INTERNATIONAL HANDBOOK OF UNIVERSITIES

2014

twenty-fifth edition

Volume 2

INTERNATIONAL ASSOCIATION OF UNIVERSITIES
INTERNATIONAL UNIVERSITIES BUREAU

palgrave macmillan

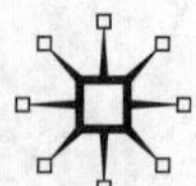

Edited by the IAU/UNESCO Information Centre on Higher Education, International Association of Universities
Director: Isabelle Turmaine
Manager, Reference Publications: Béatrice Inglisian

IAU ISBN 978-92-9002-199-5

First published 2013 by
PALGRAVE MACMILLAN

Palgrave Macmillan in the UK is an imprint of Macmillan Publishers Limited, registered in England, company number 785998, of Houndmills, Basingstoke, Hampshire RG21 6XS.

Palgrave Macmillan in the US is a division of St Martin's Press LLC, 175 Fifth Avenue, New York, NY 10010.

Palgrave Macmillan is the global academic imprint of the above companies and has companies and representatives throughout the world.

Palgrave® and Macmillan® are registered trademarks in the United States, the United Kingdom, Europe and other countries.

ISBN 978-1-137-29372-5
ISSN 0074-6215

This book is printed on paper suitable for recycling and made from fully managed and sustained forest sources. Logging, pulping and manufacturing processes are expected to conform to the environmental regulations of the country of origin.

A catalogue record for this book is available from the British Library.

A catalog record for this book is available from the Library of Congress.

CONTENTS

PREFACE

The International Association of Universities and its IAU/UNESCO Information Centre on Higher Education are pleased to present the Twenty-fifth edition of the *International Handbook of Universities*, which offers updated, comprehensive information on universities and university-level institutions worldwide.

The *Handbook* was first published by the International Association of Universities in 1959 in response to the growing demand for authoritative information about higher education institutions worldwide. It has grown considerably over the years in both the quantity and the quality of its entries. Today, it includes over 17,500 institutions extracted from the lists provided by the competent authorities or academic bodies in over 180 countries and territories, their websites or official documents. The *Handbook* also comprises basic information on the education system of all countries and two indexes (institutions and fields of study). The differentiation between university/ university-level and other higher education institutions is based on the degrees/ diplomas delivered by the institution, a university/university-level institution being an institution offering at least a postgraduate degree or a professional diploma in four years or more.

The compilation of the *Handbook* involves working on documents in many languages, covering a wide range of continuously evolving systems of higher education. Every effort has been made to ensure that the entries are as comprehensive as possible and that the information is accurate. The IAU/UNESCO Information Centre on Higher Education is indebted to those many universities/university-level institutions, governmental agencies and academic bodies which have provided material for this edition in order to make it a unique and authoritative source of information. Where information was not available in time for inclusion, entries have remained the same as in the previous edition. The date of the last update is indicated at the bottom of each entry. Comments and corrections to help to improve the next edition of the *Handbook* are most welcome at: centre@iau-aiu.net

The full wealth of data held by the IAU/UNESCO Information Centre - including the information in the *Handbook*, as well as more comprehensive data on higher education systems and credentials offered in over 180 countries - is available at www.whedonline.com, the World Higher Education Database (WHED) Online. Free single-user access is available to all purchasers of the Handbook for 12 months following the publication date, and offers users the opportunity to search and browse the information with ease and convenience. For multiple user access please contact onlinesales@palgrave.com. WHED is also available as a CD-Rom[1].

The production of the *Handbook* and of WHED is part of the drive by the International Association of Universities to provide access to information on higher education worldwide. The quarterly scholarly Journal Higher Education Policy[2] provides a deeper and more analytical understanding of higher education policy worldwide.

[1] World Higher Education Database CD-Rom, IAU, Palgrave Macmillan (see p. xviii).
[2] Higher Education Policy, Palgrave Macmillan (see p. xviii).

GUIDE TO THE ENTRIES

This edition of the *International Handbook of Universities* comprises entries for over 17,500 universities and university-level institutions in over 180 countries and territories.

COUNTRY CHAPTERS

A short presentation of the education system based upon the information provided by the appropriate higher education authorities in the countries concerned or found on their official website or documentation is provided for each country. It comprises a short description of the overall structure of the higher education system; the different stages of study; the admission requirements (including for foreign students); the quality assurance/recognition system; and information on national bodies responsible for higher education. The designations employed for countries and territories are those in use in the United Nations system and do not imply any expression of opinion with regard to their status or the delimitations of their frontiers.

INSTITUTIONAL ENTRIES

Entries are selected on the basis of the information contained in the listings provided by the appropriate higher education authorities in the countries concerned or found on their official websites. Questionnaires are then sent to those degree-granting institutions which offer at least a post-graduate degree and/or a professional diploma in four years or more to obtain more detailed information. The inclusion or omission of an institution, therefore, does not imply any judgement on the part of the IAU/UNESCO Information Centre on Higher Education as to the status or quality of that institution.

Membership of a higher education institution in the International Association of Universities is indicated by preceding its name. Higher education institutions wishing to become members should contact: iau@iau-aiu.net.

The institutional entries within each country are generally listed within Public and Private Sections, where relevant, with their postal address and telecommunication, email and website information. The name of each institution is given first in English, followed by the name in the national language(s), where appropriate. Where available, the names and full contact details of the Academic Head, the Chief Administrative Officer, and the Director of International Relations are given.

The lists of faculties, colleges, departments, schools, institutes, etc., are intended primarily as a general guide to the academic structure of the institution of which they form a part. They normally include the various fields of study offered (standardized list). The names of their heads are provided where available. This information is followed by a brief description of the history and structure of the institution and, where available, by information on co-operation programmes with institutions in other countries.

Admission requirements are usually listed for courses leading to a first degree or similar qualification. Special requirements for admission to studies leading to higher degrees and specialized diplomas are indicated where appropriate.

The names of degrees, diplomas and professional qualifications are generally given in the language of the country concerned. Fields and duration of studies are indicated when available. Tuition fees, library holdings, special facilities and student services available in each university are also indicated when provided.

Overall Academic Staff (including Staff with Doctorates) and Student Enrolment statistics complete the entry and include a breakdown of number of foreign students and part-time, evening and distance education students, if available. A breakdown by Men and Women for both Academic Staff and Students is also given where available.

LIST OF FIELDS OF STUDY

The complete list of fields of study used in the *Handbook* is provided to help users in their search of the field of study index.

INDEXES

An index to higher education institutions which comprises the name of each institution in English, in the national language (when available) and the alternative name (when appropriate) is provided at the end of the *Handbook*.

An index to fields of study is also provided to allow for searches of institutions providing courses in a specific specialty.

INTERNATIONAL HANDBOOK OF UNIVERSITIES

2014

twenty-fifth edition

Volume 2

Indonesia

STRUCTURE OF HIGHER EDUCATION SYSTEM

Description:

There are several types of institutions: universities, both private and public, which are recognized by the Ministry of National Education; institutes and teacher training institutes (Institut Keguruan dan Ilmu Pendidikan or IKIPs) which rank as universities with full degree granting status; Islamic institutes, which have the same rank as universities but come under the Ministry of Religious Affairs; schools (Sekolah Tinggi), both public and private, which offer academic and professional university level education in one particular discipline; single faculty academies which offer Diploma/Certificate technician level courses at public and private levels; and polytechnics, which are attached to universities and provide sub degree junior technician training. The Ministry of National Education, through the Directorate General of Higher Education, exercises authority over both state and private institutions. State institutions are financed by the central government, although provincial governments may also provide funds.

Stages of studies:

University level first stage: *Sarjana (S1)*
The Sarjana (Strata Satu) is awarded after four years of full-time study at a recognized university, institute or school. Students must obtain at least 144 credits. For Medicine, Dentistry, Veterinary Science, Pharmacy and Engineering, an additional two to six semesters must be added. Degree certificates usually bear the inscription Sarjana followed by the subject.

University level second stage: *Magister (S2)*
The Magister (Strata Dua) is awarded after a further two years' study plus research. Some 36-50 credits beyond S1 are required to graduate.

University level third stage: *Doktor (S3)*
The Doktor (Strata Tiga) takes another three years beyond the Magister. The Doktor degree is the highest award conferred by Indonesian universities or institutes. There is a residential requirement for 2 years and students must pass the examinations that are organized every year to check their research progress.

ADMISSION TO HIGHER EDUCATION

Admission to university-level studies:

Name of secondary school credential required: Sekolah Menengah Atas
Entrance exam requirements: Students must sit for the National Entrance Examination (Ujian Masuk Perguruan Tinggi Negeri). There are two options: Social Sciences (IPS) and Natural Sciences (IPA).

RECOGNITION OF STUDIES

Quality assurance system:

The National Accreditation Agency for Higher Education is responsible for the development and implementation of the accreditation system for higher education programmes.

Bodies dealing with recognition:

Badan Akreditasi Nasional Perguruan Tinggi - BAN-PT (National Accreditation Agency for Higher Education)

Komplek Ditjen Mandikdasmen Depdiknas RI,
Gedung D Lantai 1 Jl. RS. Fatmawati,
Cipete
Jakarta, Selatan 12410

Tel: +62(21) 7694 403
Fax: +62(21) 766 8690
EMail: sekretariat.banpt@kemdikbud.go.id
WWW: http://ban-pt.kemdiknas.go.id

NATIONAL BODIES

Kementerian Pendidikan dan Kebudayaan (Ministry of Education and Culture)

Minister: Muhammad Nuh
Jalan Jenderal Sudirman Senayan
Jakarta 10270
EMail: pengaduan@kemdikbud.go.id
WWW: http://www.kemdiknas.go.id

Direktorat Jenderal Pendidikan Tinggi (Directorate-General of Higher Education)

Director: Djoko Santoso
Gedung D, Jln. Raya Jend Sudirman Pintu I
Senayan Jakarta 10270
Tel: +62(21) 579 46105
Fax: +62(21) 573 1466
EMail: dikti@dikti.go.id
WWW: http://www.dikti.go.id/
Role of national body: Executing authority for both public and private higher education institutions.

Data for academic year: 2008-2009
Source: IAU from Widya Mandala Catholic University Surabaya, 2008 (Bodies, 2012)

INSTITUTIONS

PUBLIC INSTITUTIONS

AIRLANGGA UNIVERSITY

Universitas Airlangga (UNAIR)
Campus C, Jl. Mulyorejo, Surabaya, 60115 Jawa Timur
Tel: +62(31) 591-4042 +62(31) 591-2546
Fax: +62(31) 598-1841 +62(31) 593-9934
EMail: sekretaris_ua@unair.ac.id
Website: http://www.unair.ac.id

Rector: Fasich
Tel: +62(31) 599-4887, Fax: +62(31) 598-1841
EMail: rektor@unair.ac.id

Vice-Rector for General Administration: Mohammad Nasih
Tel: +62(31) 592-4122, Fax: +62(31) 594-3238
EMail: warek2@unair.ac.id

International Relations: Ketut Satrya Wibawa, Head of International Office and Partnership
Tel: +62(31) 596-6864, Fax: +62(31) 591-5551
EMail: international@unair.ac.id

Faculties

Dentistry *(Campus A)* (Dental Hygiene; Dental Technology; Dentistry; Oral Pathology; Orthodontics; Periodontics) *Dean*: Coen Pramono D.; **Economics and Business** *(Campus B)* (Accountancy; Banking; Economics; Hotel Management; Management; Management Systems; Marketing; Secretarial Studies; Taxation) *Dean*: Muslich Anshori; **Fisheries and Marine** *(Campus C)* (Fishery; Marine Science and Oceanography) *Dean*: Sri Subekti; **Humanities** *(Campus B)* (English; History; Indonesian; Japanese; Literature) *Dean*: Aribowo; **Law** *(Campus B)* (Commercial Law; Criminal Law; Government; Law; Notary Studies; Public Law) *Dean*: Muchammad Zaidun; **Medicine** *(Campus A)* (Anaesthesiology; Anatomy; Biochemistry; Biology; Cardiology; Dermatology; Forensic Medicine and Dentistry; Gynaecology and Obstetrics; Histology; Immunology; Medical Parasitology; Medical Technology; Medicine; Microbiology; Neurology; Ophthalmology; Orthopaedics; Otorhinolaryngology; Paediatrics; Parasitology; Pathology; Pharmacology; Physical Therapy; Physiology; Plastic Surgery; Pneumology; Psychiatry and Mental Health; Radiology; Rehabilitation and Therapy; Sports; Surgery; Traditional Eastern Medicine; Tropical Medicine; Urology; Venereology) *Dean*: Agung Pranoto; **Nursing** *(Campus C)* (Nursing) *Dean*: Purwaningsih; **Pharmacy** *(Campus B)* (Pharmacy) *Dean*: Umi Athijah; **Psychology** *(Campus B)* (Industrial and Organizational Psychology; Psychology) *Dean*: Seger Handoyo; **Public Health** *(Campus C)* (Behavioural Sciences; Demography and Population; Epidemiology; Health Administration; Nutrition; Occupational Health; Public Health) *Dean*: Tri Martiana; **Science and Technology** *(Campus C)* (Automation and Control Engineering; Biochemistry; Biology; Biomedical Engineering; Biotechnology; Chemistry; Environmental Engineering; Environmental Studies; Information Technology; Mathematics; Physics) *Dean*: Win Darmanto; **Social and Political Sciences** *(Campus B)* (Administration; Anthropology; Communication Studies; Human Resources; International Relations; Library Science; Political Sciences; Public Administration; Social Sciences; Sociology; Tourism) *Dean*: I. Basis Susilo; **Veterinary Medicine** *(Campus C)* (Agricultural Business; Animal Husbandry; Biology; Meat and Poultry; Veterinary Science; Water Science) *Dean*: Romziah Sidik

Institutes

Educational Studies and Development (Education; Educational Research; Educational Sciences) *Head*: Widji Soerati; **Research and Community Services** *(Campus B)* (Social and Community Services) *Head*: Djoko Agus Purwanto; **Tropical Diseases** (Tropical Medicine) *Head*: Nasronudin

Programmes

Postgraduate *(Campus B)* (Accountancy; Economics; Health Sciences; Islamic Studies; Law; Medicine; Natural Sciences; Pharmacy; Psychology; Social Sciences; Veterinary Science) *Director*: Sri Hayati

Research Centres

Avian Influenza *Head*: Chairul Nidom; **Demography** (Demography and Population) *Head*: Moh. Adib; **Dengue/DHF** *Head*: Soegeng Soegijanto; **Diare - Cholera** *Head*: Eddy Bagus Wasito; **Economics, Business and Accounting** (Accountancy; Business Administration; Economics) *Head*: Eny Kusreni; **Empowerment and Women's Studies** (Women's Studies) *Head*: Emy Susanti; **Empowerment of Community Performance** *Head*: Cholichul Hadi; **Empowerment of the Coastal Territory and Marine** (Coastal Studies; Marine Science and Oceanography) *Head*: Moch. Amin Alamsjah; **Entomology** (Entomology) *Head*: Subagyo Yotopranoto; **Environment** (Environmental Studies) *Head*: Agoes Soegianto; **Ethics** (Ethics) *Head*: Soedibjo HP; **Hepatisis** *Head*: Soetjipto; **HIV** *Head*: Nasronudin; **Human Genetics** (Genetics) *Head*: Moch. Soekry Erfan; **Human Rights** (Human Rights) *Head*: Bambang Budiono; **Immuno-histo-chemistry** (Chemistry; Histology; Immunology) *Head*: Juliati Hood; **Leprosy** *Head*: Indropo Agusni; **Malaria** *Head*: Bariah Ideham; **National Identity and Nationality Studies** *Head*: Ajar Triharsono; **Proteomic** *Head*: Ni Nyoman Tri Puspaningsih; **Research and Community Development on Life Sciences** (Biological and Life Sciences) *Head*: Djoko Agus Purwanto; **Research and Community Development on Social Sciences** (Social Sciences) *Head*: Sri Iswati; **Social Welfare** (Social Welfare) *Head*: Tjipto Suwandi; **Stem Cell** *Head*: Fedik A. Rantam; **Tissue Engineering** (Textile Technology) *Head*: Suhartono Putra; **Traditional Medicine Development** (Traditional Eastern Medicine) *Head*: Sukardiman; **Transmission Electron Microscope** *Head*: Ketut Sudiana; **Tuberculosis** *Head*: Ni Made Mertaniasih

History: Founded 1954 as State university by merger of faculties of Medicine and Dentistry, formerly faculties of the University of Indonesia, and Faculty of Law, formerly faculty of Gadjah Mada University . The teachers' College at Malang and the faculty of letters in Denpasar, Bali were formerly parts of Airlangga University, then seperated as Malang Teachers' College and University of Udayana, Bali. Since 1961, faculty of Economics joined Airlangga University as the Surabaya Higher Institution of Economics and further faculties developed - most recent was faculty of letter founded 1996. Acquired present status of autonomous state supported university (BHMN) 2010.

Governing Bodies: Majelis Wali Amanah (University Council)

Academic Year: September to June (September-December; January-March; April-June)

Admission Requirements: Secondary school certificate (Sekolah Menengah Umum, SMU) or equivalent and entrance examination

Fees: (Rupiahs): Undergraduate, Life Sciences, 1.25m.-70m. per semester; Social Sciences, 800,000-5m.

Main Language(s) of Instruction: Indonesian; English (20%); International Classes, English

International Co-operation: With universities in Europe (Belgium; Bulgaria; Cyprus; Finland; Germany; Liechstenstein; Netherlands; Poland; Spain) and Asia (Bangladesh; Bhutan; India; Nepal; Pakistan). Also participates in the Erasmus Mundus programme.

Accrediting Agencies: Badan Akreditasi Nasional (National Accreditation Board); Association to Advance Collegiate Schools of Business (AACSB); World Federation for Medical Education (WFME)

Degrees and Diplomas: *Diploma*: D1, 1 yr; D3, 3 yrs; *Sarjana (S1)*: Professional, 5-6 yrs; *Sarjana (S1)*: Undergraduate, 4 yrs; *Magister (S2)*: 2 yrs; *Doktor (S3)*: 3 yrs. Also Specialist Degrees

Student Services: Academic counselling, Canteen, Cultural centre, Employment services, Foreign student adviser, Health services, Language programs, Social counselling, Sports facilities

Student Residential Facilities: Available on campus (dormitories: 191 rooms, 594 beds)

Special Facilities: Hospital; Tropical Diseases Hospital

Libraries: Central Library; Internet, journals and e-books.

Publications: Administrasi dan Kebijakan Kesehatan *(quarterly)*; Berkala Ilmiah Kependudukan *(3 per annum)*; Berkala Ilmu Kesehatan Kulit dan Kelamin *(3 per annum)*; Dialetika; Folia Medica Indonesiana, Medical Journal *(quarterly)*; Indonesian Journal of Clinical Pathology and Medical Laboratory *(3 per annum)*; Indonesian Journal of Social Sciences *(quarterly)*; Insan Media Psikologi *(3 per annum)*; Journal Matematika dan Ilmu Pengetahuan Alam *(quarterly)*; Jurnal Biomorfologi *(3 per annum)*; Jurnal Global dan Strategis *(biannually)*; Jurnal Ilmiah Perikanan dan Kelautan *(3 per annum)*; Jurnal Masyarakat Kebudayaan dan Politik; Jurnal Ners *(annually)*; Jurnal Oftalmologi Indonesia *(3 per annum)*; Jurnal Penelitian Dinamika Sosial *(3 per annum)*; Jurnal Penelitian Media Eksakta *(3 per annum)*; Karakter Bangsa (Jurnal Ilmiah Kebangsaan dan Keindonesian) *(3 per annum)*; Kesehatan Lingkungan *(biannually)*; Majalah Ekonomi *(quarterly)*; Majalah Farmasi Airlangga, Airlangga Journal of Pharmacy *(3 per annum)*; Majalah Ilmu Faal Indonesia *(3 per annum)*; Majalah Kedokteran Gigi, Dental Journal *(quarterly)*; Masyarakat Kebudayaan dan Politik *(quarterly)*; Media Gizi Indonesia *(biannually)*; Media Kedokteran Hewan *(3 per annum)*; Mozaik, Journal of Humanism *(annually)*; The Indonesian Journal of Public Health *(3 per annum)*; Veterineria Medika *(quarterly)*; Yuridika *(biannually)*

Press or Publishing House: Airlangga University Press

Academic Staff *2009-2010*	MEN	WOMEN	**TOTAL**
FULL-TIME	779	749	**1,528**
PART-TIME	–	–	**342**
STAFF WITH DOCTORATE			
FULL-TIME	–	–	**377**
PART-TIME	–	–	**72**
Student Numbers *2009-2010*			
All (Foreign Included)	10,823	15,460	**26,283**
FOREIGN ONLY	–	–	**269**

Last Updated: 08/04/11

ANDALAS UNIVERSITY

Universitas Andalas (UNAND)

Kampus Limau Manis, Padang, 25163 Sumatera Barat
Tel: +62(751) 71-301 +62(751) 71-181
Fax: +62(751) 71-301 +62(751) 71-085
EMail: rektor@unand.ac.id
Website: http://www.unand.ac.id

Rector: Musliar Kasim

Faculties

Agricultural Technology (Agricultural Engineering; Crop Production); **Agriculture** (Agricultural Business; Agricultural Engineering; Agriculture; Environmental Engineering); **Animal Husbandry** (Animal Husbandry); **Arts and Humanities** (Arts and Humanities; English; History; Indonesian; Japanese; Literature; Native Language); **Economics** (Accountancy; Development Studies; Economics; Finance; Management; Marketing; Secretarial Studies); **Engineering** (Civil Engineering; Electrical Engineering; Environmental Engineering; Industrial Engineering; Information Technology; Mechanical Engineering); **Law** (Law); **Mathematics and Natural Sciences** (Biology; Chemistry; Mathematics; Mathematics and Computer Science; Natural Sciences; Physics; Systems Analysis); **Medicine** (Medicine; Nursing; Psychology; Public Health); **Pharmacy** (Pharmacy); **Social and Political Sciences** (Anthropology; Communication Studies; International Relations; Political Sciences; Public Administration; Social Sciences; Sociology)

Institutes

Research

Programmes

Postgraduate Studies (Accountancy; Agricultural Engineering; Agronomy; Anatomy; Animal Husbandry; Biology; Biomedicine; Chemistry; Civil Engineering; Dermatology; Development Studies; Economics; Engineering; Environmental Studies; Gynaecology and Obstetrics; History; Law; Management; Mathematics; Mechanical Engineering; Neurology; Ophthalmology; Otorhinolaryngology; Paediatrics; Pathology; Pharmacy; Physics; Plant and Crop Protection; Pneumology; Public Health; Regional Planning; Rural Planning; Sociology; Soil Science; Surgery)

Further Information: Special courses for foreign students

History: Founded 1956, incorporating previously existing colleges. A State institution under the supervision of the Department of Education and Culture.

Academic Year: August to July (August-January; February-July)

Admission Requirements: Secondary school certificate (Sekolah Menengah Atas, SMA)

Main Language(s) of Instruction: Indonesian

Degrees and Diplomas: *Diploma*: 3 yrs; *Sarjana (S1)*: 4 yrs; *Magister (S2)*: 2 yrs; *Doktor (S3)*: 4 yrs

Student Services: Academic counselling, Canteen, Employment services, Health services, Nursery care, Social counselling, Sports facilities

Student Residential Facilities: Yes

Libraries: 51,082 vols

Publications: Majalah Universitas Andalas; Mediterna

Student Numbers *2010-2011*: Total: c. 23,000

Last Updated: 19/05/11

BANDUNG INSTITUTE OF TECHNOLOGY

Institut Teknologi Bandung (ITB)

Jalan Tamansari 64, Bandung, 40116 Jawa Barat
Tel: +62(22) 250-0935
Fax: +62(22) 250-0935
EMail: wrkma@pusat.itb.ac.id
Website: http://www.itb.ac.id

Rector: Akhmaloka (2010-2014)
Tel: +62(22) 250-8517, Fax: +62(22) 423-1792
EMail: rector@itb.ac.id

Vice-Rector for Communication, Partnership and Alumni: Hasanuddin Z. Abidin
Tel: +62(22) 250-0935, Fax: +62(22) 250-0935

International Relations: Edwan Kardena, Director of Partnership and International Relations
Tel: +62(22) 424-0250, Fax: +62(22) 424-0250
EMail: kardena@pusat.itb.ac.id

Faculties

Art and Design (Communication Studies; Design; Fine Arts; Handicrafts; Industrial Design; Interior Design; Visual Arts) *Dean*: Biranul Anas Zaman; **Civil and Environmental Engineering** (Civil Engineering; Environmental Engineering; Marine Engineering; Road Engineering) *Dean*: Saptahari Mudjiana S. Poetra; **Earth Sciences and Technology** (Geological Engineering; Marine Science and Oceanography; Meteorology) *Dean*: Lambok Hutasoit; **Industrial Technology** (Applied Physics; Chemical Engineering; Engineering; Industrial Engineering) *Dean*: Dwiwahju Sasongko; **Mathematics and Natural Sciences** (Astronomy and Space Science; Chemistry; Mathematics; Physics) *Dean*: Pudji Astuti Waluyo; **Mechanical and Aerospace Engineering** (Aeronautical and Aerospace Engineering; Materials Engineering; Mechanical Engineering) *Dean*: Andi Isra Mahyuddin; **Mining and Petroleum Engineering** (Geological Engineering; Metallurgical Engineering; Mining Engineering; Petroleum and Gas Engineering) *Dean*: Sudarto Notosiswoyo

Graduate Schools

ITB *Dean*: Ofyar Z. Tamin

Schools

Architecture, Planning and Policy Development (Architecture; Development Studies; Police Studies; Regional Planning; Tourism; Town Planning; Transport and Communications; Transport Management; Urban Studies) *Dean*: Iwan Sudrajat; **Business and Management** (Business and Commerce; Management) *Dean*: Dermawan Wibisono; **Electrical Engineering and Informatics** (Computer Engineering; Electrical Engineering; Information Technology; Power Engineering; Telecommunications Engineering) *Dean*: Adang Suwandi Ahmad; **Life Sciences and Technology** (Biological and Life Sciences; Biology; Microbiology) *Dean*: Intan Ahmad Musmeinan; **Pharmacy** (Pharmacology; Pharmacy) *Dean*: Tutus Dusdinar Kartawinata

Further Information: Also campus at Jl. Ganesha 10

History: Founded 1920 as Technische Hogeschool by Dutch Government. Part of University of Gadjah Mada 1945-1959. Acquired present status and title 1959.

Governing Bodies: Board of Trustees, Academic Senate, Board of Professors, Board of Audit, Rector and Vice-Rectors

Academic Year: August to July (August-December; January-May; June-July)

Admission Requirements: High school certificate or equivalent

Fees: (US Dollars): 17,500 for a study period of eight semesters.

Main Language(s) of Instruction: Indonesian, English

International Co-operation: With universities in Austria; Australia; Belgium; Canada; Czech Republic; Denmark; France; Germany; Japan; Korea; Malaysia; Netherlands; Norway; Poland; Russian Federation; Singapore; Sweden; Taiwan; Thailand; United Kingdom; USA

Accrediting Agencies: National Accreditation Board

Degrees and Diplomas: *Sarjana (S1)*: Art; Science; Engineering, 4 yrs; *Magister (S2)*: Art; Science; Engineering, a further 2 yrs; *Doktor (S3)*: Art; Science; Engineering, 3 yrs

Student Services: Academic counselling, Canteen, Cultural centre, Employment services, Foreign student adviser, Foreign Studies Centre, Health services, Language programs, Nursery care, Social counselling, Sports facilities

Student Residential Facilities: For 419 students

Special Facilities: Art Gallery. Observatory. Exhibition Building. Cinema. Convention Hall, Video Conference Room.

Libraries: Central Library, printed material, 225,565 vols; 850 subscriptions to periodicals; E-books, 72,452 titles; E-journals, 85,338 titles

Publications: Asian Journal of Technology Management *(biannually)*; Berita Penelitian dan Pengabdian Kepada Masyarakat, Monthly Bulletin published by the Institute for Research and Community Services *(monthly)*; Business Review, MBA Business Review *(quarterly)*; ITB Proceedings, Selected Research Papers *(quarterly)*; Jurnal Bidang Ilmu Teknik, Journal of Engineering Science *(biannually)*; Jurnal Bidang Matematika dan Sains, Journal of Science *(biannually)*; Jurnal Bidang Seni Rupa dan Desain, Journal of Visual Arts and Design *(3 per annum)*; Jurnal Bidang Teknologi Komunikasi dan Informasi, Journal of Information and Communication Technology *(biannually)*; Jurnal Fisika Indonesia, Indonesian Journal of Geophysics published by the Association of Indonesian Physicists *(quarterly)*; Jurnal Geoaplika, Journal of Earth Sciences *(quarterly)*; Jurnal Manajemen Teknologi, Journal of Technology Management *(biannually)*; Jurnal Perencanaan Wilayah dan Kota, Journal of Urban and Regional Planning *(quarterly)*; Jurnal Teknik Sipil, Journal of Civil Engineering *(quarterly)*; Majalah Ilmiah Teknik Elektro, Scientific Journal of Electrical Engineering *(quarterly)*

Press or Publishing House: Unit Usaha Penunjang Penerbit ITB

Academic Staff *2009-2010*	MEN	WOMEN	**TOTAL**
FULL-TIME	815	210	**1,025**
STAFF WITH DOCTORATE			
FULL-TIME	601	138	**739**
Student Numbers *2009-2010*			
All (Foreign Included)	12,126	6,755	**18,881**
FOREIGN ONLY	102	106	**208**

Last Updated: 07/04/11

BENGKULU UNIVERSITY

Universitas Bengkulu (UNIB)

Jalan Raya Kandang Limun, Bengkulu, 38371 Bengkulu
Tel: +62(736) 25-764
Fax: +62(736) 20-653
Website: http://www.unib.ac.id

Rector: Zainal Muktamar EMail: muktamar1950@yahoo.com

Vice-Rector: Fahrrurozi

Centres

Public Services and Extension (Public Administration); **Research** (Demography and Population; Environmental Studies; Rural Studies; Women's Studies)

Faculties

Agriculture (Agricultural Business; Agricultural Economics; Agricultural Engineering; Agriculture; Agronomy; Animal Husbandry; Economics; Forest Products; Forestry; Industrial Engineering; Marine Science and Oceanography; Plant and Crop Protection; Plant Pathology; Soil Science); **Economics** (Accountancy; Civics;

Communication Studies; Development Studies; Economics; English; Management; Religion); **Education and Teacher Training** (Biology; Chemistry; Education; Educational and Student Counselling; Educational Sciences; English; Foreign Languages Education; Health Education; Indonesian; Literature; Mathematics Education; Native Language Education; Physical Education; Physics; Preschool Education; Primary Education; Science Education; Teacher Training); **Engineering** (Civil Engineering; Computer Engineering; Electrical Engineering; Mechanical Engineering); **Law** (Administrative Law; Civil Law; Commercial Law; Comparative Law; Criminal Law; Criminology; Economics; English; Environmental Management; Ethics; Finance; Government; Heritage Preservation; Human Rights; Indonesian; Insurance; International Law; Islamic Law; Labour Law; Law; Natural Sciences; Private Law; Religious Education; Taxation); **Mathematics and Natural Sciences** (Biology; Chemistry; Mathematics; Physics); **Social and Political Sciences** (Administration; Communication Studies; Government; Journalism; Library Science; Political Sciences; Public Administration; Secretarial Studies; Social Sciences; Social Welfare; Sociology)

Programmes

Postgraduate Studies (Business Education; Civil Law; Comparative Law; Criminal Law; Development Studies; Environmental Management; Environmental Studies; Government; Indonesian; Law; Management; Native Language Education; Natural Resources; Political Sciences; Public Administration; Rural Planning; Technology Education; Town Planning)

History: Founded 1982.

Academic Year: September to August (September-January; February-August)

Admission Requirements: Secondary school certificate (Sekolah Menengah Atas, SMA) and entrance examination

Fees: (Rupiahs): c. 200,000-425,000

Main Language(s) of Instruction: Indonesian

Degrees and Diplomas: *Diploma*: 2-3 yrs; *Sarjana (S1)*: 4 yrs; *Magister (S2)*: Development Planning; Indonesian; Law; Management; Management of Natural Resources and Environment; Public Administration; Technology Education, a further 2 yrs

Student Services: Academic counselling, Canteen, Employment services, Health services, Language programs, Sports facilities

Student Residential Facilities: Yes

Special Facilities: Auditorium

Libraries: c. 77,000 vols

Publications: Agrosia, Journal on Agronomy and related studies *(biannually)*; Jurnal Ilmu Pertanian Indonesia, Journal on Agricultural Sciences *(biannually)*; Jurnal Penelitian, Journal on Social Sciences *(biannually)*; Triadik, Journal on Education and Human Rights *(biannually)*

Last Updated: 04/07/11

BOGOR AGRICULTURAL UNIVERSITY

Institut Pertanian Bogor (IPB)

Jl. Raya Darmaga, Kampus IPB Darmaga, Bogor, 16680 Jawa Barat

Tel: +62(251) 8622-642

Fax: +62(251) 8622-708

EMail: humas_se@ipb.ac.id

Website: http://www.ipb.ac.id

Rector: Herry Suhardiyanto (2008-)
Tel: +62(251) 8622-634 EMail: rektor@ipb.ac.id

International Relations: Rinekso Soekmadi

Centres

Coastal and Marine Resources (Coastal Studies; Marine Biology); **Development Studies** (Development Studies); **Environmental Studies** (Environmental Studies); **Food and Nutrition Policy** (Food Science; Nutrition); **Marine Commodities** (Marine Biology); **Primate Studies** (Zoology); **Traditional Food Studies** (Food Science); **Tropical Biodiversity** (Biological and Life Sciences); **Tropical Biology** (Biological and Life Sciences); **Tropical Fruits** (Tropical Agriculture); **Women's Studies** (Women's Studies)

Faculties

Agricultural Technology (Agricultural Engineering; Agricultural Equipment; Civil Engineering; Environmental Engineering; Food Science; Food Technology; Harvest Technology; Industrial Engineering; Mechanical Engineering); **Agriculture** (Agriculture; Agronomy; Biotechnology; Botany; Crop Production; Entomology; Horticulture; Information Management; Landscape Architecture; Natural Resources; Plant and Crop Protection; Plant Pathology; Regional Planning; Soil Management; Soil Science; Water Management); **Animal Science** (Agricultural Management; Animal Husbandry; Cattle Breeding; Nutrition); **Economics and Management** (Agricultural Economics; Development Studies; Economics; Environmental Management; Management; Natural Resources; Regional Planning; Rural Planning); **Fishery and Marine Science** (Aquaculture; Coastal Studies; Fishery; Marine Engineering; Marine Science and Oceanography; Natural Resources; Production Engineering; Water Management; Water Science); **Forestry** (Environmental Studies; Forest Management; Forest Products; Forestry; Natural Resources; Surveying and Mapping); **Human Ecology** (Child Care and Development; Community Health; Consumer Studies; Ecology; Family Studies; Nutrition; Rural Studies); **Mathematics and Natural Sciences** (Analytical Chemistry; Applied Mathematics; Biochemistry; Biology; Biophysics; Chemistry; Computer Science; Environmental Engineering; Geophysics; Mathematics; Meteorology; Microbiology; Natural Sciences; Physics; Statistics); **Veterinary Science** (Anatomy; Animal Husbandry; Entomology; Food Science; Microbiology; Parasitology; Pathology; Pharmacology; Physiology; Public Health; Veterinary Science)

Graduate Divisions

Multidisciplinary Studies (Biotechnology; Environmental Management; Ethnology; Natural Resources)

Institutes

Research

Programmes

Biodiversity Conservation *(Professional Master's Programme)* (Ecology; Plant and Crop Protection); **Estate Plantation** *(Professional Master's Programme)* (Botany); **Food Security Management** *(Professional Master's Programme)* (Food Science); **Food Technology** *(Professional Master's Programme)* (Food Technology); **Horticulture** *(Professional Master's Programme)*; **Information Technology** *(Professional Master's Programme)* (Information Technology; Library Science); **Information Technology for Natural Resources Management** *(Professional Master's Programme)* (Environmental Management; Information Technology; Natural Resources); **Management and Business** *(Professional Master's Programme)* (Business Administration; Management); **Management and Regional Development** *(Professional Master's Programme)* (Development Studies; Management; Regional Planning; Regional Studies); **Seed Technology** *(Professional Master's Programme)*; **Small and Medium-Scale Industries** *(Professional Master's Programme)*

Further Information: Also Information Media Production, Computer Centre, Experimental Fields, Integrated Chemistry Laboratory, Language Training Centre

History: Founded 1963, the only Indonesian higher education institution dedicated exclusively to Agriculture, Natural Resources and Environmental Development.

Academic Year: September to June (September-January; February-June)

Admission Requirements: Secondary school certificate and entrance examination

Degrees and Diplomas: *Sarjana (S1)*: 4 yrs; *Magister (S2)*: a further 2 yrs; *Doktor (S3) (PhD)*: a further 3 yrs. Also Professional Master's Programmes

Student Services: Academic counselling, Cultural centre, Employment services, Foreign student adviser, Health services, Social counselling, Sports facilities

Student Residential Facilities: For c. 20,000 students

Special Facilities: Botanical Garden. Marine Centre. Education Forest. Agricultural Field Station

Publications: International Journal of Tropical Agriculture (IJTA); Journal Agrotek; Journal AINI; Journal Ilmu Pertanian Indonesia (JIPI)

Press or Publishing House: Pariwara

Last Updated: 06/05/11

BRAWIJAYA UNIVERSITY

Universitas Brawijaya (UB)

Jalan Veteran, Malang, 65145 East Java
Tel: +62(341) 551-611 +62(341) 575-777
Fax: +62(341) 565-420 +62(341) 575-814
EMail: ksln@brawijaya.ac.id
Website: http://www.brawijaya.ac.id

Rector: Yogi Sugito (2006-)
Tel: +62(341) 575-777, Ext. 100 EMail: rektor@brawijaya.ac.id

Vice-Rector, Academic Affairs: Bambang Suharto

Vice-Rector, Administration and Finance: Warkum Sumitro
Tel: +62(341) 575-777, Ext. 105 EMail: bauk@brawijaya.ac.id

International Relations: Ifar Subagiyo, Coordinator of Cooperation
Tel: +62(341) 575-777, Ext. 125 EMail: ifars@brawijaya.ac.id

Centres

Brawijaya Information Technology Services *(BITS)* (Information Technology); **Computer** (Computer Science); **E-Learning Development** (Distance Education; Educational Sciences; Educational Technology); **Language** (Food Science); **Language and Literature** (Arabic; Chinese; English; French; Japanese; Literature; Modern Languages); **Library** (Library Science); **Religious Education** (Asian Religious Studies; Christian Religious Studies; Islamic Studies; Religious Education)

Faculties

Administration (Business Administration; Finance; Government; Industrial and Production Economics; Information Management; Information Technology; Leadership; Management; Marketing; Public Administration; Regional Planning); **Agricultural Technology** (Agricultural Business; Agricultural Engineering; Agriculture; Technology); **Agriculture** (Agricultural Business; Agricultural Economics; Agricultural Engineering; Agriculture; Agronomy; Biotechnology; Coastal Studies; Development Studies; Environmental Studies; Horticulture; Marine Science and Oceanography; Natural Resources; Plant and Crop Protection; Plant Pathology; Sociology; Soil Conservation; Soil Management; Soil Science; Town Planning; Water Management; Water Science); **Animal Husbandry** (Agricultural Business; Animal Husbandry; Cattle Breeding; Veterinary Science); **Cultural Studies** (English; French; Japanese); **Economics** (Accountancy; Agricultural Business; Agricultural Management; Banking; Demography and Population; Development Studies; Economics; Finance; Human Resources; Islamic Studies; Management); **Engineering** (Architecture; Civil Engineering; Electrical Engineering; Electronic Engineering; Energy Engineering; Hydraulic Engineering; Industrial Engineering; Mechanical Engineering; Regional Planning; Software Engineering; Structural Architecture; Town Planning; Transport Engineering); **Fishery and Marine Sciences** (Fishery; Marine Science and Oceanography; Water Management; Water Science); **Law** (Administrative Law; Commercial Law; Criminal Law; Law; Notary Studies); **Mathematics and Natural Sciences** (Biology; Chemistry; Computer Engineering; Computer Science; Geophysics; Mathematics; Molecular Biology; Physics; Statistics); **Medicine** (Anaesthesiology; Anatomy; Biomedicine; Cardiology; Dentistry; Dermatology; Forensic Medicine and Dentistry; Gynaecology and Obstetrics; Health Administration; Health Education; Medicine; Midwifery; Neurology; Nursing; Ophthalmology; Orthopaedics; Otorhinolaryngology; Paediatrics; Pathology; Pharmacy; Pneumology; Radiology; Surgery); **Social and Political Sciences** (Clinical Psychology; Communication Studies; Cultural Studies; Developmental Psychology; Educational Psychology; Government; Industrial and Organizational Psychology; International Relations; Mass Communication; Peace and Disarmament; Political Sciences; Psychology; Public Relations; Social Studies; Sociology)

Institutes

Educational Studies and Development (Development Studies; Distance Education; Education; Educational Administration; Educational Research; Higher Education; Pedagogy; Vocational Education); **Research and Public Service** (Biology; Demography and Population; Environmental Studies; Gender Studies; Natural Resources; Public Administration; Social Sciences; Technology); **Research** (Biology; Demography and Population; Environmental Studies; Gender Studies; Social Sciences)

Programmes

Postgraduate Studies (Accountancy; Administrative Law; Agricultural Business; Agricultural Economics; Agricultural Engineering; Agriculture; Anatomy; Animal Husbandry; Banking; Biomedicine; Biotechnology; Botany; Business Administration; Cattle Breeding; Chemistry; Civil Engineering; Coastal Studies; Commercial Law; Communication Studies; Criminal Law; Demography and Population; Development Studies; Ecology; Economics; Electrical Engineering; Energy Engineering; Engineering; Environmental Studies; Finance; Fishery; Government; Health Administration; Horticulture; Human Resources; Immunology; Industrial Engineering; Information Management; Information Technology; Islamic Studies; Law; Leadership; Management; Marine Science and Oceanography; Marketing; Mathematics; Mechanical Engineering; Medicine; Microbiology; Molecular Biology; Natural Resources; Natural Sciences; Parasitology; Pharmacology; Physics; Plant and Crop Protection; Political Sciences; Public Administration; Regional Planning; Social and Preventive Medicine; Social Sciences; Sociology; Soil Management; Soil Science; Structural Architecture; Town Planning; Toxicology; Transport Engineering; Water Management; Water Science)

History: Founded 1957 by municipal authorities as a private university, became State university 1963.

Academic Year: September to August

Admission Requirements: Secondary school certificate (Sekolah Menengah Atas, SMA)

Main Language(s) of Instruction: Indonesian; English

Accrediting Agencies: National Accrediting Agency (Badan Akreditasi Nasional) of Indonesian Education Department

Degrees and Diplomas: *Sarjana (S1)*: 4 yrs; *Magister (S2) (MS)*: a further 2 yrs; *Doktor (S3) (Dr.)*: 3 yrs following Sarjana

Student Services: Academic counselling, Canteen, Cultural centre, Employment services, Foreign student adviser, Health services, Language programs, Nursery care, Social counselling, Sports facilities

Student Residential Facilities: For 500 students

Special Facilities: Internet access centre

Libraries: 108,383 vols; 212,881 documents (CDs, Videos, etc.)

Publications: Administrator, Administrative Sciences *(monthly)*; Agrivita, Agricultural Journal *(quarterly)*; Febra, Economic Sciences *(monthly)*; Habitat, Agricultural Journal *(quarterly)*; Info-Food, Food Technology *(bimonthly)*

Press or Publishing House: Brawijaya University Press

Academic Staff *2009-2010*: Total: c. 1,500

Student Numbers *2009-2010*: Total: c. 30,300

Last Updated: 19/05/11

CENDERAWASIH UNIVERSITY

Universitas Cenderawasih (UNCEN)

Kampus Baru Waena, PO Box 422, Waena, Jayapura, Papua
Tel: +62(967) 572-108
Fax: +62(967) 572-102
EMail: ict@uncend.ac.id
Website: http://www.uncend.ac.id

Rector: Balthazar Kambuaya Tel: +62(967) 572-108

Faculties

Agriculture (Agricultural Economics; Agriculture; Agronomy; Animal Husbandry; Fishery; Forestry); **Economics** (Accountancy; Development Studies; Economics; Management); **Education and Teacher Training** (Art Education; Biology; Chemistry; Civics; Education; Educational and Student Counselling; English; Foreign Languages Education; Geography; Geography (Human); Health Education; History; Indonesian; Literature; Mathematics Education; Native Language Education; Natural Sciences; Parks and Recreation; Physical Education; Physics; Primary Education; Science Education; Social Sciences; Teacher Training); **Engineering** (Civil Engineering; Electrical Engineering; Engineering; Mechanical Engineering; Mining Engineering); **Law** (Law); **Mathematics and Natural Sciences** (Biology; Chemistry; Mathematics; Physics); **Medicine** (Health Education; Medicine); **Public Health** (Nursing; Public Health); **Social and Political Sciences** (Administration; Anthropology; Government; International Relations; Nursing;

Political Sciences; Public Administration; Secretarial Studies; Social Sciences; Social Welfare)

Programmes

Graduate Studies (Management; Modern Languages)

History: Founded 1962. A State university under the jurisdiction of the Department of Education and Culture.

Academic Year: January to November

Admission Requirements: Secondary school certificate (Sekolah Menengah Atas, SMA) or equivalent

Main Language(s) of Instruction: Indonesian

Degrees and Diplomas: *Sarjana (S1)*; *Magister (S2)*: Languages; Management

Student Services: Academic counselling, Canteen, Cultural centre, Employment services, Foreign student adviser, Health services, Nursery care, Social counselling, Sports facilities

Student Residential Facilities: For c. 1,000 students

Libraries: Central Library, c. 40,000 vols

Publications: Majalah Universitas Centrawasih *(monthly)*; Seruling Mahasiswa *(quarterly)*

Press or Publishing House: Percetakan Universitas Cenderawasih

Last Updated: 05/07/11

DIPONEGORO UNIVERSITY

Universitas Diponegoro (UNDIP)

Campus Undip Tembalang, Jalan Prof. Sudarto, Semarang, 50275 Jawa Tengah
Tel: +62(24) 746-0011 +62(24) 746-0012
Fax: +62(24) 746-0013
EMail: pr4@undip.ac.id
Website: http://www.undip.ac.id

Rector: Sudharto P. Hadi EMail: rector@undip.ac.id

Vice-Rector: Hertanto Wahyu Subagio
Tel: +62(24) 746-0014, Fax: +62(24) 746-0014
EMail: pr1undip@telkom.net

International Relations: Sultana M.H. Faradz, Vice-Rector for Development and Collaboration
Tel: +62(24) 746-0017, Fax: +62(24) 746-0017

Faculties

Animal Husbandry (Agricultural Business; Agricultural Economics; Animal Husbandry; Farm Management); **Economics** (Accountancy; Development Studies; Economics; Management); **Engineering** (Architecture; Chemical Engineering; Civil Engineering; Computer Engineering; Electrical Engineering; Engineering; Environmental Engineering; Geological Engineering; Industrial Engineering; Marine Engineering; Mechanical Engineering; Regional Planning; Structural Architecture; Town Planning); **Fisheries and Marine Science** (Aquaculture; Fishery; Marine Science and Oceanography; Natural Resources); **Humanities** (Arts and Humanities; English; History; Indonesian; Library Science; Literature); **Law** (Law); **Mathematics and Natural Sciences** (Biology; Chemistry; Computer Science; Information Technology; Mathematics; Natural Sciences; Physics; Statistics); **Medicine** (Medicine; Nursing; Nutrition); **Psychology** (Psychology); **Public Health** *(Masyaraka)* (Health Administration; Health Sciences; Nutrition; Public Health); **Social and Political Sciences** (Business Administration; Communication Studies; Government; Political Sciences; Public Administration; Social Sciences)

Institutes

Educational Development and Quality Assurance (Educational Research); **Research and Community Services** (Social and Community Services)

Programmes

Postgraduate Studies (Accountancy; Agricultural Business; Architecture and Planning; Arts and Humanities; Biological and Life Sciences; Biomedicine; Chemical Engineering; Civil Engineering; Coastal Studies; Communication Studies; Community Health; Development Studies; Economics; Environmental Studies; Epidemiology; Health Sciences; Information Technology; Law; Linguistics; Management; Mechanical Engineering; Medicine; Notary Studies; Nutrition; Political Sciences; Public Administration; Public Health; Rural Planning; Structural Architecture; Town Planning; Zoology)

Units

Citizenship and Ethical Course (Ethics); **Computer** (Computer Science; Data Processing); **Entrepreneurship** (Management); **Foreign Language** (Modern Languages)

Further Information: Also campuses in Pleburan, Gunung Brintik and Teluk Awur

History: Founded 1957 as Universitas Semarang, a private Institution. Became State Institution and acquired present status 1961. Financed by the central Government.

Governing Bodies: University Council

Academic Year: September to August (September-January; February-August)

Admission Requirements: High school certificate (Sekolah Menengah Umum, SMU) and entrance examination

Main Language(s) of Instruction: Indonesian

International Co-operation: With universities in Australia, Germany, Japan, Republic of Korea, Netherlands, United Kingdom. Also participates in the Asea-Uninet Programme (Austria)

Accrediting Agencies: Department of National Education

Degrees and Diplomas: *Sarjana (S1)*: 4 yrs; *Sarjana (S1)*: Medicine (MD), 6 yrs; *Magister (S2)*: Accountancy; Architecture; Biological Sciences; Biomedicine; City Planning; Economics and Development Studies; Engineering (Chemical; Civil; Mechanical); Environmental Health; Epidemiology; Health Promotion; Humanities; Linguistics; Science History; Agribusiness; Community Nutrition; Coastal Resources; Environmental Science; Information Systems; Law; Management; Medicine; Notary Studies; Political Sciences; Public Administration; Public Health; Science Communication; Zoology, 2 yrs; *Doktor (S3)*: Architecture and Urban Planning; Civil Engineering; Coastal Resources Management; Economics; Law; Medicine; Zoology (PhD), 3-5 yrs

Student Services: Academic counselling, Canteen, Cultural centre, Employment services, Health services, Language programs, Nursery care, Social counselling, Sports facilities

Libraries: Central Library, c. 100,000 vols; Faculty Libraries

Publications: Bulletin of the University *(monthly)*; Citra Leka *(quarterly)*; FORUM *(quarterly)*; Ilmu Kelauten *(quarterly)*; Journal of Coastal Development *(quarterly)*; Jurnal Bisnis Strategi *(quarterly)*; Jurnal dan Pengembangan *(quarterly)*; Jurnal Matematika dan Komputer *(quarterly)*; Jurnal Sains dan Matematika *(quarterly)*; Kajian Sastra *(quarterly)*; Keairan *(quarterly)*; Manunggal *(monthly)*; Masalah Hukum *(quarterly)*; Masalah-Masalah Hukum *(quarterly)*; Media Ekonomi dan Bisnis *(quarterly)*; Media Komunikasi Teknik Sipil *(quarterly)*; Media Medika Indonesia *(quarterly)*; Media Medika Indonesiana *(bimonthly)*; Media/Jurnal Pengembangan Peternaken Tropic *(quarterly)*; Pilar *(quarterly)*; Reaktor *(quarterly)*; Sellula *(quarterly)*; Tata Loka *(monthly)*; Teknik *(quarterly)*; Undip Newsletter *(quarterly)*

Press or Publishing House: Diponegoro University Press Board

Last Updated: 05/07/11

GAJAH MADA UNIVERSITY

Universitas Gadjah Mada

Kampus Bulaksumur, Yogyakarta, 55281 Yogyakarta
Tel: +62(274) 588-688 +62(274) 562-011
Fax: +62(274) 565-223
EMail: setr@ugm.ac.id
Website: http://www.ugm.ac.id/

Rector: Ir. Sudjarwadi
EMail: rektor@ugm.ac.id; sudjarwadi-ugm@ugm.ac.id

Senior Vice-Rector, Education, Research, and Community Service: Retno Sunarminingsih EMail: wrsp3m@ugm.ac.id

International Relations: Rachmat Sriwijaya, Head of Office of International Affairs
Tel: +62(274) 649-1833 +62(274) 563-974,
Fax: +62(274) 552-810 EMail: head-oia@ugm.ac.id

Centres

Agroecology Studies (Agriculture; Ecology) *Director*: Erny Oedjirahajo; **Asia-Pacific Studies** (Asian Studies; Pacific Area Studies) *Director*: P.M. Laksono; **Biological Control Studies** (Biology) *Director*: Fransiscus Xaverius Wagiman; **Biotechnology** *Director*: Widya Asmara; **Clinical Pharmacology and Drug Policy Studies**

(Pharmacology; Toxicology) *Director*: Sri Suryawati; **Cultural Studies** (Cultural Studies; Social Studies) *Director*: Widya Nayati; **Economic Democracy Studies** (Economics; Social Sciences) *Director*: San Afri Awang; **Economics and Public Policy Studies** (Economics; Political Sciences; Public Administration) *Director*: Antonius Tony Prasetiantono; **Energy Studies Research** (Energy Engineering) *Director*: Jumina; **Engineering Sciences Studies** (Engineering) *Director*: Nur Yuwono; **Environmental Studies** (Environmental Studies) *Director*: Hari Kusnanto Josef; **Food and Nutrition Studies** (Food Science; Health Sciences; Nutrition) *Director*: Eni Harmayani; **German Studies** (German) *Director*: Kwartarini Wahyu Yuniarti; **Japanese Studies** (Japanese) *Director*: Irfan Dwidya Prijambada; **Korea Studies Research** (Southeast Asian Studies) *Director*: Djoko Suryo; **Land Resources Research** (Natural Resources) *Director*: Darmanto; **Logistics and Transportation Studies** (Transport and Communications; Transport Management) *Director*: Kuncoro Harto Widodo; **Natural Disaster Studies** (Safety Engineering) *Director*: Sunarto; **Pancasila Studies** (Cultural Studies; Indonesian) *Director*: Sindung Tjahyadi; **Population and Policy Studies** (Demography and Population) *Director*: Muhadjir Muhammad Darwin; **Regional Planning and Development Studies** (Development Studies) *Director*: R. Rijanta; **Religious and Cross-Cultural Studies** (Cultural Studies; Religious Studies) *Director*: Achmad Mursyidi; **Rural and Regional Development Research** (Regional Planning; Rural Studies) *Director*: Dyah Ismoyowati; **Security and Peace Research** (Peace and Disarmament) *Director*: Mohammad Mohtar Masoed; **South East Asia and Social Studies** (Asian Studies; Social Studies; Southeast Asian Studies) *Director*: Aris Arif Mundayat; **Tourism Research and Development** (Tourism) *Director*: Muhammad Baiquni; **Women's Studies** (Women's Studies) *Director*: Sri Djohar Winarlien Sugiharto

Faculties

Agricultural Technology (Agricultural Engineering; Food Science; Food Technology) *Dean*: Djagal Wiseso Marseno; **Agriculture** (Agricultural Business; Agricultural Economics; Agricultural Engineering; Agriculture; Agronomy; Aquaculture; Entomology; Fishery; Food Science; Food Technology; Microbiology; Plant Pathology; Soil Science) *Dean*: Triwibowo Yuwono; **Animal Husbandry** (Animal Husbandry; Zoology) *Dean*: Tri Yuwanta; **Biology** (Biology) *Dean*: Retno Peni Sancayaningsih; **Cultural Studies** (American Studies; Anthropology; Arabic; Archaeology; Arts and Humanities; Cultural Studies; English; Fine Arts; French; History; Indonesian; Japanese; Linguistics; Literature; Middle Eastern Studies; Native Language; Performing Arts) *Dean*: Ida Rochani; **Dentistry** (Dentistry) *Dean*: Soehardono; **Economics** (Accountancy; Development Studies; Economics; Management) *Dean*: Marwan Asri; **Engineering** (Chemical Engineering; Civil Engineering; Electrical Engineering; Engineering; Environmental Management; Geological Engineering; Industrial Engineering; Information Technology; Mechanical Engineering; Nuclear Engineering; Regional Planning; Safety Engineering; Structural Architecture; Town Planning; Transport Engineering; Water Management) *Dean*: Tumiran; **Forestry** (Forest Management; Forest Products; Forestry) *Dean*: Mohammad Na'iem; **Geography** (Environmental Studies; Geography; Geography (Human); Regional Planning; Surveying and Mapping) *Dean*: Suratman; **Law** (Commercial Law; Law) *Dean*: Marsudi Triatmodjo; **Mathematics and Natural Sciences** (Chemistry; Computer Science; Geophysics; Information Management; Mathematics; Natural Sciences; Physics; Statistics) *Dean*: Chairil Anwar; **Medicine** (Medicine; Nursing; Nutrition; Occupational Health; Public Health; Tropical Medicine) *Dean*: Ali Ghufron Mukti; **Pharmacy** (Pharmacy) *Dean*: Marchaban; **Philosophy** (Philosophy) *Dean*: Mukhtasar Syamsuddin; **Postgraduate Studies** (American Studies; Biotechnology; Comparative Religion; Cultural Studies; Demography and Population; Environmental Studies; Fine Arts; Information Management; Library Science; Media Studies; Middle Eastern Studies; Peace and Disarmament; Performing Arts; Political Sciences; Public Administration; Safety Engineering; Tourism) *Director*: Hartono; **Psychology** (Psychology) *Dean*: Faturochman; **Social and Political Sciences** (Communication Studies; Government; International Relations; Political Sciences; Public Administration; Social Sciences; Sociology) *Dean*: Pratikno; **Veterinary Medicine** (Veterinary Science) *Dean*: Bambang Sumiarto

Institutes

Learning and Community Empowerment *Chairman*: Danang Parikesit

Laboratories

Integrated Research and Testing Laboratory (Biological and Life Sciences; Chemistry; Physical Chemistry) *Chairman*: Sismindari

Further Information: Also Teaching Hospital. Cultural courses in Indonesian language; courses for foreign students; Language Training Center

History: Founded 1949 by merging of six existing Faculties. A State University.

Governing Bodies: Board of Curators; Senate

Academic Year: August to July (August-January; February-July)

Admission Requirements: Secondary school certificate (Sekolah Menengah Atas, SMA) and entrance examination

Fees: (US Dollars): 1,000-1,500 per semester

Main Language(s) of Instruction: Indonesian; English

Accrediting Agencies: National Accreditation Agency for Higher Education (Badan Akreditasi Nasional Perguruan Tinggi)

Degrees and Diplomas: *Diploma*: 3 yrs; *Sarjana (S1)*: 4 yrs; *Magister (S2)*: a further 2 yrs; *Doktor (S3)*: 3 yrs

Student Services: Academic counselling, Canteen, Cultural centre, Foreign student adviser, Health services, Social counselling, Sports facilities

Student Residential Facilities: Yes

Special Facilities: Museum: Biology; Paleoanthropology. Wanagama Forest; Tea Plantation

Libraries: Central Library, 101,221 vols

Publications: Agritech *(quarterly)*; Aspac News *(monthly)*; Berkala Ilmiah Biologi, Biology *(biannually)*; Berkala Ilmiah MIPA, Mathematics and Natural Sciences *(biannually)*; Berkala Ilmu Kedokteran, Medicine *(quarterly)*; Berkala Penelitian Pascasarjana *(quarterly)*; Buletin Kehutanan, Forestry *(quarterly)*; Buletin Peternakan, Animal Husbandry *(3 per annum)*; Dinamika Pedesaan & Kawasan *(3 per annum)*; Indonesian Journal of Biotechnology *(biannually)*; Indonesian Journal of Geography *(biannually)*; Journal of Agricultural Science *(annually)*; Journal of Economics (in Indonesian) *(3 per annum)*; Journal of Food and Nutrition Progress *(biannually)*; Journal of Medicine (in Indonesian); Jurnal Ekonomi dan Bisnis Indonesia, Economic and Business Journal *(quarterly)*; Jurnal Psikologi Indonesia, Psychology *(biannually)*; Kebijaksanaan Administrasi Publik, Public Policy Administration *(biannually)*; Majalah Energi *(quarterly)*; Majalah Farmasi Indonesia, Pharmacy *(quarterly)*; Majalah Ilmu Kedokteran Gigi, Dentistry Magazine *(3 per annum)*; Media Gama *(3 per annum)*; Media Teknik, Engineering *(quarterly)*; Pilsafat Pancasila, Pancasila Philosophy *(3 per annum)*; Populations, Community Service *(quarterly)*; Sains Veterinary *(biannually)*; Social and Political Science Journal *(3 per annum)*; Warta Pengabdian LPM UGM *(biannually)*

Press or Publishing House: Gadjah Mada University Press

Last Updated: 24/06/11

GANESHA UNIVERSITY OF EDUCATION

Universitas Pendidikan Ganesha (UNDIKSHA)

Jalan Ahmad Yani 67, Singaraja, 81116 Bali

Tel: +62(362) 22570

Fax: +62(362) 25735

EMail: humas@undiksha.ac.id

Website: http://www.undiksha.ac.id

Rector: Nyoman Sudiana

Vice-Rector: Gusti Putu Suharta

Faculties

Education; **Humanities and Social Science Education**; **Languages and Arts**; **Mathematics and Natural Sciences Education**; **Sports and Health**; **Technology and Vocational Studies** (Cooking and Catering; Electronic Engineering; Information Technology; Social Welfare; Technology Education; Welfare and Protective Services)

Degrees and Diplomas: *Sarjana (S1)*; *Magister (S2)*

Last Updated: 31/05/10

GENERAL SOEDIRMAN UNIVERSITY

Universitas Jenderal Soedirman

Jalan Prof. H. Boenyamin 708, Purwokerto, 53122 Jawa Tengah
Tel: +62(281) 635-292 +62(281) 635-293
Fax: +62(281) 631-802
EMail: kusja@unsoed.ac.id; info@unsoed.ac.id
Website: http://www.unsoed.ac.id

Rector: Sudjarwo

Vice-Rector I: Nurul Anwar

Faculties

Agriculture (Agricultural Business; Agricultural Economics; Agricultural Engineering; Agricultural Management; Agriculture; Agronomy; Biology; Environmental Studies; Fishery; Food Science; Food Technology; Natural Resources; Plant Pathology; Soil Science); **Animal Science** (Animal Husbandry; Zoology); **Economics** (Accountancy; Development Studies; Economics; Finance; International Business; Management; Secretarial Studies); **Law** (Law); **Medicine and Public Health** (Dentistry; Medicine; Nursing; Pharmacy; Public Health); **Science and Technology** (Chemistry; Civil Engineering; Computer Science; Electrical Engineering; Fishery; Geological Engineering; Industrial Engineering; Marine Science and Oceanography; Mathematics; Physics; Water Management); **Social and Political Sciences** (Chinese; Communication Studies; English; English Studies; Government; Indonesian; International Relations; Japanese; Political Sciences; Public Administration; Social Sciences; Sociology)

Programmes

Postgraduate Studies (Accountancy; Administration; Agronomy; Biology; Economics; Environmental Studies; Law; Management; Public Administration; Zoology)

Units

Applied Language Studies *(UPT Bidang)* (English)

History: Founded 1963.

Governing Bodies: Board of Regents; Senate; Faculty Councils

Academic Year: January to December (January-June; August-December)

Admission Requirements: Secondary school certificate (Sekolah Menengah Atas, SMA) and entrance examination

Main Language(s) of Instruction: Indonesian

Degrees and Diplomas: *Sarjana (S1)*: 5 yrs; *Magister (S2)*: Accounting; Agronomy; Animal science; Biology; Economics; Environmental studies; Law; Management; Public Administration

Libraries: Central Library, c. 3,500 vols; faculty libraries

Last Updated: 06/07/11

GORONTALO STATE UNIVERSITY

Universitas Negeri Gorontalo

Jln. Jenderal Sudirman 6, Kotak Pos 5, Gorontalo, 96128 Gorontalo
Tel: +62(435) 821-125
Fax: +62(435) 821-752
EMail: rektorat@ung.ac.id
Website: http://www.ung.ac.id/

Rector: Syamsu Qamar Badu

Vice-Rector Planning, Administration and Finance: Eduart Wolok

Faculties

Agriculture (Agricultural Engineering; Agriculture; Animal Husbandry; Aquaculture; Crop Production; Fishery; Food Technology); **Economics and Business** (Accountancy; Business Administration; Economics; Management; Secretarial Studies); **Education** (Education; Educational Administration; Educational and Student Counselling; Physical Education); **Engineering** (Architecture; Civil Engineering; Electrical Engineering; Electronic Engineering; Engineering; Handicrafts; Industrial Engineering; Information Management; Information Technology; Structural Architecture); **Health Sciences and Sports** (Health Sciences; Pharmacy; Physical Education; Public Health; Sports; Sports Management); **Literature and Culture** (Cultural Studies; English; Indonesian; Literature; Tourism); **Mathematics and Natural Sciences** (Biological and Life Sciences; Biology; Chemistry; Geography; Mathematics; Physics); **Social Sciences** (Accountancy; Civics; Communication Studies; Economics; Government; History; Management; Secretarial Studies)

Programmes

Postgraduate Studies (Biology; Demography and Population; Educational Administration; English; Environmental Studies; Foreign Languages Education; Mathematics Education; Physical Education; Primary Education)

History: Founded 1963 as Junior College FKIP Unsulteng. Acquired present status and title 2004.

Degrees and Diplomas: *Diploma*; *Sarjana (S1)*; *Magister (S2)*: Basic Education; Biology Education; Educational Administration; English Education; Mathematics Education; Physical Education; Population and Environment

Student Services: Academic counselling, Canteen, Cultural centre, Foreign Studies Centre, Health services, Language programs, Sports facilities

Libraries: Yes

Last Updated: 06/07/11

HALUOLEO UNIVERSITY

Universitas Haluoleo

Kampus Bumi Tridharma, Anduonohu, Kendari, 93232 Sulawesi Tenggara
Tel: +62(401) 390-106 +62(401) 390-105
Fax: +62(401) 390-006
EMail: bapsi@.unhalu.ac.id; bauk@unhalu.ac.id; priv@unhalu.ac.id
Website: http://www.unhalu.ac.id

Rector: Usman Rianse
Tel: +62(401) 390-105, Fax: +62(401) 390-403

Centres

Computer Science and Information Systems (Computer Science; Information Technology); **Ecological Studies** (Ecology); **Population Studies** (Demography and Population); **Rural Areas Development Studies** (Development Studies; Rural Studies)

Faculties

Agriculture (Agricultural Business; Agricultural Economics; Agriculture; Agronomy; Animal Husbandry; Aquaculture; Forestry; Natural Resources; Plant Pathology; Soil Science; Water Management; Water Science); **Economics** (Accountancy; Administration; Development Studies; Economics; Management); **Engineering** (Architecture; Civil Engineering; Electrical Engineering; Electronic Engineering; Engineering; Mechanical Engineering; Structural Architecture); **Fisheries and Marine Sciences** (Fishery; Marine Science and Oceanography); **Law** (Law); **Mathematics and Natural Sciences** (Biology; Chemistry; Community Health; Health Education; Mathematics; Mathematics and Computer Science; Natural Sciences; Pharmacy; Physics; Public Health); **Social and Political Sciences** (Administration; Anthropology; Government; Law; Political Sciences; Secretarial Studies; Social Sciences; Sociology); **Teacher Training and Educational Sciences** (Accountancy; Art Education; Biology; Business Education; Chemistry; Civics; Economics; Educational Psychology; Educational Sciences; English; Foreign Languages Education; Health Education; History; Humanities and Social Science Education; Indonesian; Literature; Mathematics; Mathematics Education; Native Language; Natural Sciences; Physical Education; Physics; Preschool Education; Primary Education; Regional Studies; Science Education; Social Sciences; Sports; Teacher Training)

Institutes

Community Service (Social and Community Services); **Social Research** (Social Studies)

Further Information: Also Open University

History: Founded 1964 as private institution. Acquired present status 1981. A State institution under the jurisdiction of the Department of Education and Culture.

Academic Year: July to June (July-December; January-June)

Admission Requirements: Secondary school certificate (Sekolah Lanjutan Tingkat Atas, SLTA)

Main Language(s) of Instruction: Indonesian

Degrees and Diplomas: *Diploma*: 1-3 yrs; *Sarjana (S1)*: 4 yrs; *Magister (S2) (S2)*: a further 2 yrs

Student Services: Academic counselling, Language programs

Libraries: c. 20,000 vols

Publications: Agriplus *(bimonthly)*; Gema Pendidikan *(bimonthly)*; Mimbar Academic *(bimonthly)*

Last Updated: 19/05/11

HASANUDDIN UNIVERSITY

Universitas Hasanuddin (UNHAS)

Kampus UNHAS Tamalanrea, Jalan Perintis Kemerdekaan Km.10, Makassar, 90245 South Sulawesi
Tel: +62(411) 586-200 +62(411) 584-200
Fax: +62(411) 585-188
EMail: cio@unhas.ac.id; humas@unhas.ac.id
Website: http://www.unhas.ac.id

Rector: Idrus A. Paturusi EMail: rector@unhas.ac.id

Vice-Rector for Academic Affairs: Dadang Ahmad Suriamihardja Tel: +62(411) 586-028 EMail: vicerector1@unhas.ac.id

International Relations: Dwia Aries Tina P.K., Vice-Rector for Cooperation Planning and Development
Tel: +62(411) 580-303 EMail: vicerector4@unhas.ac.id

Centres

Languages (English; Modern Languages); **Research**

Faculties

Agriculture (Agricultural Economics; Agricultural Engineering; Agriculture; Agronomy; Plant Pathology; Soil Science); **Culture and Literature** (Arabic; Archaeology; Arts and Humanities; Asian Studies; English; French; History; Indonesian; Japanese; Literature; Native Language; Tourism); **Dentistry** (Dental Technology; Dentistry); **Economics** (Accountancy; Development Studies; Economics; Management); **Engineering** (Civil Engineering; Electrical Engineering; Engineering; Geological Engineering; Industrial Engineering; Marine Transport; Mechanical Engineering; Naval Architecture; Structural Architecture); **Forestry** (Forest Management; Forest Products; Forestry); **Law** (Law); **Livestock Science** (Agricultural Economics; Animal Husbandry; Cattle Breeding; Food Science); **Marine and Fisheries** (Fishery; Marine Science and Oceanography; Water Management); **Mathematics and Natural Sciences** (Biology; Chemistry; Mathematics; Natural Sciences; Pharmacy; Physics; Statistics); **Medicine** (Medicine; Nursing); **Pharmacy** (Pharmacy); **Public Health** (Nutrition; Public Health); **Social and Political Sciences** (Anthropology; Communication Studies; Government; International Relations; Library Science; Political Sciences; Social Sciences; Sociology)

Institutes

Community Service (Social and Community Services); **Distance Learning** (Social and Community Services); **Educational Development** (Development Studies; Educational Sciences; Human Resources; Safety Engineering); **Research**

Programmes

Postgraduate Studies (Administration; Agriculture; Biomedicine; Chemistry; Communication Studies; Economics; Engineering; Environmental Studies; Farm Management; Law; Linguistics; Medicine; Modern Languages; Urban Studies)

History: Founded 1948 as Faculties of Economics and Law attached to the University of Indonesia. Acquired present status and title 1956.

Governing Bodies: University Council

Academic Year: September to June (September-January; February-June)

Admission Requirements: Secondary school certificate (Sekolah Lanjutan Atas, SLA), and entrance examination

Main Language(s) of Instruction: Indonesian

International Co-operation: Sun Moon University; Newcastle University; Kyoto University; Ehime University; Universiti Utara Malaysia

Accrediting Agencies: Department of National Education

Degrees and Diplomas: *Sarjana (S1)*; *Magister (S2)*; *Doktor (S3)*

Student Services: Academic counselling, Canteen, Cultural centre, Foreign student adviser, Handicapped facilities, Health services, Nursery care, Social counselling, Sports facilities

Student Residential Facilities: Yes

Special Facilities: Auditorium. Ranch

Libraries: Central Library, c. 150,000 vols; Faculty Libraries

Publications: Amanagappa *(3 per annum)*; Economy *(quarterly)*; Engineering *(quarterly)*; Lontara Majalah Universitas Hasanuddin *(3 per annum)*; Medical Nusantara *(3 per annum)*; Torani *(3 per annum)*

Press or Publishing House: Hasanuddin Publishing Press

Last Updated: 06/06/11

INDONESIA UNIVERSITY

Universitas Indonesia

UI Depok Campus, Jakarta, 16424 DKI Jakarta
Tel: +62(21) 786-7222
Fax: +62(21) 7884-9060
EMail: humas-ui@ui.ac.id; io-ui@ui.ac.id
Website: http://www.ui.ac.id

President: Gumilar Rusliwa Somantri Tel: +62 (21) 727-0020

Vice-President for Human Resources, Finance, and General Administration Affairs: Tafsir Nurchamid
EMail: humas-ui@ui.ac.id

Centres

Development Research (Development Studies); **Family Welfare** (Social Welfare); **Health Research** (Health Sciences); **Human Resources and Environment Research** (Environmental Studies; Human Resources); **Science and Technology Research** (Natural Sciences; Technology); **Social and Cultural Studies** (Cultural Studies; Social Studies)

Faculties

Arts and Humanities (Arabic; Archaeology; Arts and Humanities; Chinese; Dutch; English; French; Germanic Languages; History; Indonesian; Information Sciences; Japanese; Korean; Library Science; Linguistics; Literature; Philosophy; Russian; South and Southeast Asian Languages); **Computer Science** (Computer Science; Information Technology); **Dentistry** (Community Health; Dental Hygiene; Dental Technology; Dentistry; Oral Pathology; Orthodontics; Periodontics; Stomatology); **Economics** (Accountancy; Development Studies; Economics; Management; Regional Planning; Town Planning); **Engineering** (Architecture; Chemical Engineering; Civil Engineering; Computer Engineering; Electrical Engineering; Electronic Engineering; Engineering; Environmental Engineering; Industrial Engineering; Interior Design; Laser Engineering; Marine Engineering; Materials Engineering; Mechanical Engineering; Metallurgical Engineering; Naval Architecture; Structural Architecture); **Law** (Law; Notary Studies); **Mathematics and Natural Sciences** (Biology; Chemistry; Geography; Marine Science and Oceanography; Mathematics; Natural Sciences; Pharmacy; Physics); **Medicine** (Anaesthesiology; Anatomy; Biomedicine; Cardiology; Dermatology; Forensic Medicine and Dentistry; Gynaecology and Obstetrics; Medicine; Microbiology; Neurology; Nutrition; Occupational Health; Ophthalmology; Orthopaedics; Otorhinolaryngology; Paediatrics; Pathology; Pharmacology; Plastic Surgery; Pneumology; Psychiatry and Mental Health; Radiology; Rehabilitation and Therapy; Sports Medicine; Surgery; Urology); **Nursing** (Nursing); **Psychology** (Clinical Psychology; Education; Industrial and Organizational Psychology; Psychology); **Public Health** (Behavioural Sciences; Environmental Studies; Epidemiology; Health Administration; Health Education; Nutrition; Occupational Health; Public Health); **Social and Political Sciences** (Administration; Anthropology; Business Administration; Communication Studies; Criminology; Government; International Relations; Mass Communication; Political Sciences; Social Sciences; Social Welfare; Sociology)

Institutes

Research; **Social Services** (Social and Community Services)

Programmes

Education and Social Services (Educational Administration; Social and Community Services); **Justice and the Role of Law** (Ethics; Justice Administration; Law); **Postgraduate Studies - Master** (Accountancy; Administration; American Studies; Anthropology; Archaeology; Architecture; Biology; Biomedicine; Biotechnology; Chemical Engineering; Chemistry; Civil Engineering; Clinical Psychology; Communication Studies; Community Health;

Computer Science; Demography and Population; Dentistry; Economics; Electrical Engineering; Electronic Engineering; Engineering; Epidemiology; European Studies; Geography; Health Administration; History; Industrial and Organizational Psychology; Industrial Engineering; Information Sciences; Information Technology; International Relations; Islamic Studies; Laser Engineering; Law; Library Science; Linguistics; Literature; Management; Marine Science and Oceanography; Mathematics; Mechanical Engineering; Medicine; Metallurgical Engineering; Middle Eastern Studies; Notary Studies; Nursing; Nutrition; Occupational Health; Optics; Pharmacy; Philosophy; Physics; Police Studies; Political Sciences; Psychology; Public Health; Regional Planning; Social Welfare; Sociology; Structural Architecture; Town Planning; Women's Studies); **Postgraduate Studies - PhD** (Accountancy; Administration; Anthropology; Archaeology; Biology; Biomedicine; Chemical Engineering; Chemistry; Civil Engineering; Communication Studies; Computer Science; Dentistry; Economics; Electrical Engineering; Electronic Engineering; Environmental Studies; Epidemiology; History; Laser Engineering; Law; Linguistics; Literature; Management; Mechanical Engineering; Medicine; Nursing; Nutrition; Optometry; Paediatrics; Philosophy; Political Sciences; Psychology; Public Health; Sociology); **Regional Development** (Regional Planning); **Social Communication Services** (Communication Studies; Social and Community Services)

Further Information: Also Teaching Hospitals. Courses for foreign students. Study Abroad programme

History: Founded 1950, incorporating the Balai Perguruan Tinggi Republik Indonesia (Institution of Higher Learning of the Republic of Indonesia) and Universiteit van Indonesia. Faculties in Bandung, Surabaya and Makassar have since been incorporated in newly-established State universities.

Governing Bodies: Senate

Academic Year: August to July (August-January; February-July)

Admission Requirements: Secondary school certificate (Sekolah Lanjutan Atas, SLA) and entrance examination

Main Language(s) of Instruction: Indonesian

International Co-operation: With universities in Australia; Chine; Japan; Netherlands; Singapore and USA

Degrees and Diplomas: *Diploma*; *Sarjana (S1)*: 4 yrs; *Magister (S2)*: 2-3 yrs; *Doktor (S3)*: 2-3 yrs following Magister

Student Services: Academic counselling, Canteen, Cultural centre, Employment services, Foreign student adviser, Health services, Social counselling, Sports facilities

Student Residential Facilities: Yes

Special Facilities: Pathology Museum. Anatomy Museum

Libraries: Faculty libraries, c. 475,700 vols; Central Library, c. 17,150 vols

Publications: Access *(biannually)*; Buletin Ekonomi *(quarterly)*; Buletin Kedokteran *(quarterly)*; Der Schussel *(monthly)*; Economica *(monthly)*; Ekonomi dan Keuangan Indonesia *(quarterly)*; Gaung *(quarterly)*; Jurnal Administrasi Rumah Sakit; Jurnal Alumni Komunikasi *(bimonthly)*; Jurnal Antropologi *(quarterly)*; Jurnal Arabia *(biannually)*; Jurnal Ilmu Administrasi *(quarterly)*; Jurnal Ilmu Politik *(quarterly)*; Jurnal Kedokteran Gigi *(quarterly)*; Jurnal Sains Indonesia *(quarterly)*; Jurnal Sosiologi *(bimonthly)*; Jurnal Teknologi *(quarterly)*; Lintas Bahasa *(quarterly)*; Majalah Demografi Indonesia *(bimonthly)*; Majalah Hukum dan Pembangunan *(bimonthly)*; Majalah Ilmu Ilmu Sastra Indonesia *(biannually)*; Makara lembaga penelitian *(quarterly)*; Management dan Usahawan *(monthly)*; Media Aesculapius *(monthly)*; Medical Journal Indonesia *(quarterly)*; Romantika Arkeologia *(quarterly)*; Slavonik *(biannually)*; Stofzuiger (first publish); Suara Mahasiswa *(quarterly)*; Turning Point *(monthly)*; Utthana *(bimonthly)*

Press or Publishing House: University of Indonesia Press. Faculty of Economics Press. Faculty of Medicine Press

Last Updated: 05/07/11

INDONESIA UNIVERSITY OF EDUCATION

Universitas Pendidikan Indonesia (UPI)

Jalan Dr. Setiabudhi 229, Bandung, 40154 Jawa Barat
Tel: +62(22) 201-3162 +62(22) 201-3651
Fax: +62(22) 201-3651
EMail: info@upi.edu
Website: http://www.upi.edu

Rector: Sunaryo Kartadinata
Tel: +62(22) 201-3158 EMail: rektor@upi.edu

Vice-Rector: Adeng Chaedar Alwasilah EMail: pr1@upi.edu

Faculties

Business and Economy (Accountancy; Administration; Business Administration; Economics; Management); **Educational Sciences** (Curriculum; Education; Educational Administration; Educational and Student Counselling; Educational Technology; Preschool Education; Primary Education; Special Education); **Language and Art Education** (Arabic; Art Education; Dance; English; Fine Arts; Foreign Languages Education; French; German; Handicrafts; Indonesian; Japanese; Modern Languages; Music; Theatre; Visual Arts); **Mathematics and Natural Sciences Education** (Biology; Chemistry; Mathematics Education; Physics; Science Education); **Postgraduate Studies** (Administration; Curriculum; Distance Education; Education; Educational and Student Counselling; English; Health Education; Indonesian; Mathematics Education; Natural Sciences; Social Sciences); **Social Sciences Education** (Accountancy; Business Administration; Civics; Geography; History; Management; Political Sciences; Social Sciences); **Sport and Health Education** (Health Education; Physical Education; Sports); **Technical and Vocational Education** (Automotive Engineering; Civil Engineering; Construction Engineering; Electrical Engineering; Home Economics Education; Mechanical Engineering; Technology Education)

History: Founded 1954 as Higher Education Institute for Teacher Education (PIPG), became Institute of Teacher Training and Educational Sciences (IKIP) 1963 and acquired present status and title 1999.

Governing Bodies: Board of Trustees

Academic Year: September to August (September-January; February-July; July-August)

Admission Requirements: Secondary or vocational school certificate, and entrance examination

Fees: (Rupiahs): 950,000 per annum; foreign students, USD 1,300 per annum

Main Language(s) of Instruction: Indonesian

Accrediting Agencies: National Accreditation Board, International Standard Organization

Degrees and Diplomas: *Diploma*: 3 yrs; *Sarjana (S1)*; *Magister (S2)*; *Doktor (S3)*

Student Services: Academic counselling, Canteen, Cultural centre, Employment services, Foreign student adviser, Health services, Language programs, Nursery care, Social counselling, Sports facilities

Special Facilities: Biological Garden. Isola Heritage Museum. Open Theatre, Balai Pertemuan/Auditorium. Multimedia Language Laboratory

Libraries: 180,819 vols; 39,986 research papers

Publications: CIVICUS Jurnal Ilmu Politik, Hukum and PKN *(biennially)*; GEA Jurnal Geografi *(biennially)*; HISTORIA Jurnal Pendididakan Sejarah *(biennially)*; INVOTEC Jurnal Pendidikan Teknologi Kejuruan *(biennially)*; Isola Pos *(monthly)*; Jurnal Bimbingan and Konseling *(biennially)*; Jurnal Luar Sekolah *(biennially)*; Jurnal Penelitian *(3 per annum)*; Jurnal Pengabdian pada Masyarakat *(annually)*; Jurnal Pengajaran MIPA *(biennially)*; Mimbar Pendidikan *(quarterly)*

Press or Publishing House: University Press

Last Updated: 27/10/10

INDONESIAN INSTITUTE OF ART - DENPASAR

Institut Seni Indonesia Denpasar

Jalan Nusa Indah n°35, Denpasar 80235
Tel: +62(361) 227-316
Fax: +62(361) 236-100
EMail: info@isi-dps.ac.id
Website: http://www.isi-dps.ac.id

Rektor: Wayan Rai

Vice-Rector: Ketut Murdana

Faculties

Art and Design (Communication Arts; Design; Fine Arts; Handicrafts; Interior Design; Photography; Visual Arts); **Performing Arts** (Dance; Music; Performing Arts; Theatre)

Programmes
Postgraduate Studies (Design; Fine Arts; Performing Arts)

History: Founded 1967.

Degrees and Diplomas: *Sarjana (S1)*; *Magister (S2)*
Last Updated: 04/07/11

INDONESIAN INSTITUTE OF ART - SURAKARTA

Institut Seni Indonesia Surakarta
Jalan Ki Hajar Dewantara n°19, Kentingan, Jebres, Surakarta 57126
Tel: +62(271) 647-658
Fax: +62(217) 646-175
EMail: direct@isi-ska.ac.id
Website: http://www.isi-ska.ac.id

Rector: T. Slamet Suparno
Vice-Rector: Sri Rochana

Faculties
Fine Arts and Design (Design; Fine Arts); **Performing Arts** (Dance; Ethnology; Film; Music; Performing Arts; Radio and Television Broadcasting; Theatre)

Programmes
Postgraduate Studies
Last Updated: 02/03/10

INDONESIAN INSTITUTE OF ART - YOGYAKARTA

Institut Seni Indonesia Yogyakarta (ISI YOGYAKARTA)
PO Box 1210, Jl. Parangtritis Km. 65, Sewon Bantul, 55001 Yogyakarta
Tel: +62(274) 379-133 +62(274) 373-659
Fax: +62(274) 371-233
EMail: arts@isi.ac.id
Website: http://www.isi.ac.id

Rector: A.M. Hermien Kusmayati Tel: +62(274) 518-839

Vice-Rector I: Agus Burhan

International Relations: Syafruddin, Vice-Rector III

Faculties
Fine Arts (Communication Arts; Crafts and Trades; Design; Fine Arts; Graphic Arts; Handicrafts; Interior Design; Painting and Drawing; Sculpture; Visual Arts); **Performing Arts** (Acting; Dance; Display and Stage Design; Jazz and Popular Music; Music; Music Education; Music Theory and Composition; Musicology; Performing Arts; Theatre; Writing); **Recording and Media Arts** (Cinema and Television; Film; Media Studies; Photography; Radio and Television Broadcasting)

Programmes
Postgraduate Studies (Cultural Studies; Fine Arts; Media Studies; Performing Arts; Tourism; Visual Arts)

History: Founded 1984, by the merging of ASRI Art Academy, ASTI Dance Academy and AMI Music Academy. ISI Yogyakarta has become the largest Arts Institution in Indonesia, operates under its own Statute and Bylaws, which is funded by Government grants.

Governing Bodies: Senate

Academic Year: September to August (September-February; March-August)

Admission Requirements: Senior high school certificate and entrance examination

Main Language(s) of Instruction: Indonesian

Degrees and Diplomas: *Diploma*; *Sarjana (S1)*: 4 1/2 yrs; *Magister (S2)*; *Doktor (S3)*

Student Services: Academic counselling, Canteen, Foreign student adviser, Foreign Studies Centre, Language programs, Sports facilities

Special Facilities: Art Centre, Art Gallery. Auditorium. Studios.

Libraries: Central Library, c. 36,000 vols (23,000 titles)

Publications: Journal Ekspresi, Indonesia articles for the research's result of arts *(quarterly)*; Journal SENI, English Articles for Knowledge of Arts and Artwork Creation *(quarterly)*
Last Updated: 04/07/11

INDONESIAN SCHOOL OF ART - BANDUNG

Sekolah Tinggi Seni Indonesia Bandung
Jalan Buah Batu 212, Bandung 40265
Tel: +62(22) 731-4982
Fax: +62(22) 730-3021
EMail: stsi@stsi-bdg.ac.id
Website: http://www.stsi-bdg.ac.id

Direktor: Enoh

Programmes
Dance (Dance); **Fine Arts** (Fine Arts; Handicrafts); **Theatre** (Theatre); **Traditional Music Art** (Music; Performing Arts)

Degrees and Diplomas: *Sarjana (S1)*
Last Updated: 06/05/11

INDONESIAN SCHOOL OF ART - PADANG PANJANG

Sekolah Tinggi Seni Indonesia Padang Panjang
Jalan Bundo Kandung 35, Padang Panjang, 27128 Sumatera Barat
Tel: +62(752) 82077
Fax: +62(752) 82803
EMail: stsi_pdpanjang@hotmail.com

Direktor: Daryusti

Programmes
Art Creation and Assessment (Fine Arts); **Dance** (Dance); **Handicrafts** (Handicrafts); **Music** (Music); **Television and Film** (Cinema and Television); **Theatre** (Performing Arts)

Degrees and Diplomas: *Sarjana (S1)*; *Magister (S2)*
Last Updated: 01/06/10

JAMBI UNIVERSITY

Universitas Jambi
Kampus Pinang Masak, Mendalo Darat Km 15, Jambi, 63661 Jambi
Tel: +62(741) 583-377
Fax: +62(741) 583-111
EMail: unja@unja.ac.id
Website: http://www.unja.ac.id

Rector: Kemas Arsyad Somad Tel: +62(741) 583-255

Centres
Computer (Computer Science); **Research**; **Social Services** (Social and Community Services)

Faculties
Agriculture (Agricultural Business; Agricultural Economics; Agricultural Engineering; Agriculture; Agronomy; Plant and Crop Protection; Plant Pathology; Soil Science); **Animal Husbandry** (Agricultural Economics; Animal Husbandry; Nutrition); **Economics** (Accountancy; Development Studies; Economics; Management; Marketing; Taxation); **Education and Teacher Training** (Biology; Chemistry; Economics; Educational and Student Counselling; Educational Sciences; English; Foreign Languages Education; Health Education; Indonesian; Literature; Management; Mathematics Education; Native Language Education; Physics; Preschool Education; Primary Education; Science Education; Secondary Education; Sports; Teacher Training); **Law** (Administrative Law; Civil Law; Commercial Law; Criminal Law; International Law; Law; Public Law); **Medicine** (Medicine)

History: Founded 1963. A State institution under the jurisdiction of the Ministry of Education and Culture.

Academic Year: August to July (August-December; January-July)

Admission Requirements: Senior high school certificate (Sekolah Menengah Tingkat Atas, SLTA)

Main Language(s) of Instruction: Indonesian

Degrees and Diplomas: *Diploma*: 2-3 yrs; *Sarjana (S1)*: 5 yrs; *Magister (S2)*: Commercial Law; Criminal Law; Development Studies; Government Law; Management; Management Education; Education Environment

Special Facilities: Art Gallery.

Libraries: Central Library, c. 94,000 vols

Publications: Berita Universitas Jambi (magazine); Economic and Development Journal; Journal Penelitian Universitas Jambi (journal); Justitia (law journal)

Last Updated: 06/07/11

JEMBER UNIVERSITY

Universitas Jember (UNEJ)

PO Box 159, Jalan Kalimantan, Kampus Tegal Boto, Jember, 68121 Jawa Timur
Tel: +62(331) 330-334
Fax: +62(331) 339-029
EMail: baak@unej.ac.id; humas@unej.ac.id
Website: http://www.unej.ac.id

Rector: Tarsicius Sutikto (2007-)
Tel: +62(331) 337-422, Fax: +62(331) 337-422
EMail: rektor@unej.ac.id

Vice-Rector for Academic Affairs: Agus Subekti
EMail: pr1@unej.ac.id

International Relations: Kahar Muzakhar, Head of International Office and Collaboration EMail: internationaloffice@unej.ac.id

Departments

Nursing (Nursing); **Pharmacy** (Pharmacy)

Faculties

Agricultural Technology (Agricultural Engineering; Crop Production); **Agriculture** (Agricultural Economics; Agriculture; Agronomy; Plant Pathology; Soil Science); **Dentistry** (Dentistry); **Economics** (Accountancy; Administration; Development Studies; Economics; Management; Secretarial Studies); **Engineering** (Civil Engineering; Electrical Engineering; Engineering; Mechanical Engineering); **Law** (Administrative Law; Civil Law; Commercial Law; Criminal Law; Law); **Letters** (English; History; Indonesian; Literature); **Mathematics and Natural Sciences** (Biology; Chemistry; Mathematics; Natural Sciences; Physics); **Medicine** (Medicine; Tropical Medicine); **Public Health** (Public Health); **Social and Political Sciences** (Administration; Business Administration; International Relations; Political Sciences; Public Administration; Social Sciences; Social Welfare; Taxation; Tourism); **Teacher Training and Educational Sciences** (Art Education; Biology; Educational Sciences; English; History; Indonesian; Mathematics Education; Modern Languages; Natural Sciences; Physics; Primary Education; Science Education; Social Sciences; Teacher Training)

Programmes

Postgraduate (Administration; Agricultural Business; Agronomy; Economics; Law; Management)

History: Founded 1957 as a private University, affiliated to Brawijaja University 1963, acquired present status and title 1964. A State institution under the jurisdiction of the Department of National Education.

Academic Year: August to July (August-January; February-July)

Admission Requirements: Secondary school leaving certificate (Sekolah Menengah Umum, SMU) or equivalent, and entrance examination

Fees: (Rupiahs): c. 650,000-1.25m. per annum; admission fee for new students: 2m.-10m.

Main Language(s) of Instruction: Indonesian

International Co-operation: With Universities in USA., Philippines and Japan

Accrediting Agencies: Board of National Accreditation; Directorate General of Higher Education

Degrees and Diplomas: *Diploma*: 3 yrs; *Sarjana (S1)*: 3 yrs; *Magister (S2)*: 2 yrs; *Doktor (S3)*: 3 yrs

Student Services: Academic counselling, Canteen, Cultural centre, Employment services, Foreign student adviser, Foreign Studies Centre, Handicapped facilities, Health services, Language programs, Nursery care, Social counselling, Sports facilities

Student Residential Facilities: Yes

Libraries: Central Library, c. 220,000 vols

Publications: Agrijurnal: Jurnal Ilmu-ilmu Pertanian, Agricultural Publication *(biannually)*; Agroteknologi, Agricultural Technology Publication *(biannually)*; Aspirasi, Social publication *(quarterly)*; Bidedukasi: Jurnal biologi dan pembelajarannya, Educational publication *(biannually)*; Biomedis: Jurnal Ilmu Kedokteran dan Kesehatan, Medical Publication *(biannually)*; Ecpose: informatif, aktual, dan ilmiah, Economic publication *(quarterly)*; Hukum dan Masyarakat: Majalah ilmiah, Law Publication *(quarterly)*; IKESMA: Jurnal Ilmu Kesehatan Masyarakat, Public Health Publication *(biannually)*; JIBS: Jurnal ilmu bahasa dan sastra, Letters Publication *(biannually)*; Jurnal Akuntansi: Universitas Jember, Economic Publication *(biannually)*; Jurnal Bisnis dan Manajemen, Economic publication *(quarterly)*; Jurnal Ilmu Dasar, Basic Science publication *(biannually)*; Jurnal Ilmu ekonomiki, Economic Publication *(quarterly)*; Jurnal Ilmu Pengetahuan Sosial, Educational publication *(biannually)*; Jurnal Pendidikan Ekonomi, Educational publication *(biannually)*; Jurnal Pengendalian Hayati, Agricultural Publication *(biannually)*; Jurnal Rekayasa, Engineering Publication *(biannually)*; Jurnal Social Budaya dan Politik, Social publication *(biannually)*; Jurnal Teknik Pertanian, Agriculture Technology Publication *(biannually)*; Kultur: Jurnal sosial humaniora, Social Publication *(biannually)*; Lingua Franca: Jurnal ilmiah bahasa, pebelajarannya, Educational publication *(biannually)*; Majalah Ilmiah matematika dan statistika, Basic Science publication *(annually)*; Pancaran Pendidikan: Majalah ilmiah, Education publication *(quarterly)*; Rengganis: jurnal kajian dan Gender, Social Publication *(biannually)*; ROTOR: Jurnal Ilmiah teknik mesin, Engineering Publication *(biannually)*; Saintifika: Jurnal Ilmu Pend MIPA dan MIPA, Educational publication *(quarterly)*; Semiotika (Jurnal Ilmu Sastra dan Linguistik), Letters Publication *(quarterly)*; Spirulina: Jurnal Penelitian, Kesehatan dan Farmasi, Puublication of the Medicine and Pharmacy Research Institutes *(quarterly)*; STOMATOGNATIC: Jurnal Ilmu Kedokteran Gigi UNEJ, Dentistry Publication *(biannually)*; Tegalboto: Majalah Mahasiswa Universitas Jember, Student Association Publication *(quarterly)*

Press or Publishing House: Jember University Press

Last Updated: 06/06/11

LAMBUNG MANGKURAT UNIVERSITY

Universitas Lambung Mangkurat

PO Box 219, Jalan Brigjen H. Hasan Basry, Banjarmasin, 70123 Kalimantan Selatan
Tel: +62(511) 330-5195
Fax: +62(511) 330-5195
EMail: unlambjm@telkom.net
Website: http://www.unlam.ac.id/

Rector: Muhammad Ruslan

Faculties

Agriculture (Agricultural Business; Agricultural Management; Agronomy; Cattle Breeding; Plant and Crop Protection; Soil Science); **Economics** (Economics); **Engineering** (Chemical Engineering; Civil Engineering; Construction Engineering; Machine Building; Mining Engineering); **Fisheries** (Fishery; Natural Resources; Water Management); **Forestry** (Forest Management; Forest Products; Forestry); **Law** (Law); **Mathematics and Physical Science** (Mathematics; Physics); **Medicine** (Medicine; Public Health); **Social and Political Science** (Administration; Business Administration; Government)

Programmes

Area Development; **Education and Training**; **Entrepreneurship Development** (Management); **Field Practice and Business**; **Graduate Studies** (Agricultural Economics; Agronomy; Civil Engineering; Fishery; Foreign Languages Education; Forestry; Indonesian; Law; Literature; Management; Native Language; Public Administration); **Public Services** (Social and Community Services); **Science and Technology Applications** (Technology); **Women's Empowerment and Women's Roles** (Women's Studies)

Research Centres

Area Development; **Culture and Society**; **Environment Studies** (Environmental Studies); **Gambut and Swamp Area Studies**; **Gender Studies** (Gender Studies); **Human Rights Studies** (Human Rights); **Population Studies** (Demography and Population)

History: Founded 1958 by the Lambung Mangkurat Foundation, became a State university 1960.

Academic Year: September to July (September-January; February-July)

Admission Requirements: Secondary school certificate (Sekolah Menengah Atas, SMA) and entrance examination

Fees: (Rupiahs): c. 510,000-600,000

Main Language(s) of Instruction: Indonesian

Degrees and Diplomas: *Diploma*: 1-3 yrs; *Sarjana (S1)*: 4-5 yrs; *Magister (S2)*: 1-3 yrs

Student Residential Facilities: Yes

Libraries: Central Library, c. 44,600 vols

Publications: Agro Scientiae; Borneo; Fish Scientiae; Kalimantan Scientie; Mitafor; Orientasi; UNLAM Review; Vidya Karya; Wira Martas

Press or Publishing House: Media Kampus; Kopma (Koperasi Mahasiswa)

Last Updated: 06/06/11

LAMPUNG UNIVERSITY

Universitas Lampung (UNILA)

Jalan Prof. Dr. Sumantri Brojonegoro No.1, Bandar Lampung, 35145 Lampung
Tel: +62(721) 702-673 +62(721) 701-609
Fax: +62(721) 702-767
EMail: info@unila.ac.id
Website: http://www.unila.ac.id

Rector: Sugeng P. Harianto EMail: rektor@unila.ac.id

Vice-Rector II: Sulastri Ramli EMail: pr2@unila.ac.id

International Relations: Anshori Djausal, Vice-Rector IV EMail: pr4@unila.ac.id

Faculties

Agricultural Sciences (Agricultural Business; Agricultural Economics; Agricultural Engineering; Agriculture; Animal Husbandry; Communication Studies; Fishery; Forest Management; Harvest Technology; Plant and Crop Protection; Plant Pathology; Soil Science); **Economics** (Accountancy; Development Studies; Economics; Management); **Engineering** (Chemical Engineering; Civil Engineering; Electrical Engineering; Engineering; Mechanical Engineering); **Law** (Law); **Mathematics and Natural Sciences** (Mathematics; Natural Sciences); **Medicine** *(Preparatory)* (Medicine); **Social and Political Sciences** (Political Sciences; Social Sciences); **Teacher Training and Educational Science** (Arts and Humanities; Chemistry; Civics; Education; English; Foreign Languages Education; Geography; Health Education; History; Humanities and Social Science Education; Indonesian; Literature; Mathematics Education; Modern Languages; Natural Sciences; Physics; Primary Education; Science Education; Social Sciences; Sports; Teacher Training)

History: Founded 1961 as a branch of Sriwijaya University, acquired present status 1965. A State institution responsible to the Department of National Education, Republic of Indonesia.

Governing Bodies: Senate

Academic Year: August to July (August-December; February-July)

Admission Requirements: Secondary school certificate (Sekolah Lanjutan Tingkat Atas (SLTA)

Main Language(s) of Instruction: Indonesian

International Co-operation: With universities in France, Japan, Netherlands, United Kingdom and USA

Accrediting Agencies: National Accrediting Board (Badan akreditasi Nasional)

Degrees and Diplomas: *Diploma*; *Sarjana (S1)*; *Magister (S2)*; *Doktor (S3)*: Medicine

Student Services: Academic counselling, Canteen, Cultural centre, Employment services, Foreign student adviser, Foreign Studies Centre, Health services, Language programs, Social counselling

Special Facilities: Mosque; Student Activities Centre; Internet Centre

Libraries: Central Library, c. 3,600 vols; branch libraries, c. 78,000 exp.

Publications: Agritep, Journal on Agricultural Technology *(biennially)*; Agrotropika, Journal on Tropical Crops *(biennially)*; Hama dan Penyakit Tumbuhan, Journal on Pest and Disease *(biennially)*; Jurna Reformasi Hukum, Journal on Law Enforcement and Reformation *(biennially)*; Jurnal Aksara, Journal on Literature *(biennially)*; Jurnal Akuntansi dan Keuangan, Journal on Accounting and Finance *(biennially)*; Jurnal Bisnis dan Manajem, Journak on Business and Management *(biennially)*; Jurnal Educandum, Journal on Education *(biennially)*; Jurnal Ekonomi dan Bisnis, Journal on Economics and Business *(biennially)*; Jurnal Ilmu Pendidikan, Journal on Teaching *(biennially)*; Jurnal Justisia *(biennially)*; Jurnal Pendidikan dan Pembelajaran, Journal on Education and Teaching *(biennially)*; Jurnal Pendidikan IPS, Journal on Jumanities and Education *(biennially)*; Jurnal Pendidikan MIPA, Journal on Maths and Natural Sciences Teaching *(biennially)*; Komunitas, Journal on Communication Sciences *(biennially)*; Rekayasa, Journal on Engineering *(biennially)*; Sains dan Teknologi, Journal on Natural Sciences *(biennially)*; Sosioekonomika, Journal on Agricultural Social Sciences and Economics *(biennially)*; Tanah Tropika, Journal on Tropical Soils *(biennially)*; Teknologi dan Industri, Journal on Post Harvest Technology *(biennially)*

Press or Publishing House: Unit Pelaksana Teknis (UPT) Percetakan

Last Updated: 06/06/11

MALIKUSSALEH UNIVERSITY

Universitas Malikussaleh (UM)

Jalan Tengku Cik Ditiro 26, Lancang Garam, Lhokseumawe, Aceh
Tel: +62(645) 41-373
Fax: +62(645) 44-450
EMail: info@unimal.ac.id
Website: http://www.unimal.ac.id

Rector: Apridar (2006-) Tel: +62(645) 41-373

Assistant Rector I: Ferri Safriwardy

International Relations: Z. Iskandar, Assistant Rector IV

Faculties

Agriculture (Agricultural Business; Agriculture; Agronomy; Aquaculture); **Economics** (Accountancy; Business Administration; Economics; Management; Secretarial Studies); **Engineering** *(Samudera)* (Chemical Engineering; Civil Engineering; Computer Engineering; Electrical Engineering; Industrial Engineering; Information Technology; Mechanical Engineering; Structural Architecture); **Law** *(Umar)* (Law); **Social and Political Sciences** (Administration; Anthropology; Communication Studies; Political Sciences; Social Sciences; Sociology)

History: Founded 1989 and named after King Samudra Pasai Al-Malikussaleh. Acquired present status 2001.

Governing Bodies: Kabupaten Government Lhokseumawe

Admission Requirements: Senior high school certificate and Technical high school certificate

Main Language(s) of Instruction: Indonesian

Accrediting Agencies: Badan Akreditasi Nasional

Degrees and Diplomas: *Diploma*; *Sarjana (S1)*

Special Facilities: Computer Network; Application computer; CAD/CAM; Civil and Drawing Laboratories

Libraries: 3,171 vols

Publications: Emabis Journal, Economics *(quarterly)*; Pade Journal, Agriculture *(quarterly)*; Sainteks Journal, Engineering *(quarterly)*; Suloh Journal, Law *(quarterly)*; Suwa Journal, Social and Political Sciences *(quarterly)*; Voice Malikussaleh, Magazine *(quarterly)*

Last Updated: 06/06/11

MANADO STATE UNIVERSITY

Universitas Negeri Manado

Jalan Kampus UNIMA Tondano Tataaran, Tondano, Sulawesi Utara
Tel: +62(431) 321-845
Fax: +62(431) 321-866
EMail: admin@unima.ac.id
Website: http://www.unima.ac.id

Rector: Philoteus Edwin Tuerah

Vice-Rector I: Joppy Liando

Faculties

Economics (Administration; Economics; Management; Marketing; Public Administration); **Education** (Asian Religious Studies; Economics; Education; Education of the Handicapped; Educational and Student Counselling; Educational Sciences; Geography; Geography (Human); Health Education; History; Leisure Studies; Parks and

Recreation; Physical Education; Primary Education; Religious Education; Special Education; Sports; Sports Management; Teacher Training); **Engineering** (Civil Engineering; Electrical Engineering; Engineering; Mechanical Engineering; Technology; Wood Technology); **Languages and Literature** (Arts and Humanities; Dance; English; Fine Arts; French; German; Indonesian; Japanese; Literature; Modern Languages; Music; Native Language; Theatre); **Mathematics and Natural Sciences** (Biology; Chemistry; Mathematics; Natural Sciences; Physics); **Social Sciences** (Civics; Government; Law; Psychology; Social Sciences; Sociology); **Sport and Health Education** (Health Education; Physical Education; Sports)

Programmes

Postgraduate Studies (Biology; Chemistry; Educational Administration; Geography; Indonesian; Physics; Public Administration)

History: Founded 1955 as Institut Keguruan dan Ilmu Pendidikan Manado (IKIP Manado), acquired present status and title 1999.

Governing Bodies: Higher Education Senate

Academic Year: July to August

Admission Requirements: High school certificate and entrance examination

Main Language(s) of Instruction: Indonesian

Degrees and Diplomas: *Sarjana (S1)*: 4-7 yrs; *Magister (S2)*: Biology; Educational Administration; Indonesian Education; Public Administration

Student Services: Academic counselling, Canteen, Cultural centre, Foreign student adviser, Health services, Language programs, Social counselling, Sports facilities

Student Residential Facilities: Yes

Special Facilities: Laboratory. Arboretum

Libraries: Central and Faculty Libraries

Publications: Educational Journal *(annually)*; IKIP Manado Journal, Research Reports by Lecturers and Students *(annually)*

Last Updated: 07/07/11

MATARAM UNIVERSITY

Universitas Mataram (UNRAM)

Jl. Majapahit 62, Mataram, 83125 Nusa Tenggara Barat
Tel: +62(370) 633-007
Fax: +62(370) 636-041
EMail: rektor@unram.ac.id
Website: http://www.unram.ac.id

Rector: Mansur Ma'shum (2001-) Tel: +62(370) 633-004

Vice-Rector: Syahdan

Faculties

Agriculture (Agricultural Business; Agricultural Economics; Agricultural Engineering; Agriculture; Agronomy; Crop Production; Fishery; Forestry; Horticulture; Plant and Crop Protection; Soil Science); **Economics** (Accountancy; Development Studies; Economics; Management; Taxation; Tourism); **Education and Teacher Training** (Art Education; Biology; Chemistry; Civics; Education; English; Foreign Languages Education; Humanities and Social Science Education; Indonesian; Mathematics; Mathematics Education; Native Language Education; Natural Sciences; Physics; Science Education; Social Sciences; Teacher Trainers Education; Teacher Training); **Engineering** (Civil Engineering; Electrical Engineering; Engineering; Mechanical Engineering); **Law** (Administrative Law; Civil Law; Commercial Law; Constitutional Law; Criminal Law; Labour Law; Law; Taxation)); **Livestock** (Animal Husbandry; Nutrition); **Mathematics and Natural Sciences** (Biology; Chemistry; Mathematics; Nautical Science; Physics); **Medicine** (Medicine)

Programmes

Postgraduate Studies (Accountancy; Economics; Law; Management; Native Language Education; Natural Resources; Science Education)

Further Information: Also research centres and institutes

History: Founded 1962, acquired present status and title 2003. A public university under the jurisdiction of the Department of Education and Culture.

Academic Year: September to June (September-January; February-June)

Admission Requirements: Secondary school certificate (Sekolah Lanjutan Atas, SLA) and entrance examination

Main Language(s) of Instruction: Indonesian

International Co-operation: With universities in Australia

Accrediting Agencies: Badan Akreditasi Nasional (National Accrediting Board)

Degrees and Diplomas: *Diploma (D3)*: 3 yrs; *Diploma (D2)*: 2 yrs; *Sarjana (S1)*: 4 yrs; *Magister (S2)*: Accountancy; Dryland Resource Management; Economics; Indonesian Language Education; Law; Management; Management of Animal Resources; Science Education, 2 yrs

Student Services: Academic counselling, Canteen, Employment services, Health services, Language programs, Nursery care, Social counselling, Sports facilities

Student Residential Facilities: Yes

Libraries: Central Library, c. 80,720 vols

Publications: Agroteksos, Articles in the field of Agriculture, in Indonesian *(quarterly)*; Bovine, Articles in the field of Animal Husbandry, in Indonesian *(biannually)*; Distribusi dan Marginal, Articles in the field of Economics, in Indonesian *(quarterly)*; Gema Rinjani, Articles in the field of Education, in Indonesian *(biannually)*; Jati Suara, Articles in the field of Law, in Indonesian *(quarterly)*; Komunitas, Articles in the field of Economics *(quarterly)*; Piramida, Articles in the field of Demography and Social Sciences *(quarterly)*; Qryza, Articles in various fields of study, in Indonesian *(quarterly)*; Research Journal of Mataram University, Articles on various fields of study in Indonesian and English *(quarterly)*

Press or Publishing House: University Mataram Press

Last Updated: 06/07/11

MULAWARMAN UNIVERSITY

Universitas Mulawarman

PO Box 1068, Kampus Gunung Kelua 5, Samarinda, 75119 Kalimantan Timur
Tel: +62(541) 741-118
Fax: +62(541) 732-870
Website: http://www.unmul.ac.id

Rector: Achmad Ariffien Bratawinata

Vice-Rector: Maman Sutisna

Faculties

Agriculture (Agricultural Business; Agricultural Economics; Agricultural Engineering; Agriculture; Agronomy; Crop Production; Horticulture; Plant Pathology; Soil Science; Tropical Agriculture; Water Management); **Economics** (Accountancy; Business Administration; Development Studies; Economics; Management; Secretarial Studies); **Engineering** (Agricultural Engineering; Chemical Engineering; Civil Engineering; Engineering; Environmental Engineering; Industrial Engineering; Mining Engineering); **Fishery and Marine Science** (Aquaculture; Fishery; Marine Science and Oceanography; Natural Resources); **Forestry** (Forestry; Tropical Agriculture; Wood Technology); **Law** (Law); **Mathematics and Natural Science** (Biology; Chemistry; Mathematics; Natural Sciences; Physics; Statistics)); **Medicine** (Health Education; Medicine); **Pharmacy** (Pharmacy); **Public Health** (Public Health); **Social and Political Sciences** (Administration; Business Administration; Communication Studies; Government; International Relations; Political Sciences; Psychology; Public Administration; Social Sciences); **Teacher Training and Educational Sciences** (Biology; Chemistry; Civics; Economics; Educational and Student Counselling; Educational Sciences; English; Foreign Languages Education; Health Education; Indonesian; Leisure Studies; Literature; Mathematics Education; Native Language Education; Natural Sciences; Parks and Recreation; Physical Education; Physics; Preschool Education; Primary Education; Science Education; Social Sciences; Teacher Training)

Programmes

Postgraduate Studies (Economics; Educational Administration; English; Environmental Studies; Foreign Languages Education; Forestry; Management; Public Administration; Tropical Agriculture)

History: Founded 1962. A State institution under the jurisdiction of the Department of Education and Culture.

Governing Bodies: Board of Advisors

Academic Year: January to December (January-June; July-December)

Admission Requirements: Secondary school certificate (Sekolah Menengah Atas, SMA) and entrance examination

Main Language(s) of Instruction: Indonesian

Degrees and Diplomas: *Diploma*; *Sarjana (S1)*: 4-7 yrs; *Sarjana (S1)*: Engineering (Insinjur), 5 yrs; *Magister (S2)*: Economics; Educational Administration; English Education; Environmental Sciences; Forestry; Management; Public Administration; Wet Tropical Agriculture; *Doktor (S3)*: Forestry

Libraries: Central Library, c. 17,500 vols; faculty libraries, c. 15,580

Publications: Berita Unmul; Frontir; Research Reports

Press or Publishing House: Pusat Percetakan Unmul

Last Updated: 06/07/11

OPEN UNIVERSITY

Universitas Terbuka (UT)

PO Box 6666, Jalan Cabe Raya, Pondok Cabe, Ciputat-Tangerang, 15418 Jawa Barat
Tel: +62(21) 749-0941
Fax: +62(21) 749-0147
EMail: info@p2m.ut.ac.id
Website: http://www.ut.ac.id/

Rector: Tian Belawati
Tel: +62(21) 740-1585 EMail: rektor@mail.ut.ac.id

Vice-Rector: Yuni Tri Hewindati

Faculties

Economics (Accountancy; Development Studies; Economics; Management); **Education and Teacher Training** (Civics; Education; Educational Sciences; English; Foreign Languages Education; Indonesian; Mathematics Education; Modern Languages; Native Language Education; Preschool Education; Primary Education; Science Education; Teacher Training); **Graduate Studies** (Administration; Fishery; Management; Marine Science and Oceanography; Mathematics; Public Administration); **Mathematics and Natural Sciences** (Agricultural Business; Agriculture; Biology; Communication Studies; Environmental Studies; Food Science; Food Technology; Mathematics; Statistics); **Social and Political Sciences** (Business Administration; Communication Studies; English; Government; Library Science; Public Administration; Social Problems; Social Sciences; Sociology; Taxation; Translation and Interpretation)

History: Founded 1984.

Governing Bodies: Senate

Academic Year: August to July

Admission Requirements: Senior high school certificate

Main Language(s) of Instruction: Indonesian

Accrediting Agencies: Badan Akreditasi Nasional of the Department of Education and the ICDE Standard Agency (ISA)

Degrees and Diplomas: *Diploma*; *Sarjana (S1)*; *Magister (S2)*. Also Certificate

Student Services: Academic counselling, Canteen, Health services, Sports facilities

Libraries: Central Library. 27 local libraries at regional offices

Publications: Jurnal Pendidikan Terbuka dan Jarak Jauh, Issues on open and distance learning *(biannually)*; Komunica, (Popular science and social study publication) *(quarterly)*

Last Updated: 07/06/11

PADANG STATE UNIVERSITY

Universitas Negeri Padang (UNP)

Jalan Prof Dr Hamka, Kampus Air Tawar, Padang, 25131 Sumatra Barat
Tel: +62(751) 705-3902
Fax: +62(751) 705-5628
EMail: info@unp.ac.id
Website: http://www.unp.ac.id

Rector: Z. Mawardi Effendi

Vice-Rector I: Yanuar Kiram

International Relations: Alizamar, Vice-Rector III

Faculties

Ecomomics (Accountancy; Development Studies; Economics; Management); **Education** (Biology; Chemistry; Economics; Education; Educational Administration; Educational and Student Counselling; Educational Technology; Geography (Human); Health Education; History; Leisure Studies; Mathematics Education; Modern Languages; Parks and Recreation; Physical Education; Physics; Preschool Education; Primary Education; Special Education; Sports; Sports Management); **Engineering** (Automotive Engineering; Civil Engineering; Computer Science; Construction Engineering; Cosmetology; Electrical Engineering; Electronic Engineering; Engineering; Mechanical Engineering; Mining Engineering; Tourism; Welfare and Protective Services); **Languages, Literature and Arts** (Art Education; Communication Arts; Communication Studies; Dance; Design; English; Indonesian; Information Sciences; Library Science; Literature; Modern Languages; Music; Theatre; Visual Arts); **Mathematics and Natural Sciences** (Biology; Chemistry; Geography; Mathematics; Natural Sciences; Physics; Statistics); **Social Sciences** (Anthropology; Civics; Economics; Government; Psychology; Public Administration; Social Sciences; Social Studies); **Sports** (Leisure Studies; Sports; Sports Management)

Programmes

Postgraduate Studies (Economics; Education; Educational Administration; Educational and Student Counselling; Educational Technology; Environmental Studies; Foreign Languages Education; Humanities and Social Science Education; Native Language Education; Preschool Education; Primary Education)

History: Founded 1954 as College of Teacher Education (PTPG). Acquired present status and title 1997.

Degrees and Diplomas: *Diploma*; *Sarjana (S1)*; *Magister (S2)*: Economics; Management; Educational Guidance and Counselling; Educational Technology; Educational Administration; Basic Education; Social Sciences Education; Languages Education; Environmental Education; *Doktor (S3)*: Education

Last Updated: 07/07/11

PADJADJARAN UNIVERSITY

Universitas Padjadjaran

Jalan Dipati Ukur 35, Bandung, 40132 Jawa Barat
Tel: +62(22) 250-3271 +62(22) 250-1976
Fax: +62(22) 250-1976
EMail: info@unpad.ac.id; unpad@unpad.ac.id
Website: http://www.unpad.ac.id

Rector: Ganjar Kurnia EMail: rektor@unpad.ac.id

Vice-Rector, Academics: Husein Hernadi Bahti
EMail: pr1@unpad.ac.id

Vice-Rector, Administration and Finance: Rina Indiastuti
EMail: pr2@unpad.ac.id

International Relations: Zulrizka Iskandar, Vice-Rector, Cooperation EMail: pr4@unpad.ac.id

International Relations: Zulrizka Iskandar, Vice-Rector IV, Cooperation EMail: pr4@unpad.ac.id

Faculties

Agriculture (Agricultural Business; Agricultural Economics; Agricultural Engineering; Agriculture; Agronomy; Crop Production; Food Technology; Forestry; Horticulture; Pest Management; Plant and Crop Protection; Plant Pathology; Soil Science; Water Management); **Agroindustrial Technology** (Agricultural Engineering; Food Technology; Industrial Management); **Arts and Humanities** (Arabic; Chinese; Cultural Studies; Documentation Techniques; English; French; German; History; Indonesian; Japanese; Linguistics; Literature; Museum Studies; Native Language; Philology; Publishing and Book Trade; Russian); **Communication** (Advertising and Publicity; Communication Studies; Information Sciences; Journalism; Library Science; Public Relations; Radio and Television Broadcasting); **Dentistry** (Dental Technology; Dentistry; Oral Pathology; Orthodontics; Periodontics; Surgery); **Economics** (Accountancy; Development Studies; Economics; International Business; Management; Marketing; Taxation); **Fishery and Marine Science** (Aquaculture; Environmental Management; Fishery;

Marine Science and Oceanography; Natural Resources); **Geological Engineering** (Energy Engineering; Geological Engineering; Geology; Mineralogy; Mining Engineering; Natural Resources; Water Management); **Law** (Law; Notary Studies); **Livestock** (Agricultural Business; Agricultural Economics; Animal Husbandry; Cattle Breeding; Food Technology; Nutrition; Zoology); **Mathematics and Natural Sciences** (Analytical Chemistry; Applied Physics; Biology; Chemistry; Computer Engineering; Electronic Engineering; Geology; Geophysics; Industrial Chemistry; Information Management; Information Technology; Mathematics; Natural Sciences; Pharmacy; Physics; Statistics); **Medicine** (Anaesthesiology; Anatomy; Cardiology; Dermatology; Endocrinology; Forensic Medicine and Dentistry; Gynaecology and Obstetrics; Medicine; Microbiology; Neurology; Oncology; Ophthalmology; Orthopaedics; Otorhinolaryngology; Paediatrics; Pathology; Psychiatry and Mental Health; Radiology; Rehabilitation and Therapy; Surgery; Urology); **Nursing** (Nursing); **Pharmacy** (Pharmacy); **Psychology** (Psychology); **Social and Political Sciences** (Administration; Anthropology; Business Administration; Development Studies; Finance; Government; International Relations; Political Sciences; Public Administration; Social Sciences; Social Welfare; Sociology)

Institutes
Community Service (Social and Community Services)

Programmes
Postgraduate Studies (Accountancy; Administration; Agricultural Economics; Agricultural Engineering; Agriculture; Agronomy; Anthropology; Business Administration; Chemistry; Communication Studies; Cultural Studies; Economics; Environmental Studies; Geological Engineering; International Relations; Law; Literature; Management; Medicine; Midwifery; Notary Studies; Nursing; Pharmacy; Political Sciences; Psychology; Public Administration; Public Health; Social Studies; Social Welfare; Sociology; Soil Science; Statistics; Zoology)

Research Institutes
Demography (Demography and Population); **Health** (Health Sciences); **Human and Environmental Resources** (Environmental Management; Human Resources); **Legal Development**; **Natural Resources and Environment** (Environmental Management; Environmental Studies; Natural Resources); **Society and Culture** (Cultural Studies); **Technology** (Technology); **Women's Studies** (Women's Studies)

Further Information: Also Jatinagor-Sumedang Kampus, Teaching Hospitals (RSHS, Cicendo Eye Hospital), Polytechnic Education Development Center for Agriculture, Courses for foreign students (UPT Pusat Pelayanan Kebahasaan)

History: Founded 1952 as Independent University, a private institution with faculties of law and economics. Amalgamated with State Teacher Training College, founded 1954, to become Padjadjaran State University 1957.

Governing Bodies: Senate; Board of Curators

Academic Year: February to November (February-July; August-January)

Admission Requirements: Secondary school certificate and entrance examination

Main Language(s) of Instruction: Indonesian

Degrees and Diplomas: *Diploma*: 3 yrs; *Sarjana (S1)*: 4 yrs; *Magister (S2)*: Accountancy; Public Administration; Business Administration; Political Sciences; Social Studies; Sociology; Communication Sciences; Social Welfare; Psychology; Law; Notary Studies; Anthropology; Cultural Studies; Environmental Studies; Medicine; Public Health; Nursing; Midwifery; Geological Engineering; Agricultural Technology; Chemistry; Pharmacy; Applied Statistics; Agricultural Economics; Agronomy; Soil Science; Animal Science; Economics; Management, a further 2 yrs; *Doktor (S3)*: Medicine; Geological Engineering; Chemistry; Agriculture; Animal Sciences; Economics; Administration; International Relations; Sociology; Social Welfare; Psychology; Law; Literature, a further 3 yrs. Also Specialist programmes

Student Services: Academic counselling, Canteen, Cultural centre, Employment services, Foreign student adviser, Health services, Sports facilities

Student Residential Facilities: Yes

Special Facilities: Biological Garden. Agriculture Practice Area

Libraries: Central Library and faculty libraries, c. 110,000 vols

Publications: Arts Journal; Dental Journal; Journal of Agriculture; Journal of Law and Social Science; Medical Journal and Magazine; Padjadjaran University Scientific Journal

Last Updated: 08/07/11

PALANGKA RAYA UNIVERSITY

Universitas Palangka Raya

Jalan Hendrik Timang, Komplek Unpar, Palangka Raya, 73111A
Kalimantan Tengah
Tel: +62(536) 322-6878
Fax: +62(536) 322-1722
EMail: info@upr.ac.id; unparpalangkaraya@gmail.com
Website: http://www.upr.ac.id

Rector: Henry Singarasa EMail: rektor@upr.ac.id

Vice-Rector, Administration and Finance: Ciptadi

Vice-Rector, Academic: Kumpiady Widen

Faculties
Agriculture (Agricultural Business; Agricultural Economics; Agricultural Engineering; Agriculture; Agronomy; Aquaculture; Environmental Studies; Fishery; Forest Management; Forestry; Soil Science; Water Management); **Economics** (Accountancy; Development Studies; Economics; Government; Management; Political Sciences; Public Administration; Sociology); **Education and Teacher Training** (Biology; Chemistry; Civics; Construction Engineering; Economics; Education; Educational Administration; Educational and Student Counselling; Educational Sciences; English; Foreign Languages Education; Government; Humanities and Social Science Education; Indonesian; Leisure Studies; Literature; Mathematics Education; Mechanical Engineering; Native Language Education; Natural Sciences; Parks and Recreation; Physical Education; Physics; Preschool Education; Primary Education; Science Education; Social Sciences; Technology Education); **Engineering** (Architecture; Civil Engineering; Engineering; Information Technology; Mining Engineering; Structural Architecture); **Law** (Law); **Medical Education** (Health Education; Medicine)

Programmes
Postgraduate Studies (Education; English; Environmental Management; Environmental Studies; Foreign Languages Education; Management; Natural Resources)

History: Founded 1963. A State institution under the jurisdiction of the Department of Education and Culture.

Academic Year: July to June (July-December; January-June)

Admission Requirements: Secondary school certificate (Sekolah Menengah Atas, SMA) and entrance examination

Fees: According to parents' income

Main Language(s) of Instruction: Indonesian

Degrees and Diplomas: *Diploma*: 1-3 yrs; *Sarjana (S1)*: 5 yrs; *Magister (S2)*: Management; Out of School Education; Englich Education; Natural Resources and Environmental Management

Student Residential Facilities: Yes

Libraries: Central Library

Publications: The Heavenly Voice *(monthly)*

Last Updated: 08/07/11

PAPUA STATE UNIVERSITY

Universitas Negeri Papua

Jalan Gunung Salju, Amban Manokwari Papua, Manokwari 98314
Tel: +62(986) 211-974 +62(986) 211-982
Fax: +62(986) 211-455
Website: http://www.unipa.ac.id

Rector: Y.P. Karafir

Assistant Rector I: Marlyn N. Lekitoo

Faculties
Agriculture and Agricultural Engineering (Agricultural Business; Agricultural Engineering; Agriculture; Agronomy; Horticulture; Plant Pathology; Soil Science); **Animal Husbandry, Fishery and Marine Science** (Animal Husbandry; Fishery; Marine Science and Oceanography); **Arts and Humanities** (English; Literature); **Economics** (Development Studies; Economics); **Forestry** (Forest Management;

Forest Products; Wood Technology); **Mathematics and Natural Sciences** (Biology; Chemistry; Geological Engineering; Mathematics; Mining Engineering; Petroleum and Gas Engineering; Physics)

Programmes

Computer Science (Computer Science)

History: Founded 2000.

Degrees and Diplomas: *Diploma*; *Sarjana (S1)*; *Magister (S2)*: Agriculture; Zoology

Last Updated: 26/02/10

PATTIMURA UNIVERSITY

Universitas Pattimura

Jalan Ir. M. Putuhena Kampus Poka Unpatti, Ambon 97116

Tel: +62(911) 322-626

Fax: +62(911) 322-628

EMail: humas@unpatti.ac.id

Website: http://www.unpatti.ac.id

Rector: Hendrik Bernardus Tetelepta

Vice-Rector: Jacob William Ajawaila

Faculties

Agriculture (Agricultural Business; Agricultural Engineering; Agriculture; Animal Husbandry; Crop Production; Forestry; Soil Science); **Economics** (Accountancy; Development Studies; Economics; Management); **Education and Teacher Training** (Biology; Chemistry; Civics; Economics; Educational and Student Counselling; Educational Sciences; English; Geography; Geography (Human); German; Government; History; Indonesian; Leisure Studies; Mathematics Education; Natural Sciences; Parks and Recreation; Physical Education; Physics; Primary Education; Science Education; Teacher Trainers Education); **Engineering** (Engineering; Industrial Engineering; Marine Engineering; Mechanical Engineering); **Fishery and Marine Science** (Agricultural Business; Aquaculture; Fishery; Marine Science and Oceanography); **Law** (Law); **Mathematics and Natural Sciences** (Biology; Chemistry; Mathematics; Physics); **Social and Political Sciences** (Government; Political Sciences; Public Administration; Social Sciences; Sociology)

Programmes

Postgraduate Studies (Economics; Law; Marine Science and Oceanography; Sociology; Soil Science)

History: Founded 1962.

Degrees and Diplomas: *Diploma*; *Sarjana (S1)*; *Magister (S2)*: Soil Science; Marine Science; Economics; Sociology; Legal Studies

Last Updated: 08/07/11

RIAU UNIVERSITY

Universitas Riau (UNRI)

Kampus Binawidya Simpang Baru, Pekanbaru, 28131 Riau

Tel: +62(671) 63-266 +62(671) 63-277

Fax: +62(671) 63-279

Website: http://www.unri.ac.id

Rector: Aslahuddin Jalil

Tel: +62(671) 63-279, Fax: +62(671) 63-266

Vice-Rector I: Suwardi Mulyadi

Vice-Rector IV: Adhy Prayitno

Faculties

Agriculture (Agricultural Economics; Agriculture; Agronomy; Food Technology; Pest Management); **Economics** (Accountancy; Development Studies; Economics; Management; Taxation); **Education** (Art Education; Biology; Chemistry; Civics; Education; Educational Sciences; English; Foreign Languages Education; History; Indonesian; Literature; Mathematics; Mathematics Education; Natural Sciences; Physics; Primary Education; Science Education; Social Sciences; Teacher Trainers Education; Teacher Training); **Engineering** (Chemical Engineering; Civil Engineering; Electrical Engineering; Engineering; Mechanical Engineering); **Fisheries and Marine Science** (Agricultural Economics; Fishery; Marine Science and Oceanography; Water Management); **Law** (Law); **Medicine** (Medicine); **Science and Mathematics** (Biology; Chemistry; Mathematics; Natural Sciences; Physics); **Social and Political Sciences** (Administration; Government; International Relations; Political Sciences; Social Sciences; Sociology)

Schools

Nursing (Nursing)

History: Founded 1962.

Academic Year: July to June (July-December; January-June)

Admission Requirements: Secondary school certificate (Sekolah Menengah Umum, SMU) and entrance examination

Main Language(s) of Instruction: Indonesian

Accrediting Agencies: Badan Akreditasi Nasional (BAN)

Degrees and Diplomas: *Diploma*; *Sarjana (S1)*; *Magister (S2)*

Student Services: Academic counselling, Canteen, Employment services, Health services, Language programs, Nursery care, Social counselling, Sports facilities

Libraries: c. 7,210 vols

Last Updated: 06/06/11

SAM RATULANGI UNIVERSITY

Universitas Sam Ratulangi

Kampus Unsrat, Bahu, Manado, 95115 Sulawesi Utara

Tel: +62(431) 863-886

Fax: +62(431) 822-568

EMail: teknik@unsrat.ac.id

Website: http://www.unsrat.ac.id

Rector: Donald A. Rumokoy EMail: pti@unsrat.ac.id

Vice-Rector: Boetje Herry Moningka

Faculties

Agriculture (Agricultural Economics; Agricultural Engineering; Agriculture; Agronomy; Plant Pathology; Soil Science); **Animal Husbandry** (Animal Husbandry; Nutrition); **Arts and Humanities** (Arts and Humanities; English; German; History; Indonesian; Literature); **Economics** (Accountancy; Banking; Development Studies; Economics; Finance; Management); **Engineering** (Architecture; Civil Engineering; Electrical Engineering; Engineering; Mechanical Engineering); **Fisheries and Marine Science** (Fishery; Marine Science and Oceanography; Water Management); **Law** (Law); **Mathematics and Natural Sciences** (Biology; Chemistry; Mathematics; Natural Sciences); **Medicine** (Dentistry; Medicine); **Social and Political Sciences** (Anthropology; Business Administration; Communication Studies; Government; Political Sciences; Social Sciences; Sociology)

Programmes

Postgraduate Studies (Agronomy; Civil Engineering; Community Health; Development Studies; Economics; Law; Linguistics; Management; Water Science)

History: Founded 1961. A State institution under the jurisdiction of the Department of Education and Culture.

Academic Year: January to December (January-June; July-December)

Admission Requirements: Secondary school certificate (Sekolah Lanjutan Atas, SLA)

Main Language(s) of Instruction: Indonesian

Degrees and Diplomas: *Diploma*: 2-3 yrs; *Sarjana (S1)*: 5 yrs; *Magister (S2)*: a further 3 yrs; *Doktor (S3)*

Student Residential Facilities: Yes

Libraries: Central Library, c. 70,000 vols

Publications: Dedikasi; Kalawarta Unscrat; Majalah Sam Ratulangi

Last Updated: 01/03/10

SEBELAS MARET UNIVERSITY

Universitas Sebelas Maret (UNS)

Jalan Ir. Sutami 36A, Kentingan, Surakarta, 57126 Jawa Tengah

Tel: +62(271) 642-283 +62(271) 646-655

Fax: +62(271) 646-655

EMail: rektor@uns.ac.id

Website: http://www.uns.ac.id

Rector: Ravik Karsidi

Head, Bureau of Academic Administration: Sriyanto

International Relations: Syafi'I, Coordinator of International Cooperation
Tel: +62(271) 633-961, Fax: +62(271) 633-961
EMail: syafii@uns.ac.id

Centres

Biotech and Biodiversity (Biological and Life Sciences; Biotechnology); **Constitution and Human Rights Study**; **Disaster Study** (Safety Engineering); **Entrepreneurship Development** (Management); **Environmental Studies** (Environmental Studies); **Food, Nutrition and Health of the Society Development** (Food Science; Health Sciences; Nutrition; Public Health); **Gender Research and Development** (Gender Studies; Women's Studies); **Information and Rural Development**; **Intellectual Property Right Development** (Private Law); **Population Research** (Demography and Population); **Public and Students Empowerment**; **Region Development and Village Research** (Regional Planning); **Regional and Rural Research and Development** (Development Studies; Rural Planning); **Rehabilitation and Remediation Research** (Rehabilitation and Therapy); **Sexual Study**; **Sport RDC** (Sports); **Technology and Industrial Collaboration**; **Tourism** (Development Studies; Tourism)

Faculties

Agriculture (Agricultural Economics; Agriculture; Agronomy; Animal Husbandry; Soil Science); **Economics** (Accountancy; Development Studies; Economics; Management); **Engineering** (Architecture; Chemical Engineering; Civil Engineering; Engineering; Industrial Engineering; Mechanical Engineering); **Law** (Law); **Letters and Fine Arts** (Design; Fine Arts; History; Linguistics; Literature; Modern Languages; Philology); **Mathematics and Natural Sciences**; **Medicine** (Environmental Studies; Medicine; Occupational Health); **Social and Political Sciences** (Government; Mass Communication; Political Sciences; Public Administration; Social Sciences; Sociology); **Teacher Training and Education** (Art Education; Biology; Chemistry; Civics; Construction Engineering; Economics; Education; Education of the Handicapped; Educational Sciences; Fine Arts; Geography; Health Education; History; Mathematics Education; Mechanical Engineering; Natural Sciences; Physics; Social Sciences; Sports; Teacher Training; Technology; Vocational Education)

Institutes

Education Development (Education); **Research and Community Service** (Social and Community Services)

Programmes

Postgraduate Studies (Accountancy; Agricultural Business; Agronomy; Biology; Civil Engineering; Communication Studies; Community Health; Cultural Studies; Demography and Population; Development Studies; Economics; Education; Educational Technology; English; English Studies; Environmental Studies; Family Studies; Foreign Languages Education; History; Indonesian; Law; Linguistics; Management; Mass Communication; Mathematics Education; Mechanical Engineering; Medicine; Native Language Education; Natural Sciences; Nutrition; Physics; Public Administration; Science Education; Sociology; Sports)

History: Founded 1976, incorporating nine existing Institutions. A State Institution.

Academic Year: August to July (August-January; February-July)

Admission Requirements: Secondary school certificate (Sekolah Menengah Atas, SMA)

Fees: (Rupiahs): c. 660,000 per semester (Laboratory and Administrative costs are not included)

Main Language(s) of Instruction: Indonesian

International Co-operation: SEAMEO Regional Open Learning Centre (SEAMOLEC); with Universities in Australia (La Trobe University, Central Queensland University, James Cook University, Southern Queensland University, Curtin University), Indonesia (IEMS Belanda), China (College of Chinese Language and Culture, Jinan University China, Guangdong University of Foreign Studies, South China University of Tropical Agriculture, and Chinese Academy of Tropical Agricultural Sciences, Guangxi University of Nationalities, Zhangjiang Normal University, the Branch of Exterior Treatment of Traditional Chinese Medicine Association), Finland (Satakunta Polytechnic), France (University of La Rochelle), Malaysia (UNITAR University Utara Malaysia (UUM), German-Malaysian Institute (GMU) and MTS CNC System Singapore/Malaysia), United Kingdom (the University of Sheffield), Japan (Tottori University); Federal Research Centre for Nutrition and Food (BFE), ENED (International Education Center for Energy Solutions), Global Medic Network SDN.BHD Malaysia, ASTARI (Asosiasi Teknologi Adiguna Rusia Indonesia)

Accrediting Agencies: Department of National Education

Degrees and Diplomas: *Diploma*: Civil Engineering; Mechanical Engineering; Chemistry Engineering; Agricultural Products Technology; Agribusiness; Banking and Finance; Computer Science; Pharmacy (DIII); Hygiene and Working Safety; Accountancy; Taxation; Marketing Management; Industrial Management; International Business; English; Chinese; Tour and Travel Business; Visual Community Design; Applied Communication; Administration Management; Library Science (DIII), 3 yrs; *Diploma*: Elementary Teacher Education; Kindergarten Teacher Education (DII), 2 yrs; *Diploma*: Midwifery; Occupational Health (DIV), 4 yrs; *Sarjana (S1)*: Agriculture; Agrotechnology; Agribusiness; Science and Food Technology; Husbandry, 4 yrs; *Sarjana (S1)*: Biology Education; Civil Engineering Education; Mechanical Engineering Education; Sports, Health and Recreation Education; Sport Coaching Education; Sociology and Anthropology Education; Elementary Teacher Education; Guidance Counseling; Economics; Development Studies; Management; Accountancy; Engineering; Civil Engineering; Architecture; Industrial Engineering; Mechanical Engineering; Chemical Engineering; Planology; Law; Letters and Fine Arts; Indonesian; Javanese; English; History; Fine Arts; Visual Communication Design; Interior Design; Crafts/Sculpture; Mathematics; Natural Sciences; Chemistry; Biology; Physics; Computer Sciences; Medicine; Psychology; Social Sciences; Political Sciences; Communication Studies; Sociology; Public Administration; Teacher Training; Education; Special Education; Civics Education; History Education; Geography Education; Economics Education; Indonesian Education; English Education; Fine Arts Education; Mathematics Education; Physics Education; Chemistry Education; *Magister (S2)*: Communication Science; Agronomy; Development Communication; Law; Nutrition; Public Administration; Biology; Economic Science and Development Study; English Education; Civil Engineering; Accountancy; Cultural Studies; Sociology (S2); History Education; Linguistics; Environmental Science; Population and Environmental Education; Sports; Educational Technology; Magister Management; Family Medicine; Mathematics Education; Indonesian Education; Natural Science Education (S2), 2 yrs; *Doktor (S3)*: Linguistics; Law; Indonesian Education; Development Communication; Economic Science (S3), 4 yrs. Also Expertise/vocational Programmes in Automotive Engineering, Mechanical Industrial Engineering, Electronic Engineering, Civil Engineering, Interior & Exterior Design Education, Accountancy Education, Taxation Education, Information Technology Education. Medical Specialist Programmes in Obstetrics & Gynaecology; Othopedics & Traumatic Science; Psychiatry; Surgery; Lungs Disease Science; Internal Disease Science; Ear, Node & Throat Science; Pediatrics; Neurology; Dermatology and Venereology; Ophtalmology

Student Services: Academic counselling, Canteen, Cultural centre, Foreign student adviser, Health services, Language programs, Sports facilities

Student Residential Facilities: Yes

Special Facilities: Computer Centre; Central Laboratory; Medical Centre

Libraries: Central Library, c. 171,000 vols

Publications: Agritexts; Agro Sains; Alchemy; Arsitektura; Biodiversitas; Bioedukasi; Biofarmasi; Biosmart; Bioteknology; Caraka Tani; Diakronik; Dwijawacana; Ekuilibrium; Etnografi; Gema Teknik; Gradasi; Haluan Sastra Budaya; Jurnal Bahasa, Sastra and Studi Indonesia; Justicia, Law Publication; Linguistik Jawa; Math-info; Media Fisika; Media Teknik Sipil; Mekanik; MIPS.; Nexus; Nuansa Indonesia; Paedagogia; Performa; Peternakan; PKn Progresif; Sainmart; Sains; Sains Tanah; Saintika; SEPA

Press or Publishing House: University Press

Last Updated: 07/06/11

SEMARANG STATE UNIVERSITY

Universitas Negeri Semarang (UNNES)

Sekaran, Gunungpati, Semarang, 50229 Central Java
Tel: +62(24) 850-8081
Fax: +62(24) 850-8082
EMail: unnes@unnes.ac.id; humas@unnes.ac.id
Website: http://www.unnes.ac.id

Rector: Sudijono Sastroatmodjo (2006-) EMail: rektor@unnes.ac.id

Vice-Rector for General Affairs: Wahyono
Tel: +62(24) 850-8002 EMail: why-unnes@yahoo.com

International Relations: Abdurrahman Faridi, International Relations Officer Tel: +62(24) 850-8004 EMail: pakdur@yahoo.co.id

Centres

Community Service; **Teaching and Profession** (Teacher Training)

Faculties

Economics (Accountancy; Administration; Development Studies; Economics; Management); **Education** (Education; Educational and Student Counselling; Educational Technology; Preschool Education; Primary Education; Special Education); **Engineering** (Architecture; Chemical Engineering; Civil Engineering; Computer Engineering; Construction Engineering; Cooking and Catering; Electronic Engineering; Engineering; Fashion Design; Information Technology; Mechanical Engineering; Structural Architecture); **Languages and Arts** (Arabic; Communication Arts; Dance; English; Fine Arts; Foreign Languages Education; French; Indonesian; Japanese; Literature; Modern Languages; Music; Music Education; South and Southeast Asian Languages; Visual Arts); **Law** (Law); **Mathematics and Natural Sciences** (Biology; Chemistry; Computer Science; Mathematics; Natural Sciences; Physics; Statistics); **Social Sciences** (Anthropology; Civics; Geography (Human); History; Sociology); **Sports Sciences** (Parks and Recreation; Physical Education; Public Health; Sports; Sports Management)

Programmes

Postgraduate Studies (Curriculum; Educational Administration; Educational Technology; English; Foreign Languages Education; Humanities and Social Science Education; Indonesian; Mathematics Education; Native Language Education; Natural Sciences; Physical Education; Primary Education; Science Education; Sports)

Research Centres

Arts and Humanities, Education, Natural Sciences, Social Sciences and Technology

History: Founded 1965 as Semarang Teachers College (IKIP), acquired present status and title 1999.

Governing Bodies: Board of Trustees; University Senate

Academic Year: September to August (September-February; March-August)

Admission Requirements: Graduation from high school or equivalent and entrance examination

Fees: (Rupiahs): Admission, c. 5m.; tuition, c. 360,000 per semester; foreigners, c. 1.8m. per semester

Main Language(s) of Instruction: Indonesian (Bahasa Indonesian)

International Co-operation: With USAID; UNESCO; USINTEC; PASIAD TURKI; UPSI Malaysia

Accrediting Agencies: Badan Akreditasi Nasional Perguruan Tinggi (National Board for Higher Education Accreditation)

Degrees and Diplomas: *Diploma*: Sciences, 3-5 yrs; *Sarjana (S1)*: Education; Sciences, 4-7 yrs; *Magister (S2)*: Curriculum Development; Basic Education; Social Sciences Education; English Language Education; Dramatic Arts, Dance and Music Education; Indonesian Education; Education (Natural Sciences; Mathematics); Physical Education; Educational Guidance and Counselling; Research and Evaluation of Education; Educational Administration;, a further 2-5 yrs; *Doktor (S3)*: Education (Sports; Management; Languages), a further 2-5 yrs

Student Services: Academic counselling, Canteen, Cultural centre, Employment services, Foreign student adviser, Health services, Language programs, Nursery care, Social counselling, Sports facilities

Student Residential Facilities: Two dormitories

Special Facilities: Sport Centre; Media and Learning Resource Centre; Teleconference

Libraries: University Library, c. 130,000 vols

Publications: Abdimas (Journal of Community Services), Reports and articles on community service programs *(annually)*; Jurnal Penelitian (Research Journal), Reports and articles on research programmes *(biennially)*; Kompas Mahasiswa, Scientific articles written by students *(quarterly)*; Lembaran Ilmu Kependidikan (Journal of Education), Scientific articles written by lecturers *(quarterly)*

Press or Publishing House: UNNES Press (University press and publisher)

Academic Staff *2009-2010*	MEN	WOMEN	TOTAL
FULL-TIME	–	–	**1,000**
PART-TIME	–	–	**50**
STAFF WITH DOCTORATE			
FULL-TIME	–	–	**90**
PART-TIME	5	–	**c. 5**
Student Numbers *2009-2010*			
All (Foreign Included)	10,900	13,900	**24,800**

Last Updated: 06/06/11

SEPULUH NOVEMBER INSTITUTE OF TECHNOLOGY

Institut Teknologi Sepuluh November

Kampus ITS Keputih Sukolilo, Surabaya, 60111 Jawa Timur
Tel: +62(31) 599-4251Ext. 1224 +62(31) 592-3411 (direct)
Fax: +62(31) 592-3411 +62(31) 594-3358
EMail: int_off@its.ac.id; bpsi@its.ac.id
Website: http://www.its.ac.id

Rector: Triyogi

Vice-Rector: Arif Junaidy

Faculties

Civil Engineering and Planning (Architecture; Civil Engineering; Environmental Engineering; Industrial Design; Rural Planning; Surveying and Mapping; Town Planning); **Industrial Technology** (Chemical Engineering; Computer Engineering; Electrical Engineering; Industrial Engineering; Materials Engineering; Mechanical Engineering; Physical Engineering); **Information Technology**; **Marine Engineering** (Marine Engineering; Naval Architecture); **Mathematics and Natural Sciences** (Biology; Chemistry; Mathematics; Physics; Statistics); **Postgraduate Studies** (Chemical Engineering; Chemistry; Civil Engineering; Electronic Engineering; Environmental Engineering; Industrial Design; Information Technology; Management Systems; Marine Engineering; Mathematics; Mechanical Engineering; Physics; Statistics; Structural Architecture)

Institutes

Research

Research Centres

Computer Science and Information (Computer Science; Information Technology); **Energy** (Energy Engineering); **Industry** (Industrial Engineering); **Materials and Basic Sciences** (Materials Engineering; Natural Sciences); **Marine Engineering** (Marine Engineering); **Population and Environment** (Demography and Population; Environmental Studies)

History: Founded 1957. Acquired present status and title 1960.

Governing Bodies: Senate

Academic Year: January to December (January-July; August-December)

Admission Requirements: Secondary school certificate (Sekolah Menengah Atas, SMA), and entrance examination (Seleksi Penerimaan Mahasiswa Baru/SPMB)

Main Language(s) of Instruction: Indonesian

Degrees and Diplomas: *Diploma (A.Md; SSt.)*; *Sarjana (S1) (ST; S.Kom; Ssi.)*; *Magister (S2) (MT; MMT; Msi.; M.Kom)*; *Doktor (S3) (Dr.)*

Student Services: Academic counselling, Canteen, Cultural centre, Employment services, Health services, Social counselling, Sports facilities

Student Residential Facilities: For c. 10,000 students; Guest House

Special Facilities: Multi Purposes Hall/Graha ITS (5,000 seats); 168 laboratories

Libraries: Perpustakaan Pusat, 170,878 vols

Publications: IPTEK, Scientific Journal; Jurnal Purifikasi, Scientific Journal; Jurnal Tehnik Mesin, Scientific Journal

Press or Publishing House: ITS Press
Last Updated: 02/03/10

SRIWIJAYA UNIVERSITY

Universitas Sriwijaya

Jalan Raya Palembang, Prabumulih, Km.32, Indralaya, 30662
South Sumatera
Tel: +62(711) 580-169
Fax: +62(711) 580-644
EMail: baak@unsri.ac.id
Website: http://www.unsri.ac.id

Rector: Badia Perizade Tel: +62(711) 580-073

Vice-Rector: Zulkifli Dahlan Tel: +62(711) 580-358

International Relations: A. Hamid Rasyid, Vice-Rector for External Affairs Tel: +62(711) 580-357

Faculties
Agriculture (Agricultural Business; Agricultural Economics; Agricultural Engineering; Agriculture; Agronomy; Aquaculture; Fishery; Food Science; Nutrition; Plant and Crop Protection; Plant Pathology; Soil Science); **Computer Science** (Computer Engineering; Computer Science; Information Technology); **Economics** (Accountancy; Development Studies; Economics; Management; Secretarial Studies); **Education and Teacher Training** (Accountancy; Biology; Chemistry; Civics; Economics; Educational and Student Counselling; Educational Sciences; English; Foreign Languages Education; Government; Health Education; History; Indonesian; Literature; Mathematics Education; Mechanical Engineering; Native Language Education; Natural Sciences; Physical Education; Physics; Preschool Education; Primary Education; Science Education; Social Sciences; Teacher Training; Technology Education); **Engineering** (Architecture; Chemical Engineering; Civil Engineering; Electrical Engineering; Engineering; Mechanical Engineering; Mining Engineering; Structural Architecture); **Law** (Law); **Mathematics and Natural Sciences** (Biology; Chemistry; Marine Science and Oceanography; Mathematics; Natural Sciences; Physics); **Medicine** (Anatomy; Child Care and Development; Dental Technology; Dentistry; Gynaecology and Obstetrics; Medicine; Neurology; Nursing; Ophthalmology; Pathology; Public Health; Surgery); **Public Health** (Environmental Studies; Finance; Health Administration; Human Resources; Nutrition; Occupational Health; Public Health; Transport Management); **Social and Political Sciences** (Government; Political Sciences; Public Administration; Social Sciences; Sociology)

Research Centres
Development Studies (Development Studies); **Energy Studies** (Energy Engineering); **Environmental Studies** (Environmental Studies); **Population Studies** (Demography and Population); **Regional Planning** (Regional Planning); **Social Sciences and Culture** (Cultural Studies; Gender Studies; Social Sciences); **Water Treatment** (Water Science); **Women's Studies** (Women's Studies)

History: Founded 1953, acquired present status 1960. A State institution under the jurisdiction of the Department of Education and Culture.

Governing Bodies: Board of Regents; Senate

Academic Year: July to May (July-December; January-May). Also Summer session (June-August)

Admission Requirements: Secondary school certificate (Sekolah Menengah Atas, SMA) and entrance examination

Main Language(s) of Instruction: Indonesian

International Co-operation: With Universiti Utara Malaysia (UUM)

Accrediting Agencies: National Accreditation Board

Degrees and Diplomas: *Diploma*: 3 yrs; *Sarjana (S1)*: 4-5 yrs; *Magister (S2)*: Agricultural Business; Biomedicine; Engineering (Chemical, Civil, Mechanical); Crop Science; Economics; Educational Technology; Language Education; Law; Management; Mathematics Education; Notary Studies; Population; Public Administration; Environmental Management, a further 2 yrs; *Doktor (S3)*: Agriculture; Economics; Environmental Sudies; Law, 3 yrs

Student Services: Academic counselling, Canteen, Cultural centre, Employment services, Health services, Language programs, Social counselling, Sports facilities

Student Residential Facilities: Dormitory

Special Facilities: Art Gallery. Biological Garden. Movie Studio

Libraries: University Library, c. 170,000 vols

Publications: Agria *(biannually)*; Emperika *(biannually)*; Forum Kependidikian *(quarterly)*; Jurnal Ilmiah MIPA *(biannually)*; Jurnal Sains *(biannually)*; Rekayasa Sriwijaya *(biannually)*; Simbur Cahaya *(biannually)*; Sriwijaya *(biannually)*; Tanaman Tropis *(biannually)*; University and faculty magazines *(biannually)*

Press or Publishing House: Penerbit and Percetakan Universitas Sriwijaya
Last Updated: 08/07/11

STATE ISLAMIC UNIVERSITY SUNAN KALIJAGA

Universitas Islam Negeri Sunan Kalijaga

Jalan Marsda Adisucipto, Yogyakarta, 55281 Yogyakarta
Tel: +62(274) 589-621
Fax: +62(274) 586-117
EMail: admisi@uin-suka.ac.id
Website: http://www.uin-suka.ac.id

Rector: Musa Asy'arie (2010-2014)

Vice-Rector, Administration: H. Nizar

International Relations: Siswanto Masruri, Vice-Rector, Cooperation

Faculties
Adab (Arabic; Information Sciences; Islamic Studies; Library Science); **Dakwah** (Islamic Studies; Psychology; Social Studies); **Postgraduate Studies** (Islamic Studies; Islamic Theology; Religion); **Science and Technology** (Biology; Chemistry; Industrial Engineering; Information Technology; Mathematics; Mathematics Education; Physics); **Social Sciences and Humanities** (Arts and Humanities; Communication Studies; Psychology; Social Sciences; Sociology); **Shariah and Law** (Civil Law; Criminal Law; Family Studies; Islamic Law; Islamic Studies; Law); **Tarbiyah and Teacher Training** (Arabic; Biology; Chemistry; Islamic Studies; Mathematics Education; Physics; Science Education); **Ushuluddin, Religious Studies, and Islamic Thought** (Comparative Religion; Islamic Theology; Philosophy; Religious Studies)

History: Founded 1951 as IAIN (State Institute of Islamic Studies), acquired present status and title in 2004.

Degrees and Diplomas: *Sarjana (S1)*
Last Updated: 05/07/11

STATE UNIVERSITY OF JAKARTA

Universitas Negeri Jakarta (UNJ)

Jalan Rawamangun Muka, Jakarta, 13220 DKI Jakarta
Tel: +62(21) 489-3726 +62(21) 489-0046
Fax: +62(21) 489-3726
EMail: unj@unj.ac.id; administrator@unj.ac.id
Website: http://www.unj.ac.id

Rector: Bedjo Sujanto (2009-2014) EMail: unj@unj.ac.id

Vice-Rector: Zainal Rafli

Faculties
Economics (Accountancy; Administration; Management); **Education** (Education of the Handicapped; Educational Administration; Educational and Student Counselling; Educational Psychology; Educational Sciences; Educational Technology; Preschool Education; Primary Education; Special Education; Technology Education); **Engineering** (Civil Engineering; Clothing and Sewing; Computer Education; Construction Engineering; Cooking and Catering; Electronic Engineering; Home Economics; Information Technology; Mechanical Engineering; Technology; Welfare and Protective Services); **Languages and Arts** (Arabic; Arts and Humanities; Dance; English; Fine Arts; French; German; Handicrafts; Indonesian; Japanese; Literature; Music; Theatre); **Mathematics and Natural Sciences** (Biology; Chemistry; Mathematics Education; Natural Sciences; Physics; Science Education); **Social Sciences** (Civics; Geography (Human); Government; History; Islamic Studies; Islamic Theology; Social Sciences; Sociology); **Sports Science** (Health Education; Physical Education; Sports)

Programmes

Postgraduate Studies (Demography and Population; Educational Administration; Educational Technology; Linguistics; Management; Physical Education; Preschool Education; Primary Education; Sports; Technology Education)

History: Founded 1963. Acquired present status and title 1999.

Academic Year: July to June (July-December; January-June)

Admission Requirements: Secondary school certificate (Sekolah Lanjutan Tingkat Atas), and entrance examination

Main Language(s) of Instruction: Indonesian, English

Accrediting Agencies: Badan Akreditasi Nasional

Degrees and Diplomas: *Diploma*: 1-2 yrs; *Sarjana (S1)*: a further 2 yrs; *Magister (S2)*: Management; Physical Education; Educational Technology; Educational Administration; Primary Education; Preschool Education; Educational Evaluation; Basic Education; Education History; Lingustics; Language Education; Population and Environment, a further 2 yrs; *Doktor (S3)*: Sports Education; Educational Technology; Educational Administration; Educational Evaluation; Language Education; Population and Environment, a further 2 yrs

Student Services: Academic counselling, Canteen, Cultural centre, Employment services, Health services, Language programs, Social counselling, Sports facilities

Student Residential Facilities: Yes

Special Facilities: Studio. Art Gallery

Libraries: c. 140,000 vols (52,000 titles)

Publications: Artistika, Language and Arts Research and Development *(quarterly)*; Parameter, Research and Development in Education *(quarterly)*; Perspektif Ilmu Pendidikan, Educational Sciences Research and Development *(quarterly)*

Press or Publishing House: Percetakan Universitas Negeri Jakarta

Last Updated: 06/07/11

STATE UNIVERSITY OF MAKASSAR

Universitas Negeri Makassar (UNM)

Kampus UNM Gunungsari Baru, Jl. A. P. Pettarani, Makassar, 90222 Sulawesi Selatan
Tel: +62(411) 869-834
Fax: +62(411) 868-794
EMail: admin@unm.ac.id; rektor@unm.ac.id
Website: http://unm.ac.id

Rector: H. Arismunandar (2007-) EMail: rektor@unm.ac.id

Vice-Rector I: Sofyan Salam EMail: anwarpasau@unm.ac.id

International Relations: Nurdin Noni, Vice-Rector IV
Tel: +62(411) 868-653 EMail: mbw_unm@yahoo.com

Faculties

Art and Design (Art Education; Communication Arts; Dance; Design; Fashion Design; Fine Arts; Visual Arts); **Economics** (Accountancy; Economics; Management); **Education** (Biology; Chemistry; Curriculum; Education of the Handicapped; Educational Administration; Educational and Student Counselling; Educational Psychology; Educational Sciences; Educational Technology; Family Studies; Health Education; Leisure Studies; Mathematics Education; Parks and Recreation; Physical Education; Physics; Preschool Education; Primary Education; Social Welfare; Special Education; Sports Management; Teacher Trainers Education); **Engineering** (Automotive Engineering; Building Technologies; Civil Engineering; Construction Engineering; Electrical and Electronic Engineering; Food Technology; Information Technology; Mechanical Engineering); **Languages and Literature** (Art Education; Dance; English; Foreign Languages Education; German; Indonesian; Literature; Modern Languages; Music Education; Native Language Education); **Mathematics and Natural Sciences** (Biology; Chemistry; Geography; Mathematics Education; Physics; Science Education); **Psychology** (Psychology); **Social Sciences** (Civics; Government; Public Administration; Social Sciences; Sociology); **Sports Sciences** (Health Sciences; Physical Education; Sports)

Programmes

Postgraduate (Art Education; Biology; Chemistry; Demography and Population; Economics; Education; Educational Administration; Educational and Student Counselling; Educational Testing and Evaluation; Environmental Studies; Foreign Languages Education; Mathematics Education; Modern Languages; Native Language Education; Physical Education; Public Administration; Science Education; Social Sciences; Sociology; Sports)

History: Founded 1961 on the basis of the Faculty of Education of Hasanuddin Universityas. Attached as a branch of IKIP Yogyakarta 1964. Became IKIP Makassar 1965. Changed title to IKIP Ujung Pandang 1972. Acquired university status and present title 1999.

Academic Year: September to April (September-December;January-April)

Admission Requirements: High school certificate

Main Language(s) of Instruction: Indonesian

Degrees and Diplomas: *Diploma (A.Ma.)*: 3 yrs; *Sarjana (S1) (S.Pd.; S.S.; S.Si.; S.E.)*: 4 yrs; *Magister (S2)*: Art Education; Languages Education; Population and Education (M.Pd.); Mathematics Education; Physical Education; Chemical Education; Biology Education; Sports; Educational Guidance and Counseeling; Educational Administration; Research and Education Evaluation; Social Sciences (M.Pd.), a further 2 yrs; *Doktor (S3)*: Public Administration; Sociology; Science Education; Economic Education; Languages Education; English Education; Population and Environmental Education

Student Services: Academic counselling, Canteen, Health services, Language programs, Social counselling, Sports facilities

Press or Publishing House: Baban Penerbit UNM

Last Updated: 07/07/11

STATE UNIVERSITY OF MALANG

Universitas Negeri Malang (UM)

Jalan Semarang 5, Malang, 65145 Jawa Timur
Tel: +62(341) 551-312
Fax: +62(341) 551-921
EMail: info@um.ac.id
Website: http://www.um.ac.id

Rector: Suparno

Vice-Rector I: Kusmintardjo

Faculties

Economics (Accountancy; Development Studies; Economics; Management; Marketing); **Education** (Biology; Chemistry; Curriculum; Educational Administration; Educational and Student Counselling; Educational Psychology; Educational Technology; Geography; Health Education; History; Leisure Studies; Mathematics Education; Physical Education; Physics; Preschool Education; Primary Education; Special Education); **Engineering** (Automotive Engineering; Building Technologies; Civil Engineering; Computer Science; Electrical Engineering; Electronic Engineering; Food Technology; Industrial Engineering; Information Technology; Mechanical Engineering; Textile Design); **Humanities and Art** (Arabic; Art Education; Dance; Design; English; Fine Arts; German; History; Indonesian; Literature; Visual Arts); **Mathematics and Science** (Biology; Chemistry; Geography; Mathematics Education; Physics); **Postgraduate Studies** (Biology; Chemistry; Economics; Education; Educational Administration; Educational and Student Counselling; Educational Psychology; Educational Technology; Engineering; English; Foreign Languages Education; Geography; Geography (Human); Indonesian; Management; Mathematics Education; Native Language Education; Physical Education; Preschool Education; Primary Education; Vocational Education); **Social Sciences** (Administration; Civics; Government; Public Administration; Social Sciences); **Sports** (Physical Education; Sports)

History: Founded 1954.

Academic Year: July to June (July-December; February-June)

Admission Requirements: Senior high school certificate (Ijasah SMTA)

Main Language(s) of Instruction: Indonesian

Degrees and Diplomas: *Sarjana (S1)*: 4 yrs; *Magister (S2)*: Educational Technology; Education Management; Educational Guidance and Counselling; Educational Psychology; Indonesian; English; Biology Education; Economic Education; Mathematics Education, 5 yrs; *Doktor (S3)*: Educational Technology; Educational Management; Educational Guidance and Counselling; Out of School Education; Indonesian Language and Literature; English; Biology Education; Mathematics Education; Elementary

Mathematics Education; Chemistry Education; Geography Education; Vocational Education; Economic Education; Basic Education, 5 yrs

Student Services: Academic counselling, Canteen, Cultural centre, Foreign student adviser, Health services, Nursery care, Social counselling, Sports facilities

Student Residential Facilities: For c. 9,800 students

Special Facilities: Biological Garden. Movie Studio

Libraries: c. 60,000 vols

Publications: Abdi Masyarakat; Bahasa dan Sastra Indonesia; Bangunan; Bina Bimbingan; Chimera; Civicus; English Language Education; Formath; Forum Sekolah Dasar; Foton; Manajemen Pendidikan; Media Komunikasi Kimia; Nadi'l-Lughah Al-Arabiyyah; Pendidikan Geografi; Pendidikan Jasmani; Pendidikan Masyarakat; Pendidikan Nilai; Sejarah; Sekolah Dasar; Sumber Belajar; Teflin; Teknik Mesin dan Elektro; Teknologi Pendidikan; Wahana Sekolah Dasar

Press or Publishing House: IKIP Malang Press
Last Updated: 07/07/11

STATE UNIVERSITY OF MEDAN

Universitas Negeri Medan (UNIMED)

Jalan William Iskandar, Pasar V - Medan Estate, Medan, 20221 Sumatera Utara
Tel: +62(61) 661-3365 +62(61) 661-3276
Fax: +62(61) 661-4002
EMail: unimed@unimed.ac.id; sekretariat@unimed.ac.id
Website: http://www.unimed.ac.id

Rector: Syawal Gultom
Tel: +62(61) 6613-365, Fax: +62(61) 6613-319

Vice-Rector: Selamat Triono
Tel: +62(61) 6613-319, Fax: +62(61) 6613-319

International Relations: Setianna Simorangkir, Fourth Vice Rector
Tel: +62(61) 6643-469, Fax: +62(61) 6613-319
EMail: pr_empat@yahoo.com

Faculties

Economics (Accountancy; Economics; Management); **Education** (Education; Educational Administration; Educational and Student Counselling; Educational Technology; Primary Education); **Engineering** (Civil Engineering; Cooking and Catering; Cosmetology; Electrical Engineering; Engineering; Home Economics; Mechanical Engineering); **Languages and Art** (Dance; English; Fine Arts; French; German; Modern Languages; Music; Native Language; Theatre); **Mathematics and Natural Sciences** (Biology; Chemistry; Mathematics; Mathematics Education; Physics; Science Education); **Social Sciences** (Civics; Geography (Human); History); **Sport Science** (Health Education; Leisure Studies; Parks and Recreation; Physical Education; Sports; Sports Management)

Institutes

Research; **Social Development**

Programmes

Postgraduate Studies (Anthropology; Applied Linguistics; Biology; Chemistry; Demography and Population; Development Studies; Ecology; Economics; Education; Educational Administration; Educational Technology; English; Mathematics Education; Physical Education; Preschool Education; Primary Education; Social Sciences)

History: Founded 1956. Became Faculty of Education 1957, as part of the North Sumatra University. Became Faculty of Education of IKIP Jakarta 1963. Became IKIP Medan 1968 after integration. Became University of Medan and acquired present status 1999.

Academic Year: September to June (September-January; February-June)

Admission Requirements: Ijazah SMU, SMK or MAN (respectively, high school, vocational school or Islamic high school certificates)

Main Language(s) of Instruction: Indonesian, English

Degrees and Diplomas: *Diploma*: 2-3 yrs; *Sarjana (S1)*: 4 yrs; *Magister (S2)*: Economics; Social Anthropology; Mathematics Education; Physical Education; Chemical Education; Biology Education; Educational Technology; Educational Administration; Basic Education; Applied English Linguistics, a further 2 yrs; *Doktor (S3)*: Educational Administration

Student Services: Academic counselling, Canteen, Cultural centre, Employment services, Foreign student adviser, Foreign Studies Centre, Health services, Language programs, Nursery care, Social counselling, Sports facilities

Special Facilities: Art Gallery; Laboratories; Auditorium.

Libraries: Central Library, c. 49,000 vols

Publications: Jurnal BAHAS *(quarterly)*; Jurnal FEKOS *(quarterly)*; Jurnal Geomedia *(quarterly)*; Jurnal Ilmu Keolahragaan *(quarterly)*; Jurnal Ilmu Pendidikan *(quarterly)*; Jurnal Pendidikan Teknik dan Kejuruan *(quarterly)*; Jurnal Penelitian Bidang Pendidikan, Educational Research Journal *(quarterly)*; Jurnal Pengabdian Pada Masyarakat *(quarterly)*; Jurnal Sains Indonesia, Indonesian Science Journal *(quarterly)*; Jurnal Saintika *(quarterly)*; Jurnal Tabularasa *(quarterly)*; Jurnal Visi Ekonomi *(quarterly)*; Majalah Bina Teknik *(quarterly)*; Pelangi Pendidikan *(quarterly)*; Telaah Akuntansi *(quarterly)*

Press or Publishing House: UNIMED Press
Last Updated: 07/07/11

SUMATERA UTARA UNIVERSITY

Universitas Sumatera Utara (USU)

Jalan Dr. T. Mansoer 9, Kampus USU, Medan, 20155 Sumatera Utara
Tel: +62(61) 814-033 +62(61) 811-212
Fax: +62(61) 811-633 +62(61) 811-822
Website: http://www.usu.ac.id/

Rector: Syahril Pasaribu (2010-2014) EMail: syahril@usu.ac.id

Executive Secretary: Lian Dalimunthe
EMail: mldalimunthe@yahoo.co.id

International Relations: Ningrum Natasya Sirait
EMail: ningrum@indosat.net.id

Faculties

Agriculture (Agricultural Economics; Agricultural Engineering; Agriculture; Agronomy; Animal Husbandry; Forestry; Plant and Crop Protection; Plant Pathology; Soil Science); **Arts and Humanities** (Arabic; Arts and Humanities; English; History; Indonesian; Japanese; Library Science; Literature; Musicology; Tourism); **Dentistry** (Dentistry); **Economics** (Accountancy; Development Studies; Economics; Finance; Management; Secretarial Studies); **Engineering** (Architecture; Chemical Engineering; Civil Engineering; Electrical Engineering; Engineering; Industrial Engineering; Mechanical Engineering); **Law** (Law); **Mathematics and Natural Sciences** (Analytical Chemistry; Biology; Chemistry; Computer Science; Mathematics; Natural Sciences; Pharmacy; Physics; Science Education; Statistics); **Medicine** (Medicine; Nursing); **Public Health** (Public Health); **Social and Political Sciences** (Administration; Anthropology; Government; Mass Communication; Political Sciences; Social Sciences; Social Welfare; Sociology; Taxation)

Schools

Postgraduate Studies

History: Founded 1952. A State institution.

Governing Bodies: Board of Trustees, Academic Senate, Rectors, Professor Council, Audit Board.

Academic Year: January to December (January-June; August-December)

Admission Requirements: Secondary school certificate (Sekolah Menengah Atas, SMA. or Sekolah Lanjutan Tingkat Atas, SLA)

Fees: (Rupiahs): 1m-50m. per annum

Main Language(s) of Instruction: Indonesian

International Co-operation: With Malaysian and Thai universities (Indonesian Malaysia Thailand - Growth Triangle (IMT-GT))

Accrediting Agencies: National Accreditation Bureau (BAN - PT)

Degrees and Diplomas: *Diploma*: Business Administration, 2-3 yrs; *Sarjana (S1)*: Agriculture (Insinjur); Dentistry; Economics; Engineering (Insinjur); Hukum, law; Letters; Science; Social Science, 4-6 yrs; *Magister (S2)*: a further 2-4 yrs; *Doktor (S3)*: Law, Agriculture, Linguistics, Urban Development, Environmental Management, 3-6 yrs; *Doktor (S3)*: Medicine, 7-8 yrs

Student Services: Canteen, Cultural centre, Employment services, Foreign student adviser, Health services, Language programs, Social counselling, Sports facilities

Student Residential Facilities: Yes

Libraries: c. 500,000 vols; e-journal, 12,000 titles.

Press or Publishing House: USU Press

Academic Staff *2010-2011*	MEN	WOMEN	TOTAL
FULL-TIME	948	684	**1,632**
STAFF WITH DOCTORATE			
FULL-TIME	–	–	**298**
Student Numbers *2010-2011*			
All (Foreign Included)	–	–	**35,510**

Last Updated: 26/10/10

SURABAYA STATE UNIVERSITY

Universitas Negeri Surabaya

Kampus IKIP, Jalan Ketintang, Surabaya, 60231 Jawa Timur
Tel: +62(31) 8280-009 +62(31) 8280-383
Fax: +62(31) 8280-804
EMail: rektor@unesa.ac.id
Website: http://www.unesa.ac.id

Rector: Muchlas Samani (2010-2014)

Vice-Rector I: Kisyani Laksono

International Relations: Nurhasan, Vice-Rector IV

Faculties

Education (Curriculum; Education of the Handicapped; Educational Administration; Educational and Student Counselling; Educational Sciences; Preschool Education; Primary Education; Special Education); **Engineering** (Civil Engineering; Construction Engineering; Electrical Engineering; Engineering; Fashion Design; Food Technology; Home Economics; Mechanical Engineering); **Graduate Studies** (Art Education; Cultural Studies; Economics; Education; Educational Administration; Educational Technology; Foreign Languages Education; Humanities and Social Science Education; Mathematics Education; Modern Languages; Native Language Education; Physical Education; Preschool Education; Primary Education; Science Education; Social Studies; Special Education; Sports); **Languages and Art** (Art Education; Chinese; Crafts and Trades; Dance; English; Fine Arts; Foreign Languages Education; German; Graphic Arts; Graphic Design; Indonesian; Japanese; Literature; Modern Languages; Music Education; Native Language; Native Language Education; South and Southeast Asian Languages; Theatre); **Mathematics and Natural Sciences** (Biology; Chemistry; Mathematics; Mathematics Education; Physics; Science Education); **Social Sciences** (Administration; Civics; Economics; Geography; Government; History; Social Sciences); **Sport Sciences** (Health Sciences; Physical Education; Sports)

History: Founded 1964 as IKIP Surabaya. Acquired present status and title 1999.

Degrees and Diplomas: *Sarjana (S1)*; *Magister (S2)*: Culture and Art Education; Social Studies Education; Economic Education; Basic Education; Educational Administration; Educational Technology; Special Education; Physical Education; Mathematics Education; Science Education; Vocational Education; *Doktor (S3)*: Mathematics Education; Languages Education; Sport Sciences

Last Updated: 07/07/11

IAU SYIAH KUALA UNIVERSITY

Universitas Syiah Kuala

Kopelma Darussalam, Banda Aceh, 23111 Aceh
Tel: +62(651) 755-1242 +62(651) 755-1237 +62(651) 755-2730
Fax: +62(651) 755-1241 +62(651) 755-2730 +62(651) 755-4229
Website: http://www.unsyiah.ac.id

Rector: Darni M. Daud (2006-) EMail: rektor@unsyiah.ac.id

International Relations: Darusman Rusin, Vice-Rector, Cooperation Affairs EMail: pr4@unsyiah.ac.id

Faculties

Agriculture (Agricultural Economics; Agricultural Engineering; Agriculture; Agronomy; Animal Husbandry; Plant and Crop Protection; Plant Pathology; Social Sciences); **Economics** (Accountancy; Banking; Business Administration; Economics; Finance; Management; Taxation); **Engineering** (Architecture; Architecture and Planning; Chemical Engineering; Civil Engineering; Electrical and Electronic Engineering; Electrical Engineering; Engineering); **Law** (Law); **Mathematics and Natural Sciences** (Biological and Life Sciences; Biology; Chemistry; Marine Science and Oceanography; Mathematics; Mathematics and Computer Science; Natural Sciences; Physics); **Medicine** (Dentistry; Medicine; Nursing; Psychology); **Sociology and Political Sciences** (Anthropology; Communication Studies; Political Sciences; Sociology); **Teacher Training and Educational Sciences** (Art Education; Biology; Civics; Dance; Economics; English; Foreign Languages Education; History; Household Management; Humanities and Social Science Education; Indonesian; Law; Linguistics; Mathematics Education; Music Education; Physical Education; Science Education; Sports; Teacher Training); **Veterinary Medicine** (Veterinary Science)

History: Founded 1959 as Faculty of economics attached to Universitas Sumatera Utara, Medan. Became State university 1961.

Governing Bodies: Board of Trustees

Academic Year: February to December (February-June; September-February)

Admission Requirements: Secondary school certificate (Sekolah Menengah Atas, SMA) and entrance examination

Main Language(s) of Instruction: Indonesian

Degrees and Diplomas: *Sarjana (S1)*: 4 yrs; *Magister (S2)*: 2 yrs; *Doktor (S3)*: 3 yrs

Student Residential Facilities: For c. 3.000 students

Special Facilities: Academic Activity Centre; Union Students Centre; Computer Center; Islamic Centre; Language Centre; University Farms

Libraries: University Library System, c. 150,000 vols

Publications: Warta Unsyiah *(monthly)*

Press or Publishing House: Badan Penerbitan dan Percetakan Unsyiah (Syiah Kuala University Press)

Last Updated: 17/06/10

TADULAKO UNIVERSITY

Universitas Tadulako (UNTAD)

Kampus Bumi Tadulako Tondo, Palu, 94118 Sulawesi Tengah
Tel: +62(451) 422-611
Fax: +62(451) 422-611
EMail: sisdiksat@palu.wasantara.net.id
Website: http://www.untad.ac.id/

Rector: Sahabuddin Mustapa
Tel: +62(451) 453-776, Fax: +62(451) 422-355

Vice-Rector: Dahlia Syuaib

International Relations: Aiyen EMail: aiyen@untad.ac.id

Faculties

Agriculture (Agricultural Economics; Agriculture; Agronomy; Animal Husbandry; Fishery; Nutrition; Plant Pathology) *Dean*: Muh. Basir Cyio; **Economics** (Accountancy; Development Studies; Economics; Management) *Dean*: Patta Tope; **Engineering** (Civil Engineering; Construction Engineering; Electrical Engineering; Engineering; Mechanical Engineering) *Dean*: Hasanuddin Azikin; **Forestry** (Forest Management; Forest Products; Forestry) *Dean*: Akhbar; **Law** (Constitutional Law; Criminal Law; Law) *Dean*: Idham Chalid; **Postgraduate Studies** *Dean*: Indrianto Kadekoh; **Science** (Medicine; Public Health) *Dean*: Achmad Ramadan; **Social and Political Sciences** (Government; Political Sciences; Public Administration; Sociology) *Dean*: Maddukelleng; **Teacher Training and Educational Sciences** (Biology; Chemistry; Civics; Curriculum; Education; English; History; Indonesian; Mathematics Education; Modern Languages; Physics; Primary Education; Science Education; Teacher Training) *Dean*: Hasan Basri

Laboratories

Agricultural Sciences and Animal Husbandry (Agricultural Engineering; Agriculture; Animal Husbandry; Fishery; Forestry) *Director*: Muslimin; **Architecture** (Architecture; Engineering Drawing and Design; Interior Design) *Director*: Pudji Astutiek; **Civil Engineering** (Construction Engineering; Hydraulic Engineering; Road Engineering; Soil Science; Transport Engineering) *Director*: Sance Lipu; **Economics and Accountancy** (Accountancy; Economics) *Director*: Muh. Ramli Nuntung; **Educational and Teaching**

Sciences (Biology; Chemistry; Educational Sciences; Mathematics; Physics; Teacher Training) *Director*: Jos Ohoiwutum; **Polytechnics** (Electronic Engineering; Engineering; Machine Building) *Director*: Muhammad Iqbal; **Social Studies** (Political Sciences; Social Sciences) *Director*: Paulus Kero Lolo

History: Founded 1981, incorporating Universitas Tadulako and IKIP Ujung Pandang Cabang Palu. A State institution under the jurisdiction of the Department of Education and Culture.

Academic Year: July to June (July-December; January-June)

Admission Requirements: Secondary school certificate (Sekolah Menengah Atas, S.M.A.) and entrance examination

Fees: (Rupiahs): Undergraduate, 500,000 per semester; Postgraduate, 4m. per semester

Main Language(s) of Instruction: Indonesian

Degrees and Diplomas: *Diploma*: 3-5 yrs; *Sarjana (S1)*: 4-7 yrs; *Magister (S2)*: 2-3 yrs

Student Services: Academic counselling, Canteen, Employment services, Health services, Language programs, Social counselling, Sports facilities

Student Residential Facilities: Yes

Special Facilities: Auditorium. Islamic Studies Centre

Libraries: c. 23,650 vols

Publications: Gagasan, Magazine *(biannually)*; Mektek *(monthly)*; Perspektif *(biennially)*

Academic Staff *2010-2011*	MEN	WOMEN	**TOTAL**
FULL-TIME	803	364	**1,167**
STAFF WITH DOCTORATE			
FULL-TIME	125	34	**159**
Student Numbers *2010-2011*			
All (Foreign Included)	10,431	9,816	**20,247**

Last Updated: 07/04/11

TANJUNGPURA UNIVERSITY

Universitas Tanjungpura

Jalan A. Yani, Pontianak, 78124 Kalimantan Barat
Tel: +62(561) 736-439 +62(561) 743-464
Fax: +62(561) 739-630 +62(561) 739-636
EMail: webmaster@untan.ac.id; untan@gerbang.untan.ac.id
Website: http://www.untan.ac.id/

Rector: Thamrin Usman (2011-2015)
EMail: Thamrin_Usman@yahoo.com

Vice-Rector: Saeri Sagiman

Faculties

Agriculture (Agricultural Economics; Agriculture; Agronomy; Soil Science); **Economics** (Accountancy; Development Studies; Economics; Management); **Engineering** (Civil Engineering; Electrical Engineering); **Forestry** (Forestry); **Law** (Law); **Mathematics and Natural Sciences** *(Preparative)* (Mathematics; Natural Sciences); **Medicine** (Medicine); **Social and Political Sciences** (Administration; Political Sciences; Sociology); **Teacher Training and Educational Sciences** (Education; Educational Sciences; English; Mathematics Education; Natural Sciences; Primary Education; Social Sciences; Teacher Training)

Programmes

Postgraduate Studies (Agricultural Business; Civil Engineering; Economics; Educational Administration; Electrical Engineering; Government; Indonesian; Law; Management; Natural Sciences; Political Sciences; Social Sciences; Sociology)

History: Founded 1965.

Academic Year: July to June (July-December; January-June)

Admission Requirements: Secondary school certificate (Sekolah Menengah Atas, SMA)

Main Language(s) of Instruction: Indonesian

Degrees and Diplomas: *Diploma*: 1-3 yrs; *Sarjana (S1)*: 4-7 yrs; *Magister (S2)*

Last Updated: 07/06/11

TIRTAYASA SULTAN AGENG UNIVERSITY

Universitas Sultan Ageng Tirtayasa

Jalan Raya Jakarta Km 4, Serang, 42118 Banten
Tel: +62(254) 280-330
Fax: +62(254) 281-254
EMail: info@untirta.ac.id
Website: http://www.untirta.ac.id/

Rector: Rahman Abdullah

Vice-Rector: Sudendi

Faculties

Economics; **Engineering** (Chemical Engineering; Civil Engineering; Educational Technology; Electrical Engineering; Engineering; Industrial Engineering; Metallurgical Engineering); **Political and Social Sciences** (Communication Studies; Government; Law; Political Sciences; Social Sciences); **Teacher Training and Educational Sciences** (Education; Educational Sciences; English; Indonesian; Mathematics Education; Primary Education; Teacher Training)

Degrees and Diplomas: *Sarjana (S1)*; *Magister (S2)*

Last Updated: 04/05/10

TRUNOJOYO UNIVERSITY

Universitas Trunojoyo

PO Box 2, Kampus Unijoyo, Jalan Raya Telang, Kamal Bangkalan, Madura
Tel: +62(31) 3011-146 +62(31) 5345-570
Fax: +62(31) 3011-506 +62(31) 5316-359
EMail: humas@trunojoyo.ac.id
Website: http://www.trunojoyo.ac.id/

Rector: Ariffin Fax: +62(31) 301-3280
EMail: rektor@trunojoyo.ac.id

Faculties

Agriculture (Agriculture; Agronomy) *Dean*: Kaswan Bademi; **Economics** (Economics; Management) *Dean*: Muhammad Nizarulalim; **Engineering** (Engineering) *Dean*: Suprapto; **Law** (Law) *Dean*: Yudy Widagdo; **Social Science and Cultural studies** (Cultural Studies; Social Sciences; Social Studies) *Dean*: Suryo Trisaksono

History: Founded 2001.

Degrees and Diplomas: *Diploma*: 3 yrs; *Sarjana (S1)*: 4 yrs

Student Services: Academic counselling, Cultural centre, Employment services, Health services, Language programs, Sports facilities

Libraries: Yes

Last Updated: 15/12/10

UDAYANA UNIVERSITY

Universitas Udayana

Kampus Bukit Jimbaran, Denpasar, 80361 Bali
Tel: +62(361) 701-954 +62(361) 704-845
Fax: +62(361) 701-907
EMail: info@unud.ac.id
Website: http://www.unud.ac.id/

President: I. Made Bakta
Tel: +62(361) 703-140 EMail: rektor@unud.ac.id

Vice-President: Komang Gde Bendesa

International Relations: Made Suastra, Vice President for Cooperation and Information Affairs

Departments

Tourism (Communication Studies; Tourism; Transport Management)

Faculties

Agriculture (Agricultural Economics; Agricultural Engineering; Agriculture; Agronomy; Plant Pathology; Soil Science); **Animal Husbandry** (Agricultural Business; Agricultural Economics; Agricultural Management; Animal Husbandry; Biochemistry; Food Science; Food Technology; Nutrition; Soil Science); **Arts and Humanities** (Anthropology; Archaeology; Arts and Humanities; English; History; Indonesian; Japanese; Literature; Tourism); **Economics** (Accountancy; Development Studies; Economics; Finance; Management; Marketing; Taxation); **Engineering** (Architecture;

Civil Engineering; Electrical Engineering; Engineering; Mechanical Engineering; Structural Architecture); **Law** (Administrative Law; Civil Law; Commercial Law; Constitutional Law; Criminal Law; Criminology; Human Rights; International Law; Islamic Law; Labour Law; Law); **Mathematics and Natural Sciences** (Biology; Chemistry; Computer Science; Mathematics; Natural Sciences; Pharmacy; Physics); **Medicine and Health Sciences** (Alternative Medicine; Biochemistry; Biomedicine; Cardiology; Endocrinology; Ergotherapy; Gerontology; Gynaecology and Obstetrics; Haematology; Immunology; Information Management; Medicine; Nutrition; Oncology; Physiology; Pneumology; Rehabilitation and Therapy; Urology); **Social and Political Sciences** (Political Sciences; Public Administration; Social Sciences; Sociology); **Veterinary Medicine** (Anatomy; Pharmacology; Pharmacy; Physiology; Veterinary Science; Wildlife)

Programmes

Agricultural Technology (Agricultural Engineering; Crop Production; Food Science; Food Technology); **Postgraduate Studies** (Agricultural Business; Agriculture; Animal Husbandry; Arid Land Studies; Biomedicine; Biotechnology; Civil Engineering; Cultural Studies; Development Studies; Economics; Embryology and Reproduction Biology; Engineering; Environmental Studies; Industrial Design; Law; Linguistics; Management; Physiology; Sports; Tourism)

History: Founded 1962 incorporating former Faculty of Letters, founded 1950 and attached to Airlangga University. A State Institution.

Governing Bodies: Senate

Academic Year: February to November (February-June; July-November)

Admission Requirements: Secondary school certificate (Sekolah Menengah Atas, SMA)

Main Language(s) of Instruction: Indonesian

Accrediting Agencies: Department of Education and Culture

Degrees and Diplomas: *Sarjana (S1)*: 5 yrs; *Sarjana (S1)*: Engineering (Insinjur), 5 yrs; *Sarjana (S1)*: Medicine, 7 yrs; *Magister (S2)*: Agribusiness; Animal Husbandry; Civil Engineering; Tourism; Linguistics; Cultural Studies; Ergonomics and Work Physiology; Sport Physiology; Reproduction Medicine; Law; Management; Developmental Economics; Agricultural Biotechnology; Dry Land Agriculture; Environmental Studies; *Doktor (S3)*: Agricultural Sciences; Animal Sciences; Economics; Linguistics; Cultural Studies; Biomedical Sciences

Student Services: Canteen, Health services, Language programs, Sports facilities

Student Residential Facilities: Yes

Libraries: Central Library, Faculty Libraries, total, 40,000 vols

Publications: Majalah Ilmiah Universitas Udayana (Scientific Publication)

Last Updated: 08/07/11

YOGYAKARTA STATE UNIVERSITY

Universitas Negeri Yogyakarta (UNY)

Kampus IKIP, Karangmalang, Yogyakarta, 55281 Yogyakarta

Tel: +62(274) 586-168

Fax: +62(274) 565-500

EMail: humas@uny.ac.id

Website: http://www.uny.ac.id

Rector: Rochmat Wahab
Tel: +62(274) 512-192, Fax: +62(274) 565-500
EMail: rochmat_wb@uny.ac.id; arwahab@yahoo.com

Vice-Rector, Academic Affairs: Nurfina Aznam

Faculties

Education (Curriculum; Education; Education of the Handicapped; Educational Administration; Educational and Student Counselling; Educational Psychology; Educational Technology; Preschool Education; Primary Education; Special Education; Teacher Training); **Engineering** (Automotive Engineering; Civil Engineering; Clothing and Sewing; Construction Engineering; Cooking and Catering; Electrical and Electronic Engineering; Food Technology; Home Economics; Mechanical Engineering; Technology); **Languages and Art** (Dance; English; Fashion Design; Fine Arts; French; German; Handicrafts; Indonesian; Literature; Music; Native Language; Painting and Drawing; Performing Arts; South and Southeast Asian Languages); **Mathematics and Natural Sciences** (Biology; Chemistry; Mathematics; Natural Sciences; Physics; Science Education); **Social Sciences and Economics** (Accountancy; Administration; Civics; Economics; Geography (Human); History; Management; Marketing; Public Administration; Secretarial Studies; Social Sciences; Sociology); **Sports Sciences** (Health Education; Leisure Studies; Parks and Recreation; Physical Education; Sports; Sports Management)

Programmes

Postgraduate Studies (Educational Administration; Educational Technology; Educational Testing and Evaluation; Preschool Education; Primary Education; Science Education; Special Education; Technology Education; Vocational Education)

History: Founded 1964 as IKIP Yogyakarta. Acquired present status and title 1999.

Admission Requirements: Ijazah SMU (certificate of Senior High School) and entrance examination

Main Language(s) of Instruction: Indonesian, English

Accrediting Agencies: Badan Akreditasi Nasional

Degrees and Diplomas: *Sarjana (S1)*; *Magister (S2)*: Educational Technology; Vocational Education; Science Education; Mathematics Education; Educational Administration; Out of School Education; Educational Research and Evaluation; Basic Education; Social Sciences Education; Applied Linguistics; Sport Science; *Doktor (S3)*: Educational Technology; Vocational Education; Science Education; Educational Management; Educational Research and Evaluation

Student Services: Academic counselling, Canteen, Cultural centre, Employment services, Foreign student adviser, Health services, Language programs, Nursery care, Sports facilities

Student Residential Facilities: Yes

Libraries: Central and Faculty Libraries

Publications: Cakrawala Pendidikan *(quarterly)*; Jurnal Kependidikan *(3 per annum)*; Jurnal Limu Pengetahuan, dan Humaniora *(3 per annum)*

Last Updated: 07/07/11

PRIVATE INSTITUTIONS

17 AUGUST 1945 UNIVERSITY BANYUWANGI

Universitas 17 Agustus 1945 Banyuwangi

Jalan Adi Sucipto 26, Banyuwangi, 68416 Jawa Timur

Tel: +62(333) 411-248

Fax: +62(333) 424-980

EMail: untagbwi@plasa.com

Rector: Sugihartoyo

Faculties

Agriculture (Agricultural Economics; Agronomy; Fishery); **Economics** (Accountancy; Management); **Educational Sciences and Teacher Training** (Biology; Education; English; Foreign Languages Education; History); **Engineering** (Agricultural Engineering; Civil Engineering; Engineering; Industrial Engineering); **Law** (Law); **Social and Political Sciences** (Administration; Government; Public Administration) *Dean*: Sri Rahayu

History: Founded 1980 by the 17 August 1945 National Education Foundation. A private institution under the supervision of the Department of Education and Culture.

Academic Year: September to August (September-February; March-August)

Admission Requirements: Senior high school certificate (Sekolah Lanjutan Atas, SLA)

Main Language(s) of Instruction: Indonesian

Degrees and Diplomas: *Sarjana (S1)*: 4 yrs

Student Services: Academic counselling, Canteen, Cultural centre, Sports facilities

Libraries: University Library, c. 3,800 vols

Last Updated: 22/06/11

17 AUGUST 1945 UNIVERSITY CIREBON

Universitas 17 Agustus 1945 Cirebon (UNTAG CIREBON)
Jalan Perjuangan 17, Cirebon, 45135 Jawa Barat
Tel: +62(231) 231-745 +62(231) 230-845
Fax: +62(231) 485-345
EMail: untag@indonet.id

Rector: Djalil Idris Saputra

Ketua: Iman Taufik

Faculties

Administration (Business Administration; Government; Hotel Management; Public Administration) *Dean*: Ade Setiadi; **Agriculture** (Agriculture; Fishery) *Dean*: R.A. Maghfur; **Economics** (Accountancy; Management) *Dean*: H.A. Djalil Idris; **Engineering** (Electrical Engineering; Engineering; Mechanical Engineering) *Dean*: Soedigto Soegondo; **Law** (Law) *Dean*: Didi Nursidi

History: Founded 1962 by the 17 August 1945 National Education Foundation. A private institution under the supervision of the Department of Education and Culture.

Fees: (Rupiahs): 1.2m. per annum

Degrees and Diplomas: *Diploma*: 3 yrs; *Sarjana (S1)*; *Magister (S2)*: Administration

Libraries: 11,668 vols

Last Updated: 09/02/09

17 AUGUST 1945 UNIVERSITY JAKARTA

Universitas 17 Agustus 1945 Jakarta (UNTAG)
Jalan Sunter Permai Raya, Sunter Agung, Podomoro, Jakarta Utara, 14350 DKI Jakarta
Tel: +62(21) 6410-287 +62(21) 685-666
Fax: +62(21) 6410-287
Website: http://www.untag-jkt.org

Rector: Thomas N. Peea

Ketua: Lodewijk Aroean

Programmes

Administration (Business Administration; Government; Public Administration); **Engineering** (Civil Engineering; Electrical Engineering; Engineering; Mechanical Engineering); **Law** (Law); **Management and Accountancy** (Accountancy; Management); **Pharmacy** (Pharmacy); **Social and Political Sciences** (Communication Studies; Government; International Relations; Political Sciences; Public Administration; Social Sciences)

History: Founded 1952 by the 17 August 1945 National Education Foundation. A private institution under the supervision of the Department of Education and Culture.

Academic Year: September to August (September-February; March-August)

Admission Requirements: Secondary school certificate (Sekolah Lanjutan Atas, SLA)

Main Language(s) of Instruction: Indonesian

Degrees and Diplomas: *Diploma*; *Sarjana (S1)*: 4 yrs; *Magister (S2)*: Law, a further 2 yrs; *Doktor (S3)*: Law

Student Services: Academic counselling, Canteen, Cultural centre, Health services, Social counselling, Sports facilities

Libraries: c. 8,530 vols

Publications: Journal Ilmiah (Scientific Journal)

Last Updated: 11/07/11

17 AUGUST 1945 UNIVERSITY SAMARINDA

Universitas 17 Agustus 1945 Samarinda
PO 1052, Jalan Ir. Juanda 80, Samarinda, 75124 Kalimantan Timur
Tel: +62(541) 743-390
Fax: +62(541) 761-113
Website: http://www.untag-smd.ac.id/

Rector: Eddy Soegiarto

Vice-Rector for Public administration: Benny E. Mochtar
EMail: awangfaroek@bilingtri.com

International Relations: Pinaringan Sujalu, Vice-Rector for Student Affairs

Faculties

Agriculture (Agricultural Engineering; Agriculture; Agronomy; Forest Management); **Economics** (Accountancy; Economics; Management); **Engineering** (Architecture; Civil Engineering; Engineering; Structural Architecture); **Law** (Law); **Social and Political Sciences** (Political Sciences; Psychology; Public Administration; Social Sciences)

History: Founded 1965 by the 17 August 1945 National Education Foundation. Acquired present status 2002. A private institution under the supervision of the Department of Education and Culture.

Governing Bodies: August 17 1945 Foundation Samarinda

Admission Requirements: Senior High School Certificate; Vocational School Certificate

Main Language(s) of Instruction: Indonesian

Degrees and Diplomas: *Sarjana (S1)*: 5 yrs

Student Services: Academic counselling, Canteen, Cultural centre, Employment services, Foreign student adviser, Foreign Studies Centre, Handicapped facilities, Health services, Language programs, Social counselling, Sports facilities

Special Facilities: None

Libraries: Yes

Press or Publishing House: LPPM

Last Updated: 22/06/11

17 AUGUST 1945 UNIVERSITY SEMARANG

Universitas 17 Agustus 1945 Semarang
Jalan Pawiyatan Luhur Bhendan Duwur, Semarang, 50133 Jawa Tengah
Tel: +62(24) 844-1771
Fax: +62(24) 844-1772
EMail: untag@untagsmg.ac.id
Website: http://www.untagsmg.ac.id

Rector: Wijaya

Vice-Rector I: Bambang Joyo Supeno

International Relations: Nur Bagyo Utomo, Vice-Rector IV

Faculties

Agricultural Production Technology (Fishery; Food Science; Food Technology; Packaging Technology); **Economics** (Accountancy; Economics; Finance; Management Systems; Marketing; Taxation); **Engineering** (Architecture; Chemical Engineering; Civil Engineering; Structural Architecture); **Law** (Commercial Law; Criminal Law; Government; Law; Political Sciences); **Social and Political Sciences** (Administration; Banking; Business Administration; English; Finance; Government; Human Resources; Indonesian; Insurance; International Business; Public Relations)

Programmes

Graduate Studies (Administration; Law; Management)

History: Founded 1963 by the 17 August 1945 National Education Foundation. A private institution under the supervision of the Department of Education and Culture.

Academic Year: September to July (September-January; February-July)

Admission Requirements: Secondary school certificate (Sekolah Lanjutan Atas, SLA) and entrance examination

Main Language(s) of Instruction: Indonesian

Degrees and Diplomas: *Diploma*: 3 yrs; *Sarjana (S1)*: 5 yrs; *Magister (S2)*: Administration; Law; Management

Libraries: Total, c. 4,100 vols

Last Updated: 11/07/11

17 AUGUST 1945 UNIVERSITY SURABAYA

Universitas 17 Agustus 1945 Surabaya (UNTAG SURABAYA)
Jalan Semolowaru 45, Surabaya, 60118 Jawa Timur, East Java
Tel: +62(31) 593-1800
Fax: +62(31) 592-6714
EMail: humas@untag-sby.ac.id; info@untag.ac.id
Website: http://www.untag-sby.ac.id/

Rector: Ida Aju Brahmasari (2009-2014)
Tel: +62(31) 593-7038, Fax: +62(31) 592-7817
EMail: iabrahmasari@yahoo.com

Chairperson: Mangapul Silalahi Tel: +62(31) 594-9447

International Relations: Andik Matulessy, Assistant to the Rector on Academic and International Relations Affairs
Fax: +62(31) 592-7817 EMail: pakandik@hotmail.com

Faculties

Arts and Humanities (Arts and Humanities; English; Japanese; Literature; Modern Languages) *Dean*: Sukarno HS; **Economics** (Accountancy; Development Studies; Economics; Management) *Dean*: Nono Supriyadi; **Engineering** (Architecture; Civil Engineering; Computer Engineering; Computer Science; Electrical Engineering; Engineering; Industrial Engineering; Mechanical Engineering; Structural Architecture) *Dean*: Muaffaq Achmad Jani; **Food Technology** (Food Technology) *Dean*: Tatan Satryo; **Law** (Law) *Dean*: Adianto Martodijono; **Postgraduate Studies** *Dean*: Rudy Handoko; **Psychology** (Psychology) *Dean*: Adnani Budi Utami; **Social and Political Sciences** (Business Administration; Communication Studies; Public Administration) *Dean*: IGN Anom Maruta

History: Founded 1956 by the 17 August 1945 National Education Foundation. Acquired present status and title 1958.

Governing Bodies: 17 August 1945 National Education Foundation

Academic Year: August to July (August-January; February-July)

Admission Requirements: Senior high school certificate

Fees: (Rupiahs): 5m. per annum (2.5m. per semester)

Main Language(s) of Instruction: Indonesian

Accrediting Agencies: Department of Education and Culture, National Accreditation Board of Higher Education

Degrees and Diplomas: *Sarjana (S1)*: Social Sciences; Agricultural Technology; Economics; Law; Arts; Psychology; Engineering (S.Soc; STp; SE; SH; SS; S.Psi; ST), 4-5 yrs; *Magister (S2)*: Engineering; Management; Social Sciences; Psychology; Law (MT; MM; M.Si; MH), a further 2 yrs; *Doktor (S3)*: Economics; Law; Public and Business Administration (Dr), a further 3-5 yrs

Student Services: Academic counselling, Canteen, Cultural centre, Employment services, Foreign student adviser, Health services, Language programs, Social counselling, Sports facilities

Student Residential Facilities: Yes

Special Facilities: Laboratory (Engineering; Language; Technology; Computer; Biochemistry; Psychology; Communication; Lecture Theatre; Law Firm)

Libraries: c. 30,000 vols

Publications: Dinamika, Public and Business Administration *(biannually)*; Ekonomi dan Bisnis, Economics and Business *(biannually)*; Humanika, Social Sciences *(biannually)*; Journal of Research, University Journal *(biannually)*; Parafrase, Language, Literature, Culture *(biannually)*; Phenomenan, Psychology *(biannually)*; Saintek, Engineering *(biannually)*; Teknika, Engineering *(biannually)*

Press or Publishing House: Untag Press

Academic Staff *2009-2010*	MEN	WOMEN	**TOTAL**
FULL-TIME	207	93	**300**
PART-TIME	31	9	**40**
STAFF WITH DOCTORATE			
FULL-TIME	34	10	**44**
PART-TIME	5	4	**9**
Student Numbers *2009-2010*			
All (Foreign Included)	2,287	1,322	**3,609**
FOREIGN ONLY	1	1	**2**

Last Updated: 07/04/11

19 NOVEMBER UNIVERSITY KOLAKA

Universitas 19 November Kolaka
Jalan Pemuda 339, Kolaka 93514
Tel: +62(405) 21132
Fax: +62(405) 24028

Rector: Azhari

Ketua: Buhari Matta Msi

Programmes

Engineering; **Agriculture** (Animal Husbandry; Fishery); **English** (English); **Indonesian Language and Literature** (Indonesian; Literature; Modern Languages); **Information Technology** (Information Technology); **Law**; **Mathematics**; **Public Administration** (Public Administration)

Degrees and Diplomas: *Sarjana (S1)*
Last Updated: 27/04/10

ABDURACHMAN SALEH UNIVERSITY

Universitas Abdurachman Saleh
Jalan PB Sudirman 7, Situbondo, Jawa Timur
Tel: +62(338) 671-191
Website: http://www.unarssitubondo.org/

Rector: Hadi Wijono

Vice-Rector II: Edy Kusnadi

Vice-Rector I: Winasis Yulianto

Faculties

Agriculture (Agricultural Economics; Agriculture); **Economics** (Management); **English** (English); **Law** (Law); **Social and Political Sciences** (Administration; Government; Public Administration)

History: Founded 1981.

Degrees and Diplomas: *Sarjana (S1)*

Libraries: c. 2,220 vols
Last Updated: 23/06/11

ABDURRAB UNIVERSITY

Universitas Abdurrab
Jalan Riau Ujung 73, Tampan, Pekanbaru, 28292 Riau
Tel: +62(761) 38762
Fax: +62(761) 859-839

Rector: Tabrani Rab

Ketua: Syaiful Rab

Programmes

Engineering (Engineering); **Government** (Political Sciences); **International Relations** (International Relations); **Pharmacy and Food Science** (Food Science; Pharmacy); **Physical Therapy** (Physical Therapy); **Science** (Natural Sciences); **Social Sciences** (Communication Studies; Psychology)

Degrees and Diplomas: *Sarjana (S1)*
Last Updated: 27/04/10

ABULYATAMA UNIVERSITY

Universitas Abulyatama
Jl. Blang Bintang Km. 85, Lampo Keude, Banda Aceh, 23372 Nangroeh Aceh Darussalam
Tel: +62(651) 23699 +62(651) 34488
Fax: +62(651) 21255

Rector: Burhanuddin Salim

Ketua: H. Rusli Bintang

Faculties

Agriculture (Agricultural Business; Agricultural Engineering; Agronomy; Animal Husbandry); **Economics** (Accountancy; Management); **Engineering** (Chemical Engineering; Civil Engineering; Electrical and Electronic Engineering; Engineering Management; Industrial Engineering; Mechanical Engineering); **Fishery** (Aquaculture; Fishery; Natural Resources; Water Management); **Information Management** (Information Management); **Law** (Law); **Public Health** (Medicine; Midwifery; Nursing; Public Health); **Teacher Training and Educational Sciences** (Biology; Chemistry; Civics; Educational Sciences; English; Foreign Languages Education; Health Education; Indonesian; Literature; Mathematics Education; Native Language Education; Parks and Recreation; Physical Education; Physics; Science Education; Social Sciences; Sports)

History: Founded 1983.

Degrees and Diplomas: *Diploma*: 3 yrs; *Sarjana (S1)*

Libraries: c. 4,300 vols
Last Updated: 23/06/11

ADHI TAMA INSTITUTE OF TECHNOLOGY SURABAYA

Institut Teknologi Adhi Tama Surabaya (ITATS)

Jalan Arief Rachman Hakim 100, Surabaya, 60117 Jawa Timur
Tel: +62(31) 594-5043
Fax: +62(31) 599-4620
EMail: purek1@itats.ac.id; pr1.itats@gmail.com
Website: http://www.itats.ac.id

Rector: Hadi Setiyawan
Tel: +62(31) 594-5043 Ext. 803, Fax: +62(31) 599-4620

Ketua: Abdul Zikri

Faculties

Civil and Planning Engineering (Architecture and Planning; Civil Engineering; Environmental Engineering; Industrial Design; Regional Planning); **Industrial Engineering** (Chemical Engineering; Electrical Engineering; Geology; Industrial Engineering; Mechanical Engineering; Mining Engineering); **Information Technology** (Computer Science; Information Technology); **Marine Technology** (Marine Engineering; Marine Transport)

History: Founded 1963. Acquired present status and title 1985.

Governing Bodies: Yayasan Foundation

Admission Requirements: Secondary school certificate

Main Language(s) of Instruction: Indonesian

Accrediting Agencies: National Accreditation Agency

Degrees and Diplomas: *Sarjana (S1)*: 4 yrs; *Magister (S2)*: Environmental Engineering; Industrial Engineering

Student Services: Academic counselling, Canteen, Employment services, Health services, Language programs, Nursery care, Social counselling, Sports facilities

Special Facilities: Laboratory; Mosque; Computer and Internet facilities

Libraries: Literature on Engineering and Architecture, 25,000 titles

Publications: Journal IPTEK, Research in Science and Technology *(quarterly)*

Press or Publishing House: IPTEK

Last Updated: 11/07/11

ADI BUANA PGRI UNIVERSITY

Universitas PGRI Adi Buana

Jalan Ngagel Dadi IIIB/37,
Surabaya 60245
Tel: +62(31) 504-1097
Fax: +62(31) 504-2804
EMail: unipa@unipasby.ac.id; admin@unipasby.ac.id
Website: http://www.unipasby.ac.id

Rector: Sutijono (2006-)

Ketua: Masini Atmadji

Faculties

Economics (Accountancy; Economics; Management); **Educational Sciences and Teacher Training** (Art Education; Civics; Educational and Student Counselling; English; Family Studies; Indonesian; Literature; Mathematics Education; Modern Languages; Sports); **Industrial Engineering** (Electrical Engineering; Industrial Engineering) *Dean*: Budi Priyo Sembado; **Mathematics and Natural Sciences** (Biology; Mathematics; Natural Sciences; Statistics); **Planning and Civil Engineering** (Civil Engineering; Environmental Engineering; Regional Planning; Town Planning); **Postgraduate Studies** (Education)

Programmes

Midwifery (Midwifery)

History: Founded 1998.

Fees: (Rupiahs): 1,275,000 per annum

Degrees and Diplomas: *Sarjana (S1)*; *Magister (S2)*

Libraries: 23,979 vols

Last Updated: 04/02/09

ADVENTIST UNIVERSITY OF INDONESIA

Universitas Advent Indonesia (UNAI)

Jalan Kolonel Masturi No. 288 Parongpong, Bandung, 40067 Java Barat
Tel: +62(22) 2700-247
Fax: +62(22) 2700-162
EMail: vppr@unai.edu
Website: http://www.unai.edu

President: Canadian Z. Panjaitan (2002-) Tel: +62(22) 2700-161

Vice-President for Financial Affairs: Sumurung Purba

Vice-President for Academic Affairs: Marlinda Siahaan

Faculties

Economics (Accountancy; Management; Secretarial Studies); **Education** (English; Mathematics); **Information Technology** (Computer Science; Information Technology); **Mathematics and Natural Sciences** (Biology; Pharmacy); **Nursing** (Nursing); **Philosophy and Religion** (Philosophy; Religion)

Programmes

Postgraduate Studies (Management; Theology)

History: Founded 1948 as Seminary by the Indonesian Union Mission of Seventh-Day Adventists, became college 1962 and acquired present status and title 1982. A private institution under the supervision of the Department of Education and Culture.

Academic Year: August to May (August-December; January-May)

Admission Requirements: Secondary school certificate (Surat Tanda Tamat Belajar)

Fees: (Rupiahs): 6,800,000 per semester including board and lodging

Main Language(s) of Instruction: Indonesian

Accrediting Agencies: Adventist Accreditation Association (AAA), National Accrediting Body of Indonesia (BAN)

Degrees and Diplomas: *Diploma*: 3 yrs; *Sarjana (S1)*: 4 yrs; *Magister (S2)*: 2 yrs

Student Services: Academic counselling, Canteen, Health services, Social counselling, Sports facilities

Student Residential Facilities: Yes; dormitories

Libraries: c. 26,830 vols

Academic Staff *2009-2010*	MEN	WOMEN	**TOTAL**
FULL-TIME	51	31	**82**
PART-TIME	5	2	**7**
STAFF WITH DOCTORATE			
FULL-TIME	14	4	**18**
PART-TIME	5	1	**6**
Student Numbers *2009-2010*			
All (Foreign Included)	660	671	**1,331**
FOREIGN ONLY	10	3	**13**

Last Updated: 27/10/10

AHMAD DAHLAN UNIVERSITY

Universitas Ahmad Dahlan (UAD)

Jalan Kapas No. 9, Semaki, Yogyakarta, 55166 DI Yogyakarta
Tel: +62(274) 563-515 +62(274) 511-830
Fax: +62(274) 564-604
EMail: info@uad.ac.id
Website: http://www.uad.ac.id

Rector: H. Kasiyarno (2007-)
EMail: kasiyarno@uad.ac.id; kasi_uad@yahoo.com

Vice-Rector for Resources Management: Uswatun Khasanah

Vice-Rector for Student Affairs: H. Muchlas

Faculties

Economics (Accountancy; Development Studies; Economics; Management); **Education and Teacher Training** (Biology; Civics; Education; Educational and Student Counselling; English; Foreign Languages Education; Government; Indonesian; Mathematics Education; Native Language Education; Physics; Science Education; Teacher Training); **Graduate Studies** (English; Foreign Languages Education; Pharmacy; Physics; Psychology); **Industrial Technology** (Chemical Engineering; Computer Engineering; Electrical Engineering; Industrial Engineering); **Islamic Studies** (Arabic;

Islamic Studies); **Law** (Law); **Letters** (Arts and Humanities; English; Indonesian); **Mathematics and Natural Sciences** (Biology; Information Technology; Mathematics; Natural Sciences; Physics); **Pharmacy** (Pharmacy); **Psychology** (Clinical Psychology; Developmental Psychology; Educational Psychology; Experimental Psychology; Industrial and Organizational Psychology; Psychology; Social Psychology); **Public Health** (Public Health)

History: Founded 1960 as Muhammadiyah Institute of Education and Teacher School. Acquired present status and title 1994.

Admission Requirements: High school certificate, transcript for Diploma and Diploma Certificate, transcript for Magister

Fees: (Rupiahs): 3m. per semester

Main Language(s) of Instruction: Indonesian

International Co-operation: With universities in China, Malaysia, USA, Saudi Arabia and Iran

Degrees and Diplomas: *Diploma*: 1 yr (D1); 3 yrs (D3); *Sarjana (S1)*: 4 yrs; *Magister (S2)*: 2 yrs

Student Services: Academic counselling, Canteen, Cultural centre, Employment services, Foreign student adviser, Health services, Language programs, Social counselling, Sports facilities

Press or Publishing House: UAD Press

Last Updated: 23/06/11

AKI UNIVERSITY

Universitas Aki

Jalan Pemuda 95-97, Semarang, 50139 Jawa Tengah
Tel: +62(24) 355-2555
Fax: +62(24) 355-2111
Website: http://www.unaki.ac.id

Rector: Harto Listijo

Ketua: Handoko Soerjanto

Programmes

Accountancy and Management (Accountancy; Management); **English** (English); **Information Technology** (Information Technology); **Psychology** (Psychology)

Degrees and Diplomas: *Sarjana (S1)*

Last Updated: 28/04/10

AKPRIND INSTITUTE OF SCIENCE AND TECHNOLOGY YOGYAKARTA

Institut Sains dan Teknologi AKPRIND Yogyakarta (ISTA)

Jalan Kalisahak 28, Komplek Balapan, Tromol Pos 45, Yogyakarta, 55222 DI Yogyakarta
Tel: +62(274) 563-029
Fax: +62(274) 563-847
EMail: ista@indo.net.id
Website: http://www.akprind.ac.id

Rector: Sudarsono Tel: +62(274) 544-700

Vice-Rector: Amir Hamzah

Faculties

Industrial Technology (Chemical Engineering; Computer Engineering; Electrical Engineering; Industrial Engineering); **Mathematics and Science** (Computer Science; Information Technology; Mathematics); **Mineral Technology** (Environmental Engineering; Geological Engineering)

History: Founded 1972. Acquired present status and title 1987.

Governing Bodies: Foundation of Pembina Potensi Pembanguan

Academic Year: September to August

Admission Requirements: Senior high school certificate

Main Language(s) of Instruction: Indonesian

Accrediting Agencies: National Accredition Board

Degrees and Diplomas: *Diploma*: 3-4 yrs; *Sarjana (S1)*: 4-5 yrs

Student Services: Academic counselling, Canteen, Employment services, Health services, Language programs, Sports facilities

Student Residential Facilities: Yes

Libraries: Institute and Department Libraries

Publications: Academia ISTA, Science and Technology *(biannually)*; Buletin ISTA, Scientific Experience and Research *(annually)*

Last Updated: 11/07/11

AL-AMIN UNIVERSITY

Universitas Al-Amin

Jalan Pendidikan 27, Remu Utara, Sorong, 98416 Papua
Tel: +62(951) 322-382
Fax: +62(951) 326-162

Rector: Hermanto

Ketua: Abdul Rauf Abu

Programmes

Agriculture (Agriculture; Agronomy; Fishery; Forestry; Harvest Technology; Water Management); **Education** (English; Foreign Languages Education; Mathematics Education); **Engineering** (Agricultural Engineering; Civil Engineering; Industrial Engineering); **Law** (Administrative Law; Law); **Political and Social Sciences** (Administration; Government; Public Administration; Sociology)

History: Founded as Sekolah Tinggi Administrasi Al Amin Sorong.

Degrees and Diplomas: *Sarjana (S1)*

Last Updated: 23/06/11

AL-ASYARIAH MANDAR UNIVERSITY

Universitas Al-Asyariah Mandar

Jalan Budi Utomo 2, Manding, Polewali, 91315 Sulawesi Barat
Tel: +62(428) 21038
Fax: +62(428) 21038

Rector: Muhammad Syibli Sahabuddin

Ketua: Hajaniah

Programmes

Agriculture; **Communication Studies** (Communication Studies); **Government** (Government); **Indonesian** (Indonesian; Literature; Modern Languages); **Information Technology** (Information Technology); **Mathematics** (Mathematics); **Pancasila and Civic Education**; **Public Health** (Public Health)

Degrees and Diplomas: *Sarjana (S1)*

Last Updated: 28/04/10

AL-AZHAR UNIVERSITY

Universitas Al-Azhar

Jalan Pintu Air IV No. 214, Medan, 20142 Sumatera Utara
Tel: +62(61) 836-1911 +62(61) 836-1811
Fax: +62(61) 836-1711

Rector: M. Sinto

Ketua: H. Abdul Manan Muis

Programmes

Agriculture (Agricultural Engineering; Agronomy; Soil Science); **Engineering** (Civil Engineering; Electrical Engineering; Engineering; Industrial Engineering); **Law** (Law); **Management and Accountancy** (Accountancy; Management)

History: Founded 1983.

Degrees and Diplomas: *Sarjana (S1)*

Last Updated: 23/06/11

AL-GHIFARI UNIVERSITY

Universitas Al-Ghifari

Jalan Cisaranten Kulon 140, Bandung, 40293 Jawa Barat
Tel: +62(22) 783-5813
Fax: +62(22) 783-5845
EMail: unfari.bdg@gmail.com

Rector: Deden Suhendar

Ketua: Saepudin Djajarahmat

Programmes

Agroindustrial Technology (Agricultural Engineering); **English Literature** (English); **Food Technology** (Food Technology); **International Relations** (International Relations); **Management**; **Pharmacy** (Pharmacy); **Public Administration** (Public Administration)

Degrees and Diplomas: *Sarjana (S1)*

Last Updated: 27/04/10

ALKHAIRAAT UNIVERSITY

Universitas Alkhairaat

Jalan Diponegoro 39, Palu, 94221 Sulawesi Tengah
Tel: +62(451) 461-123
Fax: +62(451) 460-949

Rector: Lukman

Ketua: H. Fadel Muhammad

Programmes
Agriculture (Agricultural Business; Agricultural Engineering; Agriculture; Agronomy; Fishery); **Arts and Humanities** (Arabic; Indonesian; Literature); **Economics** (Economics; Management); **Education** (Health Education; Mathematics Education; Native Language Education)

History: Founded 1963.

Degrees and Diplomas: *Sarjana (S1)*
Last Updated: 23/06/11

AL-MUSLIM UNIVERSITY

Universitas Al-Muslim

Jl Tengku Abdurrahman 37, Matangglumpangdua, Bireuen, Banda Aceh
Tel: +62(644) 41126
Website: http://www.umuslim.ac.id/

Rektor: Idris Amiruddin

Vice-Rector, Administration and Finance: Hamid Marwan

Faculties
Agriculture (Agricultural Business; Agricultural Engineering; Agronomy; Animal Husbandry; Aquaculture); **Computer Science** (Computer Science; Information Management; Information Technology); **Economics** (Economics); **Education and Teacher Training** (Biology; Education; English; Foreign Languages Education; Geography; Geography (Human); Indonesian; Mathematics Education; Native Language Education; Physics; Primary Education; Teacher Training); **Engineering** (Architecture; Civil Engineering; Structural Architecture); **Social and Political Sciences** (Political Sciences; Social Sciences)

Programmes
Midwifery (Midwifery)

History: Founded 2003 as Sekolah Tinggi Pertanian Al-Muslim Peusangan.

Degrees and Diplomas: *Diploma*; *Sarjana (S1)*
Last Updated: 23/06/11

AL-QUR'AN UNIVERSITY OF SCIENCE

Universitas Sains Al-Qur'an

Jl. Raya Kalibeber Km. 3, Mojotengah, Wonosobo, 56351 Jawa Tengah
Tel: +62(286) 321-873
Fax: +62(286) 323-737
EMail: humas@unsiq.ac.id; unsiqwonosobo@yahoo.com
Website: http://unsiq.ac.id

Rector: Zamakhsyari Dhofier

Ketua: Soeprapto

Faculties
Civil Engineering (Architecture and Planning; Civil Engineering) *Dean*: Abriyani Sulistiawan; **Economics** (Accountancy; Economics; Management) *Dean*: Bambang Hargono; **Industrial Engineering** *Dean*: Agus Suryatin; **Information Sciences** (Information Management; Information Sciences; Information Technology) *Dean*: Muatohar; **Literature** (English; Literature) *Dean*: Widyastuti Purbaningrum

Degrees and Diplomas: *Diploma*; *Sarjana (S1)*
Last Updated: 05/02/09

ALWASAHIYAH UNIVERSITY

Universitas Alwashliyah

Jalan Sisingamangaraja Km. 55, Medan, 20147 Sumatera Utara
Tel: +62(61) 786-8270
Fax: +62(61) 786-8270

Rector: Syahrin

Ketua: Aziddin

Faculties
Agriculture; **Economics** (Accountancy; Development Studies; Economics; Management); **Engineering** (Civil Engineering; Electrical and Electronic Engineering; Engineering; Mechanical Engineering); **Law** (Law)

History: Founded 1986.

Degrees and Diplomas: *Diploma*: 3 yrs; *Sarjana (S1)*
Last Updated: 13/02/09

AL-WASHLIYAH LABUHAN BATU UNIVERSITY

Universitas Al-washliyah Labuhan Batu

Jalan H. Adam Malik, Rantauprapat, Sumatera Utara
EMail: univalab@yahoo.co.id
Website: http://univalabuhanbatu.wordpress.com/

Rector: Bukhari

Ketua: Usman Ahmad

Programmes
Biology (Biology); **English** (English); **Indonesian** (Indonesian); **Information Technology** (Information Technology); **Management** (Management); **Mathematics** (Mathematics)

Degrees and Diplomas: *Sarjana (S1)*
Last Updated: 28/04/10

AMIR HAMZAH UNIVERSITY

Universitas Amir Hamzah

Jalan Pancing Pasar V, Medan, 20221 Sumatera Utara
Tel: +62(61) 614-160
Fax: +62(61) 614-160
EMail: amirhamzah_univ_medan@yahoo.co.id

Rector: H. Tarmizi

Ketua: Chairuddin

Faculties
Agriculture (Agricultural Engineering; Agronomy) *Dean*: Madjid Damanik; **Economics** (Accountancy; Economics; Management) *Dean*: Pardamean Hutasuhut; **Engineering** (Civil Engineering; Electrical Engineering; Engineering; Mechanical Engineering) *Dean*: Subakti; **Law** (Law) *Dean*: Tarmizi

History: Founded 1980. A private institution under the supervision of the Department of Education and Culture.

Fees: (Rupiahs): 600,000 per annum

Degrees and Diplomas: *Sarjana (S1)*

Libraries: 1,886 vols
Last Updated: 07/01/09

ANDI JEMMA UNIVERSITY PALOPO

Universitas Andi Jemma Palopo

Jalan Sultan Hasanudin 13, Palopo
Tel: +62(471) 24-506
Fax: +62(471) 22-005

Ketua: Muhammad Iskandar

Ketua: H. Ahmar Mallawa

Faculties
Agriculture (Agricultural Economics; Agronomy); **Economics** (Development Studies; Economics; Finance; Management); **Engineering** (Engineering); **Fishery** (Fishery; Natural Resources; Water Science); **Forestry** (Forest Management; Sericulture); **Social and Political Sciences** (Administration; Government; Political Sciences; Social Sciences)

History: Founded 1995.

Degrees and Diplomas: *Sarjana (S1)*
Last Updated: 07/01/09

ANTAKUSUMA UNIVERSITY

Universitas Antakusuma
Pangkalan Bun, Kotawaringin Barat

Programmes

Accountancy (Accountancy); **Agriculture** (Agriculture); **Economics** (Economics); **Engineering** (Civil Engineering; Engineering); **Law** (Law); **Management** (Management)

Degrees and Diplomas: *Sarjana (S1)*
Last Updated: 28/04/10

ARTHA WACANA CHRISTIAN UNIVERSITY KUPANG

Universitas Kristen Artha Wacana Kupang (UKAW)
Kotak Pos 147, Jalan Adisucipto Oesapa, Kupang, East Nusa Tenggara
Tel: +62(380) 881-584 +62(380) 881-677
Fax: +62(380) 881-677
EMail: ukaw@kupang.wasantara.net.id

Rector: Dekker Mauboi

Ketua: Robert Riwu Kaho Tel: +62(380) 881-050

International Relations: James Adam, Vice-Rector for Academic Affairs EMail: james@kupang.wasantara.net.id

Faculties

Agriculture *Dean*: Jimmy Dethan; **Economics** *Dean*: Damaris Koli; **Fishery** *Dean*: Ayub Meko; **Law** *Dean*: Otlief Wewo; **Philosophy and Theology** *Dean*: Fred Djara Wellem; **Teacher Training and Educational Sciences** *Dean*: Mesach Beeh

History: Founded 1985.

Fees: (Rupiahs): 1,3m. per annum

Main Language(s) of Instruction: Indonesian

Degrees and Diplomas: *Diploma*: 3 yrs; *Sarjana (S1)*: Theology; Education; Law; Fishery; Agriculture; Economics, 4-5 yrs

Student Services: Academic counselling, Canteen, Foreign student adviser, Health services, Language programs, Sports facilities

Student Residential Facilities: Yes

Special Facilities: Agriculture, Fishery and Biology Laboratory

Libraries: 23,377 vols

ASAHAN UNIVERSITY

Universitas Asahan
Jalan Ahmad Yani Kisaran, Kisaran, 21222 Sumatera Utara
Tel: +62(623) 42-643
Fax: +62(623) 43-599

Rector: Darma Bakti

Vice-Rector: Hasruddin

Faculties

Agriculture (Agriculture; Agronomy) *Dean*: Anwar Nasution; **Economics** (Development Studies; Economics; Management) *Dean*: Syafaruddin Nasution; **Engineering** (Civil Engineering; Engineering); **Law** (Law)

History: Founded 1985.

Fees: (Rupiahs): 500,000 per annum

Degrees and Diplomas: *Sarjana (S1)*

Libraries: 1,938 vols
Last Updated: 07/01/09

ATMA JAYA CATHOLIC UNIVERSITY OF INDONESIA

Universitas Katolik Indonesia Atma Jaya (UNIKA ATMAJAYA)
Gedung B Lantai 1, Jalan Jenderal Sudirman 51, Jakarta, 12930 DKI Jakarta
Tel: +62(21) 572-7615
Fax: +62(21) 570-8811
EMail: rek@atmajaya.ac.id; pr@atmajaya.ac.id
Website: http://www.atmajaya.ac.id

Rector: F.G. Winarno (2003-) Tel: +62(21) 570-8797

Vice-Rector I: Magdalena Surjaningsih Halim

Ketua: J. Kristiadi

Faculties

Biotechnology (Biochemistry; Biotechnology; Cell Biology; Chemistry; Ecology; Fishery; Food Technology; Genetics; Immunology; Information Technology; Microbiology; Molecular Biology; Physics; Physiology; Virology); **Business Administration and Communication Sciences** (Administration; Anthropology; Communication Studies; English; Human Resources; International Business; Marketing; Media Studies; Public Relations; Social Psychology; Sociology; Statistics; Tourism); **Economics** (Accountancy; Development Studies; Economics; Management); **Education and Teacher Training** (Education; Educational Administration; Educational and Student Counselling; Educational Psychology; English; Foreign Languages Education; Pedagogy; Primary Education; Religious Education; Teacher Training; Theology); **Engineering** (Computer Science; Electrical Engineering; Electronic Engineering; Industrial Engineering; Mechanical Engineering; Power Engineering; Software Engineering; Telecommunications Engineering); **Law** (Civil Law; Commercial Law; Constitutional Law; Criminal Law; Ethics; Human Rights; International Law); **Medicine** (Anaesthesiology; Anatomy; Applied Chemistry; Applied Physics; Behavioural Sciences; Biochemistry; Biology; Biomedicine; Cardiology; Child Care and Development; Community Health; Embryology and Reproduction Biology; Endocrinology; Ethics; Forensic Medicine and Dentistry; Gastroenterology; Haematology; Histology; Immunology; Medicine; Microbiology; Midwifery; Neurology; Nutrition; Ophthalmology; Parasitology; Pathology; Pharmacology; Physiology; Public Health; Radiology; Surgery); **Psychology** (Anthropology; Clinical Psychology; Cognitive Sciences; Educational Psychology; Ethics; Industrial and Organizational Psychology; Leadership; Philosophical Schools; Philosophy; Psychiatry and Mental Health; Social Psychology)

Programmes

Magister and Doctoral Studies (Industrial and Organizational Psychology; Linguistics; Management; Psychology)

History: Founded 1960. A private institution under the supervision of the Department of Education and Culture.

Academic Year: August to July (August-January; February-July)

Admission Requirements: High School certificate or equivalent

Main Language(s) of Instruction: Indonesian, English

Accrediting Agencies: (Badan Akreditasi Nasional/National Accreditation Board) BAN

Degrees and Diplomas: *Sarjana (S1)*: 4-8 sem; *Magister (S2)*: Applied English Linguistics; Management; Professional Psychology (M.M.), $1\frac{1}{2}$-$2\frac{1}{2}$ sem; *Doktor (S3)*: Applied English Linguistics (Dr.), 4 sem

Student Services: Academic counselling, Canteen, Cultural centre, Employment services, Health services, Language programs, Nursery care, Social counselling, Sports facilities

Special Facilities: Anatomy Museum. Educational Studio

Libraries: Central Library, c. 90,000 vols; Research Centre, 16,000; Language Institute, 9,000; Library of Medicine Department, 3,700

Publications: Atma Nan Jaya *(3 per annum)*; Warta Atma Jaya *(biennially)*
Last Updated: 22/07/11

ATMA JAYA MAKASSAR UNIVERSITY

Universitas Atma Jaya Makassar (UAJM)
Jalan Tanjung Alang 23, Makassar, 90244 Sulawesi Selatan
Tel: +62(411) 871-038 +62(411) 871-733
Fax: +62(411) 870-294
EMail: uajm@uajm.ac.id
Website: http://www.uajm.ac.id

Rector: Felix Layadi (2009-2015)

Vice-Rector: Jeremias Mathias Leda

Faculties

Economics (Economics; Management); **Engineering** (Civil Engineering; Computer Science; Electrical Engineering; Mechanical Engineering); **Information Technology** (Information Technology); **Law** (Civil Law; Commercial Law; Criminal Law; International Law; Law)

History: Founded 1980 by lay-Catholics in collaboration with the local Catholic Church (Archdiocese of Ujung Pandang). Run by Atma Jaya Ujung Pandang Higher Learning Foundation.

Governing Bodies: Board of Trustees

Academic Year: September to July (September-February; March-July)

Admission Requirements: Secondary school certificate (Sekolah Menengah Atas, SMA) or foreign equivalent

Fees: (Rupiahs): c. 3.5m. per annum

Main Language(s) of Instruction: Indonesian

Accrediting Agencies: Indonesian Education and Culture Department

Degrees and Diplomas: *Sarjana (S1)*: 4-7 yrs

Student Services: Academic counselling, Canteen, Employment services, Language programs, Social counselling, Sports facilities

Student Residential Facilities: For c. 3,000 students

Libraries: University Library, c. 7,450 vols

Publications: Pembangunan Wilayah dan Masyarakat; Simak

Academic Staff *2009-2010*	**TOTAL**
FULL-TIME	**70**
PART-TIME	c. **100**
Student Numbers *2009-2010*	
All (Foreign Included)	c. **1,600**

Last Updated: 23/06/11

ATMA JAYA YOGYAKARTA UNIVERSITY

Universitas Atma Jaya Yogyakarta (UAJY)

Jalan Babarsari 44, Yogyakarta, 55281 DI Yogyakarta
Tel: +62(274) 487-711
Fax: +62(274) 487-748
EMail: khsp@mail.uajy.ac.id
Website: http://www.uajy.ac.id

Rector: Rogatianus Maryatmo Tel: +62(274) 487-711 Ext. 1210

Vice-Rector, Finance, Human Resources and Infrastructure: Theresia Anita Christiani

Vice-Rector, Academic Affairs: Ignatius Pramana Yuda

Faculties

Biotechnology (Biology; Biotechnology); **Economics** (Accountancy; Economics; Management); **Engineering** (Architecture; Civil Engineering; Computer Engineering; Engineering; Industrial Engineering; Structural Architecture); **Industrial Technology** (Computer Science; Industrial Engineering); **Law** (Law); **Postgraduate Studies** (Architecture; Civil Engineering; Construction Engineering; Information Technology; Law; Management); **Social and Political Sciences** (Communication Studies; Sociology)

History: Founded 1965. A private institution under the supervision of the Department of Education and Culture.

Academic Year: September to June (September-January; February-June)

Admission Requirements: Secondary school certificate (Sekolah Menengah Umum, SMU) and entrance examination

Fees: (Rupiahs): c. 1.1m.-1.5m. per semester. Also variable costs per credit hour

Main Language(s) of Instruction: Indonesian. English (Civil Engineering, Industrial Engineering and Management)

International Co-operation: With universities in Thailand, Australia, Philippines, France and India.

Accrediting Agencies: National Accreditation Board, National Education Department

Degrees and Diplomas: *Sarjana (S1)*: 4 yrs; *Magister (S2)*: Management; Law; Civil Engineering; Information Technology; Digital Architecture

Student Services: Academic counselling, Canteen, Cultural centre, Sports facilities

Special Facilities: Audio-Visual Studio, Laboratories

Libraries: c. 70,000 vols in Indonesian; c. 32,000 in other languages

Publications: BIOTA, Biology Faculty *(quarterly)*; Jurnal Fisip, Social and Political Science Faculty *(3 per annum)*; Jurnal Teknik Sipil, Civil Engineering Study Programme *(biennially)*; Jurnal Teknologi Industri, Industrial Technology Faculty *(3 per annum)*; Justitia et Pax, Law Faculty *(biennially)*; Kinerja, Graduate Programme *(biennially)*; MODUS, Economics Faculty *(biennially)*

Press or Publishing House: Atma Jaya Yogyakarta Publishing

Last Updated: 23/06/11

AZZAHRA UNIVERSITY

Universitas Azzahra

Jalan Jatinegara Barat 144, Jakarta Selatan,
11220 Dki Jakarta
Tel: +62(21) 280-0646
Fax: +62(21) 280-0647

Rector: Tarmizi Taher

Ketua: Safri Nurmantu

Faculties

Business Administration (Accountancy; Business Administration; Management; Public Administration); **Engineering** (Civil Engineering; Electrical Engineering; Engineering; Industrial Engineering; Structural Architecture); **Finance and Banking** (Banking; Finance); **Law** (Law); **Psychology**

Degrees and Diplomas: *Sarjana (S1)*

Last Updated: 13/01/09

BAITURRAHMAH UNIVERSITY

Universitas Baiturrahmah (UNBRAH)

Jl. By Pass Km 15, Aie Pacah, Padang,
25176 Sumatera Barat
Tel: +62(751) 463-069
Fax: +62(751) 463-068
EMail: rectorat@unbrah.ac.id
Website: http://www.unbrah.ac.id

Rector: Firdaus Rivai (1997-)
Tel: +62(751) 705-3570 EMail: firdaus_unbrah@yahoo.com

Secretary: Dartman Djamaris Tel: +62(751) 776-102

International Relations: Nazaruddin Bakar, Vice-Rector

Faculties

Dentistry (Dentistry) *Dean*: Rama Potranto; **Economics** (Accountancy; Management) *Dean*: Yandi Sukri; **Medicine** *Dean*: Amir Muslim Malik; **Public Health** *Dean*: Winardi Zainudin

Programmes

Midwifery (Midwifery) *Head*: Zufriasriaty Syahrizal; **Radiodiagnostic and Therapy** (Radiology) *Head*: Oktavia Puspita Sari

History: Founded 1979.

Governing Bodies: Yayasan Pendidikan Baiturrahmah

Academic Year: September to June (September-January; February-June)

Admission Requirements: Secondary school certificate and entrance examination

Fees: (Rupiahs): Medicine, 110m.; Dentistry 60m.; Public Health, 12m.; Midwifery, 20m.; Radiodiagnostic, 20m.

Main Language(s) of Instruction: Indonesian

Accrediting Agencies: National Accreditation Board

Degrees and Diplomas: *Diploma*: Midwifery; Radiodiagnostic, 3 yrs; *Sarjana (S1)*: Dentistry, 5 yrs; *Sarjana (S1)*: Economics; *Sarjana (S1)*: Medicine, 6 yrs; *Sarjana (S1)*: Public Health, 4 yrs

Student Services: Academic counselling, Canteen, Health services, Language programs

Special Facilities: Hospital

Libraries: Central Library, 5,000 vols

Publications: Jurnal Universitas Baiturrahmah, Health and Economic Matters (in Indonesian) *(quarterly)*

Academic Staff *2010-2011*	MEN	WOMEN	TOTAL
FULL-TIME	92	108	200
PART-TIME	263	225	488
STAFF WITH DOCTORATE			
FULL-TIME	5	2	7
PART-TIME	18	3	21
Student Numbers *2010-2011*			
All (Foreign Included)	985	2,301	3,286

Last Updated: 08/04/11

BAKRIE UNIVERSITY

Universitas Bakrie

Gelanggang Mahasiswa Soemantri Brojonegoro Suite GF, Jalan. HR Rasuna Said Kav C-22, Kuningan, Jakarta Selatan, DKI Jakarta
Tel: +62(21) 526-1448
Fax: +62(21) 527-6543
Website: http://library.bakrie.ac.id

Programmes

Accountancy (Accountancy); **Communication Studies** (Communication Studies); **Computer Engineering**; **Information Technology** (Information Technology); **Management** (Management)

Degrees and Diplomas: *Sarjana (S1)*

Last Updated: 28/04/10

BALE BANDUNG UNIVERSITY

Universitas Bale Bandung

Jalan Raa Wiranatakusumah, Baleenoah, Bandung, 40258 Jawa Barat
Tel: +62(22) 594-0443
Fax: +62(22) 594-9221
Website: http://www.unibba.ac.id

Degrees and Diplomas: *Sarjana (S1)*

Last Updated: 28/04/10

BALIKPAPAN UNIVERSITY

Universitas Balikpapan (UNIBA)

Jl.Pupuk Raya, Gn. Bahagia, Balikpapan, 76114 Kalimantan Timur
Tel: +62(542) 765-442
Fax: +62(542) 764-205
EMail: info@uniba-bpn.ac.id
Website: http://www.uniba-bpn.ac.id

Rector: Ellyano S. Lasam

Vice-Rector II, Academic Affairs: Mohammad Ardi

Faculties

Economics (Accountancy; Development Studies; Economics; Management); **Engineering** (Civil Engineering; Computer Engineering; Electronic Engineering; Engineering; Mechanical Engineering; Software Engineering); **Languages and Litterature** (Cultural Studies; English; Grammar; Indonesian; Journalism; Linguistics; Literature; Modern Languages; Philosophy; Psychology; Translation and Interpretation); **Law** (Administrative Law; Anthropology; Civil Law; Commercial Law; Constitutional Law; Criminal Law; Criminology; Human Rights; International Law; Islamic Law; Labour Law; Law; Private Law)

History: Founded 1981.

Degrees and Diplomas: *Sarjana (S1)*; *Magister (S2)*

Last Updated: 12/07/11

BANDAR LAMPUNG UNIVERSITY

Universitas Bandar Lampung (UBL)

Jalan Hi Zainal Abidin Pagar Alam 26, Labuan Ratu, Bandar Lampung, Lampung
Tel: +62(721) 701-979 +62(721) 773-847
Fax: +62(721) 701-467
EMail: info@ubl.ac.id
Website: http://www.ubl.ac.id/

Rector: Muhammad Yusuf Barusman

Ketua: Sri Hayati Barusman

Faculties

Computer Science (Computer Science; Information Technology); **Economics** (Accountancy; Economics; Management; Marketing); **Engineering** (Architecture; Civil Engineering; Computer Engineering; Computer Science; Mechanical Engineering; Structural Architecture); **Law** (Law); **Postgraduate Studies** (Engineering; Law; Management); **Social and Political Sciences** (Administration; Business Administration; Communication Studies; Government; Public Administration); **Teacher Training and Education** (Education; English; Foreign Languages Education; Teacher Training)

History: Founded 1984.

Degrees and Diplomas: *Sarjana (S1)*; *Magister (S2)*: Engineering; Law; Management

Libraries: c. 17,000 vols

Last Updated: 23/06/11

BANDUNG INSTITUTE OF SCIENCE AND TECHNOLOGY

Institut Teknologi dan Sains Bandung

Jalan Ir. H. Djuanda 254, Bandung, 40135 Jawa Barat
Tel: +62(22) 250-1541
Fax: +62(22) 250-0379
EMail: office@itsb.ac.id; itsb_bandung@yahoo.co.id
Website: http://www.itsb.ac.id

Rektor: Widiadnyana Merati

Ketua: Pudji Permani

Programmes

Architecture, Regional and City Planning (Architecture; Regional Planning; Town Planning); **Environmental Engineering** (Environmental Engineering); **Geological, Mining and Petroleum Engineering** (Geological Engineering; Mining Engineering; Petroleum and Gas Engineering); **Industrial Production Design** (Industrial Design); **Interior Design** (Interior Design); **Metallurgical and Materials Engineering** (Materials Engineering; Metallurgical Engineering)

History: Founded 2001.

Degrees and Diplomas: *Sarjana (S1)*

Last Updated: 22/06/11

BANDUNG NATIONAL INSTITUTE OF TECHNOLOGY

Institut Teknologi Nasional Bandung (ITENAS)

Jalan Penghulu K.H. Hasan Mustafa 23, Bandung, 40124 Jawa Barat
Tel: +62(22) 727-2215 +62(22) 720-2892
Fax: +62(22) 720-2892
EMail: humas@itenas.ac.id
Website: http://www.itenas.ac.id

Rector: Harsono Taroepratjeka
Tel: +62(22) 727-2218, Fax: +62(22) 720-2892

Ketua: Iwan Inrawan Wiratmadja

International Relations: Rini Budiwati
Tel: +62(22) 720-8898, Fax: +62(22) 720-2892
EMail: ninik@itenas.ac.id

Faculties

Civil Engineering and Planning (Architecture; Civil Engineering; Environmental Engineering; Regional Planning; Structural Architecture; Surveying and Mapping; Town Planning); **Fine Arts and Design** (Communication Arts; Design; Fine Arts; Graphic Design; Industrial Design; Interior Design; Visual Arts); **Industrial Engineering** (Chemical Engineering; Computer Engineering; Electrical and Electronic Engineering; Engineering; Industrial Engineering; Industrial Management; Mechanical Engineering; Power Engineering; Telecommunications Engineering)

History: Founded 1972 as Akademi Teknologi Nasional. Acquired present status and title 1984.

Academic Year: August to July

Admission Requirements: High school certificate (SMU)

Main Language(s) of Instruction: Indonesian

Accrediting Agencies: National Accreditation Agency

Degrees and Diplomas: *Diploma*; *Sarjana (S1)*: 4 yrs

Student Services: Academic counselling, Canteen, Cultural centre, Health services, Language programs, Sports facilities

Libraries: Central Library and Department Library

Publications: Itenas *(quarterly)*

Academic Staff *2009-2010*: Total: c. 200

Student Numbers *2009-2010*: Total: c. 4,460

Last Updated: 22/06/11

BANDUNG RAYA UNIVERSITY

Universitas Bandung Raya (UNBAR)
Jalan Ranggagading 8, Bandung, 40116 Jawa Barat
Tel: +62(22) 426-0985
Fax: +62(22) 420-3291

Rector: Wibowo (2000-)

Ketua: Sukar Samsudi

Faculties

Agriculture (Agricultural Economics; Agriculture; Animal Husbandry; Farm Management; Harvest Technology; Horticulture; Landscape Architecture) *Dean*: Bey Permadi; **Economics** (Accountancy; Economics; Management) *Dean*: Hayati Djatmiko; **Engineering** *(Technical) Dean*: Neni Rustini; **Teacher Trainers Education** (Social Sciences; Teacher Trainers Education) *Dean*: Gatot Sutopo

History: Founded 1984.

Governing Bodies: Foundation for Universities Bandung Raya Development

Admission Requirements: High school certificate (SMU); Technical high school certificate (SMK)

Fees: (Rupiahs): 1.8m.

Main Language(s) of Instruction: Indonesian

International Co-operation: Participates in Samba project; Care International, United States

Accrediting Agencies: National Higher Education Accrediting Agency

Degrees and Diplomas: *Diploma*: Textile Technology (Industrial and Chemical), 3 yrs; *Sarjana (S1)*: Agriculture; Engineering; Economics; Education, 4 yrs

Student Services: Academic counselling, Canteen, Employment services, Nursery care, Social counselling, Sports facilities

Special Facilities: Laboratories

Libraries: Yes

Publications: Journal *(annually)*

Last Updated: 10/02/09

BANGKA BELITUNG UNIVERSITY

Universitas Bangka Belitung
Jalan Merdeka 4, Pangkalpinang, 33121
Bangka-Belitung
Tel: +62(717) 422-145
Fax: +62(717) 422-303
EMail: info@ubb.ac.id
Website: http://www.ubb.ac.id

Rector: Bustami Rahman
EMail: rektorat@ubb.ac.id; bustami@ubb.ac.id

Vice-Rector, Administration: Fauzi Amiruddin

Faculties

Agriculture, Fishery and Biology; **Economics** (Accountancy; Economics; Management); **Engineering** (Civil Engineering; Electrical Engineering; Engineering; Mechanical Engineering; Mining Engineering); **Law and Social Sciences** (Law; Social Sciences; Sociology)

History: Founded 2006.

Degrees and Diplomas: *Sarjana (S1)*

Last Updated: 28/04/10

BANGUN NUSANTARA VETERAN UNIVERSITY

Universitas Veteran Bangun Nusantara
Jalan Letjen Sujono Humardani 1, Kampus Jombor, Sukoharjo, 57521 Jawa Tengah
Tel: +62(271) 593-156
EMail: univetbantara@yahoo.com

Rector: Trisno Martono

Ketua: Soebagyo Brotosedjati

Faculties

Agriculture (Agricultural Economics; Agricultural Engineering; Agriculture; Animal Husbandry); **Educational Sciences and Teacher Training** (Biology; Civics; Educational and Student Counselling; Educational Sciences; Educational Technology; English; Geography; History; Indonesian; Literature; Mathematics Education; Science Education; Teacher Training); **Engineering** (Civil Engineering; Engineering; Industrial Engineering; Industrial Management); **Health Sciences** (Community Health); **Social and Political Sciences** (Communication Studies; Mass Communication; Political Sciences; Social Sciences)

History: Founded 1968.

Fees: (Rupiahs): 600,000 per annum

Degrees and Diplomas: *Sarjana (S1)*; *Magister (S2)*

Libraries: 11,348 vols

Last Updated: 21/04/10

BANJARMASIN ACHMAD YANI UNIVERSITY

Universitas Achmad Yani Banjarmasin
Jalan A. Yani km. 55, Komplek Stadion Lambung Mangkurat, Banjarmasin, 70249 Kalimantan Selatan
Tel: +62(511) 325-3850
Fax: +62(511) 325-3850

Rector: Zainul Arifin Noor

Ketua: Hajjah Siti Hafsah

Faculties

Administration (Administration; Government; Public Administration); **Agriculture** (Agricultural Business; Aquaculture; Fishery); **Economics** (Development Studies; Economics; Management); **Educational Science and Teacher Training** (Educational Administration; Educational and Student Counselling; Educational Sciences; Primary Education; Teacher Training)

Programmes

Engineering (Civil Engineering)

History: Founded 1983

Degrees and Diplomas: *Sarjana (S1)*

Libraries: c. 12,300 vols

Last Updated: 23/06/11

BANYUWANGI PGRI UNIVERSITY

Universitas PGRI Banyuwangi
Jalan Jend Ahmad Yani 80, Banyuwangi, 41482 Jawa Timur
Tel: +62(333) 421-593
Fax: +62(333) 428-592
EMail: uniba2007@telkom.net

Rector: Teguh Sumarno

Ketua: Nurhadi

Programmes

Biology (Biology); **Chemistry** (Chemistry); **Education** (Educational and Student Counselling; English; Foreign Languages Education; Health Education; Leisure Studies; Mathematics Education; Physical Education); **Engineering** (Agricultural Engineering; Electrical Engineering; Engineering; Mechanical Engineering); **Fishery** (Fishery); **Pancasila and Citizenship Education** (Civics; Government)

History: Founded 1976 as Institut Keguruan dan Ilmu Pendidikan (IKIP) PGRI Banyuwangi (Institute of Teacher Training and Educational Science Banyuwangi).

Degrees and Diplomas: *Sarjana (S1)*

Libraries: c. 2,700 vols

Last Updated: 30/06/11

BATAM UNIVERSITY

Universitas Batam

Jalan Kampus Abulyatama 5, Komplek UNIBA, Batam Center, Batam, 29464 Riau
Tel: +62(778) 745-5055
Fax: +62(778) 745-5054
EMail: uniba@univ-batam.ac.id
Website: http://univbatam.ac.id/

Rector: Jemmy Rumengan

Faculties

Economics (Accountancy; Management); **Engineering** (Civil Engineering; Computer Engineering; Electrical Engineering; Information Technology; Mechanical Engineering); **Law** (Law); **Medicine and Hygiene** (Health Education; Midwifery; Nursing)

History: Founded 2000.

Degrees and Diplomas: *Diploma*: 3 yrs; *Sarjana (S1)*; *Magister (S2)*: Accountancy; Law; Management

Last Updated: 12/07/11

BATURAJA UNIVERSITY

Universitas Baturaja

Jl. Ratu Penghulu 2301, Baturaja, 32115 Sumatera Selatan
Tel: +62(735) 326-122
Fax: +62(735) 326-122

Rector: Munajat

Ketua: H. Batonazar

Faculties

Agriculture (Agricultural Business; Agricultural Engineering; Agriculture; Agronomy); **Economics** (Development Studies; Economics; Management); **Education** (Education; Educational Technology; English; Foreign Languages Education; Indonesian; Literature; Native Language Education); **Engineering** (Civil Engineering; Electronic Engineering; Engineering); **Social and Political Sciences** (Communication Studies; Government; Political Sciences; Social Sciences)

History: Founded 1999.

Degrees and Diplomas: *Sarjana (S1)*

Last Updated: 12/07/11

BEKASI '45 ISLAMIC UNIVERSITY

Universitas Islam 45 Bekasi (UNISMA)

Jalan Cut Meutia 83, Bekasi, 17113 Jawa Barat
Tel: +62(21) 880-1027 +62(21) 880-8851
Fax: +62(21) 880-1192
EMail: humas@unismabekasi.ac.id
Website: http://unismabekasi.ac.id/

Rector: Nandang Najmulmunir Tel: +62(21) 880-1124

Faculties

Agriculture (Agricultural Business; Agriculture); **Communication, Literature and Linguistics** (Communication Studies; English; Linguistics; Literature); **Economics** (Banking; Economics; Finance; Management); **Educational Science and Teacher Training** (Education; Geography; Geography (Human); Parks and Recreation; Physical Education; Teacher Training); **Engineering** (Civil Engineering; Computer Engineering; Electrical Engineering; Engineering); **Islamic Religious Studies** (Economics; Education; Islamic Law; Islamic Theology); **Postgraduate Studies** (Education; Government; Islamic Studies); **Social and Political Sciences** (Administration; Government; Political Sciences; Psychology; Public Administration; Social Sciences)

History: Founded 1982.

Main Language(s) of Instruction: Indonesian

Accrediting Agencies: Badan Akreditasi Nasional

Degrees and Diplomas: *Diploma*: 3 yrs; *Sarjana (S1)*; *Magister (S2)*

Student Services: Academic counselling, Canteen, Foreign student adviser, Health services, Language programs, Sports facilities

Libraries: Main Library and 6 Faculty Libraries, 4,656 vols

Publications: BISMA, Bulletin *(monthly)*

Academic Staff *2009-2010*: Total: c. 170

Student Numbers *2009-2010*: Total: c. 3,100

Last Updated: 27/06/11

BHAKTI WIYATA KEDIRI INSTITUTE OF MEDICAL SCIENCES

Institut Ilmu Kesehatan Bhakti Wiyata Kediri

Jalan KH Wahid Hasyim 65, Kediri, 64100 Jawa Timur
Tel: +62(354) 773-299
Fax: +62(354) 771-539
Website: http://www.iikonline.com

Rector: Tarbinoe Kasmono

Ketua: Bambang Harsono Suhartono

Programmes

Health Sciences (Biology; Chemistry; Dental Technology; Dentistry; Food Science; Health Sciences; Midwifery; Nursing; Pharmacy; Physical Therapy; Public Health; Traditional Eastern Medicine)

History: Founded 2005.

Degrees and Diplomas: *Diploma*; *Sarjana (S1)*

Last Updated: 22/04/10

BHAYANGKARA JAKARTA RAYA UNIVERSITY

Universitas Bhayangkara Jakarta Raya (UBHARA JAYA)

Jalan Dharmawangsa I n° 1, Kebayoran Baru, Jakarta Selatan, 12140 DKI Jakarta
Tel: +62(21) 723-1948
Fax: +62(21) 726-7657
EMail: ubj@ubharajaya.ac.id; contact@ubharajaya.ac.id
Website: http://www.ubharajaya.ac.id

Rector: Logan Siagian

Vice-Rector, Public Administration and Finance: Tri Haryanto

Faculties

Communication Studies (Advertising and Publicity; Cinema and Television; Communication Studies; Journalism; Media Studies; Public Relations; Visual Arts); **Economics** (Accountancy; Banking; Development Studies; Economics; Finance; Human Resources; Management; Marketing); **Engineering** (Chemical Engineering; Computer Engineering; Engineering; Industrial Engineering); **Law** (Civil Law; Commercial Law; Criminal Law; Law); **Psychology** (Clinical Psychology; Developmental Psychology; Educational Psychology; Industrial and Organizational Psychology; Psychology; Psychotherapy; Social Psychology)

Programmes

Postgraduate Studies (Law; Management; Psychology)

History: Founded 1972, acquired present status 1995.

Governing Bodies: University Council

Academic Year: September to August

Main Language(s) of Instruction: Indonesian

Accrediting Agencies: Badan Akreditasi Nasional Perguruan Tinggi

Degrees and Diplomas: *Sarjana (S1)*: 4 yrs; *Magister (S2)*: Law; Management; Psychology

Student Services: Academic counselling, Canteen, Social counselling, Sports facilities

Libraries: yes

Last Updated: 13/07/11

BHAYANGKARA UNIVERSITY SURABAYA

Universitas Bhayangkara Surabaya (UBHARA SURYA)

Jalan A. Yani 114, Wonocolo, Surabaya, 60231 Jawa Timur
Tel: +62(31) 828-5602
Fax: +62(31) 828-5601
EMail: info@ubhara.ac.id; puskom@ubhara.ac.id
Website: http://www.ubhara.ac.id

Rector: Suharto

Ketua: Piter Mauritus Hutagalung

Faculties

Economics (Accountancy; Development Studies; Economics; Management); **Engineering** (Civil Engineering; Electrical Engineering; Engineering; Information Technology); **Law** (Administrative Law; Civics; Civil Law; Commercial Law; Constitutional Law; Criminal Law; Criminology; Ethics; Human Rights; International Law; Islamic Law; Labour Law; Law); **Social and Political Sciences** (Communication Studies; Government; Political Sciences; Public Administration; Social Sciences)

Programmes

Postgraduate Studies (Law; Management)

History: Founded 1982 by the prominent members of the Regional Police of East Java.

Academic Year: August to July (August-January; February-July)

Main Language(s) of Instruction: Indonesian

Degrees and Diplomas: *Sarjana (S1)*: 4 yrs; *Magister (S2)*: Law; Management

Student Services: Academic counselling, Canteen, Language programs, Social counselling, Sports facilities

Publications: SWARA *(biannually)*

Last Updated: 13/07/11

BINA DARMA UNIVERSITY

Universitas Bina Darma

Jalan Jend. A. Yani No. 12, Palembang, Sumatera Selatan
Tel: +62(711) 515-581
Fax: +62(711) 518-000 +62(711) 515-582
EMail: universitas@mail.binadarma.ac.id
Website: http://www.binadarma.ac.id

Rector: Bochari Rachman (1994-)

Ketua: Rifa Ariani

Faculties

Communication Sciences (Advertising and Publicity; Communication Studies; Journalism; Public Relations); **Computer Science** (Accountancy; Computer Engineering; Computer Networks; Computer Science; Information Management; Information Sciences; Information Technology); **Economics and Accountancy** (Accountancy; Business Administration; Management); **Engineering** (Civil Engineering; Electrical Engineering; Industrial Engineering); **Language and Literature** (English; Literature; Modern Languages); **Psychology** (Psychology); **Teacher Training and Education** (Education; Indonesian; Native Language Education; Physical Education; Teacher Training)

Programmes

Postgraduate (Educational Administration; Finance; Human Resources; Information Management; Information Technology; Management; Marketing; Software Engineering)

History: Founded as Sekolah Tinggi Ilmu Ekonomi (STIE), Sekolah Tinggi Managemen Informatika dan Komputer (STMIK) and Sekolah Tinggi Bahasa Asing (STBA) Bina Darma.

Admission Requirements: Senior High School leaving Certificate (Sekolah Menengah Atas, SMA)

Fees: (Rupiahs): Undergraduate programmes: Computer Science, 2.25 m. per semester; Economics, 2 m. per semester; Engineering, Psychology, Communication, 1.75m. per semester; Language, Literature and Teacher Training Education, 1.25 m. per semester. Graduate programmes, 2.5 m.-4.5 m.

Main Language(s) of Instruction: Indonesian

Degrees and Diplomas: *Diploma*: Business Administration; Management; Information; Computer Accountancy (D1), 1 yr; *Diploma*: Computer Engineering; Information Management (D3), 3 yrs; *Sarjana (S1)*: Economics; Computer Science; Psychology; Communication; Language and Literature; Indonesian (Bahasa); Sports (S1), 4 yrs; *Magister (S2)*: Management (Information Systems Management; Education Management; Finance; Marketing; Human Resources); Information Technology, 2 yrs

Libraries: Digital Library; Automation System

Last Updated: 24/06/11

BINUS UNIVERSITY

Universitas Bina Nusantara (BINUS)

Jl. K.H. Syahdan No. 9, Palmerah, Jakarta, 11480 DKI Jakarta
Tel: +62(21) 534-5830
Fax: +62(21) 530-0244
EMail: io@binus.edu
Website: http://www.binus.edu

Rector: Harjanto Prabowo

Manager, Rectorate Secretariat: Stephen Wahyudi Santoso
EMail: ssantoso@binus.edu

International Relations: Wayah Surya Wiroto, Vice-Rector, Students, Alumni and Collaboration Division Fax: +62(21) 530-1668
EMail: wayahsw@binus.edu

Faculties

Communication and Multimedia (Communication Studies; Graphic Design; Interior Design; Marketing; Multimedia); **Computer Studies** (Business Computing; Computer Engineering; Computer Science; Information Sciences); **Economics and Business** (Accountancy; Hotel Management; Management); **Language and Culture** (Chinese; English; Japanese); **Psychology** (Psychology); **Science and Technology** (Architecture; Civil Engineering; Industrial Engineering)

Further Information: Also Anggrek, Kijang and Syadhan campuses

History: Founded 1974.

Academic Year: September to August

Fees: (Dollars) for foreign students 870-5,300

Main Language(s) of Instruction: Indonesian and English

International Co-operation: With universities in Australia, Germany, Malaysia, Netherlands, Canada, Japan and China

Accrediting Agencies: Bandan Akreditasi Nasional (BAN-PT), SGS- inspection, verification, testing and certification services.

Degrees and Diplomas: *Diploma*: 3-4 yrs; *Sarjana (S1)*: Computer Engineering, Economics, Technology, Literature, Psychology, Communication Studies, Arts Design, 4 yrs; *Magister (S2)*: Business Administration, 2 yrs; *Magister (S2)*: Computer Engineering, Management of Information Systems, 2 years

Student Services: Academic counselling, Canteen, Employment services, Foreign student adviser, Foreign Studies Centre, Handicapped facilities, Health services, Language programs, Nursery care, Social counselling, Sports facilities

Special Facilities: Internet; Applied Technology laboratories; TV

Libraries: 19,000 vols, periodicals: 136 titles, journals: 136 titles

Academic Staff *2009-2010*	MEN	WOMEN	**TOTAL**
FULL-TIME	465	191	**656**
PART-TIME	640	308	**948**
STAFF WITH DOCTORATE			
FULL-TIME	74	12	**86**
PART-TIME	37	16	**53**
Student Numbers *2009-2010*			
All (Foreign Included)	15,609	8,380	**23,989**

Last Updated: 28/10/10

BOJONEGORO UNIVERSITY

Universitas Bojonegoro (UNIGORO)

PO Box 114, Jalan Lettu Suyitno 2, Bojonegoro, 62119 Jawa Timur
Tel: +62(353) 881-984
Fax: +62(353) 889-270
EMail: unigoro@clovermail.net
Website: http://unigoro.50webs.com

Rector: Muhammad Thalhah

Ketua: Ambarwati Sogo

Faculties

Agriculture (Agricultural Economics; Agriculture); **Economics** (Business Administration; Economic and Finance Policy; Economics); **Engineering** (Civil Engineering; Engineering); **Law** (Law); **Social and Political Sciences** (Political Sciences; Public Administration; Social Sciences)

History: Founded 1981. A private institution under the supervision of the Department of Education and Culture.
Degrees and Diplomas: *Sarjana (S1)*
Last Updated: 13/07/11

BONDOWOSO UNIVERSITY

Universitas Bondowoso

Jalan Raya Diponegoro 247, Bondowoso, Jawa Timur
Tel: +62(332) 427-022
EMail: unibo@telkom.net

Rector: Hernanik

Ketua: Muhaimin Zawawi

Faculties

Agriculture (Agricultural Economics; Agriculture) *Dean*: Matsakur; **Educational Science and Teacher Training** (Educational Sciences; Leadership; Mathematics Education; Physical Education); **Engineering**; **Law** (Law); **Social and Political Sciences**

History: Founded 1982, acquired present status 1998.

Admission Requirements: Secondary school certificate (Sekolah Menengah Atas, SMA) and entrance examination

Fees: (Rupiahs): 800,000 per annum

Main Language(s) of Instruction: Indonesian

Degrees and Diplomas: *Sarjana (S1)*: 4-5 yrs

Student Services: Academic counselling, Canteen, Social counselling, Sports facilities

Special Facilities: Observatory

Libraries: Central library, 1,558 vols

Publications: Celebrating the Foundation of University *(annually)*; Inauguration of Schooler *(biannually)*
Last Updated: 08/01/09

BORNEO TARAKAN UNIVERSITY

Universitas Borneo Tarakan

Jalan Amal Lama 1, Tarakan, 77123 Kalimantan Timur
Tel: +62(551) 550-7023
Fax: +62(551) 551-1158
EMail: ubt@borneo.ac.id
Website: http://www.borneo.ac.id/

Rector: Abdul Jabarsyah

Ketua: Ibrahim
International Relations: Herdian Syah, Vice-Rector

Faculties

Agriculture (Agricultural Business; Agricultural Engineering; Agriculture; Agronomy); **Economics** (Development Studies; Economics; Management); **Education and Teacher Training** (Biology; Educational and Student Counselling; English; Foreign Languages Education; Indonesian; Mathematics Education; Native Language Education; Primary Education); **Engineering** (Civil Engineering; Electrical and Electronic Engineering; Engineering); **Fishery and Marine Science** (Aquaculture; Fishery; Marine Science and Oceanography); **Health Sciences** (Midwifery; Nursing); **Law** (Administrative Law; Civil Law; Commercial Law; Constitutional Law; Criminal Law; Criminology; Human Rights; International Law; Islamic Law; Labour Law; Law)

History: Founded 1999.

Main Language(s) of Instruction: English, Indonesian

Degrees and Diplomas: *Sarjana (S1)*: 4-5 yrs

Student Services: Academic counselling, Canteen, Language programs, Sports facilities

Student Residential Facilities: Yes

Special Facilities: Observatory, Laboratory
Last Updated: 13/07/11

BOROBUDUR UNIVERSITY

Universitas Borobudur

Jalan Kalimalang 1, Jakarta Timur, DKI Jakarta
Tel: +62(21) 861-3877 +62(21) 861-8293
EMail: fikes@universitasborobudur.ac.id
Website: http://www.universitasborobudur.ac.id

Rektor: Basir Barthos

Vice-Rector II: Rudy Bratamenggala

Faculties

Agriculture (Agricultural Business; Agricultural Economics; Agricultural Engineering; Agriculture; Agronomy); **Computer Science** (Computer Science); **Economics** (Accountancy; Economics; Finance; Human Resources; Information Management; Management; Marketing); **Engineering** (Architecture; Civil Engineering; Computer Engineering; Engineering; Information Technology; Structural Architecture); **Health Sciences** (Health Sciences; Nursing); **Industrial Technology** (Industrial Engineering); **Law** (Law); **Psychology** (Psychology)

Programmes

Postgraduate Studies (Economics; Law; Management)

History: Founded 1983.

Degrees and Diplomas: *Diploma*; *Sarjana (S1)*; *Magister (S2)*: Law; Management; *Doktor (S3)*: Economics; Law
Last Updated: 13/07/11

BOYOLALI UNIVERSITY

Universitas Boyolali

Jalan Pandanaran 405, Boyolali, 57145 Jawa Tengah
Tel: +62(276) 321-328
Fax: +62(276) 321-328

Rector: Slamet Rahaju Wirosuparto

Ketua: Sugianto

Programmes

Accountancy (Accountancy); **Agriculture**; **Communication Studies** (Communication Studies); **Engineering** (Automotive Engineering; Chemical Engineering; Civil Engineering; Electronic Engineering; Engineering; Industrial Engineering); **Information Technology** (Information Technology); **Law** (Law); **Management** (Management)

Degrees and Diplomas: *Sarjana (S1)*
Last Updated: 28/04/10

BUDI LUHUR UNIVERSITY

Universitas Budi Luhur

Jalan Ciledug Raya, Petukangan Utara, 12260 DKI Jakarta
Tel: +62(21) 585-3753
Fax: +62(21) 585-3752
EMail: wendiu@bl.ac.id
Website: http://www.bl.ac.id

Rector: Ronny Rahman Nitibaskara EMail: ronny@bl.ac.id

Ketua: Djaetun

Vice-Rector II: Martinus Hartun Sunjata

Faculties

Communication Studies (Communication Studies); **Economics** (Accountancy; Economics; Management); **Engineering** (Architecture; Electrical Engineering; Electronic Engineering; Engineering; Structural Architecture); **Information Technology** (Computer Engineering; Information Technology); **Social and Political Sciences** (Communication Studies; International Relations; Political Sciences; Social Studies)

Programmes

Postgraduate Studies (Accountancy; Computer Science; Economics; Information Technology; Management)

History: Founded 1979 as Sekolah Tinggi Manajemen Informatika dan Komputer Budi Luhur.

Degrees and Diplomas: *Sarjana (S1)*; *Magister (S2)*: Accountancy; Computer Science; Economics; Information Technology; Management
Last Updated: 13/07/11

BUDI UTOMO INSTITUTE OF TECHNOLOGY

Institut Teknologi Budi Utomo

Jalan Raya Mawar Merah 23, Klender, Jakarta Timur, DKI Jakarta
Tel: +62(21) 861-1849 +62(21) 861-1850
Fax: +62(21) 861-3627
Website: http://itbu.ac.id

Rector: Martin Djamin

Ketua: Edy Rulyanto

Faculties

Industrial Engineering (Computer Engineering; Electrical and Electronic Engineering; Mechanical Engineering); **Planning and Civil Engineering** (Civil Engineering; Structural Architecture; Town Planning)

History: Founded 1984.

Degrees and Diplomas: *Diploma*; *Sarjana (S1)*

Libraries: c. 4,000 titles

Academic Staff *2009-2010*: Total: c. 30

Student Numbers *2009-2010*: Total: c. 230

Last Updated: 22/06/11

BUNDA MULIA UNIVERSITY

Universitas Bunda Mulia

Jalan Lodan Raya N° 2, Jakarta Pusat, 14430 Jakarta
Tel: +62(21) 690-9090
Fax: +62(21) 690-9712
EMail: bmscc@indo.net.id
Website: http://www.ubm.ac.id

Rektor: Doddy Surja Bajuadji

Ketua: Rita Djoko Susanto

Academies

Tourism (Tourism)

Faculties

Social Sciences and Humanities (Accountancy; Arts and Humanities; Chinese; Communication Studies; English; Management; Marketing; Modern Languages; Psychology; Retailing and Wholesaling; Social Sciences); **Technology and Design** (Communication Studies; Computer Engineering; Graphic Arts; Graphic Design; Industrial Engineering; Information Technology; Multimedia)

Programmes

Postgraduate Studies (Accountancy; Computer Science; Finance; Human Resources; Management; Marketing)

History: Founded 1986 as Sekolah Tinggi Manajemen Informatika dan Komputer Bunda Mulia. Acquired present title and status from the merging of STIMIK Bunda Mulia and STIE Bunda Mulia 2003.

Degrees and Diplomas: *Diploma*; *Sarjana (S1)*; *Magister (S2)*: Computer Science; Management

Last Updated: 24/06/11

BUNG HATTA UNIVERSITY

Universitas Bung Hatta

Jalan Sumatera, Ulak Karang, Padang, 25133 Sumatera Barat
Tel: +62(751) 705-1678
Fax: +62(751) 705-5475
EMail: rektorat@bunghatta.ac.id
Website: http://www.bunghatta.ac.id/

Rector: Hafrijal Syandri (2008-)

Vice-Rector I: Eko Alfarez

Vice-Rector II: Eni Kamal

International Relations: Susi Herawati, Vice-Rector III

Faculties

Arts and Humanities (English; Indonesian; Japanese; Literature); **Civil Engineering and Planning** (Architecture; Civil Engineering; Construction Engineering; Electrical Engineering; Information Technology; Regional Planning; Structural Architecture; Town Planning); **Economics** (Accountancy; Development Studies; Economics; Management); **Fisheries and Marine Sciences** (Aquaculture; Coastal Studies; Fishery; Marine Science and Oceanography; Water Science); **Industrial Engineering** (Chemical Engineering; Electronic Engineering; Industrial Engineering; Mechanical Engineering); **Law** (Law); **Teacher Training and Education** (Biology; Civics; Education; English; Indonesian; Mathematics Education; Primary Education; Teacher Training)

Programmes

Postgraduate (Architecture; Civil Engineering; Coastal Studies; Law; Management; Marine Science and Oceanography)

History: Founded 1981. Acquired present status 1998.

Governing Bodies: Bung Hatta Educational Foundation

Academic Year: September to August

Admission Requirements: Senior High School Certificate

Main Language(s) of Instruction: Indonesian

International Co-operation: With universities in Malaysia; Germany; Australia

Accrediting Agencies: National Accrediting Board

Degrees and Diplomas: *Diploma*: 3 yrs; *Sarjana (S1)*: 4 yrs; *Magister (S2)*: Civil Engineering; Architecture; Water Resources, Coastal and Marine Sciences; Management; Legal Studies, a further 2 yrs

Student Services: Academic counselling, Canteen, Cultural centre, Health services, Language programs, Sports facilities

Libraries: Yes

Academic Staff *2009-2010*	**TOTAL**
FULL-TIME	**250**
PART-TIME	**450**
STAFF WITH DOCTORATE	
FULL-TIME	**10**
PART-TIME	c. **40**

Student Numbers *2009-2010*	
All (Foreign Included)	c. **11,000**

Last Updated: 24/06/11

BUNG KARNO UNIVERSITY

Universitas Bung Karno

Jalan Kimia 20, Pegangsaan, Jakarta Pusat, DKI Jakarta
Tel: +62(21) 390-1263 +62(21) 3192-2441
Fax: +62(21) 390-1278
EMail: sekrt@ubk.ac.id
Website: http://www.ubk.ac.id/

Rector: Radi A. Gany EMail: rektor@ubk.ac.id

Vice-Rector II: Soenarto EMail: pr2@ubk.ac.id

Faculties

Agriculture (Agricultural Business; Agriculture; Agronomy; Animal Husbandry; Crop Production; Food Science); **Civil Engineering and Planning** (Architecture; Civil Engineering; Regional Planning; Structural Architecture; Town Planning); **Computer Science** (Computer Science); **Economics** (Accountancy; Development Studies; Economics; Management); **Industrial Technology** (Electrical Engineering; Industrial Engineering; Mechanical Engineering); **Law** (Law); **Social and Political Sciences** (Communication Studies; Political Sciences; Social Sciences)

History: Founded 1999.

Degrees and Diplomas: *Diploma*: 3 yrs; *Sarjana (S1)*

Last Updated: 13/07/11

CAKRAWALA UNIVERSITY

Universitas Cakrawala

Madiun

Programmes

Business Administration (Accountancy; Business Administration; Management); **Engineering**; **English**; **Information Technology** (Information Technology); **Social Sciences** (Communication Studies; Political Sciences; Social Sciences)

Degrees and Diplomas: *Sarjana (S1)*

Last Updated: 28/04/10

CHRISTIAN UNIVERSITY OF INDONESIA

Universitas Kristen Indonesia (UKI)

PO Box 6020, Jalan Mayjen Soetoyo 2, Cawang, Jakarta Timur, 13630 DKI Jakarta
Tel: +62(21) 809-2425
EMail: rmb@uki.ac.id; humas-uki@uki.ac.id
Website: http://www.uki.ac.id

Rektor: Maruli Gultom

Vice-Rector, Academic Affairs: W.B.P Simanjuntak

Ketua: Edwin Soeryadjaya

Faculties

Arts and Humanities (English; Literature); **Economics** (Accountancy; Economics; Management); **Education and Teacher Training** (Biology; Education; Educational and Student Counselling; English; Foreign Languages Education; Mathematics Education; Religious Education; Teacher Training); **Engineering** (Architecture; Civil Engineering; Electrical Engineering; Engineering; Mechanical Engineering; Structural Architecture); **Law** (Law); **Medicine** (Health Education; Health Sciences; Medicine); **Social and Political Sciences** (Communication Studies; International Relations; Political Sciences; Social Sciences)

Programmes

Graduate Studies (Educational Administration; Law)

History: Founded 1953.

Main Language(s) of Instruction: Indonesian

Degrees and Diplomas: *Diploma*: 3 yrs; *Sarjana (S1)*; *Magister (S2)*: Education Administration; Legal Studies

Student Services: Academic counselling, Canteen, Health services, Sports facilities

Last Updated: 25/07/11

CILEGON NUSANTARA UNIVERSITY OF TECHNOLOGY

Universitas Teknologi Nusantara Cilegon

Cilegon, Banten

Tel: +62(254) 378-117

Fax: +62(254) 211-9102

EMail: utn.kampus@gmail.com

Head: Usman Mulyadi

Ketua: Fransiskus Senduk

Programmes

Biology (Biology); **Business Administration** (Accountancy; Business Administration; Management); **Chemistry** (Chemistry); **Engineering** (Electrical Engineering; Engineering; Industrial Engineering); **Psychology** (Psychology)

Degrees and Diplomas: *Sarjana (S1)*

Last Updated: 28/05/10

CIPTA WACANA CHRISTIAN UNIVERSITY

Universitas Kristen Cipta Wacana

Jalan Semeru 42, Malang, 65112 Jawa Timur

Tel: +62(341) 351-456 +62(341) 343-8871

Fax: +62(341) 351-456

EMail: rektoratukcw@plasa.com

Rector: Yohanes Hadi Soesilo

Ketua: Ham Choon Hwan

Faculties

Agriculture; **Arts and Humanities** (Biology; Civics; English; Literature); **Economics**; **Engineering** (Civil Engineering; Engineering; Mechanical Engineering); **Law**; **Teacher Training and Educational Sciences** (Biology; Civics; Humanities and Social Science Education; Mathematics Education; Science Education)

History: Founded 1965.

Fees: (Rupiahs): 700,000 per annum

Degrees and Diplomas: *Sarjana (S1)*

Libraries: 5,309 vols

Last Updated: 19/01/09

COKROAMINOTO UNIVERSITY - MAKASSAR

Universitas Cokroaminoto - Makassar

Jalan Perintis Kemerderkaan Km. 11, Makassar, 90245 Sulawesi Selatan

Tel: +62(411) 582-358

Rector: Rahmat Hasanuddin

Ketua: Ma'mun Hasanuddin

Faculties

Agriculture (Agricultural Engineering) *Dean*: Ahmad Munir; **Communication Science** (Communication Studies; Public Relations) *Dean*: T. Amrullah; **Economics** (Accountancy; Economics; Management) *Dean*: Yunus Lukkas; **Engineering** (Electrical and Electronic Engineering; Power Engineering; Telecommunications Engineering) *Dean*: Muh. Tala

History: Founded 1991.

Fees: (Rupiahs): 275,000 per annum

Degrees and Diplomas: *Sarjana (S1)*

Last Updated: 08/01/09

COKROAMINOTO UNIVERSITY - PALOPO

Universitas Cokroaminoto - Palopo

Anggrek No 09B, Palopo 91921

Tel: +62(471) 221-111

EMail: uncokro_plp@yahoo.com

Rector: Abdul Rahim

Vice-Rector: Suaedi

Faculties

Agriculture (Agricultural Engineering; Agricultural Management; Agriculture); **Educational Sciences and Teachers Training** (Biology; Chemistry; Civics; Educational Sciences; English; Indonesian; Literature; Mathematics Education; Physics; Political Sciences; Science Education; Teacher Trainers Education)

History: Founded 2005.

Degrees and Diplomas: *Sarjana (S1)*

Last Updated: 08/01/09

COKROAMINOTO UNIVERSITY - YOGYAKARTA

Universitas Cokroaminoto - Yogyakarta

Jalan Perintis Kemerdekaan, Gambiran, Umbulharjo, Yogyakarta, 55161 DI Yogyakarta

Tel: +62(274) 372-274 +62(274) 378-417

EMail: info@ucy.ac.id

Website: http://www.ucy.ac.id

Rector: Halim Zulkifli

Ketua: Markhaban Fakkih

Programmes

Civil Engineering (Civil Engineering; Engineering); **Economics** (Accountancy; Banking; Economics; Islamic Studies; Management); **Islamic Studies** (Arabic; English; Indonesian; Islamic Law; Islamic Studies; Islamic Theology; Religious Education); **Law** (Law); **Pancasila and Citizenship Education** (Civics; Government)

History: Founded1979.

Degrees and Diplomas: *Sarjana (S1)*

Last Updated: 13/07/11

CORDOVA UNIVERSITY

Universitas Cordova

Jalan Pondok Pesantren 112, Taliwang, Nusa Tenggara Barat

EMail: indra.irawanlm@yahoo.co.id

Programmes

Agriculture; **Biology** (Biology); **Economic Development**; **Engineering** (Civil Engineering; Computer Engineering; Engineering; Industrial Engineering; Mining Engineering); **English**; **Government** (Government; Political Sciences)

Degrees and Diplomas: *Sarjana (S1)*

Last Updated: 28/04/10

CUT NYAK DHIEN UNIVERSITY

Universitas Cut Nyak Dhien

Jalan Jambi 59, Medan, Sumatera Utara

Tel: +62(61) 455-1815

Fax: +62(61) 453-4731

EMail: utnd@indosat.net.id

Rector: Abdullah

Ketua: Nyak Cut Sartini

Faculties

Agriculture (Agriculture; Agronomy; Animal Husbandry; Horticulture) *Dean*: Abusani Marbun; **Economics** (Accountancy; Development Studies; Economics; Law; Management) *Dean*: Zulkarnain Adi; **Engineering** (Electrical Engineering; Engineering; Mechanical Engineering) *Dean*: Teruna Jaya; **Law** *Dean*: Nurilyani Ilyas; **Pharmacy**

History: Founded 2000.

Fees: (Rupiahs): 750,000 per annum

Degrees and Diplomas: *Diploma*; *Sarjana (S1)*
Last Updated: 06/02/09

DARMA AGUNG UNIVERSITY

Universitas Darma Agung
Jalan Dr Pardede 21, Medan,
20153 Sumatera Utara
Tel: +62(61) 4535-432
Fax: +62(61) 4149-562
EMail: darmaagung@uda.ac.id; keperawatan@uda.ac.id
Website: http://www.uda.ac.id/

Rector: Binsar Panjaitan

Ketua: Sariati P. R. Siregar Br Pardede
Vice-Rector II: Lamtama Lumban Raja

Faculties

Agriculture (Agricultural Business; Agricultural Economics; Agricultural Engineering; Agricultural Management; Agronomy); **Arts and Humanities** (English; Literature; Modern Languages; Secretarial Studies); **Economics** (Accountancy; Business Administration; Business Computing; Development Studies; Economics; Management); **Education and Teacher Training** (Art Education; Educational Sciences; Educational Technology; Modern Languages; Philosophy; Religious Education; Social Sciences); **Engineering** (Bridge Engineering; Civil Engineering; Construction Engineering; Electrical Engineering; Energy Engineering; Hydraulic Engineering; Mechanical Engineering; Road Engineering; Transport Engineering); **Law** (Administrative Law; Civil Law; Constitutional Law; Law); **Nursing** (Nursing); **Social and Political Sciences** (Communication Studies; Government; Public Relations)

Programmes

Postgraduate Studies (Administration; Agricultural Business; Agricultural Management; Communication Studies; Government; Law; Management)

Further Information: Also Teaching Hospitals

History: Founded 1957. A private institution under the supervision of the Department of Education and Culture.

Governing Bodies: Yayasan

Academic Year: September to August (September-February; March-August)

Admission Requirements: Secondary school certificate (Sekolah Menengah Umum, SMU)

Main Language(s) of Instruction: Indonesian

Degrees and Diplomas: *Diploma*: 3-5 yrs; *Sarjana (S1)*: 4-7 yrs; *Magister (S2)*: Agricultural Business Management Sciences; Communication Studies; Government Science; Law; Management

Student Services: Academic counselling, Canteen, Cultural centre, Employment services, Handicapped facilities, Health services, Nursery care, Social counselling, Sports facilities

Special Facilities: Biological Garden

Libraries: General Library Hermina Napitupulu, c. 3,700 vols

Publications: Journal Universitas Darma Agung

Press or Publishing House: T.D. Pardede Press Darma Agung University
Last Updated: 13/07/11

DARMA CENDIKA SURABAYA CATHOLIC UNIVERSITY

Universitas Katolik Darma Cendika Surabaya
Jalan Deles I/29, Masuk Klampis Harapan I, Sukolilo, Surabaya, 60177 Jawa Timur
Tel: +62(31) 594-6482
Fax: +62(31) 593-9625
EMail: info@ukdc.ac.id
Website: http://www.ukdc.ac.id

Rektor: Yovita R. Pandin

Ketua: Subroto Untario

Faculties

Accountancy (Accountancy; Leadership; Management); **Architecture** (Architecture; Structural Architecture); **Industrial Engineering** (Industrial Engineering); **Law** (Law); **Management** (Management)

History: Founded 1986.

Degrees and Diplomas: *Sarjana (S1)*
Last Updated: 22/07/11

DARMA PERSADA UNIVERSITY

Universitas Darma Persada (UNSADA)
Jalan Radin Inten II, (Teruasan Casablanca),
Pondok Kelapa, Jakarta Timur, 13450 DKI Jakarta
Tel: +62(21) 864-9051 +62(21) 864-9053
Fax: +62(21) 864-9052
EMail: humas@unsada.ac.id
Website: http://www.unsada.ac.id

Rector: Kamaruddin Abdullah Tel: +62(21) 864-9059

Deputy Rector for Administrative Affairs: Sugeng Subroto Tel: +62(21) 864-9059

International Relations: Agus Sun Sugiharto, Deputy Rector for Academic Affairs EMail: gondmn@yahoo.com

Faculties

Economics (Accountancy; Finance; Human Resources; Management; Marketing; Taxation); **Engineering** (Electrical Engineering; Engineering; Industrial Engineering; Information Technology; Mechanical Engineering); **Letters** (Chinese; English; Japanese; Literature; Modern Languages); **Marine Technology** (Marine Engineering; Naval Architecture)

History: Founded 1986 by a group of Indonesian alumni of Japanese universities. Acquired present status 1998.

Governing Bodies: Board of Trustees; Melati Sakura Foundation

Academic Year: September to August

Admission Requirements: High school certificate or equivalent

Fees: (Rupiahs): 6m. per annum

Main Language(s) of Instruction: Indonesian

International Co-operation: Participates in the Hyogo University Mobility Programme in Asia and the Pacific

Accrediting Agencies: National Accrediting Board (Badan Akreditasi Nasional)

Degrees and Diplomas: *Diploma*: Japanese; Chinese; English (Amd), 3 yrs; *Sarjana (S1)*: Electrical Engineering; Mechanical Engineering; Industrial Engineering; Computer Engineering; Information system; Marine Engineering; Naval Architecture (ST); Japanese; Chinese; English (SS); Management; Accountancy (SE), 4 yrs; *Magister (S2)*: Renewable energy

Student Services: Academic counselling, Canteen, Foreign student adviser, Language programs, Sports facilities

Student Residential Facilities: None

Special Facilities: Laboratories

Libraries: University Library, c. 18,000 vols; 11,000 titles

Publications: Jurnal Ilmien Darma Persada *(quarterly)*
Last Updated: 24/06/11

DARMAJAYA INSTITUTE OF COMPUTER SCIENCE AND BUSINESS

Institut Informatika Dan Bisnis Darmajaya
Zainal Abidin Pagar Alam 93, Bandar Lampung, 35141 Lampung
Tel: +62(721) 787-214
Fax: +62(721) 700-261
EMail: info@darmajaya.ac.id
Website: http://www.darmajaya.ac.id

Rector: Andi Desfiandi

Ketua: Yoenidar Karim Alfian

Programmes

Business and Economics (Accountancy; Business Administration; Economics; Management); **Computer Science** (Computer Engineering; Computer Science; Information Technology); **Master Studies** (Information Technology; Management)

Degrees and Diplomas: *Diploma*; *Sarjana (S1)*; *Magister (S2)*

Libraries: 8,403 vols

Academic Staff *2010-2011*	MEN	WOMEN	**TOTAL**
FULL-TIME	57	49	**106**
PART-TIME	38	29	**67**
STAFF WITH DOCTORATE			
FULL-TIME	8	2	**10**
Student Numbers *2010-2011*			
All (Foreign Included)	2,148	1,166	**3,314**

Last Updated: 28/10/10

DARUL ULUM ISLAMIC SUDIRMAN UNGARAN UNIVERSITY CENTRE

Universitas Darul Ulum Islamic Centre Sudirman (UNDARIS)
Jalan Tentara Pelajar 13, Ungaran, 50514 Jawa Tengah
Tel: +62(24) 692-3180

Rector: Edi Dui Kurniati

Ketua: Hartono Kasmadi

Faculties

Animal Husbandry (Animal Husbandry; Food Science; Nutrition) *Dean*: Sutarno; **Economics** (Economics; Management) *Dean*: Edy Dwi Kurniati; **Educational Sciences and Teacher Training** (Civics; Educational Sciences; Social Sciences; Teacher Training) *Dean*: Lamijan; **Engineering** (Civil Engineering; Electrical Engineering) *Dean*: Suharyanto; **Law** (Law) *Dean*: Tri Susilowati

History: Founded 1982.

Fees: (Rupiahs): 600,000 per annum

Degrees and Diplomas: *Diploma*: 3 yrs; *Sarjana (S1)*; *Magister (S2)*: Law

Libraries: 2,464 vols

Last Updated: 09/01/09

DARUL ULUM UNIVERSITY

Universitas Darul Ulum (UNDAR)
Jalan Merdeka 29A, Jombang, 61417 Jawa Timur
Tel: +62(321) 861-141
Fax: +62(321) 861-142
EMail: undar.65@gmail.com
Website: http://www.undar.ac.id/

Rector: Ma'murotus Sadiyah EMail: eyikmr.1965@gmail.com

Faculties

Agriculture (Agricultural Business; Agricultural Engineering; Agriculture; Agronomy); **Economics** (Accountancy; Development Studies; Economics; Management); **Engineering** (Civil Engineering; Computer Science; Electrical Engineering; Engineering; Mechanical Engineering); **Islamic Religion** (Islamic Theology); **Law** (Law); **Postgraduate Studies** (Development Studies; Economics); **Psychology** (Psychology); **Social and Political Sciences** (Government; Information Management; International Relations; Political Sciences; Social Sciences); **Teacher Training and Educational Science** (Education; Educational and Student Counselling; Teacher Training)

History: Founded 1965. A private institution under the supervision of the Department of Education and Culture.

Academic Year: August to July (August-December; January-July)

Admission Requirements: Secondary school certificate

Main Language(s) of Instruction: Indonesian, Arabic

Degrees and Diplomas: *Sarjana (S1)*; *Magister (S2)*: Economics

Student Residential Facilities: Yes

Special Facilities: Campus Mosque. Biological Garden

Libraries: Central Library, c. 14,000 vols; 6 Faculty Library Units

Publications: Gelegar 4 *(monthly)*; Gema Kampus *(monthly)*; Trisula *(monthly)*

Last Updated: 24/06/11

DARUSSALAM UNIVERSITY AMBON

Universitas Darussalam Ambon
Jalan Raya Tulehu Km. 24, Ambon 97582
Tel: +62(911) 330-3422
Fax: +62(911) 330-3422
EMail: admin@darussalam.ac.id
Website: http://elearning.darussalam.ac.id

Rector: Ismael Tahir

Ketua: Latuconsina

Faculties

Agriculture (Agricultural Engineering; Agriculture; Crop Production; Forestry; Water Management); **Economics** (Accountancy; Economics; Management); **Education Teacher Training** (Biology; Chemistry; Education; Mathematics Education; Physics; Science Education); **Engineering** (Industrial Engineering; Mechanical Engineering); **Social and Political Sciences** (Government; Political Sciences; Public Administration; Social Sciences)

History: Founded 1986.

Degrees and Diplomas: *Sarjana (S1)*

Last Updated: 13/07/11

DARWAN ALI UNIVERSITY

Universitas Darwan Ali
Sampit, Kalimantan
Tel: +62(531) 21442
Fax: +62(531) 21527

Rector: Edy Mulyono

Ketua: Yuliana Siek

Programmes

Accountancy; **Agricultural Business** (Agricultural Business); **Aquaculture** (Aquaculture); **Civil Engineering** (Civil Engineering); **Information Management and Technology** (Information Management; Information Technology); **Management**

Degrees and Diplomas: *Sarjana (S1)*; *Magister (S2)*: Management

Last Updated: 28/04/10

DAYANA IHSANUDDIN UNIVERSITY BAU-BAU

Universitas Dayanu Ikhsanuddin Bau-Bau
Kampus Istana Ilmiah, Jalan Yos Sudarso No. 43, Bau-Bau, 93711 Sulawesi Tenggara
Tel: +62(402) 282-1327
Fax: +62(402) 282-6682
Website: http://www.unidayan.ac.id

Rector: Laode Muhammad Arsal

Faculties

Economics (Development Studies; Economics; Finance; Management; Regional Planning; Town Planning); **Educational Sciences and Teacher Training** (Art Education; Economics; Educational Sciences; English; History; Mathematics; Modern Languages; Natural Sciences; Social Sciences; Teacher Training); **Engineering** (Civil Engineering; Engineering; Mechanical Engineering); **Fisheries and Marine Sciences** (Fishery; Marine Science and Oceanography; Water Science); **Law** (Law); **Postgraduate Studies** (Public Administration); **Social and Political Sciences** (Government; Political Sciences; Public Administration; Sociology)

History: Founded 1982.

Main Language(s) of Instruction: Indonesian

Accrediting Agencies: National Accreditation Board

Degrees and Diplomas: *Sarjana (S1)*; *Magister (S2)*: Public Administration

Student Services: Academic counselling, Canteen, Cultural centre, Foreign student adviser, Foreign Studies Centre, Handicapped facilities, Language programs, Social counselling, Sports facilities

Libraries: 1,957 vols

Publications: Akademika *(3 per annum)*

Last Updated: 24/06/11

DE LA SALLE CATHOLIC UNIVERSITY

Universitas Katolik De La Salle

Jalan Kairagi 1 Kombos, Manado, 95111 Sulawesi Utara
Tel: +62(431) 877-510 +62(431) 871-960
Fax: +62(431) 871-972
EMail: info@delasalle.ac.id
Website: http://www.delasalle.ac.id

Rektor: Johanis Mangkey

Ketua: Agus Mangundap

Faculties

Agriculture (Agricultural Business; Agriculture); **Economics** (Accountancy; Economics; Management); **Engineering** (Computer Engineering; Electronic Engineering; Engineering; Industrial Engineering); **Law** (Law); **Mathematics and Natural Sciences** (Computer Science; Mathematics; Natural Sciences); **Nursing** (Nursing)

History: Founded 2000.

Degrees and Diplomas: *Sarjana (S1)*

Last Updated: 22/07/11

DEHASEN BENGKULU UNIVERSITY

Universitas Dehasen Bengkulu

Jalan Meranti Raya 32, Bengkulu, 38227 Bengkulu
Tel: +62(736) 22027
Fax: +62(736) 341-139

Rector: Sigit Nugroho

Ketua: Nazir Syafrie

Programmes

Business Administration; **Engineering** (Agricultural Engineering; Computer Engineering; Engineering; Food Technology); **English** (English); **Social Sciences**

Degrees and Diplomas: *Sarjana (S1)*

Last Updated: 28/04/10

DHARMAWANGSA UNIVERSITY

Universitas Dharmawangsa

Jalan Yos Sudarso 244, Medan, 20115 Sumatera Utara
Tel: +62(61) 661-3783
Fax: +62(61) 661-5190
Website: http://dharmawangsa.ac.id

Rector: Kusbianto

Ketua: Abdussalam Ibrahim

Faculties

Economics (Accountancy; Development Studies; Economics; Management); **Fishery** (Aquaculture; Fishery; Water Management); **Law** (Law); **Social and Political Sciences** (Administration; Communication Studies; Government; Public Administration)

History: Founded 1988.

Degrees and Diplomas: *Sarjana (S1)*

Last Updated: 13/07/11

DIAN NUSANTARA UNIVERSITY

Universitas Dian Nusantara

Medan, Sumatera Utara

Programmes

Accountancy (Accountancy); **Biology** (Biology); **Business Administration** (Business Administration; Management); **Communication Studies**; **Engineering** (Civil Engineering; Electrical Engineering; Engineering); **English** (English); **Information Technology** (Information Technology); **Management** (Management); **Mathematics** (Mathematics)

Degrees and Diplomas: *Sarjana (S1)*

Last Updated: 29/04/10

DIAN NUSWANTORO UNIVERSITY

Universitas Dian Nuswantoro (UDINUS)

Jalan Nakula I No. 5-11, Semarang, 50131 Jawa Tengah
Tel: +62(24) 351-7261 +62(24) 352-0165
Fax: +62(24) 352-0165
EMail: sekretariat@dinus.ac.id
Website: http://www.dinus.ac.id

Rector: Rustanti Noersasongko

Vice-Rector for Academic Affairs: Kusni Ingsih

Vice-Rector for General and Financial Affairs: Dwiarso Utomo

Faculties

Computer Science (Accountancy; Communication Studies; Computer Engineering; Computer Networks; Computer Science; Design; Information Management; Visual Arts); **Economics** (Accountancy; Economics; Management); **Engineering** (Electrical Engineering; Engineering; Industrial Engineering); **Health Sciences** (Community Health; Occupational Health; Public Health); **Languages and Literature** (Chinese; English; English Studies; Japanese; Literature)

Programmes

Postgraduate Studies (Information Technology; Management)

History: Founded as Sekolah Tinggi Manajemen Informatika dan Komputer Dian Nuswantoro. Acquired present status and title 2001 following the merger of the four colleges managed by Dian Nuswantoro Foundation: College of Informatics Management and Computer, College of Economics, College of Foreign Languages, and College of Health.

Degrees and Diplomas: *Diploma*; *Sarjana (S1)*; *Magister (S2)*: Information Technology; Management

Last Updated: 18/07/11

DJUANDA UNIVERSITY

Universitas Djuanda

Kotak Pos 35, Jalan Tol Ciawi 1, Bogor, 16720 Jawa Barat
Tel: +62(251) 824-0773
Fax: +62(251) 824-0985
EMail: admin@universitas-djuanda.ac.id
Website: http://www.universitas-djuanda.ac.id/

Rector: Martin Roestamy

Ketua: Mohammad Emnis Anwar

Faculties

Agricultural Technology (Agricultural Engineering; Food Technology; Nutrition); **Agriculture** (Agricultural Economics; Agriculture; Agronomy; Animal Husbandry; Aquaculture); **Economics** (Accountancy; Economics; Management); **Education** (Education; Primary Education); **Islamic Studies** (Economics; Islamic Studies); **Law** (Law); **Social and Political Sciences** (Administration; Communication Studies; Government; International Relations; Journalism; Public Administration)

History: Founded 1987.

Fees: (Rupiahs): 820,000 per annum

Degrees and Diplomas: *Sarjana (S1)*; *Magister (S2)*: Law

Libraries: 13,263 vols

Last Updated: 18/07/11

DR. SOETOMO UNIVERSITY

Universitas Dr. Soetomo

Jalan Semolowaru, Surabaya, Jawa Timur
Tel: +62(31) 592-5970
Fax: +62(31) 593-8935
EMail: info@unitomo.ac.id
Website: http://www.unitomo.ac.id/

Rector: Ulul Albab

Ketua: Wahyudi Noor Saleh

Faculties
Administration (Business Administration; Public Administration; Secretarial Studies); **Agriculture**; **Communication Science**; **Economics** (Accountancy; Development Studies; Economics; Management); **Educational Sciences and Teacher Training** (Art Education; Educational Sciences; Indonesian; Literature; Mathematics Education; Modern Languages; Natural Sciences; Teacher Training); **Engineering**; **Law** (Law); **Letters**; **Postgraduate Studies** (Communication Studies; Management)

History: Founded 1981. A private institution under the supervision of the Department of Education and Culture.

Academic Year: September-August

Admission Requirements: High school leaving certificate or equivalent for Diploma Degree and Sarjana Degree (S1) any discipline for Postgraduate Degree.

Fees: (Rupiahs): 2.8m. per annum

Main Language(s) of Instruction: Indonesian

Degrees and Diplomas: *Diploma*: 3 yrs; *Sarjana (S1)*: 4 yrs; *Magister (S2)*: a further 2 yrs

Libraries: Dr. Soetomo University Library, 42,173 vols

Publications: Cendekia *(quarterly)*; Dokar *(monthly)*; Media Ilmiah *(biannually)*
Last Updated: 29/04/10

DUMOGA BONE KOTAMOBAGU UNIVERSITY

Universitas Dumoga Bone Kotamobagu (UDK)

Jalan Jenderal Ahmad Yani 184, Kotamobagu, Sulawesi Utara
Tel: +62(434) 21-831
EMail: udk_kota@yahoo.co.id

Rector: Sahrun Dalie

Ketua: Jambat A. Damopolii

Faculties
Agriculture (Agricultural Economics; Agronomy) *Dean*: Ula Mamonto; **Economics** (Management) *Dean*: Erna Manoppo; **Forestry** (Forest Management; Forestry) *Dean*: Robby Rempas

History: Founded 1984.

Fees: (Rupiahs): 225,000 per annum

Degrees and Diplomas: *Sarjana (S1)*

Libraries: 1,051 vols
Last Updated: 12/01/09

DUTA WACANA CHRISTIAN UNIVERSITY

Universitas Kristen Duta Wacana

Jalan Dr. Wahidin Sudiro Husodo 5-25, Yogyakarta, 55224 Yogyakarta
Tel: +62(274) 563-929 +62(274) 513-606
Fax: +62(274) 513-235
EMail: humas@ukdw.ac.id
Website: http://www.ukdw.ac.id

Rektor: Djohan (2010-2014)

Faculties
Biology (Biological and Life Sciences; Biology; Environmental Studies; Health Sciences; Nutrition); **Economics** (Accountancy; Economics; Management); **Engineering** (Architecture; Computer Engineering; Engineering; Engineering Drawing and Design; Information Technology; Structural Architecture); **Medicine** (Medicine); **Postgraduate Studies** (Bible; Peace and Disarmament; Religious Studies; Theology); **Theology** (Theology)

History: Founded 1985.

Degrees and Diplomas: *Sarjana (S1)*; *Magister (S2)*: Theology
Last Updated: 25/07/11

DWIJENDRA UNIVERSITY

Universitas Dwijendra (UNDWI)

Jalan Kamboja n° 17, Denpasar, 80237 Bali
Tel: +62(361) 224-383 +62(361) 233-974
Fax: +62(361) 233-974
Website: http://www.dwijendra.com

Rector: Ketut Wirawan

Ketua: Ida Bagus Gede Wiyana

Faculties
Agriculture (Agricultural Business; Agricultural Economics; Agriculture); **Communication Science** (Communication Studies); **Education and Teacher Training** (Civics; Education; Indonesian; Literature; Native Language Education; South and Southeast Asian Languages); **Engineering** (Architecture; Engineering; Structural Architecture); **Law** (Law)

History: Founded 1982.

Degrees and Diplomas: *Diploma*: 3 yrs; *Sarjana (S1)*
Last Updated: 18/07/11

EKASAKTI UNIVERSITY

Universitas Ekasakti

Jalan Veteran Dalam 26B, Padang, 25113 Sumatera Barat
Tel: +62(751) 28-859 +62(751) 32-693
Fax: +62(751) 32-694
EMail: puskom@univ-ekasakti-pdg.ac.id
Website: http://www.univ-ekasakti-pdg.ac.id

Rector: H. Andi Mustari Pide EMail: rektor@univ-ekasakti-pdg.ac.id

Vice-Rector I: Agus Salim

Faculties
Agriculture (Agricultural Business; Agricultural Engineering; Agriculture; Agronomy; Soil Science); **Arts and Humanities** (Arabic; English; Literature); **Economics** (Accountancy; Economics; Management); **Engineering** (Architecture; Civil Engineering; Electrical Engineering; Engineering; Industrial Engineering; Mechanical Engineering; Structural Architecture); **Law** (Law); **Social and Political Sciences** (Administration; Communication Studies; Government; Political Sciences; Public Administration; Social Sciences)

Programmes
Education and Teacher Training (Economics; English; Foreign Languages Education; Indonesian; Information Management; Mathematics Education; Native Language Education)

History: Founded 1984.

Degrees and Diplomas: *Diploma*: 3 yrs; *Sarjana (S1)*; *Magister (S2)*: Law (Constitutional Law; Business Law)
Last Updated: 18/07/11

ESA UNGGUL UNIVERSITY

Universitas Esa Unggul

Terusan Arjuna, Tol Tomang, Kebon Jeruk, Jakarta Barat, 11510 DKI Jakarta
Tel: +62(21) 567-4223 +62(21) 568-42510
Fax: +62(21) 567-4248 +62(21) 568-2503
EMail: humas@esaunggul.ac.id
Website: http://www.esaunggul.ac.id

Rector: Arief Kusuma

Vice-Rector I: Rokiah Kusumapradja

Faculties
Communication Sciences (Advertising and Publicity; Journalism; Public Relations; Radio and Television Broadcasting); **Computer Science** (Computer Science; Information Technology); **Design and Creative Industries** (Design; Graphic Design; Industrial Design); **Economics** (Accountancy; Economics; Management); **Engineering** (Industrial Engineering; Regional Planning; Town Planning); **Health Sciences** (Health Administration; Health Sciences; Nursing; Nutrition; Public Health); **Law** (Law); **Physiotherapy** (Physical Therapy); **Psychology** (Psychology)

Programmes
Postgraduate Studies (Accountancy; Law; Management; Public Administration)

History: Founded 1993.

Degrees and Diplomas: *Diploma*: 3-4 yrs; *Sarjana (S1)*; *Magister (S2)*: Accountancy; Law; Management; Public Administration

Special Facilities: E-learning campus; Laboratory; Studio

Libraries: c. 3,400 vols
Last Updated: 27/06/11

FAJAR UNIVERSITY

Universitas Fajar

Jalan Racing Centre 101, Makassar, 90231 Sulawesi Selatan
Tel: +62(411) 459-064
Fax: +62(411) 459-065

Programmes

Architecture; **Business Administration** (Accountancy; Business Administration; Management); **Communication Studies**; **Engineering** (Chemical Engineering; Civil Engineering; Electrical Engineering; Engineering); **English** (English); **Public and International Relations** (International Relations; Public Relations); **Tourism** (Tourism)

Degrees and Diplomas: *Sarjana (S1)*
Last Updated: 29/04/10

FLORES UNIVERSITY

Universitas Flores

Jalan Soekarno 6-8, Flores, Ende, 86316 Nusa Tengarra Timur
Tel: +62(381) 21-536 +62(381) 21-094

Rector: Thomas Geba

Ketua: H. J. Gadi Djou

Faculties

Economics (Accountancy; Development Studies; Economics; Management) *Dean*: Silas Sablon Sayang; **Educational Science and Teacher Training** *Dean*: Fidelis Nong; **Engineering** (Civil Engineering; Engineering) *Dean*: Valentinus Tan; **Law** *Dean*: Yosep Separ

History: Founded 1980.

Fees: (Rupiahs): 320,000 per annum

Degrees and Diplomas: *Diploma*: 3 yrs; *Sarjana (S1)*

Libraries: 3,663 vols
Last Updated: 12/01/09

GAJAH PUTIH UNIVERSITY

Universitas Gajah Putih

Jalan Aman Dimot 10, Takengon, 24513 Aceh
EMail: ugp@yahoo.co.id

Rector: Syukur Kobath

Ketua: Armia Se

Programmes

Agriculture (Agriculture); **Communication Studies** (Communication Studies); **Economics** (Economics); **Information Technology** (Information Technology); **Management** (Management); **Public Administration** (Public Administration)

Degrees and Diplomas: *Sarjana (S1)*
Last Updated: 29/04/10

GAJAYANA UNIVERSITY MALANG

Universitas Gajayana Malang (UNIGA)

Jalan Merjosari, Dinoyo Malang, 65144 Jawa Timur
Tel: +62(341) 562-411
Fax: +62(341) 582-168
Website: http://www.unigamalang.ac.id

Rector: Rosidi Rosidi EMail: uniga@indo.net.id

Ketua Yayasan: Mohamad Saleh
Tel: +62(341) 551-576, Fax: +62(341) 551-576

Faculties

Arts and Humanities (English; Literature) *Head*: Tatiek Danti; **Computer Science** (Computer Science; Mathematics; Natural Sciences; Statistics) *Head*: Syaad Patmantara; **Economics** (Accountancy; Economics; Management) *Head*: Endang Suswati; **Engineering** (Electrical and Electronic Engineering; Engineering; Mechanical Engineering; Telecommunications Engineering) *Head*: Erfan Dahlan; **Postgraduate Studies** (Management) *Head*: Solimun; **Postgraduate Studies** (Management) *Head*: Agus Suman; **Psychology** (Psychology) *Head*: Sri Hadiati

History: Founded 1980 as AMPA (Academy of Management, Taxation and Accountancy). Became a university and acquired present status 1986.

Academic Year: September to August (September-February; March-August)

Fees: (Rupiahs): 1.8m. per annum

Main Language(s) of Instruction: Indonesian

International Co-operation: None

Accrediting Agencies: National Accreditation Body (BAN) of Indonesia

Degrees and Diplomas: *Sarjana (S1)*: Economics; Arts and Humanities; Engineering; Psychology; Computer Science; Statistics (SE; SS; ST; S.Psi; Skom; Ssi), 4 yrs; *Magister (S2)*: Management (MM), a further 2 yrs

Student Services: Academic counselling, Canteen, Cultural centre, Employment services, Foreign student adviser, Health services, Language programs, Social counselling, Sports facilities

Special Facilities: TV and Telecommunication Studios

Libraries: 24,925 vols

Publications: Journal of Economics and Management *(quarterly)*; Journal of Gajayana Management *(biennially)*; Journal of Indonesian Accounting *(biennially)*
Last Updated: 26/04/11

GALUH UNIVERSITY CIAMIS

Universitas Galuh Ciamis

Jalan Re Martadinata 150, Ciamis, 46215 Jawa Barat
Tel: +62(265) 776-787 +62(625) 771-955
EMail: unigalciamis@gmail.com
Website: http://www.universitas-galuh.ac.id

Rector: H.S. Koswara

Vice-Rector I: Oyon Saryono

Faculties

Agriculture (Agricultural Business; Agricultural Economics; Agriculture; Agronomy; Animal Husbandry); **Economics** (Accountancy; Management); **Educational Sciences and Teacher Training** (Accountancy; Art Education; Biology; Economics; Educational Sciences; English; Foreign Languages Education; Health Education; History; Indonesian; Literature; Mathematics Education; Midwifery; Native Language Education; Natural Sciences; Parks and Recreation; Physical Education; Social Sciences; Sports; Teacher Training); **Engineering** (Civil Engineering; Electrical Engineering; Engineering Management; Industrial Engineering; Mechanical Engineering); **Health Sciences** (Health Sciences; Midwifery; Nursing); **Law** (Law); **Social and Political Sciences** (Government; Political Sciences; Public Administration; Social Sciences; Social Welfare)

Programmes

Postgraduate (Educational Administration; Management)

History: Founded 1988.

Degrees and Diplomas: *Diploma*: 3 yrs; *Sarjana (S1)*; *Magister (S2)*: Educational Administration; Management

Libraries: c. 13,000 vols
Last Updated: 24/06/11

GARUT UNIVERSITY

Universitas Garut

Jalan Raya Cimanuk 285A, Tarogong, Garut, 44151 Jawa Barat
Tel: +62(262) 231-013
Fax: +62(262) 239-126
EMail: ugtlo@telkom.net

Rector: Jusman Iskandar

Ketua: H. Cecep Syarifuddin

Faculties

Agriculture (Agriculture; Agronomy; Animal Husbandry) *Dean*: Mardjiwa; **Economics** (Accountancy; Economics; Management) *Dean*: Yoesoef Adnan; **Engineering** (Business and Commerce; Engineering; Management; Telecommunications Engineering; Textile Design) *Dean*: Andiet Mahasna; **Mathematics and Natural Sciences** (Mathematics; Natural Sciences; Pharmacy) *Dean*: R.H. Maghfur; **Social and Political Sciences** (Administration; Government; Political Sciences; Social Sciences; Social Welfare; Social Work) *Dean*: Ishak Solih

History: Founded 1998.

Fees: (Rupiahs): 1m. per annum

Degrees and Diplomas: *Diploma*: 3 yrs; *Sarjana (S1)*; *Magister (S2)*: Public Administration

Libraries: 15,047 vols

Last Updated: 12/01/09

GORONTALO UNIVERSITY

Universitas Gorontalo

Jalan Jend. Sudirman No. 247 Limboto, Gorontalo, 96211 Gorontalo
Tel: +62(435) 881-369
Fax: +62(435) 880-370
EMail: ugtlo@telkom.net

Rektor: Hariadi Said

Ketua: Rustam Akili

Faculties

Agricultural (Agricultural Engineering; Agriculture) *Dean*: Syaiful Umela; **Community Health** (Community Health) *Dean*: Faisal Idrus.; **Economics** (Economics; Management) *Dean*: Rolli Paramata; **Engineering** (Civil Engineering; Engineering; Industrial Engineering; Mechanical Engineering) *Dean*: Syamsul Q Ngabito; **Political and Social Sciences** *Dean*: Robby Hunawa

History: Founded as Sekolah Tinggi Ilmu Ekonomi Dua Lima Pohala Gorontalo

Degrees and Diplomas: *Sarjana (S1)*

Academic Staff: Total: c. 500

Last Updated: 12/01/09

GRAHA NUSANTARA UNIVERSITY

Universitas Graha Nusantara

Jalan Dr Sutomo n°14, Padang Sidempuan, 22718 Sumatera Utara
Tel: +62(634) 252-92
Fax: +62(634) 283-27
EMail: ugn_psp@yahoo.com; elka_ugn@yahoo.com

Rector: Aminullah Pakpahan

Ketua: Affan Siregar

Faculties

Agriculture (Agriculture; Agronomy; Animal Husbandry) *Dean*: Saripada Harahap; **Economics** (Development Studies; Economics; Management) *Dean*: Zulkifli Harahap; **Education and Teacher Training**; **Engineering** (Civil Engineering; Engineering) *Dean*: Saripada Harahap; **Social and Political Sciences** (Administration; Government; Political Sciences; Social Sciences) *Dean*: Rasyid Nasution

History: Founded 1985.

Fees: (Rupiahs): 200,000 per annum

Degrees and Diplomas: *Sarjana (S1)*

Libraries: 1,605 vols

Last Updated: 12/01/09

GRESIK UNIVERSITY

Universitas Gresik

Jalan Arief Rakhmar Hakim 2-B, Gresik, Jawa Timur
Tel: +62(31) 398-1918
Fax: +62(31) 397-8628
EMail: univ_gresik@yahoo.co.id

Rector: Sukiyat

Ketua: Bagoes Sasmita

Faculties

Economics (Accountancy; Economics; Management); **Education and Teacher Training** (Educational Administration; Educational Sciences; Teacher Training); **Engineering** (Civil Engineering; Engineering; Mechanical Engineering); **Law**

History: Founded 1981. A private institution under the supervision of the Department of Education and Culture.

Fees: (Rupiahs): 422,000 per annum

Degrees and Diplomas: *Sarjana (S1)*

Libraries: 1,375 vols

Last Updated: 12/01/09

GUNADARMA UNIVERSITY

Universitas Gunadarma

Jalan Margonda Raya 100, Pondok Cina, Depok, 16424 DKI Jakarta
Tel: +62(21) 752-0981 +62(21) 7888-1112
Fax: +62(21) 787-2829
EMail: sektor@gunadarma.ac.id
Website: http://www.gunadarma.ac.id

Rector: Eko Sri Margianti

Vice-Rector I: Ravi A. Salim

Faculties

Arts and Humanities (English; Literature; Modern Languages); **Civil Engineering and Planning** (Architecture; Civil Engineering; Structural Architecture); **Computer Science and Information Technology** (Computer Engineering; Computer Science; Information Technology); **Economics** (Accountancy; Economics; Management); **Industrial Technology** (Computer Engineering; Electrical Engineering; Industrial Engineering; Mechanical Engineering); **Psychology** (Psychology)

Programmes

Midwifery (Midwifery); **Postgraduate Studies** (Civil Engineering; Computer Science; Economics; Electrical Engineering; English; Information Technology; Management; Management Systems; Mechanical Engineering; Psychology)

History: Founded 1981 as Academy of Science and Computer of Indonesia, and became Gunadarma Information Management and Computer College 1985. Merged with Gunadarma Economic College and acquired present status and title 1996.

Governing Bodies: Educational Foundation of Gunadarma

Academic Year: September to August (September-December; January-August)

Admission Requirements: Certificate (Ijasah), good scores of National Exams and entrance examination

Main Language(s) of Instruction: Indonesian

Accrediting Agencies: National Higher Education Accreditation Board

Degrees and Diplomas: *Diploma*: 3 yrs; *Sarjana (S1)*: 4 yrs; *Magister (S2)*: Civil Engineering; Electrical Engineering; English Literature; Management; Management Information Systems; Mechanical Engineering; Psychology; *Doktor (S3)*: Computer Science; Economics; Information Technology; Psychology

Student Services: Academic counselling, Canteen, Employment services, Health services, Language programs, Social counselling, Sports facilities

Special Facilities: Theatre. Mosque. Video Studio

Libraries: University Library, c. 50,000 vols

Publications: Ekonomi & Bisnis, Research in the fields of Economics, Management and Accountancy *(biannually)*; Informatika & Komputer, Research in the fields of Information Systems, Computer Engineering and Computer Science *(biannually)*; Psikologi, Research in the field of Psychology *(biannually)*; Sastra & Bahasa, Research in the fields of Literature and Language *(biannually)*; Teknologi & Rekayasa, Research in the fields of Engineering, Technology and Architecture *(biannually)*

Last Updated: 18/07/11

GUNUNG KIDUL UNIVERSITY

Universitas Gunung Kidul

Jl. KH. Angus Salim No. 170, Kepek, Wonosari, 55813 DI Yogyakarta
Tel: +62(274) 391-342
EMail: university_of_gk@yahoo.com

Direktor: Mustangid EMail: univ_gunungkidul@yahoo.co.id

Ketua: Suhardono

Programmes
Agriculture (Agricultural Business; Agronomy; Cattle Breeding; Fishery; Soil Science); **Engineering** (Civil Engineering; Geological Engineering); **Public Administration** (Public Administration); **Social Sciences** (Communication Studies; Economics; Social Sciences; Social Studies)

History: Founded 2001.

Degrees and Diplomas: *Sarjana (S1)*
Last Updated: 12/01/09

GUNUNG RINJANI UNIVERSITY

Universitas Gunung Rinjani

Jl. Raya Mataram Lombok Km. 50, Selong, Mataram, 83600 Nusa Tengarra Barrat
Tel: +62(376) 631-620
Fax: +62(376) 631-621
EMail: univgunungrinjani@yahoo.co.id

Rector: Ayip Rosidi

Ketua: Asrul Sani

Faculties
Agriculture *Dean*: Rizal Ahmadi; **Economics** *Dean*: Eko Prihartono; **Fishery** *Dean*: Oktova Malaputra; **Law** *Dean*: Johan Maligan

History: Founded 1996.

Fees: (Rupiahs): 475,000 per annum

Degrees and Diplomas: *Sarjana (S1)*
Last Updated: 12/01/09

HALMAHERA UNIVERSITY

Universitas Halmahera

Komplek GMIH Wari, Wari Ino, Tobelo, 97762 Maluku Utara

Programmes
Agriculture (Agricultural Engineering; Animal Husbandry; Aquaculture; Forestry); **Business Administration** (Accountancy; Business Administration; Management; Public Administration); **Government** (Government; Political Sciences); **Law**; **Mathematics** (Mathematics); **Physics** (Physics); **Primary School Teacher Education**; **Theology** (Theology)

Degrees and Diplomas: *Sarjana (S1)*
Last Updated: 29/04/10

HANG TUAH UNIVERSITY

Universitas Hang Tuah (UHT)

Jl. Arif Rahman Hakim 150, Surabaya, 60111 East Java
Tel: +62(31) 594-5894
Fax: +62(31) 594-6261
EMail: humas@hangtuah.id; kababsi@hangtuah.id
Website: http://www.hangtuah.ac.id

Rector: Sutarno
Tel: +62(31) 594-5622, Fax: +62(31) 594-5622
EMail: spoerwowidagdo@hotmail.com

Vice-Rector for Academic Affairs: I Wajan Dana Wiardjana
EMail: wr1@hangtauh.ac.id

International Relations: Hadi Sunoto, Assistant for Cooperation Affairs EMail: hadisunoto@hangtuah.ac.id

Faculties
Dentistry (Dentistry); **Engineering and Marine Sciences** (Electrical Engineering; Fishery; Marine Engineering; Marine Science and Oceanography; Naval Architecture); **Law** (Constitutional Law; Law); **Medicine** (Medicine); **Psychology** (Psychology); **Social and Political Sciences** (Political Sciences; Social Sciences)

Programmes
Maritime Education and Training (Marine Transport; Nautical Science)

History: Founded 1987 as an independent institution.

Governing Bodies: The Nala Foundation

Academic Year: September to July

Admission Requirements: Senior High school leaving certificate (Sekolah Menengah Atas, SMA) or equivalent and entrance examination

Fees: (Rupiahs): Medical and Dentistry Schools, 13.3m. for first year plus building fee 30m. and c. 12.6m. per annum for following years. Maritime Education and Training, c. 10m. for first year and c. 4.5m. for second and following years. Engineering and Marine Science, Law, Public Administration and Psychology Schools, 10.2m. for first year and c. 4.4m. for the second and following years. Postgraduate School fee, 8.m for the first semester, and 6.5m. for second and next semesters

Main Language(s) of Instruction: Indonesian

International Co-operation: With universities in Japan, Australia and the Netherlands

Accrediting Agencies: Badan Akreditasi Nasional Perguran Tinggi - BAN PT (National Acreditation Board for Higher Education)

Degrees and Diplomas: *Diploma*: Seafarers' Education and Training (ANT-III; ATT-III; A.Md.), 3 yrs; *Sarjana (S1)*: Engineering; Marine Sciences; Oceanography; Law; Administration and Psychology (S1), 4 yrs; *Sarjana (S1)*: Medicine; Dentistry (dr.; drg.), 6 yrs; *Magister (S2)*: Public Administration and Public Policy (M.A.P.), a further 18 months

Student Services: Academic counselling, Canteen, Cultural centre, Employment services, Foreign student adviser, Health services, Language programs, Social counselling, Sports facilities

Student Residential Facilities: 1 building (65 rooms)

Special Facilities: Museum; Art Gallery; Observatory; Movie Studio; Auditorium (500 seats capacity)

Libraries: Central Library and 7 Faculty Libraries

Publications: Denta, Dentistry *(biannually)*; FIA, Applied Administration Journal *(biannually)*; Hukum, Law perspective *(biannually)*; Kedokretan, Medical Journal *(biannually)*; Neptunus, Marine Sciences and Technology *(biannually)*; Perikanan, Fishery Journal *(biannually)*; Poseidon, Psychology Journal *(biannually)*; Teknik, Science and Technology Journal *(biannually)*

Press or Publishing House: Hang Tuah University Press
Last Updated: 24/06/11

HARAPAN BANGSA INSTITUTE OF TECHNOLOGY

Institut Teknologi Harapan Bangsa Bandung (ITHB)

Jalan Dipati Ukur 80-84, Bandung, 40132 Jawa Barat
Tel: +62(22) 250-6636 +62(22) 250-6604
Fax: +62(22) 250-7901
EMail: itdept@ithb.ac.id
Website: http://www.ithb.ac.id

Rector: Samuel Tarigan (2002-) EMail: samuel_tarigan@ithb.ac.id

Ketua: B. Tarigant EMail: vunie@ithb.ac.id

International Relations: Hermanto Murniadi, Director, International Programme EMail: murniadi_hermanto@ithb.ac.id

Departments
Accountancy (Accountancy); **Computer Engineering** (Computer Engineering); **Electronic Engineering** (Electronic Engineering); **Industrial Engineering** (Industrial Engineering); **Informatics Engineering** (Computer Engineering); **Information System** (Information Technology); **Management** (Management); **Visual Communication Design** (Graphic Design; Visual Arts)

Programmes
Business (Business Administration; Management); **Games and Animation Technology** (Graphic Design; Visual Arts); **Information Technology** (Information Technology)

History: Founded 2002.

Governing Bodies: Yayasan Pendidikan Petra (Petra Education Foundation); Koordinator Perguruan Tinggi Swasta Wilayah IV (KOPERTIS IV) (State Coordinator of Private Higher Learning Institution Region IV)

Admission Requirements: High school certificate (SMU), Surat Tanda Tamat Belajar, STTB) or Technical high school certificate (SMK); Ujian Akhir Nasional (UAN) Examination; National Junior Secondary Education examination scores (Nilai Ebtanas Murni, NEM)

Fees: (Rupiahs): Art/Design programmes, Development Fee (paid only once on admission), 15m.; Fixed tuition Fee, 2.5m. per semester; SKS Fee, 180,000 per credit per semester; Technical programmes, Development Fee (paid only once on admission), 13m.; Fixed tuition Fee, c. 2m. per semester; SKS Fee, 160,000 per credit per semester; Business programmes, Development Fee (paid only once on admission), 10m.; Fixed tuition Fee, 1.5m. per semester; SKS Fee, 140,000 per credit per semester. New Student Orientation Programme Fee (paid only once on admission), 530,000; Student Activities Fee, 150,000 per semester

Main Language(s) of Instruction: Indonesian

Accrediting Agencies: Badan Akreditasi Nasional Perguruan Tinggi (National Accreditation Board of Higher Education).

Degrees and Diplomas: *Diploma*: Information Technology, 3 yrs; *Sarjana (S1)*: Design (S.Des.); Engineering (S.T.), 4 yrs. Also Advanced Diplomas (Int'l Programs)

Student Services: Academic counselling, Canteen, Cultural centre, Employment services, Foreign student adviser, Foreign Studies Centre, Handicapped facilities, Health services, Language programs, Nursery care, Social counselling, Sports facilities

Student Residential Facilities: None

Special Facilities: Photography Studio; Art Gallery; Manufacturing Facilities; SDH Multiplexer facilities

Libraries: Yes. Large collections of reference books, course guides and workbooks. Free access to some academic journals. Free Internet and Wi-fi coverage.

Publications: Jurnal Telematika, National Journal, published by the institute *(biannually)*

Academic Staff *2009-2010*	MEN	WOMEN	**TOTAL**
FULL-TIME	40	18	**58**
PART-TIME	93	38	**131**
Student Numbers *2009-2010*			
All (Foreign Included)	950	493	**1,443**

Last Updated: 27/10/10

HINDU INDONESIAN UNIVERSITY

Universitas Hindu Indonesia

Jalan Sangalanit Tembau Penatih, Denpasar, 80238 Bali
Tel: +62(361) 464-700
Fax: +62(361) 464-7818
EMail: unhis1@yahoo.com

Rector: I. Bagus Gde Yudha Triguna

Ketua: Wayan Wita

Faculties

Economics *Dean*: Wayan Surtha; **Engineering** *Dean*: Nyoman Sugita; **Mathematics and Natural Sciences** *Dean*: Gede Ardana; **Religion** *Dean*: Ida Bagus Yuddha Trguna

History: Founded 1993.

Fees: (Rupiahs): 325,000 per annum

Degrees and Diplomas: *Sarjana (S1)*; *Magister (S2)*: Religious and Cultural Studies
Last Updated: 12/01/09

IBA UNIVERSITY

Universitas Iba

Jalan Mayor Ruslan, Palembang, 30113 Sumatera Selatan
Tel: +62(711) 351-364 +62(711) 350793
Fax: +62(711) 351-364 +62(711) 350-793
EMail: info@iba.ac.id
Website: http://www.iba.ac.id

Rector: Yudi Fahrian

Ketua: Rosihan Nuch Bajumi

Faculties

Agriculture (Agricultural Business; Agriculture; Agronomy; Plant Pathology; Soil Science); **Economics** (Accountancy; Economics; Management); **Engineering** (Chemical Engineering; Civil Engineering; Engineering; Mechanical Engineering); **Law** (Administrative Law; Civil Law; Criminal Law; Law)

History: Founded 1986.

Degrees and Diplomas: *Diploma*: 3 yrs; *Sarjana (S1)*
Last Updated: 18/07/11

IBN CHALDUN UNIVERSITY

Universitas Ibnu Chaldun

Jalan Pemuda I Kav. 97, Rawamangun, Jakarta Timur, 13220 DKI Jakarta
Tel: +62(21) 472-2059 +62(21) 470-2563
Fax: +62(21) 470-2564
EMail: uickita@yahoo.com

Rector: A. Hamid Suchas

Ketua: Zulfatli Ali

Faculties

Agriculture (Agriculture; Agronomy) *Dean*: Haryadi; **Communication** (Communication Studies; Journalism; Public Relations) *Dean*: Imam Tayhid; **Economics** (Economics; Management) *Dean*: Hasan Masoed; **Law** *Dean*: Soedayo Saimin; **Social and Political Sciences** *Dean*: Mustafa Kadir

History: Founded 1956 as institute, became university 1960. A private institution under the supervision of the Department of Education and Culture.

Academic Year: September to June (September-January; February-June)

Admission Requirements: Secondary school certificate (Sekolah Lanjutan Atas, SLA)

Fees: (Rupiahs): 2.35m. per annum

Main Language(s) of Instruction: Indonesian, Arabic, English

Degrees and Diplomas: *Sarjana (S1)*: 4-7 yrs

Libraries: 8,139 vols

Publications: Media UIC

IBN KHALDUN UNIVERSITY - BOGOR

Universitas Ibn Khaldun Bogor (UIKA)

Jl. K. H. Sholeh Iskandar Km.2, Kedung Badak Bogor, Bogor, 16162 West Java
Tel: +62(251) 835-6884
Fax: +62(251) 835-6884
EMail: rektor@uika-bogor.ac.id
Website: http://www.uika-bogor.ac.id/

Rector: Ramly Hutabarat (2008-)

Chairman: Chaeruddin A. Nawawi
Tel: +62(251) 832-8203, Fax: +62(251) 832-8203
EMail: ypika@uika-bogor.ac.id

International Relations: Budi Susetyo, Head of Information Resources EMail: sdi@uika-bogor.ac.id

Departments

Islamic Science *(Doctoral studies)* (Islamic Studies; Management; Religious Education)

Faculties

Economics (Accountancy; Economics; Management); **Engineering** (Civil Engineering; Computer Engineering; Electrical Engineering; Engineering; Mechanical Engineering); **Islamic Science** (Economics; Islamic Law; Islamic Studies; Islamic Theology; Religious Education); **Law** (Law); **Teaching and Educational Science** (Art Education; Educational Sciences; English; Foreign Languages Education; Teacher Training)

Programmes

Postgraduate Studies *(Master's programme)* (Islamic Studies; Management; Religious Education)

History: Founded 1961. A private institution under the supervision of the Department of Education and Culture.

Academic Year: March to February (March-August; October-February)

Admission Requirements: Secondary school certificate (Surat Menengah Atas SMA)

Fees: (Rupiahs): 3m. per annum

Main Language(s) of Instruction: Indonesian

International Co-operation: National Accreditation Board of Higher Education

Degrees and Diplomas: *Sarjana (S1)*: 4 yrs; *Magister (S2)*: 2 yrs; *Doktor (S3)*: 3 yrs

Student Services: Academic counselling, Canteen, Employment services, Language programs, Social counselling, Sports facilities

Student Residential Facilities: Yes

Special Facilities: Music Studio

Libraries: c. 1,400 vols

Publications: Andragogi, Scientific research journal of the external educational science department *(biannually)*; English Journal, Scientific research journal of the English Faculty *(biannually)*; Inovator, Scientific research journal of the Management Department of the Economics Faculty *(biannually)*; Khazanah Journal, Publication on scientific research conducted by the university's faculty *(biannually)*; Necara Keuangan, Scientific research journal of the Accountancy Department of the Economics Faculty *(biannually)*; Tadjid, Scientific research journal of the Islamic Science Faculty *(biannually)*; Teknika, Scientific research journal of the Engineering Faculty *(biannually)*; Yustisi, Scientific research journal of the Law Faculty *(biannually)*

Press or Publishing House: UIKA Press

Last Updated: 27/06/11

ICHSAN GORONTALO UNIVERSITY

Universitas Ichsan Gorontalo

Jln. Budi Utomo No. 58, Gorontalo, 96115 Gorontalo
Tel: +62(435) 831-257
EMail: unisan_grtlo@telkom.net

Rektor: Gaffar Lacokke

Ketua: Yuriko Abdussamad

Faculties

Agriculture (Agriculture; Agronomy; Harvest Technology) *Dean*: Fardi M. Siregar; **Communication**; **Economics** *Dean*: Rahmisyahri; **Engineering** (Architecture; Computer Engineering; Electronic Engineering) *Dean*: Amirrudin; **Law** (Law) *Dean*: Haslina Said

Degrees and Diplomas: *Diploma*: Accountancy; *Sarjana (S1)*

Last Updated: 13/01/09

IMMANUEL CHRISTIAN UNIVERSITY

Universitas Kristen Immanuel (UKRIM)

PO Box 4/YKAP, Jalan Solo Km 11, Yogyakarta, 57452 DI Yogyakarta
Tel: +62(274) 496-256 +62(274) 496-257
Fax: +62(274) 496-258
EMail: ukrimyk@telkom.net.id
Website: http://www.ukrim.ac.id

Rector: George Iwan Marantika

Faculties

Christian Religious Studies (Christian Religious Studies; Music); **Economics** (Accountancy; Economics; Management); **Engineering** (Civil Engineering; Engineering); **Mathematics and Natural Sciences** (Computer Science; Mathematics; Natural Sciences; Physics)

History: Founded 1982.

Degrees and Diplomas: *Diploma*: 3 yrs; *Sarjana (S1)*

Last Updated: 25/07/11

INDO GLOBAL MANDIRI UNIVERSITY

Universitas Indo Global Mandiri

Kampus A, Jalan Jendral Sudirman 629 Km. 4, Palembang, 30112 Sumatera Selatan
Tel: +62(711) 322-705
Fax: +62(711) 357-754
Website: http://www.uigm.ac.id/

Rector: Zulkardi

Ketua: Marzuki Alie

Faculties

Computer Science; **Economics** (Accountancy; Economics; Management); **Engineering** (Architecture; Civil Engineering; Engineering; Information Management; Information Technology; Regional Planning; Road Engineering; Surveying and Mapping; Town Planning); **Government Science and Culture** (Cultural Studies; Government; Political Sciences)

Degrees and Diplomas: *Sarjana (S1)*

Last Updated: 29/04/10

INDONESIA TIMUR MAKASSAR UNIVERSITY

Universitas Indonesia Timur Makassar

Jl. Rappocini Raya No.171-173, Makassar, 90222 Sulawesi Selatan
Tel: +62(411) 421-974
Fax: +62(411) 852-111

Rektor: Abdul Muin Salim

Ketua: Haruna

Faculties

Agriculture (Agriculture; Forestry; Harvest Technology) *Dean*: Syamsu Alam; **Communication Studies**; **Community Health** (Community Health; Pharmacy) *Dean*: Ridwan; **Computer Science** (Computer Science); **Economics** (Accountancy; Economics; Management) *Dean*: Hatta Saleh; **Engineering** (Architecture; Civil Engineering; Engineering) *Dean*: Tahir Hamzah; **Law** (Law) *Dean*: Joni Akbar; **Nursing** (Midwifery; Nursing) *Dean*: Abd. Haris Mahmud; **Psychology** (Psychology; Sociology) *Dean*: Rasyid Arfah; **Social and Political Sciences** *Dean*: Natsir Mahmud

Degrees and Diplomas: *Diploma*; *Sarjana (S1)*; *Magister (S2)*

Last Updated: 13/01/09

INDONESIAN AL-AZHAR UNIVERSITY

Universitas Al-Azhar Indonesia

Komplek Masjid Agung Al Azhar, Jakarta Selatan, 12110 DKI Jakarta
Tel: +62(21) 7279-2753
Fax: +62(21) 724-4767
EMail: info@uai.ac.id
Website: http://www.uai.ac.id

Rector: Zuhal

Vice-Rector, Academic Administration, Promotion and Human Resources: Muhsin Lubis

International Relations: Ahmad H. Lubis, Vice-Rector, Student Affairs, Innovation and Cooperation

Faculties

Economics (Accountancy; Banking; Finance; Human Resources; Insurance; Leadership; Management; Marketing); **Law** (Commercial Law; Law); **Modern Languages** (Arabic; Chinese; English; Indonesian; Japanese; Spanish); **Psychology and Education** (Human Resources; Psychology); **Science and Technology** (Agrobiology; Biology; Biotechnology; Computer Science; Data Processing; Electrical Engineering; Electronic Engineering; Industrial Engineering; Industrial Management; Information Technology; Software Engineering); **Social and Political Sciences** (Advertising and Publicity; Communication Studies; Graphic Design; International Relations; Journalism; Marketing; Media Studies; Political Sciences; Public Relations; Radio and Television Broadcasting)

History: Founded 2000.

Degrees and Diplomas: *Sarjana (S1)*

Last Updated: 12/07/11

INDONESIAN BAKTI UNIVERSITY

Universitas Bakti Indonesia

Banyuwangi, Java

Programmes

Biology and Chemistry (Biology; Chemistry); **Business Administration** (Accountancy; Business Administration; Management); **Engineering** (Computer Engineering; Engineering; Industrial Engineering; Information Technology); **English**; **Law** (Law); **Mathematics** (Mathematics); **Public health**

Last Updated: 31/05/10

INDONESIAN CHRISTIAN MALUKU UNIVERSITY

Universitas Kristen Indonesia Maluku

PO Box 1151, Jalan OT. Pattimaipauw, Ambon 97115
Tel: +62(911) 345-821
Fax: +32(911) 346-206
EMail: ukim_maluku@yahoo.com

Rector: Augustinus Batlajery

Ketua: F.P.B. Litaay

Faculties

Economics (Banking; Civil Engineering; Development Studies; Economics; Finance; Management); **Engineering** (Civil Engineering; Engineering); **Philosophy** (Philosophy; Protestant Theology; Religion); **Social and Political Sciences** (Political Sciences; Social Sciences; Social Welfare)

History: Founded 1985.

Fees: (Rupiahs): 1,242,000 per annum

Degrees and Diplomas: *Diploma*: 3 yrs; *Sarjana (S1)*

Libraries: 19,045 vols

Last Updated: 09/03/10

INDONESIAN COMPUTER UNIVERSITY

Universitas Komputer Indonesia (UNIKOM)

Jalan Dipati Ukur 02-114-116, Bandung, Jawa Barat
Tel: +62(22) 250-4119 +62(22) 250-3054
Fax: +62(22) 250-3371 +62(22) 253-3754
Website: http://www.unikom.ac.id

Rector: Eddy Soeryanto Soegoto
Tel: +62(22) 250-3054, Fax: +62(22) 253-3754

Vice-Rector for Administration and Finance: Moh. Tadjuddin

International Relations: Aelina Surya, Vice-Rector For Student Affairs

Faculties

Design (Communication Arts; Design; Interior Design; Visual Arts) *Dean*: Hary Lubis; **Economics** (Accountancy; Banking; Finance; Management; Marketing) *Dean*: Umi Narimawati; **Engineering and Computer Science** (Civil Engineering; Computer Engineering; Computer Science; Electrical Engineering; Engineering; Industrial Engineering; Regional Planning; Structural Architecture; Town Planning) *Dean*: Ukun Sastraprawira; **Law** (Law) *Dean*: Otje Salman Soemadiningrat; **Literary Studies** (English; Japanese; Literature) *Dean*: Mohhamad Tadjuddin; **Political and Social Sciences** (Communication Studies; Government; International Relations; Political Sciences; Public Relations; Social Sciences) *Dean*: J.M. Papasi

Programmes

Postgraduate Studies (Information Technology)

History: Founded 2000.

Governing Bodies: Science and Technology Foundation

Admission Requirements: Senior High School Graduation (Lulusan SMTA Dari Dalam Dan Luar Negeri) or foreign equivalent; entrance examination

Fees: (Rupiahs): 2m. per annum except first year, 5m.

Main Language(s) of Instruction: Indonesian

International Co-operation: With universities in Malaysia

Accrediting Agencies: National Accreditation Agency (Badan Akreditasi Nasional Perguruan Tinggi - BAN-PT)

Degrees and Diplomas: *Diploma*: 3 yrs; *Sarjana (S1)*: 4 yrs; *Magister (S2)*: Information Systems

Student Services: Academic counselling, Canteen, Language programs, Social counselling, Sports facilities

Libraries: c. 3,500 vols

Academic Staff *2008-2009*	MEN	WOMEN	**TOTAL**
FULL-TIME	–	–	**150**
PART-TIME	–	–	**120**
STAFF WITH DOCTORATE			
FULL-TIME	–	–	**80**
PART-TIME	–	–	c. **100**
Student Numbers *2008-2009*			
All (Foreign Included)	6,500	2,500	c. **9,000**
FOREIGN ONLY			**30**

Last Updated: 25/07/11

INDONESIAN DEVELOPMENT UNIVERSITY

Universitas Pembangunan Indonesia (UNPI MANADO)

Jalan Wolter Mongisidi VI No. 129, Bahu Lingkungan II, Manado, 95115 Sulawesi Utara
Tel: +62(431) 827-686
Fax: +62(431) 865-319

Direktor: Debby Rende

Ketua: F.H Rende

Faculties

Agriculture; **Engineering** (Architecture and Planning; Electronic Engineering); **Law**; **Literature**; **Social and Political Sciences** (Political Sciences)

History: Founded as Sekolah Tinggi Social Welfare Studies Manado (STIKS), acquired present title 2000.

Degrees and Diplomas: *Diploma*; *Sarjana (S1)*

Last Updated: 04/02/09

INDONESIAN INSTITUTE OF BUSINESS AND COMPUTER SCIENCE

Institut Bisnis dan Informatika Indonesia (IBII)

Jalan Yos Sudarso Kav 87, Sunter, Jakarta, 14325 DKI Jakarta
Tel: +62(21) 6530-7062
Fax: +62(21) 6530-6967
EMail: rektorat@ibii.ac.id
Website: http://www.ibii.ac.id/

Rector: Titus W. Tjandra EMail: titusj@ibii.ac.id

Head of Academic Administration: Bun Fa Liaw
EMail: liawbunfa@ibii.ac.id

International Relations: Hisar Sirait, Vice-Rector, Academic Affairs EMail: hisar@ibii.ac.id

Departments

Accountancy (Accountancy); **Business and Commerce** (Business and Commerce); **Information Management** (Information Management); **Information Technology** (Information Technology); **Management** (Management); **Mass Communication** (Mass Communication)

History: Created in 1987. Acquired current status 2005.

Governing Bodies: Rector; Vice-Rector for Academic Affairs; Vice-Rector for Human Resources; Vice-Rector for Student Affairs; Senate

Academic Year: September to June (September-February; March-June)

Main Language(s) of Instruction: Indonesian

Degrees and Diplomas: *Sarjana (S1)*: Management; Accountancy; Information Systems; Computer Science; Communication; Business Administration; *Magister (S2)*: Accountancy; Economics; Management; *Doktor (S3)*: Economics

Student Services: Academic counselling, Canteen, Employment services, Language programs, Social counselling, Sports facilities

Student Residential Facilities: none

Special Facilities: Broadcasting studio; wifi; internet centre; computer labs; language labs; on-line stock trading simulation

Libraries: yes

Publications: Jurnal Akuntansi Perusahaan, Research articles on accounting for management, audit, taxation *(3 per annum)*; Jurnal Ekonomi Perusahaan, Research articles on management in marketing, finance, entrepreneurship, human research *(3 per annum)*

Academic Staff *2008-2009*	MEN	WOMEN	TOTAL
FULL-TIME	54	26	**80**
PART-TIME	57	18	**75**
STAFF WITH DOCTORATE			
FULL-TIME	12	2	**14**
PART-TIME	1	–	**1**
Student Numbers *2008-2009*			
All (Foreign Included)	1,391	1,937	**3,328**

Evening students, 214.
Last Updated: 08/07/11

INDONESIAN INSTITUTE OF COMPUTER SCIENCE

Institut Informatika Indonesia Surabaya
Jalan Raya Sukomanunggal Jaya 3, Surabaya, Jawa Timur
Tel: +62(31) 734-6375
Fax: +62(31) 734-9324
EMail: info@iii.ac.id
Website: http://www.iii.ac.id/

Rector: Anastasia Savitri

Ketua: Indra Setiawan

Programmes

Computer Science (Computer Graphics; Computer Science; Information Management; Information Technology; Visual Arts)
History: Founded 2003.
Degrees and Diplomas: *Diploma*; *Sarjana (S1)*
Last Updated: 22/04/10

INDONESIAN INSTITUTE OF MANAGEMENT COOPERATION

Institut Manajemen Koperasi Indonesia (IKOPIN)
Kawasan Pendidikan Tinggi Jatinangor, Km. 20.5 Cikeruh, Jatinangor, 40600 Jawa Barat
Tel: +62(22) 779-8179 +62(22) 779-6033
Fax: +62(22) 779-6033
EMail: sekrek@ikopin.ac.id; lppm@ikopin.ac.id
Website: http://www.ikopin.ac.id

Rector: Rully Indrawan

Vice-Rector I: Dindin Burhanudin

International Relations: Indra Fahmi, Vice-Rector, Cooperation and Business

Faculties

Human Resources Management (Human Resources; Information Management; Management)

Programmes

Banking Management (Banking); **Business Communication Management and Guidance** (Management); **Business Management** (Business Administration; Management); **Finance Management** (Finance); **Marketing Management** (Marketing); **Postgraduate Studies** (Management); **Production Management** (Business Administration; Management; Marketing)

History: Founded 1981.

Degrees and Diplomas: *Diploma*; *Sarjana (S1)*; *Magister (S2)*: Management
Last Updated: 11/07/11

INDONESIAN INSTITUTE OF SCIENCE AND TECHNOLOGY DEVELOPMENT

Institut Sains dan Teknologi Pembangunan Indonesia
Jalan Jenderal Sudirman 42, Makassar, Sulawesi Selatan
Tel: +62(411) 312-556

Programmes

Engineering (Civil Engineering; Electronic Engineering; Engineering)

History: Founded 1987.

Degrees and Diplomas: *Sarjana (S1)*
Last Updated: 22/06/11

INDONESIAN INSTITUTE OF SCIENCE AND TECHNOLOGY MANOKWARI

Institut Sains dan Teknologi Indonesia Manokwari
Manokwari 12345

Programmes

Civil Engineering; **Computer Engineering** (Computer Engineering); **Electrical Engineering** (Electrical Engineering); **Industrial Engineering** (Industrial Engineering); **Product Design** (Production Engineering); **Regional and Town Planning** (Regional Planning; Town Planning)
Degrees and Diplomas: *Sarjana (S1)*
Last Updated: 27/04/10

INDONESIAN INSTITUTE OF TECHNOLOGY

Institut Teknologi Indonesia (I.T.I)
Jalan Raya Puspitek, Serpong, Tangerang, 15320 DKI Jakarta
Tel: +62(21) 756-0545 +62(21) 756-0345
Fax: +62(21) 756-0542
EMail: pmb@iti.ac.id
Website: http://iti.ac.id

Rektor: Isnuwardianto

Vice-Rector for Academic Affairs: Marga Alisjahbana

Programmes

Engineering (Agricultural Engineering; Automotive Engineering; Chemical Engineering; Civil Engineering; Computer Engineering; Electrical Engineering; Electronic Engineering; Engineering; Industrial Engineering; Structural Architecture); **Regional and City Planning** (Regional Planning; Town Planning)
History: Founded 1984.

Admission Requirements: Senior high school certificate

Main Language(s) of Instruction: Indonesian

Accrediting Agencies: Ministry of National Education and National Accreditation Board

Degrees and Diplomas: *Diploma*: 3 yrs; *Sarjana (S1)*: 4 yrs

Student Services: Academic counselling, Canteen, Cultural centre, Employment services, Health services, Language programs, Sports facilities

Student Residential Facilities: Yes

Libraries: Central Library, c. 11,000 titles

Publications: Technology Journal, Research and Advanced Technology *(quarterly)*

Academic Staff *2009-2010*: Total: c. 120

Student Numbers *2009-2010*: Total: c. 1,800
Last Updated: 22/06/11

INDONESIAN MANAGEMENT DEVELOPMENT INSTITUTE

Institut Pengembangan Manajemen Indonesia (IPMI)
Jl. Rawajati Timur I No. 1, Kalibata, Jakarta, 12750 DKI Jakarta
Tel: +62(21) 797-0419
Fax: +62(21) 797-0509
Website: http://www.ipmi.ac.id/

Executive Director: Budi W. Soetjipto

Programmes

Accountancy *(Non-Degree)*; **Business Management** (Management); **Economic Management** (Economics; Management); **Executive Development** *(Non-Degree)* (Business Administration; English; Management); **Finance and Investment Management** *(Graduate)* (Banking; Finance; Management); **Management** *(Graduate)* (Accountancy)

Degrees and Diplomas: *Sarjana (S1) (SE; BBA)*; *Magister (S2) (MM/MBA)*
Last Updated: 20/06/11

INDONESIAN PRAMITA UNIVERSITY

Universitas Pramita Indonesia
Jalan Kampus Pramita Binong, Tangerang, 15810 Banten
Tel: +62(21) 598-4470
Fax: +62(21) 598-4467

Rector: Hadi Subadio

Ketua: Lailan Saufina

Programmes

Architecture (Architecture; Structural Architecture); **Business Administration** (Accountancy; Banking; Finance; Management); **Communication Studies** (Communication Studies); **Engineering** (Civil Engineering; Computer Engineering; Electrical Engineering; Electronic Engineering; Engineering; Industrial Engineering); **Government** (Government; Political Sciences)

Degrees and Diplomas: *Sarjana (S1)*; *Magister (S2)*
Last Updated: 03/05/10

INDONESIAN UNIVERSITY FOR COMMUNITY DEVELOPMENT

Universitas Pembinaan Masyarakat Indonesia
Jalan Teladan 11-15, Medan, 20217 Sumatera Utara
Tel: +62(61) 736-2927 +62(61) 736-5650
Fax: +62(61) 736-2927
Website: http://www.upmi.ac.id

Rector: Syahruddin Siregar

Ketua: Nuraini Harahap

Faculties

Agriculture (Agricultural Engineering; Agricultural Management; Agronomy) *Dean*: Azwar Hamid; **Economics** (Business Administration; Economics; Management) *Dean*: Ali Rismayani; **Engineering**; **Law** (Law) *Dean*: Ali Mukti; **Social and Political Sciences** (Administration; Government; Political Sciences; Social Psychology) *Dean*: Arif Nasution

History: Founded 1979.

Fees: (Rupiahs): 750,000 per annum

Degrees and Diplomas: *Diploma*: 3 yrs; *Sarjana (S1)*

Libraries: 3,531 vols
Last Updated: 04/02/09

INDONESIAN UNIVERSITY OF INFORMATION TECHNOLOGY AND BUSINESS

Universitas Informatika dan Bisnis Indonesia
Jalan Purnawarman 34-36B, Bandung, 40117 Jawa Barat
Tel: +62(22) 426-5399
Fax: +62(22) 420-9308
EMail: e_unibi@unibi.ac.id
Website: http://www.unibi.ac.id

Rector: Bob Foster

Vice-Rector: Mohammad Deni Johansyah

Faculties

Design (Communication Arts; Design; Interior Design; Visual Arts); **Economics and Business** (Accountancy; Business Administration; Economics; Management); **Law** (Law); **Social and Political Sciences** (Communication Studies; Government; International Relations; Political Sciences; Public Relations; Secretarial Studies; Social Sciences); **Technology and Computer Science** (Business Computing; Communication Arts; Computer Engineering; Electrical Engineering; Information Management; Information Technology; Visual Arts)

Degrees and Diplomas: *Sarjana (S1)*
Last Updated: 29/04/10

INDONESIAN UNIVERSITY OF TECHNOLOGY

Universitas Teknologi Indonesia
Jalan Teuku Umar 219 A, Denpasar, 80114 Bali
Tel: +62(361) 240-077
Fax: +62(361) 240-077

Rector: Puji Suhartono

Ketua: Ida Bagus Mertha

Programmes

Agriculture (Agriculture; Animal Husbandry); **Business Administration**; **Communication Studies** (Communication Studies); **Economics**; **Engineering** (Agricultural Engineering; Civil Engineering; Computer Engineering; Engineering; Industrial Design); **English** (English); **Law**

Degrees and Diplomas: *Sarjana (S1)*
Last Updated: 28/05/10

INDRAPRASTA PGRI UNIVERSITY

Universitas PGRI Indraprasta
Jalan Nangka 58C, Tanjung Barat, Jagakarsa, 12530 Jakarta Selatan
Tel: +62(21) 781-8718
Fax: +62(21) 7883-5283
EMail: university@unindra.ac.id
Website: http://www.unindra.ac.id/

Rector: Sumaryoto

Ketua: Rusli Yunus

Faculties

Engineering, Mathematics and Natural Sciences (Architecture; Biology; Engineering; Industrial Engineering; Information Technology; Mathematics; Natural Sciences; Physics); **Language and Arts** (Communication Arts; English; Indonesian; Literature; Modern Languages; Native Language; Native Language Education; Visual Arts); **Science Education and Social Sciences**

Degrees and Diplomas: *Sarjana (S1)*; *Magister (S2)*
Last Updated: 29/04/10

INSTITUTE OF ASIAN FINANCE, BANKING, BUSINESS AND COMPUTER SCIENCE

Institut Keu Perbankan Dan Inf Asia Perbanas
Jalan Perbanas, Karet Kuningan, Setiabudi, Jakarta, 12940 Jakarta Selatan
Tel: +62(21) 522-2501
Fax: +62(21) 522-8460
EMail: sdm@stieperbanas.ac.id
Website: http://www.perbanasinstitute.ac.id/

Rector: Fatchudin

Vice-Rector: Sudarsono

Programmes

Accountancy; **Banking**; **Computer Engineering** (Computer Engineering); **Computerized Accounting** (Accountancy; Computer Science); **Finance**; **Information Technology** (Information Technology); **Management**

History: Founded 1969.

Degrees and Diplomas: *Sarjana (S1)*; *Magister (S2)*
Last Updated: 22/04/10

INSTITUTE OF SCIENCE AND TECHNOLOGY AL-KAMAL JAKARTA

Institut Sains dan Teknologi Al-Kamal (ISTA)
Jalan Raya Al-Kamal 2 Kedoya, Kebon Jeruk, Jakarta Barat, 11520 DKI Jakarta
Tel: +62(21) 581-1088
Fax: +62(21) 5830-0105
EMail: pmb@ista.ac.id
Website: http://www.ista.ac.id

Rector: Haryanto Dhanutirto

Vice-Rector, Academic Affairs: Bayong Tjasyono

International Relations: Achmad Satari

Faculties

Engineering (Chemical Engineering; Civil Engineering; Environmental Engineering; Industrial Engineering; Information Technology; Marine Engineering; Mechanical Engineering)

History: Founded 1987, acquired present status 1989.

Degrees and Diplomas: *Sarjana (S1)*
Last Updated: 05/03/10

INSTITUTE OF SCIENCE AND TECHNOLOGY PARDEDE MEDAN

Institut Sains dan Teknologi TD Pardede
Jalan Dr. TD. Pardede 8, Medan, 20153 Sumatera Utara
Tel: +62(61) 456-9877 +62(61) 453-5631
Fax: +62(61) 456-9877
EMail: info@istp.ac.id; mail@istp.ac.id
Website: http://www.istp.ac.id

Rector: Rudolf Sitorus

Ketua: Sariaty Br. Siregar Br. Pardede

Faculties
Civil Engineering and Planning (Architecture and Planning; Civil Engineering; Interior Design; Structural Architecture); **Industrial Engineering** (Electrical Engineering; Industrial Engineering; Information Management; Information Technology); **Mineral Technology** (Geological Engineering; Mineralogy; Mining Engineering)

History: Founded 1987.

Degrees and Diplomas: *Diploma*; *Sarjana (S1)*

Libraries: 2,801 titles

Last Updated: 11/07/11

INSTITUTE OF SOCIAL AND POLITICAL SCIENCES JAKARTA

Institut Ilmu Sosial dan Ilmu Politik Jakarta (IISIP)
Jalan Raya Lenteng Agung 32, Jakarta Selatan, 12610 DKI Jakarta
Tel: +62(21) 780-6223
Fax: +62(21) 781-7630
EMail: admin@iisip.ac.id
Website: http://www.iisip.ac.id

Rector: Ir. Maslina W. Hutasuhut EMail: rektor@iisip.ac.id

Faculties
Administration (Administration; Business Administration); **Communication Science** (Advertising and Publicity; Communication Studies; Journalism; Public Relations); **Social and Political Sciences** (International Relations; Political Sciences; Social Sciences; Social Welfare)

History: Founded 1983.

Academic Year: September to February

Fees: (Rupiahs): 2,340,000-10,000,000. per annum depending on faculties

Degrees and Diplomas: *Sarjana (S1)*; *Magister (S2)*

Student Services: Sports facilities

Libraries: 13,966 vols

Academic Staff *2010-2011*	MEN	WOMEN	TOTAL
FULL-TIME	27	25	**52**
PART-TIME	40	6	**46**
STAFF WITH DOCTORATE			
FULL-TIME	1	1	**2**
PART-TIME	3	3	**6**
Student Numbers *2010-2011*			
All (Foreign Included)	949	785	**1,734**

Last Updated: 28/10/10

INSTITUTE OF TEACHER TRAINING AND EDUCATIONAL SCIENCE BOJONEGORO

Institut Keguruan dan Ilmu Pendidikan (IKIP) PGRI Bojonegoro
Jalan Panglima Polim 46, Bojonegoro, 62114 Jawa Timur
Tel: +62(353) 881-046
EMail: ikipbjn@yahoo.co.id
Website: http://www.ikipbojonegoro.ac.id/

Rector: Budi Irawanto

Ketua: Ali Noeruddin

Faculties
Language and Literature Education (English; Foreign Languages Education; Indonesian; Literature; Native Language Education); **Mathematics and Natural Sciences** (Mathematics Education; Science Education); **Social Sciences Education** (Civics; Economics)

History: Founded 1986.

Degrees and Diplomas: *Sarjana (S1)*

Last Updated: 11/07/11

INSTITUTE OF TEACHER TRAINING AND EDUCATIONAL SCIENCE BUDI UTOMO MALANG

Institut Keguruan dan Ilmu Pendidikan (IKIP) Budi Utomo Malang
Jalan Simpang Arjuna 14-B, Malang, 65112 Jawa Timur
Tel: +62(341) 323-214
Fax: +62(341) 335-070
EMail: info@ikipbudiutomo.ac.id

Rector: Nurcholis Sunuyeko

Ketua: Fatah Ibrahim

Faculties
Languages and Art Education (Art Education; English; Foreign Languages Education; Indonesian; Literature); **Mathematics and Natural Sciences Education** (Biology; Mathematics Education); **Social Sciences Education** (Civics; History; Humanities and Social Science Education; Leisure Studies; Social Work; Sociology); **Sports and Health Education** (Health Education; Sports)

History: Founded 1984.

Degrees and Diplomas: *Sarjana (S1)*; *Magister (S2)*: Sport Education

Libraries: 8,770 vols

Last Updated: 11/07/11

INSTITUTE OF TEACHER TRAINING AND EDUCATIONAL SCIENCE GUNUNG SITOLI

Institut Keguruan dan Ilmu Pendidikan (IKIP) Gunung Sitoli
Jalan Yos Sudarso 118/ES, Gunung Sitoli, 22815 Sumatera Utara
Tel: +62(639) 21-616

Rector: Desman Telaumbanua

Faculties
Educational Science (Educational and Student Counselling; Educational Psychology; Educational Sciences) *Dean*: Yarnus Zebua; **Language and Art Education** (Art Education; English; Foreign Languages Education; Indonesian; Literature) *Dean*: Yustinus Mendiofa; **Mathematics and Natural Sciences Education** (Biology; Mathematics Education; Science Education) *Dean*: Bajongga Silaban; **Social Sciences Education** (Business Education; Civics; Humanities and Social Science Education) *Dean*: Bezisokki Laoli; **Technical and Vocational Education** (Building Technologies) *Dean*: Elysati Nazara

History: Founded 1965.

Fees: (Rupiahs): 500,000 per annum

Degrees and Diplomas: *Diploma*: 3 yrs; *Sarjana (S1)*

Libraries: 3,523 vols

Last Updated: 05/01/09

INSTITUTE OF TEACHER TRAINING AND EDUCATIONAL SCIENCE JEMBER

Institut Keguruan dan Ilmu Pendidikan (IKIP) PGRI Jember
Jalan Jawa 10, Jember, Jawa Timur
Tel: +62(331) 385-823
Fax: +62(331) 335-977
Website: http://www.ikip-jember.org

Rector: Moch. Arifin (2011-2015)

Ketua: Fatah Muntafa

Faculties
Educational Sciences (Educational and Student Counselling; Educational Psychology); **Mathematics and Natural Sciences Education** (Biology; Mathematics Education; Natural Sciences;

Science Education); **Social Sciences Education** (Business Education; Civics; History; Humanities and Social Science Education)

History: Founded 1979.

Fees: (Rupiahs): c. 360,000 per annum

Degrees and Diplomas: *Sarjana (S1)*

Libraries: 2,903 vols

Last Updated: 07/06/11

INSTITUTE OF TEACHER TRAINING AND EDUCATIONAL SCIENCE MADIUN

Institut Keguruan dan Ilmu Pendidikan (IKIP) PGRI Madiun (IKIP PGRI MADIUM)

Jalan Setiabudi 85, Madiun, 63118 Jawa Timur
Tel: +62(351) 462-986
Fax: +62(351) 462-986
EMail: rektorat@ikippgri-madiun.ac.id
Website: http://www.ikippgri-madiun.ac.id

Rector: H. Parji (2006-)

Ketua: H. Imam Sujudi

International Relations: Dwi Setiyadi
Tel: +62(351) 499-315 EMail: dwisetiadi@yahoo.co.id

Faculties

Education (Education; Educational and Student Counselling; Educational Sciences; Primary Education); **Electronic Engineering** (Electronic Engineering); **Languages and Arts** (English; Indonesian; Literature; Modern Languages; Native Language); **Mathematics and Science** (Biology; Mathematics; Natural Sciences; Physics); **Social Sciences** (Accountancy; Civics; Economics; History; International Economics; Political Sciences; Social Sciences)

History: Founded 1984.

Admission Requirements: Secondary school certificate and entrance examination

Fees: (Rupiahs): Registration, c. 35,000; tuition, c. 500,000 per semester

Main Language(s) of Instruction: Indonesian

Accrediting Agencies: Badan Akreditasi Nasional

Degrees and Diplomas: *Sarjana (S1) (SPd)*: 4 yrs

Student Services: Academic counselling, Canteen, Cultural centre, Health services, Language programs, Social counselling, Sports facilities

Special Facilities: Language, Biology, Physics and Engineering Laboratories

Libraries:c. 22,000 vols

Publications: Jurnal Pendidikan *(biennially)*

Academic Staff *2009-2010*: Total: c. 220

Student Numbers *2009-2010*: Total: c. 7,550

Last Updated: 20/06/11

INSTITUTE OF TEACHER TRAINING AND EDUCATIONAL SCIENCE MATARAM

Institut Keguruan dan Ilmu Pendidikan (IKIP) Mataram (IKIP)

Jalan Pemuda 59 A, Mataram, 83126 Nusa Tenggara Barat
Tel: +62(370) 632-082
Fax: +62(370) 632-082
EMail: puscom.ikipmataram@gmail.com
Website: http://ikipmataram.ac.id

Rector: Lalu Said Ruchpina (2008-)

Ketua: Lalu Ratmadji

Faculties

Educational Sciences (Education; Educational Administration; Educational and Student Counselling); **Languages Education** (English; Foreign Languages Education); **Mathematics and Natural Sciences Education** (Biology; Chemistry; Mathematics Education; Physics; Science Education; Technology Education); **Sports and Health Education** (Health Education; Sports)

History: Founded 1968 as Sangkareang Foundation.

Academic Year: September to June (September-January; February-June)

Admission Requirements: Secondary school certificate

Main Language(s) of Instruction: Indonesian

Accrediting Agencies: Ministry of National Education

Degrees and Diplomas: *Diploma*: 3 yrs; *Sarjana (S1)*: 4-5 yrs

Student Services: Academic counselling, Health services, Language programs, Nursery care, Social counselling, Sports facilities

Student Residential Facilities: None

Libraries: 4,724 vols

Publications: Jurnal Kependidikan, Journal on Educational Sciences *(biennially)*

Last Updated: 11/07/11

INSTITUTE OF TEACHER TRAINING AND EDUCATIONAL SCIENCE PGRI BALI

Institut Keguruan dan Ilmu Pendidikan (IKIP) PGRI Bali

Jalan Seroja, Tonja, Denpasar Timur, Bali
Tel: +62(361) 431-434
Fax: +62(361) 431-434

Rector: Redha Gunawan

Faculties

Language and Art Education (Art Education; Modern Languages); **Leadership and Counselling** (Educational Administration; Educational and Student Counselling); **Mathematics and Natural Sciences Education** (Mathematics Education; Natural Sciences; Science Education); **Social Sciences Education** (Humanities and Social Science Education); **Sports and Recreation Education** (Parks and Recreation; Physical Education; Sports)

History: Founded 1983.

Degrees and Diplomas: *Sarjana (S1)*

Libraries: 3,100 vols

Last Updated: 07/06/11

INSTITUTE OF TEACHER TRAINING AND EDUCATIONAL SCIENCE PGRI SEMARANG

Institut Keguruan dan Ilmu Pendidikan (IKIP) PGRI Semarang

Jalan Lontar 1, Semarang, 50125 Jawa Tengah
Tel: +62(24) 831-6377
Fax: +62(24) 844-8217
EMail: ikippgri@ikippgrismg.ac.id
Website: http://www.ikippgrismg.ac.id

Rector: S.H. Muhdi

Vice-Rector II: Tri Suyati

Faculties

Education (Education; Educational Administration; Educational and Student Counselling; Preschool Education; Primary Education); **Languages and Art Education** (English; Foreign Languages Education; Indonesian; Native Language Education; South and Southeast Asian Languages); **Mathematics and Natural Sciences** (Biology; Mathematics Education; Physics; Science Education); **Social Sciences** (Civics; Political Sciences; Social Sciences)

History: Founded 1984.

Degrees and Diplomas: *Sarjana (S1)*; *Magister (S2)*: Educational Management

Last Updated: 11/07/11

INSTITUTE OF TEACHER TRAINING AND EDUCATIONAL SCIENCE SARASWATI

Institut Keguruan dan Ilmu Pendidikan (IKIP) Saraswati

Jalan Pahlawan 2, Tabanan, 82113 Bali
Tel: +62(361) 811-267
Fax: +62(361) 811-267

Programmes

Biology (Biology); **History** (History); **Indonesian Language and Literature** (Indonesian; Literature); **Mathematics** (Mathematics); **Pancasila and Civic Education** (Civics; Government; Social Sciences)

History: Founded 1989.

Degrees and Diplomas: *Diploma*: 3 yrs; *Sarjana (S1)*

Libraries: 2,672 vols

Academic Staff *2009-2010*: Total: c. 50

Student Numbers *2009-2010*: Total: c. 1,200

Last Updated: 20/06/11

INSTITUTE OF TEACHER TRAINING AND EDUCATIONAL SCIENCE WATES

Institut Keguruan dan Ilmu Pendidikan (IKIP) Wates

Jalan Krt. Kertodinigrat 5, Margosari, Pengasih, Wates Kulonprogo, Yogyakarta, 55652 Java

Tel: +62(274) 773-283

Fax: +62(274) 773-283

EMail: ikippgriwates@yahoo.co.id

Programmes

Education (Educational and Student Counselling; Educational Sciences); **History** (History)

History: Founded 1968. Acquired present status 2003.

Degrees and Diplomas: *Sarjana (S1)*

Libraries: 1,265 vols

Academic Staff *2009-2010*: Total: c. 50

Student Numbers *2009-2010*: Total: c. 2,300

Last Updated: 20/06/11

INSTITUTE OF TEACHER TRAINING AND EDUCATIONAL SCIENCE WIDYA DARMA SURABAYA

Institut Keguruan dan Ilmu Pendidikan (IKIP) Widya Darma

Jalan Ketintang 147, Surabaya, 60243 Jawa Timur

Tel: +62(31) 828-4121

Faculties

Economics (Economics); **English** (English; Foreign Languages Education); **Indonesian Language and Literature** (Indonesian; Literature); **Mathematics Education** (Mathematics; Mathematics Education); **Pancasila and Civic Education** (Civics; Government; Political Sciences; Social Sciences)

History: Founded 1981.

Degrees and Diplomas: *Sarjana (S1)*

Libraries: 4,557 vols

Academic Staff *2009-2010*: Total: c. 50

Student Numbers *2009-2010*: Total: c. 1,200

Last Updated: 20/06/11

INTAN INSTITUTE OF AGRICULTURE

Institut Pertanian Intan

PO Box 1059, Jalan Magelang Km. 56, Yogyakarta, 55284 DI Yogyakarta

Tel: +62(274) 588-615 +62(274) 589-520

Fax: +62(274) 589-520

EMail: intaninstitut@yahoo.co.id

Website: http://institutyogyakarta.multiply.com

Rector: Setyo Indroprahasto

Faculties

Agricultural Engineering (Agricultural Engineering; Agricultural Equipment; Food Science); **Agronomy** (Agriculture; Agronomy); **Forestry** (Forestry)

History: Founded 1986, acquired present status and title 1998.

Admission Requirements: Secondary school certificate

Main Language(s) of Instruction: Indonesian

Accrediting Agencies: National Accreditation Agency

Degrees and Diplomas: *Sarjana (S1)*: 4 yrs

Student Services: Academic counselling, Canteen, Health services, Language programs

Special Facilities: Field Experimentation, Laboratory

Libraries: Central Library

Publications: Agroindustry Bulletin *(biennially)*; Gema Mahasiswa *(biennially)*

Last Updated: 20/06/11

INTERNATIONAL ARS UNIVERSITY

Universitas ARS Internasional

Jalan Sekolah Internasional 1, Antapani, Bandung, 40282 Jawa Barat

Tel: +62(22) 720-4283

Fax: +62(22) 720-4286

EMail: arsintl@indosat.net.id

Rector: Ahman Sya

Ketua: Joddy Hernandy

Programmes

Communication Studies (Communication Studies); **Design** (Communication Arts; Design; Interior Design; Visual Arts); **Engineering** (Computer Engineering; Engineering; Industrial Engineering; Information Technology); **Management** (Accountancy; Banking; Finance; Management; Management Systems; Secretarial Studies); **Nursing** (Nursing); **Public Relations** (Public Relations)

History: Founded 2000.

Degrees and Diplomas: *Diploma*; *Sarjana (S1)*; *Magister (S2)*: Management

Last Updated: 23/06/11

INTERNATIONAL UNIVERSITY BATAM

Universitas Internasional Batam

Jl. Gajah Mada, Simpang UIB, Baloi Sei Ladi, Batam, 29442 Kepulauan Riau

Tel: +62(778) 600-2999 +62(778) 743-7111

Fax: +62(778) 600-4219 +62(778) 743-7112

EMail: info@uib.edu; webmaster@uib.edu

Website: http://www.uib.edu

Rector: Handoko Karjantoro
EMail: karjanto@uib.edu; handoko.karjantoro@gmail.com

Vice Rector: Teddy Jurnali EMail: teddy@uib.edu

International Relations: Rina Shahriyani Shahrullah, Head, Academic Development Centre and Quality Assurance Centre
EMail: r.shahrullah@uib.edu

Faculties

Civil Engineering (Civil Engineering; Construction Engineering) *Head*: Atik Wahyuni; **Computer Science** (Computer Engineering; Computer Science) *Head*: Ronny Juwono; **Economics** (Accountancy; Economics; Hotel Management; Management) *Head*: Setyarini Santosa; **Industrial Engineering** (Electrical Engineering; Industrial Engineering; Information Technology) *Head*: Teddy Jurnali; **Law** (Law) *Head*: Lu Surdiman

History: Founded 2000.

Admission Requirements: Higher School Certificate; application form to Indonesian Directorate of Higher Education or Department of Education to obtain permit to study in UIB.

Fees: (Rupiahs): Non recurring fees: Registration fee, 150,000; BPP, 5m.-7m.; supporting facilities fee, 1.5m. Recurring fees: Course, 1.2m.-1.5m.; laboratory, 200,000-250,000; credit fee, 100,000-140,000/sks; Students' Fund 50,000.

Main Language(s) of Instruction: Indonesian; English

International Co-operation: With universities in United Kingdom and Singapore

Accrediting Agencies: Bada Akreditasi Nasional (National Accreditation Bureau)

Degrees and Diplomas: *Diploma (A.Md.)*: 3 yrs; *Sarjana (S1)*: Civil Engineering; Electrical Engineering; Management; Accounting; Information Systems (ST; SE; S.Kom), 3 1/2-5 yrs

Student Services: Academic counselling, Canteen, Employment services, Foreign student adviser, Health services, Language programs, Social counselling, Sports facilities

Special Facilities: Moot Court; Civil Engineering Laboratory; Information System Laboratory; Hotel Laboratory

Libraries: Collection Room; Reading Room; On-line Catalogues; Multimedia Library; Electronic Journal

Publications: CENTRE, Journal of Engineering (Civil and Electrical Engineering) *(biennially)*; Computer and Information Sciences Journal, Journal of Computer Science Faculty *(biennially)*; Journal of Accounting and Management Research, Journal of Economics Faculty *(biennially)*; Journal of Juridical Review, Journal of Law Faculty *(biennially)*

Academic Staff *2009-2010*: Total: c. 150

Student Numbers *2009-2010*: Total 1,750

Last Updated: 27/06/11

IQRA BURU UNIVERSITY

Universitas Iqra Buru

Jalan Flamboyan 21, Namlea, 97571 Maluku
Tel: +62(913) 21909
Fax: +62(913) 21909

Rector: Suyatno S. Kusuma

Ketua: Abdurrachman Tukuboya

Programmes

Agriculture (Agricultural Business; Aquaculture; Fishery; Forestry); **Economics**; **Engineering** (Civil Engineering; Engineering; Industrial Engineering); **English** (English; Literature; Modern Languages); **Indonesian** (Indonesian; Literature; Modern Languages; Native Language); **Law** (Law); **Management** (Management)

Degrees and Diplomas: *Sarjana (S1)*

Last Updated: 29/04/10

ISKANDAR MUDA UNIVERSITY

Universitas Iskandar Muda

Jalan Kampus UNIDA Surien 15, Banda Aceh, 23234 Nangroeh Aceh Darussalam
Tel: +62(651) 42-098

Rector: Agussalim

Ketua: Ahmad Amin

Faculties

Agriculture (Agriculture; Agronomy; Plant Pathology) *Dean*: Basyir Achmad; **Engineering** (Civil Engineering; Electrical Engineering; Mechanical Engineering) *Dean*: Surya Dharma; **Social and Political Sciences** (Administration; Communication Studies; Government; Political Sciences; Social Sciences; Sociology) *Dean*: Mahmud CH Aly

History: Founded 1987.

Fees: (Rupiahs): 1m. per annum

Degrees and Diplomas: *Sarjana (S1)*

Libraries: 2,635 vols

Last Updated: 13/01/09

ISLAMIC AS-SYAFIIYAH UNIVERSITY

Universitas Islam As-Syafiiyah

Jalan Raya Jatiwaringin 12, Pondok Gede, Jakarta Timur, 17411 DKI Jakarta
Tel: +62(21) 846-2361 +62(21) 848-4719
Fax: +62(21) 846-4257 +62(21) 848-4719
EMail: uia_penmaru@yahoo.com
Website: http://www.asyafiiyah.ac.id

Rector: Tutty Alawiyah

Ketua: K. H. Ali Yafie

Academies

Nursing (Nursing)

Faculties

Economics (Accountancy; Economics; Management); **Education and Teacher Training** (Art Education; Education; Educational and Student Counselling; Educational Psychology; Educational Sciences; English; Foreign Languages Education; Indonesian; Literature; Modern Languages; Native Language Education; Teacher Training); **Health Sciences** (Health Sciences; Hygiene; Nursing); **Islamic Religion** (Communication Studies; Islamic Theology; Religious Education); **Law** (Civil Law; Commercial Law; Criminal Law; International Law; Islamic Law; Law); **Science and Technology** (Biology; Computer Science; Engineering; Industrial Engineering; Mathematics; Mechanical Engineering; Operations Research)

Programmes

Postgraduate Studies (Agricultural Engineering; Islamic Studies; Law; Management)

History: Founded 1983.

Degrees and Diplomas: *Diploma*: 3 yrs; *Sarjana (S1)*; *Magister (S2)*: Agricultural Technology; Law; Management

Libraries: c. 18,000 vols

Last Updated: 18/07/11

ISLAMIC ATTAHIRIYAH UNIVERSITY

Universitas Islam Attahiriyah

Jalan Kampung Melayu Kecil III 15, Tebet, Jakarta Selatan, 12840 DKI Jakarta
Tel: +62(21) 831-8068
Fax: +62(21) 837-6126
EMail: admin@uniat.ac.id
Website: http://www.uniat.ac.id/

Rector: H. S. Suryani Tahir

Head (Acting), Bureau of General Administration of Academic and Student Affairs: Mahrus Junaidi

Faculties

Economics (Accountancy; Management); **Engineering** (Computer Networks; Engineering); **Islamic Studies** (Arabic; Islamic Law; Islamic Studies; Islamic Theology; Religion; Religious Education); **Law** (Law)

History: Founded 1969.

Degrees and Diplomas: *Sarjana (S1)*

Libraries: 5,013 vols

Last Updated: 27/06/11

ISLAMIC BALITAR UNIVERSITY

Universitas Islam Balitar

Jalan Majapahit 4, Blitar, 66139 Jawa Timur
Tel: +62(342) 813-145
Fax: +62(342) 813-145
EMail: unisba@telkom.net

Rector: Zaenal Fanani

Ketua: Tojib Hardjito

Programmes

Agriculture (Agricultural Business; Agricultural Engineering; Animal Husbandry); **Biology**; **Business Administration** (Accountancy; Business Administration; Business Computing; Management; Public Administration); **Engineering** (Civil Engineering; Computer Engineering; Engineering; Information Technology); **English**; **Law** (Law); **Pancasila and Civic Education** (Civics; Government; Political Sciences); **Social Sciences** (Communication Studies; Sociology)

Degrees and Diplomas: *Sarjana (S1)*

Last Updated: 29/04/10

ISLAMIC BATIK UNIVERSITY

Universitas Islam Batik

Jalan KH. Agus Salim 10, Surakarta, Jawat Tengah
Tel: +62(271) 714-751
Fax: +62(271) 740-160
EMail: info_uniba@yahoo.com
Website: http://www.uniba.ac.id

Rector: H. Marsyid

Faculties

Agriculture (Agricultural Business; Agriculture; Agronomy); **Economics** (Accountancy; Banking; Economics; Management); **Law** (Law); **Postgraduate Studies** (Management)

History: Founded 1983.

Main Language(s) of Instruction: Indonesian

Accrediting Agencies: BAN-PT (Badan Akreditasi Nasional)

Degrees and Diplomas: *Sarjana (S1)*; *Magister (S2)*: Management

Student Services: Academic counselling, Canteen, Language programs, Sports facilities

Libraries: 6,000 vols

Publications: Gema *(biennially)*; Paradigma, Serambi Hukum, Agronomika *(biennially)*

Last Updated: 27/06/11

ISLAMIC DARUL 'ULUM UNIVERSITY

Universitas Islam Darul 'Ulum (UNISDA)

Jalan Airlangga 3, Sukodadi, Lamongan, 62253 Jawa Timur

Tel: +62(322) 390-497

Fax: +62(322) 390-929

EMail: unisda1@yahoo.com

Website: http://www.unisda.ac.id

Rector: Afif Hasbullah (2001-) EMail: afif_rektor@plasa.com

Vice-Rector, Administration: Kirom Shodiq
EMail: siti_lpis@plasa.com

Faculties

Agriculture (Agricultural Engineering; Agricultural Management; Agriculture); **Economics** (Accountancy; Economics; Management); **Education and Teacher Training** (Education; English; Foreign Languages Education; Indonesian; Literature; Mathematics Education; Modern Languages; Native Language Education; Teacher Training); **Engineering** (Architecture; Civil Engineering; Engineering; Structural Architecture); **Islamic Theology Education** (Arabic; Islamic Studies; Islamic Theology); **Law** (Law); **Mathematics and Natural Sciences Education** (Applied Mathematics; Computer Science; Mathematics); **Social and Political Sciences** (Government; Political Sciences)

Programmes

Postgraduate Studies (Indonesian; Islamic Theology; Literature; Management; Native Language Education)

History: Founded 1986. Acquired present status 2002.

Governing Bodies: Ulum Social and Educational Foundation

Academic Year: August to July (August-January; February-July)

Main Language(s) of Instruction: Indonesian

Accrediting Agencies: Badan Akreditasi Nasional Perguruan Tinggi (BAN-PT)

Degrees and Diplomas: *Sarjana (S1)*: Law; Agriculture; Economics; Educational Sciences and Teacher Training; Engineering; Social Politics; Mathematics and Natural Sciences; Islamic Theology (SH; SE; SPd; ST; SSos; SSi; SAg), 4 yrs; *Magister (S2)*: Management; Islamic Theology; Indonesian; Native Language Education and Literature, 2 yrs

Student Services: Academic counselling, Canteen, Language programs, Social counselling, Sports facilities

Student Residential Facilities: Yes (for c. 500 male and female students)

Special Facilities: Art Gallery; Laboratory

Libraries: 18,028 vols

Press or Publishing House: UNISDA Press

Academic Staff *2009-2010*: Total: c. 150

Student Numbers *2009-2010*: Total: c. 3,000

Last Updated: 28/06/11

ISLAMIC INDRAGIRI UNIVERSITY

Universitas Islam Indragiri

Jalan Hr Subrantas 10, Tembilahan, 11111 Riau

Tel: +62(768) 324-918

Fax: +62(768) 24636

Rector: Sufian

Ketua: Syamsurizal Awi

Programmes

Agriculture (Agricultural Business; Agricultural Engineering; Agriculture; Aquaculture; Crop Production; Fishery); **Business Administration** (Accountancy; Business Administration; Management); **Engineering** (Civil Engineering; Industrial Engineering; Information Technology); **English** (English); **Food Technology** (Food Technology); **Law** (Law); **Physical Education, Health and Recreation**

Degrees and Diplomas: *Sarjana (S1)*

Last Updated: 29/04/10

ISLAMIC KALIMANTAN M.A.B. BANJARMASIN UNIVERSITY

Universitas Islam Kalimantan M.A.B. Banjarmasin

Jalan Adhiyaksa 2, Kayu Tangi RT 26, Banjarmasin, 70123 Kalimantan Selantan

Tel: +62(511) 304-592 +62(511) 304-352

Rector: M. Sanusi

Ketua: Gt. Irhamni

Faculties

Agriculture; **Economics** (Economics; Management); **Engineering**; **Social and Political Sciences**; **Teacher Training and Educational Science** (Art Education; Educational and Student Counselling; Educational Psychology; Educational Sciences; English; Foreign Languages Education)

History: Founded 1981.

Fees: (Rupiahs): 475,000 per annum

Degrees and Diplomas: *Diploma*: 3 yrs; *Sarjana (S1)*; *Magister (S2)*

Libraries: 7,165 vols

Last Updated: 29/04/10

ISLAMIC LABUHAN BATU UNIVERSITY

Universitas Islam Labuhan Batu

Jalan Padang Bulan 110, Rantau Prapat, 20114 Sumatera Utara

Tel: +62(624) 351-426

EMail: yayasan@ulb.ac.id

Rector: Rajo Makmur Siregar

Ketua: Sampiu

Faculties

Agriculture *Dean*: Ummi Kalsum; **Economics** *Dean*: Sumarna; **Educational Science and Teacher Training** *Dean*: Ismail Ritonga; **Engineering** *Dean*: Ali Safri S.

History: Founded 2000.

Degrees and Diplomas: *Sarjana (S1)*

Last Updated: 13/01/09

ISLAMIC MADURA UNIVERSITY

Universitas Islam Madura

Komplex PP Mithtahul Ulum Bettet, Pamekasan, 69351 Jawa Timur

Tel: +62(324) 321-783

Fax: +62(324) 321-783

EMail: info@uimadura.ac.id

Website: http://uimadura.ac.id

Rector: Muhammad Sahibundin

Ketua: Abd Ali Hamid

Faculties

Agriculture (Agricultural Business; Agricultural Engineering; Agriculture; Fishery; Horticulture); **Economics** (Business Administration; Economics; Management; Management Systems); **Education** (Education; English; Foreign Languages Education; Physical Education); **Engineering** (Computer Engineering; Industrial Management; Information Technology); **Islamic Studies** (Islamic Studies); **Mathematics and Natural Sciences** (Computer Science; Mathematics Education; Natural Sciences)

Programmes

Midwifery (Midwifery)

History: Founded 2002.

Degrees and Diplomas: *Diploma*; *Sarjana (S1)*

Last Updated: 21/07/11

ISLAMIC MAJAPAHIT UNIVERSITY

Universitas Islam Majapahit
Jalan Raya Jabon Km.07, Mojokerto, 61367 Jawa Timur
Tel: +62(321) 399-474
Fax: +62(321) 399-474
EMail: info@unim.ac.id
Website: http://www.unim.ac.id

Rector: H. Machmoed Zain

Ketua: Dewi Masyitoh

Faculties

Agricultural Engineering; **Economics** (Accountancy; Economics; Management); **Education** (Education; English; Foreign Languages Education; Indonesian; Mathematics Education; Native Language Education); **Engineering** (Civil Engineering; Engineering; Industrial Engineering; Information Technology); **Social and Political Sciences** (Communication Studies; Government; Political Sciences; Social Sciences)

Programmes

Midwifery (Midwifery)

History: Founded 1999.

Degrees and Diplomas: *Sarjana (S1)*
Last Updated: 21/07/11

ISLAMIC OGAN KOMERING ILIR KAYUAGUNG UNIVERSITY

Universitas Islam Ogan Komering Ilir Kayuagung
Kabupaten Oki, Sumatera Selatan
Tel: +62(712) 323-151
Fax: +62(712) 323-151
EMail: uniskikayuagung@yahoo.co.id

Rector: Harun Marzuk

Ketua: Abdul Hamid Usman

Programmes

Agriculture; **Engineering**; **English** (English); **Indonesian** (Indonesian; Literature; Native Language); **Pancasila and Civic Education** (Civics; Government; Political Sciences)

Degrees and Diplomas: *Sarjana (S1)*
Last Updated: 29/04/10

ISLAMIC SHEIKH YUSUF UNIVERSITY OF TANGERANG

Universitas Islam Syekh Yusuf Tangerang
Jalan Maulana Yusuf, Tangerang, Banten
Tel: +62(21) 552-7061 +62(21) 552-7063
Fax: +62(21) 558-1068
EMail: rektorat@unistangerang.ac.id
Website: http://www.unistangerang.ac.id

Rector: Nana Suryana

Ketua: Hudaya Latuconsina

Faculties

Economics (Accountancy; Economics; Management); **Education and Teacher Training** (Economics; Education; English; Foreign Languages Education); **Engineering** (Chemical Engineering; Civil Engineering; Computer Engineering; Engineering; Industrial Engineering); **Islamic Studies** (Islamic Studies; Islamic Theology); **Law** (Islamic Law; Law; Notary Studies); **Social and Political Sciences** (Administration; Business Administration; Communication Studies; Government; Political Sciences; Public Administration; Social Sciences)

Programmes

Postgraduate Studies (Administration; Law; Management)

History: Founded 1966 as branch of Islamic University of Jakarta, became independent 1975. A private institution under the supervision of the Department of Education and Culture.

Academic Year: September to August (September-January; February-August)

Admission Requirements: Secondary school certificate (Sekolah Menengah Tingkat Atas SMTA) and entrance examination

Main Language(s) of Instruction: Indonesian

Degrees and Diplomas: *Diploma*: 3 yrs; *Sarjana (S1)*; *Magister (S2)*: Administration, Law, Management
Last Updated: 22/07/11

ISLAMIC SULTAN AGUNG UNIVERSITY

Universitas Islam Sultan Agung
PO Box 1054/SM, Jalan Raya Kaligawe Km 4, Semarang, 50112 Jawat Tengah
Tel: +62(24) 658-3584
Fax: +62(24) 658-2455
EMail: informasi@unissula.ac.id
Website: http://www.unissula.ac.id

Rektor: Laode M. Kamaluddin

Vice-Rector I: Widiyanto

Colleges

Communication Studies (Communication Studies); **Dentistry** (Dental Technology; Dentistry; Oral Pathology; Orthodontics; Periodontics; Radiology; Stomatology); **Economics** (Accountancy; Economics; Management); **Engineering** (Civil Engineering; Electrical Engineering; Engineering; Environmental Engineering); **Industrial Engineering** (Computer Engineering; Electrical Engineering; Industrial Engineering; Information Technology); **Islamic Studies** (Arabic; Civics; Civil Law; Criminal Law; Cultural Studies; Development Studies; Educational Administration; English; Indonesian; Information Technology; Islamic Law; Koran; Law; Natural Sciences; Philosophy; Religious Studies); **Languages and Literature** (English; Literature); **Law** (Administrative Law; Civil Law; Commercial Law; Comparative Law; Constitutional Law; Criminal Law; Criminology; Information Technology; International Law; Islamic Law; Labour Law; Law; Political Sciences; Private Law); **Medicine** (Medicine); **Nursing** (Midwifery; Nursing); **Psychology** (Psychology)

Programmes

Graduate Studies (Civil Engineering; Commercial Law; Constitutional Law; Criminal Law; Electrical Engineering; Islamic Law; Law; Management)

History: Founded 1982. A private institution under the supervision of the Department of Education and Culture.

Academic Year: January to December (January-March; April-May; November-December)

Admission Requirements: Secondary school certificate (Sekolah Menengah Atas, SMA)

Main Language(s) of Instruction: Indonesian

Degrees and Diplomas: *Diploma*: 3 yrs; *Sarjana (S1)*: 5 yrs; *Magister (S2)*: Civil Engineering; Electrical Engineering; Law; Management

Libraries: 23,765 vols
Last Updated: 21/07/11

ISLAMIC UNIVERSITY AL-AZHAR OF MATARAM

Universitas Islam Al-Azhar Mataram
Jalan Bung Hatta 21, Mataram, 83233 Nusa Tenggara Barat
Tel: +62(370) 632-232

Rector: H. Abdurrahim

Faculties

Agriculture (Agricultural Business; Agricultural Economics; Agriculture) *Dean*: Rusdi Hidayat Mugroho; **Economics** (Development Studies; Economics) *Dean*: Nur Asihin Amin; **Engineering** (Civil Engineering; Engineering) *Dean*: Masnun; **Law** (Law) *Dean*: Rifai Latif; **Mathematics and Natural Sciences** (Biology; Mathematics; Natural Sciences) *Dean*: M. Maswan; **Medicine**

History: Founded 1984.

Fees: (Rupiahs): 500,000 per annum

Degrees and Diplomas: *Sarjana (S1)*

Libraries: 3,970 vols
Last Updated: 13/01/09

ISLAMIC UNIVERSITY OF BANDUNG

Universitas Islam Bandung
Jalan Tamansari 1, Bandung, 40116 Jawa Barat
Tel: +62(22) 420-3368 +62(22) 420-5546
Fax: +62(22) 426-3895
EMail: humas@unisba.ac.id
Website: http://www.unisba.ac.id

Rector: Thaufiq Siddiq Boesoirie

Head: K. H. Miftah Faridl

Faculties

Communication *Dean*: Yusuf Hamdan; **Economics**; **Engineering** *Dean*: Sri Hidayati Djoeffan; **Law** *Dean*: Ashar Hidayat; **Mathematics and Natural Sciences** *Dean*: M. Yusuf Fajar; **Medicine** (Medicine) *Dean*: Herri S. Sastramihardja; **Postgraduate Studies** *Dean*: Toto Tohir; **Psychology** *Dean*: Umar Yusuf; **Sharia (Islamic Law)** (Banking; Finance; Religious Studies) *Dean*: Muhammad Zaenuddin; **Tarbiyah** (Educational Administration; Religious Education; Teacher Training) *Dean*: Sobar Algozal; **Ushuludin** (Communication Studies; Islamic Studies; Islamic Theology; Radio and Television Broadcasting) *Dean*: Wildan bi. Yahya

History: Founded 1958. A private institution under the auspices of the Islamic Education Foundation and under the supervision of the Department of Education and Culture and Religious Affairs.

Academic Year: September to August (September-February; March-August)

Admission Requirements: Secondary school certificate (Sekolah Lanjutan Atas, SLA) and entrance examination

Fees: (Rupiahs): 1.5m. per annum

Main Language(s) of Instruction: Indonesian

Degrees and Diplomas: *Sarjana (S1)*: 4 1/2 yrs; *Magister (S2)*: Law; Education Management; Communication; Psychology, 2 yrs; *Doktor (S3)*

Student Services: Canteen, Employment services, Health services, Language programs, Sports facilities

Libraries: University Library, 17,437 vols

Publications: Mimbar *(quarterly)*

Last Updated: 25/02/10

ISLAMIC UNIVERSITY OF INDONESIA

Universitas Islam Indonesia (UII)
Jalan Kaliurang Km 145, Sleman, Yogyakarta, 55584 DI Yogyakarta
Tel: +62(274) 898-444
Fax: +62(274) 898-459
EMail: info@uii.ac.id
Website: http://www.uii.ac.id

Rector: Edy Suandi Hamid EMail: rektor@uii.ac.id

Vice-Rector: Ir. Sarwidi

Faculties

Civil Engineering and Planning (Architecture and Planning; Civil Engineering; Environmental Engineering; Structural Architecture); **Economics** (Accountancy; Development Studies; Economics; Management); **Graduate Studies** (Accountancy; Civil Engineering; Computer Engineering; Economics; Industrial Engineering; Law; Management; Psychology); **Industrial Technology** (Chemical Engineering; Computer Engineering; Electrical and Electronic Engineering; Industrial Engineering; Information Technology; Mechanical Engineering); **Islamic Studies** (Islamic Law; Islamic Studies; Islamic Theology; Religious Education); **Law** (Law); **Mathematics and Natural Sciences** (Chemistry; Mathematics; Natural Sciences; Pharmacy; Statistics); **Medicine** (Medicine); **Psychology and Social Cultural Sciences** (Communication Studies; Cultural Studies; English; Psychology; Social Sciences)

History: Founded 1945 and officially recognized under present title 1951. A private institution under the supervision of the Department of Education and Culture.

Academic Year: July to June (July-December; January-June)

Admission Requirements: Secondary school certificate

Main Language(s) of Instruction: Indonesian, English

Degrees and Diplomas: *Diploma*: 3 yrs; *Sarjana (S1)*: 4 yrs; *Magister (S2)*: Accountancy; Civil Engineering; Computer Engineering; Economics; Industrial Engineering; Law; Management; Psychology, a further 1 1/2-2 yrs; *Doktor (S3)*: Economics; Law

Student Services: Academic counselling, Canteen, Cultural centre, Employment services, Health services, Nursery care, Social counselling, Sports facilities

Publications: Unisia Journal *(quarterly)*

Press or Publishing House: UII Press

Last Updated: 18/07/11

ISLAMIC UNIVERSITY OF JAKARTA

Universitas Islam Jakarta
Jalan Balai Rakyat Utan Kayu, Jakarta, 13120 DKI Jakarta
Tel: +62(21) 856-6451
Fax: +62(21) 850-4818
EMail: informasi@uid.ac.id
Website: http://www.uid.ac.id

Rector: Razali Usman

Ketua: Rasjidi Oesman

Programmes

Arabic Language Education (Arabic; Foreign Languages Education); **Engineering** (Engineering; Industrial Engineering); **Graduate Studies** (Law; Management); **Islamic Religious Education** (Islamic Theology; Religious Education); **Law** (Law); **Management** (Management)

History: Founded 1950. A private institution under the supervision of the Department of Education and Culture.

Degrees and Diplomas: *Sarjana (S1)*; *Magister (S2)*: Law; Management

Libraries: c. 14,000 vols

Last Updated: 18/07/11

ISLAMIC UNIVERSITY OF JEMBER

Universitas Islam Jember
Jalan Kyai Mojo 101, Jember, 68133 Jawa Timur
Tel: +62(331) 488-675
Fax: +62(231) 428-732
EMail: uijember@gmail.com
Website: http://www.uij.ac.id

Rector: Achmad Zein

Ketua: Sukamto Irch

Faculties

Agriculture (Agricultural Business; Agricultural Economics; Agricultural Engineering; Agriculture; Agronomy); **Educational Science and Teacher Training** (Biology; Education; Educational and Student Counselling; English; Foreign Languages Education; Islamic Theology; Mathematics Education; Religious Education; Teacher Training); **Law** (Law); **Social and Political Sciences** (Communication Studies; Political Sciences; Social Sciences)

History: Founded 1984.

Degrees and Diplomas: *Sarjana (S1)*

Last Updated: 18/07/11

ISLAMIC UNIVERSITY OF KADIRI

Universitas Islam Kadiri
Jalan Sersan Suharmaji 38, Kediri, Jawa Timur
Tel: +62(354) 683-243
Fax: +62(354) 699-057
EMail: uniska-kediri@telkom.net
Website: http://www.uniska-kediri.ac.id

Rector: Abu Talkah

Ketua: Anwar Iskandar

Faculties

Agriculture (Agricultural Engineering; Agriculture; Agronomy; Animal Husbandry); **Economics** (Accountancy; Economics; Management); **Education and Teacher Training** (Distance Education; Education; English; Foreign Languages Education; Teacher Training); **Engineering** (Electrical and Electronic Engineering; Engineering); **Law** (Law); **Postgraduate Studies** (Agricultural Business; Law; Management)

History: Founded 1983.

Degrees and Diplomas: *Sarjana (S1)*; *Magister (S2)*: Agricultural Business; Law; Management

Libraries: 4,496 vols

Last Updated: 18/07/11

ISLAMIC UNIVERSITY OF MAKASSAR

Universitas Islam Makassar (UIM)

Jl. Perintis Kemerdekaan, Km. 9 No. 29, Makassar, 90245 Sulawesi Selatan
Tel: +62(411) 590-023 +62(411) 588-167
Fax: +62(411) 588-167 +62(411) 585-865
EMail: ui-makassar@plasa.com

Rector: Majdah Muhyddin Zain

Faculties

Agriculture (Agricultural Business; Agricultural Engineering; Agriculture) *Dean*: Musdalifah Abdullah; **Chemistry and Pharmacy** (Applied Chemistry; Pharmacy) *Dean*: Damma Salama; **Engineering** (Chemical Engineering; Computer Engineering; Computer Science; Electrical Engineering; Engineering; Industrial Engineering; Mechanical Engineering) *Dean*: Syahrir Habiba; **Literature** (Arabic; English; Indonesian; Literature) *Dean*: Kamaluddin Abunawas; **Nursing** (Nursing) *Dean*: Muhammad Syafar; **Social Sciences** (Business Administration; Communication Studies) *Dean*: Djainuddin Maggasingan

History: Founded 2000. Formerly Faculties of Religion and Agriculture (founded 1990).

Governing Bodies: Yayasan Perguruan Tinggi AL Gazali

Academic Year: September to August

Admission Requirements: Entrance examination (written and oral)

Main Language(s) of Instruction: Indonesian

International Co-operation: None

Accrediting Agencies: Ministry of Education

Degrees and Diplomas: *Sarjana (S1)*: 4-5 yrs; *Magister (S2)*: Agricultural Business; Agricultural Technology

Student Residential Facilities: None

Special Facilities: None

Libraries: Yes (Books in Indonesian and in English)

Publications: ILTEK

Last Updated: 28/06/11

ISLAMIC UNIVERSITY OF MALANG

Universitas Islam Malang (UNISMA)

Jalan Mayjen Haryono 193, Malang, 65144 Jawa Timur
Tel: +62(341) 551-932
Fax: +62(341) 552-249
EMail: humas@unisma.ac.id
Website: http://www.unisma.ac.id

Rector: Abdul Mukri Prabowo Tel: +62(341) 551-685

Ketua: Chasan Bisri Tel: +62(341) 552-752

Faculties

Administration (Accountancy; Administration; Banking; Business Administration; English; Government; Human Rights; Island Studies; Public Administration; Taxation); **Agriculture** (Agricultural Business; Agricultural Engineering; Agriculture; Agronomy; Horticulture); **Animal Husbandry** (Animal Husbandry; Cattle Breeding; Food Technology); **Economics** (Accountancy; Economics; Management); **Education and Teacher Training** (Art Education; Educational Sciences; English; Foreign Languages Education; Indonesian; Journalism; Literature; Mathematics Education; Native Language Education; Natural Sciences; Social Sciences; Teacher Training; Translation and Interpretation); **Engineering** (Civil Engineering; Construction Engineering; Electrical Engineering; Energy Engineering; Engineering; Information Technology; Mechanical Engineering; Production Engineering); **Islamic Studies** (Arabic; Educational Administration; Islamic Law; Islamic Studies; Islamic Theology; Religious Education; Teacher Training; Technology Education); **Law** (Civil Law; Criminal Law; Government; Human Rights; International Law; Law); **Mathematics and Natural Sciences** (Biology; Environmental Management; Mathematics; Natural Resources; Natural Sciences); **Medicine** (Medicine)

Programmes

Postgraduate Studies (English; Indonesian; Islamic Studies; Law; Management; Public Administration)

History: Founded 1981. A private institution.

Main Language(s) of Instruction: Indonesian

Accrediting Agencies: Department of Education and Culture

Degrees and Diplomas: *Sarjana (S1)*: 2-4 yrs; *Magister (S2)*: English; Indonesian; Islamic Studies; Law; Management; Public Administration

Student Services: Academic counselling, Canteen, Cultural centre, Employment services, Foreign Studies Centre, Handicapped facilities, Health services, Language programs, Nursery care, Social counselling, Sports facilities

Student Residential Facilities: Yes

Special Facilities: Bangkit Theatre.

Libraries: Central Library, c. 25,000 vols

Publications: Al-Bhuts Research Journal *(quarterly)*; Buana Scientific Journal *(biannually)*; Dinamika Magazine, Law *(quarterly)*; Fisa Scientific Journal, Teacher Training and Education *(quarterly)*; Idea Magazine, Islamic Studies *(quarterly)*; Mei Magazine, Economy *(quarterly)*; Pelopor Magazine, Administrative Sciences *(quarterly)*; Phenomena Magazine, Teacher Training and Education *(quarterly)*; Radix Magazine, Agriculture *(quarterly)*; Rekasatwa Magazine, Animal Husbandry *(quarterly)*; Scale Magazine, Engineering *(quarterly)*; Vicratina Scientific Journal, Islamic Studies *(quarterly)*

Last Updated: 21/07/11

ISLAMIC UNIVERSITY OF NORTH SUMATRA

Universitas Islam Sumatera Utara (UISU)

Jalan Sisingamangaraja, Teladan Kotak Pos 1217, Medan, 20217 Sumatera Utara
Tel: +62(61) 786-9790
Fax: +62(61) 786-9790 +62(61) 786-0916
EMail: info@uisu.ac.id
Website: http://www.uisu.ac.id

Rector: H. Usman

Ketua: H. Usman Pelly

Faculties

Agriculture; **Arts and Humanities**; **Economics**; **Engineering**; **Islamic Religious Studies** (Islamic Studies; Religious Studies); **Law**; **Medicine**; **Postgraduate Studies** (Law; Management); **Social and Political Sciences**; **Teacher Training and Educational Sciences** *Dean*: Maas Harahap

History: Founded 1951. A private institution under the supervision of the Department of Education and Culture for non-Islamic studies and the Department of Religion for Islamic Studies.

Academic Year: July to July (July-January; January-July)

Admission Requirements: Secondary school certificate (Sekolah Menengah Atas, SMA) or recognized foreign equivalent

Fees: (Rupiahs): 1.5m. per annum

Main Language(s) of Instruction: Indonesian

Degrees and Diplomas: *Sarjana (S1)*: 5 yrs; *Magister (S2)*: Management; Law

Libraries: 23,219 vols

Publications: Bulletin Pertamian *(3 per annum)*

Last Updated: 25/02/10

ISLAMIC UNIVERSITY OF NUSANTARA

Universitas Islam Nusantara

Jalan Soekarno Hatta No. 530, Bandung, 40286 Jawa Barat
Tel: +62(22) 750-9656
Fax: +62(22) 750-9663
EMail: info@uninus.ac.id
Website: http://www.uninus.ac.id/

Rector: Didin Wahidin

Head of Foundation: Achmad Rustandi

Faculties

Agriculture *Dean*: Rubi Robana; **Arts and Humanities** *Dean*: Suhendra Yusuf; **Communication Science** *Dean*: Subarna Tatang; **Economics** (Accountancy; Development Studies; Economics; Management) *Dean*: H. Kusmana; **Educational Sciences and Teacher Training** *Dean*: Didin Wahidin; **Engineering** *Dean*: Achmad Dimyati; **Law** (Law) *Dean*: Enjang Surachman

History: Founded 1959. A private institution under the supervision of the Department of Education and Culture.

Academic Year: August to July (August-January; February-July)

Admission Requirements: Senior high school certificate

Fees: (Rupiahs): 2.5m. per semester; 3m.-5m. per annum

Main Language(s) of Instruction: Indonesian

Accrediting Agencies: Badan Akreditasi Nasional/National Accreditation Board (BAN)

Degrees and Diplomas: *Sarjana (S1)*: 4 yrs; *Magister (S2) (MMPd)*: 2 yrs following Sarjana

Student Services: Academic counselling, Canteen, Employment services, Foreign student adviser, Language programs, Social counselling, Sports facilities

Libraries: 41,972 vols

Publications: Literat *(quarterly)*

Last Updated: 08/03/10

ISLAMIC UNIVERSITY OF RIAU

Universitas Islam Riau (UIR)

Jalan Kaharuddin Nasution 113, Perhentian Marpoyan, Pekanbaru, Riau
Tel: +62(761) 72-126 +62(761) 72-127
Fax: +62(761) 674-834
Website: http://www.uir.ac.id

Rector: Detri Karya Tel: +62(761) 674-834

Ketua/Chairman: H. A. Kadir Abbas

Faculties

Agriculture (Agricultural Economics; Agriculture; Agronomy; Fishery; Natural Resources; Water Management) *Dean*: Rosadi; **Economics** (Accountancy; Development Studies; Economics; Management) *Dean*: Syamri Syamsudin; **Educational Science and Teacher Training** (Art Education; Biology; Dance; Educational Administration; Educational Sciences; English; Health Education; Indonesian; Literature; Mathematics Education; Modern Languages; Music Education; Natural Sciences; Physical Education; Sports; Teacher Training; Theatre) *Dean*: Amjad Amir; **Engineering** (Civil Engineering; Engineering; Information Technology; Petroleum and Gas Engineering) *Dean*: Sugeng Wijono; **Islamic Studies** (Islamic Studies) *Dean*: Hamzah; **Law** (Law) *Dean*: Idris Zulherman; **Psychology** *Dean*: Syafhendri; **Social and Political Sciences** (Administration; Business Administration; Government; Political Sciences; Secretarial Studies; Social Sciences) *Dean*: Nurman

History: Founded 1962. A private institution under the supervision of the Department of Education and Culture.

Academic Year: July to June (July-December; January-June)

Admission Requirements: Secondary school certificate (Sekolah Menengah Atas, SMA)

Fees: (Rupiahs): 1,345,000 per annum

Main Language(s) of Instruction: Indonesian

Accrediting Agencies: National Accreditation Agency

Degrees and Diplomas: *Diploma*: 3 yrs; *Sarjana (S1)*: 4 yrs; *Magister (S2)*: a further 2 yrs

Student Services: Academic counselling, Canteen, Cultural centre, Foreign Studies Centre, Health services, Language programs, Social counselling, Sports facilities

Student Residential Facilities: Student Dormitory

Special Facilities: Laboratories; Experiment Stations; Art Gallery

Libraries: 20,709 vols

Publications: Dinamika Pertanian *(quarterly)*; KIAT *(quarterly)*; Mahkamah *(quarterly)*; Saintis *(quarterly)*; Siasat *(quarterly)*

Press or Publishing House: University Press

Last Updated: 08/03/10

ISTPN INSTITUTE OF SCIENCE AND TECHNOLOGY

Institut Sains Dan Teknologi ISTPN

Jalan Jenderal Sudirman 19, Padang 12345

Programmes

Architecture; **Communication**; **Engineering**; **Regional and Town Planning** (Regional Planning; Town Planning); **Science** (Biology; Chemistry; Mathematics)

Degrees and Diplomas: *Sarjana (S1)*

Last Updated: 27/04/10

JABAL GHAFUR UNIVERSITY

Universitas Jabal Ghafur

Jalan Glepui, Sigli 24163
Tel: +62(653) 212-59

Rector: Mohammad Jamil Arbi

Ketua: H. Ibrahim Risyad

Faculties

Agriculture (Agricultural Economics; Agriculture; Agronomy; Animal Husbandry; Soil Science) *Dean*: Moh. Djamin Arenbi; **Economics** (Accountancy; Banking; Finance; Management); **Engineering** (Computer Engineering); **Law** (Law) *Dean*: Dahnil; **Social and Political Sciences** (Business Administration; Government) *Dean*: Husni Ali; **Teacher Training and Educational Science** (Art Education; Biology; Chemistry; Educational and Student Counselling; Educational Sciences; English; Health Education; History; Indonesian; Literature; Mathematics Education; Physical Education; Physics; Science Education; Secretarial Studies; Sports; Teacher Training) *Dean*: M. Nasir Basri

History: Founded 1982.

Fees: (Rupiahs): 350,000 per annum

Degrees and Diplomas: *Diploma*: 3 yrs; *Sarjana (S1)*

Libraries: 3,256 vols

Last Updated: 15/01/09

JAKARTA INSTITUTE OF ARTS

Institut Kesenian Jakarta

Jalan Cikini Raya 73, Jakarta, 10330 Jakarta Pusat
Tel: +62(21) 392-4018
Fax: +62(21) 3193-4102
EMail: baak_ikj@yahoo.co.id
Website: http://www.ikj.ac.id

Rector: Gotot Prakosa EMail: dekan@fftvikj.org

Faculties

Arts (Acting; Cinema and Television; Crafts and Trades; Dance; Film; Graphic Arts; Graphic Design; Interior Design; Musicology; Painting and Drawing; Photography; Sculpture; Singing; Sound Engineering (Acoustics); Textile Design; Theatre; Visual Arts); **Film and Television** (Cinema and Television; Film; Radio and Television Broadcasting); **Fine Arts and Design** (Design; Fine Arts; Handicrafts)

History: Founded 1970.

Degrees and Diplomas: *Diploma*; *Sarjana (S1)*; *Magister (S2)*

Libraries: 5,770 vols

Academic Staff *2009-2010*: Total: c. 140

Student Numbers *2009-2010*: Total: c. 1,400

Last Updated: 20/06/11

JAKARTA UNIVERSITY

Universitas Jakarta (UNIJA)

Jalan Pulomas Barat, Villa Tarah Mas, Jakarta Timur, 13210 DKI Jakarta
Tel: +62(21) 472-2350 +62(21) 472-2354
Fax: +62(21) 472-2374

Rector: Loebby Loqman

Ketua: Nani Sutiati

Faculties

Administration (Business Administration; Government; International Relations; Political Sciences; Public Administration) *Dean*: T Rukaesih; **Engineering** (Architecture; Civil Engineering; Engineering) *Dean*: Tri Harso Karyono; **Law** *Dean*: Tjindra Parma

History: Founded 1965. A private institution under the supervision of the Department of Education and Culture.

Fees: (Rupiahs): 1.7m. per annum

Degrees and Diplomas: *Sarjana (S1)*

Libraries: 4,839 vols

Last Updated: 14/01/09

JAMBI BATANGHARI UNIVERSITY

Universitas Batanghari Jambi (UNBARI)

Jalan Slamet Riyadi, Broni, Jambi, 36000 Jambi
Tel: +62(741) 60-673
EMail: rektorat@unbari.ac.id
Website: http://www.unbari.ac.id

Rector: Fachruddin Razi

Ketua: Abdurrahman Sayoeti

Faculties

Agriculture (Agricultural Business; Agricultural Engineering; Agriculture; Agronomy; Aquaculture); **Economics and Management** (Development Studies; Economics; Management); **Education and Teacher Training** (Economics; Education; English; Foreign Languages Education; History; Indonesian; Literature; Mathematics Education; Native Language Education; Teacher Training); **Engineering** (Civil Engineering; Electrical Engineering; Engineering; Environmental Engineering); **Law** (Law)

Programmes

Postgraduate Studies (Law; Management)

History: Founded 1985.

Degrees and Diplomas: *Diploma*: 3 yrs; *Sarjana (S1)*; *Magister (S2)*: Law; Management

Libraries: 5,106 vols

Last Updated: 12/07/11

JANABADRA UNIVERSITY

Universitas Janabadra

Jalan Tentara Rakyat Mataram 55-57, Yogyakarta, 55231 DI Yogyakarta
Tel: +62(274) 561-039 +62(274) 517-251
Fax: +62(274) 561-039
Website: http://www.janabadra.ac.id

Rector: Suharjanto Tel: +62(274) 517-251

Vice-Rector for Academic Affairs: Cungki Kusdarjito
EMail: ckusdarjito@janabadra.ac.id; ckusdarjito@gy.centrin.net.id

Faculties

Agriculture (Agricultural Business; Agricultural Economics; Agricultural Engineering; Agriculture); **Economics** (Accountancy; Development Studies; Economics; Management); **Engineering** (Civil Engineering; Computer Engineering; Engineering; Mechanical Engineering); **Law** (Administrative Law; Civil Law; Commercial Law; Constitutional Law; Criminal Law; Law); **Postgraduate Studies** (Law; Management)

History: Founded 1958, by Mr Soedarisman Purwokusumo, city major of Yogyakarta at the time.

Governing Bodies: Rector, 3 vice Rectors (Academic and International Affairs, Treasury, Student Affairs), Senate (University and Faculty levels), Deans of Faculties and Heads of Departments

Academic Year: September to June

Admission Requirements: High school certificate

Fees: (Rupiahs): 1.2m. per annum

Main Language(s) of Instruction: Indonesian

Accrediting Agencies: Indonesian Accreditation Agency

Degrees and Diplomas: *Sarjana (S1)*: 4 yrs; *Magister (S2)*: Management; Law

Student Services: Academic counselling, Sports facilities

Libraries: 9,036 vols

Last Updated: 28/06/11

JAYABAYA UNIVERSITY

Universitas Jayabaya

Jalan Pulomas Selatan Kav. 23, Jakarta Timur, 13210 DKI Jakarta
Tel: +62(21) 470-0872 +62(21) 870-0874 +62(21) 870-0877
Fax: +62(21) 870-0872 +62(21) 870-0893
EMail: info@jayabaya.ac.id
Website: http://www.jayabaya.ac.id

Rector: Amir Santoso

Ketua: Yuyun Moeslim Taher

Faculties

Accountancy; **Business Administration** (Business Administration); **Civil Engineering and Planning** (Architecture and Planning; Civil Engineering) *Dean*: Eri Setia Ramadhan; **Communication Sciences** (Communication Studies; Journalism; Public Relations) *Dean*: Dewi Setiarini; **Economics** (Accountancy; Economics; Management) *Dean*: Darwis S. Gani; **Industrial Engineering** (Chemical Engineering; Electrical Engineering; Industrial Engineering; Mechanical Engineering) *Dean*: Darma Setiarini; **Information Systems, Information Management and Information Sciences**; **Law** (Commercial Law; International Law; Law) *Dean*: Yudha Bhakti; **Psychology** *Dean*: Renny Herdiani; **Social and Political Sciences** (International Relations; Political Sciences; Public Administration; Social Sciences) *Dean*: Amir Santoso

History: Founded 1958. A private institution under the supervision of the Department of Education and Culture.

Governing Bodies: Board of Trustees

Academic Year: September to July (September-February; March-July)

Admission Requirements: Secondary school certificate (Sekolah Menengah Atas, SMA)

Fees: (Rupiahs): 1.2m. per annum

Main Language(s) of Instruction: Indonesian

Degrees and Diplomas: *Diploma*: 3-4 yrs; *Sarjana (S1)*: 4-7 yrs; *Magister (S2)*: International Relations; Law; Management; *Doktor (S3)*: Law

Libraries: 25,478 vols

Last Updated: 08/03/10

JAYAPURA UNIVERSITY OF SCIENCE AND TECHNOLOGY PAPUA ABEPURA

Universitas Sains dan Teknologi Jayapura

Jalan Raya Sentani, Padang Bulan Jayapura, Abepura, 99351 Papua
Tel: +62(967) 582-550 +62(967) 581-659
EMail: suaibpapua@yahoo.com
Website: http://www.ustj.ac.id/

Rector: Ali Kastella

Vice-Rector I: Muid Fabanyo

Ketua: David Hindom

Faculties

Civil Engineering and Planning (Civil Engineering; Environmental Engineering; Regional Planning; Structural Architecture; Town Planning); **Computer Science and Management** (Computer Engineering; Computer Networks; Computer Science; Information Technology); **Health Sciences** (Health Sciences; Pharmacy); **Social and Political Sciences** (Accountancy; Communication Studies; English; Government; International Relations; Political Sciences; Social Sciences)

Programmes
Industrial Engineering and Earth Sciences (Electrical Engineering; Engineering; Geological Engineering; Geology; Industrial Engineering; Mining Engineering)

History: Founded 1991. Formerly known as Institut Sains dan Teknologi Papua Abepura Jayapura.

Degrees and Diplomas: *Diploma*; *Sarjana (S1)*

Libraries: c. 2,000 vols
Last Updated: 30/06/11

JENDERAL ACHMAD YANI UNIVERSITY

Universitas Jenderal Achmad Yani (UNJANI)
PO Box 148, Jl Terusan Jenderal Sudirman 52-53, Cimahi, 40513 Jawa Barat
Tel: +62(22) 665-6190
Fax: +62(22) 665-2069
EMail: humas@unjani.ac.id
Website: http://www.unjani.ac.id/

Rector: Edhi Tri Cahyono

Ketua: Djoko Daryatno

Faculties
Economics (Accountancy; Economics; Management); **Engineering** (Chemical Engineering; Civil Engineering; Electrical Engineering; Engineering; Industrial Engineering; Metallurgical Engineering); **Mathematics and Natural Sciences** (Chemistry; Computer Science; Mathematics; Natural Sciences; Pharmacy; Toxicology); **Medicine** (Anaesthesiology; Anatomy; Behavioural Sciences; Biochemistry; Biology; Dermatology; Epidemiology; Forensic Medicine and Dentistry; Gynaecology and Obstetrics; Health Administration; Histology; Medical Parasitology; Medicine; Neurology; Nutrition; Occupational Health; Ophthalmology; Paediatrics; Parasitology; Pathology; Pharmacology; Pharmacy; Psychiatry and Mental Health; Surgery; Venereology); **Psychology** (Psychology); **Social and Political Sciences** (Government; International Relations; Political Sciences; Public Administration; Social Sciences)

Programmes
Graduate Studies (Government)

History: Founded 1990.

Degrees and Diplomas: *Diploma*: 3 yrs; *Sarjana (S1)*; *Magister (S2)*: Government Science

Libraries: c. 11,000 vols
Last Updated: 22/07/11

KADER BANGSA PALEMBANG UNIVERSITY

Universitas Kader Bangsa Palembang
Jalan HM. Ryacudu 88, Palembang, 30129 Sumatera Selatan
Tel: +62(711) 318-311
Fax: +62(711) 519-827
EMail: info@ukb.ac.id
Website: http://www.ukb.ac.id

Rector: HT. Wathan

Ketua: Hj. Irzanita

Vice-Rector I: Ferry Presca

Faculties
Economics (Accountancy; Management); **Engineering** (Computer Engineering; Electrical Engineering; Engineering); **Health Sciences** (Health Sciences); **Law** (Law); **Nursing and Midwifery** (Midwifery; Nursing); **Pharmacy** (Pharmacy)

Programmes
Public Health (Behavioural Sciences; Epidemiology; Health Administration; Health Education; Health Sciences; Nutrition; Occupational Health; Public Health; Sports Medicine; Toxicology)

History: Founded 2001.

Degrees and Diplomas: *Sarjana (S1)*; *Magister (S2)*: Public Health

Student Services: Nursery care
Last Updated: 22/07/11

KALABAHI TRIBUANA UNIVERSITY

Universitas Tribuana Kalabahi
Jalan Singamangaraja 24, Kalabahi, Nusa Tenggara Timur
Tel: +62(386) 222-2882
Fax: +62(386) 222-2882
EMail: untrib@gmail.com

Rector: Ayub Ranoh

Ketua: Permenas Lamma Koly

Programmes
Agriculture (Agricultural Business; Agricultural Engineering; Fishery); **Chemistry** (Chemistry); **English** (English); **Information Technology** (Information Technology); **Law** (Law); **Management** (Management); **Mathematics** (Mathematics); **Theology** (Religious Education; Theology)

Degrees and Diplomas: *Sarjana (S1)*
Last Updated: 31/05/10

KALBE INSTITUTE OF TECHNOLOGY AND BUSINESS

Institut Teknologi dan Bisnis Kalbe
Jalan Letjen S. Parman Kav 76, Jakarta 11470
Tel: +62(21) 530-0951
Fax: +62(21) 535-9812
EMail: info@itbk.ac.id
Website: http://www.itbk.ac.id/

Rector: H. Masruchin

Vice-Rector: Ulani Yunus

Programmes
Accountancy (Accountancy); **Communication Studies** (Communication Studies); **Information Systems** (Information Management; Information Technology); **Information Technology** (Information Technology); **Management** (Management)

History: Formerly known as STMIK Supra (Supra School of Business and Computer Science STMIK)

Degrees and Diplomas: *Sarjana (S1)*; *Magister (S2)*
Last Updated: 22/06/11

KALTARA UNIVERSITY

Universitas Kaltara
Tanjung Selor, Kalimantan Timur

Programmes
Architecture (Architecture); **Business Administration** (Banking; Finance; Management; Public Administration); **Economics** (Economics); **Engineering**; **Science** (Chemistry; Mathematics; Physics)

Degrees and Diplomas: *Sarjana (S1)*
Last Updated: 29/04/10

KALTIM INSTITUTE OF TEACHER TRAINING AND EDUCATIONAL SCIENCE

Institut Keguruan dan Ilmu Pendidikan (IKIP) PGRI Kaltim
Jalan Suwandi Blok C 23, Samarinda, 75117 Kalimantan Timur
Tel: +62(541) 38-620

Direktor: Mohammad Kasdie

Programmes
Economics (Economics); **Physical Education and Sports** (Physical Education; Sports; Sports Management); **Technology** (Technology)

History: Founded 1979.

Degrees and Diplomas: *Diploma*; *Sarjana (S1)*
Last Updated: 20/06/11

KANJURUHAN UNIVERSITY

Universitas Kanjuruhan (UNIKAN)
Jalan Sudanco Supriadi 48, Malang, Jawa Timur
Tel: +62(341) 801-488
Fax: +62(341) 831-532
EMail: admin@ukanjuruhan.ac.id
Website: http://www.ukanjuruhan.ac.id

Rector: Hadi Sriwiyana (2000-)

Ketua: Soenarto Djojodihardjo EMail: soenarto@ukanjuruhan.ac.id

International Relations: Christea Frisdiantara, Vice Rector EMail: theo@ukanjuruhan.ac.id

Faculties
Animal Husbandry (Agricultural Business; Cattle Breeding; Economics; Nutrition; Social Studies; Zoology); **Economics** (Accountancy; Economics; Management); **Education and Teacher Training** (Civics; Economics; Educational and Student Counselling; Educational Sciences; English; Foreign Languages Education; Geography; Indonesian; Mathematics Education; Native Language Education; Physical Education; Primary Education); **Information Technology** (Information Management; Information Sciences; Information Technology); **Languages and Literature** (English; Indonesian; Japanese; Literature; Modern Languages); **Law** (Law); **Mathematics and Natural Sciences** (Information Sciences; Mathematics Education; Physics; Science Education; Technology); **Postgraduate Studies** (Social Sciences)

History: Founded 1975 as Institut Keguruan dan Ilmu Pendidikan PGRI Malang. Acquired present status and title 2001.

Admission Requirements: Senior High School Leaving Certificate (Sekolah Menengah Atas, SMA)

Fees: (Rupiahs): 965,000 per annum

Main Language(s) of Instruction: Indonesian

Accrediting Agencies: National Accreditation Body (BAN)

Degrees and Diplomas: *Diploma*: 3 yrs; *Sarjana (S1) (S.Pd; SE; SH.S.Kom; SS; S.Si; Spt)*: 4 yrs; *Magister (S2)*: Social Sciences (M.Pd.), 2 1/2 yrs

Student Services: Academic counselling, Canteen, Cultural centre, Employment services, Health services, Language programs, Social counselling, Sports facilities

Libraries: c. 16,000 vols

Publications: Inspirasi Journal *(biweekly)*; Law Enforcement Journal *(biweekly)*; Modernisasi Journal *(monthly)*; Sintagma Journal *(monthly)*

Press or Publishing House: None

Academic Staff *2009-2010*: Total: c. 320
Student Numbers *2009-2010*: Total: c. 7,000
Last Updated: 28/06/11

KAPUAS UNIVERSITY SINTANG

Universitas Kapuas Sintang (UNKA)
Jalan J. C. Oevang Oeray, Sintang, 78611 Kalimantan Barat
Tel: +62(565) 202-5244
Fax: +62(565) 202-5244

Rector: Arkanudin

Ketua: Rambu Juris Mening

Programmes
Agricultural Engineering; **Biology** (Biology); **Forestry** (Forestry); **Law** (Law); **Public Administration** (Public Administration)

History: Founded 1992.

Degrees and Diplomas: *Sarjana (S1)*
Last Updated: 28/06/11

KARIMUN UNIVERSITY

Universitas Karimun
Karimun, Riau

Programmes
Agriculture (Agricultural Business; Aquaculture; Fishery); **Business Administration**; **Communication Studies** (Communication Studies); **Engineering** (Electrical Engineering; Information Technology); **Regional and Town Planning** (Regional Planning; Town Planning)

Degrees and Diplomas: *Sarjana (S1)*
Last Updated: 29/04/10

KARO UNIVERSITY

Universitas Karo
Jalan Letjen Djamin Ginting 41, Kabanjahe, 22151 Sumatera Utara
Tel: +62(628) 20-248
Fax: +62(628) 20-248
EMail: univ.karo@yahoo.com

Rector: Meneth Ginting

Ketua: Sehat Keloko

Faculties
Agriculture (Agricultural Engineering; Agriculture; Agronomy; Plant and Crop Protection; Plant Pathology) *Dean*: Serengena Br. Karo; **Economics** (Development Studies; Economics; Management) *Dean*: Mananti Sembiring; **Educational Science and Teacher Training** (Civics; Educational Sciences; Mathematics Education; Natural Sciences; Social Sciences; Teacher Training) *Dean*: Heryanto; **Engineering** (Civil Engineering; Engineering; Engineering Management; Industrial Management) *Dean*: Hendri Ginting; **Law** (Law) *Dean*: Beritana Bangun

History: Founded 1986.

Fees: (Rupiahs): 850,000 per annum

Degrees and Diplomas: *Sarjana (S1)*

Libraries: 6,175 vols
Last Updated: 16/01/09

KARTINI UNIVERSITY

Universitas Kartini
Jalan Raya Nginden 19-23, Surabaya, Jawa Timur
Tel: +62(31) 594-4462
Fax: +62(31) 594-1954

Rector: Eman Ramelan

Ketua: Hendratno Darmosewoyo

Faculties
Agriculture (Agronomy); **Economics** (Management); **Engineering** (Industrial Engineering); **Law** (Law)

History: Founded 1982.

Fees: (Rupiahs): 360,000 per annum

Degrees and Diplomas: *Sarjana (S1)*

Libraries: 1,498 vols
Last Updated: 16/01/09

KEBANGSAAN UNIVERSITY

Universitas Kebangsaan
Jalan Terusan Halimun 37, Bandung, 40263 Jawa Barat
Tel: +62(22) 730-1987 +62(22) 972-1999
Fax: +62(22) 730-3088 +62(22) 9344-3452
EMail: univkebangsaan@yahoo.com
Website: http://www.universitaskebangsaan.ac.id/

Rektor: Suroso Iman Zadjuli

Ketua: Prabowo Subianto

Faculties
Computer Science and Information Systems (Computer Science; Information Technology); **Industrial Technology** (Computer Engineering; Electrical Engineering; Industrial Engineering; Mechanical Engineering); **Planning and Civil Engineering** (Architecture and Planning; Civil Engineering; Engineering; Environmental Engineering); **Social Sciences and Literature** (Communication Studies; English; Social Sciences)

History: Founded 1985 as Institut Teknologi Adityawarman. Acquired present status and title 2002.

Degrees and Diplomas: *Sarjana (S1)*

Libraries: 2,458 titles
Last Updated: 22/07/11

KEDIRI NUSANTARA PGRI UNIVERSITY

Universitas Nusantara PGRI Kediri
Jalan KH. A. Dahlan 76, Mojoroto, Kediri, 64112 Jawa Timur
Tel: +62(354) 771-503
Fax: +62(354) 771-576
EMail: admin@unpkediri.ac.id
Website: http://www.unpkediri.ac.id

Rector: Samari

Ketua: H. Moeljadi

Programmes
Accountancy (Accountancy); **Animal Husbandry**; **Biology** (Biology); **Economics** (Economics); **Engineering**; **English** (English); **Guidance And Counselling**; **History**; **Indonesian Language and Literature Education**; **Information Systems** (Information Technology); **Information Technology** (Information Technology); **Management** (Management); **Mathematics Education**; **Nursing** (Nursing); **Pancasila and Civic Education** (Civics; Government); **Physical Education, Health And Recreation**; **Preschool Education** (Preschool Education); **Primary Education**

History: Founded 1977 as Institut Keguruan dan Ilmu Pendidikan (IKIP) PGRI Kediri (Institute of Teacher Training and Educational Science Kediri). Acquired present title 2006.

Fees: (Rupiahs): 1,012,000 per annum

Degrees and Diplomas: *Sarjana (S1)*

Libraries: 7,016 vols

Last Updated: 22/04/10

KEDIRI UNIVERSITY

Universitas Kadiri
Jalan Selomangleng 1, Kediri, Jawa Timur
Tel: +62(354) 771-649
Fax: +62(354) 773-032
EMail: univkadiri@unik-kediri.ac.id
Website: http://www.unik-kediri.ac.id

Rektor: Djoko Rahardjo EMail: rektor@unik-kediri.ac.id

Faculties
Agriculture (Agricultural Business; Agricultural Economics; Agricultural Engineering; Agriculture; Agronomy); **Economics** (Development Studies; Economics; Management); **Engineering** (Civil Engineering; Computer Engineering; Engineering); **Law** (Administrative Law; Civil Law; Commercial Law; International Law; Islamic Law; Labour Law; Law; Political Sciences; Private Law); **Social and Political Sciences** (Accountancy; Administration; Anthropology; Civics; Demography and Population; Economics; English; Ethics; Information Management; Law; Logic; Mathematics and Computer Science; Political Sciences; Public Administration; Sociology; Statistics)

History: Founded 1980.

Degrees and Diplomas: *Sarjana (S1)*; *Magister (S2)*: Administration; Management; Law

Libraries: 4,524 vols

Last Updated: 28/06/11

KEJUANGAN '45 UNIVERSITY OF JAKARTA

Universitas Kejuangan 45 Jakarta
Jalan Dewi Sartika 307-308, Jakarta, 13630 DKI Jakarta
Tel: +62(21) 809-7771
Fax: +62(21) 809-0822

Rector: Himawan Soetanto

Vice-Rector: Gimbal Doloksaribu

Programmes
Business Administration; **Engineering** (Electrical Engineering; Engineering; Information Technology); **Government**; **Indonesian**

Degrees and Diplomas: *Sarjana (S1)*; *Magister (S2)*

Last Updated: 30/04/10

KHAIRUN UNIVERSITY

Universitas Khairun
Jalan Bandara Babullah, Ternate, 97728 Maluku
Tel: +62(921) 311-0901
Fax: +62(921) 311-0901
EMail: univkhairun_tte@yahoo.co.id

Rector: Rivai Umar

Ketua: H. M. Jusuf Abdulrahman

Faculties
Agriculture (Agriculture; Agronomy; Fishery; Natural Resources) *Dean*: Suryati Tjokrodiningrat; **Economics** (Development Studies; Economics; Management) *Dean*: Hasanuddin; **Educational Science and Teacher Training** (Art Education; Biology; Civics; Economics; English; Humanities and Social Science Education; Indonesian; Literature; Mathematics Education; Modern Languages; Physics; Primary Education; Science Education) *Dean*: Hamid Ismail; **Engineering** (Civil Engineering; Electrical and Electronic Engineering; Marine Engineering; Mechanical Engineering) *Dean*: Abjan Sofyan; **Law** *Dean*: Juhdi Taslim

History: Founded 1964. A private institution under the supervision of the Department of Education and Culture.

Academic Year: July to June (July-December; January-June)

Admission Requirements: Secondary school certificate (Sekolah Lanjutan Tinagkat Atas, SLTA) or equivalent

Fees: (Rupiahs): 350,000 per annum

Main Language(s) of Instruction: Indonesian (excludes English Department)

Degrees and Diplomas: *Sarjana (S1)*

Special Facilities: Biological Garden

Libraries: 6,106 vols

Last Updated: 19/01/09

KLABAT UNIVERSITY

Universitas Klabat (UNKLAB)
Jalan Airmadidi, Manado, 95371 Sulawesi Utara
Tel: +62(431) 891-035
Fax: +62(431) 891-036
Website: http://www.unklab.ac.id

Rector: Tommy. A. Mambu

Ketua: R. Kesaniya

Academies
Secretarial Studies (Secretarial Studies)

Faculties
Agriculture; **Computer Science**; **Economics**; **Educational Science and Teacher Training**; **Philosophy**

History: Founded 1965.

Fees: (Rupiahs): 1.9m. per annum

Accrediting Agencies: Accrediting Association of Seventh-day Adventist Schools, Colleges and Universities

Degrees and Diplomas: *Diploma*: 3 yrs; *Sarjana (S1)*

Libraries: 18,247 vols

Last Updated: 26/02/10

KRIDA WACANA CHRISTIAN UNIVERSITY

Universitas Kristen Krida Wacana (UKRIDA)
Jalan Tanjung Duren Raya 4, Jakarta, 11470 DKI Jakarta
Tel: +62(21) 566-6952
Fax: +62(21) 566-6956
EMail: puspelti@ukrida.ac.id
Website: http://www.ukrida.ac.id

Rector: Aristarchus Sukarto

Vice-Rector: Mina Sulastri

Departments
Management (Educational Administration; Finance; Management; Marketing)

Faculties
Economics (Accountancy; Management); **Engineering** (Civil Engineering; Electrical Engineering; Industrial Engineering); **Information Technology**; **Medicine** (Medicine); **Psychology** (Psychology)

History: Founded 1967 by the Indonesian Christian Church in Synod Region, West Java. A private institution under the supervision of the Department of Education and Culture.

Academic Year: August to July (August-January; February-July)

Admission Requirements: High school certificate (Sekolah Menengah Atas, SMA)

Fees: (Rupiahs): 3,737,500 per semester

Main Language(s) of Instruction: Indonesian

Degrees and Diplomas: *Sarjana (S1)*: 4 yrs; *Magister (S2)*: 2 yrs

Student Services: Academic counselling, Canteen, Employment services, Foreign student adviser, Health services, Language programs, Sports facilities

Libraries: 19,120 vols

Publications: Jurnal Akuntansi Krida Wacana, Publication of the Faculty of Economics *(quarterly)*; Jurnal Manajemen Krida Wacana, Publication of the Faculty of Economics *(quarterly)*; Meditek FK Journal, Publication of the Faculty of Medicine *(quarterly)*; Teknokrida, Publication of the Faculty of Engineering *(quarterly)*

Last Updated: 09/03/10

KRISNADWIPAYANA UNIVERSITY

Universitas Krisnadwipayana (UNKRIS)

PO Box 7774 JAT CM, Jakarta, 13077 DKI Jakarta
Tel: +62(21) 846-2229 +62(21) 846-2231
Fax: +62(21) 846-2461
EMail: humas@unkris.ac.id
Website: http://www.unkris.ac.id

Rector: Lodewijk Gultom

Ketua: Iman Santoso

Faculties
Administration *Dean*: Jack Sidabutar; **Economics** *(I) Dean*: Abdul Rivai; **Engineering**; **Law** *Dean*: Lodewik Gultom

Programmes
Administration *(Postgraduate)* (Administration) *Head*: Ari Senduperdana; **Management** *(Postgraduate)* (Management) *Head*: Prista Tarigan; **Postgraduate Studies** *(Postgraduate)* (Administration; Law; Management) *Head*: Sunaryati Hartono; **Town and Urban Planning** *(Postgraduate) Head*: Budi Tjahyadi

History: Founded 1952. A private institution under the supervision of the Department of National Education. Acquired present status 1956.

Fees: (Rupiahs): 2.8m. per annum

Main Language(s) of Instruction: Indonesian

Degrees and Diplomas: *Sarjana (S1) (SE; SH; ST; S.Sos)*: 4 yrs; *Magister (S2) (MM; MH; MT; M.Si)*: 2 yrs

Student Services: Academic counselling, Canteen, Employment services, Health services, Language programs, Nursery care, Social counselling, Sports facilities

Libraries: 100,004 vols

Last Updated: 30/04/10

KUNINGAN UNIVERSITY

Universitas Kuningan

Jalan Pramuka 67, Kuningan, 45512 Jawa Barat
Tel: +62(232) 874-824
Website: http://www.uniku.ac.id

Rector: Iskandar

Ketua: Uri Syam

Programmes
Agriculture (Forestry); **Biology**; **Business Administration**; **Economics** (Economics); **English** (English); **Indonesian** (Indonesian; Literature; Native Language); **Information Technology** (Information Technology)

Degrees and Diplomas: *Sarjana (S1)*; *Magister (S2)*

Last Updated: 30/04/10

KUPANG PGRI UNIVERSITY

Universitas PGRI Kupang

Jalan Anggaur No. 10 Naikoten I, Kupang,
Nusa Tenggara Timur
Tel: +62(380) 821-824
Fax: +62(380) 821-824
EMail: pgrintt@yahoo.com

Rector: Charles Manu

Ketua: Sulaiman Radja

Faculties
Agriculture *Dean*: Riwu Kaito; **Economics** *Dean*: P.Ch. Mauko; **Law** (Law) *Dean*: Klas; **Mathematics** *Dean*: Frans Kia Duan; **Teacher Trainers Education** (Educational and Student Counselling; English; Indonesian; Literature; Physical Education; Teacher Trainers Education) *Dean*: L. Adoe

Degrees and Diplomas: *Sarjana (S1)*

Last Updated: 21/01/09

KUTAI KARTANEGARA UNIVERSITY TENGGARONG

Universitas Kutai Kartanegara Tenggarong (UNIKARTA)

PO Box 133, Jalan Gurung Kombeng 27, Tenggarong, 75514
Kalimantan Timur
Tel: +62(541) 661-822 +62(541) 661-821
EMail: baak_unikarta@yahoo.com
Website: http://unikarta-tenggarong.net

Rector: Aswin Tel: +62(541) 661-041, Fax: +62(541) 661-030

Ketua: Teguh Budiharso

Faculties
Agriculture (Agricultural Business; Agriculture; Agronomy); **Economics** (Economics; Management); **Educational Science and Teacher Training** (Curriculum; Educational Sciences; Educational Technology; English; Teacher Training); **Engineering**; **Islamic Studies** (Islamic Studies); **Law** (Law); **Social and Political Sciences** (Government; Political Sciences; Public Administration; Social Sciences)

Programmes
Postgraduate

History: Founded 1984.

Governing Bodies: Yayasan Kutai Kartanega; Academic Council; Kutai District Government

Main Language(s) of Instruction: Indonesian, English, Arabic

Accrediting Agencies: Higher Education National Accrediting Board, Department of National Education

Degrees and Diplomas: *Diploma*: 3 yrs; *Sarjana (S1)*: 5 yrs; *Magister (S2)*. Also Ahli Madya Tehnik in Geological Engineering, 3 yrs

Student Services: Canteen, Language programs, Sports facilities

Student Residential Facilities: Yes

Libraries: Main Library, 3,745 vols

Last Updated: 09/03/10

LAKIDENDE UNIVERSITY OF UNAHAA

Universitas Lakidende Unahaa

Jalan Sultan Hasanuddin 234, Unahaa, 93461 Sulawesi Tenggara
Tel: +62(408) 21-777
Fax: +62(408) 21-777
EMail: universitaslakidende@yahoo.com.au

Rector: Gusarmin Sofyan

Ketua: H. A. Razak Porosi

Faculties

Administration (Administration; Government); **Agriculture** (Agricultural Economics; Agriculture; Agronomy); **Economics** (Economics; Management); **Educational Sciences** (English; Indonesian; Literature); **Engineering** (Civil Engineering; Engineering)

History: Founded 1996.

Fees: (Rupiahs): 1m. per annum

Degrees and Diplomas: *Sarjana (S1)*
Last Updated: 20/01/09

LAMONGAN ISLAMIC UNIVERSITY

Universitas Islam Lamongan
Jalan Veteran No. 53 A, Lamongan, 62213 Jawa Timur
Tel: +62(322) 322-158
Fax: +62(322) 324-706
EMail: pr1@unisla.ac.id
Website: http://www.unisla.ac.id

Rector: Achmad Mudlor

Vice-Rector I: Bambang Eko Muljono EMail: pr_1@unisla.ac.id

Faculties

Agriculture (Agricultural Business; Animal Husbandry; Food Science; Nutrition); **Economics** (Accountancy; Economics; Management); **Education and Teacher Training** (Education; English; Foreign Languages Education; Teacher Training); **Engineering** (Civil Engineering; Electrical Engineering; Engineering); **Fishery** (Aquaculture; Fishery; Natural Resources); **Islamic Studies** (Islamic Studies); **Law** (Law)

Programmes

Midwifery (Midwifery)

History: Founded 1991.

Degrees and Diplomas: *Sarjana (S1)*; *Magister (S2)*: Islamic Studies; Law; Management
Last Updated: 21/07/11

LANCANG KUNING UNIVERSITY

Universitas Lancang Kuning
Jalan Yos Sudarso KM. 8, Rumbai, Pekanbaru, Riau
Tel: +62(761) 53-108
Fax: +62(761) 52-248
EMail: info@unilak.ac.id
Website: http://www.unilak.ac.id

Rector: Sudi Fahmi
Ketua: Ismail Suko

Faculties

Agriculture (Agricultural Business; Agricultural Engineering; Agriculture; Agronomy); **Arts and Humanities** (English; Indonesian; Literature; Modern Languages); **Computer Science** (Computer Science; Information Technology); **Economics** (Accountancy; Economics; Management); **Education and Teacher Training** (Biology; Education; English; Foreign Languages Education; Science Education; Teacher Training); **Engineering** (Architecture; Civil Engineering; Electrical Engineering; Engineering; Structural Architecture); **Forestry** (Forest Management; Forestry); **Law** (Law); **Social and Political Sciences** (Administration; Business Administration; Government; Library Science; Public Administration)

History: Founded 1982.

Degrees and Diplomas: *Sarjana (S1)*
Last Updated: 25/07/11

LANGLANGBUANA UNIVERSITY

Universitas Langlangbuana
Jalan Karapitan 116, Bandung,
40261 Jawa Barat
Tel: +62(22) 421-8085
Fax: +62(22) 423-0601
EMail: info.unla@unla.ac.id
Website: http://www.unla.ac.id

Rector: Ali Hanafiah EMail: rektoriat@unla.ac.id

Vice-Rector, Student Affairs: Rusly ZA Nasution

Vice-Rector, Administration and Finance: Tatang Sugandi

Faculties

Economics (Accountancy; Economics; Management; Taxation); **Education and Teacher Training** (Economics; Education; Humanities and Social Science Education; Mathematics Education; Teacher Training); **Engineering** (Architecture; Civil Engineering; Computer Engineering; Electrical Engineering; Engineering; Industrial Engineering; Structural Architecture); **Law** (Civil Law; Constitutional Law; Criminal Law; Law); **Social and Political Sciences** (Administration; Communication Studies; Government; Police Studies; Political Sciences; Public Administration; Social Sciences; Social Welfare)

Programmes

Postgraduate Studies (Business Administration; Computer Networks; Criminal Law; E-Business/Commerce; Government; Information Technology; International Law; Law; Management; Political Sciences; Public Administration)

History: Founded 1982.

Degrees and Diplomas: *Diploma*: 3 yrs; *Sarjana (S1)*; *Magister (S2)*: Government Science; Information Technology; Legal Studies; Management

Libraries: 6,075 vols
Last Updated: 25/07/11

LUMAJANG UNIVERSITY

Universitas Lumajang (UNILA)
Jalan Musi No. 12, Lumajang,
67352 Jawa Timur
Tel: +62(334) 882-769

Rector: Satuki
Ketua: Rochani

Faculties

Administration (Public Administration); **Agriculture** (Agricultural Economics); **Law** (Law)

History: Founded 1983. Acquired present status 1966.

Academic Year: September to August (September-January; February-June; July- August)

Admission Requirements: High School Certificate (Ijazah and Surat Tanda Tamat Belajar (STTB) of 3 years)

Fees: (Rupiahs): 1m. per annum except for Medicine, 3m.

Main Language(s) of Instruction: Indonesian

International Co-operation: Japan; USA; ASEAN countries; Australia; China; Korea; Canada; France and European Union countries

Accrediting Agencies: National Accrediting Agency, Badan Akreditasi Nasional (BAN)

Degrees and Diplomas: *Sarjana (S1)*

Student Services: Academic counselling, Canteen, Employment services, Foreign student adviser, Health services, Language programs, Nursery care, Sports facilities

Student Residential Facilities: Yes (limited)

Libraries: yes (vols; journals; CD; online library)

Publications: Agrotoropika, Crop Sciences *(biennially)*; Sains & Teknologi *(biennially)*; Socioeconomica *(biennially)*; Tanah Tropika, Soil Sciences *(biennially)*

Press or Publishing House: Reaksi, Unila Gazette, Teknokra
Last Updated: 20/01/09

MA CHUNG UNIVERSITY

Universitas Ma Chung
Jalan Villa Puncak Tidar 01, Malang, 65151 Jawa Timur
Tel: +62(341) 550-171
Fax: +62(341) 550-175
EMail: info@machung.ac.id
Website: http://www.machung.ac.id/

Rector: Leenawaty Limantara
EMail: leenawaty.limantara@machung.ac.id

Vice-Rector: Stefanus Yufra Menahen Taneo
EMail: stefanus.yufra@machung.ac.id

Programmes

Accounting (Accountancy); **English** (English); **Industrial Engineering** (Industrial Engineering); **Information Technology** (Information Technology); **Management** (Management)

Degrees and Diplomas: *Sarjana (S1)*

Libraries: Yes

Academic Staff *2010-2011*	MEN	WOMEN	TOTAL
FULL-TIME	34	24	**58**
PART-TIME	13	2	**15**
STAFF WITH DOCTORATE			
FULL-TIME	4	1	**5**
PART-TIME	1	1	**2**
Student Numbers *2010-2011*			
All (Foreign Included)	577	469	**1,046**

Last Updated: 26/10/10

MADAKO TOLI-TOLI UNIVERSITY

Universitas Madako Toli-Toli
Jalan Madako No. 01, Tolitoli, 94514 Sulawesi Tengah
Tel: +62(453)21-582
Fax: +62(453)21-582

Direktor: Iskandar A. Nasir

Ketua: Nursidah K. Batilan

Faculties

Agriculture (Agriculture; Cattle Breeding; Harvest Technology) *Dean*: Agus Burhan; **Animal Husbandry** *Dean*: Hardiyan; **Education** (Education; Educational Technology; English) *Dean*: Zainal Daud; **Engineering** (Architecture and Planning; Civil Engineering; Engineering) *Dean*: Santoso; **Fishery** *Dean*: Gusman; **Law** (Administrative Law; Law) *Dean*: Sinyo Mokodompit; **Social and Political Sciences** (Government; Political Sciences; Public Administration; Social Sciences) *Dean*: M.T. Masyhur

Degrees and Diplomas: *Sarjana (S1)*
Last Updated: 20/01/09

MADURA UNIVERSITY

Universitas Madura (UNIRA)
Jalan Raya Panglegur KM. 35, Pamekasan, 69300 Jawa Timur
Tel: +62(324) 322-231
Fax: +62(324) 327-418
Website: http://www.unira-pmk.net

Rector: H. Amiril

Ketua: Kadarisman Sastrodiwirjo

Faculties

Administration (Administration; Government); **Agriculture** (Agriculture; Animal Husbandry); **Economics** (Accountancy; Economics; Management); **Educational Science and Teacher Training** (Art Education; Curriculum; Educational Sciences; Educational Technology; Indonesian; Literature; Mathematics Education; Modern Languages; Science Education); **Engineering** (Civil Engineering; Computer Engineering; Engineering; Environmental Engineering) *Dean*: Wahyu Yuwana; **Law** (Law)

History: Founded 1978. A private institution under the supervision of the Department of Education and Culture.

Fees: (Rupiahs): 480,000 per annum

Degrees and Diplomas: *Sarjana (S1)*

Libraries: 6,582 vols
Last Updated: 20/01/09

MAHAPUTRA MUHAMMAD YAMIN UNIVERSITY

Universitas Mahaputra Muhammad Yamin
Jalan Raya Koto Baru 7, Kodya Solok, 27321 Sumatera Barat
Tel: +62(755) 20-565

Rector: Syafri Syafei

Vice-Rector: Syahro Ali Akbar

Faculties

Agriculture; **Economics**; **Educational Science and Teacher Training**; **Engineering**; **Law**

Further Information: Branch in Koto Baru

History: Founded 1984.

Fees: (Rupiahs): 720,000 per annum

Degrees and Diplomas: *Sarjana (S1)*

Libraries: 4,063 vols
Last Updated: 30/04/10

MAHASARASWATI DENPASAR UNIVERSITY

Universitas Mahasaraswati Denpasar
Jalan Kamboja N° 11A, Denpasar, 80233 Bali
Tel: +62(361) 227-019
EMail: info@unmas.ac.id
Website: http://unmas.ac.id

Rector: Tjokorda Istri Sri Ramaswati

Ketua: I. Gusti Gede Anom

Faculties

Agriculture (Agricultural Economics; Agriculture; Agronomy; Plant Pathology) *Dean*: Nyoman Raka; **Dentistry** (Dentistry); **Economics** (Accountancy; Development Studies; Economics; Management); **Educational Science and Teacher Training** (Art Education; Biology; Educational and Student Counselling; Educational Sciences; Educational Technology; English; History; Humanities and Social Science Education; Indonesian; Literature; Mathematics Education; Modern Languages; Science Education; Teacher Training); **Engineering** (Civil Engineering; Engineering; Rural Planning; Town Planning); **Law** (Law)

History: Founded 1961. A private institution under the supervision of the Department of Education and Culture.

Academic Year: August to July (August-January; February to July)

Admission Requirements: Secondary school certificate (Sekolah Menengah Atas, SMA) or equivalent, and entrance examination

Fees: (Rupiahs): 600,000 per annum

Main Language(s) of Instruction: Indonesian, English

Degrees and Diplomas: *Diploma*: 3 yrs; *Sarjana (S1)*: 4 yrs

Special Facilities: Language Laboratory

Libraries: Central Library, 7,645 vols

Publications: Mahawidya *(quarterly)*
Last Updated: 10/02/09

MAHASARASWATI MATARAM UNIVERSITY

Universitas Mahasaraswati Mataram
Jalan Kali Brantas Karang Sukun, Mataram, 83121 Nusa Tenggara Barat
Tel: +62(370) 623-785

Rector: Putu Karismawan

Ketua: Ida Made Semadi

Faculties

Agriculture (Agricultural Business; Agriculture) *Dean*: Made Suma Wedastra; **Economics** *Dean*: Nyoman Karyawan; **Engineering** (Civil Engineering; Engineering) *Dean*: Gde Sudantha; **Law** (Law) *Dean*: Gede Kusmayadi

History: Founded1981.

Fees: (Rupiahs): 920,000 per annum

Degrees and Diplomas: *Sarjana (S1)*

Libraries: 1,594 vols
Last Updated: 20/01/09

MAHENDRADATA UNIVERSITY

Universitas Mahendradatta
Jalan Ken Arok 12, Denpasar, 80236 Bali
Tel: +62(361) 434-827

Rector: Jimmy Z. Soputan (1987-)

Ketua: Ayu Suwitri Wedastera Suyasa

Faculties

Administration (Public Administration) *Dean*: Gst Nyoman Oka; **Industrial Engineering** (Industrial Engineering) *Dean*: H. Nurianto; **Law** (Law) *Dean*: Wayan Wisadnya; **Management** (Management) *Dean*: Ni Wayan Suartini

Further Information: Also a Law, Social and Cultural Advisory Bureau

History: Founded 1963 as Universitas Maheen. Acquired present title 1984. A State institution under the jurisdiction of the Department of Education and Culture.

Governing Bodies: Board of Advisors

Academic Year: July to June

Admission Requirements: Secondary school certificate (Sekolah Menengah Atas, SMA) and entrance examination

Fees: (Rupiahs): 600,000 per annum

Main Language(s) of Instruction: Indonesian

Degrees and Diplomas: *Sarjana (S1)*: 4 yrs; *Magister (S2)*

Libraries: 5,989 vols

Publications: Scientific Bulletin/Journal *(quarterly)*

Press or Publishing House: Penerbitan Pusat UNMAR (Central Publicity Mahaendradatta University)

Last Updated: 20/01/09

MAJALENGKA UNIVERSITY

Universitas Majalengka

Jalan KH Abdul Halim 103, Majalengka, 45418 Jawa Barat

Tel: +62(233)281-496

Fax: +62(233)281-496

Rector: Abdul Yunus

Ketua: H. Wardja

Programmes

Agriculture (Agricultural Business; Agricultural Engineering; Animal Husbandry); **Business Administration**; **Engineering** (Civil Engineering; Engineering; Industrial Engineering); **English** (English; Modern Languages); **Indonesian**; **Information Technology**; **Physical Education, Health and Recreation** (Leisure Studies; Parks and Recreation; Physical Education; Sports); **Social Sciences** (Communication Studies; International Relations)

Degrees and Diplomas: *Sarjana (S1)*; *Magister (S2)*

Last Updated: 30/04/10

MAKASSAR '45 UNIVERSITY

Universitas '45 Makassar

Jalan Urip Sumoharjo Km. 4, Makassar, Sulawesi Selatan

Tel: +62(411) 452-901 +62(411) 452-789

Fax: +62(411) 454-628

Website: http://www.univ45.ac.id/

Rector: Abu Hamid (2007-)

Vice-Rector Academic: Abduh Natsir

Faculties

Agriculture (Agricultural Economics; Agriculture; Agronomy; Animal Husbandry; Aquaculture; Fishery; Food Science) *Head*: Mir Alam; **Arts and Humanities** (English; Indonesian; Literature) *Dean*: Himan; **Economics** (Development Studies; Economics; Public Administration) *Dean*: Thamrin Abduh; **Engineering** (Architecture and Planning; Chemical Engineering; Civil Engineering; Information Management) *Dean*: Natsir Abduh; **Law** (Law) *Dean*: Ruslan Renggang; **Medicine** (Medicine); **Political and Social Sciences** (Political Sciences; Sociology) *Dean*: Syamsuddin Maldun

Last Updated: 05/01/09

MAKASSAR INSTITUTE OF ARTS

Institut Kesenian Makassar

Jalan Sungai Saddang 15, Makassar, 90142 Sulawesi Selatan

Tel: +62(411) 12345

EMail: kampusikm@gmail.com; infoikm@yahoo.com

Programmes

Cosmetology; **Dance**; **Interior Design**; **Music**; **Photography**; **Television and Film** (Cinema and Television); **Visual Communication Design** (Graphic Arts; Graphic Design; Visual Arts)

Degrees and Diplomas: *Sarjana (S1)*

Last Updated: 22/04/10

MALAHAYATI UNIVERSITY

Universitas Malahayati (UMALA)

Jalan Pramuka 27, Kemeling, Bandar Lampung, 35153 Lampung

Tel: +62(721) 271-112

Fax: +62(721) 271-119

EMail: uni_mal@telkom.net

Website: http://www.univ-malahayati.ac.id/

Rector: Mustofa Usman

Ketua: H. Rusli Bintang

Faculties

Economics (Accountancy; Economics; Management) *Dean*: Marsum Ahmadi; **Engineering** (Civil Engineering; Engineering; Environmental Engineering; Industrial Engineering; Industrial Management; Mechanical Engineering) *Dean*: Agusnardi Basyid; **Medicine** (Medicine; Nursing; Public Health)

History: Founded 1994.

Governing Bodies: Koordinator Perguruan Tinggi Swasta Wilayah II - Palembang

Academic Year: September to August

Admission Requirements: Senior high school certificate (Sekolah Menengah Umum)

Fees: (Rupiahs): 3m. per semester

Degrees and Diplomas: *Diploma*; *Sarjana (S1)*: 4-7 yrs

Student Services: Academic counselling, Canteen, Cultural centre, Employment services, Health services, Language programs, Nursery care, Sports facilities

Special Facilities: Observatory. Laboratories, including Language Laboratory

Libraries: yes

Last Updated: 20/01/09

MALANG INSTITUTE OF AGRICULTURE

Institut Pertanian Malang

Jalan Soekarno-Hatta, Malang, 65142 Jawa Timur

Tel: +62(341) 495-541

Fax: +62(341) 485-539

EMail: webmaster@ipm.ac.id

Rector: R.B. Ainurasyid

Vice-Rector: Hasyim

Faculties

Agricultural Business (Agricultural Business; Agricultural Economics; Agriculture); **Agricultural Technology** (Agricultural Engineering); **Forestry** (Forestry)

History: Founded 1984.

Degrees and Diplomas: *Sarjana (S1)*

Libraries: 4,275 titles

Last Updated: 11/07/11

MALANG NATIONAL INSTITUTE OF TECHNOLOGY

Institut Teknologi Nasional Malang (ITN MALANG)

Jalan Bendungan Sigura-gura 2, Jalan Raya Karanglo Km-2, Malang, 65145 Jawa Timur
Tel: +62(341) 551-951 +62(341) 551-431
Fax: +62(341) 553-015
EMail: humas@itn.ac.id; itn@itn.ac.id
Website: http://www.itn.ac.id

Rector: Djiwo Soeparno
Tel: +62(341) 551-431 EMail: rektor@itn.ac.id

Vice-Rector for Administration and Finance: Mulyadi Lalu
EMail: wr1@itn.ac.id

Faculties

Civil Engineering and Planning (Architecture; Civil Engineering; Construction Engineering; Earth Sciences; Environmental Engineering; Regional Planning; Structural Architecture; Town Planning); **Industrial Technology** (Chemical Engineering; Electrical Engineering; Engineering; Industrial Engineering; Information Technology)

Programmes

Postgraduate Studies (Civil Engineering; Industrial Engineering)

History: Founded 1969 as college of Technology. Acquired present status and title 1981.

Admission Requirements: Senior High school certificate (Ijasah)

Main Language(s) of Instruction: Indonesian

Accrediting Agencies: National Accreditation Board

Degrees and Diplomas: *Diploma*: 3 1/2 yrs; *Sarjana (S1)*: 4 1/2-6 yrs; *Magister (S2)*: Civil Engineering; Industrial Engineering, a further 2-4 yrs

Student Services: Academic counselling, Canteen, Cultural centre, Employment services, Handicapped facilities, Health services, Language programs, Sports facilities

Student Residential Facilities: None

Special Facilities: Architecture and Urban Planning Studios

Libraries: Central Library, c. 80,000 vols

Publications: Jurnal IPTEK *(3 per annum)*

Press or Publishing House: HRO

Academic Staff *2009-2010*: Total: c. 170

Student Numbers *2009-2010*: Total: c. 4,300

Last Updated: 22/06/11

MARANATHA CHRISTIAN UNIVERSITY

Universitas Kristen Maranatha

Jalan Prof. Drg. Suria Sumantri 65, Bandung, 40164 West Java
Tel: +62(22) 201-2186 +62(22) 200-3450
Fax: +64(22) 201-5154
EMail: humas@maranatha.edu
Website: http://www.maranatha.edu

Rector: Septoratno Siregar
Tel: +62(22) 200-3449 EMail: rektor@maranatha.edu

Vice-Rector I: Rudy Wawolumaja

Faculties

Arts and Humanities (Chinese; English; Japanese; Literature; Modern Languages); **Economics** (Accountancy; Economics; Information Technology; Management); **Engineering** (Civil Engineering; Computer Engineering; Electrical Engineering; Engineering; Industrial Engineering; Information Technology); **Fine Arts and Design** (Communication Arts; Design; Fine Arts; Interior Design; Visual Arts); **Information Technology** (Information Technology); **Law** (Commercial Law; Law; Notary Studies); **Medicine** (Anatomy; Biochemistry; Biology; Chemistry; Community Health; Dentistry; Forensic Medicine and Dentistry; Gynaecology and Obstetrics; Histology; Medicine; Microbiology; Neurology; Ophthalmology; Paediatrics; Parasitology; Pathology; Physiology; Public Health; Surgery); **Postgraduate Studies** (Business Administration; Management; Psychology); **Psychology** (Clinical Psychology; Developmental Psychology; Industrial and Organizational Psychology; Psychology; Psychotherapy; Social Psychology; Social Sciences)

Further Information: Also Teaching Hospital. Centre for Psychological Testing

History: Founded 1965. Supported by Synodes of GKP and GKI.

Governing Bodies: Yayasan Perguruan Tinggi Kristen Maranatha (YPTK)

Academic Year: September to August

Admission Requirements: High school certificate (Ijazah Sekolah Menengah Umum), or recognized foreign equivalent

Main Language(s) of Instruction: Indonesian

Accrediting Agencies: National Accreditation Board

Degrees and Diplomas: *Diploma (D3)*; *Sarjana (S1) (S3)*; *Magister (S2)*: Accountancy; Management; Psychology

Student Services: Academic counselling, Canteen, Employment services, Health services, Language programs, Social counselling, Sports facilities

Special Facilities: Theatre

Publications: Majalah Ilmiah Maranatha, Scientific and Social Paper *(quarterly)*

Last Updated: 25/07/11

MATARAM '45 UNIVERSITY

Universitas '45 Mataram

Jalan Imam Bonjol Tohpati, Cakranegara Utara -NTB, Mataram, Nusa Tenggara Barat
Tel: +62(370) 627-915

Rector: Sakdullah Hammid

Ketua: Alwan Widjaya

Faculties

Agriculture *Dean*: Pending D. Permana; **Civil Engineering** (Civil Engineering); **Fishery** (Fishery; Water Management); **Forestry** (Forest Management; Forest Products; Forestry); **Law** (Administrative Law; Law; Private Law; Public Law); **Social and Political Sciences**

History: Founded 1983 by '45 Struggler Foundation.

Fees: (Rupiahs): 600,000 per annum

Main Language(s) of Instruction: Indonesian

Accrediting Agencies: Higher Education of National Education Department

Degrees and Diplomas: *Diploma*: Forest Conservation, 3 yrs; *Sarjana (S1)*: 5 yrs

Student Services: Academic counselling, Canteen, Cultural centre, Employment services, Social counselling, Sports facilities

Special Facilities: Computer centre

Libraries: Central Library; libraries of the faculties, 4,025 vols

Last Updated: 06/01/09

MATHLA'UL ANWAR UNIVERSITY

Universitas Mathla'ul Anwar

Jalan Raya Labuan Km 23, Cikaliung Sodong Saketi, Pandeglang, 42273 Banten
Tel: +62(253) 401-307
Fax: +62(253) 401-307

Rektor: Herman Haeruman

Ketua: Irsyad Djuwaeli

Faculties

Economics (Economics); **Engineering** (Engineering); **Mathematics and Natural Sciences** (Mathematics; Natural Sciences); **Public Health** (Pharmacy; Public Health); **Social Sciences** (Communication Studies; Government; Information Management); **Teacher Training and Educational Sciences** (Indonesian; Mathematics Education; Modern Languages; Teacher Training)

History: Founded Sekolah Tinggi Ilmu Ekonomi Mathla'ul Anwar

Degrees and Diplomas: *Diploma*; *Sarjana (S1)*

Last Updated: 20/01/09

MAYJEN SUNGKONO UNIVERSITY

Universitas Mayjen Sungkono
Jalan Irian Jaya 4, Mojokerto, 61321 Jawa Timur
Tel: +62(321) 323-143
Website: http://unimas.ac.id

Rector: H. Tirtohadi

Ketua: H. Bagoes Sasmito

Faculties

Administration (Administration; Business Administration) *Dean*: F.G. Wahyana; **Agriculture** (Agricultural Business; Agricultural Economics; Agriculture) *Dean*: Trimurti; **Economics** (Business Administration; Economics; Management) *Dean*: H. Soetikno; **Law** (Law) *Dean*: Eka Darmono

Programmes

Midwifery (Midwifery)

History: Founded 1981.

Fees: (Rupiahs): 360,000 per annum

Degrees and Diplomas: *Sarjana (S1)*

Libraries: 1,584 vols

Last Updated: 20/01/09

MEDAN AREA UNIVERSITY

Universitas Medan Area (UMA)
Jalan Kolam 1, Medan, 20223 Sumatera Utara
Tel: +62(61) 820-1994
Fax: +62(61) 822-6331
EMail: uma001@indosat.net.id
Website: http://www.universitasmedanarea.com

Rector: Ali Ya'cub Matondang

Ketua: Siti Mariani Harahap

Faculties

Agriculture; **Biology**; **Economics**; **Engineering**; **Graduate Studies** (Agricultural Business; Law; Psychology; Public Administration); **Law** (Law); **Psychology** (Industrial and Organizational Psychology; Psychology); **Social and Political Sciences** (Administration; Communication Studies; Government; Journalism; Public Administration; Public Relations)

History: Founded 1983.

Admission Requirements: High school certificate (Ijazah, SMU;SMK)

Fees: (Rupiahs): 1m. per annum

Main Language(s) of Instruction: Indonesian

Degrees and Diplomas: *Sarjana (S1)*: 4-5 yrs; *Magister (S2)*

Student Services: Academic counselling, Canteen, Employment services, Health services, Nursery care, Sports facilities

Student Residential Facilities: Yes

Libraries: 16,052 Vols

Publications: Warta Universitaria *(quarterly)*

Press or Publishing House: UMA Press

Last Updated: 06/02/09

MEDAN INSTITUTE OF TECHNOLOGY

Institut Teknologi Medan (ITM)
Jalan Gedung Arca 52, Medan, 20217 Sumatera Utara
Tel: +62(61) 736-3771
Fax: +62(61) 734-7954
EMail: itm@itm.ac.id
Website: http://www.itm.ac.id

Rektor: Mastri Mahrizal EMail: masrimahrizal@yahoo.com

International Relations: Eka Onwardana
EMail: onwarda@yahoo.com

Faculties

Industrial Engineering (Chemical Engineering; Computer Science; Electrical Engineering; Engineering; Industrial Engineering); **Mining Engineering** (Geological Engineering; Mining Engineering); **Planning and Civil Engineering** (Architecture and Planning; Civil Engineering; Mechanical Engineering)

History: Founded 1963, acquired present status 1985.

Academic Year: July to June

Admission Requirements: Secondary school certificate (Sekolah Lajutan Atas, SLTA; Sekolah Menengah Atas, SMA)

Main Language(s) of Instruction: Indonesian

Accrediting Agencies: Badan Akreditasi Nasional (B.A.N)

Degrees and Diplomas: *Sarjana (S1) (ST)*: 4 1/2 yrs

Student Services: Academic counselling, Canteen, Employment services, Health services, Language programs, Social counselling, Sports facilities

Libraries: c. 4,200 vols

Publications: Saintek ITM *(quarterly)*

Academic Staff *2009-2010*: Total: c. 130

Student Numbers *2009-2010*: Total: c. 2,350

Last Updated: 22/06/11

MEGOU PAK TULANG BAWANG UNIVERSITY

Universitas Megou Pak Tulang Bawang
Jalan Lintas Timur, Tulang Bawang, Menggala, 79117 Lampung
Tel: +62(828) 757-2713
EMail: megoupaktb@yahoo.com

Rector: Ratu Betta Rudibyani

Ketua: Bupati Tulang Bawang

Programmes

Business Administration; **Engineering** (Agricultural Engineering; Civil Engineering; Electrical Engineering; Engineering; Industrial Engineering); **Information Technology**; **International Relations** (International Relations); **Law** (Law)

Degrees and Diplomas: *Sarjana (S1)*

Last Updated: 30/04/10

MERCU BUANA UNIVERSITY

Universitas Mercu Buana (UMB)
Jalan Raya Meruya Selatan, Kembangan, Jakarta Barat, 11650 DKI Jakarta
Tel: +62(21) 584-0816
Fax: +62(21) 584-0813
EMail: umb@mercubuana.ac.id
Website: http://www.mercubuana.ac.id

Rector: H. Suharyadi (1997-)

Ketua: H. Probosutedjo

Faculties

Agriculture (Agricultural Economics; Agriculture; Agronomy) *Dean*: Rachmad Soebiapradja; **Architecture and Town Planning** *Dean*: Zainal Abidin Shahab; **Business Administration** (Accountancy; Business Administration; Management) *Dean*: Hadri Mulya; **Industrial Engineering** (Computer Engineering; Electrical Engineering; Engineering; Industrial Engineering) *Dean*: Erry Rimawan; **Information Sciences** (Advertising and Publicity; Communication Studies; Information Sciences; Journalism; Public Relations) *Dean*: Henny S. Widyaningsih

Programmes

Management *(Master program)* (Management) *Director*: Laode Kamaluddin

History: Founded 1985. The Institution is based on the State philosophy of Pancasila (meaning Five Principles), 1945 Constitution of Republic Indonesia, and Tri Dharma Perguruan Tingg (the 3 services of the University, namely Teaching, Research and Community Service).

Admission Requirements: High school certificate, transcript and entrance examination

Accrediting Agencies: Badan Akreditasi Nasional

Degrees and Diplomas: *Sarjana (S1)*: 4-5 yrs (9 sem); *Magister (S2)*: a further 2 yrs

Student Services: Academic counselling, Canteen, Employment services, Health services, Language programs, Sports facilities

Student Residential Facilities: None

Special Facilities: Laboratories (Language, Photography, Industrial, Computer, etc). Architecture Studio

Libraries: Central Library

Publications: DIGNA, Research Tabloid *(quarterly)*; FORUM, Economics Tabloid *(quarterly)*; TAJUK, Agricultural Tabloid *(quarterly)*

Last Updated: 14/01/09

MERCU BUANA UNIVERSITY OF YOGYAKARTA

Universitas Mercu Buana Yogyakarta (UMBY)
Jalan Wates Km 10, Yogyakarta, 55753 Yogyakarta
Tel: +62(274) 798-212 +62(274) 795-802
Fax: +62(274) 798-213
Website: http://mercubuana-yogya.ac.id/

Rector: Djoko Wahyono

Ketua: Probosutedjo

Faculties

Agricultural Production Technology (Food Technology) *Dean*: Bisnu A. Yuliente; **Agriculture** (Agronomy; Animal Husbandry); **Economics** (Accountancy; Development Studies; Economics; Management) *Dean*: Hasim As'ari; **Engineering** (Electronic Engineering; Engineering) *Dean*: Sasongko F. Nadi; **Psychology** (Psychology) *Dean*: M. Masrun

History: Founded 1986 as Universitas Wangsa Manggala Di Yogyakarta (Wangsa Manggala University of Yogyakarta). Acquired present title 2008.

Governing Bodies: Wangsa Manggala Foundation

Academic Year: August to July (August-January; February-July)

Admission Requirements: High school certificate

Fees: (Rupiahs): 200,000 (US$: 21) per month

Main Language(s) of Instruction: Indonesian

Accrediting Agencies: Asia Foundation, Gadjah Mada University, Government

Degrees and Diplomas: *Sarjana (S1)*: 4-5 yrs; *Magister (S2)*: Psychology

Student Services: Academic counselling, Canteen, Health services, Language programs, Sports facilities

Special Facilities: Experimental Farm

Libraries: c. 25,000 vols; periodical subscriptions

Publications: Buletin Pertanian dan Peternakan, Agriculture *(biannually)*; Insight, Psychology *(biannually)*; Psikonomi, Economics, Psychology *(biannually)*

Last Updated: 09/03/10

MERDEKA UNIVERSITY MADIUN

Universitas Merdeka Madiun
Jalan Serayu, Tromol Pos 12, Madiun, 63133 Jawa Timur
Tel: +62(351) 464-427
Fax: +62(351) 497-058
EMail: baa@unmer-madiun.ac.id
Website: http://www.unmer-madiun.ac.id

Rector: Suwito Sugiyanto

Ketua: H. Suhendro

Faculties

Agriculture (Agricultural Economics; Agricultural Engineering; Agriculture; Agronomy; Forest Management); **Economics** (Accountancy; Development Studies; Economics; Management); **Engineering** (Civil Engineering; Computer Engineering; Engineering; Mechanical Engineering); **Law** (Law); **Social and Political Sciences** (Administration; Communication Studies; Government; Political Sciences; Social Sciences)

History: Founded 1979. A private institution under the supervision of the Department of Education and Culture.

Fees: (Rupiahs): 300,000 per annum

Degrees and Diplomas: *Diploma*; *Sarjana (S1)*

Libraries: 6,891 vols

Last Updated: 20/01/09

MERDEKA UNIVERSITY MALANG

Universitas Merdeka Malang
Jalan Trs. Raya Dieng 62-64, Malang, 65146 Jawa Timur
Tel: +62(341) 568-395
Fax: +62(341) 564-994
EMail: webmaster@unmer.ac.id
Website: http://www.unmer.ac.id

Rector: Kridawati Sadhana

Ketua: Toegino Soekarno

Faculties

Economics (Accountancy; Banking; Development Studies; Economics; Finance; Management); **Engineering** (Architecture; Civil Engineering; Electrical Engineering; Engineering; Industrial Engineering; Mechanical Engineering); **Information Technology**; **Law** (Law); **Political and Social Sciences** (Business Administration; Communication Studies; Government; Political Sciences; Public Administration; Social Sciences); **Postgraduate** (Economics; Law; Management; Public Administration; Social Sciences; Social Studies); **Psychology** (Psychology)

History: Founded 1964.

Academic Year: February to September (February-March; August-September)

Admission Requirements: Secondary school certificate (Sekolah Menengah Atas, SMA) or senior high school certificate

Fees: (Rupiahs): 1.52m. per annum

Main Language(s) of Instruction: Indonesian

Degrees and Diplomas: *Diploma*; *Sarjana (S1)*; *Magister (S2)*; *Doktor (S3)*

Student Services: Academic counselling, Foreign student adviser, Foreign Studies Centre, Health services, Language programs, Sports facilities

Libraries: 39,385 vols

Publications: Biocure *(annually)*

Last Updated: 21/01/09

MERDEKA UNIVERSITY PASURUAN

Universitas Merdeka Pasuruan
Jalan Ir. H. Juanda 68, Pasuruan, Jawa Timur
Tel: +62(343) 421-783
Fax: +62(343) 413-619
EMail: merdekapas@telkom.net; unmerpass@telkom.net

Rector: S. Pramono

Ketua: H. Sunarto

Faculties

Agriculture (Agricultural Engineering; Agriculture; Agronomy); **Economics** (Economics; Management); **Law** (Law)

History: Founded 1985.

Fees: (Rupiahs): 600,000 per annum

Degrees and Diplomas: *Sarjana (S1)*

Libraries: 2,805 vols

Last Updated: 10/02/09

MERDEKA UNIVERSITY PONOROGO

Universitas Merdeka Ponorogo
Jalan Pacar 30, Ponorogo
Tel: +62(352) 481-123
Fax: +62(352) 481-123
EMail: unmerpo@plasa.com

Rector: Suratno

Ketua: Nur Taslim

Faculties

Agriculture (Agriculture; Agronomy); **Law** (Law); **Social and Political Sciences** (Administration; Government; Political Sciences; Social Sciences)

History: Founded 1963.

Fees: (Rupiahs): 781,250 per annum

Degrees and Diplomas: *Sarjana (S1)*

Libraries: 2,875 vols
Last Updated: 21/01/09

MERDEKA UNIVERSITY SURABAYA

Universitas Merdeka Surabaya
Jalan Ketintang Madya VII, Surabaya, Jawa Timur
Tel: +62(31) 828-7318

Rector: Surti Yustiyanti

Ketua: Muchtar

Faculties
Agriculture (Agriculture; Agronomy); **Economics**; **Engineering** (Structural Architecture); **Law** (Law)

History: Founded 1984.

Fees: (Rupiahs): 400,000 per annum

Degrees and Diplomas: *Sarjana (S1)*

Libraries: 1,991 vols
Last Updated: 21/01/09

METHODIST UNIVERSITY OF INDONESIA

Universitas Methodist Indonesia
Jalan Hang Tuah 8, Medan, 20152 Sumatera Utara
Tel: +62(61) 453-6735 +62(61) 457-7670
Fax: +62(61) 456-7533
EMail: umimdn01@indosat.net.id
Website: http://www.umi-mdn.edu

Rector: Thomson Nadapdap EMail: rektorat_umimdn@yahoo.co.id

Ketua: Hotland Butarbutar

Faculties
Agriculture (Agricultural Economics; Agriculture; Agronomy); **Arts and Humanities** (Arts and Humanities; English; Literature); **Computer Engineering**; **Economics**; **Medicine** (Medicine)

History: Founded 1965. A private institution under the supervision of the Department of National Education of Indonesia.

Governing Bodies: Board of Trustees

Admission Requirements: Secondary school certificate

Fees: (Rupiahs): 1,925,000 per annum

Main Language(s) of Instruction: Indonesian, English

Accrediting Agencies: National Accreditation Board

Degrees and Diplomas: *Sarjana (S1)*: 4 yrs

Student Services: Academic counselling, Canteen, Cultural centre, Employment services, Health services, Language programs, Social counselling, Sports facilities

Special Facilities: Yes

Libraries: 10,881 vols

Publications: Majalah Ilmiah Universitas Methodist *(3 per annum)*
Last Updated: 06/02/09

MINAESA INSTITUTE OF TECHNOLOGY

Institut Teknologi Minaesa (ITM)
Jalan Stadion Selatan Walian, Tomohon, 95439 Sulawesi Utara
Tel: +62(431) 354-520
Fax: +62(431) 315-9197
EMail: itm-tomohon@itm-t.ac.id
Website: http://www.itm-t.ac.id

Rector: Herdianto Lantemona EMail: rektorat-itm@telkom.net

Ketua: J. Turang

Programmes
Architectural Engineering (Structural Architecture); **Computer Engineering** (Computer Engineering); **Electrical Engineering** (Electrical Engineering); **Industrial Engineering**; **Marine Engineering** (Marine Engineering)

History: Founded 1987.

Degrees and Diplomas: *Sarjana (S1)*
Last Updated: 11/07/11

MOCHAMMAD SROEDJI UNIVERSITY

Universitas Mochammad Sroedji
Jalan Sriwijaya 32, Jember, 68127 East Java
Tel: +62(331) 334-130
Fax: +62(331) 333-721
EMail: univ.mochsroedji@telkom.net

Rector: Sandjaya

Ketua: Murdijanto Purbangkoro

Faculties
Agriculture (Agricultural Economics; Agriculture; Agronomy); **Economics** (Development Studies; Economics; Management); **Educational Science and Teacher Training** (Educational and Student Counselling; Educational Sciences; Teacher Training); **Engineering** (Civil Engineering; Engineering); **Law** (Law); **Social and Political Sciences** (Public Administration)

History: Founded 1981.

Fees: (Rupiahs): 960,000 per annum

Degrees and Diplomas: *Sarjana (S1)*

Libraries: 18,450 vols
Last Updated: 13/01/09

MPU TANTULAR UNIVERSITY

Universitas MPU Tantular
Jalan Cipinang Besar 2, Jakarta Timur, 13410 DKI Jakarta
Tel: +62(21) 856-2011 +62(21) 819-7386
EMail: info@mputantular.ac.id
Website: http://www.mputantular.ac.id

Rector: Djoko Irianto

Ketua: KRHT. T. Sinambela Kusumonagoro

Faculties
Communication Studies (Communication Studies); **Computer Engineering** (Computer Education); **Economics** (Accountancy; Banking; Finance; Management) *Dean*: Wilter Silitonga; **Industrial Engineering** (Engineering Management; Industrial Engineering; Industrial Management; Mechanical Engineering) *Dean*: Syarifudin Tandiangan; **Law** (Law) *Dean*: Sri Hartati; **Marine Engineering**; **Planning and Civil Engineering** (Architecture and Planning; Civil Engineering) *Dean*: Monang Sinambela

History: Founded 1984.

Fees: (Rupiahs): 1.3m. per annum

Degrees and Diplomas: *Diploma*: 3 yrs; *Sarjana (S1)*

Libraries: 3,575 vols
Last Updated: 09/03/10

MUARA BUNGO UNIVERSITY

Universitas Muara Bungo
Jalan Lintas Sumatera Km 6, Sungai Binjai, Muara Bungo, 37215 Jambi
Tel: +62(747) 323-310
Fax: +62(747) 323-310

Rector: Husin

Ketua: Usman Hasan

Programmes
Agriculture; **Business Administration** (Accountancy; Management); **Engineering**; **English**; **Government** (Government)

Degrees and Diplomas: *Sarjana (S1)*
Last Updated: 30/04/10

MUHAMMADIYAH BUTON UNIVERSITY

Universitas Muhammadiyah Buton (UMB)
Jalan M. Husni Thamrin No. 30, Bau-Bau, 93712 Sulawesi Tenggara
Tel: +62(402) 270-37
Fax: +62(402) 270-38

Rector: Andi M. Syahir baso

Ketua: Muhammad Bahar

Faculties
Agriculture (Agricultural Engineering; Agriculture); **Economics**; **Engineering** (Civil Engineering; Engineering); **Law** (Law); **Literature** (Indonesian; Literature); **Social and Political Sciences** (Political Sciences; Social Studies); **Teacher Training**

Degrees and Diplomas: *Diploma*; *Sarjana (S1)*
Last Updated: 21/01/09

MUHAMMADIYAH MALUKU UTARA UNIVERSITY

Universitas Muhammadiyah Maluku Utara
Jalan Monomutu 10, Kelurahan TanahRaja, Ternate Selatan, 97716 Malaku
Tel: +62(921) 326-136
Fax: +62(921) 326-136
EMail: ummu_ternate@telkom.net

Rector: Kasman H.I. Ahmad

Ketua: Djafar Umar

Faculties
Agriculture *Dean*: Kahar Jamaludin; **Community Health** (Community Health; Sociology) *Dean*: Ali R. Aalbar; **Economics** *Dean*: Usam M. Fadjim; **Engineering** (Engineering) *Dean*: Rosdiati Ibrahim; **Mathematics and Natural Sciences** (Mathematics; Natural Sciences) *Dean*: Wahid Umar; **Social and Political Sciences** (Administrative Law; Government; Political Sciences; Social Sciences) *Dean*: Rusli Sibua

Degrees and Diplomas: *Sarjana (S1)*; *Magister (S2)*: Administration
Last Updated: 09/03/10

MUHAMMADIYAH PROF. DR. HAMKA UNIVERSITY

Universitas Muhammadiyah Prof. Dr. Hamka (UHAMKA)
Jalan Limau II Blok B-5, Kebayoran Baru, Jakarta Selatan, 12130 DKI Jakarta
Tel: +62(21) 720-8177 +62(21) 722-2886
Fax: +62(21) 739-1226
EMail: uhamka@uhamka.ac.id; uhamka@centrin.net.id
Website: http://www.uhamka.ac.id

Rector: Suyatno

Ketua: Din Syamsuddin

Faculties
Economics (Accountancy; Economics; Management); **Engineering** (Computer Engineering; Engineering; Engineering Drawing and Design; Telecommunications Engineering); **Health Science**; **Islamic Religion** (Islamic Studies; Religious Studies); **Mathematics and Natural Sciences** (Biology; Mathematics Education; Pharmacy; Physics); **Political and Social Sciences** (Communication Studies; Political Sciences; Social Sciences) *Dean*: Novi Andayani Praptiningsih; **Psychology** (Psychology); **Teacher Training and Education Science** (Educational Sciences; English; Geography; History; Indonesian; Japanese; Literature; Philosophy; Preschool Education; Sociology; Teacher Training)

Programmes
Postgraduate

History: Founded 1957 as Muhammadiyah Institute of Teacher Training and Educational Science Jakarta. Acquired present status and title 1997.

Admission Requirements: Secondary school certificate and entrance examination

Fees: (Rupiahs): 5.25m. per annum

Main Language(s) of Instruction: Indonesian

Accrediting Agencies: National Accreditation Committee of Education and Culture of Indonesia (BAN)

Degrees and Diplomas: *Diploma (D3)*: 3-5 yrs; *Sarjana (S1)*: Educational and Student Counselling, Management, Accountancy, Computer Engineering, Electronic Engineering, Pharmacy, Community Health, Communications Studies, Islamic studies, 4-7 yrs; *Magister (S2)*: 2-5 yrs

Student Services: Academic counselling, Canteen, Employment services, Foreign student adviser, Health services, Language programs, Social counselling, Sports facilities

Special Facilities: Laboratories, Movie Studio

Libraries: Central library
Last Updated: 10/02/09

MUHAMMADIYAH UNIVERSITY OF ACEH

Universitas Muhammadiyah Aceh
Jalan Muhammadiyah 91, Bathoh Lueng Bata, Banda Aceh, 23245 Nangroeh Aceh Darussalam
Tel: +62(651) 31-583
Fax: +62(651) 34-092

Rector: Muharrir Asy'Ary

Ketua: Suardi Saidi

Faculties
Economics (Accountancy; Economics; Management) *Dean*: Idrus Hayat; **Engineering** (Architecture; Civil Engineering; Engineering) *Dean*: Zaidi Idris; **Law** (Law) *Dean*: Yusuf Hasan; **Mathematics and Natural Sciences** (Biology; Chemistry; Mathematics and Computer Science; Natural Sciences) *Dean*: Makmur M. Zein; **Psychology** (Psychology); **Public Health** (Public Health) *Dean*: Anwar

History: Founded 1987.

Fees: (Rupiahs): 800,000 per annum

Degrees and Diplomas: *Diploma*; *Sarjana (S1)*

Libraries: 3,013 vols
Last Updated: 21/01/09

MUHAMMADIYAH UNIVERSITY OF BENGKULU

Universitas Muhammadiyah Bengkulu
PO Box 118, Jalan Bali Kodya, Bengkulu, 38119 Bengkulu
Tel: +62(736) 22-765
Fax: +62(736) 26-161
Website: http://www.umb.ac.id

Rector: Khairil

Ketua: Chairuddin

Faculties
Agriculture (Agricultural Business; Agricultural Economics; Agriculture; Animal Husbandry; Nutrition) *Dean*: Edi Efrita; **Economics** (Accountancy; Economics; Management) *Dean*: Onsardi; **Educational Science and Teacher Training** (Art Education; Biology; Economics; Educational Administration; Educational Sciences; Educational Technology; English; Indonesian; Literature; Mathematics Education; Modern Languages; Natural Sciences) *Dean*: Mardan; **Engineering** (Computer Engineering; Electronic Engineering; Engineering); **Health Sciences**; **Islamic Studies** *Dean*: Surohim; **Social and Political Sciences** (Civics; Communication Studies; Government; Political Sciences; Public Administration; Social Sciences; Sociology)

History: Founded 1970.

Fees: (Rupiahs): 840,000 per annum

Degrees and Diplomas: *Diploma*: 3 yrs; *Sarjana (S1)*

Libraries: 5,236 vols
Last Updated: 21/01/09

MUHAMMADIYAH UNIVERSITY OF CIREBON

Universitas Muhammadiyah Cirebon (UMC)
Jalan Tuparev 70 A, Cirebon, 45153 Jawa Barat
Tel: +62(231) 233-159 +62(231) 209-608
Fax: +62(231) 209-608
EMail: info@umc.ac.id; rektorat@umc.ac.id

Rector: Khaerul Wahadin

Programmes
Economics (Accountancy; Economics; Management); **Education** (Chemistry; Education; English; Foreign Languages Education; Mathematics Education; Primary Education; Science Education); **Engineering** (Computer Science; Industrial Engineering; Regional Planning; Town Planning); **Nursing** (Nursing); **Social and Political**

Sciences (Communication Studies; Government; Political Sciences; Public Relations; Social Sciences)

History: Founded 2000.

Main Language(s) of Instruction: Indonesian

Accrediting Agencies: Badan Akreditasi Nasional (BAN)/National Accreditation Board)

Degrees and Diplomas: *Sarjana (S1)*: all fields, 4 yrs

Student Services: Academic counselling, Canteen, Employment services, Language programs, Social counselling, Sports facilities

Special Facilities: Laboratories for computing, chemistry, physics, photography, language

Libraries: yes

Last Updated: 01/08/11

MUHAMMADIYAH UNIVERSITY OF GORONTALO

Universitas Muhammadiyah Gorontalo

Jalan Prof Dr Aloei Saboe 1, Gorontalo, 96115 Gorontalo

Tel: +62(435) 825-510

Fax: +62(435) 825-510

EMail: um_gorontalo@yahoo.co.id

Rector: Nani Tuloli

Ketua: Marthen A. Taha

Programmes

Agriculture (Agricultural Business; Animal Husbandry; Aquaculture); **Arabic** (Arabic; Literature; Modern Languages); **Economics** (Economics); **English** (English; Literature; Modern Languages); **Geography** (Geography); **Information Technology** (Information Technology); **Public Administration** (Public Administration)

Degrees and Diplomas: *Sarjana (S1)*

Last Updated: 30/04/10

MUHAMMADIYAH UNIVERSITY OF GRESIK

Universitas Muhammadiyah Gresik

Jalan Sumatra 101, Gresik, 61121 Jawa Timur

Tel: +62(31) 395-1414

Fax: +62(31) 395-2585

EMail: info@umg.ac.id

Website: http://www.umg.ac.id

Rector: Sarwo Edy

Ketua: Daniel Mohammad Rosyid

Faculties

Agriculture (Agricultural Engineering; Agriculture; Agronomy); **Economics** (Accountancy; Management); **Educational Science and Teacher Training** (Accountancy; Educational Sciences; English; Mathematics Education; Teacher Training); **Engineering** (Computer Engineering; Electronic Engineering; Industrial Engineering; Information Technology); **Fishery** (Fishery); **Psychology** (Psychology)

History: Founded 1980.

Fees: (Rupiahs): 1,916,000 per annum

Degrees and Diplomas: *Sarjana (S1)*

Libraries: 4,738 vols

Last Updated: 21/01/09

MUHAMMADIYAH UNIVERSITY OF JAKARTA

Universitas Muhammadiyah Jakarta (UMJ)

Jalan KH. Ahmad Dahlan Cirendeu Ciputat, Jakarta Selatan, 15419 DKI Jakarta

Tel: +62 740-1894 +62 749-2862

Fax: +62 743-0756

EMail: info@umj.ac.id

Website: http://www.umj.ac.id

Rector: Masyithon

Ketua: Masykur Wiratmo

International Relations: M. Muhammadi Tel: +62 746-0746

Faculties

Agriculture (Agriculture; Agronomy); **Economics** (Accountancy; Economics; Management); **Engineering** (Architecture; Automation and Control Engineering; Chemical Engineering; Civil Engineering; Computer Science; Electrical Engineering; Engineering; Industrial Engineering; Mechanical Engineering; Medical Technology); **Islamic Studies** (Islamic Studies; Islamic Theology; Religious Education); **Law** (Civil Law; Criminal Law; History of Law; International Law; Islamic Law; Law); **Medicine and Health Sciences** (Hygiene; Medicine; Public Health; Social and Preventive Medicine); **Postgraduate Studies**; **Social and Political Sciences** (Communication Studies; International Studies; Political Sciences; Social Sciences)

History: Founded 1955. A private institution.

Academic Year: September to August (September-January; February-August)

Admission Requirements: Senior high school certificate

Main Language(s) of Instruction: Indonesian

Accrediting Agencies: Department of Education and Culture

Degrees and Diplomas: *Diploma*; *Sarjana (S1)*: 4-4 1/2 yrs; *Magister (S2)*: Management, a further 2-2 1/2 yrs

Student Services: Academic counselling, Canteen, Language programs, Social counselling, Sports facilities

Special Facilities: Observatory

Libraries: c. 53,000 vols

Last Updated: 21/01/09

MUHAMMADIYAH UNIVERSITY OF JEMBER

Universitas Muhammadiyah Jember

Jalan Karimata 49, Jember, 68121 Jawa Timur

Tel: +62 (331) 336-728

Fax: +62 (331) 337-957

EMail: uniska-kediri@telkom.net

Rector: Yusnan Arigayo

Ketua: Aminullah El Hadi

Faculties

Economics (Accountancy; Economics; Management); **Educational Science and Teacher Training** (Educational Sciences; English; Indonesian; Mathematics Education; Modern Languages; Teacher Training); **Law** (Law); **Psychology** (Psychology); **Social and Political Sciences** (Government; Political Sciences; Social Sciences)

History: Founded 1981. A private institution under the supervision of the Department of Education and Culture.

Academic Year: February to January (February-July; September-January)

Fees: (Rupiahs): 750,000 per annum

Main Language(s) of Instruction: Indonesian

Degrees and Diplomas: *Sarjana (S1)*

Special Facilities: Biological Garden. Movie Studio. English Laboratory. Technology Laboratory

Libraries: 24,542 vols

Publications: Natural Sciences and Engineering Journal *(biannually)*; Social Sciences Journal *(biannually)*

Last Updated: 13/01/09

MUHAMMADIYAH UNIVERSITY OF KENDARI

Universitas Muhammadiyah Kendari (UMK)

Jln. K.h. Ahmad Dahlan No. 10, Kendari, 93118 Sulawesi Tenggara

Tel: +62(401) 393-641

Fax: +62(401) 393-641

EMail: unismuh_kdi@yahoo.com

Rector: Abdullah Alhadza

Ketua: Din Syamsuddin

Faculties

Agriculture *Dean*: Bambang Indro Yuwono; **Economics** (Management) *Dean*: Hasan Aedy; **Engineering** *Dean*: Ishak Kadir; **Fishery** (Fishery) *Dean*: Mu. Irwan Yusuf; **Islamic Studies** *Dean*: Nur Alim; **Law** *Dean*: Muh. Jufri Dewa; **Social and Political Sciences** (Government) *Dean*: Jamaluddin Hos; **Teacher Trainers**

Education (Child Care and Development; Educational Administration; Teacher Training) *Dean*: Hilaluddin Hanafi

History: Founded 2001.

Governing Bodies: Executive Body

Academic Year: September to September (September-Februar-y;February-September)

Admission Requirements: Senior High School Certificate (Ijazah Sekolah Lanjutan Atas)

Fees: (Rupiahs): 1m.-1.5m.

Main Language(s) of Instruction: Indonesian

Degrees and Diplomas: *Diploma*: Early Childhood Education (A.Md.), 2 yrs; *Sarjana (S1)*: 4 yrs; *Sarjana (S1)*: Primary Islamic Teacher Training (A.Md.), 2 yrs

Student Services: Academic counselling, Canteen, Employment services, Health services, Language programs, Social counselling

Libraries: 2,042 titles; 4,539 vols

Publications: Jurnal Sumber Daya Insani, Scientific journal written by Muhammadiyah University of Kendari's lecturers *(biennially)*

MUHAMMADIYAH UNIVERSITY OF KUPANG

Universitas Muhammadiyah Kupang

Jalan K.H. Ahmad Dahlan 17, Wali Kota Baru, Kupang, 82558 Nusa Tenggara Timur

Tel: +62(380) 833-693 +62(380) 833-692

Fax: +62(380) 28333

EMail: unmuhkupang@plasa.com

Rector: Markotib

Ketua: Idrus Lamaya

Faculties

Economics *Dean*: Syahlan Kamahi; **Educational Science and Teacher Training** *Dean*: Wakidi; **Fishery** (Fishery) *Dean*: Eddy Sanyoto; **Social and Political Sciences** *Dean*: Abubakar Iskandar

History: Founded 1987.

Fees: (Rupiahs): 700,000 per annum

Degrees and Diplomas: *Diploma*: 3 yrs; *Sarjana (S1)*

Libraries: 5,282 vols

Last Updated: 21/01/09

MUHAMMADIYAH UNIVERSITY OF LAMPUNG

Universitas Muhammadiyah Lampung

Jalan Za Pagaralam N°14, Bandar Lampung, Lampung

Tel: +62(721) 701-246

Fax: +62(721) 701-246

Rector: Irwan Amrullah

Ketua: Muswardi Taher

Faculties

Engineering (Electrical Engineering; Engineering) *Dean*: Sugeng Dwiono; **Psychology** (Psychology) *Dean*: Tabrani Aris; **Social and Political Sciences** (Communication Studies; Government) *Dean*: Adenan

History: Founded 1987.

Fees: (Rupiahs): 590,000 per annum

Degrees and Diplomas: *Sarjana (S1)*

Libraries: 1,280 vols

Last Updated: 21/01/09

MUHAMMADIYAH UNIVERSITY OF LUWUK BANGGAI

Universitas Muhammadiyah Luwuk Banggai

Jalan KH Ahmad Dahlan No 79, Luwuk, 94711 Sulawesi Tengah

Tel: +62(461) 23-452

Fax: +62(461) 21-725

EMail: unismuhluwuk@yahoo.co.id

Website: http://www.unismuhluwuk.ac.id/

Rector: Amelia Zainita (2009-) EMail: lia_amz@yahoo.com

Kepala Baak: Muhammad Gifari Sono

Faculties

Agriculture (Agricultural Business; Agriculture; Agronomy); **Economics** (Economics; Management); **Engineering** (Civil Engineering; Engineering; Industrial Engineering); **Fishery** (Fishery); **Islamic Religion** (Religious Education); **Law** (Law); **Social and Political Sciences** (Communication Studies; Government; Political Sciences; Social Sciences)

History: Founded 1999.

Governing Bodies: Yayasan Perguruan Tinggi Universitas Muhammadiyak Luwuk

Admission Requirements: Ijazah and transcript SMU/SMK/sederajat

Fees: (Rupiahs):100,000-400,000 per semester

Main Language(s) of Instruction: Indonesian

Accrediting Agencies: BAN-PT

Degrees and Diplomas: *Sarjana (S1)*: Agriculture; Economics; Engineering; Fishery; Islamic Religion; Law; Social and Political Sciences

Student Services: Academic counselling, Employment services, Foreign Studies Centre, Language programs, Sports facilities

Special Facilities: Laboratories (Fishery; Computer; Languages; Communications)

Libraries: Yes

Academic Staff *2010-2011*	MEN	WOMEN	**TOTAL**
FULL-TIME	95	52	**147**
PART-TIME	–	–	**9**
Student Numbers *2010-2011*			
All (Foreign Included)	2,000	2,304	**4,304**

Last Updated: 26/10/10

MUHAMMADIYAH UNIVERSITY OF MAGELANG

Universitas Muhammadiyah Magelang

Jalan Tidar 21, Magelang, 56126 Jawa Tengah

Tel: +62(293) 362-082

Fax: +62(293) 361-004

EMail: humas@ummgl.ac.id

Website: http://www.ummgl.ac.id

Ketua: Achmadi

Rector: Cholil Badawi

Faculties

Economics (Accountancy; Economics; Management) *Dean*: Hamron Zubadi; **Educational Science and Teacher Training** (Educational and Student Counselling; Educational Sciences; Preschool Education; Teacher Training) *Dean*: Tawil; **Engineering** (Computer Engineering; Engineering; Industrial Engineering) *Dean*: Bambang Purwanggoro; **Law** (Law) *Dean*: Haniyatun

Further Information: Kampus 2Branch in Jl. Mayjend, Magelang

History: Founded 1964. A private institution under the supervision of the Department of Education and Culture, and affiliated to the Muhammadiyah Education Chamber.

Governing Bodies: Board of Trustees

Academic Year: September to June (September-January; Fabruary-June)

Admission Requirements: High school certificate (Ijazah Sekolah Lanjutan Tingkat Atas SLTA)

Fees: (Rupiahs): 1,425,000 per annum

Main Language(s) of Instruction: Indonesian

Degrees and Diplomas: *Diploma*; *Sarjana (S1)*: 1-4 yrs

Student Services: Academic counselling, Canteen, Cultural centre, Health services, Social counselling, Sports facilities

Libraries: 6,639 vols

Publications: Refleksi *(biannually)*

Last Updated: 21/01/09

MUHAMMADIYAH UNIVERSITY OF MAKASAR

Universitas Muhammadiyah Makasar
Jalan Sultan Alauddin 259, Makasar 90221
Tel: +62(411) 866-972
Fax: +62(411) 865-588
EMail: admin@unismuh.ac.id
Website: http://www.unismuh.ac.id

Rector: Irwan Akib

Ketua: Djamaluddin Amin

Faculties

Agriculture (Agricultural Economics; Development Studies; Fishery; Water Management; Water Science) *Dean*: Syaiful Saleh; **Economics** (Accountancy; Development Studies; Economics; Finance) *Dean*: Amide Budi; **Educational Science and Teacher Training** (Art Education; Curriculum; Educational Sciences; Educational Technology; English; Indonesian; Literature; Modern Languages; Primary Education; Teacher Training) *Dean*: Natsir Hamdat; **Engineering** (Civil Engineering; Engineering; Irrigation) *Dean*: Kaimuddin Mahmud; **Medicine** (Medicine); **Social and Political Science** (Administration; Government; Public Administration; Social Sciences; Social Welfare; Sociology) *Dean*: Agussalim Munada

History: Founded 1963. A private institution under the supervision of the Department of Education and Culture.

Academic Year: August to July (August-January; February-July)

Fees: (Rupiahs): 450,000 per annum

Main Language(s) of Instruction: Indonesian

Degrees and Diplomas: *Diploma*: 2 yrs; *Sarjana (S1)*: 4 yrs; *Magister (S2)*

Libraries: 4,299 vols

Last Updated: 21/01/09

MUHAMMADIYAH UNIVERSITY OF MALANG

Universitas Muhammadiyah Malang (UMM)
Jalan Raya Tlogo Mas, Malang, 65113 Jawa Timur
Tel: +62(341) 463-513
Fax: +62(341) 460-782
EMail: webmaster@umm.ac.id
Website: http://www.umm.ac.id

Rector: H. Muhadjir Effendy

Ketua: H. A. Malik Fajar

Faculties

Agriculture and Animal Husbandry (Agricultural Economics; Agricultural Engineering; Agriculture; Agronomy; Animal Husbandry; Fishery; Forestry); **Economics** (Accountancy; Banking; Development Studies; Economics; Finance; Management); **Educational Science and Teacher Training** (Art Education; Biology; Civics; Educational Sciences; Educational Technology; English; Humanities and Social Science Education; Indonesian; Literature; Mathematics Education; Modern Languages; Science Education; Teacher Training); **Engineering** (Civil Engineering; Electrical Engineering; Engineering; Industrial Engineering; Mechanical Engineering); **Health Sciences** (Nursing; Pharmacy); **Islamic Studies** (Islamic Studies); **Law** (Law); **Medicine** (Medicine); **Psychology** (Psychology); **Social and Political Sciences** (Communication Studies; Government; Political Sciences; Social Sciences; Social Welfare; Sociology)

Programmes

Postgraduate Studies (Agricultural Business; Education; Islamic Studies; Law; Management; Sociology)

History: Founded 1965. A private institution of the Muhammadiyah Foundation and under the supervision of the Department of Education and Culture.

Governing Bodies: Senate

Academic Year: September to August (September-March; April-August)

Fees: (Rupiahs): 4,000,000 per annum

Main Language(s) of Instruction: Indonesian, English, Arabic

Degrees and Diplomas: *Diploma*; *Sarjana (S1)*: 4-5 yrs; *Magister (S2)*; *Doktor (S3)*

Student Residential Facilities: For c. 9,000 students

Libraries: 171,417 vols

Publications: 'Bestari' Journals

Academic Staff *2009-2010*	MEN	WOMEN	TOTAL
FULL-TIME	343	226	**569**
PART-TIME	224	188	**412**
Student Numbers *2009-2010*			
All (Foreign Included)	–	–	**18,561**

Last Updated: 28/10/10

MUHAMMADIYAH UNIVERSITY OF MATARAM

Universitas Muhammadiyah Mataram
Jalan Kh. A. Dahlan 1, Pegesangan, Mataram, Nusa Tenggara Barat
Tel: +62(370) 633-723
Fax: +62(370) 641-906
EMail: um_mataram@telkom.net
Website: http://www.unmuhmataram.com

Rector: Agufsian Wahab

Ketua: Lalu Mudjitahid

Faculties

Agriculture (Agricultural Engineering; Agriculture); **Educational Science and Teacher Training** (Art Education; Educational Sciences; English; Geography; Humanities and Social Science Education; Modern Languages; Teacher Training); **Engineering** (Civil Engineering; Engineering); **Social and Political Sciences** (Administration; Business Administration; Government; Political Sciences; Public Administration; Social Sciences)

History: Founded 1980. A private institution under the supervision of the Department of Education and Culture.

Academic Year: August to July (August-February; March-July)

Admission Requirements: Secondary school certificate (Sekolah Menengah Atas, SMA)

Fees: (Rupiahs): 350,000 per annum

Main Language(s) of Instruction: Indonesian

Degrees and Diplomas: *Sarjana (S1)*

Libraries: 8,495 vols

Publications: Ulul Albab *(quarterly)*

Last Updated: 02/02/09

MUHAMMADIYAH UNIVERSITY OF METRO

Universitas Muhammadiyah Metro
Jalan Ki Hajar Dewantara 116, Metro, 34111 Lampung
Tel: +62(725) 42-445 +62(725) 42-454
Fax: +62(725) 42-445
EMail: um_metro@plasa.com
Website: http://www.ummetro.ac.id

Rector: H. Marzuki Noor

Ketua: Masnuni Roi

Faculties

Economics (Accountancy; Economics; Information Management; Management) *Dean*: Bambang Suhada; **Educational Science and Teacher Training** (Biology; Curriculum; Educational and Student Counselling; Educational Sciences; Educational Technology; History; Mathematics Education; Natural Sciences; Physics; Primary Education; Teacher Training) *Dean*: Triyono Wisnutomo; **Engineering** (Civil Engineering; Engineering; Mechanical Engineering) *Dean*: Shantory; **Islamic Studies** (Islamic Studies); **Law** (Law)

History: Founded 1991.

Fees: (Rupiahs): 510,000 per annum

Degrees and Diplomas: *Sarjana (S1)*

Libraries: 5,293 vols

Last Updated: 02/02/09

MUHAMMADIYAH UNIVERSITY OF NORTH SUMATRA

Universitas Muhammadiyah Sumatera Utara (UMSU)
Jalan Mukhtar Basri 3, Glugur Darat II, Medan, 20238 Sumatera Utara
Tel: +62(61) 661-1233
EMail: rektor@umsu.ac.id
Website: http://www.umsu.ac.id

Rector: Bahdin Nur Tanjung

Ketua: Dalail Ahmad

Faculties

Agriculture (Agricultural Economics; Agricultural Engineering; Agriculture; Agronomy; Plant Pathology) *Dean*: Bukhari Sibuea; **Economics**; **Educational Sciences and Teacher Training**; **Engineering**; **Law**; **Social and Political Sciences**

History: Founded 1957. A private institution under the supervision of the Department of Education and Culture.

Fees: (Rupiahs): 549,500 per annum

Degrees and Diplomas: *Diploma*: 3 yrs; *Sarjana (S1)*; *Magister (S2)*: Law

Libraries: 7,513 vols
Last Updated: 06/02/09

MUHAMMADIYAH UNIVERSITY OF PALANGKA RAYA

Universitas Muhammadiyah Palangka Raya
Jalan RTA Milono Km. 1.5, Palangka Raya, 73111 Kalimantan Tengah
Tel: +62(536) 22-184

Rector: Jairi

Ketua: H.E. Lambung

Faculties

Agriculture (Agriculture; Agronomy; Forestry); **Educational Sciences** (Accountancy; Educational and Student Counselling; Educational Psychology; Educational Sciences; Social Sciences); **Engineering** (Civil Engineering; Engineering); **Social and Political Sciences** (Business Administration; Government; Political Sciences; Public Administration; Social Sciences; Social Welfare)

History: Founded 1987.

Fees: (Rupiahs): 186,000 per annum

Degrees and Diplomas: *Sarjana (S1)*
Last Updated: 02/02/09

MUHAMMADIYAH UNIVERSITY OF PALEMBANG

Universitas Muhammadiyah Palembang
Jalan Jend. A. Yani 13, Ulu, Palembang, 30263 Sumatera Selatan
Tel: +62(711) 513-022
Fax: +62(711) 513-078
EMail: info@umpalembang.ac.id; idris_ump@yahoo.co.id
Website: http://www.umpalembang.ac.id/

Rector: Muhammad Idris

Ketua: H.M. Soeripto EMail: admin@umpalembang.ac.id

Faculties

Agriculture (Agricultural Economics; Agricultural Engineering; Agriculture; Agronomy; Forest Management; Water Management) *Dean*: Minwal; **Economics** (Accountancy; Economics; Management; Marketing) *Dean*: Hatta Wazol; **Educational Science and Teacher Training** (Art Education; Biology; Educational Administration; Educational Sciences; English; History; Indonesian; Mathematics Education; Modern Languages; Natural Sciences; Social Sciences; Teacher Training) *Dean*: Husein Fattah; **Engineering** (Architecture; Chemical Engineering; Civil Engineering; Electrical Engineering; Engineering) *Dean*: Arief Karim; **Law** (Law) *Dean*: Maramis; **Medicine** (Medicine)

History: Founded 1979.

Fees: (Rupiahs): 2.5m. per annum

Degrees and Diplomas: *Diploma*: 3 yrs; *Sarjana (S1)*; *Magister (S2)*: Law, Management

Libraries: 14,423 vols
Last Updated: 02/02/09

MUHAMMADIYAH UNIVERSITY OF PALU

Universitas Muhammadiyah Palu
Kampus UMP Bumi Nyiur, Jalan Hang Tuah 29, Palu, Sulawesi Tengah
Tel: +62(451) 25-627

Rector: Aminun P. Omolu

Ketua: Sudirman Rais

Faculties

Agriculture *Dean*: Abd. Hadid; **Community Health** (Community Health); **Economics** (Banking; Economics; Finance; Management) *Dean*: Ali Supriadi; **Educational Science and Teacher Training** *Dean*: Asri Hene; **Engineering** *Dean*: Dahlan Ahmad; **Law** (Law) *Dean*: Idham Chalid; **Social and Political Sciences** (Business Administration; Political Sciences; Social Sciences; Sociology) *Dean*: Ahmad Basir Toana

History: Founded 1983.

Fees: (Rupiahs): 512,500 per annum

Degrees and Diplomas: *Diploma*: 3 yrs; *Sarjana (S1)*

Libraries: 1,562 vols
Last Updated: 09/03/10

MUHAMMADIYAH UNIVERSITY OF PARE-PARE

Universitas Muhammadiyah Pare-Pare
Jalan Jend. Ahmad Yani Km. 6 Lapadde, Pare-Pare, 91111 Sulawesi Selatan
Tel: +62(421) 22-757
Fax: +62(421) 22-757

Rector: Syarifuddin Yusuf

Ketua: Djamaluddin Idris

Faculties

Agriculture (Agricultural Business; Agricultural Economics; Agriculture; Agronomy; Animal Husbandry); **Economics** (Accountancy); **Educational Sciences** (Distance Education; Educational Sciences; English; Mathematics Education); **Engineering**

History: Founded as Sekolah Tinggi Keguruan dan Ilmu Pendidikan Muhammadiyah Pare-Pare

Degrees and Diplomas: *Sarjana (S1)*; *Magister (S2)*: Agribusiness
Last Updated: 02/02/09

MUHAMMADIYAH UNIVERSITY OF PONOROGO

Universitas Muhammadiyah Ponorogo
Ponorogo, 63471 Jawa Timur
Tel: +62(352) 481-124
Fax: +62(352) 461-796
EMail: akademik@umpo.ac.id
Website: http://www.umpo.ac.id

Rector: Sulton Tel: +62(352) 481-124, Fax: +62(352) 461-796

Ketua: Zainun Shofwan

Faculties

Economics (Accountancy; Banking; Development Studies; Finance; Management); **Engineering** (Computer Science; Electronic Engineering; Mechanical Engineering); **Health Sciences** (Midwifery; Nursing); **Islamic Religion** (Islamic Studies); **Social and Political Sciences** (Communication Studies; Government; Social Welfare); **Teaching and Educational Science** (Civics; Education; Mathematics Education; Modern Languages) *Head*: Eko Herry

History: Founded 1982.

Fees: (Rupiahs): 640,000 per annum

Main Language(s) of Instruction: Indonesian, English

Accrediting Agencies: Badan Akreditasi Nasional Perguruan Tinggi (BAN - PT)

Degrees and Diplomas: *Diploma (A.Ma.)*: 3 yrs; *Diploma (A.Md.)*: 3 yrs; *Sarjana (S1)*: 4 yrs

Student Services: Canteen, Cultural centre, Health services, Language programs, Sports facilities

Student Residential Facilities: Yes

Libraries:c. 17,000 vols

Academic Staff *2010-2011*	MEN	WOMEN	**TOTAL**
FULL-TIME	90	60	**150**
STAFF WITH DOCTORATE			
FULL-TIME	3	–	3
Student Numbers *2010-2011*			
All (Foreign Included)	1,762	1,809	**3,571**

Last Updated: 26/10/10

MUHAMMADIYAH UNIVERSITY OF PONTIANAK

Universitas Muhammadiyah Pontianak

Jalan Achmad Yani 111, Pontianak, 78124 Kalimantan Barat
Tel: +62(561) 737-278
Fax: +62(561) 764-571

Rector: Abdussamad

Ketua: Hamka Siregar

Faculties

Agriculture; **Economics**; **Education** (Chemistry; Primary Education); **Engineering**; **Health Sciences** (Community Health)

History: Founded 1990.

Fees: (Rupiahs): 800,000 per annum

Degrees and Diplomas: *Sarjana (S1)*

Last Updated: 02/02/09

MUHAMMADIYAH UNIVERSITY OF PURWOKERTO

Universitas Muhammadiyah Purwokerto

PO Box 202, Jalan Raya Dukuh Waluh, Purwokerto, 53182 Jawa Tengah
Tel: +62(281) 636-751
Fax: +62(281) 637-239
EMail: info@ump.ac.id
Website: http://www.ump.ac.id

Rector: Syamsuhadi

Ketua: Badi Nguzaman

Departments

Nursing (Nursing); **Public Health** (Community Health; Public Health) *Head*: Iksan Mujahid

Faculties

Agriculture (Agricultural Economics; Agriculture; Agronomy); **Arts and Humanities** (English; Literature); **Economics** (Accountancy; Economics; Management; Marketing); **Educational Sciences and Teacher Training** (Biology; Civics; Educational Sciences; English; Geography; History; Literacy Education; Mathematics Education; Preschool Education; Primary Education; Science Education; Teacher Training); **Engineering** (Chemical Engineering; Civil Engineering; Electronic Engineering; Engineering); **Fishery and Oceanography** (Botany; Fishery; Marine Science and Oceanography); **Law** (Law); **Muslim Religion** (Islamic Studies; Islamic Theology; Preschool Education; Primary Education; Religious Education; Religious Studies); **Pharmacy** (Pharmacy); **Psychology** (Psychology)

History: Founded 1965 as Institut Keguruan dan Ilmu Pendidikan Muhammadiyah, Purwokerto. Acquired present status and title 1995.

Fees: (Rupiahs): 900,000 per annum

Main Language(s) of Instruction: Indonesian

Accrediting Agencies: National Accreditation Board

Degrees and Diplomas: *Diploma*: 3 yrs; *Sarjana (S1)*: 5 yrs

Student Services: Academic counselling, Canteen, Cultural centre, Employment services, Foreign student adviser, Handicapped facilities, Health services, Language programs, Nursery care, Social counselling, Sports facilities

Libraries: 10,321 vols

Publications: Journal *(biennially)*

Last Updated: 10/02/09

MUHAMMADIYAH UNIVERSITY OF PURWOREJO

Universitas Muhammadiyah Purworejo

Jalan K.H. A. Dahlan 3, Purworejo, 54111 Jawa Tengah
Tel: +62(275) 321-494
EMail: info@um-pwr.ac.id
Website: http://www.um-pwr.ac.id

Rector: Mohammad Fakhrudin

Ketua: Noorwachid Soejoti

Faculties

Agriculture; **Animal Husbandry**; **Economics**; **Educational Science** (Automotive Engineering; Business and Commerce; Curriculum; Educational Sciences; Educational Technology; English; History; Indonesian; Literature; Mathematics Education; Physics); **Engineering**

History: Founded 1964 as Institut Keguruan dan Ilmu Pendidikan Muhammadiyah Purworejo. Acquired present status 1994.

Fees: (Rupiahs): 1.2m. per annum

Degrees and Diplomas: *Diploma*: 3 yrs; *Sarjana (S1)*

Libraries: 9,355 vols

Last Updated: 11/02/09

MUHAMMADIYAH UNIVERSITY OF RIAU

Universitas Muhammadiyah Riau

Pekanbaru, Riau

Programmes

Accountancy (Accountancy); **Communication Studies**; **Economics**; **Engineering** (Automotive Engineering; Engineering; Industrial Engineering); **Finance and Banking** (Banking; Finance); **Information Technology** (Information Technology); **Nursing** (Nursing); **Science**

Degrees and Diplomas: *Sarjana (S1)*

Last Updated: 30/04/10

MUHAMMADIYAH UNIVERSITY OF SEMARANG

Universitas Muhammadiyah Semarang

Jalan Kedungmundu Raya N° 18, Semarang, 50273 Jawa Tengah
Tel: +62(24) 767-40296
Fax: +62(24) 767-40291
EMail: info@unimus.ac.id
Website: http://www.unimus.ac.id

Rector: Susanto

Ketua: Musman Tholib

Faculties

Economics (Accountancy; Economics; Management); **Engineering** (Electrical Engineering; Engineering; Mechanical Engineering); **Industrial Engineering** (Food Technology; Industrial Engineering); **Letters** (Arts and Humanities; English; Literature); **Mathematics and Natural Sciences** (Mathematics and Computer Science; Natural Sciences; Statistics); **Public Health** (Medicine; Midwifery; Nursing; Nutrition; Public Health)

History: Founded 1999.

Fees: (Rupiahs): 800,000 per annum

Degrees and Diplomas: *Diploma*: 3 yrs; *Sarjana (S1)*

Last Updated: 11/02/09

MUHAMMADIYAH UNIVERSITY OF SIDOARJO

Universitas Muhammadiyah Sidoarjo (UMSIDA)

Jalan Mojopahit 666B, Sidoarjo, 61215 Jawa Timur
Tel: +62(31) 894-5444
Fax: +62(31) 894-9333
EMail: puskom@umsida.ac.id; umsidoarjo@umsida.ac.id
Website: http://www.umsida.ac.id

Rector: Achmad Jainuri Tel: +62(31) 894-1809

Ketua: Mohammad Rusdi

Faculties

Agriculture (Agriculture; Agronomy; Homeopathy); **Economics** (Accountancy; Economics; Management); **Engineering** (Computer Engineering; Electrical Engineering; Engineering; Industrial Engineering; Mechanical Engineering); **Islamic Education** (Arabic; Islamic Studies); **Psychology**; **Social and Political Sciences** (Communication Studies; Political Sciences; Public Administration; Social Sciences)

Programmes

Postgraduate Studies

Further Information: Campus II: Jl. Raya Gelam 250 Candi - Sidoarjo

History: Founded 1989 as former Sekolah Tinggi Muhammadiyah Sidoarjo.

Governing Bodies: Majelis Pendidikan Tinggi; Pimpinan Pusat Muhammadiyah

Academic Year: August to July

Admission Requirements: High School Certificate

Fees: (Rupiahs): 2m. per annum

Main Language(s) of Instruction: Indonesian

Accrediting Agencies: Badan Akreditasi Nasional

Degrees and Diplomas: *Diploma*; *Sarjana (S1)*: 4 yrs; *Magister (S2)*

Student Services: Academic counselling, Canteen, Employment services, Health services, Language programs, Social counselling, Sports facilities

Student Residential Facilities: None

Libraries: c. 10,000 vols

Publications: Halaqa, Journal of Islamic Studies *(biannually)*; Iktisadia, Journal of Economics *(biannually)*; Kalamsiasi, Journal of Social and Political Science *(biannually)*; Nabatia, Journal of Agriculture *(biannually)*; Teknolojia, Journal of Engineering *(biannually)*

Press or Publishing House: Universitas Muhammadiyah Sidoarjo Press (UMSIDA Press)

Last Updated: 11/02/09

MUHAMMADIYAH UNIVERSITY OF SUKABUMI

Universitas Muhammadiyah Sukabumi

Jalan R Syamsudin SH 54, Sukabumi, 43113 Jawa Barat

Tel: +62(266) 218-345

Fax: +62(266) 218-342

EMail: info@ummi.ac.id; info.ummi@gmail.com

Website: http://www.ummi.ac.id/

Rector: Asmawi Zainul

Ketua: Akhlan Husen

Programmes

Accountancy (Accountancy); **Agricultural Business** (Agricultural Business); **Aquatic Resources**; **Biology** (Biology); **Business Administration** (Business Administration); **Chemistry** (Chemistry); **Civil Engineering** (Civil Engineering); **English**; **Indonesian** (Indonesian; Literature; Modern Languages); **Information Technology** (Information Technology); **Nursing** (Nursing); **Public Administration** (Public Administration); **Taxation**

Degrees and Diplomas: *Sarjana (S1)*

Last Updated: 30/04/10

MUHAMMADIYAH UNIVERSITY OF SURABAYA

Universitas Muhammadiyah Surabaya

Jalan Sutorejo 59, Surabaya, 60113 Jawa Timur

Tel: +62(31) 381-1966

Fax: +62(31) 381-3096

Rector: Zainuddin Maliki

Ketua: M. Sulthon Amien

Faculties

Economics (Accountancy; Economics; Management); **Educational Sciences and Teacher Training** (Art Education; Biology; Civics; Education; Educational Sciences; English; Humanities and Social Science Education; Indonesian; Literature; Mathematics Education; Modern Languages; Natural Sciences; Psychology); **Engineering** (Architecture; Civil Engineering; Computer Engineering; Electrical Engineering; Engineering; Marine Engineering; Mechanical Engineering); **Law**; **Nursing** (Nursing)

History: Founded 1984.

Fees: (Rupiahs): 1.5m. per annum

Main Language(s) of Instruction: Indonesian

Degrees and Diplomas: *Diploma*; *Sarjana (S1)*

Student Services: Academic counselling, Canteen, Language programs, Sports facilities

Libraries: 8,325 vols

Last Updated: 02/02/09

MUHAMMADIYAH UNIVERSITY OF SURAKARTA

Universitas Muhammadiyah Surakarta

A. Yani Tromol Pos 1, Pabelan, Surakarta, 57102 Jawa Tengah

Tel: +62(271) 717-417

Fax: +62(271) 715-448

EMail: ums@ums.ac.id

Website: http://www.ums.ac.id

Rector: Bambang Setiaji EMail: b_setiaji@ums.ac.id

Vice-Rector I: Muhammad Musiyam Tel: +62(271) 619-181

Faculties

Communication and Information (Communication Studies; Information Sciences; Information Technology); **Economics** (Accountancy; Development Studies; Economics; Management); **Education and Teacher Training** (Accountancy; Biology; Civics; Education; English; Foreign Languages Education; Geography; Indonesian; Literature; Mathematics Education; Native Language; Native Language Education; Preschool Education; Teacher Training); **Engineering** (Architecture; Chemical Engineering; Civil Engineering; Electrical Engineering; Engineering; Industrial Engineering; Mechanical Engineering; Structural Architecture); **Geography** (Geography); **Health Sciences** (Community Health; Medicine; Nursing; Nutrition; Physical Therapy; Public Health); **Islamic Studies** (Islamic Law; Islamic Studies; Psychology; Religious Education); **Law** (Administrative Law; Civics; Civil Law; Commercial Law; Constitutional Law; Consumer Studies; Criminal Law; Criminology; English; Environmental Studies; Ethics; Government; Human Rights; International Law; Islamic Law; Islamic Studies; Labour and Industrial Relations; Labour Law; Law; Political Sciences; Private Law; Social Sciences); **Nursing** (Nursing); **Pharmacy** (Pharmacy); **Psychology** (Psychology)

Programmes

Postgraduate Studies (Civil Engineering; Education; Islamic Law; Islamic Studies; Law; Literature; Management; Modern Languages; Political Sciences; Psychology; Religious Education)

Further Information: Also 2 Professional Programmes (Ners Profession Programme and Pharmacist programme); an International Programme in Mechanical Engineering; 3 Twinning programmes in Law and Islamic Law, Psychology and Islamic Education, Psychology and Islamic Theology.

History: Founded 1981. A private institution under the supervision of the Department of Education and Culture.

Academic Year: February to January (February-July; August-January)

Admission Requirements: Secondary school certificate and entrance examination

Main Language(s) of Instruction: Indonesian

Degrees and Diplomas: *Sarjana (S1)*: 4 yrs; *Magister (S2)*: Civil Engineering; Educational Administration; Language Assessment; Legal Studies; Management; Psychology, a further 2 yrs; *Doktor (S3)*: Law

Student Services: Academic counselling, Canteen, Cultural centre, Employment services, Foreign student adviser, Foreign Studies Centre, Health services, Language programs, Nursery care, Sports facilities

Student Residential Facilities: Yes (Hajjah Nurriyah Sobron Islamic Boarding House; Student apartments)

Special Facilities: Computer Centre and Internet; Laboratories (Natural and Social Sciences); Art Gallery; Biological Garden; Music Studio; Drama and Film Theatres

Libraries: Central Library, 121,661 vols; 3,508 journals; 4,355 magazines; 11,174 research papers; 308 research reports; 778 final tasks

Publications: Benefit, Publication of the Faculty of Economy *(biennially)*; Daya Saing, Publication of the Magister of Management Postgraduate Programme *(biennially)*; Dinamika, Publication of the Faculty of Engineering *(biennially)*; Empirika, Publication fo the Faculty of Economy *(biennially)*; Forum Geografi, Publication of the Faculty of Geography *(biennially)*; Gelagar, Publication of the Faculty of Engineering *(quarterly)*; Humaniora, Publication of the Centre for Research and Community Services *(biennially)*; Humanity, Publication of the Language Centre *(biennially)*; Indigenous, Publication of the Faculty of Psychology *(biennially)*; Info, Muhammadiyah University Press *(monthly)*; Infokes, Publication of the Faculty of Health Science *(biennially)*; Jurnal Akuntansi, Publication of the Faculty of Economy *(biennially)*; Jurnal Ekonomi Pembangunan, Publication of the Faculty of Economy *(biennially)*; Jurnal Ilmu Hukum, Publication of the Faculty of Law *(biennially)*; Kajian Linguistik dan Sastra D.H. Mibas, Local and Indonesian Language Publication of the Faculty of Teacher Training and Education *(quarterly)*; Pabelan Pos, Publication of the Faculty of Engineering *(monthly)*; Pharmacon, Publication of the Faculty of Pharmacy *(biennially)*; Profetika, Publication of the Magister of Islamic Studies Postgraduate Programme *(biennially)*; Shobron, Publication of Hajja Nuriyah Shobron *(biennially)*; Suhuf, Publication of the Faculty of Islamic Studies *(quarterly)*; Varidika, Publication of the Faculty of Teacher Training and Education *(quarterly)*; Warta, Publication of the Centre for Research and Community Services *(biennially)*

Press or Publishing House: Muhammadiyah University Press
Last Updated: 01/08/11

MUHAMMADIYAH UNIVERSITY OF TANGERANG

Universitas Muhammadiyah Tangerang
Jalan Perintis Kemerdekaan I/33, Cikokol, Tangerang, 15118 Banten
Tel: +62(21) 5579-3251
Fax: +62(21) 5579-3251

Programmes

Business Administration (Accountancy; Management); **Communication Studies** (Communication Studies); **Engineering** (Civil Engineering; Electrical Engineering; Industrial Engineering); **English**; **Government**; **Indonesian** (Indonesian; Literature; Modern Languages); **Information Technology** (Information Technology); **Law**; **Mathematics**; **Midwifery**; **Nursing** (Nursing)

Degrees and Diplomas: *Sarjana (S1)*
Last Updated: 30/04/10

MUHAMMADIYAH UNIVERSITY OF TAPANULI SELETAN

Universitas Muhammadiyah Tapanuli Seletan
Jalan Sutan Mohd. Arif 32, Padang Sidempuan, Sumatera Utara
Tel: +62(682) 21-696

Rector: Ali Akbar Sagala

Faculties

Agriculture (Agricultural Economics; Agriculture; Agronomy; Plant Pathology); **Economics** (Accountancy; Economics); **Educational Science and Teacher Training** (Art Education; Biology; Chemistry; Curriculum; Educational and Student Counselling; Educational Psychology; Educational Sciences; English; History; Mathematics Education; Modern Languages; Physics; Science Education; Teacher Training); **Law** (Law); **Social and Political Sciences** (Administration; Government; Political Sciences; Social Sciences)

History: Founded 1983.

Fees: (Rupiahs): 727,500 per annum

Degrees and Diplomas: *Diploma*: 3 yrs; *Sarjana (S1)*

Libraries: 6,705 vols
Last Updated: 02/02/09

MUHAMMADIYAH UNIVERSITY OF WEST SUMATRA

Universitas Muhammadiyah Sumatera Barat (UMSB)
Jalan Pasir Kandang Kec. Koto Tangah, Padang, Sumatera Barat
Tel: +62(751) 481-645 +62(751) 482-274
EMail: info@umsb.ac.id
Website: http://www.umsb.ac.id

Rector: Shofwan Karim Elha

Vice-Rector: Ansofino

Faculties

Agriculture (Agricultural Business; Agricultural Engineering; Agriculture); **Economics** (Accountancy; Economics; Management); **Education and Teacher Training** (Education; Indonesian; Mathematics Education; Native Language; Native Language Education; Teacher Training); **Engineering** (Civil Engineering; Electrical Engineering; Engineering; Mechanical Engineering); **Forestry** (Forest Management; Forest Products; Forestry); **Health Sciences and Mathematics** (Health Administration; Health Sciences; Mathematics; Nursing); **Islamic Studies** (Islamic Law; Islamic Studies; Islamic Theology; Religious Education); **Law** (Law); **Tourism** (Tourism)

History: Founded 1985.

Governing Bodies: Department of National Education. Department of Religion

Main Language(s) of Instruction: Indonesian

Accrediting Agencies: Badah Akreditasi Nasonal Perguruan Tinggi (BAN PT)

Degrees and Diplomas: *Sarjana (S1)*: 4 yrs

Student Services: Academic counselling, Employment services, Social counselling, Sports facilities

Publications: Menara
Last Updated: 01/08/11

MUHAMMADIYAH UNIVERSITY OF YOGYAKARTA

Universitas Muhammadiyah Yogyakarta
Jalan Lingkar Selatan Tamantirto 17, Kasihan Bantul, Yogyakarta, 55183 DI Yogyakarta
Tel: +62(274) 387-656
EMail: umy@umy.ac.id
Website: http://www.umy.ac.id

Rector: Dasron Hamid

Ketua: Rosyad Sholeh

Faculties

Agriculture; **Economics** (Accountancy; Development Studies; Economics; Management); **Engineering**; **Graduate Studies**; **Islamic Studies**; **Law** (Law); **Medicine** (Dentistry; Medicine; Nursing); **Social and Political Sciences**

History: Founded 1981.

Fees: (Rupiahs): 1.2m. per annum

Degrees and Diplomas: *Sarjana (S1)*; *Magister (S2)*

Libraries: 17,605 vols
Last Updated: 02/02/09

MURIA KUDUS UNIVERSITY

Universitas Muria Kudus (UMK)
PO Box 53, Kampus Gondang, Bae, Kudus, 59324 Jawa Tengah
Tel: +62(291) 438-229
Fax: +62(291) 437-198
EMail: muria@umk.ac.id
Website: http://umk.ac.id

Rector: Sarjadi (2004-) Tel: +62(291) 438-229 Ext.103

Vice-Rector III: Hendy Hendro

Vice-Rector II: Iskandar Wibawa
Tel: +62(291) 438-229 Ext.105, Fax: +62(291) 437-198

Faculties

Agriculture (Agricultural Engineering; Agronomy); **Economics** (Accountancy; Economics; Management); **Education and Teacher Training** (Educational and Student Counselling; English; Foreign Languages Education); **Engineering** (Computer Engineering; Electrical and Electronic Engineering; Engineering; Information Technology; Mechanical Engineering); **Law** (Criminal Law; Justice Administration; Law); **Postgraduate Studies** (Law; Management)

Programmes

Psychology (Psychology)

History: Founded 1980. A private institution under the supervision of the Department of National Education.

Admission Requirements: Secondary school certificate

Main Language(s) of Instruction: Indonesian, English

Accrediting Agencies: National Board Accreditation

Degrees and Diplomas: *Diploma*: 3 yrs; *Sarjana (S1)*: 4 yrs; *Magister (S2)*: Management; Law

Student Services: Academic counselling, Canteen, Foreign student adviser, Foreign Studies Centre, Health services, Language programs, Social counselling, Sports facilities

Special Facilities: Movie Studio; Language Laboratory; Computer Laboratory; Mosque

Libraries: c. 11,600 vols; 120 journals; 2,400 magazines

Publications: MAWAS, Scientific magazine *(biennially)*; PEKA, Student magazine *(biennially)*

Last Updated: 29/06/11

MUSAMUS UNIVERSITY OF MERAUKE

Universitas Musamus Merauke

Jalan Kamizaun, Mopah Lama, Merauke 99600
EMail: info@unimmer.ac.id
Website: http://www.unimmer.ac.id/

Rector: Philipus Betaubun

Vice-Rector: Daud Andang Pasalli

Faculties

Agriculture (Agricultural Business; Agricultural Engineering; Agriculture; Animal Husbandry); **Economic and Social Policy** (Accountancy; Economics; Management; Public Administration); **Engineering** (Architecture; Civil Engineering; Electrical Engineering; Engineering; Information Technology; Structural Architecture)

Degrees and Diplomas: *Sarjana (S1)*

Last Updated: 03/05/10

MUSI RAWAS UNIVERSITY

Universitas Musi Rawas

Jalan Subkoss Garuda 1, Lubuk Linggau, 31611 Sumatera Selatan
Tel: +62(733) 324-083
Fax: +62(733) 324-083

Programmes

Accountancy (Accountancy); **Agriculture** (Agricultural Business; Agricultural Engineering; Agricultural Equipment); **Animal Husbandry** (Animal Husbandry); **Civil Engineering** (Civil Engineering); **Government** (Government; Political Sciences); **Public administration**

Degrees and Diplomas: *Sarjana (S1)*

Last Updated: 03/05/10

MUSLIM NUSANTARA AL-WASHLIYAH UNIVERSITY

Universitas Muslim Nusantara Al-Washliyah

Jalan Garu II 98, Medan, Sumatera Utara
Tel: +62(61) 786-7044
Fax: +62(61) 786-2747
EMail: admin@umnaw.com
Website: http://www.umnaw.com

Rector: Sri Sulistyawati

Ketua: Aziddin

Faculties

Agriculture (Agricultural Economics; Agriculture); **Economics** (Accountancy; Economics; Management); **Educational Science and Teacher Training** (Civics; Economics; Educational and Student Counselling; Educational Sciences; Educational Technology; English; Indonesian; Literature; Mathematics Education; Physics; Teacher Training); **Law**; **Literature** (Literature); **Pharmacy** (Pharmacy)

History: Founded 1996.

Fees: (Rupiahs): 500,000 per annum

Degrees and Diplomas: *Diploma*; *Sarjana (S1)*

Libraries: 20,580 vols

Last Updated: 06/01/09

MUSLIM UNIVERSITY OF INDONESIA

Universitas Muslim Indonesia (UMI)

Jalan Urip Sumoharjo 225, Makassar, 90121 Sulawesi Selatan
Tel: +62(411) 873-018
Fax: +62(411) 870-093
EMail: mm@umi.ac.id
Website: http://www.umi.ac.id/

Rector: Muhammad Nasir Hamzah

Ketua: Mukhtar Noer Jaya

Faculties

Agriculture *Dean*: Sudirman Numbu; **Arts and Humanities** *Hafidz*: Usman Ismail; **Community Health** *Dean*: Feny Hadju; **Computer Science** *Dean*: Dirgahayu Andi Lantara; **Economics** (Accountancy; Business Administration; Development Studies; Economics; Human Resources; Management) *Dean*: Hamzah Chatib; **Engineering** (Architecture; Automotive Engineering; Civil Engineering; Electrical Engineering; Energy Engineering; Mechanical Engineering; Metallurgical Engineering; Telecommunications Engineering) *Dean*: Winarno Arifin; **Fishery** (Fishery; Marine Science and Oceanography; Water Management) *Dean*: Tansil; **Industrial Engineering** (Chemical Engineering; Engineering Management; Industrial Engineering; Industrial Management) *Dean*: Amin Saleh; **Law** (Law) *Dean*: Abd. Latif; **Medicine** *Dean*: Ibrahim Abd. Samad

Programmes

Postgraduate Studies (Coastal Studies; Economics; Law; Management) *Head*: Natsir Hamzah

Further Information: Also Jalan Kakatua 27

History: Founded 1954. A private institution under the supervision of the Department of Education and Culture.

Fees: (Rupiahs): 1,225,000 per annum

Degrees and Diplomas: *Diploma*: 3 yrs; *Sarjana (S1)*; *Magister (S2)*: Management; *Doktor (S3)*: Law; Management

Libraries: 48,031 vols

Last Updated: 02/02/09

NAHDLATUL ULAMA UNIVERSITY

Universitas Nahdlatul Ulama

Jalan Dr. Wahidin 5/VI Penumping, Surakarta, Jawa Tengah
Tel: +62(271) 717-954
Fax: +62(271) 720-146
EMail: unusurakarta@yahoo.com

Rector: Mufrod Teguh Mulyo

Ketua: Suparman Ibrahim Abdullah

Faculties

Agriculture (Agricultural Economics; Agricultural Engineering; Agriculture; Forest Management) *Dean*: Windi Atmaka; **Economics** (Accountancy; Economics; Management; Marketing) *Dean*: Heriyanta Budi Utama; **Engineering** (Mechanical Engineering; Rural Planning; Town Planning) *Dean*: Aries Himawanto; **Law** (Law) *Dean*: Abdul Latief; **Mathematics and Natural Sciences** (Statistics) *Dean*: Siswandari

History: Founded 2000.

Degrees and Diplomas: *Diploma*: 3 yrs; *Sarjana (S1)*

Last Updated: 11/02/09

NAHDLATUL WATHAN UNIVERSITY OF MATARAM

Universitas Nahdlatul Wathan Mataram
Jalan Kaktus 1-3, Mataram, 82137 Nusa Tenggara Barat
Tel: +62(370) 641-275

Rector: Mustamuiuddin Ibrahim

Ketua: Siti Raehanun Z. Abdul Majid

Faculties
Administration; **Agriculture**; **Animal Husbandry** (Animal Husbandry; Nutrition); **Arts and Humanities**; **Mathematics and Natural Sciences**

Programmes
Pharmacy

History: Founded 1987.

Fees: (Rupiahs): 200,000 per annum

Degrees and Diplomas: *Sarjana (S1)*

Libraries: 1,539 vols
Last Updated: 02/02/09

NAROTAMA UNIVERSITY

Universitas Narotama (UNNAR)
Jalan Arief Rahman Hakim 51, Surabaya, 60117 Jawa Timur
Tel: +62(31) 594-6404
Fax: +62(31) 593-1213
EMail: humas@narotama.ac.id
Website: http://www.narotama.ac.id/

Rector: R. Djoko Soemadijo (1990-)
Tel: +62(31) 131-5231 EMail: rektor@narotama.ac.id

Ketua: Iswachyu Dhaniarti

International Relations: Erna Andajani Tel: +62(81) 134-0814

Faculties
Civil Engineering (Civil Engineering; Construction Engineering; Transport Engineering); **Computer Engineering** (Computer Engineering); **Economics** (Economics); **Law** (Law); **Mining Engineering**; **Postgraduate Studies** (Law; Management)

History: Founded 1981. A private institution under the supervision of the Department of Education and Culture.

Admission Requirements: Senior high school certificate

Fees: (Rupiahs): Undergraduate, 700,000-1m. per semester; postgraduate, 5m.

Main Language(s) of Instruction: Indonesian

Accrediting Agencies: National Accreditation Council

Degrees and Diplomas: *Sarjana (S1)*: 3-4 yrs; *Magister (S2)*: Management; Law, a further 2 yrs

Student Services: Academic counselling, Canteen, Language programs, Social counselling, Sports facilities

Special Facilities: Computer and Civil Engineering Laboratories

Libraries: Main Library
Last Updated: 11/02/09

NATIONAL INSTITUTE OF SCIENCE AND TECHNOLOGY

Institut Sains dan Teknologi Nasional (ISTN)
Jalan Moh. Kahfi II, Srengseng Indah, Jagakarsa, Jakarta Selatan, 12640 DKI Jakarta
Tel: +62(21) 727-0090 +62(21) 727-0091
Fax: +62(21) 786-6955
EMail: admin@istn.ac.id
Website: http://www.istn.ac.id

Rector: G. Suprayitno
Vice-Rector: Budi Santoso

Faculties
Engineering (Electronic Engineering; Engineering; Industrial Engineering; Mechanical Engineering); **Mathematics and Natural Sciences** (Mathematics; Pharmacy; Physics); **Planning and Civil Engineering** (Architecture; Civil Engineering; Structural Architecture)

History: Founded 1950. Acquired present status and title 1985.

Degrees and Diplomas: *Sarjana (S1)*; *Magister (S2)*: Electronic Engineering; Industrial Engineering; Mechanical Engineering

Libraries: 15,660 titles

Academic Staff *2009-2010*: Total: c. 200

Student Numbers *2009-2010*: Total: c. 3,120
Last Updated: 20/06/11

NATIONAL UNIVERSITY

Universitas Nasional (UNAS)
Jalan Sawo Manila Pejaten, Pasar Minggu, Jakarta, 12510 DKI Jakarta
Tel: +62(21) 780-6700
Fax: +62(21) 780-2718
EMail: info@unas.ac.id
Website: http://www.unas.ac.id

Rector: El Amry Bermawi Putera
Tel: +62(21) 7023-7621, Fax: +62(21) 780-2719

Ketua: Ibrahim Abdullah
Tel: +62(21) 780-8150 EMail: miharbi_03@yahoo.com

International Relations: Umar Said, Assistant to the Rector
Tel: +62(21) 780-2173 EMail: intl_department@unas.ac.id

Academies
Accountancy *(National)*; **Foreign Languages** (English; Korean) *Director*: Haerudin Sudibya; **Tourism** (Hotel Management; Tourism) *Director*: Ridwan Duchlun

Faculties
Agriculture (Agriculture; Agronomy) *Dean*: Tri Waluyo; **Arts and Humanities** *Dean*: Faldy Rasyidie; **Biology** *Dean*: Tatang Mitra Setia; **Economics** (Accountancy; Economics; Management) *Dean*: Moch. Rum Alim; **Engineering and Science** *Dean*: Idris Kusuma; **Law** (Law); **Social and Political Sciences** *Dean*: Hasto Atmodjo Suroyo

Programmes
Postgraduate

History: Founded 1949, acquired present status and title 1953. A private institution under the supervision of the Department of Education and Culture. Receives some financial support from the central and municipal governments.

Academic Year: September to August (September-March; March-August)

Admission Requirements: Secondary school certificate (Sekolah Menengah Atas, SMA) or equivalent

Fees: (Rupiahs): 2.85m. per annum

Main Language(s) of Instruction: Indonesian, English, Japanese

Degrees and Diplomas: *Diploma (D3)*; *Sarjana (S1)*: 4 yrs; *Magister (S2)*: a further 2 yrs

Student Services: Academic counselling, Canteen, Language programs, Sports facilities

Special Facilities: Green House. Laboratorium

Libraries: 13,600 vols

Publications: Berita Universitas Nasional *(monthly)*; Biologica *(annually)*; Ilmu dan Budaya *(quarterly)*; Politika *(annually)*
Last Updated: 09/03/10

NATIONAL UNIVERSITY OF EDUCATION

Universitas Pendidikan Nasional (UNDIKNAS)
Jalan Bedugul No.39, Sidakarya, Denpasar, 80225 Bali
Tel: +62(361) 723-868
Fax: +62(361) 723-077
EMail: info@undiknas.ac.id
Website: http://www.undiknas.ac.id

Rector: I Gede Sri Darma (2005-)

Deputy Rector I: Ida Bagus Raka Suardana
EMail: ajikraka@yahoo.com

International Relations: I Nyoman Budiana, Deputy Rector IV
EMail: budiana_ny@yahoo.com

Faculties

Economics (Accountancy; Development Studies; Economics; Management); **Engineering** (Civil Engineering; Electrical Engineering; Engineering; Mechanical Engineering); **Law** (Civil Law; Criminal Law; Law); **Postgraduate Studies** (Management; Public Administration); **Social and Political Sciences** (Administration; Political Sciences; Social Sciences)

History: Founded 1969 as Banking Academy. Became Institute of Finance 1977. Acquired present status and title 1984.

Governing Bodies: Foundation of Pendiknas Denpasar

Admission Requirements: High school graduation

Fees: (Rupiahs): 12m. per annum

Main Language(s) of Instruction: Indonesian

Accrediting Agencies: National Accreditation Board (Badan Akreditasi Nasional)

Degrees and Diplomas: *Sarjana (S1)*: 4 yrs; *Magister (S2)*: Law; Management; Public Administration, 18 months

Student Services: Academic counselling, Canteen, Employment services, Health services, Language programs, Sports facilities

Libraries: c. 50,000 vols

Publications: Journal of Accountancy *(1-2 per annum)*; Journal of Management *(1-2 per annum)*

Press or Publishing House: University of National Education Press

Last Updated: 30/06/11

NATIONAL VETERAN DEVELOPMENT UNIVERSITY OF EAST JAVA

Universitas Pembangunan Nasional Veteran Jawa Timur (UPN VETERAN JATIM)

Jalan Raya Rungkut Madya Gunung Anyar, Surabaya, 60294 Jawa Timur

Tel: +62(31) 870-6369

Fax: +62(31) 870-6372

EMail: humas@upnjatim.ac.id

Website: http://www.upnjatim.ac.id

Rector: Teguh Soedarto

Vice-Rector: Djohan Mashudi

Faculties

Agriculture (Agricultural Business; Agriculture; Agronomy; Economics; Plant and Crop Protection; Soil Science) *Dean*: Cholid Ridhlo; **Civil Engineering and Planning** (Architecture and Planning; Civil Engineering; Environmental Engineering) *Dean*: Edi Mulyadi; **Economics** (Accountancy; Development Studies; Economics; Management) *Dean*: Dany Ichsanudin; **Industrial Engineering** (Chemical Engineering; Computer Engineering; Food Technology; Industrial Engineering; Information Technology) *Dean*: Bambang Wahyudi; **Law** (Law) *Dean*: Ibnu Hadjar; **Postgraduate Studies** (Accountancy; Agricultural Business; Law; Management) *Dean*: Zainal Abidin; **Social and Political Sciences** (Business Administration; Communication Studies; Public Administration) *Dean*: Didik Tranggono

History: Founded 1959, acquired present status and title 1994.

Governing Bodies: Department of Defence

Admission Requirements: Senior high school certificate

Fees: (Rupiahs): Undergraduate, 2.67m. per annum; graduate, 15m.

Main Language(s) of Instruction: Indonesian, English

International Co-operation: With universities in Philippines and Netherlands.

Accrediting Agencies: Directorate General of Higher Education of Indonesia

Degrees and Diplomas: *Sarjana (S1)*: 4 yrs; *Magister (S2)*: a further 2 yrs

Student Services: Academic counselling, Canteen, Cultural centre, Employment services, Health services, Language programs, Social counselling, Sports facilities

Publications: Agricultural Bulletin *(quarterly)*; Agriculture Science Research Journal *(quarterly)*; Economics Science Reseach Journal *(quarterly)*; Engineering Science Research Journal

Last Updated: 04/02/09

NGURAH RAI UNIVERSITY

Universitas Ngurah Rai

Jalan Padma Penatih, Denpasar Timur, 80238 Bali

Tel: +62(361) 462-617

EMail: ft_unr@yahoo.com

Rector: Tjokorda Gede Atmadja

Ketua: Nyoman Sura Aditanaya

Faculties

Administration (Public Administration); **Economics** (Development Studies; Economics; Management); **Engineering** (Civil Engineering; Structural Architecture); **Law** (Law)

History: Founded 1979. A private institution under the supervision of the Department of Education and Culture.

Fees: (Rupiahs): 550,000 per annum

Degrees and Diplomas: *Sarjana (S1)*; *Magister (S2)*

Libraries: 8,332 vols

Last Updated: 03/02/09

NOMMENSEN (HKBP) UNIVERSITY

Universitas HKBP Nommensen (UHN)

Jalan Sutomo No.4, Medan, 20234 Sumatera Utara

Tel: +62(61) 456-5635 +62(61) 452-2922

Fax: +62(61) 457-1426

EMail: uhn@nommensen.org

Website: http://www.nommensen.org

Rector: Jongkers Tampubolon (2006-)
Tel: +62(61) 452-2922, Fax: +62(61) 457-1426
EMail: jtampubolon@yahoo.com

International Relations: Pohan Panjaitan, Vice-Rector for Development, National and International Relations
EMail: pohanpanjaitan@yahoo.com.au

Faculties

Agriculture (Agricultural Economics; Agricultural Engineering; Agriculture; Agronomy; Crop Production; Geology); **Animal Husbandry** (Animal Husbandry); **Economics** (Accountancy; Development Studies; Economics; Management); **Engineering** (Civil Engineering; Electrical Engineering; Engineering; Mechanical Engineering); **Language and Arts** (Arts and Humanities; English; Musical Instruments; Musicology; Religious Music); **Law** (Law); **Medicine** (Ethics; Medicine); **Postgraduate Studies** (English; Foreign Languages Education; Management); **Psychology** (Clinical Psychology; Educational Psychology; Industrial and Organizational Psychology; Psychology; Social Psychology); **Social and Political Sciences** (Business Administration; Management; Political Sciences; Public Administration; Public Relations; Secretarial Studies; Social Sciences; Taxation); **Teacher Training and Education** (Accountancy; Christian Religious Studies; Civics; Economics; Education; Educational and Student Counselling; English; German; Indonesian; Mathematics Education; Physics; Science Education; Teacher Training)

History: Founded 1954. A private institution under the supervision of the Department of Education and Culture.

Academic Year: September to July (September-February; March-July)

Admission Requirements: Certificate of Senior High Schools (Sekolah Lanjutan Atas, SLA)

Fees: (Rupiahs): 3m.-4.5m. per annum

Main Language(s) of Instruction: Indonesian

Degrees and Diplomas: *Diploma*: 3 yrs; *Sarjana (S1)*: 4-5 yrs; *Magister (S2)*: English Education; Management, a further 2 yrs

Student Services: Academic counselling, Canteen, Health services, Sports facilities

Special Facilities: 23 Ha Ranch for Agriculture and Animal Husbandry Expertise and Training Centre

Libraries: Nommensen University Library, c. 25,000 vols, c. 11,000 titles; 2 public magazines with 60 vols, 8 scientific magazines with 100 vols and 3 journals with 15 vols. Also Batak Studies Library.

Publications: Visi, Scientific Magazine *(quarterly)*; Warta Nommensen, University Public Magazine *(quarterly)*

Last Updated: 24/06/11

NORTH SULAWESI UNIVERSITY OF TECHNOLOGY

Universitas Teknologi Sulawesi Utara

Jalan Piere Tendean Komplek Megamas Smart 12, Manado, 95122 Sulawesi Utara
Tel: +62(431) 332-7170
Fax: +62(431) 861-328
EMail: stie_harapankasih@yahoo.com

Rector: Karolinus M. Senduk

Ketua: Fransiskus Senduk

Programmes

Business Administration; **Communication Studies**; **Economics**; **Engineering** (Agricultural Engineering; Civil Engineering; Electrical Engineering; Environmental Engineering; Industrial Engineering); **Regional and City Planning** (Regional Planning; Town Planning)

Degrees and Diplomas: *Sarjana (S1)*

Last Updated: 28/05/10

NUKU UNIVERSITY

Universitas Nuku

Jl. Pahlawan Nuku No.1, Soasio, Maluku Utara, 97812 Maluku
Tel: +62(921) 61-126

Rector: Hasanuddin

Ketua: Djafar Yunus

Faculties

Agriculture and Forestry; **Economics**; **Engineering**; **Marine Science** (Marine Science and Oceanography); **Social and Political Sciences**

Degrees and Diplomas: *Sarjana (S1)*

Last Updated: 03/02/09

NURTANIO UNIVERSITY OF BANDUNG

Universitas Nurtanio Bandung

Jalan Pajajaran 219, Lanud Husein Sastranegara, Bandung, 40174 Jawa Barat
Tel: +62(22) 603-4484 +62(22) 601-1076
Fax: +62(22) 542-0486
EMail: unnur@unnur.ac.id; webmaster@unnur.ac.id
Website: http://www.unnur.ac.id

Rector: Abdul Madjid

Vice-Rector: Hidayat EMail: hidayat@unnur.ac.id

International Relations: Melia Eka Lestiani, Vice Dean
Tel: +62(81) 56-03-95-98 EMail: mlestiani@yahoo.com

Faculties

Computer Science and Informatics (Computer Engineering; Information Technology); **Economics** (Accountancy; Economics; Management); **Engineering** (Aeronautical and Aerospace Engineering; Air Transport; Electrical Engineering; Engineering; Engineering Management; Industrial Engineering); **Social and Political Sciences** (Administration; Business Administration; Government; Political Sciences; Public Administration; Social Sciences; Transport Management)

History: Founded 1999.

Governing Bodies: Rector assisted by three Vice Rectors and four Faculties Deans

Academic Year: September to July (September-January; February-July)

Admission Requirements: Senior High School Certificate and entrance examination

Fees: (Rupiahs): 1.7m. per annum

Main Language(s) of Instruction: Indonesian

Accrediting Agencies: Ministry of Education

Degrees and Diplomas: *Diploma (D3)*: 3 yrs; *Sarjana (S1) (S1)*: 4 yrs; *Magister (S2)*: Administration, 2 yrs

Student Services: Academic counselling, Canteen, Cultural centre, Employment services, Language programs, Social counselling, Sports facilities

Special Facilities: Aircraft workshop

Libraries: 7,500 vols

Academic Staff *2009-2010*: Total: c. 140

Student Numbers *2009-2010*: Total: c. 1,100

Last Updated: 29/06/11

NUSA BANGSA UNIVERSITY

Universitas Nusa Bangsa (UNB)

Jl. KH. Solen Iskandar Km 4, Cimanggu Tanah Sareal, Bogor, 16166 Jawa Barat
Tel: +62(251) 834-0217 +62(251) 753-3680
Fax: +62(251) 753-5605
EMail: nusabangsa@unb.ac.id
Website: http://www.unb.ac.id

Rector: Barijadi Prawirosastro (2007-)

Ketua: P. Soeryo Suwarno
Tel: +62(21) 726-0744 EMail: ypkmk_nus@indo.net.id

International Relations: Nurarifin S. Muhibat, Head of Students Academics and Administration
EMail: NurarifinSMuhibat@yahoo.co.id

Faculties

Agriculture (Agricultural Business; Agricultural Economics; Agriculture; Agronomy); **Economics** (Accountancy; Economics; Finance; Health Administration; Human Resources; Management; Marketing); **Forestry** (Ecology; Forest Management; Forest Products; Forestry; Natural Resources); **Mathematics and Natural Sciences** (Biology; Chemistry; Mathematics; Natural Sciences); **Postgraduate Studies** (Economics; Management)

History: Founded 1987.

Fees: (Rupiahs): 3.5m. per semester

Main Language(s) of Instruction: Indonesian

International Co-operation: With university in the Netherlands

Accrediting Agencies: National Accreditation Board, Ministry of Education

Degrees and Diplomas: *Diploma*: 2 yrs; *Sarjana (S1)*: 4-5 yrs; *Magister (S2)*: Economic Science and Development; Management, a further 2 yrs

Student Services: Academic counselling, Canteen, Language programs, Sports facilities

Student Residential Facilities: Yes

Libraries: c. 7,500 vols

Publications: Journal, Journal of Agriculture, Economics, Science and Forestry *(biannually)*

Academic Staff *2009-2010*	**TOTAL**
FULL-TIME	c. **70**
Student Numbers *2009-2010*	
All (Foreign Included)	c. **460**

Part-time students, 310.

Last Updated: 29/06/11

NUSA LONTAR ROTE UNIVERSITY

Universitas Nusa Lontar Rote

Kompleks Unstar, Mokdale Ba'a, Kabupaten Rote Ndao, 85111 Nusa Tenggara Timur
Tel: +62(380) 871-087

Rector: Jamin Habid

Ketua: Christiene Fanggidae

Faculties

Agriculture; **Aquaculture** (Aquaculture); **Education** (Biological and Life Sciences; English; Geography; History); **Engineering** (Civil Engineering; Mechanical Engineering); **Law** (Law); **Management** (Management)

History: Founded 2001.

Degrees and Diplomas: *Sarjana (S1)*

Last Updated: 03/02/09

NUSA NIPA UNIVERSITY

Universitas Nusa Nipa
Jalan Kesehatan 3, Maumere, 86111 Nusa Tenggara Timur

Rector: Wilhelm Djulei Conterius

Ketua: Sabinus Nabu

Programmes

Agriculture (Agricultural Engineering; Fishery); **Architecture** (Architecture; Structural Architecture); **Business Administration** (Accountancy; Management); **Communication Studies** (Communication Studies); **Engineering**; **Nursing** (Nursing); **Psychology**

Degrees and Diplomas: *Sarjana (S1)*
Last Updated: 03/05/10

NUSA TENGGARA BARAT UNIVERSITY

Universitas Nusa Tenggara Barat
Jl. Pemuda No. 20, Mataram, 83125 Nusa Tenggara Barat
Tel: +62(370) 628-411 +62(370) 623-928
Fax: +62(370) 628-411

Rektor: Bernardus Sore

Ketua: Lalu Azhar

Programmes

Arts (Crafts and Trades; Dance; Theatre); **Economics** (Economics; Management); **Engineering** (Architecture; Civil Engineering; Mining Engineering; Structural Architecture); **Forestry** (Forestry); **Public Health** (Health Sciences; Public Health); **Veterinary Science** (Veterinary Science)
History: Founded 1999.

Admission Requirements: High School Certificate

Main Language(s) of Instruction: Indonesian

Degrees and Diplomas: *Diploma*: 3 yrs; *Sarjana (S1)*: 5 yrs

Student Services: Academic counselling, Canteen, Cultural centre, Employment services, Handicapped facilities, Health services, Nursery care, Sports facilities
Last Updated: 29/06/11

NUSANTARA INSTITUTE OF BUSINESS

Institut Bisnis Nusantara
Jalan DI Panjaitan 24, Jakarta 13340
Tel: +62(21) 856-4932
Fax: +62(21) 856-4937
EMail: info@ibn.ac.id
Website: http://www.ibn.ac.id/

Programmes

Accountancy (Accountancy); **Communication Studies** (Communication Studies); **Company Management** (Business Administration); **Computer Systems**; **English Literature** (English; English Studies; Literature); **Information Systems** (Information Technology); **Management** (Management); **Marketing Management**

Degrees and Diplomas: *Diploma*; *Sarjana (S1)*; *Magister (S2)*
Last Updated: 22/04/10

NUSANTARA MULTIMEDIA UNIVERSITY

Universitas Multimedia Nusantara
Jl. Boulevard Gading Serpong, Tangerang, Banten
Tel: +62(21) 5422-0808
Fax: +62(21) 5422-0800
EMail: pmb@unimedia.ac.id
Website: http://www.umn.ac.id/

Rector: Yohanes Surya

Vice-Rector, Administration: Andrey Andoko

Faculties

Art and Design; **Communication**; **Communication and Information Technology** (Computer Engineering; Information Technology); **Economics** (Accountancy; Economics; Finance; Human Resources; Management; Marketing)

Degrees and Diplomas: *Sarjana (S1)*
Last Updated: 03/05/10

NUSANTARA TIMBUL UNIVERSITY

Universitas Timbul Nusantara
Jalan Mandala Utara 33-34, Tomang, Jakarta Barat, 11440 DKI Jakarta
Tel: +62(21) 560-2637
Fax: +62(21) 560-4658
EMail: utira@utira-ibek.ac.id
Website: http://utira-ibek.ac.id/

Rector: Laurence A. Manullang EMail: biro.rektorat@yahoo.com

Faculties

Communication Studies (Communication Studies; Public Relations); **Economics** (Accountancy; Economics; Finance; International Business; Management; Marketing); **Engineering** (Computer Engineering; Computer Networks; Construction Engineering; Engineering; Structural Architecture; Transport Engineering; Water Management); **Fishing and Marine Science** (Fishery; Marine Science and Oceanography); **Law** (Commercial Law; International Law; Law); **Mathematics and Biology** (Biology; Mathematics)

Programmes

Graduate Studies (Accountancy; Finance; Information Management; International Business; Management)

Degrees and Diplomas: *Sarjana (S1)*; *Magister (S2)*
Last Updated: 31/05/10

NUSANTARA UNIVERSITY MANADO

Universitas Nusantara Manado
Jalan Sudirman 2, Manado, 95111 Sulawesi Utara
Tel: +62(431) 847-380
Fax: +62(431) 867-039
EMail: admin@nusantara.ac.id
Website: http://www.nusantara.ac.id

Rector: Yosias Eldrich Teddy Manueke

Assistant Rector I: Merry Ratar

Faculties

Agriculture; **Arts and Humanities** *Dean*: G. Warow; **Economics** *Dean*: E.P. Heydemans; **Engineering** *Dean*: E.P. Heidemans
History: Founded 1995.

Fees: (Rupiahs): 760,000 per annum

Degrees and Diplomas: *Diploma*: 3 yrs; *Sarjana (S1)*
Last Updated: 03/02/09

PADANG INSTITUTE OF TECHNOLOGY

Institut Teknologi Padang
Jalan Gajah Mada Kandis Nanggalo, Padang, 25143 Sumatera Barat
Tel: +62(751) 705-5202
Fax: +62(751) 444-842
Website: http://www.itp.ac.id

Faculties

Civil Engineering and Planning (Civil Engineering; Regional Planning; Surveying and Mapping; Town Planning); **Industrial Engineering** (Electrical Engineering; Industrial Engineering; Information Technology; Materials Engineering; Mechanical Engineering)

History: Founded 1973 as Padang Academy of Engineering (ATP). Acquired present title 2002.

Degrees and Diplomas: *Diploma*; *Sarjana (S1)*
Last Updated: 11/07/11

PAKUAN UNIVERSITY

Universitas Pakuan
PO Box 452, Jalan Pakuan, Ciheuleut, Bogor, 16144 Jawa Barat
Tel: +62(251) 312-206
Fax: +62(251) 356-927
EMail: unpak@indo.net.id
Website: http://www.unpak.ac.id/

Rector: Bibin Rubini Tel: +62(251) 373-337

Vice-Rector, Academic: Oding Sunardi

Faculties
Arts and Humanities (Arts and Humanities; English; Indonesian; Japanese; Literature); **Economics** (Accountancy; Economics; Management); **Educational Sciences and Teacher Training** (Art Education; Biology; Education; Educational Sciences; English; Indonesian; Mathematics Education; Modern Languages; Natural Sciences; Primary Education; Teacher Training); **Engineering**; **Law** (Law); **Mathematics and Natural Sciences** (Biology; Chemistry; Mathematics and Computer Science; Natural Sciences)

Programmes
Postgraduate (Biology; Educational Administration; Environmental Studies; Law; Management)

History: Founded 1961 as Universitas Bogor, merged 1977 with other private Colleges in Bogor, renamed Universitas Pakuan 1980. A private institution under the supervision of the Department of Education and Culture.

Governing Bodies: Kartika Siliwangi Foundation

Academic Year: September to July (September-January; March-July)

Admission Requirements: Senior high school certificate (Sekolah Menengah Umum)

Fees: (Rupiahs): 700,000 per annum

Main Language(s) of Instruction: Indonesian

Accrediting Agencies: National Board of Accreditation

Degrees and Diplomas: *Sarjana (S1)*: 4 yrs; *Magister (S2)*

Student Services: Academic counselling, Canteen, Cultural centre, Health services, Language programs, Sports facilities

Special Facilities: Experimental Farm. Performing Arts Studio

Libraries: Central Library, 25,421 vols

Publications: Majalah Hukum *(biannually)*; Majalah Pakuan *(biannually)*

Last Updated: 26/02/10

PALANGKA RAYA CHRISTIAN UNIVERSITY

Universitas Kristen Palangka Raya
Jalan RTA. Milono Km. 85, Palangka Raya, Kalimantan Tengah
Tel: +62(536) 22-205
Fax: +62(536) 24-212

Rector: Bambang TK Garang

Ketua: Halind Ardi

Faculties
Animal Husbandry (Animal Husbandry; Nutrition) *Dean*: Samara Massaw; **Engineering** (Civil Engineering; Engineering) *Dean*: Patris L. Sera; **Fishery** (Fishery; Water Management) *Dean*: Suwar J. Binti; **Social and Political Sciences** (Government; Political Sciences; Social Sciences) *Dean*: Elman D. Dangan

History: Founded 1987.

Fees: (Rupiahs): 800,000 per annum

Degrees and Diplomas: *Sarjana (S1)*

Libraries: 2,278 vols

Last Updated: 09/03/10

PALANGKA RAYA PGRI UNIVERSITY

Universitas PGRI Palangka Raya
Jalan Hiu Putih Tjilik Riwut Km. 7, Palangka Raya, 73112 Kalimantan Tengah
Tel: +62(536) 322-0778

Rector: Suriansyah Murhaini

Ketua: Dinus Biem

Faculties
Agriculture (Agricultural Business; Agriculture; Forestry); **Education and Teacher Training** (Educational Sciences; Geography; Geography (Human); Health Education; History; Leisure Studies; Physical Education; Social Sciences; Teacher Training); **Law** (Law); **Social and Political Sciences** (Political Sciences; Social Sciences; Sociology)

History: Founded 1990.

Degrees and Diplomas: *Sarjana (S1)*

Last Updated: 30/06/11

PALAPA INSTITUTE OF SCIENCE AND TECHNOLOGY

Institut Sains dan Teknologi Palapa
Jalan Batu Permata Tlogomas, Malang, Jawa Timur
Tel: +62(341) 582-134

Programmes
Engineering (Chemical Engineering; Computer Engineering; Industrial Engineering; Mechanical Engineering); **Statistics** (Statistics)

History: Founded 2000.

Degrees and Diplomas: *Sarjana (S1)*

Libraries: 1,089 titles

Last Updated: 22/06/11

PALEMBANG PGRI UNIVERSITY

Universitas PGRI Palembang
Jalan Jend. A. Yani, Lorong Gotong Royong 9/10, Ulu Darat, Palembang, Sumatera Selatan
Tel: +62(711) 510-043
Fax: +62(711) 514-782
EMail: info@univpgri-palembang.ac.id; univ_pgriplg@plasa.com
Website: http://www.univpgri-palembang.ac.id/

Rector: Syarwani Ahmad (2009-2014)
EMail: adm@univpgri-palembang.ac.id

Chief of Foundation: Aidil Fitrisyah
Tel: +62(711) 514-783, Fax: +62(711) 516-557

International Relations: Nangssari Ahmad
Tel: +62(711) 362-963 EMail: nangsariahmad@ymail.com

Faculties
Civil Engineering (Chemical Engineering; Civil Engineering; Electrical Engineering; Engineering); **Economics** (Accountancy; Economics; Management); **Fishery** (Fishery); **Language Education** (Modern Languages); **Mathematics and Natural Sciences** (Mathematics; Natural Sciences); **Teacher Training and Education** (Accountancy; Dance; Education; Educational and Student Counselling; English; Foreign Languages Education; Geography; History; Indonesian; Mathematics Education; Music Education; Physics; Teacher Training; Theatre)

History: Founded as Sekolah Tinggi Keguruan dan Ilmu Pendidikan PGRI Palembang 1984. Acquired present title and status 2000.

Governing Bodies: YPLP - PT PGRI Sumsel

Academic Year: September to August

Admission Requirements: Senior High School Certificate

Fees: (Rupiahs): 4.8m. per annum

Main Language(s) of Instruction: Indonesian

Accrediting Agencies: Directorate of Higher Education

Degrees and Diplomas: *Diploma (Amd)*: 3 yrs; *Sarjana (S1)*: 4 yrs; *Magister (S2)*: 3 yrs

Student Services: Academic counselling, Canteen, Cultural centre, Health services, Language programs, Nursery care, Sports facilities

Student Residential Facilities: Yes

Special Facilities: Laboratories

Libraries: c. 18,000 vols

Publications: Media Teknik, Publication of the the Engineering Faculty Articko *(1-2 per annum)*; Ripteksi, Publication of the Articko Research Centre *(1-2 per annum)*; Sainmatika, Publication of the Faculty of Mathematics and Natural Sciences *(1-2 per annum)*; Wahana Didaktika, Publication of the Faculty of Teacher Training and Education *(3 per annum)*; Wahana Ekonomika, Publciation of the Faculty of Economics *(1-2 per annum)*

Academic Staff *2008-2009*	MEN	WOMEN	TOTAL
FULL-TIME	104	170	274
PART-TIME	240	334	574
STAFF WITH DOCTORATE			
FULL-TIME	4	1	5
PART-TIME	7	2	9

Student Numbers *2008-2009*			
All (Foreign Included)	4,537	8,556	13,093
FOREIGN ONLY	-	-1	0

Part-time students, 848.

Last Updated: 26/10/10

PALEMBANG UNIVERSITY

Universitas Palembang (UNPAL)

Jalan Dharmapala 1A, Bukit Besar, Palembang, 30139 Sumatera Selatan
Tel: +62(711) 440-650 +62(711) 442-318
Fax: +62(711) 442-318

Rector: Zulkifli Sadarisman Mukti

Vice-Rector, Academic Affairs: Joni Philep Rompas

International Relations: Burlian Hasani, Director, Public Relations

Faculties

Agriculture (Agriculture; Agronomy); **Economics** (Economics; Finance; Human Resources; Management; Marketing); **Engineering** (Civil Engineering; Electrical Engineering; Engineering); **Law** (Law)

History: Founded 1981, acquired present status 1982.

Governing Bodies: Yayasan Perguruan Tinggi Palembang (YPTP)

Academic Year: September to June (September-January; February-June)

Admission Requirements: Secondary school certificat (SMU)

Main Language(s) of Instruction: Indonesian

Accrediting Agencies: Badan Akreditasi Nasional Perguruan Tinggi (BAN-PT)

Degrees and Diplomas: *Sarjana (S1)*: 4 yrs

Student Services: Academic counselling, Canteen, Social counselling, Sports facilities

Special Facilities: Agriculture and Technical Laboratory. Computer Laboratory. Green House

Libraries: Main Library

Last Updated: 29/06/11

PAMULANG UNIVERSITY

Universitas Pamulang (UNPAM)

Jln. Surya Kencana 1, Pamulang Barat - Pamulang, Tangerang, 15417 Banten
Tel: +62(21) 743-1067 +62(21) 741-2566
Fax: +62(21) 741-2566
EMail: info@unpam.ac.id
Website: http://unpam.ac.id/

Rector: Muhammed Sugeng Hidayat

Head of Academic Administration: Buchori Nuriman

International Relations: Ari Andarsyah

Programmes

Engineering (Chemical Engineering; Electrical Engineering; Information Technology; Mechanical Engineering); **Languages and Literature** (English; Indonesian; Literature; Native Language); **Law** (Law); **Management** (Accountancy; Management; Secretarial Studies); **Mathematics and Computer Science** (Computer Science; Mathematics); **Postgraduate Studies** (Management); **Social and Political Sciences** (Civics; Government)

History: Founded 2000.

Governing Bodies: Sasmita Foundation

Admission Requirements: High School Certificate; Entrance Examination

Fees: (Rupiahs): 1.8m. per semester

Main Language(s) of Instruction: Indonesian; English

Accrediting Agencies: National Accrediting Agency (Badan Akreditasi Nasional Perguruan Tinggi - BAN PT)

Degrees and Diplomas: *Diploma (D3)*: 3 yrs; *Sarjana (S1) (S1)*: 4 1/2 yrs; *Magister (S2)*: Management

Student Services: Academic counselling, Canteen, Foreign student adviser, Social counselling, Sports facilities

Special Facilities: Movie Studio; Hospital

Libraries: c. 5,600 vols

Publications: Mejalah/jurnal (Journals)

Academic Staff *2009-2010*: Total: c. 310

Student Numbers *2009-2010*: Total: c. 8,700

Last Updated: 29/06/11

PANCA BHAKTI UNIVERSITY

Universitas Panca Bhakti (UPB)

Jalan Komplek Yos. Sudarso, Pontianak, 78113 Kalimantan Barat
Tel: +62(561) 772-677
Fax: +62(561) 774-442
EMail: mail@upb.ac.id
Website: http://upb.ac.id

Rector: Irene A. Muslim

Ketua: Rihat Natsir Silalahi

Faculties

Agriculture (Agricultural Business; Agricultural Engineering; Agriculture); **Economics** (Accountancy; Economics; Management); **Engineering**; **Law**

History: Founded 1983.

Fees: (Rupiahs): 380,000 per annum

Degrees and Diplomas: *Sarjana (S1)*

Libraries: 4,624 vols

Last Updated: 03/02/09

PANCA MARGA UNIVERSITY

Universitas Panca Marga

Jalan Yos Sudarso, Pabean Dringu, Probolinggo, 67271 Jawa Timur
Tel: +62(335) 422-715
Fax: +62(335) 427-923
EMail: upm_probolinggo@telkom.net

Rector: Ngatimun

Ketua: Sugeng Irawan

Faculties

Agriculture (Agriculture; Agronomy); **Arts and Humanities**; **Economics** (Accountancy; Economics; Management); **Education** (Civics; Education); **Engineering** (Electrical Engineering; Engineering; Industrial Engineering; Mechanical Engineering); **Law**; **Social and Political Sciences**

History: Founded 1984.

Fees: (Rupiahs): 480,000 per annum

Degrees and Diplomas: *Sarjana (S1)*

Libraries: 3,717 vols

Last Updated: 03/02/09

PANCASAKTI UNIVERSITY

Universitas Pancasakti

Jalan A Mangerangi 73, Makassar, 90223 Sulawesi Selatan
Tel: +62(411) 871-306
Fax: +62(411) 837-247

Rector: Syaharuddin Nawi

Ketua: Nophand Shahnyb

Faculties

Agricultural Technology *Dean*: Asdi Marzoeki; **Community Health** (Community Health); **Mathematics and Natural Sciences** (Biology; Chemistry; Mathematics; Natural Sciences; Pharmacy; Physics) *Dean*: Hasyim Barium; **Social and Political Sciences** (Communication Studies; Government; Political Sciences; Public Relations; Social Sciences) *Dean*: Muh Nasir Mahmud

History: Founded 1987.

Fees: (Rupiahs): 562,000 per annum

Degrees and Diplomas: *Sarjana (S1)*
Last Updated: 03/05/10

PANCASAKTI UNIVERSITY OF TEGAL

Universitas Pancasakti Tegal
Jalan Pancasila N° 2, Tegal 52122
Tel: +62(283) 351-082 +62(283) 351-267
EMail: upstegal@gmail.com; bapsikups@telkom.net
Website: http://www.upstegal.ac.id

Rector: Tri Jaka Kartana

Ketua: Imawan Sugiharto

Faculties

Economics (Accountancy; Economics; Management; Taxation); **Educational Science and Teacher Training** (Art Education; Civics; Economics; Educational and Student Counselling; Educational Psychology; Educational Sciences; English; Foreign Languages Education; Indonesian; Literature; Mathematics Education; Native Language Education; Teacher Training; Technology Education; Vocational Education); **Engineering and Industrial**; **Fishery** (Aquaculture; Fishery); **Law**; **Social and Political Sciences**

History: Founded 1980.

Academic Year: September to July (September-December; February-August)

Admission Requirements: Secondary school certificate (Sekolah Menengah Atas, SMA)

Fees: (Rupiahs): 1m. per annum

Main Language(s) of Instruction: Indonesian

Degrees and Diplomas: *Diploma*: 3 yrs; *Sarjana (S1)*

Libraries: 9,408 vols

Last Updated: 11/02/09

PANCASILA UNIVERSITY

Universitas Pancasila
Jalan Srengseng Sawah, Pasar Minggu, Jakarta, 12640 Jakarta Selatan
Tel: +62(21) 727-0086
Fax: +62(21) 727-1868
EMail: info@univpancasila.ac.id
Website: http://www.univpancasila.ac.id

Rector: Hendratno Edie Toet (2004-)
Tel: +62(21) 788-80315, Fax: +62(21) 788-80315

Vice-Rector: Suharso Tel: +62 (21) 787-1325

International Relations: W.P Napitupulu, Director Postgraduate Programmes Tel: +62(21) 788-80312

Faculties

Communication Studies (Communication Studies); **Economics** (Accountancy; Management) *Dean*: Trirahayu Dewi; **Engineering** (Architecture; Civil Engineering; Electrical Engineering); **Law** (Law) *Dean*: Herlina Indah; **Pharmacy** (Chemistry; Pharmacy) *Dean*: Redja I Wayan; **Psychology**

Programmes

Postgraduate Studies (Accountancy; Law; Management; Mechanical Engineering; Pharmacy)

History: Founded 1966. A private institution under the supervision of the Department of Education and Culture.

Academic Year: September to August (September-January; February-August)

Admission Requirements: Secondary school certificate (Sekolah Menengah)

Fees: (US Dollars): c. 500-700 per semester

Main Language(s) of Instruction: Indonesian

Degrees and Diplomas: *Diploma*: 3 yrs; *Sarjana (S1)*: 4-7 yrs; *Magister (S2)*: 2 yrs; *Doktor (S3)*: 3 yrs. Also Application Course on Mining and Oil and Gas Taxation

Student Services: Academic counselling, Canteen, Employment services, Health services, Language programs, Sports facilities

Special Facilities: Language Laboratories

Libraries: Faculty libraries, total, 82,409 vols

Publications: Bulletin Fakultas Farmasi *(monthly)*; Humaniora Sains and Tecnology; Journal Fakultas Teknik *(monthly)*; Retorika Fakultas Hukum *(monthly)*; Suara Ekonomi *(monthly)*

Press or Publishing House: Pancasila Press

Last Updated: 28/01/09

PANDANARAN UNIVERSITY

Universitas Pandanaran (UPAND SEMARANG)
Jalan Kelud Raya 2, Semarang, 50237 Jawa Tengah
Tel: +62(24) 841-3061

Rector: Djoko Marsudi

Ketua: Harini Krisniati

Faculties

Economics (Accountancy; Economics; Management) *Dean*: G.B. Pakpahan; **Engineering** (Electrical Engineering; Engineering; Environmental Engineering) *Dean*: Dwi Rahadi; **Industrial Engineering** *Dean*: Herry Santosa; **Planning and Civil Engineering** (Architecture and Planning; Civil Engineering) *Dean*: Triarso; **Social and Political Sciences** (Business Administration; Communication Studies; Political Sciences; Social Sciences) *Dean*: R. Susilo

History: Founded 1996.

Fees: (Rupiahs): 750,000 per annum

Main Language(s) of Instruction: Indonesian

Degrees and Diplomas: *Diploma*: 3 yrs; *Sarjana (S1)*: 4 yrs

Student Services: Academic counselling, Canteen, Sports facilities

Libraries: 1,028 vols

Publications: Buku Pedoman UNPAND *(annually)*

Press or Publishing House: Suara Merdeka; Jawa Pos

Last Updated: 03/02/09

PANJI SAKTI UNIVERSITY OF SINGARAJA

Universitas Panji Sakti Singaraja (UNIPAS)
Jalan Bisma 22, Singaraja, 81116 Bali
Tel: +62(368) 23-588
Fax: +62(368) 21-108

Rector: Made Metera
Tel: +62(368) 23-588 EMail: metera@telkom.net

Ketua: Ketut Rindjin

Faculties

Agriculture; **Economics**; **Educational Sciences and Teacher Training**; **Law**; **Social and Political Sciences**

History: Founded 1985.

Academic Year: August to July

Fees: (Rupiahs): 1m. per annum

Main Language(s) of Instruction: Indonesian

Accrediting Agencies: National Accreditation Board, BAN (Badan Akreditasi Nasional)

Degrees and Diplomas: *Sarjana (S1)*: Economics (SE) (Sarjana Ekonomi); Law (SH) (Sarjana Hukum), 4 years; *Sarjana (S1)*: Public Administration (S.SOS) (Sarjana Ilmu Sosial), 4 yrs

Student Services: Academic counselling, Canteen, Language programs, Social counselling, Sports facilities

Libraries: 4,000 vols

Publications: Journal Widyatech, Science and Technology Journal

Last Updated: 03/02/09

PAPUA CHRISTIAN UNIVERSITY

Universitas Kristen Papua
Jalan F Kalasuat, Malanu, Sorong, 94512 Papua
Website: http://www.ukip.ac.id/

Rector: Sasmoko

Ketua: Sophian Andi

Programmes

Agricultural Business (Agricultural Business); **Animal husbandry** (Animal Husbandry); **Biology**; **Christian Religious Education** (Christian Religious Studies; Religious Education); **Engineering**;

Fishery (Fishery); **Law** (Law); **Management** (Management); **Mathematics**; **Theology** (Theology)

Degrees and Diplomas: *Sarjana (S1)*

Last Updated: 30/04/10

PAPUA YAPIS UNIVERSITY

Universitas Yapis Papua

Jalan Sam Ratulangi 11, Jayapura, 99115 Papua
Tel: +62(967)550-355
Fax: +62(967)537-985
EMail: admin@uniyap.ac.id
Website: http://www.uniyap.ac.id

Rector: Muhdi B. Ibrahim

Ketua: Zubeir D. Hussein

Programmes

Accountancy (Accountancy); **Aquaculture**; **Government** (Government; Political Sciences); **Law** (Law); **Management**; **Public Administration**

Degrees and Diplomas: *Sarjana (S1)*; *Magister (S2)*

Last Updated: 31/05/10

PARAHYANGAN CATHOLIC UNIVERSITY

Universitas Katolik Parahyangan (UNPAR)

Jalan Ciumbuleit 94, Bandung, 40141 Jawa Barat
Tel: +62(22) 203-2655, Ext. 114 +62(22) 203-2576
Fax: +62(22) 203-1110
EMail: humas@home.unpar.ac.id
Website: http://www.unpar.ac.id

Rektor: Cecilia Lauw Giok Swan EMail: rektorat@home.unpar.ac.id

Vice-Rector for Organization and Human Resources: Ismadi Santoso Bekti EMail: ismadi@home.unpar.ac.id

Vice-Rector for Academic Affairs: Paulus P. Rahardjo

Vice-Rector for Student Affairs: Laurentius Tarpin

Faculties

Economics (Accountancy; Development Studies; Economics; Management); **Engineering** (Architecture; Civil Engineering; Engineering; Structural Architecture); **Industrial Technology** (Chemical Engineering; Industrial Engineering); **Information Technology and Sciences** (Computer Science; Information Sciences; Information Technology; Mathematics; Physics); **Law** (Commercial Law; Law; Notary Studies); **Philosophy** (Philosophical Schools; Philosophy; Religious Studies); **Social and Political Sciences** (Business Administration; International Relations; Public Administration)

Programmes

Doctoral Studies (Architecture; Civil Engineering; Economics; Law; Structural Architecture); **Magister Studies** (Architecture; Chemical Engineering; Civil Engineering; Industrial Engineering; Law; Management; Social Sciences; Structural Architecture; Theology)

Further Information: Also Mandarin and Japanese Language Courses

History: Founded 1955 as Academy of Commerce, reorganized 1958 and acquired present title and status 1961. A private institution under the supervision of the Department of Education and Culture.

Academic Year: September to June (September-January; February-June)

Admission Requirements: Secondary school certificate (Sekolah Menengah Atas, SMA) and entrance examination

Main Language(s) of Instruction: Indonesian

Degrees and Diplomas: *Diploma*: 3 yrs; *Sarjana (S1)*: 4 yrs; *Magister (S2)*: Architecture; Chemical Engineering; Civil Engineering; Industrial Engineering; Laws; Management; Social Sciences; Theology, 2 yrs; *Doktor (S3)*: Architecture; Civil Engineering; Economics; Laws, 3 yrs

Student Services: Academic counselling, Employment services, Foreign student adviser, Handicapped facilities, Health services, Language programs, Social counselling, Sports facilities

Student Residential Facilities: Guest House

Libraries: University Library, c. 100,000 vols

Publications: Bina Ekonomi *(biannually)*; Integral *(3 per annum)*; Melintas *(biannually)*; Pacis *(biannually)*; Potensia *(biannually)*; Pro Justitia *(quarterly)*; Profil *(biannually)*; Teknik Sipil *(biannually)*

Last Updated: 22/07/11

PARAMADINA UNIVERSITY

Universitas Paramadina (UPM)

Jl. Gatot Subroto Kav. 97-99, Mampang, Jakarta Selatan, 12790 DKI Jakarta
Tel: +62(21) 791-81188
Fax: +62(21) 799-3375
EMail: info@paramadina.ac.id
Website: http://www.paramadina.ac.id

Rector: Anies R. Baswedan EMail: rector@paramadina.ac.id

Vice-Rector for Operational and Finance: Bima Priya Santosa EMail: bima.santosa@paramadina.ac.id

International Relations: Wijayanto, Vice-Rector for Student Affairs, Cooperation and Fellowship
EMail: wijayanto@paramadina.ac.id

Divisions

Design and Visual Communication (Communication Arts; Design; Visual Arts) *Director*: Giland Cempaka; **Industrial Design** (Industrial Design); **Information Technology** (Information Technology) *Director*: Ivonne Mangula; **International Relations** (International Relations) *Director*: Rizki Damayanti; **Management** (Management) *Director*: Iin Mayasari; **Philosophy and Religion** (Philosophy; Religion) *Director*: Abdul Muis; **Psychology** (Psychology) *Director*: Alfikalia

Graduate Schools

Business (Business Administration; Business and Commerce) *Director*: Sugeng Purwanto; **Communication** (Communication Studies) *Director*: Ketut Wijanarko; **Diplomacy** (International Relations)

History: Founded 1994.

Academic Year: September to August

Fees: (Rupiahs): 6.5m. per semester

Main Language(s) of Instruction: Indonesian

International Co-operation: With universities in Australia, Belgium, New Zealand and USA

Accrediting Agencies: National Accrediting Board, Badan Akreditasi Nasional

Degrees and Diplomas: *Sarjana (S1)*: 4 yrs; *Magister (S2)*: 2 yrs

Student Services: Academic counselling, Canteen, Cultural centre, Employment services, Foreign student adviser, Health services, Language programs, Sports facilities

Student Residential Facilities: None

Special Facilities: Audiovisual Studio; Photography Studio; Design Workshop; South East Asia Peace Laboratory; Psychological Laboratory; Computer Laboratory.

Libraries: 10,000 vols

Publications: Ekonomica Madani, Economy-Management Issues *(1-2 per annum)*; Jurnal Universitas Paramadina, Multi-disciplinary journal *(quarterly)*

Academic Staff *2009-2010*	MEN	WOMEN	TOTAL
FULL-TIME	34	24	**58**
PART-TIME	87	56	**143**
STAFF WITH DOCTORATE			
FULL-TIME	7	3	**10**
PART-TIME	10	2	**12**
Student Numbers *2009-2010*			
All (Foreign Included)	750	874	**1,624**

Last Updated: 22/11/10

PASIM NATIONAL UNIVERSITY

Universitas Nasional Pasim (UNAS PASIM)

JL. Dr Djundjunan No 167, Bandung, 40174 Jawa Barat
Tel: +62(22) 601-7486
Fax: +62(22) 602-0433
EMail: informasi@pasim.ac.id
Website: http://www.pasim.ac.id

Rektor: Mohammad Baharun

Ketua: DesfitriadyDesfitriady

Faculties

Computer Science (Computer Engineering; Computer Science; Industrial Engineering; Information Management; Information Sciences); **Economics** (Accountancy; Business Administration; Industrial Management; Management; Taxation); **Litterature**; **Psychology** (Psychology)

History: Founded 2001 as Universitas Nasional YPKP Bandung.Acquired present title 2007.

Degrees and Diplomas: *Diploma*; *Sarjana (S1)*

Last Updated: 03/02/09

PASIR PANGARAIAN UNIVERSITY

Universitas Pasir Pangaraian

Jalan Tuanku Tambusai, Kumu Desa Rambah, Pasir Pengaraian, 28457 Riau
Tel: +62(761) 91-525
Fax: +62(761) 91-525

Programmes

Agriculture (Agricultural Business; Agricultural Engineering; Agricultural Equipment; Agriculture); **Architecture** (Architecture; Structural Architecture); **Business Administration** (Accountancy; Business Administration; Management); **Engineering** (Civil Engineering; Construction Engineering; Engineering); **Midwifery** (Midwifery)

Degrees and Diplomas: *Sarjana (S1)*

Last Updated: 03/05/10

PASUNDAN UNIVERSITY

Universitas Pasundan (UNPAS)

Jl. Dr. Setiarudi 193, Bandung, Jawa Barat
Tel: +62(22) 202-1440 +62(22) 202-1436
Fax: +62(22) 200-9267
EMail: humas@unpas.ac.id
Website: http://www.unpas.ac.id/

Rector: Didi Turmudzi (2002-) EMail: rektorat@unpas.ac.id

Vice-Rector I: Eddy Jusup

International Relations: Lily Satari Satari, Vice-Rector for Cooperation Affairs

Faculties

Arts and Literature (Communication Arts; English; Film; Literature; Music; Photography; Visual Arts); **Economics** (Accountancy; Business Administration; Economics; Management); **Education and Teacher Training** (Biology; Economics; Education; Mathematics Education; Primary Education); **Engineering** (Engineering; Environmental Engineering; Food Technology; Industrial Engineering; Information Technology); **Law** (Law); **Social and Political Sciences** (Administration; Civics; Government; International Relations; Political Sciences; Public Administration; Social Sciences)

Institutes

Islamic Mission Development Studies *(LPPSI)* (Islamic Studies); **Public Service** *(LPM)*; **Research** *(LEMLIT)*; **Sundanese Culture** *(LBS)* (Islamic Studies; Mathematics and Computer Science; Technology)

Programmes

PhD Studies (Management; Social Sciences); **Postgraduate Studies** (Administration; Food Technology; Industrial Engineering; Industrial Management; Law; Management; Mathematics Education)

History: Founded 1960. A private institution under the supervision of the Department of Education and Culture.

Admission Requirements: Senior High School Certificate

Fees: (Rupiahs): 2.5m. per semester

Main Language(s) of Instruction: Indonesian

International Co-operation: With Universities in China

Degrees and Diplomas: *Diploma*: 3 yrs; *Sarjana (S1)*: 4 yrs; *Magister (S2)*: Administration and Public Policy; Food Technology; Industrial Engineering; Legal Studies; Management; Mathematics Education, 2 yrs; *Doktor (S3)*: Management; Social Sciences, 4 yrs

Student Services: Academic counselling, Canteen, Cultural centre, Employment services, Foreign student adviser, Health services, Language programs, Nursery care, Social counselling, Sports facilities

Student Residential Facilities: Dormitory

Libraries: 120,800 vols; Digital Library

Publications: Journal *(1-2 per annum)*

Last Updated: 29/06/11

PATRIA ARTHA UNIVERSITY

Universitas Patria Artha

Makassar, Sulawesi Selatan

Programmes

Business Administration (Accountancy; Business Computing; Management); **Engineering**; **Nursing** (Midwifery; Nursing); **Public Health** (Public Health)

Degrees and Diplomas: *Sarjana (S1)*; *Magister (S2)*

Last Updated: 03/05/10

PAUL CHRISTIAN UNIVERSITY OF INDONESIA

Universitas Kristen Indonesia Paulus (UKIP)

Jalan Perintis Kemerdekaan Km. 13, Daya, Makassar, 90243 Sulawesi Selatan
Tel: +62(411) 586-748 +62(411) 588-702
Fax: +62(411) 586-187
EMail: ukipsal@indosat.net.id

Rector: Pasapan Pasolong

Ketua: Litha Brent

Faculties

Agriculture (Agricultural Business; Agriculture; Aquaculture; Forest Management; Horticulture) *Dean*: Paul Gunadi; **Economics** (Accountancy; Development Studies; Economics; Management; Marketing); **Engineering** (Chemical Engineering; Civil Engineering; Computer Engineering; Electrical and Electronic Engineering; Mechanical Engineering) *Dean*: Robert Mangonton; **Law** (Law) *Dean*: Agustina Andilolo

History: Founded 1963. A private institution under the supervision of the Department of Education depending wholly on student fees.

Governing Bodies: Yayasan Pendidikan Intelegentsia Kristen Indonesia Paulus

Academic Year: September to July

Admission Requirements: High school certificate

Fees: (Rupiahs): 1,365,000 per annum

Main Language(s) of Instruction: Indonesian

Accrediting Agencies: Badan Akreditasi Nasional

Degrees and Diplomas: *Sarjana (S1)*: 4-5 yrs; *Magister (S2)*

Student Services: Academic counselling, Canteen, Language programs, Sports facilities

Libraries: 7,516 vols

Last Updated: 19/01/09

PAWYATAN DAHA UNIVERSITY

Universitas Pawyatan Daha

Jalan Soekarno - Hatta 49, Kediri, 64182 Jawa Timur
Tel: +62(354) 683-044
Fax: +62(354) 683-044

Rector: Prijo Santoso

Ketua: Jatim Mulyono

Faculties

Administration; **Economics** (Accountancy; Economics; Management); **Engineering** (Electrical Engineering; Engineering; Mechanical Engineering); **Law**

History: Founded 1986.

Fees: (Rupiahs): 946,000 per annum

Degrees and Diplomas: *Sarjana (S1)*

Libraries: 8,333 vols

Last Updated: 03/02/09

PEKALONGAN UNIVERSITY

Universitas Pekalongan

Jalan Merbabu 12, Pekalongan, 51115 Jawa Tengah
Tel: +62(285) 421-096
Fax: +62(285) 411-429
EMail: lppm_unikal@telkom.net
Website: http://www.unikal.ac.id

Rector: Husain Haikal

Ketua: Menifas Zubayr

Faculties

Agriculture *Dean*: Pudjiati Syarif; **Community Health** *Dean*: Rahardjo Sujono Putra; **Economics** *Dean*: Zahro; **Fishery** (Aquaculture; Fishery) *Dean*: Bahrus Sykirin; **Law** (Law) *Dean*: Esmara Sugeng

History: Founded 1982. A private institution under the supervision of the Department of Education and Culture.

Fees: (Rupiahs): 1.05m. per semester

Accrediting Agencies: National Accreditation Board (Badah Akreditasi Nasonal Perguruan Tinggi (BAN PT))

Degrees and Diplomas: *Sarjana (S1) (SE; SH; SPI; SP)*: 5 yrs

Libraries: 8,818 vols

Last Updated: 03/02/09

PELITA HARAPAN UNIVERSITY

Universitas Pelita Harapan

Jl. M.H. Thamrin Boulevard, Tangerang, 15811 Banten
Tel: +62(21) 546-0901
Fax: +62(21) 546-0910
EMail: infomhs@uph.edu
Website: http://www.uph.edu

Executive Vice-Chancellor/President: Gary A. Miller
EMail: gary.miller@uph.edu

Vice-President for Finance and Administration: Ferliana Suminto EMail: ferliana.suminto@staff.uph.edu

International Relations: Natalia Fifi Budiman, Director
EMail: natalia.budiman@uph.edu

Conservatories

Music (Music) *Dean*: Johnny Rep Awondatu

Faculties

Computer Science (Computer Engineering; Computer Science; Information Technology) *Dean*: Gunawan Putrodojojo; **Design and Planning** (Architecture; Civil Engineering; Communication Arts; Interior Design; Visual Arts) *Dean*: Felia Srinaga; **Industrial Technology** (Electrical Engineering; Food Technology; Industrial Engineering) *Dean*: Herman Y. Kanalebe; **Liberal Arts** (Arts and Humanities) *Dean*: Rini Wahyuningsih; **Medicine** (Medicine) *Dean*: Eka Julianta W.; **Psychology** (Psychology) *Dean*: Sri Lanawati; **Science and Mathematics** (Applied Mathematics; Biology; Biotechnology; Mathematics; Physics) *Dean*: Petrus Widjaja; **Social and Political Sciences** (Communication Studies; International Relations; Political Sciences; Social Sciences) *Dean*: Aleksius Jemadu

Schools

Business (Accountancy; Business Administration; Business and Commerce; Management) *Dean*: Adrianus Mooy; **Education** (English; Literature; Modern Languages; Teacher Trainers Education; Teacher Training) *Dean*: Connie Rasilim; **Graduate Programmes** (Accountancy; Civil Engineering; Communication Studies; Computer Science; Hotel and Restaurant; Hotel Management; Industrial Engineering; Information Technology; Journalism; Law; Management; Nursing; Radio and Television Broadcasting; Tourism) *Dean*: Juanna Judith; **Law** (Law) *Dean*: Bintan R. Saragih; **Nursing** (Nursing) *Dean*: Jane Freyana; **Tourism** (Hotel and Restaurant; Hotel Management; Tourism) *Dean*: Demson R.H. Gultom

History: Founded 1994.

Academic Year: July to June

Fees: (Rupiahs): 30m. per annum

Main Language(s) of Instruction: Indonesian, English

Degrees and Diplomas: *Sarjana (S1)*; *Magister (S2)*; *Doktor (S3)*

Student Services: Academic counselling, Canteen, Employment services, Foreign student adviser, Health services, Language programs, Sports facilities

Student Residential Facilities: Yes

Libraries: c. 65,000 vols

Last Updated: 07/04/11

PELITA HARAPAN UNIVERSITY OF MEDAN

Universitas Pelita Harapan Medan

Medan, Sumatera Utara

Programmes

Business Administration (Accountancy; Management); **Communication Studies** (Communication Studies); **Design**; **Engineering and Technology**; **Law** (Law)

Degrees and Diplomas: *Sarjana (S1)*

Last Updated: 03/05/10

PELITA HARAPAN UNIVERSITY OF SURABAYA

Universitas Pelita Harapan Surabaya (UPH SURABAYA)

Jalan A. Yani 288, Surabaya, 60234 Jawa Timur
Tel: +62(31) 5825-1007 +62(31) 5825-1010
Fax: +62(31) 5825-1020
EMail: infomhs@uphsurabaya.ac.id
Website: http://www.uphsurabaya.ac.id/

President: Jonathan Parapak (2008-) EMail: parapak@uph.edu

Vice-President: Januar Heryanto
EMail: januar.heryanto@gmail.com

International Relations: Louie Divinagracia, Dean of Business School EMail: louie_divinagracia@yahoo.com

Faculties

Computer Science (Computer Science; Information Technology) *Dean*: Kuswara Setiawan; **Economics** (Accountancy; Economics; Management) *Dean*: Louie Divinagracia; **Engineering** (Industrial Engineering; Information Technology) *Dean*: John Batubara; **Law** (Commercial Law; Law) *Dean*: Sari Mandiana; **Postgraduate Studies - Law** (Law; Management) *Dean*: Sari Mandiana; **Postgraduate Studies - Management** (Management) *Dean*: Louie Divinagracia; **Psychology** (Psychology) *Dean*: Januar Heryanto

Schools

Creative Industry (Industrial Engineering)

History: Founded 2007.

Admission Requirements: High school certificate and report from grade 10 and 11.

Fees: (Rupiahs): 5.7-7.2 per semester

Main Language(s) of Instruction: Indonesian, English

International Co-operation: With universities in Australia; Taiwan; Switzerland and USA

Accrediting Agencies: Higher Education Directorate, National Department of Education

Degrees and Diplomas: *Sarjana (S1)*: Management; Accountancy; Information Systems; Industrial Engineering; Law; Psychology, 4 yrs; *Magister (S2)*: Law; Management, 2 yrs

Student Services: Academic counselling, Canteen, Employment services, Health services, Language programs, Social counselling, Sports facilities

Student Residential Facilities: Aryaduta Apartments

Special Facilities: Laboratories

Libraries: c. 5,600 vols

Publications: Campus Asia Magazine

Academic Staff *2009-2010*	MEN	WOMEN	TOTAL
FULL-TIME	14	12	**26**
PART-TIME	31	24	**55**
STAFF WITH DOCTORATE			
FULL-TIME	17	21	**38**
PART-TIME	2	1	**3**
Student Numbers *2009-2010*			
All (Foreign Included)	308	333	**641**

Last Updated: 26/04/11

PEMBANGUNAN PANCA BUDI UNIVERSITY

Universitas Pembangunan Panca Budi (UNPAB)
PO Box 1099, Jalan Jend. Gatot Subroto, Km 45, Medan, 20122 Sumatera Utara
Tel: +62(61) 845-5571
Fax: +62(61) 451-4808
EMail: unpab@pancabudi.org; admin@pancabudi.org
Website: http://www.pancabudi.ac.id

Rector: Muhammad Isa Indrawan (1997-)

Assistant Rector: Abdullah Syafi'I Fax: +61(61) 451-4808 EMail: syafii@pancabudi.org

International Relations: Marianieke Putri, International Relation Officer EMail: admin@pancabudi.org

Faculties

Agriculture (Agriculture; Agronomy); **Economics** (Accountancy; Development Studies; Economics; Management); **Engineering** (Architecture; Computer Engineering; Electrical Engineering; Engineering; Structural Architecture); **Law** (Law)

History: Founded 1961. A private institution under the supervision of the Department of Education and Culture.

Academic Year: September to June (September-January; February-June)

Admission Requirements: Secondary school certificate (Sekolah Lanjutan Tingkat Atas, SLTA)

Fees: (Rupiahs): 1m. per annum

Main Language(s) of Instruction: Indonesian

Accrediting Agencies: Badan Akreditasi Nasional (Board of National Accreditation)

Degrees and Diplomas: *Diploma (D3)*: 3 yrs; *Sarjana (S1)*: 5 yrs; *Magister (S2)*: Law

Student Services: Academic counselling, Canteen, Employment services, Health services, Nursery care, Sports facilities

Student Residential Facilities: Yes

Special Facilities: Biological Garden. Movie Studio

Libraries: c. 10,600 vols

Publications: Collarbone Community *(1-2 per annum)*; Learned Scholar *(1-2 per annum)*; Public Lecture *(1-2 per annum)*; Research *(1-2 per annum)*

Academic Staff *2007-2008*	MEN	WOMEN	TOTAL
FULL-TIME	121	78	**199**
Student Numbers *2007-2008*			
All (Foreign Included)	2,568	1,221	**3,789**

Last Updated: 30/06/11

PEPABRI UNIVERSITY OF MAKASSAR

Universitas Pepabri Makassar
Jalan Gunung Batu Putih 38A, Makassar 90223
Tel: +62(411) 873-773
Fax: +62(411) 857-672

Rector: Tommy Sinar Surya

Ketua: Bachtiar

Faculties

Administration (Business Administration; Government; Public Administration); **Engineering** (Architecture); **Social and Political Sciences** (Criminology; Government; Social Sciences)

History: Founded 1978.

Fees: (Rupiahs): 400,000 per annum

Degrees and Diplomas: *Diploma*: 3 yrs; *Sarjana (S1)*

Libraries: 1,602 vols

Last Updated: 04/02/09

PERSADA INDONESIAN YAI UNIVERSITY

Universitas Persada Indonesia YAI
Jalan Imam Bonjol 72, Jakarta, 10310 DKI Jakarta
Tel: +62(21) 451-2954 +62(21) 451-2958
EMail: upi@yai.ac.id
Website: http://www.yai.ac.id

Rector: Yudi Yulius EMail: yayasan@yai.ac.id

Ketua: Yulius Sjukur

Faculties

Agriculture; **Economics**; **Industrial Engineering**; **Planning and Civil Engineering**; **Psychology** (Educational Psychology; Industrial and Organizational Psychology; Psychology)

History: Founded 1985.

Fees: (Rupiahs): 1.03m. per annum

Degrees and Diplomas: *Diploma*: 3 yrs; *Sarjana (S1)*; *Magister (S2)*; *Doktor (S3)*: Accountancy; Management; Psychology

Libraries: 6,160 vols

Last Updated: 04/02/09

PESANTREN TINGGI DARUL ULUM UNIVERSITY

Universitas Pesantren Tinggi Darul Ulum (UNIPDU)
Kompleks PP Darul Ulum, Peterongan, Jombang, 61481 Jawa Timur
Tel: +62(321) 861-097 +62(321) 873-655
Fax: +62(321) 866-631 +62(321) 876-771
EMail: humas@unipdu.ac.id; puskom@unipdu.ac.id
Website: http://www.unipdu.ac.id

Rector: Ahmad Zahro EMail: puskom@unipdu.ac.id

Vice-Rector: Muhammad Zainuddin Tel: +62(321) 865-703

International Relations: Muhammad Zulfikar, Vice-Rector Tel: +62(321) 866-631

Faculties

Administration (Administration; Business Administration; Public Administration); **Engineering** (Computer Graphics; Computer Networks; Industrial Engineering; Information Technology; Multimedia; Software Engineering; Telecommunications Engineering); **Health Sciences** (Midwifery; Nursing); **Islamic Studies** (Islamic Law; Islamic Studies; Islamic Theology; Primary Education; Religious Education; Secondary Education); **Languages and Literature** (English; Japanese; Literature); **Mathematics and Natural Sciences** (Applied Mathematics; Mathematics; Statistics)

Programmes

Postgraduate Studies (Educational Administration; Islamic Studies)

History: Founded 2001 through merger of the independent College of Nursing, College of Midwifery, College of Islamic Studies, College of modern languages that became faculties of the University.

Governing Bodies: Yayasan Pesantren Tinggi Darul Ulum

Academic Year: September to August (September-January; February-August)

Admission Requirements: Senior High School Certificate or Vocational School Certificate (Ijazah SMA/SMK)

Main Language(s) of Instruction: Indonesian; English

International Co-operation: With the British Council (UK) and the Indonesian Australian Language Foundation (Australia)

Accrediting Agencies: Badan Akreditasi Nasional (BAN)

Degrees and Diplomas: *Diploma*: 3 yrs; *Sarjana (S1)*: 4-5 yrs; *Magister (S2)*: a further 2 yrs

Student Services: Academic counselling, Canteen, Cultural centre, Health services, Language programs, Sports facilities

Student Residential Facilities: Female Dormitories; Male Dormitories

Special Facilities: IT Laboratory; Language Laboratory; Auditorium; Grand Mosque

Libraries: Main Library; Library of Health Science; Library of Language and Arts

Last Updated: 30/06/11

PETRA CHRISTIAN UNIVERSITY

Universitas Kristen Petra

Siwalankerto 121-131, Tromolpos 5304, Surabaya, 60236 Jawa Timur

Tel: +62(31) 843-9040 +62(31) 298-3190

Fax: +62(31) 843-6418

EMail: info@petra.ac.id

Website: http://www.petra.ac.id

Rector: Rolly Intan (2009-2013) EMail: rector@peter.petra.ac.id

Executive Secretary: Thomas Santoso

Faculties

Art and Design (Communication Arts; Design; Interior Design; Visual Arts); **Arts and Humanities** (Chinese; English Studies; Literature); **Civil Engineering and Planning** (Architecture; Civil Engineering); **Communication** (Communication Studies); **Economics** (Accountancy; Hotel Management; International Business; Management; Marketing; Tourism); **Industrial Technogy** (Computer Science; Electrical Engineering; Industrial Engineering)

Programmes

Graduate Studies (Architecture; Construction Engineering; Geological Engineering; Management)

History: Founded 1961 by the 'Petra' Association for Christian Education and Instruction. A private institution under the supervision of the Department of Education and Culture.

Governing Bodies: Foundation; Senate

Academic Year: September to July (September-January; March-July)

Admission Requirements: Secondary school certificate (Sekolah Menengah Umum, SMU) and entrance examination

Fees: (Rupiahs): 5.840,000 per annum

Main Language(s) of Instruction: Indonesian. Also English in some departments.

Accrediting Agencies: National Accreditation Board

Degrees and Diplomas: *Diploma*; *Sarjana (S1)*; *Magister (S2)*

Student Services: Academic counselling, Canteen, Cultural centre, Employment services, Foreign student adviser, Handicapped facilities, Health services, Social counselling

Special Facilities: Movie Studio, Photo Gallery, Auditorium

Libraries: Central Library, 173,877 vols; Audio Visual, 8,895 vols; Serials, 819 vols

Publications: Accountancy and Finance Journal *(biannually)*; Architecture Journal *(biannually)*; Dwi Pekan *(bimonthly)*; Electrical Journal *(biannually)*; Industrial Journal *(biannually)*; Informatic Journal *(biannually)*; 'Kata', Linguistic and Literature Journal *(biannually)*; Majalah 'Genta' *(quarterly)*; Management and Entrepreneur Journal *(biannually)*; Mechanical Journal *(biannually)*; 'Nirmana', Design, Communication and Visual Arts *(biannually)*; Sipil Journal, Journal Keilmuan and Penerapan Teknkik Sipil *(biannually)*; Tabloid 'Peduli' *(quarterly)*

Press or Publishing House: University Press

Academic Staff *2010-2011*	MEN	WOMEN	TOTAL
FULL-TIME	168	123	**291**
PART-TIME	90	61	**151**
STAFF WITH DOCTORATE			
FULL-TIME	17	5	**22**
PART-TIME	16	2	**18**
FOREIGN ONLY	5	7	**12**

Evening students, 46.

Last Updated: 27/10/10

PRESIDENT UNIVERSITY

Universitas Presiden

Jababeka Education Park, Jalan Ki Hajar Dewantara, Kota Jababeka, Bekasi, 17550 Jawa Barat

Tel: +62(21) 8910-9762

Fax: +62(21) 8910-9768

EMail: enrollment@president.ac.id

Website: http://www.president.ac.id

Rector: Ermaya Suradinata

Vice-Rector: Matias Zakaria

Faculties

Business and International Relations (Business Administration; International Relations); **Communication and Multimedia** (Computer Graphics; Public Relations); **Computing** (Information Technology); **Economics** (Accountancy; Economics; Management); **Engineering** (Electrical Engineering; Industrial Engineering); **Law** (Commercial Law; International Law; Law)

History: Founded 2001 as School of Engineering. Acquired present status 2004.

Governing Bodies: Yayasan Universitas Presiden

Fees: (Dollars) 7,500 per annum

Main Language(s) of Instruction: English

Accrediting Agencies: Ministry of Education

Degrees and Diplomas: *Sarjana (S1)*

Student Services: Academic counselling, Canteen, Employment services, Foreign student adviser, Foreign Studies Centre, Health services, Language programs, Nursery care, Social counselling, Sports facilities

Student Residential Facilities: Yes

Libraries: Yes

Academic Staff *2010-2011*	MEN	WOMEN	TOTAL
FULL-TIME	64	45	**109**
STAFF WITH DOCTORATE			
FULL-TIME	12	8	**20**

Student Numbers *2010-2011*			
All (Foreign Included)	1,128	1,103	**2,231**
FOREIGN ONLY	84	98	**182**

Last Updated: 28/10/10

PRESTON INDONESIAN UNIVERSITY

Universitas Preston Indonesia

Jalan Kapten Muslim 92, Medan, Sumatera Utara

Tel: +62(61) 845-6194

Fax: +62(61) 811-5128

Programmes

Business Administration (Management); **Communication Studies** (Communication Studies); **Economics**; **Engineering** (Agricultural Engineering; Chemical Engineering; Engineering; Industrial Engineering; Safety Engineering); **English** (English); **Japanese** (Japanese); **Public Relations** (Public Relations); **Science**

Degrees and Diplomas: *Sarjana (S1)*

Last Updated: 03/05/10

PRIMA INDONESIAN UNIVERSITY

Universitas Prima Indonesia (UNPRI)

Jalan Belanga 1, Medan, 20118 Sumatera Utara

EMail: contact@unprimdn.com

Website: http://www.unprimdn.com

Rector: Djakobus Tarigan

Vice-Rector: Monang Panjaitan

Faculties

Agriculture; **Dentistry**; **Economics**; **Engineering and Computer Science**; **Law** (Law); **Medicine** (Medicine); **Nursing and Midwifery** (Midwifery; Nursing); **Psychology** (Psychology); **Public Health** (Public Health); **Teacher Training and Education**

Degrees and Diplomas: *Sarjana (S1)*

Last Updated: 03/05/10

PROF. DR. HAZAIRIN SH UNIVERSITY

Universitas Prof. Dr. Hazairin SH
Jalan Jend. A. Yani 1, Bengkulu, 38115 Bengkulu
Tel: +62(736) 21-536
Fax: +62(736) 01-950

Rector: Pakri

Ketua: Syakum Lair

Faculties

Agriculture *Dean*: Djatmiko; **Economics** *Dean*: Syafrudin; **Educational Science and Teacher Training** *Dean*: Anuar Hamidi; **Engineering** *Dean*: Aminudin; **Law** *Dean*: Laily Ratna; **Social and Political Sciences** *Dean*: Mulyadi

History: Founded 1984.

Fees: (Rupiahs): 400,000 per annum

Degrees and Diplomas: *Diploma*: 2-3 yrs; *Sarjana (S1)*; *Magister (S2)*

Libraries: 7,667 vols

Last Updated: 03/05/10

PROF. DR. MOESTOPO (BERAGAMA) UNIVERSITY

Universitas Prof. Dr. Moestopo (Beragama)
Jalan Hanglekir 1/8 Blok, H. Kebayoran Baru, Jakarta, 12120 DKI Jakarta
Tel: +62(21) 739-5333
Fax: +62(21) 725-2682
EMail: admin@moestopo.ac.id
Website: http://www.moestopo.ac.id

Rector: H. Sunarto
Tel: +62(21) 724-8517 EMail: rektorat@moestopo.ac.id

Vice-Rector (Academic): Soenardi Dwidjosusastro

International Relations: Beya Indriati Tel: +62(21) 722-0269

Faculties

Communication Sciences *Dean*: Sunarto; **Dentistry** (Dentistry) *Dean*: Endang Jeniati; **Economics** (Accountancy; Economics; Management); **Social and Political Science** (International Relations; Political Sciences; Public Administration; Social Sciences)

Programmes

Postgraduate Studies

Further Information: Campus II : Jl.Bintaro Permai Raya No.3 Jakarta Selatan

History: Founded 1958 as School of Dentistry, became university 1962. A private institution under the supervision of the Department of Education and Culture.

Governing Bodies: Foundation

Academic Year: September to August

Admission Requirements: Secondary school certificate (Sekolah Menengah Atas, SMA)

Fees: (Rupiahs): 2m.-8m. per semester

Main Language(s) of Instruction: Indonesian

Accrediting Agencies: National Accreditation Board

Degrees and Diplomas: *Sarjana (S1)*: Dentistry; Social and Political Sciences; Economics; Communication Studies, 4 yrs; *Magister (S2)*: Management; Public Administration; Communication Studies, a further 2 yrs. Also Postgraduate certificate in Dentistry

Student Services: Academic counselling, Employment services, Health services, Nursery care

Student Residential Facilities: Yes

Libraries: Four Libraries: Dentistry, Social and Political Science, Economics, and Communication Studies

Publications: Jurnal Ilmiah dan Teknologi Kedokteran Gigi/ Scientific and Technology Journal in Dentistry *(quarterly)*; Jurnal Ilmu Social dan Ilmu Politik/ Journal of Social and Political Science *(quarterly)*; Jurnal Manajemen dan Akuntansi/ Journal of Management and Accountancy *(quarterly)*; Wacana- Jurnal Ilmiah Ilmu Komunikasi/ Wacana, Scientific Journal in Communication *(quarterly)*

Last Updated: 11/02/09

PROKLAMASI '45 UNIVERSITY - UNIVERSITY OF PETROLEUM

Universitas Proklamasi '45 (UP45)
Jalan Proklamasi 1 Babarsari, Depok, Sleman, Yogyakarta, 55281 DI Yogyakarta
Tel: +62(274) 485-517
Fax: +62(274) 486-008
Website: http://www.up45.ac.id

Rector: Mohammad Dawam Rahardjo (2008-)
Tel: +62(274) 485-517 EMail: laurenup45@yahoo.com

Ketua: Lana Saria

International Relations: Bambang Irsanto, Vice-Rector
Tel: +62 818181615 EMail: be_l@yahoo.com

Centres

Energy Studies (Energy Engineering) *Director*: Nabiel Mavrim; **Research and Social Empowerment** (Social Studies) *Director*: Feguh Presetya

Faculties

Economics (Economics; Management) *Dean*: Edi Rismiyanto; **Engineering** (Engineering; Mechanical Engineering; Petroleum and Gas Engineering) *Dean*: Soelarso Pani; **Law** (Law) *Dean*: Sobirin Malian; **Psychology** (Educational Psychology; Psychology) *Dean*: Bimono; **Social and Political Sciences** (Administration; Political Sciences; Social Sciences) *Dean*: Purnomo

History: Founded 1964. A private institution under the supervision of the Department of Education and Culture.

Governing Bodies: UP45 Foundation

Fees: (Rupiahs): 1.2m. per annum

Main Language(s) of Instruction: Indonesian

Accrediting Agencies: Badan Akreditasi Nasional (National Accreditation Board)

Degrees and Diplomas: *Sarjana (S1)*

Student Services: Academic counselling

Student Residential Facilities: None

Libraries: c. 6,820 vols

Academic Staff *2010-2011*	MEN	WOMEN	**TOTAL**
FULL-TIME	69	38	**107**
STAFF WITH DOCTORATE			
FULL-TIME	1	–	**1**
Student Numbers *2010-2011*			
All (Foreign Included)	436	149	**585**
FOREIGN ONLY	87	28	**115**

Evening students, 142.

Last Updated: 05/01/11

PURWAKARTA UNIVERSITY

Universitas Purwakarta
Jalan Letjen Basuki Rahmat 25, Purwakarta, 41112 Jawa Barat
Tel: +62(264) 207-809
Fax: +62(264) 207-809
EMail: info@unpur.ac.id
Website: http://www.unpur.ac.id

Rector: Dey Ravena (2010-2014)

Programmes

Business Administration (Accountancy; Public Administration); **Communication Studies** (Communication Studies); **Engineering and Technology**; **Law** (Law); **Physics** (Physics)

Degrees and Diplomas: *Sarjana (S1)*

Last Updated: 03/05/10

PUTERA BATAM UNIVERSITY

Universitas Putera Batam
Jalan Letjen R Soeprapto, Muka Kuning, Batam, 29433 Riau
Tel: +62(778) 364-035
EMail: upb@puterabatam.ac.id
Website: http://www.upbatam.ac.id

Rector: Adji Djojo

Vice-Rector, Administration: Fifi

Programmes
Communication Studies (Communication Studies); **Computer Science** (Computer Science; Information Technology); **Economics** (Accountancy; Management); **Engineering**; **Language and Literature** (English; Literature; Modern Languages); **Law** (Law); **Mathematics and Biology** (Biology; Mathematics); **Public Administration** (Public Administration)

Degrees and Diplomas: *Diploma*; *Sarjana (S1)*
Last Updated: 03/05/10

PUTRA INDONESIA 'YPTK' UNIVERSITY OF PADANG

Universitas Putra Indonesia YPTK Padang
Jalan Raya Lubuk Bangalung, Padang, 25221 Sumatera Barat
Tel: +62(751) 72-427 +62(751) 77-666 +62(751) 73-000
Fax: +62(751) 71-913
EMail: yptk@indosat.net.id
Website: http://www.yptk.ac.id

Rector: Sarjon Dafit

Ketua: Herman Nawas

Faculties
Civil Engineering; **Computer Science** (Computer Education; Computer Science; Information Management); **Economics** (Accountancy; Economics; Management); **Industrial Engineering** (Electronic Engineering; Industrial Engineering); **Psychology** (Psychology)

Programmes
Design

History: Founded as Sekolah Tinggi Manajemen dan Informatika YPTK Padang.

Degrees and Diplomas: *Sarjana (S1)*; *Magister (S2)*
Last Updated: 10/03/10

PUTRA INDONESIAN UNIVERSITY OF EDUCATION

Universitas Pendidikan Putra Indonesia (UNPI CIANJUR)
Jalan Dr. Muwardi 66 Bypass, Cianjur 43215
Tel: +62(272) 262-604
Fax: +62(272) 272-074
EMail: unpicianjur@yahoo.com; yppi_unpi@yahoo.com

Head: Dudih A Zuhud

Ketua: Yuyun Moeslim Taher

Faculties
Agriculture (Agricultural Business; Agricultural Economics; Agricultural Engineering); **Arts and Humanities** (Communication Studies; English; Literature); **Economics** (Accountancy; Economics; Management); **Engineering** (Civil Engineering; Computer Engineering; Industrial Engineering; Information Management; Information Technology)

History: Founded 2001, as Akademi Manajemen Informatika dan Komputer AMIK.

Degrees and Diplomas: *Diploma*: Information Management; English; *Sarjana (S1)*
Last Updated: 04/02/09

QUALITY UNIVERSITY

Universitas Quality
Jalan Letjen Jamin Ginting 41, Kabanjahe, Medan, Sumatera Utara
Tel: +62(628) 324-750

Programmes
Agriculture (Agricultural Business; Agricultural Engineering); **Economics** (Economics); **Engineering**; **Law**; **Management** (Management); **Mathematics Education**; **Pancasila and Civic Education** (Civics; Government; Political Sciences)

Degrees and Diplomas: *Sarjana (S1)*
Last Updated: 03/05/10

RAJA ALI HAJI MARITIME UNIVERSITY

Universitas Maritim Raja Ali Haji (UMRAH)
PO Box 155, Jalan Politeknik Senggarang, Tanjung Pinang, 29125 Riau
Tel: +62(771) 700-1550
Fax: +62(771) 703-8999
EMail: email@umrah.ac.id
Website: http://umrah.ac.id/

Rector: Maswardi M. Amin

Ketua: Suhajar Diantoro

Faculties
Aquatic Resources Management (Marine Biology); **Economics** (Economics); **Education** (Education; Pedagogy); **Engineering** (Engineering); **Marine Science and Fishery** (Fishery; Marine Science and Oceanography); **Social Sciences and Political Science**

Degrees and Diplomas: *Sarjana (S1)*
Last Updated: 30/04/10

RATU SAMBAN UNIVERSITY

Universitas Ratu Samban
Jl. Jend. Sudirman No. 87, Arga Makmur, 38611 Bengkulu Utara
Tel: +62(737) 522-631
Fax: +62(737) 521-120
EMail: unras@bengkulu-utara.go.id

Rector: Syafrudin

Ketua: Bakarudin Jamal

Programmes
Agronomy (Agronomy); **Cattle Breeding** (Cattle Breeding); **Civil Engineering**; **Communication Studies** (Communication Studies); **Community Health**; **Development Studies**; **Fishery**; **Forestry**; **Mechanical Engineering** (Mechanical Engineering); **Nursing** (Nursing); **Public Administration** (Public Administration)

Degrees and Diplomas: *Sarjana (S1)*
Last Updated: 05/02/09

RESPATI INDONESIAN UNIVERSITY

Universitas Respati Indonesia (URINDO)
Jalan Bambu Apus I n° 3, Cipayung, Jakarta Timur, 13890 DKI Jakarta
Tel: +62(21) 845-4731
Fax: +62(21) 845-7628
EMail: urindo@indo.net.id
Website: http://www.urindo.ac.id

Rector: Does Sampoerno

Ketua: Mugiarti

Faculties
Administration Science *Dean*: Rakiman; **Agriculture** *Dean*: Notorianto; **Computer Science** (Business Computing; Computer Science; Information Management); **Economics** *Dean*: Suparso; **Health Sciences**

Programmes
Postgraduate Studies

History: Founded 1986.

Fees: (Rupiahs): 920,000 per annum

Degrees and Diplomas: *Diploma*: 3 yrs; *Sarjana (S1)*; *Magister (S2)*

Libraries: 1,434 vols
Last Updated: 14/01/09

RESPATI UNIVERSITY OF YOGYAKARTA

Universitas Respati Yogyakarta
Jalan Laksda Adisutjipto Km 65, Sleman, Yogyakarta, 55555 DI Yogyakarta
Tel: +62(274) 488-781
Fax: +62(274) 489-780
EMail: unriyo@respati.ac.id
Website: http://www.respati.ac.id/

Rector: Widodo Suparno

Vice-Rector: Sari Sundari

Faculties

Health Sciences (Hygiene; Midwifery; Nursing; Nutrition; Public Health); **Science and Technology** (Electrical Engineering; Information Management; Information Technology)

Programmes

Social and Economic Sciences (Accountancy; Communication Studies; English; International Relations; Literature; Modern Languages)

Degrees and Diplomas: *Diploma*; *Sarjana (S1)*

Last Updated: 03/05/10

RONGGOLAWE PGRI UNIVERSITY

Universitas PGRI Ronggolawe

Jalan Manunggal 61, Tuban, 62314 Jawa Timur

Tel: +62(356) 322-233

Fax: +62(356) 331-578

Website: http://unirow.ac.id

Rector: Hadi Tugur

Ketua: Ngarbi

Faculties

Education and Teacher Training (Biology; Education; English; Foreign Languages Education; Indonesian; Literature; Mathematics Education; Native Language Education; Preschool Education; Primary Education; Science Education; Teacher Training); **Engineering** (Computer Science; Engineering; Industrial Engineering); **Fisheries and Marine Science** (Aquaculture; Fishery; Marine Science and Oceanography; Natural Resources); **Social and Political Sciences** (Civics; Communication Studies; Economics; Government; Journalism; Political Sciences; Public Relations)

History: Founded 1978 as Institut Keguruan dan Ilmu Pendidikan (IKIP) PGRI Tuban (Institute of Teacher Training and Educational Science Tuban). Acquired present status and title 2007.

Admission Requirements: Secondary school certificate

Main Language(s) of Instruction: Indonesian

Degrees and Diplomas: *Sarjana (S1) (SPd)*: 4 yrs

Student Services: Canteen, Sports facilities

Libraries: Main Library

Distance students, 313.

Last Updated: 30/06/11

SAHID UNIVERSITY

Universitas Sahid (USAMID)

Jalan Prof. Dr. Soepomo, SH. N°84, Jakarta Selatan, 12870 DKI Jakarta

Tel: +62(21) 831-2815 +62(21) 835-1763

Fax: +62(21) 835-4763

Website: http://www.usahid.ac.id

Rector: Styastie Sumitro Remi Tel: +62(251) 321-557

Ketua: Nugroho Sukamdani

Faculties

Agriculture (Agricultural Business; Food Technology; Horticulture) *Dean*: Giyatmi; **Communication Studies** (Business and Commerce; Communication Studies; Information Sciences; Journalism; Social Studies); **Economics** *Dean*: Juana Yudith Huliselan; **Engineering** (Engineering; Environmental Engineering; Food Technology; Industrial Engineering; Mechanical Engineering) *Dean*: Farhat Umar; **Law**

History: Founded 1983 as Academy for Hotel and Tourism. Acquired present status and title 1988. The Institution has been recognized as pioneer of higher education in the fields of Tourism and Entrepreneurship.

Governing Bodies: Board of Directors; Rector; Senate

Admission Requirements: High school certificate (with cumulative grade (GPA) of 7 on a scale of 10), and entrance examination

Fees: (Rupiahs): 3m. per annum

Main Language(s) of Instruction: Indonesian

Accrediting Agencies: Ministry of Education and Culture; Board of National Accreditation for Higher Education

Degrees and Diplomas: *Diploma*; *Sarjana (S1)*: 5 yrs; *Magister (S2)*: a further 2 yrs; *Doktor (S3)*: Communication Studies

Student Services: Academic counselling, Canteen, Health services, Language programs, Sports facilities

Student Residential Facilities: Yes

Special Facilities: Computer Centre. Broadcasting Laboratory. Lecture Rooms. Auditorium

Libraries: 5,422 vols

Publications: Jurnal Manajemen Expose *(quarterly)*; Majalah Ilmiah Ilmu Dan Wisata *(quarterly)*

Last Updated: 10/03/10

SAHID UNIVERSITY OF SURAKARTA

Universitas Sahid Surakarta

Jl. Adisucipto 154, Surakarta, Jawa Tengah

Tel: +62(271) 743-493

EMail: baak_usahid@yahoo.com

Website: http://usahidsolo.ac.id/

Rector: Sujoko

Ketua: Sri Huning Anwariningsih

Programmes

Agricultural Industry; **Agrobusiness**; **Business Administration** (Business Administration); **Communication Studies** (Communication Studies); **Computer Engineering**; **Environmental Engineering** (Environmental Engineering); **Food Technology**; **Industrial Engineering**; **Interior Design** (Interior Design); **Psychology**; **Visual Communication and Design** (Design; Visual Arts)

Degrees and Diplomas: *Sarjana (S1)*

Last Updated: 10/03/10

SAINT THOMAS CATHOLIC UNIVERSITY

Universitas Katolik Santo Thomas (UNIKA ST. THOMAS)

Jalan Setia Budi 479-F, Tanjung Sari, Medan, 20132 Sumatera Utara

Tel: +62(61) 821-0161

Fax: +62(61) 821-3269

EMail: info@ust.ac.id

Website: http://www.ust.ac.id

Rector: Elias Semangat Sembiring

Ketua: Paulinus Simbolon EMail: mar39@indosat.net.id

Programmes

Agriculture (Agricultural Business; Agricultural Engineering; Agriculture; Agronomy); **Computer Science and Information Systems** (Computer Science; Information Management; Information Technology); **Economics** (Accountancy; Management); **Engineering** (Architecture; Civil Engineering; Structural Architecture); **English**; **Law** (Criminal Law; Law); **Philosophy of Science** (Philosophy)

History: Founded 1984.

Academic Year: September to August

Accrediting Agencies: National Accreditation Body

Degrees and Diplomas: *Diploma*: Accountancy; Management; Information System; Computer Accountancy (D3), 3 yrs; *Sarjana (S1)*: Agronomy; THP; SEP; Accountancy; Management; Civil Engineering; Architecture; Law; Literature; Computer Science; Information System (S1), 4 yrs

Student Services: Academic counselling, Canteen, Health services, Sports facilities

Libraries: c. 26,000 vols

Publications: Media Unika, Scientific Articles from lecturers *(bimonthly)*; Warta Unika, Information on the University *(monthly)*

Academic Staff *2009-2010*: Total: c. 170

Student Numbers *2009-2010*: Total: c. 2,900

Last Updated: 28/06/11

SAMAWA UNIVERSITY

Universitas Samawa

Jalan Raya Sering, Sumbawa Besar, 84313 Nusa Tenggara Barat
Tel: +62(371) 21-236 +62(371) 626-848
Fax: +62(371) 625-848

Rector: Syaifuddin Iskandar

Ketua: Chairuddin Imbik

Faculties

Agriculture (Agricultural Engineering; Agriculture; Agronomy; Animal Husbandry; Aquaculture) *Dean*: Zainuddin Syamsu; **Economics** (Banking; Development Studies; Economics; Finance) *Dean*: Muhammading; **Educational Science** (Educational Sciences; Educational Technology; Mathematics Education; Natural Sciences; Physics) *Dean*: Gusti Made Sulindra; **Engineering** (Civil Engineering; Engineering; Mechanical Engineering) *Dean*: Sukiman Ibrahim; **Social and Political Sciences** (Administration; Government; Political Sciences; Social Sciences) *Dean*: Arief

History: Founded as Sekolah Tinggi Keguruan dan Ilmu Pendidikan Sumbawa Besar, acquired present name and status 1975.

Fees: (Rupiahs): 400,000 per annum

Degrees and Diplomas: *Diploma*: Civil Engineering; Mechanical Engineering, 3 yrs; *Sarjana (S1)*

Libraries: 1,150 vols
Last Updated: 05/02/09

SAMUDRA LANGSA UNIVERSITY

Universitas Samudra Langsa

Jalan Iskandar Muda 3-4, Langsa, 24415 Nangroeh Aceh Darussalam
Tel: +62(641) 21-443
EMail: unsam_lgs@yahoo.co.id
Website: http://www.unsam.info

Rector: Bachtiar Harum

Ketua: Azman Usmanuddin

Faculties

Agriculture (Agricultural Economics; Agriculture; Agronomy) *Dean*: Amir Hamzah; **Economics** (Development Studies; Economics; Management) *Dean*: Zulkifli Ua; **Educational Science and Teacher Training** (Art Education; Biology; Education; Educational Sciences; English; Foreign Languages Education; History; Mathematics Education; Social Sciences; Teacher Training) *Dean*: Bachtiar Yacob; **Engineering** (Civil Engineering; Engineering; Industrial Engineering; Industrial Management; Mechanical Engineering) *Dean*: Zulkifli; **Law** (Law)

History: Founded 1972.

Fees: (Rupiahs): 750,000 per annum

Degrees and Diplomas: *Sarjana (S1)*

Libraries: 4,402 vols
Last Updated: 05/02/09

SANATA DHARMA UNIVERSITY OF YOGYAKARTA

Universitas Sanata Dharma Yogyakarta (USD)

Jl. Gejayan Mrican, Tromol Pos 29, Yogyakarta, 55002 D.I. Yogyakarta
Tel: +62(274) 513-301 +62(274) 513-352
Fax: +62(274) 562-383
EMail: humas@staff.usd.ac.id
Website: http://www.usd.ac.id

Rector: Paulus Wiryono Priyotamtama (2006-)
EMail: rektor@staff.usd.ac.id

Treasurer of Sanatha Dharma Foundation: H. van Opzeeland
EMail: yayasan@staff.usd.ac.id

International Relations: Paulus Sarwoto, Head of Cooperation and International Affairs Bureau EMail: sar@staff.usd.ac.id

Faculties

Arts and Humanities *Dean*: Fr. B. Alip; **Economics** *Dean*: Alex Kahu Lantum; **Graduate Studies** (Cultural Studies; English; Religion; Theology) *Dean*: Baskara T. Wardaya; **Pharmacy** (Pharmacy) *Dean*: Rita Suhadi; **Psychology** (Psychology) *Dean*: Paulus Eddy Suhartanto; **Science and Technology** (Computer Engineering; Electrical Engineering; Information Technology; Mathematics; Mechanical Engineering; Physics) *Dean*: Greg Heliarko; **Teacher Training and Education** (Accountancy; Economics; Educational and Student Counselling; Educational Sciences; English; Foreign Languages Education; History; Indonesian; Literature; Mathematics Education; Physics; Religious Education; Teacher Training) *Dean*: T. Sarkim; **Theology** *Dean*: A. Sudiardja

History: Founded 1955. Became Sanata Dharma Faculty for Teacher Training and Education 1958. Acquired independence and autonomy and became Sanata Dharma Institute for Teacher Training and Education 1965. Acquired present status and title 1993.

Governing Bodies: Rector; Vice Rectors for Academic, Administrative and Student Affairs; Bureau of Academic Administration

Academic Year: August to June (August-December; February-June)

Admission Requirements: For international students admission to undergraduate program: High school certificate and TOEFL score of 450 (institutional)

Fees: (Rupiahs): Admission fees, 100,000; tuition fees, 3.5m.-4m. per semester; academic and facilities development fees (only for the first semester), 5m.-15m.; 7.6m. per annum; student visa conversion and administration fees, 3.5m.

Main Language(s) of Instruction: Indonesian; English

International Co-operation: With universities in Australia, United Kingdom, Netherlands, Philippines, Singapore, USA.

Accrediting Agencies: National Accreditation Organization, Minister of National Education Indonesia

Degrees and Diplomas: *Diploma*: Elementary Teacher Training and Mechatronics, 2-3 yrs; *Sarjana (S1)*: Pharmacy; Science and Technology; Economics; Psychology; Arts and Humanities; Teacher Training and Education, 4 yrs; *Magister (S2)*: English Studies; Religious and Cultural Studies, a further 2 yrs. Also Professional degree in Pharmacy (Apt. Pharmacist Profession), 1 yr.

Student Services: Academic counselling, Canteen, Cultural centre, Employment services, Foreign student adviser, Handicapped facilities, Health services, Language programs, Nursery care, Social counselling, Sports facilities

Student Residential Facilities: Realino Residence

Special Facilities: Verhaar Documentation; Self Access Centre; Laboratories (Journalism, Mutlimedia, Micro teaching, Mechanics, Electricity, Robotics, Information, Pharmacy, Mathematics, Physics, Psychology, Language and Economics).

Libraries: 120,000 vols; 508 journals; 25 daily; 250 CD-Rom

Publications: Antisipasi, Journal of Economics *(3 per annum)*; ELT, Journal of English Language and Teaching *(biennially)*; Gatra, Journal of Indonesian Language and Literature Teaching *(biennially)*; Phenomena, Journal of English Language and Literature *(quarterly)*; Retorika, Journal of Cultural Studies *(3 per annum)*; Sigma, Journal of Science and Technology Media *(quarterly)*; Sintesa, Journal of Indonesian Language and Literature *(biennially)*; Suksma, Journal of Psychology *(3 per annum)*; Teknika, Journal of Mechanical, Mechatronic and Electical Engineering *(quarterly)*; Widya Dharma, Journal of Education *(quarterly)*

Press or Publishing House: Penerbitan Universitas Sanata Dharma (Sanata Dharma University Press)
Last Updated: 28/01/09

SANG BUMI RUWA JURA UNIVERSITY

Universitas Sang Bumi Ruwa Jurai (USBRJ)

Jalan Imam Bonjol 468, Bandar Lampung, 35145 Lampung
Tel: +62(721) 265-734 +62 0721-257838
Fax: +62(721) 257-838
Website: http://www.usbrj.ac.id

Rector: Nanang Iskandar Fauzie

Vice-Rector: Kisro Edi

Ketua: Harris Hasyim

Faculties

Economics (Management) *Dean*: Salim Samil; **Engineering**; **Law** *Dean*: Adnan Rauf; **Social and Political Sciences** (Public Administration) *Dean*: Embih Ibrahim

Degrees and Diplomas: *Sarjana (S1)*

Student Services: Academic counselling, Canteen, Sports facilities

Special Facilities: Language Laboratory. Basic Physics Laboratory

Libraries: Yes

Publications: Gemaar *(quarterly)*

Last Updated: 05/02/09

SANGGA BUANA UNIVERSITY

Universitas Sangga Buana

Jalan. P.H. Hasan Mustopa No. 68, Bandung, 40124 West Java

Tel: +62(22) 720-1756

Fax: +62(22) 720-1756

EMail: adm@usbypkp.ac.id; promosi@usbypkp.com

Website: http://www.usbypkp.ac.id

Rektor: Deden Sutisna

Ketua: H. Supriyadi

Faculties

Communication Science and Administration (Administration; Business Administration; Communication Studies); **Economics** (Accountancy; Banking; Economics; Finance; Management); **Engineering** (Civil Engineering; Computer Engineering; Electrical Engineering; Engineering; Industrial Engineering; Information Technology)

History: Founded 1970. Acquired present status and title 2006, after the merging of Sekolah Tinggi Ilmu Ekonomi YPKP and Sekolah Tinggi Teknik YPKP

Degrees and Diplomas: *Sarjana (S1)*

Last Updated: 30/06/11

SARI PUTRA UNIVERSITY AT TOMOHON

Universitas Sari Putra Tomohon (UNSRIT)

Jl. Kakaskasen II Komp Wihara, Surya Dharma, Tomohon, 95362 Sulawesi Utara

Tel: +62(431) 356-7127

Fax: +62(431) 315-7126

EMail: saripurra_university@yahoo.com

Rector: Dharma Surya Mahastavira (2009-2013)
Tel: +62(431) 315-7127

Ketua: Fanny Runtuwene

Faculties

Agriculture (Agriculture; Agronomy; Harvest Technology) *Dean*: Cyres A.L.D. Bujung; **Economics** (Accountancy; Economics; Management) *Dean*: Joost Rumampuk; **Engineering** (Architecture; Civil Engineering; Computer Engineering; Engineering; Information Technology) *Dean*: Don Kabo; **Fishery** (Fishery; Marine Biology) *Dean*: Johnny Wenno; **Nursing** (Nursing) *Dean*: Moudy Lombogia; **Social Studies** (Communication Disorders; Social Studies) *Dean*: Adrie B.J. Supit

History: Founded 1999.

Admission Requirements: Ijazah SMA Sederajat

Fees: (Rupiahs): 5m. per annum

Main Language(s) of Instruction: Indonesian

International Co-operation: Rumah Sakit Jantung Jakarta, RSU Marsuki Mahdi Bogor

Accrediting Agencies: National Accreditation Board (BAN-PT)

Degrees and Diplomas: *Sarjana (S1)*: Architecture; Engineering (ST); Management Accountancy (SE); *Sarjana (S1)*: Civil Engineering; Computer Engineering (ST), 4 yrs

Student Services: Academic counselling, Canteen, Health services, Nursery care, Social counselling, Sports facilities

Libraries: Yes

Publications: Jurnal Sariputra *(quarterly)*

Academic Staff *2009-2010*	MEN	WOMEN	TOTAL
FULL-TIME	40	25	**65**
PART-TIME	50	40	**90**
Student Numbers *2009-2010*			
All (Foreign Included)	645	850	**1,495**

Last Updated: 05/11/10

SARJANAWIYATA TAMANSISWA UNIVERSITY

Universitas Sarjanawiyata Tamansiswa

Jalan Kusumanegara 157, Yogyakarta, 55165 DI Yogyakarta

Tel: +62(274) 562-265 +62(274) 377-120

Fax: +62(274) 547-042

EMail: info@ustjogja.ac.id

Website: http://www.ustjogja.ac.id

Rector: Djohar

Vice-Rector: Hazairin Eko Prasetyo

Faculties

Agriculture (Agricultural Business; Agricultural Equipment; Agriculture); **Economics** (Accountancy; Economics; Management); **Engineering** (Civil Engineering; Industrial Engineering); **Psychology** (Psychology); **Teacher Training and Educational Sciences** (Educational Sciences; English; Family Studies; Indonesian; Literature; Mathematics Education; Mechanical Engineering; Painting and Drawing; Physics; Teacher Training)

Programmes

Postgraduate Studies (Educational Administration; Educational Research; English; Management)

History: Founded 1955. A private institution under the supervision of the Ministry of National Education.

Academic Year: September to August

Admission Requirements: Secondary school certificate (Sekolah Menengah Atas, SMA)

Fees: (Rupiahs): 500,000 per annum

Main Language(s) of Instruction: Indonesian, English

Degrees and Diplomas: *Diploma*: 2-3 yrs; *Sarjana (S1)*: 4-7 yrs; *Magister (S2)*: 2-4 yrs

Student Services: Academic counselling, Canteen, Cultural centre, Employment services, Foreign student adviser, Health services, Social counselling, Sports facilities

Student Residential Facilities: Yes

Special Facilities: Kirti Griya Museum

Libraries: 38,975 vols

Publications: Semiotika, Languages, Art *(biennially)*; Wacana Akademika, Education, Engineering, Agriculture *(biennially)*

Academic Staff	MEN	WOMEN	TOTAL
STAFF WITH DOCTORATE			
FULL-TIME	14	5	**19**
PART-TIME	10	4	**14**
Student Numbers *2010-2011*			
All (Foreign Included)	2,099	2,238	**4,337**

Last Updated: 27/10/10

SATRIA MAKASSAR UNIVERSITY

Universitas Satria Makassar

Jalan Veteran Selatan 316, Makassar, 90135 Sulawesi Selatan

Tel: +62(411) 875-037

Fax: +62(411) 875-037 +62(411) 876-161

EMail: satriamakassar@yahoo.com

Rector: Waty Rosmawaty Natzir

Ketua: Etty Roslely Natzir

Programmes

Communication Sciences (Communication Studies); **Computer Science** (Computer Science); **Engineering** (Engineering; Industrial Engineering; Mechanical Engineering; Structural Architecture); **English** (English; Literature); **Forestry** (Forestry); **Law** (Law)

History: Founded 1985.

Main Language(s) of Instruction: Indonesian, English

Accrediting Agencies: Badan Akreditasi Nasional Perguruan Tinggi (BAN-PT)

Degrees and Diplomas: *Diploma*: 3 yrs; *Sarjana (S1)*: 4 yrs; *Magister (S2)*: Communication Sciences

Student Services: Academic counselling, Canteen, Foreign Studies Centre, Handicapped facilities, Health services, Language programs, Nursery care, Sports facilities

Libraries: 1,650 vols
Last Updated: 30/06/11

SATYA NEGARA UNIVERSITY OF INDONESIA

Universitas Satya Negara Indonesia (USNI)

Jalan Arteri Pondok Indah 11, Kebayoran Lama Utara, Jakarta Selatan, 12240 DKI Jakarta
Tel: +62(21) 739-8393 +62(21) 739-9394
Fax: +62(21) 720-0352
EMail: humas@usni.ac.id
Website: http://www.usni.ac.id

Rector: L. Poltak Sinambela

Ketua: Sutan Raja D. L. Sitorus

Faculties

Economics (Accountancy; Business Administration; Economics; Management) *Dean*: Usten Sitorus; **Engineering** (Environmental Engineering; Information Management; Information Technology) *Dean*: Tambar Manurung; **Fishery** (Fishery) *Dean*: Chandra Kirana; **Social and Political Sciences** (Communication Studies; International Relations; Social Welfare) *Dean*: Salten Raja Guguk

History: Founded 1987, acquired present title 1990.

Governing Bodies: Yayasan Abdi Karya

Academic Year: September to August

Admission Requirements: Secondary School Certificate

Fees: (Rupiahs): 1.4m. per annum

Main Language(s) of Instruction: Indonesian, English

Accrediting Agencies: National Accreditation Agency for Higher Education

Degrees and Diplomas: *Diploma*: 3 yrs; *Sarjana (S1)*: 4 yrs; *Magister (S2)*: Management

Student Services: Academic counselling, Canteen, Employment services, Health services, Language programs, Social counselling, Sports facilities

Libraries: Central Library, 9,369 vols

Publications: Scientific Journal of USNI, Research reports *(quarterly)*

Press or Publishing House: USNI Press
Last Updated: 11/03/10

SATYA WACANA CHRISTIAN UNIVERSITY

Universitas Kristen Satya Wacana (UKSW/SWCU)

Jalan Diponegoro 52-60, Salatiga, 50711 Jawa Tengah
Tel: +62(298) 326-362 +62(298) 326-363 +62(298) 321-433
Fax: +62(298) 21-433
EMail: ieo@uksw.edu
Website: http://www.uksw.edu

Rector: John A. Titaley (2009-2013)
Tel: +62(298) 21-212 Ext. 452 EMail: rektor@uksw.edu

Deputy Rector for Finance and Administration Affairs: S.E. Marwata

International Relations: Martha Nandari S. Handoko, Deputy Rector for Institutional Relations and Internationalisation

Colleges

Professional Studies (Chemical Engineering; Chemistry; Computer Engineering; Computer Science; Information Technology; Management; Public Relations; Secretarial Studies; Tourism) *Director*: Lina Sinatra

Faculties

Agriculture (Agricultural Business; Agriculture; Agronomy) *Dean*: Rukmadi Warsito; **Biology** (Biology; Environmental Management; Marine Biology; Microbiology) *Dean*: Agna Sulis Krave; **Economics** (Accountancy; Economics; Management) *Dean*: Usil Sis Sucahyo; **Education and Teacher Training** (Civics; Economics; Education; History; Physics; Psychology; Teacher Training) *Dean*: Kusjadi; **Engineering** (Computer Science; Electrical Engineering) *Dean*: Budihardja Murtianta; **Information Technology** (Information Technology) *Dean*: Danny Manongga; **Languages and Arts** (Arts and Humanities; English; Modern Languages) *Dean*: Urip Sutiyono; **Law** (Law) *Dean*: Johannes Daniel Zacharias; **Performing Arts** (Music; Performing Arts) *Dean*: Adriani Karyanto; **Psychology** (Psychology) *Dean (Acting)*: Sutriyono; **Science and Mathematics** (Chemistry; Mathematics; Physics) *Dean*: H.Ignatus Agus Kristijanto; **Social Sciences and Politics** (Communication Studies; Political Sciences; Social Sciences; Sociology) *Dean*: Kutut Suwondo; **Theology** (Religion; Theology) *Dean*: Daniel Nuhamara

Programmes

Doctoral Level Studies (Development Studies; Religion) *Director*: Daniel Daud Kameo; **Master Level Studies** (Biological and Life Sciences; Development Studies; Education; Management; Religion) *Director*: Daniel Daud Kameo

History: Founded 1956 by the Board of Higher Education for Indonesian Christian Teachers, which later became the Faculty of Education and Christian Teacher's Training in 1959. Also renamed Universitas Kristen Satya Wacana (UKSW) or Satya Wacana Christian University (SWCU) 1959.

Governing Bodies: Board of Trustees

Academic Year: 2 semesters: August to July (August-December; February-July). 3 terms: September to August (September-December; January-April; May-August)

Admission Requirements: Senior high school certificate (Surat Tanda Tamat Belajar)

Fees: (Rupiahs): 1.3m. per semester

Main Language(s) of Instruction: Indonesian

International Co-operation: With universities in USA, Netherlands, Australia, Germany, Japan.

Accrediting Agencies: National Accreditation Board

Degrees and Diplomas: *Diploma*: Professional Studies, 2-3 yrs; *Sarjana (S1)*: 4 yrs; *Magister (S2)*: Management, Development Studies, Societal Religion; Applied Biology, a further 2 yrs; *Doktor (S3)*: Development Studies; Societal Religion, a further 2 yrs

Student Services: Academic counselling, Canteen, Employment services, Foreign student adviser, Health services, Language programs, Sports facilities

Student Residential Facilities: Yes

Libraries: c. 120,000 vols

Publications: Agric *(quarterly)*; Dian Ekonomi *(biannually)*; Justitia *(quarterly)*; Kritis *(quarterly)*; Satya Widya *(quarterly)*

Press or Publishing House: Percetakan Satya Wacana Lestari Jaya
Last Updated: 26/02/10

SATYA WIYATA MANDALA UNIVERSITY

Universitas Satya Wiyata Mandala

Jalan Sutamsu SH, Kalibobo, Nabire, 98801 Papua
Tel: +62(984) 21-757
Fax: +62(984) 21-757

Rector: Didimus Mote

Ketua: L.A. Titaheluw

Programmes

Agriculture; **Business Administration**; **Education**; **Engineering** (Computer Engineering; Engineering; Industrial Engineering); **Government**

Degrees and Diplomas: *Sarjana (S1)*
Last Updated: 04/05/10

SATYAGAMA UNIVERSITY

Universitas Satyagama

Jalan Kamal Raya 2A, Cengkareng, Jakarta Barat, 11730 DKI Jakarta
Tel: +62(21) 545-2377 +62(21) 545-2378
Fax: +62(21) 543-91-3254
EMail: info@satyagama.ac.id
Website: http://www.satyagama.ac.id

Rector: Soenardjo Wirjoprawiro

Ketua: Makmuri Muchlas

Faculties

Agricullture *Dean*: Soepadiyo Mangoen Soekardjo; **Economics** *Dean*: Hedra Halwani; **Engineering** *Dean*: M. Suyoko; **Industrial Engineering** *Dean*: Suprapedi; **Law** *Dean*: Fachrudin Dinyati; **Social and Political Sciences** (Government; International Relations; Political Sciences; Public Relations; Social Sciences) *Dean*: Sis Mockajat

History: Founded 1988.

Fees: (Rupiahs): 2.11m. per anum

Degrees and Diplomas: *Diploma*: 3 yrs; *Sarjana (S1)*; *Magister (S2)*; *Doktor (S3)*: Governement Administration

Last Updated: 14/01/09

SAWERIGADING UNIVERSITY OF MAKASSAR

Universitas Sawerigading Makassar

Jalan Kandea I 27, Makassar, 90156 Sulawesi Selatan

Tel: +62(411) 329-561

Fax: +62(411) 334-554

Rector: Muhammad Hasyim

Ketua: Lagaligo Syahadat

Faculties

Arts and Humanities; **Engineering**; **Law**; **Social and Political Sciences**

History: Founded 1943.

Fees: (Rupiahs): 530,000 per annum

Degrees and Diplomas: *Sarjana (S1)*

Last Updated: 11/02/09

SEMARANG UNIVERSITY

Universitas Semarang (USM)

Jalan Soekarno-Hatta, Troglosari, Semarang, 50196 Jawa Tengah

Tel: +62 (24) 670-2757

Fax: +62 (24) 670-2272

EMail: univ-smg@idola.net.id

Website: http://www.usm.ac.id

Rector: Pahlawansjah Harahap Tel: +62 (24) 670-3668

Vice-Rector, Administration: Andy Kridasusila

International Relations: Priyo Bintoro, Vice-Rector

Faculties

Agricultural Technology and Animal Science (Agricultural Engineering; Animal Husbandry; Zoology); **Economics** (Accountancy; Economics; Management); **Engineering** (Civil Engineering; Electrical Engineering); **Information Technology and Communications** (Communication Studies; Information Technology); **Law** (Law); **Psychology** (Psychology)

Programmes

Postgraduate Studies (Management)

History: Founded 1987.

Admission Requirements: General high school certificate and entrance examination

Main Language(s) of Instruction: Indonesian

Accrediting Agencies: National Accreditation Board of DGHE; Directorate General Higher Education (Ministry of National Education)

Degrees and Diplomas: *Diploma*: 3 yrs; *Sarjana (S1)*: 4 yrs; *Magister (S2)*: Management

Student Services: Academic counselling, Canteen, Cultural centre, Employment services, Language programs, Sports facilities

Student Residential Facilities: None

Libraries: Yes

Publications: Journal of Social and Cultural Dynamics *(biennially)*; SAINTEKS *(3 per annum)*

Press or Publishing House: Semarang University Press

Last Updated: 30/06/11

SERAMBI MEKKAH UNIVERSITY

Universitas Serambi Mekkah (USM)

Jalan Tengku Imam Leung Bata Bathoh, Banda Aceh, 23249 Nangroeh Aceh Darussalam

Tel: + 62(651) 26-160

Fax: + 62(651) 22-471

Website: http://www.serambimekkah.ac.id/

Rector: Musafir Kumar

Vice-Rector: T. Makmur

Faculties

Agriculture (Agricultural Engineering; Agricultural Equipment; Agriculture; Food Technology; Nutrition); **Economics** (Accountancy; Economics; Management); **Education and Teacher Training** (Biology; Chemistry; English; Foreign Languages Education; History; Indonesian; Leisure Studies; Literature; Mathematics Education; Native Language Education; Physical Education; Physics; Primary Education; Social Welfare; Teacher Training); **Engineering** (Chemical Engineering; Computer Science; Environmental Engineering; Industrial Engineering); **Health Sciences** (Environmental Studies; Health Sciences; Public Health; Welfare and Protective Services)

History: Founded 1985 as Sekolah Tinggi Teknologi Pertanian Serambi Mekkah

Admission Requirements: Secondary school certificate

Main Language(s) of Instruction: Indonesian and English

Accrediting Agencies: National Accreditation Board (BAN-PT)

Degrees and Diplomas: *Sarjana (S1)*: 4 yrs

Student Services: Canteen, Sports facilities

Publications: Serambi Ilmu, Science of Education *(biennially)*

Last Updated: 01/07/11

SERANG RAYA UNIVERSITY

Universitas Serang Raya

Serang, Banten

Tel: +62(254) 208-266

EMail: stmikserang@stmik-serang.ac.id

Rector: Hamdan

Ketua: Mulya Rahayu

Faculties

Communication (Communication Studies); **Economics** (Accountancy; Banking; Business Computing; Economics; Finance; Management; Marketing; Public Administration); **Engineering** (Chemical Engineering; Civil Engineering; Computer Engineering; Engineering; Industrial Engineering); **Information Technology** (Information Technology); **Social and Political Sciences**

History: Founded 2008 following the merger of two colleges namely STMIK and STIE Serang.

Degrees and Diplomas: *Sarjana (S1)*

Last Updated: 04/05/10

SETIA BUDI MANDIRI UNIVERSITY

Universitas Setia Budi Mandiri

Jalan Jend Abdul Haris Nasution, Medan, 20142 Sumatera Utara

Tel: +62(61) 836-4427

Fax: +62(61) 836-4526

Website: http://www.usbm.ac.id

Rector: Daniel Sitanggang

Ketua: Arnold Budiman

Faculties

Computer Science (Computer Science; Information Technology); **Economics**; **Engineering**; **Law** (Law); **Mathematics and Chemistry** (Chemistry; Mathematics); **Teacher Training and Educational Sciences**

Degrees and Diplomas: *Sarjana (S1)*; *Magister (S2)*

Last Updated: 04/05/10

SETIA BUDI UNIVERSITY OF SURAKARTA

Universitas Setia Budi Surakarta

Jalan Letjen Sutoyo, Surakarta 57127
Tel: +62(271) 852-518
Fax: +62(271) 853-275
EMail: info@setiabudi.ac.id; usbsolo@yahoo.com
Website: http://www.setiabudi.ac.id

Rector: Hutomo Surachmanto

Ketua: Winarso Soerjolegowo

Faculties

Biology (Biology); **Economics** (Economics); **Engineering**; **Pharmacy**; **Psychology** (Psychology)

History: Founded 1997.

Fees: (Rupiahs): 3.63m. per annum

Degrees and Diplomas: *Diploma*: 3 yrs; *Sarjana (S1)*; *Magister (S2)*: Pharmacy

Libraries: 2,081 vols

Last Updated: 11/02/09

SILIWANGI UNIVERSITY OF TASIKMALAYA

Universitas Siliwangi Tasikmalaya

PO Box 164, Jalan Siliwangi 24, Tasikmalaya, 46115 Jawa Barat
Tel: +62(265) 333-092 +62(265) 330-634
Fax: +62(265) 325-812
Website: http://www.unsil.ac.id

Rector: Muhammad Numan Somantri

Ketua: Oman Roesman

Faculties

Agriculture (Agricultural Business; Agricultural Economics; Agriculture; Agronomy; Fishery); **Economics** (Accountancy; Banking; Development Studies; Economics; Finance; Hotel Management; Management); **Educational Science and Teacher Training** (Art Education; Biology; Business Education; Educational Sciences; English; Geography; Health Education; History; Indonesian; Literature; Mathematics Education; Physical Education; Social Sciences); **Engineering** (Civil Engineering; Electrical Engineering; Engineering); **Public Health**

History: Founded as branch of Institute of Teacher Training and Education, Bandung. Acquired present status and title 1979. A private institution under the supervision of the Department of Education and Culture.

Academic Year: August to June (August-December; February-June)

Admission Requirements: Secondary school certificate (Sekolah Lanjutan Tingkat Atas, SLTA)

Fees: (Rupiahs): 2m. per annum

Main Language(s) of Instruction: Indonesian

Degrees and Diplomas: *Diploma*: 3 yrs; *Sarjana (S1)*; *Sarjana (S1)*: Engineering (Insinjur), 5 yrs; *Magister (S2)*

Libraries: Central Library, 11,722 vols

Last Updated: 21/04/10

SIMALUNGUN UNIVERSITY

Universitas Simalungun

Jalan Sisingamangaraja Barat, Pematang Siantar, 21139 Sumatera Utara
Tel: +62(622) 24-670
Fax: +62(622) 430-071
Website: http://www.usi.ac.id

Rector: Ulung Napitu

Ketua: Laden Damanik

Faculties

Agriculture (Agricultural Business; Agricultural Economics; Agricultural Engineering; Agriculture; Agronomy; Forest Management); **Economics** (Development Studies; Economics; Management); **Educational Science and Teacher Training** (Biology; Chemistry; Civics; English; Foreign Languages Education; History; Mathematics Education; Physics; Science Education; Social Sciences); **Engineering** (Civil Engineering; Engineering; Mechanical Engineering; Rural Planning; Town Planning); **Law** (Law)

History: Founded 1966. A private institution under the supervision of the Department of Education and Culture.

Governing Bodies: Simalungun University Foundation

Academic Year: August to June (August-January; March-June)

Admission Requirements: Secondary school certificate (Sekolah Menengah Atas, SMA)

Fees: (Rupiahs): 500,000 per annum

Main Language(s) of Instruction: Indonesian

Degrees and Diplomas: *Sarjana (S1)*: 4-7 yrs; *Magister (S2)*

Libraries: 3,500 vols

Last Updated: 05/02/09

SINGAPERBANGSA UNIVERSITY

Universitas Singaperbangsa (UNSIKA)

Jalan H. S. Ronggowaluyo Teluk Jambe, Karawang, 41361 Jawa Barat
Tel: +62(267) 641-177
Fax: +62(267) 641-367
EMail: uni_singaperbangsa@yahoo.com

Rector: Dadang Fakhruddin Tel: +62(267) 642-582

Ketua: Tayo Tarmadi

International Relations: Dadang Danugiri, Vice-Rector

Faculties

Agriculture (Agricultural Engineering; Agriculture; Agronomy); **Computer Science** (Computer Science); **Economics** (Accountancy; Economics; Management); **Education and Teacher Training** (Education; English; Foreign Languages Education; Mathematics Education; Parks and Recreation; Physical Education; Teacher Training); **Engineering** (Engineering; Industrial Engineering; Mechanical Engineering); **Law** (Law); **Social and Political Sciences** (Communication Studies; Government; Political Sciences; Social Sciences)

Programmes

Midwifery (Midwifery); **Postgraduate Studies** (Management)

History: Founded 1982.

Accrediting Agencies: BAN - PT

Degrees and Diplomas: *Diploma*: 3 yrs; *Sarjana (S1)*: 4 yrs; *Magister (S2)*: Management

Student Services: Academic counselling, Canteen, Cultural centre, Employment services, Language programs, Nursery care, Social counselling, Sports facilities

Student Residential Facilities: Dormitory

Libraries: 1,475 vols

Academic Staff *2009-2010*: Total: c. 190
Student Numbers *2009-2010*: Total: c. 2,800
Last Updated: 01/07/11

SINTUWU MAROSO POSO UNIVERSITY

Universitas Sintuwu Maroso Poso

Jalan Pulau Timor 1, Poso Sulawesi Tengah, 94619 Sulawesi Tengah
Tel: +62(452) 21257 +62(452) 21737
Fax: +62(452) 324-242
Website: http://unsimar.ac.id

Rector: Lefrand Mango

Ketua: Amdjad Lawasa

Vice-Rector, Administration: M. Panjili

Faculties

Agriculture; **Arts and Humanities**; **Economics**; **Educational Sciences and Teacher Training**; **Engineering**; **Law**; **Social and Political Sciences**

History: Founded 1986.

Fees: (Rupiahs): 800,000 per annum

Degrees and Diplomas: *Sarjana (S1)*

Libraries: 3,614 vols
Last Updated: 05/02/09

SISINGAMANGARAJA XII TAPANULI UNIVERSITY UTARA DI SIBORONG-BORONG

Universitas Sisingamangaraja XII Tapanuli Utara Di Siborong-Borong

Jalan Sisingamangaraja XII N° 9, Silangit, Siborong-Borong, 22474 Sumatera Utara
Tel: +62(633) 41-017

Rector: Parsaoran Parapat

Ketua: Panggabean

Faculties
Agriculture (Agricultural Economics; Agricultural Engineering; Agriculture; Agronomy); **Economics** (Economics; Management); **Educational Science and Teacher Training** (Civics; Educational Sciences; English; Foreign Languages Education; Mathematics Education; Science Education; Social Sciences; Teacher Training); **Engineering** (Civil Engineering; Engineering; Industrial Engineering); **Law**

History: Founded 1996.

Fees: (Rupiahs): 550,000 per annum

Degrees and Diplomas: *Sarjana (S1)*

Libraries: 2,363 vols
Last Updated: 05/02/09

SISINGAMANGARAJA XII UNIVERSITY

Universitas Sisingamangaraja XII

Jalan Perintis Kemerdekaan 9, Medan, 20235 Sumatera Utara
Tel: +62(61) 414-6659
Fax: +62(61) 453-9642

Rector: Mangara Lumban Tobing

Ketua: Panggabean

Faculties
Agriculture (Agricultural Economics; Agronomy) *Dean*: A. Manurung; **Arts and Humanities** (Arts and Humanities; English; Literature) *Dean*: H. Panggabean; **Computer Engineering and Secretarial Studies** (Computer Engineering; Secretarial Studies); **Economics** (Accountancy; Economics; Finance; Management; Secretarial Studies) *Dean*: A. Pasaribu; **Engineering** (Computer Engineering; Engineering) *Dean*: Tomib S. Cholia; **Law** *Dean*: Sagala; **Mathematics and Natural Sciences** (Mathematics); **Social and Political Sciences** (Communication Studies; Journalism; Political Sciences; Public Relations; Social Sciences)

History: Founded 1984.

Fees: (Rupiahs): 600,000 per annum

Degrees and Diplomas: *Diploma*: 3 yrs; *Sarjana (S1)*

Libraries: 8,478 vols
Last Updated: 05/02/09

SJAKHYAKIRTI UNIVERSITY

Universitas Sjakhyakirti

Jl. Sultan Muhammad Mansyur 32 Ilir, Kebon Gede, Palembang, 30145 Sumatera Selatan
Tel: +62(711) 358-320
Fax: +62(711) 364-300
Website: http://www.sjakhyakirti.ac.id

Rector: Zaidan Nawawi

Ketua: Guntur M. Ali

Faculties
Administration (Administration; Government); **Agriculture** (Agricultural Economics; Agriculture; Agronomy); **Economics**; **Law**

History: Founded 1980.

Fees: (Rupiahs): 500,000 per annum

Degrees and Diplomas: *Sarjana (S1)*

Libraries: 2,253 vols
Last Updated: 05/02/09

SLAMET RIYADI UNIVERSITY OF SURAKARTA

Universitas Slamet Riyadi Surakarta

Jalan Sumpah Pemuda 18, Banjarsari, Surakarta, 57136 Jawa Tengah
Tel: +62(271) 854-270
Fax: +62(271) 854-670
EMail: rektor@unisri.ac.id
Website: http://www.unisri.ac.id

Rector: Kapti Rahayu Kuswanto

Ketua: Saino Harsomadyono

Faculties
Agricultural Technology *Dean*: Linda Kurniawati; **Agriculture** (Agriculture; Agronomy) *Dean*: Riyo Samekto; **Economics** *Dean*: Untung Sriwidodo; **Education and Teacher Training** (Civics; Education; Educational and Student Counselling; Philosophy; Teacher Training) *Dean*: Sri Nugrahaningsih; **Law** *Dean*: Budi Maknawi; **Social and Political Sciences** (Administration; Communication Studies; Journalism; Political Sciences; Public Relations; Social Sciences) *Dean*: M. Winarti

Programmes
Postgraduate Studies (Law; Management; Public Administration)

History: Founded 1980. A private institution under the supervision of the Department of Education and Culture.

Academic Year: July to June (July-December; January-June)

Admission Requirements: Secondary school certificate (Sekolah Menengah Atas, SMA) and entrance examination

Fees: (Rupiahs): 1m. per annum

Main Language(s) of Instruction: Indonesian

Accrediting Agencies: General Directorate of Higher Education in Indonesia

Degrees and Diplomas: *Sarjana (S1)*: 4-7 yrs; *Magister (S2)*

Student Services: Academic counselling, Canteen, Health services, Language programs, Sports facilities

Student Residential Facilities: Yes

Libraries: Central Library, 11,929 vols

Publications: Jurnal Ilmu Sosial Dan Humaniora, Social Sciences and Humanities *(biannually)*; Jurnal Ilmu-Ilmu Pertanian, Agriculture *(biannually)*

Last Updated: 05/02/09

SOEGIJAPRANATA CATHOLIC UNIVERSITY

Universitas Katolik Soegijapranata Semarang (UNIKA SOEPRA)

Jalan Pawiyatan Luhur IV/1, Bendan Dhuwur, Semarang, 50234 Central Java
Tel: +62(24) 844-1555
Fax: +62(24) 844-5265
EMail: unika@unika.ac.id; humas@unika.ac.id
Website: http://www.unika.ac.id

Rector: Yohanes Budi Widianarko

Vice-Rector I: Angelina Ika Rahutami

International Relations: Vincent Aryanto, Vice-Rector for international Cooperation and Development
EMail: vincent_aryanto@unika.ac.id

Faculties
Agricultural Technology (Agricultural Engineering; Food Technology) *Head*: Ita Sulistyawati; **Architecture and Design** (Architecture; Design) *Head*: Albertus Sidharta; **Arts and Humanities** (Arts and Humanities; English; Literature) *Head*: Heny Hartono; **Economics** (Accountancy; Business Administration; Economics; Management; Taxation) *Head*: Andreas Lako; **Electronic Engineering / Industrial Technology** (Electronic Engineering; Industrial Engineering) *Head*: Leonardus Heru; **Engineering** (Civil Engineering; Engineering) *Head*: Retno Susilorini; **Law** (Law) *Head*: Valentinus Suroto; **Psychology** (Psychology) *Head*: Dewi Setyorini

Programmes
Postgraduate Studies (Architecture; Environmental Management; Food Technology; Law; Management; Psychology; Structural Architecture; Town Planning)

History: Founded 1982. A private institution under the supervision of the Ministry of National Education.

Governing Bodies: Sandjojo Foundation, Board of Trustees

Academic Year: August to July (August-January; February-July)

Admission Requirements: Secondary school certificate (Sekolah Menengah Atas, SMA) and entrance examination; GMAT/GRE and TOEFL scores.

Fees: (Rupiahs): undergraduate, 10m.; graduate, 23m. per annum

Main Language(s) of Instruction: Indonesian and English (Bilingual)

International Co-operation: With institutions in the Netherlands, Taiwan, Thailand, United Kingdom, United States

Accrediting Agencies: Indonesian Board of Accreditation

Degrees and Diplomas: *Sarjana (S1)*: 4 yrs; *Magister (S2)*: Architecture (Structural Architecture); Environmental and Urban Planning; Food Technology; Legal Studies; Management; Psychology, a further 2 yrs

Student Services: Academic counselling, Canteen, Cultural centre, Employment services, Foreign student adviser, Foreign Studies Centre, Health services, Language programs, Social counselling, Sports facilities

Student Residential Facilities: Small dormitory

Special Facilities: Soegijapranata Memorial Centre; Movie Studio

Libraries: c. 320,000 vols; periodicals; digital library

Publications: CELT, Journal of English Culture and Language *(3 per annum)*; Journal of Civil Engineering *(3 per annum)*

Press or Publishing House: Soegijapranata Catholic University Press

Last Updated: 25/07/11

SOERJO UNIVERSITY

Universitas Soerjo

Jalan Cepu Km 3, Ngawi, 63217 Jawa Timur
Tel: +62(351) 749-358
EMail: unsoer@telkom.net

Rector: Cipto Dradjajati

Ketua: Harsono

Faculties

Agriculture (Agriculture; Agronomy); **Economics** (Accountancy; Economics; Management); **Engineering** (Civil Engineering; Engineering; Mechanical Engineering); **Law** (Law); **Social and Political Sciences** (Government; Political Sciences; Social Sciences)

History: Founded 1981. A private institution under the supervision of the Department of Education and Culture.

Fees: (Rupiahs): 447,000 per annum

Degrees and Diplomas: *Sarjana (S1)*

Libraries: 1,881 vols

Last Updated: 05/02/09

SORONG VICTORY UNIVERSITY

Universitas Victory Sorong

Jalan Basuki Rahmat Km 115, Kelurahan Klasaman, Sorong, 98416 Papua
EMail: unvic_sorong@yahoo.com

Rector: Marthinus Salama

Ketua: Edward Kalami

Programmes

Agriculture (Agriculture; Animal Husbandry; Forestry); **Business Administration** (Accountancy; Management; Public Administration); **Economics** (Economics); **Engineering** (Electrical Engineering; Geological Engineering); **English** (English); **Indonesian** (Indonesian; Literature); **Information Technology** (Information Technology)

Degrees and Diplomas: *Sarjana (S1)*

Last Updated: 31/05/10

SOUTHEASTERN SULAWESI UNIVERSITY

Universitas Sulawesi Tenggara (UNSULTRA)

Kepten Piere Tendean, No 109A, Lepo-Lepo, Kendari, 93121 Sulawesi Tenggara
Tel: +62(401) 328-447
Fax: +62(401) 329-596
EMail: uchyunsultra@yahoo.co.id

Rector: Muhammad Ichlas Mappilawa

Ketua: Ali Mazi

Faculties

Agriculture *Dean*: La Panga; **Economics** *Dean*: Sahyunu; **Engineering** *Dean*: Zulkarnain Sikuru; **Law** (Law) *Dean*: Suriani B.T. Tollo; **Social and Political Sciences** *Dean*: Muh Nur

History: Founded 1986. Acquired present status 1987.

Governing Bodies: Foundation Yayasan Pendidikan Tinggi Sulawesi Tenggara - YPTST

Academic Year: September to July

Admission Requirements: Surat Tanda Tamat Belajar (STTB) and entrance examination

Fees: (Rupiahs): 400,000 per semester

Main Language(s) of Instruction: Indonesian

Degrees and Diplomas: *Sarjana (S1)*: 4 yrs

Student Services: Academic counselling, Canteen, Employment services, Language programs, Social counselling, Sports facilities

Student Residential Facilities: None

Libraries: Yes

Publications: Ilmu Amalia *(biennially)*

Last Updated: 05/02/09

STIKUBANK UNIVERSITY

Universitas Stikubank

Jl. Tri Lomba Juang No. 1, Semarang, Jawa Tengah
Tel: +62(24) 831-1668 +62(24) 845-1976
Fax: +62(24) 844-3240
EMail: info@unisbank.ac.id
Website: http://www.unisbank.ac.id

Rector: Bambang Suko Priyono

Ketua: W.T. Handoko

Faculties

Economics; **Engineering**; **Information Technology**; **Language and Cultural Studies** (Cultural Studies; English; English Studies; Literature); **Law**

Degrees and Diplomas: *Diploma*; *Sarjana (S1)*; *Magister (S2)*

Last Updated: 21/04/10

STIPER INSTITUTE OF AGRICULTURE

Institut Pertanian Stiper (INSTIPER)

Jalan Nangka II, Kampus Stiper Depok, Maguwoharjo, Sleman, Yogyakarta
Tel: +62(274) 885-479
Fax: +62(274) 885-479
EMail: instiper@indosat.net.id
Website: http://www.instiper.ac.id

Rector: Purwadi

Vice-Rector: Harsawardana

Faculties

Agricultural Technology *Dean*: Siti Achadiah Muchyidin; **Agriculture** (Agricultural Economics; Agriculture; Agronomy; Crop Production) *Dean*: Sundoro Sastrowiratmo; **Forestry** (Forestry; Wood Technology) *Dean*: Sambas Sabarnurdin

History: Founded 1958 as Estate Crop Staff School. Became School of Agriculture 1985, and acquired present status and title 1987.

Governing Bodies: Foundation of Estate Crop Staff School

Admission Requirements: Secondary school certificate and entrance examination

Fees: (Rupiahs): 475,000 per semester (or US$ 4,700)

Main Language(s) of Instruction: Indonesian

Accrediting Agencies: National Accrediting Agency

Degrees and Diplomas: *Sarjana (S1)*: 4 yrs; *Magister (S2)*

Student Services: Academic counselling, Canteen, Employment services, Health services, Nursery care, Sports facilities

Special Facilities: Estate Crop Experimental Farm, Mangrove Experimental Farm, Pilot Plant

Libraries: yes

Publications: Buletin Ilmiah INSTIPER, INSTIPER Scientific Journal *(biannually)*

Last Updated: 01/03/10

SUBANG UNIVERSITY

Universitas Subang

Jalan RA Kartini KM 3, Subang, 41285 Jawa Barat

Tel: +62(260) 411-415

Fax: +62(260) 415-677

EMail: info@unsub.ac.id

Website: http://www.unsub.ac.id

Rector: Yossi Adiwisastra

Ketua: Komir Bastaman

Faculties

Administration (Administration; Business Administration; Public Administration); **Agriculture** (Agricultural Business; Agricultural Engineering); **Communication Studies**; **Computer Science** (Computer Science; Information Technology); **Engineering**; **Law** (Law); **Teacher Training and Education** (Education; English; Mathematics; Mathematics Education; Physical Education; Sports; Teacher Training)

Degrees and Diplomas: *Sarjana (S1)*

Last Updated: 04/05/10

SULAWESI UNIVERSITY OF TECHNOLOGY

Universitas Teknologi Sulawesi

Jalan Monginsidi Baru 11, Makassar, Sulawesi Selatan

Tel: +62(411) 458-059

Fax: +62(411) 458-059

EMail: uts.makassar@yahoo.co.id

Rector: Ridwan Borahima

Ketua: Frans Senduk

Programmes

Business Administration (Accountancy; Management); **Chemistry**; **Engineering** (Agricultural Engineering; Civil Engineering; Electrical Engineering; Engineering; Environmental Engineering; Industrial Engineering); **Political Sciences**; **Social Welfare** (Social Welfare)

Degrees and Diplomas: *Sarjana (S1)*

Last Updated: 28/05/10

SULTAN FATAH UNIVERSITY

Universitas Sultan Fatah

Jl. Sultah Fatah No. 83, Demak, 59516 Jawa Tengah

Tel: +62(291) 681-024

EMail: unisfat_baak@yahoo.co.id

Rector: Nor Kholis

Ketua: Suseno

Programmes

Architecture Engineering (Architecture and Planning; Structural Architecture); **Business Administration** (Business Administration); **Civil Engineering** (Civil Engineering); **Communication Studies** (Communication Studies); **Computer Engineering** (Computer Engineering; Computer Science; Information Technology); **Economic and Development Studies** (Development Studies; Economics); **Electronic Engineering** (Electrical Engineering; Electronic Engineering); **Industrial Engineering** (Industrial Engineering); **Mechanical Engineering** (Mechanical Engineering); **Public Administration** (Public Administration); **Social Sciences and Economics** (Economics; Social Sciences)

Degrees and Diplomas: *Sarjana (S1)*

Last Updated: 05/02/09

SUNAN BONANG UNIVERSITY

Universitas Sunan Bonang

Jalan Dr. Wahidin Sudiro Husodo 798, Tuban, 62313 Jawa Timur

Tel: +62(361) 22-025

Rector: Soekarman

Ketua: Bambang Sugeng Wahono

Faculties

Agriculture (Agriculture; Agronomy; Animal Husbandry); **Engineering** (Civil Engineering; Engineering); **Law** (Law)

History: Founded 1982.

Fees: (Rupiahs): 240,000 per annum

Degrees and Diplomas: *Sarjana (S1)*

Last Updated: 06/02/09

SUNAN GIRI SURABAYA UNIVERSITY

Universitas Sunan Giri Surabaya (UNSURI)

Jalan Brigjen Katamso II, Waru Sidoarjo, Surabaya, 61256 Jawa Timur

Tel: +62(31) 853-2477

Fax: +62(31) 854-2563

EMail: info@ppsunsuri.ac.id; unsurisby@yahoo.com

Website: http://www.ppsunsuri.ac.id

Rector: Bisri Affandi

Ketua: H.A. Saerozi

Faculties

Economics (Economics; Management); **Engineering** (Civil Engineering; Engineering; Mechanical Engineering); **Law**; **Social and Political Sciences**

Programmes

Postgraduate Studies *Director*: Mushcin

History: Founded 1976. A private institution under the supervision of the Department of Education and Culture.

Fees: (Rupiahs): 1,625,000 per annum

Degrees and Diplomas: *Sarjana (S1)*; *Magister (S2)*

Libraries: 1,098 vols

Last Updated: 15/01/09

SURABAYA '45 UNIVERSITY

Universitas '45 Surabaya (UNPATMA)

Jalan Mayjen Sungkono 106, Surabaya, 60256 Jawa Timur

Tel: +62(31) 561-1214

Fax: +62(31) 563-3905

EMail: unpatma_sby@yahoo.com

Rector: Masriel Djamaloes

Faculties

Economics (Accountancy; Economics; Management; Tourism); **Engineering** (Computer Engineering; Industrial Engineering; Mechanical Engineering); **Psychology** (Psychology)

History: Founded 1985.

Admission Requirements: Secondary school certificate and entrance examination

Main Language(s) of Instruction: Indonesian

Degrees and Diplomas: *Sarjana (S1)*

Student Services: Academic counselling, Canteen, Employment services, Health services, Nursery care, Social counselling, Sports facilities

Libraries: 2,526 vols

Last Updated: 22/06/11

SURABAYA CIPUTRA UNIVERSITY

Universitas Ciputra Surabaya

UC Town, CitraLand, Surabaya, 60219 Jawa Timur

Tel: +62(31) 745-1699

Fax: +62(31) 745-1698

EMail: info@ciputra.ac.id

Website: http://www.ciputra.ac.id

Rector: Tony Antonio

Faculties
Information Technology (Information Technology; Multimedia; Software Engineering); **Interior Design and Architecture** (Architecture; Interior Design); **International Business Management** (International Business; Management); **Psychology** (Psychology); **Tourism and Hotel Management** (Hotel Management; Tourism); **Visual Communication Design**

Degrees and Diplomas: *Sarjana (S1)*
Last Updated: 28/04/10

SURABAYA INSTITUTE OF TECHNOLOGY DEVELOPMENT

Institut Teknologi Pembangunan Surabaya
Jalan Balongsari Praja V N°1, Surabaya, 60186 Jawa Timur
Tel: +62(31) 502-2959
Fax: +62(31) 502-2961
Website: http://www.itps-sby.ac.id

Programmes
Engineering (Chemical Engineering; Electrical Engineering; Engineering; Environmental Engineering; Industrial Engineering; Mechanical Engineering); **Planning and Civil Engineering** (Civil Engineering; Town Planning)

History: Founded 1981.

Degrees and Diplomas: *Sarjana (S1)*

Libraries: 3,570 titles
Last Updated: 22/06/11

SURABAYA UNIVERSITY

Universitas Surabaya (UBAYA)
Ngagel Jaya Selatan 169, Surabaya, 60284 East Java
Tel: +62(31) 298-1005 +62(31) 298-1300
Fax: +62(31) 298-1018 +62(31) 298-1301
EMail: humas@ubaya.ac.id; oia@ia.ubaya.ac.id
Website: http://www.ubaya.ac.id

Rector: Joniarto Parung EMail: rektorat@ubaya.ac.id

Vice-Rector: Nemuel Daniel Pah

International Relations: Adi Tedjaksuma
EMail: atedjakusuma@ia.ubaya.ac.id

Faculties
Biotechnology (Biotechnology); **Business and Economics** (Accountancy; Banking; Business Administration; Economics; Finance; Hotel and Restaurant; Human Resources; Information Sciences; International Business; Management; Marketing; Tourism); **Engineering** (Automation and Control Engineering; Chemical Engineering; Computer Engineering; Computer Graphics; Computer Networks; Electrical Engineering; Electronic Engineering; Environmental Engineering; Industrial Design; Industrial Engineering; Information Sciences; Information Technology; Maintenance Technology; Multimedia; Polymer and Plastics Technology; Production Engineering; Safety Engineering; Technology; Telecommunications Engineering); **Law** (Administrative Law; Civil Law; Commercial Law; Constitutional Law; Criminal Law; Government; International Law; Law); **Pharmacy** (Anatomy; Biochemistry; Biotechnology; Microbiology; Pharmacology; Pharmacy; Plant Pathology; Toxicology); **Postgraduate Studies** (Accountancy; Clinical Psychology; Industrial and Organizational Psychology; Law; Management; Notary Studies; Pharmacy; Psychology); **Psychology** (Clinical Psychology; Developmental Psychology; Educational Psychology; Industrial and Organizational Psychology; Psychology; Social Psychology); **UBAYA Polytechnic** (Accountancy; English; Management; Marketing; Secretarial Studies; Taxation)

History: Founded 1968. A private institution positioned to be a leading University in the Asia-Pacific Region.

Governing Bodies: Yayasan Universitas Surabaya

Academic Year: August to July (August-January; February-July)

Admission Requirements: Secondary school certificate (Sekolah Menengam Umum - SMU), and entrance examination

Fees: (US Dollars): 1,100 per semester

Main Language(s) of Instruction: Indonesian

International Co-operation: Participates in Faculty Exchange Programme; Student Exchange Programme; Study Abroad Programme; Visiting Professorship; Volunteering Programme; Joint Research Collaboration

Accrediting Agencies: National Accrediting Board of Indonesia

Degrees and Diplomas: *Diploma*: 3 yrs; *Sarjana (S1)*: 3 1/2-4 yrs; *Magister (S2)*: Accountancy; Clinical Pharmacy; Law; Management; Notary; Professional Psychology, a further 1-2 yrs

Student Services: Academic counselling, Canteen, Cultural centre, Employment services, Foreign student adviser, Foreign Studies Centre, Health services, Language programs, Nursery care, Social counselling, Sports facilities

Special Facilities: The International Village

Libraries: c. 100,500 vols (including online journals)

Publications: Anima, Psychology *(quarterly)*; Buletin Pusat Studi Lingkungan, Environmental Studies *(quarterly)*; Buletin Pusham Ubaya, Human Rights Studies *(quarterly)*; East Java Business Review (EJBR), Business and Industry Studies *(monthly)*; Ekonomi Bisnis, Business and Economics *(quarterly)*; Jurnal Dinamika HAM, Human Rights Studies *(biannually)*; Jurnal Teknologi Industri dan Informasi, Engineering *(quarterly)*; The Office of International Affairs, Ubaya Newsletter, International cooperation and activities *(quarterly)*; Unitas, Research Reports *(biannually)*; Yustika, Law *(biannually)*

Press or Publishing House: Warta Ubaya
Last Updated: 01/07/11

SURABAYA UNIVERSITY OF TECHNOLOGY

Universitas Teknologi Surabaya
Jalan Ngagel 89, Surabaya, 60131 Jawa Timur
Tel: +62(31) 502-7460
Fax: +62(31) 502-7460

Rector: Yuliati

Ketua: Bambang Soetedjo

Programmes
Business Administration; **English**; **Law** (Law)
Degrees and Diplomas: *Sarjana (S1)*; *Magister (S2)*
Last Updated: 28/05/10

SURAKARTA CHRISTIAN UNIVERSITY

Universitas Kristen Surakarta
Jalan Robert Wolter Monginsidi 36-38, Margoyudan, Surakarta, 57134 Jawa Tengah
Tel: +62(271) 637-145
Fax: +62(271) 637-145
EMail: info@uks.ac.id
Website: http://www.uks.ac.id

Rektor: Suwitadi Kusumodilogo

Ketua: Widya Notodirya

Programmes
Christian Religious Education (Christian Religious Studies; Pastoral Studies; Religious Education); **Economics** (Accountancy; Economics; Management); **Engineering** (Computer Engineering; Engineering; Environmental Engineering)

History: Founded 1996.

Degrees and Diplomas: *Sarjana (S1)*; *Magister (S2)*: Christian Religious Education
Last Updated: 25/07/11

SURAKARTA UNIVERSITY

Universitas Surakarta
Jalan Raya Palur Km. 5, Surakarta, 57772 Jawa Tengah
Tel: +62(271) 825-117
EMail: info@unsa.ac.id
Website: http://www.unsa.ac.id

Rector: M.M. Margono

Ketua: Roch Mulyani

Faculties
Arts and Humanities (English; Literature); **Economics** *Dean*: Sulistyo; **Engineering** *Dean*: Djoko Kuncoro; **Law** *Dean*: Bernard K. Tanya; **Social and Political Sciences** *Dean*: Suraji

History: Founded 1995.

Fees: (Rupiahs): 1.57m. per annum

Degrees and Diplomas: *Diploma*: 3 yrs; *Sarjana (S1)*
Last Updated: 21/04/10

SURAPATI UNIVERSITY

Universitas Surapati
Jalan Dewi Sartika 184A, Cawang, Jakarta Timur, 13640 DKI Jakarta
Tel: +62(21) 809-4403
Fax: +62(21) 809-1129

Rector: Nurhayati Muchtar

Ketua: Salim Chalifah

Faculties

Economics (Accountancy; Economics; Management) *Dean*: Abdurrahman; **Industrial Engineering** (Electrical Engineering; Industrial Engineering) *Dean*: Samsul Ariet; **Mathematics and Natural Sciences** (Mathematics; Natural Sciences; Physics) *Dean*: Nurwati

History: Founded 1983.

Fees: (Rupiahs): 1.2m. per annum

Degrees and Diplomas: *Sarjana (S1)*; *Magister (S2)*
Last Updated: 14/01/09

SURYADARMA UNIVERSITY

Universitas Suryadarma
Jl. Protokol Halim Perdana Kusuma, Jakarta, 13610 DKI Jakarta
Tel: +62(21) 809-3475 +62(21) 800-9246
Fax: +62(21) 800-9246
EMail: pps@unsurya.ac.id
Website: http://www.unsurya.ac.id

Rector: Martono Kunarso

Ketua: Sutrisno

Faculties

Economics; **Engineering**; **Planning and Civil Engineering**; **Social and Political Sciences**

History: Founded 1999.

Degrees and Diplomas: *Sarjana (S1)*; *Magister (S2)*
Last Updated: 11/02/09

SURYAKANCANA UNIVERSITY

Universitas Suryakancana
Jalan Pair Gede Raya, Cianjur, 43216 Jawa Barat
Tel: +62(263) 263-270
EMail: suryakancanacianjur@yahoo.co.id

Rector: Erman Husein

Ketua: M. Djunaedi

Faculties

Agriculture (Agricultural Economics; Agriculture; Crop Production; Fishery); **Engineering** (Engineering; Environmental Engineering; Industrial Engineering; Information Technology); **Law** (Law); **Teacher Trainers Education** (Government; Indonesian; Literature; Mathematics; Sports; Teacher Trainers Education)

History: Founded as Sekolah Tinggi Hukum Surya Kencana.

Degrees and Diplomas: *Sarjana (S1)*; *Magister (S2)*
Last Updated: 06/02/09

SUTOMO UNIVERSITY

Universitas Sutomo
Deli Serdang, Sumatera Utara

Programmes

Business Administration (Accountancy; Management; Public Administration); **Engineering** (Computer Engineering; Electrical Engineering; Engineering; Information Technology; Structural Architecture); **Government** (Government); **Law** (Law); **Science** (Biology; Chemistry; Mathematics; Physics)

Degrees and Diplomas: *Sarjana (S1)*
Last Updated: 05/05/10

SWADAYA GUNUNG JATI UNIVERSITY

Universitas Swadaya Gunung Jati
Jalan Pemuda 32, Sartika, Cirebon, 45132 Jawa Barat
Tel: +62(321) 206-558
Fax: +62(231) 236-742
Website: http://unswagati-crb.ac.id

Rector: Djakaria Machmud

Vice-Rector: Abdul Rozak

Faculties

Agriculture (Agricultural Business; Agricultural Economics; Agricultural Engineering; Agriculture; Agronomy); **Economics** (Accountancy; Development Studies; Economics; Management); **Education and Teacher Training** (Accountancy; Art Education; Civics; Curriculum; Educational Administration; Educational Research; Educational Sciences; Educational Testing and Evaluation; English; Foreign Languages Education; Indonesian; Islamic Theology; Linguistics; Literature; Mathematics Education; Native Language Education; Religious Education; Science Education; Social Sciences; Teacher Training; Writing); **Engineering** (Civil Engineering; Engineering); **Law** (Administrative Law; Civil Law; Commercial Law; Comparative Law; Constitutional Law; Criminal Law; Criminology; Ethics; Human Rights; Indonesian; Insurance; International Law; Islamic Law; Islamic Studies; Islamic Theology; Labour Law; Law; Private Law; Social Sciences); **Medicine** (Anatomy; Biochemistry; Biology; Cardiology; Community Health; Embryology and Reproduction Biology; Genetics; Histology; Medicine; Physiology; Public Health); **Social and Political Sciences** (Administration; Communication Studies; Government; Political Sciences; Public Administration; Social Sciences)

History: Founded 1961.

Degrees and Diplomas: *Diploma*: 3 yrs; *Sarjana (S1)*; *Magister (S2)*: Agronomy; Indonesian; Law; Administration

Libraries: 12,532 vols
Last Updated: 01/07/11

SWISS GERMAN UNIVERSITY

Universitas Swiss German (SGU)
Campus BSD City, Bumi Serpong Damai, 15321 Island of Java
Tel: +62(21) 537-6221
Fax: +62(21) 537-6201
EMail: info@sgu.ac.id
Website: http://www.sgu.ac.id

Rector: Jürgen Grüneberg (2010-) EMail: rector@sgu.ac.id

Vice-Rector for Academic Affairs: Marsudi K. Kisworo
EMail: marsudi.kisworo@sgu.ac.id

Vice-Rector: Ketut Tejawibawa

International Relations: Intje Kreeft, Relations Officer
EMail: intje.kreeft@sgu.ac.id

Faculties

Business Administration (Accountancy; Business Administration; Hotel Management; Modern Languages; Tourism); **Engineering** (Electrical and Electronic Engineering; Electronic Engineering; Engineering; Industrial Engineering; Materials Engineering; Mechanical Engineering); **Information Technology** (Information Technology); **Law** (Law); **Life Sciences**; **Social Sciences**

Programmes

Accountancy (Accountancy); **Biomedical Engineering** (Biomedical Engineering); **Business Administration**; **Business Administration (with Business Language)** (Business Administration; Modern Languages); **Business Administration for Hotel and Tourism Mangement** (Business Administration; Hotel Management; Tourism); **Business Engineering**; **Business Informatics** (Business Computing); **Communication and Public Relations** (Public Relations); **Food Technology** (Food Technology); **Information and Communication Technology** *(ICT)*; **Mechatronics Engineering** (Electronic Engineering); **Pharmaceutical Engineering** (Engineering; Pharmacy); **Software Engineering** (Software Engineering)

History: Founded 2000.

Governing Bodies: Board of Patronage; Board of Management

Academic Year: August to July

Admission Requirements: College A-level (Indonesia: SMU); English test; Entrance examination

Fees: (Rupiahs): 12m.-24m. per semester

Main Language(s) of Instruction: English

International Co-operation: With universities in Germany, Switzerland, Austria, India and Korea

Accrediting Agencies: National Accreditation Agency of the Ministry of National Education; Germany Accreditation Agency ZeVA

Degrees and Diplomas: *Sarjana (S1)*: 4 yrs; *Magister (S2)*: 2 yrs; *Doktor (S3)*: 3-4 yrs

Student Services: Academic counselling, Foreign student adviser, Language programs, Sports facilities

Special Facilities: Wireless Campus

Libraries: Scientific Library

Press or Publishing House: Mac Graw-Hill; Wiley

Last Updated: 01/03/10

TABANAN UNIVERSITY

Universitas Tabanan

Jalan Wagimin 8, Kediri, Tabanan, 82121 Bali

Tel: +62(362) 811-605

Rector: Ida Bagus Gde Wirakusuma

Ketua Yayasan: Gede Mastera

Faculties

Agriculture; **Economics**; **Law**

History: Founded 1981.

Fees: (Rupiahs): 350,000 per annum

Degrees and Diplomas: *Sarjana (S1)*

Libraries: 1,901 vols

Last Updated: 06/02/09

TAMA JAGAKARSA UNIVERSITY

Universitas Tama Jagakarsa

Jalan Letjen T.B. Simatupang 152, Jakarta Selatan, 12530 DKI Jakarta

Tel: +62(21) 789-0965

Fax: +62(21) 789-0966

EMail: info@jagakarsa.ac.id

Website: http://www.jagakarsa.ac.id/

Rector: Muhammad Noor Sembiring

Ketua: Tama Sembiring

Faculties

Communication Studies (Communication Studies); **Economics** (Accountancy; Banking; Economics; Finance); **Engineering**; **Law**; **Psychology** (Psychology); **Teacher Training and Educational Sciences** (Education; English; Indonesian; Teacher Training)

Degrees and Diplomas: *Sarjana (S1)*; *Magister (S2)*

Last Updated: 05/05/10

TAMANSISWA PADANG UNIVERSITY

Universitas Tamansiswa Padang (UNITAS)

Jalan Tamansiswa 9, Padang, Sumatera Barat

Tel: +62(751) 400-20

Fax: +62(751) 444-170

EMail: unitas-pdg@ac.id

Website: http://www.unitas-pdg.ac.id/

Rector: Nanda Utama (2003-)

Ketua: Atri Tanjung

Faculties

Agriculture (Agriculture; Agronomy; Animal Husbandry); **Economics** (Accountancy; Economics; Management); **Law** (Law)

History: Founded 1983 as Academy of Agriculture and Animal Husbandry. The name changed into Agricultural High School in 1985, and became University of Tamansiswa in 1987. Acquired present status 1989.

Main Language(s) of Instruction: Indonesian, English

International Co-operation: Yes

Accrediting Agencies: National Accreditation Board

Degrees and Diplomas: *Sarjana (S1)*: 5-6 yrs

Student Services: Health services, Sports facilities

Special Facilities: Green House; Laboratory.

Libraries: 2,779 vols

Academic Staff *2009-2010*: Total: c. 60

Student Numbers *2009-2010*: Total: c. 1,500

Last Updated: 01/07/11

TAMANSISWA UNIVERSITY PALEMBANG

Universitas Tamansiswa Palembang

Jalan Taman Siswa 261, Palembang, 30125 Sumatera Selatan

Tel: +62(711) 373-292

Fax: +62(711) 373-292

Rector: Sofyan Hassan

Ketua: Ki Bakhtiar

Faculties

Agriculture (Agriculture; Agronomy) *Dean*: Irsandi; **Economics** (Accountancy; Economics; Management) *Dean*: Bastoni Achmadsyah; **Educational Sciences and Teachers Training** (Educational Sciences; English; Mathematics Education; Teacher Trainers Education); **Engineering** (Chemical Engineering; Civil Engineering; Engineering; Mechanical Engineering) *Dean*: Ahmat Hidayat; **Law** *Dean*: Djasmaniar Mahmud; **Social and Political Sciences** (Government; Political Sciences; Social Sciences) *Dean*: Joko Siswanto

History: Founded 1987.

Fees: (Rupiahs): 900,000 per annum

Degrees and Diplomas: *Sarjana (S1)*

Libraries: 2,597 vols

Last Updated: 06/02/09

TARUMANAGARA UNIVERSITY

Universitas Tarumanagara (UNTAR)

Jalan Letjen. S. Parman 1, Jakarta, 11440 DKI Jakarta

Tel: +62(21) 567-3003 +62(21) 567-1747

Fax: +62(21) 560-4478 +62(21) 563-8337

EMail: rektor@tarumanagara.ac.id

Website: http://www.tarumanagara.ac.id/

Rector: Monty P. Satiadarma

Ketua: Singgih Dirgagunarga

Faculties

Economics (Accountancy; Economics; Management; Taxation) *Dean*: Sukrisno Agoes; **Engineering** (Civil Engineering; Industrial Engineering; Mechanical Engineering; Rural Planning; Structural Architecture; Telecommunications Engineering; Town Planning) *Dean*: Ignatius Hariyanto; **Information Technology** (Computer Science; Information Sciences; Information Technology) *Dean*: Tony Mulya; **Law** (Law) *Dean*: Gunardi; **Medicine** (Medicine) *Dean*: Tom Surjadi; **Psychology** (Psychology) *Dean*: Rostiana; **Visual Arts and Design** (Communication Arts; Interior Design; Visual Arts) *Dean*: Stephanus Dwiyanto

Programmes

Postgraduate Studies *Director*: Sofia W. Alisjahbana

History: Founded 1959. A private institution under the supervision of the Department of Education and Culture.

Academic Year: July to June (July-December; January-June)

Admission Requirements: Secondary school certificate (Sekolah Menengah Atas, SMA) and entrance examination

Fees: (Rupiahs): 3.2m. per annum

Main Language(s) of Instruction: Indonesian

Degrees and Diplomas: *Diploma*: 3 yrs; *Sarjana (S1)*: 4 yrs; *Magister (S2)*: 2 yrs; *Doktor (S3)*: 3 yrs

Student Services: Academic counselling, Canteen, Health services, Language programs, Sports facilities

Libraries: 250,406 vols

Publications: Jurnal Akuntansi *(biennially)*; Jurnal Manajemen *(biennially)*

Last Updated: 01/03/10

TELKOM INSTITUTE OF MANAGEMENT

Institut Manajemen Telkom

Jalan Gegerkalong Hilir 47, Bandung 40152
Tel: +62(22) 201-1384
Fax: +62(22) 201-1387
EMail: info@imtelkom.ac.id
Website: http://www.imtelkom.ac.id

Rector: Asep Suryana Natawiria

Vice-Rector: Jafar Sembiring

Faculties

Design and Communication Management; **Finance and Business Administration**; **Telecommunications and Media Business** (Business Administration; Media Studies; Telecommunications Engineering; Telecommunications Services)

Degrees and Diplomas: *Sarjana (S1)*; *Magister (S2)*
Last Updated: 27/04/10

TELKOM INSTITUTE OF TELECOMMUNICATIONS ENGINEERING

Institut Teknologi Telkom

Jl.Telekomunikasi Terusan Buah Batu, Bandung, 40257 West Java
Tel: +62(22) 756-4108
Fax: +62(22) 756-5200
EMail: info@ittelkom.ac.id
Website: http://www.ittelkom.ac.id

Rector: Ahmad Tri Hanuranto

Faculties

Electrical and Telecommunications Engineering (Computer Engineering; Electrical Engineering; Telecommunications Engineering); **Industry** (Industrial Engineering; Information Technology); **Informatics** (Computer Engineering; Computer Science); **Postgraduate Studies** (Computer Engineering; Electrical Engineering; Telecommunications Engineering); **Science** (Computer Science; Physical Engineering)

History: Founded 1990. Formerly known as Sekolah Tinggi Teknologi Telkom Bandung (Telkom School of Engineering).

Degrees and Diplomas: *Diploma*; *Sarjana (S1)*; *Magister (S2)*: Computer Engineering; Electrical Engineering; Telecommunications Engineering
Last Updated: 11/07/11

TENTENA CHRISTIAN UNIVERSITY

Universitas Kristen Tentena

Jalan Torulemba 21, Tentena, 94663 Sulawesi Tengah
Tel: +62(458) 21475
Fax: +62(458) 21475
EMail: unkrit.gkst@yahoo.com

Rector: Heny Hermas Lumeno

Ketua: A.R. Tobondo

Programmes

Agriculture (Agricultural Business); **Biology** (Biology); **Early Childhood Teacher Education**; **Economics**; **English** (English); **Management**; **Mathematics**; **Sociology** (Sociology)

Degrees and Diplomas: *Sarjana (S1)*
Last Updated: 30/04/10

TEUKU UMAR UNIVERSITY OF MEULABOH

Universitas Teuku Umar Meulaboh

Jalan Alue Peunyareng Kec Meurebo, Meulaboh, 23617 Aceh
Tel: +62(655) 701-2801
Fax: +62(655) 755-1188

Rector: Alfian Ibrahim

Ketua: Teuku Bustami Puteh

Programmes

Agriculture; **Communication Studies**; **Economics** (Economics; Public Administration); **Engineering**; **Public Health** (Public Health); **Sociology** (Sociology)

Degrees and Diplomas: *Sarjana (S1)*
Last Updated: 05/05/10

TIDAR UNIVERSITY OF MAGELANG

Universitas Tidar Magelang

Jalan Kapten Suparman 39, Magelang, 56116 Jawa Tengah
Tel: +62(293) 364-113 +62(293) 362-438
Fax: +62(293) 362-438
EMail: admin@utm.ac.id
Website: http://www.utm.ac.id

Rector: Cahyo Yusuf

Faculties

Agriculture (Agricultural Engineering; Agriculture; Agronomy); **Economics** (Accountancy; Development Studies; Economics); **Education and Teacher Training** (Educational Sciences; English; Foreign Languages Education; Indonesian; Literature; Native Language Education; Teacher Training); **Engineering** (Civil Engineering; Electrical Engineering; Engineering; Mechanical Engineering); **Social and Political Sciences** (Government; Political Sciences; Public Administration; Social Sciences)

History: Founded 1979. A private institution under the supervision of the Department of Education and Culture and the Municipal Authorities.

Academic Year: September to August (September-February; March-August)

Admission Requirements: Secondary school certificate (Sekolah Lanjutan Tinagkat Atas, SLTA). Transfer Study for Bachelor Degree Alumni

Main Language(s) of Instruction: Indonesian

Degrees and Diplomas: *Sarjana (S1)*: 4-7 yrs

Student Services: Academic counselling, Canteen, Cultural centre, Health services, Social counselling, Sports facilities

Student Residential Facilities: For c. 5,000 students

Libraries: c. 10,000 vols

Publications: Research Report
Last Updated: 01/07/11

TIMIKA UNIVERSITY

Universitas Timika

Jalan C. Heatubun, Timika, 99910 Papua
Tel: +62(901) 323-778
Fax: +62(901) 323-778
EMail: univtimika@gmail.com

Rector: Luky Mahakena

Ketua: Gerardus Timang

Programmes

Agricultural Business (Agricultural Business); **Communication Studies** (Communication Studies); **Psychology** (Psychology)

Degrees and Diplomas: *Sarjana (S1)*
Last Updated: 31/05/10

TIMOR UNIVERSITY

Universitas Timor (UNIMOR)

Jl. Jend. Sudirman, Kefamenanu, 85613 Timor
Tel: +62(388) 31-056
Fax: +62(388) 31-056
EMail: unimor@yahoo.co.id; unimor@telkom.net

Rector: Antonius Berkanis

Ketua: Antonius Amaunut

Programmes

Administrative Law (Administrative Law); **Agriculture**; **Biology**; **Economics and Political Sciences** (Development Studies; Economics; Government; Political Sciences); **Education and Teacher's Training** (Biology; Mathematics Education); **Management**; **Mathematics** (Mathematics); **Modern Languages** (English; Indonesian; Literature)
Last Updated: 21/01/09

TOMAKAKA UNIVERSITY

Universitas Tomakaka

Jalan. Ir. H. Juanda 44/77, Mamuju, Sulawesi

Faculties

Agriculture (Agricultural Business; Agriculture; Fishery); **Computer Science**; **Education and Teacher Training**; **Engineering** (Civil Engineering; Engineering; Structural Architecture); **Law**; **Social and Political Sciences** (Political Sciences; Public Administration; Social Sciences)

Degrees and Diplomas: *Sarjana (S1)*

Last Updated: 31/05/10

TOMOHON CHRISTIAN UNIVERSITY OF INDONESIA

Universitas Kristen Indonesia Tomohon (UKIT)

Kampus UKIT Kotak POS 34, Jalan Kakaskasen III, Tomohon, 95362 Sulawesi Utara

Tel: +62(436) 351-145 +62(436) 351-183

Fax: +62(436) 351-145

Rector: Hein Arina

Ketua: A.Z.R. Wenas

Faculties

Agriculture (Agricultural Engineering; Agriculture; Agronomy) *Dean*: K. Sumampow; **Economy** (Accountancy; Economics; Management); **Educational Science and Teacher Training** (Art Education; Economics; Educational Sciences; English; History; Humanities and Social Science Education; Modern Languages; Teacher Training) *Dean*: W. Karauwan; **Engineering** (Architecture; Civil Engineering; Engineering) *Dean*: D. Suawa; **Law** (Law) *Dean*: D. Katuuk; **Mathematics and Natural Sciences** (Biology; Mathematics; Natural Sciences; Pharmacy; Statistics) *Dean*: O. J. Worrow; **Medicine** *Dean*: S. Rampun; **Psychology**; **Theological Philosophy** (Christian Religious Studies; Philosophy; Protestant Theology; Religion) *Dean*: M.M. Lengkong

History: Founded 1965. A private Christian University under the supervision of the Minahasa Christian Evangelical Church.

Governing Bodies: Senate; Advisory Council

Academic Year: September to July (September-January; February-July)

Admission Requirements: Secondary school certificate (Sekolah Menengah Atas, SMA) and entrance examination

Fees: (Rupiahs): 600,000 per annum

Main Language(s) of Instruction: Indonesian

Degrees and Diplomas: *Sarjana (S1)*

Student Residential Facilities: Yes

Special Facilities: Experimental Farm Station

Libraries: 17,719 vols

Publications: Inspirasi *(quarterly)*

Last Updated: 19/01/09

TOMPOTIKA LUWUK BANGGAI UNIVERSITY

Universitas Tompotika Luwuk Banggai

Jalan Dewi Sartika No. 65, Luwuk Banggai, 94715 Sulawesi Tengah

Tel: +62(461) 324-027

Rector: Tongko Djafar

Ketua: Ismail Muid

Faculties

Agriculture (Agriculture; Cattle Breeding; Harvest Technology) *Dean*: Herwin Yatim; **Community Health**; **Economics** *Dean*: Masdar M. Amin; **Education** (Educational and Student Counselling; Educational Sciences; Mathematics) *Dean*: Irvan Hinelo; **Engineering** (Architecture; Civil Engineering; Engineering) *Dean*: Ferdiyanto Sugiyanto; **Law** (Law) *Dean*: Sukri Sulumin; **Social and Political Sciences** (Government; Political Sciences; Social Sciences) *Head*: H. Tajuddin Tjatjo

History: Founded as Sekolah Tinggi Keguruan dan Ilmu Pendidikan Tompotika.

Degrees and Diplomas: *Sarjana (S1)*

Last Updated: 06/02/09

TORAJA CHRISTIAN UNIVERSITY OF INDONESIA

Universitas Kristen Indonesia Toraja (UKI TORAJA)

Jalan Nusantara 12, Makale, 91811 Sulawesi Selatan

Tel: +62(423) 22-468

Fax: +62(423) 22-689

EMail: ukitoraja@yahoo.com

Rector: Albertinus Lambe

Ketua: T.R Andilolo

Faculties

Agriculture (Agriculture; Agronomy) *Dean*: Yusuf Limbongan; **Animal Husbandry** (Animal Husbandry) *Dean*: Aris Somba; **Economics** (Business Administration; Economics; Management) *Dean*: Elisabeth Pali; **Engineering** (Architecture; Civil Engineering; Engineering; Mechanical Engineering) *Dean*: Marthen Luther Paembonan; **Teacher Training and Educational Sciences** (Curriculum; Educational Sciences; Educational Technology; English; Indonesian; Mathematics Education; Primary Education; Secondary Education; Teacher Training; Technology Education) *Dean*: Dan Mangoki

History: Founded 1967 as Teacher Training College. Acquired university status 1992.

Admission Requirements: High School Diploma

Fees: (Rupiahs): 875,000 per semester

Main Language(s) of Instruction: Indonesian

Degrees and Diplomas: *Diploma*; *Sarjana (S1)*

Student Services: Academic counselling, Canteen, Health services, Language programs, Social counselling

Special Facilities: Laboratories of Languages, Basic Physics, Civil Engineering, Mechanical Engineering, Agriculture; Green House; Pigs Barn

Libraries: c. 11,000 vols

Last Updated: 19/01/09

TRI TUNGGAL UNIVERSITY

Universitas Tri Tunggal

Jalan Kalijudan 34-b, Surabaya, 60285 Jawa Timur

Tel: +62(31) 381-0792

Fax: +62(31) 381-8237

Rector: Untung Supriadi

Vice-Rector: Rugaya

Faculties

Economics (Accountancy; Economics; Management); **Educational Science and Teacher Training** (Civics; Educational Sciences; Political Sciences; Social Sciences); **Engineering** (Engineering; Industrial Engineering); **Law** (Law)

History: Founded 1983.

Fees: (Rupiahs): 180,000 per annum

Degrees and Diplomas: *Sarjana (S1)*

Libraries: 1,699 vols

Last Updated: 06/02/09

TRIBHUWANA TUNGGA DEWI UNIVERSITY

Universitas Tribhuwana Tungga Dewi

Jl. Telaga Warna Bloc C, Tlogomas, Malang 65144

Tel: +62(341) 565-500

Fax: +62(341) 565-522

EMail: unitri@hotmail.com

Rector: Wani Hadi Utomo

Ketua: Bambang Guritno

Faculties

Agriculture (Agricultural Business; Agricultural Economics; Agricultural Engineering; Agriculture; Crop Production); **Animal Husbandry** (Animal Husbandry; Cattle Breeding); **Economics** (Accountancy; Economics; Management); **Engineering** (Chemical Engineering; Civil Engineering; Engineering); **Fishery** (Fishery); **Industrial Engineering** (Industrial Engineering); **Nursing** (Nursing); **Social and Political Sciences** (Government; Political Sciences; Social Sciences)

Degrees and Diplomas: *Sarjana (S1)*; *Magister (S2)*
Last Updated: 06/02/09

TRIDHARMA UNIVERSITY

Universitas Tridharma

Jalan A. Wahab Syachranie 7, Batu Ampar, Balikpapan, 76123
Kalimantan Timur
Tel: +62(542) 436-650

Rector: Achmad
Ketua: Sudarmi Aisyah

Faculties

Economics (Accountancy; Economics; Management); **Educational Science and Teacher Training** (Biology; Educational Sciences; English; Mathematics; Science Education; Teacher Training); **Engineering** (Civil Engineering; Electrical Engineering; Engineering; Mechanical Engineering; Petroleum and Gas Engineering); **Law** (Law); **Social and Political Sciences** (Administration; Government; Political Sciences; Social Sciences)

History: Founded 1978. A private institution under the supervision of the Department of Education and Culture.

Fees: (Rupiahs): 600,000 per annum

Degrees and Diplomas: *Diploma*: 3 yrs; *Sarjana (S1)*

Libraries: 2,927 vols
Last Updated: 06/02/09

TRIDINANTI UNIVERSITY OF PALEMBANG

Universitas Tridinanti Palembang (UTP)

Jalan Kapten Marzuki 2446, Kamboja, Palembang, 30145
Sumatera Selatan
Tel: +62(711) 355-961 +62(711) 358-566
Fax: +62(711) 355-961
Website: http://www.tridinanti.ac.id

Rector: Ir. Edizal (2003-)

Vice-Rector: Rusman Roni

Faculties

Agriculture (Agricultural Business; Agricultural Engineering; Agronomy); **Economics** (Accountancy; Banking; Economics; Finance; Management; Marketing); **Education and Teacher Trainiing** (Education; English; Foreign Languages Education; Indonesian; Native Language Education; Teacher Training); **Engineering** (Architecture; Civil Engineering; Electrical Engineering; Electronic Engineering; Engineering; Industrial Engineering; Industrial Management; Mechanical Engineering; Production Engineering; Structural Architecture; Telecommunications Engineering)

Programmes

Postgraduate (Management)
History: Founded 1984.
Main Language(s) of Instruction: Indonesian
Accrediting Agencies: Badan Akreditasi Nasional (BAN)
Degrees and Diplomas: *Diploma*: 3 yrs; *Sarjana (S1)*: 4 yrs; *Magister (S2)*: Management, 18 months
Student Services: Academic counselling, Canteen, Employment services, Language programs, Sports facilities
Special Facilities: Convention Hall
Libraries: c. 16,000 vols.
Publications: Journal *(quarterly)*
Last Updated: 01/07/11

TRISAKTI UNIVERSITY

Universitas Trisakti (USAKTI)

Jalan Kiyai Tapa N°1, Grogol, Jakarta, 11440 DKI Jakarta
Tel: +62(21) 560-2575 +62(21) 560-2573
Fax: +62(21) 567-3001
EMail: sekun@trisakti.ac.id; universitas@trisakti.ac.id
Website: http://www.trisakti.ac.id

Rector: Thoby Mutis (1998-)
Tel: +62(21) 560-5833, Fax: +62(21) 560-5833

Vice-Rector: Yuswa Zainuri Basri

Faculties

Civil Engineering and Planning (Architectural and Environmental Design; Architecture; Civil Engineering; Construction Engineering; Industrial Design; Interior Design; Structural Architecture); **Dentistry** *(Campus B)* (Dentistry); **Economics** *(Campus A)* (Accountancy; Development Studies; Economics; Management); **Industrial Technology** *(Campus A)* (Computer Science; Electrical Engineering; Industrial Engineering; Mechanical Engineering); **Landscape Architecture and Environmental Technology** *(Campus A)* (Environmental Engineering; Landscape Architecture; Regional Planning; Town Planning); **Law** *(Campus A)* (Administrative Law; Civil Law; Criminal Law; Human Rights; Law; Public Law); **Medicine** *(Campus B)* (Medicine); **Mineral Technology and Energy Engineering** *(Campus A)* (Energy Engineering; Geological Engineering; Mining Engineering; Petroleum and Gas Engineering); **Visual Arts and Design** *(Campus A)* (Communication Arts; Design; Management; Photography; Visual Arts)

Schools

Business (Business Administration); **Graduate Studies** *(Campus A)* (Civil Engineering; Economics; Electrical Engineering; Law; Management)

History: Founded 1965. A private institution under the supervision of the Department of Education and Culture.

Governing Bodies: Board of Trustees

Academic Year: September to August (September-February; March-August)

Admission Requirements: Secondary school certificate

Fees: (Rupiah): 1.68m.-4.55m. per semester

Main Language(s) of Instruction: Indonesian

International Co-operation: With universities in Finland, Australia, Netherlands.

Degrees and Diplomas: *Diploma*: Taxation; *Sarjana (S1)*: 4-7 yrs; *Magister (S2)*: 2 yrs; *Doktor (S3)*: Economics; Management; Civil Engineering; Law

Student Services: Academic counselling, Canteen, Cultural centre, Employment services, Health services, Language programs, Social counselling, Sports facilities

Special Facilities: Radio Broadcasting Studio; Theatre; Mosque; Auditorium; Museum; Art Gallery

Libraries: c. 15,000 vols; Journals, CD-Roms, Video

Publications: Warta Usakti *(monthly)*

Press or Publishing House: University Press
Last Updated: 11/02/09

TRUNAJAYA UNIVERSITY OF BONTANG

Universitas Trunajaya Bontang

Jalan Achmad Yani N°14 Rt 55, Tromol Pos 2, Bontang, 75311
Kalimantan Timur
Tel: +62(548) 511-6443
EMail: unijaya_btg@yahoo.co.id

Rector: Chainul Rahman

Ketua: Soedarmi Aisyah

Faculties

Economics (Accountancy; Economics; Management) *Dean*: Tata Sudirman; **Engineering** (Electrical Engineering; Engineering; Mechanical Engineering) *Dean*: Wayan Sudarma; **Law** (Law) *Dean*: Sukardi

History: Founded 1990.

Fees: (Rupiahs): 400,000 per annum

Degrees and Diplomas: *Sarjana (S1)*
Last Updated: 06/02/09

TULANG BAWANG UNIVERSITY OF LAMPUNG

Universitas Tulang Bawang Lampung
PO Box 109, Jalan Gajah Mada 34 Kota Baru, Bandar Lampung, 35121 Lampung
Tel: +62(721) 252-686
Fax: +62(721) 257-108
EMail: info@utb.ac.id
Website: http://www.utb.ac.id/

Rector: Mohammad Machrus

Ketua: Muhammad T. Perkasa Putra

Faculties
Engineering (Engineering; Industrial Engineering) *Dean*: Suprapto Nitiharjo; **Law** (Law) *Dean*: Damiri Thajib; **Mathematics and Natural Sciences** (Mathematics; Natural Sciences; Pharmacy) *Dean*: Muhaimin; **Social and Political Sciences** (Administration; Business Administration; Communication Studies; Government; Political Sciences; Social Sciences) *Dean*: Mieke Rahayu

History: Founded 1999.

Fees: (Rupiahs): 600,000 per annum

Degrees and Diplomas: *Sarjana (S1)*

Libraries: 5,886 vols

Last Updated: 06/02/09

TULUNGAGUNG UNIVERSITY

Universitas Tulungagung
Jalan Ki Mangunsarkoro Beji, Tulungagung, 66230 Jawa Timur
Tel: +62(355) 322-145
Fax: +62(355) 320-396
EMail: kampusunita@telkom.net

Rector: Eko Sugiono

Ketua: Tukidjo

Faculties
Agriculture (Agricultural Economics); **Economics** (Accountancy; Economics; Management); **Law** (Law); **Social and Political Sciences** (Administration; Government; Political Sciences; Social Sciences)

Programmes
Midwifery (Midwifery)

History: Founded 1984.

Fees: (Rupiahs): 500,000 per annum

Degrees and Diplomas: *Sarjana (S1)*

Libraries: 1,367 vols

Last Updated: 06/02/09

TUNAS PEMBANGUNAN UNIVERSITY

Universitas Tunas Pembangunan (UTP)
Jalan Balekambang Lor 1, Surakarta, 57139 Jawa Tengah
Tel: +62(271) 726-728
Fax: +62(271) 739-048
EMail: utp_slo@utp.ac.id
Website: http://www.utp.ac.id

Rector: Ongko Cahyono

Ketua: Ahmad Nangsari

Faculties
Agriculture (Agricultural Business; Agricultural Economics; Agriculture; Agronomy); **Economics** (Accountancy; Economics; Management); **Educational Science and Teacher Training** (Educational and Student Counselling; Educational Psychology; Educational Sciences; Physical Education; Sports Management; Teacher Training); **Engineering** (Architecture; Civil Engineering; Engineering; Marine Engineering)

Institutes
Experiment and Public Service

History: Founded 1980. A private institution under the supervision of the Department of Education and Culture.

Main Language(s) of Instruction: Bahasa Indonesian

Accrediting Agencies: Badan Akreditasi Nasional Perguruan Tinggi (BAN PT)

Degrees and Diplomas: *Sarjana (S1)*: Civil Engineering; Architecture; Agronomy; Agribusiness; Management; Accountancy; Sports and Health Education; Leadership and Counselling, 4 yrs

Student Services: Academic counselling, Canteen, Employment services, Health services, Nursery care, Social counselling, Sports facilities

Special Facilities: Laboratory

Libraries: c. 18,000 vols

Publications: Agrineca, Publication of Agricultural Experiments Reports written by staff and Students *(biennially)*; Geneswara, Publication of Reports on Civil Engineering and Architecture *(biennially)*; Patria, Publication of Economic Experiments Reports written by staff and Students *(biennially)*; Spirit, Publication of Educational Service and Teacher Training *(biennially)*

Last Updated: 01/07/11

UNIVERSITY OF THE RAIU ISLANDS

Universitas Riau Kepulauan
Jalan Batu Aji Baru, Batu Aji, Batam, 29422 Kepulauan Riau
Tel: +62(778) 392-752
Fax: +62(778) 391-868

Rector: Amarullah Nasution

Ketua: Erli Hamimah

Faculties
Economics; **Engineering** (Civil Engineering; Electrical Engineering; Industrial Engineering; Mechanical Engineering; Structural Architecture); **Science Teacher Training and Education** (Biology; Education; English; History; Mathematics; Mathematics Education; Teacher Training)

History: Founded 1993 as College School of Economics Batam (STIE Batam). Acquired present status and title 2006.

Degrees and Diplomas: *Sarjana (S1)*

Last Updated: 04/05/10

VETERAN INSTITUTE OF TEACHER TRAINING AND EDUCATIONAL SCIENCE JAWA TENGAH

Institut Keguruan dan Ilmu Pendidikan (IKIP) Veteran Jawa Tengah
Jalan Pawiyatan Luhur IV, 17 Bendan Duwur, Semarang, 50233 Jawa Tengah
Tel: +62(24) 316-105
Fax: +62(24) 316-105
EMail: ikipvet@yahoo.com

Direktor: Sukoco

Ketua: Agus Wijaya Suyitno

Programmes
Educational Technology (Educational Technology; Preschool Education; Primary Education); **Engineering** (Engineering); **Geography** (Geography); **History** (History); **Leadership** (Leadership); **Social Sciences** (Social Sciences)

History: Founded 1967.

Fees: (Rupiahs): 750,000 per annum

Degrees and Diplomas: *Sarjana (S1)*

Libraries: 3,774 vols

Last Updated: 09/02/09

VETERAN NATIONAL DEVELOPMENT UNIVERSITY OF JAKARTA

Universitas Pembangunan Nasional Veteran Jakarta (UPN 'VETERAN' JAKARTA)
Jalan RS. Fatmawati, Pondok Labu, Jakarta, 12450 DKI Jakarta
Tel: +62(21) 765-6971 +62(21) 765-6904
Fax: +62(21) 769-2860
EMail: puskom@upnvj.ac.id
Website: http://www.upnvj.ac.id

Rector: Busiman Djoko Said Tel: +62(21) 758-18738

Ketua: Bambang Pranowo

Faculties

Computer Science (Computer Engineering; Computer Science; Information Management; Information Technology); **Economics** (Accountancy; Banking; Business and Commerce; Economics; Finance; Management; Taxation); **Industrial Technology** (Industrial Engineering; Marine Engineering; Mechanical Engineering); **Law** (Law); **Medicine**; **Social and Political Sciences** (Business Administration; Communication Studies; International Relations)

Further Information: Also Teaching Hospital

History: Founded 1963.

Governing Bodies: Yayasan Kajuangan Panglima Besar Sudirman (YKPBS)

Academic Year: September to July

Admission Requirements: School certificate and entrance examination

Fees: (Rupiahs): 3.2m. per annum

Main Language(s) of Instruction: Indonesian, English

International Co-operation: With universities in the Netherlands, Japan and USA

Accrediting Agencies: National Accreditation Board

Degrees and Diplomas: *Diploma*; *Sarjana (S1)*: 4 yrs; *Magister (S2)*: a further 2 yrs

Student Services: Academic counselling, Canteen, Cultural centre, Employment services, Health services, Language programs, Nursery care, Social counselling, Sports facilities

Special Facilities: Observatory. Radio Station. Laboratory

Libraries: Central Library and Faculty Libraries

Publications: Bina Widya, Research Magazine *(quarterly)*

Press or Publishing House: ASPIRASI

Last Updated: 04/02/09

VETERAN NATIONAL DEVELOPMENT UNIVERSITY OF YOGYAKARTA

Universitas Pembangunan Nasional Veteran Yogyakarta (UPNYK)

Jalan Lingkar Utara 104, Condong Catur, Depok, Sleman, 55283 Daerah Istimewa Yogyakarta
Tel: +62(274) 486-733
Fax: +62(274) 486-400
EMail: info@upnyk.ac.id
Website: http://www.upnyk.ac.id

Rector: Didit Welly Udjianto
Tel: +62(274) 486-402 EMail: didiwelly_upn@yahoo.com

Vice-Rector: Sari Bahagiarti EMail: saribk@plasa.com

International Relations: Widayati, Head of Cooperation and Communication Office EMail: widabambang@yahoo.com

Faculties

Agriculture (Agricultural Business; Agricultural Engineering) *Dean*: Abdul Rizal; **Economics** (Accountancy; Economics; Management) *Dean*: Sujatmiko; **Industrial Technology** (Chemical Engineering; Industrial Engineering; Information Technology) *Dean*: Nur Idrianti; **Mineral Technology** (Environmental Engineering; Geological Engineering; Geophysics; Mining Engineering; Petroleum and Gas Engineering) *Dean*: Koesnaryo; **Social and Political Sciences** (Business Administration; Communication Studies; International Relations; Law; Political Sciences; Social Sciences) *Dean*: Asep Saepudin

Programmes

Chemical Engineering (Chemical Engineering) *Head*: Zubaidi Achmad

Schools

Postgraduate (Agricultural Business; Economics; Geological Engineering; Industrial Engineering; Management; Mining Engineering) *Director*: Sutanto

History: Founded 1958 by Defence Ministry. Status changed from Government to private services 1994.

Governing Bodies: Yayasan Kesejahteraan Pendidikan dari Perumahan (YKPP)

Academic Year: September to June (September-January; February-June)

Admission Requirements: Senior high school certificate

Fees: (Rupiahs): 2.75m. per annum for graduate degrees.

Main Language(s) of Instruction: Indonesian

International Co-operation: With universities in Malaysia, Japan, Thailand, Czech Republic and Australia.

Accrediting Agencies: National Accreditation Board

Degrees and Diplomas: *Diploma*: Chemical Engineering, 3-4 yrs; *Sarjana (S1)*: Agricultural Business; Agricultural Technology (S.P.); Communications Science; Business Administration Science (S.Sos.); Economic Management; Accountancy; Economic and Development Studies (S.E.); Industrial Engineering; Information Technology; Chemical Engineering; Geological Engineering; Petroleum Engineering; Mining Engineering; Environmental Engineering; Geophysical Engineering (S.T.); International Relations Science (S.I.P.), 4-5 yrs; *Magister (S2)*: Agribusiness Management (M.A.); Economic Management (M.M.); Geological Engineering; Mining Engineering (M.T.), 2-3 yrs

Student Services: Academic counselling, Canteen, Employment services, Health services, Language programs, Sports facilities

Student Residential Facilities: Yes

Special Facilities: English Language Studio; Computer Centre; Laboratory for Natural Sciences; Geotechnology and Minerals Museum; Green House.

Libraries: University Library and Department Libraries

Publications: Buletin Ekonomi, Economic Bulletin *(quarterly)*; Info Kampus, University/Campus Magazine *(monthly)*; Journal of Agrivet, Agronomy Journal *(quarterly)*; Journal of Dinamika Sosial, Agricultural Economics Journal *(biannually)*; Journal of Eksergi, Industrial Technology Journal *(biannually)*; Journal of Ilmu Komunikasi, Communication Science Journal *(quarterly)*; Journal of Opsi, Industrial Engineering Journal *(quarterly)*; Journal of Paradigma, Social and Political Sciences Journal *(quarterly)*; Journal of Tanah Dan Air, Soil Sciences Journal *(biannually)*; Journal of Teknologi Mineral, Geo Science Journal *(quarterly)*; Wimaya, University Journal *(biannually)*

Press or Publishing House: UPN Press

Academic Staff *2009-2010*	MEN	WOMEN	**TOTAL**
FULL-TIME	–	–	**367**
STAFF WITH DOCTORATE			
FULL-TIME	65	18	**83**
Student Numbers *2009-2010*			
All (Foreign Included)	8,732	3,730	**12,462**
FOREIGN ONLY	–	–	**55**

Evening students, 7.

Last Updated: 05/11/10

VETERAN UNIVERSITY OF THE REPUBLIC OF INDONESIA

Universitas Veteran Republik Indonesia

Jalan G. Bawakaraeng 72, Makassar, 90145 Sulawesi Selatan
Tel: +62(411) 334-426
Fax: +62(411) 494-596

Rector: Umar Tirtaraharja

Ketua: Waris Nur

Faculties

Community Heath (Community Health); **Economics** (Accountancy; Management); **Educational Science and Teacher Training** (Biology; Civics; Curriculum; Educational Sciences; Educational Technology; History; Mathematics Education; Science Education); **Engineering** (Computer Engineering; Engineering; Mechanical Engineering; Mining Engineering); **Social and Political Sciences** (Administration; Communication Studies; Government; Journalism; Political Sciences; Social Sciences)

History: Founded 1960. A private institution under the supervision of the Department of Education and Culture.

Fees: (Rupiahs): 400,000 per annum

Degrees and Diplomas: *Diploma*; *Sarjana (S1)*

Libraries: 9,868 vols

Last Updated: 09/02/09

WAHID HASYIM UNIVERSITY

Universitas Wahid Hasyim

Jalan Menoreh Tengah X/22, Semarang, 50236 Jawa Tengah
Tel: +62(24) 850-5680 +62(24) 850-5681
Fax: +62(24) 850-5680
EMail: unwahas@yahoo.com

Rector: Ahmad Rofiq

Ketua: Soewanto

Faculties

Agriculture (Agricultural Economics; Agriculture; Animal Husbandry) *Dean*: Sri Wahyuningsih; **Economics** (Accountancy; Economics; Management) *Dean*: Dahlawi Imron; **Engineering** (Chemical Engineering; Electronic Engineering; Engineering; Mechanical Engineering) *Dean*: Bambang Pramusinto; **Law** (Law); **Pharmacy** (Pharmacy) *Dean*: Siti Musinah; **Social and Political Sciences** (International Relations; Political Sciences; Social Sciences) *Dean*: Adib Fatoni

History: Founded 2000.

Degrees and Diplomas: *Diploma*: 3 yrs; *Sarjana (S1)*
Last Updated: 21/04/10

WANITA INTERNATIONAL UNIVERSITY

Universitas Wanita Internasional

Bandung, Jawa Barat

Programmes

Business Administration (Business Administration; International Relations); **Communication Studies**; **Computer Engineering**; **Design**; **Political Sciences**; **Science**

Degrees and Diplomas: *Sarjana (S1)*
Last Updated: 31/05/10

WARMADEWA UNIVERSITY

Universitas Warmadewa

Jalan Terompong 24, Tanjungbungkak, Denpasar, 80235 Bali
Tel: +62(361) 223-858
Fax: +62(361) 235-073
EMail: unwar@telkom.co.id
Website: http://www.warmadewa.ac.id/

Rector: Made Sukarsa (2011-2015)
EMail: loso_made@yahoo.ac.id

Ketua: Gede Oka Wisnumurti Tel: +62(361) 247-331

Faculties

Agriculture (Agricultural Engineering; Agriculture; Agronomy; Animal Husbandry; Aquaculture; Fishery; Marine Science and Oceanography); **Economics** (Accountancy; Development Studies; Economics; Management); **Engineering** (Architecture; Civil Engineering; Engineering; Structural Architecture); **Law** (Commercial Law; Constitutional Law; Criminal Law; Law; Public Law); **Literature** (English; Literature; Modern Languages); **Medical Education** (Health Education; Medicine); **Social and Political Sciences** (Administration; Government; Information Management; Information Technology; Political Sciences; Public Administration; Public Relations; Social Sciences)

History: Founded 1984.

Admission Requirements: Secondary school certificate

Fees: (Rupiahs): 1.6m. per annum

Main Language(s) of Instruction: Indonesian

Accrediting Agencies: Ban PT

Degrees and Diplomas: *Sarjana (S1)*: 4 yrs

Student Services: Academic counselling, Canteen, Health services, Language programs, Social counselling, Sports facilities

Special Facilities: Laboratories (Computer ; Management; Accountancy; Banking)

Libraries: 13,062 vols

Publications: Research Institution Journals *(1-2 per annum)*

Academic Staff *2009-2010*: Total: c. 250

Student Numbers *2009-2010*: Total: c. 2,000
Last Updated: 04/07/11

WESTERN SULAWESI UNIVERSITY

Universitas Sulawesi Barat

Jalan Baharuddin Lopa, Majene, 91412 Sulawesi Selatan
Tel: +62(422) 22-559

Rector: Abdul Muin Liwa

Ketua: Ma'mun Hasanuddin

Programmes

Agriculture (Agriculture); **Economics** (Economics); **Engineering** (Civil Engineering; Engineering); **Mathematics** (Mathematics); **Nursing** (Nursing); **Political Sciences and International Relations** (International Relations; Political Sciences)

Last Updated: 04/05/10

WIDYA DHARMA UNIVERSITY

Universitas Widya Dharma

Jalan Ki Hajar Dewantara, Klaten, Jawa Tengah
Tel: +62(272) 322-363
Website: http://www.unwidha.ac.id

Rector: Sumargana

Ketua: H. Basuki

Faculties

Agricultural Technology (Agricultural Engineering); **Computer Science** (Computer Science; Information Management); **Economics** (Accountancy; Economics; Management); **Education and Teacher Training** (Biology; Civics; English; Foreign Languages Education; Geography; Geography (Human); Indonesian; Literature; Mathematics Education; Modern Languages; Native Language Education; Physics; Science Education; South and Southeast Asian Languages); **Engineering** (Civil Engineering; Electrical Engineering; Engineering); **Psychology** (Psychology)

Programmes

Graduate Studies (English; Foreign Languages Education; Indonesian; Native Language Education; South and Southeast Asian Languages)

History: Founded 1969 as Teacher Training and Education Institute Education Foundation. Acquired present status and title 1994.

Degrees and Diplomas: *Diploma*; *Sarjana (S1)*; *Magister (S2)*

Libraries: c. 9,000 vols
Last Updated: 04/07/11

WIDYA GAMA MAHAKAM UNIVERSITY OF SAMARINDA

Universitas Widya Gama Mahakam Samarinda (UWIGAMA)

Jalan K. H. Wahid Hasyim, Samarinda, Kalimantan Timur
Tel: +62(541) 736-572

Rector: Ismet Bra

Ketua: Husni Basran

Faculties

Administration (Administration; Government); **Agriculture**; **Community Health** (Community Health); **Economics**; **Law** (Law)

History: Founded 1985.

Fees: (Rupiahs): 420,000 per annum

Degrees and Diplomas: *Diploma*: 3 yrs; *Sarjana (S1)*

Libraries: 5,458 vols
Last Updated: 09/02/09

WIDYA GAMA UNIVERSITY OF MALANG

Universitas Widya Gama Malang (UWIGAMA)

Jalan Borobudur 12-35, Malang, 65128 Java
Tel: +62(341) 491-648
Fax: +62(341) 403-103
EMail: humas@widyagama.ac.id; akademik@widyagama.ac.id
Website: http://www.widyagama.ac.id/

Rector: Muryati

Ketua: Mukthie Fadjar

Faculties

Agriculture (Agricultural Economics; Agricultural Engineering; Agriculture; Agronomy; Food Technology); **Economics** (Accountancy; Management); **Engineering** (Civil Engineering; Electrical Engineering; Engineering; Industrial Engineering; Mechanical Engineering; Power Engineering; Telecommunications Engineering); **Law** (Civil Law; Commercial Law; Criminal Law; Law)

History: Founded 1971, acquired present status and title 1998.

Governing Bodies: Indonesia Education Builder Foundation

Admission Requirements: Secondary school certificate

Fees: (Rupiahs): 2.69m. per annum

Main Language(s) of Instruction: Indonesian

Degrees and Diplomas: *Diploma*; *Sarjana (S1)*: 4 yrs; *Magister (S2)*: Management; Law

Student Services: Academic counselling, Canteen, Cultural centre, Employment services, Health services, Language programs, Social counselling, Sports facilities

Special Facilities: Observatory. Laboratory. Garden/Green House. Auditorium

Libraries: Central Library, 38,392 vols

Publications: Widya Humanika Journal *(biannually)*; Widya Teknika Journal *(biannually)*

Press or Publishing House: ASPIRASI

Last Updated: 02/02/09

WIDYA KARTIKA UNIVERSITY

Universitas Widya Kartika

Jalan Sutorejo Prima Utara II No. 1, Surabaya, 60112 Jawa Timur

Tel: +62(31) 592-2403

Fax: +62(31) 592-5790

EMail: info@widyakartika.ac.id

Website: http://www.widyakartika.ac.id

Rector: Willianto Ismadi (2001-)

Vice-Rector: Muliadi Tedjasukmana

International Relations: Mekawarti Marina, Corporate Secretary EMail: mekarwatimarina@hotmail.com

Faculties

Economics; **Engineering** (Civil Engineering; Computer Engineering; Electrical and Electronic Engineering); **Modern Languages**

History: Founded 1986.

Governing Bodies: Yayasan, Senate

Academic Year: September to July

Admission Requirements: Secondary school certificate (Sekolah Menengah Umum) and entrance examination

Fees: (Rupiahs): 1.9m. per semester

Main Language(s) of Instruction: Indonesian

Degrees and Diplomas: *Sarjana (S1)*: 4 yrs

Student Services: Academic counselling, Canteen, Employment services, Health services, Language programs, Nursery care, Sports facilities

Special Facilities: Drawing Studios, Workshops, Laboratories

Libraries: Central Library

Publications: Jurnal Ilmjah Universitas Yidya Kartika *(3 per annum)*

Last Updated: 09/02/09

WIDYA KARYA CATHOLIC UNIVERSITY

Universitas Katolik Widya Karya (UNIKA W.K.)

PO Box 121, Jalan Bondowoson 02, Malang, 65115 Jawa Timur

Tel: +62(341) 553-171 +62(341) 560-956

Fax: +62(341) 560-056

EMail: widyakarya@widyakarya.ac.id

Website: http://www.widyakarya.ac.id/

Rector: Matheus Agung Christiputra

Ketua: Yohannes Sumartono

Faculties

Agriculture (Agricultural Business; Agricultural Engineering; Agriculture); **Economics** (Accountancy; Economics; Management; Secretarial Studies); **Engineering** (Civil Engineering; Engineering; Information Management); **Law** (Law)

History: Founded 1982. A private institution under the supervision of the Department of Education and Culture.

Admission Requirements: High school certificate and entrance examination

Main Language(s) of Instruction: Indonesian

Accrediting Agencies: BAN (National Accreditation Body)

Degrees and Diplomas: *Diploma*: 3 yrs; *Sarjana (S1)*

Student Services: Academic counselling, Health services, Nursery care, Sports facilities

Libraries: Central Library

Publications: Wawasan *(biennially)*

Last Updated: 28/06/11

WIDYA MANDALA CATHOLIC UNIVERSITY OF MADIUN

Universitas Katolik Widya Mandala Madiun (WIMA MADIUN)

PO Box 16, Jalan Manggis 15-17, Madiun, 63131 Jawa Timur

Tel: +62(351) 453-328 +62(351) 463-311

Fax: +62(351) 453-167

EMail: universitas@widyamandala.ac.id

Website: http://www.widyamandala.ac.id

Rektor: Bernardinus Justisianto (2006-)
Tel: +62(81) 335414800 EMail: justisianto@yahoo.com

Chairman of the Widya Mandala Madiun Foundation: F.X. Hardi Aswinarno Tel: +62(858) 50509994 EMail: modiaswin@yahoo.com

Faculties

Arts and Humanities (English; Literature) *Dean*: Mikael Obat Depari; **Economics** (Accountancy; Economics; Management) *Dean*: Sri Rustiyaningsih; **Education and Teacher Training** (Education; Educational and Student Counselling; Indonesian; Mathematics Education; Native Language Education; Teacher Training) *Dean*: M. Sayekti; **Engineering** (Engineering; Industrial Engineering) *Dean*: Al. Tommy Hendrawan; **Mathematics and Natural Sciences** (Biology; Mathematics) *Dean*: Leo Eladisa Ganjari; **Psychology** (Psychology) *Dean*: Apollo

History: Founded 1960. Acquired present status 1991.

Governing Bodies: National Education State Department, c.q. Kopertis VII (State Coordinator of Private Higher Learning, Region VII, Eastern Jawa)

Academic Year: September to July

Admission Requirements: High school certificate

Fees: (Rupiahs): 3.25m. (US Dollars, 345) per annum

Main Language(s) of Instruction: Indonesian

Accrediting Agencies: Badan Akreditasi Nasional/National Accreditation Board (BAN)

Degrees and Diplomas: *Sarjana (S1)*

Student Services: Academic counselling, Canteen, Sports facilities

Special Facilities: Micro Teaching Room; Multimedia Information Centre

Libraries: 22,300 vols

Publications: Widya Warta *(biennially)*

Last Updated: 25/07/11

WIDYA MANDALA CATHOLIC UNIVERSITY OF SURABAYA

Universitas Katolik Widya Mandala Surabaya (WIMA)

Jalan Dinoyo 42-44, Surabaya, 60265 Jawa Timur

Tel: +62(31) 567-8478

Fax: +62(31) 561-0818

EMail: info@mail.wima.ac.id; bau@mail.wima.ac.id

Website: http://www.wima.ac.id/

Rector: Soewandi Ami (2003-)
Tel: +62(31) 567-8478, Ext. 126 EMail: rektor@mail.wima.ac.id

Vice-Rector II: Adriana Anggorowati
Tel: +62(31) 567-8478, Ext. 128 EMail: warek2@mail.wima.ac.id

International Relations: Kuncoro Foe, Vice-Rector I
Tel: +62(31) 567-8478, Ext. 127 EMail: warek1@mail.wima.ac.id

Faculties

Agricultural Technology (Agricultural Engineering; Food Science; Food Technology); **Business** (Accountancy; Management); **Education and Teacher Training** (English; Foreign Languages Education; Mathematics Education; Physics; Science Education); **Engineering** *(Kalijudan)* (Chemical Engineering; Electrical Engineering; Engineering; Industrial Engineering); **Medicine** (Medicine); **Nursing** (Nursing); **Pharmacy** (Biochemistry; Biotechnology; Botany; Cell Biology; Chemistry; Cosmetology; Immunology; Mathematics; Microbiology; Organic Chemistry; Pharmacology; Pharmacy; Toxicology; Virology); **Philosophy** (Anthropology; Ethics; Island Studies; Logic; Metaphysics; Philosophy; Philosophy of Education; Psychology; Religious Studies; Sociology); **Postgraduate Studies** (English; Foreign Languages Education; Management); **Psychology** (Psychology)

Programmes

Communication Studies (Communication Studies)

History: Founded 1960, acquired present status and title 2004. A private Institution.

Governing Bodies: Board of Trustees

Academic Year: August to July

Admission Requirements: Secondary school certificate (SMA)

Fees: (Rupiahs): 12m. per annum

Main Language(s) of Instruction: Indonesian, English

International Co-operation: With universities in Australia, Thailand, Netherlands, China, Canada, Norway

Accrediting Agencies: National Accreditation Council

Degrees and Diplomas: *Diploma*: Accountancy, 3 yrs; *Sarjana (S1)*: 4 yrs; *Magister (S2)*: Management; English Education; *Doktor (S3)*: Management

Student Services: Academic counselling, Canteen, Employment services, Language programs, Social counselling, Sports facilities

Student Residential Facilities: None

Special Facilities: Music Room; Chapel; Radio Station and Television Station

Libraries: c. 88,000 vols

Publications: Alfa-T *(biannually)*; Magister Scientiae *(biannually)*; Manuver *(annually)*; Psy Magz *(biannually)*; Wafema *(biannually)*; Warta Medica *(biannually)*; Warta Widya Mandala *(quarterly)*; Zigma *(biannually)*

Academic Staff *2009-2010*	TOTAL
FULL-TIME	220
PART-TIME	160
STAFF WITH DOCTORATE	
FULL-TIME	30
PART-TIME	c. 20
Student Numbers *2009-2010*	
All (Foreign Included)	c. 6,650

Evening students, 450.

Last Updated: 25/07/11

WIDYA MANDIRA CATHOLIC UNIVERSITY OF KUPANG

Universitas Katolik Widya Mandira Kupang
Jalan Jenderal A. Yani 50-52, Kupang, 85225 Nusa Tenggara Timur
Tel: +62(380) 833-395
Fax: +62(380) 831-194
EMail: info@unwira.ac.id
Website: http://www.unwira.ac.id

Rector: Yulius Yasinto

Vice-Rector for Administration and Finance: Wilhelmus Ngete

Faculties

Economics (Accountancy; Development Studies; Economics; Management); **Education and Teacher Training** (Biology; Chemistry; Education; Educational and Student Counselling; English; Foreign Languages Education; Mathematics Education; Physical Education; Science Education; Teacher Training); **Engineering** (Civil Engineering; Engineering; Structural Architecture); **Law** (Law); **Mathematics and Natural Sciences** (Biology; Chemistry; Mathematics; Natural Sciences); **Philosophy** (Christian Religious Studies; Philosophical Schools; Philosophy; Religion); **Social and Political Sciences** (Communication Studies; Government; Political Sciences; Public Administration; Social Sciences)

Programmes

Magister Studies (Management)

History: Founded 1982.

Degrees and Diplomas: *Diploma*: 3 yrs; *Sarjana (S1)*; *Magister (S2)*: Management

Last Updated: 22/07/11

WIDYA MATARAM UNIVERSITY OF YOGYAKARTA

Universitas Widya Mataram Yogyakarta (UWMY)
Ndalem Mangkubumen Kt. III/237, Yogyakarta, 55132 DI Yogyakarta
Tel: +62(274) 374-352 +62(274) 381-722
Fax: +62(274) 381-722
Website: http://www.widyamataram.ac.id/

Rector: Bandul Sunjoto

Chairman: Sultan Hamengkubuwono

International Relations: Martadani Noor, Assistant Rector for Division of Cooperation and Public Relations

Faculties

Agricultural Engineering; **Economics**; **Engineering**; **Law**; **Social and Political Sciences**

History: Founded 1982.

Governing Bodies: Board of Mataram Yogyakarta Foundation (Umbrella organisation); Daily Board of Mataram Yogyakarta Foundation; University Senate; Management of University (Rector, Dean, Assistants Dean, Head of Academic and Students Affairs, Head of Human Resources and Financial); Management of Units; Board of Students

Academic Year: December to November (December-April; June-November)

Admission Requirements: High School Certificate; Entrance Examination

Fees: (Rupiahs): 3m. for first semester; 1m. for second semester

Main Language(s) of Instruction: Indonesian

Degrees and Diplomas: *Sarjana (S1)*: 3 1/2-4 yrs

Student Services: Academic counselling, Canteen, Cultural centre, Employment services, Foreign student adviser, Foreign Studies Centre, Health services, Language programs, Nursery care, Social counselling, Sports facilities

Special Facilities: Chemical Laboratory; Computer Laboratory; Drawing Studio; Workshop Room; Architecture Studio; Engineering Laboratory; Juridical Laboratory; Social Laboratory

Libraries: 6,923 vols; 15 journal titles; 3,000 titles file research; 5 newspapers

Publications: Padma Sri Krisna, University Journal; Populika, Journal of Social and Political Sciences; Pranata, Journal of Law and Sciences

Last Updated: 22/04/10

WIDYA PUTRA UNIVERSITY

Universitas Wijaya Putra
Jalan Raya Benowo 1-3, Surabaya, 60197 Jawa Timur
Tel: +62(31) 741-3061
Fax: +62(31) 740-4405

Rector: Budi Endarto

Ketua: Saleh Soegiyanto

Faculties
Agriculture; **Economics**; **Engineering**; **Law**; **Letters**; **Social and Political Sciences**

History: Founded 1981.

Fees: (Rupiahs): 441,000 per annum

Degrees and Diplomas: *Sarjana (S1)*; *Magister (S2)*

Libraries: 4,378 vols

Last Updated: 09/02/09

WIDYATAMA UNIVERSITY

Universitas Widyatama (UTAMA)

Jln. Cikutra 204 A, Bandung, 40124 Jawa Barat

Tel: +62(22) 727-4010

Fax: +62(22) 727-4010

EMail: rektorat@widyatama.ac.id

Website: http://www.widyatama.ac.id

Rector: Mame Slamet Sutoko (2005-)
Tel: +62(22) 720-6713 EMail: mame@widyatama.ac.id

Vice-Rector for Planning and Development: Uman Hardi
EMail: usman.hardi@widyatama@ac.id

International Relations: Cristiana Victoria Martha Davidescu, Vice Rector for Operational and InternationalAffairs
Tel: +62(22) 720-6713 EMail: cristiana.victoria@widyatama.ac.id

Faculties
Business and Management (Business Administration; Management); **Economics** (Accountancy; Economics); **Engineering** (Computer Engineering; Engineering; Industrial Engineering; Information Technology); **Languages** (English; Japanese); **Visual Communication and Design** (Communication Arts; Graphic Design; Multimedia; Visual Arts)

Graduate Schools
Management (Management)

History: Founded 1973 as Bandung School of Economics. Acquired present title and status 2001.

Governing Bodies: Senate, Recorate, Dean, Heads of Study Programmes

Academic Year: Sept - Jan; Feb - July

Admission Requirements: Secondary school certificate.

Fees: (Rupiahs): 10,000.00 per annum

Main Language(s) of Instruction: Indonesian

International Co-operation: with institutions in France, Philippines, Germany, Malaysia, Switzerland, USA, Japan, Austria.

Accrediting Agencies: National Accreditation Board, Badan Akreditasi Nasional (BAN) and TÜV

Degrees and Diplomas: *Diploma*: 3-4 yrs; *Sarjana (S1)*; *Magister (S2)*

Student Services: Academic counselling, Canteen, Employment services, Foreign student adviser, Foreign Studies Centre, Health services, Language programs, Sports facilities

Student Residential Facilities: none

Special Facilities: Campus TV

Libraries: 28,364 vols; digital collection; audio/film collection; periodicals

Publications: Business Management and Economics *(quarterly)*

Academic Staff *2010-2011*	MEN	WOMEN	TOTAL
FULL-TIME	101	72	**173**
PART-TIME	99	38	**137**
STAFF WITH DOCTORATE			
FULL-TIME	17	8	**25**
PART-TIME	18	4	**22**
Student Numbers *2010-2011*			
All (Foreign Included)	3,078	2,365	**5,443**
FOREIGN ONLY	3	1	**4**

Evening students, 246.

Last Updated: 27/09/11

WIJAYA KUSUMA UNIVERSITY OF PURWOKERTO

Universitas Wijaya Kusuma Purwokerto

Kampus Karangsalam, Purwokerto, 53152 Jawa Tengah

Tel: +62(281) 635-889

Fax: +62(281) 634-611

EMail: info@unwiku.ac.id

Website: http://www.unwiku.ac.id

Rector: Kaboel Suwardi

Ketua: Poedjatman Priambodo

Faculties
Animal Husbandry; **Economics**; **Engineering**; **Law**; **Social and Political Sciences**

History: Founded 1980. A private institution under the supervision of the Department of Education and Culture.

Academic Year: September to August (September-February; March-August)

Admission Requirements: Secondary school certificate (Sekolah Menengah Atas, SMA) and entrance examination

Fees: (Rupiahs): 1.15m. per annum

Main Language(s) of Instruction: Indonesian

Accrediting Agencies: National Accreditation Board, Badan Akreditasi Nasional Perguruan Tinggi (BAN PT)

Degrees and Diplomas: *Diploma*: 3 yrs; *Sarjana (S1)*: 4 yrs

Student Services: Academic counselling, Canteen, Cultural centre, Health services, Language programs, Sports facilities

Libraries: 6,668 vols

Publications: Bovine, Animal Production *(quarterly)*; Management and Business

Last Updated: 16/01/09

WIJAYA KUSUMA UNIVERSITY OF SURABAYA

Universitas Wijaya Kusuma Surabaya

Jalan Dukuh Kupang XXV/54, Surabaya, 60225 Jawa Timur

Tel: +62(31) 567-7577

Fax: +62(31) 567-9791

EMail: wijayakusuma@telkom.net

Website: http://www.wijayakusumasby.ac.id

Rector: Soedijono

Ketua: Asri Soebarijati

Faculties
Agriculture; **Economics**; **Engineering** *Dean*: Miftahul Huda; **Language and Science**; **Law**; **Medicine**; **Postgraduate Studies** (Accountancy; Agricultural Business; Law); **Social and Political Sciences**

History: Founded 1981.

Fees: (Rupiahs): 1m. per annum

Degrees and Diplomas: *Diploma*; *Sarjana (S1)*; *Magister (S2)*

Libraries: 12,370 vols

Last Updated: 09/02/09

WINAYA MUKTI UNIVERSITY

Universitas Winaya Mukti

Jalan Winaya Mukti, Jatinangor, Sumedang, 45363 Jawa Barat

Tel: +62(261) 796-964

Fax: +62(261) 796-964

EMail: yayasan@unwim.ac.id; unwim@unwim.ac.id

Website: http://www.unwim.ac.id

Rector: Endang Sufiadi

Ketua: Sonny Djoko Santoso

Faculties
Agriculture (Agricultural Economics; Agricultural Management; Agronomy); **Economics** (Accountancy; Economics; Management); **Engineering** (Architecture and Planning; Civil Engineering; Engineering; Environmental Engineering; Industrial Engineering; Regional Planning; Surveying and Mapping; Town Planning); **Forestry** (Forest Management; Forest Products; Forestry)

History: Founded 1990.

Fees: (Rupiahs): 600,000 per annum

Degrees and Diplomas: *Diploma*: 3 yrs; *Sarjana (S1)*; *Magister (S2)*

Libraries: 13,262 vols

Last Updated: 22/04/10

WIRALODRA UNIVERSITY

Universitas Wiralodra (UNWIR)

Jalan Raya Singaraja Km. 3, Indramayu, Jawa Barat

Tel: +62(234) 275-946

Fax: +62(234) 275-946

Rector: Djunaedi Tohidin

Ketua: Dunadi Saroni

Faculties

Agriculture (Agricultural Economics; Agriculture; Fishery); **Community Health**; **Economics** (Development Studies; Economics; Management); **Educational Science and Teacher Training** (Art Education; Educational Administration; Educational Sciences; English; Foreign Languages Education; Indonesian; Literature; Mathematics Education; Science Education; Teacher Training); **Engineering** (Civil Engineering; Engineering); **Law** (Law)

History: Founded 1982.

Fees: (Rupiahs): 285,000 per annum

Main Language(s) of Instruction: Indonesian; English

Degrees and Diplomas: *Diploma*: Fishery, 3 yrs; *Sarjana (S1)*: 4-5 yrs

Student Services: Academic counselling, Cultural centre, Employment services, Foreign student adviser, Foreign Studies Centre, Language programs, Social counselling, Sports facilities

Special Facilities: Computer and Language Centre

Libraries: 4,294 vols

Last Updated: 09/02/09

WIRARAJA UNIVERSITY

Universitas Wiraraja

Jalan Raya Sumenep Km. 5, Sumenep 69451

Tel: +62(328) 664-272

Fax: +62(328) 673-088

EMail: univwiraraja@yahoo.com

Rector: Ida Ekawati

Ketua: Kurniadi Widjaja

Faculties

Administration; **Agriculture**; **Economics**; **Education**; **Engineering**; **Law**; **Nursing** (Nursing)

Programmes

Midwifery (Midwifery)

Fees: (Rupiahs): 360,000 per annum

Degrees and Diplomas: *Sarjana (S1)*

Libraries: 1,055 vols

Last Updated: 09/02/09

WIRASWASTA UNIVERSITY OF INDONESIA

Universitas Wiraswasta Indonesia

Jl. Jagakarsa Raya, Pasar Minggu, Jakarta Selatan, 13210 DKI Jakarta

Tel: +62(21) 831-2209 +62(21) 831-2210

Fax: +62(21) 831-2209

Rector: Baron A. Tirtamaja

Ketua: Halim Soesanto Tirtamadja

Faculties

Economics (Economics; Management) *Dean*: Tien Kartika; **Engineering** *Dean*: Maskur Effendi; **Law** *Dean*: Luhut Pangaribuan

History: Founded 1983.

Fees: (Rupiahs): 500,000 per annum

Degrees and Diplomas: *Sarjana (S1)*

Last Updated: 14/01/09

WISNUWARDHANA UNIVERSITY

Universitas Wisnuwardhana

Jalan Danau Sentani 99, Malang, 65139 Jawa Timur

Tel: +62(341) 713-604

Fax: +62(341) 713-603

Rector: Sukowiyono

Ketua: Bagoes Sasmito

Faculties

Agriculture; **Economics**; **Educational Science and Teacher Training**; **Engineering**; **Law**; **Psychology**

History: Founded 1981. A private institution under the supervision of the Department of Education and Culture.

Fees: (Rupiahs): 900,000 per annum

Degrees and Diplomas: *Sarjana (S1)*; *Magister (S2)*

Libraries: 5,377 vols

Last Updated: 09/02/09

W.R. SUPRATMAN UNIVERSITY

Universitas W.R. Supratman

Jalan A. Rachman Hakim 14, Surabaya, 60111 Jawa Timur

Tel: +62(31) 594-5452

Fax: +62(31) 592-3815

EMail: tiunipra@yahoo.com

Rector: Achmad Baktir

Ketua: Budi Kartono

Faculties

Economics (Economics); **Engineering** (Engineering); **Social and Political Sciences** (Business Administration; Public Administration)

History: Founded 1985.

Fees: (Rupiahs): 900,000 per annum

Degrees and Diplomas: *Sarjana (S1)*; *Magister (S2)*

Libraries: 2,705 vols

Last Updated: 09/02/09

YAPIS BIAK INSTITUTE OF SOCIAL AND POLITICAL SCIENCES

Institut Ilmu Sosial dan Ilmu Politik Yapis Biak

Jalan S. Condronegoro, Distrik Samofa, Biak, 98117 Papua

Tel: +62 (981) 22788

Fax: +62 (981) 24068

EMail: iisipyapisbiak@gmail.com

Website: http://www.iisipyapisbiak.com/

Rector: Hamdan

Ketua: Marsam

Programmes

Business Administration (Business Administration); **Communication Studies** (Communication Studies); **Government** (Government); **Political Sciences**; **Public Administration** (Public Administration); **Sociology** (Sociology)

History: Founded 2006. Previously known as STIA Yapis Biak.

Degrees and Diplomas: *Sarjana (S1)*

Last Updated: 22/04/10

YARSI UNIVERSITY

Universitas Yarsi

Jalan Letjen Suprapto, Cempaka Putih, Jakarta Pusat, 10510 DKI Jakarta

Tel: +62(21) 420-6674 +62(21) 420-6676

Fax: +62(21) 424-3171

EMail: rektorat@yarsi.ac.id

Website: http://www.yarsi.ac.id

Rector: Abdul Salam M. Sofro

Vice-Rector III: Ardin Amir

Vice-Rector I: Isna Indrawati

Faculties

Economics (Accountancy; Applied Mathematics; Banking; English; Finance; Human Resources; Indonesian; Management; Marketing);

Information Technology (Computer Engineering; Information Technology; Library Science); **Law** (Civil Law; Commercial Law; Law); **Medicine** (Anatomy; Behavioural Sciences; Biology; Cardiology; Cell Biology; Community Health; Dentistry; Endocrinology; Environmental Studies; Gerontology; Gynaecology and Obstetrics; Immunology; Medicine; Molecular Biology; Neurology; Nutrition; Religion; Surgery); **Psychology** (Anthropology; Behavioural Sciences; Clinical Psychology; Educational Psychology; English; Ethics; Genetics; Gerontology; Indonesian; Industrial and Organizational Psychology; Islamic Theology; Logic; Philosophy; Psychiatry and Mental Health; Psychology; Religion; Sociology; Statistics)

History: Founded 1967.

Degrees and Diplomas: *Diploma*; *Sarjana (S1)*; *Magister (S2)*: Management

Libraries: c. 9,600 vols

Last Updated: 04/07/11

YOGYAKARTA PGRI UNIVERSITY OF YOGYAKARTA

Universitas PGRI Yogyakarta Di Yogyakarta

Kotak Pos 1123, Jalan PGRI I 117, Sonosewu, Yogyakarta, DI Yogyakarta

Tel: +62(274) 376-808 +62(274) 373-038

EMail: fakti@upy.ac.id; webmaster@upy.ac.id

Website: http://www.upy.ac.id

Rector: Sri Pawiti

Vice-Rector: Ahmad Riyadi

Faculties

Agriculture; **Economics**; **Educational Science and Teacher Training**; **Engineering**

History: Founded as Institut Keguruan dan Ilmu Pendidkan PGRI Yogyakarta, acquired present name and status 1997.

Fees: (Rupiahs): 700,000 per annum

Degrees and Diplomas: *Sarjana (S1)*

Libraries: 3,745 vols

Last Updated: 04/02/09

YOGYAKARTA UNIVERSITY OF TECHNOLOGY

Universitas Teknologi Yogyakarta

Jl. Ring Road Utara Jombor, Sleman, DI Yogyakarta

Tel: +62(274) 623-310

Fax: +62(274) 623-306

EMail: info@uty.ac.id

Website: http://www.uty.ac.id

Rector: Bambang Hartadi

Vice-Rector, Research and Cooperation: Emita W. Astami

Vice-Rector, Administration, Finance and General Affairs: Yunus Indra Purnama

Faculties

Economics (Accountancy; Economics; Management); **Literature and Cultural Studies** (Cultural Studies; English; English Studies; Japanese; Literature); **Psychology** (Psychology); **Science and Engineering** (Civil Engineering; Computer Engineering; Computer Networks; Industrial Engineering; Information Management; Information Technology; Regional Planning; Town Planning)

Programmes

Graduate Studies (Management)

History: Founded 1968.

Degrees and Diplomas: *Diploma*; *Sarjana (S1)*; *Magister (S2)*: Management

Last Updated: 01/07/11

YOS SUDARSO UNIVERSITY

Universitas Yos Sudarso

Jalan Dukuh Kupang Barat I/216, Surabaya, 60252 Jawa Timur

Tel: +62(31) 568-9805

Rector: Bahtiar Prabowo

Ketua: Bagoes Sasmito

Faculties

Economics; **Engineering**; **Law**

History: Founded 1981.

Fees: (Rupiahs): 635,000 per annum

Degrees and Diplomas: *Sarjana (S1)*

Libraries: 1,539 vols

Last Updated: 09/02/09

YUDHARTA PASURUAN UNIVERSITY

Universitas Yudharta Pasuruan

Jln. Pesantren Ngalah 16, Pasuruan, 67162 Jawa Timur

Tel: +62(343) 611-186

EMail: baak@yudharta.ac.id

Website: http://www.yudharta.ac.id

Rector: Mohammad Shochib

Ketua: Sholihuddin

Vice-Rector: Wiwin Fachrudin Yusuf

Faculties

Administration; **Agricultural Engineering** (Agricultural Business; Fishery; Harvest Technology); **Engineering** (Civil Engineering; Engineering; Industrial Engineering; Information Technology; Mechanical Engineering); **Psychology** (Psychology)

Degrees and Diplomas: *Sarjana (S1)*

Last Updated: 09/02/09

Iran (Islamic Republic of)

STRUCTURE OF HIGHER EDUCATION SYSTEM

Description:

Higher education is provided by public and private comprehensive universities, specialized universities, universities of technology, medical universities, and teacher training centres.

Stages of studies:

University level first stage: *Bachelor's degree (Karshenasi); Continuous Master degree*

The Bachelor's degree is conferred after four to five years' study or two years after the Associate degree. The Bachelor's degree requires 130 to 140 credit units. The continuous Master degree is offered in Dentistry, Medicine, Pharmacy and Veterinary Medicine as well as in some other fields and requires the completion of 210-290 units and a dissertation.

University level second stage: *Master degree (Karshenasi Arshad)*

The postgraduate qualification of Master's degree in Arts and Science is generally conferred after two years' study beyond the Bachelor's degree. Students must sit for an entrance examination, pass 13 general and 32 to 36 semester units. It is either by coursework or research (in this case, students must prepare a thesis (dissertation) and defend it successfully before the advisory committee).

University level third stage: *Doctorate*

The Doctorate is offered at the professional level (Medicine, Dentistry, Pharmacy, Veterinary Medicine) and is the level of a Ph.D. In Dentistry, Pharmacy and Veterinary Medicine, studies last for 6 years. Ph. D. programmes are divided into educational and research phases. The educational phase comprises a Master's degree and passing an entrance examination.

Distance higher education:

Distance education is provided by both public and private institutions. It is provided by payam-e-nour.

ADMISSION TO HIGHER EDUCATION

Admission to university-level studies:

Name of secondary school credential required: Diplom-e-Motevasete

Entrance exam requirements: National Entrance Examination

Numerus clausus/restrictions: Some fields of study are completely segregated. In addition, 60% of places are allocated according to merit/locality factors.

Foreign students admission:

Definition of foreign student: Foreign students are defined as non citizens enrolled in education programmes in a host country. Thus, some permanent residents are included.

Entrance exam requirements: Foreign students must hold a Secondary School Leaving Certificate with a minimum average of 62.5% for studies leading to a Bachelor's Degree. For postgraduate studies they must have a minimum of 3 out of 4. Candidates who do not meet the requirements must take additional classes.

Entry regulations: Students must have a visa which can be delivered by the Immigration Office, provided admission into a university has been accepted.

Language requirements: Courses in Persian (12 months) are organized for foreign students.

RECOGNITION OF STUDIES

Quality assurance system:

The Ministry issues the patent for establishing any kind of higher education institution.

Bodies dealing with recognition:

Institute for Research and Planning in Higher Education

No.1, Golfam St., Africa Ave
Tehran
Tel: +98(21) 2201 0616-18
Fax: +98(21) 6640 4272
EMail: institute@irphe.ir
WWW: http://www.irphe.ir

NATIONAL BODIES

Ministry of Science, Research and Technology

Minister: Kamran Daneshju
Tehran
WWW: http://www.msrt.ir/

Minister of Health Medicine & Medical Education

Minister: Marzieh Vahid Dastjerdi
Tehran

Institute for Research and Planning in Higher Education

No.1, Golfam St., Africa Ave
Tehran
Tel: +98(21) 2201 0616-18
Fax: +98(21) 6640 4272
EMail: institute@irphe.ir
WWW: http://www.irphe.ir

Data for academic year: 2008-2009
Source: IAU from the Bureau for Scientific and International Cooperation, Ministry of Education; and the Iranian Centre for Research and Planning in Higher Education, 2008 (Bodies, 2012)

INSTITUTIONS

PUBLIC INSTITUTIONS

AHVAZ JONDISHAPOUR UNIVERSITY OF MEDICAL SCIENCES (AUMS)

PO Box 61355-45, Central Building, Golestan Avenue, Ahvaz
Tel: +98(611) 333-9092
Fax: +98(611) 333-5200
EMail: administrator@aums.ac.ir
Website: http://www.ajums.ac.ir

Chancellor: Mansour Soltanzadeh
EMail: AJUMS_President@ajums.ac.ir

Vice-Chancellor for Academic Affairs: Mohammadhosain Sarmast Shoshtari EMail: Amoozeshi@ajums.ac.ir

Faculties

Dentistry (Dentistry); **Health and Hygiene Sciences** (Health Sciences; Hygiene); **Medicine** *(Dezful)* (Medicine); **Medicine** (Medicine); **Nursing** *(Abadan)* (Nursing); **Nursing and Midwifery** (Midwifery; Nursing); **Paramedical Sciences** (Paramedical Sciences); **Paramedical Sciences** *(Behbahan)* (Paramedical Sciences) *Dean*: M.H. Mousavi-Nasab; **Pharmacy** (Pharmacy); **Rehabilitation and Therapy** (Physical Therapy; Rehabilitation and Therapy)

History: Founded 1955. Formerly part of Shahid Shamran University (former Jondi-Shapur University).

Main Language(s) of Instruction: Farsi, English

Degrees and Diplomas: *Kardani (Associate degree)*: 2 yrs; *Karshebasi (Bachelor's degree) (BA)*: 4 yrs; *Karshenasi Arshad (Master's degree) (MA)*: a further 2 yrs; *Doctorate (PhD)*

Libraries: 5,000 volumes

Last Updated: 03/07/08

ALLAMEH TABATABA'I UNIVERSITY

PO Box 14155-8473, Karimkhan Zand Street, Tehran
Tel: +98(21) 4473-7561
Fax: +98(21) 4473-7562
EMail: research-vp@atu.ac.ir
Website: http://atu.ac.ir

President: Seyed Sadroddin Shariati (2008-)
EMail: president@atu.ac.ir

International Relations: Fariborz Dortaj, Vice-President, Research

Faculties

Economics (Computer Science; Econometrics; Economics; Statistics); **Education and Psychology** (Clinical Psychology; Educational Psychology; Educational Sciences; Physical Education; Psychometrics); **Law and Political Sciences** (International

Relations; Law; Political Sciences); **Management and Accountancy** (Accountancy; Management; Public Administration; Tourism); **Persian Literature and Foreign Languages** (Arabic; English; French; Literature; Persian); **Social Sciences** (Communication Studies; Social Policy; Social Sciences; Social Welfare; Sociology)

Institutes

Insurance *(ECO)* (Insurance)

History: Founded 1984, incorporating 22 previously existing universities, faculties, colleges, and institutes.

Academic Year: October to June

Admission Requirements: Secondary school certificate and entrance examination

Main Language(s) of Instruction: Farsi

Degrees and Diplomas: *Karshebasi (Bachelor's degree) (BA; BSc)*: 4 yrs; *Karshenasi Arshad (Master's degree) (MA; MSc)*: 2 yrs; *Doctorate (PhD)*: 3 yrs

Student Services: Academic counselling, Canteen, Cultural centre, Foreign student adviser, Handicapped facilities, Health services, Language programs, Nursery care, Social counselling, Sports facilities

Libraries: Central Library, c. 48,000 vols; libraries of the faculties

Last Updated: 30/11/11

ALZAHRA UNIVERSITY

Vanak, Tehran 1993891176
Tel: +98(21) 8805-8940
Fax: +98(21) 8803-5187
EMail: Publer@alzahra.ac.ir
Website: http://www.alzahra.ac.ir

Chancellor: Mahboubeh Mobasheri (2006-)
Tel: +98(21) 8803-2721, Fax: +98(21) 8803-0673
EMail: mobasheri@alzahra.ac.ir; office@alzahra.ac.ir; ranavard@alzahra.ac.ir

Vice-Chancellor: Mahdi Pedram Tel: +98(21) 8804-7078

International Relations: Azam Sazvar, Director
Tel: +98(21) 8805-8925, Fax: +98(21) 8803-0652
EMail: office@alzahra.ac.ir

Centres

Literature, Languages and History (Arabic; English; French; History; Persian; Translation and Interpretation) *Dean*: Azam Sazvar; **Women's Research** (Educational Sciences; Family Studies; Psychology; Social Sciences; Women's Studies) *Head*: Shekoofeh Golkhoo

Faculties

Art (Graphic Arts; Handicrafts; Industrial Design; Painting and Drawing; Textile Design); **Education and Psychology** (Education; Educational Administration; Educational Psychology; Library Science); **Engineering and Technology** (Computer Engineering; Engineering; Industrial Engineering; Software Engineering; Technology); **Literature, Languages and History** (Arabic; English; French; History; Persian; Translation and Interpretation); **Physical Education and Sports** (Physical Education; Sports); **Social Sciences and Economics** (Accountancy; Economics; Management; Social Sciences); **Theology** (Islamic Studies; Koran; Theology)

History: Founded 1964 as Iran Girls' College. Acquired present status and title 1975. The only university for women in the country.

Academic Year: September to July (September-February; February-July)

Admission Requirements: Secondary school certificate and entrance examination

Main Language(s) of Instruction: Farsi

Degrees and Diplomas: *Karshebasi (Bachelor's degree) (BSc; BA)*: 4 yrs; *Karshenasi Arshad (Master's degree) (MSc; MA)*: a further 2-3 yrs; *Doctorate (PhD)*

Student Services: Academic counselling, Cultural centre, Health services, Nursery care, Social counselling, Sports facilities

Student Residential Facilities: Yes

Special Facilities: Kamaleddin Behzad Art Gallery

Libraries: Central Library, c. 55,000 vols

Publications: Gelve-ye Honar, Magazine on Arts *(quarterly)*; Journal of Humanities *(quarterly)*; Journal of Science *(quarterly)*

Last Updated: 30/11/11

AMIRKABIR UNIVERSITY OF TECHNOLOGY - TEHRAN POLYTECHNIC (AUT)

PO Box 15825-4413, Opposite Somaye Street, Hafez Ave., Tehran 15914
Tel: +98(21) 64540-1
Fax: +98(21) 641-3969
EMail: webmaster@aut.ac.ir
Website: http://www.aut.ac.ir

Chancellor: Alireza Rahai

Centres

Energy Research and Process Design (Energy Engineering); **Food Industry** (Food Technology); **Industrial Engineering and Productivity** (Industrial Engineering; Information Management; Maintenance Technology; Systems Analysis); **New Technology Research** (Automation and Control Engineering; Production Engineering; Robotics; Technology); **Textile Industry and Synthetic Fibre** (Textile Technology)

Departments

Mathematics and Computer Science (Mathematics and Computer Science); **Aerospace Engineering** (Aeronautical and Aerospace Engineering); **Biomedical Engineering** (Biomedical Engineering); **Chemical Engineering** (Chemical Engineering); **Civil and Environmental Engineering** (Civil Engineering; Environmental Engineering; Hydraulic Engineering; Water Management); **Computer Engineering and Information Technology** (Artificial Intelligence; Computer Engineering; Information Technology; Software Engineering); **Electrical Engineering** (Electrical Engineering) *Division Head*: azandarina; **Industrial Engineering and Management Systems** (Industrial Engineering; Mechanics); **Maritime Engineering** (Marine Engineering; Naval Architecture); **Mechanical Engineering** (Mechanical Engineering); **Mining and Metallurgical Engineering** (Metallurgical Engineering; Mining Engineering); **Nuclear Engineering and Physics** (Applied Physics; Atomic and Molecular Physics; Nuclear Engineering; Nuclear Physics; Physics); **Polymer Engineering and Colour Technology** (Chemical Engineering); **Textile Engineering** (Textile Technology)

Groups

Physical Education *(Mahshar Branch)* (Physical Education); **Chemistry** *(Mahshar Branch)* (Chemistry); **Culture and Human Science** *(Mahshar Branch)* (Islamic Studies; Literature; Persian; Theology); **Language** *(Mahshar Branch)* (English; Modern Languages)

Further Information: Also Tafresh, Bandar Abbas and Mahshahr Campuses

History: Founded 1958 as Tehran Polytechnic, acquired present status and title 1979.

Governing Bodies: Board of Trustees

Academic Year: September to June (September-January; February-June)

Admission Requirements: Secondary school certificate and national entrance examination for undergraduate programme and MSc degree. Amirkabir University entrance examination for PhD

Fees: None

Main Language(s) of Instruction: Farsi

Degrees and Diplomas: *Karshebasi (Bachelor's degree) (BA; BSc)*: 4 yrs; *Karshenasi Arshad (Master's degree) (MA; MSc)*: a further 2 yrs; *Doctorate (PhD)*: 4 yrs

Student Services: Academic counselling, Canteen, Cultural centre, Foreign student adviser, Health services, Nursery care, Social counselling, Sports facilities

Student Residential Facilities: Yes

Libraries: Central Library, c. 80,000 vols. Departmental libraries, c. 31,000 vols

Publications: Amirkabir Journal of Science and Technology *(quarterly)*

Press or Publishing House: Amirkabir Publishing Institute

Last Updated: 17/02/12

ARAK UNIVERSITY

PO Box 379, Arak 38156
Tel: +98(861) 777-400-4
Fax: +98(861) 777-4031
EMail: p-r@araku.ac.ir
Website: http://www.araku.ac.ir

President: Sadeghi Sarabi Tel: +98(861) 771-446

Colleges

Agriculture and Natural Resources (Agricultural Equipment; Agriculture; Animal Husbandry; Environmental Studies; Horticulture; Plant and Crop Protection; Water Science); **Engineering** (Chemical Engineering; Civil Engineering; Computer Engineering; Electrical Engineering; Materials Engineering; Mechanical Engineering); **Human Sciences** (Arabic; Arts and Humanities; English; History; Persian; Physical Education; Social Sciences; Theology; Translation and Interpretation); **Science** (Biology; Chemistry; Mathematics; Natural Sciences; Physics)

History: Founded 1971. Acquired present status and title 1996.

Academic Year: September to July (September-January; February-July)

Admission Requirements: Secondary school certificate and entrance examination

Main Language(s) of Instruction: Farsi

Degrees and Diplomas: *Karshebasi (Bachelor's degree) (BSc; BA)*: 4 yrs; *Karshenasi Arshad (Master's degree) (MA;MSc)*: a further 2 yrs

Student Services: Canteen, Cultural centre, Health services, Nursery care, Social counselling, Sports facilities

Student Residential Facilities: For c. 3,000 students

Special Facilities: Zoology Museum

Libraries: Central Library, 48,011 vols (in Persian); 14,063 (in English); 3,457 (in Arabic)

Press or Publishing House: Arak University Publications
Last Updated: 30/11/11

ARAK UNIVERSITY OF MEDICAL SCIENCES

Shahid Shiroodi Street, Arak
Tel: +98(861) 3135-760
Fax: +98(861) 3134-766
EMail: Info@arakmu.ac.ir
Website: http://www.arakmu.ac.ir/
Chancellor: Majid Ramezani

Schools

Health Sciences (Health Sciences; Occupational Health); **Medicine** (Medicine); **Nursing** *(Khomein)* (Nursing); **Nursing** *(Saveh)* (Nursing); **Nursing and Midwifery** (Midwifery; Nursing); **Paramedical Sciences** (Paramedical Sciences)

History: Founded 1987, acquired present status and title 1990.

Academic Year: September to June

Main Language(s) of Instruction: Farsi

Degrees and Diplomas: *Kardani (Associate degree)*: 2 yrs; *Karshebasi (Bachelor's degree) (BA)*: 4 yrs; *Karshenasi Arshad (Master's degree)*; *Doctorate*
Last Updated: 30/11/11

ARAK UNIVERSITY OF TECHNOLOGY

18 Fallahpour Street, Sepahbod Gharani Avenue, Tehran
Tel: +98(21) 24003 +98(21) 22048
Fax: +98(21) 882-7156
EMail: am_hajati@iustarak.ac.ir
Website: http://www.arakut.ac.ir/index.php?slc_lang=en&sid=1

President: Abbas Pak EMail: a.pak @ iustarak.ac.I

Departments

Civil Engineering (Civil Engineering); **Electrical Engineering** (Electrical Engineering); **Mechanical Engineering** (Mechanical Engineering); **Mining Engineering** (Mining Engineering)

History: Founded 1990.

Main Language(s) of Instruction: Farsi

Degrees and Diplomas: *Karshebasi (Bachelor's degree)*

Libraries: Yes
Last Updated: 17/02/12

ARDABIL UNIVERSITY OF MEDICAL SCIENCES (AR-U-M-S)

University Street, Shorabil, Ardabil 56197
Tel: +98(451) 335-1020
Fax: +98(451) 335-1053
EMail: webmaster@arums.ac.ir
Website: http://www.arums.ac.ir/

President: Farhad Pourfarzi

Departments

Anatomy (Anatomy; Embryology and Reproduction Biology; Histology); **Biochemistry** (Biochemistry); **Health Sciences** (Health Sciences); **Medicine** (Anaesthesiology; Cardiology; Dermatology; Epidemiology; Gastroenterology; Medicine; Nephrology; Paediatrics; Parasitology; Pathology; Psychiatry and Mental Health; Surgery; Urology; Virology); **Nursing and Midwifery** (Midwifery; Nursing); **Paramedical Sciences** (Paramedical Sciences); **Parasitology** (Immunology; Microbiology; Parasitology); **Physiology and Biophysics** (Biophysics; Physiology)

History: Founded 1993.

Fees: None

Main Language(s) of Instruction: Farsi, English

Degrees and Diplomas: *Kardani (Associate degree)*: 2 yrs; *Karshebasi (Bachelor's degree) (BA)*: 4 yrs; *Doctorate*: 7 yrs

Student Services: Academic counselling, Canteen, Cultural centre, Employment services, Health services, Language programs, Nursery care, Social counselling, Sports facilities

Student Residential Facilities: Yes

Special Facilities: Observatory. Movie studio

Libraries: c. 19,610 vols

Publications: Scientific Bulletin
Last Updated: 17/02/12

ART UNIVERSITY OF ISFAHAN

Isfahan
Tel: +98(311) 624-9836
Fax: +98(311) 634-9841
Website: http://www.aui.ac.ir/default.aspx

President: Farhang Mozaffar

Programmes

Architecture (Architecture; Architecture and Planning); **Fine Arts** (Handicrafts; Painting and Drawing)

History: Founded 1974 as Farabi University. Acquired present status and title 1999.

Main Language(s) of Instruction: Farsi

Degrees and Diplomas: *Karshebasi (Bachelor's degree) (BA)*: 4 yrs; *Karshenasi Arshad (Master's degree) (MA)*: a further 2 yrs
Last Updated: 17/02/12

ARTESH UNIVERSITY OF MEDICAL SCIENCES

Dr. Fatemi Avenue West, Shahid Etemadzadeh Avenue, Tabriz
Tel: +98(21) 628-000
Fax: +98(21) 802-6846

Chancellor: Seyyed Abolghasem Mousavi

Faculties

Medicine

BAAKHTARAN UNIVERSITY OF MEDICAL SCIENCES

PO Box 67145, Baakhtaran 1619

Faculties

Medicine (Medicine)

Degrees and Diplomas: *Karshebasi (Bachelor's degree)*; *Professional Doctorate*; *Karshenasi Arshad (Master's degree)*
Last Updated: 17/02/12

BABOL UNIVERSITY OF MEDICAL SCIENCES

PO Box 47176-41367, Ganje Afrooze Ave, Babol, Mazandaran
Tel: +98(111) 229-4720
Fax: +98(111) 222-7667
EMail: info@mubabol.ac.ir
Website: http://www.mubabol.ac.ir

Chancellor: Ebrahim Mekaniki
Tel: +98(111) 222-9015 EMail: chancellor@mubabol.ac.ir

Secretary-General: Alinaghi Rezaie

International Relations: Ali Bijani

Faculties

Nursing and Midwifery *(Amol City) Dean*: Abolfazl Hashemi

Schools

Allied Medical Sciences *Director*: Parvin Sajadi; **Dentistry** (Dentistry); **Medicine** (Anaesthesiology; Cardiology; Dermatology; Endocrinology; Gastroenterology; Gynaecology and Obstetrics; Medicine; Nephrology; Ophthalmology; Orthopaedics; Paediatrics; Pathology; Psychiatry and Mental Health; Radiology; Rheumatology; Surgery; Tropical Medicine); **Nursing** *(Ramsor City)* (Midwifery; Nursing); **Nursing and Midwifery** (Midwifery; Nursing)

History: Founded 1983. Acquired present status 1986. Previously part of Mazandaran University.

Academic Year: September to August

Admission Requirements: University entrance examination

Fees: None except for evening studies

Main Language(s) of Instruction: Farsi

Accrediting Agencies: Ministry of Health and Medical Education

Degrees and Diplomas: *Kardani (Associate degree)*: 2 yrs; *Karshebasi (Bachelor's degree) (BA)*: 4 yrs; *Doctorate (PhD)*. GP 7 yrs

Student Services: Academic counselling, Canteen, Cultural centre, Employment services, Health services, Language programs, Nursery care, Social counselling, Sports facilities

Student Residential Facilities: Yes

Libraries:c. 13,000 vols

Publications: Babol Medical Journal *(quarterly)*
Last Updated: 17/02/12

BAQIYATALLAH MEDICAL SCIENCES UNIVERSITY

Baghyatollahelazam Hospital, Mollasara Avenue, Vanak Square, Tehran
Tel: +98(21) 215-4461
Fax: +98(21) 803-7673
Website: http://www.bmsu.ac.ir

President: Jafar Aslani

Faculties

Medicine (Medicine); **Nursing** (Nursing); **Public Health** (Health Sciences; Public Health)

History: Founded 1994.

Main Language(s) of Instruction: Farsi, English

Degrees and Diplomas: *Kardani (Associate degree)*: 2 yrs; *Karshebasi (Bachelor's degree) (BA)*: 4 yrs; *Karshenasi Arshad (Master's degree) (MA)*: a further 2 yrs; *Doctorate (PhD)*

Student Services: Health services, Nursery care, Sports facilities

Special Facilities: Observatory; Movie studio

Libraries: Electronic library and documentation centre
Last Updated: 17/02/12

BIRJAND UNIVERSITY OF MEDICAL SCIENCES

Moallem Street, Birjand 97178
Tel: +98(561) 4430-075
Fax: +98(561) 4430-076
EMail: Public-r@bums.ac.ir
Website: http://www.bums.ac.ir/

President: Morad Hashem Zehi

Faculties

Health Sciences (Health Sciences); **Medicine** (Medicine); **Nursing** (Gynaecology and Obstetrics; Nursing)

History: Founded 1986 as Faculty. Acquired present status and title 1993.

Academic Year: September to July

Admission Requirements: Secondary school certificate and entrance examination

Fees: None

Main Language(s) of Instruction: Farsi

Degrees and Diplomas: *Kardani (Associate degree)*: 2 yrs; *Karshebasi (Bachelor's degree) (BA)*: 4 yrs; *Doctorate*: 7 yrs. Also Undergraduate Diplomas, 2-3 yrs

Student Services: Academic counselling, Health services, Social counselling, Sports facilities

Student Residential Facilities: Yes

Libraries: Total, 20,062 vols

Publications: Journal of Medical University of Birjand *(quarterly)*
Last Updated: 17/02/12

IAU BU-ALI SINA UNIVERSITY (BASU)

University Bvd, Hamadan 65175-4161
Tel: +98(811) 827-3001 +98(811) 827-3952
Fax: +98(811) 827-2046
EMail: ico@basu.ac.ir
Website: http://www.basu.ac.ir

President: Mohammad Ali Zolfigol (2008-) EMail: zolfi@basu.ac.ir

Vice-Chancellor, Administration and Finance: Ali Yalfani
Tel: +98(811) 827-8899, Fax: +98(811) 827-3126
EMail: ali_yalfani@yahoo.com

International Relations: Ali AKbar Sabziparvar, Director of International Cooperation Office
Tel: +98(811) 827-3001, Fax: +98(811) 827-3001
EMail: swsabzi@basu.ac.ir

Faculties

Agriculture (Agricultural Education; Agricultural Equipment; Agronomy; Biotechnology; Crop Production; Horticulture; Irrigation; Plant and Crop Protection; Plant Pathology; Soil Science; Water Science; Zoology); **Art and Architecture** (Archaeology; Architecture; Fine Arts; Graphic Arts); **Chemistry** (Chemistry); **Civil Engineering** *(Kaboodrahang)* (Civil Engineering); **Economics and Social Science** (Accountancy; Business and Commerce; Economics; Law; Psychology; Social Sciences); **Engineering** (Civil Engineering; Computer Engineering; Electrical Engineering; Energy Engineering; Geological Engineering; Hydraulic Engineering; Industrial Engineering; Mechanical Engineering; Power Engineering; Software Engineering; Thermal Engineering); **Industrial Engineering** *(Toyserkan)* (Industrial Engineering); **Literature and Humanities** (Ancient Civilizations; Ancient Languages; Arabic; Business and Commerce; Economics; Educational Sciences; French; Islamic Studies; Law; Literature; Modern Languages; Persian; Physical Education; Psychology; Social Sciences; Sports; Theology); **Management and Accountancy** *(Razan)* (Accountancy; Management); **Physical Education** *(Nahavand)* (Physical Education; Sports); **Science** (Biology; Ecology; Geology; Mathematics; Natural Sciences; Physics)

Further Information: Branches in Nahavand City

History: Founded 1973.

Academic Year: September to July (Sept-Jan; Feb-July)

Admission Requirements: Secondary school certificate and entrance examination

Fees: None for Iranian students; Overseas students, (US Dollars): 4,000 (Bachelors), 6,000 (PhD)

Main Language(s) of Instruction: Farsi

Accrediting Agencies: Ministry of Science, Research and Technology

Degrees and Diplomas: *Karshebasi (Bachelor's degree)*: Agricultural Education and Extension; Soil Science; Plant and Crop Protection; Agricultural Bio-Technology; Agronomy and Plant Breeding; Horticultural Science; Animal Science; Agricultural Machinery (BSc; BA); Electrical Engineering; Industrial Engineering;

Hydraulic Engineering; Material Engineering; Computer Engineering; Mechanical Engineering; Veterinary Medicine; Theology and Islamic Science; Physical Education and Sport Science (BSc; BA); French Language; Islamic Education; Persian Language and Literature; Education Science; Arabic Language and Literature; Archaeological Language and Culture; Foreign Languages and Linguistics (BSc; BA); Irrigation Science; Fine Arts; Archaeology; Graphic Arts; Architecture; Applied Chemistry; Analytical Chemistry; Inorganic Chemistry; Organic Chemistry; Physical Chemistry; Civil Engineering,; Geological Engineering (BSc; BA); Plant Biology; Zoology; Geology; Physics; Mathematics; Ecology; Law; Social Science; Economics; Business; Commerce; Psychology; Accounting (BSc; BA), 4 yrs; *Karshenasi Arshad (Master's degree)*: Agricultural Engineering; Soil Mechanics Engineering; Geology; Chemistry; Soil Conservation; Geological Engineering (MSc; MA); Literature; Physics; Sport Science; Economics; Computer Engineering; Civil Engineering; Mechanical Engineering; Biotechnology; Animal Science (MSc; MA), a further 2 yrs; *Doctorate*: Chemistry; Mechanical Engineering; Geotechnical Engineering; Soil Science; Ecology (PhD), up to 4 yrs

Student Services: Academic counselling, Canteen, Cultural centre, Foreign student adviser, Health services, Nursery care, Social counselling, Sports facilities

Student Residential Facilities: For 3,000 students

Special Facilities: Film Studio; Museum of Natural History; Museum of Geology; educational and research farms.

Libraries: Central library and reference documents; Subject libraries (Engineering, Science, Agriculture, Art and Architecture, Human Science, Chemistry).

Publications: Quarterly of Agricultural Research *(quarterly)*

Academic Staff *2009-2010*	MEN	WOMEN	**TOTAL**
FULL-TIME	328	41	**369**
PART-TIME	15	–	**15**
STAFF WITH DOCTORATE			
FULL-TIME	239	22	**261**
PART-TIME	12	–	**12**
Student Numbers *2009-2010*			
All (Foreign Included)	3,822	5,103	**8,925**
FOREIGN ONLY	7	1	**8**

Part-time students, 227. **Evening students**, 2,374.

Last Updated: 01/12/11

BUSHEHR PORT UNIVERSITY OF MEDICAL SCIENCES

PO Box 3631, Moalem Street, Bushehr, Bushehr
Tel: +98(771) 253-1933
Fax: +98(771) 252-3123
EMail: admin@bpums.ac.ir
Website: http://www.bpums.ac.ir

Chancellor: Abdul Ali Ebrahimi (2005-) Tel: +98(771) 171-5515

Vice-Chancellor: Morad Ali Fooladvand
Tel: +98(771) 252-6189, Fax: +98(771) 252-5800
EMail: mfooladvand39@yahoo.com

International Relations: Davood Issazadeh, International Relations Officer Tel: +98(771) 172-5292

Faculties

Medicine (Medicine); **Nursing and Midwifery** (Midwifery; Nursing); **Paramedical Sciences** (Paramedical Sciences); **Public Health Sciences** (Health Sciences)

History: Founded 1983 and until 1987 was Narjes School of Nursing and Midwifery. From 1988 until 1990 it was the Junior College of Allied Health Services, Nursing and Midwifery. In 1991 became a full faculty of medicine before obtaining current status and title in 1995.

Governing Bodies: University Council

Academic Year: September to June

Admission Requirements: Secondary school certificate and entrance examination

Fees: none

Main Language(s) of Instruction: Farsi

Degrees and Diplomas: *Kardani (Associate degree)*: Anaesthesiology, Laboratory Sciences, Operating Room Nursing, Midwifery, Environmental Health, Family Health, 2 yrs; *Karshebasi (Bachelor's degree)*: Nursing, Midwifery, Library Science (BA), 4 yrs; *Doctorate*: Medicine (MD), 7 yrs. Also diploma in Nursing, Health Sciences and Midwifery, 2 1/2 yrs

Student Services: Academic counselling, Canteen, Cultural centre, Foreign student adviser, Health services, Language programs, Nursery care, Social counselling, Sports facilities

Student Residential Facilities: Residential facilities for male and female students as well as couples

Special Facilities: Computer Centre, Language Laboratory

Libraries: 5 libraries with c. 100.00 vols in English and Farsi

Publications: Laymer, Medical information *(quarterly)*; Teb-e-Jonoob, Medical and academic information *(quarterly)*

Last Updated: 01/12/11

CIVIL AVIATION TECHNOLOGY COLLEGE (CATC)

Meaaraj Street, Mehrabad International Airport, Tehran 13445-418
Tel: +98(21) 660 25125
Fax: +98(21) 660 19426
EMail: webmaster@catc.ac.ir
Website: http://www.catc.ac.ir/

Dean of College: Mohammad Reza Habibi (2004-)
Tel: +98(21) 660 22512 EMail: habibi@catc.ac.ir

Deputy of Education: Mohammad Reza Akbari
Tel: +98(21) 610 22851, Fax: +98(21) 660 29765
EMail: akbari@catc.ac.ir

International Relations: Javad Parastari, Head of International Relations Tel: +98(21) 660 22677 EMail: parastari@catc.ac.ir

Departments

Air Traffic Services (Air Transport); **Aircraft Repair and Maintenance** (Aeronautical and Aerospace Engineering); **Aviation Communication**; **Computer** (Computer Science); **Electronics** (Aeronautical and Aerospace Engineering; Electronic Engineering)

History: Founded 1949. Also known as College of Aviation Industry. Specialised training centre for Aviation Industry following guidelines set by International Civil Aviation Organisation (ICAO).

Academic Year: September to December; December to June.

Admission Requirements: Two groups: (Academic entry), Secondary school diploma and Iranian university entrance exam. (Free entry), college entrance exam for students with diploma in mathematics or science for admission to two-year course.

Fees: For Academic entrants, daily courses are free, evening courses have a fixed charge of 100 US dollars. For those passing the free entrance exam, the cost of a two-year course is 4,000 US dollars.

Main Language(s) of Instruction: Farsi, English

Degrees and Diplomas: *Kardani (Associate degree)*: 2 yrs; *Karshebasi (Bachelor's degree)*: Aircraft Maintenance; Electronics; Air Traffic Control, 4 yrs

Student Services: Academic counselling, Canteen, Cultural centre, Foreign student adviser, Health services, Language programs, Nursery care, Social counselling, Sports facilities

Special Facilities: English language laboratories.

Libraries: Yes

Last Updated: 01/12/11

IAU DAMGHAN UNIVERSITY

PO Box 36715-364, Cheshmeh Ali Road, Damghan, 3671641167 Semnan
Tel: +98(232) 526-2595
Fax: +98(232) 526-2595
EMail: international@du.ac.ir
Website: http://www.du.ac.ir

President: Ali Haghighi Asl (2007-) EMail: Haghighi@du.ac.ir

International Relations: Abdolali Basiri, Head of International & Scientific Cooperation Office EMail: basiri@du.ac.ir

Schools
Biology (Biology); **Chemistry** (Analytical Chemistry; Applied Chemistry; Chemistry; Inorganic Chemistry; Organic Chemistry; Physical Chemistry); **Geology** (Geology; Paleontology); **Mathematics and Computer Science** (Applied Mathematics; Mathematics; Mathematics and Computer Science; Statistics); **Physics** (Astrophysics; Nuclear Physics; Physics; Solid State Physics)

History: Founded 1989. Previously known as Damghan University of Basic Sciences.

Governing Bodies: Board of Trustees, University Council

Academic Year: October - January; February - July

Admission Requirements: Secondary school certificate and entrance examination

Fees: (US Dollars): 200-1,000 per term

Main Language(s) of Instruction: Persian, English

International Co-operation: with institutions in Russia

Degrees and Diplomas: *Karshebasi (Bachelor's degree) (BSc)*: 4-5 yrs; *Karshenasi Arshad (Master's degree) (MSc)*: a further 2 yrs; *Doctorate*

Student Services: Academic counselling, Canteen, Cultural centre, Employment services, Health services, Language programs, Nursery care, Social counselling, Sports facilities

Student Residential Facilities: for 2,000 students

Libraries: c. 40,000 vols

Academic Staff *2011-2012*	MEN	WOMEN	**TOTAL**
FULL-TIME	63	163	**226**
STAFF WITH DOCTORATE			
FULL-TIME	74	11	**85**
Student Numbers *2011-2012*			
All (Foreign Included)	1,051	2,140	**3,191**

Evening students, 892.

Last Updated: 29/09/11

DR SHARIATY TECHNICAL COLLEGE

Daneshkade St, South Misaq Ave, Tehran
Tel: +98(21) 5500-3335
Fax: +98(21) 5500-3339
EMail: support@shariaty.ac.ir
Website: http://www.shariaty.ac.ir

Schools
Administrative Science (Accountancy; Administration; Health Administration; Health Education; Secretarial Studies); **Architecture** (Architecture); **Art** (Fine Arts); **Fashion and Textile** (Fashion Design; Handicrafts; Textile Design; Textile Technology); **Sports Education** (Physical Education; Sports); **Technical Sciences** (Computer Science; Electrical Engineering; Electronic Engineering; Industrial Design)

History: Created in 1983 as an undergraduate college for women. Currently offers undergraduate courses for women and postgraduate courses for both men and women.

Degrees and Diplomas: *Kardani (Associate degree)*; *Karshebasi (Bachelor's degree)*; *Karshenasi Arshad (Master's degree)*

Last Updated: 27/08/10

FARABI COLLEGE OF SCIENCE AND TECHNOLOGY

Tehran

Colleges
Science and Technology

Degrees and Diplomas: *Karshebasi (Bachelor's degree) (BA)*: 4 yrs; *Karshenasi Arshad (Master's degree) (MA)*: a further 2 yrs

FASA UNIVERSITY OF MEDICAL SCIENCES

Daneshgahe Pezeshki Fasa
Fasa 74615-168
Tel: +98(731) 222-7093
Fax: +98(731) 222-7091
EMail: khademianmh@msn.com
Website: http://www.fums.ac.ir

Chancellor: Gholam Reza Hatam (1996-)
EMail: Hatam25@hotmail.com

Vice-Chancellor for Administration and Logistics: Mohammad Houssain Khademian Tel: +98(731) 222-7094

International Relations: Tayebah Allahpanahzadeh
EMail: tayallap@yahoo.com

Colleges
Nursing (Nursing)

Departments
Anatomy (Anatomy); **Biochemistry** (Biochemistry); **Medicine Internship** (Medicine); **Microbiology** (Microbiology); **Paediatrics** (Paediatrics); **Physiology** (Physiology); **Surgery** (Surgery)

History: Founded 1977. Formerly Fasa Medical College.

Academic Year: September to July

Admission Requirements: Secondary school certificate and entrance examination

Fees: Free for Iranian nationals

Main Language(s) of Instruction: Farsi, English

Degrees and Diplomas: *Kardani (Associate degree)*: 2 yrs; *Karshebasi (Bachelor's degree) (BA)*: 4 yrs

Student Services: Academic counselling, Canteen, Cultural centre, Foreign student adviser, Health services, Language programs, Nursery care, Social counselling, Sports facilities

Student Residential Facilities: Yes

Libraries:c. 14,000 vols

FERDOWSI UNIVERSITY OF MASHHAD (FUM)

University Campus, Azadi Square, University Paradise, Mashhad, 9177948974 Khorasan Razavi
Tel: +98(511) 878-8990
Fax: +98(511) 878-4849
EMail: coff@ferdowsi.um.ac.ir
Website: http://www.um.ac.ir

President: Ali Reza Ashouri (2005-)
Tel: +98(511) 842-4587, Fax: +98(511) 840-3461
EMail: ch@ferdowsi.um.ac.ir

International Relations: Abedin Vahedian, Director (2007-)
Tel: +98(511) 883-6037, Fax: +98(511) 883-6056
EMail: intr@ferdowsi.um.ac.ir

Centres
Higher Education *(Shirvan)* (Plant and Crop Protection)

Colleges
Agriculture (Agricultural Economics; Agricultural Equipment; Agriculture; Agronomy; Animal Husbandry; Biotechnology; Food Science; Plant and Crop Protection; Plant Pathology; Soil Science; Water Science)

Faculties
Architecture and Urban Planning (Architecture; Town Planning; Urban Studies); **Arts** *(Neyshabour)* (Archaeology; Fine Arts; Graphic Design; Painting and Drawing; Sculpture); **Economics and Business Administration** (Accountancy; Administration; Economics; Law; Management; Political Sciences); **Education and Psychology** (Clinical Psychology; Curriculum; Education; Educational Administration; Library Science; Preschool Education; Psychology); **Engineering** (Chemical Engineering; Civil Engineering; Computer Engineering; Electrical Engineering; Engineering; Materials Engineering; Mechanical Engineering); **Letters and Humanities** (Arabic; English; French Studies; Geography; History; Linguistics; Persian; Russian; Social Sciences); **Natural Resources and Environment** (Arid Land Studies; Environmental Management; Natural Resources; Water Science); **Physical Education** (Physical Education); **Science** (Biology; Chemistry; Geology; Natural Sciences; Physics); **Theology** (Esoteric Practices; Islamic Law; Islamic Studies; Koran; Religion); **Veterinary Medicine** (Veterinary Science)

Research Centres
Botany (Botany; Plant and Crop Protection; Vegetable Production)

Schools

Mathematics (Mathematics; Statistics)

History: Founded 1937 as State School of Hygiene, became Faculty of Medicine 1949, and university 1956. A State institution responsible to the Ministry of Culture and Higher Education.

Academic Year: September to June (September-February; February-June)

Admission Requirements: Secondary school certificate and entrance examination

Main Language(s) of Instruction: Farsi

Accrediting Agencies: Ministry of Science, Research and Technology

Degrees and Diplomas: *Kardani (Associate degree)*: 2 yrs; *Karshebasi (Bachelor's degree) (BA; BSc)*: 4 yrs; *Karshenasi Arshad (Master's degree) (MA; MSc)*: a further 2 yrs; *Doctorate (PhD)*

Student Services: Academic counselling, Canteen, Cultural centre, Foreign student adviser, Health services, Nursery care, Social counselling, Sports facilities

Student Residential Facilities: Dormitories

Special Facilities: Zoology Museum. Herbarium

Libraries: Literature and Humanities, 90,000 vols; Education and Psychology, 26,300; Agriculture, 12,000; Engineering, 15,000; Sciences, 650,000; Central Library, 35,000

Publications: Faculty of Agriculture Periodicals *(quarterly)*; Faculty of Economics and Administration Periodicals *(quarterly)*; Faculty of Education and Psychology Periodicals *(quarterly)*; Faculty of Engineering Periodicals *(quarterly)*; Faculty of Literature and Humanities Periodicals *(quarterly)*; Faculty of Science Periodicals *(quarterly)*; Faculty of Theology and Islamic Studies Periodicals *(quarterly)*

Press or Publishing House: University Press

Last Updated: 02/12/11

GONABAD UNIVERSITY OF MEDICAL SCIENCES

Iman Khomeini Avenue, Farmandari Square, Gonabad 96916
Tel: +98(5359) 2328
Fax: +98(5359) 3815
EMail: info@gmu.ac.ir
Website: http://www.gmu.ac.ir

Chancellor: Mohammad Ghahramani (1993-)

Faculties

Medicine (Medicine); **Nursing and Midwifery** (Midwifery; Nursing); **Paramedical Sciences** (Paramedical Sciences)

History: Founded 1985 as Gonabad College of Nursing and Midwifery, acquired present status 1993.

Academic Year: September to June

Main Language(s) of Instruction: Farsi, English

Degrees and Diplomas: *Kardani (Associate degree)*: 2 yrs; *Karshebasi (Bachelor's degree) (BA)*: 4 yrs

Libraries: c. 6,000 vols

Last Updated: 15/12/08

GORGAN UNIVERSITY OF AGRICULTURE AND NATURAL RESOURCES

PO Box 386, Shahid Beheshti Street, Gorgan
Tel: +98(171) 222-0028
Fax: +98(171) 222-5989
EMail: guasnr@gau.ac.ir
Website: http://www.gau.ac.ir

President: Ramin Rahmani Tel: +98(171) 222-4080

Colleges

Agriculture *(Gonbad)* (Agriculture); **Agronomy** (Agricultural Engineering; Agronomy); **Fisheries and Environmental Sciences** (Environmental Studies; Fishery); **Science** (Natural Sciences); **Wood, Pulp and Forestry Sciences** (Forestry; Paper Technology; Wood Technology)

Research Centres

Forestry (Forestry)

History: Founded 1957 as College of Rangeland and Forestry, became Faculty of Natural Resources of Mazandaran University 1986. Acquired present status and title 1992.

Academic Year: September to July (September-December; February-July)

Admission Requirements: Secondary school certificate and entrance examination

Main Language(s) of Instruction: Farsi

Degrees and Diplomas: *Kardani (Associate degree)*: 2 yrs; *Karshebasi (Bachelor's degree) (BSc)*: 4 yrs; *Karshenasi Arshad (Master's degree) (MSc)*: a further 2 yrs following Bachelor; *Doctorate (PhD)*: a further 4 yrs following Master

Student Services: Academic counselling, Canteen, Cultural centre, Employment services, Foreign student adviser, Handicapped facilities, Health services, Language programs, Nursery care, Social counselling, Sports facilities

Student Residential Facilities: Yes

Special Facilities: Wildlife Museum. Botanical Garden. Computer Training Centre

Libraries: Central Library, c. 30,000 vols

Publications: Scientific Journal (Journal of Agricultural Sciences and Natural Resources) *(quarterly)*

Press or Publishing House: Central Publishing House

Last Updated: 16/12/08

GORGAN UNIVERSITY OF MEDICAL SCIENCES

PO Box 665, Sary-Gorgan Avenue 2nd Km, Gorgan 49165
Tel: +98(171) 222-4540
Fax: +98(171) 222-4551

Chancellor: Aref Salehi (1994-)

Faculties

Medicine (Medicine); **Nursing and Midwifery** *(Booye)* (Midwifery; Nursing); **Paramedical Sciences** (Paramedical Sciences)

History: Founded 1967 as Bouyeh Faculty of Nursing and Midwifery, acquired present status and title 1992.

Main Language(s) of Instruction: Farsi, English

Degrees and Diplomas: *Kardani (Associate degree)*: 2 yrs; *Karshebasi (Bachelor's degree) (BA)*: 4 yrs; *Doctorate (PhD)*

Libraries:c. 12,000 vols

Publications: Journal of Gorgan University of Medical Sciences

GUILAN UNIVERSITY OF MEDICAL SCIENCES (GUMS)

Namjoo Avenue, Rasht 41625
Tel: +98(131) 322-1282
Fax: +98(131) 322-7070
EMail: info@gums.ac.ir
Website: http://www.gums.ac.ir

President: Hasan Behboodi
Tel: +98(131) 322-9282 EMail: behboodi@gums.ac.ir

Vice-Chancellor for Education: Mir Mohammad Jalali
EMail: mmjalali@gums.ac.ir

Faculties

Dentistry (Dentistry); **Medicine** (Anaesthesiology; Anatomy; Biochemistry; Biophysics; Cardiology; Community Health; Dermatology; Gynaecology and Obstetrics; Immunology; Medicine; Neurology; Ophthalmology; Orthopaedics; Otorhinolaryngology; Paediatrics; Pathology; Pharmacology; Physiology; Psychiatry and Mental Health; Radiology; Surgery; Urology); **Nursing and Midwifery** *(Shahid Beheshti)* (Midwifery; Nursing); **Nursing and Midwifery** *(Langeroud)* (Midwifery; Nursing); **Nursing and Midwifery** (Midwifery; Nursing)

Research Centres

Gastro-intestinal and Liver Diseases *(GLDRC)* (Gastroenterology; Hepatology); **Haematology** (Haematology)

Schools

Health (Health Sciences)

History: Founded 1985. Previously part of the University of Gilan.

Academic Year: September to June

Main Language(s) of Instruction: Farsi

Degrees and Diplomas: *Kardani (Associate degree)*: 2 yrs; *Karshebasi (Bachelor's degree) (BA)*: 4 yrs; *Karshenasi Arshad (Master's degree) (MA)*: a further 2 yrs; *Doctorate (PhD)*

Libraries: 55,182 vols

Last Updated: 02/12/11

HAMADAN UNIVERSITY OF MEDICAL SCIENCES AND HEALTH SERVICES

Shariaty Street, Hamadan, 518 Hamadan
Tel: +98(81) 827-8810
EMail: info@umsha.ac.ir
Website: http://www.umsha.ac.ir

Chancellor: Abbas Zamanyan (2002-)
Tel: +98(81) 252-0683, Fax: +98(81) 252-0773

Executive Director: Saeed Bashiran
Tel: +98(81) 252-0402, Fax: +98(81) 252-0401

International Relations: Gholamhossein Sadri
Fax: +98(81) 252-0428
EMail: ghsadri2000@yahoo.com; sadri@umsha.ac.ir

Faculties

Dentistry (Dentistry); **Health Sciences** (Health Sciences); **Medicine** (Medicine); **Nursing and Midwifery** (Midwifery; Nursing); **Paramedical Sciences** (Paramedical Sciences)

Further Information: Also Teaching Hospitals in: Imam, Ekbatan, Fatemeiah, Sina, Mobasher Kashani

History: Founded 1986. Previously part of Bou Ali Sina University.

Governing Bodies: Trustees appointed by Iranian President; University Council

Academic Year: September to May (September-January; January-May)

Admission Requirements: Secondary education certificate (Diploma) and entrance examination

Main Language(s) of Instruction: Farsi

Degrees and Diplomas: *Kardani (Associate degree)*: Science, 2 yrs; *Karshebasi (Bachelor's degree)*: Science (BA), 4 yrs; *Karshenasi Arshad (Master's degree)*: Science (MA), a further 2 yrs; *Doctorate*: Dentistry (DDS), 6 yrs; *Doctorate*: Medicine (MD), 7 yrs; *Doctorate*: Science, a further 3-4 yrs. Also High Diploma in Sciences, 2 yrs

Student Services: Canteen, Cultural centre, Employment services, Health services, Language programs, Social counselling, Sports facilities

Student Residential Facilities: Yes

Special Facilities: Movie studio

Libraries: Central Library, 33,000 vols, 12 specialized libraries

Publications: Journal of Public Health Sciences; Scientific Journal *(biannually)*

Last Updated: 17/12/08

HIGHER EDUCATION CENTRE FOR PUBLIC ADMINISTRATION

Tehran
Tel: +98(21) 889-0930-9
Fax: +98(21) 889-3887

Programmes

Public Administration (Public Administration)

Degrees and Diplomas: *Karshebasi (Bachelor's degree) (BA)*: 4 yrs; *Karshenasi Arshad (Master's degree) (MA)*: a further 2 yrs

HIGHER EDUCATION INSTITUTION OF IRANIAN BANKING

Tehran
Tel: +98(21) 284-9091
Fax: +98(21) 284-2618

Programmes

Banking (Banking)

Degrees and Diplomas: *Karshebasi (Bachelor's degree) (BA)*: 4 yrs; *Karshenasi Arshad (Master's degree) (MA)*: a further 2 yrs

HORMOZGAN UNIVERSITY

Ayatollah Ghafari Street, Bandar Abbas, Hormozgan
Tel: +98(761) 334-0121-5
Fax: +98(761) 333-7322
Website: http://www.hormozgan.ac.ir

President: J. Kambozia (1998-) Tel: +98(761) 399-90

Centres

Persian Gulf Studies (Middle Eastern Studies)

Faculties

Civil Engineering (Civil Engineering); **Industrial Engineering and Management** (Industrial Engineering; Industrial Management); **Mathematics** (Mathematics); **Mechanical Engineering** (Mechanical Engineering); **Persian Language and Literature and Humanities** (Arts and Humanities; Persian); **Physics** (Physics)

History: Founded 1992.

Academic Year: September to June (September-January; January-June)

Admission Requirements: Secondary school certificate and entrance examination

Fees: None

Main Language(s) of Instruction: Farsi, English

Degrees and Diplomas: *Karshebasi (Bachelor's degree) (BA; BSc)*: 4 yrs

Student Services: Canteen, Cultural centre, Social counselling, Sports facilities

Student Residential Facilities: For c. 100 students

Libraries: Central Library, 13,000 vols

Publications: Hormozgan *(quarterly)*

Last Updated: 15/12/08

HORMOZGAN UNIVERSITY OF MEDICAL SCIENCES (HUMS)

PO Box 3838, Shahid Chamran Blvd, Banda Abbas
Tel: +98(761) 333-7190
Fax: +98(761) 333-5009
EMail: bmch@hums.ac.ir; hums@hums.ac.ir
Website: http://www.hums.ac.ir

Chancellor: Abdolmahdi Araghizade (1998-)
Tel: +98(761) 333-4275, Fax: +98(761) 333-1991
EMail: araghizadeh@hums.ac.ir

Vice-Chancellor for Education and Research: Omid Safa
EMail: osafa@hums.ac.ir

Schools

Health (Health Sciences); **Medicine** (Medicine); **Nursing and Midwifery** (Midwifery; Nursing)

History: Founded 1983. Formerly Bandar Abbas University of Medical Sciences.

Academic Year: September to June

Main Language(s) of Instruction: Farsi, English

Degrees and Diplomas: *Kardani (Associate degree)*: 2 yrs; *Karshebasi (Bachelor's degree) (BA)*: 4 yrs; *Doctorate (PhD)*

Libraries:c. 8,000 vols

Last Updated: 17/12/08

ILAM UNIVERSITY

Daneshgah Ilam (IU)
Pajoohesh St., Ilam 69315-516
Tel: +98(841) 223-4850-54
Fax: +98(841) 222-7010
EMail: union.office@mail.ilam.ac.ir; intoffice@mail.ilam.ac.ir
Website: http://www.ilam.ac.ir/

Public Relations Officer: Aref Hashemi
Tel: +98(841) 222-7029, Fax: +98(841) 222-7029
EMail: arefhashemi@ilam.ac.ir

International Relations: Mahmoud Samaie
Tel: +98(841) 222-7061, Fax: +98(841) 222-7061
EMail: m.samaie@ilam.ac.ir

Colleges

Veterinary Medicine (Veterinary Science)

Faculties

Agriculture (Agricultural Equipment; Agriculture; Agronomy; Crop Production; Forestry; Horticulture; Vegetable Production); **Fundamental Science**; **Humanities, Science and Literature** (Accountancy; Arabic; Arts and Humanities; Economic and Finance Policy; Economics; English; Islamic Theology; Koran; Literature; Management; Persian; Philosophy; Social Sciences); **Technical Engineering** (Architecture; Civil Engineering; Computer Engineering; Computer Networks; Construction Engineering; Environmental Engineering; Road Engineering; Software Engineering)

History: Created 1985 as a Veterinary College - branch of Razi University. Acquired current status 2000.

Academic Year: September to July

Admission Requirements: Secondary school leaving certificate, entrance exam.

Fees: (Rials): 2,750,000 per semester, Masters; 700,000 per semester, Bachelors

Main Language(s) of Instruction: Farsi

Accrediting Agencies: Ministry of Science, Research and Technology

Degrees and Diplomas: *Karshebasi (Bachelor's degree) (Karshenasi)*: 4; *Karshenasi Arshad (Master's degree) (Karshenasi Arshad)*: 2; *Doctorate*

Student Services: Academic counselling, Cultural centre, Employment services, Health services, Nursery care, Social counselling, Sports facilities

Libraries: On-line Library

Academic Staff *2009-2010*: Total 136

STAFF WITH DOCTORATE: Total 74

Student Numbers *2009-2010*: Total 3,722

Evening students, 1,264.

Last Updated: 17/02/12

ILAM UNIVERSITY OF MEDICAL SCIENCES

Keshvari Square, Azadi Avenue, Ilam 69314
Tel: +98(841) 333-4060
Fax: +98(841) 333-4080
Website: http://www.medilam.ac.ir

Chancellor: A. Kaikhavandi (1991-)

Faculties

Medicine (Medicine); **Nursing and Midwifery** (Midwifery; Nursing); **Paramedical Sciences** (Paramedical Sciences)

Schools

Health (Health Sciences)

History: Founded 1986 as Faculty, acquired present status and title 1995.

Academic Year: September to June

Main Language(s) of Instruction: Farsi

Degrees and Diplomas: *Kardani (Associate degree)*: 2 yrs; *Karshebasi (Bachelor's degree) (BA)*: 4 yrs; *Karshenasi Arshad (Master's degree) (MA)*: a further 2 yrs; *Doctorate (PhD)*

Libraries: 7,720 vols

Publications: Ilam UMS Journal

IMAM KHOMEINI INTERNATIONAL UNIVERSITY

Daneshgahe Beynolmelalie Imam Khomeini (IKIU)

Imam Khomeini Boulevard, Qazvin 3414916818
Tel: +98(281) 3780041-2
Fax: +98(281) 3780-043
EMail: office@ikiu.ac.ir; pr.office@ikiu.ac.ir
Website: http://www.ikiu.ac.ir/

President: Abdolali Alebooyeh (2010-) EMail: president@ikiu.ac.ir

Deputy for Education: Seyed Mohammad Hakak

International Relations: Mohammad Hosseini Moghadam, Director of International Scientific and Collaboration Office
EMail: int.office@ikiu.ac.ir

Centres

Persian Language

Faculties

Architecture and Urbanism (Architecture; Heritage Preservation; Urban Studies); **Basic Sciences** (Chemistry; Geology; Mathematics; Natural Sciences; Physics; Statistics); **Islamic Theology and Knowledge** (Islamic Theology); **Literature and Humanities** (Arabic; Arts and Humanities; English; Persian; Philosophy; Translation and Interpretation); **Social Sciences** (Accountancy; Industrial Management; Law; Physical Education; Political Sciences; Psychology; Sports); **Technical Sciences and Engineering** (Agricultural Engineering; Civil Engineering; Computer Engineering; Electrical Engineering; Engineering; Materials Engineering; Mechanical Engineering; Mining Engineering; Technology)

History: Founded 1983.

Main Language(s) of Instruction: Farsi

International Co-operation: With universities in Russia; Turkey; India; Sudan; Malaysia; Afghanistan; Pakistan

Degrees and Diplomas: *Karshebasi (Bachelor's degree) (BA; BSc)*: 4 yrs; *Karshenasi Arshad (Master's degree) (MA; MSc)*: a further 2 yrs; *Doctorate*. Also Associate Degree

Student Services: Academic counselling, Canteen, Cultural centre, Foreign student adviser, Foreign Studies Centre, Health services, Language programs, Nursery care, Social counselling, Sports facilities

Libraries: Central Library

Student Numbers *2010-2011*: Total 6,877

Last Updated: 28/03/11

INSTITUTE FOR ADVANCED STUDIES IN BASIC SCIENCES, ZANJAN (IASBS)

PO Box 45195-1159, Zanjan 45195
Tel: +98(241) 415-2259
Fax: +98(241) 424-9023
EMail: iasbs_z@iasbs.ac.ir
Website: http://www.iasbs.ac.ir

Director: Yousef Sobouti (1992-)
Tel: +98(241) 424-9872 EMail: sobouti@iasbs.ac.ir

Deputy Director: Mohammad Reza Khajehpour
Tel: +98(241) 424-9874 EMail: pour@iasbs.ac.ir

International Relations: Ra'na Moghanlou
Tel: +98(241) 415-2255 EMail: moghanlou@iasbs.ac.ir

Departments

Biological Sciences (Biochemistry; Biology; Biophysics; Cell Biology; Molecular Biology); **Chemistry** (Analytical Chemistry; Chemistry; Inorganic Chemistry; Organic Chemistry; Physical Chemistry); **Earth Sciences** (Earth Sciences; Geophysics); **Information Technology** (Information Sciences; Information Technology); **Mathematics** (Applied Mathematics; Mathematics); **Physics** (Applied Physics; Astronomy and Space Science; Astrophysics; Optics; Physics; Solid State Physics)

History: Founded 1991.

Governing Bodies: Board of Trustees

Admission Requirements: High school diploma

Fees: Bachelor of Science (Yes); Master's and Doctorate Degree (None)

Main Language(s) of Instruction: Farsi, English

International Co-operation: With universities in France; Germany; United Kingdom; India; Italy; Hungary and Sweden

Accrediting Agencies: Ministry of Science, Research and Technology

Degrees and Diplomas: *Karshebasi (Bachelor's degree)*: Information Technology, 4-6 yrs; *Karshenasi Arshad (Master's degree)*: Chemistry; Geophysics; Mathematics; Physics (MS), 2-3 yrs; *Doctorate*: Chemistry; Mathematics; Physics (PhD), 3-4 yrs

Student Services: Academic counselling, Canteen, Language programs, Nursery care, Sports facilities

Student Residential Facilities: Yes

Special Facilities: Observatory

Libraries: Specialized Library, c. 18,000 vols

Last Updated: 02/12/11

INTERNATIONAL CENTRE FOR SCIENCE AND TECHNOLOGY AND ENVIRONMENTAL SCIENCES

Kerman
Tel: +98(341) 226-1771
Fax: +98(341) 226-1770
Website: http://www.icst.ac.ir/international/

Institutes

Energy (Energy Engineering); **Environmental Sciences** (Biotechnology; Ecology; Environmental Studies); **Materials and Metallurgy** (Materials Engineering; Metallurgical Engineering); **Photonics** (Laser Engineering; Nanotechnology)

History: Founded 1996.

Degrees and Diplomas: *Karshenasi Arshad (Master's degree) (MSc)*; *Doctorate (PhD)*

Last Updated: 02/12/11

IRAN UNIVERSITY OF MEDICAL SCIENCES AND HEALTH SERVICES

Daneshgah-e Oloom Pezeshki va Khadamat-e Behdashti Darmani-e Iran (IUMS)

P.O. Box 15875-6171, Crossroads of Shahid Hemmat and Shahid Chamran Expressways, Tehran 1449614535
Tel: +98(21) 8805-2263
Fax: +98(21) 8805-4393
EMail: ofintrel@iums.ac.ir
Website: http://www.iums.ac.ir/

Chancellor: Seyed Ali Abtahi
Tel: +98(21) 8805-2234, Fax: +98(21) 8805-2235

Vice-Chancellor for Academic Affairs: S.J. Esmaeil
Tel: +98(21) 8805-2239, Fax: +98(21) 8805-2240

Director, Office of Public Relations: Ahmad Joneidi Jafari
Tel: +98(21) 8805-2238, Fax: +98(21) 8805-8675
EMail: pubrel@iums.ac.ir

International Relations: Mohsen Asadi-Lari, Director, Office of International Relations

Institutes

Endocrinology and Metabolism (Endocrinology); **Psychiatry** *(Teheran)* (Behavioural Sciences; Clinical Psychology; Psychiatry and Mental Health)

Research Centres

Cellular and Molecular Sciences *(CMSRC)* (Biomedicine; Cell Biology; Molecular Biology); **Medical Laboratory Sciences Research and Education** (Laboratory Techniques); **Otorhinolaryngology - Head and Neck Surgery** (Otorhinolaryngology; Surgery)

Research Institutes

Medical History, Islamic and Complementary Medicine (Ethics; Medicine)

Schools

Allied Medical Sciences (Anaesthesiology; Laboratory Techniques; Paramedical Sciences; Radiology); **Management and Medical Information Science** (Health Administration; Information Management; Statistics); **Medicine** (Medicine); **Nursing and Midwifery** (Midwifery; Nursing); **Public Health** (Environmental Studies; Health Education; Nutrition; Occupational Health; Public Health); **Rehabilitation Sciences** (Occupational Therapy; Optometry; Orthopaedics; Physical Therapy; Speech Therapy and Audiology)

Further Information: Also 10 Teaching Hospitals

History: Founded 1974 through the merger of several Health and Medical Centres as well as Iran Medical Centre and Ayatollah Taleghani School of Medicine after the newly formed Ministry of Health 1986. A State institution affiliated to the Ministry of Health and Medical Education.

Governing Bodies: Board of Trustees; University Council; Administrative Board

Academic Year: September to July (September-February; March-July)

Admission Requirements: Secondary school certificate and entrance examination

Fees: None

Main Language(s) of Instruction: Farsi

Degrees and Diplomas: *Kardani (Associate degree) (AS)*: 2 yrs; *Karshebasi (Bachelor's degree) (BS)*: 4 yrs; *Karshenasi Arshad (Master's degree) (MS)*: 3 yrs; *Doctorate (PhD)*: 3 yrs; *Doctorate*: Medicine (MD), 7 yrs

Student Services: Academic counselling, Canteen, Foreign Studies Centre, Language programs, Social counselling, Sports facilities

Student Residential Facilities: For 2500dents

Libraries: 45,244 vols; 3,681 periodicals; 14,825 theses and dissertations

Publications: Annals of Iranian Medicine, Medical Education and Research *(quarterly)*; Five Star Doctor, Continuing education *(quarterly)*; Iran Journal of Nursing *(quarterly)*; Iranian Journal of Pharmacology and Therapeutics, Online *(quarterly)*; Journal of IUMS *(quarterly)*; Journal of Medical Management *(quarterly)*; Journal of the Medical Laboratory Sciences Research Centre *(quarterly)*; Medical Education *(quarterly)*; Rehabilitation Message *(quarterly)*; Thought and Behaviour, Research, Psychology and Psychiatry *(quarterly)*

Last Updated: 01/12/11

IRAN UNIVERSITY OF SCIENCE AND TECHNOLOGY (IUST)

Hengum Street, Resalat Square, Tehran 1684613114
Tel: +98(21) 772-40303
Fax: +98(21) 774-91031
EMail: interiust@iust.ac.ir
Website: http://www.iust.ac.ir

Chancellor: Mohammad Saeed Jabalameli (2006-)
Tel: +98(21) 772-40400, Fax: +98(21) 772-40405
EMail: chancellor@iust.ac.ir

Vice-Chancellor for Administration and Financial Affairs: Bijan Ghaffari Tel: +98(21) 772-40411 EMail: bijan_ghafary@iust.ac.ir

International Relations: Hadi Khoramishad, Director, Office of International and Scientific Cooperation
EMail: khoramishad@iust.ac.ir

Campuses

IUST Arak Branch (Electrical Engineering; Mechanical Engineering; Mining Engineering; Power Engineering; Surveying and Mapping); **IUST Behshahr Branch** (Applied Mathematics; Computer Engineering; Industrial Engineering; Software Engineering)

Centres

Centre of Excellence for Advanced Matetials Processing (Materials Engineering); **Centre of Excellence for Fundamental Studies in Structural Engineering** (Structural Architecture); **Centre of Excellence for Power Systems Automation and Operation** (Automation and Control Engineering); **E-Learning** (Architecture; Chemical Engineering; Chemistry; Computer Engineering; Industrial Engineering; Information Technology; Physical Chemistry; Software Engineering; Systems Analysis; Urban Studies)

Departments

Chemistry (Analytical Chemistry; Chemistry; Inorganic Chemistry; Organic Chemistry; Physical Chemistry); **Foreign Languages** (English; Foreign Languages Education); **Islamic Studies** (Islamic Studies; Persian; Theology); **Physical Education** (Physical Education)

Research Centres

Asphalt Mixtures and Bitumen (Materials Engineering); **Automotive Engineering** (Automotive Engineering); **Cement**; **Electronics** (Electronic Engineering); **Green Research Centre** (Ecology; Environmental Management; Environmental Studies); **Information Technology** (Information Technology); **Iran Aluminium** (Materials Engineering); **Iran Composite Institute**; **IUST Technology Incubator** (Technology); **Transport** (Transport and Communications)

Schools

Architecture and Environmental Design (Architecture; Industrial Design; Regional Planning; Town Planning); **Automotive Engineering** (Automotive Engineering); **Chemical Engineering** (Chemical Engineering; Engineering Management; Inorganic Chemistry; Thermal Physics); **Civil Engineering** (Civil Engineering; Construction Engineering; Engineering Management; Hydraulic Engineering; Seismology; Soil Science; Transport Engineering; Water Science); **Computer Engineering** (Artificial Intelligence; Computer Engineering; Electronic Engineering; Information Technology; Software Engineering); **Electrical Engineering** (Automation and Control Engineering; Biomedical Engineering; Computer Engineering; Electrical Engineering; Electronic Engineering; Power Engineering); **Industrial Engineering** (Engineering Management; Industrial Engineering; Management; Systems Analysis); **Mathematics** (Applied Mathematics; Mathematics; Statistics); **Mechanical Engineering** (Aeronautical and Aerospace Engineering; Automation and Control Engineering; Energy Engineering; Mechanical Engineering; Mechanics; Metal Techniques; Physics); **Metallurgy and Materials Engineering** (Ceramics and Glass Technology; Materials Engineering; Metallurgical Engineering); **Physics** (Atomic and Molecular Physics; Nuclear Physics; Physics; Solid State Physics); **Railway Engineering** (Railway Engineering; Railway Transport; Safety Engineering)

History: Founded 1929 as technical school, acquired present status and title 1978. A State institution responsible to the Ministry of Science, Research and Technology.

Governing Bodies: Board of Trustees

Academic Year: September to June (September-January; February-June)

Admission Requirements: Secondary school certificate and national entrance examination

Fees: For e-learning and evening programmes.

Main Language(s) of Instruction: Farsi

International Co-operation: With institutions in Australia, China, France, Germany, India, Italy, Japan, Russian Federation, Tajikistan, Ukraine, UK.

Accrediting Agencies: Ministry of Science, Research and Technology

Degrees and Diplomas: *Karshebasi (Bachelor's degree)*: Architecture (BArch); Science; Engineering (BSc), 4-6 yrs; *Karshenasi Arshad (Master's degree)*: Architecture (MArch); Science; Engineering (MSc), a further 2-3 yrs; *Doctorate*: Engineering; Science; Architecture (PhD), a further 4-5 yrs

Student Services: Academic counselling, Canteen, Cultural centre, Foreign student adviser, Foreign Studies Centre, Handicapped facilities, Health services, Language programs, Nursery care, Social counselling, Sports facilities

Student Residential Facilities: Female, male and family dormitories.

Special Facilities: Masjid. Amphitheatre. Museum. Movie Studio. Counselling Centre. Online book store

Libraries: c. 42,800 publications; c. 11,000 journals; 15,000 digital books; 15 satellite libraries

Publications: Comprehensive English Bulletin of University *(annually)*; International Journal of Civil Engineering, in English *(quarterly)*; International Journal of Engineering, in Farsi and English *(quarterly)*; Iranian Journal of Electrical Engineering, in English *(quarterly)*; Iranian Journal of Materials Science and Engineering, in English *(quarterly)*; Proceedings, For each department; Research News, in Farsi *(annually)*

Press or Publishing House: University Central Publication Centre

Academic Staff *2009-2010*	MEN	WOMEN	**TOTAL**
FULL-TIME	341	23	**364**
STAFF WITH DOCTORATE			
FULL-TIME	303	16	**319**
Student Numbers *2011-2012*			
All (Foreign Included)	–	–	**12,189**

Note: statistics for main campus.

Last Updated: 02/12/11

ISFAHAN UNIVERSITY OF MEDICAL SCIENCES

Daneshgahe Oloom Pezeshki Isfahan (IUMS)

Hezar Jerib Avenue, Azadi Square, Isfahan, 81745 Isfahan

Tel: +98(311) 668-5141

Fax: +98(311) 668-5145

EMail: webmaster@mui.ac.ir

Website: http://www.mui.ac.ir

Chancellor: Sh. Shirani (2005-)
Tel: +98(311) 792-2011 EMail: shirani@mui.ac.ir

Administrative Officer: Mehran Harirchian
Tel: +98(311) 792-2118

International Relations: Amir Zargarzadeh
Tel: +98(311) 792-3077 EMail: international@mui.ac.ir

Faculties

Dentistry (Dentistry); **Health Sciences** (Epidemiology; Health Education; Health Sciences; Nutrition; Occupational Health); **Management and Medical Information** (Management); **Medicine** (Medicine); **Nursing and Midwifery** (Midwifery; Nursing); **Pharmacy and Pharmaceutical Sciences** (Biochemistry; Pharmacology; Pharmacy; Toxicology); **Rehabilitation Sciences** (Occupational Therapy; Orthopaedics; Physical Therapy; Rehabilitation and Therapy)

History: Founded 1986. Previously part of the University of Isfahan (1946-1985).

Governing Bodies: Board of Trustees

Academic Year: September to July

Admission Requirements: High school certificate and national entrance examination

Fees: None

Main Language(s) of Instruction: Farsi

Accrediting Agencies: Ministry of Health and Medical Education

Degrees and Diplomas: *Kardani (Associate degree)*: 2 yrs; *Karshebasi (Bachelor's degree) (BA; BS)*: 4 yrs; *Karshenasi Arshad (Master's degree)*: Parasitology, Microbiology, Immunology, Histiology, Anatomy, Physiology, Medical Physics, Medical Technology, Midwifery, Biochemistry, Environmental Engineering, Public Health, Nursing (MS), 2-3 yrs; *Doctorate*: Dentistry (DDS); Pharmacy (PharmD), 6 yrs; *Doctorate*: Environmental Health, Microbiology, Parasitology, Anatomy, Physiology, Pharmacology, Pharmaceutics, Pharmacognosy, Biochemistry, Medical Chemistry (PhD), a further 3-5 yrs; *Doctorate*: Medicine (MD), 7 yrs

Student Services: Academic counselling, Canteen, Cultural centre, Employment services, Foreign student adviser, Foreign Studies Centre, Handicapped facilities, Health services, Language programs, Nursery care, Social counselling, Sports facilities

Student Residential Facilities: Yes

Libraries: 17 Libraries, total, 26,741 vols; 1,113 periodicals

Publications: Atherosclerosis *(quarterly)*; Dental Research Journal *(quarterly)*; Journal of Dentistry *(quarterly)*; Journal of Health *(quarterly)*; Journal of Isfahan Medical School, Original Research Articles *(quarterly)*; Journal of Management and Information in Health *(quarterly)*; Journal of Research in Behaviourial Sciences *(quarterly)*; Journal of Research in Medical Sciences, Original Articles *(quarterly)*; Journal of Research in Pharmaceutical Sciences; Journal of Research in Rehabilitation *(quarterly)*

Last Updated: 01/12/11

ISFAHAN UNIVERSITY OF TECHNOLOGY (IUT)

Isfahan 84154
Tel: +98(311) 391-2210
Fax: +98(311) 391-3112
EMail: Evp@of.iut.ac.ir
Website: http://www.iut.ac.ir

President: Gholam-Reza Ghorbani
Tel: +98(311) 391-3200, Fax: +98(311) 391-2345

Colleges

Agriculture (Agricultural Equipment; Agriculture; Agronomy; Animal Husbandry; Food Science; Plant and Crop Protection; Soil Science)

Departments

Chemical Engineering (Chemical Engineering); **Chemistry** (Chemistry); **Civil Engineering** (Civil Engineering; Environmental Engineering); **Electrical and Computer Engineering** (Computer Engineering; Electrical Engineering); **Industrial Engineering** (Industrial Engineering; Industrial Management); **Materials Engineering** (Materials Engineering); **Mathematical Sciences** (Mathematics); **Mechanical Engineering** (Mechanical Engineering); **Mining Engineering** (Mining Engineering); **Natural Resources** (Environmental Studies; Fishery; Natural Resources; Water Management); **Physics** (Physics); **Textile Engineering** (Textile Technology)

Research Centres

Electrical and Computer Engineering (Computer Engineering; Electrical Engineering); **Sub-sea Studies** (Marine Science and Oceanography)

History: Founded 1974. A State institution responsible to the Ministry of Higher Education and Culture.

Academic Year: October to June (October-January; February-June)

Admission Requirements: Secondary school certificate and entrance examination

Fees: None

Main Language(s) of Instruction: Farsi

Degrees and Diplomas: *Karshebasi (Bachelor's degree) (BA; BSc)*: 5 yrs; *Karshenasi Arshad (Master's degree) (MA; MSc)*: a further 2 yrs; *Doctorate (PhD)*

Student Residential Facilities: Yes

Libraries: Central Library, c. 451,000 vols

Last Updated: 02/12/11

JAHROM UNIVERSITY OF MEDICAL SCIENCES

Shahid M. Motahari Street, Jahrom
Tel: +98(791) 444-7760
Fax: +98(791) 444-9003
EMail: info@jums.ac.ir
Website: http://www.jums.ac.ir

Chancellor: Bahram Hasanshahi (1993-)

Faculties

Dentistry (Dentistry); **Health Sciences** (Health Sciences); **Medicine** (Medicine); **Nursing and Midwifery** (Midwifery; Nursing); **Paramedical Sciences** (Paramedical Sciences); **Pharmacy** (Pharmacy)

Further Information: Shahid Motahari Hospital, Shahid Motahari Polyclinic, 5 Health Centres in Towns and 17 Health Centres in Villages

History: Founded 1978.

Academic Year: September to June

Main Language(s) of Instruction: Farsi

Degrees and Diplomas: *Kardani (Associate degree)*: 2 yrs; *Doctorate (PhD)*

Libraries: 6,476 vols

KASHAN UNIVERSITY OF MEDICAL SCIENCES AND HEALTH SERVICES

PO Box 87155-111, 15th Khordad Square, Abazar Street, Kashan
Tel: +98(361) 444-3022-5
Fax: +98(361) 555-6112
EMail: setad@kaums.ac.ir
Website: http://www.kaums.ac.ir

Chancellor: Mohammad Hossein A'arabi
EMail: presidentoffice@kaums.ac.ir

Vice-Chancellor for Logistics: Mehrdad Farzandipour
Tel: +98(361) 444-055 EMail: logistic@kaums.ac.ir

Faculties

Health Sciences (Health Sciences; Occupational Health; Public Health); **Medicine** (Medicine); **Nursing and Midwifery** (Midwifery; Nursing); **Paramedical Sciences** (Anaesthesiology; Laboratory Techniques; Paramedical Sciences; Radiology)

Further Information: Also 5 Teaching Hospitals. Part-time courses in Medical Sciences

History: Founded 1986. Acquired present status and title 1993.

Governing Bodies: Board of Governors

Academic Year: September to June

Admission Requirements: Secondary school certificate and entrance examination

Fees: None

Main Language(s) of Instruction: Farsi, English

Degrees and Diplomas: *Kardani (Associate degree)*: Sciences, 2 yrs; *Karshebasi (Bachelor's degree)*: Sciences (BA), 4 yrs; *Professional Doctorate*: Medicine, 7 yrs

Student Services: Health services, Language programs, Social counselling, Sports facilities

Student Residential Facilities: For c. 1,080 students

Libraries: Central Library, c. 20,790 vols

Publications: Fyze, Scientific Journal *(quarterly)*

Last Updated: 02/12/11

KERMAN MEDICAL UNIVERSITY (KUMS)

Jomhori Islami Boulevard, Kerman, 76175-584 Kerman
Tel: +98(341) 211-3192-4
Fax: +98(341) 211-3195
EMail: info@kmu.ac.ir
Website: http://www.kmu.ac.ir

Chancellor: Iraj Sharifi (1999-)
Tel: +98(341) 213-025 EMail: sharifi@kmu.ac.ir

Vice-Chancellor for Administrative Affairs: Mohammad Malakoutian Tel: +98(341) 214-930, Fax: +98(341) 213-708

International Relations: Maryam Nazaryan
Tel: +98(341) 214-538, Fax: +98(341) 212-794

Faculties

Dentistry (Dentistry); **Health Sciences** (Health Sciences); **Management and Information Science** (Information Sciences; Management); **Medicine** (Medicine); **Nursing** *(Jiroft: Fereidoon Afzali)* (Nursing); **Nursing** *(Bam: Abbas Abbaszadeh)* (Nursing); **Nursing and Midwifery** (Midwifery; Nursing); **Paramedical Sciences** (Paramedical Sciences); **Pharmacy** (Pharmacy)

Research Centres

Diabetes Research; **Medicine** (Medicine)

History: Founded 1977. Previously part of Martyr Bahonar University. Acquired present status 1986.

Academic Year: September to June

Main Language(s) of Instruction: Farsi

Degrees and Diplomas: *Kardani (Associate degree)*: 2 yrs; *Karshebasi (Bachelor's degree) (BA)*: 4 yrs; *Karshenasi Arshad (Master's degree) (MA)*: 6 yrs; *Doctorate (PhD)*

Student Services: Canteen, Sports facilities

Student Residential Facilities: Yes

Special Facilities: Movie studio

Libraries: c. 20,000 vols; 500 journal titles

Publications: Journal of Kerman University of Medical Sciences *(quarterly)*
Last Updated: 02/12/11

KERMANSHAH UNIVERSITY OF MEDICAL SCIENCES

Shaheed Beheshti Boulevard, Kermanshah 67146
Tel: +98(831) 835-4434
Fax: +98(831) 835-6433
EMail: administration@kums.ac.ir
Website: http://www.kums.ac.ir

Chancellor: Samad Nourizad

Schools

Dentistry (Dentistry); **Health** (Epidemiology; Health Sciences; Nutrition; Occupational Health; Public Health; Statistics); **Medicine** (Medicine); **Nursing** (Midwifery; Nursing); **Paramedics** (Anaesthesiology; Laboratory Techniques; Radiology); **Pharmacy** (Pharmacology)

History: Founded 1974.

Academic Year: September to June
Main Language(s) of Instruction: Farsi

Degrees and Diplomas: *Kardani (Associate degree)*: 2 yrs; *Karshebasi (Bachelor's degree) (BA)*: 4 yrs; *Karshenasi Arshad (Master's degree) (MA)*: a further 2 yrs; *Doctorate (PhD)*

Libraries: Central Library

Publications: Journal of Kermanshah College of N.M. and Paramedicine
Last Updated: 02/12/11

K.N. TOOSI UNIVERSITY OF TECHNOLOGY

Daneshgah-e-Khajeh Nassir-o-diné Toosi (KNTU)
PO Box 15875-4416, 470 Mirdamad Avenue West, Tehran 19697
Tel: +98(21) 8888-1003
Fax: +98(21) 8888-2997
EMail: oisc@kntu.ac.ir
Website: http://www.kntu.ac.ir

President: Majid Ghassemi
Tel: +98(21) 8888-3001, Fax: +98(21) 8879-7469
EMail: ghasemi@kntu.ac.ir

Vice-Chancellor for Academic Affairs: Saadn Zokaie
Tel: +98(21) 8879-7280, Fax: +98(21) 8888-1065
EMail: szokaei@eetd.kntu.ac.ir

International Relations: Hamid Taghirad, Director, Office of International and Scientific Cooperation
Tel: +98(21) 8888-1003, Fax: +98(21) 8888-1003
EMail: taghirad@kntu.ac.ir;

Faculties

Aerospace Engineering (Aeronautical and Aerospace Engineering; Astronomy and Space Science); **Civil Engineering** (Civil Engineering; Hydraulic Engineering; Marine Engineering; Road Engineering; Road Transport; Soil Science; Water Science); **Electrical Engineering** (Automation and Control Engineering; Biomedical Engineering; Computer Engineering; Electrical Engineering; Electronic Engineering; Power Engineering; Telecommunications Engineering); **Geodesy and Geomatics** (Earth Sciences; Measurement and Precision Engineering; Surveying and Mapping); **Industrial Engineering** (E-Business/Commerce; Industrial Engineering; Systems Analysis; Technology); **Mechanical Engineering** (Automotive Engineering; Electronic Engineering; Energy Engineering; Materials Engineering; Mechanical Engineering; Production Engineering); **Science** (Chemistry; English; Mathematics; Physical Education; Physics)

Research Centres

Boilers Technology; **Chemistry** (Chemistry); **Communication** (Communication Studies); **Control and Robotics** (Automation and Control Engineering; Robotics); **Materials Behaviour**; **Water Resources** (Water Management)

History: Founded 1928 as Institute of Communications. Acquired present title 1984.

Governing Bodies: Board of Trustees; University Council

Academic Year: September to June (September-February; February-June)

Admission Requirements: Secondary school certificate and entrance examination (Diplom & Konkoor)

Main Language(s) of Instruction: Farsi, English

International Co-operation: With universities in United Kingdom, Netherlands, Russian Federation, Germany and France. Also cooperates with IAESTE

Degrees and Diplomas: *Karshebasi (Bachelor's degree)*: Science; Engineering (BA; BSc) (Karshenasi), 4 yrs; *Karshenasi Arshad (Master's degree)*: Science; Engineering (MA; MSc) (Karshenasi Arshad), a further 1 1/2-2 1/2 yrs; *Doctorate*: Science; Engineering (PhD), 3-5 yrs

Student Services: Academic counselling, Canteen, Cultural centre, Employment services, Health services, Social counselling, Sports facilities

Student Residential Facilities: For c. 1,000 students

Special Facilities: Computer Centre

Libraries: Total: c. 67,000 vols

Publications: Olum-o-Mohandesi-e-Nasir *(quarterly)*

Press or Publishing House: K.N.Toosi University Publishing House
Last Updated: 04/04/08

KURDISTAN UNIVERSITY OF MEDICAL SCIENCES

Pasdaran Avenue, Sanandaj 66-35-494
Tel: +98(871) 328-7101
Fax: +98(871) 323-3600
Website: http://www.muk.ac.ir

Chancellor: Hamid Derafshi (1993-)

Schools

Health Sciences (Health Sciences); **Medicine** (Medicine); **Nursing and Midwifery** (Midwifery; Nursing); **Paramedical Sciences** (Paramedical Sciences)

History: Founded 1986 as Institute, became College 1989 and acquired present status and title 1992.

Main Language(s) of Instruction: Farsi

Degrees and Diplomas: *Kardani (Associate degree)*: 2 yrs; *Karshebasi (Bachelor's degree) (BA)*: 4 yrs; *Doctorate (PhD)*

Libraries: c. 8,000 vols

Publications: Journal of Kurdistan University of Medical Sciences; Scientific Quarterly (Student Scientific Research Centre)
Last Updated: 05/12/11

LORESTAN UNIVERSITY

PO Box 465, Falakol' Aflak Street, Khoramabad
Tel: +98(661) 250-58-9
Fax: +98(661) 227-82
Website: http://www.lu.ac.ir/

Chancellor: Reza Sadeghi Sarabi

Faculties

Agriculture (Agriculture; Agronomy; Animal Husbandry; Natural Resources; Plant and Crop Protection); **Basic Science** (Biology; Chemistry; Geology; Mathematics; Natural Sciences; Physics); **Literature and Humanities** (Arts and Humanities; English; History; Literature; Persian); **Veterinary Medicine** (Veterinary Science)

History: Founded 1977.

Main Language(s) of Instruction: Farsi

Degrees and Diplomas: *Kardani (Associate degree)*: 2 yrs; *Karshebasi (Bachelor's degree) (BA; BSc)*: 4 yrs; *Karshenasi Arshad (Master's degree) (MA; MSc)*: a further 2 yrs
Last Updated: 17/12/08

LORESTAN UNIVERSITY OF MEDICAL SCIENCES

Shafa Street, Khoramabad 68138
Tel: +98(661) 221-49 +98(661) 220-30
Fax: +98(661) 220-30
EMail: publicrelation@lums.ac.ir
Website: http://www.lums.ac.ir

Chancellor: Qodratollah Shams Khorramabadi

Faculties

Health Sciences (Health Sciences); **Medicine** (Medicine); **Nursing** *(Aligoodarz)* (Nursing); **Nursing and Midwifery** (Midwifery; Nursing); **Pharmacy** (Pharmacy)

History: Founded 1991.

Academic Year: September to July

Main Language(s) of Instruction: Farsi, English

Degrees and Diplomas: *Kardani (Associate degree)*: 2 yrs; *Karshebasi (Bachelor's degree) (BA)*: 4 yrs; *Doctorate (PhD)*

Libraries: c. 5,000 vols

Publications: Quarterly Journal

Last Updated: 17/12/08

MALEK ASHTAR UNIVERSITY OF TECHNOLOGY

Isfahan
EMail: international@mut.ac.ir
Website: http://www.mut.ac.ir

Faculties

Aerospace Engineering (Aeronautical and Aerospace Engineering); **Applied Sciences** (Applied Chemistry; Applied Mathematics; Applied Physics); **Electrical and Electronic Engineering** (Electrical and Electronic Engineering); **Information, Communication and Security Technologies** (Communication Studies; Information Technology; Safety Engineering); **Management and Industrial Engineering** (Industrial Engineering; Management); **Marine Sciences and Engineering** (Marine Engineering; Marine Science and Oceanography); **Materials and Manufacturing Technologies** (Materials Engineering)

History: Founded 1986.

Main Language(s) of Instruction: Farsi

Degrees and Diplomas: *Karshebasi (Bachelor's degree)*; *Karshenasi Arshad (Master's degree)*; *Doctorate*

Last Updated: 19/12/08

MASHHAD UNIVERSITY OF MEDICAL SCIENCES

Daneshgahe Oloom Pezeshki Mashhad (MUMS)
PO Box 91735-346, Daneshgah Street, Mashhad, Khorasan
Tel: +98(511) 841-2081-3
Fax: +98(511) 841-3006
EMail: Presidentoffice@mums.ac.ir
Website: http://www.mums.ac.ir

President: Mahmood Mohammadzade Shabestari
Tel: +98(511) 841-3007 EMail: ShabestariM@mums.ac.ir

Vice-Chancellor for Education: Farshid Abedi
EMail: AbediF@mums.ac.ir

Faculties

Dentistry (Dentistry; Oral Pathology; Orthodontics; Paediatrics; Periodontics; Radiology; Surgery); **Medicine** (Anaesthesiology; Cardiology; Dermatology; Gynaecology and Obstetrics; Medicine; Neurology; Pathology; Psychiatry and Mental Health; Radiology); **Nursing and Midwifery** (Anaesthesiology; Midwifery; Nursing); **Paramedical Sciences** (Optometry; Paramedical Sciences; Radiology); **Pharmacy** (Pharmacology; Pharmacy)

Further Information: Faculties of Torbat, Neyshabour and Bojnoured are supervised by MUMS

History: Founded 1949. Previously part of the University of Mashhad.

Academic Year: September to June

Admission Requirements: High school diploma and pass in Higher Education National Exam held by the Iranian Ministry of Higher Education

Main Language(s) of Instruction: Farsi

International Co-operation: With universities in USA, China, France and Canada.

Accrediting Agencies: Ministry of Health Medicine and Medical Education

Degrees and Diplomas: *Kardani (Associate degree)*: Operating Room Technician; Anaesthesiology; Health Sciences; Medical Record; Radiology; Lab Technology; Emergency Technician, 2 yrs; *Karshebasi (Bachelor's degree)*: Nursing; Midwifery; Optometry; Health Sciences; Lab Technology; Radiology (BA), 4 yrs; *Karshenasi Arshad (Master's degree)*: Nursing (Education Management); Paediatrics; Psychiatric and Community Health; Midwifery (Education and Maternity Health); Biophysics; Parasitology; Anatomy; Physiology; Microbiology; Toxicology (MA), 2 yrs; *Doctorate*: Dental Surgery (DDS), 6 yrs; *Doctorate*: Medicine (MD), 7 yrs; *Doctorate*: Parasitology; Anatomy; Physiology; Immunology; Pharmacology; Biophysics; Drug Biotechnology (PhD), 3 yrs; *Doctorate*: Pharmacy (PharmD), 5 yrs

Student Services: Academic counselling, Canteen, Cultural centre, Employment services, Foreign student adviser, Foreign Studies Centre, Handicapped facilities, Health services, Language programs, Nursery care, Social counselling, Sports facilities

Student Residential Facilities: Yes (Female students: 770; Male students: 600)

Special Facilities: Computer room

Libraries: c. 200,913 vols, c. 1,095 journals

Publications: Computer in Medicine *(quarterly)*; Iranian Journal of Basic Medical Sciences *(quarterly)*; Journal of Mashhad Dental School *(quarterly)*; Medical Journal *(quarterly)*; Secrets of living healthy *(quarterly)*; The Iranian Journal of Obstetrics, Gynaecology and Infertility *(biannually)*; The Iranian Journal of Otorhinolaryngology *(biannually)*; The Scientific and Research Journal of Mashhad Nursing-Midwifery School *(quarterly)*

Last Updated: 01/12/11

MAZANDARAN UNIVERSITY

Daneshgahe Mazandaran (UMZ)
PO Box 416, Pasdaran Street, Babolsar 47415
Tel: +98(11252) 32091-95
Fax: +98(11252) 32017-33702
EMail: webadmin@umz.ac.ir
Website: http://www.umz.ac.ir

Chancellor: Ahmad Ahmadpour Kasgari
Tel: +98(11252) 325-00 EMail: ahmadpour@umz.ac.ir

Faculties

Art and Architecture (Architecture; Handicrafts; Town Planning); **Basic Sciences** (Analytical Chemistry; Applied Chemistry; Applied Mathematics; Biology; Chemistry; Inorganic Chemistry; Mathematics; Natural Sciences; Organic Chemistry; Physical Chemistry; Physics; Polymer and Plastics Technology; Statistics); **Chemistry** (Analytical Chemistry; Chemistry; Inorganic Chemistry; Organic Chemistry); **Economics and Administration** (Accountancy; Business Administration; Economics; Industrial Management); **Engineering and Technology** (Chemical Engineering; Civil Engineering; Electronic Engineering; Engineering; Mechanical Engineering; Power Engineering); **Humanities and Social Sciences** (Accountancy; Anthropology; Arts and Humanities; Business and Commerce; Criminal Law; Economics; English; Geography; Industrial Management; Islamic Theology; Koran; Law; Literature; Management; Persian; Physical Education; Private Law; Social Sciences); **Law and Political Science** (Law; Political Sciences); **Physical Education and Sports** (Physical Education; Sports); **Theology** (Islamic Law; Islamic Theology; Koran; Theology); **Veterinary Medicine** (Veterinary Science)

History: Founded 1979 incorporating previously existing institutions in the Province. A State institution responsible to the Ministry of Higher Education and Culture.

Governing Bodies: University Council

Academic Year: September to June

Admission Requirements: Secondary school certificate and entrance examination

Main Language(s) of Instruction: Farsi

Degrees and Diplomas: *Kardani (Associate degree)*: Agricultural Equipment, 2 yrs; *Karshebasi (Bachelor's degree)*: Accountancy; Chemical Engineering; Civil Engineering; Electronic Engineering; Power Engineering; Mechanical Engineering; Biology; Chemistry; Mathematics; Statistics; Physics; Farsi; English; Physical Education; Industrial Management; Economics; Law (BSc; BA); Geography; Social Sciences; Koran; Islamic Theology; Agriculture; Agronomy; Animal Husbandry; Horticulture; Irrigation; Plant Pathology; Soil Sciences; Agricultural Equipment; Forestry; Fishery; Water Management; Handicrafts; Town Planning (BSc; BA), 4 yrs; *Karshenasi Arshad (Master's degree)*: Agriculture; Agronomy; Animal Husbandry; Mechanical Engineering; Chemical Engineering; Electronic Engineering; Power Engineering; Civil Engineering; Environmental Engineering; Economics; Private Law; Criminal Law; Accountancy; Management; Forestry (MSc; MA); Water Management; Irrigation; Chemistry; Mathematics; Physics (MSc; MA), a further 2 yrs; *Doctorate*: Analytical Chemistry; Physical Chemistry; Organic Chemistry; Economics (PhD), 4 yrs

Student Services: Academic counselling, Canteen, Cultural centre, Handicapped facilities, Health services, Language programs, Social counselling, Sports facilities

Student Residential Facilities: Yes

Special Facilities: Observatory. Movie Studios

Libraries: Central Library, c. 55,000 vols; also faculty libraries

Publications: Journal of Humanities and Social Sciences *(quarterly)*

Press or Publishing House: Mazandaran University Press

Last Updated: 01/12/11

MAZANDARAN UNIVERSITY OF MEDICAL SCIENCES

Valie-Asr Boulevard, Sari, 4815733971 Mazandaran
Tel: +98(151) 226-2140
Fax: +98(151) 226-2370
EMail: jmums@mazums.ac.ir
Website: http://www.mazums.ac.ir/

Chancellor: Mohammad Mahdi Nasehi

Faculties

Health Sciences (Health Sciences); **Nursing and Midwifery** (Midwifery; Nursing); **Paramedical Sciences** (Paramedical Sciences); **Pharmacy** (Pharmacy)

Schools

Medicine (Medicine)

History: Founded 1988. Acquired present status 1995.

Admission Requirements: Secondary school certificate and entrance examination

Main Language(s) of Instruction: Farsi

Degrees and Diplomas: *Karshebasi (Bachelor's degree) (BD)*: 4 yrs; *Professional Doctorate*: Medicine (MD), 7 yrs; *Karshenasi Arshad (Master's degree) (MSc)*: 2 yrs; *Doctorate*: Pharmacy (PhD), 6 yrs

Student Services: Academic counselling, Health services, Language programs, Sports facilities

Libraries: Yes

Publications: Journal of Mazandaran University of Medical Sciences *(biennially)*; Mazandaran Journal of Medicine *(quarterly)*

Last Updated: 05/12/11

PAYAME NOOR UNIVERSITY (DISTANCE EDUCATION) (PNU)

PO Box 19395-4697, Lashkarak Road, Tehran, 19395 Tehran
Tel: +98(21) 244-2042
Fax: +98(21) 244-1511
EMail: webmaster@pnu.ac.ir
Website: http://www.pnu.ac.ir

President: Hassan Ziari
Tel: +98(21) 244-0925, Fax: +98(21) 244-2052

Faculties

Agricultural Sciences (Agricultural Economics; Agricultural Equipment; Agriculture; Animal Husbandry; Biotechnology; Environmental Engineering; Fishery; Food Science; Rural Planning; Soil Science; Water Science); **Art and Media** (Ceramic Art; Fine Arts; Glass Art; Handicrafts; Interior Design; Journalism; Library Science; Media Studies; Painting and Drawing; Photography; Public Relations; Textile Design; Town Planning); **Economics and Social Sciences** (Accountancy; Business Administration; Economics; Political Sciences; Public Administration; Social Sciences; Tourism); **Engineering** (Engineering; Information Technology); **Humanities** (Arabic; Arts and Humanities; Education; English; Geography; Handicrafts; Islamic Studies; Literature; Modern Languages; Persian; Physical Education; Primary Education; Psychology; Translation and Interpretation); **Science** (Applied Physics; Biology; Chemistry; Computer Science; Geology; Mathematics; Natural Sciences; Statistics); **Theology and Islamic Sciences** (Criminal Law; Criminology; Ethics; Islamic Law; Islamic Studies; Koran; Law; Philosophy; Private Law; Religious Education)

Further Information: Also Overseas Centre

History: Founded 1988 as the unique distance learning institution in the country. A State institution whose degrees are all recognized and have the same status as those of other State universities. 217 Local Study Centres and Units throughout the country.

Governing Bodies: Board ot Trustees; University Council

Academic Year: September to June (September-January; January-June)

Admission Requirements: Secondary school certificate and entrance examination

Main Language(s) of Instruction: Farsi

Degrees and Diplomas: *Kardani (Associate degree)*: 2-5 yrs; *Karshebasi (Bachelor's degree)*: Accountancy; Business Administration; Economics; Education; Translation and Interpretation (English); English; Psychology; Human Geography; Law; Library Science; Persian; Physical Education; Sport Sciences; Public Administration; Social Sciences; Theology (BA; BSc); Biology; Chemistry; Computer Engineering; Computer Sciences; Geology; Handicraft; Mathematics; Physics; Statistics (BA; BSc), 2-10 yrs; *Karshenasi Arshad (Master's degree)*: Biological and Life Sciences; Chemistry; Education; Linguistics; Psychology; Geography; Rural Planning; International Law; Islamic Philosophy; Mathematics; Nahj-ol-Balagheh studies (MA; MSc); Persian; Physics; Physical Education; Sport Sciences; Public Administration (MA; MSc), 3-5 yrs; *Doctorate*: Education (Distance Education), International Law; Persian (PhD), 3-9 yrs

Student Services: Academic counselling, Canteen, Cultural centre, Foreign student adviser, Foreign Studies Centre, Health services, Language programs, Nursery care, Social counselling, Sports facilities

Special Facilities: Audio-Visual Media Centre

Libraries: Central Library; Local Study Centres Libraries, total, c. 1,300,000 vols

Publications: Peyke Noor Journal *(quarterly)*

Last Updated: 05/12/11

PERSIAN GULF UNIVERSITY

Shahid Mahini Street, Bushehr, 75168 Bushehr
Tel: +98(771) 454-5187 +98(771) 422-2011
Fax: +98(771) 454-5188
EMail: Intl_pres@pgu.ac.ir; intl_ofic@pgu.ac.ir
Website: http://www.pgu.ac.ir/

President: Hassan Tajik (2005-) EMail: Tajik@pgu.ac.ir

Director: Ali Dezhgahi-Pour

International Relations: Gholamreza Dehdashti
Tel: +98(771) 422-2026 EMail: dehdashti@pgu.ac.ir

Faculties

Agriculture and Natural Resources *(Borazjan)* (Fishery; Horticulture; Plant and Crop Protection); **Arts and Architecture** (Architecture; Town Planning); **Engineering** (Chemical Engineering; Civil

Engineering; Construction Engineering; Electrical Engineering; Mechanical Engineering; Naval Architecture; Telecommunications Engineering); **Humanities** (Accountancy; Arabic; English; History; Industrial Management; Information Management; Library Science; Management); **Marine Science and Technology** (Fishery; Marine Science and Oceanography; Naval Architecture); **Sciences** (Analytical Chemistry; Chemistry; Inorganic Chemistry; Mathematics; Organic Chemistry; Physical Chemistry; Physics; Statistics)

Research Centres

Persian Gulf Studies and Research (Biotechnology; Environmental Studies; Fishery) *Head*: Mohammad Ali San'ati

History: Founded 1991 under management of Shiraz University and was renamed Bushehr University in 1994. Obtained current name in 1996 due to its geographic location on the coast of the Persian Gulf

Governing Bodies: Ministry of Science, Research and Teaching

Academic Year: September to June (September-January; February-June)

Admission Requirements: Secondary school certificate and entrance examination

Fees: (Rials): None for day students; 3,000,000 per session for evening students; US$ 1,000 per session for foreign students

Main Language(s) of Instruction: Farsi, English

International Co-operation: With universities in Russia, Britain, Yemen

Accrediting Agencies: Ministry of Science, Research and Technology

Degrees and Diplomas: *Karshebasi (Bachelor's degree)*: Engineering, Literature, Humanities, Arts (BA; BSc), 4 yrs; *Karshenasi Arshad (Master's degree)*: Structural Engineering, Physical Chemistry, Organic Chemistry, Inorganic Chemistry, Analytical Chemistry (MSc), a further 2 yrs

Student Services: Academic counselling, Canteen, Cultural centre, Employment services, Foreign student adviser, Foreign Studies Centre, Handicapped facilities, Health services, Language programs, Nursery care, Social counselling, Sports facilities

Student Residential Facilities: Yes (two dormitories for male students, five for female students plus five residential complexes for staff) guest house; hotel and club

Libraries: c. 8,000 vols

Press or Publishing House: Persian Gulf University Press

Last Updated: 05/12/11

PETROLEUM UNIVERSITY OF TECHNOLOGY

Central Building, 569 Hafez Avenue, Tehran 15996
Tel: +98(21) 880-7689
Fax: +98(21) 880-4272
EMail: info@put.ac.ir
Website: http://www.put.ac.ir

Chancellor: Gholam Reza Rashed

Faculties

Chemical and Petrochemical Engineering *(Abadan)* (Chemical Engineering; Petroleum and Gas Engineering); **Marine Sciences** *(Mahmood-Abad)* (Marine Science and Oceanography; Nautical Science); **Petroleum Engineering** *(Ahwaz)* (Automation and Control Engineering; Health Sciences; Petroleum and Gas Engineering; Safety Engineering)

Institutes

Engineering and Technology *(Isfahan)* (Engineering; Technology)

History: Founded 1939 as Abadan Institute of Technology. Under the jurisdiction of the Ministry of Petroleum.

Main Language(s) of Instruction: Farsi

International Co-operation: With universities in France; Norway; Australia; Saudi Arabia; United States; United Kingdom

Degrees and Diplomas: *Karshebasi (Bachelor's degree) (BSc)*: 4 yrs; *Karshenasi Arshad (Master's degree) (MSc)*: a further 2 yrs

Last Updated: 05/12/11

QAZVIN UNIVERSITY OF MEDICAL SCIENCES

Shahid Bahonar Boulevard, Qazvin, Qazvin Iran
Tel: +98(281) 333-6001-5
Fax: +98(281) 333-6007
EMail: info@qums.ac.ir
Website: http://www.qums.ac.ir

Chancellor (Acting): A.A. Zinaloo
Tel: +98(281) 333-3400, Fax: +98(281) 333-1300
EMail: chancellor@qums.ac.ir

Schools

Dentistry (Dentistry); **Medicine** (Medicine); **Nursing and Midwifery** (Midwifery; Nursing); **Paramedical Sciences** *(Junior)* (Paramedical Sciences)

History: Founded 1985.

Governing Bodies: University President

Academic Year: September to June

Admission Requirements: High school certificate in experimental sciences and entrance examination

Fees: (Rials): 836,687 per semester

Main Language(s) of Instruction: Farsi

Accrediting Agencies: Ministry of Health and Medical Education

Degrees and Diplomas: *Kardani (Associate degree)*: 2 yrs; *Karshebasi (Bachelor's degree) (BA)*: 4 yrs; *Doctorate (DDS; BS)*: 6-7 yrs

Student Services: Academic counselling, Canteen, Cultural centre, Foreign student adviser, Health services, Language programs, Social counselling, Sports facilities

Student Residential Facilities: Yes

Special Facilities: Movie studio

Libraries: c. 25,700 vols

Publications: Computing in Medicine and Biology; Final Research Reports (62 titles); Manual of Introductory Clinical Medicine; Scientific Journal

Last Updated: 17/12/08

QOM UNIVERSITY OF MEDICAL SCIENCES

PO Box 3534 Shahid Lavasani Avenue, Qom
Tel: +98(251) 771-3550
Fax: +98(251) 36767
EMail: qsms@noavor.com

Programmes

Medicine (Medicine)

Degrees and Diplomas: *Kardani (Associate degree)*: 2 yrs; *Karshebasi (Bachelor's degree) (BA)*: 4 yrs

Last Updated: 15/12/08

RAFSANJAN UNIVERSITY OF MEDICAL SCIENCES

Iman Ali Boulevard, Rafsanjan, Kerman
Tel: +98(391) 822-0091
Fax: +98(391) 822-0092
EMail: info@rums.ac.ir
Website: http://www.rums.ac.ir

President: Abbas Esmaeil

Faculties

Dentistry (Dentistry); **Medicine** (Biochemistry; Medicine); **Nursing** (Anaesthesiology; Laboratory Techniques; Midwifery; Nursing)

Further Information: Also Teaching Hospitals

History: Founded 1986, started as a medical college, acquired present status and title1993.

Academic Year: September to June (September-February; February-June)

Admission Requirements: Secondary school diploma and certificate and entrance examination

Fees: None

Main Language(s) of Instruction: Farsi

Degrees and Diplomas: *Kardani (Associate degree)*: Midwifery, Science Laboratoty, Anaesthesiology, 2 yrs; *Karshebasi (Bachelor's degree)*: Nursing (BS), 4 yrs; *Karshenasi Arshad (Master's degree)*: Biochemistry (MS), 2 yrs; *Doctorate*: Dentistry (MD); Medicine (MD), 7 yrs

Student Services: Academic counselling, Cultural centre, Employment services, Foreign student adviser, Health services, Nursery care, Social counselling, Sports facilities

Special Facilities: Anatomy Museum; Observatory

Publications: Scientific Journal of RUMS, Scientific, original articles *(quarterly)*

Last Updated: 05/12/11

RAZI UNIVERSITY

Azadi Square, Kermanshah 67155
Tel: +98(831) 422-8439
Fax: +98(831) 428-7393
EMail: info@razi.ac.ir
Website: http://www.razi.ac.ir

Chancellor: Mohammad Mehdi Khodaei
EMail: chancellor@razi.ac.ir

Vice-Chancellor for Administrative Affairs: Hossein Sheisi
EMail: sheisi@razi.ac.ir

Schools

Agriculture (Agriculture; Animal Husbandry; Irrigation; Plant and Crop Protection); **Chemistry** (Analytical Chemistry; Applied Chemistry; Chemistry; Inorganic Chemistry; Organic Chemistry); **Engineering** (Architecture; Chemical Engineering; Civil Engineering; Computer Engineering; Electrical Engineering; Mechanical Engineering); **Literature and Humanities** (Arabic; Arts and Humanities; English; Geography; Islamic Studies; Literature; Persian; Theology); **Physical Education** (Physical Education; Rehabilitation and Therapy; Sports Management); **Science** (Biology; Chemistry; Mathematics; Natural Sciences; Physics; Statistics); **Social Sciences** (Social Sciences); **Social Sciences** (Accountancy; Economics; Library Science; Political Sciences; Sociology); **Veterinary Medicine** (Biology; Food Science; Pathology; Veterinary Science); **Veterinary Science** (Veterinary Science)

History: Founded 1972 as Kermanshah Faculty of Science. Acquired present status and title 1974. A State institution responsible to the Ministry of Culture and Higher Education.

Academic Year: September to June (September-January; February-June)

Admission Requirements: Secondary school certificate and entrance examination

Main Language(s) of Instruction: Farsi

Degrees and Diplomas: *Kardani (Associate degree)*: 2 yrs; *Karshebasi (Bachelor's degree) (BA; BSc)*: 4 yrs; *Karshenasi Arshad (Master's degree) (MA; MSc)*: a further 2 yrs; *Doctorate (PhD)*: a further 2 yrs

Special Facilities: Natural History Museum

Libraries: Central Library

Press or Publishing House: Razi University Publishing House

Last Updated: 05/12/11

SABZEVAR UNIVERSITY OF MEDICAL AND HEALTH SERVICES

PO Box 107, Sabzevar
Tel: +98(571) 267-00
Fax: +98(571) 215-23
Website: http://www.medsab.ac.ir

Director: Mohammad Javad Namazi (1994-)

Faculties

Dentistry (Dentistry); **Health Sciences** (Health Sciences); **Medicine** (Medicine); **Nursing and Midwifery** (Midwifery; Nursing); **Paramedical Sciences** (Paramedical Sciences); **Pharmacy** (Pharmacy)

Further Information: Also 3 Teaching Hospitals

History: Founded 1986 as part of Mashhad University, acquired present status and title 1993.

Academic Year: September to June (September-January; February-June)

Admission Requirements: Secondary school certificate and entrance examination

Main Language(s) of Instruction: Farsi

Degrees and Diplomas: *Kardani (Associate degree)*: 2 yrs; *Karshenasi Arshad (Master's degree) (MA)*: a further 2 yrs

Student Services: Academic counselling, Cultural centre, Employment services, Handicapped facilities, Health services, Nursery care, Social counselling, Sports facilities

Student Residential Facilities: For c. 250 students

Libraries: 10,500 vols

SAHAND UNIVERSITY OF TECHNOLOGY

PO Box 51335-1996, Sahand New Town, East Azarbaijan
Tel: +98(412) 322-4957
Fax: +98(412) 322-4950
EMail: adminoffice@sut.ac.ir
Website: http://www.sut.ac.ir

Chancellor: Mohammad Reza Chenaghlou
EMail: mrchenaghlou@sut.ac.ir

Vice Chancellor of Financial Affairs: Ali Reza Tabatabaei-Nejad
Tel: +98(412) 322-5341, Fax: +98(412) 322-3867
EMail: tabatabaei@sut.ac.ir

International Relations: Mohammad Hossein Hekmat-Shoar
EMail: hekmatshoar@sut.ac.ir

Faculties

Basic Science (Applied Mathematics; Atomic and Molecular Physics; Mathematics; Mechanical Engineering; Physics; Solid State Physics); **Chemical Engineering** (Chemical Engineering; Industrial Engineering; Petroleum and Gas Engineering); **Civil Engineering** (Civil Engineering; Marine Engineering); **Electrical Engineering** (Bioengineering; Electrical Engineering; Power Engineering; Telecommunications Engineering); **Material Engineering** (Materials Engineering; Metallurgical Engineering); **Mining Engineering** (Mining Engineering); **Polymer Engineering** (Polymer and Plastics Technology)

Research Centres

Environmental Engineering (Environmental Engineering); **Hydrometeorology and Earthquake** (Meteorology; Seismology); **Mineral Processing** (Mineralogy); **Nano Structured Materials** (Nanotechnology); **Petroleum Research Centre** (Petroleum and Gas Engineering); **Polymer Material** (Polymer and Plastics Technology; Technology)

History: Founded 1989.

Academic Year: September to June (September-February; February-June)

Admission Requirements: Secondary school certificate with university entrance test

Main Language(s) of Instruction: Farsi, English

International Co-operation: with Regina University, Canada

Accrediting Agencies: Ministry of Science, Research and Technology

Degrees and Diplomas: *Karshebasi (Bachelor's degree)*: Chemical Engineering; Electrical Engineering; Materials Engineering; Mining Engineering (Ba; BSc); *Karshenasi Arshad (Master's degree)*: Chemical Engineering; Electrical Engineering; Materials Engineering; Mining Engineering (MA; MSc); *Doctorate*: Chemical Engineering; Civil Engineering (PhD)

Student Services: Academic counselling, Canteen, Cultural centre, Handicapped facilities, Health services, Language programs, Social counselling, Sports facilities

Student Residential Facilities: For 732 male students and 213 female students.

Special Facilities: Art Gallery. Movie Theatre

Libraries: Off and on-line databases. Books in Farsi and English

Last Updated: 05/12/11

SCHOOL OF ECONOMIC AFFAIRS

Tehran
Tel: +98(21) 641-4322-3
Fax: +98(21) 641-9716

Programmes

Economics (Economics)

Degrees and Diplomas: *Kardani (Associate degree)*: 2 yrs; *Karshebasi (Bachelor's degree) (BA)*: 4 yrs; *Karshenasi Arshad (Master's degree)*

Last Updated: 20/02/12

SCHOOL OF INTERNATIONAL RELATIONS OF THE MINISTRY OF FOREIGN AFFAIRS

Tehran
Tel: +98(21) 280-2744
Fax: +98(21) 280-2742
EMail: info@sir.ac.ir
Website: http://www.sir.ac.ir

Programmes

International Relations (International Relations)

Degrees and Diplomas: *Karshebasi (Bachelor's degree) (BA)*: 4 yrs; *Karshenasi Arshad (Master's degree) (MA)*: a further 2 yrs

SEMNAN UNIVERSITY OF MEDICAL SCIENCES

PO Box 35195-163, Sadi Sq., Molavi Blvd, Semnan
Tel: +98(231) 332-0112; +98(231) 332-1622
Fax: +98(231) 311-2379; +98(231) 322-1622
EMail: info@sem-ums.ac.ir
Website: http://www.sem-ums.ac.ir

Chancellor: Rashidy Pour Ali
Tel: +98(231) 332-1622, Fax: +98(231) 311-2379
EMail: med_Semnan@Kumesh.irost.net

Vice-Chancellor for Research and Education: Malek Mojtaba
Tel: +98(231) 444-0225, Fax: +98(231) 444-0225
EMail: Der@Sem-ums.ar.ir

Faculties

Health *(Damaghan)* (Health Sciences; Occupational Health; Public Health); **Medicine** (Immunology; Medicine; Microbiology; Parasitology; Pathology; Pharmacology); **Nursing and Paramedicine** (Nursing; Paramedical Sciences); **Rehabilitation Sciences** (Rehabilitation and Therapy)

History: Founded 1988.

Academic Year: September to June

Main Language(s) of Instruction: Farsi

Degrees and Diplomas: *Kardani (Associate degree)*; *Karshebasi (Bachelor's degree) (BA)*; *Doctorate (PhD)*

Libraries: c. 20,000 vols

Last Updated: 05/12/11

SHAHED UNIVERSITY

Daneshgahe Shahed

PO Box 15875-5794, North Kargar Avenue 115, Tehran, 14179 Tehran
Tel: +98(21) 641-8857 +98(21) 641-9410
Fax: +98(21) 641-8422
EMail: admin@shahed.ac.ir
Website: http://www.shahed.ac.ir

President: Mahmood Noorisafa (1998-) Tel: +98(21) 641-9713

Vice-Chancellor for Administrative and Financial Affairs: Seyyed Mostafa Kiaie Tel: +98(21) 641-9439

International Relations: Seyyed Kazem Forootan
Tel: +98(21) 831-4744, Fax: +98(21) 831-4743

Faculties

Agriculture *(Ramsar-Mazandaran Province)* (Agricultural Engineering; Agriculture; Agronomy; Horticulture; Plant and Crop Protection); **Art** (Communication Arts; Fine Arts; Painting and Drawing); **Dentistry** (Dentistry); **Engineering** (Biomedical Engineering; Computer Engineering; Electronic Engineering; Engineering; Power Engineering; Software Engineering; Technology; Telecommunications Engineering); **Human Sciences** (Arts and Humanities; Business Administration; Business and Commerce; Clinical Psychology; Educational Sciences; Government; Industrial Management; Islamic Theology; Law; Library Science; Management; Psychology; Social and Community Services; Social Sciences; Theology); **Medicine** (Medicine); **Nursing** (Midwifery; Nursing); **Science** (Applied Mathematics; Biology; Molecular Biology; Natural Sciences; Physics; Solid State Physics; Zoology)

Further Information: Also Shahid Mostafa Khomeini Training Hospital; Hazrat Zeinab Training Hospital and Shahid Mohammad Montazeri Dentistry Training Clinic

History: Founded 1989. Acquired present status 1996.

Academic Year: September to June

Admission Requirements: Secondary school certificate and entrance examination

Fees: None

Main Language(s) of Instruction: Farsi

Degrees and Diplomas: *Karshebasi (Bachelor's degree) (BA)*: 4 yrs; *Karshebasi (Bachelor's degree)*: Sciences and Engineering (BSc), 4 yrs; *Karshenasi Arshad (Master's degree) (MA)*: a further 2 yrs; *Doctorate*: Dentistry (DDM), 7 years; *Doctorate*: Medicine (MD), 7 yrs

Student Services: Academic counselling, Canteen, Cultural centre, Health services, Social counselling, Sports facilities

Student Residential Facilities: Yes

Libraries: Central Library of Shahed University, 85,071 vols

Publications: Daneshvar *(quarterly)*; Scientific-Research Journal of Shahed University

Press or Publishing House: Shahed University Press and Publishing House

Last Updated: 01/12/11

SHAHID ABBASPOUR POWER AND WATER UNIVERSITY OF TECHNOLOGY

Daneshgah Sanat Aab va Bargh (PWUT)

Vafadar Expressway, Shahid Abbaspour, Tehran 16765-1719
Tel: +98(21) 7731-2780
Fax: +98(21) 7731-0425
EMail: pwut@pwut.ac.ir
Website: http://www.pwut.ac.ir/

President: Ali Akbar Afzalian EMail: Afzalian@pwut.ac.ir

Faculties

Electrical and Computer Engineering (Computer Engineering; Electrical Engineering; Electronic Engineering; Power Engineering); **Management and Economics** (Economics; Management); **Mechanical and Energy Systems Engineering** (Energy Engineering; Materials Engineering); **Water and Environmental Engineering** (Civil Engineering; Environmental Engineering; Water Management)

History: Founded 1970 as Power and Water Institute of Technology. Obtained current title and status 2003.

Governing Bodies: Ministry of Energy; Ministry of Science, Research and Technology.

Academic Year: September to February; February to June

Admission Requirements: Iranian National Diploma and entrance exam.

Fees: Free for home students admitted by entrance exam.

Main Language(s) of Instruction: Farsi

Accrediting Agencies: Ministry of Science, Research and Technology.

Degrees and Diplomas: *Karshebasi (Bachelor's degree)*: Engineering (BSc), 4 yrs; *Karshenasi Arshad (Master's degree)*: Engineering (MSc), 2 yrs; *Doctorate*

Student Services: Academic counselling, Canteen, Cultural centre, Employment services, Health services, Language programs, Nursery care, Social counselling, Sports facilities

Student Residential Facilities: Self-catering residence on campus.

Special Facilities: Film studio.

Last Updated: 01/12/11

SHAHID BAHONAR UNIVERSITY OF KERMAN

Daneshgahe Shahid Bahonar-e-Kerman (SBUK)

PO Box 76169-133 Afzalipour Square, Afzalipour Campus, Kerman, 7616914111 Kerman

Tel: +98(341) 322-0041-5

Fax: +98(341) 322-0065

EMail: sbuk@mail.uk.ac.ir

Website: http://www.uk.ac.ir

Chairman: Ahmad Amiri Khorasani EMail: amiri@mail.uk.ac.ir

Colleges

Agriculture *(Jiroft)* (Agriculture; Animal Husbandry; Plant and Crop Protection); **Higher Education** *(Bam)* (Higher Education)

Faculties

Agriculture (Agriculture); **Arts** (Architectural Restoration; Architecture; Art Education; Handicrafts; Painting and Drawing; Weaving); **Arts and Humanities** (Arts and Humanities; English; Islamic Studies; Library Science; Literature; Persian; Social Sciences; Translation and Interpretation); **Business Administration and Economics** (Accountancy; Administration; Economics); **Engineering** (Chemical Engineering; Civil Engineering; Computer Engineering; Engineering; Industrial Engineering; Mechanical Engineering; Metallurgical Engineering; Mining Engineering); **Mathematics and Computer Science** (Computer Science; Mathematics); **Mineral Industry** *(Zarand)* (Mineralogy; Mining Engineering); **Physical Education and Sports** (Physical Education; Sports); **Science** (Biology; Chemistry; Geology; Physics); **Technology** *(Sirjan)* (Technology); **Veterinary Medicine** (Food Science; Public Health; Veterinary Science)

Research Centres

Horticulture and Dates (Horticulture); **Mathematics** *(Mahani)* (Mathematics); **Persian Language and Culture** (Cultural Studies; Persian); **Social Sciences** (Social Sciences)

History: Founded 1974. Acquired present status 1978.

Governing Bodies: Board of Governors

Academic Year: September to June (September-January; February-June)

Admission Requirements: High school certificate

Fees: (Rials) Evening courses: 200,000-1,200,000 per term

Main Language(s) of Instruction: Farsi

Degrees and Diplomas: *Kardani (Associate degree)*: 2 yrs; *Karshebasi (Bachelor's degree)*: Arts; Literature (BA); Science; Mathematics; Humanities; Agriculture; Engineering (BSc), 4 yrs; *Karshenasi Arshad (Master's degree)*: Civil Engineering; Mathematics; Veterinary Medicine; Physics; Geology; Mechanical Engineering; Mining Engineering; Electrical Engineering; Metallurgical Engineering; Chemistry; Physics (MSc; MA), a further 2 yrs; *Doctorate*: Mathematics; Civil Engineering; Mechanical Engineering; Geology; Chemistry; Literature; Physics (PhD), 4 yrs

Student Services: Academic counselling, Canteen, Cultural centre, Employment services, Foreign Studies Centre, Handicapped facilities, Language programs, Nursery care, Social counselling, Sports facilities

Special Facilities: Geological Museum; Natural History Museum

Libraries: Central Library, c. 70,000 vols; Engineering, c. 26,000; Letters and Humanities, c. 13,000; Physical Education, c. 3,500

Publications: Journal of the Faculty of Letters and Humanities *(quarterly)*

Last Updated: 01/12/11

IAU SHAHID BEHESHTI UNIVERSITY (SBU)

P.O. Box 19395-4716, Evin Square, Tehran 1983963113

Tel: +98(21) 299-01

Fax: +98(21) 224-31818

EMail: info@sbu.ac.ir

Website: http://www.sbu.ac.ir

President: Ahmad Shaabani (2007-)
Tel: +98(21) 2990-2222, Fax: +98(21) 2243-1602
EMail: president@mail.sbu.ac.ir

Vie-President for Administration and Finance: Behrooz Dorri
EMail: finvp@mail.sbu.ac.ir

International Relations: Hossein Pourahmadi, Director of International Relations
Tel: +98(21) 2243-1877, Fax: +98(21) 2243-1878
EMail: h-pourahmadi@sbu.ac.ir

Faculties

Architecture and Urban Planning (Architecture; Construction Engineering; Landscape Architecture; Town Planning); **Arts and Humanities** (Arabic; Chinese; English; French; German; History; Persian; Philosophy; Social Sciences); **Biological Sciences** (Botany; Marine Biology; Microbiology; Zoology); **Earth Sciences** (Earth Sciences; Geography; Geology); **Economics and Political Science** (Economics; Political Sciences); **Education and Psychology** (Education; Educational and Student Counselling; Physical Education; Psychology); **Electrical and Computer Engineering** (Computer Engineering; Electrical Engineering; Electronic Engineering); **Law** (Criminal Law; Criminology; International Law; Islamic Law; Law; Private Law; Public Law); **Management and Accountancy** (Accountancy; Administration; Business Administration; Finance; Industrial Management; Management; Public Administration); **Mathematical Sciences** (Computer Science; Mathematics; Statistics); **New Technologies Engineering** (Astronomy and Space Science; Biotechnology; Energy Engineering; Nanotechnology; Paper Technology); **Physical Education and Sports Science** (Physical Education; Physiology; Sports Management); **Science** (Biology; Chemistry; Natural Sciences; Nuclear Engineering; Physics); **Theology and Religions** (Islamic Theology; Philosophy; Religion; Theology)

History: Founded 1959. Formerly, the National University of Iran.

Academic Year: September to July (September-January; February-July)

Admission Requirements: Secondary school certificate and entrance examination

Main Language(s) of Instruction: Farsi

Degrees and Diplomas: *Karshebasi (Bachelor's degree) (BA; BSc)*: 4 yrs; *Karshenasi Arshad (Master's degree) (MA; MSc)*: a further 2 yrs; *Doctorate (PhD)*: a further 2-3 yrs

Student Services: Academic counselling, Canteen, Cultural centre, Foreign student adviser, Health services, Nursery care, Social counselling, Sports facilities

Student Residential Facilities: Yes

Libraries: Central Library, c. 105,000 vols; Mathematics and Science, c. 4,400 vols; Science, c. 10,400 vols; Architecture, c. 12,300 vols; Economics, 14,255 vols; Law, c. 14,200 vols; Arts and Humanities, c. 34,750; Education, c. 10,540; Administration Science, 4,625 vols; Electronics and Computer Science, c. 5,500 vols; Earth Science, c. 11,300 vols; Biology, 6,155 vols

Publications: Journal of Administrative Sciences; Journal of Civil Research; Journal of Earth Science; Journal of Economics; Journal of Law Researches; Journal of Literature, Humanities and Architecture; Soffeh, Journal of Architecture

Last Updated: 05/12/11

SHAHID BEHESHTI UNIVERSITY OF MEDICAL SCIENCES

PO Box 4739-19395, Evin Street, Shahid Chamran Exp. Way, Tehran 4739

Tel: +98(21) 240-1022 +98(21) 2243-9900

Fax: +98(21) 240-0052

EMail: webmaster@sbmu.ac.ir

Website: http://www.sbmu.ac.ir

Chancellor: Hassan Abolghasemi
EMail: chancellor@sbmu.ac.ir; dr_a_zali@yahoo.com

Vice-Chancellor for Academic Affairs: Seyed Abass Safavi Naeeni

Centres

Eye Research *Director*: Mohammad-Ali Javadi

Research Centres

Cell and Molecular Biology *Director*: Ahmad Hosseini; **Dentistry** *Director*: Mohammad-Reza Saffavi; **Endocrinology** *Director*: Fereidoun Azizi; **Gastroenterology and Liver Transplant** *Director*: Mohammad-Reza Zali; **Neuroscience** *Director*: Fereshteh Motamedi; **Skin** *Director*: Parviz Toosi; **Urology and Nephrology** *Director*: Abbas Bassiri

Research Institutes

Nutrition and Food Technology *Director*: Nasser Kalantari

Schools

Dentistry (Dentistry); **Health, Safety and Environment** (Health Sciences; Public Health); **Medicine** (Anatomy; Biochemistry; Bioengineering; Immunology; Medicine; Microbiology; Parasitology; Physiology); **Nursing and Midwifery** (Anaesthesiology; Midwifery; Nursing); **Nutrition and Food Technology** (Dietetics; Food Technology; Nutrition); **Paramedical Sciences** (Medical Technology; Radiology); **Pharmacy** (Pharmacy; Toxicology); **Public Health** (Epidemiology; Health Sciences; Occupational Health; Public Health); **Rehabilitation** (Occupational Therapy; Optometry; Physical Therapy; Speech Therapy and Audiology); **Traditional Medicine** (Ethics; Medicine; Pharmacology)

History: Founded 1961 as Melli University, acquired present title 1986.

Governing Bodies: Board of Trustees

Academic Year: September to June

Admission Requirements: Secondary school certificate and entrance examination

Main Language(s) of Instruction: Farsi

Degrees and Diplomas: *Kardani (Associate degree)*: 3 yrs; *Karshebasi (Bachelor's degree)*: 6 yrs; *Karshenasi Arshad (Master's degree)*: a further 2 yrs; *Doctorate (PhD)*: 4-5 yrs; *Doctorate*: Medicine (MD), 6 yrs

Student Services: Academic counselling, Canteen, Cultural centre, Health services, Language programs, Nursery care, Social counselling, Sports facilities

Special Facilities: Movie Studio

Libraries: Total, 74,894 vols; 10,320 subscriptions to periodicals

Publications: Bina, Research Journal *(quarterly)*; Iranian Journal of Endocrinology and Metabolism, Research (Endocrinology) *(quarterly)*; Iranian Journal of Infectious Disease and Tropical Medicine, Research *(quarterly)*; Iranian Journal of Plastic and Reconstructive Surgery, Research *(quarterly)*; Journal of the Dental School, Research *(quarterly)*; Journal of the Faculty of Medicine, Research *(quarterly)*; Pejouhandeh, Research *(quarterly)*; Tanaffos (Respiration), Research *(quarterly)*; The Iranian Journal of Urology, Research *(quarterly)*; Yakhteh, Research (Anatomy) *(quarterly)*

Last Updated: 18/07/08

SHAHID CHAMRAN UNIVERSITY

Golestan Boulevard, Ahvaz 83151-61355
Tel: +98(611) 333-0010-19
Fax: +98(611) 336-0017
EMail: info@scu.ac.ir
Website: http://www.cua.ac.ir

Chancellor: Mortaza Zargar Shooshtari (2006-)
Tel: +98(611) 333-2041, Fax: +98(611) 333-2044
EMail: zargar@scu.ac.ir

Vice-Chancellor for Administrative and Financial Affairs: Siamak Vahdatinia (2008-)
Tel: +98(611) 2910, Fax: +98(611) 2910 EMail: public@scu.ac.ir

International Relations: Hossein Shokouhi, Director, International and Scientific Cooperation Office
Tel: +98(611) 336-7008, Fax: +98(611) 333-2618
EMail: shokouhi_hossein@yahoo.com

Faculties

Agriculture *Dean*: Majid Nabipour; **Arts** *Dean*: Mansour Kollahkaj; **Economics and Social Sciences** (Accountancy; Economics; Law; Social Sciences) *Dean*: Amir Hossain Nabavi; **Education and Psychology** (Clinical Psychology; Education; Educational Psychology; Educational Technology; Industrial and Organizational Psychology; Information Sciences; Library Science; Preschool Education; Primary Education; Psychology) *Dean*: Mortaza Kokabi; **Engineering** (Architecture; Civil Engineering; Computer Engineering; Electrical Engineering; Electronic Engineering; Engineering; Heating and Refrigeration; Hydraulic Engineering; Mechanical Engineering; Metallurgical Engineering; Power Engineering; Software Engineering) *Dean*: Mahmood Joorabian; **Geological Sciences** (Geography; Geology; Geophysics) *Dean*: Bahram Alizadeh; **Literature and Humanities** (English; French; Geography; History; Literature; Native Language; Persian; Town Planning; Translation and Interpretation) *Dean*: Ali Movahed; **Mathematical Sciences and Statistics** (Applied Mathematics; Computer Science; Mathematics; Mathematics Education; Statistics) *Dean*: Habib Harizavi; **Natural Resources** *Dean*: Mohammad Faraji; **Physical Education and Sports Science** (Physical Education; Sports; Sports Management; Sports Medicine) *Dean*: A. Hamid Habibi; **Sciences** *Dean*: Manochehr Chitsazan; **Theology and Islamic Studies** (Arabic; Islamic Law; Islamic Studies; Islamic Theology; Koran) *Dean*: Ali Matoory; **Veterinary Medicine** *Dean*: Masoud Ghorbanpoor; **Water Science Engineering** (Environmental Management; Irrigation; Marine Science and Oceanography; Water Management)

History: Founded 1955 as a College of Agriculture. Renamed Jondi-Shapour University and acquired present title 1981.

Governing Bodies: Board of Trustees

Academic Year: September to June (September-January; February-June)

Admission Requirements: Secondary school certificate and entrance examination

Main Language(s) of Instruction: Farsi

International Co-operation: with institutions in France, Iraq, Denmark, Germany. Participates in Erasmus.

Degrees and Diplomas: *Kardani (Associate degree)*: 2 yrs; *Karshebasi (Bachelor's degree) (BA; BSc)*: 4 yrs; *Karshenasi Arshad (Master's degree) (MA; MSc)*: a further 2-3 yrs; *Doctorate (PhD)*: a further 4 yrs. Also: Veterinary Medical Doctorate (DVM), 4 yrs

Student Services: Academic counselling, Canteen, Cultural centre, Foreign student adviser, Foreign Studies Centre, Health services, Language programs, Nursery care, Social counselling, Sports facilities

Student Residential Facilities: For c. 3,660 students

Special Facilities: Museum of Natural History and Science, Central Laboratory, Computer laboratories, Audio-Visual Centre, Botanical Gardens

Libraries: Central Library, 500,000 vols; 2,900 periodical subscriptions; libraries of the colleges. Books in Farsi, English, French, and Arabic

Publications: Iranian Veterinary Journal *(quarterly)*; Journal of Economic Review *(quarterly)*; Journal of Education and Psychology, separate editions in Education and Psychology *(quarterly)*; Journal of Human Development *(quarterly)*; Journal of the Faculty of Letters and Humanities *(quarterly)*; Journal of Theology and Islamic Sciences *(quarterly)*; University Journal of Science *(quarterly)*

Press or Publishing House: Shahid Chamran University Publishing Centre

Last Updated: 24/02/09

SHAHID RAJAEE TEACHER TRAINING UNIVERSITY

Lavizan, Tehran 16788
Tel: +98(21) 229-70030
Fax: +98(21) 229-70033
EMail: sru@sru.ac.ir
Website: http://www.srttu.edu

Chancellor: Abbas Haghollahi EMail: haghollahi@srttu.edu

International Relations: Reza Zamen EMail: rzamen@srttu.edu

Colleges

Civil Engineering (Architecture; Civil Engineering; Surveying and Mapping; Wood Technology) *Head*: Shahram Vosough; **Electrical Engineering** *Head*: Ali Akbar Motie Birjandi; **Humanities and Physical Education** (Arts and Humanities; English; Modern Languages; Physical Education) *Head*: Gholamali Ahmadi; **Mechanical Engineering** (Automotive Engineering; Industrial Design;

Mechanical Engineering; Metallurgical Engineering; Production Engineering) *Head*: Gholamhassan Payganeh; **Science** (Chemistry; Mathematics; Physics) *Head*: Hamid Mesgarani

History: Founded 1980 as Enghelab-e- Islami. Later became Enghelabe-Islami Higher Education center. In 1992, a technical and vocational college was established for teachers. Acquired current status and title in 1997.

Academic Year: September to June

Main Language(s) of Instruction: Farsi

Accrediting Agencies: Ministry of Science, Research and Technology

Degrees and Diplomas: *Kardani (Associate degree)*: 2 yrs; *Karshebasi (Bachelor's degree) (BA)*: 4 yrs; *Karshenasi Arshad (Master's degree) (MA)*: a further 2 yrs

Student Services: Academic counselling, Canteen, Cultural centre, Health services, Nursery care, Social counselling, Sports facilities

Student Residential Facilities: Yes

Publications: Teaching and Technology Quarterly

Last Updated: 17/12/08

SHAHID SADOUGHI UNIVERSITY OF MEDICAL SCIENCES AND HEALTH SERVICES

PO Box 734, Bou Ali Avenue, Yazd
Tel: +98(351) 824-5442
Fax: +98(351) 824-5446
Website: http://www.ssu.ac.ir

President: Ahmad Ha'erian

Research Centres

Cardiovascular (Cardiology); **Diabetes** (Diabetology; Endocrinology); **Education Development** (Education); **Infertility** *(Postgraduate)* (Embryology and Reproduction Biology; Genetics; Gynaecology and Obstetrics)

Schools

Dentistry (Dental Hygiene; Dentistry; Oral Pathology; Orthodontics); **Health Sciences** (Health Education; Health Sciences; Occupational Health; Public Health; Social and Preventive Medicine); **Medicine** (Anaesthesiology; Anatomy; Biochemistry; Cardiology; Dermatology; Gynaecology and Obstetrics; Medicine; Natural Sciences; Ophthalmology; Orthopaedics; Pathology; Pharmacology; Physiology; Surgery); **Paramedical Sciences** (Anaesthesiology; Medical Technology; Paramedical Sciences; Radiology)

History: Founded 1989, acquired present title and status 1994.

Admission Requirements: Secondary school certificate and entrance examination

Main Language(s) of Instruction: Farsi

Degrees and Diplomas: *Kardani (Associate degree)*: 2 yrs; *Karshebasi (Bachelor's degree) (BA)*: 4 yrs; *Doctorate*: Medicine (MD), 6 yrs

Student Services: Academic counselling, Cultural centre, Health services, Language programs, Nursery care, Social counselling, Sports facilities

Student Residential Facilities: Yes

Libraries: 70,000 vols

Publications: Medical Article (Original Review and Case Report); Shahid Sadoughi Yazd Medical Sciences *(quarterly)*

Last Updated: 17/12/08

SHAHID SATTARI AVIATION UNIVERSITY

Tehran
Tel: +98(21) 669-3442
Fax: +98(21) 669-3442

Programmes

Aviation (Air Transport)

History: Founded 1986.

Degrees and Diplomas: *Kardani (Associate degree)*: 2 yrs; *Karshebasi (Bachelor's degree) (BA)*: 4 yrs; *Karshenasi Arshad (Master's degree) (MA)*: a further 2 yrs

SHAHREKORD UNIVERSITY (SKU)

PO Box 115, Shahrekord, 88186/34141 Chaharmahal Bakhtiari
Tel: +98(381) 442-4401-6
Fax: +98(381) 442-4412
EMail: info@sku.ac.ir
Website: http://www.sku.ac.ir

President: Esmaeil Asadi EMail: asadi-es@agr.sku.ac.ir

Faculties

Agriculture (Agricultural Engineering; Agricultural Equipment; Agriculture; Animal Husbandry; Crop Production; Irrigation; Plant and Crop Protection; Soil Science); **Basic Sciences** (Biology; Chemistry; Genetics; Mathematics; Natural Sciences; Physics; Plant Pathology); **Letters and Humanities** (Archaeology; Islamic Studies; Law; Literature; Persian; Physical Education; Sports); **Natural Resources and Geosciences** (Aquaculture; Environmental Studies; Fishery; Forestry; Water Management); **Technology and Engineering** (Civil Engineering; Electrical Engineering; Materials Engineering; Mechanical Engineering); **Veterinary Medicine** (Veterinary Science)

Research Institutes

Animal Embryo Technology *Director*: Abolfazl Shirazi

History: Founded 1977. Acquired present status 2004.

Main Language(s) of Instruction: Farsi

Degrees and Diplomas: *Kardani (Associate degree)*: 2 yrs; *Karshebasi (Bachelor's degree) (BA; BSc)*: 4 yrs; *Karshenasi Arshad (Master's degree) (MA; MSc)*: 2 yrs; *Doctorate (PhD)*

Student Services: Academic counselling, Canteen, Cultural centre, Employment services, Health services, Language programs, Nursery care, Social counselling, Sports facilities

Student Residential Facilities: Yes

Libraries: Yes

Last Updated: 06/12/11

SHAHREKORD UNIVERSITY OF MEDICAL SCIENCES (SKUMS)

PO Box 618-8815713471, Ayatollah Kashani Street, Shahrekord, 88184 Chahar Mahal and Bakhtiari
Tel: +98(381) 333-4580 +98(381) 333-4590
Fax: +98(381) 333-4588
EMail: pajoohesh@skums.ac.ir
Website: http://www.skums.ac.ir

Chancellor: Mahdi Mahmoodzade
EMail: drmahmoodzadeh@yahoo.com

Administrative Officer: Hedayat Shirzad

International Relations: Abolghasem Sharifi
Tel: +98(381) 2222-664, Fax: +98(381) 2221-669

Faculties

Health Sciences *Dean*: Mohammad Reza Zahedi; **Medicine and Paramedical Sciences** (Medicine; Paramedical Sciences) *Dean*: Reza Khadivi; **Nursing and Midwifery** (Medical Auxiliaries; Midwifery; Nursing) *Dean*: Mohammad Rahimi

History: Founded 1986.

Governing Bodies: University Council

Academic Year: September to June

Admission Requirements: Secondary school certificate and entrance examination

Fees: (Rials): 250,000-350,000 per term

Main Language(s) of Instruction: Farsi

Degrees and Diplomas: *Kardani (Associate degree)*: Paramedical Sciences (AD), 2 yrs; *Karshebasi (Bachelor's degree)*: Nursing; Midwifery (BS), 4 yrs; *Karshenasi Arshad (Master's degree)*: Microbiology; Parasitology (MS), a further 2 yrs; *Doctorate*: Medicine (MD), 7 yrs

Student Services: Academic counselling, Canteen, Cultural centre, Health services, Language programs, Nursery care, Sports facilities

Student Residential Facilities: Yes

Libraries: 14,404 vols (in English); 41,626 vols (in Farsi); 40 periodical subscriptions

Publications: Journal of Shahrekord University of Medical Sciences

SHAHROOD UNIVERSITY OF MEDICAL SCIENCES

Shohada Avenue, Shahrood 36184
Tel: +98(2731) 333-1850 +98(2731) 333-4012
Fax: +98(2731) 333-4090
EMail: mushahrood@farabi.dmr.or.ir
Website:http: //www.shmu.ac.ir

Chancellor: M. E. Ajami (1985-)

Faculties

Dentistry (Dentistry); **Health Sciences** (Health Sciences); **Medicine** (Medicine); **Nursing and Midwifery** (Midwifery; Nursing); **Paramedical Sciences** (Paramedical Sciences); **Pharmacy**

History: Founded 1975.

Academic Year: October to September

Main Language(s) of Instruction: English

Degrees and Diplomas: *Kardani (Associate degree)*: 2 yrs; *Karshebasi (Bachelor's degree) (BA)*: 4 yrs

Libraries: 9,645 vols

Last Updated: 15/12/08

SHAHROOD UNIVERSITY OF TECHNOLOGY

Daneshgahe Sanati Shahrood

7th tir Square, Shahrood, 36155-316 Semnan
Tel: +98(273) 333-2204-9
Fax: +98(273) 333-6006
EMail: webmaster@shahrood.ac.ir; support@shahroodut.ac.ir
Website: http://www.shahroodut.ac.ir/

President: Ali Morad Zadeh
Tel: +98(273) 628-6416 EMail: amoradzadeh@shahrood.ac.ir

Vice-Chancellor, Administration and Finance: Ali Moradzadeh
Tel: +98(273) 333-4932, Fax: +98(273) 333-6006
EMail: amoradzadeh@shahrood.ac.ir

International Relations: Mohammad Reza Amerion
Tel: +98(273) 334-3500 EMail: amerianuk@yahoo.co.uk

Schools

Agricultural Engineering (Agricultural Engineering; Agriculture; Agronomy; Crop Production; Irrigation; Soil Science); **Chemistry** (Analytical Chemistry; Chemistry; Inorganic Chemistry; Organic Chemistry); **Civil and Architectural Engineering** (Architecture; Civil Engineering); **Electrical, Electronic and Robotic Engineering** (Automation and Control Engineering; Electronic Engineering; Power Engineering; Robotics); **Geosciences** (Geology; Hydraulic Engineering; Petroleum and Gas Engineering); **Industrial Engineering and Management** (Accountancy; Industrial Engineering; Management); **Information Technology and Computer Engineering** (Artificial Intelligence; Computer Engineering; Information Technology; Software Engineering); **Mathematics** (Mathematics); **Mechanical Engineering** (Mechanical Engineering); **Mining, Petroleum and Geophysics Engineering** (Geophysics; Mining Engineering; Petroleum and Gas Engineering)

History: Founded 1973 as Mining School. Became Complex 1987 and Shahrood University 1993. Acquired present status and title 2002.

Governing Bodies: University Council; Administrative Board

Academic Year: September to July

Admission Requirements: Secondary school certificate and entrance examination

Fees: (Rials): 1.2m per term, evening students only

Main Language(s) of Instruction: Farsi

Degrees and Diplomas: *Kardani (Associate degree)*: 2 yrs; *Karshebasi (Bachelor's degree) (BA; BSc)*: 4 yrs; *Karshenasi Arshad (Master's degree) (MA; MSc)*: a further 2-3 yrs; *Doctorate*: Mining Engineering (PhD), a further 3 yrs following Master's

Student Services: Academic counselling, Canteen, Cultural centre, Employment services, Health services, Language programs, Nursery care, Social counselling, Sports facilities

Student Residential Facilities: Yes

Libraries: Central Library, c. 50,000 vols

Last Updated: 01/12/11

SHARIF UNIVERSITY OF TECHNOLOGY (SUT)

PO Box 11365-8639, Azadi Avenue, Tehran
Tel: +98(21) 6600-5419
Fax: +98(21) 6601-2983
EMail: oisc@sharif.edu
Website: http://www.sharif.edu

President: Reza Roosta Azad
Tel: +98(21) 6600-5210, Fax: +98(21) 6600-5310
EMail: roosta@sharif.ir

Centres

Computing (Computer Science); **Engineering Graphics** (Engineering Drawing and Design); **Islamic Studies** (Islamic Studies); **Languages** (Linguistics; Modern Languages)

Departments

Aerospace Engineering (Aeronautical and Aerospace Engineering); **Chemical and Petroleum Engineering** (Chemical Engineering; Food Technology; Petroleum and Gas Engineering); **Chemistry** (Analytical Chemistry; Applied Chemistry; Chemistry; Inorganic Chemistry; Organic Chemistry; Physical Chemistry); **Civil Engineering** (Civil Engineering; Construction Engineering; Environmental Engineering; Seismology; Water Management); **Computer Engineering** (Artificial Intelligence; Computer Engineering; Computer Science; Robotics; Software Engineering); **Electrical Engineering** (Automation and Control Engineering; Biomedical Engineering; Electrical Engineering; Electronic Engineering; Power Engineering; Telecommunications Engineering); **Industrial Engineering** (Industrial Engineering; Management; Systems Analysis); **Materials Science and Engineering** (Engineering; Materials Engineering; Metallurgical Engineering); **Mathematical Sciences** (Applied Mathematics; Mathematics); **Mechanical Engineering** (Aeronautical and Aerospace Engineering; Mechanical Engineering; Nuclear Engineering); **Physics** (Physics)

Graduate Schools

Management and Economics (Economics; Management) *Chairman*: M. Najmi

Research Centres

Advanced Information and Communication Technology (Information Technology; Software Engineering) *Director*: H. R. Rabiee; **Advanced Manufacturing** (Industrial Engineering) *Director*: M. Tahmoures; **Biochemical and Bioenvironmental Studies** (Biochemistry; Biotechnology) *Director*: R. Roosta Azad; **Design, Robotics and Automation** *(Centre of Excellence)* (Automation and Control Engineering; Electronic Engineering; Mechanical Engineering; Robotics) *Director*: A. Meghdari; **Earthquake Engineering** (Earth Sciences) *Chairperson*: M. T. Kazemi; **Electronics** (Electronic Engineering) *Director*: M. Tabiani; **Energy** (Energy Engineering) *Director*: Y. Sabouhi; **Green Card Project** *(Green Card Project)* (Environmental Studies) *Director*: Ali Reza Tavakoli; **Water and Energy** (Energy Engineering; Marine Engineering; Water Management) *Director*: Seyed Jamal-eddin Hashemian

Research Institutes

Transport Studies (Transport Engineering) *Director*: H. Pourzahedi

History: Founded 1965. Acquired present title 1979. A State institution responsible to the Ministry of Science, Research and Technology.

Governing Bodies: Board of Trustees

Academic Year: September to May (September-January; February-May)

Admission Requirements: Secondary school certificate and entrance examination

Fees: None for local students

Main Language(s) of Instruction: Farsi, English

International Co-operation: With universities in Japan; France; United Kingdom; Germany; Italy; Sweden, and other countries

Degrees and Diplomas: *Karshebasi (Bachelor's degree) (BA; BSc)*: 4 yrs; *Karshebasi (Bachelor's degree)*: Engineering, 4 yrs; *Karshenasi Arshad (Master's degree) (MA; MSc)*: a further 2-3 yrs following Bachelor's Degree; *Karshenasi Arshad (Master's degree)*: Engineering, a further 2-3 yrs following Bachelor's Degree; *Doctorate (PhD)*: a further 2-4 yrs following Master's Degree; *Doctorate*: Engineering, a further 3-4 yrs following Master's Degree

Student Services: Academic counselling, Canteen, Cultural centre, Foreign student adviser, Health services, Language programs, Nursery care, Social counselling, Sports facilities

Student Residential Facilities: Yes

Special Facilities: Workshops. Auditoriums; Art Gallery. Observatory. Movie studio

Libraries: Central Library, c. 168,000 vols; 570 CD Rom Databases; 30,000 microforms

Publications: Research Proceedings *(other/irregular)*; Scientia Iranica, International Journal of Science and Technology. In English *(quarterly)*; 'Sharif', Research, New Technologies, Higher Education. In Farsi *(quarterly)*

Press or Publishing House: SUP (Sharif University Press)

Last Updated: 06/12/11

SHIRAZ UNIVERSITY (SU)

Jomhoori Eslami Blvd, Shiraz, 71946-84471 Fars

Tel: +98 711 628 641 617

Fax: +98 711 628 6419

EMail: suiro@shirazu.ac.ir

Website: http://www.shirazu.ac.ir

Chancellor: Mohammad Moazzeni (2010-)
Tel: +98(711) 628-64(16-17), Fax: +98(711) 628-6419
EMail: chancellor@shirazu.ac.ir

Vice-Chancellor for Financial and Administrative Affairs: Seyed Mohammad Zebarjad Sex
Tel: +98(711) 628-6434, Fax: +98(711) 628-6435

International Relations: Farahnaz Farahmond Far, Director
Tel: +98(711) 646-0430, Fax: +98(711) 628-6446
EMail: suro@shirazu.ac.ir

Centres

Population Studies (Demography and Population); **Radiation Protection** (Safety Engineering); **Solar Energy** (Energy Engineering)

Colleges

Engineering (Chemical Engineering; Civil Engineering; Computer Engineering; Electrical and Electronic Engineering; Engineering; Materials Engineering; Mechanical Engineering; Petroleum and Gas Engineering)

Divisions

International *(Qeshm)*

Schools

Agriculture *(Shiraz)* (Agricultural Economics; Agricultural Education; Agriculture; Animal Husbandry; Crop Production; Farm Management; Horticulture; Irrigation; Plant and Crop Protection; Soil Science); **Agriculture** *(Darab)* (Agricultural Management; Irrigation; Natural Resources; Plant and Crop Protection; Water Management); **Art and Architecture** (Architecture; Handicrafts; Town Planning); **Economics, Management, and Social Sciences** (Accountancy; Economics; Management; Social Sciences; Sociology); **Education and Psychology** (Clinical Psychology; Curriculum; Educational Administration; Educational Psychology; Physical Education; Primary Education; Special Education); **Humanities and Literature** (Accountancy; Arts and Humanities; Economics; History; Library Science; Linguistics; Literature; Management; Modern Languages; Persian; Social Sciences); **Law and Political Science** (Criminal Law; International Law; Islamic Law; Law; Political Sciences; Public Law); **Literature and Humanities** (Arabic; History; Linguistics; Literature; Modern Languages; Persian); **Science** (Biology; Chemistry; Geology; Mathematics; Natural Sciences; Physics; Statistics); **Veterinary Medicine** (Food Science; Hygiene; Public Health; Veterinary Science)

History: Founded 1946. College of Medicine detached 1986 to form separate University.

Academic Year: September to June (September-January; February-June)

Admission Requirements: Secondary school certificate and competitive entrance examination

Main Language(s) of Instruction: Farsi, English

International Co-operation: Participates in Erasmus programmes

Degrees and Diplomas: *Kardani (Associate degree)*: 2 yrs; *Karshebasi (Bachelor's degree)*: Agriculture; Nursing, 4 yrs; *Karshebasi (Bachelor's degree)*: Engineering, 5 yrs; *Karshenasi Arshad (Master's degree)*: Agriculture; Biochemistry; Biology; Chemistry; Economics; Engineering; English; Mathematics; Microbiology; Physics; *Doctorate*: Agriculture (PhD); Basic Sciences (PhD); Engineering (PhD); Humanities (PhD), 4 yrs; *Doctorate*: Dentistry (PhD); Veterinary Medicine (PhD), 6 yrs

Student Services: Academic counselling, Canteen, Cultural centre, Foreign student adviser, Foreign Studies Centre, Health services, Language programs, Nursery care, Social counselling, Sports facilities

Special Facilities: Natural History and Technology Museum. Naranjestan Museum. Eram Botanical Garden. Buruni Observatory

Libraries: Central Library, c. 120,000 vols (English); c. 30,000 (Farsi). Also College Libraries

Publications: Economics; Iranian Agricultural Journal; Iranian Journal of Science and Technology; Iranian Journal of Veterinary Research; Religious Thought/Journal of Social Sciences and Humanities

Press or Publishing House: Markaze Nashr, Shiraz University Publishing Office

Last Updated: 06/12/11

SHIRAZ UNIVERSITY OF MEDICAL SCIENCES (SUMS)

PO Box 71345-1849, Zand Avenue, Shiraz

Tel: +98(71) 235-7598

Fax: +98(71) 230-4366

EMail: ejraeia@sums.ac.ir

Website: http://www.sums.ac.ir

President: Mohammad Hadi Imanieh Tel: +98(71) 332-366

Faculties

Health and Nutrition *(Lar)* (Epidemiology; Health Administration; Health Sciences; Occupational Health; Public Health); **Nursing and Midwifery** (Anaesthesiology; Midwifery; Nursing); **Paramedical Sciences** *(Gerash Hazrat-e-Emam Sadegh)* (Anaesthesiology; Laboratory Techniques); **Pharmacy** (Analytical Chemistry; Biochemistry; Chemistry; Organic Chemistry; Pharmacy; Physics; Physiology; Toxicology)

Research Centres

Cancer (Oncology); **Gastroenterology-Hepatology** (Gastroenterology; Hepatology); **Medicinal and Natural Products Chemistry** (Chemistry); **Transplant** *(Shiraz)*

Schools

Management and Medical Information Sciences (Health Administration; Management); **Medicine** *(Shiraz)* (Anaesthesiology; Anatomy; Biochemistry; Cardiology; Community Health; Dermatology; Gynaecology and Obstetrics; Immunology; Medicine; Oncology; Ophthalmology; Paediatrics; Parasitology; Pathology; Pharmacology; Psychiatry and Mental Health; Radiology; Rehabilitation and Therapy; Surgery; Virology); **Paramedical Sciences** (Laboratory Techniques; Paramedical Sciences; Radiology); **Rehabilitation** (Physical Therapy; Rehabilitation and Therapy)

History: Founded 1950 as Medical School of the University of Shiraz. Became an independent University in 1988.

Governing Bodies: Board of Trustees; University Council

Academic Year: September to June (September-January; February-June)

Admission Requirements: Secondary school certificate and entrance examination

Fees: (Rials): Foreign students, c. 3m. per annum

Main Language(s) of Instruction: Farsi

Degrees and Diplomas: *Kardani (Associate degree)*: 2 yrs; *Karshebasi (Bachelor's degree) (BA)*: 4 yrs; *Karshenasi Arshad (Master's degree) (MA)*; *Doctorate (PhD)*: a further 4 yrs; *Doctorate*: Medicine (M.D.), 6-7 yrs

Student Services: Academic counselling, Canteen, Cultural centre, Foreign student adviser, Handicapped facilities, Health services, Nursery care, Social counselling, Sports facilities

Libraries: Alameh-Tabatabae Library

Publications: Iranian Journal of Medical Science

Last Updated: 06/12/11

SHIRAZ UNIVERSITY OF TECHNOLOGY

P.O. Box. 71555-313, Moddares Boulevard, Shiraz
Tel: +98(71) 17262102
Fax: +98(71) 17262102
Website: http://www.sutech.ac.ir

President: M. Moghadasi

Departments

Chemical Engineering; **Civil Engineering** (Civil Engineering); **Electrical and Electronic Engineering** (Electrical and Electronic Engineering); **Information Technology**; **Science** (Natural Sciences)

History: Founded 2004.

Main Language(s) of Instruction: Farsi

Degrees and Diplomas: *Karshebasi (Bachelor's degree)*; *Karshenasi Arshad (Master's degree)*

Last Updated: 19/12/08

SISTAN AND BALUCHISTAN UNIVERSITY

P.O.Box 98155-987, Zahedan
Tel: +98(541) 244-5981
Fax: +98(541) 244-6888
EMail: intl_ofic@usb.ac.ir
Website: http://www.usb.ac.ir

Chancellor and President: Ahmad Akbari
Tel: +98(541) 447-010 EMail: aakbari@hamoon.usb.ac.ir

Faculties

Administration and Accountancy (Accountancy; Administration); **Art and Architecture** (Anthropology; Architecture; Fine Arts; Handicrafts; Painting and Drawing; Restoration of Works of Art; Weaving); **Economics** (Accountancy; Agricultural Economics; Business and Commerce; Economics; Industrial and Production Economics; Public Administration); **Engineering** *(Shahid Nikbakht)* (Chemical Engineering; Civil Engineering; Electrical Engineering; Engineering; Materials Engineering; Mechanical Engineering); **Geography and Environmental Planning** (Environmental Management; Geography); **Literature and Humanities** (Arts and Humanities; Literature); **Mathematics** (Mathematics); **Physical Education** (Physical Education); **Psychology and Educational Sciences** (Educational Sciences; Psychology); **Science** (Chemistry; Geology; Mathematics; Natural Sciences; Physical Chemistry; Physics); **Theology** (Theology)

Further Information: Also Saravan Campus

History: Founded 1975. A State institution responsible to the Ministry of Science, Research and Technology.

Academic Year: September to July (September-February; February-July)

Admission Requirements: Secondary school certificate and national entrance examination

Main Language(s) of Instruction: Farsi

Degrees and Diplomas: *Kardani (Associate degree)*: 2 yrs; *Karshebasi (Bachelor's degree) (BA; BSc)*: 4 yrs; *Karshenasi Arshad (Master's degree) (MA; MSc)*: a futher 2 yrs; *Doctorate (PhD)*: 4 yrs following Master's Degree

Student Services: Academic counselling, Canteen, Cultural centre, Employment services, Foreign student adviser, Handicapped facilities, Health services, Language programs, Nursery care, Social counselling, Sports facilities

Student Residential Facilities: Yes

Libraries: c. 160,000 vols in Farsi, Urdu, Arabic; c. 120,000 vols in English

Publications: Journal of Arts and Humanities *(quarterly)*; Journal of Sciences and Engineering *(quarterly)*

Last Updated: 06/12/11

TABRIZ UNIVERSITY OF MEDICAL SCIENCES

Daneshgah-e-Oloom Pzezshki-e-Tabriz (TBZMED)
Daneshgah Street, Tabriz, 51664 Azarbaijan
Tel: +98(411) 334-6147 +98(411) 334-6103
Fax: +98(411) 334-2761
EMail: chancellor@tbzmed.ac.ir
Website: http://www.tbzmed.ac.ir

Chancellor: Ahmad-Reza Khalili (2007-)

Vice-Chancellor: Alireza Javadzadeh
Tel: +98(411) 335-5934, Fax: +98(411) 335-9670
EMail: Logist.vs@tbzmed.ac.ir

Vice-Chancellor for Research: Abdolhassan Kazemi
EMail: iro@tbzmed.ac.ir; Rhassan5628@yahoo.com

International Relations: Amir-Afshin Khaki
Tel: +98(411) 334-1249, Fax: +98(411) 334-4280
EMail: Dr.aakhaki@yahoo.com

Schools

Advanced Biomedical Sciences (Bioengineering; Biomedicine; Biotechnology; Molecular Biology; Nanotechnology); **Dentistry** (Dental Hygiene; Dental Technology; Dentistry; Oral Pathology; Orthodontics; Periodontics); **Health and Nutrition** (Health Sciences; Nutrition; Public Health); **Medicine** (Anaesthesiology; Anatomy; Biochemistry; Community Health; Dermatology; Forensic Medicine and Dentistry; Gynaecology and Obstetrics; Immunology; Medicine; Neurology; Ophthalmology; Orthopaedics; Parasitology; Pathology; Physiology; Psychiatry and Mental Health; Radiology; Surgery; Urology; Virology); **Nursing and Midwifery** (Midwifery; Nursing); **Paramedical Sciences** (Paramedical Sciences); **Pharmacy** (Chemistry; Pharmacology; Pharmacy; Toxicology); **Rehabilitation** (Physical Therapy; Rehabilitation and Therapy)

Further Information: Also 3 research centres

History: Founded 1949 as part of the University of Tabriz. Acquired present status 1986.

Academic Year: September to June

Admission Requirements: Secondary school certificate and entrance examination

Fees: None

Main Language(s) of Instruction: Farsi

Degrees and Diplomas: *Kardani (Associate degree)*: 2 yrs; *Karshebasi (Bachelor's degree)*: Public Health; Environmental Health; Laboratory Sciences; Radiology; Anaesthesia; Nutrition; Library and Medical Information Science; Nursing; Midwifery; Physiotherapy (BA), 4 yrs; *Professional Doctorate*: Medicine; Dentistry; Pharmacy, 7 yrs; *Karshenasi Arshad (Master's degree)*: Biochemistry; Histology; Pharmaceutics; Pharmacology; Nutrition; Nursing (PhD); Biochemistry; Physiology; Dissection; Medical Sciences; Medical Physics; Microbiology; Parasitology; Nutrition; Midwifery; Nursing (MA), a further 3 yrs. Also 'Residency' (3 yrs), and Sub-speciality programmes in Heart Surgery; Thorax Surgery; Lung Diseases; Haematology

Student Services: Academic counselling, Cultural centre, Handicapped facilities, Health services, Language programs, Nursery care, Social counselling, Sports facilities

Special Facilities: Medical History Museum; Observatory

Publications: Dentistry Journal *(quarterly)*; Medical Journal *(quarterly)*; Nursing Journal *(quarterly)*; Pharmaceutical Journal *(quarterly)*

Last Updated: 01/12/11

TARBIAT MOALLEM UNIVERSITY

Daneshgahe Tarbeeat Moallem (TTUT)
49 Mofateh Avenue, Tehran 15719-14911
Tel: +98(21) 883-29220-4
Fax: +98(21) 888-30857
EMail: info@saba.tmu.ac.ir
Website: http://www.tmu.ac.ir

President: Abdoljavad Taherizade Tel: +98(21) 888-25010

Faculties

Chemistry (Chemistry); **Engineering** (Civil Engineering; Engineering; Environmental Engineering; Industrial Engineering; Information Technology); **Letters and Humanities** (Arabic; Arts and Humanities; Geography; History; Islamic Studies; Literature; Modern Languages; Persian; Philosophy; Social Sciences; Sociology; Theology); **Mathematics and Computer Engineering** (Computer Engineering; Mathematics; Mathematics and Computer Science; Statistics); **Physical Education and Sports** (Physical Education; Sports); **Psychology and Educational Sciences** (Educational Sciences; Psychology); **Science** (Biology; Geology; Physics)

Institutes

Foreign Languages (Modern Languages)

Research Institutes

Education (Educational Sciences); **Mathematics** (Mathematics)

Further Information: Also campus in Karaj

History: Founded 1919, became Teacher Training College 1932. Acquired present status and title 1974. A State institution responsible to the Ministry of Science, Research and Technology.

Governing Bodies: University Council; Administrative Board

Academic Year: September to June (September-January; February-June)

Admission Requirements: Secondary school certificate and entrance examination

Fees: None

Main Language(s) of Instruction: Farsi

International Co-operation: With universities in Ukraine, Syria, Kyrgyzstan.

Degrees and Diplomas: *Kardani (Associate degree)*: 2 yrs; *Karshebasi (Bachelor's degree) (BA; BSc)*: 4 yrs; *Karshenasi Arshad (Master's degree) (MA; MSc)*: a further 2 yrs; *Doctorate (PhD)*: a further 4 yrs

Student Services: Canteen, Health services, Language programs, Nursery care, Social counselling, Sports facilities

Student Residential Facilities: Yes (dormitory for students, houses for staff)

Libraries: 250,000 vols

Publications: Journal of Applied Linguistics *(quarterly)*; Journal of Educational Research *(quarterly)*; Journal of Science *(quarterly)*; Journal of the Faculty of Human Sciences and Literature *(quarterly)*

Press or Publishing House: University Press

Last Updated: 02/12/11

TARBIAT MOALLEM UNIVERSITY OF AZARBAIJAN (TMUA)

Tabriz, 5375171379 East Azarbaijan
Tel: +98(41) 243-27500
Website: http://www.azaruniv.ac.ir

President: Mohammad Aminfard (2007-)
EMail: intl_pres@azaruniv.ac.ir

Vice-President: Ja'far Amjadi EMail: j.amjadi@azaruniv.ac.ir

International Relations: Ali Akbar Shirizadeh, Director of International Relations EMail: intl_ofic@azaruniv.ac.ir

Faculties

Education (Family Studies; Library Science; Physical Education; Psychology); **Humanities** (Arabic; English; Literature; Persian); **Information Technology** (Information Technology); **Science** (Agriculture; Biology; Botany; Chemistry; Mathematics; Physics); **Theology** (Arabic; Islamic Studies; Islamic Theology; Koran; Theology)

History: Founded 1988. Former Branch of Tehran Tarbiat Moallem University. Acquired current title and status 2001.

Governing Bodies: Board of Trustees; Executive Committee; University Council

Academic Year: September to June (September-January; February-June)

Admission Requirements: Secondary school certificate and entrance examination

Fees: None

Main Language(s) of Instruction: Farsi

International Co-operation: With universities in Azarbaijan, Russia, Japan.

Accrediting Agencies: Ministry of Science, Research and Technology of Iran

Degrees and Diplomas: *Karshebasi (Bachelor's degree)*: English Literature; Persian Literature; Arabic Literature; Physical Education; Psychology; Family Studies; Philosophy; Quranic Sciences; Religions; Islamic History and Civilization; Chemistry; Physics; Pure Mathematics; Applied Mathematics; Biology; Agriculture; Electrical Engineering; Mechanics; Civil Engineering; Botany, 4 yrs; *Karshenasi Arshad (Master's degree)*: English Teaching; English Literature; Psychology; Persian Literature; Arabic Literature; Religious Studies; Mathematics; Chemistry; Physics; Electrical Engineering; Civil Engineering, a further 2 yrs; *Doctorate*: Persian Literature; Mathematics; Physics (PhD)

Student Services: Academic counselling, Canteen, Cultural centre, Health services, Social counselling, Sports facilities

Student Residential Facilities: Separate male and female dormitories.

Special Facilities: Art gallery

Libraries: Central Library, 55,000 vols

Publications: Journal of Literature and Humanities, Articles in the domain of Persian language and literature. *(quarterly)*

Academic Staff *2009-2010*	MEN	WOMEN	TOTAL
FULL-TIME	136	13	**149**
STAFF WITH DOCTORATE			
FULL-TIME	35	7	**42**
Student Numbers *2009-2010*			
All (Foreign Included)	2,246	3,468	**5,714**

Part-time students, 174. **Evening students**, 2,216.

Last Updated: 18/03/10

TARBIAT MOALLEM UNIVERSITY OF SABZEVAR

PO Box 397, Enghelab Avenue, Sahebazaman Square, Sabzevar, 9618676115 Khorasan
Tel: +98(571) 264-4427
Fax: +98(571) 264-1950
EMail: webmaster@sttu.ac.ir
Website: http://www.sttu.ac.ir

Chancellor: S. Abolfazl Alavi (1995-) Tel: +98(571) 264-5337

Executive Director: Abdorrahim Askari
Tel: +98(571) 264-4430, Fax: +98(571) 264-7430

International Relations: Hoseyn Vafaii, Head Office
Tel: +98(571) 264-1954

Boards Of Study

Arabic Literature (Arabic) *Head*: Akbari Saheb Ali; **Architecture** *Head*: Maasumi Masihollah; **Biology** *Head*: Hosseini S. Abolfazl; **Educational Sciences** (Educational Sciences) *Head*: Yamini Mohammed; **Electrical Engineering** *Head*: Baghiinezhad Majid; **English Language and Literature** (English) *Head*: Ghapanchi Zargham; **Environmental Sciences and Technology** *Head*: Ghelichi Zahra; **Geography** (Geography) *Head*: Zangene Asadi Mohammad Ali; **Islamic Sciences** *Head*: Siyanati Hassan; **Materials Engineering and Technical Studies** *Head*: Kuroji Bahman; **Mathematics** (Mathematics) *Head*: Efati Sohrab; **Persian Literature** (Persian) *Head*: Khjeim Ahmad; **Physics** (Physics) *Head*: Azadegan Behnam; **Theology** (Theology) *Head*: Vahid Hamid

Faculties

Arts and Humanities (Arts and Humanities; Literature) *Dean*: Jaafari Sani Hossein; **Basic Sciences** (Natural Sciences) *Dean*: Gholizadeh Abdollah

History: Founded 1986.

Academic Year: September to July (September-January; February-July)

Admission Requirements: Secondary school certificate and entrance examination

Main Language(s) of Instruction: Farsi

Degrees and Diplomas: *Kardani (Associate degree)*: 2 yrs; *Karshebasi (Bachelor's degree) (BA; BSc)*: 4 yrs; *Karshenasi Arshad (Master's degree) (MA; MSc)*: a further 2 yrs

Student Services: Academic counselling, Canteen, Cultural centre, Health services, Language programs, Nursery care, Social counselling, Sports facilities

Libraries: 27,567 vols

IAU TARBIAT MODARES UNIVERSITY

Daneshgahe Tarbiat Modares (TMU)

PO Box 14115-111, Chamran Expressway and Jalal Al'Ahmad Intersection, Tehran 14117-13116
Tel: +98(21) 8288 0000
Fax: +98(21) 8288 3132
EMail: intl@modares.ac.ir
Website: http://www.modares.ac.ir

Chancellor: Bijan Ranjbar (2010-)
Tel: +98(21) 8288-2005, Fax: +98(21) 8800-6544
EMail: ranjbarb@modares.ac.ir

Vice-Chancellor for Finance and Administrative Affairs: Assadollah Kordnaeij
Tel: +98(21) 8288-2008, Fax: +98(21) 8801-1918
EMail: naiej@modares.ac.ir

International Relations: Naser Khaji, Director of International Scientific Collaborations Office
Tel: +98(21) 8288-3128, Fax: +98(21) 8822-0307
EMail: nkhaji@modares.ac.ir

Centres

Biotechnology Products *(Centre of Excellence) Director*: Seyed Abbas Shojaolsadati; **Chemical Engineering Process Products** *(Centre of Excellence) Director*: Ali Haghtalab; **Integrated Pest and Disease Management of Oil Crops** *(Centre of Excellence) Director*: Saeid Moharramipour; **Recycling and Losses of Strategic Agricultural Products** *(Centre of Excellence) Director*: Barat Ghobadian

Faculties

Agriculture *(Karaj City)* (Agricultural Business; Agricultural Education; Agricultural Equipment; Agronomy; Animal Husbandry; Crop Production; Entomology; Food Science; Food Technology; Horticulture; Hydraulic Engineering; Irrigation; Meat and Poultry; Plant Pathology; Soil Science; Water Management; Water Science) *Dean*: Ebrahim Pourjam; **Arts and Architecture** (Acting; Engineering Management; Fine Arts; Graphic Design; Literature; Painting and Drawing; Regional Planning; Theatre) *Dean*: Motjaba Ansari; **Basic Sciences** (Analytical Chemistry; Atomic and Molecular Physics; Chemistry; Geological Engineering; Geology; Inorganic Chemistry; Organic Chemistry; Petrology; Physical Chemistry; Physics; Solid State Physics) *Dean*: Ali Uromeie; **Biological Sciences** (Biochemistry; Biology; Biophysics; Biotechnology; Genetics; Plant Pathology) *Dean*: Khosro Khajeh; **Chemical Engineering** (Biotechnology; Chemical Engineering; Polymer and Plastics Technology) *Dean*: Seyed Abbas Shojaosadati; **Civil and Environmental Engineering** (Environmental Engineering; Geological Engineering; Hydraulic Engineering; Marine Engineering; Road Engineering; Seismology; Transport Engineering) *Dean*: Mahmoud Saffarzadeh; **Electrical and Computer Engineering** (Automation and Control Engineering; Biomedical Engineering; Computer Engineering; Electronic Engineering; Information Technology; Power Engineering; Telecommunications Engineering) *Dean*: Mohsen Moghaddam; **Engineering** (Aeronautical and Aerospace Engineering; Ceramics and Glass Technology; Design; E-Business/Commerce; Energy Engineering; Engineering Management; Industrial Engineering; Information Technology; Materials Engineering; Mechanical Engineering; Metallurgical Engineering; Mineralogy; Mining Engineering; Production Engineering) *Dean*: Amir Abdollahzadeh; **Humanities** (Arabic; Archaeology; Education; Educational Sciences; English; French; Geography; History; Islamic Studies; Koran; Law; Linguistics; Literature; Persian; Philosophy; Physical Education; Political Sciences; Psychology; Russian; Sociology; Sports; Women's Studies) *Dean*: Reza Akbari; **Management and Economics** (Accountancy; Economics; Information Management; Information Technology; Library Science; Management) *Dean*: Seyed Hamid Khodadad Hoseini; **Mathematical Sciences** (Applied Mathematics; Computer Science; Mathematics; Statistics) *Dean*: Ali Iranmanesh; **Medical Sciences** (Anatomy; Biochemistry; Biotechnology; Botany; Entomology; Genetics; Haematology; Health Education; Immunology; Medical Technology; Medicine; Midwifery; Nursing; Occupational Health; Physical Therapy; Physics; Physiology; Psychology; Virology) *Dean*: Abdolamir Allameh; **Natural Resources and Marine Sciences** *(Norr City)* (Environmental Management; Fishery; Forestry; Marine Science and Oceanography; Natural Resources; Paper Technology; Water Management; Wood Technology) *Dean*: Seyed Hamid Reza Sadeghi

Institutes

Economic Studies *(North Tehran)* (Agricultural Economics; Economic and Finance Policy; Economics) *Director*: Hossein Sadeghi; **International Research on Persian Language and Literature** (International Studies; Literature; Persian) *Director*: Naser Nikobakhi; **Management and Development of Technology** (Industrial Engineering; Management; Production Engineering) *Director*: Khodadad Hosseini

Research Centres

African Studies (African Studies; Cultural Studies) *Director*: Ali Reza Mehrabi; **Iran Management and Productivity Study Center** *Director*: Ahmad Ali Khaef; **Iran Power System Engineering Research Center** *(IPSERC)* (Power Engineering) *Director*: Hossein Seifi; **Persian Language and Literature** (Literature; Persian) *Director*: Ebrahim Khodayar; **Religious Culture and Thought Research Center** (Ethics; Philosophy; Religious Education; Theology) *Director*: Mohammad Roohi

Research Groups

Chabahar Studies Center *Director*: Hasan Asilian e Mahabadi; **Environmental Research Group** *Director*: Shamsedin Niknamy

Research Institutes

Economics (Agricultural Economics; Economics; Regional Planning; Town Planning) *Director*: Ali Mohammad Ahmadi; **Information Technology** (Information Technology; Telecommunications Engineering) *Director*: Seyed Kamal Charsooghi; **Water Engineering** (Hydraulic Engineering; Water Management) *Director*: Seyed Ali Akbar Salehi Neishabory

History: Founded 1982 as School, acquired present status and title 1986. A graduate institution.

Governing Bodies: University chancellor; Vice-Chancellor for Academic Affairs; Vice-Chancellor for Research Affairs; Vice-Chancellor for Support and Human Resource Affairs; Vice-Chancellor for Student Affairs; Vice-Chancellor for Cultural Affairs; Director for Office of International and Scientific Collaborations

Academic Year: September to June (September-January; February-June)

Admission Requirements: Undergraduate degree for Master's programme. Master's degree for PhD programme.

Fees: (Rial): 7,000,000 to 18,000,000 for overseas students only.

Main Language(s) of Instruction: Farsi

International Co-operation: with IAESTE (The International Association for the Exchange of Students for Technical Experience).

Accrediting Agencies: Ministry of Science, Research and Technology

Degrees and Diplomas: *Karshenasi Arshad (Master's degree)*: Resources and Marine Sciences (Master's degree), 2-3 yrs; *Doctorate (PhD)*: 4-6 yrs

Student Services: Academic counselling, Canteen, Cultural centre, Employment services, Foreign student adviser, Foreign Studies Centre, Handicapped facilities, Health services, Language programs, Nursery care, Social counselling, Sports facilities

Student Residential Facilities: Yes

Special Facilities: Movie Studio

Libraries:c. 190,000 vols; c. 1,500 periodical subscriptions.

Publications: Africa Research *(quarterly)*; Hydraulics *(quarterly)*; International Journal of Natural Resources and Marine Sciences; Journal of Economic Research *(quarterly)*; Literary Criticism, Journal of the Research Center for Persian Language & Literature *(quarterly)*; Modares Biological Sciences and Technology Journal; Modares Civil Engineering *(quarterly)*; Modares Human Sciences and Management Research in Iran *(quarterly)*; Modares Human Sciences and Spatial Planning *(quarterly)*; Modares Journal of Comparative Law *(quarterly)*; Modares Journal of Electrical Engineering *(quarterly)*; Modares Journal of Mechanical Engineering *(quarterly)*; Modares Journal of Medical Sciences, Pathobiology journal. *(quarterly)*; Multi disciplinary Journals of the Faculty of Humanities; Organizational Resources Management Research *(quarterly)*; Social Sciences *(quarterly)*; The International Journal of Humanities of the Islamic Republic of Iran, in Arabic *(quarterly)*; The International Journal of Humanities of the Islamic Republic of Iran, in English *(quarterly)*; The Journal of Agricultural Science and Technology; The Journal of Comparative Language & Literature Research *(quarterly)*; The Modares Semiannual Art Journal *(quarterly)*

Press or Publishing House: Tarbiat Modares University Press

Academic Staff *2011-2012*	MEN	WOMEN	**TOTAL**
FULL-TIME	884	384	**1,268**
STAFF WITH DOCTORATE			
FULL-TIME	2	1	**3**
Student Numbers *2011-2012*			
All (Foreign Included)	4,121	2,731	**6,852**
FOREIGN ONLY	76	34	**110**

Distance students, 510. **Evening students**, 527.

Last Updated: 08/11/11

TEHRAN UNIVERSITY OF MEDICAL SCIENCES AND HEALTH SERVICES

Daneshgahe Olome Pezeshki va Khadamate Behdashti Darmani Tehran (TUMS)

No. 23, Dameshgh Str., Vali-e Asr Str,
Tehran 14167
Tel: +98(21) 66405666
Fax: +98(21) 66419541
EMail: chancellor@tums.ac.ir
Website: http://www.tums.ac.ir

Chancellor: Bagher Larijani (2005-)
Tel: +98(21) 6640-5666, Fax: +98(21) 6641-9537

Vice-Chancellor for Research: Akbar Fotouhi
Tel: +98(21) 8898-7381 +98(21) 8898-7382,
Fax: +98(21) 8898-9664 EMail: afotouhi@tums.ac.ir

International Relations: M.S. Ghasemi, Director of International Relations and Accreditation EMail: m-ghasemi@tums.ac.ir

Campuses

International (Dentistry; Health Administration; Medicine; Midwifery; Nursing; Occupational Therapy; Optometry; Pharmacy; Physical Therapy; Speech Therapy and Audiology)

Institutes

Cancer *(CRCI)* (Oncology); **Public Health Research** (Health Sciences; Public Health)

Research Centres

Addiction Sciences (Psychiatry and Mental Health; Toxicology); **Audiology** (Speech Therapy and Audiology); **Basic Medical Sciences** (Medicine); **Bioinformatics** (Biology; Computer Science); **Brain and Spinal Injury Studies** (Rehabilitation and Therapy); **Cancer** (Oncology); **Dentistry** (Dentistry); **Digestive Diseases** (Gastroenterology); **Ear Nose Throat Studies** *(ENT)* (Otorhinolaryngology); **Endocrinology and Metabolism** (Endocrinology); **Environmental Research** (Environmental Studies); **Haematology, Oncology and Blood and Marrow Transplant** (Haematology; Oncology); **Heart Diseases** (Cardiology); **HIV** (Virology); **Immunology, Asthma and Allergy** (Immunology); **Iranian Tissue Bank** (Medicine); **Medical History and Ethics** (Ethics; Medicine); **Medical Nanotechnology** (Medicine; Nanotechnology); **Medical Plant Reasearch** *(MPRC)* (Medicine); **Neuroscience** (Neurosciences); **Nuclear Medicine** (Medicine); **Ophthalmology** (Ophthalmology); **Pharmaceutical Sciences** (Pharmacy); **Psychiatry and Psychology** (Psychiatry and Mental Health; Psychology); **Reproductive Health** *(Vali-e-Asr)* (Embryology and Reproduction Biology); **Rheumatology** (Rheumatology); **Science and Technology in Medicine** (Biomedical Engineering); **Skin Diseases and Leprosy** (Dermatology); **Sports Medicine** (Sports Medicine); **Trauma and Surgery** *(Sina)* (Surgery); **Urology** (Urology)

Schools

Allied Medical Sciences (Anaesthesiology; Health Administration; Medical Auxiliaries; Paramedical Sciences); **Dentistry** (Dental Technology; Dentistry; Oral Pathology; Orthodontics); **Medicine** (Anaesthesiology; Anatomy; Biochemistry; Biophysics; Cardiology; Dermatology; Forensic Medicine and Dentistry; Genetics; Gynaecology and Obstetrics; Health Sciences; Immunology; Medicine; Microbiology; Neurology; Occupational Health; Ophthalmology; Orthopaedics; Otorhinolaryngology; Paediatrics; Pathology; Pharmacology; Physiology; Psychiatry and Mental Health; Radiology; Surgery; Tropical Medicine); **Nursing and Midwifery** (Midwifery; Nursing); **Pharmacy** (Pharmacology; Pharmacy; Toxicology); **Public Health** *(Postgraduate)* (Health Administration; Health Education; Health Sciences; Public Health); **Rehabilitation** (Physical Therapy; Rehabilitation and Therapy; Speech Therapy and Audiology)

Further Information: Also 16 Teaching Hospitals

History: Founded 1934. Acquired present status 1986.

Governing Bodies: Board of Trustees

Academic Year: September to June (September-January; February-June)

Admission Requirements: Secondary school certificate and entrance examination

Fees: None for Iranian students. Vary according to programmes for foreigners

Main Language(s) of Instruction: Farsi, English

International Co-operation: With universities in Austria; France; Canada; Germany; Sweden; South Africa; United Kingdom; Pakistan; Armenia; Spain; Syria; Tajikistan; Bahrain; Kyrgyztan; Qatar; Japan; Indonesia; Malaysia. Participates in the WHO, UNESCO, ISESCO, UNFPA, UNICEF, ICO, FIWU, AAU, IAU, EMRO, ECHO programmes

Accrediting Agencies: Ministry of Health Medicine and Medical Education

Degrees and Diplomas: *Kardani (Associate degree)*: Dentistry, Allied Medical Sciences, 2 yrs; *Karshebasi (Bachelor's degree)*: Nursing, Rehabilitation Medicine, Allied Medical Sciences (BS), 4 yrs; *Karshenasi Arshad (Master's degree)*: Public Health (MPH), 1-2 yrs; *Karshenasi Arshad (Master's degree)*: Public Health, Nursing, Rehabilitation Medicine, Allied Medical Sciences (MS), a further 2 yrs; *Doctorate*: Dentistry (DDS), 2 yrs; *Doctorate*: Medicine (MD), 7 yrs; *Doctorate*: Medicine, Rehabilitation, Nursing, Pharmacy, Public Health (PhD), 2 yrs following Master's Degree; *Doctorate*: Pharmacy (PharmD), 6 yrs. Specialisation 2-6 yrs

Student Services: Academic counselling, Canteen, Cultural centre, Employment services, Foreign student adviser, Foreign Studies Centre, Handicapped facilities, Health services, Language programs, Nursery care, Social counselling, Sports facilities

Student Residential Facilities: 11 dormitories for boys, 6 dormitories for girls, 1 dormitory for couples

Special Facilities: National Museum of History of Medical Sciences.

Libraries: 40 Libraries. 81,300 Farsi books, 85,299 English books

Publications: Acta Medica Iranica *(quarterly)*; Audiology *(biannually)*; Daroo, Related to Pharmacy and Biomedical Sciences *(quarterly)*; Hayat, Journal of the Faculty of Nursing and Midwifery *(quarterly)*; Iranian Journal of Diabetes and Lipid Disorders *(quarterly)*; Iranian Journal of Environmental Health Science and Engineering *(quarterly)*; Iranian Journal of Nuclear Medicine *(quarterly)*; Iranian Journal of Paediatrics *(biannually)*; Iranian Journal of Public Health *(quarterly)*; Iranian Journal of Radiology *(biannually)*; Journal of Dentistry *(quarterly)*; Journal of School of Public Health and

Institute of Public Health Research *(quarterly)*; Journal of the Faculty of Medicine *(quarterly)*

Last Updated: 01/12/11

THE UNIVERSITY OF GUILAN

Daneshgah Guilan

PO Box 1841, Rasht, 41625 Guilan

Tel: +98(131) 323-2806

Fax: +98(131) 323-2806

EMail: int@guilan.ac.ir

Website: http://www.guilan.ac.ir

President: Abdollah Hatamzadeh (2010-)

International Relations: Afshar Mohammadian Mansour, Director, International Relations

Faculties

Agriculture (Agricultural Equipment; Agriculture; Agronomy; Animal Husbandry; Forestry; Horticulture; Irrigation; Plant and Crop Protection); **Arts and Architecture** (Architecture; Fine Arts; Graphic Design; Music; Town Planning); **Engineering** (Civil Engineering; Electronic Engineering; Engineering; Mechanical Engineering; Textile Technology); **Humanities** (Arabic; Cultural Studies; English; Geography; History; Industrial Management; Law; Persian; Political Sciences; Psychology; Russian); **Mathematical Sciences** (Applied Mathematics; Mathematics; Statistics); **Natural Resources** (Aquaculture; Forestry; Natural Resources; Water Management); **Physical Education** (Physical Education); **Science** (Analytical Chemistry; Animal Husbandry; Applied Chemistry; Biology; Chemistry; Inorganic Chemistry; Nuclear Physics; Organic Chemistry; Physical Chemistry; Physics; Solid State Physics)

History: Founded 1976.

Academic Year: September to July (September-January; February-July)

Admission Requirements: Secondary school certificate and entrance examination

Main Language(s) of Instruction: Farsi

International Co-operation: Cooperation with the Universities of the Caspian Region

Degrees and Diplomas: *Karshebasi (Bachelor's degree) (BA; BSc)*: 4 yrs; *Karshenasi Arshad (Master's degree) (MA; MSc)*: a further $2\frac{1}{2}$ yrs; *Doctorate*

Student Services: Academic counselling, Canteen, Cultural centre, Employment services, Foreign student adviser, Foreign Studies Centre, Handicapped facilities, Health services, Language programs, Social counselling, Sports facilities

Student Residential Facilities: For c. 1,500 students

Special Facilities: Natural History Museum

Libraries: 290,000 vols; 794 periodical subscriptions; electronic networks (ACS, Science Direct, OUP, IOP, ISI Knowledge, Mathscinet, EBSCO

Press or Publishing House: Enteshارat Daneshgah-e-Guilan

Academic Staff *2009-2010*	TOTAL
FULL-TIME	407
PART-TIME	24
STAFF WITH DOCTORATE	
FULL-TIME	407
Student Numbers *2009-2010*	
All (Foreign Included)	9,400

Last Updated: 22/08/11

TRAINING BUREAU FOR INDUSTRIAL MANAGEMENT

Tehran

Tel: +98(21) 204-1081 +98(21) 205-2095

Fax: +98(21) 201-3408

EMail: info@imior.com

Programmes

Industrial Management

Degrees and Diplomas: *Karshenasi Arshad (Master's degree) (MA)*

UNIVERSITY OF APPLIED SCIENCES AND TECHNOLOGY

751 Enghelab eslami Ave, Tehran

Tel: +98(21) 82779

Fax: +98(21) 888-08987

Website: http://www.uast.ac.ir

Chancellor: Ali A. Tofigh (1993-)

Centres

Agriculture (Agriculture); **Basic Sciences and Services**; **Industrial Technology** (Industrial Engineering); **Technical Sciences** (Technology)

History: Founded 1992.

Main Language(s) of Instruction: Farsi

UNIVERSITY OF ART, TEHRAN

PO Box 14155-6464, Tehran

Tel: +98(21) 895-4601-5

Fax: +98(21) 895-4609

EMail: international-office@art.ac.ir

Website: http://www.art.ac.ir

President: Mohammad Reza Hafezi (1995-)

Colleges

Applied Arts (Handicrafts; Industrial Design; Textile Design; Weaving); **Architecture and Town Planning** (Architecture; Town Planning); **Cinema and Theatre** (Cinema and Television; Theatre); **Music** (Music); **Visual Arts** (Graphic Design; Painting and Drawing; Photography; Sculpture)

History: Founded 1980.

Academic Year: September to June (September-December; February-June)

Admission Requirements: Secondary school certificate

Main Language(s) of Instruction: Farsi

Degrees and Diplomas: *Karshebasi (Bachelor's degree) (BA)*: 4 yrs; *Karshenasi Arshad (Master's degree) (MA)*: a further 2 yrs; *Doctorate (PhD)*: a further 5 yrs

Student Services: Canteen, Cultural centre, Foreign student adviser, Handicapped facilities, Health services

Student Residential Facilities: For c. 2,200 students

Special Facilities: Farabi Arts Centre

Libraries: Central Library

Publications: Arts *(quarterly)*

Press or Publishing House: Publication Centre

UNIVERSITY OF BIRJAND (U OF B)

PO Box 97175/615, Shokatabad Campus, Birjand, Khorasan

Tel: +98(561) 223-4803-4

Fax: +98(561) 223-0009

EMail: contact@birjand.ac.ir

Website: http://www.birjand.ac.ir

President: Mohammad Reza Miri (2006-)
Tel: +98(561) 250-2008, Fax: +98(561) 250-2009
EMail: mmiri@bums.ac.ir

Director for Administrative and Financial Affairs: G. R. Zamani
Tel: +98(561) 223-0516, Fax: +98(561) 223-0515
EMail: gzamani@birjand.ac.ir

International Relations: Reza Pazhouhesh
Tel: +98(561) 250-2516, Fax: +98(561) 250-2515

Faculties

Agriculture (Agriculture; Agronomy; Irrigation; Zoology); **Arts and Humanities** (Education; History; Literature; Physical Education); **Engineering** (Computer Engineering; Electrical Engineering; Engineering; Materials Engineering; Mechanical Engineering); **Fine Arts** (Archaeology; Fine Arts); **Science** (Chemistry; Geology; Mathematics; Natural Sciences; Physics; Statistics)

History: Founded 1976, acquired present status 1991.

Academic Year: September to July (September-February; February-July)

Admission Requirements: Secondary school certificate and national entrance examination

Main Language(s) of Instruction: Farsi

International Co-operation: With University of Osmanieh, India and Brunel University, United Kingdom

Accrediting Agencies: Ministry of Science, Research and Technology

Degrees and Diplomas: *Kardani (Associate degree)*: Arts; Engineering; Agriculture; Fine Arts, 2 yrs; *Karshebasi (Bachelor's degree)*: Science; Arts and Humanities; Engineering; Agriculture (BA; BSc), 4 yrs; *Karshenasi Arshad (Master's degree)*: Science; Arts and Humanities; Engineering; Agriculture (MA; MSc), a further 2 yrs; *Doctorate*: Science; Engineering, 4-6 yrs

Student Services: Academic counselling, Canteen, Cultural centre, Employment services, Health services, Language programs, Social counselling, Sports facilities

Student Residential Facilities: For 5,000 students

Special Facilities: Movie Studio, Observatory

Libraries: Central Library and 4 Faculty Libraries

Last Updated: 20/02/12

UNIVERSITY OF ISFAHAN

Daneshgah-e-Isfahan (UI)

Hezar Jarib Street, Darvaze Shiraz, Isfahan 81746-73441
Tel: +98(311) 793-2001 +98(311) 793-2002 +98(311) 793-040
Fax: +98(311) 668-7396 +98(311) 668-2910
EMail: int-office@ui.ac.ir
Website: http://www.ui.ac.ir

Chancellor: Mohamad Hossein Ramesht Tel: +98(311) 793-2002

Vice-Chancellor: Hossein Harsij
Tel: +98(311) 793-2003, Fax: +98(311) 668-7396
EMail: harsij@ase.ui.ac.ir

International Relations: Arash Shahin, Director
Tel: +98(311) 793-2039, Fax: +98(311) 668-2910

Faculties

Administrative Sciences and Economics (Accountancy; Economics; Law; Management; Political Sciences); **Educational Sciences and Psychology** (Education; Educational and Student Counselling; Educational Sciences; Library Science; Psychology); **Engineering** (Biomedical Engineering; Biotechnology; Chemical Engineering; Civil Engineering; Computer Engineering; Electronic Engineering; Information Technology; Mechanical Engineering; Surveying and Mapping); **Foreign Languages** (Arabic; English; French; German; Linguistics); **Literature and Humanities** (Geography; History; Koran; Literature; Persian; Philosophy; Social Sciences; Theology); **Mathematics and Computer Science** *(Khansar Institute of Higher Education)* (Applied Mathematics; Computer Engineering; Computer Science; Mathematics; Statistics); **Physical Education and Sports Science** (Physical Education); **Science** (Biology; Chemistry; Geology; Mathematics; Physics; Statistics)

History: Founded 1946 as College. Became a State university and acquired current status 1958. Faculty of Medicine became a seperate entity in 1986.

Governing Bodies: Ministry of Science and Technology

Academic Year: September to July

Admission Requirements: Secondary school diploma and university entrance examination.

Fees: No fees required for home students. Fees for overseas students vary according to region.

Main Language(s) of Instruction: Farsi

International Co-operation: With universities in Germany, France, Jordan, Syria, Italy, Sweden, Canada and other countries.

Accrediting Agencies: Ministry of Science, Research and Technology

Degrees and Diplomas: *Karshebasi (Bachelor's degree) (BA; BSc)*: 4-5 yrs; *Karshenasi Arshad (Master's degree) (MA; MSc)*: a further 2 -3 yrs; *Doctorate (PhD)*: a further 4-5 yrs

Student Services: Academic counselling, Canteen, Cultural centre, Employment services, Foreign student adviser, Handicapped facilities, Health services, Language programs, Nursery care, Social counselling, Sports facilities

Student Residential Facilities: Yes

Special Facilities: Geology Museum; Biology Museum; Movie Studio; University Memorial Museum

Libraries: Central Library; Faculty libraries and department libraries, total, 438,063 vols (in Farsi, Arabic, English, French, German, Armenian)

Publications: Comparative Theology, Journal of the Faculty of Literature and Humanities *(biannually)*; Geography and Environmental Planning, Journal of the Faculty of Literature and Humanities *(quarterly)*; Geography Research, Journal of the Faculty of Literature and Humanities *(quarterly)*; Historical Research, Journal of the Faculty of Literature and Humanities *(quarterly)*; International Economics, Journal of the Faculty of Administrative Sciences and Economics *(biannually)*; Iranian Journal of Petrology, Journal of the Faculty of Engineering *(quarterly)*; Iranian Journal of Plant Biology, Journal of the Faculty of Sciences *(biannually)*; Journal of Financial Accounting Research, Journal of the Faculty of Administrative Sciences and Economics *(biannually)*; Journal of Metaphysics, Journal of the Faculty of Literature and Humanities *(quarterly)*; Journal of Persian Language and Literature (GOHARE GOYA), Journal of the Faculty of Literature and Humanities *(quarterly)*; Journal of Regional and Urban Planning, Journal of the Faculty of Literature and Humanities *(quarterly)*; Journal of Research in Linguistics, Journal of the Faculty of Foreign Languages *(quarterly)*; Practical Sociology, Journal of the Faculty of Literature and Humanities *(quarterly)*; Research on Persian Language Literature, Journal of the Faculty of Literature and Humanities *(quarterly)*; Researches in Sedimentology and Cryptology, Journal of the Faculty of Sciences *(quarterly)*; Taxonomy and Biosystematics, Journal of the Faculty of Sciences *(biannually)*

Press or Publishing House: Isfahan University Publishing House

Academic Staff *2009-2010*	MEN	WOMEN	**TOTAL**
FULL-TIME	494	391	**885**
STAFF WITH DOCTORATE			
FULL-TIME	436	58	**494**
Student Numbers *2009-2010*			
All (Foreign Included)	5,342	10,152	**15,494**
FOREIGN ONLY	61	8	**69**

Part-time students, 285. **Distance students**, 125. **Evening students**, 4,902.

Last Updated: 01/12/11

UNIVERSITY OF KASHAN (UOK)

Km 6, Ravand Bvd, Kashan, 87317-51167 Isfahan
Tel: +98(361) 591-2125
Fax: +98(361) 555-2930
EMail: isco@kashanu.ac.ir
Website: http://www.kashanu.ac.ir

Chancellor: Abbas Ketabi (2011-)
Tel: +98(361) 591-2100 EMail: chancellor@kashanu.ac.ir

Administrative Officer: Mahdi Mohammadzadeh
EMail: proffice@kashanu.ac.ir

International Relations: Javad Safaei Ghomi, Head, International Relations EMail: safaei@kashanu.ac.ir

Faculties

Architecture and Arts (Archaeology; Architecture; Fine Arts; Handicrafts; Textile Design; Textile Technology); **Chemistry** (Analytical Chemistry; Chemistry; Inorganic Chemistry; Organic Chemistry; Physical Chemistry); **Earth Sciences and Natural Resources** (Earth Sciences; Natural Resources; Water Management); **Engineering** (Chemical Engineering; Civil Engineering; Computer Engineering; Electrical Engineering; Environmental Engineering; Mechanical Engineering; Mining Engineering); **Humanities** (Arabic; Education; Educational Sciences; English; Islamic Law; Islamic Theology; Koran; Literature; Persian; Philosophy; Physical Education; Psychology; Religion; Social Sciences; Sports; Traditional Eastern Medicine); **Mathematics and Statics** (Applied Mathematics; Mathematics; Statistics); **Physics** (Physical Engineering; Physics; Science Education; Solid State Physics)

Institutes

Energy (Energy Engineering); **Essential Oils** (Botany); **Nanoscience and Nanotechnology** (Nanotechnology)

Research Centres

Carpet (Handicrafts; Textile Design; Textile Technology); **Kashan** (Literature; Native Language)

History: Founded 1973, became Teacher Training University 1989. Acquired present status and title1994.

Governing Bodies: University Council

Academic Year: September to July (September-February; February-July)

Admission Requirements: National Entrance Exam (Kunkur)

Main Language(s) of Instruction: Farsi

International Co-operation: with institutions in Iraq and Afghanistan

Accrediting Agencies: Ministry of Science, Research and Technology

Degrees and Diplomas: *Karshebasi (Bachelor's degree)*: 4 yrs; *Karshenasi Arshad (Master's degree)*: Chemistry; Engineering; Science; Humanities; Architecture and Arts; Natural Resources and Earth Science, a further 2 yrs following Bachelor's; *Doctorate*. Also Higher National Diploma

Student Services: Academic counselling, Canteen, Cultural centre, Employment services, Foreign student adviser, Foreign Studies Centre, Handicapped facilities, Health services, Language programs, Nursery care, Social counselling, Sports facilities

Student Residential Facilities: Yes

Libraries: 172,000 vols in Persian; 44,500 vols in English; 455 Persion periodical subscriptions; 55 English periodical subscriptions.

Publications: Hadith Studies, The study of the Prophet Mohammad and his progeny's sayings *(quarterly)*; Kashan Shenakht, The study of Kashan city *(annually)*; Mysticism Studies, The study of Islamic and Mysticism *(quarterly)*

Academic Staff *2011-2012*	MEN	WOMEN	**TOTAL**
FULL-TIME	184	14	**198**
PART-TIME	168	52	**220**
STAFF WITH DOCTORATE			
FULL-TIME	150	11	**161**
PART-TIME	68	2	**70**
Student Numbers *2011-2012*			
All (Foreign Included)	2,765	3,555	**6,320**
FOREIGN ONLY	29	16	**45**

Distance students, 266. **Evening students**, 1,796.

Last Updated: 26/03/12

UNIVERSITY OF KURDISTAN

PO Box 416, Pasdaran Street, Sanandaj, 66135 Kurdistan
Tel: +98(871) 666-0066
Fax: +98(871) 662-4002
EMail: uok.ac.@uok.ac.ir
Website: http://www.uok.ac.ir

Chancellor: Jahanshir Amini EMail: JAmini@uok.ac.ir

Vice-Chancellor for Academic Affairs: Ghorban Ali Sadegi EMail: gsadeghi@uok.ac.ir

Faculties

Agriculture (Agricultural Economics; Agricultural Engineering; Agriculture; Agronomy; Animal Husbandry; Horticulture; Plant and Crop Protection; Water Science); **Art and Architecture** (Architecture; Fine Arts; Urban Studies); **Engineering** (Civil Engineering; Electronic Engineering; Engineering; Industrial Engineering; Technology) *Dean*: Habibollah Daniali; **Literature and Social Sciences** (Accountancy; Arabic; Arts and Humanities; Business Administration; Education; Educational Sciences; English; Law; Literature; Management; Persian; Physical Education; Psychology); **Natural Resources** (Earth Sciences; Environmental Studies; Fishery; Forestry; Geography; Water Management); **Science** (Chemistry; Geology; Mathematics; Physics)

History: Founded 1974. Acquired present status 1991.

Admission Requirements: Secondary school certificate

Main Language(s) of Instruction: Farsi

Accrediting Agencies: Ministry of Science, Research and Technology

Degrees and Diplomas: *Kardani (Associate degree)*: 2 yrs; *Karshebasi (Bachelor's degree) (BA; BSc)*: 4 yrs; *Karshenasi Arshad (Master's degree) (MSc; MA)*: a further 2 yrs; *Doctorate (PhD)*: 4 yrs

Student Services: Canteen, Health services, Nursery care, Sports facilities

Libraries: Central Library

Last Updated: 06/12/11

UNIVERSITY OF MOHAGHEGH ARDEBILI

PO Box 179, University Street, Ardabil 56199-11367
Tel: +98(451) 551-0133
Fax: +98(451) 551-0133
EMail: intl_office@uma.ac.ir
Website: http://www.uma.ac.ir

President: Masoud Ganji (2009-) EMail: mganji@uma.ac.ir

Vice-Chancellor: Jabraeil Razmjou EMail: razmjou@uma.ac.ir

International Relations: Roya Rassizadeh, Director, International Relations Office EMail: intl_ofic@uma.ac.ir

Faculties

Agriculture (Agricultural Engineering; Agricultural Equipment; Agronomy; Animal Husbandry; Biotechnology; Crop Production; Entomology; Horticulture; Plant and Crop Protection; Soil Science); **Engineering** (Architecture; Chemical Engineering; Civil Engineering; Computer Engineering; Electrical Engineering; Engineering; Software Engineering); **LIterature and Foreign Languages** *(Namin)* (Archaeology; Geography; Literature; Persian; Psychology; Religion; Sports; Tourism); **Science** (Applied Chemistry; Biology; Crop Production; Mathematics; Physics; Statistics)

History: Founded 1978 as branch of Tabriz University, became independent 1993 as Ardebil University, and acquired present title 1996.

Governing Bodies: University Council

Academic Year: October to January; February to June

Admission Requirements: Secondary school certificate and entrance examination

Fees: None

Main Language(s) of Instruction: Farsi

Degrees and Diplomas: *Karshebasi (Bachelor's degree) (BA; BSc)*: 4 yrs; *Karshenasi Arshad (Master's degree)*; *Doctorate*

Student Services: Academic counselling, Canteen, Cultural centre, Employment services, Foreign student adviser, Health services, Language programs, Nursery care, Sports facilities

Student Residential Facilities: Yes

Libraries: Central Library, 37,000 vols

Academic Staff *2010-2011*	MEN	WOMEN	**TOTAL**
FULL-TIME	167	10	**177**
Student Numbers *2010-2011*			
All (Foreign Included)	3,726	4,618	**8,344**

Last Updated: 11/10/11

UNIVERSITY OF SCIENCE AND CULTURE

Daneshgah Elm va Farhang

Ashrafi Esfahani Boulevard, Park Street, PO Box 13145-871, Tehran 1461968151
Tel: +98(21) 4423-8171-5
Fax: +98(21) 4421-4750
EMail: info@usc.ac.ir
Website: http://www.usc.ac.ir/

President: Mohammad Hossein Imani Khoshkhoo (2011-) Tel: +98(21) 4421-4745-46, Fax: +98(21) 4421-4750 EMail: imanikhoshkoo@usc.ac.ir

Vice-President, Administration: Hasan Sheybani Tel: +98(21) 4421-4755 EMail: sheybani@usc.ac.ir

International Relations: Ahmad Moallem, Director, International Relations Tel: +98(21) 4423-8171, Ext. 230 EMail: amoallem@usc.ac.ir

Departments

Basic Sciences (Biology; Statistics)

Faculties

Arts and Architecture (Architecture; Graphic Arts; Interior Design; Painting and Drawing; Structural Architecture; Textile Design; Visual Arts); **Engineering and Technology** (Civil Engineering; Computer Engineering; Electrical Engineering; Engineering; Industrial Engineering; Software Engineering; Technology); **Humanities** (Accountancy; Art Management; Business Administration; Clinical Psychology; Cultural Studies; Industrial Management; Law; Social Studies)

History: Created 1993 by the Iranian Academic Center for Education, Culture and Research (ACECR) with special permit by the Ministry of Science, Research and Technology, Iran as Jahad Daneshgahi Higher Education Institution. Acquired current title and status 2005.

Governing Bodies: Board of Trustees

Academic Year: October to July

Admission Requirements: Secondary school certificate and entrance examination

Fees: (Rials): 9,000,000 (c. $1,000) per annum

Main Language(s) of Instruction: Farsi

International Co-operation: With universities in Malaysia, Thailand and United Kingdom

Accrediting Agencies: Academic Center for Education, Culture and Research (ACECR)

Degrees and Diplomas: *Karshebasi (Bachelor's degree)*: Accounting; Applied-Scientific Accounting; Clinical Psychology; Cultural-Artistic Management; Industrial Management; Law; Statistics; Architecture Engineering; Clothing Design; Fabric Design; Graphics; Interior Architecture; Painting; Visual Arts; Civil Engineering; Computer Engineering; Computer Software Technology Engineering; Electrical Engineering; Industrial Engineering, 4 yrs; *Karshenasi Arshad (Master's degree)*: Art Research; Civil Engineering (Earthquake); Civil Engineering (Structure); Financial Engineering; Industrial Engineering; Clinical Psychology (Family Therapy Approach); Cultural-Social Studies; Law (Private); MBA (Strategic Management); Biology (Zoology), 2 yrs; *Doctorate*: Incipient Biology, 4 yrs

Student Services: Academic counselling, Cultural centre, Employment services, Health services, Language programs, Nursery care, Social counselling, Sports facilities

Student Residential Facilities: None

Special Facilities: Equipped laboratories and workshops; Graphic workshops equipped with computers, VCRs, TV sets, light desks, and slide projectors; Photography laboratories

Libraries: Central and three specialized branch libraries equipped with CDs in various scientific fields and internet, and the latest scientific sources and valid scientific magazines (national and international) by being connected to the valid scientific websites.

Last Updated: 26/10/11

UNIVERSITY OF SEMNAN

Daneshgah-e-Semnan

PO Box 35195-363, Mowlawi Boulevard, Motahari Square, Semnan, 35196-45399 Semnan

Tel: +98(231) 332-3088 +98(231) 333-1665

Fax: +98(231) 332-1005

EMail: admin@semnan.ac.ir

President: Ali Kheirodin
Tel: +98(231) 332-8860 EMail: akheirodin@semnan.ac.ir

Faculties

Art (Architecture; Handicrafts; Video); **Engineering** (Chemical Engineering; Civil Engineering; Electronic Engineering; Metallurgical Engineering; Power Engineering); **Humanities** (Arabic; Business Administration; Educational Administration; English; Persian; Theology); **Science** (Chemistry; Mathematics; Physics); **Teacher Training** *(Mahdi Shahr)* (Mathematics; Mathematics Education); **Veterinary Medicine** *(Shahmirzad)* (Laboratory Techniques; Veterinary Science)

History: Founded 1974 as school, became Educational Complex 1990, and acquired present status and title 1993.

Governing Bodies: Board of Managers

Academic Year: September to June (September-January; February-June)

Admission Requirements: Secondary school certificate and entrance examination

Main Language(s) of Instruction: Farsi

Degrees and Diplomas: *Kardani (Associate degree)*: 2 yrs; *Karshebasi (Bachelor's degree) (BA; BSc)*: 4 yrs; *Karshebasi (Bachelor's degree)*: Engineering, 4 yrs; *Karshenasi Arshad (Master's degree) (MA; MSc)*: a further 2 yrs; *Karshenasi Arshad (Master's degree)*: Engineering (M.Sc), a further 2 yrs

Student Services: Academic counselling, Canteen, Cultural centre, Employment services, Health services, Social counselling, Sports facilities

Student Residential Facilities: Yes

Libraries: Central Library; Library of Humanities; Library of Teacher Training; Library of Veterinary Medicine

Last Updated: 01/12/11

UNIVERSITY OF SOCIAL WELFARE AND REHABILITATION SCIENCES, TEHRAN

Koodakyar Avenue, Daneshgah Street, Evin, Tehran 19834

Tel: +98(21) 222180008

Fax: +98(21) 22180121

EMail: international_affairs@uswr.ac.ir

Website: http://www.uswr.ac.ir

Chancellor: Mohamad Taghi Joghataii (1993-)

Faculties

Nursing and Midwifery (Midwifery; Nursing); **Psychology** (Psychology); **Rehabilitation Sciences** (Health Sciences; Occupational Health; Occupational Therapy; Physical Therapy; Rehabilitation and Therapy)

History: Founded 1992. Affiliated to the State Welfare Organisation.

Governing Bodies: University Executive Council

Academic Year: September to June (September-January; February-June)

Admission Requirements: Secondary school certificate

Main Language(s) of Instruction: Farsi

Degrees and Diplomas: *Karshebasi (Bachelor's degree) (BA)*: 4 yrs; *Karshenasi Arshad (Master's degree) (MA)*: a further 2 yrs; *Doctorate (PhD)*

Student Services: Academic counselling, Canteen, Cultural centre, Employment services, Foreign student adviser, Foreign Studies Centre, Handicapped facilities, Health services, Language programs, Nursery care, Social counselling, Sports facilities

Libraries: c. 9,570 vols and c. 3,260 vols in English

Publications: Iranian Rehabilitation Journal

Last Updated: 06/12/11

UNIVERSITY OF TABRIZ

Daneshgahe Tabriz

PO Box 711-51664, 29 Bahman Boulevard, Tabriz, 5166614766 Eastern Azerbaijan

Tel: +98(411) 334-0080-9

Fax: +98(411) 334-4013

EMail: webmaster@tabrizu.ac.ir

Website: http://www.tabrizu.ac.ir

President: Parviz Ajideh (2012-) EMail: Parviz-333@yahoo.com

Vice-Chancellor for Financial Affairs: Hamid Reza Ghassemzadeh Tel: +98(411) 334-1302 EMail: Ghassemzadeh@tabrizu.ac.ir

International Relations: Farahmand Farrokhi
Tel: +98(411) 335-5994 EMail: International@tabrizu.ac.ir

Centres

Astronomical Research and Observatory *(Khajeh Nassir Aldin)* (Astronomy and Space Science); **Geographical Research** (Geography; Geology; Hydraulic Engineering; Meteorology; Regional Planning; Regional Studies; Rural Studies; Urban Studies)

Colleges

Technical *(Marand)* (Civil Engineering; Construction Engineering; Engineering; Surveying and Mapping)

Faculties

Agriculture (Agricultural Economics; Agricultural Equipment; Agriculture; Agronomy; Animal Husbandry; Crop Production; Food Science; Food Technology; Forestry; Horticulture; Irrigation; Plant and Crop Protection; Plant Pathology; Soil Science); **Civil Engineering** (Civil Engineering; Hydraulic Engineering; Road Engineering; Structural Architecture; Surveying and Mapping; Transport Engineering); **Education and Psychology** (Clinical Psychology; Education; Educational Technology; Library Science; Physical Education; Psychology); **Electrical and Computer Engineering** (Electrical Engineering; Electronic Engineering; Engineering; Power Engineering; Telecommunications Engineering); **Humanities and Social Sciences** (Architecture; Arts and Humanities; Economics; Geography; History; Law; Social Sciences; Town Planning); **Mathematics** (Applied Mathematics; Computer Science; Mathematics; Statistics); **Mechanical Engineering** (Hydraulic Engineering; Materials Engineering; Mechanical Engineering; Mechanics; Metallurgical Engineering; Production Engineering; Transport Engineering); **Natural Sciences** (Biological and Life Sciences; Botany; Geology; Natural Sciences; Zoology); **Persian Literature and Foreign Languages** (Cultural Studies; English; French; Islamic Studies; Persian; Philosophy); **Physics** (Astrophysics; Atomic and Molecular Physics; Mathematical Physics; Nuclear Physics; Physics; Solid State Physics); **Veterinary Medicine** (Laboratory Techniques; Veterinary Science)

Research Centres

Social Sciences (Social Sciences)

Research Institutes

Applied Physics and Astrophysical Research (Applied Physics; Astronomy and Space Science; Astrophysics; Laser Engineering; Solid State Physics)

Schools

Engineering Emerging Technologies (Electronic Engineering; Mechanical Engineering; Nanotechnology)

Further Information: Also Teaching and Research Centre of Khalat Poushan affiliated to the Faculty of Agriculture

History: Founded 1946 as the Azerbaycan University (University of Azerbaijan). Faculty of Medicine and Pharmacy detached in 1986 to inform an independent university. A State-run institution responsible to the Iranian Ministry of Science, Research and Technology.

Governing Bodies: University Directorate; Board of Trustees

Academic Year: September to June (September-January; February-June)

Admission Requirements: Secondary school certificate and competitive entrance examination

Fees: None

Main Language(s) of Instruction: Farsi

Accrediting Agencies: Iranian Ministry of Science, Research and Technology

Degrees and Diplomas: *Kardani (Associate degree)*: 2 yrs; *Karshebasi (Bachelor's degree) (BA; BSc)*: 4 yrs; *Karshenasi Arshad (Master's degree) (MA; MSc)*: a further 2 yrs; *Doctorate (PhD)*: a further 3-4 yrs

Student Services: Academic counselling, Canteen, Cultural centre, Employment services, Foreign student adviser, Handicapped facilities, Health services, Nursery care, Social counselling, Sports facilities

Student Residential Facilities: For 5400 single and 210 married students

Special Facilities: Khadjeh Nassir-Aldin Observatory and Planetarium

Libraries: Central Library, 93,619 vols; faculty libraries, total, 227,200

Publications: Journal of Agricultural Science *(quarterly)*; Journal of Faculty of Engineering *(quarterly)*; Journal of Faculty of Humanities and Social Sciences *(quarterly)*; Pazhoohesh, Research publication *(biannually)*

Last Updated: 02/12/11

UNIVERSITY OF TEHRAN

Daneshgahe Tehran (UT)

Enghelab Street, Tehran 14174
Tel: +98(21) 6111-2500
Fax: +98(21) 6111-2699
EMail: international@ut.ac.ir
Website: http://www.ut.ac.ir

President: Farhad Rahbar (2008-)
Tel: +98(21) 6611-2500, Fax: +98(21) 6646-2349
EMail: president@ut.ac.ir

Vice-President for Finance and Administration: Seyed Mohammad Moghimi Tel: +98(21) 6640-5046, Fax: +98(21) 6640-4848

International Relations: Mohammad A. Mousavi, Vice-President, International Tel: +98(21) 6664-9807, Fax: +98(21) 6649-8873

Centres

Electrotechnology (Electronic Engineering) *Director*: Parviz Jabeh Dar Maralani; **International Studies** (International Studies); **Law and Criminology Research** *(Graduate)* (Criminology; Law); **Living with Desert** *(International Research Centre)* (Arid Land Studies) *Director*: Hassan Ahmadi; **Persian Studies** *(International)* (Linguistics; Literature; Persian) *Head*: M. Shahidi

Colleges

Agriculture and Natural Resources *(Karaj)* (Agricultural Economics; Agricultural Education; Agricultural Engineering; Agricultural Equipment; Agriculture; Agronomy; Animal Husbandry; Biotechnology; Food Science; Food Technology; Horticulture; Irrigation; Plant and Crop Protection; Soil Science); **Engineering** (Chemical Engineering; Civil Engineering; Electrical Engineering; Engineering; Industrial Engineering; Mechanical Engineering; Metallurgical Engineering; Mining Engineering; Surveying and Mapping) *Dean*: Mahmod Ahmad abadi; **Fine Arts** (Architecture; Fine Arts; Music; Performing Arts; Theatre; Urban Studies; Visual Arts) *Dean*: Mohsen Habibi; **Science** (Biology; Chemistry; Computer Science; Geology; Mathematics; Natural Sciences; Physics) *Dean*: Ali Maghari

Faculties

Arts and Humanities (Arabic; Archaeology; Arts and Humanities; Classical Languages; Education; Geography; History; Linguistics; Literature; Persian; Philosophy) *Dean*: Manochehre Akbari; **Economics** (Economics) *Dean*: Seyed Mansor Khalili Araghi; **Environmental Studies** (Environmental Studies) *Dean*: Gholam Reza Nabi Bidhendi; **Foreign Languages** (English; French; German; Indic Languages; Italian; Japanese; Modern Languages; Russian; Urdu) *Dean*: Farideh Alavi; **Law and Political Science** (Criminal Law; Criminology; International Relations; Islamic Law; Law; Political Sciences; Private Law; Public Law) *Dean*: Abbas Karimi; **Management** *(Karaj)* (Administration; Management) *Dean*: Seyed Reza Javadin; **Physical Education and Sports Science** (Physical Education; Sports) *Dean*: Mahmod Godarzi; **Psychology and Education** (Educational Administration; Educational Sciences; Psychology) *Dean*: Gholam Ali Afroz; **Social Sciences** (Anthropology; Communication Studies; Demography and Population; Social Sciences; Social Welfare) *Dean*: Gholam Reza Jamshidiha; **Theology and Islamic Studies** (Cultural Studies; History of Religion; Islamic Studies; Islamic Theology; Religious Studies) *Dean*: Mohammad Reza Emam; **Veterinary Medicine** (Veterinary Science) *Dean*: Parviz Tajik

Institutes

Archaeology (Archaeology) *Director*: Haiedeh Laleh; **Biochemistry and Biophysics** (Biochemistry; Biophysics) *Director*: Ali Akbar Sabori; **Geophysics** (Geophysics; Seismology) *Director*: Farhang Ahmadi Ghivi

Research Centres

Arts and Culture (Cultural Studies; Fine Arts) *Head*: Piroz Hanachi; **History of Science** (History; Natural Sciences) *Head*: Ahmad Badkobeh Hazaveh

Further Information: Also Higher Education Complexes at Abour-eihan and Ghom and Encyclopaedia Institute (Dahkhoda)

History: Founded 1934 as an autonomous institution, responsible to the Ministry of Higher Education and Culture. Received Charter of Independence 1941. Faculty of Medicine detached 1986 to form separate University.

Academic Year: September to June (September-January; January-June)

Admission Requirements: Secondary school certificate and competitive entrance examination

Fees: (US Dollars): Foreign students, 2,000-4,000 per annum

Main Language(s) of Instruction: Farsi

Degrees and Diplomas: *Karshebasi (Bachelor's degree) (BA; BSc)*: 4-6 yrs; *Karshenasi Arshad (Master's degree) (MA; MSc)*: a further 2 1/2-4 1/2 yrs; *Doctorate (PhD)*

Student Services: Academic counselling, Canteen, Cultural centre, Employment services, Foreign student adviser, Foreign Studies Centre, Handicapped facilities, Health services, Language programs, Nursery care, Social counselling, Sports facilities

Student Residential Facilities: Yes

Special Facilities: Museum of Zoology and Entomology

Libraries: Central Library, c. 450,000 vols

Press or Publishing House: Tehran University Press

Last Updated: 16/12/08

UNIVERSITY OF ZABOL

PO Box 98615-538, Jahad Square, Zabol
Tel: +98(542) 223-2112-18
Fax: +98(542) 222-6765
EMail: info@zabol.ac.ir
Website: http://www.uoz.ac.ir

Vice-Chancellor: Ali Reza Shahriyari
Tel: +98(542) 223-2017, Fax: +98(542) 223-2017
EMail: Nimaaryan2002@yahoo.com

International Relations: Ali Shahraki
Tel: +98(542) 225-0480, Fax: +98(542) 225-0480
EMail: shahraki66@yahoo.co.uk

Colleges

Veterinary Science (Laboratory Techniques; Veterinary Science)

Faculties

Agriculture (Agricultural Economics; Agronomy; Animal Husbandry; Food Science; Irrigation; Plant and Crop Protection); **Art and Architecture** (Archaeology; Architecture; Handicrafts; Weaving); **Arts and Humanities** (Arabic; Arts and Humanities; Geography (Human); History; Islamic Studies; Literature; Oriental Languages; Persian; Theology; Urdu); **Engineering** (Civil Engineering; Computer Science; Electrical Engineering; Engineering; Mechanical Engineering); **Natural Resources** (Environmental Studies; Fishery; Natural Resources; Paper Technology; Wood Technology); **Science** (Biology; Chemistry; Mathematics; Physics)

Research Centres

Agriculture (Agricultural Management; Animal Husbandry; Botany; Crop Production; Fishery; Fruit Production; Harvest Technology; Meat and Poultry; Soil Science; Vegetable Production; Veterinary Science)

History: Founded 1979 as Agriculture Junior College. Became Zabol University 1999.

Academic Year: September to July

Admission Requirements: Secondary school certificate and entrance examination

Fees: None; evening students (US Dollars): 2,000 per semester

Main Language(s) of Instruction: Farsi

International Co-operation: With universities in Italy, Pakistan, Afghanistan and Germany.

Accrediting Agencies: Ministry of Science, Research and Technology

Degrees and Diplomas: *Kardani (Associate degree)*: Agronomy and Plant Breeding; Animal Husbandry; Archaeology; Architecture; Civil Engineering; Electrical Engineering; Mechanical Engineering; Veterinary Science (ASc), 2 yrs; *Karshebasi (Bachelor's degree)*: Agriculture; Natural Resources; Law; Natural Sciences; Arts; Computer Science; Literature; Humanities; Veterinary Science (BA; BSc), 4 yrs; *Karshenasi Arshad (Master's degree)*: Agricultural Economics; Agronomy; Animal Husbandry; Botany; Entomology (MA; MSc), 2 yrs

Student Services: Academic counselling, Canteen, Cultural centre, Employment services, Foreign student adviser, Foreign Studies Centre, Handicapped facilities, Health services, Language programs, Nursery care, Social counselling, Sports facilities

Student Residential Facilities: Yes

Special Facilities: Wildlife Museum; Zoological Gardens

Libraries: 60,000 vols (English, Farsi, Arabic); 400 periodicals (English, Farsi, Arabic)

Publications: Journal of Agricultural Sciences and Natural Resources *(quarterly)*

Last Updated: 06/12/11

URMIA UNIVERSITY

Urmia, 57135 West Azerbaijan
Tel: +98(441) 344-8131-3
Fax: +98(441) 344-3443
EMail: Chancellor@urmia.ac.ir
Website:http: //www.urmia.ac.ir

President: Hasaan Sedghi (2001-) Tel: +98(441) 345-5209

Vice-Chancellor for Personnel and Finance: Gholamreza Mansoorfar Tel: +98(441) 344-5420

International Relations: Jirair Carapetian
Tel: +98(441) 277-0555, Fax: +98(441) 277-9559
EMail: J.carapetian@mail.urmia.ac.ir

Faculties

Agriculture (Agricultural Equipment; Agriculture; Agronomy; Animal Husbandry; Food Science; Horticulture; Irrigation; Plant and Crop Protection; Soil Science); **Arts** (Architecture; Painting and Drawing; Town Planning); **Economics** (Accountancy; Economics; Management); **Engineering** (Architecture; Civil Engineering; Computer Engineering; Electrical and Electronic Engineering; Engineering; Mechanical Engineering; Mining Engineering; Rural Planning); **Literature** (Education; Educational Sciences; English; History; Modern Languages; Persian; Physical Education); **Natural Resources** (Forestry; Natural Resources); **Science** (Biology; Botany; Chemistry; Geology; Mathematics; Physics); **Veterinary Medicine** (Nutrition; Veterinary Science)

History: Founded 1965 as College of Agriculture, became university 1976. School of Medicine was detached 1985 to form separate University. There are three campuses.

Governing Bodies: University Board

Academic Year: September to July (September-February; February-July)

Admission Requirements: High school diploma (Diplomé dabirestam) and national entrance examination

Fees: None

Main Language(s) of Instruction: Farsi

International Co-operation: With universities in Azerbaijan, Australia, Iraq, Canada.

Accrediting Agencies: Ministry of Science, Research and Technology

Degrees and Diplomas: *Kardani (Associate degree)*: Rural Development; Veterinary Medicine, 2 yrs; *Karshebasi (Bachelor's degree)*: Agriculture; Engineering; Literature; Sciences (BSc; BA), 4 yrs; *Professional Doctorate*: Veterinary Medicine (DVM), 6 yrs; *Professional Doctorate*: Veterinary Science (DVSc), 3-4 yrs; *Karshenasi Arshad (Master's degree)*: Agriculture; Engineering; Sciences (MSc; MA), a further 2 yrs; *Doctorate*: Electronics; Biology (PhD), a further 3-4 yrs

Student Services: Academic counselling, Canteen, Health services, Social counselling, Sports facilities

Student Residential Facilities: For c. 3,500 students

Special Facilities: Geology Museum

Libraries: Total, 58,000 vols (38,000 in Farsi; 20,000 in other languages)

Last Updated: 18/12/08

URMIA UNIVERSITY OF MEDICAL SCIENCES

PO Box 1138, Dhjahad Avenue, Urmia 57147
Tel: +98(441) 222-6020
Fax: +98(441) 222-1841
EMail: info@umsu.ac.ir
Website: http://www.umsu.ac.ir

President: Ali Taqizadeh Afshari Tel: +98(441) 223-2296

Faculties

Dentistry (Dentistry); **Medicine** (Medicine); **Nursing and Midwifery** (Midwifery; Nursing); **Paramedical and Health Sciences** (Health Sciences; Paramedical Sciences); **Pharmacy** (Pharmacy)

History: Founded 1986. Previously part of the University of Urmia.

Academic Year: October to September (October-February; March-September)

Admission Requirements: Secondary school certificate or equivalent and entrance examination

Main Language(s) of Instruction: Farsi

Degrees and Diplomas: *Pre-University Certificate*: 2 yrs; *Kardani (Associate degree)*: Lab Sciences, Operating Theatre Technology, Occupational Health, Environmental Health, Family Health, Anaesthesiology, Radiology, 2 yrs; *Karshebasi (Bachelor's degree)*: Nursing, Midwifery, Environmental Health (BA), 4 yrs; *Professional Doctorate*: Medicine (MD), 7 yrs; *Karshenasi Arshad (Master's degree) (MA)*: a further 2 yrs. Also Diploma of Specialization

Student Services: Academic counselling, Canteen, Health services, Language programs, Nursery care, Sports facilities

Libraries: 14,000 vols

Publications: Urmia Medical Journal *(quarterly)*

Last Updated: 18/12/08

URMIA UNIVERSITY OF TECHNOLOGY

Band Highway, Urmia, West Azarbijan
Tel: +98(441) 3554180
Fax: +98(441) 3554184
Website: http://www.uut.ac.ir

Schools

Chemical Engineering (Chemical Engineering); **Computer Engineering** (Computer Engineering); **Industrial Engineering** (Industrial Engineering); **Information Technology** (Information Technology); **Mechanical Engineering** (Mechanical Engineering)

Main Language(s) of Instruction: Farsi

Degrees and Diplomas: *Kardani (Associate degree)*; *Karshebasi (Bachelor's degree)*; *Karshenasi Arshad (Master's degree)*; *Doctorate*

Last Updated: 19/12/08

VALI-E-ASR UNIVERSITY

PO Box 518, Shahid Ghafari Street, Rafsanjan
Tel: +98(391) 522-7416-18
Fax: +98(391) 522-7419
EMail: Pup_rel@vru.ac.ir
Website: http://www.vru.ac.ir

President: A. Bahrampour (1992-)

Programmes

Agriculture (Agriculture)

History: Founded 1992.

Degrees and Diplomas: *Kardani (Associate degree)*: 2 yrs; *Karshebasi (Bachelor's degree) (BA; BSc)*: 4 yrs; *Karshenasi Arshad (Master's degree) (MA; MSc)*: a further 2 yrs

YASUJ UNIVERSITY

PO Box 353, Yasuj 75914
Tel: +98(741) 222-3474 +98(741) 222-3188
Fax: +98(741) 222-3822
Website: http://www.yu.ac.ir

Director: Mohsen Askarian (1996-) Tel: +98(741) 217-12

Faculties

Agriculture (Agricultural Education; Agriculture; Animal Husbandry; Crop Production; Irrigation; Plant and Crop Protection; Soil Science); **Engineering** (Chemical Engineering; Civil Engineering; Materials Engineering; Mechanical Engineering); **Natural Resources** (Natural Resources); **Science** (Natural Sciences); **Social Sciences and Humanities** (Arts and Humanities; Social Sciences)

History: Founded 1983, acquired present status 1996.

Academic Year: September to June (September-January; February-June)

Admission Requirements: Secondary school certificate

Main Language(s) of Instruction: Farsi

Degrees and Diplomas: *Kardani (Associate degree)*: 2 yrs; *Karshebasi (Bachelor's degree)*: Agronomy; Animal Husbandry; Chemistry; Civil Engineering; Mathematics; Mechanics; Physics; Plant Protection, 4 yrs

Last Updated: 15/12/08

YASUJ UNIVERSITY OF MEDICAL SCIENCES

Motahari Boulevard, Yasuj 75914
Tel: +98(741) 222-7229
Fax: +98(741) 222-5689
Website: http://www.yums.ac.ir

Chancellor: Shahin Mohammad Sade (1994-)

Faculties

Dentistry (Dentistry); **Health Sciences** (Health Sciences); **Medicine** (Medicine); **Nursing and Midwifery** (Midwifery; Nursing); **Paramedical Studies** (Paramedical Sciences); **Pharmacy** (Pharmacy)

History: Founded 1990.

Academic Year: September to June

Main Language(s) of Instruction: Farsi

Degrees and Diplomas: *Kardani (Associate degree)*: 2 yrs; *Karshebasi (Bachelor's degree) (BA)*: 4 yrs; *Doctorate (PhD)*

Libraries: 13,045 vols

Publications: Armaghan Danesh

YAZD UNIVERSITY

Daneshgahe Yazd (YAZDUNI)

Yazd, 89195-741 Yazd
Tel: +98(351) 725-0119
Fax: +98(351) 725-0119
EMail: publicrelation@yazduni.ac.ir
Website: http://www.yazduni.ac.ir

President: Seyyed Ali Mohammad Mirmohammadi Meybodi
Tel: +98(351) 725-0111, Fax: +98(351) 725-6210
EMail: president-office@yazduni.ac.ir

Vice President for Finance and Admininstration: Mohammad Hossein Hakimi Meibodi EMail: mhakimi@yazduni.ac.ir

Departments

Theology (Theology)

Faculties

Art and Architecture (Architecture; Painting and Drawing; Town Planning); **Engineering** (Civil Engineering; Computer Engineering; Electronic Engineering; Industrial Engineering; Mechanical Engineering; Mining Engineering; Textile Technology); **Humanities** (Accountancy; Arts and Humanities; Business Administration; Economics; English; Geography; History; Industrial Management; Information Sciences; Islamic Studies; Library Science; Literature; Persian; Political Sciences; Religion; Theology); **Natural Resources and Desert Studies** (Arid Land Studies; Environmental Engineering; Forestry; Natural Resources; Soil Science; Water Management); **Science** (Chemistry; Computer Science; Mathematics; Natural Sciences; Physics; Statistics)

History: Founded 1988.

Academic Year: September to July (September-January; February-July)

Admission Requirements: Secondary school certificate and national entrance examination

Fees: (Rials): Evening students, 200,000 per term

Main Language(s) of Instruction: Farsi

International Co-operation: With universities in Austria, Russian Federation, France, Canada

Degrees and Diplomas: *Karshebasi (Bachelor's degree)*: Arts and Humanities (MA); Science; Chemistry; Mathematics; Physics (BSc), 4 yrs; *Karshenasi Arshad (Master's degree)*: Humanities; English Language; Farsi; Geography; Science; Engineering (MSc; MA); *Doctorate*: Persian Language and Literature (PhD)

Student Services: Academic counselling, Canteen, Cultural centre, Employment services, Foreign student adviser, Handicapped facilities, Health services, Nursery care, Social counselling, Sports facilities

Student Residential Facilities: Yes

Libraries: Central Library

Press or Publishing House: Publishing House

Last Updated: 02/12/11

YAZD UNIVERSITY OF MEDICAL SCIENCES

PO Box 734, Safaeieh, Bouali Street, Safaeeyeh, Yazd
Tel: +98(351) 454-45
Fax: +98(351) 454-46

Chancellor: Mohammadreza Besharati

Faculties

Dentistry (Dentistry); **Health Sciences** (Health Sciences); **Medicine** (Medicine); **Nursing and Midwifery** (Midwifery; Nursing); **Paramedical Sciences** (Paramedical Sciences)

History: Founded 1983 as Faculty, acquired present status and title 1986.

ZABOL UNIVERSITY OF MEDICAL SCIENCES

Ester Ferdosi Street, Zabol
Fax: +98(5421) 3943

Chancellor: Mokhary Ghasem

Faculties

Dentistry (Dentistry); **Health Sciences** (Health Sciences); **Medicine** (Medicine); **Nursing and Midwifery** (Midwifery; Nursing); **Paramedical Sciences** (Paramedical Sciences); **Pharmacy** (Pharmacy)

Libraries: 5,744 vols

ZAHEDAN UNIVERSITY OF MEDICAL SCIENCES (ZUMS)

Zahedan, 98135 Sistan and Balouchistan
Tel: +98(241) 9413
Fax: +98(241) 3973
Website: http://www.zdmu.ac.ir

Chancellor: Masoud Salehi Tel: +98(541) 322-8110

Faculties

Dentistry (Dental Hygiene; Dentistry; Oral Pathology); **Health Sciences** (Health Sciences); **Medicine** (Anaesthesiology; Medicine; Ophthalmology; Paediatrics; Radiology; Surgery); **Nursing and Midwifery** (Midwifery; Nursing); **Paramedical Sciences** (Anaesthesiology; Laboratory Techniques; Optics; Physical Therapy; Radiology)

History: Founded 1976.

Academic Year: September to June

Admission Requirements: Secondary school certificate and entrance examination

Main Language(s) of Instruction: Farsi

Degrees and Diplomas: *Kardani (Associate degree)*: 2 yrs; *Karshebasi (Bachelor's degree)*: Nursing, Midwifery, Optometry, Physical Therapy (BA), 4 yrs; *Professional Doctorate*: Dentistry and Stomatology (DDS), 6 yrs; *Professional Doctorate*: Medicine (MD), 7 yrs. Also Degrees of Specialization

Student Services: Foreign student adviser, Foreign Studies Centre, Sports facilities

Libraries: Central Library c. 25,000 vols. Also six College Libraries and six Hospital Libraries

Publications: Tabib-e-shargh, Scientific Journal *(quarterly)*

Last Updated: 18/12/08

ZANJAN UNIVERSITY

PO Box 45195-313, Zanjan
Tel: +98(241) 528-5151
Fax: +98(241) 8583100
EMail: master@mail.znu.ac.ir
Website: http://www.znu.ac.ir

President: Mohsen Afsharchi
Tel: +98(241) 528-3081 EMail: afsharchim@znu.ac.ir

Vice-President (Financial Affairs): MohammadReza Yaftian
Tel: +98(241) 528-3080 EMail: admin-fina@znu.ac.ir

Faculties

Agriculture (Agricultural Education; Agriculture; Agronomy; Animal Husbandry; Horticulture; Plant and Crop Protection; Soil Science); **Arts and Humanities** (Accountancy; Arts and Humanities; Business Administration; English; Geography; Islamic Studies; Islamic Theology; Literature; Persian; Philosophy; Physical Education; Social Sciences; Theology); **Engineering** (Architecture; Civil Engineering; Computer Engineering; Electrical Engineering; Engineering; Mechanical Engineering; Surveying and Mapping); **Science** (Biology; Chemistry; Geology; Mathematics; Natural Sciences; Physics)

History: Founded 1975 as Higher School for Agriculture & Animal Science. Acquired present status 1991.

Governing Bodies: Research Council

Academic Year: September to June (September to February; February to June)

Admission Requirements: High school diploma and national entrance examination

Fees: None

Main Language(s) of Instruction: Farsi

Accrediting Agencies: Ministry of Science, Research and Technology

Degrees and Diplomas: *Kardani (Associate degree)*: Computer Science; Mechanical Engineering; Architecture; Surveying and Mapping; Physics, 2 yrs; *Karshebasi (Bachelor's degree) (BA; BSc)*: 4 yrs; *Karshenasi Arshad (Master's degree)*: Chemistry; Physics; Mathematics; Civil Engineering; Electrical Engineering; Animal Husbandry; Geography (MSc; MA), 2 yrs; *Doctorate*: Chemistry, Physics (PhD), 4 yrs

Student Services: Academic counselling, Canteen, Cultural centre, Handicapped facilities, Health services, Language programs, Nursery care, Social counselling, Sports facilities

Student Residential Facilities: Yes

Special Facilities: Museum; Movie Studio

Libraries: Central Library and Faculty Libraries.

Last Updated: 06/12/11

ZANJAN UNIVERSITY OF MEDICAL SCIENCES (ZUMS)

Azadi Boulevard, Imam Street, Zanjan 45154
Tel: +98(241) 322-0761
Fax: +98(241) 322-0861
EMail: executive@zums.ac.ir; webmaster@zums.ac.ir
Website: http://www.zums.ac.ir

Chancellor: Mohammad Khani

Faculties

Allied Health Sciences (Health Sciences; Occupational Health; Paramedical Sciences); **Medicine** (Medicine); **Nursing** *(Abahar City)* (Nursing); **Nursing and Midwifery** (Midwifery; Nursing)

History: Founded 1987 as College of Nursing. Acquired present status 1988.

Academic Year: September to July

Admission Requirements: Secondary school certificate and entrance examination

Main Language(s) of Instruction: Farsi

Degrees and Diplomas: *Kardani (Associate degree)*: 2 yrs; *Karshebasi (Bachelor's degree) (BA)*: 4 yrs; *Doctorate*: Medicine, 6 yrs

Student Services: Academic counselling, Canteen, Cultural centre, Health services, Nursery care, Social counselling, Sports facilities

Student Residential Facilities: Yes

Libraries: Central Library, 10,500 vols; Paramedical, 5,743; Nursing and Midwifery, 7,441 vols

Publications: Journal of Zanjan University of Medical Sciences and Health Services *(quarterly)*

PRIVATE INSTITUTIONS

ADIBAN HIGHER EDUCATION INSTITUTE

Garmsar, 35815-179 Semnan
Tel: +98(232) 4239-083
Fax: +98(232) 4239-097
EMail: info@adiban.ac.ir
Website: http://www.adiban.ac.ir/

President: Mohammad Taghi Mokhtari (2006-)
EMail: mokhtari@adiban.ac.ir

Manager, Public Relations: Mehdi Alireza
EMail: alireza@adiban.ac.ir

International Relations: Mohammad Hossein Rohani, Deputy, International Relations EMail: rohani@adiban.ac.ir

Departments

Computer Science (Computer Engineering; Computer Science; Software Engineering); **Electronic Engineering** (Electronic Engineering); **Information and Communication Technology** (Electrical Engineering; Information Technology; Telecommunications Engineering); **Statistics** (Statistics)

History: Founded 2006.

Academic Year: October to June

Admission Requirements: High School Diploma, entrance exam.

Fees: (Rials): 7,000,000 per annum

Main Language(s) of Instruction: Farsi

Degrees and Diplomas: *Karshebasi (Bachelor's degree)*: Electrical Engineering; ICT and Electronic Engineering; Computer Engineering; Software Engineering; Statistics (BSc), 4 yrs

Student Services: Academic counselling, Canteen, Cultural centre, Handicapped facilities, Health services, Language programs, Nursery care, Social counselling, Sports facilities

Student Residential Facilities: For 100 students

Special Facilities: Laboratories; Movie Studio

Libraries: c. 5,000 vols.

Academic Staff *2009-2010*	MEN	WOMEN	**TOTAL**
FULL-TIME	15	12	**27**
PART-TIME	3	–	**3**
STAFF WITH DOCTORATE			
FULL-TIME	4	1	**5**
PART-TIME	2	–	**2**
Student Numbers *2009-2010*			
All (Foreign Included)	853	747	**1,600**

Last Updated: 26/08/10

AL-MUSTAFA INTERNATIONAL UNIVERSITY (MIU)

P.O. Box 439, Mo'alem Street, Qom 439
Tel: +98(251) 717-2415
Fax: +98(251) 717-2222
EMail: info@miu.ac.ir
Website: http://miu.ac.ir/

President: Ali-Reza A'arafi (2002-)
Tel: +98(251) 717-2616, Fax: +98(251) 717-2222
EMail: ar_aarafi@miu.ac.ir

International Relations: Abdulmajid Hakimelahi, Director, International Affairs and Public Relations
Tel: +98(251) 717-7616, Fax: +98(251) 717-2222
EMail: am_hakimelahi@miu.ac.ir

Faculties

Humanities (Arts and Humanities; Economics; Education; History; Law; Management; Modern Languages; Social Studies); **Islamic Studies** (Islamic Law; Islamic Studies; Islamic Theology; Koran; Theology)

History: Created in 1986 as the International Centre for Islamic Studies. Acquired current title and status 2008.

Governing Bodies: Board of Governors

Academic Year: Sept to June

Admission Requirements: Entrance examination.

Fees: None - all students are sponsored

Main Language(s) of Instruction: Arabic, Persian. Some courses in English

Accrediting Agencies: Ministry of Science, Research and Technology

Degrees and Diplomas: *Karshebasi (Bachelor's degree)*; *Karshenasi Arshad (Master's degree)*; *Doctorate*. Also: Post doctorate, 5 yrs

Student Services: Academic counselling, Canteen, Cultural centre, Employment services, Foreign student adviser, Foreign Studies Centre, Handicapped facilities, Health services, Language programs, Nursery care, Social counselling, Sports facilities

Student Residential Facilities: Yes - for all single students; some married accommodation also available

Special Facilities: Film studio

Libraries: c. 500,000 vols; 531 periodical subscriptions.

Academic Staff *2010-2011*	MEN	WOMEN	**TOTAL**
FULL-TIME	1,329	70	**1,399**
PART-TIME	2,374	122	**2,496**
STAFF WITH DOCTORATE			
FULL-TIME	127	11	**138**
PART-TIME	86	12	**98**
Student Numbers *2010-2011*			
All (Foreign Included)	13,596	8,064	**21,660**
FOREIGN ONLY	13,074	7,947	**21,021**

Distance students, 215.

Last Updated: 20/05/11

ARADAN HIGHER EDUCATION INSTITUTE

Enghelab Blvd, Aradan, 35861-548 Semnan
Tel: +98(232) 4543-884
Fax: +98(232) 4543-883
EMail: info@aradan.ac.ir
Website: http://www.aradan.ac.ir/

Head of Institution: Ali Daneshvar (2004-)
EMail: daneshvarkiyan@yahoo.com

Assistant to Head: Ali Yazdani

Departments

Accounting (Accountancy); **Computer Software Engineering** (Computer Engineering; Software Engineering); **Finance Management** (Business Administration; Finance); **Urban Construction Engineering** (Architecture; Civil Engineering; Construction Engineering)

History: Created 2004.

Academic Year: October to June

Admission Requirements: High school diploma

Fees: (Euro): 900 per annum

Main Language(s) of Instruction: Farsi, English

Accrediting Agencies: Ministry of Science, Research and Technology

Degrees and Diplomas: *Kardani (Associate degree)*: Architecture and Urban Construction; Computer Engineering, 2 yrs; *Karshebasi (Bachelor's degree)*: Computer Software Engineering; Finance Management; Accountancy, 4 yrs

Student Services: Academic counselling, Canteen, Cultural centre, Employment services, Health services, Language programs, Social counselling, Sports facilities

Academic Staff *2009-2010*	MEN	WOMEN	TOTAL
FULL-TIME	14	6	**20**
Student Numbers *2009-2010*			
All (Foreign Included)	318	407	**725**

Last Updated: 30/08/10

AZARBAIJAN ACCOUNTING AND MANAGEMENT HIGHER EDUCATION INSTITUTION

Tabriz
Tel: +98(41) 208-020 +98(41) 313-100
Fax: +98(21) 321-013

Programmes

Accountancy and Management (Accountancy; Management)

Degrees and Diplomas: *Kardani (Associate degree)*: 2 yrs; *Karshebasi (Bachelor's degree) (BA; BSc)*: 4 yrs; *Karshenasi Arshad (Master's degree) (MA; MSc)*: a further 2 yrs

BAQIR AL-OLUM UNIVERSITY

Qom 37185-787
Tel: +98(251) 291-0105
Fax: +98(251) 291-0133
Website: http://www.bou.ac.ir

Rector: Muhammad Javad Arasta EMail: arasta@bou.ac.ir

Administrative and Financial Director: Najaf Hedayatizadeh

International Relations: Khosrow Taqadosi, International Relations Officer

Colleges

Foreign Languages (English; Foreigners Education)

Departments

Islamic History (Islamic Studies); **Islamic Teachings** (Islamic Studies; Islamic Theology); **Islamic Theology and Philosophy** (Islamic Theology; Philosophy); **Political Science** (Political Sciences); **Social Sciences** (Social Sciences)

History: Created 1991. Acquired current name 2005

Academic Year: Sep-Jan; Feb-June

Main Language(s) of Instruction: Farsi, Arabic, English

Degrees and Diplomas: *Karshebasi (Bachelor's degree) (BA)*: 4 yrs; *Karshenasi Arshad (Master's degree) (MA)*: a further 2 yrs; *Doctorate*

Student Services: Academic counselling, Canteen, Health services, Language programs, Social counselling, Sports facilities

Publications: Aayeen of Hikmah (Practice of Wisdom) *(quarterly)*; Farhang-e-Pajuhesh (Culture of Research) *(biannually)*; History of Islam *(quarterly)*; Political Sciences *(quarterly)*

Academic Staff *2011-2012*	MEN	WOMEN	TOTAL
FULL-TIME	109	6	**115**
STAFF WITH DOCTORATE			
FULL-TIME	15	–	**15**
Student Numbers *2011-2012*			
All (Foreign Included)	275	94	**369**
FOREIGN ONLY	5	–	**5**

Part-time students, 400.
Last Updated: 26/09/11

ERSHAD DAMAVAND INSTITUTE OF HIGHER EDUCATION

24 Shohadaye Jandarmeri St, Abureyhan St, Enghelab Avenue, Tehran
Tel: +98(21) 6648-3602
Fax: +98(21) 6648-3608
EMail: info@ershad-damavand.ac.ir
Website: http://www.eud.ir

President: Seyyed Kazem Akrami (1995-)
EMail: Dr.Akrami@ershad-damavand.ac.ir

Vice chancellor, Education: Khosrou Ghanbari Tehrani
EMail: Dr.Tehrani@ershad-damavand.ac.ir

International Relations: Sharareh Mirchi, International Relations Officer
EMail: mirchi@ershad-damavand.ac.ir; Sh_mirchi383@yahoo.com

Departments

Accounting (Accountancy); **English Language** (English; Translation and Interpretation); **Industrial Engineering** (Industrial Engineering); **Law** (Law); **Management** (Industrial Management; Management)

History: Founded 1996

Academic Year: Sep - Jan; Feb - June

Admission Requirements: High School Diploma and entrance examination

Fees: (US Dollars): 350$ per annum

Main Language(s) of Instruction: Persian

Degrees and Diplomas: *Kardani (Associate degree)*: Management; *Karshebasi (Bachelor's degree)*: Management; Business; Accounting; Law; Industrial Engineering; English; *Karshenasi Arshad (Master's degree)*: Industrial Business Management

Student Services: Academic counselling, Cultural centre, Employment services, Foreign student adviser, Health services, Language programs, Nursery care, Social counselling, Sports facilities

Academic Staff *2011-2012*	MEN	WOMEN	TOTAL
FULL-TIME	110	60	**170**
STAFF WITH DOCTORATE			
FULL-TIME	60	30	**90**
Student Numbers *2011-2012*			
All (Foreign Included)	818	1,617	**2,435**

Last Updated: 29/09/11

FATEMIEH QOM UNIVERSITY OF MEDICAL SCIENCES

Qom

Programmes

Medicine

Degrees and Diplomas: *Karshebasi (Bachelor's degree)*; *Doctorate*

IMAM REZA UNIVERSITY

Mashhad
Tel: +98(511) 842-6038
Fax: +98(511) 843-6660
EMail: sabet@imamreza.or.ir
Website: http://www.imamreza.ac.ir/

Degrees and Diplomas: *Karshebasi (Bachelor's degree) (BA)*: 4 yrs
Last Updated: 15/12/08

IMAM SADIQ UNIVERSITY

Modiriat Bridge, Chamran Expressway, Tehran 14655-159
Tel: +98(21) 8809-4001
Fax: +98(21) 8809-3484
EMail: isu@isu.ac.ir
Website: http://www.isu.ac.ir

President: Mohammad Reza Mahdavi Kani (1983-)

Vice-president for Research: Asghar Eftekhari
EMail: eftekhari_asg@yahoo.com

International Relations: Mahmoud Karimi EMail: karimii@isu.ir

Departments

Arabic Language (Arabic) *Director*: Adnan Lajevardi; **Foreign Languages** (Modern Languages)

Faculties

Islamic Studies and Economics (Economics; Islamic Studies); **Islamic Studies and Law** (Islamic Law; Islamic Studies; Law); **Islamic Studies and Management** (Islamic Studies; Management); **Islamic Studies and Political Science** (Islamic Studies; Political Sciences); **Islamic Studies, Culture and Communications**

(Communication Studies; Cultural Studies; Islamic Studies); **Theology, Islamic Studies and Guidance** (Islamic Studies; Theology)

History: Founded 1982.

Admission Requirements: Diploma

Main Language(s) of Instruction: Farsi

Degrees and Diplomas: *Karshebasi (Bachelor's degree) (BA)*: 4 yrs; *Karshenasi Arshad (Master's degree) (MA)*: a further 2 yrs; *Doctorate (PhD)*: a further 4 yrs

Student Services: Academic counselling, Canteen, Cultural centre, Health services, Language programs, Social counselling, Sports facilities

Libraries: Yes

Last Updated: 17/12/08

ISLAMIC AZAD UNIVERSITY

Daneshgah-e Azad-e-Islami (IAU)

PO Box 1666637611, N°. 159, 7th Boostan St., Pasdaran Avenue, Tehran
Tel: +98(21) 2256-5149
Fax: +98(21) 2258-6222
EMail: info@intl.iau.ir
Website: http://www.intl.iau.ir/

President: Farhad Daneshjoo (2012-)
Tel: +98(21) 2256-5149, Fax: +98(21) 2254-7787

Director-General, International and Public Relations: Majid Setoudeh Tel: +98(21) 2276-0208 EMail: setoudeh@intl.iau.ir

International Relations: Hossein Sadeghi Shoja, Vice-President of International Affairs Tel: +98(21) 2257-4370

Faculties

Agricultural Engineering and Natural Resources (Agricultural Economics; Agricultural Engineering; Agronomy; Environmental Engineering; Fishery; Food Science; Food Technology; Forestry; Horticulture; Irrigation; Natural Resources; Plant Pathology; Soil Science; Water Science); **Art** (Acting; Architectural and Environmental Design; Architectural Restoration; Architecture; Graphic Arts; Graphic Design; Handicrafts; Industrial Design; Music; Painting and Drawing; Photography; Restoration of Works of Art; Textile Design; Theatre); **Engineering** (Aeronautical and Aerospace Engineering; Bioengineering; Biomedical Engineering; Chemical Engineering; Civil Engineering; Computer Engineering; Construction Engineering; Electrical and Electronic Engineering; Energy Engineering; Environmental Engineering; Hydraulic Engineering; Industrial Engineering; Marine Engineering; Materials Engineering; Mechanical Engineering; Metallurgical Engineering; Mining Engineering; Nuclear Engineering; Polymer and Plastics Technology; Power Engineering; Software Engineering; Soil Science; Telecommunications Engineering; Transport Engineering); **Humanities** (Accountancy; African Languages; Arabic; Archaeology; Banking; Business and Commerce; Economics; Educational Sciences; English; Finance; French; Geography; German; History; Industrial Management; Italian; Library Science; Linguistics; Literature; Management; Persian; Philosophy; Physical Education; Psychology; Public Administration; Russian; Social Sciences; Spanish; Translation and Interpretation); **Law and Political Science** (Criminal Law; International Law; International Relations; Law; Political Sciences; Private Law; Public Law; Regional Studies); **Medicine** (Dentistry; Laboratory Techniques; Medicine; Midwifery; Nursing; Nutrition; Pharmacology); **Science**

Further Information: Also 350 campuses. For complete list of campuses see http://www.intl.iau.ir/intbr.html

History: Founded 1982. A private university.

Academic Year: September to September

Admission Requirements: High school certificate or university diploma

Main Language(s) of Instruction: Farsi

Accrediting Agencies: Supreme Council of the Cultural Revolution

Degrees and Diplomas: *Kardani (Associate degree)*: 2 yrs; *Karshebasi (Bachelor's degree) (BA; BSc)*: 4 yrs; *Karshenasi Arshad (Master's degree) (MSc; MA)*: a further 2 yrs; *Doctorate (PhD)*

Student Services: Academic counselling, Canteen, Cultural centre, Employment services, Foreign student adviser, Handicapped facilities, Health services, Language programs, Nursery care, Social counselling, Sports facilities

Student Residential Facilities: Provided by all campuses

Libraries: Each campus has its own library facilities

Publications: Bassirat (Vision), Social Sciences; Danesh Nameh *(quarterly)*; Economies and Management *(quarterly)*; Ensan-va-Andishe (Man and Thought), Cultural, Literary and Social Issues; Jelvegahe-do-payam, Social Conscience and Discipline; Journal of Agricultural Sciences; Journal of Basic Sciences; Journal of Medical Sciences; Nedaye-Golestan, Sociology and Theology; Pazhoheshnameh, Projects Reports; Peyke-Dime, Scientific, Political, Cultural, Artistic and Sport Sciences; Rah-avar, Scientific Research Issues *(quarterly)*; Scientific and Research Periodical; Scientific and Research Periodical on Medical Research; Scientific Letters of Research; Scientific Research Journal on Management Issues; Sokhane-Ashna, Cultural and Social Issues *(quarterly)*; Yeganeh, Journal of Humanities *(quarterly)*; Zakaria Razi, Scientific, Cultural, Literary, Geographical and Basic Science

Press or Publishing House: IAU Press

Student Numbers *2012-2013*: Total 1,400,000
Last Updated: 14/02/13

ISLAMIC AZAD UNIVERSITY - TEHRAN MEDICAL BRANCH

Daneshgahe Azad Eslami, Vahed-e Pezeshki Tehran

PO Box 19395/1495, khaghani st, shariati Ave, Tehran, 19168 Tehran
Tel: +98(21) 200-6660
EMail: iautmu@iautmu.ac.ir
Website: http://www.iautmu.ac.ir

Dean: Ahmad Firouzan

Schools

Medicine (Medicine) *Dean*: Seyed Hossain Yahyavi; **Nursing and Midwifery** (Midwifery; Nursing); **Paramedicine** (Paramedical Sciences); **Public Health** (Health Sciences; Public Health)

History: Founded 1983, acquired present status and title 1985.

Academic Year: September to June

Admission Requirements: Secondary school certificate

Main Language(s) of Instruction: Farsi

Degrees and Diplomas: *Karshebasi (Bachelor's degree)*: Nursing, Midwifery, 4 yrs; *Karshenasi Arshad (Master's degree)*: Nursing, 4 yrs; *Doctorate*: Medicine, 7 yrs. Also Postgraduate diploma (2 yrs)

Student Services: Academic counselling, Canteen, Cultural centre, Employment services, Foreign student adviser, Foreign Studies Centre, Handicapped facilities, Health services, Language programs, Nursery care, Social counselling, Sports facilities

Libraries: c. 20,000 vols

Publications: Medical Science Magazine

Last Updated: 01/12/11

KAR HIGHER EDUCATION INSTITUTE

11, 12th Ave, Ahmad Qasir St., Tehran
Tel: +98(21) 8850-0970
Website: http://www.kar.ac.ir/

President: Mohammad Rabiei EMail: rabiei@kar.ac.ir

Programmes

Business Administration (Accountancy; Business Administration; Labour and Industrial Relations; Public Administration); **Engineering** (Engineering; Industrial Engineering; Industrial Management; Production Engineering; Textile Technology); **Law** (Law)

History: Created 1995.

Degrees and Diplomas: *Kardani (Associate degree)*: 2 yrs; *Karshebasi (Bachelor's degree)*: 4 yrs; *Karshenasi Arshad (Master's degree)*: a further 2 yrs

Last Updated: 27/09/11

KHAYYAM HIGHER EDUCATION INSTITUTE

1st Fallahi Street - Fallahi Blvd., Mashhad 9189747178
Tel: +98(511) 622-1777
Website: http://www.khayyam.ac.ir

Faculties

Architecture (Architecture); **Engineering** (Engineering); **Humanities** (Arts and Humanities); **Science** (Natural Sciences)

Degrees and Diplomas: *Kardani (Associate degree)*: 2 yrs; *Karshebasi (Bachelor's degree) (BA)*: 4 yrs; *Karshenasi Arshad (Master's degree) (MA)*: a further 2 yrs

Last Updated: 02/12/11

MAZANDARAN UNIVERSITY OF SCIENCE AND TECHNOLOGY

Babol, Mazandaran
Tel: +98(111) 229-1205-9
Fax: +98(111) 229-0118
EMail: a_sheikh@ustmb.ac.ir
Website: http://en.ustmb.ac.ir

Chancellor: Abdolreza Sheikholeslami

Vice-President of Education and Student Welfare: Babak Shirazi
EMail: babak@ustmb.ac.ir

Departments

Business Administration (Business Administration); **Civil Engineering** (Civil Engineering); **Computer and IT Engineering** (Computer Engineering; Information Technology); **Electrical Engineering** (Electrical Engineering); **Industrial Engineering** (Industrial Engineering)

History: Founded 1992.

Degrees and Diplomas: *Karshebasi (Bachelor's degree) (BA)*: 4 yrs; *Karshenasi Arshad (Master's degree) (MA)*: a further 2 yrs

Libraries: Yes

Last Updated: 02/12/11

MOFID UNIVERSITY

Qom
Tel: +98(251) 625-761-3
Fax: +98(251) 927-395
EMail: info@mofidu.ac.ir
Website: http://www.mofidu.ac.ir

Chancellor: Abdolkarim Mousavi Ardebili

Departments

Economics (Economics); **English Translation** (English; Translation and Interpretation); **Koran** (Islamic Theology); **Law** (Law); **Philosophy** (Philosophy); **Political Science**

History: Founded 1989.

Main Language(s) of Instruction: Farsi

Degrees and Diplomas: *Karshebasi (Bachelor's degree) (BA)*: 4 yrs; *Karshenasi Arshad (Master's degree) (MA)*: a further 2 yrs; *Doctorate*

Last Updated: 17/12/08

RAJA UNIVERSITY

Noruzian Avenue, Quazvin
Tel: +98(281) 367-7101
Fax: +98(281) 368-5406
EMail: university@raja.ac.ir
Website: http://www.raja.ac.ir/

President: Jahangir Biyabani (1995-)
Tel: +98(281) 367-7105, Fax: +98(281) 367-7105
EMail: jbiabani@raja.ac.ir

International Relations: Hamid Reza Malek Mohammadi, Head, International Relations
Tel: +98(281) 367-7105, Fax: +98(281) 367-7105
EMail: malekmohammadi@raja.ac.ir; Malekgl@yahoo.com

Faculties

Accounting (Accountancy; Taxation); **Economics** (Banking; Economics); **Engineering** (Civil Engineering; Computer Engineering; Electronic Engineering; Engineering; Industrial Engineering; Information Technology; Software Engineering; Telecommunications Engineering); **Management** (Management)

History: Founded 1995 as Raja Higher Education Centre. Acquired current status 2005.

Admission Requirements: Secondary school certificate and entrance exam.

Main Language(s) of Instruction: Persian

Degrees and Diplomas: *Karshebasi (Bachelor's degree)*: Economics; Information Technology; Management, 4 yrs; *Karshenasi Arshad (Master's degree)*: Accounting; Engineering, 2 1/2 yrs

Student Services: Academic counselling, Canteen, Cultural centre, Employment services, Foreign student adviser, Foreign Studies Centre, Handicapped facilities, Health services, Language programs, Social counselling, Sports facilities

Libraries: c. 17,380 vols; 42 periodical subscriptions;

Academic Staff *2011-2012*	MEN	WOMEN	**TOTAL**
FULL-TIME	30	22	**52**
STAFF WITH DOCTORATE			
FULL-TIME	5	–	**5**
Student Numbers *2011-2012*			
All (Foreign Included)	1,492	2,645	**4,137**
FOREIGN ONLY	8	2	**10**

Last Updated: 11/03/13

RAZAVI UNIVERSITY OF ISLAMIC SCIENCES

Holy Shrine of Imam Reza, Mashhad
Tel: +98(511) 221-8990
Fax: +98(511) 222-6844
Website: http://www.imamreza.net

Departments

Arabic Language and Literature (Arabic; Literature); **English** (English); **Fiqh and Usul** (Islamic Studies); **Islamic Philosophy and Theology** (Islamic Theology; Philosophy); **Koranic Sciences** (Koran); **Law** (Islamic Law); **Persian Language and Literature**

History: Founded 1984.

Main Language(s) of Instruction: Farsi

Degrees and Diplomas: *Karshebasi (Bachelor's degree) (BA)*: 4 yrs; *Karshenasi Arshad (Master's degree) (MA)*: a further 2 yrs

Last Updated: 17/12/08

SADJAD INSTITUTE OF HIGHER EDUCATION (SIHE)

Iraj Miriza 62, Mashhad, Khorasan Razavi
Tel: +98(511) 602-9000
Fax: +98(511) 602-9100
EMail: info@sadjad.ac.ir
Website: http://www.sadjad.ac.ir/

President: Ali Haerian Ardakani (2006-)
Tel: +98(511) 602-9111, Fax: +98(511) 602-9110
EMail: ahaerian@sadjad.ac.ir

President's Office Administrator: Maliheh Zakeri
Tel: +98(511) 602-9111, Fax: +95(511) 602-9110

International Relations: Morteza Afsari, International Relations Officer
Tel: +98(511) 602-9000, Fax: +95(511) 602-9110
EMail: m.afsari@sadjad.ac.ir

Departments

Civil Engineering (Civil Engineering) *Head*: Hasan Haji-Kazemi; **Computer Engineering and Information Technology** (Computer Engineering; Information Technology; Software Engineering); **Electrical Engineering** (Electrical Engineering; Electronic Engineering); **Industrial Engineering** (Industrial Engineering)

History: Founded 1993. Obtained status 1996.

Governing Bodies: Board of Trustees

Academic Year: September to February; February to July

Admission Requirements: High School Diploma (for undergraduate and technical programmes); Bachelor's Degree (for postgraduate programmes). Must also sit the Iranian National Entrance Exam.

Fees: (Rials): 3,500,000 (350 US$) per semester

Main Language(s) of Instruction: Farsi

Degrees and Diplomas: *Kardani (Associate degree)*: Electronics, Information and Communication Technology, 2 yrs; *Karshebasi (Bachelor's degree)*: Electronic Engineering; Telecommunication Engineering; Power Engineering; Control Systems Engineering; Software Engineering; Hardware Engineering; Information Technology; Industrial Engineering, 4 yrs; *Karshenasi Arshad (Master's degree)*: 2 yrs

Student Services: Academic counselling, Canteen, Cultural centre, Handicapped facilities, Health services, Language programs, Nursery care, Social counselling, Sports facilities

Student Residential Facilities: One student dormitory

Libraries: 6,700 vols; 20 periodical subscriptions; online services

Last Updated: 05/12/11

SHAHID MOTAHARI INSTITUTE

Tehran
Tel: +98(21) 366-166-9
Fax: +98(21) 363-738

Degrees and Diplomas: *Karshebasi (Bachelor's degree) (BA)*: 4 yrs; *Karshenasi Arshad (Master's degree) (MA)*: a further 2 yrs; *Doctorate (PhD)*

SHEIKHBAHAEE UNIVERSITY

1 Fereshteh Avenue, Isfahan 817935296
Tel: +98(311) 681-6760
Fax: +98(311) 681-6767
EMail: info@shbu.ac.ir
Website: http://www.shbu.ac.ir

Chancellor: Jafar Zafarani (2005-)
Tel: +98(311) 681-6769, Fax: +98(311) 681-6767
EMail: Danaee@shbu.ac.ir

Vice-Chancellor, Academic Affairs: M. Hassan Tahririan
Tel: +98(311) 681-6768

International Relations: Ali Akbar Mohammadi, International Relations Officer
Tel: +98(311) 681-0008 EMail: mohammadi@shbu.ac.ir

Faculties

Engineering (Computer Engineering; Electrical Engineering; Information Technology; Software Engineering; Town Planning); **Foreign Languages** (English; Foreign Languages Education; Translation and Interpretation); **Management** (Business Administration; Industrial Management; Tourism); **Mathematical and Computer Sciences** (Applied Mathematics; Computer Science; Statistics)

History: Founded 1994. Previously known as Sheikh Baha'i Higher Education Institution. Acquired current title and status 2006.

Academic Year: September to June.

Admission Requirements: Iranian National University Entrance Exam.

Main Language(s) of Instruction: Farsi

Degrees and Diplomas: *Kardani (Associate degree)*: Tourism, 2 yrs; *Karshebasi (Bachelor's degree)*: Applied Mathematics; Computer Science; Statistics; Urban Planning; Computer Engineering (Hardware/Software); Information Technology; Electrical Engineering; Electronic Engineering (BSc); English Literature; Teaching English as a Foreign Language; Translation; Business Administration; Industrial Management; Tourism Management; Tourist Services (BA), 4 yrs; *Karshenasi Arshad (Master's degree)*: Computer Engineering (Software); Applied Mathematics; Fiscal Mathematics (MSc); Teaching English as a Foreign Language; Translation (MA)

Student Services: Academic counselling, Cultural centre, Social counselling, Sports facilities

Student Residential Facilities: Female residence.

Libraries: 2 libraries.

Publications: Sheikh Baha'i University Research Bulletin, Research papers *(biannually)*

Last Updated: 06/10/08

SHOMAL UNIVERSITY

Daneshgah Shomal
P.O.Box 731, Amol, Mazandaran
Tel: +98(121) 212 27 20
Fax: +98(121) 550-3755
EMail: intl@shomal.ac.ir
Website: http://www.shomal.ac.ir/

President: Abassali Rostami (2006-)
Tel: +98(121) 220-3639, Fax: +98(121) 220-3755
EMail: rostami@umz.ac.ir

Vice President, Administration and Finance: Malak Mohammad Gholami
Tel: +98(121) 220-3728, Fax: +98(121) 220-3755
EMail: mm.gholami@shomal.ac.ir

International Relations: Julia Sedighi, Head of International Affairs
Tel: +98(121) 220-3756, Fax: +98(121) 220-3756
EMail: jpayne_63@yahoo.com

Faculties

Humanities and Social Sciences (Accountancy; Business Administration; Industrial Management; Law; Management); **Physical Education and Sports Science** (Physical Education; Sports); **Technology and Engineering** (Architecture; Building Technologies; Chemical Engineering; Civil Engineering; Computer Engineering; Electronic Engineering; Engineering; Environmental Engineering; Food Science; Food Technology; Information Technology; Natural Resources; Software Engineering)

History: Created 1996. Acquired present status 2008.

Governing Bodies: Board of Founders; Board of Trustees

Academic Year: October to January; January to July; July to September

Admission Requirements: High School Diploma; National University Entrance Exam

Fees: (Rials): 1,158,300 to 3,400.00 per semester, depending on level

Main Language(s) of Instruction: Farsi

Accrediting Agencies: Ministry of Science, Technology and Research

Degrees and Diplomas: *Karshebasi (Bachelor's degree)*: Chemical Engineering; Food Industries; Computer Engineering; Software Engineering; Industrial Engineering; Producation, Programming and System Analysis; Natural Resources; Environmental Engineering; Electronic Engineering, 4 yrs; *Karshebasi (Bachelor's degree)*: Civil Engineering; Accountancy; Law; Industrial Management; Business Management; Physical Education and Sports Science (4 yrs); *Karshenasi Arshad (Master's degree)*: Physical Education; Management; Physical Education and Sports Science; Industrial Engineering; Management and Systems (2 yrs)

Student Services: Academic counselling, Canteen, Cultural centre, Foreign student adviser, Health services, Language programs, Social counselling, Sports facilities

Special Facilities: Auditorium with full stage lightning, surround sound.

Libraries: 17,650 vols (Farsi); 3,000 vols (English); 150 periodical subscriptions (Farsi and English)

Academic Staff *2008-2009*	MEN	WOMEN	**TOTAL**
FULL-TIME	52	3	**55**
PART-TIME	7	–	**7**
STAFF WITH DOCTORATE			
FULL-TIME	3	–	**3**
PART-TIME	–	–	**9**
Student Numbers *2008-2009*			
All (Foreign Included)	3,054	2,247	**5,301**

Last Updated: 17/02/12

TABARESTAN HIGHER EDUCATIONAL INSTITUTE

Khazar St., 17 Shahrivar Ave, Chalous, Mazandaran
Tel: +98(21) 8809-9414
Fax: +98(21) 8837-1841
EMail: info@tabarestan.ac.ir
Website: http://www.tabarestan.ac.ir

President: Afrasiab Amiri (2010-)
EMail: president@tabarestan.ac.ir

Public Realations Manager: Hamid Yazdani Abyaneh
EMail: publicrelation@tabarestan.ac.ir

International Relations: Maryam Maleknejad, Internationamal Relations Manager EMail: malekl@tabarestan.ac.ir

Faculties

Engineering (Computer Engineering; Engineering; Telecommunications Engineering); **Humanities** (Accountancy; Geography; Law; Management; Psychology); **Science** (Biology; Chemistry; Mathematics; Natural Sciences; Physics)

History: Created 1996.

Governing Bodies: University Council

Academic Year: Sept - Dec; Feb - July

Admission Requirements: High School Diploma and Entrance Examination

Main Language(s) of Instruction: Persian

International Co-operation: with institutions in New Zealand

Accrediting Agencies: Ministry of Science, Research and Technology

Degrees and Diplomas: *Karshebasi (Bachelor's degree)*: Computer Engineering; Software Engineering; Computer Science; Applied Mathematics; Business Administration; Psychology; Accounting; Law; Geography; Urban Planning, 4 yrs; *Karshenasi Arshad (Master's degree)*: Geography, a further 2 yrs

Student Services: Academic counselling, Canteen, Cultural centre, Employment services, Handicapped facilities, Health services, Language programs, Social counselling, Sports facilities

Student Residential Facilities: Yes

Libraries: c. 15,000 vols; 33 journal subscriptions

Academic Staff *2010-2011*: Total 327

Student Numbers *2010-2011*: Total 3,200

Last Updated: 02/08/11

UNIVERSITY COLLEGE OF NABI AKRAM

Daneshgah-e-Nabi Akram (UCNA)

1283 Rah Ahan Blvd, PO Box 51385-1488, Tabriz, 5183918993
East Azerbaijan
Tel: +98(411) 442-4154
Fax: +98(411) 444-2095
EMail: info@ucna.ac.ir
Website: http://www.ucna.ac.ir

Chancellor, Chairman of the Founding Board: Seyed Mohammad Reza Milani Hosseini (1996-) EMail: drmilani@iust.ac.ir

Vice-Chancellor: Seyyed Mahmood Milani Hosseini
EMail: milani@ucna.ac.ir

Faculties

Fine Arts (Acting; Architecture; Computer Graphics; Theatre; Visual Arts); **Humanities** (Business Administration; Information Sciences; Library Science; Management; Translation and Interpretation; Writing); **Technology and Engineering** (Engineering; Technology)

History: Founded 1996.

Governing Bodies: Founding Board, Board of Trustees, Chancellor, Vice-Chancellor, Deputy of Educational Affairs, Deputy of Human Resources and Financial Affairs, Deputy of Cultural and Student Affairs, Deans of Faculties

Academic Year: September - December; January - April; June - July

Admission Requirements: High School Diploma (completion of 12 years secondary education); National University Entrance Exam (Konkoor)

Fees: (Rials): 7,000,000 per annum

Main Language(s) of Instruction: Farsi

International Co-operation: with institutions in Azerbaijan

Degrees and Diplomas: *Karshebasi (Bachelor's degree)*: Architecture; Visual Communications;Theatre Acting; Theatre Directing; Management; Library and Information Science; English to Persian Translation (BA); Information Technology Engineering; Software Engineering (BSc), 4 yrs; *Karshenasi Arshad (Master's degree)*: Visual Communications; Artificial Intelligence and Robotics (MA; MSc), 2 yrs. Also: Advanced Diploma (2 yrs)

Student Services: Academic counselling, Canteen, Cultural centre, Handicapped facilities, Health services, Nursery care, Social counselling, Sports facilities

Publications: Linguistics Seasonal, Scientific journal in linguistics *(quarterly)*

Last Updated: 01/12/11

UNIVERSITY OF QOM

Qom
Tel: +98(251) 293-1771-3
Fax: +98(251) 293-5684
EMail: info@qom.ac.ir
Website: http://www.qom.ac.ir/

President: Ahmad Beheshti

Faculties

Electronic Education (Law); **Islamic Theology** (Islamic Law; Islamic Theology; Koran; Philosophy); **Law** (Criminal Law; Law; Private Law); **Letters and Humanities**; **Science** (Applied Mathematics; Astronomy and Space Science; Physics); **Technology and Engineering** (Architecture; Civil Engineering; Computer Engineering; Industrial Engineering; Information Technology)

History: Founded 1979 as The High Educational and Legal School of the Seminarians. Acquired present status and title 1997.

Main Language(s) of Instruction: Farsi

Degrees and Diplomas: *Karshebasi (Bachelor's degree) (BA)*: 4 yrs; *Karshenasi Arshad (Master's degree) (MA)*: a further 2 yrs; *Doctorate (PhD)*

Last Updated: 05/12/11

Iraq

STRUCTURE OF HIGHER EDUCATION SYSTEM

Description:

Higher education is provided by State universities, technical institutes and private colleges. Apart from the private colleges, institutions are all financed by the State. Other institutions of higher education exist under different ministries.

Stages of studies:

University level first stage:

Higher technical education is offered in technical institutes and technical colleges offering Technical Diplomas (2 years), Technical Bachelors (4 years) and Technical Masters (2 years) covering up to 60 fields of specialization in Engineering, Administration, Applied Arts, agricultural and medical subjects. They are governed by the Foundation of Technical Education (FTE).

Most academic Bachelor's degree courses last for four years.

University level second stage: *Master's degree*

The Master's degree is conferred after two years' study (one by tuition, one by research leading to a thesis) beyond the Bachelor's degree. Students must have obtained at least 65 % at the Bachelor's degree. Specialized institutions also confer a Higher Diploma in some medical fields. Students must hold a Bachelor's degree in the same field and have obtained an average mark of over 65%. Courses last for two years.

University level third stage: *Doctorate*

The Doctorate (PhD) is conferred after a further three years' study beyond the Master's degree, with one year of coursework and two years of thesis preparation. Some specialized institutes also offer a two-year Postgraduate Higher Diploma.

ADMISSION TO HIGHER EDUCATION

Admission to university-level studies:

Name of secondary school credential required: Sixth Form Baccalaureat

For entry to: Minimum score: 50% for Institutes; 60% for Colleges

RECOGNITION OF STUDIES

Quality assurance system:

All universities in Iraq are recognized, including private universities and colleges.

Bodies dealing with recognition:

Ministry of Higher Education and Scientific Research

Baghdad

EMail: mc_mohesr@mohesr.gov.iq

WWW: http://www.mohesr.gov.iq

NATIONAL BODIES

Ministry of Higher Education and Scientific Research

Minister: Ali Mohammed Hussein Al-Adib

Director, International Relations: Layla Esa Salim

Baghdad
EMail: mc_mohesr@mohesr.gov.iq
WWW: http://www.mohesr.gov.iq
Role of national body: Responsible for tertiary education.

Data for academic year: 2011-2012
Source: IAU from MoHESR/Baghdad, 2011. Bodies 2012.

INSTITUTIONS

PUBLIC INSTITUTIONS

AL-ANBAR UNIVERSITY

PO Box 55431, Baghdad
Tel: +964(1) 817-8849 +964(1) 543-3813
Fax: +964(1) 887-8849
EMail: anbar_university@yahoo.com
Website: http://www.uoanbar.edu.iq/index.en.htm

President: Khalil Ibrahim Al Dulaimi

Colleges
Agriculture (Agricultural Economics; Agriculture; Animal Husbandry; Crop Production; Food Science; Horticulture; Soil Science; Water Science); **Arts** (Arabic; English; Geography (Human); History; Mass Communication; Media Studies; Sociology); **Computer** (Computer Science; Information Technology); **Dentistry** (Community Health; Dentistry; Oral Pathology; Orthodontics; Periodontics; Radiology; Social and Preventive Medicine; Surgery); **Economics and Administration** *(Ramadi)* (Accountancy; Administration; Economics; Public Administration); **Economics and Administration** *(Faluja)* (Administration; Economics; Public Administration); **Education** *(for women)* (Arabic; Biology; Chemistry; Education; Educational and Student Counselling; English; Geography; Geography (Human); History; Islamic Studies; Islamic Theology; Koran; Religious Education); **Education - Humanities** (Arabic; Education; English; Geography (Human); History; Koran); **Education - Pure Sciences** (Biology; Chemistry; Mathematics; Physics; Science Education); **Education - Qaim** (Arabic; Islamic Studies; Islamic Theology; Koran; Religious Education); **Engineering** (Civil Engineering; Electrical Engineering; Engineering; Mechanical Engineering; Water Science); **Islamic Sciences** *(Faluja)* (Arabic; Islamic Law; Law); **Islamic Sciences** *(Ramadi)* (Islamic Studies; Islamic Theology; Koran); **Law and Political Sciences** *(Faluja)* (Administrative Law; Civil Law; Commercial Law; Constitutional Law; Criminal Law; Criminology; Economics; Human Rights; International Law; Islamic Law; Labour Law; Law; Private Law); **Law and Political Sciences** *(Ramadi)* (Islamic Law; Law; Political Sciences); **Medicine** (Medicine); **Physical Education** (Physical Education; Sports); **Science** (Biology; Botany; Chemistry; Environmental Studies; Geology; Industrial Chemistry; Microbiology; Organic Chemistry; Physics; Physiology; Solid State Physics); **Veterinary Medicine** (Anatomy; Biochemistry; Embryology and Reproduction Biology; Histology; Parasitology; Pathology; Pharmacology; Physiology; Surgery; Veterinary Science)

History: Founded 1987.

Academic Year: September to June (September-January; February-June)

Admission Requirements: Secondary school certificate or equivalent

Accrediting Agencies: Ministry of Higher Education and Scientific Research

Degrees and Diplomas: *Bachelor's Degree*; *Master's Degree*; *Higher Diploma*; *Doctorate*
Last Updated: 22/09/11

AL-MUSTANSIRIYAH UNIVERSITY

Al-Jami'at Al-Mustansiriyah
PO Box 14022, Palestine Street, Al-Waziriyah, Baghdad
Tel: +964(1) 416-8500
Fax: +964(1) 885-3122
EMail: info@uomustansiriyah.edu.iq
Website: http://www.uomustansiriyah.edu.iq/

President: Ihsan Al-Qurashi

Centres
Computer (Computer Science); **Development of Teaching Methods** (Pedagogy); **Middle East Studies** (Middle Eastern Studies); **Modern Languages** (Modern Languages); **Teaching Arabic to Foreigners** (Foreign Languages Education)

Colleges
Arts (Arts and Humanities; Library Science; Modern Languages; Psychology); **Basic Education** (Education); **Dentistry** (Dentistry); **Economics and Administration** (Administration; Economics); **Education** (Education); **Engineering** (Engineering); **Law** (Law); **Medicine** (Medicine); **Pharmacy** (Pharmacy); **Physical Education** (Physical Education); **Political Sciences** (Political Sciences); **Science** (Biology; Chemistry; Mathematics; Natural Sciences; Physics)

Institutes
National and Social Studies (Social Studies)

History: Founded 1963 by the Republic of Iraq Teachers' Union. Merged by government decree with Al-Sha'b University 1964 to form University College and became part of University of Baghdad. Granted independent status as a private University 1965. Became a State institution 1974. Financed by the government.

Academic Year: September to June (September-January; February-June)

Admission Requirements: Secondary school certificate or equivalent

Main Language(s) of Instruction: Arabic, English

Degrees and Diplomas: *Technical Diploma*: Arts; *Bachelor's Degree*: Arts; Science, 4 yrs; *Master's Degree*: Arts, 1 1/2-3 yrs following Bachelor's Degree; *Master's Degree*: Science, 1 1/2-3 yrs following Bachelor's Degree; *Doctorate*: Science (PhD). Also postgraduate Diplomas, 2 yrs

Student Residential Facilities: Yes

Libraries: Central Library, c. 120,000 vols; libraries of the Colleges and Institutes

Publications: Al-Mustansiriyah Journal of Science; Al-Mustansiriyah Literary Review; Journal of Administration and Economics; Journal of Education
Last Updated: 21/09/11

AL-MUTHANNA UNIVERSITY

Samawa, Al Muthanna
EMail: admin@uoalmuthana.edu.iq
Website: http://www.uoalmuthana.edu.iq/

Rector: Aqeel Moslem Abdulhussein Al-Hajjoo (2011-)
EMail: info@uoalmuthana.edu.iq

Faculties

Agriculture (Agriculture; Animal Husbandry; Crop Production; Plant and Crop Protection; Soil Science; Water Science); **Economics and Administration** (Accountancy; Banking; Economics; Finance); **Education** (Arabic; Education; Geography; Geography (Human); History; Koran; Science Education); **Engineering** (Chemical Engineering; Civil Engineering; Engineering); **Medicine** (Medicine); **Physical Education** (Physical Education); **Science** (Biology; Chemistry; Environmental Management; Environmental Studies; Mathematics and Computer Science; Physics)

History: Created 2007.

Admission Requirements: Certificate of Secondary Education.

Fees: Day studies, free; evening studies (Iraqi Dinars): 300,000-500,000 per annum

Main Language(s) of Instruction: Arabic, English

Degrees and Diplomas: *Bachelor's Degree*: Education; Science; Engineering; Agriculture; Medicine; Physical Education; Management and Economics; *Master's Degree*: Science (Biology); Arabic Language; History; Agricultural Sciences

Student Services: Academic counselling, Canteen, Health services, Language programs, Nursery care, Social counselling, Sports facilities

Libraries: General library and faculty libraries

Academic Staff *2009-2010*	MEN	WOMEN	**TOTAL**
FULL-TIME	691	163	**854**
STAFF WITH DOCTORATE			
FULL-TIME	241	43	**284**
Student Numbers *2009-2010*			
All (Foreign Included)	2,575	2,168	**4,743**

Last Updated: 25/10/11

AL-NAHRAIN UNIVERSITY

PO Box 64074, Al-Jadiriyah, Baghdad
Tel: +964(1) 778-8786 +964(1) 778-2564
Fax: +964(1) 778-0297
EMail: alnahrin_online@yahoo.com
Website: http://www.alnahrain-university.com

President: Mohammad Jabir Ali
EMail: nahrain.president@yahoo.com

Faculties

Economics and Administration (Administration; Business Administration; Economics); **Engineering** (Chemical Engineering; Civil Engineering; Computer Engineering; Electronic Engineering; Laser Engineering; Medical Technology; Structural Architecture; Telecommunications Engineering); **Information Technology** (Information Technology); **Law** (Private Law; Public Law); **Medicine** (Anatomy; Biochemistry; Chemistry; Community Health; Gynaecology and Obstetrics; Medicine; Microbiology; Paediatrics; Pathology; Pharmacology; Physiology; Surgery); **Political Sciences** (Economics; International Studies; Political Sciences); **Science** (Biotechnology; Chemistry; Computer Science; Mathematics; Physics)

Institutes

Embryo Research and Infertility Treatment (Embryology and Reproduction Biology)

Research Centres

Biotechnology (Biotechnology)

Further Information: Campuses in in Al-Jadriya and Kadhimiya (Baghdad)

History: Founded 1987 as Saddam Hussein University. Renamed 2004.

Academic Year: September to June (September-January; February-June)

Admission Requirements: Secondary school certificate or equivalent

Student Services: Health services, Sports facilities

Student Residential Facilities: Yes

Libraries: Yes
Last Updated: 22/09/11

AL-QADISIYA UNIVERSITY

PO Box 88, Diwaniyah, Al-Qadisiya
Tel: +964 7801024027
EMail: info@qadissuni.edu.iq
Website: http://www.qadissuni.edu.iq

President: Imad A. Al-Jawaheri (2005-)
EMail: imadaljawaheri@yahoo.com

President Assistant/Administrative Assistant: Abdulkareem Umrani

International Relations: Jaafar Jotheri, Director of Scholarships and Cultural Relations Department
Tel: +964 781801829747 EMail: jafarjotheri@yahoo.com

Colleges

Administration and Economics (Accountancy; Administration; Economics; Management; Statistics); **Agriculture** (Agriculture; Crop Production; Soil Science; Water Science); **Arts** (Arabic; Archaeology; Geography (Human); Psychology; Sociology); **Computer Science and Mathematics** (Computer Science; Information Technology; Mathematics; Statistics); **Engineering** (Chemical Engineering; Civil Engineering; Engineering; Mechanical Engineering); **Law** (Law); **Medicine** (Biochemistry; Gynaecology and Obstetrics; Medicine; Microbiology; Paediatrics; Surgery); **Physical Education** (Physical Education; Sports; Sports Management); **Science** (Biology; Chemistry; Environmental Management; Environmental Studies; Physics); **Veterinary Medicine** (Anatomy; Microbiology; Pathology; Physiology; Public Health; Surgery; Veterinary Science)

History: Founded 1988. An public institution under the supervision of the Ministry of Higher Education and Scientific Research.

Governing Bodies: University Council

Academic Year: September to June

Admission Requirements: Secondary school certificate or equivalent

Fees: None

Main Language(s) of Instruction: English and Arabic

International Co-operation: None

Degrees and Diplomas: *Bachelor's Degree (BA; BSc)*: 4 yrs; *Master's Degree (MA; MSc)*; *Doctorate (PhD)*: 3 yrs

Student Services: Academic counselling, Health services, Social counselling, Sports facilities

Special Facilities: Al-Qadisiyah museum. Arabian Horse Centre

Libraries: Central library, 27,000 vols

Publications: Al-Qadisiyah for Human Sciences *(quarterly)*; Al-Qadisiyah for Science *(quarterly)*

Academic Staff *2010-2011*	MEN	WOMEN	**TOTAL**
FULL-TIME	653	278	**931**
STAFF WITH DOCTORATE			
FULL-TIME	233	52	**285**
Student Numbers *2010-2011*			
All (Foreign Included)	5,865	5,577	**11,442**

Evening students, 5,519.
Last Updated: 26/10/11

COLLEGE OF ALEMAM ALAADAM

Baghdad, Alaadamya
Tel: +964(1) 425-1700
Fax: +964(1) 425-6521
EMail: co_alemam_alaadm@yahoo.com; tasjeel_au@yahoo.com

Dean: Makki Hussain Hamdan

Departments

Arabic (Arabic); **Law** (Islamic Law); **Religion** (Religion)

History: Created 1997 acquired status 2008.

Governing Bodies: College Council

Admission Requirements: Preparatory school certificate.

Fees: None

Main Language(s) of Instruction: Arabic, English

Degrees and Diplomas: *Bachelor's Degree*; *Master's Degree*; *Doctorate*

Student Services: Academic counselling, Canteen, Cultural centre, Employment services, Nursery care, Social counselling, Sports facilities

Libraries: 10,000 vols.

Academic Staff *2009-2010*	MEN	WOMEN	TOTAL
FULL-TIME	116	14	**130**
STAFF WITH DOCTORATE			
FULL-TIME	50	2	**52**

Student Numbers *2009-2010*			
All (Foreign Included)	1,215	300	**1,515**

Last Updated: 12/04/10

HAWLER MEDICAL UNIVERSITY

Zankoy Hawleri Pezishki
PO Box 178, Erbil, Kurdistan
Tel: +964(66) 227-3384 +964(66) 227-3382
Fax: +964(66) 227-3382 +964(66) 253-2429
EMail: info@hmu.edu.iq
Website: http://www.hmu.edu.iq

President: Pishtewan Hashim Al-Bazzaz
EMail: pishtewan.bazzaz@hmu.edu.iq

International Relations: Abubakir M. Saleh, Head, International Relations EMail: Abubakir.majeed@hmu.edu.iq

Centres

Medical Research (Environmental Management; Environmental Studies; Epidemiology; Molecular Biology; Nutrition; Oncology; Pharmacy) *General Director*: Saleem S. Qader

Colleges

Dentistry (Dental Hygiene; Dental Technology; Dentistry; Oral Pathology; Orthodontics; Periodontics; Stomatology; Surgery) *Dean*: Ziwar Ahmed Al-Qassab; **Medicine** (Anatomy; Biochemistry; Biophysics; Community Health; Forensic Medicine and Dentistry; Gynaecology and Obstetrics; Histology; Microbiology; Paediatrics; Pathology; Pharmacology; Physiology; Psychiatry and Mental Health; Surgery) *Dean*: Ali A. Al-Dabbagh; **Nursing** (Anatomy; Biochemistry; Biology; Child Care and Development; Computer Science; English; Epidemiology; Health Administration; Medicine; Microbiology; Nursing; Nutrition; Paediatrics; Pathology; Pharmacology; Physiology; Psychology; Rehabilitation and Therapy; Surgery) *Dean*: Vian Afan Naqashbandi; **Pharmacy** (Analytical Chemistry; Applied Physics; Biochemistry; Biology; Chemistry; Community Health; Computer Science; Histology; Industrial Chemistry; Inorganic Chemistry; Mathematics; Microbiology; Organic Chemistry; Pathology; Pharmacology; Pharmacy; Physiology; Toxicology) *Dean*: Abdulqader Aziz Hassan

History: Founded 2005 incorporating four colleges of Salahaddin University.

Degrees and Diplomas: *Bachelor's Degree*: Dentistry (BDS); Pharmacy (BSc), 5 yrs; *Bachelor's Degree*: Medicine (BChB), 6 yrs; *Bachelor's Degree*: Nursing (BSc), 4 yrs; *Master's Degree*: Basic Sciences, 2 yrs; *Higher Diploma*: Clinical Sciences, 2 yrs; *Doctorate*: Basic Sciences (PhD), 3 yrs

Libraries: c. 60,500 vols; 20,000 periodical subscriptions

Academic Staff *2010-2011*	MEN	WOMEN	TOTAL
FULL-TIME	243	148	**391**

Student Numbers *2010-2011*			
All (Foreign Included)	853	755	**1,608**
FOREIGN ONLY	72	45	**117**

Last Updated: 06/06/11

IRAQI COMMISSION FOR COMPUTERS AND INFORMATICS

Baghdad
Tel: +964(1) 719-2391
EMail: icci@icci.edu.iq; icci_mohe@yahoo.com
Website: http://www.icci.edu.iq/

Head of Commission: Imad H. Al-Hussaini

Associate Dean for Administrative Affairs: Zaydon Abd-AlKarem Tel: +964 7702-932400 EMail: zaidoon-52@yahoo.com

International Relations: Rabab A. Ahmood, Head of International Relations Department Tel: +964 771-2797981

Centres

Information Technology (Software Engineering)

Institutes

Postgraduate Studies (Computer Science; Information Technology)

History: Created 1972. Acquired status 2001. Part of the Ministry of Higher Education and Scientific Research; as well as proposing policies and plans, and offering advice in the field of information technology and informatics, the Commission also conducts research and applicable studies in the field of informatics and grants degrees and diplomas in related computer science fields.

Academic Year: October to July

Admission Requirements: Higher Diploma and Master's degree, Bachelor's degree; Ph.D, Master's degree in related field.

Fees: No fee.

Main Language(s) of Instruction: Arabic, English

Degrees and Diplomas: *Master's Degree*: Computer Science, 2 yrs; *Higher Diploma*: Computer Science, 1 yr; *Doctorate*: Computer Science, 3 yrs

Student Services: Academic counselling, Canteen, Cultural centre, Employment services, Health services, Language programs, Nursery care, Social counselling, Sports facilities

Student Residential Facilities: No

Libraries: 623 theses; 1,254 scientific books; 281 science journals

Publications: Eye of Informatics, Newspaper *(biweekly)*

Academic Staff *2011-2012*	MEN	WOMEN	TOTAL
FULL-TIME	182	179	**361**
STAFF WITH DOCTORATE			
FULL-TIME	4	3	**7**
PART-TIME	2	1	**3**

Last Updated: 27/07/12

KARBALA UNIVERSITY

PO Box 1152, Karbala
Tel: +964(32) 321-364
EMail: info@uokerbala.edu.iq
Website: http://www.uokerbala.edu.iq/

President: Mufeed J. Ewadh (2004-)
EMail: mufeed55@hotmail.com

Faculties

Agriculture (Agriculture); **Business and Economics** (Administration; Business Administration; Economics); **Education** (Education); **Engineering** (Engineering); **Islamic Sciences** (Islamic Studies); **Law** (Law); **Medicine** (Medicine); **Pharmacy** (Pharmacy); **Physical Education** (Physical Education); **Science** (Mathematics and Computer Science; Natural Sciences); **Veterinary Science** (Veterinary Science)

History: Founded 2002.

Academic Year: September to June

Main Language(s) of Instruction: Arabic; English for Medicine and Pharmacy programmes

International Co-operation: With universities in United Kingdom, Algeria and Canada

Accrediting Agencies: Ministry of Higher Education and Scientific Research

Degrees and Diplomas: *Bachelor's Degree*; *Master's Degree*

Student Services: Academic counselling, Canteen, Cultural centre, Employment services, Foreign student adviser, Foreign Studies Centre, Health services, Language programs, Social counselling, Sports facilities

Special Facilities: Internet Centre; E-library.

Libraries: Yes

Publications: Journal of Kerbala University, Both Arabic and English scientific articles

Press or Publishing House: University Press

Last Updated: 22/09/11

KIRKUK UNIVERSITY

Baghdad Road, Kirkuk
Tel: +964(50) 418-531
EMail: kirkuk_univ@uokirkuk.edu.iq; kirkuk_univ@yahoo.com
Website: http://www.uokirkuk.edu.iq/

President: Hussein Hassan Omar Khanqah
EMail: prof_h_khunaka@yahoo.com

Assistant Rector for Administrative Affairs: Mohamed Ibrahim Ahmed Al-Naimi

Colleges

Agriculture (Agriculture; Animal Husbandry; Horticulture); **Business and Economics** (Administration; Management; Statistics); **Education** (Arabic; Education; English; Foreign Languages Education; Geography; Geography (Human); History; Koran; Kurdish; Native Language Education; Physical Education; Turkish); **Engineering** (Civil Engineering; Mechanical Engineering; Petroleum and Gas Engineering); **Nursing** (Nursing); **Science** (Biological and Life Sciences; Biology; Chemistry; Mathematics and Computer Science; Physics)

Faculties

Law (Law); **Medicine** (Anatomy; Applied Chemistry; Biochemistry; Medicine; Microbiology; Physiology; Surgery)

History: Founded 2003. Started off with four colleges and grew into seven colleges, including twenty departments.

Governing Bodies: Presidential Council of the University

Admission Requirements: Adadiyah (Secondary School Leaving Certificate)

Fees: (Iraqi Dinars): Evening courses, 200,000 - 250,000 per annum. All other courses free

Main Language(s) of Instruction: Arabic and English

Degrees and Diplomas: *Bachelor's Degree*; *Master's Degree*

Student Services: Academic counselling, Canteen, Sports facilities

Libraries: One central library plus individual college libraries

Publications: Kirkuk University Journal: Humanities, Academic Studies and Research in Humanities *(other/irregular)*; Kirkuk University Journal: Scientific Studies, Scientific Studies and Research *(other/irregular)*

Last Updated: 22/09/11

KOYA UNIVERSITY

Zankoy Koya

University Campus, Koya, Erbil, Kurdistan KO50 1001
Tel: +964(7480) 127-028
EMail: info@koyauni.ac
Website: http://koyauni.ac

President: Khidir Masum Hawrami (2005-)
Tel: +964(770) 234-4444
EMail: khawrami@koyauni.ac; khawrami@gmail.com

Vice-President for Scientific Affairs: Sherzad Al-Talabani

Vice-President for Administrative and Financial Affairs: Jawad Faqe Ali

International Relations: Hoshang Farooq Jawad, International Relations Officer
Tel: +964(770) 158-5866 EMail: hoshang.farooq@gmail.com

Faculties

Education (Education; Educational Psychology; Educational Sciences; Modern Languages; Science Education; Sports; Teacher Training); **Engineering** (Architecture; Chemical Engineering; Civil Engineering; Computer Engineering; Engineering; Geological Engineering; Information Technology; Petroleum and Gas Engineering; Structural Architecture) *Dean*: Fuad Mohamed Khoshnaw; **Humanities and Social Sciences** (Arabic; Arts and Humanities; Economics; English; French; Geography (Human); History; Islamic Studies; Islamic Theology; Kurdish; Law; Management; Modern Languages; Religious Studies; Social Sciences; Sociology; Turkish); **Science and Health** (Biology; Chemistry; Clinical Psychology; Forestry; Genetics; Health Sciences; Mathematics; Microbiology; Physics) *Dean*: Shwan Kamal Rashid

Research Centres

Education (Education); **Engineering** (Engineering); **Humanities and Social Sciences** (Arts and Humanities; Social Sciences); **Science and Health** (Health Sciences; Natural Sciences)

Schools

Basic Education (Modern Languages; Science Education); **Computer Engineering** (Computer Engineering; Information Technology); **Educational Sciences** (Educational Psychology; Educational Sciences; Teacher Training); **Engineering** (Architecture; Civil Engineering; Engineering; Geological Engineering; Structural Architecture); **Health** (Clinical Psychology; Genetics; Health Sciences; Microbiology); **Languages** (Arabic; English; French; Kurdish; Modern Languages; Turkish); **Law and Management** (Law; Management); **Petroleum and Chemical Engineering** (Chemical Engineering; Petroleum and Gas Engineering); **Religious Studies** (Islamic Studies; Islamic Theology; Religious Studies); **Science** (Biology; Chemistry; Forestry; Mathematics; Physics); **Social Sciences** (Geography (Human); History; Social Sciences; Sociology); **Sport Education** (Physical Education; Sports)

History: Founded 2003 incorporating the three colleges of Education, Law and Islamic Studies of the University of Sulaimany.

Governing Bodies: University Council

Admission Requirements: High School Certificate

Fees: No fees - government funded.

Main Language(s) of Instruction: English, Kurdish and Arabic

International Co-operation: with institutions in Portugal, Turkey, United Kingdom and USA

Accrediting Agencies: Ministry of Higher Education and Scientific Research

Degrees and Diplomas: *Bachelor's Degree*: 4 yrs; *Bachelor's Degree*: Architecture, 5 yrs; *Master's Degree (MA/MSc)*: minimum 2 yrs; *Doctorate (PhD)*: minimum 3 yrs

Student Services: Academic counselling, Canteen, Cultural centre, Employment services, Foreign student adviser, Health services, Language programs, Nursery care, Social counselling, Sports facilities

Student Residential Facilities: 100 apartments, 50 houses (for university staff)

Special Facilities: Internet centre. Art Gallery. Movie Studio

Libraries: 62,000 vols. 3,000 periodical subscriptions

Publications: Koya University Scientific Journal, Sciences *(biannually)*; Koya University Scientific Journal, Humanities and Science *(quarterly)*

Academic Staff *2010-2011*	MEN	WOMEN	TOTAL
FULL-TIME	595	65	**660**
PART-TIME	37	23	**60**
STAFF WITH DOCTORATE			
FULL-TIME	205	25	**230**
PART-TIME	60	21	**81**
Student Numbers *2010-2011*			
All (Foreign Included)	1,945	1,750	**3,695**
FOREIGN ONLY	50	30	**80**

Last Updated: 17/06/11

MISAN UNIVERSITY

Rusafa Street 52, Amarah, Maysan
EMail: int@mail.uomisan.edu.iq
Website: http://uomisan.edu.iq/

President: Muayad Faisal Raba (2008-)
EMail: choffic@uomisan.edu.iq

President's Assistant for Administrative Affairs: Amer Zeghair Mchaisen EMail: vich.ad@uomisan.edu.iq

Colleges

Basic Education (Arabic; Art Education; Education; English; Mathematics Education; Primary Education; Religious Education; Science Education; Social Sciences); **Education** (Arabic; Biology; English; Foreign Languages Education; Geography; Geography (Human); History; Mathematics Education; Native Language Education); **Law** (Law); **Management and Economics** (Business Administration; Economics); **Medicine** (Medicine); **Science** (Analytical Chemistry; Anatomy; Biology; Chemistry; Microbiology;

Organic Chemistry; Physical Chemistry; Physics); **Sport Education** (Physical Education; Sports)

History: Founded 2007.

Degrees and Diplomas: *Bachelor's Degree*; *Master's Degree*
Last Updated: 22/09/11

THE ISLAMIC UNIVERSITY - BAGHDAD

PO Box 7366 Haifa post office, Al-Athmia, Baghdad
Tel: 964(1) 425-3271
Fax: 964(1) 425-3246
EMail: islamicuniversitybag@yahoo.com

President: Zeyad M. Al-Ani

Administrative Officer: Anmar Ahmad Mohammad

International Relations: Khalid Abd-Alkareem

Colleges

Art (Arabic; English; History; Holy Writings; Islamic Studies; Koran; Literature) *Dean*: Abdullah Hassan Hamid; **Basic Education** (Anatomy; Arabic; Biological and Life Sciences; Chemistry; Computer Education; Computer Science; Cultural Studies; Education; History; Holy Writings; Islamic Studies; Koran; Literature; Physics; Social Sciences) *Dean*: Adnan Ali Kharmosh; **Economics and Administration** (Accountancy; Banking; Business Administration; Economics; Finance; Statistics) *Dean*: Hekmat Faris Taan; **Education** *(for girls)* (Arabic; Education; English; Foreign Languages Education; History; Holy Writings; Islamic Law; Koran; Native Language Education; Religious Education) *Dean*: Omar Majeed Abd Al-Ani; **Law** (Law) *Dean*: Ziyad Hamad Abbas Sumaidaie; **Media** (Communication Studies; Journalism; Media Studies; Photography; Public Relations; Radio and Television Broadcasting) *Dean*: Myaser Mohammad Yunus; **Religion** (Comparative Religion; Islamic Theology; Religion; Religious Studies) *Dean*: Subhi Fendi Khdir; **Sharia** (Economics; Islamic Law; Law; Political Sciences) *Dean*: Abd El-Munem Khalil Al-Hiti

Research Centres

Islamic Studies (Islamic Studies)

History: Founded 1989.

Admission Requirements: Secondary school certificate

Fees: None

Main Language(s) of Instruction: Arabic

Degrees and Diplomas: *Bachelor's Degree*: 4 yrs; *Master's Degree*: 2 yrs; *Doctorate*: 3 yrs

Student Services: Canteen, Health services, Sports facilities

Libraries: Central library

Publications: Islamic Studies

Press or Publishing House: University Press

Academic Staff *2010-2011*	MEN	WOMEN	**TOTAL**
FULL-TIME	411	111	**522**
STAFF WITH DOCTORATE			
FULL-TIME	–	–	**283**
Student Numbers *2010-2011*			
All (Foreign Included)	6,641	4,390	**11,031**

Last Updated: 17/06/11

THI-QAR UNIVERSITY

Al-Nasiriyah, Thi-Qar 0096442
Tel: +964(1) 224-3598 +964(780) 139-7994 (mobile)
EMail: university_of_thi_qar@yahoo.com
Website: http://english.thiqaruni.org

Chancellor: Ali Esmail Al-Snafi EMail: aboahmad61@yahoo.com

Colleges

Agriculture (Agriculture; Animal Husbandry; Crop Production); **Arts** (Arabic; Geography; Geography (Human); Koran); **Economics and Administration** (Public Administration; Statistics); **Education** (Arabic; Biology; Computer Science; Education; English; Foreign Languages Education; Geography; Geography (Human); History; Mathematics Education; Native Language Education; Science Education); **Engineering** (Civil Engineering; Electrical Engineering; Engineering; Mechanical Engineering); **Law** (Law; Private Law; Public Law); **Mathematics and Computer Science** (Mathematics and Computer Science); **Medicine** (Anatomy; Applied Chemistry; Applied Physics; Behavioural Sciences; Biochemistry; Biology; Community Health; Computer Science; Dermatology; Embryology and Reproduction Biology; Ethics; Forensic Medicine and Dentistry; Gynaecology and Obstetrics; Histology; Human Rights; Microbiology; Ophthalmology; Orthopaedics; Otorhinolaryngology; Paediatrics; Pathology; Pharmacology; Physiology; Psychiatry and Mental Health; Surgery); **Nursing** (Anatomy; Biochemistry; Epidemiology; Human Rights; Microbiology; Nursing; Nutrition; Paediatrics; Pharmacology; Physiology; Political Sciences; Psychiatry and Mental Health); **Physical Education** (Physical Education); **Science** (Biology; Chemistry; Physics)

History: Founded 2002.

Degrees and Diplomas: *Bachelor's Degree*; *Master's Degree*
Last Updated: 22/09/11

UNIVERSITY OF BABYLON

Jami'at Babil
PO Box 4, Hilla City, Babylon
Tel: +964(30)-249-551 +964(760) 100-6256
EMail: uniheadoffice@uobabylon.edu.iq
Website: http://www.uobabylon.edu.iq/

President: Nabeel Hashim Al-A'raji (2005-)
Tel: +964(770) 710-5060

Vice-Chancellor, Administrative Affairs: Jawad Kadhim AL-Janabi EMail: vcadmoffice@uobabylon-uni.com

International Relations: Abdul Ameer Alwash
EMail: Acadaffairs@babylon.uni.com

Colleges

Administration and Economics (Administration; Economics); **Agriculture** (Agriculture); **Arts** (Arts and Humanities); **Basic Education** (Education; Teacher Training); **Computer Technology** (Computer Engineering); **Dentistry** (Dentistry); **Education** *(Safi Al-Deen)* (Education); **Education** *(IBN Hayyaan)* (Education); **Engineering** *(Babylon)* (Engineering); **Fine Arts Education** *(Babylon, Hilla City Center)* (Art Education); **Koranic Studies** (Koran); **Law** (Law); **Medicine** *(Babylon, Hilla City Center)* (Medicine); **Metallurgical Engineering** (Metallurgical Engineering); **Nursing** (Nursing); **Pharmacy** (Pharmacy); **Physical Education** (Physical Education); **Science** (Mathematics and Computer Science; Natural Sciences); **Science for Girls** (Mathematics and Computer Science; Natural Sciences); **Veterinary Medicine** (Veterinary Science)

Further Information: Also 3 Teaching Hospitals

History: Founded 1991.

Governing Bodies: University Council, comprising Deans of Colleges, President Assistants, Faculty Members, Representatives of Teachers Union and National Union of Iraqi students

Academic Year: September to June

Admission Requirements: Secondary school certificate or equivalent

Fees: None

Main Language(s) of Instruction: Arabic, English

International Co-operation: With Koria Foundation for Advanced Studies. Also participates in DAD and DILPH programmes

Degrees and Diplomas: *Bachelor's Degree*: Administration and Economics; Agriculture; Arts; Computer Technology; Engineering; Koranic Studies; Metallurgical Engineering; Nursing; Pharmacy; Science; Science for Girls; Veterinary Medicine (BSc); Arts; Basic Education; Education; Fine Arts Education; Law; Physical Education (BA), 4 yrs; *Bachelor's Degree*: Dentistry, 5 yrs; *Bachelor's Degree*: Medicine (MBChB), 6 yrs; *Master's Degree*: Science, Art and Education, a further 2 yrs; *Doctorate*: Science and Arts (PhD), a further 3 yrs

Student Services: Academic counselling, Canteen, Cultural centre, Health services, Language programs, Nursery care, Social counselling, Sports facilities

Libraries: General Library. College Libraries. Department Libraries

Publications: Al-Furat Magazine of the College of Agriculture; Babylon Magazine for Historical and Civilized Studies; Babylon Magazine for Physical Sciences & Physical Education; Investigator Magazine of the College of Law; Iraqi and National Magazine of the College of Science; Iraqi Magazine of Mechanical and Material

Engineering of the College of Engineering; Journal of Babylon University; Magazine for Fiscal, Administrative and Economic Studies of the College of Administration and Economics; Magazine of Babylon University; Magazine of Human Sciences of the College of Education/Safi -al-deen; Medical Magazine of the College of Medicine; Nabo Magazine of Fine Arts

Academic Staff *2010-2011*	MEN	WOMEN	**TOTAL**
FULL-TIME	1,311	1,570	**2,881**
STAFF WITH DOCTORATE			
FULL-TIME	501	103	**604**
Student Numbers *2010-2011*			
All (Foreign Included)	7,101	9,927	**17,028**

Last Updated: 21/07/11

UNIVERSITY OF BAGHDAD

Al- Jadrriya compound, Baghdad
Tel: +964(1) 778-8501
Fax: +964(1) 778-3592
EMail: info@uobaghdad.edu.iq; baghdadunv2@yahoo.com
Website: http://uobaghdad.edu.iq/

President: Mosa Jawad Al-Mosawe

Centres

Computer (Computer Science); **Development and Continuing Education** (Continuing Education); **Educational Studies and Psychological Research** (Educational Sciences; Psychology); **International Studies** (International Studies); **Market Research and Consumer Protection** (Consumer Studies); **Natural History Research** (Natural Sciences); **Revival of Arabic Scientific Heritage**

Colleges

Administration and Economics (Administration; Economics); **Agriculture** (Agriculture); **Arts** (Archaeology; Arts and Humanities; Islamic Studies; Journalism; Media Studies; Modern Languages; Psychology; Sociology); **Dentistry** (Dentistry); **Education** *(Ibn-Alhatham)* (Education); **Education for Girls** (Education); **Education** *(Ibn-Rushd)* (Education); **Engineering and Architecture** *(Also Alkwarismic)* (Architecture; Engineering); **Fine Arts** (Fine Arts); **Islamic Science and Shari'a** (Islamic Law; Islamic Studies); **Languages** (Modern Languages); **Law and Political Science** (Law; Political Sciences); **Media Studies** (Media Studies); **Medicine** *(Alkindi)* (Medicine); **Medicine** (Medicine); **Nursing** (Nursing); **Pharmacy** (Pharmacy); **Physical Education** *(for women)* (Physical Education); **Physical Education** (Physical Education); **Science** (Mathematics and Computer Science; Natural Sciences); **Veterinary Medicine** (Veterinary Science)

Higher Institutes

Accountancy and Finance (Accountancy; Finance)

Institutes

Genetic Engineering and Biotechnology (Biotechnology; Genetics); **Laser** *(for postgraduate studies)* (Laser Engineering); **Urban and Regional Planning** (Regional Planning; Town Planning)

History: Founded 1958 as a State university incorporating existing colleges established between 1908 and 1952. Branches in Mosul and Basrah detached to form separate universities 1967. Reorganized 1969 when ten colleges were merged to form four new Colleges of Law and Political Science, Administration and Economics, Arts, and Agriculture and Veterinary Medicine. In 1970 placed under the authority of the Ministry of Higher Education and Scientific Research. Financed by the government.

Governing Bodies: University Council

Academic Year: September to May (September-January; February-May)

Admission Requirements: Secondary school certificate or equivalent

Fees: None

Main Language(s) of Instruction: Arabic, English

Degrees and Diplomas: *Bachelor's Degree*: Arts (BA), 4 yrs; *Bachelor's Degree*: Sciences (BSc), 4-6 yrs; *Master's Degree*: Arts (MA), 2 yrs; *Master's Degree*: Science (MSc), 2 yrs following Bachelor's Degree; *Doctorate*: Medicine, 6 yrs

Student Residential Facilities: Yes

Special Facilities: Natural History Museum

Libraries: Central Library, c. 270,000 vols; libraries of the colleges and institutes

Publications: College Bulletins

Press or Publishing House: University Press

Last Updated: 21/09/11

UNIVERSITY OF BASRAH

Jami'at Al-Basrah
PO Box 49, Basrah
Tel: +964(1) 886-8520
Fax: +964(1) 886-8520
EMail: basrahuniv123@yahoo.com; info@uobasrah.edu.iq
Website: http://www.uobasrah.edu.iq/

President: Sahel Najim EMail: chancellery@uobasrah.edu.iq

Centres

Arab Gulf Studies (Middle Eastern Studies); **Arabic Language** (Arabic); **Basrah Studies**; **English Language** (English); **Iranian Studies** (Middle Eastern Studies); **Marine Sciences** (Marine Science and Oceanography); **Modern Languages** (Modern Languages); **Polymer** (Polymer and Plastics Technology); **Teaching Methods Development** (Educational Technology; Pedagogy)

Colleges

Administration and Economics (Accountancy; Administration; Economics; Statistics) *Dean*: Yosif Al-Assad; **Agriculture** (Agriculture; Animal Husbandry; Crop Production; Fishery; Food Technology; Horticulture; Soil Science) *Dean*: Shakier Aday; **Arts** (Arabic; Arts and Humanities; English; Geography; Philosophy) *Dean*: Dawood Al-Rubaie; **Dentistry** (Dentistry) *Dean*: Abdul Jabar Manury; **Education** (Education) *Dean*: Ameen Al-Silamy; **Engineering** (Engineering) *Dean*: Abass Abass; **Fine Arts** (Painting and Drawing; Sculpture; Theatre) *Dean*: Sabah Al-Shaia; **Historical Studies** (History) *Dean*: Rabab Al-Sudan; **Law and Policy** (Law) *Dean*: Aqeel Jasim; **Medicine** (Medicine) *Dean*: Thamir Al-Hamdan; **Nursing** (Nursing) *Dean*: Abdul Hussein Mohammed; **Pharmacy** (Pharmacy) *Dean*: Sahkier Al-Nima; **Physical Education** (Physical Education) *Dean*: Mohammed Hassein; **Science** (Mathematics and Computer Science; Natural Sciences) *Dean*: Mohammed Al-Assidi; **Veterinary Medicine** (Veterinary Science) *Dean*: Basil Abass

History: Founded 1964, comprising colleges forming part of the University of Baghdad. Became independent university 1967. Under the jurisdiction of the Ministry of Higher Education and Scientific Research and financed by the government.

Governing Bodies: University Council

Academic Year: September to June (September-January; February-June)

Admission Requirements: Secondary school certificate or equivalent

Fees: None

Main Language(s) of Instruction: Arabic, English

Degrees and Diplomas: *Bachelor's Degree*: Arts (BA); Science (BSc), 4 yrs; *Bachelor's Degree*: Medicine and Surgery (MB, ChB), 6 yrs; *Bachelor's Degree*: Veterinary Medicine and Surgery (BVMS), 5 yrs; *Master's Degree*: Arts (MA); Science (MSc), 2-4 further yrs; *Master's Degree*: Business Administration and Economics (MSc); *Higher Diploma*: Engineering; Medicine, 1 yr; *Doctorate*: Administration and Economics; Agriculture; Arts; Education; Engineering; Fine Arts; Law and Policy; Medicine; Physical Education; Science; Veterinary Medicine; Historical Studies (PhD)

Student Services: Academic counselling, Canteen, Cultural centre, Health services, Language programs, Social counselling, Sports facilities

Student Residential Facilities: For c. 3,500 students

Special Facilities: Natural History Museum

Libraries: Central Library, 187,194 vols; 10 specialized libraries, c. 594,000 vols

Publications: Basrah Art Journal; Basrah Journal of Agricultural Sciences; Basrah Journal of Medicine; Basrah Journal of Science *(biannually)*; Basrah Journal of Surgery *(biannually)*; Basrah Journal of Veterinary Research; Centre for Arab Gulf Studies Journal *(biannually)*; Engineering Journal; Iranian Studies Journal *(biannually)*; Iraqi Journal of Aquaculture; Iraqi Journal of Engineering Electrons; Iraqi Journal of Marine Science *(biannually)*; Journal of Basrah Studies; Journal of Date Plam; Journal of Economic Science; Journal of Historical Studies; Mesopotamian Journal of Marine Science

Press or Publishing House: Publishing House of Basrah University

Academic Staff *2010-2011*	MEN	WOMEN	**TOTAL**
FULL-TIME	1,694	869	**2,563**
Student Numbers *2010-2011*			
All (Foreign Included)	8,117	10,975	**19,092**

Last Updated: 21/07/11

UNIVERSITY OF DIYALA

Baquba-Diyala
Tel: +964(25) 532-360
EMail: hq.university@uodiyala.edu.iq; diyala_university@yahoo.com; relations@uodiyala.edu.iq
Website: http://www.uodiyala.edu.iq/

President (Acting): Mahmood Shakir Rasheed Al-Juboory
EMail: president@uodiyala.edu.iq

Colleges

Administration and Economics (Administration; Economics; Statistics); **Agriculture** (Agriculture; Animal Husbandry; Horticulture); **Basic Education** (Arabic; Art Education; Computer Education; Computer Science; Education; Educational and Student Counselling; English; Foreign Languages Education; Geography; Geography (Human); History; Mathematics; Mathematics Education; Native Language Education; Physical Education; Science Education); **Education - Al Asma'e** (Arabic; Educational Sciences; English; Foreign Languages Education; Geography; Geography (Human); History; Islamic Law; Native Language Education); **Education - Al Razi** (Biology; Chemistry; Computer Science); **Engineering** (Civil Engineering; Computer Engineering; Electronic Engineering; Mechanical Engineering; Power Engineering; Telecommunications Engineering); **Islamic Science** (Islamic Law; Islamic Theology); **Law and Political Sciences** (Law; Political Sciences); **Medicine** (Anatomy; Chemistry; Community Health; Gynaecology and Obstetrics; Medicine; Microbiology; Paediatrics; Pathology; Pharmacology; Physiology; Surgery); **Physical Education** (Physical Education); **Science** (Biology; Chemistry; Computer Science; Mathematics; Physics); **Veterinary Medicine** (Anatomy; Medicine; Microbiology; Pathology; Pharmacology; Physiology; Public Health; Surgery; Veterinary Science)

History: Founded 1999.

Admission Requirements: Adadiyah (Secondary School Leaving Certificate) and no more than 24 years old.

Fees: None

Main Language(s) of Instruction: Arabic and English

International Co-operation: Yes

Degrees and Diplomas: *Bachelor's Degree*; *Master's Degree*; *Doctorate*

Student Services: Academic counselling, Canteen, Cultural centre, Employment services, Health services, Language programs, Nursery care, Sports facilities

Student Residential Facilities: Yes

Special Facilities: Yes

Libraries: Yes

Publications: Al Afaak Al Jadida *(monthly)*

Press or Publishing House: University Press of Diyala

Academic Staff *2010-2011*: Total 942
STAFF WITH DOCTORATE: Total 302
Student Numbers *2010-2011*: Total 14,782
Last Updated: 18/05/11

UNIVERSITY OF DUHOK

Zankuya Duhok (UOD)
PO Box 78, Iraq-Zakho Road, Duhok, Kurdistan
Tel: +964 (62) 722-22-92 +964(750) 455-13-44
Fax: +44(870) 132-73-96
EMail: relations@uod.ac; vprel@uod.ac
Website: http://www.uod.ac

President: Asmat M. Khalid (1992-)
Tel: +32(48) 445-76-54, Fax: +44(870) 132-7369
EMail: president@dohukuni.net; asmat.khalid@yahoo.com

International Relations: Rund Hammoudi
Tel: +964 62 722 7060 EMail: rund.hammoudi@uod.ac

Faculties

Agriculture and Forestry (Agriculture; Animal Husbandry; Forestry; Horticulture; Natural Sciences; Plant and Crop Protection; Soil Science; Water Science); **Educational Sciences** (Education; Educational Sciences; Physical Education; Primary Education); **Engineering and Applied Sciences** (Earth Sciences; Engineering); **Humanities** (Administration; Arts and Humanities; Economics; Law; Political Sciences); **Medical Sciences** (Dentistry; Medicine; Nursing; Pharmacy); **Science** (Biology; Chemistry; Computer Science; Mathematics; Physics); **Veterinary Medicine** (Anatomy; Biochemistry; Biology; Chemistry; Food Science; Genetics; Histology; Immunology; Meat and Poultry; Parasitology; Pathology; Pharmacology; Physiology; Surgery; Toxicology; Veterinary Science; Virology; Zoology)

Higher Institutes

Planning (Agricultural Management; Educational Administration; Environmental Management; Forest Management; Health Administration; Natural Resources; Public Administration; Rural Planning; Statistics; Surveying and Mapping; Town Planning; Water Management; Water Science)

Programmes

Graduate Studies (Accountancy; Administration; Animal Husbandry; Arabic; Banking; Biochemistry; Biology; Biophysics; Business Administration; Chemistry; Computer Engineering; Computer Science; Economics; Education; Electrical Engineering; Engineering; English; Finance; Forestry; Geography (Human); History; Horticulture; Kurdish; Management; Mathematics; Mathematics Education; Medicine; Microbiology; Natural Resources; Physics; Physiology; Plant and Crop Protection; Psychology; Regional Planning; Soil Science; Sports; Statistics; Surgery; Town Planning; Veterinary Science; Water Management; Water Science)

Schools

Administration and Economics (Accountancy; Administration; Banking; Business Administration; Economics; Finance; Management); **Arts** (English; Geography (Human); History; Kurdish; Native Language; Theatre); **Basic Education** *(Duhok)* (Education; English; Foreign Languages Education; Mathematics Education; Native Language Education; Preschool Education; Social Studies); **Basic Education** *(Akre)* (Arabic; Education; Social Sciences); **Dentistry** (Dentistry); **Earth Sciences and Geoinformatics** (Earth Sciences); **Engineering** (Architecture; Civil Engineering; Computer Engineering; Electrical Engineering; Engineering; Natural Resources; Structural Architecture; Water Management); **Law and Politics** (Administrative Law; Civil Law; Commercial Law; Constitutional Law; Criminal Law; Criminology; History of Law; Human Rights; International Law; Islamic Law; Labour Law; Law; Political Sciences; Private Law); **Medicine** (Anatomy; Biochemistry; Community Health; Gynaecology and Obstetrics; Medicine; Microbiology; Paediatrics; Pathology; Physiology; Surgery); **Nursing** (Nursing); **Pharmacy** (Pharmacy); **Physical Education** (Anatomy; Physical Education; Sports)

Further Information: Also Faculty of Humanities/ Evening Studies

History: Founded 1992.

Academic Year: September to June

Admission Requirements: Secondary school certificate or equivalent

Degrees and Diplomas: *Bachelor's Degree*: 4 yrs; *Bachelor's Degree*: Medicine, 6 yrs; *Bachelor's Degree*: Veterinary Studies; Architectural Engineering, 5 yrs; *Master's Degree*: Agriculture (Horticulture; Forestry; Animal Production; Plant Protection; Water and Soil Sciences); Economics; Business Management;

Accountancy; Financial and Banking Sciences; Arts (English Language; History; Kurdish Language; Geography); Medicine; Veterinary Medicine (Surgery and Medicine); Physical Education (Science and Athletic Games); Education (Biology; Chemistry; Computer Science; Mathematics; Physics; Psychology; History; Arabic Language; Engineering (Electrical and Computer; Water Resources); Planning; *Higher Diploma*: Biophysics; Biochemistry; Microbiology; Medical Physiology; Medicine; Surgery, 2 yrs; *Higher Diploma*: Education (Biology; Chemistry; Physics; Computer Science); General Administration; Statistics, 1 yr; *Doctorate*: Agriculture (Horticulture; Forestry; Animal Production); Physical Education (Science and Athletic Games); Medicine; Education (Biology; Psychology); Arts (History); Veterinary Medicine (Surgery and Medicine) (PhD), at least 3 further 3 yrs. Also medical postgraduate diploma

Libraries: c. 88,000 vols

Publications: Journal of Dohuk University; Sun Shine, Newspaper in English; Vejen, Monthly student journal

Last Updated: 23/09/11

UNIVERSITY OF KUFA

Jami'at Al-Kufa

Al-Najaf 21, Kufa
Tel: +964(1) 333-4603
Fax: +964(33) 886-7170
EMail: Info@kuiraq.com; Mail@kuiraq.com
Website: http://www.uokufa.edu.iq/ar/

President: Aqeel A. Yaseen Al-kufi EMail: president@kuiraq.com

Vice-President for Administration: Adel Hussaien Al-Baghdadi

Centres

Academic Teaching and Training (Educational Testing and Evaluation; Teacher Training); **Informatics for Research and Rehabilitation**; **Kufa Studies** (History; Religious Studies)

Colleges

Administration and Economics (Accountancy; Administration; Banking; Business Administration; Economics; Finance; Statistics); **Agriculture** (Animal Husbandry; Biochemistry; Botany; Crop Production; Food Science; Horticulture; Plant and Crop Protection; Plant Pathology; Soil Science; Water Science); **Arts** (Arabic; English; Fine Arts; Geography (Human); History; Philosophy; Social Studies); **Basic Education** (Arabic; Education; Koran; Religious Education); **Dentistry** (Dentistry; Oral Pathology; Orthodontics; Surgery); **Education** (Art Education; Computer Education; Education; English; Foreign Languages Education); **Education** *(for women)* (Arabic; Biology; Chemistry; Computer Education; Computer Science; Education; Geography; History; Koran; Mathematics; Physical Education; Physics; Psychology; Sports); **Engineering** (Civil Engineering; Electrical Engineering; Engineering; Mechanical Engineering; Metallurgical Engineering; Natural Resources; Water Science); **Jurisprudence** *(Al Fqh)* (Islamic Law; Islamic Studies); **Law and Political Sciences** (Law; Political Sciences; Public Law); **Mathematics and Computer Science** (Computer Graphics; Computer Networks; Data Processing; E-Business/Commerce; Information Technology; Mathematics and Computer Science; Nanotechnology; Software Engineering); **Medicine** (Biochemistry; Gynaecology and Obstetrics; Health Sciences; Medicine; Microbiology; Paediatrics; Pathology; Pharmacology; Physiology); **Nursing** (Nursing); **Pharmacy** (Anatomy; Applied Chemistry; Biology; Computer Science; Health Sciences; Histology; Mathematics; Organic Chemistry; Pharmacology; Pharmacy); **Physical Education** (Physical Education); **Science** (Biology; Chemistry; Ecology; Physics); **Veterinary Medicine** (Anatomy; Meat and Poultry; Physiology; Veterinary Science)

History: Founded 1988.

Governing Bodies: University Council

Academic Year: September to June (September-January; February-June)

Admission Requirements: Secondary school certificate or equivalent

Fees: None

Main Language(s) of Instruction: Arabic, English

Degrees and Diplomas: *Bachelor's Degree*: Medicine (MBCHB), 6 yrs; *Bachelor's Degree*: Science, Agriculture, Art, Pharmacy, Engineering, Economics (BSc; BA), 4 yrs; *Master's Degree*: Science, Education, Arts (MSc; MA), a further 2 yrs; *Higher Diploma*: Medicine, Surgery, Paediatrics, 1 further yr; *Doctorate*: Arabic, History, Philosophy, Biology, Bacteriology, Pharmacy (PhD), a further 3-4 yrs

Student Services: Canteen, Cultural centre, Employment services, Foreign Studies Centre, Health services, Sports facilities

Student Residential Facilities: For c. 1,750 students

Special Facilities: Botanical Garden

Libraries: The Central Library (with Sub-libraries in each college), Total: c. 400,000 vols

Publications: Al-Kufa Journal *(biannually)*; Journal of Kufa College of Medicine *(annually)*

Last Updated: 02/05/12

UNIVERSITY OF KURDISTAN - HEWLER

30 Meter Avenue, Erbil, Kurdistan
Tel: +964(66) 223-8665
Fax: +964(66) 223-8661
EMail: info@ukh.ac; ukhadmission@ukh.ac
Website: http://www.ukh.ac

Vice-Chancellor: Khaled Salih (2012-)

Academic Registrar: Sue Rouf EMail: suerouf@gmail.com

Departments

Applied Social Sciences (Social Sciences; Sociology); **Business and Management** (Business and Commerce; Economic History; Finance; Management; Public Administration); **Computer Science and Engineering** (Computer Engineering; Computer Science); **Natural Resources Engineering and Management** (Hydraulic Engineering; Mining Engineering; Natural Resources; Petroleum and Gas Engineering; Water Science); **Politics and International Relations** (International Relations; Political Sciences)

History: Created 2006.

Degrees and Diplomas: *Bachelor's Degree*: Computer Science; Computer Engineering; Applied Social Sciences; Business and Management; Natural Resources Engineering and Management; Politics and International Relations; *Master's Degree*: Business and Management; Politics and International Relations; *Doctorate*

Academic Staff *2010-2011*	MEN	WOMEN	TOTAL
FULL-TIME	18	6	**24**
PART-TIME	12	3	**15**
PART-TIME	1	1	**2**
Student Numbers *2010-2011*			
All (Foreign Included)	242	172	**414**
FOREIGN ONLY	16	10	**26**

Last Updated: 06/06/11

UNIVERSITY OF MOSUL

Jami'at Al-Mosul

Al-Majmoaa Al-Thaqafia, Mosul
Tel: +964(60) 810-733
Fax: +964(60) 815-066
Website: http://uomosul.edu.iq

President: Obay S. Al-Dewachi (2004-)
Tel: +964(60) 815-066
EMail: president@uomosul.edu.iq; obaydewachi@yahoo.com

Vice-president for Administrative Affairs: Adnan M. Alsaffawi
Tel: +964(60) 817-115
EMail: vpadmin@uomosul.edu.iq; unmoadm@yahoo.com

International Relations: Nazar Qibi, Vice-president for Scientific Affairs
Tel: +964(60) 813-238
EMail: vpscie @uomosul.edu.iq; vpscie@yahoo.com

Centres

Computer (Computer Science) *Director*: Qutaiba Ibrahim Ali Saleh; **Dams and Water Resources Research** (Water Management) *Director*: Salem Al-Naqeeb; **Environment and Pollution** (Environmental Studies) *Director*: Sati Al-Rawi; **Mosul Studies** (Heritage Preservation; History) *Director*: Thanoon Altaee; **Regional Studies** (Middle Eastern Studies) *Director*: Ibrahim Al-Allaf; **Remote Sensing** (Surveying and Mapping) *Director*: Hekmat Subhi Yousif Al-Daghastani

Colleges

Agriculture and Forestry (Agriculture; Forestry) *Dean*: Nahil Mohammed Ali Suliaman; **Archeology** (Archaeology) *Dean*: Ali Yassin; **Arts** (Arts and Humanities; History; Modern Languages; Translation and Interpretation) *Dean*: Mohamed Al-Azzawi; **Basic Education** (Education) *Dean*: Fadhil Ibrahim; **Computer and Mathematical Sciences** (Mathematics and Computer Science) *Dean*: Thafer Ramadan; **Dentistry** (Dentistry) *Dean*: Tahani Al-Sondook; **Economics and Administration** (Administration; Economics) *Dean*: Fawaz Al-Dulaimy; **Education** (Education) *Dean*: Abdul Wahid Thanon; **Education for Girls** (Education) *Dean*: Khawola Al-Flayeh; **Electronic Engineering** (Electronic Engineering) *Dean*: Basel Shoker; **Engineering** (Engineering) *Dean*: Farook Khalil Amouri; **Environmental Science and Technology** (Environmental Engineering; Environmental Studies) *Dean*: Moath Hamid; **Fine Arts** (Fine Arts) *Dean*: Hamid Ibrahim Al-Rashdi; **Islamic Science** (Islamic Studies) *Dean*: Abdullah Fathi Dhahir; **Law** *(Tamim)* (Law) *Dean*: Akram Mohmoud; **Medicine** (Anatomy; Biochemistry; Medicine; Physiology) *Dean*: Muzahim Fattah Mohamood; **Natural Sciences** (Natural Sciences) *Dean*: Ihssan Mostafa; **Ninevah Medicine** (Anatomy; Biochemistry; Medicine; Physiology) *Dean*: Faris Al-Sawaf; **Nursing** (Nursing) *Dean*: Subhi Hussain; **Pharmacy** (Pharmacy) *Dean*: Basil Mohammad Yahya Al-khyate; **Physical Education** (Physical Education; Sports) *Dean*: Yassin Mohamed Ali; **Political Science** (International Relations; Political Sciences; Public Administration) *Dean*: Mufeed Thanoon; **Veterinary Medicine** (Veterinary Science) *Dean*: Fouad Kasim Mohammad

History: Founded 1967, comprising colleges which were formerly part of the University of Baghdad. A State institution financed by the government.

Governing Bodies: University Council

Academic Year: September to June (September-January; February-June)

Main Language(s) of Instruction: Arabic in Humanitarian sciences, English and Arabic in Science colleges

Degrees and Diplomas: *Bachelor's Degree*: Architecture, Engineering, Pharmacy; Dentistry (BSc); Veterinary Medicine (BVMS), 5 yrs; *Bachelor's Degree*: Arts and Humanities (BA); Science, Engineering, Education, Agriculture, Administration (BSc), 4 yrs; *Bachelor's Degree*: Medicine (MBCh.B), 6 yrs; *Master's Degree*: Arts (MA); Science, Arts and Humanities (MSc; MA), 2 yrs following Bachelor's Degree; *Doctorate (PhD)*: 3 yrs following Master's Degree

Student Services: Academic counselling, Canteen, Cultural centre, Health services, Nursery care, Sports facilities

Student Residential Facilities: Yes

Special Facilities: Museum; Student's Centre; Al-Muntada Al-Ilmi Centre; Stadium; Cisco Academy Centre

Libraries: Central Library (Main Campus); Ibn-Khaldoon Library (Second Campus); Colleges libraries

Publications: ADAB Al-Rafidain *(quarterly)*; Al-Rafidain Development *(quarterly)*; Al-Rafidain Agriculture Journal *(quarterly)*; Al-Rafidain Dental Journal *(biannually)*; Al-Rafidain Engineering Journal *(quarterly)*; Al-Rafidain Journal for rights *(quarterly)*; Al-Rafidain Journal for the Sporting Sciences *(quarterly)*; Al-Rafidain Journal of Computer Sciences and Mathematics *(biannually)*; Al-Rafidain Sciences Journal *(quarterly)*; Annals of the College of Medicine Mosul *(biannually)*; College of Basic Education Researches Journal *(monthly)*; Iraqi Journal for Geology *(annually)*; Iraqi Journal of Pharmacy *(3 per annum)*; Iraqi Journal of Statistical Sciences IRQ.J.S.S. *(biannually)*; Iraqi Journal of Veterinary Sciences *(biannually)*; Journal of Education and Sciences *(quarterly)*; Journal of Regionalism Studies *(quarterly)*; Journal of the Mosul Studies *(quarterly)*

Academic Staff *2009-2010*	MEN	WOMEN	TOTAL
FULL-TIME	2,787	1,555	**4,342**
STAFF WITH DOCTORATE			
FULL-TIME	1,340	447	**1,787**
Student Numbers *2009-2010*			
All (Foreign Included)	21,283	14,483	**35,766**

Evening students, 6,322.

Last Updated: 19/05/11

UNIVERSITY OF SALAHADDIN

Zankoy Salahaddin

Karkuk Street, Runaki 235 n323, Erbil, Kurdistan
Tel: +964(66) 265-0821
Fax: +964(66) 222-6627
EMail: p.s@suh-edu.com
Website: http://www.suh-edu.com

President: Ahmad Anwar Dezaye (2009-)
Tel: +964 7504 481025 EMail: ahmeddezaye@suh-edu.com

Vice-President for Administration and Finance Affairs: Muhamad Rashed Mukhtar
Tel: +964(66) 223-0480 EMail: m.mochtar@suh-edu.com

International Relations: Mohammed Aziz, Director, International Relations
Tel: +964 7504 622954 EMail: mohammedaziz953@suh-edu.com

Faculties

Administration and Economics (Accountancy; Administration; Banking; Economics; Finance; Statistics); **Agriculture** (Agriculture; Animal Husbandry; Crop Production; Food Technology; Plant and Crop Protection; Soil Science; Water Management; Water Science); **Arts** (Archaeology; Geography (Human); History; Information Sciences; Philosophy; Social Sciences; Sociology; Tourism); **Basic Education** (English; Kurdish; Mathematics; Mathematics Education; Natural Sciences; Preschool Education; Science Education; Sociology; Teacher Training); **Basic Education in Soran** (English; Kurdish; Mathematics; Natural Sciences; Sociology; Teacher Training); **Education in Soran** (Arabic; English; Kurdish; Mathematics; Natural Sciences; Sociology; Teacher Training); **Engineering** (Civil Engineering; Electrical Engineering; Mechanical Engineering; Software Engineering; Structural Architecture; Water Management); **Fine Arts** (Cinema and Television; Cultural Studies; Music; Painting and Drawing; Theatre); **Graduate Studies** *(MSc and PHD programmes)*; **Humanities Education** (Arabic; Education; Educational Administration; Educational Psychology; Educational Sciences; English; Geography; Kurdish; Psychology); **Language in Soran** (Arabic; English; French; Kurdish; Persian); **Languages** (Arabic; English; French; Kurdish; Modern Languages; Persian; Translation and Interpretation); **Law and Political Sciences** (Law; Political Sciences); **Law in Soran** (Law; Political Sciences); **Physical Education** (Physical Education; Sports); **Science Education** (Biology; Chemistry; Computer Education; Computer Science; Mathematics; Mathematics Education; Physics; Science Education); **Science** (Biological and Life Sciences; Biology; Chemistry; Environmental Studies; Geology; Mathematics; Physics); **Shari'a and Islamic Studies** (Islamic Law; Islamic Studies; Islamic Theology; Religion)

Further Information: Also evening faculties: Administration and Economics, Arts; Languages; Law and Political Sciences

History: Founded 1968 as University of Sulaymaniyah, an independent state institution financed by the government; acquired present status and title 1981.

Governing Bodies: University Council

Academic Year: September to June (September-February; February-June)

Admission Requirements: Secondary school certificate or equivalent

Main Language(s) of Instruction: English, Kurdish, Arabic

Degrees and Diplomas: *Bachelor's Degree*: 4-5 yrs; *Master's Degree*; *Doctorate*

Student Residential Facilities: Yes

Libraries: Central Library, 245,208 vols; libraries of the colleges

Press or Publishing House: University Press

Student Numbers *2012-2013*: Total: c. 23,000
Last Updated: 14/03/13

UNIVERSITY OF SULAIMANY

Zankoy Sulaimany

Sulaimany
Tel: +964(207) 810-0308
Fax: +964(870) 169-6314
EMail: uos.relations@univsul.net
Website: http://www.univsul.org/

President: Ali Saeed Mohammad EMail: presidency@univsul.net

Vice-President for Administration Affairs: Bakhtyar Mohammed Ameen EMail: bakhtyar.ameen@univsul.net

Faculties

Agriculture (Agriculture; Agronomy; Animal Husbandry; Food Science; Food Technology; Horticulture; Soil Science; Water Science); **Education and Politics** *(Chamchamal)* (Education; Political Sciences; Social Sciences); **Engineering** (Construction Engineering; Electrical Engineering; Engineering; Irrigation; Structural Architecture); **Languages and Humanities** (Arts and Humanities; Modern Languages); **Law, Politics and Administration** (Administration; Law; Political Sciences); **Medical Sciences** (Dentistry; Medicine; Nursing; Pharmacy; Veterinary Science); **Physical and Basic Education** (Education; Physical Education); **Science and Education Sciences** (Biology; Chemistry; Computer Science; Geology; Mathematics; Mathematics Education; Physics)

Schools

Administration and Economics (Accountancy; Administration; Economics; Statistics); **Basic Education** *(Chamchamal)* (Education; Science Education); **Basic Education** (Computer Education; Education; English; Foreign Languages Education; Mathematics Education; Physical Education; Preschool Education; Social Sciences); **Dentistry** (Anatomy; Biology; Biophysics; Chemistry; Dentistry; Histology; Microbiology; Oral Pathology; Orthodontics; Pathology; Periodontics; Pharmacology; Physiology; Radiology; Social and Preventive Medicine; Surgery); **Education** *(Chamchamal)* (Arabic; Curriculum; Education; Educational Psychology; English; Foreign Languages Education; Kurdish; Native Language Education; Philosophy; Psychology; Social Psychology); **Educational Sciences** (Educational Sciences; Mathematics; Mathematics Education; Physics; Science Education); **Fine Arts** (Ceramic Art; Fine Arts; Painting and Drawing; Sculpture); **Humanities** (Arts and Humanities; Geography (Human); History; Island Studies; Media Studies; Sociology); **Islamic Sciences** (Islamic Studies; Philology; Religion); **Languages** (English; Kurdish; Modern Languages); **Law and Politics** (Administrative Law; Civil Law; Commercial Law; Constitutional Law; Criminal Law; Criminology; Economic and Finance Policy; Economics; Human Rights; International Law; International Relations; Law; Political Sciences; Private Law; Public Law; Public Relations); **Medicine** (Anatomy; Applied Physics; Biochemistry; Biology; Chemistry; Community Health; Computer Science; Dermatology; Embryology and Reproduction Biology; Forensic Medicine and Dentistry; Gynaecology and Obstetrics; Histology; Medicine; Microbiology; Neurology; Ophthalmology; Orthopaedics; Otorhinolaryngology; Paediatrics; Parasitology; Pathology; Pharmacology; Physiology; Plastic Surgery; Psychology; Radiology; Surgery; Urology); **Nursing** (Nursing); **Pharmacy** (Pharmacy); **Physical Education** (Physical Education); **Political and Social Sciences** *(Chamchamal)* (Political Sciences; Social Sciences); **Science** (Biology; Chemistry; Computer Science; Geology; Mathematics; Physics); **Veterinary Medicine** (Anatomy; Histology; Medicine; Microbiology; Pathology; Surgery; Veterinary Science)

Further Information: Also Scientific and Agricultural Laboratories. Teaching Hospital

History: Founded 1968.

Degrees and Diplomas: *Bachelor's Degree*; *Master's Degree*; *Higher Diploma*; *Doctorate (PhD)*

Libraries: c. 42,000 vols; 3,540 periodicals

Publications: Journal of Sulaimany Medical College, Research results; Zankoy Sulaimany, Research results
Last Updated: 23/09/11

UNIVERSITY OF TECHNOLOGY

Al-Jami'at Al-Technologia (UOT)

Al Sinah Street, Baghdad
Tel: +964(1) 719-9446
Fax: +964(1) 774-6532
EMail: thakafiya@yahoo.com
Website: http://www.uotechnology.edu.iq/

President: Kahtan Khalaf Al-Khazraji Fax: +964(1) 719-9446

Vice-President for Scientific Affairs: Ahmed Ali Moosa

Departments

Applied Sciences (Applied Mathematics; Applied Physics; Biochemistry; Laser Engineering; Materials Engineering; Mathematics; Natural Sciences; Physics); **Architectural Engineering** (Architecture; Structural Architecture; Town Planning); **Building and Construction Engineering** (Bridge Engineering; Construction Engineering; Environmental Engineering; Irrigation; Road Engineering; Sanitary Engineering); **Chemical Engineering** (Chemical Engineering; Petroleum and Gas Engineering); **Computer Engineering and Information Technology** (Computer Engineering; Information Technology; Software Engineering); **Computer Science** (Artificial Intelligence; Computer Science; Information Technology; Software Engineering); **Control and Systems Engineering** (Automation and Control Engineering; Computer Engineering; Electrical Engineering; Mechanical Engineering; Systems Analysis); **Electrical and Electronic Engineering** (Electrical and Electronic Engineering); **Electro-Mechanical Engineering** (Electrical Engineering; Mechanical Engineering); **Laser Engineering and Electronic Optics** (Laser Engineering; Optics); **Materials Engineering** (Materials Engineering); **Mechanical and Equipment Engineering** (Automotive Engineering; Heating and Refrigeration; Mechanical Engineering); **Petroleum Engineering** (Petroleum and Gas Engineering); **Production Engineering and Metallurgy** (Industrial Engineering; Metallurgical Engineering; Production Engineering)

History: Founded 1960, and attached to the University of Baghdad 1969 as College of Engineering, became independent with present title and status 1975. A State institution financed by the Government.

Academic Year: September to July (September-January; February-July)

Admission Requirements: Secondary school certificate

Fees: None

Main Language(s) of Instruction: Arabic, English

Degrees and Diplomas: *Bachelor's Degree*: Engineering and Applied Sciences (BSc), 4-5 yrs; *Master's Degree*: Engineering and Applied Sciences (MSc), a further 2 yrs; *Higher Diploma*: Engineering and Applied Sciences; *Doctorate*: Engineering and Applied Sciences (PhD), a further 3 yrs

Student Services: Academic counselling, Canteen, Health services, Social counselling, Sports facilities

Student Residential Facilities: Yes

Special Facilities: Movie studio

Libraries: c. 30,000 vols

Publications: Engineering and Technology

Press or Publishing House: University Press
Last Updated: 21/09/11

UNIVERSITY OF TIKRIT (UOT)

PO Box 42, Tikrit, Salah Addin
Tel: +964(882) 1641112012
EMail: tu@tikrituniversity.edu.iq; tikrituniversity@hotmail.com

President: Ali S. Hussein Al-Jubori

Vice-President for Academic Affairs: Thamer A. Zahwan

Vice-President for Administrative Affairs: Adnaan Jayed Zaydaan

International Relations: Maan M. Aubed, Director, Office of Scholarships, International and Cultural Relations

Colleges

Administration and Economics (Accountancy; Banking; Business Administration; Economics; Finance) *Dean*: Sami Dyab Mahal;

Agriculture (Agricultural Economics; Agricultural Education; Agriculture; Animal Husbandry; Food Science; Food Technology; Horticulture; Plant and Crop Protection) *Dean*: Abdulkarim Uraibi Sabaa; **Archaeology** (Archaeology) *Dean*: Tawfeeq Khalaf Yaseen; **Arts and Humanities** (Arabic; Arts and Humanities; English; French; Geography (Human); History; Mass Communication; Media Studies; Translation and Interpretation) *Dean*: Khalid Abid Harbi; **Dentistry** (Dentistry) *Dean*: Mohammed Sharif Abdullah; **Education** *(Samarra)* (Arabic; Biology; Chemistry; English; History; Islamic Studies; Koran; Mathematics) *Dean*: Mahmoud Al-Samarrai; **Education** *(for women)* (Arabic; Biology; Chemistry; Education; Educational Psychology; Educational Sciences; English; Geography; Geography (Human); History; Koran; Mathematics; Psychology) *Dean*: Ahmed Khalaf Ghanam; **Education** *(co-educational)* (Arabic; Biology; Chemistry; Education; Educational Psychology; Educational Sciences; English; Geography; History; Islamic Studies; Koran; Mathematics; Physics; Psychology) *Dean*: Talab Sabar Mahal; **Engineering** (Chemical Engineering; Civil Engineering; Electrical Engineering; Engineering; Environmental Engineering; Mechanical Engineering) *Dean*: Farok Mnsour Mahdi; **Islamic Law (Shariaa)** (Islamic Law) *Dean*: Farmaan Ismail Ibrahim; **Islamic Sciences** (Islamic Law; Islamic Studies; Islamic Theology) *Dean*: Hatim Ahmed Abass; **Law** (Law) *Dean*: Amir Ayash Abid; **Mathematics and Computer Science** (Computer Science; Mathematics) *Dean*: Saeed Hussein Ali Althallab; **Medicine** (Anatomy; Community Health; Gastroenterology; Gynaecology and Obstetrics; Medicine; Microbiology; Paediatrics; Pathology; Pharmacology; Physiology; Surgery) *Dean*: Wisam Suhail Najim; **Petroleum Engineering** (Automation and Control Engineering; Computer Engineering; Petroleum and Gas Engineering) *Dean*: Mizhir Mahdi Ibrahim Salih; **Pharmacy** (Pharmacology; Pharmacy; Toxicology) *Dean*: Ali Ibraheem Khaleel; **Physical Education** (Physical Education) *Dean*: Mahmoud Abdullah Ahmed; **Political Sciences** (Government; Political Sciences) *Dean*: Latif Karim Mohammed; **Science** *(co-educational)* (Biology; Chemistry; Geology; Physics) *Dean*: Imaad Taha Bakir; **Veterinary Science** (Veterinary Science) *Dean*: Ayad Hameed

History: Founded 1987.

Academic Year: September to June (September-January; February-June)

Admission Requirements: Secondary school certificate or equivalent

Fees: None

Main Language(s) of Instruction: Arabic and English

International Co-operation: With universities in Syria, India, Malaysia, Turkey, United Kingdom and USA

Accrediting Agencies: Ministry of Higher Education and Scientific Research

Degrees and Diplomas: *Bachelor's Degree*: 4 yrs; *Master's Degree*: 2 yrs; *Doctorate*: 3 yrs

Student Services: Academic counselling, Cultural centre, Employment services, Health services, Nursery care, Social counselling, Sports facilities

Student Residential Facilities: Yes

Libraries: Central and college libraries

Publications: The Regional Magazine for Educational and Psychological Sciences *(annually)*; Tikrit Magazine for Agricultural Sciences *(annually)*; Tikrit Magazine for Engineering Sciences *(annually)*

Academic Staff *2010-2011*	MEN	WOMEN	**TOTAL**
FULL-TIME	1,343	349	**1,692**
Student Numbers *2010-2011*			
All (Foreign Included)	6,725	5,741	**12,466**

Last Updated: 19/05/11

WASSIT UNIVERSITY

Wassit-Kut
EMail: presidency@uowasit.edu.iq
Website: http://en.uowasit.edu.iq/

President: Jawad Matar Al-Moussawi

Colleges

Basic Education (Education; Educational Technology; Information Technology; Philosophy of Education; Primary Education; Teacher Training); **Engineering** (Civil Engineering; Electrical Engineering; Engineering; Mechanical Engineering); **Management and Economics** (Accountancy; Administration; Economics; Management; Statistics); **Medicine** (Medicine)

Faculties

Agriculture (Agriculture; Animal Husbandry; Crop Production); **Arts** (Arabic; Arts and Humanities; Cultural Studies; Information Technology; Modern Languages; Oriental Studies; Philosophy; Social Sciences); **Education** (Curriculum; Education; Educational Administration; Educational and Student Counselling; Educational Psychology; Educational Technology; Teacher Training); **Law** (Human Rights; Law); **Science** (Mathematics and Computer Science; Natural Sciences)

Further Information: Also Centre of Computing and Information, and Cultural and Healthy Center for Women

History: Founded 2003.
Last Updated: 22/09/11

PRIVATE INSTITUTIONS

AL-MANSOUR UNIVERSITY COLLEGE

PO Box 69005, Baghdad 12906
Tel: +964(1) 718-9469
Fax: +964(1) 718-9471
EMail: info@muc.edu.iq
Website: http://www.muc.edu.iq/

President: Abdul Rasul A. Jasim (2008-)
Tel: +964(1) 718-9471 EMail: abdulrasulj@hotmail.com

International Relations: Waleed Kima, Head of Public Relations Department EMail: w.kirma@yahoo.com

Departments

Banking and Commercial Sciences (Accountancy; Banking; Business Administration; Business and Commerce; Commercial Law; Insurance; Taxation); **Business Administration** (Accountancy; Business Administration; Communication Studies; Computer Science; Finance; Management; Marketing); **Computer Communication Engineering** (Computer Engineering; Computer Graphics; Computer Networks; Mathematics); **Computer Science and Information Systems** (Artificial Intelligence; Computer Graphics; Computer Science; Information Management; Information Technology; Operations Research; Statistics); **Computer Technology Engineering** (Computer Engineering); **English** (English); **Law** (Administrative Law; Civil Law; Commercial Law; Constitutional Law; Criminal Law; Criminology; History of Law; International Law; Islamic Law; Labour Law; Law; Public Law; Taxation); **Software Engineering** (Computer Networks; Multimedia; Software Engineering)

History: Founded 1988.

Degrees and Diplomas: *Bachelor's Degree*: Commercial and Banking Sciences; Business Administration; Law (BA); Software Engineering; Computer Engineering; Computer Science; Information Systems (BSc), 4 yrs

Libraries: 1,500 vols; 271 periodical subscriptions

Student Numbers *2012-2013*: Total: c. 3,750
Last Updated: 05/03/13

AL-RAFIDAIN UNIVERSITY COLLEGE

PO Box 46036, Baghdad, Al-Risafa
EMail: info@coalrafidain.edu.iq
Website: http://www.coalrafidain.edu.iq/

Dean: Mahmood Aboo
Tel: +964 7901 913866 EMail: dean@coalrafidain.edu.iq

Internal Relations Officer: Abdulkarim Al-Mazidi
Tel: +964 7901 643462
EMail: abdulkarimalmazedi@coalrafidain.edu.iq

International Relations: Enas Al-Klaibawi
Tel: +954 7811 758477 EMail: dr.enas.salih@coalrafidain.edu.iq

Departments

Accounting (Accountancy); **Air Conditioning and Refrigeration Polyechnics** (Heating and Refrigeration); **Business Administration** (Business Administration); **Computer and Telecommunications Engineering** (Computer Engineering; Telecommunications Engineering); **Computer Engineering** (Computer Engineering); **Computer Information Systems** (Computer Science; Information Sciences); **Computer Science** (Computer Science); **Dentistry** (Dentistry); **Law** (Law); **Operations Research** (Management; Operations Research); **Software Engineering** (Software Engineering); **Statistics and Informatics** (Information Management; Statistics)

History: Created 1988. Acquired status 2009.

Governing Bodies: University Council

Academic Year: September to June

Admission Requirements: Secondary school certificate (Baccalaureat).

Fees: (Iraqi Dinars): c. 11/2 million per annum

Main Language(s) of Instruction: Arabic, English

Degrees and Diplomas: *Bachelor's Degree (BSc; BA; BEng)*: 4 yrs; *Bachelor's Degree*: Dentistry (BDMS), 5 yrs

Student Services: Academic counselling, Canteen, Cultural centre, Health services, Language programs, Social counselling, Sports facilities

Student Residential Facilities: none

Special Facilities: Workshops, computer centre, conference room

Libraries: 1,187 books, 201 periodicals, 508 journals

Publications: The Journal of Al-Rafidain University College of Sciences *(quarterly)*

Academic Staff *2009-2010*	MEN	WOMEN	TOTAL
FULL-TIME	183	81	**264**
PART-TIME	40	6	**46**
STAFF WITH DOCTORATE			
FULL-TIME	63	7	**70**
PART-TIME	16	–	**16**

Student Numbers *2009-2010*			
All (Foreign Included)	6,644	3,159	**9,803**
FOREIGN ONLY	25	9	**34**

Evening students, 2,767.

Last Updated: 04/01/11

AMERICAN UNIVERSITY OF IRAQ - SULAIMANI

Building No. 7, Street 10, Quarter 410 Ablakh Area, Sulaimani
Tel: +964 (53) 330-1011
EMail: info@auis.edu.iq; admissions@auis.edu.iq
Website: http://auis.edu.iq

President and Provost: Athanasios Moulakis

Centres

Peace and Security Studies (Peace and Disarmament); **Regional Studies** (Regional Studies); **Study of Ancient Mesopotamia** (Ancient Civilizations)

Programmes

Business Administration (Business Administration); **Engineering** (Engineering); **Environmental Science** (Environmental Studies); **Information Systems and Technology** (Conducting; Information Technology); **International Studies** (International Studies)

History: Founded 2007.

Degrees and Diplomas: *Bachelor's Degree*

Last Updated: 23/09/11

Ireland

STRUCTURE OF HIGHER EDUCATION SYSTEM

Description:

The Irish higher education and training system comprises of a range of higher education institutions – Universities, Institutes of Technology and other nationally recognised institutions and independent higher education colleges. Universities are financed for the most part by the State in the form of annual grants-in-aid and non-recurrent grants for capital expenditure, in a proportion of the order of 90%, as well as by student fees, endowments, and private donations. Each university has its own governing body and exercises full control over its finances. Colleges are composed of faculties and departments.

Stages of studies:

University level first stage: *Bachelor's degree*

The main stage of higher education leads to a Bachelor's degree, which may, in certain cases, also be a professional qualification (Professional degree). The length of study generally varies between three and four years. The Bachelor's degree may be awarded as an Ordinary degree (3 years in duration), an Honours degree (3-4 years in duration). In Veterinary Medicine, Architecture and Dentistry, studies last for five years. Medicine takes six years.

University level second stage: *Master's degree/Post Graduate Diploma*

The second stage of higher education consists of more advanced (graduate) studies and leads to the Master's degree. These studies last for a minimum of one year after the award of the Bachelor's degree. Candidates who attend a course of study and/or present a thesis based on research are awarded a Master's degree.

University level third stage: *Doctorate*

A further three to four years of study after the Master's degree is normally required for the PhD degree.

University level fourth stage: *Higher Doctorate*

A Higher Doctorate may be awarded, after a minimum of five years (usually longer), following the award of the first Doctorate, for original work already published.

Distance higher education:

Oscail -The National Distance Education Centre - is located on the campus of Dublin City University and offers a range of undergraduate, postgraduate and continuing professional education programmes.

ADMISSION TO HIGHER EDUCATION

Admission to university-level studies:

Name of secondary school credential required: Leaving Certificate (Ardteistmeireacht)

For entry to: All higher education institutions.

Numerus clausus/restrictions: Places are allocated in order of merit depending on the Leaving Certificate grades, on the basis of points score.

Other admission requirements: Applicants for postgraduate courses must make direct applications to the college of their choice.

Foreign students admission:

Entrance exam requirements: Foreign students must have, as a minimum, qualifications equivalent to GCE with at least 2 subjects at Advanced level with high grades (at least Grade C) plus 4 other subjects at Ordinary level.

Entry regulations: Entry and residence regulations in Ireland vary according to the person's country of origin. Students who are nationals of another EU Member State and who enter the Republic from any place (other than the UK) must present themselves to the Immigration Officer at the port or airport of entry with the following documents: valid passport; evidence of acceptance as a student at a college or higher education institution; evidence of the ability to meet their needs for the period of study.

Health requirements: Health visa required

RECOGNITION OF STUDIES

Quality assurance system:

The Higher Education and Training Awards Council validates courses in non-university higher education institutions and grants and confers awards upon those who successfully take approved courses.

Bodies dealing with recognition:

NARIC, National Qualifications Authority of Ireland/Údarás Náisiúnta Cáilíochtaí na hÉireann

Chairperson: Paul Haran
Chief Executive Officer: Padraig Walsh
Manager of Operations: Niamh Lenehan
5th Floor
Jervis House
Jervis Street
Dublin 1
Tel: +353(1) 887 1500
Fax: +353(1) 887 1595
EMail: info@nqai.ie
WWW: http://www.nqai.ie/

Services provided and students dealt with: Responsible for development and implementation of the Irish National Framework of Qualifications. Also responsible, as the Irish NARIC, for the academic recognition of foreign qualifications in Ireland.

NATIONAL BODIES

Department of Education and Skills/An Roinn Oideachais agus Scileanna

Minister: Ruairí Quinn
Marlborough Street
Dublin 1
Tel: +353(1) 889 6400
EMail: info@education.gov.ie
WWW: http://www.education.ie/

Higher Education Authority - HEA/An tÚdarás Um Ard-Oideachas

Chief Executive: Tom Boland
Brooklawn House, Crampton Ave., Shelbourne Road
Dublin 4
Tel: +353(1) 231 7100
Fax: +353(1) 231 7172
EMail: info@hea.ie
WWW: http://www.hea.ie

Role of national body: Responsible for the founding of universities and tertiary level institutions and their development to meet the needs of the community.

Higher Education and Training Awards Council/Comhairle na nDámhachtainí Ardoideachais agus Oiliuna

Chairperson: W.J. (Séamus) Smyth
26/27 Denzille Lane
Dublin 2
Tel: +353(1) 631 4567
Fax: +353(1) 631 4577

EMail: info@hetac.ie
WWW: http://www.hetac.ie
Role of national body: HETAC is the qualifications awarding body for third-level education and training institutions outside the university sector.

Irish Universities' Association - IUA/Cumann Ollscoileanna Eireann
President: Brian MacCraith
Chief Executive: Ned Costello
48 Merrion Square
Dublin 2
Tel: +353(1) 676 4948
Fax: +353(1) 662 2815
EMail: info@iua.ie
WWW: http://www.iua.ie
Role of national body: IUA is the representative body of the Heads of the seven Irish universities.

Data for academic year: 2011-2012
Source: IAU from the National Qualifications Authority of Ireland, 2012.

INSTITUTIONS

ALL HALLOWS COLLEGE

Grace Park Road, Drumcondra, Dublin 9
Tel: +353(1) 837-3745
Fax: +353(1) 837-7642
EMail: info@allhallows.ie
Website: http://www.allhallows.ie

President: Patrick McDevitt EMail: pmcdevitt@allhallows.ie

Vice-President for Student Life and Pastoral care: John Joe Spring EMail: jjspring@allhallows.ie

Programmes

Applied Christian Spirituality *(Postgraduate)* (Christian Religious Studies); **Ecology and Religion** *(Postgraduate)* (Ecology; Religion); **Humanities: Pastoral Theology** *(Adult Learning BA for Personal and Professional Development)* (Arts and Humanities; Pastoral Studies; Theology); **Leadership and Pastoral Care** *(Postgraduate)* (Leadership; Pastoral Studies); **Management for Community and Voluntary Services** *(Postgraduate)* (Management); **Research Studies** (Christian Religious Studies; Pastoral Studies); **Social Justice and Public Policy** *(Postgraduate)* (Social Policy); **Supervisory Practice** *(Postgraduate)* (Religious Studies); **Theology and English Literature** (English; Literature; Theology); **Theology and Philosophy** (Philosophy; Theology); **Theology and Psychology** (Psychology; Theology)

History: Founded 1842. A college of the Dublin City University.

Main Language(s) of Instruction: English

International Co-operation: With universities in USA, Germany. Also participates in ERASMUS Programme.

Accrediting Agencies: Dublin City University

Degrees and Diplomas: *Ordinary Bachelor Degree*: Theology and Philosophy; Theology and Psychology; Theology and English Literature; Pastoral Theology; *Masters Degree*: Applied Christian Spirituality; Ecology and Religion; Leadership and Pastoral Care; Management for Community and Voluntary Services; Social Justice and Public Policy; Supervisory Practice; *Doctoral Degree*. Also Research Master

Student Residential Facilities: On-campus accommodation for Sabbatical Programmes

Libraries: c. 22,000 vols. 120 periodical titles

Last Updated: 10/02/12

AMERICAN COLLEGE DUBLIN (AMCD)

2, Merrion Square, Dublin 2
Tel: +353(1) 676-8939
Fax: +353(1) 676-8941
EMail: info@amcd.ie
Website: http://www.amcd.ie

President: Donald E. Ross
Tel: +353(1) 662-0281, Fax: +353(1) 662-1896
EMail: president@amcd.ie

Director of Administrative Services: Mary Monahan

Departments

Business (Accountancy; Business Administration; Finance; International Business); **Hospitality Management** (Hotel Management; Public Relations); **Liberal Arts** (American Studies; History; Irish; Literature)

History: Founded 1993 as a branch of Lynn University, Boca Ratón. Provides international education by combining traditions of American and Irish educational systems.

Governing Bodies: Board of Trustees

Academic Year: September to May (September-December; January-May)

Admission Requirements: Irish Leaving Certificate with grade Cs in two higher level subjects and four ordinary or higher level subjects, or equivalent. US Nationals, minimum academic requirements with SAT score of at least 1000. TOEFL 500 (paper based) or 173 (computer based) or IELTS 5.5

Fees: (Euros): Undergraduate fees, 5,000 per annum for EU students and non-European students, 7,000; Postgraduate fees, 8,000 for all students

Main Language(s) of Instruction: English

Accrediting Agencies: Higher Education and Training Awards Council (HETAC); Middle States Commission on Higher Education (MSCHE)

Degrees and Diplomas: *Ordinary Bachelor Degree*; *Honours Bachelor Degree*; *Higher Diploma*; *Masters Degree*. Alos Certificate and Diploma

Student Services: Academic counselling, Canteen, Cultural centre, Employment services, Foreign student adviser, Social counselling, Sports facilities

Student Residential Facilities: Yes

Special Facilities: Oscar Wilde House. Museum

Libraries: 'Rooney' Library, 11,000 vols

Last Updated: 10/02/12

ATHLONE INSTITUTE OF TECHNOLOGY

Institiúid Teicneolaíochta Bhaile Átha Luain (AIT)

Dublin Road, Athlone, Co. Westmeath
Tel: +353(90) 646-8000
Fax: +353(90) 646-8148
EMail: info@ait.ie
Website: http://www.ait.ie

President: Ciarán Ó Catháin
Tel: +353(90) 646-8101, Fax: +353(90) 642-4417
EMail: cocathain@ait.ie

Registrar: Joseph Ryan
Tel: +353(90) 646-8106 EMail: josephryan@ait.ie

International Relations: Mary Simpson, Director of International Relations Tel: +353(90) 642-4562 EMail: international@ait.ie

Departments

Adult and Continuing Education (Accountancy; Business Administration; Child Care and Development; Chinese; Computer Science; Cosmetology; Design; Education; Engineering; English; Fine Arts; French; German; Hotel and Restaurant; Leisure Studies; Management; Modern Languages; Occupational Health; Parks and Recreation; Physical Therapy; Psychology; Psychotherapy; Social and Community Services; Social Work; Spanish; Sports Management; Teacher Training; Tourism)

Schools

Business Studies (Accountancy; Business Administration; Business Computing; Computer Science; Design; Law; Music Education); **Engineering** (Civil Engineering; Computer Engineering; Construction Engineering; Electronic Engineering; Engineering; Maintenance Technology; Mechanical Engineering; Mechanical Equipment and Maintenance; Mineralogy; Polymer and Plastics Technology; Software Engineering; Technology); **Humanities and Hospitality Studies** (Arts and Humanities; Business Administration; Child Care and Development; Communication Arts; Continuing Education; Cooking and Catering; Design; Hotel and Restaurant; Hotel Management; Law; Leisure Studies; Media Studies; Parks and Recreation; Peace and Disarmament; Psychiatry and Mental Health; Service Trades; Social Problems; Social Studies; Sports Management; Tourism; Visual Arts); **Science** (Biochemistry; Biological and Life Sciences; Biology; Botany; Dentistry; Ecology; Genetics; Gerontology; Health Sciences; Microbiology; Molecular Biology; Natural Sciences; Neurology; Nursing; Nutrition; Oral Pathology; Pharmacology; Pharmacy; Physics; Physiology; Psychiatry and Mental Health; Toxicology; Veterinary Science; Welfare and Protective Services; Zoology)

History: Founded 1970.

Fees: (Euro): Undergraduate tuition fee, 868-5,252 per annum for EU students and 8,000 per annum for non-EU students; Postgraduate tuition fee, 3,500-6,820 per annum and for non-EU students.

Main Language(s) of Instruction: English

International Co-operation: With universities in France; Germany; Spain; Poland; China

Degrees and Diplomas: *Advanced Certificate*; *Higher Certificate*; *Ordinary Bachelor Degree*; *Honours Bachelor Degree*; *Higher Diploma*; *Masters Degree*; *Post Graduate Diploma*: Advanced Social Care Practice. Also Technician Course; Undergraduate Certificate and Diploma; Undergraduate and Postgraduate Special Purpose Awards; Executive MBA programme

Student Services: Academic counselling, Canteen, Employment services, Foreign student adviser, Foreign Studies Centre, Handicapped facilities, Health services, Language programs, Social counselling, Sports facilities

Student Residential Facilities: None

Libraries: Yes

Last Updated: 22/02/12

BURREN COLLEGE OF ART

Newton Castle, Ballyvaughan, Co.Clare
Tel: +353(65) 707-7200
Fax: +353(65) 707-7201
EMail: anna@burrencollege.ie
Website: http://www.burrencollege.ie

President: Mary Hawkes-Greene

Dean and Director of Graduate Studies: Timothy Emlyn Jones

Programmes

Fine Arts (Fine Arts)

History: Founded 1993.

Governing Bodies: Advisory Council

Fees: (Euro): Master programme,17,035 per annum

International Co-operation: With unviersities in U.S.A.

Degrees and Diplomas: *Ordinary Bachelor Degree*; *Masters Degree*; *Doctoral Degree (PhD)*. Also Post-Baccalaureate Certificate

Student Services: Sports facilities

Special Facilities: Art Studios; Gallery; Photographic Studio; Sculpture Workshop; Seminar and Tutorial Rooms; Art Supplies Shop

Libraries: c. 6,000 vols

Last Updated: 10/02/12

COLLEGE OF COMPUTER TRAINING (CCT)

30 - 34 Westmoreland St., Dublin 2, 2 Dublin
Tel: +353(1) 633-3444
Fax: +353(1) 633-3446
EMail: info@cct.ie
Website: http://www.cct.ie/

Director: Neil Gallagher

Programmes

Business Administration (Business Administration); **Computer Engineering** (Computer Engineering; Information Technology; Software Engineering)

International Co-operation: UK, USA, France, Germany, Spain, Netherlands, Denmark, Bulgaria, Russia, India, Brazil.

Degrees and Diplomas: *Higher Certificate*; *Ordinary Bachelor Degree*; *Masters Degree*; *Post Graduate Diploma*

Libraries: Yes

Last Updated: 29/02/12

CORK INSTITUTE OF TECHNOLOGY

Institiúid Teicneolaíochta Chorcaí (CIT)

Rossa Avenue, Bishopstown, Cork
Tel: +353(21) 432-6100
Fax: +353(21) 454-5343
EMail: info@cit.ie; admissions@cit.ie
Website: http://www.cit.ie

President: Brendan Murphy

Registrar and Vice President for Academic Affairs: Barry O'Connor Tel: +353(21) 432-6465 EMail: barry.oconnor@cit.ie

International Relations: Margaret Mulderrig, International Officer Tel: +353(21) 4326-689, Fax: +353(21) 4326-685
EMail: margaret.mulderrig@cit.ie

Colleges

Art and Design (Art Education; Art Therapy; Ceramic Art; Communication Arts; Design; Fine Arts; Glass Art; Journalism; Media Studies; Multimedia; Painting and Drawing; Photography; Public Relations; Sculpture; Textile Design; Video; Visual Arts); **Maritime Studies** *(National)* (Marine Engineering; Marine Science and Oceanography; Marine Transport; Nautical Science; Transport Management)

Faculties

Business and Humanities (Accountancy; Arts and Humanities; Business Administration; Cooking and Catering; Education; Food Science; Hotel and Restaurant; Information Sciences; Leisure Studies; Management; Marketing; Parks and Recreation; Psychology;

Psychotherapy; Social and Community Services; Social Sciences; Social Studies; Tourism); **Engineering and Science** (Analytical Chemistry; Applied Physics; Architecture; Astronomy and Space Science; Automation and Control Engineering; Bioengineering; Biological and Life Sciences; Biomedical Engineering; Biomedicine; Biotechnology; Chemical Engineering; Chemistry; Civil Engineering; Computer Networks; Computer Science; Construction Engineering; Electrical Engineering; Electronic Engineering; Energy Engineering; Engineering; Environmental Engineering; Environmental Studies; Food Science; Health Sciences; Heating and Refrigeration; Industrial Engineering; Information Management; Information Technology; Instrument Making; Mathematics; Mechanical Engineering; Metal Techniques; Nutrition; Pharmacy; Physics; Robotics; Safety Engineering; Software Engineering; Structural Architecture; Surveying and Mapping; Transport Engineering)

Schools

Music (Music; Musical Instruments; Singing; Technology; Theatre)

History: Founded 1978.

Governing Bodies: Institute Executive Board (IEB); Governing Body; Academic Council;

Admission Requirements: Irish Leaving Certificate

Main Language(s) of Instruction: English

Degrees and Diplomas: *Higher Certificate*; *Ordinary Bachelor Degree*; *Honours Bachelor Degree*; *Higher Diploma*; *Masters Degree*; *Doctoral Degree*. Also Undergradaute Certificates; Special Purpose Awards; Minor or Supplemental Awards

Libraries: c. 65,000 vols

Academic Staff *2010-2011*	**TOTAL**
FULL-TIME	**824**
PART-TIME	**233**
Student Numbers *2010-2011*	
All (Foreign Included)	c. **12,000**

Part-time students, 6,000.

Last Updated: 22/02/12

DUBLIN BUSINESS SCHOOL (DBS)

13-14 Aungier Street, Dublin 2
Tel: +353(1) 417-7500
Fax: +353(1) 417-7543
EMail: admissions@dbs.ie; international@dbs.ie
Website: http://www.dbs.edu

Chief Executive Officer: Gerry Muldowney

Courses

Professional Evening Diploma (Accountancy; Advertising and Publicity; Business Administration; Cinema and Television; Commercial Law; Criminology; Finance; Human Resources; Information Technology; International Business; Journalism; Labour Law; Law; Management; Marketing; Media Studies; Psychology; Public Relations; Social Sciences; Taxation; Toxicology)

Schools

Arts (Arts and Humanities; Cultural Studies; Film; Journalism; Literature; Media Studies; Psychology; Psychotherapy; Social Sciences; Social Studies; Theatre; Toxicology); **Business** (Accountancy; Advertising and Publicity; Banking; Business Administration; Business Computing; Finance; Human Resources; Information Management; Information Sciences; Information Technology; Journalism; Leisure Studies; Library Science; Management; Marketing; Media Studies; Parks and Recreation; Psychology; Public Relations; Retailing and Wholesaling); **Law** (Business Administration; Commercial Law; Law); **Professional Accountancy** (Accountancy)

History: Founded 1975 as Accountancy and Business College, . Incorporated LSB College 2000, acquired present status 2003, amalgamed with Portobello College 2007.

Admission Requirements: Leaving Certificate

Fees: (Euro): Bachelor: 5,200 per annum; Master and Postgraduate Diplomas: 4,750-7,700 depending on programmes

Main Language(s) of Instruction: English

Degrees and Diplomas: *Higher Certificate*; *Ordinary Bachelor Degree*; *Honours Bachelor Degree*; *Higher Diploma*; *Masters Degree*. Also Undergraduate Professional Programmes, 1 yr; Evening Diplomas; MBA

Student Services: Academic counselling, Sports facilities

Libraries: c. 50,000 vols; 194 print journals; 750 e-books; 45,000 full-text electronic journals

Student Numbers *2011-2012*: Total: c. 9,000

Last Updated: 13/02/12

DUBLIN CITY UNIVERSITY

Ollscoil Chathair Bhaile Átha Cliath (DCU)

Glasnevin, Dublin 9
Tel: +353(1) 700-5000 +353(1) 700-5338
Fax: +353(1) 836-0830
EMail: public.affairs@dcu.ie; registry@dcu.ie
Website: http://www.dcu.ie

President: Brian MacCraith (2010-)
Tel: +353(1) 700-5666, Fax: +353(1) 700-5888
EMail: brian.maccraith@dcu.ie

Vice-President and Registrar: Anne Scott
Tel: +353(1) 700-8271, Fax: +353(1) 700-5042
EMail: anne.scott@dcu.ie; registrar@dcu.ie

Centres

Communication Technology and Culture Research (Cultural Studies; Telecommunications Engineering) *Director*: Paschal Preston; **Language Technology** *(National)* (Speech Studies) *Director*: Josef van Genabith; **Oscail- Distance Learning**; **Sensor Research** *(BEST)* (Biological and Life Sciences; Nanotechnology) *Director*: Dermot Diamond; **Software Engineering** (Software Engineering) *Director*: Robert Cochran; **Telecommunications Research** *(TELTEC)* (Telecommunications Services) *Director*: Tommy Curran

Faculties

Engineering and Computing (Computer Science; Electronic Engineering; Mechanical Engineering; Production Engineering; Software Engineering) *Dean*: Jim Dowling; **Humanities and Social Sciences** (Arts and Humanities; Communication Studies; Cultural Studies; Government; Irish; Law; Modern Languages) *Dean*: Eithne Guilfoyle; **Science and Health** (Biotechnology; Chemistry; Health Sciences; Mathematics; Natural Sciences; Nursing; Physics; Sports) *Dean*: Malcolm Smyth

Institutes

Cellular Biotechnology *(National)* (Biological and Life Sciences; Cell Biology) *Director*: Martin Clynes

Laboratories

Laser Plasma Research (Laser Engineering) *Director*: Edin T. Kennedy; **Optical Sensors** (Optical Technology) *Director*: Brian MacCraith; **Optronics Ireland** (Electronic Engineering) *Director*: Martin Henry; **Plasma Research** (Physics) *Director*: Miles Turner; **Surface Physics** (Physics) *Director*: Gregory Hughes

Schools

Business (Accountancy; Finance; International Business; Modern Languages)

Further Information: A traditional and Distance Education Institution.

History: Founded 1975 as National Institute for Higher Education, Dublin. First students admitted 1980. Became Dublin City University through legislation enacted June 1989. Receives financial support from the Government.

Governing Bodies: Governing Body, appointed by the Irish Government, consisting of Chairman, Chancellor, University President and 34 ordinary members (including staff and student representatives)

Academic Year: October to May (October-January; February-May)

Admission Requirements: Irish Leaving Certificate with 3 grade Cs in two higher level subjects and 3 grade Ds in four ordinary or higher level subjects (which must include Mathematics and either English or Irish)

Fees: (Euros): EU students, 5,917-8,410 per annum depending on programmes; non-EU, 10,653-15,145; postgraduate, EU students, 6,196-13,200; Non-EU, 6,196-19,200

Main Language(s) of Instruction: English

International Co-operation: With universities and institutions of higher education in Austria, Bangladesh, Belgium, Bulgaria, Canada, Chile, China, Croatia, Czech Republic, Denmark, Estonia, Finland, France, Germany, Greece, Italy, Japan, Latvia, Lithuania, Malawi, Netherlands, Norway, Poland, Portugal, Romania, Russian Federation, Slovak Republic, Spain, Sweden, Switzerland, Taiwan, Tanzania, United Kingdom, USA. Also participates in ERASMUS/ SOCRATES Programme

Degrees and Diplomas: *Ordinary Bachelor Degree*; *Honours Bachelor Degree*; *Higher Diploma*; *Masters Degree*; *Post Graduate Diploma*; *Doctoral Degree*. Also Undergraduate Certificate; Foundation Programme; Pre-Masters Programmes; Professional Postgraduate Diplomas and Doctoral Programmes.

Student Services: Academic counselling, Canteen, Employment services, Foreign student adviser, Foreign Studies Centre, Handicapped facilities, Health services, Language programs, Nursery care, Social counselling, Sports facilities

Student Residential Facilities: Yes

Special Facilities: Student Centre, "The Hub"; Disability Service; Arts Centre, "The Helix"

Libraries: Main Library, c. 250,000 vols

Publications: Journal of Higher Education Studies *(3 per annum)*

Student Numbers *2010-2011*: Total 11,126

Part-time students, 1,564. **Distance students**, 780.

Last Updated: 27/02/12

DUBLIN INSTITUTE OF TECHNOLOGY

Institiúid Teicneolaíochta Átha Cliath (DIT)

143-149 Rathmines Road, Dublin 6

Tel: +353(1) 402-3000

Fax: +353(1) 402-3399

EMail: president@dit.ie

Website: http://www.dit.ie

President: Brian Norton (2003-2013)
Tel: +353(1) 402-7134, Fax: +353(1) 402-7099

Head of Public Affairs: Melda Slattery
Tel: +353(1) 402-7138, Fax: +353(1) 402-7099
EMail: melda.slattery@dit.ie

International Relations: Noel O'Connor, Director, Student Affairs
Tel: +353(1) 867-6075, Fax: +353(1) 402-3429
EMail: robert.flood@dit.ie

Colleges

Arts and Tourism (Advertising and Publicity; Applied Linguistics; Chinese; Cooking and Catering; Criminology; Cultural Studies; Design; Film; Fine Arts; Food Technology; French; German; Health Administration; History; Irish; Italian; Journalism; Law; Leisure Studies; Literature; Media Studies; Modern Languages; Music; Music Education; Photography; Printing and Printmaking; Radio and Television Broadcasting; Russian; Social Sciences; Spanish; Theatre; Tourism; Visual Arts); **Business** (Accountancy; Business Administration; Chinese; Finance; Human Resources; International Business; Management; Marketing; Retailing and Wholesaling; Service Trades); **Engineering and Built Environment** (Architecture; Architecture and Planning; Building Technologies; Civil Engineering; Construction Engineering; Electrical Engineering; Electronic Engineering; Engineering; Environmental Management; Industrial Engineering; Mechanical Engineering; Real Estate; Structural Architecture; Telecommunications Engineering; Transport Engineering); **Sciences and Health** (Biological and Life Sciences; Biomedicine; Chemistry; Computer Science; Environmental Studies; Food Science; Health Sciences; Mathematics; Optometry; Pharmacy; Physics; Software Engineering)

History: Founded 1887. Acquired present status 1992 through merge of six colleges of higher education.

Academic Year: September to August

Admission Requirements: Irish Leaving Certificate or equivalent

Fees: (Euros) EU students: 750 per annum; Non-EU students 11,000 per annum.

Main Language(s) of Instruction: English

Accrediting Agencies: With institutions in France; Germany; Spain; Netherlands; USA

Degrees and Diplomas: *Higher Certificate*; *Ordinary Bachelor Degree*; *Honours Bachelor Degree*; *Masters Degree*; *Post Graduate Diploma*; *Doctoral Degree*. Also undergraduate Certificate; Mature Students Access Course; Part-time doctoral Degree.

Student Services: Academic counselling, Canteen, Employment services, Foreign student adviser, Handicapped facilities, Health services, Language programs, Social counselling, Sports facilities

Student Residential Facilities: None

Libraries: 6 campus libraries, c. 350,000 vols; 35,000 journal titles

Last Updated: 21/02/12

DUNDALK INSTITUTE OF TECHNOLOGY

Institiúid Teicneolaíochta, Dhún Dealgan (DKIT)

Dublin Road, Dundalk, Co. Louth

Tel: +353(42) 937-0200

Fax: +353(42) 937-0201

EMail: info@dkit.ie

Website: http://www.dkit.ie

President: Denis Cummins EMail: Denis.Cummins@dkit.ie

International Relations: Jane Daly, International Administrator
EMail: jane.daly@dkit.ie

Centres

Lifelong Learning (Arts and Humanities; Business Administration; Computer Science; Engineering; Health Sciences; Law)

Schools

Business and Humanities (Accountancy; Administration; Arts and Humanities; Business Administration; Cooking and Catering; Cultural Studies; Finance; Hotel and Restaurant; Information Sciences; International Business; Leadership; Management; Marketing; Native Language Education; Performing Arts; Public Relations; Social Work); **Engineering** (Automotive Engineering; Building Technologies; Business Administration; Civil Engineering; Construction Engineering; Electrical and Electronic Engineering; Electrical Engineering; Electronic Engineering; Energy Engineering; Engineering; Engineering Management; Environmental Engineering; Industrial Design; Mechanical Engineering; Service Trades; Surveying and Mapping); **Informatics, Music and Creative Media** (Computer Engineering; Computer Networks; Computer Science; Film; Information Management; Information Technology; Mass Communication; Mathematics; Mathematics and Computer Science; Multimedia; Music; Musical Instruments; Musicology; Software Engineering; Video); **Nursing, Midwifery, Health Studies and Applied Sciences** (Agriculture; Biology; Child Care and Development; Environmental Studies; Health Sciences; Midwifery; Nursing; Pharmacy; Psychiatry and Mental Health; Social Policy; Veterinary Science)

History: Founded 1970.

Governing Bodies: Governing Body; Academic Council; Executive Board; Academic Management and Planning Committee; Operations and Support Services Management Committee; Student Council

Admission Requirements: Leaving Certificate

Main Language(s) of Instruction: English

Degrees and Diplomas: *Ordinary Bachelor Degree*; *Honours Bachelor Degree*; *Higher Diploma*; *Masters Degree*; *Post Graduate Diploma*; *Doctoral Degree*. Also Undergraduate Certificates and Diplomas, 1-2 yrs; Executive MBA

Student Services: Canteen

Libraries: c. 50,000 vols

Last Updated: 24/02/12

DÚN LAOGHAIRE INSTITUTE OF ART, DESIGN AND TECHNOLOGY (IADT)

Kill Avenue, Dún Laoghaire, Co. Dublin

Tel: +353(1) 239-4000

Fax: +353(1) 239-4700

EMail: info@iadt.ie

Website: http://www.iadt.ie

President: Annie Doona (2011-2016)

Schools

Business and Humanities (Art Management; Business Administration; Cultural Studies; English; Management; Media Studies; Writing); **Creative Arts** (Cinema and Television; Communication Arts; Design; Display and Stage Design; Film; Photography; Radio and Television Broadcasting; Visual Arts); **Creative Technologies** (Communication Studies; Computer Engineering; Computer Science; Cultural Studies; English; Information Technology; Media Studies; Multimedia; Psychology; Software Engineering)

History: Founded 1997.

Admission Requirements: Irish Leaving Certificate or equivalent

Main Language(s) of Instruction: English

Degrees and Diplomas: *Ordinary Bachelor Degree*; *Honours Bachelor Degree*; *Masters Degree*; *Post Graduate Diploma*. Also Undergraduate Certificate

Special Facilities: ICT Office

Libraries: Yes

Last Updated: 14/02/12

FROEBEL COLLEGE OF EDUCATION

Coláiste Oideachais Froebel

Sion Hill, Blackrock, Co. Dublin

Tel: +353(1) 288-8520

Fax: +353(1) 288-0618

EMail: admin@froebel.ie

Website: http://www.froebel.ie

President: Marie McLoughlin (2008-)
EMail: marie.mcloughlin@froebel.ie

Head of Administration: Peter Kenny
Tel: +353(1) 211-2025 EMail: Peter.Kenny@froebel.ie

International Relations: Máire Nic an Bhaird, Co-ordinator of International Programme
Tel: +353(1) 200-0168 EMail: Maire.NicanBhaird@froebel.ie

Programmes

Early Childhood in Teaching and Learning *(Part-time)* (Pre-school Education; Teacher Training); **Education** (Education); **Education** *(Mature)* (Education); **Primary Education** *(Postgraduate)* (Primary Education); **Special Education** *(Postgraduate)* (Special Education)

History: Founded 1943. Acquired present status 1976.

Admission Requirements: Irish Leaving Certificate

Main Language(s) of Instruction: English

International Co-operation: Participates in the Socrates-Erasmus Programme

Degrees and Diplomas: *Ordinary Bachelor Degree*: Education; Education (Mature); *Honours Bachelor Degree*: Early Childhood - Teaching and Learning (part-time); *Higher Diploma*: Primary Education; *Post Graduate Diploma*: Special Education

Libraries: 19,000 vols

Last Updated: 13/02/12

GALWAY-MAYO INSTITUTE OF TECHNOLOGY

Institiúid Teicneolaíochta na Gaillimhe-Maigh Eo (GMIT)

Dublin Road, Galway

Tel: +353(91) 753-161

Fax: +353(91) 751-107

EMail: info@gmit.ie

Website: http://www.gmit.ie

President: Michael Carmody (2011-)
Tel: +353(91) 742-223, Fax: +353(91) 751-144
EMail: president@gmit.ie

Registrar: Michael Hannon
Tel: +353(91) 742-723 EMail: michael.hannon@gmit.ie

International Relations: Dennis Murphy, Head of International Relations Tel: +353(91) 742-765 EMail: dennis.murphy@gmit.ie

Campuses

Castlebar (Accountancy; Arts and Humanities; Business Administration; Business Computing; Computer Science; Construction Engineering; Design; Education; European Languages; Finance; Fine Arts; Heritage Preservation; Information Technology; Maintenance Technology; Mathematics; Nursing; Psychiatry and Mental Health; Psychology; Social Studies; Technology); **Letterfrack** (Design; Industrial Design; Technology Education; Wood Technology)

Schools

Business *(Galway)* (Accountancy; Administration; Agricultural Business; Business Administration; Information Management; Information Sciences); **Engineering** *(Galway)* (Building Technologies; Civil Engineering; Electrical and Electronic Engineering; Electrical Engineering; Electronic Engineering; Engineering; Industrial Engineering; Mechanical Engineering); **Hotel** *(Galway)* (Cooking and Catering; Hotel and Restaurant; Tourism); **Humanities** (Arts and Humanities; Design; Film; Fine Arts; French; German; Heritage Preservation; Irish; Modern Languages; Radio and Television Broadcasting; Religious Studies; Spanish; Theology; Translation and Interpretation); **Science** *(Galway)* (Agricultural Management; Biological and Life Sciences; Business Computing; Chemistry; Computer Science; Environmental Management; Forensic Medicine and Dentistry; Information Technology; Instrument Making; Marine Biology; Mathematics; Mathematics and Computer Science; Media Studies; Medicine; Natural Sciences; Pharmacy; Physics; Software Engineering)

Further Information: Also campus in Cluain Mhuire.

History: Founded 1972 as Regional Technical College Galway. Acquired present status 1998.

Governing Bodies: Governing Body; Academic Council; Executive Board; Management Group

Fees: (Euro): EU undergraduate students: 1,500, postgraduate: 4,019-6,250; Non UE students: 5,500-10.000 depending on programmes

International Co-operation: With universities in China, Saudi Arabia, U.S.A., Australia, Thailand, India. Participates in Erasmus programme

Degrees and Diplomas: *Higher Certificate*; *Ordinary Bachelor Degree*; *Honours Bachelor Degree*; *Higher Diploma*; *Masters Degree*; *Post Graduate Diploma*; *Doctoral Degree*. Also Undergraduate Certificates; Professional Programme in Accountancy

Student Services: Academic counselling, Canteen, Employment services, Foreign student adviser, Handicapped facilities, Health services, Language programs, Social counselling, Sports facilities

Special Facilities: IT Services

Libraries: c. 100,000 vols; 500 print journals; 8,500 electronic journals

Last Updated: 23/02/12

GARDA COLLEGE

Templemore, Tipperary

Tel: +353(504) 35400

EMail: College_admin@garda.ie

Website: http://www.gardacollegelms.ie/

Faculties

Crime and Operational Training; **Leadership and Management Development** (Leadership; Management); **Police Studies** (Police Studies)

Programmes

Education, Training and Development (Education)

Degrees and Diplomas: *Ordinary Bachelor Degree*. Also a Post-Graduate Diploma in Executive Leadership delivered in conjunction with the Michael Smurfit Business School, University College Dublin

Last Updated: 06/03/12

GRAFTON COLLEGE OF MANAGEMENT SCIENCES

7 Gardiner Row, 1 Dublin

Tel: +353(1) 872-6597

Fax: +353 (1) 872-6599

EMail: info@graftoncollege.ie

Website: http://www.graftoncollege.ie

Programmes
Business Administration (Business Administration; Finance; Leadership; Management; Marketing)

Further Information: Alsos campuses in London and Islamabad (Pakistan)

International Co-operation: With Coventry University (UK)

Degrees and Diplomas: *Ordinary Bachelor Degree*; *Masters Degree*.

Last Updated: 29/02/12

GRIFFITH COLLEGE DUBLIN (GCD)

South Circular Road, Dublin 8
Tel: +353(1) 415-0400
Fax: +353(1) 454-9265
EMail: admissions@gcd.ie
Website: http://www.gcd.ie

President: Diarmuid Hegarty

Faculties
Computing (Communication Arts; Computer Networks; Computer Science; Design; Information Management; Media Studies; Multimedia; Software Engineering; Telecommunications Engineering; Visual Arts); **Journalism and Media Communications** (Ethics; Journalism; Law; Media Studies; Public Relations; Radio and Television Broadcasting; Sociology)

Graduate Schools
Business (Accountancy; Finance; International Business; Management)

Programmes
Education Training *(Griffith)* (Education; Educational Sciences)

Schools
Accountancy *(Professional)* (Accountancy); **Law** (Commercial Law; Constitutional Law; Criminal Law; Human Rights; International Law; Law; Public Law); **Music and Drama** *(Leinster)* (Conducting; Music; Music Education; Music Theory and Composition; Musical Instruments)

History: Founded 1974.

Fees: (Euro): Full-time tuition for European students, 2,000-7,500; Non-European students, 7,000-11,000. Part-time, 2,800-6,500.

Main Language(s) of Instruction: English

Degrees and Diplomas: *Honours Bachelor Degree*; *Masters Degree*; *Post Graduate Diploma*. Also Undergraduate Diploma and Professional Diploma; MBA

Student Services: Canteen, Sports facilities

Student Residential Facilities: Griffith College Halls of Residence (GHR)

Libraries: c. 15,000 journals

Student Numbers *2009-2010*: Total: c. 8,000

Last Updated: 20/02/12

GRIFFITH COLLEGE CORK (GCC)

Cove Street, Sullivan's Quay, Cork
Tel: +353(21) 450-7027
Fax: +353(21) 450-7659
EMail: registrar@gcc.ie
Website: http://www.gcc.ie/index.jsp

President: Diarmuid Hegarty EMail: director@gcc.ie

Courses
Accountancy *(Professional)* (Accountancy; Finance; International Business); **Professional Evening** (Advertising and Publicity; Business Administration; Human Resources; Management; Public Relations)

Faculties
Business (Accountancy; Business Administration; Finance; Marketing); **Design** (Design; Interior Design); **Journalism and Media Courses** (Journalism; Media Studies); **Law** (Law)

Graduate Schools
Law (Commercial Law; Human Rights; International Law; Law)

Programmes
Evening Courses (Accountancy; Business Administration; Computer Science; Journalism; Law; Media Studies; Music; Psychology; Theatre); **Short-Term Courses** (Accountancy; Business Computing; Computer Science; Secretarial Studies)

Schools
Law *(Professional)* (Law)

History: Founded 1884 as Skerry's College. Acquired present title 2005.

Fees: (Euro): 2,750-6,500

Degrees and Diplomas: *Higher Certificate*; *Ordinary Bachelor Degree*; *Honours Bachelor Degree*; *Higher Diploma*; *Masters Degree*. Also Certificate in Business in Intercultural Studies -Levl 6 Foundation; Undergraduate Certificate in Administration and Office Skills.

GRIFFITH COLLEGE LIMERICK (GCL)

31/32 Upper William Street, Limerick
Tel: +353(61) 310-031 +353(61) 310-043
Fax: +353(61) 310-059
EMail: info@gcl.ie
Website: http://www.gcl.ie

President: Diarmuid Hegarty

Courses
Corporate Training; **Part-time Studies** (Accountancy; Advertising and Publicity; Business Administration; Business Computing; Child Care and Development; Dietetics; Electrical and Electronic Engineering; Graphic Design; Human Resources; Labour Law; Law; Leadership; Management; Marketing; Nutrition; Public Relations; Secretarial Studies)

Faculties
Administration (Administration); **Business** (Advertising and Publicity; Business Administration; Hotel and Restaurant; Human Resources; Leadership; Management; Marketing; Public Relations); **Computing** (Computer Science; Graphic Design; Marketing; Media Studies); **Engineering** (Electrical and Electronic Engineering; Engineering; Industrial Engineering); **Humanities** (Arts and Humanities; Child Care and Development; Dietetics; Nutrition; Psychology; Social Studies)

Schools
Accountancy *(Professional)* (Accountancy; Business Administration; Finance)

History: Founded as the Mid West Business Institute. Acquired present status and title 2006.

Degrees and Diplomas: *Higher Certificate*; *Ordinary Bachelor Degree*; *Honours Bachelor Degree*; *Higher Diploma*; *Post Graduate Diploma*. Also Undergraduate Certificates; MBA

Special Facilities: Computer Rooms; Engineering Lab Facilities Computer Rooms Computer facilities include two modern centrally networked computer rooms with internet access, printers, wireless routers for use with laptops and state-of-the-art software required for the various Computing, Information Technology and Engineering courses that are delivered at the College. Both computer rooms are equipped with ceiling mounted high-beam projectors. Engineering Labs

HIBERNIA COLLEGE

2 Clare Street, Dublin 2
Tel: +353(1) 661-0168
Fax: +353(1) 661-0162
EMail: info@hiberniacollege.net; academicaffairs@hiberniacollege.net
Website: http://www.hiberniacollege.net

President: Seán M. Rowland

Registrar: Naomi Jackson

Schools
Education (Distance Education; Education; Educational Technology; Primary Education; Secondary Education; Teacher Training); **Health Sciences** (Health Sciences; Pharmacy); **Management and Law** (Commercial Law; International Law; Law; Management)

Further Information: Also campuses in London and Westport

History: Founded in 2001, Hibernia College is Ireland's first nationally accredited third level online College, offering flexible web-enabled learning opportunities to students and organizations in Ireland and internationally.

Degrees and Diplomas: *Higher Diploma*; *Masters Degree*. Also Professional Diploma in Post Primary Education

Last Updated: 20/02/12

ICD BUSINESS SCHOOL

BPP House, 5 Lad Lane, 2 Dublin
Website: http://www.icd.ie/

Programmes

Accountancy (Accountancy); **Business Administration and Management** (Business Administration; Management); **Finance** (Finance)

Degrees and Diplomas: *Honours Bachelor Degree*; *Higher Diploma*

Last Updated: 29/02/12

INSTITUTE OF BUSINESS AND TECHNOLOGY

Forster Way, Swords, Dublin 1
Tel: +353(1) 807-5055
Fax: +353(1) 807-5056
EMail: info@ibat.ie
Website: http://www.ibat.ie/

Director: Shane Ormsby

Programmes

Information Technology (Information Technology); **Accountancy** (Accountancy); **Marketing** (Marketing)

Degrees and Diplomas: *Higher Certificate*; *Ordinary Bachelor Degree*; *Honours Bachelor Degree*; *Masters Degree (MBA)*

Last Updated: 29/02/12

INSTITUTE OF TECHNOLOGY BLANCHARDSTOWN

Institiúid Teicneolaíochta Baile Bhlainséir (ITB)
Blanchardstown Road North, Blanchardstown, 15 Dublin
Tel: +353(1) 885-1000
Fax: +353(1) 885-1001
EMail: info@itb.ie
Website: http://www.itb.ie

President: Mary Meaney EMail: Mary.Meany@itb.ie

Registrar: Margaret Davis

Schools

Business and Humanities (Accountancy; Business Administration; Child Care and Development; Finance; Modern Languages; Social and Community Services; Social Work; Sports Management); **Informatics and Engineering** (Computer Engineering; Computer Science; Electronic Engineering; Engineering; Horticulture; Information Technology; Mechanical Engineering; Multimedia)

History: Founded 1999.

Admission Requirements: Leaving Certificate

Fees: (Euro): Tuition Fee, 868-2,450 per annum fro EU students; 8,895 per annum for non-EU students

Main Language(s) of Instruction: English

International Co-operation: Participates in the Erasmus programme

Degrees and Diplomas: *Higher Certificate*; *Ordinary Bachelor Degree*; *Honours Bachelor Degree*; *Higher Diploma*; *Masters Degree*

Student Services: Academic counselling, Health services, Social counselling, Sports facilities

Special Facilities: Lecture Theatres; Computer Laboratories; Language Laboratories

Libraries: Yes

Last Updated: 22/02/12

INSTITUTE OF TECHNOLOGY CARLOW

Institiúid Teicneolaíochta Ceatharlach
Kilkenny Road, Carlow
Tel: +353(59) 917-5000
Fax: +353(59) 917-5005
EMail: info@itcarlow.ie
Website: http://www.itcarlow.ie/

President: Patricia Mulcahy
Tel: +353(59) 917-5001 EMail: patricia.mulcahy@itcarlow.ie

Registrar: Brian Bennett EMail: brian.bennett@itcarlow.ie

International Relations: Patricia Rochford, Administrator, International Department - EU
Tel: +353(59) 917-5090 EMail: patricia.rochford@itcarlow.ie

International Relations: Flynn Rosemary, Administrator, International Department - Non-EU
Tel: +353(59) 917-5205 EMail: rosemary.flynn@itcarlow.ie

Campuses

Wexford (Architecture; Arts and Humanities; Business Administration; Child Care and Development; Communication Arts; Design; E-Business/Commerce; Graphic Design; Management; Marketing; Mass Communication; Media Studies; Social Studies)

Schools

Business and Humanities (Accountancy; Arts and Humanities; Business Administration; Child Care and Development; Communication Studies; Design; Human Resources; Industrial Design; International Business; Law; Management; Marketing; Media Studies; Public Relations; Social and Community Services; Social Studies; Social Work; Sports; Sports Management); **Engineering** (Aeronautical and Aerospace Engineering; Architecture; Building Technologies; Civil Engineering; Construction Engineering; Electronic Engineering; Energy Engineering; Engineering; Mechanical Engineering; Surveying and Mapping); **Science** (Applied Chemistry; Biological and Life Sciences; Biology; Computer Networks; Computer Science; Environmental Studies; Forensic Medicine and Dentistry; Health Sciences; Information Technology; Natural Sciences; Pharmacy; Physiology; Rehabilitation and Therapy; Software Engineering; Sports; Sports Medicine)

Further Information: Also campus in Wicklow

History: Founded 1970.

Main Language(s) of Instruction: English

Degrees and Diplomas: *Higher Certificate*; *Ordinary Bachelor Degree*; *Honours Bachelor Degree*; *Masters Degree*; *Doctoral Degree*

Student Services: Academic counselling, Health services, Social counselling, Sports facilities

Special Facilities: Multi-Media Centre; Learning Resource Centre; Engineering Technology Building

Libraries: Yes

Academic Staff *2009-2010*: Total: c. 200
Student Numbers *2009-2010*: Total: c. 4,000
Last Updated: 22/02/12

INSTITUTE OF TECHNOLOGY SLIGO

Institiúid Teicneolaíochta Sligeach
Ash Lane, Sligo
Tel: +353(71) 9155-222
Fax: +353(71) 9160-475
EMail: info@itsligo.ie
Website: http://www.itsligo.ie

President: Terri Scott Tel: +353(71) 9155-201

Registrar: Brendan McCormack
Tel: +353(71) 9155-294 EMail: mccormack.brendan@itsligo.ie

International Relations: Eileen Curley Fax: +353(71) 9155-384 EMail: curley.eileen@itsligo.ie

Schools

Business and Humanities (Accountancy; Administration; Arts and Humanities; Business Administration; Computer Engineering; Computer Networks; Computer Science; Data Processing; Design; Finance; Fine Arts; Information Sciences; International Business;

Leisure Studies; Marketing; Modern Languages; Multimedia; Parks and Recreation; Performing Arts; Preschool Education; Public Relations; Social Studies; Social Work; Software Engineering; Tourism); **Engineering** (Architecture; Civil Engineering; Construction Engineering; Electronic Engineering; Engineering; Interior Design; Mechanical Engineering; Surveying and Mapping); **Science** (Archaeology; Biomedicine; Biotechnology; Business Administration; Energy Engineering; Environmental Management; Environmental Studies; Fishery; Forensic Medicine and Dentistry; Health Sciences; Natural Sciences; Occupational Health; Pharmacy; Physiology; Public Health; Safety Engineering)

Further Information: A traditional, open and distance learning education institution.

History: Founded 1970.

Admission Requirements: Six subjects in the Leaving Certificate at a minimum level of Grade D3. For Honours Degree two of higher level papers, Grade C3 or better, English or Irish, and Mathematics must be Higher Level Mathematics. All subjects must be obtained at one sitting

Fees: (Euro) Undergraduate Tuition Fees, 1,368-2,950 per annum for EU Citizens and 9,000 per annum for International (Non-EU) Citizens; Postgraduate Tuition Fees, 4,019 per annum for EU Citizens and 10,000 per annum for International (Non-EU) Citizens.

Accrediting Agencies: Higher Education and Training Award Council (HETAC)

Degrees and Diplomas: *Higher Certificate*; *Ordinary Bachelor Degree*; *Honours Bachelor Degree*; *Masters Degree*; *Post Graduate Diploma*; *Doctoral Degree*. Also Postgraduate Special Purpose Award

Student Services: Sports facilities

Student Residential Facilities: Student Accommodation (2,100 beds).

Libraries: Yes

Academic Staff *2009-2010*: Total: c. 600
Student Numbers *2009-2010*: Total: c. 5,800
Last Updated: 24/02/12

INSTITUTE OF TECHNOLOGY TALLAGHT

Institiúid Teicneolaíochta Tamhlacht

Tallaght, Dublin 24
Tel: +353(1) 404-2000
Fax: +353(1) 404-2700
EMail: info@ittdublin.ie
Website: http://www.it-tallaght.ie/

International Officer: Alison Hawkins
EMail: Alison.Hawkins@ittdublin.ie

President: Pat MacLaughlin
Tel: +353(1) 404-2110 EMail: pat.mclaughlin@ittdublin.ie

Registrar: John Vickery
Tel: +353(1) 404-2220 EMail: john.vickery@ittdublin.ie

Schools

Business and Humanities (Accountancy; Advertising and Publicity; Arts and Humanities; Business Administration; Business Computing; Cooking and Catering; European Studies; Finance; Hotel and Restaurant; Management; Marketing; Multimedia; Social Work; Tourism); **Engineering** (Electronic Engineering; Energy Engineering; Engineering; Environmental Engineering; Mechanical Engineering); **Science and Computing** (Biological and Life Sciences; Biology; Chemistry; Computer Science; Forensic Medicine and Dentistry; Health Sciences; Information Management; Information Sciences; Information Technology; Pharmacy; Sports)

History: Founded 1992.

Main Language(s) of Instruction: English

International Co-operation: Participates in ERASMUS

Degrees and Diplomas: *Higher Certificate*; *Ordinary Bachelor Degree*; *Honours Bachelor Degree*; *Masters Degree*

Student Residential Facilities: Yes

Libraries: Yes

Academic Staff *2010-2011*: Total: c. 400
Student Numbers *2010-2011*: Total: c. 3,700
Last Updated: 24/02/12

INSTITUTE OF TECHNOLOGY TRALEE

Institúid Teicneolaíochta Trá Lí

Clash, Tralee, Co. Kerry
Tel: +353(66) 714-5600
Fax: +353(66) 712-5711
EMail: info@ittralee.ie
Website: http://www.ittralee.ie

President: Oliver Murphy (2010-)
Tel: +353(66) 714-5625 EMail: president@ittralee.ie

Registrar: Michael Hall
Tel: +353(66) 714-5619 EMail: Michael.Hall@staff.ittralee.ie

International Relations: Lila O'Donnell, International Officer
EMail: Lila.ODonnell@staff.ittralee.ie

Schools

Business and Humanities (Arts and Humanities; Business Administration; Child Care and Development; Cooking and Catering; French; German; Hotel and Restaurant; Hotel Management; Information Sciences; Information Technology; Media Studies; Modern Languages; Multimedia; Music; Radio and Television Broadcasting; Social and Community Services; Social Sciences; Social Work; Spanish; Technology; Tourism); **Engineering and Construction Studies** (Agricultural Engineering; Agricultural Management; Building Technologies; Civil Engineering; Construction Engineering; Engineering; Management; Mechanics; Production Engineering; Service Trades; Surveying and Mapping); **Science and Computing** (Applied Chemistry; Biological and Life Sciences; Biology; Computer Engineering; Computer Networks; Computer Science; Cosmetology; Educational Technology; Environmental Studies; Forensic Medicine and Dentistry; Health Sciences; Information Technology; Leadership; Leisure Studies; Mathematics; Mathematics and Computer Science; Nursing; Pharmacy; Physical Education; Psychiatry and Mental Health; Software Engineering; Sports; Wildlife)

History: Founded 1977. Acquired present status 1993.

Governing Bodies: Governing Body; Academic Council; Executive Council

Academic Year: September to June

Admission Requirements: Irish Leaving Certificate or equivalent

Fees: (Euros) EU students none; Non-EU students 8,000-12,000 per annum depending on course

Main Language(s) of Instruction: English

International Co-operation: Participates in Socrates/Erasmus

Accrediting Agencies: HETAC

Degrees and Diplomas: *Higher Certificate*; *Ordinary Bachelor Degree*; *Honours Bachelor Degree*; *Higher Diploma*; *Masters Degree*; *Post Graduate Diploma*; *Doctoral Degree*. Also Professional Certificates; Undergraduate Certificates; Minor Award Diploma; Special Purpose Award

Student Services: Academic counselling, Canteen, Employment services, Foreign student adviser, Foreign Studies Centre, Handicapped facilities, Health services, Language programs, Social counselling, Sports facilities

Student Residential Facilities: Yes

Special Facilities: Kerry Technology Park

Libraries: c. 60,000 vols

Last Updated: 24/02/12

IRISH COLLEGE OF HUMANITIES AND APPLIED SCIENCES (ICHAS)

Walton House, Lonsdale Road, National Technology Park, Castletroy, Limerick
Tel: +353(61) 216-288
Fax: +353(61) 330-459
EMail: info@ichas.ie
Website: http://www.ichas.ie

President: Maria Carmody

Registrar: Suzanne O Callaghan

Institutes

Childcare and Humanities (Arts and Humanities; Child Care and Development); **Counselling and Psychotherapy** (Development Studies; Health Sciences; Leadership; Management; Psychotherapy; Social Studies); **Open Learning**

History: ICHAS has evolved from the National Counselling and Psychotherapy Institute of Ireland, which was founded in 1999.

Accrediting Agencies: Higher Education and Training Awards Council (HETAC)

Degrees and Diplomas: *Honours Bachelor Degree*; *Masters Degree*

Last Updated: 01/03/12

IRISH MANAGEMENT INSTITUTE (IMI)

Sandyford Road, Dublin 18
Tel: +353(1) 207-8400
Fax: +353(1) 295-5147
EMail: info@imi.ie
Website: http://www.imi.ie

Chief Executive: Tom McCarthy (2004-)

Programmes

Advanced Negotiation Skills (Business Administration); **Advanced Skills of Management** (Management); **Business** (Business Administration); **Business Finance** (Business Administration; Finance); **Business Research Project** (Business Administration); **Cloud Strategy** (Business Computing); **Communicating For Performance** (Communication Studies); **Essential Skills of Management** (Management); **Executive Coaching** (Human Resources); **Finance for Non-Financial Managers** (Finance; Management); **Front Line Management Foundation Skills** (Management); **Henley MBA** (Behavioural Sciences; Business Administration; Finance; Leadership; Management); **High Impact Leadership** (Leadership); **Leadership** (Leadership); **Leadership and Motivation** (Leadership); **Management** (Management); **Management Practice** (Behavioural Sciences; Finance; Industrial and Organizational Psychology; Information Technology; Management); **Managing People** (Management); **Marketing Strategy with Digital Marketing** (Marketing); **Master Trainer** (Management); **Mini MBA** (Business Administration; Finance; Leadership; Management; Marketing); **Organisational Behaviour** (Behavioural Sciences; Economic and Finance Policy; Economics; Human Resources; Industrial and Organizational Psychology; Management; Political Sciences; Social Psychology; Social Sciences; Sociology; Statistics); **Senior Executive** (Business Administration); **Strategic HR Management** (Human Resources; Management); **Strategy and Innovation** (Business Administration); **Training That Gets Results** (Management)

History: Founded 1952.

Governing Bodies: Council; Board; Chief Executive

Main Language(s) of Instruction: English

Degrees and Diplomas: *Masters Degree*. Also IMI Undergraduate Diploma; Professional Porgrammes in Business and Management; Henley MBA, jointly delivered with the Henley Business School (UK).

Libraries: c. 18,000 journals

Last Updated: 24/02/12

KIMMAGE DEVELOPMENT STUDIES CENTRE (KDSC)

Kimmage Manor, Whitehall Road, Dublin 12
Tel: +353(1) 406-4386 +353(1) 406-4380
Fax: +353(1) 406-4388
EMail: info@kimmagedsc.ie
Website: http://www.kimmagedsc.ie

Executive Director: Paddy Reilly

Programmes

Development Studies (Adult Education; Anthropology; Development Studies; Environmental Studies; Gender Studies; Leadership; Management; Peace and Disarmament; Political Sciences; Sociology); **Dryland Policy and Climate Change Adaptation** (Development Studies; Economics; Environmental Studies; Natural Resources; Peace and Disarmament; Sociology)

History: Founded 1974 as an institution specializing in facilitating education and training courses for development professionals. Acquired new status 2006.

Governing Bodies: Board of Directors

Degrees and Diplomas: *Ordinary Bachelor Degree*; *Masters Degree*; *Post Graduate Diploma*

Libraries: Yes

Last Updated: 24/02/12

LETTERKENNY INSTITUTE OF TECHNOLOGY

Institiúid Teicneolaíochta Leitir Ceanainn (LYIT)

Port Road, Letterkenny, Co. Donegal
Tel: +353(74) 918-6000
Fax: +353(74) 918-6005
EMail: Reception@lyit.ie
Website: http://www.lyit.ie

President: Paul Hannigan
Tel: +353(74) 918-6012, Fax: +353(74) 918-6011
EMail: paul.hannigan@lyit.ie

Registrar: Danny Brennan
Tel: +353(74) 918-6012, Fax: +353(74) 918-6101
EMail: danny.brennan@lyit.ie

International Relations: Dermot Cavanagh
EMail: dermot.cavanagh@lyit.ie

Departments

Business (Accountancy; Business Administration; Leadership; Management; Marketing; Sports Management); **Civil Engineering and Construction** (Architecture; Civil Engineering; Construction Engineering; Energy Engineering; Fire Science; Safety Engineering); **Computing** (Business Computing; Computer Engineering; Computer Networks; Computer Science; Information Technology; Multimedia; Telecommunications Engineering); **Continuing Education** (Accountancy; Business Administration; Chinese; Computer Science; Cooking and Catering; Design; Finance; Food Science; Higher Education; Hotel and Restaurant; Irish; Law; Management; Marketing; Nursing; Pharmacy; Philosophy; Photography; Public Administration; Software Engineering; Spanish; Tourism; Video); **Design and Creative Media** (Design; Graphic Design; Media Studies); **Electronic and Mechanical Engineering** (Computer Engineering; Design; Electronic Engineering; Energy Engineering; Mechanical Engineering); **Gastronomy and Culinary Arts** (Cooking and Catering; Food Science; Hygiene); **Hospitality and Tourism** (Hotel and Restaurant; Management; Marketing; Tourism); **Law and Humanities** (Arts and Humanities; French; German; International Business; Law; Modern Languages; Spanish); **Nursing and Health Studies** (Health Sciences; Nursing; Psychiatry and Mental Health; Social Studies); **Science** (Biological and Life Sciences; Food Science; Forensic Medicine and Dentistry; Nutrition; Pharmacy; Veterinary Science)

Further Information: Also campus at Shore Road, Killybegs

Governing Bodies: Governing Body; Academic Council

Admission Requirements: Leaving Certificate or equivalent

Main Language(s) of Instruction: English

Degrees and Diplomas: *Higher Certificate*; *Ordinary Bachelor Degree*; *Honours Bachelor Degree*; *Higher Diploma*; *Masters Degree*; *Post Graduate Diploma*. Also Undergraduate Certificates and Diplomas; Minor Awards.

Student Services: Academic counselling, Handicapped facilities, Health services, Social counselling

Libraries: Yes

Academic Staff *2009-2010*: Total: c. 350

Student Numbers *2009-2010*: Total: c. 3,000

Last Updated: 23/02/12

LIMERICK INSTITUTE OF TECHNOLOGY (LIT)

Moylish Park, Limerick
Tel: +353(61) 208-208
Fax: +353(61) 208-209
EMail: information@lit.ie
Website: http://www.lit.ie/

President: Maria G. Hinfelaar
Tel: +353(61) 208-233 EMail: Maria.Hinfelaar@lit.ie

Registrar: Terry Twomey

Schools

Art and Design *(LSAD)* (Art Education; Ceramic Art; Communication Arts; Design; Fashion Design; Fine Arts; Media Studies; Painting and Drawing; Printing and Printmaking; Sculpture); **Business and Humanities** (Accountancy; Arts and Humanities; Business Administration; Cooking and Catering; Finance; Hotel and Restaurant; Law; Management; Marketing; Social Work; Sports Management; Taxation); **LIT Tipperary** (Accountancy; Art Therapy; Business Administration; Computer Engineering; Computer Science; Education; Energy Engineering; Environmental Management; Finance; French; German; Information Technology; Irish; Leadership; Management; Marketing; Media Studies; Modern Languages; Multimedia; Natural Resources; Psychology; Social and Community Services; Social Sciences; Software Engineering; Sports; Technology); **Science, Engineering and Information Technology** (Agricultural Engineering; Applied Chemistry; Automation and Control Engineering; Automotive Engineering; Biology; Biotechnology; Business Administration; Business Computing; Chemistry; Computer Networks; Computer Science; E-Business/Commerce; Electrical and Electronic Engineering; Electrical Engineering; Electronic Engineering; Energy Engineering; Engineering; Environmental Studies; Forensic Medicine and Dentistry; Information Technology; Management; Mechanical Engineering; Multimedia; Music; Pharmacy; Production Engineering; Road Engineering; Software Engineering; Sound Engineering (Acoustics); Systems Analysis; Technology; Transport Engineering; Video); **The Built Environment** (Building Technologies; Civil Engineering; Construction Engineering; Energy Engineering; Environmental Engineering; Environmental Management; Safety Engineering; Surveying and Mapping)

Further Information: Also Clare Street, Ennis, George's Quay, Clonmel, and Thrules Campuses

History: Founded 1975 as Limerick Technical College. Transformed into Limerick College of Art, Commerce and Technology (Limerick CoACT) to include the newly established Limerick School of Art and Design, the School of Professional Studies, located on O'Connell Avenue 1980. Became Regional Technical College in 1993. Upgraded to Institute of Technology 1997. Merged with Tipperary Institute 2011.

Governing Bodies: Governing Body; Academic Council

Fees: (Euro): 2,250 per annum

Main Language(s) of Instruction: English

International Co-operation: Participates in the Erasmus programme.

Degrees and Diplomas: *Higher Certificate*; *Ordinary Bachelor Degree*; *Honours Bachelor Degree*; *Higher Diploma*; *Masters Degree*; *Post Graduate Diploma*; *Doctoral Degree*. Also Undergraduate Diploma and Certificates; Professional Certification (Cisco); Professional National Traineeship in Professional; Apprenticeship programmes.

Student Services: Health services, Sports facilities

Student Residential Facilities: Yes

Special Facilities: Theatre; Computer Services Department

Libraries: Yes

Last Updated: 27/02/12

MARINO INSTITUTE OF EDUCATION

Coláiste Mhuire Marino (MIE)
Griffith Avenue, Dublin 9
Tel: +353(1) 805-7700
Fax: +353(1) 833-5290
EMail: info@mie.ie
Website: http://www.mie.ie

President: Anne O'Gara EMail: Anne.OGara@mie.ie

Registrar: Stuart Garvie EMail: Stuart.Garvie@mie.ie

Programmes

Education *(Professional)* (Education); **Education Studies** (Adult Education; Art Education; Education; Educational Sciences); **Primary Education** *(Postgraduate)* (Primary Education); **Spirituality and Leadership in Education** *(Postgraduate)* (Education; Leadership; Religious Education)

History: Founded 1904.

Fees: (Euro): Tuition fees, 4,500 for undergraduate programmes.

Main Language(s) of Instruction: English

Degrees and Diplomas: *Ordinary Bachelor Degree*; *Honours Bachelor Degree*; *Higher Diploma*; *Post Graduate Diploma*

Student Services: Canteen

Student Residential Facilities: Yes

Special Facilities: ICT Facilities

Libraries: c. 30,000 vols

Last Updated: 13/02/12

MATER DEI INSTITUTE OF EDUCATION (MDI)

Clonliffe Road, Dublin 3
Tel: +353(1) 808-6500 +353(1) 808-6518
Fax: +353(1) 837-0776
EMail: info@materdei.dcu.ie; admissions@materdei.dcu.ie
Website: http://www.materdei.ie

Director: Andrew G. McGrady Tel: +353(1) 295-6165

Academic Registrar: Annabella Stover

International Relations: Stephen Stewart, International Programme Co-Ordinator

Schools

Education (Art Education; Education; Teacher Training) *Head*: Andrew McGrady; **Humanities** (Arts and Humanities; English; History; Irish; Music; Philosophy) *Head*: Michael Hinds; **Theology** (Bible; Christian Religious Studies; Ethics; Religion; Theology) *Head*: Paul Tighe

History: Founded 1996. Acquired present status 1999. A College of Dublin City University

Admission Requirements: Irish Leaving Certificate or equivalent

Fees: (Euro): Master's Programmes: 5,990 per annum for EU students. Non-EU fees are double the EU fees.

Main Language(s) of Instruction: English

Degrees and Diplomas: *Ordinary Bachelor Degree*; *Honours Bachelor Degree*; *Masters Degree*; *Doctoral Degree (PhD)*

Student Services: Canteen, Sports facilities

Student Residential Facilities: None

Special Facilities: ICT facilities

Libraries: Yes

Last Updated: 20/02/12

NATIONAL COLLEGE OF IRELAND (NCIRL)

Mayor Street, Dublin 1
Tel: +353(1) 4498-500 +353(1850) 221-721
Fax: +353(1) 4972-200
EMail: info@ncirl.ie
Website: http://www.ncirl.ie

President: Philip Matthews
Tel: +353(1) 4498-636 EMail: pmatthews@ncirl.ie

Registrar: John McGarrigle
Tel: +353(1) 4498-514 EMail: jmcgarrigle@ncirl.ie

International Relations: Nicola Carroll, Head of International Office
Tel: +353(1) 4498-653 EMail: nicola.carroll@ncirl.ie

Schools

Business (Accountancy; Advertising and Publicity; Business Administration; Finance; Human Resources; Labour and Industrial Relations; Labour Law; Management; Marketing; Public Relations; Technology); **Computing** (Business Computing; Computer Science; E-Business/Commerce; Educational Technology; Information Sciences; Information Technology; Software Engineering; Teacher Training)

History: Founded 1951 as The Catholic Workers College. Became National College of Industrial Relations (NCIR) 1966. Acquired present status and title 1998.

Main Language(s) of Instruction: English

International Co-operation: Higher Education and Training Awards Council (HETAC)

Degrees and Diplomas: *Higher Certificate*; *Ordinary Bachelor Degree*; *Honours Bachelor Degree*; *Higher Diploma*; *Masters Degree*; *Post Graduate Diploma*; *Doctoral Degree*. Also Part-time Undergraduate (Diplomas, Certificates, Higher Certificates, Ordinary and Honours Bachelors) and Postgraduate (Higher Diplomas, Masters, Postgraduate Diplomas, and Doctoral Degrees) Programmes.

Student Services: Academic counselling, Canteen, Health services, Social counselling, Sports facilities

Student Residential Facilities: 53 apartments (286 separate study bedrooms).

Special Facilities: Lecture Theatre (270 seats); Computer Laboratories and Studio Classrooms; Lecture Hall;

Libraries: Norma Smurfit Library, c. 56,000 vols; 255 paper periodical subscriptions and over 64,400 online subscriptions.

Last Updated: 27/02/12

IAU NATIONAL UNIVERSITY OF IRELAND

Ollscoil na hÉireann (NUI)

49 Merrion Square, Dublin 2
Tel: +353(1) 439-2424
Fax: +353(1) 439-2466
EMail: registrar@nui.ie
Website: http://www.nui.ie

Vice-Chancellor: Hugh Brady (2012-)
Tel: +353(1) 439-2424, Fax: +353(1) 439-2466

History: Founded 1908, incorporating existing colleges in Dublin, Cork, and Galway, as constituent Colleges. Under the Universitites Act 1997, the University was restructured to comprise four constituent Universities, i.e. University College, Dublin / National University of Ireland; University College, Cork / National University of Ireland, Cork; National University of Ireland, Galway; National University of Ireland, Maynooth. The University has five recognized Colleges, i.e. The Royal College of Surgeons in Ireland; The National College of Art and Design; St. Angela's College, Sligo, Shannon College of Hotel Management, and Institute of Public Administration.

Governing Bodies: Senate, comprising 40 members

Admission Requirements: NUI Matriculation: Leaving certificate examination, with passes in 6 subjects, selected according to faculty requirements; at least 2 subjects must be at higher level

Main Language(s) of Instruction: English

Degrees and Diplomas: *Ordinary Bachelor Degree*: Agricultural Science; Architecture; Arts; Civil Law; Commerce; Dairy Science; Dental Surgery; Engineering; Law; Medicine, Surgery, Obstetrics; Music; Nursing; Physiotherapy; Public Administration; Radiography; Science; Social Science; Technology; Veterinary Medicine; *Honours Bachelor Degree*: Arts; Science; *Higher Diploma*; *Masters Degree*: Agricultural Science; Animal Science; Applied Science; Architectural Science; Architecture, Rural Development; Arts; Business Studies; Commerce; Counselling; Dairy Science; Education; Engineering; Industrial Engineering; Law; Library and Information Studies; Management Science; Medical Science, Dentistry; Obstetrics; hilosophy, (in Medieval or Irish Studies); Psychological Science; Public Administration; Public Health; Regional and Urban Planning; Science; Science (Agriculture); Science (Dairy Science); Social Science; Surgery; Veterinary Medicine; *Post Graduate Diploma*; *Doctoral Degree*: Economic Science; Law; Literature; Medicine; Music; Science. Also Undergraduate Diplomas and Certificates; Honorary Degrees

Student Services: Academic counselling, Canteen, Cultural centre, Employment services, Foreign student adviser, Handicapped facilities, Health services, Language programs, Nursery care, Social counselling, Sports facilities

Last Updated: 27/07/12

COLÁISTE SAN AINGEAL, SLIGEACH
ST. ANGELA'S COLLEGE

Lough Gill, Sligo
Tel: +353(71) 9143-580
Fax: +353(71) 9144-585
EMail: admin@stangelas.nuigalway.ie
Website: http://www.stangelas.nuigalway.ie/

President: Anne Taheny EMail: ataheny@stacs.edu.ie

Registrar: Declan Courell
Tel: +353(71) 9195-516
EMail: dcourell@stacs.edu.ie; dcourell@stangelas.nuigalway.ie

Centres

Life Long Learning (Health Sciences; Leadership; Management; Midwifery; Nursing; Rehabilitation and Therapy; Social and Community Services); **Special Educational Needs Inclusion and Diversity** (Education; Special Education)

Departments

BA (Economics; Environmental Studies; Family Studies; Social Studies); **Education** (Biology; Child Care and Development; Economics; Education; Educational Administration; Family Studies; Foreign Languages Education; Home Economics; Home Economics Education; Pastoral Studies; Religious Education; Special Education; Technology; Theology); **Home Economics** (Biology; Business Administration; Chemistry; Child Care and Development; Economics; Education; Family Studies; Fashion Design; Food Science; Food Technology; Home Economics; Home Economics Education; Irish; Management; Physics; Primary Education; Religious Education; Science Education; Textile Design); **Nursing and Health Studies** (Ethics; Health Sciences; Nursing; Psychiatry and Mental Health; Public Health; Rehabilitation and Therapy)

History: Founded as a training college for teachers of Home Economics. Became a Recognized College of the National University of Ireland 1978. Under the direction of the Ursuline Order. Became College of the National University of Ireland (Galway) January 2006.

Admission Requirements: Irish Leaving Certificate with matriculation requirements, and competitive entrance examination

International Co-operation: With universities in Wales, Denmark, Finland, Norway, France, Austria, Malta and Germany. Participates in the Erasmus Programme

Degrees and Diplomas: *Honours Bachelor Degree*; *Higher Diploma*; *Masters Degree*; *Post Graduate Diploma*. Also Undergraduate Certificates and Diplomas

Libraries: A total of c. 20.000 vols and subscriptions to over 250 academic journals

Student Numbers *2010-2011*: Total: c. 900

NATIONAL UNIVERSITY OF IRELAND, GALWAY
OLLSCOIL NA HÉIREANN, GAILLIMH (NUI GALWAY/ OÉGAILLIMH)

University Road, Galway, Connaught
Tel: +353(91) 524-411
Fax: +353(91) 524-176
EMail: info@nuigalway.ie
Website: http://www.nuigalway.ie

President: James J. Browne (2008-2018)
Tel: +353(91) 492-110, Fax: +353(91) 524-176
EMail: president@nuigalway.ie

Director of Marketing and Communications: Caroline Loughnane
Tel: +353(91) 49 5851, Fax: +353(91) 49 4582
EMail: caroline.loughnane@nuigalway.ie

International Relations: Anna Cunningham, Director of International Relations
Tel: +353(91) 492-277, Fax: +353(91) 495-551
EMail: international@nuigalway.ie

Centres

Astronomy (Astronomy and Space Science); **Chromosome Biology** *(CCB)* (Biology); **Clinical Health Services Research and**

Development *(CCHSRD)* (Health Sciences); **Computational Algebra** *(De Brún)* (Mathematics; Mathematics and Computer Science); **Crystallography** (Crystallography); **High End Computing** *(Irish - ICHEC)* (Computer Science); **Integrated Development of Agricultural and Rural Institutions** (Agriculture; Development Studies); **Nanoscale Biophotonics** (Nanotechnology; Physics); **Occupational Health and Safety Engineering and Ergonomics** (Occupational Health; Safety Engineering)

Colleges

Arts, Social Sciences and Celtic Studies (Archaeology; Arts and Humanities; Celtic Languages and Studies; Classical Languages; Cultural Studies; Education; English; Film; French; Geography; German; History; Irish; Italian; Journalism; Literature; Media Studies; Philosophy; Political Sciences; Psychology; Sociology; Spanish; Women's Studies); **Business, Law and Public Policy** (Accountancy; Business Administration; Business Computing; Economics; Finance; Human Rights; Law; Management; Management Systems; Marketing); **Engineering and Informatics** (Biomedical Engineering; Civil Engineering; Electrical and Electronic Engineering; Electronic Engineering; Engineering; Hydraulic Engineering; Information Technology; Mechanical Engineering); **Medicine, Nursing and Health Sciences** (Anaesthesiology; Anatomy; Computer Science; Gynaecology and Obstetrics; Medicine; Midwifery; Nursing; Occupational Therapy; Paediatrics; Pathology; Pharmacology; Physiology; Podiatry; Psychiatry and Mental Health; Public Health; Radiology; Rehabilitation and Therapy; Speech Therapy and Audiology; Surgery; Virology); **Science** (Applied Mathematics; Biochemistry; Biology; Botany; Chemistry; Computer Science; Earth Sciences; Information Technology; Marine Science and Oceanography; Mathematical Physics; Mathematics; Mathematics and Computer Science; Microbiology; Natural Sciences; Physics; Statistics; Zoology)

Institutes

Lifecourse (Child Care and Development; Family Studies; Gerontology; Law); **Prostate Cancer** (Oncology); **Ryan** (Energy Engineering; Environmental Studies; Marine Science and Oceanography)

Laboratories

Salmonella Reference (Epidemiology; Public Health)

Research Centres

Applied Photonics *(LightHOUSE)* (Laser Engineering; Optical Technology; Optics); **Bioethical Research and Analysis** *(COBRA)* (Ethics); **Bioinformatics** (Biological and Life Sciences; Computer Science); **Biomedical Engineering Science** *(National Centre)* (Biomedical Engineering); **Child and Family** (Family Studies; Social Policy; Social Problems; Social Studies; Social Welfare; Sociology); **Climate and Air Pollution Studies** *(C-CAPS)* (Environmental Studies; Meteorology); **Combustion Chemistry** (Chemistry); **Complex Systems** *(CORE)* (Biological and Life Sciences; Computer Science; Economics; Physics; Statistics); **Disability Law and Policy** *(CDLP)*; **Energy** *(ERC)* (Energy Engineering; Environmental Studies); **Health Promotion** (Health Sciences); **Innovation and Structural Change** (Business and Commerce; Management; Management Systems); **Irish Centre for Human Rights** (Human Rights); **Irish Centre for Rural Transformation and Sustainability** *(ICERTS)* (Rural Studies); **Irish Centre for Social Gerontology** *(ICSG)* (Gerontology; Social and Community Services); **Irish Studies** (Celtic Languages and Studies; Irish); **Laser Applications** *(National - NCLA)* (Laser Engineering); **Marine Law and Ocean Policy** (Coastal Studies; Marine Science and Oceanography; Maritime Law); **Occupational and Life Stress** (Occupational Therapy; Psychology; Social Psychology); **Pain Research**; **Power Electonics** *(PERC)* (Power Engineering); **Social Sciences** *(SSRC)* (Social Sciences); **Women's Studies** (Women's Studies)

Research Groups

Alimentary Glycoscience *(Research Cluster)* (Food Science); **Applied Optics** (Computer Graphics; Optics); **Atmospheric Science** (Meteorology); **Palaeoenvironmentology** (Environmental Studies; Paleontology)

Research Institutes

Digital Enterprise Research *(DERI)*; **Humanities and Social Studies** *(Moore)* (Arts and Humanities; Social Studies); **Regenerative Medicine** *(REMEDI)* (Rehabilitation and Therapy)

Research Units

Clinical Research Facility Galway (Biological and Life Sciences; Statistics); **Computer Integrated Manufacturing** *(CIMRU)* (Industrial Engineering); **Development Education** *(Research Network)* (Development Studies; Education); **Economics of Social Policy** *(ESPRU)* (Economics; Social Policy); **Environmental and Natural Resource Economics** (Economics; Environmental Studies; Natural Resources); **Micromechanics** (Mechanics)

Schools

Film and Digital Media *(Huston)* (Film; Media Studies)

Units

Network of Excellence for Functional Biomaterials *(NFB)* (Biological and Life Sciences; Materials Engineering)

History: Founded 1845 as Queen's College, Galway. In 1908 became an University College, Galway, under a Constituent College of the newly-established National University of Ireland. Acquired present status and title under Universities Act 1997.

Governing Bodies: Udarás na hOllscoile (The University Governing Authority), comprising the President and Registrar and Deputy-President ex officio, 2 persons nominated by the National University of Ireland, 5 professors/associate professors, 5 other academic staff, 3 other employees elected by the respective categories, 3 students (at least 1 postgraduate), 3 nominees of selected external organizations, 4 graduates elected by the graduates, 7 representatives of local authorities and 3 members nominated by the Minister for Education and Science and 1 nominee from artistic/cultural interests.

Academic Year: September to June (Terms: September-December; January-March; April-June; Semesters: (all except Medicine and first year) September-December; January-June)

Admission Requirements: Irish Leaving Certificate with matriculation requirements, or equivalent. Minimum age of entry is 16 3/4

Fees: (Euros): Undergraduate, 5,220 - 7,573 per annum for home and EU students; non-EU students, 12,000 - 29,000 per annum

Main Language(s) of Instruction: English, Irish

International Co-operation: ERASMUS programme; Year Abroad programme; Junior Year Abroad (programme for North American students) Details of the arrangements for co-operation may be obtained on request from the International Affairs Office.

Degrees and Diplomas: *Ordinary Bachelor Degree*; *Honours Bachelor Degree*; *Higher Diploma*; *Masters Degree*; *Post Graduate Diploma*; *Doctoral Degree*

Student Services: Academic counselling, Canteen, Cultural centre, Employment services, Foreign student adviser, Foreign Studies Centre, Handicapped facilities, Health services, Language programs, Nursery care, Social counselling, Sports facilities

Student Residential Facilities: Yes

Special Facilities: James Mitchell Geology Museum; University Art Gallery; Frank Imbusch Observatory.

Libraries: James Hardiman Library, c. 300,000 vols

Publications: ROPES, Review of postgraduate studies in English *(annually)*

Press or Publishing House: Galway University Press

NATIONAL UNIVERSITY OF IRELAND, MAYNOOTH
OLLSCOIL NA HÉIREANN, MÁ NUAD (NUI MAYNOOTH)

Maynooth, Co. Kildare
Tel: +353(1) 708-3868
Fax: +353(1) 708-6113
EMail: admissions@nuim.ie; international.office@nuim.ie
Website: http://www.nuim.ie

President: Philip Nolan (2011-)
Tel: +353(1) 708-3893, Fax: +353(1) 628-6583
EMail: president@nuim.ie

Vice President, Registrar: Aidan Mulkeen
EMail: resistrars.office@nuim.ie

International Relations: Henry Wayne, Director of International Education
Tel: +353(1) 708-6230, Fax: +353(1) 708-6113
EMail: wayne.henry@nuim.ie

Faculties

Arts, Celtic Studies and Philosophy (Ancient Civilizations; Celtic Languages and Studies; Chinese; English; French; German; Irish; Media Studies; Music; Philosophy; Spanish; Theatre); **Science and Engineering** (Biology; Chemistry; Computer Science; Electronic Engineering; Mathematical Physics; Mathematics; Physics; Psychology; Statistics); **Social Sciences** (Accountancy; Anthropology; Business and Commerce; Design; Economics; Education; Finance; Geography; Law; Social Studies; Sociology)

Research Institutes

An Foras Feasa (Heritage Preservation; Irish); **Callan Institute** (Computer Science; Information Sciences; Information Technology); **Edward M Kennedy Institute for Conflict Intervention** (Peace and Disarmament); **Hamilton Institute** (Biology; Biotechnology; Information Technology; Mathematics); **Innovation Value Institute** (Information Management; Information Technology); **Institute of Immunology** (Immunology); **National Centre for Geocomputation** (Surveying and Mapping); **National Institute for Regional and Spatial Analysis** (Economic and Finance Policy; Geography (Human); Social Studies)

Further Information: Also campus in Kilkenny

History: Founded 1795 as St. Patrick's College, became Pontifical University 1896 and incorporated by charter as a Recognized College of the National University of Ireland 1910. Acquired present status and title under Universities Act 1997.

Academic Year: September-January; February-June

Admission Requirements: Irish Leaving Certificate with matriculation or equivalent international qualification. English language requirements for overseas students.

Fees: (Euros): please see university website

Main Language(s) of Instruction: English

International Co-operation: Participates in the SOCRATES/ ERASMUS programme

Accrediting Agencies: National University of Ireland

Degrees and Diplomas: *Honours Bachelor Degree*; *Higher Diploma*; *Masters Degree*; *Post Graduate Diploma*; *Doctoral Degree*

Student Services: Academic counselling, Canteen, Employment services, Foreign student adviser, Handicapped facilities, Health services, Language programs, Nursery care, Social counselling, Sports facilities

Student Residential Facilities: for c. 900 students; overseas students are guaranteed accommodation.

Special Facilities: National Science Museum

Libraries: 465,000 vols in John Paul II Library and over 10,000 vols in the Russell Library; 80,000 periodical subscriptions; e-resources, 43,000 online journals and 300,000 e-books; access to electronic networks, access to a campus wireless network through the University.

Academic Staff *2012-2013*	**TOTAL**
FULL-TIME	**230**
STAFF WITH DOCTORATE	
FULL-TIME	**212**
Student Numbers *2012-2013*	
All (Foreign Included)	**8,882**
FOREIGN ONLY	**1,014**

INSTITUTE OF PUBLIC ADMINISTRATION (IPA)

57-61 Lansdowne Road, Ballsbridge, Dublin 4
Tel: +353(1) 240-3600
Fax: +353(1) 668-9135
EMail: information@ipa.ie
Website: http://www.ipa.ie

Director-General: Brian Cawley EMail: bcawley@ipa.ie

Assistant Director General and Registrar: Michael Mulreany EMail: mmulreany@ipa.ie

International Relations: Nicolas Marcoux, International Services Manager EMail: nmarcoux@ipa.ie

Programmes

Training and Organisational Development (Accountancy; Finance; Government; Health Administration; Human Resources; Information Technology; Leadership; Management)

Schools

Government and Management *(Whitaker)* (Accountancy; Administrative Law; Business Administration; Commercial Law; Computer Science; Criminal Law; Economic and Finance Policy; Economics; European Studies; Finance; Government; Health Administration; Human Resources; Information Technology; Justice Administration; Labour Law; Law; Leadership; Management; Marketing; Political Sciences; Public Administration)

Further Information: Vergemount Hall, Clonskeagh, Dublin 4

History: Founded 1957. Became a recognized College of the National University of Ireland 2001.

Fees: (Euro): Undergraduate programmes : 2,780-2,980; Postgraduate : 5,000-10.000 depending on programmes

Degrees and Diplomas: *Honours Bachelor Degree*; *Masters Degree*; *Post Graduate Diploma*; *Doctoral Degree*: Governance. Also Undergraduate Diplomas and Certificates; Professional Certificate in Governance

Libraries: Yes

SHANNON COLLEGE OF HOTEL MANAGEMENT

Shannon International Airport, Co. Clare
Tel: +353(61) 712-210
Fax: +353(61) 475-160
EMail: info@shannoncollege.com
Website: http://www.shannoncollege.com

Director: Phillip J. Smyth
EMail: phillipjsmyth@shannoncollege.com

Registrar: Kate O'Connell
Tel: +353(61) 712-363 EMail: kateoconnell@shannoncollege.com

Programmes

Business Studies in International Hotel Management (Business Administration; Hotel Management; International Business; Management); **Commerce** *(with NUI Diploma in International Hotel Management)* (Business and Commerce; Hotel Management; International Business; Management)

History: Founded 1951. Granted recognized College of the National University of Ireland status 2000.

Fees: (Euro): Tuition fee for international students, 32,500 for Bachelor's degrees and 4,990 for certificates; Free Fees for Irish and other EU Students

Degrees and Diplomas: *Honours Bachelor Degree*. Also Certificates in English Language

Academic Staff *2009-2010*	**TOTAL**
FULL-TIME	c. **27**
Student Numbers *2009-2010*	
All (Foreign Included)	c. **360**
FOREIGN ONLY	**182**

THE MILLTOWN INSTITUTE

Milltown Park, Sandford Road, Ranelagh, Dublin 6
Tel: +353(1) 277-6300
Fax: +353(1) 269-2528
EMail: info@milltown-institute.ie
Website: http://www.milltown-institute.ie

President (Acting): Finnbar Clancy
Tel: +353(1) 277-6314
EMail: president@milltown-institute.ie; fclancy@milltown-institute.ie

Academic Registrar (Acting): Santiago Sia
Tel: + 353(1) 277-6342 EMail: registrar@milltown-institute.ie

Faculties

Philosophy (Philosophy); **Theology and Spirituality** (Canon Law; Holy Writings; Missionary Studies; Pastoral Studies; Theology)

History: Founded 1968. Became Recognised College of the National University of Ireland 2005.

Governing Bodies: Board of Trustees; Governing Authority

Academic Year: September to April

Admission Requirements: Level 6 Cambridge English, Leaving Certificate

Fees: (Euro): Certificates, 800-850 per annum; Degrees, 2,400-4,750 per annum; Licenciate, 7,150 per annum.

Main Language(s) of Instruction: English

International Co-operation: With institutions in Belgium and Germany

Accrediting Agencies: NUI and HETAC

Degrees and Diplomas: *Ordinary Bachelor Degree*; *Masters Degree*; *Doctoral Degree*. Also Undergraduate Certificates and Diploma; and Licenciate, equivalent to a civil Master's degree; Undergraduate and Postgraduate Awards

Student Services: Canteen

Student Residential Facilities: None

Special Facilities: Computer services

Libraries: Jesuit Library; c. 137,000 vols

Publications: Milltown Studies *(biennially)*

ROYAL COLLEGE OF SURGEONS IN IRELAND

COLÁISTE RÍOGA NA MÁINLEÁ IN ÉIRINN (RCSI)

123 St. Stephen's Green, Dublin 2
Tel: +353(1) 402-2100
Fax: +353(1) 402-2458
EMail: info@rcsi.ie
Website: http://www.rcsi.ie

President: Eilis McGovern (2010-)

Chief Executive and Registrar: Kelly Cathal
EMail: chiefexecutive@rcsi.ie

Faculties

Dentistry (Dentistry); **Nursing and Midwifery** (Midwifery; Nursing); **Radiologists** (Radiology); **Sports and Exercise Medicine** (Sports)

Institutes

Leadership (Health Administration; Leadership; Management); **RCSI Research** (Cardiology; Cell Biology; Chemistry; Genetics; Health Administration; Medicine; Molecular Biology; Neurology; Oncology; Public Health; Surgery); **Surgery - The Colles** (Medical Technology; Surgery)

Schools

Medicine (Anaesthesiology; Anatomy; Biochemistry; Biology; Chemistry; Epidemiology; Forensic Medicine and Dentistry; Gynaecology and Obstetrics; Medicine; Microbiology; Neurology; Ophthalmology; Orthopaedics; Otorhinolaryngology; Paediatrics; Pathology; Pharmacology; Physics; Physiology; Psychiatry and Mental Health; Radiology; Surgery); **Nursing** (Nursing); **Pharmacy** (Health Administration; Pharmacy); **Physiotherapy** (Gerontology; Neurology; Physical Therapy); **Postgraduate Studies** (Ethics; Leadership; Nursing; Pharmacy; Physical Therapy; Surgery)

Further Information: Also Medical University of Dubai (http://www.rcsidubai.com) and Medical University of Bahrain (http://www.rcsi-mub.com).

History: Founded 1784, became Recognized College of the National University of Ireland 1997. A private institution financially dependent on its own endowments, voluntary donations and small income.

Governing Bodies: Council of University

Fees: (Euro): 2,000-6,710 per annum

Main Language(s) of Instruction: English

Degrees and Diplomas: *Ordinary Bachelor Degree*; *Masters Degree*; *Post Graduate Diploma*; *Doctoral Degree*. Also Undergraduate Programmes; Graduate Entry Programme (GEP); Professional Postgraduate Certificate.

Libraries: 75,000 vols; special collections including 20,000 rare books

Academic Staff *2010-2011*: Total: c. 800

Student Numbers *2010-2011*: Total 3,384

THE NATIONAL COLLEGE OF ART AND DESIGN

COLÁISTE NAISIÚNTA EALAINE IS DEARTHA (NCAD)

100 Thomas Street, Dublin 8
Tel: +353(1) 636-4200
Fax: +353(1) 636-4207
EMail: fios@ncad.ie
Website: http://www.ncad.ie

Director: Declan McGonagle (2008-)
Tel: +353(1) 636-4261, Fax: +353(1) 636-4267
EMail: lynchm@ncad.ie

Faculties

Design (Art History; Ceramic Art; Communication Arts; Fashion Design; Fine Arts; Glass Art; Graphic Design; Industrial Design; Textile Design; Visual Arts); **Education** (Art Education; Design; Photography; Visual Arts); **Fine Arts** (Fine Arts; Media Studies; Painting and Drawing; Printing and Printmaking; Sculpture); **First Year Core Studies** (Ceramic Art; Communication Arts; Design; Education; Fashion Design; Fine Arts; Glass Art; Handicrafts; Textile Design; Visual Arts); **Visual Culture** (Art History; Design; Film; Fine Arts)

History: Founded 1746. Became a Recognized College of the National University of Ireland 1996.

Academic Year: September to June

Admission Requirements: Leaving Certificate examination or approved equivalent is 2 subjects at Grades A1 - C3 on Higher Level papers and 4 other subjects at Grades A1 - D3 on Ordinary or Higher Level papers, in NUI recognised subjects.

Fees: (Euros): c. 5,800 per annum

Main Language(s) of Instruction: English

International Co-operation: With universities in Europe, New England.

Accrediting Agencies: National University of Ireland

Degrees and Diplomas: *Ordinary Bachelor Degree*; *Honours Bachelor Degree*; *Higher Diploma*; *Masters Degree*; *Post Graduate Diploma*; *Doctoral Degree*. Also Professional Professional Diploma

Student Services: Academic counselling, Canteen, Employment services, Foreign Studies Centre, Handicapped facilities, Health services, Language programs, Social counselling

Student Residential Facilities: None

Libraries: c. 81,000 vols; c. 300 periodical subscriptions; National Irish Visual Arts Library (NIVAL)

Publications: Thought Lines

UNIVERSITY COLLEGE CORK

COLÁISTE NA HOLLSCOILE CORCAIGH (NUI CORK - UCC)

Cork
Tel: +353(21) 490-3000
Fax: +353(21) 427-3072
EMail: registrar@ucc.ie
Website: http://www.ucc.ie

President: Michael Murphy
Tel: +353(21) 490-3623, Fax: +353(21) 427-5006
EMail: president@ucc.ie

Registrar and Vice-President for Academic Affairs: Paul Giller
Tel: +353(21) 490-2257 EMail: vpacademic@ucc.ie

International Relations: Marita Foster, International Education Officer (Acting) Tel: +353(21) 490-4722 EMail: m.foster@ucc.ie

Centres

Alimentary Pharmabiotic (Biological and Life Sciences); **Analytical and Biological Chemistry** (Analytical Chemistry; Chemistry); **Aquaculture and Fisheries Development** (Aquaculture; Fishery); **Atlas of Irish Names**; **Atmospheric Chemistry** (Chemistry); **Business Information Systems** (Business Computing; Information Sciences); **Clinical Trials in Rare Diseases** *(European)* (Medicine); **Coastal and Marine Resources** (Coastal Studies; Natural Resources); **Coding and Cryptography**; **Constraint Computation** *(Cork)* (Computer Science); **Co-operative Studies** (Business Administration); **Counselling and Health Studies** (Health Sciences; Psychology); **Criminal Justice and Human Rights**

(Criminal Law; Human Rights); **Efficient Embedded Digital Signal Processing** *(EEDSP)* (Medical Technology); **Eldermet** (Biological and Life Sciences; Microbiology); **Electronic Corpus of Irish Literature and History** (History; Literature); **Famine** *(International)*; **Financial Services Innovation** (Finance); **Food Health Ireland** (Food Science; Health Sciences); **Forest Ecology** (Ecology; Forest Biology; Forestry); **Health and Diet Research** *(HRB)* (Dietetics; Health Sciences); **Hydraulics and Maritime Research** (Hydraulic Engineering; Marine Science and Oceanography); **Informatics Research** *(Boole Centre)* (Mathematics; Mathematics and Computer Science); **Investment Research** (Business Administration); **LOCUS – Irish Placenames and Title Names**; **Maternal and Child Enquiries** (Child Care and Development; Psychology); **Migration Studies** *(Irish)* (Demography and Population); **National Adult Nutrition Survey** (Nutrition); **National Cancer Registry** (Oncology); **National Perinatal Epidemiology** (Epidemiology); **Sustainable Livelihoods**; **Unified Computing** (Computer Science)

Colleges

Arts, Celtic Studies and Social Sciences (Archaeology; Art History; Arts and Humanities; Asian Studies; Celtic Languages and Studies; Classical Languages; Education; English; Ethnology; Folklore; French; Geography; German; History; Irish; Italian; Literature; Modern Languages; Music; Philosophy; Physical Education; Political Sciences; Preschool Education; Primary Education; Psychology; Religion; Social Sciences; Social Studies; Sociology; Spanish; Theatre); **Business and Law** (Accountancy; Business Administration; Business and Commerce; Civil Law; Criminal Law; Economics; Family Studies; Finance; Food Science; French; Government; Human Rights; Information Sciences; International Law; Irish; Law; Management; Marketing; Private Law; Statistics); **Medicine and Health** (Anatomy; Dentistry; Epidemiology; Gynaecology and Obstetrics; Health Sciences; Medicine; Midwifery; Nursing; Occupational Therapy; Paediatrics; Pathology; Pharmacology; Pharmacy; Physiology; Psychiatry and Mental Health; Public Health; Radiology; Rehabilitation and Therapy; Speech Therapy and Audiology; Surgery); **Science, Engineering and Food Science** (Architecture; Astrophysics; Biochemistry; Biological and Life Sciences; Chemical Engineering; Chemistry; Civil Engineering; Computer Science; Earth Sciences; Electrical and Electronic Engineering; Energy Engineering; Engineering; Environmental Engineering; Environmental Management; Environmental Studies; Food Science; Genetics; Information Technology; Mathematics; Microbiology; Nutrition; Physics)

Groups

NeuroScience *(Cork)* (Neurosciences)

Institutes

Biosciences Research (Biological and Life Sciences); **Environmental Research** (Environmental Management); **Social Science in the 21st Century** (Social Sciences); **Tyndall** *(National)* (Biological and Life Sciences; Chemistry; Computer Science; Electrical and Electronic Engineering; Engineering; Mathematics; Microelectronics; Physics)

Research Centres

Biomerit (Biological and Life Sciences); **Cancer** *(Cork)* (Oncology); **Cancer Biology at UCC** (Biology; Oncology); **Folklore** *(The Northside Folklore Project)* (Folklore); **Health Information Systems** (Information Sciences); **Oral Health Services** (Oral Pathology); **Vascular Biology** (Biology; Cardiology)

Research Groups

Human Factors (Information Technology; Software Engineering); **Neonatal Brain** (Neurology)

Units

BioTransfer (Food Science); **Cleaner Production Promotion** (Environmental Studies); **Food Industry Training** (Food Science; Food Technology); **Informatic Research in Sustainable Engineering** *(IRUSE)* (Architectural and Environmental Design; Civil Engineering); **Photonics Systems Group** (Physics)

History: Founded 1849 as Queen's College Cork. Incorporated by charter as constituent College of National University of Ireland 1908. Acquired present status and title under the Universities Act 1997.

Governing Bodies: Governing Body, comprising 40 members and a Chairperson. Its membership includes President and ex-officio senior officers, academic and non-academic members of staff, nominees of government and local authorities

Academic Year: October to September

Admission Requirements: Irish Leaving Certificate with matriculation, or equivalent, and competitive examination

Fees: (Euros): 4,855-22,365 per annum

Main Language(s) of Instruction: English

International Co-operation: Participates in the SOCRATES programme

Degrees and Diplomas: *Ordinary Bachelor Degree*; *Honours Bachelor Degree*; *Higher Diploma*; *Masters Degree*; *Post Graduate Diploma*; *Doctoral Degree*. Also Undergraduate Diplomas and Certificates; Postgraduate Professional Diplomas

Student Services: Academic counselling, Canteen, Cultural centre, Employment services, Foreign student adviser, Foreign Studies Centre, Handicapped facilities, Health services, Language programs, Nursery care, Social counselling, Sports facilities

Student Residential Facilities: Yes

Special Facilities: Computing and language facilities. Crawford Observatory

Libraries: Boole Library, c. 700,000 titles (of which approximately 200,000 are e-books)

Press or Publishing House: Cork University Press

Academic Staff *2009-2010*	**TOTAL**
FULL-TIME	**c. 2,800**
Student Numbers *2010-2011*	
All (Foreign Included)	**c. 18,820**
FOREIGN ONLY	**2,000**

UNIVERSITY COLLEGE DUBLIN, BELFIELD

AN COLAISTE OLLSCOILE, BAILE ATHA CLIATH

Belfield, Dublin 4
Tel: +353(1) 716-7777
Fax: +353(1) 269-4409
EMail: info@ucd.ie
Website: http://www.ucd.ie

President: Hugh Brady (2004-)
Tel: +353(1) 716-1,618; +353(1) 716-1704,
Fax: +353(1) 716-1170 EMail: president@ucd.ie

Registrar and Vice-President for Academic Affairs: Mark Rogers
Tel: +353(1) 716-1404, Fax: +353(1) 716-1169
EMail: officeoftheregistrar@ucd.ie; edel.ward@ucd.ie

International Relations: Erik Lithander, Director of International Affairs
Tel: +353(1) 716-8500, Fax: +353(1) 716-1165
EMail: international@ucd.ie

Centres

Clinical Research (Medicine); **Dublin Academic Medical** *(DAMC)* (Medicine); **Sensor Web Technologies** *(CLARITY)* (Surveying and Mapping); **Synthesis and Chemical Biology** (Biology; Chemistry); **Systems Biology** *(Ireland)* (Biology)

Colleges

Agriculture, Food Science and Veterinary Science (Agricultural Business; Agricultural Management; Agriculture; Animal Husbandry; Crop Production; Dairy; Food Science; Forestry; Horticulture; Nutrition; Veterinary Science); **Arts and Celtic Studies** (Archaeology; Archiving; Art History; Arts and Humanities; Celtic Languages and Studies; Classical Languages; Cultural Studies; English; Film; Folklore; French; French Studies; German; Germanic Studies; History; Irish; Italian; Linguistics; Literature; Modern Languages; Music; Portuguese; Spanish; Theatre); **Business and Law** (Business Administration; Business and Commerce; Commercial Law; Criminal Law; Criminology; Economics; European Union Law; Finance; French; History; Human Rights; International Business; Law; Philosophy; Political Sciences); **Engineering and Architecture** (Architecture; Bioengineering; Chemical Engineering; Civil Engineering; Electrical and Electronic Engineering; Electrical Engineering; Electronic Engineering; Engineering; Environmental

Engineering; Landscape Architecture; Materials Engineering; Mathematics; Mechanical Engineering; Physics; Structural Architecture; Telecommunications Engineering); **Health Sciences** (Biology; Demography and Population; Environmental Studies; Epidemiology; Food Science; Health Sciences; Medicine; Midwifery; Nursing; Occupational Health; Physical Therapy; Psychiatry and Mental Health; Public Health; Rehabilitation and Therapy; Sports); **Human Sciences** (Economics; Education; Environmental Management; Geography; Information Sciences; International Relations; Library Science; Philosophy; Political Sciences; Psychology; Social Policy; Social Sciences; Social Welfare; Sociology); **Science** (Biological and Life Sciences; Biology; Biomedical Engineering; Biomedicine; Chemistry; Computer Science; Environmental Studies; Geology; Mathematics; Molecular Biology; Physics)

Institutes

American Studies *(Clinton)* (American Studies); **Biomolecular and Biomedical Research** *(Conway)*; **British Irish Studies** (Anthropology; Cultural Studies; Social Sciences); **Claude Shannon** (Mathematics); **Confucius/Irish Institute for Chinese Studies** (Chinese); **Earth** (Earth Sciences); **Food and Health** (Food Science; Health Sciences); **Global Irish** (Irish); **Humanities of Ireland**; **Micheál Ó'Cléirigh** (Cultural Studies; History); **Sport and Health** *(National)* (Health Sciences; Sports); **Study of Social Change** *(Geary)* (Social Studies); **The Charles** (Dermatology); **Urban** *(Ireland)* (Urban Studies)

Laboratories

Complex and Adaptive Systems (Biology; Computer Science; Mathematics; Meteorology; Nanotechnology; Statistics); **National Virus Reference** (Virology)

Research Centres

Bioresources (Energy Engineering; Environmental Engineering); **Electricity** (Electrical Engineering); **Irish Social Science Data Archive** *(ISSDA)* (Social Sciences); **Irish Virtual Research Library and Archive** *(IVRLA)*; **James Joyce** (Literature)

History: Founded 1854 as Catholic University of Ireland, became college of Royal University of Ireland 1879. Incorporated by charter as constituent College of the National University of Ireland 1908. Acquired present status and title under the Universities Act 1997.

Governing Bodies: Council, comprising the President (ex officio), the Registrar, 3 members appointed by the government, 3 members appointed by the Senate of the National University of Ireland, 6 members elected by the Academic Council, 3 graduates, 4 student representatives, the Lord Mayor of the City of Dublin (ex officio), 3 members elected by Organizations, 8 members elected by General Council of County Councils, and 8 co-opted members

Academic Year: September to April (September-December; January-March; April)

Admission Requirements: Irish Leaving Certificate with matriculation, or equivalent. Students must be 17 years of age or over

Fees: (Euros):Students who qualify for "free fees" 878; EU students, c. 1,500-8,000 per annum, according to field of study; foreign students, 5,000-25,000 depending on degree

Main Language(s) of Instruction: English

International Co-operation: Participates in the SOCRATES and TEMPUS programmes with over 150 European universities and institutions of higher education

Degrees and Diplomas: *Higher Certificate*; *Ordinary Bachelor Degree*; *Honours Bachelor Degree*; *Higher Diploma*; *Masters Degree*; *Post Graduate Diploma*; *Doctoral Degree*. Also undergraduate Certificates and Diplomas, 1-2 yrs; Professional Certificates and Diplomas; MBA Programmes

Student Services: Academic counselling, Canteen, Cultural centre, Employment services, Foreign student adviser, Handicapped facilities, Health services, Nursery care, Social counselling, Sports facilities

Student Residential Facilities: For c. 2,700 students

Special Facilities: Classics Museum; Oakmount Creche

Libraries: Main Library, c. 800,000 vols; special collections

Press or Publishing House: UCD Press

Academic Staff *2009-2010*	**TOTAL**
FULL-TIME	c. **2,500**
Student Numbers *2010-2011*	
All (Foreign Included)	c. **25,000**
FOREIGN ONLY	**5,000**

NEW MEDIA TECHNOLOGY COLLEGE

13 Harcourt Street, 2 Dublin
Tel: +353(1) 478-0905
Fax: +353 (1) 478-0922
EMail: info@nmtc.ie
Website: http://www.nmtc.ie/

Programmes

Digital Film and Animation (Film); **Graphic design and Journalism** (Graphic Design; Journalism); **Performing Arts** (Music; Performing Arts); **Photography** (Photography)

International Co-operation: With London Metropolitan University, City & Guilds

Degrees and Diplomas: *Masters Degree*. Masters Degree programmes are accredited by London Metropolitan University. Also 2-year BTEC Higher National Diploma and 1-year FETAC (Level 5 & 6) Certificate

Last Updated: 01/03/12

PONTIFICAL UNIVERSITY, ST PATRICK'S COLLEGE

Coláiste Phádraig, Má Nuad
Maynooth, Kildare
Tel: +353(1) 708-4700
Fax: +353(1) 708-3959
EMail: President@spcm.ie
Website: http://www.maynoothcollege.ie

President: Hugh G. Connolly EMail: presoff@may.ie

Vice-President and Registrar: Michael Mullaney
Tel: +353(1) 708-3988 EMail: michael.mullaney@spcm.ie

Centres

Liturgy *(National)* (Pastoral Studies; Theology)

Faculties

Canon Law (Canon Law); **Philosophy** (Arts and Humanities; Philosophy); **Theology** (Arts and Humanities; Communication Studies; Missionary Studies; Pastoral Studies; Religion; Religious Music; Theology)

History: Founded 1795 as the National Seminary for Ireland.

Governing Bodies: Board of Trustees

Admission Requirements: Leaving Certificate or equivalent

Fees: (Euros) 3,100-9,600 per annum

Main Language(s) of Instruction: English

International Co-operation: Participates in the ERASMUS Programme

Degrees and Diplomas: *Higher Diploma*; *Masters Degree*; *Post Graduate Diploma*; *Doctoral Degree*. Also Baccalaureate; Licenciate degree; Undergraduate Certificate

Student Services: Academic counselling, Canteen, Handicapped facilities, Health services, Nursery care, Sports facilities

Student Residential Facilities: 2 Hostels: Divine Word Hostel (for male and female mature students) and St Catherine's Hostel (for male students).

Libraries: John Paul II Library c. 440,000 vols; c. 38,000 journals; 190,000 eBooks

Last Updated: 13/02/12

ROYAL IRISH ACADEMY OF MUSIC

Ceol Acadamh Ríoga na hÉireann
36-38 Westland Row, Dublin 2
Tel: +353(1) 676-4412
Fax: +353(1) 662-2798
EMail: info@riam.ie
Website: http://www.riam.ie

Director: Deborah Kelleher

Registrar: Anthony Madigan

Faculties

Keyboard (Musical Instruments); **Musicianship** (Music Education); **Strings** (Music; Music Education; Musical Instruments); **Vocal Studies** (Opera; Singing; Speech Studies; Theatre); **Wind, Brass and Percussion** (Musical Instruments)

History: Founded 1848.

Main Language(s) of Instruction: English

Degrees and Diplomas: *Ordinary Bachelor Degree*; *Masters Degree*; *Doctoral Degree*. Also undegraduate Diploma and Certificates

Libraries: Yes

Last Updated: 13/02/12

SAINT NICHOLAS MONTESSORI COLLEGE IRELAND (SNMCI)

16 Adelaide Street, Dún Laoghaire
Tel: +353(1) 280-6064
Fax: +351(1) 284-4764
EMail: info@snmci.ie
Website: http://www.snmci.ie

Director: Aileen O' Brien EMail: aileen@snmci.ie

Administration Manager: Bernie Gilsenan EMail: bernie@snmci.ie

Programmes

Early Childhood Montessori Education (Arts and Humanities; Communication Studies; Cultural Studies; Education; Management; Psychology; Teacher Training; Writing); **Montessori Education** (Cultural Studies; Education; Irish; Preschool Education; Psychology; Special Education)

History: Founded 1970.

Fees: (Euro): 4,500-5,610 per programme.

Main Language(s) of Instruction: English

International Co-operation: Participates in the Erasmus/Socrates Programme

Accrediting Agencies: HETAC

Degrees and Diplomas: *Ordinary Bachelor Degree*; *Honours Bachelor Degree*; *Higher Diploma*

Special Facilities: Computer rooms

Libraries: Yes

Last Updated: 29/02/12

ST. PATRICK'S, CARLOW COLLEGE

College Street, Carlow
Tel: +353(59) 915-3200
Fax: +353(59) 914-0248
EMail: infocc@carlowcollege.ie; registrarcc@carlowcollege.ie
Website: http://www.carlowcollege.ie

President: Caoimhín Ó Néill EMail: kevinoneill@carlowcollege.ie

Admissions officer: Ciara Morgan
EMail: cmorgan@carlowcollege.ie

Courses

Therapeutical Child Care *(Postgraduate)* (Child Care and Development; Rehabilitation and Therapy)

Departments

Humanities (Arts and Humanities; Catholic Theology; Celtic Languages and Studies; Communication Studies; Cultural Studies; English; English Studies; History; Holy Writings; Irish; Literature; Philosophy; Psychology; Theology); **Social Studies** (Social and Community Services; Social Studies; Social Work)

History: Founded 1782.

Admission Requirements: Leaving Certificate

Fees: (Euro): Tuition Fees, 4,392-4,642.

Main Language(s) of Instruction: English

International Co-operation: With universities in the USA

Accrediting Agencies: Higher Education and Training Awards Council (HETAC)

Degrees and Diplomas: *Ordinary Bachelor Degree*; *Honours Bachelor Degree*; *Masters Degree*. Also part-time A.C.C.S. (Accumulation of Credits and Certification of Subjects) courses.

Libraries: Fr Paul Brophy Library, c. 14,000 vols.

Last Updated: 29/02/12

ST PATRICK'S COLLEGE (STPATS)

Cathedral Street, Thurles, Co. Tipperary
Tel: +353(504) 212-01
Fax: +353(504) 237-35
EMail: office@stpats.ie
Website: http://www.stpats.ie

President: Thomas Fogarty EMail: tfogarty@stpats.ie

Registrar: Paula Hourigan EMail: phourigan@stpats.ie

Departments

Business Studies (Accountancy; Business Administration; Economics; Finance; International Business; Management; Marketing); **Education** (Curriculum; Education; Educational Sciences; Educational Technology; Pedagogy; Teacher Training); **Irish Studies** (Irish); **Religious Studies** (Anthropology; Christian Religious Studies; Ethics; History of Religion; Holy Writings; Pastoral Studies; Religion; Religious Studies; Theology)

History: Founded 1837.

Fees: (Euro): 2,250 per annum

Degrees and Diplomas: *Honours Bachelor Degree*: Education, Business Studies and Religious Studies; Education, Irish and Religious Studies. Also Non-degree programmes in Irish Language

Student Services: Canteen, Sports facilities

Special Facilities: IT Facilities; Study Rooms

Libraries: c. 25,000 vols; 434 journals

Last Updated: 21/02/12

ST. PATRICK'S COLLEGE, DRUMCONDRA, A COLLEGE OF DUBLIN CITY UNIVERSITY

Coláiste Phádraig, Droim Conrach (SPD)

Drumcondra, Dublin 9
Tel: +353(1) 884-2000
Fax: +353(1) 837-6197
EMail: internationalaffairs@spd.dcu.ie
Website: http://www.spd.dcu.ie

President: Pauric Travers
Tel: +353(1) 884-2006, Fax: +353(1) 836-7613
EMail: presidents.office@spd.dcu.ie

Registrar: Olivia Bree
Tel: +353(1) 884-2020 EMail: Mary.McMahon@spd.dcu.ie

International Relations: Bernie Donnelly, International Affairs Administrator
Tel: +353(1) 884-2214, Fax: +353(1) 837-6197
EMail: Bernie.Donnelly@spd.dcu.ie

Faculties

Education (Biology; Civics; Development Studies; Education; Human Rights; Literacy Education; Mathematics Education; Religious Education; Religious Studies; Special Education; Teacher Trainers Education; Teacher Training); **Humanities** (English; French; Geography; History; Irish; Mathematics; Music)

History: Founded 1875. Became designated college of Dublin City University 1993 in accordance with an institutional linkage agreement.

Academic Year: October to June

Admission Requirements: Leaving Certificate

Main Language(s) of Instruction: English

International Co-operation: Participates in Socrates/Erasmus

Accrediting Agencies: Dublin City University

Degrees and Diplomas: *Ordinary Bachelor Degree*; *Honours Bachelor Degree*; *Masters Degree*; *Post Graduate Diploma*; *Doctoral Degree*. Also Undergraduate and Postgraduate Certificates in Religious Studies

Student Services: Academic counselling, Canteen, Employment services, Foreign student adviser, Handicapped facilities, Health services, Language programs, Nursery care, Social counselling, Sports facilities

Student Residential Facilities: Student residences for c. 300 students

Special Facilities: Lecture theatres; Teaching and seminar rooms; College chapel; Auditorium; IT facilities; Education Resource Centre; Art rooms; Language lab; Belvedere House; St. Patrick's Primary School; Drumcondra Education Centre; Educational Research Centre; Educational Disadvantage Centre; National Induction Programme for Teachers (NIPT); College Creche

Libraries: Cregan Library

Publications: Irish Journal of Education; Studia Hibernica

Student Numbers *2011-2012*: Total: c. 2,500
Last Updated: 13/02/12

THE CHURCH OF IRELAND COLLEGE OF EDUCATION (CICE)

96 Upper Rathmines Road, Dublin 6
Tel: +353(1) 497-0033
Fax: +353(1) 497-1932
EMail: info@cice.ie
Website: http://www.cice.ie

Principal: Anne Lodge EMail: alodge@cice.ie

Programmes

Education (Curriculum; Education; Educational Technology; English; Information Technology; Irish; Mathematics; Teacher Training); **Special Needs** *(Postgraduate)* (Education; Educational Administration; Educational Technology; Primary Education; Psychology; Special Education; Teacher Training)

History: Founded 1811.

Degrees and Diplomas: *Ordinary Bachelor Degree*: Education; *Post Graduate Diploma*: Special Education

Student Residential Facilities: 72 single bedrooms; two three-bedroom houses

Special Facilities: Archives; The Plunket Museum of Irish Education; The Reading Centre

Libraries: c. 30,000 vols
Last Updated: 29/02/12

THE HONORABLE SOCIETY OF KING'S INNS

Henrietta Street, Dublin 1
Tel: +353(1) 874-4840
Fax: +353(1) 872-6048
EMail: info@kingsinns.ie
Website: http://www.kingsinns.ie

Dean: Mary Faulkner EMail: mfaulkner@kingsinns.ie

Registrar: Marcella Higgins EMail: marcella.higgins@kingsinns.ie

Programmes

Barrister-at-Law *(Professional)* (Civil Law; Criminal Law; Ethics; Law); **Lawyer - Linguistics and Legal Translation** (Law; Linguistics; Translation and Interpretation); **Legal Practice thourgh Irish** (Irish; Law); **Legal Studies** (Administrative Law; Commercial Law; Constitutional Law; Criminal Law; European Union Law; Human Rights; Law); **Legal Translation** (Law; Translation and Interpretation); **Legislative Drafting** (Law; Writing)

History: Founded 1541. The oldest institution of legal education in Ireland. It governs entry to the profession of barrister-at-law.

Admission Requirements: Approved law degree and entrance examination

Main Language(s) of Instruction: English

Degrees and Diplomas: *Post Graduate Diploma*. Also 2-year Barrister-at-Law Degree following approved Law degree or the Society's Diploma in Legal Studies; Advanced Diplomas.

Libraries: c. 100,000 vols
Last Updated: 29/02/12

THE OPEN TRAINING COLLEGE (OTC)

Prospect Hall, Willowfield Park, Goatstown, Dublin 14
Tel: +353(1) 298-8544
Fax: +353(1) 298-7004
EMail: info.otc@smh.ie
Website: http://www.opentrainingcollege.com

Director: Karen Finnerty EMail: kfinnerty.otc@smh.ie

Courses

Apllied Management (Management); **Applied Social Studies (Disability)** (Social Studies); **Continuing Professional Development** (Health Sciences; Management); **Supported Employment** (Education; Social Work; Teacher Training)

History: Founded 1992. The Open Training College is a part of St. Michael's House (provides services for children and adults with an intellectual disability and their families in the Greater Dublin Area).

Admission Requirements: Leaving Certificate

Main Language(s) of Instruction: English

Accrediting Agencies: Higher Education and Training Awards Council (HETAC); National University of Ireland, Galway; Further Education and Training Awards Council (FETAC)

Degrees and Diplomas: *Higher Certificate*; *Ordinary Bachelor Degree*; *Honours Bachelor Degree*. Also Undergraduate Certificates and Diplomas; Professional Development Programmes.

Student Numbers *2011-2012*: Total: c. 2,600
Last Updated: 29/02/12

THE ROYAL COLLEGE OF PHYSICIANS IN IRELAND (RCPI)

Frederick House, 19 South Frederick Street, Dublin 2
Tel: +353 (1) 863-9700
Fax: +353 (1) 672-4707
EMail: college@rcpi.ie
Website: http://www.rcpi.ie

President: John Crowe (2011-)

Registrar: Frank Murray

Faculties

Irish Committee on Higher Medical Training (Cardiology; Dermatology; Endocrinology; Gastroenterology; Gerontology; Gynaecology and Obstetrics; Haematology; Histology; Immunology; Medicine; Microbiology; Nephrology; Neurological Therapy; Neurology; Occupational Health; Oncology; Paediatrics; Pathology; Pharmacology; Public Health; Rehabilitation and Therapy; Respiratory Therapy; Rheumatology; Urology); **Occupational Medicine** (Occupational Health); **Paediatrics** (Paediatrics); **Pathology** (Haematology; Immunology; Microbiology; Neurological Therapy; Neurology; Pathology); **Public Health Medicine** (Medicine; Public Health)

Institutes

Obstetricians and Gynaecologists (Gynaecology and Obstetrics)

History: Founded 1654.

Governing Bodies: Council; Executive Committee; Deanery; Standing Committees

Main Language(s) of Instruction: English

Accrediting Agencies: Recognised by the Medical Council of Ireland

Degrees and Diplomas: Diplomas; Short-term Professional Development Courses; Postgraduate Professional Training Programmes; Higher Specialist Training Programmes; Masterclass programmes.
Last Updated: 29/02/12

THE UNIVERSITY OF DUBLIN, TRINITY COLLEGE DUBLIN

Coláiste na Tríonóide, Baile Átha Cliath (TCD)

College Green, Dublin 2
Tel: +353(1) 896-1000
Fax: +353(1) 677-2694
EMail: admissions@tcd.ie
Website: http://www.tcd.ie

Provost: Patrick Prendergast (2011-)
Tel: +353(1) 896-4362, Fax: +353(1) 896-2303
EMail: provost@tcd.ie

Secretary to the College: Anne FitzGerald
Tel: +353(1) 8961-123, Fax: +353(1) 6710-037
EMail: secretary@tcd.ie

International Relations: John McPartland
Tel: +353(1) 608-3150, Fax: +353(1) 677-1698
EMail: international@tcd.ie; john.mcpartland@tcd.ie

Faculties

Arts, Humanities and Social Sciences (Ancient Civilizations; Archaeology; Art History; Arts and Humanities; Business Administration; Celtic Languages and Studies; Commercial Law; Communication Studies; Comparative Law; Cultural Studies; Economics; Education; English; European Studies; European Union Law; Film; Finance; French; Gender Studies; Germanic Studies; Greek (Classical); History; Home Economics; International Business; Irish; Islamic Studies; Italian; Jewish Studies; Latin; Law; Linguistics; Literature; Management; Medieval Studies; Modern Languages; Music; Music Education; Music Theory and Composition; Philosophy; Political Sciences; Psychology; Religion; Russian; Slavic Languages; Social Policy; Social Sciences; Social Studies; Social Work; Sociology; Spanish; Speech Studies; Theatre; Theology; Women's Studies); **Engineering, Mathematics and Science** (Biochemistry; Botany; Chemistry; Civil Engineering; Computer Science; Electrical Engineering; Electronic Engineering; Engineering; Environmental Engineering; Environmental Studies; Genetics; Geography; Geology; Immunology; Mathematics; Mechanical Engineering; Microbiology; Natural Sciences; Physics; Production Engineering; Statistics; Structural Architecture; Zoology); **Health Sciences** (Anatomy; Biological and Life Sciences; Dental Hygiene; Dentistry; Dietetics; Gerontology; Gynaecology and Obstetrics; Haematology; Health Administration; Health Sciences; Histology; Immunology; Medicine; Microbiology; Midwifery; Nursing; Nutrition; Occupational Therapy; Oral Pathology; Paediatrics; Pathology; Periodontics; Pharmacology; Pharmacy; Physical Therapy; Physiology; Psychiatry and Mental Health; Public Health; Radiology; Rehabilitation and Therapy; Surgery)

History: Founded and incorporated 1592 by Royal Charter as 'mater universitatis'. Trinity College is the sole Constituent College of the University of Dublin. Financially supported by the Department of Education and Science.

Governing Bodies: Board; University Council.

Academic Year: September to July (September-December; January-March; April-July)

Admission Requirements: Irish Leaving Certificate or equivalent

Fees: Enquiries should be addressed directly to the Fees Office, Trinity College

Main Language(s) of Instruction: English

International Co-operation: Collaboration with industry. Special arrangements with universities in North America and Europe. Also participates in the Socrates programme with most of the EU countries

Degrees and Diplomas: *Ordinary Bachelor Degree*; *Honours Bachelor Degree*; *Higher Diploma*; *Masters Degree*; *Post Graduate Diploma*; *Doctoral Degree*. Also Undergraduate Diploma; MBA

Student Services: Academic counselling, Canteen, Foreign student adviser, Handicapped facilities, Health services, Nursery care, Social counselling, Sports facilities

Student Residential Facilities: For 1,740 students

Special Facilities: Weingreen Museum of Biblical Antiquities; Anatomy Museum; Geology Museum; Zoology Museum; Herbarium

Libraries: Trinity College Library, c. 4.5m vols; 30,000 electronic journals and nearly 300,000 online books

Publications: Hermathena, Literary and Scientific Papers *(biannually)*

Academic Staff *2010-2011*	MEN	WOMEN	**TOTAL**
FULL-TIME	–	–	**676**
Student Numbers *2009-2010*			
All (Foreign Included)	6,555	10,252	**16,807**
FOREIGN ONLY	–	–	**3,361**

Part-time students, 2,180.
Last Updated: 27/02/12

THE UNIVERSITY OF LIMERICK, MARY IMMACULATE COLLEGE

Ollscoil Luimnigh, Coláiste Mhuire Gan Smál (MIC)

South Circular Road, Limerick
Tel: +353(61) 204-300
Fax: +353(61) 313-632
Website: http://www.mic.ul.ie

President: Michael Hayes
Tel: +353(61) 204-589, Fax: +353(61) 204-392
EMail: president@mic.ul.ie

Registrar: Eugene Wall
Tel: + 353(61) 204-993, Fax: + 353(61) 204-921
EMail: eugene.wall@mic.ul.ie

Faculties

Arts (Arts and Humanities; Communication Studies; English; French; Geography; German; History; Irish; Literature; Mathematics and Computer Science; Media Studies; Modern Languages; Music; Philosophy; Psychology; Religious Studies; Theology); **Education** (Adult Education; Art Education; Continuing Education; Education; Educational Psychology; Educational Sciences; Humanities and Social Science Education; Mathematics Education; Pedagogy; Physical Education; Preschool Education; Religious Education; Sociology; Special Education)

History: Founded 1898 to train primary school teachers. Became Recognised College of the National University of Ireland 1974 and established a link with the University of Limerick 1992.

Governing Bodies: Governing Body; Academic Council; College Management Committee; Faculty Management Committees; Interview Board

Admission Requirements: Leaving Certificate

Accrediting Agencies: University of Limerick

Degrees and Diplomas: *Ordinary Bachelor Degree*; *Honours Bachelor Degree*; *Masters Degree*; *Post Graduate Diploma*; *Doctoral Degree*. Also Undergraduate Diploma and Certificates.

Student Residential Facilities: Yes

Libraries: Yes

Student Numbers *2010-2011*: Total: c. 3,000
Last Updated: 29/02/12

UNIVERSITY OF LIMERICK

Ollscoil Luimnigh (UL)

Limerick
Tel: +353(61) 202-700
Fax: +353(61) 330-316
EMail: admissions@ul.ie
Website: http://www.ul.ie

President: Don Barry
Tel: +353(61) 202-021, Fax: +353(61) 330-027
EMail: president@ul.ie

Vice President Academic and Registrar: Paul McCutcheon
Tel: +353(61) 330-027 EMail: vpa@ul.ie

International Relations: Josephine Page, Manager, International Education Division
Tel: +353(61) 213-520 EMail: josephine.page@ul.ie

Centres

Active Management of Lifelong Ageing *(CAMLA)* (Gerontology); **Advancement of Mathematical Education in Technology** (Mathematics Education; Technology); **Applied Biomedical Engineering** (Biomedical Engineering); **Applied Biostatistics Consulting** (Biological and Life Sciences; Computer Science; Statistics); **Applied Language Studies** (Applied Linguistics; Arts and Humanities; Linguistics; Modern Languages); **Biostatistics** (Biological and Life Sciences; Statistics); **Criminal Justice** (Criminal Law); **Efficient Use of Energy, Conservation and Sustainable Industrial Resources Management** (Energy Engineering; Industrial Engineering); **Environmental Research** (Environmental Studies); **European Studies** (European Studies); **Historical Research** (History); **Information and Knowledge Management** (Information Management); **Interaction Design** (Design); **Irish**

Software Engineering *(LERO)* (Software Engineering); **Irish-German Studies** (Cultural Studies; German; Germanic Studies; Irish); **MACSI - Mathematics Applications Consortium for Science and industry** (Applied Mathematics); **Pre-Hospital Research** *(CPR)* (Health Sciences); **Tourism Policy Studies** *(National)* (Tourism); **Ubuntu - the Teacher Education for Sustainable Development Network and the Irish Regional Centre of Expertise in Education for Sustainable Development** (Development Studies; Education; Teacher Training)

Faculties

Arts, Humanities and Social Sciences (Accountancy; Art History; Arts and Humanities; Commercial Law; Criminal Law; Cultural Studies; Dance; Development Studies; Distance Education; Economics; English; European Studies; European Union Law; Film; French; Gender Studies; German; Government; History; Human Rights; Insurance; International Law; International Relations; International Studies; Irish; Journalism; Law; Media Studies; Modern Languages; Music; Native Language Education; Peace and Disarmament; Political Sciences; Psychology; Public Administration; Social Sciences; Social Studies; Sociology); **Education and Health Sciences** (Biological and Life Sciences; Business Education; Chemistry; Clinical Psychology; Education; Educational Technology; Health Education; Health Sciences; Leadership; Mathematics Education; Medicine; Midwifery; Music Education; Nursing; Occupational Therapy; Physical Education; Physical Therapy; Physics; Psychiatry and Mental Health; Psychology; Rehabilitation and Therapy; Respiratory Therapy; Science Education; Sociology; Sports; Surgery; Technology Education; Toxicology; Vocational Education); **Science and Engineering** (Aeronautical and Aerospace Engineering; Animal Husbandry; Applied Physics; Architecture; Biochemistry; Biological and Life Sciences; Biomedical Engineering; Business Computing; Chemistry; Civil Engineering; Computer Engineering; Computer Graphics; Computer Networks; Computer Science; Construction Engineering; Design; Electronic Engineering; Energy Engineering; Engineering; Environmental Studies; Health Sciences; Industrial Chemistry; Industrial Design; Information Sciences; Materials Engineering; Mathematics; Mechanical Engineering; Multimedia; Music; Natural Sciences; Physics; Production Engineering; Safety Engineering; Software Engineering; Statistics; Technology; Telecommunications Engineering; Wood Technology)

Groups

Biocomputing and Developmental Systems (Biological and Life Sciences; Computer Science); **Hardware Digital Signals and Systems** (Computer Engineering); **Nanostructured Patterned Materials and Application** (Materials Engineering; Nanotechnology); **Wireless Research Centre** (Telecommunications Engineering)

Institutes

Materials and Surface Science (Energy Engineering; Environmental Engineering; Materials Engineering; Medical Technology; Transport Engineering); **Study of Knowledge in Society** *(ISKS)* (Social Studies)

Research Centres

Automation (Automation and Control Engineering); **Building Physics** (Building Technologies; Physics); **Business** *(Graduate)* (Business Administration; Economics; Government; Management; Marketing; Public Administration; Tourism); **Circuit and Systems** (Electrical and Electronic Engineering); **Composites** (Materials Engineering); **Data Communications Security** (Data Processing; Telecommunications Engineering); **Digital Media and Arts** (Communication Arts; Media Studies; Visual Arts); **Enterprise** (Business Administration; Management); **Euro-Asia** (Asian Studies; Business Administration; Cultural Studies; European Studies; International Business; International Economics; International Relations; International Studies; Linguistics; Political Sciences; Social Studies); **Food Science** (Food Science); **John Holland** (Computer Engineering); **Limerick Hub of The National Physiotherapy Research Network** (Physical Therapy); **Localisation**; **Microelectronics and Semiconductor** (Electronic Engineering; Microelectronics); **Mobile and Marine Robotic** (Robotics); **PE PAYS** (Physical Education; Sports); **Social Issues** *(CSI-R)* (Social Problems); **Telecommunications** (Telecommunications Engineering); **Wireless Access** (Telecommunications Engineering)

Research Groups

Control Engineering (Automation and Control Engineering); **Design for Testability** (Design); **Ergonomics** (Safety Engineering); **International and Commercial Economic Law** (Commercial Law; Economics; International Law); **Material and Automation Technology** (Automation and Control Engineering; Materials Engineering); **Optical Fibre Sensor** (Electronic Engineering); **Social Research and Policy** (Social Policy; Social Sciences); **Women's Studies** (Women's Studies)

Research Institutes

Stokes (Mechanical Engineering; Mechanics)

Research Units

Biomechanics (Biological and Life Sciences; Mechanics); **Curriculum Evaluation and Policy** (Curriculum)

Schools

Business *(Kemmy - KBS)* (Accountancy; Air Transport; Business Administration; Business Computing; Economics; European Studies; Finance; French; German; Health Administration; Human Resources; Industrial and Organizational Psychology; Information Sciences; Insurance; International Business; Japanese; Law; Management; Marketing; Mathematics; Modern Languages; Psychology; Social Psychology; Sociology; Taxation; Tourism; Transport Management)

History: Founded 1972 as National Institute for Higher Education, Limerick. Became University of Limerick through legislation enacted June 1989. Receives financial support from the Government.

Governing Bodies: Governing Authority, comprising 34 members appointed in accordance with the Universities Act, 1,997, and drawn from the University and the community at large

Academic Year: September to June (September-January; February-June)

Admission Requirements: Irish Leaving Certificate or approved equivalent

Fees: (Euros): EU Residents, 673-4,937 per annum; non-EU, 2,160-20,787

Main Language(s) of Instruction: English

International Co-operation: With universities in Australia, Brazil, Uruguay,Canada, China, Japan, New Zealand, Singapore, South Korea, Thailand and the USA. Participates in the Erasmus programme.

Degrees and Diplomas: *Ordinary Bachelor Degree*; *Honours Bachelor Degree*; *Masters Degree*; *Post Graduate Diploma*; *Doctoral Degree*. Also Undergraduate Certificate and Diploma; Corporate MBA; Professional Diplomas.

Student Services: Academic counselling, Canteen, Cultural centre, Employment services, Foreign student adviser, Handicapped facilities, Health services, Language programs, Nursery care, Social counselling, Sports facilities

Student Residential Facilities: Accommodation for 2,401 students and 24 faculty

Special Facilities: National Self-Portrait Collection of Ireland. Watercolour Society of Ireland Permanent Collection. Collection of 18th and 19th century Irish Painting. The Richard Wood Collection of Irish Landscape Paintings. The O'Malley Sculpture Collection. The Helen Hooker O'Malley Roelofs Sculpture Collection. The Irish American Cultural Institute's O'Malley Collection; 222 Laboratories

Libraries: Information Systems Division incorporating Campus Library, 324,300 print vols; 311,000 electronic vols; 62,800 periodical subscriptions, including more than 6,100 peer-reviewed journals.

Press or Publishing House: University of Limerick Press

Academic Staff *2011-2012*	**TOTAL**
FULL-TIME	c. **1,400**
Student Numbers *2011-2012*	
All (Foreign Included)	c. **12,000**
FOREIGN ONLY	**2,500**

Part-time students, 1,700.

Last Updated: 28/02/12

WATERFORD INSTITUTE OF TECHNOLOGY

Institiúid Teicneolaíochta Phort Láirge
Cork Road, Waterford, Co. Waterford
Tel: +353(51) 302-000
Fax: +353(51) 378-292
EMail: info@wit.ie
Website: http://www.wit.ie

President (Acting): Tony McFeely
Tel: +353(51) 302-015 EMail: tmcfeely@wit.ie; president@wit.ie

Registrar: Derek O'Byrne
Tel: +353(51) 845-535 EMail: dobyrne@wit.ie

Schools

Business (Accountancy; Administration; Business and Commerce; E-Business/Commerce; Economics; Finance; Human Resources; International Business; Management; Marketing; Retailing and Wholesaling); **Education** (Adult Education; Air Transport; Continuing Education; Education; Health Education; Higher Education; Literacy Education; Management); **Engineering** (Architecture; Automotive Engineering; Building Technologies; Civil Engineering; Construction Engineering; Electrical Engineering; Electronic Engineering; Engineering; Mechanical Engineering; Production Engineering; Surveying and Mapping); **Health Sciences** (Health Sciences; Nursing; Parks and Recreation; Psychology; Sports; Sports Management); **Humanities** (Arts and Humanities; Child Care and Development; Cooking and Catering; Criminal Law; Design; Fine Arts; Heritage Preservation; Hotel and Restaurant; Law; Marketing; Modern Languages; Music; Performing Arts; Psychology; Social Studies; Social Work; Sports; Tourism; Visual Arts); **Science** (Agriculture; Biological and Life Sciences; Biology; Business Administration; Business Computing; Chemistry; Computer Engineering; Computer Science; Educational Technology; Food Science; Forestry; Health Sciences; Horticulture; Information Technology; Mathematics; Mathematics and Computer Science; Multimedia; Natural Sciences; Nursing; Pharmacy; Physics; Software Engineering)

History: Founded 1970 as as Waterford Regional Technical College. Acquired present status 1998.

Governing Bodies: Executive Board

Accrediting Agencies: Higher Education and Training Awards Council (HETAC)

Degrees and Diplomas: *Higher Certificate*; *Ordinary Bachelor Degree*; *Honours Bachelor Degree*; *Higher Diploma*; *Masters Degree*; *Post Graduate Diploma*; *Doctoral Degree*. Also Executive MBA

Libraries: Yes

Student Numbers *2010-2011*: Total: c. 6,000

Part-time students, 3,000.

Last Updated: 24/02/12

Israel

STRUCTURE OF HIGHER EDUCATION SYSTEM

Description:

Higher education is provided by universities, non-university institutions offering instruction in specific fields (e.g. Technology, Arts and Teacher Training, para-medical schools) and academic courses in regional colleges for which universities are academically responsible. Higher education comes under the direct jurisdiction of the Council for Higher Education which is responsible for the accreditation and authorization of higher education institutions to award degrees. Non-university institutions are usually only authorized to award Bachelors' degrees and in some cases Master's degrees.

Higher education institutions are autonomous in the conduct of their academic and administrative affairs. Most of them receive public funds and supplement their finances with tuition and student fees. Yet, some institutions do not receive any government support.

Stages of studies:

University level first stage: *Undergraduate*

The first stage usually requires three years' study, with some exceptions, such as Architecture, Dentistry, Engineering, Law, Medicine, Nursing, Pharmacy, Physiotherapy, Veterinary Medicine. Each department structures its programme in a logical pattern of introductory and theoretical coursework, followed by specialized, advanced study. Much of the work in the second and third years can be considered as advanced upper level work in which pro-seminars and seminars are required. Single and dual major programmes are offered in many departments. Students usually register for approximately 10 annual hours in each department (approximately 40 semester hours). Degrees based on the dual major or single major programmes are viewed equally. Bachelor's degrees in Arts, Law, Science, Fine Art, Music and Education are awarded by the universities and colleges. Students studying for a Bachelor's degree at those universities that offer a Teacher's Certificate Programme may begin during their third year. On completing their additional year of Teaching Certificate studies, they will be awarded both a Bachelor's degree and a Teacher's Certificate, entitling them to teach from pre-primary school onwards.

University level second stage: *Graduate Studies*

The length and structure of Master's degree programmes vary according to the field of study, the department or the institution. It usually lasts between 2 and 3 years. Students admitted with course deficiencies are required to complete supplementary coursework which extends throughout the programme. This may include: lectures, seminars, laboratory work, theoretical or practical research, a thesis and a comprehensive final examination. Admission requirements are: A Bachelor's degree from a recognized university with a grade average of 75-80. Some departments may require more or less than the stated minimum grade average. Some may require entrance examinations or interviews. Two programmes are generally offered: A-coursework and a thesis, which give access to further study at the doctoral level; or B-additional coursework and no thesis. B does not permit to continue at the doctoral level, but there are some mechanisms which allow students to change from one programme to another. A Master's degree in Arts, Social Sciences, Science, Engineering, Law, Public Health and Library Science is awarded by the universities and some academic colleges. A Diploma in Criminology and Librarianship is also awarded.

University level third stage: *Postgraduate Studies*

This stage represents the highest level of academic work and is only offered by universities. The doctoral programme extends over a minimum period of two years after the Master's degree. The doctoral thesis is expected to make a substantial and original contribution to the advancement of science. A Master's degree with a grade average of 80 and above and a grade of at least 90 on the Master's thesis are usually required. A direct doctoral programme for exceptional students with a Bachelor's degree and a grade of 90 or above in their major subject and of 80 in other course work is also offered. The first year of the Master's degree is accelerated and, if high achievement is maintained, the student may bypass the second year of the Master's degree and proceed directly to doctoral studies.

Distance higher education:

Distance education is provided by the Open University of Israel which offers courses leading to a Bachelor's degree and Master's degree which may be taken at the student's own pace. The Open University is a full university-level accredited institution.

ADMISSION TO HIGHER EDUCATION

Admission to university-level studies:

Name of secondary school credential required: Bagrut

Minimum score/requirement: Bagrut - 20-25 units

For entry to: All institutions of higher learning except the Open University

Alternatives to credentials: Candidates over 30 years of age may be accepted to some departments on the basis of PET results. Pre-academic programmes.

Entrance exam requirements: Psychometric Entrance Test (PET) for all degree studies, with minimum mark determined by each institution, faculty or department.

Numerus clausus/restrictions: Medicine: national quota is divided among the institutions; Dental medicine; Veterinary medicine; Engineering (some fields); Management; Psychology.

Foreign students admission:

Definition of foreign student: A student having completed secondary-school studies or one or more years of university studies outside Israel; anyone requesting admission on the basis of educational documents issued outside Israel.

Entrance exam requirements: Foreign students should have qualifications equivalent to the Israeli Bagrut. The pre-academic year for foreign students who do not hold the equivalent High School Certificate is determined by individual institutions. Initiation and orientation programmes are organized by Departments of Overseas Students in institutions.

Entry regulations: A student visa or a temporary resident visa is required.

Language requirements: Good knowledge of Hebrew is essential. Most reading lists require a strong passive knowledge of English. Intensive language courses in Hebrew are available. A special one-year language preparatory course is also available. Initiation and orientation programmes are organized by Departments of Overseas Students in institutions of higher learning.

RECOGNITION OF STUDIES

Quality assurance system:

The Council for Higher Education is responsible for the recognition of all academic institutions in Israel. Each institution awards degrees on the basis of the authority extended by the Council of Higher Education.
In regulated professions like accounting, law, medicine, engineering, a designed competent authority is responsible for giving the authorization to exercise the relevant profession (in addition to the diploma).
In non regulated professions, the diploma from a recognized higher education institution will usually be accepted by employees.
If the academic certificate was handed by a foreign institution, then an academic evaluation from the Ministry of Education will be needed.

Bodies dealing with recognition:

Gaf LeHa'arahat Tearim Academi'im miHu"l (Department for Evaluation of Foreign Academic Degrees (Israeli ENIC))

Director: Tzipy Weinberg
Ministry of Education,
Lev Ram Building (room #110),
2 Devora Haneviah Street
Jerusalem 91911
Tel: +972(2) 560 2853
Fax: +972(2) 560 3876
EMail: diplomot@education.gov.il

Special provisions for recognition:

Recognition for university level studies: All applicants must submit complete official academic documents together with their application form to the specific university

For access to advanced studies and research: All applicants must submit complete official academic documents together with their application form to the specific university

For exercising a profession: Applicants must present relevant documents to the appropriate services: for all medical professions, the Ministry of Health; for engineers, architects and social workers, the Ministry of Labour and Social Welfare. Lawyers must address themselves to the Israel Bar Association and accountants to the Council of Accountants.

NATIONAL BODIES

Council for Higher Education - CHE

Minister of Education, Chairman: Gideon Sa'ar
Director General: Moshe Vigdor
PO Box 4037
Jerusalem 91040
Tel: +972(2) 567 9911
Fax: +972(2) 567 9955
EMail: info@che.org.il
WWW: http://www.che.org.il

Role of national body: The Council for Higher Education is a corporation which was established by the Council for Higher Education Law, 1958-5718, with the aim of being the national institution for higher education in Israel.

Quality Assessment Unit (CHE)

Head: Michal Neumann
38 Keren Hayesod Street
Jerusalem 91040
Tel: +972(2) 566 9938
Fax: +972(2) 561 1914
EMail: adi@che.org.il
WWW: http://www.che.org.il/template/default_e.aspx?PageId=297

Role of national body: In June 2003 the Council for Higher Education (CHE) decided to establish a system for quality assessment of Israeli higher education with the aim of:

- Improving the quality of higher education in Israel;
- Strengthening the awareness to the quality assessment process and developing internal mechanisms in the institutions of higher education, that would continually evaluate the academic quality;
- Ensuring the continual integration of the Israeli academic system within the global academic systems.

Data for academic year: 2010-2011
Source: IAU from the website of the Council for Higher Education, Jerusalem (Israel) 2010. Bodies, 2012.

INSTITUTIONS

PUBLIC INSTITUTIONS

ACHVA COLLEGE

D.N. Shikmim 79800
Tel: +972(8) 8580-044
Fax: +972(8) 8501-447
EMail: tzelgov@achva.ac.il
Website: http://www.achva.ac.il

President: Joseph Tzelgov Tel: +972(8) 8588-193

Director: Shoshana Millet
Tel: +972(8) 8588-001 EMail: millet@macam.ac.il

Programmes
Early Childhood Education (Preschool Education); **Educational Systems Management** (Educational Administration); **Elementary Education** (Primary Education); **English** (English); **Junior High School Education** (Secondary Education); **Special Education** (Education of the Handicapped; Special Education)

Accrediting Agencies: Council for Higher Education

Degrees and Diplomas: *Bachelor's Degree*: Early Childhood Education; Elementary Education; English; Junior-High School Education; Special Education (BEd); *Master's Degree*: Educational Systems Management (MEd)

Last Updated: 30/11/11

ARIEL UNIVERSITY

Ariel 40700
Tel: +972(3) 906-6153
Fax: +972(3) 906-7440
EMail: pres@ariel.ac.il
Website: http://www.ariel.ac.il/

President: Yehuda Danon (2012-)

International Relations: Michael Zinigrad, Rector, Head of International Affairs Tel: +972(3) 906-6281 EMail: rector@ariel.ac.il

Faculties

Engineering (Biotechnology; Chemical Engineering; Civil Engineering; Electrical and Electronic Engineering; Industrial Engineering; Industrial Management; Mechanical Engineering); **Natural Sciences** (Applied Physics; Biochemistry; Biology; Mathematics and Computer Science; Molecular Biology; Natural Sciences); **Social Sciences and Humanities** (Anthropology; Arts and Humanities; Behavioural Sciences; Criminology; Economics; Jewish Studies; Political Sciences; Psychology; Social Sciences; Social Work; Sociology)

Schools

Architecture (Architecture); **Communications**; **Health Sciences** (Health Administration; Nutrition; Physical Therapy; Speech Therapy and Audiology)

History: Founded 1982. Previously known as The College of Judea and Samaria, then as Ariel University Center of Samaria.

Governing Bodies: Board of Governors; Executive Committee

Fees: (Shekel): 12,000 per annum

Main Language(s) of Instruction: Hebrew

Accrediting Agencies: Council for Higher Education

Degrees and Diplomas: *Bachelor's Degree*: Architecture (BArch); Behavioural Sciences; Economics; Business Administration; Social Work; Health Administration; Speech Therapy; Liberal Arts; Criminology; Sociology & Anthropology; Psychology; Middle East & Political Sciences; Communication (BA); Electrical and Electronic Engineering; Chemical Engineering and Biotechnology; Industrial Engineering and Industrial Management; Civil Engineering; Mechanical and Mechatronics Engineering (BSc); Nutrition; Mathematical & Computer Science; Biological Chemistry; Molecular Biology; Applied Physics; Medical Physics-Imaging (BSc); Physical Therapy (B.P.T.); *Master's Degree*: Psychology; Social Work; Electrical Engineering & Electronics; Business Administration (MA / MSc / MBA)

Student Services: Academic counselling, Canteen, Employment services, Handicapped facilities, Nursery care, Social counselling, Sports facilities

Student Residential Facilities: Dormitories

Libraries: c. 160,000 vols

Publications: Functional Differential Equations; Judea and Samaria Research Studies, A journal of Study and Analisys of Social Issues; Moreshet Israel, A journal for the Study of Judaism, Zionism and Eretz-Israel; Social Issues in Israel

Student Numbers *2012-2013*: Total 10,500
Last Updated: 11/03/13

BAR-ILAN UNIVERSITY

Ramat-Gan 52900
Tel: +972(3) 5318-111
Fax: +972(3) 5352-423
EMail: biuspoke@mail.biu.ac.il
Website: http://www.biu.ac.il

President: Moshe Kaveh
Tel: +972(3) 531-8536, Fax: +972(3) 535-2423

Director-General: Haim Glick (2008-)
Tel: +972(3) 531-8530 EMail: director-general.office@mail.biu.ac.il

International Relations: Yona Tillman, Director, Public Relations and International Affairs
Tel: +972(3) 531-8191, Fax: +972(3) 534-9136
EMail: tillmany@mail.biu.ac.il

Centres

Land of Israel Studies *(David & Jemina Jeselsohn)* (Middle Eastern Studies)

Faculties

Exact Sciences (Chemistry; Mathematics; Mathematics and Computer Science; Optometry; Physics); **Humanities** (Arabic; Classical Languages; Comparative Literature; English; French Studies; Information Sciences; Music; Philosophy; Translation and Interpretation; Writing); **Jewish Studies** (Bible; Hebrew; History; Jewish Studies; Judaic Religious Studies; Middle Eastern Studies); **Law** (Law); **Life Sciences** (Biological and Life Sciences; Biology; Biomedicine; Botany; Cell Biology; Environmental Engineering; Optometry; Physiology); **Social Sciences** (Anthropology; Business Administration; Criminology; Economics; Education; Geography; Government; Journalism; Political Sciences; Psychology; Social Work; Sociology)

Foundations

English Literature *(Lewis Family)*

Programmes

American Literature *(J.M. Kaplan)* (American Studies); **Public Communications** *(Philip Slomowitz)* (Communication Studies)

Research Centres

Alzheimer's Disease *(William Farber)* (Medicine); **Cell Scan for the Early Detection of Cancer** *(Jerome Schottenstein)* (Oncology); **Commercial Law** (Commercial Law); **Defence and Peace Economics** (Peace and Disarmament); **Dyslexia and Reading Disorders** *(Haddad)* (Education of the Handicapped); **Family** *(Kukin)* (Family Studies); **Holocaust Literature** (Jewish Studies); **International Policy and Communications** (International Relations; International Studies); **Israel-Diaspora Relations** *(Shlomo Argov)* (International Relations); **Israeli Economy and Society** *(Schnitzer Foundation)* (Economics; Jewish Studies); **Jerusalem Studies** *(Ingeborg Rennert)* (Jewish Studies); **Jewish Education in the Diaspora** *(Lookstein)* (Jewish Studies); **Latin American Development** (Latin American Studies); **Life Sciences Applied Research** *(Dr. Jaime Lusinchi)* (Biological and Life Sciences); **Medical Diagnostics** *(Gonda Goldschmied)* (Medicine); **Midrasha for Women** (Jewish Studies); **Nuclear Magnetic Resonance** *(NMR)* (Nuclear Physics); **Religious Anthropology** *(Jacob Taubes)* (Anthropology); **Strategic Studies** *(Begin-Sadat (BESA))* (Military Science; Peace and Disarmament); **Study and Dissemination of Oral Law** *(Naftal)* (Law); **Study of Developmental Disorders in Infants and Young Children** *(Fanny and Edward Baker)* (Developmental Psychology); **Study of Mountainous Areas in Judea and the Etzion Bloc** (Mountain Studies); **Study of Women in Judaism** *(Fanya Gottesfeld Heller)* (Women's Studies); **Teaching of Sciences** (Science Education); **Yiddish Culture** *(Rena Costa)* (Jewish Studies)

Research Institutes

Advanced Technology *(Pearl and Jack Resnick)* (Technology); **Advanced Torah Studies** (Holy Writings); **Advancement of Religious Education** *(Stern)* (Religious Art); **Assyriology** *(Samuel Noah Kramer)* (Ancient Civilizations); **Cancer, AIDS and Immunology** *(CAIR)* (Oncology); **Comparative Law** (Comparative Law); **Computerized Data in Jewish Studies** (Jewish Studies); **Economic Structures of Jewish Communities** (Jewish Studies); **Economics** (Economics); **Economy of Israel** *(David J. Azrieli)* (Economics); **European Community** (European Studies); **History of Jewish Bible** (Bible); **History of Oriental Jewry** (Jewish Studies; Oriental Studies); **History of the Land of Israel and its Settlements** *(Rivlin)* (History; Jewish Studies); **Jewish Thought** *(Rabbi Carlebach)* (Jewish Studies); **Lexicography** (Terminology); **Literature of the People of Israel** *(Baruch Kurzweil)* (Jewish Studies; Literature); **Mathematical Sciences** *(Abraham Gelbart)* (Mathematics); **Post-Talmudic Halakhic** (Judaic Religious Studies); **Religious Zionism** (Judaic Religious Studies); **Shoah** *(Leona and Arnold Finkler)* (Jewish Studies); **Sociology of Ethnic Groups** (Sociology)

History: Founded 1955. The University combines secular and religious studies and is recognized by the Ministry of Education. The State provides 60% of the budget. Regional Colleges: Ashkelon; Safed; Western Galilee (Yad Natan); Jordan Valley (Tzemach); Yehuda and Shomron (Ariel).

Governing Bodies: Senate; Global Board of Trustees, composed mainly of members from the USA, but also from Israel, Canada, Australia, Europe and South Africa; Executive Council

Academic Year: November to June (November-February; March-June)

Admission Requirements: Secondary school certificate (Teudat Bagrut) or equivalent, and entrance examination

Fees: (Shekels): 11,095 per annum

Main Language(s) of Instruction: Hebrew, English

International Co-operation: With over 50 universities in Europe, USA, Russian Federation, India, Japan and China

Accrediting Agencies: Council for Higher Education

Degrees and Diplomas: *Bachelor's Degree*: Arts (BA); Law (LLB); Science (BSc), 3-4 yrs; *Diploma*: Hotel Management and Tourism; Journalism and Communications, Librarianship, Translation and Interpreting; Local Government; Music Therapy; Optometry; Teaching; *Master's Degree*: Arts (MA), a further 1-2 yrs following Bachelor's Degree; *Master's Degree*: Law, a further 1-2 yrs following Bachelor's Degree; *Master's Degree*: Science (MSc), a further 1-2 yrs following Bachelor; *Master's Degree*: Social Work, a further 1-2 yrs following Bachelor; *Doctorate (PhD)*: a further 2-3 yrs

Student Services: Academic counselling, Foreign student adviser, Handicapped facilities

Student Residential Facilities: Yes

Special Facilities: Carl Alexander Floersheim Museum of Jewish Art and Judaica

Libraries: Wurzweiler Library, c. 1 m vols; department libraries; rare Judaica manuscripts and first editions

Publications: Bar Ilan Law Studies *(biannually)*; Criticism and Interpretation *(biannually)*; Democratic Culture *(biannually)*; Hebrew Computational Linguistics *(biannually)*; Philosophia *(annually)*

Press or Publishing House: Bar-Ilan University Press

Academic Staff *2009-2010*: Total: c. 1,350

Student Numbers *2009-2010*: Total: c. 31,700

Last Updated: 30/11/11

BEIT-BERL ACADEMIC COLLEGE

Doar Beit Berl 44905
Tel: +972(9) 7476-333
Fax: +972(9) 7454-104
EMail: dinamr@beitberl.ac.il
Website: http://www.beitberl.ac.il

President: Tamar Ariav

Academies

Academic Institute for the Training of Arab Teachers *(AITAT)* (Teacher Training)

Schools

Art *(Hamidrasha)* (Art Education; Film); **Education** (Arabic; Bible; Biology; Chemistry; Civics; Computer Science; Curriculum; Ecology; Educational Administration; English; Geography; Hebrew; History; Jewish Studies; Literature; Mathematics; Preschool Education; Primary Education; Secondary Education; Social Sciences; Special Education); **Government and Social Policy** *(Hamidrasha Hamidrasha Hamidrasha Hamidrasha Hamidrasha Hamidrasha Hamidrasha Hamidrasha Hamidrasha Hamidrasha)* (Anthropology; Criminology; Gender Studies; Government; Information Management; Leadership; Library Science; Public Administration; Social Policy; Sociology)

International Co-operation: With universities in Poland, Germany, Czech Republic, Turkey

Accrediting Agencies: Council for Higher Education

Degrees and Diplomas: *Bachelor's Degree*: Art; Early Childhood Education; Elementary Education; High School Education; Non-Formal Education (BEd), 4 yrs; *Master's Degree*: Education Counseling (MEd)

Academic Staff *2009-2010*: Total: c. 700

Student Numbers *2009-2010*: Total: c. 8,000

Last Updated: 30/11/11

BEN-GURION UNIVERSITY OF THE NEGEV

Universitat Ben Gurion Ba-Negev (BGU)
PO Box 653, Beer-Sheva 84105
Tel: +972(8) 6461-111
Fax: +972(8) 6472-891
EMail: oiaa@bgu.ac.il
Website: http://www.bgu.ac.il

President: Rivka Carmi (2006-) EMail: president@bgu.ac.il

Rector: Zvi Hacohen
Tel: +972(8) 6477-786, Fax: +972(8) 6479-434
EMail: rector@bgu.ac.il

Director-General: David Bareket
Tel: +972(8) 6461-226, Fax: +972(8) 6479-333
EMail: bareket@bgu.ac.il

International Relations: Moshe Amir, Director, International Academic Affairs Tel: +972(8) 6477-679 EMail: tivoli@bgu.ac.il

Faculties

Business and Management *(Guilford Glazer)* (Behavioural Sciences; Business Administration; Economics; Health Administration; Hotel Management; Management; Public Administration; Tourism); **Engineering Sciences** (Biomedical Engineering; Biotechnology; Chemical Engineering; Computer Engineering; Construction Engineering; Electrical and Electronic Engineering; Energy Engineering; Environmental Engineering; Industrial Engineering; Information Sciences; Information Technology; Materials Engineering; Mechanical Engineering; Nuclear Engineering; Safety Engineering; Software Engineering; Telecommunications Engineering); **Health Sciences** (Anatomy; Biochemistry; Epidemiology; Gerontology; Health Administration; Health Sciences; Immunology; Medical Technology; Medicine; Microbiology; Nursing; Pharmacology; Pharmacy; Physical Therapy; Physiology; Public Health; Virology); **Humanities and Social Sciences** (Accountancy; Ancient Civilizations; Anthropology; Archaeology; Art History; Arts and Humanities; Behavioural Sciences; Bible; Biology; Cognitive Sciences; Economics; Education; English; Environmental Studies; Geography; Hebrew; History; Jewish Studies; Linguistics; Literature; Mathematics Education; Media Studies; Middle Eastern Studies; Modern Languages; Philosophy; Political Sciences; Psychology; Science Education; Social Sciences; Social Work; Sociology; Statistics; Technology Education); **Natural Sciences** (Biological and Life Sciences; Biotechnology; Chemistry; Computer Science; Ecology; Environmental Studies; Geology; Mathematics; Mathematics and Computer Science; Optical Technology; Physics)

Institutes

Desert Research *(Jacob Blaustein)* (Arid Land Studies; Biotechnology; Energy Engineering; Environmental Engineering; Natural Resources; Water Management)

Research Institutes

Study of Israel and Zionism (Jewish Studies)

Schools

Desert Studies *(Albert Katz International)* (Arid Land Studies; Hydraulic Engineering; Water Science); **Advanced Graduate Studies** *(Kreitman)*; **Continuing Education** (Continuing Education) *Director*: Mira Efraty

Further Information: Also branches in Eilat and Sede Boqer.

History: Founded 1964 as the University of the Negev. Acquired present title 1973. In 2000, the Eliat Regional College (located in the city of Eliat) became an external campus of Ben-Gurion University

Governing Bodies: Board of Governors; University Senate

Academic Year: October to June (October-January; February-June)

Admission Requirements: High School Diploma (or equivalent). Psychometric test and Hebrew language proficiency. Admission to the M.D. program in International Health is administered through Columbia University, Faculty of Health Sciences, New York,NY.

Fees: (Shekels): 10,000 per annum

Main Language(s) of Instruction: Hebrew

International Co-operation: With universities in Austria, Australia, Ukraine, Italy, Argentina, USA, Ethiopia, Bulgaria, Brazil, Guatemala, Germany, South Africa, Honduras, Venezuela, Mexico, China, Spain, Chile, Czech Republic, France, Canada, Kenya, Romania, Russia, Thailand, Turkey. Member of Regional/ International Networks/ Programs: Community of Mediterranean Universities (CMU).

Accrediting Agencies: Council for Higher Education

Degrees and Diplomas: *Bachelor's Degree*: Arts (BA); Emergency Medical Services (BEMS); Medical Laboratory Sciences (BMedLabSc); Science (BSc); Social Work (BSW), 3 yrs; *Bachelor's Degree*: Engineering (BSc); Nursing (BN); Pharmacy (BPharm); Physiotherapy (BPT), 4 yrs; *Master's Degree*: Arts, Gerontology

(MA); Business Administration (MBA); Medical Sciences (MMedSc); Public Health (MPH); Science; Engineering (MSc), a further 2 yrs; *Master's Degree*: Health Administration (MHA); Nursing (MN), 2 yrs; *Doctorate*: Medicine; International Medicine (MD), 6 yrs; *Doctorate*: Philosophy (PhD), 4-6 yrs

Student Services: Academic counselling, Canteen, Cultural centre, Employment services, Foreign student adviser, Foreign Studies Centre, Handicapped facilities, Health services, Language programs, Nursery care, Social counselling, Sports facilities

Student Residential Facilities: Yes

Special Facilities: Baron Art Gallery

Libraries: The Zalman Aranne Central Library, 900,000 vols (not including bound journals). Medical Library, 30,000 vols. Desert Research Library, 13,000 vols

Publications: Geography Research Forum *(biannually)*; HAGAR, International Social Science Journal; Israel Studies; ISSR-Israel Social Science Research Journal *(biannually)*; JAMA'A, Interdisciplininary Journal for the Study of the Middle East; MIKAN, Research Journal of Hebrew Literature; Shvut, Studies in Russian and East European Jewish History and Culture

Press or Publishing House: Ben Gurion University of the Negev Press

Last Updated: 09/12/11

BEZALEL ACADEMY OF ART AND DESIGN

PO Box 24046, Mount Scopus, Jerusalem 91240
Tel: +972(2) 5893-333
Fax: +972(2) 5823-094
EMail: mail@bezalel.ac.il
Website: http://www.bezalel.ac.il

President: Arnon Zuckerman

Deputy President for Academic Affairs: Yaara Bar-On

International Relations: Liv Sperber, Student Exchange Director
EMail: ir@bezalel.ac.il

Departments

Ceramic and Glass Design (Ceramic Art; Glass Art); **Fine Arts** *(Blanche and Romie Shapiro)* (Fine Arts); **History and Theory** (History); **Industrial Design** *(Benjamin Swig)* (Industrial Design); **Jewelry and Fashion** (Fashion Design; Jewelry Art); **Photography, Video and Computerized Imaging** (Photography; Video); **Screen Based Art** (Film; Media Studies; Video); **Visual Communication** *(Rothschild Caesarea Foundation)* (Advertising and Publicity; Communication Arts)

Accrediting Agencies: Council for Higher Education

Degrees and Diplomas: *Bachelor's Degree*: Art; Photography; Ceramic Design; Gold and Silversmithing; Graphic Design; Industrial Design; Architecture; Screen Based Arts; *Master's Degree*: Fine Arts; Industrial Design. Belazel is also authorized to register students in a programme leading to a Master of Fine Arts degree (MFA) in Arts, in conjunction with the Hebrew University of Jerusalem

Libraries: The Mildred and Philip Gutkin Center; Slides Library

Last Updated: 30/11/11

DAVID YELLIN COLLEGE OF EDUCATION

PO Box 3578, Beit Hakerem, Jerusalem 91035
Tel: +972(2) 6558-111
Fax: +972(2) 6521-548
EMail: michalgo@dyellin.ac.il
Website: http://www.dyellin.ac.il/

Administrative Director: Margalit Matityahu

International Relations: Michal Goshczini, Director of the Resource Development and Public Relations Department
Tel: +972(2) 6558-174

Programmes

Education (Preschool Education; Primary Education; Secondary Education; Special Education; Teacher Training)

History: Founded 1913 as College for Hebrew Teachers.

Accrediting Agencies: Council for Higher Education

Degrees and Diplomas: *Bachelor's Degree*: Early Childhood Education; Elementary Education; Junior-High School Education; Special Education (Bed), 4 yrs; *Master's Degree*: Instruction & Learning (MEd)

Student Numbers *2009-2010*: Total: c. 3,500

Last Updated: 30/11/11

HOLON INSTITUTE OF TECHNOLOGY (HIT)

PO Box 305, 52 Golomb Street, Holon 58102
Tel: +972(3) 5026-666
Fax: +972(3) 5026-720
Website: http://www.hit.ac.il/

President: Gideon Langholz (2007-)
Tel: +972(3) 5026-501, Fax: +972(3) 5026-510
EMail: president_office@hit.ac.il

Vice-President: Josiah Kahane
Tel: +972(3) 5026-680, Fax: +972(3) 5026-598
EMail: kahane@hit.ac.il

International Relations: Benny Alon, Director, Communication and Public Affairs Division
Tel: +972(3) 5026-727, Fax: +972(3) 5029-729
EMail: beni@hit.ac.il

Departments

Instructional Systems Technology (Pedagogy; Systems Analysis; Technology)

Faculties

Design (Design; Industrial Design; Interior Design); **Engineering** (Electrical and Electronic Engineering); **Management of Technology** (Engineering Management; Management); **Sciences** (Applied Mathematics; Computer Science)

History: Founded 1969 as University Institute of Technology. Functionned under the auspices of Tel-Aviv University for over two decades. Its graduates received Tel-Aviv University's B.Sc degree in Technological Education as well as Teacher's Certificate. Acquired present status and title, 1999.

Governing Bodies: Board of Governors. Executive Committee

Admission Requirements: High School Matriculation Certificate. Psychometric Entrance Test

Fees: (Shekels): 11,636 per annum

Main Language(s) of Instruction: Hebrew

International Co-operation: With Universities in EEC, USA, Japan

Accrediting Agencies: Council for Higher Education

Degrees and Diplomas: *Bachelor's Degree*: Applied Mathematics for Industry (BSc); Computer Science (BA), 3 yrs; *Bachelor's Degree*: Electrical and Electronic Engineering; Communication Engineering (BSc); Industrial Design; Interior Design; Visual Communications Design, 4 yrs; *Master's Degree*: Management Systems; Electrical and Electronics Engineering; Communication Engineering (MSc), 2 yrs

Student Services: Academic counselling, Canteen, Employment services, Foreign student adviser, Social counselling

Special Facilities: Design Gallery

Libraries: Central Library, c. 55,000 titles in Exact Sciences, Engineering, Social Sciences, Philosophy, Humanities and Arts. Prof.Nathan Rotenstreich Collection: a rare and unique collection of 5,000 items in Philosophy, Jewish Philosophy and other fields of knowledge.

Publications: Journal of Science & Engineering *(annually)*

Last Updated: 08/12/11

JERUSALEM COLLEGE OF TECHNOLOGY - MACHON LEV

PO Box 16031, 21 Avaad Haleumi St., Givat Mordechai, Jerusalem 91160
Tel: +972(2) 6751-111
Fax: +972(2) 6751-068
EMail: pr@jct.ac.il
Website: http://www.jct.ac.il

President: Noah Dana-Picard
Tel: +972(2) 6751-106 EMail: president@jct.ac.il

Rector: Menachem Steiner
Tel: +972(2) 6751-115 EMail: rector@jct.ac.il

Departments

Applied Mathematics (Applied Mathematics); **English** (English); **Science and Technology Teaching** (Science Education; Technology Education)

Schools

Engineering (Applied Physics; Computer Science; Electronic Engineering; Industrial Engineering; Industrial Management; Software Engineering); **Industrial Management** *(Bernard and Miriam Hochstein)* (Accountancy; Business Administration; Engineering Management; Industrial Management; Information Management; Marketing); **Life and Health Sciences** (Health Sciences; Nursing)

Accrediting Agencies: Council for Higher Education

Degrees and Diplomas: *Bachelor's Degree*: Physical Engineering; Electronic Engineering; Optical Engineering; Computer Science; Accountancy; Information Science; Management; Marketing; Applied Sciences; Industrial Engineering and Management; Applied Physics; Medical Engineering; Software Eng.; *Master's Degree*: Business Administration (MBA)

KIBBUTZIM COLLEGE OF EDUCATION, TECHNOLOGY AND ARTS - THE SCHOOL OF ARTS AND TECHNOLOGY

Namir Road 149, Tel Aviv 62507
Tel: +972(3) 6901-200
Fax: +972(3) 6996-459
EMail: smkb@smkb.ac.il
Website: http://www.smkb.ac.il/

Programmes

Education (Dance; Education; Environmental Studies; Mathematics Education; Music Education; Physical Education; Preschool Education; Primary Education; Secondary Education; Special Education)

Further Information: Also campuses in Antigonus and Kalisher.

History: Founded 1939. Merged with the Kibbutzim College of Education and Teacher's College of Technology, 2008, became Kibbutzim College of Education, Technology and the Arts.On January 1, 2008, the Teachers College of Technology merged with the Kibbutzim College, and became the Arts and Technology School of the Kibbutzim College of Education, Technology and the Arts.

Accrediting Agencies: Council for Higher Education

Degrees and Diplomas: *Bachelor's Degree*: Dance and Movement; Early Childhood Education; Elementary Education; Junior-High School Education; Kindergarten Education; Music and Movement; Physical Education and Movement; Special Education (BEd); *Master's Degree*: Environmental Education; Education; Mathematics Education (MEd)

Last Updated: 09/12/11

OPEN UNIVERSITY OF ISRAEL

Ha'Universita Ha'Petuha

PO Box 808, 108 Ravutski Street, Raanana 43107
Tel: +972(9) 7780-778
Fax: +972(9) 7780-780
EMail: infodesk@openu.ac.il.
Website: http://www.openu.ac.il

President: Hagit Messer-Yaron
Tel: +972(9) 7782-200, Fax: +972(9) 7780-643

Director-General: Amit Streit
Tel: +972(9) 7782-247, Fax: +972(9) 7780-266

International Relations: Elissa Allerhand
Tel: +972(9) 7781-833, Fax: +972(9) 7780-666
EMail: elissa@openu.ac.il

Departments

Education and Psychology (Education; Psychology); **History, Philosophy and Judaic Studies** (History; Jewish Studies; Philosophy); **Literature, Language and Arts** (Art History; Film; Linguistics; Literature; Music; Theatre); **Management and Economics** (Economics; Management); **Mathematics and Computer Science** (Computer Science; Industrial Engineering; Industrial Management; Mathematics); **Natural Sciences** (Biological and Life Sciences; Chemistry; Geology; Meteorology; Natural Sciences; Physics); **Sociology, Political Science and Communication** (International Relations; Mass Communication; Political Sciences; Sociology)

History: Founded 1974 to provide distance education. Instruction is given through written course/textbooks and the University has four regional campuses and over 70 Study Centres and local colleges throughout the country.

Governing Bodies: Council; Executive Committee; Academic Committee; Faculty Council

Academic Year: October to June (October-January; February-June). Also summer semester (July-August)

Admission Requirements: No formal admission requirements but must meet the rigorous requirements of the Open University. Students are evaluated only on their achievements within the Open University and not on prior attainments. Proficiency in Hebrew is essential

Main Language(s) of Instruction: Hebrew

International Co-operation: With universities in France, United Kingdom, Korea, Costa Rica, Swaziland. Also assistance to countries wishing to establish Open University systems, especially in Asia, Eastern Europe, Latin America and Africa.

Accrediting Agencies: Council for Higher Education

Degrees and Diplomas: *Bachelor's Degree*: Humanities; Social Sciences; Accountancy; Computer Science; Economics; Mathematics; Natural Sciences; Life Sciences; Industrial Engineering and Management (BA; BSc); *Master's Degree*: Biological Thought (MA); Business Administration; Computer Science; Cultural Studies; Democracy Studies (Interdisciplinary); Education (Learning Technologies and Learning Systems) (M.A.). Dual disciplinary BA degrees with combinations in the fields of Management, Economics, Political Science, Sociology, Education (Curriculum and Instruction Studies; Learning Disabilities), Behavioural Sciences and Psychology, History, Mathematics, Computer Science. Interdisciplinary degrees: Economics and Computer Science; Economics and Mathematics; Life Sciences and Management; Natural Sciences and Biotechnology; Chemistry and Life Sciences; Chemistry and Management; Chemistry and Education; Life Sciences and Economics; Life Sciences and Management; Psychology and Life Sciences; Management and Computer Science; Mathematics and Education; Psychology and Computer Science. Degree of Bachelor of Arts, at least 108 credits, which may be taken at the student's own pace

Student Services: Academic counselling, Employment services, Foreign student adviser, Handicapped facilities, Language programs, Sports facilities

Special Facilities: Three Studios for Open University broadcasts of interactive lessons (two broadcast via cable and a conference studio) to 40 classrooms throughout the country. Websites for all courses. Two Cultural Centres in Tel Aviv and Zichron Yakov

Libraries: Electronic library (23 bibliographical databases, 26 full text databases, 26,219 digital periodicals, 380 e-books); Media library (7,700 video and audio cassettes); Print collection (60,000 vols). Also 70 branches of the Library throughout Israel. Cooperation with other university libraries.

Press or Publishing House: The Publishing House of the Open University of Israel

Academic Staff *2009-2010*	**TOTAL**
FULL-TIME	**150**
PART-TIME	**250**
STAFF WITH DOCTORATE	
FULL-TIME	**100**
PART-TIME	**c. 90**

Student Numbers *2009-2010*	
All (Foreign Included)	**c. 48,000**
FOREIGN ONLY	**7,800**

Part-time students, 25,000.

Last Updated: 08/12/11

ORANIM, THE SCHOOL OF EDUCATION OF THE KIBBUTZ MOVEMENT

Tivon Post 36006
Tel: +972(4) 9838-811
Fax: +972(4) 9530-488
EMail: yacaro@kvgeva.org.il
Website: http://www.oranim.ac.il

President: Yair Caro
Tel: +972(4) 9838-802 EMail: yairc@oranim.ac.il

General Director: Michael Ofer
Tel: +972(4) 9838-803 EMail: mike@oranim.ac.il

International Relations: Kari Smith

Centres

Community Leadership *(Shdemot)* (Jewish Studies) *Director*: Michael Mensky

Faculties

Arts and Humanities and Social Science (Arts and Humanities) *Head*: Arnon Medzini; **Graduate Studies** *Head*: Neima Barzel; **Science Education** (Chemistry; Computer Education; Education; Mathematics Education; Physics; Science Education) *Head*: Efrat Shimshoni; **Teacher Training** (Preschool Education; Primary Education; Secondary Education; Special Education; Teacher Training) *Head*: Michal Golan

Accrediting Agencies: Council for Higher Education

Degrees and Diplomas: *Bachelor's Degree*: Arts and Humanities (BA); Science Education (BSc); *Master's Degree*: Education and Teacher Training, Language Education (Med)

OROT ISRAEL COLLEGE

Elkana, D.N. Harei Ephraim 44814
Tel: +972(3) 9061-234
Fax: +972(3) 9362-288
EMail: development@orot.ac.il
Website: http://www.orot.ac.il

Head: Neriah Rabbi Gutel (2004-)
Tel: +972(3) 9064-422 EMail: gutel@orot.ac.il

Director: Asher Parshani
Tel: +972(3) 9061-212 EMail: orot@macam.ac.il

Rector: Elazar Touitou
Tel: +972(3) 9061-202 EMail: eladina@netvision.net.il

Programmes

Education (Education); **Rabbinical Literature** (Jewish Studies)

Further Information: Also campus in Rechovot

History: Founded 1979 as a religious-academic institution of higher education for women. Previously known as Orot Israel College of Education

Governing Bodies: Academic Council and Board of Directors.

Academic Year: September to June

Admission Requirements: Matriculation and psychometric test.

Fees: (Shekels): 11,128 per annum

Main Language(s) of Instruction: Hebrew

International Co-operation: With universities in USA and Ukraine.

Accrediting Agencies: Council for Higher Education

Degrees and Diplomas: *Bachelor's Degree*: High School Education; Special Education; Preschool Education (BEd); *Master's Degree*: Rabbinical Literature (MEd)

Student Services: Academic counselling, Canteen, Foreign student adviser, Foreign Studies Centre, Language programs, Nursery care, Social counselling, Sports facilities

Student Residential Facilities: Dormitories

Special Facilities: Computer centre. Pedagogical resource centre. Computerized linguistic laboratory. Science laboratory. Auditorium. Broadcasting studio.

Libraries: Computerized Library, c. 60,000 vols

Academic Staff *2009-2010*: Total: c. 330
Student Numbers *2009-2010*: Total: c. 1,500
Last Updated: 08/02/10

RUPPIN ACADEMIC CENTER

Emek Hefer 40250
Tel: +972(9) 8983-030
Fax: +972(9) 8983-090
EMail: info@ruppin.ac.il
Website: http://www.ruppin.ac.il

President: Shosh Arad

Director General: Zvika Levin

Schools

Engineering (Biomedical Engineering; Computer Engineering; Electrical Engineering; Engineering; Industrial Management); **Marine Science and Marine Enviromnent** (Marine Biology; Marine Science and Oceanography); **Social Sciences and Management**

Accrediting Agencies: Council for Higher Education

Degrees and Diplomas: *Bachelor's Degree*: Computer Engineering; Industrial Engineering & Management; Oceanography & Marine Environment (BSc); Economics & Accounting; Business Administration; Behavioural Sciences; Economics & Administration (BA); *Master's Degree*: Business Administration; Immigration and Social Integration (MA / MBA)

Student Residential Facilities: Yes

Special Facilities: Computer centre

Libraries: Yes

Last Updated: 08/02/10

SHENKAR COLLEGE OF ENGINEERING AND DESIGN

Pernick Building, 12 Anna Frank Street, Ramat-Gan 52526
Tel: +972(3) 6110-000
Fax: +972(3) 7521-141
EMail: info@shenkar.ac.il
Website: http://www.shenkar.ac.il

President: Yuli Tamir EMail: e@shenkar.ac.il

General Manager: Dror Kaveh
Tel: +972(3) 6110-037, Fax: +972(3) 7518-247
EMail: dror@shenkar.ac.il

International Relations: Varda Kalmar
EMail: vardak@shenkar.ac.il

Faculties

Design (Design; Fashion Design; Graphic Design; Industrial Design; Interior Design; Jewelry Art; Textile Design); **Engineering**; **Multidisciplinary Art** (Fine Arts)

International Co-operation: With universities in the United States; Europe, India and South America

Accrediting Agencies: Council for Higher Education

Degrees and Diplomas: *Bachelor's Degree*: Chemical Engineering; Electronics Engineering; Industrial Engineering & Management; Plastic Engineering; Software Engineering (BSc); Fashion; Graphic Design; Industrial Design; Jewelry; Structural & Environmental Design; Textile (BDes); Textile; Software Engineering; Industrial Engineering & Management (BTech); *Master's Degree*

Last Updated: 23/01/12

IAU TECHNION-ISRAEL INSTITUTE OF TECHNOLOGY

Technion-Machon Technologi Le' Israel

Technion City, Haifa 32000
Tel: +972(4) 8292-111
Fax: +972(4) 8325-537
EMail: svpr@technion.ac.il
Website: http://www.technion.ac.il

President: Peretz Lavie (2009-2013)
Tel: +972(4) 8292-595, Fax: +972(4) 8292-000
EMail: president@technion.ac.il

Director of Public Affairs and Ressource Development: Danny Shapiro
Tel: +972(4) 829-2578, Fax: +972(4) 823-5195
EMail: parddir@dp.technion.ac.il

International Relations: Anat Rafaeli, Deputy Senior VP for International Academic Relations
Tel: +972(4) 8293-532, Fax: +972(4) 8293-773
EMail: dsvpiar@technion.ac.il

Centres

Continuing Education and External Studies; **Pre-University Education**

Faculties

Aerospace Engineering (Aeronautical and Aerospace Engineering); **Architecture and Town Planning** (Architecture; Industrial Design; Regional Planning; Town Planning); **Biology** (Biology; Biotechnology; Cell Biology; Endocrinology; Genetics; Molecular Biology; Physiology; Virology); **Biomedical Engineering** (Bioengineering; Biomedical Engineering); **Biotechnology and Food Engineering** (Biotechnology; Food Technology; Nutrition; Toxicology); **Chemical Engineering** (Bioengineering; Chemical Engineering; Environmental Engineering); **Chemistry** *(Schulich)* (Chemistry); **Civil and Environmental Engineering** (Agricultural Engineering; Civil Engineering; Construction Engineering; Environmental Engineering; Structural Architecture; Transport Engineering; Water Science); **Computer Science** (Computer Science); **Education in Technology and Science** (Biology; Chemistry; Computer Science; Educational Technology; Electrical Engineering; Environmental Studies; Mathematics; Physics; Science Education; Technology Education); **Electrical Engineering** (Electrical Engineering); **Humanities and Arts** (Arabic; Arts and Humanities; Chinese; Fine Arts; French; German; Hebrew; Italian; Judaic Religious Studies; Literature; Music; Performing Arts; Philosophy; Political Sciences; Russian; Social Sciences; Spanish); **Industrial Engineering and Management** *(William Davidson)* (Industrial and Organizational Psychology; Industrial Engineering; Industrial Management; Statistics); **Materials Engineering** (Materials Engineering); **Mathematics** (Mathematics); **Mechanical Engineering** (Mechanical Engineering); **Medicine** (Medicine); **Physics** (Physics)

Institutes

Advanced Studies in Science and Technology *(Samuel Neaman Institute)* (Science Education; Technology); **Medical Sciences Research** (Health Sciences); **Nanothechnology** *(Russell Berrie)*; **National Building Research**; **Solid State**; **Space Research**; **Transportation Research**; **Water Research** (Water Science)

Programmes

Enviromental Engineering; **Quality Assurance and Reliability**

History: Founded 1912, opened 1924. An independent institution. The government meets 75% of the operational costs and provides 50% of the budget for building and development.

Governing Bodies: Board of Governors, comprising members from Israel and abroad including representatives of the government, and representatives of students and academic staff

Academic Year: October to July (October-February; March-July)

Admission Requirements: Secondary school certificate (Teudat Bagrut) or equivalent, and entrance examination

Fees: (Shekels): Undergraduate, c. 9,360 per annum

Main Language(s) of Instruction: Hebrew

Accrediting Agencies: Council for Higher Education

Degrees and Diplomas: *Bachelor's Degree*: Architecture (B.Arc or B.LA), 4-5 yrs; *Bachelor's Degree*: Biology (B.A.); Chemistry (B.A.); Computer Science (B.A.); Mathematics (B.A.); Physics (B.A.), 3 yrs; *Bachelor's Degree*: Computer Science (B.Sc.); Engineering (B.Sc.); Mathematics (B.Sc.), 4 yrs; *Master's Degree*: Science (MSc), a further 2 yrs; *Doctorate*: Medicine, 7 yrs; *Doctorate*: Philosophy (PhD); Science (DSc); Science and Technology (DScTech), a further 2-3 yrs

Student Services: Academic counselling, Canteen, Cultural centre, Employment services, Foreign student adviser, Health services, Nursery care, Social counselling, Sports facilities

Student Residential Facilities: For c. 4,000 students

Special Facilities: Museum for Science and Development of Technology

Libraries: Central Library, 18 departmental libraries, over 1,000,000 vols, 10,500 current periodicals

Publications: Research Reports *(biannually)*; Synopses of D.Sc., Ph.D., and M.Sc.theses *(annually)*

Press or Publishing House: Technion Printing Department

Academic Staff *2009-2010*: Total: c. 830

Student Numbers *2009-2010*: Total: c. 12,450

Last Updated: 09/12/11

TEL AVIV UNIVERSITY

Universitat Tel Aviv

PO Box 39040, Ramat-Aviv 69978
Tel: +972(3) 6408-111
Fax: +972(3) 6407-174
EMail: tauinfo@post.tau.ac.il
Website: http://www.tau.ac.il

President: Joseph Klafter

Faculties

Arts *(David and Yolanda Katz)* (Architecture; Art History; Cinema and Television; Music; Theatre); **Engineering** *(Iby and Aladar Fleischman)* (Biomedical Engineering; Electrical Engineering; Engineering; Environmental Engineering; Industrial Engineering; Mechanical Engineering; Nanotechnology); **Exact Sciences** *(Raymond and Beverly Sackler)* (Astronomy and Space Science; Chemistry; Computer Science; Geophysics; Mathematics; Natural Sciences; Physics; Statistics); **Humanities** *(Lester and Sally Entin)* (African Studies; American Studies; Ancient Civilizations; Arabic; Archaeology; Bible; Classical Languages; Cultural Studies; East Asian Studies; English; French; Gender Studies; Geography; History; Islamic Studies; Jewish Studies; Linguistics; Middle Eastern Studies; Philosophy; Publishing and Book Trade); **Law** *(Buchmann)* (Law); **Life Sciences** *(George S. Wise)* (Biological and Life Sciences; Biotechnology; Botany; Ecology; Microbiology; Zoology); **Management** (Accountancy; Business Administration; Management); **Medicine** *(Sackler)* (Anaesthesiology; Anatomy; Cardiology; Cell Biology; Dermatology; Epidemiology; Genetics; Gynaecology and Obstetrics; Medicine; Neurological Therapy; Oncology; Ophthalmology; Orthopaedics; Otorhinolaryngology; Paediatrics; Pathology; Pharmacology; Physiology; Psychiatry and Mental Health; Public Health; Rehabilitation and Therapy; Surgery); **Social Sciences** *(Gershon H. Gordon)* (Communication Studies; Economics; Labour and Industrial Relations; Labour Law; Political Sciences; Psychology; Public Administration; Social Sciences; Sociology)

Schools

Dentistry *(Maurice and Gabriela Goldschleger)* (Dentistry; Oral Pathology; Orthodontics; Surgery); **Education** *(Jaime and Joan Constantiner)* (Education); **Environmental Studies** *(Porter)* (Environmental Studies); **Social Work** *(Bob Shapell)* (Social Work)

Further Information: Also Student Exchange Programmes, Hebrew Studies Unit, Preparatory Programme (Mechina)

History: Founded1953 as a municipal institution, incorporating the former School of Law and Economics, established 1935, the Institute of Natural Sciences, and the Institute of Jewish Studies. Became University 1956. An autonomous institution with independent organizational status. 70% of income provided by the government.

Governing Bodies: Board of Governors; Executive Council; Academic Senate

Academic Year: October to June (October-January; March-June)

Admission Requirements: Secondary school certificate (Teudat Bagrut) or recognized foreign equivalent, and entrance examination; psychometric examination or SAT; satisfactory knowledge of Hebrew

Fees: (Shekels): c. 11,600 per annum

Main Language(s) of Instruction: Hebrew

International Co-operation: With universities in Europe and North and South America

Accrediting Agencies: Council for Higher Education

Degrees and Diplomas: *Bachelor's Degree*: Arts (BA); Communication Disorders; Fine Arts (BFA); Law (LLB); Music (BMus);

Physical Therapy (BPT); Science (BSc); Social Work (BSW), 3-4 yrs; *Master's Degree*: Arts (MA); Business Administration (MBA); Communication Disorders; Fine Arts (MFA); Jewish Law (MA); Law (LLM); Management Sciences (MSM); Music; Science (MSc); Social Work, a further 1-2 yrs; *Doctorate*: in all disciplines (PhD); *Doctorate*: Law (LLD), 2 yrs following Master's Degree; *Doctorate*: Medicine (MD), 7 yrs

Student Services: Academic counselling, Canteen, Employment services, Foreign student adviser, Handicapped facilities, Health services, Social counselling, Sports facilities

Student Residential Facilities: For c. 1,000 students

Special Facilities: Zoology Museum. Art Gallery. Experimental Zoological and Botanical Garden

Libraries: The Brender-Moss Library for Social Sciences and Management; The David J. Light La Library; The Elias Sourasky Central Library (Humanities and Arts mainly); The Gitter-Smolarz Library of Life Sciences and Medicine; The Neiman Library of Exact Sciences and Engineering

Publications: Estudios Interdisciplinarios de América Latina *(biannually)*; Hasifrut *(quarterly)*; Iunei Mishpat *(monthly)*; Mediterranean Historical Review *(biannually)*; Middle East Contemporary Survey *(annually)*; Middle East Record *(annually)*

Academic Staff *2009-2010*: Total: c. 1,000

Student Numbers *2009-2010*: Total: c. 14,000

Last Updated: 09/12/11

TEL-HAI COLLEGE

Upper Galilee 12210
Tel: +972(4) 8181-785
Fax: +972(4) 8181-787
EMail: amnonleshem@adm.telhai.ac.il
Website: http://www.telhai.ac.il

President: Yona Chen

International Relations: Amnon Leshem, Vice President, External Relations & Development

Faculties

Humanities and Social Sciences (Arts and Humanities; Behavioural Sciences; Economics; Education; Management; Psychology; Social Sciences; Social Work); **Science and Technology**

Institutes

Arts (Ceramic Art; Fine Arts; Jewelry Art)

History: Founded 1996.

Main Language(s) of Instruction: Hebrew

Accrediting Agencies: Council for Higher Education

Degrees and Diplomas: *Bachelor's Degree*: Biotechnology; Environmental Studies; Nutrition; Computer Science (BSc); Education; Social Work; Economics;Inter-disciplinary Studies; Management; Computer Science (BA); *Master's Degree*: Biotechnology, MSc; *Master's Degree*: Social Work (MA)

Student Residential Facilities: For 500 students

Libraries: Yes

Last Updated: 09/12/11

THE ACADEMIC COLLEGE OF TEL AVIV, YAFFO

PO Box 16131, 4 Antokolsky Street, Tel Aviv 64044
Tel: +972(3) 5211-844
Fax: +972(3) 5211-872
EMail: info@mta.co.il
Website: http://www.mta.ac.il

President: Nehemia Friedland (2004-) EMail: nehemia@mta.ac.il

Schools

Behavioural Sciences (Behavioural Sciences); **Computer Science** (Mathematics and Computer Science); **Governement and Society** (Government); **Management and Economics** (Economics; Management)

History: Founded 1994.

Admission Requirements: High school diploma, Psychometric examination

Fees: (Shekels): 9,400 per annum

Main Language(s) of Instruction: Hebrew

Accrediting Agencies: Council for Higher Education

Degrees and Diplomas: *Bachelor's Degree*: Social Studies; Political Science; Behavioural Sciences; Economics; Management; Computer Science (BA or BSc), 3 yrs; *Master's Degree*: Computer Science; Psychology (MSc or MA), 2 yrs

Student Services: Academic counselling, Canteen, Employment services, Handicapped facilities, Social counselling

Last Updated: 02/02/10

THE HADASSAH COLLEGE JERUSALEM

PO Box 1114, 37 Haneviim Street, Jerusalem 91010
Tel: +972(2) 6291-911
Fax: +972(2) 6250-619
EMail: info@hadassah.ac.il
Website: http://www.hadassah.ac.il

President: Nava Ben Zvi

Departments

English (English)

Schools

Computer Science (Computer Engineering; Computer Science; Electrical and Electronic Engineering; Management; Mathematics; Social Sciences; Software Engineering); **Design and Communication** (Communication Studies; Industrial Design; Photography); **Health and Life Sciences** (Anatomy; Biochemistry; Biology; Biotechnology; Cell Biology; Chemistry; Endocrinology; Genetics; Immunology; Inorganic Chemistry; Laboratory Techniques; Microbiology; Molecular Biology; Optometry; Organic Chemistry; Parasitology; Pathology; Pharmacology; Physical Chemistry; Physiology; Virology); **Management** (Health Administration; Hotel Management)

Accrediting Agencies: Council for Higher Education

Degrees and Diplomas: *Bachelor's Degree*: Communication Disorders; Computer Science (BA); Medical Laboratory Studies (BTech); Optometry; *Master's Degree*: Computer Science; Optometry. The College has also received permission to advertise and register students in a program leading to a Bachelor's degree in Medical and Environmental Sciences (B.A.) and in Biotechnology (B.Sc.).

Last Updated: 09/12/11

THE HEBREW UNIVERSITY OF JERUSALEM

Ha'Universita Ha'Ivrit Bi'Yerushalayim

Mount Scopus, Jerusalem 91905
Tel: +972(2) 5882-111
Fax: +972(2) 5811-023
EMail: rector@savion.huji.ac.il
Website: http://www.huji.ac.il

President: Menahem Ben-Sasson (2009-)
EMail: menahemb@savion.huji.ac.il

Vice-President and Director-General: Elhanan HaCohen
Tel: +972(2) 5882-908, Fax: +972(2) 5828-547
EMail: elhananh@savion.huji.ac.il

Rector: Sarah Stroumsa EMail: stroums@vms.huji.ac.il

International Relations: Carmi Gillon, Vice-President for External Relations
Tel: +972(2) 5881-188, Fax: +972(2) 5826-360
EMail: carmig@savion.huji.ac.il

Centres

Citizenship, Democracy and Civil Education *(Gilo) Director*: Dan Avron; **Dead Sea Scrolls and Associated Literature** *(Orion) Director*: Esther Chazon; **General and Tumour Immunology** *(Lautenberg) Director*: Eitan Yefe-Nof; **Geographical Information Systems** *Director*: Ronen Kadmon; **German History** *(Richard Koebner) Director*: Moshe Zimmerman; **Herbarium of Middle Eastern Flora**; **History and Philosophy of Science, Technology and Medicine** *(Sidney M. Edelstein) Director*: Itamar Pitowsky; **Industrial Development** *(Gal-Edd) Director*: Niron Hashai; **International Retail and Marketing** *(K Mart) Director*: David Mazursky;

Islamic Studies *(The Nehemia Levzion) Director*: Reuven Amitai; **Jewish Art** *Director*: Rina Talgam; **Jewish Studies in Russian** *(The Chais) Director*: Alexander Kulik; **Marine Biogeochemistry** *(Moshe Shilo) Director*: Yehuda Cohen; **Nanoscience and Nanotechnology** *Director*: Uri Banin; **Neural Computation** *(Interdisciplinary) Director*: Idan Segev; **Photosynthesis Research** *(Minerva Avron) Director*: Joseph Hirschberg; **Studies of Visual Transduction** *(Kühne-Minerva) Director*: Baruch Minke; **Study and Research in Psycholanalysis** *(Sigmund Freud) Director*: Gaby Shefler; **Study and Treatment of Alzheimer's Disease and Related Topics** *(Harry Stern National) Director*: Bernard Lerer; **Study of Antisemitism** *(Vidal Sassoon - International) Director*: Robert Wistrich; **Study of Christianity** *Director*: David Satran; **Study of German Culture and Literature** *(Franz Rosenzweig) Director*: Paul Mendes Flohr; **Study of Infectious and Tropical Diseases** *(Sanford F. Kuvin) Dierctor*: Joseph Shlomai; **Study of Jewish Languages and Literature** (Jewish Studies) *Director*: Moshe Bar-Asher; **Study of Light Speed Included Processes** *(Knune Minerva Farkas) Director*: Sanford Ruhman; **Study of Normal Child and Adolescent Development** *(Lewin) Director*: Ruth Butler; **Study of Pain** *Director*: Yair Sharav; **Study of Sephardi and Oriental Jewry** *(Misgav Yerushalaim) Director*: Meir Buzaglo; **Study of Zionism, the Yishuv and the History of Israel** *(Bernard Cherrick) Director*: Uzi Revhun; **University Teaching of Jewish Civilization** *(International) Director*: Yom Tov Assis; **Women's Studies** *(Lafer) Director*: Tamar El-Or; **Zigi and Lisa Daniel Swiss** *Director*: Yaacov Abr Siamn Tov

Faculties

Agriculture, Food and Environment *(The Robert H. Smith)* (Agricultural Economics; Agricultural Management; Agriculture; Animal Husbandry; Biotechnology; Crop Production; Entomology; Environmental Studies; Food Science; Horticulture; Hotel Management; Natural Resources; Nutrition; Plant and Crop Protection; Soil Science; Vegetable Production; Veterinary Science; Water Science); **Dentistry** *(Ein Karem Campus)* (Dentistry; Orthodontics; Periodontics; Surgery); **Humanities** (African Studies; American Studies; Ancient Languages; Archaeology; Art History; Arts and Humanities; Asian Studies; Bible; Central European Studies; Classical Languages; Cognitive Sciences; Comparative Literature; Comparative Religion; East Asian Studies; Eastern European Studies; Education; English; History; Jewish Studies; Linguistics; Literature; Middle Eastern Studies; Modern Languages; Musicology; Philosophy); **Law** (Criminology; European Union Law; History of Law; Human Rights; Labour Law; Law); **Medicine** *(Ein Karem Campus)* (Biochemistry; Genetics; Medicine; Molecular Biology; Nursing; Occupational Health; Oncology; Pharmacy; Public Health); **Science** *(Givat Ram Campus)* (Applied Physics; Behavioural Sciences; Biochemistry; Biological and Life Sciences; Chemistry; Computer Science; Earth Sciences; Ecology; Engineering; Environmental Studies; Genetics; Mathematics; Natural Sciences; Physics; Plant and Crop Protection; Software Engineering); **Social Sciences** (Anthropology; Communication Studies; Demography and Population; Economics; Geography; International Relations; Political Sciences; Psychology; Social Sciences; Sociology; Statistics)

Institutes

Advanced Studies *Director*: Eliezer Rabinovii; **Advancement of Peace** *(Harry S. Truman)* (Peace and Disarmament); **Communication** *(Smart Family Foundation)* (Communication Studies) *Director*: Menachem Blondheim; **Dental Science** *Director*: Yona Sela; **Economic, Social and Political Research** *(Levi Eshkol)* (Economics; Political Sciences; Sociology) *Director*: Gad Wolsfeld; **European Studies** (European Studies) *Director*: Bianca Kuhnel; **International Relations** *(Leonard Davis)* (International Relations) *Director*: Raymond Cohen; **Legislative Research and Comparative Law** *(Harry and Michael Sacher)* (Comparative Law; Law) *Director*: Shimon Shetreet; **Psychobiology** *(National - Israel) Director*: Bernard Lerer; **Study of Jewish Communities in the East** *(Ben-Zwi) Director*: Haggai Ben-Shamai

Research Centres

Agricultural Economy *Director*: Israel Finkelshtain; **Agriculture** *(Kennedy Leigh) Director*: Alexander Vanstein; **Bee** *(Benjamin Triwaks) Director*: Sharon Shafir; **Business Administration** *(Recanati) Director*: Yishai Yafe; **Computer Sciences** *(G. W. Leibnitz Minerva) Director*: Leo Joskowich; **Dental Implant** *(Niznick) Director*: David Kohavi; **Dental Materials and Aesthetics in Dentistry** *(Ronald E. Goldstein DDS) Director*: Ervin Weiss; **Diabetes** *Director*: Shlomo Sasson; **Dutch Jewry** (Jewish Studies) *Director*: Yosef Kaplan; **Environmental Studies** *(Multi-Disciplinary)*; **Experimental Medicine and Cancer** *(Huvert H. Humphrey) Director*: Shulamit Katzan; **Folklore** (Labour and Industrial Relations) *Director*: Galit Hasan-Rokem; **Germania-Judaica**; **Groundwater** *(Leo Picard) Director*: Yechezkel Mualem; **History and Culture of Polish Jews** *Director*: Israel Bartal; **History of Hebrew** *(The Eliezer Ben-Yehudah)*; **Jewish Music** *Director*: Edwin Serussi; **Jewish Oral Traditions** *Director*: Aharon Maman; **Jewish Studies** *(Scholion Interdisciplinary) Director*: Israel J. Yuval; **Molecular Dynamics** *(Fritz Haber) Director*: Avinoam Ben-Shaul; **Neurodegenerative Disease** *(Roland)*; **Romanian Jewry** *Director*: Ezra Fleischer; **Russian and East European Jewry** *(Leonid Nevzlin) Director*: Israel Bartal; **Social Sciences** *(Shaine) Director*: Amalia Oliver; **The Hebrew University Bible Project**; **Trauma** *Director*: Avi Rivkind

Research Institutes

Innovation in Education *(National Council of Jewish Women)*; **Jewish History** *(Ben-Zion Dinur)* (History; Jewish Studies) *Director*: Emmanuel Etkes; **Jewish Law** *(Israel Matz) Director*: Gideon Libson

Schools

Business Administration *(Jerusalem)* (Business Administration); **Computer Science and Engineering** *(Givat Ram Campus)* (Computer Science; Software Engineering); **Education** (Education); **International** *(Rothberg)* (Jewish Studies; Modern Languages; Natural Sciences; Social Sciences); **Nursing** *(Henrietta Szold-Hadassah-Hebrew)* (Nursing); **Nutritional Sciences** *(Rehovot)* (Dietetics; Nutrition); **Occupational Therapy** *(Hadassah-Hebrew)* (Occupational Therapy); **Pharmacy** *(Ein Karem Campus)* (Pharmacy); **Public Health and Community Medicine** *(Ein Karem Campus)* (Public Health); **Social Work and Social Welfare** *(Paul Baerwald)* (Social Welfare; Social Work); **Veterinary Medicine** *(Koret)* (Veterinary Science)

History: Founded 1918 and opened on Mount Scopus 1925. Transferred to Central Jerusalem 1948 when Mount Scopus was cut off from Jewish section of the city. Construction of Givat Ram campus started 1954, completed 1958. Mount Scopus campus reopened 1967, and the return of the student body and staff was completed 1981. Also campuses in Rehovot (Agriculture), and Ein Karem, Jerusalem (Medical Sciences). A private Institution financially supported by the Government, tuition fees and donations.

Governing Bodies: Board of Governors of 530 members and composed of representatives of Jewish communities in all parts of the world; Executive Committee, comprising 40 members; Academic Senate

Academic Year: October to June (October-January; February-June)

Admission Requirements: Secondary school certificate (Bagrut) or recognized foreign equivalent, and Psychometric entrance examination

Fees: (Shekels): c. 11,600 per annum

Main Language(s) of Instruction: Hebrew

International Co-operation: With universities in North and South America, Europe, Eastern Asia and Australia

Accrediting Agencies: Council for Higher Education

Degrees and Diplomas: *Bachelor's Degree*: 3 yrs; *Diploma*: 1 yr; *Master's Degree*: a further 2 yrs; *Master's Degree*: Business Administration (MBA), 4 semesters; *Doctorate*: at least 2 yrs following Master; *Doctorate*: Dental Medicine (DMD); Medicine (MD), 6 yrs; *Doctorate*: Veterinary Medicine (DMV), 4 yrs following at least 2 yrs in related fields

Student Services: Academic counselling, Canteen, Employment services, Foreign student adviser, Foreign Studies Centre, Handicapped facilities, Health services, Language programs, Nursery care, Social counselling, Sports facilities

Student Residential Facilities: For c. 6,000-6,500 students

Special Facilities: Spielberg Jewish Film Archives. 2 Botanical Gardens. Marine Research Laboratory at Eilat (external research station). Desert Ecosystem Field Stations. Educational Television and Movie Studio. Medium-Size Particle Accelerator

Libraries: Jewish National and University Library, c. 5m. vols; 8 libraries, c. 3m. Vols: Humanities and Social Sciences Library.

Agricultural Library, Berman Medical Library; Harman Science Library, Mathematics and Computer Science Library; Archaeology Library; Education and Social Work Library, Law Library.

Publications: ACTA-Analysis of Current Trends in Antisemitism, Research papers on current issues related to antisemitism, in English *(3 per annum)*; Aleph: Historical Studies in Science and Judaism *(annually)*; Antisemitism International, Research Journal in English *(annually)*; Edah Velashon, Publication of the Hebrew University Jewish Oral Traditions Research Centre, in Hebrew *(annually)*; Hispania Judaica Bulletin, History, Culture, Thought, Literature, Art and Language of Jews in the Iberian Peninsula in English *(annually)*; Israel Law Review, In English *(3 per annum)*; Italia - Research in the History, Culture and Literature of the Jews of Italy, multi-lingual (English, Hebrew, Italian, French, etc.) *(annually)*; Iyyun, Journal of Philosophy (twice a year in Hebrew and twice a year in English) *(quarterly)*; Jerusalem Studies in Arabic and Islam, Study of classical Islam, Arabic language and literature, the origin of Islamic institutions and the interaction between Islam and other civilizations, mostly in English, also contributions in French, German and Arabic *(annually)*; Jerusalem Studies in Hebrew Language, In Hebrew *(annually)*; Jerusalem Studies in Hebrew Literature, in Hebrew *(annually)*; Jerusalem Studies in Jewish Folklore, in Hebrew *(annually)*; Jerusalem Studies in Jewish Thought, in Hebrew *(annually)*; Jews in Russia Eastern Europe, Published in English in cooperation with Leaonid Nevzlin Research Centre *(biannually)*; Journal of Experimental Criminology, In English *(quarterly)*; Mishpatim, Publication on Law, in English and Hebrew *(3 per annum)*; Partial Answers, Journal of Literature and the History of Ideas, in English *(biannually)*; Perspectives, Humanistic Studies, in particular - Literature, History and Arts, in French *(annually)*; Politika, Journal of Israeli Political Science and International Relations that addresses timely issues affecting both Israel and the world, in Hebrew *(biannually)*; QAEDEM: Monographs of the Institute of Archaeology, Scientific Publication of excavation reports and other studies in archaeology of Israel. In English *(1-2 per annum)*; QEDEM Reports, Scientific Publication of excavation reports of archaeological sites in Israel. In English *(1-2 per annum)*; Shnaton - Annual for Biblical and Ancient Near Eastern Studies, in Hebrew *(annually)*; Shnaton Hamishpat Haivri, Jewish Law, in Hebrew; Studies in Contemporary Jewry, Published in English, in Conjunction with Oxford University Press *(annually)*; Tarbiz, Jewish Studies, in English *(quarterly)*

Press or Publishing House: The Magnes Press

Academic Staff *2009-2010*	**TOTAL**
FULL-TIME	**1,500**
STAFF WITH DOCTORATE	
FULL-TIME	c. **1,200**
Student Numbers *2009-2010*	
All (Foreign Included)	c. **23,500**
FOREIGN ONLY	**1,050**

Last Updated: 04/02/10

THE JERUSALEM ACADEMY OF MUSIC AND DANCE

Ha'Akademia Lemusica ve Lmachol Byerushalyim

Campus Givat Ram, Jerusalem 91904
Tel: +972(2) 6759-911
Fax: +972(2) 6527-713
EMail: schul@jamd.ac.il
Website: http://www.jamd.ac.il

President: Ilan Schul (2003-)
Tel: +972(2) 6512-824, Fax: +972(2) 6527-713

Director-General: Micha Tal
Tel: +972(2) 6759-903 EMail: michat@jamd.ac.il

International Relations: Tamar Millo, Director of International Relations
Tel: +972(2) 6759-924, Fax: +972(2) 6527-713
EMail: tamarm@jamd.ac.il

Faculties

Composition, Conducting and Music Education (Conducting; Music Education; Music Theory and Composition); **Dance** (Dance); **Performing Arts** (Music Theory and Composition; Musical Instruments; Singing)

History: Created 1932 as The Conservatory of Music. Obtained current title and status 1947.

Accrediting Agencies: Council for Higher Education

Degrees and Diplomas: *Bachelor's Degree*: Music; Music Education; Dance, 4 yrs; *Master's Degree*: Music, 2 yrs

Libraries: 20,000 vols. 60,000 music scores. 35 periodical subscriptions.

Last Updated: 30/11/11

THE KAYE COLLEGE OF EDUCATION

PO Box 13001, Yehuda HaLevy Street, Beer-Sheva 84100
Tel: +972(8) 6402-777
Fax: +972(8) 6413-020
Website: http://www.kaye.ac.il/

President: Lea Kozminsky EMail: leako@macam.ac.il

Executive Director: Taly Ben Israel

Schools

Advanced Studies (Educational and Student Counselling); **Education** (Education)

Accrediting Agencies: Council for Higher Education

Degrees and Diplomas: *Bachelor's Degree*: Early Childhood Education; Elementary Education; Junior-High School Education; Special Education; Art Education; Physical Education; Kindergarten Education (BEd); *Master's Degree*: Education Counseling (MEd)

Last Updated: 09/02/10

THE ZINMAN COLLEGE OF PHYSICAL EDUCATION AND SPORT SCIENCES AT THE WINGATE INSTITUTE

Wingate Post Office, Netanya 42902
Tel: +972(9) 8639-550
Fax: +972(9) 8650-960
EMail: wincol@wincol.ac.il
Website: http://www.wincol.ac.il/

President: Michael Sagiv (1998-)
Tel: +972(9) 8639-205 EMail: sagiv@wincol.ac.il

International Relations: Mike Garmise
Tel: +972(9) 8639-272 EMail: garmize@wincol.ac.il

Programmes

Education

History: Founded 1944. Acquired present status and title 1984. Situated in the Wingate Institute.

Admission Requirements: Matriculation certificate and psychometric examination

Main Language(s) of Instruction: Hebrew

Accrediting Agencies: Council for Higher Education

Degrees and Diplomas: *Bachelor's Degree*: Education (BEd), 4 yrs; *Master's Degree*: Physical Education (MPE), a further 2 yrs

Student Services: Academic counselling, Canteen, Handicapped facilities, Health services, Sports facilities

Student Residential Facilities: Yes.

Libraries: c. 55,000 vols

Publications: BIT'NUA (Movement), Journal of Physical Education Sciences *(3 per annum)*

Last Updated: 03/02/10

UNIVERSITY OF HAIFA

Universitat Haifa

Mount Carmel, Haifa 31905
Tel: +972(4) 8240-111
Fax: +972(4) 8342-101
EMail: info@mail.uhaifa.org
Website: http://www.haifa.ac.il

President: Aaron Ben-Ze'ev EMail: abenzeev@univ.haifa.ac.il

Rector: David Faraggi
Tel: +972(4) 8240-405 EMail: dfaraggi@univ.haifa.ac.il

Departments

Physical Education (Physical Education)

Faculties
Education (Education; Educational and Student Counselling; Mathematics Education; Special Education; Teacher Training); **Humanities** (Arabic; Archaeology; Art Education; Bible; Comparative Literature; Cultural Studies; English; French; Hebrew; History; Information Sciences; Jewish Studies; Philosophy; Theatre); **Law** (Law); **Natural Sciences** (Biology; Marine Biology; Mathematical Physics; Mathematics; Science Education; Teacher Training); **Social Sciences** (Anthropology; Communication Studies; Computer Science; Economics; Geography; Management; Natural Resources; Political Sciences; Psychology; Sociology; Statistics); **Social Welfare and Health Studies** (Communication Disorders; Gerontology; Occupational Therapy; Physical Therapy; Social Sciences; Social Work)

Graduate Schools
Business (Business and Commerce)

Schools
Graduate Studies *Dean*: Gideon Fishman; **Marine Sciences** *(Leon H. Charney)* (Marine Science and Oceanography)

History: Founded 1963 as University Institute of Haifa under an agreement between the municipal authorities of Haifa and the Hebrew University, Jerusalem. Became an accredited autonomous institution 1972. Receives financial support from the government.

Governing Bodies: Board of Governors; Executive Committee; Senate of the Faculty

Academic Year: October to July (October-March; March July)

Admission Requirements: Secondary school matriculation certificate (Teudat Bagrut) or equivalent, and Psychometric entrance examination

Main Language(s) of Instruction: Hebrew

International Co-operation: With universities in USA; Germany; Mediterranean institutions.

Accrediting Agencies: Council for Higher Education

Degrees and Diplomas: *Bachelor's Degree*: Arts and Humanities; Education; Fine Arts (BA), 3-4 yrs; *Diploma*: Librarianship; Museology; Teaching, 2 yrs; *Master's Degree*: Arts; Social Sciences; Science (MA/MSc), a further 2-3 yrs; *Doctorate*: Arts; Social Sciences; Mathematics (PhD), a further 3-4 yrs

Student Services: Academic counselling, Canteen, Cultural centre, Foreign student adviser, Foreign Studies Centre, Handicapped facilities, Health services, Language programs, Social counselling, Sports facilities

Student Residential Facilities: Yes

Special Facilities: Edith and Reuben Hecht Museum of Archaeology. Ghez Holocaust Art Collection. Art Gallery. Videoconference Studio

Libraries: Younes and Soraya Nazarian Library, c. 800,000 vols; Library of Wydra Shipping and Aviation Research Institute, c. 3,000; Law Library

Publications: Dapim B'Hinoch, Hebrew *(annually)*; Hok Umimshal (Law and Government) *(annually)*; Israel Shipping, Hebrew, with comprehensive English summary *(annually)*; Jewish History, English *(annually)*; Michmanim (Treasures), Archeology Publication of the Hecht Museum *(annually)*

Press or Publishing House: Haifa University Press

Last Updated: 09/12/11

WEIZMANN INSTITUTE OF SCIENCE

Machon Weizmann Lemada

PO Box 26, Rehovot 76100

Tel: +972(8) 9342-111 +972(8) 9343-111

Fax: +972(8) 9344-107

EMail: academic.affairs@weizmann.ac.il

Website: http://www.weizmann.ac.il

President: Daniel Zajfman (2006-)

Tel: +972(8) 9343-951, Fax: +972(8) 9344-100

EMail: daniel.zajfman@weizmann.ac.il

Vice-President for Finance and Administration: Isaac Shariv

Departments
Science Teaching (Science Education)

Faculties
Biochemistry (Biochemistry; Genetics; Plant and Crop Protection); **Biology** (Biology; Cell Biology; Immunology; Molecular Biology); **Chemistry** (Chemistry); **Mathematics and Computer Science** (Mathematics and Computer Science); **Physics** (Physics) *Dean*: Yosef Nir

Schools
Graduate *(Feinberg) Dean*: Lia Addadi

History: Founded 1934 as Daniel Sieff Research Institute, renamed 1949. A private institution, under the supervision of the Council for Higher Education. Financially supported by the government, research grants and contracts, gifts and bequests.

Governing Bodies: Board of Governors

Academic Year: October to September (October-February, March-June, July-September)

Admission Requirements: For Master of Science, an excellent BSc from an accredited university in Israel or abroad; for Doctor of Philosophy, an excellent MSc from an accredited university in Israel or abroad; Letters of reference (at least 2); a personal interview; GRE (general & and subject test) + TOEFL may be required

Fees: None

Main Language(s) of Instruction: English

Accrediting Agencies: Council for Higher Education

Degrees and Diplomas: *Master's Degree*: Science (MSc), 2 yrs; *Doctorate (PhD)*: a further 4 1/2 yrs

Student Services: Academic counselling, Canteen, Cultural centre, Foreign student adviser, Sports facilities

Student Residential Facilities: Yes

Special Facilities: The Weizmann House. The Weizmann Archives. The Levinson Visitors Centre. The Clore Garden of Science

Libraries: Total, c. 250,000 vols

Publications: Interface *(biennially)*; List of Current Research Projects, Online at : http://www.weizmann.ac.il/acadaff/Current Research/ *(weekly)*; Scientific Activities, Online at : http://www.weizmann.ac.il/acadaff/Scientific Activities/ *(annually)*

Last Updated: 09/12/11

PRIVATE INSTITUTIONS

COLLEGE OF MANAGEMENT ACADEMIC STUDIES

Hamaslool Ha'akademi shel Hamichlala Leminhal (COMAS)

7 Yitchak Rabin Boulevard, Rishon Lezion 75190

Tel: +972(3) 963-4403

Fax: +972(3) 963-4493

EMail: rdas@colman.ac.il

Website: http://www.colman.ac.il

President: Seev Neumann

Tel: +972(3) 963-4402 EMail: seevne@hdq.colman.ac.il

Departments
Computer Science (Computer Science; Mathematics and Computer Science); **Interior Design** (Interior Design)

Graduate Schools
Business Studies (Business Administration; Business and Commerce; Finance; Human Resources; Management; Marketing)

Research Institutes
Applied Economics *(Moshe Sanbar)* (Economics); **Conflict Resolution and Mediation** (Peace and Disarmament); **Human Factors in Road Safety** (Road Transport)

Schools
Behavioural Sciences (Behavioural Sciences); **Business Administration**; **Economics** (Economics; Finance; Marketing); **Law** *(Haim Striks)* (Criminology; Law); **Media Studies** *(Tel-Aviv campus)* (Advertising and Publicity; Communication Studies; Media Studies)

History: Founded 1977. Acquired present status 1986.

Governing Bodies: Board of Trustees

Academic Year: October to September

Admission Requirements: Secondary school certificate or equivalent. Psychometric, English, Mathematics and Logic examinations for some programmes

Fees: (Shekels): c. 25,000 per annum

Main Language(s) of Instruction: Hebrew

Accrediting Agencies: Council for Higher Education

Degrees and Diplomas: *Bachelor's Degree*: Business Administration (BB); Media Studies; Behavioural Sciences; Economics and Management; Computer Science (BA), 3 yrs; *Bachelor's Degree*: Interior Design (BDes(Int)), 4 yrs; *Bachelor's Degree*: Law (LLB), 3 1/2 yrs; *Master's Degree*: Business Administration; Interior Design (MBA); Counceling and Organisational Development; Behavioural Sciences (MA); Law; Criminology (LLM), a further 2 yrs

Student Services: Academic counselling, Canteen, Employment services, Handicapped facilities, Social counselling

Student Residential Facilities: No

Libraries: Three libraries

Publications: Al Hagova, Journal on Higher Education Teaching in Israel *(annually)*; Hamishpat, Law Journal *(biannually)*; Kaveret, Journal of the Department of Behavioural Sciences *(biannually)*

Student Numbers *2009-2010*: Total 12,000

LEVINSKY COLLEGE OF EDUCATION

PO Box 48130, Tel Aviv
Tel: +972(3) 6902-444
Fax: +972(3) 6993-546
Website: http://www.levinsky.ac.il

Programmes

Education (Education; Music Education; Preschool Education; Secondary Education; Teacher Training)

Degrees and Diplomas: *Bachelor's Degree*: Education; *Master's Degree*: Education

Last Updated: 12/02/10

MACHON LANDER

PO Box 34353, Olam Umlo'o 8, Givat Shaul, 91343 Jerusalem
Tel: +972(2) 6599-333 +972(73) 220-4204
Fax: +972(2) 6528-859
EMail: rsassoon@lander.ac.il
Website: http://www.lander.ac.il

Program Director: Rabbi Robbie Sassoon
Tel: +972(73) 220-4216

Schools

Business Administration (Business Administration); **Jewish Studies**

History: Founded 2002.

Degrees and Diplomas: *Bachelor's Degree*: Business Administration (BA); *Master's Degree*: Jewish Studies (MA)

Last Updated: 12/02/10

NETANYA ACADEMIC COLLEGE

1 University Street, Kiryat Yitzhak Rabin, Netanya 42365
Tel: +972(9) 8607-777
Fax: +972(9) 8607-799
Website: http://www.netanya.ac.il

President: Zvi Arad
Tel: +972(9) 8607-710 EMail: aradtzvi@netanya.ac.il

Rector: Bernard Pinchuk EMail: pinchuk@netanya.ac.il

International Relations: David Altman, Vice President for Development Tel: +972(9) 8607-779 EMail: daltman@netanya.ac.il

Schools

Banking and Finance *(Mike Feldman)* (Banking; Finance); **Behavioural Sciences** (Anthropology; Behavioural Sciences; Psychology; Sociology); **Business Administration** (Business Administration; Management) *Dean*: Yehoshua Lieberman; **Communications and Media** (Journalism; Mass Communication; Media Studies); **Computer Science and Mathematics** (Computer Science; Mathematics) *Dean*: Amos Israeli; **Insurance and Business Administration** *(Ernst & Margot Hamburger)* (Business Administration; Insurance); **Law** (Law)

History: Founded 1995.

Governing Bodies: Board of Trustees; Acadmic Council (Senate)

Academic Year: October to September

Admission Requirements: High School diploma (86 pt. average)

Fees: (Shekels): 25,000 per annum

Main Language(s) of Instruction: Hebrew, English

Accrediting Agencies: Council for Higher Education

Degrees and Diplomas: *Bachelor's Degree*: Business Administration; Behavioural Sciences; Insurance; Communication Studies; Banking; Finance (BA); *Bachelor's Degree*: Computer Science; Mathematics (BSc), 3 yrs; *Bachelor's Degree*: Law (LLB), 3 1/2 yrs; *Master's Degree*: Business Administration; Finance; Marketing; Management (MBA), a further 2 yrs; *Master's Degree*: Communications; Organizational Behaviour; Information System (MA); Law; Commercial Law (LLM)

Student Services: Academic counselling, Canteen, Employment services, Foreign student adviser, Handicapped facilities, Sports facilities

Student Residential Facilities: None

Libraries: 75,000 vols.; 60 databases

Publications: Law Review *(biannually)*

Academic Staff *2009-2010*	MEN	WOMEN	TOTAL
FULL-TIME	65	15	**80**
PART-TIME	90	70	**160**
STAFF WITH DOCTORATE			
FULL-TIME	60	10	**70**
PART-TIME	70	50	c. **120**
Student Numbers *2009-2010*			
All (Foreign Included)	–	–	c. **4,000**

Part-time students, 50. **Evening students**, 230.

Last Updated: 09/12/11

ONO ACADEMIC COLLEGE (OAC)

PO Box 759, 104 Zahal Street, Kiryat Ono 55000
Tel: +972(3) 5311-888
Fax: +972(3) 5356-120
EMail: info@ono.ac.il
Website: http://www.ono.ac.il/

Chancellor: Moshe Ben Horin
Tel: +972(3) 5311-840 EMail: leas@ono.ac.il

Faculties

Business Administration (Accountancy; Advertising and Publicity; Business Administration; Finance; Human Resources; Marketing; Systems Analysis); **Health Professions** (Communication Disorders; Communication Studies; Occupational Therapy)

Schools

Law (Administrative Law; Civil Law; Commercial Law; Constitutional Law; Fiscal Law; Labour Law; Law; Public Law)

History: Founded 1995 as Israeli Center for Academic Studies. Acquired present title 2004.

Accrediting Agencies: Council for Higher Education

Degrees and Diplomas: *Bachelor's Degree*: Business Administration (BA); Law (LLB); Occupational Therapy; Communications Sciences and Disorders; *Master's Degree*: Business Administration (MBA)

Student Numbers *2009-2010*: Total: c. 8,500

Last Updated: 09/12/11

PERES ACADEMIC CENTER

PO Box 328, Hanevi'im 8, Rehovot 76120
Tel: +972(8) 9390-520
Fax: +972(8) 9390-519

Programmes

Business Administration (Business Administration)

Degrees and Diplomas: *Bachelor's Degree*: Business Administration; Behavioral sciences; *Master's Degree*: Business Administration
Last Updated: 12/02/10

SCHECHTER INSTITUTE OF JEWISH STUDIES

PO Box 16080, 4 Avraham Granot Street, Jerusalem 91160
Tel: +972(2) 747-800-600
Fax: +972(2) 679-0840
EMail: pr@schechter.ac.il
Website: http://www.schechter.edu

President: David Golinkin

Institutes

Jewish Studies (Jewish Studies)

Degrees and Diplomas: *Master's Degree*: Jewish Studies
Last Updated: 12/02/10

SHA'AREI MISHPAT - THE COLLEGE OF LEGAL STUDIES

PO Box 261, Hod Hasharon 45101
Tel: +972(9) 7405-799 +972(9) 7750-337
Fax: +972(9) 7405-782
EMail: info@mishpat.ac.il
Website: http://www.mishpat.ac.il

Programmes

Law

History: Founded 1995.

Accrediting Agencies: Council for Higher Education

Degrees and Diplomas: *Bachelor's Degree*: Law (LLB); *Master's Degree*

THE CENTER FOR ACADEMIC STUDIES: MANAGEMENT-EDUCATION-SOCIETY

Rehov HaYotzrim 2, Or Yehuda
Tel: +972(3) 735-4444
Fax: +972(3) 735-4445
Website: http://www.mla.ac.il

Programmes

Business Administration (Business Administration); **Education** (Education)

Degrees and Diplomas: *Bachelor's Degree*: Business Administration; Psychology; Education; *Master's Degree*: Education; Educational Counseling; Business Administration
Last Updated: 12/02/10

THE INTERDISCIPLINARY CENTER (IDC)

PO Box 167, Kanfei Nesharim Street, Herzliya 46150
Tel: +972(9) 9527-272
Fax: +972(9) 9567-392
EMail: rishum@idc.ac.il
Website: http://www.idc.ac.il

President: Uriel Reichman EMail: president@idc.ac.il

Schools

Business *(Arison)* (Business Administration; Finance; Information Technology; Management; Marketing); **Communications** *(Samy Ofer)* (Communication Arts; Communication Studies); **Computer Science** *(Efi Arazi)* (Computer Science); **Government, Diplomacy and Strategy** *(Lauder)* (Government; International Relations; Political Sciences); **International Studies** *(Raphael Recanati)* (International Studies); **Law** *(Radzyner)* (Law); **Psychology** (Psychology)

Units

English as a Foreign Language (English)

Accrediting Agencies: Council for Higher Education

Degrees and Diplomas: *Bachelor's Degree*: Business Administration; Computer Sciences; Government; Communication; Psychology (BA); Law (LLB); *Master's Degree*: Business Administration (MBA); Computer Science (MSc); Government (MA-pending); Law (LLM)

Student Services: Academic counselling, Sports facilities

Libraries: Marc Rich Library
Last Updated: 09/12/11

Italy

STRUCTURE OF HIGHER EDUCATION SYSTEM

Description:

Higher education is provided by universities, technical universities, university institutes, as well as by a wide range of academies, higher institutes/schools, especially, but not exclusively, in the artistic sector, and by a number of professional training institutions in a variety of fields related to commerce, e-technologies, fashion, industry, etc. Most of the existing university institutions were established directly by the State, while a limited number, originally set up by private entities, were later recognized by the relevant Ministry. At present (2008-2009), the university system includes 95 university institutions.
From 1989 to 1999, the Ministry of Universities and Scientific Research (MURST) was responsible for university education, some sectors of non-university education (interpretation and translation, psychotherapy) and the allocation of funds to the state universities and the private universities that had conformed with the structure of the public sector (i.e. legally-recognized university institutions). The main advisory bodies for university education are the National University Council (CUN), the University Student National Council (CNSU) in which the representatives of the various categories of university staff and students participate, and the Conference of Italian University Rectors (CRUI). In the same decade (1989-99), the supervision and development of primary and secondary education were entrusted to the Ministero della Pubblica Istruzione (MPI) (Ministry of Education), whereas responsibility for the non-university sector of higher education was shared between the Ministry for the National Cultural Heritage (institutions and programmes in conservation and restoration) and MPI (institutions for fine and applied arts, dance, drama, and music, as well as, since 1998-99, all FIS programmes (higher integrated technical education). In 1999, the reform of the artistic sector (drama, dance and music) was entrusted to MURST (Law 508/99). More recently, the new Ministry of Education, Universities and Research (MIUR) was established and all the financial resources, staff and functions of the former MPI and MURST were transferred there. The merging of the two ministries took place in 2001.
Degree programmes are structured in credits (crediti formativi universitari-CFU at universities and crediti formativi accademici-CFA at AFAM institutions). A CFU or CFA corresponds to a minimum of 25 hours of work, time for personal study included. The average annual workload of a full-time student is usually fixed at 60 credits.

Stages of studies:

University level first stage: *First Cycle/Laurea*
Undergraduate studies consist of Corsi di Laurea (CL) (first degree courses) which aim at guaranteeing students an adequate command of general scientific methods and contents as well as specific professional skills. The general access requirement is the Italian school leaving qualification, the Diploma di Superamento dell'Esame di Stato conclusivo dei Corsi di Istruzione Secondaria Superiore. Equivalent foreign qualifications may also be accepted. Admission to individual degree courses may be subject to specific requirements. First degree courses last for three years. The Laurea-L (first degree) is awarded to undergraduates who have obtained 180 credits.

University level second stage: *Second Cycle*
Graduate studies include Corsi di Laurea Specialistica (CLS) and Corsi di Master Universitario di 1° livello (CMU1).
1) CLS provide graduates with an advanced level of education to exercise highly qualified activities in specific areas. Access to CLS is through the Italian first degree (L) or an equivalent foreign degree and the course lasts for two years. The final degree, the Laurea Specialistica- LS (second degree) is awarded to graduates who have obtained a total of 300 credits, including those of the first degree that have been recognized for access to the CLS (maximum 180). The writing of an original dissertation is also compulsory. A limited number of CLS regulated by specific EU directives (in Dentistry, Human Medicine, Veterinary Medicine) share the following features: access is through the Italian school leaving certificate or an equivalent foreign qualification, admission is always subject to an entrance examination; the course lasts for 5 years (6 in Human Medicine).
2) CMU1 consist in advanced scientific courses or higher continuing education studies that are open to holders of a Laurea-L or an equivalent foreign degree. Admission may be subject to additional conditions. The length of the

course is a minimum of one year. The degree of Master Universitario di 1° livello - MU1 (first level university Master's) is awarded to graduates who have obtained at least 60 credits. The latest legal provisions on university education have changed the name of the Laurea Specialistica into "Laurea Magistrale" (LM), the related programme into "Corsi di Laurea Magistrale" (CLM) and "Corsi di Laurea Magistrale a ciclo unico" (CLMu) in Dentistry, Medicine and Veterinary Medicine.

University level third stage: *Third Cycle*
Postgraduate studies include Corsi di Dottorato di Ricerca-CDR (research doctorate programmes), Corsi di Specializzazione-CS (specialization courses) and Corsi di Master Universitario di 2° livello-CMU2 (second level university Master's degree courses).
1) CDR train postgraduates for very advanced scientific research or professional appointments at the highest level: they use suitable teaching methodologies such as updated technologies, study periods abroad, internships in specialized research centres. Access is based on an Italian second degree (LS/LM) or a comparable foreign qualification recognized as suitable and admission is subject to the passing of very competitive examinations. The official length of the programme is a minimum of three years. Students must write an original dissertation to be awarded the Dottorato di Ricerca-DR.
2) CS provide postgraduates with the knowledge and skills required for the practice of highly qualified professions. They may only be established in application of specific Italian laws or EU directives. Access is based on the LS/LM (second degree) or a comparable foreign qualification recognized as suitable. Admission may be subject to additional conditions. Courses last from two to 5/6 years in the health sector.
3) CMUs consist in advanced scientific courses or higher continuing education courses which are open to holders of an LS/LM or a comparable foreign qualification recognized as suitable. Admission may be subject to additional conditions. Studies last for a minimum of one year. The Master Universitario di 2° livello-MU2 is awarded to postgraduates who have obtained a minimum of 60 credits.

Distance higher education:
The Consorzio Nettuno is an official university-business consortiumwhich provides distance higher education. Made up of a number of universities and public companies, it offers open education programmes that mainly lead to the award of DUs. The Consorzio FOR.COM, a non-profit body recognised by MURST (DM 9.10.97) is the result of cooperation between certain Italian and foreign universities. Within its educational offer, it is worth mentioning new 3-year Laurea programmes as well as post-laurem courses (Master's, specialization courses, other advanced programmes). ICON (Italian Culture on the Net) is a consortium made up of 24 Italian universities. The main seat is at the State University of Pisa. Legally established in 1999, ICON aims to promote and disseminate the Italian language, civilization and culture worldwide. At present, it offers a Laurea programme in Italian Language and Culture for Foreigners.
There are also two open universities (decree 17.4.03): Guglielmo Marconi Open University (Università telematica Guglielmo Marconi) and Tel.m.a Open University (Università telematica Tel.m.a)

ADMISSION TO HIGHER EDUCATION

Admission to university-level studies:

Name of secondary school credential required: Diploma dell' Esame di Stato conclusivo dei Corsi di Istruzione Secondaria Superiore

Minimum score/requirement: 60/100

For entry to: All universities (since 1998-99)

Name of secondary school credential required: Maturità

Minimum score/requirement: 36

For entry to: All universities (before 1998-99)

Numerus clausus/restrictions: Some programmes are regulated by a numerus clausus (e.g. Architecture, Dentistry, Medicine, Surgery, Veterinary Medicine) which is determined every year by the Academic Senate of the University. Individual universities may also decide to limit admission according to place availability, facilities and services.

Foreign students admission:

Definition of foreign student: A foreign student is a person who is not a permanent resident of Italy and is enrolled at an Italian higher education institution

Quotas: Yes.

Entrance exam requirements: EU applicants : they are subject to the same conditions as Italians. For admission to degree programmes regulated by numerus clausus they have to pass a selective entrance exam. Non-EU applicants: They are admitted to and enrolled in any degree course according to quotas which vary from one institution and degree programme to the other.

Entry regulations: An entry visa, residence permit and financial guarantee are required.

Language requirements: Good knowledge of Italian. International students must pass an Italian language exam prior to matriculation. Universities organize language courses.

RECOGNITION OF STUDIES

Quality assurance system:

Contents of individual degree courses are determined autonomously by universities. Individual institutions, however, in doing so have to adopt several general requirements fixed at national level in relation to groups (classi) of similar degree programmes. These national requirements may not bind more than 2/3 of each curriculum. Degree programmes which share the same objectives and same fundamental types of teaching/learning activities are organized in groups called classi di appartenenza (classes of degree programmes).

Bodies dealing with recognition:

Centro di Informazione sulla Mobilità e le Equivalenze Accademiche - CIMEA (Information Centre on Academic Mobility and Equivalence)

Deputy Director: Luca Lantero
Viale XXI Aprile, 36
Roma 00162
Tel: +39(06) 8632 1281
Fax: +39(06) 8632 2845
EMail: cimea@fondazionerui.it
WWW: http://www.cimea.it

NATIONAL BODIES

Ministero dell' Istruzione, dell'Università e della Ricerca - MiUR (Ministry of Education, University and Research)

Minister: Franceso Profumo
Piazza Kennedy, 20
Roma 00144
Fax: +39 6 9772 7351
EMail: urp@miur.it
WWW: http://www.miur.it

Consiglio Universitario Nazionale - CUN (National University Council)

President: Andrea Lenzi
Secretary-General: Fabio Naro
Piazzale Kennedy 20
Roma 00144
Tel: +39(06) 9772 7502
Fax: +39(06) 9772 6031
WWW: http://www.cun.it/
Role of national body: Elected body carrying out advisory functions.

Comitato Nazionale di Valutazione del Sistema Universitario (National Committee for the Assessment of the University System)
President: Luigi Biggeri
MiUR
P.le Kennedy, 20
Roma 00144
Tel: +39(06) 9772 6401
Fax: +39(06) 9772 6480
EMail: valuniv@miur.it
WWW: http://www.cnvsu.it/
Role of national body: Fixes the general criteria for the assessment of university activity.

Conferenza dei Rettori delle Università Italiane - CRUI (Italian University Rectors' Conference)
President: Marco Mancini
Palazzo Rondanini
Piazza Rondanini, 48 - I
Roma 00186
Tel: +39(06) 684 411
Fax: +39(06) 6844 1399
EMail: segreteria@crui.it
WWW: http://www.crui.it
Role of national body: Association of the state and private universities, the CRUI investigates and analyzes issues regarding the university system.

Data for academic year: 2006-2007
Source: IAU from Italian NARIC-ENIC, CIMEA de la Fondazione Rui, 2006 (Bodies, 2012)

INSTITUTIONS

PUBLIC INSTITUTIONS

ALDO MORO UNIVERSITY OF BARI

Università degli studi di Bari Aldo Moro
Piazza Umberto I, 1, 70121 Bari
Tel: +39(080) 571-1111
Fax: +39(080) 571-4641
EMail: urp@urp.uniba.it
Website: http://www.uniba.it

Rettore: Corrado Petrocelli
Tel: +39 080 5714271, Fax: +39 080 5714697
EMail: rettore@uniba.it

Direttore Amministrativo: Giorgio de Santis
Tel: +39 080 5714221, Fax: +39 080 5714639
EMail: g.desantis@diramm.uniba.it

Faculties
Agriculture (Agriculture; Food Science; Food Technology; Forestry); **Biotechnology** (Biomedicine; Biotechnology; Pharmacology); **Economics** (Economics; Industrial Management; Marketing; Statistics); **Education** (Education; Primary Education); **Foreign Languages and Literature** (Foreign Languages Education; Literature; Modern Languages); **Humanities and Philosophy** (Archaeology; Art History; Arts and Humanities; Heritage Preservation; History; Literature; Multimedia; Philology; Philosophy; Social Sciences); **Law** (Law); **Mathematics, Physics and Natural Sciences** (Anatomy; Biology; Biotechnology; Chemistry; Computer Science; Earth Sciences; Geology; Mathematics; Pharmacology; Physics); **Medicine and Surgery** (Dental Technology; Dentistry; Medicine; Surgery); **Pharmacy** (Pharmacy); **Political Science** (Political Sciences); **Veterinary Medicine** (Veterinary Science)

Further Information: Also branch in Taranto

History: Founded 1924 with Faculty of Medicine. A State institution enjoying administrative autonomy.

Governing Bodies: Senato Accademico; Consiglio di Amministrazione

Academic Year: November to October

Admission Requirements: Secondary school certificate (classical, scientific or technical high school), or qualification as primary school teacher

Main Language(s) of Instruction: Italian

International Co-operation: Participates in Socrates, Erasmus, and Leonardo da Vinci programmes.

Degrees and Diplomas: *Laurea (triennale)*; *Laurea Magistrale*; *Laurea Specialistica*; *Master di 1° Livello*; *Master di 2° Livello*; *Dottorato di Ricerca*

Student Services: Academic counselling, Canteen, Employment services, Foreign student adviser, Handicapped facilities, Health services, Sports facilities

Student Residential Facilities: Yes

Special Facilities: Archaeology Museum. Cinema. Theatre

Libraries: Libraries of faculties and institutes including Law, c. 120,000 vols; Economics and Commerce, c. 60,000; Humanities and Philosophy, c. 35,000; Agriculture, c. 8,000; Science, c. 18,000; Medicine and Surgery, c. 5,000; Engineering, c. 12,000

Publications: Annals of the Faculty of Agriculture; Annals of the Faculty of Economics and Commerce; Annals of the Faculty of Engineering; Annals of the Faculty of Foreign Languages and Literature; Annals of the Faculty of Humanities and Philosophy; Annals of the Faculty of Law

Last Updated: 20/10/11

AMEDEO AVOGADRO UNIVERSITY OF EASTERN PIEMONTE

Università degli studi del Piemonte Orientale Amedeo Avogadro

Via Duomo 6, 13100 Vercelli, VC
Tel: +39(0161) 261-500
Fax: +39(0161) 210-729
EMail: da@rettorato.unipmn.it
Website: http://www.unipmn.it

Rettore: Paolo Luciano Garbarino
Tel: +39 0161 261 500 EMail: rettore@unipmn.it

Direttore Amministrativo: Pasquale Mastrodomenico
Tel: +39 0161 261550

International Relations: Alberto Cuttica
Tel: +39 0161 261517, Fax: +39 0161 211358
EMail: alberto.cuttica@rettorato.unipmn.it

Faculties

Economics *(Novarra)* (Economics); **Humanities and Philosophy** (Literature; Modern Languages; Philology; Philosophy); **Law** *(Alessandria)* (Law); **Mathematics, Physics, and Natural Sciences** *(Alessandria)* (Mathematics; Natural Sciences; Physics); **Medicine, Surgery and Health Studies** *(Novara)* (Health Sciences; Medicine; Surgery); **Pharmacy** *(Novara)* (Pharmacy); **Political Science** *(Alessandria)* (Political Sciences)

History: Founded 1998.

Governing Bodies: Senato accademico; Consiglio di Amministrazione

Admission Requirements: Secondary school certificate (maturità)

Fees: (Euros): 485-1,453, depending on income

International Co-operation: With universities in Austria, Belgium, Finland, Germany, the Netherlands, Poland, Portugal, Romania, Spain, Sweden, UK, USA

Degrees and Diplomas: *Diploma di Laurea*: Arts and Humanities; Economics; Law; Mathematics, Physics and Natural Sciences; Medicine and Surgery; Pharmacy; Political Sciences, 3 yrs; *Diploma di Specializziazione*: Medicine and Surgery, 4-6 yrs; *Laurea Magistrale*; *Laurea Specialistica*: Law; Mathematics, Physics and Natural Sciences; Political Science, a further 2 yrs; *Laurea Specialistica*: Medicine and Surgery, 6 yrs; *Laurea Specialistica*: Pharmacy, 5 yrs; *Master di 1° Livello*: Arts and Humanities, 1yr; *Master di 1° Livello*: Economics; Law; Political Science, 1 yr; *Master di 2° Livello*: Mathematics, Physics and Natural Sciences; Medicine and Surgery, 2 yrs; *Dottorato di Ricerca*

Student Services: Academic counselling, Cultural centre, Employment services, Foreign student adviser, Handicapped facilities, Language programs, Social counselling, Sports facilities

Student Residential Facilities: Yes

Special Facilities: Humanities Laboratories; Law Laboratories; Medical Laboratories; Scientific Laboratories.

Libraries: Libraries of faculties and departments

Last Updated: 05/10/11

CA' FOSCARI UNIVERSITY OF VENICE

Università Ca' Foscari di Venezia

Dorsoduro 3246, 30123 Venezia
Tel: +39(041) 234-7066
Fax: +39(041) 234-8321
EMail: urp@unive.it; international.networks
Website: http://www.unive.it

Rettore: Carlo Carraro (2009-)
Tel: +39(041) 234-8211 EMail: ccarraro@unive.it; rettore@unive.it

Direttore Administrativo: Alberto Scuttari
Tel: +39(041) 234-8311, Fax: +39(041) 234-8350
EMail: alberto.scuttari@unive.it

International Relations: Mario Magliari, Head, International Relations, a.i.
Tel: +39(041) 234-7560, Fax: +39(041) 234-7576
EMail: mario.magliari@unive.it

Colleges

Ca' Foscari International College (Albanian; Arabic; Armenian; Baltic Languages; Catalan; Chemistry; Chinese; Comparative Politics; Computer Science; Cultural Studies; Czech; Economics; English; Environmental Management; French; German; Greek; Hebrew; Heritage Preservation; Hindi; History; Information Technology; International Business; Italian; Japanese; Korean; Literature; Management; Persian; Philosophy; Polish; Portuguese; Restoration of Works of Art; Romance Languages; Romanian; Russian; Serbocroatian; Slavic Languages; Social and Community Services; Spanish; Swedish; Tibetan; Translation and Interpretation; Turkish; Urdu)

Departments

Asian and North African Studies (Arabic; Armenian; Chinese; Eurasian and North Asian Languages; Foreign Languages Education; Hebrew; Hindi; History of Religion; Japanese; Korean; Linguistics; Persian; Religious Studies; Sanskrit; Tibetan; Translation and Interpretation; Turkish; Urdu; Writing); **Economics** (Econometrics; Economic and Finance Policy; Economic History; Economics; Finance; Human Resources; Industrial and Production Economics; Insurance; International Economics; Labour and Industrial Relations; Marketing); **Environmental Sciences, Informatics, and Statistics** (Chemistry; Computer Science; Earth Sciences; Environmental Studies; Information Management; Information Technology; Laboratory Techniques; Marine Science and Oceanography; Mathematics; Statistics); **Humanities** (Ancient Civilizations; Anthropology; Archaeology; Classical Languages; Comparative Literature; Contemporary History; Geography (Human); History; Library Science; Medieval Studies; Modern History; Prehistory; Religious Art); **Linguistics and Comparative Cultural Studies** (Albanian; Armenian; Baltic Languages; Bulgarian; Catalan; Cultural Studies; Czech; English; Foreign Languages Education; French; German; Greek; Italian; Linguistics; Polish; Portuguese; Romance Languages; Romanian; Russian; Serbocroatian; Slavic Languages; Spanish; Swedish; Translation and Interpretation; Writing); **Management** (Accountancy; Administration; Business and Commerce; Finance; Labour and Industrial Relations; Management); **Molecular Sciences and Nanosystems** (Chemistry; Laboratory Techniques; Materials Engineering; Metallurgical Engineering); **Philosophy and Cultural Heritage** (Heritage Preservation; Philosophy)

Graduate Schools

Ca' Foscari Graduate School (Ancient Civilizations; Archaeology; Art History; Asian Studies; Business and Commerce; Chemistry; Cultural Studies; Economics; Educational Sciences; Environmental Studies; European Union Law; Linguistics; Medieval Studies; Modern History; Modern Languages; North African Studies; Philology; Philosophy)

Schools

Sustainability of Environmental and Tourism Systems (Environmental Studies; Tourism); **Asian Studies and Business Management** (Arabic; Armenian; Asian Studies; Chinese; Hebrew; Hindi; International Studies; Japanese; Management; Marketing; North African Studies; Persian; Turkish); **Ca' Foscari Challenge School** *(CFCS)* (Business Administration; Civil Security; Cultural Studies; Eastern European Studies; Education of the Handicapped; Environmental Management; Ethics; Finance; Foreign Languages Education; Health Administration; House Arts and Environment; Information Management; International Studies; Labour Law; Marketing; Mass Communication; Public Administration; Social Problems; Social Welfare; Sports Management; Tourism; Transport Management; Waste Management); **Ca' Foscari Summer School** *(CFSS)* (Behavioural Sciences; Communication Arts; East Asian Studies; Education of the Handicapped; English; Environmental Studies; Finance; Handicrafts; Journalism; Landscape Architecture; Leadership; Leisure Studies; Management; Marketing; Painting and Drawing; Social Psychology; Theatre; Town Planning; Urban Studies; Writing); **Cultural Production and Conservation of the Cultural Heritage** (Art History; Heritage Preservation; Museum Management; Performing Arts; Restoration of Works of Art); **Economics, Languages, and Entrepreneurship** (Communication Arts; International Business; International Economics; International Studies; Leadership; Management; Translation and Interpretation); **International Relations** (Comparative Politics; International Relations); **Social Work and Public Policies** (Social Policy; Social Work)

History: Founded in 1868 as "Regia Scuola Superiore di Economia e Commercio", the institution acquired the status of University in 1935. It is a national institution financially supported by the Italian Government, and is endowed with administrative autonomy.

Governing Bodies: Rettore; Senato Accademico; Consiglio di Amministrazione

Academic Year: November to October

Admission Requirements: School-leaving qualification conferred on completion of a minimum of 12 years of secondary education.

Fees: (Euro): c. 1,500 per annum.

Main Language(s) of Instruction: Italian, English

International Co-operation: with institutions in Europe, Russian Federation, Northern Africa, USA, Latin America, India, China, Japan, South Corea. Also participates in Erasmus, Erasmus Mundus and Leonardo Programmes.

Degrees and Diplomas: *Laurea (triennale)*; *Laurea Magistrale*: all fields (MA/MSc), 2 yrs; *Master di 1° Livello*: all fields (MU), 1 yr; *Master di 2° Livello*: all fields (MU), 1 yr; *Dottorato di Ricerca*: all fields (PhD), 3 yrs. Also: Advanced training courses and specialising training courses.

Student Services: Academic counselling, Canteen, Cultural centre, Employment services, Foreign student adviser, Foreign Studies Centre, Handicapped facilities, Health services, Language programs, Social counselling, Sports facilities

Student Residential Facilities: Yes

Libraries: 15 Libraries; 994,392 vols; 3,436 periodicals; 5,148 online periodicals.

Publications: Annali di Ca' Foscari, Literary research journal *(biannually)*; Ricerche economiche, Economics research *(quarterly)*

Academic Staff *2010-2011*	TOTAL
FULL-TIME	488
PART-TIME	25
STAFF WITH DOCTORATE	
FULL-TIME	268
Student Numbers *2010-2011*	
All (Foreign Included)	19,397

Last Updated: 20/09/12

EUROPEAN UNIVERSITY INSTITUTE (EUI)

Badia Fiesolana, Via dei Roccettini 9, 50014
San Domenico di Fiesole, FI
Tel: +39(55) 4685 373
Fax: +39(55) 4685 444
Website: http://www.eui.eu

President: Marise Cremona
Tel: +39(55) 4685310, Fax: +39(55) 4685312
EMail: marise.cremona@eui.eu

Secretary General: Pasquale Ferrara
Tel: +39(55) 4685313, Fax: +39(55) 468544
EMail: pasquale.ferrara@eui.eu

Departments

Economics (Economics); **History and Civilization** (History); **Law** (Law); **Political and Social Sciences** (Political Sciences; Social Sciences)

Programmes

Max Weber *(MWP)* (Social Sciences)

Research Centres

Robert Schuman *(RSCAS)* (European Studies)

History: Founded 1976.

Main Language(s) of Instruction: English

Degrees and Diplomas: *Master di 2° Livello*; *Dottorato di Ricerca*

Libraries: Research Library in economics, history, law, political and social sciences

Last Updated: 09/11/12

GABRIELE D'ANNUNZIO UNIVERSITY OF CHIETI AND PESCARA

Università degli studi Gabriele d'Annunzio di Chieti e Pescara

Via dei Vestini 31, 66013 Chieti
Tel: +39(0871) 3551
Fax: +39(0871) 355-6007
EMail: segreteriarettore@unich.it
Website: http://www.unich.it

Rettore: Franco Cuccurullo (1997-)
Tel: +39(0871) 355-6164 EMail: rettore@unich.it

Direttore Amministrativo: Marco Napoleone
Tel: +39(0871) 355-6003, Fax: +39(0871) 552-319
EMail: genman@unich.it

Faculties

Architecture (Architecture; Building Technologies; Design); **Economics** *(Pescara)* (Business Administration; Business and Commerce; Economics; European Union Law); **Educational Sciences** (Educational Sciences); **Foreign Languages and Literature** *(Pescara)* (Literature; Modern Languages; Translation and Interpretation); **Humanities and Philosophy** (Arts and Humanities; Heritage Preservation; Literature; Philosophy; Social Work); **Management** (Management); **Mathematics, Physics, and Natural Sciences** (Earth Sciences; Mathematics; Natural Sciences; Physics); **Medicine and Surgery** (Anaesthesiology; Biomedical Engineering; Cardiology; Criminology; Dentistry; Dermatology; Dietetics; Ergotherapy; Forensic Medicine and Dentistry; Gastroenterology; Gerontology; Gynaecology and Obstetrics; Journalism; Laboratory Techniques; Medicine; Neurological Therapy; Nursing; Oncology; Ophthalmology; Orthodontics; Orthopaedics; Paediatrics; Physical Therapy; Psychiatry and Mental Health; Radiology; Rheumatology; Sports Medicine; Surgery; Urology; Venereology); **Pharmacy** (Pharmacology; Pharmacy); **Psychology** (Psychology); **Social Sciences** (Social Sciences); **Sports** (Sports)

Further Information: Also 26 institutes of the different faculties

History: Founded as a private institution 1961 with the support of various local and municipal authorities. Received State recognition 1965. Under the supervision of the Ministry of Education. Financed by an Inter-provincial Consortium consisting of the local and municipal authorities of Pescara, Chieti, and Teramo.

Governing Bodies: Consiglio di Amministrazione; Senato Accademico

Academic Year: November to October

Admission Requirements: Secondary school certificate (maturità) or foreign equivalent

Main Language(s) of Instruction: Italian

International Co-operation: Participates in the Socrates/Erasmus programme with 18 institutions

Degrees and Diplomas: *Laurea (triennale)*; *Attestato/Diploma di Perfezionamento*; *Diploma di Specializziazione*; *Laurea Magistrale*; *Laurea Specialistica*: Medicine and Surgery, 6 yrs; *Master di 1° Livello*; *Master di 2° Livello*; *Dottorato di Ricerca*

Student Services: Canteen, Sports facilities

Libraries: Yes

Publications: Collections of the Faculties of Medicine

Last Updated: 24/10/11

INTERNATIONAL SCHOOL FOR ADVANCED STUDIES

Scuola internazionale superiore di studi avanzati (SISSA)

via Bonomea, 265, 34136 Trieste
Tel: +39(040) 3787-111
Fax: +39(040) 3787-249
EMail: info@sissa.it
Website: http://www.sissa.it

Direttore: Guido Martinelli
Tel: +39(040) 378-7581, Fax: +39(040) 378-7466
EMail: guido.martinelli@sissa.it

Direttore Amministrativo: Luca Bardi
Tel: +39(040) 378-7201, Fax: +39(040) 378-7429
EMail: luca.bardi@sissa.it

Sections

Astrophysics (Astronomy and Space Science) *Head*: Luigi Danese; **Cognitive Neurosciences** (Neurosciences) *Head*: Mathew Diamond; **Functional Analysis and Applications** (Physics) *Head*: Gianni Dalmaso; **Mathematical Physics** (Mathematical Physics) *Head*: Boris Dubrovin; **Neurobiology** (Biophysics) *Head*: Enrico Cherubini; **Statistical and Biological Physics** *Head*: Paolo Carloni; **Theory of Condensed Matter** (Physics) *Head*: Erio Tosatti; **Theory of Elementary Particles** (Physics) *Head*: Serguey Petcov

History: Founded 1978. A postgraduate institute for teaching and research with complete autonomy concerning its teaching, scientific, administrative and disciplinary activities.

Governing Bodies: Senato Accademico; Consiglio di Amministrazione

Academic Year: November to October

Admission Requirements: Laurea or equivalent, and entrance examination

Main Language(s) of Instruction: English

International Co-operation: With universities in Argentina; Australia; Austria; Belgium; Chile; Croatia; Czech Republic; France; Germany; Hungary; India; Iran; Israel; Japan; Mexico; Poland; Serbia; Slovak Republic; South Africa; Spain; Sweden; Switzerland; United Kingdom; United States

Degrees and Diplomas: *Laurea Magistrale*; *Dottorato di Ricerca (PhD)*: 3-4 yrs

Student Services: Canteen, Handicapped facilities, Health services, Language programs

Libraries: SISSA Library, 20,000 vols; 18,000 bound journals; 300 current print subscriptions; c. 5,000 electronic subscriptions
Last Updated: 04/10/11

ITALIAN INSTITUTE OF HUMANITIES

Istituto italiano di scienze umane (SUM)
Palazzo Strozzi, Piazza degli Strozzi, 50123 Firenze
Tel: +39 055-2673300
Fax: +39 055-2673350
EMail: segreteria@sumitalia.it
Website: http://www.sumitalia.it

Director: Mario Citroni (2010-)

History: Founded 2005. Institute of advanced doctoral studies with a special statute from 2005.

Governing Bodies: Interim Committee

Main Language(s) of Instruction: Italian

Degrees and Diplomas: *Master di 1° Livello*; *Dottorato di Ricerca*. Also post-doctorate courses.

ITALIAN UNIVERSITY LINE (IUL)

Via Michelangela Buonarroti 10, 50122 Firenze
Tel: +39 055 2380504
EMail: info@iuline.it
Website: http://www.iuline.it

Rettore: Michele Corsi EMail: corsi@unimc.it

Faculties

Educational Sciences (Educational Sciences)

History: Founded 2005. Joint collaboration between Indire Institute, University of Milan-Bicocca, University of Florence, University of Lumsa-Rome, University of Macerata, University of Palermo and De Agostini publishers.

Governing Bodies: Governing Council; Board of Directors

Admission Requirements: Diploma dell Esame di Stato following higher secondary education

Main Language(s) of Instruction: Italian

Degrees and Diplomas: *Laurea (triennale)*: 3 yrs; *Master di 1° Livello*: 1 yr
Last Updated: 24/10/11

ITALIAN UNIVERSITY SPORT AND MOVEMENT - ROME

Università degli studi di Roma Foro Italico (IUSM)
Piazzale Lauro De Bosis 15, 00194 Roma
Tel: +39 06-36733501
Fax: +39 06-3613065
EMail: paolo.parisi@uniroma4.it
Website: http://www.uniroma4.it

Rettore: Paolo Parisi Tel: +39 06 36733503

Faculties

Human Movement and Sports Sciences (Health Sciences; Sports)

History: Founded 1958 as Italian Sport Academy.

Main Language(s) of Instruction: Italian

Degrees and Diplomas: *Laurea (triennale)*; *Laurea Magistrale*; *Master di 1° Livello*; *Master di 2° Livello*; *Dottorato di Ricerca*
Last Updated: 21/10/11

IUAV UNIVERSITY OF VENICE

Università IUAV di Venezia (IUAV)
Santa Croce 191, Tolentini, 30135 Venezia
Tel: +39(041) 257-1111
Fax: +39(041) 257-1760
EMail: inforientamento@iuav.it
Website: http://www.iuav.it

Rettore: Amerigo Restucci (2009-)
Tel: +39(041) 522-1119 EMail: rettore@iuav.it

Direttore Amministrativo: Aldo Tommasin
Tel: +39(041) 257-1712, Fax: +39(041) 257-1780
EMail: direttore.amministrativo@iuav.it

Faculties

Architecture (Architecture; Building Technologies; Landscape Architecture; Urban Studies); **Art and Design** (Fashion Design; Industrial Design; Performing Arts; Theatre; Visual Arts); **Town and Regional Planning** (Regional Planning; Town Planning)

History: Founded 1926. Acquired present status and title 2000.

Governing Bodies: Consiglio di Amministrazione; Senato Accademico

Admission Requirements: Secondary school certificate (Maturitá)

Main Language(s) of Instruction: Italian

Degrees and Diplomas: *Laurea (triennale)*; *Laurea Magistrale*; *Laurea Specialistica*: Architecture; History of Architecture; Product Design; Visual and Multimedia Design; Visual Arts, a further 2 yrs; *Master di 1° Livello*: Cultural Studies, 1 yr; *Master di 2° Livello*: Development, Management and Conservation of Industrial Property; Planning and Environmental Policy Evaluation; Town and Regional Planning in Developing Countries, 1 yr following Laurea Specialistica; *Dottorato di Ricerca*: Art; Design; Architectural Composition; History of Architecture; Town Planning; Territorial Public Policy

Student Services: Academic counselling, Canteen, Foreign student adviser, Sports facilities

Student Residential Facilities: Yes

Libraries: Central Library
Last Updated: 24/10/11

MAGNA GRÆCIA UNIVERSITY OF CATANZARO

Università degli studi di Catanzaro Magna Græcia
Viale Europa - Campus di Germaneto, 88100 Catanzaro
Tel: +39 961-709729; 800-453444
EMail: orientamento@unicz.it
Website: http://www.unicz.it

Rettore: Aldo Quattrone
Tel: +39 0961-3694134, Fax: +39 0961-3694112

Direttore Amministrativo: Luigi Grandinetti
Tel: +39 0961-3694146, Fax: +39 0961-3694069
EMail: diramm@unicz.it

Faculties

Law; **Medicine and Surgery** (Medicine; Surgery); **Pharmacy** (Pharmacy)

History: A University already existed in the 19th century, but was abolished in 1923. In 1979, it was founded again as a branch of the University of Reggio Calabria. Officially established in Catanzaro in 1998.

Governing Bodies: Rettore; Consiglio di Ammistrazione; Senato Accademico

Admission Requirements: Secondary school certificate (maturità)

Fees: (Euros): 239,19-751.80 per annum

Main Language(s) of Instruction: Italian

International Co-operation: With universities in Spain; France; Germany; Netherlands; Slovak Republic; Hungary; Albania; Lybia; United Kingdom; United States; Portugal; Austria; Czech Republic

Degrees and Diplomas: *Laurea (triennale)*; *Laurea Magistrale*; *Laurea Specialistica*: Computer Engineering; Biomedical Engineering; Economics; Law; Social Sciences; Biotechnology, 2 yrs; *Laurea Specialistica*: Medicine; Pharmacy; Odonthology; Veterinary Science, 5-6 yrs; *Master di 1° Livello*; *Master di 2° Livello*; *Dottorato di Ricerca*: Medicine; Law; Pharmacy; Biotechnology; Computer Engineering; Biomedical Engineering, 3-4 yrs

Student Services: Academic counselling, Cultural centre, Employment services, Foreign student adviser, Handicapped facilities, Language programs, Sports facilities

Student Residential Facilities: None

Special Facilities: None

Libraries: Yes

Last Updated: 05/10/11

MEDITERRANEAN UNIVERSITY OF REGGIO CALABRIA

Università degli studi Mediterranea di Reggio Calabria
Via Zecca 4, 89125 Reggio di Calabria
Tel: +39 0965-26047
Fax: +39 0965-332201
EMail: amministrazione@pec.unirc.it
Website: http://www.unirc.it

Rettore: Massimo Giovannini (2010-2014)
EMail: massimo.giovannini@unirc.it

Direttore Amministrativo: Antonio Romeo
Tel: +39 0965-3695365, Fax: +39 0965-27901
EMail: diramm@unirc.it

Faculties

Agriculture (Agriculture; Agronomy; Environmental Studies; Forestry); **Architecture** (Architecture; Heritage Preservation; Town Planning); **Engineering** (Civil Engineering; Electronic Engineering; Environmental Engineering; Structural Architecture; Telecommunications Engineering); **Law** (Administrative Law; Civil Law; Law)

History: Founded 1982.

Governing Bodies: Senato Accademico; Consiglio di Amministrazione

Academic Year: November to October

Admission Requirements: Secondary school certificate (maturità)

Main Language(s) of Instruction: Italian

International Co-operation: Participates in the Erasmus, Comett and Tempus programmes

Degrees and Diplomas: *Laurea (triennale)*; *Laurea Magistrale*; *Laurea Specialistica*: Engineering; Architecture and Planning; Agriculture; Law, a further 2 yrs; *Master di 1° Livello*; *Master di 2° Livello*; *Dottorato di Ricerca*

Student Services: Sports facilities

Libraries: Yes

Last Updated: 24/10/11

PARTHENOPE UNIVERSITY OF NAPLES

Università degli studi di Napoli Parthenope
Via Ammiraglio Acton 38, 80133 Napoli
Tel: +39(081) 547-5111
Fax: +39(081) 552-1485
EMail: direzione.amministrativa@uniparthenope.it
Website: http://www.uniparthenope.it

Rettore: Claudio Quintano (2010-)
Tel: +39(081) 547-5327, Fax: +39(081) 547-5329
EMail: rettore@uniparthenope.it

Direttore Amministrativo: Livia Mauro

Faculties

Economics (Business Administration; Business and Commerce; Economics; Marketing; Tourism; Transport Economics); **Engineering** (Civil Engineering; Environmental Engineering; Industrial Engineering; Telecommunications Engineering); **Law** (Administration; Law); **Science and Technology** (Computer Science; Environmental Studies; Marine Science and Oceanography; Meteorology); **Sports Science** (Sports; Sports Management)

History: Founded 1920 as Istituto Universitario Navale. Acquired present name 2001.

Governing Bodies: Senato Accademico; Consiglio Di Amministrazione

Academic Year: November-October

Admission Requirements: Diploma di scuola Media Superiore

Fees: Tuition fee is dependent on family's income.

Main Language(s) of Instruction: Italian

International Co-operation: With universities in France, Spain, Germany, Belgium, Austria.

Accrediting Agencies: Erasmus Agency

Degrees and Diplomas: *Diploma di Laurea*: Administration and Control; Administration Sciences; Business Economy; Commercial Economy; Informatics; Law; Logistics and Transportation; Management of the International Enterprises; Management of the-Tourist Enterprises; Motor Sciences; Nautical Sciences; Oceanography and Meteorology; Statistics and Computer Science for the Management of the Enterprises; Telecommunication Engineering; Weather and Territory Based Engineering; Weather Sciences, 3 yrs; *Diploma di Specializziazione*: Secondary Education, 2 yrs; *Laurea Specialistica*: International Business; Management; Science for Preventive and Adaptive Engines; Statistics for Business; Telecommunication Engineering, a further 2 yrs; *Master di 1° Livello*: Auditing and Administrative Management; Computer Systems Management for Enterprises; Economy and Business Management for the Human Development; Management of Innovation of the Tourist Services; Organization and Scholastic Direction of the Institution, 1 yr; *Master di 2° Livello*; *Dottorato di Ricerca*: Economic-Business Doctrines and Government for Enterprises; Economics; Economics of Food Resources; Statistics Applied to the Territory, 3 yrs

Student Services: Canteen, Handicapped facilities, Sports facilities

Publications: Annali della Facoltà di Scienze e Tecnologie, Scientific journal of faculty *(annually)*

Last Updated: 23/03/11

POLYTECHNIC OF TURIN

Politecnico di Torino (POLITO)
Corso Duca degli Abruzzi 24, 10129 TO Torino
Tel: +39(011) 564-6155
Fax: +39(011) 564-6160
EMail: international.relations@polito.it
Website: http://www.polito.it

Rettore: Francesco Profumo (2005-)
Tel: +39(011) 564-6300, Fax: +39(011) 564-6399
EMail: rettore@polito.it

Direttore Amministrativo: Maria Schiavone
Tel: +39(011) 564-6183 EMail: sda@polito.it

Faculties

Architecture I (Architecture; Graphic Design; Industrial Design); **Architecture II** (Architectural Restoration; Architecture; Art History; Landscape Architecture; Town Planning); **Engineering I** *(Mondovì,*

Biella, Alessandria) (Aeronautical and Aerospace Engineering; Biomedical Engineering; Chemical Engineering; Civil Engineering; Construction Engineering; Electrical Engineering; Energy Engineering; Engineering; Environmental Engineering; Management Systems; Materials Engineering; Mechanical Engineering; Nuclear Engineering); **Engineering III - Information Technology** *(Aosta, Modovì, Ivrea)* (Information Technology); **Engineering IV** (Economics; Industrial Engineering; Management)

Graduate Schools

Civil Engineering and Architecture *Director*: Mario Rasetti

History: Founded 1859 as School of Engineering, became Politecnico 1906. A public university enjoying administrative autonomy. Financially supported by the State and other regional bodies and self-funding.

Governing Bodies: Consiglio di Amministrazione; Senato Accademico

Academic Year: October to September (October-February; March-September)

Admission Requirements: Secondary school certificate (Esame di Maturità) or recognized foreign equivalent

Fees: (Euros): Undergraduate students, c. 1,500

Main Language(s) of Instruction: Italian

International Co-operation: With universities in France, other European Union countries, Mediterranean Area and Latin America. Also participates in the Socrates programme

Accrediting Agencies: Ministero dell'Istruzione, dell'Università e della Ricera (Comitato per la Valutazione del Sistema Universitario)

Degrees and Diplomas: *Laurea (triennale)*; *Laurea Magistrale*; *Laurea Specialistica*: Architecture; Engineering, a further 2 yrs; *Master di 1° Livello*: Architecture; Engineering, a further yr following Laurea; *Master di 2° Livello*: Architecture; Engineering, a further yr following Laurea Specialistica; *Dottorato di Ricerca*: Architecture; Engineering, 3 yrs

Student Services: Academic counselling, Canteen, Cultural centre, Employment services, Foreign student adviser, Foreign Studies Centre, Handicapped facilities, Health services, Language programs, Sports facilities

Student Residential Facilities: Yes

Libraries: 4 general libraries and 16 sector libraries: total, 268,320 vols

Last Updated: 03/10/11

POLYTECHNIC UNIVERSITY OF THE MARCHES

Università politecnica delle Marche

Piazza Roma 22, 60121 Ancona
Tel: +39(071) 2201
Fax: +39(071) 220-2324
EMail: relazioni.esterne@univpm.it
Website: http://www.univpm.it

Rettore: Marco Pacetti
Tel: +39(071) 220-2212, Fax: +39(071) 220-2213
EMail: rettore@univpm.it

Direttore Amministrativo: Luisiana Sebastianelli
EMail: luisiana.sebastianelli@univpm.it

Faculties

Agriculture (Agriculture; Environmental Studies; Food Science; Food Technology; Forestry; Oenology; Viticulture); **Economics** (Business Administration; Business Education; Economics; Finance; Social and Community Services); **Engineering** (Architecture; Automation and Control Engineering; Biomedical Engineering; Building Technologies; Civil Engineering; Electronic Engineering; Engineering; Engineering Management; Industrial Engineering; Landscape Architecture; Mechanical Engineering; Telecommunications Engineering); **Medicine and Surgery** (Gynaecology and Obstetrics; Laboratory Techniques; Medicine; Nursing; Orthodontics; Radiology; Surgery); **Science** (Biology; Biotechnology; Environmental Studies; Marine Biology)

Further Information: Also Italian courses for foreign students (October-June)

History: Founded 1969 as a private University, became a State institution (Università degli Studi di Ancona) enjoying administrative autonomy 1970. Acquired present title 2003.

Governing Bodies: Senato Accademico; Consiglio di Amministrazione

Academic Year: November to October

Admission Requirements: Secondary school certificate (maturità)

Main Language(s) of Instruction: Italian

Degrees and Diplomas: *Laurea (triennale)*; *Diploma di Specializziazione*; *Diploma di Specializziazione*; *Laurea Magistrale*; *Laurea Specialistica*; *Master di 1° Livello*: 1-2 yrs; *Master di 2° Livello*: 1-2 yrs; *Dottorato di Ricerca*: 3 yrs

Student Services: Academic counselling, Employment services, Foreign Studies Centre, Handicapped facilities, Language programs, Sports facilities

Libraries: Faculty Libraries

Last Updated: 24/10/11

SAINT ANNA SCHOOL OF ADVANCED STUDIES OF PISA

Scuola Superiore S. Anna di studi universitari e di perfezionamento

Piazza Martiri della Libertà 33, 56127 Pisa
Tel: +39 050 883111
Fax: +39 050 883296
EMail: diramm@sssup.it
Website: http://www.sssup.it/

Direttore: Maria Chiara Carrozza
Tel: +39 050-883305, Fax: +39 050-883296
EMail: chiara.carrozza@sssup.it

Direttore Amministrativo: David Vannozzi
Tel: +39 050-883370, Fax: +39 050-883212

Departments

Experimental and Applied Sciences (Agriculture; Engineering; Medicine; Natural Sciences) *Dean*: Enrico Bonari; **Social Sciences** (Economics; Law; Management; Political Sciences; Social Sciences) *Dean*: Fabrizio Bulckaen

History: Founded 1987.

Governing Bodies: Senato Accademico; Consiglio di Amministrazione

Academic Year: November to October

Admission Requirements: Competitive entrance examination following secondary school certificate (maturità)

Main Language(s) of Instruction: Italian

Degrees and Diplomas: *Laurea Magistrale*; *Laurea Specialistica*: 3 yrs; *Master di 1° Livello*; *Master di 2° Livello*; *Dottorato di Ricerca*: 3 yrs

Student Services: Canteen, Cultural centre, Employment services, Foreign student adviser, Handicapped facilities, Language programs, Sports facilities

Student Residential Facilities: Yes

Libraries: Central Library

Last Updated: 05/10/11

SECOND UNIVERSITY OF NAPLES

Seconda Università degli Studi di Napoli

Viale Beneduce 10, 80138 Caserta
Tel: +39 0823-329988
Fax: +39 0823-327589
EMail: rettoratoce@unina2.it
Website: http://www.unina2.it/

Rettore: Francesco Rossi
Tel: +39 0823-274901, Fax: +39 0823-327589

Direttore Amministrativo: Vincenzo Lanza
Tel: +39 0815-666457, Fax: +39 0815-666456
EMail: uffservgen@unina2.it

Faculties

Architecture *(Aversa)* (Architecture; Fashion Design; Industrial Design); **Economics** *(Capua)* (Business and Commerce; Economics; Finance; International Studies; Management; Marketing; Tourism); **Engineering** *(Aversa)* (Aeronautical and Aerospace Engineering; Civil Engineering; Computer Engineering; Electronic Engineering; Engineering; Environmental Engineering; Mechanical Engineering); **Law** *(Santa Maria Capua Vetere)* (International Relations; Law); **Letters and Philosophy** *(Santa Maria Capua Vetere)* (Archaeology; Art History; Arts and Humanities; Literature; Restoration of Works of Art; Tourism); **Mathematical, Physical, and Natural Sciences** *(Caserta)* (Biology; Mathematics; Natural Sciences; Physics); **Medicine and Surgery** *(Caserta)* (Biotechnology; Dentistry; Medicine; Nursing; Orthopaedics; Physical Therapy; Podiatry; Surgery); **Pharmacy for the Environment and Health** *(Caserta)* (Biotechnology; Environmental Studies; Pharmacy); **Political Science and Advanced European and Mediterranean Studies** *(Jean Monnet)* (European Studies; Mediterranean Studies; Political Sciences); **Psychology** *(Caserta)* (Psychology)

Research Centres

Computer Science and Biotechnology *(CRISCEB)* (Biotechnology; Computer Science); **Human Rights** *(CIRDUA, Santa Maria Capua Vetere)* (Human Rights)

Further Information: Also Policlinico

History: Founded 1992 to decongest the University of Naples "Federico II".

Governing Bodies: Consiglio di Amministrazione; Senato Accademico; Collegio dei Revisori dei Conti

Academic Year: November to October (November-February; February-October)

Admission Requirements: Secondary school certificate (maturità)

Fees: (Euros): 250-650 per annum, according to parents' income

Main Language(s) of Instruction: Italian

International Co-operation: With universities in Europe

Degrees and Diplomas: *Laurea (triennale)*; *Laurea Magistrale*; *Master di 1° Livello*; *Master di 2° Livello*; *Dottorato di Ricerca*: 3-4 yrs

Student Services: Academic counselling, Employment services, Handicapped facilities, Health services, Sports facilities

Special Facilities: Anatomy Museum

Libraries: Faculty Libraries

Publications: Scientific Activities *(annually)*

Last Updated: 05/10/11

SUOR ORSOLA BENINCASA UNIVERSITY

Università degli studi Suor Orsola Benincasa

via Santa Caterina da Siena, 37, 80135 Napoli

Tel: +39 081-2522$,570; 081-2522111

Fax: +39 081-421363

EMail: sc.form@unisob.na.it

Website: http://www.unisob.na.it

Rettore: Lucio d'Alessandro

Administrative Officer: Antonio Cunzio

Faculties

Arts and Humanities (Ancient Civilizations; Archaeology; Art History; Cultural Studies; Heritage Preservation; Medieval Studies; Modern Languages; Restoration of Works of Art); **Educational Sciences** (Educational Sciences; Social and Community Services; Teacher Training); **Law** (Law)

History: Founded 1891, acquired present status 1901.

Main Language(s) of Instruction: Italian

Degrees and Diplomas: *Laurea (triennale)*; *Diploma di Specializziazione*; *Diploma di Specializziazione*: Art History; *Laurea Magistrale*; *Master di 1° Livello*; *Master di 2° Livello*; *Dottorato di Ricerca*

Student Services: Academic counselling, Language programs, Social counselling

Special Facilities: Archaeological Laboratories; Botanical Laboratories; Multimedia Laboratories.

Libraries: c. 130.000 vols

Last Updated: 24/10/11

TEACHER TRAINING SCHOOL OF PISA

Scuola normale superiore di Pisa

Piazza dei Cavalieri 7, 56126 Pisa

Tel: +39 050-509111

Fax: +39 050-563513

EMail: d.lalli@sns.it

Website: http://www.sns.it

Direttore: Fabio Beltram (2010-)
Tel: +39 050-509215, Fax: +39 050-509101
EMail: direttore@sns.it

Faculties

Arts (Ancient Civilizations; Archaeology; Art History; Arts and Humanities; History; Linguistics; Literature; Paleontology; Philosophy); **Science** (Biological and Life Sciences; Biology; Chemistry; Mathematics; Natural Sciences; Physics)

History: Founded 1813.

Admission Requirements: Competitive exams

Main Language(s) of Instruction: Italian

Degrees and Diplomas: *Dottorato di Ricerca*

Libraries: c. 500,000 vols

Last Updated: 05/10/11

TECHNICAL UNIVERSITY OF BARI

Politecnico di Bari

Via Amendola 126/B, 70126 Bari

Tel: +39(080) 596-2111

Fax: +39(080) 596-2510

EMail: diramm@poliba.it

Website: http://www.poliba.it

Rettore: Nicola Costantino
Tel: +39(080) 596-2508 EMail: rettore@poliba.it

Direttore Amministrativo: Antonino Di Guardo

Faculties

Architecture (Architecture; Industrial Design); **Engineering** (Construction Engineering; Electrical and Electronic Engineering; Hydraulic Engineering; Mathematics; Physics; Road Engineering); **Engineering** *(Taranto)* (Civil Engineering; Environmental Engineering; Industrial Engineering)

History: Founded 1990.

Main Language(s) of Instruction: Italian

Degrees and Diplomas: *Laurea (triennale)*; *Diploma di Specializzazione*; *Laurea Magistrale*; *Laurea Specialistica*

Last Updated: 03/10/11

TECHNICAL UNIVERSITY OF MILAN

Politecnico di Milano

Piazza Leonardo da Vinci 32, 20133 Milano

Tel: +39 02-23991

Fax: +39 02-23992206

EMail: cri.relint@polimi.it

Website: http://www.polimi.it

Rettore: Giovanni Azzone
Tel: +39 02-23994359, Fax: +39 02-23994205
EMail: giovanni.azzone@polimi.it

Schools

Architecture and Society (Architectural and Environmental Design; Architecture; Regional Planning; Town Planning); **Civil Architecture** (Architecture; Structural Architecture); **Civil, Environmental and Territorial Engineering** (Civil Engineering; Engineering; Environmental Engineering; Regional Planning); **Engineering/Architecture** (Architecture; Building Technologies; Construction Engineering; Engineering; Structural Architecture); **Industrial Engineering** (Aeronautical and Aerospace Engineering; Energy Engineering; Engineering; Mechanical Engineering; Transport Engineering); **Industrial Processing Engineering** (Chemical Engineering; Electrical Engineering; Engineering; Materials Engineering; Nanotechnology); **Information Engineering** (Automation and Control Engineering; Computer Engineering; Electronic Engineering; Engineering; Information Technology; Telecommunications Engineering); **Systems Engineering** (Biomedical Engineering;

Management; Mathematics; Physical Engineering; Production Engineering)

History: Founded 1863 as Reale Istituto Tecnico Superiore. Acquired present status and title 1934.

Governing Bodies: Consiglio di Amministrazione; Senato Accademico

Academic Year: September to June (September-January; March-June)

Admission Requirements: Secondary school certificate (maturità) or foreign equivalent

Fees: (Euros): 130-1,680 per annum according to family income

Main Language(s) of Instruction: Italian, English

International Co-operation: Participates in Socrates and Erasmus programmes. Also cooperation agreements with universities outside the European Union

Degrees and Diplomas: *Laurea (triennale)*; *Laurea Magistrale*; *Laurea Specialistica*: a further 2 yrs; *Master di 1° Livello*; *Master di 2° Livello*; *Dottorato di Ricerca*: a further 3 yrs

Student Services: Academic counselling, Canteen, Employment services, Foreign student adviser, Foreign Studies Centre, Handicapped facilities, Language programs, Sports facilities

Student Residential Facilities: Yes

Libraries: Engineering, 170,000 vols; Architecture, 35,700 vols; Libraries of the Institutes, 239,250 vols

Last Updated: 03/10/11

UNITELMA SAPIENZA UNIVERSITY

Università telematica UNITELMA SAPIENZA (UNITELMA)

Via di Santa Caterina da Siena n°57, 00186 Roma
Tel: +39(06) 6919-0797
Fax: +39(06) 679-2048
EMail: segreteriastudenti@unitelma.it
Website: http://www.unitelma.it

Rettore: Aniello Cimitile EMail: aniello.cimitile@unitelma.it

Faculties

Economics (Economics); **Law** (Law)

History: Founded 2004.

Main Language(s) of Instruction: Italian

Degrees and Diplomas: *Laurea (triennale)*; *Laurea Specialistica*; *Master di 1° Livello*; *Master di 2° Livello*

Last Updated: 24/10/11

UNIVERSITY FOR FOREIGNERS - PERUGIA

Università per stranieri di Perugia

Palazzo Gallenga, Piazza Fortebraccio 4, 06122 Perugia
Tel: +39(075) 574-61
Fax: +39(075) 573-2014
EMail: orientam@unistrapg.it
Website: http://www.unistrapg.it

Rettore: Stefania Giannini
Tel: +39(075) 574-6240, Fax: +39(075) 573-0901
EMail: rettore@unistrapg.it

Direttore Amministrativo: Antonella Bianconi
Tel: +39 075 5746215, Fax: +39 075 5732014
EMail: diramm@unistrapg.it

Centres

MERIDIUM (Mediterranean Studies)

Faculties

Italian Language and Culture (Advertising and Publicity; International Studies; Italian)

Research Centres

Water Resources and Documentation Centre *(Warredoc)* (Water Science)

History: Founded 1925.

Governing Bodies: Consiglio di Amministrazione, comprising 23 members; Senato Accademico, comprising 19 members

Academic Year: October to September

Admission Requirements: Secondary school certificate (maturità) or equivalent

Main Language(s) of Instruction: Italian

International Co-operation: Participates in the Socrates/Erasmus, Tempus-Phare, Tempus-Tacis, Progetto Lingua Italiana programmes

Degrees and Diplomas: *Laurea (triennale)*; *Laurea Magistrale*; *Master di 1° Livello*; *Master di 2° Livello*; *Dottorato di Ricerca*

Student Services: Canteen, Cultural centre, Foreign student adviser, Health services, Social counselling, Sports facilities

Student Residential Facilities: Yes

Special Facilities: Museums. Theatres. Cinemas

Libraries:c. 80,000 vols

Press or Publishing House: Guerra-Edizioni

Last Updated: 24/10/11

UNIVERSITY FOR FOREIGNERS - SIENA

Università per stranieri di Siena (USS)

Via Pantaneto 45, 53100 Siena, Si
Tel: +39(0577) 240-115
Fax: +39(0577) 270-630
EMail: info@unistrasi.it
Website: http://www.unistrasi.it

Rettore: Massimo Vedovelli
Tel: +39 0577 240162/163, Fax: +39 0577 270630
EMail: rettore@unistrasi.it

Direttore Amministrativo: Alessandro Balducci
Tel: +39 0577 240170, Fax: +39 0577 281030
EMail: aagg@unistrasi.it

Departments

Humanities (Arts and Humanities; Comparative Literature; Linguistics; Literature; Native Language)

Faculties

Italian Language and Culture (Foreign Languages Education; Italian; Linguistics; Literature; Native Language)

History: Founded 1917. Aims to spread knowledge of the Italian language and culture. It offers courses for both students and teachers.

Governing Bodies: Academic Board; Managing Board

Academic Year: October to June (October-January; March-June)

Admission Requirements: Secondary school certificate (maturità)

Main Language(s) of Instruction: Italian

International Co-operation: With universities in United Kingdom, France, Germany, Spain, Belgium, Finland and Greece.

Degrees and Diplomas: *Laurea (triennale)*; *Diploma di Specializziazione*: Teaching italian as a Foreign Language, 2 yrs; *Laurea Magistrale*; *Laurea Specialistica*: Textual Competence for Publishing; Linguistic Sciences for International Communication, 2 yrs; *Master di 1° Livello*; *Master di 2° Livello*; *Dottorato di Ricerca*

Student Services: Canteen, Foreign Studies Centre, Language programs, Sports facilities

Student Residential Facilities: For c. 1,000 students

Special Facilities: Multimedia Room. Movie Studio. Language Laboratories. Film Collection

Libraries: Central Library

Publications: Si&Na, (Studies of Linguistics and Didactics)

Last Updated: 24/10/11

UNIVERSITY OF BASILICATA

Università degli studi della Basilicata

Via Nazario Sauro 85, 85100 Potenza
Tel: +39(0971) 201-111
Fax: +39(0971) 202-110
EMail: cisit@unibas.it
Website: http://www.unibas.it

Rettore: Mauro Fiorentino
Tel: +39 0971 202106-3, Fax: +39 0971 202102
EMail: rettore@unibas.it

Direttore Amministrativo: Lorenzo Bochicchio
Tel: +39 0971 202107, Fax: +39 0971 202110
EMail: direzione@unibas.it

Faculties

Agriculture (Agricultural Management; Agriculture; Animal Husbandry; Crop Production; Food Science; Forestry; Oenology); **Architecture** (Architecture); **Arts and Philosophy** (Archaeology; Arts and Humanities; Literature; Modern Languages; Philosophy; Primary Education); **Economics** (Business Administration; Commercial Law; Economics; Private Law); **Engineering** (Civil Engineering; Electronic Engineering; Engineering; Environmental Engineering; Mechanical Engineering); **Mathematics, Physics and Natural Sciences** (Biotechnology; Chemistry; Geology; Mathematics; Natural Sciences; Physics); **Pharmacy** (Pharmacy); **Teacher Training** (Teacher Training)

History: Founded 1982.

Governing Bodies: Senato Accademico

Academic Year: October to June

Admission Requirements: Secondary school certificate

Main Language(s) of Instruction: Italian

International Co-operation: With universities in Belgium, Germany, Greece, Spain, France, Austria, Portugal, Sweden, Czech Republic, Hungary, Poland and Romania.

Degrees and Diplomas: *Diploma di Laurea*: Agricultural Management; Animal Husbandry; Arts and Humanities; Chemistry; Communication Arts; Computer Science; Food Technology; Forestry; Environmental Studies; Geology; Mathematics; Modern Languages; Cultural Studies, 3 yrs; *Diploma di Specializziazione*; *Laurea Specialistica*; *Laurea Specialistica*: Civil Engineering; Mechanical Engineering; Engineering Management, 5 yrs; *Dottorato di Ricerca*

Student Services: Cultural centre, Foreign student adviser, Handicapped facilities, Sports facilities

Student Residential Facilities: Yes

Libraries: 70,000 vols

Publications: Annali della Facoltà di Lettere e Filosifia *(annually)*

Last Updated: 20/10/11

UNIVERSITY OF BERGAMO

Università degli studi di Bergamo
Via Salvecchio 19, 24129 Bergamo
Tel: +39(035) 205-2111
Fax: +39(035) 243-054
EMail: relint@unibg.it
Website: http://www.unibg.it

Rettore: Stefano Paleari (2009-)
Tel: +39(035) 205-2226, Fax: +39(035) 243-054
EMail: rettore@unibg.it

Direttore Amministrativo: Giuseppe Giovanelli
Tel: +39(035) 205-2610, Fax: +39(035) 2052-862
EMail: direttore.amministrativo@unibg.it

International Relations: Paola Riva
Tel: +39(035) 205-2830, Fax: +39(035) 2052-838
EMail: paola.riva@unibg.it

Faculties

Economics and Business Administration (Banking; Business Administration; Business and Commerce; Business Computing; Commercial Law; Economics; International Business); **Educational Studies** (Arts and Humanities; Behavioural Sciences; Clinical Psychology; Educational Psychology; Educational Sciences; Literature; Museum Studies; Pedagogy; Psychology; Sociology; Special Education); **Engineering** *(Dalmine)* (Computer Science; Construction Engineering; Engineering; Management; Mechanical Engineering; Textile Technology; Transport Management); **Foreign Languages and Literature** (Educational Sciences; Heritage Preservation; Literature; Mass Communication; Modern Languages; Tourism); **Human Sciences** (Aesthetics; Ancient Civilizations; Anthropology; Art History; Arts and Humanities; Cinema and Television; Comparative Literature; Cultural Studies; Development Studies; English; French; Geography (Human); German; History; Human Rights; Latin; Latin American Studies; Library Science; Linguistics; Literature; Music; Performing Arts; Philology; Religion; Spanish; Theatre; Visual Arts); **Law** (Law)

History: Founded 1968. Acquired present status 1990.

Main Language(s) of Instruction: Italian

International Co-operation: Participates in Erasmus and Leonardo

Degrees and Diplomas: *Laurea (triennale)*; *Laurea Magistrale*; *Laurea Specialistica*: Economics; Law; Pedagogy; Translation and Interpretation; *Master di 1° Livello*; *Master di 2° Livello*: Anthropology; E-Business; Writing; Management; Finance; Energy Engineering; *Dottorato di Ricerca*

Student Services: Academic counselling, Canteen, Employment services, Foreign student adviser, Language programs, Sports facilities

Libraries: 200,000 vols

Last Updated: 20/10/11

UNIVERSITY OF BOLOGNA

Università di Bologna
Via Zamboni 33, 40126 Bologna
Tel: +39(051) 209-9111
Fax: +39(051) 209-9779
Website: http://www.unibo.it

Rettore: Ivano Dionigi (2009-)
Tel: +39(051) 209-9942 EMail: segrettore@unibo.it

Direttore Amministrativo: Giuseppe Colpani
Tel: +39(051) 209-9934, Fax: +39(051) 209-9268
EMail: segdamm@unibo.it

International Relations: Carla Salvaterra, Vice Rector for International Relations
Tel: +39(051) 209-9960 EMail: prorettore.salvaterra@unibo.it

Faculties

Agriculture (Agriculture; Agronomy; Animal Husbandry; Biotechnology; Food Technology; Forest Products; Forestry; Oenology; Plant and Crop Protection; Viticulture; Zoology); **Architecture** *(Aldo Rossi)* (Architecture); **Economics** *(Rimini)* (Business and Commerce; Economics); **Economics** (Actuarial Science; Business Administration; Business and Commerce; Economics; Tourism); **Economics** *(Forlì Campus)* (Business and Commerce; Economics); **Education** (Education; Education of the Handicapped; Educational Sciences; Teacher Training); **Engineering** *(Cesana Campus)* (Automation and Control Engineering; Chemical Engineering; Civil Engineering; Computer Engineering; Electrical Engineering; Electronic Engineering; Energy Engineering; Environmental Engineering; Mechanical Engineering; Telecommunications Engineering); **Engineering** (Aeronautical and Aerospace Engineering; Biomedical Engineering; Chemical Engineering; Civil Engineering; Computer Science; Construction Engineering; Electrical Engineering; Electronic Engineering; Environmental Engineering; Management Systems; Mechanical Engineering; Nuclear Engineering; Telecommunications Engineering); **Foreign Languages and Literature** (Literature; Modern Languages); **Humanities and Philosophy** (Archaeology; Arts and Humanities; Communication Studies; Fashion Design; Fine Arts; Greek; History; Journalism; Latin; Literature; Music; Performing Arts; Philosophy); **Industrial Chemistry** (Analytical Chemistry; Industrial Chemistry; Inorganic Chemistry; Organic Chemistry; Physical Chemistry); **Law** (Canon Law; Civil Law; Commercial Law; Criminal Law; European Union Law; Fiscal Law; History of Law; International Law; Islamic Law; Labour Law; Law; Public Administration); **Mathematics, Physics, and Natural Sciences** (Analytical Chemistry; Astronomy and Space Science; Biology; Biotechnology; Chemistry; Computer Science; Environmental Studies; Geology; Information Sciences; Mathematics; Natural Sciences; Nautical Science; Physics); **Medicine and Surgery** (Biotechnology; Cardiology; Dental Hygiene; Dentistry; Dermatology; Endocrinology; Forensic Medicine and Dentistry; Gastroenterology; Gerontology; Gynaecology and Obstetrics; Hygiene; Laboratory Techniques; Medicine; Microbiology; Neurology; Nursing; Ophthalmology; Orthopaedics; Paediatrics; Physical Therapy; Podiatry; Psychiatry and Mental Health; Rheumatology; Sports Medicine; Surgery; Urology; Venereology; Virology); **Pharmacy** (Biotechnology; Cosmetology; Food Technology; Pharmacology; Pharmacy; Toxicology); **Political Science** *(Roberto Ruffilli)* (Criminology; Eastern European Studies; International Relations; Political Sciences); **Political Science** (Human Rights; International Relations; International Studies; Labour and Industrial Relations; Political Sciences; Social Policy); **Preservation of Cultural Heritage** *(Ravenna*

Campus) (Heritage Preservation); **Psychology** (Psychology); **Sports Science** (Sports); **Statistics** (Business Computing; Demography and Population; Public Administration; Statistics); **Veterinary Medicine** (Animal Husbandry; Biotechnology; Veterinary Science)

Schools

Modern Languages for Interpreters and Translators

Further Information: Also 10 postgraduate schools and courses of the different Faculties. Sede in Buenos Aires (Argentina)

History: Founded 11th century with Faculties of Law and Arts. Faculty of Science developed 17th century. Acquired present status 1802. A State Institution enjoying administrative autonomy. Financially supported by the State and by other bodies.

Governing Bodies: Consiglio di Amministrazione; Senato Accademico; Giunta di Ateneo

Academic Year: October to September

Admission Requirements: Secondary school certificate (maturità) or recognized foreign equivalent

Main Language(s) of Instruction: Italian; some international courses taught in English

International Co-operation: Participation in EU programmes: LLP-Erasmus (students and academic staff mobility with almost all of European countries); Erasmus Mundus; EMECW; Atlantis Eu-U.S:, Eu-Canada; Alfa; TempusIV; Eu-Australia,Japan and New Zeland; Agreements of Cooperation and Overseas programmes (for students and staff mobility) with countries all over the world: Argentina, Australia, Brazil, Canada, China, Colombia, India, Iran, Japan, Mexico; Lybia, Mali, New Zeland, Russia, Sudan, Taiwan, Puerto Rico, Peru, Tunisia, Tanzania, Ukraina, USA, Uruguay.

Degrees and Diplomas: *Laurea (triennale)*; *Diploma di Specializziazione*; *Laurea Magistrale*: 2 yrs; *Laurea Specialistica*: Architecture; Dentistry; Pharmacy; Veterinary Medicine, 5 yrs; *Laurea Specialistica*: Surgery, 6 yrs; *Master di 1° Livello*; *Master di 2° Livello*; *Dottorato di Ricerca*: all fields (PhD). Also Vocational Master courses (after Bachelor) in Business Administration; Computer Science; Arts; Restoration; Museum Studies; Food Sciences; Development Studies; Law; Tourism; Public Administration; Horticulture; Finance; Journalism; Engineering; Mass Communication; Health Administration; Mathematics; Educational Sciences; Social Sciences; Gender Studies and Technology. Vocational Master courses (after Master) in Medicine and Psychology; Business and Commerce; Architecture and Planning; Political and Social Sciences; Law; Humanities; Engineering.Also 11 international master's programmes and 7 vocational master's programmes taught in English.

Student Services: Academic counselling, Canteen, Foreign Studies Centre, Handicapped facilities, Language programs, Sports facilities

Student Residential Facilities: Yes, plus accommodation support services.

Special Facilities: 16 university museums.

Libraries: Central Library, c. 1,250,000; 72 department and faculty libraries; 20.000 e-periodicals, over 250 electronic databases.

Student Numbers *2012-2013*: Total 83,000
Last Updated: 14/03/13

UNIVERSITY OF BRESCIA

Università degli studi di Brescia
Piazza del Mercato 15, 25121 Brescia
Tel: +39(030) 298-81
Fax: +39(030) 298-8329
EMail: speranza@eco.unibs.it
Website: http://www.unibs.it

Rettore: Sergio Pecorelli
Tel: +39(030) 298-8201, Fax: +39(030) 298-8329
EMail: segr_ret@amm.unibs.it

Faculties

Economics (Business Administration; Civil Law; Economics; Labour Law; Mathematics; Social Sciences; Statistics); **Engineering** (Building Technologies; Chemistry; Civil Engineering; Electronic Engineering; Engineering; Materials Engineering; Mathematics; Mechanical Engineering; Physics); **Law** (Law); **Medicine and Surgery** (Biomedical Engineering; Biomedicine; Dentistry; Gynaecology and Obstetrics; Medicine; Nursing; Physical Therapy; Surgery)

Further Information: Also Teaching Hospital (Ospedali civili di Brescia); 19 Research Centres

History: Founded 1982. A State institution enjoying administrative autonomy.

Governing Bodies: Consiglio di Amministrazione; Senato Accademico

Academic Year: October to June (October-February; March-June)

Admission Requirements: Secondary school certificate (maturità) or recognized foreign equivalent

Main Language(s) of Instruction: Italian

International Co-operation: Participates in the Socrates/Erasmus programme

Degrees and Diplomas: *Laurea (triennale)*; *Laurea Magistrale*; *Master di 1° Livello*; *Master di 2° Livello*; *Dottorato di Ricerca*

Student Services: Academic counselling, Canteen, Cultural centre, Sports facilities

Student Residential Facilities: Yes

Libraries: Central Interfaculty Library; Engineering; Medicine and Surgery.

Last Updated: 20/10/11

UNIVERSITY OF CAGLIARI

Università degli studi di Cagliari
Via Università 40, 09124 Cagliari
Tel: +39(070) 6751
Fax: +39(070) 669-425
EMail: rettore@unica.it
Website: http://www.unica.it

Rettore: Giovanni Melis
Tel: +39 070.659670 - 070.664052, Fax: +39 070. 669425

Direttore Amministrativo: Fabrizio Cherchi
Tel: +39 070 675.2304, Fax: +39 070 658895
EMail: fcherchi@amm.unica.it

International Relations: Angela Carreras
EMail: acarreras@amm.unica.it

Faculties

Architecture (Architecture; Heritage Preservation); **Economics** (Business Administration; Business and Commerce; Economics; Labour and Industrial Relations; Tourism); **Engineering** (Architecture; Chemical Engineering; Construction Engineering; Electrical Engineering; Electronic Engineering; Environmental Engineering; Hydraulic Engineering; Mechanical Engineering; Mining Engineering; Town Planning; Transport Engineering); **Foreign Languages and Literature** (Modern Languages); **Law** (Law); **Mathematics, Physics, and Natural Sciences** (Biology; Chemistry; Geology; Mathematics; Natural Sciences; Physics); **Medicine and Surgery** (Cardiology; Dental Technology; Forensic Medicine and Dentistry; Gastroenterology; Gerontology; Gynaecology and Obstetrics; Medicine; Nursing; Paediatrics; Physical Therapy; Psychiatry and Mental Health; Radiology; Rehabilitation and Therapy; Rheumatology; Speech Therapy and Audiology; Sports Medicine; Surgery; Urology); **Pharmacy** (Pharmacology; Pharmacy; Toxicology); **Philosophy and Humanities** (Archaeology; Art History; Italian; Literature; Medieval Studies; Modern History; Philosophy; Tourism); **Political Science** (Administration; Economics; Law; Political Sciences; Public Administration); **Teacher Training** (Pedagogy; Physical Therapy; Psychology; Teacher Training)

History: Founded 1607 by Bull of Pope Paul V, confirmed by Philip III of Spain in 1620. A State institution enjoying administrative and academic autonomy. Financed by the State.

Governing Bodies: Senato Accademico, comprising 10 members; Consiglio di Amministrazione, comprising 29 members

Academic Year: November to October

Admission Requirements: Secondary school certificate (maturità)

Main Language(s) of Instruction: Italian

International Co-operation: Participates in the Erasmus and Lingua programmes

Degrees and Diplomas: *Laurea (triennale)*; *Laurea Magistrale*; *Laurea Specialistica*: Dentistry, 5 yrs; *Laurea Specialistica*: Medicine and Surgery, 6 yrs; *Master di 1° Livello*; *Master di 2° Livello*; *Dottorato di Ricerca*

Special Facilities: Museum of Anthropology; Museum of Geology; Museum of Natural Sciences. Observatory. Botanical Garden

Libraries: Faculty libraries

Publications: Annali Facoltà di Lettere e Filosofia; Annali Facoltà Economia e Commercio; Rassegna Medica Sarda; Rendiconti Seminario Scienze; Studi Economico-giuridici; Studi Sardi

Last Updated: 20/10/11

UNIVERSITY OF CALABRIA

Università degli studi della Calabria (UNICAL)

Via Pietro Bucci, 87036 Arcavacata di Rende

Tel: +39(0984) 4911

Fax: +39(0984) 493-616

Website: http://www.unical.it

Rettore: Giovanni Latorre (2007-)
Tel: +39(0984) 403-876, Fax: +39(0994) 493-896
EMail: rettore@unical.it

Direttore Amministrativo: Bruna Adamo
Tel: +39(0984) 493-938 EMail: diramm@unical.it

International Relations: Palma Siniscalchi
Tel: +39(0984) 493-756 EMail: relest@amministrazione.unical.it

Faculties

Economics (Actuarial Science; Business Administration; Economics; Public Administration; Statistics; Tourism); **Engineering** (Civil Engineering; Computer Science; Construction Engineering; Environmental Engineering; Mechanical Engineering); **Humanities and Philosophy** (Arts and Humanities; Heritage Preservation; History; Modern Languages; Music; Performing Arts; Philosophy; Primary Education); **Mathematics, Physics, and Natural Sciences** (Biology; Chemistry; Geology; Mathematics; Natural Sciences; Physics; Primary Education); **Pharmacy, Food and Health Sciences** (Food Science; Pharmacology; Pharmacy; Toxicology); **Political Science** (Political Sciences; Social Work)

History: Founded 1972.

Governing Bodies: Senato Accademico; Consiglio di Amministrazione; Comitato di Coordinamento e Programmazione

Academic Year: October to June (October-January; March-June)

Admission Requirements: Secondary school certificate (maturità)

Main Language(s) of Instruction: Italian

International Co-operation: With universities in Albania; China; Canada; Germany; United Kingdom; USA; Russian Federation; France; Spain; Eastern Europe

Degrees and Diplomas: *Laurea (triennale)*; *Diploma di Laurea*: 3 yrs; *Diploma di Specializziazione*; *Laurea Magistrale*; *Laurea Specialistica*: 5 yrs; *Master di 1° Livello*; *Master di 2° Livello*; *Dottorato di Ricerca*: a further 2-3 yrs

Student Services: Academic counselling, Canteen, Cultural centre, Employment services, Handicapped facilities, Health services, Language programs, Social counselling, Sports facilities

Student Residential Facilities: For 3,000 students

Special Facilities: Botanical Garden; Radio and Television Centre; Arts and Music Centre

Libraries: Biblioteca Centrale, Biblioteca di Area Umanistica, Biblioteca di Area Economico-Giuridica, Biblioteca di Area Tecnico-Scientifica

Press or Publishing House: Centro Editoriale e Librario, Universitá della Calabria

Last Updated: 20/10/11

UNIVERSITY OF CAMERINO

Università degli studi di Camerino (UNICAM)

Via del Bastione 2, 62032 Camerino

Tel: +39(0737) 4011

Fax: +39(0737) 402-007

EMail: diramm@unicam.it

Website: http://www.unicam.it

Rettore: Fulvio Esposito
Tel: +39(0737) 402-003, Fax: +39 (0737) 402-007
EMail: segreteria.rettore@unicam.it

Direttore Amministrativo: Luigi Tapanelli
Tel: +39(0737) 402-005, Fax: +39(0737) 402-007

International Relations: Francesca Magni, Responsabile
Tel: +39 0737 404-601, Fax: +39 0737 404-610
EMail: francesca.magni@unicam.it

Faculties

Architecture (Architecture; Industrial Design); **Law** (Civil Law; Economics; Forensic Medicine and Dentistry; History of Law; Law; Political Sciences; Private Law; Public Law; Social Studies); **Mathematics, Physics, and Natural Sciences** (Biology; Chemistry; Computer Science; Environmental Management; Geology; Mathematics; Natural Sciences; Physics; Surveying and Mapping); **Pharmacy** (Pharmacology; Pharmacy); **Veterinary Medicine** (Dairy; Meat and Poultry; Veterinary Science)

History: Founded as Collegio dei Dottori 1336 by Bull of Pope Benedetto XII, formally recognized as university 1727 by Bull of Pope Benedetto XIII, and 1753 by Charter of Emperor Francis I of Lorraine who conferred on the Rector the title of Count (which is still used). Closed except for chair of Law by Napoleon. Re-established by Pope Pius VII 1816, and finally reorganized by Bull of Pope Leo XII. Recognized as a free university by decree 1861, confirmed 1923. Became a State institution 1958, enjoying administrative autonomy.

Governing Bodies: Senato Accademico; Consiglio di Amministrazione

Academic Year: November to October

Admission Requirements: Secondary school certificate (maturità) (classical or scientific), or in some fields, technical secondary certificate

Main Language(s) of Instruction: Italian

Degrees and Diplomas: *Laurea (triennale)*; *Laurea Magistrale*; *Master di 1° Livello*; *Master di 2° Livello*; *Dottorato di Ricerca*

Student Residential Facilities: Yes

Libraries: Libraries of the Departments

Publications: Medicina Legale-Quaderni Cameriti; Studi geologici cameriti.

Press or Publishing House: Centro Stampa

Last Updated: 20/10/11

UNIVERSITY OF CASSINO

Università degli studi di Cassino

Via Guglielmo Marconi 10, 03043 Cassino

Tel: +39(0776) 2991

Fax: +39(0776) 310-562

EMail: diramm@unicas.it

Website: http://www.unicas.it

Rettore: Ciro Attaianese
Tel: +39 0776 2993208 EMail: rettore@unicas.it

Direttore Amministrativo: Ascenzo Farenti
Tel: +39 0776 2993230

Faculties

Arts and Philosophy (Arts and Humanities; Communication Studies; Educational Sciences; Heritage Preservation; Literature; Modern Languages; Philology; Philosophy; Social Policy); **Economics** (Business Administration; Business and Commerce; Economics; Food Technology); **Engineering** (Civil Engineering; Electrical Engineering; Mechanical Engineering; Telecommunications Engineering); **Law** (Law); **Sports Sciences** (Sports)

History: Founded 1979. A State institution enjoying administrative autonomy.

Governing Bodies: Senato Accademico; Consiglio di Amministrazione

Academic Year: November to October

Admission Requirements: Secondary school certificate (maturità)

Main Language(s) of Instruction: Italian

International Co-operation: With universities in Germany, United Kingdom, France, Spain

Degrees and Diplomas: *Laurea (triennale)*; *Laurea Magistrale*; *Laurea Specialistica*; *Master di 1° Livello*; *Master di 2° Livello*; *Dottorato di Ricerca*: 4-5 yrs

Student Services: Academic counselling, Employment services, Handicapped facilities, Language programs, Social counselling, Sports facilities

Libraries: Yes

Last Updated: 20/10/11

UNIVERSITY OF CATANIA

Università degli studi di Catania

Piazza dell'Università 2, 95124 Catania
Tel: +39 095 7307111
Fax: +39 095 325194
EMail: uri@unict.it
Website: http://www.unict.it

Rettore: Antonino Recca (2006-)
Tel: +39 095 321112, Fax: +39 095 325194 EMail: rettore@unict.it

Direttore Amministrativo: Lucio Maggio

Faculties

Agriculture *(Catania, Caltagirone, Nicosia, Ragusa)* (Agricultural Business; Agricultural Engineering; Agricultural Equipment; Agricultural Management; Agriculture; Food Science; Food Technology; Tropical Agriculture); **Architecture** *(Siracusa)* (Architecture; Construction Engineering; Structural Architecture); **Arts and Philosophy** *(Catania, Siracusa, Enna)* (Archaeology; Arts and Humanities; Italian; Literature; Pedagogy; Philosophy; Psychology); **Economics** (Administration; Agricultural Business; Business Administration; Business and Commerce; Economics; Human Resources; Labour and Industrial Relations; Management; Tourism); **Educational Sciences** *(Catania, Enna, Piazza Armerina)* (Developmental Psychology; Education; Educational Psychology; Educational Sciences; Preschool Education; Psychology; Psychometrics; Tourism); **Engineering** *(Catania, Enna)* (Architecture; Automation and Control Engineering; Building Technologies; Civil Engineering; Computer Engineering; Computer Science; Construction Engineering; Electrical Engineering; Electronic Engineering; Energy Engineering; Engineering; Environmental Engineering; Management; Mechanical Engineering; Rural Planning; Structural Architecture; Telecommunications Engineering); **Foreign Languages and Literature** *(Catania, Ragusa)* (American Studies; Canadian Studies; Communication Studies; Cultural Studies; English; European Languages; French; German; Greek; Hispanic American Studies; Modern Languages; Russian; Spanish); **Law** (Administrative Law; Commercial Law; Criminal Law; European Union Law; International Law; Law); **Mathematics, Physics, and Natural Sciences** (Applied Mathematics; Applied Physics; Biological and Life Sciences; Chemistry; Computer Science; Ecology; Environmental Engineering; Environmental Studies; Geology; Geophysics; Heritage Preservation; Mathematics; Natural Resources; Natural Sciences; Physics; Restoration of Works of Art); **Medicine and Surgery** (Anaesthesiology; Dental Hygiene; Dentistry; Dietetics; Medicine; Physical Therapy; Radiology; Rehabilitation and Therapy; Sports Medicine; Surgery); **Pharmacy** (Chemistry; Homeopathy; Pharmacology; Pharmacy; Toxicology); **Political Science** *(Catania, Caltanissetta, Modica)* (Government; History; International Relations; Political Sciences; Public Administration; Public Relations; Social Work; Sociology)

Further Information: Also 48 Research Departments of the Faculties

History: Founded 1434 as Siciliae Studiorum Generale by Decree of King Alfonso of Aragon. Under the jurisdiction of the Ministry of Public Instruction, but enjoys administrative autonomy.

Governing Bodies: Consiglio di Amministrazione (Administrative Council); Senato Accademico (Academic Senate)

Academic Year: October to July

Admission Requirements: Secondary school certificate (maturità). Qualifications from appropriate technical or industrial schools also recognized for admission to Faculties of Economics, Commerce and Agriculture

Main Language(s) of Instruction: Italian

Degrees and Diplomas: *Laurea (triennale)*; *Laurea Magistrale*; *Laurea Specialistica (LS)*; *Master di 1° Livello*; *Master di 2° Livello*; *Dottorato di Ricerca (DR)*: 3-4 yrs

Student Services: Academic counselling, Canteen, Foreign student adviser, Foreign Studies Centre, Handicapped facilities, Language programs, Sports facilities

Student Residential Facilities: 8 student halls of residence

Special Facilities: Zoology Museum, Biological Garden, Observatory

Libraries: Faculty libraries

Last Updated: 20/10/11

UNIVERSITY OF FERRARA

Università degli studi di Ferrara (UNIFE)

Via Savonarola 9/11, 44100 Ferrara
Tel: +39 0532 293111
Fax: +39 0532 248927
EMail: rettore@unife.it
Website: http://www.unife.it

Rettore: Pasquale Nappi

Direttore Amministrativo: Roberto Polastri

Faculties

Architecture (Architecture; Industrial Design); **Economics** (Business Administration; Economics; Finance; International Business; Public Administration); **Engineering** (Automation and Control Engineering; Civil Engineering; Computer Engineering; Electrical and Electronic Engineering; Electronic Engineering; Engineering; Environmental Engineering; Materials Engineering; Mechanical Engineering; Telecommunications Engineering); **Humanities** (Arts and Humanities; Cinema and Television; Communication Studies; Educational Sciences; Literature; Modern Languages; Multimedia; Music; Performing Arts; Philosophy; Tourism); **Law** (Administrative Law; Commercial Law; Criminal Law; Law; Public Administration); **Mathematics, Physics, and Natural Sciences** (Applied Mathematics; Architectural Restoration; Astrophysics; Biology; Biotechnology; Cell Biology; Chemistry; Computer Science; Ecology; Environmental Studies; Geology; Heritage Preservation; Mathematics; Meteorology; Molecular Biology; Natural Resources; Natural Sciences; Physics); **Medicine and Surgery** (Biomedical Engineering; Dentistry; Dietetics; Gynaecology and Obstetrics; Laboratory Techniques; Medical Technology; Medicine; Nursing; Ophthalmology; Physical Therapy; Radiology; Rehabilitation and Therapy; Speech Therapy and Audiology; Surgery); **Pharmacy** (Botany; Cosmetology; Dietetics; Pharmacology; Pharmacy)

History: Founded 1391 as Studium Generale by Bull of Pope Boniface IX with Faculties of Law, Arts and Theology. Closed in 1394, the institution was re-opened in 1402. Became Università dello Stato Pontificio 1598. Reformed 1771 by Pope Clement XIV. Became an independent institution 1860. A private university which became a national university 1942.

Governing Bodies: Senato Accademico

Academic Year: November to October

Admission Requirements: Secondary school certificate (maturità)

Main Language(s) of Instruction: Italian

International Co-operation: With universities in Spain; Sweden; Netherlands; France

Degrees and Diplomas: *Laurea (triennale)*; *Laurea Magistrale*; *Laurea Specialistica*; *Master di 1° Livello*; *Master di 2° Livello*; *Dottorato di Ricerca*: a further 3 yrs following Laurea Specialistica

Student Services: Academic counselling, Canteen, Cultural centre, Employment services, Foreign student adviser, Handicapped facilities, Social counselling, Sports facilities

Student Residential Facilities: Some

Special Facilities: Natural History Museum; Mineralogy and Geology Museum. Theatre

Last Updated: 20/10/11

UNIVERSITY OF FLORENCE

Università degli studi di Firenze

Piazza San Marco 4, 50121 Firenze
Tel: +39(055) 27571
Fax: +39(055) 264-194
EMail: direttore.amministrativo@unifi.it
Website: http://www.unifi.it

Rettore: Alberto Tesi
Tel: +39(055) 275-7211, Fax: +39(055) 275-7429
EMail: rettore@unifi.it

Direttore Amministrativo: Giovanni Colucci
Tel: +39(055) 275-7357, Fax: +39(055) 215-782

Faculties

Agriculture (Agricultural Economics; Agricultural Engineering; Agriculture; Agronomy; Animal Husbandry; Biological and Life Sciences; Chemistry; Crop Production; Earth Sciences; Environmental Studies; Farm Management; Fishery; Food Science; Forest Management; Forestry; Horticulture; Meteorology; Physics; Soil Science; Tropical Agriculture; Water Science); **Architecture** (Architectural and Environmental Design; Architectural Restoration; Architecture; Landscape Architecture; Regional Planning; Structural Architecture; Town Planning); **Arts and Humanities** (Archaeology; Archiving; Art History; Arts and Humanities; Classical Languages; Comparative Literature; Design; Documentation Techniques; Heritage Preservation; History; Library Science; Linguistics; Literature; Mass Communication; Modern Languages; Music; Native Language; Performing Arts; Philosophy; Theatre); **Economics** (Accountancy; Actuarial Science; Agricultural Economics; Banking; Business Administration; Business and Commerce; Civil Law; Commercial Law; Demography and Population; Economics; European Union Law; Finance; Geography (Human); History; Hotel Management; Human Resources; Industrial Management; Institutional Administration; Insurance; International Business; Labour and Industrial Relations; Labour Law; Management; Management Systems; Marketing; Mathematics; Mathematics and Computer Science; Modern Languages; Public Administration; Retailing and Wholesaling; Service Trades; Social Sciences; Sociology; Statistics; Tourism; Transport Economics); **Educational Sciences** (Adult Education; Anthropology; Behavioural Sciences; Cognitive Sciences; Education; Educational Sciences; Philosophy; Preschool Education; Primary Education; Psycholinguistics; Secondary Education; Social Sciences; Sociology; Special Education; Teacher Trainers Education); **Engineering** (Automation and Control Engineering; Bioengineering; Biomedical Engineering; Civil Engineering; Computer Engineering; Electrical and Electronic Engineering; Energy Engineering; Engineering; Engineering Management; Environmental Engineering; Industrial Engineering; Information Technology; Materials Engineering; Mechanical Engineering; Physical Engineering; Production Engineering; Safety Engineering; Surveying and Mapping; Transport and Communications); **Law** (Air and Space Law; Canon Law; Civil Law; Commercial Law; Comparative Law; Criminal Law; Criminology; Economics; European Union Law; History of Law; Human Rights; International Law; International Studies; Labour Law; Law; Maritime Law; Notary Studies; Philosophy; Political Sciences; Public Law); **Mathematics, Physics, and Natural Sciences** (Actuarial Science; Anthropology; Applied Mathematics; Artificial Intelligence; Astronomy and Space Science; Astrophysics; Biological and Life Sciences; Chemistry; Computer Science; Earth Sciences; Heritage Preservation; Marine Science and Oceanography; Mathematics; Meteorology; Museum Studies; Natural Sciences; Physics; Statistics; Systems Analysis); **Medicine and Surgery** (Biological and Life Sciences; Biomedicine; Dental Technology; Dentistry; Forensic Medicine and Dentistry; Health Administration; Medical Auxiliaries; Medical Parasitology; Medicine; Midwifery; Nursing; Optometry; Pharmacy; Podiatry; Public Health; Radiology; Rehabilitation and Therapy; Surgery; Treatment Techniques); **Pharmacy** (Chemistry; Pharmacy); **Political Science** (Administration; Behavioural Sciences; Business Administration; Cognitive Sciences; Commercial Law; Communication Studies; Comparative Law; Demography and Population; Economics; European Union Law; Geography (Human); History; History of Law; Human Rights; Industrial Management; Information Sciences; Institutional Administration; International Business; International Law; International Relations; Journalism; Labour and Industrial Relations; Labour Law; Law; Management Systems; Media Studies; Political Sciences; Psychology; Public Administration; Public Law; Sociology; Urban Studies); **Psychology** (Psychology)

Further Information: Also Teaching Hospitals

History: Founded 1321 as Studium Generale by the Republic of Florence. Recognized by Bull of Pope Clement VII 1349 and by Royal Decree of Charles IV 1364. Transferred to Pisa 1472, but law and medicine continued to be taught in Florence. Reorganized as Istituto di Studi Superiori Pratici e di Perfezionamento 1859. The institution became autonomous 1872 and was granted full university status 1924. Under the jurisdiction of the Ministry of Public Instruction and financially supported by the State.

Governing Bodies: Consiglio di Amministrazione (Board of Directors), comprising 15 members; Senato Accademico (Senate), comprising 23 members

Academic Year: October to May

Admission Requirements: Secondary school certificate (maturità), and entry examination for most Degree and Diploma Courses

Main Language(s) of Instruction: Italian

International Co-operation: With universities in Cape Verde, Egypt, Ethiopia, Morocco, Mozambique, South Africa, Tunisia, Zimbabwe, USA, Argentina, Spain, Bolivia, Brazil, Chile, Colombia, Cuba, Honduras, Mexico, Paraguay, Peru, Uruguay, Venezuela, Canada, Hong kong, China, Japan, India, Taiwan, Thailand, Jordan, Iran, Israel, Palestine, Australia, France, Germany, Switzerland, United Kingdom, Greece, Albania, Belarus, Serbia and Montenegro, Bulgaria, Croatia, Estonia, Latvia, Macedonia, Poland, Romania, Russian Federation, Ukraine, Hungary. Also participates in the Socrates/ Erasmus Programme.

Degrees and Diplomas: *Laurea (triennale)*; *Diploma di Specializzazione*: 3-5 yrs; *Laurea Magistrale*; *Master di 1° Livello*; *Master di 2° Livello*; *Dottorato di Ricerca*: a further 3 yrs

Student Services: Academic counselling, Canteen, Cultural centre, Foreign student adviser, Foreign Studies Centre, Language programs, Sports facilities

Student Residential Facilities: For c. 900 students

Special Facilities: Natural History Museum

Libraries: Faculty libraries, c. 3m. vols

Publications: Advances in Horticulture Science; Bolletino del Dipartimento di Urbanistica e Planificazione del Territorio; Cariologia, International Journal of Cytology, Cysistematics and Cytogenetics; Ethnology, Ecology and Evolution; Firenze e Architettura; Global Bioethics; International Journal of Anthropology; Marshall Studies Bulletin; Medioevo e Rinascimento; Phitopatologia Mediterranea

Press or Publishing House: Firenze University Press

Last Updated: 20/10/11

UNIVERSITY OF FOGGIA

Università degli studi di Foggia (UNIFG)
Via Gramsci 89-91, 71100 Foggia
Tel: +39(0881) 338311
Fax: +39(0881) 709262
EMail: g.lovallo@unifg.it
Website: http://www.unifg.it

Rettore: Giuliano Volpe
Tel: +39(0881) 338-446, Fax: +39(0881) 338-449

Direttore Amministrativo: Costantino Quartucci
Tel: +39 0881 338444-338445, Fax: +39 0881 338442
EMail: c.quartucci@unifg.it

International Relations: Giovanni Lovallo, Responsabile
Tel: +39 0881 338337 EMail: r.sarao@unifg.it

Faculties

Agriculture (Agriculture; Crop Production; Food Science; Food Technology); **Economics** (Business Administration; Economics; Tourism); **Humanities and Philosophy** (Anthropology; Archaeology; Classical Languages; History; Literature; Philology; Philosophy; Social Sciences); **Law** (Law); **Medicine and Surgery** (Biochemistry; Endocrinology; Gynaecology and Obstetrics; Laboratory Techniques; Medicine; Nursing; Physical Therapy; Psychology; Surgery); **Teacher Training** (Teacher Training)

Further Information: Also 6 Laboratories

History: Founded 1991. Acquired present status and title 1999.

Governing Bodies: Consiglio di Amministrazione; Consiglio Accademico

Admission Requirements: Secondary school certificate

International Co-operation: Participates in the Socrates/Erasmus and Leonardo programmes

Degrees and Diplomas: *Laurea (triennale)*; *Diploma di Specializziazione*; *Laurea Magistrale*; *Master di 1° Livello*; *Master di 2° Livello*; *Dottorato di Ricerca*: a further 3 yrs

Student Services: Academic counselling, Canteen, Sports facilities

Student Residential Facilities: Yes

Libraries: Main Library; Faculty of Agriculture Library; Faculty of Medicine and Surgery Library, Faculty of Humanities, Faculty of Economics and Faculty of Law

Last Updated: 20/10/11

UNIVERSITY OF GENOA

Università degli studi di Genova

Via Balbi 5, 16126 Genova
Tel: +39(010) 209-91
Fax: +39(010) 209-9227
EMail: info@unige.it
Website: http://www.unige.it

Rettore: Giacomo Deferrari (2008-2014)
Tel: +39(010) 209-9221, Fax: +39(010) 209-5786
EMail: rettore@balbi.unige.it

Direttore Amministrativo: Rosa Gatti
Tel: +39(010) 209-9223, Fax: +39(010) 209-9310
EMail: direttore@balbi.unige.it

International Relations: Maria Traino, Head of International Activities Service
Tel: +39 010 209-9646, Fax: +39 010 209-5605
EMail: relint@unige.it

Faculties

Architecture (Architectural and Environmental Design; Architecture; Landscape Architecture; Structural Architecture); **Economics** (Business Administration; Economic and Finance Policy; Economics); **Engineering** (Chemical Engineering; Energy Engineering; Engineering; Information Sciences; Systems Analysis; Transport Engineering); **Foreign Languages and Literature** (Literature; Modern Languages; Translation and Interpretation); **Humanities and Philosophy** (Ancient Civilizations; Anthropology; Archaeology; Arts and Humanities; Ethnology; Fine Arts; Medieval Studies; Modern History; Performing Arts; Philosophy); **Law** (History of Law; Law; Private Law; Public Law); **Mathematics, Physical and Natural Sciences** (Applied Mathematics; Chemistry; Environmental Studies; Industrial Chemistry; Information Sciences; Mathematics; Natural Resources; Natural Sciences; Physics); **Medicine and Surgery** (Dentistry; Endocrinology; Genetics; Gynaecology and Obstetrics; Health Sciences; Medical Technology; Medicine; Neurology; Oncology; Ophthalmology; Paediatrics; Psychology; Rehabilitation and Therapy; Surgery); **Pharmacy** (Biomedicine; Pharmacy); **Political Science** (European Studies; Political Sciences; Social Sciences); **Teacher Training** (Teacher Training)

History: Founded 1471 by Bull of Pope Sixtus IV, degrees recognized by Emperor Maximilian I 1496. Acquired university status and reorganized 1773. Under the jurisdiction of the Ministry of Universities and Scientific and Technological Research, but enjoys administrative autonomy. Financially supported by the State.

Governing Bodies: Senato Accademico; Consiglio di Amministrazione

Academic Year: November to October

Admission Requirements: Secondary school certificate (maturità) or equivalent

Main Language(s) of Instruction: Italian

International Co-operation: Participates in LLP Erasmus, Erasmus Mundus, Socrates, Tempus, Jean Monnet, Alfa programmes and the 7th Framework programme 2007-2013

Degrees and Diplomas: *Laurea (triennale)*; *Diploma di Specializziazione*; *Laurea Magistrale*: Archiving and Library Science; Cultural Studies; Classical Litterature and Civilization; Modern Litterature and Civilization; Philosophical Methodology; Performing Arts; Research History Methodology; Archaelogy; Modern Languages and Litterature; Environmental Science; Telecommunications Engineering; Electrical Engineering; Electronic Engineering; Engineering Management; Computer Engineering; Mechanical Engineering; Marine Engineering; International Relations; Physics; Computer Science; Industrial Design; Economics; Marine Management and Economics; Management; Environmental Engineering; Telecommunications Engineering; Electrical Engineeering; Electronic Engineering; Engineering Management; Computer Engineering; Mechanical Engineering; Marine Engineering; Bioengineering; Transport Engineering Water Engineering; Construction Engineering; Jurisprudence; Social Work; Labour Law; Political Science; International Relations; Public Administration; Letters and Philosophy, 2 yrs; *Laurea Specialistica*: Mathematics; Biology; Chemical Engineering; Translation; Training Science; Psychology; Pedagogy; Pgysics; Computer Science; Mathematics; Biology; Chemical Engineering, 2 yrs; *Master di 1° Livello*; *Master di 2° Livello*; *Dottorato di Ricerca*: Architecture; Pharmacy; Chemistry and Pharmacology; Medicine; Surgery; Odontotics and Protheses, 3 yrs

Student Services: Academic counselling, Canteen, Cultural centre, Employment services, Foreign student adviser, Foreign Studies Centre, Handicapped facilities, Health services, Language programs, Sports facilities

Student Residential Facilities: Yes

Special Facilities: Botanical Garden

Libraries: Faculty libraries

Publications: Genuense Athenaeum *(biannually)*; Organi Percorsi Formativi *(annually)*

Last Updated: 20/10/11

UNIVERSITY OF INSUBRIA

Università degli studi dell' Insubria

Via Ravasi 2, 21100 Varese
Tel: +39(0332) 219-001
Fax: +39(0332) 219-009
Website: http://www.uninsubria.it

Rettore: Renzo Dionigi (2008-) Fax: +39 0332 219009
EMail: rettore@uninsubria.it; renzo.dionigi@uninsubria.it

Direttore Amministrativo: Marino Balzani Fax: +39 0332 219029
EMail: marino.balzani@uninsubria.it

International Relations: Federico Raos, Responsabile
Tel: +39 0332 219340, Fax: +39 0332 219349
EMail: relint@uninsubria.it

Faculties

Economics (Banking; Business Administration; Economics; Finance; Management); **Law** *(Como)* (Law); **Mathematics, Physics and Natural Sciences** *(Como)* (Chemistry; Environmental Studies; Mathematics; Physics); **Mathematics, Physics and Natural Sciences** *(Varese)* (Biology; Biotechnology; Computer Science; Ecology; Environmental Studies); **Medicine and Surgery** (Medicine; Surgery)

Institutes

Law *(Como)* (Law) *Head*: Giorgio Luraschi

Research Centres

Internationalisation of Local Economics (Business Administration) *Director*: Gioacchino Garofoli; **Local Histories and Cultural Diversities** (Arts and Humanities; Social Sciences) *Director*: Claudia Storti Storchi; **Natural Sciences** *(Lake of Varese) Director*: Davide Calamari; **Neurosciences** (Health Sciences; Natural Sciences) *Director*: Daniela Parolaro; **Non Linear and Complex Systems** (Natural Sciences; Physics) *Director*: Giulio Casati; **Thoracic Surgery** (Health Sciences) *Director*: Lorenzo Dominioni

History: Founded 1998.

Governing Bodies: Senato Accademico, Consiglio di Amministrazione, Nucleo di Valutazione

Academic Year: October to September

Admission Requirements: Diploma di Maturità

Fees: (Euros): 595-2,500 per annum

Main Language(s) of Instruction: Italian

International Co-operation: With universities in Spain, France, Poland, United Kingdom, Denmark, Germany, Belgium, Lithuania, Norway, Greece, Switzerland, Portugal, Poland, Brazil, Spain, France, USA.

Degrees and Diplomas: *Laurea (triennale)*; *Laurea Magistrale*; *Laurea Specialistica*: Economics; Law; Natural Sciences; Biology; Mathematics; Physics; Chemistry; Medicine and Surgery; Dentistry

(DLS), 2 yrs; *Master di 1° Livello*; *Master di 2° Livello*; *Dottorato di Ricerca*: Physics; Chemistry; Biology; Medicine; Law; Economics; Political and Social Sciences (DS), a further 3-4 yrs

Student Services: Academic counselling, Employment services, Foreign student adviser, Handicapped facilities, Language programs, Social counselling, Sports facilities

Libraries: Four Libraries

Last Updated: 20/10/11

UNIVERSITY OF L'AQUILA

Università degli studi dell'Aquila

Piazza Vincenzo Rivera 1, 67100 L'Aquila

Tel: +39(0862) 431-111

Fax: +39(0862) 412-948

EMail: filippo.delvecchio@cc.univaq.it

Website: http://www.univaq.it

Rettore: Ferdinando di Orio
Tel: +39 086 2432092, Fax: +39 086 2412948
EMail: rettore@cc.univaq.it

Direttore Amministrativo: Pietro Di Benedetto
Tel: +39 086 2432081, Fax: +39 086 2412948
EMail: pietro.dibenedetto@cc.univaq.it

International Relations: Anna Tozzi
Tel: +39 0862 432762, Fax: +39 0862 432763
EMail: anna.tozzi@univaq.it

Faculties

Biotechnology (Biomedicine; Biotechnology); **Economics** (Business Administration; Business and Commerce; Commercial Law; Cultural Studies; Economics; Environmental Studies; Management; Tourism); **Educational Sciences** (Education; Educational Psychology; Educational Sciences; Environmental Studies; Preschool Education; Primary Education; Teacher Trainers Education; Teacher Training); **Engineering** (Architecture; Automation and Control Engineering; Building Technologies; Chemical Engineering; Civil Engineering; Electrical Engineering; Electronic Engineering; Engineering; Engineering Management; Environmental Engineering; Information Technology; Mechanical Engineering; Structural Architecture; Telecommunications Engineering; Town Planning); **Humanities and Philosophy** (Arts and Humanities; Classical Languages; Communication Studies; Comparative Religion; Comparative Sociology; Cultural Studies; Environmental Studies; European Languages; Heritage Preservation; History; Italian; Literature; Modern Languages; Music; Performing Arts; Philosophy; Theatre); **Mathematics, Physics and Natural Sciences** (Applied Mathematics; Applied Physics; Astronomy and Space Science; Astrophysics; Biological and Life Sciences; Biology; Biotechnology; Chemical Engineering; Chemistry; Computer Science; Environmental Studies; Materials Engineering; Mathematics; Microbiology; Natural Sciences; Organic Chemistry; Physics); **Medicine and Surgery** (Biomedicine; Dental Hygiene; Dentistry; Gynaecology and Obstetrics; Medicine; Nursing; Ophthalmology; Physical Therapy; Psychiatry and Mental Health; Public Health; Rehabilitation and Therapy; Social Work; Surgery); **Sports Science** (Physical Education; Sports; Sports Management)

History: Founded 1952. A State institution enjoying administrative autonomy.

Academic Year: November to October

Admission Requirements: Secondary school certificate (maturità)

Main Language(s) of Instruction: Italian

Degrees and Diplomas: *Laurea (triennale)*; *Laurea Magistrale*; *Laurea Specialistica*: Dentistry, 5 yrs; *Laurea Specialistica*: Medicine; Surgery, 6 yrs; *Laurea Specialistica*: Structural Architecture; Physics; Computer Science; Mathematics; Applied Mathematics; Astrophysics; Biotechnology, a further 2 yrs; *Master di 1° Livello*; *Master di 2° Livello*; *Dottorato di Ricerca*

Student Services: Canteen, Sports facilities

Student Residential Facilities: For c. 160 students

Special Facilities: Archeology collection

Libraries: Faculty of Economics Library, c. 18,000 vols; Faculty of Engineering Library, c. 18,000 vols; Faculty of Humanities and Philosophy Library, c. 120,000 vols and 1,500 videos; Faculty of Medicine and Surgery Library, c. 20,000 vols; Faculty of Educational Sciences, c. 6,000 vols; Faculty of Mathematics, Physics and Natural Science Library, c. 43,000 vols

Last Updated: 20/10/11

UNIVERSITY OF MACERATA

Università degli studi di Macerata

Piaggia dell'Università 11, 62100 Macerata

Tel: +39(0733) 2581

Fax: +39(0733) 258-2688

EMail: cri@unimc.it

Website: http://www.unimc.it

Rettore: Luigi Lacchè
Tel: +39(0733) 258.2410-2610-2822, Fax: +39(0733) 258-2688
EMail: rettore@unimc.it

Direttore Amministrativo: Mauro Giustozzi
Tel: +39(0733) 258-2411, Fax: +39(0733) 258-2689
EMail: direzioneamministrativa@unimc.it

Faculties

Communication Sciences (Communication Studies; Information Sciences; Mathematics and Computer Science; Performing Arts); **Cultural Heritage** (Cultural Studies; Heritage Preservation); **Educational Sciences** (Education; Educational Sciences; Mathematics and Computer Science); **Humanities and Philosophy** (Archaeology; Arts and Humanities; Fine Arts; History; Mathematics and Computer Science; Modern Languages; Philosophy); **Law** (Law; Public Administration; Social and Community Services); **Political Science** (Economics; Political Sciences)

Institutes

Civil Law (Civil Law); **Classical Philology** *(Carlo Tibiletti)* (Philology); **Forensic Medicine and Insurance** (Forensic Medicine and Dentistry; Insurance); **History** (History); **History, Philosophy of Law and Ecclesiastical Law** (History of Law); **International and European Union Law** (European Union Law; International Law); **Law and Legal Proceedings** (Law); **Roman Law** *(Luigi Raggi)* (Law)

History: Founded 1290 as School of Law. Recognized as a University, Studium Generale, by Papal Bull of Pope Paul III 1540.

Governing Bodies: Consiglio di Amministrazione, comprising 28 members; Senato Accademico

Academic Year: October to November

Admission Requirements: Secondary school certificate (maturità)

Main Language(s) of Instruction: Italian

International Co-operation: Participates in the Socrates/Erasmus programme (Spain, Germany, France and Scandinavian countries)

Degrees and Diplomas: *Laurea (triennale)*; *Diploma di Specializziazione*: Syndicate Law, 2 yrs; *Laurea Magistrale*; *Laurea Magistrale*; *Master di 1° Livello*; *Master di 2° Livello*; *Dottorato di Ricerca*

Student Services: Academic counselling, Canteen, Cultural centre, Employment services, Foreign student adviser, Foreign Studies Centre, Handicapped facilities, Health services, Language programs, Social counselling, Sports facilities

Student Residential Facilities: Yes

Special Facilities: Movie Studio. Museum. Art Gallery

Libraries: Centro d'Ateneo per i servizi bibliotecari

Publications: Annali della Facoltà di Giurisprudenza; Annali della Facoltà di Lettere e Filosofia *(annually)*; Annali della Facoltà di Scienze Politiche

Press or Publishing House: Centro Stampa, Università degli Studi Macerata

Last Updated: 20/10/11

UNIVERSITY OF MESSINA

Università degli studi di Messina

Piazza Pugliatti 1, 98122 Messina

Tel: +39(090) 7161

Fax: +39(090) 717-762

Website: http://www.unime.it

Rettore: Francesco Tomasello (1995-)
Tel: +39(090) 676-4559, Fax: +39(090) 676-4274
EMail: rettorato@unime.it

Direttore Amministrativo: Giuseppe Cardile
Tel: +39 090 6764291, Fax: +39 090 6764240

Faculties

Economics (Banking; Business Administration; Business and Commerce; Commercial Law; Economics; Labour Law; Law); **Engineering** (Civil Engineering; Electronic Engineering; Engineering; Materials Engineering); **Humanities and Philosophy** (Arts and Humanities; Heritage Preservation; Literature; Modern Languages; Philosophy; Translation and Interpretation); **Law** (Labour Law; Law); **Mathematics, Physics, and Natural Sciences** (Biology; Chemistry; Computer Science; Mathematics; Natural Sciences; Physics); **Medicine and Surgery** (Anaesthesiology; Cardiology; Criminology; Dental Hygiene; Dentistry; Dermatology; Dietetics; Endocrinology; Gastroenterology; Gerontology; Gynaecology and Obstetrics; Laboratory Techniques; Medicine; Neurology; Nursing; Oncology; Ophthalmology; Orthopaedics; Pharmacology; Physical Therapy; Podiatry; Psychiatry and Mental Health; Radiology; Speech Therapy and Audiology; Surgery); **Pharmacy** (Pharmacology; Pharmacy); **Political Science** (Administration; Communication Studies; Law; Political Sciences; Public Administration; Social Work); **Statistical Sciences** (Demography and Population; Statistics); **Teacher Training** (Classical Languages; Educational Sciences; German; Literacy Education; Modern Languages; Pedagogy; Slavic Languages; Teacher Training); **Veterinary Medicine** (Cattle Breeding; Veterinary Science; Zoology)

History: Founded 1598 and recognized by Bull of Pope Paul III. Closed by the Spaniards 1678, re-opened 1838.

Governing Bodies: Consiglio di Amministrazione; Senato Accademico

Academic Year: September to July (September-february; February-July)

Admission Requirements: Secondary school certificate (maturità)

Main Language(s) of Instruction: Italian

International Co-operation: Participates in the Socrates and Erasmus programmes

Degrees and Diplomas: *Laurea (triennale)*; *Diploma di Specializzazione*; *Laurea Magistrale*; *Laurea Specialistica*: Medicine and Surgery, 6 yrs; *Laurea Specialistica*: Veterinary Medicine, 5 yrs; *Dottorato di Ricerca*

Student Services: Academic counselling, Canteen, Foreign student adviser, Sports facilities

Student Residential Facilities: Yes

Libraries: Yes

Publications: Atti dell'Accademia Peloritana dei Pericolanti

Last Updated: 20/10/11

UNIVERSITY OF MILAN

Università degli studi di Milano
Via Festa del Perdono 7, 20122 Milano
Tel: +39(02) 503-111
Fax: +39(02) 5031-2627
EMail: direzione.amministrativa@unimi.it
Website: http://www.unimi.it

Rettore: Enrico Decleva
Tel: +39(02) 5031-2000, Fax: +39(02) 5031-2508
EMail: rettore@unimi.it

Direttore Amministrativo: Alberto Silvani
Tel: +39 02 503.12020, Fax: +39 02 503.13255

Faculties

Agriculture (Agricultural Engineering; Agricultural Equipment; Agricultural Management; Agriculture; Biochemistry; Biotechnology; Botany; Chemistry; Cooking and Catering; Dairy; Earth Sciences; Ecology; Environmental Studies; Food Science; Food Technology; Mountain Studies; Oenology; Plant and Crop Protection; Viticulture); **Humanities and Philosophy** (Communication Studies; Cultural Studies; Environmental Studies; Heritage Preservation; History; Literature; Modern Languages; Philosophy); **Law** (Administrative Law; Civil Law; Commercial Law; Comparative Law; Constitutional Law; Criminal Law; European Union Law; History of Law; International Law; Labour Law; Law; Public Law); **Mathematics, Physics, and Natural Sciences** *(Computer Science and Information Technology in Crema)* (Applied Chemistry; Applied Mathematics; Biological and Life Sciences; Biotechnology; Chemical Engineering; Chemistry; Computer Science; Electronic Engineering; Environmental Studies; Geology; Industrial Chemistry; Information Sciences; Information Technology; Mathematics; Musical Instruments; Natural Sciences; Physics; Sound Engineering (Acoustics); Telecommunications Engineering); **Medicine and Surgery** (Biomedicine; Biotechnology; Cardiology; Dental Hygiene; Dental Technology; Dentistry; Endocrinology; Gastroenterology; Gerontology; Gynaecology and Obstetrics; Hygiene; Laboratory Techniques; Medical Technology; Medicine; Midwifery; Neurological Therapy; Neurology; Nursing; Nutrition; Occupational Health; Occupational Therapy; Oncology; Ophthalmology; Orthopaedics; Pathology; Pharmacology; Physical Therapy; Physiology; Podiatry; Psychiatry and Mental Health; Public Health; Radiology; Rehabilitation and Therapy; Rheumatology; Social and Preventive Medicine; Speech Therapy and Audiology; Surgery); **Pharmacy** (Biotechnology; Homeopathy; Pharmacology; Pharmacy; Toxicology); **Political Science** (Administration; Communication Studies; Economics; European Studies; Human Resources; International Relations; Political Sciences; Social Sciences; Sociology); **Sport and Physical Training** (Physical Education; Sports); **Veterinary Medicine** (Animal Husbandry; Biotechnology; Cattle Breeding; Dairy; Food Science; Pathology; Veterinary Science)

Further Information: Also 49 departments and 100 postgraduate schools, mainly in Medicine and Para-medicine; 77 Research Centres; 72 Research Doctorates

History: Founded 1924. Under the jurisdiction of the Ministry of Universities and Scientific and Technological Research but enjoys administrative autonomy.

Governing Bodies: Senato Accademico; Consiglio di Amministrazione

Academic Year: October to September

Admission Requirements: Secondary school certificate (maturità)

Main Language(s) of Instruction: Italian

International Co-operation: With universities worldwide. Also participates in the Socrates, Tempus, Leonardo, Alfa programmes, and has 400 research and teaching collaboration agreements with universities abroad.

Degrees and Diplomas: *Laurea (triennale)*; *Laurea Magistrale*; *Laurea Specialistica*: Computer Science; Food Science; Information and Communications Technology; International Relations; Pharmaceutical Chemistry and Technology; Pharmacy; Social Science; Veterinary Medicine, a further 2 yrs; *Laurea Specialistica*: Dentistry, 5 yrs; *Laurea Specialistica*: Medicine and Surgery, 6 yrs; *Master di 1° Livello*; *Master di 2° Livello*; *Dottorato di Ricerca*: Agricultural and Geological Sciences; Biological Sciences; Classics, Philology, Literature and Art History; Economic, Statistical, Political and Sociological Sciences; History, Philosophy, Pedagogy and Psychology; Law; Mathematical, Physical, Chemical and Information Sciences; Medical Sciences; Pharmaceutical and Pharmacological Sciences; Veterinary Sciences, 3 yrs

Student Services: Academic counselling, Employment services, Foreign student adviser, Foreign Studies Centre, Handicapped facilities, Social counselling, Sports facilities

Student Residential Facilities: Yes

Special Facilities: Zoology Museum. Observatory

Libraries: Yes

Press or Publishing House: University Press

Last Updated: 20/10/11

UNIVERSITY OF MILAN-BICOCCA

Università degli studi di Milano-Bicocca
Piazza dell'Ateneo Nuovo 1, 20126 Milano
Tel: +39(02) 64481
Website: http://www.unimib.it

Rettore: Marcello Fontanesi
Tel: +39(02) 6448-6010, Fax: +39(02) 6448-6005
EMail: marcello.fontanesi@unimib.it

Direttore Amministrativo: Candeloro Bellantoni
Tel: +39 02 6448 6032 EMail: candeloro.bellantoni@unimib.it

Faculties

Economics (Banking; Business Administration; Economics; Finance; Marketing); **Educational Sciences** (Education; Teacher

Training); **Law** (Law); **Mathematics, Physics and Natural Sciences** (Astrophysics; Biology; Biotechnology; Chemistry; Computer Science; Environmental Studies; Geology; Mathematics; Optometry; Physics); **Medicine and Surgery** (Medicine; Surgery); **Psychology** (Psychology); **Sociology** (Sociology); **Statistics** (Statistics)

History: Founded 1998 as Second University of Milan. Acquired present status 1999.

Main Language(s) of Instruction: Italian

Degrees and Diplomas: *Laurea (triennale)*; *Diploma di Specializziazione*; *Laurea Magistrale*; *Master di 1° Livello*; *Master di 2° Livello*; *Dottorato di Ricerca*

Student Residential Facilities: Yes

Libraries: Yes

Last Updated: 20/10/11

UNIVERSITY OF MODENA AND REGGIO EMILIA

Università degli studi di Modena e Reggio Emilia

Via Università 4, 41100 Modena

Tel: +39(059) 2056511

Fax: +39(059) 218-661

EMail: direttore@unimore.it

Website: http://www.unimore.it/

Rettore: Aldo Tomasi (2008-) Fax: +39(059) 245-156
EMail: rettore@unimore.it

Direttore Amministrativo: Stefano Ronchetti
Tel: +39 059 205 6453 EMail: ronchetti.stefano@unimore.it

International Relations: Gabriella Brancolini, Responsabile
Tel: +39 059 205 6571, Fax: +39 059 205 6566
EMail: uri@unimore.it

Faculties

Agriculture (Agricultural Engineering; Agriculture; Food Technology); **Arts and Philosophy** (Anthropology; Arts and Humanities; Cultural Studies; History; Linguistics; Modern Languages; Philosophy); **Bioscience and Biotechnology** (Biological and Life Sciences; Biotechnology; Pharmacology; Public Health); **Communication and Economics** (Communication Studies; Economics); **Economics** *(Marco Biagi)* (Economics; Finance; Marketing); **Engineering** *(Enzo Ferrari)* (Civil Engineering; Electronic Engineering; Engineering; Environmental Engineering; Materials Engineering; Mechanical Engineering); **Engineering** *(Reggio Emilia)* (Electronic Engineering; Engineering; Environmental Engineering; Mechanical Engineering); **Law** (Law; Public Administration); **Mathematics, Physics, and Natural Sciences** (Applied Mathematics; Biology; Chemistry; Computer Science; Earth Sciences; Geology; Mathematics; Natural Sciences; Physics); **Medicine and Surgery** (Medicine; Surgery); **Pharmacy** (Pharmacy)

Further Information: Also site in Reggio Emilia, Via A. Allegri, 9 - 42100 Reggio Emilia - Tel. +39 0522 522604

History: Founded 1175 as a School of Law. A State institution enjoying administrative autonomy.

Governing Bodies: Consiglio di Amministrazione; Senato Accademico

Academic Year: November to October

Admission Requirements: Secondary school certificate (maturità) or, in some fields, Technical school diploma

Main Language(s) of Instruction: Italian

International Co-operation: Participates in the Socrates and Erasmus programmes

Degrees and Diplomas: *Laurea (triennale)*; *Laurea Magistrale*; *Laurea Specialistica*; *Master di 1° Livello*; *Master di 2° Livello*; *Dottorato di Ricerca*

Student Residential Facilities: Yes

Special Facilities: Anatomy Museum; Zoology Museum; Mineralogy Museum

Libraries: Faculty libraries: Economics and Commerce, c. 23,000 vols; Law, c. 60,800 vols; Institute of Mathematics, c. 8,900 vols

Last Updated: 20/10/11

UNIVERSITY OF MOLISE

Università degli studi del Molise

Via F. de Sanctis, s/n, 86100 Campobasso

Tel: +39(0874) 4041

Fax: +39(0874) 418-295

EMail: relazint@unimol.it

Website: http://www.unimol.it

Rettore: Giovanni Cannata (2005-)
Tel: +39(0874) 404-422, Fax: +39(0784) 418-295
EMail: rettore@unimol.it

Direttore Amministrativo: Vincenzo Lucchese
Tel: +39(0874) 404-304, Fax: +39(0874) 418-373
EMail: direttore@unimol.it

International Relations: Loredana di Rubbo
Tel: +39(0874) 404-768, Fax: +39(0874) 404-258

Centres

Management *(Unimol)* (Private Administration; Public Administration) *Director*: Francesco Testa; **Teacher Training** *(G.A. Glozza)* (Education; Teacher Training) *Head*: Guido Gili

Departments

Agro-industrial, Environmental and Microbiological Sciences (Agriculture; Environmental Studies; Fishery; Forestry; Microbiology) *Principal*: Raffaele Coppola; **Animal, Plant and Environmental Sciences** (Animal Husbandry; Applied Chemistry; Biochemistry; Botany; Environmental Studies; Zoology) *Principal*: Giuseppe Rotundo; **Economics, Management and Social Sciences** (Business Administration; Economics; English; Geography; History; Management; Philosophy; Social Sciences) *Principal*: Alberto Petrucci; **Health Sciences** (Biochemistry; Genetics; Hygiene; Molecular Biology; Nutrition; Pathology; Pharmacology; Physiology) *Principal*: Guido Maria Grasso; **Historical, Human and Social Sciences** *Principal*: Angelo Saporiti; **Juridical, Social and Administrative Sciences** (Administration; Labour Law; Law; Social Sciences) *Principal*: Rocco Favale; **Science and Technology for the Environment and Territory** *(Isernia)* (Biochemistry; Chemistry; Environmental Engineering; Environmental Studies; Geology; Regional Planning) *Principal*: Vincenzo De Felice

Faculties

Agriculture (Agriculture; Agronomy; Crop Production; Food Science; Forestry; Soil Science); **Economics** (Business Administration; Economics; Political Sciences; Social Sciences; Social Work; Tourism); **Engineering** (Civil Engineering; Construction Engineering); **Health Sciences** (Sports); **Human and Social Sciences** (Advertising and Publicity; Archaeology; Arts and Humanities; Communication Studies; Cultural Studies; Heritage Preservation; Literature); **Law** (Administration; Law); **Mathematics, Physics and Natural Sciences** *(Isernia)* (Biology; Cell Biology; Environmental Studies; Forestry; Mathematics and Computer Science; Molecular Biology; Natural Sciences); **Medicine and Surgery** (Medicine; Surgery)

History: Founded 1982.

Governing Bodies: Consiglio di Amministrazione; Senato Accademico

Academic Year: November to October with semestrial division

Admission Requirements: Secondary school certificate (maturità)

Fees: (Euros): 670-775

Main Language(s) of Instruction: Italian

International Co-operation: Participates in the Socrates, Leonardo programmes

Degrees and Diplomas: *Laurea (triennale)*; *Laurea Magistrale*: a further 2 yrs; *Master di 1° Livello*: 1 yr; *Master di 2° Livello*: 2 yrs; *Dottorato di Ricerca*: 2 yrs

Student Services: Academic counselling, Canteen, Foreign student adviser, Sports facilities

Libraries: Yes

Student Numbers *2011-2012*: Total 10,000

Last Updated: 05/10/11

UNIVERSITY OF NAPLES FEDERICO II

Università degli studi di Napoli Federico II
Corso Umberto 1, 40, 80138 NA Napoli
Tel: +39(081) 253-1111
EMail: orientamento@unina.it
Website: http://www.unina.it

Rettore: Massimo Marrelli
Tel: +39(081) 253-7200, Fax: +39(081) 253-7278
EMail: rettore@unina.it

Direttore administrativo: Maria Luigia Liguori
Tel: +39(081) 253-7251 EMail: diramm@unina.it

International Relations: Antonietta Attanasio, Responsabile
Tel: +39 081 2537102, Fax: +39 081 2537110
EMail: antonietta.attanasio@unina.it

Faculties

Agriculture (Agriculture; Agrobiology; Agronomy; Biotechnology; Food Science; Forestry; Oenology; Plant and Crop Protection; Vegetable Production; Viticulture); **Architecture** (Architectural and Environmental Design; Architecture; Industrial Design; Parks and Recreation; Restoration of Works of Art; Town Planning); **Biotechnology** (Biotechnology; Food Science); **Economics** (Accountancy; Business Administration; Business and Commerce; Commercial Law; Economics; Management; Statistics); **Engineering** (Aeronautical and Aerospace Engineering; Chemical Engineering; Civil Engineering; Computer Science; Construction Engineering; Electrical and Electronic Engineering; Engineering Management; Environmental Engineering; Materials Engineering; Mechanical Engineering; Naval Architecture; Telecommunications Engineering); **Humanities and Philosophy** (Archaeology; Art History; Arts and Humanities; European Studies; Heritage Preservation; History; Literature; Modern Languages; Philology; Philosophy; Psychology; Religious Studies; Social Work); **Law** (Administrative Law; Canon Law; Civil Law; Commercial Law; Criminal Law; Labour Law; Law); **Mathematics, Physics and Natural Sciences** (Aquaculture; Astrophysics; Biotechnology; Chemistry; Computer Science; Environmental Studies; Geology; Geophysics; Industrial Chemistry; Mathematics; Natural Sciences; Physics); **Medicine and Surgery** (Anaesthesiology; Biotechnology; Cardiology; Dental Hygiene; Dermatology; Dietetics; Forensic Medicine and Dentistry; Gastroenterology; Gynaecology and Obstetrics; Hygiene; Laboratory Techniques; Medical Technology; Medicine; Neurological Therapy; Nursing; Nutrition; Oncology; Ophthalmology; Orthodontics; Orthopaedics; Otorhinolaryngology; Paediatrics; Physical Therapy; Psychiatry and Mental Health; Radiology; Rehabilitation and Therapy; Rheumatology; Speech Therapy and Audiology; Sports Medicine; Surgery; Toxicology; Urology; Virology); **Pharmacy** (Biotechnology; Pharmacology; Pharmacy); **Political Science** (Administration; Econometrics; International Relations; International Studies; Political Sciences; Public Administration; Social Policy; Statistics); **Sociology** (Development Studies; Health Administration; Mass Communication; Social Policy; Sociology); **Veterinary Medicine** (Animal Husbandry; Biotechnology; Food Science; Meat and Poultry; Veterinary Science)

Further Information: Also University Hospital www.policlinico.unina.it

History: Founded 1224 as Studium Generale by Frederick II. Dissolved 1229 and re-established 1234. Transferred to Salerno 1252 but returned to Naples 1258. Acquired present title 1987.

Governing Bodies: Consiglio di Amministrazione; Senato Accademico

Academic Year: September to June (September-January; March-June)

Admission Requirements: Secondary school certificate (maturità)

Main Language(s) of Instruction: Italian

International Co-operation: With universities in Europe, Middle and Far-East, USA and South America

Degrees and Diplomas: *Laurea (triennale)*; *Laurea Magistrale*; *Laurea Specialistica*: Chemical and Technological Pharmaceutics; Pharmacy; Construction Engineering/ Architecture; Electrical Engineering; Electronic Engineering; Informatic Engineering; Materials Engineering; Odontology and Dental Technology; Telecommunication Engineering; Veterinary Medicine, 5 yrs; *Laurea Specialistica*: Medicine and Surgery, 6 yrs; *Master di 1° Livello*; *Master di 2° Livello*; *Dottorato di Ricerca*

Student Services: Academic counselling, Cultural centre, Employment services, Handicapped facilities, Health services, Language programs, Social counselling, Sports facilities

Student Residential Facilities: For c. 350 students

Special Facilities: Museo Botanico "Orazio Comes"; Museo "Orto Botanico di Portici"; Museo Anatomo - Zootecnico "Tito Manlio Bettini"; Museo di Mineralogia "Antonio Parascandolo"; Museo di Entomologia "Filippo Silvestri"; Museo delle Macchine Agricole "Carlo Santini"; Museo Agronomico

Libraries: Faculty and institute libraries

Last Updated: 20/10/11

UNIVERSITY OF NAPLES - L'ORIENTALE

Università degli studi di Napoli L'Orientale
Via Chiatamone 61/62, 80121 Napoli
Tel: 039 081 7643230
EMail: tutor@unior.it
Website: http://www.unior.it

Rettore: Lida Viganoni
Tel: +39 081-7642264, Fax: +39 081-6909115
EMail: rettorato@iuo.it

Direttore Amministrativo: Giuseppe Giunto
Tel: +39 081-7643230, Fax: +39 081-6909112
EMail: diramm@unior.it

Centres

Archaeology *(Interdepartmental)* (Archaeology) *Dean*: B. D'Agostino

Faculties

Arts and Philosophy (African Languages; Ancient Civilizations; Arabic; Archaeology; Arts and Humanities; Chinese; Christian Religious Studies; Comparative Literature; Cultural Studies; Eastern European Studies; Literature; Modern History; Music; Oriental Studies; Philology; Philosophy; Religion); **Foreign Languages and Literature** (American Studies; European Languages; Literature; Modern Languages); **Islamic and Mediterranean Studies** (African Languages; African Studies; Islamic Studies; Mediterranean Studies); **Political Science** (International Relations; Political Sciences)

Further Information: Also Italian Language courses for Erasmus students

History: Founded 1732. Became a State University 1957.

Governing Bodies: Senato Accademico; Consiglio di Amministrazione

Academic Year: October to June(October-January; March-June)

Admission Requirements: Secondary school certificate (maturità) or foreign equivalent

Main Language(s) of Instruction: Italian

Degrees and Diplomas: *Laurea (triennale)*; *Diploma di Specializziazione*; *Laurea Magistrale*; *Master di 1° Livello*; *Master di 2° Livello*; *Dottorato di Ricerca*

Student Services: Academic counselling, Canteen, Cultural centre, Employment services, Foreign student adviser, Sports facilities

Student Residential Facilities: Yes

Special Facilities: International Observatory; Audiovisual Centre; Centre of Archeological Research

Libraries: 7 specialized Libraries

Last Updated: 21/10/11

UNIVERSITY OF PADUA

Università degli studi di Padova
Via VIII Febbraio 2, 35122 PD Padova
Tel: +39(049) 827-5111
Fax: +39(049) 827-3009
EMail: rettore@unipd.it
Website: http://www.unipd.it

Rettore: Giuseppe Zaccaria (2009-)
Tel: +39(049) 827-3001, Fax: +39(049) 827-3009

Direttore Amministrativo: Giuseppe Barbieri
Tel: +39 049 8273014, Fax: +39 049 8273022
EMail: direttore.amministrativo@unipd.it

Faculties

Agriculture (Agricultural Management; Agriculture; Agronomy; Animal Husbandry; Crop Production; Entomology; Food Science; Forest Products; Forestry; Oenology; Parks and Recreation; Plant and Crop Protection; Plant Pathology; Rural Studies); **Economics** (Business and Commerce; Economics; Management); **Engineering** (Biomedical Engineering; Chemical Engineering; Civil Engineering; Computer Science; Construction Engineering; Electrical Engineering; Electronic Engineering; Engineering; Environmental Engineering; Machine Building; Materials Engineering; Mechanical Engineering; Telecommunications Engineering; Urban Studies); **Humanities and Philosophy** (Archaeology; Arts and Humanities; Communication Studies; History; Leisure Studies; Literature; Modern Languages; Philosophy; Slavic Languages); **Law** (Commercial Law; Labour Law; Law); **Mathematics, Physics and Natural Sciences** (Astronomy and Space Science; Biotechnology; Chemical Engineering; Chemistry; Computer Science; Geology; Materials Engineering; Mathematics; Natural Sciences; Nuclear Physics; Physics); **Medicine and Surgery** (Anaesthesiology; Dentistry; Dietetics; Gynaecology and Obstetrics; Hygiene; Laboratory Techniques; Medicine; Nursing; Ophthalmology; Physical Therapy; Psychiatry and Mental Health; Radiology; Speech Therapy and Audiology; Surgery); **Pharmacy** (Chemistry; Pharmacology; Pharmacy); **Political Science** (European Union Law; Finance; Human Rights; International Business; Political Sciences; Public Administration); **Psychology** (Educational Psychology; Psychoanalysis; Psychology; Psychometrics); **Statistics** (Demography and Population; Statistics); **Teacher Training** (Communication Studies; Educational Sciences; Library Science; Pedagogy; Teacher Training); **Veterinary Medicine** (Veterinary Science)

Institutes

Nuclear Physics *(INFN)* (Nuclear Physics)

History: Founded 1222. A State institution enjoying administrative autonomy.

Governing Bodies: Consiglio di Amministrazione; Senato Accademico

Academic Year: November to October

Admission Requirements: Secondary school certificate (maturità) or equivalent

Main Language(s) of Instruction: Italian

International Co-operation: With universities in Europe; Japan; Tunisia; Sudan; Burkina Faso; USA; Argentina; Brazil; Ecuador; Chile; Australia

Degrees and Diplomas: *Laurea (triennale)*; *Diploma di Specializziazione*: 2 further yrs; *Laurea Magistrale*; *Laurea Specialistica*; *Master di 1° Livello*; *Master di 2° Livello*; *Dottorato di Ricerca*

Student Services: Academic counselling, Canteen, Sports facilities

Student Residential Facilities: Some

Special Facilities: Anthropology Museum; Ethnology Museum. Botanic Garden. Astronomic Observatory. Antique Archives

Libraries: Central Library; American Library; faculty libraries

Publications: Scienza e Cultura

Last Updated: 21/10/11

UNIVERSITY OF PALERMO

Università degli studi di Palermo

Palazzo Steri, 90133 Palermo
Tel: +39 091 6075111
Fax: +39 091 6529124
EMail: rettore@unipa.it
Website: http://www.unipa.it

Rettore: Roberto Lagalla
Tel: +39 091 334139/331929, Fax: +39 091 6110448

Direttore Amministrativo: Antonio Valenti
Tel: +39(091) 607-5713, Fax: +39(091) 334-210
EMail: diramm2@unipa.it

Faculties

Agriculture (Agriculture; Agronomy; Entomology; Forest Biology; Forestry; Oenology; Plant Pathology; Viticulture; Zoology); **Architecture** (Architecture and Planning; Industrial Design; Parks and Recreation; Town Planning; Urban Studies); **Economics** (Business Administration; Business and Commerce; Econometrics; Economics; Labour Law; Statistics); **Educational Training** (Advertising and Publicity; Anthropology; Communication Studies; Education; Educational Sciences; Human Rights; Psychology)); **Engineering** (Aeronautical and Aerospace Engineering; Chemical Engineering; Civil Engineering; Computer Science; Construction Engineering; Electrical Engineering; Electronic Engineering; Engineering; Environmental Engineering; Management; Mechanical Engineering; Nuclear Engineering); **Humanities and Philosophy** (Ancient Civilizations; Anthropology; Archaeology; Arts and Humanities; Fine Arts; Greek; Heritage Preservation; History; Latin; Linguistics; Literature; Modern Languages; Musicology; Performing Arts; Philosophy; Social and Community Services); **Law** (Criminal Law; European Union Law; Labour Law; Law; Private Law; Public Administration); **Mathematics, Physics, and Natural Sciences** (Biology; Chemistry; Computer Science; Environmental Studies; Geological Engineering; Geology; Mathematics; Natural Sciences; Physics); **Medicine and Surgery** (Anaesthesiology; Dentistry; Dietetics; Forensic Medicine and Dentistry; Gerontology; Gynaecology and Obstetrics; Health Sciences; Medicine; Nursing; Ophthalmology; Physical Therapy; Psychiatry and Mental Health; Radiology; Speech Therapy and Audiology; Sports Medicine; Surgery; Urology); **Pharmacy** (Pharmacology; Pharmacy); **Political Science** (Administration; Business Administration; Institutional Administration; Political Sciences; Private Administration; Public Administration); **Sports Science** (Sports; Sports Management; Sports Medicine)

History: Founded 1779 as Academy, became University by Royal Decree 1806. A State institution enjoying administrative autonomy.

Governing Bodies: Senato Accademico 24 members, Consiglio di Amministrazione 17 members

Academic Year: November to October

Admission Requirements: Secondary school certificate (maturità) or recognized equivalent

Main Language(s) of Instruction: Italian

International Co-operation: With universities in Austria, Belgium, Switzerland, Czech Republic, Germany, Denmark, Spain, France, Greece, Hungary, Ireland, Lithuania, Norway, Netherlands, Portugal, Poland, Romania, Sweden, Finland, Slovenia and United Kingdom. Also participates in Erasmus programme.

Degrees and Diplomas: *Laurea (triennale)*; *Diploma di Specializziazione*; *Laurea Magistrale*; *Laurea Specialistica*: Architecture; Pharmacology; Pharmacy; Structural Architecture; Orthodontics and Dentistry, 5 yrs; *Laurea Specialistica*: Environmental Management; Regional Planning; Law; Social Work; Arts and Humanities; Pedagogy; Physics; Information Sciences; Administration Management; European Studies, 2 yrs; *Laurea Specialistica*: Medicine and Surgery, 6 yrs; *Master di 1° Livello*; *Master di 2° Livello*; *Dottorato di Ricerca*: a further 3-4 yrs

Student Services: Canteen, Handicapped facilities, Sports facilities

Student Residential Facilities: For 970 students

Special Facilities: Paleontology Museum. Observatory; Zoology; Botanical Parks

Libraries: Faculty libraries, total, c. 471,000 vols

Publications: Ateneo Palermitano *(monthly)*

Last Updated: 21/10/11

UNIVERSITY OF PARMA

Università degli studi di Parma

Via Università 12, 43121 Parma
Tel: +39(0521) 902-111
Fax: +39(0521) 032-111
EMail: urp@unipr.it
Website: http://www.unipr.it

Rettore: Gino Ferretti (2000-)
Tel: +39(0521) 034-200, Fax: +39(0521) 904-357
EMail: rettore@unipr.it; ferretti@ied.unipr.it

International Relations: Alessandro Bernazzoli, International Relations Officer Tel: +39(0521) 034-037 EMail: relint@unipr.it

Faculties

Agriculture (Agricultural Economics; Biochemistry; Biology; Chemistry; Consumer Studies; Food Science; Food Technology; Oenology; Vegetable Production); **Architecture** (Architecture; Building Technologies; Industrial Design); **Economics** (Business and Commerce; Economics; Finance; International Economics; Marketing); **Engineering** (Civil Engineering; Computer Engineering; Electronic Engineering; Engineering Management; Environmental Engineering; Mechanical Engineering; Telecommunications Engineering); **Humanities and Philosophy** (Archaeology; Behavioural Sciences; Communication Studies; Cultural Studies; Heritage Preservation; Italian; Leisure Studies; Library Science; Literature; Media Studies; Modern Languages; Philosophy; Psychology); **Law** (Law; Social and Community Services; Social Work); **Mathematics, Physics, and Natural Sciences** (Biology; Biotechnology; Chemistry; Computer Science; Ecology; Environmental Studies; Geology; Heritage Preservation; Industrial Chemistry; Materials Engineering; Mathematics; Mathematics and Computer Science; Natural Sciences; Packaging Technology; Physics); **Medicine and Surgery** (Dentistry; Gynaecology and Obstetrics; Laboratory Techniques; Medical Auxiliaries; Medicine; Midwifery; Nursing; Ophthalmology; Optometry; Physical Therapy; Speech Therapy and Audiology; Surgery); **Pharmacy** (Alternative Medicine; Chemistry; Pharmacy); **Veterinary Medicine** (Animal Husbandry; Food Technology; Veterinary Science)

Research Centres

Communication Studies (Communication Studies); **Computer Science** (Computer Science); **Environmental Education** (Environmental Studies); **Language Studies** (Modern Languages)

History: Founded 962. A State institution enjoying administrative autonomy.

Governing Bodies: Consiglio di Amministrazione; Senato Accademico

Academic Year: October to May

Admission Requirements: Secondary school certificate (maturità)

Main Language(s) of Instruction: Italian

Degrees and Diplomas: *Laurea (triennale)*; *Laurea Magistrale*; *Laurea Specialistica*: 2 yrs following Laurea, or 5-6 yrs; *Master di 1° Livello*: following Laurea; *Master di 2° Livello*: following Laurea specialistica; *Dottorato di Ricerca*: following Laurea specialistica

Student Services: Academic counselling, Canteen, Cultural centre, Employment services, Foreign student adviser, Foreign Studies Centre, Handicapped facilities, Language programs, Social counselling, Sports facilities

Student Residential Facilities: For 550 students

Special Facilities: Museo de Scienze Naturali. Centro Studi Archivio della Comunicazione (CSAC). Orto botanico. Museo Paleontologico Parmense; Museo di Mineralogia; Collezione di Strumenti 'Macedonio Melloni'; Museo Anatomico; Museo dell'Istituto di Anatomia Umana Normale

Libraries: Faculty libraries: Medicine, 106,556 vols; Economics, c. 140,000; Law, 125,715; Veterinary Medicine, 36,995; Science, Pharmacy, 8,419; Architecture and Engineering,12,470; Humanities, 208,758

Publications: Acta Biomedica; Acta Naturalia; Annali della Facoltà di Economia (studi e ricerche); Annali della Facoltà di Lettere; Annali della Facoltà di Veterinaria; La Collana della Facoltà di Giurisprudenza; Quaderni di Storia dell'Arte (Collana); Rivista di Matematica; Studi Parmensi

Student Numbers *2012-2013*: Total 28,791
Last Updated: 14/03/13

UNIVERSITY OF PAVIA

Università degli studi di Pavia
Strada Nuova 65, 27100 Pavia
Tel: +39(0382) 9811
Fax: +39(0382) 984-529
EMail: emdir01@unipv.it
Website: http://www.unipv.it

Rettore: Angiolino Stella (2005-)
Tel: +39(0382) 984-202 EMail: rettore@unipv.it

Direttore Amministrativo: Giuseppino Molinari
Tel: +39 0382 984204-5, Fax: +39 0382 984634
EMail: direttore.amministrativo@unipv.it

International Relations: Gianni Vaggi
Tel: +39 0382-984223, Fax: +39 0382-984287

Faculties

Economics (Business Administration; Economics; Management); **Engineering** (Architecture; Chemical Engineering; Civil Engineering; Electronic Engineering; Engineering; Mechanical Engineering); **Humanities and Philosophy** (Arts and Humanities; Literature; Modern Languages; Philosophy; Psychology); **Law** (Law); **Mathematics, Physics, and Natural Sciences** (Environmental Studies; Geology; Mathematics; Natural Sciences; Physics); **Medicine and Surgery** (Dentistry; Medicine; Nursing; Surgery); **Musicology** *(Cremona)* (Music; Music Theory and Composition; Musicology); **Pharmacy** (Pharmacy); **Political Science** (Political Sciences; Social Sciences)

History: Founded 825 as School of Law, recognized as University, Studium Generale, 1361 by Emperor Charles IV. A State institution enjoying administrative autonomy.

Governing Bodies: Senato; Consiglio di Administrazione; Consiglio di Facoltà

Academic Year: November to October

Admission Requirements: Secondary school certificate (maturità) or equivalent

Main Language(s) of Instruction: Italian

International Co-operation: Participates in the Erasmus, Isep, Tempus programmes, and in the Coimbra Group

Degrees and Diplomas: *Laurea (triennale)*; *Diploma di Specializziazione*; *Laurea Magistrale*; *Laurea Specialistica*: Applied Chemistry; Archives and Library Science; Business Law; Business Management; Chemistry and Pharmaceutical Technology; Economics; European and American Cultures; History of Art; Modern Philology; Musicology; Pharmacy; Theoretical and Applied Linguistics, a further 2 yrs; *Laurea Specialistica*: Dentistry and Dental Prothesis, 5 yrs; *Laurea Specialistica*: Medicine; Surgery, 6 yrs; *Master di 1° Livello*; *Master di 2° Livello*; *Dottorato di Ricerca*: All fields. Also Inter-faculty and Inter-university courses. Laurea in Mechanical Engineering with the Polytechnic of Milan

Student Services: Academic counselling, Canteen, Cultural centre, Foreign student adviser, Handicapped facilities, Language programs, Sports facilities

Student Residential Facilities: Yes

Special Facilities: History of the University Museum. Archaeological Museum. Anatomy Museum. Zoological Museum. Mineralogical Museum. Geological Museum. Botanical Garden

Libraries: Central University; libraries of the faculties and departments

Publications: Atheneum *(biannually)*; Atti Istituto Botanico e Laboratorio Crittogamico *(annually)*; Atti Ticinensi di Scienze della Terra *(annually)*; Autografo *(3 per annum)*; Avocetta *(biannually)*; Basic and Applied Histochemistry *(quarterly)*; Diritto Finanziario e Scienza delle Finanze *(quarterly)*; Epidemiologia e Scienze Sanitarie Applicate *(biannually)*; Haematologica *(monthly)*; Il Confronto Letterario *(biannually)*; Il Politico *(quarterly)*; Microbiologica *(annually)*; Selecta Paediatrica *(annually)*

Press or Publishing House: Centro Stampa Universitario
Last Updated: 21/10/11

UNIVERSITY OF PERUGIA

Università degli studi di Perugia
Piazza della Università 1, 06100 Perugia
Tel: +39(075) 5851
Fax: +39(075) 585-2067
EMail: gestione@unipg.it
Website: http://www.unipg.it

Rettore: Francesco Bistoni
Tel: +39 075 5852224, Fax: +39 075 5852359
EMail: rettore@unipg.it

Direttore Administrativo: Angela Maria Lacaita
Tel: +39 075 5852123, Fax: +39 075 5852207
EMail: director@unipg.it

International Relations: Cinzia Rampini, Responsabile
Tel: +39 075 5852219 EMail: cinzia@unipg.it

Faculties

Agriculture (Agriculture; Agronomy; Animal Husbandry; Crop Production; Food Science; Oenology; Viticulture); **Economics**

(Business Administration; Economics; Statistics; Tourism); **Engineering** (Architectural Restoration; Civil Engineering; Electronic Engineering; Environmental Engineering; Materials Engineering; Mechanical Engineering; Telecommunications Engineering); **Humanities and Philosophy** (Communication Studies; Heritage Preservation; Linguistics; Literature; Modern Languages; Philology; Philosophy; Translation and Interpretation); **Law** (History of Law; Law; Private Law; Public Law); **Mathematics, Physics and Natural Sciences** (Astronomy and Space Science; Biology; Chemistry; Computer Science; Geology; Mathematics; Natural Sciences; Physics); **Medicine and Surgery** (Anaesthesiology; Dental Hygiene; Dentistry; Dietetics; Forensic Medicine and Dentistry; Gerontology; Gynaecology and Obstetrics; Laboratory Techniques; Medicine; Nursing; Physical Therapy; Podiatry; Psychiatry and Mental Health; Radiology; Speech Therapy and Audiology; Sports Medicine; Surgery; Urology); **Pharmacy** (Pharmacology; Pharmacy); **Political Science** (Linguistics; Political Sciences; Social and Community Services); **Teacher Training** (Educational Sciences; Italian; Modern Languages; Teacher Training); **Veterinary Medicine** (Veterinary Science)

History: Founded 1200, recognized as university, Studium Generale, by Pope Clement V 1308. A State institution.

Governing Bodies: Consiglio di Amministrazione; Senato Accademico

Academic Year: November to October

Admission Requirements: Secondary school certificate (maturità) or foreign equivalent

Main Language(s) of Instruction: Italian

Degrees and Diplomas: *Laurea (triennale)*; *Laurea Magistrale*; *Laurea Specialistica*: Medicine and Surgery, 6 yrs; *Laurea Specialistica*: Veterinary Medicine and Surgery, 5 yrs; *Master di 1° Livello*; *Master di 2° Livello*; *Dottorato di Ricerca*: 3-4 yrs

Student Residential Facilities: Yes

Libraries: Central Library, c. 150,000 vols; libraries of the faculties, c. 231,000; Classical Studies, c. 23,000 vols

Publications: Annali della Facoltà di-Giurisprudenza; Annali Italiani di Dermatologia e Clinica Sperimentale; Economia e Commercio; La Salute Umana; Lettere e Filosofia; L'Università; Medicina e Chirurgia; Medicina veterinaria; Prosopon; Rivista di Idrobiologia; Scienze agrare; Scienze politiche

Last Updated: 21/10/11

UNIVERSITY OF PISA

Università degli studi di Pisa
Lungarno Pacinotti 43, 56126 Pisa
Tel: +39(050) 221-2111
Fax: +39(050) 408-34
EMail: segr.rettore@unipi.it
Website: http://www.unipi.it

Rettore: Massimo Mario Augello
Tel: +39(050) 221-2175, Fax: +39(050) 424-46
EMail: rettore@unipi.it

Direttore Amministrativo: Riccardo Grasso
Tel: +39(050) 2212-112, Fax: +39(050) 2212-160
EMail: dir.amm@adm.unipi.it

International Relations: Enrico Giaccherini, Vice-Rector for International Relations
Tel: +39 050 2212175, Fax: +39 050 42446
EMail: e.giaccherini@unipi.it

Centres

Interdisciplinary Research *(E. Piaggio)* (Mathematics); **Linguistics** *(Interdepartmental)* (Linguistics)

Faculties

Agriculture (Agriculture; Biotechnology; Chemistry; Oenology; Plant and Crop Protection; Viticulture); **Economics** (Banking; Business Administration; Business and Commerce; Economics; Finance; Marketing); **Engineering** (Aeronautical and Aerospace Engineering; Building Technologies; Chemical Engineering; Civil Engineering; Electrical and Electronic Engineering; Engineering; Information Sciences; Information Technology; Mechanical Engineering; Nuclear Engineering; Telecommunications Engineering); **Foreign Languages and Literature** (Literature; Modern Languages); **Humanities and Philosophy** (Archaeology; Art History; Arts and Humanities; Cinema and Television; Communication Studies; Heritage Preservation; History; Library Science; Literature; Music; Philosophy; Theatre); **Law** (Law); **Mathematics, Physics and Natural Sciences** (Biology; Computer Science; Environmental Studies; Geology; Materials Engineering; Mathematics; Natural Sciences; Physics); **Medicine and Surgery** (Dentistry; Medicine; Surgery); **Pharmacy** (Pharmacy); **Political Science** (Political Sciences); **Veterinary Medicine** (Animal Husbandry; Veterinary Science)

Research Centres

Complex Systems; **Natural History**

History: Founded 1343 as Studium Generale by decree of Pope Clement VI. A State institution enjoying administrative autonomy. Financially supported by the State.

Governing Bodies: Consiglio di Amministrazione; Senato Accademico

Academic Year: November to October

Admission Requirements: Secondary school certificate (maturità)

Main Language(s) of Instruction: Italian

Degrees and Diplomas: *Laurea (triennale)*; *Laurea Magistrale*; *Laurea Specialistica*: a further 2 yrs following Laurea; *Laurea Specialistica*: Medicine, 6 yrs; *Master di 1° Livello*; *Master di 2° Livello*; *Dottorato di Ricerca*: a further 3 yrs following Laurea Specialistica and thesis

Student Services: Academic counselling, Canteen, Cultural centre, Foreign student adviser, Health services, Sports facilities

Student Residential Facilities: Yes

Special Facilities: Museum of Natural and Territorial Sciences. Collection of Drawings and Prints in the History of Art Department. AnatomyCollections (Istituto di Anatomia Umana Normale). Museum and Institute of Morbid Anatomy. Botanical Museum and Gardens. Archaeological Antiquarium. Egyptology Collection. Departmental Centre for the Preservation and Study of Scientific Instruments

Libraries: University libraries, c. 600,000 vols; Bibliographic heritage, c. 900,000 vols

Publications: Pubblicazioni scientifiche *(annually)*

Press or Publishing House: Plus-Pisa University Press

Last Updated: 21/10/11

UNIVERSITY OF ROME LA SAPIENZA

Sapienza Università di Roma
Piazzale Aldo Moro 5, 00185 Roma
Tel: +39(06) 49911
Fax: +39(06) 4991-0382
EMail: urp@uniroma1.it
Website: http://www.uniroma1.it

Rettore: Luigi Frati (2008-)
Tel: +39(06) 4991-0292, Fax: +39(06) 4991-0382
EMail: rettore@uniroma1.it

Direttore Amministrativo: Carlo Musto d'Amore
Tel: +39(06) 4991-0311 +39(06) 4991-0602,
Fax: +39(06) 4991-0698 EMail: carlo.mustodamore@uniroma1.it

International Relations: Antonella Cammisa
Tel: +39(06) 4991-0745, Fax: +39(06) 4991-0978
EMail: antonella.cammisa@uniroma1.it

Faculties

Architecture *(Valle Giulia)* (Architecture; Industrial Design; Landscape Architecture; Urban Studies); **Architecture** *(Ludovico Quaroni)* (Architectural Restoration; Architecture; Environmental Studies; Industrial Design; Landscape Architecture; Parks and Recreation; Town Planning); **Civil and Industrial Engineering** (Aeronautical and Aerospace Engineering; Automation and Control Engineering; Building Technologies; Chemical Engineering; Civil Engineering; Computer Engineering; Computer Science; Construction Engineering; Electrical Engineering; Electronic Engineering; Energy Engineering; Environmental Engineering; Hydraulic Engineering; Management; Mechanical Engineering; Structural Architecture;

Telecommunications Engineering; Transport Engineering); **Economics** (Banking; Business Administration; Commercial Law; Economics; Finance; Insurance; International Economics; Political Sciences; Social Welfare; Tourism); **Law** (Comparative Law; Criminal Law; Human Rights; International Law; Law; Private Law; Public Law); **Mathematics, Physics, and Natural Sciences** (Agricultural Business; Agrobiology; Applied Chemistry; Applied Mathematics; Applied Physics; Astronomy and Space Science; Astrophysics; Biological and Life Sciences; Biotechnology; Chemistry; Computer Networks; Computer Science; Environmental Studies; Geology; Heritage Preservation; Industrial Chemistry; Information Technology; Mathematics; Natural Sciences; Physics); **Medicine and Dentistry** (Dentistry; Medicine); **Medicine and Psychology** (Medicine; Psychology); **Pharmacy and Medicine** (Medicine; Pharmacy); **Philosophy, Letters, Humanities and Oriental Studies** (American Studies; Ancient Civilizations; Art History; Cinema and Television; Classical Languages; Cultural Studies; Dance; Documentation Techniques; European Studies; History; Italian; Linguistics; Literature; Oriental Studies; Performing Arts; Philology; Philosophy; Religion; Theatre); **Political Science, Sociology and Communication** (Communication Studies; Development Studies; Economic and Finance Policy; Economics; Government; International Relations; International Studies; Political Sciences; Sociology); **Psychology I** (Cognitive Sciences; Developmental Psychology; Industrial and Organizational Psychology; Pathology; Psychology); **Psychology II** (Developmental Psychology; Educational Psychology; Industrial and Organizational Psychology; Psychology; Social Psychology); **Sociology** (Communication Studies; Human Resources; Social Sciences; Sociology); **Statistics** (Business Computing; Demography and Population; Economics; Finance; Information Technology; Insurance; Sociology; Statistics)

Schools

Aerospace Engineering (Aeronautical and Aerospace Engineering); **Archive and Library Sciences** (Archiving; Heritage Preservation; Library Science)

History: Founded 1303 by Pope Boniface VIII. Acquired present status 1935. A State institution enjoying administrative autonomy. Financially supported by the State.

Governing Bodies: Senato Accademico; Consiglio di Amministrazione

Academic Year: November to October

Admission Requirements: School leaving certificate (Diploma di Scuola media di 2° Grado)

Fees: (Euros): 336-1,291 per annum

Main Language(s) of Instruction: Italian

International Co-operation: With universities in Europe; Latin America; USA; Asia; Mediterranean region

Accrediting Agencies: Ministry of Education, University and Research

Degrees and Diplomas: *Laurea (triennale)*; *Laurea Magistrale*; *Laurea Specialistica*: a further 2 yrs; *Master di 1° Livello*: All fields, 1 yr following Laurea Specialistica; *Master di 2° Livello*: All fields, 2 yrs following Laurea Specialistica; *Dottorato di Ricerca*: 3 yrs

Student Services: Canteen, Cultural centre, Handicapped facilities, Health services, Sports facilities

Student Residential Facilities: For 1,440 students, awarded subject to family income

Special Facilities: 41 Museums

Libraries: 93 libraries

Publications: Publications of the departments and institutes

Last Updated: 03/10/11

UNIVERSITY OF ROME TOR VERGATA

Università degli studi di Roma Tor Vergata

Via Orazio Raimondo 18, 00173 Roma

Tel: +39(06) 72591

Fax: +39(06) 723-4368

EMail: rettore@uniroma2.it

Website: http://www.uniroma2.it

Rettore: Renato Lauro (2008-)
Tel: +39(06) 723-5404, Fax: +39(06) 723-5980

Faculties

Economics (Administration; Business and Commerce; Business Computing; Economics; Finance; Taxation); **Engineering** (Civil Engineering; Computer Science; Construction Engineering; Electronic Engineering; Environmental Engineering; Management Systems; Mechanical Engineering; Medical Technology; Telecommunications Engineering); **Humanities and Philosophy** (Arts and Humanities; Dance; Greek; Heritage Preservation; Latin; Literature; Modern Languages; Music; Philosophy); **Law** (Human Rights; Labour Law; Law); **Mathematics, Physics, and Natural Sciences** (Biology; Biotechnology; Communication Studies; Mass Communication; Mathematics; Natural Sciences; Physics); **Medicine and Surgery** (Anaesthesiology; Cardiology; Criminology; Dermatology; Dietetics; Forensic Medicine and Dentistry; Gerontology; Gynaecology and Obstetrics; Laboratory Techniques; Medicine; Nursing; Nutrition; Ophthalmology; Orthopaedics; Paediatrics; Physical Therapy; Plastic Surgery; Podiatry; Psychiatry and Mental Health; Radiology; Speech Therapy and Audiology; Sports Medicine; Surgery; Urology; Venereology)

History: Founded 1979 by law; courses started 1982.

Main Language(s) of Instruction: Italian

Degrees and Diplomas: *Laurea (triennale)*; *Laurea Magistrale*; *Master di 1° Livello*; *Master di 2° Livello*; *Dottorato di Ricerca*

Libraries: Yes

Publications: Quaderni di Tor Vergata

Last Updated: 21/10/11

UNIVERSITY OF SALENTO

Università del Salento

Piazza Tancredi, 7, 73100 Lecce

Tel: +39(0832) 291-111

EMail: direzione.amministrativa@unisalento.it

Website: http://www.unisalento.it/web/guest/home_page

Rettore: Domenico Laforgia
Tel: +39(0832) 2585, Fax: +39(0832) 292-204
EMail: rettore@unisalento.it

Direttore Amministrativo: Emilio Miccolis
Tel: +39 0832 292210-292396, Fax: +39 0832 292212-292219
EMail: emilio.miccolis@unisalento.it

Faculties

Arts and Humanities (Arts and Humanities; Development Studies; Philosophy; Social Studies); **Cultural Heritage** (Cultural Studies; Heritage Preservation); **Economics** (Business Administration; Business and Commerce; Cultural Studies; Economic and Finance Policy; Economics; Environmental Management; Finance; Marketing); **Educational Sciences** (Educational Sciences; Pedagogy; Social Sciences; Social Studies; Sociology); **Engineering** (Computer Engineering; Engineering; Management; Materials Engineering; Mechanical Engineering); **Foreign Languages and Literature** (Literature; Modern Languages); **Industrial Engineering** (Industrial Engineering); **Law** (Law); **Mathematics, Physics, and Natural Sciences** (Applied Mathematics; Biology; Biotechnology; Environmental Studies; Mathematics; Natural Sciences; Physics); **Social, Political and Territorial Sciences** (Political Sciences; Social Sciences; Sociology)

History: Founded 1966. A State institution enjoying administrative autonomy. Previously known as Università degli studi di Lecce. Acquired current title 2006.

Governing Bodies: Senato Accademico; Consiglio di Amministrazione (maturitá)

Academic Year: November to October

Admission Requirements: Secondary school certificate

Main Language(s) of Instruction: Italian

Degrees and Diplomas: *Laurea (triennale)*; *Attestato/Diploma di Perfezionamento*: 1 yr; *Diploma di Specializziazione*: a further yr; *Laurea Magistrale*; *Laurea Specialistica*; *Master di 1° Livello*; *Master di 2° Livello*; *Dottorato di Ricerca*

Student Residential Facilities: Yes

Libraries: Central Library, c. 90,000 vols

Publications: Publications of the Institutes and Departments

Last Updated: 24/10/11

UNIVERSITY OF SALERNO

Università degli studi di Salerno (UNISA)
Via Ponte Don Melillo, Mercato S, Severino, 84084 Fisciano
Tel: +39(089) 966-111
Fax: +39(089) 966-246
EMail: ueri@seda.unisa.it
Website: http://www.unisa.it

Rettore: Raimondo Pasquino (2001-)
Tel: +39(089) 966-001, Fax: +39(089) 966-116
EMail: segrrett@unisa.it

Direttore Amministrativo: Giuseppe Paduano
Tel: +39(089) 966-006 EMail: diramm@seda.unisa.it

Faculties

Economics (Business and Commerce; Economics; Statistics); **Engineering** (Chemical Engineering; Civil Engineering; Electrical Engineering; Engineering; Mechanical Engineering); **Foreign Languages and Literature** (Literature; Modern Languages); **Humanities and Philosophy** (Arts and Humanities; Communication Studies; Heritage Preservation; Literature; Philosophy; Sociology); **Law** (Law); **Mathematics, Physics and Natural Sciences** (Biology; Computer Science; Environmental Management; Mathematics; Natural Sciences; Physics); **Medicine and Surgery** (Medicine; Surgery); **Pharmacy** (Pharmacy); **Political Science** (Administration; International Relations; Political Sciences); **Teacher Training** (Education; Teacher Training)

History: Founded 1944. Acquired present status 1968.

Governing Bodies: Senato Accademico; Consiglio di Amministrazione

Academic Year: November to October

Admission Requirements: Secondary school certificate (Diploma di Scuola Superiore)

Main Language(s) of Instruction: Italian

International Co-operation: With universities in USA, Spain, France, Russian Federation, Colombia, Brazil, Malta and Ukraine.

Degrees and Diplomas: *Laurea (triennale)*; *Laurea Magistrale*; *Master di 1° Livello*: 2 yrs; *Master di 2° Livello*; *Dottorato di Ricerca*: 3 yrs

Student Services: Canteen, Foreign student adviser, Handicapped facilities, Health services, Language programs, Sports facilities

Student Residential Facilities: Yes

Libraries: Central Library and Scientific Library

Publications: Collana Scientifica delle Pubblicazioni dell'Università di Salerno *(monthly)*

Last Updated: 21/10/11

UNIVERSITY OF SANNIO

Università degli studi del Sannio
Palazzo S. Domenico, Piazza Guerrazzi 1,
82100 Benevento
Tel: +39(0824) 305-001
Fax: +39(0824) 43-021
EMail: amministrazione@cert.unisannio.it
Website: http://www.unisannio.it

Rettore: Filippo Bencardino
Tel: +39 0824 305002, Fax: +39 0824 43021
EMail: rettore@unisannio.it

Direttore Amministrativo: Gaetano Telesio
Tel: +39 0824 305010, Fax: +39 0824 23648
EMail: direzione.amministrativa@unisannio.it

International Relations: Lorella Maria Teresa Canzoniero
Tel: +39 0824 305454, Fax: +39 0824 23648
EMail: ufficio.ricerca@unisannio.it

Faculties

Economics (Economics); **Engineering** (Automation and Control Engineering; Civil Engineering; Computer Engineering; Energy Engineering; Telecommunications Engineering); **Law** (Law; Political Sciences; Statistics); **Mathematics, Physics and Natural Sciences** (Biology; Biotechnology; Geology; Mathematics; Physics)

History: Founded 1998.

Main Language(s) of Instruction: Italian

Degrees and Diplomas: *Laurea (triennale)*; *Laurea Magistrale*; *Laurea Specialistica*; *Master di 1° Livello*; *Master di 2° Livello*; *Dottorato di Ricerca*

Libraries: Yes

Last Updated: 20/10/11

UNIVERSITY OF SASSARI

Università degli studi di Sassari
Piazza Università 21, 07100 Sassari
Tel: +39(079) 228-211
Fax: +39(079) 228-816
EMail: rettore@uniss.it
Website: http://www.uniss.it

Rettore: Attilio Mastino (2009-) Tel: +39(079) 228-211

Direttore Amministrativo: Guido Crocci Tel: +39(079) 228-822

International Relations: Savio Domenico Regaglia, International Relations Officer
Tel: +39(079) 229-787, Fax: +39(079) 229-979
EMail: relint@uniss.it

Faculties

Agriculture (Agriculture; Biotechnology; Environmental Studies; Food Technology; Forestry; Viticulture); **Architecture** (Architecture; Design; Town Planning); **Economics** (Economics; Management; Tourism); **Foreign Languages and Literature** (Literature; Modern Languages); **Humanities and Philosophy** (Anthropology; Archaeology; Arts and Humanities; Communication Studies; Educational Sciences; Heritage Preservation; Literature; Philosophy; Social Policy); **Law** (Law); **Mathematics, Physics, and Natural Sciences** (Biology; Biotechnology; Environmental Management; Environmental Studies; Mathematics; Natural Sciences; Physics); **Medicine and Surgery** (Medicine; Surgery); **Pharmacy** (Pharmacy); **Political Science** (Political Sciences); **Veterinary Medicine** (Veterinary Science)

History: Founded 1562 as Studium Generale and recognized by Bull of Pope Paul V. Established as University 1617, reorganized 1766. A State institution enjoying administrative autonomy.

Governing Bodies: Consiglio di Amministrazione; Senato Accademico

Academic Year: November to October

Admission Requirements: Secondary school certificate (maturità) or for some fields, Technical School Diploma

Main Language(s) of Instruction: Italian

International Co-operation: Participates in the Erasmus programme, co-operation with developing countries

Degrees and Diplomas: *Laurea (triennale)*; *Laurea Magistrale*; *Laurea Specialistica*: Chemistry and Pharmacology; Pharmacy; Veterinary Medicine; Orthodontics and Dental Technology, 5 yrs; *Laurea Specialistica*: Medicine and Surgery, 6 yrs; *Master di 1° Livello*; *Master di 2° Livello*; *Dottorato di Ricerca*

Student Services: Handicapped facilities, Health services, Language programs, Sports facilities

Student Residential Facilities: Yes

Special Facilities: Botanical Garden

Libraries: Yes

Student Numbers *2011-2012*: Total 13,659

Last Updated: 21/10/11

UNIVERSITY OF SIENA

Università degli studi di Siena
Via Banchi di Sotto 55, 53100 Siena
Tel: +39(0577) 232-403
Fax: +39(0577) 232-392
EMail: uri@unisi.it
Website: http://www.unisi.it

Rettore: Angelo Riccaboni
Tel: +39(0577) 232-206, Fax: +39(0577) 232-202
EMail: rettore@unisi.it

International Relations: Annalisa Poggialini, Head of International Relations
Tel: +39(0577) 232-403 EMail: annalisa.poggialini@unisi.it

Faculties

Economics (Banking; Business Administration; Econometrics; Economics; Environmental Management; Finance; International Business; International Economics; Tourism); **Engineering** (Automation and Control Engineering; Computer Engineering; Engineering; Telecommunications Engineering); **Humanities and Philosophy** *(Arezzo)* (Ancient Civilizations; Archaeology; Art History; Educational Sciences; Heritage Preservation; History; Literature; Modern Languages; Philosophy); **Humanities and Philosophy** (Anthropology; Archaeology; Art History; Classical Languages; Communication Studies; History; Literature; Modern Languages; Philosophy); **Law** (Law); **Mathematics, Physics, and Natural Sciences** (Biology; Chemistry; Geology; Heritage Preservation; Mathematics; Natural Sciences; Physics; Physiology); **Medicine and Surgery** (Biophysics; Cosmetology; Dental Hygiene; Dentistry; Dermatology; Dietetics; Forensic Medicine and Dentistry; Gastroenterology; Gynaecology and Obstetrics; Laboratory Techniques; Medicine; Microbiology; Nursing; Nutrition; Ophthalmology; Osteopathy; Paediatrics; Physical Therapy; Psychiatry and Mental Health; Radiology; Rheumatology; Speech Therapy and Audiology; Sports Medicine; Surgery; Toxicology; Urology; Virology); **Pharmacy** (Alternative Medicine; Cosmetology; Criminal Law; Forensic Medicine and Dentistry; International Law; Labour Law; Nutrition; Organic Chemistry; Pharmacology; Pharmacy; Public Law; Statistics); **Political Science** (Political Sciences; Social Work)

History: Founded 1240 but traces its history to a school of Roman Law, 1056. Recognized as Studium Generale, confirmed by Frederick II 1248, and Pope Innocent IV 1252. Became a State institution 1859. A State institution enjoying administrative autonomy. Financially supported by the State, the Municipality and the Province of Siena, and other bodies.

Governing Bodies: Consiglio di Amministrazione; Senato Accademico

Academic Year: October to June (October-January; March-June)

Admission Requirements: Secondary school certificate (maturità)

Main Language(s) of Instruction: Italian

Degrees and Diplomas: *Laurea (triennale)*; *Laurea Magistrale*; *Laurea Specialistica*: Dentistry, 5 yrs; *Laurea Specialistica*: Medicine and Surgery, 6 yrs; *Master di 1° Livello*; *Master di 2° Livello*; *Dottorato di Ricerca*

Student Services: Academic counselling, Canteen, Cultural centre, Handicapped facilities, Social counselling, Sports facilities

Student Residential Facilities: Yes

Special Facilities: Accademia dei Fisiocritici

Libraries: Central Libraries of the Faculties; Libraries of the Institutes

Student Numbers *2012-2013*: Total 19,769

Last Updated: 14/03/13

UNIVERSITY OF TERAMO

Università degli studi di Teramo

Viale Crucioli 120, 64100 Teramo
Tel: +39(0861) 2661
Fax: +39(0861) 245-350
EMail: info@unite.it
Website: http://www.unite.it

Rettore: Rita Tranquilli Leali (2009-)
Tel: +39(0861) 266-285 EMail: rettore@unite.it

Direttore Amministrativo: Luigi Renzullo
Tel: +39(0861) 266-214 EMail: lrenzullo@unite.it

Faculties

Agriculture (Food Science; Food Technology; Oenology; Viticulture); **Communication Science** (Communication Studies); **Law** (History of Law; Law; Private Law; Public Law); **Political Science** (Political Sciences); **Veterinary Medicine** (Veterinary Science)

History: Founded 1993.

Governing Bodies: Consiglio di Amministrazione; Senato Accademico

Admission Requirements: Secondary school certificate (maturità) and entrance examination

Main Language(s) of Instruction: Italian

International Co-operation: Participates in the Socrates/Erasmus programmes

Degrees and Diplomas: *Laurea (triennale)*; *Laurea Magistrale*; *Master di 1° Livello*; *Master di 2° Livello*; *Dottorato di Ricerca*

Student Services: Academic counselling, Canteen, Foreign student adviser, Language programs, Sports facilities

Student Residential Facilities: Yes

Last Updated: 21/10/11

UNIVERSITY OF THE VALLEY OF AOSTA

Università della Valle d'Aosta

Strada Cappuccini 2A, 11100 Aosta
Tel: +39(0165) 306711
EMail: info@univda.it
Website: http://www.univda.it

Rettore: Pietro Passerin d'Entreves
Tel: +39(0165) 306-730, Fax: +39(0165) 306-749
EMail: u-rettorato@univda.it

Faculties

Economics and Business Administration (Administrative Law; Business Administration; Commercial Law; Economics); **Language and Communication** (Communication Studies; Cultural Studies; English; French; Italian; Portuguese; Spanish); **Political Science and International Relations** (European Union Law; International Law; International Relations; Modern History; Political Sciences; Private Law; Public Law; Sociology); **Psychology** (Psychology); **Teacher Training** (Educational Sciences; Preschool Education; Primary Education)

History: Founded 2000.

Main Language(s) of Instruction: Italian

Degrees and Diplomas: *Laurea (triennale)*; *Laurea Magistrale*; *Laurea Specialistica*; *Master di 1° Livello*; *Master di 2° Livello*

Libraries: Yes

Last Updated: 24/10/11

UNIVERSITY OF TRENTO

Università degli studi di Trento

Via Belenzani 12, 38100 Trento
Tel: +39(0461) 881-111
Fax: +39(0461) 881-258
EMail: orienta@unitn.it
Website: http://www.unitn.it

Rettore: Davide Bassi (1996-)
Tel: +39(0461) 881-121, Fax: +39(0461) 881-247
EMail: rettore@unitn.it

Direttore Amministrativo: Marco Tomasi
Tel: +39 0461 881240, Fax: +39 0461 881258
EMail: direzione.generale@unitn.it

Faculties

Arts and Philosophy (Comparative Literature; Heritage Preservation; History; Modern Languages; Philology; Philosophy); **Cognitive Science** *(Rovereto)* (Social Sciences); **Economics** (Business Administration; Business Computing; International Business; International Studies; Law; Management; Social Studies); **Engineering** (Architecture; Civil Engineering; Environmental Engineering; Food Technology; Industrial Engineering; Materials Engineering; Mechanical Engineering; Metallurgical Engineering; Production Engineering; Telecommunications Engineering); **Law** (European Union Law); **Mathematical, Physical and Natural Sciences** (Biotechnology; Computer Science; Mathematics; Physics); **Sociology** (Social Work; Sociology)

History: Founded 1962 as private Istituto Superiore di Scienze Sociali by the Istituto Trentino di Cultura. Recognized by the State 1966 and became Libera Università 1972. Acquired status and title 1982. A State Institution enjoying administrative autonomy. Acquired present status 1995.

Governing Bodies: Consiglio di Amministrazione (Board of Directors); Senato Accademico (Univrersity Senate)

Academic Year: November to October

Admission Requirements: Secondary school certificate (maturità) or recognized foreign equivalent

Main Language(s) of Instruction: Italian

Degrees and Diplomas: *Laurea (triennale)*; *Laurea Magistrale*; *Laurea Specialistica*: a furhetr 2 yrs; *Master di 1° Livello*; *Master di 2° Livello*; *Dottorato di Ricerca*: a further 3 yrs

Student Services: Canteen, Cultural centre, Foreign student adviser, Foreign Studies Centre, Handicapped facilities, Language programs, Sports facilities

Student Residential Facilities: Yes

Libraries: Central Library; Library of Arts and Philosophy; Library of Engineering; Library of Science; Library of Rovereto Branch

Last Updated: 21/10/11

UNIVERSITY OF TRIESTE

Università degli studi di Trieste

Piazzale Europa 1, 34127 Trieste
Tel: +39(040) 558-7111
Fax: +39(040) 558-3093
EMail: rettore@univ.trieste.it
Website: http://www.units.it

Rettore: Francesco Peroni
Tel: +39(040) 558-3001, Fax: +39(040) 558-3000

Faculties

Architecture (Architecture; Architecture and Planning); **Economics** (Business Administration; Economics; Marketing; Statistics); **Education** (Communication Studies; Education; Teacher Training); **Engineering** (Chemical Engineering; Civil Engineering; Electrical and Electronic Engineering; Engineering; Environmental Engineering; Materials Engineering; Mechanical Engineering; Naval Architecture); **Humanities and Philosophy** (Archaeology; Art History; History; Literature; Modern Languages; Philosophy); **Law** (Law); **Mathematics, Physics and Natural Sciences** (Biology; Chemistry; Information Technology; Mathematics; Natural Sciences; Physics); **Medicine and Surgery** (Biomedical Engineering; Biotechnology; Dentistry; Gynaecology and Obstetrics; Medicine; Nursing; Physical Therapy; Radiology; Rehabilitation and Therapy; Surgery); **Pharmacy** (Pharmacy); **Political Science** (Administration; Political Sciences); **Psychology** (Psychology)

Schools

Modern Languages, Translation and Interpretation (Arabic; Chinese; Cultural Studies; Dutch; English; French; German; Literature; Portuguese; Russian; Slavic Languages; Spanish; Translation and Interpretation)

Further Information: Also Teaching Hospitals

History: Founded 1877 on private initiative as College of Commerce. Transformed by Italian Government into Institute of Economics and Commerce 1920, awarded university status 1924, but not established unitl 1945. Faculty of Humanities and Philosophy created 1943 on the intiative of the academic staff and subsequently granted formal recognition. A state institution enjoying administrative and didactic autonomy.

Governing Bodies: Senato accademico; Consiglio di Amministrazione

Academic Year: November to October

Admission Requirements: Secondary school certificate (maturità) or foreign equivalent

Main Language(s) of Instruction: Italian

International Co-operation: With universities in EU countries; Danube and Balkan Region; Alps-Adriatic countries; Central and Eastern European countries; North and South America; China; Australia. Runs a Fulbright Chair. Also participates in Socrates, Erasmus, Leonardo da Vinci programmes. Member of the Santander Group European Network and CEI network.

Degrees and Diplomas: *Laurea (triennale)*; *Diploma di Specializziazione*; *Laurea Magistrale*; *Laurea Specialistica*: 2 yrs; *Master di 1° Livello*: 1 yr; *Master di 2° Livello*: 1 yr; *Dottorato di Ricerca*: 3 yrs

Student Services: Academic counselling, Cultural centre, Sports facilities

Student Residential Facilities: Yes

Special Facilities: Antarctica Museum. Observatory

Libraries: c. 880,000 vols.

Publications: Research Directory *(biennially)*

Press or Publishing House: EUT (Trieste University Press)

Last Updated: 21/10/11

UNIVERSITY OF TURIN

Università degli studi di Torino

Via Verdi 8, 10124 Torino
Tel: +39(011) 670-6111
Fax: +39(011) 670-2218
EMail: info@unito.it
Website: http://www.unito.it

Rettore: Ezio Pelizzetti (2004-)
Tel: +39(011) 6702200/2201, Fax: +39(011) 6702218
EMail: rettore@unito.it

Direttore Amministrativo: Loredano Segreto
Tel: +39 011 6702066, Fax: +39 011 6702230
EMail: loredana.segreto@unito.it

Faculties

Agriculture (Agricultural Economics; Agricultural Engineering; Agriculture; Agronomy; Forestry; Zoology); **Economics** (Banking; Business and Commerce; Economics; Insurance); **Foreign Languages and Literature** (Literature; Modern Languages); **Humanities and Philosophy** (Archaeology; Archiving; Arts and Humanities; Communication Studies; Cultural Studies; Heritage Preservation; History; Library Science; Literature; Philosophy); **Law** (Law); **Mathematics, Physics, and Natural Sciences** (Computer Science; Geology; Mathematics; Natural Sciences; Optometry; Physics); **Medicine and Surgery** *(Torino)* (Medicine; Surgery); **Medicine and Surgery** *(S.Luigi Gonzaga)* (Medicine; Surgery); **Pharmacy** (Pharmacy); **Political Science** (Political Sciences); **Psychology** (Psychology); **Teacher Training** (Teacher Training); **Veterinary Medicine** (Veterinary Science)

Schools

Management

History: Founded 1404 by Benedetto XIII. Reorganized and re-established 1713. A State institution enjoying administrative autonomy. Financially supported by the State and local public funds.

Governing Bodies: Consiglio di Amministrazione; Senato Accademico

Academic Year: November to October

Admission Requirements: Secondary school certificate (maturità) or equivalent

Main Language(s) of Instruction: Italian

International Co-operation: Participates in the Erasmus programme

Degrees and Diplomas: *Laurea (triennale)*; *Laurea Magistrale*; *Laurea Specialistica*: Agriculture; Economics; Foreign Languages and Literature; Law; Arts and Humanities; Philosophy; Mathematics; Physics; Natural Sciences; Political Science; Psychology; Teacher Training; Management, 2 yrs; *Laurea Specialistica*: Medicine, 6 yrs; *Laurea Specialistica*: Pharmacy; Dentistry; Veterinary Science, 5 yrs; *Master di 1° Livello*: 1 yr; *Master di 2° Livello*: 1 yr; *Dottorato di Ricerca*: Agriculture; Economics; Foreign Languages and Literature; Law; Arts and Humanities; Philosophy; Mathematics; Physics; Natural Sciences; Political Science; Psychology; Teacher Training; Management; Medicine; Pharmacy; Veterinary Science; Dentistry, 3 yrs

Student Services: Handicapped facilities, Social counselling

Student Residential Facilities: Yes

Special Facilities: Anthropology Museum; Geology Museum; Zoology Museum;Criminal Anthropology Museum

Libraries: Libraries of the Faculties

Last Updated: 21/10/11

UNIVERSITY OF TUSCIA

Università degli studi della Tuscia
Via Santa Maria in Gradi 4, 01100 Viterbo
Tel: +39(0761) 3571
Fax: +39(0761) 325-785
EMail: rettore@unitus.it
Website: http://www.unitus.it

Rettore: Marco Mancini
Tel: +39(0761) 324-687, Fax: +39(0761) 325-785
EMail: marco_manci@libero.it

Direttore Amministrativo: Giovanni Cucullo

International Relations: Stefano Grego
Tel: +39(0761) 357-329, Fax: +39(0761) 357-919
EMail: relint@unitus.it

Faculties

Agriculture (Agricultural Engineering; Agriculture; Animal Husbandry; Biotechnology; Crop Production; Development Studies; Ecology; Environmental Studies; Food Science; Food Technology; Forestry; Oenology; Plant and Crop Protection; Rural Planning; Rural Studies; Wood Technology); **Cultural Heritage** (Archaeology; Architectural Restoration; Archiving; Art History; Heritage Preservation; Library Science; Multimedia; Museum Studies; Restoration of Works of Art); **Economics** (Business and Commerce; Economics; Finance; Labour and Industrial Relations; Labour Law); **Foreign Languages and Literature** (Literature; Modern Languages; Philology; Translation and Interpretation); **Mathematics, Physics and Natural Sciences** (Agrobiology; Biological and Life Sciences; Biotechnology; Cell Biology; Environmental Studies; Marine Biology; Marine Science and Oceanography; Mathematics; Molecular Biology; Natural Sciences; Physics; Water Science); **Political Science** (Political Sciences)

History: Founded 1979. A State institution enjoying administrative autonomy. Financially supported by the State. Campuses in: Monterotondo; Cittaducale; Velletri (Wine Production).

Governing Bodies: Senato Academico; Consiglio di Amministrazione

Academic Year: November to October

Admission Requirements: Secondary school certificate (maturità)

Main Language(s) of Instruction: Italian

International Co-operation: Participates in the Socrates, Erasmus, Comett and Tempus programmes

Degrees and Diplomas: *Laurea (triennale)*; *Laurea Magistrale*; *Master di 1° Livello*; *Master di 2° Livello*; *Dottorato di Ricerca*

Student Services: Academic counselling, Canteen, Cultural centre, Foreign student adviser, Handicapped facilities, Sports facilities

Student Residential Facilities: Yes

Special Facilities: Botanical Gardens. Experimental Farm. Vocational Alpine Training Centre

Libraries: Libraries of the Faculties of Agriculture and Foreign Languages and Literature

Last Updated: 20/10/11

UNIVERSITY OF UDINE

Università degli studi di Udine
Palazzo Florio, 33100 Udine
Tel: +39(0432) 556-111
Fax: +39(0432) 507-715
EMail: archivio@uniud.it
Website: http://www.uniud.it

Rettore: Cristiana Compagno (2008-2013)
Tel: +39(0432) 556-250, Fax: +39(0432) 556-259
EMail: rettore@uniud.it

Direttore Amministrativo: Clara Coviello
Tel: +39(0432) 556-280, Fax: +39(0432) 556-309
EMail: clara.coviello@uniud.it

Faculties

Agriculture *(FAAG)* (Agriculture; Biotechnology; Environmental Studies; Food Technology; Oenology; Viticulture); **Economics** *(FAEC)* (Banking; Business Administration; Business and Commerce; Business Computing; Economics; Finance); **Engineering** *(FAIN)* (Architecture; Civil Engineering; Electronic Engineering; Engineering; Environmental Engineering; Industrial Engineering; Mechanical Engineering); **Foreign Languages and Literature** *(FALI)* (German; Modern Languages; Oriental Languages; Oriental Studies; Public Relations; Translation and Interpretation); **Humanities and Philosophy** *(FALE)* (Archaeology; Archiving; Arts and Humanities; Cinema and Television; Classical Languages; Heritage Preservation; History; Library Science; Music; Philosophy); **Law** *(FAGI)* (Law); **Mathematics, Physics, and Natural Sciences** *(FAMA)* (Computer Science; Mathematics; Natural Sciences; Physics; Statistics); **Medicine and Surgery** *(FAAM)* (Biotechnology; Gynaecology and Obstetrics; Laboratory Techniques; Medicine; Nursing; Physical Therapy; Radiology; Surgery); **Teacher Training** *(FASE)* (Teacher Training); **Veterinary Medicine** *(FAVE)* (Veterinary Science)

Further Information: Also Italian summer courses for foreign students.

History: Founded 1978, incorporating faculties previously attached to the University of Trieste. A State institution enjoying administrative autonomy. Financially supported by the State.

Governing Bodies: Consiglio di Amministrazione; Senato Accademico

Academic Year: September to August

Admission Requirements: Secondary school certificate (maturità)

Main Language(s) of Instruction: Italian

International Co-operation: Participates in the Socrates, Tempus and Leonardo programmes

Degrees and Diplomas: *Laurea (triennale)*; *Diploma di Specializzazione*; *Laurea Magistrale*; *Laurea Specialistica*: a further 2 yrs; *Master di 1° Livello*: 1 yr following Laurea Specialistica; *Master di 2° Livello*; *Dottorato di Ricerca*: 3 yrs

Student Services: Canteen, Foreign student adviser, Foreign Studies Centre, Handicapped facilities, Language programs

Student Residential Facilities: For 700 students

Special Facilities: Art Galleries. Observatory. Biological Garden

Libraries: Faculty Libraries, c. 114,823 vols; libraries of the institutes, 137,342

Publications: La Ricerca Informa *(monthly)*

Last Updated: 21/10/11

UNIVERSITY OF VERONA

Università degli studi di Verona
Via S. dell'Artigliere 8, 37129 Verona
Tel: +39(045) 809-8111
Fax: +39(045) 809-8255
EMail: ufficio.rettorato@ateneo.univr.it
Website: http://www.univr.it

Rettore: Alessandro Mazzucco
Tel: +39 045 8028253, Fax: +39 045 8028255
EMail: alessandro.mazzucco@univr.it

Direttore Amministrativo: Antonio Salvini
Tel: +39 045 8028211, Fax: +39 045 8028255
EMail: antonio.salvini@univr.it

International Relations: Elisa Silvestri Nazzaro, Direttore
Tel: +39 045 8028283, Fax: +39 045 8028592
EMail: mara.olivetti@univr.it

Centres

European Documentation; **Linguistics** (Linguistics); **Strategic Planning and Evaluation**

Faculties

Economics (Accountancy; Business Administration; Economics; Food Technology; International Business); **Education** (Education); **Humanities and Philosophy** (Arts and Humanities; Communication Studies; Educational Sciences; Heritage Preservation; Journalism; Philosophy; Publishing and Book Trade); **Law** (Law); **Mathematics, Physical and Natural Sciences** (Agricultural Engineering; Computer Science; Information Sciences; Mathematics; Natural Sciences; Physics); **Medicine and Surgery** (Biomedical

Engineering; Dental Hygiene; Dentistry; Gynaecology and Obstetrics; Medicine; Nursing; Paramedical Sciences; Psychiatry and Mental Health; Rehabilitation and Therapy; Surgery); **Modern Languages and Literature** (Literature; Modern Languages); **Sports** (Sports)

Further Information: Also special Training School for Cardiocirculatory Physiopathologists

History: Founded 1959 as Faculty of the University of Padua, acquired present status 1982.

Governing Bodies: Senato Accademico

Academic Year: October to September

Admission Requirements: Secondary school certificate (maturità)

Main Language(s) of Instruction: Italian

International Co-operation: Participates in the Socrates/Erasmus, Leonardo da Vinci, Jean Monnet Action, Fifth Framework programmes. Several bilateral agreements have been signed in the area of didactic and research cooperation with European and non-European institutions

Degrees and Diplomas: *Laurea (triennale)*; *Attestato/Diploma di Perfezionamento*; *Diploma di Specializzazione*; *Laurea Magistrale*; *Laurea Specialistica*; *Master di 1° Livello*; *Master di 2° Livello*; *Dottorato di Ricerca*

Libraries: Central Libraries 'Frinzi', 210,000 vols; 'Meneghetti', 49,000 vols

Press or Publishing House: University Press

Last Updated: 21/10/11

UNIVERSITY ROMA TRE

Università degli studi Roma Tre

Via Ostiense 161, 00154 Roma
Tel: +39(06) 570-671
Fax: +39(06) 5706-7300
EMail: dir_amm@uniroma3.it
Website: http://www.uniroma3.it

Rettore: Guido Fabiani (1993-)
Tel: +39 06 57067403, Fax: +39 06 57067300
EMail: rettore@uniroma3.it

Direttore Amministrativo: Pasquale Basilicata
Tel: +39 06 57067356, Fax: +39 06 57067266

International Relations: Valentina Feliciello, Responsabile
Tel: +39 06 57067325, Fax: +39 06 57067740
EMail: feliciel@uniroma3.it

Faculties

Architecture (Architecture; Architecture and Planning; Town Planning); **Economics** *("Federico Caffè")* (Business Administration; Economics; Finance; Management); **Education** (Educational Sciences); **Engineering** (Aeronautical and Aerospace Engineering; Civil Engineering; Computer Engineering; Electrical and Electronic Engineering; Engineering; Mechanical Engineering); **Humanities and Philosophy** (Arts and Humanities; Cinema and Television; Cultural Studies; Dance; History; Linguistics; Literature; Modern Languages; Multimedia; Music; Performing Arts; Philosophy; Religion; Social Sciences; Theatre); **Law** (Law); **Mathematics, Physics and Natural Sciences** (Biology; Geology; Mathematics; Mathematics and Computer Science; Physics); **Political Science** (International Relations; Political Sciences; Public Administration)

History: Founded 1992.

Governing Bodies: Senato Accademico; Consiglio di Amministrazione

Academic Year: September to June (September-Februrary; March-June)

Admission Requirements: High School Diploma (diplome di scuola superiore). Test for many courses

Main Language(s) of Instruction: Italian

International Co-operation: Participates in the Socrates/Erasmus programmes. Bilateral agreements with institutions in the Mediterranean Area, Latin America, North America, Australia and China

Degrees and Diplomas: *Laurea (triennale)*; *Laurea Magistrale*; *Laurea Specialistica*: Economics; Education; Engineering; Humanities; Law; Natural Sciences; Political Science, a further 2 yrs; *Master di 1° Livello*: 1 yr; *Master di 2° Livello*; *Dottorato di Ricerca*: Architecture; Economics; Education; Engineering; Humanities; Law; Natural Sciences; Political Science, 3 yrs

Student Services: Academic counselling, Canteen, Employment services, Foreign student adviser, Handicapped facilities, Health services, Language programs, Social counselling, Sports facilities

Special Facilities: Language Centre

Libraries: Yes

Last Updated: 24/10/11

PRIVATE INSTITUTIONS

BIO-MEDICAL CAMPUS UNIVERSITY OF ROME

Università Campus Bio-Medico di Roma

Via Longoni 83, 00155 Roma
Tel: +39(06) 225-411
Fax: +39(06) 2254-1456
EMail: info@unicampus.it
Website: http://www.unicampus.it

Rector: Vincenzo Lorenzelli
Tel: +39(06) 2254-1304, Fax: +39(06) 2254-1456
EMail: v.lorenzelli@unicampus.it

Segretario Generale: Alessandro Pernigo
EMail: l.aglietti@unicampus.it

Faculties

Engineering (Biomedical Engineering; Chemical Engineering; Industrial Engineering); **Medicine and Surgery** (Medicine; Surgery)

History: Founded 1991 as Libero Istituto Universitario Campus Bio-Medico. Became Libera Universita Campus Bio-Medico 1997. Acquired present status and title 2001.

Academic Year: October to June (October-January; March-June)

Admission Requirements: Secondary school certificate (maturità), diploma and entrance examination

Fees: (Euros): c. 1,700-5,420 per annum

Main Language(s) of Instruction: Italian

Degrees and Diplomas: *Laurea (triennale)*; *Laurea Magistrale*; *Master di 1° Livello*; *Master di 2° Livello*; *Dottorato di Ricerca*

Last Updated: 05/10/11

CARLO BO UNIVERSITY OF URBINO

Università degli studi Carlo Bo di Urbino

Via Saffi, 2, 61029 Urbino
Tel: +39(0722) 3501
Fax: +39(0722) 329-186
EMail: diramm@uniurb.it
Website: http://www.uniurb.it

Rettore: Stefano Pivato
Tel: +39(0722) 305-343, Fax: +39(0722) 305-347
EMail: rettore@uniurb.it

Direttore Amministrativo: Luigi Botteghi
Tel: +39(0722) 305-416, Fax: +39(0722) 305-347

Faculties

Economics (Administration; Business and Commerce; Business Computing; Economics; Environmental Management; Finance; International Business; Management Systems; Marketing; Private Administration); **Foreign Languages and Literature** (Arabic; Chinese; English; French; Literature; Portuguese; Russian; Spanish); **Humanities and Philosophy** (Archaeology; Art History; Arts and Humanities; Cultural Studies; Fashion Design; Heritage Preservation; Library Science; Philosophy); **Law** (Commercial Law; Development Studies; International Relations; Law); **Pharmacy** (Chemistry; Dietetics; Pharmacy; Technology; Traditional Eastern Medicine); **Physical Education and Health** (Health Sciences; Physical Education; Sports); **Political Science** (Administration; International Studies; Management; Political Sciences); **Science and Technology** (Biochemistry; Biology; Biotechnology; Computer Science; Geology; Natural Sciences); **Sociology** (Advertising and

Publicity; Performing Arts; Sociology); **Teacher Training** (Pedagogy; Teacher Training)

History: Founded 1506 as College of Law by Guidobaldo I of Montefeltro, Duke of Urbino. Recognized by Bull of Pope Julius II 1507 and authorized to award the title of Doctor 1566. Formally recognized as a university by the Sacred Congregation of Studies 1826, and by Royal decree 1862. Recognized as Libera Università 1923. A non State institution enjoying administrative autonomy. Financially supported by State and provincial subventions, and tuition fees.

Governing Bodies: Consiglio di Amministrazione; Senato Accademico

Academic Year: October to September

Admission Requirements: Secondary school certificate (maturità) or equivalent

Main Language(s) of Instruction: Italian

Degrees and Diplomas: *Laurea (triennale)*; *Laurea Magistrale*; *Laurea Specialistica*; *Master di 1° Livello*; *Master di 2° Livello*; *Dottorato di Ricerca*

Student Residential Facilities: For c. 1,400 students

Libraries: Humanities Library, c. 370,000 vols; Law and Politics, c. 120,000; Economics and Sociology, c. 70,000; Science, c. 42,000

Publications: Documents de Travail - Sez. A, B, C, D, E, F, Semiotics; Fonti e Documenti, History; Hemeneutica, Philosophy; Le Carte, History; Notizie da Palazzo Albani, Art Review; Quaderni dell'Istituto di Filosofia; Quaderni di Hermeneutica, Philosophy; Quaderni Urbinati di Cultura Classica, Philology; Storie Locali, History; Studi Urbinati - B, History, Philosophy and Literature; Studi Urbinati - A, Law and Economics

Last Updated: 05/10/11

CARLO CATTANEO UNIVERSITY

Università Carlo Cattaneo (LIUC)

Corso Matteotti 22, 21053 Castellanza
Tel: +39 0331-5721
Fax: +39 0331-572320
EMail: info@liuc.it
Website: http://www.liuc.it

Rettore: Andrea Taroni
Tel: +39 0331-572214, Fax: +39 0331-572260

Faculties

Economics (Business Administration; Economics; Management); **Engineering** (Engineering; Production Engineering); **Law** (Criminal Law; Law)

History: Founded 1991 by the Industrial Association of the Province of Varese (UNIVA).

Governing Bodies: Senato Accademico; Consiglio di Facolta; Consiglio di Amministrazione

Academic Year: September to July (September-February; February-July)

Admission Requirements: Secondary school certificate (Maturità) or equivalent

Fees: (Euros): 4,530 per annum

Main Language(s) of Instruction: Italian, English

International Co-operation: With universities in Europe, United States; Canada; Australia; Argentina; China; Japan; India; Ecuador

Accrediting Agencies: Ministry for University Education and Research

Degrees and Diplomas: *Laurea (triennale)*; *Laurea Magistrale*; *Master di 1° Livello*: Law, Economics, Engineering, 1 yr; *Master di 2° Livello*; *Dottorato di Ricerca*: Economics, 3 yrs

Student Services: Academic counselling, Canteen, Employment services, Foreign student adviser, Foreign Studies Centre, Handicapped facilities, Language programs, Social counselling

Student Residential Facilities: For 400 students

Libraries: Mario Rostoni Library, c. 40,000 vols

Publications: LIUC Papers *(monthly)*

Last Updated: 05/10/11

CATHOLIC UNIVERSITY OF THE SACRED HEART

Università Cattolica del Sacro Cuore (UCSC)

Largo Agostino Gemelli 1, 20123 Milano
Tel: +39(02) 7234-5801
Fax: +39(02) 7234-5806
EMail: rel.internazionali@unicatt.it
Website: http://www.unicatt.it

Rettore: Lorenzo Ornaghi (2002-)
Tel: +39(02) 7234-2288, Fax: +39(02) 7234-2704
EMail: rettore@unicatt.it

Direttore Administrativo: Marco Elefanti

Faculties

Agriculture *(Piacenza Cremona)* (Agriculture; Food Science; Food Technology; Forestry; Viticulture); **Bank, Financial and Insurance Sciences** (Banking; Finance; Insurance); **Economics** *(Piacenza)* (Business Administration; Economics); **Economics** *(Milan, Rome)* (Economics; Management); **Foreign Languages and Literature** *(Milan, Brescia)* (Arabic; Chinese; English; French; Literature; Modern Languages; Portuguese; Russian; Spanish); **Humanities and Philosophy** *(Milan, Brescia)* (Aesthetics; Anthropology; Archaeology; Art History; Arts and Humanities; Classical Languages; History; Linguistics; Literature; Philology; Philosophy); **Law** *(Piacenza)* (Law); **Law** (Law); **Linguistics and Foreign Literature** (Linguistics; Literature); **Mathematics, Physical and Natural Sciences** *(Brescia)* (Mathematics; Natural Sciences; Physics); **Medicine and Surgery** *(Rome)* (Medicine; Surgery); **Political Science** (Political Sciences); **Psychology** (Psychology); **Sociology** *(Milan, Brescia, Piacenza)* (Sociology); **Teacher Training** *(Milan, Brescia, Piacenza)* (Teacher Training)

History: Founded 1920 by decree of the Sacred Congregation of Education and recognized by the Italian Government 1924. The degrees and diplomas awarded by the University are formally recognized by the State.

Governing Bodies: Consiglio di Amministrazione; Senato Accademico

Academic Year: October to September

Admission Requirements: Secondary school certificate (maturità), teacher's diploma or technical school diploma, or foreign equivalent

Fees: (Euros) 1,500-5,000 per annum. Depends on family income

Main Language(s) of Instruction: Italian

International Co-operation: Participates in Socrates-Erasmus; Comenius; Minerva; Lingua; Erasmus Mundus; Leonardo Da Vinci; Alfa; Alban; Tempus; Esprit; VII Framework Programmes, European Social Foundation

Degrees and Diplomas: *Laurea (triennale)*; *Laurea Magistrale*; *Laurea Specialistica*: 2 yrs; *Master di 1° Livello*; *Master di 2° Livello*; *Dottorato di Ricerca*: 3 yrs

Student Services: Academic counselling, Canteen, Cultural centre, Employment services, Foreign Studies Centre, Handicapped facilities, Health services, Language programs, Nursery care, Social counselling, Sports facilities

Student Residential Facilities: Yes

Libraries: University Library, Milan c. 1,206,356 vols; Rome, c. 251,000 vols

Publications: Aegyptus - Rivista italiana di egittologia e di papirologia *(biannually)*; Aevum - Rassegna di Scienze storiche linguistiche e filologiche *(3 per annum)*; Aevum Antiquum *(annually)*; Analisi di scienze religiose *(annually)*; Annali di storia moderne e contemporanea *(annually)*; Archivio di Psicologia, Neurologia e Psichiatria *(quarterly)*; Bollettino dell'Archivio per la Storia del movimento sociale cattolico in Italia *(3 per annum)*; Comunicazioni Sociali *(3 per annum)*; JUS Rivista di Scienze Giuridiche *(quarterly)*; La Rivista del Clero Italiano *(monthly)*; L'analisi linguistica e letteraria *(biannually)*; Medicina e morale; Presenza *(quarterly)*; Rivista di Filosofia Neoscolastica *(quarterly)*; Rivista Internazionale di Scienze Sociali *(quarterly)*; Studi di Sociologia *(quarterly)*; Vita e Pensiero *(monthly)*

Press or Publishing House: Editrice 'Vita e Pensiero'

Academic Staff *2009-2010*: Total: c. 1,400

Student Numbers *2009-2010*: Total: c. 42,000

Last Updated: 05/10/11

DANTE ALIGHIERI UNIVERSITY FOR FOREIGNERS OF REGGIO DI CALABRIA

Università per stranieri Dante Alighieri di Reggio Calabria
Via del Torrione, 95, 89125 Reggio di Calabria
Tel: +39(0965) 31-25-93
EMail: info@unistrada.it
Website: http://www.unistrada.it

Rettore: Salvatore Berlingo EMail: rettore@unistrada.it

Faculties

Society and Formation of the Mediterranean Area (Mediterranean Studies)

Schools

Italian Language and Culture for Foreigners (Italian)

History: Founded 1984. Acquired present status 2007.

Main Language(s) of Instruction: Italian

Degrees and Diplomas: *Laurea (triennale)*; *Laurea Magistrale*; *Master di 1° Livello*; *Master di 2° Livello*

Last Updated: 05/10/09

E-CAMPUS TELEMATIC UNIVERSITY

Università Telematica e-Campus
Via Isimbardi 10, 22060 Novedrate
Tel: +39(31) 7942500
EMail: info@uniecampus.it
Website: http://www.uniecampus.it

Rettore: Lanfranco Rosati

Faculties

Arts (Design; Fashion Design; Literature; Music); **Economics** (Banking; Business and Commerce; Economics); **Engineering** (Automation and Control Engineering; Civil Engineering; Computer Engineering; Energy Engineering; Environmental Engineering; Industrial Engineering); **Law** (Law); **Psychology** (Psychology)

History: Founded 2006.

Main Language(s) of Instruction: Italian

Degrees and Diplomas: *Laurea (triennale)*; *Laurea Magistrale*; *Master di 1° Livello*; *Master di 2° Livello*

Libraries: Yes

Last Updated: 24/10/11

EUROPEAN UNIVERSITY OF ROME

Università Europea di Roma
Via degli Aldobrandeschi 190, 00163 Roma
Tel: +39(06) 6652-7936
EMail: info@unier.it
Website: http://www.universitaeuropeadiroma.it

Rettore: Paolo Scarafoni EMail: rettorato@unier.it

Programmes

Economics and Business Administration (Business Administration; Economics; Finance; Management); **History** (History; History of Religion); **Law** (Law); **Psychology** (Psychology)

History: Founded 2004.

Main Language(s) of Instruction: Italian

Degrees and Diplomas: *Laurea (triennale)*; *Laurea Magistrale*; *Master di 1° Livello*; *Master di 2° Livello*; *Dottorato di Ricerca*

Last Updated: 05/10/09

FREE UNIVERSITY OF BOZEN - BOLZANO

Libera Università di Bolzano
Via della Mostra 4, 39100 Bolzano
Tel: +39(0471) 011-000
Fax: +39(0471) 011-009
EMail: info@unibz.it
Website: http://www.unibz.it

Rettore: Walter Lorenz
Tel: +39(0471) 010-203, Fax: +39(0471) 010-209
EMail: rectorate@unibz.it

Faculties

Computer Science (Computer Engineering; Computer Science); **Design and Art** (Design); **Education** *(Brixen/Bressanone)* (Education; Teacher Training); **Science and Technology** (Agricultural Economics; Agriculture; Industrial Engineering; Mechanical Engineering; Production Engineering)

Schools

Economics and Management (Business Administration; Economics; Management; Sports; Tourism)

History: Founded 1997 as a private, state recognized university. As a central-European, internationally-oriented educational establishment it acts as an important link between the German and Italian cultural and economic spheres. Most of the teaching staff have an international professional background.

Governing Bodies: University Council; University Senate

Admission Requirements: Secondary school certificate (maturità). Good knowledge of two of the three languages in which lessons are conducted (Italian, German and English)

Fees: (Euros): 950 per annum for EU students; 2,000 for non EU

Main Language(s) of Instruction: Italian, German, English

International Co-operation: Participates in Socrates/Erasmus; Leonardo Da Vinci; Project Softworld; EU-Canada programmes and programme for cooperation in Higher Education and Training

Degrees and Diplomas: *Laurea (triennale)*; *Laurea Magistrale*; *Master di 1° Livello*; *Master di 2° Livello*; *Dottorato di Ricerca*

Student Services: Academic counselling, Canteen, Employment services, Foreign student adviser, Handicapped facilities, Language programs

Student Residential Facilities: Yes

Special Facilities: Movie Studio

Libraries: University Libraries in Bozen/Bolzano and in Brixen/Bressanone

Last Updated: 30/09/09

FREE UNIVERSITY OF ENNA KORE

Libera Università degli Studi di Enna Kore
Cittadella Universitaria, 94100 Enna
Tel: +39 0935-53636
Fax: +39 0935-41789
EMail: rettore@unikore.it
Website: http://www.unikore.it/

Rettore: Giovanni Puglisi
Tel: +39 0935-536200, Fax: +39 0935-41789

Faculties

Arts and Communication (Archaeology; Journalism; Multimedia); **Economics and Social Sciences** (Economics; Political Sciences; Social Sciences; Tourism); **Engineering and Architecture** (Aeronautical and Aerospace Engineering; Civil Engineering; Environmental Engineering; Telecommunications Engineering); **Law** (Law); **Movement and Well-being** (Sports); **Psychology and Education** (Clinical Psychology; Cultural Studies; Modern Languages; Psychology)

Programmes

Psychology and Educational Sciences (Educational Sciences; Modern Languages; Psychology)

History: Founded 2004.

Main Language(s) of Instruction: Italian

Degrees and Diplomas: *Laurea (triennale)*; *Laurea Magistrale*: Archeology; Economics; Tourism; *Laurea Specialistica*: Telecommunications; *Dottorato di Ricerca (new system)*

Last Updated: 27/01/12

GIUSTINO FORTUNATO ONLINE UNIVERSITY

Università telematica Giustino Fortunato
Viale Raffaele Delcogliano, 12, 82100 Benevento
Tel: +39(0824) 31-60-57
EMail: info@unifortunato.eu
Website: http://www.unifortunato.it

Rettore: Augusto Fantozzi (2009-)

Faculties
Law (Commercial Law; Law)

History: Founded 2006.

Main Language(s) of Instruction: Italian

Degrees and Diplomas: *Laurea (triennale)*; *Laurea Magistrale*; *Master di 1° Livello*; *Master di 2° Livello*

Libraries: Yes

Last Updated: 24/10/11

GUGLIELMO MARCONI UNIVERSITY

Università degli studi Guglielmo Marconi
Via Plinio 44, 00193 Roma
Tel: +39(06) 377-2551
EMail: info@unimarconi.it
Website: http://www.unimarconi.it

Rettore: Alesandra Briganti EMail: rettore@unimarconi.it

Centres
Life Sciences (Biological and Life Sciences)

Faculties
Applied Science and Technology (Applied Chemistry; Applied Mathematics; Applied Physics; Computer Science; Surveying and Mapping; Technology); **Economics** (Economics); **Education** (Education; Educational Sciences; Educational Technology; Pedagogy); **Humanities** (Arts and Humanities; Cultural Studies; Modern Languages); **Law** (Law); **Political Science** (International Relations; Political Sciences; Public Administration; Social Sciences; Social Work)

History: Founded 2004. First recognized Open University.

Main Language(s) of Instruction: Italian

Degrees and Diplomas: *Laurea (triennale)*; *Diploma di Specializziazione*; *Laurea Magistrale*; *Master di 1° Livello*; *Master di 2° Livello*; *Dottorato di Ricerca*

Last Updated: 24/10/11

GUIDO CARLI FREE INTERNATIONAL UNIVERSITY OF SOCIAL STUDIES

Libera Università internazionale degli study sociali Guido Carli (LUISS)
Viale Pola 12, 00198 Roma
Tel: +39 06-852251
Fax: +39 06-85225354
EMail: orientamento@luiss.it
Website: http://www.luiss.it

Rettore: Massimo Egidi
Tel: +39 06-85225221, Fax: +39 06-8412954
EMail: rettore@luiss.it

Faculties
Economics (Business Administration; Economics; Law; Social Sciences) *Dean*: Franco Fontana; **Law** (Business Administration; Law) *Dean*: Marcello Foschini; **Political Science** (Communication Studies; Information Sciences; International Studies; Labour and Industrial Relations; Law; Political Sciences; Social Sciences) *Dean*: Gian Candido De Martin

Schools
Business; **Government** (Government); **Journalism** (Journalism); **Legal Profession**

History: Founded 1966, acquired present status 1978. A private Institution operated and financed by the Associazione Internazionale Pro Deo.

Governing Bodies: Consiglio di Amministrazione; Consiglio di Facoltà

Academic Year: October to September

Admission Requirements: Secondary school certificate (maturità) or foreign equivalent

Fees: (Euros): c. 5,220 per annum

Main Language(s) of Instruction: Italian and English

International Co-operation: Participates in the Socrates/Erasmus programme. Bilateral agreements with European institutions

Degrees and Diplomas: *Laurea (triennale)*; *Laurea Magistrale*; *Laurea Specialistica*: Economics; Law; Political Science (LS), 2 yrs; *Master di 1° Livello*; *Master di 2° Livello*; *Dottorato di Ricerca*

Student Services: Academic counselling, Canteen, Employment services, Foreign student adviser, Foreign Studies Centre, Handicapped facilities, Health services, Language programs, Sports facilities

Student Residential Facilities: Yes

Libraries: Central Library, c. 118,000 vols; 2,133 periodicals; Institute Libraries

Publications: Filosofia e questioni pubbiche, Political Theory; Luiss International Journal, International Academic Activity and Research

Press or Publishing House: Luiss Edizioni

Last Updated: 03/10/11

HUMAN SCIENCES ONLINE UNIVERSITY

Universita telematica delle Scienze Umane - UNISU
Via Casalmonferrato 2/B, 00182 Roma
EMail: info@unisu.it
Website: http://www.unisu.it

Presidente: Stefano Ranucci

Faculties
Economics (Economics); **Education and Training** (Educational Sciences); **Law** (Law); **Political Science** (Political Sciences)

History: Founded 2006.

Main Language(s) of Instruction: Italian

Degrees and Diplomas: *Laurea (triennale)*; *Laurea Magistrale*; *Master di 1° Livello*

Last Updated: 24/10/11

IMT-INSTITUTE FOR ADVANCED STUDIES LUCCA

Scuola IMT (istituzioni, mercati, tecnologie) di alti studi di Lucca
vi San Micheletto 3, 55100 Lucca
Tel: +39 0583-4326561
Fax: +39 0583-4326565
EMail: info@imtlucca.it
Website: http://www.imtlucca.it/

Direttore: Fabio Pammolli
Tel: +39 0583-4326551, Fax: +39 0583-4326560
EMail: direttore@imtlucca.it

Programmes
Computer Science and Engineering; **Economics, Markets, Institutions**; **Political Systems and Institutional Change**; **Technology and Management of Cultural Heritage**

History: IMT was founded as independent institution in November 2005 by way of a partnership between four leading Italian universities and the Fondazione Lucchese per l'Alta Formazione e la Ricerca (FLAFR), a private foundation in Lucca which aims to promote social and economic growth in Italy via higher education.

Main Language(s) of Instruction: Italian

Degrees and Diplomas: *Dottorato di Ricerca*

Student Residential Facilities: 1 Main Residence - 12 rooms (for short term guests).49 apartments for students and IMT guests.

Special Facilities: 1 canteen.

Libraries: Yes

Last Updated: 04/10/11

INTERNATIONAL TELEMATIC UNIVERSITY UNINETTUNO

Università telematica internazionale UNINETTUNO
Corso Vittorio Emanuele II, 39, 00186 Roma
EMail: info@uninettunouniversity.net
Website: http://www.uninettunouniversity.net

Rettore: Maria Amata Garito EMail: garito@uninettuno.it

Faculties
Arts (Archaeology; Art History; Arts and Humanities; Heritage Preservation; Library Science; Literature); **Communication Science** (Advertising and Publicity; Communication Studies; Journalism; Media Studies; Modern Languages); **Economics** (Business Administration; Business and Commerce; Economics; Management); **Engineering** (Civil Engineering; Computer Engineering; Management Systems; Telecommunications Engineering); **Law** (Law); **Psychology** (Psychology)

History: Founded 2005.

Main Language(s) of Instruction: Italian

Degrees and Diplomas: *Laurea (triennale)*; *Master di 1° Livello*

Last Updated: 24/10/11

IULM UNIVERSITY OF LANGUAGES AND COMMUNICATION

Libera Università di Lingue e Comunicazione IULM
Via Carlo Bo 1, 20143 Milano
Tel: +39(02) 8914-11
Fax: +39(02) 8914-12266
EMail: international.office@iulm.it
Website: http://www.iulm.it

Rettore: Giovanni Puglisi (2010-2015)
Tel: +39(02) 8914-12415
EMail: rettore@iulm.it; giovanni.puglisi@iulm.it

International Relations: Raffaella Angelucci, Head of International Relations Office Tel: +39(02) 8914-12395

Faculties
Art and Cultural Heritage (Art History; Art Management; Heritage Preservation); **Communication, Public Relations and Advertising** (Advertising and Publicity; Cinema and Television; Communication Studies; Marketing; Mass Communication; Media Studies; Public Relations); **Interpretation, Modern Languages, Literature and Culture** (Cultural Studies; Literature; Modern Languages; Translation and Interpretation); **Tourism, Events and Regions** (Regional Studies; Tourism)

Research Institutes
Arts, Cultures and Comparative Literatures (Comparative Literature; Fine Arts; History; Modern Languages; Translation and Interpretation) *Director*: Paolo Proeitti; **Communication Studies** (Advertising and Publicity; Cinema and Television; Communication Studies; Multimedia; Public Relations; Sociology) *Director*: Alberto Abruzzese; **Consumption and Business Communication** (Administration; Business Administration; Consumer Studies; Psychology; Sociology) *Director*: Paolo Moderato; **Economics and Marketing** (Economics; Information Technology; Marketing; Tourism) *Director*: Emanuele Invernizzi; **Human and Environmental Sciences** (Environmental Studies; Philosophy; Psychology; Sociology) *Director*: Marco Villamira; **Law, Communication and Information Sciences** *(Alessandro Migliazza)* (Communication Studies; History; Law) *Director*: Guido Formigoni

Further Information: Also Centre for Research and Development; Observatory of Media no Limits and Road Safety; Observatory of Humanities Laboratory. Branch in Rome

History: Founded 1968 as Istituto Universitario di Lingue Moderne (IULM). Acquired present title and status 1998.

Governing Bodies: Consiglio di Amministrazione; Senato Accademico; Consiglio di Facoltà; Giunta di Ateneo

Academic Year: September to June

Admission Requirements: Secondary school certificate (maturità) or equivalent

Fees: (Euros): 3,926-7,620 per annum

Main Language(s) of Instruction: Italian

International Co-operation: Participates in the LLP/Erasmus and Leonardo programmes.

Degrees and Diplomas: *Laurea (triennale)*; *Laurea Magistrale*: Brand, Fashion and Design: Strategies and Communication; Consumer and Trade Marketing; Television, Cinema and New Media; Tourism and Culture: Promotion and Management; Arts, Heritage and Markets; Specialised Translation and Conference Interpreting, 2 yrs; *Master di 1° Livello*: Communication for International Relations; Management of Creative Processes; Journalism; Tourism Management; Management of Social, Political and Institutional Communication; Italian Fashion, Design and Luxury Product Management and Communication; Food Culture and Marketing; Old and Rare Book Management, 1-2 yrs; *Dottorato di Ricerca*: Communication & New Technologies; Economics, Marketing & Business Communication; Comparative Literature; Literature, Culture & Europe: History, Writing & Translation; Aegean Languages And Culture; Human Interaction: Consumer Psychology, Behaviour & Communication

Student Services: Academic counselling, Canteen, Employment services, Foreign student adviser, Handicapped facilities, Health services, Language programs

Student Residential Facilities: Yes

Special Facilities: Language Laboratories; Multimedia Centre

Libraries:c. 145,000 vols; 1,000 journal subscriptions; 6,000 a/v items; online booking service; multimedia and audiovisuals room

Publications: Lingua e letteratura *(biannually)*

Student Numbers *2012-2013*: Total 4,495
Last Updated: 14/03/13

JEAN MONNET FREE MEDITERRANEAN UNIVERSITY

Libera Università Mediterranea Jean Monnet (LUM)
Strada statale 100 km. 18, Casamassima, 70010 Bari
Tel: +39 080-6978250
Fax: +39 080-6977122
EMail: info@lum.it; scozia@lum.it
Website: http://www.lum.it

Rettore: Emanuele Degennaro
Tel: +39 080-6978111 EMail: rettorato@lum.it; edg@lum.it

Direttore Amministrativo: Felice Gnagnarella

International Relations: Giuseppe Arlacchi, Head of International Affairs Office EMail: parlacchi@tiscali.it

Faculties
Economics (Economics; Management); **Law** (Law)

History: Founded 1995.

Main Language(s) of Instruction: Italian

Degrees and Diplomas: *Laurea (triennale)*; *Laurea Magistrale*; *Laurea Specialistica*; *Master di 1° Livello*; *Master di 2° Livello*; *Dottorato di Ricerca*

Libraries: c. 11,000 vols; 100 periodicals
Last Updated: 03/10/11

LEONARDO DA VINCI ONLINE UNIVERSITY

Università telematica Leonardo da Vinci
Palazzo dei Baroni, Piazza San Rocco 4, 66010 Torrevecchia Teatina
EMail: info@unidav.it
Website: http://www.unidav.it/

Presidente: Fabio Capani

Faculties
Cultural Studies (Cultural Studies); **Education** (Education; Educational Psychology; Pedagogy; Teacher Training); **Management** (Management)

History: Founded on the initiative of the Università Gabriele d'Annunzio di Chieti-Pescara.

Main Language(s) of Instruction: Italian

Degrees and Diplomas: *Laurea (triennale)*; *Laurea Magistrale*; *Master di 1° Livello*; *Master di 2° Livello*
Last Updated: 24/10/11

LUIGI BOCCONI UNIVERSITY

Università commerciale Luigi Bocconi
Via Sarfatti 25, 20136 Milano
Tel: +39(02) 583-61
Fax: +39(02) 5836-2195
EMail: orienta.trienni@unibocconi.it
Website: http://www.unibocconi.it

Rettore: Guido Tabellini (2008-)
Tel: +39(02) 5836-2199 EMail: guido.tabellini@unibocconi.it

Departments

Accountancy (Accountancy); **Decision Sciences**; **Economics** *(Ettore Bocconi)* (Comparative Law; Economic History; Economics; Statistics); **Finance** (Finance); **Law** *(Angelo Sraffa)* (Law); **Management and Technology** (Management); **Marketing** (Marketing); **Public Management** (Public Administration)

History: Founded 1902, an autonomous institution recognized by the State.

Governing Bodies: Consiglio di Amministrazione; Consiglio di Facoltà

Academic Year: September to June (September-February; February-June)

Admission Requirements: Secondary school certificate (maturità) or foreign equivalent

Fees: (Euros): depending on family income, c. 8,300

Main Language(s) of Instruction: Italian; English

International Co-operation: Participates in the Programme of International Management (P.I.M.) and Commmunity of European Management Schools(CEMS)

Degrees and Diplomas: *Laurea (triennale)*; *Laurea Magistrale*; *Laurea Specialistica*: 2 yrs; *Master di 1° Livello*: 1 yr; *Master di 2° Livello*; *Dottorato di Ricerca*: 3 yrs

Student Services: Academic counselling, Canteen, Employment services, Foreign student adviser, Foreign Studies Centre, Language programs, Sports facilities

Student Residential Facilities: Yes

Libraries: Central Library, 600,000 vols

Publications: Commercio, Finanza Marketing e Produzione; Economia e Management; Economia e Politica Industriale; Economia Internazionale delle Fonti di Energia; Giornale degli Economisti e Annali di Economia; Rivista Internazionale delle Scienze Economiche e Commerciali; Sviluppo e Organizzazione

Press or Publishing House: EGEA Spa

Last Updated: 05/10/11

LUMSA UNIVERSITY

LUMSA - Libera Università Maria Ss. Assunta (LUMSA)

Via della Traspontina 21, 00193 Roma
Tel: +39 06 684221
Fax: +39 06 6878357
EMail: lumsa@lumsa.it
Website: http://www.lumsa.it

Rettore: Giuseppe Dalla Torre (1992-)
Tel: +39 06 684221, Fax: +39 06 68422236
EMail: rettorato@lumsa.it

Administrative Director: Giannina Di Marco
Tel: +39 06-684221, Fax: +39 06-68422246

Faculties

Education Sciences (Child Care and Development; Education; Educational Sciences; Educational Technology; Primary Education; Psychology; Social and Community Services); **Humanities** *(Also Scuola di Specializzazione in Storia dell'Arte Medievale e Moderna)* (Advertising and Publicity; Arts and Humanities; Communication Studies; Literature; Modern Languages; Philosophy; Tourism); **Law** (Administration; Banking; Economic and Finance Policy; Human Resources; Law; Political Sciences; Public Administration)

Further Information: Also Campuses in Palermo, Taranto, Caltanissetta and Gubio

History: Founded 1939 as Istituto Universitario "Mari SS. Assunta". Acquired present status 1991.

Governing Bodies: Consiglio di Amministrazione; Senato Accademico; Consigli di Facoltà; Consigli di corso di laurea

Academic Year: October to May

Admission Requirements: Secondary school certificate (Maturità)

Fees: (Euros): 1,070-3,900 per annum according to parents' income

Main Language(s) of Instruction: Italian

International Co-operation: With universities in Latin and North America. Also participates in the Socrates/Erasmus exchange programmes with 130 universities in Europe.

Degrees and Diplomas: *Laurea (triennale)*; *Laurea Magistrale*; *Laurea Specialistica*: Business Administration; International Law; Communication and Cultural Production; Communication Studies; Advertising and New Medias; Editing and Journalism; International Relations Language; Linguistics; Economics; Finance and Insurance; Education and Training Management; Social Services and Political Management; Clinical, Educational and Developmental Psychology, a further 2 yrs; *Master di 1° Livello*; *Master di 2° Livello*; *Dottorato di Ricerca*

Student Services: Academic counselling, Canteen, Cultural centre, Employment services, Foreign student adviser, Foreign Studies Centre, Handicapped facilities, Language programs, Social counselling, Sports facilities

Student Residential Facilities: Yes

Libraries: c. 110,000 vols

Publications: Collana di Giurisprudenza, Faculty of Law Journal *(other/irregular)*; Quaderni della LUMSA *(other/irregular)*; Rivista Nuovi Studi Politici, Faculty of Law Journal *(quarterly)*

Last Updated: 03/10/11

LUSPIO UNIVERSITY

Università degli Studi Internazionali di Roma (LUSPIO)

Via dell Sette Chiese 139, 00145 Roma
Tel: +39 06-510777406
Fax: +39 06-5122416
EMail: orientamento@luspio.it
Website: http://www.luspio.it

Rettore: Giuseppe Acocella
Tel: +39 06-510777234, Fax: +39 06-5122416
EMail: rettore@luspio.it

Faculties

Economics (Economics); **Interpretation and Translation** (Translation and Interpretation); **Political Science** (Political Sciences)

History: Founded 1996. The Istituto has a distinctive network structure comprising the Universities of Bologna, Firenze, Milano-Bicocca, Napoli "Federico II", Napoli "L'Orientale", Napoli "Suor Orsola Benincasa", Roma "La Sapienza" and Siena.

Main Language(s) of Instruction: Italian

International Co-operation: With universities in Malta, Russia, United States, Romania, Libya, Thailand

Degrees and Diplomas: *Laurea (triennale)*; *Laurea Magistrale*; *Master di 1° Livello*; *Master di 2° Livello*; *Dottorato di Ricerca*

Last Updated: 03/10/11

MERCATORUM UNIVERSITY

Universitas Mercatorum

Via Appia Pignatelli, 62, 00178 Roma
Tel: +39(06) 78-05-23-27
EMail: segreteria@unimercatorum.it
Website: http://www.unimercatorum.it

Rettore: Giorgio Marbach

Faculties

Business Administration (Business Administration)

History: Founded 2006.

Main Language(s) of Instruction: Italian

Degrees and Diplomas: *Laurea (triennale)*; *Laurea Magistrale*; *Master di 1° Livello*; *Master di 2° Livello*

Last Updated: 24/10/11

PEGASO TELEMATIC UNIVERSITY

Università telematica Pegaso

Via Vittoria Colonna 14, 80121 Napoli
Website: http://www.unipegaso.it

Rettore: Riccardo Fragnito

Faculties

Humanities (Educational Sciences); **Law** (Law)

History: Founded 2006.

Main Language(s) of Instruction: Italian

Degrees and Diplomas: *Laurea (triennale)*; *Laurea Magistrale*; *Master di 1° Livello*; *Master di 2° Livello*

Last Updated: 24/10/11

SAN RAFFAELE UNIVERSITY ROME

Università San Raffaele Roma

Via Val Cannuta 247, 20138 Roma

Website: http://www.unisanraffaele.gov.it

Rettore: Giuseppe Rotilio

Faculties

Agrarian Sciences; **Architecture and Industrial Design** (Architecture; Fashion Design); **Sports Science**

History: Founded 2006 as Università telematica Internazionale.

Main Language(s) of Instruction: Italian

Degrees and Diplomas: *Laurea (triennale)*; *Laurea Magistrale*; *Master di 1° Livello*; *Master di 2° Livello*; *Dottorato di Ricerca*

Last Updated: 24/10/11

UNIVERSITY OF GASTRONOMIC SCIENCES

Università di Scienze gastronomiche

Piazza Vittorio Emanuele 9,

12060 Pollenzo-Bra

Tel: +39(0172) 458-511

EMail: info@unisg.it

Website: http://www.unisg.it

Rettore: Piercarlo Grimaldi (2011-) EMail: rettore@unisg.it

Programmes

Gastronomy (Cooking and Catering)

History: Founded 2004 by the international Slow Food Association in collaboration with the regional authorities of Piedmont and Emilia-Romagna.

Main Language(s) of Instruction: Italian

Degrees and Diplomas: *Laurea (triennale)*: Gastronomic Sciences, 3 yrs; *Laurea Magistrale*; *Master di 1° Livello*: Gastronomic Sciences and Quality Products; Food Culture, 1 yr

Last Updated: 24/10/11

VITA-SALUTE SAN RAFFAELE UNIVERSITY

Università Vita-Salute San Raffaele

Via Olgettina 58, 20132 Milano

Tel: +39(02) 2643-2794 +39(02) 2643-3897

Fax: +39(02) 2643-3809

EMail: amministrazione@unisr.it

Website: http://www.unisr.it

Rettore: Luigi Maria Verzè

Tel: +39 02-26432243, Fax: +39 02-26432170

EMail: uhsr.rettorato@hsr.it

General Director: Raffaella Voltolini

Tel: +39 02-26433802, Fax: +39 02-26433803

EMail: uhsr.direzionegen@hsr.it

International Relations: Simona Manetti

Tel: +39 02-26433688, Fax: +39 02-26433809

EMail: manetti.simona@hsr.it

Faculties

Medicine and Surgery (Medicine; Surgery); **Philosophy** (Philosophy); **Psychology** (Psychology)

History: Founded 1996.

Governing Bodies: Board of Directors

Admission Requirements: Secondary school certificate (maturità)

Main Language(s) of Instruction: Italian

Degrees and Diplomas: *Laurea (triennale)*; *Diploma di Specializziazione*: Medical Sciences; *Laurea Magistrale*; *Laurea Specialistica*: Medicine; Surgery (Doctor), 6 yrs; *Master di 1° Livello*; *Master di 2° Livello*; *Dottorato di Ricerca*

Student Services: Academic counselling, Canteen, Foreign student adviser, Foreign Studies Centre, Sports facilities

Libraries: 40,000 Journals, 5,000 vols, 2,000 Theses

Last Updated: 24/10/11

Jamaica

STRUCTURE OF HIGHER EDUCATION SYSTEM

Description:

In Jamaica, higher education is offered in universities and other tertiary level institutions. Tertiary institutions operating in Jamaica are either private or public. Public institutions are those financed by the government with different levels of funding depending on the type of institutions. Private institutions do not receive financing or scholarships from the government. The public institutions serve different functions and can be classified as: teacher training college, theological college, technical college, community college, specialist training college and multi-purpose college. Also, there are a number of universities, one of which is the regional University of the West Indies (UWI) with a campus in Jamaica. Some higher education institutions are at the university level; others are local and public (UWI, UTECH) or local and private. There are also overseas 'offshore' universities which have been granted a license to operate in Jamaica. The non-university institutions represent the majority of the higher education sector. These are all public institutions and include teachers colleges, community colleges, a technical and vocational training institute and specialist colleges that train public servants. Additionally, there are private theological/bible colleges, business colleges, schools of nursing and midwifery, colleges of professional studies, and various technical institutes. Some of the community colleges are also multi-purpose institutions as they offer teacher education along with other programmes. Most of the programmes offered by non-university institutions are below baccalaureate degree level. However, these institutions also offer some baccalaureate and postgraduate degrees, in collaboration with universities, both local and foreign-based, in addition to diplomas and certificates.
Programmes offered by the higher education institutions vary by the type of institution. There are a considerable number of private institutions which offer certain Degree programmes recognized and accredited by the University Council of Jamaica. The teachers colleges offer non-degree programmes and award a diploma in Teaching. Some also provide certification in other fields. The community colleges offer diplomas, certificates, Associate degrees as well as Bachelor's degrees. The Bachelor's degrees are presented jointly with local and foreign institutions. The community colleges have outreach centres in various parts of the island and have full-time, part-time, day and evening programmes which range from general academic upgrading to Pre-University and Professional and Para-professional courses.
During the last decade, access to tertiary level education has increased considerably due to the services being provided by offshore universities. These universities have been granted a license to operate in Jamaica.

Stages of studies:

University level first stage: *Undergraduate*
The first stage of higher education leads to the Bachelor's degree, or to a professional qualification. Bachelor's degrees normally take three years (four when part-time).

University level second stage: *Postgraduate*
The second stage of higher education leads to higher degrees. The Master's degree requires two years' study and the submission of a thesis or a research paper (e.g. Master of Social Work). Medical specialization leading to a Master's degree is available in a range of specialties after four years of an approved internship.

University level third stage: *Doctorate*
The third stage leads, after three years' study following upon the Master's degree, to a Doctorate (PhD). Candidates are required to submit a thesis. Professional qualifications in the form of a Diploma may be obtained in one year following certain degrees or qualifications.

University level fourth stage: *Professorship (Honorary)*
This title is awarded by the universities of the region to graduates who have excelled in a particular field and have published books or articles. This stage does not necessarily follow upon the third stage of higher education. It may follow the second. Duration varies according to performance.

ADMISSION TO HIGHER EDUCATION

Admission to university-level studies:

Name of secondary school credential required: Caribbean Secondary Education Certificate

Minimum score/requirement: Entry with this exam is highly competitive and may be determined by the grade or level of passes achieved.

Name of secondary school credential required: General Certificate of Education 'A' Level

Minimum score/requirement: Passes in five subjects in in CSEC (including Math and English) or GCE 'O' Level and two or three at advanced 'A' Level.

For entry to: Bachelor's degree programmes

Alternatives to credentials: CSEC or GCSE-level equivalent ('O' levels in five subjects) and a preliminary year's study. Other equivalent qualifications as approved by the University.

Other admission requirements: Students must have passed CSEC/GCE "O" levels. English is required at the regional level.

RECOGNITION OF STUDIES

Bodies dealing with recognition:

Caribbean Accreditation Authority for Education in Medicine and other Health Professions - CAAM-HP

Executive Director: Lorna Parkins
P.O. Box 5167
Kingston 6
Tel: +1(876) 927 4765
Fax: +1(876) 906 6781
EMail: lorna.parkins@caam-hp.org
WWW: http://www.caam-hp.org/

NATIONAL BODIES

Ministry of Education

Minister: Ronald Thwaites
2a National Heroes Circle
Kingston 4
Tel: +1(876) 9221 400/1
EMail: webmaster@moec.gov.jm
WWW: http://www.moeyc.gov.jm
Role of national body: To administer, finance and coordinate public institutions and regulate the private ones.

University Council of Jamaica

Chairman: Burchell Whiteman
Executive Director: Yvonnette Marshall
6b Oxford Road
Kingston 5
Tel: +1(876) 929 7299 +1(876) 906 8012
Fax: +1(876) 929 7312
EMail: info@ucj.org.jm
WWW: http://www.ucj.org.jm/
Role of national body: Statutory body established to increase availability of university-level training through the accreditation of programmes offered by other tertiary institutions.

Caribbean Area Network for Quality Assurance in Tertiary Education – CANQATE

President: Yvonnette Marshall
Secretary: Nicole Manning

C/o University Council of Jamaica, 6b Oxford Road
Kingston, 5 Saint Andrew
Tel: +1(876) 929 7299
Fax: +1(876) 929 7312
EMail: info@canqate.org
WWW: http://www.canqate.org/

Role of national body: The Caribbean Area Network for Quality Assurance in Tertiary Education was established as a sub-network of the International Network for Quality Assurance Agencies in Higher Education (INQAAHE). The aims and objectives of CANQATE are compatible with those of INQAAHE whose principal purpose is to "enable members to share information about the maintenance, evaluation, accreditation and improvement of higher education and to disseminate good practices in the field of Quality Assurance".

Data for academic year: 2006-2007
Source: IAU from Ministry of Education, Youth and Culture (MOEYC), 2006 (Bodies, 2012)

INSTITUTIONS

PUBLIC INSTITUTIONS

CHURCH TEACHERS' COLLEGE

40 Manchester Road, Mandeville, Manchester
Tel: +1(876) 962 2662
Fax: +1(876) 962 0525
EMail: ctcmand@cwjamaica.com
Website: http://www.ctc.edu.jm

Principal: Garth Anderson

Programmes
Early Childhood Education (Preschool Education); **Education Leadership** (Educational Administration); **Mathematics Education** *(Master's Programme)* (Mathematics Education); **Primary Spanish Education** (Primary Education); **Secondary Education** (Computer Education; Computer Science; Geography; Humanities and Social Science Education; Literacy Education; Mathematics; Mathematics Education; Physical Education; Religious Education; Science Education; Secondary Education)

History: Creadted 1965.

Degrees and Diplomas: *Diploma*: Early Childhood Education; Spanish for Primary Schools; Secondary Education; *Bachelor's Degree*: Education (Mathematics, Physical, Religious, Computer Science, Spanish, Geography, Social Sciences); Primary Education; Literacy Education (Bachelor of Education); *Master's Degree*: Mathematics Education. Also offers EdD and MEd in Educational Leadership with Temple University, USA.
Last Updated: 07/06/12

MICO UNIVERSITY COLLEGE

1A Marescaux Road, Kingston, 5 St Andrew
Tel: +1876 929 5260
Fax: +1876 926 2238
EMail: mico@jol.com.jm
Website: http://www.themicouniversitycollege.edu.jm

President: Claude Packer

Faculties
Humanities; **Liberal Arts and Education** (Education; Library Science; Literature; Modern Languages; Physical Education; Special Education); **Science and Technology** (Biology; Chemistry; Computer Science; Family Studies; Industrial Engineering; Information Technology; Mathematics Education; Physics)

History: Founded 1836. Acquired present status 2006.

Degrees and Diplomas: *Bachelor's Degree*; *Master's Degree*
Last Updated: 20/10/09

THE UNIVERSITY OF THE WEST INDIES (UWI)

Mona Campus, Kingston, 7 St Andrew
Tel: +1(876) 927-1661
Fax: +1(876) 977-1422
EMail: oadmin@uwimona.edu.jm
Website: http://www.uwi.edu.jm/

Vice-Chancellor: Eon Nigel Harris (2004-)
Tel: +1(876) 927-2406, Fax: +1(876) 927-0253
EMail: vcoff@uwimona.edu.jm; enigel.harris@uwimona.edu.jm

Director of Administration/University Registrar: Dawn-Marie Defour-Gill (2006 to present)
Tel: +1(858) 665 3330, Fax: +1(858) 645 6396
EMail: dawn-marie.defour@sta.uni.edu

International Relations: Sharan Singh, Director, International Office (2009 to present)
Tel: +1(868) 662 2002 +1(868) 662 4280, Fax: +1(868) 662 6930
EMail: sharan.singh@sta.uni.edu

Centres
Marine Sciences

Faculties
Humanities and Education (Arts and Humanities; Communication Studies; Education; English; French; German; History; Information Sciences; Library Science; Linguistics; Mass Communication; Philosophy; Spanish); **Law** (Civil Law; Commercial Law; Criminal Law; Labour Law; Law; Public Law); **Medical Sciences** (Anatomy; Dental Hygiene; Dentistry; Gynaecology and Obstetrics; Medicine; Microbiology; Paediatrics; Pathology; Pharmacology; Pharmacy; Psychiatry and Mental Health; Radiology; Social and Preventive Medicine; Surgery; Veterinary Science); **Pure and Applied Sciences** (Actuarial Science; Biological and Life Sciences; Chemistry; Computer Science; Earth Sciences; Mathematics; Natural Sciences; Physics); **Social Sciences** (Economics; Political Sciences; Psychology; Social Sciences; Sociology)

Institutes
Social and Economic Studies *(Sir Arthur Lewis)* (Economics; Social Policy)

Schools
Business *(Mona)* (Business Administration); **Continuing Education** (Accountancy; Business Administration; Education; Information Sciences; Psychology; Public Administration; Social Sciences)

Further Information: Cave Hill (Barbados), St Augustine (Trinidad and Tobago).

History: Founded 1948; incorporated by Royal Charter 1962. The University is supported by and serves 15 different territories in the

West Indies. An international institution recognized worldwide for its scholarship in Science, Medicine, Social Sciences, Agriculture and Humanities.

Governing Bodies: Council; Senate

Academic Year: August to May (August-December; January-May). Also Summer School, June-July

Admission Requirements: Completion of secondary school education General Certificate of Education for most Faculties

Fees: Cave Hill Campus, (Barbados Dollars): 4,626-13,750 per annum; Mona Campus, (Jamaican Dollars): 116-786 per annum; St Augustine Campus, (Trinidad and Tobago Dollars): 11,800-15,400 per annum

Main Language(s) of Instruction: English

International Co-operation: Programmes for staff and students with several external institutions, including the ACU Split Site Scholarships, for academic links, and Fullbright-Laspau Scholarship programme to pursue postgraduate studies

Accrediting Agencies: General Medical Council, Council for Legal Education, Joint Board of Moderators for Civil Engineering, Institution of Mechanical Engineers, Institution of Electrical Engineers, The Royal Institute of Chartered Surveyors, Institution of Chemical Engineers

Degrees and Diplomas: *Bachelor's Degree*: Social Sciences; Medical Sciences; Natural Sciences; Humanities; Law; Engineering (BSc; BA; LLB), 3-4 yrs; *Master's Degree*: Social Sciences; Medical Sciences; Natural Sciences; Humanities; Law; Engineering (MA; MSc; MPhil), a further 1-2 yrs; *Doctorate*: Social Sciences; Medical Sciences; Natural Sciences; Humanities; Law; Engineering (DPhil), 3-4 yrs following Master's. Also Postgraduate Diploma in: Social Sciences; Medical Sciences; Natural Sciences; Humanities; Law; Engineering

Student Services: Academic counselling, Canteen, Cultural centre, Employment services, Handicapped facilities, Health services, Language programs, Social counselling, Sports facilities

Student Residential Facilities: Yes

Special Facilities: Radio Station (Mona); Performing Arts Theatre (Mona and St. Augustine)

Libraries: Main General Libraries; Science Library; Medical Library; Documentation Centre (Education); Law Library; Library of the Spoken Word

Press or Publishing House: The University Press

Last Updated: 19/10/09

UNIVERSITY OF TECHNOLOGY (UTECH)

237 Old Hope Road, Kingston, 6 St Andrew
Tel: +1876 927-1680
Fax: +1876 977-4388; +1876 927-1925
EMail: regist@utech.edu.jm
Website: http://www.utech.edu.jm

President: Errol Morrison (2007-) Fax: +1876 977 6645

Vice-President and Registrar: Dianne Mitchell
Tel: +1876 512-2034, Fax: +1876 970-2095

Centres

Graduate Studies and Research *Director*: Adelani Ogunrinade

Faculties

Built Environment (Architecture and Planning; Building Technologies; Surveying and Mapping); **Business and Management** (Business and Commerce; Management); **Education and Liberal Studies** (Behavioural Sciences; Caribbean Studies; Communication Studies; Education; French; German; Japanese; Social Sciences; Spanish); **Engineering and Computing** (Computer Science; Engineering); **Health and Applied Science** (Child Care and Development; Health Sciences; Medical Technology; Natural Sciences; Nursing; Nutrition; Pharmacy); **Law**

History: Founded 1958 as Jamaica Institute of Technology, acquired present status and title 1995.

Governing Bodies: Council; Academic Board

Academic Year: August to July

Admission Requirements: 5 CXC (Caribbean Examination Council) subjects including Mathematics and English Language

Main Language(s) of Instruction: English

Accrediting Agencies: University Council of Jamaica

Degrees and Diplomas: *Bachelor's Degree*: administrative management; banking and financial services; business administration; human resources management (BEng), 4 yrs; *Bachelor's Degree*: architectural studies (BBA); computing; education (technical); education (vocational); electrical engineering; mechanical engineering (BA); food service management; integrated planning; tourism; health science; pharmacy (BEng); *Master's Degree*: architecture (MArch). + postgraduate diploma in education

Student Residential Facilities: Some

Special Facilities: Sculpture Park

Libraries: Calvin McKain Library, c. 85,000 vols; c. 550 journal titles

Publications: Focus on Architecture; President's Report *(annually)*; Review of the Academic Year

Last Updated: 19/10/09

PRIVATE INSTITUTION

NORTHERN CARIBBEAN UNIVERSITY

Manchester Road, Mandeville, Manchester
Tel: +1876 962-2204
Fax: +1876 962-0075
EMail: info@ncu.edu.jm
Website: http://www.ncu.edu.jm

President: Herbert J. Thompson (1990-)
Tel: +1876 962-1,685; +1876 523-2045, Fax: +1876 962-6870
EMail: president@ncu.edu.jm

Vice-President for Academic Administration: Beverley Cameron
Tel: +1875 523 2031-2 EMail: bcameron@ncu.edu.jm

Colleges

Arts and General Studies (English; Fine Arts; French; Geography; History; Law; Mass Communication; Music; Political Sciences; Social Studies; Sociology; Spanish); **Business and Hospitality Management** (Accountancy; Business Administration; Business and Commerce; Finance; Human Resources; Information Sciences; Management; Marketing); **Natural and Applied Sciences**; **Teacher Education and Behavioural Sciences** (Educational and Student Counselling; Educational Psychology; Family Studies)

Schools

Religion and Theology (New Testament; Religion; Theology)

History: Founded 1919 as West Indies College. Acquired present status and title 1999.

Degrees and Diplomas: *Associate Degree*; *Bachelor's Degree*; *Master's Degree*: Education; Public Health; Biology; Counselling Psychology; Business Administration; *Doctorate*

Last Updated: 19/10/09

Japan

STRUCTURE OF HIGHER EDUCATION SYSTEM

Description:

Higher education is provided by universities, junior colleges, colleges of technology, as well as specialized schools. These institutions may be national, public or private. The Ministry of Education, Culture, Sports, Science and Technology (MEXT) must approve the foundation of higher education institutions. Universities include one or more faculties offering 4-year courses in a variety of subjects. Junior colleges and colleges of technology do not grant university-level qualifications, but students holding the title of Associate may pursue their studies at universities.

Stages of studies:

University level first stage: *Undergraduate level (first stage)*
Higher education consists of a 4-year course (six years in Medicine, Veterinary Medicine, Dentistry and Pharmaceutics). Applicants to national and public universities must take a national examination (the "National Center Exam") before passing entrance examinations. A credit system is used, with the minimum requirement for graduation set at 124 credits (except Medicine, Dentistry and Pharmaceutical studies). The degree awarded at the end of the first stage is the Bachelor's degree (Gakushi).

University level second stage: *Graduate level (second stage, specialization)*
Specialization takes place in postgraduate schools (daigaku-in), which do not exist in every university, and leads after two years to a postgraduate diploma or Master's degree (Shushi). It requires a number of additional credits, a research thesis and a final examination. Postgraduate studies in the field of medical sciences lead directly to a Doctor's degree.

University level third stage: *Postgraduate level (third stage, further specialization and personal research)*
The third stage leads to the highest university degree, the Doctor's Degree (Hakase). Studies last for a minimum of three years following the Shushi (four years in Medicine, Dentistry and Pharmaceutical studies). PhD candidates must submit a thesis and undergo a final examination. The Katei-Hakase (Doctorate by course work) is conferred on those who graduate from a graduate school programme and the Ronbun-Hakase (Doctorate by dissertation) is conferred on those who successfully submit a dissertation.

Distance higher education:
The University of the Air (Hoso Daigaku) was established in 1983 under government auspices. It is a degree-granting institution that uses radio, television and other media. It promotes collaboration with other private and public universities by increasing mutual recognition of earned credits, by developing the exchange of teaching staff, and by making broadcast materials available to other universities.

ADMISSION TO HIGHER EDUCATION

Admission to university-level studies:

Name of secondary school credential required: Kotogakko Sotsugyo Shomeisho

For entry to: Universities and junior colleges

Entrance exam requirements: Scholastic achievement tests, including the nation-wide entrance examination ("National Center Test") administered by the National Centre for University Entrance Examinations. At the undergraduate level, an entrance examination is required at all universities. Examinations usually consist of a written test and an interview.

Foreign students admission:

Entrance exam requirements: Foreign students over the age of 18 from countries where school education lasts for 10 or 11 years are eligible to enter higher education institutions after they complete any of the "courses of preliminary study for university entrance" authorized by MEXT. They must take an entrance examination.

Entry regulations: A visa granting foreign student status must be obtained before entering Japan.

Language requirements: Japanese courses (one to one-and-a-half years) are available at some private universities or private Japanese language schools to upgrade students' knowledge of Japanese.

RECOGNITION OF STUDIES

Quality assurance system:

Mandatory self-evaluation.
Since 2004, all universities must evaluate the state of their education and research activities, organizational management and facilities and equipment and publish the results of the evaluation.
National Quality Assurance Framework.
Various regulations stipulate the minimum standards and desirable goals and duties of universities. peer review by specialist assure that application to establish universities meet the standards. Quality assurance and accreditation associations certified by the Ministry check the self-evaluations provided by universities.

Bodies dealing with recognition:

National Institution for Academic Degrees and University Evaluation - NIAD-UE

President: Tomoyuki Nogami
1-29-1 Gakuen-nishimachi, Kodaira-shi
Tokyo 187-8587
Tel: +81(42) 307 1500
Fax: +81(42) 307 1552
WWW: http://www.niad.ac.jp/english/index.html

Japan Institution for Higher Education Evaluation - JIHEE

4-2-11 Kudankita, Chiyoda-ku
Tokyo 102-0073
Tel: +81(3) 5211 5131
Fax: +81(3) 5211 5132
WWW: http://www.jihee.or.jp/index.html

NATIONAL BODIES

Ministry of Education, Culture, Sports, Science and Technology - MEXT

Minister: Makiko Tanaka
3-2-2 Kasumigaseki, Chiyoda-ku
Tokyo 100-8959
Tel: +81(3) 5253 4111
Fax: +81(3) 3772 4111
WWW: http://www.mExt.go.jp/
Role of national body: The Ministry is responsible for education, culture, sports, science and technology policies.

Kokuritu Kyoiku Seisaku kenkyu Sho (National Institute for Educational Policy Research)

Director-General: Haruki Ozaki
3-2-2 Kasumigaseki, Chiyoda-ku
Tokyo 100-8951
Tel: +81(3) 6733 6833
EMail: info@nier.go.jp
WWW: http://www.nier.go.jp

Daigaku Kijun Kyokai (Japan University Accreditation Association)

President: Hiromi Naya
2-7-13 Ichigayasadohara, Shinjuku-ku
Tokyo 162-0842
Tel: +81(3) 5228 2020

Fax: +81(3) 5228 2323
EMail: info@juaa.or.jp
WWW: http://www.juaa.or.jp

Kokuritsu Daigaku Kyokai (The Japan Association of National Universities)
President: Junichi Hamada
2-1-2 Hitotsubashi
Chiyoda-ku
Tokyo 101-0003
Tel: +81(3) 4212 3506
Fax: +81(3) 4212 3509
EMail: info@janu.jp
WWW: http://www.janu.jp

Nihon Shiritsu Daigaku Renmei (The Japan Association of Private Universities and Colleges - JAPUC)
President: Atsushi Seike
Shigaku-kaikan Bekkan Bldg.,
4-2-25 kudan-kita, Chiyoda-ku
Tokyo 102-0073
Tel: +81(3) 3262 2420
Fax: +81(3) 3262 2441
EMail: info@shidairen.or.jp
WWW: http://www.shidairen.or.jp/
Role of national body: The Japan Association of Private Universities and Colleges was established in 1951. It comprises private universities and colleges offering four-year/six-year academic programs.

Nihon Shiritsu Daigaku Kyokai (Association of Private Universities of Japan)
Secretary-General: Hidebumi Koide
Chairman: Sunao Onuma
Shigakukaikan Bekkan 9F, 4-2-25, Kudankita, Chiyodaku
Tokyo 102-0073
Tel: +81(3) 3261 7048
Fax: +81(3) 3261 0769
WWW: http://www.shidaikyo.or.jp/
Role of national body: Established on 7 December 1946 as the National Union of Private colleges. The present name was adopted on 26 March 1948.

Data for academic year: 2010-2011
Source: IAU from MEXT (Documentation) 2010. Bodies updated 2012.

INSTITUTIONS

ADVANCED INSTITUTE OF INDUSTRIAL TECHNOLOGY

Sangyou Gijutsu Daigakuin Daigaku
1-10-40 Higashiooi, Shinagawa-ku,
Tokyo 140-0011
Tel: +81(3) 3472-7831
Fax: +81(3) 3472-2790
EMail: info@aiit.ac.jp
Website: http://aiit.ac.jp/english/
President: Shintaro Ishijima

Graduate Divisions
Industrial Technology (Industrial Design; Industrial Engineering; Information Technology)
History: Founded 2006.
Degrees and Diplomas: *Shushi*
Last Updated: 12/02/09

AICHI BUNKYO UNIVERSITY

Aichi Bunkyo Daigaku
5969-3 Nenjo-Zaka, Komaki-shi, Aichi 485-8565
Tel: +81(568) 78-2211
Fax: +81(568) 78-2240
EMail: bunkyo@abu.ac.jp
Website: http://www.abu.ac.jp
President: Shin Sakata

Faculties
Chinese Language and Literature (Chinese; Literature); **English and American Languages and Literature** (American Studies;

English; Literature); **Indian Studies and Buddhism** (Asian Religious Studies; Asian Studies); **Japanese Language and Literature** (Japanese; Literature)

Degrees and Diplomas: *Gakushi*: 4 yrs

AICHI GAKUIN UNIVERSITY

Aichi Gakuin Daigaku

Araike 12, Iwasaki-cho, Nisshin-shi, Aichi 470-0195
Tel: +81(56) 1731-111
Fax: +81(56) 1735-889
Website: http://www.agu.ac.jp/

President: Hideto Ohno (2010-)

Centres

Data Processing (Data Processing); **Foreign Language Audio-Visual Education** (Educational Technology; Foreign Languages Education); **International Studies** (International Studies)

Departments

Liberal Arts (Arts and Humanities)

Faculties

Arts and Humanities (Arts and Humanities; Asian Religious Studies; Cultural Studies; History; International Studies; Psychology); **Commerce** (Business and Commerce); **Information and Policy Studies** (Information Sciences); **Law**; **Management** (Management); **Psychological and Physical Sciences** (Physics; Psychology)

Graduate Schools

Arts and Humanities (Arts and Humanities; Asian Religious Studies; Cultural Studies; English Studies; History; Psychology); **Commerce** (Business and Commerce); **Dentistry** (Dentistry); **Law** (Law); **Management** (Management); **Policy Studies** (Insurance)

Institutes

Cultural Studies (Cultural Studies); **Foreign Languages** (Modern Languages); **Zen Studies**

Research Institutes

Business Administration (Business Administration); **Law and Religion** (Law; Religion); **Management**; **Marketing and Distribution** (Marketing; Sales Techniques)

Schools

Dentistry (Dentistry)

Further Information: Also Japanese language courses for foreign students. University Dental Hospital. Psychological Clinic

History: Founded 1950 as Junior College, acquired present status 1953.

Academic Year: April to March (April-September; September-March)

Admission Requirements: Graduation from high school and entrance examination

Main Language(s) of Instruction: Japanese

International Co-operation: For overseas English Studies with Queensland University (Australia), Illinois University (USA) and University of Edinburgh (UK)

Degrees and Diplomas: *Gakushi*: Arts (Bungakushi); Commerce (Shogakushi); Law (Hogakushi), 4 yrs; *Gakushi*: Dentistry; *Hakase*: Arts (Bungakuhakushi); Commerce (Shogakuhakushi); Law (Hogakuhakushi), a further 5 yrs; *Hakase*: Dental Sciences

Student Services: Foreign student adviser, Language programs, Sports facilities

Special Facilities: Dental Hospital

Libraries: 826,217 vols

Publications: Foreign Languages and Literature *(annually)*; Journal of Aichi Gakuin University Dental Society *(quarterly)*; Journal of the Zen Research Institute *(annually)*; The Aichi Gakuin Law Review *(quarterly)*; The Business Review *(quarterly)*; The Journal of Aichi Gakuin University (Humanities and Sciences) *(quarterly)*; Transactions of the Institute of Cultural Studies *(annually)*

Last Updated: 14/06/10

AICHI GAKUSEN UNIVERSITY

Aichi Gakusen Daigaku

1 Shiotori, Oike-cho, Toyota-shi, Aichi 471-8532
Tel: +81(565) 35-1313
Fax: +81(565) 35-1677
EMail: nyushi@gakusen.ac.jp
Website: http://www.gakusen.ac.jp

President: Akira Terabe

Programmes

Business Administration (Business Administration); **Home Economics** (Home Economics)

History: Founded 1966.

Degrees and Diplomas: *Gakushi*: 4 yrs

Last Updated: 29/10/08

AICHI INSTITUTE OF TECHNOLOGY

Aichi Kogyo Daigaku

1247 Yachigusa, Yakusa-cho, Toyota-shi, Aichi 470-0392
Tel: +81(565) 48-8121
Fax: +81(565) 48-0277
EMail: koho@office.aitech.ac.jp
Website: http://www.aitech.ac.jp

Programmes

Engineering *(Graduate)* (Civil Engineering; Construction Engineering; Production Engineering); **Engineering** *(Undergraduate)*

History: Founded 1912 as Denki Kogaku Koshujo, became Junior College 1954. Acquired present status 1959.

International Co-operation: With universities in China

Degrees and Diplomas: *Gakushi*; *Shushi*; *Hakase*

Student Services: Foreign student adviser, Foreign Studies Centre

Libraries: c. 270,000 vols

Academic Staff *2007-2008*	**TOTAL**
FULL-TIME	**140**
PART-TIME	c. **220**
Student Numbers *2007-2008*	
All (Foreign Included)	c. **6,700**

Last Updated: 28/10/08

AICHI MEDICAL UNIVERSITY

Aichi Ika Daigaku

21 Yazako Karimata, Nagakute-cho, Aichi-gun, Aichi 480-1195
Tel: +81(52) 264-4811
Fax: +81(561) 62-4866
EMail: soumu@aichi-med-u.ac.jp
Website: http://www.aichi-med-u.ac.jp/index.html

President: Nobuo Kato

Centres

Data Processing (Data Processing); **Radioisotope Research** (Organic Chemistry)

Colleges

Nursing (Nursing)

Graduate Schools

Medicine (Medicine); **Nursing**

Institutes

Gerontology (Gerontology); **Industrial Health Sciences** (Health Sciences); **Molecular Science of Medicine** (Molecular Biology); **Physical Fitness, Sports Medicine and Rehabilitation** (Rehabilitation and Therapy; Sports Medicine)

Schools

Medicine (Medicine; Pathology; Physiology; Social and Preventive Medicine; Surgery)

Further Information: Also University Hospital

History: Founded 1971. A private Institution.

Governing Bodies: University Foundation

Academic Year: April to March (April-October; October-March)

Admission Requirements: Graduation from high school or equivalent or foreign equivalent, and entrance examination

Main Language(s) of Instruction: Japanese

International Co-operation: With universities in USA

Degrees and Diplomas: *Gakushi*: Medicine; *Hakase*: Medical Sciences

Student Services: Foreign student adviser, Health services, Sports facilities

Libraries: Medical Information Centre and Library, c. 171,000 vols

Publications: Bulletin of Liberal Arts and Science *(annually)*; Journal of the Aichi Medical University Association *(quarterly)*

Last Updated: 28/10/08

AICHI MIZUHO COLLEGE

Aichi Mizuho Daigaku

86-1 Haiwa, Hiratobashi-cho, Toyota-shi, Aichi 470-0394
Tel: +81(565) 43-0111
Fax: +81(565) 46-5220
Website: http://amc.mizuho-c.ac.jp

Programmes

Human Sciences (Environmental Studies; Social Sciences)

History: Founded 1993.

Degrees and Diplomas: *Gakushi*: 4 yrs

Student Residential Facilities: Yes

Special Facilities: Computer Centre

Libraries: 37,000 vols

Last Updated: 29/10/08

AICHI PREFECTURAL COLLEGE OF NURSING AND HEALTH

Aichi Kenritsu Kango Daigaku

Togoku, Kamishidami, Moriyama-ku, Nagoya-shi, Aichi 463-8502
Tel: +81(52) 736-1401
Fax: +81(52) 736-1415
EMail: www@aichi-nurs.ac.jp
Website: http://www.aichi-nurs.ac.jp

Programmes

Nursing

History: Founded 1995.

Degrees and Diplomas: *Gakushi*; *Shushi*

Academic Staff *2007-2008*: Total: c. 60

Student Numbers *2007-2008*: Total: c. 360

Last Updated: 28/10/08

AICHI PREFECTURAL UNIVERSITY

Aichi Kenritsu Daigaku

Ibaragabasama, Kumabari, Nagakute-cho, Aichi-gun, Aichi 480-1198
Tel: +81(561) 641-111
Fax: +81(561) 641-101
EMail: jim@bur.aichi-pu.ac.jp
Website: http://www.aichi-pu.ac.jp

President: Masao Mori EMail: mori@bur.aichi-pu.ac.jp

Secretary-General: Shibata Kazuo

International Relations: Shibata Kasuo

Faculties

Arts and Humanities (Arts and Humanities; Asian Studies; Cultural Studies; Education; English; Japanese; Parks and Recreation; Preschool Education; Primary Education; Protective Services; Social Welfare); **Foreign Studies** (American Studies; Chinese; English; European Languages; French; French Studies; German; Germanic Studies; Latin American Studies; Spanish); **Information Sciences and Technology**

Graduate Schools

Information Sciences and Technology (Information Sciences; Information Technology); **International Cultural Studies** (Cultural Studies; International Studies)

History: Founded 1950, acquired present status 1966.

Academic Year: April to March

Fees: (Yen): Registration, 282,000; Tuition, 496,800

Main Language(s) of Instruction: Japanese

Degrees and Diplomas: *Gakushi*: 4 yrs; *Shushi*: 2 yrs; *Hakase*: 3 yrs

Student Services: Academic counselling, Canteen, Employment services, Foreign student adviser, Handicapped facilities, Health services, Language programs, Nursery care, Social counselling, Sports facilities

Special Facilities: Computer room, Audiovisual room, Auditorium

Libraries: University Library, c. 430,000 vols

Publications: Bulletin of Foreign Studies *(annually)*; Bulletin of Information Science and Technology *(annually)*; Bulletin of Letters *(annually)*

Last Updated: 28/10/08

AICHI PREFECTURAL UNIVERSITY OF FINE ARTS AND MUSIC

Aichi Kenritsu Geijutsu Daigaku

1-1 Sagamine, Yazako, Nagakute-cho, Aichi-gun, Aichi 480-1194
Tel: +81(561) 62-1180
Fax: +81(561) 62-0083
Website: http://www.aichi-fam-u.ac.jp

Faculties

Fine Arts (Ceramic Art; Design; Fine Arts; Painting and Drawing; Sculpture); **Music** (Music; Musicology)

History: Founded 1966.

Main Language(s) of Instruction: Japanese

Degrees and Diplomas: *Gakushi*; *Shushi*

Libraries: 84,079 vols

AICHI SANGYO UNIVERSITY

Aichi Sangyo Daigaku

12-5 Harayama, Oka-cho, Okazaki-shi, Aichi 444-0005
Tel: +81(564) 484-511
Fax: +81(564) 484-940
EMail: info@asu.ac.jp
Website: http://www.asu.ac.jp

Programmes

Business Administration (Business Administration); **Crafts and Design**

History: Founded 1992.

Degrees and Diplomas: *Gakushi*: 4 yrs

Academic Staff *2007-2008*	**TOTAL**
FULL-TIME	**60**
PART-TIME	**c. 80**

Student Numbers *2007-2008*	
All (Foreign Included)	**c. 1,220**

Last Updated: 29/10/08

AICHI SHUKUTOKU UNIVERSITY

Aichi Shukutoku Daigaku (ASU)

9 Katahira, Nagakute, Nagakute-cho, Aichi-gun, Aichi 480-1197
Tel: +81(561) 62-4111
Fax: +81(561) 63-1977
EMail: kouhou@asu.aasa.ac.jp
Website: http://www.aasa.ac.jp

Faculties

Arts and Humanities (Arts and Humanities; Education; English; Information Sciences; Japanese; Library Science); **Business**; **Communication Studies** (Chinese; Communication Studies; English; Japanese; Psychology); **Creativity and Culture** (Cultural Studies; English; Media Studies; Modern Languages); **Medical Welfare**; **Studies on Contemporary Society** (Architecture and Planning; Media Studies; Social Sciences; Social Studies; Town Planning)

Graduate Schools

Arts and Humanities (Arts and Humanities; English; Information Sciences; Japanese; Library Science; Literature); **Business** (Accountancy; Business and Commerce); **Creativity and Culture** (Cultural Studies; International Studies; Modern Languages; Writing); **Global Culture and Communication** (Communication Studies; Cultural Studies; English; Eurasian and North Asian Languages; Linguistics); **Medical Welfare**; **Psychology** (Psychology); **Studies on Contemporary Society** (Architectural and Environmental Design; Cultural Studies; International Studies; Media Studies; Social Studies; Sociology; Town Planning)

Further Information: Also Center for Education of Health Sciences; Multimedia Resource Centre

History: Founded 1975. Faculty of Communication and Faculty of Creativity and Culture founded 2000.

Governing Bodies: Aichi Shukutoku Gakuen

Academic Year: April to March (April-July; October-March)

Admission Requirements: Graduation from high school or equivalent

Main Language(s) of Instruction: Japanese; English

International Co-operation: With universities in USA, China, Australia, United Kingdom and Republic of Korea

Degrees and Diplomas: *Gakushi*: Arts (Gendaishakai gakushi); Arts (Bungakushi); Communication; Arts, 4 yrs; *Shushi*: Arts (Gendai Shakai); Arts (Bungakushushi); Communication, a further 2 yrs; *Hakase*: Arts (Gendai Shakai); Arts (Bungakuhakushi); Communication, a further 2-3 yrs

Student Services: Academic counselling, Canteen, Employment services, Foreign student adviser, Foreign Studies Centre, Handicapped facilities, Health services, Language programs, Nursery care, Social counselling, Sports facilities

Student Residential Facilities: Yes

Special Facilities: Recording and Editing Studio; Multimedia Resource Centre; Socio-media centre; Multi-media laboratory

Libraries: University Library (Nagakute) 176,937 vols; University Library (Hoshigaoka) 113,185 vols

Publications: Bulletin of Aichi Shukutoku University *(annually)*; Evergreen *(annually)*; Intercultural Communication Studies *(annually)*; Journal of Library and Information Science *(annually)*; Language and Literature (Japan) *(annually)*; Language Communication Studies *(annually)*; Studies in Contemporary Society *(annually)*

Academic Staff *2007-2008*	**TOTAL**
FULL-TIME	**200**
PART-TIME	**390**
STAFF WITH DOCTORATE	
FULL-TIME	**c. 60**
Student Numbers *2007-2008*	
All (Foreign Included)	**c. 6,800**
FOREIGN ONLY	**60**

Last Updated: 28/10/08

AICHI TOHO UNIVERSITY

Aichi Toho Daigaku

3-11 Heiwagaoka, Meito-ku, Nagoya 465-8515
Tel: +81(52) 782-1241
Fax: +81(52) 781-0931
Website: http://www.aichi-toho.ac.jp/english/

Faculties

Business Administration (Business Administration); **Human Studies** (Child Care and Development; Health Sciences)

History: Founded 2001 as Toho Gakuen Daigaku (Toho Gakuen University). Acquired present title 2007.

International Co-operation: With Universities in USA

Degrees and Diplomas: *Gakushi*

Student Services: Cultural centre, Sports facilities

Last Updated: 03/02/09

AICHI UNIVERSITY

Aichi Daigaku

1-1 Machihata-cho, Toyohashi-shi, Aichi 441-8522
Tel: +81(532) 47-4131
Fax: +81(532) 47-4144
EMail: inted@aichi-u.ac.jp
Website: http://www.aichi-u.ac.jp

President: Motohiko Sato

Centres

Chinese Studies *(International Center)*; **Regional Cooperation** *(San-En-Nanshin Center)*

Faculties

Business Administration (Accountancy; Business Administration; Finance); **Economics** (Economics); **International Communication**; **Law** (Law); **Letters** (Arts and Humanities; Sociology); **Modern Chinese Studies** (Chinese; South Asian Studies)

Institutes

International Affairs (International Relations; International Studies); **Managerial Research** (Management)

Research Institutes

Community Studies (Urban Studies); **Industry in Chubu District** (Industrial Engineering)

Further Information: One year Japanese language course for foreign students

History: Founded 1946.

Governing Bodies: Board of Directors

Academic Year: April to March (April-September; September-March)

Admission Requirements: Graduation from high school and entrance examination

Main Language(s) of Instruction: Japanese

International Co-operation: With universities in Australia; China; France; Germany; Republic of Korea; Thailand; United Kingdom and USA

Degrees and Diplomas: *Gakushi*: Economics; Letters; International Communication; Law; Business Administration; Modern Chinese Studies, 4 yrs; *Shushi*: Economics; Humanities; International Communication; Business Administration; Chinese Studies, a further 2 yrs; *Hakase*: Economics; Humanities; Business Administration; Chinese Studies; Law, a further 3 yrs. Graduate School of Law: Professional degree course, 2 yrs (Law learner), 3 yrs (Non Law learner). Graduate School of Accounting and Finance: Professional degree course, 2 yrs (Accounting)

Student Services: Nursery care

Special Facilities: Comprehensive Chinese-Japanese Dictionary Editing Center. Toa Dobunshoin University Memorial Center

Libraries: 1,492,539 vols

Publications: Journal of the Association of Economic Sciences *(3 per annum)*; Journal of the Association of Managerial Sciences *(biannually)*; Journal of the Institute of International Affairs *(biannually)*; Journal of the Managerial Research Institute *(biannually)*; Memoirs of the Community Research Institute *(annually)*; Memoirs of the Institute of International Affairs *(biannually)*; Memoirs of the Managerial Research Institute *(biannually)*; Memoirs of the Research Institute of Industry in Chubu District *(biannually)*

Last Updated: 27/10/08

AICHI UNIVERSITY OF EDUCATION

Aichi Kyoiku Daigaku

1 Hirosawa, Igaya-cho, Kariya-shi, Aichi-ken 448-8542
Tel: +81(566) 26-2178
Fax: +81(566) 26-2170
EMail: gakusei@auecc.aichi-edu.ac.jp
Website: http://www.aichi-edu.ac.jp

President: Masahisa Matsuda

Secretary-General: Itsuro Tomioka

Faculties

Education (Arts and Humanities; Child Care and Development; Education; Educational Psychology; Educational Sciences; English;

Environmental Studies; Fine Arts; Health Education; Information Sciences; Japanese; Mathematics Education; Natural Sciences; Primary Education; Science Education; Secondary Education; Social Sciences; Social Studies; Special Education)

Graduate Schools

Education

History: Founded as School 1873, reorganized 1949 and acquired present title 1966.

Academic Year: April to March (April-September; October-March)

Admission Requirements: Graduation from high school or foreign equivalent, and entrance examination

Main Language(s) of Instruction: Japanese

International Co-operation: With universities in USA, China, Thailand

Degrees and Diplomas: *Gakushi*: Education, 4 yrs; *Shushi*: Education, a further 2 yrs

Student Services: Academic counselling, Canteen, Cultural centre, Employment services, Foreign student adviser, Handicapped facilities, Health services, Language programs, Nursery care, Social counselling, Sports facilities

Student Residential Facilities: For c. 300 students

Libraries: c. 694,000 vols

Publications: Bulletin, Research paper *(annually)*

Academic Staff *2007-2008*: Total: c. 150

Student Numbers *2007-2008*: Total: c. 4,200

Last Updated: 28/10/08

AICHI UNIVERSITY OF TECHNOLOGY

Aichi Kouka Daigaku

50-2 Manori Nishihasama-cho, Gamagori-shi, Aichi 443-0047

Tel: +81(533) 68-1135

Fax: +81(533) 68-0352

EMail: nyushi@aut.ac.jp

Website: http://www.aut.ac.jp

Programmes

Engineering (Automation and Control Engineering; Automotive Engineering; Computer Engineering; Electronic Engineering; Engineering; Mechanical Engineering; Robotics)

History: Founded 2000.

Degrees and Diplomas: *Gakushi*: 4 yrs

Student Services: Academic counselling, Social counselling

Special Facilities: Computer Centre

Libraries: c. 700,000 vols

Last Updated: 29/10/08

AIKOKU GAKUEN UNIVERSITY

Aikoku Gakuen Daigaku

1532 Yotsukaido, Yotsukaido-shi, Chiba 284-0005

Tel: +81(43) 424-4410

Fax: +81(43) 424-4322

Website: http://www.aikoku-u.ac.jp/

Programmes

Human and Cultural Sciences

History: Founded 1998.

International Co-operation: With institutions in Republic of Korea, China, Sudan

Degrees and Diplomas: *Gakushi*: 4 yrs

Student Residential Facilities: Yes

Special Facilities: Computer Centre

Libraries: c. 17,200 vols.

Academic Staff *2007-2008*	**TOTAL**
FULL-TIME	**10**
PART-TIME	c. **10**
Student Numbers *2007-2008*	
All (Foreign Included)	c. **200**

Last Updated: 29/10/08

AKITA INTERNATIONAL UNIVERSITY

Kokusai Kyouyou Daigaku

193-2 Okutsubakidai, Yuwa-Tsubakigawa, Akita-shi, Akita 010-1211

Tel: +81(18) 886-5900

Fax: +81(18) 886-5910

EMail: info@aiu.ac.jp

Website: http://www.aiu.ac.jp

President: Mineo Nakajima

Executive Officer: Keisuke Yoshio EMail: k-yoshio@aiu.ac.jp

Faculties

Basic Education; **English for Academic Purposes** *(EAP)*; **Global Business** (International Business)

History: Founded 2004.

Academic Year: April to March (April-August; September-March)

Degrees and Diplomas: *Gakushi*: 4 yrs; *Shushi*

Student Services: Sports facilities

Academic Staff *2007-2008*	**TOTAL**
FULL-TIME	**50**
PART-TIME	c. **40**
Student Numbers *2007-2008*	
All (Foreign Included)	c. **560**

Last Updated: 29/10/08

AKITA PREFECTURAL UNIVERSITY

Akita Kenritsu Daigaku

241-7 Kaidobata Nishi, Shimoshinjo Nakano, Akita 010-0195

Tel: +81(18) 872-1500

Fax: +81(18) 872-1670

EMail: adma1@akita-pu.ac.jp

Website: http://www.akita-pu.ac.jp

President: Shunichi Kobayashi

Faculties

Bioresources Sciences *(Also Graduate School;Akita Campus/ Ogata Campus)* (Agricultural Business; Biology; Biotechnology); **Systems Science and Technology** *(Also Graduate School; Honjo Campus)*

History: Founded 1999.

Degrees and Diplomas: *Gakushi*: Bioresources Science; Agriculture; Technology; *Shushi*: Bioresources Science; Technology; *Hakase*: Bioresources Science; Technology

Last Updated: 29/10/08

AKITA UNIVERSITY

Akita Daigaku

1-1, Tegata Gakuen-machi, Akita-shi, Akita 010-8502

Tel: +81(18) 889-2258

Fax: +81(18) 832-5364

EMail: ryugaku@jimu.akita-u.ac.jp

Website: http://www.akita-u.ac.jp

President: Noboru Yoshimura

Centres

Co-operative Research (Engineering; Information Sciences; Technology); **Data Processing** (Data Processing); **Educational Research and Practice** (Educational Sciences); **Radio Isotope** (Organic Chemistry)

Colleges

Allied Medical Science (Nursing; Occupational Therapy; Physical Therapy)

Departments

Advanced Studies in Special Education for the Mentally Handicapped (Education of the Handicapped; Special Education)

Faculties

Education and Humanities (Cultural Studies; Education; Environmental Studies; Modern Languages); **Engineering and Resources Science** (Engineering; Natural Resources; Technology)

Institutes
Materials Resources Research (Geology; Materials Engineering)

Research Laboratories
Animal Facilities for Experimental Medicine; **Central Research**

Schools
Medicine (Forensic Medicine and Dentistry; Medicine; Pharmacy; Public Health; Radiology; Surgery)

Further Information: Also University Hospital

History: Founded 1949, incorporating Akita Shihan Gakko (Normal School), founded 1875, Akita Kozan Senmon Gakko (Mining College) 1910, Akita Seinen Shihan Gakko (Normal School for Youth Education) 1944, and Igakubu (School of Medicine) 1970. Responsible to the Ministry of Education, Science, Sports and Culture.

Governing Bodies: Hyogikai (University Council)

Academic Year: April to March (April-September; October-March)

Admission Requirements: Graduation from high school or foreign equivalent, and entrance examination

Main Language(s) of Instruction: Japanese

International Co-operation: With universities in China, Australia and USA

Degrees and Diplomas: *Gakushi*: Education and Humanities; Engineering and Resource Science, 4 yrs; *Gakushi*: Medicine, 6 yrs; *Shushi*: Education; Engineering; Resources Science, a further 2 yrs; *Hakase*: Engineering and Resource Science, 3 yrs following Shushi; *Hakase*: Medical Sciences, a further 3-4 yrs

Student Services: Academic counselling, Canteen, Cultural centre, Employment services, Foreign student adviser, Foreign Studies Centre, Health services, Language programs, Nursery care, Social counselling, Sports facilities

Student Residential Facilities: Yes

Special Facilities: Mineral Industry Museum

Libraries: University Library, Medical School Library : 501,000 vols

Publications: Akita Igaku *(quarterly)*; Akita University *(annually)*; Memoirs of the Faculty of Education and Humanities *(annually)*; Reports of Research Institute of Natural Resources, Materials and Global Environments *(annually)*; Scientific and Technical Reports of the Faculty of Engineering and Resource Science *(annually)*

Last Updated: 28/10/08

AOMORI CHUO GAKUIN UNIVERSITY

Aomori Chuo Gakuin Daigaku
12 Kanda, Yokouchi, Aomori-shi, Aomori 030-0132
Tel: +81(17) 728-0131
Fax: +81(17) 738-8333
EMail: international@aomoricgu.ac.jp
Website: http://www.aomoricgu.ac.jp

Programmes
Law (Law); **Management**

History: Founded 1998.

International Co-operation: With universities in China, USA and Philippines

Degrees and Diplomas: *Gakushi*: 4 yrs

Student Services: Sports facilities

Special Facilities: Computer Centre

Libraries: 56,400 vols.

Last Updated: 29/10/08

AOMORI PUBLIC COLLEGE

Aomori Kouritsu Daigaku
153-4 Yamazaki, Goshizawa, Aomori-shi, Aomori 030-0196
Tel: +81(177) 64-1555
Fax: +81(177) 64-1544
EMail: entrance@nebuta.ac.jp
Website: http://www.nebuta.ac.jp

Programmes
Business Administration (Business Administration); **Economics** (Economics)

History: Founded 1993.

Main Language(s) of Instruction: Japanese

International Co-operation: With universities in USA and Russian Federation

Degrees and Diplomas: *Gakushi*; *Shushi*

Libraries: 124,546 vols

Last Updated: 29/10/08

AOMORI UNIVERSITY

Aomori Daigaku
2-3-1 Kobata, Aomori-shi, Aomori 030-0943
Tel: +81(177) 38-2001
Fax: +81(177) 38-0143
EMail: jimukyoku@aomori-u.ac.jp
Website: http://www.aomori-u.ac.jp/

Programmes
Education (Education; Environmental Studies; Teacher Training); **Environmental Sciences**; **Social Welfare** (Social Welfare); **Sociology** (Sociology); **System Science and Engineering** (Computer Engineering; Electronic Engineering; Engineering; Information Technology)

Further Information: Also Preparatory Japanese Language Course

History: Founded 1968.

International Co-operation: With universities in USA, France and Armenia

Degrees and Diplomas: *Gakushi*; *Shushi*

Student Services: Language programs

Libraries: 130,000 vols

Last Updated: 29/10/08

AOMORI UNIVERSITY OF HEALTH AND WELFARE

Aomori Kenritsu Hoken Daigaku (AUHW)
Mase 58-1, Hamadate, Aomori-shi, Aomori 030-8505
Tel: +81(17) 765-2000
Fax: +81(17) 765-2188
EMail: webmaster@auhw.ac.jp
Website: http://www.auhw.ac.jp

Centres
Research Training

Faculties
Health Sciences (Nursing; Physical Therapy; Social Sciences; Social Welfare)

History: Founded 1999.

Degrees and Diplomas: *Gakushi*: 4 yrs

Libraries: c. 67,000 vols

Last Updated: 29/10/08

AOYAMA GAKUIN UNIVERSITY

Aoyama Gakuin Daigaku
4-4-25 Shibuya, Shibuya-ku, Tokyo 150-8366
Tel: +81(3) 3409-8156
Fax: +81(3) 3409-7923
EMail: iec-office@iec.aoyama.ac.jp
Website: http://www.aoyama.ac.jp/en/

President: Kenichi Semba

Centres
Information Science Research (Artificial Intelligence; Computer Science; Information Management; Information Technology)

Graduate Schools
Business (Business Administration; Business and Commerce; Management); **Culture and Creative Studies** (Cultural Studies); **Economics** (Economics); **International Management** (Business Administration; International Business; Management); **International Politics, Economics and Communication** (International Economics; International Relations; International Studies); **Law** (Commercial Law; Law; Private Law; Public Law); **Literature** (American

Studies; English; French; History; Japanese; Literature; Modern Languages); **Professional Accountancy** (Accountancy); **Science and Engineering** (Engineering; Mathematics and Computer Science; Natural Sciences); **Social Informatics** (Computer Science)

Institutes

Research (Arts and Humanities; Business Administration; Chemistry; Christian Religious Studies; Economics; Engineering; International Studies; Law; Physics)

Laboratories

Foreign Languages (Modern Languages)

Schools

Business *(Undergraduate)* (Business Administration; Business and Commerce; Marketing); **Culture and Creative Studies** *(Undergraduate)* (Cultural Studies); **Economics** *(Undergraduate)* (Econometrics; Economic and Finance Policy; Economic History; Economics; Environmental Studies; Finance; Geography; Industrial and Production Economics; International Economics; Social Welfare; Taxation; Transport Economics); **Education, Psychology and Human Studies** *(Undergraduate)* (Education; Humanities and Social Science Education; Psychology); **International Politics, Economics and Communication** *(Undergraduate)* (Accountancy; Administration; African Studies; American Studies; Asian Studies; Banking; Business and Commerce; Commercial Law; Communication Studies; Data Processing; Development Studies; Econometrics; Economic and Finance Policy; Economics; English; European Studies; Finance; Government; Human Resources; Industrial and Production Economics; Industrial Management; Insurance; International Business; International Economics; International Relations; Labour and Industrial Relations; Management; Marketing; Middle Eastern Studies; Pacific Area Studies; Political Sciences; Religious Studies; Taxation; Translation and Interpretation; Writing); **Law** *(Undergraduate)* (Administrative Law; Air and Space Law; Civil Law; Commercial Law; Comparative Law; Constitutional Law; Criminal Law; European Union Law; History of Law; Human Rights; International Law; Labour Law; Law; Maritime Law; Public Law); **Literature** *(Undergraduate)* (Adult Education; Ancient Civilizations; Archaeology; Art History; Classical Languages; Comparative Literature; Continuing Education; Curriculum; Education; Education of the Handicapped; Educational Administration; Educational Sciences; Educational Testing and Evaluation; English; Ethics; Foreign Languages Education; French; Greek; Higher Education; History; Humanities and Social Science Education; International and Comparative Education; Japanese; Latin; Library Science; Linguistics; Literature; Medieval Studies; Modern History; Modern Languages; Museum Management; Pedagogy; Philosophy; Philosophy of Education; Preschool Education; Primary Education; Religious Education; Secondary Education; Translation and Interpretation; Writing); **Science and Engineering** *(Undergraduate)* (Aeronautical and Aerospace Engineering; Analytical Chemistry; Applied Chemistry; Applied Physics; Artificial Intelligence; Atomic and Molecular Physics; Automation and Control Engineering; Automotive Engineering; Bioengineering; Biomedical Engineering; Chemistry; Computer Science; Electronic Engineering; Energy Engineering; Engineering; Engineering Drawing and Design; Environmental Engineering; Hydraulic Engineering; Industrial Chemistry; Industrial Engineering; Inorganic Chemistry; Machine Building; Materials Engineering; Mathematics; Measurement and Precision Engineering; Mechanical Engineering; Metallurgical Engineering; Microelectronics; Natural Sciences; Nuclear Engineering; Nuclear Physics; Optics; Organic Chemistry; Physical Chemistry; Physical Engineering; Physics; Power Engineering; Production Engineering; Software Engineering; Solid State Physics; Statistics; Surveying and Mapping; Systems Analysis; Thermal Physics); **Social Informatics** *(Undergraduate)* (Computer Science)

Further Information: Also campus in Sagamihara

History: Founded 1904 as seminary tracing origin to School founded 1874. Acquired present status 1949. Graduate School established 1952.

Governing Bodies: Rijikai (Board of Trustees); Daigaku Kyogikai (University Council)

Academic Year: April to March (April-July; September-February)

Admission Requirements: Graduation from high school (Sotsugyo Shomeisho) or foreign equivalent, and entrance examination

Fees: (Yen): c. 1.2m.-1.7m. per annum

Main Language(s) of Instruction: Japanese

International Co-operation: With universities in USA, UK, Australia, Canada, China, Korea, Russia, Thailand, France, Germany and 17 other countries

Degrees and Diplomas: *Gakushi*: 4 yrs; *Shushi*: a further 2 yrs; *Hakase*: 3 yrs following Shushi

Student Services: Academic counselling, Canteen, Employment services, Foreign student adviser, Foreign Studies Centre, Handicapped facilities, Health services, Language programs, Social counselling, Sports facilities

Student Residential Facilities: For 68 men and 94 women students

Libraries: Total, c. 1,730,000 vols

Publications: Aoyama Business Journal *(annually)*; Journal of Business Administration *(quarterly)*; Journal of Culture and Creative Studies; Journal of Economics *(quarterly)*; Journal of General Education *(annually)*; Journal of History; Journal of International Politics, Economics and Business *(quarterly)*; Journal of Professional Accountancy; Journal of Social Informatics; Law Journal *(quarterly)*; Law School Journal; Thought Currents in English Literature

Academic Staff *2011*	**TOTAL**
FULL-TIME	**554**
PART-TIME	**1,540**
Student Numbers *2011*	
All (Foreign Included)	c. **20,000**

Last Updated: 04/01/12

ASAHI UNIVERSITY

Asahi Daigaku

1851 Hozumi, Hozumi-cho, Motosu-gun, Gifu 501-0296
Tel: +81(58) 329-1111
Fax: +81(58) 329-1025
EMail: w-admin@alice.asahi-u.ac.jp; nyuusi@alice.asahi-u.ac.jp
Website: http://www.asahi-u.ac.jp

President: Katsuyuki Ohtomo

Centres

Computer Science (Computer Science); **Japanese Language and Culture** (Cultural Studies; Japanese); **Teacher Training** (Teacher Training)

Institutes

Industry and Information; **Law** (Law); **Marketing** (Marketing)

Schools

Business Administration (Business Administration; Information Management); **Dentistry** (Dentistry); **Law** (Law)

Further Information: Also Asahi University Hospital; Murakami Memorial Hospital

History: Founded 1971 as Gifu College of Dentistry. Acquired present status and title 1985.

Governing Bodies: Board of Trustees

Academic Year: April to March (April-September; September-March)

Admission Requirements: Graduation from high school or equivalent, and entrance examination

Main Language(s) of Instruction: Japanese

Degrees and Diplomas: *Gakushi*: Business Administration; Law, 4 yrs; *Gakushi*: Dentistry, 6 yrs; *Shushi*: Business Administration; Law, a further 2 yrs; *Hakase*: Business Administration, Information Management; Business Planning; Law, 3 yrs following Shushi; *Hakase*: Dentistry, a further 4 yrs

Student Services: Academic counselling, Canteen, Cultural centre, Employment services, Foreign Studies Centre, Health services, Language programs, Social counselling, Sports facilities

Student Residential Facilities: Yes

Libraries: Library of Asahi University, 292,000 vols

Publications: Asahi Business Review; Asahi Law Review; International Trade Law Studies; Journal of Gifu Dental Society

Last Updated: 29/10/08

ASAHIKAWA MEDICAL COLLEGE

Asahikawa Ika Daigaku

Midorigaoka Higashi 2-1-1-1, Asahikawa-shi, Hokkaido 078-8510
Tel: +81(166) 65-2111
Fax: +81(166) 65-5533
EMail: digakuin@jimu.asahikawa-med.ac.jp
Website: http://www.asahikawa-med.ac.jp

President: Akitoshi Yoshida

Vice-President, General and Financial Affairs: Susumu Ohta

Courses

General Education; **Nursing** (Nursing)

Research Departments

Cells and Organs (Cell Biology; Surgery); **Defence Mechanisms** (Immunology); **Human Ecology** (Ecology); **Integrative Control of Biological Functions** (Biological and Life Sciences)

Schools

Medicine (Anaesthesiology; Analytical Chemistry; Biochemistry; Dermatology; Forensic Medicine and Dentistry; Gynaecology and Obstetrics; Health Sciences; Immunology; Medicine; Microbiology; Neurology; Ophthalmology; Orthopaedics; Otorhinolaryngology; Paediatrics; Parasitology; Pathology; Pharmacology; Physiology; Psychiatry and Mental Health; Radiology; Surgery; Urology)

Further Information: Also Graduate School (Master and Doctor courses)

History: Founded 1973. Graduate course established 1979.

Academic Year: April to March (April-September; October-March)

Admission Requirements: Graduation from senior high school or equivalent, and entrance examination

Main Language(s) of Instruction: Japanese

Degrees and Diplomas: *Gakushi*: 6 yrs; *Shushi*; *Hakase*: a further 4 yrs

Libraries: c. 140,000 vols

Publications: Asahikawa Medical College *(annually)*

Last Updated: 29/10/08

ASAHIKAWA UNIVERSITY

Asahikawa Daigaku

3-23-113 Nagayama, Asahikawa-shi, Hokkaido 079-8501
Tel: +81(166) 48-3121
Fax: +81(166) 48-8718
EMail: nyushi@asahikawa-u.ac.jp
Website: http://www.asahikawa-u.ac.jp

Programmes

Economics (Economics); **Political Sciences** *(Graduate)*

History: Founded 1968.

Governing Bodies: Board of Directors

Academic Year: April to March

Admission Requirements: Graduation from high school or equivalent

Main Language(s) of Instruction: Japanese

Degrees and Diplomas: *Gakushi*: Economics, 4 yrs; *Shushi*: Regional Policy and Planning, a further 2 yrs

Student Services: Academic counselling, Canteen, Employment services, Foreign student adviser, Health services, Language programs, Social counselling, Sports facilities

Special Facilities: Regional Research Institute. Education Center for Information Literacy

Libraries: 200,910 vols

Publications: The Annual Report of the Regional Research Institute *(annually)*; The Journal of Asahikawa University *(biannually)*

Last Updated: 29/10/08

ASHIKAGA INSTITUTE OF TECHNOLOGY

Ashikaga Kogyo Daigaku

268-1 Omae, Ashikaga-shi, Tochigi 326-8558
Tel: +81(284) 62-0605
Fax: +81(284) 62-5009
EMail: aithome@ashitech.ac.jp
Website: http://www.ashitech.ac.jp

President: Izumi Ushiyama

Divisions

General Education (English; Mathematics; Physics)

Faculties

Engineering (Architecture; Civil Engineering; Electrical and Electronic Engineering; Engineering; Industrial Engineering; Information Management; Mechanical Engineering)

Graduate Schools

Engineering (Architecture; Civil Engineering; Construction Engineering; Electrical and Electronic Engineering; Engineering; Environmental Engineering; Information Sciences; Mechanical Engineering; Production Engineering; Structural Architecture)

History: Founded 1967.

Main Language(s) of Instruction: Japanese

International Co-operation: With universities in China and USA

Degrees and Diplomas: *Gakushi*; *Shushi*; *Hakase*

Student Services: Foreign student adviser, Sports facilities

Libraries: 131,052 vols

Last Updated: 25/03/11

ASHIYA UNIVERSITY

Ashiya Daigaku

13-22 Rokurokuso-cho, Ashiya-shi, Hyogo 659-8511
Tel: +81(797) 23-0661
Fax: +81(797) 23-1901
EMail: nyushi@ashiya-u.ac.jp
Website: http://www.ashiya-u.ac.jp

Faculties

Education (Educational Sciences; Teacher Training)

History: Founded 1964 as private co-educational institution. Graduate studies established 1968.

Governing Bodies: Board of Regents

Academic Year: April to March (April-July; Octorber-March)

Admission Requirements: Graduation from high school or equivalent, and entrance examination

Main Language(s) of Instruction: Japanese

Degrees and Diplomas: *Gakushi*: Education; Philosophy, 4 yrs; *Shushi*: Education, a further 2 yrs; *Hakase*: Education, 3 yrs following Shushi

Student Services: Academic counselling, Canteen, Employment services, Nursery care, Sports facilities

Special Facilities: Audio-visual room

Libraries: c. 235,000 vols (in Japanese and other languages)

Publications: Ashiya Daigaku Ronso; The Report on the International Conference on Vocational Guidance

Press or Publishing House: Ashiya University Press

Last Updated: 29/10/08

ASIA UNIVERSITY

Ajia Daigaku

5-24-10 Sakai, Musashino-shi, Tokyo 180-8629
Tel: +81(422) 36-3255
Fax: +81(422) 36-4869
EMail: koryu@asia-u.ac.jp
Website: http://www.asia-u.ac.jp/english

Faculties

Business Administration (Accountancy; Business Administration; Finance; Management; Marketing); **Economics** (Economics; Political Sciences; Social Studies; Statistics); **International Relations** (Asian Studies; Cultural Studies; Economics; International Relations; International Studies; Law; Modern Languages; Political Sciences; Social Studies); **Law** (Civil Law; Commercial Law; Criminal Law; History of Law; International Law; Law)

Graduate Schools

Asian and International Business Strategy (International Business); **Economics** (Econometrics; Economic History; Economics; Finance; Fiscal Law; International Economics); **Law** (Civil Law; Criminal Law; Law; Public Law)

Further Information: Also Japanese language courses for foreign students

History: Founded 1941, acquired present status and title 1955.

Governing Bodies: Board of Directors

Academic Year: April to March (April-September; October-March)

Admission Requirements: Graduation from high school or equivalent

Main Language(s) of Instruction: Japanese

International Co-operation: With universities in USA, China and Indonesia

Degrees and Diplomas: *Gakushi*: 4 yrs; *Shushi*: a further 2 yrs; *Hakase*: 3 yrs following Shushi

Student Services: Language programs

Student Residential Facilities: Yes

Libraries: 550,000 vols

Publications: Publications of the faculties and departments

Academic Staff *2007-2008*: Total: c. 480

Student Numbers *2007-2008*: Total: c. 6,300

Last Updated: 28/10/08

ATOMI UNIVERSITY

Atomi Gakuen Joshi Daigaku
1-9-6 Nakaro, Niiza-shi, Saitama 352-8501
Tel: +81(48) 478-3333
Fax: +81(48) 479-8418
EMail: d-nyushi@atomi.ac.jp
Website: http://www.atomi.ac.jp

Programmes

Arts and Humanities (Aesthetics; American Studies; Art History; Arts and Humanities; Cultural Studies; English; Japanese; Literature)

History: Founded 1969.

Degrees and Diplomas: *Gakushi*

AZABU UNIVERSITY

Azabu Daigaku
1-17-71 Fuchinobe, Sagamihara-shi, Kanagawa 229-8501
Tel: +81(42) 754-7111
Fax: +81(42) 754-7661
EMail: www-box@azabu-u.ac.jp
Website: http://www.azabu-u.ac.jp

Colleges

Environmental Health (Environmental Management; Environmental Studies)

Graduate Schools

Environmental Health (Environmental Studies; Health Sciences)

Institutes

Biosciences

Research Centres

High-Tech

Schools

Life and Environmental Sciences (Biological and Life Sciences; Environmental Studies; Food Science; Medical Technology); **Veterinary Medicine** *(Also Graduate School)* (Biotechnology; Veterinary Science; Zoology)

Further Information: Also Veterinary Teaching Hospital

History: Founded 1890 as School, became College 1950.

Academic Year: April to March (April-October; October-March)

Admission Requirements: Graduation from high school or equivalent, and entrance examination

Main Language(s) of Instruction: Japanese, English

Degrees and Diplomas: *Gakushi*: 4 yrs; *Shushi (Juigakushushi)*: a further 2 yrs; *Hakase*. Also Eiseikensagishi, Certificate in Public Hygiene, 2 yrs

Student Residential Facilities: Yes

Libraries: c. 154,600 vols

Last Updated: 29/10/08

BAIKA WOMEN'S UNIVERSITY

Baika Joshi Daigaku
2-19-5 Shukunosho, Ibaraki-shi, Osaka 567-8578
Tel: +81(726) 43-8642
Fax: +81(726) 43-6137
EMail: intraff@baika.ac.jp
Website: http://www.baika.ac.jp

Colleges

Junior Studies (Cooking and Catering; Crafts and Trades; Design; English; Japanese)

Faculties

Contemporary Human Studies (Child Care and Development; Environmental Studies; Health Sciences; Psychology; Social Welfare); **Cultural and Expression Studies** (English; Information Sciences; Japanese; Literature; Media Studies)

History: Founded 1878 as School, acquired present status and title 1964. A private Christian Liberal Arts College for Women.

Governing Bodies: Board of Trustees

Academic Year: April to March (April-September; October-March)

Admission Requirements: Graduation from high school and entrance examination

Main Language(s) of Instruction: Japanese, English

International Co-operation: With universities in USA; United Kingdom; China; Canada; Korea and Australia.

Accrediting Agencies: Japanese University Accreditation Association (JUAA)

Degrees and Diplomas: *Gakushi*; *Shushi*; *Hakase*

Student Services: Academic counselling, Canteen, Employment services, Foreign student adviser, Foreign Studies Centre, Handicapped facilities, Health services, Social counselling, Sports facilities

Student Residential Facilities: Yes

Libraries: c. 300,000 vols

Publications: Kami-Hikoki, Children's Literature Department *(annually)*; Puck, Baika Review, English and American Literature Department *(annually)*

Last Updated: 25/03/11

BAIKO GAKUIN UNIVERSITY

Baiko Gakuin Daigaku (BGU)
1-1-1 Kouyoucho, Shimonoseki-shi, Yamaguchi 750-8511
Tel: +81(832) 27-1020
Fax: +81(832) 27-1120
EMail: baiko-u@baiko.ac.jp; president@uv.baiko.ac.jp
Website: http://www.baiko.ac.jp

Divisions

Arts and Humanities (American Studies; Chinese; English; Japanese; Library Science; Literature; Museum Studies; Psychology; Teacher Trainers Education)

Research Centres

Modern Foreign Languages Education (Foreign Languages Education); **Regional Cultural Anthropology** (Anthropology; Regional Studies)

Schools

Modern Communication (Communication Studies)

History: Founded in 1872 as a Christian School for Women by American missionaries. Co-educational from 2001.

Governing Bodies: Board of Trustees; Board of Councillors

Academic Year: April to March (April-July; September-March)

Admission Requirements: Graduation from high school

Main Language(s) of Instruction: Japanese

Degrees and Diplomas: *Gakushi*: Japanese Literature; English; English and American Literature (BA); Modern Communication (BA), 4 yrs; *Shushi*: Japanese Literature; English; English and

American Literature (MA), a further 2 yrs; *Hakase*: Japanese Literature; English; English and American Literature (PhD), 3 yrs following Shushi

Student Services: Academic counselling, Canteen, Cultural centre, Employment services, Foreign student adviser, Foreign Studies Centre, Handicapped facilities, Health services, Language programs, Social counselling, Sports facilities

Student Residential Facilities: For 120 students

Special Facilities: Regional Cultural Anthropology Research Museum

Libraries: University Library, c. 189,000 vols

Publications: Journal *(annually)*; Studies in English Literature *(annually)*; Studies in Japanese Literature *(annually)*; Studies in Modern Communication *(annually)*

Last Updated: 29/10/08

BEPPU UNIVERSITY

Beppu Daigaku

82 Kitaishigaki, Beppu-shi, Oita 874-8501
Tel: +81(977) 67-0101
Fax: +81(977) 66-9696
EMail: bu-adm@beppu-u.ac.jp
Website: http://www.beppu-u.ac.jp

Faculties

Food and Nutrition (Food Science; Nutrition); **Humanities** (Arts and Humanities; Cultural Studies; English; History; Japanese; Literature; Social Sciences)

Research Institutes

Asian History and Culture (Asian Studies; Cultural Studies; History); **Cultural Properties** (Cultural Studies); **Japanese Language and Literature**; **Regional Community Studies** (Regional Studies)

History: Founded 1950.

International Co-operation: With universities in Republic of Korea, China and Taiwan

Degrees and Diplomas: *Gakushi*; *Shushi*; *Hakase*

Student Services: Language programs, Sports facilities

Libraries: c. 219,000 vols

Last Updated: 29/10/08

BIWAKO SEIKEI SPORT COLLEGE

Biwako Seikei Supotsu Daigaku

1204 Bidokoro, Kitahira, Shiga-cho, Shiga-gun, Shiga 520-0503
EMail: nyu@osaka-seikei.ac.jp
Website: http://www.bss.ac.jp/

Departments

Athletic Sport (Sports; Sports Management); **Sport for Life**

Degrees and Diplomas: *Gakushi*

Last Updated: 13/02/09

BUKKYO UNIVERSITY

Bukkyo Daigaku

96 Kitahananobo-cho, Murasakino, Kita-ku, Kyoto-shi, Kyoto 603-8301
Tel: +81(75) 491-2141
Fax: +81(75) 495-5724
EMail: kokusai@bukkyo-u.ac.jp
Website: http://www.bukkyo-u.ac.jp

President: Ryuzen Fukuhara

Graduate Schools

Education (Clinical Psychology; Education); **Literature**; **Social Welfare** (Social Welfare); **Sociology** (Sociology)

Schools

Education; **Health Sciences** (Health Sciences; Occupational Therapy; Physical Therapy); **Literature** (Arts and Humanities; Asian Religious Studies; Chinese; English; History; Japanese); **Social Welfare** (Social Welfare); **Sociology** (Sociology)

Further Information: Also Japanese language courses for foreign students. Correspondence courses.

History: Founded 1887 as Jodo-shugaku Honko, became Special School of Buddhism (Bukkyo Senmon Gakko) 1913, accredited as College 1949 and became University 1967.

Governing Bodies: Jodoshu-Kyoiku-shidan (Education Foundation established by the Jodo Shu Sect of Buddhism)

Academic Year: April to March (April-September; October-March)

Admission Requirements: Graduation from high school or equivalent

Main Language(s) of Instruction: Japanese

International Co-operation: With universities in Republic of Korea, China and Vietnam

Degrees and Diplomas: *Gakushi*: 4 yrs; *Shushi*: a further 2 yrs; *Hakase*

Student Services: Language programs

Student Residential Facilities: Yes

Libraries: University Library, 806,400 vols

Publications: Journal of Letters; Journal of Sociology; Memoirs of the Postgraduate Research Institution; The Bukkyo Daigaku Kenkyukiyo (Journal)

Last Updated: 29/10/08

BUNKA FASHION GRADUATE UNIVERSITY

Bunka Fasyon Daigakuin Daigaku

3-22-1 Yoyogi, Shibuya-ku, Tokyo 151-8521
Tel: +81(3) 3299-2701
Fax: +81(3) 3299-2714
Website: http://www.bfgu-bunka.ac.jp

Programmes

Fashion Design (Fashion Design)

History: Founded 2006.

Degrees and Diplomas: *Shushi*

Last Updated: 12/02/09

BUNKA WOMEN'S UNIVERSITY

Bunka Joshi Daigaku

1196 Kamekubo, Oimachi, Iruma-gun, Saitama 356-8533
Tel: +81(3) 3299-2311
Fax: +81(3) 3299-2637
Website: http://www.bunka.ac.jp

President: Sunao Onuma

Faculties

Art and Design (Architectural and Environmental Design; Design; Fine Arts; Graphic Arts; Graphic Design; Interior Design); **Fashion Science** (Fashion Design); **Liberal Arts and Sciences**

History: Founded 1964.

Academic Year: April to March (April-October; October-March)

Admission Requirements: Graduation from high school or equivalent, and entrance examination

Main Language(s) of Instruction: Japanese

International Co-operation: With universities in USA, China and Germany

Degrees and Diplomas: *Gakushi*; *Shushi*; *Hakase*

Student Services: Foreign student adviser

Special Facilities: Bunka Gakuen Costume Museum

Libraries: 320,500 vols

Last Updated: 30/10/08

BUNKYO GAKUIN UNIVERSITY

Bunkyo Gakuin Daigaku

1-91-1 Mukogaoka, Bunkyo-ku, Tokyo 113-8668
Tel: +81(3) 3814-1661
Fax: +81(3) 5684-4836
EMail: suwa@ell.u-bunkyo.ac.jp; mimura@ba.u-bunkyo.ac.jp
Website: http://www.u-bunkyo.ac.jp

President: Akiko Shimada

Faculties

Business Administration (Accountancy; Business Administration; Finance; Information Management; Management; Taxation); **Foreign Studies**; **Health Science Technology**; **Human Studies** (Child Care and Development; Education; Psychology; Social Sciences; Social Welfare; Social Work)

Further Information: Also campuses in Fujimino and Hongo

History: Founded 1991.

International Co-operation: With universities in Australia; Canada; China; Malaysia; New Zealand and USA

Degrees and Diplomas: *Gakushi*; *Shushi*

Special Facilities: Computer Centre

Libraries: 182,708 vols.

Last Updated: 30/10/08

BUNKYO UNIVERSITY

Bunkyo Daigaku

3-2-17 Hatanodai Shinagawa-ku, Tokyo 142-0064
Tel: +81(3) 3783-5511
Fax: +81(3) 3783-8300
EMail: h.iec@stf.bunkyo.ac.jp
Website: http://www.bunkyo.ac.jp

President: Yukako Ohashi

Director: Hiroo Masuda

International Relations: Hiroko Yamazaki, Chair, International Exchange Centre

Faculties

Education *(Also Graduate School)* (Educational Psychology; Pedagogy; Primary Education; Psychology; Secondary Education) *Dean*: Yukako Ohashi; **Human Sciences** *(Also Graduate School)* (Psychology; Social Sciences) *Dean*: Susumu Fujimori; **Information and Communication** *(Also Graduate School)* (Business Administration; Information Sciences; Information Technology; Public Relations) *Dean*: Hitoshi Takeda; **International Studies** *(Also Graduate School)* (Communication Studies; International Relations) *Dean*: Nobuo Shiino; **Language and Literature** *(Also Graduate School)* (Chinese; English; Japanese) *Dean*: Kiyoshi Hasegawa

Further Information: Also Foreign Student Department in Koshigaya Campus, Women's Junior College in Shonan Campus.

History: Founded 1927 as Rissho Women's Vocational School. Acquired present title 1976.

Governing Bodies: Bunkyo University Foundation

Academic Year: April to March

Admission Requirements: Graduation from high school

Main Language(s) of Instruction: Japanese

International Co-operation: With universities in Australia; China; Germany; Republic of Korea; New Zealand; Thailand and USA

Accrediting Agencies: Japanese Universities Accreditation Association

Degrees and Diplomas: *Gakushi*: Education; Human Sciences; Language and Literature; Information and Communications; International Studies (BA), 4 yrs; *Shushi*: Human Sciences; Language and Culture; Information and Communications; International Cooperation (MA), a further 2 yrs; *Hakase*: Clinical Psychology (PhD), 2 yrs following Shushi

Student Services: Academic counselling, Canteen, Cultural centre, Employment services, Foreign student adviser, Foreign Studies Centre, Handicapped facilities, Health services, Language programs, Social counselling, Sports facilities

Student Residential Facilities: Yes

Special Facilities: Yatsugatake Lodge (vacation accommodation)

Libraries: Koshigaya Library, Shonan Library, 585,000 vols

Publications: Bulletin of Institute of Educational Research, and others

Last Updated: 25/03/11

BUNRI UNIVERSITY OF HOSPITALITY

Seibu Bunri Daigaku

311-1 Kashiwabara-Shinden, Sayama-shi, Saitama-shi, Saitama 350-1336
Tel: +87(42) 954-7575
Fax: +87(42) 954-7511
EMail: koho@bunri-c.ac.jp
Website: http://www.bunri-c.ac.jp

President: Hideki Sato

Faculties

Service Management

History: Founded 1999.

International Co-operation: With universities in USA

Degrees and Diplomas: *Gakushi*

Special Facilities: Audiovisual Learning Centre

Libraries: c. 31,000 vols.

Last Updated: 02/02/09

BUNSEI UNIVERSITY OF ART

Bunsei Geijutsu Daigaku

4-8-15 Kamitomatsuri, Utsunomiya-shi, Tochgi 320-0058
Tel: +81(28) 625-6888
Fax: +81(28) 625-6822
EMail: kouhou@art.bunsei.ac.jp
Website: http://www.bunsei.ac.jp

President: Kenji Ueno

Programmes

Art (Aesthetics; Art History; Ceramic Art; Painting and Drawing; Sculpture; Textile Technology; Visual Arts)

Schools

Graduate Studies

Further Information: Also 2 campuses

History: Founded 1972.

Degrees and Diplomas: *Gakushi*; *Shushi*

Last Updated: 30/10/08

CHIBA INSTITUTE OF SCIENCE

Chiba Kagaku Daigaku (CIS)

3 Shimicho, Choshi-shi, Chiba 288-0025
Tel: +81(47) 9 30-4517
Fax: +81(47) 9 30-4518
EMail: jim@edu.kake.ac.jp; intl@cis.ac.jp
Website: http://ww.cis.ac.jp

Faculties

Pharmaceutical Science (Pharmacology); **Risk and Crisis Management** (Insurance)

History: Founded 2004.

Degrees and Diplomas: *Gakushi*

CHIBA INSTITUTE OF TECHNOLOGY

Chiba Kogyo Daigaku (CIT)

2-17-1 Tsudanuma, Narashino-shi, Chiba 275-0016
Tel: +81(47) 478-0245
Fax: +81(47) 478-3344
EMail: nyushi@it-chiba.ac.jp
Website: http://www.it-chiba.ac.jp

Faculties

Engineering (Architecture; Biological and Life Sciences; Civil Engineering; Electrical Engineering; Electronic Engineering; Environmental Studies; Industrial Design; Measurement and Precision Engineering; Mechanical Engineering; Metallurgical Engineering); **Information and Computer Science** (Computer Engineering; Computer Networks; Computer Science; Information Technology); **Social Systems Science** (Chemistry; Information Management; Management; Mathematics; Natural Sciences; Physics; Social Sciences)

History: Founded 1942 in Machida City, Tokyo, as Koa Engineering College. Moved to Kimitsu-machi, Chiba, 1946, and to Narashino-shi, Chiba 1950, and reorganized as Chiba Institute of Technology.

Governing Bodies: Board of Trustees

Academic Year: April to March (April-October; October-March)

Admission Requirements: Graduation from high school or equivalent, and entrance examination

Main Language(s) of Instruction: Japanese

International Co-operation: With universities in China, USA, Canada, France and Poland

Degrees and Diplomas: *Gakushi*: 4 yrs; *Shushi*: a further 2 yrs; *Hakase*: a further 3 yrs

Student Services: Academic counselling, Canteen, Employment services, Nursery care, Sports facilities

Libraries: 250,000 vols

Publications: Chiba Kogyo Daigaku Kenkyu Houkoku (Research Reports) *(annually)*

Last Updated: 30/10/08

CHIBA KEIZAI UNIVERSITY

Chiba Keizai Daigaku

3-59-5 Todoroki-cho, Inage-ku, Chiba-shi, Chiba 263-0021
Tel: +81(43) 253-9111
Fax: +81(43) 254-6600
Website: http://www.cku.ac.jp

Programmes

Economics (Economics)

History: Founded 1988.

Main Language(s) of Instruction: Japanese

Degrees and Diplomas: *Gakushi*; *Shushi*

Student Services: Sports facilities

Libraries: 170,000 vols

CHIBA UNIVERSITY

Chiba Daigaku

1-33 Yayoi-cho, Inage-ku, Chiba-shi, Chiba 263-8522
Tel: +81(43) 251-1111
Fax: +81(43) 290-2041
EMail: kokusai@office.chiba-u.jp
Website: http://www.chiba-u.ac.jp

President: Yasushi Saito (2008-)
Tel: +81(43) 290-2040, Fax: +81(43) 290-2011
EMail: bgp2002@office.chiba-u.ac.jp

Secretary-General: Takeo Fukushima

International Relations: Takeshi Tokuhisa, Vice-President for Research and International Affairs
Tel: +81(43) 290-2008, Fax: +81(43) 290-2064
EMail: tokuhisa@office.chiba-u.jp

Centres

Chemical Analysis (Chemistry) *Director*: Tsutomu Ishikawa; **Education and Research in Nursing Practice** (Nursing) *Director*: Tadashi Kitaike; **Environment, Health and Field Sciences** *Director*: Hiroshi Amano; **Environmental Remote Sensing** (Surveying and Mapping; Technology) *Director*: Fumihiko Nishio; **Forensic Mental Health** (Forensic Medicine and Dentistry) *Director*: Masaomi Iyo; **Frontier Science** *Director*: Nobuo Ueno; **General Education** *Director*: Akihide Kitamura; **International Research and Education** (Foreigners Education; Modern Languages) *Director*: Akikazu Ando; **Language Education** (Foreign Languages Education; Modern Languages; Native Language Education) *Director*: Itaru Shimazu; **Preventive Medical Science** (Social and Preventive Medicine) *Director*: Chisato Mori; **Radioisotope Research** (Radiology) *Director*: Yasushi Arano; **Research Training and Guidance in Educational Practice** *Director*: Shigeru Amagasa; **Sustainable Tourism Creation** *Director*: Yasunori Nishimura

Faculties

Education (Education; Nursing; Preschool Education; Primary Education; Secondary Education; Special Education) *Dean*: Takashi Tamura; **Engineering** (Applied Chemistry; Architecture; Biomedical Engineering; Computer Graphics; Electrical and Electronic Engineering; Engineering; Environmental Engineering; Industrial Design; Information Sciences; Materials Engineering; Mechanical Engineering; Urban Studies) *Dean*: Hiroshi Noguchi; **Horticulture** *(Matsudo)* (Agricultural Business; Crop Production; Environmental Studies; Horticulture; Landscape Architecture) *Dean*: Masao Kikuchi; **Law and Economics** (Economics; Law) *Dean*: Muneyuki Shindo; **Letters** (Arts and Humanities; Behavioural Sciences; Cultural Studies; History; Modern Languages) *Dean*: Sukeyuki Miura; **Pharmaceutical Sciences** (Pharmacy) *Dean*: Tsutomu Ishikawa; **Science** (Biology; Chemistry; Earth Sciences; Natural Sciences; Physics) *Dean*: Takashi Tsuji

Graduate Schools

Advanced Integration Science *Dean*: Hiroyuki Kobayashi; **Education** (Education) *Dean*: Takashi Tamura; **Horticulture** (Horticulture) *Dean*: Masao Kikuchi; **Humanities and Social Sciences** (Arts and Humanities) *Dean*: Akimasa Miyake; **Medical and Pharmaceutical Sciences** *Dean*: Toshiharu Horie; **Medicine** *(Inohana)* (Medicine) *Dean*: Takeshi Tokuhisa; **Nursing** (Nursing) *Dean*: Emi Mori; **Pharmaceutical Sciences** (Medicine; Pharmacy) *Dean*: Tsutomu Ishikawa; **Science** (Engineering; Horticulture; Natural Sciences; Technology) *Dean*: Takashi Tsuji

Institutes

Media and Information Technology (Data Processing; Information Technology; Media Studies) *Director*: Nobuhiro Isezaki

Laboratories

Venture Business *Director*: Kyoichi Saito

Research Centres

Biomedical Sciences *(Inohana)* (Genetics) *Director*: Toshinori Nakayama; **Frontier Medical Engineering** *Director*: Yoichi Miyake; **Marine Biosystems Research** *Director*: Susumu Okitsu; **Medical Mycology** (Botany) *Director*: Yuzuru Mikami; **Medicinal Resources** *Director*: Hiromitsu Takayama

Schools

Law (Law) *Dean*: Toshio Fujii

Further Information: Also University Hospital

History: Founded 1949 as a State University incorporating Chiba Medical College, Chiba Normal School, Chiba Youth Normal School, Tokyo Industrial College, and Chiba Agricultural College. Graduate School established 1955.Acquired present status 2004.

Governing Bodies: Hyogikai (University Council), Yakuinkai

Academic Year: April to March (April-September; October-March)

Admission Requirements: Graduation from high school or equivalent or foreign equivalent, and entrance examination

Fees: (Yen): Registration, 282,000; tuition, 535,800 (Undergraduate), 535,800 (Master's programme), 520,800 (Doctoral programme)

Main Language(s) of Instruction: Japanese

Degrees and Diplomas: *Gakushi*: 4-6 yrs; *Shushi*: a further 2 yrs; *Hakase*: a further 3-4 yrs

Student Services: Academic counselling, Canteen, Cultural centre, Employment services, Foreign student adviser, Foreign Studies Centre, Handicapped facilities, Health services, Language programs, Nursery care, Social counselling, Sports facilities

Student Residential Facilities: For 218 students

Special Facilities: University Farms; Laboratory Animal Centre

Libraries: University Library, c. 1.4m vols, 16,066 electronic journal titles

Publications: Annual Report of Marine Biosystems Research Centre *(annually)*; Annual Report of Research Centre for Pathogenic Fungi and Microbial Toxicoses *(annually)*; Bulletin of Faculty of Horticulture *(annually)*; Bulletin of the Faculty of Education, Chiba University *(annually)*; Economics Journal of Chiba University *(quarterly)*; Journal of Humanities; Journal of Law and Politics *(quarterly)*; Journal of School of Nursing *(annually)*; List of Research Publications, School of Medicine; Record of Research Activities, Faculty of Pharmaceutical Science *(biannually)*; Research Activities and Interests of Faculty of Engineering *(biannually)*; Technical Bulletin of Faculty of Horticulture *(annually)*; Technical Reports of Mathematical Sciences

Student Numbers *2011-2012*: Total 14,576
Last Updated: 20/11/08

CHIBA UNIVERSITY OF COMMERCE

Chiba Shoka Daigaku
1-3-1 Konodai, Ichikawa-shi, Chiba 272-8512
Tel: +81(47) 372-4111
Fax: +81(47) 375-1101
EMail: somu-1@cuc.ac.jp
Website: http://www.cuc.ac.jp/

President: Haruo Shimada EMail: yharada@cuc.ac.jp

International Relations: Yoshitake Hashimoto, Chief, Student Affairs Section Fax: +81(47) 375-1603 EMail: y-hashi@cuc.ac.jp

Faculties

Commerce and Economics (Business and Commerce; Economics; Management) *Dean*: Shinji Ogura; **Policy Informatics** (Computer Science) *Dean*: Toshiaki Izeki

Graduate Schools

Commerce (Business and Commerce) *Head*: Yasunori Takagi; **Economics** (Economics) *Head*: Kiichi Kageyama; **Policy Informatics** *Head*: Toshiaki Izeki; **Policy Studies** *Head*: Hiroshi Kato

Institutes

Economics Research (Economics) *Director*: Saburo Ota

History: Founded 1928 as Sugamo College of Commerce, became Sugamo College of Economics 1944. Acquired present title 1950.

Governing Bodies: Board of Trustees

Academic Year: April to March (April-September; October-March)

Admission Requirements: Graduation from high school or equivalent or foreign equivalent, and entrance examination

Fees: (Yen): 801,900 per annum for entering the Faculty of Commerce and Economics; 828,000 for the Faculty of Policy Informatics.

Main Language(s) of Instruction: Japanese

Degrees and Diplomas: *Gakushi*: 4 yrs; *Shushi*: a further 2 yrs; *Hakase (PhD)*: a further 3 yrs

Student Services: Academic counselling, Canteen, Foreign student adviser, Handicapped facilities, Health services, Nursery care, Sports facilities

Libraries: c. 580,000 vols

Publications: Konodai Bulletin of Economic Studies *(annually)*; The Journal of Chiba University of Commerce *(quarterly)*; The Review of Chiba University of Commerce *(quarterly)*
Last Updated: 20/08/09

CHIKUSHI JOGAKUEN UNIVERSITY

Chikushi Jogakuen Daigaku
2-12-1 Ishizaka, Dazaifu-shi, Fukuoka 818-0192
Tel: +81(92) 925-3511
Fax: +81(92) 924-4369
EMail: exam@chikushi-u.ac.jp
Website: http://www.chikushi.ac.jp

Faculties

Literature

History: Founded 1988.

Degrees and Diplomas: *Gakushi*
Last Updated: 30/10/08

CHITOSE INSTITUTE OF SCIENCE AND TECHNOLOGY

Chitose Kagaku Gijutsu Daigaku (CIST)
758-65 Vivi, Chitose, Hokkaido 066-8655
Tel: +81(123) 27-6001
Fax: +81(123) 27-6007
EMail: nyushi@mail.chitose.ac.jp
Website: http://www.chitose.ac.jp

President: Hiroyuki Sasabe
Tel: +81(123) 27-6001, Fax: +81(123) 27-6007

Director: Takaaki Koyatsu

Programmes

Science and Technology *(Faculty of Photonics Sciences)* (Applied Physics; Biomedical Engineering; Electronic Engineering; Information Sciences; Materials Engineering; Optical Technology; Technology) *Dean*: Keiichi Mito

Schools

Graduate Studies

History: Founded 1998.

Degrees and Diplomas: *Gakushi*; *Shushi*; *Hakase*

Student Services: Academic counselling, Canteen, Employment services, Foreign student adviser, Social counselling, Sports facilities

Student Residential Facilities: None

Special Facilities: TV Studio

Libraries: 23,210 vols.
Last Updated: 30/10/08

CHUBU GAKUIN UNIVERSITY

Chubu Gakuin Daigaku
4909-3 Kurachi, Seki-shi, Gifu 501-3993
Tel: +81(575) 242-211
Fax: +81(575) 240-077
EMail: nyushi@jimu.chubu-gu.ac.jp
Website: http://www.chubu-gu.ac.jp

Graduate Schools

Social Welfare

Programmes

Social Welfare and Human Development *(Undergraduate)*

History: Founded 1997.

Degrees and Diplomas: *Gakushi*; *Shushi*

Libraries: c. 86,000 vols
Last Updated: 30/10/08

CHUBU UNIVERSITY

Chubu Daigaku
1200 Matsumoto-cho, Kasugai-shi, Aichi 487-8501
Tel: +81(568) 51-1111
Fax: +81(568) 51-1141
EMail: koho@office.chubu.ac.jp
Website: http://www.chubu.ac.jp

President: Okitsugu Yamashita (2005-) Fax: +81(568) 51-4001 EMail: okitsugu@isc.chubu.ac.jp

Secretary-General: Toyoshige Tanaka

Centres

Data Processing (Data Processing; Information Technology); **Innovation Production Engineering** (Production Engineering); **Language** (Linguistics; Modern Languages); **Lifelong Learning**; **Media Education** (Media Studies); **Physical Education and Activities** (Physical Education)

Colleges

Bioscience and Biotechnology (Biochemistry; Biology; Biotechnology; Food Science; Nutrition); **Business Administration and Information Sciences** *(Graduate)* (Business Administration; Information Sciences; Management); **Contemporary Education**; **Engineering** *(Graduate)* (Applied Chemistry; Architecture; Civil Engineering; Computer Science; Electrical Engineering; Electronic Engineering; Engineering; Mechanical Engineering); **Humanities** (Communication Studies; English; Geography (Human); History; Japanese; Psychology); **International Studies** *(Graduate)* (Cultural Studies; International Relations; International Studies); **Life and Health Sciences** (Biological and Life Sciences; Biomedicine; Health Sciences; Nursing)

Graduate Schools

Bioscience and Biotechnology *(Master's and Doctoral courses)* (Biological and Life Sciences; Biotechnology); **Business Administration and Information Sciences** *(Master's and Doctoral courses)* (Business Administration; Information Sciences; Management); **Engineering** *(Master's and Doctoral courses)* (Applied Chemistry; Computer Science; Construction Engineering; Electrical Engineering;

Electronic Engineering; Engineering; Mechanical Engineering); **Global Human Sciences** *(Master's and Doctoral courses)* (Cultural Studies; Geography (Human); History; International Relations; Modern Languages; Psychology)

Research Institutes

Advanced Studies *(Chubu Institute)*; **Biological Functions** (Biological and Life Sciences; Biology); **Contemporary Education**; **Global Human Sciences** (Social Sciences); **Industry and Economics** (Economics; Industrial Engineering); **Information Sciences** (Information Sciences); **Life and Health Sciences** (Biological and Life Sciences; Health Sciences); **Production Engineering**; **Science and Technology Research** (Natural Sciences; Technology)

Further Information: Also Japanese language and culture programme. Study abroad programme

History: Founded 1938 as School, became College 1962, Institute 1964, and acquired present status 1984. Graduate School established 1972. A private institution governed by the Chubu University Educational Foundation.

Governing Bodies: Board of Trustees

Academic Year: April to March (April-September; October-March)

Admission Requirements: Graduation from high school or foreign equivalent, and entrance examination

Main Language(s) of Instruction: Japanese

International Co-operation: With universities in USA; Australia; Malaysia; Sweden; Germany; France; Lithuania; Republic of Korea; China and Morocco

Degrees and Diplomas: *Gakushi*: 4 yrs; *Shushi*: a further 2 yrs; *Hakase*: 3 yrs following Shushi

Student Services: Foreign student adviser, Health services, Language programs, Sports facilities

Student Residential Facilities: Yes

Libraries: Central Library, 550,000 vols

Publications: International Studies, Research Institute for International Studies *(annually)*; Journal of Information Sciences *(annually)*; Journal of the College of Humanities *(annually)*; Journal of the College of International Studies *(biannually)*; Journal of the Research Institute for Industry and Economics *(annually)*; Journal of the Research Institute for Science and Technology *(annually)*; Memoirs of the College of Engineering, Chubu University *(annually)*; The Journal of the College of Business Administration and Information Science *(biannually)*

Last Updated: 20/11/08

CHUGOKU GAKUEN UNIVERSITY

Chugoku Gakuen Daigaku

83 Niwase, Okayama-shi, Okayama 701-0197
Tel: +81(86) 293-1100
Fax: +81(86) 293-3993
Website: http://www.cjc.ac.jp

Faculties

Contemporary Life Science (Biological and Life Sciences)

History: Founded 2001.

Degrees and Diplomas: *Gakushi*

CHUKYO GAKUIN UNIVERSITY

Chukyo Gakuin Daigaku

1-104 Sendanbayashi, Nakatsugawa-shi, Gifu 509-6192
Tel: +81(573) 663-121
Fax: +81(573) 667-722
Website: http://www.chukyogakuin-u.ac.jp

Programmes

Business Administration

History: Founded 1993.

Degrees and Diplomas: *Gakushi*

Special Facilities: Multimedia resource centre

Libraries: 55,000 vols

CHUKYO UNIVERSITY

Chukyo Daigaku

101-2 Yagoto Honmachi, Showa-ku, Nagoya-shi, Aichi 466-8666
Tel: +81(52) 832-2151
Fax: +81(52) 835-7119
EMail: ic@mng.chukyo-u.ac.jp
Website: http://www.chukyo-u.ac.jp

President: Kaoru Kitagawa

Schools

Contemporary Sociology (Social Sciences; Sociology); **Economics** (Economics); **English Languages** (American Studies; Cultural Studies; English; English Studies); **Health and Sports Sciences** (Health Sciences; Sports); **Information Sciences and Technology** (Information Sciences; Information Technology); **International Liberal Studies** (Economics; Environmental Studies; Geography; History; Law; Literature; Modern Languages; Natural Sciences; Philosophy; Political Sciences; Sociology; Sports); **Law** (Administrative Law; Civil Law; Commercial Law; Constitutional Law; Criminal Law; International Law; Law); **Letters**; **Management** (Business and Commerce; Management); **Policy Design** (Business Administration; Economics; Law; Political Sciences; Social Sciences); **Psychology** (Clinical Psychology; Psychology)

Further Information: Also Graduate Schools and Research Institutes

History: Founded 1927 as Chukyo Commercial High School, became Junior College 1954, acquired present status 1956.

Academic Year: April to March

Admission Requirements: Graduation from high school or recognized equivalent, and entrance examination. Provision is made for the recognition of foreign qualifications

Main Language(s) of Instruction: Japanese

International Co-operation: With universities in USA, China and Australia

Degrees and Diplomas: *Gakushi*: 4 yrs; *Shushi*; *Hakase*

Student Services: Foreign student adviser, Foreign Studies Centre, Health services, Language programs, Social counselling, Sports facilities

Special Facilities: Audio-visual centre

Libraries: University Library, 1,263,622 vols

Publications: Journals

Last Updated: 30/10/08

CHUO UNIVERSITY

Chuo Daigaku

742-1 Higashinakano, Hachioji-shi, Tokyo 192-0393
Tel: +81(42) 674-2211
Fax: +81(42) 674-2214
EMail: intlcent2@tamajs.chuo-u.ac.jp
Website: http://www.chuo-u.ac.jp

President: Tadahiko Fukuhara (2011-)
Tel: +81(426) 74-2112, Fax: +81(426) 74-2158

Secretary-General: Michito Kubota

International Relations: Masahik Omura, Director of International Center

Faculties

Commerce (Accountancy; Banking; Business Administration; Business and Commerce; Finance; Marketing); **Economics** (Economics; Environmental Studies; Information Sciences; International Economics; Public Administration); **Law** (International Business; International Law; Law; Political Sciences); **Letters** (American Studies; Arts and Humanities; Asian Studies; Chinese; Computer Science; Cultural Studies; Education; English; English Studies; History; Japanese; Literature; Native Language; Philosophy; Psychology; Sociology; Western European Studies); **Policy Studies** (Cultural Studies; Political Sciences); **Science and Engineering** (Applied Chemistry; Civil Engineering; Computer Engineering; Electrical and Electronic Engineering; Electrical Engineering; Electronic Engineering; Engineering; Industrial Engineering; Information Sciences; Information Technology; Mathematics; Measurement and

Precision Engineering; Mechanical Engineering; Mechanics; Physics; Telecommunications Engineering)

Graduate Schools

Commerce; **Economics**; **International Accounting** *(Professional)*; **Law** *(Chuo Law School - Professional)*; **Law** *(Chuo Law School)*; **Letters** (African Studies; American Studies; Asian Studies; Chinese; Cultural Studies; Education; English; English Studies; French; German; History; Japanese; Literature; Native Language; Philosophy; Psychology; Sociology; Western European Studies); **Policy Studies**; **Public Policy** (Public Administration); **Science and Engineering** (Applied Chemistry; Civil Engineering; Computer Engineering; Electrical and Electronic Engineering; Industrial Engineering; Information Technology; Mathematics; Measurement and Precision Engineering; Physics; Telecommunications Engineering); **Strategic Management** *(Professional)* (Management); **Strategic Management** *(Chuo Graduate School)* (Management)

Institutes

Business Research (Business and Commerce); **Comparative Law in Japan** (Comparative Law)

Further Information: Also Korakuen and Ichigaya campuses

History: Founded 1885 as English Law School, recognized as University 1903. Reorganized 1949.

Governing Bodies: Hyogiinkai (Board of Trustees); Rijikai (Board of Directors)

Academic Year: April to March (April-September; September-March)

Admission Requirements: Graduation from high school or foreign equivalent, and entrance examination

Main Language(s) of Instruction: Japanese

International Co-operation: With universities in Australia; Belgium; China; Croatia; Denmark; France; Germany; Indonesia; Italy; Republic of Korea; Netherlands; New Zealand; Philippines; Russian Federation; Sweden; Switzerland; Taiwan; Thailand; United Kingdom; USA and Vietnam

Degrees and Diplomas: *Gakushi*: Arts (Bungaku); Arts in Education (Kyoikugaku); Commerce (Shogaku); Economics (Keizaigaku); Engineering (Kogaku); History (Shigaku); Law (Hogaku); Philosophy (Tetsugaku); Policy studies (Sogoseisaku); Science (Rigaku); Sociology (Shakaigaku), 4 yrs; *Shushi*: Arts (Bungaku); Commerce (Shogaku); Economics (Keizaigaku); Education (Kyoikugaku); Engineering (Kogaku); Finance (MBA) (Senmonshoku); History (Shigaku); International Accounting (MBA) (Kokusaikaikei); Law (Hogaku); Philosophy (Tetsugaku); Policy Studies (Sogoseisaku); Political Science (Seijigaku); Professional Accounting (MBA) (Kaiei (Senmonshoku)); Psychology (Shinrigaku); Public Policy (Kokyoseisakugaku); Science (Rigaku); Socioinformatics (Shakaijohogaku); Sociology (Shakaigaku), a further 2 yrs; *Hakase*: Accounting (Kaikeigaku); Arts (Bungaku); Business Administration (Keieigaku); Commerce (Shogaku); Economics (Keizaigaku); Education (Kyoikugaku); Engineering (Kogaku); Finance (Kinyugaku); History (Shigaku); Juris Doctor (Homu (Senmonshoku)); Law (Hogaku); Philosophy (Tetsugaku); Policy Studies (Sogoseisaku); Political Science (Seijigaku); Psychology (Shinrigaku); Science (Rigaku); Socioinformatics (Shakaijohogaku); Sociology (Shakaigaku), a further 3 yrs

Student Services: Academic counselling, Canteen, Employment services, Foreign student adviser, Foreign Studies Centre, Handicapped facilities, Health services, Language programs, Social counselling, Sports facilities

Libraries: Central Library; Graduate Library; Science and Engineering Library; total, 1,993,861 vols

Publications: Annual of German Culture *(annually)*; Bulletin of French Studies *(annually)*; Bulletin of Graduate Studies *(annually)*; Bulletin of the Faculty of Science and Engineering *(annually)*; Chuo Review *(quarterly)*; Comparative Law Review *(quarterly)*; English Language and Literature *(annually)*; Journal of Commerce *(bimonthly)*; Journal of Economics *(bimonthly)*; Journal of Liberal Arts *(annually)*; Journal of Pedagogics *(annually)*; Journal of Policy and Culture *(annually)*; Journal of the Faculty of Literature *(annually)*; The Chuo Law Review *(monthly)*

Press or Publishing House: Shuppan-bu (Publishing Office)

Student Numbers *2012-2013*: Total: c. 27,648

Last Updated: 18/12/08

CHUOGAKUIN UNIVERSITY

Chuogakuin Daigaku

451 Kujike, Abiko-shi, Chiba 270-1196

Tel: +81(471) 836-501-514

Fax: +81(471) 836-532

Website: http://www.cgu.ac.jp

Courses

Commerce *(Graduate)*

Faculties

Commerce (Accountancy; Business Administration; Business and Commerce; Economics; Information Sciences; International Business); **Law** (Commercial Law; Law; Public Administration)

Degrees and Diplomas: *Gakushi*. Also graduate course in Commerce

Libraries: 220,000 vols

Last Updated: 30/10/08

DAIDO INSTITUTE OF TECHNOLOGY

Daido Kogyo Daigaku

10-3 Takiharu-cho, Minami-ku, Nagoya-shi, Aichi 457-8530

Tel: +81(52) 612-6111

Fax: +81(52) 612-5623

EMail: ditgakum@daido-it.ac.jp

Website: http://www.daido-it.ac.jp

President: Akira Sawaoka

General Manager: Hishiro Tanaka

International Relations: Kouichi Amaike

Graduate Schools

Technology (Construction Engineering; Electrical and Electronic Engineering; Engineering; Environmental Engineering; Materials Engineering; Mechanical Engineering)

Schools

Engineering (Architectural and Environmental Design; Architecture; Civil Engineering; Computer Engineering; Electrical and Electronic Engineering; Engineering; Mechanical Engineering; Robotics); **Informatics**; **Liberal Arts and Sciences** (Arts and Humanities; Biological and Life Sciences; Engineering; Information Sciences; Modern Languages; Natural Sciences; Social Sciences)

History: Founded 1964.

Academic Year: April to March

Fees: (Yen): Engineering, 1.5m. per annum; Informatics, 1.43m. per annum

Main Language(s) of Instruction: Japanese

International Co-operation: With universities in Denmark; Germany; United Kingdom and USA

Degrees and Diplomas: *Gakushi*; *Shushi*; *Hakase*

Student Services: Sports facilities

Libraries: 206,592 vols

Last Updated: 30/10/08

DAIICHI COLLEGE OF PHARMACEUTICAL SCIENCES

Daiichi Yakka Daigaku

22-1 Tamagawa-cho, Minami-ku, Fukuoka-shi, Fukuoka 815-8511

Tel: +81(92) 541-0161

Fax: +81(92) 553-5698

Website: http://www.daiichi-cps.ac.jp

Programmes

Pharmacy (Pharmacy)

History: Founded 1960.

Degrees and Diplomas: *Gakushi*

DAIICHI UNIVERSITY, COLLEGE OF TECHNOLOGY

Daiichi Kogyo Daigaku

1-10-2 Chuo, Kokubu-shi, Kagoshima 899-4395
Tel: +81(995) 45-0640
EMail: admit@daiichi-koudai.ac.jp
Website: http://www.daiichi-koudai.ac.jp

Programmes

Technology (Technology)

Degrees and Diplomas: *Gakushi*

DAITO BUNKA UNIVERSITY

Daito Bunka Daigaku

1-9-1 Takashimadaira, Itabashi-ku, Tokyo 175-8571
Tel: +81(3) 5399-7323
Fax: +81(3) 5399-7823
EMail: dbuinter@daito.ac.jp
Website: http://www.daito.ac.jp

Faculties

Business Administration (Business Administration; Business Computing; Computer Science; Management); **Economics** *(Undergraduate and graduate programmes)* (Economics); **Foreign Languages** *(Undergraduate and graduate programmes)* (Chinese; English; Japanese); **International Relations** (Cultural Studies; International Relations; International Studies); **Law** (Law; Political Sciences); **Literature** *(Undergraduate and graduate programmes)* (American Studies; Chinese; Education; English; Japanese; Literature); **Social-Human Environmental Sciences** (Environmental Management; Environmental Studies); **Sports and Health Sciences** (Health Sciences; Sports)

Graduate Schools

Asian Area Studies (Asian Studies)

Schools

Law *(Undergraduate and graduate programmes)* (Law)

Further Information: Also Japanese language programme for foreign students

History: Founded 1923 as College, became University 1949.

Governing Bodies: Rijikai (Board of Trustees)

Academic Year: April to March (April-September; October-March)

Admission Requirements: Graduation from high school or equivalent or foreign equivalent, and entrance examination

Main Language(s) of Instruction: Japanese

International Co-operation: With universities in USA, China and Australia

Degrees and Diplomas: *Gakushi*: 4 yrs; *Shushi*: a further 2 yrs; *Hakase*: 3 yrs following Shushi

Student Services: Language programs

Libraries: 1,300,000 vols

Press or Publishing House: Daito Bunka University Publishing House

Last Updated: 31/10/08

DEN-EN CHOFU UNIVERSITY

Den-en Chofu Gakuen Daigaku

3-4-1 Higashiryurigaoka, Aso-ku, Kawasaki-shi, Kanagawa 215-8542
Tel: +81(44) 966-9211
Fax: +81(44) 955-4345
Website: http://www.dcu.ac.jp

Faculties

Human Welfare (Child Care and Development; Family Studies; Nursing; Social Welfare; Social Work; Welfare and Protective Services)

History: Founded 2002.

Degrees and Diplomas: *Gakushi*

Last Updated: 31/10/08

DOHO UNIVERSITY

Doho Daigaku

7-1 Inabaji-cho, Nakamura-ku, Nagoya-shi, Aichi 453-8540
Tel: +81(52) 411-1111
Fax: +81(52) 411-0333
EMail: nyushi@doho.ac.jp
Website: http://www.doho.ac.jp/

Faculties

Arts and Humanities (Arts and Humanities; Asian Religious Studies; Cultural Studies; Japanese; Linguistics; Literature); **Social Welfare** (Child Care and Development; Social Welfare)

Schools

Graduate Studies

History: Founded 1921. Acquired present status 1950.

Degrees and Diplomas: *Gakushi*; *Shushi*

Libraries: c. 170,000 vols

Last Updated: 31/10/08

DOHTO UNIVERSITY

Doto Daigaku

7-1 Ochiishi-cho, Mombetsu-shi, Hokkaido 094-8582
Tel: +81(1582) 4-8101
Website: http://www.dohto.ac.jp

Chancellor: Jun Sakurai

Faculties

Fine Arts (Architectural and Environmental Design; Architecture; Communication Arts; Communication Studies; Design; Fine Arts; Interior Design); **Management** (Information Management; Management; Regional Planning; Sports Management); **Social Welfare** (Child Care and Development; Education; Psychology; Social Welfare)

Further Information: Also Sapporo and Mombetsu campuses

History: Founded 1978.

Degrees and Diplomas: *Gakushi*

Libraries: c. 110,000 vols

Last Updated: 31/10/08

DOKKYO UNIVERSITY

Dokkyo Daigaku

1-1 Gakuen-cho, Soka-shi, Saitama 340-0042
Tel: +81(489) 42-1111
Fax: +81(489) 41-6621
EMail: info@ml.dokkyo.ac.jp
Website: http://www.dokkyo.ac.jp

President: Ko Kajiyama

Faculties

Economics *(Undergraduate and graduate programmes)* (Economics; Management); **Foreign Languages** *(Undergraduate and graduate programmes)* (English; French; German; Modern Languages); **International Liberal Arts** (Arts and Humanities); **Law** *(Undergraduate and graduate programmes)* (International Law; Law; Political Sciences)

Further Information: Also Japanese language courses for foreign students

History: Founded 1964. Forms part of Dokkyo Gakuen (Dokkyo Group of Academic Institutions), founded 1883 as School for the Association of German Studies.

Academic Year: April to March (April-September; September-March)

Admission Requirements: Graduation from senior high school or equivalent, and entrance examination

Main Language(s) of Instruction: Japanese

Degrees and Diplomas: *Gakushi*: Economics (Keizaigakushi); Foreign Languages (Bungakushi); Law (Hogakushi), 4 yrs; *Shushi*: Economics (Keizaigakushushi); Foreign Languages, German, English, French (Bungakushushi); Law (Hogakushushi); *Hakase*:

Foreign Languages, German, English (Bungakuhakushi); Law (Hogakuhakushi)

Student Residential Facilities: For women students

Special Facilities: German Expressionism Collection of Dokkyo University

Libraries: Central Library, c. 690,000 vols

Publications: Bulletin of Liberal Arts *(annually)*; Dokkyo International Journal *(annually)*; Dokkyo News *(monthly)*; English Studies *(annually)*; Etudes françaises *(annually)*; Forschungsbericht Germanistik *(annually)*; Law Review *(annually)*; Studies in Economics *(annually)*; University Journal *(annually)*

Last Updated: 31/10/08

DOKKYO UNIVERSITY SCHOOL OF MEDICINE

Dokkyo Ika Daigaku

880 Kitakobayashi, Mibu-machi, Shimotsuga-gun, Tochigi 321-0293
Tel: +81(282) 86-2108
Fax: +81(282) 86-5678
EMail: gakusei@dokkyomed.ac.jp
Website: http://www.dokkyomed.ac.jp

Schools

Medicine *(Also graduate school)* (Anaesthesiology; Anatomy; Biochemistry; Cardiology; Cell Biology; Dermatology; Endocrinology; Forensic Medicine and Dentistry; Gastroenterology; Gynaecology and Obstetrics; Haematology; Hygiene; Immunology; Medicine; Microbiology; Molecular Biology; Neurology; Oncology; Ophthalmology; Orthopaedics; Otorhinolaryngology; Paediatrics; Pathology; Pharmacology; Physiology; Pneumology; Psychiatry and Mental Health; Public Health; Radiology; Rehabilitation and Therapy; Surgery; Urology; Zoology); **Nursing** (Nursing)

History: Founded 1972. Forms part of the Dokkyo Gakuen (Dokkyo Group of Academic Institutions), founded 1883 as School for the Association of German Studies.

Main Language(s) of Instruction: Japanese

Degrees and Diplomas: *Gakushi*; *Hakase*

Student Services: Health services, Language programs, Sports facilities

Libraries: 210,000 vols

Last Updated: 31/10/08

DOSHISHA UNIVERSITY

Doshisha Daigaku

Imadegawa-dori, Kamigyo-ku, Kyoto-shi, Kyoto 602-8580
Tel: +81(75) 251-3260
Fax: +81(75) 251-3057
EMail: ji-kksai@mail.doshisha.ac.jp
Website: http://www.doshisha.ac.jp

President: Eiji Hatta (2004-)
Tel: +81(75) 251-3110, Fax: +81(75) 251-3075

Vice-President for Academic Affairs: Nobuhiro Tabata

International Relations: Yasuhiro Kuroki, Vice-President for International Affairs

Centres

American Studies (American Studies) *Director*: Naoki Kameda; **Christian Culture** (Christian Religious Studies) *Director*: Makoto Mizutani; **Japanese Language and Culture** (Japanese) *Dean*: Nobuyuki Yamauchi

Faculties

Commerce (Business and Commerce) *Dean*: Hideo Fujiwara; **Culture and Information Sciences** (Cultural Studies; Information Sciences) *Dean*: Masakatsu Murakami; **Economics** (Economics) *Dean*: Yoshiaki Shikano; **Health and Sports Sciences** *Dean*: Yoshihiko Fujisawa; **Law** (Law; Political Sciences) *Dean*: Michio Tsuchida; **Letters** (Aesthetics; Art History; Cultural Studies; English; Japanese; Philosophy; Psychology) *Dean*: Nobuyoshi Saito; **Life and Medical Sciences** *Dean*: Yoshiaki Watanabe; **Policy Studies** *Dean*: Tatsushi Mayama; **Science and Engineering** (Chemical Engineering; Computer Engineering; Electrical Engineering; Electronic Engineering; Engineering; Environmental Studies; Information Management; Information Sciences; Mechanical Engineering; Molecular Biology) *Dean*: Takashi Matsuoka; **Social Studies** (Communication Studies; Journalism; Labour and Industrial Relations; Media Studies; Social Studies; Social Welfare; Sociology) *Dean*: Mitsuo Ishida

Graduate Schools

American Studies (American Studies) *Dean*: Naoki Kameda; **Business** *(Professional Graduate Course) Dean*: Harukiyo Hasegawa; **Commerce** (Business and Commerce); **Economics**; **Engineering** (Applied Chemistry; Computer Engineering; Electrical Engineering; Engineering; Environmental Engineering; Mechanical Engineering); **Law** *(Professional Graduate Course) Dean*: Mitsunori Fukada; **Letters**; **Life and Medical Sciences** (Biological and Life Sciences; Medicine); **Policy and Management** (Insurance; Management) *Dean*: Tatsuro Niikawa; **Theology** (Bible; History of Religion; Theology)

Institutes

Humanities and Social Sciences (Arts and Humanities; Social Sciences) *Director*: Yu Kamitani; **Language and Culture** (Cultural Studies; Modern Languages) *Director*: Hisao Nakamura; **Science and Engineering Research** (Engineering; Science Education) *Director*: Akira Hayashida

Schools

Law (Law) *Dean*: Masao Okumura; **Theology** (Theology) *Dean*: Makoto Hara

Further Information: Also summer programmes and study abroad programmes

History: Founded 1875 as a Doshisha English School, became College 1912, reorganized 1920 and 1949. Financed by student fees and donations.

Governing Bodies: Rijikai (Board of Trustees); Hyogikai (University Council); Buchokai (Deans' Council)

Academic Year: April to March (April-September; October-March)

Admission Requirements: Graduation from high school or equivalent, or foreign equivalent, and entrance examination

Fees: (Yen): 1,074,000-1,543,000 per annum

Main Language(s) of Instruction: Japanese

International Co-operation: With universities in Argentina; Australia; Austria; Canada; Chile; China; Czech Republic; Egypt; Finland; France; Germany; Indonesia; Israel; Italy; Jordan; Korea; Mexico; Nepal; Netherlands; New Zealand; Norway; Philippines; Poland; Spain; Sweden; Syria; Thailand; United Kingdom; USA

Degrees and Diplomas: *Gakushi*: 4 yrs; *Shushi*: a further 2 yrs; *Hakase*: 3 yrs following Shushi

Student Services: Academic counselling, Canteen, Employment services, Foreign student adviser, Handicapped facilities, Health services, Language programs, Social counselling, Sports facilities

Student Residential Facilities: Yes

Special Facilities: Historical Museum. International Center

Libraries: University Library (Imadegawa campus), 588,611 vols; Learned Memorial Library (Kyotanabe campus), 207,821 vols; Faculty and Institute libraries, 1,419,883 vols

Publications: Annual of Philosophy; Annual report of Cultural Studies; Annual Report of the School of Museology; Bulletin of the Centre for Japanese Language; Doshisha American Studies; Doshisha Danso; Doshisha Journal of Health and Sport Sciences; Doshisha Journal of Library and Information Science; Doshisha Literature; Doshisha Psychological Review; Doshisha Review of Sociology; Doshisha Studies in English; Doshisha Studies in Language and Culture; Journal of Education and Culture; Neesima Studies; Science and Engineering Review of Doshisha; SHURYU; Social Science Review; Studies in Christianity; Studies in Cultural History; Studies in Humanities; Studies in the Christian Religion; The Doshisha Law Review; The Doshisha University Economic Review; The Social Sciences; The Society of Aesthetics and Science of Arts; The Study of Christianity and Social Problems; World Wide Business Review

Last Updated: 31/10/08

DOSHISHA WOMEN'S COLLEGE OF LIBERAL ARTS

Doshisha Joshi Daigaku (DWCLA)
Kyotanabe-shi, Kyoto 610-0395
Tel: +81(774) 65-8811
Fax: +81(774) 65-8460
EMail: examstaff@dwc.doshisha.ac.jp; koho-t@dwc.doshisha.ac.jp
Website: http://www.dwc.doshisha.ac.jp

President: Hiroo Kaga

Faculties

Contemporary Social Studies (Child Care and Development; Social Studies); **Human Life and Science** (Biological and Life Sciences; Food Science; Nutrition); **Liberal Arts** (Arts and Humanities; English Studies; Information Sciences; Japanese; Literature; Media Studies; Music)

History: Founded as School 1876, acquired present status 1949.

Governing Bodies: Board of Trustees

Academic Year: April to March (April-September; October-March)

Admission Requirements: Graduation from high school or equivalent, and entrance examination

Fees: (Yen) Undergraduate, 1,142,500-1,597,500; Graduate, 774,000-892,000 per annum

Main Language(s) of Instruction: Japanese

Accrediting Agencies: Daigaku Kijun Kyokai

Degrees and Diplomas: *Gakushi*: Home Economics (Seikatsukagaku); Information and Media; Letters (Bungaku); Music (Ongaku); Social Studies (Shakai), 4 yrs; *Shushi*: a further 2-4 yrs; *Hakase*: 3 yrs following Shushi

Student Services: Canteen, Employment services, Handicapped facilities, Health services, Social counselling, Sports facilities

Student Residential Facilities: For 224 students

Libraries: College Library, 465,000 vols

Publications: Asphodel *(annually)*; Bulletin of Institute for Interdisciplinary Studies of Culture *(annually)*; Doshisha Home Economics *(annually)*; Nihongo Nihon Bungaku *(annually)*

Last Updated: 25/03/11

EDOGAWA UNIVERSITY

Edogawa Daigaku
474 Komaki, Nagareyama-shi, Chiba 270-0198
Tel: +81(471) 520-660 +81(471) 529-871
Fax: +81(471) 542-490 +81(471) 534-596
Website: http://www.edogawa-u.ac.jp

Departments

Business Design; **Environmental Information**; **Mass Communication**; **Sociology and Human Studies**

History: Founded 1990.

Degrees and Diplomas: *Gakushi*

EHIME PREFECTURAL UNIVERSITY OF HEALTH SCIENCES

Ehime Kenritsu Iryo Gijutsu Tanki Daigaku
543 Takooda, Tobe-cho, Iyo-gun, Ehime 791-2101
Tel: +81(89) 958-2111
Fax: +81(89) 958-2177
EMail: info@ehime-chs.ac.jp
Website: http://www.ehime-chs.ac.jp

Faculties

Health Sciences (Health Sciences; Medical Technology; Nursing)

History: Founded 2004.

Degrees and Diplomas: *Gakushi*

Libraries: c. 71,700 vols

Publications: Bulletin of Ehime Prefectural University of Health Sciences

Last Updated: 31/10/08

EHIME UNIVERSITY

Ehime Daigaku
10-13 Dogo-Himata, Matsuyama-shi, Ehime 790-8577
Tel: +81(89) 927-9157
Fax: +81(89) 927-9171
EMail: ryugaku@stu.ehime-u.ac.jp
Website: http://www.ehime-u.ac.jp

President: Masayuki Komatsu

Faculties

Agriculture (Agricultural Engineering; Agriculture; Agrobiology; Environmental Engineering; Environmental Management; Forestry; Natural Resources); **Education** (Education; Education of the Handicapped; Educational Research; Preschool Education; Primary Education; Secondary Education; Teacher Training); **Engineering** (Applied Chemistry; Civil Engineering; Computer Science; Electrical and Electronic Engineering; Engineering; Environmental Engineering; Materials Engineering; Mechanical Engineering); **Law and Letters** (Arts and Humanities; Business Administration; Cultural Studies; Economics; Law; Literature; Modern Languages; Regional Studies); **Science** (Applied Chemistry; Applied Mathematics; Applied Physics; Biology; Chemistry; Earth Sciences; Materials Engineering; Mathematics and Computer Science; Natural Sciences; Physics; Statistics)

Schools

Medicine (Anaesthesiology; Anatomy; Biochemistry; Dentistry; Dermatology; Forensic Medicine and Dentistry; Gynaecology and Obstetrics; Hygiene; Immunology; Medicine; Microbiology; Neurology; Nursing; Ophthalmology; Otorhinolaryngology; Paediatrics; Parasitology; Pathology; Pharmacology; Physiology; Public Health; Radiology; Surgery; Urology)

Further Information: Also centres, research centres and laboratories

History: Founded 1949, incorporating Ehime Normal School, founded 1943, Matsuyama Higher School, 1919, Ehime Youth Normal School, 1944, Niihama Technical College, 1939, and Matsuyama Agricultural College, 1949.

Governing Bodies: Hyogikai (University Council), comprising the dean and 2 professors of each faculty

Academic Year: April to March (April-September; October-March)

Admission Requirements: Graduation from high school or equivalent and entrance examination

Main Language(s) of Instruction: Japanese

International Co-operation: With universities in China, USA and France

Degrees and Diplomas: *Gakushi*: Agriculture (Nogakushi); Arts (Bungakushi); Education (Kyoikugakushi); Engineering (Kogakushi); Law (Hogakushi); Science (Rigakushi); Social sciences (Shakaigakushi), 4 yrs; *Shushi*: Agriculture (Nogakushushi); Engineering (Kogakushushi); Law (Hogakushushi); Science (Rigakushushi), a further 2 yrs; *Hakase*: Agriculture (Nogahakushi), 4 yrs following Shushi; *Hakase*: Medical Sciences, a further 4 yrs

Student Services: Language programs, Sports facilities

Student Residential Facilities: Yes

Libraries: Central and branch libraries, total, 1,200,000 vols

Last Updated: 31/10/08

ELISABETH UNIVERSITY OF MUSIC

Erizabeto Ongaku Daigaku
4-15 Nobori-cho, Naka-ku, Hiroshima 730-0016
Tel: +81(82) 221-0918
Fax: +81(82) 221-0947
EMail: exam01@eum.ac.jp
Website: http://www.eum.ac.jp

President: Hideaki Nakamura

Faculties

Music *(Undergraduate and graduate divisions)* (Conducting; Music; Music Education; Music Theory and Composition; Musical Instruments; Musicology; Religious Music; Singing)

History: Founded 1948 as School, became Junior College 1952, acquired present status 1963. Division of Graduate Studies opened 1991. Recognized by the Ministry of Education, Science and Culture. Affiliated to the Pontificio Istituto di Musica Sacra in Rome. Directed by the Society of Jesus.

Governing Bodies: Board of Trustees

Academic Year: April to March (April-September; September-March)

Admission Requirements: Graduation from high school or equivalent, and entrance examination

Main Language(s) of Instruction: Japanese

Degrees and Diplomas: *Gakushi*: Fine Arts, Sacred Music (Geijutsugakushi); Fine Arts (Geijutsugakushi), 4 yrs; *Shushi*: Fine Arts (Geijutsushushi), a further 2 yrs; *Hakase*

Student Services: Academic counselling, Employment services, Foreign student adviser, Handicapped facilities, Sports facilities

Student Residential Facilities: For c. 100 women students

Libraries: University Library, c. 125,000 vols

Publications: Arts et Mystica (Review) *(annually)*; Research Bulletin *(annually)*

Academic Staff *2007-2008*	TOTAL
FULL-TIME	30
PART-TIME	c. 130
Student Numbers *2007-2008*	
All (Foreign Included)	c. 490

Last Updated: 31/10/08

FERRIS UNIVERSITY

Ferisu Jogakuin Daigaku

37 Yamate-cho, Naka-ku, Yokohama-shi, Kanagawa 231-8651
Tel: +81(45) 662-4521
Fax: +81(45) 662-6102
EMail: univ-nys@ferris.ne.jp
Website: http://www.ferris.ac.jp

Colleges

Music *(Undergraduate and graduate divisions)* (Music; Musicology; Singing)

Faculties

Global and Inter-cultural Studies *(Undergraduate and graduate divisions)* (Cultural Studies; Education; Finance; Geography (Human); History; Social Studies; Welfare and Protective Services); **Humanities** *(Undergraduate and graduate divisions)* (Arts and Humanities; Communication Studies; Cultural Studies; Education; English; Finance; History; Japanese; Literature; Modern Languages; Social Studies; Translation and Interpretation)

Further Information: Also summer language programmes with: Towson State University; Bath College; IIK, Jena; Tsinghua University, Beijing

History: Founded 1965. Acquired present status and title 1997.

Governing Bodies: Board of Directors

Academic Year: April to January (April-July; October-January)

Admission Requirements: Graduation from high school or equivalent, and entrance examination

Main Language(s) of Instruction: Japanese

International Co-operation: With universities in USA, Republic of Korea and Philippines

Degrees and Diplomas: *Gakushi*: 4 yrs; *Shushi*: a further 2 yrs; *Hakase*: 3 yrs following Shushi

Student Services: Academic counselling, Employment services, Foreign student adviser, Foreign Studies Centre, Language programs, Nursery care, Social counselling, Sports facilities

Special Facilities: Ferris Hall (Concert Hall)

Libraries: c. 300,000 vols

Publications: Ferris Studies (College of Music vol.1-vol.2) *(annually)*

Last Updated: 31/10/08

FUJI TOKOHA UNIVERSITY

Fuji Tokoha Daigaku

325 Obuchi, Fuji-shi, Shizuoka 417-0801
Tel: +81(545) 36-1133
Fax: +81(545) 36-2651
Website: http://www.fuji-tokoha-u.ac.jp

Colleges

Distribution Economics (Economics); **Environment and Disaster Research**

Institutes

Environment and Disaster Research (Environmental Engineering; Safety Engineering); **Technology** *(Fudo)*

History: Founded 1999.

Degrees and Diplomas: *Gakushi*

Libraries: c. 100,000 vols

Publications: Fuji Tokoha University Journal

Last Updated: 31/10/08

FUJI UNIVERSITY

Fuji Daigaku

450-3 Shimoneko, Hanamaki-shi, Iwate 025-0025
Tel: +81(198) 23-6221
Fax: +81(198) 23-5818
EMail: fujiuniv.n@gmail.com
Website: http://www.fujidai.net/

Programmes

Business Law (Commercial Law; Law); **Economics** (Economics); **Management**

History: Founded 1965.

Degrees and Diplomas: *Gakushi*

Last Updated: 31/10/08

FUJI WOMEN'S UNIVERSITY

Fuji Joshi Daigaku

Nishi 2-chome, Kita 16-jo, Kita-ku, Sapporo-shi, Hokkaido 001-0016
Tel: +81(11) 736-0311
Fax: +81(11) 709-8541
EMail: nyushi@fujijoshi.ac.jp
Website: http://www.fujijoshi.ac.jp

President: Generoso Florez

Faculties

Human Life Sciences *(Hanakawa Campus)* (Child Care and Development; Education; Food Science; Nutrition; Social Sciences); **Humanities** *(Sapporo Campus)* (Arts and Humanities; English; Japanese)

History: Founded 1961.

Degrees and Diplomas: *Gakushi*; *Shushi*

Libraries: c. 307,000 vols

Last Updated: 31/10/08

FUJITA HEALTH UNIVERSITY

Fujita Hoken Eisei Daigaku

1-92 Dengakugakubo, Kutsukake-cho, Toyoake-shi, Aichi 470-1192
Tel: +81(562) 93-2401
Fax: +81(562) 93-4597
Website: http://www.fujita-hu.ac.jp

President: Hiroshi Nakano
Tel: +81(562) 93-2620, Fax: +81(562) 93-4593

Faculties

Health Sciences (Health Sciences; Medical Technology; Nursing; Radiology; Rehabilitation and Therapy); **Medicine** (Medicine)

Graduate Schools

Health Sciences (Medical Technology; Nursing; Radiology); **Medicine** (Biomedicine; Medicine; Public Health; Surgery)

Institutes

Biochemistry *(Fujita Memorial Nanakuri)* (Biochemistry); **Comprehensive Medical Sciences** (Biochemistry; Cell Biology; Genetics; Immunology; Molecular Biology)

Further Information: Also Fujita Health University Hospital

History: Founded 1964.

Governing Bodies: Board of Directors

Academic Year: April to March (April-July; September-December; January-March)

Admission Requirements: Graduation from high school or equivalent and entrance examination

Fees: (Yen): Registration, 300,000-1m.; tuition, Medicine, 7,006,000 (1st yr); 5,706,000 (2nd-6th yr) per annum; Health Sciences, 1,356,000 or 1,406,000 (Nursing and Rehabilitation) (1st yr); 1,506,000 or 1,556,000 (Nursing and Rehabilitation) (2nd-4th yr) per annum

Main Language(s) of Instruction: Japanese

Accrediting Agencies: Japan University Accreditation Association

Degrees and Diplomas: *Gakushi*: Igaku, Medicine, 6 yrs; *Gakushi*: Medical Technology; Nursing; Radiology; Rehabiltation, 4 yrs; *Shushi*: Medical Technology, Nursing, Radiology, a further 2 yrs; *Hakase*: Medicine, a further 4 yrs

Student Services: Canteen, Employment services, Health services, Language programs, Social counselling, Sports facilities

Student Residential Facilities: Yes

Libraries: Central Library,101,289 vols (Japanese); 84,846 vols (foreign languages); periodicals: 480 publications (Japanese); 594 publications (foreign languages)

Publications: Bulletin of the Fujita Medical Society *(biennially)*

Last Updated: 31/10/08

FUKUI PREFECTURAL UNIVERSITY

Fukui Kenritsu Daigaku

4-1-1 Kenjojima, Matsuoka-cho, Yoshida-gun, Fukui 910-11
Tel: +81(776) 61-6000
Fax: +81(776) 61-6011
EMail: nyusi@fpu.ac.jp
Website: http://www.fpu.ac.jp

Faculties

Biotechnology; **Economics**; **Nursing and Social Welfare**

Graduate Schools

Bioscience and Biotechnology (Biotechnology; Marine Biology); **Economics and Business Administration**; **Nursing and Social Welfare**

Research Institutes

Regional Economics (Economics)

Further Information: Also Obama campus

History: Founded 1992.

Main Language(s) of Instruction: Japanese

Degrees and Diplomas: *Gakushi*; *Shushi*; *Hakase*

Libraries: c. 303,000 vols

Last Updated: 03/11/08

FUKUI UNIVERSITY OF TECHNOLOGY

Fukui Kogyo Daigaku

3-6-1 Gakuen, Fukui-shi, Fukui 910-8505
Tel: +81(776) 22-8111
Fax: +81(776) 29-7891
EMail: kouhou@ccmails.fukui-ut.ac.jp
Website: http://www.fukui-ut.ac.jp

President: Masahiro Johno

Departments

Applied Nuclear Technology; **Construction and Architectural Engineering**; **Construction and Civil Engineering** (Civil Engineering; Construction Engineering); **Electrical and Electronic Engineering** (Electrical and Electronic Engineering; Engineering); **Environmental and Biotechnological Frontier Engineering** (Bioengineering; Environmental Engineering); **Management Science**; **Mechanical Engineering** (Mechanical Engineering); **Space Communication Engineering**

Schools

Graduate Studies

History: Founded 1965.

Academic Year: April to March (April-September; September-March)

Admission Requirements: Graduation from high school and entrance examination

Main Language(s) of Instruction: Japanese

International Co-operation: With universities in China and Republic of Korea

Degrees and Diplomas: *Gakushi*: Engineering (Kogakushi), 4 yrs; *Shushi*; *Hakase*

Student Services: Sports facilities

Student Residential Facilities: Yes

Libraries: 158,000 vols

Last Updated: 03/11/08

FUKUOKA DENTAL COLLEGE

Fukuoka Shika Daigaku

2-15-1 Tamura, Sawara-ku, Fukuoka-shi, Fukuoka 814-0193
Tel: +81(92) 801-0411
Fax: +81(92) 801-3678
EMail: kikaku@college.fdcnet.ac.jp
Website: http://www.fdcnet.ac.jp

President: Takeshi Honda

Colleges

Dentistry (Biochemistry; Bioengineering; Biology; Cell Biology; Dental Hygiene; Dental Technology; Dentistry; Medicine; Oral Pathology; Otorhinolaryngology; Pathology; Public Health; Surgery); **Health Sciences**

Graduate Schools

Dentistry

Further Information: Also College Hospital

History: Founded 1972.

Degrees and Diplomas: *Gakushi*; *Hakase*

Student Services: Foreign student adviser, Social counselling, Sports facilities

Libraries: c. 140,000 vols

Last Updated: 06/11/08

FUKUOKA INSTITUTE OF TECHNOLOGY

Fukuoka Kogyo Daigaku (FIT)

3-30-1 Wajirohigashi, Higashi-ku, Fukuoka-shi, Fukuoka 811-0295
Tel: +81(92) 606-3131
Fax: +81(92) 606-8923
EMail: staff@fit.ac.jp
Website: http://www.fit.ac.jp

President: Kaoru Yamafuji Tel: +81(92) 606-2211

Faculties

Engineering (Electrical Engineering; Electronic Engineering; Environmental Engineering; Information Technology; Materials Engineering; Mechanical Engineering); **Information Engineering** (Automation and Control Engineering; Communication Studies; Computer Engineering; Computer Science; Industrial Engineering); **Social and Environmental Studies** (Business Administration; Environmental Studies; Law; Social Sciences)

Further Information: Also graduate school

History: Founded 1963.

Academic Year: April to March (two semesters)

Admission Requirements: Secondary school certificate

Fees: (Yen): 1,097,000 per annum

Main Language(s) of Instruction: Japanese

International Co-operation: With universities in Australia, China, Republic of Korea and USA

Degrees and Diplomas: *Gakushi*: 4 yrs; *Shushi*: a further 2 yrs; *Hakase*: 3 yrs following Shushi

Student Services: Academic counselling, Canteen, Employment services, Handicapped facilities, Nursery care, Social counselling

Student Residential Facilities: Yes

Special Facilities: Monotsukuri Centre

Libraries: 249,614 vols

Publications: Reports of Computer Science Laboratory, Fukuoka Institute of Technology *(annually)*; Reports of the Electronics Research Laboratory, Fukuoka Institute of Technology *(annually)*; Research Bulletin of Fukuoka Institute of Technology *(biennially)*

Last Updated: 05/11/08

FUKUOKA INTERNATIONAL UNIVERSITY

Fukuoka Kokusai Daigaku

4-16-1 Gojo, Daizaifu-shi, Fukuoka 818-0193
Tel: +81(92) 922-4034
Fax: +81(92) 922-6453
EMail: koryu@fukuoka-int-u.ac.jp
Website: http://www.fukuoka-int-u.ac.jp/

Programmes

International Studies

History: Founded 1998.

International Co-operation: With institutions in USA, Australia and China

Degrees and Diplomas: *Gakushi*

Libraries: 130,000 vols.

Last Updated: 06/11/08

FUKUOKA JO GAKUIN UNIVERSITY

Fukuoka Jo Gakuin Daigaku

3-42-1 Osa, Minami-ku, Fukuoka-shi, Fukuoka 811-1313
Tel: +81(92) 581-1492
Fax: +81(92) 575-4456
EMail: nyushi@fukujo.ac.jp
Website: http://www.fukujo.ac.jp/

Faculties

Human Relations (Communication Studies; Psychology; Social Sciences; Sociology); **Humanities** (American Studies; Arts and Humanities; Asian Studies; Computer Graphics; Cultural Studies; Education; English; European Studies; Japanese; Music; Performing Arts; Regional Studies)

Graduate Schools

Human Sciences (Social Sciences)

History: Founded 1990.

Degrees and Diplomas: *Gakushi*; *Shushi*

Last Updated: 05/11/08

FUKUOKA PREFECTURAL UNIVERSITY

Fukuoka Kenritsu Daigaku

4395 Ita, Tagawa-shi, Fukuoka 825-8585
Tel: +81(947) 422-118
Fax: +81(947) 426-171
EMail: kyomu@fukuoka-pu.ac.jp
Website: http://www.fukuoka-pu.ac.jp

President: Hajime Nawata

Graduate Schools

Human and Social Sciences

Schools

Human and Social Sciences (Pedagogy; Psychology; Social Welfare; Sociology); **Nursing** (Nursing)

History: Founded 1992.

Degrees and Diplomas: *Gakushi*; *Shushi*

Last Updated: 05/11/08

FUKUOKA SOCIAL MEDICAL WELFARE UNIVERSITY

Fukuoka Iryo Fukushi Daigaku

3-10-10 Gojo, Dazaifu-shi, Fukuoka 818-0194
Tel: +81(92) 918-6511
Fax: +81(92) 918-6510

President: Yasuhisa Tsuzuki

Faculties

Social Welfare and Human Services (Clinical Psychology; Social and Community Services; Social Welfare)

History: Founded 2002 as Daiichi Fukushi Daigaku (Daiichi Welfare University). Acquired present title 2008.

Degrees and Diplomas: *Gakushi*

FUKUOKA UNIVERSITY

Fukuoka Daigaku

8-19-1 Nanakuma, Jonan-ku, Fukuoka-shi, Fukuoka 814-0180
Tel: +81(92) 871-6631
Fax: +81(92) 862-4431
EMail: kokusai@adm.fukuoka-u.ac.jp
Website: http://www.fukuoka-u.ac.jp

President: Takuya Eto
Tel: +81(92) 871-6631, Fax: +81(92) 862-4431

Faculties

Commerce *(Also evening and graduate school)* (Business and Commerce; International Business; Management); **Economics** *(Also graduate school)*; **Engineering** *(Also graduate school)* (Architecture; Chemical Engineering; Civil Engineering; Computer Science; Construction Engineering; Electrical Engineering; Electronic Engineering; Mechanical Engineering); **Humanities** *(Also graduate school)* (Clinical Psychology; Cultural Studies; East Asian Studies; Education; English; French; German; History; Japanese; Literature); **Law** *(Also graduate school)*; **Medicine** *(Also graduate school)* (Medicine; Nursing); **Pharmacy** *(Also graduate school)* (Pharmacology; Pharmacy); **Science** *(Also graduate school)* (Applied Mathematics; Applied Physics; Chemistry; Earth Sciences; Nanotechnology); **Sports and Health Science** *(Also graduate school)* (Health Sciences; Sports; Sports Medicine)

Further Information: Also junior high, high school and Nursing school.

History: Founded 1934 as Fukuoka Higher Commercial School, acquired present status 1949. Present title adopted 1956.

Governing Bodies: Board of Regents

Academic Year: April to March (April-July; October-March)

Admission Requirements: Graduation from high school or foreign equivalent, and entrance examination

Fees: (Yen): 799,710-8,623,710 per annum

Main Language(s) of Instruction: Japanese

International Co-operation: With universities in USA, United Kingdom, Republic of Korea, China, Taiwan, Nepal, Indonesia, Philipines, Australia, France, Italy, Belgium and Brazil.

Degrees and Diplomas: *Gakushi*: Commerce; Economics; Engineering; Humanities; Law; Medicine; Pharmaceutical Sciences; Science; Sports and Health Science, 4 yrs; *Shushi*: Commerce; Economics; Engineering; Humanities; Law; Medicine; Pharmaceutical Sciences; Science; Sports and Health Science, a further 2 yrs; *Hakase*: Commerce; Economics; Engineering; Humanities; Law; Medicine; Pharmaceutical Sciences; Science; Sports and Health Science, 3 yrs following Shushi

Student Services: Foreign student adviser, Foreign Studies Centre, Language programs, Sports facilities

Student Residential Facilities: Yes

Libraries: 1,600,000 vols

Publications: Journals (Law, Economics, Commercial Sciences, Humanities, Medicine, Physical Education, Technological Sciences, Pharmaceutical Sciences)

Last Updated: 03/11/08

FUKUOKA UNIVERSITY OF ECONOMICS

Fukuoka Keizai Daigaku

3-11-25 Gojo, Dazaifu-shi, Fukuoka-shi, Fukuoka 818-0197
Tel: +81(92) 922-5131
EMail: admit@daiichi-ue.ac.jp

President: Yasduhisa Tsuzuki

Programmes

Economics (Economics)

History: Founded 1968. Formerly known as Daiichi Keizai Daigaku (Daiichi University, College of Economics).

Degrees and Diplomas: *Gakushi*

FUKUOKA UNIVERSITY OF EDUCATION

Fukuoka Kyoiku Daigaku

729-1 Akama, Munakata-shi, Fukuoka 811-4192
Tel: +81(940) 35-1200
Fax: +81(940) 35-1700
EMail: ryugak01@fukuoka-edu.ac.jp
Website: http://www.fukuoka-edu.ac.jp

President: Shinishi Terao

Faculties

Education (Art Education; Cultural Studies; Education; Education of the Handicapped; English; Foreign Languages Education; Health Education; Home Economics; Japanese; Mathematics; Modern Languages; Music Education; Physical Education; Science Education; Social Studies; Social Welfare; Special Education; Technology Education)

Graduate Schools

Education (Art Education; Education; English; Health Education; Home Economics Education; Mathematics Education; Music Education; Natural Sciences; Physical Education; Primary Education; Science Education; Secondary Education; Social Studies; Special Education; Technology Education)

Programmes

Postgraduate Diploma

Further Information: Also Japanese language courses for foreign students

History: Founded 1943, reorganized 1949.

Academic Year: April to March (April-October; October-March)

Admission Requirements: Graduation from high school and entrance examination

Main Language(s) of Instruction: Japanese

Degrees and Diplomas: *Gakushi*: 4 yrs; *Shushi*: a further 2 yrs

Libraries: Central Library c. 500,000 vols

Last Updated: 24/03/11

FUKUOKA WOMEN'S UNIVERSITY

Fukuoka Joshi Daigaku

1-1-1 Kasumigaoka, Higashi-ku, Fukuoka-shi, Fukuoka 813-8529
Tel: +81(92) 661-2411
Fax: +81(92) 661-2415
EMail: webmasters@fwu.ac.jp
Website: http://www.fwu.ac.jp

President: Makoto Takagi

Faculties

Human Environmental Science *(Undergraduate and graduate programmes)* (Environmental Studies; Health Sciences; Nutrition); **Literature** *(Undergraduate and graduate programmes)* (Arts and Humanities; English; Japanese; Literature)

History: Founded 1950.

Academic Year: April to March

Admission Requirements: Graduation from high school and entrance examination

Main Language(s) of Instruction: Japanese

Degrees and Diplomas: *Gakushi*; *Shushi*: a further 2-3 yrs; *Hakase*

Student Services: Academic counselling, Health services, Sports facilities

Libraries: c. 143,000 vols

Last Updated: 24/03/11

FUKUSHIMA MEDICAL UNIVERSITY

Fukushima Kenritsu Ika Daigaku

1 Hikarigaoka, Fukushima-shi, Fukushima 960-1295
Tel: +81(24) 548-2111
Fax: +81(24) 549-7712
EMail: info@fmu.ac.jp
Website: http://www.fmu.ac.jp/index.html

President: Shin-ichi Kikuchi

Vice-President: Seiichi Takenoshita

Schools

Medicine *(Also graduate school)* (Anaesthesiology; Anatomy; Arts and Humanities; Biochemistry; Biological and Life Sciences; Biology; Chemistry; Dermatology; Forensic Medicine and Dentistry; Gynaecology and Obstetrics; Hygiene; Mathematics; Medicine; Microbiology; Modern Languages; Neurology; Ophthalmology; Otorhinolaryngology; Paediatrics; Pathology; Pharmacology; Physics; Physiology; Psychiatry and Mental Health; Public Health; Radiology; Social and Preventive Medicine; Social Sciences; Statistics; Surgery; Urology); **Nursing** *(Also graduate school)*

History: Founded 1952.

Academic Year: April to March (April-October; October-March)

Admission Requirements: Graduation from high school and entrance examination

Main Language(s) of Instruction: Japanese

Degrees and Diplomas: *Gakushi*: Medicine, 6 yrs; *Shushi*: Medicine; *Hakase*: Medicine, 4 yrs

Student Services: Sports facilities

Student Residential Facilities: For c. 40 students

Special Facilities: Medical Museum

Libraries: 173,700 vols

Publications: Fukushima Igaku Zassi *(bimonthly)*; Journal *(quarterly)*

Last Updated: 28/03/12

FUKUSHIMA UNIVERSITY

Fukushima Daigaku

1 Kanayagawa, Fukushima-shi, Fukushima 960-1296
Tel: +81(24) 548-5151
Fax: +81(24) 548-3180
EMail: hpc@fukushima-u-ac-jp
Website: http://www.fukushima-u.ac.jp/

President: Osamu Nittono

Faculties

Administration and Social Sciences (Administration; Cultural Studies; Law; Social and Community Services; Social Sciences); **Economics and Business Administration** (Business Administration; Economics; International Economics); **Human Development and Culture** (Cultural Studies; Development Studies; Fine Arts; Social Sciences; Sports); **Symbiotic Systems Science** (Arts and Humanities; Engineering; Environmental Management; Social Sciences)

Graduate Schools

Economics (Business Administration; Economic History; Economics; Industrial Engineering; Information Technology; International Economics); **Education** (Art Education; Clinical Psychology; Education; Japanese; Music Education; Physical Education; Social Studies); **Public Policy and Regional Administration** (Administration; Public Administration; Regional Planning); **Symbiotic Systems Science and Technology** (Technology)

History: Founded 1949.

Academic Year: April to March (April-September; October-March)

Admission Requirements: Graduation from high school or equivalent or foreign equivalent, and entrance examination

Main Language(s) of Instruction: Japanese

Degrees and Diplomas: *Gakushi*: 4 yrs; *Shushi*: a further 2 yrs

Student Services: Health services, Language programs, Social counselling, Sports facilities

Special Facilities: Observatory

Libraries: 790,000 vols

Publications: Annual Report of the Research Centre for Lifelong Learning and Education; Bulletin of the Healthcare Centre; Bulletin of the Research and Guidance Centre of Teaching Practice; Faculty Bulletins; Journal of Administrative and Social Sciences; Journal of Commerce, Economics and Economic History; Regional Studies
Last Updated: 28/03/12

FUKUYAMA HEISEI UNIVERSITY

Fukuyama Heisei Daigaku

117-1 Syouto, Kamiiwanari, Miyuki-cho, Fukuyama-shi, Hiroshima 720-0001
Tel: +81(849) 72-5001
Fax: +81(849) 72-7771
EMail: shomu@heisei-u.ac.jp
Website: http://www.heisei-u.ac.jp

Programmes
Management

Schools
Business Administration

History: Founded 1994.

Degrees and Diplomas: *Gakushi*; *Shushi*

Student Services: Sports facilities

Special Facilities: Computer Centre

Libraries: c. 50,000 vols.

FUKUYAMA UNIVERSITY

Fukuyama Daigaku

1 Sanzo, Gakuen-cho, Fukuyama-shi, Hiroshima 729-0292
Tel: +81(849) 36-2111
Fax: +81(849) 36-2213
EMail: shomu@fucc.fukuyama-u.ac.jp
Website: http://www.fukuyama-u.ac.jp

President: Taizo Muta

Vice-President: Ryuusuke Yoshihara

Faculties
Economics (Economics; International Economics; Taxation) *Dean*: Isao Ookubo; **Engineering** (Architecture; Civil Engineering; Electrical and Electronic Engineering; Engineering; Information Technology; Mechanical Engineering) *Dean*: Kazuo Kobayashi; **Human Cultures** (Cultural Studies; Information Sciences; Media Studies; Psychology) *Dean*: Fumiko Matsuda; **Life Science and Biotechnology** (Biological and Life Sciences; Biotechnology; Marine Science and Oceanography) *Dean*: Kiyoshi Satouchi; **Pharmacy** (Biology; Pharmacology; Pharmacy) *Dean*: Satoshi Hibino

Graduate Schools
Economics *Head*: Ryuusuke Yoshihara; **Engineering** *Head*: Yoshihiro Furue; **Pharmacy** (Pharmacology; Pharmacy) *Head*: Tsuyoshi Goromaru

Further Information: Also Intensive Japanese Programme (IJP) for students of sister universities, held for one month a year. Intensive English Programme (IEP) at UCR (sister university), for one month a year

History: Founded 1975, consisted of the Faculties of Economics and Engineering. Faculty of Pharmacy and Pharmaceutical Sciences added 1983.

Governing Bodies: Board of Regents

Academic Year: April to March (April-September; September-March)

Admission Requirements: Graduation from high school or equivalent, or foreign equivalent and entrance examination

Main Language(s) of Instruction: Japanese

Degrees and Diplomas: *Gakushi*: Economics; Engineering; Pharmacy, 4 yrs; *Shushi*: Economics; Engineering; Pharmacy, a further 2 yrs; *Hakase*: Engineering; Pharmacy, 3 yrs following Shushi

Student Services: Sports facilities

Student Residential Facilities: For c. 185 students

Libraries: 300,000 vols

Publications: Annual Report of the Faculty of Pharmacy and Pharmaceutical Sciences *(annually)*; Bulletin of the Research Centre for Human Science; Journal of the Faculty of Liberal Arts; Report of the Research Institute of Marine Bioresources; Scientific Report of the Japan Research Institute of Industrial Science; The Fukuyama Economic Review; The Memoirs of the Faculty of Engineering
Last Updated: 06/11/08

FUTURE UNIVERSITY - HAKODATE

Kouritu Hakodate Mirai Daigaku

116-2 Kamedanakano-cho, Hakodate-shi, Hokkaido
Tel: +81(138) 34-6444
Fax: +81(138) 34-6383
EMail: edu@fun.ac.jp
Website: http://www.fun.ac.jp

President: Hideyuki Nakashima

Departments
Complex Systems; **Media Architecture** (Media Studies)

Schools
Systems Information Sciences *(Also graduate school)* (Information Sciences; Media Studies; Telecommunications Engineering)

History: Founded 2000.

Degrees and Diplomas: *Gakushi*; *Shushi*; *Hakase*

Student Services: Sports facilities

Libraries: 34,560 vols.

GAKUSHUIN UNIVERSITY

Gakushuin Daigaku

1-5-1 Mejiro, Toshima-ku, Tokyo 171-8588
Tel: +81(3) 3986-0221
EMail: webmaster@gakushuin.ac.jp
Website: http://www.gakushuin.ac.jp/univ/

President: Norihiko Fukui (2007-)
Tel: +91(3) 3986-0221, Fax: +81(3) 5992-9246

International Relations: Ken Mizuno, Director, Centre for International Exchange Fax: +81(3) 5992-1025

Centres
Computer (Computer Science); **Foreign Language Teaching and Research** (Arts and Humanities; Chinese; English; Foreign Languages Education; French; German; Literature); **Oriental Cultures**; **Sports and Health Sciences** (Health Sciences; Sports)

Faculties
Economics (Business Administration; Economics; Management); **Law** (Law; Political Sciences); **Letters** (Arts and Humanities; English; Foreign Languages Education; French; German; History; Japanese; Literature; Philosophy; Psychology); **Science** (Chemistry; Mathematics; Natural Sciences; Physics)

Graduate Schools
Economics (Economics); **Humanities** (Arts and Humanities; English; French; German; History; Japanese; Philosophy; Psychology); **Law** (Law); **Management**; **Political Studies**; **Science** (Chemistry; Mathematics; Physics)

Institutes
Biomolecular Science; **Museum of History** (Archiving; Documentation Techniques)

Research Institutes
Economics and Management (Economics; Management); **Humanities**; **Oriental Cultures** (Asian Studies)

History: Founded 1877 as School, financed by the Imperial Ministry of Education. Became University 1949. A private Institution financed by student fees and donations.

Governing Bodies: University Council; Board of Trustees

Academic Year: April to March (April-September; September-March)

Admission Requirements: Graduation from high school or equivalent and entrance examination

Fees: (Yen): Registration, 300,000; tuition, 871,300-1,315,800 per annum

Main Language(s) of Instruction: Japanese

Degrees and Diplomas: *Gakushi*: Law; Political Studies; Economics; Management; Arts; Science, 4 yrs; *Shushi*: Law; Political Studies; Economics; Management; Arts; Science, a further 2 yrs; *Hakase*: Law; Philosophy; Science, 3 yrs following Shushi

Student Services: Canteen, Employment services, Foreign student adviser, Foreign Studies Centre, Handicapped facilities, Health services, Social counselling, Sports facilities

Libraries: c. 1,480,000 vols

Publications: Gakushuin Economic Papers *(quarterly)*; Gakushuin Review of Law and Politics; Gakushuin University Studies *(annually)*; The Annual Collection of Essays and Studies (Faculty of Letters) *(quarterly)*

Last Updated: 09/02/09

GAKUSHUIN WOMEN'S COLLEGE

Gakushuin Joshi Daigaku

3-20-1 Toyama, Shinjuku-ku, Tokyo 162-8650

Tel: +81(3) 3203-1906

Fax: +81(3) 3203-8873

EMail: gwc-fsc@gakushuin.ac.jp

Website: http://www2.gwc.gakushuin.ac.jp

Departments

English Communications; **Intercultural Communications** (Applied Linguistics; Architecture; Communication Studies; Eastern European Studies; Education; English; Environmental Studies; Film; German; Heritage Preservation; History; International Economics; International Relations; Journalism; Linguistics; Literature; Management; Media Studies; Political Sciences; Theatre); **Japanese Studies** (Aesthetics; Art History; Biochemistry; Clinical Psychology; Computer Science; Cultural Studies; Environmental Studies; Health Sciences; Information Sciences; Japanese; Library Science; Linguistics; Medieval Studies; Modern History; Physics; Sociology; Sports)

Schools

Graduate Studies

History: Founded 1998.

Academic Year: Two semesters from April to January (April-August; September-January)

Fees: (Yen): first year, 1.35m. per annum; subsequent years, 1.05m. per annum.

Degrees and Diplomas: *Gakushi*; *Shushi*

Last Updated: 06/11/08

GIFU COLLEGE OF NURSING

Gifu Kenritsu Kango Daigaku

3047-1 Egira-cho, Hashima-shi, Gifu 501-6295

Tel: +81(58) 397-2300

Fax: +81(58) 397-2302

EMail: kanri@gifu-cn.ac.jp

Website: http://www.gifu-cn.ac.jp

President: Konishi Michiko

Programmes

Nursing (Arts and Humanities; Child Care and Development; English; Health Sciences; Information Management; Japanese; Midwifery; Natural Sciences; Nursing; Social Welfare)

History: Founded 2000.

Academic Year: April to March (April-September; October-March)

Admission Requirements: Completion of the entire senior-high school course or 12 years of regular school education or equivalent.

Fees: (Yen): entrance examination fee, 17,000; Admission fee: for Gifu Prefecture residents, 226,000; for others 338,000; Tuition 520,800.

Degrees and Diplomas: *Gakushi*

Student Services: Sports facilities

Special Facilities: Audi-visual room; multi-media room

Libraries: c. 14,000 vols.

Last Updated: 24/03/11

GIFU KEIZAI UNIVERSITY

Gifu Keizai Daigaku

5-50 Kitagata-cho, Ogaki-shi, Gifu 503-8550

Tel: +81(584) 77-3511

Fax: +81(584) 81-7807

EMail: nyushi@gifu-keizai.ac.jp

Website: http://www.gifu-keizai.ac.jp

President: Hiroshi Kurokawa

Faculties

Business Administration (Business Administration); **Economics** (Economics; Social and Community Services; Welfare and Protective Services)

Graduate Schools

Business Administration

Schools

Business Administration (Business Administration; Information Management; Multimedia)

History: Founded 1967.

Degrees and Diplomas: *Gakushi*; *Shushi*

Libraries: c. 310,000 vols

Last Updated: 06/11/08

GIFU PHARMACEUTICAL UNIVERSITY

Gifu Yakka Daigaku

5-6-1 Mitahora-higashi, Gifu-shi, Gifu 502-8585

Tel: +81(58) 237-3931

Fax: +81(58) 237-5979

EMail: kyomu@gifu-pu.ac.jp

Website: http://www.gifu-pu.ac.jp

Institutes

Biological Pharmacy (Biotechnology; Pharmacy)

Programmes

Pharmaceutical Sciences *(Undergraduate and graduate programmes)* (Pharmacology; Pharmacy; Production Engineering; Public Health)

History: Founded 1932 as Municipal Senmon Gakko of Pharmacy. Acquired present status and title 1946.

Academic Year: April to March (April-September; October-March)

Admission Requirements: Graduation from high school or equivalent, and entrance examination

Main Language(s) of Instruction: Japanese

International Co-operation: With universities in Australia; Brazil; China; Italy; Spain and USA

Degrees and Diplomas: *Gakushi*: Pharmacy (Yakugakushi), 4 yrs; *Shushi*: Pharmacy (Yakugakushushi), a further 2 yrs; *Hakase*: Pharmacy (Yakugakuhakushi), 3 yrs following Shushi

Special Facilities: Herbal Garden; Experimental Farm; Kawashima Memorial Experimental Farm at Nenohara

Libraries: 69,000 vols

Publications: Annual Proceedings *(annually)*

Last Updated: 06/11/08

GIFU SHOTOKU GAKUEN UNIVERSITY

Gifu Shotoku Gakuen Daigaku

2078 Takakuwa, Yanaizu-cho, Hashima-gun, Gifu 501-6174
Tel: +81(58) 279-0804
Fax: +81(58) 279-4171
EMail: nory@ha.shotoku.ac.jp/
Website: http://www.ha.shotoku.ac.jp/

Centres

Buddhist Study (Asian Religious Studies)

Programmes

Economic Information; **Education** (Education; Japanese; Pre-school Education; Primary Education; Secondary Education; Social Studies); **Foreign Languages**; **International Culture**

Research Centres

Communication Technology; **Education** (Education)

History: Founded 1963 by Shin Buddhist priests (Nishi Honganji Temple), and named after Prince Shotokum (AD 574-622). Known as Shokotu Gakuen Gifu Kyoiku Daigaku/Gifu University for Education and Languages until 1998.

Fees: (Yen): 200,000 per annum

International Co-operation: With institutions in China, Canada, New Zealand

Degrees and Diplomas: *Gakushi*; *Shushi*

Special Facilities: Computer Centre

Libraries: 230,000 vols.
Last Updated: 06/11/08

GIFU UNIVERSITY

Gifu Daigaku

1-1 Yanagido, Gifu-shi, Gifu 501-1193
Tel: +81(58) 230-1111
Fax: +81(58) 230-1410
EMail: direcent@cc.gifu-u.ac.jp; president@cc.gifu-u.ac.jp
Website: http://www.gifu-u.ac.jp

President: Hideki Mori

Faculties

Applied Biological Science *Dean*: Yoshinori Furuta; **Education** (Art Education; Biology; Chemistry; Continuing Education; Earth Sciences; Economics; Education; Education of the Handicapped; Educational Psychology; English; Geography; Geography (Human); Health Education; History; Home Economics Education; Japanese; Law; Mathematics Education; Music Education; Philosophy; Physical Education; Physics; Primary Education; Psychology; Science Education; Secondary Education; Social Studies; Special Education; Teacher Training; Technology) *Dean*: Yoshinori Furuta; **Engineering** (Applied Chemistry; Biomedical Engineering; Chemistry; Civil Engineering; Computer Engineering; Electrical and Electronic Engineering; Engineering; Environmental Engineering; Information Sciences; Materials Engineering; Mechanical Engineering) *Dean*: Minoru Miwa; **Regional Studies** (Regional Studies) *Dean*: Masataka Takemori

Graduate Schools

Agricultural and Veterinary Sciences *(United)* (Agricultural Management; Agrobiology; Biological and Life Sciences; Veterinary Science) *Dean*: Yoshinoko Shinoda; **Agriculture** (Agriculture; Biological and Life Sciences) *Dean*: Yoshihiko Furuta; **Education** (Education; Special Education) *Dean*: Yoshinori Furuta; **Engineering** (Applied Chemistry; Civil Engineering; Computer Engineering; Electronic Engineering; Engineering; Environmental Engineering; Information Technology; Materials Engineering; Mechanical Engineering; Natural Resources) *Dean*: Minoru Miwa; **Medicine** (Medicine; Physiology; Social and Preventive Medicine; Surgery) *Dean*: Hiroyuki Shimizu; **Regional Studies** (Regional Studies) *Dean*: Masataka Takemori

Schools

Medicine (Anaesthesiology; Anatomy; Biochemistry; Cardiology; Cell Biology; Dermatology; Diabetology; Endocrinology; Epidemiology; Forensic Medicine and Dentistry; Gastroenterology; Gerontology; Gynaecology and Obstetrics; Health Education; Immunology; Medicine; Microbiology; Neurology; Nursing; Oncology; Ophthalmology; Orthopaedics; Otorhinolaryngology; Paediatrics; Parasitology; Pharmacology; Pharmacy; Physiology; Psychiatry and Mental Health; Radiology; Rheumatology; Social and Preventive Medicine; Sports Medicine; Surgery; Traditional Eastern Medicine; Urology) *Dean*: Naomi Kondo

History: Founded 1949, incorporating Gifu Normal College founded 1875, and Gifu College of Agriculture and Forestry founded 1924. Faculty of Engineering of Gifu Prefectural University attached 1952. Gifu Prefectural College of Medicine attached 1964 as Faculty of Medicine.

Governing Bodies: Hyogikai (University Council)

Academic Year: April to March (April-September; October-March)

Admission Requirements: Graduation from high school or equivalent or foreign equivalent, and entrance examination

Fees: (Yen): Undergraduate, 520,800 for tuition, 282,000 for admission, 17,000 for entrance examination. Graduate, 520,800 for tuition, 282,000 for admission, 30,000 for entrance examination. Research Student, 28,900 per month, 84,600 for admission, 9,800 for entrance examination

Main Language(s) of Instruction: Japanese

Degrees and Diplomas: *Gakushi*: Agriculture; Education; Engineering; Regional Studies, 4 yrs; *Gakushi*: Medicine, 6 yrs; *Shushi*: Agriculture; Education; Engineering; Regional Studies, a further 2 yrs; *Hakase*: Agricultural Sciences; Kogakuhakushi, engineering, 3 yrs following Shushi; *Hakase*: Medicine; Veterinary Science, a further 4 yrs

Student Services: Canteen, Employment services, Foreign student adviser, Foreign Studies Centre, Health services

Student Residential Facilities: Yes

Special Facilities: Gifu Local Museum

Libraries: Central Libray, 906,522 vols

Publications: Faculty Research Report, Agriculture *(annually)*; Faculty Research Report, Education *(annually)*; Faculty Research Report, Engineering *(annually)*; Faculty Research Report, General Education *(annually)*; Faculty Research Report, Medicine *(annually)*
Last Updated: 24/03/11

GIFU UNIVERSITY OF MEDICAL SCIENCES

Gifu Iryou Kagaku Daigaku

795-1 Azanagamine, Hiraa, Seki-shi, Gifu 501-3882
EMail: jinno4@jinno.ac.jp
Website: http://www.jinno.ac.jp

Departments

Health Sciences (Medical Technology; Midwifery; Nursing; Radiology)

History: Founded 2006.

Degrees and Diplomas: *Gakushi*
Last Updated: 13/02/09

GIFU WOMEN'S UNIVERSITY

Gifu Joshi Daigaku

80 Taromaru, Gifu-shi, Gifu 501-2592
Tel: +81(58) 229-2211
Fax: +81 (58) 229-2222
EMail: nagako@gijodai.ac.jp
Website: http://www.gijodai.ac.jp

Departments

Creativity and Culture *(Undergraduate and graduate programmes)* (Cultural Studies; Fine Arts); **Elementary Education**; **Housing and Design** (Home Economics; House Arts and Environment; Interior Design); **Human Life Sciences** *(Undergraduate and graduate programmes)* (Biological and Life Sciences); **Nutrition and Food Science**

Further Information: Also special Japanese curriculum for foreign students

History: Founded 1968.

Main Language(s) of Instruction: Japanese

Degrees and Diplomas: *Gakushi*; *Shushi*

Student Services: Sports facilities

Libraries: 110,000 vols
Last Updated: 06/11/08

GLOBIS MANAGEMENT SCHOOL

Gurobisu Keiei Daigakuin Daigaku

Sumitomo Fudosan Kojimachi Bldg., 5-1, Niban-cho, Chiyoda-ku, Tokyo 102-0084
Fax: +81(3) 5275-3787
EMail: imba@globis.ac.jp
Website: http://mba.globis.ac.jp/

President: Yoshito Hori

Programmes

Management (Accountancy; Business Administration; Finance; Human Resources; Leadership; Management; Marketing)

Further Information: Campuses in Osaka and Nagoya

History: Founded 2006.

Degrees and Diplomas: *Shushi*

Last Updated: 12/02/09

GRADUATE INSTITUTE FOR ENTREPRENEURIAL STUDIES

Jigyou Souzou Daigakuin Daigaku

3-1-46 Yoneyama, Chuo-ku, Niigata-shi, Niigata 950-0916
Website: http://www.jigyo.ac.jp

Courses

Entrepreneurial Studies *(Professional Degree Course)* (Business Administration; Management)

Further Information: Also Tokyo and Nagaoka campuses

History: Founded 2006.

Degrees and Diplomas: *Shushi*

Last Updated: 13/02/09

GRADUATE SCHOOL OF FILM PRODUCING

Eiga Senmon Daigakuin Daigaku

3-40-6 Honmachi, Shibuya-ku, Tokyo 151-0071
Tel: +81(3) 5365-3399
Fax: +81(3) 3370-2223
EMail: producer@toho-univ.ac.jp
Website: http://www.toho-univ.ac.jp

Programmes

Film Producing (Accountancy; Cinema and Television; Cultural Studies; Economics; English; Film; Finance; Law; Marketing; Public Administration)

History: Founded 2006.

Degrees and Diplomas: *Gakushi*; *Shushi*

Last Updated: 12/02/09

GUNMA PREFECTURAL COLLEGE OF HEALTH SCIENCES

Gunma Kenritsu Kenmin Kenko Kagaku Daigaku (GCHS)

323-1 Kamiokicho, Maebashi-shi, Gunma, Gunma 371-0052
Tel: +81(27) 235-1211
Fax: +81(27) 235-2501
EMail: info@gchs.ac.jp
Website: http://www.gchs.ac.jp

President: Kunio Doi

Schools

Nursing (Medical Technology; Nursing); **Radiological Technology** (Medical Technology; Radiology)

History: Founded 1992.

Main Language(s) of Instruction: Japanese

Degrees and Diplomas: *Gakushi*. Also offers Associate Bachelor's degree.

Last Updated: 24/03/11

GUNMA PREFECTURAL WOMEN'S UNIVERSITY

Gunma Kenritsu Joshi Daigaku

1395-1 Kaminote Tamamura, Sawa-gun, Gunma 370-1193
Tel: +81(270) 65-8511
Fax: +81(270) 65-9538
EMail: soumu@gpwu.ac.jp
Website: http://www.gpwu.ac.jp

President: Kenji Tomioka

Departments

Aesthetics and Art History; **English Literature**; **International Studies** (International Studies); **Japanese Literature**

History: Founded 1980.

Academic Year: April to March

Admission Requirements: Graduation from high school or 12 yrs education

Main Language(s) of Instruction: Japanese

Degrees and Diplomas: *Gakushi*: 4 yrs; *Hakase*: a further 2 yrs

Student Services: Academic counselling, Canteen, Employment services, Handicapped facilities, Health services, Nursery care, Social counselling, Sports facilities

Special Facilities: Fine Arts Studio. Art Gallery. Auditorium

Libraries: 100,000 vols

Publications: Bulletin of Gunma Prefectural Women's University *(annually)*

Last Updated: 24/03/11

GUNMA UNIVERSITY

Gunma Daigaku

4-2 Aramaki-Machi, Maebashi-shi, Gunma 371-8510
Tel: +81(27) 220-7627
Fax: +81(27) 220-7630
Website: http://www.gunma-u.ac.jp

President: Kuniaki Takata
Tel: +81(27) 220-7000, Fax: +81(27) 220-7012

Executive Director: Seiji Ozawa
Tel: +81(27) 220-7530 EMail: ozawas@jimu.gunma-u.ac.jp

International Relations: Yasuhiko Tamura
Tel: +81(27) 220-7505, Fax: +81(27) 220-7630
EMail: tamura@si.gunma-u.ac.jp

Faculties

Education (Art Education; Biological and Life Sciences; Education; Education of the Handicapped; Educational Research; Fine Arts; Health Sciences; Information Sciences; Modern Languages; Music Education; Natural Sciences; Preschool Education; Primary Education; Secondary Education; Social Sciences; Teacher Training); **Engineering** (Bioengineering; Chemical Engineering; Chemistry; Civil Engineering; Computer Engineering; Computer Science; Electrical and Electronic Engineering; Engineering; Engineering Management; Environmental Engineering; Materials Engineering; Mechanical Engineering; Production Engineering); **Medicine** (Health Sciences; Medicine); **Social and Information Studies** (Economics; Government; Information Sciences; Public Administration; Social Sciences; Social Studies)

Graduate Schools

Education (Curriculum; Development Studies; Education; Educational Research; Educational Sciences; Teacher Training); **Engineering** (Bioengineering; Chemical Engineering; Chemistry; Civil Engineering; Computer Engineering; Computer Science; Electrical and Electronic Engineering; Engineering; Environmental Engineering; Materials Engineering; Mechanical Engineering; Production Engineering); **Medicine** (Health Sciences; Medicine; Pathology; Social and Preventive Medicine; Surgery); **Social and Information Sciences** (Information Sciences; Social Sciences)

Institutes

Molecular and Cellular Regulation (Cell Biology; Genetics; Molecular Biology; Physiology)

History: Founded 1949, incorporating Gunma Normal School, founded 1876, Kiryu Technical College, 1915, and Maebashi Medical College, 1943. Responsible to the Ministry of Education, Science, Sports and Culture.

Academic Year: April to March (April-September; October-March)

Admission Requirements: Graduation from high school or equivalent, and entrance examination

Fees: (Yen) Tuition: 535,800 per annum; Registration: 282,000 per annum; 17,000 for application per annum

Main Language(s) of Instruction: Japanese

International Co-operation: With universities in Canada; USA; Colombia; Nicaragua; China; Republic of Korea; Taiwan; Indonesia; Thailand; Bangladesh; India; Australia; France; Italy; Slovenia; United Kingdom

Degrees and Diplomas: *Gakushi*: Education; Engineering; Health Sciences; Nursing; Social and Information Studies, 4 yrs; *Gakushi*: Medicine, 6 yrs; *Shushi*: Education; Engineering; Health Sciences; Social and Information Studies, 2 yrs following Gakushi; *Hakase*: Engineering; Health Sciences, 3 yrs; *Hakase*: Medical Sciences, 4 yrs

Student Services: Academic counselling, Canteen, Employment services, Foreign student adviser, Foreign Studies Centre, Health services, Language programs, Social counselling, Sports facilities

Student Residential Facilities: Yes

Libraries: 673,483 vols

Last Updated: 24/03/11

GUNMA UNIVERSITY OF SOCIAL WELFARE

Gunma Shakai Fukushi Daigaku

191-1 kawamagarimachi, Maebashi-shi, Gunma 371-0823

Tel: +81(27) 253-0294

Fax: +81(27) 253-0294

EMail: info@shoken-gakuen.ac.jp

Website: http://www.shoken-gakuen.ac.jp

Faculties

Social Welfare

Graduate Schools

Social Welfare (Social Welfare)

History: Founded 2002.

Degrees and Diplomas: *Gakushi*; *Shushi*

HACHINOHE INSTITUTE OF TECHNOLOGY

Hachinohe Kogyo Daigaku (HIT)

88-1 Obiraki, Myo, Hachinohe-shi, Aomori 031-8501

Tel: +81(178) 25-3111

Fax: +81(178) 25-1966

EMail: www-admin@hi-tech.ac.jp

Website: http://www.hi-tech.ac.jp

President: Shigetaka Fujita

Centres

Liberal Arts and Technology (Arts and Humanities; Technology)

Departments

Architectural Engineering; **Chemical Engineering and Biological Environment** (Biology; Chemical Engineering; Environmental Studies); **Electronic Intelligence and Systems** (Electronic Engineering); **Mechanical Systems and Information Technology** (Electronic Engineering; Information Technology; Mechanical Engineering); **System and Information Engineering**

Faculties

Environmental and Civil Engineering (Civil Engineering; Environmental Engineering)

Schools

Graduate Studies

History: Founded 1972.

International Co-operation: With universities in China

Degrees and Diplomas: *Gakushi*; *Shushi*; *Hakase*

Student Services: Health services, Language programs, Sports facilities

Libraries: 123,000 vols

Last Updated: 25/03/11

HACHINOHE UNIVERSITY

Hachinohe Daigaku

13-98 Mihono, Hachinohe-shi, Aomori 031-8588

Tel: +81(178) 25-2711

Website: http://www.hachinohe-u.ac.jp

Programmes

Business and Commerce (Business and Commerce); **Health Sciences** (Health Sciences)

Degrees and Diplomas: *Gakushi*

HAGOROMO UNIVERSITY OF INTERNATIONAL STUDIES

Hagoromo Kokusai Daigaku

1-89-1 Hamaderaminamimachi, Sakai-shi, Osaka 592-8344

Tel: +81(72) 265-7000

Fax: +81(72) 265-7005

EMail: info@hagoromo.ac.jp

Website: http://www.hagoromo.ac.jp

Programmes

International Studies

History: Founded 2002.

Degrees and Diplomas: *Gakushi*

HAKODATE UNIVERSITY

Hakodate Daigaku

51-1 Takaoka-cho, Hakodate-shi, Hokkaido 042-0955

Tel: +81(138) 57-1181

Fax: +81(138) 57-0298

Website: http://www.hakodate-u.ac.jp

Programmes

Business and Commerce (Business and Commerce)

History: Founded 1965.

Degrees and Diplomas: *Gakushi*

HAKUOH UNIVERSITY

Hakuoh Daigaku

1117 Daigyoji, Oyama-shi, Tochigi 323-8585

Tel: +81(285) 22-1111

Fax: +81(285) 22-0800

EMail: nyushi@hakuoh.ac.jp

Website: http://hakuoh.jp/english/index.html

President: Mayumi Moriyama

Faculties

Business Management (Accountancy; Business Administration; Business and Commerce; Information Management; International Business); **Education** (Child Care and Development; Education; Physical Education; Preschool Education; Primary Education); **Law** (International Law; Law)

Schools

Graduate Studies (Business Administration; Law)

History: Founded 1986.

Degrees and Diplomas: *Gakushi*; *Shushi*

Last Updated: 07/11/08

HAMAMATSU GAKUIN UNIVERSITY

Hamamatsu Gakuin Daigaku

3-2-3 Nunohashi, Hamamatsu-shi, Shizuoka 432-8012

Tel: +81(53) 450-7000

Fax: +81(53) 450-7110

EMail: nyushi@hgu.ac.jp

Website: http://www.hgu.ac.jp

History: Founded 2004.

Degrees and Diplomas: *Gakushi*

HAMAMATSU UNIVERSITY SCHOOL OF MEDICINE

Hamamatsu Ika Daigaku
1-20-1 Handayama, Hamamatsu-shi,
Shizuoka 431-3192
Tel: +81(53) 435-2111
Fax: +81(53) 433-7290
Website: http://www.hama-med.ac.jp

President: Toshihko Terao
Tel: +81(53) 435-2100, Fax: +81(53) 435-2112
EMail: terao@hama-med.ac.jp

Vice-President: Osamu Suzuki Tel: +81(53) 435-2233

International Relations: Arata Ichiyama, Director, Education and International Exchange EMail: ichiyama@hama-med.ac.jp

Centres
Photon Medical Research

Faculties
Medicine (Anaesthesiology; Anatomy; Anthropology; Biochemistry; Biological and Life Sciences; Biology; Chemistry; Community Health; Dentistry; Dermatology; English; Ethics; Forensic Medicine and Dentistry; Gynaecology and Obstetrics; Japanese; Mathematics; Medicine; Ophthalmology; Orthopaedics; Otorhinolaryngology; Pathology; Pharmacology; Physics; Physiology; Psychiatry and Mental Health; Psychology; Radiology; Social and Preventive Medicine; Surgery; Urology); **Nursing** (Nursing)

History: Founded 1974.

Governing Bodies: Kyojukai (University Council)

Academic Year: April to March (April-September; October-March)

Admission Requirements: Graduation from high school or equivalent or foreign equivalent, and entrance examination

Main Language(s) of Instruction: Japanese

International Co-operation: With universities in China, Republic of Korea, Germany

Degrees and Diplomas: *Gakushi*: Medicine, 6 yrs; *Gakushi*: Nursing, 4 yrs; *Shushi*: Nursing, a further 2 yrs after Gakushi; *Hakase*: Medicine, a further 4 yrs after Gakushi

Student Services: Foreign student adviser

Student Residential Facilities: Yes

Libraries: 130,900 vol
Last Updated: 07/11/08

HANAZONO UNIVERSITY

Hanazono Daigaku
8-1 Tsubonouchi-cho, Nishinokyo, Nakagyo-ku,
Kyoto-shi, Kyoto 604-8456
Tel: +81(75) 811-5181
Fax: +81(75) 823-0580
EMail: nyushi@hanazono.ac.jp
Website: http://www.hanazono.ac.jp

President: Kosan Abe

Faculties
Letters (Asian Religious Studies; History; Japanese; Literature; Religion; Social Studies); **Social Welfare**

Further Information: Also Graduate School

History: Founded 1872.

Main Language(s) of Instruction: Japanese

Degrees and Diplomas: *Gakushi*; *Shushi*

Libraries: 210,000 vols
Last Updated: 07/11/08

HANNAN UNIVERSITY

Hannan Daigaku
5-4-33 Amami Higashi, Matsubara-shi,
Osaka 580-8502
Tel: +81(72) 332-1224
Fax: +81(72) 336-2633
EMail: info-kokusai@hannan-u.ac.jp
Website: http://www.hannan-u.ac.jp

President: Sinichi Otsuki

Faculties
Business (Accountancy; Banking; Business and Commerce; Finance; International Business; International Economics); **Economics** (Agricultural Economics; Commercial Law; Constitutional Law; Economic History; Economics); **International Communication** (Asian Studies; Chinese; Communication Studies; Cultural Studies; English; Environmental Studies; Ethics; European Studies; Geography (Human); Heritage Preservation; History; International Economics; International Law; International Relations; Japanese; Mass Communication; Modern Languages; Psychology; Religion; Social Psychology; Tourism); **Management Information** (Accountancy; E-Business/Commerce; Information Management; Information Sciences; Information Technology; Management; Management Systems; Marketing; Multimedia)

Schools
Graduate Studies (Accountancy; Artificial Intelligence; E-Business/Commerce; Economics; Finance; Information Management; Information Sciences; Information Technology; International Business; International Economics; International Relations; Management; Marketing; Multimedia; Small Business; Statistics; Taxation)

Degrees and Diplomas: *Gakushi*; *Shushi*
Last Updated: 07/11/08

HEALTH SCIENCES UNIVERSITY OF HOKKAIDO

Hokkaido Iryo Daigaku (HSUH)
1757 Kanazawa, Tobetsu-cho, Ishikari-gun 061-0293
Tel: +81(1332) 31-211
Fax: +81(1332) 31-669
EMail: nice@hoku-iryo-u.ac.jp
Website: http://www.hoku-iryo-u.ac.jp

Centres
Animals Laboratories; Network Information

Faculties
Pharmaceutical Sciences (Applied Chemistry; Biochemistry; Chemistry; Immunology; Microbiology; Pharmacology; Pharmacy; Toxicology)

Graduate Schools
Dentistry (Dental Hygiene; Dental Technology; Dentistry); **Nursing and Social Services** (Clinical Psychology; Nursing; Social and Community Services; Social Work); **Pharmaceutical Sciences** (Applied Chemistry; Biochemistry; Chemistry; Pharmacy; Physiology); **Psychology** (Clinical Psychology; Communication Disorders; Psychology)

Research Institutes
Health Sciences

Schools
Dentistry (Dental Hygiene; Dental Technology; Dentistry); **Nursing and Social Services** (Health Sciences; Nursing; Social and Community Services; Social Work); **Psychology** *(Sapporo, Ainosato Area. Department of Clinical Psychology, of Communication Disorders)* (Clinical Psychology; Communication Disorders; Psychology; Rehabilitation and Therapy; Speech Therapy and Audiology)

History: Founded 1974.

Governing Bodies: Higashi Nippon Gakuen

Academic Year: April to March (April-September; October-March)

Admission Requirements: Graduation from high school and entrance examination

Fees: (Yens): 1.05m.-4m. per annum

Main Language(s) of Instruction: Japanese

International Co-operation: With universities in China and Canada

Accrediting Agencies: Japanese University Accreditation Association

Degrees and Diplomas: *Gakushi*: Clinical Psychology (BS) (Rinsho Shinrigakushi); Communication Disorders (BS); Nursing (BN); Pharmacy (Bpharm) (Yakugakushi); Social Work (BS) (Iryo Fukushigakushi), 4 yrs; *Gakushi*: Dentistry (DDS) (Shigakushi), 6 yrs; *Shushi*: Clinical Psychology (MS) (Rinsho Shinrigakushushi); Nursing (MSN) (Kangogakushushi); Pharmacy (Mpharm) (Yakugakushushi); Social Work (MSW) (Rinsho Fukushigakushushi), a further 2 yrs; *Hakase*: Dental Sciences (PhD) (Shigakuhakushi), 5 yrs following Gakushi; *Hakase*: Nursing (PhD) (Kangogakuhakushi); Pharmacy (PhD) (Yakugakuhakushi); Social Work (PhD) (Rinsho Fukushigakuhakushi), 3 yrs following Shushi

Student Services: Academic counselling, Canteen, Employment services, Handicapped facilities, Health services, Social counselling, Sports facilities

Student Residential Facilities: None.

Special Facilities: Medicinal Botanic Garden. Dental Hospital. Medical and Dental Clinic

Libraries: 215,000 vols, 2,240 periodicals, 3,640 audiovisual materials.

Last Updated: 20/11/08

HEIAN JOGAKUIN ST. AGNES' SCHOOL

Heian Jogakuin St. Agnes Daigaku

5-81-1 Nampeidai, Takatsuki-shi, Osaka 569-1092

Tel: +81(72) 693-2311

Fax: +81(72) 696-4919

Website: http://www.heian.ac.jp

Departments

Home Science (Child Care and Development; Environmental Studies); **International Studies**

History: Founded 1950.

Degrees and Diplomas: *Gakushi*

HEISEI COLLEGE OF MUSIC

Heisei Ongaku Daigaku

1658 Takigawa, Mifune-cho, Kamimashiki-gun, Kumamoto 861-3295

Tel: +81(96) 282-0506

Fax: +81(96) 282-7800

EMail: info@heisei-music.ac.jp

Website: http://www.heisei-music.ac.jp

Programmes

Music (Music)

History: Founded 2001.

Degrees and Diplomas: *Gakushi*

HEISEI INTERNATIONAL UNIVERSITY

Heisei Kokusai Daigaku (HIU)

2000 Otateno, Mizubuka, Kazo-shi, Saitama 347-8504

Tel: +81(480) 66-2100

Fax: +81(480) 65-2101

EMail: somu@hiu.ac.jp

Website: http://www.hiu.ac.jp

Programmes

Law

History: Founded 1996.

Degrees and Diplomas: *Gakushi*

Student Services: Language programs, Sports facilities

Libraries: Total, c. 64,200 vols.

HIGASHI NIPPON INTERNATIONAL UNIVERSITY

Higashi Nippon Kokusai Daigaku

37 Suganezawa, Taira-Kamata, Iwaki-shi, Fukushima 970-8567

Tel: +81(246) 350-001

Fax: +81(246) 259-188

Website: http://www.tonichi-kokusai-u.ac.jp

Faculties

Economic Informatics

Schools

Social and Environmental Services (Environmental Management; Environmental Studies; Social and Community Services; Social Welfare)

History: Founded 1995.

Degrees and Diplomas: *Gakushi*

Libraries: 73,000 vols

HIGASHI OSAKA COLLEGE

Higashi Osaka Daigaku

3-1-1 Nishitsutsumi Gakuencho, Higashiosaka-shi, Osaka 577-8567

Tel: +81(6) 6782-2824

Fax: +81(6) 6782-2896

Website: http://www.higashiosaka.ac.jp

History: Founded 2002.

Degrees and Diplomas: *Gakushi*

HIJIYAMA UNIVERSITY

Hijiyama Daigaku

4-1-1 Ushita Shin-machi, Higashi-ku, Hiroshima-shi, Hiroshima 732-8509

Tel: +81(82) 229-0121

Fax: +81(82) 229-3033 +81(82) 229-5100

EMail: hijim@hijiyama-u.ac.jp

Website: http://www.hijiyama-u.ac.jp

Courses

Fine Arts; **Preschool Education**

Departments

Comprehensive Human Life Studies *(Junior College)* (Arts and Humanities; Physical Education); **Culture and Administration** *(Regional)*; **Early Childhood Education** *(Junior College)* (Arts and Humanities; Preschool Education); **European and American Languages and Cultures**; **Fine Arts** *(Junior College)*; **Japanese Language and Culture**; **Mass Communication**; **Social and Clinical Psychology**

Faculties

Contemporary Culture (Cultural Studies)

Graduate Schools

Communication; **Languages and Culture** (Arts and Humanities)

History: Founded 1994.

Degrees and Diplomas: *Gakushi*; *Shushi*

HIMEJI DOKKYO UNIVERSITY (DOKKYO GROUP)

Himeji Dokkyo Daigaku

7-2-1 Kami-Ono, Himeji-shi, Hyogo 670-8524

Tel: +81(792) 23-2211

Fax: +81(792) 85-0352

EMail: kikaku@himeji-du.ac.jp

Website: http://www.himeji-du.ac.jp

Faculties

Economics, Management and Information Sciences (Business Administration; Computer Science; Economics; Information Sciences; Management); **Law** (Law; Political Sciences); **Literature, Linguistics and Area Studies** (Chinese; English; European Languages; German; Japanese; Modern Languages; Oriental Languages; Pedagogy); **Medicine and Pharmacy**

History: Founded 1987. Forms part of the Dokkyo Gakuen (Dokkyo Group of Academic Institution), founded 1883 as School for the Association of German Studies.

Admission Requirements: Graduation from high school and entrance examination

Main Language(s) of Instruction: Japanese

International Co-operation: With universities in Australia, USA and Republic of Korea

Degrees and Diplomas: *Gakushi*; *Shushi*

Student Services: Health services, Language programs, Sports facilities

Libraries: 320,000 vols

Last Updated: 19/11/08

HIROSAKI GAKUIN UNIVERSITY

Hirosaki Gakuin Daigaku

13-1 Minori-cho, Hirosaki-shi, Aomori-shi, Aomori 036-8577

Tel: +81(172) 34-5211

Website: http://www.hirogaku-u.ac.jp

Programmes

Arts and Humanities (Arts and Humanities)

Degrees and Diplomas: *Gakushi*

HIROSAKI UNIVERSITY

Hirosaki Daigaku

1 Bunkyo-cho, Hirosaki-shi, Aomori 036-8560

Tel: +81(172) 36-2111

Fax: +81(172) 39-3919

EMail: ryugaku@cc.hirosaki-u.ac.jp; webmaster@cc.hirosaki-u.ac.jp

Website: http://www.hirosaki-u.ac.jp/

President: Masahiko Endo

Faculties

Agriculture and Life Sciences (Agriculture; Agronomy; Biochemistry; Biological and Life Sciences; Biology; Biotechnology; Chemistry; Environmental Studies; Horticulture); **Education** (Education; Education of the Handicapped; Teacher Training); **Humanities** (Arts and Humanities; Business and Commerce; Cultural Studies; Economics; Information Management; Information Sciences; Social Sciences); **Science and Technology** (Computer Engineering; Earth Sciences; Electronic Engineering; Engineering; Environmental Studies; Information Technology; Materials Engineering; Mathematics; Natural Sciences; Technology)

Graduate Schools

Agricultural Sciences *(United Graduate School)* (Agriculture)

Programmes

Graduate Studies *(Graduate)*

Schools

Medicine (Medicine; Pathology; Physiology; Social and Preventive Medicine; Surgery)

Further Information: Also Japanese language courses for foreign students

History: Founded 1949 as a new system national university incorporating Hirosaki High School, founded 1920, Aomori Normal School 1943, Young Men's Normal School 1944, Hirosaki College of Medicine 1948, and Aomori College of Medicine.

Governing Bodies: Board of Directors; Board of Trustees

Academic Year: April-March (April-September; October-March)

Admission Requirements: Graduation from high school or equivalent or foreign equivalent, and entrance examination

Main Language(s) of Instruction: Japanese

Degrees and Diplomas: *Gakushi*: Agriculture (Nogakushi); Arts (Bungakushi); Economics (Keizaigakushi); Education (Kyoikugakushi); Science (Rigakushi), 4 yrs; *Gakushi*: Medicine, 6 yrs; *Shushi*: a further 2 yrs; *Hakase*: a further 4 yrs

Student Residential Facilities: For c. 670 students

Libraries: 855,940 vols

Publications: Faculty Bulletins *(annuall*

Last Updated: 19/11/08

HIROSHIMA BUNKYO WOMEN'S COLLEGE

Hiroshima Bunkyo Joshi Daigaku

1-2-1 Kabehigashi, Asakita-ku, Hiroshima-shi, Hiroshima 731-0295

Tel: +81(82) 814-3191

Fax: +81(82) 815-6801

EMail: koho@h-bunkyo.ac.jp

Website: http://www.h-bunkyo.ac.jp/koho/

Programmes

Education and Social Sciences (Education; Social Sciences; Social Studies; Social Welfare); **Japanese and Modern Languages** *(Graduate)* (English; European Languages; Japanese; Literature; Modern Languages; Oriental Languages)

History: Founded 1966.

Academic Year: April to March (April-September; October-March)

Admission Requirements: Graduation from high school and entrance examination

Main Language(s) of Instruction: Japanese

Degrees and Diplomas: *Gakushi*: Arts (Bungakushi), 4 yrs; *Shushi*: Arts (Bungakushushi), a further 2 yrs. Also Teaching Qualifications

Student Services: Foreign student adviser, Health services, Sports facilities

Student Residential Facilities: For c. 280 students

Libraries: 175,000 vols

Publications: Hiroshima Bunkyo Women's College Bulletin *(annually)*; Lilium Bunkyo Japanese Literature *(annually)*

HIROSHIMA CITY UNIVERSITY

Hiroshima Shiritsu Daigaku

3-4-1 Ozuka-Higashi, Asa-Minami-Ku, Hiroshima-shi, Hiroshima 731-3194

Tel: +81(82) 830-1500

Fax: +81(82) 830-1656

EMail: kyomu@office.hiroshima-cu.ac.jp; www-admin@hiroshima-cu.ac.jp

Website: http://www.hiroshima-cu.ac.jp

Faculties

Art; **Information Sciences** (Artificial Intelligence; Computer Engineering; Computer Networks; Computer Science; Information Sciences; Information Technology); **International Studies** (Cultural Studies; International Economics; International Studies; Political Sciences)

Graduate Schools

Art; **Information Sciences** (Artificial Intelligence; Computer Engineering; Computer Networks; Computer Science; Information Sciences; Information Technology); **International Studies** (International Studies)

Further Information: Also Hiroshima Peace Institute.

History: Founded 1994.

International Co-operation: With universities in China, USA and Germany

Degrees and Diplomas: *Gakushi*; *Shushi*; *Hakase*

Student Services: Language programs, Sports facilities

Special Facilities: Language Centre; Information Processing Centre; Museum of Art

Libraries: c. 220,340 vols

Last Updated: 20/11/08

HIROSHIMA INSTITUTE OF TECHNOLOGY

Hiroshima Kogyo Daigaku

2-1-1 Miyake, Saeki-ku, Hiroshima-shi, Hiroshima 731-5193

Tel: +81(82) 921-3121

Fax: +81(82) 921-8934

EMail: nyushi@jim.it-hiroshima.ac.jp; info@it-hiroshima.ac.jp

Website: http://www.it-hiroshima.ac.jp

President: Kazuhiro Mori

Faculties
Applied Information Sciences (Computer Science; Health Sciences; Information Management; Information Sciences); **Engineering** (Civil Engineering; Electrical Engineering; Electronic Engineering; Engineering; Information Technology; Mechanical Engineering; Structural Architecture); **Environmental Studies** (Architectural and Environmental Design; Environmental Studies)

Graduate Schools
Engineering *(Master and Doctoral programmes)* (Artificial Intelligence; Civil Engineering; Electronic Engineering; Environmental Studies; Information Technology; Mechanical Engineering; Structural Architecture)

History: Founded 1963.

Governing Bodies: Board of Trustee

Academic Year: April to March (April-September; October-March)

Admission Requirements: Graduation from high school or equivalent, and entrance examination

Main Language(s) of Instruction: Japanese

International Co-operation: With universities in USA

Degrees and Diplomas: *Gakushi*: Engineering, 4 yrs; *Shushi*: a further 2 yrs; *Hakase*: Engineering, 3 yrs following Shushi

Student Services: Cultural centre, Nursery care, Sports facilities

Student Residential Facilities: For c. 980 students

Libraries: 236,000 vols

Publications: Research Bulletin *(annually)*

Last Updated: 19/11/08

HIROSHIMA INTERNATIONAL UNIVERSITY

Hiroshima Kokusai Daigaku

555-36, Kurose Gakuendai, Higashi Hiroshima City, Hiroshima-shi, Hiroshima 724-0695
EMail: webmaster@ofc.hirokoku-u.ac.jp
Website: http://www.hirokoku-u.ac.jp

Faculties
Engineering (Architectural and Environmental Design; Communication Studies; Engineering; Information Technology; Mechanics; Robotics; Structural Architecture); **Health and Welfare** (Health Administration; Health Sciences; Physical Therapy; Social and Community Services); **Health Sciences** (Health Sciences; Medical Technology; Physical Therapy; Radiology; Sanitary Engineering); **Nursing** (Nursing); **Pharmaceutical Sciences** (Pharmacy); **Psychological Sciences** (Clinical Psychology; Communication Studies; Design; English; Psychology)

Graduate Schools
Integrated Human Sciences; **Nursing**; **Socio-Infrastructural Technologies** (Architectural and Environmental Design; Communication Studies; Information Technology; Structural Architecture)

Further Information: Also campuses in Kure and Hiroshima.

History: Founded 1998.

Degrees and Diplomas: *Gakushi*; *Shushi*; *Hakase*

Libraries: 117,000 vols

Last Updated: 20/11/08

HIROSHIMA JOGAKUIN UNIVERSITY

Hiroshima Jogakuin Daigaku

4-13-1 Ushita-Higashi, Higashi-ku, Hiroshima-shi, Hiroshima 732-0063
Tel: +81(82) 228-0386
Fax: +81(82) 227-4502
EMail: kokusai@gaines.hju.ac.jp
Website: http://www.hju.ac.jp

Faculties
Human Life Sciences (Cultural Studies; Dietetics; Food Science; Home Economics; Information Technology; Nutrition; Psychology; Social Sciences); **Literature** (Arts and Humanities; Civics; Cultural Studies; English; Geography; History; Japanese; Literature; Social Studies)

Graduate Schools
Human Life Sciences (Information Sciences; Social Sciences); **Languages and Cultures**

History: Founded 1932. Acquired present title 1949.

Degrees and Diplomas: *Gakushi*; *Shushi*; *Hakase*

Last Updated: 19/11/08

HIROSHIMA-KOKUSAI GAKUIN UNIVERSITY

Hiroshima Kokusai Gakuin Daigaku

6-20-1 Nakano, Aki-ku, Hiroshima-shi, Hiroshima-shi, Hiroshima 739-0321
Tel: +81(82) 820-2524
Fax: +81(82) 820-2526
EMail: nyuushi@office.hkg.ac.jp
Website: http://www.hkg.ac.jp

Faculties
Engineering (Computer Science; Electrical Engineering; Electronic Engineering; Mechanical Engineering)

Graduate Schools
Engineering (Automation and Control Engineering; Electrical Engineering; Electronic Engineering; Materials Engineering; Mechanical Engineering)

Schools
Contemporary Sociology (Social Welfare; Sociology)

History: Founded 1967. Formerly known as Hiroshima-Denki Institute of Technology until 1999.

Degrees and Diplomas: *Gakushi*; *Shushi*; *Hakase*

Student Services: Sports facilities

Libraries: 2 libraries with 175,500 vols.

Last Updated: 20/11/08

HIROSHIMA PREFECTURAL UNIVERSITY

Hiroshima Kenritsu Daigaku

562 Nanatsuka-cho, Shobara-shi, Hiroshima 727-0023
Tel: +81(824) 741-000
Fax: +81(824) 740-191
Website: http://www.hiroshima-pu.ac.jp

Schools
Bioresources; **Business**

History: Founded 1988.

Degrees and Diplomas: *Gakushi*; *Shushi*; *Hakase*

Last Updated: 19/11/08

HIROSHIMA SHUDO UNIVERSITY

Hiroshima Shudo Daigaku

1-1-1 Ozukahigashi, Asaminami-ku, Hiroshima-shi, Hiroshima 731-3195
Tel: +81(82) 830-1103
Fax: +81(82) 830-1303
EMail: kokusai@js.shudo-u.ac.jp
Website: http://www.shudo-u.ac.jp

Faculties
Commerce (Business Administration; Business and Commerce; International Business); **Economics** (Business Computing; Economics; Finance; International Economics); **Human Environmental Studies** (Environmental Management; Environmental Studies); **Humanities and Sciences** (Arts and Humanities; Education; English; Literature; Natural Sciences; Psychology; Social Sciences; Sociology); **Law** (Administration; Commercial Law; English; International Relations; Law; Political Sciences; Public Law)

Further Information: Also Japanese language and culture courses for foreign students

History: Founded 1952 as Junior College, acquired present status and title 1973.

Academic Year: April to March (April-July; October-March)

Admission Requirements: Graduation from high school and entrance examination

Fees: (Yen): Undergraduate: registration fee: 280,000 per annum; tuition: 727,000 per annum; graduate: registration: 280,000 per annum; tuition: 557,000 per annum

Main Language(s) of Instruction: Japanese

International Co-operation: With universities in Republic of Korea; USA; Canada; Australia; United Kingdom; China; New Zealand

Degrees and Diplomas: *Gakushi*: Commerce; Humanities and Human Sciences; Law; Economics; Human Environmental Studies, 4 yrs; *Shushi*: Law; Humanities; Commerce; Economics, a further 2 yrs; *Hakase*: Business and Commerce; Economics; Humanities, 3 yrs following Shushi

Student Services: Academic counselling, Canteen, Employment services, Foreign student adviser, Foreign Studies Centre, Handicapped facilities, Health services, Social counselling, Sports facilities

Special Facilities: Computer Centre; Language Laboratory

Libraries: c. 708,613 vols

Publications: Journal of Economic Sciences *(biennially)*; Papers of the Research Society of Commerce and Economics; Shudo Law Review; Studies in Humanities and Sciences

HIROSHIMA UNIVERSITY

Hiroshima Daigaku

3-2 Kagamiyana, 1-chome, Higashi-Hiroshima, Hiroshima 739-8511
Tel: +81(824) 22-7111
Fax: +81(824) 24-6020
EMail: admin@hiroshima-u.ac.jp
Website: http://www.hiroshima-u.ac.jp

President: Toshimasa Asahara

Executive Vice-President (General Affairs): Tomomitsu Kawamoto

International Relations: Hideo Kadowaki, Chief Manager
EMail: inquiry@office.hiroshima-u.ac.jp

Centres

Astrophysical Science *(Hiroshima)* (Astrophysics); **Beijing Research**; **Collaborative Research**; **Community Cooperation**; **Natural Science**; **Study of International Cooperation in Education** (International and Comparative Education); **Synchrotron Radiation** *(Hiroshima) Director*: Masaki Taniguchi

Faculties

Applied Biological Sciences; **Dentistry** *Dean*: Takashi Takata; **Economics** (Business and Commerce; Data Processing; Econometrics; Economics; Management) *Dean*: Toshitaka Fukiharu; **Education**; **Engineering** (Biotechnology; Chemical Engineering; Electrical Engineering; Environmental Engineering; Mechanical Engineering); **Integrated Arts and Science** (Arts and Humanities; Behavioural Sciences; Cultural Studies; Environmental Studies; Foreign Languages Education; Information Sciences; Modern Languages; Natural Sciences; Regional Studies; Social Sciences); **Law** (International Relations; Law; Political Sciences; Private Law; Public Law) *Dean*: Hiromi Nishimura; **Letters**; **Medicine** *Dean*: Nobuoki Kohno; **Pharmacy** (Pharmacy) *Dean*: Shigeru Ota; **Science** (Biology; Chemistry; Earth Sciences; Mathematics; Physics)

Graduate Schools

Advanced Science of Matter *Dean*: Takeo Jo; **Biomedical Sciences** (Biomedical Engineering; Dentistry; Medicine; Pharmacy) *Dean*: Tetuji Okamoto; **Biosphere Sciences** (Environmental Management; Environmental Studies) *Dean*: Muneharu Esaka; **Education** (Continuing Education; Curriculum; Education; Educational Sciences; Higher Education; Modern Languages; Psychology; Science Education; Social Studies; Special Education) *Dean*: Masaki Sakakoshi; **Engineering** (Chemical Engineering; Chemistry; Engineering; Environmental Engineering; Information Technology; Mechanical Engineering) *Dean*: Yasuo Yamane; **Health Sciences** *Dean*: Yoshito Tanaka; **Integrated Arts and Sciences** *Dean*: Osamu Kashihara; **International Development and Cooperation** (Cultural Studies; Development Studies; Regional Planning) *Dean*: Hideo Ikeda; **Letters** (Archaeology; Chinese; Cultural Studies; Geography; Heritage Preservation; History; Literature; Philosophy) *Dean*: Kazuto Tominaga; **Science** *Dean*: Hiroshi Shimizu; **Social Sciences** *Dean*: Shoichi Tomioka

Institutes

Foreign Language Research and Education (Modern Languages); **Peace Science** (Peace and Disarmament); **Wasted Waters Treatment**

Research Institutes

Higher Education *Director*: Shinichi Yamamoto; **Nano Devices and Bio Systems** (Nanotechnology; Systems Analysis) *Director*: Takamaro Kikkawa; **Radiation Biology and Medicine** (Biology; Environmental Studies; Molecular Biology; Nuclear Engineering; Social and Preventive Medicine) *Director*: Fumio Suzuki

Further Information: Also Hiroshima University Hospital

History: Founded 1949, incorporating an existing University and seven colleges. Hiroshima Higher Normal School founded in 1902 and the former Hiroshima University in 1929. Postgraduate courses and Faculty of Medicine established 1953.

Governing Bodies: Board of Directors

Academic Year: April to March (April-September; October-March)

Admission Requirements: Graduation from high school or recognized equivalent

Fees: (Yen): Tuition and fees, 535,800 per annum

Main Language(s) of Instruction: Japanese

Degrees and Diplomas: *Gakushi*: 4 yrs; *Gakushi*: Dentistry; Medicine, 6 yrs; *Shushi*: a further 2 yrs; *Hakase*: 3 yrs following Shushi. Also First Professional, a further 4 yrs

Student Residential Facilities: For 690 students

Special Facilities: Training and Research Vessel 'Toyoshio-Maru' Kure Marine. University Farm

Libraries: Central Library and faculty libraries, total, 3m. vols

Publications: Annual Report of Research Centre for Regional Geography; Bulletin of the Faculty of Education-Hiroshima University; Bulletin of the Faculty of Engineering; Bulletin of the Hiroshima University Faculty of School Education; Bulletin of the Institute for Cultural Studies of the Seto Inland Sea; Hiroshima Economic Review; Hiroshima Economic Studies; Hiroshima Journal of Mathematics Education; Hiroshima Journal of Medical Sciences; Hiroshima Law Journal; Hiroshima Mathematical Journal *(3 per annum)*; Hiroshima Peace Science *(annually)*; Hiroshima University Studies-Faculty of Letters *(annually)*; Journal of International Cooperation in Education; Journal of International Development and Cooperation; Journal of Science of the Hiroshima University, Series A (Physics and Chemistry), Series B, Division 1 (Zoology), Series B, Division 2 (Botany), Series C (Earth and Planetary Sciences); Journal of the Faculty of Applied Biological Science; Proceedings of the Research Institute for Radiation Biology and Medicine; Reports of the Miyajima Natural Botanical Garden (Miyajima Shizen Shokubutsu Jikkensho Ronbunshu, Japanese and English); Science Reports; Studies in Area Culture; Studies in Culture and Humanities; Studies in Language and Culture; Studies in Social Sciences; The Economic Studies; The Journal of Hiroshima University Dental Society

Last Updated: 19/11/08

HIROSHIMA UNIVERSITY OF ECONOMICS

Hiroshima Keizai Daigaku

5-37-1 Gion, Asa Minami-ku, Hiroshima-shi, Hiroshima 731-0192
Tel: +81(82) 871-1002
Fax: +81(82) 871-3063
EMail: int-sc@hue.ac.jp
Website: http://www.hue.ac.jp

President: Kouichi Maekawa
Tel: +81(82) 871-1000, Fax: +81(82) 871-1005

Departments

Business Administration; **Business Information System** (Business and Commerce; Information Management); **Economics**; **Media Business** (Business and Commerce; Information Management); **Regional Economies** (Economics; Regional Studies)

Graduate Schools

Economics *(Master and Doctoral programmes)*

History: Founded 1907 as High School, acquired present status and title 1967.

Governing Bodies: Board of Directors

Academic Year: April to March (April-September; October-March)

Admission Requirements: Graduation from high school or foreign equivalent and entrance examination

Fees: (Yen): 900,000 per annum

Main Language(s) of Instruction: Japanese

International Co-operation: Participates in the Network of International Business and Economic Schools (19 universities in 16 countries)

Degrees and Diplomas: *Gakushi*: Economics (Keizaigakushi,), 4 yrs; *Shushi*: Economics (Keizaigakushushi), a further 2 yrs; *Hakase*: Economics (Keizaigakuhakushi), 3 yrs following Shushi

Student Services: Academic counselling, Canteen, Employment services, Foreign student adviser, Foreign Studies Centre, Health services, Language programs, Social counselling, Sports facilities

Student Residential Facilities: Yes

Special Facilities: Rare Books Collection

Libraries: Central Library, c. 340,000 vols

Publications: Journal of Economics and Business *(quarterly)*; Journal of Humanities, Social and Natural Sciences *(quarterly)*

Last Updated: 25/03/11

HITOTSUBASHI UNIVERSITY

Hitotsubashi Daigaku

2-1 Naka, Kunitachi-shi, Tokyo 186-8601
Tel: +81(42) 580-8000
Fax: +81(42) 580-8006
EMail: gakuchositu3@ad.hit-u.ac.jp
Website: http://www.hit-u.ac.jp

President: Susumu Yamauchi
Tel: +81(42) 580-8001, Fax: +81(42) 580-8016

Secretary-General: Masao Kaneda Tel: +81(42) 580-8003

Graduate Schools

Commerce and Management (Business Administration; Business and Commerce; Management) *Dean*: Hirotaka Yamauchi; **Economics** (Economics) *Dean*: Katsuto Tanaka; **International and Public Policy** *Director*: Ryo Oshiba; **International Corporate Strategy** (Finance; Law; Management; Political Sciences) *Chairman*: Hirotaka Takeuchi; **Language and Society** (Linguistics; Social Studies) *Chairman*: Yasuo Sano; **Law** (Law) *Dean*: Seigo Mori; **Social Sciences** (Social Sciences) *Dean*: Osamu Watanabe

Institutes

Economics Research (Economics) *Director*: Noriyuki Takayama; **Innovation Research** *Director*: Sadao Nagaska

Schools

Law *Dean*: Akira Goto

Further Information: Also student exchange programmes in Japanese studies and counselling

History: Founded 1875 as Institute of Business Training. Became Tokyo University of Commerce 1920. Reorganized and present title adopted 1949.

Governing Bodies: Board of Councillors

Academic Year: April to March (April-September; October-March)

Admission Requirements: Graduation from high school or equivalent, and entrance examination

Fees: (Yen): Registration, 282,000; tuition, 535,800 per annum

Main Language(s) of Instruction: Japanese

Degrees and Diplomas: *Gakushi*: Commerce; Economics; Law; Social Sciences, 4 yrs; *Shushi*: Arts; Economics; Law; Management; Social Sciences, a further 2 yrs; *Shushi*: Business Law; Public Policy; *Hakase*: Business Law; Economics; Law; Management; Philosophy; Social Sciences, 3 yrs following Shushi; *Hakase*: Commerce, a further 3 yrs following Shushi

Student Services: Academic counselling, Employment services, Foreign student adviser, Foreign Studies Centre, Handicapped facilities, Health services, Social counselling, Sports facilities

Student Residential Facilities: For 793 students (including foreign students), and for 33 foreign researchers

Libraries: Kunitachi Main Library, c. 1,7m. vols; Centre for Historical Social Science Literature, c. 68,700 vols

Publications: Economic Research Series, in Western languages *(annually)*; Economic Research Series, in Japanese *(annually)*; Gengo Bunka-Cultura Philologica *(annually)*; Gengo Shakai: The Journal of the Graduate School of Language and Society *(annually)*; Hitotsubashi Annual of Sport Studies *(annually)*; Hitotsubashi Bulletin of Social Sciences *(3 per annum)*; Hitotsubashi Business Journal *(quarterly)*; Hitotsubashi Journal of Arts and Sciences *(annually)*; Hitotsubashi Journal of Arts and Sciences *(annually)*; Hitotsubashi Journal of Commerce and Management *(annually)*; Hitotsubashi Journal of Economics *(biannually)*; Hitotsubashi Journal of Law and Politics *(annually)*; Hitotsubashi Journal of Social Studies *(biannually)*; Journal of the Centre for Student Exchange *(annually)*; The Economic Journal *(quarterly)*; The Hitotsubashi Journal of Commerce and Management *(biannually)*; The Hitotsubashi Journal of Economics *(biannually)*; The Hitotsubashi Journal of Law and International Studies *(3 per annum)*

Last Updated: 24/03/11

HOKKAI-GAKUEN UNIVERSITY

Hokkai Gakuen Daigaku (HGU)

1-40, 4-chome, Asahi-machi, Toyohira-ku, Sapporo-shi, Hokkaido 062-8605
Tel: +81(11) 841-1161
Fax: +81(11) 824-3141
Website: http://www.hokkai-s-u.ac.jp/index.html

President: Toshimitsu Asakura (2005-) EMail: asakura@hgu.jp

Secretary-General: Atsushi Yoshida
EMail: a-yoshi@tyhr.hookai-s-u-ac.jp

International Relations: Takafumi Kurihara, Administrative Assistant, Academic and International Relations
EMail: kurihara@tyhr.hokkai-s-u.ac.jp

Centres

Development Policy Studies (Development Studies) *Head*: Kazutaka Takahara

Faculties

Business Administration (Behavioural Sciences; Business Administration; Information Management) *Dean*: Hiroyuki Takagi; **Economics** (Economics) *Dean*: Masayuki Kobayashi; **Engineering** (Civil Engineering; Computer Engineering; Electrical and Electronic Engineering) *Dean*: Yoshio Tani; **Humanities** (Arts and Humanities; Cultural Studies) *Dean*: Chihiro Oishio; **Law** (Law; Political Sciences) *Dean*: Naonori Mukaida

Graduate Schools

Business Administration (Business Administration) *Chair*: Yutaka Hayakawa; **Economics** (Economics) *Chair*: Naoto Kosaka; **Engineering** *Chair*: Takashi Kuwahara; **Law** *Chair*: Fumito Komiya; **Literature** (Arts and Humanities; Cultural Studies; Literature) *Chair*: Tadao Hama

Schools

Law *(Graduate School)* (Law) *Chair*: Osamu Maruyama

History: Founded 1887 as English Language School, became College 1950 and University 1952.

Academic Year: April to March (April-September; October-March)

Admission Requirements: Graduation from high school or recognized equivalent, and entrance examination

Main Language(s) of Instruction: Japanese

Degrees and Diplomas: *Gakushi*: 4 yrs; *Shushi*: a further 2 yrs; *Hakase*: 3 yrs following Shushi

Student Services: Canteen, Employment services, Health services, Language programs, Sports facilities

Libraries: 803,060 vols; 9,200 periodicals

Publications: Gakuen-Ronshu, The Journal of Hokkai-Gakuen University *(quarterly)*; Hogaku-Kenkyu, The Journal of the Faculty of Law *(quarterly)*; Jinbun-Ronshu, Studies in Culture *(3 per annum)*; Kaihatsu Ronshu, The Journal of Development Policy Studies *(biannually)*; Keiei-Ronshu, Journal of Business Administration *(quarterly)*; Keizai-Ronshu, The Journal of Economics *(quarterly)*; Kougakubu-Kenkyu-Houkoku, Bulletin of the Faculty of Engineering *(annually)*

Last Updated: 20/11/08

HOKKAI SCHOOL OF COMMERCE

Hokkai Shoka Daigaku
6-6-10 Toyohira, Toyohira-Ku, Sapporo-shi, Hokkaido 062-8607
Tel: +81(11) 841-1161
Fax: +81(11) 824-0801
Website: http://www.hokkai.ac.jp

President: Masao Morimoto

Faculties

Commerce (Business and Commerce; International Business; Tourism)

History: Founded 1977 as Hokkai Gakuen Kitami Daigaku (Hokkai-Gakuen University of Kitami).

Degrees and Diplomas: *Gakushi*

Last Updated: 20/11/08

HOKKAIDO BUNKYO UNIVERSITY

Hokkaido Bunkyo Daigaku
196-1 Koganemachi, Eniwa, Hokkaido 061-1408
Tel: +81(123) 34-0160
Fax: +81(123) 34-1640
EMail: nyushi@do-bunkyodai.ac.jp
Website: http://www.do-bunkyodai.ac.jp

Programmes

Human Sciences; Literature, Linguistics and Area Studies *(Undergraduate and graduate programmes)* (Chinese; Communication Studies; Cultural Studies; English; Japanese; Linguistics; Literature; Modern Languages)

History: Founded 1999.

International Co-operation: With China, Australia, New Zealand and Russian Federation

Degrees and Diplomas: *Gakushi*; *Shushi*

Student Services: Sports facilities

Student Residential Facilities: For International Students

Libraries: 85,000 vols.

Last Updated: 20/11/08

HOKKAIDO INFORMATION UNIVERSITY

Hokkaido Joho Daigaku (HIU)
59-2 Nishinopporo, Ebetsu-shi, Hokkaido 069-8585
Tel: +81(11) 385-4411
Fax: +81(11) 384-0134
Website: http://www.do-johodai.ac.jp

Faculties

Business Administration and Information Sciences; **Information Media**

Graduate Schools

Business Administration and Information Science

Schools

Distance/Satellite Education (Business Administration; Computer Engineering; Information Technology)

History: Founded 1989.

Admission Requirements: 12-year formal education

Fees: (Yen): Faculty of Business Administration and Information Sciences, 1.22m.-1.28m. per annum; Faculty of Information Media, 1.26m.

Main Language(s) of Instruction: Japanese

International Co-operation: With universities in China and USA

Degrees and Diplomas: *Gakushi (BA)*: 4 yrs; *Shushi (MA)*: a further 2 yrs

Student Services: Academic counselling, Canteen, Employment services, Foreign student adviser, Handicapped facilities, Social counselling, Sports facilities

Libraries: 114,030 vols

Publications: Memoirs of Hokkaido Information University

HOKKAIDO INSTITUTE OF TECHNOLOGY

Hokkaido Kogyo Daigaku
4-1, 7-15 Maeda, Teine-ku, Sapporo-shi, Hokkaido 006-8585
Tel: +81(11) 681-2161
Fax: +81(11) 681-3622
EMail: nyushi@hit.ac.jp
Website: http://www.hit.ac.jp

President: Yasunobu Nishi

Centres

Cold Regions Research

Departments

Applied Electronics; **Architecture** (Architecture); **Civil Engineering** (Civil Engineering); **Electrical Engineering** (Electrical Engineering); **Industrial Engineering** (Industrial Engineering); **Mechanical Engineering** (Computer Engineering; Mechanical Engineering)

Further Information: Also 260 laboratories

History: Founded 1967.

Main Language(s) of Instruction: Japanese

International Co-operation: With universities in Finland

Degrees and Diplomas: *Gakushi*; *Shushi*; *Hakase*

Student Services: Language programs

Libraries: 124,000 vols

Last Updated: 25/03/11

HOKKAIDO PHARMACEUTICAL UNIVERSITY SCHOOL OF PHARMACY

Hokkaido Yakka Daigaku
7-1 Katsuraoka-cho, Otaru-shi, Hokkaido 047-0264
Tel: +81(134) 62-5111
Fax: +81(134) 62-5161
EMail: info@hokuyakudai.ac.jp
Website: http://www.hokuyakudai.ac.jp

President: Eiji Owada (2002-)

Graduate Schools

Pharmaceutical Sciences

Schools

Pharmaceutical Sciences (Biological and Life Sciences; Biology; Chemistry; Community Health; Mathematics; Modern Languages; Pharmacology; Pharmacy; Physics; Public Health; Toxicology)
Dean: Kazuo Ichihara

History: Founded 1974.

Governing Bodies: Board of Trustees

Academic Year: April to March (April-September; September-March)

Admission Requirements: Graduation from high school and entrance examination

Main Language(s) of Instruction: Japanese

Degrees and Diplomas: *Gakushi*: Pharmacy (Yakugakushi), 4 yrs; *Shushi*: Pharmacy (Yakugakushushi), a further 2 yrs; *Hakase*: Pharmacy (Yakugakuhakushi), 3 yrs following Shushi

Student Services: Sports facilities

Student Residential Facilities: Yes

Libraries: 65,765 vols

Last Updated: 21/11/08

HOKKAIDO UNIVERSITY

Hokkaido Daigaku (HOKUDAI)
Nishi 5 Kita 8, Kita-ku, Sapporo-shi, Hokkaido 060-0808
Tel: +81(11) 706-8027
Fax: +81(11) 706-8036
EMail: info@oia.hokudai.ac.jp
Website: http://www.hokudai.ac.jp

President: Keizo Yamaguchi (2013-)
Tel: +81(11) 706-8027, Fax: +81(11) 706-8036
EMail: global@oia.hokudai.ac.jp

International Relations: Masani Gomita, Director, Division of International Relations (2008-)
Tel: +81(11) 706-8027, Fax: +81(11) 706-8036
EMail: global@oia.hokudai.ac.jp

Centres

Advanced Research on Energy Conversion Materials (Energy Engineering) *Director*: Kazuya Kurokawa; **Field Science Centre for Northern Biosphere** (Environmental Studies) *Director*: Kaichiro Sasa; **Health Administration** (Health Administration) *Director*: Manabu Musashi; **Information Initiative Centre** (Computer Science; Information Technology; Multimedia) *Director*: Tsuyoshi Yamamoto; **Instrumental Analysis** *Director*: Toshiaki Miura; **Research and Development in Higher Education** (Higher Education) *Director*: Minoru Wakita

Graduate Schools

Agriculture (Agriculture; Animal Husbandry; Forestry) *Dean*: Akihito Hattori; **Dental Medicine** (Dentistry) *Dean*: Masamitsu Kawanami; **Economics and Business Administration** (Business Administration; Economics) *Dean*: Kazuo Machino; **Education** (Education) *Dean*: Osamu Aoki; **Engineering** (Engineering) *Dean*: Takashi Mikami; **Environmental Science** (Earth Sciences; Environmental Studies) *Dean*: Toshio Iwakuma; **Fisheries Sciences** (Fishery) *Dean*: Akihiro Hara; **Health Sciences** *Dean*: Seiichi Kobayashi; **Information Science and Technology** *Dean*: Masanori Koshiba; **International Media, Communication and Tourism Studies** *Dean*: Shuichi Sugiura; **Law** (Law) *Dean*: Nobuhisa Segawa; **Letters** (Arts and Humanities) *Dean*: Tsuneko Mochizuki; **Life Science** (Biological and Life Sciences) *Dean*: Akira Matsuda; **Medicine** (Medicine) *Dean*: Ken-ichi Honma; **Public Policy** *Dean*: Takao Sasaki; **Science** (Natural Sciences) *Dean*: Keizo Yamaguchi; **Veterinary Medicine** (Veterinary Science) *Dean*: Takashi Umemura

Institutes

Genetic Medicine (Genetics; Medicine) *Director*: Toshimitsu Uede; **Low Temperature Science** *Director*: Akira Kouchi; **Radioisotope Science** (Organic Chemistry) *Director*: Nagara Tamaki

Laboratories

Meme Media Laboratory (Media Studies; Robotics; Software Engineering) *Director*: Yuzuru Tanaka

Research Centres

Advanced Tourism Studies (Tourism) *Director*: Shuzo Ishimori; **Ainu and Indigenous Studies** *Director*: Teruki Tsunemoto; **Catalysis** (Chemistry) *Director*: Wataru Ueda; **Creative Research Initiative 'Sousei'** *Director*: Hisatake Okada; **Environmental Nano and Bio Engineering** (Bioengineering; Environmental Engineering; Nanotechnology) *Director*: Yoshimasa Watanabe; **Environmental Preservation** (Environmental Management) *Director*: Masaya Sawamura; **Experimental Research in Social Sciences** *Director*: Toshio Yamaguchi; **Hokkaido University Archives** *Director*: Masaaki Hemmi; **Integrated Quantum Electronics** (Electronic Engineering) *Director*: Takashi Fukui; **Integrative Mathematics** *Director*: Ichiro Tsuda; **Language Learning** *Director*: Yutaka Eguchi; **Research and Education Centre for Brain Drain** *Director*: Shinya Kuriki; **Slavic Studies** (Slavic Languages) *Director*: Akihiro Iwashita; **Sustainability Science** *Director*: Takao Sasaki; **Zoonosis Control** *Director*: Hiroshi Kida

Research Institutes

Electronic Science (Electronic Engineering) *Director*: Keiji Sasaki; **Information Law and Policy** *Director*: Yoshiyuki Tamura

Further Information: Also Medical, Dental, and Veterinary Hospitals; Training Ships

History: Founded 1876 as school, became Sapporo Agricultural College 1876. Became part of Tohuku Imperial University in Sendai 1907-1918. Renamed Hokkaido University 1947. Acquired present status of National University Corporation Hokkaido University 2004.

Governing Bodies: Management Council

Academic Year: April to March (April-September; October-March)

Admission Requirements: Graduation from high school or recognized equivalent (Daiken), and entrance examination (Center Shiken)

Fees: (Yen): 535,800 per annum

Main Language(s) of Instruction: Japanese

International Co-operation: With universities in China; Republic of Korea; New Zealand; Germany; France; Russian Federation; USA; Taiwan; Australia; Switzerland; United Kingdom; Finland; Hungary; Canada; Indonesia; Thailand; Nepal; Malaysia; Sri Lanka; Zambia; Austria; Netherlands; Spain; Sweden; Poland; Italy; South Africa; Brazil; Bangladesh; Nepal; Singapore; Ukraine; etc.

Degrees and Diplomas: *Gakushi*: Agriculture; Economics and Business Administration; Education; Engineering; Fisheries Science; Health Sciences; Law; Letters; Nursing; Pharmaceutical Science; Science, 4 yrs; *Gakushi*: Dental Medicine; Medicine; Veterinary Medicine, 6 yrs; *Shushi*: Agriculture; Economics and Business Administration; Education; Engineering; Environmental Sciences; Fisheries Sciences; Health Sciences; Information Science and Technology; International Media and Communication; Law; Letters; Life Sciences; Medical Sciences; Nursing; Public Policy; Science; Tourism Studies, a further 2 yrs; *Hakase*: Agriculture; Economics and Business Administration; Education; Engineering; Environmental Sciences; Fisheries Sciences; Information Science and Technology; International Media and Communication; Law; Letters; Life Sciences; Science, a further 3 yrs following Shushi; *Hakase*: Dental Medicine; Medicine; Veterinary Medicine, a further 4 yrs following shushi. The Graduate School of Medicine, Dental Medicine and Veterinary Medicine do not offer Master's Programme. The School of Pharmaceutical Sciences does not offer Master's and Doctor's programmes

Student Services: Academic counselling, Canteen, Cultural centre, Employment services, Foreign student adviser, Foreign Studies Centre, Health services, Social counselling, Sports facilities

Student Residential Facilities: Yes

Special Facilities: Research and Clinical Centre for Child Development. Akkeshi Marine Biological Research Station. Botanic Garden. University Forests. Livestock Farm. Training Ships 'Oshoromaru', 'Hokusei-maru'. Institute of Seismology and Volcanology. Experimental Station for Medicinal Plant Studies. Sea-Ice Research Laboratory. Electronics Instruments Laboratory. Centre for Virus Vector Development. Institute for Animal Experiment. Dental Hospital. Experimental Farms. Veterinary Teaching Hospital. Advanced Institute for Law and Politics. University Museum

Libraries: Central Library, 1,697,713 vols; North Library, 338,966 vols

Publications: A Brief Sketch of Hokkaido University, English, Chinese, Korean *(annually)*; Hokkaido University Newsletter, English, Chinese *(biannually)*; Hokudai Jiho, Japanese *(monthly)*; Profile of Hokkaido University, English, Chinese, Korean *(annually)*

Student Numbers *2011-2012*: Total: c. 18,195
Last Updated: 28/03/13

HOKKAIDO UNIVERSITY OF EDUCATION

Hokkaido Kyoiku Daigaku

5-3-1-3 Ainosato, Kita-ku, Sapporo-shi, Hokkaido 002-8501
Tel: +81(11) 778-0265
Fax: +81(11) 778-0634
EMail: ryugaku@sap.hokkyodai.ac.jp
Website: http://www.hokkyodai.ac.jp

President: Kenji Honma

Centres

Research and Guidance for Teaching Practice (Pedagogy)

Faculties

Education (Art Education; Art Management; Art Therapy; Curriculum; Design; Education; English; Fine Arts; Handicrafts; Health Education; Home Economics Education; Japanese; Mathematics Education; Media Studies; Music Theory and Composition; Musical Instruments; Nursing; Painting and Drawing; Physical Education; Science Education; Sculpture; Sports; Teacher Training; Technology Education)

Graduate Schools

Education

Further Information: Also campuses in Asahikawa, Kushiro, Hakodate and Iwamizawa

History: Founded 1949.

Academic Year: April to March (April-September; October-March)

Admission Requirements: Graduation from high school and entrance examination

Main Language(s) of Instruction: Japanese

Degrees and Diplomas: *Gakushi*: Education (Kyoikugakushi), 4 yrs; *Shushi*: Education (Kyoikugakushushi), a further 2 yrs

Student Residential Facilities: Yes

Libraries: 998,529 vols

Publications: Bulletin of Rural Education Institute; Reports of the Taisetsusan Institute of Science; Studies of Teaching Methods

Last Updated: 24/03/11

HOKURIKU UNIVERSITY

Hokuriku Daigaku

1-1 Taiyogaoka, Kanazawa-shi, Ishikawa 920-1180

Tel: +81(76) 229-1161

Fax: +81(76) 229-1393

EMail: iec@hokuriku-u.ac.jp; koho@hokuriku-u.ac.jp

Website: http://www.hokuriku-u.ac.jp

Faculties

Pharmaceutical Sciences (Medicine; Pharmacology; Pharmacy; Traditional Eastern Medicine)

Graduate Schools

Pharmaceutical Research

Schools

Future Learning (Chinese; Communication Studies; English; Law)

Further Information: Also Japanese language courses for foreign students

History: Founded 1975.

Academic Year: April to March (April-September; October-March)

Admission Requirements: Graduation from high school and entrance examination

Main Language(s) of Instruction: Japanese

International Co-operation: With universities in China, USA and Republic of Korea

Degrees and Diplomas: *Gakushi*: 4 yrs; *Shushi*: a further 2 yrs; *Hakase*: 3 yrs following Shushi

Student Services: Foreign student adviser, Health services, Language programs, Sports facilities

Libraries: Central Library, 232,310 vols

Last Updated: 21/11/08

HOKUSEI GAKUEN UNIVERSITY

Hokusei Gakuen Daigaku

2-3-1 Oyachi Nishi, Atsubetusu-ku, Sapporo-shi, Hokkaido 004-8631

Tel: +81(11) 891-2731

Fax: +81(11) 892-6097

EMail: soumu@hokusei.ac.jp

Website: http://www.hokusei.ac.jp

Faculties

Economics (Commercial Law; Economics; Information Management; Management); **Humanities** (Arts and Humanities; English; English Studies; Psychology; Social Work); **Social Welfare** (Social Welfare; Social Work)

Graduate Schools

Economics; **Literature** (Communication Studies; Cultural Studies; Linguistics; Literature); **Social Welfare** (Clinical Psychology; Psychology; Social Welfare)

History: Founded 1887 as School by an American missionary, acquired present status 1962. Financed by tuition fees, Government grant and donations.

Governing Bodies: Board of Trustees

Academic Year: April to March (April-September; October-March)

Admission Requirements: Graduation from high school or equivalent, and entrance examination

Main Language(s) of Instruction: Japanese

International Co-operation: With universites in USA, China and United Kingdom

Degrees and Diplomas: *Gakushi*: 4 yrs; *Shushi*: a further 2 yrs; *Hakase*: 3 yrs following Shushi

Student Services: Employment services, Foreign student adviser, Foreign Studies Centre, Handicapped facilities, Health services, Language programs, Nursery care, Social counselling, Sports facilities

Libraries: 360,000 vols

Publications: Hokusei Ronshu *(annually)*

Last Updated: 21/11/08

HOKUSHO UNIVERSITY

Hokusho Daigaku

23 Bunkyodai, Ebetsu-shi, Hokkaido 069-8511

Tel: +81(11) 386-8011

Fax: +81(11) 387-1542

EMail: kokusaic@hokusho-u.ac.jp

Website: http://www.hokusho-u.ac.jp

Programmes

Lifelong Learning Education (Fine Arts; Management; Multimedia; Music; Psychiatry and Mental Health; Sports); **Social Welfare** (Clinical Psychology; Health Education; Nursing; Social and Community Services; Welfare and Protective Services); **Social Welfare** *(Graduate)*

History: Founded 1997. Renamed Hokkaido Asai Gakuen University and acquired present status 2000. Formerly known as Asai Gakuen Daigaku (Asai Gakuen University). Acquired present title 2007.

Degrees and Diplomas: *Gakushi*; *Shushi*

Libraries: Total, c. 164,000 vols

Last Updated: 29/10/08

HOSEI UNIVERSITY

Hosei Daigaku

2-17-1, Fujimi, Chiyoda-ku, Tokyo 102-8160

Tel: +81(3) 3264-9315

Fax: +81(3) 3238-9873

EMail: ic@hosei.ac.jp; ic@fujimi.hosei.ac.jp

Website: http://www.hosei.ac.jp

President: Toshio Masuda

Vice-President: Akira Hamamura

Faculties

Bioscience and Applied Chemistry; **Business Administration** (Business Administration; Marketing); **Computer and Information Sciences**; **Economics**; **Economics** (Economics; International Economics); **Engineering** (Chemical Engineering; Civil Engineering; Electrical and Electronic Engineering; Engineering; Industrial Engineering; Materials Engineering; Mechanical Engineering); **Engineering and Design** (Architectural and Environmental Design; Civil Engineering; Engineering; Environmental Engineering; Structural Architecture); **Global and Interdisciplinary Studies**; **Humanity and Environment** (Biological and Life Sciences; Cultural Studies; Environmental Studies; Ethics; Fine Arts; History; Philosophy; Psychology); **Intercultural Communication**; **Law** (Law; Political Sciences); **Letters** (English; Geography (Human); History; Japanese; Philosophy; Psychology); **Lifelong Learning and Career Studies** (Cultural Studies; Japanese); **Science and Engineering** (Computer Engineering; Electrical and Electronic Engineering; Industrial Engineering; Mechanical Engineering); **Social Policy and Administration** (Administration; Social Policy; Social Sciences; Sociology); **Social Sciences**

Graduate Schools

Art and Technology; **Business Administration**; **Computer and Information Sciences**; **Engineering** (Architecture; Civil Engineering; Computer Engineering; Electrical Engineering; Engineering; Information Management; Information Technology; Materials Engineering; Mechanical Engineering; Structural Architecture); **Environmental Management**; **Humanities**; **Intercultural Communication**; **Japan Studies** *(International)*; **Law**; **Policy Science**; **Politics** (Political Sciences); **Regional Policy Design**; **Social Well-being Studies**; **Sociology** (Sociology)

Further Information: Ichigaya, Tama and Konagei campuses. Also professional schools (Law; Innovation Management; Accountancy)

History: Founded 1880 as Tokyo Hogakusha (Tokyo School of Law), combined in 1889 with Tokyo French School to become Wafutsu Horitsu Gakko (School of Japanese and French Law). Became College 1903 and acquired present status 1949.

Governing Bodies: University Council; Board of Trustees

Academic Year: April to March (April-July; September-March)

Admission Requirements: Graduation from high school or equivalent, or foreign equivalent, and entrance examination

Main Language(s) of Instruction: Japanese

International Co-operation: With universities in USA, United Kingdom and Australia

Degrees and Diplomas: *Gakushi*: 4 yrs; *Shushi*: a further 2 yrs; *Hakase*: 3 yrs following Shushi

Student Services: Foreign student adviser, Health services, Language programs, Sports facilities

Student Residential Facilities: For foreign scholars

Libraries: University Library ; branch libraries: 1,680,000 vols

Publications: Bungakubu-kiyou (Bulletin of Faculty of Letters); Daigakuin-kiyou (Graduate School Bulletin); Hogakubu kenkyushubo (College of Engineering Bulletin); Hogaku-shirin (Law and Political Sciences Review); Keiei-shirin (Business Journal); Keizaishirin (The Hosei University Economic Review); Many research reports published by affiliated institutions; Shakai-rodo-Kendyu (Society and Labour)

Press or Publishing House: Hosei University Press

Last Updated: 21/11/08

HOSHI UNIVERSITY

Hoshi Yakka Daigaku

2-4-41 Ebara, Shinagawa-ku, Tokyo 142-8501
Tel: +81(3) 3786-1011
Fax: +81(3) 3787-0036
EMail: somu@hoshi.ac.jp
Website: http://www.hoshi.ac.jp

Faculties

Pharmaceutical Sciences (Pharmacology; Pharmacy)

History: Founded 1911.

Academic Year: April to March (April-September; October-March)

Admission Requirements: Graduation from high school and entrance examination

Main Language(s) of Instruction: Japanese

Degrees and Diplomas: *Gakushi*; *Shushi*; *Hakase*

Student Services: Academic counselling, Canteen, Employment services, Handicapped facilities, Health services, Nursery care, Social counselling, Sports facilities

Libraries: c. 102,800 vols

Publications: Hoshi Yakka Daigaku Kiyo (Proceedings) *(annually)*

Last Updated: 21/11/08

HYOGO UNIVERSITY

Hyogo Daigaku

2301 Shinzaike Hiraoka-cho, Kakogawa-shi, Hyogo 675-0101
Tel: +81(794) 27-5111
Fax: +81(794) 27-5112
Website: http://www.hyogo-dai.ac.jp

Faculties

Economics and Information Sciences (Economics; Information Sciences); **Health Sciences** (Health Sciences)

Schools

Graduate Studies

History: Founded 1995.

Degrees and Diplomas: *Gakushi*; *Shushi*

Last Updated: 21/11/08

HYOGO UNIVERSITY OF HEALTH SCIENCES

Hyogo Iryou Daigaku

1-1 Mukogawa-cho, Nishinomiya-shi, Hyogo 663-8501
Tel: +81(798) 45-6163
Fax: +81(798) 45-6168
EMail: kenkyuka@hyo-med.ac.jp
Website: http://www.hyo-med.ac.jp

Departments

Medicine (Medicine; Public Health; Rehabilitation and Therapy; Surgery; Treatment Techniques)

History: Founded 1971. Medical Society of Hyogo College of Medicine established in 1975. In 1978, the institution obtained the Accreditation of Graduate Education of Medicine.

Governing Bodies: Board of Directors

Academic Year: April to March (April-September; October-March)

Admission Requirements: Graduation from high school and entrance examination

Fees: (Yen): First year, c. 8,8m.; each following year, c. 6,0m.

Main Language(s) of Instruction: Japanese

Degrees and Diplomas: *Gakushi*: Medicine (MD), 6 yrs; *Hakase*: Medical Sciences (DMSc), a further 4 yrs

Student Residential Facilities: Yes

Special Facilities: Institute for Advanced Medical Sciences

Libraries: c. 166,000 vols

Publications: Acta Medica Hyogoensia *(annually)*

HYOGO UNIVERSITY OF TEACHER EDUCATION

Hyogo Kyoiku Daigaku

942-1 Shimokume, Yashiro-cho, Kato-gun, Hyogo 673-1494
Tel: +81(795) 44-2011
Fax: +81(795) 44-2009
EMail: office-kikaku-k@hyogo-u.ac.jp
Website:http: //www.hyogo-u.ac.jp/

President: Kajisa Tetsuya

Programmes

Education and Teacher Training *(Pre-school, Primary levels and Graduate)* (Education; Preschool Education; Primary Education; Teacher Training); **Education of the Handicapped** (Education of the Handicapped; Special Education)

History: Founded 1978.

Governing Bodies: University Council

Academic Year: April to March (April-September; October-March)

Main Language(s) of Instruction: Japanese

International Co-operation: With universities in China, Republic of Korea, New Zealand, Thailand and USA

Degrees and Diplomas: *Gakushi*; *Shushi*; *Hakase*

Student Services: Academic counselling, Canteen, Employment services, Foreign student adviser, Foreign Studies Centre, Health services, Language programs, Social counselling, Sports facilities

Student Residential Facilities: Yes

Libraries: 318,882 vols

Last Updated: 24/03/11

IBARAKI CHRISTIAN UNIVERSITY

Ibaraki Kirisutokyo Daigaku

6-11-1 Omika-cho, Hitachi-shi, Ibaraki 319-1295
Tel: +81(294) 52-3215
Fax: +81(294) 53-5864
EMail: nyushi@icc.ac.jp
Website: http://www.icc.ac.jp

President: Mihoko Komatsu

Colleges

Life Sciences; **Literature** (Bible; Cultural Studies; Education; English; European Languages; Modern Languages; Religious Studies); **Nursing** (Nursing)

Graduate Schools

Literature (Education; English; Linguistics)

History: Founded 1967.

Main Language(s) of Instruction: Japanese

Degrees and Diplomas: *Gakushi*; *Shushi*

Libraries: 103,660 vols

Last Updated: 25/03/11

IBARAKI PREFECTURAL UNIVERSITY OF HEALTH SCIENCES

Ibaraki Kenritsu Iryou Daigaku

4669-2 Ami, Ami-machi, Inashiki-gun, Ibaraki-shi, Osaka 300-0394
Tel: +81(298) 88-4000
Fax: +81(298) 40-2301
EMail: webmaster@ipu.ac.jp
Website: http://www.ipu.ac.jp

Programmes

Health Sciences (Health Sciences); **Nursing** (Nursing); **Occupational Therapy** (Occupational Therapy); **Physical Therapy** (Physical Therapy); **Radiology** (Radiology)

History: Founded 1995.

Degrees and Diplomas: *Gakushi*; *Shushi*

Last Updated: 07/01/09

IBARAKI UNIVERSITY

Ibaraki Daigaku

2-1-1 Bunkyo, Mito-shi, Ibaraki 310-8512
Tel: +81(29) 228-8111
Fax: +81(29) 228-8019
EMail: ib-kouhou@mx.ibaraki.ac.jp
Website: http://www.ibaraki.ac.jp

President: Yukio Ikeda Tel: +81(29) 228-8002

Centres

Co-operative Research and Development *(Hitachi-campus)* (Development Studies); **Education and Research in Lifelong Learning** (Continuing Education); **Gene Research**; **Health** (Health Sciences); **Information Technology** *(Hitachi-campus)* (Information Technology); **Instrumental Analysis**; **University Education** (Higher Education); **Water Environment Studies** (Environmental Studies; Water Management)

Colleges

Agriculture *(Ami-campus)* (Agriculture; Biotechnology); **Education** *(Mito-campus)* (Education; Nursing; Special Education); **Engineering** *(Hitachi-campus)* (Civil Engineering; Computer Science; Electrical Engineering; Electronic Engineering; Engineering; Information Sciences; Materials Engineering; Mechanical Engineering; Systems Analysis; Town Planning); **Humanities** *(Mito-campus)* (Arts and Humanities; Communication Studies; Social Sciences); **Science** *(Mito-campus)* (Environmental Studies; Mathematics; Natural Sciences)

Institutes

Arts and Culture *(Izura)* (Fine Arts); **Regional Studies** *(Regional Institute)* (Regional Studies)

History: Founded 1949.

Governing Bodies: Senate

Academic Year: April to March (April-September; October-March)

Admission Requirements: Graduation from high school or recognized equivalent, and entrance examination

Main Language(s) of Instruction: Japanese

International Co-operation: With universities in USA, Philippines, China and Republic of Korea

Degrees and Diplomas: *Gakushi*: Agriculture; Arts; Communication; Education; Engineering; Science; Social Sciences, 4 yrs; *Shushi*: Agriculture; Arts; Education; Engineering; Science, a further 2 yrs; *Hakase*: Agriculture; Arts; Engineering; Science, 3 yrs following Shushi

Student Services: Academic counselling, Canteen, Employment services, Foreign student adviser, Foreign Studies Centre, Health services, Nursery care, Sports facilities

Student Residential Facilities: For c. 520 students and c. 70 foreign students

Special Facilities: Izura (Institute of Arts and Culture)

Libraries: University Library, c. 940,000 vols

Last Updated: 07/01/09

INSTITUTE OF ADVANCED MEDIA ARTS AND SCIENCES

Joho Kagaku Geijutsu Daigakuin Daigaku (IAMAS)

3-95, Ryoke-cho, Ogaki-shi, Gifu 503-0014
Tel: +81(584) 75-6600
Fax: +81(584) 75-6637
EMail: info@iamas.ac.jp
Website: http://www.iamas.ac.jp/index_E.html

President: Atsuhito Sekiguchi

Faculties

Advanced Media Arts and Sciences (Information Technology; Media Studies; Multimedia)

History: Founded 2001. Part of IAMAS with the International Academy of Media Arts and Sciences.

Degrees and Diplomas: *Shushi*

Last Updated: 24/03/11

INSTITUTE OF INFORMATION SECURITY

Joho Sekyuriti Daigakuin Daigaku

2-14-1 Tsuruyasho, Kanagawa-ku, Tokohama-shi, Kanagawa 221-0835
Tel: +81(45) 311-7784
Fax: +81(45) 311-6871
EMail: iisecc@iwasaki.ac.jp
Website: http://www.iisec.ac.jp

Programmes

Information Security

History: Founded 2004.

Degrees and Diplomas: *Gakushi*

Last Updated: 13/02/09

INSTITUTE OF TECHNOLOGISTS

Monotsukuri Daigaku

333 Maeya, Gyoda-shi, Saitama 361-0038
Tel: +81(48) 564-3200 +81(48) 564-3816
Fax: +81(48) 564-3201
EMail: info@iot.ac.jp
Website: http://www.iot.ac.jp

Departments

Building Technology (Civil Engineering; Construction Engineering; Structural Architecture; Wood Technology); **Manufacturing Technology**

History: Founded 2001.

Degrees and Diplomas: *Gakushi*

Libraries: 28,000 vols

Last Updated: 07/01/09

INTERNATIONAL BUDO UNIVERSITY

Kokusai Budo Daigaku

841 Shinkan, Katsuura-shi, Chiba 299-5295
Tel: +81(470) 73-4111
Fax: +81(470) 73-4148
EMail: kokusai@budo-u.ac.jp
Website: http://www.budo-u.ac.jp

Divisions

Budo; **International Sports Culture** (Physical Education; Sports); **Physical Education** (Physical Education); **Sports Trainers** (Physical Education; Sports)

Faculties

Physical Education (Physical Education; Sports)

History: Founded 1984.

Main Language(s) of Instruction: Japanese
Degrees and Diplomas: *Gakushi*
Student Services: Academic counselling, Canteen, Employment services, Foreign student adviser, Foreign Studies Centre, Health services, Language programs, Nursery care, Sports facilities
Libraries: 80,000 vols
Last Updated: 13/01/09

INTERNATIONAL CHRISTIAN UNIVERSITY

Kokusai Kirisutokyo Daigaku (ICU)
3-10-2 Osawa, Mitaka-shi, Tokyo 181-8585
Tel: +81(422) 33-3043
Fax: +81(422) 33-3355
EMail: dia@icu.ac.jp
Website: http://www.icu.ac.jp

President: Junko Hibiya (2012-)
Tel: +81(422) 33-3005 EMail: president@icu.ac.jp
International Relations: Shaun Malarney, Dean, International Affairs Tel: +81(422) 33-3043, Fax: +81(422) 33-3764

Colleges

Liberal Arts (American Studies; Anthropology; Archaeology; Arts and Humanities; Asian Studies; Biology; Business Administration; Chemistry; Communication Studies; Computer Science; Cultural Studies; Development Studies; Economics; Education; Fine Arts; Foreign Languages Education; Gender Studies; History; Information Sciences; International and Comparative Education; International Relations; Japanese; Law; Linguistics; Literature; Mathematics; Media Studies; Modern Languages; Music; Native Language Education; Peace and Disarmament; Philosophy; Physics; Political Sciences; Psychology; Religion; Social Sciences; Sociology) *Dean*: William Steele

Divisions

Humanities (Archaeology; Arts and Humanities; Ethics; Literature; Music; Philosophy; Religion) *Chair*: Naoki Onishi; **International Studies** (Communication Studies; Comparative Sociology; Cultural Studies; International Business; International Economics; International Relations; International Studies; Linguistics) *Chair*: John C. Maher; **Languages** *Chair*: Junko Hibiya; **Natural Sciences** (Biology; Chemistry; Information Sciences; Mathematics; Physics) *Chair*: Kazuo Kitahara; **Social Sciences** (Anthropology; Business Administration; Economics; History; Law; Political Sciences; Social Sciences; Sociology) *Chair*: Yoshimichi Someya

Graduate Schools

Comparative Culture (Cultural Studies) *Chair*: Atsushi Tanaka; **Education** (Education) *Chair*: Machiko Tomiyama; **Natural Sciences** (Natural Sciences) *Chair*: Robert W. Ridge; **Public Administration** (Public Administration) *Chair*: Takashi Kibe

Institutes

Advanced Studies in Clinical Psychology (Clinical Psychology) *Director*: Hidefumi Kotani; **Asian Cultural Studies** (Asian Studies; Cultural Studies) *Director*: Kenneth R. Robinson; **Educational Research and Service** (Educational Research; Social Sciences) *Director*: David W. Rackham; **Gender Studies** *Director*: Norie Takazawa; **Peace Research** (Peace and Disarmament) *Director*: Toshiki Mogami; **Social Sciences** (Peace and Disarmament; Social Sciences) *Director*: Vosse Wilhelm; **Study of Christianity and Culture** (Christian Religious Studies) *Director*: Anri Morimoto

Programmes

English Language *(ELP)* (English) *Director*: William Harshbarger; **Japanese Language** *(JLP)* (Japanese) *Director*: Machiko Netsu; **Physical Education** (Physical Education) *Director*: Nobuyuki Matsuoka

Research Centres

Japanese Language Education *Director*: Masayoshi Hirose

Further Information: Also summer courses in Japanese language. Study abroad programme in : USA; Canada; Chile; China; Taiwan; South Korea; Philippines; Thailand; Vietnam; UK; Italy; Spain; Netherlands; Belgium; France; Germany; Austria; Russia; Lithuania; Hungary; Czech Republic; Denmark; Sweden; Finland; Iceland, Ghana, South Africa; New Zealand and Australia

History: Founded 1949.
Governing Bodies: Board of Trustees; Board of Councellors; University Management Committee; University Senate
Academic Year: April to March (April-June; September-November; December-March)
Admission Requirements: Graduation from high school and entrance examination; admittance in April. Foreign students: graduation from high school (completion of 12 yrs of education) and documentary screening; admittance in September. TOEFL and SAT required.
Fees: (Yen): Registration, 150,000 (One-Year-Regular), 300,000 (Regular); tuition, 1,359,000 per annum
Main Language(s) of Instruction: Japanese, English
Degrees and Diplomas: *Gakushi*: 4 yrs; *Shushi*: a further 2 yrs; *Hakase*: 3 yrs following Shushi
Student Services: Academic counselling, Canteen, Employment services, Foreign student adviser, Health services, Language programs, Social counselling, Sports facilities
Student Residential Facilities: For c. 300 students
Special Facilities: Hachiro Yuasa Memorial Museum (Archaeology and Folk Art)
Libraries: c. 670,000 vols; 2,100 periodical titles
Publications: Asian Cultural Studies *(annually)*; Christianity and Culture *(annually)*; Educational Studies *(annually)*; Journal of Social Science *(biannually)*; Language Research Bulletin *(annually)*

Student Numbers *2011-2012*: Total: c. 3,000
Last Updated: 09/12/08

INTERNATIONAL COLLEGE FOR POSTGRADUATE BUDDHIST STUDIES

Kokusai Bukkyogaku Daigakuin Daigaku (ICABS)
5-3-23 Toranomon, Minato-ku, Tokyo 105-0001
Tel: +81(3) 3434-6953
Fax: +81(3) 3578-1205
EMail: icabs@icabs.ac.jp; student@icabs.ac.jp
Website: http://www.icabs.ac.jp

President: Imanishi Junkichi

Graduate Colleges

Buddhist Studies
History: Founded 1995.
Governing Bodies: Gakko Hajin Kokusai Bukkyo Gakuin
Academic Year: April to March (April-September; October-March)
Admission Requirements: Gakushi (Bachelor's degree)
Fees: (Yen): Registration, 300,000; tuition 600,000 per annum
Main Language(s) of Instruction: Japanese
Degrees and Diplomas: *Shushi (MA)*: 2 yrs following Gakushi; *Hakase (PhD)*: 3 yrs following Shushi
Student Services: Health services
Libraries: 93,000 vols
Publications: Journal of the International College for Postgraduate Buddhist Studies *(annually)*
Last Updated: 25/03/11

INTERNATIONAL PACIFIC UNIVERSITY

Kan Taiheiyou Daigaku
721 Kannonji, Seito, Okayama 709-0863
Tel: +81(86) 958-0200
Fax: +81(86) 958-0282
EMail: yuchida@ipu-japan.ac.jp
Website: http://www.ipu-japan.ac.jp

President: Akiro Otomo

Faculties

Education for Future Generations (Educational Administration; International and Comparative Education; Preschool Education); **Physical Education**
History: Founded 2007.

Degrees and Diplomas: *Gakushi*
Last Updated: 13/02/09

INTERNATIONAL UNIVERSITY OF HEALTH AND WELFARE

Kokusai Iryo Fukushi Daigaku

2600-1 Kitakanemaru, Otawara-shi, Tochigi 324-8501
Tel: +81(287) 243-000
Fax: +81(287) 243-100
EMail: nyushi@iuhw.ac.jp; www-admin@iuhw.ac.jp
Website: http://www.iuhw.ac.jp/

President: Shuichi Tani

Graduate Schools

Health and Welfare Sciences *(Also Research Institute, Okawa Campus)* (Health Sciences; Social Welfare; Welfare and Protective Services)

Schools

Health and Welfare (Health Administration; Health Sciences; Social and Community Services); **Health Sciences**; **Nursing and Rehabilitation Sciences** *(Odawara Campus)* (Nursing; Rehabilitation and Therapy); **Pharmacy** (Pharmacology; Pharmacy); **Rehabilitation Sciences** *(Fukuoka)* (Rehabilitation and Therapy)

History: Founded 1995.

Degrees and Diplomas: *Gakushi*; *Hakase*

Last Updated: 13/01/09

INTERNATIONAL UNIVERSITY OF JAPAN

Kokusai Daigaku (IUJ)

777 Kokusai-cho, Minami-Uonuma-shi, Niigata 949-7277
Tel: +81(25) 779-1104
Fax: +81(25) 779-1188
EMail: info@iuj.ac.jp
Website: http://www.iuj.ac.jp

President: Masakatsu Mori
Tel: +81(25) 779-1453, Fax: +81(25) 779-1184

Centres

Global Communications (Communication Studies) *Director*: Shumpei Kumon

Graduate Schools

International Management (Business Administration; E-Business/Commerce; International Business) *Dean*: Philip Sugai; **International Relations** (Development Studies; International Relations) *Dean*: Takahiro Akita

Programmes

E-Business Management *Director*: Jay Rajasekera; **English** *(Intensive)*; **Japanese Language** (Japanese)

Research Institutes

IUJ *Director*: Ippei Yamazawa

History: Founded 1982 with a mission to provide graduate level education in English to develop future leaders in the global society. It is supported by the Japanese industrial, financial and educational communities and by local community of Urasa.

Governing Bodies: Board of Trustees; Board of Councilors; University Council

Academic Year: September to August

Admission Requirements: University degree at Bachelor level or equivalent

Main Language(s) of Instruction: English

International Co-operation: With universities in USA; Canada; China; Hong Kong; Indonesia; Republic of Korea; Philippines; Singapore; Taiwan; Thailand; Belgium; Denmark; Finland; France; Germany; Italy; Netherlands; Norway; Spain; Switzerland; Turkey; United Kingdom and Australia

Accrediting Agencies: Ministry of Education, Culture, Sports, Science and Technology (MEXT)

Degrees and Diplomas: *Shushi*: E-Business Management (MEBM), 1 yr; *Shushi*: International Management (MBA); International Relations, International Development and International Peace Studies (MA), 2 yrs

Student Services: Academic counselling, Canteen, Employment services, Foreign student adviser, Health services, Language programs, Social counselling, Sports facilities

Student Residential Facilities: Yes

Libraries: c. 120,000 vols

Last Updated: 25/03/11

INTERNATIONAL UNIVERSITY OF KAGOSHIMA

Kagoshima Kokusai Daigaku

8850 Shimofukomoto-cho, Kagoshima-shi, Kagoshima 891-0191
Tel: +81(99) 261-3211
Fax: +81(99) 261-3299
EMail: koruou@ofc.iuk.ac.jp
Website: http://www.iuk.ac.jp

Faculties

Economics (Banking; Business Administration; Economics; Finance; Labour Law; Management); **Education**; **Intercultural Studies**; **Welfare Society** (Child Care and Development; Psychology; Social Studies; Social Welfare; Sociology; Tourism; Welfare and Protective Services)

Schools

Graduate Studies (Cultural Studies; Economics; Welfare and Protective Services)

History: Founded 1990. Formerly known as Kagoshima Keizai Daigaku/Kagoshima Keizai University.

Degrees and Diplomas: *Gakushi*; *Shushi*; *Hakase*

Last Updated: 09/01/09

ISHIKAWA PREFECTURAL NURSING UNIVERSITY

Ishikawa Kenritsu Kango Daigaku

7-1 Aza-Nakanuma, Takamatsu, Kahoku-gun, Ishikawa 929-1212
Tel: +81(76) 281-8300
Fax: +81(76) 281-8319
EMail: office@ishikawa-nu.ac.jp
Website: http://www.ishikawa-nu.ac.jp

Departments

Nursing (Arts and Humanities; Nursing)

History: Founded 2000.

Degrees and Diplomas: *Gakushi*; *Shushi*; *Hakase*

Libraries: c. 50,000 vols.

Last Updated: 08/01/09

ISHINOMAKI SENSHU UNIVERSITY

Ishinomaki Senshu Daigaku

1 Shinmito Minamisakai, Ishinomaki-shi, Miyagi 986-8580
Tel: +81(225) 22-7711
Fax: +81(225) 22-7710
EMail: nyushi@isenshu-u.ac.jp
Website: http://www.isenshu-u.ac.jp

Faculties

Business Administration (Accountancy; Business Administration; Management; Management Systems); **Graduate Studies**; **Science and Engineering** (Biological and Life Sciences; Biotechnology; Electronic Engineering; Engineering; Environmental Studies; Materials Engineering; Mathematics and Computer Science; Mechanical Engineering)

History: Founded 1989.

International Co-operation: With universities in USA and Mongolia

Degrees and Diplomas: *Gakushi*; *Shushi*; *Hakase*

Student Services: Employment services, Foreign student adviser, Foreign Studies Centre, Health services, Sports facilities

Libraries: 130,390 vols

IWAKI MEISEI UNIVERSITY

Iwaki Meisei Daigaku

5-5-1 Chuodai-iino, Iwaki-shi, Fukushima 970-8551
Tel: +81(246) 29-5111
Fax: +81(246) 29-5105
EMail: imu@iwakimu.ac.jp
Website: http://www.iwakimu.ac.jp

President: Takeshi Sekiguchi

Colleges

Humanities (American Studies; Arts and Humanities; Cultural Studies; English; Japanese; Literature; Psychology; Sociology); **Science and Engineering** (Biological and Life Sciences; Computer Science; Electronic Engineering; Environmental Engineering; Environmental Studies; Mechanical Engineering; Natural Sciences)

Faculties

Pharmacy (Pharmacology; Pharmacy)

Graduate Schools

Humanities (Arts and Humanities; English; Japanese; Literature; Modern Languages; Sociology); **Science and Engineering** (Engineering; Natural Sciences)

History: Founded 1987. Acquired present status 2001.

Main Language(s) of Instruction: Japanese

Degrees and Diplomas: *Gakushi*; *Shushi*; *Hakase*

Libraries: 180,000 vols

Last Updated: 25/03/11

IWATE MEDICAL UNIVERSITY

Iwate Ika Daigaku

19-1 Uchimaru, Morioka-shi,
Iwate 020-8505
Tel: +81(19) 651-5111
Fax: +81(19) 651-8055
EMail: webmaster@iwate-med.ac.jp
Website: http://www.iwate-med.ac.jp

Centres

Cyclotron Research; **Heart Research**

Faculties

Dentistry (Dentistry); **Liberal Arts and Sciences**; **Medicine** (Medicine)

History: Founded 1928 as Iwate Medical College, acquired University status 1952. Faculty of Dentistry added 1965.

Academic Year: April to March (April-September; November-March)

Admission Requirements: Graduation from high school or equivalent, and entrance examination

Main Language(s) of Instruction: Japanese

Degrees and Diplomas: *Gakushi*: Dentistry; Medicine, 6 yrs; *Hakase*: Dentistry; Medical Sciences, a further 4 yrs

Student Services: Sports facilities

Student Residential Facilities: Yes

Libraries: 262,210 vols

Publications: Dental Journal of Iwate Medical University *(quarterly)*; Journal of Iwate Medical Association *(bimonthly)*

Last Updated: 09/01/09

IWATE PREFECTURAL UNIVERSITY

Iwate Kenritsu Daigaku

152-52 Takizawa-aza-Sugo, Takizawa, Iwate-gun,
Iwate 020-0173
Tel: +81(019) 694-2014
Fax: +81(019) 694-2035
EMail: webmaster@iwate-pu.ac.jp
Website: http://www.iwate-pu.ac.jp

President: Yoshihisa Nakamura

Faculties

Nursing (Nursing); **Policy Studies** (Political Sciences); **Social Welfare** (Social Welfare); **Software and Information Science**

Graduate Schools

Policy Studies (Political Sciences)

Schools

Graduate Studies (Information Sciences; Nursing; Social Welfare; Software Engineering)

History: Founded 1998.

International Co-operation: With universities in China

Degrees and Diplomas: *Gakushi*; *Shushi*; *Hakase*

Libraries: 210,000 vols

Last Updated: 24/03/11

IWATE UNIVERSITY

Iwate Daigaku

3-18-8 Ueda, Morioka-shi, Iwate 020-8550
Tel: +81(19) 621-6000
Fax: +81(19) 621-6065
EMail: sshomu@iwate-u.ac.jp
Website: http://www.iwate-u.ac.jp

President: Katsumi Fujii

Faculties

Agriculture (Agriculture; Agronomy; Crop Production; Food Science; Forestry; Horticulture; Soil Science; Veterinary Science; Water Science); **Education** (Education; Primary Education; Secondary Education; Special Education); **Engineering** (Applied Chemistry; Civil Engineering; Computer Science; Electrical and Electronic Engineering; Engineering; Environmental Engineering; Information Sciences; Materials Engineering; Mechanical Engineering; Molecular Biology); **Humanities and Social Sciences** (Arts and Humanities; Behavioural Sciences; Cultural Studies; Economics; Environmental Studies; Law; Social Sciences)

History: Founded 1949.

Academic Year: April to March

Admission Requirements: Graduation from high school and entrance examination

Fees: (Yen): 478,800 per annum

Main Language(s) of Instruction: Japanese

Accrediting Agencies: Ministry of Education, Culture, Sports, Science and Technology

Degrees and Diplomas: *Gakushi*: Agriculture; Education; Engineering; Humanities and Social Sciences, 4 yrs; *Shushi*: Agriculture; Education; Humanities and Social Sciences, a further 2 yrs; *Hakase*: Engineering, 3 yrs following Shushi

Student Services: Academic counselling, Canteen, Employment services, Foreign student adviser, Health services, Language programs, Social counselling, Sports facilities

Student Residential Facilities: Yes

Special Facilities: Botanical Garden

Libraries: c. 840,700 vols

Publications: Arutesu Liberales, Academic Reports of Faculty of Humanities and Social Sciences *(biannually)*; Iwatedaigaku Gijutsubu Hokoku, Academic Reports of Faculty of Engineering *(annually)*; Kyoikugakubu Kenkyu Nenpo, Academic Reports of Faculty of Education *(biannually)*

Last Updated: 08/01/09

JAPAN ADVANCED INSTITUTE OF SCIENCE AND TECHNOLOGY

Hokuriku Sentan Kagaku Gijutsu Daigakuin Daigaku (JAIST)

1-1 Asahidai, Nomi, Ishikawa 923-1292
Tel: +81(761) 51-1111
Fax: +81(761) 51-1959
EMail: kokusai@jaist.ac.jp
Website: http://www.jaist.ac.jp

President: Takuya Katayama

Secretary-General: Masanobu Ito

Centres

Distance Learning Research *Director*: Toshiya Ando; **Health Care** *Director*: Takio Hayashi; **Highly Dependable Embedded Systems Technology Research** *Director*: Koichiro Ochimizu; **Information Sciences** (Information Sciences) *Director*: Teruo Matsuzawa; **Intellectual Property (IP) Operation** *Director*: Kazuyoshi Yamamoto; **Internet Research** (Computer Networks) *Director*: Koichiro Ochimizu; **Knowledge Science** *Director*: Kazushi Nishimoto; **Nano-Materials and Technology** (Nanotechnology) *Director*: Shintaro Sasaki; **Regional Innovation** *Director*: Susumu Kunifuji; **Research and Investigation of Advanced Science and Technology** *Director*: Kazuyoshi Yamamoto; **Trustworthy e-Society Research** *Director*: Akira Shimazu

Laboratories

Venture Business *Director*: Kazuyoshi Yamamoto

Schools

Information Sciences (Artificial Intelligence; Computer Engineering; Computer Networks; Information Sciences; Software Engineering) *Dean*: Koichiro Ochimizu; **Knowledge Science** (Arts and Humanities; Biology; Cognitive Sciences; Development Studies; Economics; Engineering; Leadership; Natural Sciences; Philosophy; Social Sciences) *Dean*: Susumu Kunifuji; **Materials Science** (Biological and Life Sciences; Biology; Biotechnology; Chemistry; Materials Engineering; Nanotechnology; Physics) *Dean*: Hideki Matsumura

History: Founded 1990 as School of Information Science; School of Materials Science organized 1991 and School of Knowledge Science organized 1996. A University of graduate education and research in Science and Technology.

Governing Bodies: Senate

Academic Year: April to March (April-September; October-March)

Admission Requirements: University degree at Bachelor level

Main Language(s) of Instruction: Japanese; English (doctoral course)

International Co-operation: Academic exchanges agreements with over 50 institutions in 17 foreign countries including Republic of Korea, China and Vietnam

Degrees and Diplomas: *Shushi*: 1-2 yrs; *Hakase*: 2-3 yrs

Student Services: Academic counselling, Canteen, Employment services, Health services, Language programs, Sports facilities

Student Residential Facilities: For 599 students

Libraries: Institute Library, 126,000 vols

Publications: JAIST *(biannually)*

Last Updated: 21/11/08

JAPAN COLLEGE OF SOCIAL WORK

Nihon Shakaijigyo Daigaku

3-1-30 Takeoka, Kiyose-shi, Tokyo 204-8555

Tel: +81(424) 92-6111

Fax: +81(424) 92-6816

Website: http://www.jcsw.ac.jp

Programmes

Welfare and Community Services *(Also Graduate Programme)* (Social and Community Services; Social Welfare; Social Work)

History: Founded 1946.

International Co-operation: With universities in Republic of Korea, Thailand and USA

Degrees and Diplomas: *Gakushi*; *Shushi*; *Hakase*

Student Services: Language programs, Sports facilities

Libraries: 191,433 vols

Last Updated: 27/01/09

JAPAN LUTHERAN COLLEGE

Ruteru Gakuin Daigaku (JLC)

3-10-20 Osawa, Mitaka-shi, Tokyo 181-0015

Tel: +81(422) 31-4611

Fax: +81(422) 33-6405

EMail: koho@luther.ac.jp

Website: http://www.luther.ac.jp

Departments

Christian Studies; **Clinical Psychology**; **Social Work** (Social Welfare; Social Work)

Graduate Schools

Integrated Human Studies

History: Founded 1963 as Japan Lutheran Theological College. Acquired present title 1996 and status 2001.

Degrees and Diplomas: *Gakushi*; *Shushi*

JAPAN WOMEN'S COLLEGE OF PHYSICAL EDUCATION

Nihon Joshi Taiiku Daigaku

8-19-1 Kita-karasuyama, Setagaya-ku, Tokyo 157-8565

Tel: +81(3) 3300-2250 +81(3) 3300-2256

Fax: +81(3) 3308-7244

EMail: gakuseika@jwcpe.ac.jp

Website: http://www.jwcpe.ac.jp

President: Kazuyuki Takahashi

Faculties

Sports and Health Sciences (Child Care and Development; Dance; Sports; Sports Management; Sports Medicine)

Graduate Schools

Sports Science (Sports)

History: Founded 1922.

Main Language(s) of Instruction: Japanese

Degrees and Diplomas: *Gakushi*; *Shushi*

Student Services: Foreign student adviser, Health services, Social counselling, Sports facilities

Libraries: c. 128,000 vols

Last Updated: 27/01/09

JAPAN WOMEN'S UNIVERSITY

Nihon Joshi Daigaku (JWU)

2-8-1 Mejirodai, Bunkyo-ku, Tokyo 112-8681

Tel: +81(3) 3943-3131

EMail: n-abroad@atlas.jwu.ac.jp

Website: http://www.jwu.ac.jp

President: Yoshiko Arikawa (2009-)

Secretary-General: Kyoko Shimada

International Relations: Michiko Ohtsuka, Dean of Students

Divisions

Correspondence Courses (Child Care and Development; Food Science; House Arts and Environment; Nutrition)

Faculties

Home Economics (Child Care and Development; Clothing and Sewing; Food Science; House Arts and Environment; Household Management; Nutrition) *Dean*: Kazuto Sato; **Humanities** (English; History; Japanese) *Dean*: Rikiya Nishiyama; **Integrated Arts and Social Sciences** *(Kawasaki City)* (Arts and Humanities; Cultural Studies; Education; Psychology; Social Sciences; Social Studies; Social Welfare) *Dean*: Yoshio Katagiri; **Science** (Biology; Chemistry; Mathematics; Physics) *Dean*: Yoshiko Kubo

Graduate Schools

Home Economics (Child Care and Development; Clothing and Sewing; Food Science; House Arts and Environment; Nutrition; Social Welfare) *Chairperson*: Hiromi Tokoyama; **Human Life Science** (Development Studies; House Arts and Environment) *Chairperson*: Hiromi Tokoyama; **Humanities** (English; History; Japanese) *Chariperson*: Goro Minamoto; **Integrated Arts and Social Sciences** *(Kawasaki City)* (Cultural Studies; Education; Psychology; Social Studies; Social Welfare) *Chairperson*: Tadaaki Yamada; **Science** (Biology; Mathematics; Physics) *Chairperson*: Hajime Imai

Institutes

Research (Educational Research; History; Philosophy) *Head*: Noriko Shimada

Research Institutes

Women's Career *Head*: Masami Iwata

History: Founded 1901 as Liberal Arts College, became University 1948. Faculty of Integrated Arts and Social Sciences established 1990. Faculty of Science established 1992. A private institution for women. Mainly financed by tuition fees.

Governing Bodies: Board of Trustees

Academic Year: April to March (April-September; September-March)

Admission Requirements: Graduation from senior high school or foreign equivalent, and entrance examination

Fees: (Yen): 640,000-840,000 per annum

Main Language(s) of Instruction: Japanese

International Co-operation: With universities in Afghanistan; Australia; Canada; Republic of Korea; Slovenia; United Kingdom and USA

Degrees and Diplomas: *Gakushi*: Education (BA) (Kyoikugaku); Home Economics (BHE) (Kaseigaku); Humanities (BA) (Bungaku); Humanities and Cultures (BA) (Bungaku); Psychology (BA) (Shinrigaku); Science (BS) (Rigaku); Social Welfare (BS.S) (Shakaifukushigaku); Sociology (BA) (Shakaigaku), 4 yrs; *Shushi*: Education (MA) (Kyoikugaku); Home Economics (MHE) (Kaseigaku); Humanities (MA) (Bungaku); Psychology (MA) (Shinrigaku); Science (MS) (Rigaku); Social Welfare (MS.S) (Shakaifukushigaku); Sociology (MS.S) (Shakaigaku), a further 2 yrs; *Hakase*: 3 yrs following Shushi; *Hakase*: Contemporary Society Studies (PhD) (Gakujutu); Education (PhD) (Kyoikugaku); Human Life Science (PhD) (Gakujutu); Humanities (PhD) (Bungaku); Psychology (PhD) (Shinrigaku); Science (PhD) (Rigaku); Social Welfare (PhD) (Shakaifukushigaku), 3 yrs following upon Shushi

Student Services: Academic counselling, Canteen, Employment services, Foreign student adviser, Foreign Studies Centre, Handicapped facilities, Health services, Language programs, Nursery care, Social counselling, Sports facilities

Student Residential Facilities: For 206 students

Special Facilities: Naruse Memorial Hall: Museum maintains and exhibits articles on and about Japan Women's University (educational concepts of the founder, historical study on education for women, etc)

Libraries: University Library, 773,011 vols

Publications: Journals of the faculties *(annually)*; Journals of the Graduate Schools *(annually)*

Last Updated: 05/05/09

JAPANESE RED CROSS TOYOTA COLLEGE OF NURSING

Nihon Sekijuji Toyota Kango Daigaku

12-33 Nanamagari, Hakusancho, Toyota-shi, Aichi 471-8565
Tel: +81(565) 36-5111
Fax: +81(565) 37-8558
EMail: info@rctoyota.ac.jp
Website: http://www.rctoyota.ac.jp

Departments

Nursing

History: Founded 2004.

Degrees and Diplomas: *Gakushi*

Last Updated: 27/01/09

J. F. OBERLIN UNIVERSITY

Obirin Daigaku

3758 Tokiwa-machi, Machida-shi, Tokyo 194-0294
Tel: +81(42) 797-2661 +81(42) 797-1542
Fax: +81(42) 797-0132
EMail: intl@obirin.ac.jp
Website: http://www.obirin.ac.jp

President: Takayasu Mitani EMail: gakucho@obirin.ac.jp

International Relations: Hiroaki Hatayama, Vice President for Strategic Planning and International Relations
Tel: +81(42) 797-0817 EMail: hatayama@obirin.ac.jp

Colleges

Business Administration (Business Administration; Hotel and Restaurant; Hotel Management; Information Technology; International Business; Leisure Studies; Marketing; Tourism); **Business Management** (Air Transport; Business Administration; Hotel and Restaurant; International Business; Management; Marketing; Service Trades; Tourism); **Health and Welfare**; **Liberal Arts** (Arts and Humanities; Biology; Chemistry; Earth Sciences; Economics; Education; Ethics; Geography; History; Law; Literature; Mathematics; Modern Languages; Natural Sciences; Physics; Political Sciences; Psychology; Religion; Social Sciences; Sociology); **Performing and Visual Arts** (Film; Music; Performing Arts; Theatre; Visual Arts)

Graduate Schools

International Studies

Institutes

Confucius (Chinese; Modern Languages); **Japanese Languages and Culture**

History: Founded 1946 as Obirin Gakuen (Obirin University). Changed english name 2006.

International Co-operation: With universities in Australia; Brazil; Canada; China; Czech Republic; Egypt; India; Thailand; United Kingdom; USA; New Zealand; Netherlands; Denmark; Chile; Norway; Iceland; Korea; Vietnam; Philippines; Bangladesh

Accrediting Agencies: Japanese University Accreditation Association

Degrees and Diplomas: *Gakushi (BA)*; *Shushi (MA)*; *Hakase (PhD)*

Student Services: Academic counselling, Canteen, Employment services, Foreign Studies Centre, Health services, Language programs, Social counselling, Sports facilities

Libraries: 480,000 vols

Student Numbers *2012-2013*: Total 8,595

Last Updated: 14/02/13

JICHI MEDICAL UNIVERSITY

Jichi Ika Daigaku

3311-1 Yakushiji, Shimotsuke-shi, Tochigi 329-0498
Tel: +81(285) 442-111
Fax: +81(285) 443-625
EMail: kokusai@jichi.ac.jp
Website: http://www.jichi.ac.jp

President: Fumimaro Takaku (1996-)

Chairman: Hiromasa Yoshida

International Relations: Masayuki Suzukawa
Tel: +81(285) 587-395, Fax: +81(285) 440-919
EMail: eccmsuzu@jichi.ac.jp

Faculties

Medicine *(Research)* (Medicine) *Dean*: Fumimaro Takaku; **Nursing** (Nursing) *Dean*: Mitsuko Mito

History: Founded 1972.

Governing Bodies: Board of Trustees

Academic Year: April to March

Admission Requirements: Graduation from high school and entrance examination

Main Language(s) of Instruction: Japanese

Degrees and Diplomas: *Gakushi*: Medicine (MD) (Igaku-gakushi), 6 yrs; *Gakushi*: Nursiing (Kangogaku-gakushi), 4 yrs; *Shushi*: Medicine (Ikagaku-shushi); Nursing (Kango-shushi), 2 yrs; *Hakase*: Medicine (PhD) (Igaku-hakushi), 4 yrs

Student Services: Canteen, Foreign student adviser, Health services, Sports facilities

Student Residential Facilities: Yes

Libraries: 227,494 vols

Publications: Jichi Medical University Journal *(annually)*

JIN-AI UNIVERSITY

Jinai Daigaku

3-1-1 Ohde-cho, Takefu, Fukui 915-8586
Tel: +81(778) 27-2010
Fax: +81(778) 27-1990
EMail: nyusi@jindai.ac.jp
Website: http://www.jindai.ac.jp

President: Tan Sonoda

Programmes

Psychology and Communication (Communication Studies; Psychology)

History: Founded 2001 with the aim of promoting an education based on Buddhist philosophy.

Degrees and Diplomas: *Gakushi*

Special Facilities: Computer Centre

Libraries: 50,000 vols

Last Updated: 09/01/09

JISSEN WOMEN'S UNIVERSITY

Jissen Joshi Daigaku

4-1-1 Osakaue, Hino-shi, Tokyo 191-8510

Tel: +81(42) 585-8817

Fax: +81(42) 585-8818

EMail: webmaster@jissen.ac.jp

Website: http://www.jissen.ac.jp

Departments

Aesthetics and Art History (Aesthetics; Art History); **Clothing Science** (Textile Technology); **English Communications** (English; Literature); **Food Science** (Food Science); **Japanese Communications** (Japanese; Literature)

Faculties

Human Life Sciences (Biological and Life Sciences; Dietetics; Environmental Studies; Food Science; Health Sciences; Social Sciences); **Humanities and Social Sciences**; **Literature** (Aesthetics; Art History; English; Japanese; Literature)

Institutes

Japanese Arts and Literature (Fine Arts; Japanese; Literature)

History: Founded 1899.

Governing Bodies: Board of Trustees

Academic Year: April to March (April-September; October-March)

Admission Requirements: Graduation from high school and entrance examination

Main Language(s) of Instruction: Japanese

Degrees and Diplomas: *Gakushi*: Letters (Bungakushi); Science (Rigakushi), 4 yrs; *Shushi*: a further 2 yrs; *Hakase*: 3 yrs following Shushi

Student Services: Academic counselling, Employment services, Health services, Social counselling

Student Residential Facilities: Yes

Libraries: 400,000 vols

Last Updated: 09/01/09

JOBU UNIVERSITY

Jobu Daigaku

634-1 Toyazuka-machi, Isesaki, Gunma 372-8588

Tel: +81(270) 32-1010

Fax: +81(270) 32-1021

EMail: nyushi@jobu.ac.jp; webmaster@jobu.ac.jp

Website: http://www.jobu.ac.jp

Programmes

Business Administration; **Business Information Sciences** (Business and Commerce; Management Systems); **Management Information Sciences**

History: Founded 1968.

Main Language(s) of Instruction: Japanese

Degrees and Diplomas: *Gakushi*; *Shushi*

Student Services: Employment services, Language programs, Sports facilities

Libraries: 124,704 vols

Last Updated: 09/01/09

JOETSU UNIVERSITY OF EDUCATION

Joetsu Kyoiku Daigaku

1 Yamayashiki-machi, Joetsu-shi, Niigata 943-8512

Tel: +81(25) 521-3299

Fax: +81(25) 521-3621

EMail: ryugaku@juen.ac.jp

Website: http://www.juen.ac.jp

President: Yaichi Wakai

Centres

Demonstration and Research on the Handicapped (Education of the Handicapped); **Educational Research and Development** (Educational Research); **Health** (Health Sciences); **Research and Training in Educational Information**; **Skills Training** (Fine Arts; Modern Languages; Music)

Departments

Early Childhood and Special Education; **Fine Arts and Music** (Fine Arts; Music); **Languages** (Modern Languages); **Physical Education, Home Economics and Industrial Arts** (Home Economics; Industrial Arts Education; Physical Education); **School Education** (Education); **Science** (Natural Sciences); **Social Studies** (Social Studies)

History: Founded 1978.

Academic Year: April to March (April-September; October-March)

Admission Requirements: Graduation from high school

Main Language(s) of Instruction: Japanese

Degrees and Diplomas: *Gakushi*: 4 yrs; *Shushi*: a further 2 yrs

Libraries: c. 264,301 vols

Last Updated: 24/03/11

JOSAI INTERNATIONAL UNIVERSITY

Josai Kokusai Daigaku

1 Gumyo, Togane-shi, Chiba 283-8555

Tel: +81(475) 55-8800

Fax: +81(475) 55-8811

EMail: admis@jiu.ac.jp

Website: http://www.jiu.ac.jp

President: Noriko Mizuta

Faculties

Humanities and Social Sciences (Cultural Studies; Humanities and Social Science Education; Women's Studies); **Management and Information Sciences**; **Media Studies**; **Pharmaceutical Sciences**; **Social Work Studies** (Social Work; Welfare and Protective Services)

Graduate Schools

Business Design; **Humanities** (Cultural Studies; International Business; Social Welfare; Women's Studies); **Management and Information Sciences** (Business Administration; Management)

History: Founded 1992.

Degrees and Diplomas: *Gakushi*; *Shushi*; *Hakase*

Libraries: 100,000 vols

Last Updated: 09/01/09

JOSAI UNIVERSITY

Josai Daigaku

1-1 Keyakidai, Sakado-shi, Saitama 350-0295

Tel: +81(492) 71-7711

Fax: +81(492) 86-4477

EMail: webmaster2006@josai.ac.jp

Website: http://www.josai.ac.jp

President: Yasunori Morimoto

Faculties

Business Administration *(Also Graduate School)*; **Contemporary Policy Studies** (Business Administration; Economics; Law; Political Sciences); **Economics** *(Also Graduate School)* (Economics); **Pharmaceutical Sciences** *(Also Graduate School)* (Pharmacology; Pharmacy); **Science** *(Also Graduate School)* (Chemistry; Mathematics)

Programmes
Japanese Studies

History: Founded 1965.

Academic Year: April to March (April-September; October-March)

Admission Requirements: Graduation from high school and entrance examination

Main Language(s) of Instruction: Japanese

Degrees and Diplomas: *Gakushi*: 4 yrs; *Shushi*: a further 2 yrs

Libraries: 380,000 vols
Last Updated: 09/01/09

JOSHIBI UNIVERSITY OF ART AND DESIGN

Joshi Bijutsu Daigaku
1900 Asamizo-dai, Sagamihara-shi, Kanagawa 228-8538
Tel: +81(42) 778-6627
Fax: +81(42) 778-6649
EMail: itn@joshibi.ac.jp
Website: http://www.joshibi.ac.jp

Programmes
Art and Design *(Also Graduate School)*

History: Founded as Private Women's School of Fine Arts 1900. Renamed Women's Academy of Fine Arts 1929 and Women's College of Fine Arts 1949. Acquired present title 2001.

Degrees and Diplomas: *Gakushi*; *Shushi*
Last Updated: 09/01/09

JUMONJI UNIVERSITY

Jumonji Gakuen Joshi Daigaku
2-1-28 Sugasawa, Niiza-shi, Saitama 352-8501
Tel: +81(48) 477-0603
Fax: +81(48) 477-9123
EMail: fsc@jumonji-u.ac.jp
Website: http://www.jumonji-u.ac.jp

President: Masashi Miyamaru

Faculties
Human Life; **Social and Information Sciences** (Communication Studies; Information Sciences; Social Sciences)

History: Founded 1922.

Degrees and Diplomas: *Gakushi*
Last Updated: 09/01/09

JUNTENDO UNIVERSITY

Juntendo Daigaku
2-1-1 Hongo, Bunkyo-ku, Tokyo 113-8421
Tel: +81(3) 3813-3111
Fax: +81(3) 3814-9100
Website: http://www.juntendo.ac.jp/english/index.html

President: Eiki Kominami

International Relations: Tadashi Kagami, Senior Advisor, Admissions EMail: quagami@med.juntendo.ac.jp

Graduate Schools
Health and Sports Science *(Imba-gun, Chiba Prefecture)* (Health Education; Physical Education; Public Health; Sports; Sports Management; Sports Medicine; Teacher Training) *Dean*: Jun-Ichiro Aoki; **Health Care and Nursing** *(Urayasu City, Chiba Prefecture)* (Nursing) *Dean*: Keiko Inatomi; **Medicine** *Dean*: Eiki Kominami

Institutes
Environmental and Gender-specific Medicine (Medicine)

Research Centres
Allergy *(Atopy)*

Research Institutes
Pathophysiology and Illnesses of the Aged (Gerontology; Pathology; Physiology)

Schools
Health and Sports Science *(Imba-gun, Chiba Prefecture)* (Health Education; Physical Education; Public Health; Sports; Sports Management; Sports Medicine; Teacher Training) *Dean*: Keisuke Sawaki; **Health Care and Nursing** *(Urayasu City, Chiba Prefecture)* (Nursing) *Dean*: Keiko Inatomi; **Medicine** (Anaesthesiology; Anatomy; Biochemistry; Cardiology; Dermatology; Endocrinology; Epidemiology; Forensic Medicine and Dentistry; Gastroenterology; Haematology; Health Administration; Immunology; Medicine; Nephrology; Neurology; Ophthalmology; Otorhinolaryngology; Paediatrics; Parasitology; Pathology; Pharmacology; Physiology; Plastic Surgery; Psychiatry and Mental Health; Public Health; Radiology; Respiratory Therapy; Rheumatology; Surgery; Urology) *Dean*: Yasuhiko Tomino

Further Information: Also six hospitals

History: Founded 1838. Acquired present status 1951.

Governing Bodies: Board of Trustees

Academic Year: April to March

Admission Requirements: Graduation from high school and entrance examination

Fees: (Yen): School of Medicine: 4.7m. per annum; School of Health and Sports Science: 1.39m.; School of Health Care and Nursing, 1.55m. per annum; Graduate Schools, 550,000-600,000 per annum

Main Language(s) of Instruction: Japanese

Accrediting Agencies: Ministry of Education, Culture, Sports, Science and Technology; Japan University Accreditation Association

Degrees and Diplomas: *Gakushi*: Medicine (Igaku), 6 yrs; *Gakushi*: Nursing (Kango); Physical Education (Taiikui), 4 yrs; *Shushi*: Nursing (Kango), 2 yrs; *Shushi*: Physical Education (Taiiku), a further 2 yrs; *Hakase*: Medicine (Igaku), 4 yrs; *Hakase*: Physical Education (Taiiku), 2 yrs

Student Services: Academic counselling, Canteen, Employment services, Foreign student adviser, Health services, Nursery care, Social counselling, Sports facilities

Student Residential Facilities: Yes

Libraries: 4 libraries

Publications: Bulletin of Health and Physical Education *(annually)*; Journal of Health Care and Nursing *(annually)*; Juntendo Medical Journal *(bimonthly)*
Last Updated: 09/01/09

KAETSU UNIVERSITY

Kaetsu Daigaku
2-8-4, Hanakoganeiminami-cho, Kodaira-shi, Tokyo 187-8578
Tel: +81(424) 66-3711
Fax: +81(424) 63-1778
EMail: info@kaetsu.ac.jp; nyushi@kaetsu.ac.jp
Website: http://www.kaetsu.ac.jp

President: Hirsohi Kato (2008-)

Colleges
Business Communication; **Management and Economics** (Accountancy; Business Computing; Commercial Law; Ecology; Law; Management; Modern Languages)

History: Founded 2001.

Degrees and Diplomas: *Gakushi*
Last Updated: 09/01/09

KAGAWA NUTRITION UNIVERSITY

Joshi Eiyo Daigaku
3-9-21 Chiyoda, Sakado-shi, Saitama 350-0288
Tel: +81(492) 84-6245
Fax: +81(492) 84-6410
EMail: knuintlo@eiyo.ac.jp
Website: http://www.eiyo.ac.jp

President: Yoshiko Kagawa

International Relations: Shigeji Miyagi

Departments
Health and Nutrition *(Evening courses)*

Graduate Schools
Nutrition and Health Sciences

Schools

Nutrition Sciences (Food Science; Health Sciences; Nursing; Nutrition)

History: Founded 1961, incorporating Kagawa Nutrition School founded 1939, and Junior College 1950.

Governing Bodies: Board of Directors

Academic Year: April to March (April-July; October-March)

Admission Requirements: Graduation from high school or equivalent, and entrance examination. Japanese language proficiency certified at Level 1 of the Japanese Proficiency Test

Main Language(s) of Instruction: Japanese

International Co-operation: With universities in Australia

Degrees and Diplomas: *Gakushi*: 4 yrs; *Shushi*: a further 2 yrs; *Hakase*: 3 yrs following Shushi

Student Services: Academic counselling, Canteen, Cultural centre, Employment services, Foreign student adviser, Foreign Studies Centre, Handicapped facilities, Health services, Social counselling, Sports facilities

Student Residential Facilities: Yes

Special Facilities: Agricultural Garden

Libraries: College Library, 90,400 vols

Publications: Joshi Eiyo-Daigaku Kiyo (Scientific Report of the College) *(annually)*

Press or Publishing House: Joshi Eiyo Daigaku Shuppanbu (Women's College, Publishing Division)

Last Updated: 09/01/09

KAGAWA PREFECTURAL COLLEGE OF HEALTH SCIENCES

Kagawa Kenritsu Hoken Iryo Daigaku

281-1 Hara, Mure-cho, Kita-gun 761-0123

Tel: +81(87) 870-1212

Fax: +81(87) 870-1202

Website: http://www.pref.kagawa.jp/daigaku

Departments

Medical Technology; **Nursing** (Nursing)

History: Founded 2004.

Degrees and Diplomas: *Gakushi*

Libraries: Yes

Last Updated: 09/01/09

KAGAWA UNIVERSITY

Kagawa Daigaku

1-1, Saiwai-cho, Takamatsu-shi, Kagawa 760-8521

Tel: +81(87) 832-1149

Fax: +81(87) 832-1155

EMail: soryugat@jim.ao.kagawa-u.ac.jp; kokusait@jim.ao.kagawa-u.ac.jp

Website: http://www.kagawa-u.ac.jp

President: Masahiko Ichii

Faculties

Agriculture *(Also Graduate School)* (Agriculture; Biochemistry; Biological and Life Sciences; Food Science); **Economics** *(Also Graduate School)* (Business Administration; Economics; Regional Studies; Social Studies); **Education** *(Also Graduate School)* (Education; Education of the Handicapped; Pedagogy; Psychology); **Engineering** *(Also Graduate School)* (Construction Engineering; Engineering; Information Technology; Materials Engineering; Mechanical Engineering; Safety Engineering); **Law** *(Also Graduate School)* (Law); **Medicine** *(Also Graduate School)*

Graduate Schools

Law *(Kagawa-Ehime Universities Graduate School)*; **Management** (Management)

Further Information: Also Japanese language courses for foreign students. Centre for Educational Research and Teacher Development

History: Founded 1949. Merged with Kagawa Medical University 2003. Acquired present status 2004.

Governing Bodies: Yakuinkai (University Council); Advisory Board, comprising the president and six trustees

Academic Year: April to March (April-October; October-March)

Admission Requirements: Graduation from high school or equivalent, and entrance examination

Main Language(s) of Instruction: Japanese

International Co-operation: With universities in China and Thailand

Degrees and Diplomas: *Gakushi*: Agriculture (Nogakushi); Economics (Keizaigakushi); Education (Kyoikugakushi); Engineering (Kogakushi); Law (Hogakushi); Nursing (Kangogakushi), 4 yrs; *Gakushi*: Medicine, 6 yrs; *Shushi*: Agriculture (Nogakushushi); Economics (Keizaigashushi); Education (Kyoikugakushushi); Engineering (Kogakushushi); Law (Hogakushushi); Nursing (Kangogakushushi), a further 2 yrs; *Hakase*: Engineering (Kogakuhakushi), a further 3 yrs; *Hakase*: Medicine, a further 4 yrs

Student Services: Canteen, Employment services, Foreign student adviser, Foreign Studies Centre, Handicapped facilities, Health services, Language programs, Nursery care, Sports facilities

Special Facilities: University Hospital. Central Office for Creation and Transfer of Intellectual Property. University Farm. Marine Environmental Research Station

Libraries: 938,554 vols

Publications: Memoirs of Faculty of Agriculture; Memoirs of Faculty of Education; Technical Bulletin of Faculty of Agriculture

Last Updated: 09/01/09

KAGOSHIMA IMMACULATE HEART UNIVERSITY

Kagoshima Junshin Joshi Daigaku

2365 Amatatsu-cho, Sendai-shi, Miyagi 895-0011

Tel: +81(996) 23-5311

Fax: +81(996) 23-5030

EMail: foreign@jundai.k-junshin.ac.jp

Website: http://www.k-junshin.ac.jp/jundai/

President: Michiko Inai

Faculties

International Human Studies (Child Care and Development; International Studies); **Nursing and Nutrition** (Nursing; Nutrition)

History: Founded 1994.

Degrees and Diplomas: *Gakushi*

Last Updated: 09/01/09

KAGOSHIMA UNIVERSITY

Kagoshima Daigaku

1-21-24 Korimoto, Kagoshima-shi, Kagoshima 890-8580

Tel: +81(99) 285-7325

Fax: +81(99) 285-7328

EMail: ryugaku1@kuasmail.kuas.kagoshima-u.ac.jp

Website: http://www.kagoshima-u.ac.jp

President: Hiroki Yoshida

Tel: +81(99) 285-7000, Fax: +81(99) 285-7001

Faculties

Agriculture (Agriculture; Biochemistry; Biomedicine; Environmental Engineering; Technology; Veterinary Science); **Education** (Continuing Education; Education; Special Education); **Engineering** (Applied Chemistry; Architecture; Bioengineering; Chemical Engineering; Civil Engineering; Computer Science; Electrical and Electronic Engineering; Engineering; Marine Engineering; Marine Science and Oceanography; Mechanical Engineering); **Fisheries** (Fishery); **Law, Economics and Humanities** (Arts and Humanities; Economics; Law; Social Policy); **Medicine** (Medicine); **Science** (Biochemistry; Biomedicine; Biophysics; Chemistry; Computer Science; Earth Sciences; Mathematics; Natural Sciences; Physics)

Graduate Schools

Agricultural Sciences *(United)*; **Agriculture**; **Clinical Psychology** (Clinical Psychology); **Education** (Education); **Fisheries** (Fishery); **Health Sciences** (Health Sciences); **Humanistic-Sociological**

Sciences; **Medical and Dental Sciences** (Dentistry; Medicine); **Science and Engineering** (Computer Science; Engineering; Natural Sciences)

Schools
Dentistry (Dentistry); **Law**

Further Information: Also experimental farm. Veterinary hospital. 2 training ships

History: Founded 1949, incorporating seven high schools, Kagoshima Normal School, Kagoshima Youth Normal School, Kagoshima College of Agriculture and Forestry, and Kagoshima College of Fishery.

Governing Bodies: Hyogikai (University Council)

Academic Year: April to March (April-September; October-March)

Admission Requirements: Graduation from high school or equivalent, or foreign equivalent, and entrance examination

Main Language(s) of Instruction: Japanese

International Co-operation: With universities in the Republic of Korea, China and Australia

Degrees and Diplomas: *Gakushi*: 4 yrs; *Gakushi*: Dentistry (Shigaku); Medicine (Igaku); Veterinary Medicine, 6 yrs; *Shushi*: a further 2 yrs; *Hakase*: 3 yrs following Shushi; *Hakase*: Dental Science; Medical Sciences; Veterinary Medicine, a further 4 yrs

Student Services: Academic counselling, Canteen, Employment services, Foreign student adviser, Foreign Studies Centre, Health services, Language programs, Nursery care, Social counselling, Sports facilities

Student Residential Facilities: For students and Foreign Researchers

Libraries: Central Library; Faculty of Medicine; Faculty of Fisheries: 1,289,686 vols

Last Updated: 09/01/09

KAMAKURA WOMEN'S UNIVERSITY

Kamakura Joshi Daigaku

6-1-3 Ofuna, Kamakura-shi, Kanagawa 247-8512
Tel: +81(467) 44-2111
Fax: +81(467) 44-7131
Website: http://www.kamakura-u.ac.jp

Programmes
Home Economics (Home Economics)

History: Founded 1943. Acquired present title 1959.

Degrees and Diplomas: *Gakushi*

Last Updated: 09/01/09

KANAGAWA DENTAL COLLEGE

Kanagawa Shika Daigaku

82 Inaoka-cho, Yokusuka-shi, Kanagawa 238-8580
Tel: +81(46) 825-1500
Fax: +81(46) 822-8801
EMail: nyushi@kdcnet.ac.jp
Website: http://www.kdcnet.ac.jp

Programmes
Dentistry (Dentistry)

History: Founded 1964.

Academic Year: April to March (April-July; September-December; January-February)

Admission Requirements: Graduation from high school or equivalent, and entrance examination

Main Language(s) of Instruction: Japanese

Degrees and Diplomas: *Gakushi*: 6 yrs; *Hakase*

Student Services: Sports facilities

Student Residential Facilities: Yes

Libraries: 131,936 vols

Publications: Kanagawa Shigaku

Last Updated: 09/01/09

KANAGAWA INSTITUTE OF TECHNOLOGY

Kanagawa Koka Daigaku (KAIT)

1030 Shimo-ogino, Atsugi-shi, Kanagawa 243-0292
Tel: +81(46) 291-3313
Fax: +81(46) 291-3314
EMail: ic@kait.jp
Website: http://www.kait.jp

Departments
Applied Chemistry (Analytical Chemistry; Applied Chemistry; Biochemistry; Bioengineering; Chemical Engineering; Environmental Engineering; Industrial Chemistry; Inorganic Chemistry; Organic Chemistry); **Electrical and Electronic Engineering** (Electrical and Electronic Engineering; Microelectronics; Optical Technology; Sound Engineering (Acoustics); Telecommunications Engineering); **Information and Computer Science** (Artificial Intelligence; Computer Engineering; Computer Science; Optical Technology; Software Engineering); **Mechanical Engineering** (Energy Engineering; Industrial Engineering; Materials Engineering; Measurement and Precision Engineering; Mechanical Engineering); **Network Engineering** (Computer Networks; Software Engineering; Telecommunications Engineering); **Systems Design Engineering** (Automation and Control Engineering; Automotive Engineering; Industrial Design; Safety Engineering); **Welfare Systems Engineering** (Artificial Intelligence; Automation and Control Engineering; Welfare and Protective Services)

History: Founded 1975 as Ikutoku Technical University. Acquired present title 1988.

Academic Year: April to March (April-September; October-March)

Admission Requirements: Graduation from high school

Main Language(s) of Instruction: Japanese

Degrees and Diplomas: *Gakushi*: 4 yrs; *Shushi*: a further 2 yrs; *Hakase*: 3 yrs following Shushi

Student Services: Canteen, Employment services, Foreign Studies Centre, Health services, Social counselling, Sports facilities

Libraries: c. 200,000 vols

Publications: Research Reports, Part A, Humanities and Social Sciences; Part B, Science and Technology *(annually)*

Last Updated: 09/01/09

KANAGAWA UNIVERSITY

Kanagawa Daigaku (KU)

3-27-1 Rokkakubashi, Kanagawa-ku, Yokohama-shi, Kanagawa 221-8686
Tel: +81(45) 481-5661
Fax: +81(45) 491-7915
EMail: kohou-web@kanagawa-u.ac.jp
Website: http://www.kanagawa-u.ac.jp

Faculties
Business Administration *(Also Graduate School)* (Business Administration; International Business; International Economics; Management); **Economics** *(Also Graduate School and Evening Division)* (Business and Commerce; Economics; International Business); **Engineering** *(Also Graduate School and Evening Division)* (Applied Chemistry; Architecture; Electrical Engineering; Industrial Engineering; Industrial Management; Mechanical Engineering); **Foreign Languages** *(Also Graduate School)* (Chinese; English; Modern Languages; Spanish); **Human Sciences**; **Law** *(Also Graduate School and Evening Division)* (Government; Law); **Science** *(Also Graduate School)* (Biological and Life Sciences; Information Sciences; Materials Engineering)

Graduate Schools
History and Folklore Studies (Folklore; History)

Institutes
Economics and Foreign Trade (Economics; International Business); **Humanities Research** (Arts and Humanities); **International Business and Management** (International Business; Management); **Legal Studies** (Law); **Study of Japanese Folk Culture** (Cultural Studies; Folklore; History; Japanese); **Technological Research** (Technology)

Research Institutes
Integrated Science Research (Mathematics and Computer Science)

History: Founded 1928. Acquired present status and title 1949.

Academic Year: April to March (April-September; October-March)

Admission Requirements: Graduation from high school or equivalent, and entrance examination

Main Language(s) of Instruction: Japanese

International Co-operation: With universities in China, USA, Canada, United Kingdom, Thailand, Germany.

Degrees and Diplomas: *Gakushi*: Business Administration; Economics; Engineering; Law; Literature; Public Administration; Science; Trade, 4 yrs; *Shushi*: Business Administration; Economics; Engineering; Historical and Folklore Studies; Law; Literature; Science, a further 2 yrs; *Hakase*: Business Administration; Economics; Engineering; History and Folklore Studies; Law; Literature; Science, 3 yrs following Shushi

Student Services: Academic counselling, Employment services, Foreign student adviser, Health services, Social counselling, Sports facilities

Student Residential Facilities: Yes

Libraries: c. 960,000 vols.

Publications: Jinmon Kenkyu (Studies in Humanities); Kanagawa Daigaku Hyoron (Kanagawa University Review); Kanagawa Daigaku Jomin Bunka Shosho (Study of Japanese Folk Culture Series); Kanagawa Hogaku (Review of Law and Politics); Keizai-Boeki-Kenkyu (Studies in Economics and Trades); Kenkyu Nenpo (Annual Report); Kogaku Kenkyusho Shoho (Science Reports of Research Institute for Engineering; Kokusai Keiei Ronshu (International Business Administration Series); Shokei Ronso (Review of Economics and Commerce)

Last Updated: 09/01/09

KANAGAWA UNIVERSITY OF HUMAN SERVICES

Kanagawa Kenritsu Hoken Fukushi Daigaku

1-10-1 Heiseicho, Yokosuka-shi, Kanagawa 238-8522

Tel: +82(46) 828-2500

Fax: +82(46) 828-2501

EMail: info@kuhs.ac.jp

Website: http://www.kuhs.ac.jp

Programmes

Food Science *(Also graduate programme)*; **Medicine** *(Also graduate programme)* (Medicine; Occupational Therapy; Physical Therapy); **Nursing** *(Also graduate programme)* (Nursing); **Social Welfare** *(Also graduate programme)*

History: Founded 2003.

Degrees and Diplomas: *Gakushi*; *Shushi*

Last Updated: 09/01/09

KANAZAWA COLLEGE OF ART

Kanazawa Bijutsu Kougei Daigaku

5-11-1 Kodatsuno, Kanazawa-shi, Ishikawa 920-8656

Tel: +81(76) 262-3531

Fax: +81(76) 262-6594

EMail: admin@kanazawa-bidai.ac.jp

Website: http://www.kanazawa-bidai.ac.jp

Faculties

Art (Aesthetics; Art History; Ceramic Art; Crafts and Trades; Design; Fine Arts; Industrial Design; Metal Techniques; Painting and Drawing; Sculpture; Visual Arts)

Research Institutes

Art (Art History; Fine Arts; Metal Techniques; Painting and Drawing)

History: Founded 1946 as Senmon Gakko, became Junior College 1950, acquired present status 1955.

Governing Bodies: Kyojukai (Faculty Council)

Academic Year: April to March (April-September; October-March)

Admission Requirements: Graduation from high school or foreign equivalent, and entrance examination

Main Language(s) of Instruction: Japanese

Degrees and Diplomas: *Gakushi*: Arts (Bungakushi), 4 yrs; *Shushi*: Arts (Bungakushushi), a further 2 yrs; *Hakase*: Arts (Bungakuhakushi), 3 yrs following Shushi

Student Services: Academic counselling, Employment services, Health services, Social counselling, Sports facilities

Libraries: c. 93,200 vols

Publications: Kanazawa Bijutsu Kogei Daigaku Gakuho (Bulletin) *(annually)*

Last Updated: 09/01/09

KANAZAWA GAKUIN UNIVERSITY

Kanazawa Gakuin Daigaku

10 Sue-machi, Kanazawa-shi, Ishikawa 920-1392

Tel: +81(762) 229-1181

Fax: +81(762) 229-1352

EMail: nyushi@kanazawa-gu.ac.jp

Website: http://www.kanazawa-gu.ac.jp

President: Hiroto Ishida

Graduate Schools

Humanities

Programmes

Business Administration and Information Sciences *(Also graduate school)* (Business Administration; Computer Networks; E-Business/Commerce; Information Sciences); **Fine Arts and Informatics** (Cultural Studies; Design; Fine Arts; Handicrafts; Heritage Preservation; Information Sciences); **Literature** (Cultural Studies; Japanese; Literature)

History: Founded 1987.

Degrees and Diplomas: *Gakushi*; *Shushi*; *Hakase*

Last Updated: 12/01/09

KANAZAWA INSTITUTE OF TECHNOLOGY

Kanazawa Kogyo Daigaku (KIT)

7-1 Ohgigaoka, Nonoichi-machi, Ishikawa 921-8501

Tel: +81(76) 294-6725

Fax: +81(76) 294-6718

EMail: skomori@neptune.kanazawa-it.ac.jp

Website: http://www.kanazawa-it.ac.jp

President: Ken-ichi Ishikawa (1994-)
Tel: +81(76) 248-1100
EMail: ishikawa@neptune.kanazawa-it.ac.jp

Managing Director: Yoshio Izumiya
EMail: frogs@neptune.kanazawa-it.ac.jp

International Relations: Jun Fudano, Director, Office of International Programmes
Tel: +81(76) 294-6725, Fax: +81(76) 294-6718
EMail: fudanoj1@neptune.kanazawa-it.ac.jp

Colleges

Bioscience and Chemistry; **Engineering**; **Environmental Engineering and Architecture**; **Information Science and Human Communication**

Divisions

Architecture *(College of Environmental Engineering and Architecture)* (Architectural and Environmental Design; Architecture; Structural Architecture) *Professor*: Toshihide Mori; **Bioscience and Chemistry** *(College of Bioscience and Chemistry)* *Professor*: Eiji Kusano; **Electrical Engineering** *(College of Engineering)* (Electrical and Electronic Engineering; Information Technology; Telecommunications Engineering) *Professor*: Ryoichi Hanaoka; **Environmental Engineering** *(College of Environmental Engineering and Architecture)* (Civil Engineering; Environmental Engineering) *Professor*: Ippei Nakamura; **Informatics, Science and Human Communications** *(College of Information Science and Human Communication)* (Computer Science; Management Systems; Media Studies) *Professor*: Toshiyuki Yamamoto; **Information and Computer Science** *(College of Information Science and Human Communication)* (Computer Science; Information Sciences) *Professor*: Nobuo Tsuda; **Mechanical Engineering** *(College of Engineering)* (Aeronautical and Aerospace Engineering; Mechanical Engineering; Robotics) *Professor*: Zenjiro Yajima

Graduate Schools

Engineering (Engineering); **Psychology** (Psychology)

Programmes

Architecture *(Graduate School of Engineering)* (Architecture; Structural Architecture) *Professor*: Toshihide Mori; **Bioscience and Appllied Chemistry** *(Graduate School of Engineering)* (Applied Chemistry; Biological and Life Sciences) *Professor*: Eiji Kusano; **Business Architecture** *(Graduate School of Engineering)* (Architecture) *Professor*: Akinori Tsuchiya; **Civil and Environmental Engineering** *(Graduate School of Engineering)* (Civil Engineering; Environmental Engineering) *Professor*: Ippei Nakamura; **Clinical Psychology** *(Graduate School of Psychology)* (Clinical Psychology) *Professor*: Haruo Tada; **Electrical and Electronic Engineering** *(Graduate School of Engineering) Professor*: Ryoichi Hanaoka; **English Language** *(Academic Fondations Programme)* (English) *Professor*: Braksdale Lewis; **Humanities and Social Sciences** *(Academic Fondations Programme)* (Arts and Humanities; Social Sciences) *Professor*: Motohiro Fujimoto; **Information and Computer Engineering** *(Graduate School of Engineering) Professor*: Nobuo Tsuda; **Liberal Arts and Professional Development** *(Graduate School of Engineering)* (Arts and Humanities) *Professor*: Jun Fudano; **Mathematics and Science for Engineering** *(Academic Fondations Programme)* (Engineering; Mathematics) *Professor*: Katsuhiko Aoki; **Mechanical Engineering** *(Graduate School of Engineering)* (Mechanical Engineering) *Professor*: Zenjiro Yajima; **Practical Engineering Education** *(Academic Fondations Programme)* (Engineering) *Professor*: Eiichi Sentoku; **Synthesized Engineering** *(Graduate School of Engineering)* (Engineering) *Professor*: Osamu Ueda; **System Design Engineering** *(Graduate School of Engineering)* (Computer Engineering) *Professor*: Hideo Jingu; **Systems for Intellectual Creation** *(Graduate School of Engineering) Professor*: Koichiro Kato

Research Laboratories

Advanced Materials Processing *Professor*: Kazuhiro Shintani; **Advanced Materials Science Research and Development** *Professor*: Hidehito Nanto; **Advanced Optical Electromagnetic Field Science** (Optical Technology; Optics) *Professor*: Ryoichi Hanaoka; **Affective Design Engineering** *Professor*: Hideo Jingu; **Applied Electronics** *Professor*: Hisashi Kato; **Applied Ethics Center for Engineering and Science**; **Architectural Archives** *Professor*: Kakugyo Chiku; **Disaster and Environment Science** (Environmental Management; Environmental Studies) *Professor*: Hideo Takabatake; **Environmental Research** *(Institute)* (Environmental Studies) *Professor*: Yu Komatsu; **Future Design** *Professor*: Brown Azby; **Future Machine Technology** (Technology) *Professor*: Nobuaki Kobayashi; **Genome Biotechnology** (Biotechnology; Genetics) *Professor*: Shinichi Ohashi; **Human Information Systems** *Professor*: Tetsuo Kawahara; **Information Technological Frontier** (Information Technology) *Professor*: Hiroshi Nagase; **Integrated Technological Systems** *Professor*: Isao Kimpara; **Intellectual Creation and Management** *Professor*: Yuji Tanahashi; **Intellectual Property Science** *Professor*: Kazunari Sugimitsu; **Internet Technology Frontier** (Computer Networks) *Professor*: Shinmi Hattori; **Japan Studies** *Professor*: Takafusa Hiraizumi; **Materials Systems** *Professor*: Yasushi Miyano; **Media Informatics** *Professor*: Takashi Kusaka; **Optoelectronic Device System** *(R&D Centre) Professor*: Tadatsugu Minami; **Psychological Sciences** (Psychology) *Professor*: Toru Shiotani; **Regional Planning** (Regional Planning) *Professor*: Ichiro Mizuno; **Social and Industrial Management Systems** (Management Systems) *Professor*: Kazuyoshi Ishii; **Telecommunications Technology** (Telecommunications Engineering) *Professor*: Shin-ichi Betsudan

Further Information: Also KIT/MIT, KIT/UMD joint research laboratories and KIT/Macquarie University Brain Science research laboratory

History: Founded 1965. Graduate School established 1978.

Governing Bodies: Board of Directors

Academic Year: April to March

Admission Requirements: Graduation from high school and entrance examination

Fees: (Yen): c. 1.4m. per annum

Main Language(s) of Instruction: Japanese

Degrees and Diplomas: *Gakushi*: Engineering; Information Science; Science and Engineering, 4 yrs; *Shushi*: Engineering; Information Science; Science and Engineering, a further 2 yrs; *Hakase*: Engineering; Information Science; Science and Engineering (Kogakuhakushi), 3 yrs following Shushi

Student Services: Academic counselling, Canteen, Cultural centre, Employment services, Foreign student adviser, Handicapped facilities, Health services, Language programs, Nursery care, Social counselling, Sports facilities

Special Facilities: Yumekobo; Multimedia Workshop; Sakai Memorial Hall

Libraries: c. 417,000 vols; he Dawn of Science and Technology (Rare Books Collection); Popular Music Collection, c. 200,000 vols

Publications: KIT Progress, Research developments and achievements *(1-2 per annum)*

Press or Publishing House: Kanazawa Institute of Technology Press (KIT Press)

Student Numbers *2012-2013*: Total 7,197

Last Updated: 25/02/13

KANAZAWA MEDICAL UNIVERSITY

Kanazawa Ika Daigaku (KMU)

1-1 Daigaku, Uchinada-machi, Kahoku-gun, Ishikawa 920-0293

Tel: +81(76) 286-2211

Fax: +81(76) 286-2373

EMail: kouryu-c@kanazawa-med.ac.jp

Website: http://www.kanazawa-med.ac.jp

President: Yuishi Yamada

Institutes

Medical Research (Cell Biology; Genetics; Medicine; Molecular Biology; Virology)

Schools

Medicine (Medicine); **Nursing**

Further Information: University Hospital

History: Founded 1972. Graduate School established 1984.

Governing Bodies: Board of Directors

Academic Year: April to March

Admission Requirements: Graduation from high school and entrance examination

Fees: (Yen): c. 6,000,000 per annum

Main Language(s) of Instruction: Japanese

Degrees and Diplomas: *Gakushi*: Medicine (M.D.), 6 yrs; *Hakase*: Medical Sciences (Ph.D.), a further 4 yrs

Student Services: Academic counselling, Canteen, Health services, Social counselling, Sports facilities

Student Residential Facilities: Yes

Special Facilities: University Hospital, 938 beds

Libraries: Central Library, c. 200,000 vols

Publications: Journal of Kanazawa Medical University *(quarterly)*

Press or Publishing House: Kanazawa Medical University Press

Last Updated: 12/01/09

KANAZAWA SEIRYO UNIVERSITY

Kanazawa Seiryo Daigaku

101 Ushi, Gosho-machi, Kanazawa-shi, Ishikawa 920-8620

Tel: +81(76) 353-3924

Fax: +81(76) 353-3995

EMail: skokusai@kanazawa-eco.ac.jp

Website: http://www.kanazawa-eco.ac.jp

Departments

Business Communication (Business and Commerce; Cultural Studies; Economics; Information Technology; International Business; International Law; Management; Modern Languages); **Economics** (Economics)

History: Founded 1967 as Kanazawa College of Economics.

Degrees and Diplomas: *Gakushi*

Libraries: 3 libraries, total, c. 108,000 vols

Last Updated: 12/01/09

KANAZAWA UNIVERSITY

Kanazawa Daigaku
Kakuma-machi, Kanazawa, Ishikawa 920-1192
Tel: +81(76) 264-5111
Fax: +81(76) 234-4010
EMail: now@kanazawa-u.ac.jp
Website: http://www.kanazawa-u.ac.jp

President: Shin-ichi Nakamura (2008-2014)
Tel: +81(76) 264-6196, Fax: +81(76) 234-4014
EMail: hisyo@adm.kanazawa-u.ac.jp

International Relations: Kazuo Miyasaka, Deputy Director of Global Affairs Support Office (2010-)
Tel: +81(76) 264-5244, Fax: +81(76) 234-4043
EMail: kokukou@adm.kanazawa-u.ac.jp

Centres

Advanced Science Research (Natural Sciences) *Director*: Hirofumi Mori; **Environment Preservation** *Director*: Hiroyuki Nakamura; **Health Service** (Health Sciences) *Director*: Mitsuru Furukawa; **Higher Education Research** *Director*: Toru Aono; **Information Media** (Media Studies) *Director*: Masayoshi Iwahara; **Innovation** *Director*: Nobuo Yoshikuni; **International Student** (International Studies) *Director*: Masaru Kitaura; **Regional Collaboration** (Regional Studies) *Director*: Takashi Nakanishi

Colleges

Human and Social Sciences (Arts and Humanities; Development Studies; Economics; International Studies; Law; Regional Studies; Social Sciences; Teacher Training) *Dean*: Kazuo Katagiri; **Medical, Pharmaceutical and Health Sciences** *Dean*: Hiroshi Yamamoto; **Science and Engineering** *Dean*: Shintaro Nakao

Graduate Schools

Education (Art Education; Education; Education of the Handicapped; English; Foreign Languages Education; Health Education; Home Economics Education; Humanities and Social Science Education; Japanese; Mathematics Education; Music Education; Native Language Education; Physical Education; Science Education; Technology Education) *Dean*: Hideaki Ookubo; **Human and Socio-Environment Studies** (Arts and Humanities; Social Sciences; Social Studies; Sociology) *Dean*: Hideo Inoue; **Law** (Law) *Director*: Shigeki Ojima; **Medical Science** (Cardiology; Environmental Studies; Health Sciences; Medicine; Neurosciences; Oncology) *Dean*: Yasuni Nakanuma; **Natural Science and Technology** (Biological and Life Sciences; Biology; Chemistry; Civil Engineering; Computer Engineering; Computer Science; Earth Sciences; Electrical Engineering; Environmental Engineering; Environmental Studies; Health Sciences; Materials Engineering; Mathematics; Mechanical Engineering; Mechanics; Natural Sciences; Pharmacy; Physics; Technology) *Dean*: Hajime Ishida

Institutes

Foreign Languages (Modern Languages) *Director*: Takayoshi Yabuchi; **Nature and Environmental Technology** (Environmental Engineering) *Director*: Koji Nakamura

Programmes

Frontier Science *(Organisation)* (Natural Sciences) *Director*: Isamu Nagano

Research Centres

Child Mental Development (Child Care and Development) *Director*: Haruhiro Higashida

Research Institutes

Cancer (Cell Biology; Medicine; Molecular Biology; Oncology) *Director*: Hiroshi Satou

Further Information: Also University Hospital

History: Founded 1949, incorporating four high schools, Ishikawa Normal School, Ishikawa Youth Normal School, Kanazawa Higher Normal School, Kanazawa Medical College, and Kanazawa Technological College.

Governing Bodies: Yakuinkai (Executive Board)

Academic Year: April to March (April-October; October-March)

Admission Requirements: Graduation from high school or equivalent or foreign equivalent, and entrance examination

Fees: (Yen): Tuition, 535,800 per annum

Main Language(s) of Instruction: Japanese

International Co-operation: With universities in China; India; Republic of Korea; Taiwan; Thailand; Indonesia; Egypt; Australia; Czech Republic; Finland; France; Germany; Ireland; Poland; Russian Federation; Slovak Republic; United Kingdom and USA

Degrees and Diplomas: *Gakushi*: 4 yrs; *Gakushi*: Pharmacy; Medicine (Igakushi), 6 yrs; *Shushi*: a further 2 yrs; *Hakase*: 3 yrs; *Hakase*: Neuroscience; Cancer Medicine; Cardiovascular Medicine; Environmental Science, 4 yrs. The Law Graduate School also offers a Homu-Hakase (Senmonshoku) diploma in 3 yrs.

Student Services: Academic counselling, Canteen, Employment services, Foreign student adviser, Foreign Studies Centre, Handicapped facilities, Health services, Language programs, Sports facilities

Student Residential Facilities: Yes

Special Facilities: University Museum

Libraries: Main Library and 3 branch libraries

Publications: Acanthus News *(3 per annum)*; Advanced Scientific Research *(annually)*; Annual Report of Noto Marine Laboratory Institute of Nature and Environmental Technology, Kanazawa University *(annually)*; Annual Report of the Center for Archaeological Research, the University of Kanazawa *(annually)*; Bulletin of the Faculty of Human Sciences, Institute of human and social sciences, Kanazawa University *(annually)*; Cancer Research Institute Report *(3 per annum)*; COM. CLUB *(annually)*; Doctoral Course Bulletin of the Graduate school of Medical Sciences Kanazawa University *(annually)*; Foreign Language Institute Journal *(annually)*; Human and Socio-environmental Studies *(biannually)*; Info. Core Press *(quarterly)*; International Student Center News *(annually)*; International Student Centre Research Bulletin *(annually)*; Journal of the Juzen Medical Society, Doctoral Course Bulletin of the Graduate school of Medical Sciences Kanazawa University *(quarterly)*; Kanazawa Law Review *(annually)*; Kanazawa University Data *(annually)*; Kanazawa University Economic Review *(biannually)*; Kanazawa University Museum Newsletter *(biannually)*; Outline of Kanazawa University *(annually)*; Outline of Kanazawa University Library *(biennially)*; Studies and Essays History and Archaeology; Studies and Essays Language and Literature *(annually)*

Last Updated: 28/03/12

KANDA UNIVERSITY OF INTERNATIONAL STUDIES

Kanda Gaigo Daigaku (KUIS)
1-4-1 Wakaba, Mihama-ku, Chiba-shi, Chiba 261-0014
Tel: +81(43) 273-1320
Fax: +81(43) 273-1197
EMail: japanese@kanda.kuis.ac.jp; prdept@kanda.kuis.ac.jp
Website: http://www.kandagaigo.ac.jp/kuis/

Departments

Chinese (Chinese; Modern Languages; Oriental Languages) *Professor*: Keiichi Tsukamoto; **English** (English; European Languages; Modern Languages) *Professor*: Yasushi Sekiya; **International Communication** (Communication Studies) *Professor*: Kazuei Tokado; **Korean** (Korean; Modern Languages; Oriental Languages) *Professor*: Noboru Hamanaka; **Languages and Culture** (Business Administration; Cultural Studies; Modern Languages) *Professor*: Hiroshi Nagai; **Spanish** (European Languages; Modern Languages; Spanish) *Professor*: Koichiro Yaginuma

Faculties

Foreign Languages (Modern Languages)

Graduate Schools

Language Science (Linguistics; Pedagogy) *Professor*: Takeo Saito

Institutes

Intercultural Communication (Communication Studies; Cultural Studies); **Japanese Studies** (Japanese; Linguistics; Oriental Languages; Pedagogy); **Language Research and Education** (Linguistics; Modern Languages; Pedagogy)

Programmes

Japanese Language and Culture (Cultural Studies; Japanese) *Assistant Professor*: S.K Fan

History: Founded 1987.

Governing Bodies: Sano Educational Foundation

Academic Year: April to January (April-July; September-January)

Admission Requirements: Graduation from High School

Fees: (Yen): Registration, 250,000; tuition, 890,000

Main Language(s) of Instruction: Japanese, English, Chinese, Spanish

International Co-operation: With universities in China, Republic of Korea and USA. Also participates in UMAP Programme

Accrediting Agencies: Ministry of Education, Culture, Sports, Science and Technology

Degrees and Diplomas: *Gakushi*: Chinese; English; International Communication; Korean; Languages and Culture; Spanish, 4 yrs; *Shushi*: English Linguistics and Pedagogy; Japanese Linguistics and Pedagogy, a further 2 yrs; *Hakase*: Language Science, 3 yrs following Shushi

Student Services: Academic counselling, Canteen, Cultural centre, Employment services, Foreign student adviser, Health services, Language programs, Social counselling, Sports facilities

Student Residential Facilities: For women

Libraries: c. 100,000 vols

Publications: Intercultural Communications *(annually)*; Kotoba to Bunka (Language and Culture); Studies in Linguistics and Language Teaching *(annually)*

Last Updated: 12/01/09

KANSAI GAIDAI UNIVERSITY

Kansai Gaikokugo Daigaku

16-1 Nakamiyahigashino-cho, Hirakata-shi, Osaka 573-1001
Tel: +81(72) 856-1721
Fax: +81(72) 855-5552
EMail: inquiry@kansaigaidai.ac.jp
Website: http://www.kansaigaidai.ac.jp

President: Sadato Tanimoto

Programmes

Business Administration (Business Administration); **Fine Arts** (Business Administration; Ceramic Art; Fine Arts; Painting and Drawing); **Religion** (Religion); **Social Sciences, Arts and Humanities** (Asian Studies; Cultural Studies; Economics; English; History; International Relations; Japanese; Literature; Oriental Languages; Political Sciences; Spanish)

Further Information: Also junior college. Japanese language courses for foreign students

History: Founded 1945.

Academic Year: September to June (September-December; January-March; March-June)

International Co-operation: With universities in USA, Australia and Canada

Degrees and Diplomas: *Gakushi*; *Shushi*; *Hakase*

Student Services: Academic counselling, Foreign Studies Centre, Health services, Sports facilities

Student Residential Facilities: For foreign students

Libraries: 411,225 vols

KANSAI MEDICAL UNIVERSITY

Kansai Ika Daigaku

10-15 Fumizono-cho, Moriguchi-shi, Osaka 570-8506
Tel: +81(6) 992-1001
Fax: +81(6) 992-1409
EMail: gakumu@takii.kmu.ac.jp
Website: http://www.kmu.ac.jp

Colleges

Nursing (Nursing)

Faculties

Medicine (Medicine)

Graduate Schools

Medicine (Medicine)

Further Information: Also 4 Teaching Hospitals

History: Founded 1928 as Osaka Women's Medical School, became Osaka Women's Medical College 1947, and Kansai Medical School 1954 (co-educational).

Governing Bodies: Board of Trustees

Academic Year: April to March (April-August; September-December; January-March)

Admission Requirements: Graduation from high school or equivalent, and entrance examination

Main Language(s) of Instruction: Japanese

Degrees and Diplomas: *Gakushi*: Medicine, 6 yrs; *Hakase*: Medicine, a further 4 yrs

Student Services: Canteen, Health services, Sports facilities

Student Residential Facilities: For c. 800 students

Libraries: 159,660 vols

Publications: Kansai Medical University Journal

Last Updated: 12/01/09

KANSAI UNIVERSITY

Kansai Daigaku

3-3-35 Yamate-cho, Suita-shi, Osaka 564-8680
Tel: +81(6) 6368-1121
Fax: +81(6) 6330-3027
EMail: kokusai@jm.kansai-u.ac.jp
Website: http://www.kansai-u.ac.jp

President: Harushige Kusumi

Vice-President (Academic Affairs): Yasuhisa ICHIHARA Ichihara

Faculties

Commerce (Business and Commerce; Finance) *Dean*: Mikiyoshi Hirose; **Economics** (Economics) *Dean*: Katsuhiko Kitagawa; **Engineering** *Dean*: Tetsuaki Tsuchido; **Informatics** (Computer Science) *Dean*: Shin'ichi Kitani; **Law** (Law) *Dean*: Yasuhisa Ichihara; **Letters** (German) *Dean*: Jun Oku; **Policy Studies** *Dean*: Nobuo Kochu; **Sociology** (Industrial and Organizational Psychology) *Dean*: Isamu Kuroda

Institutes

Economic and Political Studies (Economics; Political Sciences) *Director*: Shouichi Hashimoto; **Foreign Language Education and Research** *Director*: Taichi Usami; **Human Rights Studies** (Human Rights) *Director*: Yoshikazu Tanaka; **Legal Studies** (Law; Political Sciences) *Director*: Nobuo Kochu; **Organization for Research and Development of Innovative Science and Technology** (Engineering; Technology) *Director*: Kenkichi Ohba; **Oriental and Occidental Studies** (History) *Director*: Seiji Hashimoto

Schools

Accountancy *Director*: Kenji Shiba; **Law** (Law) *Director*: Kei'ichi Yamanaka

Further Information: All Faculties have attached graduate schools

History: Founded 1886 as Kansai Law School, became Kansai University 1905. Acquired present status 1948.

Governing Bodies: Board of Trustees

Academic Year: April to March (April-September; October-March)

Admission Requirements: Graduation from high school or equivalent, and entrance examination

Fees: (Yen): Registration, 260,000; tuition, 670,000 per annum

Main Language(s) of Instruction: Japanese

Degrees and Diplomas: *Gakushi*: Commerce (Shogaku); Computer Science (Johogaku); Economics (Keizaigaku); Engineering (Kogaku); Law (Hogaku); Letters (Bungaku); Sociology (Shakaigaku), 4 yrs; *Shushi*: Commerce (Shogaku); Computer Science (Johogaku); Economics (Keizaigaku); Engineering (Kogaku); Foreign Languages Education (Gaikokugo Kyoikugaku); Law (Hogaku); Letters (Bungaku); Sociology (Shakaigaku), a further 2 yrs; *Hakase*: Commerce (Shogaku); Economics (Keizaigaku); Engineering (Kogaku); Law (Hogaku); Letters (Bungaku); Sociology (Shakaigaku), at least 3 yrs following Shushi; *Hakase*: Computer Science (Johogaku)

Student Services: Academic counselling, Canteen, Employment services, Foreign student adviser, Foreign Studies Centre, Handicapped facilities, Health services, Language programs, Nursery care, Social counselling, Sports facilities

Student Residential Facilities: For 283 students

Special Facilities: Museum. Information Technology Centre. Extension Reed Centre.

Libraries: University Library, c. 2.02 m. vols

Publications: Bungaku Ronshu, Essays and Studies by members of Faculty of Letters; Gien, Industrial Technology; Hogaku Kenkyusho Kenkyu Shoho *(annually)*; Hogaku Ronshu, Law Review *(bimonthly)*; Johokenkyu, Informatics Research *(quarterly)*; Keizai Ronshu, Economic Review *(bimonthly)*; Keizai-Seiji Kenkyusho Kenkyu Shoho, Economic and Political Studies; Kogaku Kenkyu Hokoku, Technology Reports; Kogaku to Gijutsu, Engineering and Technology; Review of Business and Commerce *(annually)*; Review of Economics *(annually)*; Review of Law and Politics *(annually)*; Shakaigaku Kiyo, Journal of Sociological Research; Shogaku Ronshu, Business Review; Tozaigakujutsu Kenkyusho Kiyo, Bulletin of Institute of Oriental and Occidental Studies *(annually)*

Press or Publishing House: University Press

Last Updated: 25/03/11

KANSAI UNIVERSITY OF INTERNATIONAL STUDIES

Kansai Kokusai Daigaku

1-18 Aoyama, Shijimicho, Miki-shi, Hyogo 673-0521

Tel: +81(794) 84-3505

Fax: +81(794) 84-3562

EMail: iec@kuins.ac.jp

Website: http://www.kuins.ac.jp

Faculties

Business Management (Administration; Business Administration; Management); **Humanities** (Arts and Humanities; Asian Studies; Behavioural Sciences; Chinese; Communication Studies; English; French; Korean; Pacific Area Studies; Thai Languages)

History: Founded 1998.

Degrees and Diplomas: *Gakushi*

Libraries: Yes.

Last Updated: 12/01/09

KANSAI UNIVERSITY OF SOCIAL WELFARE

Kansai Fukushi Daigaku

380-3 Shinden, Ako-shi, Hyogo 678-0255

Tel: +81(791) 462-525

Fax: +81(791) 462-526

EMail: kusw-info@kusw.ac.jp

Website: http://www.kusw.ac.jp

Programmes

Social Welfare (Social Welfare; Social Work)

History: Founded 1997.

Degrees and Diplomas: *Gakushi*

Last Updated: 12/01/09

KANTO GAKUEN UNIVERSITY

Kanto Gakuen Daigaku

200 Fujiagu-cho, Ota-shi, Gunma-ken 373-8515

Tel: +81(276) 32-7800

Fax: +81(276) 31-2708

EMail: kohouniv@kanto-gakuen.ac.jp

Website: http://www.kanto-gakuen.ac.jp

President: Kazumi Yamano (2000-)

Secretary-General: Kazuhisa Shimozu

International Relations: Chowa Takezoe
Tel: +81(276) 32-7905, Fax: +81(276) 32-3382
EMail: cyowa_takezoe@kanto-gakuen.ac.jp

Departments

Economics (Business Administration; Economics) *Dean*: Sumio Hyugaji; **Law** (Law) *Dean*: Yoshitada Kawauchi

Graduate Schools

Economics *(Master)* (Economics) *Dean*: Sumio Hyugaji; **Law** *(Master)* (Law) *Dean*: Yoshitada Kawauchi

History: Founded 1976 as Department of Economics, added Graduate School of Business Administration and Economics 1981. Added Department of Law 1990 and Graduate School of Law 1994.

Governing Bodies: Gakkohoujin Kanto Gakuen

Academic Year: April to March (April-September; September-March)

Admission Requirements: Graduation from High School or equivalent and entrance examination

Fees: (Yen): Registration, 614,000; tuition, 665,000 per annum

Main Language(s) of Instruction: Japanese

Degrees and Diplomas: *Gakushi*: Business Administration; Economics; Law, 4 yrs; *Shushi*: Economics; Law, a further 2 yrs

Student Services: Academic counselling, Canteen, Employment services, Health services, Language programs, Sports facilities

Special Facilities: Malthus Papers Museum

Libraries: c. 217,000 vols

Publications: Journal of Economics *(annually)*; Journal of Law *(biannually)*; Journal of Liberal Arts *(annually)*

KANTO GAKUIN UNIVERSITY

Kanto Gakuin Daigaku

4834 Mutsuura-cho, Kanazawa-ku, Yokohama-shi, Kanagawa 236-8501

Tel: +81(45) 786-7015

Fax: +81(45) 786-7043

EMail: intlcent@kanto-gakuin.ac.jp

Website: http://www.kanto-gakuin.ac.jp

Colleges

Economics (Business Administration; Economics); **Engineering** (Architecture; Civil Engineering; Electrical and Electronic Engineering; Engineering; Environmental Engineering; Industrial Chemistry; Mechanical Engineering); **Humanities** (Arts and Humanities; English; Literature; Sociology); **Law** (Law; Political Sciences)

Institutes

Architectural and Environmental Engineering *(Osawa Memorial)* (Architecture; Environmental Engineering; Structural Architecture); **Cultural Science** (Cultural Studies); **Economics and Business Administration** *(Graduate)* (Business Administration; Economics); **Engineering** *(Graduate)* (Architecture; Civil Engineering; Electrical Engineering; Engineering; Industrial Chemistry; Mechanical Engineering); **Humanities** *(Graduate)* (Arts and Humanities; English; Sociology); **Japanese Protestant History** (Religious Studies); **Law** *(Graduate)* (Law; Political Sciences); **Legal Research** (Law); **Technology** (Technology)

Schools

Engineering (Architecture; Civil Engineering; Electrical Engineering; Engineering; Industrial Chemistry; Mechanical Engineering)

Further Information: Also English language and Cultural programmes

History: Founded 1949 with Colleges of Engineering and Economics, but tracing the origins to Baptist Theological Seminary 1884.

Governing Bodies: Board of Trustees

Academic Year: April to January (April-July; September-January)

Admission Requirements: Graduation from high school and entrance examination

Main Language(s) of Instruction: Japanese

International Co-operation: With universities in USA and United Kingdom

Degrees and Diplomas: *Gakushi*: 4 yrs; *Shushi*: a further 2 yrs; *Hakase*: 3 yrs following Shushi

Student Services: Academic counselling, Canteen, Employment services, Foreign student adviser, Health services, Language programs, Social counselling, Sports facilities

Libraries: University Library, 1,123,000 vols. Collection of Classical English Economics and Philosophy. Theology Collection

Publications: Bulletin of Kanto Gakuin University *(quarterly)*; Journal of Science and Humanities *(annually)*; Journal of Technological Research (Engineering) *(biannually)*; Jurisconsultus *(annually)*; Kamariya Life and Letters *(annually)*; Memoirs of the Economic Postgraduate Course of Kanto Gakuin University *(annually)*; Poetry Kanto *(annually)*; Quarterly Journal of Economics *(quarterly)*; School of Law; Transactions of the Institute of Humanities *(annually)*
Last Updated: 12/01/09

KAWAMURA GAKUEN WOMEN'S UNIVERSITY

Kawamura Gakuen Joshi Daigaku
1133 Sageto, Abiko-shi, Chiba 270-1138
Tel: +81(4) 7183-0114
Fax: +81(4) 7183-9015
EMail: postmaster@kgwu.ac.jp
Website: http://www.kgwu.ac.jp

Programmes

Cultural Studies (Cultural Studies; Environmental Studies; Japanese; Tourism); **Education** (Education; Information Sciences; Teacher Training); **Liberal Arts** (Arts and Humanities; English; History; Japanese; Linguistics; Literature; Psychology)

History: Founded 1988.

Degrees and Diplomas: *Gakushi*; *Shushi*
Last Updated: 12/01/09

KAWASAKI MEDICAL SCHOOL

Kawasaki Ika Daigaku
577 Matsushima, Kurashiki-shi,
Okayama 701-0192
Tel: +81(86) 462-1111
Fax: +81(86) 464-1019
EMail: gakumu@med.kawasaki-m.ac.jp
Website: http://www.kawasaki-m.ac.jp/med

Programmes

Anatomy (Anatomy); **Biochemistry**; **Medicine** (Medicine); **Physiology** (Physiology)

History: Founded 1970.

Governing Bodies: Board of Trustees

Academic Year: April to March (April-July; September-December; January-March)

Admission Requirements: Graduation from high school and entrance examination

Main Language(s) of Instruction: Japanese

Degrees and Diplomas: *Gakushi*: Medicine, 6 yrs; *Hakase*: Medicine, a further 4 yrs

Student Services: Health services, Language programs, Sports facilities

Student Residential Facilities: Yes

Special Facilities: Gendai-Igakukyoiku Hakubutsu-Ken (Medical Museum)

Libraries: 175,000 vols

Publications: Medical Journal *(quarterly)*
Last Updated: 12/01/09

KAWASAKI UNIVERSITY OF MEDICAL WELFARE

Kawasaki Iryo Fukushi Daigaku
288 Matsushima, Kurashiki-shi,
Okayama 701-0193
Tel: +81(86) 462-1111
Fax: +81(86) 462-1193
EMail: iec@mw.kawasaki-m.ac.jp
Website: http://www.kawasaki-m.ac.jp/mw/

Faculties

Health and Welfare (Health Sciences; Nursing; Psychology; Welfare and Protective Services); **Health and Welfare Services Administration** (Health Administration; Health Sciences; Welfare and Protective Services); **Health Science and Technology** (Health Sciences; Medical Technology; Nutrition; Occupational Therapy; Ophthalmology; Physical Therapy; Rehabilitation and Therapy; Speech Therapy and Audiology; Sports Medicine)

Graduate Schools

Health and Welfare (Health Sciences; Nursing; Psychology; Social Work; Welfare and Protective Services); **Health Science and Technology** (Health Administration; Health Sciences; Nutrition; Rehabilitation and Therapy; Sports Medicine)

History: Founded 1991.

Main Language(s) of Instruction: Japanese

Degrees and Diplomas: *Gakushi*; *Shushi*; *Hakase*

Libraries: 162,993 vols

KEIAI UNIVERSITY

Keiai Daigaku
1-5-21 Anagawa, Chiba-shi, Chiba 263-8588
Tel: +81(43) 284-2486
Fax: +81(43) 284-2558
EMail: nyushi@u-keiai.ac.jp
Website: http://www.u-keiai.ac.jp

Faculties

Economics (Business Administration; Economics)

Schools

International Studies (Environmental Studies; International Relations; International Studies; Political Sciences; Regional Studies)

History: Founded 1966.

Degrees and Diplomas: *Gakushi*
Last Updated: 12/01/09

KEIO UNIVERSITY

Keio Gijuku Daigaku
2-15-45 Mita, Minato-ku, Tokyo 108-8345
Tel: +81(35) 453-4511 +81(35) 427-1541
Fax: +81(35) 427-7640
EMail: m-koho@adst.keio.ac.jp
Website: http://www.keio.ac.jp/index-en.html

President: Atsushi Seike (2009-)
Tel: +81(35) 427-1541, Fax: +81(35) 441-7640
EMail: president@info.keio.ac.jp

International Relations: Naoyuki Agawa, Vice-President, International Collaboration, International Alumni Relations, Strategic Planning (2009) Tel: +81(35) 427-1541, Fax: +81(35) 441-7640

Centres

Arts and Arts Administration (Art Management); **Fukuzawa Memorial Centre for Modern Japanese Studies** *(Fukuzawa Memorial)* (Cultural Studies); **Health** (Health Sciences); **Integrated Medical Research** *(Shinanomachi Campus)* (Medicine); **International Studies** (International Studies); **Japanese Studies** (Japanese); **Laboratory of Science and Technology** *(Yagami Campus)*; **Sports Medicine Research** (Sports Medicine); **Teacher Training** (Teacher Training)

Faculties

Business and Commerce (Business and Commerce); **Economics** (Economics); **Environment and Information Studies** *(Shonan Fujisawa Campus)* (Environmental Studies); **Law** (Law; Political Sciences); **Letters** (Arts and Humanities); **Nursing and Medical Care** *(Shonan Fujisawa Campus)*; **Pharmacy** (Pharmacy); **Policy Management** *(Shonan Fujisawa Campus)* (Leadership); **Science and Technology** *(Yagami Campus)* (Natural Sciences; Technology)

Graduate Schools

Business Administration *(Hiyoshi Campus)* (Business Administration); **Business and Commerce** (Business and Commerce); **Economics** (Economics); **Health Management** *(Shonan Fujisawa Campus)*; **Human Relations**; **Law**; **Letters** (Arts and Humanities); **Media and Governance** *(Shonan Fujisawa Campus)* (Government; Media Studies); **Medicine** *(Shinanomachi Campus)* (Medicine); **Science and Technology** *(Yagami Campus)* (Natural Sciences; Technology)

Institutes
Advanced Biosciences (Biological and Life Sciences); **Cultural and Linguistic Studies** (Cultural Studies; Linguistics); **Digital and Media Content**; **East Asian Studies** (Regional Studies); **Economic Observatory** (Economics; Industrial Management); **Media and Communications Research** (Communication Studies; Media Studies); **Oriental Classics** (Oriental Studies); **Physical Education** *(Hiyoshi Campus)* (Physical Education); **Research Institute at SFC** *(Keio, SFC)*

Research Centres
Foreign Languages Education *(Hiyoshi Campus)* (Foreign Languages Education); **Liberal Arts** *(Hiyoshi Campus)*

Research Institutes
Global Security *(G-SEC)*

Schools
Business *(Hiyoshi Campus)*; **Correspondence Courses** (Arts and Humanities; Economics; Law); **Foreign Languages** (Modern Languages); **Law** (Law); **Medicine** *(Shinanomachi Campus)* (Medicine)

Further Information: Also University Hospital and Rehabilitation Centre

History: Founded 1858 as private School to teach Dutch; became private University 1890. Graduate divisions opened 1906. School of Medicine founded 1917 followed by the opening of University Hospital 1920; Faculty of Engineering (1944); School of Library Science (1951); Business School (1962); Shonan Fujisawa Campus (Faculty of Policy Management and Faculty of Environmental Information opened 1990); Graduate School of Media and Governance (1994); Faculty of Nursing and Medical Care (2001); Law School (2004). Merged with Kyoritsu Yakka Daigaku (Kyoritsu College of Pharmacy) 2008.

Governing Bodies: Board of Councillors; Board of Trustees

Academic Year: April to March (April-July; September-February)

Admission Requirements: Graduation from high school or recognized equivalent, and entrance examination

Main Language(s) of Instruction: Japanese

International Co-operation: With universities in USA; United Kingdom; France; Germany; China; Republic of Korea; Australia; Russian Federation

Degrees and Diplomas: *Gakushi*: Arts; Engineering; Law; Science, 4 yrs; *Gakushi*: Medicine, 6 yrs; *Shushi*: Arts; Business Administration; Law; Media and Governance; Science, a further 2 yrs; *Hakase*: Law (Juris Doctor), a further 2-3 yrs; *Hakase*: Medical Sciences, a further 4 yrs; *Hakase*: Philosophy (PhD), 3 yrs following Shushi

Student Services: Academic counselling, Canteen, Cultural centre, Employment services, Foreign student adviser, Foreign Studies Centre, Handicapped facilities, Health services, Language programs, Social counselling, Sports facilities

Libraries: Mita Media Center ; Hiyoshi Media Center ; Medical Information and Media Center ; Media Center for Science and Technology ; Shonan Fujisawa Campus Media Center. 4,641,695 vols

Publications: Studies, journals and monographs of the various University units

Last Updated: 16/06/09

KEISEN UNIVERSITY

Keisen Jogakuen Daigaku
2-10-1 Minamino, Tama-shi, Tokyo 206-0032
Tel: +81(42) 376-8217
Fax: +81(42) 376-8218
EMail: nyushi@keisen.ac.jp
Website: http://www.keisen.ac.jp/univ/

Faculties
Human and Social Studies *(Also graduate school)* (Environmental Studies; International Studies; Social Studies); **Humanities** *(Also graduate school)* (American Studies; Arts and Humanities; Cultural Studies; English; European Studies; Japanese; Social Studies)

History: Founded 1988.

Degrees and Diplomas: *Gakushi*; *Shushi*

Last Updated: 12/01/09

KEIWA COLLEGE

Keiwa Gakuen Daigaku
1270 Tomizuka, Shibata-shi,
Niigata 957-8585
Tel: +81(254) 26-3636
Fax: +81(254) 26-3646
EMail: nyushi@keiwa-c.ac.jp
Website: http://www.keiwa-c.ac.jp

Programmes
Community and Social Welfare (Social Welfare; Urban Studies); **English Culture and Communication** (Communication Studies; Cultural Studies; English); **International Cultural Studies** (Cultural Studies; International Studies)

History: Founded 1991.

Degrees and Diplomas: *Gakushi*

Last Updated: 12/01/09

KENICHI OHMAE GRADUATE SCHOOL OF BUSINESS

Bijinesu Burekusuru Daigakuin Daigaku
Fujisoft Building 19F, 3 Kanda Neribei-cho,
Chiyoda-ku, Tokyo
Tel: +81(3) 5860-5531
EMail: bbtuniv@ohmae.ac.jp
Website: http://www.ohmae.ac.jp

Dean: Kenichi Ohmae

Departments
Management

History: Founded 2005.

Degrees and Diplomas: *Shushi*

Last Updated: 12/02/09

KIBI INTERNATIONAL UNIVERSITY

Kibi Kokusai Daigaku
8 Iga-machi, Takahashi-shi,
Okayama 716
Tel: +81(866) 22-9189
Fax: +81(866) 22-8133
EMail: koho@kiui.ac.jp; intleaff@kiui.ac.jp
Website: http://kiui.jp/pc/english

President: Kazuhiro Fujita

Schools
Cultural Properties Studies; **Health Sciences** (Health Sciences; Nursing; Occupational Therapy; Physical Therapy); **International Environmental Management**; **Psychology** (Clinical Psychology; Psychology); **Social Studies** (Business Administration; Business and Commerce; International Studies; Social Studies; Sociology); **Social Welfare** (Child Care and Development; Social Welfare)

History: Founded 1990.

Governing Bodies: Takahashi Educational Institution

Academic Year: April to March (April-September; September-March)

Admission Requirements: Graduation from high school or equivalent

Main Language(s) of Instruction: Japanese

International Co-operation: With universities in USA, China and Brazil

Degrees and Diplomas: *Gakushi*: 4 yrs; *Shushi*: a further 2 yrs; *Hakase*: 3 yrs following Shushi

Student Services: Academic counselling, Canteen, Cultural centre, Employment services, Foreign student adviser, Social counselling, Sports facilities

Student Residential Facilities: For c. 650 students

Libraries: 110,000 vols

Last Updated: 12/01/09

KINJO GAKUIN UNIVERSITY

Kinjo Gakuin Daigaku
2-1723 Omori, Moriyama-ku, Nagoya-shi,
Aichi 463-8521
Tel: +81(52) 798-0180
Fax: +81(52) 798-4453
EMail: ciep@kinjo-u.ac.jp
Website: http://www.kinjo-u.ac.jp

Colleges

Contemporary Society and Culture (Cultural Studies; International Studies; Regional Studies; Social Studies; Social Work; Sociology); **Human Life and Environment**; **Human Sciences** (Art Therapy; Child Care and Development; Clinical Psychology; Psychology); **Humanities** (Cultural Studies; English; Japanese; Modern Languages); **Pharmacy** (Pharmacy)

Graduate Schools

Human Ecology (Consumer Studies; Development Studies; Ecology); **Humanities** (English; Japanese; Linguistics; Literature; Sociology)

Further Information: Also Centres for Christianity

History: Founded 1889. Acquired present status and title 1949.

Academic Year: April to January (April-July; September-January)

Admission Requirements: Graduation from high school

Main Language(s) of Instruction: Japanese

International Co-operation: International exchange programmes

Degrees and Diplomas: *Gakushi*: 4 yrs; *Shushi*: a further 1-2 yrs; *Hakase*: 2-3 yrs following Shushi

Student Services: Academic counselling, Canteen, Cultural centre, Employment services, Foreign student adviser, Foreign Studies Centre, Handicapped facilities, Health services, Language programs, Nursery care, Social counselling, Sports facilities

Student Residential Facilities: Yes

Special Facilities: TV Studio. Multimedia

Libraries: 470,200 vols

Publications: Studies in British and American Literature *(annually)*; Studies in Family and Consumer Sciences *(annually)*; Studies in Human Sciences *(annually)*; Studies in Humanities *(annually)*; Studies in Japanese Literature *(annually)*; Studies in Social Sciences *(annually)*

Last Updated: 12/01/09

KINJO UNIVERSITY

Kinjo Daigaku
1200 Kasama-machi, Matto,
Ishikawa 924-8511
Tel: +81(76) 276-4400
Fax: +81(76) 275-4316
EMail: daigaku@kinjo.ac.jp
Website: http://www.kinjo.ac.jp

Faculties

Health Sciences (Health Sciences; Physical Therapy); **Social Work** (Social Welfare; Social Work)

History: Founded 2000.

Degrees and Diplomas: *Gakushi*

Student Services: Sports facilities

Student Residential Facilities: Yes

Special Facilities: Computer Centre

Libraries: 58,000 vols.

Last Updated: 12/01/09

KINKI UNIVERSITY

Kinki Daigaku
3-4-1 Kowakae, Higashiosaka-shi, Osaka 577-8502
Tel: +81(6) 6721-2332
Fax: +81(6) 6729-2387
EMail: koho@msa.kindai.ac.jp
Website: http://www.kindai.ac.jp

Centres

Agriculture Research (Agricultural Engineering); **Animal Development Biotechnology** (Biotechnology; Zoology); **Blood Pressure Research**; **Human Rights** (Human Rights); **Legal and Industrial Information**; **Life Science Research** (Biological and Life Sciences); **Pharmaceutical Research and Technology** (Pharmacology; Pharmacy; Technology)

Graduate Schools

Advanced Technology (Technology); **Commerce**; **Industrial Technology** (Industrial Engineering)

Institutes

Atomic Energy Research (Atomic and Molecular Physics; Energy Engineering); **Health and Sports Sciences** (Health Sciences; Sports); **Oriental Medicine** (Traditional Eastern Medicine)

Laboratories

Environmental Sciences (Environmental Studies); **Ethnology Research** (Ethnology); **Fisheries** (Fishery); **Science and Engineering Research** (Engineering; Mathematics and Computer Science)

Schools

Agriculture *(Also graduate school)* (Agriculture; Applied Chemistry; Chemistry; Fishery; Food Science; Management; Nutrition); **Biological Sciences and Technology** *(Also graduate school)* (Biotechnology; Electronic Engineering; Genetics; Information Technology; Mechanical Engineering; Mechanics); **Business Administration** (Accountancy; Business Administration; Marketing); **Economics** *(Also graduate school)* (Business Administration; Business and Commerce; Economics; International Economics; Public Administration); **Engineering** *(Hiroshima)* (Architecture; Chemistry; Computer Science; Electronic Engineering; Engineering; Environmental Engineering; Industrial Engineering; Management Systems; Mechanical Engineering); **Engineering** *(Kyusyu)* (Architecture; Computer Engineering; Electrical Engineering; Engineering; Industrial Chemistry; Industrial Design; Industrial Engineering; Management); **Humanities and Engineering** (Arts and Humanities; Engineering); **Law** *(Also graduate school)* (Business Administration; Law); **Literature, Art and Cultural Studies** *(Also graduate school)* (Cultural Studies; Fine Arts; Literature); **Medicine** *(Also graduate school)* (Medicine); **Pharmaceutical Sciences** *(Also graduate school)* (Pharmacy); **Science and Engineering** *(Also graduate school (Interdisciplinary))* (Applied Chemistry; Architecture; Biological and Life Sciences; Chemistry; Civil Engineering; Computer Science; Electrical Engineering; Electronic Engineering; Environmental Engineering; Industrial Engineering; Mathematics; Mechanical Engineering; Metallurgical Engineering; Natural Sciences; Nuclear Engineering; Physics; Technology)

Further Information: Also Special Department for Foreign Studies

History: Founded 1925.

Academic Year: April to March (April-September; October-March)

Admission Requirements: Graduation from high school or foreign equivalent, and entrance examination

Main Language(s) of Instruction: Japanese

International Co-operation: With universities in USA, Canada and United Kingdom

Degrees and Diplomas: *Gakushi*: Agriculture; Business Management; Commercial Science; Economics; Engineering; Law; Literature; Medicine; Pharmacy; Science; *Shushi*: Agriculture; Commercial Science; Culture Studies; Economics; Engineering; Law; Literature; Medicine; Pharmacy; Science, 2 yrs; *Hakase*: Agriculture; Commercial Science; Economics; Engineering; Law; Pharmacy; Science

Student Services: Foreign student adviser, Health services, Language programs, Sports facilities

Libraries: c. 2,165,000 vols

Publications: Acta Medica; Bulletin of Faculty of Pharmacy; Journal of Faculty of Science and Engineering; Jurisprudence; Memoirs of Faculty of Agriculture; Proceedings of Commerce and Economics Faculty; Science and Technology

Last Updated: 12/01/09

KIO UNIVERSITY

Kio Daigaku

4-2-2 Umami-naka, Kryo-cho, Kitakatsuragi-gun, Nara 635-0832
Tel: +81(745) 54-1601
Fax: +81(745) 54-1600
EMail: nyusi@kio.ac.jp
Website: http://www.kio.ac.jp

Faculties

Health Sciences (Health Sciences)

History: Founded 2003.

Degrees and Diplomas: *Gakushi*

Publications: Bulletin of Kio University
Last Updated: 12/01/09

KITAKYUSHU UNIVERSITY

Kitakyushu Daigaku

4-2-1 Kitagata, Kokuraminami-ku, Kitakyushu-shi, Fukuoka 802-8577
Tel: +81(93) 964-4022
Fax: +81(93) 964-4020
EMail: k-kikaku@kitakyu-u.ac.jp
Website: http://www.kitakyu-u.ac.jp

President: Toshifumi Yada

Faculties

Economics and Business Administration *(Also graduate school)* (Business Administration; Economics); **Environmental Engineering** *(Also graduate school)* (Architectural and Environmental Design; Environmental Engineering; Environmental Management; Information Sciences; Media Studies); **Foreign Studies** (Chinese; Cultural Studies; English; European Languages; International Relations; International Studies; Modern Languages; Oriental Languages); **Humanities** (Arts and Humanities; Cultural Studies); **Law** *(Also graduate school)* (Law; Public Administration)

Graduate Schools

Social Systems Studies (Cultural Studies; East Asian Studies; Economics; Modern Languages; Regional Studies)

Further Information: Also Hibikino Campus

History: Founded 1946.

Governing Bodies: Hyogikai (University Council)

Academic Year: April to March (April-September; October-March)

Admission Requirements: Graduation from high school or foreign equivalent, and entrance examination

Main Language(s) of Instruction: Japanese

International Co-operation: With universities in Australia, United Kingdom and China

Degrees and Diplomas: *Gakushi*: 4 yrs; *Shushi*: a further 2 yrs; *Hakase*

Student Services: Language programs, Sports facilities

Libraries: c. 445,800 vols

Publications: Bulletin of the Faculty of Foreign Languages *(biannually)*; Journal of the Faculty of Economics *(biannually)*; Law and Public Affairs *(biannually)*; Letters *(biannually)*; Studies in Kitakyushu Society *(annually)*; Trade and Industry *(annually)*
Last Updated: 24/03/11

KITAMI INSTITUTE OF TECHNOLOGY

Kitami Kogyo Daigaku

165 Koen-cho, Kitami-shi, Hokkaido 090-8507
Tel: +81(157) 26-9106
Fax: +81(157) 26-9117
EMail: kenkyu05@desk.kitami-it.ac.jp
Website: http://www.kitami-it.ac.jp

President: Koichi Ayuta (2008-)
Tel: +81(157) 26-9107, Fax: +81(157) 26-9113

Courses

Humanities (Arts and Humanities; Social Sciences)

Departments

Biotechnology and Environmental Chemistry (Applied Chemistry; Biotechnology; Chemistry; Environmental Engineering); **Civil and Environmental Engineering** (Civil Engineering; Environmental Engineering; Physical Engineering); **Computer Science** (Applied Mathematics; Artificial Intelligence; Computer Science; Engineering Management); **Electrical and Electronic Engineering** (Electrical and Electronic Engineering); **Materials Science and Engineering** (Chemistry; Materials Engineering); **Mechanical Engineering** (Mechanical Engineering)

Further Information: Also Japanese language courses for foreign students

History: Founded 1960 as Kitami Junior College of Technology, reorganized 1966 as Kitami Institute of Technology. Graduate School established 1984. Graduate school reorganised as Master's Program and Doctoral Program.

Academic Year: April to March (April-September; October-March)

Admission Requirements: Graduation from high school and entrance examination

Fees: (Yen): 496,800 per annum

Main Language(s) of Instruction: Japanese

Degrees and Diplomas: *Gakushi*: Engineering (Kogakushi), 4 yrs; *Shushi*: Engineering (Kogakushushi,), a further 2 yrs; *Hakase*: Engineering (Kogakuhakushi), a further 3 yrs

Student Services: Academic counselling, Canteen, Employment services, Foreign student adviser, Foreign Studies Centre, Handicapped facilities, Health services, Language programs, Social counselling, Sports facilities

Student Residential Facilities: Yes

Libraries: Total, c. 171,000 vols

Publications: Research Bulletin *(biannually)*
Last Updated: 12/01/09

KITASATO UNIVERSITY

Kitasato Daigaku

5-9-1 Shirokane, Minato-ku, Tokyo 108-8641
Tel: +81(3) 3444-6161
Fax: +81(3) 3444-2530
EMail: www@kitasato-u.ac.jp
Website: http://www.kitasato-u.ac.jp

President: Shiba Tadayoshi

Colleges

Health and Hygiene *(Kitasato Junior College)* (Health Sciences; Hygiene); **Liberal Arts and Sciences**

Graduate Schools

Fisheries Sciences (Fishery); **Fundamental Life Sciences**; **Infection Control Sciences** (Epidemiology); **Medical Sciences** (Medicine); **Nursing**; **Pharmaceutical Sciences** (Pharmacy); **Science**; **Veterinary Medicine and Animal Sciences** (Veterinary Science; Zoology)

Schools

Allied Health Sciences (Health Sciences); **Fisheries Sciences**; **Medicine** (Medicine); **Nursing**; **Pharmacy**; **Science**; **Veterinary Medicine**; **Veterinary Medicine and Animal Sciences**

History: Founded 1962 as College, became University 1964. Financially supported by the Kitasato Gakuen Foundation.

Governing Bodies: Board of Directors

Academic Year: April to March (April-August; September-March)

Admission Requirements: Graduation from high school and entrance examination

Main Language(s) of Instruction: Japanese

Degrees and Diplomas: *Gakushi*: Agriculture; Fisheries Sciences; Science; Physical Therapy; Speech Therapy; Clinical Engineering; Nursing; Hygiene Technology; Occupational Therapy; Orthoptics; Radiological Technology, 4 yrs; *Gakushi*: Medicine; Veterinary Medicine, 6 yrs; *Gakushi*: Pharmaceutical Sciences, 4-6 yrs; *Shushi*: Pharmaceutical Sciences; Biostatistics; Fisheries Sciences; Science; Clinical Pharmacy; Agriculture; Nursing; Life Sciences; Medical Sciences; Infection Control Sciences; Medical Technology, 2 yrs; *Hakase*: Medicine; Veterinary Medicine, 4 yrs; *Hakase*:

Pharmaceutical Sciences; Biostatistics; Agriculture; Nursing; Life Sciences; Clinical Pharmaceutical Sciences; Medical Sciences; Fisheries Sciences; Science; Infection Control Sciences, 3 yrs

Libraries: 558,195 vols

Publications: Kitasato Archives of Experimental Medicine

KOBE CITY COLLEGE OF NURSING

Kobeshi Kango Daigaku

3-4 Gakuen-nishi-machi, Nishi-ku, Kobe-shi, Hyogo 651-2103
Tel: +81(78) 794-8080
Fax: +81(78) 794-8086
Website: http://www.kobe-ccn.ac.jp

President: Kiyoko Ikegawa

Programmes
Nursing

History: Founded 1996.

Degrees and Diplomas: *Gakushi*
Last Updated: 12/01/09

KOBE CITY UNIVERSITY OF FOREIGN STUDIES

Kobeshi Gaikokugo Daigaku

9-1 Gakuen-higashi-machi, Nishi-ku, Kobe-shi, Hyogo 651-2187
Tel: +81(78) 794-8121
Fax: +81(78) 792-9020
EMail: info@office.kobe-cufs.ac.jp
Website: http://www.kobe-cufs.ac.jp

President: Yoshio Yukida

Faculties
Foreign Studies *(Undergraduate and graduate programmes)* (Chinese; Cultural Studies; English; European Languages; International Relations; International Studies; Japanese; Linguistics; Modern Languages; Oriental Languages; Oriental Studies; Russian; Spanish)

Institutes
Foreign Studies

History: Founded 1946 as school, acquired university status 1949.

Academic Year: April to March (April-September; October-March)

Admission Requirements: Graduation from high school or equivalent or foreign equivalent, and entrance examination

Main Language(s) of Instruction: Japanese

Degrees and Diplomas: *Gakushi*: 4 yrs; *Shushi*; *Hakase*

Libraries: c. 380,000 vols

Publications: Annual Report of Research Institute for Foreign Studies *(annually)*; Foreign Studies Pamphlet; Kobe Municipal College Journal
Last Updated: 12/01/09

KOBE COLLEGE

Kobe Jogakuin Daigaku (KC)

4-1 Okadayama, Nishinomiya-shi, Hyogo 662-8505
Tel: +81(798) 51-8585
Fax: +81(798) 51-8535
EMail: dean@mail.kobe-c.ac.jp
Website: http://www.kobe-c.ac.jp

Institutes
Research

Schools
Human Sciences *(Also graduate school)* (Arts and Humanities; Behavioural Sciences; Psychology); **Letters** *(Also graduate school)* (Arts and Humanities; Cultural Studies; English; European Languages; Japanese; Modern Languages; Oriental Languages; Sociology); **Music** *(Also graduate school)* (Dance; Music; Singing)

History: Founded 1875 as School, became College 1891, acquired present status and title 1948.

Governing Bodies: Board of Trustees

Academic Year: April to March (April-September; October-March)

Admission Requirements: Graduation from high school or foreign equivalent, and entrance examination

Main Language(s) of Instruction: Japanese

Degrees and Diplomas: *Gakushi*: English Literature (BA); Human Sciences (BA); International Studies (BA); Music (BA), 4 yrs; *Shushi*: English Literature (MA); Human Sciences (MA); International Studies (MA); Music (MA); Sociology (MA), a further 2 yrs; *Hakase*: Human Sciences (PhD); Letters (PhD), 3 yrs following Shushi

Student Services: Academic counselling, Employment services, Foreign student adviser, Health services, Language programs, Social counselling

Student Residential Facilities: For 179 students

Libraries: c. 390,000 vols

Publications: Joseigaku Hyoran, Research Publication by Institute for Women's Studies *(annually)*; Ronshu (Studies) *(quarterly)*
Last Updated: 12/01/09

KOBE DESIGN UNIVERSITY

Kobe Geijutsu Koka Daigaku (KDU)

8-1-1 Gakuen-nishi-machi, Nishi-ku, Kobe-shi, Hyogo 651-2196
Tel: +81(78) 794-2112
Fax: +81(78) 794-5027
EMail: international@kobe-du.ac.jp
Website: http://www.kobe-du.ac.jp

President: Takahito Saiki EMail: president@kobe-du.ac.jp

Departments
Environmental Design; **Fashion and Textile Design**; **Media Arts**; **Plastic Arts** (Handicrafts; Painting and Drawing; Sculpture); **Product Design**; **Visual Design**

Divisions
Arts and Design (Design; Fine Arts); **Integrated Arts**; **Integrated Design**

Graduate Schools
Design Research (Design)

Schools
Arts and Design; **Design**; **Progressive Arts**

History: Founded 1989.

Governing Bodies: Tanioka Educational Foundation

Academic Year: April to March (April-September; October-March)

Admission Requirements: Graduation from high school (Katogakko) or recognized equivalent and entrance examination

Fees: (Yen): Registration, 150,000 per annum; tuition, 950,000 per annum

Main Language(s) of Instruction: Japanese

International Co-operation: With universities in Asia, Pacific countries and United Kingdom

Degrees and Diplomas: *Gakushi*: 4 yrs; *Shushi*: a further 2 yrs; *Hakase*: 3 yrs

Student Services: Academic counselling, Canteen, Employment services, Foreign student adviser, Foreign Studies Centre, Nursery care, Social counselling, Sports facilities

Special Facilities: Environmental Design Studio; Product Design Studio; Visual Communication Design Studio; Fashion and Textile Design Studio; Media Arts Studio; Plastic Arts Studio; Computer Laboratory

Libraries: c. 100,000 vols

Publications: Bulletin, Theses and Work of Academic Faculty *(annually)*; Series of Graduate School Lectures, Guest Speaker's lecture reports *(annually)*
Last Updated: 12/01/09

KOBE GAKUIN UNIVERSITY

Kobe Gakuin Daigaku

518 Arise, Ikawadani-cho, Nishi-ku, Kobe-shi, Hyogo-ken 651-2180
Tel: +81(78) 974-1551
Fax: +81(78) 974-5689
EMail: kgu@j.kobegakuin.ac.jp
Website: http://www.kobegakuin.ac.jp

President: Toyoki Okada

Faculties

Business Administration; **Economics** (Business Administration; Economics; International Economics); **Humanities and Science** (Arts and Humanities; Behavioural Sciences; Cultural Studies; Natural Sciences; Psychology); **Law** (International Law; International Relations; Law); **Nutrition** (Dietetics; Nutrition); **Pharmaceutical Sciences** (Pharmacology; Pharmacy); **Rehabilitation** (Occupational Therapy; Physical Therapy; Rehabilitation and Therapy)

Graduate Schools

Economics and Business Administration (Business Administration; Economics); **Food and Medical Sciences** (Dietetics; Food Science; Health Sciences; Pharmacology; Toxicology); **Humanities and Science** (Arts and Humanities; Behavioural Sciences; Cultural Studies; Natural Sciences; Psychology); **Law** (International Law; International Relations; Law); **Law Practices**; **Nutrition** (Dietetics; Nutrition); **Pharmaceutical Sciences** (Pharmacology; Pharmacy)

Further Information: Also exchange student programmes (1 yr)

History: Founded 1966.

Academic Year: April to March (April-September; October-March)

Admission Requirements: Graduation from high school or equivalent or foreign equivalent, and entrance examination

Fees: (Yen): 460,000-875,500 per semester

Main Language(s) of Instruction: Japanese

International Co-operation: With universities in Australia and United Kingdom. Also participates in the HUMAP (Hyogo Mobility in Asia and the Pacific) programme

Degrees and Diplomas: *Gakushi*: Business Administration (Keieigaku); Economics (Keizsaigaku); Human Psychology (Ningen Shinrigaku); Humanities (Jinbungaku); International Economics (Kokusai Keizaigaku); International Relations and Law (Kokusai Kankei Hogaku); Law (Horitsugaku); Nutrition (Eiyogaku); Occupational Therapy (Sagyo Ryohogaku); Pharmaceutical Sciences (Yakugaku); Physical Therapy (Rigaku Ryohogaku), 4 yrs; *Shushi*: Business Administration (Keieigaku); Economics (Keizaigaku); Human Studies (Ningen Bunkagaku); International Relations and Law (Kokusai Kankei Hogaku); Law (Hogaku); Nutrition (Eiyogaku); Pharmaceutical Sciences (Yakugaku), a further 2 yrs; *Hakase*: Business Administration (Keieigaku); Economics (Keizaigaku); Human Studies (Ningen Bunkagaku); International Relations and Law (Kokusai Kankei Hogaku); Law (Horitsugaku); Nutrition (Eiyogaku); Pharmaceutical Sciences (Yakugaku); Philosophy (Gakujutsu), 3 yrs following Shushi. Also Homu Hakushi (a further 2 or 3 yrs) in Law

Student Services: Academic counselling, Canteen, Cultural centre, Employment services, Foreign student adviser, Foreign Studies Centre, Handicapped facilities, Health services, Language programs, Nursery care, Social counselling, Sports facilities

Student Residential Facilities: Yes

Special Facilities: Yakuso-en: Herbal Garden

Libraries: 861,086 vols

Publications: Bulletin of Humanities and Sciences *(biannually)*; Economic Papers *(quarterly)*; Law and Politics Review *(quarterly)*; Memoirs of the Faculty of Pharmaceutical Sciences *(other/irregular)*

Last Updated: 12/01/09

KOBE INSTITUTE OF COMPUTING/ GRADUATE SCHOOL OF INFORMATION TECHNOLOGY

Kobe Joho Daigakuin Daigaku (KIC)
2-2-7 Kano-cho, Chuo-ku, Kobe-shi, Hyogo
Tel: +81(78) 262-7715
Fax: +81(78) 262-7737
Website: http://www.kic.ac.jp

President: Hatsukazu Tanaka

Graduate Schools

Information Technology (Information Technology; Software Engineering)

History: Founded 2005.

Degrees and Diplomas: *Shushi*

Last Updated: 13/02/09

KOBE INTERNATIONAL UNIVERSITY

Kobe Kokusai Daigaku
5-1-1-Manabigaoka, Tarumi-ku, Kobe-shi, Hyogo 655-0004
Tel: +81(78) 845-3131
Fax: +81(78) 845-3600
EMail: nyushi@kobe-kiu.ac.jp
Website: http://www.kobe-kiu.ac.jp

Departments

Economics and Business Administration (Business Administration; Economics; International Business); **Urban Environment and Tourism** (International Studies; Tourism; Urban Studies)

Further Information: Also Foundation Course

Degrees and Diplomas: *Gakushi*

Last Updated: 12/01/09

KOBE KAISEI COLLEGE

Kobe Kaisei Joshi Gakuin Daigaku
2-7-1 Aotani-cho, Nada-ku, Kobe-shi, Hyogo 657-0805
Tel: +81(78) 801-2277
Fax: +81(78) 801-5190
EMail: kaiseiweb@kaisei.ac.jp
Website: http://www.kaisei.ac.jp

Programmes

Arts and Humanities (Arts and Humanities)

Degrees and Diplomas: *Gakushi*

Last Updated: 12/01/09

KOBE PHARMACEUTICAL UNIVERSITY

Kobe Yakka Daigaku
4-19-1 Motoyamakita-machi, Higashinada-ku, Kobe-shi, Hyogo 658
Tel: +81(78) 453-0031
Fax: +81(78) 435-2080
EMail: info@kobepharma-u.ac.jp
Website: http://www.kobepharma-u.ac.jp

Programmes

Pharmaceutical Sciences *(Also graduate programme)*

Further Information: Also18 laboratories

History: Founded 1930.

Academic Year: April to March (April-July; September-March)

Admission Requirements: Graduation from high school or equivalent and entrance examination

Main Language(s) of Instruction: Japanese

Degrees and Diplomas: *Gakushi*: Pharmacy, 4 yrs; *Shushi*: Pharmacy, a further 2 yrs; *Hakase*: Pharmacy, 3 yrs following Shushi

Student Services: Sports facilities

Student Residential Facilities: Yes

Libraries: 102,345 vols

Last Updated: 12/01/09

KOBE SHINWA WOMEN'S UNIVERSITY

Kobe Shinwa Joshi Daigaku
7-13-1 Suzurandai-kitamachi, Kita-ku, Kobe-shi, Hyogo 651-1111
Tel: +81(78) 591-1651
Fax: +81(78) 591-3113
EMail: nyushi@kobe-shinwa.ac.jp
Website: http://www.kobe-shinwa.ac.jp

Programmes

Education *(Also graduate programme)* (Education; Physical Education; Preschool Education; Primary Education); **International Studies**; **Psychology** *(Also graduate programme)* (Psychology); **Social Welfare** (Social Welfare)

Degrees and Diplomas: *Gakushi*; *Shushi*
Last Updated: 12/01/09

KOBE SHOIN WOMEN'S UNIVERSITY

Kobe Shoin Joshi Gakuin Daigaku

1-2-1 Shinohara-obanoyama-cho, Nada-ku, Kobe-shi, Hyogo 657-0015
Tel: +81(78) 882-6122
Fax: +81(78) 882-5032
EMail: kokusai@shoin.ac.jp
Website: http://www.shoin.ac.jp

Programmes

Food Science; **Home Sciences** (Home Economics); **Literature, Linguistics and Area Studies** *(Also graduate programme)* (English; Japanese; Linguistics; Literature)

History: Founded 1966.
Degrees and Diplomas: *Gakushi*; *Shushi*; *Hakase*
Last Updated: 12/01/09

KOBE SHUKUGAWA GAKUIN UNIVERSITY

Kobe Syukugawa Gakuin Daigaku

1-3-11 Minato-jima, Chuo-Ku, Kobe-shi, Hyogo 650-0045
Website: http://www.kobeshukugawa.ac.jp

President: Masaharu Goto

Schools

Tourism
Degrees and Diplomas: *Gakushi*
Last Updated: 25/03/11

KOBE UNIVERSITY

Kobe Daigaku

1-1 Rokkodai-cho, Nada-ku, Kobe-shi, Hyogo 657-8501
Tel: +81(78) 881-1212
Fax: +81(78) 803-5049
EMail: intl-relatations@kobe-u.ac.jp
Website: http://www.kobe-u.ac.jp

President: Hideki Fukuda (2009-)
Tel: +81(78) 803-5282, Fax: +81(78) 803-5009

International Relations: Hitoshi Matsumura, Head of International Affairs Planning Division
Tel: +81(78) 803-5044, Fax: +81(78) 803-5049
EMail: intl-relations@office.kobe-u.ac.jp

Faculties

Agriculture *(Graduate School)* (Agricultural Economics; Agricultural Engineering; Agriculture; Environmental Studies; Natural Resources) *Dean*: Chiharu Nakamura; **Economics** *(Graduate School)* (Economics) *Dean*: Yasuhide Tanaka; **Engineering** *(Graduate School)* (Architecture; Chemical Engineering; Civil Engineering; Computer Engineering; Computer Science; Electrical and Electronic Engineering; Engineering; Mechanical Engineering; Structural Architecture; Systems Analysis) *Dean*: Masayuki Morimoto; **Health Sciences** *(Graduate School, Suma-ku)* (Health Sciences) *Dean*: Yuichi Ishikawa; **Human Development and Environment** *(Graduate School)* (Behavioural Sciences; Education; Environmental Studies; Health Administration; Health Education; Health Sciences; Psychology; Social Sciences) *Dean*: Tsutomu Aoki; **Humanities** *(Graduate School)* (Arts and Humanities; Cognitive Sciences; Cultural Studies; History; Literature; Philosophy; Social Studies) *Dean*: Mamoru Sasaki; **Intercultural Studies** *(Graduate School)* (Communication Studies; Cultural Studies; Social Studies) *Dean*: Kyohei Mizuta; **Law** *(Graduate School)* (Administrative Law; Civil Law; Commercial Law; Comparative Law; Constitutional Law; Criminal Law; Fiscal Law; Government; History of Law; Human Rights; International Law; Justice Administration; Labour Law; Law; Political Sciences) *Dean*: Hiroshi Yamamoto; **Maritime Sciences** *(Graduate School, Fukaeminami-cho)* (Marine Engineering; Marine Science and Oceanography; Marine Transport; Transport Management) *Dean*: Hiroshi Ishida; **Science** *(Graduate School)* (Biology; Chemistry; Earth Sciences; Mathematics; Physics) *Dean*: Yasunari Higuchi

Graduate Schools

International Cooperation Studies (Development Studies; Economics; International Law; International Studies; Law; Regional Studies) *Dean*: Motoki Takahashi

Research Centres

Biosignal Research (Cell Biology; Molecular Biology) *Director*: Ushio Kikkawa; **Environmental Genomics** *Director*: Mitsuru Sasaki; **Inland Seas** *(Tsuna-gun)* (Biochemistry; Environmental Studies; Marine Biology; Marine Science and Oceanography) *Director*: Hiroshi Kawai; **Molecular Photoscience** (Biochemistry; Molecular Biology) *Director*: Keisuke Tominaga; **Promotion of Higher Education** *(Institute) Director*: Hiromoto Usui; **Urban Safety and Security** *Director*: Yasuo Ariki

Research Institutes

Economics and Business Administration (Business Administration; Economics; International Business; International Economics) *Director*: Ryuzo Miyao

Schools

Business Administration *(Graduate School)* (Accountancy; Business Administration; Business and Commerce; Finance; Human Resources; Management; Marketing; Transport and Communications; Transport Economics) *Dean*: Yutaka Kato; **Medicine** *(Chuo-ku; Graduate School)* (Biomedicine; Medicine) *Dean*: Yoshimi Takai

Units

Collaborative Research and Technology Development *Director*: Shigehito Deki; **Environmental Management** *Director*: Yasukiyo Ueda; **Information Science and Technology** (Computer Education; Computer Networks; Software Engineering) *Director*: Makoto Kaburagi; **International Student** *(Education for foreign students)* (Asian Studies; Japanese; Linguistics; Native Language; Native Language Education) *Director*: Yasuhiro Nakanishi; **Languages and Communication** *(School)* (Communication Studies; Modern Languages) *Director*: Yoshio Miki; **Supports to Research and Education Activities** *Director*: Hiroshi Yamagata

Further Information: Also Experimental Farm. Medical Centre for Student Health. University Hospital. Office for the Promotion of International Exchange. EU Institute in Japan, Kansai

History: Founded 1902, integrating Kobe University of Economics, Hyogo Normal and Junior Normal Schools, Kobe College of Technology and Himeji High School. Acquired present status and title 1949. Integrated Kobe University of Mercantile Marine 2003.

Academic Year: April to March (April-September; October-March)

Admission Requirements: Graduation from high school or equivalent or foreign equivalent, and entrance examination

Fees: (Yen): 535,800 per annum

Main Language(s) of Instruction: Japanese

Degrees and Diplomas: *Gakushi*: 4 yrs; *Gakushi*: Health Sciences, 4 yrs; *Gakushi*: Medicine, 6 yrs; *Shushi*: a further 2 yrs; *Hakase*: 3 yrs following Shushi; *Hakase*: Medicine, a further 4 yrs. Also Professional Degrees in Business Administration (2 yrs) and Law (3 yrs)

Student Services: Academic counselling, Canteen, Cultural centre, Employment services, Foreign student adviser, Foreign Studies Centre, Handicapped facilities, Health services, Language programs, Social counselling, Sports facilities

Student Residential Facilities: Yes

Libraries: Central and branch Libraries, 2,012,829 vols in Japanese and Chinese; 1,511,855 vols in foreign languages

Publications: Bulletin of Health Sciences Kobe *(annually)*; Discussion Papers (Business Administration) *(other/irregular)*; Discussion Papers (Economics) *(other/irregular)*; GSICS Working Papers Series *(other/irregular)*; Kobe Economic and Business Review *(annually)*; Kobe Journal of Mathematics *(biannually)*; Kobe Journal of Medical Sciences *(monthly)*; Kobe University Economic Review *(annually)*; Kobe University Law Review *(annually)*; Research Arena *(quarterly)*

Student Numbers *2011-2012*: Total 16,730
Last Updated: 28/04/10

KOBE UNIVERSITY OF FASHION AND DESIGN

Kobe Fasshon Zokei Daigaku

2-1-50 Meinan-cho, Akashi-shi, Hyogo 673-0001
Tel: +81(78) 927-0771
Fax: +81(78) 927-0774
EMail: international@kobe-fashion.ac.jp
Website: http://www.kobe-fashion.ac.jp/international/index.shtml

Programmes

Design (Design; Fashion Design; Interior Design)

Degrees and Diplomas: *Gakushi*

Last Updated: 13/02/09

KOBE WOMEN'S UNIVERSITY

Kobe Joshi Daigaku

2-1 Aoyama, Higashi-suma, Suma-ku, Kobe-shi, Hyogo 654-8585
Tel: +81(78) 731-4416
Fax: +81(78) 732-5161
Website: http://www.yg.kobe-wu.ac.jp/wu/index.html

Faculties

Home Economics (Dietetics; Home Economics); **Literature** (Education; English; History; Japanese; Literature; Social Welfare)

History: Founded 1950, reorganized 1966.

Governing Bodies: Rijikai (Executive Assembly); Hyogiinkai (Representative Conference)

Academic Year: April to March (April-September; October-March)

Admission Requirements: Graduation from high school or equivalent or foreign equivalent, and entrance examination

Fees: (Yen): 500,000 per semester

Main Language(s) of Instruction: Japanese

International Co-operation: With universities in USA, United Kingdom and China

Accrediting Agencies: Japanese University Accreditation Association

Degrees and Diplomas: *Gakushi*: 4 yrs; *Shushi*: 2 further yrs; *Hakase*: 3 yrs following Shushi

Student Services: Employment services, Health services, Sports facilities

Student Residential Facilities: Yes

Libraries: 223,918 vols

Last Updated: 12/01/09

KOBE YAMATE UNIVERSITY

Kobe Yamate Daigaku

6-5-2 Nakayamate-douri, Chuou-ku, Kobe-shi, Hyogo 650-0004
Tel: +81(78) 371-8000
Fax: +81(78) 371-4938
EMail: sky@kobe-yamate.ac.jp
Website: http://www.kobe-yamate.ac.jp

Programmes

Environmental Studies (Cultural Studies; Environmental Studies)

History: Founded 1999.

Degrees and Diplomas: *Gakushi*

Student Services: Cultural centre, Sports facilities

Libraries: 180,000 vols.

Last Updated: 12/01/09

KOCHI UNIVERSITY

Kochi Daigaku

2-5-1 Akebono-cho, Kochi-shi, Kochi 780-8520
Tel: +81(88) 844-8643
Fax: +81(88) 844-8033
EMail: gs05@jimu.kochi-u.ac.jp
Website: http://www.kochi-u.ac.jp

President: Yusuke Sagara

Faculties

Agriculture *(Also graduate school)* (Aquaculture; Environmental Engineering; Forestry; Natural Resources; Tropical Agriculture); **Education** *(Also graduate school)* (Curriculum; Education; Teacher Training); **Humanities and Economics** *(Also graduate school)* (Communication Studies; Economics; Humanities and Social Science Education; International Studies; Social Sciences); **Science** *(Also graduate school)* (Applied Chemistry; Applied Physics; Chemistry; Environmental Engineering; Geology; Information Sciences; Materials Engineering; Mathematics; Natural Sciences; Physics)

Graduate Schools

Agricultural Sciences *(with Ehime University)* (Biological and Life Sciences; Environmental Management; Natural Resources); **Kuroshio Science** *(Doctoral Course)* (Environmental Studies; Health Sciences; Marine Science and Oceanography; Medicine; Natural Resources)

Schools

Medicine *(Also graduate school)* (Biomedicine; Medicine; Neurosciences; Nursing; Social and Preventive Medicine)

Further Information: Also Japanese language courses for foreign students. University farm. University forest. Centre for Research and Training of Teachers

History: Founded as national university 1949, incorporating Kochi High School founded 1923, Kochi Normal School, 1874, and Kochi Youth Normal School, 1923. Merged with Kochi Ika Daigaku 2003.

Governing Bodies: Hyogikai (University Council); Faculty Meeting

Academic Year: April to March (April-October; October-March)

Admission Requirements: Graduation from high school or recognized equivalent, and entrance examination

Main Language(s) of Instruction: Japanese

Degrees and Diplomas: *Gakushi*: Agriculture; Arts; Economics; Education; Science, 4 yrs; *Gakushi*: Medicine; *Shushi*: Agriculture; Science, a further 2 yrs; *Hakase*: Agriculture, 3 yrs following Shushi; *Hakase*: Medicine. Also Teaching Qualitication, 4 yrs

Student Residential Facilities: Yes

Special Facilities: Earthquake Observatory

Libraries: c. 583,760 vols

Publications: Reports of USA Marine Biological Station *(annually)*; Research Reports of Faculty of Agriculture *(annually)*; Research Reports of Faculty of Education *(annually)*; University Research Reports *(annually)*

Last Updated: 12/01/09

KOCHI UNIVERSITY OF TECHNOLOGY

Kochi Koka Daigaku

185 Miyanokuchi, Tosayamada-cho, Kochi-shi, Kochi 782-8502
Tel: +81(887) 531-111
Fax: +81(887) 572-000
EMail: international@mlsv.kochi-tech.ac.jp
Website: http://www.kochi-tech.ac.jp

President: Taketo Sakuma

Programmes

Engineering *(Undergraduate and graduate programmes)* (Electronic Engineering; Engineering; Environmental Engineering; Information Technology; Management; Mechanical Engineering)

History: Founded 1997.

Degrees and Diplomas: *Gakushi*; *Shushi*; *Hakase*

Last Updated: 12/01/09

KOGAKKAN UNIVERSITY

Kogakkan Daigaku

1704 Kodakujimoto-cho, Ise-shi, Mie 516-8555
Tel: +81(596) 22-0201
Fax: +81(596) 27-1704
EMail: kyomu@kogakkan-u.ac.jp
Website: http://www.kogakkan-u.ac.jp

Programmes

History *(Also graduate programme)*; **Literature, Linguistics and Area Studies** *(Also graduate programme)* (Japanese; Linguistics; Literature); **Religion** *(Also graduate programme)* (Religion); **Social Welfare** *(Also graduate programme)* (Social Welfare)

History: Founded 1882 by Imperial order, became National College 1903 and University 1940. Re-established 1962.

Academic Year: April to March (April-October; October-March)

Admission Requirements: Graduation from high school or equivalent, and entrance examination

Main Language(s) of Instruction: Japanese

Degrees and Diplomas: *Gakushi*; *Shushi*; *Hakase*

Student Residential Facilities: Yes

Libraries: 282,000 vols

Publications: Bulletin *(annually)*

Last Updated: 12/01/09

KOGAKUIN UNIVERSITY

Kogakuin Daigaku

1-24-2 Nishi-Shinjuku, Shinjuku-ku, Tokyo 163-8677
Tel: +81(3) 3340-0130
Fax: +81(3) 3340-5304
EMail: nyushi@cc.kogakuin.ac.jp
Website: http://www.kogakuin.ac.jp

President: Hirofumi Miura (2003 -)
EMail: miura@cc.kogakuin.ac.jp

Dean of Academic Affairs: Mitsuhiro Udagawa
Tel: +81(3) 3340-0547, Fax: +81(3) 3342-5304
EMail: udagawa@cc.kogakuin.ac.jp

International Relations: Mitsunobu Sato, Director, Centre of International Affairs
Tel: +81(3) 3340-0849 EMail: ft10302@ns.kogakuin.ac.jp

Centres

Basic Study Support; **Engineering Clinic Programme** (Engineering); **Information Science**; **Techno Creation**

Faculties

Engineering *(Evening Programme)* (Architecture; Chemical Engineering; Computer Science; Engineering; Mechanical Engineering; Media Studies; Telecommunications Engineering); **Engineering** (Applied Chemistry; Architectural and Environmental Design; Architecture and Planning; Computer Engineering; Electrical Engineering; Engineering; Environmental Engineering; Information Technology; Materials Engineering; Mechanical Engineering; Telecommunications Engineering); **Global Engineering** (Engineering; Mechanical Engineering); **Informatics**

Graduate Schools

Graduate Studies (Applied Chemistry; Architecture; Chemical Engineering; Computer Science; Electrical and Electronic Engineering; Mechanical Engineering)

Research Centres

Collaborative *(Open Research Center)*; **Environmental and Earthquake Engineering** (Environmental Engineering; Seismology); **Nano-Structure Surfaces and Interfaces** (Nanotechnology); **Smart Machine and Micro and Bio Systems**

Research Institutes

Science and Technology

History: Founded 1887 as Technical School, reorganized as University 1949.

Governing Bodies: Board of Trustees

Academic Year: April to March (April-September; October-March)

Admission Requirements: Graduation from high school or recognized equivalent, and entrance examination

Fees: (Yen): Day Programme: 1.3m. per annum and admission fee, 250,000 for the first year; Evening Programme: 780,000 and admission fee of 100,000; Master Course: 890,000 and admission fee of 250,000; Doctoral Course: 890,000 and admission fee of 250,000

Main Language(s) of Instruction: Japanese

International Co-operation: With universities in China; Finland; France; Germany; Ireland; Spain; Taiwan and USA

Degrees and Diplomas: *Gakushi*: 4 yrs; *Shushi*: 2 yrs; *Hakase*: 3 yrs

Student Services: Academic counselling, Canteen, Employment services, Health services, Sports facilities

Special Facilities: Creative Activity Studio

Libraries: University Library, 45,000 vols

Publications: Research Report (Part A, Engineering) *(biennially)*; Research Report (Part B, General Culture) *(biennially)*

KOKUGAKUIN UNIVERSITY

Kokugakuin Daigaku

4-10-28 Higashi, Shibuya-ku, Tokyo 150-8440
Tel: +81(3) 5788-7061
Fax: +81(3) 5778-7062
EMail: kokusai@kokugakuin.ac.jp
Website: http://www.kokugakuin.ac.jp

Faculties

Economics (Business Administration; Economics); **Law** (Law); **Letters** (Arts and Humanities; Chinese; Cultural Studies; History; Japanese; Modern Languages; Museum Studies; Natural Sciences; Philosophy; Physical Education; Sports); **Shinto Studies** (Religious Studies)

Institutes

Japanese Culture and Classics (Japanese)

History: Founded 1882 as Institute for Japanese Classics (Koten-Koukyusho), acquired present title 1919. Reorganized 1948. Graduate School established 1951.

Governing Bodies: Board of Trustees

Academic Year: April to March (April-September; October-March)

Admission Requirements: Graduation from high school or recognized equivalent, and entrance examination

Main Language(s) of Instruction: Japanese

Accrediting Agencies: Ministry of Education, Culture, Sports, Science and Technology

Degrees and Diplomas: *Gakushi*: Economics (Keizaigakushi); Law (Hogakushi); Letters (Bungakushi), 4 yrs; *Shushi*: Economics (Keizaigakushushi); Law (Hogakushushi); Letters (Bungakushushi), a further 2 yrs; *Hakase*: Economics (Keizaigakuhakushi); Law (Hogakuhakushi); Letters (Bungakuhakushi), 3 yrs following Shushi. Also Teaching Qualifications and Certificate in Librarianship

Student Services: Canteen, Employment services, Health services, Language programs, Social counselling, Sports facilities

Student Residential Facilities: For c. 200 male students

Special Facilities: Archaeological Museum. Museum of Shinto Studies

Libraries: c. 1,289,382 vols

Publications: Kokugakuin Daigaku Kiyo (Transactions of Kokugakuin Graduate School); Kokugakuin Hogaku (Journal of Faculty of Law); Kokugakuin Keizaigaku (Journal of Faculty of Economics); Kokugakuin Zasshi (Journal); Nihonbunka-Kenkyusho-Kiyo (Transactions of Institute for Japanese Culture and Classics)

Last Updated: 12/01/09

KOKUSHIKAN UNIVERSITY

Kokushikan Daigaku

4-28-1 Setagaya, Setagaya-ku, Tokyo 154-8515
Tel: +81(3) 5481-3206
Fax: +81(3) 5481-5672
EMail: intrel@kokushikan.ac.jp; ic@kokushikan.ac.jp
Website: http://www.kokushikan.ac.jp

President: Katsuhiko Wakabayashi

International Relations: Yasuyoshi Okada

Centres

Asia-Japan Research (Asian Studies); **Information Sciences**; **Lifelong Learning**; **Wellness Research**

Faculties

Engineering (Architecture; Civil Engineering; Electrical Engineering; Engineering; Environmental Engineering; Information Technology; Mechanical Engineering); **International Studies - 21st Century Asian Studies** (Asian Studies; International Studies); **Law** (Commercial Law; Law); **Letters** (Archaeology; Asian Studies; Chinese; Education; Environmental Studies; Ethics; Geography; History; Japanese; Literature; Primary Education); **Physical Education** (Physical Education; Sports; Sports Medicine); **Political**

Science and Economics (Business Administration; Economics; Political Sciences)

Institutes

Accountancy Research (Accountancy); **Budo and Moral Education Research**; **Cultural Studies on Ancient Iraq** (Ancient Civilizations; Middle Eastern Studies); **Economics Research** (Economics); **Engineering Research**; **Law Research** (Comparative Law); **Physical Education Research** (Physical Education); **Study of Politics** (Political Sciences)

History: Founded 1917.

Governing Bodies: Board of Directors

Academic Year: April to March (April-July; September-March)

Admission Requirements: Please consult http://www.kokushikan.ac.jp/english/contents/admission/admission.html

Main Language(s) of Instruction: Japanese

Degrees and Diplomas: *Gakushi*: Political Science; Economics; Business Administration; Sport and Physical Education; Martial Arts; Sport and Medical Science; Engineering; Law; Literature; Asian Studies (BA), 4 yrs; *Shushi*: Political Science; Economics; Business Administration; Sport Science; Engineering; Law; Human Sciences; Interdisciplinary Intellectual Property Laws; Business Communication; Japanese Language Education; Cultural Heritage (MA; MSc), 2 yrs; *Hakase*: Economics; Business Administration; Sport Science; Engineering; Law; Human Sciences, 3 yrs

Student Residential Facilities: For c. 300 Men and c. 50 Women students

Libraries: c. 699,540 vols

Publications: Al-Rafidan, Journal of Western Asiatic Studies; Annual Reports of Health, Physical Education and Sport Science *(annually)*; Bulletin of the Institute of Economic Studies; Bulletin of the Science and Engineering Research Institute; Bu-Toku; Butoku-Kiyo; Collection of Papers on Elementary Education; Keiei Keiri, Management and Accountancy; Kokushi; Kokushikan Comparative Law Review; Kokushikan Daigaku Chirigaku Hokoku; Kokushikan Hogaku, Kokushikan Law Review; Kokushikan Law Review; Kokushikan Studies in Japanese Literature; Kokushikan Tetsugaku; Kyoikugaku Ronso; Kyoyo-Ronshu, Liberal Arts Review; Memoirs of the Kokushikan University Center for Information Science; Seikei Ronso, Review of Politics and Economics; Seikei Ronso (Politics and Economics Review) *(biannually)*; Seikyoken Review; Student Law Journal; Studies on Foreign Languages and Cultures; The Graduate School Law Review; The Kokushikan-Shigaku, Kokushikan Society of Sport Science; Transactions of the Academic Society of the Humanities; Transactions of the Faculty of Engineering

Last Updated: 13/01/09

KOMAZAWA UNIVERSITY

Komazawa Daigaku

1-23-1 Komazawa, Setagaya-ku, Tokyo 154-8525

Tel: +81(3) 3702-9730

Fax: +81(3) 3702-9721

Website: http://www.komazawa-u.ac.jp

President: Rentaro Ikeda (2006-)

Secretary-General: Masahiro Takahashi

International Relations: Hiroyuki Akashi, Director
Tel: +81(3) 3702-9730, Fax: +81(3) 3702-9721
EMail: kokusaicenter@komazawa-u.ac.jp

Faculties

Arts and Sciences *(Also graduate division)*; **Buddhism** (Asian Religious Studies) *Dean*: Shudo Ishii; **Business Administration** *(Also graduate division)* (Business Administration) *Dean*: Shigeru Hatori; **Economics** *(Also graduate division)* (Business and Commerce; Economics) *Dean*: Shuji Kosugi; **Global Media Studies** (Media Studies) *Dean*: Nobuo Saito; **Health Sciences** (Radiology) *Dean*: Masaki Koyama; **Law** *(Also graduate division)* (Law; Political Sciences) *Dean*: Sanae Urata; **Letters** (Arts and Humanities; English; European Languages; Geography; History; Japanese; Literature; Modern Languages; Oriental Languages; Psychology; Sociology) *Dean*: Masahiro Takagi

Graduate Divisions

Commerce (Business and Commerce); **Legal Research and Training** (Law)

Institutes

Accountancy (Accountancy); **Applied Geography** (Geography); **Comparative Buddhist Literature** (Asian Religious Studies; Comparative Literature); **Legal Research** (Law; Religious Studies); **Mass Communication** (Mass Communication); **Zen** (Asian Religious Studies); **Zen Buddhism and Economics** (Asian Religious Studies; Economics)

History: Founded 1582.

Academic Year: April to March (April-July; September-December; January-March)

Admission Requirements: Graduation from high school and entrance examination

Fees: (Yen): 860,000-1.26m. per annum

Main Language(s) of Instruction: Japanese

Degrees and Diplomas: *Gakushi*: Buddhist Studies; Business Administration; Commerce; Economics; English and American Literature; Geography; Global Media; History; Japanese Literature; Law; Political Science; Psychology; Radiological Sciences; Sociology; Zen Buddhist Studies, 4 yrs; *Shushi*: Buddhism; Business Administration; Commerce; Economics; English and American Literature; Geography; Japanese History; Japanese Literature; Private Law; Psychology; Public Law; Sociology, a further 2 yrs; *Hakase*: Buddhism; Business Management; Commerce; Economics; English and American Literature; Geography; Japanese History; Japanese Literature; Private Law; Psychology; Public Law; Sociology, 3 yrs following Shushi; *Hakase*: Legal Research and Training, 2-3 yrs following Shushi

Student Services: Academic counselling, Canteen, Employment services, Foreign student adviser, Foreign Studies Centre, Health services, Language programs, Sports facilities

Special Facilities: Museum of Zen Buddhist Culture

Libraries: c. 1,113,807 vols

Publications: Bunka, Komazawa University Journal of Culture; Journal of Buddhist Studies; Journal of Department of Radiology, Komazawa Junior College; Journal of English Literature, Komazawa Junior College; Journal of Health Sciences of Komazawa University; Journal of Komazawa Junior College; Journal of Radiological Sciences of Komazawa University; Journal of the Faculty of Buddhism; Journal of the Faculty of Economics; Journal of the Faculty of Foreign Languages; Journal of the Faculty of Law of Komazawa University; Journal of the Faculty of Letters; Komazawa Annual Report of Psychology; Komazawa Business Review; Komazawa Business Studies; Komazawa Educational Review; Komazawa Japanese Literature; Komazawa Journal of Geography; Komazawa Journal of Sociology; Komazawa Junior College Journal of Buddhism; Komazawa Law and Political Science Review; Komazawa Law Journal; Regional Reviews; Studies in British and American Literature; The Economic Review of Komazawa University; The Journal of the Historical Association of Komazawa; The Komazawa Junior College Review of Japanese Literature; The Komazawa University Journal of Health and Physical Education; The Revue of Foreign Languages

KOMAZAWA WOMEN'S UNIVERSITY

Komazawa Joshi Daigaku

238 Sakahama, Inagi-shi, Tokyo 206-8511

Tel: +81(42) 350-7111

Fax: +81(42) 350-7112

EMail: kouhou@komajo.ac.jp

Website: http://www.komajo.ac.jp/uni/

Programmes

Crafts and Design (Design; Handicrafts); **Home Science** (Home Economics); **International Studies** (Cultural Studies; International Studies); **Japanese Culture** *(Also graduate programme)* (Cultural Studies; Japanese)

History: Founded 1993.

Degrees and Diplomas: *Gakushi*; *Shushi*. Also special Japanese language and culture classes for foreign students.

Student Services: Sports facilities

Special Facilities: Audio-visual section

Libraries: c. 102,000 vols

Last Updated: 13/01/09

KONAN UNIVERSITY

Kounan Daigaku
8-9-1 Okamoto, Higashinada-ku, Kobe-shi, Hyogo 658-8501
Tel: +81(78) 431-4341
Fax: +81(78) 435-2306
EMail: hpmaster@konan-u.ac.jp
Website: http://www.konan-u.ac.jp

President: Yoshimi Sugimura (2006-)

International Relations: Kuniko Uemura
Tel: +81(78) 452-1641, Fax: +81(78) 435-2557
EMail: kiec@adm.konan-u.ac.jp

Centres
Business Law *Director*: Satoshi Negishi; **Counseling** (Educational and Student Counselling) *Director*: Kenichi Mizuno; **Education and Research in Information Sciences** (Information Sciences) *Director*: Yasuo Nunokami; **Education and Research in Sport and Health Science** (Health Sciences; Physical Education; Sports) *Director*: Yutaka Katsura; **General Studies** (Arts and Humanities; International Relations; Social Studies) *Director*: Kensuke Hiroyama; **Teacher Education** (Teacher Training) *Director*: Naoya Tsuzome

Divisions
Frontier Research *Director*: Yoshiyuki Shigematsu

Faculties
Business Administration (Business Administration) *Dean*: Junji Nishimura; **Economics** (Economics) *Dean*: Hitoshi Kobayashi; **Law** (Law) *Dean*: Hidekazu Nishida; **Letters** (Cultural Studies; English; History; Japanese; Literature; Social Sciences; Sociology) *Dean*: Hiroyasu Kotani; **Science and Engineering** (Applied Chemistry; Biology; Chemistry; Computer Engineering; Information Sciences; Natural Sciences; Physics) *Dean*: Toshihiko Shigematsu

Graduate Schools
Accountancy (Accountancy) *Director*: Teruyuki Kawasaki; **Humanities** (Arts and Humanities; English; Literature; Sociology) *Director*: Saburo Morita; **Law** *Dean*: Gishu Watanabe; **Natural Sciences** (Biology; Chemistry; Information Sciences; Natural Sciences; Physics; Systems Analysis) *Director*: Akira Sugimura; **Social Sciences** (Business Administration; Economics; Law; Social Sciences) *Director*: Junji Nishimura

Institutes
Business Innovation (Business and Commerce) *Director*: Yoshihiro Nakata; **Economics and Business Administration** (Business Administration; Economics) *Director*: Kazutoshi Watanabe; **Frontier Institute for Biomolecular Engineering Research** (Chemistry) *Director*: Naoki Sugimoto; **Human Sciences** (Clinical Psychology) *Director*: Shigeyuki Mori; **Language and Culture** (Chinese; Cultural Studies; English; French; German; Korean; Modern Languages) *Director*: Tomi Harada; **Research** *Director*: Kaneaki Arimura

Further Information: Also courses for foreign students. The Year-in-Konan Program. Intensive languages courses. Introductory Japanese studies courses

History: Founded 1919 as College, acquired present status 1951.

Governing Bodies: Board of Trustees

Academic Year: April to March (April-September; October-March)

Admission Requirements: Graduation from high school or equivalent or foreign equivalent, and entrance examination

Fees: (Yen): 706,000 per annum; Science, 1,037,000

Main Language(s) of Instruction: Japanese

International Co-operation: With institutions in USA; United Kingdom; Canada; Australia; New Zealand; France; Germany; China and Republic of Korea

Degrees and Diplomas: *Gakushi*: Business Administration; Economics; Law; Letters; Science; Sociology, 4 yrs; *Shushi*: Accountancy; Business Administration; Economics; Letters; Science; Sociology, a further 2 yrs; *Hakase*: Business Administration; Letters; Science; Sociology, 3 yrs following Shushi; *Hakase*: Law, 3 yrs

Student Services: Academic counselling, Canteen, Cultural centre, Employment services, Foreign student adviser, Foreign Studies Centre, Health services, Language programs, Nursery care, Social counselling, Sports facilities

Special Facilities: Cyber Library

Libraries: University Library, c. 850,000 vols

Publications: "Konan University /Clinical Psychology Report", Counseling Center of Konan University *(annually)*; "Language and Culture", The Journal of the Institute for Language and Culture *(annually)*; "Mental Crises and Clinical Knowledge", Konan institute of Human Science *(annually)*; Annual Report, Series of General Institute *(annually)*; Annual Review (Letters) *(annually)*; Bulletin of the Research Institute *(annually)*; Business Review *(quarterly)*; EBA Letter, Economics & Business Administration *(3 per annum)*; EBA Report, Economics & Business Administration *(annually)*; Economic Papers *(quarterly)*; Law Review *(quarterly)*; Memoirs of Konan University Science and Engineering *(biennially)*; Zephyr Nishikaze, Institute for Language and Culture *(3 per annum)*

KONAN WOMEN'S UNIVERSITY

Konan Joshi Daigaku (KWU)
2-23, 6 Morikita-machi, Higashinada-ku, Kobe-shi, Hyogo 658-0001
Tel: +81(78) 431-0391
Fax: +81(78) 431-5888
EMail: tai@konan-wu.ac.jp
Website: http://www.konan-wu.ac.jp

President: Yoshihiro Tsubouchi

Faculties
Arts and Humanities (Arts and Humanities; English; Environmental Studies; French; International Studies; Japanese; Sociology)

Graduate Schools
Arts and Humanities (Arts and Humanities; Education; English; French; Japanese; Linguistics; Literature; Psychology; Sociology)

History: Founded 1955 as Junior College, acquired present status and title 1964.

Governing Bodies: Konan Women's Academy

Academic Year: April to March (April-September; October-March)

Admission Requirements: Graduation from high school or equivalent, or foreign equivalent and entrance examination

Main Language(s) of Instruction: Japanese

International Co-operation: With universities in China, Republic of Korea and France

Degrees and Diplomas: *Gakushi*: 4 yrs; *Shushi*: a further 2 yrs; *Hakase*: 3 yrs following Shushi

Student Services: Academic counselling, Foreign student adviser, Health services, Sports facilities

Student Residential Facilities: For c. 110 students

Special Facilities: Media Centre; Ashihara Auditorium

Libraries: Central Library (Abe Memorial Library), c. 310,700 vols

Publications: Konan Women's University 'Research' *(annually)*

Last Updated: 14/01/09

KORIYAMA WOMEN'S UNIVERSITY

Koriyama Joshi Daigaku
3-25-2 Kasei, Koriyama-shi, Fukushima 963-8503
Tel: +81(24) 932-4848
Fax: +81(24) 932-6748
EMail: admin@koriyama-kgc.ac.jp
Website: http://www.koriyama-kgc.ac.jp

Schools
Home Economics *(Also graduate programme)* (Food Science; Home Economics; Nutrition)

History: Founded 1947.

Degrees and Diplomas: *Gakushi*; *Shushi*; *Hakase*

Student Services: Employment services, Foreign student adviser, Health services, Social counselling, Sports facilities

Libraries: 100,000 vols

KOSHIEN UNIVERSITY

Koshien Daigaku

10-1 Momijigaoka, Takarazuka-shi, Hyogo 665-0006
Tel: +81(797) 87-5111
Fax: +81(797) 87-5666
EMail: info@koshien.ac.jp
Website: http://www.koshien.ac.jp

Programmes

Arts and Humanities *(Also graduate school)* (Arts and Humanities; Cultural Studies; Psychology); **Business Administration and Information Sciences** *(Also graduate school)* (Business Administration; Information Sciences); **Nutrition** *(Also graduate school)* (Food Science; Nutrition)

History: Founded 1967.

Main Language(s) of Instruction: Japanese

International Co-operation: With universities in China and Republic of Korea

Degrees and Diplomas: *Gakushi*; *Shushi*; *Hakase*

Libraries: 99,440 vols

Last Updated: 10/03/08

KOYASAN UNIVERSITY

Koyasan Daigaku

385 Koyasan, Koya-cho, Ito-gun, Wakayama 648-0280
Tel: +81(736) 56-2921
Fax: +81(736) 56-2746
EMail: kyomu@koyasan-u.ac.jp
Website: http://www.koyasan-u.ac.jp

Faculties

Literature (Arts and Humanities; Asian Religious Studies; Social Work; Sociology)

Institutes

Esoteric Buddhist Culture (Asian Religious Studies)

History: Founded 1886 as Kogi Daigakurin for the Shingon Sect of Esoteric Buddhism. Became University 1926.

Academic Year: April to March (April-September; September-March)

Admission Requirements: Graduation from high school or equivalent, and entrance examination

Main Language(s) of Instruction: Japanese

Degrees and Diplomas: *Gakushi*: 4 yrs; *Shushi*: a further 2 yrs; *Hakase*: 3 yrs following Shushi. Also Degree in Esoteric Buddhism

Student Services: Sports facilities

Special Facilities: Scripture Museum; Sculpture Museum; Museum of Religious Art

Libraries: c. 286,000 vols

Publications: Journal *(annually)*; Mikkyo Bunka (The Culture of Esoteric Buddhism) *(quarterly)*

Last Updated: 14/01/09

KUMAMOTO GAKUEN UNIVERSITY

Kumamoto Gakuen Daigaku

2-5-1 Oe, Kumamoto-shi, Kumamoto 862-8680
Tel: +81(96) 364-5161 +81(96) 366-3230
Fax: +81(96) 363-1289 +81(96) 372-4112
EMail: ipkgu@kumagaku.ac.jp
Website: http://www.kumagaku.ac.jp

President: Tadashi Sakamoto

Centres

Foreign Languages (Chinese; English; Korean; Modern Languages)

Faculties

Commerce (Business and Commerce; Management; Tourism); **Economics** (Commercial Law; Economics; International Economics); **Foreign Languages** (East Asian Studies; English; Modern Languages); **Social Welfare** (Child Care and Development; Environmental Studies; Family Studies; Social Welfare)

Institutes

Economics and Business (Business and Commerce; Economics); **Foreign Affairs** (International Business); **Social Welfare** (Social Welfare)

History: Founded 1942 as Institute of Oriental Languages, became University of Commerce 1954. Acquired present status 1990 and present title 1994.

Academic Year: April to February (April-July; September-February)

Admission Requirements: Graduation from high school

Main Language(s) of Instruction: Japanese

International Co-operation: With universities in Australia; Canada; China; Republic of Korea; New Zealand; United Kingdom; USA and Vietnam

Degrees and Diplomas: *Gakushi*: 4 yrs; *Shushi*: 2 yrs

Student Services: Employment services, Language programs, Social counselling, Sports facilities

Libraries: 700,000 vols

Publications: Daigaku Yoran *(annually)*; Icho Namiki *(other/irregular)*

KUMAMOTO HEALTH SCIENCES UNIVERSITY

Kumamoto Hoken Kagaku Daigaku

325 Izumimachi, Kumamoto-shi, Kumamoto 861-5598
Tel: +81(96) 275-2111
Fax: +81(96) 245-3126
EMail: nyushi@kumamoto-hsu.ac.jp
Website: http://www.kumamoto-hsu.ac.jp

Programmes

Health Sciences (Health Sciences)

History: Founded 2002.

Degrees and Diplomas: *Gakushi*

Publications: Journal of Health Sciences

Last Updated: 14/01/09

KUMAMOTO UNIVERSITY

Kumamoto Daigaku

2-39-1 Kurokami, Kumamoto-shi, Kumamoto 860-8555
Tel: +81(96) 344-2111
Fax: +81(96) 342-3110
EMail: sos-somu@jimu.kumamoto-u.ac.jp
Website: http://www.kumamoto-u.ac.jp

President: Isao Taniguchi Tel: +81(96) 342-3113

Director-General: Masaharu Choki Tel: +81(96) 342-3112

International Relations: Tomomichi Ono, Vice-President Tel: +81(96) 342-2021

Centres

AiDS Research (Medicine) *Director*: Masafumi Takiguchi; **Cooperative Research** *(Mashiki-machi, Kamimashiki-gun, Kumamoto-ken) Director*: Hiroyoshi Ikuno; **International Student** *Director*: Takashi Hiyama; **Lifelong Learning** *Director*: Haruo Yanagi; **Marine Environment Studies** (Marine Science and Oceanography) *Director*: Akinori Uchino; **Multimedia and Information Technologies** (Information Technology; Multimedia) *Director*: Tsuyoshi Usagawa

Faculties

Education (Art Education; Biological and Life Sciences; Curriculum; Education; English; Health Education; Industrial Engineering; Japanese; Mathematics; Music; Music Education; Natural Sciences; Physical Education; Primary Education; Secondary Education; Social Studies; Special Education) *Dean*: Shoichi Ishihara; **Engineering** (Applied Chemistry; Architecture; Biochemistry; Civil Engineering; Computer Science; Construction Engineering; Electrical Engineering; Engineering; Environmental Engineering; Materials Engineering; Mathematics; Mechanical Engineering) *Dean*: Isao Taniguchi; **Law** (Civil Law; Law; Public Law) *Dean*: Yataro Yoshinaga; **Letters** (Archaeology; Arts and Humanities; Communication Studies; East Asian Studies; History; Information Sciences; Literature; Social Sciences) *Dean*: Masato Mori; **Medical and Pharmaceutical Sciences** (Medicine; Pharmacy) *Dean*: Shinji Harada; **Science** (Biological and Life Sciences; Chemistry; Earth

Sciences; Mathematics; Natural Sciences; Physics) *Dean*: Mitsuhiko Khono

Graduate Schools

Science and Technology (Natural Sciences; Technology) *Chairman*: Katsuhiko Sugawara; **Social and Cultural Sciences** *Chairman*: Yasutoshi Yukawa

Institutes

Molecular Embryology and Genetics (Genetics; Molecular Biology) *Director*: Tetsuya Taga; **Resource Development and Analysis** (Biological and Life Sciences) *Director*: Hideyuki Saya

Research Centres

Higher Education (Educational Research) *Director*: Yoshitaka Hase; **Shock Wave and Condensed Matter** (Physics) *Director*: Shigeru Ito

Schools

Law (Law) *Dean*: Itaru Yamanaka; **Medicine** (Anatomy; Cell Biology; Histology; Immunology; Laboratory Techniques; Medicine; Microbiology; Molecular Biology; Neurology; Nursing; Pathology; Pharmacology; Psychiatry and Mental Health; Radiology; Surgery) *Dean*: Kiyoshi Siga; **Pharmacy** (Applied Chemistry; Biological and Life Sciences; Pharmacology; Pharmacy) *Dean*: Masato Odagiri

History: Founded 1949 incorporating five high schools, founded 1886, Kumamoto College of Technology (1906), Kumamoto Normal School (1874), Kumamoto Pharmacy College (1885), and Kumamoto Medical College (1896). A national university corporation financed by the Ministry of Education, Culture, Sports, Science, and Technology.

Governing Bodies: Hyogikai (University Council)

Academic Year: April to March (April-September; October-March)

Admission Requirements: Graduation from high school or equivalent, and entrance examination

Fees: (Yen): Registration, 282,000; tuition, 520,800 per annum

Main Language(s) of Instruction: Japanese

Degrees and Diplomas: *Gakushi*: Education; Engineering; Health Sciences; Health Sciences; Law; Letters; Nursing; Pharmacy; Science, 4 yrs; *Shushi*: Clinical Pharmacy; Education; Engineering; Law; Letters; Pharmacy; Philosophy; Public Economics; Science, a further 2 yrs; *Hakase*: Law; Engineering; Medical Science; Pharmacy; Philosophy; Science, a further 3 yrs; *Hakase*: Medical Sciences, 4 yrs

Student Services: Academic counselling, Canteen, Employment services, Foreign student adviser, Foreign Studies Centre, Handicapped facilities, Health services, Language programs, Social counselling, Sports facilities

Student Residential Facilities: Yes

Special Facilities: Medicinal Plant Garden (Faculty of Pharmaceutical Sciences)

Libraries: University Library and 2 branch libraries

Publications: Bulletin of Centre for Education and Guidance *(annually)*; Calanus *(annually)*; Journal of Culture and Humanities *(quarterly)*; Journal of Mathematics *(annually)*; Journal of Science *(other/irregular)*; Kumamoto Hogaku (Journal of Law) *(quarterly)*; Medical Journal *(quarterly)*; Memoirs of the Faculty of Education *(biannually)*; Memoirs of the Faculty of Engineering *(biannually)*; Physics Reports *(quarterly)*; Technical Reports *(quarterly)*

Last Updated: 24/03/11

KUNITACHI COLLEGE OF MUSIC

Kunitachi Ongaku Daigaku

5-5-1 Kashiwa-cho, Tachikawa-shi, Tokyo 190-8520

Tel: +81(42) 535-0321

Fax: +81(42) 535-2313

Website: http://www.kunitachi.ac.jp

President: Noriko Takano

Centres

Collection for Organology; **Media** (Media Studies)

Faculties

Music (Child Care and Development; Music Education; Musical Instruments; Musicology; Singing)

Graduate Schools

Music

Institutes

Music Research

History: Founded 1926 as Tokyo School of Music, acquired present status and title 1950.

Governing Bodies: Board of Directors

Academic Year: April to March (April-September; October-March)

Admission Requirements: High school degree and entrance examination

Main Language(s) of Instruction: Japanese

Degrees and Diplomas: *Gakushi*: Music, 4 yrs; *Shushi*: Music, a further 2 yrs

Student Services: Academic counselling, Canteen, Employment services, Handicapped facilities, Language programs, Nursery care, Sports facilities

Student Residential Facilities: Yes

Special Facilities: Musical Arts Centre. Gakkigaku Shiryokan (Organ Collection)

Libraries: Central Library, 160,000 vols; 120,000 vols of music, and 70,000 audio-visual materials

Publications: Kunitachi College of Music Journal *(annually)*; Kunitachi College of Music Research Institute Bulletin *(annually)*

KURASHIKI SAKUYO UNIVERSITY

Kurashiki Sakuyo Daigaku

3515 Tamashima-Nagao, Kurashiki-shi, Okayama 710-0292

Tel: +81(86) 523-0888

Fax: +81(86) 523-0811

EMail: ota@ksu.ac.jp

Website: http://www.ksu.ac.jp

Programmes

Education; **Food Science**; **Music** (Conducting; Music; Music Theory and Composition; Musical Instruments)

History: Founded 1966.

Degrees and Diplomas: *Gakushi*

Last Updated: 14/01/09

KURASHIKI UNIVERSITY OF SCIENCE AND THE ARTS

Kurashiki Geijutsu Kagaku Daigaku

2640 Nishinoura, Tsurajima-cho, Kurashiki-shi, Okayama 712-8505

Tel: +81(86) 440-1111

Fax: +81(86) 440-1126

EMail: koho@hq.kusa.ac.jp

Website: http://www.kusa.ac.jp

Programmes

Business and Management *(Undergraduate)*; **Chemistry** *(Graduate)*; **Culture and Information Sciences** *(Graduate)*; **Tourism** *(Undergraduate)* (Tourism)

History: Founded 1995.

Degrees and Diplomas: *Gakushi*; *Shushi*; *Hakase*

Last Updated: 14/01/09

KURE UNIVERSITY

Kure Daigaku

1-1-1 Gohara Manabinooka, Kure-shi, Hiroshima 737-0182

Tel: +81(823) 703-300

Fax: +89(823) 703-311

EMail: yoshinori@ondo.kure-u.ac.jp

Website: http://www.kure-u.ac.jp

Programmes

Nursing (Nursing); **Social Information Science** (Information Sciences; Social Sciences)

History: Founded 1995. Integrated Risshikan Daigaku/Risshikan University 2003.

Degrees and Diplomas: *Gakushi*; *Shushi*; *Hakase*

Last Updated: 14/01/09

KURUME INSTITUTE OF TECHNOLOGY

Kurume Kogyo Daigaku

2228 Kamitsu-machi, Kurume-shi, Fukuoka 830-0052
Tel: +81(942) 22-2345
Fax: +81(942) 21-8770
EMail: shomu@cc.kurume-it.ac.jp
Website: http://www.kurume-it.ac.jp

President: Tatsuo Ozaki

Departments

Architecture and Building Services Engineering (Construction Engineering; Structural Architecture); **Education and Creation Engineering** (Engineering); **Environmental Symbiosis Engineering** (Environmental Engineering); **Information and Network Engineering**; **Mechanical Systems Engineering**; **Transport Mechanical Engineering**

Programmes

Bekka

History: Founded 1976.

Degrees and Diplomas: *Gakushi*; *Shushi*

Libraries: c. 112,000 vols

Last Updated: 25/03/11

KURUME UNIVERSITY

Kurume Daigaku

67 Asahi-machi, Kurume-shi, Fukuoka 830-0011
Tel: +81(94) 235-3311 +81(94) 231-7511
Fax: +81(94) 232-5191 +81(94) 231-7718
EMail: kikakukouhou@kurume-u.ac.jp
Website: http://www.kurume-u.ac.jp

President: Michiaki Yakushiji

Faculties

Commerce (Business and Commerce); **Economics** (Economics); **Law** (International Law; Law); **Literature** (Arts and Humanities; Cultural Studies; Social Welfare)

Graduate Schools

Business Administration (Business Administration); **Comparative Studies of International Cultures and Societies** (Comparative Sociology; Cultural Studies; International Studies); **Law** *(Graduate and Professional School)*; **Medicine** (Medicine); **Psychology**

Schools

Medicine (Medicine; Nursing)

Further Information: Also research institutes

History: Founded 1928 as Kyushi Medical School, reorganized as University 1950 and incorporated the School of Commerce.

Governing Bodies: Board of Trustees; University Council

Academic Year: April to March (April-August; September-December; January-March)

Admission Requirements: Graduation from high school and entrance examination

Main Language(s) of Instruction: Japanese

International Co-operation: With universities in China, United Kingdom and USA

Degrees and Diplomas: *Gakushi*: 4 yrs; *Gakushi*: Medicine, 6 yrs; *Hakase*: a further 4 yrs

Student Services: Employment services, Foreign student adviser, Health services, Sports facilities

Student Residential Facilities: Yes

Libraries: c. 680,000 vols

Publications: Industrial and Economic Studies; Journal of Kurume Medical Association; Kurume Medical Journal

Last Updated: 14/01/09

KUSHIRO PUBLIC UNIVERSITY OF ECONOMICS

Kushiro Koritsu Daigaku

4-1-1 Ashino, Kushiro-shi, Hokkaido 085-8585
Tel: +81(154) 373-211
Fax: +81(154) 373-287
Website: http://www.kushiro-pu.ac.jp

Departments

Business Administration (Business Administration); **Economics**

History: Founded 1988.

Degrees and Diplomas: *Gakushi*. Also Teaching Certificate

Last Updated: 14/01/09

KWANSEI GAKUIN UNIVERSITY

Kwansei Gakuin Daigaku

1-1-155 Uegahara, Nishinomiya-shi, Hyogo 662-8501
Tel: +81(798) 546-115
Fax: +81(798) 510-954
EMail: ipd@kwansei.ac.jp; ciec@kwansei.ac.jp
Website: http://www.kwansei.ac.jp

President: Sugihara Soichi
Tel: +81(798) 546-100, Fax: +81(798) 510-954

Chancellor: Ichiro Yamauchi

International Relations: Tadahisa Oshika, Dean, International Programmes EMail: ipd@kwansei.ac.jp

Centres

Information and Media Studies (Information Sciences; Media Studies); **Language**

Graduate Schools

Language, Communication and Culture (Communication Studies; Cultural Studies; Modern Languages); **Law**

Institutes

Business and Accountancy; **Industrial Research** (Industrial Management); **Integrated Communication Research and Development** (Communication Studies; Development Studies)

Research Centres

Teachers Development

Schools

Business Administration *(Also Graduate School)* (Accountancy; Business Administration; Finance; International Business; Marketing); **Economics** *(Also Graduate School)* (Economics); **Humanities** *(Also Graduate School)* (Aesthetics; American Studies; Arts and Humanities; Asian Studies; Education; Educational Psychology; English; Ethics; European Studies; Fine Arts; French; Geography (Human); German; History; Japanese; Linguistics; Philosophy; Psychology; Regional Studies); **Law and Politics** *(Also Graduate School)* (Law; Political Sciences); **Policy Studies** *(Also Graduate School)* (Ecology; Environmental Management; Information Technology; International Studies; Urban Studies); **Science and Technology** *(Kobe-Sanda; Also Graduate School)* (Biology; Chemistry; Information Technology; Mathematics; Natural Sciences; Physics; Technology); **Sociology and Social Work** *(Also Graduate School)* (Environmental Studies; Journalism; Mass Communication; Media Studies; Social Psychology; Social Welfare; Social Work; Sociology); **Theology** *(Also Graduate School)* (Theology)

Further Information: Also international programmes and courses for foreign students; study abroad programmes in 25 colleges and universities in North America, Europe, Asia, and Australia

History: Founded 1889 by Methodist Episcopal Church, South (USA). Accredited as College 1912, acquired University status 1932. An independent private institution financed mainly by student fees (entrance/tuition) and Government support.

Governing Bodies: Board of Trustees

Academic Year: April to March (April-September; October-March)

Admission Requirements: Graduation from high school or foreign equivalent, and entrance examination

Main Language(s) of Instruction: Japanese

International Co-operation: With universities in Australia, Canada, China, Denmark, France, Germany, Republic of Korea, United Kingdom and USA

Degrees and Diplomas: *Gakushi*: Business Administration; Economics; Humanities; Law; Policy Studies; Science; Sociology; Theology, 4 yrs; *Shushi*: Business Administration; Economics; Humanities (Philosophy, Aesthetics, Psychology, Education, Japanese History, Western History, Japanese Literature, English

Literature, French Literature, German Literature); Law; Policy Studies; Science (Physics, Chemistry); Shogakushushi, Business Administration; Sociology (Sociology, Social Welfare); Theology, a further 2 yrs; *Hakase*: Business Administration; Economics; Humanities; Law; Policy Studies; Science; Sociology; Theology, 3 yrs following Shushi

Student Services: Employment services, Foreign Studies Centre, Handicapped facilities, Health services, Language programs, Sports facilities

Libraries: University Library, c. 1.1m. vols. Kobe-Sanda branch c. 120,000 vols

Publications: Humanities Review *(quarterly)*; Journal of Business Administration *(quarterly)*; Journal of Economic Studies; Journal of Law and Politics; Journal of Policy Studies; Law Review; Social Studies; Studies in English, French, German, Christianity, Physical Education *(annually)*; Theological Studies *(biannually)*

Last Updated: 14/01/09

KWASSUI WOMEN'S COLLEGE

Kwassui Joshi Daigaku

1-50 Higashi-yamate-machi, Nagasaki-shi, Nagasaki 850-8515

Tel: +81(95) 820-6024

Fax: +81(95) 820-6024

EMail: intersec@kwassui.ac.jp

Website: http://www.kwassui.ac.jp

Faculties

Health Studies (Health Sciences) *Head*: Yoshiro Tsuji; **Humanities** (Arts and Humanities; English; European Languages; International Relations; Literature; Modern Languages) *Head*: Tetsuo Yamaguchi; **Music** (Education; Music Theory and Composition; Musical Instruments; Performing Arts; Rehabilitation and Therapy; Singing) *Head*: Kozaburo Kushido

Graduate Schools

Graduate Studies (English; Literature; Modern Languages) *Head*: Kazumi Manabe

History: Founded 1879.

Governing Bodies: Kwassui Gakuin

Academic Year: April to March (April-September; October-March)

Admission Requirements: Secondary school certificate

Fees: (Yen): first year, c. 930,000; second to fourth year, c. 630,000

Main Language(s) of Instruction: Japanese

International Co-operation: With universities in USA and China

Accrediting Agencies: Ministry of Education, Culture, Sports, Science and Technology

Degrees and Diplomas: *Gakushi*: 4 yrs; *Shushi*: English Literature; Modern Languages, 2 yrs

Student Services: Academic counselling, Canteen, Employment services, Foreign student adviser, Foreign Studies Centre, Language programs, Social counselling, Sports facilities

Student Residential Facilities: Yes

Libraries: c. 240,000 vols

Publications: Bulletin of Kwassui Women's College/ Junior College *(annually)*

Last Updated: 14/01/09

KYOEI UNIVERSITY

Kyoei Daigaku

4158 Uchimaki, Kasukabe-shi, Saitama 344-0051

Tel: +81(48) 755-2932

Fax: +81(48) 755-3198

EMail: webmaster@kyoei.ac.jp; kyoumu@kyoei.ac.jp

Website: http://www.kyoei.ac.jp

Programmes

International Business Management (International Business; Management)

History: Founded 2001.

Degrees and Diplomas: *Gakushi*

Publications: Journal of Kyoei University

Last Updated: 14/01/09

KYORIN UNIVERSITY

Kyorin Daigaku

Mitaka Campus, 6-20-2 Shinkawa, Mitaka-shi, Tokyo 181-8611

Tel: +81(422) 44-0611

Fax: +81(422) 44-0892

EMail: koho@kyorin-u.ac.jp

Website: http://www.kyorin-u.ac.jp

President: Yutaka Atomi

Tel: +81(422) 47-5511, Fax: +81(422) 49-3361

Faculties

Foreign Studies (Chinese; English; European Languages; International Studies; Japanese; Modern Languages; Oriental Languages; Pacific Area Studies; Tourism) *Dean*: Katsuji Torio; **Health Sciences** (Health Sciences; Medical Technology; Nursing) *Director*: Takaaki Fujiwara; **Medicine** (Medicine) *Dean*: Yutaka Atomi; **Social Sciences** (Accountancy; Business Administration; Ecology; Economics; Environmental Studies; Finance; International Business; International Economics; Law; Management; Political Sciences; Public Administration; Social Policy; Social Welfare)

Graduate Schools

Health Sciences (Health Sciences; Medical Technology; Nursing) *Dean*: Takaaki Fujiwara; **International Cooperation Studies and Development** (Development Studies; International Relations) *Director*: Hiroshi Chiba; **Medicine** (Medicine) *Director*: Yutaka Atomi

Schools

Nursing (Nursing) *Director*: Kiyoshi Kitamoto

Further Information: Also University Hospital. Japanese training course

History: Founded 1966 as College, became University 1970.

Governing Bodies: Board of Trustees

Academic Year: April to March (April-September; October-March)

Admission Requirements: Graduation from high school or foreign equivalent, and entrance examination

Fees: (Yen): 450,000-3m. per annum (tuition fees)

Main Language(s) of Instruction: Japanese

International Co-operation: With universities in Taiwan, China, Hong Kong, Indonesia, Korea, Thailand, Vietnam, Peru, Australia and United Kingdom

Degrees and Diplomas: *Gakushi*: Foreign Studies; General Policy Studies; Health Sciences, 4 yrs; *Gakushi*: Medicine, 6 yrs; *Shushi*: Health Sciences, 2 yrs; *Shushi*: International Cooperation Studies, a further 2 yrs; *Hakase*: Health Sciences; International Cooperation Studies, 3 yrs following Shushi; *Hakase*: Medical Sciences, 4 yrs following Gakushi

Student Services: Academic counselling, Canteen, Employment services, Foreign student adviser, Foreign Studies Centre, Handicapped facilities, Health services, Language programs, Social counselling, Sports facilities

Special Facilities: Hospital

Libraries: c. 450,000 vols

Publications: Journal of Arts and Sciences *(annually)*; Journal of Kyorin Medical Society *(quarterly)*; Journal of Social Sciences *(quarterly)*; Kyorin University Review *(annually)*

Last Updated: 25/03/11

KYORITSU WOMEN'S UNIVERSITY

Kyoritsu Joshi Daigaku

2-2-1 Hitotsubashi, Chiyoda-ku, Tokyo 101-8433

Tel: +81(3) 3237-2436

Fax: +81(3) 3237-2620

EMail: yumin@sakura.kyoritsu-wu.ac.jp

Website: http://www.kyoritsu-wu.ac.jp

Programmes

Arts (Arts and Humanities; Cultural Studies; English; European Languages; Fine Arts; French; Japanese; Literature; Modern Languages; Oriental Languages); **Comparative Literature and Cultural Studies** *(Graduate)* (Comparative Literature; Cultural Studies); **Design and Home Science** (Design; Fine Arts; Home Economics; Nutrition); **Japanese and International Studies** (American Studies; Chinese; European Studies; Japanese; Oriental Studies)

History: Founded 1886 as School, became College 1925, and University 1949.

Academic Year: April to March (April-September; October-March)

Admission Requirements: Graduation from high school or equivalent, and entrance examination

Main Language(s) of Instruction: Japanese

International Co-operation: With universities in USA, United Kingdom and France

Degrees and Diplomas: *Gakushi*: 4 yrs; *Shushi*; *Hakase*

Student Services: Sports facilities

Libraries: 531,000 vols

Publications: Bulletin

Last Updated: 14/01/09

KYOTO BUNKYO UNIVERSITY

Kyoto Bunkyo Daigaku

80 Senzoku, Makishima-cho, Uji-shi, Kyoto 611-0041
Tel: +81(774) 23-3121
Fax: +81(774) 25-2498
EMail: nyushi@po.kbu.ac.jp
Website: http://www.kbu.ac.jp

Institutes

Cultural and Human Research (Cultural Studies; Social Sciences)

Programmes

Clinical Psychology (Clinical Psychology); **Cultural Anthropology** (Anthropology; Cultural Studies); **Human Sciences** (Social Sciences)

History: Founded 1996.

International Co-operation: With institutions in Canada

Degrees and Diplomas: *Gakushi*; *Shushi*

Special Facilities: Computer Centre

Libraries: c 62,000 vols

Last Updated: 14/01/09

KYOTO CITY UNIVERSITY OF ARTS

Kyoto Shiritsu Geijutsu Daigaku

13-6 Kutsukake-cho, Oe, Nishigyo-ku, Kyoto-shi, Kyoto 610-1197
Tel: +81(75) 332-0701
Fax: +81(75) 332-0709
EMail: www-admin@kcua.ac.jp
Website: http://www.kcua.ac.jp

Faculties

Fine Arts (Ceramic Art; Design; Fine Arts; Handicrafts; Painting and Drawing; Sculpture; Textile Design); **Music** (Music; Music Theory and Composition; Musical Instruments; Singing)

History: Founded 1880.

Academic Year: April to March (April-October; October-March)

Admission Requirements: Graduation from high school or equivalent, and entrance examination

Main Language(s) of Instruction: Japanese

Degrees and Diplomas: *Gakushi (Geijutsugakushi)*: 4 yrs; *Shushi*

Libraries: c. 91,300 vols

Publications: Ken-kyu-kiyo *(annually)*

Last Updated: 14/01/09

KYOTO COLLEGE OF GRADUATE STUDIES FOR INFORMATICS

Kyoto Joho Daigakuin Daigaku (KCGI)

7 Monzen-cho, Tanaka, Sakyo-ku, Kyoto 606-8225
Tel: +81(75) 711-0161
Fax: +81(75) 722-2283
EMail: admissions@kcg.ac.jp
Website: http://www.kcg.edu

President: Toshiharu Hasegawa

Programmes

Information Technology (Information Technology); **Web Business Technology**

History: Founded 2004.

Degrees and Diplomas: *Shushi*

Last Updated: 14/01/09

KYOTO GAKUEN UNIVERSITY

Kyoto Gakuen Daigaku

Nanjo Otani, Sogabe-cho, Kameoka-shi, Kyoto 621-8555
Tel: +81(771) 22-2001
Fax: +81(771) 29-2269
EMail: nyushi@kyotogakuen.ac.jp
Website: http://www.kyotogakuen.ac.jp

Faculties

Bioenvironmental Science (Biological and Life Sciences; Biotechnology; Environmental Studies); **Business Administration and Management** *(Also Graduate School)* (Business Administration; Management); **Economics** *(Also Graduate School)* (Economics); **Human and Cultural Studies** *(Also Graduate School)* (Communication Studies; Cultural Studies); **Law** *(Also Graduate School)* (Law)

Schools

Graduate Studies (Arts and Humanities; Business Administration; Commercial Law; Economics; Social Sciences)

History: Founded 1969.

International Co-operation: With universities in USA

Degrees and Diplomas: *Gakushi*; *Shushi*

Student Services: Foreign student adviser, Foreign Studies Centre, Language programs, Sports facilities

Libraries: 250,000 vols

Last Updated: 14/01/09

KYOTO INSTITUTE OF TECHNOLOGY

Kyoto Kogei Seni Daigaku (KIT)

Hashigami-cho, Matsugasaki, Sakyo-ku, Kyoto-shi, Kyoto 606-8585
Tel: +81(75) 724-7132
Fax: +81(75) 724-7710
EMail: ab7131c@adm.kit.ac.jp
Website: http://www.kit.ac.jp

President: Yoshimichi Ejima Tel: +81(75) 724-7001

Director-General: Makoto Kinoshita Tel: +81(75) 724-7002

International Relations: Tsutomu Yoshii Tel: +81(75) 724-7127

Centres

Bioresource Field Science (Entomology; Plant and Crop Protection) *Director*: Koji Ikura; **Cooperative Research** *Director*: Masayoshi Yamada; **Drosophila Genetic Resource** *Director*: Masatoshi Yamamoto; **Environmental Science** (Environmental Studies) *Director*: Sadao Miki; **Fibre and Textile Science** (Textile Technology) *Director*: Yoshiharu Kimura; **Health Care Service** (Health Administration) *Director*: Kengo Nagaoka; **Incubation** *Director*: Kunihiko Tajima; **Information Science** *Director*: Koichiro Wakasugi; **Instrumental Analysis** *Director*: Naoto Tsutsumi; **Manufacturing Technology** (Production Engineering) *Director*: Norio Takakura

Faculties

Science and Technology (Architecture; Biology; Chemistry; Computer Engineering; Design; Electronic Engineering; Engineering; Information Sciences; Materials Engineering; Mechanical Engineering; Molecular Biology) *Dean*: Kiyoshi Shibayama

Laboratories

Radioisotope (Radiology) *Director*: Akira Murakami; **Venture** *(Graduate School) Director*: Hiroyuki Hamada

Further Information: Also Japanese language courses for foreign students

History: Founded 1949 incorporating Kyoto College of Industry, founded 1902 and Kyoto College of Textile Fibres, 1899.

Governing Bodies: Executive Board

Academic Year: April to March (April-October; October-March)

Admission Requirements: Graduation from high school or equivalent and entrance examination

Fees: (Yen): 535,800 per annum

Main Language(s) of Instruction: Japanese

Degrees and Diplomas: *Gakushi*: Agriculture; Engineering, 4 yrs; *Shushi*: Agriculture; Architectural Design; Engineering, a further 2 yrs; *Hakase*: 3 yrs following Shushi

Student Services: Academic counselling, Canteen, Employment services, Foreign student adviser, Foreign Studies Centre, Health services, Language programs, Social counselling, Sports facilities

Student Residential Facilities: Yes

Special Facilities: Museums and Archives

Libraries: University Library, c. 362,000 vols

Publications: Bulletin of the Faculty of Textile Science *(annually)*; KIT International Journal *(annually)*; Memoirs of the Faculty of Engineering and Design *(annually)*

KYOTO KOKA WOMEN'S UNIVERSITY

Kyoto Koka Joshi Daigaku

38 Kadono-cho, Nishikyogoku, Ukyo-ku, Kyoto-shi, Kyoto 615-0882
Tel: +81(75) 325-5304
Fax: +81(75) 325-5307
EMail: kj@bbs.koka.ac.jp
Website: http://www.koka.ac.jp

President: Masamichi Ichigo

Faculties

Literature (English; International Studies; Japanese; Modern Languages)

Programmes

Human Sciences

History: Founded 1944 as Koka Women's University. Acquired present status 1964.

Main Language(s) of Instruction: Japanese

Degrees and Diplomas: *Gakushi*; *Shushi*

Libraries: c. 150,000 vols

Last Updated: 14/01/09

KYOTO NOTRE DAME UNIVERSITY

Kyoto Notoru Damu Joshi Daigaku

1 Minami-Nonogami-cho, Shimogamo, Sakyo-ku, Kyoto-shi, Kyoto 606-0847
Tel: +81(75) 706-3746
Fax: +81(75) 706-3749
EMail: international@notredame.ac.jp
Website: http://www.notredame.ac.jp/int/english/

Departments

Cross-Cultural Studies; **English Language and Literature** (English); **Home Science and Welfare** (Home Economics; Welfare and Protective Services); **Psychology** (Psychology)

Graduate Schools

Humanities and Social Sciences (Arts and Humanities; Cultural Studies; Home Economics; Social Sciences; Welfare and Protective Services); **Psychology** (Clinical Psychology; Educational Psychology; Psychology)

History: Founded 1961. Acquired present title 2002.

Degrees and Diplomas: *Gakushi*; *Shushi*

Last Updated: 14/01/09

KYOTO PHARMACEUTICAL UNIVERSITY

Kyoto Yakka Daigaku

5 Nakauchi-cho, Misasagi, Yamashina-ku, Kyoto-shi, Kyoto 607-8412
Tel: +81(75) 595-4600
Fax: +81(75) 595-4750
EMail: gakusei@mb.kyoto-phu.ac.jp
Website: http://www.kyoto-phu.ac.jp

President: Ken-ichi Inui

Centres

Frontier Research in Medical Science

Institutes

Molecular and Cellular Biology for Pharmaceutical Sciences

Programmes

Pharmacy (Biology; Chemistry; Pharmacology; Pharmacy)

History: Founded 1884 as a private German School, became College 1919. Reorganized and acquired present title 1949.

Governing Bodies: Rijikai (Board of Directors)

Academic Year: April to March (April-October;October-February)

Admission Requirements: Graduation from high school or equivalent or foreign equivalent, and entrance examination

Main Language(s) of Instruction: Japanese

Degrees and Diplomas: *Gakushi*: Pharmacy (Yakugakushi), 4 yrs; *Shushi*: Science in Pharmacy (Yakugakushushi), a further 2 yrs; *Hakase*: Science in Pharmacy (Yakugakuhakushi), 3 yrs following Shushi

Student Services: Sports facilities

Student Residential Facilities: For c. 50 women students

Special Facilities: Botanical Garden

Libraries: 106,099 vols

Last Updated: 25/03/11

KYOTO PREFECTURAL UNIVERSITY

Kyoto Furitsu Daigaku

1-5 Hangi-cho, Shimogamo, Sakyo-ku, Kyoto-shi, Kyoto 606-8522
Tel: +81(75) 703-5101 +81(75) 703-5144
Fax: +81(75) 703-5149 +81(75) 703-2474
EMail: nyushi@kpu.ac.jp
Website: http://www.kpu.ac.jp

President: Go Takeba

Programmes

Agriculture and Natural Sciences (Agriculture; Biological and Life Sciences; Biology; Chemistry; Forestry); **Architecture, Food Science and Nutrition** (Architectural and Environmental Design; Food Science; Nutrition); **Arts and Humanities** (Arts and Humanities; Chinese; Cultural Studies; English; History; Japanese; Literature; Modern Languages; Oriental Languages); **Social Welfare** (Social Welfare)

History: Founded 1895.

Academic Year: April to March (April-October; October-March)

Admission Requirements: Graduation from high school or equivalent, and entrance examination

Main Language(s) of Instruction: Japanese

Degrees and Diplomas: *Gakushi*: 4 yrs; *Shushi*; *Hakase*

Student Services: Sports facilities

Libraries: 330,000 vols

Publications: Agriculture; Humanistic Science; Living Science and Welfare; Natural Science; Scientific Reports

KYOTO PREFECTURAL UNIVERSITY OF MEDICINE

Kyoto Furitsu Ika Daigaku

465 Kajii-cho, Kawaramachi-dori Hirokoji-agaru, Kamigyo-ku, Kyoto-shi, Kyoto 602-0841
Tel: +81(75) 251-5111
Fax: +81(75) 211-7093
EMail: kikaku01@koto.kpu-m.ac.jp
Website: http://www.kpu-m.ac.jp

President: Hisakazu Yamagishi

Research Institutes

Neurological Diseases and Geriatrics (Gerontology; Neurological Therapy; Neurology)

Schools

Medicine (Medicine)

History: Founded 1872 as hospital, became Medical School 1880, acquired university status 1922. Reorganized 1949 and 1955.

Academic Year: April to March (April-September; September-January; January-March)

Admission Requirements: Graduation from high school and entrance examination

Main Language(s) of Instruction: Japanese

Degrees and Diplomas: *Gakushi*: Medicine, 6 yrs; *Hakase*: Medicine, a further 4 yrs

Libraries: University Library, 100,000 vols

Publications: Kyoto Furitsu Ikadaigaku Fasshi

KYOTO SAGA UNIVERSITY OF ARTS

Kyoto Saga Geijutsu Daigaku

1, Gotoh-cho, Saga, Ukyo-kyu, Kyoto 616-8362

Tel: +81(75) 684-7858

Fax: +81(75) 881-7133

Website: http://www.kyoto-saga.ac.jp

President: Ikuo Miyoshi

Faculties

Arts

Graduate Schools

Art and Design

History: Founded 2001.

Degrees and Diplomas: *Gakushi*; *Shushi*

Special Facilities: Audio-visual room.

Libraries: c. 88,000 vols.

Last Updated: 14/01/09

KYOTO SANGYO UNIVERSITY

Kyoto Sangyo Daigaku

Motoyama, Kamigamo, Kita-ku, Kyoto-shi, Kyoto 603-8555

Tel: +81(75) 705-1408

Fax: +81(75) 705-1412

EMail: kayoko@star.kyoto-su.ac.jp

Website: http://www.kyoto-su.ac.jp

President: Ichiro Fujioka

Faculties

Business Administration (Business Administration); **Cultural Studies** (Cultural Studies; International Studies); **Economics** (Economics); **Engineering** (Biotechnology; Computer Engineering; Engineering; Information Technology; Telecommunications Engineering); **Foreign Languages** (Chinese; English; Foreign Languages Education; French; German; Linguistics); **Law** (Law); **Science** (Computer Science; Mathematics; Physics)

Institutes

Comprehensive Research

Research Institutes

Advanced Technology; **Japanese Culture**; **World Affairs** (International Relations)

Schools

Graduate Studies (Economics; Engineering; Law; Management; Mathematics; Modern Languages; Natural Sciences; Physics)

History: Founded 1965.

Governing Bodies: Board of Directors

Academic Year: Autumn semester: (October-March); Spring semester: (April-September)

Admission Requirements: Graduation from high school or equivalent, and entrance examination

Fees: (Yen): 889,000-1,323,000 per annum

Main Language(s) of Instruction: Japanese

International Co-operation: With universities in the USA, Germany, Spain, Italy, Taiwan, United Kingdom; New Zealand; Indonesia; Russian Federation; Mexico

Degrees and Diplomas: *Gakushi*: 4 yrs; *Shushi*: a further 2 yrs; *Hakase*: 3 yrs following Shushi

Student Services: Academic counselling, Canteen, Cultural centre, Employment services, Foreign student adviser, Foreign Studies Centre, Handicapped facilities, Health services, Language programs, Social counselling, Sports facilities

Student Residential Facilities: Yes

Special Facilities: Koyama Hall. Koyama Stadium

Libraries: Central Library, and faculties libraries, total, c. 1m. vols

Publications: Institute Bulletins *(monthly)*; Institute Bulletins *(quarterly)*

Last Updated: 25/03/11

KYOTO SEIKA UNIVERSITY

Kyoto Seika Daigaku (KSU)

137 Kino-cho, Iwakura, Sakyo-ku, Sakyo-ku, Kyoto 606-8588

Tel: +81(75) 702-5199

Fax: +81(75) 705-4028

EMail: ksuinted@kyoto-seika.ac.jp

Website: http://www.kyoto-seika.ac.jp/eng

President: Shigeaki Tsubouchi

Vice-President: Atsuhiko Musashi

Faculties

Art (Ceramic Art; Cinema and Television; Fine Arts; Media Studies; Painting and Drawing; Printing and Printmaking; Sculpture; Textile Design; Video) *Dean*: Kojii Sagawa; **Design** *Dean*: Shojun Matsutani; **Humanities** (Arts and Humanities; Cultural Studies; Environmental Studies; Media Studies; Social Studies) *Dean*: Keiji Washio; **Manga** (Painting and Drawing) *Dean*: Keichi Makino

History: Founded 1968 as a private two-year College with Departments of Arts and English. In 1979 introduced fully accredited and distinctive 4-yr undergraduate courses in the Faculty of Arts. Faculty of Humanities enrolled its first students 1989. Masters programmes introduced 1991. Doctorate programmes introduced 2003.

Governing Bodies: Kino-Gakuen

Academic Year: April to March

Fees: (Yens): Humanities, undergraduate, 567,600 per annum, 2nd year, 572,600; Art, undergraduate, 812,200; 2nd year, 807,200

Main Language(s) of Instruction: Japanese

International Co-operation: With universities in Australia; Finland; Germany; Malawi; Netherlands; Republic of Korea; Thailand; United Kingdom and USA

Accrediting Agencies: Ministry of Education, Culture, Sports, Science and Technology (MEXT)

Degrees and Diplomas: *Gakushi*: Art (BA); Humanities (BA), 4 yrs; *Shushi*: Art (MA); Humanities (MA), a further 2 yrs; *Hakase*: Art (PhD)

Student Services: Academic counselling, Canteen, Cultural centre, Employment services, Foreign student adviser, Foreign Studies Centre, Handicapped facilities, Health services, Language programs, Social counselling, Sports facilities

Student Residential Facilities: For exchange and overseas students

Special Facilities: Art Galleries. A-V Center. Off-campus seminar houses.

Libraries: c. 225,000 vols

Publications: Kinohyoron, Social criticism *(annually)*; Kyoto Seika Daigaku Kiyou, Journal of Kyoto Seika University *(biennially)*

Last Updated: 25/03/11

KYOTO SOSEI UNIVERSITY

Kyoto Sosei Daigaku

3370 Nishi Kotanigaoka, Fukuchiyama-shi, Kyoto 620-0886

Tel: +81(773) 24-7100

Fax: +81(773) 24-7170

EMail: info@kyoto-sosei.ac.jp

Website: http://www.kyoto-sosei.ac.jp

Departments

Information Management (Information Management)

History: Founded 1999.

Degrees and Diplomas: *Gakushi*

Special Facilities: Media Centre.
Last Updated: 14/01/09

KYOTO TACHIBANA UNIVERSITY

Kyoto Tachibana Daigaku

34 Yamada-cho, Oyake, Yamashina-ku, Kyoto-shi, Kyoto 607-8175
Tel: +81(75) 571-1111
Fax: +81(75) 571-4122
EMail: adm@mx.tachibana-u.ac.jp
Website: http://www.tachibana-u.ac.jp

President: Keisuke Aoki

Faculties

Contemporary Business (Architectural and Environmental Design; Cultural Studies; Interior Design; Management; Tourism; Town Planning); **Literature** (Child Care and Development; Cultural Studies; English; Heritage Preservation; History; Japanese; Literature; Modern Languages); **Nursing** (Nursing)

Graduate Schools

Graduate Studies (Cultural Studies; English; History; Japanese; Literature; Nursing)

History: Founded 1967 as Tachibana Women's University. Renamed Kyoto Tachibana Women's University 1988. Acquired present title 2005.

Main Language(s) of Instruction: Japanese

International Co-operation: With universities in Australia, USA, China, Canada, United Kingdom, Taiwan and New Zealand

Degrees and Diplomas: *Gakushi*; *Shushi*; *Hakase*

Libraries: c. 140,000 vols
Last Updated: 25/03/11

KYOTO UNIVERSITY

Kyoto Daigaku

Yoshida-Honmachi, Sakyo-ku, Kyoto-shi, Kyoto 606-8501
Tel: +81(75) 753-7531
Fax: +81(75) 753-2042
EMail: renkei@www.admin.kyoto-u.ac.jp
Website: http://www.kyoto-u.ac.jp/en

President: Hiroshi Matsumoto (2008-2014)
Tel: +81(75) 753-2005, Fax: +81(75) 753-2091

Executive Vice-President for General Affairs, Personnel and Public Relations: Tamae Ohnishi
Tel: +81(75) 753-2003 EMail: koryu52@mail.adm.kyoto-u.ac.jp

International Relations: Masao Tsukamoto, Director
Tel: +81(75) 753-2019, Fax: +81(75) 753-2042

Centres

Advanced Biomedical Engineering Research Unit (Biomedical Engineering) *Director*: Shinzaburo Ito; **African Area Studies** (African Studies) *Director*: Itaru Ohta; **Career-Path Promotion Unit for Young Life Scientists** (Biochemistry; Cell Biology; Genetics; Physiology) *Director*: Yo-ichi Nabeshima; **Computing and Media Studies** *Director*: Michihiko Minoh; **Counselling** (Educational and Student Counselling) *Director*: Kenji Aoki; **Cultural Heritage Studies** (Cultural Studies; Heritage Preservation) *Director*: Mahito Uehara; **Ecological Research** (Ecology) *Director*: Junji Takabayashi; **Environment Preservation** (Environmental Management) *Director*: Masahiro Kawasaki; **Field Science Education and Research** (Coastal Studies; Ecology; Forest Biology; Marine Biology) *Director*: Yoshihisa Shirayama; **Fundamental Chemisty** *(Fukui Institute)* (Chemistry) *Director*: Shigeyoshi Sakaki; **Innovative Collaboration** *Director*: Keisuke Makino; **Integrated Area Studies** (Cultural Studies) *Director*: Koji Tanaka; **International** (International Studies) *Director*: Junichi Mori; **Kokoro Research** *Director*: Sakiko Yoshikawa; **Low Temperature and Materials Science** *Director*: Satoru Maegawa; **Nano-Medicine Merger Education Unit** *(Nishikyo-ku, Kyoto-shi)* (Nanotechnology) *Director*: Masahiro Hiraoka; **Pioneering Research Unit for Next Generation** *Director*: Hirotake Moriyama; **Promotion of Excellence in Higher Education** (Curriculum; Educational Research; Higher Education) *Director*: Tsunemi Hiraoka; **Radiation Biology** (Biology) *Director*: Kenshi Komatsu; **Radioisotope Research** (Radiology) *Director*: Hideo Saji; **Unit for Global Leaders in Advanced Engineering and Pharmaceutical Sciences** *(Nishikyo-ku, Kyoto-shi)* *Director*: Shinsuke Morisawa; **Unit for Synergetic Studies for Space** *(Uji-shi, Kyoto)* (Astronomy and Space Science) *Director*: Katsuji Koyama; **Wildlife Research** (Cognitive Sciences; Wildlife; Zoology) *Director*: Genichi Idani

Faculties

Agriculture (Agricultural Engineering; Agriculture; Biological and Life Sciences; Biotechnology; Environmental Engineering; Environmental Management; Food Science; Forestry; Natural Resources) *Dean*: Shogo Okumura; **Economics** (Business Administration; Economics) *Dean*: Kimio Morimune; **Education** (Education; Educational Sciences) *Dean*: Satoji Yano; **Engineering** (Computer Science; Electrical and Electronic Engineering; Engineering; Industrial Chemistry; Mathematics; Structural Architecture) *Dean*: Koichiro Oshima; **Integrated Human Studies** (Social Sciences) *Dean*: Toshitaka Hori; **Law** (Law) *Dean*: Masanori Shiyake; **Letters** (Social Sciences) *Dean*: Naoyuki Osaka; **Medicine** (Health Sciences; Medicine) *Dean*: Masao Mitsuyama; **Pharmaceutical Sciences** (Pharmacy; Toxicology) *Dean*: Nobuyuki Itoh; **Science** (Astronomy and Space Science; Biology; Chemistry; Earth Sciences; Mathematics; Natural Sciences; Physics) *Dean*: Shigeki Kato

Graduate Schools

Agriculture (Agriculture; Agronomy; Biological and Life Sciences; Biotechnology; Environmental Engineering; Forestry; Horticulture; Natural Resources) *Dean*: Shogo Okumura; **Asian and African Area Studies** *Dean*: Shuhei Shimada; **Biostudies** *Dean*: Eisuke Nishida; **Economics** *Dean*: Kimio Morimune; **Education** *Dean*: Satoji Yano; **Energy Science** *Dean*: Takeshi Yao; **Engineering** *(Nishikyo-ku, Kyoto-shi)* (Aeronautical and Aerospace Engineering; Applied Chemistry; Architecture; Chemical Engineering; Civil Engineering; Electrical Engineering; Electronic Engineering; Engineering; Environmental Engineering; Materials Engineering; Mechanical Engineering; Molecular Biology; Natural Resources; Nuclear Engineering; Polymer and Plastics Technology; Structural Architecture) *Dean*: Koichiro Oshima; **Global Environmental Studies** *Dean*: Shintaro Kobayashi; **Government** *Dean*: Makoto Oishi; **Human and Environmental Studies** *Dean*: Toshitaka Hori; **Informatics** *Dean*: Shinji Tomita; **Law** (Law; Political Sciences) *Dean*: Masanori Shiyake; **Letters** (Behavioural Sciences; Cultural Studies; History; Literature; Philology; Philosophy) *Dean*: Naoyuki Osaka; **Management** (Business Administration; Management) *Dean*: Tatsuhiko Nariu; **Medicine** (Health Sciences; Medicine; Public Health) *Dean*: Masao Mitsuyama; **Pharmaceutical Sciences** (Biological and Life Sciences; Biomedicine; Chemistry; Organic Chemistry; Pharmacy; Physical Chemistry) *Dean*: Nobuyuki Itoh; **Science** (Astronomy and Space Science; Biological and Life Sciences; Chemistry; Earth Sciences; Mathematics; Physics) *Dean*: Shigeki Kato

Institutes

Advanced Energy *(Uji-shi, Kyoto)* *Director*: Yukio Ogata; **Chemical Research** *(Uji-shi, Kyoto)* (Applied Chemistry; Biochemistry; Chemistry) *Director*: Norihiro Tokitoh; **Disaster Prevention Research** *(Uji-shi, Kyoto)* (Civil Engineering; Coastal Studies; Meteorology; Seismology) *Director*: Kazuhiro Ishihara; **Economic Research** (Economics; Educational Administration; Public Administration) *Director*: Kazuo Nishimura; **Frontier Medical Sciences** (Biological and Life Sciences; Biomedicine; Medical Technology) *Director*: Shimon Sakaguchi; **Integrated Cell-Material Sciences** (Cell Biology) *Director*: Norio Nakatsuji; **Mathematical Sciences** (Mathematics) *Director*: Masaki Kashiwara; **Primate Research** *(Inuyama-shi, Aichi)* (Behavioural Sciences; Cell Biology; Ecology; Molecular Biology; Psychology) *Director*: Tetsuro Matsuzawa; **Research in Humanities** *Director*: Bunkyo Kin; **Research Reactor** *(Sennan-gun, Osaka)* (Nuclear Engineering; Nuclear Physics; Safety Engineering) *Director*: Seiji Shiroya; **Southeast Asian Studies** (Cultural Studies; Economics; Environmental Studies; Political Sciences; Southeast Asian Studies) *Director*: Kosuke Mizuno; **Sustainability Science** *(Uji-shi, Kyoto)* (Development Studies) *Director*: Satoshi Konishi; **Sustainable Humanosphere** *(Uji-shi, Kyoto)* (Nuclear Physics; Physics) *Director*: Shuichi Kawai; **Theoretical Physics** (Applied Physics; Astronomy and Space Science; Physics) *Director*: Tohru Eguchi; **Virus Research** (Cell Biology; Genetics; Molecular Biology; Oncology; Virology) *Director*: Ryoichiro Kageyama

Laboratories

Venture Business Laboratory *Director*: Kazumi Matsushige

Further Information: Also Teaching Hospital. Experimental farm. University forests

History: Founded 1897 as Kyoto Imperial University with Colleges of Law, Science and Engineering, Medicine and Letters. Colleges renamed faculties 1919, and acquired present title 1947.

Governing Bodies: Yakuinkai (Board of Directors)

Academic Year: April to March (April-September; October-March)

Admission Requirements: Graduation from high school or equivalent or foreign equivalent, and entrance examination

Fees: (Yen): Undergraduate, Graduate: Registration, 282,000, tuition, 535,800 per annum. Law School: Registration, 282,000, tuition, 804,000 per annum

Main Language(s) of Instruction: Japanese

International Co-operation: With universities in Australia, Austria, Belgium, Canada, China, Czech Republic, France, Germany, Indonesia, Israel, Italy, Republic of Korea, Laos, Malaysia, Mexico, Netherlands, New Zealand, Russian Federation, Singapore, Sudan, Switzerland, Thailand, United Kingdom, USA and Vietnam

Degrees and Diplomas: *Gakushi*: 4 yrs; *Shushi*: a further 2 yrs; *Hakase*: 3 yrs following Shushi

Student Services: Academic counselling, Canteen, Employment services, Foreign student adviser, Foreign Studies Centre, Handicapped facilities, Health services, Language programs, Nursery care, Social counselling, Sports facilities

Student Residential Facilities: Yes

Special Facilities: University Museum. University Archives. University Hospital, Centre for Women Researchers

Libraries: Central library and faculty libraries, total, 6,344,681 vols

Publications: Kyoto University *(annually)*; Kyoto University Bulletin *(biannually)*; Periodicals of the Faculties, Institutes and Centres *(other/irregular)*; Raku-yu *(biannually)*

Academic Staff *2008-2009*	MEN	WOMEN	TOTAL
FULL-TIME	4,201	1,796	**5,997**
PART-TIME	4,297	3,309	**7,606**
Student Numbers *2008-2009*			
All (Foreign Included)	18,360	5,683	**24,043**
FOREIGN ONLY	787	549	**1,336**

Last Updated: 08/12/08

KYOTO UNIVERSITY OF ART AND DESIGN

Kyoto Zokei Geijutsu Daigaku

2-116 Uryuyama, Kita-shikarawa, Sakyo-ku, Kyoto-shi, Kyoto 606-8271

Tel: +81(75) 791-9122

Fax: +81(75) 791-9127

Website: http://www.kyoto-art.ac.jp

Programmes

Art (Architectural and Environmental Design; Ceramic Art; Cultural Studies; Design; Fashion Design; Fine Arts; Graphic Arts; Handicrafts; Heritage Preservation; Painting and Drawing; Performing Arts; Sculpture; Visual Arts)

History: Founded 1991.

Degrees and Diplomas: *Gakushi*; *Shushi*; *Hakase*

KYOTO UNIVERSITY OF EDUCATION

Kyoto Kyoiku Daigaku

1 Fukakusa-Fujinomori-cho, Fushimi-ku, Kyoto-shi, Kyoto 612-8522

Tel: +81(75) 644-8100

Fax: +81(75) 644-8113

EMail: intel@kyokyo-u.ac.jp

Website: http://www.kyokyo-u.ac.jp

Centres

Data Processing (Data Processing); **Educational Research and Training** (Educational Research); **Environmental Education** (Environmental Studies)

Faculties

Education (Education; Educational Sciences; Special Education; Teacher Training)

History: Founded 1876 as Kyoto Prefectural Normal School, acquired present title 1949.

Governing Bodies: Faculty meeting

Academic Year: April to March (April-July; October-March)

Admission Requirements: Graduation from high school, or foreign equivalent, and entrance examination

Fees: (Yen): 496,800 per annum

Main Language(s) of Instruction: Japanese

International Co-operation: With universities in Australia, Canada, China, Germany, Republic of Korea and Thailand

Accrediting Agencies: Japan University Accreditation Association

Degrees and Diplomas: *Gakushi*: 4 yrs; *Shushi*: a further 2 yrs

Student Services: Academic counselling, Canteen, Employment services, Foreign student adviser, Handicapped facilities, Health services, Language programs, Social counselling, Sports facilities

Student Residential Facilities: For c. 400 students

Libraries: Yes

Publications: Bulletin of Kyoto University of Education *(biennially)*

Last Updated: 14/01/09

KYOTO UNIVERSITY OF FOREIGN STUDIES

Kyoto Gaikokugo Daigaku

6 Kasame-cho, Saiin Ukyo-ku, Kyoto-shi, Kyoto 615-8558

Tel: +81(75) 322-6043

Fax: +81(75) 322-6243

EMail: oips@kufs.ac.jp

Website: http://www.kufs.ac.jp

President: Takeshi Matsuda (2010-)
Tel: +81(75) 322-6710, Fax: +81(75) 322-6751
EMail: gakujimo@kufs.ac.jp

International Relations: Toshiki Kumagai, Director, Office of International Programmes (2004-)
Tel: +81(75) 322-6043, Fax: +81(75) 322-6243

Faculties

Foreign Studies (Chinese; English; French; German; Italian; Japanese; Portuguese; Spanish) *Dean*: Tetsuo Kubo

Institutes

Language and Peace Research *(International)* (Linguistics; Peace and Disarmament) *Director*: Toru Horikawa; **Latin-American Studies** *(Kyoto)* (History; Latin American Studies; Linguistics) *Head*: Kishiro Ogaki

Further Information: Also Japanese course for overseas students. Study Abroad programmes in USA, UK, Australia, Canada, Argentina, France, Switzerland, Brazil, China, Mexico, Spain, Belgium, Germany, Portugal

History: Founded 1947 as College, acquired present status and title 1959.

Governing Bodies: Board of Directors

Academic Year: April to March (April-September; September-March)

Admission Requirements: Graduation from high school or equivalent and entrance examination

Fees: (Yen): 700,000 (Spring: 410,000; Autumn: 290,000)

Main Language(s) of Instruction: Japanese

International Co-operation: With universities in USA, United Kingdom and Australia

Degrees and Diplomas: *Gakushi*: Arts (BA), 4 yrs; *Shushi*: Arts (MA) (Bungakushushi), a further 2 yrs

Student Services: Academic counselling, Canteen, Foreign student adviser, Foreign Studies Centre, Handicapped facilities, Health services, Social counselling, Sports facilities

Student Residential Facilities: College Residence (20 rooms for international students)

Libraries: Central Library, 506,190 vols

Academic Staff *2008-2009*	**TOTAL**
FULL-TIME	**137**
PART-TIME	**391**
Student Numbers *2010-2011*	
All (Foreign Included)	**4,053**

Last Updated: 09/12/08

KYOTO WOMEN'S UNIVERSITY

Kyoto Joshi Daigaku (KWU)

35 Kitahiyoshi-cho, Imakumano, Higashiyama-ku, Kyoto-shi, Kyoto 605-8501
Tel: +81(75) 531-7054
Fax: +81(75) 531-7222
EMail: kokusai@kyoto-wu.ac.jp
Website: http://www.kyoto-wu.ac.jp

President: Shigeo Kawamoto
Tel: +81(75) 531-7030, Fax: +81(75) 531-7077

Faculties

Arts and Humanities (Applied Linguistics; English; History; Japanese; Linguistics; Literature; Museum Studies); **Home Economics** (Biochemistry; Dietetics; Fashion Design; Food Science; Food Technology; Interior Design; Medical Auxiliaries; Nutrition; Rehabilitation and Therapy; Social Welfare; Textile Design); **Human Development and Education**; **Study of Contemporary Society**

History: Founded 1920 as Women's College, acquired present status 1949.

Academic Year: April to March (April-September; October-March)

Admission Requirements: High school certificate or foreign equivalent, and entrance examination

Fees: (Yen): 1,046,000 per annum

Main Language(s) of Instruction: Japanese

Degrees and Diplomas: *Gakushi (BA; BS)*: 4 yrs; *Shushi (MA; MS)*: a further 2 yrs; *Hakase*: Japanese; English; History; Education and Psychology; Living Environment; Public Spheres Studies (Ph.D), 3 yrs following Shushi

Student Services: Academic counselling, Canteen, Employment services, Handicapped facilities, Health services, Language programs, Social counselling, Sports facilities

Student Residential Facilities: For c. 850 students

Special Facilities: Concert Hall

Libraries: University Library, c. 762,000 vols

Publications: Bulletin of the Faculty of Human Development and Education *(annually)*; English Literature Review *(annually)*; Gendai Shakai Kenkyu: Contemporary Society *(annually)*; Joshidai Kokubun, Journal of Department of Japanese Literature *(biannually)*; Journal of Apparel and Space Design *(annually)*; Journal of Food Science *(annually)*; Journal of Humanities *(annually)*; Journal of Living and Welfare *(annually)*; Shiso, Journal of Historical Studies *(annually)*; The Shizen Kagaku Ronso, Journal of the Society of Natural Sciences and Physical Education *(annually)*

Last Updated: 25/03/11

KYUSHU DENTAL COLLEGE

Kyushu Shika Daigaku

2-6-1 Manazuru, Kokurakitaku, Kitakyushu-shi, Fukuoka 803-8580
Tel: +81(93) 582-1131
Fax: +81(93) 582-6000
EMail: admin@kyu-dent.ac.jp
Website: http://www.kyu-dent.ac.jp

Faculties

Dentistry (Dentistry)

Graduate Schools

Dentistry (Dental Hygiene; Dental Technology; Dentistry; Oral Pathology; Surgery)

History: Founded 1914. Acquired present status 2006.

Governing Bodies: Kyojukai (Faculty Council)

Academic Year: April to March (April-October; October-March)

Admission Requirements: Graduation from high school or foreign equivalent, and entrance examination

Main Language(s) of Instruction: Japanese

International Co-operation: With universities in China and Republic of Korea

Degrees and Diplomas: *Gakushi*: Dentistry, 6 yrs; *Hakase*: Dental Sciences, a further 4 yrs

Student Services: Sports facilities

Libraries: 87,768 vols

Publications: Journal; Kiyo (Research Papers)

Last Updated: 16/01/09

KYUSHU INSTITUTE OF INFORMATION SCIENCES

Kyushu Joho Dagaiku

6-3-1 Saifu, Dazaifu, Dazaifu-shi, Fukuoka 818-0117
Tel: +81(92) 928-4000
Fax: +81(92) 928-3200
EMail: nyushi@kiis.ac.jp
Website: http://www.kiis.ac.jp

President: Takashi Aso

Departments

Information Sciences (Information Sciences); **Management** (Management)

History: Founded 1998.

Degrees and Diplomas: *Gakushi*

Special Facilities: Computer Centre

Libraries: c/c. 506,000 vols.

Last Updated: 14/01/09

KYUSHU INSTITUTE OF TECHNOLOGY

Kyushu Kogyo Daigaku

1-1 Sensui-cho Tobata-ku, Kitakyushu-shi, Fukuoka 804-8550
Tel: +81(94) 884-3000
Fax: +81(94) 884-3015
Website: http://www.kyutech.ac.jp

President: Morio Matsunaga

Faculties

Computer Science and Systems Engineering (Computer Engineering; Computer Science); **Engineering** (Engineering)

Graduate Schools

Computer Science and Systems Engineering (Computer Engineering; Computer Science); **Engineering** (Engineering); **Life Science and Systems Engineering** (Biological and Life Sciences; Computer Engineering)

Further Information: Also Ilzuka and Wakamatsu campuses. Japanese language courses for foreign students

History: Founded 1907 as Meiji Senmon Gakko, a private Institution. Became National Institution 1921. Acquired present status and title 1949.

Academic Year: April to March (April-October; October-March)

Admission Requirements: Graduation from high school or recognized equivalent and entrance examination

Main Language(s) of Instruction: Japanese

Degrees and Diplomas: *Gakushi*: Engineering, 4 yrs; *Shushi*: Engineering, a further 2 yrs; *Hakase*: Engineering, Mechanical Engineering, a further 3 yrs

Student Residential Facilities: Yes

Libraries: University Library, c. 515,800 vols

Publications: Annual Bulletin (Faculty of Engineering; Faculty of Computer Science and System Engineering and Graduate School of Life Science and Systems Engineering)

Last Updated: 24/03/11

KYUSHU INTERNATIONAL UNIVERSITY

Kyushu Kokusai Daigaku (KIU)

1-6-1 Hirano, Yahatahigashi-ku, Kitakyushu-shi, Fukuoka 805-8512
Tel: +81(93) 671-8910
Fax: +81(93) 671-9035
EMail: admission@kiu.ac.jp
Website: http://www.kiu.ac.jp

Departments

Economics (Economics; Management); **International Studies and Business** (Asian Studies; International Business; Regional Studies); **Law** (Law)

Graduate Schools

Business and Environment; **Legal Studies**

History: Founded 1947. Acquired present status 1950.

Academic Year: April to March (April-September; October-March)

Admission Requirements: Graduation from high school and entrance examination

Fees: (Yen): 820,000 per annum; foreign students, 520,000

Main Language(s) of Instruction: Japanese

International Co-operation: With universities in China, Republic of Korea, Taiwan, Indonesia, India and Thailand

Degrees and Diplomas: *Gakushi*: 4 yrs; *Shushi*: a further 2 yrs

Student Services: Academic counselling, Canteen, Cultural centre, Employment services, Foreign student adviser, Foreign Studies Centre, Handicapped facilities, Health services, Language programs, Social counselling, Sports facilities

Student Residential Facilities: Exchange Students Dorms

Libraries: Science Information System

Publications: KIU Journal of Economics and Business *(3 per annum)*; Kokusai Shogakubu Bulletin *(3 per annum)*; Kyushu International University Law Journal *(3 per annum)*; Kyushu International University Studies of Liberal Arts *(3 per annum)*

KYUSHU KYORITSU UNIVERSITY

Kyushu Kyoritsu Daigaku

1-8 Jiyugaoka, Yahatanishi-ku, Kitakyushu-shi, Fukuoka 807-8585
Tel: +81(93) 693-3305
Fax: +81(93) 603-8186
EMail: nyushi@kyukyo-u.ac.jp
Website: http://www.kyukyo-u.ac.jp

Programmes

Economics (Business Administration; Economics); **Engineering** (Architectural and Environmental Design; Civil Engineering; Construction Engineering; Electrical and Electronic Engineering; Engineering; Environmental Engineering; Information Technology; Mechanical Engineering; Robotics)

History: Founded 1965.

Degrees and Diplomas: *Gakushi*; *Shushi*; *Hakase*

Last Updated: 16/01/09

KYUSHU LUTHERAN COLLEGE

Kyushu Ruteru Gakuin Daigaku (KLC)

3-12-16 Kurokami, Kumamoto-shi, Kumamoto 860-8520
Tel: +81(96) 343-1600
Fax: +81(96) 343-0354
EMail: koho@klc.ac.jp
Website: http://www.klc.ac.jp

Programmes

Global Communication (Communication Studies); **Humanities** (Arts and Humanities); **Psychology and Development** (Development Studies; Psychology); **Social Action** (Social Work)

History: Founded 1997.

Degrees and Diplomas: *Gakushi*

Last Updated: 16/01/09

KYUSHU NUTRITION AND WELFARE UNIVERSITY

Kyushu Eiyo Fukushi Daigaku

5-1-1 Shimoitozu, Kokurakita-ku, Kitakyushu-shi, Fukuoka 803-8511
Tel: +81(93) 561-2136
Fax: +81(93) 561-9728
EMail: fujino@knwu.ac.jp
Website: http://www.knwu.ac.jp

Faculties

Food and Nutrition

History: Founded 2001.

Degrees and Diplomas: *Gakushi*

Libraries: Yes.

Last Updated: 16/01/09

KYUSHU SANGYO UNIVERSITY

Kyushu Sangyo Daigaku (KSU)

2-3-1 Matsukadai, Higashi-ku, Fukuoka 813-8503
Tel: +81(92) 673-5050
Fax: +81(92) 673-5599
Website: http://www.ip.kyusan-u.ac.jp

President: Takashi Sago

Secretary-General: Kazuyuki Kuwamura

International Relations: Masayasu Tanaka, General Manager
Tel: +81(92) 673-5548, Fax: +81(92) 673-5611
EMail: mtanaka@ip.kyusan-u.ac.jp

Centres

Academic Frontier Research; **Advanced Instruments** (Engineering); **Computing and Networking** (Computer Networks; Computer Science); **Health and Sports Science** (Health Sciences; Sports); **Landscape Research**; **Language Education and Research** (Foreign Languages Education; Native Language Education)

Faculties

Commerce (Business and Commerce; Tourism); **Economics** (Economics); **Engineering** (Applied Chemistry; Architecture; Biochemistry; Civil Engineering; Electrical Engineering; Engineering; Information Sciences; Mechanical Engineering; Robotics); **Fine Arts** (Art History; Ceramic Art; Design; Fine Arts; Handicrafts; Painting and Drawing; Photography; Sculpture; Textile Design); **Information Science**; **International Studies of Culture** (Clinical Psychology; Cultural Studies; International Studies; Regional Studies); **Management** (Industrial Management; International Business; Management)

Research Institutes

Industrial Management (Industrial Management)

Further Information: Also Special English and Japanese programmes for foreign students. Study Abroad programmes

History: Founded 1960, acquired present status 1963.

Governing Bodies: Nakamura Sangyo Gakuen (Academic juridical organization)

Academic Year: April to March (April-August; September-March)

Admission Requirements: Graduation from high school or equivalent or foreign equivalent, and entrance examination

Fees: (Yen): 743,000-1,256,000

Main Language(s) of Instruction: Japanese

International Co-operation: With universities in China; France; Republic of Korea; United Kingdom and USA

Degrees and Diplomas: *Gakushi*: Commerce; Economics; Engineering; Fine Arts; Information Science; International Studies of Culture; Management, 4 yrs; *Shushi*: Commerce; Economics; Engineering; Fine Arts; Information Science; International Studies of Culture; Management, a further 2 yrs; *Hakase*: Commerce; Economics; Engineering; Fine Arts; Information Science; Management, 3 yrs following Shushi; *Hakase*: International Studies of Culture, 5 yrs following Gakushi

Student Services: Academic counselling, Canteen, Employment services, Foreign student adviser, Foreign Studies Centre,

Handicapped facilities, Health services, Language programs, Social counselling, Sports facilities

Student Residential Facilities: For 203 students

Special Facilities: Art Gallery. Art Museum. Kakiemon-style Kiln. Virtual Studio

Libraries: 806,691 vols

Publications: Kogakukai-Shi, Essays on Technology; Kokusai Bunka Gakubu-kiyo, Journal of International Cultural Studies; Shokei-Ronso, Essays on Commerce and Finance

Last Updated: 16/01/09

KYUSHU UNIVERSITY

Kyushu Daigaku

6-10-1 Hakozaki, Higashi-ku, Fukuoka 812-8581

Tel: +81(92) 642-2111

Fax: +81(92) 642-2113

EMail: intlkoryu@jimu.kyushu-u.ac.jp

Website: http://www.kyushu-u.ac.jp

President: Setsuo Arikawa (2008-)

Director-General: Kenji Hayata

International Relations: Hirofumi NIshi, Director, International Affairs Division Tel: +81(92) 642-7093, Fax: +81(92) 642-4242

Centres

Accelerator and Beam Applied Science *Director*: Tetsuo Noro; **Advanced Instrumental Analysis** *Director*: Toshihiko Imato; **Advanced Medical Innovation** *(CAMI) Director*: Makoto Hashizume; **Advanced Research in Drug Creation** *Director*: Kazuhide Inoue; **Art, Science and Technology Center for Cooperative Research** *(KASTEC) Director*: Hiroto Yasuura; **Asian Conservation Ecology** *Director*: Tetsukazu Yahara; **Bio-architecture** *Director*: Tetsuo Kondo; **Biotron Application** *Director*: Ken Matsuoka; **Environment and Safety** *Director*: Kiyoshi Ikemizu; **Epigenome Network Research Center** *Director*: Hiroyuki Sasaki; **EU Centre** *(EUIJ-Kyushi) Director*: Machiko Hachiya; **Future Chemistry** *Director*: Masahiro Goto; **Human Proteome Research Center** *Director*: Keiichi Nakayama; **INAMORI Frontier Research Center** *Director*: Yukio Fujiki; **Incubation Center for Advanced Medical Science** *(ICAMS) Director*: Ryoichi Takayanagi; **Institute of Tropical Agriculture** *Director*: Kiyoshi Kurosawa; **Integrated Kansei Design Center** *Director*: Etsuo Genda; **Intellectual Property and Private International Law** *Director*: Toshiyuki Kono; **International Center for Space Weather Science and Education** *Director*: Kiyofumi Yumoto; **International Education Center** *Director*: Kazuo Ogata; **International Research Center for Hydrogen Energy** *Director*: Kazunari Sasaki; **International Research Center for Molecular Systems** *Director*: Nobuo Kimizuka; **Itoh Research Center for Plasma Turbulence** *Director*: Sanae Itoh; **Japan-Egypt Cooperation in Science and Technology** *Director*: Hiroshi Furukawa; **Kyushu University Archives** *Director*: Yoshiaki Kawamoto; **Laboratory for Ionized Gas and Laser Research** *Director*: Kiichiro Uchino; **Low Temperature Center** *Director*: Kazuo Funaki; **Material Management Center** *Director*: Satoru Kuhara; **Natural Disaster Information Center of Western Japan** *Director*: Kenichi Tsukahara; **Next-Generation Fuel Cell Research Center** *Director*: Kazunari Sasaki; **Nucleotide Pool Research Center** *Director*: Yusaku Nakabeppu; **Organic Photonics and Electronics Research** *Director*: Chihaya Adachi; **Plasma Nano-interface Engineering** *Director*: Masaharu Shiratani; **Radioisotope Center** *Director*: Yoshitaka Tanaka; **Research and Education Center of Carbon Resources** *Director*: Jun-ichiro Hayashi; **Research Center for Advanced Biomechanics** *Director*: Renshi Sawada; **Research Center for Advanced Immunology** *Director*: Yoshinori Fukui; **Research Center for Cancer Stem Cell** *Director*: Koichi Akashi; **Research Center for Education in Health Care Systems** *Director*: Satoshi Morimoto; **Research Center for Environment and Developmental Medical Sciences** *Director*: Toshiro Hara; **Research Center for Korean Studies** *Director*: Takatoshi Matsubara; **Research Center for Steel** *Director*: Setsuo Takaki; **Research Center for Synchrotron Light Applications** *Director*: Yasutake Teraoka; **Research Institute of Superconductor Science and Systems** *(RISS) Director*: Keiji Enpuku; **Research Laboratory for High Voltage Electron Microscopy** *Director*: Sho Matsumura; **Risk Science Research Center** *Director*: Yasuyuki Shimohigashi; **Robert T.Huang Entrepreneurship Center** *(QREC) Director*: Toru Tanigawa; **Science,Technology and Innovation Policy Studies** *Director*: Akiya Nagata; **Synthetic Systems Biology Research Center** *Director*: Masahiro Okamoto; **System LSI Research Center** *Director*: Akira Fukuda; **Yunus and Shiiki Social Business Center** *(SBRC) Director*: Hiroto Yasuura

Faculties

Agriculture (Agricultural Education; Agriculture; Biological and Life Sciences; Biotechnology) *Dean*: Atsushi Yoshimura; **Arts and Science** (Arts and Humanities; Natural Sciences) *Director*: Shunichi Maruno; **Dental Science** (Dentistry) *Dean*: Akifumi Akamine; **Design** (Communication Arts; Design) *Dean*: Shinnichi Ishimura; **Economics** (Business Administration; Economics; Engineering Management; International Economics) *Dean*: kenji Yamamoto; **Engineering** (Aeronautical and Aerospace Engineering; Applied Chemistry; Applied Physics; Chemical Engineering; Civil Engineering; Earth Sciences; Environmental Engineering; Marine Engineering; Materials Engineering; Mechanical Engineering; Nuclear Engineering) *Dean*: Sunao Yamada; **Engineering Sciences** (Energy Engineering; Engineering; Materials Engineering) *Dean*: Hideharu Nakashima; **Human Environmental Studies** (Architecture; Education; Urban Studies) *Dean*: Yuji Hakoda; **Humanities** (History; Literature; Modern Languages; Philosophy) *Dean*: Michiaki Takayama; **Information Sciences and Electrical Engineering** (Electrical and Electronic Engineering; Information Sciences; Information Technology) *Dean*: Rin-ichiro Taniguchi; **Languages and Cultures** (Cultural Studies; Linguistics) *Dean*: Michio Tokumi; **Law** (Criminal Law; International Law; Justice Administration; Law; Polish; Private Law; Public Law) *Dean*: Ichiro Sako; **Mathematics** (Mathematics) *Dean*: Masanobu Kaneko; **Medical Sciences** (Health Education; Health Sciences; Medicine; Molecular Biology) *Dean*: Mitsuo Katano; **Pharmaceutical Sciences** (Medicine; Pharmacology) *Dean*: Kazuhide Inoue; **Science** (Astronomy and Space Science; Biology; Chemistry; Earth Sciences; Physics) *Dean*: Makoto Araatono; **Social and Cultural Studies** (Cultural Studies; Environmental Studies; Social Studies) *Dean*: Hideo Hattori

Graduate Schools

Bioresources and Bioenvironmental Sciences (Agricultural Economics; Biotechnology; Environmental Studies; Natural Resources) *Dean*: Atsushi Yoshimura; **Dental Science** (Dental Hygiene; Dental Technology; Dentistry) *Dean*: Akifumi Akamine; **Design** (Design) *Dean*: Shinnichi Ishimura; **Economics** *(Kyushu University Business School, QBS)* (Business Administration; Economics; Management) *Dean*: Kenji Yamamoto; **Engineering** (Aeronautical and Aerospace Engineering; Applied Physics; Biochemistry; Chemistry; Civil Engineering; Earth Sciences; Environmental Engineering; Marine Engineering; Materials Engineering; Mechanical Engineering; Nuclear Engineering) *Dean*: Sunao Yamada; **Engineering Sciences** (Earth Sciences; Electronic Engineering; Energy Engineering; Environmental Engineering) *Dean*: Hideharu Nakashima; **Human-Environment Studies** (Architecture; Behavioural Sciences; Clinical Psychology; Education; Health Sciences; Urban Studies) *Dean*: Yuji Hakoda; **Humanities** (Geography; History; Literature; Modern Languages; Philosophy) *Dean*: Michiaki Takayama; **Information Sciences and Electrical Engineering** (Electrical and Electronic Engineering; Information Sciences; Information Technology) *Dean*: Rin-ichiro Taniguchi; **Integrated Frontier Sciences** (Automotive Engineering; Library Science) *Dean*: Yoshitsugu Morita; **Law** (Law; Political Sciences) *Dean*: Ichiro Sako; **Law** *(Professional)* (Law) *Dean*: Hidetake Akamatsu; **Mathematics** (Mathematics) *Dean*: Masanobu Kaneko; **Medical Sciences** (Health Administration; Health Sciences) *Dean*: Mitsuo Katano; **Pharmaceutical Sciences** (Pharmacy) *Dean*: Kazuhide Inoue; **Sciences** (Chemistry; Earth Sciences; Physics) *Dean*: Makoto Aratono; **Social and Cultural Studies** (International Studies; Japanese) *Dean*: Hideo Hattori; **Systems Life Sciences** (Biological and Life Sciences) *Dean*: Keiji Iramina

Institutes

Advanced Study *Director*: Yoh Iwasa

Research Institutes

Applied Mechanics *Director*: Yuji Ohya; **Bioregulation** *Director*: Hiroyuki Sasaki; **Carbon-Neutral Energy Research** *(International) Director*: Petros Sofronis; **Health Sciences** *Director*: Shuzo Kumagai; **Information Technology** *Director*: Mutsumi Aoyagi; **Materials Chemistry and Engineering** *Director*: Hideo Nagashima; **Mathematics for Industry** *Director*: Masato Wakayama

Schools

Agriculture *(Undergraduate)* (Agriculture; Natural Resources) *Dean*: Atsushi Yoshimura; **Dentistry** *(Undergraduate)* (Dental

Hygiene; Dental Technology; Dentistry) *Dean*: Akifumi Akamine; **Design** *(Undergraduate)* (Communication Arts; Design; Environmental Engineering; Industrial Design) *Dean*: Shinnichi Ishimura; **Economics** *(Undergraduate)* (Business and Commerce; Economics) *Dean*: Kenj Yamamoto; **Education** *(Undergraduate)* (Education) *Dean*: Hirofumi Minami; **Engineering** *(Undergraduate)* (Aeronautical and Aerospace Engineering; Architecture; Civil Engineering; Computer Science; Earth Sciences; Electrical Engineering; Energy Engineering; Marine Engineering; Materials Engineering; Mechanical Engineering) *Dean*: Sunao Yamada; **Law** *(Undergraduate)* (Law) *Dean*: Ichiro Sako; **Letters** *(Undergraduate)* (Arts and Humanities) *Dean*: Michiaki Takayama; **Medicine** *(Undergraduate)* (Biomedicine; Health Sciences; Medicine) *Dean*: Mitsuo Katano; **Pharmaceutical Sciences** *(Undergraduate)* (Pharmacy) *Dean*: Kazuhide Inoue; **Science** *(Undergraduate)* (Biology; Chemistry; Earth Sciences; Mathematics; Physics) *Dean*: Makoto Aratono

Further Information: Also 2 Teaching Hospitals. University farm. University forests. University archives

History: History: Founded 1903 as Fukuoka College of Medicine of Kyoto Imperial University. Established 1911 as Kyushu Imperial University. Acquired present status 1947. Integrated Kyushu Geijutsu Koka Daigaku/Kyushu Institute of Design 2003

Governing Bodies: Hyogikai (University Council)

Academic Year: April to March (April-September; October-March)

Admission Requirements: Graduation from upper secondary school or foreign equivalent, and entrance examination

Fees: (Yen): 535,800 per annum

Main Language(s) of Instruction: Japanese

Degrees and Diplomas: *Gakushi*: Arts; Arts and Science; Education; Law; Economics; Science; Biomedical Science; Nursing; Health Sciences; Pharmaceutical Sciences; Medical Sciences; Engineering; Design (Bachelor's Degree), 4 yrs; *Gakushi*: Clinical Pharmacy (Bachelor's Degree); Medicine; Dental Surgery (Doctor), 6 yrs; *Shushi*: Arts; Science; Engineering; Law; Economics; Mathematics; Mathematics Administration; System Life Sciences; Medical Sciences; Nursing Science; Health Sciences; Pharmaceutical Sciences (Master's Degree); Design; Design Strategy; Philosophy; Information Science; Science and Engineering; Kansei Science; Automotive Science; Library Science (Master's Degree), a further 2 years; *Hakase*: Literature; Philosophy; Science; Engineering; Law; Economics; Mathematics; Design; Information Science; Kansei Science; Automotive Science; Education; Psychology; Pharmaceutical Science; Medical Science; Agricultural Science; Health Science, a further 3 years; *Hakase*: Medical Science; Dental Science; Clinical Dentistry; Clinical Pharmacy, a further 4 years; *Hakase*: Science; Engineering; Philosophy, a further 5 years

Student Services: Academic counselling, Canteen, Employment services, Foreign student adviser, Foreign Studies Centre, Health services, Language programs, Nursery care, Sports facilities

Student Residential Facilities: Yes

Special Facilities: International Student Centre; Kyushu University Museum; Kyushu University Hospital

Libraries: University Library, 957,043 vols; Medicine Library, 345,909 vols; Design Library, 176,197 vols; Chikushi Library, 144,740 vols; Ito Library, 951,647 vols; other institutions, 1,532,170 vols

Publications: Kyudai News *(quarterly)*

Academic Staff *2011-2012*	**TOTAL**
FULL-TIME	**4,118**
Student Numbers *2011-2012*	
All (Foreign Included)	**18,925**
FOREIGN ONLY	**1,931**

Last Updated: 29/10/12

KYUSHU UNIVERSITY OF HEALTH AND WELFARE

Kyushu Hoken Fukushi Daigaku

1714-1 Yoshino-machi, Nobeoka-shi, Miyazaki 882-8508
Tel: +81(982) 23-5555
Fax: +81(982) 23-5530
EMail: kouhou@phoenix.ac.jp
Website: http://www.phoenix.ac.jp

President: Miyako Kake

Faculties

Health Sciences (Health Sciences); **Pharmaceutical Sciences** (Pharmacology; Pharmacy); **Social Welfare**

History: Founded 1999.

Degrees and Diplomas: *Gakushi*

Publications: Journal of Kyushu University of Health and Welfare

Last Updated: 14/01/09

KYUSHU UNIVERSITY OF NURSING AND SOCIAL WELFARE

Kyushu Kango Fukushi Daigaku

Tomio 888, Tamana-shi, Kumamoto 865-0062
Tel: +81(968) 75-1800
Fax: +81(968) 75-1811
EMail: webmaster@kyushu-ns.ac.jp
Website: http://www.kyushu-ns.ac.jp

President: Takuro Kobayashi

Faculties

Nursing and Social Welfare (Nursing; Social Welfare; Welfare and Protective Services)

History: Founded 1998.

Degrees and Diplomas: *Gakushi*

Publications: Memoirs of Kyushu University of Nursing and Social Welfare

KYUSHU WOMEN'S UNIVERSITY

Kyushu Joshi Daigaku

1-1 Jiyagaoka, Yahatanishi-ku, Kitakyushu-shi, Fukuoka 807-8586
Tel: +81(93) 693-3277
Fax: +81(93) 603-9816
EMail: nyushi@kwuc.ac.jp
Website: http://www.kwuc.ac.jp

President: Hiroyuki Fukuhara

Faculties

Home Economics (Home Economics; Nutrition); **Humanities** (Arts and Humanities; Education; Nursing; Primary Education; Psychology)

History: Founded 1962.

Degrees and Diplomas: *Gakushi*

Last Updated: 25/03/11

MAEBASHI INSTITUTE OF TECHNOLOGY

Maebashi Kouka Daigaku

460-1 Kamisadori-machi, Maebashi-shi, Gunma 371-0816
Tel: +81(27) 265-0111
Fax: +81(27) 265-3837
EMail: jimu@maebashi-it.ac.jp
Website: http://www.maebashi-it.ac.jp

Programmes

Engineering

History: Founded 1997.

Degrees and Diplomas: *Gakushi*; *Shushi*

Last Updated: 16/01/09

MAEBASHI KYOAI GAKUEN COLLEGE

Kyoai Gakuen Maebashi Kokusai Daigaku

1154-4 Koyahara-shi, Maebashi-shi, Gunma 379-2192
Tel: +81(27) 266-7576
Fax: +81(27) 266-7576
EMail: mkc@ct.kyoai.ac.jp
Website: http://www.kyoai.ac.jp

Programmes

International Social Studies

History: Founded 1999.

International Co-operation: With Universities in USA and China

Degrees and Diplomas: *Gakushi*

Student Services: Academic counselling, Foreign student adviser, Foreign Studies Centre, Social counselling, Sports facilities

Special Facilities: Computer Centre

Libraries: 44,614 vols.

Last Updated: 14/01/09

MATSUMOTO DENTAL UNIVERSITY

Matsumoto Shika Daigaku

1780 Gobara-Hirooka, Shiojiri-shi, Nagano 399-0781

Tel: +81(263) 523-100

Fax: +81(263) 523-285

Website: http://www.mdu.ac.jp

Graduate Schools

Dental Medicine (Dentistry)

Schools

Dentistry (Dentistry)

History: Founded 1972.

Degrees and Diplomas: *Gakushi*; *Hakase*

MATSUMOTO UNIVERSITY

Matsumoto Daigaku

2095-1 Niimura, Matsumoto-shi, Nagano 390-1295

Tel: +81(263) 48-7200

Fax: +81(263) 48-7290

EMail: mgkouhou@matsu.ac.jp

Website: http://www.matsumoto-u.ac.jp

President: Gyou Sumiyoshi

Departments

Business Administration (Business Administration; Tourism)

Faculties

Human Health Sciences

History: Founded 2002.

Degrees and Diplomas: *Gakushi*

Publications: Matsumoto University Kenkyukiyou; The Journal of Matsumoto University

Last Updated: 16/01/09

MATSUYAMA SHINONOME COLLEGE

Matsuyama Shinonome Joshi Daigaku

3-2-1 Kuwabara, Matsuyama-shi, Ehime 790-8531

Tel: +81(89) 931-6211

Fax: +81(89) 934-9055

EMail: info@shinonome.ac.jp; yuka@shinonome.ac.jp

Website: http://www.shinonome.ac.jp

Programmes

Humanities (Communication Studies; Cultural Studies; Education; International Studies; Japanese; Linguistics; Literature; Philosophy; Psychology; Social Sciences; Social Welfare; Sociology)

History: Founded 1992.

Degrees and Diplomas: *Gakushi*

Student Services: Sports facilities

Special Facilities: Audio-visual room

Libraries: 181,387 vols.

Last Updated: 21/01/09

MATSUYAMA UNIVERSITY

Matsuyama Daigaku

4-2 Bunkyo-cho, Matsuyama-shi, Ehime 790-8578

Tel: +81(89) 925-7111

Fax: +81(89) 926-7565 +81(89) 926-7156

EMail: mu-kokusai@matsuyama-u.jp

Website: http://www.matsuyama-u.ac.jp

Faculties

Business Administration (Accountancy; Business Administration; Business and Commerce); **Economics** (Economics); **Humanities** (Arts and Humanities; English; European Languages; Linguistics; Literature; Modern Languages; Sociology); **Law** (Law); **Pharmaceutical Sciences**

Graduate Schools

Graduate Studies (Business Administration; Communication Studies; Economics; Modern Languages; Sociology)

History: Founded 1923 as Matsuyama Higher Commercial School, acquired present status 1949 and present title 1989.

Governing Bodies: Board of Trustees

Academic Year: April to March (April-September; October-March)

Admission Requirements: Graduation from high school and entrance examination

Main Language(s) of Instruction: Japanese

International Co-operation: With universities in Republic of Korea

Degrees and Diplomas: *Gakushi*: 4 yrs; *Shushi*: a further 2 yrs; *Hakase*: 3 yrs following Shushi

Student Services: Foreign student adviser, Sports facilities

Libraries: 712,828 vols

Publications: Journal of Language and Culture *(biannually)*

Last Updated: 21/01/09

MEIJI GAKUIN UNIVERSITY

Meiji Gakuin Daigaku

1-2-37 Shirokane-dai, Minato-ku, Tokyo 108-8636

Tel: +81(3) 5421-5152

Fax: +81(3) 5421-5458

EMail: cicet@mguad.meijigakuin.ac.jp

Website: http://www.meijigakuin.ac.jp/index_en.html

President: Haruki Onishi

Centres

Liberal Arts

Faculties

Economics *(Also graduate school)* (Business Administration; Economics); **International Studies** *(Also graduate school; Yokohama)* (International Studies); **Law** *(Also graduate school)* (Law; Political Sciences); **Letters** *(Also graduate school)* (Arts and Humanities; Education; English; French; Literature; Psychology); **Psychology** *(Also graduate school)* (Psychology); **Sociology and Social Work** *(Also graduate school)* (Social Work; Sociology)

Institutes

Christian Research (Christian Religious Studies); **Foreign Language Education** (Modern Languages); **General Education** (Education); **Industry and Economy** *(Research)* (Industrial and Production Economics); **International Peace Research** *(PRIME)* (Peace and Disarmament); **International Studies** (International Studies); **Language and Culture** (Cultural Studies; Modern Languages); **Law Research** (Law); **Sociology and Social Work** (Social Work; Sociology)

Further Information: Also semester and academic year curriculum in Japan and Asian studies for short-term exchange Institutions

History: Founded 1877 as private Protestant College. Reorganized as University 1949. Also Campus in Yokohama 1986.

Governing Bodies: Board of Trustees

Academic Year: April to March (April-September; October-March)

Admission Requirements: Graduation from high school and entrance examination

Main Language(s) of Instruction: Japanese

Degrees and Diplomas: *Gakushi*: 4 yrs; *Shushi*: a further 2 yrs; *Hakase*: 3 yrs following Shushi

Student Services: Employment services, Foreign student adviser, Foreign Studies Centre, Health services

Libraries: c. 852,000 vols

Publications: Bulletin of Faculties

Last Updated: 21/01/09

MEIJI PHARMACEUTICAL UNIVERSITY

Meiji Yakka Daigaku
2-522-1 Noshio, Kiyose, Tokyo 204-8588
Tel: +81(424) 95-8611
Fax: +81(424) 95-8612
EMail: gakusei@my-pharm.ac.jp
Website: http://www.my-pharm.ac.jp

President: Akinori Kubo

Graduate Schools

Pharmaceutical Sciences (Health Sciences; Pharmacy)

Schools

Pharmacy (Biology; Chemistry; Pharmacology; Pharmacy)

History: Founded 1902 as Tokyo Pharmaceutical School. Acquired present title 1998.

Main Language(s) of Instruction: Japanese

Degrees and Diplomas: *Gakushi*; *Shushi*; *Hakase*

Libraries: c. 135,000 vols
Last Updated: 21/01/09

MEIJI UNIVERSITY

Meiji Daigaku
1-1 Kanda Surugadai, Chiyoda-ku, Tokyo 101-8301
Tel: +81(3) 3296-4545
Fax: +81(3) 3296-4360
EMail: ico@mics.meiji.ac.jp
Website: http://www.meiji.ac.jp

President: Hiromi Naya (2004-)
Tel: +81(3) 3296-4013, Fax: +81(3) 3296-4353

Secretary-General: Yukio Fujita

International Relations: Etsuko Katsu, Vice-President, International EMail: etsuko@isc.meiji.ac.jp

Centres

Clinical Psychology; **Computer Science** (Computer Science); **Intellectual Properties**

Graduate Schools

Education and Facilities (Agricultural Economics; Agriculture; Anthropology; Applied Chemistry; Arts and Humanities; Biological and Life Sciences; Business and Commerce; Civil Law; Economics; Education; Engineering; English; French; Geography (Human); German; History; Information Technology; Japanese; Law; Mathematics; Physics; Political Sciences; Sociology; Theatre); **Global Business** (Accountancy; Business Administration; Finance; Management; Marketing); **Governance Studies**; **Professional Accountancy** (Accountancy)

Institutes

Humanities (Arts and Humanities); **Science and Technology** (Natural Sciences; Technology); **Social Sciences** (Social Sciences)

Schools

Agriculture (Agricultural Economics; Agriculture; Applied Chemistry; Biological and Life Sciences); **Arts and Letters** (American Studies; Archaeology; Asian Studies; English; English Studies; French; French Studies; Geography; German; Germanic Studies; History; Japanese; Literature; Media Studies; Social Psychology; Theatre); **Business Administration** (Accountancy; Business Administration; Public Administration); **Commerce** (Business and Commerce); **Global Japanese Studies**; **Information and Communication** (Communication Studies; Information Sciences); **Law** (Law; Private Law; Public Law); **Political Science and Economics** (Economics; Political Sciences); **Science and Technology** (Chemistry; Computer Science; Engineering; Mathematics; Natural Sciences; Physics; Technology)

History: Founded 1881 as Meiji Law School, became University 1903. Reorganized 1925 and 1949.

Governing Bodies: Board of Trustees

Academic Year: April to March (April-September; October-March)

Admission Requirements: Graduation from high school or equivalent, and entrance examination

Main Language(s) of Instruction: Japanese

International Co-operation: With universities in Australia; Austria; Canada; China; France; Germany; Republic of Korea; Lao PDR; Malaysia; New Zealand; Sweden; Taiwan; United Kingdom; USA and Vietnam

Degrees and Diplomas: *Gakushi*: 4 yrs; *Shushi*: a further 2 yrs; *Hakase*: 3 yrs following Shushi

Student Services: Academic counselling, Canteen, Cultural centre, Employment services, Foreign Studies Centre, Handicapped facilities, Health services, Language programs, Sports facilities

Special Facilities: Archaeological Museum; Commercial Museum; Museum of Criminology

Libraries: Total, c. 2,120,000 vols

Publications: Journal of the Historical Association of Meiji University *(biannually)*; Law Review *(quarterly)*; Meiji Business Review *(3 per annum)*; Research Reports of the Faculty of Engineering *(annually)*; Review of Economics and Political Science *(3 per annum)*; Studies in Literature *(biannually)*
Last Updated: 21/01/09

MEIJI UNIVERSITY OF INTEGRATIVE MEDICINE

Meiji Kokusai Iryo Daigaku
Hiyoshi-cho, Funai-gun, Kyoto 629-0392
Tel: +81(771) 72-1181
Fax: +81(771) 72-0326
EMail: exam@muom.meiji-u.ac.jp
Website: http://www.meiji-u.ac.jp

Centres

Medical Education and Research (Medicine)

Schools

Acupuncture and Moxibustion *(Also graduate school)* (Acupuncture); **Judo Seifuku Therapy** (Physical Therapy); **Nursing**

History: Founded 1983 as Meiji Shinkyu Daigaku (Meiji University of Oriental Medicine). Acquired present title 2008.

Main Language(s) of Instruction: Japanese

Degrees and Diplomas: *Gakushi*; *Shushi*; *Hakase*

Student Services: Sports facilities

Libraries: c. 64,770 vols
Last Updated: 21/01/09

MEIJO UNIVERSITY

Meijo Daigaku
1-501 Shiogamaguchi, Tempaku, Nagoya-shi, Aichi 468-8502
Tel: +81(52) 832-1151
Fax: +81(52)833-1753
EMail: kouhou@ccmails.meijo-u.ac.jp
Website: http://www.meijo-u.ac.jp

Faculties

Agriculture (Agriculture; Agrobiology; Biochemistry); **Business Management** (Business Administration; Business and Commerce; International Business); **Economics** (Economics); **Humanities** (Arts and Humanities); **Law** (Law); **Pharmacy** (Health Sciences; Pharmacology; Pharmacy); **Science and Technology** (Architecture; Civil Engineering; Construction Engineering; Electrical and Electronic Engineering; Environmental Engineering; Mathematics and Computer Science; Mechanical Engineering; Natural Sciences; Technology; Transport Engineering); **Urban Science** (Urban Studies)

Graduate Schools

Graduate Studies (Agriculture; Biological and Life Sciences; Building Technologies; Business Administration; Business and Commerce; Civil Engineering; Construction Engineering; Economics; Electrical and Electronic Engineering; Engineering; Environmental Management; Environmental Studies; Law; Mathematics; Mechanical Engineering; Pharmacy; Social Sciences; Structural Architecture; Technology; Urban Studies)

History: Founded 1926 as Nagoya School of Science and Engineering. Acquired present status and title 1949.

Academic Year: April to March

Main Language(s) of Instruction: Japanese

International Co-operation: With universities in China, USA and Republic of Korea

Degrees and Diplomas: *Gakushi*: 4 yrs; *Shushi*: a further 2 yrs; *Hakase*

Student Services: Language programs

Libraries: c. 973,000 vols

Last Updated: 21/01/09

MEIKAI UNIVERSITY

Meikai Daigaku

1-1 Keyakidai, Sakado-shi, Saitama 350-0283

Tel: +81(49) 285-5511

Fax: +81(49) 286-0294

EMail: koho999@meikai.ac.jp

Website: http://www.meikai.ac.jp

President: Toshikazu Yasui

Faculties

Dentistry (Dental Hygiene; Dental Technology; Dentistry; Oral Pathology; Periodontics; Pharmacy); **Economics** *(Urayasu-shi)* (Economics); **Hospitality and Tourism Management** (Tourism); **Languages and Cultures** *(Urayasu-shi)* (Chinese; Cultural Studies; English; Japanese); **Real Estate Science** *(Urayasu-shi)* (Real Estate)

Graduate Schools

Applied Linguistics (Linguistics); **Dentistry** (Dentistry); **Economics**; **Real Estate Science** (Real Estate)

Further Information: Also Meikai University Hospital

History: Founded 1970 as Josai Dental University, acquired present title 1988.

Academic Year: April to March (April-September; October-March)

Admission Requirements: Graduation from high school and entrance examination

Fees: (Yen): Registration, 140,000-230,000; tuition, 504,000-938,000; Dentistry, registration, 500,000, tuition, 3.9m. per annum

Main Language(s) of Instruction: Japanese

Degrees and Diplomas: *Gakushi*: Dentistry (Sigaku), 6 yrs; *Gakushi*: Economics (Keizaigaku); Languages and Cultures (Nihongogaku); Languages and Cultures (Eibeigogaku); Languages and Cultures (Chugokugogaku); Real Estate Sciences (Fudosangaku), 4 yrs; *Shushi*: Applied Linguistics (Oyogengogaku); Economics (Keizaigaku); Real Estate Sciences (Fudosangaku), a further 2 yrs; *Hakase*: Dental Sciences (Shigaku), a further 4 yrs

Student Services: Academic counselling, Canteen, Cultural centre, Employment services, Foreign student adviser, Health services, Social counselling, Sports facilities

Student Residential Facilities: Shiseiryo (Dormitory, Faculty of Dentistry)

Libraries: Library (Urayasu Campus), 174,472 vols. Library of Dentistry (Sakado Campus), c. 132,200 vols

Publications: Meikai Economic Review *(annually)*; Meikai Japanese Language Journal *(annually)*; Meikai Journal, Faculty of languages and Cultures *(annually)*; Meikai Roundtable in Applied Linguistics *(annually)*; Meikai Studies in Real Estate Sciences *(annually)*; Meikai University Dental Journal *(biennially)*; The Journal of Arts and Sciences *(annually)*

Last Updated: 21/01/09

MEIO UNIVERSITY

Meio Daigaku

1220-1 Birmata, Nago-shi, Okinawa 905-8585

Tel: +81(980) 542-111

Fax: +81(980) 540-077

Website: http://www.meio-u.ac.jp

President: Eiki Senaha (2006-)

Faculties

Human Health (Health Sciences; Nursing; Sports); **International Studies** (Business and Commerce; Cultural Studies; Education; English; Information Sciences; International Studies; Japanese; Modern Languages; Primary Education)

Graduate Schools

Graduate Studies (Cultural Studies; Environmental Studies; Information Sciences; Management; Modern Languages; Social Studies; Tourism)

History: Founded 1994.

Degrees and Diplomas: *Gakushi*; *Shushi*

Last Updated: 21/01/09

MEISEI UNIVERSITY

Meisei Daigaku

2-1-1 Hodokubo, Hino-shi, Tokyo 191-8506

Tel: +81(42) 591-5111

Fax: +81(42) 591-8181

EMail: kyoumuka@gad.meisei-u.ac.jp

Website: http://www.meisei-u.ac.jp

President: Tetsuo Ogawa

Graduate Schools

Graduate Studies (Arts and Humanities; Economics; Engineering; Information Sciences)

Schools

Art and Design (Design; Fine Arts); **Economics**; **Humanities** *(Hino)* (Arts and Humanities; Education; Educational Psychology; English; International Studies; Literature; Pedagogy; Psychology; Social Sciences; Sociology; Welfare and Protective Services); **Information Science** *(Ome)*; **Japanese and Culture** *(Ome)*; **Science and Engineering** *(Hino)*

History: Founded 1964.

Main Language(s) of Instruction: Japanese

International Co-operation: With universities in USA and China

Degrees and Diplomas: *Gakushi*; *Shushi*; *Hakase*

Student Services: Cultural centre, Sports facilities

Libraries: 813,520 vols

Last Updated: 21/01/09

MEJIRO UNIVERSITY

Mejiro Daigaku

4-31-1 Nakaochiai, Shinjuku-ku, Tokyo 161-8539

Tel: +81(3) 5996-3117

Fax: +81(3) 5996-3247

EMail: colkoho@mejiro.ac.jp

Website:http: //www.mejiro.ac.jp

President: Koki Sato

Faculties

Business Administration; **Foreign Languages Studies** (Chinese; English; Korean; Modern Languages); **Health Sciences** (Biological and Life Sciences; Occupational Therapy; Physical Therapy; Speech Therapy and Audiology); **Human Sciences** (Media Studies; Psychology; Social Sciences; Welfare and Protective Services); **Humanities** (Cultural Studies; Modern Languages; Social Studies); **Nursing** (Nursing); **Studies on Contemporary Society** (Media Studies; Social and Community Services; Social Studies)

Graduate Schools

Business Administration; **International Studies** (Cultural Studies; International Studies); **International Studies**; **Psychology**; **Psychology** (Clinical Psychology; Psychology); **Social Welfare Services** (Social and Community Services; Social Welfare)

History: Founded 1994.

Degrees and Diplomas: *Gakushi*; *Shushi*; *Hakase*

Last Updated: 21/01/09

MIE CHUKYO UNIVERSITY

Mie Chukyo Daigaku

1846 Kubo-cho, Matsusaka-shi, Mie 515-8511

Tel: +81(598) 29-1122

Fax: +81(598) 29-1014

EMail: nyushi@mie-chukyo-u.ac.jp

Website: http://www.mie-chukyo-u.ac.jp

Departments
Political Sciences and Economics (Political Sciences; Regional Planning)

Graduate Schools
Political Science (Political Sciences)

History: Founded 1982 as Matsusaka Daigaku (Matsusaka University). Acquired present title 2005.

Main Language(s) of Instruction: Japanese

Degrees and Diplomas: *Gakushi*; *Shushi*; *Hakase*

Student Services: Employment services, Social counselling, Sports facilities

Libraries: 200,000 vols
Last Updated: 21/01/09

MIE PREFECTURAL COLLEGE OF NURSING

Mie Kenritsu Kango Daigaku
1-1-1 Yumegaoka, Tsu-shi, Mie 514-0116
Tel: +81(59) 233-5600
Fax: +81(59) 233-5666
EMail: kandai@pref.mie.jp
Website: http://www.mcn.ac.jp

Programmes
Nursing

History: Founded 1997.

Degrees and Diplomas: *Gakushi*: 4 yrs; *Shushi*: 2 yrs
Last Updated: 21/01/09

MIE UNIVERSITY

Mie Daigaku
1515 Kamihama-cho, Tsu-shi, Mie 514-8507
Tel: +81(59) 232-1211 +81(59) 232-9057
Fax: +81(59) 231-9000 +81(59) 231-9058
EMail: ryugaku@ab.mie-u.ac.jp
Website: http://www.mie-u.ac.jp

President: Atsumasa Uchida

Faculties
Bioresources (Agricultural Engineering; Aquaculture; Biochemistry; Biological and Life Sciences; Biotechnology; Environmental Engineering; Forest Products; Marine Biology; Natural Resources); **Education** (Art Education; Education; Education of the Handicapped; Health Education; Home Economics Education; Mathematics Education; Music Education; Native Language Education; Physical Education; Preschool Education; Primary Education; Science Education; Secondary Education; Social Studies; Technology Education); **Engineering** (Architecture; Chemical Engineering; Electrical and Electronic Engineering; Engineering; Information Technology; Materials Engineering; Mechanical Engineering; Systems Analysis); **General Education**; **Humanities, Law and Economics** (American Studies; Arts and Humanities; Asian Studies; Cultural Studies; Economics; Environmental Studies; European Studies; Law; Literature; Mediterranean Studies; Modern Languages; Regional Studies; Social Sciences)

Programmes
Agriculture *(Special Programme)* (Agriculture; Crop Production; Food Science; Horticulture)

Schools
Medicine (Medicine)

Further Information: Also Japanese courses for foreign students

History: Founded 1949, incorporating Mie Normal School, founded 1875, Mie Agriculture and Forestry College, 1921, and Mie Normal School for Youth School Teachers, 1925.

Governing Bodies: Administration Bureau

Academic Year: April to March

Admission Requirements: Graduation from high school and entrance examination

Main Language(s) of Instruction: Japanese

Degrees and Diplomas: *Gakushi*: 4 yrs; *Gakushi*: Medicine, 6 yrs; *Shushi*: a further 2 yrs; *Hakase*: 3 yrs following Shushi

Student Services: Health services, Language programs, Sports facilities

Student Residential Facilities: Yes

Libraries: 912,280 vols

Publications: Annals of the Institute of Tractor Research and Testing; Bulletin of the Faculty of Bioresources; Bulletin of the Faculty of Education; Bulletin of the Institute for Experimental Farming; Bulletin of the Mie University Forests; Mie Medical Journal; Report of Environmental Science; Report of the Centre for Educational Research and Practice; Research Reports of the Faculty of Engineering; The Journal of Law and Economics
Last Updated: 24/03/11

MIMASAKA UNIVERSITY

Mimasaka Daigaku
32 Kamigawara, Tsuyama-shi, Okayama 708-8511
Tel: +81(868) 22-5770
Fax: +81(868) 23-6936
EMail: kouhou@mimasaka.ac.jp
Website: http://www.mimasaka.ac.jp

Programmes
Architecture; **Education** (Child Care and Development; Education; Special Education); **Food Science** (Food Science); **Special Needs and Social Welfare** (Social Welfare)

History: Founded 1967 as Mimasaka Women's College.

Degrees and Diplomas: *Gakushi*
Last Updated: 21/01/09

MINAMI KYUSHU COLLEGE

Minami Kyushu Daigaku
Hibariga-oka, Takanabe-cho, Koyu-gun, Miyazaki 884-0911
Tel: +81(983) 23-0793
Fax: +81(983) 22-3444
Website: http://www.nankyudai.ac.jp

President: Yoshio Shibuya

Programmes
Horticulture (Horticulture)

History: Founded 1967. Acquired present status 1967.

Degrees and Diplomas: *Gakushi*

MINOBUSAN UNIVERSITY

Minobusan Daigaku
3567 Minobu-cho, Yamanashi-shi, Yamanashi 409-2597
Tel: +81(556) 62-0107
Fax: +81(556) 62-0727
EMail: info@min.ac.jp
Website: http://www.min.ac.jp

Programmes
Buddhism

History: Founded 1995.

Degrees and Diplomas: *Gakushi*
Last Updated: 21/01/09

MIYAGI GAKUIN WOMEN'S COLLEGE

Miyagi Gakuin Joshi Daigaku (MGU)
9-1-1 Sakuragaoka, Aoba-ku, Sendai-shi, Miyagi 981-8557
Tel: +81(22) 279-1311
Fax: +81(22) 279-7566
EMail: ircenter@mgu.ac.jp
Website: http://www.mgu.ac.jp

President: Yasuhiro Yoshizaki (2005-)
Secretary-General (Acting): Fumio Ise
International Relations: Masayoshi Kumagai
Tel: +81(22) 279-5908, Fax: +81(22) 279-4953

Departments

Cultural Studies (Cultural Studies) *Chair*: Shirou Tanaka; **Developmental and Clinical Studies** *Chair*: Takashi Ishikawa; **English Language and Literature** (English; European Languages; Literature; Modern Languages) *Chair*: Chris Huston; **Food and Nutritional Science** (Food Science; Home Economics; Nutrition) *Chair*: Fumiyuki Takehisa; **International Studies** *Chair*: Yuko Yagi; **Japanese Literature** (Japanese; Literature; Modern Languages; Oriental Languages) *Chair*: Hiroshi Ikari; **Living and Cultural Science** *Chair*: Motoya Hayashi; **Music** (Music) *Chair*: Tomoko Sumikawa

History: Founded 1886. Acquired present status 1949.

Governing Bodies: Board of Trustees

Academic Year: April to March

Admission Requirements: Graduation from senior high school or foreign equivalent, and entrance examination

Fees: (Yen): 865,000-1,468,500

Main Language(s) of Instruction: Japanese

International Co-operation: With universities in Australia; China; Republic of Korea; United Kingdom and USA

Degrees and Diplomas: *Gakushi*: 4 yrs; *Shushi*: English Language and Literature, Japanese Language and Literature, Humanities and Cultural Studies, a further 2 yrs

Student Services: Academic counselling, Canteen, Employment services, Foreign student adviser, Handicapped facilities, Health services, Language programs, Nursery care, Social counselling, Sports facilities

Student Residential Facilities: For 87 students

Special Facilities: Audio-visual Rooms, Computer Rooms, Language Laboratories

Libraries: 322,349 vols

MIYAGI UNIVERSITY

Miyagi Daigaku

1 Gakuen, Taiwa-cho, Miyagi-ken 981-3298

Tel: +81(22) 377-8222

Fax: +81(22) 377-8282

EMail: admin@myu.ac.jp

Website: http://www.myu.ac.jp

President: Shohken Mawatari

Schools

Food, Agricultural and Environmental Sciences (Agriculture; Environmental Studies; Food Science); **Nursing** *(Also graduate school)*; **Project Design** *(Also graduate school)*

History: Founded 1997.

Degrees and Diplomas: *Gakushi*; *Shushi*

Libraries: c. 55,000 vols.

Last Updated: 21/01/09

MIYAGI UNIVERSITY OF EDUCATION

Miyagi Kyoiku Daigaku

Aza-Aoba, Aramaki, Aoba-Ku, Sendai-shi, Miyagi 980-0845

Tel: +81(22) 214-3654

Fax: +81(22) 214-3935 +81(22) 214-3621

EMail: center@ipc.miyakyo-u.ac.jp

Website: http://www1.miyakyo-u.ac.jp/english

President: Kosuke Takahashi

Centres

Data Processing (Data Processing); **Education Counselling** (Educational and Student Counselling); **Environmental Education** (Environmental Studies)

Programmes

Lifelong Education; **Special Education** (Special Education); **Teacher Training** (Teacher Training)

Further Information: Also Japanese language courses for foreign students

History: Founded 1965 as National University providing training courses for teachers previously given at Tohoku Daigaku. Financed by the State.

Governing Bodies: Faculty Meeting; Administration Office

Academic Year: April to March (April-September; October-March)

Admission Requirements: Graduation from senior high school or foreign equivalent, and entrance examination

Main Language(s) of Instruction: Japanese

International Co-operation: With universities in Australia, United Kingdom and China

Degrees and Diplomas: *Gakushi*: 4 yrs; *Shushi*: a further 2 yrs

Student Services: Academic counselling, Canteen, Cultural centre, Employment services, Foreign student adviser, Foreign Studies Centre, Handicapped facilities, Health services, Language programs, Social counselling, Sports facilities

Student Residential Facilities: For c. 240 men and c. 140 women students

Libraries: University Library, c. 330,000 vols

Publications: Annual Reports of Science Education Research Institute *(annually)*; Bulletin of Miyagi University of Education *(annually)*

Last Updated: 24/03/11

MIYAZAKI INDUSTRIAL ADMINISTRATIVE UNIVERSITY

Miyazaki Sangyo Keiei Daigaku

100 Maruo, Furujo-cho, Miyazaki-shi, Miyazaki 880-0931

Tel: +81(985) 523-111

Fax: +81(985) 548-609

EMail: nyushi@po.miyasankei-u.ac.jp

Website: http://www.miyasankei-u.ac.jp

Programmes

Business Administration (Business Administration); **Economics** (Economics); **Law** (Law)

History: Founded 1987.

Degrees and Diplomas: *Gakushi*

Last Updated: 21/01/09

MIYAZAKI INTERNATIONAL COLLEGE

Miyazaki Kokusai Daigaku

1405 Kano, Kiyotake-cho, Miyazaki-shi, Miyazaki 889-1605

Tel: +81(985) 855-931

Fax: +81(985) 843-396

Website: http://www.miyazaki-mic.ac.jp

President: Masayuki Kumamoto

Programmes

Education (Education; Health Education; Physical Education; Teacher Training); **General Sciences**; **Humanities** (Art History; Arts and Humanities; Environmental Studies; History; Literature; Philosophy; Religion); **Languages**; **Social Sciences** (Anthropology; Economics; Environmental Studies; Political Sciences; Psychology; Social Sciences; Sociology)

History: Founded 1994.

Degrees and Diplomas: *Gakushi*

Last Updated: 25/03/11

MIYAZAKI MUNICIPAL UNIVERSITY

Miyazaki Koritsu Daigaku

1-1-2 Funazuka, Miyazaki-shi, Miyazaki 880-8520

Tel: +81(985) 20-2000

Fax: +81(985) 20-4820

EMail: nyusi@miyazaki-mu.ac.jp

Website: http://www.miyazaki-mu.ac.jp

Faculties

Humanities (Arts and Humanities; Communication Studies; English; Information Technology)

History: Founded 1993.

Main Language(s) of Instruction: Japanese

Degrees and Diplomas: *Gakushi*

Last Updated: 21/01/09

MIYAZAKI PREFECTURAL NURSING UNIVERSITY

Miyazaki Kenritsu Kango Daigaku
2203 Komogasako-otsu, Gujibun, Miyazaki-shi, Miyazaki 880-0924
Tel: +81(985) 597-7700
Fax: +81(985) 597-7771
Website: http://www.mpu.ac.jp

President: Hiroko Usui

Programmes

Nursing

History: Founded 1997.

Degrees and Diplomas: *Gakushi*
Last Updated: 21/01/09

MOMOYAMA GAKUIN UNIVERSITY

Momoyama Gakuin Daigaku
1-1 Manabino, Izumi, Osaka 594-1198
Tel: +81(725) 54-3131
Fax: +81(725) 54-3215
EMail: kokusai@andrew.ac.jp
Website: http://www.andrew.ac.jp

President: Kichizo Akashi Fax: +81(725) 54-3202
EMail: gaku-ji@andrew.ac.jp

Faculties

Arts and Humanities (American Studies; Arts and Humanities; Cultural Studies; English; Literature); **Business Administration** (Accountancy; Business Administration; Management; Marketing); **Economics** (Computer Science; Economics; Statistics); **Law** (Civil Law; Criminal Law; Law); **Sociology** (Political Sciences; Social Welfare; Sociology)

History: Founded 1884. Acquired present status 1959.

Governing Bodies: Momoyama Gakuin Institute

Admission Requirements: Secondary school certificate

Fees: (Yen): 1m. per annum

Main Language(s) of Instruction: Japanese

International Co-operation: With universities in Canada, Australia, United Kingdom, Republic of Korea, Taiwan and USA

Degrees and Diplomas: *Gakushi*: 4 yrs; *Shushi*: 2 yrs; *Hakase*: 3 yrs

Student Services: Academic counselling, Canteen, Cultural centre, Employment services, Foreign student adviser, Foreign Studies Centre, Handicapped facilities, Health services, Language programs, Social counselling, Sports facilities

Student Residential Facilities: Yes

Publications: Bulletin *(annually)*; St Andrew's Cross *(quarterly)*
Last Updated: 25/03/11

MORIOKA COLLEGE

Morioka Daigaku
808 Sunagome, Takizawa, Iwate-gun, Iwate 020-0183
Tel: +81(19) 688-5555
Fax: +81(19) 688-5577
EMail: mcnyushi@morioka-u.ac.jp
Website: http://www.morioka-u.ac.jp

Programmes

Education and Literature (Cultural Studies; Education; English; International Studies; Japanese; Linguistics; Literature)

History: Founded 1981.

Degrees and Diplomas: *Gakushi*
Last Updated: 21/01/09

MUKOGAWA WOMEN'S UNIVERSITY

Mukogawa Joshi Daigaku (MWU)
6-46 Ikebiraki-cho, Nishinomiya-shi, Hyogo 663-8558
Tel: +81(798) 47-1212 +81(798) 45-3523
Fax: +81(798) 45-3560 +81(798) 45-3562
EMail: britesox@mwu.mukogawa-u.ac.jp
Website: http://www.mukogawa-u.ac.jp

President: Naosuke Itoigawa

Graduate Schools

Arts and Humanities; **Clinical Education**; **Human Environmental Sciences**; **Pharmaceutical Sciences**

Institutes

Aesthetics in Everyday Life (Aesthetics); **Biosciences** (Biological and Life Sciences); **Developmental and Clinical Psychology** (Clinical Psychology; Developmental Psychology); **Education** (Educational Sciences); **Educational Computing Research** (Computer Science); **Linguistic Cultural Studies** (Cultural Studies; Linguistics)

Programmes

Arts and Humanities *(1 yr, Graduate)*; **Music** *(1 yr, Graduate)*

Schools

General Education; **Human Environmental Sciences** (Dietetics; Environmental Studies; Food Science; Information Sciences; Nutrition); **Letters** (Arts and Humanities; English; Health Sciences; Human Resources; Japanese; Literature; Physical Education; Primary Education; Sports); **Music** (Musical Instruments; Singing); **Pharmaceutical Sciences** (Pharmacology)

Further Information: Also Study Abroad Programme with Mukogawa Fort Wright Institute, Spokane, WA

History: Founded 1949

Governing Bodies: Board of Directors (Educational Corporation Mukogawa Gakuin), comprising 7 members

Academic Year: April to March (April-July; September-December). Also Special Winter Session, January-March

Admission Requirements: Graduation from senior high school or foreign equivalent, and entrance examination

Main Language(s) of Instruction: Japanese

International Co-operation: With universities in USA and Australia

Accrediting Agencies: Japanese University Accreditation Association

Degrees and Diplomas: *Gakushi*: 4 yrs; *Shushi*: a further 2 yrs; *Hakase*: 3 yrs following Shushi

Student Services: Academic counselling, Canteen, Cultural centre, Employment services, Foreign student adviser, Handicapped facilities, Health services, Sports facilities

Student Residential Facilities: For c. 580 students

Special Facilities: Art and Antique Gallery. Koe Memorial Auditorium. Koshien Hall Botanical Garden. Japanese Garden with Tea Ceremony House

Libraries: Central Library, Pharmaceutical Science Branch Library : 550,000 vols

Publications: Bulletins; Research Reports
Last Updated: 21/01/09

MURORAN INSTITUTE OF TECHNOLOGY

Muroran Kogyo Daigaku (MURORANIT)
27-1 Mizumoto-cho, Muroran-shi, Hokkaido 050-8585
Tel: +81(143) 46-5000 +81(143) 46-5024
Fax: +81(143) 46-5032
EMail: renkei@mmm.muroran-it.ac.jp; kikaku@mmm.muroran-it.ac.jp
Website: http://www.muroran-it.ac.jp/index-e.html

President: Kazuhiko Satoh

Centres

Aerospace Research; **Cooperative Research and Development** (Development Studies); **Environmental Science and Disaster Mitigation** *(CEDAR)*; **Health Administration** (Health Administration); **Instrumental Analysis**; **Multimedia Aided Education** (Educational Technology; Multimedia); **Satellite Venture Business Laboratory**

Departments

Applied Chemistry (Bioengineering; Biological and Life Sciences; Chemical Engineering; Chemistry); **Civil Engineering and Architecture** (Architecture and Planning; Civil Engineering; Construction Engineering; Environmental Engineering; Town Planning); **Common Subject** (Arts and Humanities; Linguistics; Mathematics; Social Sciences); **Computer Science and Systems Engineering** (Artificial Intelligence; Computer Engineering; Computer Science; Information Technology); **Electrical and Electronic Engineering** (Electrical Engineering; Electronic Engineering); **Materials Science and Engineering** (Applied Physics; Materials Engineering); **Mechanical Systems Engineering** (Aeronautical and Aerospace Engineering; Automation and Control Engineering; Mechanical Engineering; Production Engineering; Thermal Engineering)

Faculties

Engineering (Applied Chemistry; Architecture; Arts and Humanities; Civil Engineering; Computer Engineering; Computer Science; Electrical and Electronic Engineering; Linguistics; Materials Engineering; Mathematics; Mechanical Engineering; Social Sciences)

Graduate Schools

Chemical and Materials Engineering *(Graduate)* (Chemical Engineering; Materials Engineering; Physical Engineering); **Civil and Environmental Engineering** *(Graduate)* (Architecture and Planning; Civil Engineering; Earth Sciences; Environmental Engineering; Geological Engineering; Structural Architecture); **Doctoral Courses**; **Master's Courses** (Aeronautical and Aerospace Engineering; Applied Chemistry; Applied Physics; Architecture; Artificial Intelligence; Automation and Control Engineering; Bioengineering; Chemical Engineering; Chemistry; Civil Engineering; Computer Engineering; Computer Science; Construction Engineering; Electrical and Electronic Engineering; Electrical Engineering; Environmental Engineering; Materials Engineering; Mechanical Engineering; Production Engineering; Telecommunications Engineering; Thermal Engineering; Urban Studies); **Production and Information Systems Engineering** *(Graduate)* (Aeronautical and Aerospace Engineering; Automation and Control Engineering; Computer Engineering; Electrical and Electronic Engineering; Energy Engineering; Information Technology; Instrument Making; Mechanical Engineering; Production Engineering; Thermal Engineering); **Science for Composite Function**

Further Information: All departments are divisions of the Faculty of Engineering. Also Japanese studies for foreign students

History: Founded 1949, incorporating the Civil Engineering Department of Sapporo Agricultural College, founded 1887, and Muroran Higher Technical School (1939).

Governing Bodies: Yakuinkai (Executive Committee)

Academic Year: April to March (April-September; October-March)

Admission Requirements: Graduation from high school or equivalent, and entrance examination

Main Language(s) of Instruction: Japanese

International Co-operation: With universities in Australia; China; Finland; Germany; Republic of Korea; Russian Federation; Spain; Thailand and USA

Degrees and Diplomas: *Gakushi*: Engineering, 4 yrs; *Shushi*: Engineering, a further 2 yrs; *Hakase*: Engineering, 3 yrs following Shushi. Gakushi equivalent to Bachelor; Shushi equivalent to Master; Hakase equivalent to Doctorate

Student Services: Academic counselling, Foreign student adviser, Health services, Language programs, Social counselling, Sports facilities

Student Residential Facilities: Yes

Libraries: Total, 308,442 vols

Publications: Memoirs *(annually)*

Last Updated: 24/03/11

MUSASHI UNIVERSITY

Musashi Daigaku

1-26-1 Toyotama-kami, Nerima-ku,
Tokyo 176-8534
Tel: +81(3) 5984-3886
Fax: +81(3) 5984-4065
EMail: isc@sec.musashi.ac.jp
Website: http://www.musashi.ac.jp

President: Kazuyuki Hirabayashi

Secretary-General: Sadanori Yuasa

International Relations: Masahiko Masuda

Faculties

Economics (Economics; Finance; Management); **Humanities** (American Studies; Asian Studies; English Studies; European Studies); **Sociology** (Media Studies; Social Sciences; Social Studies; Sociology)

History: Founded 1921 as Musashi High School, became College 1949, acquired present status 1969.

Governing Bodies: Board of Trustees

Academic Year: April to March (April-September; October-March)

Admission Requirements: Graduation from high school or equivalent, and entrance examination

Fees: (Yen): 680,000 per annum

Main Language(s) of Instruction: Japanese

Degrees and Diplomas: *Gakushi*: Arts (Bungakushi); Economics (Keizaigakushi), 4 yrs; *Shushi*: Economics (Keizaigakushushi), a further 2 yrs; *Hakase*: Economics (Keizaigakuhakushi), 3 yrs following Shushi

Student Residential Facilities: Yes

Special Facilities: Audio-Visual and Foreign Language Centre. Centre for Computer Education. Musashi University Research Institute

Libraries: c. 573,790 vols

Publications: Journal (Economics); Journal (Human and Cultural Sciences)

MUSASHINO ACADEMIA MUSICAE

Musashino Ongaku Daigaku

1-13-1 Hazawa, Nerima-ku,
Tokyo 176-8521
Tel: +81(3) 3992-1121
Fax: +81(3) 3991-7599
Website: http://www.musashino-music.ac.jp

Faculties

Music (Music Education; Music Theory and Composition; Musical Instruments; Musicology; Singing)

History: Founded 1929 as Musashino School of Music. Officially recognized by the Government 1932. Acquired present status 1949. Financially self-supporting.

Governing Bodies: Board of Trustees

Academic Year: April to March (April-September; October-March)

Admission Requirements: Graduation from high school and entrance examination

Main Language(s) of Instruction: Japanese

Degrees and Diplomas: *Gakushi*: Music (B.Mus), 4 yrs; *Shushi*: Music; Musicology (M.Mus), a further 2 yrs; *Hakase*: Music; Musicology (D.Mus), a further 3 yrs. Also Teaching Qualifications

Student Services: Academic counselling, Canteen, Employment services, Foreign student adviser, Health services, Language programs, Social counselling, Sports facilities

Student Residential Facilities: For c. 1,120 students

Special Facilities: Musashino Ongaku Daigaku Gakki-Hakubutsukan (Instrument Museum)

Libraries: Central Library, 200,000 vols

Publications: Gakusei no rombun (Collection of theses) *(annually)*; Kenkyu Kiyo (Research Bulletin)

MUSASHINO ART UNIVERSITY

Musashino Bijutsu Daigaku (MAU)

1-736 Ogawa-cho, Kodaira-shi, Tokyo 187-8505
Tel: +81(42) 341-5011
Fax: +81(42) 342-5193
EMail: kokusai@musabi.ac.jp
Website: http://www.musabi.ac.jp/

President: Masataka Nakano

International Relations: Tadanori Nagasawa
Tel: +81(423) 42-6037

Departments
Architecture (Architecture and Planning); **Arts Policy and Management** (Art Management); **Design Informatics** (Computer Graphics); **Imaging Arts and Sciences** (Cinema and Television; Computer Graphics; Photography; Theatre); **Industrial, Interior, and Craft Design** (Handicrafts; Industrial Design; Interior Design); **Japanese Painting** (Painting and Drawing); **Painting** (Painting and Drawing); **Scenography, Display, and Fashion Design** (Display and Stage Design; Fashion Design); **Science of Design** (Design; Graphic Design; Visual Arts); **Sculpture** (Sculpture); **Visual Communication Design** (Graphic Design)

History: Founded 1929 as Art School, acquired University status 1962.

Governing Bodies: Board of Directors; Board of Trustees

Academic Year: April to March (April-July; September-March)

Admission Requirements: Graduation from high school or equivalent, and entrance examination. Provision is made for the recognition of foreign qualifications

Fees: (Yen): Registration, 360,000; tuition, 1.5m. per annum

Main Language(s) of Instruction: Japanese

International Co-operation: With institutions in France, Finland, United Kingdom and Italy

Degrees and Diplomas: *Gakushi*: 4 yrs; *Shushi*: a further 2 yrs; *Hakase (PhD)*: a further 3 yrs

Special Facilities: Museum Library

Libraries: University Library, c. 220,000 vols

Publications: Bulletin of Museum Library *(annually)*

Press or Publishing House: University Press

Last Updated: 21/01/09

MUSASHINO GAKUIN UNIVERSITY

Musashino Gakuin Daigaku
860 Kamihirose, Sayama-shi,
Saitama 350-1321
Tel: +81(42) 954-6131
Fax: +81(42) 954-6134
EMail: kokusai@musa.ac.jp
Website: http://www.musashino.ac.jp/university/

Graduate Schools
International Communication (Communication Studies; International Studies)

Programmes
Business; **Cultural Studies** (Cultural Studies); **Human Sciences**

History: Founded 2004.

Degrees and Diplomas: *Gakushi*; *Shushi*

Publications: The Bulletin of Musashino Gakuin University

Last Updated: 26/01/09

MUSASHINO UNIVERSITY

Musashino Daigaku
1-1-20 Shin-machi, Nishi-Tokyo, Tokyo 202-8585
Tel: +81(424) 68-3111
Fax: +81(424) 68-3154
EMail: nyushi@musashino-u.ac.jp
Website: http://www.musashino-u.ac.jp

President: Osamu Terasaki

Faculties
Human Studies (Architectural and Environmental Design; Child Care and Development; Environmental Studies; Social Studies; Social Welfare); **Literature** (Cultural Studies; English; European Languages; Humanities and Social Science Education; Japanese; Literature; Modern Languages; Oriental Languages); **Nursing**; **Pharmacy** (Pharmacy); **Political Sciences and Economics**

Schools
Graduate Studies

History: Founded 1950 as Musashino Women's Junior College. Known as Musashino Joshi Daigaku/Musashino Women's University until 2003.

Academic Year: April to March

Fees: (Yen): Tuition, 700,000; other expenses, 230,000

Main Language(s) of Instruction: Japanese

International Co-operation: With universities in Canada, USA, China and Republic of Korea

Degrees and Diplomas: *Gakushi*: 4 yrs; *Shushi*; *Hakase*

Student Services: Academic counselling, Canteen, Employment services, Foreign student adviser, Foreign Studies Centre, Language programs, Sports facilities

Student Residential Facilities: Yes

Libraries: c. 300,000 vols

Last Updated: 26/01/09

NAGAHAMA INSTITUTE OF BIO-SCIENCE AND TECHNOLOGY

Nagahama Baio Daigaku
1266 Tamuracyo, Nagahama-shi, Shiga 526-0829
Tel: +81(749) 64-8100
Fax: +81(749) 64-8140
EMail: jim@nagahama-i-bio.ac.jp
Website: http://www.nagahama-i-bio.ac.jp

Programmes
Bio-Science and Technology

Degrees and Diplomas: *Gakushi*

Last Updated: 26/01/09

NAGANO COLLEGE OF NURSING

Naganoken Kango Daigaku (NCN)
1694 Akaho, Komagane-shi, Nagano-shi, Nagano 399-4117
Tel: +81(265) 81-5100
Fax: +81(265) 81-1256
EMail: webmaster@nagano-nurs.ac.jp
Website: http://www.nagano-nurs.ac.jp

Programmes
Arts and Humanities (Arts and Humanities); **Nursing** (Nursing); **Social and Natural Sciences** (Natural Sciences; Social Sciences)

History: Founded 1995.

Degrees and Diplomas: *Gakushi (BScN)*; *Shushi (MSN)*; *Hakase (PhD)*

Libraries: c. 35,800 vols.

NAGANO UNIVERSITY

Nagano Daigaku
Shimonogo 658-1, Ueda-shi, Nagano 386-1298
Tel: +81(268) 39-0001
Fax: +81(268) 39-0002
EMail: kouhou@nagano.ac.jp
Website: http://www.nagano.ac.jp

President: Rikio Shimada

Faculties
Social Sciences (Business Administration; Chinese; Communication Studies; Cultural Studies; English; Environmental Studies; French; German; Information Management; Information Sciences; Information Technology; Media Studies; Modern Languages; Natural Sciences; Philosophy; Physical Education; Social Sciences); **Social Welfare**

History: Founded 1966.

Degrees and Diplomas: *Gakushi*

Last Updated: 26/01/09

NAGAOKA INSTITUTE OF DESIGN

Nagaoka Zokei Daigaku
197 Miyazeki-machi, Nagaoka-shi, Niigata 940-2088
Tel: +81(258) 213-311
Fax: +81(258) 213-312
EMail: nyushi@nagaoka-id.ac.jp
Website: http://www.nagaoka-id.ac.jp

Departments

Architecture and Environmental Design (Architectural and Environmental Design; Interior Design; Landscape Architecture); **Industrial Design** (Handicrafts; Industrial Design; Textile Design); **Visual Communication Design** (Communication Arts; Design; Photography; Visual Arts)

History: Founded 1994.

Degrees and Diplomas: *Gakushi*; *Shushi*; *Hakase*

Last Updated: 26/01/09

NAGAOKA UNIVERSITY OF TECHNOLOGY

Nagaoka Gijutsu Kagaku Daigaku

1603-1, Kamitomioka-machi, Nagaoka-shi, Niigata 940-2188

Tel: +81(258) 46-6000

EMail: koho@jcom.nagaokaut.ac.jp

Website: http://www.nagaokaut.ac.jp

President: Koichi Niihara

Graduate Schools

Engineering *(Doctoral programme)*; **Management of Technology** *(Professional Degree Course)* (Information Technology; Safety Engineering)

Schools

Engineering *(Also Master's programme)* (Bioengineering; Civil Engineering; Electrical and Electronic Engineering; Engineering; Environmental Engineering; Information Technology; Materials Engineering; Mechanical Engineering)

Further Information: Also research programmes

History: Founded 1976.

Academic Year: April to March (April-August; September-December; January-March)

Admission Requirements: Graduation from high school and entrance examination

Main Language(s) of Instruction: Japanese

International Co-operation: With universities in China, Korea and Thailand

Degrees and Diplomas: *Gakushi*: 4 yrs; *Shushi*: a further 2 yrs; *Hakase*

Student Services: Academic counselling, Employment services, Foreign student adviser, Health services, Language programs, Sports facilities

Student Residential Facilities: For c. 360 students

Libraries: 138,500 vols

Last Updated: 24/03/11

NAGASAKI INSTITUTE OF APPLIED SCIENCES

Nagasaki Sogo Kagaku Daigaku

536 Aba-machi, Nagasaki-shi, Nagasaki 851-0193

Tel: +81(95) 839-3111

Fax: +81(95) 839-0584

EMail: pr@nias.ac.jp

Website: http://www.nias.ac.jp

Programmes

Architecture (Architecture; Structural Architecture); **Business Administration** (Administration; Business Administration); **Computer Science**; **Engineering** (Computer Engineering; Electrical Engineering; Electronic Engineering; Engineering; Engineering Drawing and Design; Marine Engineering; Mechanical Engineering; Naval Architecture); **Environmental Management**; **Information Technology**

History: Founded 1942, became College of Shipbuilding 1965 and recently acquired new title.

Governing Bodies: Board of Trustees; Council

Academic Year: April to March (April-October; October-March)

Admission Requirements: Graduation from high school and entrance examination

Main Language(s) of Instruction: Japanese

International Co-operation: With universities in China

Degrees and Diplomas: *Gakushi*: Engineering (Kogakushi), 4 yrs; *Shushi*: a further 2 yrs

Student Services: Cultural centre, Language programs, Sports facilities

Libraries: 172,000 vols

Publications: Bulletin *(biannually)*; Studies of Peace Culture *(annually)*

Last Updated: 26/01/09

NAGASAKI INTERNATIONAL UNIVERSITY

Nagasaki Kokusai Daigaku

2825-7 Huis Ten Bosch-cho, Sasebo-shi, Nagasaki-shi, Nagasaki 859-3298

Tel: +81(956) 39-2020

Fax: +81(956) 39-3111

EMail: miz@niu.ac.jp

Website: http://www.niu.ac.jp

Faculties

Health Management; **Human Sociology** (Arts and Humanities; International Studies; Social Sciences; Social Work; Tourism)

History: Founded 2000.

Admission Requirements: Applicants must be 18 year old as of March 31 in the year of entry and must possess Grade 2 (or equivalent) or above of the Japanese Language Ability Test (JLAT); also entrance examination.

Fees: (Yen): entrance examination fee, 10,000; first year, 795,000 per annum for overseas students.

Degrees and Diplomas: *Gakushi*

Last Updated: 26/01/09

NAGASAKI JUNSHIN CATHOLIC UNIVERSITY

Nagasaki Junshin Daigaku (NJCU)

253 Mitsuyama-machi, Nagasaki-shi, Nagasaki 852-8558

Tel: +81(95) 846-0084

Fax: +81(95) 846-0737 +81(95) 849-1694

EMail: nyushikoho@n-junshin.ac.jp

Website: http://www.n-junshin.ac.jp/

Faculties

Humanities

History: Founded 1994.

Admission Requirements: Graduation from high school and entrance examination

Main Language(s) of Instruction: Japanese

International Co-operation: With universities in USA, China and Europe

Degrees and Diplomas: *Gakushi*: Arts and Humanities, 4 yrs; *Shushi*: Arts and Humanities, a further 2 yrs; *Hakase*: Arts and Humanities

Student Services: Academic counselling, Canteen, Cultural centre, Employment services, Foreign student adviser, Foreign Studies Centre, Handicapped facilities, Health services, Language programs, Nursery care, Social counselling, Sports facilities

Student Residential Facilities: Yes

Special Facilities: Nagasaki Junshin Catholic University Museum

Libraries: University Library,150.00 vols

Publications: Academic Research Series *(annually)*; Collection of Academic Studies on the History of Nagasaki *(annually)*; Junshin Journal of Human Studies, Academic Papers by Faculty Members *(annually)*; Series of Humanistic Culture Studies *(annually)*; Series of Nagasaki Junshin Lectures, Institution of Christian Culture in Nagasaki *(annually)*

Last Updated: 26/01/09

NAGASAKI UNIVERSITY

Nagasaki Daigaku

1-14 Bunkyo-machi, Nagasaki-shi, Nagasaki 852-8521

Tel: +81(95) 847-1111

Fax: +81(95) 844-5491

EMail: www_admin@ml.nagasaki-u.ac.jp

Website: http://www.nagasaki-u.ac.jp/index_en.html

President: Shigeru Katamine (2008-)

Centres
Education Research and Training (Educational Research); **Educational Research for Lifelong Learning** (Continuing Education; Curriculum; Educational Testing and Evaluation; Higher Education) *Director*: Tatsuro Obara; **Frontier Life Sciences** (Biomedicine; Genetics; Organic Chemistry) *Director*: Hiroshi Sato; **International Collaborative Research**; **Joint Research** *Director*: Mutsuhisa Furukawa; **Total Human Education and Child Welfare** *Director*: Kotako Kamizono

Faculties
Engineering (Applied Chemistry; Automation and Control Engineering; Chemistry; Civil Engineering; Computer Engineering; Computer Science; Construction Engineering; Electrical and Electronic Engineering; Energy Engineering; Engineering; Environmental Engineering; Information Sciences; Materials Engineering; Mechanical Engineering; Production Engineering; Software Engineering; Telecommunications Engineering) *Dean*: Jun Oyama; **Environmental Studies** *Dean*: Tadashi Sakuma; **Fisheries** (Aquaculture; Biochemistry; Fishery; Marine Science and Oceanography) *Dean*: Hideaki Nakata; **General Economics** (Accountancy; Business Administration; Communication Studies; Econometrics; Economic and Finance Policy; Economics; International Economics; Leadership; Management Systems; Regional Studies) *Dean*: Tadashi Tojo; **Teacher Education** (Biological and Life Sciences; Cultural Studies; Education; Educational Psychology; Fine Arts; Health Sciences; Information Technology; Natural Sciences; Preschool Education; Primary Education; Secondary Education; Teacher Training) *Dean*: Tateo Hashimoto

Graduate Schools
Biomedical Sciences (Biomedicine; Epidemiology; Medicine; Pharmacology; Pharmacy) *Dean*: Masao Tomonaga; **Economics** (Economics; Leadership; Management; Management Systems) *Dean*: Tadashi Tojo; **Education** (Curriculum; Education) *Dean*: Tateo Hashimoto; **Science and Technology** (Computer Science; Electrical Engineering; Environmental Engineering; Environmental Management; Environmental Studies; Fishery; Marine Science and Oceanography; Materials Engineering; Mechanical Engineering) *Dean*: Masahiro Ishida

Institutes
Atomic Bomb Disease; **East China Sea Research** *Director*: Kazumi Matsuoka; **Tropical Medicine** (Microbiology; Tropical Medicine) *Dean*: Yoshiki Aoki

Research Centres
Higher Education *(Research and Development Centre)* (Educational Research; Higher Education) *Director*: Hirotoshi Fukunaga; **Tropical Infections** *(Animal Research Centre)* (Tropical Medicine); **Tropical Infectious Diseases** (Tropical Medicine)

Schools
Dentistry (Dentistry; Oral Pathology) *Dean*: Atsushi Rokutanda; **Medicine** (Community Health; Health Sciences; Medicine; Nursing; Occupational Therapy; Physical Therapy; Social and Preventive Medicine) *Dean*: Shigeru Kono; **Pharmaceutical Sciences** (Pharmacy; Toxicology) *Dean*: Yoshihiro Matsumura

Further Information: Also University Hospital of Medicine and Dentistry. Training Ships (Nagasaki-maru and Kakuyo-maru)

History: Founded 1949 following merger of Nagasaki University with Nagasaki Medical College, the College of Pharmaceutical Science of Nagasaki Medical College, Nagasaki College of Economics, Nagasaki Normal School, Nagasaki Youth Normal School, and Nagasaki High School. Incorporated as National University Corporation 2004.

Governing Bodies: Hyogikai (University Council)

Academic Year: April to March (April-September; October-March)

Admission Requirements: Secondary school certificate or equivalent and entrance examination

Fees: (Yen): 800,000 per annum (including admission fee)

Main Language(s) of Instruction: Japanese

International Co-operation: About 70 cooperation agreements with universities and other institutions in China; Republic of Korea; Taiwan; Thailand; Indonesia; etc.

Degrees and Diplomas: *Gakushi*: Dentistry; Medical Sciences, 6 yrs; *Gakushi*: Economics; Education; Engineering; Environmental Studies; Fishery; Pharmaceutical Sciences, 4 yrs; *Gakushi*: Health Sciences; *Shushi*: Biomedical Sciences; Economics; Education; Science and Technology, 2 yrs; *Hakase*: Biomedical Sciences (Medical and Dental Sciences; Infection Research; Life Sciences and Radiation Research), 4 yrs; *Hakase*: Biomedical Sciences (Pharmaceutical Sciences); Economics; Science and Technology, 3 yrs

Student Services: Academic counselling, Canteen, Cultural centre, Employment services, Foreign student adviser, Foreign Studies Centre, Handicapped facilities, Health services, Language programs, Social counselling, Sports facilities

Student Residential Facilities: International House (two in two different locations, exclusively for international students)

Special Facilities: Medicinal Plants Garden; Seaside Training Centre; Shimabara Training Centre

Libraries: Main Library, Medical Library; Economics Branch Library and Faculty Libraries, total (vols and periodicals), 968,918

Publications: Acta Medica Nagasakiensia; Annual Journal of Economics *(annually)*; Annual Report of the Institute of Tropical Medicine *(annually)*; Annual Report of the Research Institute of Southeast Asia; Annual Report of the School of Dentistry *(annually)*; Bulletin of the Faculty of Education; Bulletin of the Faculty of Fisheries *(annually)*; Bulletin of the School of Allied Medical Sciences, Japanese/English; Journal of Business and Economics; Journal of Environmental Studies; Nagasaki Igakkai Zasshi; Report of the Faculty of Engineering *(annually)*; Study Series on Southeast Asia; Tropical Medicine *(quarterly)*

Last Updated: 26/01/09

NAGASAKI UNIVERSITY OF FOREIGN STUDIES

Nagasaki Gaikokugo Daigaku
3-15-1 Yokoo, Nagasaki-shi, Nagasaki 851-2196
Tel: +81(95) 840-2000
Fax: +81(95) 840-2001
Website: http://www.nagasaki-gaigo.ac.jp

Departments
International Communication (Communication Studies; International Studies)

Faculties
Foreign Languages (Modern Languages)

History: Founded 2000.

Degrees and Diplomas: *Gakushi*

Publications: The Journal of Nagasaki University of Foreign Studies

NAGASAKI WESLEYAN UNIVERSITY

Nagasaki Uesureyan Daigaku
1057 Eida, Isahaya, Nagasaki-shi, Nagasaki 854-0081
Tel: +81(957) 26-1234
Fax: +81(957) 26-2063
EMail: iec@nwjc.ac.jp; koho@wesleyan.ac.jp
Website: http://www.wesleyan.ac.jp

Departments
Human Service and Community Development (Communication Studies; Education; Psychology; Social and Community Services)

Faculties
Contemporary Social Studies

History: Founded 1999.

Degrees and Diplomas: *Gakushi*

Last Updated: 26/01/09

NAGOYA BUNRI UNIVERSITY

Nagoya Bunri Daigaku
365 Maeda, Inazawa-cho, Inazawa-shi, Aichi 492-8520
Tel: +81(587) 23-2400
Fax: +81(587) 21-2844
EMail: nyushika@nagoya-bunri.ac.jp
Website: http://www.nagoya-bunri.ac.jp

Colleges
Food, Nutrition, Care and Welfare (Food Science; Nutrition)

Faculties
Health and Human Life (Health Sciences); **Information Culture**

History: Founded 1999.

Degrees and Diplomas: *Gakushi*

Student Services: Foreign student adviser, Sports facilities

Libraries: c. 67,000 vols.

Last Updated: 26/01/09

NAGOYA CITY UNIVERSITY

Nagoya Shiritsu Daigaku

1 Kawasumi, Mizuho-cho, Mizuho-ku, Nagoya-shi, Aichi 467-8601
Tel: +81(52) 853-8023 +81(52) 853-8020
Fax: +81(52) 841-7428
EMail: shingaku@adm.nagoya-cu.ac.jp
Website: http://www.nagoya-cu.ac.jp

President: Hitoo Nishino

Colleges
General Education (Arts and Humanities; Education; Health Education; Modern Languages; Natural Sciences; Physical Education; Social Sciences)

Faculties
Economics *(Also graduate school)* (Business Administration; Economics); **Pharmaceutical Sciences** *(Also graduate school)* (Pharmacology; Pharmacy)

Institutes
Natural Sciences *(Also graduate school)* (Natural Sciences)

Schools
Design and Architecture *(Also graduate school)*; **Humanities and Social Sciences** *(Also graduate school)*; **Medicine** *(Also graduate school)* (Health Sciences; Medicine); **Nursing** *(Also graduate school)* (Nursing)

Further Information: Also University Hospital. Japanese language courses for foreign students

History: Founded 1950, incorporating Nagoya Pharmaceutical School, founded 1931, and Nagoya Women's Medical College, founded 1943.

Governing Bodies: Hyogikai (Board of Trustees); Kyogikai (Council); Kyojukai (Faculty Council)

Academic Year: April to March (April-October; October-March)

Admission Requirements: Graduation from high school or equivalent or foreign equivalent, and entrance examination

Main Language(s) of Instruction: Japanese

International Co-operation: With universities in Australia, USA and Germany

Degrees and Diplomas: *Gakushi*: Arts (Bungakushi); Economics (Keizaigakushi); Medicine; Pharmacy (Yakugakushi), 4 yrs; *Shushi*: Economics (Keizaigakushushi); Pharmacy (Yakugakushushi), a further 2 yrs; *Hakase*: Economics (Keizaigakuhakushi); Pharmacy (Yakugakuhakushi), 3 yrs following Shushi; *Hakase*: Medicine, a further 4 yrs

Student Services: Language programs

Student Residential Facilities: For Nursing School students

Libraries: c. 850,000 vols

Publications: Bulletin of College of General Education, Natural Sciences Section *(annually)*; Faculty of Pharmacy Annual Report; Nagoya Medical Journal *(quarterly)*; Oikonomika *(quarterly)*; Studies in Social Sciences and Humanities

Last Updated: 26/01/09

NAGOYA COLLEGE OF MUSIC

Nagoya Ongaku Daigaku

7-1 Inabaji-cho, Nakamura-ku, Nagoya-shi, Aichi 453-8540
Tel: +81(52) 411-1111 +81(52) 411-1129
Fax: +81(52) 413-2300
EMail: stdnt_on@doho.ac.jp
Website: http://www.meion.ac.jp/

Faculties
Music (Dance; Jazz and Popular Music; Music; Music Education; Music Theory and Composition; Musical Instruments; Musicology; Opera; Singing; Theatre)

Programmes
Music *(Graduate)* (Music; Music Education; Music Theory and Composition; Musical Instruments; Musicology; Singing)

History: Founded 1976.

Main Language(s) of Instruction: Japanese

Degrees and Diplomas: *Gakushi*; *Shushi*

Last Updated: 26/01/09

NAGOYA GAKUIN UNIVERSITY

Nagoya Gakuin Daigaku

1350 Kamishinano-cho, Seto-shi, Aichi 480-1298
Tel: +81(561) 42-0350
Fax: +81(561) 42-1147
EMail: kouryuu-center@ngu.ac.jp
Website: http://www.ngu.jp

Faculties
Commerce (Business and Commerce); **Economics** (Economic and Finance Policy; Economics); **Foreign Studies** (Chinese; English; Foreign Languages Education)

Graduate Schools
Economics and Business Administration (Business Administration; Economics); **Foreign Languages** (Chinese; English)

Institutes
Japanese Studies (Japanese)

History: Founded 1964.

Governing Bodies: Board of Trustees

Academic Year: April to March

Admission Requirements: Graduation from high school

Fees: (Yen): Undergraduate, 978,000-1,113m. per annum; graduate, 740,000 per annum; Institute for Japanese Studies, 620,000 per annum

Main Language(s) of Instruction: Japanese

Accrediting Agencies: Ministry of Education, Culture, Sports, Science and Technology

Degrees and Diplomas: *Gakushi*: 4 yrs; *Shushi*: a further 2 yrs; *Hakase*: 3 yrs following Shushi

Student Services: Academic counselling, Canteen, Employment services, Foreign student adviser, Handicapped facilities, Health services, Language programs, Nursery care, Social counselling, Sports facilities

Student Residential Facilities: Yes

Special Facilities: TV Studio. Computer-Assisted Language Laboratory

Libraries: c. 320,000 vols

Publications: Journal of Nagoya Gakuin University, Social Sciences and Natural Sciences *(other/irregular)*

Press or Publishing House: Cosmorama

Last Updated: 26/01/09

NAGOYA INSTITUTE OF TECHNOLOGY

Nagoya Kogyo Daigaku

Gokiso-cho, Showa-ku, Nagoya-shi, Aichi 466-8555
Tel: +81(52) 735-5079
Fax: +81(52) 735-5621
EMail: international@ml.nitech.ac.jp
Website: http://www.nitech.ac.jp

President: Takahashi Minoru

Vice-President: Hidetaka Umehara

Departments
Architecture and Design (Architectural and Environmental Design; Architecture; Design; Environmental Engineering); **Civil Engineering and Systems Management** (Civil Engineering; Environmental Engineering; Town Planning; Transport Engineering); **Computer Science** (Computer Networks; Computer Science); **Electrical and**

Electronic Engineering; **Environmental and Materials Engineering** (Environmental Engineering; Materials Engineering; Nanotechnology); **Life and Materials Engineering** (Applied Chemistry; Biochemistry; Bioengineering; Materials Engineering; Molecular Biology; Polymer and Plastics Technology); **Mechanical Engineering** (Applied Mathematics; Applied Physics; Computer Engineering; Computer Science; Energy Engineering; Measurement and Precision Engineering; Mechanical Engineering)

Graduate Schools

Engineering

Further Information: Also Japanese language courses for foreign students

History: Founded 1905 as Nagoya Higher Technical School. Merged with Aichi Prefectural College of Technology. Became national institute 1949.

Academic Year: April to March (April-September; October-March)

Admission Requirements: Graduation from high school or equivalent, or foreign equivalent, and entrance examination

Main Language(s) of Instruction: Japanese

International Co-operation: Exchange and joint research agreements with 31 universities abroad

Degrees and Diplomas: *Gakushi*: Engineering, 4 yrs; *Shushi*: Engineering, 2 yrs; *Hakase*: Engineering, 3 yrs

Student Services: Health services, Language programs, Sports facilities

Student Residential Facilities: Yes

Libraries: 467,724 vols

Publications: ;

Last Updated: 24/03/11

NAGOYA KEIZAI UNIVERSITY

Nagoya Keizai Daigaku

61-1 Uchikubo, Inuyama-shi, Aichi 484-8504

Tel: +81(568) 670-511

EMail: nyugakukoho@kan.nagoya-ku.ac.jp

Website: http://www.nagoya-ku.ac.jp

Programmes

Accountancy; **Economics** (Economics); **Law** (Commercial Law; Law); **Management** (Management)

History: Founded 1999.

Degrees and Diplomas: *Gakushi*; *Shushi*; *Hakase*

Last Updated: 26/01/09

NAGOYA SANGYO UNIVERSITY

Nagoya Sangyo Daigaku

3255-5 Araicho, Owariasashi-shi, Aichi 488-8711

Tel: +81(561) 55-5101

Fax: +81(561) 55-0515

Website: http://www.nagoya-su.ac.jp

Faculties

Economics (Economics); **Environment and Information Management** (Environmental Management; Environmental Studies; Information Management)

History: Founded 2000.

Degrees and Diplomas: *Gakushi*

Libraries: Yes.

Last Updated: 26/01/09

NAGOYA UNIVERSITY

Nagoya Daigaku

Furo-cho, Chikusa-ku, Nagoya-shi, Aichi 464-8601

Tel: +81(52) 789-2044

Fax: +81(52) 789-2045

Website: http://www.nagoya-u.ac.jp

President: Michinari Hamaguchi (2009-)

Tel: +81(52) 789-2002, Fax: +81(52) 789-2005

Director-General: Makoto Takahashi

Centres

Asian Legal Exchange (Law; Political Sciences) *Director*: Masanori Aikyo; **Bioscience and Biotechnology** (Biochemistry; Biomedicine; Biophysics; Biotechnology) *Director*: Michihiro Kobayashi; **Chronological Research** *Director*: Kazuhiro Suzuki; **Co-operative Research in Advanced Science and Technology** (Artificial Intelligence; Environmental Engineering; Materials Engineering; Systems Analysis) *Director*: Goro Obinata; **Developmental Clinical Psychology and Psychiatry** (Child Care and Development; Clinical Psychology) *Director*: Shuji Honjo; **Education for International Students** (Cultural Studies; Japanese) *Director*: Mitsuo Ezaki; **Gene Research** (Genetics) *Director*: Masahiro Ishiura; **Health, Physical Fitness and Sports** (Health Education; Health Sciences; Sports) *Director*: Kiyoshi Shimaoka; **Higher Education** *Director*: Kazuhisha Todayama; **Hydrospheric Atmospheric** (Biochemistry; Environmental Studies; Geophysics; Marine Biology; Marine Science and Oceanography; Waste Management; Water Science) *Director*: Hiroshi Uyeda; **Information Media Studies** (Media Studies) *Director*: Ichiro Yamamoto; **Information Technology** (Information Technology) *Director*: Toyohide Watanabe; **International Cooperation in Agricultural Education** *Director*: Hiroyuki Takeya; **Letters** (Arts and Humanities) *Dean*: Ken Machida; **Materials Science** *Director*: Kazuyuki Tatsumi; **Radioisotope Research** (Radiology) *Director*: Kunihide Nishizawa

Faculties

Languages and Culture (Applied Linguistics; Chinese; Cultural Studies; Dutch; English; French; German; Greek; Indonesian; International Studies; Italian; Korean; Latin; Modern Languages; Portuguese; Regional Studies; Russian; Spanish) *Dean*: Kenji Kondo

Graduate Schools

Bio-agricultural Sciences (Bioengineering; Biological and Life Sciences) *Dean*: Tsukasa Matsuda; **Economics** (Economics; Industrial Management) *Dean*: Yuko Arayama; **Education and Human Development** (Development Studies; Education; Educational Sciences; Psychology) *Dean*: Moriki Terada; **Engineering** (Aeronautical and Aerospace Engineering; Applied Chemistry; Applied Physics; Biotechnology; Chemical Engineering; Civil Engineering; Computer Engineering; Computer Science; Energy Engineering; Engineering; Mechanical Engineering; Nanotechnology) *Dean*: Nobuhiko Sawaki; **Environmental Studies** (Architecture; Earth Sciences; Environmental Engineering; Environmental Studies; Social Studies) *Dean*: Yoshitsugu Hayashi; **Information Sciences** (Computer Science; Media Studies; Natural Sciences; Social Sciences) *Dean*: Kiyoshi Agusa; **International Development** (Communication Studies; International Studies) *Dean*: Yoshihiko Nishimura; **Languages and Cultures** (Cultural Studies; Japanese) *Dean*: Kenji Kondo; **Law** (Law; Political Sciences) *Dean*: Yoshiharu Matsuura; **Mathematics** (Mathematics) *Dean*: Yukihiko Namikawa; **Medicine** (Cell Biology; Community Health; Medicine; Molecular Biology; Nursing; Occupational Therapy; Physical Therapy; Radiology) *Dean*: Yasuo Sugiura; **Science** (Astrophysics; Biological and Life Sciences; Materials Engineering) *Dean*: Iwao Ohmine

Institutes

Advanced Research (Arts and Humanities; Natural Sciences) *Director*: Keiichiro Kitazumi; **Eco Topia Science** *Director*: Tsuneo Matsui; **Environmental Medicine** (Neurosciences) *Director*: Itsuo Kodama; **Liberal Arts and Science** (Arts and Humanities; Natural Sciences) *Director*: Yuji Wakao; **Solar Terrestrial Environment** (Astronomy and Space Science) *Director*: Ryoichi Fujii

Schools

Agricultural Science (Agriculture; Biological and Life Sciences; Environmental Studies) *Dean*: Tsukasa Matsuda; **Economics** (Business Administration; Economic and Finance Policy; Economic History; Economics) *Dean*: Yuko Arayama; **Education** (Development Studies; Education) *Dean*: Moriki Terada; **Engineering** (Aeronautical and Aerospace Engineering; Architecture; Bioengineering; Chemical Engineering; Civil Engineering; Electrical and Electronic Engineering; Engineering; Information Technology; Mechanical Engineering; Physics) *Dean*: Nobuhiko Sawaki; **Informatics and Science** *Dean*: Mitsuru Sano; **Law** (Law; Political Sciences) *Dean*: Yoshiharu Matsuura; **Letters** (Arts and Humanities) *Dean*: Ken Machida; **Medicine** (Health Sciences; Medicine) *Dean*: Michinari Hamaguchi; **Science** (Biology; Chemistry; Earth

Sciences; Mathematics; Natural Sciences; Physics) *Dean*: Takao Kondo

Further Information: Also University Hospital

History: Founded 1871 as Medical School. Became Nagoya Medical College 1931 and Nagoya Imperial University 1939, renamed Nagoya University 1947 and restarted as a University under the new educational system 1949 and reorganized as a National university Corporation 2004.

Governing Bodies: Board of Trustees; Administrative Council; Education and Research Council

Academic Year: April to March (April-September; October-March)

Admission Requirements: Graduation from high school or recognized equivalent, and entrance examination

Fees: (Yen): 535,800 per annum

Main Language(s) of Instruction: Japanese

International Co-operation: With Universities in China, Laos, Thailand, Indonesia, Republic of Korea, USA, United Kingdom, Germany, France, and Australia. Also participates in Seameo, Searca, AC21(Academic Consortium) programmes

Degrees and Diplomas: *Gakushi*: Agricultural Sciences; Arts; Economics; Education; Engineering; Informatics and Science; Law; Science (Medical Technology); Nursing; Occupational Therapy; Physical Therapy; Radiological Technology, 4 yrs; *Gakushi*: Medical Doctor; Medical Sciences, 6 yrs; *Shushi*: Agricultural Sciences; Architecture; Arts; Business Administration; Economics; Engineering; Environmental Studies; Geography; Information Science; Law; Letters; Psychology; Science; Sociology, a further 2 yrs; *Hakase*: Agricultural Sciences; Economics; Education; Educational Psychology; Engineering; Geography; History; Law; Letters; Philosophy; Science; Sociology, 3 yrs following Shushi; *Hakase*: Medicine Sciences, a further 4 yrs

Student Services: Academic counselling, Canteen, Employment services, Foreign student adviser, Foreign Studies Centre, Handicapped facilities, Health services, Language programs, Social counselling, Sports facilities

Student Residential Facilities: Yes

Special Facilities: Nagoya University Furukawa Museum

Libraries: Central Library, 1,043,880 vols; other libraries, 1,842,661 vols

Publications: Bulletin *(biennially)*; Journals; Memoirs; Proceedings; Scientific Reports

Press or Publishing House: Nagoya University Press

Last Updated: 24/03/11

NAGOYA UNIVERSITY OF ARTS

Nagoya Geijutsu Daigaku

280 Kumanosho, Shikatsu-cho, Nishikasugai-gun, Aichi 481-8503
Tel: +81(568) 240-315
Fax: +81(568) 240-317
EMail: nua-adm@tcp-ip.or.jp
Website: http://www.nua.ac.jp

Schools

Art *(Also postgraduate and research programme)*; **Design** *(Also postgraduate and research programme)*; **Human Development** (Development Studies); **Music** *(Also postgraduate and research programme)* (Jazz and Popular Music; Music; Music Education; Music Theory and Composition; Musical Instruments; Musicology; Singing)

Degrees and Diplomas: *Gakushi*; *Shushi*

Last Updated: 26/01/09

NAGOYA UNIVERSITY OF ARTS AND SCIENCES

Nagoya Gakugei Daigaku (NUAS)

57 Takenoyama, Iwasakicho, Nisshin-shi, Aichi 470-0196
Tel: +81(561) 75-7111
Fax: +81(561) 73-8539
EMail: na-info@ml.nakanishi.ac.jp
Website: http://www.nuas.ac.jp

Programmes

Crafts and Design (Architectural and Environmental Design; Communication Arts; Design; Fashion Design; Graphic Design; Handicrafts; Industrial Design; Interior Design; Textile Design; Visual Arts); **Food Science** (Food Science; Nutrition); **Visual and Performing Arts** (Cinema and Television; Performing Arts; Photography; Visual Arts)

History: Founded 2002.

Degrees and Diplomas: *Gakushi*

Last Updated: 26/01/09

NAGOYA UNIVERSITY OF COMMERCE AND BUSINESS ADMINISTRATION

Nagoya Shoka Daigaku

4-4 Sagamine, Komenoki-cho, Nisshin-shi, Aichi 470-0193
Tel: +81(561) 73-2111
Fax: +81(561) 73-1202
EMail: nyushi@nucba.ac.jp
Website: http://www.nucba.ac.jp

President: Hiroshi Kurimoto Fax: +81(561) 75-2430
EMail: hiroshi@nucba.ac.jp

Faculties

Accounting and Finance (Accountancy; Banking; Finance; Taxation); **Business Administration** (Business Administration; Economics; Management; Marketing); **Economics** (Economics); **Foreign Languages and Asian Studies** (Asian Studies; Chinese; Communication Studies; Cultural Studies; English; Indonesian; International Studies; Korean; Modern Languages; Thai Languages; Translation and Interpretation; Vietnamese); **Marketing** (Marketing)

History: Founded 1935, acquired present status 1953. International College founded 1982. Faculty of Foreign Languages and Asian Studies founded 1998.

Governing Bodies: Board of Trustees

Academic Year: April to February (April-July; September-February)

Admission Requirements: Graduation from high school and entrance examination

Fees: (Yens): Faculty of Foreign Language and Faculty of Accounting and Finance: 1,432,000 per annum; Faculty of Management and Information Science: 1,392,000 per annum; Faculty of Business Administration: 1,342.00 per annum

Main Language(s) of Instruction: Japanese, English

International Co-operation: With universities in United Kingdom, China and Thailand

Degrees and Diplomas: *Gakushi*: Accounting and Finance (BA); Asian Studies, English Communication (BA); Commerce and Business Administration (BA), 4 yrs; *Shushi*: Management Information Sciences (MBA), a further 2 yrs. Also Diploma in Cross Cultural Studies, and Teaching Qualifications, 2 yrs

Student Services: Academic counselling, Canteen, Employment services, Foreign student adviser, Health services, Language programs, Sports facilities

Special Facilities: Centre for Tomorrow; Intelligent School (IS) Building; Centre for Global Communication (CGC); Fushimi Downtown Campus; Tokyo Satellite Campus

Libraries: Central Information Centre, c. 220,000 vols

Publications: NUCB Journal of Economics and Management *(biannually)*; NUCB Journal of Language, Culture and Communication *(biannually)*

NAGOYA UNIVERSITY OF FOREIGN STUDIES

Nagoya Gaikokugo Daigaku (NUFS)

57 Takenoyama, Iwasaki-cho, Nisshin-shi, Aichi 470-0197
Tel: +81(5617) 41-111
Fax: +81(5617) 51-723
EMail: info@nic-nagoya.or.jp
Website: http://www-e.nufs.ac.jp

President: Osamu Mizutani Tel: +81(5617) 5-1770

Director of Administrative Affairs: Takeru Yamakawa

International Relations: Hiroko Chinen Quackenbush

Graduate Schools

International Studies (Chinese; French; International Relations; Japanese; Pedagogy) *Dean*: Minoru Kawakita

Institutes

Japanese Language (East Asian Studies; Japanese) *Director*: Kazuko Nakajima

Schools

Contemporary International Studies (Accountancy; English; Finance; International Business; Journalism; Management; Marketing; Tourism; Translation and Interpretation) *Dean*: Toshinori Tamai; **Foreign Languages** *Dean*: Kazuhiko Matsuno

History: Founded 1988.

Governing Bodies: Nakanishi Educational Foundation

Admission Requirements: Japanese Language Proficiency Test or Japanese as a Foreign Language (score: 210 and higher) + Japan and the World (score: 4 and higher); Graduation from high school or equivalent for undergraduates, graduation from university for postgraduates.

Fees: (Yen): Undergraduates, 965,500 per annum (200,000 for 1st year entrance fee); Postgraduates, 725,500 per annum (100,000 for entrance fee) - 30% reduction for overseas students studying at their own expense is applied to tuition fees.

Main Language(s) of Instruction: Japanese, English.

International Co-operation: With universities in USA, Australia, China, United Kingdom, Korea, Canada, France, New Zealand, Belgium, Vietnam, Mexico

Degrees and Diplomas: *Gakushi*: English; French; Chinese; Intenational Studies; Global Business (BA), 4 yrs; *Shushi*: English and English Language Education; French and French Language Education; Chinese and Chinese Language Education; Japanese and Japanese Language Education; International Relations; Global Business; Online Language Education (MA), a further 2 yrs; *Hakase*: English Linguistics and Pedagogy; Japanese Linguistics and Pedagogy; International Cultural Studies (PhD), 3 yrs following Shushi

Student Services: Academic counselling, Canteen, Employment services, Foreign student adviser, Foreign Studies Centre, Health services, Language programs, Social counselling, Sports facilities

Student Residential Facilities: For foreign students

Libraries: c. 200,000 vols

Publications: Journal of School of Foreign Languages; Journal of School of Global Business and Economics

Press or Publishing House: Nogoya University of Foreign Studies Press

Last Updated: 26/01/09

NAGOYA WOMEN'S UNIVERSITY

Nagoya Joshi Daigaku

4-30 Shioji-cho, Mizuho-ku, Nagoya-shi, Aichi 467-8507

Tel: +81(52) 852-1111

Fax: +81(52) 852-7470

Website: http://www.nagoya-wu.ac.jp

Chancellor: Ichiro Koshihara

Faculties

Human Life and Environmental Sciences (Biological and Life Sciences; Environmental Studies; Food Science; Nutrition; Social Welfare); **Literature** (Child Care and Development; Literature; Modern Languages; Preschool Education; Primary Education)

Graduate Schools

Human Life Science; **Humanities** (Child Care and Development; Communication Studies; Cultural Studies; Educational Psychology; Modern Languages; Preschool Education)

History: Founded 1964.

Degrees and Diplomas: *Gakushi*; *Shushi*; *Hakase*

Last Updated: 26/01/09

NAGOYA ZOKEI UNIVERSITY OF ART AND DESIGN

Nagoya Zokei Daigaku

6004 Nenjozaka, Komaki-shi, Aichi 485-8563

Tel: +81(568) 79-1111

Fax: +81(568) 79-1070

Website: http://www.nzu.ac.jp

President: Yukiya Takakita

Programmes

Art and Design (Design; Fine Arts)

History: Founded 1989 as Nagoya Zokei Geijutu Daigaku . Acquired present title 2008.

Degrees and Diplomas: *Gakushi*

Last Updated: 26/01/09

NAKAMURA GAKUEN UNIVERSITY

Nakamura Gakuen Daigaku (NGU)

5-7-1 Befu, Jonan-ku, Fukuoka-shi, Fukuoka 814-0198

Tel: +81(92) 851-2531

Fax: +81(92) 841-7762 +81(92) 851-2539

EMail: nyushi@cc.nakamura-u.ac.jp

Website: http://www.nakamura-u.ac.jp

Faculties

Business, Marketing and Distribution *(Also graduate school)* (Business Administration; Business and Commerce; Marketing); **Human Development** *(Also graduate school)* (Child Care and Development; Education; Preschool Education); **Nutrition** *(Also graduate school)* (Health Sciences; Nutrition; Public Health)

History: Founded 1965.

Academic Year: April to March (April-July; September-March)

Admission Requirements: Graduation from high school and entrance examination

Main Language(s) of Instruction: Japanese

International Co-operation: With universities in China and USA

Degrees and Diplomas: *Gakushi*: 4 yrs; *Shushi*: a further 2 yrs

Student Services: Academic counselling, Canteen, Cultural centre, Employment services, Foreign student adviser, Health services, Social counselling, Sports facilities

Student Residential Facilities: Yes

Libraries: 182,000 vols

Last Updated: 26/01/09

NANZAN UNIVERSITY

Nanzan Daigaku

18 Yamazato-cho, Showa-ku, Nagoya-shi, Aichi 466-8673

Tel: +81(52) 832-3112

Fax: +81(52) 833-6985

EMail: n-somu@nanzan-u.ac.jp

Website: http://www.nanzan-u.ac.jp

President: Michael Calmano, S.V.D. (2008-)
Tel: +81(52) 832-3113, Fax: +81(52) 832-0666
EMail: gaku-kohu@nanzan-u.ac.jp

Director: Hajime Makita EMail: makita@nanzan-u.ac.jp

International Relations: Akira Tsuchiya, Head, Centre for International Education Office
Tel: +81(52) 832-3123, Fax: +81(52) 832-5490
EMail: cie-office@nanzan-u.ac.jp

Centres

Japanese Studies *(for Foreign students)* (Japanese) *Director*: Noboru Kinoshita

Faculties

Business Administration (Accountancy; Business Administration; Finance; Human Resources; Marketing) *Dean*: Yoshiaki Kaoru; **Economics** (Economics) *Dean*: Yoshikazu Arai; **Foreign Studies** (Arts and Humanities; Cultural Studies; Modern Languages; Social Sciences) *Dean*: Hiroshi Fujimoto; **Humanities** (Arts and Humanities) *Dean*: Shinzo Sakai; **Law** (Law) *Dean*: Izumi Okada; **Mathematical Sciences and Information Engineering** *(Seto Campus)* (Information Technology; Mathematics and Computer Science; Operations Research; Transport and Communications) *Dean*: Atsuo Suzuki; **Policy Studies** *(Seto Campus)* (Administration; History;

International Studies; Political Sciences; Social Policy; Sociology) *Dean*: Michio Fujiwara

Institutes

Anthropology (Anthropology; Cultural Studies; Ethnology; Folklore) *Director*: Manabu Watanabe; **Religion and Culture** (Cultural Studies; Philosophy; Religion) *Director*: Paul Swanson; **Social Ethics** (Arts and Humanities; Ethics; Human Rights; Law; Social Problems; Sociology) *Director*: Masao Maruyama

Research Centres

American Studies (American Studies) *Director*: Masaki Kawashima; **Asian-Pacific Studies** (Asian Studies; Pacific Area Studies) *Director*: Yasuko Kobayashi; **European Studies** (European Studies) *Director*: Minoru Tanaka; **Human Relations** (Social Sciences) *Director*: Toshimitsu Tsumura; **Latin American Studies** (Latin American Studies) *Director*: Takahiro Kato; **Legal Practice Education and Research** (Law) *Director*: Yoshio Kato; **Linguistics** (Linguistics) *Director*: Mamoru Saito; **Management Studies** (Accountancy; Business and Commerce; Finance; Human Resources; Management) *Director*: Koichi Saito; **Mathematical Sciences and Information Engineering** (Computer Engineering; Computer Networks; Operations Research; Statistics; Telecommunications Engineering) *Director*: Masanori Fushimi

History: Founded 1932 as Nanzan Middle School for Boys by the Society of the Divine Word, acquired present status 1949.

Governing Bodies: Board of Directors

Academic Year: April to March (April-July; September-February)

Admission Requirements: Graduation from high school or foreign equivalent, and entrance examination

Fees: (Yen): First year, 1,265,200; subsequent years, 953,000

Main Language(s) of Instruction: Japanese

International Co-operation: With universities in USA; Thailand; Republic of Korea; Indonesia; Philippines; China; Malaysia; United Kingdom; Germany; Sweden; Spain; Australia; France; Canada and Netherlands

Accrediting Agencies: Japan University Accreditation Association

Degrees and Diplomas: *Gakushi*: Humanities; Foreign Studies; Economics; Business Administration; Law; Policy Studies; Mathematical Sciences and Information Engineering, 4 yrs; *Shushi*: Humanities; International Area Studies; Economics; Business Administration; Arts in Management; Policy Studies; Mathematical Sciences and Information Engineering, a further 2 yrs; *Hakase*: Humanities; Economics; Business Administration; Policy Studies; Mathematical Sciences and Information Engineering, 3 yrs following Shushi. Also Homu Hakushi in Law (3 yrs)

Student Services: Academic counselling, Canteen, Cultural centre, Employment services, Foreign student adviser, Foreign Studies Centre, Handicapped facilities, Health services, Language programs, Social counselling, Sports facilities

Student Residential Facilities: For 357 students

Special Facilities: Museum of Anthropology

Libraries: Central Library, 683,669 vols; Nagoya Library, 638,940 vols; Seto Library, 75,903 vols; Institute Libraries, 98,895 vols

Publications: Academia-Humanities and Social Sciences *(biannually)*; Academia-Literature and Language *(biannually)*; Academia-Mathematical Sciences and Information Engineering *(annually)*; Academia-Natural Science, Health and Physical Education *(annually)*; Asian Folklore Studies *(biannually)*; Bulletin of the Center for International Education, Nanzan University *(annually)*; Bulletin of the Nanzan Centre for Asia-Pacific Studies *(annually)*; Bulletin of the Nanzan Centre for European Studies *(annually)*; Bulletin of the Nanzan Institute for Religion and Culture (in English) *(annually)*; Bulletin of the Nanzan Institute for Religion and Culture (in Japanese) *(annually)*; Human Relations *(annually)*; Japanese Journal of Religious Studies *(biannually)*; Nanzan Journal of American Studies *(annually)*; Nanzan Journal of Economic Studies *(3 per annum)*; Nanzan Law Review *(quarterly)*; Nanzan Linguistics *(annually)*; Nanzan Management Review *(3 per annum)*; Nanzan Review of Theological Studies *(annually)*; Nanzan Studies on Japanese Language and Culture *(annually)*; Perspectivas Latinoamericanas *(annually)*; Society and Ethics *(biannually)*

Student Numbers *2010-2011*: Total: c. 10,426

Last Updated: 09/12/08

NARA INSTITUTE OF SCIENCE AND TECHNOLOGY

Nara Sentan Kagakugijyutsu Daigakuin Daigaku (NAIST)

8916-5 Takayama-cho, Ikoma-shi, Nara 630-0101

Tel: +81(743) 72-5937

Fax: +81(743) 72-5939

EMail: intc@ad.aist-nara.ac.jp

Website: http://www.naist.jp

President: Akira Isogai

Tel: +81(743) 72-5000, Fax: +81(743) 72-5009

Centres

Information Technology (Software Engineering; Telecommunications Engineering)

Graduate Schools

Biological Sciences; **Information Science**; **Materials Science**

Research Centres

Advanced Science and Technology (Educational Research; Industrial Engineering; Multimedia; Natural Sciences; Technology); **Genetic Information** (Genetics; Molecular Biology); **Materials Science** (Design; Materials Engineering)

History: Founded 1991. A postgraduate educational and research institution.

Governing Bodies: Academic Senate

Academic Year: April to March

Admission Requirements: University Degree

Fees: (Yen): Registration, 282,000 per annum; Tuition, 520,800 per annum

Main Language(s) of Instruction: Japanese

Degrees and Diplomas: *Shushi*: 2 yrs; *Hakase*: 3 yrs

Student Services: Academic counselling, Canteen, Employment services, Foreign student adviser, Foreign Studies Centre, Handicapped facilities, Health services, Language programs, Nursery care, Social counselling, Sports facilities

Student Residential Facilities: Yes

Libraries: Digital Library

Last Updated: 24/03/11

NARA MEDICAL UNIVERSITY

Nara Kenritsu Ika Daigaku

840 Shijo-cho, Kashihara-city, Nara 634-8521

Tel: +81(744) 22-3051

Fax: +81(744) 25-7657

EMail: soumuka@naramed-u.ac.jp

Website: http://www.naramed-u.ac.jp

President: Osamu Yoshida

Secretary-General: Nobuhiko Yasukawa

Schools

Medicine *(Also graduate school)* (Anatomy; Biochemistry; Biology; Chemistry; English; German; Health Sciences; Information Sciences; Mathematics; Medicine; Neurosciences; Parasitology; Pathology; Philosophy; Physical Education; Physics; Physiology; Statistics); **Nursing** (Midwifery; Nursing)

Further Information: Also University Hospital

History: Founded 1945 by Nara Prefecture.

Academic Year: April to March (April-July; September-December; January-March)

Admission Requirements: Graduation from high school and entrance examination

Main Language(s) of Instruction: Japanese

International Co-operation: With Chiang Mai University in Thailand

Degrees and Diplomas: *Gakushi*: Medicine, 6 yrs; *Hakase*: Medicine, a further 4 yrs

Libraries: c. 172,000 vols

Publications: Journal of Nara Medical Association

Last Updated: 26/01/09

NARA PREFECTURAL UNIVERSITY

Nara Kenritsu Daigaku

10 Funahashi-cho, Nara-shi, Nara 630-8258
Tel: +81(742) 22-4978
Fax: +81(742) 22-4991
Website: http://www.narapu.ac.jp

Programmes

Business and Commerce; **Regional Promotion** (Economics; Tourism)

History: Founded 1990.

Main Language(s) of Instruction: Japanese

Degrees and Diplomas: *Gakushi*

Student Services: Sports facilities

Last Updated: 26/01/09

NARA SANGYO UNIVERSITY

Nara Sangyo Daigaku

3-12-1 Tatsunokita, Sango-cho, Ikomo-gun, Nara 636-8503
Tel: +81(745) 73-7800
Fax: +81(745) 72-0822
EMail: jimu@nara-su.ac.jp
Website: http://www.nara-su.ac.jp

Programmes

Economics (Economics); **Law** (Law)

History: Founded 1984.

Degrees and Diplomas: *Gakushi*

Last Updated: 26/01/09

NARA UNIVERSITY

Nara Daigaku

1500 Misasagi-cho, Nara-shi, Nara 631-8502
Tel: +81(742) 44-1251
Fax: +81(742) 41-0650
EMail: somu@aogaki.nara-u.ac.jp
Website: http://www.nara-u.ac.jp

Colleges

Liberal Arts *(Also graduate school)* (Arts and Humanities; Health Sciences; Modern Languages; Sports)

Divisions

Distance Education (Archiving; Cultural Studies; Library Science)

Faculties

Letters *(Also graduate school)* (Arts and Humanities; Cultural Studies; Geography (Human); History; Japanese; Literature; Modern Languages; Oriental Languages); **Sociology** *(Also graduate school)* (Clinical Psychology; Psychology; Sociology)

History: Founded 1969 as a college of four Departments (Literature, Japanese Literature, History and Geography). Acquired present status 1988.

Governing Bodies: Nara Daigaku Educational Foundation

Academic Year: April to March

Admission Requirements: High school graduation or equivalent diploma and entrance examination

Fees: (Yen): 980,000 per annum

Main Language(s) of Instruction: Japanese

Degrees and Diplomas: *Gakushi*: 4 yrs; *Shushi*: a further 2 yrs

Student Services: Academic counselling, Canteen, Handicapped facilities, Nursery care, Social counselling

Libraries: Central Library, c. 320,000 vols

Publications: Graduate School Research Annual Report, Faculty research papers *(annually)*; Memoirs of Nara University, Faculty research papers *(annually)*

Last Updated: 26/01/09

NARA UNIVERSITY OF EDUCATION

Nara Kyoiku Daigaku

Takabatake-cho, Nara-shi, Nara 630-8528
Tel: +81(742) 27-9111 +81(742) 27-9148
Fax: +81(742) 27-9141 +81(742) 27-9146
EMail: ryugaku@nara-edu.ac.jp
Website: http://www.nara-edu.ac.jp

Centres

Educational Research and Development (Educational Research; Educational Technology; Pedagogy); **Natural Environment Education**

Faculties

Education *(Also graduate school and postgraduate course)* (Art Education; English; Health Education; Home Economics Education; Japanese; Mathematics Education; Music Education; Native Language Education; Physical Education; Preschool Education; Primary Education; Science Education; Secondary Education; Social Studies; Sports; Technology Education)

Research Centres

Special Needs Education

Further Information: Also Japanese language courses for foreign students

History: Founded 1949, incorporating Nara Normal School and Nara Youth Normal School, acquired present title 1966.

Academic Year: April to March (April-September; October-February)

Admission Requirements: Graduation from high school or equivalent or foreign equivalent and entrance examination

Main Language(s) of Instruction: Japanese

International Co-operation: With universities in USA, Germany and Republic of Korea

Degrees and Diplomas: *Gakushi*: Education, 4 yrs; *Shushi*: Education, a further 2 yrs

Student Services: Employment services, Foreign Studies Centre, Language programs, Sports facilities

Student Residential Facilities: For c. 235 students

Libraries: c. 300,000 vols

Publications: Bulletins *(annually)*

Last Updated: 26/01/09

NARA WOMEN'S UNIVERSITY

Nara Joshi Daigaku

Kitawoyahigashi-machi, Nara-shi, Nara 630-8506
Tel: +81(742) 20-3204
Fax: +81(742) 20-3205
EMail: soumu@cc.nara-wu.ac.jp
Website: http://www.nara-wu.ac.jp/index-e.html

President: Seishi Noguchi (2009-)
Tel: +81(742) 20-3724, Fax: +81(742) 20-3205

International Relations: Yujiro Baba, Head, International and Research Cooperation Office
Tel: +81(742) 20-3725, Fax: +81(742) 20-3205

Faculties

Arts and Humanities (Arts and Humanities; Education); **Human Life and Environment** (Environmental Studies; Home Economics; Social Sciences; Technology); **Science** (Mathematics and Computer Science; Natural Sciences)

Graduate Schools

Humanities and Sciences (Arts and Humanities; Education; Home Economics; Mathematical Physics; Natural Sciences; Social Sciences)

History: Founded 1908 as the Nara Higher Normal College for Women, became National University 1949. Reorganized as National University Corporation 2004.

Governing Bodies: Board of Directors

Academic Year: April to March (April-September; October-March)

Admission Requirements: Graduation from high school or equivalent or foreign equivalent, and entrance examination

Fees: (Yen): 535,800 per annum

Main Language(s) of Instruction: Japanese

International Co-operation: With universities in Afghanistan; Australia; Austria; Bangladesh; Belgium; China; France; Germany; Italy; Republic of Korea; Poland; Russian Federation; Taiwan; United Kingdom; USA and Vietnam

Degrees and Diplomas: *Gakushi*: Letters; Science; Human Life and Environment, 4 yrs; *Shushi*: Letters; Science; Human Life and Environment; Home Economics; Philosophy, a further 2 yrs; *Hakase*: Letters; Science; Philosophy; Social Sciences; Human Life and Environment; Computer Science, 3 yrs following Shushi

Student Services: Academic counselling, Canteen, Employment services, Foreign student adviser, Foreign Studies Centre, Handicapped facilities, Health services, Social counselling, Sports facilities

Student Residential Facilities: For 500 students

Special Facilities: Computing and Networking Centre

Libraries: University Library, 519,879 vols

Publications: Annual Report of the Graduate School of Humanities and Sciences *(annually)*; Annual Report on Research and Education, Faculty of Letters *(annually)*; Research Journal of Living Science *(biannually)*

Academic Staff *2008-2009*	MEN	WOMEN	**TOTAL**
FULL-TIME	–	–	**372**
STAFF WITH DOCTORATE			
FULL-TIME	–	–	**153**
Student Numbers *2008-2009*			
All (Foreign Included)	–	2,817	**2,817**
FOREIGN ONLY	–	125	**125**

Last Updated: 09/12/08

NARUTO UNIVERSITY OF EDUCATION

Naruto Kyoiku Daigaku

748, Nakajima, Takashima, Naruto-cho, Naruto-shi, Tokushima 772-8502

Tel: +81(88) 687-6000

Fax: +81(88) 687-6040

EMail: kg.kokusai@jim.naruto-u.ac.jp

Website: http://www.naruto-u.ac.jp/

President: Yuzo Tanaka

Centres

Data Processing (Data Processing); **Health Service**; **Training for Practical Skills** (Fine Arts; Music; Physical Education; Speech Studies)

Faculties

Arts (Fine Arts; Music; Teacher Trainers Education); **Health and Life Sciences** (Health Education; Health Sciences; Home Economics; Industrial Arts Education; Physical Education; Teacher Trainers Education); **Language and Social Sciences** (Foreign Languages Education; Native Language Education; Science Education; Social Sciences; Teacher Trainers Education); **Natural Sciences** (Mathematics; Natural Sciences; Teacher Trainers Education); **School Education** (Child Care and Development; Curriculum; Development Studies; Education of the Handicapped; Educational Administration; Educational and Student Counselling; Teacher Trainers Education)

Research Centres

School Education (Educational and Student Counselling; Educational Technology; Teacher Trainers Education)

History: Founded 1981. The University participated as a constituent School in the Joint Graduate School (PhD programme) in Science of School Education 1996, Hyogo University of Education.

Governing Bodies: University Senate, Professorial Council, Committee for Graduate School of Education

Academic Year: April to March (April-July; August-November; December-March)

Admission Requirements: Graduation from high school or recognized equivalent and entrance examination. Japanese Language Proficiency Test for international students

Fees: (Yen): Registration, 282,000; tuition, 520,800 per annum

Main Language(s) of Instruction: Japanese

International Co-operation: With universities in USA, Germany, Republic of Korea, China, Australia, South Africa

Degrees and Diplomas: *Gakushi*: Education, 4 yrs; *Shushi*: Education, a further 2 yrs

Student Services: Academic counselling, Canteen, Employment services, Foreign student adviser, Health services, Social counselling, Sports facilities

Student Residential Facilities: Yes

Libraries: University Library, Children's Library, total c. 288,430 vols

Publications: Research Bulletins *(annually)*

Last Updated: 24/03/11

NATIONAL GRADUATE INSTITUTE FOR POLICY STUDIES

Seisaku Kenkyu Daigakuin Daigaku

7-22-1 Roppongi, Minato-ku,
Tokyo 106-8677

Tel: +81(3) 6439-6000

Fax: +81(3) 6439-6010

EMail: admissions@grips.ac.jp

Website: http://www.grips.ac.jp

President: Tatsuo Hatta

International Relations: Takashi Fukushima, Vice-President, Director International Development Studies

Graduate Schools

Policy Studies (Cultural Studies; Development Studies; Economics; Educational Sciences; Finance; International Studies; Japanese; Leadership; Public Administration; Regional Studies)

History: Founded 1997.

Degrees and Diplomas: *Shushi*; *Hakase*

Last Updated: 12/02/09

NATIONAL INSTITUTE OF FITNESS AND SPORTS IN KANOYA

Kanoya Taiiku Daigaku

1 Shiromizu-cho, Kanoya-shi,
Kagoshima 891-2393

Tel: +81(994) 46-4111

Fax: +81(994) 46-2831

EMail: kyoumu2@nifs-k.ac.jp

Website: http://www.nifs-k.ac.jp

President: Tetsuo Fukunaga (2008-)

Centres

Foreign Languages (Modern Languages); **Marine Sports** (Sports)

Colleges

Physical Education *(Also graduate school)* (Physical Education; Sports)

History: Founded 1981.

Academic Year: April to March (April-November; December-March)

Admission Requirements: Graduation from high school or recognized equivalent, and entrance examination

Main Language(s) of Instruction: Japanese

International Co-operation: With universities in China and Republic of Korea

Degrees and Diplomas: *Gakushi*: 4 yrs; *Shushi*: a further 2 yrs; *Hakase*

Student Services: Employment services, Health services, Language programs, Social counselling, Sports facilities

Student Residential Facilities: For c. 350 students

Libraries: 105,795 vols

Last Updated: 12/01/09

NIHON BUNKA UNIVERSITY

Nihon Bunka Daigaku

977 Katakura-cho, Hachioji-shi,
Tokyo 192-8526
Tel: +81(426) 365-211
Website: http://www.nihonbunka-u.ac.jp

History: Founded 1978.

Degrees and Diplomas: *Gakushi*

NIHON FUKUSHI UNIVERSITY

Nihon Fukushi Daigaku

Okuda, Mihama-cho, Chita-gun, Aichi-ken, Mihama-shi, Chiba 470-3295
Tel: +81(569) 87-2214
Fax: +81(569) 87-2314
EMail: kokusai@n-fukushi.ac.jp
Website: http://www.n-fukushi.ac.jp

President: Sachio Kato

Centres
Clinical Psychological Research (Clinical Psychology); **Lifelong Education** (Continuing Education)

Colleges
Human Services *(Takahama)* (Occupational Therapy; Social and Community Services; Social Sciences; Social Welfare); **Social Services** *(Chuo)* (Social and Community Services; Social Welfare)

Faculties
Economics (Economics; Management); **Healthcare Management** (Development Studies; Health Administration; Management); **Social and Information Sciences (SIS)** *(Handa Campus)* (Information Sciences; Information Technology; Social Sciences); **Social Welfare** (Health Education; Humanities and Social Science Education; Social Welfare)

Graduate Schools
International Social Development *(Distance Education)* (Development Studies); **Management Development and Information Systems** (Information Sciences; Management Systems); **Social Welfare** (Social Welfare)

Institutes
Alternative Systems of Social Welfare and Development (Development Studies; Social and Community Services; Social Sciences; Social Welfare); **Chita Hanto Regional Development** *(Handa Campus)* (Heritage Preservation; Regional Planning)

Research Centres
Psychology (Psychology)

Research Institutes
System Sciences *(Handa Campus)* (Social and Community Services; Systems Analysis)

History: Founded 1953, acquired present status and title 1957.

Governing Bodies: Nihon Fukushi Educational Group, Board of Trustees

Academic Year: April to March (April-September; October-March)

Admission Requirements: Graduation from high school and entrance examination (in Japanese Language)

Main Language(s) of Instruction: Japanese

International Co-operation: With universities in Canada, Philippines, Australia, Malaysia, China, Republic of Korea

Degrees and Diplomas: *Gakushi*: Economics; Health and Human Services; Healthcare and Business Management; Social and Information Sciences; Social Welfare; Welfare Clinical Psychology Studies; *Shushi*: Clinical Psychology; Development Studies; Human Environment Information Technology; Management Development; Social Welfare; Welfare Management; *Hakase*: Human Environment Information Studies; Management Development; Social Welfare

Student Services: Academic counselling, Canteen, Employment services, Foreign student adviser, Foreign Studies Centre, Handicapped facilities, Health services, Social counselling, Sports facilities

Student Residential Facilities: For 240 students

Special Facilities: Cultural Hall, Budo-jo (Martial Arts Facility)

Libraries: Mihama Campus Library; Handa Campus Library and Nagoya Campus Library

Publications: Annual Bulletin of Institute of Alternative Systems of Social Welfare Sciences and Development; Bulletin of Nihon Fukushi University; Chiiki to Rinsho, Bulletin of the Clinical Psychological Research Center; Chita Hanto no Rekishi to Genzai, Annual Report of the Institute of Chita Regional Development; Fukushi Kenkyu, Bulletin of the Faculty of Social Welfare; Journal of Economic Studies, Bulletin of the Faculty of Economics

Last Updated: 25/03/11

NIHON PHARMACEUTICAL UNIVERSITY

Nihon Yakka Daigaku

10281 Korumo, Inamachi, Kita-adachi-gun, Saitama-shi, Saitama 362-0806
Tel: +81(48) 721-1155
Fax: +81(48) 721-6718
Website: http://www.nihonyakka.jp/index.html

Schools
Pharmaceutical Sciences (Pharmacology; Pharmacy)

History: Founded 2004.

Degrees and Diplomas: *Gakushi*

Special Facilities: Medicinal Plants Garden; Experimental Animal Centre; Instrumental Analyses Centre.

NIHON UNIVERSITY

Nihon Daigaku

4-8-24 Kudan-Minami, Chiyoda-ku, Tokyo 102-8275
Tel: +81(3) 5275-8116
Fax: +81(3) 5275-8315
EMail: ils@nihon-u.ac.jp
Website: http://www.nihon-u.ac.jp

President: Kichibee Otsuka (2011-)

Director of Academic Affairs: Michiharu Okano
EMail: okano.michiharu@nihon-u.ac.jp

International Relations: Makoto Ishigaki, Chief, International Liaison Section EMail: ishigaki.makoto@nihon-u.ac.jp

Colleges
Art (Cinema and Television; Design; Film; Fine Arts; Literature; Music; Photography; Radio and Television Broadcasting; Theatre); **Bioresource Sciences** (Agricultural Engineering; Animal Husbandry; Biological and Life Sciences; Biotechnology; Chemistry; Development Studies; Environmental Engineering; Food Science; Forest Products; Forestry; Marine Science and Oceanography; Plant and Crop Protection; Veterinary Science); **Commerce** (Accountancy; Business Administration; Business and Commerce); **Economics** (Economics; Finance; Industrial Management); **Engineering** (Applied Chemistry; Architecture; Biology; Chemical Engineering; Civics; Computer Science; Electrical and Electronic Engineering; Mechanical Engineering); **Humanities and Science** (Biology; Chemistry; Chinese; Computer Science; Education; English; Geography; German; History; Japanese; Literature; Mathematics; Philosophy; Physical Education; Physics; Psychology; Sociology; Systems Analysis); **Industrial Technology** (Applied Chemistry; Architecture; Civil Engineering; Computer Engineering; Construction Engineering; Electrical and Electronic Engineering; Industrial Engineering; Industrial Management; Mechanical Engineering); **International Relations** (International Relations); **Law** (Commercial Law; Economics; Journalism; Law; Political Sciences; Public Administration); **Pharmacy** (Pharmacy); **Science and Technology** (Aeronautical and Aerospace Engineering; Applied Chemistry; Architecture; Civics; Computer Science; Electrical Engineering; Electronic Engineering; Marine Engineering; Marine Science and Oceanography; Materials Engineering; Mathematics; Mechanical Engineering; Physics; Transport Engineering)

Divisions
Distance Education (Business and Commerce; Economics; English; History; Japanese; Law; Literature; Political Sciences)

Graduate Schools

Art (Design; Fine Arts; Literature; Music; Performing Arts; Visual Arts); **Bioresource Sciences** (Biological and Life Sciences; Environmental Engineering; Environmental Management; Natural Resources); **Business** *(Master's Programme only)* (Management) *Division Head*: Sezai; **Business Administration** (Accountancy; Business Administration; Business and Commerce); **Dentistry** *(Doctor's programme only)* (Dentistry); **Dentistry (Matsudo)** *(Doctor's programme only)* (Dentistry); **Economics** (Economics); **Engineering** (Architecture; Civil Engineering; Computer Engineering; Electrical and Electronic Engineering; Materials Engineering; Mechanical Engineering); **Industrial Technology** (Applied Chemistry; Architecture; Civil Engineering; Electrical and Electronic Engineering; Engineering Management; Mechanical Engineering); **Integrated Basic Sciences** (Chemistry; Mathematics; Mathematics and Computer Science; Physics); **Intellectual Property** *(Professional Course)*; **International Relations** (International Relations); **Journalism and Media** (Journalism; Media Studies); **Law** (Political Sciences; Private Law; Public Law); **Literature and Social Sciences** (Chinese; Education; English; German; History; Japanese; Literature; Philosophy; Psychology; Sociology); **Medicine** *(Doctor's programme only)* (Community Health; Medicine; Pathology; Physiology; Surgery); **Pharmacy** (Pharmacy); **Science and Technology** (Aeronautical and Aerospace Engineering; Applied Chemistry; Architecture; Civil Engineering; Computer Science; Electrical Engineering; Electronic Engineering; Geography; Marine Engineering; Marine Science and Oceanography; Materials Engineering; Mathematics; Mechanical Engineering; Physics; Real Estate; Transport Engineering); **Social and Cultural Studies** (Cultural Studies; Economics; International Economics; Political Sciences); **Veterinary Medicine** *(Doctor's Program Only)* (Veterinary Science)

Schools

Dentistry (Dentistry); **Dentistry (Matsudo)** (Dentistry); **Law** *(Professional Course)* (Law); **Medicine** (Medicine); **Pharmacy** (Pharmacy)

History: Founded 1889 as Nihon Horitsu Gakko (Nihon Law School). Title changed to Nihon Daigaku 1903, acquired present status 1949.

Governing Bodies: Board of Trustees

Academic Year: April to March (April-September; October-March)

Admission Requirements: Graduation from high school or equivalent or foreign equivalent, and entrance examination

Main Language(s) of Instruction: Japanese

Degrees and Diplomas: *Gakushi*: Dentistry; Medicine; Pharmacy; Veterinary Medicine, 6 yrs; *Gakushi*: Law; Literature; Sociology; Education; Physical Education; Psychology; Geography; Science; Economics; Commerce; Arts; International Relations; Engineering; Bioresource Science, 4 yrs; *Shushi*: Intellectual Property (Professional Shushi); International Relations; Engineering; Bioresource Sciences; Business; International Political Science and Economics; Culture and Communication Studies; Human Science; Liberal Arts; Law; Political Science; Journalism and Media; Literature; Sociology; Education; Psychology; Science; Economics; Commerce; Arts, a further 2 yrs; *Hakase*: Dentistry; Medicine; Pharmacy; Veterinary Medicine, 4 yrs after Shushi; *Hakase*: Law (JD) (Professional Hakase), 2 - 2 yrs after Gakushi; *Hakase*: Law; Political Science; Literature; Sociology; Education; Psychology; Science; Economics; Commerce; Arts; International Relations; Engineering; Bioresource Sciences; Social and Cultural Studies; Liberal Arts (Doctorate), 3 yrs after Shushi

Student Residential Facilities: Yes

Special Facilities: Museum

Libraries: Central Library; College libraries; total, c. 5,900,000 vols

Publications: Annual Reports of The Institute of Information Sciences; Artistic Works, College of Art, Nihon University; Bulletin of Liberal Arts and Sciences, Nihon University School of Medicine; Comparative Law; Hogaku Kenkyu Nenpo, The Graduate School Law Review; Hogaku Kiyo, Journal of the Law Institute; Information Science Studies; International Journal of Oral-Medical Sciences, Research Institute of Oral Science; Journal of College of Industrial Technology, Nihon University; Journal of Intellectual Property; Journal of Oral Science; Journal of the College of Engineering, Nihon University; Journal of The College of International Relations, Nihon University; Journal of the Research Institute of Science and Technology, College of Science and Technology, Nihon University; Journalism and Media; Keikaken Reports, Reports of the Research Institute of Economic Science; Keizai Shushi, Nihon University Economic Review; Kiyo; Nihon Daigaku Seibutsushigenkagakubu ei Kenkyu, Proceeding of the Life Science Research Center, College of Bioresource Sciences; Nihon Daigaku Seibutsushigenkagakubu Sogokenkyujyo Kenkyugyosekishu, Proceeding of the General Research Institute, College of Bioresources; Nihon Daigaku Tushinkyouikubu Kenkyu Kiyou, Bulletin of the Correspondence Division, Nihon University; Nihon Hogaku, Law journal; Nihon University Business Research; Nihon University GSSC Journal, The Bulletin of the Graduate School of Social and Cultural Studies, Nihon University; Nihon University Law Review; Nihon University of Journal of Business; Nihon University of Journal of Humanities and Sciences; Omon Ronso; Proceedings of The Institute of Natural Sciences Nihon University; Report of The Research Institute of Industrial Technology, Nihon University; Report of The Research Institute of Sciences for Living, College of International Relations, Nihon University; Research Bulletin in Liberal Arts, Bulletin of the Research Institute of Economic Science, College of Economics, Nihon University; Research in Arts, College of Art, Nihon University; Sangyo Keiei Kenkyu, Journal of Business Research; Seikei Kenkyu, Studies in Political Science and Economics; Shoho, Institute Newsletter; Studies in Humanities and Social Sciences; Studies in International Relations, College of International Relations, Nihon University; Survey Report on Business Administration Trends; The Nihon University Journal of Medicine; The Study of Accounting; The Study of Business and Industry; Transactions of Nihon University School of Dentistry; Yakugakubu Kenkyu Kiyou, Bulletin of the School of Pharmacy

Academic Staff *2009-2010*	MEN	WOMEN	**TOTAL**
FULL-TIME	2,483	451	**2,934**
PART-TIME	3,078	762	**3,840**
Student Numbers *2011-2012*			
All (Foreign Included)	–	–	**81,100**

Last Updated: 25/10/11

NIHONBASHI GAKKAN UNIVERSITY

Nihonbashi Gakkan Daigaku (NGU)

1225-6 Kashiwa, Kashiwa-shi, Chiba 277-0005
Tel: +81(4) 7167-8655
Fax: +81(4) 7163-0096
EMail: admission@nihonbashi.ac.jp; student-center@nihonbashi.ac.jp
Website: http://www.nihonbashi.ac.jp

Faculties

Human Cultural Sciences and Business Administration (Business Administration)

History: Founded 2000.

Degrees and Diplomas: *Gakushi*

Academic Staff: Total 900
Last Updated: 27/01/09

NIIGATA COLLEGE OF NURSING

Niigata Kenritsu Kango Daigaku

240 Shinnancho, Joetsu-shi, Niigata-shi, Niigata 943-0147
Tel: +81-25-526-2811
Fax: +81-25-526-2815
EMail: soumu@niigata-cn.ac.jp
Website: http://www.niigata-cn.ac.jp/index.htm

President: Takashi Watanabe

Programmes

Nursing *(Also Graduate Programme)* (Anatomy; Community Health; Gerontology; Information Sciences; Midwifery; Nursing; Physiology; Psychiatry and Mental Health; Public Health; Social Sciences)

History: Founded 2002.

Degrees and Diplomas: *Gakushi*; *Shushi*

Libraries: c. 50,000 vols

Last Updated: 24/03/11

NIIGATA INSTITUTE OF TECHNOLOGY

Niigata Koka Daigaku
1719 Fujihashi, Kashiwazaki, Niigata-shi, Niigata 945-1195
Tel: +81(257) 22-8111
Fax: +81(257) 22-8112
EMail: nyuushi@adm.niit.ac.jp
Website: http://www.niit.ac.jp

Faculties

Engineering (Applied Chemistry; Architecture; Automation and Control Engineering; Biotechnology; Civil Engineering; Electronic Engineering; Information Technology; Mechanical Engineering)

Graduate Schools

Technology (Biochemistry; Civil Engineering; Energy Engineering; Engineering; Environmental Engineering; Information Technology; Materials Engineering; Mechanical Engineering; Telecommunications Engineering)

History: Founded 1995.

Academic Year: April to March (April-September; October-March)

International Co-operation: With universities in China and Republic of Korea

Degrees and Diplomas: *Gakushi*; *Shushi*; *Hakase*

Student Services: Academic counselling, Employment services, Sports facilities

Libraries: c. 40,000 vols

NIIGATA SANGYO UNIVERSITY

Niigata Sangyo Daigaku
4730 Karuigawa, Kashiwazaki-shi, Niigata 945-1393
Tel: +81(257) 24-6655
Fax: +81(257) 22-1300
EMail: nyushi@office.nsu.ac.jp
Website: http://www.nsu.ac.jp

Departments

Economics (Economics); **Humanities**

History: Founded 1988.

Degrees and Diplomas: *Gakushi*

Student Services: Foreign student adviser, Sports facilities

Special Facilities: Two computer laboratories.

Libraries: c. 120,000 vols.

Last Updated: 28/01/09

NIIGATA SEIRYO UNIVERSITY

Niigata Seiryo Daigaku
1-5939 Suido-cho, Niigata-shi, Niigata 951-8121
Tel: +81(25) 266-0127
Fax: +81(25) 267-0053
EMail: ao4@n-seiryo.ac.jp
Website: http://www.n-seiryo.ac.jp/

President: Fujio Shimizu

Departments

Nursing (Nursing); **Social Welfare and Psychology** (Psychology; Social Welfare)

Degrees and Diplomas: *Gakushi*

Student Services: Cultural centre, Sports facilities

Libraries: 110,000 vols; Audio-Visual Centre

Last Updated: 28/01/09

NIIGATA UNIVERSITY

Niigata Daigaku
8050, Ikarashi 2-nocho, Niigata-shi, Niigata 950-2181
Tel: +81(25) 223-6161
Fax: +81(25) 262-6539
EMail: info@adm.niigata-u.ac.jp; kokusai@adm.niigata-u.ac.jp
Website:http: //www.niigata-u.ac.jp/

President: Fumitake Gejyo (2002-)

Centres

Co-operative Research (Biotechnology; Communication Studies; Computer Education; Electronic Engineering; Mechanics); **Instrumental Analysis**; **Integrated Data Processing** (Data Processing); **Radioisotope** (Radiophysics)

Faculties

Agriculture (Agriculture; Agrobiology; Biological and Life Sciences; Chemistry; Environmental Studies; Production Engineering); **Dentistry** (Dentistry; Oral Pathology); **Economics** (Business Administration; Economics); **Education** (Education; Preschool Education; Primary Education; Secondary Education); **Engineering** (Architecture; Chemical Engineering; Chemistry; Civil Engineering; Computer Engineering; Electrical and Electronic Engineering; Engineering; Materials Engineering; Mechanical Engineering; Production Engineering; Technology); **Humanities** (Arts and Humanities; Behavioural Sciences; Communication Studies; Cultural Studies; Information Sciences; Philosophy); **Law** (Law); **Medicine** (Health Sciences; Medicine); **Science** (Biology; Chemistry; Environmental Studies; Geology; Mathematics; Natural Sciences; Physics)

Graduate Schools

Education (Curriculum; Education); **Health Sciences**; **Law** (Law); **Medical and Dental Sciences** (Biomedicine; Dentistry; Medicine); **Modern Society and Culture** (Cultural Studies; Development Studies; Economics; International Studies; Japanese; Law; Social Sciences; Sociology); **Science and Technology** (Biological and Life Sciences; Botany; Computer Engineering; Electronic Engineering; Energy Engineering; Environmental Management; Environmental Studies; Food Science; Information Sciences; Mathematics; Natural Sciences; Production Engineering; Technology); **Technology** (Technology)

Institutes

Brain Research; **Faculty Development Research**; **Hazards in Snowy Areas Research** (Environmental Studies); **Transdisciplinary Research**

Further Information: Also Medical Hospital. Dental Hospital

History: Founded 1945 as National University. Became National University Corporation 2004.

Governing Bodies: Kyouiku Kenkyu Hyogikai (University Council of Education and Research)

Academic Year: April to March (April-September; October-March)

Admission Requirements: Graduation from high school or equivalent or foreign equivalent, and entrance examination

Fees: (Yen): 520,800 per annum

Main Language(s) of Instruction: Japanese

Degrees and Diplomas: *Gakushi*: Agriculture; Arts; Economics; Education; Engineering; Law; Science, 4 yrs; *Gakushi*: Dentistry; Medicine, 6 yrs; *Shushi*: Agriculture; Arts; Economics; Education; Engineering; Law; Science, a further 2 yrs; *Hakase*: Agriculture; Engineering; Philosophy; Science, 3 yrs following Shushi; *Hakase*: Dental Sciences; Medicine Sciences, a further 4 yrs

Student Services: Academic counselling, Canteen, Cultural centre, Employment services, Foreign student adviser, Foreign Studies Centre, Health services, Language programs, Social counselling, Sports facilities

Student Residential Facilities: For 564 students

Libraries: University Libraries, 1,672,410 vols

Publications: Acta Medica at Biologica *(biannually)*; Agriculture and Forestry Studies; Annual Report of the Brain Research Institute *(annually)*; Annual Report of the Research Institute for Hazards in Snowy Areas *(annually)*; Annual Report of the University Medical Hospital *(annually)*; Bulletin of Centre for Educational Research and Practice *(annually)*; Humanistic Studies *(biannually)*; Journal of Commerce; Journal of Economics; Journal of General Education; Journal of Law and Politics; Journal of the Study of Modern Society and Culture *(biennially)*; Letters from the University Library *(quarterly)*; Memoirs of the Faculty of Agriculture; Memoirs of the Faculty of Education; News from the School of Dentistry; Niigata Dental Journal *(biannually)*; Niigata Medical Journal *(monthly)*; Report of the Sado Marine Biological Station; Research Report of the Faculty of Engineering; Science Reports, Series A-E

Last Updated: 28/01/09

NIIGATA UNIVERSITY OF HEALTH AND WELFARE

Niigata Iryo Fukushi Daigaku (NUHW)

1398 Shimamicho, Niigata-shi, Niigata 950-3198
Tel: +81(25) 257-4455
Fax: +81(25) 257-4456
EMail: info@nuhw.ac.jp; nyuusi@nuhw.ac.jp
Website: http://www.nuhw.ac.jp

Faculties

Health Sciences (Health Sciences; Nursing; Nutrition; Sports); **Medical Technology** (Medical Technology; Occupational Therapy; Physical Therapy; Speech Therapy and Audiology); **Social Welfare** (Social Welfare)

Graduate Schools

Health and Welfare

History: Founded 2001.

Degrees and Diplomas: *Gakushi*; *Shushi*; *Hakase*

Libraries: Yes.

Publications: Niigata Journal of Health and Welfare

Last Updated: 28/01/09

NIIGATA UNIVERSITY OF INTERNATIONAL AND INFORMATION STUDIES

Niigata Kokusai Joho Daigaku

3-1-1 Mizukino, Niigata-shi, Niigata-shi, Niigata 950-2292
Tel: +81(25) 239-3111
Fax: +81(25) 239-3690
EMail: kouhouweb@nuis.ac.jp
Website: http://www.nuis.ac.jp

Programmes

Information Culture (Information Sciences); **Information System**

History: Founded 1994.

International Co-operation: With universities in USA, China, Republic of Korea, Russia

Degrees and Diplomas: *Gakushi*

Student Services: Canteen, Language programs, Sports facilities

Libraries: c. 75,000 vols.

NIIGATA UNIVERSITY OF MANAGEMENT

Niigata Keiei Daigaku

2909-2 Kibo-ga-oka, Kamo-shi, Niigata 959-13
Tel: +81(256) 53-3000
Fax: +81(256) 53-4544
EMail: gakumuka@duck.niigataum.ac.jp
Website: http://www.niigataum.ac.jp

Programmes

Business Information Systems (Business Administration; Information Technology; Management)

History: Founded 1994.

Degrees and Diplomas: *Gakushi*

Last Updated: 28/01/09

NIIGATA UNIVERSITY OF PHARMACY AND APPLIED LIFE SCIENCES

Niigata Yakka Daigaku (NUPALS)

5-13-2 Kamishin'ei-cho, Niigata-shi, Niigata 950-2081
Tel: +81(250) 25-5000
Fax: +81(250) 25-5021
Website: http://www.nupals.ac.jp

Programmes

Graduate (Biological and Life Sciences; Medicine; Pharmacology; Pharmacy); **Undergraduate** (Biological and Life Sciences; Food Science; Pharmacology; Pharmacy)

History: Founded 1977. Known as Niigata College of Pharmacy until 2002.

Academic Year: April to March

Admission Requirements: Graduation from high school or equivalent

Main Language(s) of Instruction: Japanese

Degrees and Diplomas: *Gakushi*: 4 yrs; *Shushi*: a further 2 yrs; *Hakase*: 3 yrs following Shushi

Student Services: Canteen, Employment services, Health services, Social counselling, Sports facilities

Libraries: c. 85,400 vols

Publications: Bulletin *(annually)*

Last Updated: 28/01/09

NIPPON BUNRI UNIVERSITY

Nippon Bunri Daigaku

1727 Ichigi, Oita-shi, Oita 870-0397
Tel: +81(97) 592-1600
Fax: +81(97) 592-3482
EMail: kokusai@nbu.ac.jp
Website: http://www.nbu.ac.jp

Programmes

Graduate (Aeronautical and Aerospace Engineering; Electronic Engineering; Environmental Studies; Information Sciences; Mechanical Engineering); **Undergraduate** (Aeronautical and Aerospace Engineering; Architecture; Civil Engineering; Computer Science; Electronic Engineering; Information Sciences; Information Technology; Mechanical Engineering)

History: Founded 1967. Acquired present status 1982.

Degrees and Diplomas: *Gakushi*; *Shushi*

Last Updated: 28/01/09

NIPPON DENTAL UNIVERSITY

Nippon Shika Daigaku

1-9-20 Fujimi, Chiyoda-ku, Tokyo 102-8159
Tel: +81(3) 3261-8311 +81(3) 3261-8400
Fax: +81(3) 3261-8086
Website: http://www.ndu.ac.jp

President: Sen Nakahara

Schools

Dentistry *(Also Graduate School)* (Dental Hygiene; Dental Technology; Dentistry)

Further Information: Also campus in Niigata

History: Founded 1907 as Private Kyoritsu Dental School. Reorganized and acquired present name 1949. Graduate School added 1960.

Governing Bodies: Board of Regents

Academic Year: April to March (April-September; October-March)

Admission Requirements: Graduation from high school or equivalent, and entrance examination

Main Language(s) of Instruction: Japanese

International Co-operation: With universities in USA, China and Thailand

Degrees and Diplomas: *Gakushi*: Dentistry, 6 yrs; *Hakase*: Dentistry, a further 4 yrs

Student Services: Sports facilities

Student Residential Facilities: For women students

Special Facilities: Institution of Dental History

Libraries: c. 250,000 vols

Publications: Bulletin *(annually)*; Odontology *(bimonthly)*

Last Updated: 28/01/09

NIPPON INSTITUTE OF TECHNOLOGY

Nippon Kogyo Daigaku

4-1 Gakuendai, Miyashiro-machi, Minamisaitama-gun, Saitama 345-8501
Tel: +81(480) 34-4111
Fax: +81(480) 33-7678
EMail: nyu-shi@nit.ac.jp
Website: http://www.nit.ac.jp

President: Akira Yanagisawa
Tel: +81(480) 33-7501, Fax: +81(480) 33-7476

Faculties
Engineering

Graduate Schools
Engineering (Architecture; Computer Engineering; Electrical Engineering; Information Technology; Mechanical Engineering; Structural Architecture); **Management of Technology** (Engineering Management)

History: Founded 1967. Graduate School established 1982.

Academic Year: April to March (April-September; October-March)

Admission Requirements: Graduation from high school or technical high school, and entrance examination

Main Language(s) of Instruction: Japanese

Degrees and Diplomas: *Gakushi*: Engineering (Kogakushi), 4 yrs; *Shushi*: Engineering (Kogakushushi), a further 2 yrs; *Hakase*: Engineering (Kogakuhakushi), 3 yrs following Shushi

Special Facilities: Museum of Industrial Technology

Libraries: c. 210,000 vols

Publications: Research Reports *(quarterly)*

Last Updated: 28/01/09

NIPPON MEDICAL SCHOOL

Nihon Ika Daigaku

1-1-5 Sendagi, Bunkyo-ku, Tokyo 113-8602
Tel: +81(3) 3822-2131
Fax: +81(3) 3824-7712
EMail: kokusai@nms.ac.jp
Website: http://www.nms.ac.jp

Faculties
Medicine (Gerontology; Immunology; Medicine; Science Education)

Schools
Medicine *(Postgraduate)* (Community Health; Pathology; Physiology; Surgery)

History: Founded 1904 as School, became College 1912, acquired present status 1925.

Governing Bodies: Board of Trustees

Academic Year: April to March (April-July; September-December; January-March)

Admission Requirements: Graduation from high school and entrance examination

Main Language(s) of Instruction: Japanese

International Co-operation: With univerisities in China and Thailand

Degrees and Diplomas: *Gakushi*: Medicine, 6 yrs; *Hakase*: Medicine, a further 4-6 yrs

Student Services: Foreign Studies Centre

Student Residential Facilities: Yes

Libraries: 150,000 vols

Publications: Journal *(bimonthly)*

Last Updated: 28/01/09

NIPPON SPORT SCIENCE UNIVERSITY

Nippon Taiiku Daigaku (NSSU)

1-1 Fukazawa 7-chome, Setagaya-ku, Tokyo 158-8508
Tel: +81(3) 5706-0900
Fax: +81(3) 5706-0912
EMail: international@nittaidai.ac.jp
Website: http://www.nittai.ac.jp

President: Takushiro Ochiai (2007-)
Tel: +81(3) 5706-0921, Fax: +81(3) 5706-0949

Executive Director: Kiyoshi Otani
Tel: +81(3) 5706-0921, Fax: +81(3) 5706-0949

International Relations: Hiroshi Kiyota, Vice President, Dean, Faculty of Sport Science
Tel: +81(3) 5706-0923, Fax: +81(3) 5706-0949

Departments
Physical Education and Early Childhood Education *(Women's Junior College of NSSU)* (Health Sciences; Physical Education; Preschool Education; Sports) *Dean*: Osamu Murakami

Faculties
Sports Science *(Yokohama)* (Art Education; Health Sciences; Performing Arts; Physical Education; Social Welfare; Sports; Sports Management) *Dean*: Hiroshi Kiyota

Graduate Schools
Health and Sport Science *Dean*: Takeshi Takahashi

History: Founded 1891 as School, became university 1949.

Governing Bodies: Educational Foundation of Nippon Taiikukai.

Academic Year: April to March (April-September; October-March)

Admission Requirements: Graduation from high school or equivalent, and entrance examination

Main Language(s) of Instruction: Japanese

International Co-operation: With universities in Germany, China, Republic of Korea

Accrediting Agencies: Japan Institution for Higher Education Evaluation (JIHEE); Japan University Accreditation Association (JUAA); National Institution for Academic Degrees and University Evaluation (NIAD-UE); Japan Association for College Accreditation (JACA)

Degrees and Diplomas: *Tankidaigakushi*: Taiiku (Associate Degree), 2 yrs; *Gakushi*: Physical Education, 4 yrs; *Shushi*: Health and Sports Sciences (Master's Degree), a further 2 yrs; *Hakase*: Health and Sports Sciences (PhD), 3 yrs following Shushi

Student Services: Academic counselling, Canteen, Employment services, Foreign student adviser, Health services, Language programs, Nursery care, Social counselling, Sports facilities

Student Residential Facilities: 4 dormitories

Special Facilities: Research Institute for Sport Science, Sports Training Centre, Office of Athletics

Libraries: Two libraries, 411,397 vols

Publications: Bulletin of Nippon Sports Sciences University *(biannually)*

Academic Staff *2008-2009*	MEN	WOMEN	TOTAL
FULL-TIME	133	26	**159**
PART-TIME	159	51	**210**
STAFF WITH DOCTORATE			
FULL-TIME	28	1	**29**
Student Numbers *2008-2009*			
All (Foreign Included)	3,842	2,062	**5,904**
FOREIGN ONLY	9	4	**13**

Part-time students, 49.

Last Updated: 06/07/09

NIPPON VETERINARY AND LIFE SCIENCE UNIVERSITY

Nihon Jui Chikusan Daigaku

1-7-1 Kyonan-cho, Musashino-shi, Tokyo 180
Tel: +81(422) 31-4151
Fax: +81(422) 33-2094
Website: http://www.nvlu.ac.jp

Faculties
Applied Life Sciences (Animal Husbandry; Biological and Life Sciences; English; Environmental Management; Food Science; Food Technology; Physics; Zoology); **Veterinary Medicine**

Graduate Schools
Veterinary Science (Veterinary Science)

History: Founded 1881. Formerly known as Nippon Veterinary and Animal Sciences University.

Academic Year: April to March

Admission Requirements: Graduation from high school

Main Language(s) of Instruction: Japanese

Degrees and Diplomas: *Gakushi*: 6 yrs; *Hakase*: a further 4 yrs

Student Services: Sports facilities

Libraries: c. 94,000 vols
Last Updated: 27/01/09

NISHIKYUSHU UNIVERSITY

Nishikyushu Daigaku
4490-9 Oaza-Osaki, Kanzaki-machi, Kanzaki-gun, Saga 842-8585
Tel: +81(952) 524-4191
Fax: +81(952) 524-4194
EMail: nky-info@nisikyu-u.ac.jp
Website: http://www.nisikyu-u.ac.jp

Programmes

Health and Social Welfare (Health Sciences; Home Economics; Nutrition; Social Welfare)

History: Founded 1968.

Degrees and Diplomas: *Gakushi*; *Shushi*

NISHINIPPON INSTITUTE OF TECHNOLOGY

Nishinippon Kogyo Daigaku
1-11 Aratsu, Kanda-machi, Miyako-gun, Fukuoka 800-0394
Tel: +81(930) 23-1491
Fax: +81(930) 24-7900
EMail: nyushi@nishitech.ac.jp
Website: http://www.nishitech.ac.jp

Programmes

Engineering (Engineering)

History: Founded 1967.

Degrees and Diplomas: *Gakushi*
Last Updated: 28/01/09

NISHOGAKUSHA UNIVERSITY

Nishogakusha Daigaku
6-16 Sanban-cho, Chiyoda-ku, Tokyo 102-8336
Tel: +81(3) 3261-7423
Fax: +81(3) 3261-8904
EMail: icenter1@nishogakusha-u.ac.jp
Website: http://www.nishogakusha-u.ac.jp

Faculties

Arts and Humanities (Chinese; Japanese; Literature; Modern Languages; Oriental Languages; Philosophy); **International Political Science and Economics** (International Economics; International Studies)

History: Founded 1877.

International Co-operation: With universities in China, Australia and Taiwan

Degrees and Diplomas: *Gakushi*; *Shushi*; *Hakase*

Libraries: 280,000 vols
Last Updated: 28/01/09

NORTH ASIA UNIVERSITY

North Asia Daigaku
46-1 Morisawa, Tezakura, Shimokita, Akita-shi, Akita 010-8515
Tel: +81(188) 363-313
EMail: koho@nau.ac.jp
Website: http://www.nau.ac.jp/eng/

President: Ken Koizumi

Faculties

Economics (Accountancy; Business Administration; Economics; Finance; Management); **Law** (Law; Tourism)

History: Founded 1953. Formerly known as Akita Keizai Hoka Daigaku (Akita University of Economics and Law). Acquired present title 2007.

Degrees and Diplomas: *Gakushi*: Economics; Law, 4 yrs
Last Updated: 29/10/08

IAU NOTRE DAME SEISHIN UNIVERSITY

Notoru Damu Seishin Joshi Daigaku (NDSU)
2-16-9 Ifuku-cho, Okayama-shi, Okayama 700-8516
Tel: +81(86) 252-7145
Fax: +81(86) 252-5099
EMail: apoffice@pluto.ndsu.ac.jp
Website: http://www.ndsu.ac.jp

President: Takako Frances Takagi (2001-)
EMail: prof4@pluto.ndsu.ac.jp

Head of Administration: Yoshihiro Suzuki

International Relations: Yoshiji Hirose, Head of International Communication Section, Student Affairs Division
Tel: +81(86) 252-5719, Fax: +81(86) 252-5719
EMail: exch1@pluto.ndsu.ac.jp

Departments

Child Welfare *(This department belongs to the faculty of Human Life Sciences) Head*: Kaneyoshi Ishihara; **Contemporary Sociological Studies** (Folklore; History; Sociology) *Head*: Hiromi Kojima; **English Language and Literature** *(This department belongs to the Faculty of Literature)* (English; Linguistics; Literature) *Head*: Masuko Adachi; **Food and Human Nutrition** *(This department belongs to the Faculty of Human Life Sciences)* (Food Science; Nutrition) *Head*: Yasushi Hayashi; **Human Living Sciences** *(This department belongs to the Faculty of Human Life Sciences) Head*: Yasutsugu Ueda; **Japanese Language and Literature** *(This department belongs to the Faculty of Literature) Head*: Susumu Hiroshima

Faculties

Human Life Sciences (Child Care and Development; Food Science; Nutrition; Social Sciences); **Literature**

Graduate Schools

Human Life Sciences; **Literature**

History: Founded 1949 by the Sisters of Notre Dame de Namur.

Governing Bodies: Notre Dame Seishin School Corporation

Academic Year: April to March

Admission Requirements: Graduation from high school or recognized foreign equivalent and entrance examination for foreign students

Fees: (Yen): Tuition, 560,000 per annum

Main Language(s) of Instruction: Japanese

Degrees and Diplomas: *Teaching Certificate*; *Gakushi*: 4 yrs; *Shushi*: a further 2 yrs; *Hakase*: a further 3 yrs

Student Services: Academic counselling, Canteen, Employment services, Foreign student adviser, Foreign Studies Centre, Handicapped facilities, Health services, Language programs, Social counselling, Sports facilities

Student Residential Facilities: Yes

Libraries: 303,796 vols

Academic Staff *2008-2009*	MEN	WOMEN	**TOTAL**
FULL-TIME	53	46	**99**
PART-TIME	75	36	**111**
Student Numbers *2008-2009*			
All (Foreign Included)	–	–	**2,276**

Last Updated: 09/12/08

OBIHIRO UNIVERSITY OF AGRICULTURE AND VETERINARY MEDICINE

Obihiro Chikusan Daigaku
Nishi 2-11, Inada-cho, Obihiro-shi, Hokkaido 080-8555
Tel: +81(155) 49-5115
Fax: +81(155) 49-5319
EMail: rgk@obihiro.ac.jp
Website: http://www.obihiro.ac.jp

President: Hideyuki Nagasawa Tel: +81(155) 49-5210

Departments

Animal Medical Science *(Doctoral)* (Zoology); **Environmental Hygiene** (Environmental Studies; Hygiene); **Food Hygiene** *(Doctoral)* (Food Science; Hygiene)

Divisions
Animal Science and Production (Animal Husbandry; Zoology); **Veterinary Medicine** (Veterinary Science)

Graduate Schools
Agricultural Science *(Iwate University, Doctoral)* (Agriculture; Natural Resources); **Veterinary Science** *(Gifu University, Doctoral)* (Veterinary Science)

Programmes
Agro-Environmental Science *(Graduate, Master)* (Agriculture; Environmental Studies); **Animal and Food Hygiene** *(Graduate, Master)* (Animal Husbandry; Zoology); **Animal Production and Agricultural Economics** *(Graduate, Master)*; **Biological Resource Science** *(Graduate, Master)* (Biological and Life Sciences; Natural Resources)

Research Centres
Protozoan Diseases *(National)*

Further Information: Also Japanese language courses for foreign students

History: Founded 1941 as Technical School of Veterinary Science, became College of Veterinary Science and Animal Production 1944, College of Agricultural Science 1946 and University 1949.

Governing Bodies: Faculty Council

Academic Year: April to March (April-September; October-March)

Admission Requirements: Graduation from high school or equivalent, and entrance examination

Main Language(s) of Instruction: Japanese

Degrees and Diplomas: *Gakushi*: Agriculture, 4 yrs; *Gakushi*: Veterinary Medicine, 6 yrs; *Shushi*: a further 2 yrs; *Hakase*: 3-4 yrs following Shushi

Student Residential Facilities: Yes

Libraries: 192,680 vols

Publications: Research Bulletin

Last Updated: 24/03/11

OCHANOMIZU UNIVERSITY

Ochanomizu Joshi Daigaku

2-1-1 Otsuka, Bunkyo-ku, Tokyo 112-8610
Tel: +81(3) 5978-5106
Fax: +81(3) 5978-5978
EMail: info@cc.ocha.ac.jp
Website: http://www.ocha.ac.jp

President: Sawako Hanyu

Director-General of Administration: Hiroshi Akiyama

International Relations: Seitoku Minagawa, Executive Assistant Director, International and Scientific Research Affairs Division

Centres
Health Care (Health Sciences; Public Health) *Director*: Yutaka Morita

Faculties
Human Life and Environmental Science (Biological and Life Sciences; Clinical Psychology; Cultural Studies; Environmental Studies; Family Studies; Food Science; Nutrition; Social Sciences) *Dean*: Tamie Kaino; **Letters and Education** (Art History; Arts and Humanities; Chinese; Cultural Studies; Dance; Educational Sciences; English; Ethics; French; Geography (Human); History; Japanese; Modern Languages; Music; Performing Arts; Philosophy; Psychology; Social Sciences; Sociology) *Dean*: Nobuko Uchida; **Science** (Biology; Chemistry; Information Sciences; Mathematics; Natural Sciences; Physics) *Dean*: Fumiaki Shibata

Graduate Schools
Humanities and Science (Arts and Humanities; Mathematics; Natural Sciences; Philosophy; Social Sciences) *Dean*: Yukiko Hirano

Institutes
Environmental Science for Human Life (Environmental Studies; Food Science; Health Sciences; Nutrition) *Director*: Kazuo Kondoh; **Gender Studies** (Gender Studies) *Director*: Kaoru Tachi

Laboratories
International Student Centre (Foreigners Education) *Director*: Yasuko Sasaki

History: Founded 1874 as School, became National University 1949.

Governing Bodies: Yakuinkai (University Council)

Academic Year: April to March (April-July; September-March)

Admission Requirements: Graduation from high school or equivalent or foreign equivalent and entrance examination

Fees: (Yen): 520,800 per annum

Main Language(s) of Instruction: Japanese

International Co-operation: With universities in Australia, China, Republic of Korea, Taiwan, United Kingdom, France, Russia Federation and Germany

Degrees and Diplomas: *Gakushi*: Human Life and Environmental Sciences; Letters and Education; Science, 4 yrs; *Shushi*: Human Life and Environmental Sciences (MA); Humanities (MA); Philosophy (MA); Science (MA); Social Sciences (MA), a further 2 yrs; *Hakase (PhD)*: 3 yrs following Shushi. PhD awarded in all fields included in graduate school

Student Services: Canteen, Cultural centre, Employment services, Foreign Studies Centre, Health services, Sports facilities

Student Residential Facilities: For 479 students

Libraries: University Library, 616,106 vols

Publications: Natural Sciences Report *(biannually)*; Studies in Arts and Culture *(annually)*

Last Updated: 01/09/09

OHKA GAKUEN UNIVERSITY

Oukagakuen Daigaku

12-1 Nanamagari, Taihei-cho, Toyota-shi, Aichi 471-0057
Tel: +81(565) 35-3131
Fax: +81(565) 35-3137
EMail: nyushi@ohkagakuen-u.ac.jp; webmaster@ohkagakuen-u.ac.jp
Website: http://www.ohkagakuen-u.ac.jp

Faculties
Early Childhood Care and Education; **Humanities** (Arts and Humanities; Cultural Studies)

Schools
Graduate Studies (Arts and Humanities; Cultural Studies; Social Sciences)

History: Founded 1998.

Degrees and Diplomas: *Gakushi*; *Shushi*

Publications: Bulletin of Ohkagakuen University; Cosmos

Last Updated: 28/01/09

O-HARA COLLEGE OF BUSINESS

O-Hara Gakuen (OCB)

1-2-10 Nishikanda, Chiyoda-ku, Tokyo 101-8351
Tel: +81 (3) 3234-6374
Fax: +81 (3) 3234-6361
EMail: info@o-hara.ac.jp
Website: http://www.o-hara.ac.jp

President: Fumio Kubo (1999-)
Tel: +81 (3) 3234-6374, Fax: +81 (3) 3234-6361
EMail: kubo@o-hara.ac.jp

General Manager: Tatsushi Abe (1995-)
Tel: +81 (3) 3234-6374, Fax: +81 (3) 3234-6361
EMail: t_abe@o-hara.ac.jp

International Relations: Shinsuke Nishihara, General Manager (1991-)
Tel: +81 (3) 3234-6374, Fax: +81 (3) 3234-6361
EMail: nishihara@o-hara.ac.jp

Colleges
Accounting (Accountancy; Taxation) *General Manager*: Shinsuke Nishihara; **Business Administration** (Business Administration; Business and Commerce; Private Administration; Public Administration) *General Manager*: Masahiro Iwgami; **IT Business** *General*

Manager: Nobuhiro Miyazawa; **Law and Regulations** *General Manager*: Masahiro Iwagami; **Medical Care** (Health Administration; Social Welfare; Sports Medicine) *General Manager*: Naoe Mitutomo; **Sports Science** (Sports; Sports Management; Sports Medicine) *General Manager*: Tetu Ozawa

Graduate Schools
Accounting *General Manager*: Yasuaki Aoki

Further Information: 23 campuses in Japan. Some campuses have all the above colleges; others have certain of these colleges

History: Founded 1957as O-Hara Boki School specialising in Accountancy; Fully accredited in 2006

Governing Bodies: Board of Directors

Academic Year: April to March

Admission Requirements: (Undergraduate): Secondary School Certificate (Sotsugyo-shosho) plus entrance examination; (Graduate School): BA plus entrance examination

Fees: (Yen): c. 1m. per annum

Main Language(s) of Instruction: Japanese

Accrediting Agencies: Ministry of Education, Culture, Sports, Science and Technology (MEXT)

Degrees and Diplomas: *Senmonshi*: 2 yrs; *Kodo-Senmonshi*: 4 yrs; *Shushi*: Accountacy (MA), a further 2 yrs

Student Services: Academic counselling, Canteen, Employment services, Foreign student adviser, Handicapped facilities, Health services, Language programs, Sports facilities

Student Residential Facilities: Limited residential facilities

Press or Publishing House: O-Hara Press

OHU UNIVERSITY
Ou Daigaku

31-1 Misumido, Tomita-machi, Koriyama-shi, Fukushima 963-8611
Tel: +81(24) 932-8931
Fax: +81(24) 933-7372
EMail: info@ohu-u.ac.jp
Website: http://www.ohu-u.ac.jp

Programmes
Dentistry (Dentistry); **Pharmacy** (Pharmacology; Pharmacy); **Social Sciences, Arts and Humanities** (Cultural Studies; English; European Languages; French; Japanese; Linguistics; Literature; Modern Languages)

History: Founded 1972.

Main Language(s) of Instruction: Japanese

Degrees and Diplomas: *Gakushi*; *Shushi*

Libraries: 190,000 vols

Last Updated: 28/01/09

OITA UNIVERSITY
Oita Daigaku

700 Dannoharu, Oita-shi, Oita 870-1192
Tel: +81(97) 554-7473
Fax: +81(97) 554-6069
EMail: tankoury@oita-u.ac.jp
Website: http://www.oita-u.ac.jp

President: Tadashi Hano
Tel: +81(97) 554-7402, Fax: +81(97) 554-7414

International Relations: Yuko Sato, Head, Academic Cooperation Office Tel: +81(97) 554-7429, Fax: +81(97) 554-7437

Centres
Community Research (Urban Studies); **Data Processing** (Information Management); **Development of University Education** *(Support Center)* (Higher Education); **Health Sciences** (Health Sciences); **Research and Development** (Development Studies)

Faculties
Economics (Economics; Sociology); **Education and Welfare Science** (Educational Sciences; Regional Studies; Special Education; Teacher Training); **Engineering** (Chemical Engineering; Computer Engineering; Electrical and Electronic Engineering; Environmental Engineering; Materials Engineering; Production Engineering); **Medicine**

Graduate Schools
Economics (Economics; Sociology); **Education** (Education); **Engineering** (Chemical Engineering; Computer Engineering; Electrical and Electronic Engineering; Environmental Engineering; Materials Engineering; Production Engineering); **Medicine** (Anatomy; Biochemistry; Ecology; Medicine; Nursing; Physiology); **Social Service Administration** (Regional Studies)

Institutes
Science Research

Laboratories
Venture Business (Business Administration)

Research Centres
Human Welfare (Welfare and Protective Services); **Lifelong Learning** (Continuing Education)

Further Information: Also University Hospital

History: Founded 1949 as a National University under the new educational system incorporating the Oita College of Economics, Oita Normal School, and Oita Normal School for Youth Education. Graduate School of Economics founded 1977, Graduate School of Education 1992, Graduate School of Engineering 1995, and Graduate School of Social Service Administration 2002. Merged with Oita Medical University 2003.

Governing Bodies: University Council

Academic Year: April to March (April-September; October-March)

Admission Requirements: Graduation from high school or equivalent or foreign equivalent, and entrance examination

Fees: (Yen): Registration, 282,000; tuition, 520,800 per annum

Main Language(s) of Instruction: Japanese

International Co-operation: With universities in USA, United Kingdom, China, Republic of Korea, Netherlands, Germany, Dominican Republic and Portugal

Degrees and Diplomas: *Teaching Certificate*: Teacher Training, Disabled Children's School Level); Teacher Training, Kindergarten Level; Teacher Training, Primary Level; Teacher Training, Secondary Level; *Gakushi*: Economics; Education; Engineering; Medicine, 4 yrs; *Shushi*: Economics; Education; Engineering; Medicine, 2 yrs following Gakushi; *Hakase*: Engineering, 3 yrs following Shushi; *Hakase*: Medicine, 3 yrs follwing Shushi

Student Services: Canteen, Employment services, Foreign Studies Centre, Health services, Sports facilities

Student Residential Facilities: Yes

Libraries: University Library, c. 741,000 vols

Publications: Academic Bulletin *(annually)*; Bulletin of the Research Institute of Economics *(annually)*; Reports of the Faculty of Engineering *(annually)*; Research Bulletin of Faculty of Education *(annually)*

Last Updated: 24/03/09

OITA UNIVERSITY OF NURSING AND HEALTH SCIENCES
Oita Kenritsu Kango Kagaku Daigaku

2944-9 Megusuno, Notsuharu, Oita-shi, Oita 870-1201
Tel: +81(97) 586-4303
Fax: +81(97) 586-4370
EMail: info@oita-nhs.ac.jp
Website: http://www.oita-nhs.ac.jp

President: Tomoko Kusama

Departments
Basic Nursing Sciences; **Clinical Nursing**; **Health Sciences** (Biology; Clinical Psychology; Computer Science; Health Sciences; Modern Languages; Sports; Statistics); **Public Health Nursing** (Community Health; Health Administration; Nursing; Public Health)

Programmes
Graduate Studies (Biological and Life Sciences; Community Health; Epidemiology; Gerontology; Health Administration; Midwifery; Nursing; Physiology; Psychiatry and Mental Health; Public Health; Radiology; Statistics)

History: Founded 1998.

Degrees and Diplomas: *Gakushi*; *Shushi*; *Hakase*

Student Services: Language programs, Sports facilities
Libraries: c. 25,580 vols; Media Centre.
Last Updated: 28/01/09

OKAYAMA GAKUIN UNIVERSITY

Okayama Gakuin Daigaku

787 Akuri, Kurashiki-shi, Okayama-shi, Okayama 710-8511
Tel: +81(86) 428-2651
Fax: +81(86) 429-0323
EMail: owc@owc.ac.jp
Website: http://www.owc.ac.jp

Departments

Food and Nutrition; **Human Communication**

Degrees and Diplomas: *Gakushi*

Special Facilities: Language Laboratory.

Libraries: Yes.

OKAYAMA PREFECTURAL UNIVERSITY

Okayama Kenritsu Daigaku

111 Kuboki, Soja-shi, Okayama 719-1197
Tel: +81(866) 94-2111
Fax: +81(866) 94-2196
EMail: kendai@ad.oka-pu.ac.jp
Website: http://www.oka-pu.ac.jp

Programmes

Computer Science and Systems Engineering (Computer Engineering; Computer Science; Electronic Engineering; Information Technology; Mechanical Engineering; Telecommunications Engineering); **Design** (Design; Handicrafts; Industrial Design; Visual Arts); **Health and Welfare** (Health Sciences; Nursing; Nutrition; Social Welfare)

History: Founded 1993.

Main Language(s) of Instruction: Japanese

Degrees and Diplomas: *Gakushi*; *Shushi*; *Hakase*

OKAYAMA SHOKA UNIVERSITY

Okayama Shoka Daigaku

2-10-1 Tsushima-Kyo-machi, Okayama-shi, Okayama 700-8601
Tel: +81(86) 252-0642
Fax: +81(86) 255-6947
EMail: nyusi@osu.ac.jp
Website: http://www.osu.ac.jp

Faculties

Commerce (Business Administration; Business and Commerce; Information Sciences; Tourism); **Law and Economics** (Economics; Law)

History: Founded 1965.

Governing Bodies: Kibi Gakuen Foundation

Academic Year: April to March

Main Language(s) of Instruction: Japanese

International Co-operation: With universities in China, Australia, United Kingdom and Northern Ireland

Degrees and Diplomas: *Gakushi*: 4 yrs; *Shushi*: a further 2 yrs

Student Services: Academic counselling, Canteen, Employment services, Foreign student adviser, Health services, Language programs, Nursery care, Social counselling, Sports facilities

Student Residential Facilities: Yes

Libraries: University Library, 300,000 vols
Last Updated: 28/01/09

OKAYAMA UNIVERSITY

Okayama Daigaku

1-1-1 Tsushima-Naka, Okayama-shi, Okayama 700-8530
Tel: +81(86) 252-1111
Fax: +81(86) 254-6104
EMail: kokusai@adm.okayama-u.ac.jp
Website: http://www.okayama-u.ac.jp

President: Kyozo Chiba (2005-)

Director-General: Kenji Kajiwara

International Relations: Ryo Tabohashi
Tel: +81(86) 251-7036, Fax: +81(86) 254-6104
EMail: kokusai@cc.okayama-u.ac.jp

Faculties

Agriculture (Biochemistry; Biology; Botany; Crop Production; Environmental Management; Zoology); **Economics** (Accountancy; Econometrics; Economics; Management; Social Policy; Social Studies); **Education** (Art Education; Education; Education of the Handicapped; Educational Administration; Educational Psychology; Foreign Languages Education; Health Education; Home Economics Education; Humanities and Social Science Education; Mathematics Education; Music Education; Native Language Education; Physical Education; Primary Education; Science Education; Technology Education); **Engineering** (Applied Chemistry; Biological and Life Sciences; Biotechnology; Computer Engineering; Electrical and Electronic Engineering; Information Technology; Mechanical Engineering; Telecommunications Engineering); **Environmental Science and Technology** (Civil Engineering; Environmental Engineering; Environmental Management; Environmental Studies; Mathematics and Computer Science); **Law** (Civil Law; Comparative Law; International Law; Political Sciences; Public Law); **Letters** (American Studies; Amerindian Languages; Arts and Humanities; Asian Studies; Behavioural Sciences; European Languages; European Studies; History; Oriental Languages; Philosophy); **Pharmaceutical Sciences** (Medicine; Pharmacology; Pharmacy); **Science** (Biology; Chemistry; Earth Sciences; Mathematics; Physics)

Graduate Schools

Environmental Science (Development Studies; Environmental Engineering; Environmental Studies); **Health Sciences**; **Humanities and Social Sciences** (Cultural Studies; Social Sciences; Social Studies); **Medicine, Dentistry and Pharmaceutical Sciences**; **Natural Sciences and Technology** (Biochemistry; Biological and Life Sciences; Biotechnology; Chemistry; Earth Sciences; Electronic Engineering; Mathematics; Mechanical Engineering; Molecular Biology; Physics; Telecommunications Engineering)

Institutes

Study of the Earth's Interior

Research Institutes

Institute for Bioresources

Schools

Dentistry; **Law**; **Medicine** (Anaesthesiology; Biology; Child Care and Development; Environmental Studies; Epidemiology; Ethics; Forensic Medicine and Dentistry; Health Sciences; Immunology; Medicine; Neurosciences; Oncology; Paediatrics; Pathology; Physics; Social and Preventive Medicine)

Further Information: Also University Hospitals (Dentistry and Medicine). Shikata, Higashiyama, Hirai, Kurashiki and Misasa campuses.

History: Founded 1949 as National University, incorporating Okayama Medical School, affiliated Medical College, Sixth National Higher School, Okayama Normal School, Okayama Youth Normal School, and Okayama Prefectural College of Agriculture. Agricultural Biological Research Institute added in 1951, and Faculty of Engineering established 1960.

Governing Bodies: Hyogikai (University Council), Yakuinkai (Board of Directors)

Academic Year: April to March (April-September; October-March)

Admission Requirements: Graduation from high school or recognized equivalent, and entrance examination

Fees: (Yen): 535,900 per annum

Main Language(s) of Instruction: Japanese

International Co-operation: With universities in China, Republic of Korea, Thailand, Australia, United Kingdom, USA, Turkey, France, Germany, Italy, Poland, and Serbia and Montenegro

Degrees and Diplomas: *Gakushi*: 4-6 yrs; *Shushi*: a further 2 yrs; *Hakase*: 3-4 yrs following Shushi

Student Services: Academic counselling, Canteen, Employment services, Foreign student adviser, Foreign Studies Centre, Health services, Language programs, Nursery care, Sports facilities

Student Residential Facilities: Yes

Libraries: Main Library, 1,574,145 vols; Medical School, 262,730 vols; Research Institute for Bioresources, 181,323 vols; other libraries, 5,844 vols

Publications: Acta Medica Okayama *(bimonthly)*; Bulletin of School of Education *(3 per annum)*; Contributions from the Ushimado Marine Laboratory; Faculty of Engineering, Okayama University; Journal of Humanities and Social Sciences *(biannually)*; Journal of the Faculty of Letters *(biannually)*; Mathematical Journal *(annually)*; Nogaku Kenkyu *(annually)*; Okayama Economic Review *(quarterly)*; Okayama Law Journal *(quarterly)*; Okayama-Igakkai-Zasshi *(bimonthly)*; Reports of the Research Laboratory for Surface Science *(annually)*; Scientific Reports of the Faculty of Agriculture *(biannually)*; Technical Report of ISEI *(annually)*

Last Updated: 28/01/09

OKAYAMA UNIVERSITY OF SCIENCE

Okayama Rika Daigaku (OUS)

1-1 Ridai-cho, Okayama-shi, Okayama 700-0005

Tel: +81(86) 252-3161

Fax: +81(86) 252-4040

Website: http://www.ous.ac.jp

President: Kotaro Kake (2001-)

International Relations: Masaji Nishino, Director
EMail: yamada@edu.kake.ac.jp

Faculties

Engineering (Applied Chemistry; Computer Engineering; Electronic Engineering; Engineering; Information Technology; Mechanical Engineering) *Director*: Manmoto Yoshinori; **Informatics** (Geophysics; Information Sciences; Mathematical Physics; Mathematics and Computer Science; Physical Engineering) *Director*: Eiji Yamamoto; **Science** (Applied Chemistry; Applied Mathematics; Applied Physics; Biochemistry; Biological and Life Sciences) *Director*: Tsukio Ohtani

Graduate Schools

Engineering; **Informatics**; **Science**

History: Founded 1962, acquired present status 1964.

Governing Bodies: Kake Educational Group (Kake Educational Institution and Takahashi Educational Institution Boards)

Academic Year: April to March (April to October; October-March)

Admission Requirements: Graduation from high school or equivalent, entrance examination (OUS's test) and test of proficiency in Japanese.

Fees: (Yen): 1,440,000 per annum; 220,000 for 1st entrance fee.

Main Language(s) of Instruction: Japanese

International Co-operation: With universities in USA, China, United Kingdom, Republic of Korea

Degrees and Diplomas: *Gakushi*: Engineering; Informatics; Science, 4 yrs; *Shushi*: Engineering; Informatics; Science, a further 2 yrs; *Hakase*: Engineering; Informatics; Science. Also Teaching credentials, Certification for Curatorship, Certification as a Technician for Sanitary Control, Certification for Food Sanitation.

Student Services: Academic counselling, Canteen, Employment services, Foreign student adviser, Foreign Studies Centre, Health services, Language programs, Social counselling, Sports facilities

Student Residential Facilities: Yes

Special Facilities: Museum. Movie Studio.

Libraries: 3 main libraries

Publications: Ridai-tsushin *(other/irregular)*

OKINAWA CHRISTIAN UNIVERSITY

Okinawa Kirisutokyo Gakuin Daigaku

777 Onaga, Nishihara-cho, Nakagami-gun, Okinawa 903-0207

Tel: +81(98) 946-1231

Fax: +81(98) 946-1241

EMail: somu@ocjc.ac.jp

Website: http://www.ocjc.ac.jp

President: Randolph H. Thrasher

Departments

Communication Skills (Communication Studies; Cultural Studies; Education; English; Information Sciences; International Business; Statistics; Welfare and Protective Services)

History: Founded 2004.

Governing Bodies: Board of Trustees; Board of Councillors

Degrees and Diplomas: *Gakushi*; *Shushi*

Publications: Journal of Okinawa Christian University

Last Updated: 28/01/09

OKINAWA INTERNATIONAL UNIVERSITY

Okinawa Kokusai Daigaku (OIU)

2-6-1 Ginowan, Ginowan-shi, Okinawa 901-2701

Tel: +81(98) 892-1111

Fax: +81(98) 893-3271

EMail: entchr@okiu.ac.jp; pubchr@okiu.ac.jp

Website: http://www.okiu.ac.jp

President: Moritake Tomikawa

Colleges

Economics and Environmental Policy (Economics; Environmental Studies); **Global and Regional Culture**; **Industry and Information Sciences**; **Law** (Administration; Law)

Graduate Schools

Law (Civil Law; Criminal Law; Law; Public Law); **Regional Business and Economics** (Accountancy; Business and Commerce; Economics; Industrial and Production Economics; Management; Regional Studies); **Regional Culture** (American Studies; Clinical Psychology; Cultural Studies; English; English Studies; History; Modern Languages; Prehistory; Regional Studies; Social Welfare; Sociology)

History: Founded 1972.

Governing Bodies: Riji-kai (Board of Trustees)

Academic Year: April to March (April-September; October-March)

Admission Requirements: Graduation from high school

Fees: (Yen): 969,300 per annum

Main Language(s) of Instruction: Japanese

Degrees and Diplomas: *Gakushi*: British and American Languages and Cultures; Business Administration; Cultural Sociology; Economics; Environmental Policy; Industry and Information Sciences; Japanese Culture; Law; Psychology; Social Welfare, 4 yrs; *Shushi*: Clinical Psychology; Commerce; Economics; Law; Literature; Social Welfare; Sociology, 2 yrs

Student Services: Academic counselling, Canteen, Employment services, Foreign student adviser, Foreign Studies Centre, Handicapped facilities, Health services, Language programs, Nursery care, Social counselling, Sports facilities

Libraries: c. 330,000 vols

Last Updated: 28/01/09

OKINAWA PREFECTURAL COLLEGE OF NURSING

Okinawa Kenritsu Kango Daigaku

1-24-1, Yogi, Naha, Okinawa 902-0076

Tel: +82(98) 833-8800

Fax: +82(98) 833-5133

Website: http://www.okinawa-nurs.ac.jp

President: Miwako Noguchi

Programmes

Nursing (Child Care and Development; Community Health; Gerontology; Health Administration; Midwifery; Nursing; Public Health)

History: Founded 1999.

Degrees and Diplomas: *Gakushi*; *Shushi*; *Hakase*

Libraries: Yes.

Publications: OPCN Journal; Synthesizer

Last Updated: 28/01/09

OKINAWA PREFECTURAL UNIVERSITY OF ARTS

Okinawa Kenritsu Geijutsu Daigaku

1-4 Tonokura-cho, Shuri Naha-shi, Okinawa 903-8602
Tel: +81(98) 882-5000
Fax: +81(98) 882-5033
EMail: okiarts@okigei.ac.jp
Website: http://www.okigei.ac.jp

President: Koji Asaoka (2003-)

Faculties

Arts and Crafts (Crafts and Trades; Design; Fine Arts; Painting and Drawing; Sculpture); **Music Arts** *(Also Japanese Music)* (Music; Musicology; Singing; Theatre)

Graduate Schools

Cultural Arts *(MA)* (Cultural Studies; Fine Arts); **Formative Arts** *(MA: Daily Life Design; Environmental Design; Comparative Art Studies)* (Aesthetics; Visual Arts); **Music Arts** *(MA: Music Performance Arts)* (Music; Musicology; Performing Arts; Theatre)

Further Information: Also intensive Japanese language courses for foreign students

History: Founded 1986.

Academic Year: April to March (April-September; October-March)

Admission Requirements: Graduation from high school or recognized equivalent, and entrance examination

Main Language(s) of Instruction: Japanese

International Co-operation: With universities in United Kingdom, Germany and China

Degrees and Diplomas: *Gakushi*: 4 yrs; *Shushi*: a further 2 yrs; *Hakase*: 3 yrs following Shushi

Student Services: Canteen, Cultural centre, Employment services, Foreign student adviser, Handicapped facilities, Health services, Social counselling, Sports facilities

Special Facilities: Concert Hall

Libraries: 67,630 vols

Publications: Bulletin *(annually)*

OKINAWA UNIVERSITY

Okinawa Daigaku

555 Kokuba, Naha-shi, Okinawa 902-8521
Tel: +81(98) 832-1768
Fax: +81(98) 831-8650
EMail: admission@okinawa-u.ac.jp
Website: http://www.okinawa-u.ac.jp

Departments

International Communication (Asian Studies; Chinese; Communication Studies; English; History); **Law and Economics** (Economics; Law; Management); **Welfare and Culture** (Cultural Studies; Health Sciences; Human Resources; Social Welfare; Sports)

Schools

Graduate Studies (Administration; East Asian Studies; Regional Studies)

History: Founded 1961.

Degrees and Diplomas: *Gakushi*; *Shushi*

Last Updated: 28/01/09

ONOMICHI UNIVERSITY

Onomichi Daigaku

1600 Hisayamadacho, Onomichi-shi, Hiroshima-shi, Hiroshima 722-8506
Tel: +81(84) 822-8311
Fax: +81(84) 822-5460
EMail: jimukyok@onomichi-u.ac.jp
Website: http://www.onomichi-u.ac.jp

President: Hideyuki Adachi

Vice-President: Saburo Kurata

Departments

Japanese Literature

Faculties

Artistic Culture (Cultural Studies; Fine Arts); **Economics, Management and Information Science** (Accountancy; Administration; Chinese; Computer Science; Economics; English; French; German; Health Sciences; Information Sciences; Italian; Management; Mathematics; Natural Sciences; Social Sciences; Sports)

History: Founded 2001.

Degrees and Diplomas: *Gakushi*; *Shushi*

Libraries: Yes.

Publications: Onomichi University Keizai Jyoho Ronsyu, Bulletin of Onomichi University's Faculty of Artistic Culture

Last Updated: 28/01/09

OSAKA CITY UNIVERSITY

Osaka Shiritsu Daigaku

3-3-138 Sugimoto, Sumiyoshi-ku, Osaka-shi, Osaka 558-8585
Tel: +81(6) 6605-3453
Fax: +81(6) 6605-2058
EMail: gakujutu@ado.osaka-cu.ac.jp
Website: http://www.osaka-cu.ac.jp/

President: Yoshiki Nishizawa
Tel: +81(6) 6605-2000, Fax: +81(6) 6692-1295

Faculties

Business *(Also Graduate School)* (Business Administration; Business and Commerce); **Economics** *(Also Graduate School)* (Economic and Finance Policy; Economics); **Engineering** *(Also Graduate School)* (Applied Chemistry; Applied Physics; Architecture; Artificial Intelligence; Building Technologies; Civil Engineering; Electrical Engineering; Engineering; Environmental Engineering; Information Technology; Mechanical Engineering); **Human Life Science** *(Also Graduate School)*; **Law** *(Also Graduate School)* (Law; Private Law; Public Law); **Literature and Human Sciences** *(Also Graduate School)* (Asian Studies; Behavioural Sciences; Cultural Studies; Education; Geography; History; Literature; Philosophy; Psychology; Social Sciences; Sociology); **Science** *(Also Graduate School)* (Biology; Chemistry; Earth Sciences; Mathematics; Natural Sciences; Physics)

Graduate Schools

Creative Cities

Schools

Medicine *(Also Graduate School)* (Medicine); **Nursing** *(Also Graduate School)* (Nursing)

Further Information: Also University Hospital

History: Founded 1949, incorporating Osaka University of Commerce, Osaka City Technical College, Institute of Economic Research of Osaka City, and Osaka City Women's College. Osaka City Medical School incorporated 1955.

Governing Bodies: Hyogikai (University Council)

Academic Year: April to March (April-September; October-March)

Admission Requirements: Graduation from high school or recognized equivalent or foreign equivalent, and entrance examination

Main Language(s) of Instruction: Japanese

Degrees and Diplomas: *Gakushi*: 4-6 yrs; *Shushi*: a further 2 yrs; *Hakase*: 3-4 yrs following Shushi

Student Services: Academic counselling, Canteen, Cultural centre, Employment services, Foreign student adviser, Foreign Studies Centre, Handicapped facilities, Health services, Language programs, Sports facilities

Special Facilities: Botanical Garden

Libraries: Central Library, 2m. vols and 9,000 periodical titles

Publications: Business Review *(annually)*; Economy Journal *(bimonthly)*; Journal of Economics, in Japanese *(quarterly)*; Journal of Geoscience; Journal of Law and Politics, in Japanese *(quarterly)*; Memoirs of the Faculty of Engineering *(annually)*; Osaka City Medical Journal *(biannually)*; Osaka Journal of Mathematics *(quarterly)*; Quarterly Journal of Economic Studies, in Japanese

(quarterly); Studies in Humanities, in japanese *(annually)*; University Bulletin
Last Updated: 24/03/11

OSAKA COLLEGE OF MUSIC

Osaka Ongaku Daigaku

1-1-8 Shonai-Saiwai-machi, Toyonaka-shi, Osaka 561-8555
Tel: +81(6) 6334-2131
Fax: +81(6) 6333-0286
EMail: info-nyushi@daion.ac.jp; kikaku@daion.ac.jp
Website: http://www.daion.ac.jp

President: Takayoshi Nakamura (2006-)

Administrative Director: Yoshio Nakaue

Departments

Composition (Music Theory and Composition; Musicology); **Instrumental Music** (Musical Instruments); **Vocal Music** (Singing)

Graduate Schools

Composition (Music; Music Theory and Composition; Musicology); **Instrumental Music** (Music; Musical Instruments); **Vocal Music** (Opera; Singing)

History: Founded 1915 as Osaka School of Music, became High School 1948, Junior College 1951. Acquired present status 1958.

Governing Bodies: Board of Directors, comprising 15 members; University Council, comprising 30 members

Academic Year: April to March (April-September; October-March)

Admission Requirements: Graduation from high school or foreign equivalent, and entrance examination

Main Language(s) of Instruction: Japanese

Degrees and Diplomas: *Gakushi*: Fine Arts; Music (BA), 4 yrs; *Shushi*: Fine Arts; Music (MA), a further 2 yrs

Student Services: Academic counselling, Canteen, Employment services, Health services, Nursery care, Social counselling

Student Residential Facilities: For women students

Special Facilities: Museum of Musical Instruments. College Opera House

Libraries: Central Library, 129,000 vols; 42,000 music-related items

Publications: Muse, Bulletin *(monthly)*; Music Research *(annually)*

OSAKA DENTAL UNIVERSITY

Osaka Shika Daigaku (ODU)

8-1 Kuzuhahanazozno-cho, Hirakata-shi, Osaka-shi, Osaka 573-1121
Tel: +81(72) 864-3111
Fax: +81(72) 864-3000
Website: http://www.osaka-dent.ac.jp

President: Takayoshi Kawazoe

Colleges

Dental Hygiene *Director*: Kazuhiko Yao; **Dental Technology** (Dental Technology; Dentistry) *Director*: Kazuhiko Suese

History: Founded 1911, acquired present status 1952.

Academic Year: April to March (April-June; September-December; January-March)

Admission Requirements: Graduation from high school and entrance examination

Main Language(s) of Instruction: Japanese

International Co-operation: With universities in China, Republic of Korea and Australia

Degrees and Diplomas: *Gakushi*: Dental Surgery, 6 yrs; *Hakase*: Dental Sciences, a further 4 yrs

Student Services: Academic counselling, Canteen, Employment services, Handicapped facilities, Health services, Language programs, Nursery care, Social counselling, Sports facilities

Libraries: 150,000 vols

Last Updated: 28/03/11

OSAKA ELECTRO-COMMUNICATIONS UNIVERSITY

Osaka Denkitsushin Daigaku (OECU)

18-8 Hatsu-cho, Neyagawa-shi, Osaka 572-8530
Tel: +81(72) 824-1131
Fax: +81(72) 825-4589
EMail: nyushi@isc.osakac.ac.jp
Website: http://www.osakac.ac.jp

Faculties

Biomedical Engineering (Biomedical Engineering); **Engineering** (Applied Physics; Automation and Control Engineering; Computer Science; Electronic Engineering; Engineering; Information Sciences; Materials Engineering; Mechanical Engineering; Telecommunications Engineering); **Information Science and Arts** (Media Studies; Video)

Graduate Schools

Engineering (Applied Physics; Automation and Control Engineering; Computer Science; Electronic Engineering; Information Sciences; Mechanical Engineering)

History: Founded 1961.

Main Language(s) of Instruction: Japanese

Degrees and Diplomas: *Gakushi*: Computer Science; Engineering; General Studies, 4 yrs; *Shushi*: Computer Science; Engineering; General Studies, a further 2 yrs; *Hakase*: Engineering, a further 3 yrs; *Hakase*: General Studies, 3 yrs

Student Services: Canteen, Cultural centre, Sports facilities

Libraries: 264,338 vols

Last Updated: 28/01/09

OSAKA GAKUIN UNIVERSITY

Osaka Gakuin Daigaku

2-36-1 Kishibe-Minami, Suita-shi, Osaka 564-8511
Tel: +81(6) 6381-8434
Fax: +81(6) 6382-4363
EMail: www-admin@uta.osaka-gu.ac.jp
Website: http://www.osaka-gu.ac.jp

President: Yoshiyasu Shirai (1977-)

Divisions

Correspondence Studies (Communication Studies)

Faculties

Business Administration (Administration; Business Administration; Tourism); **Corporate Intelligence**; **Distribution and Communication Sciences** (Communication Studies); **Economics** (Economics); **Foreign Languages** (English; German; Modern Languages); **Informatics**; **International Studies** (International Studies); **Law**

Graduate Schools

Commerce (Business and Commerce); **Computer Science**; **Economics** (Economics); **International Studies** (International Studies); **Law** (Law); **Legal Profession**

History: Founded 1962 as Junior College, acquired present status 1963. Postgraduate studies introduced 1967.

Governing Bodies: Board of Trustees

Academic Year: April to March (April-September: October-March)

Admission Requirements: Graduation from secondary school and entrance examination

Fees: (Yen): Tuition, 1.71m.-1.84m. per annum

Main Language(s) of Instruction: Japanese

International Co-operation: With universities in USA, United Kingdom, France, Germany, New Zealand, Sweden, Thailand and China

Degrees and Diplomas: *Gakushi*: 4 yrs; *Shushi*: a further 2 yrs; *Hakase*: 3 yrs following Shushi

Student Services: Academic counselling, Canteen, Employment services, Handicapped facilities, Health services, Language programs, Social counselling, Sports facilities

Student Residential Facilities: For 275 students

Special Facilities: Media Centre (Audiovisual Facility). Gakuin Island Seminar House. Sertiyama Seminar House. MELOP (Media Laboratory of Phoenix)

Libraries: Shirai Memorial Library, 980,000 vols

Publications: Foreign Linguistic and Literary Studies *(biannually)*; International Studies *(biannually)*; Journal of Distribution, Communication and Administration *(quarterly)*; Osaka Gakuin Corporate Intelligence Journal *(3 per annum)*; Osaka Gakuin Law Journal *(biannually)*; The Bulletin of the Cultural and Natural Sciences in Osaka Gakuin University *(biannually)*; The Osaka Gakuin Journal of Economics *(biannually)*

Last Updated: 29/01/09

OSAKA INSTITUTE OF TECHNOLOGY

Osaka Kogyo Daigaku (OIT)

5-16-1 Omiya, Asahi-ku, Osaka-shi, Osaka 535-8585
Tel: +81(6) 6954-4097
Fax: +81(6) 6953-9496
EMail: shomu@ofc.oit.ac.jp
Website: http://www.oit.ac.jp

President: Masataka Inoue Fax: +81(6) 6952-3403

Faculties

Engineering *(Also Graduate School)* (Applied Chemistry; Architecture; Bioengineering; Civil Engineering; Design; Electrical and Electronic Engineering; Engineering; Environmental Engineering; Information Technology; Landscape Architecture; Mechanical Engineering; Structural Architecture; Technology; Telecommunications Engineering; Town Planning); **Information Science and Technology** *(Also Graduate School)* (Computer Networks; Computer Science; Information Sciences; Information Technology; Media Studies); **Intellectual Property** *(Also Graduate School)*

Further Information: Also Graduate Course in Engineering and Information Science and Studies Programmes (American, Chinese)

History: Founded 1922 as Kansai College of Engineering, acquired present status 1949.

Governing Bodies: Board of Trustees

Academic Year: April to March (April-September; October-March)

Admission Requirements: Graduation from high school or equivalent, and entrance examination

Fees: (Yen): Registration, 150,000-250,000; tuition, 1.28m. per annum; graduate, 1.11m.-1.21m. per annum

Main Language(s) of Instruction: Japanese

International Co-operation: With universities in China, Indonesia, Republic of Korea, Mexico and USA

Degrees and Diplomas: *Gakushi*: Engineering (Kogakushi); Information Science (Johokagakushi); Intellectual Property, 4 yrs; *Shushi*: Engineering (Kogakushushi); Information Science (Johokagakushushi); Intellectual Property, a further 2 yrs; *Hakase*: Engineering (Kogakuhakushi); Information Science (Johokagakuhakushi), 3 yrs following Shushi

Student Services: Academic counselling, Canteen, Employment services, Foreign student adviser, Health services, Social counselling, Sports facilities

Student Residential Facilities: Yes

Special Facilities: Computer Centre; New Materials Research Centre

Libraries: c. 570,000 vols

Publications: Series for Liberal Arts (Memoirs), Japanese, English *(biannually)*; Series for Science and Technology (Memoirs), Japanese, English *(biannually)*

Press or Publishing House: Oyodo

Last Updated: 29/01/09

OSAKA INTERNATIONAL UNIVERSITY

Osaka Kokusai Daigaku

3-50-1 Sugi, Hirakata-shi, Osaka 573-0192
Tel: +81(72) 858-1616
Fax: +81(72) 858-0897
EMail: iec@oiu.ac.jp
Website: http://www.oiu.ac.jp/

President: Goro Okuda

Faculties

Management and Information Science (Information Sciences; Management); **Politics, Economics and Law** (Economics; Law; Political Sciences)

Graduate Schools

Management and Information Science (Information Sciences; Management); **Social Sciences** (Economics; International Studies; Social Sciences)

Institutes

International Relations (International Relations)

Further Information: Also School of Japanese studies for foreign students

History: Founded 1988. Incorporated Osaka International University for Women 2002.

Governing Bodies: Osaka International Educational Foundation

Academic Year: April to March

Admission Requirements: Graduation from high school or equivalent, or foreign equivalent, with a minimum of 12 yrs of schooling, and entrance examination

Main Language(s) of Instruction: Japanese

International Co-operation: With universities in USA, Republic of Korea and China

Degrees and Diplomas: *Gakushi*: 4 yrs; *Shushi*: a further 2 yrs; *Hakase*: 3 yrs following Shushi

Student Services: Academic counselling, Canteen, Cultural centre, Employment services, Foreign student adviser, Health services, Language programs, Nursery care, Social counselling, Sports facilities

Libraries: 260,000 vols

Last Updated: 29/01/09

OSAKA JOGAKUIN COLLEGE

Osaka Jogakuin Daigaku

2-26-54 Tamatsukuri, Chuo-ku, Osaka 540-0004
Tel: +81(6) 6761-9371
EMail: webmaster@wilmina.ac.jp
Website: http://www.wilmina.ac.jp/ojc

Programmes

English (English); **International Collaboration, Management and Communication; Religious Studies** (Religious Studies)

History: Founded 1968. Acquired present status 2004.

Degrees and Diplomas: *Gakushi*

Last Updated: 29/01/09

OSAKA MEDICAL COLLEGE

Osaka Ika Daigaku

2-7 Daigaku-machi, Takatsuki-shi, Osaka 569-8686
Tel: +81(726) 83-1221
Fax: +81(726) 81-3723
EMail: hpinfo2@poh.osaka-med.ac.jp
Website: http://www.osaka-med.ac.jp

President: Minoru Ueki

Faculties

Medicine *(Also Graduate School)* (Anaesthesiology; Anatomy; Applied Chemistry; Biology; Chemistry; Dermatology; Forensic Medicine and Dentistry; Gynaecology and Obstetrics; Hygiene; Mathematics; Medicine; Microbiology; Modern Languages; Neurosciences; Ophthalmology; Orthopaedics; Otorhinolaryngology; Paediatrics; Pathology; Pharmacology; Philosophy; Physics; Physiology; Psychology; Public Health; Radiology; Surgery; Urology)

History: Founded 1927 as Osaka Professional High School of Medicine. Acquired present status and title 1952.

Governing Bodies: Board of Directors

Academic Year: April to March (April-August; September-December; January-March)

Admission Requirements: Graduation from high school or equivalent, and entrance examination

Main Language(s) of Instruction: Japanese

Degrees and Diplomas: *Gakushi*: Medicine, 6 yrs; *Hakase*: Medicine, a further 4 yrs

Student Services: Cultural centre, Sports facilities

Special Facilities: Nakayama International Medical and Clinical Exchange Centre

Libraries: c. 210,000 vols

Publications: Bulletin; Journal

Last Updated: 29/01/09

OSAKA OHTANI UNIVERSITY

Osaka Ohtani Daigaku

3-11-1 Nishikiori-kita, Tondabayashi-shi, Osaka 584-8540

Tel: +81(721) 24-0775

Fax: +81(721) 24-0775

Website: http://www.osaka-ohtani.ac.jp

President: Muneharu Kusaba

Director, Administration: Moriya Shibahara

International Relations: Sachiko Oka, Chairperson, International Exchange Committee

Faculties

Education and Social Welfare *Dean*: Yuko Okazaki; **Human and Social Sciences** (Business and Commerce; Community Health; Information Sciences; Social Psychology; Social Sciences; Sports); **Literature** (Archaeology; Art History; Cultural Studies; English; Folklore; History; Japanese; Native Language; Native Language Education) *Dean*: Hiroshi Mori; **Pharmacy** *Dean*: Keiichi Tanaka

History: Founded 1966. Known as Ohtani Women's University/ Otani Joshi Daigaku until 2006.

Academic Year: April to March (April-July; October-March)

Admission Requirements: Japanese Language Proficiency Test, Level 1 or 2

Fees: (Yen): Registration, 320,000-400,000 (Pharmacy); tuition, 1.08m.-1.78m. (Pharmacy) per annum

Main Language(s) of Instruction: Japanese

Accrediting Agencies: Ministry of Education, Culture, Sports, Science and Technology

Degrees and Diplomas: *Gakushi*: Literature; Education and Social Welfare; Human and Social Sciences, 4 yrs; *Gakushi*: Pharmacy, 6 yrs; *Shushi*: Cultural Properties; Japanese Language and Literature; English and American Language and Literature, a further 2 yrs; *Hakase*: 2-3 yrs following Shushi

Student Services: Academic counselling, Canteen, Employment services, Foreign student adviser, Handicapped facilities, Health services, Nursery care, Social counselling, Sports facilities

Student Residential Facilities: For 88 students

Special Facilities: Museum

Libraries: Total, 403,881 vols

Publications: Bulletin *(annually)*

OSAKA PREFECTURE UNIVERSITY

Osaka Furitsu Daigaku

1-1 Gakuen-cho, Sakai-shi, Osaka 599-8531

Tel: +81(72) 252-1161

Fax: +81(72) 254-9900

Website: http://www.osakafu-u.ac.jp

President: Taketoshi Okuno
Tel: +81 (72) 254-9100, Fax: +81 (72) 254-9941

Secretary-General: Kazuo Izumi
Tel: +81 (72) 254-9100, Fax: +81 (72) 254-9941
EMail: izumi@osakafu-u.ac.jp

Faculties

Liberal Arts and Science (Arts and Humanities; Biology; Chemistry; Chinese; Computer Science; Earth Sciences; English; French; German; Koran; Mathematics; Modern Languages; Natural Sciences; Physics; Russian)

Schools

Comprehensive Rehabilitation (Nutrition; Occupational Therapy; Physical Therapy); **Economics** *(Also Graduate School)* (Business Administration; Business and Commerce; Commercial Law; Econometrics; Economics; Finance; International Economics; Small Business; Statistics; Taxation); **Engineering** *(Also Graduate School)* (Aeronautical and Aerospace Engineering; Applied Chemistry; Chemical Engineering; Computer Science; Electronic Engineering; Engineering; Information Management; Marine Engineering; Materials Engineering; Mathematics; Mechanical Engineering; Physics); **Humanities and Social Sciences** *(Also Graduate School)* (Arts and Humanities; Cultural Studies; Modern Languages; Social Sciences; Social Welfare); **Life and Environmental Sciences** *(Also Graduate School)*; **Nursing** *(Also Graduate School)* (Nursing); **Science** *(Also Graduate School)* (Astrophysics; Biology; Chemistry; Information Sciences; Inorganic Chemistry; Mathematics; Organic Chemistry; Physics)

Further Information: Also Teaching Hospital and Pedagogical Farm

History: Founded 1949 as Naniwa University, incorporating Osaka Technical College, Osaka Youth Normal School, Osaka Prefectural College of Chemical Engineering, Osaka College of Veterinary Medicine and Zoology, and Osaka Prefecture College of Agriculture. Present title adopted 1955. Incorporated Osaka Women's University and Osaka Prefectural College of Nursing 2005.

Governing Bodies: University Council Meeting

Academic Year: April to March (April-September; October-March)

Admission Requirements: Graduation from high school or recognized equivalent, and entrance examination

Fees: (Yen): 496,800 per annum

Main Language(s) of Instruction: Japanese

International Co-operation: With universities in USA, China, France and Republic of Korea

Accrediting Agencies: Japan University Accreditation Association

Degrees and Diplomas: *Gakushi*: Agriculture (Nogakushi); Economics (Keizaigakushi); Engineering (Kogakushi); Liberal Arts (Kyoyogakushi); Nursing (Kangogakushi); Rehabilitation (Rihabiriteishon); Sociology (Shakaigakushi), 4 yrs; *Gakushi*: Veterinary Medicine (Juigakushi), 6 yrs; *Shushi*: Agriculture (Nogakushushi); Economics (Keizaigakushushi); Engineering (Kogakushushi); Nursing (Kangakushushi); Philosophy (Gakujutsushushi), a further 2 yrs; *Hakase*: Agriculture (Nogakuhakushi); Economics (Keizaigakuhakushi); Engineering (Kogakuhakushi), 3 yrs following Shushi; *Hakase*: Nursing (Kangogakuhakushi), a further s yrs

Student Services: Academic counselling, Employment services, Health services, Social counselling, Sports facilities

Student Residential Facilities: Yes

Libraries: Central library; Science Information Centre

Publications: Research Report *(annually)*

Last Updated: 24/03/11

OSAKA SANGYO UNIVERSITY

Osaka Sangyo Daigaku (OSU)

3-1-1 Nakagaito, Daito-shi, Osaka 574-8530

Tel: +81(72) 875-3001

Fax: +81(72) 871-9765

EMail: nyushi@cnt.osaka-sandai.ac.jp

Website: http://www.osaka-sandai.ac.jp

President: Masanori Kagotani

Colleges

General Education (Arts and Humanities; English; Natural Sciences; Social Sciences)

Faculties

Business Management (Accountancy; Business Administration; Management); **Economics** (Economics; International Economics); **Engineering** (Architectural and Environmental Design; Civil Engineering; Electrical and Electronic Engineering; Engineering; Environmental Engineering; Information Technology; Mechanical Engineering; Telecommunications Engineering; Transport Engineering); **Human Environment** (Cultural Studies; Environmental Management; Town Planning; Urban Studies)

Graduate Schools

Business Administration; **Economics** (Economics; International Economics); **Engineering** (Architectural and Environmental Design; Civil Engineering; Electronic Engineering; Engineering; Environmental Engineering; Information Technology; Mechanical

Engineering; Production Engineering; Telecommunications Engineering); **Human Environment**

History: Founded 1928.

Main Language(s) of Instruction: Japanese

International Co-operation: With univerisities in China, Republic of Korea and Taiwan

Degrees and Diplomas: *Gakushi*; *Shushi*; *Hakase*

Student Services: Language programs, Sports facilities

Special Facilities: Multimedia studio

Libraries: 400,000 vols

Last Updated: 29/01/09

OSAKA SEIKEI UNIVERSITY

Osaka Seikei Daigaku

1-25-1 Choshi, Nagaokakyo-shi, Kyoto 617-0844

Tel: +81(6) 6829-2500

Fax: +81(6) 6829-2509

EMail: sou@osaka-sekei.ac.jp; nyu@osaka-seikei.ac.jp

Website: http://www.osaka-seikei.ac.jp

Faculties

Art and Design (Design; Fine Arts); **Business Administration** (Business Administration)

History: Founded 2003.

Degrees and Diplomas: *Gakushi*

OSAKA SHOIN WOMEN'S UNIVERSITY

Osaka Shoin Joshi Daigaku

4-2-26 Hishiya-nishi, Higashi, Osaka-shi, Osaka 577-8550

Tel: +81(6) 6723-8181

Fax: +81(6) 6723-8438

Website: http://www.osaka-shoin.ac.jp

Programmes

Graduate (Food Science; Nutrition; Psychology); **Undergraduate**

History: Founded 1917. Acquired present status 1949.

Degrees and Diplomas: *Gakushi*; *Shushi*

Last Updated: 29/01/09

OSAKA UNIVERSITY

Kokuritsu Daigaku Hojin Osaka Daigaku

1-1 Yamadaoka, Suita-shi, Osaka 565-0871

Tel: +81(6) 6877-5111

Fax: +81(6) 6879-7106

EMail: kokusai-ina@ml.office.osaka-u.ac.jp

Website: http://www.osaka-u.ac.jp

President: Toshio Hirano (2011-)

International Relations: Kenzo Abe, Head, International Relations

Centres

Advanced Medical Engineering and Informatics *Director*: Yoshihisa Kurachi; **Advanced Science and Innovation** (Automation and Control Engineering; Bioengineering; Biomedical Engineering; Business and Commerce; Chemical Engineering; Computer Engineering; Electrical and Electronic Engineering; Energy Engineering; Environmental Engineering; Materials Engineering) *Director*: Akio Baba; **Biotechnology** *(International Centre)* (Biotechnology; Molecular Biology) *Director*: Satoshi Harashima; **Cyber Media Centre** *Director*: Haruo Takemura; **Education and Research** *(Bangkok, Gröningen and San Francisco Overseas Centres)*; **Global Collaboration Centre** *Director*: Eisei Kurimoto; **Health Care Centre** (Public Health) *Director*: Toshiki Moriyama; **International Student** *Director*: Toru Kikuno; **Japanese Language and Culture** (Japanese) *Director*: Shunsuke Okunishi; **Laser Engineering** (Applied Physics; Energy Engineering; Laser Engineering; Nuclear Physics) *Director*: Kunioki Mima; **Low Temperature Centre** (Electronic Engineering; Physics) *Director*: Seizo Morita; **Nakanoshima Centre** *Director*: Hiroshi Takeda; **Quantum Science and Technology under Extreme Conditions** *Director*: Kazumasa Miyake; **Renovation of Instruments for Science and Technology** *Director*: Toshio Kasai; **Study of Communication-Design** *Director*: Satoshi Kinsui; **Study of Finance and Insurance** (Finance; Insurance) *Director*: Hideo Nagai; **Sustainability Design Centre** *Director*: Akio Baba

Faculties

Medicine (Health Sciences; Medicine) *Dean*: Toshio Hirano

Graduate Schools

Dentistry (Dentistry; Oral Pathology; Stomatology) *Dean*: Toshiyuki Yoneda; **Economics** (Business and Commerce; Economics; Management) *Dean*: Takeshi Abe; **Engineering** (Applied Chemistry; Applied Physics; Architecture; Biotechnology; Electrical Engineering; Electronic Engineering; Energy Engineering; Environmental Engineering; Industrial Management; Information Technology; Materials Engineering; Measurement and Precision Engineering; Mechanical Engineering) *Dean*: Akio Baba; **Engineering Science** (Bioengineering; Materials Engineering; Mechanical Engineering) *Dean*: Yoshito Tobe; **Frontier Biosciences** (Biology; Biomedical Engineering; Nanotechnology; Neurosciences) *Dean*: Fujio Murakami; **Human Sciences** (Anthropology; Behavioural Sciences; Philosophy; Psychology; Social Studies; Sociology) *Dean*: Toshiaki Miura; **Information Sciences and Technology** (Applied Mathematics; Computer Networks; Computer Science; Information Sciences; Information Technology; Multimedia; Physics) *Dean*: Makoto Imase; **International Public Policy** (International Studies) *Dean*: Fumio Tokotani; **Language and Culture** (Cultural Studies; Linguistics; Modern Languages) *Dean*: Haruyuki Kanasaki; **Law** (Law) *Dean*: Tadaki Matsukawa; **Law and Politics** (Law; Political Sciences) *Dean*: Toshimitsu Nakao; **Letters** (Cultural Studies) *Dean*: Atsushi Egawa; **Medicine** (Health Sciences; Medicine; Pathology; Physiology; Social and Preventive Medicine) *Dean*: Toshio Hirano; **Pharmaceutical Sciences** (Pharmacology; Pharmacy) *Dean*: Motomasa Kobayashi; **Science** (Astronomy and Space Science; Biological and Life Sciences; Chemistry; Earth Sciences; Mathematics; Physics) *Dean*: Kiyoshi Higashijima

Institutes

Higher Education Research and Practice (Higher Education) *Director*: Mayumi Kudo

Research Centres

Environmental Preservation *Director*: Naoto Cyatani; **Nuclear Physics** *(Research Centre) Director*: Tadafumi Kishimoto; **Radioisotope Research** (Nuclear Engineering) *Director*: Shigenori Iwai; **Solar Energy Chemistry** (Applied Chemistry) *Director*: Kazunari Ohgaki; **Ultra-High Voltage Electron Microscopy** (Electronic Engineering; Metallurgical Engineering) *Director*: Hirotaro Mori; **WPI Immunology Frontier** (Immunology) *Director*: Shizuo Akira

Research Institutes

Joining and Welding (Metal Techniques) *Director*: Kiyoshi Nogi; **Microbial Disease** (Microbiology) *Director*: Hitoshi Kikutani; **Protein Research** (Biochemistry) *Director*: Saburo Aimoto; **Scientific and Industrial Research** (Engineering; Information Sciences; Natural Sciences) *Director*: Akihito Yamaguchi; **Social and Economic Research** (Econometrics; Economics; Finance; International Economics; Social Studies) *Director*: Fumio Ohtake; **World Languages** *Director*: Akira Takahashi

Schools

Dentistry (Dentistry) *Dean*: Toshiyuki Yoneda; **Economics** (Business and Commerce; Economics) *Dean*: Takeshi Abe; **Engineering** *Dean*: Akio Baba; **Engineering Science** *Dean*: Yoshito Tobe; **Foreign Studies** (International Studies) *Dean*: Takashi Sugimoto; **Human Sciences** (Anthropology; Behavioural Sciences; Education; Environmental Studies; Philosophy; Psychology; Social Studies; Sociology) *Dean*: Toshiaki Miura; **Law** *Dean*: Toshimitsu Nakao; **Letters** *Dean*: Atsushi Egawa; **Pharmaceutical Sciences** *Dean*: Motomasa Kobayashi; **Science** *Dean*: Kiyoshi Higashijima

Further Information: Also short-term student exchange programme. OUSSEP, OUSSEP-Maple and FrontierLab@OsakaU programmes

History: Founded 1931 as Osaka Imperial University, with Faculties of Medicine and Science. The academic origins of humanities schools trace back to Kaitokudo, a general education school for Osaka citizens, founded 1724. The Faculty of Medicine traces its origin to the Tekijuku, a Dutch studies school, founded 1838. Osaka Engineering College incorporated as Faculty 1933. Title changed to Osaka University 1947. Acquired present status 1949. From April 2004, all of Japan's national universities have become national corporations/semi-national universities. Merged with Osaka University of Foreign Studies October 2007.

Governing Bodies: Board of Trustees; Administrative Council; Education and Research Council

Academic Year: April to March (April-September; October-March)

Admission Requirements: Graduation from high school or recognized equivalent, and entrance examination

Fees: (Yen): Registration, 282,000; tuition, 535,800 per annum

Main Language(s) of Instruction: Japanese

International Co-operation: 69 Inter-University agreements with universities in Australia; Belgium; Canada; China; Denmark; Finland; France; Germany; Indonesia; Republic of Korea; Mexico; Mongolia; Netherlands; Peru; Philippines; Spain; Sweden; Switzerland; Taiwan; Thailand; United Kingdom; USA and Vietnam

Degrees and Diplomas: *Gakushi*: Arts; Human Sciences; Foreign Studies; Law; Economics; Science; Nursing; Health Sciences; Pharmaceutical Sciences; Engineering, 4 yrs; *Gakushi*: Dental Surgery; Pharmacy; Medicine, 6 yrs; *Shushi*: Arts; Philosophy; Human Sciences; Law; Economics; Applied Economics; Business Administration; Science; Medical Sciences; Science in Nursing; Health Sciences; Pharmaceutical Sciences; Pharmaceutical Clinical Sciences; Engineering; Arts in Language and Culture; International Studies; Human Sciences; Japanese Studies; International Public Policy; Information Science and Technology, 2-3 yrs following Gakushi; *Hakase*: 3 yrs following Shushi; *Hakase*: Philosophy in Language and Culture, International Studies, Human Sciences, in Japanese Studies, in International Public Policy, 3 yrs following Shushi; *Hakase*: Philosophy in Medical Sciences; Science in Nursing; Health Sciences; Philosophy in Dental Science, 4 yrs following 6 yrs Gakushi. Also Homu Hakase, 2 yrs following Gakushi: Juris Doctor

Student Services: Academic counselling, Canteen, Cultural centre, Employment services, Foreign student adviser, Foreign Studies Centre, Handicapped facilities, Health services, Nursery care, Social counselling, Sports facilities

Student Residential Facilities: Yes

Special Facilities: University Hospital, Dental Hospital, Museum of Osaka University; Kaitokudo for the 21st Century; Nakanoshima Center; Convention Center

Libraries: Main Library and Branch Libraries, total 3,897,502 vols; 70,000 periodicals

Publications: Annual Progress Report on Laser Fusion Programmes *(annually)*; Annual Report of Research Centre for Molecular Thermodynamics *(annually)*; Annual Reports of the International Centre for Biotechnology, CD Rom *(annually)*; Discussion Papers, http://www.iser.osaka-u.ac.jp; Medical Journal of Osaka University; Memoirs of the Institute for Protein Research; Memoirs of the Institute of Scientific and Industrial Research; Osaka Economic Papers; Osaka Journal of Mathematics *(quarterly)*; Osaka University Annual Report *(annually)*; Osaka University Laboratory of Nuclear Studies Annual Report *(annually)*; Osaka University Law Journal *(annually)*; Osaka University Prospectus *(annually)*; RCNP Annual Report *(annually)*; Science Reports; Studies in Language and Culture; Transactions of JWRI

Press or Publishing House: Osaka University Press; Publicity and University-Community Collaboration Office

Student Numbers *2011-2012*: Total 23,702
Last Updated: 15/03/13

OSAKA UNIVERSITY OF ARTS

Osaka Geijutsu Daigaku

Higashiyama, Kanan-cho, Minamikawachi-gun, Osaka 585-8555
Tel: +81(721) 93-6583
Fax: +81(721) 93-5360
EMail: nyusi@osaka-geidai.ac.jp
Website: http://www.osaka-geidai.ac.jp

Departments

Architecture (Architecture); **Art Planning**; **Broadcasting** (Radio and Television Broadcasting); **Crafts** (Crafts and Trades); **Design** (Design); **Environmental Planning** (Environmental Management); **Fine Arts** (Fine Arts); **Literary Arts** (Literature); **Music Education** (Music Education); **Music Performance** (Music); **Musicology** (Musicology); **Photography** (Photography); **Theatre** (Theatre); **Visual Concept Planning** (Visual Arts)

Graduate Schools

Creative Arts; **Science of Arts**

History: Founded 1964.

Academic Year: April to March April-September; October-March)

Admission Requirements: Graduation from high school and entrance examination

Main Language(s) of Instruction: Japanese

Degrees and Diplomas: *Gakushi*: Arts, 4 yrs; *Shushi*: Creative Arts; Science of Art, 2 yrs; *Hakase*: Science of Art, 3 yrs. Also Diplomas

Libraries: c. 300,000 vols
Last Updated: 29/01/09

OSAKA UNIVERSITY OF COMMERCE

Osaka Shogyo Daigaku (OUC)

4-1-10 Mikuriya Sakae-machi, Higashiosaka-shi, Osaka 577-8505
Tel: +81(6) 6781-0381
Fax: +81(6) 6781-8438
EMail: nyugaku@oucow.daishodai.ac.jp
Website: http://ouc.daishodai.ac.jp

President: Ichiro Tanioka (1997-)
Tel: +81(6) 6781-0381, Fax: +81(6) 6781-4476
EMail: xxichiro@daishodai.ac.jp

Secretary-General: Yuji Sakamoto
EMail: sakamoto@oucow.daishodai.ac.jp

International Relations: Shujiro Sumikawa, Director

Colleges

Business Administration *Dean*: Yasusi Nakano

Departments

Commerce (Business and Commerce) *Head*: Tatsuaki Minakata; **Economics** (Economics) *Head*: Keiichi Maeda; **Management** *Head*: Masahiko Ohashi; **Public Management** *Head*: Kojiro Iida

Faculties

Business Administration *Dean*: Takako Nishimura; **Economics** (Economics; Finance; International Economics) *Dean*: Masaroni Shiota

Graduate Schools

Regional Policy Studies (Business and Commerce; Economic and Finance Policy) *Director*: Takao Katayama

History: Founded 1928, acquired present status 1949.

Governing Bodies: Board of Directors

Academic Year: April-March (April-September; September-March)

Admission Requirements: Graduation from high school or equivalent, and entrance examination

Fees: (Yen): 1m. per annum

Main Language(s) of Instruction: Japanese

Accrediting Agencies: Ministry of Education, Culture, Sports, Science and Technology

Degrees and Diplomas: *Gakushi*: Business Administration; Economics, 4 yrs; *Shushi*: Regional Policy Study, a further 2 yrs; *Hakase*: Regional Policy Study, 3 yrs following Shushi. Also Graduate Programme, 1 yr

Student Services: Academic counselling, Canteen, Cultural centre, Employment services, Foreign student adviser, Health services, Language programs, Nursery care, Social counselling, Sports facilities

Student Residential Facilities: For 72 students

Special Facilities: Museum of Commercial History; Institute of Regional Studies; Institute of Amusement Industry Studies

Libraries: c. 400,000 vols

Publications: Shodai Ronshu, Collection of Research Reports and Essays *(quarterly)*

Last Updated: 09/12/08

OSAKA UNIVERSITY OF ECONOMICS

Osaka Keizai Daigaku

2-2-8 Osumi, Higashiyodogawa-ku, Osaka-shi, Osaka 533-8533
Tel: +81(6) 6328-2431
Fax: +81(6) 6370-5497
Website: http://www.osaka-ue.ac.jp

President: Mitsutoshi Tokunaga

Faculties

Business Administration *(Also Graduate School)* (Business Administration; Commercial Law); **Economics** *(Also Graduate School)* (Economics; Regional Planning); **Human Sciences** *(Also Graduate School)*; **Information Management** *(Also Graduate School)* (Finance; Information Management)

Institutes

Research in Economic History of Japan (Economics; History); **Small Business Research and Business Administration** (Business Administration; Small Business)

History: Founded 1932 as Naniwa College of Commerce. Became Showa College of Commerce 1935. Acquired present status 1949. Graduate School added 1966.

Academic Year: April to March (April-September; October-March)

Admission Requirements: Graduation from high school or foreign equivalent, and entrance examination

Main Language(s) of Instruction: Japanese

International Co-operation: With universities in China, Republic of Korea and Sweden and USA

Degrees and Diplomas: *Gakushi*: Business Administration; Economics; Information Management, 4 yrs; *Shushi*: Economics; Business Administration; Business Information Systems; Human Sciences, a further 2 yrs; *Hakase*: Economics, 3 yrs following Shushi

Student Services: Employment services, Foreign student adviser, Health services, Language programs, Social counselling, Sports facilities

Libraries: 616,894 vols

Publications: Chushokigyo Kiho *(quarterly)*; Keiei-Keizai, Business Economics *(annually)*; Kyoyobu Kiho *(annually)*; Osaka Keidai Ronshu, Journal of Osaka University of Economics *(bimonthly)*

Last Updated: 28/03/11

OSAKA UNIVERSITY OF ECONOMICS AND LAW

Osaka Keizai Hoka Daigaku

6-10 Gakuoniji, Yao-shi, Osaka 581-8511
Tel: +81(72) 941-8211
Fax: +81(72) 943-7035
EMail: nyushi@keiho-u.ac.jp
Website: http://www.keiho-u.ac.jp

Faculties

Economics (Business Administration; Business and Commerce; Economics; Management); **Law** (Administration; Consumer Studies; Environmental Studies; Law; Management; Social Welfare)

History: Founded 1971.

Degrees and Diplomas: *Gakushi*

Last Updated: 29/01/09

OSAKA UNIVERSITY OF EDUCATION

Osaka Kyoiku Daigaku

4-698-1 Asahigaoka, Kashiwara-shi, Osaka 582-8582
Tel: +81(729) 78-3299
Fax: +81(729) 78-3316
EMail: isc@cc.osaka-kyoiku.ac.jp
Website: http://www.osaka-kyoiku.ac.jp

President: Akio Nagao

Departments

Arts and Science (Cultural Studies; Environmental Studies; Fine Arts; Health Sciences; Humanities and Social Science Education; Information Sciences; Mathematics; Mathematics and Computer Science; Music; Natural Sciences; Social Sciences; Sports); **Education** *(Also Graduate School)* (Art Education; Cultural Studies; Education; Engineering; English; European Languages; Health Education; Home Economics Education; International Studies; Japanese; Mathematics Education; Modern Languages; Music Education; Nursing; Oriental Languages; Physical Education; Preschool Education; Primary Education; Science Education; Secondary Education; Social Sciences; Special Education; Technology Education)

History: Founded 1874.

Academic Year: April to March (April-September; October-March)

Admission Requirements: Secondary school certificate or equivalent, and entrance examination

Main Language(s) of Instruction: Japanese, English

Degrees and Diplomas: *Teaching Certificate*; *Gakushi*: 4 yrs; *Shushi*: a further 2 yrs

Libraries: 805,000 vols

Publications: Memoirs

Last Updated: 29/01/09

OSAKA UNIVERSITY OF HEALTH AND SPORT SCIENCES

Osaka Taiiku Daigaku

1-1 Asashirodai, Kumatori-cho, Sennan-gun, Osaka 590-0496
Tel: +81(724) 53-7022
Fax: +81(724) 53-8818
Website: http://www.ouhs.ac.jp

President: Hirohide Nagayoshi

Schools

Health and Sports Sciences *(Also Graduate School)* (Educational and Student Counselling; Educational Psychology; Health Sciences; Physical Education; Sports; Sports Management); **Health and Welfare Sciences** *(Also Graduate School)*

History: Founded 1965.

Academic Year: April to March (April-September; September-March)

Admission Requirements: Graduation from high school and entrance examination

Main Language(s) of Instruction: Japanese

Degrees and Diplomas: *Gakushi*: 4 yrs; *Shushi*; *Hakase*. Also Graduate Programme, 1 yr

Last Updated: 29/01/09

OSAKA UNIVERSITY OF HUMAN SCIENCES

Osaka Ningen Kagaku Daigaku

1-4-1 Shojaku, Settsu-shi, Osaka 566-8501
Tel: +81(6) 6381-3000
Fax: +81(6) 6381-3502
Website: http://www.ohs.ac.jp

President: Sho Ogiya

Faculties

Human Sciences (Social Sciences)

History: Founded 2001.

Degrees and Diplomas: *Gakushi*

OSAKA UNIVERSITY OF PHARMACEUTICAL SCIENCES

Osaka Yakka Daigaku

4-20-1 Nasahara, Takatsuki-shi, Osaka 569-1094
Tel: +81(72) 690-1000
Fax: +81(72) 690-1005
EMail: spoksman@gly.oups.ac.jp
Website: http://www.oups.ac.jp

Departments

Pharmaceutical Sciences *(4-year Programme; also Graduate School)*; **Pharmacy** *(6-year Programme)* (Pharmacy)

History: Founded 1904.

Main Language(s) of Instruction: Japanese

Degrees and Diplomas: *Gakushi*; *Shushi*; *Hakase*

Student Services: Sports facilities

Special Facilities: Medicinal Plants Garden

Libraries: c. 89,000 vols

Last Updated: 29/01/09

OSAKA UNIVERSITY OF TOURISM

Osaka Kanko Daigaku

5-3-1, Okubominami, Kumatori-cho, Sennan-gun, Osaka-shi, Osaka 590-0493

Tel: +81(724) 53-8222

Fax: +81(724) 53-1451

EMail: webmaster@tourism.ac.jp

Website: http://www.tourism.ac.jp/en/index.html

Courses

Foreign Language; **Hotel Industry Management**; **International Tourism** (Tourism); **Leisure**; **Tourism Culture** (Cultural Studies; Geography; Media Studies; Museum Studies; Public Relations; Tourism); **Travel Industry Management**

History: Founded 2000. Formerly known as Osaka Meijo Daigaku (Osaka Meijo University).

Fees: (Yen): first year, 1.33m.; 855,000 for International Students

Degrees and Diplomas: *Gakushi*

Last Updated: 29/01/09

OTANI UNIVERSITY

Otani Daigaku

Kamifusa-cho, Koyama, Kita-ku, Kyoto-shi, Kyoto 603-8143

Tel: +81(75) 432-3131

Fax: +81(75) 411-8153

EMail: acexchg@otani.ac.jp; nyushi-c@sec.otani.ac.jp

Website: http://www.otani.ac.jp

President: Sensho Kimura (2004-)

Faculties

Letters (Anthropology; Asian Religious Studies; Chinese; Clinical Psychology; Cultural Studies; East Asian Studies; Education; English; Ethics; German; History; History of Religion; Japanese; Literature; Philosophical Schools; Philosophy; Religious Studies; Social Welfare; Sociology)

Graduate Schools

Letters (Asian Religious Studies; Asian Studies; Cultural Studies; Education; Philosophy; Sociology)

Further Information: Also Junior College

History: Founded as College 1665, became University 1904. Reorganized and present title adopted 1949.

Governing Bodies: Shinshu Otani Gakuen

Academic Year: April to March (April-September; October-March)

Admission Requirements: Graduation from high school or equivalent or foreign equivalent, and entrance examination

Main Language(s) of Instruction: Japanese

International Co-operation: With universities in China; Republic of Korea and USA

Degrees and Diplomas: *Gakushi*: Letters, 4 yrs; *Shushi*: Letters, a further 2 yrs; *Hakase*: Letters, a further 3 yrs

Student Services: Canteen, Cultural centre, Employment services, Foreign student adviser, Foreign Studies Centre, Health services, Social counselling, Sports facilities

Student Residential Facilities: Yes

Special Facilities: Multi Media Studio

Libraries: University Library, 725,000 vols

Publications: Annual Memoirs of the Otani University Shin Buddhist Comprehensive Research Institute, Academic Journal *(annually)*; Annual Report of Research at Otani University, Academic Journal *(annually)*; The Otani Gakuho, Academic Journal *(biannually)*

OTARU UNIVERSITY OF COMMERCE

Otaru Shoka Daigaku

3-5-21 Midori, Otaru-shi, Hokkaido 047-8501

Tel: +81(134) 27-5200

Fax: +81(134) 27-5213

EMail: inl@otaru-uc.ac.jp

Website: http://www.otaru-uc.ac.jp

Departments

Commerce (Accountancy; Banking; Business Administration; Business and Commerce; Communication Studies; English; Finance; Human Resources; Insurance; International Business; Management; Marketing); **Economics** (Banking; Econometrics; Economic History; Economics; Finance; International Economics; Statistics); **Information and Management Sciences** (Information Management; Information Sciences; Management; Mathematics and Computer Science; Operations Research; Statistics); **Law** (Administrative Law; Civil Law; Commercial Law; Constitutional Law; Criminal Law; International Law; Labour Law; Law)

Further Information: Also teacher's training programme in Commerce

History: Founded 1910 as School, acquired present status and title 1949.

Academic Year: April to March (April-September; October-March)

Admission Requirements: Graduation from high school or recognized equivalent, and entrance examination

Fees: (Yen): Entrance, 282,000; tuition, 520,800 per annum

Main Language(s) of Instruction: Japanese, English

Degrees and Diplomas: *Gakushi*: 4 yrs; *Shushi*: a further 2 yrs; *Hakase*

Student Services: Academic counselling, Canteen, Employment services, Foreign student adviser, Handicapped facilities, Health services, Social counselling, Sports facilities

Libraries: University Library, c. 444,000 vols

Publications: The Economic Journal *(quarterly)*; The Journal of Liberal Arts *(biannually)*

Last Updated: 29/01/09

OTEMAE UNIVERSITY

Otemae Daigaku

6-42 Ochayasho-cho, Nishinomiya-shi, Hyogo 662-8552

Tel: +81(798) 34-6331

Fax: +81(798) 32-5040

Website: http://www.otemae.ac.jp

President: Koji Kawamoto EMail: kawamoto@otemae.ac.jp

Faculties

Humanities (Arts and Humanities; Comparative Literature; Cultural Studies; English; European Languages; Fine Arts; Handicrafts; History; Literature; Media Studies; Modern Languages; Oriental Studies; Visual Arts); **Socio-Cultural Studies** (Architectural and Environmental Design; Business and Commerce; Cultural Studies; Environmental Studies; Information Sciences; Media Studies; Psychology)

Graduate Schools

Comparative Culture (Cultural Studies)

Institutes

History Research (History); **Intercultural Studies** (Cultural Studies; Regional Studies)

History: Founded 1966 as Otemae University for Women. Acquired present title 2000.

Academic Year: April to March

Admission Requirements: Graduation from High School or equivalent

Main Language(s) of Instruction: Japanese

International Co-operation: With universities in United Kingdom and USA

Degrees and Diplomas: *Gakushi*: 4 yrs; *Shushi*; *Hakase*

Student Services: Sports facilities

Libraries: c. 200,000 vols

Publications: Otemae Winds *(1-2 per annum)*

Last Updated: 29/01/09

OTEMON GAKUIN UNIVERSITY

Otemon Gakuin Daigaku

2-1-15 Nishiai, Ibaraki-shi, Osaka 567-8502
Tel: +81(726) 41-9608
Fax: +81(726) 43-9414
EMail: admit@jimu.otemon.ac.jp
Website: http://www.otemon.ac.jp

President: Masayuki Ochiai

Centres

Australian Studies (Pacific Area Studies)

Faculties

Economics *(Also Graduate School)* (Economics; International Economics); **International Liberal Arts** (Arts and Humanities; Asian Studies; Chinese; Cultural Studies; English; European Languages; Literature; Modern Languages; Oriental Studies; Sociology); **Management** *(Also Graduate School)* (Management; Marketing); **Psychology** (Psychology); **Sociology** (Sociology)

Graduate Schools

Letters

Institutes

Educational Research (Educational Research)

History: Founded 1966.

Academic Year: April to March (April-September; October-March)

Admission Requirements: Graduation from high school or equivalent, or foreign equivalent, and entrance examination

Main Language(s) of Instruction: Japanese, English

International Co-operation: With universities in China, Australia, India, Germany and USA

Degrees and Diplomas: *Gakushi*: 4 yrs; *Shushi*: a further 2 yrs; *Hakase*

Student Services: Canteen, Employment services, Foreign student adviser, Foreign Studies Centre, Health services, Language programs, Social counselling, Sports facilities

Libraries: c. 450,000 vols

Publications: Faculty of Letters Journal *(annually)*; Otemon Economic Journal *(quarterly)*; Otemon Economic Studies *(annually)*; The Otemon Journal of Australian Studies

Last Updated: 28/03/11

OTSUMA WOMEN'S UNIVERSITY

Otsuma Joshi Daigaku

12 Sanban-cho, Chiyoda-ku, Tokyo 102-8357
Tel: +81(3) 5275-6074
Fax: +81(3) 3261-8119
Website: http://www.otsuma.ac.jp

Faculties

Comparative Culture *(Tama Campus, Tama-shi, Tokyo)*; **Home Economics** *(Sayama Campus, Iruma-shi, Saitama-ken)* (Child Care and Development; Clothing and Sewing; Food Science; Home Economics); **Human Relations** *(Tama Campus, Tama-shi, Tokyo)* (Social Psychology; Social Welfare; Social Work; Sociology); **Language and Literature** *(Sayama campus, Iruma-shi, Saitama-ken)* (English; Japanese; Literature; Modern Languages); **Social Information Studies** *(Tama Campus, Tama-shi, Tokyo)* (Information Management; Information Sciences; Information Technology)

Institutes

Human Life Sciences

Further Information: Sayama Campus (Iruma-shi, Saitama-ken); Tama Campus (Tama-shi, Tokyo)

History: Founded 1908 as School for Needlework and Handicrafts, became Junior College 1942, and acquired present status 1992.

Governing Bodies: Board of Trustees; Board of Councillors

Academic Year: April to March (April-September; September-March)

Admission Requirements: Graduation from high school and entrance examination

Main Language(s) of Instruction: Japanese

Accrediting Agencies: Ministry of Education, Culture, Sports, Science and Technology

Degrees and Diplomas: *Gakushi*: 4 yrs; *Shushi*: a further 2 yrs; *Hakase*: 2 yrs following Shushi. Also Teaching Graduation

Student Services: Academic counselling, Canteen, Employment services, Health services, Social counselling, Sports facilities

Student Residential Facilities: Dormitories (Kagaryo: c. 660, Sayamadaiyo: c. 560)

Special Facilities: Data Processing Education Centre; Education Engineering Development Room, Draft/text Research Institute

Libraries: Central Library, Tama Library, Sayama Library: c. 400,000 vols

Publications: Ostuma Journal, Journal of the Otsuma Women's University English Language and Literature Association *(annually)*; Ostuma Kokubun, Journal of Ostuma Women's University Japanese Language and Literature Association *(annually)*; Seien, Journal of the Otsuma Women's University Home Economics Association *(annually)*

Last Updated: 30/01/09

POOLE GAKUIN UNIVERSITY

Puru Gakuin Daigaku

4-5-1 Makizukadai, Sakai-shi, Osaka-shi, Osaka 590-0114
Tel: +81(72) 292-7201
Fax: +81(72) 293-5525
EMail: poole@poole.ac.jp
Website: http://www.poole.ac.jp

Faculties

Intercultural Studies (Arts and Humanities; Chinese; Cultural Studies; French; German; Italian; Japanese; Korean; Regional Studies)

Graduate Schools

Intercultural Studies

History: Founded 1879. Added a women's junior college with a program in English and literature 1950. Moved to Saikai 1982. Acquired present status 1995.

Academic Year: April to March (April-September; October-March)

Fees: (Yen): Secretarial Studies, Junior College: 1.4m. per annum; Intercultural Studies, Undergraduate Program: 1.25m. per annum; Intercultural Studies, Graduate Program: 900,000 per annum

International Co-operation: With universities in Republic of Korea, China, Nepal, United Kingdom, Canada, Australia, Myanmar, Philippines and Indonesia

Degrees and Diplomas: *Gakushi*; *Shushi*

Student Services: Canteen, Sports facilities

Student Residential Facilities: Dormitories outside campus.

Libraries:c. 120,500 vols

Last Updated: 30/01/09

PREFECTURAL UNIVERSITY OF HIROSHIMA

Kenritsu Hiroshima Daigaku

1-1-71 Ujina-higashi, Minami-ku, Hiroshima-shi, Hiroshima 734-8558
Tel: +81(82) 251-5178
Fax: +81(82) 251-9181
Website: http://www.pu-hiroshima.ac.jp/

Programmes

Biology *(Graduate)*; **Environmental Sciences** *(Undergraduate)* (Environmental Studies); **Humanities** *(Undergraduate)* (Arts and Humanities; Cultural Studies; Environmental Studies); **Humanities** *(Graduate)*; **Social Welfare** *(Graduate)*; **Social Welfare** *(Undergraduate)*

History: Founded 2005, incorporating Hiroshima Joshi Daigaku (Hiroshima Women's University).

Degrees and Diplomas: *Gakushi*; *Shushi*; *Hakase*
Last Updated: 19/11/08

PREFECTURAL UNIVERSITY OF KUMAMOTO

Kumamoto Kenritsu Daigaku

3-1-100 Tsukide, Kumamoto-shi, Kumamoto 862-8502
Tel: +81(96) 383-2929
Fax: +81(96) 384-6765
EMail: rep-puk@pu-kumamoto.ac.jp
Website: http://www.pu-kumamoto.ac.jp

President: Michihiro Sugano (2000-)

Secretary-General: Akimichi Etoh

International Relations: Kazuhiko Fukatsu, Dean of Student Affairs

Centres

Foreign Language Education (Modern Languages)

Faculties

Administration (Administration); **Environmental and Symbiotic Sciences** (Architecture; Ecology; Environmental Studies; Food Science; Health Sciences); **Letters** (Arts and Humanities; English; European Languages; Japanese; Literature; Modern Languages; Oriental Languages)

Graduate Schools

Administration (Administration); **Environmental and Symbiotic Sciences** (Environmental Studies); **Language and Literature** (English; Japanese; Literature)

History: Founded 1947, acquired present status 1994.

Academic Year: April to March (April-September; October-March)

Admission Requirements: Graduation from high school or equivalent

Main Language(s) of Instruction: Japanese

Degrees and Diplomas: *Gakushi*: 4 yrs; *Shushi*: a further 2 yrs; *Hakase (PhD)*: 3 yrs following Shushi

Student Services: Academic counselling, Canteen, Employment services, Foreign student adviser, Handicapped facilities, Health services, Nursery care, Social counselling, Sports facilities

Libraries: c. 320,000 vols

Publications: Faculty Journal, Academic Journal *(quarterly)*
Last Updated: 14/01/08

RAKUNO GAKUEN UNIVERSITY

Rakuno Gakuen Daigaku

582-1 Bunkyodai-Midorimachi, Ebetsu-shi, Hokkaido 069-8501
Tel: +81(11) 386-1111
Fax: +81(11) 386-1214
EMail: koho@rakuno.ac.jp
Website: http://www.rakuno.ac.jp

Programmes

Graduate; Undergraduate (Agricultural Economics; Environmental Studies; Food Science; Veterinary Science)

History: Founded 1933 as Hokkaido Dairy Farming School, acquired present status 1959.

Academic Year: April to March (April-September; October-March)

Admission Requirements: Graduation from high school or equivalent, or foreign equivalent and entrance examination

Main Language(s) of Instruction: Japanese

Degrees and Diplomas: *Gakushi*: Agriculture (Nogakushi), 4 yrs; *Gakushi*: Veterinary Medicine, 6 yrs; *Shushi*: Agriculture (Nogakushushi), a further 2 yrs; *Hakase*: Agriculture (Nogakuhakushi), 3 yrs following Shushi; *Hakase*: Veterinary Medicine, 4 yrs after Juigakushi

Student Services: Academic counselling, Employment services, Foreign student adviser, Health services, Social counselling, Sports facilities

Student Residential Facilities: For c. 410 students

Special Facilities: Research and Teaching Farm

Libraries: 271,926 vols

Publications: Journal of Rakuno Gakuen University *(annually)*
Last Updated: 30/01/09

REITAKU UNIVERSITY

Reitaku Daigaku

2-1-1 Hikarigaoka, Kashiwa-shi, Chiba 277-8686
Tel: +81(471) 73-3601
Fax: +81(471) 73-1100
EMail: riec@reitaku-u.ac.jp
Website: http://www.reitaku-u.ac.jp

President: Osamu Nakayama

Colleges

Modern Languages (Chinese; English; European Languages; German; Japanese; Modern Languages; Oriental Languages)

Graduate Schools

Japanese and Oriental Languages *(Graduate Programme)* (Japanese; Linguistics; Modern Languages; Oriental Languages)

Schools

Economics and Business Administration (Administration; Business Administration; Economics; Information Technology; International Business; International Economics; Management; Public Administration)

History: Founded 1935.

International Co-operation: With universities in Australia; China; Germany; Taiwan; United Kingdom and USA

Degrees and Diplomas: *Gakushi*; *Shushi*; *Hakase*

Student Services: Language programs, Sports facilities

Student Residential Facilities: Yes

Libraries: 454,592 vols
Last Updated: 30/01/09

RIKKYO UNIVERSITY

Rikkyo Daigaku

3-34-1 Nishi Ikebukuro, Toshima-ku, Tokyo 171-8501
Tel: +81(3) 3985-2255
Fax: +81(3) 3985-2825
Website: http://www.rikkyo.ac.jp

President: Tomoya Yoshioka (2010-2014)
Tel: +81(3) 3985-2201, Fax: +81(3) 3985-2825

International Relations: Herbert Donovan, International Liaison Officer
Tel: +81(3) 3985 2204, Fax: +81(3) 3985 2825
EMail: donovan@rikkyo.ac.jp

Centres

Asian Area Studies (Asian Studies); **Business Creator Promotion** (Business and Commerce); **Educational Testing and Psychological Consulting**; **General Curriculum Development** (Cultural Studies; Education; Modern Languages; Natural Sciences; Physical Education; Social Sciences); **Popular Culture Studies** *(Edogawa Rampo Memorial Center)* (Cultural Studies)

Colleges

Arts *(Also Graduate School)* (American Studies; Arts and Humanities; Christian Religious Studies; Cultural Studies; Education; Educational Psychology; Educational Research; English; French; German; History; Japanese; Literature; Primary Education; Psychology; Special Education; Theology; Writing); **Business** *(Also Graduate School)* (Business Administration; Business and Commerce; International Business); **Community and Human Services** *(Also Graduate School)* (Social and Community Services; Social Work; Sports); **Contemporary Psychology** *(Also Graduate School)* (Psychology); **Economics** *(Also Graduate School)* (Accountancy; Economic and Finance Policy; Economics; Finance); **Intercultural Communication** (Chinese; Communication Studies; Cultural Studies; English; French; German; Koran; Spanish); **Law and Politics** *(Also Graduate School)* (Commercial Law; International Law; Law; Political Sciences; Private Law; Public Law); **Science** *(Also Graduate School)* (Biological and Life Sciences; Chemistry; Mathematics; Natural Sciences; Physics); **Sociology** *(Also Graduate School)* (Communication Studies; Cultural Studies; Media Studies;

Sociology); **Tourism** *(Also Graduate School)* (Communication Studies; Cultural Studies; Tourism)

Graduate Schools

Business Administration; **Christian Studies**; **Social Design** (Business Administration; Management)

Institutes

Atomic Energy (Atomic and Molecular Physics); **Business Law Studies** *(Rikkyo Institute)* (Commercial Law); **Christian Education** *(JICE)* (Christian Religious Studies); **Church Music** *(Rikkyo Institute)* (Religious Music); **English Language Education** *(St. Paul's Institute)* (English); **Global Urban Studies** *(Rikkyo Institute)* (Urban Studies); **Japanese Studies** (Asian Studies; East Asian Studies; Japanese); **Latin American Studies** (Latin American Studies); **Leadership Studies** (Leadership); **Legal Practice Studies** *(Rikkyo Institute)*; **Peace and Community Studies** *(Rikkyo Institute)* (Peace and Disarmament; Urban Studies); **Social Welfare** (Social Welfare); **Tourism** (Tourism); **Wellness** *(Rikkyo Institute)*

Research Centres

Amusement; **Extermophile Information**; **Future Molecules** (Biology; Molecular Biology); **Measurement in Advanced Science**; **Sustainable Development** (Development Studies)

Research Institutes

American Studies (American Studies); **Economics** *(Rikkyo Research Institute)*

Further Information: Also Rikkyo Gender Forum

History: Founded 1874 by Bishop Channing Moore Williams of the Episcopal Church of the USA. Acquired University status 1883. Administration taken over by the Japanese 1920. Reorganized and became co-educational 1949. Graduate School established 1951.

Governing Bodies: Board of Trustees; Council of Deans

Academic Year: April to March (April-September; October-January)

Admission Requirements: Graduation from high school or equivalent, and entrance examination

Main Language(s) of Instruction: Japanese

International Co-operation: With universities in USA, China and Germany

Degrees and Diplomas: *Gakushi*: Law and Political Science (Hogakushi); Letters (Bungakushi); Science (Rigakushi), 4 yrs; *Shushi*: Economics (Keizaigakushushi); Law and Political Science (Hogakushushi); Letters (Bungakushushi); Science (Rigakushushi); Sociology (Shakaigakushushi); Systematic Theology (Shingakushushi), a further 2-4 yrs; *Hakase*: Economics (Keizaigakuhakushi); Law and Political Science (Hogakuhakushi); Letters (Bungakuhakushi); Science (Rigakuhakushi); Sociology (Shakaigakuhakushi); Systematic Theology (Shingakuhakushi), 3-6 yrs following Shushi

Student Services: Academic counselling, Foreign student adviser, Language programs, Sports facilities

Student Residential Facilities: For women students

Libraries: University and branch libraries,1,709,453 vols

Publications: Arts and Letters (Eibei-Bungaku) *(annually)*; Christian Studies (Kirisutokyo Gaku); Journal of Applied Sociology *(biannually)*; Journal of Historical Studies *(biannually)*; Journal of Japanese Literature *(biannually)*; Rikkyo Quarterly *(quarterly)*; St Paul's Journal of Law and Politics (Rikkyo Hogaku) *(annually)*; St. Paul's Economic Journal *(quarterly)*

Student Numbers *2008-2009*: Total 18,538

Last Updated: 30/01/09

RISSHO UNIVERSITY

Rissho Daigaku

4-2-16 Osaki, Shinagawa-ku, Tokyo 141-8602
Tel: +81(3) 3492-6649
Fax: +81(3) 5487-3347
EMail: oinet@ris.ac.jp
Website: http://www.ris.ac.jp

Departments

Nichiren Buddhist Studies (Asian Religious Studies)

Faculties

Buddhist Studies *(Research)* (Asian Religious Studies); **Business Administration** (Business Administration); **Economics** (Economics); **Geo-Environmental Science** (Environmental Management; Geography); **Law** (Law); **Letters** (History; Literature; Philosophy; Sociology); **Psychology** (Clinical Psychology; Psychology); **Social Welfare** (Social Welfare; Welfare and Protective Services)

Graduate Schools

Business Administration Research (Business Administration); **Economic Research** (Economics); **Geo-Environmental Science Research** (Environmental Studies); **Law Research** (Law); **Literary Research** (Literature); **Psychology Reasearch**; **Social Welfare Research** (Social Welfare)

Further Information: Also Kumagaya Campus

History: Founded 1904 as Buddhist College, became University 1924, incorporating the College. Acquired present status 1949. Financed by the Nichiren Sect.

Academic Year: April to January (April-July; September-January)

Admission Requirements: Graduation from high school or equivalent or foreign equivalent, and entrance examination

Main Language(s) of Instruction: Japanese

International Co-operation: With universities in China; Republic of Korea; New Zealand and USA

Degrees and Diplomas: *Gakushi*: 4 yrs; *Shushi*: 2 yrs following Gakushi; *Hakase*: 3 yrs following Shushi

Student Services: Canteen, Health services, Social counselling, Sports facilities

Student Residential Facilities: Yes

Special Facilities: Rissho Oriental Bell Museum. Ishibashi Tanzan Memorial Auditorium

Libraries: University Library and faculty libraries, total, c. 863,000 vols

Publications: Bungakuburonso (Journal of Faculty of Letters); Eibungakuronko (Critical Studies in English Literature); Keizaigakukiho (Quarterly Report of Economics); Kokugokokubungaku (Journal of Japanese Philology and Literature); Osakigakuho (Journal of Nichiren and Buddhist Studies); Risshochiri (Geographical Journal); Risshoshigaku (Historical Research Report); Shakaigakuronso (Critical Studies in Sociology); Tetsugakuronso (Critical Studies in Philosophy)

Last Updated: 30/01/09

RITSUMEIKAN ASIA PACIFIC UNIVERSITY

Ritsumeikan Ajia Taiheiyou Daigaku (APU)

Academic Outreach Office, 1-1 Jumonjibaru, Beppu-shi, Oita 874-8577
Tel: +81(977) 78-1101
Fax: +81(977) 78-1102
EMail: intl@apu.ac.jp
Website: http://www.apu.ac.jp

President: Shun Korenaga
Tel: +81(977) 78-1101, Fax: +81(977) 78-1102

Dean, Academic Affairs: Edgar Porter
Tel: +81(977) 78-1101, Fax: +81(977) 78-1102
EMail: porter@apu.ac.jp

International Relations: Nao Oshima, Manager, Academic Outreach Office
Tel: +81(977) 78-1101, Fax: +81(977) 78-1102
EMail: noo07219@apu.ac.jp

Colleges

Asia Pacific Studies (Comparative Sociology; Cultural Studies; Development Studies; Environmental Management; International Studies) *Dean*: Yamagami Susumu; **International Management** (Accountancy; Finance; International Business; Management; Marketing) *Dean*: Namba Masanori

Graduate Schools

Asia Pacific Studies (Asian Studies; Economics; Environmental Management; International Relations; Pacific Area Studies; Tourism) *Dean*: Yamagami Susumu; **Management** (Finance; International Business; Management; Marketing) *Dean*: Namba Masanori

History: Founded 2000, part of Ritsumeikan Trust.

Governing Bodies: Ritsumeikan Academy

Academic Year: Spring semester, April-July; Fall semester, October-January

Admission Requirements: Has completed a standard 12 years of education outside Japan or be at least 18 years of age and hold an International Baccalaureate Diploma or other qualification (course completion certificate) recognized by APU. Japanese basis applicants: A score of 240 points or more for level 1, or 280 points or more for level 2 on the Japanese Language Proficiency Test (JLPT). English basis applicants: A score of 500 points or more of the paper-based TOEFL (or 173 and 61 for computer-based and internet-based respectively), or a score of 5.5 or higher on the IELTS (Academic).

Fees: (Yen): Admission fees: 130,000 per annum. First year: 1,265,000; second year: 1,401,000; third year: 1,414,000; fourth year: 1,140,000 yen

Main Language(s) of Instruction: Japanese and English

International Co-operation: The Ritsumeikan Trust has established cooperative relations with 337 universities and institutions in 56 countries and regions of the world (as of January 2008). Based on this network, APU offers various partnership projects, including exchange programmes for study abroad, language training programmes, joint research and interactive programmes for students and faculty members. The academic network consists of universities, institutions, companies, NPOs, national governments, local governments, international institutions and prominent researchers worldwide. Student exchange is also done through the International Student Exchange Program (ISEP)

Accrediting Agencies: Ministry of Education, Culture, Sports, Science and Technology (MEXT)

Degrees and Diplomas: *Gakushi*: Business Administration (APM); Social Sciences (APS), 3-4 yrs; *Shushi*: Business Administration (MBA); Science in Asia Pacific Studies (APS); Science in International Cooperation Policy (ICP), 1 1/2-2 yrs; *Hakase*: Philosophy in Asia Pacific Studies (APS), 2-3 yrs

Student Services: Academic counselling, Canteen, Cultural centre, Employment services, Foreign student adviser, Foreign Studies Centre, Handicapped facilities, Health services, Language programs, Social counselling, Sports facilities

Student Residential Facilities: AP House (for c. 1,300 students)

Libraries: 2,792,194 vols; 1,706 subscriptions to periodicals; access to 58 electronic networks (Oxford University Press, JSTOR, etc)

Publications: Crossroads, Annual University Handbook *(annually)*; Polyglossia, Articles on language education; research articles; reports on language teaching practices; book reviews and translations of research articles in languages other than English and Japanese *(biannually)*; Ritsumeikan Journal of Asia Pacific Studies, The 'RCAPS Journal' mainly features papers on Asia Pacific studies *(3 per annum)*

Last Updated: 29/03/11

RITSUMEIKAN UNIVERSITY

Ritsumeikan Daigaku

56-1 Toji-in, Kita-machi, Kita-ku, Kyoto-shi, Kyoto 603-8577
Tel: +81(75) 465-1111 +81(75) 465-8230
Fax: +81(75) 465-8160
EMail: kokusai@st.ritsumei.ac.jp
Website: http://www.ritsumei.jp/index_j.html

President: Kawaguchi Kiyofumi

Departments

International Relations *(Graduate Programme)*; **Political Science**; **Social Sciences** (Social Sciences); **Sociology** *(Graduate Programme)* (Sociology)

Faculties

Arts and Humanities (Arts and Humanities; Geography; History; Literature; Philosophy); **Business Administration** (Business Administration); **Economics** (Economics); **International Relations** (International Relations); **Law** (Law); **Science and Engineering** (Biological and Life Sciences; Biotechnology; Chemistry; Civil Engineering; Computer Science; Electrical and Electronic Engineering; Engineering; Environmental Engineering; Mathematics; Mechanical Engineering; Natural Sciences; Physics; Robotics)

Institutes

Cultural Research (Cultural Studies); **Science and Engineering Research** (Engineering; Mathematics and Computer Science)

Further Information: Suzaku, Kinugasa and Biwako-Kusatsu campuses

History: Founded 1900 as a College of Law and Politics, renamed Ritsumeikan College 1913. Reorganized 1948 as a private University.

Governing Bodies: Board of Trustees; University Council

Academic Year: April to March (April-September; October-March)

Admission Requirements: Graduation from high school and entrance examination

Main Language(s) of Instruction: Japanese

International Co-operation: With universities in USA, China and Taiwan

Degrees and Diplomas: *Gakushi*: Arts; Economics; Engineering; Law; Science, 4 yrs; *Shushi*: Arts; Economics; Engineering; Law; Science, a further 2 yrs; *Hakase*: Arts; Economics; Engineering; Law; Science, 3 yrs following Shushi

Student Services: Academic counselling, Language programs, Sports facilities

Student Residential Facilities: For c. 435 students

Libraries: 2,600,000 vols

Publications: Journals of the Faculties and Research Institutes

Last Updated: 30/01/09

RYOTOKUJI UNIVERSITY

Ryotokuji Daigaku

40 Gaiku Akemi, Urayasu-shi, Chiba 279-0014
Fax: +81(47) 380-0447
EMail: info@ryotokuji-u.ac.jp
Website: http://www.ryotokuji-u.ac.jp

Faculties

Japanese Culture and Arts (Cultural Studies; Fine Arts; Painting and Drawing)

History: Founded 2006.

Degrees and Diplomas: *Gakushi*

Last Updated: 12/02/09

RYUKOKU UNIVERSITY

Ryukoku Daigaku

67 Tsukamoto-cho, Fukakusa, Fushimi-ku, Kyoto 612-8577
Tel: +81(75) 642-1111 +81(75) 645-7898
Fax: +81(75) 642-8876 +81(75) 645-2020
EMail: ric@rnoc.fks.ryukoku.ac.jp
Website: http://www.ryukoku.ac.jp

President: Dosho Wakahara

Centres

Ryukoku Extension *(Seta Campus)*

Faculties

Business Administration *(Also Graduate School)* (Business Administration); **Economics** *(Also Graduate School)* (Economics); **Intercultural Communication** *(Seta Campus; Also Graduate School)*; **Law** *(Also Graduate School)* (Law); **Letters** *(Omiya Campus; Also Graduate School)* (Arts and Humanities; Asian Religious Studies; English; History; Japanese; Literature; Philosophy); **Science and Technology** *(Seta Campus; Also Graduate School)* (Applied Mathematics; Computer Science; Electronic Engineering; Information Sciences; Materials Engineering; Mechanical Engineering; Natural Sciences; Systems Analysis; Technology); **Sociology** *(Seta Campus; Also Graduate School)* (Sociology)

Institutes

Buddhist Cultural Studies *(Omiya Campus)* (Asian Religious Studies; Cultural Studies); **Science and Technology** *(Seta Campus, Joint Research)* (Natural Sciences; Technology); **Social and Cultural Research** *(Seta Campus)* (Cultural Studies; Social Studies); **Social Sciences Research** (Social Sciences)

Further Information: Also special courses for foreign students: Japanese Culture and Language Program (JCLP) and Janapese and Asian Studies Program (JAS)

History: Founded 1639 as Buddhist Seminary, became College 1900 and University 1922. The University is supported by the Honpa Hongawanji denomination and has 3 campuses: Fukakusa and Omya in Kyoto, and Seta in Shiga Prefecture.

Governing Bodies: Board of Trustees

Academic Year: April to March (April-September; October-March)

Admission Requirements: Graduation from high school or recognized foreign equivalent, and entrance examination

Main Language(s) of Instruction: Japanese

International Co-operation: With universities in China, Australia and USA

Degrees and Diplomas: *Gakushi*: 4 yrs; *Shushi*: a further 2 yrs and thesis; *Hakase*: 3 yrs following Shushi, and thesis

Student Services: Academic counselling, Employment services, Foreign student adviser, Handicapped facilities, Health services, Language programs, Social counselling, Sports facilities

Student Residential Facilities: Yes

Libraries: Kukakusa Library, Omiya Library, Seta Library: 1,500,000 vols

Publications: Bulletin of Institute of Buddhist Cultural Studies; Bulletin of the Research Institute for Social Sciences *(annually)*; Journal of Business Studies; Journal of Economic Studies; Journal of Education; Journal of English Language and English Literature.; Journal of Humanities and Sciences; Journal of Japanese History; Journal of Religious Law; Journal of Ryukoku University; Journal of Studies in Shin Buddhism; Law Review; Philosophical Review

Last Updated: 30/01/09

RYUTSU KEIZAI UNIVERSITY

Ryutsu Keizai Daigaku (RKU)

120 Hirahata, Ryugasaki-shi, Ibaraki 301-8555
Tel: +81(297) 64-0001
Fax: +81(297) 64-0011
EMail: ipc@rku.ac.jp; ees@rku.ac.jp
Website: http://www.rku.ac.jp

Centres

Data Processing (Data Processing); **Languages and Cultural Exchange** (Cultural Studies; Foreign Languages Education); **Physical Education** (Physical Education)

Departments

Japanese Language

Faculties

Distribution and Logistics Systems (Transport Management); **Economics** (Business Administration; Economics) *Dean*: Tomio Koikeda; **Law**; **Sociology** (Sociology; Tourism)

Institutes

RKU Logistics

History: Founded 1965 under the auspices of Nippon Express, an International transportation and distribution Company.

Governing Bodies: Council of Trustees

Academic Year: April to March (April-September; October-March)

Admission Requirements: Graduation from high school and entrance examination

Main Language(s) of Instruction: Japanese

Degrees and Diplomas: *Gakushi*: Distribution and Logistics Systems; Economics; Law; Management; Sociology, 4 yrs. Also Graduate Course in: Economics, Sociology, 5 yrs; Distribution and Logistics Systems, 2 yrs

Student Residential Facilities: Yes

Libraries: 290,000 vols

Publications: RKU Hougaku *(biannually)*; RKU Logistics Journal *(biannually)*; RKU Ronshu *(quarterly)*; RKU Ryutsu Johogakubu Kiyo *(biannually)*; RKU Shakaigakubu Ronso *(biannually)*

Press or Publishing House: Ryutsu Keizai University Press

SAGA UNIVERSITY

Saga Daigaku

1 Honjo-machi, Saga-shi, Saga 840-8502
Tel: +81(952) 28-8168
Fax: +81(952) 28-8819
EMail: studenta@cc.saga-u.ac.jp
Website: http://www.saga-u.ac.jp

President: Takao Hotokebuchi

Centres

Coastal Bioenvironment (Coastal Studies; Environmental Studies); **Computer and Network** (Computer Engineering; Computer Networks; Computer Science); **Joint Research and Development**; **Research and Development of Higher Education** (Higher Education); **Synchrotron Light Application**

Faculties

Agriculture *(Also Graduate School)* (Agriculture; Applied Chemistry; Biological and Life Sciences; Coastal Studies; Environmental Studies; Food Science); **Culture and Education** *(Also Graduate School)* (Crafts and Trades; Cultural Studies; Education; Environmental Studies; International Studies); **Economics** *(Also Graduate School)* (Business Administration; Economics; Law); **Medicine** *(Also Graduate School)* (Anatomy; Biological and Life Sciences; Biology; Community Health; Forensic Medicine and Dentistry; Genetics; Immunology; Medicine; Nursing; Oncology; Social and Preventive Medicine; Toxicology); **Science and Engineering** *(Also Graduate School)* (Applied Chemistry; Chemistry; Civil Engineering; Electrical and Electronic Engineering; Engineering; Information Sciences; Mathematics; Mathematics and Computer Science; Mechanical Engineering; Natural Sciences; Physics)

Institutes

Lowland Technology; **Ocean Energy**

Laboratories

Venture Business

Research Centres

Experimental Science (Analytical Chemistry; Biochemistry; Bioengineering; Organic Chemistry)

Further Information: Also Japanese language courses for foreign students

History: Founded 1949 as National University incorporating former Normal Schools. Incorporated Saga Ika Daigaku/Saga Medical School 2003.

Academic Year: April to March (April-October; October-March)

Admission Requirements: Graduation from high school or equivalent or foreign equivalent, and entrance examination

Main Language(s) of Instruction: Japanese

International Co-operation: With universities in Republic of Korea, China and USA

Degrees and Diplomas: *Gakushi*: Agriculture (Nogakushi); Economics (Keizaigakushi); Education (Kyoikugakushi); Engineering; Nursing; Science (Rigakushi), 4 yrs; *Gakushi*: Medicine, 6 yrs; *Shushi*: Agriculture (Nogakushushi), a further 2 yrs; *Shushi*: Nursing, 2 yrs following Gakushi; *Hakase*: Medicine, 4 yrs following Igakushi

Student Services: Academic counselling, Employment services, Foreign Studies Centre, Health services, Language programs, Sports facilities

Student Residential Facilities: Yes

Libraries: c. 707,000 vols

Publications: Faculty journals

Last Updated: 24/03/11

SAGAMI WOMEN'S UNIVERSITY

Sagami Joshi Daigaku

2-1-1 Buhkyo, Sagamihara-shi, Kanagawa 228-8533
Tel: +81(427) 421-411
Fax: +81(427) 421-732
Website: http://www.sagami-wu.ac.jp

Programmes

Arts and Humanities (Arts and Humanities); **Natural Sciences**

History: Founded 1900. Acquired present status 1949.

Degrees and Diplomas: *Gakushi*

SAITAMA GAKUEN UNIVERSITY

Saitama Gakuen Daigaku
1510 Kizoro, Kawaguchi-shi, Saitama 333-0831
Tel: +81(48) 294-1110
Fax: +81(48) 294-0294
EMail: nyushi@saigaku.ac.jp
Website: http://www.saigaku.ac.jp

History: Founded 2001.

Degrees and Diplomas: *Gakushi*

SAITAMA INSTITUTE OF TECHNOLOGY

Saitama Kogyo Daigaku (Osato-gun) (SIT)
1690 Fusaiji, Fukaya, Saitama 369-0293
Tel: +81(48) 585-2521
Fax: +81(48) 585-2523
Website: http://www.sit.ac.jp

Faculties

Engineering (Applied Chemistry; Computer Science; Electronic Engineering; Mechanical Engineering) *Dean*: Sinji Kumagai; **Human and Social Studies** (Psychology; Social Studies) *Dean*: Atuhiko Narita

Graduate Schools

Engineering (Applied Chemistry; Computer Science; Electronic Engineering; Materials Engineering; Mechanical Engineering) *Head*: S. Uchiyama; **Human and Social Studies** *Head*: Hiroaki Naki

History: Founded 1976.

Academic Year: April to March (April-September; October-March)

Main Language(s) of Instruction: Japanese

Accrediting Agencies: Japan University Accreditation Association

Degrees and Diplomas: *Gakushi*: Engineering; Human and Social Studies, 4 yrs; *Shushi*: Engineering; Human and Social Studies, 2 yrs following Gakushi; *Hakase*: Engineering, 3 yrs

Student Services: Academic counselling, Canteen, Employment services, Handicapped facilities, Health services, Language programs, Social counselling, Sports facilities

Special Facilities: Advanced Science Research Laboratory

Libraries: 140,000 vols

Publications: Bulletin of the Faculty of Human and Social Studies, SIT *(annually)*; Journal of the Faculty of Engineering, SIT *(annually)*

SAITAMA MEDICAL SCHOOL

Saitama Ika Daigaku
38 Morohongo, Morayama-machi, Iruma-gun, Saitama-shi, Saitama 350-0495
Tel: +81(492) 76-1110
Fax: +81(492) 95-2784
EMail: postmaster@saitama-med.ac.jp
Website: http://www.saitama-med.ac.jp

Faculties

Health and Medical Care (Biomedical Engineering; Health Sciences; Medical Technology; Nursing); **Medicine** (Medicine)

Graduate Schools

Medicine (Biomedicine; Medicine; Social and Preventive Medicine)

Further Information: Also University Hospital

History: Founded 1972.

Governing Bodies: Board of Trustees

Academic Year: April to March (April-July; September-December; January-March)

Admission Requirements: Graduation from high school and entrance examination

Main Language(s) of Instruction: Japanese

Degrees and Diplomas: *Gakushi*: Medicine (MD), 6 yrs; *Hakase*: Medical Sciences (PhD), a further 4 yrs

Student Services: Academic counselling, Canteen, Health services, Nursery care

Libraries: 230,000 vols

Publications: Saitama Igaku Zasshi (Journal) *(quarterly)*

Last Updated: 30/01/09

SAITAMA PREFECTURAL UNIVERSITY

Saitama Kenritsu Daigaku
820 Sannomiya, Koshigaya, Saitama-shi, Saitama 343-8540
Tel: +81(48) 971-0500
Fax: +81(48) 973-4807
Website: http://www.spu.ac.jp

President: Susumu Sato

Schools

Health and Social Services (Behavioural Sciences; Health Sciences; Laboratory Techniques; Nursing; Occupational Therapy; Physical Therapy; Social Work)

History: Founded 1999.

Degrees and Diplomas: *Gakushi*

Libraries: c. 90,000 vols.

Last Updated: 24/03/11

SAITAMA UNIVERSITY

Saitama Daigaku
255 Shimo-Okubo, Sakura-ku, Saitama-shi, Saitama 338-8570
Tel: +81(48) 858-9624
Fax: +81(48) 858-9675
Website: http://www.saitama-u.ac.jp

President: Yoshihiko Kamii

Centres

Cooperative Research *Director*: Susumu Takada; **Geosphere Research Institute** (Earth Sciences) *Director*: Kunio Watanabe; **Information Technology** (Computer Engineering) *Director*: Hitoshi Maekawa; **Molecular Analysis and Life Science** (Chemical Engineering) *Director*: Kinji Inoue

Faculties

Economics (Business and Commerce; Development Studies; Economics) *Dean*: Yoshihiko Kamii; **Education** (Special Education; Teacher Training) *Dean*: Haruyoshi Shibuya; **Engineering** (Bioengineering; Civil Engineering; Computer Engineering; Electrical and Electronic Engineering; Materials Engineering; Mechanical Engineering) *Dean*: Masaaki Kawahashi; **Liberal Arts** (Cultural Studies; Philosophy; Sociology) *Dean*: Jun Sekiguchi; **Science** (Biological and Life Sciences; Chemistry; Mathematics; Physics) *Dean*: Takeo Machida

Graduate Schools

Cultural Science *Dean*: Jun Sekiguchi; **Economic Science** (Economics) *Dean*: Yoshihiko Kamii; **Education** *(The United Graduate School of Education Tokyo Gakugei University (Doctoral course))* *Dean*: Haruyoshi Shibuya; **Science and Engineering** (Biological and Life Sciences; Chemistry; Civil Engineering; Environmental Engineering; Mathematics; Mechanical Engineering; Physics) *Dean*: Yuzuru Husimi

History: Founded 1949, incorporating Urawa High School, Saitama Youth School and Saitama Teachers College. Reorganized 1965.

Academic Year: April to March (April-September; October-March)

Admission Requirements: Graduation from high school or equivalent, and entrance examination

Fees: (Yen): 535,800 per annum

Main Language(s) of Instruction: Japanese

Accrediting Agencies: Ministry of Education, Culture, Sports, Science and Technology

Degrees and Diplomas: *Gakushi*: 4 yrs; *Shushi*: a further 2 yrs; *Hakase*: 3 yrs following Shushi

Student Services: Academic counselling, Canteen, Cultural centre, Employment services, Foreign student adviser, Foreign Studies Centre, Handicapped facilities, Health services, Language programs, Social counselling, Sports facilities

Student Residential Facilities: Yes

Libraries: 758,521 vols; serials, 19,265 titles

Publications: Bulletin *(annually)*
Last Updated: 24/03/11

SAKUSHIN GAKUIN UNIVERSITY

Sakushin Gakuin Daigaku
908 Takeshita-machi, Utsunomiya-shi, Tochigi 321-3295
Tel: +81(28) 667-7111
Fax: +81(28) 667-7110
EMail: soum@sakushin-u.ac.jp
Website: http://www.sakushin-u.ac.jp

President: Takashi Morotomi (2002-)
EMail: morotomi@sakushin-u.ac.jp

Secretary-General: Yuji Ishizaki

Faculties

Business Administration (Accountancy; Business Administration; Finance; Information Technology; Management) *Dean*: Kimito Nasuno; **Community Development** (Business and Commerce; Law; Political Sciences; Public Administration; Town Planning) *Dean*: Toyohiki Inoue; **Human and Cultural Sciences** *Dean*: Masayuki Matsuda

Schools

Graduate Studies

History: Founded 1989.

Governing Bodies: Funada Kyoikukai

Academic Year: April to March

Admission Requirements: Graduation from high school and entrance examination

Fees: (Yen): 1,210,000 per annum

Main Language(s) of Instruction: Japanese

Degrees and Diplomas: *Gakushi (BA)*: 4 yrs; *Shushi (MD)*; *Hakase (PhD)*

Student Services: Academic counselling, Canteen, Employment services, Language programs, Social counselling, Sports facilities

Libraries: 190,000 vols

SANNO INSTITUTE OF MANAGEMENT - SANNO UNIVERSITY

Sanno Daigaku - Sangyo Noritsu Daigaku
1573 Kamikasuya, Isehara-shi, Kanagawa 259-1197
Tel: +81(463) 92-2211
Fax: +81(463) 93-0554
EMail: nyushi@mi.sanno.ac.jp
Website: http://www.sanno.ac.jp/english/index.html

Graduate Schools

Sanno (Business Administration; Information Management; Information Sciences; Management)

Schools

Information Oriented Management (Information Sciences; Management) *Dean*: Minami Miyauchi; **Management** *Dean*: Yosuke Naito

Further Information: Also Jiyugaoka and Daikanyama campuses

History: Founded 1979.

Academic Year: April to March

Admission Requirements: Graduation from high school

Fees: (Yen): First year, 1,346,700; following years, 1,004,500

Main Language(s) of Instruction: Japanese

Accrediting Agencies: Ministry of Education, Culture, Sports, Science and Technology

Degrees and Diplomas: *Gakushi*: 4 yrs; *Shushi*

Student Services: Academic counselling, Canteen, Employment services, Foreign student adviser, Foreign Studies Centre, Handicapped facilities, Health services, Language programs, Nursery care, Social counselling, Sports facilities

Libraries: c. 216,000 vols
Last Updated: 30/01/09

SANYO GAKUEN UNIVERSITY

Sanyo Gakuen Daigaku
1-14-1 Hirai, Okayama-shi, Okayama 703-8501
Tel: +81(83) 272-6254
Fax: +81(83) 273-3226
EMail: nyushi@sguc.ac.jp
Website: http://www.sguc.ac.jp

Programmes

Intercultural Studies (Cultural Studies)

History: Founded 1994.

Degrees and Diplomas: *Gakushi*
Last Updated: 30/01/09

SAPPORO CITY UNIVERSITY

Sapporo Shiritsu Daigaku
Kita 11 Nishi 13, Chuo-ku, Sapporo-shi, Sapporo 060-0011
Tel: +81(11) 592-2371
Fax: +81(11) 592-2374
EMail: gakusei@scu.ac.jp/english/
Website: http://www.scu.ac.jp/english/

President: Akira Harada

Secretary-General: Suteshige Ikeda

Vice-President: Keiko Nakamura

Schools

Design *Dean*: Keisuke Yoshida; **Nursing** *Dean*: Keiko Nakamura

History: Founded 2006.

Degrees and Diplomas: *Gakushi*
Last Updated: 12/02/09

SAPPORO GAKUIN UNIVERSITY

Sapporo Gakuin Daigaku
11 Bunkyodai, Ebetsu-shi, Hokkaido 069-8555
Tel: +81(11) 386-8111
Fax: +81(11) 386-8113
EMail: kyoumu@ims.sgu.ac.jp
Website: http://www.sgu.ac.jp

President: Akiko Fuse

Faculties

Commerce (Business and Commerce); **Economics** (Economics); **Humanities** (English; European Languages; Literature; Modern Languages; Psychology; Social Sciences); **Law** (Law); **Social Information** (Social Studies)

Schools

Graduate Studies (Clinical Psychology; Law; Psychology; Regional Planning)

History: Founded 1946.

International Co-operation: With universities in USA, Republic of Korea and China

Degrees and Diplomas: *Gakushi*; *Shushi*

Student Services: Health services, Language programs, Social counselling, Sports facilities

Libraries: 443,000 vols
Last Updated: 02/02/09

SAPPORO INTERNATIONAL UNIVERSITY

Sapporo Kokusai Daigaku
4-1-4-1 Kiyota, Kiyota-ku, Sapporo-shi, Hokkaido 004-8602
Tel: +81(11) 881-8844
Fax: +81(11) 885-3370
EMail: kyomuka@ed.siu.ac.jp
Website: http://www.siu.ac.jp

Departments

Regional Studies; **Tourism** (Tourism)

Schools

Humanities

History: Founded 1993. Known as Seishu Joshi Daigaku (Seishu Women's University) until 1997.

International Co-operation: With universities in Canada, China and Republic of Korea

Degrees and Diplomas: *Gakushi*; *Shushi*

Student Services: Employment services, Foreign student adviser, Language programs, Social counselling, Sports facilities

Libraries: c. 200,000 vols

Last Updated: 02/02/09

SAPPORO MEDICAL UNIVERSITY

Sapporo Ika Daigaku

South 1 West 17, Chuo-ku, Sapporo-shi, Hokkaido 060-8556
Tel: +81(11) 611-2111
Fax: +81(11) 613-7134
EMail: kouhou@sapmed.ac.jp
Website: http://web.sapmed.ac.jp/

President: Kazuaki Shimamoto
Tel: +81(11) 631-0777, Fax: +81(11) 613-3485

Graduate Schools
Medicine

Institutes
Cancer (Oncology); **Health Sciences** (Health Sciences; Nursing; Occupational Therapy; Physical Therapy)

Schools
Marine Biomedicine (Marine Biology)

History: Founded 1950.

Academic Year: April to March (April-October; October-March)

Admission Requirements: Graduation from high school or recognized equivalent, and entrance examination

Main Language(s) of Instruction: Japanese

International Co-operation: With universities in Canada and USA

Degrees and Diplomas: *Gakushi*: Medicine, 6 yrs; *Hakase*: Medicine, a further 3-4 yrs

Student Services: Sports facilities

Student Residential Facilities: For c. 50 students

Special Facilities: Medical Museum. University Hospital

Libraries: c. 232,000 vols

Publications: Journal of Liberal Arts and Sciences Sapporo Medical College *(annually)*; Sapporo Medical Journal *(bimonthly)*; Tumour Research *(annually)*

Last Updated: 24/03/11

SAPPORO UNIVERSITY

Sapporo Daigaku

3-1-3-7 Nishioka, Toyohira-ku, Sapporo-shi, Hokkaido 062-8520
Tel: +81(11) 852-1181
Fax: +81(11) 856-8280
Website: http://www.sapporo-u.ac.jp

Faculties
Business Administration *(Also Graduate School)* (Business Administration; Industrial Management; Information Management); **Cultural Studies** *(Also Graduate School)* (Cultural Studies; Japanese); **Economics** *(Also Graduate School)* (Economics); **Foreign Languages** *(Also Graduate School)* (English; European Languages; Modern Languages; Russian); **Law** *(Also Graduate School)* (Law)

History: Founded 1967.

Main Language(s) of Instruction: Japanese

International Co-operation: With universities in USA, Australia and Canada

Degrees and Diplomas: *Gakushi*; *Shushi*

Student Services: Health services, Sports facilities

Libraries: c. 563,000 vols

Last Updated: 30/01/09

SEIAN UNIVERSITY OF ART AND DESIGN

Seian Zokei Daigaku

4-3-1 Ohginosato-higashi, Otsu-shi, Shiga 520-0248
Tel: +81(77) 574-2111
Fax: +81(77) 574-2120
EMail: info@seian.ac.jp; nyushi@seian.ac.jp
Website: http://www.seian.ac.jp

Programmes
Art and Design (Design; Fine Arts)

History: Founded 1993.

Degrees and Diplomas: *Gakushi*

Last Updated: 02/02/09

SEIGAKUIN UNIVERSITY

Seigakuin Daigaku (SEIG)

1-1 Tosaki, Ageo-shi, Saitama 362-8585
Tel: +81(48) 781-0031
Fax: +81(48) 762-2962
EMail: info@seigakuin-univ.ac.jp
Website: http://www.seig.ac.jp

Head: Mitsuharu Akudo
Tel: +81(48) 781-0925 EMail: presoffice@seigakuin-univ.ac.jp

Faculties
Human Welfare (Biological and Life Sciences; Child Care and Development; Clinical Psychology; Educational Sciences; Environmental Studies; Psychology; Social Welfare; Sociology); **Humanities**; **Political Sciences and Economics**

Graduate Schools
American-European Cultural Studies (American Studies; Christian Religious Studies; Cultural Studies; English; Ethics; European Studies; History); **Politics and Policy Studies** (Government; Political Sciences; Social Policy; Taxation)

History: Founded 1988.

Governing Bodies: Board of Directors; Board of Councillors

Academic Year: April to March (April-July; September-March)

Admission Requirements: Graduation from high school and entrance examination

Fees: (Yen): 100,000,000 per annum

Main Language(s) of Instruction: Japanese

International Co-operation: With universities in USA, United Kingdom and Australia

Degrees and Diplomas: *Gakushi*: 4 yrs; *Shushi*: 2 yrs following Gakushi; *Hakase*: 3 yrs following Shushi. Kyoin Menkyo (Teaching Certificate) for Kindergarten, Middle School and High School; Toshokan Shisho (Librarian Certificate)

Student Services: Academic counselling, Canteen, Employment services, Foreign student adviser, Handicapped facilities, Health services, Language programs, Social counselling, Sports facilities

Special Facilities: Seminar House (Karuizawa)

Libraries: 256,838 vols; Japanese and Foreign Language periodicals; tape, video and CD facilities; Internet

Publications: Seigakuin Journal, Academic Research

Press or Publishing House: Seigakuin University Press

Last Updated: 02/02/09

SEIJO UNIVERSITY

Seijo Daigaku

6-1-20 Seijo, Setagaya-ku, Tokyo 157-8511
Tel: +81(3) 3482-1181 +81(3) 3482-6020
Fax: +81(3) 3484-2698 +81(3) 3482-1213
EMail: kokusai@seijo.ac.jp
Website: http://www.seijo.ac.jp

President: Mazumi Shimizu

Faculties
Arts and Literature *(Also Graduate School)* (Aesthetics; Art History; Cultural Studies; English; European Studies; Film; Fine Arts;

Japanese; Mass Communication; Musicology; Theatre); **Economics** *(Also Graduate School)* (Business Administration; Economics); **Law** *(Also Graduate School)* (Law); **Social Innovation** (Psychology; Sociology)

History: Founded 1917 as Elementary School, became High School 1926, acquired University status 1950.

Governing Bodies: Seijo Gakuen (Board of Directors), comprising 15 members

Academic Year: April to March (April-September; September-March)

Admission Requirements: Graduation from high school or foreign equivalent, and entrance examination

Main Language(s) of Instruction: Japanese

International Co-operation: With universities in USA, France and Belgium

Degrees and Diplomas: *Gakushi*: Arts (Bungakushi); Economics (Keizaigakushi); Law (Hogakushi), 4 yrs; *Shushi*: Arts (Bungakushushi); Economics (Keizaigakushushi); Law (Hogakushushi), a further 2 yrs; *Hakase*: 3 yrs following Shushi

Student Services: Academic counselling, Canteen, Employment services, Health services, Language programs, Social counselling, Sports facilities

Libraries: University Library, 670,000 vols

Publications: English Monographs *(annually)*; Kokubungaku Ronshu (Monographs on Japanese Literature and Language, annually)); Minzokugaku Kenkyujo Kiyo (Folklore Studies) *(annually)*; Seijo Bungei (Arts and Literature) *(quarterly)*; Seijo Daigaku Keizai Kenkyu (Economic Studies) *(quarterly)*; Seijo Law Journal

Last Updated: 02/02/09

SEIJOH UNIVERSITY

Seijoh Daigaku

2-172 Fukinodai, Tokai-Shi, Aichi-gun, Aichi 476-8588
Tel: +81(52) 601-6000
Fax: +81(52) 601-6010
EMail: webmaster@seijoh-u.ac.jp
Website: http://www.seijoh-u.ac.jp/en/en_index.html

Faculties

Business Administration; **Rehabilitation and Care** (Occupational Therapy; Physical Therapy)

History: Founded 2002.

Degrees and Diplomas: *Gakushi*

Last Updated: 02/02/09

SEIKEI UNIVERSITY

Seikei Daigaku

3-3-1 Kichijoji-Kitamachi, Musashino-shi, Tokyo 180-8633
Tel: +81(422) 37-3533
Fax: +81(422) 37-3864
EMail: nyushi@jim.seikei.ac.jp
Website: http://www.seikei.ac.jp/university/

President: Yoichi Kamejima

Centres

Asian and Pacific Studies (Asian Studies; Pacific Area Studies)

Faculties

Economics (Business Administration; Economics; Management); **Humanities** (Arts and Humanities; Cultural Studies; English; European Languages; Japanese; Literature; Modern Languages; Oriental Languages; Social Sciences); **Law** (Law; Political Sciences); **Science and Technology** (Applied Physics; Electrical Engineering; Electronic Engineering; Engineering; Industrial Chemistry; Industrial Engineering; Information Sciences; Mechanical Engineering)

Graduate Schools

Business (Business and Commerce); **Economics** (Economics); **Engineering** (Applied Physics; Electrical and Electronic Engineering; Engineering; Industrial Chemistry; Information Sciences; Mechanical Engineering); **Humanities** (Arts and Humanities; Cultural Studies; English; European Languages; Japanese; Literature; Modern Languages; Oriental Languages; Social Sciences); **Law and Political Sciences** (Law; Political Sciences)

Schools

Law *(Graduate)*

Further Information: Also Centre for International Exchange

History: Founded 1949.

Governing Bodies: Board of Trustees; Faculty Meetings

Academic Year: April to March (April-September; October-March)

Admission Requirements: Graduation from high school, and entrance examination

Main Language(s) of Instruction: Japanese

International Co-operation: With universities in Australia, USA and United Kingdom

Degrees and Diplomas: *Gakushi*: Arts (Bungakushi); Economics (Keizaigakushi); Engineering (Kogakushi); Law (Hogakushi), 4 yrs; *Shushi*: a further 2 yrs; *Hakase*: 3 yrs following Shushi

Student Services: Academic counselling, Canteen, Cultural centre, Employment services, Foreign student adviser, Health services, Language programs, Social counselling, Sports facilities

Libraries: 773,000 vols

Publications: Bulletin of Seikei University; Journal of the Faculty of Economics; Proceedings of the Faculty of Engineering; Proceedings of the Faculty of Letters; The Seikei Japanese Literature; The Seikei Legal Sciences

Last Updated: 28/03/11

SEINAN GAKUIN UNIVERSITY

Seinan Gakuin Daigaku

6-2-92, Nishijin, Sawara-ku, Fukuoka-shi, Fukuoka 814-8511
Tel: +81(92) 823-3346
Fax: +81(92) 823-3334
EMail: intleduc@seinan-gu.ac.jp
Website: http://www.seinan-gu.ac.jp

Departments

Commerce (Business Administration; Business and Commerce); **Economics** (Economics; International Economics); **Human Sciences** (Education; Social Welfare); **Intercultural Studies** (Cultural Studies); **Law** (International Law; International Relations; Law; Political Sciences); **Literature** (Cultural Studies; English; French; International Studies; Literature; Modern Languages; Preschool Education); **Theology** (Christian Religious Studies; Theology)

Schools

Graduate (Business Administration; Cultural Studies; Economics; English; French; International Studies; Law; Literature)

Further Information: Also International Division (courses in English); Junior Year Study Abroad Programme

History: Founded 1916 by the Southern Baptist Missionaries as School, acquired present status 1949.

Governing Bodies: Board of Trustees

Academic Year: April to March (April-September; October-March)

Admission Requirements: Graduation from high school or equivalent, and entrance examination

Fees: (Yen): 720,000 per annum

Main Language(s) of Instruction: Japanese

Degrees and Diplomas: *Gakushi*: Arts (Bungakushi), 4 yrs; *Shushi*: Business Administration; Economics; Law; Letters, a further 2 yrs; *Hakase*: 3 yrs following Shushi

Student Services: Academic counselling, Canteen, Cultural centre, Employment services, Foreign student adviser, Health services, Nursery care, Social counselling, Sports facilities

Student Residential Facilities: For 130 students

Libraries: c. 720,000 vols; Theology, 60,000 vols

Publications: Academic Research Bulletin; Commercial Journal; Economic Journal; English Language and Literature; French Language and Literature; International Cultures; Law Journal; Studies in Theology; Study in Education and Welfare

Last Updated: 02/02/09

SEINAN JO GAKUIN UNIVERSITY

Seinan Jo Gakuin Daigaku

1-3-5 Ibori, Kokura-kita-ku, Kitakyushu-shi, Fukuoka 803-0835
Tel: +81(93) 583-5123
Fax: +81(93) 583-5614
EMail: nyusi@seinan-jo.ac.jp
Website: http://www.seinan-jo.ac.jp

Programmes

Health and Welfare (Social Welfare)

History: Founded 1994.

Degrees and Diplomas: *Gakushi*

SEIREI CHRISTOPHER UNIVERSITY

Seirei Kurisutofa Daigaku

3543 Mikatabara-cho, Hamamatsu-shi, Shizuoka 433-8558
Tel: +81(53) 439-1400
Fax: +81(53) 439-1406
EMail: cl-entrance@admin.seirei.ac.jp
Website: http://www.seirei.ac.jp

Schools

Nursing *(Undergraduate and graduate programmes)* (Midwifery; Nursing); **Rehabilitation Sciences** *(Undergraduate and graduate programmes)*; **Social Work** *(Undergraduate and graduate programmes)* (Social Work)

History: Founded 1992 as Seirei Kurisutofa Kango Daigaku (Seirei Christopher College of Nursing). Acquired present title 2006.

Degrees and Diplomas: *Gakushi*; *Shushi*; *Hakase*

Last Updated: 02/02/09

SEISA UNIVERSITY

Seisa Daigaku

5-14 Ryokusen-cho, Ashibetsu-shi, Hokkaido 075-0163
Tel: +81(120) 59-3104
EMail: info@seisa.ac.jp; kyomu@seisa.ac.jp
Website: http://www.seisa.ac.jp

President: Kaoru Yamaguchi

Faculties

Life Network Sciences *(Basic Introductory Courses)*

Programmes

Education *(Advanced Courses)*; **Environmental Studies** *(Advanced Courses)*; **International Relations** *(Advanced Courses)*

Degrees and Diplomas: *Gakushi*

SEISEN JOGAKUIN COLLEGE

Seisen Jogakuin Daigaku

2-120-8 Uwano, Nagano-shi, Nagano 381-0085
Tel: +81(26) 295-5665
Fax: +81(26) 295-6420
EMail: info@seisen-jc.ac.jp
Website: http://www.seisen-jc.ac.jp

Colleges

Early Childhood Education and International Communication *(Tandai)* (Business Administration; Communication Studies; Cultural Studies; Education; English; Information Sciences)

Faculties

Human Studies

History: Founded 2003.

Degrees and Diplomas: *Gakushi*

Student Services: Canteen, Sports facilities

Special Facilities: Music room; Marian Hall; Tea ceremony room; Chapel; Fine Arts room.

Libraries: Yes.

SEISEN UNIVERSITY

Seisen Joshi Daigaku

3-16-21 Higashi Gotanda, Shinagawa-ku, Tokyo 141-8642
Tel: +81(3) 3447-5551
Fax: +81(3) 3447-5493
EMail: nyushi@seisen-u.ac.jp
Website: http://www.seisen-u.ac.jp

Departments

Cultural History (Cultural Studies; History); **English Language and Literature** (English); **Global Citizenship Studies**; **Japanese Language and Literature** (Japanese); **Spanish Language and Literature** (Spanish); **Studies on Global Citizenship**

Graduate Schools

Humanities (Arts and Humanities; Cultural Studies; Linguistics; Literature; Modern Languages)

Research Institutes

Christian Culture; **Cultural Studies** (Cultural Studies); **Language Education** (English; Japanese; Spanish)

History: Founded 1950. A Catholic Liberal Arts Women's University.

Academic Year: April to March (April-September; October-March)

Admission Requirements: Graduation from high school and entrance examination

Main Language(s) of Instruction: Japanese

International Co-operation: With universities in United Kingdom, Spain, China, Taiwan, Phillipines, Canada, and USA

Accrediting Agencies: Ministry of Education, Culture, Sports, Science and Technology

Degrees and Diplomas: *Gakushi*: 4 yrs; *Shushi*: a further 2 yrs; *Hakase*

Student Services: Foreign Studies Centre, Sports facilities

Libraries: 280,000 vols

Publications: Bulletin of Seisen University; Bulletin of Seisen University Research Institute for Cultural Science; Journal of the Institute of Christian Culture Seisen University; Papers in Language, Thought and Culture Seisen University Graduate School; Sesen Bun-en

Last Updated: 02/02/09

SEITOKU UNIVERSITY

Seitoku Daigaku

550 Iwase, Matsudo-shi, Chiba 271-8555
Tel: +81(47) 365-1111
Fax: +81(47) 363-1401
EMail: kikaku@seitoku.ac.jp
Website: http://www.seitoku.jp

President: Hiroaki Kawanami

Administrative Director: Makoto Yoshida

International Relations: Hirozumi Kawanami, Vice-President

Faculties

Child Studies; **Humanities**; **Music** (Music; Music Theory and Composition; Musical Instruments; Musicology; Performing Arts)

Graduate Schools

Graduate Studies (American Studies; Child Care and Development; Cultural Studies; European Studies; Music; Music Theory and Composition; Nutrition; Psychology)

History: Founded 1990. Graduate School 1998.

Governing Bodies: Executive Board

Academic Year: April to March

Admission Requirements: Secondary school certificate and entrance examination

Fees: (Yen): 1,180,000-1,429,000 per annum

Main Language(s) of Instruction: Japanese

Accrediting Agencies: Japan University Accreditation Association

Degrees and Diplomas: *Gakushi*: Child Studies; Social Welfare; Psychology; Lifelong Education; Business Management; English Linguistics; Nutritional Science; Music, 4 yrs; *Shushi*: Child Studies;

Psychology; Japanese Culture; British and American Cultures; Music; Music Therapy; Nutritional Science; *Hakase*: Child Studies; Psychology; Japanese Culture; British and American Cultures; Music; Nutritional Science. Also Associate Degree (2 yrs)

Student Services: Canteen, Cultural centre, Employment services, Health services, Language programs, Sports facilities

Student Residential Facilities: Yes

Libraries: Kawanami Memorial Library, total, c. 380,000 vols

Publications: Bulletin of Seitoku University, Academic Articles *(annually)*; Bulletin of the Junior College Seitoku University, Academic Articles *(annually)*

Press or Publishing House: Seitoku Times 'Wa'

SEIWA COLLEGE

Seiwa Daigaku

7-54 Okadayama, Nishinomiya-shi, Hyogo 662-0827
Tel: +81(798) 52-0724
Fax: +81(798) 52-0974
EMail: nyushi@seiwa-u.ac.jp
Website: http://www.seiwa-u.ac.jp

Schools

Education (Child Care and Development; Education); **Humanities** (American Studies; Arts and Humanities; Christian Religious Studies; European Studies)

History: Founded 1880.

Governing Bodies: Board of Trustees

Academic Year: April to February (April-July; October-February)

Admission Requirements: Graduation from high school or equivalent, and entrance examination

Main Language(s) of Instruction: Japanese

International Co-operation: With universities in USA

Degrees and Diplomas: *Gakushi*: 4 yrs; *Shushi*: a further 2 yrs; *Hakase*: 2-3 yrs following Shushi

Student Services: Academic counselling, Canteen, Cultural centre, Employment services, Foreign student adviser, Handicapped facilities, Health services, Social counselling, Sports facilities

Student Residential Facilities: Yes

Libraries: 154,298 vols

Publications: Seiwa College Bulletin

SEIWA UNIVERSITY

Seiwa Daigaku

3-4-5 Higashiota, Kisarazu-shi, Chiba 292-8555
Tel: +81(438) 30-5555
Fax: +81(438) 30-5550
EMail: nyushi@seiwa-univ.ac.jp
Website: http://www.seiwa-univ.ac.jp

Faculties

Law

History: Founded 1994.

Degrees and Diplomas: *Gakushi*

Student Services: Sports facilities

Special Facilities: Multimedia PC room; Audio-visual room; Yukio Memorial Hall.

Libraries: c. 43,440 vols

Publications: Seiwa Bulletin; Seiwa Law Study

SENDAI SHIRAYURI WOMEN'S COLLEGE

Sendai Shirayuri Joshi Daigaku

6-1 Honda-cho, Izumi-ku, Sendai-shi, Miyagi 981-3107
Tel: +81(22) 372-3254
Fax: +81(22) 375-4343
EMail: nyushi@sendai-shirayuri.ac.jp
Website: http://www.sendai-shirayuri.ac.jp

Faculties

Human Sciences (Child Care and Development; Cultural Studies; Development Studies; Food Science; Health Sciences; International Studies; Nutrition; Social Sciences; Social Welfare)

History: Founded 1996.

Degrees and Diplomas: *Gakushi*

Last Updated: 02/02/09

SENDAI UNIVERSITY

Sendai Daigaku

2-2-18 Funaoka-Minami, Shibata-gun, Miyagi-Ken 989-1693
Tel: +81(224) 55-1121
Fax: +81(224) 57-2769
Website: http://www.scn.ac.jp

President: Masataka Mukai

Faculties

Health and Welfare (Health Sciences; Social Welfare); **Physical Education** (Physical Education); **Sports Nutrition** (Nutrition; Sports)

History: Founded 1967.

Degrees and Diplomas: *Gakushi*; *Shushi*

Student Services: Sports facilities

Libraries: 66,799 vols

SENRI KINRAN UNIVERSITY

Senri Kinran Daigaku

5-25-1 Fujisirodai, Suita-shi, Osaka 565-0873
Tel: +81(6) 6872-0639
Fax: +81(6) 6872-7724
EMail: int@kinran.ac.jp
Website: http://www.kinran.ac.jp

Departments

Information and Communication (Communication Studies; Information Sciences)

Faculties

Human Life Sciences (Biological and Life Sciences)

History: Founded 2003.

Degrees and Diplomas: *Gakushi*

SENSHU UNIVERSITY

Senshu Daigaku

3-8-1 Kandajimbo-cho, Chiyoda-ku, Tokyo 101-8425
Tel: +81(3) 3265-6821
Fax: +81(3) 3265-3649
Website: http://www.senshu-u.ac.jp

President: Yoshihiro Hidaka (2004-)
Tel: +81(44) 911-1252, Fax: +81(44) 900-7803
EMail: president@isc.senshu-u.ac.jp

Associate Chairman: Hideo Mishima
Tel: +81(3) 3265-6218, Fax: +81(3) 3265-7848

International Relations: Mamoru Obayashi, Dean
Tel: +81(44) 911-1250, Fax: +81(44) 911-1243
EMail: iaffairs@acc.senshu-u.ac.jp

Graduate Schools

Business Administration (Business Administration; Information Management) *Dean*: Michiharu Sakurai; **Commerce** (Accountancy; Business and Commerce) *Dean*: Shigemi Matsubara; **Economics** (Economics) *Dean*: Toshihiko Machida; **Humanities** (English; Geography; History; Japanese; Literature; Philosophy; Psychology; Sociology) *Dean*: Tanjiro Suzuki; **Law** *Dean*: Atsushi Furukawa

Schools

Business Administration (Business Administration) *Dean*: Katsuomi Uota; **Commerce** (Accountancy; Business and Commerce; Finance; Labour and Industrial Relations; Marketing) *Dean*: katsuaki Onishi; **Economics** (Economics; International Economics) *Dean*: Susumu Sakai; **Law** (Law) *Dean*: Buntoku Kohata; **Legal Affairs** *(Professional)* (Law) *Dean*: Yoshio Hidaka; **Literature** (English; Geography; Histology; Japanese; Literature; Philosophy; Psychology; Sociology) *Dean*: Toshio Araki; **Network and Information** *Dean*: Minoru Sakamoto

Further Information: Also 12 Research Institutes. Affiliated institutions: Ishinomaki Senshu University and Hokkaido College, Senshu University.

History: Founded 1880 as School, became Senshu Daigaku 1913, recognized as private University 1922. Reorganized 1949.

Governing Bodies: Board of Trustees; Board of Councilors

Academic Year: April to March (April-July; September-March)

Admission Requirements: Graduation from high school or foreign equivalent, and entrance examination

Fees: (Yen): Undergraduate 1,134,000-1,365,000 per annum, graduate, 839,000-1,422,000

Main Language(s) of Instruction: Japanese

International Co-operation: With universities in USA; China; United Kingdom; Republic of Korea; Vietnam; Mongolia; Ireland; Germany; France; Spain; New Zealand; Australia and Mexico.

Degrees and Diplomas: *Gakushi*: Business Administration; Commerce; Economics; Law; Letters, 4 yrs; *Shushi*: Business Administration; Commerce; Economics; Law; Letters, a further 2 yrs; *Hakase*: Business Administration; Commerce; Economics; Law; Letters, 3 yrs following Shushi; *Hakase*: Legal Affairs, 3-4 yrs following Gakushi

Student Services: Academic counselling, Canteen, Employment services, Foreign student adviser, Foreign Studies Centre, Handicapped facilities, Health services, Language programs, Nursery care, Social counselling, Sports facilities

Student Residential Facilities: Yes.

Libraries: 1,543,958 vols.

Publications: Annual Bulletin of Accounting Studies *(annually)*; Annual Bulletin of Social Science *(annually)*; Annual Bulletin of the Association of Natural Sciences *(annually)*; Annual Bulletin of the Humanities *(annually)*; Annual Bulletin of the Institute of Sports, Physical Education and Recreation *(annually)*; Business Review *(annually)*; Economics Bulletin *(annually)*; Journal of Law and Political Science *(annually)*; Studies in Humanities *(annually)*

Last Updated: 02/02/09

SENZOKU GAKUEN COLLEGE OF MUSIC

Senzoku Gakuen Ongaku Daigaku
2-3-1 Hisamoto, Takatsu-ku, Kawasaki-shi, Kanagawa 213-8580
Tel: +81(44) 856-2955
Fax: +81(44) 856-2968
Website: http://www.senzoku.ac.jp

Programmes

Advanced Sound Technology and Engineering (Sound Engineering (Acoustics)); **Choral Music** (Singing); **Conducting** (Conducting); **Music**; **Opera** (Opera)

History: Founded 1967.

Governing Bodies: Board of Directors

Academic Year: April to March (April-September; October-March)

Admission Requirements: Graduation from high school or foreign equivalent and entrance examination

Fees: (Yen): Registration, 3.52m.; tuition, 1,685,000 per annum

Main Language(s) of Instruction: Japanese

Degrees and Diplomas: *Gakushi*: 4 yrs; *Shushi*

Student Residential Facilities: Residential facilities for 70 students

Libraries: Fuzokutoshokan (Central Library), c. 153,000 vols

Publications: Senzoku ronso (Memoirs) *(annually)*

Last Updated: 02/02/09

SETSUNAN UNIVERSITY

Setsunan Daigaku
17-8 Ikedanaka-machi, Neyagawa-shi, Osaka 572-8508
Tel: +81(72) 839-9104
Fax: +81(72) 826-5100
EMail: nyushika@ofc.setsunan.ac.jp
Website: http://www.setsunan.ac.jp

President: Mitsunori Imai Tel: +81(72) 839-9100

Chairman of the Board: Masao Sakaguchi

Faculties

Business Administration and Information *(Also Graduate School)* (Business Administration; Information Sciences); **Engineering** *(Also Graduate School)* (Architecture; Civil Engineering; Electrical Engineering; Electronic Engineering; Engineering; Engineering Management; Environmental Engineering; Industrial Engineering; Mechanical Engineering; Structural Architecture; Systems Analysis); **Foreign Studies/International Languages and Cultures** *(Also Graduate School)* (Chinese; Cultural Studies; English; French; German; Indonesian; Modern Languages; Spanish); **Law** *(Also Graduate School)* (Law; Political Sciences); **Pharmaceutical Sciences** *(Also Graduate School)* (Environmental Studies; Health Sciences; Pharmacy)

Further Information: Also Studies programmes (American, Mexican, Indonesian, Chinese)

History: Founded 1922 as Kansai Technical Institution, acquired present status and title 1975.

Governing Bodies: Board of Trustees

Academic Year: April to March (April-September; October-March)

Admission Requirements: Graduation from high school or equivalent, and entrance examination

Fees: (Yen): Registration, 250,000 per annum; Pharmacy, 450,000 per annum; tuition, undergraduate, 960,000-1.74m. per annum; graduate, 870,000-1.01m. per annum

Main Language(s) of Instruction: Japanese

International Co-operation: With universities in USA, Mexico and China

Degrees and Diplomas: *Gakushi*: 4 yrs; *Shushi*: a further 2 yrs; *Hakase*: 3 yrs following Shushi

Student Services: Canteen, Employment services, Health services, Language programs, Social counselling, Sports facilities

Student Residential Facilities: Yes

Libraries: c. 580,000 vols

Publications: Journal of Business Administration and Information *(biannually)*; Setsunan Journal of Humanities and Social Sciences *(annually)*; Setsunan Law Journal *(biannually)*

Last Updated: 02/02/09

SHIBAURA INSTITUTE OF TECHNOLOGY

Shibaura Kogyo Daigaku
3-9-14 Shibaura, Minato-ku, Tokyo 108-8548
Tel: +81(3) 5476-3127
Fax: +81(3) 5476-2949
EMail: kokusai@ow.shibaura-it.ac.jp
Website: http://www.shibaura-it.ac.jp

President: Ayao Tsuge
Tel: +81(3) 5476-3137, Fax: +81(3) 5476-3175

Colleges

Engineering *Dean*: Tomohiko Kamimura; **Systems Engineering** *Dean*: Takashi Komeda

Graduate Schools

Engineering *Dean*: Masato Murakami; **Engineering Management** *Dean*: Takashi Watanabe

History: Founded 1927. Acquired present status 1949.

Governing Bodies: Board of Directors

Academic Year: April to January (April-July; September-January)

Admission Requirements: Graduation from high school and entrance examination

Fees: (Yen): Tuition, 899,000-990,000 per annum

Main Language(s) of Instruction: Japanese

Degrees and Diplomas: *Gakushi*: Engineering (Kogakushi), 4 yrs; *Shushi*: a further 2 yrs; *Hakase*: 3 yrs following Shushi

Student Services: Academic counselling, Canteen, Employment services, Foreign student adviser, Foreign Studies Centre, Handicapped facilities, Health services, Nursery care, Social counselling, Sports facilities

Libraries: c. 284,584 vols

Publications: Human Technology *(annually)*

Last Updated: 02/02/09

SHIGA UNIVERSITY

Shiga Daigaku

1-1-1 Banba, Hikone-shi, Shiga 522-8522
Tel: +81(749) 27-1172
Fax: +81(749) 27-1174
EMail: koho@biwako.shiga-u.ac.jp
Website: http://www.shiga-u.ac.jp

President: Takamitsu Sawa

Centres

Data Processing (Data Processing); **Education Research and Practice** *(Otsu-shi)* (Teacher Training); **Environmental Education and Lake Science** *(Otsu-shi)* (Environmental Studies; Limnology); **Joint Research** (Industrial Engineering); **Lifelong Learning Research** *(Otsu-shi)*

Faculties

Economics (Economics) *Dean*: Nakakazu Konishi; **Education** *(Otsu-shi)* (Education) *Dean*: Eiji Yoshikawa

Graduate Schools

Economics (Economics) *Dean*: Nakakazu Konishi; **Education** *(Otsu-shi)* (Education) *Dean*: Eiji Yoshikawa

Institutes

Economics and Business Research (Business and Commerce; Economics)

Research Centres

Sustainability and Environment

Further Information: Also Japanese courses for foreign students. Study abroad programmes

History: Faculty of Education Founded 1874 as Shiga Normal School. Faculty of Economics founded 1922 as Hikone Commercial College. Present status and title acquired 1949.

Academic Year: April to March (April-September; October-March)

Admission Requirements: Graduation from high school (Koto Gakko)

Fees: (Yen): Registration, 282,000; tuition, 496,800 per annum. Research, registration, 84,600; tuition, 27,600 per month

Main Language(s) of Instruction: Japanese

International Co-operation: With universities in China, USA, Thailand and Australia

Degrees and Diplomas: *Gakushi*: Economics (Keizaigakushi); Education (Kyoikugakushi), 4 yrs; *Shushi*: Economics (Keizaishushi); Education (Kyoikushushi), a further 1-2 yrs; *Hakase*: Economics; Education

Student Services: Academic counselling, Canteen, Cultural centre, Employment services, Foreign student adviser, Foreign Studies Centre, Handicapped facilities, Health services, Language programs, Social counselling, Sports facilities

Student Residential Facilities: Yes

Special Facilities: Archives Museum

Libraries: Central Library, Japanese and Chinese, 412,847 vols; Western Languages, 128,097 vols

Publications: Hikone Ronso, Economics *(biennially)*; Kenkyu-Nenpo, Annals of Human and Social Sciences *(annually)*; Kyoiku-Gakubu Kiyo, Memoirs of Faculty of Education *(annually)*; Shiga-Eibun-Gakkai-Ronbunshu, English Studies Journal *(biennially)*

Last Updated: 02/02/09

SHIGA UNIVERSITY OF MEDICAL SCIENCE

Shiga Ika Daigaku

Seta, Tsukinowa-cho, Otsu-shi, Shiga 520-2192
Tel: +81(77) 548-2111
Fax: +81(77) 543-8659
EMail: aiura@belle.shiga-med.ac.jp
Website: http://www.shiga-med.ac.jp

President: Tadao Bamba (2008-)
Tel: +81(77) 548-2000, Fax: +81(77) 548-2001
EMail: kikkawa@belle.shiga-med.ac.jp

Director, General Affairs: Shigeki Wakabayashi
Tel: +81(77) 548-2003

International Relations: Teruo Tokura, Head, Research Cooperation Division Tel: +81(77) 548-2013

Faculties

Medicine *(Also Graduate School)* (Anatomy; Anthropology; Behavioural Sciences; Biochemistry; Biology; Cell Biology; Chemistry; English; Forensic Medicine and Dentistry; Genetics; German; Health Sciences; Mathematics; Medicine; Microbiology; Molecular Biology; Neurosciences; Pathology; Pharmacology; Philosophy; Physics; Physiology; Social and Preventive Medicine; Sociology) *Dean*: Iwao Ohkubo; **Nursing** *Dean*: Kaoru Takigawa

History: Founded 1974. Graduate School established 1981.

Academic Year: April to March (April-September; October-March)

Admission Requirements: Graduation from high school and entrance examination

Fees: (Yen): 434,800

Main Language(s) of Instruction: Japanese

Degrees and Diplomas: *Gakushi*: Medicine (Igakushi), 6 yrs; *Gakushi*: Nursing, 4 yrs; *Shushi*: Nursing, a further 2 yrs; *Hakase*: Medicine (Igaku-Hakushi), a further 4 yrs

Student Services: Academic counselling, Canteen, Employment services, Foreign student adviser, Handicapped facilities, Health services, Language programs, Social counselling, Sports facilities

Student Residential Facilities: Yes

Libraries: Two libraries, total c. 593,000 vols

Publications: Bulletin of Shiga University of Medical Science *(annually)*

Press or Publishing House: Shiga University of Medical Science

Last Updated: 02/02/09

IAU SHIGAKKAN UNIVERSITY

Shigakkan Daigaku

55 Nakouyama, Yokone-machi, Obu-shi, Aichi 474-8651
Tel: +81(562) 46-1291
Fax: +81(562) 46-1313
EMail: m_gakuch@sgk.ac.jp
Website: http://www.sgk.ac.jp/

President: Kuniko Tanioka (1986-)
Tel: +81(562) 46-1293, Fax: +81(562) 46-1298
EMail: ktanioka@sgk.ac.jp

Secretary-General: Toshio Okada
Tel: +81(562) 46-1291, Fax: +81(562) 46-1298
EMail: t-okada@sgk.ac.jp

International Relations: Kenichi Yoshimoto
EMail: yoshiken@sgk.ac.jp

Departments

Child Education and Health (Child Care and Development); **Nutrition** (Nutrition); **Sport and Fitness** (Sports)

Faculties

Wellness (Health Education; Health Sciences; Sports)

History: Founded 1905 as Sewing School, known as Chukyo Joshi Daigaku (Chukyo Women's University) in 1963. Acquired current title and became co-educational 1 April 2010.

Governing Bodies: Gakkouhoujin Chukyo Joshidaigaku

Academic Year: April to March

Fees: (Yen): 1,159,000-1,213,000 per annum

Main Language(s) of Instruction: Japanese

Degrees and Diplomas: *Gakushi*: 4 yrs; *Shushi*: a further 2 yrs

Student Services: Academic counselling, Canteen, Employment services, Foreign student adviser, Health services, Language programs, Nursery care, Social counselling, Sports facilities

Student Residential Facilities: Yes

Libraries: 149,759 vols

Academic Staff *2008-2009*	**TOTAL**
FULL-TIME	**60**
PART-TIME	**111**
Student Numbers *2010-2011*	
All (Foreign Included)	**1,088**

Last Updated: 07/07/11

SHIGAKUKAN UNIVERSITY

Shigakukan Daigaku

1904 Uchi, Hayato-cho, Aira-gun, Kagoshima 899-5194
Tel: +81(995) 43-1111
Fax: +81(995) 43-1114
EMail: entrance@shigakukan.ac.jp
Website: http://www.shigakukan.ac.jp

Faculties

Humanities (Arts and Humanities; Clinical Psychology; Cultural Studies); **Law** (Law)

History: Founded 1979.

Degrees and Diplomas: *Gakushi*

Academic Staff *2007-2008*	**TOTAL**
FULL-TIME	**50**
PART-TIME	c. **70**
Student Numbers *2007-2008*	
All (Foreign Included)	c. **930**

Last Updated: 02/02/09

SHIKOKU GAKUIN UNIVERSITY

Shikoku Gakuin Daigaku

3-2-1 Bunkyo-cho, Zentsuji-shi, Kagawa 765-8505
Tel: +81(877) 62-2111
Fax: +81(877) 62-2225
EMail: ninobuyu@sg-u.ac.jp
Website: http://www.sg-u.ac.jp

Faculties

Arts and Humanities (Arts and Humanities; Education; English; European Languages; Modern Languages); **Social Sciences** (Social Welfare; Sociology)

History: Founded 1950 on the initiative of American Presbyterian missionaries as School, became Junior College 1959, acquired present status 1962.

Governing Bodies: Board of Trustees; College Council

Academic Year: April to March (April-September; October-February)

Admission Requirements: Graduation from high school and entrance examination

Main Language(s) of Instruction: Japanese

International Co-operation: With universities in USA, Republic of Korea and Philippines

Degrees and Diplomas: *Teaching Certificate*; *Gakushi*: Arts (Bungakushi), 4 yrs; *Shushi*: Arts in Social Welfare (Bungakushushi), a further 2 yrs

Student Services: Social counselling, Sports facilities

Student Residential Facilities: Yes

Libraries: c. 200,000 vols

Publications: Karashidane *(annually)*; Ronshu (Studies) *(annually)*

SHIKOKU UNIVERSITY

Shikoku Daigaku

123-1 Furukawa, Ojin-cho, Tokushima-shi, Tokushima 771-1192
Tel: +81(886) 665-1300
Fax: +81(886) 665-8037
EMail: oip@shikoku-u.ac.jp
Website: http://www.shikoku-u.ac.jp

President: Noboru Fukuoka

Chair: Ichiro Satoh

International Relations: Shigeyoshi Aoki
EMail: aokig@shikoku-u.ac.jp

Faculties

Human Life Sciences *Dean*: Yukio Yoshimura; **Literature** (Arts and Humanities; Cultural Studies; English; Japanese; Modern Languages) *Dean*: Hiroshi Shirai; **Management and Information Science** *Dean*: Yoshitane Shinohara

History: Founded 1925 as Tokusima School of Sewing. Gone through several processes and changes and became Shikoku University 2004.

Admission Requirements: High School diploma or equivalent; Japanese Language proficiency

Fees: (Yen): 1,002,420-1,148,230 per annum

Main Language(s) of Instruction: Japanese

Degrees and Diplomas: *Gakushi*: Literature; Management and Information Sciences; Human Life Science, 4 yrs; *Shushi*: Management and Information Sciences; *Hakase*: Management and Information Sciences

Student Services: Academic counselling, Canteen, Employment services, Foreign student adviser, Handicapped facilities, Health services, Nursery care, Social counselling, Sports facilities

Student Residential Facilities: 2 women's residences.

Special Facilities: Art gallery. Movie studio.

Libraries: 1 main library.

Publications: Bulletin of Shikoku University *(annually)*

Last Updated: 02/02/09

SHIMANE UNIVERSITY

Shimane Daigaku

1060 Nishikawatsu-cho, Matsue-shi, Shimane 690-8504
Tel: +81(852) 32-6106
Fax: +81(852) 32-6481
EMail: gak-ryugaku@jn.shimane-u.ac.jp
Website: http://www.shimane-u.ac.jp

President: Yuichi Honda

Faculties

Education (Art Education; Biological and Life Sciences; Cultural Studies; Education; Educational Psychology; Environmental Studies; Health Education; Mathematics Education; Music Education; Native Language Education; Physical Education; Primary Education; Psychology; Science Education; Social Studies); **Law and Literature** (Cultural Studies; Economics; Law; Literature; Native Language; Social Studies); **Life and Environmental Science** (Agriculture; Biological and Life Sciences; Biology; Biotechnology; Development Studies; Ecology; Environmental Studies; Forestry; Marine Biology; Regional Studies); **Medicine** (Medicine; Nursing); **Science and Engineering** *(Interdisciplinary)* (Automation and Control Engineering; Earth Sciences; Electronic Engineering; Engineering; Engineering Management; Materials Engineering; Mathematics and Computer Science; Natural Resources)

Graduate Schools

Education; **Law and Literature** (Arts and Humanities; Cultural Studies; Japanese; Law; Native Language; Social Sciences); **Life and Environmental Science**; **Medicine**; **Science and Engineering** (Automation and Control Engineering; Earth Sciences; Electronic Engineering; Engineering Management; Materials Engineering; Mathematics and Computer Science; Natural Resources)

Further Information: Also University farms and forests. Special programme for International Students in Science and Engineering

History: Founded as National University 1949, incorporating Matsue Higher School, Shimane Teachers' Training School, and Shimane Youth Normal School. Graduate School established 1971. Merged with Shimane Medical University (Shimane Ika Daigaku) 2003.

Governing Bodies: Hyogikai (University Council)

Academic Year: April to March (April-September; October-March)

Admission Requirements: Graduation from high school or recognized equivalent or foreign equivalent, and entrance examination

Main Language(s) of Instruction: Japanese

International Co-operation: With universities in China, USA and Republic of Korea

Degrees and Diplomas: *Gakushi*: Law and Economics; Socio-Cultural Studies; Language and Culture; Education; Medicine; Nursing; Science and Engineering; Life and Environmental Science, 4 yrs; *Shushi*: Law and Economics; Socio-Cultural Studies; Language and Culture; Education; Medicine; Nursing; Science and Engineering; Science; Engineering; Life and Environmental Science, a further 2 yrs; *Hakase*: Medicine; Science; Engineering; Law

Student Services: Academic counselling, Employment services, Foreign student adviser, Handicapped facilities, Health services, Social counselling, Sports facilities

Student Residential Facilities: Yes

Libraries: University Library, c. 873,000 vols

Publications: Bulletin of the Faculty of Agriculture; English Education and English Studies; Geological Reports of Shimane University; Journal of Early Childhood Education; Journal of Economics; Journal of Social Studies Education; Laguna; Literature; Literature and Social Science; Memoirs of the Faculty of Education (Educational Science); Memoirs of the Faculty of Law and Literature (Shimane Law Review); Memoirs of the Faculty of Science; Natural Sciences; Research for Educational Practice; Studies of the San'in Region

Last Updated: 02/02/09

SHIMONOSEKI CITY UNIVERSITY

Shimonoseki Shiritsu Daigaku

2-1-1 Daigaku-cho, Shimonoseki-shi, Yamaguchi 751-8510
Tel: +81(83) 252-0288
Fax: +81(83) 252-8099
EMail: international@shimonoseki-cu.ac.jp
Website: http://www.shimonoseki-cu.ac.jp

Programmes

Graduate (International Business); **Undergraduate** (Business and Commerce; International Business; Management)

History: Founded 1956. Acquired present status 1962.

Degrees and Diplomas: *Gakushi*; *Shushi*

Last Updated: 02/02/09

SHINSHU UNIVERSITY

Shinshu Daigaku

3-1-1 Asahi, Matsumoto-shi, Nagano 390-8621
Tel: +81(263) 35-4600
Fax: +81(263) 34-6481
EMail: kenkyou@jm.shinshu-u.ac.jp
Website: http://www.shinshu-u.ac.jp

President: Kiyohito Yamasawa Tel: +81(263) 37-2100

International Relations: Yutaka Karasawa
Tel: +81(263) 37-3482, Fax: +81(263) 37-3484
EMail: kyutaka@gipmc.shinshu-u.ac.jp

Centres

General Data Processing *(Nagano City)*; **General Education** (Education); **Health, Safety and Environmental Management** (Environmental Management; Health Sciences)

Faculties

Agriculture *(Also Graduate School)* (Agriculture; Biological and Life Sciences; Biotechnology; Food Science; Forestry); **Arts** *(Also Graduate School)* (Arts and Humanities; Communication Studies; Cultural Studies; Social Sciences); **Economics** (Economics; Law; Public Administration); **Education** *(Also Graduate School; Nagano City)* (Education; Educational and Student Counselling; Physical Education; Special Education; Teacher Training); **Engineering** *(Nagano City)* (Architecture; Chemical Engineering; Civil Engineering; Electrical and Electronic Engineering; Engineering; Environmental Studies; Information Technology; Materials Engineering; Mechanical Engineering; Technology); **Science** (Biology; Chemistry; Environmental Studies; Geology; Mathematics; Natural Sciences; Physics); **Textile Science and Technology** *(Also Graduate School; Ueda City)* (Biology; Machine Building; Materials Engineering; Mechanical Engineering; Polymer and Plastics Technology; Technology; Textile Technology)

Institutes

Mountain Studies (Mountain Studies)

Research Centres

Cooperative; **Educational Programmes** (Educational Research) *Director*: Yoshitaka Tamaki; **Genes** *(Ueda City)* (Genetics); **Inland Water Environment** (Environmental Studies; Water Science)

Schools

Allied Medical Sciences (Medical Technology; Nursing; Occupational Therapy; Physical Therapy); **Law** *(Graduate)* (Law); **Medicine** *(Also Graduate School)* (Medicine)

History: Founded 1949, incorporating previously existing regional Colleges and Institutes.

Governing Bodies: Board of Trustees

Academic Year: April to March (April-September; October-March)

Admission Requirements: Graduation from high school or recognized equivalent or foreign equivalent, and entrance examination

Fees: (Yen): Registration, 282,000; tuition, 520,800 per annum

Main Language(s) of Instruction: Japanese

International Co-operation: With universities in China, Republic of Korea, Thailand, USA, United Kingdom, India, Indonesia, Australia, Poland, France, Germany and Belgium

Degrees and Diplomas: *Gakushi*: Bungakushi, Arts; Keizaigakushi, Economics; Kyoikugakushi, Education; Rigakushi, Science; Nogakushi, Agriculture; Kogakushi, Engineering, 4 yrs; *Gakushi*: Medicine, 6 yrs; *Shushi*: Bungakushushi, Arts; Nogakushushi, Agriculture; Kogakushushi, Engineering; Keizaigakushi, Economics; Kyoikugakushi, Education; Rigakushi, Science, a further 2 yrs; *Hakase*: Medical Sciences, a further 4 yrs; *Hakase*: Nogakushushi, Agriculture; Gakujutsuhakushi, Philosophy, a further 3 yrs following Shushi

Student Services: Academic counselling, Canteen, Employment services, Foreign student adviser, Foreign Studies Centre, Handicapped facilities, Health services, Language programs, Social counselling, Sports facilities

Student Residential Facilities: Matsumoto and Nagano International Houses

Libraries: Main library, 773,682 vols in Japanese, 367,099 in foreign languages; 5 branch Libraries

Last Updated: 02/02/09

SHIRAYURI COLLEGE

Shirayuri Joshi Daigaku

1-25 Midorigaoka, Chofu-shi, Tokyo 182-8525
Tel: +81(3) 3326-5050
Fax: +81(3) 3326-4550
EMail: nyuko@shirayuri.ac.jp
Website: http://www.shirayuri.ac.jp

Departments

Child Studies *(Also Graduate School)* (Arts and Humanities; Child Care and Development; Clinical Psychology; Developmental Psychology; Literature; Social Sciences); **English Language and Literature** *(Also Graduate School)* (English; Literature); **French Language and Literature** *(Also Graduate School)* (French; Literature); **Japanese Language and Literature** *(Also Graduate School)* (Japanese; Literature)

Graduate Departments

Language and Literature

Further Information: Also Special Unit, Developmental Psychology Clinical Centre

History: Founded 1898 as School, acquired present status and title 1965.

Governing Bodies: Board of Trustees

Academic Year: April to March (April-September; October-March)

Admission Requirements: Graduation from senior high school, or recognized foreign equivalent, and entrance examination

Main Language(s) of Instruction: Japanese

International Co-operation: With universities in USA, France and United Kingdom

Accrediting Agencies: Japanese University Accreditation Association

Degrees and Diplomas: *Gakushi*: 4 yrs; *Shushi*: a further 2 yrs; *Hakase*: 3 yrs following Shushi

Student Services: Academic counselling, Canteen, Cultural centre, Employment services, Foreign student adviser, Health services, Social counselling, Sports facilities

Student Residential Facilities: For c. 70 students

Libraries: Shirayuri Joshi Daigaku Toshokan (Shirayuri College Library), 210,000 vols

Publications: Kannazuki (Japanese Language and Literature) *(annually)*; Korobokkuru (Child Development and Juvenile Culture) *(annually)*; Lilia Candia (French Language and Literature) *(annually)*; Sella (English Language and Literature) *(annually)*; Shirayuri Jido Bunka (Juvenile Culture and Literature) *(annually)*

Last Updated: 02/02/09

SHITENNOJI UNIVERSITY

Shitennoji Daigaku

3-2-1 Gakuenmae, Habikino-shi, Osaka-shi, Osaka 583-8501

Tel: +81(72) 956-3181

Fax: +81(72) 956-6011

EMail: info@shitennoji.ac.jp

Website: http://www.shitennoji.ac.jp/ibu/index.html

Divisions

Junior College (Child Care and Development; Education; English; Health Sciences; Home Economics)

Graduate Schools

Human Sociology (Arts and Humanities; Social Welfare)

Schools

Humanities and Social Sciences (Arabic; Arts and Humanities; Asian Religious Studies; Education; English; Japanese; Social Welfare; Sociology)

History: Founded 1967 as Shitennoji Joshi Daigaku/Shitennoji Women's University. Renamed Shitennoji Kokusai Bukkyo Daigaku/ International Buddhist University 1981. Acquired present title 2008.

Academic Year: Two semesters from April to March or September to August.

International Co-operation: With universities in Germany, England, Taiwan, China, USA, Australia, Tunisia, Canada, New Zealand, France.

Degrees and Diplomas: *Gakushi*; *Shushi*; *Hakase*

Student Services: Sports facilities

Special Facilities: Computer Lab; Audio-visual Room

Libraries: c. 170,000 vols

SHIZUOKA EIWA GAKUIN UNIVERSITY

Shizuoka Eiwa Gakuin Daigaku

1769 Ikeda, Shizuoka-shi, Shizuoka 422-8545

Tel: +81(54) 261-9201

Fax: +81(54) 263-4763

EMail: info@shizuoka-eiwa.ac.jp

Website: http://www.shizuoka-eiwa.ac.jp

Departments

Community and Social Welfare (Social and Community Services; Social Welfare); **Contemporary Communications and Food Science**; **Humanities and Social Sciences**

History: Founded 2002.

Degrees and Diplomas: *Gakushi*

Last Updated: 02/02/09

SHIZUOKA INSTITUTE OF SCIENCE AND TECHNOLOGY

Shizuoka Rikoka Daigaku

2200-2 Toyosawa, Fukuroi-shi, Shizuoka 437-8555

Tel: +81(538) 45-0111

Fax: +81(583) 45-0110

EMail: kouhou@ob.sist.ac.jp

Website: http://www.sist.ac.jp

Faculties

Comprehensive Informatics (Artificial Intelligence; Computer Engineering; Computer Networks; Software Engineering); **Science and Technology** (Aeronautical and Aerospace Engineering; Automotive Engineering; Biochemistry; Biological and Life Sciences; Biology; Electrical and Electronic Engineering; Engineering; Information Technology; Materials Engineering; Mechanical Engineering; Microbiology; Molecular Biology; Natural Sciences)

Graduate Schools

Graduate Studies (Engineering; Management)

History: Founded 1991.

Degrees and Diplomas: *Gakushi*; *Shushi*

Last Updated: 03/02/09

SHIZUOKA SANGYO UNIVERSITY

Shizuoka Sangyo Daigaku

1572-1 Owara-machi, Iwata-shi, Shizuoka 438-0043

Tel: +81(538) 370-191

Fax: +81(538) 368-809

Website: http://www.ssu.ac.jp

President: Mayumi Otsubo

Colleges

Business Administration (Administration; Business Administration); **Information Science and Technology** (Information Sciences; Information Technology)

History: Founded 1994.

Degrees and Diplomas: *Gakushi*

Last Updated: 03/02/09

SHIZUOKA UNIVERSITY

Shizuoka Daigaku

836 Ohya, Suruga-ku, Shizuoka-shi, Shizuoka 422-8529

Tel: +81(54) 238-4996

Fax: +81(54) 238-5041

EMail: koho@gene1.adb.shizuoka.ac.jp

Website: http://www.shizuoka.ac.jp

President: Oki Naotaka (2007-)

Faculties

Agriculture (Agriculture; Applied Chemistry; Biochemistry; Biological and Life Sciences; Environmental Engineering; Forest Products; Forestry); **Education** (Art Education; Continuing Education; Education; Education of the Handicapped; Science Education; Teacher Trainers Education; Teacher Training); **Engineering** (Chemical Engineering; Computer Engineering; Electrical and Electronic Engineering; Engineering; Materials Engineering; Mechanical Engineering); **Humanities and Social Sciences** (Arts and Humanities; Economics; Law; Literature; Modern Languages; Social Sciences; Sociology); **Informatics** (Computer Science; Information Sciences); **Science** (Biology; Chemistry; Earth Sciences; Geology; Mathematics; Physics)

Graduate Schools

Agricultural Sciences, Doctoral course *(United Graduate School, Gifu University)*; **Agriculture, Master's course** (Agriculture; Applied Chemistry; Biological and Life Sciences; Biology; Environmental Studies; Forest Products; Forestry; Veterinary Science); **Education, Master's course** (Art Education; Education; English; Health Education; Home Economics; Japanese; Mathematics Education; Music Education; Physical Education; Science Education; Secondary Education; Social Studies; Technology); **Engineering, Master's course** (Business Administration; Computer Engineering; Electrical and Electronic Engineering; Engineering; Materials Engineering; Mechanical Engineering); **Humanities and Social Sciences, Master's course** (Anthropology; Arts and Humanities; Economics; Linguistics; Literature; Psychology; Social Sciences; Sociology); **Informatics, Master's course** (Information Sciences); **Law** *(Shizuoka Law School; Professional Degree course)* (Law); **Science and Technology, Educational Division, Doctoral course** (Bioengineering; Electronic Engineering; Energy Engineering; Environmental Engineering; Information Sciences; Information Technology; Nanotechnology); **Science, Master's course**

Further Information: Also Hamamatsu Campus. Japanese language courses for foreign students

History: Founded 1949.

International Co-operation: With universities in Australia; Canada; China; France; Germany; Hungary; Republic of Korea; Poland; Russian Federation; Slovak Republic; Sweden; Thailand and USA

Degrees and Diplomas: *Gakushi*: Agriculture; Arts; Economics; Education; Engineering; Informatics; Law; Science; Sociology; *Shushi*: Agriculture; Arts; Clinical Human Sciences; Economics; Education; Engineering; Informatics; Law; Science; *Hakase*: Agriculture; Engineering; Informatics; Science (PhD)

Student Services: Academic counselling, Health services, Language programs, Social counselling, Sports facilities

Student Residential Facilities: Dormitories; Katayama-Ryo, Yuhou-Ryo (Shizuoka), Ataksuki-Ryo (Hamamatsu), Shizuoka and Hamamatsu Internationa l Residence

Libraries: 1,154,102 vols

Last Updated: 02/02/09

SHIZUOKA UNIVERSITY OF ARTS AND CULTURE

Shizuoka Bunka Geijutsu Daigaku (SUAC)

1794-1 Noguchicho, Hamamatsu-shi, Shizuoka 430-8533
Tel: +81(53) 457-6111 +81(53) 457-6113
Fax: +81(53) 457-6123
EMail: kikaku@suac.ac.jp
Website: http://www.suac.ac.jp

Head: Kenichi Fujita

Faculties

Cultural Policy and Management *(Also Graduate School)* (Art Management; Cultural Studies; International Studies; Regional Studies); **Design** *(Also Graduate School)* (Architectural and Environmental Design; Fine Arts; Industrial Design)

History: Founded 2000.

Degrees and Diplomas: *Gakushi*; *Shushi*

Last Updated: 02/02/09

SHIZUOKA UNIVERSITY OF WELFARE

Shizuoka Fukushi Daigaku

549-1 Honnakane, Yaizu-shi, Shizuoka 425-8611
Tel: +81(54) 623-7000
Fax: +81(54) 623-7453
EMail: siryo@suw.ac.jp
Website: http://www.suw.ac.jp

Programmes

Social Welfare

History: Founded 1992.

Degrees and Diplomas: *Gakushi*

SHOBI UNIVERSITY

Shobi Gakuen Daigaku

1373 Toyodahon, Kawagoe, Saitama-shi, Saitama 350-1118
Tel: +81(492) 46-2700
Fax: +81(492) 46-2531
EMail: j-info@shobi-u.ac.jp; iec@shobi-u.ac.jp
Website: http://www.shobi-u.ac.jp

Faculties

Multimedia and Arts; **Policy Management**

Further Information: Also campuses in Kawagoe and Saitama.

History: Founded 2000.

Degrees and Diplomas: *Gakushi*: Music; Policy Studies; *Shushi*: Musical Arts; Policy and Administration

Student Services: Cultural centre, Sports facilities

Student Residential Facilities: Dormitories in Saitama and Tokyo areas.

Libraries: 2 libraries, c. 114,000 vols.

Last Updated: 03/02/09

SHOIN UNIVERSITY

Shoin Daigaku

9-1 Morinosatowakamiya, Atsugi-shi, Kanagawa 243-0124
Tel: +81(46) 247-1511
Fax: +81(46) 247-4234
EMail: webmaster@shoin-u.ac.jp
Website: http://www.shoin-u.ac.jp

Departments

Business Management; **Cross-cultural Communication** (Communication Studies)

Faculties

Business Administration and Culture

Institutes

Business Administration and Culture; **Information and Administration**

History: Founded 2000 as Shoin Joshi Daigaku (Shoin Women's University). Acquired present title 2004.

Degrees and Diplomas: *Gakushi*

Last Updated: 03/02/09

SHOKEI COLLEGE

Shokei Daigaku

2155-7 Nirenoki, Shimizu-machi, Kumamoto-shi, Kumamoto 860-8538
Tel: +81(96) 338-8840
Fax: +81(96) 338-9301
EMail: dnyutshi@shokei-gakuen.ac.jp
Website:http: //www.shokei-gakuen.ac.jp/shokeicol/

Programmes

Arts and Humanities (Arts and Humanities; English; Japanese)

History: Founded 1975.

Degrees and Diplomas: *Gakushi*

Last Updated: 03/02/09

SHOKEI GAKUIN COLLEGE

Shokei Gakuin Daigaku

4-10-1 Yurigaoka, Natori-shi, Miyagi 981-1295
Tel: +81(22) 383-0111 +81(22) 381-3333
Fax: +81(22) 383-0130 +81(22) 381-3335
EMail: kikaku@shokei.ac.jp
Website: http://ap.shokei.jp/

Executive-Director: Masana Kato

Faculties

Comprehensive Human Sciences *(Also Graduate School)* (Arts and Humanities)

History: Founded 2003.

Degrees and Diplomas: *Gakushi*

Last Updated: 03/02/09

SHONAN INSTITUTE OF TECHNOLOGY

Shonan Koka Daigaku

1-1-25 Tsujidonishikaigan, Fujisawa-shi, Kanagawa 251-8511
Tel: +81(466) 34-4021 +81(466) 30-0200
Fax: +81(466) 34-4022
EMail: nyushika@center.shonan-it.ac.jp
Website: http://www.shonan-it.ac.jp

President: Toshio Tanimoto

Faculties

Engineering (Computer Science; Electrical Engineering; Engineering; Industrial Design; Information Sciences; Materials Engineering; Mechanical Engineering)

Schools

Graduate Studies (Electrical Engineering; Information Technology; Materials Engineering; Mechanical Engineering)

History: Founded 1963.

Main Language(s) of Instruction: Japanese

International Co-operation: With universities in USA, Germany and Australia

Degrees and Diplomas: *Gakushi*; *Shushi*; *Hakase*

Student Services: Employment services, Health services, Social counselling, Sports facilities

Libraries: c. 135,000 vols
Last Updated: 03/02/09

SHOWA ACADEMIA MUSICAE

Showa Ongaku Daigaku

1-11-1 Kamiasao Asao-ku, Kawasaki-shi, Kanagawa 215-8558
Tel: +81(44) 953-1121
Fax: +81(44) 953-1311
EMail: info@tosei-showa-music.ac.jp
Website: http://www.tosei-showa-music.ac.jp

Faculties
Music (Art Management; Music; Music Theory and Composition; Musical Instruments; Singing)

History: Founded 1984.

Degrees and Diplomas: *Gakushi*; *Shushi*
Last Updated: 03/02/09

SHOWA PHARMACEUTICAL UNIVERSITY

Showa Yakka Daigaku (SPU)

3-3165 Higashitamagawagakuen, Machida-shi, Tokyo 194-8543
Tel: +81(42) 721-1511
Fax: +81(42) 721-1588
EMail: webmaster@shoyaku.ac.jp
Website: http://www.shoyaku.ac.jp

Faculties
Pharmaceutical Sciences *(Also Graduate School)* (Organic Chemistry; Pharmacology; Pharmacy)

History: Founded 1930 as Showa Women's Senmon Gakko of Pharmacy, acquired present status 1950.

Main Language(s) of Instruction: Japanese

Degrees and Diplomas: *Gakushi*; *Shushi*; *Hakase*

Student Services: Sports facilities

Libraries: 130,000 vols
Last Updated: 03/02/09

SHOWA UNIVERSITY

Showa Daigaku

1-5-8 Hatanodai, Shinagawa-ku, Tokyo 142-8555
Tel: +81(3) 3784-8000
Fax: +81(3) 3784-8012
EMail: homepage@ic.showa-u.ac.jp
Website: http://www.showa-u.ac.jp

Colleges
Medical Radiology; **Nursing**

Graduate Schools
Graduate Studies (Dentistry; Medicine; Pharmacy)

Research Institutes
Molecular Oncology

Schools
Dentistry (Dentistry); **Medicine** (Medicine; Pathology; Physiology; Social and Preventive Medicine; Surgery); **Nursing and Rehabilitation Sciences** (Nursing; Occupational Therapy; Physical Therapy; Rehabilitation and Therapy); **Pharmaceutical Sciences**

History: Founded 1928 as Medical College, became full Medical School 1952 and acquired present status 1964.

Academic Year: April to March (April-October; October-March)

Admission Requirements: Graduation from high school and entrance examination

Main Language(s) of Instruction: Japanese

Degrees and Diplomas: *Gakushi*: Medicine, 6 yrs; *Gakushi*: Pharmaceutical Sciences (Yakugakushi), 4 yrs; *Hakase*: Medicine, a further 4 yrs

Student Services: Sports facilities

Libraries: 260,595 vols

Publications: Journal of the Showa Medical Association
Last Updated: 03/02/09

SHOWA WOMEN'S UNIVERSITY

Showa Joshi Daigaku (SWU)

1-7 Taishido, Setagaya-ku, Tokyo 154-8533
Tel: +81(3) 3411-5111
Fax: +81(3) 3411-5171
EMail: ico@swu.ac.jp
Website: http://www.swu.ac.jp

President: Mariko Bando

Faculties
Human and Social Sciences (Architectural and Environmental Design; Clinical Psychology; Economics; Education; Educational Psychology; Environmental Studies; Industrial and Organizational Psychology; Literature; Media Studies; Political Sciences; Primary Education; Psychology; Social Psychology; Social Welfare; Social Work; Sociology); **Human Life and Environmental Sciences** (Architectural and Environmental Design; Architecture; Design; Ecology; Food Science; Nutrition)

Graduate Schools
Human Life Sciences (Architectural and Environmental Design; Cultural Studies; Psychology; Social Sciences; Social Welfare); **Letters** (American Studies; English; European Languages; Japanese; Literature; Modern Languages; Oriental Languages)

Research Institutes
International Culture (Cultural Studies; International Studies); **Modern Culture** (Cultural Studies); **Psychological Studies** (Psychology); **Women's Culture** (Cultural Studies; Women's Studies)

Schools
Human Life Sciences (Communication Studies; Cultural Studies; English; History; Japanese; Literature)

Further Information: Also Showa Boston Study Abroad programmes and Showa Boston Summer Session programmes

History: Founded 1920 as College, acquired present status 1949.

Academic Year: April to March (April-July; October-March)

Admission Requirements: Graduation from high school and entrance examination

Fees: (Yen): 1.45m.-1.56m. per annum

Main Language(s) of Instruction: Japanese

International Co-operation: With universities in Australia, Republic of Korea, China, Vietnam, Cambodia and USA

Degrees and Diplomas: *Gakushi*: 4 yrs; *Shushi*: a further 1-2 yrs; *Hakase*: 3 yrs following Shushi

Student Services: Academic counselling, Canteen, Employment services, Health services, Sports facilities

Student Residential Facilities: For 800 students

Special Facilities: Koyo Museum. Hitomi Memorial Hall

Libraries: c. 327,000 vols, 12,300 periodicals

Publications: Gakuen *(monthly)*; Josei Bunka Kenkyujo Kiyo, Women's Culture *(biannually)*; Kokusai Bunka Kenkyujo Kiyo, International Culture *(annually)*; Seikatsu Shinri Kenkyujo Kiyo, Practical Psychology *(annually)*
Last Updated: 03/02/09

SHUCHIIN UNIVERSITY

Shuchiin Daigaku

70 Nishi-jouuke, Mukaijima, Fushimi-ku, Kyoto 612-8156
Tel: +81(75) 604-5600
Fax: +81(75) 604-5610
EMail: office@shuchiin.ac.jp
Website: http://www.shuchiin.ac.jp

Programmes
Buddhism (Asian Religious Studies; Social Welfare)

Degrees and Diplomas: *Gakushi*
Last Updated: 03/02/09

SHUJITSU UNIVERSITY

Shujitsu Daigaku

1-6-1 Nishigawara, Okayama-shi, Okayama 703-8516
Tel: +81(86) 271-8111
Fax: +81(86) 271-8222
EMail: i-center@shujitsu.ac.jp
Website:http: //www.shujitsu.ac.jp

Faculties

Humanities (Arts and Humanities; English; History; Japanese; Literature)

Schools

Pharmacy (Pharmacy)

History: Founded 1979 as Shujitsu Joshi Daigaku (Shujitsu Women's University). Acquired present title 2003.

Main Language(s) of Instruction: Japanese

International Co-operation: With universities in China, UK, Australia

Degrees and Diplomas: *Gakushi*; *Shushi*

SHUKUTOKU UNIVERSITY

Shukutoku Daigaku

200 Daiganji-cho, Chuo-ku, Chiba-shi, Chiba 260-8701
Tel: +81(43) 265-7331
Fax: +81(43) 265-8310
EMail: aochiba@soc.shukutoku.ac.jp
Website: http://www.shukutoku.ac.jp

Colleges

Cross-Cultural Communication and Business (Business Administration; Communication Studies; Cultural Studies); **Sociology** (Social Welfare; Sociology)

Graduate Schools

Social Welfare (Social Welfare)

Institutes

Social Welfare Studies (Social Welfare)

Further Information: Also Study Abroad programmes. Intensive Language Training and Intensive English Training programmes

History: Founded 1965 by Rev. Yoshinobo Hasegawa. A second campus in Saitama added 1996.

Governing Bodies: Board of Directors; Board of Councillors

Academic Year: April to February (April-July; September-February)

Main Language(s) of Instruction: Japanese

Degrees and Diplomas: *Gakushi*: 4 yrs; *Shushi*: a further 2 yrs; *Hakase*: at least 3 yrs following Shushi

Student Services: Academic counselling, Canteen, Cultural centre, Employment services, Foreign student adviser, Handicapped facilities, Health services, Social counselling, Sports facilities

Student Residential Facilities: For c. 60 women students

Libraries: 242,700 vols

Publications: Annual Research Report *(3 per annum)*; Bulletin *(annually)*; Clinical Studies *(annually)*; Cross-Cultural Business and Cultural Studies *(biannually)*; Graduate School Bulletin *(annually)*

SHUMEI UNIVERSITY

Shumei Daigaku

1-1 Daigaku-cho, Yachiyo-shi, Chiba 276
Tel: +81(47) 488-2111
Fax: +81(47) 488-8290
Website: http://www.shumei-u.ac.jp

Programmes

International Economics and Political Sciences (International Economics; Political Sciences); **International Relations**

History: Founded 1988 as Yachiyo Kokusai Daigaku (Yachiyo International University).

Degrees and Diplomas: *Gakushi*

Libraries: 80,000 vols

Last Updated: 03/02/09

SOAI UNIVERSITY

Soai Daigaku

4-4-1 Nanko-Naka, Suminoe-ku, Osaka-shi, Osaka 559-0033
Tel: +81(6) 6612-5900
Fax: +81(6) 6612-2993
Website: http://www.soai.ac.jp

Faculties

Human Development (Development Studies; Social Sciences); **Humanities**; **Music** (Music)

Degrees and Diplomas: *Gakushi*. Also one year postgraduate programme in Music

Last Updated: 03/02/09

SOJO UNIVERSITY

Sojo Daigaku

4-22-1 Ikeda, Kumamoto-shi, Kumamoto 860
Tel: +81(96) 326-3111
Fax: +81(96) 326-3000
Website: http://www.sojo-u.ac.jp

Faculties

Art; **Biotechnology and Life Sciences** (Biological and Life Sciences; Biotechnology; Microbiology); **Computer and Information Sciences**; **Engineering**; **Pharmaceutical Sciences** (Applied Chemistry; Biochemistry; Biophysics; Microbiology; Oncology; Organic Chemistry; Pharmacology; Pharmacy)

History: Founded 1965 as Junior College, became Kumamoto Institute of Technology recognized by the Government 1967. Graduate School established 1982. Acquired present title 2000.

Governing Bodies: Board of Directors; Senate

Academic Year: April to March (April-September; October-March)

Admission Requirements: Graduation from high school and entrance examination

Main Language(s) of Instruction: Japanese

Degrees and Diplomas: *Gakushi*: 4 yrs; *Shushi*: a further 2 yrs; *Hakase*: 3 yrs following Shushi. Also Teaching Diplomas

Libraries: c. 140,000 vols

Publications: Bulletin

Last Updated: 03/02/09

SOKA UNIVERSITY

Soka Daigaku

1-236 Tangi-cho Hachioji, Tokyo 192-0003
Tel: +81(42) 691-8200
Fax: +81(42) 691-2039
EMail: intloff@soka.ac.jp
Website: http://www.soka.ac.jp

President: Hideo Yamamoto (2007-)
Tel: +81(42) 691-9481, Fax: +81(42) 691-9847

Centres

World Languages

Faculties

Business Administration (Business Administration); **Economics** (Economics); **Education** (Education; Primary Education); **Engineering** (Bioengineering; Engineering; Environmental Engineering; Information Sciences); **Law** (Law); **Letters** (Arts and Humanities)

Graduate Schools

Economics (Business Administration; Economics); **Engineering** (Bioengineering; Engineering; Environmental Engineering); **Law** (Law); **Letters** (Arts and Humanities; Education; English; Sociology)

Programmes

Intensive Japanese Studies (Japanese)

Research Institutes

Comparative Study of Cultures; **Education on Ultimate Facts in Law Schools**; **International Research for Advanced Buddhology** (Asian Religious Studies); **Japanese Language** (Japanese); **Life Sciences** (Biological and Life Sciences); **Peace Research Studies** (Peace and Disarmament); **Soka Education Research** (Educational Research)

History: Founded 1971. Graduate Schools established 1975.

Governing Bodies: Soka University Corporation; Board of Trustees

Academic Year: April to March (April-July; September-March)

Admission Requirements: Graduation from high school or equivalent or foreign equivalent, and entrance examination

Main Language(s) of Instruction: Japanese, English

Degrees and Diplomas: *Teaching Certificate*; *Gakushi*: Business Administration; Economics; Education; Engineering; Law; Letters, 4 yrs; *Shushi*: Economics; Law; Letters, a further 2 yrs; *Hakase*: 3 yrs following Shushi

Student Residential Facilities: For c. 1,000 students

Libraries: Central Library, 870,000 vols

Publications: Bulletin of the Educational Society *(quarterly)*; Journal of Business Administration *(quarterly)*; Sociologica *(quarterly)*; Soka Economic Studies *(quarterly)*; Soka Law Journal *(quarterly)*; Studies in English Language and Literature *(quarterly)*

Last Updated: 03/02/09

SONODA WOMEN'S UNIVERSITY

Sonoda Gakuen Joshi Daigaku

7-29-1 Minami-Tsukaguchi-cho, Amagasaki-shi, Hyogo 661-8521
Tel: +81(06) 6429-1291
Fax: +81(06) 6429-1326
EMail: iec@sonoda-u.ac.jp
Website: http://www.sonoda-u.ac.jp

Programmes

Cross-Cultural Studies

History: Founded 1966.

Degrees and Diplomas: *Gakushi*

Last Updated: 03/02/09

SOPHIA UNIVERSITY

Jochi Daigaku

7-1 Kioicho, Chiyoda-ku, Tokyo 102-8554
Tel: +81(3) 3238-4018
Fax: +81(3) 3238-3262
Website: http://www.sophia.ac.jp/eng/e_top

President: Tadashi Takizawa (2011-)
Tel: +81(3) 3238-3131, Fax: +81(3) 3238-3137
EMail: mayo_okano@cl.sophia.ac.jp

International Relations: Angela Yiu, Vice-President for Academic Exchange Tel: +81(3) 3238-3521, Fax: +81(3) 3238-3554

Faculties

Economics (Business Administration; Economics) *Dean*: Tetsuo Sugimoto; **Foreign Studies** (Cultural Studies; International Studies; Linguistics; Modern Languages) *Dean*: Kensaku Yoshida; **Human Sciences** *Dean*: Misako Ogino; **Humanities** (Arts and Humanities; History; Journalism; Philosophy) *Dean*: Akira Oshima; **Law** (Law) *Dean*: Nobuyuki Tsuji; **Liberal Arts** (Arts and Humanities; Business Administration; Cultural Studies; Social Sciences) *Dean*: Richard Gardner; **Science and Technology** (Chemistry; Communication Studies; Engineering; Information Sciences; Mathematics; Physics) *Dean*: Toru Tamiya; **Theology** (Theology) *Dean*: Tsutomu Sakuma

Institutes

American and Canadian Studies (American Studies; Canadian Studies) *Director*: Tomoyuki Ino; **Asian Cultures** (Asian Studies) *Director*: Masatoshi Kisaichi; **Christian Culture** (Asian Religious Studies; Christian Religious Studies) *Director*: Koji Matsuoka; **Comparative Culture** (Cultural Studies) *Director*: James Farrer; **European Cultural Studies** (European Studies) *Director*: Masaharu Nakamura; **Global Environmental Studies** *Director*: Hiroshi Kito; **Ibero-American Studies** (Latin American Studies) *Director*: Kotaro Horisaka; **Linguistic Institute for International Communication** (Communication Studies; International Studies; Linguistics) *Director*: Kensaku Yoshida; **Medieval Thought** (Medieval Studies) *Director*: Naoko Sato; **Social Justice Studies** (Social Problems) *Director*: Tsutomu Kanayama

Research Centres

Nanotechnology (Nanotechnology) *Director*: Katsumi Kishino

History: Founded 1913 as College, recognized as University 1928. Graduate School added 1951. The University is a private Institution directed by the Society of Jesus. Financed from tuition and service fees, grants from public and private bodies, and donations.

Governing Bodies: Board of Trustees

Academic Year: April to March (April-September; Mid-September-March)

Admission Requirements: Graduation from high school or foreign equivalent, and entrance examinations conducted by the University

Fees: (Yen): Registration, 270,000; tuition, 692,000-1,017,000

Main Language(s) of Instruction: Japanese, English, Latin (Faculty of Theology)

International Co-operation: With universities in 30 countries

Accrediting Agencies: Monbu Kagaku Sho (Ministry of Education, Culture, Sports, Science and Technology)

Degrees and Diplomas: *Gakushi*: 4 yrs; *Shushi*: a further 2 yrs; *Hakase*: 3 yrs following Shushi

Student Services: Academic counselling, Canteen, Cultural centre, Employment services, Foreign student adviser, Handicapped facilities, Health services, Nursery care, Social counselling, Sports facilities

Student Residential Facilities: For 141 Men and 172 Women students (all off-campus)

Libraries: Central Library, 1,027,629 vols; Law School Library, 19,615 vols; Shakujii Library, 125,356 vols

Publications: Beiträge zur Deutschen Literatur *(annually)*; Catholic Studies *(biannually)*; Communications Research *(annually)*; Cosmopolis *(annually)*; English Literature and Language *(annually)*; Foreign Studies Journal *(annually)*; Historical Studies *(annually)*; Japanese Literature Journal *(annually)*; Journal of Global Environmental Studies *(annually)*; Lingua *(annually)*; Monumenta Nipponica *(quarterly)*; Philosophical Anthropology *(annually)*; Philosophy Journal *(annually)*; Physical Education at Sophia *(annually)*; Revue d'Etudes françaises *(annually)*; Sophia *(quarterly)*; Sophia Economics Journal *(biannually)*; Sophia Education Journal *(annually)*; Sophia International Review *(annually)*; Sophia Law Journal *(annually)*; Sophia Psychology Journal *(annually)*; Sophia Sci-Tech *(annually)*; Sophia Sociology Journal *(annually)*

Last Updated: 03/06/11

ST. CATHERINE UNIVERSITY

Sei Katarina Daigaku

660 Hojo, Hojo-shi, Ehime 799-2496
Tel: +81(89) 993-0702
Fax: +81(89) 993-0900
EMail: nyushi@catherine.ac.jp
Website: http://www.catherine.ac.jp

President: Jovino San Miguel

Faculties

Health and Welfare Human Services (Health Sciences; Social Welfare; Social Work; Sports; Sports Management)

History: Founded 1987.

Degrees and Diplomas: *Gakushi*

Last Updated: 02/02/09

ST. LUKE'S COLLEGE OF NURSING

Seiruka Kango Daigaku

10-1 Akashi-cho, Chuo-ku, Tokyo 104-0044
Tel: +81(3) 3543-6391
Fax: +81(3) 5565-1626
Website: http://www.slcn.ac.jp

President: Toshiko Ibe

Faculties

Nursing (Arts and Humanities; Child Care and Development; Community Health; English; Ethics; Gerontology; Health Education; Information Sciences; Midwifery; Nursing; Psychiatry and Mental Health; Psychology; Sociology)

Further Information: Also St Luke's International Hospital, Summer English Program at McGill University

History: Founded 1920 as School, became College 1964. Financially supported by tuition fees and Government subsidies.

Governing Bodies: Board of Directors

Academic Year: April to March (April-September; October-February)

Admission Requirements: Graduation from high school or equivalent, and entrance examination

Main Language(s) of Instruction: Japanese

Degrees and Diplomas: *Gakushi*: Nursing (Kangogakushi), 4 yrs (Transfer students with RN, 2 yrs); *Shushi*: Nursing (Kangogashushi), a further 2 yrs; *Hakase*: 3 yrs following Shushi

Libraries: 65,000 vols

Publications: Kiyo (Treatise)

Last Updated: 02/02/09

ST. MARIANNA UNIVERSITY SCHOOL OF MEDICINE

Sei Marianna Ika Daigaku

2-16-1, Sugao, Miyamae-ku, Kawasaki-shi, Kanagawa 216-8511
Tel: +81(44) 977-8111
Fax: +81(44) 977-5542
EMail: admin@marianna-u.ac.jp
Website: http://www.marianna-u.ac.jp

Institutes

Intractable Disease Treatment Research (Treatment Techniques)

Schools

Medicine (Medicine; Social and Preventive Medicine)

Further Information: Also 3 Hospitals

History: Founded 1971 by the St. Marianna Foundation.

Academic Year: April to March

Admission Requirements: Graduation from high school or foreign equivalent, and entrance examination

Main Language(s) of Instruction: Japanese

Degrees and Diplomas: *Gakushi*: Medicine, 6 yrs; *Hakase*: Medicine, a further 4 yrs

Student Services: Academic counselling, Canteen, Health services, Social counselling, Sports facilities

Libraries: c. 183,660 vols

Publications: The St. Marianna Medical Journal *(bimonthly)*

ST. THOMAS UNIVERSITY

Sei Tomasu Daigaku

2-18-1 Nakoji, Amagasaki-shi, Hyogo 661-8530
Tel: +81(6) 6491-5100
Fax: +81(6) 6491-7120
EMail: stujmail@st.thomas.ac.jp
Website: http://www.st.thomas.ac.jp/

President: Stephen M. Ryan

Faculties

Interpersonal and Cross-cultural Understanding (Cultural Studies; Development Studies; English; English Studies; Social Sciences); **Letters** *(Graduate programme)* (American Studies; Arts and Humanities; English; Linguistics; Literature; Religion; Religious Studies)

History: Founded 1962 as Eichi Daigaku (Eichi University). Acquired present title 2007.

Main Language(s) of Instruction: Japanese

International Co-operation: With universities in USA, Spain and France

Degrees and Diplomas: *Gakushi*; *Shushi*; *Hakase*

Student Services: Language programs, Sports facilities

Libraries: 224,370 vols

Last Updated: 28/03/11

SUGINO FASHION COLLEGE

Sugino Fukushoku Daigaku

4-6-19 Kamiosaki, Shinagawa-ku, Tokyo 141-8652
Tel: +81(3) 3491-8151
Fax: +81(3) 3491-8136
EMail: info@sugino.ac.jp
Website: http://www.sugino.ac.jp

Programmes

Fashion (Fashion Design)

History: Founded 1950. Acquired present status 1964. Known as Sugino Joshi Daigaku (Sugino Women's College) until 2002.

Degrees and Diplomas: *Gakushi*

Last Updated: 03/02/09

SUGIYAMA JOGAKUEN UNIVERSITY

Sugiyama Jogakuen Daigaku

17-3 Hoshigaoka-motomachi, Chikusa-ku, Nagoya-shi, Aichi 464-8662
Tel: +81(52) 781-1186 +81(52) 781-5674
Fax: +81(52) 781-4466 +81(52) 781-2038
EMail: ciep@sugiyama-u.ac.jp
Website: http://www.sugiyama-u.ac.jp

Graduate Schools

Human Sciences (Clinical Psychology; Education; Sociology); **Life Studies** (Food Science; Nutrition; Social Sciences)

Research Centres

Human Nutrition (Nutrition)

Schools

Cross-Cultural Studies (English; European Languages; European Studies; Japanese; Literature; Modern Languages; Oriental Languages; Oriental Studies); **Culture-Information Studies** (Behavioural Sciences; Communication Studies; Cultural Studies; Information Sciences; Linguistics; Social Studies); **Education**; **Human Sciences** (Arts and Humanities; Social Sciences); **Life Studies** (Food Science; Nutrition); **Modern Management** (Business and Commerce; International Business; Management)

History: Founded 1905.

Governing Bodies: Board of Trustees

Academic Year: April to March (April-October; October-March)

Admission Requirements: Graduation from high school and entrance examination

Main Language(s) of Instruction: Japanese

International Co-operation: Co-operation with universities in Australia and United Kingdom

Degrees and Diplomas: *Gakushi*: Arts (Bungakushi); Science (Rigakushi), 4 yrs; *Shushi*: Science, 2 yrs

Student Services: Language programs

Student Residential Facilities: For c. 40 students

Libraries: 357,454 vols

Publications: Journal *(annually)*

Last Updated: 03/02/09

SURUGADAI UNIVERSITY

Surugadai Daigaku

698 Azu, Hanno-shi, Saitama 357-8555
Tel: +81(429) 72-1124
Fax: +81(429) 72-1139
EMail: nyushi@surugadai.ac.jp
Website: http://www.surugadai.ac.jp

President: Norihiko Narita

Faculties

Contemporary Cultures (Cultural Studies); **Cultural Information Resources** (Cultural Studies; Information Management; Library Science); **Economics** (Business Administration; Economics; Information Sciences; Management); **Law** (Law)

Graduate Schools

Cultural Information Resources; **Economics** (Business Administration; Economics; Information Sciences; Management); **Law** (Law)

History: Founded 1987.

Governing Bodies: School Corporation

Academic Year: April to March

Admission Requirements: Graduation from high school, or equivalent

Fees: (Yen): 1.2m. per annum

Main Language(s) of Instruction: Japanese

International Co-operation: With universities in Australia, China, Germany, United Kingdom and USA

Degrees and Diplomas: *Gakushi*: 4 yrs; *Shushi*: a further 2 yrs

Student Services: Academic counselling, Canteen, Employment services, Foreign student adviser, Health services, Social counselling, Sports facilities

Libraries: c. 250,000 vols

Publications: Bulletin of the Faculty of Cultural Information Resources, Surugadai University *(biannually)*; Bulletin of the Institute for Economic Research *(annually)*; Comparative Law and Culture *(annually)*; Surugadai Economic Studies *(biannually)*; Surugadai Journal of Law and Politics *(biannually)*; Surugadai University Studies *(biannually)*

Last Updated: 03/02/09

SUZUKA INTERNATIONAL UNIVERSITY

Suzuka Kokusai Daigaku

663-222 Koriyama-cho, Suzuka-shi, Mie 510-0298
Tel: +81(593) 72-2121
Fax: +81(593) 72-2827
EMail: nyushi-kt@m.suzuka-iu.ac.jp
Website: http://www.suzuka-iu.ac.jp

President: Takashi Hori

Faculties

International Human Studies *(Also Graduate Programme)*

History: Founded 1994.

Main Language(s) of Instruction: Japanese

Degrees and Diplomas: *Gakushi*; *Shushi*

Student Services: Academic counselling, Employment services, Foreign student adviser, Language programs, Social counselling

Libraries: 65,000 vols

Last Updated: 03/02/09

SUZUKA UNIVERSITY OF MEDICAL SCIENCE

Suzuka Iryo Kagaku Daigaku (SUMS)

1001-1 Kishioka-cho, Suzuka-shi, Mie 510-0293
Tel: +81(593) 83-8991
Fax: +81(593) 83-9666
EMail: s-hase@suzuka-u.ac.jp
Website: http://www.suzuka-u.ac.jp

Centres

Medical Imaging (Medical Technology; Radiology)

Faculties

Acupuncture and Moxibustion (Acupuncture); **Health Sciences** (Health Sciences; Nutrition; Radiology); **Medical Engineering** (Engineering; Medical Technology); **Pharmaceutical Sciences**

Graduate Schools

Health Sciences (Health Sciences)

Institutes

Traditional Chinese Medicine (Traditional Eastern Medicine)

History: Founded 1991.

Degrees and Diplomas: *Gakushi*; *Hakase*

Last Updated: 03/02/09

TAISEI GAKUIN UNIVERSITY

Taisei Gakuin Daigaku

1060-1 Hirao, Mihara-cho, Minamikawachi-gun 587-8555
Tel: +81(72) 362-3731
Fax: +81(72) 362-0598
EMail: nyushi@tgu.ac.jp
Website: http://www.tgu.ac.jp

Faculties

Human Studies (Social Sciences); **Information Management** (Information Management)

History: Founded 1998. Known as Minami Osaka Daigaku (Southern Osaka University) until 2003.

Degrees and Diplomas: *Gakushi*

Publications: Bulletin of Taisei Gakuin University, (common with attached Junior College)

TAISHO UNIVERSITY

Taisho Daigaku

3-20-1 Nishisugamo, Toshima-ku, Tokyo 170-8470
Tel: +81(3) 3918-7311
Fax: +81(3) 5394-3037
EMail: info@mail.tais.ac.jp
Website: http://www.tais.ac.jp

President: Eiki Hoshino (2003-)

Secretary-General: Shodo Enomoto

International Relations: Shinro Chiba, Director, International Programmes Centre

Faculties

Human Studies (Arts and Humanities; Asian Religious Studies; Clinical Psychology; Social Welfare); **Literature** (History; International Studies; Japanese; Literature)

Research Institutes

Comprehensive Studies of Buddhism (Asian Religious Studies); **Counselling**

Schools

Graduate Studies

Further Information: Also Course for Training of Buddhist Priests. Japanese Language Programme for foreign students

History: Founded 1926, reorganized 1949.

Governing Bodies: Senate

Academic Year: April to March (April-September; October-March)

Admission Requirements: Graduation from high school or equivalent, and entrance examination

Main Language(s) of Instruction: Japanese

Degrees and Diplomas: *Gakushi*; *Shushi*; *Hakase*

Libraries: 561,367 vols

Publications: Taisho Daigaku Daigakuin Kenkyuronshu (Journal of the Graduate School of Taisho University) *(annually)*; Taisho Daigaku Kenkyu Kiyo (Memoirs of Taisho University) *(annually)*

Press or Publishing House: Taisho University Press

TAKACHIHO UNIVERSITY

Takachiho Daigaku

2-19-1 Omiya, Suginami-ku, Tokyo 168-8508
Tel: +81(3) 3313-0148
Fax: +81(3) 3313-9034
EMail: nyuushi@gac.takachiho.ac.jp; adc@gac.takachiho.ac.jp
Website: http://www.takachiho.ac.jp

Programmes

Business Management; **Commerce** (Business and Commerce); **Human Sciences** (Social Sciences)

Further Information: Also Master's and Doctoral programmes

History: Founded 1903. Formerly known as Takashiho Shoka Daigaku (Takachiho College of Commerce).

Main Language(s) of Instruction: Japanese

International Co-operation: With universities in USA and Taiwan

Degrees and Diplomas: *Gakushi*; *Shushi*; *Hakase*

Student Services: Employment services, Health services, Language programs, Social counselling, Sports facilities

Libraries: 240,000 vols

Last Updated: 03/02/09

TAKAMATSU UNIVERSITY

Takamatsu Daigaku

960 Kasuga-cho, Takamatsu-shi, Kagawa 761-0194
Tel: +81(87) 841-3255
Fax: +81(87) 841-3064
EMail: nyushi@takamatsu-u.ac.jp; admin@takamatsu-u.ac.jp
Website: http://www.takamatsu-u.ac.jp

Programmes

Business Administration (Business Administration; Industrial Management; Management Systems)

History: Founded 1995.

Degrees and Diplomas: *Gakushi*; *Shushi*

Last Updated: 03/02/09

TAKAOKA UNIVERSITY OF LAW

Takaoka Hoka Daigaku

307-3 Toidekokudai, Takaoka-shi, Toyama 939-1193
Tel: +81(766) 633-388
Fax: +81(766) 636-410
EMail: koho@takaoka.ac.jp
Website: http://www.takaoka.ac.jp

Programmes

Law (Law)

History: Founded 1989.

Degrees and Diplomas: *Gakushi*

Last Updated: 03/02/09

TAKARAZUKA UNIVERSITY OF ARTS AND DESIGN

Takarazuka Zokei Geijutsu Daigaku

7-27 Tsutsujigaoka, Hanayashiki, Takarazuka-shi, Hyogo 665-0803
Tel: +81(727) 56-1231
Fax: +81(727) 58-7869
EMail: info@takara-univ.ac.jp
Website: http://www.takara-univ.ac.jp

Divisions

Fine Arts (Fine Arts; Painting and Drawing; Sculpture); **Industrial Design**; **Media Arts and Art Information**

History: Founded 1986. Graduate courses started 1993.

Governing Bodies: Kansai Joshi Gakuen Institution

Academic Year: April to March

Admission Requirements: Graduation from high school

Main Language(s) of Instruction: Japanese

Degrees and Diplomas: *Gakushi*: Design; Fine Arts, 4 yrs; *Shushi*: Design, 2 yrs; *Shushi*: Fine Arts, a further 2 yrs; *Hakase*: Design, 3 yrs; *Hakase*: Fine Arts, 3 yrs following Shushi

Student Services: Academic counselling, Canteen, Employment services, Health services, Nursery care, Social counselling, Sports facilities

Special Facilities: Computer Centre. Movie Studio

Libraries: 40,000 vols

Publications: Artes, (Bulletin of Takarazuka University of Arts and Design) *(annually)*

TAKASAKI CITY UNIVERSITY OF ECONOMICS

Takasaki Keizai Daigaku (TCUE)

1300 Kaminamie-machi, Takasaki-shi, Gumma 370-0801
Tel: +81(27) 344-6265
Fax: +81(27) 343-4830
Website: http://www.tcue.ac.jp

President: Itaru Kogure (2006-)

Secretary-General: Masaharu Ishiduka

Faculties

Economics (Business Administration; Economics) *Dean*: Nobuo Ishi; **Regional Policy** (Regional Studies) *Dean*: Noboru Omiya

Schools

Graduate Studies

History: Founded 1957.

Governing Bodies: University Council

Academic Year: April to March

Admission Requirements: Graduation from high school and entrance examination

Fees: (Yen): 925,665 per annum

Main Language(s) of Instruction: Japanese

International Co-operation: With universities in Australia; Germany; Ireland and USA

Degrees and Diplomas: *Gakushi*: Economics; Regional Policy, 4 yrs; *Shushi*: 2 yrs following Gakushi; *Hakase (PhD)*: 3 yrs

Student Services: Academic counselling, Canteen, Employment services, Foreign student adviser, Health services, Nursery care, Social counselling

Student Residential Facilities: Yes

Publications: Bulletin of the Institute for Research in Regional Economy; The Economics Journal of Takasaki City University of Economics

Student Numbers *2008*	MEN	WOMEN	TOTAL
All (Foreign Included)	2,803	1,220	**4,023**

Last Updated: 03/02/09

TAKASAKI UNIVERSITY OF HEALTH AND WELFARE

Takasaki Kenko Fukushi Daigaku

37-1 Nakaohrui-machi, Takasaki-shi, Gunma 370-0033
Tel: +81(27) 352-1290
Fax: +81(27) 353-2055
EMail: info@takasaki-u.ac.jp
Website: http://www.takasaki-u.ac.jp

Programmes

Graduate (Biological and Life Sciences; Computer Science; Food Science; Health Sciences; Information Sciences; Nutrition; Social Welfare; Social Work; Welfare and Protective Services); **Undergraduate** (Computer Science; Food Science; Health Sciences; Information Sciences; Information Technology; Nutrition; Pharmacy; Social Welfare; Social Work; Welfare and Protective Services)

History: Founded 2001.

Degrees and Diplomas: *Gakushi*; *Shushi*; *Hakase*

Last Updated: 03/02/09

TAKUSHOKU UNIVERSITY

Takushoku Daigaku

3-4-14 Kohinata, Bunkyo-ku, Tokyo 112-8585
Tel: +81(3) 3947-2261
Fax: +81(3) 3947-5333
EMail: web_int@ofc.takushoku-u.ac.jp
Website: http://www.takushoku-u.ac.jp

Faculties

Commerce (Business Administration; Business and Commerce); **Engineering** (Computer Science; Electronic Engineering; Engineering; Industrial Design; Information Sciences; Mechanical Engineering); **Foreign Studies** (Chinese; English; European Languages; Modern Languages; Oriental Languages; Spanish); **International Studies** (International Studies); **Political Science and Economics** (Economics; Political Sciences)

Graduate Schools

Commerce (Business and Commerce); **Economics** (Economics); **Engineering**; **Language Education**

Institutes

International Cooperation Studies *(Also Graduate School)* (International Studies)

Further Information: Also 13 Research Institutes

History: Founded 1900.

Academic Year: April to March

Admission Requirements: Graduation from high school and entrance examination

Main Language(s) of Instruction: Japanese

Degrees and Diplomas: *Gakushi*: 4 yrs; *Shushi*: a further 2 yrs; *Hakase*

Student Services: Academic counselling, Canteen, Employment services, Foreign student adviser, Foreign Studies Centre, Health services, Language programs, Nursery care, Social counselling, Sports facilities

Student Residential Facilities: For overseas students

Libraries: c. 420,000 vols

Publications: Kaigai Jijo, Journal of World Affairs *(monthly)*; Takushoku Daigaku Ronshu *(biennially)*

Last Updated: 03/02/09

TAMA ART UNIVERSITY

Tama Bijutsu Daigaku (TAU)

2-1723 Yarimizu, Hachioji-shi, Tokyo 192-0394
Tel: +81(426) 76-8611
Fax: +81(426) 76-2935
EMail: pro@tamabi.ac.jp
Website: http://www.tamabi.ac.jp

President: Yoshihide Seita

Faculties

Art and Communication *(Evening Division)* (Design; Film; Fine Arts; Performing Arts); **Art and Design** (Architectural and Environmental Design; Ceramic Art; Ceramics and Glass Technology; Design; Environmental Studies; Fine Arts; Glass Art; Graphic Arts; Graphic Design; Japanese; Metal Techniques; Painting and Drawing; Printing and Printmaking; Sculpture; Textile Design)

History: Founded as a private School 1935, became College 1947 and acquired University level 1953.

Governing Bodies: Board of Directors; Council; Faculty Meeting

Academic Year: April to February (April-September; October-February)

Admission Requirements: Graduation from high school and entrance examination

Fees: (Yen): Faculty of Arts and Design, c. 1.7m. per annum; Faculty of Art and Communication, c. 1.2m. per annum

Main Language(s) of Instruction: Japanese

International Co-operation: With universities in China; Republic of Korea; Finland; Thailand and USA

Degrees and Diplomas: *Gakushi*: 4 yrs; *Shushi*: 2 yrs; *Hakase*: 3 yrs

Student Services: Academic counselling, Canteen, Cultural centre, Employment services, Foreign Studies Centre, Handicapped facilities, Health services, Language programs, Social counselling, Sports facilities

Special Facilities: Art Museum; Media Centre

Libraries: University Libraries, c. 180,000 vols

Publications: Tama Art University Bulletin *(annually)*

Last Updated: 03/02/09

TAMA UNIVERSITY

Tama Daigaku

4-1-1 Hijirigaoka, Tama-shi, Tokyo 206-0022
Tel: +81(42) 337-7111
Fax: +81(42) 337-7100
Website: http://www.tama.ac.jp

President: Iwao Nakatani

Schools

Global Studies (Computer Networks; English; International Relations; Japanese; Leadership); **Management and Information Sciences** *(Also Graduate School)*

Further Information: Also Shinagawa and Meguro campuses

History: Founded 1989.

Academic Year: April to March

Admission Requirements: Graduation from high school and entrance examination

Main Language(s) of Instruction: Japanese

Degrees and Diplomas: *Gakushi*: 4 yrs; *Shushi*: a further 2 yrs; *Hakase*: 3 yrs following Shushi

Libraries: 44,960 vols

TAMAGAWA UNIVERSITY

Tamagawa Daigaku

6-1-1 Tamagawa Gakuen, Machida-shi, Tokyo 194-8610
Tel: +81(42) 739-8111
Fax: +81(42) 739-8795
EMail: koho@tamagawa.ac.jp
Website: http://www.tamagawa.ac.jp

President: Yoshiaki Obara (1994-)
EMail: kokusai@tamagawa.ac.jp

International Relations: Sadao Takashi, Executive Director for Higher Education; Director, Center for University International Programs
Tel: +81(42) 739-8660, Fax: +81(42) 739-8661
EMail: kokusai@tamagawa.ac.jp

Colleges

Agriculture (Agriculture; Biological and Life Sciences; Environmental Studies; Natural Resources); **Arts** (Media Studies; Performing Arts; Visual Arts); **Arts and Sciences** (Arts and Humanities; Natural Sciences; Social Sciences); **Business Administration; Education** (Child Care and Development; Education); **Engineering** (Engineering; Management Systems; Mechanical Engineering; Software Engineering; Technology); **Humanities** (Arts and Humanities; Cultural Studies; International Studies; Social Sciences)

Departments

Correspondence Courses

Research Institutes

Education (Educational Research)

History: Founded 1929 as Tamagawa Academy, became University 1949.

Governing Bodies: Board of Directors

Academic Year: April to March (April-July; September-March)

Admission Requirements: Graduation from senior high school or equivalent or foreign equivalent, and entrance examination

Main Language(s) of Instruction: Japanese

Degrees and Diplomas: *Gakushi*: 4 yrs; *Shushi*: a further 2 yrs; *Hakase*: 3 yrs following Shushi

Special Facilities: Kyoiku Hakubutsu Shiryokan

Libraries: c. 850,000 vols

Publications: Mitsubachi Kagaku (Honeybee Science Report) *(quarterly)*; Shohou *(annually)*; Zenjin *(monthly)*

Student Numbers *2012-2013*: Total 7,658

Last Updated: 19/02/13

TEIKYO HEISEI UNIVERSITY

Teikyo Heisei Daigaku

2289-23 Oyatsu, Uruido, Ichihara-shi, Chiba 290-0193
Tel: +81(436) 74-3920
Fax: +81(436) 74-7871
EMail: nyushi@thu.ac.jp
Website: http://www.thu.ac.jp

Faculties

Health Care (Alternative Medicine; Nursing); **Medical Science for Health** (Occupational Therapy; Physical Therapy; Speech Therapy and Audiology); **Pharmaceutical Sciences** (Pharmacology)

Graduate Schools

Informatics (Applied Mathematics; Artificial Intelligence; Software Engineering; Statistics)

Schools

Informatics (Computer Science; Information Management; Information Technology; Management Systems)

History: Founded 1987 as Teikyo University of Technology. Forms part of Teikyo University Group.

Academic Year: April to January (April-July; September-January)

Admission Requirements: Graduation from high school and entrance examination

Main Language(s) of Instruction: Japanese, English

Degrees and Diplomas: *Gakushi*; *Shushi*

Student Services: Academic counselling, Employment services, Nursery care, Sports facilities

Libraries: c. 100,000 vols

Last Updated: 03/02/09

TEIKYO UNIVERSITY

Teikyo Daigaku
2-11-1 Kaga, Itabashi-ku, Tokyo 173-8605
Tel: +81(3) 3579-5901
Fax: +81(3) 3579-5715
EMail: teikyoip@med.teikyo-u.ac.jp
Website: http://www.teikyo-u.ac.jp

President: Yoshihito Okinaga

Faculties

Economics *(Hachioji City, Tokyo; Also Graduate School)* (Economics); **Language Studies** *(For foreign students, Hachioji City, Tokyo)* (Japanese); **Law** *(Hachioji City, Tokyo; Also Graduate School)* (Law); **Liberal Arts** *(Hachioji City, Tokyo; Also Graduate School)* (Arts and Humanities; Education; English; History; Psychology; Sociology); **Medical Technology** *(Also Faculty of Fukuoka Medical Technology and Graduate School)* (Medical Technology; Optical Technology; Optics); **Medicine** *(Also Graduate School)* (Medicine); **Pharmaceutical Sciences** *(Sagamiko City, Kanagawa; Also Graduate School)* (Biochemistry; Biophysics; Chemistry; Pharmacy; Physics); **Science and Engineering** *(Utsunomiya City, Tochigi; Also Graduate School)* (Biochemistry; Biomedicine; Biophysics; Engineering; Information Sciences; Materials Engineering; Natural Sciences)

Further Information: Also 3 Teaching Hospitals

History: Founded 1966.

Governing Bodies: Board of Trustees; Board of Directors or Councillors

Academic Year: April to January (April-July; September-January)

Admission Requirements: Graduation from high school and entrance examination

Main Language(s) of Instruction: Japanese, English

International Co-operation: With universities in USA, United Kingdom and Republic of Korea

Degrees and Diplomas: *Gakushi*: Economics; Engineering; Law; Liberal Arts; Orthoptics; Pharmacy; Science, 4 yrs; *Gakushi*: Medicine, 6 yrs; *Shushi*: a further 2 yrs; *Hakase*: 3 yrs following Shushi; *Hakase*: Medicine, 4 yrs following Igakushi

Student Services: Academic counselling, Canteen, Employment services, Foreign student adviser, Foreign Studies Centre, Handicapped facilities, Health services, Language programs, Nursery care, Sports facilities

Libraries: c. 885,000 vols

Last Updated: 03/02/09

TEIKYO UNIVERSITY OF SCIENCE AND TECHNOLOGY

Teikyo Kagaku Daigaku
2525 Yatsusawa, Uenohara-cho, Kitatsuru-gun, Yamanashi 409-0193
Tel: +81(554) 63-4411
Fax: +81(554) 63-4430
EMail: www@ntu.ac.jp
Website: http://www.ntu.ac.jp

Departments

Biosciences (Biochemistry; Biomedicine; Biophysics); **Ecological Materials** (Ecology); **Electronics and Information Science** (Electronic Engineering; Information Sciences); **Management Systems** (Management Systems); **Science and Engineering** (Engineering; Natural Sciences)

History: Founded 1989.

Academic Year: April to March (April-September; October-March)

Admission Requirements: Graduation from high school and entrance examination

Main Language(s) of Instruction: Japanese, English, German

Degrees and Diplomas: *Gakushi*: Engineering (Kogakushi); Science (Rigakushi), 4 yrs; *Shushi*

Libraries: 100,000 vols

TENRI UNIVERSITY

Tenri Daigaku
1050 Somanouchi-cho, Tenri-shi, Nara 632-8510
Tel: +81(743) 63-1515 +81(743) 63-9005
Fax: +81(743) 63-7388
EMail: koryu@sta.tenri-u.ac.jp
Website: http://www.tenri-u.ac.jp

Faculties

Health, Budo and Sports Studies; **Human Studies** (Clinical Psychology; Comparative Religion; Psychology; Religious Studies; Welfare and Protective Services); **International Cultural Studies** (American Studies; Asian Studies; Chinese; Cultural Studies; English; European Studies; French; German; Indonesian; Japanese; Korean; Russian; Spanish; Thai Languages); **Letters** (Arts and Humanities; Cultural Studies; History; Japanese; Literature)

History: Founded 1925. Acquired present status 1949.

Degrees and Diplomas: *Gakushi*. Also graduate programme in Human Clinical Studies

Last Updated: 03/02/09

TENSHI COLLEGE

Tenshi Daigaku
1-30 Higashi 3, Kita 13-jo, Higashi-ku, Sapporo-shi, Hokkaido 065-0013
Tel: +81(11) 741-1051
Fax: +81(11) 741-1077
Website: http://www.tenshi.ac.jp

Schools

Graduate Studies; **Nursing and Nutrition** (Nursing; Nutrition)

History: Founded 2000.

Degrees and Diplomas: *Gakushi*; *Shushi*

TEZUKAYAMA GAKUIN UNIVERSITY

Tezukayama Gakuin Daigaku
2-1823 Imakuma, Osakasaya-mashi, Osaka 589-8585
Tel: +81(723) 650-865
Fax: +81(723) 655-628
Website: http://www.tezuka-gu.ac.jp

President: Motoi Minagawa

Programmes

Arts and Humanities (Arts and Humanities; Literature)

History: Founded 1966.

Degrees and Diplomas: *Gakushi*

TEZUKAYAMA UNIVERSITY

Tezukayama Daigaku
7-1-1 Tezukayama, Nara-shi, Nara 631-8501
Tel: +81(742) 48-9358
Fax: +81(742) 48-9135 +81(742) 48-8137
EMail: kokusai@jimu.tezukayama-u.ac.jp; webmaster@tezukayama-u.ac.jp
Website: http://www.tezukayama-u.ac.jp

Faculties

Business Administration (Business Administration); **Economics** (Economics); **Humanities**; **Law and Policy** (Law; Political Sciences)

History: Founded 1964.

Main Language(s) of Instruction: Japanese

Degrees and Diplomas: *Gakushi*; *Shushi*; *Hakase*

Student Services: Employment services, Foreign Studies Centre, Language programs, Sports facilities

Libraries: 590,000 vols

Last Updated: 03/02/09

THE GRADUATE UNIVERSITY FOR ADVANCED STUDIES

Sogo Kenkyu Daigakuin Daigaku
1560-35 Aza-kanmon, Kamiyamaguchi, Hayama-cho, Miura-gun, Kanagawa 240-0193
Tel: +81(46) 858-1500
Fax: +81(46) 858-1541
EMail: kokusai@soken.ac.jp
Website: http://www.soken.ac.jp

President: Naoyuki Takahata

Schools

Advanced Sciences (Biological and Life Sciences); **Cultural and Social Studies** (Cultural Studies; History; Japanese; Modern Languages; Oriental Languages; Oriental Studies; Regional Studies; Social Studies); **High Energy Accelerator Science** (Nuclear Physics); **Life Sciences** (Biological and Life Sciences; Biology; Genetics; Molecular Biology; Physiology); **Multidisciplinary Science** (Computer Science; Statistics); **Physical Sciences** (Astronomy and Space Science; Nuclear Physics; Physics)

History: Founded 1988. A postgraduate institution operating in close collaboration with inter-university research institutes.

Governing Bodies: University Council, Faculty Councils

Academic Year: April to February (April-September; October-February)

Admission Requirements: Five-year doctor course, university degree; three-year doctor course, Master degree or foreign equivalent

Main Language(s) of Instruction: Japanese; English

International Co-operation: With Byelorussian State University (Belarus); Sofia University St. Kliment Ohridski (Bulgaria); Collège doctoral franco-japonais; Fudan University and The University of Science and Tecnology (China)

Degrees and Diplomas: *Hakase*: at least 3 yrs

Special Facilities: Inter-university Research Institutes: National Museum of Ethnology, Osaka; International Research Centre for Japanese Studies; Kyoto; National Museum of Japanese History, Chiba; National Institute of Multimedia Education, Chiba; National Institute of Japanese Literature, Tokyo; Institute for Molecular Science, Aichi; National Astronomical Observatory, Tokyo; National Institute for Fusion Science, Gifu; Institute of Space and Astronautical Science, Kanagawa; Accelerator Laboratory, Ibaraki; Institute of Materials Structure Science, Ibaraki; Institute of Particle and Nuclear Studies, Ibaraki; The Institute of Statistical Mathematics, Tokyo; National Institute of Polar Research, Tokyo; National Institute of Informatics, Tokyo; National Institute of Genetics, Shizuoka; National Institute for Basic Biology, Aichi; National Institute for Physiological Sciences, Aichi

Libraries: 33,200 vols

Last Updated: 03/02/09

THE JAPANESE RED CROSS COLLEGE OF NURSING

Nihon Sekijuji Kango Daigaku
4-1-3 Hiroo, Shibuya-ku, Tokyo 150-0012
Tel: +81(3) 3409-0875
Fax: +81(3) 3409-0589
EMail: info@redcross.ac.jp
Website: http://www.redcross.ac.jp

President: Hadama Etsuko

Colleges

Nursing *(Also Graduate School)* (Child Care and Development; Health Sciences; Midwifery; Nursing; Psychiatry and Mental Health)

Further Information: Also Musashino Campus

History: Founded 1986.

Main Language(s) of Instruction: Japanese

Degrees and Diplomas: *Gakushi*; *Shushi*; *Hakase*

Libraries: 53,285 vols

Last Updated: 27/01/09

THE JAPANESE RED CROSS HIROSHIMA COLLEGE OF NURSING

Nihon Sekijuji Hiroshima Kango Daigaku
1-2 Ajiradai-Higashi, Hatsukaichi-shi, Hiroshima 738-0052
Tel: +81(829) 20-2800
Fax: +81(829) 20-2801
EMail: soumu@jrchcn.ac.jp
Website: http://www.jrchcn.ac.jp

President: Sachie Shindo

Programmes

Nursing *(Also Graduate School)* (Law; Nursing)

History: Founded 2000.

Degrees and Diplomas: *Gakushi*; *Shushi*

Publications: Bulletin of the Japanese Red Cross Hiroshima College of Nursing; Report of the Japanese Red Cross Hiroshima College of Nursing "Futaba"; Voluntary Evaluation and Assessment Report

Last Updated: 27/01/09

THE JAPANESE RED CROSS KYUSHU INTERNATIONAL COLLEGE OF NURSING

1-1 Asty, Munakata-shi, Fukuoka 811-4157
Tel: +81(940) 35-7008
Fax: +81(940) 35-7021
EMail: info@jrckicn.ac.jp
Website: http://www.jrckicn.ac.jp

President: Etsuko Kita

Departments

Nursing

History: Founded 2001.

Degrees and Diplomas: *Gakushi*; *Shushi*

Special Facilities: Information Processing Hall

Publications: Breeze from Munakata

Last Updated: 25/09/08

IAU THE JIKEI UNIVERSITY SCHOOL OF MEDICINE

Tokyo Jikei Ika Daigaku
3-25-8 Nishi-shinbashi, Minato-ku, Tokyo 105-8461
Tel: +81(33) 433-1111
Fax: +81(33) 435-6128
Website: http://www.jikei.ac.jp

President: Satoshi Kurihara (2001-)
Tel: +81(3) 3433-1111, Ext. 2104 EMail: kurihara@jikei.ac.jp

International Relations: Kurihiko Fukuda, Chairman, International Exhange Programme Tel: +81(33) 433-1111

Centres

Continuing Medical Education; Medical Information

Institutes

Medical Sciences (Health Sciences)

Laboratories

Space Medicine

Schools

Medicine (Medicine); **Nursing** (Nursing)

History: Founded 1881 as School of Medicine, became College 1921. Acquired University status 1952.

Governing Bodies: Board of Directors

Academic Year: April to March (April-July; September-December; January-March)

Admission Requirements: Graduation from high school or equivalent, and entrance examination

Main Language(s) of Instruction: Japanese

Degrees and Diplomas: *Gakushi*: Medicine, 6 yrs; *Gakushi*: Nursing (Kangogakushi), 4 yrs; *Hakase*: Medicine, a further 4 yrs

Special Facilities: Hyohon-kan (Medical Museum); Jikei Historical Collection

Libraries: 315,400 vols

Publications: Jikeikai Medical Journal (in English) *(quarterly)*; Kyoiku Kenkyu Nenpo (Annual Report of Education and Research, in Japanese) *(annually)*; Research Activities (in English) *(annually)*; Tokyo Jikeikai Ika Daigaku Zasshi (in Japanese) *(bimonthly)*

Last Updated: 04/04/08

THE OPEN UNIVERSITY OF JAPAN

Hoso Daigaku (OUJ)

2-11 Wakaba, Mihama-Ku, Chiba-shi, Chiba 261-8586

Tel: +81(43) 276-5111

Fax: +81(43) 298-4378

EMail: kokusai@u-air.ac.jp

Website: http://www.u-air.ac.jp

President: Norihito Tambo

Faculties

Liberal Arts (Arts and Humanities; Economics; Natural Resources; Natural Sciences; Social Studies; Social Welfare)

Graduate Schools

Arts and Science (Clinical Psychology; Cultural Studies; Education; Environmental Studies; Information Sciences)

Further Information: Also 49 Study centres throughout Japan

History: Founded 1983 as Open and Distance Institution with own broadcasting station to provide the general public with an opportunity for College-level education. Digital broadcast via telecommunication satellite, supplementing the ground transmission using radio and TV, covering only the Kanto area, began 1998. Now programmes are accessible from every part of Japan. Formerly known as the University of the Air.

Governing Bodies: Board of Trustees

Academic Year: April to March (April-September; October-March)

Admission Requirements: Graduation from high school or foreign equivalent (no entrance examination)

Main Language(s) of Instruction: Japanese

Degrees and Diplomas: *Gakushi*: 4-10 yrs; *Shushi*

Student Services: Health services

Libraries: c. 201,000 vols

Publications: On Air *(quarterly)*

Press or Publishing House: The Society for the Promotion of the University of the Air (Hoso Daigaku Kyoiku Shinkokai)

Last Updated: 21/11/08

THE UNIVERSITY OF DIGITAL CONTENT

Dejitaru Hariuddo Daigaku

Akihabara Daibiru 7th Floor, 1-18-13 Sotokanda, Chiyoda-ku, Tokyo 101-0021

Tel: +81(3) 5297-5787

Fax: +81(3) 5297-5788

EMail: daigaku@dhw.ac.jp

Website: http://www.dhw.ac.jp

Colleges

Digital Arts

History: Founded 2005.

Degrees and Diplomas: *Gakushi*; *Shushi*

Last Updated: 13/02/09

THE UNIVERSITY OF HUMAN ENVIRONMENTS

Ningen Kankyo Daigaku

6-2, Kamisanbonmatsu Motojuku, Okazaki, Aichi-gun, Aichi 444-3505

Tel: +81(564) 48-7811

Fax: +81(564) 48-7814

EMail: koho@uhe.ac.jp

Website: http://www.uhe.ac.jp

Divisions

Historical and Cultural Environments (Crafts and Trades; Cultural Studies; Handicrafts; History; Japanese); **Human Environments** (Economics; Environmental Management; Environmental Studies; Town Planning); **Mental Environments** (Communication Studies; Cultural Studies; Psychology; Social Sciences)

History: Founded 2000.

Degrees and Diplomas: *Gakushi*; *Shushi*

Last Updated: 28/01/09

THE UNIVERSITY OF NIIGATA REHABILITATION GRADUATE SCHOOL

Niigata Rihabiritesyon Daigakuin Daigaku

2-16 Kaminoyama, Murakami, Niigata 958-0053

Tel: +81(254) 56-8292

Fax: +81(254) 56-8291

EMail: office@nrgs.ac.jp

Website: http://www.nrgs.ac.jp

Programmes

Rehabilitation (Laboratory Techniques; Radiology; Rehabilitation and Therapy)

History: Founded 2007.

Degrees and Diplomas: *Shushi*

Last Updated: 13/02/09

THE UNIVERSITY OF SHIMANE

Shimane Kenritsu Daigaku

2433-2 Nobara-cho, Hamada-shi, Shimane 697-0016

Tel: +81(855) 24-2200

Fax: +81(855) 24-2208

EMail: us@admin.u-shimane.ac.jp

Website: http://www.u-shimane.ac.jp

President: Shigeaki Uno

Departments

Multidisciplinary Studies

Graduate Schools

Development Studies (Accountancy; Administration; Anthropology; Development Studies; Economics; Law; Management; Sociology); **Northeast Asia (NEA) Studies**

History: Founded 2000.

Degrees and Diplomas: *Gakushi*; *Shushi*; *Hakase*

Last Updated: 13/02/09

IAU THE UNIVERSITY OF TOKYO

Tokyo Daigaku

7-3-1 Hongo, Bunkyo-ku, Tokyo 113-8654

Tel: +81(3) 5841-0297

Fax: +81(3) 5689-7344

EMail: intpl-a@ml.adm.u-tokyo.ac.jp

Website: http://www.u-tokyo.ac.jp

President: Junichi Hamada (2009-) Tel: +81(3) 5841-0297

International Relations: Masashi Haneda, Vice-President Tel: +81(3) 5841-0297

Centres

Artifacts in Engineering *(Kashiwa Campus) Director*: Kazuro Kageyama; **Asian Natural Environmental Science** *Director*: Taizo Hogetsu; **Cryogenic Research** (Applied Physics; Heating and Refrigeration) *Director*: Kazushi Kanoda; **Elementary Particle Physics** *(International Centre)* (Physics) *Director*: Sachio Komamiya; **Environmental Science** (Environmental Studies) *Director*: Masanori Owari; **Health Service** (Health Sciences) *Director*

(Acting): Makoto Asashima; **Information Technology** (Information Technology) *Director*: Akinori Yonezawa; **Radioisotope** (Radiology) *Director*: Hajime Tokuda; **Research and Development of Higher Education** (Educational Research; Educational Sciences; Higher Education) *Director*: Kazuo Okamoto; **Spatial Information Science** *(Kashiwa Campus)* (Aeronautical and Aerospace Engineering) *Director*: Ryosuke Shibasaki; **Very Large Scale Integration (VLSI) Design and Education** *Director*: Kunihiro Asada

Colleges

Arts and Science, Junior Division *(Komaba I Campus)* (Anthropology; Arts and Humanities; Astronomy and Space Science; Biology; Chemistry; Chinese; Classical Languages; Computer Science; Cultural Studies; Earth Sciences; Economics; Educational Sciences; English; French; Geography (Human); German; Graphic Design; Health Sciences; History; International Relations; Japanese; Korean; Latin American Studies; Law; Mathematics; Modern Languages; Philosophy; Physics; Political Sciences; Psychology; Russian; Sociology; Spanish; Sports; Statistics) *Dean*: Norimichi Kojima; **Arts and Science, Senior Division** (American Studies; Anthropology; Asian Studies; Behavioural Sciences; Biological and Life Sciences; Cognitive Sciences; Cultural Studies; East Asian Studies; Eastern European Studies; European Studies; Geography (Human); Information Sciences; International Relations; Mathematics; Modern Languages; Social Studies; Western European Studies) *Dean*: Norimichi Kojima

Faculties

Agriculture (Agricultural Economics; Agriculture; Applied Chemistry; Aquaculture; Bioengineering; Biological and Life Sciences; Biology; Biotechnology; Environmental Engineering; Environmental Management; Forest Biology; Natural Resources; Veterinary Science; Zoology) *Dean*: Shin-ichi Shogenji; **Economics** (Business Administration; Economic History; Economics; Finance; Statistics) *Dean*: Motoshige Itoh; **Education** (Curriculum; Education; Educational Administration; Educational Psychology; Educational Sciences; Health Education; Philosophy; Physical Education; Social Sciences; Teacher Training) *Dean*: Motohisa Kaneko; **Engineering** (Aeronautical and Aerospace Engineering; Applied Chemistry; Applied Mathematics; Applied Physics; Architecture; Biotechnology; Chemical Engineering; Chemistry; Civil Engineering; Electrical and Electronic Engineering; Engineering; Information Technology; Materials Engineering; Measurement and Precision Engineering; Mechanical Engineering; Metallurgical Engineering; Systems Analysis; Telecommunications Engineering) *Dean*: Kazuo Hotate; **Law** (Law; Political Sciences; Private Law; Public Law) *Dean*: Masahito Inouye; **Letters** *Dean*: Masao Tachibana; **Medicine** (Anatomy; Biochemistry; Biology; Biomedical Engineering; Cell Biology; Forensic Medicine and Dentistry; Gerontology; Gynaecology and Obstetrics; Health Sciences; Immunology; Medicine; Microbiology; Molecular Biology; Neurosciences; Nursing; Occupational Health; Paediatrics; Pathology; Pharmacology; Physiology; Radiology; Social and Preventive Medicine; Surgery) *Dean*: Takao Shimizu; **Pharmaceutical Sciences** (Biology; Chemistry; Genetics; Immunology; Microbiology; Neurosciences; Oncology; Organic Chemistry; Pharmacology; Pharmacy; Physical Chemistry) *Dean*: Yuichi Sugiyama; **Science** (Applied Physics; Astronomy and Space Science; Astrophysics; Biochemistry; Biological and Life Sciences; Biophysics; Chemistry; Earth Sciences; Environmental Studies; Information Sciences; Mathematics; Physics) *Dean*: Masayuki Yamamoto

Graduate Schools

Agricultural and Life Sciences *Dean*: Shin-ichi Shogenji; **Arts and Science** *(Komaba I Campus)* (American Studies; Anthropology; Behavioural Sciences; Biological and Life Sciences; Biology; Canadian Studies; Cognitive Sciences; Comparative Politics; Cultural Studies; East Asian Studies; Eastern European Studies; European Studies; Information Sciences; International Relations; International Studies; Islamic Studies; Japanese; Korean; Latin American Studies; Linguistics; Literature; Modern Languages; Natural Sciences; Pacific Area Studies; Social Studies) *Dean*: Norimichi Kojima; **Economics** (Economic and Finance Policy; Economic History; Economics; Finance; Management; Statistics) *Dean*: Motoshige Itoh; **Education** (Clinical Psychology; Curriculum; Education; Educational Administration; Educational Psychology; Educational Research; Educational Sciences; Health Sciences; Higher Education; Social Sciences; Teacher Training) *Dean*: Motohisa Kaneko; **Engineering** *Dean*: Kazuo Hotate; **Frontier Sciences** *(Kashiwa Campus)* (Biological and Life Sciences; Computer Science; Cultural Studies; Energy Engineering; Engineering; Environmental Engineering; Environmental Studies; International Studies; Materials Engineering; Medicine; Social Sciences) *Dean*: Yoshiyuki Amemiya; **Humanities and Sociology** (American Studies; Arts and Humanities; Asian Studies; Cultural Studies; European Studies; Japanese; Korean; Social Studies; Sociology) *Dean*: Masao Tachibana; **Information Science and Technology** (Applied Mathematics; Applied Physics; Computer Science; Information Sciences; Information Technology; Physics; Telecommunications Engineering) *Dean*: Isao Shimoyama; **Interdisciplinary Information Studies** *Dean*: Shunya Yoshimi; **Law and Politics** *Dean*: Masahito Inouye; **Mathematical Sciences** *(Komaba I Campus)* (Mathematics) *Dean*: Toshiyuki Katsura; **Medicine** (Biology; Biomedical Engineering; Cell Biology; Embryology and Reproduction Biology; Gerontology; Health Sciences; Immunology; Medicine; Microbiology; Molecular Biology; Neurosciences; Nursing; Pathology; Public Health; Radiology; Social and Preventive Medicine; Surgery) *Dean*: Takao Shimizu; **Pharmaceutical Sciences** (Biology; Chemistry; Pharmacology; Pharmacy) *Dean*: Yuichi Sugiyama; **Public Policy** *Dean*: Yoshitsugu Kanemoto; **Science** (Astronomy and Space Science; Biochemistry; Biological and Life Sciences; Biophysics; Chemistry; Earth Sciences; Physics) *Dean*: Masayuki Yamamoto

Institutes

Historiography (Ancient Books; Cultural Studies; East Asian Studies; Medieval Studies; Modern History) *Director*: Yoshinori Yokoyama; **Industrial Science** *(Komaba II Campus)* (Computer Engineering; Energy Engineering; Environmental Engineering; Inorganic Chemistry; Machine Building; Materials Engineering; Measurement and Precision Engineering; Physical Engineering) *Director*: Masafumi Maeda; **Medical Science** *(Shirokane Campus)* (Biochemistry; Cell Biology; Genetics; Health Sciences; Immunology; Microbiology; Molecular Biology; Oncology) *Director*: Motoharu Seiki; **Molecular and Cellular Biosciences** *(Promotion of Independence for Young Investigators)* (Biology; Cell Biology; Molecular Biology) *Director*: Atsushi Miyajima; **Oriental Culture** (Asian Studies; Oriental Studies) *Director*: Teruo Sekimeto; **Social Sciences** (Economics; Law; Political Sciences; Social Sciences; Sociology) *Director*: Akio Komorida; **Solid State Physics** *(Kashiwa Campus)* (Laboratory Techniques; Nanotechnology; Physics; Solid State Physics) *Director*: Yasuhiro Iye

Laboratories

Intelligent Modelling (Computer Engineering) *Director*: Kazuo Hotate; **Komaba Open Laboratory** *(Open Laboratory, Komaba II Campus)* *Director*: Kenjiro Miyano

Research Centres

Advanced Science and Technology *(Komaba II Campus)* (Applied Chemistry; Biochemistry; Biology; Cognitive Sciences; Electronic Engineering; Energy Engineering; Environmental Engineering; Finance; Information Sciences; Law) *Director*: Kenjiro Miyano; **Biotechnology** (Biomedicine; Biotechnology) *Director*: Yasuo Igarashi; **Climate System** *(Kashiwa Campus)* (Meteorology) *Director*: Teruyuki Nakajima; **Medical Education** *(IRCME, International Centre)* (Medicine) *Director*: Kazuhiko Yamamoto

Research Institutes

Cosmic Ray Research *(Kashiwa Campus)* (Applied Physics; Astrophysics; Physics) *Director*: Takaaki Kajita; **Earthquake Research** (Architecture; Civil Engineering; Earth Sciences; Safety Engineering; Seismology) *Director*: Shuhei Okubo; **Ocean Research** *(Nakano Campus)* (Biology; Chemistry; Ecology; Fishery; Geophysics; Marine Science and Oceanography; Meteorology; Microbiology; Physiology) *Director*: Mutsumi Nishida

Further Information: Also Japanese language courses for international students, international researchers and their spouses

History: Established 1877, amalgamating several institutions that had existed from the 18th and the early 19th centuries. Renamed Imperial University and then Tokyo Imperial University before becoming Tokyo Daigaku (University of Tokyo) again in 1947. Incorporated as National University Corporation in 2004.

Governing Bodies: Yakuinkai (Board of Directors)

Academic Year: April to March (April-September; October-March)

Admission Requirements: High school diploma or equivalent and entrance examination

Fees: (Yen): Enrolment fee, 282,000; tuition, undergraduate and graduate (excluding Law School), 535,800, Law School students, 804,000 per annum

Main Language(s) of Instruction: Japanese

International Co-operation: With universities in Argentina; Australia; Austria; Belgium; Brazil; Brunei; Canada; Chile; China; Colombia; Croatia; Denmark; Egypt; Ethiopia; Finland; France; Georgia; Germany; Greece; Hungary; India; Indonesia; Iran; Italy; Republic of Korea; Malaysia; Mexico; Mongolia; Morocco; Netherlands; New Zealand; Norway; Philippines; Portugal; Russian Federation; Serbia; Singapore; Slovenia; Sri Lanka; Sweden; Switzerland; Taiwan; Thailand; Turkey; United Kingdom; USA and Vietnam

Degrees and Diplomas: *Senmonshi*: Juris Doctor; Public Policy; *Gakushi*: Agriculture; Arts; Economics; Education; Engineering; Health Sciences; Laws; Liberal Arts; Science; Pharmaceutical Sciences, 4 yrs; *Gakushi*: Medicine (Igakushi); Veterinary Science (Juigakushi), 6 yrs; *Shushi*: Agriculture; Advanced Social and International Studies; Area Studies; Arts and Sciences (Information Studies); Economics; Education; Engineering; Environmental Studies; European Studies; Human Security Studies; Health Science; Information Science and Technology; Integrated Bioscience; Interdisciplinary Cultural Studies; International Studies; Language and Information Sciences; Laws; Letters; Multidisciplinary Sciences; Mathematical Science; Medical Science; Pharmaceutical Science; Psychology; Social Psychology; Socio-information and Communication Studies; Sociology; Science; Sustainability Science, a further 2 yrs; *Hakase*: Agriculture; Advanced Social and International Studies; Area Studies; Economics; Education; Engineering; Environmental Studies; Health Science; Human Security Studies; Information Studies; Information Science and Technology; Integrated Biosciences; Interdisciplinary Cultural Studies; International Studies; Language and Information Science; Laws; Letters; Multidisciplinary Sciences; Mathematical Sciences; Pharmaceutical Science; Philosophy; Psychology; Social Psychology; Socio-information and Communication Studies; Sociology; Science; Sustainability Science, 3 yrs following Shushi; *Hakase*: Veterinary Science; Medicine; Medical Science, a further 4 yrs. Also Senmonshoku, Nuclear Engineering, 1 yr following first degree

Student Services: Academic counselling, Canteen, Employment services, Foreign student adviser, Foreign Studies Centre, Handicapped facilities, Health services, Nursery care, Social counselling, Sports facilities

Student Residential Facilities: Yes

Special Facilities: University Museum. Botanical Garden

Libraries: Central Libraries and other department libraries, total, c. 8,700,000 vols

Publications: Activity Report, The Institute for Solid State Physics *(annually)*; Activity Report of the VLSI Design and Education Centre *(annually)*; Advanced Social and International Studies, Graduate School of Arts and Sciences *(annually)*; Annual Bulletin of the Faculty of Education *(annually)*; Annual Bulletin of the Graduate School of Education *(annually)*; Annual Report, Institute of Medical Science *(annually)*; Annual Report of Activities of the Health Service Centre *(annually)*; Annual Report of Interfaculty Initiative in Information Studies, Graduate School of Interdisciplinary Information Studies *(annually)*; Annual Report of the Biotechnology Research Centre *(annually)*; Annual Report of the Earthquake Research Institute *(annually)*; Annual Report of the Institute for Cosmic Ray Research *(annually)*; Annual Report of the Institute of Engineering Innovation, Graduate School of Engineering *(annually)*; Annual Report of the Institute of Molecular and Cellular Biosciences *(annually)*; Annual Report of the Intelligent Modeling Laboratory, Computer Engineering *(annually)*; Bulletin, The University Museum; Bulletin of the Earthquake Research Institute *(quarterly)*; Bulletin of the Graduate School of Agricultural and Life Sciences, Faculty of Agriculture; Bulletin of the International Centre *(annually)*; Bunseiken Journal *(3 per annum)*; CIC Newsletter, Ocean Research Institute *(annually)*; CNS Annual Report, Centre for Nuclear Studies, Graduate School of Science *(annually)*; Coastal Marine Science, International Coastal Research Centre, Ocean Research Institute *(annually)*; CPAS Newsletter, Graduate School of Arts and Sciences *(biannually)*; Frontier, Graduate School of Arts and Sciences *(annually)*; 'Gakkan Gakufu' Newsletter, Interfaculty Initiative in Information Studies, Graduate School of Interdisciplinary Information Studies *(annually)*; Graduate School of Information Science and Technology, The University of Tokyo *(annually)*; Institute of Industrial Science, The University of Tokyo *(annually)*; Interdisciplinary Cultural Studies, Graduate School of Arts and Sciences *(annually)*; International Centre News *(3 per annum)*; Journal of Mathematical Sciences, Graduate School of Mathematical Sciences *(quarterly)*; Keizaigaku Ronshu (Journal of Economics), Graduate School of Economics *(quarterly)*; Komaba 20xx (Annual Report on Staff Achievements), Graduate School of Arts and Sciences *(annually)*; Kyoyo Gabuku Ho (The Newsletter of the College of Arts and Sciences), Graduate School of Arts and Science; Language and Information Sciences, Graduate School of Arts and Sciences *(annually)*; Language, Information, Text, Graduate School of Arts and Sciences *(annually)*; Material Reports, The University Museum; Memoirs of the Institute of Oriental Culture *(annually)*; Odysseus: Proceedings of the Graduate Department of Area Studies, Graduate School of Arts and Sciences *(annually)*; Oriental Culture, Institute of Oriental Culture *(annually)*; Pacific and American Studies, Graduate School of Arts and Sciences; Preliminary Report of the Hakuho-Maru Cruise, Ocean Research Institute *(other/irregular)*; RCAST News, Newsletter introducing researchers, research activities and outcomes, etc. *(quarterly)*; Shakaikagaku Kenkyu (Journal of Social Science), Institute of Social Science *(bimonthly)*; Social Science Japan Journal, Institute of Social Science *(biannually)*; The Archive for Philosophy and the History of Science, Graduate School of Arts and Sciences; The Komaba Journal of Area Studies, Graduate School of Arts and Sciences *(annually)*; The Proceedings of the Foreign Language Sections, Graduate School of Arts and Sciences; The Tokyo Journal of Medical Sciences, Graduate School of Medicine *(annually)*; The University of Tokyo School of Engineering *(biennially)*; Tokyo Daigaku Shiryo Hensan-jo Ho, Report of the Activities of the Historiographical Institute *(annually)*; Tokyo Daigaku Shiryo Hensan-jo Kenkyu Kiyo, Research Report of the Historiographical Institute *(annually)*

Press or Publishing House: University of Tokyo Press

Student Numbers *2012-2013*: Total 28,206

Last Updated: 10/12/08

TOHO COLLEGE OF MUSIC

Toho Ongaku Daigaku

84 Imaizumi, Kawagoe-shi, Saitama 350-0015

Tel: +81(492) 352-157

Website: http://www.toho-music.ac.jp

Programmes

Music (Music)

History: Founded 1965.

Academic Year: April to March (April-September; October-March)

Admission Requirements: Graduation from high school or equivalent or foreign equivalent

Main Language(s) of Instruction: Japanese

Degrees and Diplomas: *Gakushi*: Bungakushi, arts, 4 yrs. Also Graduate Course, 1 yr

TOHO GAKUEN GRADUATE SCHOOL OF MUSIC

Toho Gakuen Daigakuin Daigaku

1884-17 Kurehamachi, Toyama-shi, Toyama 930-0138

Tel: +81(76) 434-6800

Fax: +81(76) 434-6666

Website: http://www.tohomusic.ac.jp

President: Tsuyoshi Tsutsumi

Graduate Schools

Music

History: Founded 1999.

Degrees and Diplomas: *Shushi*: 2 yrs

TOHO GAKUEN SCHOOL OF MUSIC

Toho Gakuen Daigaku

1-41-1 Wakaba-cho, Chofu-shi, Tokyo 182-8510

Tel: +81(03) 3307-4101

Fax: +81(03) 3307-4354

Website: http://www.tohomusic.ac.jp

President: Tsuyoshi Tsutsumi

Programmes

Music (Conducting; Music; Music Theory and Composition; Musical Instruments; Musicology; Singing)

History: Founded 1955. Acquired present status 1961.

Degrees and Diplomas: *Gakushi*

Last Updated: 03/02/09

TOHO UNIVERSITY

Toho Daigaku

5-21-16 Omori-nishi, Ota-ku, Tokyo 143-8540

Tel: +81(3) 3762-4151

Fax: +81(3) 3768-0660 +81(3) 3762-7180

EMail: daijimu@jim.toho-u.ac.jp

Website: http://www.toho-u.ac.jp

Faculties

Medicine *(Also Graduate School)* (Anatomy; Medicine; Social and Preventive Medicine; Surgery); **Pharmaceutical Sciences** *(Also Graduate School)* (Pharmacology; Pharmacy); **Science** *(Also Graduate School)* (Biology; Chemistry; Information Sciences; Natural Sciences; Physics)

History: Founded 1925 as Imperial Women's Medical College, became private University 1947.

Academic Year: April to March (April-July; September-December; January-March)

Main Language(s) of Instruction: Japanese

International Co-operation: With universities in USA, United Kingdom and Australia

Degrees and Diplomas: *Gakushi*: Medicine, 6 yrs; *Gakushi*: Pharmacy (Yakugakushi); Science (Rigakushi), 4 yrs; *Hakase*: a further 4 yrs

Student Services: Sports facilities

Student Residential Facilities: Yes

Libraries: c. 423,000 vols

Publications: Toho Medical Journal (Toho Igakukai Zasshi) *(monthly)*

Last Updated: 03/02/09

TOHOKU BUNKA GAKUEN UNIVERSITY

Tohoku Bunka Gakuen Daigaku

6-45-16 Kunimi, Aoba-ku, Sendai-shi, Miyagi 981-8551

Tel: +81(22) 233-3310

Fax: +81(22) 233-7941

EMail: nyugaku@office.tbgu.ac.jp

Website: http://www.tbgu.ac.jp

Programmes

Medical Science and Welfare (Medicine; Occupational Therapy; Physical Therapy; Social Work; Welfare and Protective Services); **Policy Management** (Management); **Science and Technology** (Environmental Engineering; Environmental Management; Information Technology)

History: Founded 1999.

Degrees and Diplomas: *Gakushi*; *Shushi*

Student Services: Cultural centre, Sports facilities

Special Facilities: Computer Centre

Libraries: 48,088 vols.

Last Updated: 04/02/09

TOHOKU FUKUSHI (WELFARE) UNIVERSITY

Tohoku Fukushi Daigaku

1-8-1 Kunimi, Aoba-ku, Sendai-shi, Miyagi 981-8522

Tel: +81(22) 233-3111

Fax: +81(22) 233-3113

EMail: nyushi@tfu-mail.tfu.ac.jp

Website: http://www.tfu.ac.jp

Programmes

Buddhist Social Education *(Research)* (Religious Education); **Public Administration** *(Research)* (Public Administration); **Social Welfare** (Social Welfare)

History: Founded 1958. Acquired present status 1962.

Governing Bodies: Board of Directors; Board of Trustees

Academic Year: April to March (April-September; October-March)

Admission Requirements: Graduation from high school or equivalent or foreign equivalent, and entrance examination

Main Language(s) of Instruction: Japanese

Degrees and Diplomas: *Gakushi*: Sociology (Shakaigakushi), 4 yrs; *Shushi*: Sociology (Shakaigakushushi), a further 2 yrs. Also Professional Qualifications

Student Services: Sports facilities

Special Facilities: Keisuke Serizawa's Collection of African Folk Materials

Libraries: 210,000 vols

Publications: Bulletin *(annually)*

TOHOKU GAKUIN UNIVERSITY

Tohoku Gakuin Daigaku

1-3-1 Tsuchitoi, Aoba-ku, Sendai-shi, Miyagi 980-8511

Tel: +81(22) 264-6425

Fax: +81(22) 264-6515

EMail: ico@tscc.tohoku-gakuin.ac.jp

Website:http: //www.tohoku-gakuin.ac.jp

President: Nozomu Hoshimiya (2004-)
Tel: +81(22) 264-6421, Fax: +81(22) 264-3030
EMail: nozomu@tscc.tohoku-gakuin.ac.jp

Vice-president: Noboru Sekiya Tel: +81(22) 264-6426

International Relations: Michiko Oda

Centres

Audio-Visual (Cinema and Television); **Counselling**

Faculties

Economics (Economics); **Engineering** *(Tagajo City)* (Engineering); **Law** (Law); **Letters** (Arts and Humanities); **Liberal Arts** (Arts and Humanities)

Graduate Schools

Economics (Business Administration; Economics); **EngineeringEngineering** *(Tagajo City)* (Applied Physics; Civil Engineering; Electrical Engineering; Mechanical Engineering; Technology); **Human Informatics** (Computer Science); **Law** (Law); **Letters** (Cultural Studies; English; Literature); **Professional Legal Studies**

Institutes

Accountancy Research (Accountancy); **Business and Management** (Business and Commerce; Management); **Christianity and Culture** (Christian Religious Studies; Cultural Studies); **Computer Science** (Computer Science); **Education** (Education); **English Language and Literature** (English; Literature); **Environmental Protection Engineering** (Environmental Engineering); **European Culture** (Cultural Studies; European Studies); **Law and Political Science** (Law; Political Sciences); **North Japan Culture** (Cultural Studies); **Religious Music** (Religious Music); **Social Welfare Research** (Social Welfare)

Further Information: Tsuchitoi, Tagajo and Izumi campuses

History: Founded 1886 as Sendai Theological Seminary, acquired present title 1949.

Academic Year: April to March (April-September; October-March)

Admission Requirements: Graduation from high school and entrance examination

Main Language(s) of Instruction: Japanese

Degrees and Diplomas: *Gakushi*: 4 yrs; *Shushi*: a further 2 yrs; *Hakase*: 3 yrs following Shushi

Student Services: Academic counselling, Canteen, Cultural centre, Employment services, Foreign student adviser, Foreign Studies Centre, Handicapped facilities, Health services, Language programs, Nursery care, Social counselling, Sports facilities

Student Residential Facilities: Yes

Libraries: University Library, 909,000 vols

Publications: Journals *(annually)*

Last Updated: 04/04/08

TOHOKU INSTITUTE OF TECHNOLOGY

Tohoku Kogyo Daigaku (TIT)
35-1 Kasumi-cho, Yagiyama, Taihaku-ku, Sendai-shi, Miyagi 982-8577
Tel: +81(22) 229-1151
Fax: +81(22) 228-2781 +81(22) 228-1813
EMail: nyushi@tohtech.ac.jp
Website: http://www.tohtech.ac.jp

President: Yasuji Sawada

Vice-President: Hiroshi Konno

Centres
Human Sciences; **Teacher Training** (Teacher Training)

Departments
Architecture (Architecture; Structural Architecture); **Civil Engineering** (Civil Engineering); **Creative Design**; **Electronics and Intelligent System** (Artificial Intelligence; Electronic Engineering); **Environmental Information Engineering** (Environmental Engineering); **Industrial Design** (Industrial Design); **Information and Communication Engineering** (Information Technology; Telecommunications Engineering); **Life Design for Safety and Amenity**; **Management and Communication**

Graduate Schools
Engineering (Architecture; Civil Engineering; Electronic Engineering; Engineering; Environmental Engineering; Industrial Engineering; Structural Architecture; Telecommunications Engineering)

History: Founded 1964.

Academic Year: April to March

Admission Requirements: Graduation from high school and entrance examination

Main Language(s) of Instruction: Japanese

Accrediting Agencies: Ministry of Education, Culture, Sports, Science and Technology

Degrees and Diplomas: *Gakushi*: Engineering, 4 yrs; *Shushi*: Engineering, a further 2 yrs; *Hakase*: Engineering, a further 3 yrs

Student Services: Canteen, Employment services, Health services, Language programs, Nursery care, Social counselling, Sports facilities

Libraries: 177,680 vols; 1,620 periodicals

Publications: Memoirs of the Tohoku Institute of Technology, (Ser. I: Science and Engineering) *(annually)*; Memoirs of the Tohoku Institute of Technology, (Ser. II: Humanities and Social Sciences) *(annually)*

Last Updated: 04/02/09

TOHOKU PHARMACEUTICAL UNIVERSITY

Tohoku Yakka Daigaku
4-4-1 Komatsushima, Aoba-ku, Sendai-shi, Miyagi 981-8558
Tel: +81(22) 234-4181
Fax: +81(22) 275-2013
EMail: shomuka@tohoku-pharm.ac.jp
Website: http://www.tohoku-pharm.ac.jp

Programmes
Cancer Research (Oncology); **Pharmaceutical Sciences** (Chemical Engineering; Hygiene; Pharmacology; Pharmacy)

History: Founded 1939 as School, became College 1949.

Academic Year: April to March (April-September; October-March)

Admission Requirements: Graduation from high school or equivalent or foreign equivalent, and entrance examination

Main Language(s) of Instruction: Japanese

Degrees and Diplomas: *Gakushi*: Pharmacy (Yakugakushi), 4 yrs; *Shushi*: Pharmacy (Yakugakushushi), a further 2 yrs; *Hakase*: Pharmacy (Yakugakuhakushi), 3 yrs following Shushi

Student Services: Sports facilities

Libraries: 94,000 vols

Last Updated: 04/02/09

TOHOKU SEIKATSU BUNKA COLLEGE

Tohoku Seikatsu Bunka Daigaku
1-18 Nijinooka, Izumi-ku, Sendai-shi, Miyagi 981-8585
Tel: +81(22) 272-7513
Fax: +81(22) 301-5602
EMail: dkyomu@mishima.ac.jp
Website: http://www.mishima.ac.jp

Departments
Home Economics (Home Economics)

History: Founded 1958. Formerly known as Mishima Gakuen Joshi Daigaku.

Degrees and Diplomas: *Gakushi*

Last Updated: 04/02/09

TOHOKU UNIVERSITY

Tohoku Daigaku
2-1-1 Katahira, Aoba-ku, Sendai-shi, Miyagi 980-8577
Tel: +81(22) 217-4844
Fax: +81(22) 217-4846
EMail: kokusai@bureau.tohoku.ac.jp
Website: http://www.tohoku.ac.jp

President: Akihisa Inoue EMail: hisyo@bureau.tohoku.ac.jp

Vice President, International Student Exchange and Graduate School Education: Osamu Hashimoto

International Relations: Hiroyuki Uchiyama, Directtor, International Affairs Department

Centres
Cyclotron and Radioisotope; **Gene Research**; **Higher Education Research**; **Information Synergy**; **Interdisciplinary Research**; **International Student** (Educational and Student Counselling; Japanese); **Low Temperature Science**; **New Industry Creation Hatchery**; **Northeast Asian Studies** *(Interdisciplinary)*

Faculties
Agriculture (Agriculture; Biological and Life Sciences; Environmental Management; Natural Resources) *Dean*: Akihiko Kudo; **Arts and Letters** (Arts and Humanities; Development Studies; History of Societies; Linguistics; Social Sciences) *Dean*: Junsuke Hara; **Dentistry** (Dentistry; Stomatology) *Dean*: Takashi Sasano; **Economics** (Business Administration; Economics; Management) *Dean*: Yoshihiko Tsukuda; **Education** (Educational Sciences) *Dean*: Toru Hosokawa; **Engineering** (Aeronautical and Aerospace Engineering; Applied Chemistry; Applied Physics; Architecture; Artificial Intelligence; Biomedical Engineering; Building Technologies; Chemical Engineering; Civil Engineering; Earth Sciences; Electrical and Electronic Engineering; Energy Engineering; Engineering; Geology; Materials Engineering; Measurement and Precision Engineering; Metallurgical Engineering; Telecommunications Engineering) *Dean*: Tatsuo Uchida; **Law** (International Law; Law; Political Sciences; Public Law) *Dean*: Kaoru Inaba; **Medicine** (Health Sciences; Medicine; Rehabilitation and Therapy) *Dean*: Masayuki Yamamoto; **Pharmaceutical Sciences** (Biological and Life Sciences; Chemistry; Pharmacy) *Dean*: Akira Naganuma; **Science** (Astronomy and Space Science; Biology; Chemistry; Environmental Studies; Geology; Geophysics; Mathematics; Mineralogy; Petroleum and Gas Engineering; Physics) *Dean*: Kimio Hanawa

Graduate Schools
Educational Informatics *(Education and Research Divisions)* *Dean*: Shinichi Watabe; **Environmental Studies** (Chemistry; Cultural Studies; Earth Sciences; Energy Engineering; Environmental Engineering; Materials Engineering) *Dean*: Shoji Taniguchi; **Information Sciences** (Information Sciences; Mathematics and Computer Science; Social Sciences) *Dean*: Takao Nishizeki; **International Cultural Studies** (Communication Studies; Cultural Studies; Economics; Linguistics; Literature; Modern Languages) *Dean*: Naoki Ishihata; **Life Sciences** (Biological and Life Sciences; Environmental Studies; Neurosciences) *Director*: Toshio Iijima

Institutes
Development, Ageing and Cancer (Biology; Genetics; Medicine; Neurology; Oncology; Physiology); **Electrical Communication Research** (Computer Science; Electrical Engineering;

Telecommunications Engineering); **Fluid Science** (Mechanics; Physics); **Materials Research**; **Multi-disciplinary Research for Advanced Materials** (Automation and Control Engineering; Engineering; Materials Engineering)

Further Information: All Faculties have attached graduate schools

History: Founded 1907 as Tohoku Imperial University, incorporating College of Science, Sendai, and branch School of Sapporo Agricultural College, Hokkaido. Reorganized as National University 1949. Reorganized as National University Corporation and incorporated College of Medical Sciences Tohoku University 2004.

Governing Bodies: Yakuinkai (Board of Directors)

Academic Year: April to March (April-September; October-March)

Admission Requirements: Graduation from high school or equivalent or foreign equivalent, and entrance examination

Fees: (Yens): 520,800 per annum

Main Language(s) of Instruction: Japanese

Degrees and Diplomas: *Gakushi*: Arts and Humanities; Education; Law; Economics; Science; Pharmaceutical Sciences; Engineering; Agriculture, 4 yrs; *Gakushi*: Dentistry; Medicine, 6 yrs; *Shushi*: Arts and Humanities; Education; Law; Economics; Science; Medicine; Pharmaceutical Sciences; Engineering; Agriculture; International Cultural Studies; Information Sciences; Life Sciences, a further 2 yrs; *Hakase*: Arts and Humanities; Education; Law; Economics; Science; Pharmaceutical Sciences; Engineering; Agriculture; International Cultural Studies; Information Sciences; Life Sciences, 3 yrs following Shushi; *Hakase*: Dental Sciences; Medicine Sciences, a further 4 yrs

Student Services: Academic counselling, Canteen, Foreign student adviser, Foreign Studies Centre, Health services, Language programs

Student Residential Facilities: Rooms for Domestic Students, 654, for Foreign Students, 220, for Foreign Researchers, 34.

Special Facilities: University Museum, University Farm, University Archives, Kawatabi Seminar Centre, One Million Volt Electron Microscope Laboratory, Environment Conservation Centre, Archaeological Research Centre, Venture Business Laboratory

Libraries: University Library, c. 2,500,000 vols; Medical Library, c. 408,000 vols; Engineering Library, c. 305,000 vols; Agricultural Library, c. 127,000 vols; Kita-Aobayama Library, c. 361,000 vols

Publications: Annual Report of the Economic Society *(quarterly)*; Annual Research Bulletin of the Graduate School of Pharmaceutical Sciences *(annually)*; CYRIC Annual Report *(annually)*; Faculty of Engineering *(annually)*; Interdisciplinary Information Sciences *(biennially)*; New Industry Creation Hatchery Centre *(biennially)*; Northeast Asian Studies *(annually)*; Research Report of the Laboratory of Nuclear Science *(annually)*; Tohoku Geophysical Journal *(3 per annum)*; Tohoku Journal of Experimental Medicine *(monthly)*; Tohoku Mathematical Journal *(quarterly)*; Tohoku University Bulletin *(annually)*

Last Updated: 04/02/09

TOHOKU UNIVERSITY OF ART AND DESIGN

Tohoku Geijutsu Koka Daigaku

200 Kamisakurada, Yamagata-shi, Yamagata 990-9530
Tel: +81(23) 627-2011
Fax: +81(23) 627-2154
EMail: nyushi@aga.tuad.ac.jp
Website: http://www.tuad.ac.jp

President: Tetsuo Matsumoto

Vice-President: Tatsuo Miyajima

Graduate Schools

Art and Design (Architectural and Environmental Design; Art History; Cultural Studies; Design; Handicrafts; Heritage Preservation; Painting and Drawing; Sculpture)

Schools

Art; **Design**

History: Founded 1992.

Degrees and Diplomas: *Gakushi*; *Shushi*

Last Updated: 04/02/09

TOHOKU UNIVERSITY OF COMMUNITY SERVICE AND SCIENCE

Tohoku Koeki Bunka Daigaku

3-5-1 Iimoriyama, Sakata, Yamagata-shi, Yamagata 998-8580
Tel: +81(234) 41-1111
Fax: +81(234) 41-1133
EMail: begin@koeki-u.ac.jp
Website: http://www.koeki-u.ac.jp

Departments

Community Services and Science (Business Administration; Computer Science; English; Environmental Studies; Social Sciences)

Schools

Community Services and Science

History: Founded 2001.

Degrees and Diplomas: *Gakushi*; *Shushi*; *Hakase*

Student Services: Cultural centre, Sports facilities

Libraries: c. 20,000 vols.

Last Updated: 04/02/09

TOHOKU WOMEN'S UNIVERSITY

Tohoku Joshi Daigaku

1-2-1 Toyohara, Hirosaki-shi, Aomori 036-8154
Tel: +81(172) 332-289
Website: http://www.tojo.ac.jp

Programmes

Home Economics (Home Economics)

Degrees and Diplomas: *Gakushi*

TOHWA UNIVERSITY

Tohwa Daigaku

1-1-1 Chikushigaoka, Minami-ku, Fukuoka-shi, Fukuoka 815-8510
Tel: +81(92) 541-1511
Fax: +81(92) 552-2707
EMail: office@tohwa-u.ac.jp
Website: http://www.tohwa-u.ac.jp

Programmes

Engineering (Engineering)

Degrees and Diplomas: *Gakushi*

TOIN UNIVERSITY OF YOKOHAMA

Toin Yokohama Daigaku

1614 Kurogane-cho, Aoba-ku, Yokohama-shi, Kanagawa 225-8502
Tel: +81(45) 971-1411
Fax: +81(45) 975-5295
EMail: kikaku@cc.toin.ac.jp
Website: http://www.toin.ac.jp

Centres

Biomedical Engineering (Biochemistry; Bioengineering; Cell Biology; Molecular Biology; Pharmacology)

Faculties

Biomedical Engineering; **Culture and Sport Policy**; **Engineering** *(Also Graduate School)* (Electronic Engineering; Engineering; Information Technology; Materials Engineering; Mechanical Engineering; Robotics); **Law** *(Also Graduate School)* (Law)

History: Founded 1988.

Main Language(s) of Instruction: Japanese

International Co-operation: With universities in USA, China and Germany

Degrees and Diplomas: *Gakushi*; *Shushi*; *Hakase*

Student Services: Academic counselling, Social counselling

Libraries: c. 140,000 vols

Last Updated: 04/02/09

TOKAI GAKUEN UNIVERSITY

Tokai Gakuen Daigaku

2-901 Nakahira, Tenpaku-ku, Nagoya-shi, Aichi 468-8514
Tel: +81(52) 801-1204
Fax: +81(52) 804-1044
EMail: koho@tokaigakuen-u.ac.jp
Website: http://www.tokaigakuen-u.ac.jp

Faculties

Human Health; **Humanities** (Arts and Humanities); **Management**

History: Founded 1995.

Degrees and Diplomas: *Gakushi*

Last Updated: 04/02/09

TOKAI GAKUIN UNIVERSITY

Tokai Gakuin Daigaku

Kirino-cho Naka, Kakamigahara-shi, Gifu-Ken 504-8511
Tel: +81(58) 389-2200
Fax: +81(58) 389-2205
EMail: nyushi@hm.tokaijoshi-u.ac.jp
Website: http://www.tokaigakuin-u.ac.jp

Graduate Schools

English and American Culture (American Studies; Cultural Studies; English Studies; Linguistics; Literature)

Programmes

Art and Language (Linguistics; Literature; Social Sciences); **Social Services and Welfare** (Social and Community Services; Social Welfare)

History: Founded 1981. Known as Tokai Joshi Daigaku (Tokai Women's University) until 2007.

Governing Bodies: Kamiya Gakuen Educational Trust

Academic Year: April to March

Main Language(s) of Instruction: Japanese

Degrees and Diplomas: *Gakushi (BA)*: 4 yrs; *Shushi (MA)*: a further 2 yrs

Student Services: Academic counselling, Canteen, Employment services, Language programs, Social counselling, Sports facilities

Student Residential Facilities: Yes

Libraries: c. 20,000 vols

Last Updated: 04/02/09

TOKAI UNIVERSITY

Tokai Daigaku

Shonan Campus, 1117 Kitakaname, Hiratsuka, Kanagawa 259-1292
Tel: +81(463) 581-211
Fax: +81(463) 352-458
EMail: info@tsc.u-tokai.ac.jp; iadt@yyg.u-tokai.ac.jp
Website: http://www.u-tokai.ac.jp

President: Tatsuro Matsumae Tel: +81(463) 581-211, Ext. 2010

Vice-Chancellor, Administration: Tateo Adachi

Graduate Schools

Agriculture *(Kyushu area; Master's programme)* (Agriculture); **Arts** *(Tokyo area; Master's programme)* (Design; Fine Arts; Music); **Bioscience** *(Doctoral programme)*; **Design** *(Hokkaido area; Master's programme)*; **Earth and Environmental Science** *(Doctoral programme)* (Earth Sciences; Environmental Engineering; Environmental Studies); **Economics** *(Tokyo area; Doctoral programme)* (Economics); **Engineering** *(Tokyo area; Master's programme)* (Aeronautical and Aerospace Engineering; Civil Engineering; Computer Engineering; Construction Engineering; Electrical and Electronic Engineering; Engineering; Industrial Chemistry; Information Sciences; Information Technology; Management; Mechanical Engineering; Metallurgical Engineering; Optical Technology; Structural Architecture; Telecommunications Engineering); **Health Sciences** *(Tokyo area; Master's programme)* (Health Sciences; Nursing; Social Work); **High-Technology for Human Welfare** *(Tokyo area; Master's programme)* (Bioengineering; Biomedical Engineering; Communication Studies; Information Technology; Materials Engineering); **Human Environmental Studies** *(Tokyo area; Master's programme)* (Environmental Studies); **Industrial Engineering** *(Kyushu area; Master's programme)* (Architecture; Civil Engineering; Industrial Engineering; Information Technology; Production Engineering; Structural Architecture); **Law** *(Tokyo area; Doctoral programme)* (Law); **Letters** *(Tokyo area; Doctoral programme)* (Arts and Humanities; Communication Studies; English; History; Japanese); **Marine Science and Technology** *(Tokyo area; Master's programme)* (Fishery; Marine Engineering; Marine Science and Oceanography); **Medicine** *(Tokyo area; Master's and Doctoral programmes)* (Medicine); **Physical Education** *(Tokyo area; Master's programme)*; **Political Science** *(Tokyo area; Doctoral programme)* (Political Sciences); **Regional Development Studies** *(Hokkaido area; Master's programme)*; **Science** *(Tokyo area; Master's programme)*; **Science and Engineering** *(Hokkaido area; Master's programme)*; **Science and Technology** *(Doctoral programme)*

Schools

Agriculture *(Aso Campus)* (Agriculture; Botany; Zoology); **Art and Technology** *(Asahikawa Campus)* (Architectural and Environmental Design; Design; Fine Arts); **Biological Science and Engineering** *(Sapporo Campus)*; **Business Studies** *(Kumamoto Campus)*; **Engineering** *(Shonan Campus)* (Aeronautical and Aerospace Engineering; Air Transport; Applied Chemistry; Architecture; Biochemistry; Building Technologies; Civil Engineering; Construction Engineering; Electrical and Electronic Engineering; Energy Engineering; Engineering; Materials Engineering; Measurement and Precision Engineering; Mechanical Engineering; Optical Technology); **Health Sciences** *(Isehara Campus)*; **High-Technology for Human Welfare** *(Numazu Campus)* (Applied Chemistry; Biological and Life Sciences; Biomedical Engineering; Communication Studies; Information Technology); **Humanities and Culture** *(Shonan Campus)* (Arts and Humanities; Cultural Studies; Design; Development Studies; Environmental Studies; Fine Arts; International Studies; Music; Natural Resources; Social Welfare); **Industrial Engineering** *(Kumamoto Campus)*; **Information and Design Engineering** *(Yoyogi Campus)*; **Information and Telecommunication Engineering** *(Takanawa Campus)* (Computer Engineering; Computer Networks; Information Technology; Telecommunications Engineering); **Information Science and Technology** *(Shonan Campus)*; **International Cultural Relations** *(Sapporo Campus)* (Communication Studies); **Law** *(Shonan Campus)* (Commercial Law; International Law; Law); **Letters** *(Shonan Campus)*; **Marine Science and Technology** *(Shimizu Campus)*; **Medicine** *(Isehara Campus)* (Medicine); **Physical Education** *(Shonan Campus)*; **Political Science and Economics** *(Shonan Campus)* (Business Administration; Economics; Political Sciences); **Science** *(Shonan Campus)* (Chemistry; Mathematics; Physics)

Further Information: Also Professional Graduate Schools (Embedded Technology and Law School). Japanese language course for foreign students and shipboard training. Campuses in: Tokyo (Shonan, Takanawa, Numazu, Yoyogi, Isehara and Shimizu), Hokkaido (Sapporo and Asahikawa), and Kyushu (Kumamoto and Aso)

History: Founded 1942 as Aerial Science College, recognized 1946 as Tokai University, and officially authorized by the Ministry of Education. From 2008, Tokai Daigaku (Tokai University) Kyushu Tokai Daigaku (Kyushu Tokai University) and Hokkaido Tokai Daigaku (Hokkaido Tokai University) were integrated under one banner as Tokai University.

Governing Bodies: Board of Trustees

Academic Year: April to March (April-September; October-March)

Admission Requirements: Graduation from high school and entrance examination

Fees: (Yen): Registration and tuition, 1,522,200-1,959,200 per annum; Medicine, 10,951,200

Main Language(s) of Instruction: Japanese

International Co-operation: With universities in Bulgaria, Russia, Thailand, Hungary, Germany, France, United Kingdom, Spain, USA, China, Australia, Canada, Denmark, Finland, Kenya, Laos, Malaysia, New Zealand, Norway, Vietnam, Republic of Korea, Philippines, Taiwan, Brazil

Accrediting Agencies: Ministry of Education, Culture, Sports, Science and Technology

Degrees and Diplomas: *Gakushi*: 4 yrs; *Gakushi*: Medicine, 6 yrs; *Shushi*: a further 2 yrs; *Hakase*: 3 yrs following Shushi

Student Services: Academic counselling, Canteen, Cultural centre, Employment services, Foreign student adviser, Foreign Studies Centre, Handicapped facilities, Health services, Language programs, Social counselling, Sports facilities

Student Residential Facilities: For foreign students

Special Facilities: Marine Science Museum; Natural History Museum; Mtsumae Museum; Bosei Maru research and training vessels

Libraries: Shonan, Yoyogi, Isehara, Shimizu and Numazu libraries, total, 2,032,474 vols

Last Updated: 21/11/08

TOKIWA UNIVERSITY

Tokiwa Daigaku (TU)

1-430-1 Miwa, Mito-shi, Ibaraki 310-8585

Tel: +81(29) 232-2511

Fax: +81(29) 231-6078

EMail: intlco@tokiwa.ac.jp

Website: http://www.tokiwa.ac.jp

President: Isato Takagi Tel: +81(29) 232-2611

Colleges

Applied International Studies (American Studies; Business and Commerce; English Studies; International Business; International Relations); **Community Development** (Development Studies; Regional Studies; Social and Community Services); **Human Sciences** (Communication Studies; Education; Health Sciences; Nutrition; Psychology; Sociology)

Schools

Graduate Studies (Development Studies; Psychology; Social Psychology; Social Sciences; Urban Studies)

History: Founded 1983.

Governing Bodies: Tokiwa School Corporation

Academic Year: April to January (April-July; September-January)

Admission Requirements: High school diploma or equivalent

Fees: (Yen): 1.24m. per annum

Main Language(s) of Instruction: Japanese

International Co-operation: With universities in USA

Degrees and Diplomas: *Gakushi*: 4 yrs; *Shushi*: a further 2 yrs; *Hakase*: 3 yrs following Shushi

Student Services: Academic counselling, Canteen, Employment services, Foreign student adviser, Foreign Studies Centre, Handicapped facilities, Health services, Language programs, Social counselling, Sports facilities

Student Residential Facilities: Yes

Libraries: c. 290,000 vols

Publications: Community Development Studies *(annually)*; Human Science *(biennially)*; Tokiwa International Studies Journal *(annually)*

Last Updated: 04/02/09

TOKIWAKAIGAKUEN UNIVERSITY

Tokiwakaigakuen Daigaku

1-4-12 Kirehigashi, Hirano-ku, Osaka 547-0021

Tel: +81(6) 4302-8880

Fax: +81(6) 4302-8884

EMail: info@sftokiwakai.ac.jp

Website: http://www.sftokiwakai.ac.jp

Programmes

International Communication (Communication Studies; International Relations)

History: Founded 1999.

International Co-operation: With Universities in China; Australia; USA

Degrees and Diplomas: *Gakushi*

Student Services: Cultural centre, Sports facilities

TOKOHA GAKUEN UNIVERSITY

Tokoha Gakuen Daigaku

1-22-1 Sena, Shizuoka-shi, Shizuoka 420-0911

Tel: +81(54) 263-1125

Fax: +81(54) 263-2750

EMail: inexpr@tokoha-u.ac.jp

Website: http://www.tokoha-u.ac.jp

Faculties

Education (Education; Primary Education); **Foreign Studies** (Communication Studies; Cultural Studies; English; International Business; International Studies; Modern Languages; Spanish)

Schools

Graduate Studies

History: Founded 1980.

Degrees and Diplomas: *Gakushi*; *Shushi*

Last Updated: 04/02/09

TOKUSHIMA BUNRI UNIVERSITY

Tokushima Bunri Daigaku

1-8 Terashimahon-cho, Tokushima-shi, Tokushima 770-8560

Tel: +81(886) 22-0097

Fax: +81(886) 26-2998

EMail: kokusai@tokushima.bunri-u.ac.jp

Website: http://www.bunri-u.ac.jp

Faculties

Engineering *(Also Graduate School)* (Artificial Intelligence; Bioengineering; Computer Engineering; Electronic Engineering; Engineering; Environmental Engineering; Information Sciences; Mechanical Engineering; Nanotechnology; Robotics); **Human Life Sciences** (Food Science; Home Economics; Information Technology; Nutrition; Psychology; Social Sciences; Social Welfare; Welfare and Protective Services); **Literature** *(Also Graduate School)* (American Studies; Communication Studies; Cultural Studies; English; European Languages; International Relations; Japanese; Literature; Modern Languages; Oriental Languages); **Music** *(Also Postgraduate one-year courses)* (Music; Musical Instruments; Singing); **Pharmaceutical Sciences** *(Kagawa Campus; Also Graduate School)* (Pharmacology; Pharmacy); **Pharmaceutical Sciences** *(Also Graduate School)* (Pharmacology; Pharmacy); **Policy Studies** *(Also Graduate School)* (Political Sciences)

Graduate Schools

Home Economics (Environmental Studies; Food Science; Home Economics; Social Sciences; Social Studies)

History: Founded 1895, acquired present status 1966.

Academic Year: April to March

Admission Requirements: Graduation from high school and entrance examination

Main Language(s) of Instruction: Japanese

International Co-operation: With universities in Canada, USA and Australia

Degrees and Diplomas: *Gakushi*: 4 yrs; *Shushi*: a further 2 yrs; *Hakase*

Student Services: Foreign Studies Centre, Sports facilities

Libraries: c.623,000 vols

Last Updated: 04/02/09

TOKUYAMA UNIVERSITY

Tokuyama Daigaku

843-4-2 Kume-Kurigasako, Tokuyama-shi, Yamaguchi 745-8566

Tel: +81(834) 282-088

Fax: +81(834) 282-088

EMail: kokusai@tokuyama-u.ac.jp

Website: http://www.tokuyama-u.ac.jp

Faculties

Economics (Economics); **Welfare and Information** (Social Welfare)

History: Founded 1971.

Degrees and Diplomas: *Gakushi*
Last Updated: 04/02/09

TOKYO CHRISTIAN UNIVERSITY

Tokyo Kirisutokyo Daigaku
3-301-5-1 Uchino, Inzai-shi, Chiba 270-1347
Tel: +81(476) 46-1131
Fax: +81(476) 46-1405
EMail: acts@tci.ac.jp
Website: http://www.tci.ac.jp

President: Masanori Kurasawa

Programmes

Bible (Bible); **Church History**; **Japanese Studies** (Communication Studies; Cultural Studies; East Asian Studies; History; Religion; South Asian Studies; Southeast Asian Studies); **Languages**; **Liberal Arts**; **Missiology**; **Practical Theology** (Theology); **Systematic Theology** (Theology)

History: Founded 1990.

Degrees and Diplomas: *Gakushi*
Last Updated: 05/02/09

TOKYO CITY UNIVERSITY

Tokyo Shiritsu Daigaku
1-28-1 Tamazutsumi, Setagaya-ku, Tokyo 158-8557
Tel: +81(3) 3703-3111
Fax: +81(3) 5707-2222
EMail: sangaku@tcu.ac.jp
Website: http://www.tcu.ac.jp/english/index.html

President: Hideo Nakamura (2004-)

Faculties

Engineering; **Environmental and Information Studies**; **Human Life Sciences** (Biological and Life Sciences; Child Care and Development; Social Sciences); **Knowledge Engineering**; **Urban Life Studies** (Urban Studies)

Graduate Schools

Engineering; **Environmental and Information Studies**

History: Founded 1929 as Technical School, became Institute 1949. Known as Musashi Kogyo Daigaku (Musashi Institute of Technology) until April 2009.

Academic Year: April to March (April-October; October-March)

Admission Requirements: Graduation from high school or recognized equivalent or foreign equivalent, and entrance examination

Fees: (Yen): 1.19m.-1.34m. per annum, according to Faculty

Main Language(s) of Instruction: Japanese

Degrees and Diplomas: *Gakushi*: Environmental Studies; Information Sciences; Mechanical Engineering; Mechanical Systems Engineering; Electrical and Electronic Engineering; Electronics and Communication Engineering; Computer Science and Media Engineering; Architecture; Civil Engineering; Systems Information Engineering; Environmental Energy Engineering, 4 yrs; *Shushi*: Environmental and Information Studies; Mechanical Engineering; Mechanical Systems Engineering; Electrical Engineering; Architecture; Civil Engineering; Systems Information Engineering (Industrial Engineering); Energy Science and Nuclear Engineering, a further 2 yrs; *Hakase*: Environmental and Information Studies; Mechanical Engineering; Mechanical Systems Engineering; Electrical Engineering; Architecture; Civil Engineering; Systems Information Engineering (Industrial Engineering); Energy Science and Nuclear Engineering (Kogakuhakushi), 3 yrs following Shushi

Student Services: Academic counselling, Canteen, Employment services, Foreign student adviser, Handicapped facilities, Health services, Social counselling, Sports facilities

Special Facilities: Centre for Information Studies. Information Processing Centre. Research and advanced research centres, special and advanced research laboratories

Libraries: c. 325,000 vols

Publications: MI-TECH Quarterly *(quarterly)*

TOKYO COLLEGE OF MUSIC

Tokyo Ongaku Daigaku
3-4-5 Minami-Ikebukuro, Toshima-ku, Tokyo 171-8540
Tel: +81(3) 3982-3186
Fax: +81(3) 3986-2883
EMail: admissions@tokyo-ondai.ac.jp
Website: http://www.tokyo-ondai.ac.jp

President: Yoshio Unno

Programmes

Music (Conducting; Music; Music Theory and Composition; Musical Instruments; Opera; Singing)

History: Founded 1907.

Main Language(s) of Instruction: Japanese

Degrees and Diplomas: *Gakushi*; *Shushi*

Libraries: Total, c. 160,000 vols
Last Updated: 05/02/09

TOKYO DENKI UNIVERSITY

Tokyo Denki Daigaku
2-2 Kanda-Nishikicho, Chiyoda-ku, Tokyo 101-8457
Tel: +81(3) 5280-3511
Fax: +81(3) 5280-3599
EMail: nyushi@jim.dendai.ac.jp
Website: http://www.dendai.ac.jp

President: Katsuhisa Furuta

Centres

Multimedia Resource and Library Science (Library Science; Multimedia); **Research Collaboration**

Graduate Schools

Advanced Science and Technology *(Doctoral programme)*; **Engineering** *(Master's programme)* (Engineering); **Information Environment** *(Master's programme)* (Information Sciences); **Science and Engineering** *(Master's programme)* (Engineering)

Institutes

Construction Technology Research (Construction Engineering); **Technology Research** (Technology)

Laboratories

Applied Superconductivity Research

Schools

Engineering (Applied Chemistry; Electrical and Electronic Engineering; Engineering; Information Technology; Mechanical Engineering); **Engineering** *(Evening Division)*; **Information Environment** (Architectural and Environmental Design; Communication Studies; Computer Engineering; Computer Networks; Information Management; Information Sciences; Information Technology; Media Studies); **Science and Engineering** (Biological and Life Sciences; Civil Engineering; Engineering; Environmental Engineering; Information Technology; Mechanical Engineering; Natural Sciences); **Science and Technology for the Future Life**

Further Information: Also Courses for foreign students. Study Abroad programmes in USA

History: Founded 1907 as evening Institute of Electrical and Mechanical Technology. Became Higher Technical School 1939 and College 1949. Two Campuses: Hatoyama (Saitama), and Chiba.

Academic Year: April to March (April-September; October-March)

Admission Requirements: Graduation from high school or equivalent, and entrance examination

Main Language(s) of Instruction: Japanese

International Co-operation: With universities in USA, China and Republic of Korea

Degrees and Diplomas: *Gakushi*: Engineering (Kogakushi); Science (Rigakushi), 4 yrs; *Shushi*: a further 3 yrs; *Hakase*: 3 yrs following Shushi

Student Services: Academic counselling, Canteen, Employment services, Health services, Sports facilities

Student Residential Facilities: For c. 260 students

Libraries: c. 357,000 vols

Publications: Library Reports *(annually)*; Research Reports *(annually)*

Press or Publishing House: The University Press

Last Updated: 04/02/09

TOKYO DENTAL COLLEGE

Tokyo Shika Daigaku

1-2-2, Masago, Chiba-shi, Chiba 261-8502
Tel: +81(43) 270-3764
Fax: +81(43) 270-3765
EMail: ip@tdc.ac.jp
Website: http://www.tdc.ac.jp

Dean: Yuzuru Kaneko

Head, Administration: Takao Nagai

International Relations: Takashi Inoue, Professor, Director of International Programme
Tel: +81(43) 270-3753, Fax: +81(43) 270-3756

Colleges

Dentistry (Dentistry) *Dean*: Yuzuru Kaneko

History: Founded 1890 as Takayama Dental School, acquired present title and status 1907. Reorganized 1950.

Governing Bodies: Board of Trustees; Faculty Assembly; Faculty Council

Academic Year: April to March (April-September; October-March)

Admission Requirements: Graduation from high school and entrance examination

Fees: (Yen): 3m. per annum

Main Language(s) of Instruction: Japanese

Degrees and Diplomas: *Gakushi*: Dentistry, 6 yrs; *Hakase*: Dentistry, 4 yrs

Student Services: Academic counselling, Canteen, Employment services, Health services, Social counselling, Sports facilities

Special Facilities: Historical Museum; Observatory; Oral Health Science Center; Laboratory of Brain Research

Libraries: College Library, c. 198,000 vols; branch libraries, c. 14,820

Publications: Bulletin of Tokyo Dental College *(quarterly)*; Shikwa Gakuho *(biennially)*

Last Updated: 05/02/09

TOKYO FUTURE UNIVERSITY

Tokyo Mirai Daigaku

34-12 Senju, Akebono-cho, Adaki-chu, Tokyo 120-0023
Tel: +81(3) 5813-2525
Fax: +81(3) 5813-2529
EMail: info@tokyomirai.ac.jp
Website: http://www.tokyomirai.ac.jp

President: Takashi Sakamoto

Departments

Psychology (Child Care and Development; Psychology)

History: Founded 2007.

Degrees and Diplomas: *Gakushi*

Last Updated: 13/02/09

TOKYO GAKUGEI UNIVERSITY

Tokyo Gakugei Daigaku

4-1-1 Nukui-Kitamachi, Koganei-shi, Tokyo 184-8501
Tel: +81(42) 329-7111 +81(42) 329-7763
Fax: +81(42) 329-7114 +81(42) 329-7765
EMail: ryuugaku@u-gakugei.ac.jp
Website: http://www.u-gakugei.ac.jp

President: Yasuhiko Washiyama (2003-) Tel: +81(42) 329-7111

Faculties

Education (Education; Educational Sciences; Special Education; Teacher Training)

Further Information: Also Japanese language courses for foreign students

History: Founded 1949, incorporating Tokyo First, Second, and Third Normal Schools, and Youth Normal School, founded between 1873 and 1937.

Governing Bodies: National University Corporation Tokyo Gakugei University

Academic Year: April to March (April-September; October-March)

Admission Requirements: Graduation from high school (undergraduate), from university with Bachelor's Degree (Master), with Master's Degree (Doctor) or recognized equivalent or foreign equivalent, and entrance examination

Main Language(s) of Instruction: Japanese

International Co-operation: Exchange agreements with universities in Australia; China; France; Germany; Indonesia; Philippines; Republic of Korea; Sweden; Taiwan; Tanzania; Thailand and USA

Degrees and Diplomas: *Gakushi*: Arts (Kyouyo); Education (Kyouiku), 4 yrs; *Shushi*: Education (Kyouiku); Philosophy (Gakujutsu), a further 2 yrs; *Hakase*: Education (Kyouikugaku); Philosophy (Gakujutsu), 3 yrs following Shushi

Student Services: Academic counselling, Canteen, Employment services, Foreign student adviser, Foreign Studies Centre, Handicapped facilities, Health services, Language programs, Social counselling, Sports facilities

Student Residential Facilities: Yes

Special Facilities: Art Hall

Libraries: University Library, 864,087 vols

Press or Publishing House: University Press

Last Updated: 04/02/09

TOKYO INSTITUTE OF TECHNOLOGY

Tokyo Kogyo Daigaku

2-12-1 E3 Ookayama, Meguro-ku, Tokyo 152-8550
Tel: +81(3) 5734-2975
Fax: +81(3) 5734-3661
EMail: hyo.koh.sya@jim.titech.ac.jp
Website: http://www.titech.ac.jp

President: Kenichi Iga (2007-)
Tel: +81(3) 5734-2039, Fax: +81(3) 5734-3446
EMail: president@titech.ac.jp

International Relations: Ichiro Okura, Executive Vice-President (2007-)
Tel: +81(3) 5734-2039, Fax: +81(3) 5734-3446
EMail: vicepresident1@titech.ac.jp

Graduate Schools

Bioscience and Biotechnology *(5 Departments, Yokohama City)* (Bioengineering; Biological and Life Sciences; Biomedical Engineering; Molecular Biology) *Dean*: Shigehisa Hirose; **Decision Science and Technology** *(4 Departments)* (Industrial Engineering; Industrial Management; Social Sciences) *Dean*: Noboru Hidano; **Information Science and Engineering** *(3 Departments)* (Computer Science; Environmental Engineering; Information Sciences; Mathematics and Computer Science; Mechanical Engineering) *Dean*: Sadaoki Furui; **Innovation Management** *(2 Departments)* (Engineering Management) *Dean*: Takao Enkawa; **Interdisciplinary Science and Engineering** *(11 Departments, Yokohama City)* (Applied Chemistry; Applied Physics; Artificial Intelligence; Chemistry; Computer Engineering; Electronic Engineering; Energy Engineering; Environmental Engineering; Information Technology; Materials Engineering; Mechanical Engineering; Systems Analysis) *Dean*: Yoshinao Mishima; **Science and Engineering** *(20 Departments)* (Aeronautical and Aerospace Engineering; Applied Chemistry; Automation and Control Engineering; Ceramics and Glass Technology; Chemical Engineering; Chemistry; Civil Engineering; Communication Studies; Construction Engineering; Development Studies; Earth Sciences; Electrical and Electronic Engineering; Electronic Engineering; Materials Engineering; Mathematics; Mechanical Engineering; Metallurgical Engineering; Nuclear Engineering; Nuclear Physics; Physics; Polymer and Plastics Technology; Structural Architecture; Systems Analysis; Telecommunications Engineering) *Dean*: Ken Okazaki

Research Centres

Biological Resources and Informatics; **Carbon Recycling and Energy** (Chemistry); **Educational Facilities**; **Foreign Language Research and Teaching** (Foreign Languages Education); **Frontier Research**; **Global Scientific Information and Computing** (Computer Engineering; Information Technology); **Low Temperature Physics** (Physics); **Quantum Nanoelectronics** (Nanotechnology); **Research and Development of Educational Technology** (Educational Technology); **Research for Educational Facilities**; **Research on Carbon Recycling and Energy**; **Volcanic Fluid Research**

Research Laboratories

Chemical Resources *(Yokohama City)* (Applied Chemistry; Chemistry; Inorganic Chemistry; Laboratory Techniques; Molecular Biology; Natural Resources; Organic Chemistry) *Director*: Masasuke Yoshida; **Materials and Structures** *(Yokohama City)* (Building Technologies; Materials Engineering; Nanotechnology; Structural Architecture) *Director*: Ken-ichi Kondou; **Nuclear Reactors** (Energy Engineering; Nuclear Engineering; Safety Engineering) *Director*: Masanori Aritomi; **Precision and Intelligence** *(Yokohama City)* (Bioengineering; Biomedical Engineering; Information Sciences; Information Technology; Materials Engineering; Mechanical Engineering; Microelectronics) *Director*: Kourou Kobayashi

Schools

Bioscience and Biotechnology *(2 Departments, Yokohama City)* (Bioengineering; Biological and Life Sciences; Biotechnology) *Dean*: Shigehisa Hirose; **Engineering** *(16 Departments)* (Aeronautical and Aerospace Engineering; Applied Chemistry; Architecture and Planning; Automation and Control Engineering; Chemical Engineering; Civil Engineering; Computer Science; Construction Engineering; Electrical and Electronic Engineering; Environmental Engineering; Industrial Engineering; Inorganic Chemistry; Mechanical Engineering; Metallurgical Engineering; Organic Chemistry; Polymer and Plastics Technology; Structural Architecture; Systems Analysis) *Dean*: Ken Okazaki; **Science** *(5 Departments)* (Chemistry; Earth Sciences; Information Sciences; Mathematics; Physics) *Dean*: Makoto Oka

History: Founded 1881 as Tokyo Shokko Gakko (Tokyo Vocational School), acquired present status and title 1929, under direct control of the Ministry of Education, Culture, Sports, Science and Technology.

Governing Bodies: Board of Directors; Management Committee; Educational and Research Council

Academic Year: April to March (April-September; October-March)

Admission Requirements: Graduation from high school or recognized equivalent and entrance examination

Fees: (Yens): Registration, 282,000; tuition, 535,800 per annum

Main Language(s) of Instruction: Japanese, English

International Co-operation: Participates in the Young Scientist Exchange Programme (YSEP). Joint Graduate Course Programme between Tokyo Tech (Tokyo Institute of Technology) and Tsinghua University (China)

Accrediting Agencies: National Institution for Academic Degrees and University Evaluation (NIAD-UE)

Degrees and Diplomas: *Gakushi*: Engineering; Science, 4 yrs; *Shushi*: Engineering; Science; Arts, a further 2 yrs; *Hakase*: Engineering; Science; Management of Technology (MOT); Philosophy (PhD), 3 yrs following Shushi. Also Gijutukeiei Shushi in Management of Technology (2 yrs)

Student Services: Academic counselling, Canteen, Cultural centre, Employment services, Foreign student adviser, Foreign Studies Centre, Handicapped facilities, Health services, Language programs, Social counselling, Sports facilities

Student Residential Facilities: 5 dormitories for students, 2 dormitories for students and researchers, and international house for researchers.

Special Facilities: Kusatsu-Shirane Volcano Observatory. Museum of Evolving Earth. The Centennial Hall. Venture Business Laboratory. Experiment Waste Liquid Disposal Facility. International House. The 70th Anniversary Auditorium. Extracurricular Bildg. 1-4. Network Communication Training Room. Research Centre for Urban Infrastructure. International Student Centre.

Libraries: Institute Library, 801,228 vols (including 7,591 e-journals)

Publications: Annual List of Faculty and Staff Publications *(annually)*

Last Updated: 10/12/08

TOKYO INTERNATIONAL UNIVERSITY

Tokyo Kokusai Daigaku (TIU)

1-13-1 Matoba-Kita, Kawagoe-shi, Saitama-shi, Saitama 350-1197
Tel: +81(492) 32-1111
Fax: +81(492) 32-1119
EMail: kouhou@tiu.ac.jp
Website: http://www.tiu.ac.jp

President: Tsugio Tajeri

Graduate Schools

Applied Sociology *(Master's course)* (Sociology); **Business and Commerce** *(Master's and Doctoral courses)* (Business and Commerce); **Clinical Psychology** *(Master's and Doctoral courses)* (Clinical Psychology); **Economics** *(Master's and Doctoral courses)* (Economics); **International Relations** *(Master's Course)* (International Relations)

Schools

Business and Commerce (Accountancy; Business and Commerce; Finance; International Business; Marketing); **Economics** (Economics; International Economics); **Human and Social Sciences**; **International Relations** (International Relations; Journalism; Radio and Television Broadcasting); **Language Communication**

Further Information: Also affiliated Japanese Language School

History: Founded 1965 as the International College of Commerce and Economics. A private institution emphasizing international Education.

Governing Bodies: Kaneko Educational Foundation

Academic Year: April to March (April-July; September-December; January-March)

Admission Requirements: Secondary school certificate or equivalent and entrance examination

Fees: (Yen): Admission, 230,000; tuition and fee, 1.02m. per annum

Main Language(s) of Instruction: Japanese

International Co-operation: With universities in USA, Republic of Korea, China, Germany, United Kingdom and Sweden

Degrees and Diplomas: *Gakushi*: Accountancy (BA); Behavioural Sciences (BA); Business and Commerce (BA); Distribution and Marketing (BA); Economics (BA); Human Relations (BA); Industrial Relations (BA); Interdisciplinary Studies (BA); International Business (BA); International Economics (BA); International Politics and Economics (BA); International Relations (BA); International Studies; International Broadcasting and Journalism (BA); Sociology (BA), 4 yrs; *Shushi*: Economics (MA); International Relations (MA); Psychology (MA); Sociology (MA), a further 2 yrs; *Hakase*: Business and Commerce; Economics; Clinical Psychology (PhD), 3 yrs following Shushi

Student Services: Canteen, Employment services, Handicapped facilities, Nursery care, Sports facilities

Libraries: Taizo Kaneko Library, 600,000 vols

Last Updated: 28/03/11

TOKYO JOGAKKAN COLLEGE

Tokyo Jogakkan Daigaku

1105 Tsuruma, Machida-shi, Tokyo 194-0004
Tel: +81(42) 796-1145
Fax: +81(42) 799-2652
EMail: a-info@m.tjk.ac.jp
Website: http://www.tjk.ac.jp

Programmes

Liberal arts and International Studies (Anthropology; Arts and Humanities; Biological and Life Sciences; Chinese; Communication Studies; Cultural Studies; Curriculum; East Asian Studies; Economic and Finance Policy; Educational Psychology; English; European Studies; Gender Studies; History; Information Sciences; Information Technology; International Relations; International

Studies; Japanese; Linguistics; Management; Pedagogy; Psychology; Religion; Sociology; South Asian Studies; Southeast Asian Studies; Sports; Women's Studies)

History: Founded 2002.

Degrees and Diplomas: *Gakushi*

Last Updated: 04/02/09

TOKYO JUNSHIN WOMEN'S COLLEGE

Tokyo Junshin Joshi Daigaku

2-600 Takiyama-cho, Hachioji-shi, Tokyo 192-0011
Tel: +81(426) 92-0326
Fax: +81(426) 92-5551
EMail: koho@t-junshin.ac.jp
Website: http://www.t-junshin.ac.jp

Faculties

Modern Culture

History: Founded 1996.

Degrees and Diplomas: *Gakushi*

Last Updated: 04/02/09

TOKYO KASEI GAKUIN UNIVERSITY

Tokyo Kasei Gakuin Daigaku

2600 Aihara-machi, Machida-shi, Tokyo 194-0292
Tel: +81(42) 782-9811
Fax: +81(42) 782-9880
EMail: nyushi@kasei-gakuin.ac.jp
Website: http://www.kasei-gakuin.ac.jp

Faculties

Home Economics; Humanities

Programmes

Human Life Sciences *(Graduate)*

History: Founded 1963.

Main Language(s) of Instruction: Japanese

Degrees and Diplomas: *Gakushi*; *Shushi*

Student Services: Academic counselling, Health services, Social counselling, Sports facilities

Student Residential Facilities: Yes

Libraries: c. 240,000 vols

Last Updated: 04/02/09

TOKYO KASEI UNIVERSITY

Tokyo Kasei Daigaku (TKU)

1-18-1 Kaga, Itabashi-ku, Tokyo 173-8602
Tel: +81(3) 3961-1983 +81(3) 3961-5228
Fax: +81(3) 3961-1736
EMail: nyushi@tokyo-kasei.ac.jp
Website: http://www.tokyo-kasei.ac.jp

Faculties

Home Economics (Child Care and Development; Clothing and Sewing; Environmental Studies; Home Economics; Nutrition); **Humanities** *(Sayama City)* (Arts and Humanities; Education; English; Psychology)

History: Founded 1881. The Institution is playing a very important role in Women's education in Japan.

Governing Bodies: Board of Trustees

Academic Year: April to March

Admission Requirements: Graduation from high school or equivalent

Main Language(s) of Instruction: Japanese

Degrees and Diplomas: *Gakushi*: 4 yrs; *Shushi*; *Hakase*

Student Services: Academic counselling, Canteen, Employment services, Foreign student adviser, Foreign Studies Centre, Handicapped facilities, Health services, Social counselling, Sports facilities

Student Residential Facilities: Yes

Special Facilities: Museum

Libraries: c. 282,000 vols

Publications: Bulletin of Research, Institution of Domestic Science *(annually)*; Bulletin of Tokyo Kasei University *(annually)*

Last Updated: 04/02/09

TOKYO KEIZAI UNIVERSITY

Tokyo Keizai Daigaku

1-7-34, Minami-cho, Kokubunji-shi, Tokyo 185-8502
Tel: +81(42) 328-7711
Fax: +81(42) 328-7770
EMail: ieo@tku.ac.jp
Website: http://www.tku.ac.jp

President: Shigekazu Kukita (2008-)

Faculties

Business Administration (Business Administration; Marketing); **Communication Studies** (Communication Studies; Social Sciences); **Contemporary Law** (Law); **Economics** (Economics; International Economics)

Further Information: Also Graduate Schools in fields of study offered in Faculties

History: Founded 1900 as Okura Commerce School, became University 1949. Graduate School established 1970. Japan's first Faculty of Communication Studies 1995. Formerly known as Tokyo College of Economics.

Governing Bodies: Board of Trustees; Board of Councillors

Academic Year: April to March (April-July; October-March)

Admission Requirements: Graduation from high school or equivalent, and entrance examination

Fees: (Yen): Registration, 100,000; tuition, 785,000 per annum

Main Language(s) of Instruction: Japanese

International Co-operation: With universities in Australia; China; Germany; Republic of Korea; New Zealand; United Kingdom and USA

Degrees and Diplomas: *Gakushi*: Business Administration; Communication Studies; Economics; Law; Marketing and Distribution, 4 yrs; *Shushi*: Business Administration; Communication Studies; Economics, a further 2 yrs; *Hakase*: Business Administration; Communication Studies; Economics, 3 yrs following Shushi

Student Services: Academic counselling, Canteen, Cultural centre, Employment services, Foreign student adviser, Handicapped facilities, Health services, Language programs, Social counselling, Sports facilities

Student Residential Facilities: Dormitory (174 rooms)

Special Facilities: Media Studio.

Libraries: c. 650,000 vols

Publications: Journal of Communication Studies *(biennially)*; Journal of Humanities and Natural Sciences *(biennially)*; Journal of Tokyo Keizai University *(quarterly)*; Tokyo Keizai Law Review *(biennially)*

Press or Publishing House: Tokyo Keizai Daigaku-hó

Last Updated: 04/02/09

TOKYO MEDICAL UNIVERSITY

Tokyo Ika Daigaku (TMU)

6-1-1 Shinjuku, Shinjuku-ku, Tokyo 160-8402
Tel: +81(3) 3351-6141
Fax: +81(3) 3226-7030
Website: http://www.tokyo-med.ac.jp

President: Masahiko Usui
Tel: +81(3) 3354-6141, Fax: +81(3) 3226-7030

Faculties

Medicine (Anatomy; Medicine; Social and Preventive Medicine; Surgery)

Schools

Nursing

History: Founded 1916.

Governing Bodies: Board of Regents

Academic Year: April to March (April-August; September-December; January-March)

Admission Requirements: Graduation from high school and entrance examination

Fees: (Yen): 3,471,000 per annum

Main Language(s) of Instruction: Japanese

International Co-operation: With institutions in USA, United Kingdom, Sweden, France, Denmark, Austria, Hungary, China, Egypt

Accrediting Agencies: Ministry of Education, Culture, Sports, Science and Technology

Degrees and Diplomas: *Gakushi*: Medicine (Igakushi), 6 yrs; *Hakase*: Medicine (Igaku-Hakushi), 4 yrs following Igakushi

Student Services: Academic counselling, Canteen, Foreign student adviser, Health services, Nursery care

Student Residential Facilities: Dormitory for undergraduate men.

Libraries: 232,117 vols

Publications: Journal of Tokyo Medical University, Peer-reviewed journal on all aspects of medicine *(biennially)*

Last Updated: 28/03/11

TOKYO MEDICAL AND DENTAL UNIVERSITY

Tokyo Ikashika Daigaku
1-5-45 Yushima, Bunkyo-ku, Tokyo 113-8510
Tel: +81(3) 3813-6111 +81(3) 5283-5891
Fax: +81(3) 5803-0105 +81(3) 5283-5855
EMail: iss.adm@tmd.ac.jp
Website: http://www.tmd.ac.jp

President: Takashi Ohyama
Tel: +81(3) 5803-5000, Fax: +81(3) 5803-0100

Colleges
Liberal Arts and Sciences

Faculties
Dentistry (Dentistry); **Medicine** (Health Sciences; Medicine) *Dean*: Morio Koike

Graduate Schools
Biomedical Science *(PhD programme)*; **Health Sciences** (Biological and Life Sciences; Community Health; Health Education; Health Sciences; Nursing); **Medicine and Dentistry**

Further Information: Also Japanese language courses for foreign students

History: Founded 1946.

Governing Bodies: Hyogikai (University Council)

Academic Year: April to March (April-October; October-March)

Admission Requirements: Graduation from high school or recognized equivalent, and entrance examination

Main Language(s) of Instruction: Japanese

International Co-operation: With universities in USA, China and Republic of Korea

Degrees and Diplomas: *Gakushi*: 6 yrs; *Hakase*: a further 4 yrs

Student Services: Language programs, Sports facilities

Libraries: 326,913 vols

Publications: Bulletins *(quarterly)*; Report of the Institute for Medical and Dental Engineering *(annually)*

Last Updated: 04/02/09

TOKYO METROPOLITAN UNIVERSITY

Syuto Daigaku Tokyo (TMU)
1-1 Minami-Ohsawa, Hachioji-shi, Tokyo 192-0397
Tel: +81(426) 77-1111
Fax: +81(426) 77-1221
Website: http://www.tmu.ac.jp

President: Jun-ichi Nishizawa

Secretary-General: Kazuyuki Hirai

Divisions
Urban Policy (Town Planning; Urban Studies)

Faculties
Health Sciences; **System Design**; **Urban Environmental Sciences** (Applied Chemistry; Architectural and Environmental Design; Architecture; Architecture and Planning; Civil Engineering; Environmental Engineering; Geography (Human); Tourism; Urban Studies); **Urban Liberal Arts** (Arts and Humanities; Economics; Engineering; Law; Natural Sciences; Social Sciences; Urban Studies)

Graduate Schools
Human Health Sciences (Behavioural Sciences; Biochemistry; Food Science; Health Sciences; Neurosciences; Nursing; Nutrition; Occupational Therapy; Physical Therapy; Physiology; Radiology; Sports); **Humanities**; **Science and Engineering** (Biological and Life Sciences; Chemistry; Electrical and Electronic Engineering; Information Sciences; Mathematics; Mechanical Engineering; Physics); **Social Sciences** (Accountancy; Business Administration; Economic History; Industrial Engineering; Law; Leadership; Management; Management Systems; Marketing; Political Sciences); **System Design**; **Urban Environmental Sciences** (Applied Chemistry; Architectural and Environmental Design; Architecture; Civil Engineering; Construction Engineering; Environmental Engineering; Geography; Geography (Human); Geology; Meteorology; Social and Community Services; Structural Architecture; Tourism; Town Planning; Urban Studies)

Schools
Business Administration (Accountancy; Business Administration; Economic History; Economics; Industrial Engineering; Management; Marketing); **Humanities and Social Sciences** (American Studies; Anthropology; Archaeology; Arts and Humanities; Asian Studies; Cultural Studies; English Studies; European Studies; French Studies; Germanic Studies; History; Literature; Modern Languages; Pedagogy; Philosophical Schools; Philosophy; Psychology; Social Studies; Social Welfare; Sociology; Visual Arts); **Law and Politics** (Administrative Law; Constitutional Law; International Law; Law; Political Sciences; Public Law); **Science and Engineering** (Biological and Life Sciences; Chemistry; Electrical and Electronic Engineering; Engineering; Mathematics; Mechanical Engineering; Natural Sciences; Physics)

History: Founded 1949, incorporating 6 former Colleges. Graduate Schools established 1953. Known as Tokyo Toritsu Daigaku until 2005. Tokyo Toritsu Kagaku Gijutsu Daigaku (Tokyo Metropolitan Institute of Technology), Tokyo Toritsu Hoken Kagaku Daigaku (Tokyo Metropolitan College of Health Sciences) and Shuto Daigaku Tokyo (Tokyo Metropolitan University) incorporated 2005.

Governing Bodies: Hyogikai (University Council); Kyojukai (Faculty Councils)

Academic Year: April to March (April-September; October-March)

Admission Requirements: Graduation from high school or equivalent and entrance examination

Fees: (Yen): 496,800 per annum

Main Language(s) of Instruction: Japanese

Degrees and Diplomas: *Gakushi*: Economics (Keizaigakushi); Engineering (Kogakushi); Law (Hogakushi); Science (Rigakushi); Social Sciences and Humanities (Bungakushi), 4 yrs; *Shushi*: Economics (Keizaigakushushi); Engineering (Kogakushushi); Law (Hogakushushi); Science (Rigakushushi); Social Sciences and Humanities (Bungakushushi), a further 2 yrs; *Hakase*: 3 yrs following Shushi

Student Services: Canteen, Health services, Sports facilities

Student Residential Facilities: Yes

Special Facilities: Makino Herbarium

Libraries: Central Library, c. 1,3m. vols

Publications: Geographical Reports; Hogakkai (Journal of Law and Political Science); Jinbungakuho (Journal of Social Sciences and Humanities); Keizai to Keizaigaku (Journal of Economics); Memoirs of Graduate School of Engineering; Ogasawara Kenkyu (Ogasawara Research); Ogasawara Nenpo; Sogo Toshi Kenkyu (Comprehensive Urban Studies)

TOKYO POLYTECHNIC UNIVERSITY

Tokyo Kogei Daigaku
9-5 Honcho 2-chome, Nakano-ku, Tokyo 164
Tel: +81(3) 3372-1321
Fax: +81(3) 3372-1330
EMail: nyushi@t-kougei.ac.jp
Website: http://www.t-kougei.ac.jp

President: Shin'ichiro Wakao

Faculties

Arts *(Also Graduate School)* (Arts and Humanities; Communication Studies; Design; Media Studies; Photography; Social Sciences; Sports; Visual Arts); **Engineering** *(Also Graduate School)* (Computer Graphics; Computer Science; Electronic Engineering; Information Technology; Media Studies)

History: Founded 1923 as Konishi Professional School of Photography. Acquired present title 1977.

Academic Year: April to March (April-September; September-March)

Admission Requirements: Graduation from high school and entrance examination

Main Language(s) of Instruction: Japanese

Degrees and Diplomas: *Gakushi*: Engineering (Kogakushi), 4 yrs; *Shushi*: Engineering (Kogakushushi), a further 2 yrs; *Hakase*: Engineering

Libraries: 162,000 vols

Publications: Bulletin *(annually)*

TOKYO SEITOKU UNIVERSITY

Tokyo Seitoku Daigaku

2014 Nakadaiyatsu, Hoshina, Yachiyo-shi, Chiba 276-0013
Tel: +81(47) 488-1000
Fax: +81(47) 480-5160
EMail: info@tsu.ac.jp
Website: http://www.tokyoseitoku.ac.jp

Departments

International Languages and Cultures (Cultural Studies; Modern Languages); **Traditional Japanese Culture** (Cultural Studies; Japanese)

Faculties

Psychology

Graduate Schools

Clinical Psychology (Clinical Psychology)

History: Founded 1993.

Degrees and Diplomas: *Gakushi*; *Shushi*

Last Updated: 05/02/09

TOKYO UNIVERSITY AND GRADUATE SCHOOL OF SOCIAL WELFARE

Tokyo Fukushi Daigaku (TUSW)

4-23-1 Higashi-Ikebukuro, Toshima-ku, Tokyo 170-8426
Tel: +81(3) 3987-6602
Fax: +81(3) 3987-8403
Website: http://www.tokyo-fukushi.ac.jp

President: Tatsuya Matsubara

Institutes

Japanese (Japanese)

Programmes

Social Welfare (Clinical Psychology; International Studies; Social Welfare; Social Work)

Schools

Education; **Psychology** (Child Care and Development; Psychology); **Social Welfare** *(Also Graduate School)* (Child Care and Development; Clinical Psychology; Gerontology; Preschool Education; Psychiatry and Mental Health; Social Welfare; Social Work)

Further Information: Also Summer Study Programme in USA

History: Founded 2000.

International Co-operation: With Universities in USA

Degrees and Diplomas: *Gakushi*; *Shushi*; *Hakase*

Student Services: Sports facilities

Special Facilities: Computer Laboratory

Libraries: c. 32,000 vols.

Last Updated: 04/02/09

TOKYO UNIVERSITY OF AGRICULTURE

Tokyo Nogyo Daigaku

1-1-1 Sakuragaoka, Setagaya-ku, Tokyo 156-8502
Tel: +81(3) 5477-2207 +81(3) 5477-2560
Fax: +81(3) 5477-2613 +81(3) 5477-2635
EMail: tuacip@nodai.ac.jp
Website: http://www.nodai.ac.jp

President: Kanju Ohsawa

Faculties

Agriculture (Agriculture; Zoology); **Applied Bio-Science** (Applied Chemistry; Biology; Biotechnology; Food Science; Nutrition); **Bio-industry** (Aquaculture; Food Science; Food Technology); **International Agriculture and Food Studies** (Agriculture; Food Science); **Regional Environmental Science** (Environmental Engineering; Forestry; Landscape Architecture; Production Engineering)

History: Founded 1891 as College, became University 1925.

Governing Bodies: Tokyo University of Agriculture Educational Corporation

Academic Year: April to March (April-September; October-March)

Admission Requirements: Competitive entrance examination following graduation from high school. Proficiency in Japanese

Main Language(s) of Instruction: Japanese

International Co-operation: With universities in Asia; North America; South America and Europe

Degrees and Diplomas: *Gakushi*: Agricultural Science; Applied Bio-science; Regional Environment Science; International Agriculture and Food Studies; Business Science, 4 yrs; *Shushi*: a further 2 yrs; *Hakase*: 3 yrs following Shushi

Student Services: Academic counselling, Canteen, Employment services, Foreign student adviser, Health services, Social counselling, Sports facilities

Student Residential Facilities: For 372 students

Special Facilities: Food and Agriculture Museum; Miyako Subtropical Farm; Atsugi Farm; Fuji Farm; Abashiri Farm; Okutama Practice Forest

Libraries: 700,000 vols

Publications: General Education Journal *(quarterly)*; Memoirs *(quarterly)*; Nogaku Shuho (Agricultural Journal) *(annually)*

Press or Publishing House: Tokyo University of Agriculture Press

TOKYO UNIVERSITY OF AGRICULTURE AND TECHNOLOGY

Tokyo Noko Daigaku (TUAT)

3-8-1 Harumi-cho, Fuchu-shi, Tokyo 183-8538
Tel: +81(42) 364-5506
Fax: +81(42) 364-5898
EMail: koho2@cc.tuat.ac.jp
Website: http://www.tuat.ac.jp

President: Hidefumi Kobatake
Tel: +81(42) 367-5909, Fax: +81(42) 367-5910

Director-General: Masahiro Hashimoto Tel: +81(42) 364-3317

International Relations: Takahiko Ono, Vice-President for Public Relations and International Affairs
Tel: +81(42) 367-5512 EMail: koshukan@cc.tuat.ac.jp

Faculties

Agriculture (Agricultural Economics; Agricultural Engineering; Agriculture; Biochemistry; Ecology; Environmental Engineering; Environmental Studies; Farm Management; Forestry; Molecular Biology; Natural Resources; Natural Sciences; Social Sciences; Veterinary Science; Welfare and Protective Services) *Dean*: Yasuhiro Arima; **Engineering** *(Koganei-shi, Tokyo)* (Applied Chemistry; Applied Physics; Biological and Life Sciences; Biotechnology; Chemical Engineering; Communication Studies; Computer Science; Electrical and Electronic Engineering; Engineering; Environmental Engineering; Information Sciences; Mechanical Engineering; Organic Chemistry; Polymer and Plastics Technology; Technology) *Dean*: Akinori Koukitu

Graduate Schools

Agricultural Science *Dean*: Yasushisa Kunimi; **Agriculture** *Dean*: Yasuhiro Arima; **Bio-Applications and Systems Engineering**

(Koganei-shi, Tokyo) (Engineering; Natural Sciences) *Dean*: Masanori Okazaki; **Technology** *(Koganei-shi, Tokyo)* (Engineering; Natural Sciences; Technology) *Dean*: Hideo Kameyama

Further Information: Also research centres and institutes; Japanese language courses for foreign students

History: Founded 1874, acquired present status 1949.

Governing Bodies: Ministry of Education, Culture, Sports, Science and Technology

Academic Year: April to March (April-October; October-March)

Admission Requirements: Graduation from high school or recognized equivalent and entrance examination

Fees: (Yen): 496,800 per annum

Main Language(s) of Instruction: Japanese

International Co-operation: With universities in China and USA

Degrees and Diplomas: *Gakushi*: Agriculture (Nogakushi); Technology (Kogakushi), 4 yrs; *Shushi*: Agriculture; Science (Gakujutsushushi), a further 2 yrs; *Hakase*: Agriculture; Science (Gakujutsuhakase); Technology (Kogakuhakase), a further 3 yrs

Student Services: Canteen, Foreign student adviser, Foreign Studies Centre, Health services, Language programs, Sports facilities

Student Residential Facilities: Yes

Special Facilities: Textile Museum, Field Science Centre and Veterinary Clinic

Libraries: c. 534,600 vols

Last Updated: 05/02/09

TOKYO UNIVERSITY OF CAREER DEVELOPMENT

LEC Tokyo Rigaru Maindo Daigaku

2-2-15 Misaki-cho, Chiyoda-ku, Tokyo
EMail: mail@lec.ac.jp
Website: http://www.lec.ac.jp/english/

President: Katsuo Sorimachi

Schools

Career Development (Accountancy; Administration; Business Administration; Insurance; Law; Management; Public Administration; Real Estate; Small Business; Social Welfare)

Further Information: Also campuses in Osaka.

History: Founded 1979 as Tokyo Legal Mind. Acquired present status and title 2004.

Fees: (Yen): admission fee, 160,000; tuition, 730,000-900,000 per annum.

Degrees and Diplomas: *Gakushi*

Last Updated: 16/01/09

TOKYO UNIVERSITY OF FOREIGN STUDIES

Tokyo Gaikokugo Daigaku

3-11-1 Asahi-cho, Fuchu-shi, Tokyo 183-8534
Tel: +81(42) 330-5183
EMail: ryugakuseika@tufs.ac.jp
Website: http://www.tufs.ac.jp

President: Ikuo Kameyama

Faculties

Foreign Studies (American Studies; Arabic; Chinese; Cultural Studies; Czech; East Asian Studies; Eastern European Studies; English; European Studies; Filipino; French; German; Hindi; Indonesian; International Studies; Italian; Japanese; Korean; Literature; Malay; Modern Languages; Mongolian; Oriental Studies; Persian; Polish; Portuguese; Russian; South Asian Studies; Southeast Asian Studies; Spanish; Thai Languages; Turkish; Urdu; Vietnamese) *Dean*: Toshihiro Takagaki

Graduate Schools

Area and Culture Studies (Cultural Studies; International Studies; Linguistics; Modern Languages; Regional Studies) *Dean*: Tadahiko Wada

Research Institutes

Languages and Cultures of Asia and Africa (African Languages; African Studies; Asian Studies)

Further Information: Also Japanese Language Center for International Students

History: Founded 1899.

Academic Year: April to March (April-October; October-March)

Admission Requirements: Graduation from high school or foreign equivalent, and entrance examination

Main Language(s) of Instruction: Japanese

Degrees and Diplomas: *Gakushi*: 4 yrs; *Shushi*; *Hakase*

Libraries: c. 722,000 vols

Publications: Area and Culture Studies

TOKYO UNIVERSITY OF INFORMATION SCIENCES

Tokyo Joho Daigaku

4-1 Onaridai, Wakaba-ku, Chiba-shi, Chiba 265-8501
Tel: +81(43) 236-1408
Fax: +81(43) 236-2215
EMail: tju@affrs.tuis.ac.jp
Website: http://www.tuis.ac.jp

Faculties

Informatics *(Also Graduate School)* (Business Administration; Business and Commerce; Computer Networks; Cultural Studies; Information Sciences; Information Technology; Media Studies; Social Studies; Software Engineering)

History: Founded 1988.

Academic Year: April to March (April-September; October-March)

Admission Requirements: Graduation from high school or recognized equivalent, and entrance examination

Main Language(s) of Instruction: Japanese

Degrees and Diplomas: *Gakushi*: 4 yrs; *Shushi*: a further 2 yrs; *Hakase*: a further 3 yrs

Student Services: Employment services, Language programs, Sports facilities

Libraries: c. 130,000 vols

Publications: Keiei Johoi Kagaku (Management Information Science)

Last Updated: 04/02/09

TOKYO UNIVERSITY OF MARINE SCIENCE AND TECHNOLOGY

Tokyo Kaiyo Daigaku (TUMSAT)

4-5-7 Konan, Minato-ku, Tokyo 108-8477
Tel: +81(3) 5463-0436
Fax: +81(3) 5463-0437
EMail: g-ryuu@s.kaiyodai.ac.jp
Website: http://www.kaiyodai.ac.jp

President: Masaji Matsuyama
Tel: +81(3) 5463-0350, Fax: +81(3) 5463-0425

Departments

Food Science and Technology *(in Faculty of Marine Science)* (Food Science; Food Technology); **Logistics and Information Engineering** *(in Faculty of Marine Science)* (Economics; Engineering; Information Technology; Management; Transport Management); **Marine Biosciences** *(in Faculty of Marine Science)*; **Marine Electronics and Mechanical Engineering** *(in Faculty of Marine Science)* (Automation and Control Engineering; Mechanical Engineering; Power Engineering); **Marine Policy and Culture** *(in Faculty of Marine Science)* (Cultural Studies; International Studies; Marine Engineering; Marine Science and Oceanography; Maritime Law; Marketing); **Maritime Systems Engineering** *(in Faculty of Marine Science)* (Automation and Control Engineering; Information Management; Information Technology; Management; Marine Engineering; Mechanical Engineering); **Ocean Sciences** *(in Faculty of Marine Science)* (Environmental Engineering; Environmental Studies; Marine Biology; Marine Science and Oceanography)

Faculties

Marine Science (Agriculture; Engineering; Natural Sciences; Social Sciences) *Dean*: Masaji Matsuyama; **Marine Technology** (Information Technology; Marine Engineering; Nautical Science; Transport Management) *Dean*: Kohei Ohtsu

Graduate Schools

Applied Marine Biosciences; **Applied Marine Environmental Studies** (Management Systems; Marine Biology; Marine Engineering; Marine Science and Oceanography; Marine Transport; Natural Resources); **Food Science and Technology**; **Marine Environmental Studies** (Environmental Engineering; Environmental Studies; Marine Biology; Marine Science and Oceanography; Maritime Law); **Marine Life Sciences** (Aquaculture; Biology; Demography and Population; Ecology; Fishery; Health Administration; Limnology; Marine Biology; Microbiology); **Marine System Engineering**; **Maritime Technology and Logistics** (Economics; Information Technology; Marine Engineering; Transport Management)

Further Information: Also Japanese language courses for foreign students

History: Founded 2003 following merger of Tokyo Suisan Daigaku (Tokyo University of Fisheries), founded 1888 and Tokyo Shusen Daigaku (Tokyo University of Mercantile Marine), founded 1875.

Academic Year: April to March (April-October; October-March)

Admission Requirements: Graduation from high school or recognized equivalent

Fees: (Yens): 520,800 per annum; Admission fee, 282,000 (first year only)

Main Language(s) of Instruction: Japanese

International Co-operation: With universities in Republic of Korea; China; Netherlands; USA; Norway; Indonesia; Canada; United Kingdom; Brazil; Thailand; Turkey; Iceland; Philippines; Egypt; Australia; United Arab Emirates; Russian Federation; Sweden; Serbia and Montenegro; Spain

Degrees and Diplomas: *Gakushi*: Engineering (BE); Marine Science, 4 yrs; *Shushi*: Engineering (ME), a further 2 yrs; *Shushi*: Marine Science (MS), a further 2 yrs; *Hakase*: Engineering (PhD); Marine Science (PhD), a further 3 yrs

Student Services: Academic counselling, Canteen, Foreign student adviser, Handicapped facilities, Health services, Language programs, Social counselling, Sports facilities

Student Residential Facilities: For c. 800 students

Special Facilities: Fisheries Museum, Centennial Museum

Libraries: University Library, c. 478,000 vols

Last Updated: 25/03/11

TOKYO UNIVERSITY OF PHARMACY AND LIFE SCIENCES

Tokyo Yakka Daigaku

1432-1 Horinouchi, Hachioji-shi, Tokyo 192-0392

Tel: +81(426) 76-5111

Fax: +81(426) 75-3095

EMail: support@bus.toyaku.ac.jp

Website: http://www.toyaku.ac.jp

Graduate Schools

Graduate Studies (Biological and Life Sciences; Pharmacy)

Schools

Pharmacy (Pharmacy)

History: Founded 1880 as School, acquired present status and title 1949.

Academic Year: April to March (April-September; October-March)

Admission Requirements: Graduation from high school and entrance examination. Special provisions for foreign students with similar qualifications

Fees: (Yen): Pharmacy: 2,189,000 per annum; Life Sciences: 1,901,000 per annum

Main Language(s) of Instruction: Japanese

Degrees and Diplomas: *Gakushi*: Pharmacy; Life Sciences, 4 yrs; *Shushi*: Pharmacy; Life Sciences, a further 2 yrs; *Hakase*: Pharmacy; Life Sciences, 3 yrs following Shushi

Student Residential Facilities: Yes

Libraries: c. 107,040 vols

Publications: Annual Report of School of Pharmacy and TUPLS *(annually)*; School of Life Sciences, Tokyo University of Pharmacy and Life Sciences (Annual Report) *(annually)*; The Journal of Tokyo University of Pharmacy and Lifes Sciences *(annually)*

Last Updated: 05/02/09

TOKYO UNIVERSITY OF SCIENCE

Tokyo Rika Daigaku (TUS)

1-3 Kagurazaka, Shinjuku-ku, Tokyo 162-8601

Tel: +81(3) 3260-4271

Fax: +81(3) 3260-4370

EMail: intlexchg@admin.tus.ac.jp

Website: http://www.tus.ac.jp

President: Akira Fujishima
Tel: +81(3) 3260-4271, Fax: +81(3) 3260-4370

Secretary-General: Jun Hatano

Senior Advisor, International Affairs: Tadanori Mizoguchi
EMail: mizoguchi_tadanori@admin.tus.ac.jp

International Relations: Michinori Yoshidome, Manager, International Exchange Office
Tel: +81(3) 5228-8726, Fax: +81(3) 5228-8727
EMail: soshi@admin.tus.ac.jp

Faculties

Engineering I (Architecture; Electrical Engineering; Engineering; Industrial Chemistry; Management; Mechanical Engineering) *Dean*: Tsunehiro Manabe; **Engineering II** (Architecture; Electrical Engineering; Engineering; Management) *Dean*: Noriaki Masui; **Industrial Science and Technology** *(Noda Campus, Chiba)* (Biological and Life Sciences; Electronic Engineering; Materials Engineering) *Dean*: Hiroshi Fukuda; **Pharmaceutical Sciences** *(Noda Campus, Chiba)* (Pharmacology; Pharmacy) *Dean*: Hiroyuki Oshima; **Science and Technology** *(Noda Campus, Chiba)* (Administration; Architecture; Biology; Chemistry; Civil Engineering; Electrical Engineering; Industrial Engineering; Information Sciences; Mathematics; Mechanical Engineering; Physics) *Dean*: Masanori Ohya; **Science I** (Applied Chemistry; Applied Mathematics; Applied Physics; Chemistry; Information Sciences; Mathematics; Physics) *Dean*: Iwao Hashimoto; **Science II** (Chemistry; Mathematics; Natural Sciences; Physics) *Dean*: Hiroshi Niizuma

Research Centres

Advanced Materials (Natural Sciences; Technology) *Director*: Masahiko Abe; **Drug Delivery System** *Director*: Hiroshi Terada; **Fire Science and Technology** *Director*: Takao Wakamatsu; **Genome and Drug Research** (Natural Sciences; Pharmacy) *Director*: Sei-ichi Tanuma; **Green Photo-Science and Technology** (Natural Sciences; Technology) *Director*: Izumi Nakai; **Holistic Computational Science** (Computer Science) *Director*: Hiroshi Kawamura; **Human Support Engineering** (Robotics; Technology) *Director*: Hiroshi Kobayashi; **IR Free Electron Laser Research** (Laser Engineering; Natural Sciences) *Director*: Kouichi Tsukiyama; **Nanoparticle Health Science** (Biological and Life Sciences; Environmental Studies) *Director*: Ken Takeda; **Nanoscience and Nanotechnology** (Nanotechnology; Natural Sciences) *Director*: Iwao Miyamoto; **Polyscale Technology Research** *Director*: Atsuo Yasumori; **Quantum Life Information Science** (Biological and Life Sciences; Computer Science) *Director*: Masanori Ohya; **Tissue Engineering** (Biology; Engineering; Technology) *Director*: Yasuhiro Tomooka

Research Institutes

Biological Sciences (Biological and Life Sciences) *Director*: Ryo Abe; **Research-Education Organization for Information Science and Technology** (Information Sciences; Technology Education) *Head*: Masanori Ohya; **Science and Technology** *(Noda Campus, Chiba)* (Natural Sciences; Technology) *Head*: Yoshimasa Nihei

Schools

Management *(Kuki Campus, Saitama)* (Management) *Dean*: Noboru Harada

Further Information: Kagurazaka Campus, Tokyo; Noda Campus, Chiba; Oshamambe Campus, Hokkaido; Kuki Campus, Saitama. Also Sister Universities in Yamaguchi and Suwa

History: Founded 1881 as College, reorganized and became University 1949.

Governing Bodies: Board of Trustees

Academic Year: April to March (April-September; September-March)

Admission Requirements: Graduation from high school or recognized equivalent, and entrance examination

Fees: (Yen): 715,000 - 2.07m. (including entrance fees)

Main Language(s) of Instruction: Japanese

International Co-operation: With universities in Bulgaria; China; Germany; France; India; Indonesia; Italy; Poland; Romania; Thailand; United Kingdom and USA

Accrediting Agencies: Ministry of Education, Culture, Sports, Science and Technology

Degrees and Diplomas: *Gakushi*: Engineering; Management; Science, 4 yrs; *Gakushi*: Pharmacy, 4-6 yrs; *Shushi*: a further 2 yrs; *Hakase*: 3 yrs following Shushi

Student Services: Academic counselling, Canteen, Employment services, Foreign student adviser, Health services, Sports facilities

Special Facilities: Science and Technology Museum, Seminar House

Libraries: University Library, 1,066,023 vols

Publications: Ridai Science Forum *(monthly)*

Last Updated: 12/04/10

TOKYO UNIVERSITY OF SCIENCE, YAMAGUCHI

Yamaguchi Tokyo Rika Daigaku

1-1-1 Daigakudori, Onoda-shi, Yamaguchi-shi, Yamaguchi 756-0884

Tel: +81(836) 883-500

Fax: +81(836) 883-400

Website: http://www.yama.tus.ac.jp/

Programmes

Engineering and Computer Science (Computer Science; Electronic Engineering; Engineering); **Natural Sciences and Mathematics** (Mathematics; Natural Sciences)

History: Founded 1995.

Academic Year: April to March (April-September; October-March)

Main Language(s) of Instruction: Japanese

Degrees and Diplomas: *Gakushi*

Last Updated: 11/02/09

TOKYO UNIVERSITY OF TECHNOLOGY

Tokyo Koka Daigaku

1401-1 Katakura-cho, Hachioji-shi, Tokyo 192-0982

Tel: +81(42) 637-2111

Fax: +81(42) 637-2112

EMail: int-info@so.teu.ac.jp

Website: http://www.teu.ac.jp

Graduate Schools

Bionics, Computer and Media Sciences (Computer Science; Management; Media Studies)

Schools

Bioscience and Biotechnology (Biological and Life Sciences; Biotechnology; Cosmetology; Environmental Studies; Food Science; Medical Technology); **Computer Science** (Computer Engineering; Computer Networks; Computer Science; Robotics; Software Engineering); **Media Sciences** (Electronic Engineering; Information Technology; Sociology)

History: Founded 1986. Formerly known as Tokyo Engineering University.

Academic Year: April to March

Admission Requirements: Graduation from high school and entrance examination

Main Language(s) of Instruction: Japanese

Degrees and Diplomas: *Gakushi*: 4 yrs; *Shushi*: a further 2 yrs; *Hakase*: 3 yrs following Shushi

Student Services: Academic counselling, Employment services, Foreign student adviser, Handicapped facilities, Health services, Social counselling, Sports facilities

Libraries: 60,000 vols

Publications: Sciences and Culture: The Journal of Tokyo Engineering University *(annually)*

Last Updated: 05/02/09

TOKYO UNIVERSITY OF THE ARTS

Tokyo Geijutsu Daigaku

12-8 Ueno Koen, Taito-ku, Tokyo 110-8714

Tel: +81(50) 5525-2013

Fax: +81(50) 5525-2479

EMail: toiawase@ml.geidai.ac.jp

Website: http://www.geidai.ac.jp

President: Ryôhei Miyata

Secretary-General: Yoshiyuki Otawa

Faculties

Fine Arts (Aesthetics; Architecture; Art History; Crafts and Trades; Design; Painting and Drawing; Sculpture) *Dean*: Kijo Rokkaku; **Music** *Dean*: Ueda Katsumi

Schools

Graduate Studies (Film; Fine Arts; Heritage Preservation; Multimedia; Music)

Further Information: Also Japanese language courses for foreign students

History: Founded 1949, incorporating Tokyo School of Fine Arts and Tokyo School of Music established 1887.

Governing Bodies: Yakuinkai (Board of Officials); Faculty Councils

Academic Year: April to March (April-September; October-March)

Admission Requirements: Graduation from high school or foreign equivalent, and entrance examination

Main Language(s) of Instruction: Japanese

Degrees and Diplomas: *Gakushi*: 4 yrs; *Shushi*: a further 2 yrs; *Hakase*: 3 yrs following Shushi

Special Facilities: University Art Museum; Sogakudo Concert Hall

Libraries: c. 488,000 vols

Last Updated: 25/03/11

TOKYO WOMEN'S CHRISTIAN UNIVERSITY

Tokyo Joshi Daigaku

2-6-1 Zempukuji, Suginami-ku, Tokyo 167-8585

Tel: +81(3) 5382-6267

Fax: +81(3) 5382-6531

EMail: o-board@office.twcu.ac.jp

Website: http://www.twcu.ac.jp

President: Masako Sanada EMail: president@office.twcu.ac.jp

Colleges

Arts and Science (Arts and Humanities; Economics; English; History; Japanese; Literature; Mathematics; Philosophy; Psychology; Sociology); **Culture and Communication** (Communication Studies; Cultural Studies; Modern Languages)

Graduate Schools

Culture and Communication (Communication Studies; Cultural Studies); **Humanities and Sciences** (Arts and Humanities; Cultural Studies; Social Sciences); **Science** (Mathematics)

Institutes

Comparative Cultural Studies (Cultural Studies); **Women's Studies** (Women's Studies)

History: Founded 1918 as College, became University 1948. Graduate School established 1971. College of Culture and Communication established 1988.

Governing Bodies: Board of Trustees; University Council

Academic Year: April to March (April-September; September-March)

Admission Requirements: Graduation from high school or equivalent, and entrance examination

Fees: (Yen): Registration, 300,000; tuition, 930,000 per annum

Main Language(s) of Instruction: Japanese

Degrees and Diplomas: *Gakushi*: Arts; Culture and Communication; Science, 4 yrs; *Shushi*: Arts; Culture and Communication; Science, a further 2 yrs; *Hakase*: Cultural Studies; Human Sciences; Science, 3 yrs following Shushi

Student Services: Academic counselling, Canteen, Employment services, Foreign Studies Centre, Health services, Social counselling

Student Residential Facilities: Yes

Special Facilities: Christian Centre; Centre for Information Science; Centre for Audio-Visual Education

Libraries: c. 600,000 vols

Publications: Annals of Institute for Comparative Studies of Culture *(annually)*; Essays and Studies *(biannually)*; Essays and Studies in British and American Literature *(annually)*; Historica *(annually)*; Japanese Literature *(annually)*; Science Reports *(annually)*; Sociology and Economics *(annually)*; Studies in Language and Culture *(annually)*; University Bulletin *(quarterly)*

Last Updated: 28/03/11

TOKYO WOMEN'S COLLEGE OF PHYSICAL EDUCATION

Tokyo Joshi Taiiku Daigaku

4-30-1 Fujimidai, Aoyagi, Kunitachi-shi, Tokyo 186-8668

Tel: +81(42) 572-4131

Fax: +81(42) 576-2397

Website: http://www.twcpe.ac.jp

Programmes

Physical Education and Sports (Physical Education; Sports)

Degrees and Diplomas: *Gakushi*

Last Updated: 04/02/09

TOKYO WOMEN'S MEDICAL UNIVERSITY

Tokyo Joshi Ika Daigaku (TWMU)

8-1 Kawada-cho, Shinjuku-ku, Tokyo 162-8666

Tel: +81(3) 3353-8111

Fax: +81(3) 3353-6793

Website: http://www.twmu.ac.jp

President: Shunichi Miyazaki

Faculties

Medicine (Medicine); **Nursing** (Nursing)

Further Information: Also 3 Research Institutes and Centres, and 2 Hospitals

History: Founded in 1900 by Dr. Yayoi Yoshioka as a Medical School, became College in 1951 and University in 1998.

Governing Bodies: Board of Trustees

Academic Year: April to March (April-July; September-December; January-March)

Admission Requirements: Graduation from high school or foreign equivalent, and entrance examination

Fees: (Yen): 2,8m. per annum

Main Language(s) of Instruction: Japanese

Degrees and Diplomas: *Gakushi*: Medicine (MD), 6 yrs; *Gakushi*: Nursing (BSN), 4 yrs; *Shushi*: Nursing (MSN), 2 yrs (Postgraduate course); *Hakase*: Medical Sciences (PhD), 4 yrs (Postgraduate course)

Student Services: Academic counselling, Foreign student adviser, Foreign Studies Centre, Health services, Language programs, Nursery care, Social counselling, Sports facilities

Special Facilities: Yayoi Memorial Hall

Libraries: Tokyo Women's Medical University Library, c. 232,500 vols

Publications: Bulletin of Medical Research Institute *(annually)*; Bulletin of Tokyo Women's Medical University School of Nursing *(annually)*; Journal of Tokyo Women's Medical University *(monthly)*

Last Updated: 04/02/09

TOKYO ZOKEI UNIVERSITY

Tokyo Zokei Daigaku

1556 Utsunuki-machi, Hachioji-shi, Tokyo 192-0992

Tel: +81(426) 37-8111

Fax: +81(426) 37-8110

EMail: nyugakukouhou@zokei.ac.jp

Website: http://www.zokei.ac.jp

Departments

Art and Design (Fashion Design; Film; Fine Arts; Graphic Design; Industrial Design; Interior Design; Media Studies; Painting and Drawing; Photography; Sculpture; Textile Design)

Schools

Graduate Studies (Design; Fine Arts)

History: Founded 1966.

Degrees and Diplomas: *Gakushi*; *Shushi*

Last Updated: 05/02/09

TOMAKOMAI KOMAZAWA UNIVERSITY

Tomakomai Komazawa Daigaku

521-293 Nishikioka, Tomakomai-shi, Hokkaido 059-1292

Tel: +81(144) 61-3460

Fax: +81(144) 61-3339

EMail: komamail@t-komazawa.ac.jp

Website: http://www.t-komazawa.ac.jp

Courses

Buddhist Culture (Asian Religious Studies; Cultural Studies); **Comparative Culture** (Cultural Studies; Japanese; Literature; Social Studies); **Computer Communication** (Computer Science; Information Technology); **Corporate Culture**; **English Communication**; **English Culture** (Cultural Studies; Modern Languages); **Local Hokkaido Culture** (Cultural Studies; History); **Non-language Communication** (Communication Arts; Communication Studies; Cultural Studies)

History: Founded 1998.

Fees: (Yen): First year, 790,000 per annum; second year, 590,000 per annum.

Degrees and Diplomas: *Gakushi*; *Shushi*

Last Updated: 05/02/09

TOTTORI UNIVERSITY

Tottori Daigaku

4-101 Minami-koyama-cho, Tottori-shi, Tottori 680-8550

Tel: +81(857) 31-5056

Fax: +81(857) 31-5056

EMail: kokuko-gaku@tottori-u.ac.jp

Website: http://www.tottori-u.ac.jp

President: Takayuki Nose EMail: gakucho@adm.tottori-u.ac.jp

Centres

Arid Land Research (Agronomy; Ecology; Hydraulic Engineering; Irrigation; Meteorology); **Data Processing** (Data Processing); **Educational Practical Study and Teaching** (Pedagogy); **Health Sciences** (Health Sciences); **Joint Research and Development** (Development Studies); **Laboratory Animal Research**; **Molecular and Cell Genetics** (Cell Biology; Genetics; Molecular Biology)

Colleges

Medical Care Technology (Medical Technology)

Faculties

Agriculture (Agricultural Management; Agriculture; Bioengineering; Environmental Engineering; Environmental Studies; Forestry; Information Sciences; Production Engineering; Veterinary Science); **Engineering** (Aeronautical and Aerospace Engineering; Applied Mathematics; Applied Physics; Biotechnology; Chemistry; Civil Engineering; Electrical and Electronic Engineering; Engineering; Engineering Drawing and Design; Information Technology; Materials Engineering; Mechanical Engineering); **Medicine** (Anatomy; Biological and Life Sciences; Cell Biology; Health Sciences; Medicine; Microbiology; Molecular Biology; Neurology; Nursing; Pathology; Pharmacology; Physiology; Social and Preventive Medicine; Surgery); **Regional Sciences** (Japanese; Modern Languages; Oriental Languages; Regional Studies; Social Studies)

Graduate Schools
Agriculture *(United Graduate School)*; **Veterinary Science** *(United Graduate School, Yamaguchi University)*

Institutes
Neurological Sciences (Neurosciences); **Radioisotope** (Radiology)

Further Information: Also University Hospital. Experimental farms and forests. Veterinary Hospital. Japanese language courses for foreign students

History: Founded 1949 incorporating College of Agriculture and Forestry, founded 1920, College of Medicine, 1948, and Normal School.

Academic Year: April to March (April-September; October-March)

Admission Requirements: Graduation from high school or equivalent or foreign equivalent, and entrance examination

Main Language(s) of Instruction: Japanese

International Co-operation: With universities in China, Republic of Korea and Mexico

Degrees and Diplomas: *Gakushi*: Agriculture (Nogakushi); Education (Kyoyogakushi); Engineering (Hogakushi); Life science, 4 yrs; *Gakushi*: Medical Sciences; Veterinary Science, 6 yrs; *Shushi*: Agriculture (Nogakushushi); Education (Kyoikugakushushi); Engineering (Kogakushushi); Life science (Seimeikagakushushi), a further 2 yrs; *Hakase*: Agriculture (Nogakuhakushi); Engineering (Hogakuhakushi), 3 yrs following Shushi; *Hakase*: Medical Sciences; Veterinary Science, a further 4 yrs

Student Services: Academic counselling, Employment services, Health services, Language programs, Social counselling, Sports facilities

Student Residential Facilities: Yes

Special Facilities: University Hospital

Libraries: 610,425 vols

Publications: Arid Land Research Center; Bulletin of Tottori University Forests *(annually)*; Journal of the Faculty of Agriculture *(annually)*; Journal of the Faculty of Education *(biannually)*; Reports of the Faculty of Engineering *(annually)*; Yonago Acta Medica *(quarterly)*; Yonago Igaku Zasshi *(bimonthly)*

Last Updated: 05/02/09

TOTTORI UNIVERSITY OF ENVIRONMENTAL STUDIES

Tottori Kankyo Daigaku
1-1-1 Wakabadai Kita, Tottori-shi, Tottori 698-1111
Tel: +81(857) 38-6700
Fax: +81(857) 38-6709
EMail: nyushi@kankyo-u.ac.jp
Website: http://www.kankyo-u.ac.jp

Programmes
Environmental Studies; **Information Studies** (Information Sciences)

History: Founded 2001.

International Co-operation: With Universities in New Zealand; Republic of Korea; China

Degrees and Diplomas: *Gakushi*

TOYAMA PREFECTURAL UNIVERSITY

Toyama Kenritsu Daigaku
5180 Kurokawa, Kosugi-machi, Imizu-gun, Toyama-shi, Toyama 939-0398
Tel: +81(766) 56-7500
Fax: +81(766) 56-6182
EMail: web-admin@pu-toyama.ac.jp
Website: http://www.pu-toyama.ac.jp

President: Masato Tanaka

Colleges
Technology

Faculties
Engineering *(Also Graduate School)* (Arts and Humanities; Automation and Control Engineering; Biotechnology; Computer Science; Electronic Engineering; Information Technology; Mechanical Engineering; Telecommunications Engineering)

History: Founded 1990.

Degrees and Diplomas: *Gakushi*; *Shushi*; *Hakase*

Student Services: Sports facilities

Special Facilities: Audio-visual room.

Libraries: c. 164,000 vols.

Last Updated: 06/02/09

TOYAMA UNIVERSITY OF INTERNATIONAL STUDIES

Toyama Kokusai Daigaku
65-1 Higashikuromaki, Oyama-cho, Kaminiikawa-gun, Toyama 930-1292
Tel: +81(76) 483-8000
Fax: +81(76) 483-8008
EMail: iec@tuins.ac.jp
Website: http://www.tuins.ac.jp

Faculties
Contemporary Society (Business Administration; Business and Commerce; Environmental Studies; Information Technology; Tourism); **Humanities**

History: Founded 1990.

Degrees and Diplomas: *Gakushi*

TOYO EIWA UNIVERSITY

Toyo Eiwa Jogakuin Daigaku
32 Miho-cho, Midori-ku, Yokohama-shi, Kanagawa 226-0015
Tel: +81(45) 922-5512
Fax: +81(45) 922-6641
EMail: nyushi@toyoeiwa.ac.jp
Website: http://www.toyoeiwa.ac.jp

President: Hiroshi Akuto

Faculties
Human Sciences (Child Care and Development; Clinical Psychology; Family Studies; Health Sciences; Psychology; Social Psychology; Social Sciences); **Social Sciences** (Social Sciences)

Graduate Schools
Graduate Studies (Child Care and Development; Clinical Psychology; International Relations; Preschool Education; Social Sciences)

History: Founded 1989. Graduate School added 1993.

Governing Bodies: Administrative Council

Academic Year: April to January (April-July; September-January)

Admission Requirements: Graduation from high school, or equivalent

Main Language(s) of Instruction: Japanese, English

International Co-operation: With universities in USA and Republic of Korea

Degrees and Diplomas: *Gakushi*: Human Sciences (Bungakushi); Social Sciences (Bungakushi), 4 yrs; *Shushi*: a further 2 yrs

Student Services: Academic counselling, Health services, Language programs, Social counselling, Sports facilities

Libraries: University Library, c. 200,000 vols

Last Updated: 06/02/09

TOYO GAKUEN UNIVERSITY

Toyo Gakuen Daigaku
1660 Hiregasaki, Nagareyama-shi, Chiba 270-0161
Tel: +81(4) 7150-3001
Fax: +81(4) 7150-3345
EMail: kokusai-koho@of.tyg.jp
Website: http://www.toyogakuen-u.ac.jp

President: Naomichi Ichinowatari

Faculties
Business Administration; **Humanities**

History: Founded 1992.

Degrees and Diplomas: *Gakushi*
Last Updated: 06/02/09

TOYO UNIVERSITY

Toyo Daigaku
5-28-20 Hakusan, Bunkyo-ku,
Tokyo 112-8606
Tel: +81(3) 3945-7557 +81(3) 3945-7272
Fax: +81(3) 3942-2489 +81(3) 3945-7607
EMail: ipo@hakusrv.toyo.ac.jp
Website: http://www.toyo.ac.jp

President: Makio Takemura
Tel: +81(3) 3945-7208, Fax: +81(3) 3945-7238

Faculties

Business Administration (Accountancy; Business Administration; Finance; Marketing); **Economics** (Economics; International Economics); **Engineering** *(Kawagoe-shi)* (Applied Chemistry; Architecture; Civil Engineering; Computer Engineering; Computer Science; Electronic Engineering; Engineering; Environmental Engineering; Information Technology; Mechanical Engineering; Robotics; Telecommunications Engineering); **Human Life Design**; **Law** *(Asaka-shi)* (Commercial Law; Law); **Life Sciences** (Biological and Life Sciences); **Literature** *(Asaka-shi)* (Chinese; Education; English; History; Japanese; Literature; Modern Languages; Pedagogy; Philosophical Schools; Philosophy); **Regional Development Studies** *(Itakura)* (Development Studies; Regional Studies; Tourism); **Sociology** *(Asaka-shi)* (Communication Studies; Media Studies; Social Psychology; Social Welfare; Sociology)

Graduate Schools

Business Administration (Accountancy; Business Administration; Finance; Marketing); **Economics** (Economics); **Engineering** (Applied Chemistry; Electronic Engineering; Engineering; Environmental Engineering; Environmental Management; Information Management); **Law** *(Professional)*; **Law** (Law; Private Law; Public Law); **Life Sciences** (Biological and Life Sciences); **Literature** (Asian Religious Studies; Education; English; History; Japanese; Literature; Philosophical Schools; Philosophy); **New Sciences** *(Interdisciplinary)*; **Regional Development Studies** (Development Studies; Regional Studies; Tourism); **Sociology** (Social Psychology; Sociology); **Welfare Society Design** (Social Welfare)

Research Institutes

Asian Cultures (Asian Studies); **Human Sciences** (Social Sciences); **Industrial Technology** (Technology); **Oriental Studies** (Oriental Studies); **Regional Vitalization Studies** (Development Studies; Regional Studies); **Social Sciences**

Further Information: Also academic programmes for foreign students

History: Founded 1887 as 'Tetsugaku-kan' (Academy of Philosophy). Became University and acquired present title 1906.

Governing Bodies: Board of Trustees

Academic Year: April to March (April-September; October-March)

Admission Requirements: Graduation from high school or equivalent and entrance examination

Main Language(s) of Instruction: Japanese

International Co-operation: With universities in China; France; Germany; Ireland; Republic of Korea and USA

Degrees and Diplomas: *Gakushi*: 4 yrs; *Shushi*: a further 1-2 yrs; *Hakase (PhD)*: 2-3 yrs following Shushi

Student Services: Academic counselling, Canteen, Employment services, Foreign student adviser, Foreign Studies Centre, Health services, Language programs, Social counselling, Sports facilities

Libraries: 1,230,000 vols

Publications: Archives *(monthly)*
Last Updated: 28/03/11

TOYOHASHI SOZO COLLEGE

Toyohashi Sozo Daigaku
20-1 Matsushita, Ushikawa-cho, Toyohashi-shi, Aichi 440-8511
Tel: +81(532) 54-9725
Fax: +81(532) 54-9726
EMail: kouhou@sozo.ac.jp
Website: http://www.sozo.ac.jp

Faculties

Management and Information Sciences (Accountancy; Computer Networks; Information Sciences; Management; Media Studies; Software Engineering)

Graduate Schools

Business (Business and Commerce)

History: Founded 1983 as Junior College. Acquired present status and title 1996.

Degrees and Diplomas: *Gakushi*; *Shushi*

Student Services: Cultural centre, Sports facilities

Special Facilities: Computer Centre

TOYOHASHI UNIVERSITY OF TECHNOLOGY

Toyohashi Gijutsu Kagaku Daigaku (TUT)
1-1 Hibarigaoka, Tempaku-cho, Toyohashi-shi, Aichi 441-8580
Tel: +81(532) 44-6577
Fax: +81(532) 44-6547
EMail: ryugaku@office.tut.ac.jp
Website: http://www.tut.ac.jp

President: Yoshiyuki Sakaki

Centres

Engineering Education Development *(International Cooperation)* (Engineering); **Information and Media**; **International Student** (Education); **Language** (Linguistics; Modern Languages); **Physical Fitness, Sports and Health** (Health Education; Physical Education; Sports); **Venture Business** *(Incubation Centre)*

Departments

Architecture and Civil Engineering (Architecture; Civil Engineering); **Ecological Engineering** (Biological and Life Sciences; Biotechnology); **Electrical and Electronic Engineering** (Electrical and Electronic Engineering); **Humanities, Management Science and Engineering** (Arts and Humanities; Engineering; Management); **Information and Computer Sciences** (Computer Engineering; Information Technology); **Knowledge-based Information Engineering** (Computer Science; Information Technology); **Materials Science** (Materials Engineering); **Mechanical Engineering** (Mechanical Engineering); **Production Systems Engineering** (Production Engineering)

Laboratories

Civil and Environmental Engineering (Civil Engineering; Environmental Engineering); **Cryogenic Research**; **Information and Communication** (Information Technology; Telecommunications Engineering); **Natural Energy Research** (Energy Engineering); **Radiation** (Information Technology; Nuclear Engineering); **Venture Business**

Research Centres

Collaborative Regional Planning and Design (Regional Planning); **Cooperative Research Facility**; **Electron Device**; **Future Technology** (Technology); **Future Vehicle**; **Intelligent Sensing System**; **Interdisciplinary Future Environment Ecological Design** (Ecology; Environmental Studies)

History: Founded 1976. Graduate School established 1980. Doctoral Programme established 1986 and reorganized 1995. Turned into independent administrative entity as a National University Corporation 2004.

Governing Bodies: Daigiinkai (University Council)

Academic Year: April to March (April-July; August-November; December-March)

Admission Requirements: Graduation from high school and entrance examination

Fees: (Yen): 535,800 per annum

Main Language(s) of Instruction: Japanese

International Co-operation: With universities in China, Republic of Korea and Indonesia

Accrediting Agencies: Ministry of Education, Culture, Sports, Science and Technology

Degrees and Diplomas: *Gakushi*: Engineering (Kogakushi), 4 yrs; *Shushi*: Engineering (Kogakushushi), a further 2 yrs; *Hakase*: Engineering (Kogakuhakase), 3 yrs following Shushi

Student Services: Academic counselling, Canteen, Foreign student adviser, Foreign Studies Centre, Health services, Language programs, Social counselling, Sports facilities

Student Residential Facilities: For c. 500 students

Libraries: 187,000 vols

Last Updated: 25/03/11

TOYOTA TECHNOLOGICAL INSTITUTE

Toyota Kogyo Daigaku (TTI)

2-12 Hisakata, Tempaku-ku, Nagoya-shi, Aichi 468-8511

Tel: +81(52) 802-1111

Fax: +81(52) 809-1721

EMail: tti-gakusei@toyota-ti.ac.jp

Website: http://www.toyota-ti.ac.jp

President: Akira Ikushima

Faculties

Education; **Engineering** (Engineering; Systems Analysis) *Dean*: Yutaka Iino; **Foreign Languages**; **Health and Physical Education**; **Information Technology and Automation and Control Engineering** *Dean*: Hajime Kitagawa

Graduate Schools

Engineering

History: Founded 1981.

Academic Year: April to March (April-September; October-March)

Admission Requirements: Graduation from high school or equivalent, and entrance examination

Fees: (Yen): Tuition, 496,800; Graduate School of Engineering, 792,180 per annum

Main Language(s) of Instruction: Japanese

Degrees and Diplomas: *Gakushi*: Engineering (Kogakushi), 4 yrs; *Shushi*: Engineering (Kogakushushi), 2 yrs; *Hakase*: Engineering (Kogakuhakushi), 3 yrs following Shushi

Student Services: Academic counselling, Canteen, Employment services, Health services, Social counselling, Sports facilities

Student Residential Facilities: Yes

Special Facilities: Semi-Conductor Centre

Libraries: c. 64,000 vols

Publications: ADVANCE *(bimonthly)*; Nenpou Kenkyukatsudou *(annually)*

Last Updated: 06/02/09

TSUDA COLLEGE

Tsuda Juku Daigaku

2-1-1 Tsuda-machi, Kodaira-shi, Tokyo 187-8577

Tel: +81(42) 342-5111

Fax: +81(42) 341-2444

EMail: webadmin@tsuda.ac.jp

Website: http://www.tsuda.ac.jp

President: Masako Iino

Tel: +81(42) 342-5116, Fax: +81(42) 342-5116

Centres

Audiovisual (Cinema and Television; Video); **Computer** (Computer Science); **Open Research** (Cultural Studies; International Studies); **Wellness** (Welfare and Protective Services)

Departments

English (American Studies; Communication Studies; English; English Studies; Linguistics; Literature); **International and Cultural Studies** (Comparative Sociology; Cultural Studies; International Economics; International Law; International Studies); **Mathematics and Computer Science** (Applied Mathematics; Mathematics and Computer Science)

Institutes

International and Cultural Studies (Cultural Studies; International Studies); **Mathematics and Computer Science** (Mathematics and Computer Science); **Research in Language and Culture**

History: Founded 1900 as School, acquired present status 1948.

Governing Bodies: Board of Trustees; Council

Academic Year: April to March (April-July; October-March)

Admission Requirements: Graduation from high school or equivalent, and entrance examination

Fees: (Yen): Registration, 300,000; tuition, 795,000-875,000

Main Language(s) of Instruction: Japanese

Degrees and Diplomas: *Gakushi*: English Literature; Mathematics; Physics; Science, 4 yrs; *Shushi*: International Studies; Literature; Science, a further 2 yrs; *Hakase*: International Studies; Literature; Science, 3 yrs following Shushi

Student Services: Academic counselling, Canteen, Employment services, Foreign student adviser, Foreign Studies Centre, Health services, Nursery care, Social counselling, Sports facilities

Student Residential Facilities: Yes

Libraries: College Library, c. 310,000 vols

Publications: Study of International Relations *(annually)*

Last Updated: 06/02/09

TSUKUBA GAKUIN UNIVERSITY

Tsukuba Gakuin Daigaku

3-1 Azuma, Tsukuba-shi, Ibaraki-shi, Osaka 305-0031

Tel: +81(298) 58-4815

Fax: +81(298) 58-7388

EMail: office@cs.kasei.ac.jp

Website: http://www.tsukuba-g.ac.jp

Faculties

Information and Communication

History: Founded 1996 as Tokyo Kasei Gakuin Tsukuba Joshi Daigaku (Tokyo Kasei Gakuin Tsukuba Women's University). Acquired present title 2005.

International Co-operation: With universities in USA.

Degrees and Diplomas: *Gakushi*

Libraries: c. 75,000 vols.

Last Updated: 04/02/09

TSUKUBA INTERNATIONAL UNIVERSITY

Tsukuba Kokusai Daigaku

6-20-1 Manabe, Tsuchiura-shi, Ibaraki-shi, Osaka 300-0051

Tel: +81(29) 826-6000

Fax: +81(29) 826-6937

EMail: tiutjob@beige.ocn.ne.jp

Website: http://www.ktt.ac.jp/tiu/

Departments

Industrial Research (Industrial Engineering); **Social Services** (Social and Community Services)

History: Founded 1994.

Degrees and Diplomas: *Gakushi*

Student Services: Sports facilities

Special Facilities: Audio-visual room.

TSUKUBA UNIVERSITY OF TECHNOLOGY

Tsukuba Gijutsu Daigaku (NTUT)

Amakubo 4-3-15, Tsukuba-shi, Ibaraki 305-8520

Tel: +81(29) 852-2931

Fax: +81(29) 858-9312

Website: http://www.tsukuba-tech.ac.jp/en/

President: Naoki Ohnuma

Faculties

Health Sciences; **Industrial Technology** (Architectural and Environmental Design; Architecture and Planning; Artificial Intelligence; Computer Engineering; Computer Networks; Computer Science; Ecology; Electrical Engineering; Electronic Engineering; Environmental Engineering; Industrial Design; Information Sciences; Information Technology; Interior Design; Mechanical Engineering; Multimedia; Polymer and Plastics Technology; Regional Planning; Robotics; Social Welfare; Telecommunications Engineering; Thermal Engineering; Town Planning)

History: Founded 2005.

Degrees and Diplomas: *Gakushi*

Last Updated: 12/02/09

TSURU UNIVERSITY

Tsuru Bunka Daigaku
3-8-1 Tahara, Tsuru-shi, Yamanashi 402-8555
Tel: +81(554) 43-4341
Fax: +81(554) 43-4347
EMail: kokusai@tsuru.ac.jp
Website: http://www.tsuru.ac.jp

Colleges

Humanities *(Also graduate studies)* (Arts and Humanities; Cultural Studies; English; Japanese; Primary Education; Sociology)

History: Founded 1955.

Main Language(s) of Instruction: Japanese

Degrees and Diplomas: *Gakushi*; *Shushi*

Student Services: Health services, Language programs, Social counselling

Student Residential Facilities: Yes

Libraries: c. 316,000 vols

Last Updated: 06/02/09

TSURUMI UNIVERSITY

Tsurumi Daigaku
2-1-3 Tsurumi, Tsurumi-ku, Yokohama-shi, Kanagawa 230-8501
Tel: +81(45) 581-1001
Fax: +81(45) 584-4588
Website: http://www.tsurumi-u.ac.jp

President: Keiji Yanagisawa (2005-)
Tel: +81(45) 574-8600, Fax: +81(45) 574-8687

Institutes

Buddhist Culture (Asian Religious Studies)

Schools

Dental Medicine *(Also Graduate School)* (Dentistry); **Literature** *(Also Graduate School)* (American Studies; Archiving; Comparative Literature; Cultural Studies; English; Information Sciences; Japanese; Library Science; Literature)

History: Founded 1924 as School, became Junior College 1953, acquired present status and title 1963.

Governing Bodies: Board of Trustees

Academic Year: April to March (April to September; October to March)

Admission Requirements: Graduation from high school or recognized equivalent, and entrance examination

Main Language(s) of Instruction: Japanese

International Co-operation: With universities in Republic of Korea

Degrees and Diplomas: *Gakushi*: Dentistry (MD), 6 yrs; *Gakushi*: Literature, 4 yrs; *Shushi*: Literature, a further 2 yrs; *Hakase*: Dentistry (PhD (DSc)), 4 yrs following Shigakushi; *Hakase*: Literature (PhD), 3 yrs follwing Shushi

Student Services: Employment services, Health services, Sports facilities

Student Residential Facilities: For c. 170 women students

Special Facilities: Tsurumi University Hospital

Libraries: c. 600,000 vols

Publications: Bulletin of the Institute of Buddhist Culture *(annually)*; Bulletin of Tsurumi University *(annually)*

UBE FRONTIER UNVERSITY

Ube Furontia Daigaku
2-1-1 Bunkyo-dai, Ube-shi, Yamaguchi 755-0805
Tel: +81(836) 38-0500
Fax: +81(836) 38-0600
EMail: info@frontier-u.jp
Website: http://www.frontier-u.jp/frontier/univ/english/index.html

President: Hiroshi Takeshita

Programmes

Humanities and Social Sciences (Environmental Studies; Psychiatry and Mental Health; Psychology; Social Studies; Social Welfare; Social Work)

History: Founded 2001.

Degrees and Diplomas: *Gakushi*; *Shushi*

Last Updated: 06/02/09

UENO GAKUEN UNIVERSITY

Ueno Gakuen Daigaku
4-24-12 Higashiueno, Taito-ku, Tokyo 110-8642
Tel: +81(3) 3842-1021
Fax: +81(3) 3843-7548
Website: http://www.uenogakuen.ac.jp

President: Hiro Ishibashi

Faculties

Music and Cultural Studies (Cultural Studies; Music; Music Education; Musical Instruments; Musicology; Singing)

History: Founded 1952. Acquired present status 1958.

Degrees and Diplomas: *Gakushi*. Also 1-year Postgraduate Diploma programmes

Last Updated: 06/02/09

UNITED NATIONS UNIVERSITY (UNU)

5–53–70 Jingumae, Shibuya-ku, Tokyo 150-8925
Tel: +81 3 5467 1212
Fax: +81 3 3499 2828
Website: http://unu.edu

Rector: David Malone (2013-)
EMail: rector@unu.edu; masuda@unu.edu

Executive Officer, Office of the Rector: Max Bond
EMail: bond@unu.edu

Further Information: 15 institutes and programmes in 13 countries (Belgium, Canada, China, Finland, Germany, Ghana, Iceland, Japan, Malaysia, Spain, The Netherlands, United States of America, Venezuela) and administrative and services units in Tokyo (headquarters), Bonn, Kuala Lumpur, New York and Paris.

History: Founded 1973.

Main Language(s) of Instruction: English

Degrees and Diplomas: *Shushi*: Geography of Environmental Risks and Human Security;Public Policy and Human Development;Environmental Governance with Specialization in Biodiversity;Sustainability, Development and Peace (MSc); *Hakase*: Development Economics;Sustainability Science;ICT for Sustainable Development;Economics and Governance (PhD)

Libraries: Library of the United Nations University

Last Updated: 09/11/12

UNIVERSITY OF AIZU

Aizu Daigaku
Kamiiawase 90, Ikkimachi-tsuruga, Aizuwakamatsu-shi, Fukushima 965-8580
Tel: +81(242) 37-2500
Fax: +81(242) 37-2528
EMail: sad-aas@u-aizu.ac.jp
Website: http://www.u-aizu.ac.jp

President: Shigeaki Tsunoyama
Tel: +81(242) 37-2525, Fax: +81(242) 37-2757

Graduate Schools

Computer Science and Engineering (Computer Engineering; Computer Science; Information Technology) *Dean*: Satoshi Okawa

Schools

Computer Science and Engineering

History: Founded 1993.

Academic Year: April to March

Admission Requirements: Upper secondary school leaving certificate (Kotogakko Sotsugyo Shomeisho)

Main Language(s) of Instruction: Japanese, English

Accrediting Agencies: Government of Fukushima Prefecture

Degrees and Diplomas: *Gakushi*: Computer Science; Engineering, 4 yrs; *Shushi*: Computer Science; Engineering, a further 2 yrs; *Hakase*: Computer Science; Engineering, 3 yrs following Shushi

Student Services: Canteen, Employment services, Handicapped facilities, Health services, Sports facilities

Special Facilities: University-Business Innovation Centre

Libraries: Books, c. 89,000 vols; periodicals, c. 950 titles

Publications: Journal of the School of Computer Science and Engineering, Research activities of the Faculty members *(annually)*

Last Updated: 28/10/08

UNIVERSITY OF CREATION, ART, MUSIC AND SOCIAL WORK

Sozo Gakuen Daigaku

2-3-6 Yachiyo-Machi, Takasaki-shi, Gunma 370-0861
Tel: +81(27) 328-6111
Fax: +81(27) 322-2103
EMail: souzou@tacc.ac.jp
Website: http://souzou.ac.jp/

Departments

Creative Arts (Fine Arts; Music) *Dean*: Shin Miyashita; **Social Work** (Social Work)

History: Founded 2004.

Admission Requirements: Applicants must be 18 years old, hold a Baccalaureate degree or equivalent or have accomplished 12 years of formal education. Foreign students should also have taken the Standard University Entrance Exam for Private Foreign Students and level 1 or Japanese Proficiency Test.

Fees: (Yen): Entrance fee, 200,000; First term (April), 510,000; Second term (September), 490,000

Degrees and Diplomas: *Gakushi*

Student Residential Facilities: Student Dormitories

Special Facilities: Suikin Sogakudo Concert Hall; Ethnic Instruments Museum; Sanpukuan Museum.

Libraries: Bruno Taut Reference Library.

UNIVERSITY OF EAST ASIA

Toa Daigaku

2-1 Ichinomiya gakuen-cho, Shimonoseki-shi, Yamaguchi 751-8503
Tel: +81(832) 56-1111
Fax: +81(832) 56-9577
EMail: jimu@po.pios.cc.toua-u.ac.jp
Website: http://www.toua-u.ac.jp

Programmes

Graduate; **Undergraduate** (Computer Engineering; Design; Food Technology; Mechanical Engineering)

History: Founded 1974.

Main Language(s) of Instruction: Japanese

Degrees and Diplomas: *Gakushi*; *Shushi*; *Hakase*

Student Services: Academic counselling, Health services, Language programs, Social counselling, Sports facilities

Student Residential Facilities: Yes

Libraries: c. 110,000 vols

Last Updated: 03/02/09

UNIVERSITY OF ELECTRO-COMMUNICATIONS

Denki Tsushin Daigaku

1-5-1 Chofugaoka, Chofu-shi, Tokyo 182-8585
Tel: +81(424) 43-5014 +81(424) 43-5115
Fax: +81(424) 43-5108 +81(424) 43-5116
EMail: www-admin@uec.ac.jp
Website: http://www.uec.ac.jp/

Centres

Co-operative Research; **Data Processing** (Data Processing); **Instrumental Analysis**; **Satellite Venture Business Laboratories** (Telecommunications Engineering); **Space Radio Observatory** *(Sugadaira)*

Faculties

Electro-Communications *(Undergraduate and graduate programmes)* (Applied Chemistry; Applied Physics; Artificial Intelligence; Communication Studies; Computer Engineering; Computer Science; Electronic Engineering; Information Technology; Mechanical Engineering)

Graduate Schools

Information Systems (Computer Science; Information Technology; Media Studies; Social Sciences)

Institutes

Laser Science (Laser Engineering)

Further Information: Also student exchange programmes

History: Founded 1918 by Wireless Association, transferred to Ministry of Communications 1942 and to Ministry of Education 1948. Re-established as University 1949. Junior Technical College established 1953, Graduate School of Electro-Communications 1965, and Graduate School of Information 1992.

Academic Year: April to March (April-September; October-March)

Admission Requirements: Graduation from high school and entrance examination

Main Language(s) of Instruction: Japanese

International Co-operation: With universities in Australia, China and Canada

Degrees and Diplomas: *Gakushi*: Engineering (Kogakushi), 4 yrs; *Shushi*: Engineering (Kogakushushi); Science (Rigakushi), a further 2 yrs; *Hakase*: Engineering (Kogakuhakushi); Science (Rigakuhakushi), 3 yrs following Shushi

Student Services: Academic counselling, Canteen, Cultural centre, Employment services, Foreign student adviser, Foreign Studies Centre, Health services, Language programs, Social counselling, Sports facilities

Student Residential Facilities: For 167 students

Special Facilities: Observatory

Libraries: University Library, 403,669 vols

Publications: Annual Report of Research *(annually)*; Report of Annual Research Works *(annually)*; Reports *(biannually)*

Last Updated: 31/10/08

UNIVERSITY OF FUKUI

Fukui Daigaku

3-9-1 Bunkyo, Fukui-shi, Fukui 910-8507
Tel: +81(776) 23-0500
Fax: +81(776) 27-8518
Website: http://www.fukui-u.ac.jp

President: Masaru Fukuda EMail: funivtop@sec.icpc.fukui-u.ac.jp

Centres

Advanced Research Support; **Cooperative Research in Science and Technology**; **Innovative Research and Creative Leading Education**; **Integrated Research for Educational Practice** (Education); **Interdisciplinary Studies**; **Nature Education**; **Research and Education for Regional Environment**; **Research and Education Programme for Life Sciences** (Biological and Life Sciences); **Venture Business Laboratory** (Technology)

Faculties

Education and Regional Studies (Administration; Art Education; Cultural Studies; Ecology; Education of the Handicapped; Educational Sciences; Foreign Languages Education; Humanities and Social Science Education; Native Language Education; Physical Education; Regional Studies; Social Studies; Special Education; Teacher Training; Technology Education); **Engineering** (Applied Chemistry; Applied Physics; Architecture; Artificial Intelligence; Biotechnology; Civil Engineering; Electrical and Electronic Engineering; Engineering; Information Sciences; Materials Engineering; Mechanical Engineering); **Medical Sciences** (Medicine; Nursing)

Graduate Schools

Education *(Master Programe)* (Education; Education of the Handicapped; Pedagogy; Primary Education; Secondary Education); **Engineering** *(Master and Doctoral Programmes)*; **Medical Sciences** *(Master and Doctoral programmes)* (Anatomy; Biochemistry; Ecology; Medicine; Nursing; Physiology)

Research Centres

Biomedical Imaging (Biomedical Engineering); **Development of Far-infrated Region**

History: Founded 1949 incorporating Fukui Normal School, Fukui Youth Normal School, and Fukui Technical Senmon Gakko. Financed by the State through the Ministry of Education, Culture, Sports, Science and Technology (MEXT). Merged with Fukui Ika Daigaku/ Fukui Medical University 2003.

Academic Year: April to March (April-September; October-March)

Admission Requirements: Graduation from high school or equivalent and entrance examination

Fees: (Yen): Registration, 282,000; tuition, 535,800 per annum

Main Language(s) of Instruction: Japanese

International Co-operation: With universities in Australia; Bangladesh; China; Germany; India; Republic of Korea; Mongolia; Poland; Russian Federation; Thailand; USA; France; Canada; Bulgaria; Sweden; Taiwan; Indonesia and United Arab Emirates

Accrediting Agencies: Ministry of Education, Culture, Sports, Science and Technology (MEXT).

Degrees and Diplomas: *Teaching Certificate*: Teacher Training, Elementary Level; Teacher training, Handicapped Children; Teacher Training, Kindergarten; Teacher Training, Lower Secondary Level; Teacher training, Secondary Level, 4 yrs; *Gakushi*: Education; Engineering; Medical Science; Nursing; Regional and Cultural Studies; Regional and Social Studies, 4 yrs; *Gakushi*: Medical Science; Medicine, 6 yrs; *Shushi*: Education; Engineering; Medical Science; Nursing, a further 2 yrs; *Hakase*: Engineering, 3 yrs following Shushi; *Hakase*: Medical Science; Medicine, a further 4 yrs

Student Services: Academic counselling, Canteen, Employment services, Foreign student adviser, Foreign Studies Centre, Handicapped facilities, Health services, Language programs, Nursery care, Social counselling, Sports facilities

Student Residential Facilities: Yes (accommodation for overseas students)

Libraries: c. 571,000 vols

Publications: Basic Material *(annually)*; Fukui Daigaku Gakuho Report *(monthly)*

Last Updated: 31/10/08

UNIVERSITY OF HAMAMATSU

Hamamatsu Daigaku

1230 Miyakoda-cho, Hamamatsu-shi, Shizuoka-shi, Shizuoka 431-2102

Tel: +81(53) 428-3511

Fax: +81(53) 428-2900

Website: http://www.hamamatsu-u.ac.jp/

Faculties

Administration and Informatics (Administration; Computer Science); **Health Promotional Science**; **International Economics** (Child Care and Development; Clinical Psychology; Development Studies; Education; International Economics; Nutrition)

History: Founded 1988 as Tokoha Gakuen Hammatsu Daigaku. Acquired present title 1998.

International Co-operation: With universities China, Sweden and USA; also summer home-stay program in Australia (three weeks)

Degrees and Diplomas: *Gakushi*; *Shushi*

Student Services: Sports facilities

Libraries:c. 123,000 vols.

Last Updated: 07/11/08

UNIVERSITY OF HUMAN ARTS AND SCIENCES

Ningen Sougou Kagaku Daigaku

1288 Magome, Iwatsuki-shi, Saitama 339-8539

Tel: +81(48) 749-6111

Fax: +81(48) 749-6110

EMail: admin@human.ac.jp

Website: http://www.human.ac.jp

Programmes

Human Arts and Sciences (Arts and Humanities; Behavioural Sciences; Chinese; English; Environmental Studies; Health Sciences; Home Economics; Japanese; Literature; Modern Languages; Multimedia; Natural Sciences; Psychology; Social Studies)

History: Founded 2000.

Degrees and Diplomas: *Gakushi*

Libraries: 9,290 vols.

Last Updated: 28/01/09

UNIVERSITY OF HYOGO

Hyogo Kenritsu Daigaku

Administrative Office, 1-3-3, Higashikawasaki-cho, Chuo-ku, Kobe-shi, Hyogo 650-0044

Tel: +81(78) 367-8600

Fax: +81(78) 362-0650

EMail: u-hyogo@pref.hyogo.jp

Website: http://www.u-hyogo.ac.jp

President: Nobuaki Kumagai

Colleges

Nursing Art and Science *(Also Graduate School)* (Nursing)

Graduate Schools

Applied Informatics (Communication Studies; Computer Networks; Information Sciences)

Institutes

Natural and Environmental Sciences

Laboratories

Advanced Science and Technology for Industry (Industrial Engineering)

Research Institutes

Economics and Business Administration *(LASTI)* (Business Administration; Economics); **Nursing Care for People and Community** (Nursing)

Schools

Business Administration *(Also Graduate School)* (Business Administration); **Economics** *(Also Graduate School)* (Economics; International Economics); **Engineering** *(Also Graduate School)* (Chemical Engineering; Computer Engineering; Computer Science; Electrical Engineering; Engineering; Materials Engineering; Mechanical Engineering); **Human Science and Environment** *(Also Graduate School)* (Cultural Studies; Ecology; Environmental Studies; Regional Planning; Social Sciences); **Science** *(Also Graduate School)*

History: Founded 2004 incorporating Kobe University of Commerce (founded 1929), Himeji Institute of Technology (founded 1949), and the College of Nursing Art and Science, Hyogo (founded 1993).

Admission Requirements: Graduation from high school or equivalent, and entrance examination

Main Language(s) of Instruction: Japanese

Degrees and Diplomas: *Gakushi*: 4 yrs; *Shushi*: a further 2 yrs; *Hakase*: 3 yrs following Shushi

Student Services: Employment services, Health services, Social counselling, Sports facilities

Last Updated: 07/01/09

UNIVERSITY OF KOCHI

Kochi Joshi Daigaku

5-15 Eikokuji-cho, Kochi-shi, Kochi 780-8515

Tel: +81(88) 873-2156

Fax: +81(88) 873-8515

EMail: wwwadmin@cc.kochi-wu.ac.jp

Website: http://www.kochi-wu.ac.jp

Faculties

Cultural Studies (Cultural Studies; English; Japanese); **Human Life and Environmental Science** (Environmental Studies; Health Sciences); **Nursing** *(Ike)* (Nursing); **Social Welfare** *(Ike)* (Social Welfare)

Graduate Schools

Human Health Sciences *(Doctoral)*; **Human Life** (Health Sciences); **Nursing** *(Ike)* (Nursing)

History: Founded 1949. Acquired present title 2011.

Academic Year: April to March

Main Language(s) of Instruction: Japanese, English

International Co-operation: With universities in USA

Degrees and Diplomas: *Gakushi*: 4 yrs; *Shushi*: a further 2 yrs; *Hakase*

Student Residential Facilities: Yes

Libraries: University Library, 240,000 vols

Publications: Bulletin of Kochi Women's University *(annually)*

Last Updated: 24/03/11

UNIVERSITY OF MARKETING AND DISTRIBUTION SCIENCES

Ryutsu Kagaku Daigaku

3-1 Gakuen-nishimachi, Nishi-ku, Kobe-shi, Hyogo 651-21
Tel: +81(78) 794-3095
Fax: +81(78) 794-3094
EMail: nyushi@red.umds.ac.jp
Website: http://www.umds.ac.jp

President: Junzo Ishii

Centres

Information Studies

Faculties

Commerce (Business Administration; Business and Commerce; Finance; Marketing); **Information Science and Technology** (Economics; Information Sciences; Information Technology; Management); **Services Industries** (Public Health; Social and Community Services; Tourism)

Graduate Schools

Marketing and Distribution Sciences (Business and Commerce; Marketing)

Schools

Business *(Nakauchi)*

History: Founded 1988.

Admission Requirements: 12 years education and/or graduate of (senior) high school or equivalent

International Co-operation: With universities in China, Taiwan, Republic of Korea

Degrees and Diplomas: *Gakushi*; *Shushi*; *Hakase*

Student Services: Foreign Studies Centre, Sports facilities

Libraries: c. 165,000 vols.

Last Updated: 30/01/09

UNIVERSITY OF MIYAZAKI

Miyazaki Daigaku

1-1 Gakuen Kibanadai-nishi, Miyazaki-shi, Miyazaki-shi, Miyazaki 889-2192
Tel: +81(985) 58-7111
Fax: +81(985) 58-2886
EMail: kokusai@of.miyazaki-u.ac.jp
Website: http://www.miyazaki-u.ac.jp

President: Tatsuo Suganuma Tel: +81(985) 58-7100

Secretary-General: Kiyoshi Ootani
EMail: ootani@of.miyazaki-u.ac.jp

International Relations: Yukifumi Nawa, Vice-President
EMail: fukur@of.miyazaki-u.ac.jp

Faculties

Agriculture (Agricultural Engineering; Agriculture; Animal Husbandry; Biochemistry; Biological and Life Sciences; Environmental Studies; Veterinary Science) *Dean*: Sho-ichiro Kobaye; **Education and Culture** (Cultural Studies; Education; Rural Studies; Social Studies) *Dean*: Toshimi Saduka; **Engineering** (Applied Chemistry; Applied Physics; Civil Engineering; Computer Science; Electrical and Electronic Engineering; Engineering; Environmental Engineering; Mechanical Engineering; Systems Analysis) *Dean*: Chikahisa Honda; **Medicine** *(Miyazaki Medical College) Dean*: Hiroshi Kannan

Further Information: Also Japanese language courses for foreign students. University Hospital and Hospital for Domestic Animals

History: Founded 1949 incorporating Miyazaki Agricultural College, Miyazaki Normal College, Miyazaki Youth Normal College. New Miyazaki University, "University of Miyazaki" was established following integration of Miyazaki Ika Daigaku/ Miyazaki Medical College October 2003.

Academic Year: April to March (April-September; October-March)

Admission Requirements: Graduation from high school or recognized equivalent, and entrance examination

Fees: (Yen): 535,800 per annum

Main Language(s) of Instruction: Japanese

International Co-operation: With universities in Republic of Korea, China, Thailand, Philippines, Indonesia, Slovenia, United Kingdom, Australia, New Zealand, USA, Argentina, Poland, Vietnam and Mongolia

Degrees and Diplomas: *Gakushi*: Agriculture; Education; Engineering; Liberal Arts; Nursing, 4 yrs; *Gakushi*: Medicine; Veterinary, 6 yrs; *Shushi*: Agriculture; Education; Engineering; Medicine; Nursing, a further 2 yrs; *Hakase*: Engineering, a further 3 yrs; *Hakase*: Medicine (Igaku-Hakushi), a further 4 yrs

Student Services: Academic counselling, Canteen, Employment services, Foreign student adviser, Health services, Language programs, Sports facilities

Student Residential Facilities: Yes

Special Facilities: Agricultural Museum

Libraries: Central Library; faculty libraries; total, 596,444 vols

Publications: Bulletin of Faculty of Agriculture *(annually)*; Bulletin of Faculty of Education and Culture *(annually)*; Bulletin of Faculty of Engineering *(annually)*

Last Updated: 25/03/11

UNIVERSITY OF NAGASAKI

Nagasaki Kenritsu Daigaku

123 Kawashimo-cho, Sasebo-shi, Nagasaki 858-8580
Tel: +81(956) 47-2191
Fax: +81(956) 47-6941
Website: http://www.nagasakipu.ac.jp

President: Zenji Ishimura (1997-)

Departments

Distribution and Business Administration (Business Administration; Information Management; Information Sciences; Information Technology; Marketing); **Economics** (Economics; International Economics); **Regional Policy**

Graduate Schools

Economics (Economic and Finance Policy; Economic History; Economics; Management)

History: Founded 1967. An institution under the juridiction of Nagasaki prefecture. Formerly known as Nagasaki Kenritsu Daigaku (Nagasaki Prefectural University). Acquired present title 2008 following merger with Kenritsu Nagasaki Siboruto Daigaku (Siebold University of Nagasaki).

Academic Year: April to March

Admission Requirements: Graduation from high school and entrance examinations, one in Japanese

Main Language(s) of Instruction: Japanese

International Co-operation: With universities in China

Degrees and Diplomas: *Gakushi*: 4 yrs; *Shushi*: a further 2 yrs

Student Services: Academic counselling, Canteen, Cultural centre, Employment services, Foreign student adviser, Handicapped facilities, Health services, Language programs, Nursery care, Social counselling, Sports facilities

Libraries: c. 212,000 vols

Last Updated: 12/01/09

UNIVERSITY OF NIIGATA PREFECTURE

Niigata Kenritsu Daigaku
471 Ebigase, Higashi-ku, Niigata-shi, Niigata 950-8680
Tel: +81(25) 270-1300
Fax: +81(25) 270-5173
EMail: unp@unii.ac.jp; iabe@unii.ac.jp
Website: http://www.unii.ac.jp/

President: Takashi Inoguchi (2009-) EMail: inoguchi@unii.ac.jp

Secretary General: Takashi Kato
Tel: +81(25) 270-1312 EMail: tkato@unii.ac.jp

International Relations: Ichiro Abe, Manager, International Exchange Office Tel: +81(25) 368-8373 EMail: iabe@unii.ac.jp

Faculties

Human Life Studies (Child Care and Development; Dietetics; Nutrition; Welfare and Protective Services); **International Studies and Regional Development** (Development Studies; International Studies; Regional Studies)

History: Created 2009. First cohort graduated 2013.

Governing Bodies: Board of Trustees

Academic Year: Apr to Sept; Oct to March

Admission Requirements: High school graduation certificate (Kotogakko Sotsugyo Shomeisho) or equivalent.

Fees: (Yen): Tuition 535,800 (per annum); Admission fee 564,000 (one-off fee paid at admission)

Main Language(s) of Instruction: Japanese

Accrediting Agencies: MEXT

Degrees and Diplomas: *Gakushi*: International Studies; Regional Development; Child Studies; Nutrition, 4 yrs

Student Services: Academic counselling, Canteen, Employment services, Foreign student adviser, Foreign Studies Centre, Handicapped facilities, Health services, Language programs, Nursery care, Social counselling, Sports facilities

Student Residential Facilities: None

Publications: Journal of International Studies and Regional Development, Research Journal *(annually)*; Ningen Seikatsu gaku kenkyu, Research Journal *(annually)*

Academic Staff *2011-2012*	MEN	WOMEN	**TOTAL**
FULL-TIME	48	32	**80**
PART-TIME	87	61	**148**
STAFF WITH DOCTORATE			
FULL-TIME	20	14	**34**
PART-TIME	22	9	**31**
Student Numbers *2011-2012*			
All (Foreign Included)	203	794	**997**

Last Updated: 28/08/12

UNIVERSITY OF OCCUPATIONAL AND ENVIRONMENTAL HEALTH

Sangyo Ika Daigaku
1-1 Iseigaoka, Yahata-nishi-ku, Kitakyushu-shi, Fukuoka 807-8555
Tel: +81(93) 603-1611
Fax: +81(93) 601-3446
Website: http://www.uoeh-u.ac.jp

President: Akio Shigematsu (2005-)

Secretary-General: Eiichi Kaneko

Centres

Occupational Health Training (Occupational Health)

Graduate Schools

Medical Sciences (Medicine)

Institutes

Industrial Ecological Sciences (Ecology; Occupational Health)

Schools

Health Sciences (Nursing; Social and Preventive Medicine); **Medicine** (Medicine)

Further Information: Also University Hospital

History: Founded 1978. Graduate School established 1984.

Governing Bodies: Board of Directors

Academic Year: April to March (April-September; October-March)

Admission Requirements: Graduation from high school and entrance examination

Fees: (Yen): 802,800-5m. per annum

Main Language(s) of Instruction: Japanese

Degrees and Diplomas: *Gakushi*: Environmental Management; Nursing, 4 yrs; *Gakushi*: Medicine, 6 yrs; *Hakase*: Environmental Management, a further 4 yrs. Also Diplomas and Certificates

Student Services: Academic counselling, Canteen, Cultural centre, Employment services, Health services, Social counselling, Sports facilities

Student Residential Facilities: For c. 226 women students

Special Facilities: University Hospital

Libraries: 117,964 vols

Publications: Journal of UOEH *(quarterly)*

UNIVERSITY OF SHIGA PREFECTURE

Shiga Kenritsu Daigaku
2500 Hassaka-cho, Hikone-shi, Shiga 522-8533
Tel: +81(749) 28-8200
Fax: +81(749) 28-8470
EMail: webmaster@usp.ac.jp
Website: http://www.usp.ac.jp

President: Lake Biwa

Schools

Engineering *(Also Graduate School)*; **Environmental Sciences** *(Also Graduate School)*; **Human Cultures** *(Also Graduate School)*; **Human Nursing** *(Also Graduate School)* (Nursing)

History: Founded 1995.

Degrees and Diplomas: *Gakushi*; *Shushi*; *Hakase*

Last Updated: 02/02/09

UNIVERSITY OF SHIZUOKA

Shizuoka Kenritzu Daigaku
52-1 Yada, Shizuoka-shi, Shizuoka 422-8526
Tel: +81(54) 264-5007
Fax: +81(54) 264-5199
EMail: nyus@gm.u-shizuoka-ken.ac.jp
Website: http://www.u-shizuoka-ken.ac.jp

President: Masachika Suzuki

Faculties

International Relations *(Also Graduate School)* (International Relations; International Studies)

Institutes

Environmental Sciences *(Also Graduate School)* (Environmental Studies)

Schools

Administration and Informatics *(Also Graduate School)* (Administration; Computer Science); **Food and Nutritional Sciences** *(Also Graduate School)* (Food Science; Nutrition); **Nursing** *(Also Graduate School)* (Nursing); **Pharmaceutical Sciences** *(Also Graduate School)* (Pharmacology; Pharmacy)

Further Information: Also Japanese language courses for foreign students

History: Founded 1987, incorporating the existing three Prefectural Colleges (Shizuoka College of Pharmacy, Shizuoka Women's College, and Shizuoka Women's Junior College).

Academic Year: April to March (April-September; October-March)

Admission Requirements: Graduation from high school or recognized equivalent or foreign equivalent, and entrance examination

Main Language(s) of Instruction: Japanese

Degrees and Diplomas: *Gakushi*: 4 yrs; *Shushi*: a further 2 yrs; *Hakase*: 3 yrs following Shushi

Student Services: Employment services, Health services, Language programs, Sports facilities

Libraries: c. 336,000 vols

Last Updated: 02/02/09

UNIVERSITY OF THE RYUKYUS

Ryukyu Daigaku

1 Senbaru, Nishihara-cho, Okinawa 903-0213

Tel: +81(98) 895-8131

Fax: +81(98) 895-8102

EMail: ryryki@to.jim.u-ryukyu.ac.jp

Website: http://www.u-ryukyu.ac.jp

President: Teruo Iwamasa

Faculties

Agriculture (Agriculture; Biology; Biotechnology; Environmental Engineering; Environmental Studies; Production Engineering); **Education** (Education); **Engineering** (Architecture; Civil Engineering; Electrical and Electronic Engineering; Energy Engineering; Engineering; Information Technology; Mechanical Engineering); **Law and Letters** (Arts and Humanities; Cultural Studies; Law; Modern Languages; Social Policy); **Medicine** (Anatomy; Health Sciences; Medicine); **Science** (Biology; Chemistry; Earth Sciences; Marine Science and Oceanography; Mathematics; Natural Sciences; Physics)

Graduate Schools

Agriculture *(United Graduate School, Kagoshima University)* (Biological and Life Sciences; Marine Science and Oceanography; Production Engineering); **Education** (Crafts and Trades; Education; Educational Psychology; English; Fine Arts; Handicrafts; Health Education; Home Economics Education; Japanese; Mathematics; Music Education; Natural Sciences; Pedagogy; Physical Education; Psychology; Social Sciences; Special Education; Technology Education); **Engineering and Science** (Artificial Intelligence; Biology; Chemistry; Civil Engineering; Earth Sciences; Electrical and Electronic Engineering; Energy Engineering; Engineering; Environmental Engineering; Information Technology; Marine Science and Oceanography; Materials Engineering; Mathematics; Mechanical Engineering; Physics; Structural Architecture); **Health Sciences**; **Humanities and Social Sciences** *(Graduate Programme)* (Cultural Studies; Economics; Law; Regional Studies; Social Sciences); **Medicine** (Anaesthesiology; Anatomy; Biochemistry; Environmental Studies; Immunology; Medicine; Oncology; Pathology; Physiology; Social and Preventive Medicine; Tropical Medicine)

Further Information: Also education and research institutes

History: Founded 1950 under the authority of the United States Civil Administration, authority transferred to a Board of Trustees 1952. Transferred to control of Government of the Ryukyus 1966, and became under the jurisdiction of Japanese Ministry of Education, Science, Sports and Culture a National University 1972. Graduate School of Agriculture established 1977.

Academic Year: April to March (April-October; October-March)

Admission Requirements: Graduation from high school or equivalent, and entrance examination

Main Language(s) of Instruction: Japanese

International Co-operation: With universities in Oceania, China and Thailand

Degrees and Diplomas: *Gakushi*: Agriculture (Nogakushi); Arts in English Language and Literature (Bungakushi); Arts in Fine Arts (Bungakushi); Arts in Geography (Bungakushi); Arts in History (Bungakushi); Arts in Japanese Language and Literature (Bungakushi); Arts in Law and Political Science (Bungakushi); Civil Engineering (Kogakushi); Education in Music (Kyoikugakushi); Education in Psychology (Kyoikugakushi); Electrical Engineering (Kogakushi); Elementary Education (Kyoikugakushi); Health Sciences (Hokeneiseigakushi); Mechanical Engineering (Kogakushi); Physical Education (Kyoikugakushi); Science in Biology (Rigakushi); Science in Chemistry (Rigakushi); Science in Mathematics (Rigakushi); Science in Physics (Rigakushi); Sociology (Shakaigakushi); Vocational Education (Kyoikugakushi), 4 yrs; *Shushi*: a further 2 yrs; *Hakase*

Student Services: Academic counselling, Foreign student adviser, Foreign Studies Centre, Social counselling

Student Residential Facilities: Yes

Special Facilities: Academic Museum

Libraries: c. 952,000 vols

Last Updated: 30/01/09

UNIVERSITY OF THE SACRED HEART

Seishin Joshi Daigaku

4-3-1 Hiroo, Shibuya-ku, Tokyo 150-8938

Tel: +81(33) 407-5811

Fax: +81(35) 485-3884

EMail: wwwadmin@u-sacred-heart.ac.jp

Website: http://www.u-sacred-heart.ac.jp

President: Heiji Taranaka (2007-)

Tel: +81(33) 407-5037, Fax: +81(35) 485-0420

EMail: secretary@u-sacred-heart.ac.jp; admin@u-sacred-heart.-ac.jp

International Relations: Takayo Mukai, International Centre

Tel: +81(33) 407-5072, Fax: +81(33) 407-5917

EMail: mukai@u-sacred-heart.ac.jp

Departments

Christian Culture Research *Dean*: Tôru Endô; **Education** (Education; Educational Psychology; Primary Education; Secondary Education); **English Language and Literature** (English; English Studies; Literature); **History and Social Sciences** (History; International Studies; Social Studies); **Japanese Language and Literature** (Japanese; Literature); **Philosophy** (Philosophy)

History: Founded 1910 as Primary and High School. Teachers' Training School added 1951. Raised to College status 1948 and University status 1950. Given the right to grant Sho-gakko (State primary school Teachers' Certificate) 1957.

Governing Bodies: Board of Trustees

Academic Year: April to March (April-July; October-March)

Admission Requirements: Graduation from high school (Koto Gakko) or recognized foreign equivalent, and entrance examination

Fees: (Yen): 970,000 per annum

Main Language(s) of Instruction: Japanese, English (in some courses)

Degrees and Diplomas: *Gakushi*: Arts (BA) (Bungakushi), 4 yrs; *Shushi*: Arts (MA) (Bungakushushi), at least a further 2 yrs; *Hakase (PhD)*: at least 3 yrs following Shushi

Student Services: Academic counselling, Canteen, Cultural centre, Employment services, Foreign student adviser, Foreign Studies Centre, Handicapped facilities, Health services, Language programs, Social counselling

Student Residential Facilities: For 250 students

Libraries: Seishin Joshi Daigaku Library, 319,411 vols

Publications: Christian Cultural Institute Publications *(annually)*; Seishin Campus *(quarterly)*; Seishin Studies *(biannually)*

Academic Staff *2008-2009*	MEN	WOMEN	**TOTAL**
FULL-TIME	34	33	**67**
PART-TIME	178	149	**327**
STAFF WITH DOCTORATE			
FULL-TIME	31	25	**56**
PART-TIME	1	3	**4**
Student Numbers *2010-2011*			
All (Foreign Included)	–	–	**2,246**

Last Updated: 09/12/08

UNIVERSITY OF TOKUSHIMA

Tokushima Daigaku

2-24 Shinkura-cho, Tokushima-shi, Tokushima 770-8501

Tel: +81(88) 656-7021

Fax: +81(88) 656-7012

EMail: hibunsyok@jim.tokushima-u.ac.jp

Website: http://www.tokushima-u.ac.jp

President: Toshihiro Aono

Administrator: Takashima Takashi

EMail: ttakashi@jim.tokushima-u.ac.jp

International Relations: Toshihiko Nagata

EMail: ryugakuk@jim.tokushima-u.ac.jp

Faculties

Dentistry (Dentistry) *Dean*: Eiichi Bando; **Engineering** (Applied Mathematics; Applied Physics; Artificial Intelligence; Bioengineering; Chemical Engineering; Civil Engineering; Electrical and Electronic Engineering; Engineering; Environmental Engineering; Information Technology; Mechanical Engineering; Optical Technology) *Dean*: Yoneo Yano; **Integrated Arts and Sciences** (Asian Studies; Behavioural Sciences; Biological and Life Sciences; Chemistry; Comparative Sociology; Computer Science; Cultural Studies; Economics; Environmental Studies; European Languages; Fine Arts; Geology; Law; Mathematics; Media Studies; Modern Languages; Natural Sciences; Physics; Regional Studies; Social Sciences) *Dean*: Makoto Wada; **Medicine** (Health Sciences; Medicine; Nutrition) *Dean*: Saburo Sone; **Pharmaceutical Sciences** (Pharmacology; Pharmacy) *Dean*: Takashi Yamauchi

Graduate Schools

Advanced Technology and Science *Dean*: Yoneo Yano; **Human and Natural Environment Sciences** (Environmental Management; Environmental Studies; Psychology; Social Sciences) *Dean*: Makoto Wada; **Medical Sciences** (Health Sciences; Medicine) *Dean*: Saburo Sone; **Nutrition and Bioscience** *Dean*: Yutaka Nakaya; **Oral Sciences** *Dean*: Eiichi Bando; **Pharmaceutical Sciences** (Chemistry; Pharmacology; Pharmacy) *Dean*: Takashi Yamauchi

Institutes

Health Biosciences *(Graduate School)* (Biomedicine; Health Sciences; Nutrition; Pharmacy) *Dean*: Saburo Sone; **Technology and Science** *(Graduate School)* (Engineering) *Dean*: Yoneo Yano

Further Information: Also Japanese language courses for foreign students

History: Founded 1874 as Tokushima Kisei Normal School. Acquired present status and title 1949.

Governing Bodies: Board of Executive Directors, comprising 8 members

Academic Year: April to March (April-September; October-March)

Admission Requirements: Graduation from high school or recognized equivalent, and entrance examination

Main Language(s) of Instruction: Japanese

Degrees and Diplomas: *Gakushi*: Dentistry; Medicine, 6 yrs; *Gakushi*: Engineering; Health Sciences; Integrated Arts and Sciences; Nutrition and Bioscience, 4 yrs; *Gakushi*: Pharmacy, 4-6 yrs; *Shushi*: Advanced Technology and Science; Human and Natural Environmental Sciences; Nutrition and Bioscience; Pharmaceutical Sciences, a further 2 yrs; *Hakase*: Advanced Technology and Sciences; Nutrition and Bioscience; Pharmaceutical Sciences, a further 3 yrs; *Hakase*: Medical Sciences; Oral Sciences, a further 4 yrs

Student Residential Facilities: Yes (International House and dormitory)

Libraries: University Library, 822,000 vols (in Japanese and other languages)

Publications: Bulletin of Faculty of Engineering *(annually)*; Study Reports (Integrated Arts and Sciences) *(annually)*; The Journal of Medical Investigation *(biennially)*

UNIVERSITY OF TOYAMA

Toyama Daigaku

3190 Gofuku, Toyama-shi, Toyama 930-8555
Tel: +81(76) 445-6082
Fax: +81(76) 445-6093
EMail: ryugaku@adm.u-toyama;ac.jp
Website: http://www.u-toyama.ac.jp

President: Saito Tokuso

Centres

Cooperative Research (Education); **Education and Research of Lifelong Learning** (Computer Science); **Far Eastern Studies**; **Information Technology**; **Instrumental Analysis**; **International Student**; **Nature Study and Training**; **Water Quality Management**

Colleges

Arts, Design and Regional Business *(Takoaka)*

Faculties

Art and Design; **Economics** (Business Administration; Commercial Law; Economics); **Engineering** (Biological and Life Sciences; Electrical and Electronic Engineering; Information Technology; Materials Engineering; Mechanical Engineering); **Humanities** (Arts and Humanities; Cultural Studies; International Studies; Modern Languages); **Liberal Arts and Science** *(Sugitani Campus)*; **Medicine** (Anaesthesiology; Anatomy; Biochemistry; Dermatology; Epidemiology; Forensic Medicine and Dentistry; Gerontology; Gynaecology and Obstetrics; Immunology; Medicine; Neurosciences; Nursing; Ophthalmology; Orthopaedics; Otorhinolaryngology; Paediatrics; Pathology; Pharmacology; Psychiatry and Mental Health; Public Health; Radiology; Surgery; Urology; Virology); **Pharmacy and Pharmaceutical Sciences**; **Science** (Biology; Chemistry; Earth Sciences; Environmental Studies; Mathematics; Physics)

Graduate Schools

Economics; **Education** (Curriculum; Education); **Humanities**; **Innovative Life Science** (Biological and Life Sciences); **Medicine and Pharmaceutical Science for Education** (Medicine; Pharmacy); **Medicine and Pharmaceutical Science for Research**; **Science and Engineering for Education** (Biological and Life Sciences; Biology; Chemistry; Computer Engineering; Earth Sciences; Electrical and Electronic Engineering; Energy Engineering; Environmental Studies; Information Technology; Materials Engineering; Mathematics; Mechanical Engineering; Physics); **Science and Engineering for Research**

Laboratories

Radioisotope (Radiology); **Venture Business**

Research Centres

Hydrogen Isotope; **Low Temperature Quantum Science**

Further Information: Also Japanese language courses for foreign students

History: Founded 1949 incorporating Toyama Normal College founded 1943, Toyama High School, 1943, Takaoka Vocational School, 1944, and Toyama Normal School for Youth, 1944. Toyama Ika Yakka Daigaku (Toyama Medical and Pharmaceutical University) and Takaoka National College incorporated 2005.

Governing Bodies: National University Corporation

Academic Year: April to March (April-September; October-March)

Admission Requirements: Graduation from high school or recognized equivalent or foreign equivalent, and entrance examination

Fees: (Yen): 520,800 per annum

Main Language(s) of Instruction: Japanese

Accrediting Agencies: Ministry of Education, Culture, Sports, Science and Technology

Degrees and Diplomas: *Gakushi*: Business Administration (Keieigaku); Economics (Keizaigakushi); Economics (Law) (Hogaku); Education (Kyoiku); Engineering (Kogaku); Humanities (Bungaku); Science (Rigaku), 4 yrs; *Shushi*: Business Administration (Keieigaku); Education (Kyoikugaku); Humanities (Bungaku); Regional and Economic Policy (Keizaigaku); Science & Engineering (Rigaku); Science & Engineering (Kogaku), a further 2 yrs; *Hakase*: Science and Engineering (Rigaku), 3 yrs; *Hakase*: Science and Engineering (Kogaku), a furher 3 yrs

Student Services: Academic counselling, Canteen, Employment services, Foreign student adviser, Foreign Studies Centre, Health services, Language programs, Social counselling, Sports facilities

Student Residential Facilities: Yes

Libraries: c. 1,290,000 vols

Publications: Bulletin of Faculty of Education Toyama University *(annually)*; Bulletin of the Center for Educationnal Research and Practice Toyama University *(annually)*; Journal of the Faculty of Humanities Toyama University *(annually)*; Mathematics Journal of Toyama University *(annually)*; Memoirs of the Faculty of Education Toyama University *(annually)*; The Fudai Keizai Ronshu *(annually)*; The Journal of Economic Studies Toyama University *(annually)*

Last Updated: 06/02/09

UNIVERSITY OF TSUKUBA

Tsukuba Daigaku (UT)
1-1-1 Tennodai, Tsukuba-shi, Ibaraki 305-8577
Tel: +81(29) 853-2111
Fax: +83(29) 853-2059
EMail: koryuka@sakura.cc.tsukuba.ac.jp
Website: http://www.tsukuba.ac.jp

President: Nobuhiro Nagata (2013-)

Executive Director: Hiromochi Yoshitake Tel: +81(29) 853-2004

International Relations: Masaru Adachi, Director, Department of Global Activities Tel: +81(29) 853-2080

Centres

Academic Computing and Communications *Director*: Kozo Itano; **Admission** *Director*: Tomonori Shirakawa; **Agricultural and Forestry Research** (Agriculture; Forestry) *Director*: Naoki Sakai; **Alliance for Research on North Africa** (North African Studies) *Director*: Mitsutoshi Nakajima; **Computational Sciences** *(TARA)* (Computer Science) *Director*: Mitsuhisa Sato; **Foreign Languages** (Modern Languages) *Director*: Daisaku Ihara; **Gene Research** (Genetics) *Director*: Hiroshi Ezura; **International Student** *Director*: Kazuo Watanabe; **Laboratory Animal Resource** *Director*: Ken-ichi Yagami; **Plasma Research Centre** *(TARA) Director*: Tsuyoshi Imai; **Proton Medical Research** *Director*: Akira Matsumura; **Radioisotope** *Director*: Hiroki Oshio; **Research Facility for Science and Technology** *Director*: Kazuo Matsuuchi; **Research for Knowledge Communities** *Director*: Shigeo Sugimoto; **Research for University Studies** *Director*: Hisatoshi Suzuki; **Research on International Cooperation in Educational Development** *Director*: Hideo Nakata; **Shimoda Marine Research** *(Shimoda City) Director*: Kazuo Inaba; **Special Support Education Research** *Director*: Yoshihiro Fujiwara; **Sport and Physical Education** (Physical Education; Sports) *Director*: Ken Miyashita; **Sugadaira Montane Research** *(Ueda City) Director*: Osamu Numata; **Terrestrial Environment Research** (Environmental Studies) *Director*: Tadashi Tanaka; **Tsukuba Advanced Research Alliance** *(TARA) Director*: Akiyoshi Fukamizu; **Tsukuba Critical Path Research and Education Integrated Leading Centre** *Director*: Naoyuki Ochiai; **Tsukuba Industrial Liaison and Cooperative Research** *Director*: Shin'ichi Yuta; **Tsukuba Research for Interdisciplinary Materials Science** *Director*: Youiti Ootuka; **University Health Centre** *Director*: Morio Ohtsuka

Colleges

Agro-biological Resources Sciences (Agrobiology; Applied Chemistry; Economics; Environmental Engineering) *Dean*: Suminori Tokunaga; **Biological Sciences** (Biochemistry; Biology; Botany; Ecology; Embryology and Reproduction Biology; Genetics; Molecular Biology) *Dean*: Shinobu Satoh; **Chemistry** (Biotechnology; Chemistry; Genetics; Inorganic Chemistry; Organic Chemistry; Physical Chemistry) *Dean*: Tatsuo Arai; **Comparative Culture** (Cultural Studies; Literature; Regional Studies) *Dean*: Taiji Azegami; **Disability Sciences** *Dean*: Hisao Maekawa; **Education** (Development Studies; Education; Educational Administration; Educational Research; International and Comparative Education; Primary Education; Secondary Education) *Dean*: Kazuko Shoji; **Engineering Sciences** (Applied Physics; Electronic Engineering; Materials Engineering) *Dean*: Katsumi Kose; **Engineering Systems** (Electrical Engineering; Engineering Management; Environmental Engineering; Mechanical Engineering) *Dean*: Yutaka Abe; **Geoscience** (Geography (Human); Geology; Meteorology; Mineralogy; Paleontology; Water Science) *Dean*: Norikazu Matsuoka; **Humanities** (Archaeology; Folklore; History; Linguistics; Philosophy) *Dean*: Makoto Ito; **Information Sciences** (Artificial Intelligence; Computer Engineering; Computer Science; Information Sciences; Information Technology; Media Studies; Software Engineering) *Dean*: Yoshinori Yamaguchi; **International Studies** (Cultural Studies; Development Studies; Economics; Environmental Studies; Information Sciences; International Law; International Relations; Political Sciences) *Provost*: Yukio Fukui; **Japanese Language and Culture** (Cultural Studies; Japanese) *Dean*: Hideichi Eto; **Knowledge and Library Sciences** (Information Technology; Library Science) *Dean*: Chieko Mizoue; **Mathematics** (Mathematics; Mathematics Education) *Dean*: Seiichiro Wakabayashi; **Media Arts, Science and Technology** (Actuarial Science; Cognitive Sciences; Communication Arts; Communication Studies; Computer Engineering; Computer Networks; Information Sciences; Information Technology; Media Studies; Operations Research; Statistics) *Dean*: Kazumi Odaka; **Physics** (Biology; Biophysics; Earth Sciences; Mechanics; Physical Chemistry; Physics; Statistics; Thermal Physics) *Dean*: Naomasa Nakai; **Policy and Planning Sciences** (Economics; Management; Regional Planning; Social Studies; Town Planning) *Dean*: Reiji Obase; **Psychology** (Clinical Psychology; Educational Psychology; Psychology; Social Psychology) *Dean*: Yukio Ichitani; **Social Sciences** (Economics; Law; Political Sciences; Sociology) *Dean*: Miyoko Motozawa

Graduate Schools

Area Studies *(Master's Degree Programme) Chair*: Shigeo Osonoi; **Business Sciences** *(Master's Degree Programme)* (Business Administration; Business and Commerce; Commercial Law; Law) *Provost*: Shu Yamada; **Business Sciences** *(Doctoral Degree Programme)* (Business Administration; Business and Commerce; Commercial Law; Law) *Provost*: Shu Yamada; **Comprehensive Human Sciences** *(Doctoral Degree Programme) Provost*: Kazuhiko Shimizu; **Comprehensive Human Sciences** *(Master's Degree Programme) Provost*: Kazuhiko Shimizu; **Education** *(Master's Degree Programme) Chair*: Izumi Ohtaka; **Health and Sport Sciences** *(Master's Degree Programme) Chair*: Akira Nakagawa; **Humanities and Social Sciences** *(Master's Degree Programme)* (Cultural Studies; Economics; International Studies; Law; Modern Languages; Political Sciences) *Provost*: Yoshiki Tsuboi; **Humanities and Social Sciences** *(Doctoral Degree Programme)* (Anthropology; Asian Studies; Cultural Studies; East Asian Studies; Economics; History; International Studies; Law; Linguistics; Literature; Modern Languages; Philosophy; Political Sciences; Social Sciences) *Provost*: Yoshiki Tsuboi; **Library, Information and Media Studies** *(Doctoral Degree Programme) Provost*: Shin-ichi Nakayama; **Library, Information and Media Studies** *(Master's Degree Programme) Provost*: Shin-ichi Nakayama; **Life and Environmental Sciences** *(Master's Degree Programme)* (Agriculture; Biological and Life Sciences; Environmental Studies) *Provost*: Norio Tase; **Life and Environmental Sciences** *(Doctoral Degree Programme) Provost*: Norio Tase; **Pure and Applied Sciences** *(Master's Degree Programme)* (Applied Physics; Chemistry; Materials Engineering; Mathematics; Physics) *Provost*: Masafumi Akahira; **Pure and Applied Sciences** *(Doctoral Degree Programme)* (Applied Physics; Chemistry; Materials Engineering; Mathematics; Physics) *Provost*: Masafumi Akahira; **Systems and Information Engineering** *(Master's Degree Programme) Provost*: Jiro Tanaka; **Systems and Information Engineering** *(Doctoral Degree Programme) Provost*: Jiro Tanaka

Institutes

Agricultural and Forest Engineering (Agricultural Engineering; Agriculture; Forestry) *Chair*: Masayoshi Satoh; **Agriculture and Forestry** *Chair*: Hiroshi Honda; **Applied Biochemistry** (Biochemistry) *Chair*: Seigo Satoh; **Applied Physics** *Chair*: Katsuhiro Akimoto; **Art and Design** (Design; Fine Arts) *Chair*: Shin-ichi Tamagawa; **Basic Medical Sciences** (Health Sciences) *Chair*: Akira Shibuya; **Biological Sciences** (Biological and Life Sciences) *Chair*: Yoshihiro Shiraiwa; **Chemistry** *Chair*: Yasuhiko Yamamoto; **Clinical Medicine** *Chair*: Nobuhiro Okohchi; **Community Medicine** (Community Health; Medicine) *Chair*: Yoji Nakatani; **Disability Science** (Rehabilitation and Therapy) *Chair*: Kiyohiko Kawauchi; **Education** (Education) *Chair*: Akitoshi Teuchi; **Engineering Mechanics and Systems** (Engineering; Mechanical Engineering) *Chair*: Yuichi Ota; **Geoscience** *Chair*: Norikazu Matsuoka; **Health and Sport Sciences** (Health Sciences; Sports) *Chair*: Yoshikazu Nomura; **History and Anthropology** *Chair*: Shinpei Furuie; **Information Sciences and Electronics** (Information Sciences; Information Technology) *Chair*: Hiroyuki Kitagawa; **Library and Information Sciences** (Information Sciences; Library Science) *Chair*: Hidehiro Ishizuka; **Literature and Lingusitics** *Chair*: Yukio Hirose; **Materials Science** *Chair*: Hiroaki Suzuki; **Mathematics** *Chair*: Masahiko Miyamoto; **Modern Languages and Cultures** *Chair*: Yasuaki Kawanabe; **Nursing Sciences** (Nursing) *Chair*: Takayasu Kawaguchi; **Philosophy** (Philosophy) *Chair*: Nobuo Horiike; **Physics** *Chair*: Shinhong Kim; **Policy and Planning Sciences** *Chair*: Masato Koda; **Psychology** *Chair*: Fujio Yoshida; **Social Sciences** *Chair*: Jiro Obata

Schools

Arts and Design (Art History; Communication Arts; Design; Fine Arts) *Provost*: Kiyoshi Nishikawa; **Health and Physical Education** (Anatomy; Health Education; Physical Education; Physiology; Sports; Sports Management) *Provost*: Michiyoshi Abe; **Human Sciences** (Education; Psychology; Social Sciences) *Provost*: Kazuo

Hori; **Humanities and Culture** (Arts and Humanities; Cultural Studies) *Provost*: Norio Yamada; **Informatics** *Provost*: Yoshihiko Ebihara; **Life and Environmental Sciences** (Biological and Life Sciences; Environmental Studies) *Provost*: Yukio Kanai; **Medical Sciences** (Biochemistry; Health Sciences; Pathology; Pharmacology; Physiology) *Dean*: Osamu Urayama; **Medicine** (Biology; Medicine; Social and Preventive Medicine; Sports; Sports Management; Sports Medicine) *Dean*: Akira Hara; **Medicine and Medical Sciences** *Provost*: Fujio Otsuka; **Nursing** *Dean*: Yuka Saeki; **Science and Engineering** *Vice-Provost*: Mitsuhiro Takeuchi; **Science and Engineering** (Engineering; Mathematics; Natural Sciences) *Provost*: Masatoshi Yoshida; **Social and International Studies** *Provost*: Nohibuko Kitawaki

Further Information: Also major research institutes: the Japan Aerospace Exploration (JAXA) and the High Energy Accelerator Research Organization (KEK)

History: Founded 1872 as Normal School, later renamed Tokyo Higher Normal School, the first teachers' college in Japan. Became Tokyo University of Education in 1947. Moved to the Tsukuba area, reorganized and acquired present status and title in 1973. Merger with Toshokan Joho Daigaku (University of Library and Information Science) 2002.

Governing Bodies: Keiei-kyogikai (Administrative Council)

Academic Year: April to March (April-July; August-November; December-March)

Admission Requirements: Graduation from high school (or recognized equivalent) and entrance examination

Fees: (Yen): Registration, 282,000; tuition, 535,800 per annum

Main Language(s) of Instruction: Japanese

International Co-operation: With universities in USA; Republic of Korea; China; Thailand; Australia; France; Russian Federation; United Kingdom; Canada; etc.

Degrees and Diplomas: *Gakushi*: Agro-Biological Resources Sciences (BS); Art and Design (BA); Biological Sciences (BS); Chemistry (BS); Comparative Culture (BA); Disability Sciences (BS); Education (BA); Engineering Sciences (Bsc Eng); Geoscience (BS); Health and Physical Education (BS); Information Science (BSc Eng); International Studies (BA); Japanese Language and Culture (BA); Knowledge and Library Sciences (BS); Mathematics (BS); Media, Arts, Science and Technology (BS); Medical Sciences (BS); Nursing (BS); Physics (BS); Policy and Planning Sciences (BS); Psychology (BS); Social Sciences (BA), 4 yrs; *Gakushi*: Medicine (MD) (Igakushi); *Shushi*: Advanced Studies of Business Law (LLM); Agro-Bioresources Science and Technology (MS); Applied Physics (MEng); Art and Design (MA); Biological Sciences (MS); Business Administration (MBA); Business Administration and Public Policy (MBA); Chemistry (MS); Computer Science (MEng); Disability Sciences (MS); Economics (MA); Educational Sciences (MS); Engineering Mechanics and Energy (MEng); Environmental Sciences (MS); Frontier Science (MS); Geosciences (MS); Health and Sport Sciences (MS); Intelligent Interaction Technologies (MEng); International Area Studies (MA); International Public Policy; Kansei, Behavioural and Brain Sciences (MS); Law (JD); Library, Information and Media Studies (MS); Lifespan Development (MS); Materials Science (MEng); Mathematics (MS); Medical Sciences (MS); Modern Languages and Cultures (MA); Nursing Sciences (MS); Physics (MS); Psychology (MS); Risk Engineering (MEng); School Leadership and Professional Development (MA); Secondary Education (MA); Social Systems Engineering (MEng); Special Needs Education (MS); Sports and Health Promotion (MS); Systems Management (MS); World Heritage Studies (MA), 2 yrs; *Hakase*: Advanced Agricultural Technology and Science (PhD); Applied Physics (PhD); Appropriate Technology and Sciences for Sustainable Development (PhD); Art and Design (PhD); Bioindustrial Sciences (PhD); Biosphere Resources Science and Technology (PhD); Chemistry (PhD); Clinical Sciences (PhD); Coaching Science (PhD); Computer Science (PhD); Disability Sciences (PhD); Earth Evolution Sciences (PhD); Economics (PhD); Education (PhD); Engineering Mechanics and Energy (PhD); Frontier Science (PhD); Functional Biosciences (PhD); Geoenvironmental Sciences (PhD); Health and Sports Sciences (PhD); History and Anthropology (PhD); Human Care Science (PhD); Intelligent Interaction Technologies (PhD); Interactive Environmental Sciences (PhD); International and Advanced Japanese Studies (PhD); International Public Policy (PhD); Kansei, Behavioural and Brain Sciences (PhD); Law (PhD); Library, Information and Media Studies (PhD); Life Sciences and Bioengineering (PhD); Life System Medical Sciences (PhD); Lifespan Developmental Sciences (PhD); Literature and Linguistics (PhD); Materials Science (PhD); Materials Science and Engineering (PhD); Mathematics (PhD); Modern Languages and Cultures (PhD); Philosophy (PhD); Physical Education (PhD); Physics (PhD); Psychology (PhD); Risk Engineering (PhD); School Education (PhD); Social Systems and Management (PhD); Sports Medicine (PhD); Structural Biosciences (PhD); Sustainable Environmental Studies (PhD); Systems Management and Business Law (PhD); World Cultural Heritage Studies (PhD)

Student Services: Academic counselling, Canteen, Employment services, Foreign student adviser, Foreign Studies Centre, Handicapped facilities, Health services, Language programs, Social counselling, Sports facilities

Student Residential Facilities: For 4,196 students

Special Facilities: University of Tsukuba Gallery; University of Tsukuba Art Space, Art and Design Faculty Gallery

Libraries: Central Library, total, 2,457,258 vols; 23,001 titles

Press or Publishing House: University of Tsukuba Press

Student Numbers *2012-2013*: Total 16,685

Last Updated: 14/03/13

UNIVERSITY OF YAMANASHI

Yamanashi Daigaku

4-4-37 Takeda, Kofu-shi, Yamanashi 400-8510

Tel: +81(55) 220-8004

Fax: +81(55) 220-8799

EMail: yu-study-abroad@yamanashi.ac.jp

Website: http://www.yamanashi.ac.jp

President: Shuichiro Maeda

Centres

Co-operative Research and Development (Development Studies); **Data Processing** (Data Processing); **Health Care** (Health Sciences); **Instrumental Analysis** (Instrument Making); **Life Science Research** (Biological and Life Sciences)

Faculties

Education and Human Sciences (Cultural Studies; Education; Educational Sciences; Fine Arts; Social Studies); **Engineering** (Applied Chemistry; Biotechnology; Civil Engineering; Computer Science; Electrical and Electronic Engineering; Environmental Engineering; Information Sciences; Mechanical Engineering); **Medicine** (Health Administration; Medicine; Nursing; Pharmacy)

Graduate Schools

Education; **Medicine and Engineering** *(Interdisciplinary)* (Applied Chemistry; Biotechnology; Civil Engineering; Computer Science; Electrical and Electronic Engineering; Engineering; Environmental Engineering; Materials Engineering; Mechanical Engineering; Medical Technology; Medicine; Nursing)

Programmes

Special Education (Special Education)

Research Centres

Clean Energy (Energy Engineering)

Further Information: Also University Hospital

History: Founded 1949 incorporating Yamanashi Technical College, Yamanashi Normal School, and Yamanashi Normal School for Youth. Merged with Yamanashi Ika Daigaku (Yamanashi Medical University) 2002. Became National university corporation University of Yamanashi 2004.

Governing Bodies: Hyogikai (University Council)

Academic Year: April to March (April-September; October-March)

Admission Requirements: Graduation from high school or recognized equivalent, and entrance examination

Main Language(s) of Instruction: Japanese

Degrees and Diplomas: *Gakushi*: Education (Kyoikugakushi); Engineering (Kogakushi), 4 yrs; *Shushi*: Education (Kyoikugakushushi), a further 2 yrs; *Hakase*: Engineering (Kogakuhakushi), 3 yrs following Shushi; *Hakase*: Engineering (Kogakushushi), a further 2 yrs

Student Services: Canteen, Employment services, Foreign student adviser, Foreign Studies Centre, Health services, Language programs, Sports facilities

Student Residential Facilities: Yes

Libraries: Total, c. 587,800 vols

Publications: Bulletin of the Faculty of Education and Humanities *(3 per annum)*; Reports of the Faculty of Engineering Yamanashi University *(annually)*

Last Updated: 25/03/11

URAWA UNIVERSITY

Urawa Daigaku

3551 Osaki, Midori-ku, Saitama-shi, Saitama 336-0974
Tel: +81(48) 878-3741
Fax: +81(48) 878-3620
EMail: nyushi@urawa.ac.jp
Website: http://www.urawa.ac.jp

Faculties

Care Welfare (Social Welfare; Welfare and Protective Services); **Comprehensive Welfare** (Social Welfare; Welfare and Protective Services); **English Communication**; **Management and Information** (Information Sciences; Management)

History: Founded 2003.

Degrees and Diplomas: *Gakushi*

UTSUNOMIYA KYOWA UNIVERSITY

Utsunomiya Kyouwa Daigaku

131 Kanosaki, Kuroiso-shi, Tochigi 329-3121
Tel: +81(287) 67-3111
Fax: +81(287) 67-3112
EMail: nyuushi@kyowa-u.ac.jp
Website: http://www.kyowa-u.ac.jp

Programmes

Urban Economics (Economics; English; Information Management; Information Technology; Urban Studies)

History: Founded 1999. Formerly known as Nasu Daigaku (Nasu University).

Degrees and Diplomas: *Gakushi*

Student Services: Sports facilities

Student Residential Facilities: Yes

Libraries: c. 38,000 vols

Last Updated: 27/01/09

UTSUNOMIYA UNIVERSITY

Utsonomiya Daigaku

350 Mine-machi, Utsunomiya-shi, Tochigi 321-8505
Tel: +81(28) 649-8649
Fax: +81(28) 649-5115
EMail: plan@miya.jm.utsunomiya-u.ac.jp
Website: http://www.utsunomiya-u.ac.jp

President: Takeo Shinmura

Faculties

Agriculture (Agricultural Economics; Agriculture; Animal Husbandry; Applied Chemistry; Bioengineering; Botany; Crop Production; Environmental Engineering; Forestry; Production Engineering; Zoology); **Education** (Art Education; Ecology; Education; Education of the Handicapped; Environmental Studies; Health Education; Japanese; Mathematics Education; Music Education; Physical Education; Primary Education; Science Education; Secondary Education; Social Studies; Special Education; Sports; Teacher Training; Technology Education); **Engineering** (Applied Chemistry; Architecture; Civil Engineering; Electrical and Electronic Engineering; Energy Engineering; Engineering; Environmental Engineering; Information Sciences; Materials Engineering; Mechanical Engineering; Production Engineering); **International Studies** (Cultural Studies; International Studies; Social Studies)

Further Information: Also Japanese language courses for foreign students. University Institutes for Education and Research

History: Founded 1949 as a National University, incorporating Utsunomiya Senmon Gakko of Agriculture and Forestry founded 1922, Tochigi Normal School 1943, and Tochigi Youth Normal School 1944.

Governing Bodies: Hyogikai (University Council)

Academic Year: April to March (April-September; October-March)

Admission Requirements: Graduation from high school or equivalent or foreign equivalent, and entrance examination

Main Language(s) of Instruction: Japanese

International Co-operation: With universities in China, Thailand and Republic of Korea

Degrees and Diplomas: *Gakushi*: Agriculture (Nogakushi); Education (Kyoikugakushi); Engineering (Kogakushi), 4 yrs; *Shushi*: Agriculture (Nogakushushi); Engineering (Kogakushushi), a further 2 yrs; *Hakase*

Student Services: Employment services, Health services, Language programs, Social counselling, Sports facilities

Student Residential Facilities: For c. 420 students

Libraries: c. 585,000 vols

Publications: Bulletin of Faculty of Agriculture; Bulletin of Faculty of Education

Last Updated: 25/03/11

WAKAYAMA MEDICAL UNIVERSITY

Wakayama Kenritsu Ika Daigaku

811-1 Kimiidera, Wakayama-shi, Wakayama 641-8509
Tel: +81(73) 447-2300
Fax: +81(73) 441-0704
EMail: www-admin@wakayama-med.ac.jp
Website: http://www.wakayama-med.ac.jp

President: Kishio Nanjo

Departments

Liberal Arts and Sciences

Institutes

Advanced Medicine (Medicine)

Further Information: Also research institutes

History: Founded 1945 as Medical School, became University 1948.

Academic Year: April to March (April-July; September-December; January-March)

Admission Requirements: Graduation from high school and entrance examination

Main Language(s) of Instruction: Japanese

International Co-operation: With universities in China

Degrees and Diplomas: *Gakushi*: Medicine, 6 yrs; *Hakase*: Medicine, a further 4 yrs

Student Services: Sports facilities

Libraries: 134,987 vols

Publications: Wakayama Medical Reports *(quarterly)*

Last Updated: 09/02/09

WAKAYAMA UNIVERSITY

Wakayama Daigaku

930 Sakaedani, Wakayama-shi, Wakayama 640-8510
Tel: +81(73) 457-7524
Fax: +81(73) 457-7520
EMail: nakamura@center.wakayama-u.ac.jp
Website: http://www.wakayama-u.ac.jp

President: Akira Oda

Faculties

Economics *(Also Graduate School)* (Business Administration; Economics; Marketing); **Education** *(Also Graduate School)* (Cultural Studies; Education; English; European Languages; Fine Arts; Health Education; International Studies; Japanese; Mathematics Education; Modern Languages; Music Education; Natural Sciences; Oriental Languages; Physical Education; Social Studies); **Systems Engineering** *(Also Graduate School)* (Chemistry; Computer Science; Information Sciences; Materials Engineering; Systems Analysis); **Tourism**

Further Information: Also Japanese language courses for foreign students. Research centres and institutes

History: Founded 1871 as School, became College 1922, and University 1949.

Academic Year: April to March (April-October; October-March)

Admission Requirements: Graduation from high school or equivalent or foreign equivalent, and entrance examination

Main Language(s) of Instruction: Japanese

International Co-operation: With universities in China, USA and France

Degrees and Diplomas: *Gakushi*: 4 yrs; *Shushi*: a further 2 yrs; *Hakase*

Student Services: Academic counselling, Language programs, Sports facilities

Student Residential Facilities: Yes

Libraries: 741,768 vols

Publications: Bulletin of the Faculty of Education *(biannually)*; The Wakayama Economics Review (Keizai Riron) *(bimonthly)*

Last Updated: 06/02/09

WAKKANAI HOKUSEI GAKUEN UNIVERSITY

Wakkanai Hokusei Gakuen Daigaku (WAKHOK)

Wakabadai 1-2290-28, Wakkanai, Hokkaido 097-0013

Tel: +81(162) 32-7511

Fax: +81(162) 32 7500

EMail: international-admin@wakhok.ac.jp

Website: http://www.wakhok.ac.jp

President: Sasaki Masanori

Departments

Integrated Media *(Wakhok Main Campus)* (Computer Networks; Computer Science; Information Technology; Mathematics; Media Studies; Multimedia; Software Engineering; Telecommunications Engineering)

Further Information: Also Branch, the Tokyo Satellite, at Akihabara, Chiyoda Ward, Tokyo

History: Founded 1987. Acquired present status and title 2000.

Admission Requirements: Secondary school certificate or equivalent.

Fees: (Yen): 1,080,900 per annum.

Main Language(s) of Instruction: Japanese.

International Co-operation: With universities in Russia, China and Nepal

Accrediting Agencies: Ministry of Education, Culture, Sports, Science and Technology; Association of Private Universities of Japan.

Degrees and Diplomas: *Gakushi*. Bachelor's degree, 4 yrs.

Student Services: Academic counselling, Canteen, Cultural centre, Employment services, Foreign student adviser, Foreign Studies Centre, Handicapped facilities, Health services, Social counselling, Sports facilities

Special Facilities: Art gallery, Movie Studio, Wakhok TV Station, Auditorium Hall, Computer Labs and Research Facilities.

Libraries: Yes

Publications: Wakhok Bulletin, Set of thesis and research papers. *(biennially)*

Last Updated: 09/02/09

WAKO UNIVERSITY

Wako Daigaku

2160 Kanai-cho, Machida-shi, Tokyo 195-8585

Tel: +81(44) 988-1431

Fax: +81(44) 989-2241

EMail: nyushi@wako.ac.jp

Website: http://www.wako.ac.jp

Faculties

Economics and Business Management (Business Administration; Computer Science; Economics; Media Studies); **Human Sciences**; **Representational Studies** (Cultural Studies; Fine Arts)

Schools

Graduate Studies (Cultural Studies; Social Studies)

History: Founded 1966.

Academic Year: April to March (April-September; October-March)

Admission Requirements: Graduation from high school and entrance examination

Main Language(s) of Instruction: Japanese

Degrees and Diplomas: *Gakushi*: Bungakushi, Arts; Keizaigakushi, Economics, 4 yrs; *Shushi*

Student Residential Facilities: Yes

Libraries: c. 100,000 vols

Last Updated: 09/02/09

WASEDA UNIVERSITY

Waseda Daigaku

1-104 Totsuka-machi, Shinjuku-ku, Tokyo 169-8050

Tel: +81(3) 3202-7747

Fax: +81(3) 3202-8583

EMail: intl-ac@list.waseda.jp

Website: http://www.waseda.ac.jp/

President: Kaoru Kamata (2010-) Tel: +81(3) 3203-7747

International Relations: Shinichi Hirota, Dean of International Affairs Division

Tel: +81(3) 3203-7747 EMail: int-adm@list.waseda.jp

Graduate Schools

Accountancy (Accountancy; Business Administration); **Advanced Science and Engineering** (Applied Chemistry; Applied Physics; Biochemistry; Biological and Life Sciences; Chemistry; Electrical Engineering; Physics); **Asia-Pacific Studies**; **Commerce**; **Creative Science and Engineering** (Architecture; Civil Engineering; Environmental Engineering; Industrial Engineering; Management Systems; Mechanical Engineering; Natural Resources); **Economics** (Economics); **Education** (Curriculum; Education; Educational Sciences; English; Humanities and Social Science Education; Japanese; Mathematics Education); **Environment and Energy Engineering**; **Finance, Accounting and Law**; **Fundamental Science and Engineering** (Aeronautical and Aerospace Engineering; Applied Mathematics; Computer Engineering; Computer Science; Electronic Engineering; Mathematics; Mechanical Engineering; Multimedia); **Global Information and Telecommunication Studies**; **Human Sciences**; **Information, Production and Systems** (Computer Engineering; Information Sciences; Information Technology); **Japanese Applied Linguistics** (Applied Linguistics; Japanese); **Law** (Civil Law; Law; Public Law); **Letters, Arts and Sciences** (Arts and Humanities; Chinese; Cultural Studies; Education; English; Fine Arts; French; German; History; Japanese; Literature; Natural Sciences; Philosophical Schools; Philosophy; Psychology; Russian; Sociology); **Political Science** (Political Sciences); **Public Management** *(Okuma School)*; **Science and Engineering** (Engineering; Mathematics and Computer Science; Natural Sciences); **Social Sciences** (International Studies; Management; Political Sciences; Regional Studies; Social Sciences); **Sport Sciences** (Sports); **Teacher Education** (Education; Teacher Training)

Research Centres

Environmental Safety; **Human Services**; **International Education**; **Japanese Language**; **Open Education**

Research Institutes

Asia-Pacific Studies (Asian Studies; Pacific Area Studies); **Business Administration**; **Comparative Law**; **Comprehensive Research Organisation**; **Contemporary Political and Economic Affairs**; **Education** *(Advanced Studies)*; **Environment** (Environmental Studies); **Global Information and Telecommunications**; **Human Sciences** *(Advanced)* (Social Sciences); **Media Network**; **Science and Engineering** *(Advanced)* (Engineering; Mathematics and Computer Science; Natural Sciences); **Waseda University Archives**

Research Laboratories

Materials Science and Technology *(Kagami Memorial)*

Schools

Advanced Science and Engineering; **Commerce** *(Undergraduate)*; **Creative Science and Engineering**; **Culture, Media and Society**; **Education** *(Undergraduate)* (Cultural Studies; Education; English; Japanese; Mathematics; Natural Sciences; Social Sciences; Social Studies); **Fundamental Science and Engineering**; **Human Sciences** (Behavioural Sciences; Cognitive Sciences; Environmental Studies; Health Sciences; Social Sciences; Social Welfare); **Humanities and Social Sciences** *(Undergraduate)* (Archaeology; Art History; Chinese; Education; English; Environmental Studies; Film; French; German; Health Sciences; History; Japanese; Philosophical Schools; Philosophy; Psychology; Russian; Social Sciences; Social Welfare; Sociology; Theatre); **International Liberal Studies** (Arts and Humanities; International Studies); **Law** *(Undergraduate)* (Administrative Law; Constitutional Law; International Law; Law; Mass Communication; Public Administration; Public Law; Taxation); **Letters, Arts and Sciences I** *(Undergraduate)* (Archaeology; Art History; Arts and Humanities; Chinese; English; Film; French; German; History; Japanese; Mathematics and Computer Science; Natural Sciences; Philosophical Schools; Philosophy; Psychology; Russian; Sociology; Theatre; Writing); **Letters, Arts and Sciences II** *(Evening Divison, Undergraduate)* (Arts and Humanities; Folklore; History; Linguistics; Literature; Performing Arts; Philosophy; Religion; Social Sciences); **Political Science and Economics** *(Undergraduate)* (Economics; International Economics; Political Sciences); **Science and Engineering** *(Undergraduate)* (Applied Chemistry; Applied Physics; Architecture; Biological and Life Sciences; Biomedical Engineering; Chemistry; Civil Engineering; Computer Science; Electrical Engineering; Environmental Engineering; Information Management; Management Systems; Materials Engineering; Mathematics; Mechanical Engineering; Nanotechnology; Natural Resources; Physics); **Social Sciences**; **Sport Sciences** (Sports)

History: Founded 1882 as Tokyo Senmon Gakko (College). Acquired present title 1902. Reorganized 1949. Graduate School established 1951.

Governing Bodies: Board of Trustees; Congregation; Executive Board of Directors with the President of the University as ex officio chairman

Academic Year: April to March (April-July; September-March)

Admission Requirements: Graduation from high school or equivalent or foreign equivalent, and entrance examination

Main Language(s) of Instruction: Japanese

Degrees and Diplomas: *Gakushi*: 4 yrs; *Shushi*: a further 2 yrs; *Hakase*: 3 yrs following Shushi

Special Facilities: Tsubouchi Memorial Theatre Museum. Aizu Museum

Libraries: University Library, c. 5,200,000; Central Library, 2,3,397,000 vols

Publications: Human Science Research; Waseda Bulletin of Comparative Law; Waseda Business and Economic Studies; Waseda Commercial Journal; Waseda Economic Papers; Waseda Journal of Socio-science; Waseda Law Journal; Waseda Political Studies

Press or Publishing House: Waseda University Press

Student Numbers *2012-2013*: Total 54,113

Last Updated: 15/03/13

WAYO WOMEN'S UNIVERSITY

Wayo Joshi Daigaku

2-3-1 Konodai, Ichikawa-shi, Chiba 272-8533
Tel: +81(473) 711-111
EMail: nyushi@wayo.ac.jp
Website: http://www.wayo.ac.jp

Graduate Schools

Human Ecology; **Humanities** (English; Japanese; Literature; Modern Languages)

Research Centres

Foreign Language Education (Foreign Languages Education)

Schools

Home Economics; **Humanities**

History: Founded 1928. Acquired present title 1949.

Degrees and Diplomas: *Gakushi*; *Shushi*

Last Updated: 11/02/09

YAMAGATA PREFECTURAL UNIVERSITY OF HEALTH SCIENCES

Yamagata Kenritsu Hokeniryou Daigaku

260 Kamiyanagi, Yamagata-shi, Yamagata-shi, Yamagata 990-2212
Tel: +81(23) 686-6688
Fax: +81(23) 686-6674
EMail: webmaster@yachts.ac.jp
Website: http://www.yachts.ac.jp

Departments

Nursing; **Occupational Therapy**; **Physical Therapy** (Physical Therapy)

Programmes

General Education

History: Founded 2000.

Degrees and Diplomas: *Gakushi*; *Shushi*

Libraries: c. 51,000 vols.

YAMAGATA UNIVERSITY

Yamagata Daigaku

1-4-12 Kojirakawa-machi, Yamagata-shi, Yamagata 990-8560
Tel: +81(236) 28-4119
Fax: +81(236) 28-4125
EMail: kmryug@jm.kj.yamagata-u.ac.jp
Website: http://www.yamagata-u.ac.jp

President: Akio Yuki

Faculties

Agriculture (Biotechnology; Ecology; Environmental Studies; Natural Resources); **Education, Art and Science** (Cultural Studies; Education; Environmental Studies; Fine Arts; Food Science; Information Sciences; Nursing); **Engineering** *(Also Graduate School)* (Bioengineering; Chemical Engineering; Chemistry; Computer Science; Electrical Engineering; Engineering; Mechanical Engineering; Polymer and Plastics Technology; Technology); **Literature and Social Sciences** (Cultural Studies; Literature; Social Sciences; Social Studies); **Medicine** *(Also Graduate School)* (Anaesthesiology; Anatomy; Biology; Cardiology; Cell Biology; Community Health; Dermatology; Endocrinology; Gastroenterology; Gynaecology and Obstetrics; Immunology; Medicine; Nephrology; Neurology; Nursing; Oncology; Ophthalmology; Orthopaedics; Paediatrics; Pathology; Pharmacology; Psychiatry and Mental Health; Public Health; Radiology; Social and Preventive Medicine; Surgery; Urology); **Science** *(Also Graduate School)* (Biochemistry; Biology; Earth Sciences; Environmental Studies; Mathematics; Natural Sciences; Physics)

Graduate Schools

Education (Education); **Social and Cultural Systems**

Further Information: Also Japanese language courses for foreign students

History: Founded 1949 incorporating Yamagata High School, Yamagata Normal School, Yamagata Youth's Normal School, Yonezawa Engineering College, and Yamagata Prefectural Agriculture and Forestry College.

Governing Bodies: Hyogikai (University Council)

Academic Year: April to March (April-September; October-March)

Admission Requirements: Graduation from high school or recognized equivalent, and entrance examination

Main Language(s) of Instruction: Japanese

Degrees and Diplomas: *Gakushi*: Agriculture (Nougakushi); Economics (Keizaigakushi); Education (Kyouikugakushi); Engineering (Kougakushi); Law (Hougakushi); Literature (Bungakushi); Nursing (Kangogakushi); Policy studies (Seisakukagakushi); Science (Rigakushi), 4 yrs; *Gakushi*: Medicine (Igakushi), 6 yrs; *Shushi*: Agriculture (Nougakushushi), a further 2 yrs; *Shushi*: Arts (Bungakushushi); Education (Kyouikugakushushi); Engineering (Kougakushushi); Nursing (Kangogakushushi); Policy studies

(Seisakukagakushushi); Science (Rigakushushi), a further 2 yrs; *Hakase*: Engineering (Kougaku-hakushi); Science (Rigaku-hakushi), a further 3 yrs; *Hakase*: Medical sciences (Igaku-hakushi), 4 yrs

Student Residential Facilities: For 636 students

Special Facilities: University Museum

Libraries: Central Library, c. 1m. vols

Publications: Bulletins

Last Updated: 11/02/09

YAMAGUCHI PREFECTURAL UNIVERSITY

Yamaguchi Kenritsu Daigaku

3-2-1 Sakurabatake, Yamaguchi-shi, Yamaguchi 753-8502
Tel: +81(83) 928-0211
Fax: +81(83) 928-2251
EMail: kokusai@tokuyama-u.ac.jp
Website: http://www.yamaguchi-pu.ac.jp

President: Kensuke Esato

Faculties

Human Life Sciences (Biological and Life Sciences; Home Economics); **International Studies** (Cultural Studies; International Studies); **Nursing** (Nursing); **Social Welfare** (Social Welfare)

History: Founded 1941 as Yamaguchi Women's School, reorganized 1950 as Yamaguchi Women's College, became Yamaguchi Women's University 1975 and acquired present title 1996. Incorporated Yamanashi Kenritsu Kango Daigaku (Yamanashi College of Nursing) 2005.

Degrees and Diplomas: *Gakushi*; *Shushi*; *Hakase*

Last Updated: 11/02/09

YAMAGUCHI UNIVERSITY

Yamaguchi Daigaku

1677-1 Yoshida, Yamaguchi-shi, Yamaguchi 753-8511
Tel: +81(83) 933-5981
Fax: +81(83) 933-5029
EMail: ga142@yamaguchi-u.ac.jp
Website: http://www.yamaguchi-u.ac.jp

President: Takuya Marumoto (2006-)

Secretary-General: Masayasu Ohmoto

International Relations: Kimio Ishibashi, Director
EMail: sh031@office.cc.yamaguchi-u.ac.jp

Centres

Business Incubation Square (Business and Commerce) *Director*: Setsuo Yamamoto; **Collaborative Research** (Engineering) *Director*: Norikazu Shimizu; **Design and Products Innovation** *Director*: Hideo Ohsaka; **Media and Information Technology** (Information Technology) *Director*: Hidetoshi Miike

Faculties

Agriculture (Agriculture; Biological and Life Sciences; Environmental Studies; Veterinary Science) *Dean*: Daizo Koga; **Economics** (Business and Commerce; Economics; International Economics; Law; Management; Tourism) *Dean*: Daijirou Fujii; **Education** (Child Care and Development; Cultural Studies; Education; Information Sciences; Preschool Education; Primary Education; Secondary Education) *Dean*: Issei Yoshida; **Engineering** (Applied Chemistry; Applied Mathematics; Applied Physics; Chemical Engineering; Civil Engineering; Computer Science; Design; Electrical and Electronic Engineering; Engineering; Environmental Engineering; Materials Engineering; Mechanical Engineering; Systems Analysis) *Dean*: Fusanori Miura; **Humanities** (Arts and Humanities; History; Literature; Modern Languages; Philosophy; Social Sciences) *Dean*: Seiji Tanaka; **Medicine and Health Sciences** (Health Sciences; Medicine) *Dean*: Tsuyoshi Maekawa; **Science** (Biology; Chemistry; Earth Sciences; Information Sciences; Mathematics; Natural Sciences; Physics) *Dean*: Hiroyuki Mashiyama

Graduate Schools

Agriculture (Agriculture) *Dean*: Daizo Koga; **East Asian Studies** (East Asian Studies; Economics) *Dean*: Noriko Otani; **Economics** (Economics) *Dean*: Dajirou Fujii; **Education** (Education) *Dean*: Issei Yoshida; **Humanities** (Arts and Humanities) *Dean*: Seiji Tanaka; **Innovation and Technology** (Technology) *Dean*: Ken Kaminishi; **Medicine** *Dean*: Tsuyoshi Maekawa; **Science and Engineering** *Dean*: Fusanori Miura; **Veterinary Science** *Dean*: Toshiharu Hayashi; **Veterinary Science, Tottori University**

Institutes

East Asian Economic Affairs; **Education Research and Training** *(Integrated Centre) Director*: Tokuji Hayashi; **Venture Business Laboratory** (Management) *Director*: Setsuzo Yamamoto

Research Institutes

Science Research *Director*: Yasuo Kiso; **Time Studies** *Director*: Shoji Tsuji

History: Founded 1949 as a National University at 3 campuses.

Governing Bodies: Board of University Councillors

Academic Year: April to March

Admission Requirements: Graduation from high school and entrance examination

Fees: (Yen): 535,800 per annum

Main Language(s) of Instruction: Japanese

Degrees and Diplomas: *Gakushi*: Agriculture; Arts; Economics; Education; Engineering; Health Sciences; Law; Nursing; Science, 4 yrs; *Gakushi*: Medicine; Veterinary Medicine, 6 yrs; *Shushi*: Agriculture; Arts; Bioscience; Economics; Education; Engineering; Health Sciences; Medical Engineering Science; Philosophy; Science; Technology Management (Professional), a further 2 yrs; *Hakase*: Bioscience; Engineering; Medical Engineering Science; Philosophy; Science, 3 yrs following Shushi; *Hakase*: Medicine; Veterinary Science, 4 yrs following Shushi

Student Services: Academic counselling, Canteen, Cultural centre, Employment services, Foreign student adviser, Foreign Studies Centre, Handicapped facilities, Health services, Social counselling, Sports facilities

Student Residential Facilities: For 648 students

Special Facilities: Archaeological Museum. Museum of Commodity. University Farm. Institute of East Asian Economic Affairs. University Hospital. Intellectual Property Centre. University Evaluation Department

Libraries: Central Library, 1,264,000 vols; Medicine Library, 185,768 vols; Engineering Library, 144,855 vols

YAMAGUCHI UNIVERSITY OF HUMAN WELFARE AND CULTURE

Yamaguchi Fukushi Bunka Daigaku

5000 Urata, Chinto, Hagi-shi, Yamaguchi-shi, Yamaguchi 758-8585
Tel: +81(838)24 4000
Fax: +81(838)24 4090
EMail: info@hagi.ac.jp
Website: http://www.hagi.ac.jp

Programmes

Child Life Study (Child Care and Development); **Health Sports**; **Welfare Environment Design** (Environmental Studies; Welfare and Protective Services); **Welfare Psychology** (Psychology; Social Welfare)

History: Founded 1999 as Hagi Kokusai Daigaku (Hagi International University). Acquired present title 2007.

Degrees and Diplomas: *Gakushi*

Student Services: Sports facilities

Libraries: 69,000 vols

Last Updated: 07/11/08

YAMANASHI EIWA COLLEGE

Yamanashi Eiwa Daigaku

888 Yokonemachi, 888 Yokonemachi, Kofu-shi, Yamanashi 400-8555
Tel: +81(55) 223-6020
Fax: +81(55) 223-6025
EMail: nyushi@y-eiwa.ac.jp
Website: http://www.yamanashi-eiwa.ac.jp

President: Shigeo Kazama

Graduate Schools

Humanities and Clinical Psychology

Schools
Humanities (Arts and Humanities; Cultural Studies; English; Information Sciences; Library Science; Media Studies; Museum Studies; Psychology)

History: Founded 2002.

Degrees and Diplomas: *Gakushi*; *Shushi*

Last Updated: 28/03/11

YAMANASHI GAKUIN UNIVERSITY

Yamanashi Gakuin Daigaku

International Exchange Office, 5-7-15 Sakaori, Kofu-shi, Yamanashi 400-8575
Tel: +81(55) 224-1650
Fax: +81(55) 224-1498
Website: http://www.ygu.ac.jp

Faculties
Commerce; **Information Management**; **Law** (Administrative Law; Commercial Law; Comparative Law; Criminal Law; Fiscal Law; History of Law; Human Rights; International Law; Labour Law; Law; Maritime Law; Private Law; Public Law); **Politics and Public Administration** (Administration; Administrative Law; Educational Administration; Political Sciences; Public Administration; Town Planning)

Further Information: Also Graduate School

History: Founded 1946, acquired present status and title 1962.

Academic Year: April to March

Admission Requirements: Graduation from high school

Main Language(s) of Instruction: Japanese

International Co-operation: With universities in China, USA and Taiwan

Degrees and Diplomas: *Gakushi*: 4 yrs; *Shushi*: a further 2 yrs

Student Services: Academic counselling, Canteen, Employment services, Foreign student adviser, Foreign Studies Centre, Handicapped facilities, Language programs, Nursery care, Sports facilities

Student Residential Facilities: Yes

Libraries: 312,827 vols. Also Computer Library

Publications: Altair *(annually)*

Last Updated: 11/02/09

YAMANASHI PREFECTURAL UNIVERSITY

Yamanashi Kenritsu Daigaku

5-11-1 Iida, Kofu-shi, Yamanashi 400-0035
Tel: +81(55) 224-5261
Fax: +81(55) 228-6819
EMail: soumuka@yamanashi-ken.ac.jp
Website: http://www.yamanashi-ken.ac.jp

Faculties
Communications, Human and Social Services; Global Policy Management; Nursing

Further Information: Also Ikeda Campus

History: Founded 2005 following merger of Yamanashi Kenritsu Kango Daigaku (Yamanashi College of Nursing) and Yamnashi Women's Junior College.

Academic Year: April to March (April-September; October-March)

Main Language(s) of Instruction: Japanese

Accrediting Agencies: Ministry of Education, Culture, Sports, Science and Technology

Degrees and Diplomas: *Gakushi*: 4 yrs

Student Services: Academic counselling, Employment services, Health services, Social counselling, Sports facilities

Libraries: 162,000 vols.

Publications: Bulletin *(annually)*

Academic Staff *2007-2008*	TOTAL
FULL-TIME	100
PART-TIME	c. 170
Student Numbers *2007-2008*	
All (Foreign Included)	c. 780

Last Updated: 12/02/09

YASHIMA GAKUEN UNIVERSITY

Yashima Gakuen Daigaku

7-42 Sakuragi-cho, Nishi-ward, Yokohama-shi, Kanagawa 220-0021
Tel: +81(45) 313-5454
Fax: +81(45) 323-6961
Website: http://www.yashima.ac.jp/univ/eng/index.aspx

History: Founded 2004.

Degrees and Diplomas: *Gakushi*

YASUDA WOMEN'S UNIVERSITY

Yasuda Joshi Daigaku

6-13-1 Yasuhigashi, Asaminami-ku, Hiroshima-shi, Hiroshima 731-0153
Tel: +81(82) 878-8111
Fax: +81(82) 872-2896
EMail: gakusei.box@yasuda-u.ac.jp
Website: http://www.yasuda-u.ac.jp

Programmes
Education *(Graduate Programme)* (Education); **English and American Literature** (American Studies; English; European Languages; Literature; Modern Languages); **Humanities** (Social Sciences); **Japanese Literature** (Japanese; Literature; Modern Languages; Oriental Languages); **Literature** (Literature); **Primary Education** (Primary Education)

History: Founded 1966.

Main Language(s) of Instruction: Japanese

International Co-operation: With universities in USA, New Zealand and United Kingdom

Degrees and Diplomas: *Gakushi*; *Shushi*; *Hakase*

Student Services: Sports facilities

Libraries: 240,000 vols

Last Updated: 11/02/09

YOKKAICHI UNIVERSITY

Yokkaichi Daigaku

200 Kayo-cho, Yokkaichi-shi, Mie 512-8512
Tel: +81(593) 65-6588
Fax: +81(593) 65-6630
EMail: issc@yokkaichi-u.ac.jp
Website: http://www.yokkaichi-u.ac.jp

Faculties
Economics (Economics); **Environmental and Information Sciences; Policy Management** (Management)

History: Founded 1988.

Academic Year: April to March (April-September; October-March)

Main Language(s) of Instruction: Japanese

Degrees and Diplomas: *Gakushi*

Last Updated: 11/02/09

YOKOHAMA CITY UNIVERSITY

Yokohama Shiritsu Daigaku (YCU)

22-2 Seto, Kanazawa-ku, Yokohama-shi, Kanagawa 236-0027
Tel: +81(45) 787-2311
Fax: +81(45) 787-2316
EMail: koho@yokohama-cu.ac.jp
Website: http://www.yokohama-cu.ac.jp

President: Tsutomu Fuse

Colleges
Arts and Sciences *(International)*; **Nursing** (Nursing) *Dean*: Masato Egawa

Departments
General Education (Education) *Director*: Chikakazu Tadakoshi

Faculties
Economics and Business Administration (Business Administration; Economics) *Dean*: Yoshitada Kawauchi; **Humanities and International Studies** (American Studies; Asian Studies; European Studies; Humanities and Social Science Education; International

Relations; International Studies) *Dean*: Fumio Kaneko; **Science** (Environmental Engineering; Mathematics and Computer Science; Natural Sciences) *Dean*: Kunisuke Maki

Graduate Schools

Arts and Sciences *(International)* (Biotechnology; Business Administration; Cultural Studies; Economics; Environmental Studies; International Studies; Mathematics and Computer Science; Molecular Biology; Nanotechnology; Natural Sciences); **Medicine** (Immunology; Medicine; Neurosciences)

Institutes

Biological Research (Biology) *Director*: Kaoru Miyazaki; **Economic Research** (Economics) *Director*: Masato Oka

Schools

Medicine (Medicine; Pathology; Physiology; Surgery) *Dean*: Kenji Okuda

Further Information: Also Japanese language courses for foreign students

History: Founded 1928 as College of Commerce, acquired University status 1949 with School of Medicine and Faculty of Liberal Arts and Science added.

Academic Year: April to March (April-October; October-March)

Admission Requirements: Graduation from high school or equivalent, and entrance examination

Fees: (Yen): 496,800 per annum

Main Language(s) of Instruction: Japanese

Degrees and Diplomas: *Gakushi*: Business Administration; Economics; Letters; Science, 4 yrs; *Gakushi*: Medicine, 6 yrs; *Shushi*: Business Administration; Economics, a further 2 yrs; *Hakase*: Medicine Sciences, a further 4 yrs

Student Services: Canteen, Employment services, Foreign student adviser, Language programs, Nursery care

Libraries: c. 1,370,000 vols

Publications: Bulletin of Yokohama City University Society; The Industry and Trade *(biennially)*; The Journal of Yokohama City University *(annually)*; Yokohama Medical Bulletin

Last Updated: 12/02/09

YOKOHAMA COLLEGE OF COMMERCE

Yokohama Shoka Daigaku

4-11-1 Higashi-Terao, Tsurumiku, Yokohama-shi, Kanagawa 230-8577

Tel: +81(45) 571-3901

Fax: +81(45) 571-4125

EMail: yumiko@shodai.ac.jp

Website: http://www.shodai.ac.jp

President: Eiji Matsumoto

Faculties

Commerce (Accountancy; Business and Commerce; Crafts and Trades; Economic History; Economics; Finance; International Economics; Law; Management; Small Business; Taxation; Tourism)

History: Founded 1966, acquired present status 1968.

Degrees and Diplomas: *Gakushi*

Last Updated: 12/02/09

YOKOHAMA COLLEGE OF PHARMACY

Yokohama Yakka Daigaku

601 Matano-cho, Totuka-ku, Yokohama-shi, Kanagawa

Tel: +81(45) 859-1300

Fax: +80(45) 859-1301

EMail: toiawase@hamayaku.jp

Website: http://hamayaku.jp/index.html

Departments

Health Pharmacy (Pharmacology; Pharmacy; Traditional Eastern Medicine)

History: Founded 2006.

Degrees and Diplomas: *Gakushi*

Last Updated: 13/02/09

YOKOHAMA NATIONAL UNIVERSITY

Yokohama Kokuritsu Daigaku (YNU)

79-1 Tokiwadai, Hodogaya-ku, Yokohama-shi, Kanagawa 240-8501

Tel: +81(45) 339-3036

Fax: +81(45) 339-3039

EMail: ryugakuseika@nuc.ynu.ac.jp; international@nuc.ynu.ac.jp

Website: http://www.ynu.ac.jp

President: Kunio Suzuki

Secretary-General: Noriyuki Takeshita

Centres

Cooperative Research and Development; **Information Processing** (Information Management); **Instrumental Analysis** (Mechanical Equipment and Maintenance; Technology); **Radio-Isotope** (Chemistry; Laboratory Techniques; Natural Sciences; Physics)

Faculties

Business Administration (Accountancy; Business Administration; International Business; Management Systems) *Dean*: Shuji Mizoguchi; **Economics** (Commercial Law; Economics; International Economics) *Dean*: Yuichi Hasebe; **Education and Human Sciences** (Education; Environmental Studies; Multimedia; Social Studies) *Dean*: Yugaku Arimitsu; **Engineering** (Architecture; Chemical Engineering; Civil Engineering; Computer Engineering; Engineering; Marine Engineering; Materials Engineering; Mechanical Engineering; Physics) *Dean*: Masaki Shiratori

Graduate Schools

Education (Art Education; Education; Mathematics Education; Physical Education; Psychology; Science Education; Special Education) *Dean*: Sachio Fukuda; **Engineering** (Architecture; Chemical Engineering; Civil Engineering; Computer Engineering; Electrical Engineering; Engineering; Materials Engineering; Systems Analysis) *Dean*: Masaki Shiratori; **Environment and Information Sciences** (Environmental Studies; Information Sciences; Media Studies; Natural Sciences; Technology) *Dean*: Seiichi Inoue; **Social Sciences** *(International)* (Accountancy; Business Administration; Commercial Law; Development Studies; Economics; International Economics; International Law; International Relations; Law; Management Systems; Social Sciences) *Dean*: Hitoshi Sasai

Laboratories

Ecotechnology System (Environmental Studies) *Director*: Katsutoshi Komeya

Further Information: Also International Student Centre (Japanese language training)

History: Founded 1949 incorporating Kanagawa Normal School, founded 1876, Kanagawa Youth Normal School 1920, Yokohama Commercial College 1923, and Yokohama Technical College, 1920.

Governing Bodies: Research and Education Council

Academic Year: April to March (April-October; October-March)

Admission Requirements: Graduation from high school or equivalent or foreign equivalent, and entrance examination

Fees: (Yen): Registration, 282,000; tuition, 520,800 per annum

Main Language(s) of Instruction: Japanese

Degrees and Diplomas: *Gakushi*: Education, Economics, Business Administration, Engineering, 4 yrs; *Shushi*: Education, Economics, Business Administration, Engineering, International and Business Law, Environment Science, Information Science, Technology Management, Philosophy, a further 2 yrs; *Hakase*: Law, Engineering, Environmental Science, Information Science, Technology Management, Philosophy, International Development Studies, Economics, Business Administration, 3 yrs following Shushi

Student Services: Academic counselling, Canteen, Cultural centre, Employment services, Foreign student adviser, Foreign Studies Centre, Handicapped facilities, Health services, Language programs, Nursery care, Social counselling, Sports facilities

Student Residential Facilities: Yes

Libraries: University Library, total, c. 1,369,000 vols

Last Updated: 12/02/09

Jordan

STRUCTURE OF HIGHER EDUCATION SYSTEM

Description:

Higher education in Jordan emerged with the creation of two-year teacher training colleges in the 1950s. As for university education, it commenced by the establishment of the University of Jordan in 1962, followed by the establishment of Al-Ahliyya Amman University in 1989 as the first private university. The Ministry of Higher Education was created in 1985 to regulate and coordinate the work of the higher education sector. It is the home of the Council of Higher Education, which is in charge of establishing the higher education policy in the Kingdom. The Accreditation Commission, an independent body, accredits both private and public universities. Each university is managed by an independent board of trustees, which chooses the university president.

Stages of studies:

University level first stage: *Undergraduate level*

Bachelor's degrees normally take four years. The Bachelor's degree normally requires between 130-160 credit hours, depending on the field of study.

University level second stage: *Postgraduate level*

A Master's degree is awarded after a further two years' study following upon the Bachelor's degree. It can be obtained either by course work and a thesis (c. 24 credit hours of courses and nine credit hours of research), or by course work (c. 33 credit hours) and a comprehensive examination. Candidates should hold the Bachelor's degree with "good" as a minimum rating.

University level third stage: *Doctorate*

A Doctorate degree is awarded after three to five years of further study and the submission of an original dissertation. It requires, depending on the subject, 24 credit hours of course work and 24 credit hours of research. Candidates should hold a Master's degree with "very good" as a minimum rating.

Distance higher education:

Distance education is offered at the Jordan branch of the Arab Open University and several other universities.

ADMISSION TO HIGHER EDUCATION

Admission to university-level studies:

Name of secondary school credential required: Tawjihi

Minimum score/requirement: Minimum 85% for Medicine and Dentistry, 80% for Pharmacy and Engineering, 75% for allied health sciences, and 65% in the scientific or arts streams according to the nature of the discipline.

For entry to: Public universities

Name of secondary school credential required: Tawjihi

Minimum score/requirement: 80% for Pharmacy and Engineering in the scientific stream, 75% for allied health sciences specializations, and 55% for all other disciplines.

For entry to: Private universities

Entrance exam requirements: State Matura Exams (2+2). There are 2 compulsory exams marking the completion of the secondary education and 2 elective exams (out of a 10-subject list – kind of A-levels) for entrance at public HE Institutions. It is at national level. There is an entrance exam at HE Institutions only for study programmes requiring special skills like Sports, Arts, Architecture, some foreign languages, which is provided in the Government Act for admission to public HE Institutions. Admission at public HE Institutions is based on the total score obtained at High School GPA + the 4 grades of the State Matura Exams.

Numerus clausus/restrictions: At national level (State Matura)

Foreign students admission:

Quotas: Foreign students can apply to Jordanian public universities through the Jordanian embassy in their countries. If there is no Jordanian embassy in their countries, they can apply directly to public or private universities.

Entrance exam requirements: Recognition of the secondary education of the foreign student's country.

Health requirements: Standard ones, like for home students

RECOGNITION OF STUDIES

Quality assurance system:

The Higher Education Council approves the establishment of higher education institutions. The Ministry of Higher Education and Scientific Research recognizes the non-Jordanian higher education institutions and is responsible for issuing equivalencies of certificates. The Accreditation Council defines the regulations, supervises the performance of higher education institutions and ensures that they reach their goals through continuous evaluation of their programmes.

NATIONAL BODIES

Ministry of Higher Education and Scientific Research

Minister: Wajih Owais
P.O.Box 138
Aljbaha 11941
Tel: +962(6) 534 7671
Fax: +962(6) 534 9079
EMail: mohe@mohe.gov.jo
WWW: http://www.mohe.gov.jo

Data for academic year: 2010-2011

Source: IAU from Ministry of Higher Education and Scientific Research, Jordan, August 2010. Bodies updated 2012.

INSTITUTIONS

AJLOUN NATIONAL PRIVATE UNIVERSITY

Ajloun
Website: http://www.anpu.edu.jo

President: Mahmoud Dwairi

Colleges

Arts and Educational Sciences (Arabic; Educational and Student Counselling; Educational Psychology; Educational Sciences; Special Education); **Business Management** (Business Administration; Management); **Information Technology** (Computer Science; Information Technology); **Law** (Private Law; Public Law)

History: Created 2008. First intake 2009.

Degrees and Diplomas: *Bachelor's Degree*

Last Updated: 17/09/10

AL-AHLIYYA AMMAN UNIVERSITY

Jami'at Amman Al-Ahliyya
PO Box 183, Al Salt Road, 19328 Amman
Tel: +962(5) 350-0211
Fax: +962(6) 533-6104
EMail: info@ammanu.edu.jo
Website: http://www.ammanu.edu.jo

President: Sadeq Hamed
Tel: +962(6) 533-6033, Fax: +962(6) 533-6104
EMail: president@ammanu.edu.jo

Faculties

Architecture and Design (Architecture; Graphic Design; Interior Design); **Arts and Humanities** (English; Literature; Psychology; Special Education; Translation and Interpretation); **Engineering** (Architecture; Biomedical Engineering; Civil Engineering; Computer Engineering; Electronic Engineering); **Finance and Administrative Sciences** (Accountancy; Administration; Banking; Business Administration; Finance; Hotel Management; Management Systems; Marketing; Tourism); **Information Technology** (Computer Science; Information Technology; Software Engineering); **Law** (Law); **Nursing** (Nursing); **Pharmaceutical and Medical Sciences** (Medical Technology; Pharmacy; Speech Therapy and Audiology)

Further Information: Also Foundation Year Programme, in co-operation with British universities

History: Founded 1990.

Governing Bodies: United Jordan Company for Investment Ltd

Academic Year: September to June (September-January; February-June). Also summer session (June-August)

Admission Requirements: Secondary school certificate (Tawjihi) or equivalent

Fees: (US Dollars): 2,175-2,550 per semester

Main Language(s) of Instruction: English, Arabic

Degrees and Diplomas: *Bachelor's Degree*: Arts; Business Administration; Administrative and Financial Sciences; Computer Science; Economics; English Literature; Hotel Management; Interior Design; Law; Nursing; Science; Translation, 4 yrs; *Bachelor's Degree*: Engineering; Medical Sciences; Pharmacy; Speech Therapy and Audiology, 5 yrs; *Master's Degree*: Law, 2 yrs

Student Services: Academic counselling, Canteen, Cultural centre, Employment services, Foreign student adviser, Foreign Studies Centre, Health services, Language programs, Nursery care, Social counselling, Sports facilities

Student Residential Facilities: Female student dorms

Special Facilities: Wireless environment, Art gallery

Libraries: c. 78,200 vols

Publications: Al-Balqu'a (Journal for Research Studies)

Last Updated: 22/11/11

AL AL-BAYT UNIVERSITY

Jami'at Al Al-Bayt

PO Box 130040, Al Jubaiha, Al Albayt, 25113 Mafraq
Tel: +962(2) 629-7000
EMail: info@aabu.edu.jo
Website: http://www.aabu.edu.jo

President: Nabil Shawaqfeh
Tel: +962(2) 629-7000, Ext. 2000, Fax: +962(2) 629-7025
EMail: president@aabu.edu.jo; shawagfeh@aabu.edu.jo

Faculties

Arts and Humanities (Arabic; English; French; German; History; Italian; Literature; Spanish); **Educational Sciences** (Curriculum; Education; Educational Administration; Primary Education; Teacher Training); **Engineering** (Architecture; Civil Engineering; Surveying and Mapping); **Finance and Business Administration** (Accountancy; Banking; Economics; Finance; Public Administration); **Information Technology** *(Prince Hussein bin Abdullah)* (Computer Science; Information Technology); **Law** (Law); **Nursing** *(Princess Salma)* (Child Care and Development; Nursing); **Science** (Biological and Life Sciences; Biology; Chemistry; Computer Science; Mathematics; Physics); **Sharia** (Islamic Law; Islamic Studies)

Higher Institutes

Islamic Studies (Islamic Studies)

Institutes

Astronomy and Space Sciences (Astronomy and Space Science); **Bayt al-Hikmah** *(House of Wisdom)* (Human Rights; International Law; International Studies; Islamic Studies; Political Sciences); **Earth and Environmental Sciences** (Earth Sciences; Environmental Studies)

History: Founded 1993.

Governing Bodies: Board of Trustees; University Council; Deans' Council

Academic Year: October to June (October-January; February-June)

Admission Requirements: Secondary school certificate (Tawjihi), with an average of not less than 65% and a good command of Arabic

Main Language(s) of Instruction: Arabic for Humanities; English for Science

International Co-operation: With institutions in Malaysia, United Kingdom, USA, France, Spain, Italy.

Accrediting Agencies: Ministry of Higher Education and Scientific Research

Degrees and Diplomas: *Bachelor's Degree*: 4-5 yrs; *Master's Degree*: a further 2-3 yrs

Student Services: Academic counselling, Canteen, Health services, Language programs, Sports facilities

Student Residential Facilities: Yes

Special Facilities: Museum of Islamic Art and Architecture. Samarkand Museum. Ibn Al-Bitar Herbal Plants Unit

Libraries: Al-Hashemiyyah

Publications: Jordan Journal of Islamic Studies

Last Updated: 22/11/11

AL-BALQA' APPLIED UNIVERSITY

Jami'at Al-Balqa Al-Tatbiqiyya (BAU)

PO Box 19117, Al-Salt
Tel: +962(5) 349-1111
Fax: +962(5) 353-2743 +962(5) 353-0462
EMail: info@bau.edu.jo
Website: http://www.bau.edu.jo

President: Ekhleif Tarawneh (2010-)
Tel: +962(5) 338-231, Fax: +962(5) 339-213
EMail: etarawneh@bau.edu.jo; Tarawneh_c@yahoo.com

Vice-President for Administrative and Financial Affairs: Suleiman Al-Louzi EMail: Lawzi@bau.edu.jo

International Relations: Abdallah S. Al-Zoubi, Vice-President for Scientific Centers and International Relations

Deaneries

Scientific Research

Faculties

Agricultural Technology (Agricultural Engineering; Biotechnology; Environmental Management; Food Science; Food Technology; Natural Resources; Nutrition; Plant and Crop Protection; Water Management); **Engineering** (Civil Engineering; Electrical Engineering; Electronic Engineering; Materials Engineering; Mechanical Engineering; Metallurgical Engineering; Mining Engineering; Software Engineering; Surveying and Mapping); **Graduate Studies** (Biotechnology; Business Administration; Chemistry; Computer Science; Education; Islamic Theology; Law; Metallurgical Engineering; Mining Engineering; Regional Planning; Special Education); **Planning and Management** (Accountancy; Banking; Business Computing; Economics; Finance; Information Management; Library Science; Management; Management Systems; Regional Planning); **Science and Information Technology** *(Prince Abdullah Bin Ghazi)* (Arabic; Chemistry; English; Information Technology; Islamic Law; Islamic Theology; Mathematics; Natural Sciences; Nuclear Physics; Physical Education; Physics)

Institutes

Traditional Islamic Arts (Fine Arts; Islamic Studies)

History: Founded 1996, incorporating Amman University College for Applied Engineering 1997, and all State Community Colleges. BAU has seventeen affiliated colleges.

Admission Requirements: Secondary School Leaving Certificate (Tawjeehy)

Fees: (Jordanian Dinars): Engineering, 800 per semester; Humanities, 600 per semester (300 for Intermediate Diploma, 2 yrs)

Main Language(s) of Instruction: Arabic; English

International Co-operation: With universities in Oman; Kuwait; Yemen; Saudi Arabia; Palestine; UAE; United Kingdom and Russia. Also twinning programmes with colleges in Canada, France and England. Participates with UNESCO in the Sesame Synchrotron programme

Degrees and Diplomas: *Bachelor's Degree*: 4 yrs; *Bachelor's Degree*: Engineering (BSc), 5 yrs; *Master's Degree*: Agriculture; Administration; Engineering; Science; Physics; Chemistry (MSc), a further 2 yrs following Bachelor's Degree; *Doctorate*

Student Services: Academic counselling, Canteen, Employment services, Handicapped facilities, Health services, Language programs, Nursery care, Social counselling, Sports facilities

Student Residential Facilities: Yes

Special Facilities: Museum

Libraries: Central Library, c. 32,000 vols

Last Updated: 22/11/11

AL-ISRA UNIVERSITY

Jami'at Al-Isra Al Ahliyyah
PO Box 621286, 11622 Amman, Greater Amman
Tel: +962(6) 471-1710
Fax: +962(6) 471-1505
EMail: info@isra.edu.jo; info@iu.edu.
Website: http://www.isra.edu.jo

President: Nu'man Al-Khateeb EMail: president@isra.edu.jo

Centres

Computer (Administration; Computer Science; Finance)

Colleges

Medical Sciences (Medicine; Pharmacy)

Departments

Cultural and Public Relations, Continuing Education and Community Services (Continuing Education; Management; Public Relations; Secretarial Studies; Social and Community Services)

Faculties

Administration and Finance (Accountancy; Administration; Banking; Business Administration; Finance; Information Management; Marketing); **Arts and Humanities** (Arabic; Arts and Humanities; Education; English; Literature; Modern Languages; Translation and Interpretation); **Engineering** (Architecture; Civil Engineering; Computer Engineering; Electrical Engineering; Electronic Engineering; Engineering; Telecommunications Engineering); **Law** (Law); **Science and Information Technology** (Computer Science; Information Technology; Natural Sciences; Software Engineering)

Further Information: Also Engineering Workshop

History: Founded 1991. Acquired present status 1995.

Governing Bodies: Board of Directors, Board of Trustees, University Council, Deans Council

Academic Year: September to June (September-January; February-June). Also Summer Course, July-August

Admission Requirements: High school certificate or equivalent

Fees: (Jordanian Dinars): 35-75 per credit hour

Main Language(s) of Instruction: Arabic, English

Accrediting Agencies: Council for Higher Education - Ministry of Higher Education and Scientific Research

Degrees and Diplomas: *Bachelor's Degree*: 3-5 yrs

Student Services: Academic counselling, Canteen, Foreign student adviser, Health services, Social counselling, Sports facilities

Libraries: University Library, c. 50,000 vols; 250 periodical subscriptions; computer facilities

Publications: Al-Ma'rifah (Knowledge) *(quarterly)*; Pharmacare *(monthly)*; Translation Bulletin *(biannually)*

Last Updated: 22/11/11

AL-ZAYTOONAH UNIVERSITY OF JORDAN

Jami'at Al-Zaytoonah Alordunia Al-Khassa
PO Box 130, 11733 Amman
Tel: +962(6) 429-1511
Fax: +962(6) 429-1432
EMail: info@alzaytoonah.edu.jo
Website: http://www.zuj.edu.jo/

President: Rushdi Ali Hasan
Tel: +962(6) 429-1278, Fax: +962(6) 429-1509
EMail: president@alzaytoonah.edu.jo

Faculties

Arts (Arabic; Arts and Humanities; English; French; Graphic Arts; Teacher Training); **Economics and Administration** (Accountancy; Banking; Business Administration; Finance; Hotel Management; Information Management; Marketing; Tourism); **Law** (International Law; Law; Private Law); **Nursing** (Nursing); **Pharmacy** (Pharmacy); **Science and Information Technology** (Computer Science; Information Technology; Mathematics; Natural Sciences; Software Engineering)

History: Founded 1993.

Academic Year: October to August (October-February; February-June; June-August)

Admission Requirements: Secondary school certificate (Al Tawjihi) or equivalent

Fees: (Jordanian Dinars): 1,000-1,200 per semester

Main Language(s) of Instruction: Arabic, English

Degrees and Diplomas: *Bachelor's Degree*: 4 yrs; *Bachelor's Degree*: Pharmacy, 5 yrs; *Master's Degree (MBA)*: a further 2 yrs

Student Services: Academic counselling, Canteen, Cultural centre, Foreign student adviser, Health services, Social counselling, Sports facilities

Libraries: Yes

Last Updated: 22/11/11

AMMAN ARAB UNIVERSITY

Jami'at Amman Al-Arabiyya lil Disarat Al-Ulia
PO Box 2234, 11953 Amman
Tel: +962(6) 554-0040, Ext. 201
Fax: +962(6) 551-6103
EMail: aaugs@aau.edu.jo; reg@aau.edu.jo
Website: http://www.aau.edu.jo

President: Said Al-Tell
Tel: +962(6) 551-6124, Ext. 106 EMail: president@aau.edu.jo

Colleges

Business (Accountancy; Business Computing; Finance; Management; Management Systems; Marketing); **Computer Science** (Computer Science; Information Technology); **Education and Psychology** (Curriculum; Education; Educational Administration; Educational and Student Counselling; Educational Psychology; Psychology; Special Education); **Law** (Law; Private Law; Public Law)

History: Founded 2000.

Governing Bodies: Board of Trustees and Arab Foundation for Education, Research and Community Services

Academic Year: October to June

Fees: (Jordanian Dinars): MA: 120-140 per credit hour depening on field of studies; PhD: 180-200 per credit hour

Main Language(s) of Instruction: Arabic, English (for Specific Courses)

Accrediting Agencies: Ministry of Higher Education, Council of Higher Education

Degrees and Diplomas: *Bachelor's Degree*; *Master's Degree*; *Doctorate*

Student Services: Academic counselling, Health services

Special Facilities: Language Centre, Computer Centre

Libraries: Books, Periodicals, E Journals, CD ROMs, EBESCO, World Web

Last Updated: 22/11/11

APPLIED SCIENCE PRIVATE UNIVERSITY

Jami'at Al-Ulum Al-Tatbiqiya (ASU)
Shafa Badran, 11931 Amman
Tel: +962(6) 560-9999
Fax: +962(6) 523-2899
EMail: info@asu.edu.jo; presidentoffice@asu.edu.jo
Website: http://www.asu.edu.jo

Acting President: Shafig Al-Haddad
Tel: +962(6) 560-9990 ext 1600 EMail: vice_president@asu.edu.jo

International Relations: Mohammad H. Alomari, External Agreements Committee
Tel: +962(6) 560-9999 Ext. 1078 EMail: m_alomari@asu.edu.jo

Faculties

Allied Medical Sciences (Food Science; Natural Sciences; Nutrition); **Art and Design** (Graphic Design; Interior Design); **Arts and Humanities** (Arabic; Education; English; Fine Arts; Islamic Law; Islamic Studies; Literature; Political Sciences; Social Sciences); **Economics and Administrative Sciences** (Accountancy; Administration; Banking; Business Administration; Economics; Finance; Health Administration; Hotel Management; International Relations; Marketing; Political Sciences); **Engineering** (Architecture; Civil Engineering; Computer Engineering; Electrical Engineering; Engineering; Industrial Engineering; Mechanical Engineering;

Telecommunications Engineering); **Information Technology** (Computer Networks; Computer Science; Information Technology; Software Engineering); **Law** (Law; Private Law; Public Law); **Nursing** (Community Health; Nursing); **Pharmacy** (Pharmacology; Pharmacy)

History: Founded 1991, the largest private University in Jordan.

Governing Bodies: Board of Trustees, comprising 20 members; Arab International Company for Investment and Education (Board of Directors)

Academic Year: October to June (October-January; February-June). Also Summer Session (July to September)

Admission Requirements: Secondary school certificate (Shahadit Al-Thanaweyya Al Ama) or equivalent

Fees: (Jordanian Dinars): 45-75 per credit hour

Degrees and Diplomas: *Bachelor's Degree*: 4-5 yrs (135-182 credit hours); *Master's Degree*

Student Services: Academic counselling, Canteen, Cultural centre, Employment services, Foreign student adviser, Handicapped facilities, Health services, Social counselling, Sports facilities

Libraries: Central Library

Publications: Jordan Journal of Applied Sciences (Humanities) *(biannually)*; Jordan Journal of Applied Sciences (Natural Sciences) *(biannually)*

Student Numbers *2012-2013*: Total 8,000

Last Updated: 05/03/13

ARAB OPEN UNIVERSITY - JORDAN BRANCH (AOU/JORDAN)

PO Box 1339, 11953 Amman
Tel: +962(6) 551-4851
Fax: +962(6) 553-0813
EMail: c_sweiss@aou.edu.jo
Website: http://www.aou.edu.jo

Director: Mohammad Abu Qudais EMail: director@aou.edu.jo

Faculties

Business Studies (Business Administration; Business and Commerce; Management Systems); **Computer Studies** (Computer Science; Information Technology); **Educational Studies** (Education; Primary Education); **Language Studies** (English; Literature)

History: Founded 2001.

Governing Bodies: Rector, Vice-Rectors, Branch Directors

Academic Year: October to August (October-January; February-June; July-August)

Admission Requirements: Secondary School Certificate (Tawjihi) or equivalent.

Fees: (US Dollars): 45-60 per credit hour, other expenses, 170 per credit hour

Main Language(s) of Instruction: English; Arabic

International Co-operation: With the Open University (United Kingdom)

Accrediting Agencies: Local accreditation: Jordanian Ministry of Higher Education and Scientific Research; international accreditation: Open University Validation Service

Degrees and Diplomas: *Bachelor's Degree*: English Language and Literature, Business Administration, Information Technology and Computing; Education (Primary Education)

Student Services: Canteen, Handicapped facilities, Language programs, Social counselling

Libraries: Traditional library and online databases

Publications: The International Arab Journal of e-Technology

Last Updated: 21/11/11

COLLEGE OF EDUCATIONAL SCIENCES

Kulliyat Al-Ulum Al-Tarbawiyya

PO Box 270, Na'ur, Amman
Tel: +962(6) 420-2161
Fax: +962(6) 420-5502

President: Ahmad Subhi Ayyadi

Programmes

Education (Educational Sciences; Teacher Training)

History: Founded 1993. Under UNRWA Institute of Education, provides upgrading in teachiing qualifications to a first university degree.

Degrees and Diplomas: *Bachelor's Degree*: Education, 4 yrs

Last Updated: 16/09/10

GERMAN-JORDANIAN UNIVERSITY (GJU)

PO Box 35247, 11180 Amman
Tel: +962(6) 530-0666
Fax: +962(6) 534-1573
EMail: info@gju.edu.jo
Website: http://www.gju.edu.jo

President: Labeeb Khadra EMail: president@gju.edu.jo

Colleges

Business *(Talal Abu- Ghazaleh)* (Accountancy; Management; Transport Management)

Schools

Applied Medical Sciences (Biomedical Engineering; Chemical Engineering; Pharmacy); **Applied Natural Sciences** (Energy Engineering; Environmental Engineering; Water Management); **Architecture and Built Environment** (Architecture; Design; Interior Design; Visual Arts); **Informatics and Computing** (Computer Engineering; Computer Science); **Languages** (English; German; Translation and Interpretation); **Technical Sciences** (Industrial Engineering; Maintenance Technology; Mechanical Engineering)

History: Created in 2005 by a Royal Decree, in accordance with a Memorandum of Understanding between the Ministry of Higher Education and Scientific Research and the German Federal Ministry of Education and Research.

Degrees and Diplomas: *Bachelor's Degree*; *Master's Degree*

Last Updated: 16/09/10

IRBID NATIONAL UNIVERSITY

Jami'at Irbid Al-Ahliyya Al-Khassa

PO Box 2600, 21110 Irbid
Tel: +962(2) 705-6682 +962(2) 705-6686
Fax: +962(2) 705-6681
EMail: public_rel@inu.edu.jo
Website: http://www.inu.edu.jo

President: Mohammed Sabarini EMail: president@inu.edu.jo

Faculties

Administration and Finance (Accountancy; Banking; Business Administration; Economics; Finance; Hotel Management; Marketing; Tourism); **Arts** (Arabic; Arts and Humanities; English; Graphic Design; Literature; Translation and Interpretation); **Educational Sciences** (Educational and Student Counselling; Educational Psychology; Educational Sciences; Special Education); **Law** (Law); **Nursing** (Nursing); **Science and Information Technology** (Computer Science; Mathematics)

History: Founded 1992.

Main Language(s) of Instruction: Arabic

Degrees and Diplomas: *Bachelor's Degree (BA, BSc)*: 4 yrs

Student Services: Academic counselling, Canteen, Employment services, Foreign student adviser, Foreign Studies Centre, Health services, Language programs, Nursery care, Social counselling, Sports facilities

Libraries: 70,000 vols

Publications: Irbid Journal for Research and Studies *(quarterly)*

Last Updated: 22/11/11

JADARA UNIVERSITY

PO Box 733, 21110 Irbid
EMail: info@jadara.edu.jo
Website: http://www.jadara.edu.jo

President: Mohamd Mahmmud Al-taamneh
EMail: president@jadara.edu.jo

Faculties

Arts and Languagues (Arabic; English; Graphic Design; Information Technology; Literature; Social Sciences; Translation and Interpretation); **Economics and Business** (Accountancy; Banking; Business Administration; Business Computing; Finance; Marketing); **Education Sciences** (Educational Administration; Educational Sciences; Educational Technology; Educational Testing and Evaluation; Special Education); **Engineering** (Computer Engineering; Engineering; Telecommunications Engineering); **Law** (Law); **Science and Information Technology** (Computer Networks; Computer Science; Mathematics; Software Engineering)

History: Created 2005.

Main Language(s) of Instruction: Arabic

Degrees and Diplomas: *Bachelor's Degree*; *Master's Degree*

Libraries: Yes
Last Updated: 22/11/11

JERASH UNIVERSITY

Jami'at Jerash Al-Ahliyya Al-Khassa
PO Box 311, 26150 Jerash
Tel: +962(2) 635-0521
Fax: +962(2) 635-0520
EMail: jpu.info@jpu.edu.jo
Website: http://www.jpu.edu.jo/

President: Khalid Al-Omari (2010-)
Tel: +962 7774-24241
EMail: president@jerashun.edu.jo; komari42@hotmail.com

Director: Adel Tubeishat Tel: +962(2) 635-0521, Ext. 128

International Relations: Walid Halloush, Head of Department of International Relations
Tel: +962 7772-21012 EMail: whalloush@yahoo.com

Colleges

Agriculture (Agricultural Economics; Agriculture; Animal Husbandry; Crop Production; Food Science; Nutrition; Plant and Crop Protection; Veterinary Science); **Engineering** (Civil Engineering; Electronic Engineering; Engineering; Telecommunications Engineering)

Faculties

Arts (Arabic; English; Literature; Translation and Interpretation); **Economics and Administrative Sciences** (Accountancy; Administration; Banking; Economics; Finance); **Education** (Educational Administration; Foreign Languages Education; Teacher Training); **Law** (Law; Private Law; Public Law); **Nursing** (Nursing); **Science** (Biology; Chemistry; Computer Science; Mathematics); **Shari'a** (Islamic Law; Islamic Studies)

History: Founded 1992.

Governing Bodies: University Council

Academic Year: October to August (October-January; February-May; June-August)

Admission Requirements: Secondary school certificate or equivalent

Fees: (Jordanian Dinars): 30-55 per credit hour

Main Language(s) of Instruction: Arabic, English

Degrees and Diplomas: *Bachelor's Degree*: 8 sem; *Master's Degree*

Student Services: Academic counselling, Canteen, Cultural centre, Foreign student adviser, Foreign Studies Centre, Health services, Language programs, Nursery care, Social counselling, Sports facilities

Student Residential Facilities: For 5,000 students

Special Facilities: Biological Garden

Libraries: 70,000 vols

Publications: Jerash for Research and Studies *(biannually)*

Student Numbers *2012-2013*: Total 5,000
Last Updated: 05/03/13

JORDAN ACADEMY OF MUSIC

Al-Akadimiya Al-Urdunia Lilmusiqa
PO Box 962127, 24 Sayed Qutub Street, Shamasani, 11196 Amman
Tel: +962(6) 560-4172
Fax: +962(6) 560-6234
EMail: info@jam.edu.jo
Website: http://www.jam.edu.jo

Dean: Iyad Abdel Hafeez Hafez Moh'd EMail: dean@jam.edu.jo

Departments

Music (Music; Music Theory and Composition; Musical Instruments)

History: Founded 1989.

Degrees and Diplomas: *Bachelor's Degree*: 4 yrs
Last Updated: 21/11/11

JORDAN UNIVERSITY OF SCIENCE AND TECHNOLOGY

Jami'at Al-Ulum wa Al-Tiknolojia Al-Urdunia (JUST)
PO Box 3030, 22110 Irbid
Tel: +962(2) 720-1000
Fax: +962(2) 709-5123
EMail: just@just.edu.jo
Website: http://www.just.edu.jo

President: Abdallah Malkawi
Tel: (962) 2 720 1000, Fax: (962) 2 709 5148
EMail: prsdy@just.edu.jo

Centres

Biotechnology *(Princess Haya)* (Bioengineering; Biotechnology); **Energy** (Energy Engineering); **Nanotechnology** (Nanotechnology); **Science and Technology** *(Consultative)* (Natural Sciences; Technology); **Veterinary Medicine** (Veterinary Science)

Faculties

Agriculture (Agronomy; Animal Husbandry; Crop Production; Food Technology; Horticulture; Natural Resources; Nutrition; Plant and Crop Protection; Soil Science); **Applied Medical Sciences** (Chemistry; Dental Technology; Genetics; Haematology; Immunology; Laboratory Techniques; Microbiology; Molecular Biology; Optometry; Paramedical Sciences; Physical Therapy; Radiology; Speech Therapy and Audiology); **Architecture and Design** (Architecture; Town Planning; Urban Studies); **Computer and Information Technology** (Computer Engineering; Computer Networks; Computer Science; Information Technology; Software Engineering); **Dentistry** (Dentistry; Oral Pathology; Periodontics; Surgery); **Engineering** (Architecture; Architecture and Planning; Biomedical Engineering; Chemical Engineering; Civil Engineering; Electrical Engineering; Electronic Engineering; Industrial Engineering; Irrigation; Mechanical Engineering; Nuclear Engineering; Power Engineering; Structural Architecture; Transport and Communications; Urban Studies); **Graduate Studies** (Agriculture; Applied Chemistry; Applied Linguistics; Applied Physics; Architecture; Biology; Computer Science; Dentistry; Design; Engineering; Information Technology; Mathematics; Medicine; Nursing; Pharmacy; Veterinary Science); **Nursing** (Community Health; Midwifery; Nursing); **Pharmacy** (Medical Technology; Pharmacology; Pharmacy); **Science and Arts** (Applied Chemistry; Applied Linguistics; Applied Physics; Biological and Life Sciences; English; Genetics; Immunology; Mathematics; Microbiology; Molecular Biology; Statistics); **Veterinary Medicine** (Anatomy; Animal Husbandry; Embryology and Reproduction Biology; Histology; Hygiene; Microbiology; Pathology; Pharmacology; Physiology; Surgery; Veterinary Science)

Research Centres

Environmental Science and Technology *(Queen Rania Al-Abdullah)* (Environmental Studies); **Pharmaceutical Studies** (Pharmacology; Pharmacy)

History: Founded 1986 to train students in the fields of applied sciences.

Governing Bodies: Board of Trustees; University Council; Deans' Council

Academic Year: September to June (September-January; January-June). Also summer Semester (June-August)

Admission Requirements: Secondary school certificate (Al Tawjihi) or equivalent with different minimum requirements for each Faculty

Fees: (US Dollars): 60-215 per credit hour according to Faculty

Main Language(s) of Instruction: English

International Co-operation: With institutions in the USA, Canada, Europe, Japan, Arab countries.

Accrediting Agencies: Ministry of Higher Education

Degrees and Diplomas: *Bachelor's Degree*: Agricultural Engineering; Structures; Highway Transportation; Environment and Water Resources; Soil and Foundations; Power and Electrical Machines; Communications and Electronics; Power Engineering; Mechatronics; Production and Manufacturing; Aviation (BSc); Allied Dental Sciences; Dental Technology; Occupational Therapy; Optometry; Physiotherapy; Radiologic Technology; Nursing; Biotechnology and Genetic Engineering; Environmental Sciences; Applied Chemistry; Applied Mathematics; Applied Physics (BSc); Chemical Engineering; Irrigation and Drainage; Agricultural Machinery; Biomedical Engineering; Manufacturing Management; Computer Science and Information Systems; Medicine and Surgery; Health Administration Services; Medical Laboratory Sciences; English for Specific Purposes (BESP); Plant Production; Animal Production; Nutrition and Food Technology; Forestry and Range Management; Soil, Water and Environment; Veterinary Medicine (BSc), 4-6 yrs; *Bachelor's Degree*: Dentistry (BDS); Pharmacy (BSc), 5-7 yrs; *Bachelor's Degree*: Pharm D (BSc), 6-8 yrs; *Master's Degree*: Communications and Electronics; Mechatronics; Production and Manufacturing; Chemical Engineering; Clinical Pharmacy; Pharmaceutical Technology; Adult Health Nursing; Community and Mental Health Nursing; Applied Chemistry; Applied Biology; Plant Protection; Environment and Behaviour; Regional Planning; Urban Design; Cultural and Heritage Conservation; Housing; Structures; Highway and Transportation; Environment and Water Resources; Soil and Foundations; Power and Electrical Machines (MSc); Field Crops and Gardening; Animal Production; Soil, Water and Environment; Clinical Veterinary Medical Science; Basic Veterinary Medical Sciences, a further 2-3 yrs. Also Diplomas in Public health, Poultry Diseases, Veterinary Pathology, Artificial Insemination and Embryo Transplant, Therionology, Veterinary Surgery, Veterinary Medicine, and Higher Speciality in General Surgery, Internal Medicine, Obstetrics and Gynaecology, Paediatrics, Family Medicine, Community Medicine, Pathology, Clinical Microbiology and Immunology, Clinical Chemistry, Molecular Biology and Human Genetics, Hematology and Blood Banking

Student Services: Academic counselling, Canteen, Cultural centre, Employment services, Foreign student adviser, Foreign Studies Centre, Handicapped facilities, Health services, Language programs, Social counselling, Sports facilities

Student Residential Facilities: For Women students and university staff

Special Facilities: Agricultural Experimental Station; Museum of Veterinary Medicine; Museum of Pathology; Medicinal Plant Museum

Libraries: 155,000 vols

Last Updated: 22/11/11

KING HUSSEIN UNIVERSITY

Al-Hussein Bin Talal University (AHU)

PO Box 20, Ma'an
Tel: +962(3) 217-9000
Fax: +962(3) 217-9050
EMail: ahu@go.com.jo
Website: http://www.ahu.edu.jo

President: Taha Al-Khamis

Colleges

Archaeology, Tourism and Hotel Management (Archaeology; Hotel and Restaurant; Hotel Management; Tourism); **Arts** (Arabic; English; Library Science; Linguistics; Literature; Media Studies); **Business Administration and Economics** (Accountancy; Business Administration; Economics); **Education** (Curriculum; Education; Pedagogy; Special Education); **Engineering** (Chemical Engineering; Civil Engineering; Computer Engineering; Environmental Engineering; Mining Engineering; Telecommunications Engineering); **Information Technology** (Computer Science; Information Technology; Software Engineering); **Science** (Biology; Chemistry; Mathematics; Physics; Statistics)

Faculties

Nursing *(Princess Aysha Bint Al-Hussein)* (Nursing)

History: Founded 1999.

Governing Bodies: Board of Trustees; Deans' Council

Admission Requirements: General Secondary Certificate (Tawjeehi) minimum grade 65% for Humanities and Science and 80% for Engineering

Fees: (Jordanian Dinars): 12-40 per programme

Main Language(s) of Instruction: Arabic, English

International Co-operation: With universities in USA, United Kingdom, Australia.

Accrediting Agencies: Ministry of Higher Education and Scientific Research

Degrees and Diplomas: *Bachelor's Degree*; *Master's Degree*; *Doctorate*

Student Services: Academic counselling, Canteen, Cultural centre, Employment services, Foreign student adviser, Foreign Studies Centre, Health services, Language programs, Nursery care, Sports facilities

Special Facilities: King Abdulla I Museum

Libraries: Yes

Publications: AHU Journal for Research and Studies *(biannually)*; Al-Haq Ya'lu *(quarterly)*

Last Updated: 21/11/11

MIDDLE EAST UNIVERSITY

PO Box 42, 11610 Amman
Tel: +962(6) 479-0222
Fax: +962(6) 412-96113
EMail: info@meu.edu.jo
Website: http://www.meu.edu.jo

President: Abdel Bari Durra

Colleges

Engineering (Civil Engineering; Engineering)

Faculties

Arts (Arabic; English; Graphic Design; Literature; Political Sciences); **Business** (Accountancy; Business Administration; E-Business/Commerce; Finance; Hotel Management; Marketing; Tourism); **Educational Sciences** (Curriculum; Education; Educational Administration; Educational Technology; Special Education); **Information Technology** (Computer Science; Information Technology); **Media and Communication** (Journalism; Media Studies; Radio and Television Broadcasting)

Schools

Law (Law; Private Law; Public Law)

History: Created 2005.

Degrees and Diplomas: *Bachelor's Degree*; *Master's Degree*

Last Updated: 17/09/10

MU'TAH UNIVERSITY

Jami'at Mu'tah

PO Box 7, Karak, 61710 Mu'tah, Al-Karak
Tel: +962(3) 237-2380
Fax: +962(3) 237-5540
EMail: webmaster@mutah.edu.jo
Website: http://www.mutah.edu.jo

President: Abdelrahim A. Hunaiti (2009-)
Tel: +962(3) 237-2380, Ext 6000, Fax: +962(3) 237-2588
EMail: hunaiti@mutah.edu.jo

International Relations: Mohammad A. Abbadi, Vice President, Academic Affairs

Tel: +962(3) 237 2380, Ext 6005/6006, Fax: +962(3) 237-5540
EMail: baabbadi@mutah.edu.jo

Faculties

Agriculture (Agriculture; Animal Husbandry; Food Technology; Plant and Crop Protection); **Arts** (Arabic; English; European Languages; Literature); **Business Administration** (Accountancy; Banking; Business Administration; Economics; Finance; Management Systems; Marketing; Public Administration); **Educational Sciences** (Curriculum; Education; Educational Administration; Educational and Student Counselling; Educational Sciences; Pedagogy; Psychology; Special Education); **Engineering** (Chemical Engineering; Civil Engineering; Computer Engineering; Electrical Engineering; Engineering; Environmental Engineering; Mechanical Engineering); **Law** (Law; Private Law; Public Law); **Medicine** (Anatomy; Biochemistry; Forensic Medicine and Dentistry; Gynaecology and Obstetrics; Histology; Medicine; Microbiology; Paediatrics; Pharmacology; Physiology; Public Health; Surgery); **Nursing** (Community Health; Nursing); **Science** (Biology; Chemistry; Information Technology; Mathematics; Natural Sciences; Physics; Statistics); **Shari'ah** (Islamic Law); **Social Sciences** (Archaeology; Geography; History; Political Sciences; Psychology; Sociology; Tourism); **Sports Sciences** (Physical Education; Rehabilitation and Therapy; Sports)

History: Founded 1981. A State Institution enjoying academic and administrative autonomy. Acquired present status and title 1986.

Governing Bodies: Board of Trustees; University Council; Deans' Council

Academic Year: September to June (September-January; February to June). Also Summer Term (June-August)

Admission Requirements: Jordanian General Secondary Certificate (Tawjihi) or equivalent

Main Language(s) of Instruction: Arabic, English

Degrees and Diplomas: *Bachelor's Degree*: Accountancy (BA); Agricultural Counselling and Economics (BSc); Animal and Plant Production (BSc); Arabic Language and Literature (BA); Archaeology and Tourism (BA); Biology (BSc); Business Administration (BA); Chemical Engineering (BSc); Chemistry (BSc); Civil Engineering; Water and Environment (BSc); Computer Engineering (BSc); Computer Science; Computer Information Systems (BSc); Counselling (BA); Economics (BA); Electrical Engineering; Power and Control Engineering; Telecommunications (BSc); Electronic Engineering (BSc); English and French Languages; Literature (BA); English Language and Literature (BA); Finance and Banking; Management Systems (BA); French and English (BA); Geography (BA); History (BA); Islamic Studies; Islamic Jurisprudence (BA); Law (BA); Marketing (BA); Mathematics (BA); Mathematics Education; Science Education; English Language Education; Islamic Studies Education; Social Studies Education; Arabic Language Education; Preschool Education; Special Education (BA); Mechanical Engineering; Energy and Thermal Power; Materials and Manufacturing (BSc); Nursing (BSc); Nutrition and Food Technology; Physical Education and Rehabilitaiton (BSc); Political Science (BA); Public Administration (BA); Sociology (BA); *Medical Doctor*; *Master's Degree*: Applied Linguistics (MA); Arabic Language (MA); Archaeology (MA); Biology (MSc); Business Administration (MBA); Business and Finance Economics; Chemistry (MSc); Communication Engineering (MSc); Counselling (MA); Criminology (MA); Curriculum and Instruction: Science; Social Studies; English (MA); Economics (MA); Educational Administration (MA); Educational Psychology (MA); Engineering Management (MSc); Fiqh and Jurisprudence (MA); Geography (MA); History (MA); International Relations (MA); Law (LLM); Law and Police Science (MA); Mathematics (MSc); Measurement and Evaluation (MA); Physics (MSc); Plant Production (MA); Public Administration (MPA); Sociology (MA); Water and Environmental Engineering (MSc); *Doctorate*: Arabic Linguistic Studies (PhD); Arabic Literary Studies (PhD); Criminology (PhD); Islamic History (PhD); Modern History (PhD)

Student Services: Academic counselling, Canteen, Cultural centre, Employment services, Foreign student adviser, Foreign Studies Centre, Handicapped facilities, Health services, Language programs, Nursery care, Social counselling, Sports facilities

Student Residential Facilities: For faculty and female students

Special Facilities: Natural History Museum. Art Gallery

Libraries: Yes

Publications: Mu'tah LiL-Buhuth Wad-Dirasat (Humanities and Social Sciences, Natural and Applied Sciences Series) *(quarterly)*; The Jordanian Journal of Arabic Language and Literature

Last Updated: 22/11/11

PETRA UNIVERSITY

Jami'at Al-Petra Al-Khassa
PO Box 961343, 11196 Amman
Tel: +962(6) 579-9555
Fax: +962(6) 571-5570
EMail: info@uop.edu.jo
Website: http://www.uop.edu.jo

President: Adnan Badran EMail: president@uop.edu.jo

Faculties

Administrative and Financial Sciences (Accountancy; Banking; Business Administration; Business Computing; E-Business/Commerce; Finance; Management Systems; Marketing); **Architecture and Fine Arts** (Architecture; Fine Arts; Graphic Design; Interior Design); **Arts and Science** (Arabic; Chemistry; Educational Sciences; English; Journalism; Literature; Media Studies); **Information Technology** (Computer Networks; Computer Science; Information Technology; Software Engineering); **Pharmacy and Medical Sciences** (Biomedicine; Medical Technology; Nutrition; Pharmacology; Pharmacy)

History: Founded 1991 as Jordan University for Women. Acquired present status 2000.

Governing Bodies: Board of Trustees

Admission Requirements: Secondary school certificate with pass grade of at least 60%; Pharmacy and Architecture 80%

Fees: (Jordanian Dinars): c. 2,000-3,000 per annum

Main Language(s) of Instruction: Arabic, English

Degrees and Diplomas: *Bachelor's Degree*; *Master's Degree*

Student Services: Academic counselling, Canteen, Cultural centre, Employment services, Foreign Studies Centre, Health services, Language programs, Nursery care, Social counselling, Sports facilities

Student Residential Facilities: Yes (for female students)

Libraries: c. 45,000 vols

Publications: Al-Basair *(quarterly)*; Awraq Jamie'ya *(biennially)*

Last Updated: 22/11/11

PHILADELPHIA UNIVERSITY

Jami'at Feladelfya Al-Khassa (PU)
PO Box 1101, 19392 Amman
Tel: +962(6) 479-9000
Fax: +962(6) 479-9033
EMail: info@philadelphia.edu.jo
Website: http://www.philadelphia.edu.jo

President: Marwan Kamal (2005-)
Tel: +962(6) 479-9000 EMail: mkamal@philadelphia.edu.jo

Vice-President for Administrative and Financial Affairs: Saleh K. Abu-Obsa
Tel: +962(6) 637-4444, Fax: +962(6) 637-4440
EMail: sabuosa@philadelphia.edu.jo

International Relations: Ibrahim Badran, International Relations and Scientific Affairs
Tel: +962(6) 479-9000 EMail: ebrbadran@gmail.com

Faculties

Administrative and Financial Sciences (Accountancy; Banking; Business Administration; Finance; Hotel Management; Information Sciences; Library Science; Marketing; Tourism); **Arts** (Arabic; Development Studies; English; Graphic Design; Interior Design; Social Sciences); **Engineering** (Architecture; Civil Engineering; Computer Engineering; Electrical Engineering; Electronic Engineering; Engineering; Mechanical Engineering; Telecommunications Engineering); **Information Technology** (Business Computing; Computer Science; Information Technology; Software Engineering); **Law** (Law); **Nursing** (Nursing); **Pharmacy** (Pharmacy); **Science** (Biotechnology; Genetics; Mathematics; Natural Sciences)

History: Founded 1989, acquired present status 1991.

Governing Bodies: Board of Trustees; University Board; Council of Deans

Academic Year: October to June (October-January; February-June). Also Summer Courses (July-August)

Admission Requirements: Secondary school certificate

Fees: ((Jordanian Dinars): 50-75 per credit hour

Main Language(s) of Instruction: Arabic, English

Degrees and Diplomas: *Bachelor's Degree*: 4-5 yrs; *Master's Degree*: Computer Science; English language and Literature

Student Services: Academic counselling, Canteen, Cultural centre, Foreign student adviser, Foreign Studies Centre, Health services, Language programs, Nursery care, Social counselling, Sports facilities

Student Residential Facilities: None

Special Facilities: 3 Theatres. 2 Language Laboratories. Computer Laboratories. Design Laboratories

Libraries: 50,000 vols (Arabic); 22,000 vols (English)

Publications: Almasira Aljamiyah *(quarterly)*; Philadelphia Cultural Magazine *(annually)*

Student Numbers *2011-2012*: Total 5,960

Last Updated: 22/11/11

PRINCESS SUMAYA UNIVERSITY FOR TECHNOLOGY

Jami'at Al-Ameera Sumaya Littecknologia (PSUT)

PO Box 925819, 11941 Al-Jubaiha
Tel: +962(6) 535-9967
Fax: +962(6) 534-7295
EMail: info@psut.edu.jo
Website: http://www.psut.edu.jo

President: Issa Batarseh

Schools

Business *(King Talal)* (Business Administration); **Electrical Engineering** *(King Abdullah II)* (Computer Engineering; Electrical Engineering; Telecommunications Engineering); **Information Technology** *(King Hussein)* (Computer Graphics; Computer Science; Information Technology)

History: Founded 1991.

Admission Requirements: High School Tawjihi Certificate / the Science Stream, or a recognized equivalent certificate (such as the GCE). The minimum Tawjihi average is 60% for IT School applicants, and 80% for Engineering School applicants.

Main Language(s) of Instruction: Arabic

Accrediting Agencies: Jordanian Council for Higher Education

Degrees and Diplomas: *Bachelor's Degree*: 5 yrs

Last Updated: 22/11/11

RED SEA INSTITUTE OF CINEMATIC ARTS

PO Box 1484, Aqaba
EMail: info@rscia.edu.jo
Website: http://www.rsica.edu.jo

Programmes

Cinematic Arts (Cinema and Television; Film)

History: Founded 2008.

Accrediting Agencies: Ministry of Higher Education and Scientific Research

Degrees and Diplomas: *Master's Degree*

Last Updated: 22/11/11

TAFILA TECHNICAL UNIVERSITY (TTU)

PO Box 179, 66110 Tafila
Tel: +962(3) 225-0326
Fax: +962(3) 225-0002
EMail: webmaster@ttu.edu.jo
Website: http://www.ttu.edu.jo/

President: Yaqoub Al-Masa'feh EMail: yacoub111@yahoo.com

Colleges

Administrative & Financial Sciences (Accountancy; Banking; Business Administration; Business and Commerce; Economics; Finance); **Arts** (Arabic; Arts and Humanities; English; Social Sciences); **Educational Sciences** (Preschool Education; Primary Education; Special Education; Teacher Training); **Engineering** (Chemical Engineering; Civil Engineering; Electrical Engineering; Engineering; Geological Engineering; Mechanical Engineering; Mining Engineering); **Science** (Applied Physics; Chemistry; Information Technology; Mathematics)

History: Created 1986 as Tafila Applied University College. Acquired current status 2005.

Degrees and Diplomas: *Bachelor's Degree*. Also: Postgraduate Diploma in Education

Libraries: Yes

Last Updated: 22/11/11

THE ARAB ACADEMY FOR BANKING AND FINANCIAL SCIENCES

PO Box 13190, 11942 Amman
Tel: +962(6) 550-2900 +962(6) 550-3838
Fax: +962(6) 523-7834
EMail: aabfs@aabfs.org
Website: http://www.aabfs.org

President: Isam Zabalawi
Tel: +962(6) 550-2900 Ext. 115 EMail: president@aabfs.org

Vice-President for Financial and Administrative Affairs: Raed Jaber EMail: RJaber@aabfs.org

International Relations: Taghreed Mbaydeen, Director or Arab and International Relations EMail: TMbaydeen@aabfs.org

Centres

Banking and Financial Consultancy (Accountancy; Banking; Finance; Information Technology); **Banking and Financial Research** (Accountancy; Arabic; Banking; Insurance; Translation and Interpretation); **Certified Financiers and Bankers** (Banking; Finance); **Design and Printing** (Design; Printing and Printmaking)

Colleges

Banking and Financial Sciences *(Sana'a, Yemen Branch)* (Accountancy; Banking; Business Administration; Finance; Information Sciences; Information Technology; Management); **Banking and Financial Sciences** *(Karak, Jordan Branch)* (Accountancy; Banking; Business Administration; Finance; Information Management; Information Sciences; Information Technology; Management; Marketing); **Post-graduate Studies** *(Damascus, Syria Branch)* (Banking; Computer Networks; Computer Science; Finance; Information Technology); **Post-graduate Studies** *(Cairo, Egypt Branch)* (Accountancy; Banking; Business Administration; Finance; Information Management; Insurance; Marketing)

Deaneries

Scientific Research; **Students' Affairs**

Departments

Accountancy (Accountancy); **Banking** (Banking); **Banking** *(Islamic)* (Banking); **Business Administration** (Business Administration); **Computer Information Systems** (Information Technology); **Financial Management** (Finance); **Financial Markets** (Finance); **Management Information Systems** (Information Management; Information Technology); **Marketing** (Marketing)

Faculties

Banking and Financial Sciences *(Amman, Jordan)* (Accountancy; Banking; Finance; Management; Marketing); **Information Systems and Technology** *(Amman, Jordan)* (Computer Science; E-Business/Commerce; Information Management; Information Technology)

Institutes

Banking and Financial Training *(Cairo)* (Accountancy; Banking; Finance; Human Resources; Information Technology; Insurance; Management; Small Business); **Banking and Financial Training** *(Amman)* (Accountancy; Banking; Finance; Human Resources; Information Technology; Insurance; Management; Small Business)

Programmes
Bachelor *(Muscat, Oman Branch)*

Further Information: Also representative offices in Beirut, Tripoli, in Saudi Arabia and Tunis.

History: Founded 1988 as Arab Institute. A non-profit, pan-Arab regional Institution for the development of human resources operating at various levels in banks, financial Institutions, companies and Government departments. Emphasis on postgraduate and professional studies.

Governing Bodies: Board of Trustees

Academic Year: September to June (September-January; February-June). Summer Session (July-September)

Degrees and Diplomas: *Bachelor's Degree*: Banking and Financial Sciences; Accounting; Business Administration; Marketing; Finance & Accounting; Computer Information Systems; Information Systems Management; Information Systems & Management; *Master's Degree*: Banking and Financial Sciences; Accounting; Business Administration; Marketing; Finance & Accounting; Computer Information Systems; Information Systems Management; Information Systems & Management; *Doctorate*: Banking; Islamic Banking; Financial Management; Accounting; Computer Information Systems; Management Information Systems

Libraries: 17,300 vols and electronic library

Publications: Academy Bulletin *(quarterly)*; Journal of Banking and Financial Studies *(quarterly)*

Last Updated: 16/09/10

THE HASHEMITE UNIVERSITY

Al Jami'at Al-Hashimiyyah (HU)

PO Box 330127, 13115 Zarqa

Tel: +962(5) 390-3333

Fax: +962(5) 382-6613

EMail: huniv@hu.edu.jo

Website: http://www.hu.edu.jo

President: Kamal Bani-Hani (2012-)
EMail: k_banihani@hu.edu.jo; kamal@just.edu.jo

International Relations: Kifah Al Omari, Director of the Office of International Relations EMail: k.m.alumari@hu.edu.jo

International Relations: Marwan Obeidat, Advisor to the President for International Relations

Faculties
Allied Health Sciences (Dietetics; Medical Auxiliaries; Medical Technology; Nutrition; Occupational Therapy; Physical Therapy; Radiology); **Arts** (Arabic; Arts and Humanities; English; Literature; Social Sciences); **Childhood** *(Queen Rania)* (Child Care and Development; Preschool Education); **Economics and Administrative Sciences** (Accountancy; Banking; Economics; Finance; Management); **Educational Sciences** (Curriculum; Educational Administration; Educational Psychology; Educational Sciences); **Engineering** (Biomedical Engineering; Civil Engineering; Computer Engineering; Electrical Engineering; Engineering; Industrial Engineering; Mechanical Engineering); **Information Technology** *(Prince Al Hussein Bin Abdullah II)* (Computer Science; Information Technology; Software Engineering); **Medicine** (Medicine); **Natural Resources and Environment** (Earth Sciences; Environmental Studies; Rural Planning; Water Management); **Nursing** (Community Health; Midwifery; Nursing); **Physical Education and Sports Sciences** (Physical Education; Rehabilitation and Therapy; Sports; Sports Management); **Sciences** (Biology; Biotechnology; Chemistry; Mathematics; Physics)

Institutes
Tourism and Heritage *(Queen Rania)* (Archaeology; Cultural Studies; Heritage Preservation; Management; Museum Studies; Tourism)

History: Founded 1992.

Governing Bodies: Board of Trustees, Higher Council for Higher Education

Academic Year: September to August (September-January; February-June; June-August)

Admission Requirements: Secondary school certificate (Al-Tawjihi) or equivalent

Fees: (Jordanian Dinars): 8-45 per credit hour. Foreign students, (US Dollars), 60-75 Normal Programme; (US Dollars), 90-115 International Programme

Main Language(s) of Instruction: Arabic, English

Degrees and Diplomas: *Bachelor's Degree*: 4 yrs; *Master's Degree*

Student Services: Academic counselling, Canteen, Cultural centre, Employment services, Handicapped facilities, Health services, Social counselling, Sports facilities

Special Facilities: Learning Resources in Teacher Education

Libraries: c. 96,000 vols and Journals; Microfiles, Audio-Visual Media, Internet Titles, CD-ROM's

Student Numbers *2013*: Total 28,000

Last Updated: 12/09/12

UNIVERSITY OF JORDAN

Al-Jami'ah Al-Urdunia

Jubaiha, Queen Rania Al Abdullah Street, 11942 Amman

Tel: +962(6) 535-5000

Fax: +962(6) 535-5511

EMail: admin@ju.edu.jo

Website: http://www.ju.edu.jo

President: Ekhleif Tarawneh (2012-)
Tel: +962(6) 535-5544, Fax: +962(6) 535-5533
EMail: president@ju.edu.jo; tarawneh_c@yahoo.com

International Relations: Rami Ali, Director, Office of International Relations and Programmes
Tel: +962(6) 535-5000 Ext. 21050, Fax: +962(6) 6535 6518
EMail: ramimali@ju.edu.jo

Centres
Computer Science (Computer Science); **Documents and Manuscripts**; **Educational Development** (Health Administration; Health Sciences); **Global Development Learning Network**; **Islamic Cultural Studies** (Islamic Studies); **Languages** (Arabic; Communication Studies; English; Modern Languages); **Strategic Studies**; **Women's Studies** (Women's Studies)

Faculties
Agriculture (Agricultural Economics; Agricultural Equipment; Agriculture; Animal Husbandry; Environmental Studies; Food Technology; Horticulture; Irrigation; Nutrition; Plant and Crop Protection; Soil Science); **Art and Design** (Music; Theatre; Visual Arts); **Arts** (Arabic; Geography; History; Philosophy; Political Sciences; Psychology; Sociology); **Business** (Accountancy; Business Administration; Economics; Finance; Marketing; Public Administration); **Dentistry** (Dental Technology; Dentistry; Oral Pathology; Orthodontics; Periodontics); **Educational Sciences** (Curriculum; Educational Administration; Educational Psychology; Educational Sciences; Special Education); **Engineering and Technology** (Architecture; Chemical Engineering; Civil Engineering; Computer Engineering; Electrical Engineering; Engineering; Industrial Engineering; Mechanical Engineering; Technology); **Foreign Languages** (English; French; German; Italian; Korean; Linguistics; Literature; Modern Languages; Phonetics; Spanish); **Graduate Studies** (Agriculture; Art Education; Humanities and Social Science Education; Information Technology; International Economics; International Relations; Medical Auxiliaries; Science Education; Women's Studies); **International Studies** *(Master Program)* (International Relations; Political Sciences); **Islamic Studies (Shari'a)** (Islamic Law; Islamic Studies; Islamic Theology); **Law** (Law; Private Law; Public Law); **Medicine** (Anaesthesiology; Anatomy; Biochemistry; Community Health; Forensic Medicine and Dentistry; Gynaecology and Obstetrics; Histology; Medicine; Microbiology; Paediatrics; Pathology; Pharmacology; Physiology; Surgery); **Nursing** (Community Health; Nursing); **Pharmacy** (Pharmacology; Pharmacy); **Physical Education** (Health Education; Health Sciences; Physical Education; Sports Management); **Rehabilitation Sciences** (Occupational Therapy; Physical Therapy; Respiratory Therapy; Speech Therapy and Audiology); **Science** (Actuarial Science; Biological and Life Sciences; Chemistry; Geology; Mathematics; Physics)

Institutes

Arabic Teaching to Speakers of Other Languages *(International Institute (II-TASOL))* (Arabic); **Archaeology** (Archaeology)

Schools

Information Technology *(King Abdullah II)* (Information Technology)

Further Information: Also University of Jordan Hospital; University farm. 6 programmes in Arabic for non-native speakers

History: Founded 1962 as an independent national higher education institution.

Governing Bodies: Board of Trustees; University Council

Academic Year: October to June (October-February; February-June). Also summer session (June-August)

Admission Requirements: Secondary school certificate or recognized equivalent with a GPA of not less than 65%

Fees: (US Dollars): Foreign students, c. 70-250 per credit hour (Parallel Programmes)

Main Language(s) of Instruction: Arabic, English

Degrees and Diplomas: *Bachelor's Degree*: Humanities; Sciences, 3-4 yrs; *Bachelor's Degree*: Pharmacy; Engineering; Dentistry, 5 yrs; *Medical Doctor*: 6 yrs; *Master's Degree*: Humanities; Sciences, a further 2-3 yrs; *Doctorate*: a further 3-4 yrs

Student Services: Academic counselling, Canteen, Health services, Language programs, Nursery care, Sports facilities

Student Residential Facilities: For women students

Special Facilities: Museum of Archaeology; Museum of Zoology; Museum of Medicine; Folklore Museum; Insects Museums; Seismological Station; Marine Science Station in Aqaba

Libraries: Main Library, c. 900,000 documents

Publications: Cultural Journal 'Al-Majallah al-Thaqafiyyahq', Arabic *(quarterly)*; Dirasat (Refeered Journal), Arabic and English *(monthly)*; Profile (English)

Press or Publishing House: University Publishing House

Student Numbers *2011-2012*: Total: c. 37,000
Last Updated: 21/11/11

YARMOUK UNIVERSITY

Jami'at Al-Yarmouk (YU)

PO Box 566, Irbid
Tel: +962(2) 721-1111
Fax: +962(2) 727-4725
EMail: yarmouk@yu.edu.jo
Website: http://www.yu.edu.jo

President: Abdullah M. Al-Musa
Tel: +962(2) 727-1474 EMail: president@yu.edu.jo

International Relations: Hanan Malkawi, Vice-President
Tel: +962(2) 721-1111 Ext 2103 EMail: vice.randi@yu.edu.jo

Centres

Computer and Information Technology (Computer Science; Information Sciences); **Consultation and Community Services** (Social and Community Services); **Faculty Members Development** (Development Studies; Educational Research); **Jordanian Studies** (Cultural Studies); **Language** (Linguistics; Modern Languages); **Refugees and Displaced Persons** (Demography and Population); **Speech and Hearing** (Speech Studies; Speech Therapy and Audiology); **Theorical and Applied Physics** (Physics)

Faculties

Archaeology and Anthropology (Anthropology; Archaeology; Heritage Preservation; Tourism); **Arts** (Arabic; English; Geography; History; Journalism; Literature; Mass Communication; Modern Languages; Oriental Languages; Political Sciences; Sociology); **Economics and Administration** (Accountancy; Banking; Business Administration; Economics; Finance; Marketing; Public Administration); **Education** (Curriculum; Education; Educational Administration; Educational and Student Counselling; Educational Psychology; Teacher Training); **Engineering Technology** *(Hijjawi)* (Computer Engineering; Electrical Engineering; Electronic Engineering; Power Engineering); **Fine Arts** (Aesthetics; Art History; Ceramic Art; Fine Arts; Graphic Design; Music; Painting and Drawing); **Information Technology and Computer Science** (Computer Science; Information Technology); **Law** (Law); **Mass Communication** (Advertising and Publicity; Journalism; Mass Communication; Public Relations; Radio and Television Broadcasting); **Physical Education** (Physical Education; Sports); **Science** (Biology; Chemistry; Earth Sciences; Environmental Studies; Mathematics; Physics; Statistics); **Shari'a and Islamic Studies** (Islamic Law; Islamic Studies); **Tourism and Hotel Management** (Hotel Management; Tourism)

Units

Marine Sciences Station (Marine Science and Oceanography)

Further Information: The Language Centre offers a series of integrated programmes of Arabic as a Foreign Language (AFL)

History: Founded 1976 by Royal Decree with Faculty of Arts and Science. A State Institution enjoying academic and administrative autonomy. Largely financed by the State.

Governing Bodies: Council Higher Education; Board of Trustees; University Council; Deans Council

Academic Year: September to August (September-January; February-June; June-August)

Admission Requirements: Secondary school certificate or recognized equivalent

Fees: (Jordanian Dinars): Bachelor, 16-45 per credit hour (foreign students, US Dollars 60-112.5). Higher Studies: Master, 50-75 per credit hour, Doc. 75-90 per credit hour (foreign students, US Dollars 112.5-225)

Main Language(s) of Instruction: Arabic, English

International Co-operation: With over 110 national and international universities, higher scientific institutions and centres

Accrediting Agencies: Council of Higher Education

Degrees and Diplomas: *Bachelor's Degree*: 4-5 yrs; *Master's Degree*: a further 2-3 yrs; *Doctorate (PhD)*: 2-5 yrs

Student Services: Academic counselling, Canteen, Foreign student adviser, Handicapped facilities, Health services, Language programs, Social counselling, Sports facilities

Student Residential Facilities: For Women students from remote areas

Special Facilities: Archaeology Museum (Jordan Heritage); Natural History Museum. Radio and T.V. Studio. Greenhouse. Permanent Art Exhibition. Numismatics Gallery

Libraries: 500,000 vols in different languages, 90,000 back issues, 15,000 audiovisual materials

Publications: Abhath al-Yarmouk, Series of Humanities and Social Sciences; Literature and Language; Pure Science and Engineering; Majallat al-Yarmouk *(quarterly)*; Yarmouk Numismatics *(annually)*

Press or Publishing House: Yarmouk University Press

Student Numbers *2012-2013*: Total 34,584
Last Updated: 05/03/13

ZARQA UNIVERSITY

Jami'at Al-Zarqa' Al-Ahliyya

PO Box 2000, 13110 Zarqa
Tel: +962(5) 382-1100
Fax: +962(5) 382-1120
EMail: admin@zpu.edu.jo; regist@zpu.edu.jo
Website: http://www.zpu.edu.jo

President: Yousef Abu Addous

Faculties

Allied Medical Science (Anatomy; Biochemistry; Biological and Life Sciences; Endocrinology; Haematology; Medical Technology; Molecular Biology; Parasitology; Pathology); **Art and Design** (Graphic Design; Interior Design); **Arts** (Arabic; English; History; Journalism; Literature; Translation and Interpretation); **Economics and Administrative Sciences** (Accountancy; Banking; Business Administration; Business Computing; Economics; Finance; Information Management; Management Systems; Marketing); **Educational Sciences** (Education; Educational Sciences; Information Sciences; Library Science; Preschool Education; Primary Education); **Law** (Law); **Nursing** (Nursing); **Science and Information Technology** (Computer Science; Mathematics; Software Engineering; Systems Analysis); **Shari'a** (Islamic Law; Islamic Studies); **Technical Engineering** (Architecture; Civil Engineering; Electrical Engineering; Surveying and Mapping)

History: Founded 1994. Acquired present status 1999.

Governing Bodies: Board of Trustees

Admission Requirements: Secondary school certificate or equivalent. Minimum marks of 50% for all majors except Allied Medical Sciences

Fees: (Jordanian Dinars): Registration, 20; tuition, 30 - 60 per credit hour

Main Language(s) of Instruction: Arabic; English

Accrediting Agencies: Ministry of Higher Education

Degrees and Diplomas: *Bachelor's Degree*: 4 yrs

Student Services: Academic counselling, Canteen, Health services, Nursery care, Social counselling, Sports facilities

Libraries: Yes

Publications: Al A' Afaq (The Horizon), Cultural Magazine *(quarterly)*; IAJIT, Scientific Journal *(quarterly)*; Zarqa Journal for Research and Studies, Scientific Journal *(biannually)*

Last Updated: 22/11/11

Kazakhstan

STRUCTURE OF HIGHER EDUCATION SYSTEM

Description:

Higher education comprises universities, academies, institutes, conservatoires, higher schools and higher colleges, all considered as higher education institutions. It is provided at three levels: Bachelor's degree (Graduate Education), Master's degree and Doctor of Philosophy (PhD) (Postgraduate education). Persons of the Kazakh nationality who are citizens of other States; foreign citizens and persons without the citizenship living in the Republic of Kazakhstan can receive free higher education through the State educational grant. Citizens of the Russian Federation, Republic of Belarus, Republic of Tajikistan and the Kyrgyz Republic have the same right. Educational grants can be awarded to foreign citizens according to the international agreements ratified by the Republic of Kazakhstan.

Stages of studies:

University level first stage: *Graduate stage*
Bachelor's degrees are conferred after four years of studies.

University level second stage: *Postgraduate stage*
Master's degrees are conferred after a further two years' study beyond the Bachelor's degree.
A PhD usually lasts for a minimum of three years and is conferred after completion of a thesis based on original research.

Distance higher education:
Some 20 universities offer distance education.

ADMISSION TO HIGHER EDUCATION

Admission to university-level studies:

Name of secondary school credential required: Diplom o Technitcheskom I Professional'nom Obrazovanii

Name of secondary school credential required: Attestat o Obschem Srednem Obrazovanii

Entrance exam requirements: School graduates have to pass an exam, the Edinoe Nacional'noe Testirovanie (Unified National Testing Exam) and obtain its diploma the Certificat o Rezul'tatah EHT to enter universities.

RECOGNITION OF STUDIES

Quality assurance system:

The Ministry of Education and Science and the National Accreditation Center (ENIC-Kazakhstan) are in charge of higher education quality control.
A National System of Education Quality Evaluation was developed in 2010.

Bodies dealing with recognition:

National Accreditation Center/ ENIC Kazakhstan

19, Imanov str
Astana 010000
Tel: +7(7172) 787 160
Fax: +7(7172) 787 160
EMail: nac.edu@bk.ru
WWW: http://www.nac.edu.kz
Deals with credential recognition for entry to institution: yes

NATIONAL BODIES

Ministry of Education and Science

Minister: Bakhytzhan Zhumagulov
8, Orynbor str.
Astana 0100000
Tel: +7(7172) 742 428
Fax: +7(7172) 742 416
EMail: pressa@edu.gov.kz
WWW: http://www.edu.gov.kz

Role of national body: The main aim of the Ministry of Education and Science is the realization of state policy in the field of education and science, general scientific and methodical guidance over all educational and scientific institutions.

Data for academic year: 2010-2011
Source: IAU from the National Accreditation Center, ENIC Kazakhstan, 2010. Bodies updated 2012.

INSTITUTIONS

PUBLIC INSTITUTIONS

ACADEMICIAN E.A. BUKETOV KARAGANDA STATE UNIVERSITY

Karagandinskij Gosudarstvennyj Universitet imeni Akademika E.A. Buketova (KSU)
ul. Universiteckaja 28, 470074 Karaganda
Tel: +7(3212) 770-389
Fax: +7(3212) 770-384
EMail: root@kargu.krg.kz
Website: http://www.ksu.kz

Rector: Erkin Kinayatovich Kubeev

First Vice-Rector: Rymbek Muratovich Zhumashev
Tel: +7(3212) 770-386 EMail: zhumashev@ksu.kz

International Relations: Dinara Apijeva, Head, International Relations Tel: +7(3212) 745-595

Departments

Skill Level Raising (Arts and Humanities; Computer Science; Social Sciences)

Faculties

Biology and Geography (Biology; Ecology; Geography; Zoology); **Chemistry** (Chemistry); **Economics** (Accountancy; Economics; Finance; Management; Marketing; Public Administration; Service Trades; Tourism); **Foreign Languages** (English; French; German; Modern Languages; Philology; Translation and Interpretation); **History** (Archaeology; Ethnology; Heritage Preservation; History; International Relations; Museum Studies); **Law** (International Law; Law); **Mathematics** (Applied Mathematics; Mathematics; Mathematics and Computer Science; Mathematics Education; Mechanics); **Pedagogy and Social Work** (Pedagogy; Preschool Education; Primary Education; Psychology; Social Work); **Philology** (Foreign Languages Education; Journalism; Literature; Native Language; Philology; Russian); **Philosophy and Psychology** (Cultural Studies; Philosophy; Political Sciences; Psychology; Religious Studies; Social Sciences); **Physical Training and Sports** (Physical Education; Sports); **Physics** (Applied Physics; Electronic Engineering; Environmental Studies; Instrument Making; Materials Engineering; Physics; Power Engineering; Radiophysics; Social Welfare; Telecommunications Engineering); **Professional Arts** (Design; Fine Arts; Library Science; Painting and Drawing; Publishing and Book Trade; Transport and Communications; Vocational Education)

History: Founded 1972 as Karaganda Pedagogical Institute. Acquired present status and title 1997.

Governing Bodies: Academic Council

Academic Year: September to July

Admission Requirements: Competitive entrance examination following general or special secondary school certificate

Fees: (Tenge): 92,100 per annum

Main Language(s) of Instruction: Kazakh, Russian

International Co-operation: With universities in France, USA. Also participates in Tempus, DAAD programmes

Degrees and Diplomas: *Diplom o Vysshem Obrazovanii (Bakalavr)*: 4 yrs; *Diplom Magistra*: a further 2 yrs following Bachelor, a further yr following Specialist; *Diplom Doktora (PhD)*: by thesis

Student Services: Academic counselling, Canteen, Cultural centre, Employment services, Foreign student adviser, Health services, Language programs, Social counselling, Sports facilities

Student Residential Facilities: Yes

Special Facilities: Museum of E.A. Buketov; Museum of Archeology of Central Kazakhstan; Museum of Nature

Libraries: Total, 1,325,900 vols

Publications: Vestnik KarGU, Scientific Journal *(quarterly)*

Press or Publishing House: Karaganda State University Publishing House

Last Updated: 19/10/10

ACADEMY OF CIVIL AVIATION

Akademija Graždanskoj Aviatsii
ul. Zakarpatskaja, 44, 050093 Almaty, Almaty
Tel: +7(727) 383-89-79
Fax: +7(727) 383-89-69
EMail: colledge@agakaz.kz
Website: http://www.agakaz.kz

Rector: Kazbek Aldamzharov

Programmes

Aviation Engineering and Technology (Aeronautical and Aerospace Engineering; Air Transport; Technology); **Transport Management** (Air Transport; Transport and Communications; Transport Management)

History: Created 2000. A postgraduate institution.

Admission Requirements: Bakalvr or Diplom Spetsialista

Degrees and Diplomas: *Diplom o Vysshem Obrazovanii (Bakalavr)*; *Diplom Magistra*

Special Facilities: 6 computer rooms; internet access

Libraries: c. 147 000 vols; digital library, 270,000 documents

Academic Staff *2009-2010*: Total: c. 130
Last Updated: 18/02/10

ACADEMY OF FINANCIAL POLICE OF THE REPUBLIC OF KAZAKHSTAN

Akademija Finansovoj Politsyj Respubliki Kazakhstan
Kosshi, Akmola
Website: http://www.finpol.kz/eng/academy/about/

Rector: Ramazan Tleukhan

Programmes
Customs (Taxation); **Law** (Law); **Law Enforcement** (Police Studies)

History: Founded 1999.

Admission Requirements: Age of sixteen, with a secondary general education; mandatory special examination and medical examination at the military-medical commission of the Ministry of Internal Affairs of the Republic of Kazakhstan

International Co-operation: With universities in Ukraine and Russia.

Degrees and Diplomas: *Diplom o Vysshem Obrazovanii (Bakalavr)*; *Diplom Magistra*

Student Services: Sports facilities

Student Residential Facilities: Yes

Special Facilities: Computer labs

Libraries: 94,820 vols.

Student Numbers *2009-2010*: Total: c. 440
Last Updated: 27/10/10

ACADEMY OF PUBLIC ADMINISTRATION UNDER THE PRESIDENT OF KAZAKHSTAN

Akademija Gosudarstvennogo Upravlenija pri Presidente Respubliki Kazakhstan
Abay avenue, 33a, 010000 Astana
Tel: +7(7172) 75-32-27 +7(7172) 75-34-22
Fax: +7(7172) 75-32-45
EMail: info@apa.kz
Website: http://pa-academy.kz

Rector: Aryn Orsariyev

Institutes
Civil Servants's Retraining and Skills-upgrading (Economics; Finance; Law; Leadership; Political Sciences; Social Sciences); **Diplomacy** (Economics; History; International Relations; Law; Management; Philosophy; Political Sciences; Public Administration; Social Sciences); **Justice** (Arts and Humanities; Civil Law; Criminal Law; Social Sciences); **Public Administration Modernization** (Public Administration); **Public and Local Administration** (Administration; Economics; Finance; Human Resources; Information Technology; Management; Native Language; Public Administration)

Schools
Public Policy *(National - NSPP)* (Political Sciences)

History: Founded 1994 as National Higher School of public administration under the President of the Republic of Kazakhstan (NHSPA) on the basis of the Party School at the Central Committee of the Kazakh Soviet Socialist Republic. Became the Academy of public service under the President the Republic of Kazakhstan 1998 after merging with Institute of civil servants' retraining and skill-upgrading under the Government of the Republic of Kazakhstan. Relocated in Astana 2000. Became Academy of public administration under the President the Republic of Kazakhstan 2005 through merger of the reorganized state institutions "The Academy of public service under the President of the Republic of Kazakhstan", "The Academy of Justice at the Supreme court of the Republic of Kazakhstan" and transfer of functions of Diplomatic Academy of the republican state enterprise "Eurasian national university named after L.N.Gumilev" to newly created state body.

Degrees and Diplomas: *Diplom Magistra*; *Diplom Doktora (PhD)*
Last Updated: 27/10/10

ACADEMY OF THE COMMITTEE OF CRIMINAL-EXECUTIVE SYSTEM OF THE MINISTRY OF JUSTICE

Akademija Komiteta Ugolovno-ispolnitelnoj Sistemy Ministerstva Yustitsii
11, Abay avenue, 110005 Kostanay, Kostanay
Tel: +7(7142) 26-34-23 +7(7142) 25-58-40
Fax: +7(7142) 25-58-40
EMail: kyimjurk@mail.ru
Website: http://akuis.kz/

Commander: Kazbek Ukanov

Faculties
Distance Learning (Police Studies); **Full-time Study** (Pedagogy; Police Studies; Psychology); **Training and Retraining** (Police Studies)

Degrees and Diplomas: *Diplom o Vysshem Obrazovanii (Bakalavr)*; *Diplom Magistra*
Last Updated: 27/10/10

ACADEMY OF THE MINISTRY OF INTERNAL AFFAIRS OF THE REPUBLIC OF KAZAKHSTAN

Akademija Ministerstva Vnutrennih del Respubliki Kazahstan
29, Utepov street, 050060 Almaty
EMail: academymvd@academymvd.kz
Website: http://www.academymvd.kz/

Rector: Zhan Kenzhetayev

Departments
Administrative and Legal Policy (Administration; Law); **Civil - Legal Disciplines** (Law); **Computer Science, Special and Computer Engineering** (Computer Science); **Criminal Policy and Criminology** (Criminology; Police Studies); **Criminalistics** (Criminology); **Expert Technical Support Detection and Investigation of Crimes** (Criminology); **Kazakh Language** (Native Language); **Military and Physical Training** (Military Science; Physical Education); **Military and Special Tactical Training** (Military Science); **Organization Investigation of Crimes and Criminal Procedure** (Criminology); **Organization Operatively-search Activity and Use of Special Equipment**; **Pedagogy and Psychology** (Education; Law; Management; Pedagogy; Psychology); **Philosophy and Socio-economic Disciplines** (Economics; Philosophy; Social Sciences); **Russian and Foreign Languages** (Modern Languages; Russian); **State and Legal Disciplines** (Law)

Faculties
Distance Learning; **Full-time Study**

History: Founded 1999.

Degrees and Diplomas: *Diplom o Vysshem Obrazovanii (Bakalavr)*; *Diplom Magistra*
Last Updated: 27/10/10

ACADEMY OF THE NATIONAL SECURITY COMMITTEE OF THE REPUBLIC OF KAZAKHSTAN

Akademija Komiteta Natsionalnoj Bezopasnosti Respubliki Kazakhstan
Madi Street 1 A, Alatau Village, 040907 Almaty, Almaty
Website: http://www.knb.kz/

Rector: Adil Shayahmetov

Programmes
Law (Law); **National and Foreign Languages** (Modern Languages; Native Language)

History: Founded 1974.

Degrees and Diplomas: *Diplom o Vysshem Obrazovanii (Bakalavr)*; *Diplom Magistra*; *Diplom Doktora (PhD)*
Last Updated: 27/10/10

AKHMET YASAVI INTERNATIONAL KAZAKH-TURKISH UNIVERSITY

Meždunarodnij Kazahsko-Tureckij Universitet im. H.A. Yesevi (IKTU)

Bekzat Sattarhanov, 29, 161200 Turkistan, SKO
Tel: +7(725) 336-3848
Fax: +7(725) 336-3849
EMail: vasawiun@mktu.turkistan.kz
Website: http://www.turkistan.kz/;http://www.yesevi.edu.tr/

Rector: Lesbek Tashimov

First Vice-President: Mahir Nakip
Tel: +7(725) 336-3601, Fax: +7(725) 336-3605
EMail: mnakip@yahoo.com

International Relations: Sauranbek Jamalbekov, Head, department of international relations
Tel: +7(725) 336-3621
EMail: vanzi86@mail.ru; gainii_oshanova@mail.ru

Divisions

Economics and Law (Economics; History; Law; Native Language)

Faculties

Art (Design; Fine Arts; Painting and Drawing); **Ecology** (Agriculture; Ecology; Environmental Studies; Farm Management; Welfare and Protective Services); **Economics** (Economics; International Economics; Management; Marketing; Tourism); **History** (History; History of Societies; Political Sciences; Religious Studies; Sociology); **Law** (International Law; International Relations; Law); **Medicine** (Medicine; Traditional Eastern Medicine); **Natural Sciences** (Biology; Chemistry; Mathematics; Mechanics; Natural Sciences; Physics); **Philology** (Journalism; Linguistics; Literature; Modern Languages; Philology; Translation and Interpretation)

Further Information: Also Branches in Kentau, Almaty, Taraz and Šymkent. Polyclinic for Medical Studies, Šymkent; Kazakh and Russian courses for foreign students

History: Founded 1991, acquired present status and title 1993 by special agreement between Governments of the Republic of Kazakhstan and the Republic of Turkey.

Governing Bodies: International Board of Directors

Academic Year: September to July (September-January; February-July)

Admission Requirements: Secondary school certificate (Atestat srednem obrazovanii)

Fees: (Tenge): c. 28,800-94,600 per annum

Main Language(s) of Instruction: Kazakh, Russian, Turkish, English

International Co-operation: Erasmus Mundus; Tempus IV

Accrediting Agencies: Government of Kazakhstan; Government of Turkey

Degrees and Diplomas: *Diplom o Vysshem Obrazovanii (Bakalavr); Diplom Magistra; Diplom Doktora (PhD) (PhD)*

Student Services: Academic counselling, Canteen, Cultural centre, Employment services, Foreign student adviser, Foreign Studies Centre, Handicapped facilities, Health services, Language programs, Nursery care, Social counselling, Sports facilities

Student Residential Facilities: c. 1,300 in Student Hostels

Special Facilities: University Museum. Botanical Garden. Movie Studio. Handicraft Workshops

Libraries: Central Library, Faculty and Division Libraries, c. 480,000 vols

Publications: University Bulletin, Scientific Methodological Articles *(bimonthly)*

Press or Publishing House: Yasawi University Press

Academic Staff *2009-2010*	**TOTAL**
FULL-TIME	**1,829**
Student Numbers *2009-2010*	
All (Foreign Included)	**18,248**

Part-time students, 1,139. **Evening students,** 8,138.

Last Updated: 06/10/10

AKTOBE STATE PEDAGOGICAL INSTITUTE

Aktiubinskij Gosudarstvennyj Pedagogičeskij Institut

34, Moldagulova avenue, 030000 Aktobe, Aktobe
Tel: +8(313-2) 56-82-80
Fax: +8(313-2) 56-82-80
EMail: agpi@mail.kz

Rector: Galymzhan Nuryshev

Programmes

Pedagogy (Pedagogy)

History: Founded 1966.

Degrees and Diplomas: *Diplom o Vysshem Obrazovanii (Bakalavr); Diplom Magistra*

Last Updated: 27/10/10

AL-FARABI KAZAKH NATIONAL UNIVERSITY

Kazahskij Nacionalnij Universitet im. Al Farabi (KAZNU)

Prosp. Al Farabi 71, 050040 Almaty
Tel: +7(727) 377 33 33
EMail: anurmag@kazsu.kz
Website: http://www.kaznu.kz/

Rector: Galimkair Mutanovich Mutanov (2010-)

International Relations: Sholpan Tazabek, Manager, International Cooperation Department
Tel: +7(727) 377 33 33 ext 1166
EMail: Sholpan.Tazabek@kaznu.kz

Centres

Physical and Chemical Methods of Research and Analysis (Chemistry; Physics)

Departments

Journalism (Communication Studies; Journalism; Public Relations; Publishing and Book Trade; Radio and Television Broadcasting)

Faculties

Biology (Biology; Biophysics; Biotechnology; Cell Biology; Ecology; Fishery; Genetics; Molecular Biology; Sports); **Chemistry** (Chemistry; Ecology; Inorganic Chemistry; Organic Chemistry; Physical Chemistry); **Economics and Business** (Accountancy; Business Administration; Economics; Finance; Law; Management; Marketing); **Geography** (Ecology; Geography; Geography (Human); Meteorology; Surveying and Mapping; Tourism; Water Science); **History** (Ancient Civilizations; Archaeology; Contemporary History; Ethnology; History; Medieval Studies; Modern History; Museum Studies); **International Relations** (International Law; International Relations; Regional Studies); **Law** (Civil Law; Criminal Law; Fiscal Law; Law; Public Law); **Mechanical Mathematics** (Computer Science; Information Technology; Mathematics; Mathematics and Computer Science; Mechanics); **Oriental Studies** (Arabic; Chinese; East Asian Studies; Hindi; Japanese; Korean; Modern Languages; Persian; Philology; Regional Studies; Translation and Interpretation; Turkish; Urdu); **Philology** (Linguistics; Literature; Native Language; Philology; Russian; Translation and Interpretation); **Philosophy and Political Science** (Anthropology; Educational Administration; Pedagogy; Philosophy; Political Sciences; Psychology; Religion; Social Work; Sociology); **Physics** (Applied Physics; Astronomy and Space Science; Materials Engineering; Measurement and Precision Engineering; Nuclear Physics; Physics; Thermal Physics); **Preparatory Studies for Foreign Students** (Cultural Studies; Geography (Human); Grammar; History; Literature; Native Language; Russian)

Institutes

Combustion Problems (Chemistry; Industrial Chemistry)

Laboratories

Nanotechnology (Nanotechnology)

Research Institutes

Biology and Biotechnology Problems (Biochemistry; Biology; Biophysics; Biotechnology; Cell Biology; Genetics; Histology; Microbiology; Molecular Biology; Physiology); **Ecology Problems** (Ecology; Environmental Studies); **Experimental and Theoretical Physics** (Atomic and Molecular Physics; Electronic Engineering; Nuclear Physics; Physics; Thermal Physics); **Mathematics and**

Mechanics (Mathematics; Mechanics); **New Chemical Technologies and Materials** (Chemical Engineering; Materials Engineering)

Further Information: Also Scientific Technology Park

History: Founded 1934, became autonomous State Institution 1993, acquired present status and title 2001.

Governing Bodies: Academic Council

Academic Year: September to July (September-January; February-July)

Admission Requirements: Competitive entrance examination following general or special secondary school certificate

Fees: (US Dollars): Foreign students, 2,000-3,000 per annum

Main Language(s) of Instruction: Kazakh, Russian

International Co-operation: With universities in USA; United Kingdom; Germany; France; Spain; Poland; Egypt; Iran; Turkey; South Korea; Japan; China; CIS countries

Accrediting Agencies: Ministry of Education and Science

Degrees and Diplomas: *Diplom o Vysshem Obrazovanii (Bakalavr)*; *Diplom Magistra*; *Diplom Doktora (PhD)*

Student Services: Academic counselling, Cultural centre, Health services, Social counselling, Sports facilities

Student Residential Facilities: Yes

Special Facilities: History of the University Museum; Biology Museum; Archaeology Museum; Ethnography Museum; Paleolithic Kazakhstan Museum

Libraries: Total, 1,500,316 vols

Publications: Vestnik KazNU in 9 Branches, Scientific Publication of KazNU *(annually)*

Last Updated: 29/11/11

ALMATY INSTITUTE OF POWER ENGINEERING AND TELECOMMUNICATIONS

Almatinskij Institut Energetiki i Svjazi (AIPET)

ul. Baytursynuly 126, 480013 Almaty, Republik Kazaksthan
Tel: +7(3272) 925-740
Fax: +7(3272) 925-057
EMail: aipet@aipet.kz
Website: http://www.aipet.kz

Rector: Gumarbek Daukeyev (1997-)

Vice-Rector: Yevgeniy Malishevskiy
Tel: +7(3272) 929-981 EMail: evm@aipet.kz

Vice-Rector: Ernest Sericov
Tel: +7(3272) 925-010, Fax: +7(3272) 920-303
EMail: eas@aipet.kz

International Relations: Erkin Yakhyaev
Tel: +7(3272) 925-789, Fax: +7(3272) 925-789
EMail: fdp@aipet.kz

Centres

Information Technology (Computer Networks; Information Technology; Software Engineering; Telecommunications Engineering)

Faculties

Distance Learning and Retraining (Electronic Engineering; Power Engineering; Telecommunications Engineering; Thermal Engineering); **Electrical Engineering** (Automation and Control Engineering; Ecology; Electrical Engineering; Native Language; Occupational Health; Power Engineering; Russian; Social Sciences); **Heat Power Engineering** (Automation and Control Engineering; Economics; Industrial Engineering; Modern Languages; Physics; Power Engineering; Thermal Engineering); **Pre-Institutional Training** (History; Mathematics; Physics); **Radio Engineering and Communication** (Computer Engineering; Electronic Engineering; Engineering; Mathematics; Mechanics; Telecommunications Engineering)

History: Founded 1966 as Almaty Technological Institute, reorganized as Almaty Institute of Power Engineering 1975, and acquired present status and title 1997.

Governing Bodies: Academic Council; Council of Trustees; Rectorship; Meeting of Constituents

Academic Year: September to July

Admission Requirements: Competitive entrance examination following general or special secondary school certificate

Fees: (US Dollars): c. 1,100-1,300 per annum

Main Language(s) of Instruction: Kazakh, Russian

International Co-operation: With universities in Russian Federation. Participates in INCO-Copernicus; INTAS; Tempus-TACIS and Sixth Framework Programme of the European Community programmes

Accrediting Agencies: Ministry of Education and Science

Degrees and Diplomas: *Diplom o Vysshem Obrazovanii (Bakalavr)*; *Diplom Magistra*

Student Services: Canteen, Cultural centre, Employment services, Foreign student adviser, Health services, Language programs, Social counselling, Sports facilities

Student Residential Facilities: For 1,300 students and Hotel for 60 persons and building research

Special Facilities: Museum of Telecommunications Equipment

Libraries: Central Library, c. 400,000 vols; 7 reading halls

Publications: Power Engineering, Radiotechnology, Electronics and Communications, Scientific works *(biennially)*; Power Engineering, Telecommunications and Higher Education in Modern Conditions, Scientific works *(biennially)*

Last Updated: 08/10/10

ALMATY TECHNOLOGICAL UNIVERSITY

Almaty Tehnologiyalik Universitety

Tole bi str., 100, 050012 Almaty
Tel: +7(727) 293-52-89 +7(727) 293-52-87
Fax: +7(727) 293-52-92
EMail: atukz@mail.ru
Website: http://www.atu.kz

Rector: Kuralbek Sadibayevich Kulazhanov
Tel: +7(727) 293-52-89 EMail: rector@atu.kz

International Relations: Mereke Tankibayeva
Tel: +7(727) 293-52-87, Ext.120

Departments

Food Production (Biotechnology; Chemistry; Ecology; Food Science; Food Technology; Organic Chemistry)

Faculties

Economics and Business (Accountancy; Economics; Finance; Management; Marketing; Service Trades; Tourism); **Engineering and Information Technology** (Computer Science; Engineering; Information Sciences; Information Technology; Physical Education); **Light Industry and Design** (Design; Mathematics; Modern Languages; Physics; Technology; Textile Design)

History: Founded 1952 as Almaty Training-Consulting Branch of All-Union Extra-Mural Institute of Food Industry. Renamed Almaty Technological Institute 1996. Acquired present status and title 2001.

Main Language(s) of Instruction: Kazakh, Russian

Degrees and Diplomas: *Diplom o Vysshem Obrazovanii (Bakalavr)*: 4 yrs; *Diplom Magistra*: a further 2 yrs following Bachelor; *Diplom Doktora (PhD)*

Libraries: General fund of c. 697,000 vols

Publications: Food Technology and Service, Scientific Magazine

Academic Staff *2008-2009*	TOTAL
FULL-TIME	290
PART-TIME	130

Last Updated: 22/01/10

ASTANA MEDICAL UNIVERSITY

Medicinskij Universitet Astana (AMU)

49a, Beibitshilik Street, 010000 Astana, Akmola
Tel: +7(7172) 53-94-24
Fax: +7(7172) 53-94-24
EMail: rektorat@amu.kz
Website: http://www.amu.kz/

Rector: Zhaxybay Zhumadilov (2008-) EMail: zzhuma@mail.ru

International Relations: Damir Kozhanbayev, Head of International Cooperation EMail: damirlider@mail.ru

Faculties
Continuing Professional Development and Education (Forensic Medicine and Dentistry; Gynaecology and Obstetrics; Medical Technology; Medicine; Paediatrics; Radiology; Surgery); **General Medicine, Dentistry and Pharmacy** (Anaesthesiology; Anatomy; Biochemistry; Biology; Chemistry; Dentistry; Histology; Latin; Medicine; Native Language; Neurology; Orthopaedics; Pathology; Pharmacology; Pharmacy; Philosophy; Psychiatry and Mental Health; Russian; Sociology; Surgery); **Medicine, Paediatrics, Oriental Medicine, Biomedical and Preventive Health, and Nursing** (Alternative Medicine; Dermatology; Gynaecology and Obstetrics; Medicine; Nursing; Oncology; Ophthalmology; Otorhinolaryngology; Paediatrics; Pneumology; Radiology; Surgery; Venereology); **Public Health** (Arts and Humanities; Computer Science; Forensic Medicine and Dentistry; Hygiene; Immunology; Mathematics; Microbiology; Modern Languages; Nutrition; Physiology; Public Health; Social and Preventive Medicine; Social Sciences; Virology)

History: Founded 1964.

Degrees and Diplomas: *Diplom o Vysshem Obrazovanii (Bakalavr)*; *Diplom o Vysshem Obrazovanii (Specialist)*; *Diplom Magistra*; *Diplom Doktora (PhD)*

Libraries: 475,000 vols; 215 periodical subscriptions.

Academic Staff *2009-2010*: Total 571
STAFF WITH DOCTORATE: Total 245

Student Numbers *2009-2010*: Total 3,679

Last Updated: 28/10/10

ATYRAU INSTITUTE OF OIL AND GAS

Atyrauskij Institut Nefti i Gaza
pr. Azattyka, 1, Atyrau
Tel: +7(712-2) 35-46-54
Fax: +7(712-2) 32-95-57
EMail: aing-atr@nursat.kz
Website: http://www.aing.kz/

Rector: Tuluesh Serikov

International Relations: Islam Dzhanzakov, Pro-Rector on Scientific Work and International Relations

Faculties
Distance Learning (Distance Education; Educational Sciences); **Economics** (Accountancy; Economics; Management; Marketing; Modern Languages; Native Language; Russian; Service Trades); **Engineering** (Automation and Control Engineering; Chemical Engineering; Chemistry; Engineering; Environmental Engineering; Information Technology; Power Engineering; Safety Engineering); **Mechanics** (Arts and Humanities; Construction Engineering; History of Law; Machine Building; Materials Engineering; Mathematics; Mechanics; Transport and Communications); **Oil and Petroleum** (Geology; Geophysics; Petroleum and Gas Engineering)

History: Created 1984.

Degrees and Diplomas: *Diplom o Vysshem Obrazovanii (Bakalavr)*; *Diplom Magistra*

Last Updated: 08/10/10

B. BEISENOV KARAGANDA JURIDICAL INSTITUTE OF THE MINISTRY OF INTERNAL AFFAIRS OF THE REPUBLIC OF KAZAKHSTAN

Karagandinskij Juridičeskij Institut imeni B. Beisenova Ministerstva vnutrennih del Respubliki Kazahstan
ul. Yermekov, 124, 100009 Karagandy, Karagandy
Tel: +8(7212) 30-33-99
EMail: webmaster@kzi.kz
Website: http://kzi.kz/

Rector: Serik Erkenov

Departments
Administrative Law (Administrative Law); **Civil Law Disciplines** (Civil Law); **Criminal Law and Criminology** (Criminal Law; Criminology); **Criminal Procedure** (Criminal Law); **Criminology** (Criminology); **Language Training** (Modern Languages); **Management and Psychology** (Management; Psychology); **Military Science and Special Tactical Training** (Military Science); **Operational and Investigative Activities**; **Organisation of Crime Investigation** (Criminology); **Philosophy and Socio-economic Disciplines** (Economics; Philosophy; Social Sciences); **Phsycial Training** (Physical Education); **Special Training**; **State Legal Disciplines** (Law)

History: Founded 1969.

Degrees and Diplomas: *Diplom o Vysshem Obrazovanii (Bakalavr)*; *Diplom Magistra*

Last Updated: 29/10/10

CASPIAN STATE UNIVERSITY OF TECHNOLOGIES AND ENGINEERING NAMED AFTER SH. YESENOV

Kaspiyskij Gosudarstvennyj Universitet Tehnologij I Inžiniringa imeni ŠYesenova
50, 32-microdistrict, 130003 Aktau, Mangistau Region
Tel: +7(7292) 43-85-68
Fax: +7(7292) 43-27-56
EMail: aktsu@nursat.kz

Rector: Abdumutalip Abzhapparov

Institutes
Arts and Humanities and Natural Sciences (Arabic; Biology; Chemistry; Chinese; Foreign Languages Education; French; Geography; German; History; Information Sciences; Literature; Mathematics; Pedagogy; Philosophy; Physical Education; Physics; Psychology; Russian); **Economics and Law** (Accountancy; Economics; Finance; International Relations; Management); **Technology and Engineering** (Building Technologies; Chemical Engineering; Computer Engineering; Ecology; Geology; Marine Engineering; Mechanical Engineering; Mining Engineering; Power Engineering; Transport Engineering)

History: Founded as Aktauskij Universitet im. ŠYesenova (Sh. Yesenov Aktau State University), acquired present title 2008.

Degrees and Diplomas: *Diplom o Vysshem Obrazovanii (Bakalavr)*; *Diplom Magistra*

Academic Staff *2008-2009*	MEN	WOMEN	**TOTAL**
FULL-TIME	126	455	**581**
STAFF WITH DOCTORATE			
FULL-TIME	2	10	**12**
Student Numbers *2008-2009*			
All (Foreign Included)	3,837	3,789	**7,626**
FOREIGN ONLY	90	76	**166**

Last Updated: 18/10/10

D. SERIKBAYEV EAST KAZAKHSTAN STATE TECHNICAL UNIVERSITY

Vostočno-Kazahstanskij Gosudarstvennyj Tehničeskij Universitet im D. Serikbaeva (EKSTU)
69 A.K. Protozanov Street, 070004 Ust-Kamenogorsk
Tel: +7(723) 226-2533
Fax: +7(732) 226-7409
EMail: kanc_ektu@mail.ru
Website: http://www.ektu.kz

Rector: Galimkair Mutanovich Mutanov (2003-)
EMail: gmutanov@ektu.kz

First Vice-Rector: Ženis Kulseitov
Tel: +7(3232) 266-785 EMail: kulseitov@ektu.kz

International Relations: Aizhan Smailova, Director of Centre for International Scientific and Educational Programmes
Tel: +7(7232) 26-55-33, Fax: +7(7232) 26–25-33
EMail: ASmailova@ektu.kz

Colleges
EKSTU (Civil Engineering; Economics; Information Technology; Mechanics; Mining Engineering)

Departments
Architectural and Civil Engineering (Architecture; Building Technologies; Civil Engineering; Construction Engineering; Design; Forestry; Heating and Refrigeration; Measurement and Precision Engineering; Transport and Communications; Water Management; Wood Technology); **Economics and Management** (Accountancy; Economics; Finance; History; Law; Management; Native Language; Russian; Taxation); **Information Technology and Power Engineering** (Automation and Control Engineering; Industrial Engineering; Information Technology; Mathematics; Mathematics and Computer Science; Modern Languages; Power Engineering); **Mechanical Engineering and Transport** (Materials Engineering; Mechanical Engineering; Philosophy; Physics; Transport and Communications; Transport Management); **Military Science** (Economics; Engineering; Maintenance Technology; Military Science); **Mining and Metallurgy** (Chemistry; Environmental Studies; Geology; Metallurgical Engineering; Mining Engineering; Sports; Surveying and Mapping)

Further Information: Centres also in Zyryanovsk, Ridder, Semipalatinsk, Kurchatov, Almaty

History: Founded 1958, acquired present status 1996 and title 1997, named after D. Serikbaev.

Governing Bodies: Administrative Board

Academic Year: September to June (September-January; February-June)

Admission Requirements: Competitive entrance examinations following secondary school certificate (Atestat o srednem obrazovanii) or recognized foreign equivalent

Fees: (Tenge): 96,600-111,300 per annum

Main Language(s) of Instruction: Russian, Kazakh

International Co-operation: With universities in USA, Germany and Spain. Also participates in Tempus and IASTE programmes.

Accrediting Agencies: Ministry of Education and Science

Degrees and Diplomas: *Diplom o Vysshem Obrazovanii (Bakalavr)*; *Diplom Magistra*; *Diplom Doktora (PhD)*

Student Services: Academic counselling, Canteen, Cultural centre, Employment services, Foreign student adviser, Health services, Language programs, Nursery care, Sports facilities

Student Residential Facilities: For c. 8,000 students

Special Facilities: University Museum

Libraries: 923,467 vols, 552 periodical subscriptions

Press or Publishing House: EKTU Publishers

Academic Staff *2008-2009*	**TOTAL**
FULL-TIME	626
PART-TIME	174
Student Numbers *2008-2009*	
All (Foreign Included)	5,817

Last Updated: 18/10/10

INTERNATIONAL EDUCATIONAL CORPORATION

Meždunarodnaja Obrazovatelnaja Korporacija (IEC)

28, Ryskulbekov Street, 050043 Almaty, Almaty

Website: http://www.kazgasa.kz/

Rector: Amirlan Kussainov

Departments
Architecture (Architecture; Town Planning); **Building Technologies, Economy and Management** (Accountancy; Building Technologies; Economics; Heating and Refrigeration; Management; Materials Engineering; Safety Engineering; Surveying and Mapping; Wood Technology); **Design** (Design; Graphic Design; Industrial Design); **General (common) Natural - scientific Preparation** (Information Technology; Mathematics; Physical Education; Physics); **General Construction** (Civil Engineering; Construction Engineering; Industrial Engineering); **General Humanitarian Training** (English; Native Language; Philosophy; Political Sciences; Russian; Social Sciences; Sociology)

Degrees and Diplomas: *Diplom o Vysshem Obrazovanii (Bakalavr)*; *Diplom Magistra*; *Diplom Doktora (PhD)*

Last Updated: 29/10/10

I. ZHANSUGUROV ZHETYSU STATE UNIVERSITY

Žetysuskij Gosudarstvennyj Universitet im. I. Žansugurova (ŽHGU)

ul. I. Žansugurova 187a, 040009 Taldykorgan, Almatynskaya

Tel: +7(7282) 20-00-20

Fax: +7(7282) 22-21-94

EMail: tk_jgu@mail.ru

Website: http://vuz-zhgu.kz/

Rector: Abdimanap Bekturganov

Faculties
Art and Culture (Design; Fine Arts; Music Education; Physical Education; Sports); **Finance and Economics** (Accountancy; Economics; Finance; Management); **Humanities** (English; History; Native Language; Philology; Russian); **Law** (Civil Law; Constitutional Law; Criminal Law; Law; Philosophy; Political Sciences; Public Law); **Mathematics and Natural Science** (Biology; Chemistry; Computer Science; Ecology; Geography; Information Sciences; Information Technology; Mathematics; Mathematics Education; Physics; Science Education); **Pedagogy and Psychology** (Education; Pedagogy; Psychology; Teacher Training)

History: Founded 1972 as Taldykorgan University. Acquired present status 1994.

Governing Bodies: University Council; Scientific and Methodological Council; Council of Education

Academic Year: September to June

Admission Requirements: General or special secondary school certificate (Attestat o Srednem Obrazovanii or Diplom o Srednem Spetsialnom Obrazovanii)

Fees: (Tenge): 93,000 per annum; 46,500 per term

Main Language(s) of Instruction: Kazakh, Russian

International Co-operation: With universities in Germany, Korea and USA

Accrediting Agencies: Ministry of Education and Science

Degrees and Diplomas: *Diplom o Vysshem Obrazovanii (Bakalavr)*; *Diplom Magistra*; *Diplom Doktora (PhD)*

Student Services: Academic counselling, Cultural centre, Social counselling, Sports facilities

Student Residential Facilities: Yes

Special Facilities: History of the University Museum. Concert Hall

Libraries: Central Library

Publications: Vestnik, Scientific magazine *(annually)*

Last Updated: 25/10/10

KARAGANDA STATE INDUSTRIAL UNIVERSITY

Karagandinskij Gosudarstvennyj Industrialnyj Universitet (KMI)

30, pr. Respubliki, 101400 Temirtau, Karaganda Region

Tel: +7(7213) 915-626

Fax: +7(7213) 914-266

EMail: kgiu@mail.ru

Website: http://www.kgiu.kz/

Rector: Abdrakhman Naizabekov

Faculties
Economics (Accountancy; Economics; Management); **Engineering Technology and Automation** (Automation and Control Engineering; Chemical Engineering; Computer Engineering; Electrical Engineering; Environmental Engineering; Health Sciences; Materials Engineering; Measurement and Precision Engineering; Mechanical Engineering; Organic Chemistry; Safety Engineering; Software Engineering; Transport Engineering); **Metallurgical and Construction Engineering** (Construction Engineering; Metallurgical Engineering; Thermal Engineering)

History: Founded 1963 as Karaganda Polytechnical Institute, acquired present status and title 2006.

Academic Year: September to July

Admission Requirements: Competitive entrance examination following general or special secondary school certificate

Fees: (US Dollars): c. 800 per annum

Main Language(s) of Instruction: Kazakh, Russian

Degrees and Diplomas: *Diplom o Vysshem Obrazovanii (Bakalavr)*: 4 yrs; *Diplom Magistra*: 2 yrs; *Diplom Doktora (PhD)*: 2 yrs

Student Services: Canteen, Cultural centre, Employment services, Handicapped facilities, Health services, Language programs, Sports facilities

Student Residential Facilities: Yes

Special Facilities: Museum

Libraries: c. 290,000 vols

Publications: Republic Scientific Bulletin, In 4 branches *(biennially)*

Last Updated: 19/10/10

KARAGANDA STATE MEDICAL UNIVERSITY

Karagandinskij Gosudartsvennyj Medicinskij Universitet (KGMU)

40, Gogoly Street, 100008 Karaganda
Tel: +7(7212) 51-34-79
Fax: +7(7212) 51-89-31
EMail: info@kgmu.kz; kargmu@mail.ru
Website: http://www.kgmu.kz

Rector: Murat Teleuov
Tel: +8(7212) 513-291,
Fax: +8(3212) 513-395; +8(3212) 518-931

Vice-Rector: Zakir Bekturganov
Tel: +8(7212) 330-686; +8(7212) 513-479

International Relations: Vladimir Priz, Vice-Rector
Tel: +8(7212) 513-479

Centres

Scientific Research (Biochemistry; Histology; Hygiene; Immunology; Microbiology; Pathology; Pharmacology; Physiology)

Colleges

Paramedical Personnel (Dentistry; Medical Auxiliaries; Medicine; Midwifery; Pharmacy)

Faculties

Alternative Medicine (Acupuncture; Alternative Medicine; Homeopathy; Traditional Eastern Medicine); **Biology** (Automation and Control Engineering; Biochemistry; Biological and Life Sciences; Biology; Biophysics; Genetics; Microbiology; Molecular Biology); **Biomedicine** (Applied Chemistry; Applied Mathematics; Biochemistry; Biomedical Engineering; Biophysics; Molecular Biology; Neurosciences; Operations Research; Physical Chemistry; Physiology; Statistics; Systems Analysis); **Dentistry** (Dental Hygiene; Dentistry; Oral Pathology; Orthodontics; Periodontics; Stomatology); **Medicine** (Anaesthesiology; Anatomy; Biochemistry; Biology; Biophysics; Cardiology; Chemistry; Dentistry; Dermatology; Embryology and Reproduction Biology; Endocrinology; Epidemiology; Gastroenterology; Genetics; Gerontology; Gynaecology and Obstetrics; Haematology; Hepatology; Histology; Immunology; Inorganic Chemistry; Microbiology; Nephrology; Neurology; Neurosciences; Oncology; Ophthalmology; Organic Chemistry; Orthopaedics; Otorhinolaryngology; Paediatrics; Parasitology; Pathology; Pharmacology; Physical Therapy; Physiology; Plastic Surgery; Pneumology; Psychiatry and Mental Health; Psychotherapy; Radiology; Rheumatology; Surgery; Toxicology; Tropical Medicine; Urology; Venereology; Virology); **Paediatrics** (Paediatrics; Surgery); **Pharmacy** (Analytical Chemistry; Biotechnology; Botany; Inorganic Chemistry; Organic Chemistry; Pharmacology; Pharmacy; Physical Chemistry; Toxicology); **Postgraduate Studies** (Anaesthesiology; Cardiology; Dentistry; Dermatology; Endocrinology; Epidemiology; Genetics; Gynaecology and Obstetrics; Hygiene; Immunology; Microbiology; Neurology; Oncology; Ophthalmology; Orthopaedics; Otorhinolaryngology; Paediatrics; Parasitology; Pharmacology; Physical Therapy; Pneumology; Psychiatry and Mental Health; Radiology; Surgery; Urology; Venereology); **Public Health** (Community Health; Dietetics; Hygiene; Occupational Health; Public Health; Social and Preventive Medicine)

History: Founded 1950 as Karaganda State Medical Institute. Acquired present status and title 2009. Formerly know as Karagandy Memlekettik Medicina Akademijasy (Karaganda State Medical Academy).

Academic Year: September to July

Admission Requirements: Secondary Education Certificate (Attestat o Srednem Obrazovanii) and Common National Test (Kazakh, Russian, Languages, History of Kazakhstan, Biology, Mathematics)

Fees: (US Dollars): 2,373 per annum, foreign students, 3,035

Main Language(s) of Instruction: Kazakh, Russian, English

International Co-operation: With University of New-Mexico, School of Medicine (USA), University of Miami (USA), University of Southampton, School of Medicine (United Kingdom), Moscow Medical Academy named after I. Sechenov (Russia), Novosibirsk State Medical University (Russia), Research Institute for Medical Social Expertise and Rehabilitation (Belarus)

Accrediting Agencies: Ministry of Education and Science; Ministry of Health

Degrees and Diplomas: *Diplom o Vysshem Obrazovanii (Bakalavr)*; *Diplom Magistra*; *Diplom Doktora (PhD)*

Student Services: Academic counselling, Canteen, Cultural centre, Employment services, Foreign student adviser, Foreign Studies Centre, Handicapped facilities, Health services, Language programs, Nursery care, Social counselling, Sports facilities

Student Residential Facilities: 7 hostels for 2,050 students

Special Facilities: Museum of Anatomy. Vivarium. Research laboratories. Clinical skills Centre

Libraries: Central Library, 500,000 vols in Kazakh, Russian and English

Publications: Medicine and Ecology *(biennially)*

Press or Publishing House: University Printing House

Academic Staff *2009-2010*	MEN	WOMEN	TOTAL
FULL-TIME	144	391	**535**
PART-TIME	17	31	**48**
STAFF WITH DOCTORATE			
FULL-TIME	24	24	**48**
PART-TIME	3	1	**4**
Student Numbers *2009-2010*			
All (Foreign Included)	1,327	2,948	**4,275**
FOREIGN ONLY	217	82	**299**

Last Updated: 07/10/10

KARAGANDA STATE TECHNICAL UNIVERSITY

Karagandinskij Gosudartsvennyj Tehničeskij Universitet (KGTU)

bulvar Mira 56, 100027 Karaganda
Tel: +7(7212) 56-51-92
Fax: +7(7212) 56-03-28
EMail: kargtu@kstu.kz; pk@kstu.kz
Website: http://www.kstu.kz

Rector: Arstan Gazaliev

Faculties

Architecture and Building (Architecture; Building Technologies; Design); **Economics and Management** (Accountancy; Economics; Management; Marketing; Service Trades); **Information Technology** (Computer Engineering; Computer Science; Information Technology; Instrument Making; Software Engineering); **Machine Building** (Materials Engineering; Mechanical Engineering; Metallurgical Engineering); **Military Engineering** (Military Science); **Mining** (Biotechnology; Chemical Engineering; Geology; Mining Engineering; Organic Chemistry; Safety Engineering; Surveying and Mapping); **Power Engineering, Communication and Automation** (Automation and Control Engineering; Electronic Engineering; Heating and Refrigeration; Power Engineering; Telecommunications Engineering); **Road Transport** (Transport and Communications; Transport Management)

Further Information: Also Technological College and Technical Lyceum.

History: Founded 1953 as Karaganda Mining Institute. Reorganized 1958 and acquired present status and title 1996.

Governing Bodies: Scientific Board

Academic Year: September to June

Admission Requirements: Competitive entrance examination of National Centre of State Education Standards following general or special secondary school certificate

Fees: (US Dollars): 1,200 per annum

Main Language(s) of Instruction: Kazakh, Russian

International Co-operation: With universities in the Russian Federation. Also participates in Soros Foundation; Resource Network for Economics and Business Education; Accels; Nafsa; Tempus-Tacis; Nefems (UK); Usis; Irex; Cep; Ansys; Cad-Fem (Germany)

Degrees and Diplomas: *Diplom o Vysshem Obrazovanii (Bakalavr)*; *Diplom Magistra*; *Diplom Doktora (PhD)*

Student Services: Academic counselling, Canteen, Cultural centre, Employment services, Foreign student adviser, Health services, Language programs, Social counselling, Sports facilities

Special Facilities: University History Museum; Geological Museum

Libraries: Central Library, total, c. 1.5m. Vols

Publications: Scientific Publications *(annually)*

Academic Staff *2008-2009*	MEN	WOMEN	**TOTAL**
FULL-TIME	307	355	**662**
PART-TIME	87	15	**102**
STAFF WITH DOCTORATE			
FULL-TIME	44	3	**47**
PART-TIME	3	–	**3**
Student Numbers *2008-2009*			
All (Foreign Included)	4,351	2,571	**6,922**
FOREIGN ONLY	54	17	**71**

Part-time students, 193. **Distance students**, 814.

Last Updated: 07/10/10

KAZAKH ABYLAI KHAN UNIVERSITY OF INTERNATIONAL RELATIONS AND WORLD LANGUAGES

Abylai Khan Atyndagy Kazak Halykaralyk Katynastar Zhane Alem Tilderi Universiteti

ul. Muratbayev 200, 050022 Almaty
Tel: +7(727) 292-23-63
Fax: +7(727) 292-44-73
EMail: kazumo@ablaikhan.kz
Website: http://www.ablaikhan.kz

Rector: Salima Sagievna Kunanbayeva (2000-)
Tel: +7(727) 292-23-63

Vice-Rector for Educational Affairs: Batima Zhunagulova
Tel: +7(727) 292-63-23, Fax: +7(727) 292-44-73

International Relations: Nelly S. Asmatullayeva, Head of International Cooperation Department
Tel: +7(727) 260-12-44, Fax: +7(727) 292-44-73
EMail: asmatullayeva@ablaikhan.kz; cip@ablaikhan.kz

Faculties

Evening and Correspondence Studies (Modern Languages; Teacher Training); **Foreign Languages** (English; Modern Languages; Teacher Training); **Foreign Philology and Oriental Studies** (Linguistics; Modern Languages; Oriental Studies; Philology; Religion); **International Relations** (Arts and Humanities; Business Administration; Information Sciences; International Law; International Relations; Law; Social Sciences); **Management and International Communication** (Business Administration; Business and Commerce; International Relations; Management; Marketing; Public Relations; Service Trades; Tourism); **Translation** (Arts and Humanities; English; French; German; Modern Languages; Translation and Interpretation)

History: Founded 1941 as Teacher Training Institute of Foreign Languages. Acquired present status 1998.

Governing Bodies: Rectorate

Academic Year: September to July

Admission Requirements: Secondary school certificate (Atestat o srednem obrazovanii)

Fees: (Tenge): Undergraduate Studies, 180,000-450,000 per annum; Graduate Studies, 400,000-500,000 per annum; Doctoral Studies, 850,000-1,200,000 per annum; International Students, 30,000 per annum

Main Language(s) of Instruction: Russian, Kazakh, English, French, German

International Co-operation: With universities in USA, Egypt, Germany, France, Russian Federation, Spain, Turkey, Belgium, South Korea and New Zealand

Accrediting Agencies: Ministry of Education and Science

Degrees and Diplomas: *Diplom o Vysshem Obrazovanii (Bakalavr)*: Documentation Studies; Management; Public Relations; Marketing and Commerce; Tourism; International Law; World Economy; Regional Studies; Journalism; International Relations; Religion; Foreign Languages; Translation, 4 yrs; *Diplom Magistra*: Documentation Studies; Management; Public Relations; Marketing and Commerce; Tourism; International Law; World Economy; Regional Studies; Journalism; International Relations; Religion; Foreign Languages; Translation, 2 yrs; *Diplom Doktora (PhD)*: 3 yrs

Student Services: Academic counselling, Canteen, Cultural centre, Employment services, Foreign student adviser, Foreign Studies Centre, Health services, Language programs, Nursery care, Social counselling, Sports facilities

Student Residential Facilities: Yes

Special Facilities: Auditoriums. Language Laboratories. Videoroom. Computer rooms

Libraries: Library of foreign literature, c. 1m vols. Also 10 University Cultural Resources Centres from foreign countries

Publications: Vestnik, Scientific staff publications *(annually)*

Academic Staff *2008-2009*	**TOTAL**
FULL-TIME	**545**
PART-TIME	**59**
STAFF WITH DOCTORATE	
FULL-TIME	**244**
Student Numbers *2011-2012*	
All (Foreign Included)	**5,218**

Last Updated: 12/02/10

KAZAKH HUMANITARIAN LAW UNIVERSITY

Kazahskij Gumanitarno-Juridičeskij Universitet (KAZGJUU)

8, Korgalzhyn Road, 010000 Astana, Akmola
Tel: +7(7272) 32-33-18
Fax: +7(7272) 32-29-05
EMail: deviant_men@mail.ru; kazzan.kazgua@mail.ru
Website: http://www.kazuhl.kz/

Rector: Marat Kogamov

Centres

Business Education and Marketing Research (Arabic; Chinese; English; Human Resources; Law; Management; Marketing; Native Language); **Master's and Doctorate PhD** (Economics; International Law; Law; Sociology; Translation and Interpretation)

Faculties

Business Law (Commercial Law; International Law)

History: Founded 1994 as Kazakh State Law Institute. Acquired present title and status 2002.

Governing Bodies: Board of Departments' Directors

Academic Year: September to June

Admission Requirements: Competitive entrance examination following general or special secondary school certificate (Attestat o Srednem Obrazovanii or Diplom o Srednem Spetsialnom Obrazovanii)

Fees: (US Dollars): 1,200 per annum

Main Language(s) of Instruction: Kazakh, Russian

International Co-operation: With universities in Italy, Australia, Korea, France, Japan and Russian Federation

Degrees and Diplomas: *Diplom o Vysshem Obrazovanii (Bakalavr)*; *Diplom Magistra*; *Diplom Doktora (PhD)*

Student Services: Academic counselling, Canteen, Cultural centre, Employment services, Foreign student adviser, Foreign Studies Centre, Health services, Language programs, Social counselling, Sports facilities

Student Residential Facilities: 2 hostels (510 rooms), 60 rooms for families, 15 flats

Special Facilities: University Museum

Libraries: Total 493,173 vols

Publications: State and Law Journal *(3 per annum)*

Press or Publishing House: The University's Publishing House

Last Updated: 20/10/10

KAZAKH KURMANGAZY NATIONAL CONSERVATORY

Kazahskaja Nacionalnaja Konservatorija im. Kurmanganzy

pr. Abylay Khan, 86, 050000 Almaty
Tel: +7(727) 261-76-40
Fax: +7(727) 272-63-48
EMail: info@conservatoire.kz
Website: http://conservatoire.kz/news.php

Rector: Zhanija Yakhiyevna Aubakirova Tel: +7(727) 261-76-40

Departments

Obschevuzovskie (Arts and Humanities; Educational Technology; Social Sciences)

Faculties

Instrumental Performance (Musical Instruments); **Folk Music** (Jazz and Popular Music; Musical Instruments; Singing); **Musicology and Management** (Art Management; Educational Psychology; Music Education; Musicology); **Singing and Conducting** (Conducting; Singing)

History: Created 1944.

Admission Requirements: Diplom o Srednem Spetsialnom Obrazovanii (Secondary School Certificate) or equivalent.

Fees: (US Dollars): Full-time, 1,200; part-time, 550 (home students); Full-time, 1,800 (overseas students)

Degrees and Diplomas: *Diplom o Vysshem Obrazovanii (Bakalavr); Diplom o Vysshem Obrazovanii (Specialist); Diplom Magistra*

Last Updated: 20/10/10

KAZAKH NATIONAL PEDAGOGICAL UNIVERSITY NAMED AFTER ABAI

Kazahskij Nacionalnij Pedagogičeskij Universitet im. Abaya (AASU)

Prosp. Dostyk 13, 050010 Almaty
Tel: +7(272) 916-339
Fax: +7(272) 916-406
EMail: international@kaznpu.kz
Website: http://www.kaznpu.kz

Rector: Serik Zhaylauovich Praliyev (2008-)
Tel: +7(272) 913-326, Fax: +7(272) 913-050
EMail: rector@kaznpu.kz

Chairman, Committee for Youth Affairs: Arman Ukeevich Abdikalykov EMail: kdm519@kaznpu.kz

International Relations: Dana Temirtaevna Medeuova, Vice-Rector for International Relations
Tel: +7(272) 913-692, Fax: +7(272) 913-692

Departments

Foreign Languages (English; Modern Languages); **General Psychology** (Psychology); **Military Science** (Military Science; Psychology); **Pedagogy** (Pedagogy; Psychology); **Philosophy and Methodology of Science** (Philosophy); **Physical Culture and Sports** (Physical Education; Sports); **Political Sciences and Sociology** (Political Sciences; Sociology); **State Language** (Native Language)

Faculties

Chemistry and Biology (Biochemistry; Biology; Botany; Chemistry; Ecology; Geography; Natural Sciences; Organic Chemistry; Physiology; Psychology; Zoology); **Finance and Economics** (Accountancy; Banking; Business and Commerce; Economics; Finance; Management; Marketing; Taxation); **Geography and Environmental Studies** (Ecology; Environmental Studies; Geography; Geography (Human); Tourism); **Graphics Arts** (Art History; Dance; Design; Fine Arts; Graphic Arts; Music; Painting and Drawing); **History** (Ancient Civilizations; Contemporary History; Economics; English; Geography; History; Law; Medieval Studies; Modern History; Museum Studies; Political Sciences; Regional Studies); **International Relations and Law** (Administrative Law; Constitutional Law; Criminal Law; Criminology; English; History; History of Law; Human Rights; International Law; International Relations; Labour Law; Private Law; Public Administration; Public Law); **Philology** (Arabic; Chinese; English; German; Grammar; Japanese; Korean; Linguistics; Literature; Persian; Philology; Translation and Interpretation; Turkish); **Physical Education and Basic Military Training** (Physical Education; Sports); **Physics and Mathematics** (Applied Mathematics; Astronomy and Space Science; Computer Science; Mathematics; Mathematics Education; Mechanics; Physics); **Psychology and Pedagogy** (Pedagogy; Physical Education; Preschool Education; Primary Education; Psychology; Social Psychology; Special Education)

Schools

Preparatory Studies *(For foreign students)* (Literature; Russian)

Further Information: Also preparatory courses for foreign students in Kazakh and Russian languages

History: Founded 1928 as Kazakh State University. Renamed Kazakh State Pedagogical Institute 1930, and Almaty State University named after Abai 1991. Acquired present status and title 2003.

Governing Bodies: Research Council

Academic Year: September to June (September-December; January-June)

Admission Requirements: Competitive entrance examination following secondary school certificate

Fees: None

Main Language(s) of Instruction: Kazakh, Russian

International Co-operation: With universities in 30 countries

Accrediting Agencies: Ministry of Education and Science

Degrees and Diplomas: *Diplom o Vysshem Obrazovanii (Bakalavr); Diplom Magistra; Diplom Doktora (PhD)*

Student Services: Academic counselling, Canteen, Foreign student adviser, Health services, Social counselling, Sports facilities

Student Residential Facilities: For 2,500 students

Special Facilities: Museum of the University's history

Libraries: University Library, c. 1m. vols

Publications: Functioning Languages in the Republic of Kazakhstan *(annually)*; International Relations Problems *(annually)*; Principles of Training Teachers at the University *(annually)*; Problems of Ethnopolicy in Kazakhstan *(annually)*; Problems of Geoecology in Kazakhstan *(annually)*; Problems of Sociology *(annually)*

Press or Publishing House: University Publishing Centre

Last Updated: 21/10/10

KAZAKH NATIONAL UNIVERSITY OF AGRICULTURE

Kazahskij Nacionalnij Agrarnyj Universitet (KGAU)

prosp. Abaia 8, 050010 Almaty
Tel: +7(7272) 62-19-48
Fax: +7(7272) 64-24-09
EMail: info@kaznau.kz; info@mail.ru
Website: http://www.kaznau.kz/

Rector: Tlektes Espolov (2001-) EMail: rector@kaznau.kz

Departments

Foreign Languages (English; French; German; Modern Languages); **History and Political Science** (History; Political Sciences); **Kazakh Language** (Native Language); **Philosophy and Sociology** (Philosophy; Sociology); **Physical Education and Sport** (Physical Education; Sports); **Russian Language** (Russian)

Faculties

Agronomy, Agricultural Chemistry and Plant Protection (Agronomy; Biology; Chemistry; Ecology; Horticulture; Plant and Crop Protection; Soil Science); **Animal Health and Zootechnology** (Animal Husbandry; Biochemistry; Fishery; Food Technology; Physiology; Veterinary Science; Zoology); **Economics and Finance** (Accountancy; Agricultural Business; Banking; Economics; Finance; Law; Management; Marketing); **Energy and Information Systems** (Automation and Control Engineering; Computer Science; Electrical and Electronic Equipment and Maintenance; Energy Engineering; Information Sciences; Mathematics; Measurement and Precision Engineering; Physics; Software Engineering); **Engineering and Technology** (Agricultural Engineering; Machine Building; Maintenance Technology; Technology; Transport and Communications;

Transport Management; Vocational Education); **Forestry, Land and Water Resources** (Forest Management; Forest Products; Forestry; Hydraulic Engineering; Irrigation; Natural Resources; Surveying and Mapping; Water Management); **Veterinary Medicine and Biotechnology** (Biotechnology; Gynaecology and Obstetrics; Immunology; Microbiology; Parasitology; Pharmacology; Surgery; Veterinary Science; Virology)

History: Founded 1929 as Kazakh State Institute of Agriculture. Became Kazakh State University of Agriculture (Kazahskij Gosudarstvennyj Agrarnij Universitet) in 1996. Acquired current title and status in 2001.

Academic Year: September to July

Admission Requirements: Competitive entrance examination following general or special secondary school certificate

Fees: None

Main Language(s) of Instruction: Kazakh, Russian

Degrees and Diplomas: *Diplom o Vysshem Obrazovanii (Bakalavr)*; *Diplom o Vysshem Obrazovanii (Specialist)*; *Diplom Magistra*; *Diplom Doktora (PhD)*

Special Facilities: University History Museum; Anatomy Museum; Parasitology Museum

Libraries: c. 800,000 vols

Publications: Scientific Publications *(annually)*

Last Updated: 20/10/10

KAZAKH NATIONAL UNIVERSITY OF ARTS

Kazahskij Nacionalnij Universitet Iskusstv (KAZNUA)

33, Podeda avenue, 010000 Astana, Akmola

Tel: +7(7172) 44-37-21

Fax: +7(7172) 44-37-23

Rector: Aiman Musakhodzhayeva

Programmes

Cinema and Television (Cinema and Television); **Dance** (Dance); **Fine Arts** (Fine Arts); **Music** (Music); **Theatre** (Theatre)

History: Founded 1998.

Degrees and Diplomas: *Diplom o Vysshem Obrazovanii (Bakalavr)*; *Diplom Magistra*

Last Updated: 29/10/10

KAZAKH STATE WOMEN'S PEDAGOGICAL INSTITUTE

Kazahskij Gosudarstvennyj Ženskij Pedagogičeskij Institut

ul. Aiteke-bi 99, 050000 Almaty

Tel: +7(7272) 33-18-36

EMail: genpi@front.ru; zhenpi@mail.online.kz; zhen.nauka@mail.ru

Website: http://www.genpi.front.ru/

Rector: Shamsha Berkimbayeva

Faculties

History and Philology (History; Modern Languages; Native Language; Native Language Education; Philology; Russian); **Music Education and Culture** (Cultural Studies; Dance; Music Education; Musical Instruments); **Natural Sciences** (Biology; Chemistry; Geography; Information Technology; Mathematics; Physics); **Pedagogy and Psychology** (Pedagogy; Psychology)

History: Founded 1944.

Academic Year: September to July

Admission Requirements: Competitive entrance examination following general or special secondary school certificate

Main Language(s) of Instruction: Kazakh, Russian

Degrees and Diplomas: *Diplom o Vysshem Obrazovanii (Bakalavr) (BA)*: 4 yrs; *Diplom Magistra*: a further 3 yrs

Student Residential Facilities: Yes

Libraries: Total: c. 860,000 vols

Last Updated: 21/10/10

KAZAKH TRANSPORT AND COMMUNICATIONS ACADEMY M. TYNYSHPAEVA

Kazahskaja Akademija Transporta i Kommunikatsii im. M. Tynyshpaeva

ul. Shevchenko 97 (ug. ul. Masanchi), 050012 Almaty

Tel: +7(727) 292-09-86

Fax: +7(727) 292-57-21

EMail: info@kazatk.kz

Website: http://www.kazatk.kz/

President and Rector: Adilbek Kozhabekovich Botabekov

Faculties

Automation and Telecommunications (Automation and Control Engineering; Computer Engineering; Computer Networks; Data Processing; Electrical Engineering; Electronic Engineering; Information Technology; Software Engineering; Telecommunications Engineering); **Construction** (Civil Engineering; Construction Engineering; Road Engineering; Transport Engineering); **Economics** (Accountancy; Economics; Finance; Marketing; Tourism); **General Education** (History; Modern Languages; Native Language; Natural Sciences; Philosophy; Physical Education; Political Sciences; Russian; Sports); **Organization of Transportation and Logistics** (Transport and Communications; Transport Management); **Transport Engineering** (Measurement and Precision Engineering; Transport Engineering)

Further Information: Also Faculty of Part-time Education

History: Founded 1976.

Governing Bodies: Scientific Council

Degrees and Diplomas: *Diplom o Vysshem Obrazovanii (Bakalavr)*; *Diplom Magistra*; *Diplom Doktora (PhD)*

Libraries: Yes. Electronic catalog.

Academic Staff *2009-2010*: Total: c. 1,000

Student Numbers *2009-2010*: Total: c. 12,000

Last Updated: 20/10/10

KAZAKH T. ZHURGENOV NATIONAL ACADEMY OF ART

Kazahskaja Nacionalnaja Akademija Iskusstva im. T. Žurgenova

ul. Panfilova 127, 050000 Almaty

Tel: +7(727) 261-76-40

EMail: kaznai@art-oner.kz

Website: http://www.art-oner.kz/

Rector: Arystanbek Muhamediuly

Faculties

Choreography (Dance); **Design and Decorative Arts** (Computer Graphics; Fashion Design; Graphic Design; Handicrafts; Interior Design); **Film and Television** (Cinema and Television; Radio and Television Broadcasting); **History of Art** (Art History; Cinema and Television; Theatre); **Musical Arts** (Dance; Music; Performing Arts; Singing); **Painting and Sculpture** (Painting and Drawing; Sculpture); **Theatre Arts** (Acting; Display and Stage Design; Singing; Theatre)

History: Founded in 1977 as Almaty State Institute of Art and Performing Arts. Acquired current title and status 2001.

Degrees and Diplomas: *Diplom o Vysshem Obrazovanii (Bakalavr)*; *Diplom Magistra*; *Diplom Doktora (PhD)*

Last Updated: 20/10/10

KH. DOSMUHAMEDOV ATYRAU STATE UNIVERSITY

Atyrauskij Gosudarstvennyj Universitet im. Kh. Dosmuhamedova

Studencheskii Str., 212, 060011 Atyrau

Tel: +7(7122) 27-01-56

EMail: atyrauuniv@nursat.kz

Website: http://www.atyrauuniv.kz/

Rector: Altai Kazmagambetov

Faculties

Distance Education; **Economics, Finance and Management** (Economics; Finance; Management); **Foreign Languages** (Modern Languages; Translation and Interpretation); **Humanities** (Arts and Humanities; Geography; History; Journalism; Library Science; Literature; Native Language; Philology; Russian; Tourism); **Law** (Civil Law; Criminology; Law); **Natural Science** (Agronomy; Animal Husbandry; Biology; Chemistry; Environmental Studies; Fishery; Military Science; Physical Education; Soil Science; Sports; Water Management); **Pedagogy, Psychology and Art** (Acting; Educational Psychology; Fashion Design; Fine Arts; Graphic Design; Music Education; Pedagogy; Performing Arts; Preschool Education; Primary Education; Psychology); **Physics, Mathematics and Information Technology** (Computer Science; Mathematics; Physics)

History: Created 1950.

Degrees and Diplomas: *Diplom o Vysshem Obrazovanii (Bakalavr)*; *Diplom o Vysshem Obrazovanii (Specialist)*; *Diplom Magistra*; *Diplom Doktora (PhD)*

Last Updated: 04/02/10

K.I. SATBAYEV KAZAKH NATIONAL TECHNICAL UNIVERSITY

Kazahskij Nacionalnij Tehničeskij Universitet im K.I. Satpaeva (KAZNTU)

22 Satpaev Street, 050013 Almaty
Tel: +7(727) 292-43-04
Fax: +7(727) 292-43-04
EMail: gmoldrah@yahoo.com
Website: http://www.ntu.kz

Rector: Zheksenbek Adylov (2008-)
Tel: +7(727) 292-69-01 EMail: adilov@ntu.kz

Director: Gulnara Sarsenbayeva
Tel: +7(727) 257-71-27 EMail: sarsenbayeva@ntu.kz

Institutes

Information Technology (Computer Science; Electrical Engineering; Information Technology; Software Engineering); **Architecture and Civil Engineering** (Architecture; Biotechnology; Civil Engineering; Construction Engineering; Design; Ecology; Environmental Studies; Safety Engineering); **Automation and Telecommunication** (Automation and Control Engineering; Electronic Engineering; Telecommunications Engineering); **Economy and Business** (Accountancy; Economics; Finance; Management; Marketing; Public Administration); **Geological Prospecting** (Earth Sciences; Geological Engineering; Geophysics; Mineralogy); **High Technologies and Sustainable Development** (Chemistry; Ecology; Physics); **Machine Building** (Engineering; Machine Building; Materials Engineering; Mechanics); **Metallurgical Engineering and Polygraphy** (Metal Techniques; Metallurgical Engineering); **Oil and Gas** (Geology; Geophysics; Organic Chemistry; Petroleum and Gas Engineering)

Further Information: Also KazNTU College

History: Founded 1933 as Semipalatinsk Geological Survey Institute. Transferred to Almaty, became Kazakh Mining and Smelting Institute 1934. Became Kazakh Polytechnical Institute 1960. Tranformed into Kazakh National Technical University 1994. Acquired present title 1999. Acquired present status 2001.

Academic Year: September to July

Admission Requirements: Secondary school certificate (attestat zrelosty) and national entrance examination; national test

Fees: (Tenge): 250,000 per annum

Main Language(s) of Instruction: Kazakh, Russian

International Co-operation: With institutions in Cyprus, France, USA, China, Germany, Russia, Italy, Poland, United Kingdom, USA.

Accrediting Agencies: National Accreditation Centre of the Republic of Kazakhstan (NAC); Accreditation Agency ABET (USA); Association of Engineering Education of Russia; American University Accreditation Council (AUAC).

Degrees and Diplomas: *Diplom o Vysshem Obrazovanii (Bakalavr)*; *Diplom Magistra*; *Diplom Doktora (PhD)*: Petroleum Engineering and Petrogeology; Industrial Ecology; Metallurgical Engineering, Automation and Management of Technological Process and Production; Economics; Computer and Software Engineering; Radio Engineering, Electronics and Telecommunication; Systems Analysis, Management and Information Processing; Mechatronics and Robotics; Printing Engineering; Programming Engineering; Machine Building; Information Systems

Student Services: Academic counselling, Canteen, Cultural centre, Employment services, Foreign student adviser, Foreign Studies Centre, Health services, Language programs, Nursery care, Social counselling, Sports facilities

Student Residential Facilities: 5 campuses for over 2,000 students

Special Facilities: Museum, Art Gallery; Observatory; Technopark: Open Laboratory; Coliseum

Libraries: 2,000,000 vols; E-library.

Publications: KazNTU Vestnik, Papers on Science and Technology *(bimonthly)*

Academic Staff *2009-2010*	MEN	WOMEN	TOTAL
FULL-TIME	574	717	**1,291**
PART-TIME	82	78	**160**
STAFF WITH DOCTORATE			
FULL-TIME	373	268	**641**
PART-TIME	32	8	**40**
Student Numbers *2008-2009*			
All (Foreign Included)	9,902	5,885	**15,787**
FOREIGN ONLY	214	335	**549**

Part-time students, 200. **Distance students**, 1,279.

Last Updated: 07/10/10

KORKYT ATA KYZYLORDA STATE UNIVERSITY

Kyzylordinskij Gosudarstvennyj Universitet im. Korkyt Ata (KSU)

ul. Aiteke-bi 29a, 120014 Kyzylorda
Tel: +7(7242) 26-17-16
Fax: +7(7242) 26-27-14
EMail: ksu@korkyt.kz
Website: http://www.korkyt.kz

Rector: Baizak Momynbaev

Faculties

Agro-technical (Agricultural Engineering; Agricultural Equipment; Heating and Refrigeration; Mechanical Engineering; Mechanics; Physics; Transport and Communications); **Economics** (Accountancy; Economics; Finance; Management; Public Administration); **Engineering and Economics** *(Distance education)* (Accountancy; Agriculture; Computer Engineering; Construction Engineering; Economics; Environmental Studies; Finance; Information Sciences; Measurement and Precision Engineering; Power Engineering; Software Engineering; Transport and Communications; Water Management); **History and Law** (Ancient Civilizations; Economics; Ethnology; History; Law); **Humanities and Education** *(Distance Education)* (Archaeology; Biology; Business Administration; Chemistry; Design; Ecology; Economics; Ethnology; Fine Arts; Geography; History; Information Sciences; Journalism; Law; Literature; Mathematics; Military Science; Modern Languages; Music Education; Native Language; Pedagogy; Physical Education; Physics; Primary Education; Psychology; Russian; Sports; Translation and Interpretation; Vocational Education); **Music and Education** (Dance; Music; Music Education; Musical Instruments; Pedagogy; Psychology); **Natural History** (Biology; Chemistry; Ecology; Environmental Studies; Geography; Inorganic Chemistry; Military Science; Natural Sciences; Physical Education; Sports); **Oil and Gas** (Chemistry; Ecology; Electrical Engineering; Natural Resources; Petroleum and Gas Engineering; Safety Engineering); **Philology** (Arabic; French; German; Germanic Languages; Journalism; Literature; Native Language; Oriental Languages; Philology; Romance Languages; Russian; Translation and Interpretation; Turkish); **Physics and Mathematics** (Computer Science; Fashion Design; Fine Arts; Mathematics; Mathematics Education; Painting and Drawing; Physics; Vocational Education)

Schools

Polytechnics (Architecture; Building Technologies; Computer Engineering; Computer Science; Information Technology; Mathematics; Software Engineering; Water Management)

Further Information: Also Postgraduate studies

History: Founded 1937 as Kyzylorda Pedagogical Institute. Acquired present status and title 1998 following merger with 'I. Žahajev' Kyzylorda Polytechnical Institute (founded 1976), named after Korkyt Ata.

Governing Bodies: Academic Council; Rectorate

Academic Year: September to June (September-January; February-June)

Admission Requirements: Competitive entrance examination following secondary school certificate or special vocational school diploma, or special technical professional college diploma

Fees: (Tenge): 118,000 per annum

Main Language(s) of Instruction: Kazakh, Russian

Degrees and Diplomas: *Diplom o Vysshem Obrazovanii (Bakalavr)*; *Diplom Magistra*

Student Services: Academic counselling, Canteen, Cultural centre, Foreign student adviser, Health services, Language programs, Nursery care, Social counselling, Sports facilities

Student Residential Facilities: For 656 students

Special Facilities: University History Museum; Ethnography Museum. Art Gallery. International Centre for Study of Korkyt Ata Legacy; Computer Centre

Libraries: Total: c. 1,780,000 printed matter, including 580,000 textbooks

Publications: Vestnik of KSU, Scientific Magazine *(quarterly)*

Last Updated: 21/10/10

KOSTANAI STATE PEDAGOGICAL INSTITUTE

Kostanaiskij Gosudarstvennyj Pedagogičeskij Institut

ul. Tarana, 118, 11000 Kostanai
Tel: +7(714-2) 53-04-55
Fax: +7(714-2) 53-04-55
EMail: kgpi118@mail.ru; kspi@mail.kz
Website: http://www.kspi.kz

Rector: Kuat Maratuly Baimirzaev

Faculties

Distance Learning (Biology; Chemistry; Computer Science; Economics; Geography; History; Law; Literature; Mathematics; Modern Languages; Music Education; Native Language; Pedagogy; Physical Education; Physics; Preschool Education; Psychology; Russian; Sports; Tourism; Visual Arts; Vocational Education); **History and Art** (Art History; Economics; History; Law; Music Education; Musical Instruments; Visual Arts); **Natural Science and Mathematics** (Biology; Chemistry; Computer Science; Geography; Mathematics; Physics); **Philology** (English; French; German; Germanic Languages; Modern Languages; Native Language; Oriental Languages; Philology; Romance Languages; Russian; Turkish); **Physical Education and Sports** (Physical Education; Sports; Tourism); **Psychology and Pedagogy** (Preschool Education; Primary Education; Psychology; Special Education)

Degrees and Diplomas: *Diplom o Vysshem Obrazovanii (Bakalavr)*; *Diplom Magistra*

Last Updated: 21/10/10

KOSTANAI STATE UNIVERSITY NAMED AFTER AHMET BAITURSYNOV

Kostanaiskij Gosudarstvennyj Universitet im. Ahmet Baitursynova

ul. Baitursynova, 47, 110000 Kostanai
Tel: +7(7142) 511-195
Website: http://www.ksu.kst.kz/

Rector: Askar Nametov Myrzakhmetovich

Faculties

Agro-Biology (Agronomy; Biology; Chemistry; Ecology); **Economics** (Accountancy; Banking; Economics; Finance; Management; Marketing); **Engineering** (Agricultural Engineering; Energy Engineering; Engineering; Machine Building; Physics; Transport Engineering); **Humanities and Social Sciences** (English; German; History; Journalism; Native Language; Philology; Psychology; Russian; Translation and Interpretation); **Information Technology**; **Law** (Law); **Veterinary and Food Technology** (Biotechnology; Food Technology; Veterinary Science; Zoology)

History: Founded 1939, acquired present status and title 1992.

Academic Year: September to July

Admission Requirements: Competitive entrance examination following general or special secondary school certificate

Fees: (US Dollars): c. 1,000 per annum

Main Language(s) of Instruction: Kazakh, Russian and English

Degrees and Diplomas: *Diplom o Vysshem Obrazovanii (Bakalavr) (BA)*: 4 yrs; *Diplom o Vysshem Obrazovanii (Specialist)*; *Diplom Magistra*: A further 2 yrs; *Diplom Doktora (PhD)*

Special Facilities: University History Museum

Libraries: c. 400,000 vols

Publications: Scientific Publications *(annually)*; Vestnik Nauky

Academic Staff *2009-2010*: Total 200
STAFF WITH DOCTORATE: Total 20
Last Updated: 21/01/10

K. ZHUBANOV AKTOBE STATE UNIVERSITY

Aktiubinskij Gosudarstvennyj Universitet im. K. Žubanova

Br. Zhubanov Street, 263, 030000 Aktobe
Tel: +7(7132) 54-37-56
Fax: +7(7132) 56-78-43
EMail: zhubanov@samgau.kz; mail@samgau.kz
Website: http://www.agu.kz/

Rector: Kenžegali Kenžebaiev
Tel: +7(3132) 567-843, Fax: +7(3132) 567-843
EMail: zhubanov@mail.ru

Faculties

Economics (Accountancy; Banking; Business Administration; Economics; Finance; International Economics; Management; Marketing; Mathematics); **Foreign Languages** (German; Translation and Interpretation); **History and Philology**; **Law** (Law); **Natural Science** (Biology; Chemistry; Ecology; Psychology); **Physics and Mathematics** (Computer Science; Information Sciences; Mathematics; Physics); **Technology** (Chemical Engineering; Design; Metal Techniques; Petroleum and Gas Engineering; Transport and Communications; Transport Management)

History: Created 1966.

Degrees and Diplomas: *Diplom o Vysshem Obrazovanii (Bakalavr)*; *Diplom Magistra*; *Diplom Doktora (PhD)*

Last Updated: 12/02/10

L.N. GUMILYOV EURASIAN NATIONAL UNIVERSITY

Evrazijskij Natsionalnyj Universitet im. L.N. Gumileva (ENU)

ul. Munaitpasova 5, 010008 Astana
Tel: +8(3172) 35-38-06
Fax: +8(3172) 35-38-08
EMail: rector@enu.kz
Website: http://www.enu.kz/

Rector: Yerlan B. Sydykov (2011-) Tel: +8(7172) 35-39-00

Administrative Officer: A.Z. Ismailov

International Relations: Serik Murzakhmetovich Shaikhin, Prorektor, International Affairs Tel: +8(3172) 353-807

Faculties

Additional Education and Training; **Architecture, Design and Performing Arts** (Architecture; Design; Fine Arts); **Civil Engineering** (Building Technologies; Civil Engineering; Computer Graphics; Construction Engineering; Materials Engineering; Measurement and Precision Engineering; Surveying and Mapping; Thermal Engineering; Transport Engineering); **Economics** (Accountancy; Economics; Finance; Management; Tourism); **Information Technology** (Computer Science; Information Technology); **International Relations** (International Relations; Modern Languages; Oriental Studies; Political Sciences; Regional Studies); **Journalism and Political Science** (Political Sciences; Printing and Printmaking; Public Relations; Radio and Television Broadcasting); **Mechanics and Mathematics** (Applied Mathematics; Mathematics; Mechanics); **Natural Sciences** (Biology; Biotechnology; Chemical

Engineering; Engineering Management; Environmental Engineering; Geography; Natural Sciences); **Philology** (English; French; German; Linguistics; Literature; Modern Languages; Native Language; Philology; Russian; Translation and Interpretation); **Physics and Technics** (Electronic Engineering; Nuclear Physics; Physics; Radiophysics; Systems Analysis; Telecommunications Engineering); **Social Sciences** (Archaeology; Cultural Studies; Ethnology; History; Pedagogy; Physical Education; Psychology; Religious Studies; Social Sciences; Social Work; Sociology; Sports)

Schools

Law (Civil Law; Constitutional Law; Criminal Law; International Law; Labour Law; Law)

History: Founded 1996, acquired present title 2000.

Academic Year: September to June (September-January; February-June)

Admission Requirements: Competitive entrance examination following general or special secondary school certificate

Fees: (US Dollars): c. 500-1,000 per annum

Main Language(s) of Instruction: Kazakh, Russian

Degrees and Diplomas: *Diplom o Vysshem Obrazovanii (Bakalavr)*; *Diplom Magistra*; *Diplom Doktora (PhD)*

Student Services: Academic counselling, Canteen, Cultural centre, Health services, Social counselling, Sports facilities

Student Residential Facilities: Yes

Special Facilities: Museum of Biology. Youth Centre. Philharmonic Orchestra

Libraries: c. 1m. vols; 360 periodical subscriptions

Publications: Eurasian University Vestnik, Scientific Journal *(annually)*

Press or Publishing House: 'Eurasia'

Academic Staff *2009-2010*	**TOTAL**
FULL-TIME	**1,050**
PART-TIME	**120**
STAFF WITH DOCTORATE	
FULL-TIME	c. **360**
Student Numbers *2009-2010*	
All (Foreign Included)	c. **9,000**

Last Updated: 22/10/10

MARAT OSPANOV WESTERN KAZAKHSTAN STATE MEDICAL ACADEMY

Zapadno-Kazahstanskaja Gosudarstvennaja Medicinskaja Akademija im M. Ospanova

ul. Maresyeva 68, 030019 Aktobe
Tel: +7(7132) 563-425
Fax: +7(7132) 563-201
EMail: zkgma@mail.kz
Website: http://www.zkgma.kz/

Rector: Yerbol Bekmukhambetov (2008-)

Administrative Officer: Kulash Omarova Tel: +7(7132) 567-116

International Relations: Zhurabekova Gulmira

Departments

Child Dentistry (Dentistry; Orthodontics); **Dermatology, Venereology and Tuberculosis** (Dermatology; Pneumology; Venereology); **Epidemiology** (Epidemiology); **Faculty Pediatrics** (Paediatrics); **Faculty Surgery** (Ophthalmology; Surgery; Urology); **Faculty Therapy** (Endocrinology; Rehabilitation and Therapy); **General Practice** (Medicine; Surgery); **Gynaecology and Obstetrics** (Gynaecology and Obstetrics); **Histology** (Forensic Medicine and Dentistry; Histology); **Hospital Surgery** (Nephrology; Neurology; Surgery); **Hospital Therapy** (Medical Technology; Occupational Therapy; Pharmacology; Physical Therapy); **Hygiene** (Hygiene; Public Health); **Infectious Diseases and Childhood Infections** (Epidemiology; Paediatrics); **Oncology** (Oncology; Otorhinolaryngology); **Pediatric Surgery** (Paediatrics; Surgery); **Pharmaceutical Sciences** (Pharmacy); **Surgical and Prosthetic Dentistry** (Dental Technology; Dentistry)

History: Founded 1957 as Aktobe State Medical Institute. Renamed Aktobe State Medical Academy 1997. Acquired present status and title 2000.

Governing Bodies: Academic Council

Academic Year: September to June

Admission Requirements: Secondary school certificate and Common National Test with a minimum passing score of 60

Fees: (Tenge): 191,200 per annum

Main Language(s) of Instruction: Kazakh, Russian, English

International Co-operation: With universities in USA

Degrees and Diplomas: *Diplom o Vysshem Obrazovanii (Bakalavr)*; *Diplom Magistra*

Student Services: Academic counselling, Canteen, Cultural centre, Foreign student adviser, Foreign Studies Centre, Health services, Language programs, Social counselling, Sports facilities

Student Residential Facilities: Yes (3 hostels)

Special Facilities: Two Anatomy Museums; History of the Academy Museum

Libraries: 429,174 vols

Publications: Medical Journal of Western Kazakhstan *(quarterly)*; Medik, Newspaper *(monthly)*

Academic Staff *2008-2009*	MEN	WOMEN	**TOTAL**
FULL-TIME	188	324	**512**
STAFF WITH DOCTORATE			
FULL-TIME	–	–	**208**
Student Numbers *2008-2009*			
All (Foreign Included)	695	2,277	**2,972**

Part-time students, 80.

Last Updated: 25/10/10

M. KH. DULATY TARAZ STATE UNIVERSITY

Taraskij Gosudartsvennyj Universitet im. M.H. Dulaty (TARSU)

ul Tole bi, 60, 080012 Taraz, Jambyl
Tel: +8(7262) 45-36-64
Fax: +8(7262) 43-24-02
EMail: info@tarsu.kz
Website: http://www.tarsu.kz

Rector: Ashimzhan Suleimenovich Akhmetov (2001-)
EMail: rektor@tarsu.kz

First Vice-Rector: Tiribolsyn Omarbekuly
Tel: +8(7262) 45-36-67 EMail: omarbekov@tarsu.kz

International Relations: Seythan Koybakov, Provost for Research and International Relations
Tel: +8(7262) 42-64-01 EMail: seithan@tarazinfo.kz

Institutes

Distance Learning (Arts and Humanities; Economics; Technology); **Economics and Business** (Accountancy; Economics; Finance; Management; Marketing; Service Trades; Tourism); **Humanities and Social Sciences** (History; Journalism; Literature; Modern Languages; Native Language; Philology; Physical Education; Psychology; Russian; Sociology; Sports; Translation and Interpretation); **Law** (Civil Law; Criminology; Law; Philosophy); **Oil and Gas Mechanics** (Engineering; Mechanics; Petroleum and Gas Engineering; Power Engineering; Transport and Communications; Transport Engineering); **Postgraduate Education and Training**; **Technology and Information Systems** (Applied Mathematics; Automation and Control Engineering; Biology; Biotechnology; Chemistry; Computer Science; Design; Food Technology; Information Technology; Inorganic Chemistry; Materials Engineering; Mathematics; Measurement and Precision Engineering; Physics; Software Engineering; Textile Design); **Water Resources, Environment and Construction** (Agronomy; Architecture; Biology; Building Technologies; Construction Engineering; Environmental Engineering; Environmental Studies; Geography; Safety Engineering; Water Management)

Further Information: Also Branch in Karatau

History: Founded 1998 by the merging of Zhambyl University, Zhambyl Institute of Irrigation, Land Reclamation and

Construction and Zhambyl Technological Institute of Light and Food Industry.

Governing Bodies: University Council

Academic Year: September to July

Admission Requirements: Secondary school certificate (Atestat o srednem obrazovanii) and Certificate of United National Test

Fees: (US Dollars): 900-1,300 per annum

Main Language(s) of Instruction: Kazakh, Russian

International Co-operation: With Universities in USA, Korea, Italy, Germany, Latvia, Russia, Uzbekistan

Accrediting Agencies: Ministry of Education and Science

Degrees and Diplomas: *Diplom o Vysshem Obrazovanii (Bakalavr)*; *Diplom Magistra*; *Diplom Doktora (PhD)*

Student Services: Canteen, Cultural centre, Health services, Language programs, Sports facilities

Special Facilities: University History Museum; Art Gallery

Libraries: c. 1.5m. Vols

Publications: Materials of Scientific Conferences *(biannually)*; Vestnik, Scientific Papers *(monthly)*

Academic Staff *2009-2010*: Total 530

STAFF WITH DOCTORATE: Total 28

Student Numbers *2009-2010*: Total: c. 10,000

Last Updated: 22/10/10

M. UEZOV SOUTHERN KAZAKHSTAN STATE UNIVERSITY

Iužno-Kazahstanskij Gosudarstvennyj Universitet im. M. Auezova (M. AUESOV SKSU)

prosp. Tauke Khan 5, 160012 Shymkent
Tel: +7(7252) 535-048
Fax: +7(7252) 210-141
EMail: koncel@ukgu.kz
Website: http://www.ukgu.kz/

Rector: Valikhan Kozykeevich Bishimbaev (2007-)
Fax: +7(7252) 21-41-54

Vice Rector, Administration: Dauren Dosmakhanbetovich Tagibaev Tel: +7(7252) 21-19-68

International Relations: Tinlibek Saifutdinovich Bazhirov, Vice Rector on SWR and MC
Tel: +7(7252) 21-19-89, Fax: +7(7252) 21-19-89
EMail: tynlybek.bazhirov@gmail.com

Faculties

Agro-Industry (Agricultural Engineering; Biotechnology; Native Language; Veterinary Science; Water Management; Zoology); **Chemical Engineering** (Chemical Engineering; Chemistry; Ecology; Electronic Engineering; Environmental Management; Inorganic Chemistry; Petroleum and Gas Engineering); **Cultural Pedagogy** (Cultural Studies; Design; Ethnology; Pedagogy; Primary Education); **Distance Education** (Distance Education); **Economy and Finance** (Accountancy; Administration; Banking; Business and Commerce; Economics; Finance; Management; Marketing); **Information Technology, Telecommunication and Automatic System** (Automation and Control Engineering; Computer Engineering; Electrical Engineering; Information Technology; Mathematics and Computer Science; Modern Languages; Power Engineering; Telecommunications Engineering); **Jurisprudence and International Relations** (Civil Law; Criminal Law; International Law; International Relations; Law; Philosophy; Political Sciences; Taxation); **Light and Food Industry** (Food Technology; Heating and Refrigeration; Physics; Technology); **Mechanics and Civil Engineering** (Architecture; Civil Engineering; Design; Engineering; Industrial Engineering; Mechanics; Road Engineering; Technology; Transport Management); **Natural Pedagogical Science** (Mathematics Education; Science Education); **Philology** (English; German; Landscape Architecture; Linguistics; Literature; Modern Languages; Native Language; Native Language Education; Russian); **Sports and Tourism** (Psychology; Sports; Tourism)

History: Created in 1998 by the merger of Southern Kazakhstan Technical University (Iužno-Kazahstanskij Tehnieeskij Universitet) (1943) and Southern Kazakhstan Humanities University named after M.Auezov (Iužno-Kazahstanskij Gumanitarnij Universitet im. Auezova)(1968).

Governing Bodies: Academic Council

Academic Year: September to July

Admission Requirements: Secondary school certificate

Fees: (US Dollars): 1,800 per annum

Main Language(s) of Instruction: Kazakh; Russian

International Co-operation: With nternational Association for the Exchange of Students for Technical Experience (IAESTE), Deutscher Akademischer Austausch Dienst (DAAD), Tempus, ICCR, INSPIRE

Accrediting Agencies: Ministry of Education and Science; ASIIN - Accreditation Agency

Degrees and Diplomas: *Diplom o Vysshem Obrazovanii (Bakalavr)*; *Diplom Magistra*; *Diplom Doktora (PhD)*

Student Services: Academic counselling, Canteen, Cultural centre, Employment services, Foreign student adviser, Foreign Studies Centre, Health services, Language programs, Social counselling, Sports facilities

Student Residential Facilities: Students Hostel

Special Facilities: French Reading Room; Research Laboratories; Art Gallery; Museum; Linguistic Centre; Indian Cultural Centre

Libraries:c. 524,000 vols

Publications: South Kazakhstan's Science and Education, Journal publishing articles on all spheres of science *(bimonthly)*; Treatises of M. Auezov SKSU, Journal publishing articles on all spheres of science *(quarterly)*

Academic Staff *2009-2010*	MEN	WOMEN	**TOTAL**
FULL-TIME	674	814	**1,488**
PART-TIME	79	108	**187**
STAFF WITH DOCTORATE			
FULL-TIME	79	17	**96**
PART-TIME	24	1	**25**
Student Numbers *2009-2010*			
All (Foreign Included)	8,403	8,787	**17,190**
FOREIGN ONLY	119	131	**250**

Part-time students, 12,316. **Evening students**, 4,874.

Last Updated: 06/10/10

M. UTEMISSOV WESTERN KAZAKHSTAN STATE UNIVERSITY

Makhambet Utemissov Atyndagy Batys Kazakhstan Memlekettyk Universiteti (WKSU)

162, Dostyk avenue, 090000 Uralsk, Western Kazakhstan
Tel: +7(311-2) 51-26-32
Fax: +7(311-2) 51-26-32
EMail: zapkazgu@wksu.kz
Website: http://www.wksu.kz

Rector: Tuyakbai Rysbekov (2003-)
Tel: +7(311-2) 50-85-03 EMail: rector@wksu.kz

Vice Rector: Zakhot Mukhlisova
Tel: +7(311-2) 51-35-19, Fax: +7(311-2) 51-37-82
EMail: prorectornirms@wksu.kz

International Relations: Ainash Kenzhegalieva, Head of International Department
Tel: +7 (3112) 51-24-85, Fax: +4 (3112) 51-37-82
EMail: inter_dep@wksu.kz

Faculties

Education (Computer Science; Education; Pedagogy; Physical Education; Psychology); **History and Law** (History; International Relations; Law; Sociology); **Natural Sciences and Mathematics** (Biology; Chemistry; Computer Science; Ecology; Geography; Inorganic Chemistry; Mathematics; Natural Sciences; Organic Chemistry; Physics); **Philology** (English; Literature; Modern Languages; Native Language; Philology; Russian; Translation and Interpretation)

Institutes

Culture and Art (Dance; Library Science; Music Education; Musical Instruments; Painting and Drawing; Singing; Theatre; Visual Arts); **Economics and Management** (Accountancy; Economics; Finance; Information Sciences; Management; Marketing; Public Administration; Tourism)

History: Founded 1932. Acquired present status 2000 by merger of Western Kazakhstan Agrarian University, Western Kazakhstan Humanitarian University and Western Kazakhstan 'Dauletkerey' Institute of Arts. Acquired present title 2003, and is the oldest University in Kazakhstan

Academic Year: September to July

Admission Requirements: Competitive entrance examination following secondary school certificate (Аммесмам) or equivalent

Fees: Vary according to faculties

Main Language(s) of Instruction: Kazakh, Russian

International Co-operation: With institutions in Russia, Ukraine, Georgia, Lithuania, Azerbaijan, Israel, Germany, Spain

Accrediting Agencies: Ministry of Education and Science

Degrees and Diplomas: *Diplom o Vysshem Obrazovanii (Bakalavr)*; *Diplom Magistra*

Student Services: Academic counselling, Canteen, Cultural centre, Employment services, Foreign student adviser, Foreign Studies Centre, Health services, Language programs, Nursery care, Social counselling, Sports facilities

Student Residential Facilities: Hostels for 400 students

Special Facilities: History, Archeology, Nature, Ethnography museums

Libraries: Scientific Library, Library of the Humanities, Library of Arts, Technical and Agrarian Library

Publications: Orken, Student newspaper *(monthly)*; Vestnik, Scientific magazine *(quarterly)*

Press or Publishing House: Printing House

Last Updated: 25/10/10

NORTHERN KAZAKHSTAN UNIVERSITY NAMED AFTER M. KAZYBAEV

Severo-Kazahstanskij Gosudarstvennyj Universitet im. M. Kozybaeva (NKSU)

ul. Puškina 86, 150000 Petropavlosk
Tel: +7(7152) 493-352
Fax: +7(7152) 463-342
EMail: mail@nkzu.kz
Website: http://www.nkzu.kz/

Rector: Undassyn Ašimov (1994-) EMail: uashimov@nkzu.kz

Vice-rector of the Academic Work: Laura Kairzhanova
Tel: +7(7152) 49-31-66 EMail: lkairzhanova@mail.ru

International Relations: Aleksandr Tukachev, Pro-rector for Science and External Relations
Tel: +7(7152) 461-585, Fax: +7(7152) 461-585
EMail: atukachev@nkzu.kz

Faculties

Economics (Accountancy; Economics; Finance; Management); **Energy and Mechanical Engineering** (Electronic Engineering; Energy Engineering; Instrument Making; Mechanical Engineering; Telecommunications Engineering); **History and Law** (History; Law); **Information Technologies** (Computer Science; Information Technology; Mathematics; Physics); **Music and Pedagogics** (Design; Music; Pedagogy; Primary Education; Psychology; Singing; Speech Therapy and Audiology); **Natural Sciences and Geography** (Agriculture; Biology; Chemistry; Ecology; Geography; Natural Sciences; Organic Chemistry); **Physical Education** (Military Science; Physical Education; Sports; Tourism); **Transport and Construction Engineering** (Construction Engineering; Engineering; Transport Engineering)

Institutes

Language and Literature (English; French; German; Literature; Native Language; Philology; Russian); **Retraining and Raising the Level of Professional Skills** (Administration; Computer Science; Distance Education; English; Ethics; Higher Education; Marketing; Pedagogy; Psychology; Sports; Technology)

Further Information: Also language courses for Kazakh minorities. Agency on Energy Saving and Resources

History: Founded 1937 as Pedagogical Institute, and acquired present status 1994. Incorporated Petropavlovsk Polytechnical Institute 1996.

Governing Bodies: Academic Council

Academic Year: September to July (September-January; February-July)

Admission Requirements: Secondary school certificate (Atestat o srednem obrazovanii)

Fees: (US Dollars): 1,500 per annum

Main Language(s) of Instruction: Kazakh, Russian

International Co-operation: Participates in DAAD and IAESTE programmes

Degrees and Diplomas: *Diplom o Vysshem Obrazovanii (Bakalavr)*; *Diplom Magistra*

Student Services: Academic counselling, Canteen, Cultural centre, Employment services, Foreign Studies Centre, Health services, Language programs, Social counselling, Sports facilities

Student Residential Facilities: For 1,800 students

Special Facilities: History Museum. TV Studio "Parasat". Observatory. Student Theatre. Agricultural/Biological Station

Libraries: c. 1 million vols

Publications: Interinstitutional Bulletin *(quarterly)*; NKSU Bulletin *(quarterly)*

Press or Publishing House: Publishing Centre of Northern Kazakhstan University

Last Updated: 22/10/10

O.A. BAIKONUROV ZHEZKAZGAN UNIVERSITY

Žezkazganskij Universitet im. O.A. Baikonurova

prosp. Alashakhana 1b, 100602 Zhezkazgan
Tel: +7(7102) 73-63-24 +7(7102) 76-48-26
Fax: +7(7102) 73-60-15
EMail: univer@zhez.kz
Website: http://univer.zhez.kz/home.htm

Rector: Abdimalik Takishov

Institutes

Economics and Law (Economics; Finance; History; Law; Management; Public Law; Regional Studies); **Humanities and Pedagogy** (Arts and Humanities; Biological and Life Sciences; Biology; Computer Science; Design; English; Fine Arts; Geography; German; History; Mathematics; Native Language; Pedagogy; Philology; Philosophy; Physics; Preschool Education; Primary Education; Psychology; Russian; Technology; Vocational Education); **Mountain** (Geology; Machine Building; Metallurgical Engineering; Mining Engineering; Safety Engineering); **Technology** (Automation and Control Engineering; Construction Engineering; Heating and Refrigeration; Machine Building; Maintenance Technology; Materials Engineering; Measurement and Precision Engineering; Mechanical Engineering; Mechanics; Power Engineering; Transport and Communications)

Further Information: Also study abroad programmes

History: Founded 1961 as Technical Faculty of Karaganda Polytechnic Institute. Became Zhezkazgan Pedagogic Institute 1975 and acquired present status and title 1996.

Admission Requirements: Secondary school certificate (Atestat o srednem obrazovanii)

Fees: (Tenge): 55,000-170,000 per annum

Main Language(s) of Instruction: Kazakh, Russian, English, German

Degrees and Diplomas: *Diplom o Vysshem Obrazovanii (Bakalavr)*; *Diplom Magistra*

Student Services: Academic counselling, Canteen, Cultural centre, Foreign student adviser, Foreign Studies Centre, Health services, Language programs, Social counselling, Sports facilities

Special Facilities: Historical and Ethnographical Museum. Geological Museum

Libraries: Central Library

Last Updated: 25/10/10

PAVLODAR STATE PEDAGOGICAL INSTITUT

Pavlodarskij Gosudarstvennyj Pedagogičeskij Institut

ul. Mira, 60, 140000 Pavlodar
Tel: +7(718-2) 55-24-76
Fax: +7(718-2) 52-42-22
Website: http://www.ppi.kz/

Rector: Zhanmurza Nurmagambetov

Faculties

History, Economics and Law (Economics; History; Law; Music Education); **Natural Sciences** (Biology; Chemistry; Ecology; Geography; Science Education); **Pedagogy and Psychology** (Educational Psychology; Pedagogy; Preschool Education; Primary Education; Psychology); **Philology** (Native Language; Philology; Russian); **Physical Education and Sports** (Physical Education; Sports); **Physics and Mathematics** (Information Sciences; Mathematics; Physics)

History: Created 1962.

Degrees and Diplomas: *Diplom o Vysshem Obrazovanii (Bakalavr)*; *Diplom Magistra*

Last Updated: 18/02/10

S. AMANZHOLOV EAST KAZAKHSTAN STATE UNIVERSITY

Voštočno-Kazahstanskij Gosudarstvennyj Universitet imeni S. Amanžolova (VKGU)

34, 30-Gvardeyskoy divizii street, 070020 Ust-Kamenogorsk, Eatern Kazakhstan
Tel: +8(7232) 54-14-11
Fax: +8(7232) 54-04-07
EMail: kancelaria@vkgu.kz; kense@vkgu.kz
Website: http://www.vkgu.kz/

Rector: Beybit Mamrayev EMail: rector@vkgu.kz

Faculties

Culture and Sport (Music Education; Physical Education; Sports); **Distance Education** (Biology; Chemistry; Computer Science; Ecology; Economics; English; Finance; Geography; Government; History; Information Technology; International Relations; Journalism; Law; Literature; Mathematics; Military Science; Native Language; Pedagogy; Physical Education; Physics; Political Sciences; Preschool Education; Psychology; Russian; Sports; Vocational Education); **Economics and Business** (Accountancy; Business Administration; Economics; Finance; Government; Management; Marketing; Tourism); **Environmental and Natural Sciences** (Biology; Chemistry; Ecology; Environmental Studies; Geography); **History and International Relations** (History; International Relations; Philosophy; Political Sciences); **Mathematics, Physics and Technology** (Agricultural Engineering; Computer Science; Materials Engineering; Mathematics; Physics; Vocational Education); **Philology** (English; German; Journalism; Literature; Native Language; Philology; Russian; Translation and Interpretation); **Pre-University Training** (Marketing); **Psychology and Pedagogy** (Educational Psychology; Pedagogy; Preschool Education; Psychology; Social Work); **Public Administration and Law** (Civil Law; Criminal Law; Law; Public Administration)

History: Founded 1952.

Degrees and Diplomas: *Diplom o Vysshem Obrazovanii (Bakalavr)*; *Diplom Magistra*; *Diplom Doktora (PhD)*

Last Updated: 03/11/10

S.D. ASFENDIYAROV KAZAKH NATIONAL MEDICAL UNIVERSITY

Kazahskij Nacionalnij Meditsinskii Universitet im. S.D. Asfendijarova (KAZNMU)

ul. Tole bi, 94, 050012 Almaty
Tel: +7(727) 292-70-15 +7(727) 292-78-85 +7(727) 292-79-37
Fax: +7(727) 292-70-15
EMail: kaznmu@kaznmu.kz; icd@kaznmu.kz
Website: http://www.kaznmu.kz

Rector: Aikan Akanov EMail: a.akanov@kaznmu.kz

International Relations: Dana Abdrasheva, Head of International Cooperation Department EMail: icd@kaznmu.kz

Faculties

Dentistry (Anatomy; Dentistry; Forensic Medicine and Dentistry; Orthodontics; Stomatology; Surgery); **General Medicine** (Anatomy; Biophysics; Clinical Psychology; Forensic Medicine and Dentistry; Genetics; Histology; Medicine; Molecular Biology; Native Language; Pathology; Pharmacology; Physiology; Psychology; Russian; Statistics; Surgery); **Management** (Management); **Medical Studies** (Anatomy; Biochemistry; Forensic Medicine and Dentistry; Gynaecology and Obstetrics; Medicine; Ophthalmology; Physiology; Surgery); **Medical-prophylactic Studies** (Epidemiology; Hygiene; Nutrition; Occupational Health; Public Health); **Paediatrics** (Paediatrics); **Pharmacy** (Pharmacy)

History: Founded as Kazakh Medical Institute 1931. Renamed Almaty State Medical Institute 1961. Became Kazakh State Medical University 1996. Acquired present status and title 2001.

Governing Bodies: Ministry of Health; Ministry of Education and Sciences

Academic Year: September to July

Admission Requirements: Secondary school certificate and entrance examination

Fees: (Tenge): c. 304,900 per annum according to Faculty

Main Language(s) of Instruction: Kazakh, Russian, English

International Co-operation: With universities in Russia, Uzbekistan, Kyrgyzstan, Tadjikistan, Japan, India, Pakistan, Syria, Palestine, Jordan, Turkey, Iran

Accrediting Agencies: Ministry of Education and Science; Ministry of Health

Degrees and Diplomas: *Diplom o Vysshem Obrazovanii (Bakalavr)*; *Diplom o Vysshem Obrazovanii (Specialist)*; *Diplom Magistra*; *Diplom Doktora (PhD)*: a further 3 yrs. Also Clinical Ordinature (Residenture), 2 yrs

Student Services: Academic counselling, Canteen, Cultural centre, Employment services, Foreign student adviser, Foreign Studies Centre, Health services, Language programs, Social counselling, Sports facilities

Student Residential Facilities: Seven hostels

Special Facilities: Museum. Movie Studio

Libraries: 899,679 vols

Publications: Herald of Kazakh National Medical University, Scientific Magazine *(quarterly)*

Academic Staff *2012-2013*	**TOTAL**
FULL-TIME	**1,310**
PART-TIME	**1,080**
Student Numbers *2012-2013*	
All (Foreign Included)	**9,382**

Last Updated: 21/10/10

SEMEY STATE MEDICAL UNIVERSITY

Gosudarstvennyj Medicinskij Universitet Goroda Semei

ul. Abaia Kunanbaeva, 103, 071400 Semey, East Kazakhstan Region
Tel: +7(7222) 522-251
EMail: sgma-mail@ok.kz; iws@relkom.kz
Website: http://www.sgma.kz/

Rector: Tolebay Rakhypbekov (2007-)

Prorector: Bekbolat Zhetpisbaev

International Relations: Tasbolat Adylchanov, Prorector

Programmes
Library Science (Library Science); **Medicine** (Medicine); **Nursing** (Nursing); **Paediatrics** (Paediatrics); **Pharmacy** (Pharmacy); **Public Health** (Public Health); **Stomatology** (Stomatology); **Surgery** (Surgery)

History: Founded 1953. Acquired present status and title 2009.

Governing Bodies: Rector, prorectors and managers of structural departments

Academic Year: September to July

Admission Requirements: Competitive entrance examination following general or special secondary school certificate; personal certificate

Fees: (US Dollars): Foreign students, c. 1,000 per annum; (Tenge): 355,900 for national students

Main Language(s) of Instruction: Kazakh, Russian, English

International Co-operation: With institutions in Singapour and Japan.

Accrediting Agencies: National Academy Centre, Ministry of Republic of Kazakhstan.

Degrees and Diplomas: *Diplom o Vysshem Obrazovanii (Specialist)*: Medicine (MD); *Diplom Magistra*; *Diplom Doktora (PhD)*

Student Services: Academic counselling, Canteen, Cultural centre, Foreign Studies Centre, Health services, Language programs, Nursery care, Social counselling, Sports facilities

Special Facilities: University History Museum; Museum of Anatomy; Museum of Manšuk Mametova

Libraries: 492,369 vols

Publications: "Nauka i zdorovje", Magazine *(monthly)*; Scientific Publications *(annually)*

Academic Staff *2009-2010*	MEN	WOMEN	TOTAL
FULL-TIME	108	458	**566**
STAFF WITH DOCTORATE			
FULL-TIME	1	1	**2**
Student Numbers *2009-2010*			
All (Foreign Included)	1,096	2,805	**3,901**
FOREIGN ONLY	172	18	**190**

Last Updated: 06/10/10

SEMEY STATE PEDAGOGICAL INSTITUTE

Semipalatinskij Gosudarstvennyj Pedagogičeskij Institut (SGPI)

1, Tanibergenov street, 071410 Semey, Eastern Kazakhstan
EMail: info@sgpi.kz
Website: http://www.sgpi.kz/

Rector: Meir Yeskendirov

Faculties
History and Philology (Economics; History; Law; Literature; Modern Languages; Philology; Philosophy; Russian); **Natural Sciences** (Biology; Chemistry; Ecology; Geography; Military Science; Physical Education; Sports); **Philology of the Kazakh Language** (Literature; Native Language; Philology); **Physics and Mathematics** (Computer Science; Mathematics; Physics); **Psychology and Pedagogy** (Design; Fine Arts; Music Education; Painting and Drawing; Pedagogy; Preschool Education; Psychology; Social Work; Vocational Education)

History: Founded 1934.

Main Language(s) of Instruction: Kazakh, Russian

Degrees and Diplomas: *Diplom o Vysshem Obrazovanii (Bakalavr)*; *Diplom Magistra*

Last Updated: 03/11/10

SHAKARIM SEMEY STATE UNIVERSITY

Semipalatinskij Gosudarstvennyj Universitet imeni Šakarima (SEMGU)

20A, Glinka street, 071412 Semey, Eastern Kazakhstan
Website: http://www.semgu.kz/

Rector: Yerlan Sydykov

Departments
Agriculture (Agricultural Engineering; Agronomy; Animal Husbandry; Biology; Ecology; Environmental Studies; Farm Management; Veterinary Science); **Finance and Economics** (Accountancy; Business Administration; Economics; Finance; Management; Marketing)

Faculties
Engineering and Technology (Building Technologies; Chemistry; Engineering; Food Technology; Heating and Refrigeration; Mechanical Engineering; Mechanics; Technology); **Humanities** (English; History; Law; Literature; Modern Languages; Native Language; Philology; Philosophy; Psychology; Russian; Translation and Interpretation); **Information and Communication Technology** (Automation and Control Engineering; Computer Engineering; Design; Electrical Engineering; Graphic Design; Information Technology; Mathematics; Physical Education; Physics; Software Engineering; Surveying and Mapping; Translation and Interpretation)

History: Founded 1995.

International Co-operation: With universities in the U.S., Germany, Britain, Japan, China, Turkey , Hungary, Slovenia, Poland, Russia, Belarus, Ukraine, Baltic states, Kyrgyzstan.

Degrees and Diplomas: *Diplom o Vysshem Obrazovanii (Bakalavr)*; *Diplom o Vysshem Obrazovanii (Specialist)*; *Diplom Magistra*; *Diplom Doktora (PhD)*

Last Updated: 03/11/10

SH. UALIKHANOV KOKSHETAU STATE UNIVERSITY

Kokšetauskij Gosudarstvennyj Universitet im. Šokana Ualihanova (KOKGU)

ul. Abaja 76, 020000 Kokshetau
Tel: +7(7162) 25-55-83
Fax: +7(7162) 25-55-83
EMail: universi@kokshetau.online.kz
Website: http://kgu.kz

Rector: Shakimasharip Ibrayev Tel: +8(7162) 25-55-83

Faculties
Agro-engineering (Agricultural Engineering; Agronomy; Animal Husbandry; Construction Engineering; Crop Production; Forestry; Mechanical Engineering; Mining Engineering; Soil Science; Transport and Communications; Transport Engineering); **Economics** (Accountancy; Economics; Finance; Management; Marketing); **Education** (Biology; Biotechnology; Chemistry; Ecology; Education; Educational Technology; Geography; Pedagogy; Preschool Education; Psychology); **Foreign Languages** (English; German; Modern Languages; Philology); **History** (Economics; History; Law; Philosophy; Sociology); **Philology** (Literature; Native Language; Philology; Russian); **Physics and Mathematics** (Computer Engineering; Computer Science; Information Technology; Mathematics; Physics; Software Engineering); **Tourism, Sport and Design** (Design; Fine Arts; Physical Education; Social Work; Sports; Tourism; Vocational Education)

History: Founded 1962. Acquired present status and title 1996.

Academic Year: September to July (September-January; February-July)

Admission Requirements: Competitive entrance examination following general or special secondary school certificate (Attestat o srednem obrazovanii)

Fees: (Tenge): 95,000 per annum. Distance Education, 54,000

Main Language(s) of Instruction: Kazakh, Russian

International Co-operation: Participates in Tempus, German Academic Exchange Service (DAAD), programmes.

Degrees and Diplomas: *Diplom o Vysshem Obrazovanii (Bakalavr)*; *Diplom Magistra*

Student Services: Academic counselling, Canteen, Cultural centre, Employment services, Foreign Studies Centre, Health services, Social counselling, Sports facilities

Student Residential Facilities: For c. 5,000 students

Special Facilities: Shokan Valihanov Museum, Museum of the History of the University

Libraries: c. 600,000 vols

Publications: Scientific Publications - Valihanovskie Ctenija *(annually)*; Scientific Publications 'Vestnis' *(biannually)*
Last Updated: 21/10/10

SOUTH-KAZAKHSTAN STATE PHARMACEUTICAL ACADEMY

Iužno-Kazahstanskaja Gosudarstvennaja Farmatsevticheskaja Akademija

1, Al-Farabi Square, 160019 Shymkent
Tel: +7(3252) 408-208 +7(3252) 408-217
Fax: +7(3252) 408-222
EMail: medacadem@rambler.ru; n_jugai@mail.ru
Website: http://www.ukgma.kz/

Rector: Bahytzhan Deribsalyevich Seksenbaev

Faculties

Medicine and Pharmacy (Medicine; Midwifery; Nursing; Pharmacy; Public Health)

History: Founded 1979 as Šymkent State Medical Institute, acquired present status and title 1997. Previously known as Iužno-Kazahstanskaja Gosudarstvennaja Medicinskaja Akademija (South-Kazakhstan State Medical Academy). Acquired current title 2009.

Main Language(s) of Instruction: Kazakh, Russian

Degrees and Diplomas: *Diplom o Vysshem Obrazovanii (Bakalavr)*; *Diplom o Vysshem Obrazovanii (Specialist)*; *Diplom Magistra*

Libraries: 48,665 vols; 236 periodical subscriptions

Academic Staff *2008-2009*	MEN	WOMEN	TOTAL
FULL-TIME	174	284	**458**
PART-TIME	98	52	**150**
Student Numbers *2008-2009*			
All (Foreign Included)	1,170	2,177	**3,347**

Last Updated: 26/10/10

S. SEIFULLIN KAZAKH AGRO-TECHNICAL UNIVERSITY

Kazahskij Agrotehničeskij Universitet im. S. Seifullina (KAZATU)

Prosp. Pobedy 62, 010011 Astana
Tel: +7(7172) 317-547
Fax: +7(7172) 316-072
EMail: agun.katu@gmail.com
Website: http://www.agun.kz

President: Aitbay K. Bulashev

Faculties

Computer Systems and Vocational Training (Computer Networks; Data Processing; Software Engineering); **Agronomy** (Agronomy; Ecology; Farm Management; Forest Management; Plant and Crop Protection); **Architecture** (Architecture; Design); **Economics** (Accountancy; Business and Commerce; Economics; Finance; Industrial Management; Marketing); **Energy** (Electrical Engineering; Heating and Refrigeration; Power Engineering; Telecommunications Engineering); **Humanities** (Cultural Studies; English; French; German; History; Native Language; Philosophy; Political Sciences; Russian; Sociology); **Land Use Planning** (Real Estate; Soil Conservation; Soil Management); **Technical Studies** (Farm Management; Mechanical Engineering; Road Engineering; Transport Engineering); **Veterinary Science and Animal Breeding Technology** (Animal Husbandry; Biotechnology; Crop Production; Fishery; Food Science; Technology; Veterinary Science)

History: Founded 1957.

Academic Year: September to July

Admission Requirements: Competitive entrance examination following general or special secondary school certificate

Main Language(s) of Instruction: Kazakh, Russian

International Co-operation: Participates in Tempus, DAAD, ITEC, FAO, IREX programmes of embassies of France, USA, Germany and India

Accrediting Agencies: Ministry of Education and Science

Degrees and Diplomas: *Diplom o Vysshem Obrazovanii (Bakalavr)*; *Diplom o Vysshem Obrazovanii (Specialist)*; *Diplom Magistra*; *Diplom Doktora (PhD)*

Student Services: Canteen, Health services, Language programs, Sports facilities

Student Residential Facilities: 8 students dormitories

Special Facilities: Health Centre; Center for Computer Technology; Centre for Modern Biotechnology; Center for Economic Problems in Agricultural Development; Pavilion for new Agricultural Machinery Exhibition; Research Labs; 35 Computer Rooms (900 units); Internet Access; University Museum

Libraries: Total, c. 981.648 vols

Publications: Science Review, Scientific articles in English on agricultural issues relating to Agronomy, Architecture, Land Use Planning, Biotechnology, Veterinary Science, Energy, Economics, Technique, Comuter Systems.; Specialist, Newsletter

Press or Publishing House: University Printing House
Last Updated: 07/10/10

S. TORAIGIROV PAVLODAR STATE UNIVERSITY

Pavlodarskij Gosudarstvennyj Universitet im. S. Toraigyrova (PGU)

ul. Lomova 64, 140008 Pavlodar
Tel: +7(3182) 67-36-76
Fax: +7(3182) 67-37-01
EMail: pgu@psu.kz
Website: http://www.psu.kz

Rector: Erlan Aryn

Faculties

Agriculture Technology (Agronomy; Biotechnology; Forestry; Zoology); **Architecture and Construction** (Architecture; Construction Engineering; Design; Engineering; Environmental Studies; Food Technology); **Chemical Technology and Natural Sciences** (Biology; Chemical Engineering; Chemistry; Ecology; Geography; Natural Sciences; Physical Education; Sports; Tourism); **Distance Learning** (Automation and Control Engineering; Economics; Finance; Information Technology; Management; Power Engineering; Social Work); **Energy Engineering** (Automation and Control Engineering; Electrical Engineering; Energy Engineering; Engineering; Power Engineering; Telecommunications Engineering); **Finance and Economics** (Accountancy; Economics; Finance; Management); **History** (Archaeology; Criminal Law; Criminology; Cultural Studies; Ethnology; History; Philosophy; Political Sciences; Sociology); **Metallurgy, Machine Building and Transport** (Engineering; Machine Building; Metallurgical Engineering; Transport and Communications; Transport Engineering); **Philology, Journalism and Art** (German; Journalism; Library Science; Modern Languages; Native Language; Pedagogy; Performing Arts; Philology; Psychology; Russian; Translation and Interpretation); **Physics, Mathematics and Information Technologies** (Computer Engineering; Information Technology; Mathematics; Physics)

Further Information: Also Military Department; Distance Learning Institute, Pre-higher Education and Professional Orientation Faculty

History: Founded 1960 as Pavlodar Industrial Institute. Acquired present status and title 1996.

Governing Bodies: Scientific Council

Academic Year: September to June (September-January; February-June)

Admission Requirements: Common National Examination following secondary school certificate (Atestat o srednem obrazovanii)

Fees: (US Dollars): 400-1,500 per annum (depending on faculty)

Main Language(s) of Instruction: Russian, Kazakh

Accrediting Agencies: Ministry of Education and Science

Degrees and Diplomas: *Diplom o Vysshem Obrazovanii (Bakalavr)*; *Diplom Magistra*; *Diplom Doktora (PhD)*

Student Services: Academic counselling, Canteen, Cultural centre, Employment services, Foreign student adviser, Foreign Studies Centre, Health services, Language programs, Social counselling, Sports facilities

Student Residential Facilities: Yes

Special Facilities: Kazakh Ethnography Museum; Natural Sciences Museum

Libraries: Central Library, c. 850,000 vols

Publications: Biological Sciences in Kazahkstan *(quarterly)*; Regional Studies *(quarterly)*; Science and Technique in Kazakhstan; Science and Technology of Kazakhstan *(quarterly)*; Uchenye zapiski PGU, Scientific Journal of Pavlodar State University *(quarterly)*; Vestnik PGU
Last Updated: 22/10/10

TARAZ STATE PEDOGOGICAL INSTITUTE

Tarazskij Gosudarstvennyj Pedagogičeskij Institut
ul. Tole Bi, 62, 080000 Taraz, Jambyl
Tel: +7(726-2) 43-58-06
Fax: +7(726-2) 43-58-06
EMail: targpi@mail.ru
Website: http://tarmpi.kz/

Rector: Askar Abdualy

Faculties
Additional Pedagogical Education; **Creative Specialty** (Dance; Military Science; Music Education; Painting and Drawing; Physical Education; Vocational Education); **Distance Education**; **Education** (Pedagogy; Psychology); **History and Geography** (Ecology; Economics; Geography; History; Law; Philosophy; Political Sciences); **Natural Sciences** (Biology; Chemistry; Computer Science; Information Technology; Mathematics; Physics); **Philology** (German; Germanic Languages; Literature; Modern Languages; Native Language; Philology; Russian)

Degrees and Diplomas: *Diplom o Vysshem Obrazovanii (Bakalavr)*; *Diplom Magistra*
Last Updated: 22/10/10

THE KAZAKH ACADEMY OF SPORT AND TOURISM

Kazahskaja Akademija Sporta i Turisma
prosp. Abaia 83/85, 050022 Almaty
Tel: +7(327) 292-07-56 +7(327) 292 39-37 +7(327) 292 43-77
Fax: +7(327) 292 68-05
EMail: oursport@nursat.kz; kazast@nurzat.kz
Website: http://www.kazacademsport.kz/

President: Kairat Zakiryanov

Faculties
Olympic Sports (Physical Education; Sports); **Postgraduate Studies and Further Education** (Cooking and Catering; Hotel and Restaurant; Physical Education; Social and Community Services; Sports; Tourism); **Professional Sports and Arts** (Physical Education; Physical Therapy; Psychology; Sports; Sports Management); **Tourism** (Cooking and Catering; Hotel and Restaurant; Social and Community Services; Tourism)

Degrees and Diplomas: *Diplom o Vysshem Obrazovanii (Bakalavr)*; *Diplom o Vysshem Obrazovanii (Specialist)*; *Diplom Magistra*
Last Updated: 20/10/10

T. RYSKULOV KAZAKH ECONOMICS UNIVERSITY

Kazahskij Economičeskij Universitet imeni T. Ryskulova
55, Zhandosov street, 050035 Almaty
Tel: +7(727) 228-08-71 +7(727) 309-22-80
Website: http://www.kazeu.kz/

Rector: Ali Abishev

Faculties
Accounting and Statistics (Accountancy; Statistics); **Economics** (Economics; English; International Economics; International Relations); **Engineering and Economics** (Applied Mathematics; Business Computing; Ecology; Economics; Measurement and Precision Engineering; Natural Resources; Physical Education); **Finance** (Banking; Finance; Native Language; Russian); **Management** (Business and Commerce; Economics; Management; Marketing); **Military Science** (Accountancy; Economics; Engineering; Finance; Military Science)

History: Founded 1963.

Degrees and Diplomas: *Diplom o Vysshem Obrazovanii (Bakalavr)*; *Diplom Magistra*; *Diplom Doktora (PhD)*
Last Updated: 29/10/10

ZHANGIR KHAN WEST KAZAKHSTAN AGRO-TECHNICAL UNIVERSITY

Zapadno-Kazahstanskij Agrarno-tehničeskij Universitet im. Žangir Khana
ul. Zhangir Khana, 51, 090009 Uralsk
Tel: +8(7112) 50-10-00
Fax: +8(7112) 50-13-74
EMail: zapkazatu@wkau.kz
Website: http://www.wkau.kz/

Rector: Kazybai Bozymov

Faculties
Agronomy (Agriculture; Agronomy; Biology; Ecology; Environmental Studies; Food Technology; History; Natural Resources; Philosophy; Plant and Crop Protection); **Correspondence and Distance Learning** (Accountancy; Agronomy; Animal Husbandry; Business Administration; Construction Engineering; Ecology; Electrical Engineering; Environmental Studies; Finance; Food Technology; Forestry; Information Sciences; Instrument Making; Management; Measurement and Precision Engineering; Organic Chemistry; Petroleum and Gas Engineering; Safety Engineering; Vocational Education); **Economics and Business** (Accountancy; Business Administration; Economics; Finance; Management; Marketing); **Mechanical Engineering** (Building Technologies; Chemistry; Construction Engineering; English; German; Mechanical Engineering; Modern Languages; Petroleum and Gas Engineering); **Veterinary Medicine and Biotechnology** (Animal Husbandry; Biological and Life Sciences; Biotechnology; Fishery; Native Language; Physiology; Russian; Veterinary Science; Zoology)

Schools
Polytechnic (Agricultural Equipment; Energy Engineering; Information Sciences; Mathematics; Physics)

History: Created 1963. Reorganized into West-Kazakhstan Agrarian University 1996. Became part of West Kazakhstan State University 2000. Reorganized into the West-Kazakhstan Agrarian-Technical University 2002. Acquired present title 2003.

Degrees and Diplomas: *Diplom o Vysshem Obrazovanii (Bakalavr)*; *Diplom o Vysshem Obrazovanii (Specialist)*; *Diplom Magistra*; *Diplom Doktora (PhD)*
Last Updated: 25/10/10

PRIVATE INSTITUTIONS

ACADEMIC INNOVATIVE UNIVERSITY

Akademičeskij Innovatsionnyj Universitet
13, Baitursynov Street, 160012 Shymkent, South Kazakhstan
Tel: +8(7252) 21-29-21
EMail: aiu_1937@mail.ru
Website: http://aiu1937.kz/

Faculties
Art (Dance; Design; Graphic Design; Music); **Economics** (Economics); **History and Law** (History; Law); **Philology** (Native Language; Pedagogy; Philology); **Physics and Mathematics** (Mathematics; Physics); **Science** (Biology; Chemistry; Ecology; Mechanics); **Sport and Psychology** (Psychology; Sports)

History: Founded 1937.

Degrees and Diplomas: *Diplom o Vysshem Obrazovanii (Bakalavr)*; *Diplom Magistra*
Last Updated: 26/10/10

ACADEMY OF ECONOMICS AND LAW

Akademija Ekonomiki i Prava
13, Egizbayev street, 050060 Almaty
Tel: +7(727) 394-06-11 +7(727) 394-06-07
EMail: aep_host@rambler.ru
Website: http://www.aep.kz

Rector: Serikzhan Ospanov

Programmes

Accounting and Auditing (Accountancy); **Economics** (Economics); **Finance** (Finance); **Graduate Studies** (Economics; Law); **Law** (Law)

History: Founded 1998.

Degrees and Diplomas: *Diplom o Vysshem Obrazovanii (Bakalavr); Diplom Magistra*

Last Updated: 27/10/10

ALMATY ACADEMY OF ECONOMICS AND STATISTICS

Almatinskaja Akademija Ekonomiki i Statistiki

59, Zhandosov street, 050035 Almaty, Almaty

Tel: +7(727) 309-58-15

Fax: +7(727) 309-30-00

EMail: aesa2005@mail.ru; info@aesa.kz

Website: http://www.aesa.kz/

Rector: Valeri Korvyakov

Tel: +8(727) 309-58-15 EMail: v.korvyakov@rambler.ru

Faculties

Accounting and Auditing (Accountancy); **Economics and Management** (Economics; Management; Marketing); **Evaluation and Statistics** (Statistics); **Finance** (Finance); **Informatics** (Computer Science); **Social Sciences and Humanities** (Commercial Law; Cultural Studies; History; Law; Modern Languages; Native Language; Pedagogy; Philosophy; Political Sciences; Psychology; Russian; Sociology)

History: Founded 1997.

Degrees and Diplomas: *Diplom o Vysshem Obrazovanii (Bakalavr); Diplom Magistra*

Last Updated: 27/10/10

ALMATY HUMANITARIAN TECHNICAL UNIVERSITY

Almatinskij Gumanitarno-Tehničeskij Universitet (AGTU)

ul. Tole, 109, 050012 Almaty, Almaty

Tel: +7(727) 292-59-00

Fax: +7(727) 292-24-43

EMail: info@agtu.kz

Website: http://www.agtu.kz/

Rector: Abdukarim Serikbayev

Tel: +7(727) 292-59-00, Fax: +7(727) 292-24-43

EMail: rector@agtu.kz

Programmes

Graduate Studies (Economics; Information Technology; Law; Machine Building; Management; Power Engineering; Transport Management; Vocational Education); **Undergraduate Studies** (Accountancy; Computer Engineering; Design; Ecology; Economics; Engineering; Finance; Law; Management; Measurement and Precision Engineering; Pedagogy; Power Engineering; Primary Education; Software Engineering; Taxation; Tourism; Transport and Communications; Transport Management; Vocational Education; Wood Technology)

Further Information: Also Distance Education Programmes.

History: Founded 1997.

Admission Requirements: Certificate or diploma of basic vocational or secondary vocational school

Fees: (Tenge): Undergraduate studies: Full-time, 250,000; Part-time, 150,000. Graduate studies: 360,000.

Main Language(s) of Instruction: Kazakh, Russian

Degrees and Diplomas: *Diplom o Vysshem Obrazovanii (Bakalavr); Diplom Magistra; Diplom Doktora (PhD)*

Last Updated: 28/10/10

A. MYRZAKHMETOVA KOKSHETAU UNIVERSITY

Kokšetauskij Universitet imeni A. Myrzahmetova (KUAM)

189A, Auezov street, 020000 Kokshetau, Akmola

Tel: +7(7162) 23-02-78 +7(7162) 25-42-59 +7(7162) 25-29-78

Fax: +7(3162) 25-29-78

EMail: kuam-kokshetau@mail.kz; kuam-kokchetau@mail.ru

Website: http://kuam.forever.kz/

Rector: Sagintay Yelubayev

Departments

Economics (Accountancy; Economics; Finance; Government; Management; Tourism); **Engineering and Environment** (Advertising and Publicity; Architectural and Environmental Design; Art History; Computer Science; Design; Ecology; Engineering; Environmental Engineering; Fashion Design; Graphic Design; Industrial Design; Information Technology; Interior Design; Transport and Communications); **Faculty Correspondence**; **Humanities and Education** (History; International Relations; Pedagogy; Psychology; Social Work; Translation and Interpretation)

Schools

Law (Law)

History: Founded 2000.

Degrees and Diplomas: *Diplom o Vysshem Obrazovanii (Bakalavr); Diplom Magistra; Diplom Doktora (PhD)*

Last Updated: 03/11/10

ATYRAU ENGINEERING-HUMANITARIAN INSTITUTE

Atyrauskij Inženerno-Gumanitarnyj Institut

64, Baizhigitova street, 060014 Atyrau, Atyrau

Tel: +7(7122) 24-44-01

Fax: +7(7122) 24-44-02

EMail: unatatyrau@nursat.kz

Rector: Ersain Ikhsanov

Programmes

Arts and Humanities (Arts and Humanities); **Engineering** (Engineering)

History: Founded 2001.

Degrees and Diplomas: *Diplom o Vysshem Obrazovanii (Bakalavr); Diplom Magistra*

Last Updated: 28/10/10

BOLASHAK KARAGANDA UNIVERSITY

Karagandinskij Universitet 'Bolašak'

16, Yerubayev street, 100008 Karagandy, Karagandy

Website: http://www.kubolashak.kz/

Rector: Nurlan Dulatbekov

Faculties

Economics and Informatics (Computer Science; Economics; Finance; Information Technology; Management); **Humanities and Education** (Cultural Studies; Modern Languages; Native Language; Pedagogy; Political Sciences; Preschool Education; Psychology; Translation and Interpretation); **Law** (Civil Law; Criminal Law; Law); **Pharmacy** (Chemistry; Organic Chemistry; Pharmacy)

History: Founded 1995.

Degrees and Diplomas: *Diplom o Vysshem Obrazovanii (Bakalavr); Diplom o Vysshem Obrazovanii (Specialist); Diplom Magistra; Diplom Doktora (PhD)*

Last Updated: 29/10/10

BOLASHAK MANGISTAU INSTITUTE

Mangystauskij Institut 'Bolashak'

1, District 3B, 130001 Aktau, Mangystau

Tel: +7(7292) 50-37-30 +7(7292) 51-37-30

Fax: +7(7292) 50-45-98

EMail: Mibaktau@yandex.ru; Kunakbaeva@yandex.ru

Rector: Mukhit Kalamkaliyev

Degrees and Diplomas: *Diplom o Vysshem Obrazovanii (Bakalavr); Diplom Magistra*

Last Updated: 28/10/10

BOLASHAK UNIVERSITY

Universitet 'Bolašak'
31A, Abay avenue, 123000 Kyzylorda, Kyzylorda
Tel: +7(72422) 20-22-72
Fax: +7(72422) 20-22-80
EMail: bolashak_5@mail.ru

Rector: Umirbek Umbetov

History: Founded 1995 as branch of Moscow International University of Business and Information Technologies. Became Kyzylorda University of Economics, Statistics and Informatics 2000. Acquired present title 2002.

Degrees and Diplomas: *Diplom o Vysshem Obrazovanii (Bakalavr); Diplom Magistra*
Last Updated: 04/11/10

CASPIAN SOCIAL UNIVERSITY

Kaspiyskij Obšestvennyj Universitet (KOU)
521, Seifullin street, 050000 Almaty, Almaty
Tel: +7(727) 250-69-35 +7(727) 250-69-34
EMail: caspian@kou.kz
Website: http://www.kou.kz/

Rector: Sergey Alimov

Departments
Automation and Technology vycheslitelnoy (Automation and Control Engineering); **Economics and Management** (Administration; Economics; Management; Marketing); **Finance and Accounting** (Accountancy; Finance); **Geology, Oil and Gas** (Geology; Petroleum and Gas Engineering); **Native and Foreign Languages** (Modern Languages; Native Language; Russian); **Petroleum Engineering** (Petroleum and Gas Engineering); **Private Law** (Private Law); **Public Law** (Public Law); **Social Sciences and Humanities** (Arts and Humanities; Social Sciences)

History: Founded 1992.

Degrees and Diplomas: *Diplom o Vysshem Obrazovanii (Bakalavr); Diplom Magistra*
Last Updated: 28/10/10

CENTRAL-ASIAN UNIVERSITY

Tsentralno-Asiatskij Universitet (CAU)
60, Dzhandosov street, Almaty, 050060
Tel: +7(727) 274-74-54 +7(727) 274-74-24
Fax: +7(727) 274-01-12
EMail: info@cau.kz
Website: http://www.cau.kz/

Rector: Makash Tatimov

Faculties
Economics (Accountancy; Economics; Finance; Management; Marketing; Public Administration; Service Trades; Tourism); **Engineering** (Computer Science; Construction Engineering; Engineering; Geological Engineering; Information Technology; Mining Engineering; Petroleum and Gas Engineering; Transport Engineering; Transport Management); **Foreign Languages and International Relations** (Arabic; Chinese; English; International Relations; Translation and Interpretation; Turkish); **Law** (International Law; Justice Administration; Law)

History: Founded 1997.

Degrees and Diplomas: *Diplom o Vysshem Obrazovanii (Bakalavr); Diplom Magistra; Diplom Doktora (PhD)*
Last Updated: 06/09/11

CENTRAL KAZAKHSTAN UNIVERSITY MGTI-LINGUA

Tsentralno-Kazahstanskij Universitet MGTI-Lingva
35, boulevard Mira, 100012 Karagandy, Karagandy
Tel: +7(7212) 42-14-96 +7(7212) 42-14-96 +7(7212) 42-14-83
Fax: +7(7212) 42-14-96 +7(7212) 43-37-52
EMail: zku_mgti-lingua@mail.ru
Website: http://www.mhti-lingva.kz/

Rector: Asylbek Zhartybayev

Faculties
Economics (Accountancy; Design; Economics; Finance; Management; Marketing; Public Administration); **Social Sciences and information Technology** (Automation and Control Engineering; Information Technology; Pedagogy; Psychology; Social Work)

Institutes
Foreign Languages (Modern Languages; Translation and Interpretation)

History: Founded 1996.

Degrees and Diplomas: *Diplom o Vysshem Obrazovanii (Bakalavr); Diplom Magistra*
Last Updated: 28/10/10

D.A. KUNAEV UNIVERSITY

Universitet imeni D.A. Kunaeva
ul. Kurmangazy, 107, 050022 Almaty
Tel: +7(727) 292-98-87 +7(727) 292-98-41
Fax: +7(727) 292-98-77
EMail: kunaevun@mail.ru
Website: http://www.vuzkunaeva.kz/

Rector: Omrali Kopabayev

Faculties
Humanities and Economics (Accountancy; Business Administration; Economics; Finance; Government; History; Modern Languages; Regional Studies; Social Sciences; Translation and Interpretation); **Law** (Civil Law; Constitutional Law; Criminal Law; Criminology; International Law; Law; Police Studies)

History: Founded 1944.

Degrees and Diplomas: *Diplom o Vysshem Obrazovanii (Bakalavr); Diplom o Vysshem Obrazovanii (Specialist); Diplom Magistra; Diplom Doktora (PhD)*
Last Updated: 04/11/10

EAST KAZAKHSTAN REGIONAL UNIVERSITY

Voštočno-Kazahstanskij Regionalnyj Universitet
ul.Solnechnaya, 48, 070003 Ust-Kamenogorsk, East Kazakhstan
Tel: +7(723) 54-14-19
Fax: +7(723) 54-14-18
EMail: vkru48@mail.ru
Website: http://www.vkru.kz/

Rector: Manarbek Kylyshkanov

Departments
Economics and Business (Accountancy; Economics; Finance; Government; Management; Statistics); **Engineering, Energy and Information Systems** (Computer Engineering; Computer Science; Construction Engineering; Design; Instrument Making; Power Engineering; Software Engineering; Transport and Communications); **Intercultural Communication and Tourism** (Literature; Native Language; Psychology; Social Work; Tourism; Translation and Interpretation); **Law** (International Law; Law)

History: Founded 2001.

Degrees and Diplomas: *Diplom o Vysshem Obrazovanii (Bakalavr); Diplom Magistra*
Last Updated: 28/10/10

EURASIAN ACADEMY

Evrazijskaja Akademija
194, Dostyk avenue, 090000 Oral, Western Kazakhstan
Tel: +7(7112) 50-46-23
Fax: +7(7112) 50-46-23
EMail: zinevr@nursat.kz
Website: http://www.eurasia.edu.kz/

Rector: Isatai Ashetov

Programmes
Accounting and Audits (Accountancy); **Economics** (Economics); **Finance** (Finance); **Foreign Languages** (English; German); **Information Systems** (Information Technology); **State and Local Management** (Management); **Translation and Interpretation** (Translation and Interpretation)

History: Founded 1996.

Degrees and Diplomas: *Diplom o Vysshem Obrazovanii (Bakalavr)*; *Diplom Magistra*

Last Updated: 28/10/10

EURASIAN HUMANITARIAN INSTITUTE

Evrazijskij Gumanitarnyj Institut
ul. Zhumabayeva, 3, Astana
Tel: +7(717-2) 561-933 +7(717-2) 562-200
Fax: +7(717-2) 561-933
EMail: eagi@list.ru
Website: http://www.eagi.kz/

Rector: Amangheldy Kussaiynov (1995-)

Pro-Rector: Amangheldy Issmayilov

International Relations: Ludmila Volkova, Head of Foreign Language Department EMail: ludmila-prof.48@mail.ru

Faculties

Economics (Economics; Finance); **Education**; **Foreign Languages** (English; French; German; Translation and Interpretation); **History** (History); **Kazakh Language and Literature** (Literature; Native Language); **Law**; **Law and Economics**; **Pedagogy and Psychology**; **Primary Education** (Primary Education)

History: Created and acquired status 1995.

Governing Bodies: Council of Shareholders; Scientific Council; Rectorate

Admission Requirements: Secondary School Certificate, National Test

Fees: (Tenge): 240,000 per annum.

Main Language(s) of Instruction: Kazakh, Russian

International Co-operation: with institutions in Russian Federation.

Accrediting Agencies: National Accreditation Centre

Degrees and Diplomas: *Diplom o Vysshem Obrazovanii (Bakalavr)*; *Diplom Magistra*: Economics; Education

Student Services: Academic counselling, Canteen, Cultural centre, Employment services, Foreign student adviser, Health services, Language programs, Social counselling, Sports facilities

Student Residential Facilities: None

Libraries: Yes

Publications: Vestnic EAGI, Magazine of scientific articles *(quarterly)*; Zhas Urpak, Academic, social and leisure activities of staff *(quarterly)*

Academic Staff *2009-2010*	MEN	WOMEN	**TOTAL**
FULL-TIME	42	104	**146**
STAFF WITH DOCTORATE			
FULL-TIME	33	26	**59**
Student Numbers *2009-2010*			
All (Foreign Included)	238	694	**932**
FOREIGN ONLY	4	6	**10**

Part-time students, 1,242.

Last Updated: 20/04/10

EURASIAN INSTITUTE OF MARKETING

Evrazijskij Institut Rynka
39A, K. Ryskulov street, 050042 Almaty
Tel: +7(727) 220-28-33
Fax: +7(727) 220-02-12
EMail: info@eurazir.kz; recep_com@eurazir.kz
Website: http://www.eurazir.kz/

Rector: Aitkali Nurseit

Programmes

Accounting and Audit (Accountancy); **Economics** (Economics; International Business; International Economics); **Finance** (Banking; Finance; Insurance; Taxation); **Information Systems** (Information Technology); **Management** (Business Administration; Management; Tourism); **Marketing** (Marketing); **State and Municipal Management** (Management)

History: Founded 1993.

Degrees and Diplomas: *Diplom o Vysshem Obrazovanii (Bakalavr)*; *Diplom Magistra*

Last Updated: 28/10/10

FEMIDA JURIDICAL ACADEMY

Juridičeskaja Akademija 'Femida'
259, Pichugin street, 100009 Karagandy, Karagandy
EMail: femida_krg@mail.ru
Website: http://www.kar-femida.kz/

Rector: Bakhtybai Zhunusov Tel: +8(7212) 47-80-07

Departments

Civil and Investment Law (Civil Law; Economics; Finance; Law; Private Law); **Criminal Law and Procedure** (Criminal Law; Criminology; Law); **General Financial and Economic Disciplines** (Accountancy; Computer Science; Ecology; Economics; English; Ethics; German; History; Law; Logic; Mathematics; Native Language; Pedagogy; Philosophy; Physical Education; Political Sciences; Psychology; Russian; Sociology)

History: Founded 1997.

Degrees and Diplomas: *Diplom o Vysshem Obrazovanii (Bakalavr)*; *Diplom Magistra*

Student Residential Facilities: Hostel.

Publications: Bulletin of Themis, Newspaper; Karaganda conduct, Newspaper

Press or Publishing House: University Press

Last Updated: 29/10/10

INNOVATIVE UNIVERSITY OF EURASIA

Innovatsionnyj Evrazijskij Universitet (INEU)
Lomova, 45, 140003 Pavlodar
Tel: +7(7182) 34-47-50
Fax: +7(7182) 34-47-50
EMail: oms-pau@rambler.ru; oms@ineu.edu.kz
Website: http://www.ineu.edu.kz/

Rector: Askar Yu. Kamerbayev
Tel: +7(7182) 34-46-56 EMail: referent@ineu.edu.kz

International Relations: Evgeniy Nikitin, Vice-Rector
Tel: +7(7182) 34-56-78, Fax: +7(7182) 34-56-78
EMail: prorpau@rambler.ru

Academies

Agricultural Science *(Engineering Academy)* (Animal Husbandry); **Arts** *(Engineering Academy)* (Architecture; Design); **Business and Law** (Accountancy; Economics; Finance; Government; Journalism; Law; Management; Psychology; Taxation); **Education** *(Pedagogical Academy)* (Biotechnology; Chemistry; Economic History; Educational Psychology; English; Geography; German; History of Law; Literature; Mathematics; Native Language; Physical Education; Primary Education; Russian; Sports); **Humanities** *(Pedagogical Academy)* (Chinese; English; German; History; Native Language; Philology; Russian; Translation and Interpretation); **Natural Sciences** *(Pedagogical Academy)* (Biology; Chemistry; Computer Science; Ecology; Geography; Mathematics; Physics); **Service** *(Engineering Academy)* (Maintenance Technology; Transport and Communications; Transport Management); **Technical Science** *(Engineering Academy)* (Biotechnology; Construction Engineering; Food Technology; Heating and Refrigeration; Information Technology; Inorganic Chemistry; Machine Building; Measurement and Precision Engineering; Metallurgical Engineering; Mining Engineering; Organic Chemistry; Power Engineering; Safety Engineering; Transport Engineering)

Colleges

Economics (Finance; Management); **Information Technology** (Automation and Control Engineering; Electrical and Electronic Engineering; Heating and Refrigeration; Maintenance Technology; Power Engineering; Software Engineering); **Polytechnic** (Construction Engineering; Food Technology; Maintenance Technology; Metal Techniques)

Programmes

Aspirantura *(Postgraduate)* (Economics; Electrical and Electronic Engineering; Energy Engineering; Food Science; Food Technology; Mathematics; Metallurgical Engineering; Pedagogy; Psychology;

Russian); **Master** (Automation and Control Engineering; Biology; Biotechnology; Computer Science; Economics; Educational Psychology; Heating and Refrigeration; Information Management; Management; Measurement and Precision Engineering; Pedagogy; Philology; Power Engineering; Psychology; Safety Engineering; Sociology; Software Engineering)

Research Institutes

Energy Saving Technologies (Energy Engineering; Metallurgical Engineering; Thermal Engineering); **Social Problems** (Sociology); **Sustainable Regional Development**

History: Founded 1991, acquired present status and title 2006. Previously known as Pavlodarskij Universitet.

Governing Bodies: Board of Founders; Scientific Council; Rector's Board

Academic Year: September to June (September-January; February-June)

Admission Requirements: Competitive entrance examination following secondary school certificate (Atestat o srednem obrazovanii)

Fees: (US Dollars): c. 800-1,200 per annum

Main Language(s) of Instruction: Kazakh, Russian

International Co-operation: Joint Master programme in Renewable Energy with TEI Greece (Tempus Tacis), joint bachelor programme in Biotechnology with University of Neubrandenburg (DAAD, Germany).

Accrediting Agencies: State Certification Commission

Degrees and Diplomas: *Diplom o Vysshem Obrazovanii (Bakalavr)*: Education; Economics; Humanities; Law; Arts; Social Sciences and Business; Natural Sciences; Technical Sciences; Agricultural Sciences; Services; *Diplom o Vysshem Obrazovanii (Specialist)*: Education; Economics; Humanities; Law; Arts; Social Sciences and Business; Natural Sciences; Technical Sciences; Agricultural Sciences; Services; *Diplom Magistra*: Pedagogy and Psychology; Informatics; Geography; Philology; Sociology; Psychology; Economics; Management; Computer studies; Biology; Biotechnology; Automation and Control, a further 2 yrs; *Diplom Magistra*: Software and Hardware; Heat Engineering; Power Engineering; Life Safety and Environmental Studies; Standardization, Methodology and Certification

Student Services: Academic counselling, Canteen, Cultural centre, Employment services, Foreign student adviser, Foreign Studies Centre, Health services, Language programs, Social counselling, Sports facilities

Student Residential Facilities: Yes

Special Facilities: Museum; Technical Maintenance Station

Libraries: InEU Library

Publications: Vesnik PaU, Scientific Journal *(quarterly)*

Academic Staff *2009-2010*	MEN	WOMEN	**TOTAL**
FULL-TIME	105	291	**396**
PART-TIME	95	73	**168**
STAFF WITH DOCTORATE			
FULL-TIME	17	9	**26**
PART-TIME	11	–	**11**
Student Numbers *2009-2010*			
All (Foreign Included)	4,913	5,345	**10,258**
FOREIGN ONLY	28	14	**42**

Part-time students, 4,236. **Evening students**, 74.

Last Updated: 01/10/10

INTERNATIONAL ACADEMY OF BUSINESS

Meždunarodnaja Akademija Biznesa

ul. Rozybakieva, 227, 050060 Almaty

Tel: +7(727) 249-69-06 +7(727) 248-48-66

Fax: +7(727) 293-30-70

EMail: Info@iab.kz

Website: http://www.iab.kz/

President-Rector: Asylbek Kozhakhmetov

Tel: +7(727) 249-64-46, Fax: +7(727) 293-30-70

EMail: secretary@iab.kz

Centres

Management Development (Finance; Human Resources; Management; Marketing)

Departments

Doctor of Business Administration (Business Administration); **Higher Professional Education** (Accountancy; Cooking and Catering; Finance; Information Management; Information Sciences; Marketing; Transport Management); **International Development**; **Master of Business Administration** (Business Administration); **Monitoring and Quality Management System**

History: Created 1988 as Almaty School of Management (Almatynskaja Škola Menedžmenta). Acquired current title and status 2002.

Degrees and Diplomas: *Diplom o Vysshem Obrazovanii (Bakalavr)*; *Diplom o Vysshem Obrazovanii (Specialist)*; *Diplom Magistra*; *Diplom Doktora (PhD)*

Last Updated: 26/10/10

INTERNATIONAL BUSINESS ACADEMY

Meždunarodnaja Biznesa Academija

12, Tulepov street, 100027 Karagandy, Karagandy

Tel: +8(32-12) 42-14-35

Fax: +8(32-12) 42-14-36

EMail: yavorsky-v-v@rambler.ru

Rector: Kazbek Saginov

Programmes

International Business (International Business)

History: Founded 1996.

Degrees and Diplomas: *Diplom o Vysshem Obrazovanii (Bakalavr)*; *Diplom Magistra*

Last Updated: 28/10/10

INTERNATIONAL HUMANITARIAN-TECHNICAL UNIVERSITY

Meždunarodnij Gumanitarno-Tehničeskij Universitet

80, Baitursynov street, 160021 Shymkent, Southern Kazakhstan

Website: http://hgtu.kz/

President: Galymzhan Zhurynov

Faculties

Economics (Accountancy; Economics); **Law** (Fine Arts; Law; Physical Education; Sports); **Pedagogy** (Geography; History; Pedagogy; Philology; Psychology); **Sciences and Technology** (Biology; Chemistry; Ecology; Mathematics and Computer Science; Measurement and Precision Engineering)

Degrees and Diplomas: *Diplom o Vysshem Obrazovanii (Bakalavr)*; *Diplom Magistra*

Last Updated: 29/10/10

KAINAR UNIVERSITY

Universitet 'Kaynar' (KAINAR)

ul. Satpajeva 7a, 480013 Almaty

Tel: +8(727) 255-84-58 +8(727) 255-83-44

Fax: +8(727) 255-83-66 +8(727) 255-83-42

EMail: kainar@kazuniver.kz

Website: http://www.kazuniver.kz

Rector: Yerengaip Salipovič Omarov (1991-)

Tel: +7(3272) 620-992 EMail: yerengaipom@mail.kz

Faculties

Economics (Accountancy; Economics; Finance; Management); **Foreign Languages** (Chinese; English; French; German; Modern Languages; Spanish; Translation and Interpretation; Turkish); **Information Systems** (Computer Engineering; Computer Science; Graphic Design; Information Technology; Software Engineering); **Law** (Civil Law; Criminal Law; Economics; Law); **Pedagogy and Psychology** (Education; Pedagogy; Psychology; Social Work); **Philology, History and International Relations** (History; International Relations; Journalism; Literature; Modern Languages; Native Language; Political Sciences)

Further Information: Also branches in Akmola, Aktobe, Aktau, Pavlodar, Semei, Taraz and Šymkent

History: Founded 1991, acquired present status 1992.

Governing Bodies: University Council

Academic Year: September to June

Admission Requirements: Competitive entrance examinations following secondary school leaving certificate (Atestat o srednem obrazovanii), health certificate, military card (only for males)

Fees: (Tenge): 71,500-143,000 per annum; evening students, 35,000-85,800; correspondence students, 35,750-71,500

Main Language(s) of Instruction: Kazakh, Russian

International Co-operation: Participates in the Tempus-Tacis programme

Accrediting Agencies: Ministry of Education and Science

Degrees and Diplomas: *Diplom o Vysshem Obrazovanii (Bakalavr); Diplom Magistra*

Student Services: Academic counselling, Cultural centre, Employment services, Foreign student adviser, Foreign Studies Centre, Health services, Language programs, Nursery care, Social counselling, Sports facilities

Special Facilities: TV Studio. Department of War Affairs. Centre for European and American Studies

Libraries: Kainar University Library, c. 300,000 vols

Press or Publishing House: Kainar Publishing House

Last Updated: 25/10/10

KAINAR UNIVERSITY (SEMEY)

Universitet 'Kainar' (Semey)

152A, Chaizhunusova street, 071400 Semey, Eastern Kazakhstan
Tel: +7(7222) 56-47-79
Fax: +7(7222) 56-47-79
Website: http://www.kainar-semey.kz/

Rector: Leila Mausunbayeva
Tel: +8(7222) 52-29-14; +8(7222) 52-37-45,
Fax: +8(7222) 56-60-41 EMail: kainar_it@mail.ru

Faculties

Economics and Information Systems (Economics; Information Technology); **Humanities** (Modern Languages; Pedagogy; Psychology); **Jurisprudence** (Law)

History: Founded 1996.

Degrees and Diplomas: *Diplom o Vysshem Obrazovanii (Bakalavr); Diplom Magistra*

Last Updated: 04/11/10

KARAGANDA ECONOMICS UNIVERSITY OF KAZPOTREBSOYUZ

Karagandinskij Ekonomičeskij Universitet Kazpotrebsoyuza (KEUK)

ul. Akademiceskaya 9, 100009 Karaganda
Tel: +77(121) 441-622
Fax: +77(121) 441-632
EMail: keu@mail.pmicro.kz
Website: http://www.keu.kz

Rector: Yerkara Aimagambetov Balkaraevich (1997-)
EMail: rector@keu.kz

Pro-Rector: Kosman Abilov
Tel: +77(212) 441-563 EMail: pms@keu.kz

International Relations: Aliya Abdikarimova, International Projects Coordinator EMail: Aliyata@mail.ru

International Relations: Oksana Stepanitskaya, Head of International Office EMail: step-oks@mail.ru

Faculties

Accountancy and Finance (Accountancy; Banking; Computer Science; Economics; Finance; Insurance; Physical Education; Taxation); **Business and Law** (Law; Marketing; Social Work; Taxation; Tourism); **Economics and Management** (Economics; International Economics; Management; Mathematics; Modern Languages; Native Language; Public Administration; Russian)

Further Information: Branches in Astana, Pavlodar, Kostanai, Shymkent and Kyzylorda

History: Founded 1966, acquired present status and title 1997.

Governing Bodies: Rectorate

Academic Year: September to June

Admission Requirements: Secondary school certificate (Gosudarstvennyj obrazovatelnyj sertifikat)

Fees: (Tenge): c. 186,000 per annum (US Dollars: 1,550)

Main Language(s) of Instruction: Kazakh, Russian

International Co-operation: With universities in Russia, Ukraine, Uzbekistan, Moldova, Belorussia, Tajikistan, Kyrgystan, Germany, Austria, Italy, USA, UK

Accrediting Agencies: Ministry of Education and Science

Degrees and Diplomas: *Diplom o Vysshem Obrazovanii (Bakalavr)*: 4 yrs; *Diplom Magistra*: 2 yrs following Bakalavr; *Diplom Doktora (PhD)*

Student Services: Academic counselling, Canteen, Cultural centre, Health services, Social counselling, Sports facilities

Student Residential Facilities: 3 dormitories for 410 students

Special Facilities: Museums.

Libraries: Library, 813,849 vols, 322 titles of subscriptions and electronic resources.

Publications: KEU Bulletin *(quarterly)*

Press or Publishing House: University Printing Office

Academic Staff *2008-2009*	MEN	WOMEN	TOTAL
FULL-TIME	56	181	**237**
PART-TIME	2	12	**14**
STAFF WITH DOCTORATE			
FULL-TIME	35	66	**101**
PART-TIME	5	7	**12**
Student Numbers *2008-2009*			
All (Foreign Included)	2,905	5,752	**8,657**

Distance students, 6,535.

Last Updated: 19/10/10

KAZAKH ACADEMY OF LABOUR AND SOCIAL RELATIONS

Kazahskaja Akademija Truda i Socialnyj Otnoshenij

9, Nauryzbai batyr street, 050004 Almaty, Almaty
Tel: +7(727) 279-95-70
Fax: +7(727) 279-95-70
Website: http://www.atso.kz/

Rector: Bayan Besbayeva

Departments

Oriental and Western Languages *(Interfaculty)* (Chinese; English; French; German; Japanese; Korean; Native Language; Turkish)

Faculties

Economics (Accountancy; Computer Science; Economics; Finance; Management; Marketing; Software Engineering); **Humanities** (International Relations; Political Sciences; Psychology; Regional Studies; Social Work)

Schools

Law (Law)

History: Founded 1996.

Degrees and Diplomas: *Diplom o Vysshem Obrazovanii (Bakalavr); Diplom Magistra*

Last Updated: 29/10/10

KAZAKH-AMERICAN FREE UNIVERSITY

Kazahstansko-Amerikanskij Svobodnyj Universitet (KAFU)

Independence, 86, 070018 Ust-Kamenogorsk, East Kazakhstan
Tel: +7(7232) 23-12-53 +7(7232) 22-23-24
EMail: kafu@ok.kz
Website: http://www.kafu.kz/

President: Yerezhep Mambetkaziyev

Programmes

Doctoral Studies (Administrative Law; Business Administration; Educational Administration; International Law; Law; Leadership; Management); **Graduate Studies** (Fiscal Law; Law; Leadership;

Management); **Undergraduate Studies** (Arts and Humanities; Business Administration; Education; Engineering; Law; Service Trades; Social Sciences; Technology)

History: Founded 1994.

Degrees and Diplomas: *Diplom o Vysshem Obrazovanii (Bakalavr); Diplom Magistra; Diplom Doktora (PhD)*

Last Updated: 29/10/10

KAZAKH-BRITISH TECHNICAL UNIVERSITY

Kazahsko-Britanskij Tehničeskij Universitet (KBTU)
ul. Tole Bi, 59, 050000 Almaty
Tel: +7(327) 250-46-58
Fax: +7(327) 272-46-37
EMail: info@kbtu.kz; intoffice@kbtu.kz
Website: http://www.kbtu.kz

Rector: Iskander Kalybekovich Byeisembetov

Departments

Master's Programmes (Business Administration; Petroleum and Gas Engineering)

Faculties

Economy and Finance (Accountancy; Economics; Finance; Management); **Information Technology** (Automation and Control Engineering; Computer Engineering; Computer Science; Information Sciences; Information Technology; Software Engineering); **Petroleum and Gas Engineering** (Chemical Engineering; Chemistry; Engineering; Hydraulic Engineering; Inorganic Chemistry; Mechanics; Organic Chemistry; Petroleum and Gas Engineering; Physics)

Schools

Economics and Social Sciences *(International)* (Banking; Economics; Finance; Management)

History: Created in 2001 in conjunction with British government as a joint venture between Ministry of Education and Science and British Council.

Main Language(s) of Instruction: Russian, English

Accrediting Agencies: Ministry of Education and Science

Degrees and Diplomas: *Diplom o Vysshem Obrazovanii (Bakalavr); Diplom Magistra; Diplom Doktora (PhD)*

Student Services: Academic counselling, Canteen, Cultural centre, Foreign student adviser, Health services, Language programs, Sports facilities

Student Residential Facilities: Yes

Libraries: Yes

Last Updated: 26/10/10

KAZAKH-CHINA INSTITUTE

Kazahsko-Kitayskij Institutyj
ul. Michurina, 1A, 120008 Kyzylorda, Kyzylorda
Tel: +7(7242) 23-03-97
Fax: +7(7242) 23-02-51
EMail: kazki@kazki.kz; intern@kazki.kz
Website: http://www.kazki.kz/

Rector: Kazhdenbek Nuraliyev

Programmes

Computer Hardware and Software (Computer Engineering; Software Engineering); **Ecology** (Ecology); **Economics** (Economics); **Finance** (Finance); **Foreign Languages** (Chinese); **History** (History); **Kazakh Language and Literature** (Literature; Native Language); **Music Education** (Music Education); **Oil and Gas Business** (Business Administration; Petroleum and Gas Engineering); **Pedagogy and Methodology of Elementary Education** (Pedagogy; Primary Education); **Principles of Law and Economics** (Economics; Law)

History: Founded 1993.

International Co-operation: With institutions in China, Slovak Republic, United Kingdom, Kyrgyzstan, Uzbekistan, USA, Russia

Degrees and Diplomas: *Diplom o Vysshem Obrazovanii (Bakalavr); Diplom Magistra*

Last Updated: 02/11/10

KAZAKH ENGINEERING-TECHNICAL ACADEMY

Kazahskaja inženerno-Tehničeskaja Akademija (CITA)
22A, Zheltoksan street, 010000 Astana, Akmola
Tel: +8(7172) 32-07-94 +8(7172) 32-35-14
Fax: +8(7172) 32-01-52
EMail: kazita2008@mail.ru; of_kita@mail.ru; pk_kita@mail.ru
Website: http://www.kazita.kz/

Rector: Kanat Tulenbayev

Programmes

Engineering and Technology (Accountancy; Economics; Engineering; Information Technology; Technology)

History: Founded 1997.

Degrees and Diplomas: *Diplom o Vysshem Obrazovanii (Bakalavr); Diplom Magistra*

Last Updated: 29/10/10

KAZAKH FINANCE-ECONOMIC ACADEMY

Kazahskaja Finansovo-Ekonomičeskaja Akademija
5, Baisetova street, 071400 Semey, Eastern Kazakhstan
Tel: +7(3222) 66-02-02 +7(3222) 66-22-53
Fax: +7(3222) 66-58-13
EMail: kazfei@semsk.kz

Rector: Nadirbek Apsalyamov

Programmes

Finance and Economics (Economics; Finance)

Degrees and Diplomas: *Diplom o Vysshem Obrazovanii (Bakalavr); Diplom Magistra*

Last Updated: 29/10/10

KAZAKH-GERMAN UNIVERSITY

Kazahsko-Nemetskij Universitet (KNU)
ul. Pushkina 111/113, 050010 Almaty, Almaty
Tel: +7(727) 293-89-13
Fax: +7(727) 293-90-01
EMail: info@dku.kz
Website: http://www.dku.kz/

President and Rector: Johann W. Gerlach
Tel: +7(727) 293-89-13 -12
EMail: gerlach@dku.kz; jgerlach@zedat.fu-berlin.de

Faculties

Economics and Management (Finance; International Business; Management; Marketing); **Engineering and Ecology** (Energy Engineering; Environmental Engineering); **Engineering and Economics** (Business Computing; Transport Management); **Social Sciences** (International Relations; Regional Studies)

History: Founded 1999.

Fees: (Tenge): Bachelor programmes, 480,000 per annum for first higher education; 100,000 per annum in Second Higher Education (5 semesters). Master programmes, 600,000 per annum.

Degrees and Diplomas: *Diplom o Vysshem Obrazovanii (Bakalavr); Diplom Magistra*

Last Updated: 02/11/10

KAZAKH HUMANITARIAN JURIDICAL INNOVATIVE UNIVERSITY

Kazahskij Gumanitarno-Juridičeskij Innovatsionnyj Universitet
ul.Abaya, 94, 0714000 Semey, East Kazakhstan
Tel: +8(7222) 52-52-26 +8(7222) 56-88-40 +8(7222) 56-24-23
Fax: +8(7222) 56-59-99 +8(7222) 56-88-40
EMail: semey_urist@mail.ru
Website: http://www.semuniver.com/

Rector: Kurmanbayeva Shyryn

Faculties
Humanities (Arts and Humanities); **Information Technology and Economics** (Accountancy; Biology; Computer Science; Economics; Mathematics; Physical Education)

Schools
Law (Civil Law; Criminal Law; Law; Police Studies; Public Law)

History: Founded 1997.

Degrees and Diplomas: *Diplom o Vysshem Obrazovanii (Bakalavr); Diplom Magistra*

Student Numbers *2009-2010*: Total: c. 5,000

Last Updated: 29/10/10

KAZAKHSTAN ENGINEERING-TECHNOLOGICAL UNIVERSITY

Kazahstanskij Inženerno-Tehnologičeskij Universitet (KAZETU)

93A, Al Farabi street, 050060 Almaty, Almaty
Tel: +8(727) 269-46-48 +8(727) 269-46-42
Fax: +8(727) 269-46-40
EMail: kazetu@gmail.com; kazetu@mail.ru; kazetu@kazetu.kz
Website: http://www.kazetu.kz/

Rector: Nailya Jerembayeva

Departments
Agricultural Technology, Standardization and Certification (Horticulture; Measurement and Precision Engineering; Soil Science); **Computer Science, Automation and Telecommunications** (Automation and Control Engineering; Computer Science; Electronic Engineering; Software Engineering; Telecommunications Engineering); **Economics and Finance** (Accountancy; Finance; Marketing; Service Trades; Tourism); **Natural Sciences** (Biotechnology; Organic Chemistry); **Social Sciences and Humanities** (Economics); **Technology and Equipment of Food Production** (Food Technology; Machine Building)

History: Founded 2001.

Degrees and Diplomas: *Diplom o Vysshem Obrazovanii (Bakalavr); Diplom Magistra*

Last Updated: 02/11/10

KAZAKHSTAN INSTITUTE OF MANAGEMENT, ECONOMICS AND STRATEGIC RESEARCH

Kazahstanskij Institut Menedžmenta, Ekonomiki i Prognozirovanija (KIMEP)

Ul Abay 4, 050010 Almaty
Tel: +7(727) 237-47-57
Fax: +7(727) 270-42-33
EMail: bang@kimep.kz
Website: http://www.kimep.kz

President: Chan Young Bang
Tel: +7 (727) 270-42-00, Fax: +7 (727) 270-42-33

Executive Vice-President: Habibur Rahman
Tel: +7(272) 270-42-02 EMail: sergei@kimep.kz

International Relations: Ronald Voogdt, Director, International Relations Office
Tel: +7(272) 270-43-80, Fax: +7(272) 270-42-11
EMail: rvoogdt@kimep.kz

Centres
Language (English; French; German; Japanese; Korean; Native Language; Russian; Spanish; Turkish)

Colleges
Business Administration *(Bang)* (Accountancy; Business Administration; Finance; Hotel and Restaurant; Information Sciences; International Business; Law; Leadership; Management; Marketing; Tourism); **Social Sciences** (Economics; International Relations; Journalism; Mass Communication; Political Sciences; Public Administration; Social Sciences)

Schools
Law (International Law; Law)

History: Founded 1992 by the Decree of the President of the Republic of Kazakhstan. Acquired present status and title 2004.

Governing Bodies: Board of Trustees; KIMEP Council

Academic Year: August to May. Summer school from May-mid August

Admission Requirements: High school Diploma and English proficiency

Fees: (Tenge): 16,600-32,800 per credit per annum

Main Language(s) of Instruction: English

International Co-operation: With universities in the United Kingdom, Sweden, Germany, USA, Republic of Korea, Kyrgyzstan, Denmark, Latvia, Hungary, China, Netherlands, Slovenia, Turkey, Poland and South Africa. Also participates in Erasmus Mundus programmes

Accrediting Agencies: National Accreditation Center under the Ministry of Education and Science

Degrees and Diplomas: *Diplom o Vysshem Obrazovanii (Bakalavr)*: Accountancy; Finance; Management; Marketing; Operations Management; Information Systems; Business Administration; Accounting; Finance; Management; Marketing; Management; Information Systems; Economics; International Journalism; International Relations; Public Administration; Political Science; *Diplom Magistra*: Accountancy; Finance; Management; Marketing; Information Systems; Management; Operations Management; Business Law; Foreign Language Education; English; International Economics; Public Policy Economics; International Journalism; Mass Communication; International Relations; Public Administration; *Diplom Doktora (PhD)*: Business Administration

Student Services: Academic counselling, Canteen, Cultural centre, Employment services, Foreign student adviser, Foreign Studies Centre, Health services, Language programs, Sports facilities

Student Residential Facilities: Dormitory

Special Facilities: Student Fun Club

Libraries: c. 90,000 vols.

Publications: ; Central Asian Journal of Management, Economics and Social Research, Research publication *(annually)*

Last Updated: 21/10/10

KAZAKHSTAN MULTI-PROFILE INSTITUTE 'PARASAT'

Kazahstanskij Mnogoprofilnyj Institut 'Parasat'

88A, Satpayev street, 050046 Almaty
Tel: +7(727) 275-97-96 +7(727) 275-97-97 +7(727) 259-81-73
EMail: parasat@kmiparasat.kz
Website: http://www.kmiparasat.kz/

Rector: Vyacheslav Ugai

Faculties
Architecture and Civil Engineering *(AACI)* (Architecture; Civil Engineering); **Medical Studies** (Nursing); **Social Sciences and Humanities** (Educational Psychology; Geography; Modern Languages; Psychology; Social Sciences; Translation and Interpretation)

History: Founded 2006.

Degrees and Diplomas: *Diplom o Vysshem Obrazovanii (Bakalavr); Diplom Magistra*

Last Updated: 03/11/10

KAZAKHSTAN UNIVERSITY 'ALATAU'

Kazahstanskij Universitet 'Alatau'

184/15-17, Zhibek Zholy street, 050012 Almaty, Almaty
Tel: +7(727) 292-14-84 +7(727) 292-50-35
Fax: +7(727) 292-20-05
EMail: info@abd.kz
Website: http://www.abd.kz/?q=kk/node/335

Rector: Sergazy Dzhienkulov

Departments
Accounting and Audit (Accountancy); **Economy and Social-humanitarian Disciplines** (Design; Economics; Management; Tourism); **Finance** (Finance); **Information Technology** (Information Technology)

History: Founded 1998.

Degrees and Diplomas: *Diplom o Vysshem Obrazovanii (Bakalavr); Diplom Magistra*
Last Updated: 03/11/10

KAZAKHSTAN-RUSSIAN MEDICAL UNIVERSITY

Kazahstansko-Rossijskij Meditsinskij Universitet
71, Torekulov street, 050004 Almaty

Rector: Nurlan Dzhainakbayev

Programmes
Medicine (Medicine)

History: Founded 1992.

Degrees and Diplomas: *Diplom o Vysshem Obrazovanii (Bakalavr); Diplom Magistra*
Last Updated: 03/11/10

KAZAKHSTAN-RUSSIAN UNIVERSITY

Kazahstansko-Rossijskij Universitet (KAZRU)
8, Kabanbai batyr avenue, 010000 Astana, Akmola
Tel: +8(7172) 24-23-14 +8(7172) 24-05-54
Fax: +8(7172) 24-33-60
EMail: muh-astana@rambler.ru; liceymuldahmetov@mail.ru
Website: http://www.kazru.kz/

Rector: Abdygali Dzhandigulov

Departments
Design (Architectural and Environmental Design; Design; Graphic Design); **Economics and Accounting** (Accountancy; Economics); **Finance and Management** (Finance; Management); **Informatics and Applied Mathematics** (Applied Mathematics; Computer Science); **Kazakh and Foreign Languages** (English; French; German; Literature; Modern Languages; Native Language; Philology); **Legal Disciplines** (Law); **Political Sciences and Social-humanitarian Disciplines** (Political Sciences); **Psychology and Pedagogy** (Pedagogy; Psychology)

History: Founded 1998.

Degrees and Diplomas: *Diplom o Vysshem Obrazovanii (Bakalavr); Diplom Magistra*
Last Updated: 03/11/10

KAZAKH UNIVERSITY OF ECONOMY, FINANCE AND INTERNATIONAL TRADE

Kazahskij Universitet Ekonomiki, Finansov i Meždunarodnoj Torgovli (KAZUEFIMT)
7, Zhubakov street, 010008 Astana, Akmola
Tel: +8(7172) 37-39-04
Fax: +8(7172) 37-16-22
EMail: priemkom@mail.ru; kazeu_astana@list.ru; kazeu_astana@list.ru
Website: http://www.kuef.kz/

Rector: Gabdigapar Seyitkasimov

Faculties
Accounting and Finance (Accountancy; Banking; Finance; Information Technology; Software Engineering); **Economics and Business** (Cultural Studies; Economics; English; French; German; International Economics; Law; Management; Marketing; Native Language; Philosophy; Russian; Social Work; Sociology; Taxation; Tourism); **Evening and Distance Education** *(FVDO)* (Distance Education; Maintenance Technology; Software Engineering)

History: Founded 1999.

Degrees and Diplomas: *Diplom o Vysshem Obrazovanii (Bakalavr); Diplom Magistra; Diplom Doktora (PhD)*
Last Updated: 02/11/10

KAZAKH UNIVERSITY OF FRIENDSHIP OF NATIONS

Kazahskij Universitet Družby Narodov
32, Tole bi street, 160020 Shymkent, Southern Kazakhstan
Tel: +7(7252) 53-01-59
Fax: +7(7252) 55-81-63
EMail: info@kudn.kz; kuigu@nursat.kz
Website: http://www.kudn.kz/

Rector: Abdumusa Kuatbekov

Departments
Chemistry and Biology (Biology; Chemistry); **Economics and Finance** (Economics; Finance); **History and Geography** (Geography; History); **Jurisprudence** (Law); **Mathematics and Computer Science** (Computer Science; Mathematics; Mathematics and Computer Science); **Pedagogy and Psychology** (Pedagogy; Psychology); **Petroleum and Gas Engineering** (Petroleum and Gas Engineering); **Philology** (Philology); **Physical Education and Sports** (Physical Education; Sports); **Radioengineering, Electronics and Telecommunications Engineering** (Electronic Engineering; Telecommunications Engineering)

Degrees and Diplomas: *Diplom o Vysshem Obrazovanii (Bakalavr); Diplom Magistra*
Last Updated: 02/11/10

KAZAKH UNIVERSITY OF MEANS OF COMMUNICATION

Kazahskij Universitet Putej Soobšenija (KUPS)
32 A, Zhetysu-1 district, 050063 Almaty, Almaty
Tel: +7(727) 376-74-78
Fax: +7(727) 376-74-81
EMail: kups1@mail.ru
Website: http://www.kups.kz/

Rector: Amangeldy Omarov

Faculties
Transport Technology, Construction and Automation (Automation and Control Engineering; Building Technologies; Construction Engineering; Electrical Engineering; Mechanical Engineering; Power Engineering; Telecommunications Engineering; Transport and Communications); **Transportation Organization and Economy** (Accountancy; Economics; Finance; Management; Marketing; Taxation; Transport and Communications; Transport Management)

History: Founded 2000.

Degrees and Diplomas: *Diplom o Vysshem Obrazovanii (Bakalavr); Diplom Magistra; Diplom Doktora (PhD)*
Last Updated: 02/11/10

KAZAKH UNIVERSITY OF TECHNOLOGY AND BUSINESS

Kazahskij Universitet Tehnologij i Biznesa
54/2, Respublika avenue, Sary-Arka district, 010000 Astana, Akmola
Website: http://www.kazutb.kz/

President: Seitkassym Baibekov EMail: akutb@mail.ru

Departments
Business Technology (Cooking and Catering; Economics; Finance; Tourism); **Chemistry, Chemical Technology and Ecology** (Chemistry; Ecology; Environmental Studies; Organic Chemistry); **General Studies** (Computer Engineering; Computer Graphics; Computer Networks; Computer Science; Cultural Studies; Data Processing; English; German; History; Information Sciences; Mathematics; Native Language; Philosophy; Physics; Political Sciences; Russian; Sociology; Statistics); **Light Industry Technology and Design** (Design; Industrial Design); **Technology and**

Standardization (Biotechnology; Cooking and Catering; Food Technology; Measurement and Precision Engineering)

History: Founded 2004.

Degrees and Diplomas: *Diplom o Vysshem Obrazovanii (Bakalavr); Diplom Magistra*

Academic Staff *2009-2010*: Total 105

STAFF WITH DOCTORATE: Total 6

Last Updated: 02/11/10

KOKSHE ACADEMY

Akademija 'Kokshe' (KU)

ul. Esenberlina, 38, 020000 Kokshetau

Tel: +7(7162) 32-70-36

Fax: +7(7162) 32-70-36

EMail: idt67@mail.ru; koksheuniver@mail.kz; koksheuniver@mail.ru

Website: http://www.koksheacad.kz/

Rector: Zhanat Kassym (1993-) EMail: idt67@mail.ru

Pro-Rector, Academic: Uldai Kereeva

Tel: +7(7162) 75-02-81, Fax: +7(7162) 75-02-81

International Relations: Diana Ismailova, Vice-Rector, International Affairs EMail: idt67@mail.ru

Departments

Accounting and Auditing (Accountancy); **Design** (Design; Graphic Design; Industrial Design); **Environment and Forestry** (Ecology; Environmental Studies; Forestry; Health Sciences; Safety Engineering); **Jurisprudence** (Law); **Kazakh Language and Literature** (Literature; Native Language); **Pedagogy** (Pedagogy; Preschool Education); **Politics** (History; Political Sciences); **Psychology** (Pedagogy; Psychology); **Scientific Disciplines** (Computer Science; Econometrics; English; German; Mathematics; Physics; Russian; Statistics)

Faculties

Finance (Finance); **Physical Culture and Tourism** (Physical Education; Sports; Tourism)

History: Created in 1993. Previously known as Kokshetau University.

Admission Requirements: Unified National Exam or equivalent secondary school certificate

Fees: (Tenge): 900,000 - 110,000 per annum

Main Language(s) of Instruction: Kazakh, Russian

International Co-operation: USAid, Tempus

Degrees and Diplomas: *Diplom o Vysshem Obrazovanii (Bakalavr); Diplom Magistra*

Student Services: Academic counselling, Canteen, Cultural centre, Employment services, Foreign student adviser, Foreign Studies Centre, Health services, Language programs, Nursery care, Social counselling, Sports facilities

Special Facilities: Printing House; Ecology Centre; TV Studio; Archaeological Centre

Libraries: c. 400,000 vols. 90 Periodical subscriptions.

Academic Staff *2010-2011*: Total 148

STAFF WITH DOCTORATE: Total 51

Last Updated: 27/10/10

KOKSHETAU INSTITUTE OF ECONOMICS AND MANAGEMENT

Kokšetauskij Institut Ekonomiki i Managementa (KIEM)

ul. Žambyla 35, 020000 Kokshetau

Tel: +8(7162) 264-949 +8(7162) 264-636 +8(7162) 264-760

Fax: +8(7162) 264-828

EMail: kokshetau@kiem.kz

Website: http://www.kiem.kz

Rector: Abilmazhin Ayulov

Departments

Economics and Management (Economics; Government; Management; Marketing; Service Trades); **Financial Management and Accounting** (Accountancy; Finance; Management); **Information Systems and Computer Engineering** (Computer Engineering; Information Technology); **Socio-Humanities** (Arts and Humanities; English; Philosophy)

History: Founded 1992. Former Kokšetau Higher College of Management and Business. A private, non-profit institution.

Academic Year: September to July

Admission Requirements: Competitive entrance examinations following secondary school certificate (Atestat srednem obrazovanii)

Fees: (Tenge): 105,000 per annum

Main Language(s) of Instruction: Kazakh, Russian

International Co-operation: With universities in USA and United Kingdom

Accrediting Agencies: Ministry of Education and Science

Degrees and Diplomas: *Diplom o Vysshem Obrazovanii (Bakalavr); Diplom Magistra*

Student Services: Canteen, Cultural centre, Employment services, Health services, Language programs, Sports facilities

Special Facilities: Communication Centre; Regional Training Centre

Libraries: 25,000 volumes

Publications: KIEM *(annually)*

Press or Publishing House: Publishing House

Last Updated: 21/10/10

KOSTANAI SOCIAL TECHNICAL UNIVERSITY NAMED AFTER THE ACADEMICIAN ACADEMICIAN Z. ALDAMZHAR

Kostanaiskij Socialno-Tehničeskij Universitet imeni Akademika Z. Aldamžar (KOSSTU)

27, Gertsen street, 110000 Kostanay, Kostanay

Tel: +7(7142) 55-40-09 +7(7142) 55-42-64 +7(7142) 51-11-85

Fax: +7(7142) 55-41-42

EMail: pkkstu@mail.ru

Website: http://www.kosstu.kz/

Rector: Kadyrgali Dzhamanbalin

Faculties

Economics, Law and Management (Banking; Economics; Finance; Law; Management; Taxation); **Education** (Economics; Education; Environmental Studies; Geography; History; Law; Literature; Modern Languages; Music Education; Pedagogy; Physical Education; Psychology; Sports; Translation and Interpretation); **Technical Studies** (Computer Engineering; Computer Science; Electrical Engineering; Information Technology; Physics; Power Engineering; Software Engineering; Transport Engineering; Transport Management; Vocational Education)

Further Information: Also distance education programmes.

History: Founded 1998.

Degrees and Diplomas: *Diplom o Vysshem Obrazovanii (Bakalavr); Diplom Magistra*

Last Updated: 03/11/10

KOSTANAY ENGINEERING-PEDAGOGICAL UNIVERSITY

Kostanaiskij Inženerno-Pedagogičeskij Universitet

59, Chernyshevskii street, 110007 Kostanay, Kostanay

Rector: Sabit Ismuratov

Programmes

Engineering (Engineering); **Pedagogy** (Pedagogy)

History: Founded 1996.

Degrees and Diplomas: *Diplom o Vysshem Obrazovanii (Bakalavr); Diplom o Vysshem Obrazovanii (Specialist); Diplom Magistra*

Last Updated: 03/11/10

L.B. GONCHAROV KAZAKH AUTOMOBILE AND ROAD INSTITUTE

Kazahskij Avtodorožnyj Institut imeni L.B. Gončarova
417A, Raiymbek street, 050061 Almaty, Almaty
Tel: +7(727) 239-54-64 +7(727) 225-61-89 +7(727) 239-56-70
EMail: kazadi@kazadi.kz
Website: http://www.kazadi.kz/

Rector: Rakhimzhan Kabashev

Faculties
Automobile and Road (Accountancy; Building Technologies; Economics; Finance; Information Technology; Marketing; Road Engineering; Translation and Interpretation; Transport Engineering)

History: Founded 1944.

Degrees and Diplomas: *Diplom o Vysshem Obrazovanii (Bakalavr); Diplom Magistra*
Last Updated: 03/11/10

MIRAS UNIVERSITY

Universitet 'Miras'
2, Sapa Datka street, 160012 Shymkent, Southern Kazakhstan
Tel: +7(7252) 33-99-47
Website: http://www.miras.edu.kz/

Rector: Bolat Myrzaliyev

Faculties
Accounting and Auditing (Accountancy); **Biology** (Biology); **Chemistry** (Chemistry); **Computer Science** (Computer Science); **Computers and Software** (Computer Engineering; Software Engineering); **Customs** (Taxation); **Design** (Design); **Economics** (Economics); **Electronics and Telecommunications Engineering** (Electronic Engineering; Telecommunications Engineering); **Finance** (Finance); **Foreign languages** (Modern Languages); **History** (History); **Information Systems** (Information Technology); **Kazakh Language and Literature** (Literature; Native Language); **Law** (Law); **Management** (Management); **Pedagogy and Methodology of Elementary Education** (Pedagogy; Primary Education); **Pedagogy and Psychology** (Pedagogy; Psychology); **Professional Training**; **Tourism** (Tourism); **Translation Studies** (Translation and Interpretation)

History: Founded 1997.

Degrees and Diplomas: *Diplom o Vysshem Obrazovanii (Bakalavr); Diplom Magistra*
Last Updated: 04/11/10

M. SAPARBAYEV SOUTH KAZAKHSTAN HUMANITARIAN INSTITUTE

Iužno-Kazahstanskij Gumanitarnyj Institut imeni M. Saparbayeva
ul. 137 Madeli Kozha, 137, 160013 Shymkent, Southern Kazakhstan
Tel: +8(7252) 43-32-03
Fax: +8(7252) 53-56-95 +8(7252) 43-32-03
EMail: ukgi202@mail.ru
Website: http://ukgi.chimkent.kz/

Rector: Gulshara Saparbayeva

Faculties
Basic Military Training and Physical Education and Sports (Military Science; Physical Education; Sports); **Economics and Information Technology** (Accountancy; Economics; Finance; Information Technology)

History: Founded 1994.

Degrees and Diplomas: *Diplom o Vysshem Obrazovanii (Bakalavr); Diplom Magistra*
Last Updated: 04/11/10

NUR-MUBARAK EGYPT UNIVERSITY OF ISLAM CULTURE

Yegipetskij Universitet Islamskoi Kultury 'Nur-Mubarak'
73, Al-Farabi street, 050040 Almaty
Tel: +7(727)

Rector: Makhmud Khizhazi

Programmes
Islamic Culture (Comparative Religion; English; Islamic Studies; Literature; Teacher Training)

History: Founded 2001.

Degrees and Diplomas: *Diplom o Vysshem Obrazovanii (Bakalavr); Diplom Magistra*
Last Updated: 28/10/10

S. BAISHEV AKTOBE UNIVERSITY

Aktiubinskij Universitet imeni S. Baisheva
Br. Zhubanovyh, 302-A, 030000 Aktobe, Aktobe
Tel: +8(7132) 97-47-02 +8(7132) 45-79-48
EMail: edu_ausb@mail.kz
Website: http://ausb.kz/

Rector: Khalel Kusainov Tel: +8(7132) 97-42-02

Departments
Science and Postgraduate Education (Administration; Economics; Finance; Literature; Management; Modern Languages; Native Language; Philology; Philosophy; Public Administration; Russian)

Faculties
Economics (Accountancy; Arts and Humanities; Economics; Finance; Government; Law; Management; Pedagogy; Preschool Education; Psychology; Social Sciences; Tourism); **Humanitarian-Technical Studies** (Construction Engineering; Design; Ecology; Industrial Design; Information Sciences; Modern Languages; Natural Sciences; Petroleum and Gas Engineering; Philology; Technology; Translation and Interpretation)

History: Founded 1996.

Degrees and Diplomas: *Diplom o Vysshem Obrazovanii (Bakalavr); Diplom Magistra*
Last Updated: 27/10/10

SHYMKENT SOCIAL-PEDAGOGICAL UNIVERSITY

Šymkentskij Socialno-Pedagogičeskij Universitet
4, D. Kurmanbekov street, 160001 Shymkent, Southern Kazakhstan
Tel: +8(7252) 54-30-09
Fax: +8(7252) 56-60-40
EMail: shspu@nursat.kz
Website: http://www.shspu.kz/

Rector: Mombek Kozybakov

Faculties
Biology and Physical Education (Biology; Physical Education); **Foreign Languages** (Modern Languages); **History and Geography** (Geography; History); **Kazakh Language and Philology** (Native Language; Philology); **Management and Economics** (Economics; Management); **Pedagogy and Psychology** (Pedagogy; Psychology); **Physics, Mathematics and Computer Science** (Computer Science; Mathematics; Physics); **Visual Arts and Vocational Education** (Visual Arts; Vocational Education)

Degrees and Diplomas: *Diplom o Vysshem Obrazovanii (Bakalavr); Diplom Magistra*
Last Updated: 03/11/10

SHYMKENT UNIVERSITY

Šymkentskij Universitet
32A, Sh. Kaldayakova street, 160000 Shymkent, Southern Kazakhstan
Tel: +7(7252) 50-02-20 +7(7252) 50-03-12
EMail: shimunivers@shym.kz

Rector: Alimkul Baibulekov

Degrees and Diplomas: *Diplom o Vysshem Obrazovanii (Bakalavr); Diplom Magistra*
Last Updated: 04/11/10

SOUTH-KAZAKHSTAN PEDAGOGICAL UNIVERSITY

Iužno-Kazahstanskij Pedagogičeskij Universitet (UKPU)
13, Dzhangildin street, 160019 Shymkent, Southern Kazakhstan
EMail: ukpu_kaz@mail.ru
Website: http://www.ukpu.kz/

Rector: Abdyzhalil Akkuzov

Programmes

Graduate Studies (History; Literature; Native Language; Pedagogy; Philology; Psychology); **Undergraduate Studies** (Computer Science; Economics; Fine Arts; History; Information Sciences; Law; Mathematics; Music Education; Painting and Drawing; Pedagogy; Physical Education; Primary Education; Psychology; Sports)

History: Founded 1992.

Degrees and Diplomas: *Diplom o Vysshem Obrazovanii (Bakalavr); Diplom Magistra*
Last Updated: 04/11/10

SÜLEYMAN DEMIREL UNIVERSITY

Süleyman Demirel Atyndagy Universitet (SDU)
Toraigyrova street, 19, 480043 Almaty
Tel: +8(727) 229-77-44 +8(727) 229-77-00
Fax: +8(727) 229 77-22
EMail: info@sdu.edu.kz; internationaloffice@sdu.edu.kz
Website: http://www.sdu.edu.kz/

Rector: Akgul Mesut EMail: rector@sdu.edu.kz

International Relations: Mesut Yilmaz, Head of International Relations Office
Tel: +7(727) 229-77-00 Ext: 117, Fax: +7(727) 229-77-72
EMail: mesutyilmaz@sdu.edu.kz

Faculties

Economics (Economics; Finance; International Relations; Management; Marketing); **Engineering** (Computer Engineering; Computer Science; Information Technology; Mathematics; Software Engineering); **Philology** (Chinese; English; French; Journalism; Literature; Native Language; Philology; Russian; Translation and Interpretation; Turkish)

History: Created 1996.

Degrees and Diplomas: *Diplom o Vysshem Obrazovanii (Bakalavr); Diplom Magistra; Diplom Doktora (PhD)*

Libraries:c. 32,200 vols, 26 periodical subscriptions

Academic Staff *2008-2009*	**TOTAL**
FULL-TIME	**195**
PART-TIME	**45**
Student Numbers *2008-2009*	
All (Foreign Included)	c. **1,500**

Last Updated: 26/10/10

SYMBAT ACADEMY OF DESIGN AND TECHNOLOGY

Akademija Dizayna i Technologii 'Symbat'
65A, Zhibek Zholy avenue, 050004 Almaty, Almaty
Tel: +7(727) 273-14-41
Website: http://www.symbat.kz/

President: Sabyrkul Assanova EMail: president@symbat.kz

Programmes

Design and Technology (Design; Fashion Design)

History: Founded 1998.

Degrees and Diplomas: *Diplom o Vysshem Obrazovanii (Bakalavr); Diplom Magistra; Diplom Doktora (PhD)*
Last Updated: 27/10/10

SYRDARIYA UNIVERSITY

Universitet 'Syrdariya'
11, Auezov street, 160500 Zhetysai, Southern Kazakhstan
Tel: +8(32534) 6-30-00 +8(32534) 6-34-03
Fax: +8(32534) 6-34-03 +8(32534) 6-14-63
EMail: sirdariya@mail.ru
Website: http://www.sirdariya.ru.gg/

Rector: Abdmalik Ashirov

Faculties

Arts and Humanities (Arts and Humanities); **Biology** (Biology); **Distance Education**; **Economics** (Economics); **Fine Arts** (Fine Arts); **Philology** (Philology); **Physical Education and Sports** (Physical Education; Sports); **Physics and Mathematics** (Mathematics; Physics)

History: Founded 1998.

Degrees and Diplomas: *Diplom o Vysshem Obrazovanii (Bakalavr); Diplom o Vysshem Obrazovanii (Specialist); Diplom Magistra*
Last Updated: 04/11/10

TARAZ INNOVATIVE-HUMANITARIAN UNIVERSITY

Tarazskij Innovatsionno-Gumanitarnyj Universitet (TIGU)
190, Koigeldi street, 080000 Taraz, Jambyl
Website: http://tigu.ax3.net/

Rector: Kairat Baizhanov
Tel: +8(7262) 45-59-06, Fax: +8(7262) 45-59-98

Departments

Biology and Geography (Biology; Geography); **Physics and Informatics** (Chemistry; Computer Engineering; Computer Science; Physics; Software Engineering); **Social Sciences and Humanities** (Cultural Studies; Finance; History; Mathematics; Military Science; Native Language; Pedagogy; Philosophy; Physical Therapy; Political Sciences; Psychology; Sociology)

History: Founded 2008.

International Co-operation: With universities in the CIS countries, Germany, Japan, China and Turkey.

Degrees and Diplomas: *Diplom o Vysshem Obrazovanii (Bakalavr); Diplom Magistra*

Student Services: Language programs, Sports facilities

Special Facilities: Agrobiological Station; 3 reading rooms; 15 computer classrooms connected to the Internet; specialized accounting class; 3 e-learning rooms; Science Laboratory; Forensic Testing Grounds

Academic Staff *2009-2010*: Total 180
STAFF WITH DOCTORATE: Total 11
Last Updated: 04/11/10

TECHNICAL AND ECONOMIC ACADEMY OF CINEMA AND TELEVISION

Tehniko-Ekonomičeskaja Akademija Kino i Televidenija
108, 110 Dostyk avenue, 050100 Almaty
Tel: +7(727) 264-48-72 +7(727) 64-63-99
EMail: teact@inbox.ru

Rector: Kulyash Bolsanbek

Programmes

Cinema and Television (Cinema and Television)

History: Founded 1998.

Degrees and Diplomas: *Diplom o Vysshem Obrazovanii (Bakalavr); Diplom o Vysshem Obrazovanii (Specialist); Diplom Magistra*
Last Updated: 04/11/10

TURAN-ASTANA UNIVERSITY

Universitet 'Turan-Astana'

166/5, Pushkin street, 010000 Astana
Tel: +7(7172) 39-81-18
Fax: +7(7172) 39-81-18
EMail: info@turan-astana.kz
Website: http://www.turan-astana.kz/

Rector: Gulzhamal Dzhaparova

Faculties

Engineering and Economics (Accountancy; Computer Engineering; Design; Economics; Engineering; Finance; Government; Information Sciences; Information Technology; Management; Marketing; Service Trades; Software Engineering; Tourism); **Humanities and Law** (International Law; Law; Literature; Native Language; Psychology; Russian; Translation and Interpretation)

History: Founded 1998.

Degrees and Diplomas: *Diplom o Vysshem Obrazovanii (Bakalavr); Diplom Magistra*

Academic Staff *2009-2010*: Total 200

STAFF WITH DOCTORATE: Total 9

Student Numbers *2009-2010*: Total 3,000

Last Updated: 04/11/10

TURAN UNIVERSITY

Universitet 'Turan'

L. Chaikina 12a, 050020 Almaty
Tel: +7(727) 387-36-36
Fax: +7(727) 387-36-36
EMail: turpost_09@mail.ru; turpost@list.ru
Website: http://www.turan.edu.kz

Rector: Rakhman Alshanov

Faculties

Economics (Accountancy; Economics; Finance; Information Sciences; Management; Marketing; Service Trades); **Humanities and Law** (International Law; International Relations; Journalism; Law; Psychology; Regional Studies; Tourism; Translation and Interpretation)

History: Created 1992.

Degrees and Diplomas: *Diplom o Vysshem Obrazovanii (Bakalavr); Diplom Magistra; Diplom Doktora (PhD)*

Last Updated: 25/10/10

UNIVERSITY OF FOREIGN LANGUAGES AND PROFESSIONAL CAREER

Universitet Inostrannyh Yazykov i Delovoi Karyery

168, Kazybek bi street, 050026 Almaty
Tel: +7 (727) 379-78-94 +7 (727) 379-78-96
Fax: +7 (727) 379-78-93
EMail: ydu2006@mail.ru
Website: http://www.ydu.kz/

Rector: Khizmetli Sabri

Faculties

Economics and Administration (Accountancy; Computer Science; Economics; Finance; Management; Marketing); **Foreign Languages** (Arabic; Chinese; English; French; Japanese; Korean; Modern Languages; Translation and Interpretation; Turkish); **History and Religious Studies** (History; Religious Studies); **International Relations** (Government; International Relations; Regional Studies); **Tourism and Communications** (Journalism; Tourism)

History: Founded 2001.

Degrees and Diplomas: *Diplom o Vysshem Obrazovanii (Bakalavr); Diplom Magistra*

Last Updated: 04/11/10

UNIVERSITY OF INTERNATIONAL BUSINESS

Universitet Meždunarodnoj Biznesa (UIB)

ul. Abaja, 8a, 050010 Almaty
Tel: +7(727) 250-05-05
Fax: +7(727) 267-12-45
EMail: uib@uib.kz
Website: http://www.uib.kz/

Rector: Genadi Gamarnik EMail: gamarnik@uib.kz

Departments

Accounting and Audit (Accountancy); **Economics and Marketing** (Economics; Household Management; Marketing); **Finance and Credit** (Banking; Finance); **Information Systems** (Computer Engineering; Computer Science; Information Sciences; Software Engineering); **Languages** (English; French; German; Native Language; Russian; Spanish); **Management** (Management); **Social Arts** (Journalism; Social Welfare; Sociology)

History: Created 1993 as International Business School. Acquired current title 2001. Acquired status 2002.

Degrees and Diplomas: *Diplom o Vysshem Obrazovanii (Bakalavr); Diplom Magistra; Diplom Doktora (PhD)*

Last Updated: 26/10/10

WEST KAZAKHSTAN ENGINEERING-HUMANITARIAN UNIVERSITY

Zapadno-Kazahstanskij Inženerno-Gumanitarnyj Universitet (WKEHU)

208, Dostyk avenue, 090006 Uralsk, Western Kazakhstan
Tel: +8(7112) 50-90-67 +8(7112) 50-09-43
Fax: +8(7112) 51-18-38
EMail: wketu@mail.ru
Website: http://www.wkehu.kz/

Rector: Nurbulat Kadyrgaliyev

Departments

Business and Law (Accountancy; Business Administration; Finance; Government; Law; Management; Taxation); **Computer Science and Information Systems** (Computer Science; Information Technology); **Ecology and Biotechnology** (Animal Husbandry; Biotechnology; Ecology; Environmental Studies; Fishery; Organic Chemistry; Veterinary Science); **Petroleum Engineering and Industrial Technologies** (Industrial Engineering; Petroleum and Gas Engineering); **Social Sciences and Humanities** (History; Modern Languages; Native Language; Philosophy; Physical Education; Religious Studies; Russian; Social Sciences)

History: Founded 2008.

Degrees and Diplomas: *Diplom o Vysshem Obrazovanii (Bakalavr); Diplom o Vysshem Obrazovanii (Specialist); Diplom Magistra*

Last Updated: 04/11/10

ZHAMBYL HUMANITARIAN-TECHNICAL UNIVERSITY

Žambylskij Gumanitarno-Tehničeskij Universitet

171, Kolbasshy Koigeldi street, 080000 Taraz, Jambyl
Tel: +7(7262) 45-37-48
Fax: +7(7262) 45-68-39

Rector: Zhomart Koshkarov

History: Founded 2007.

Degrees and Diplomas: *Diplom o Vysshem Obrazovanii (Bakalavr); Diplom Magistra*

Last Updated: 04/11/10

Kenya

STRUCTURE OF HIGHER EDUCATION SYSTEM

Description:

Higher education is offered in public universities (some of them with constituent colleges), and private universities. Universities are autonomous. All administrative functions are independently managed by University Councils. Apart from universities, there are a number of post-secondary institutions offering training at diploma and certificate levels. Technical education is offered at polytechnics, institutes of technology and technical training institutes.

Stages of studies:

University level first stage: *Bachelor's degree*
Bachelor's degrees with Honours (there are no Ordinary degrees), including those in Law and Engineering, are generally obtained after four years of study; Veterinary Medicine takes five years, and Architecture and Medicine six years.

University level second stage: *Master's degree*
Master's degrees in Architecture, Humanities, Law, Commerce, Science, Engineering, Medicine and Education take between one 1/2 and three years' further study after the Bachelor's degree.

University level third stage: *Doctorate*
Holders of a Master's degree need a minimum of three years' research to obtain a PhD.

ADMISSION TO HIGHER EDUCATION

Admission to university-level studies:

Name of secondary school credential required: Kenyan Certificate of Secondary Education

Minimum score/requirement: C+ in at least ten subjects

For entry to: University

Alternatives to credentials: Under the Mature Age Scheme, candidates over 25 who do not meet entry requirements may take an entrance examination. Graduates of post-secondary institutions may be admitted to universities.

Foreign students admission:

Quotas: Admission depends on availability of places and ability to pay.

Entrance exam requirements: Foreign students should have qualifications equivalent to the Cambridge High School Certificate, GCE or East African Certificate of Education at 'A' level; special one-year courses are arranged under the Mature Age Scheme to allow students over 25 not meeting university requirements to take the entrance examination.

Entry regulations: Visas are required from countries that require visas for Kenyans.

Language requirements: Good knowledge of English is essential.

RECOGNITION OF STUDIES

Quality assurance system:

Recognition is by a Committee of the Commission for Higher Education (CHE). Experts in relevant disciplines are invited to the Committee. Private universities are established by a Charter granted by the President of Kenya upon recommendation of the Ministry of Education, following upon a recommendation of the CHE.

Special provisions for recognition:

Recognition for university level studies: University attended must be recognized in own country

For access to advanced studies and research: University attended must be recognized in own country

For exercising a profession: University attended must be recognized in own country

NATIONAL BODIES

Ministry of Higher Education, Science and Technology

Minister: Margaret Kamar
Assistant Minister, Higher Education: Kilemi Mwiria
8th to 10th floor, Jogoo House 'B'
P.o Box 9583-00200
Nairobi
Tel: +254 020 318581
Fax: +254 020 251991
EMail: info@scienceandtechnology.go.ke
WWW: http://www.scienceandtechnology.go.ke/

Role of national body: To develop higher and technical education and enhance integration of science, technology and innovation into national production systems for sustainable development.

Commission for Higher Education (CHE)

Commission Secretary/Chief Executive Officer: Everett M. Standa
PO Box 54999
Nairobi 00200
Tel: +254 020 7205000
Fax: +254 020 2021172
EMail: csoffice@che.or.ke
WWW: http://www.che.or.ke

Role of national body: To plan, budget and finance public universities; to accredit universities; to coordinate education and training in middle level colleges for the purpose of admission to universities; standardization, equivalence and recognition of qualifications; advices and recommendations to the Government on matters relating to university education.

Data for academic year: 2012-2013

Source: IAU from the Ministry of Higher Education and CHE websites, 2012

INSTITUTIONS

PUBLIC INSTITUTIONS

EGERTON UNIVERSITY (EU)

PO Box 536, Njoro
Tel: +254(37) 62282 +254(37) 62278
Fax: +254(37) 62527
EMail: info@egerton.ac.ke
Website: http://www.egerton.ac.ke/

Vice-Chancellor: J. K. Tuitoek
Tel: +254(37) 62454 EMail: vc@egerton.ac.ke

Registrar (Academic): S. F. O. Owido
Tel: +254(37) 62332, Fax: +254(37) 62213
EMail: registrar@egerton.ac.ke

Colleges

Chuka University College (Agricultural Education; Business Administration; Communication Studies; Criminology; Economics; Education; Environmental Studies; Geography; History; Home Economics; Journalism; Media Studies; Peace and Disarmament; Religious Studies; Sociology); **Kisii University College** (Actuarial Science; Agricultural Economics; Agricultural Education; Agricultural Management; Agriculture; Aquaculture; Biomedicine; Business Administration; Business and Commerce; Curriculum; Education; Educational and Student Counselling; Environmental Studies; Food Science; Hotel Management; Information Technology; Law; Management; Natural Resources; Nursing; Sales Techniques)

Faculties

Agriculture (Agriculture; Agronomy; Animal Husbandry; Botany; Horticulture; Natural Resources); **Arts and Social Sciences** (Anthropology; Arts and Humanities; Geography; History; Linguistics; Literature; Modern Languages; Philosophy; Religious Studies; Social Sciences; Sociology); **Commerce** (Accountancy; Banking; Business Administration; Business and Commerce; Finance; Human Resources; Insurance; Management); **Education and Community Studies** (Agricultural Education; Curriculum; Development Studies; Education; Educational and Student Counselling; Educational Psychology); **Engineering and Technology** (Agricultural Engineering; Automation and Control Engineering; Engineering; Environmental Engineering; Industrial Engineering; Technology; Water Science); **Environmental and Resource Development** (Environmental Studies; Geography; Natural Resources); **Health Sciences** (Health Sciences; Medicine;

Surgery); **Science** (Chemistry; Computer Science; Mathematics; Molecular Biology; Natural Sciences; Physics); **Veterinary Medicine and Surgery** (Surgery; Veterinary Science)

Institutes

Women, Gender and Development Studies (Development Studies; Gender Studies; Women's Studies)

Schools

Continuing Education (Continuing Education)

Further Information: Also Chuka, Laikipia, Kisii, Nakuru Town Campuses

History: Founded 1939 as Egerton Agricultural College, became a University College of University of Nairobi 1986, and acquired present status and title 1987.

Governing Bodies: University Council

Academic Year: September to May

Admission Requirements: Kenya Certificate of Secondary Education (KCSE) or equivalent

Main Language(s) of Instruction: English

International Co-operation: With universities in China, United Kingdom, Austria, South Africa, India, USA, Netherlands, Australia, Tanzania, Egypt

Degrees and Diplomas: *Certificate/ Diploma*: 4 yrs; *Bachelor's Degree*: 4 yrs; *Master's Degree*; *Doctor's Degree*

Student Services: Academic counselling, Canteen, Employment services, Health services, Language programs, Nursery care, Social counselling, Sports facilities

Student Residential Facilities: For over 90% of the students

Libraries: c. 150,000 vols

Publications: Egerton Journal *(annually)*

Press or Publishing House: Education Media Centre (EMC)
Last Updated: 26/06/12

INTERNATIONAL CENTRE OF INSECT PHYSIOLOGY AND ECOLOGY (ICIPE)

PO Box 30772-00100, Nairobi 00100 GPO
Tel: +254(20) 863-2000
Fax: +254(20) 863-2001 +254(20) 863-2002
EMail: icipe@icipe.org
Website: http://www.icipe.org

Director: Christian Borgemeister (2005-) EMail: dg@icipe.org

Deputy-Director: Onesmo K. Ole Moi Yoi
EMail: oolemoiyoi@icipe.org

Divisions

Animal Health (Animal Husbandry); **Environmental Health** (Environmental Studies; Health Sciences); **Human Health** (Health Sciences); **Plant Health** (Botany)

Research Departments

Behavioural and Chemical Ecology *(BCE)* (Chemistry; Ecology); **Molecular Biology and Biochemistry** (Biochemistry; Molecular Biology); **Population Ecology and Ecosystems Science** *(PEES)*

Research Units

Animal Breeding and Containment (Cattle Breeding); **Biostatistics**; **Biosystematics**; **Entomopathology** (Entomology; Pathology); **Information Technology** (Information Technology); **Laboratory Management** (Laboratory Techniques); **Molecular Biology and Biochemistry** (Biochemistry; Molecular Biology); **Social Sciences** (Social Sciences)

History: Founded 1970 as a Company. Acquired present status and title in the mid-80s. Campuses in Nairobi, Kenya West Coast, Ethiopia.

Governing Bodies: Council; ARPIS Academic Board

Fees: (US Dollars): c. 1,000 per annum. Scholarships provided for ARPIS students

Main Language(s) of Instruction: English

International Co-operation: With 30 African universities

Degrees and Diplomas: Postgraduate training at MSc and PhD levels

Student Residential Facilities: For c. 100 students

Special Facilities: Biosystematics Unit

Libraries: Information Resource Centre

Publications: Insect Science and its Applications

Press or Publishing House: ICIPE Science Press
Last Updated: 11/12/12

JOMO KENYATTA UNIVERSITY OF AGRICULTURE AND TECHNOLOGY (JKUAT)

PO Box 62000, Nairobi 00200
Tel: +254(20) 1515-2711
Fax: +254(20) 1515-2164
EMail: vc@jkuat.ac.ke; jku-lib@jkuat.ac.ke; info@jkuat.ac.ke
Website: http://www.jkuat.ac.ke

Vice-Chancellor: Mabel O. Imbuga (2008-) EMail: vc@jkuat.ac.ke

Deputy-Vice-Chancellor, Administration, Planning and Development: Francis Mwihuri Njeru
Tel: +254(67) 52-711 ext 2113 EMail: dvc@apd.jkuat.ac.ke

International Relations: Araka Davies, Corporate Communications Officer EMail: info@jkuat.ac.ke

Centres

Central Business District *(Nairobi)* (Business Administration); **Central Business District** *(Mombasa)* (Business Administration); **Information Technology** *(IT)* (Information Technology)

Colleges

Engineering and Technology (Agricultural Engineering; Civil Engineering; Computer Engineering; Electrical and Electronic Engineering; Environmental Engineering; Geological Engineering; Marine Engineering; Mechanical Engineering; Mining Engineering; Soil Science; Telecommunications Engineering; Water Science)

Faculties

Agriculture (Agriculture; Food Science; Horticulture; Rural Planning); **Engineering** (Engineering); **Science** (Actuarial Science; Biochemistry; Botany; Chemistry; Mathematics; Microbiology; Natural Sciences; Physics; Statistics; Zoology)

Institutes

Biotechnology Research (Biotechnology); **Computer Science and Information Technology** (Computer Science; Information Technology); **Energy and Environmental Technology** (Energy Engineering; Environmental Engineering); **Tropical Medicine and Infectious Diseases** (Tropical Medicine)

Schools

Architecture and Building Sciences *(SABS)* (Architecture; Building Technologies); **E-Learning** (Distance Education); **Human Resources Development** *(SHRD)* (Human Resources)

Further Information: Also Nairobi, Karen, Taita/Taveta campuses. Constituent colleges: Kimathi Institute University College; Mombasa Polytechnic University College; Kenya Multimedia University College; Meru University College of Science and Technology and Taita Taveta University College. JKUAT coordinates 32 approved centres for Continuing Education.

History: Founded 1981 as the Jomo Kenyatta College of Agriculture and Technology (JKCAT), by the government of Kenya with assistance of the Japanese government. Formally opened 1982. Became Constituent College of Kenyatta University and acquired present title 1988. Acquired present status 1994.

Governing Bodies: University Council; University Senate; University Management Board

Academic Year: March to April (March-August; September-December; January-April)

Admission Requirements: Kenya Certificate of Secondary Education (KCSE)

Fees: (Kenyan Shillings): Engineering: Undergraduate programmes, 230,096 per annum (plus an additional 9,000 for books, 18,000 for food and 40,518 for attachment), Postgraduate programmes 282,210 over two years (plus an additional 75,000 per annum for research/field work/computer lab). Architecture and Building Sciences: Undergraduate programmes, 242,720 per annum (plus an additional 9,000 for books, 18,000 for food and 6,948 for attachment), Postgraduate programmes 282,210 over two years (plus an additional 100,000 per annum for research/field work/ computer lab); Computer Science and Information Technology, Undergraduate programmes, 190,695 per annum (plus an additional 9,000 for books, 18,000 for food and 40,518 for attachment), Postgraduate programmes 503,710 over two years (plus an additional 15,000 per annum for research/field work/computer lab); Agriculture: Undergraduate programmes, 209,055 per annum (plus an additional 9,000 for books, 18,000 for food and 32,877 for attachment), Postgraduate programmes 161,500 over two years (plus an additional 150,000 per annum for research/field work/ computer lab). Science: Undergraduate programmes, 178,730 per annum (plus an additional 9,000 for books, 18,000 for food and 15,000 for attachment), Postgraduate programmes 242,210 over two years (plus an additional 50,000 per annum for research/field work/computer lab). Energy and Environmental Technologies: Postgraduate programmes, 395,710 over two years (plus an additional 150,000 per annum for research/field work/computer lab). Biotechnology: Postgraduate programmes, 456,200 over two years (plus an additional 200,000 per annum for research/field work/ computer lab). Human Resource Development: Undergraduate programmes, 159,190 per annum (plus an additional 9,000 for books, 18,000 for food and 6,948 for attachment), Postgraduate programmes 263,233 over two years. Tropical Medicine and Infectious Diseases: Undergraduate programmes, 163,100 per annum (plus an additional 9,000 for books, 18,000 for food and 23,154 for attachment), Postgraduate programmes 491,200 over two years (plus an additional 200,000 per annum for research/field work/ computer lab)

Main Language(s) of Instruction: English

International Co-operation: International Association for Exchange of Students for Technical Experience (IAESTE), Berlin-Nairobi Exchange Programme, Obihiro University, Japan and Kenya

Accrediting Agencies: Commission for Higher Education; Council for Legal Studies

Degrees and Diplomas: *Bachelor's Degree*: Architecture (B.Arch.), 6 yrs; *Bachelor's Degree*: Biomechanical and Processing Engineering; Computer Science; Computer Technology; Information Technology; Mathematics and Computer Science; Analytical Chemistry; Industrial Chemistry; Biochemistry and Molecular Biology; Botany; Zoology (B.Sc.); Commerce; Commerce and Business Administration; Business Information Technology; Purchasing and Supplies Management (B.Com.); Law (LL.B.), 4 yrs; *Bachelor's Degree*: Civil Engineering; Electrical and Electronics Engineering; Mechanical Engineering; Mechatronic Engineering; Geomatic Engineering; Electronics and Computer Engineering; Telecommunications and Information Engineering; Soil, Water and Environmental Engin.; Control and Instrumentation; Food Science; Food Science and Postharvest Technology; Food Science and Nutrition; Horticulture; Environemental Horticulture and Landscaping Tech.; Animal Health; Production and Processing; Land Resource Planning and Manag.; *Master's Degree*: Business Administration (MBA); Environmental Legislation and Management; Occupational Health and Safety; Public Health; Medicinal Chemistry; Entomology: Parasitology; Virology; Epidemiology; Molecular Medicine; Microbiology (M.Sc.); Food Science and Postharvest Technology; Food Science and Nutrition; Horticulture; Urban Design; ICT Policy and Regulation; Procurement and Logistics Management; Human Resource Management; Entrepreneurship; Biotechnology (M.Sc.); Software Engineering; Geomatic and Geospatial Information Systems; Civil Engineering; Electrical and Electronics Engineering; Mechanical Engineering; Mechatronic Engineering; Biochemistry; Botany; Zoology; Physics; Mathematics and Statistics (M.Sc.), 2 yrs; *Doctor's Degree*: Urban Design; Horticulture; Food Science and Postharvest Technology; Botany; Zoology; Physics; Mathematics and Satistics; Engineering; Public Health; Medicinal Chemistry; Entomology; Parasitology; Virology; Epidemiology; Molecular Medicine; Microbiology (Ph.D.), 3 yrs

Student Services: Academic counselling, Canteen, Foreign student adviser, Health services, Nursery care, Social counselling, Sports facilities

Student Residential Facilities: On Campus Hostels. Out-of-campus Hostels

Special Facilities: Communication Laboratories; Tissue Culture Laboratory; Greenhouses; Demonstration Farm; Foundry; Engineering Workshops; Technical Drawing Studios; Computer Laboratories with high speed internet connection

Libraries: Main Campus Library; Sub-branches in offsite campuses

Publications: Journal of Agriculture, Science and Technology (JAGST), Articles in the field of Science, Agriculture and Technology *(annually)*

Press or Publishing House: University Press

Student Numbers *2011-2012*: Total: c. 22,500

Last Updated: 11/12/12

KENYATTA UNIVERSITY (KU)

PO Box 43844-00100, Nairobi 00100
Tel: +254(20) 810-901
Fax: +254(20) 811-575
EMail: info@ku.ac.ke
Website: http://www.ku.ac.ke

Vice-Chancellor: Olive M. Mugenda (2006-)
Tel: +254(20) 812-676 EMail: mugenda@nbnet.co.ke

Deputy Vice-Chancellor (Academic): John Okumu

Colleges

Pwani University College (Archaeology; Environmental Studies; History; Philosophy; Political Sciences; Religious Studies; Sociology)

Programmes

African Virtual University and E-Learning

Schools

Agriculture and Enterprise Development (Agricultural Business; Agricultural Management; Agriculture); **Applied Human Sciences** (Dietetics; Fashion Design; Health Education; Leisure Studies; Nutrition; Physical Education); **Business** (Accountancy; Actuarial Science; Business and Commerce; Finance; Human Resources; Management; Marketing); **Economics** (Economics; Statistics); **Education** (Child Care and Development; Curriculum; Education; Educational Administration; Educational Psychology; Information Management; Public Relations; Special Education); **Engineering and Technology** (Civil Engineering; Computer Science; Electronic Engineering; Energy Engineering; Information Technology; Mechanical Engineering); **Environmental Studies** (Environmental Management; Environmental Studies); **Graduate**; **Health Sciences** (Food Science; Leisure Studies; Medicine; Nursing; Nutrition; Pathology; Public Health; Sports); **Hospitality and Tourism** (Hotel Management; Tourism); **Humanities and Social Sciences** (African Languages; Archaeology; Economics; English; Fine Arts; Geography; History; Literature; Modern Languages; Music; Philosophy; Political Sciences; Psychology; Religious Studies; Sociology); **Law** (Private Law; Public Law); **Public Health** (Community Health; Health Administration); **Pure and Applied Sciences** (Biotechnology; Engineering; Health Sciences; Information Sciences; Information Technology; Mathematics; Natural Sciences); **Visual and Performing Arts** (Dance; Design; Film; Fine Arts; Music; Theatre)

History: Founded 1965 as Kenyatta University College, acquired present status and title 1985.

Governing Bodies: Council; Senate

Academic Year: September to June

Admission Requirements: Kenya Certificate of Secondary Education (KCSE)

Fees: (Kenyan Shillings): c. 16,000 per semester; foreign students, c. 216,000 per semester; summer term, c. 8,000

Main Language(s) of Instruction: English

Degrees and Diplomas: *Bachelor's Degree*: 3-4 yrs; *Postgraduate Diploma*: Education; Public Relations, 1 yr; *Master's Degree*: a further 2 yrs; *Doctor's Degree (PhD)*: a further 3-4 yrs

Student Services: Academic counselling, Canteen, Cultural centre, Employment services, Handicapped facilities, Health services, Nursery care, Social counselling, Sports facilities

Student Residential Facilities: For c. 6,000 students

Libraries: Yes

Last Updated: 11/12/12

MASENO UNIVERSITY (MSU)

Private Bag Maseno/Busia Rd, Maseno
Tel: +254(57) 351-008 +254(57) 351-011
Fax: +254(57) 351-153
EMail: info@maseno.ac.ke
Website: http://www.maseno.ac.ke/

Vice-Chancellor: Dominic W. Makawiti (2011-)
Tel: +254(57) 351-620/2, Fax: +254(57) 351-221

Deputy-Vice-Chancellor, Academic Affairs: Madara Ogot

Colleges

Bondo University College (Actuarial Science; Astronomy and Space Science; Biology; Business Administration; Computer Science; Cultural Studies; Education; Engineering; Gender Studies; Health Sciences; Law; Mathematics; Natural Resources; Physics; Social Sciences)

Faculties

Arts and Social Sciences (African Languages; Anthropology; Archaeology; Arts and Humanities; Design; French; History; Linguistics; Literature; Media Studies; Modern Languages; Music; Performing Arts; Philosophy; Psychology; Religion; Sociology; Sports); **Education** (Curriculum; Education; Educational Administration; Educational Technology; Psychology; Special Education); **Medicine** (Dentistry; Medicine; Nursing; Pharmacology; Surgery); **Science** (Botany; Cell Biology; Chemistry; Computer Science; Genetics; Horticulture; Hotel Management; Mathematics; Molecular Biology; Natural Sciences; Physics; Plant Pathology; Statistics; Zoology)

Schools

Agriculture and Food Security (Agriculture; Food Science); **Business and Economics** (Accountancy; Business Administration; Economics; Finance; Human Resources; Management; Marketing); **Computing and Informatics** (Computer Science); **Environment and Earth Sciences** (Earth Sciences; Environmental Studies; Geography; Regional Planning; Town Planning); **Mathematics, Statistics and Actuariel Science** (Actuarial Science; Applied Mathematics; Mathematics; Statistics); **Planning and Architecture** (Architectural and Environmental Design; Regional Planning; Town Planning); **Public Health and Community Development** (Biomedicine; Community Health; Epidemiology; Health Administration); **Strategic and Development Studies** (Development Studies; International Relations; Political Sciences)

History: Founded 1990 as a Constituent College of Moi University. Acquired present status 2001.

Governing Bodies: Senate; Council

Academic Year: September to May (September-December; January-May)

Admission Requirements: Kenya Certificate of Secondary Education (KCSE), level C+ or higher grades

Main Language(s) of Instruction: English

International Co-operation: With universities in Germany; USA; South Africa; Sweden; Republic of Korea

Degrees and Diplomas: *Bachelor's Degree*: Arts; History and Archaeology; Political Science; Music; French; Horticulture; Biomedical Science and Technology; Textile Design and Merchandising; Hotel and Institutional Management; Home Science and Technology; Computer Science and Engineering; Environmental Studies; Applied Statistics; Interior Design, 4 yrs; *Postgraduate Diploma*; *Master's Degree*: Horticulture; Botany; Cell Biology; Economics and Education Planning; English; History; Literature; Zoology; Health Promotion and Internal Health (M.Sc.); Plant Pathology; Molecular Epidemiology and Biotechnology; Educational Administration; Mathematics; Community Nutrition; Hospitality (M.Sc.), a further 2 yrs; *Doctor's Degree*: Social and Cultural Studies; Biological Sciences; Physics; Mathematics; Agricultural Sciences; Environmental Sciences (Ph.D). Also Sandwich Courses

Student Services: Academic counselling, Canteen, Cultural centre, Employment services, Health services, Social counselling, Sports facilities

Student Residential Facilities: Yes

Libraries: University Library

Publications: Maseno Journal of Education, Arts and Science *(biennially)*

Press or Publishing House: Maseno University Desktop Publishing Unit

Last Updated: 26/06/12

MASINDE MULIRO UNIVERSITY OF SCIENCE AND TECHNOLOGY (MMUST)

PO Box 190, Kakamega 50100
Tel: +254(56) 31375
Fax: +254(56) 30153
EMail: vc@mmust.ac.ke
Website: http://www.mmust.ac.ke

Vice-Chancellor: Barasa Cleophas Wangila (2003-)
Tel: +254(56) 30686

Deputy Vice-Chancellor, Administration and Finance (Acting): Sibilike Makhanu
Tel: +254(56) 30784, Fax: +254(56) 30784
EMail: dvc-af@mmust.ac.ke

Centres

Disaster Management and Humanitarian Assistance (Development Studies; Engineering Management; Environmental Management; Environmental Studies; International Relations; International Studies; Peace and Disarmament; Safety Engineering)

Faculties

Education and Social Sciences (Arts and Humanities; Business Administration; Criminology; Curriculum; Education; Educational Administration; Educational Psychology; Educational Technology; Foreign Languages Education; Journalism; Leadership; Literature; Mass Communication; Mathematics Education; Native Language Education; Science Education; Social Sciences; Social Work; Swahili); **Engineering** (Civil Engineering; Electrical Engineering; Production Engineering; Structural Architecture; Telecommunications Engineering); **Science** (Botany; Chemistry; Computer Science; Food Technology; Physics; Zoology)

Schools

Graduate Studies; **Health Sciences** (Health Sciences; Nursing); **Open Learning and Continuing Education** (Adult Education; Advertising and Publicity; Agricultural Engineering; Biology; Business Administration; Chemistry; Civil Engineering; Electrical Engineering; English; Ethics; Food Technology; Information Technology; Mathematics; Mechanical Engineering; Physics; Public Relations; Structural Architecture)

History: Founded 1972 as Western College of Arts and Applied Sciences (WECO). Upgraded to a constituent college of Moi University 2002. Acquired present status and title 2007.

Governing Bodies: Council; Senate

Academic Year: September to April (September-December; January-April)

Admission Requirements: Kenya Certificate of Secondary Education (KCSE) - C+ (Plus)

Fees: (Kenyan Shillings): 60,000 per semester

Main Language(s) of Instruction: English

International Co-operation: With universities in the West Indies and Finland

Accrediting Agencies: Commission for Higher Education

Degrees and Diplomas: *Certificate/ Diploma*: Business Administration; Disaster Management (Dip), 2 yrs; *Bachelor's Degree*: Education (B.Ed.), 4 yrs; *Bachelor's Degree*: Science; Engineering; *Postgraduate Diploma*: Education; Disaster Management (PGD), 2 yrs; *Master's Degree*: Education; Engineering; Disaster Management; Science (M.Sc.; M.Ed.), 2 yrs; *Doctor's Degree*: Education; Disaster Management (Ph.D.), 3 yrs

Student Services: Academic counselling, Canteen, Employment services, Health services, Social counselling, Sports facilities

Student Residential Facilities: Three Halls of Residence for Males and one Hall for Females

Special Facilities: Botanical Garden; Science and Technology Park; Radio Station

Libraries: Yes

Publications: J-Stem Journal, Academic Refereed Papers *(annually)*

Last Updated: 26/06/12

MOI UNIVERSITY (MU)

Eldoret, Rift Valley 30100
Tel: +254(53) 43620
Fax: +254(53) 43047
EMail: vcmu@mu.ac.ke
Website: http://www.mu.ac.ke

Vice-Chancellor: Richard K. Mibey (2006-)
Tel: +254(53) 43363, Fax: +254(53) 43047
EMail: rkmibey@mu.ac.ke

Deputy Vice-Chancellor, Research and Extension: Bob Whishitemi Tel: +254(53) 43355 EMail: dvcre@mu.ac.ke

International Relations: Thomas Kipkurgat
Tel: +254(53) 43355 EMail: ipo@mu.ac.ke

Colleges

Chepkoilel University College (Actuarial Science; Agricultural Education; Agriculture; Analytical Chemistry; Animal Husbandry; Aquaculture; Biochemistry; Biotechnology; Botany; Business Administration; Civil Engineering; Computer Science; Economics; Education; Entomology; Environmental Studies; Ethnology; Fashion Design; Fishery; Food Science; Forestry; Home Economics; Horticulture; Information Technology; Mechanical Engineering; Microbiology; Parasitology; Rural Planning; Statistics; Tourism; Water Management; Wildlife); **Kabianga University College** (Accountancy; Agricultural Economics; Agricultural Management; Banking; Business Administration; Computer Science; Economics; Education; Finance; Forestry; Horticulture; Human Resources; Information Technology; Management; Marketing; Public Administration; Public Relations; Rural Planning; Statistics); **Karatina University College** (Actuarial Science; Agricultural Economics; Agriculture; Aquaculture; Biology; Biotechnology; Business Administration; Computer Science; Criminology; Earth Sciences; Economics; Education; Environmental Studies; Fishery; Food Science; Horticulture; Human Resources; Mathematics; Natural Resources; Nutrition; Physics; Tourism); **Narok University College** (Agricultural Economics; Agriculture; Animal Husbandry; Business Administration; Communication Studies; Computer Science; Crop Production; Cultural Studies; Development Studies; Economics; Education; Horticulture; Hotel Management; Human Resources; Management; Media Studies; Public Administration; Public Relations; Social Work; Statistics; Tourism; Wildlife); **Rongo University College**

Schools

Aerospace Sciences (Aeronautical and Aerospace Engineering); **Arts and Social Sciences** (Administration; African Languages; Anthropology; Cultural Studies; Ecology; Film; Geography; History; Linguistics; Literature; Modern Languages; Philosophy; Political Sciences; Psychology; Religious Studies; Social Studies; Sociology; Theatre); **Biological and Physical Sciences** (Botany; Chemistry; Computer Science; Mathematics; Microbiology; Physics; Statistics; Zoology); **Business and Economics** (Agricultural Economics; Business Administration; Business and Commerce; Economics; Hotel Management; Management; Tourism); **Dentistry** (Dentistry; Oral Pathology; Orthodontics; Periodontics; Radiology; Surgery); **Education** (Education; Educational and Student Counselling; Educational Psychology); **Engineering** (Chemical Engineering; Civil Engineering; Computer Engineering; Construction Engineering; Electrical Engineering; Engineering; Mechanical Engineering; Structural Architecture; Textile Technology); **Human Resource Development** (Communication Studies; Human Resources; Public Relations); **Information Sciences** (Archiving; Information Sciences; Library Science; Media Studies; Publishing and Book Trade); **Law** *(Annex Campus)* (Commercial Law; Law; Public Law); **Medicine** (Medicine; Nursing; Surgery); **Nursing** (Nursing); **Public Health** (Epidemiology; Health Administration; Health Sciences; Nutrition; Public Health); **Science** (Biochemistry; Chemistry; Computer Science; Mathematics; Physics)

History: Founded 1984.

Governing Bodies: Council; Senate

Academic Year: Undergraduate, August to April (August-December; January-April). Postgraduate, September to May (September-January; February-May). School of Medicine, January to December

Admission Requirements: Minimum of C+ in Kenya Certificate of Secondary Education (KCSE) or equivalent

Fees: (Kenyan Shillings): 120,000 per annum

Main Language(s) of Instruction: English

Accrediting Agencies: Commission for Higher Education

Degrees and Diplomas: *Bachelor's Degree*: Medicine (MBchB), 6 yrs; *Bachelor's Degree*: Technology; Law; Business Administration and Management; Arts; Science; Education; Engineering, 4-5 yrs; *Master's Degree*; *Doctor's Degree (PhD)*: 3-6 yrs

Student Services: Academic counselling, Canteen, Cultural centre, Employment services, Foreign student adviser, Foreign Studies Centre, Handicapped facilities, Health services, Language programs, Nursery care, Social counselling, Sports facilities

Student Residential Facilities: Yes

Libraries: Margaret Thatcher Library

Publications: Maarifa *(annually)*; The Educator *(annually)*

Press or Publishing House: Moi University Press

Last Updated: 26/06/12

UNIVERSITY OF NAIROBI (UON)

PO Box 30197, Nairobi 00100
Tel: +254(20) 318-262
Fax: +254(20) 245-566
EMail: vc@uonbi.ac.ke; postmaster@unics.gn.apc.org
Website: http://www.uonbi.ac.ke

Vice-Chancellor: George Albert Omore Magoha (2004-)
Tel: +254(20) 221-9056, Fax: +254(20) 221-6030
EMail: vc@uonbi.ac.ke

Deputy Vice-Chancellor, Academic Affairs: Jacob T. Kaimenyi
Tel: +254(20) 222-8986, Fax: +254(20) 221-4325
EMail: dvca@uonbi.ac.ke

Deputy Vice-Chancellor, Administration and Finance: Peter M.F. Mbithi
Tel: +254(20) 224-1149, Fax: +254(20) 222-6329
EMail: dvcaf@uonbi.ac.ke

International Relations: Simon E. O. Mitema, Director, International Relations EMail: esmitema@uonbi.ac.ke

Centres

Information and Communication Technology (Information Technology)

Colleges

Kenya Polytechnic University College (Architecture; Business Administration; Communication Studies; Engineering; Fashion Design; Health Sciences; Hotel Management; Information Technology; Journalism; Management; Mathematics; Media Studies; Music; Performing Arts; Printing and Printmaking; Social Studies; Statistics; Technology; Textile Design; Tourism)

Faculties

Agriculture *(Upper Kabete)* (Agricultural Business; Agriculture; Food Science; Horticulture; Plant and Crop Protection); **Arts** (Arabic; Arts and Humanities; French; Geography; History; Linguistics; Literature; Philosophy; Political Sciences; Psychology; Public Administration; Sociology); **Veterinary Medicine** *(Upper Kabete)* (Veterinary Science)

Institutes

Anthropology, Gender and African Studies (African Studies; Anthropology; Gender Studies); **Development Studies** *(IDS)* (Development Studies); **Diplomacy and International Studies** *(IDIS)* (International Relations; International Studies); **International Relations and International Studies** (International Relations; International Studies); **Nuclear Science** (Nuclear Engineering); **Population Studies and Research** *(PSRI)* (Demography and Population); **Tropical and Infectuous Diseases** (Tropical Medicine)

Schools

Arts and Design (Architecture; Design; Fine Arts); **Biological Sciences** (Botany; Zoology); **Built Environment** (Building Technologies); **Business** *(Lower Kabete)* (Business Administration; Business and Commerce; Finance; Human Resources; Marketing); **Computing and Informatics** (Computer Science); **Continuing and Distance Education** *(Kikuyu)*; **Dental Sciences** (Dentistry); **Economics** (Economics); **Education** *(Kikuyu)* (Education); **Engineering** (Aeronautical and Aerospace Engineering; Bioengineering; Civil Engineering; Construction Engineering; Electrical Engineering;

Engineering; Environmental Engineering; Mechanical Engineering); **Journalism and Mass Communication** (Journalism; Mass Communication); **Law** *(Parklands)* (Law) *Dean*: James Odek; **Mathematics** (Mathematics) *Dean*: Jamen Were; **Medicine** (Medicine) *Dean*: Charles Omwandho; **Nursing** (Nursing); **Pharmacy** (Pharmacy) *Dean*: Grace Thoithi; **Physical Sciences** (Chemistry; Geology; Meteorology; Physics) *Dean*: Lydia Njenga; **Public Health** (Public Health) *Dean*: Dismas Ongore

Further Information: Parklands, Kenya Science Campus and Kenya Polytechnic University College.

History: Founded 1956 as Royal Technical College of East Africa, became University College Nairobi 1963 and acquired present status and title 1970.

Governing Bodies: University Council; University Senate; College Academic Boards; College Management Boards; University Management Board

Academic Year: October to July

Admission Requirements: Kenya Certificate of Secondary Education (KCSE), prior to Higher School Certificate (HSC) of GCE Advanced ('A') level examinations.

Fees: (Kenyan Shillings): 80,000-450,000 per annum

Main Language(s) of Instruction: English

Degrees and Diplomas: *Bachelor's Degree*: 4-6 yrs; *Postgraduate Diploma*: 1 yr; *Master's Degree*: a further 1-3 yrs; *Doctor's Degree (PhD / DSc)*: at least 3- 5 yrs

Student Services: Academic counselling, Canteen, Cultural centre, Employment services, Foreign student adviser, Handicapped facilities, Health services, Language programs, Social counselling, Sports facilities

Student Residential Facilities: Yes

Special Facilities: Biological Garden

Libraries: c. 700,000 vols; 45,000 e-journals; 51,000 e-books

Press or Publishing House: University of Nairobi Press

Academic Staff *2010-2011*	MEN	WOMEN	TOTAL
FULL-TIME	1,232	426	**1,658**
Student Numbers *2010-2011*			
All (Foreign Included)	34,020	22,259	**56,279**
FOREIGN ONLY	348	254	**602**

Part-time students, 25,815. **Distance students**, 17,280.

Last Updated: 12/07/11

PRIVATE INSTITUTIONS

AFRICA INTERNATIONAL UNIVERSITY

P.O BOX 24686, Karen-Dagoretti Road,
Nairobi 00502
Tel: +254(20) 260-3664
Website: http://www.africainternational.edu

Graduate Schools

Theology *(Nairobi Evangelical)* (Bible; Christian Religious Studies; Missionary Studies; Theology)

Institutes

Study of African Realities (Cultural Studies; Social Studies)

Schools

Professional Studies (Business Administration; Child Care and Development; Curriculum; Education; Family Studies; Leadership; Psychology; Translation and Interpretation)

History: Founded as Nairobi Evangelical Graduate School of Theology 1977. Acquired present status and title 2011.

Degrees and Diplomas: *Bachelor's Degree*; *Master's Degree*; *Doctor's Degree*

Student Residential Facilities: Yes

Libraries: Yes

Last Updated: 27/06/12

AFRICA NAZARENE UNIVERSITY (ANU)

PO Box 53067, Ongata Rongal Area of Kajiado District, Nairobi 00200
Tel: +254(20) 252-7170
Fax: +254(20) 201-2233
EMail: info@anu.ac.ke
Website: http://www.anu.ac.ke

Vice-Chancellor: Leah Marangu (1997-)
EMail: lmarangu@anu.ac.ke'

Dean of Students: Peter Kangori

Departments

Business (Accountancy; Banking; Business Administration; Business and Commerce; Finance; Management; Marketing); **Computer Science and Information Technology** (Computer Science); **Education** (Education); **Law** (Law); **Mass Communication** (Advertising and Publicity; Journalism; Mass Communication; Public Relations; Publishing and Book Trade); **Peace and Conflict** (Peace and Disarmament); **Religion** (Bible; Christian Religious Studies; Religion; Theology)

Institutes

Open and Distance Learning (Distance Education)

History: Founded 1993. Acquired present status 2002.

Main Language(s) of Instruction: English

Degrees and Diplomas: *Bachelor's Degree*; *Postgraduate Diploma*; *Master's Degree*

Student Residential Facilities: Yes

Libraries: Grace Roles Library

Last Updated: 26/06/12

DAYSTAR UNIVERSITY

PO Box 44400, Nairobi
Tel: +254(20) 732-002
Fax: +254(20) 728-338
EMail: admissions@daystar.ac.ke
Website: http://www.daystar.ac.ke/

Vice-Chancellor: Timothy Wachira Tel: +254(20) 720-650

Deputy-Vice-Chancellor for Finance, Administration and Planning: Jomo Gatundu

Faculties

Arts and Humanities (Education; International Studies; Pastoral Studies; Peace and Disarmament; Theology); **Science, Engineering and Health** (Biomedicine; Computer Science; Electronic Engineering; Environmental Studies; Mathematics; Nursing; Physics)

Schools

Business and Economics (Accountancy; Business Administration; Business Computing; Economics; Finance; Human Resources; Management; Marketing; Sales Techniques); **Communication, Language and Performing Arts** (Communication Studies; English; French; Literature; Music; Swahili); **Human and Social Sciences** (Child Care and Development; Development Studies; Psychology)

History: Founded 1974, previously Daystar Communications, Daystar University College. Acquired present status and title 1992. Also 2 branches in Athi River and Mombassa.

Governing Bodies: Daystar Company and Daystar University Council

Academic Year: August to May

Admission Requirements: Kenya Certificate of Secondary Education grade C+, or equivalent

Fees: (Kenyan Shillings): 5,650.00 per credit hour per semester

Main Language(s) of Instruction: English

Accrediting Agencies: Commission for Higher Education

Degrees and Diplomas: *Certificate/ Diploma*: 2 yrs; *Bachelor's Degree*: Accountancy, Business Administration and Management, Economics and Marketing; Bible and Religious Studies, Communication, Community Development, English and Psychology, 4 yrs; *Master's Degree*: 2 yrs; *Doctor's Degree*

Student Services: Academic counselling, Canteen, Employment services, Foreign student adviser, Health services, Language programs, Social counselling, Sports facilities

Student Residential Facilities: For c. 1,000 students

Libraries: Agape Library. Library on each campus

Publications: Interdisciplinary Perspectives *(biannually)*

Last Updated: 26/06/12

GREAT LAKES UNIVERSITY OF KISUMU

P.O.Box 2224, Kisumu 40100
EMail: info@gluk.ac.ke
Website: http://www.gluk.ac.ke

Vice-Chancellor: Dan C.O. Kaseje

Departments
Education (Education)

Faculties
Arts and Science (Agricultural Business; Information Technology; Nutrition; Pastoral Studies; Theology); **Health Science** (Community Health; Health Sciences; Medicine; Nursing; Surgery)

Institutes
Community Health And Development *(Tropical)* (Community Health)

History: Founded 2006 from Tropical Institute of Community Health and Development founded 1998. Acquired present status and title 2006.

Degrees and Diplomas: *Certificate/ Diploma*; *Bachelor's Degree*; *Master's Degree*; *Doctor's Degree*

Student Residential Facilities: Yes

Last Updated: 26/06/12

KABARAK UNIVERSITY

PO Private Bag 20157, Nakuru-Eldama Ravine Highway, Kabarak
Tel: +254(51) 343-234/5
Fax: +254(51) 343-012
EMail: registrar@kabarak.ac.ke
Website: http://www.kabarak.ac.ke

Vice-Chancellor: Jacob Kibor
Tel: +254(51) 343028 EMail: vicechancellor@karabak.ac.ke

Registrar: Ronald Chepkilot
Tel: +254(51) 343-509 EMail: rkchepkilot@kabarak.ac.ke

Schools
Business (Business Administration; Business and Commerce; Management; Staff Development); **Law** (Law); **Science, Engineering and Technology** (Biological and Life Sciences; Computer Science; Engineering; Environmental Engineering; Mathematics; Natural Sciences; Physics; Technology; Telecommunications Engineering); **Theology Education and Arts** (Art Education; Education; Theology)

History: Founded 2002. Charter awarded 2008.

Governing Bodies: Board of Trustees; Governing Council; Board of Management; Senate

Academic Year: September to August

Admission Requirements: Kenyan Certificate of Secondary Education(KCSE) C+, Diploma

Fees: (Kenyan Shillings): 40,000

Main Language(s) of Instruction: English/Kiswahili

International Co-operation: With Liberty University in America (USA); St Jones University (UK)

Accrediting Agencies: Commission for Higher Education

Degrees and Diplomas: *Certificate/ Diploma*: Computer Science (Dip (Comp Science)); Information Technology (Dip (IT)), 2 yrs; *Bachelor's Degree*: Accounting; Finance; Human Resource Management; Marketing Management (Business Administration) (BCOMM); Business Management and Information Technology (BBMIT); Computer Science (BSc (Computer Science)); Economics (BSc (Econ)); Economics and Mathematics (BSc (Econ and Maths)); Education, Mathematics, Physics, Chemistry, Biology (BEd (Science)); Environmental Technology (BSc (Envi. Tech)); Information Technology (BIT); Mathematics and Physics, Chemistry, Botany, Zoology (BSc); Telecommunications (BSc (Telecomm)); Theology (BTh), 4 yrs; *Master's Degree*; *Doctor's Degree*

Student Services: Academic counselling, Canteen, Employment services, Handicapped facilities, Health services, Nursery care, Social counselling, Sports facilities

Student Residential Facilities: 6 hostels for 1,500 students; 53 staff houses

Libraries: Yes

Last Updated: 26/06/12

KENYA METHODIST UNIVERSITY

PO Box 267, Meru
Tel: +254(64) 31229
Fax: +254(64) 30162
EMail: info@kemu.ac.ke
Website: http://www.kemu.ac.ke

Vice-Chancellor: Alfred Mutema (2010-) EMail: vc@kemu.ac.ke

Faculties
Computing and Informatics (Business Computing; Computer Science); **Education and Social Sciences** (Communication Studies; Education; Educational and Student Counselling; Journalism; Religious Studies; Theology; Tourism); **Science and Technology** (Agriculture; Biology; Computer Science; Engineering; Mathematics)

Schools
Business and Economics (Accountancy; Business Administration; Economics; Finance; Statistics); **Medicine and Health Sciences** (Anatomy; Biochemistry; Community Health; Dietetics; Health Administration; Laboratory Techniques; Medicine; Microbiology; Nursing; Nutrition; Parasitology; Pathology; Pharmacy; Physiology; Public Health; Surgery)

History: Founded 1997. Charter awarded 2006.

Main Language(s) of Instruction: English

Degrees and Diplomas: *Bachelor's Degree*: 4 yrs; *Master's Degree*; *Doctor's Degree*

Last Updated: 11/12/12

KIRIRI WOMEN'S UNIVERSITY OF SCIENCE AND TECHNOLOGY

PO Box 49274 - 00100, Nairobi
Tel: +254(2) 444-2212
EMail: info@kwust.ac.ke
Website: http://www.kwust.ac.ke

Vice-Chancellor: Joseph Njino Kariuki

Faculties
Science (Mathematics)

Schools
Business and Management Studies (Business Administration; Management); **Computer and Information Technology** (Computer Science; Information Technology)

Further Information: Also Kasarani Campus.

History: Founded 2002.

Degrees and Diplomas: *Bachelor's Degree*: 4 yrs

Student Residential Facilities: Yes

Libraries: Yes

Last Updated: 26/06/12

MANAGEMENT UNIVERSITY OF AFRICA

P O Box 29677, Nairobi 00100
Tel: +254(20) 236-1160
EMail: mua@mua.ac.ke
Website: http://mua.ac.ke

Vice-Chancellor: Jude M. Mathooko

Schools
Management and Leadership (Business Administration; Human Resources; Leadership; Marketing)

History: Founded 1954 as Kenya Institute of Management (KIM). Acquired present status and title 2011.

Admission Requirements: Mean grade C+ (PLUS) with C in Math and English or Kiswahili

Fees: (Ksh) 102,000 per annum

Degrees and Diplomas: *Bachelor's Degree*; *Master's Degree*; *Doctor's Degree*

Last Updated: 03/07/12

MOUNT KENYA UNIVERSITY

P.O.Box 342-01000, Thika
Tel: +254(20) 208-8310
Fax: +254(20) 205-0315
EMail: info@mku.ac.ke
Website: http://www.mku.ac.ke

Vice-Chancellor: Stanley Waudo

Schools

Business and Public Management (Accountancy; Business Administration; Finance; Hotel Management; Management; Tourism); **Education** (Curriculum; Education; Preschool Education; Special Education); **Health Sciences** (Dentistry; Dietetics; Health Sciences; Laboratory Techniques; Medicine; Nutrition; Public Health; Surgery); **Law** (Law); **Nursing** (Nursing); **Pharmacy** (Pharmacy); **Pure and Applied Sciences** (Agriculture; Analytical Chemistry; Animal Husbandry; Biomedical Engineering; Biotechnology; Business Computing; Chemical Engineering; Computer Engineering; Electrical Engineering; Electronic Engineering; Energy Engineering; Food Science; Food Technology; Horticulture; Industrial Chemistry; Information Technology; Library Science; Mathematics; Software Engineering); **Social Sciences** (Criminology; Development Studies; Economics; Ethics; Government; History; Journalism; Mass Communication; Peace and Disarmament; Psychology; Social Work; Sociology)

Further Information: Campuses in Mombasa,Nairobi, Nakuru, Kitale, Kakamega, Eldoret, Nkubu (Meru), Lodwar and Kigali

History: Founded 1996 as Thika Institute of Technology . Acquired present status and title 2011.

Admission Requirements: At least KCSE mean grade C Plus

Fees: (Kshs) 1,000

Accrediting Agencies: Commission for Higher Education

Degrees and Diplomas: *Certificate/ Diploma*; *Bachelor's Degree*; *Postgraduate Diploma*; *Master's Degree*; *Doctor's Degree*

Student Residential Facilities: Yes

Libraries: Yes

Last Updated: 03/07/12

PRESBYTERIAN UNIVERSITY OF EAST AFRICA

P.O. B0x 387, Kikuyu 00902
Tel: +254(723) 799-904
EMail: info@puea.ac.ke
Website: http://puea.ac.ke

Vice-Chancellor (Acting): Paul Mungai Mbugua

Deputy Vice-Chancellor: Timothy Henry Gatara

Schools

Business and Management Studies (Accountancy; Business Administration; Finance; Human Resources; Management; Marketing); **Computer Science** (Business Computing; Computer Science); **Education** (Education; Educational and Student Counselling; Preschool Education); **Health Sciences** (Community Health; Medicine; Nursing; Occupational Therapy; Oral Pathology; Surgery); **Journalism and Mass Communication** (Communication Studies; Journalism; Mass Communication; Public Relations); **Law** (Criminology; Law); **Pure and Applied Science** (Hotel Management; Natural Sciences; Tourism); **Theology** (Pastoral Studies; Theology)

Further Information: Also Nairobi campus, St Andrews Campus and Githunguri Campus

History: Founded 1994 as The Presbyterian College. Acquired present status and title 2007.

Admission Requirements: A minimum of Grade C+ at the Kenya Certificate of Secondary Examination (KCSE) or equivalent.

Degrees and Diplomas: *Certificate/ Diploma*; *Bachelor's Degree*; *Postgraduate Diploma*; *Master's Degree*

Student Residential Facilities: Yes

Libraries: Presbyterian University of East Africa Library.

Last Updated: 03/07/12

SCOTT THEOLOGICAL COLLEGE (STC)

PO Box 49, Machakos
Tel: +254(44) 21086
Fax: +254(44) 21336
EMail: scott-theol.college@aimint.net
Website: http://www.scott.ac.ke/

Principal: Mumo Kisau EMail: Principal@scott.ac.ke

Departments

Biblical and Theological Studies (Bible; Theology); **Church Ministry and Missions**

Institutes

Church Renewal

Schools

Education (Education)

History: Founded 1962 as College of the Africa Inland Church, Kenya, acquired present status and title 1997.

Governing Bodies: Governing Council; Academic Council (Senate); Management Board

Academic Year: September to July

Admission Requirements: Kenya Certificate of Secondary Education (KCSE), C+ or above

Fees: (U.S. Dollars): 2,289 per annum; (Kenyan Shillings): 160,212 per annum

Main Language(s) of Instruction: English

Accrediting Agencies: Accreditation Council for Theological Education in Africa (ACETEA); Commission for Higher Education (CHE)

Degrees and Diplomas: *Certificate/ Diploma*: Theology (DipTh), 4 yrs; *Bachelor's Degree*: Theology (BTh), 4 yrs; *Master's Degree*. Also Certificate

Student Services: Academic counselling, Foreign student adviser, Health services, Social counselling, Sports facilities

Libraries: Yes

Publications: African Journal of Evangelical Theology, Academic Journal *(biannually)*

Last Updated: 26/06/12

ST PAUL'S UNIVERSITY

PO Private Bag, Limuru 00217
Tel: +254(20) 2020505
Fax: +254(66) 73033
EMail: pro@spu.ac.ke
Website: http://www.spu.ac.ke

Vice-Chancellor: Joseph D. Galgalo

Faculties

Business and Communication (Business Administration; Business and Commerce; Education; Information Technology; Leadership; Management); **Theology** (Christian Religious Studies; Islamic Theology; Theology)

History: Founded 1903 as St. Paul's Divinity School. Acquired present status and title 2007.

Degrees and Diplomas: *Bachelor's Degree*: Business Administration; Management; Marketing; Accounting; Communication; *Postgraduate Diploma*: Islam and Christian-Muslim Relations; *Master's Degree*: Theology; Islam and Christian-Muslim Relations; Business and Information Technology

Student Residential Facilities: Yes

Libraries: Bishop Okullu Memorial Library

Last Updated: 26/06/12

STRATHMORE UNIVERSITY

PO Box 59857, Madaraka Estate, Ole Sangale Road, City Square, Nairobi 00200
Tel: +254(20) 606-155
Fax: +254(20) 607-498
EMail: enquiries@strathmore.edu
Website: http://www.strathmore.edu

Vice-Chancellor: John Odhiambo (2008-2013)
Tel: +254(20) 606-268 EMail: jodhiambo@strathmore.edu

Deputy Vice-Chancellor (Academic Affairs): Izael Pereira Da Silva

Faculties

Information Technology (Business Computing; Computer Science; Information Technology)

Institutes

Continuing Education (Business Education; Continuing Education; Finance; Management)

Research Centres

Governance *(Strathmore)* (Ethics; Government; Leadership)

Schools

Accountancy (Accountancy); **Business** *(Strathmore)* (Business Administration; Leadership; Management); **Finance and Applied Economics** (Actuarial Science; Economics; Finance); **Hospitality and Tourism** (Cooking and Catering; Hotel Management; Tourism); **Humanities and Social Sciences** (Anthropology; Communication Studies; Development Studies; Educational Administration; Ethics; Philosophy); **Law** *(Strathmore)* (Administrative Law; Constitutional Law; International Law; Labour Law; Law); **Management and Commerce** (Business Administration; Business and Commerce; Management)

History: Founded 1961. Acquired present status 2002 and awarded charter 2008.

Academic Year: July to June

Admission Requirements: Mean Grade C+ at National Secondary School Examinations

Fees: (Kenyan Shillings): 200,000 per annum

Main Language(s) of Instruction: English

Accrediting Agencies: Commission for Higher Education

Degrees and Diplomas: *Bachelor's Degree*: 4 yrs; *Postgraduate Diploma*; *Master's Degree*: 2 yrs; *Doctor's Degree*: 3 yrs

Student Services: Academic counselling, Canteen, Employment services, Language programs, Social counselling, Sports facilities

Student Residential Facilities: No

Libraries: Yes

Press or Publishing House: Strathmore University Press

Academic Staff	MEN	WOMEN	**TOTAL**
STAFF WITH DOCTORATE			
FULL-TIME	11	1	**12**
PART-TIME	14	3	**17**
Student Numbers *2009-2010*			
All (Foreign Included)	–	–	**4,495**

Part-time students, 1,759.

Last Updated: 26/06/12

THE AGA KHAN UNIVERSITY

P.O. Box 30270-00100, 3rd Parklands Avenue, Off Limuru Road, Nairobi
Tel: +254(20) 366-2000
EMail: contactus@aku.edu
Website: http://www.aku.edu/aboutaku/akuataglance/campusesandteachingsites/eastafrica/pages/kenya.aspx

President: Firoz Rasul (2006-)

Colleges

Medical (Anaesthesiology; Gynaecology and Obstetrics; Medicine; Paediatrics; Pathology; Radiology; Surgery)

Faculties

Health Sciences (Health Sciences)

Schools

Nursing and Midwifery (Midwifery; Nursing)

History: Founded 2002.

Degrees and Diplomas: *Bachelor's Degree*: Medicine; *Master's Degree*

Libraries: Yes

Last Updated: 26/06/12

THE CATHOLIC UNIVERSITY OF EASTERN AFRICA (CUEA)

PO Box 62157, Nairobi 00200
Tel: +254(20) 891-601
Fax: +254(20) 891-261
EMail: admin@cuea.edu
Website: http://www.cuea.edu

Vice-Chancellor: Pius Rutechura (2002-)
Tel: +254(20) 890-095, Fax: +254(20) 891-261
EMail: vc@cuea.edu

International Relations: Peter Gichure, Coordinator of Academic Linkages Tel: +254(20) 891-601, Fax: +254(20) 891-261

Centres

Social Justice and Ethics (Ethics; Pastoral Studies)

Colleges

Hekima (International Relations; Pastoral Studies; Peace and Disarmament; Theology); **Tangaza** (African Studies; Communication Studies; Development Studies; Education; Media Studies; Theology)

Departments

Research

Faculties

Arts and Social Sciences (African Languages; Anthropology; Arts and Humanities; Economics; English; Geography; History; Philosophy; Political Sciences; Religious Studies; Social Sciences; Social Work; Sociology); **Commerce** (Business Administration); **Education** (Curriculum; Education; Educational Administration); **Law** (Law); **Science** (Biology; Chemistry; Computer Science; Mathematics; Physics); **Theology** (Bible; Canon Law; Pastoral Studies; Religious Studies; Theology)

Institutes

Canon Law (Canon Law)

Further Information: Also Gaba Campus, Kisumu Campus

History: Founded 1984 as the Catholic Higher Institute of Eastern Africa. Acquired present status and title 1992.

Governing Bodies: University Council; Senate; Management Board

Academic Year: August to April (August-December; January-April)

Admission Requirements: Kenya Certificate of Secondary Education (KCSE); Kenya Advanced Certificate of Education or equivalent

Fees: (Kenyan Shillings): 190,000 per annum; postgraduate, 160,000

Main Language(s) of Instruction: English

Accrediting Agencies: Commission for Higher Education

Degrees and Diplomas: *Bachelor's Degree*: Accountancy; Finance; Marketing; Business Administration; Insurance; Management (BCom), 2-4 yrs; *Bachelor's Degree*: Arts and Humanities; Social Sciences; Geography; History; Philosophy; Religious Studies; Economics; Political Science; Sociology; Anthropology; Social Work; English; Kiswahili; Education; Mathematics; Computer Science; Biology; Physics (BSc); Theology; *Bachelor's Degree*: Law (LLB), 4 yrs; *Postgraduate Diploma*: Education; Project Planning and Management (PGDE/DPM), 1 yr following Bachelor; *Master's Degree*: Education (MED); Philosophy; Religious Studies (MA); Theology, a further 2 yrs; *Master's Degree*: Mathematics; Business Administration (MBA); *Doctor's Degree*: Philosophy; Theology; Religious Studies; Education (PhD), a further 3 yrs

Student Services: Academic counselling, Canteen, Cultural centre, Employment services, Foreign student adviser, Health services, Language programs, Social counselling, Sports facilities

Libraries: Total, 60,070 vols; 11,568 periodicals

Publications: African Christian Studies *(quarterly)*; C.U.E.A., Eastern Africa Journal of Humanities and Sciences *(quarterly)*

Press or Publishing House: Catholic University of Eastern Africa Publications

Student Numbers *2010-2011*: Total: c. 6,000
Last Updated: 12/12/12

THE PAN AFRICA CHRISTIAN UNIVERSITY

P.O. Box 56875, Nairobi 00200
Tel: +254(20) 2013146
EMail: enquiries@pacuniversity.ac.ke
Website: http://www.pacuniversity.ac.ke/

Vice-Chancellor: Godfrey M. Nguru

Registrar: Anthony Mwaniki

Programmes
Bible and Theology (Bible; Theology); **Business Leadership** (Accountancy; Business Administration; Business Education; Finance; Marketing); **Counselling**

History: Founded 1978 as a Bible College. Acquired present status 2006.

Admission Requirements: A minimum of a mean grade C in the Kenya Certificate of Secondary Education (KCSE), or its equivalent.

Fees: (KShs) 44,100 per term

Degrees and Diplomas: *Bachelor's Degree*; *Postgraduate Diploma*; *Master's Degree*

Libraries: Richard Ondeng' Library

Press or Publishing House: Evangel Publishing House
Last Updated: 27/06/12

UNITED STATES INTERNATIONAL UNIVERSITY (USIU)

PO Box 14634, Thika Road Kasarani, Nairobi 00800
Tel: +254(20) 3606-000
Fax: +254(20) 3606-100
EMail: admit@usiu.ac.ke
Website: http://www.usiu.ac.ke

Vice-Chancellor: Freida Augustine Brown (1994-)
Tel: +254(20) 3606-411 EMail: fbrown@usiu.ac.ke

Deputy Vice-Chancellor, Academic Affairs: Mathew Buyu
EMail: mbuyu@usiu.ac.ke

Schools
Business *(Chandaria)* (Accountancy; Business Administration; Business and Commerce; Finance; Hotel and Restaurant; Human Resources; International Business; Management; Marketing; Tourism); **Humanities and Social Sciences** (Arts and Humanities; Clinical Psychology; Criminal Law; International Relations; Psychology); **Science and Technology** (Computer Science; Information Technology; Journalism)

History: Founded 1969. Acquired status 1999.

Governing Bodies: Board of Directors; Management Council, Faculty Senate; Staff Council; Students Affairs Council

Academic Year: September to August (September-December; January-April, May-August)

Admission Requirements: Kenya Certificate of Secondary Education (KCSE), C+ and above.TOEFL score of 550 (213 computer based) Bachelor's Degree and either GRE (Arts) or GMAT (Business) for Graduate Programmes

Fees: (Kshs) 88,650 per semester

Main Language(s) of Instruction: English

International Co-operation: With universities in USA, Japan, Spain, Sweden, Germany and China.

Accrediting Agencies: Commission for Higher Education (CHE); Western Association of Schools and Colleges (WASC), USA

Degrees and Diplomas: *Bachelor's Degree*: Business Administration; International Business; Information Systems; Information Technology; Hotel and Restaurant Management; Tourism; International Relations; Psychology; Journalism (BA); *Master's Degree*: Business Administration (MBA); International Relations; Counselling Psychology (MA); Management and Organization Development (EMOD), a further 1-2 yrs

Student Services: Academic counselling, Canteen, Employment services, Foreign student adviser, Foreign Studies Centre, Handicapped facilities, Health services, Language programs, Social counselling, Sports facilities

Student Residential Facilities: Residential Housing

Special Facilities: Computer Labs

Libraries: U.S.I.U Library and Information Center
Last Updated: 27/06/12

UNIVERSITY OF EASTERN AFRICA, BARATON

PO Box 2500-30100, Eldoret, Rift Valley
Tel: +254(20) 244-1536
EMail: registrar@ueab.ac.ke
Website: http://www.ueab.ac.ke/

Vice-Chancellor: Miriam B. Mwita

Schools
Business (Accountancy; Business and Commerce; Business Computing; Management); **Education** (Curriculum; Education; Educational Administration; Educational Psychology; Teacher Training); **Health Sciences** (Health Sciences; Laboratory Techniques; Nursing; Public Health); **Humanities and Social Sciences** (Arts and Humanities; Development Studies; English; French; Geography; History; Literature; Modern Languages; Religious Studies; Social Sciences; Swahili; Theology); **Science and Technology** (Agriculture; Biological and Life Sciences; Family Studies; Mathematics; Natural Sciences; Physics; Technology)

History: Founded 1980. Chartered by the Government 1991.

Governing Bodies: University Council

Academic Year: September to September (September-December; January-March; April-June; July-September)

Admission Requirements: Kenya Certificate of Secondary Education (KCSE), with C+ average grade in 8 subjects

Fees: (Kshs) 90,140.00 per semester

Main Language(s) of Instruction: English

Degrees and Diplomas: *Bachelor's Degree*; *Postgraduate Diploma*; *Master's Degree*: 2 yrs; *Doctor's Degree*

Student Services: Academic counselling, Canteen, Employment services, Foreign student adviser, Health services, Language programs, Social counselling, Sports facilities

Student Residential Facilities: Yes

Libraries: Central Library
Last Updated: 27/06/12

Korea (Democratic People's Republic of)

STRUCTURE OF HIGHER EDUCATION SYSTEM

Description:

Higher education is provided by universities and other institutions of higher education. All come under the responsibility of the Ministry of Education.

Stages of studies:

University level first stage:
The first stage of higher education includes three to six-year courses leading to a Bachelor's degree.

University level second stage:
The second stage leads, after three or four years' study and research, to an Associate Doctorate.

University level third stage: *Specialization and individual research*
The title of Doctor is granted, after study and research pursued over several years, to scholars who have performed scientific work of the highest value.

Distance higher education:
Correspondence courses are offered by universities and specialized schools.

ADMISSION TO HIGHER EDUCATION

Admission to university-level studies:
Name of secondary school credential required: Secondary School Leaving Certificate

NATIONAL BODIES

Ministry of Education
Minister: Kim Yong Jin
Pyongyang

Data for academic year: 1999-2000
Source: IAU, 1999 (Bodies, 2012)

INSTITUTIONS

PUBLIC INSTITUTIONS

CHAGANG UNIVERSITY
Chagang Taehak
Kanggye City, Chagang Province

Faculties
Agriculture (Agriculture); **Forestry Engineering** (Forestry); **Forestry Machinery** (Agricultural Equipment); **Forestry** (Forestry); **Horticulture** (Horticulture); **Sericulture** (Sericulture); **Veterinary Medicine and Animal Husbandry** (Animal Husbandry; Veterinary Science); **Wood Processing** (Wood Technology)

History: Founded 1970.

Governing Bodies: Instruction; Scientific Research; General Affairs

Academic Year: September to August (September-February; February-August)

Admission Requirements: Graduation from senior middle school

Main Language(s) of Instruction: Korean

Degrees and Diplomas: *Bachelor's Degree*: Engineering, 4 1/2-5 yrs; *Associate Doctorate*

Libraries: c. 130,000 vols

Publications: Gazette; Newspaper

Press or Publishing House: University Publishing House

CHA GWAN SU UNIVERSITY

Cha Gwang Su Taehak
North Pyongan Province

Faculties
Biology and Chemistry (Biology; Chemistry); **Foreign Studies** (International Studies); **History and Geography** (Geography; History); **Korean Language and Literature** (Korean); **Mathematics** (Mathematics); **Physical Education** (Physical Education); **Physics** (Physics)

History: Founded 1961.

CHANG CHOL GU UNIVERSITY

Chang Chol Gu Taehak
Pyongchon District, Pyongsong City

Faculties
Cookery (Cooking and Catering); **Management** (Management); **Tailoring** (Clothing and Sewing)

Institutes
Commercial Management (Business Administration); **Organizational Techniques** (Management); **Supply Service**

History: Founded 1970. A State institution responsible to the National Education Commission.

Governing Bodies: Instruction; Scientific Research; General Affairs

Admission Requirements: Graduation from senior middle school

Main Language(s) of Instruction: Korean

Degrees and Diplomas: *Bachelor's Degree*: Engineering, 4 1/2-5 yrs; *Associate Doctorate*

Libraries: c. 130,000 vols

Publications: Gazette; Newspaper

Press or Publishing House: University Publishing House

CHANGJASAN UNIVERSITY

Changjasan Taehak
Chagang Province

Faculties
Biochemistry (Biochemistry); **Foreign Studies** (International Studies); **Home Economics** (Home Economics); **Korean Language and Literature** (Korean; Literature); **Mathematics** (Mathematics); **Pedagogical Psychology** (Pedagogy; Psychology); **Physics** (Physics)

History: Founded 1967.

CHANGSUSAN UNIVERSITY

Changsusan Taehak
Haeju City, South Hwanghae Province

Faculties
Dentistry (Dentistry); **Koryo Medicine and Pharmacy** (Traditional Eastern Medicine); **Pharmacy** (Pharmacy)

History: Founded 1959. A State institution responsible to the National Education Commission.

Governing Bodies: Instruction; Scientific Research; General Affairs

Academic Year: September to August (September-February; February-August)

Admission Requirements: Graduation from senior middle school

Main Language(s) of Instruction: Korean

Degrees and Diplomas: *Bachelor's Degree*: 5-6 yrs; *Associate Doctorate*; *Doctorate*

Libraries: c. 200,000 vols

Publications: Gazette; Newspaper

Press or Publishing House: University Publishing House

CHINMYONG UNIVERSITY

Chinmyong Taehak
North Hamgyong Province

Faculties
Biology and Chemistry (Biology; Chemistry); **History and Geography** (Geography; History); **Korean Language and Literature** (Korean; Literature); **Mathematics** (Mathematics); **Music and Fine Arts** (Fine Arts; Music); **Physics** (Physics)

History: Founded 1948.

CHONG JUN TAEK UNIVERSITY OF ECONOMICS

Chong Jun Taek Kyongje Taehak
Wonsan City, Kangwon Province

Faculties
Commercial Management (Business Administration); **Finance; Economics** (Economics; Finance); **Materials Supply and Labour Administration** (Administration); **Planning Economics** (Economics)

History: Founded 1960. A State institution responsible to the National Education Commission.

Governing Bodies: Instruction; Scientific Research; General Affairs

Academic Year: September to August (September-February; February-August)

Admission Requirements: Graduation from senior middle school

Main Language(s) of Instruction: Korean

Degrees and Diplomas: *Bachelor's Degree*: 4 yrs; *Associate Doctorate*; *Doctorate*

Libraries: c. 120,000 vols

Publications: Gazette; Newspaper

Press or Publishing House: University Publishing House

CHONGSONG UNIVERSITY

Chongsong Taehak
Hamhung City, South Hamgyong Province

Faculties
Hygiene (Hygiene); **Koryo Medicine** (Traditional Eastern Medicine); **Medicine** (Medicine); **Stomatology** (Stomatology); **Surgery** (Surgery)

History: Founded 1946. A State institution responsible to the National Education Commission.

Governing Bodies: Instruction; Scientific Research; General Affairs

Academic Year: September to August (September-February; February-August)

Admission Requirements: Graduation from senior middle school

Main Language(s) of Instruction: Korean

Degrees and Diplomas: *Bachelor's Degree*: 5-6 yrs; *Associate Doctorate*; *Doctorate*

Libraries: c. 361,100 vols

Publications: Gazette; Newspaper

Press or Publishing House: University Publishing House

CHONRIGIL UNIVERSITY

Chonrigil Taehak
Chagang Province

Faculties
Biology and Chemistry (Biology; Chemistry); **History and Geography** (Geography; History); **Korean Language and Literature** (Korean; Literature); **Mathematics** (Mathematics); **Music and Fine Arts** (Fine Arts; Music); **Physics** (Physics)

History: Founded 1953.

CHOSON UNIVERSITY OF PHYSICAL EDUCATION

Choson Cheyuk Taehak
Tongdaewon District, Pyongyang

Programmes
Physical Education (Physical Education); **Sports** (Sports)

History: Founded 1958. A State institution responsible to the National Education Commission.

Governing Bodies: Instruction; Scientific Research; General Affairs

Academic Year: September to August (September-February; February-August)

Admission Requirements: Graduation from senior middle school

Main Language(s) of Instruction: Korean

Degrees and Diplomas: *Bachelor's Degree*: 4 yrs; *Associate Doctorate*; *Doctorate*

Libraries: c. 95,000 vols

Publications: Gazette; Newspaper

Press or Publishing House: University Publishing House

HAMBUK UNIVERSITY

Hambuk Taehak
Ranam District, Chongjin City, North Hamgyong Province

Faculties
Agriculture (Agriculture); **Farm Machinery** (Agricultural Equipment); **Pomiculture** (Crop Production); **Veterinary Medicine and Animal Husbandry** (Animal Husbandry; Veterinary Science)

History: Founded 1970. A State institution responsible to the National Education Commission.

Governing Bodies: Instruction; Scientific Research; General Affairs

Academic Year: September to August (September-February; February-August)

Admission Requirements: Graduation from senior middle school

Main Language(s) of Instruction: Korean

Degrees and Diplomas: *Bachelor's Degree*: Engineering, 4 1/2-5 yrs; *Associate Doctorate*

Libraries: c. 110,000 vols

Publications: Gazette; Newspaper

Press or Publishing House: University Publishing House

HUICHON UNIVERSITY OF TECHNOLOGY

Huichon Kongop Taehak
Huichon City, Chagang Province

Faculties
Automation Engineering (Automation and Control Engineering); **Electro-Apparatus Engineering** (Electronic Engineering); **Mechanical Engineering** (Mechanical Engineering); **Radio Engineering** (Telecommunications Engineering); **Wire Communication Engineering** (Telecommunications Engineering)

History: Founded 1959. A State institution responsible to the National Education Commission.

Governing Bodies: Instruction; Scientific Research; General Affairs

Academic Year: September to August (September-February; February-August)

Admission Requirements: Graduation from senior middle school

Main Language(s) of Instruction: Korean

Degrees and Diplomas: *Bachelor's Degree*: Engineering, 5 yrs; *Associate Doctorate*; *Doctorate*

Libraries: c. 18,000 vols

Publications: Gazette; Newspaper

Press or Publishing House: University Publishing House

INPUNG UNIVERSITY

Inpung Taehak
Kanggye City, Chagang Province

Faculties
Koryo Medicine (Traditional Eastern Medicine); **Medicine** (Medicine); **Surgery** (Surgery)

History: Founded 1969. A State institution responsible to the National Education Commission.

Governing Bodies: Instruction; Scientific Research; General Affairs

Academic Year: September to August (September-February; February-August)

Admission Requirements: Graduation from senior middle school

Main Language(s) of Instruction: Korean

Degrees and Diplomas: *Bachelor's Degree*: 5-6 yrs; *Associate Doctorate*

Libraries: c. 105,000 vols

Publications: Gazette; Newspaper

Press or Publishing House: University Publishing House

JANGSUN UNIVERSITY OF PHARMACY

Jangsu Yakhak Taehak
North Hwanghae Province

Faculties
Herbal Studies (Alternative Medicine); **Koryo Pharmacy** (Traditional Eastern Medicine); **Medical Zoology** (Veterinary Science)

History: Founded 1984.

KANG GON UNIVERSITY

Kang Gon Taehak
Sariwon City, North Hwanghae Province

Programmes
Medicine (Medicine); **Pharmacy** (Pharmacy); **Surgery** (Surgery); **Traditional Eastern Medicine** (Traditional Eastern Medicine)

History: Founded 1971. A State institution responsible to the National Education Commission.

Governing Bodies: Instruction; Scientific Research; General Affairs

Academic Year: September to August (September-February; February-August)

Admission Requirements: Graduation from senior middle school

Main Language(s) of Instruction: Korean

Degrees and Diplomas: *Bachelor's Degree*: 5-6 yrs; *Associate Doctorate*

Libraries: c. 200,000 vols

Publications: Gazette; Newspaper

Press or Publishing House: University Publishing House

KARIMCHON UNIVERSITY

Karimchon Taehak
Hyesan City, Ryangang Province

Programmes
Medicine (Medicine); **Traditional Eastern Medicine** (Traditional Eastern Medicine)

History: Founded 1971. A State institution responsible to the National Education Commission.

Governing Bodies: Instruction, Scientific Research and General Affairs

Academic Year: September to August (September-February; February-August)

Admission Requirements: Graduation from senior middle school

Main Language(s) of Instruction: Korean

Degrees and Diplomas: *Bachelor's Degree*: 5-6 yrs; *Associate Doctorate*

Libraries: c. 90,000 vols

Publications: Gazette; Newspaper

Press or Publishing House: University Publishing House

KIM CHAEK UNIVERSITY OF TECHNOLOGY

Kim Chaek Kongop Jonghap Taehak

Central District, Pyongyang

Faculties

Automatic Engineering (Engineering); **Communication** (Communication Studies); **Computer Engineering** (Computer Engineering); **Electrical Engineering** (Electrical Engineering); **Electronic Engineering** (Electronic Engineering); **Geological Prospecting** (Geological Engineering); **Heating Engineering** (Heating and Refrigeration); **Industrial Management** (Industrial Management); **Machine Building** (Machine Building); **Materials Engineering** (Materials Engineering); **Mechanical Engineering** (Mechanical Engineering); **Metallurgy** (Metallurgical Engineering); **Mining Engineering** (Mining Engineering); **Physical Engineering** (Physical Engineering); **Power-Driven Machine Engineering** (Power Engineering); **Shipbuilding** (Marine Engineering)

History: Founded 1948. A State institution responsible to the National Education Commission.

Governing Bodies: Instruction; Scientific Research; General Affairs

Academic Year: September to August (September-February; February-August)

Admission Requirements: Graduation from senior middle school

Main Language(s) of Instruction: Korean

Degrees and Diplomas: *Bachelor's Degree*: Engineering, 5 1/2 yrs; *Associate Doctorate*; *Doctorate*

Publications: Gazette; Newspaper

Press or Publishing House: University Publishing House

KIM CHOL JU UNIVERSITY OF EDUCATION

Kim Chol Ju Sabom Taehak

Pyongyang

Faculties

Arts (Fine Arts); **Biology and Chemistry** (Biology; Chemistry); **Foreign Studies** (International Studies); **History and Geography** (Geography; History); **Korean Language and Literature** (Korean; Literature); **Mathematics** (Mathematics); **Physical Education** (Physical Education); **Physics** (Physics)

History: Founded 1946.

KIM HYONG GWON UNIVERSITY OF EDUCATION

Kim Hyong Gwon Sabon Taehak

South Hamgyong Province

Faculties

Biochemistry (Biochemistry); **Foreign Studies** (International Studies); **Korean Language and Literature** (Korean); **Mathematics** (Mathematics); **Physical Education** (Physical Education); **Physics** (Physics)

History: Founded 1961.

KIM HYONG JIK UNIVERSITY OF EDUCATION

Kim Hyong Jik Sabom Taehak

Pyongyang

Faculties

Arts (Fine Arts); **Biology** (Biology); **Chemistry** (Chemistry); **Education** (Education); **Geography** (Geography); **History** (History); **Korean Language and Literature** (Korean; Literature); **Mathematics** (Mathematics); **Philosophy** (Philosophy); **Physical Education** (Physical Education); **Physics** (Physics)

History: Founded 1946.

KIM IL SUNG UNIVERSITY

Kim Il Sung Juonghap Taehak

Taesong District, Pyongyang

Faculties

Automation (Automation and Control Engineering); **Biology** (Biology); **Chemistry** (Chemistry); **Economics** (Economics); **Foreign Languages and Literature** (Modern Languages); **Geography** (Geography); **Geology** (Geology); **History** (History); **Korean Language and Literature** (Korean); **Law** (Law); **Mathematics** (Mathematics); **Philosophy** (Philosophy); **Physics** (Physics)

Institutes

Juche Philosophy (Ethics); **Social Sciences** (Social Sciences)

History: Founded 1946, reorganized 1953. A State institution responsible to the National Education Commission.

Governing Bodies: Instruction; Scientific Research; Social Science; Natural Science; General Affairs

Academic Year: September to August (September-February; February-August)

Admission Requirements: Graduation from senior middle school

Main Language(s) of Instruction: Korean

Degrees and Diplomas: *Bachelor's Degree*: 4 1/2-5 1/2 yrs; *Associate Doctorate*; *Doctorate*

Libraries: Science Library, c. 2,250,000 vols

Publications: Gazette; Newspaper

Press or Publishing House: University Publishing House

KIM JE WON UNIVERSITY

Haeju City, South Hwanghae Province

Faculties

Agriculture (Agriculture); **Agronomics** (Agronomy); **Farm Machinery** (Agricultural Equipment); **Pomiculture** (Crop Production)

Institutes

Agricultural Sciences Research; **Forest and River Protection** (Forestry); **Veterinary Medicine and Animal Husbandry** (Animal Husbandry; Veterinary Science)

History: Founded 1960. A State institution responsible to the National Education Commission.

Governing Bodies: Instruction; Scientific Research; General Affairs

Academic Year: September to August (September-February; February-August)

Admission Requirements: Graduation from senior middle school

Main Language(s) of Instruction: Korean

Degrees and Diplomas: *Bachelor's Degree*: Egineering, 41/2-5 yrs; *Associate Doctorate*; *Doctorate*

Libraries: c. 285,000 vols

Publications: Gazette; Newspaper

Press or Publishing House: University Publishing House

KIM JONG SUK UNIVERSITY OF EDUCATION

Kim Jong Suk Sabom Taehak

Ryanggang Province

Faculties

Arts (Fine Arts); **Biochemistry** (Biochemistry); **Foreign Studies** (International Studies); **History and Geography** (Geography; History); **Korean Language and Literature** (Korean); **Mathematics** (Mathematics); **Physical Education** (Physical Education); **Physics** (Physics)

History: Founded 1967.

KIM JONG TAE UNIVERSITY

Kim Jong Tae Sabon Taehak

South Hwanghae Province

Faculties

Biochemistry (Biochemistry); **Foreign Studies** (International Studies); **History and Geography** (Geography; History); **Korean Language and Literature** (Korean; Literature); **Mathematics** (Mathematics); **Physical Education** (Physical Education); **Physics** (Physics)

History: Founded 1957.

KORYO UNIVERSITY OF PHARMACY

Koryo Yakhak Taehak

Hamhung City, South Hamgyong Province

Programmes

Pharmacy (Pharmacy)

History: Founded 1968. A State institution responsible to the National Education Commission.

Governing Bodies: Instruction; Scientific Research; General Affairs

Academic Year: September to August (September-February; February-August)

Admission Requirements: Graduation from senior middle school

Main Language(s) of Instruction: Korean

Degrees and Diplomas: *Bachelor's Degree*: Engineering, 5 yrs

Libraries: c. 130,000 vols

Publications: Gazette; Newspaper

Press or Publishing House: University Publishing House

KUMGANG UNIVERSITY

Kumgang Taehak

Kangwon Province

Faculties

Arts (Arts and Humanities); **Biochemistry** (Biochemistry); **Foreign Studies** (International Studies); **History and Geography** (Geography; History); **Korean Language and Literature** (Korean; Literature); **Mathematics** (Mathematics); **Physical Education** (Physical Education); **Physics** (Physics)

History: Founded 1949.

KUMYA UNIVERSITY

Kumya Taehak

Sapo District, Hamhung City, South Hamgyong Province

Faculties

Agriculture (Agriculture); **Farm Machinery** (Agricultural Equipment); **Pomiculture** (Crop Production)

Institutes

Agricultural Scientific Research (Agriculture); **Veterinary Medicine and Animal Husbandry** (Animal Husbandry; Veterinary Science)

History: Founded 1958. A State institution responsible to the National Education Commission.

Governing Bodies: Instruction; Scientific Research; General Affairs

Academic Year: September to August (September-February; February-August)

Admission Requirements: Graduation from senior middle school

Main Language(s) of Instruction: Korean

Degrees and Diplomas: *Bachelor's Degree*: Engineering, 4 1/2-5 yrs; *Associate Doctorate*; *Doctorate*

Libraries: c. 83,000 vols

Publications: Gazette; Newspaper

Press or Publishing House: University Publishing House

KWANJE UNIVERSITY

Kwangje Taehak

Pyonghawa-Dong, Sinuiju City, Pyongan Province

Faculties

Hygiene (Hygiene); **Koryo Medicine** (Traditional Eastern Medicine); **Medicine** (Medicine); **Pharmacy** (Pharmacy); **Stomatology** (Stomatology); **Surgery** (Surgery)

History: Founded 1969. A State institution responsible to the National Education Commission.

Governing Bodies: Instruction; Scientific Research; General Affairs

Academic Year: September to August (September-February; February-August)

Admission Requirements: Graduation from senior middle school

Main Language(s) of Instruction: Korean

Degrees and Diplomas: *Bachelor's Degree*: 5-6 yrs; *Associate Doctorate*

Libraries: c. 115.00 vols

Publications: Gazette; Newspaper

Press or Publishing House: University Publishing House

KWANSO UNIVERSITY

Kwanso Taehak

North Pyongan Province

Faculties

Biochemistry (Biochemistry); **History and Geography** (Geography; History); **Korean Language and Literature** (Korean; Literature); **Mathematics** (Mathematics); **Music and Fine Arts** (Fine Arts; Music); **Physical Education** (Physical Education); **Physics** (Physics)

History: Founded 1947.

KYE UNG SAN UNIVERSITY

Kye Ung Sang Taehak

Sariwon City, North Hwanghae Province

Faculties

Agriculture (Agriculture); **Agrochemistry** (Chemistry); **Agronomy** (Agronomy); **Biology** (Biology); **Economic Plant** (Plant and Crop Protection); **Farm Machinery** (Agricultural Equipment); **Forest and River Protection** (Environmental Studies); **Land Development** (Environmental Studies); **Pomiculture** (Crop Production); **Sericulture** (Sericulture); **Veterinary Medicine and Animal Husbandry** (Animal Husbandry; Veterinary Science)

Academic Year: September to August (September-February; February-August)

Admission Requirements: Graduation from senior middle school

Main Language(s) of Instruction: Korean

Degrees and Diplomas: *Bachelor's Degree*: Engineering, 4 1/2-5 yrs; *Associate Doctorate*; *Doctorate*

Libraries: c. 365,000 vols

Publications: Gazette; Newspaper

Press or Publishing House: University Publishing House

KYONGSONG UNIVERSITY

Kyongsong Taehak

Pohang District, Chongjin City, North Hamgyong Province

Faculties

Hygiene (Hygiene); **Koryo Medicine** (Traditional Eastern Medicine); **Medicine** (Medicine); **Pharmacy** (Pharmacy); **Stomatology** (Stomatology); **Surgery** (Surgery)

Further Information: Also Research Institute

History: Founded 1948. A State institution responsible to the National Education Commission.

Governing Bodies: Instruction; Scientific Research; General Affairs

Academic Year: September to August (September-February; February-August)

Admission Requirements: Graduation from senior middle school

Main Language(s) of Instruction: Korean

Degrees and Diplomas: *Bachelor's Degree*: 5-6 yrs; *Associate Doctorate*; *Doctorate*

Publications: Gazette; Newspaper

Press or Publishing House: University Publishing House

MANPUNG UNIVERSITY

Manpung Taehak

Sinuiju City, North Pyongyang Province

Faculties

Agriculture (Agriculture); **Farm Machinery** (Agricultural Equipment); **Pomiculture** (Crop Production); **Stockraising** (Animal Husbandry)

History: Founded 1969. A State institution responsible to the National Education Commission.

Governing Bodies: Instruction; Scientific Research; General Affairs

Academic Year: September to August (September-February; February-August)

Admission Requirements: Graduation from senior middle school

Main Language(s) of Instruction: Korean

Degrees and Diplomas: *Bachelor's Degree*: Engineering, 4-5 yrs; *Associate Doctorate*

Libraries: c. 85,000 vols

Publications: Gazette; Newspaper

Press or Publishing House: University Publishing House

MYONGSIN UNIVERSITY

South Pyongan Province

Faculties

Arts (Arts and Humanities); **Biochemistry** (Biochemistry); **Foreign Studies** (International Studies); **History and Geography** (Geography; History); **Korean Language and Literature** (Korean; Literature); **Mathematics** (Mathematics); **Physical Education** (Physical Education); **Physics** (Physics)

History: Founded 1961.

NAMPO UNIVERSITY

Nampo Taehak

Waudo District, Nampo City

Faculties

Agriculture (Agriculture); **Farm Machinery** (Agricultural Equipment); **Horticulture** (Horticulture); **Pomiculture** (Crop Production)

History: Founded 1967. A State institution responsible to the National Education Commission.

Governing Bodies: Instruction; Scientific Research; General Affairs

Academic Year: September to August (September-February; February-August)

Admission Requirements: Graduation from senior middle school

Main Language(s) of Instruction: Korean

Degrees and Diplomas: *Bachelor's Degree*: Engineering, 4 1/2-5 yrs; *Associate Doctorate*

Libraries: c. 105,000 vols

Publications: Gazette; Newspaper

Press or Publishing House: University Publishing House

NAMPO UNIVERSITY OF MEDICINE

Nampo Uihak Taehak

Nampo City, South Pyongan Province

Faculties

Dentistry (Dentistry); **Medicine** (Medicine); **Pharmacy** (Pharmacy)

History: Founded 1985.

O JUNG HUP UNIVERSITY

O Jung Hup Taehak

North Hamgyong Province

Faculties

Biochemistry (Biochemistry); **Foreign Studies** (International Studies); **History and Geography** (Geography; History); **Korean Language and Literature** (Korean; Literature); **Mathematics** (Mathematics); **Musics and Fine Arts** (Fine Arts; Music); **Physics** (Physics)

History: Founded 1961.

PONGHWA UNIVERSITY

Ponghwa Taehak

Pyongsong City, South Pyongan Province

Faculties

Koryo Medicine (Traditional Eastern Medicine); **Medicine** (Medicine); **Pharmacy** (Pharmacy); **Stomatology** (Stomatology); **Surgery** (Surgery)

History: Founded 1972. A State institution responsible to the National Education Commission.

Governing Bodies: Instruction; Scientific Research; General Affairs

Academic Year: September to August (September-February; February-August)

Admission Requirements: Graduation from senior middle school

Main Language(s) of Instruction: Korean

Degrees and Diplomas: *Bachelor's Degree*: 5-6 yrs; *Associate Doctorate*

Libraries: c. 110,000 vols

Publications: Gazette; Newspaper

Press or Publishing House: University Publishing House

PYONGYANG NONGOP UNIVERSITY OF AGRICULTURE

Pyongyang Nongop Taehak

Ryongsong District, Pyongyang

Faculties

Agriculture (Agriculture); **Agrobiology** (Agrobiology); **Farm Machinery** (Agricultural Equipment); **Veterinary Medicine and Animal Husbandry** (Animal Husbandry; Veterinary Science)

History: Founded 1981. A State institution responsible to the National Education Commission.

Governing Bodies: Instruction; Scientific Research; General Affairs

Academic Year: September to August (September-February; February-August)

Admission Requirements: Graduation from senior middle school

Main Language(s) of Instruction: Korean

Degrees and Diplomas: *Bachelor's Degree*: Engineering, 4 1/2-5 yrs

Libraries: c. 55,100 vols

Publications: Gazette; Newspaper

Press or Publishing House: University Publishing House

PYONGYANG UNIVERSITY OF CINEMATICS

Pyongyang Yonguk Yonghwa Taehak

Tongdaewon District, Pyongyang

Faculties

Acting (Acting); **Cinema** (Cinema and Television); **Cinematography** (Cinema and Television); **Creation** (Fine Arts); **Direction**; **Social Sciences** (Social Sciences); **Technology** (Technology)

History: Founded 1953. A State institution responsible to the National Education Commission.

Governing Bodies: Instruction; Scientific Research; General Affairs

Academic Year: September to August (September-February; February-August)

Admission Requirements: Graduation from senior middle school

Main Language(s) of Instruction: Korean

Degrees and Diplomas: *Bachelor's Degree*: 4 yrs; *Doctorate*

Libraries: c. 100,000 vols

Publications: Gazette; Newspaper

Press or Publishing House: University Publishing House

PYONGYANG UNIVERSITY OF FINE ARTS

Pyongyang Misul Taehak

Tongdaewon District, Pyongyang

Faculties

Crafts (Crafts and Trades); **Graphic Art** (Graphic Arts); **Industrial Art** (Industrial Arts Education); **Korean Painting** (Painting and Drawing); **Painting** (Painting and Drawing); **Sculpture** (Sculpture)

Institutes

Fine Arts Research (Fine Arts)

History: Founded 1947. A State institution responsible to the National Education Commission.

Governing Bodies: Instruction; Scientific Research; General Affairs

Academic Year: September to August (September-February; February-August)

Admission Requirements: Graduation from senior middle school

Main Language(s) of Instruction: Korean

Degrees and Diplomas: *Bachelor's Degree*: 4 yrs; *Associate Doctorate*; *Doctorate*

Libraries: c. 85,000 vols

Publications: Gazette; Newspaper

Press or Publishing House: University Publishing House

PYONGYANG UNIVERSITY OF FOREIGN STUDIES

Pyongyang Oeguko Taehak

Taesong District, Pyongyang

Faculties

Education (Education); **English** (English); **French and Spanish** (French; Spanish); **Russian; Chinese; Arabic; Japanese** (Arabic; Chinese; Japanese; Russian)

Institutes

Education Theory (Education); **Simultaneous Interpretation** (Translation and Interpretation); **Training** (Teacher Training)

History: Founded 1949. A State institution responsible to the National Education Commission.

Governing Bodies: Instruction; Scientific Research; General Affairs

Academic Year: September to August (September-February; February-August)

Admission Requirements: Graduation from senior middle school

Main Language(s) of Instruction: Korean

Degrees and Diplomas: *Bachelor's Degree*: 5 yrs; *Associate Doctorate*; *Doctorate*

Libraries: c. 225,000 vols

Publications: Gazette; Newspaper

Press or Publishing House: University Publishing House

PYONGYANG UNIVERSITY OF LIGHT INDUSTRY

Pyongyang Kyonggongop Taehak

Songyo District, Pyongyang

Faculties

Chemical Engineering (Chemical Engineering); **Food Engineering** (Food Technology); **Machine Engineering** (Machine Building); **Management** (Management); **Textile Engineering** (Textile Technology)

Institutes

Food Research (Food Science); **Light Industry** (Electrical Engineering); **Paper Technology** (Paper Technology)

History: Founded 1959. A State institution responsible to the National Education Commission.

Governing Bodies: Instruction; Scientific Research; General Affairs

Academic Year: September to August (September-February; February-August)

Admission Requirements: Graduation from senior middle school

Main Language(s) of Instruction: Korean

Degrees and Diplomas: *Bachelor's Degree*: 5 yrs; *Associate Doctorate*; *Doctorate*

Libraries: c. 260,000 vols

Publications: Gazette; Newspaper

Press or Publishing House: University Publishing House

PYONGYANG UNIVERSITY OF MECHANICAL ENGINEERING

Pyongyang Kigye Taehak

Taedonggang District, Pyongyang

Faculties

Automation (Automation and Control Engineering); **Construction Machinery** (Machine Building); **Design** (Design); **Mechanical Engineering** (Mechanical Engineering)

History: A State institution responsible to the National Education Comission.

Governing Bodies: Instruction; Scientific Research; General Affairs

Academic Year: September to August (September-February; February-August)

Admission Requirements: Graduation from senior middle school

Main Language(s) of Instruction: Korean

Degrees and Diplomas: *Bachelor's Degree*: Engineering, 5 yrs; *Associate Doctorate*; *Doctorate*

Libraries: c. 310,000 vols

Publications: Gazette; Newspaper

Press or Publishing House: University Publishing House

PYONGYANG UNIVERSITY OF MEDICINE

Pyongyang Uihak Taehak

Central District, Pyongyang

Faculties

Basic Medicine (Medicine); **Clinical Medicine** (Medicine); **Hygiene** (Hygiene); **Koryo Medicine**; **Pharmacy** (Pharmacy); **Stomatology** (Stomatology)

History: Founded 1948. A State institution responsible to the National Education Commission.

Governing Bodies: Instruction; Scientific Research; General Affairs

Academic Year: September to August (September-February; February-August)

Admission Requirements: Graduation from senior middle school

Main Language(s) of Instruction: Korean

Degrees and Diplomas: *Bachelor's Degree*: 5-6 yrs; *Associate Doctorate*; *Doctorate*

Libraries: c. 265,000 vols

Publications: Gazette; Newspaper

Press or Publishing House: University Publishing House

PYONGYANG UNIVERSITY OF MUSIC AND DANCE

Pyongyang Umakmuyong Taehak
Taedonggang District, Pyongyang

Faculties
Composition (Music Theory and Composition); **Dance** (Dance); **National Instruments** (Musical Instruments); **Preparatory**; **Vocal Technique** (Singing); **Western Instruments** (Musical Instruments)

Institutes
Music and Dance (Dance; Music)

History: Founded 1948. A State institution responsible to the National Education Commission.

Governing Bodies: Instruction; Scientific Research; General Affairs

Academic Year: September to August (September-February; February-August)

Admission Requirements: Graduation from senior middle school

Main Language(s) of Instruction: Korean

Degrees and Diplomas: *Bachelor's Degree*: 4 yrs; *Associate Doctorate*

Libraries: c. 140,000 vols

Publications: Gazette; Newspaper

Press or Publishing House: University Publishing House

PYONGYANG UNIVERSITY OF RAILWAYS

Pyongyang Choldo Taehak
Hyongjesan District, Pyongyang

Programmes
Railway Engineering (Railway Engineering)

History: Founded 1959. A State institution responsible to the National Education Commission.

Governing Bodies: Instruction; Scientific Research; General Affairs

Academic Year: September to August (September-February; February-August)

Admission Requirements: Graduation from senior middle school

Main Language(s) of Instruction: Korean

Degrees and Diplomas: *Bachelor's Degree*: Engineering, 5 yrs; *Associate Doctorate*; *Doctorate*

Libraries: c. 210,000 vols

Publications: Gazette; Newspaper

Press or Publishing House: University Publishing House

PYONGYANG UNIVERSITY OF SURGERY

Pyongyang

Faculties
Dentistry (Dentistry); **Koryo Medicine** (Traditional Eastern Medicine); **Medical Sciences** (Health Sciences); **Pharmacy** (Pharmacy)

History: Founded 1985.

RI KYE SUN UNIVERSITY

Ri Kye Sun Taehak
North Hwanghae Province

Faculties
Biochemistry (Biochemistry); **Foreign Studies** (International Studies); **Korean Language and Literature** (Korean; Literature); **Mathematics** (Mathematics); **Physical Education** (Physical Education); **Physics** (Physics)

History: Founded 1953.

RI SU BOK UNIVERSITY

Ri Su Bok Taehak
South Pyongan Province

Faculties
Antibiotics Pharmacy (Pharmacy); **Chemical Machine Building** (Machine Building); **High Polymer Chemistry** (Chemistry); **Inorganic Synthetic Techniques** (Inorganic Chemistry); **Organic Synthetic Techniques** (Organic Chemistry)

History: Founded 1984.

RYANGGANG UNIVERSITY

Ryanggang Taehak
Hyesan City, Ryangang Province

Faculties
Agriculture (Agriculture); **Forestry Engineering** (Forestry); **Wood Processing** (Forest Products)

Institutes
Agricultural and Forestry Scientific Research (Agriculture; Forestry); **Stockraising** (Cattle Breeding)

History: Founded 1955. A State institution responsible to the National Education Commission.

Governing Bodies: Instruction; Scientific Research; General Affairs

Academic Year: September to August (September-February; February-August)

Admission Requirements: Graduation from senior middle school

Main Language(s) of Instruction: Korean

Degrees and Diplomas: *Bachelor's Degree*: Engineering, 4 1/2-5 yrs; *Associate Doctorate*; *Doctorate*

Libraries: c. 135,000 vols

Publications: Gazette; Newspaper

Press or Publishing House: University Publishing House

RYOMYONG UNIVERSITY

Ryomyong Taehak
North Hamgyong Province

Faculties
History and Geography (Geography; History); **Korean Language and Literature** (Korean; Literature); **Mathematics** (Mathematics); **Music and Fine Arts** (Fine Arts; Music); **Physics** (Physics)

History: Founded 1946.

SAENAL UNIVERSITY

Saenal Taehak
South Hamgyong Province

Faculties
Biochemistry (Biochemistry); **History and Geography** (Geography; History); **Korean Language and Literature** (Korean; Literature); **Mathematics** (Mathematics); **Music and Fine Arts** (Fine Arts; Music); **Physics** (Physics)

History: Founded 1961.

SANMGWANG UNIVERSITY

Samgwang Taehak
Nampo, South Pyongan Province

Faculties
Arts (Arts and Humanities); **Biochemistry** (Biochemistry); **Foreign Studies** (International Studies); **History and Geography** (Geography; History); **Korean Language and Literature** (Korean; Literature); **Mathematics** (Mathematics); **Physical Education** (Physical Education); **Physics** (Physics); **Technical Education** (Technology Education)

History: Founded 1963.

SARIWON UNIVERSITY

Sariwon Taehak
North Hwanghae Province

Faculties
History and Geography (Geography; History); **Korean Language and Literature** (Korean; Literature); **Mathematics** (Mathematics); **Music and Fine Arts** (Fine Arts; Music); **Physics** (Physics)

History: Founded 1963.

SINUIJU UNIVERSITY OF LIGHT INDUSTRY

Sinuiju Kyongkongop Taehak
Sinuiju City, North Pyongyang Province

Faculties
Chemical Engineering (Chemical Engineering); **Food Technology** (Food Technology); **Machine Engineering** (Machine Building); **Textile Engineering** (Textile Technology)

History: Founded 1982. A State institution responsible to the National Education Commission.

Governing Bodies: Instruction; Scientific Research; General Affairs

Academic Year: September to August (September-February; February-August)

Admission Requirements: Graduation from senior middle school

Main Language(s) of Instruction: Korean

Degrees and Diplomas: *Bachelor's Degree*: Engineering, 5 yrs

Libraries: c. 75,000 vols

Publications: Gazette; Newspaper

Press or Publishing House: University Publishing House

SOHAE UNIVERSITY

Sohae Taehak
Waudo District, Nampo City

Faculties
Fish Farming and Cultivation (Aquaculture); **Fisheries** (Fishery); **Mechanical Engineering** (Mechanical Engineering)

History: Founded 1977. A State institution responsible to the National Education Commission.

Governing Bodies: Instruction; Scientific Research; General Affairs

Academic Year: September to August (September-February; February-August)

Admission Requirements: Graduation from senior middle school

Main Language(s) of Instruction: Korean

Degrees and Diplomas: *Bachelor's Degree*: Engineering, 4 yrs

Libraries: c. 70,000 vols

Publications: Gazette; Newspaper

Press or Publishing House: University Publishing House

SONGDO UNIVERSITY

Songdo Taehak
Kaesong

Faculties
Arts (Arts and Humanities); **Biochemistry** (Biochemistry); **Foreign Studies** (International Studies); **History and Geography** (Geography; History); **Korean Language and Literature** (Korean; Literature); **Mathematics** (Mathematics); **Physical Training** (Physical Education); **Physics** (Physics)

History: Founded 1961.

SONGDOWON UNIVERSITY

Songdowon Taehak
Wonsan City, Kangwon Province

Faculties
Koryo Medicine (Traditional Eastern Medicine); **Koryo Pharmacy** (Traditional Eastern Medicine); **Medicine** (Medicine)

History: Founded 1971. A State institution responsible to the National Education Commission.

Governing Bodies: Instruction; Scientific Research; General Affairs

Academic Year: September to August (September-February; February-August)

Admission Requirements: Graduation from senior middle school

Main Language(s) of Instruction: Korean

Degrees and Diplomas: *Associate Doctorate*; *Doctorate*: 5 yrs

Libraries: c. 130,000 vols

Publications: Gazette; Newspaper

Press or Publishing House: University Publishing House

TONGHAE UNIVERSITY

Tonghae Taehak
Wonsan City, Kangwon Province

Faculties
Fish Farming and Cultivation (Aquaculture); **Fisheries** (Fishery); **Marine Products Processing** (Marine Biology); **Mechanical Engineering** (Mechanical Engineering)

History: Founded 1959. A State institution responsible to the National Education Commission.

Governing Bodies: Instruction; Scientific Research; General Affairs

Academic Year: September to August (September-February; February-August)

Admission Requirements: Graduation from senior middle school

Main Language(s) of Instruction: Korean

Degrees and Diplomas: *Bachelor's Degree*: Engineering, 5 yrs; *Associate Doctorate*; *Doctorate*

Libraries: c. 190,000 vols

Publications: Gazette; Newspaper

Press or Publishing House: University Publishing House

UNIVERSITY OF CHEMICAL INDUSTRY

Hwahak Kongop Taehak
Hoesang District, Hamhung City, South Hamgyong Province

Faculties
High Polymers Chemical Engineering (Chemical Engineering); **Inorganic Chemical Engineering** (Inorganic Chemistry); **Machine Engineering** (Machine Building); **Organic Chemical Engineering** (Organic Chemistry); **Silicate Engineering** (Mining Engineering)

History: Founded 1947. A State institution responsible to the National Education Commission.

Governing Bodies: Instruction; Scientific Research; General Affairs

Academic Year: September to August (September-February; February-August)

Admission Requirements: Graduation from senior middle school

Main Language(s) of Instruction: Korean

Degrees and Diplomas: *Bachelor's Degree*: Engineering, 5 yrs; *Associate Doctorate*; *Doctorate*

Libraries: c. 340,000 vols

Publications: Gazette; Newspaper

Press or Publishing House: University Publishing House

UNIVERSITY OF COAL MINING

Sokthan Kongop Taehak
Pyongsong City, South Pyongan Province

Faculties
Anthracite Engineering (Mining Engineering); **Automation** (Automation and Control Engineering); **Coal Mine Machine Engineering** (Mechanical Engineering); **Coal Mining** (Mining Engineering)

History: Founded 1968. A State institution responsible to the National Education Commission.

Governing Bodies: Instruction; Scientific Research; General Affairs

Academic Year: September to August (September-February; February-August)

Admission Requirements: Graduation from senior middle school

Main Language(s) of Instruction: Korean

Degrees and Diplomas: *Bachelor's Degree*: Engineering, 5 yrs; *Associate Doctorate*

Libraries: c. 160,000 vols

Publications: Gazette; Newspaper

Press or Publishing House: University Publishing House

UNIVERSITY OF CONSTRUCTION AND BUILDING MATERIALS

Konsol Konjae Taehak

Taedonggang District, Pyongyang

Faculties

Architectural Engineering (Architecture); **Architecture** (Architecture); **Building Machines** (Machine Building); **Building Materials** (Materials Engineering); **City Management** (Town Planning); **Civil Engineering** (Construction Engineering); **Construction** (Construction Engineering)

History: Founded 1959. A State institution responsible to the National Education Commission.

Governing Bodies: Instruction; Scientific Research; General Affairs

Academic Year: September to August (September-February; February-August)

Admission Requirements: Graduation from senior middle school

Main Language(s) of Instruction: Korean

Degrees and Diplomas: *Bachelor's Degree*: 5 yrs

Libraries: c. 150,000 vols

Publications: Gazette; Newspaper

Press or Publishing House: University Publishing House

UNIVERSITY OF GEOLOGY

Jijil Taehak

Sariwon City, North Hwanghae Province

Faculties

Geological Engineering (Geological Engineering); **Geology** (Geology); **Machine Engineering** (Machine Building); **Physical Prospecting**

History: Founded 1970. A State institution responsible to the National Education Commission.

Governing Bodies: Instruction; Scientific Research; General Affairs

Academic Year: September to August (September-February; February-August)

Admission Requirements: Graduation from senior middle school

Main Language(s) of Instruction: Korean

Degrees and Diplomas: *Bachelor's Degree*: Engineering, 5 yrs; *Associate Doctorate*; *Doctorate*

Libraries: c. 180,000 vols

Publications: Gazette; Newspaper

Press or Publishing House: University Publishing House

UNIVERSITY OF HYDRAULICS AND DYNAMICS

Suridongryok Taehak

Tonghungsan District, Hamhung City, South Hamgyong Province

Faculties

Electrical Engineering (Electrical Engineering); **Hydraulic and Port Construction Engineering** (Construction Engineering; Hydraulic Engineering); **Hydraulic Engineering** (Hydraulic Engineering); **Irrigation** (Irrigation); **Mechanical Engineering** (Mechanical Engineering)

History: Founded 1959. A State institution responsible to the National Education Commission.

Governing Bodies: Instruction;Scientific Research; General Affairs

Academic Year: September to August (September-February; February-August)

Admission Requirements: Graduation from senior middle school

Main Language(s) of Instruction: Korean

Degrees and Diplomas: *Bachelor's Degree*: Engineering, 5 yrs; *Associate Doctorate*; *Doctorate*

Libraries: c. 25,000 vols

Publications: Gazette; Newspaper

Press or Publishing House: University Publishing House

UNIVERSITY OF LIGHT INDUSTRY

Koryo Songgyungwan Taehak

Kaesong

Programmes

Textile Technology (Textile Technology)

History: Founded 1992.

UNIVERSITY OF MINING AND METALLURGICAL ENGINEERING

Kwangsan Gumsok Taehak

Pohang District, Chongjin City, North Hamgyong Province

Faculties

Automation (Automation and Control Engineering); **Coal Engineering** (Mining Engineering); **Geotechnology** (Geological Engineering); **Metallurgy** (Metallurgical Engineering); **Mineral Analysis** (Mineralogy); **Mining Machine Engineering** (Mechanical Engineering); **Mining** (Mining Engineering)

History: Founded 1959. A State institution responsible to the National Education Commission.

Governing Bodies: Instruction; Scientific Research; General Affairs

Academic Year: September to August (September-February; February-August)

Admission Requirements: Graduation from senior middle school

Main Language(s) of Instruction: Korean

Degrees and Diplomas: *Bachelor's Degree*: Engineering, 4 yrs; *Associate Doctorate*; *Doctorate*

Libraries: c. 320,000 vols

Publications: Gazette; Newspaper

Press or Publishing House: University Publishing House

UNIVERSITY OF NATIONAL ECONOMICS

Inmin Gyongje Taehak

Pyongyang

Faculties

Agricultural Management (Agricultural Management); **Finance and Banking** (Banking; Finance); **Government** (Government); **Industrial Management** (Industrial Management); **Planning**; **Statistics** (Statistics); **Trade** (Business and Commerce)

History: Founded 1946. A State institution responsible to the National Education Commission.

Governing Bodies: Instruction; Scientific Research; General Affairs

Academic Year: September to August (September-February; February-August)

Admission Requirements: Graduation from senior middle school

UNIVERSITY OF PRINTING TECHNOLOGY

Inswae Kongop Taehak

Pyongyang

Programmes

Engineering and Technology (Engineering; Technology); **Printing and Printmaking** (Printing and Printmaking)

History: Founded 1984. A State institution responsible to the Provincial Committee for Administration and Economic Guidance.

Governing Bodies: Instruction; Scientific Research; General Affairs

Academic Year: September to August(September-February; February-August)

Admission Requirements: Graduation from senior middle school

Main Language(s) of Instruction: Korean

Degrees and Diplomas: *Bachelor's Degree*: 4 yrs

UNIVERSITY OF SCIENCE

Rigwa Taehak

Pyongsong City, South Pyongan Province

Faculties

Automation (Automation and Control Engineering); **Biology** (Biology); **Chemistry** (Chemistry); **Computer Sciences** (Computer Science); **Electrical Engineering** (Electrical Engineering); **Mathematics** (Mathematics); **Mechanical Engineering** (Mechanical Engineering); **Physics** (Physics)

Further Information: Also Research Institute

History: Founded 1967. A State institution responsible to the National Education Commission.

Governing Bodies: Instruction; Scientific Research; General Affairs

Academic Year: September to August (September-February; February-August)

Admission Requirements: Graduation from senior middle school

Main Language(s) of Instruction: Korean

Degrees and Diplomas: *Bachelor's Degree*: 5 yrs; *Associate Doctorate*; *Doctorate*

Libraries: c. 255,000 vols

Publications: Gazette; Newspaper

Press or Publishing House: University Publishing House

UNIVERSITY OF SEA TRANSPORT

Haeun Taehak

Rajin City, North Hamgyong Province

Programmes

Electrical Engineering (Electrical Engineering); **Marine Engineering** (Marine Engineering); **Marine Transport** (Marine Transport); **Nautical Science** (Nautical Science)

History: Founded 1968. A State institution responsible to the National Education Commission.

Governing Bodies: Instruction; Scientific Research; General Affairs

Academic Year: September to August (September-February; February-August)

Admission Requirements: Graduation from senior middle school

Main Language(s) of Instruction: Korean

Degrees and Diplomas: *Bachelor's Degree*: Engineering, 5 yrs; *Associate Doctorate*; *Doctorate*

Libraries: c. 160,000 vols

Publications: Gazette; Newspaper

Press or Publishing House: University Publishing House

UNIVERSITY OF VETERINARY MEDICINE AND ANIMAL HUSBANDRY

Suui Chuksan Taehak

Pyongsong City, South Pyongan Province

Faculties

Animal Husbandry (Animal Husbandry); **Veterinary Science** (Veterinary Science)

History: Founded 1955. A State institution responsible to the National Education Commission.

Governing Bodies: Instruction; Scientific Research; General Affairs

Academic Year: September to August (September-February; February-August)

Admission Requirements: Graduation from senior middle school

Main Language(s) of Instruction: Korean

Degrees and Diplomas: *Bachelor's Degree*: Engineering, 5 yrs; *Associate Doctorate*; *Doctorate*

Libraries: c. 175,000 vols

Publications: Gazette; Newspaper

Press or Publishing House: University Publishing House

WONSAN UNIVERSITY OF AGRICULTURE

Wonsan Nongop Taehak

Wonsan City, Kwangwon Province

Faculties

Agricultural Machines (Agricultural Equipment); **Agriculture** (Agriculture); **Agrobiology** (Agrobiology); **Agrochemistry** (Agronomy; Chemistry); **Agronomy** (Agronomy); **Botany** (Botany); **Irrigation Engineering** (Irrigation); **Pomiculture** (Crop Production); **Sericulture** (Sericulture)

Further Information: Also 3 Research Institutes

History: Founded 1948. A State institution responsible to the National Education Commission.

Governing Bodies: Instruction; Scientific Research; General Affairs

Academic Year: September to August (September-February; February-August)

Admission Requirements: Graduation from senior middle school

Main Language(s) of Instruction: Korean

Degrees and Diplomas: *Bachelor's Degree*: Engineering, 4 1/2-5 yrs; *Associate Doctorate*; *Doctorate*

Libraries: c. 325,000 vols

Publications: Gazette; Newspaper

Press or Publishing House: University Publishing House

Korea (Republic of)

STRUCTURE OF HIGHER EDUCATION SYSTEM

Description:

The South Korean higher education system, which includes public and private institutions, is relatively centralized under the government and the Ministry of Education, Science, & Technology despite a general trend toward greater autonomy. There are 5 main types of institution: universities (public & private), junior colleges (public & private), industrial universities (public & private), education universities (public), and graduate school universities (private). There are also several online universities, ecclesiastical universities, and a public correspondence university. Most of these (over 80%) are privately owned, rely mostly on private funding, and tend to have higher tuition rates and a somewhat greater degree of autonomy from the government than public institutions, which are mainly managed by the Ministry of Education.

Stages of studies:

University level first stage: *Undergraduate universities: confer general and specialized Baccalaureate degrees*
Most higher education students enter universities that include 4-year programmes across a range of fields in Science, Humanities, Engineering, Business, etc. A few universities focus on technical subjects. Some fields require students to pass licensing exams in addition to regular coursework. Industrial universities train in 4-year programmes focused on technological areas but may also include many of the same fields as universities; priority is generally given to graduates of vocational schools. Law students currently study for four years and must pass a licensing exam; a US-style system with specialized law studies following regular undergraduate studies is likely to be adopted in the future.

University level second stage: *Graduate schools (independent and attached to universities): confer Master's degrees*
Graduate schools provide 2-3 years of study beyond the baccalaureate degree in the same field of study for students to obtain a Master's degree. Most graduate schools, including medical schools, are attached to universities. Students must submit a thesis and/or pass licensing examinations in addition to completing regular coursework. Presently medical students complete a total of 6 years of higher education and must pass a national medical examination in addition to specialized clinical practice and training. This is likely to change soon to require 8 total years of higher education.

University level third stage: *Graduate schools (independent and attached to universities): confer Doctoral degrees*
Graduate schools also provide 2-3 years of training beyond a Master's degree to obtain a Doctoral degree. Students must submit a doctoral dissertation and pass an oral or equivalent examination in addition to required coursework.

Distance higher education:
Korea National Open University, a public institution, provides distance education programmes at the national level. It offers courses for Bachelor's degrees. There are also 17 private online universities across the country offering baccalaureate-level educational programmes taken through the Internet.

ADMISSION TO HIGHER EDUCATION

Admission to university-level studies:

Name of secondary school credential required: High School Diploma

Alternatives to credentials: Credit Bank System: people can accumulate credits to earn the degree equivalent.

Entrance exam requirements: Korean scholastic achievement test (suneung).

Other admission requirements: Access to higher education is based on the composite score of the CSAT, high-school academic records, an essay test, and an interview.

Foreign students admission:

Definition of foreign student: Students from foreign countries or overseas Koreans with foreign nationality taking up courses, doing research or language studies in an accredited university or graduate school (including industrial universities, universities of education and junior colleges). However, students enrolled in distance education or evening schools are not included.

Quotas: None

Entrance exam requirements: Foreign students must hold qualifications equivalent to full secondary or high school certificate or its equivalent for graduate studies. Requirements include the following: application form, certificate of graduation, grade points average (records), two references, proof of Korean language proficiency, study plan, curriculum vitae and portfolio (for applicants in arts/physical education).

Entry regulations: Foreign students must secure standard admission issued by the president or the dean of the university where they intend to study and submit the documents to the Ministry of Justice or to an overseas Korean diplomatic mission. Applicants should secure a D2 visa for degree programmes and D4 visa for language studies.

Health requirements: None

Language requirements: Although an increasing number of universities teach classes in English (quantity and quality vary by university), students are advised to have a good knowledge of Korean.

RECOGNITION OF STUDIES

Quality assurance system:

Current quality assurance mechanisms in South Korean higher education are generally less homogenous and less compulsory than in many other countries. The Ministry of Education, Science, and Technology indirectly accredits institutions through evaluations of individual universities' compliance with government regulations and policies and provides funding accordingly. Also, evaluations of institutions and specific academic fields are conducted by several organizations, such as the Korean Council for University Education (KCUE) and the Korean Council for College Education (KCCE). The privately-owned Joongang Daily also publishes independent rankings of schools and specific academic fields every year (available in Korean at http://univ.joins.com). Individual schools also have quality assurance mechanisms such as department reviews and less formal student evaluations.

Special provisions for recognition:

Recognition for university level studies: The Korean Council for University Education (KCUE) conducts voluntary accreditations of its member universities, which include all four-year higher education institutions in the country. Two rounds of accreditations, 1994-2000 and 2001-2006, have been completed and included both comprehensive and field-specific evaluations. Although an English translation is not yet available, results can be viewed in Korean at http://eval.kcue.or.kr/. The results of the first round of evaluations were valid for seven years and the results of the second round for six years. It was intended for universities to request another evaluation once the previous one expired. Accreditation is lost if the expiration passes without a further evaluation or if the institution fails to pass the second evaluation. As of the end of 2007, the KCUE is reviewing and improving its accreditation process in anticipation of regular accreditations in the near future.

For exercising a profession: A system of licensing exists parallel to college and university degrees in many fields of study leading to professional practices. In colleges such fields include electrical engineering, cosmetology, and auto mechanics, and in universities such fields include government civil service, law, medicine, elementary and secondary teaching, engineering, and architecture. In most cases students must pass a rigorous licensing examination after completing a degree programme. For the most part, university degree programmes do not specifically prepare students for licensing exams, and thus many students spend considerable amounts of time in private tutoring during their third and fourth years of university.

NATIONAL BODIES

Gyoyuk Gwahak Gisulbu (Ministry of Education, Science and Technology - MEST)

Minister: Ju-Ho Lee
Central Government Complex, 77-6 Sejong-no, Jongno-gu
Seoul 110-760
Tel: +82(2) 6222 6118-9
Fax: +82(2) 2100 6133
WWW: http://www.mest.go.kr/

Role of national body: Oversees and coordinates human resource development policies and governs matters related to school education, lifelong education, and other academic affairs.

Hanguk Daehak Gyoyuk Heopuihoe (Korean Council for University Education - KCUE)

Chairman: Young-Gil Kim
Director, Office of Planning & Coordination: In-sung Hwang
KGIT Sangam Center 11th Fl.
Mapo-gu Sangam-dong 1601
Seoul 121-270
Tel: +82(2) 6393 5225
Fax: +82(2) 6393 5220
EMail: intl@kcue.or.kr
WWW: http://www.kcue.or.kr

Role of national body: The KCUE is responsible for: 1) professional research on the management of colleges and universities, 2) professional research on and implementation of the college entrance system, 3) provision of admissions information, 4) development of policies to increase financial support to universities, 5) development of college curricula and teaching methods, 6) conducting university evaluations, 7) making recommendations to the government on university education, and 8) implement projects commissioned by the government.

Gungnip Gukje Gyoyukwon (National Institute for International Education - NIIED)

President: Ha Tae Yoon
81 Ihwajang-gil, jongno-gu
Seoul 110-810
Tel: +82(2) 3668 1300
Fax: +82(2) 742 1064
EMail: niied@mest.go.kr
WWW: http://www.niied.go.kr/

Role of national body: Major areas of oversight of the NIIED include education of overseas Koreans, international education exchange and cooperation, overseas training of teachers and university students, selection and management of government scholarship recipients, and support services for overseas study.

Hanguk Gukje Gyoryu Jaedan (Korea Foundation)

President: Kim Woosang
Diplomatic Center Building, 10th-11th Fl.
2558 Nambusunhwanno, Seocho-gu
Seoul 137-863
Tel: +82(2) 2046 8500
Fax: +82(2) 3463 6076
EMail: webmaster@kf.or.kr
WWW: http://www.kf.or.kr

Role of national body: The Korea Foundation promotes international understanding through creative exchanges by supporting Korean studies development overseas; providing fellowships; supporting museums, exhibitions, and performances; and organizing international conferences, forums, and other exchange programs.

National Research Foundation of Korea - NRF

President: Se-Jung Oh
201 Gajeong-ro, Yuseong-gu
Daejeon 305-754

Tel: +82(42) 869-6114
Fax: +82(42) 869-6777
WWW: http://www.nrf.re.kr
Role of national body: Founded in 2009 through a merger of the Korea Science and Engineering Foundation (KOSEF), the Korea Research Foundation (KRF), and the Korea Foundation for International Cooperation of Science and Technology (KICOS). The aim of the NRF is to optimize and advance the national basic research funding system that encompasses all academic research fields.

Data for academic year: 2008-2009
Source: IAU from the Korean Council for University Education (KCUE), 2008 (Bodies, 2012)

INSTITUTIONS

PUBLIC INSTITUTIONS

ANDONG NATIONAL UNIVERSITY (ANU)

388 Seongcheon-dong, Andong-si, Gyeongbuk-do 760-749
Tel: +82(54) 841-5114
Fax: +82(54) 850-5599
EMail: panu@andong.ac.kr
Website: http://www.andong.ac.kr

President: Hee Jae Lee

International Relations: Soon-young kim
Tel: +82(54) 820-5227, Fax: +82(54) 820-5228
EMail: dkchoi@andong.ac.kr

Centres
Agricultural Development (Agriculture); **Continuing Education**; **Information and Communication**; **Language** (Modern Languages); **Physical Education**

Colleges
Arts (Fine Arts; Music; Physical Education); **Education** (Computer Education; Education; Ethics; Foreign Languages Education; Mathematics Education; Technology Education); **Engineering** (Automation and Control Engineering; Ceramics and Glass Technology; Civil Engineering; Computer Engineering; Electronic Engineering; Engineering; Environmental Engineering; Mechanical Engineering; Metallurgical Engineering; Telecommunications Engineering); **Human Ecology** (Clothing and Sewing; Ecology; Home Economics; Physical Education); **Humanities** (Arts and Humanities; Chinese; English; Ethics; Folklore; History; Korean; Literature; Oriental Studies); **Natural Sciences** (Agrobiology; Biological and Life Sciences; Biology; Botany; Chemistry; Environmental Studies; Food Science; Horticulture; Natural Sciences; Physics; Surveying and Mapping); **Social Sciences** (Accountancy; Business Administration; Economics; International Business; Law; Public Administration; Social Sciences)

Institutes
Andong Regional Social Development (Regional Planning); **Basic Sciences** (Natural Sciences); **Folklore** (Folklore); **Toegye** (Cultural Studies)

Laboratories
Instrumental Analysis

Research Institutes
Social Sciences (Social Sciences)

History: Founded 1947 as Andong Normal School. Closed 1962 and opened as Junior Teachers' College 1965. Acquired present status and title 1979. A State Institution financed by the central Government.

Academic Year: March to December (March-June; September-December)

Admission Requirements: Graduation from high school or equivalent, and entrance examination

Main Language(s) of Instruction: Korean

Degrees and Diplomas: *Bachelor's Degree*: 4 yrs; *Master's Degree*: Arts, a further 2 yrs; *Doctor's Degree*

Student Residential Facilities: Yes

Special Facilities: University Museum

Libraries: University Library, c. 110,000 vols

Publications: Andong Culture *(annually)*; Bulletin of Basic Science Research Institute *(annually)*; Research Review *(annually)*; Social Science Review *(annually)*; The Andong Moon Wha *(annually)*

Press or Publishing House: Andong National University Press

Last Updated: 02/01/09

CHANGWON NATIONAL UNIVERSITY

9 Sarim-dong, Changwon-si,
Gyeongnam-do 641-773
Tel: +82(55) 279-7000
Fax: +82(55) 283-2970
EMail: webmaster@sarim.changwon.ac.kr
Website: http://www.changwon.ac.kr/

President: Park Seong Wo

International Relations: Kyung-hoon Kim
Tel: +82(55) 279-8021, Fax: +82(55) 266-1448
EMail: cinter@sarim.changwon.ac.kr

Centres
Computer (Computer Science)

Colleges
Arts (Fine Arts; Music); **Economics and Business** (Economics; Management); **Engineering** (Engineering; Technology); **Humanities** (Arts and Humanities); **Social Sciences** (Natural Sciences)

Institutes
Industrial Management (Industrial Management); **Industrial Technology** (Industrial Engineering); **Labour Problems Research** (Labour and Industrial Relations); **Unification Research**

History: Founded 1969 as a National Teachers College, acquired present title 1982.

Academic Year: March to December (March-June; August-December)

Admission Requirements: Graduation from high school and entrance examination

Main Language(s) of Instruction: Korean

Degrees and Diplomas: *Bachelor's Degree*: 4 yrs; *Master's Degree*: a further 2 yrs; *Doctor's Degree*

Student Residential Facilities: Yes

Special Facilities: Archaeological Museum. Broadcasting Station

Libraries: Central Library, c. 105,000 vols

Publications: Bulletins (in Korean and English); Publications of the Institutes
Last Updated: 02/01/09

CHEJU NATIONAL UNIVERSITY (CNU)

1 Ara 1-dong, Cheju-si, Cheju-do 690-756
Tel: +82(64) 754-2114
Fax: +82(64) 755-6130
Website: http://www.cheju.ac.kr

President: Choong-Suk Koh
Tel: +82(64) 754-2001 +82(64) 754-2002, Fax: +82(64) 754-8583

Dean, Academic Affairs: Dae Jin Song
Tel: +82(64) 754-2003, Fax: +82(64) 755-6204
EMail: djsong@cheju.ac.kr

International Relations: Boo Chan Kim
Tel: +82(64) 754-2198, Fax: +82(64) 757-7268
EMail: bckim@cheju.ac.kr

Colleges

Agriculture and Life Sciences (Agricultural Economics; Agriculture; Animal Husbandry; Biological and Life Sciences; Biotechnology; Botany; Horticulture; Veterinary Science) *Dean*: Ji-Yong Kang; **Economics and Commerce** (Accountancy; Business Administration; Business and Commerce; Economics; Information Management; International Business; Management; Tourism) *Dean*: Sang-Soo Park; **Education** (Biology; Business Education; Computer Education; Education; English; Ethics; Foreign Languages Education; Geography; Humanities and Social Science Education; Mathematics Education; Native Language Education; Physics; Science Education; Sociology) *Dean*: Sung-Sook Moon; **Engineering** (Chemical Engineering; Computer Engineering; Electrical and Electronic Engineering; Energy Engineering; Engineering; Food Technology; Industrial Design; Mechanical Engineering; Production Engineering; Structural Architecture; Telecommunications Engineering) *Dean*: Jin-Hwan Ha; **Humanities** (Chinese; English; Fine Arts; German; History; Japanese; Korean; Literature; Music; Philosophy; Sociology) *Dean*: Kyung-whan Koh; **Law and Political Science** (Advertising and Publicity; International Relations; Journalism; Law; Political Sciences; Public Administration; Public Relations) *Dean*: Hyung-Soo Kim; **Natural Sciences** (Biology; Chemistry; Clothing and Sewing; Food Science; Home Economics; Mathematics and Computer Science; Natural Sciences; Nutrition; Physical Education; Physics; Statistics; Textile Technology) *Dean*: Young-Oh Yang; **Ocean Sciences** (Civil Engineering; Environmental Engineering; Marine Biology; Marine Engineering; Marine Science and Oceanography) *Dean*: Young-Hwa Ahn

Schools

Graduate Studies (Accountancy; Administration; Agricultural Economics; Agriculture; Architecture; Biology; Biotechnology; Business Administration; Chemistry; Chinese; Civil Engineering; Clothing and Sewing; Computer Science; Construction Engineering; Economics; Educational Administration; Educational and Student Counselling; Electrical and Electronic Engineering; Energy Engineering; Engineering; English; Environmental Engineering; Ethics; Fine Arts; Fishery; Food Science; Geography; German; Government; History; Home Economics; Horticulture; Industrial Design; Industrial Engineering; Information Management; Information Technology; International Business; International Relations; Japanese; Justice Administration; Korean; Law; Management; Marine Biology; Marine Engineering; Mathematics; Mechanical Engineering; Music; Nuclear Engineering; Nutrition; Physical Education; Physics; Political Sciences; Psychology; Public Administration; Social Studies; Sociology; Statistics; Telecommunications Engineering; Textile Technology; Tourism; Translation and Interpretation; Veterinary Science) *Dean*: Doo-khil Moon; **Medical Sciences** (Anaesthesiology; Anatomy; Biochemistry; Dermatology; Forensic Medicine and Dentistry; Gynaecology and Obstetrics; Medicine; Microbiology; Neurology; Nursing; Orthopaedics; Otorhinolaryngology; Paediatrics; Parasitology; Pathology; Pharmacology; Physiology; Plastic Surgery; Radiology; Rehabilitation and Therapy; Social and Preventive Medicine; Surgery; Urology) *Dean*: Kang-Eui Hong

History: Founded 1952 as Cheju Provincial Junior College. Became Cheju National College 1962 and acquired present status and title 1982.

Academic Year: March to February

Admission Requirements: Graduation from High School

Fees: (Won): 1.2m.-1.5m. per semester

Main Language(s) of Instruction: Korean

International Co-operation: With 18 universities in 7 countries

Accrediting Agencies: Ministry of Education

Degrees and Diplomas: *Bachelor's Degree*: 4 yrs; *Master's Degree*: a further 2-2 1/2 yrs; *Doctor's Degree*: 3 yrs

Student Services: Academic counselling, Canteen, Employment services, Foreign student adviser, Handicapped facilities, Health services, Language programs, Nursery care, Social counselling, Sports facilities

Student Residential Facilities: Yes

Special Facilities: Museum

Publications: Islander, English *(quarterly)*

Press or Publishing House: CNU Press Center
Last Updated: 02/01/09

CHEJU NATIONAL UNIVERSITY OF EDUCATION

4810 Hwabuk 1-dong, Cheju-si, Cheju-do 690-839
Tel: +82(64) 720-0900
Fax: +82(64) 755-0729
EMail: jhan@jejue.ac.kr
Website: http://www.jejue.ac.kr

President: Jong-ik Hyun

International Relations: Jung-hee Kim

Departments

Agriculture (Agriculture); **Animal Husbandry** (Animal Husbandry); **Business Administration** (Business Administration); **English Language and Literature** (English); **Fishery** (Fishery); **Food Production**; **Home Economics** (Home Economics); **Horticulture** (Horticulture); **Korean Language and Literature** (Korean); **Law** (Law); **Marine Biology** (Marine Biology); **Mathematics** (Mathematics); **Veterinary Science** (Veterinary Science)

History: Founded 1968.

Academic Year: April to March (April-September; October-March)

Admission Requirements: Graduation from high school and entrance examination

Degrees and Diplomas: *Bachelor's Degree*: Agricultural Science; Arts; Commerce; Law; Veterinary Science, 4 yrs

CHEONGJU NATIONAL UNIVERSITY OF EDUCATION

135 Sugok-dong, Heungduk-gu, Cheongju-si,
Chungbuk-do 361-712
Tel: +82(43) 299-0613
Fax: +82(43) 299-0616
EMail: aboram@cje.ac.kr
Website: http://www.cje.ac.kr

President: Soo-hwan Kim

Faculties

Education (Arts and Humanities; Curriculum; Education; Natural Sciences; Physical Education; Social Sciences)

History: Founded 1941.
Last Updated: 02/01/09

CHINJU NATIONAL UNIVERSITY OF EDUCATION

380 Shinan-dong, Chinju-si, Gyeongnam-do 660-756
Tel: +82(55) 740-1340
Fax: +82(55) 740-1349
EMail: sysop@cue.ac.kr
Website: http://www.cue.ac.kr

President: Yong-won Lee
International Relations: Jong-pyo Kang
Tel: +82(55) 740-1345, Fax: +82(55) 740-1339

Programmes

Elementary Education (Primary Education)

History: Founded 1940.
Degrees and Diplomas: *Bachelor's Degree*; *Master's Degree*
Last Updated: 02/01/09

CHONBUK NATIONAL UNIVERSITY (CBNU)

664-14 Deockjin dong 1-ga Deockjin-gu, Jeonju-si, Jeollabuk-do 561-756
Tel: +82(63) 270-2098
Fax: +82(63) 270-2099
EMail: ioffice@cbnu.edu
Website: http://www.chonbuk.ac.kr

President: Geo-Suk Suh EMail: president@chonbuk.ac.kr
International Relations: Hee-chul Lee

Centres
Advanced Image and Information Technology (Multimedia); **Computer Science** (Computer Science)

Colleges
Agriculture and Life Sciences (Agriculture; Biological and Life Sciences; Food Science; Forest Products; Horticulture; Landscape Architecture; Zoology); **Art** (Dance; Fine Arts; Industrial Design; Music); **Commerce** (Business Administration; Business and Commerce; Economics; International Business); **Economics** (Clothing and Sewing; Food Science; Home Economics Education; Textile Technology); **Education** (Biology; Chemistry; Earth Sciences; Education; English; Ethics; Fine Arts; Geography; German; History; Korean; Mathematics; Music; Physical Education; Physics; Social Studies); **Engineering** (Aeronautical and Aerospace Engineering; Automotive Engineering; Chemical Engineering; Civil Engineering; Computer Engineering; Computer Science; Electrical Engineering; Electronic Engineering; Engineering; Environmental Engineering; Industrial Engineering; Materials Engineering; Mechanical Engineering; Metallurgical Engineering; Mining Engineering; Polymer and Plastics Technology; Structural Architecture; Textile Technology); **Humanities** (Anthropology; Archaeology; Arts and Humanities; Chinese; English; French; German; History; Information Sciences; Japanese; Korean; Library Science; Philosophy; Spanish); **Law** (Law); **Natural Sciences** (Natural Sciences); **Social Sciences** (Accountancy; Business Administration; Economics; International Business; Journalism; Psychology; Public Administration; Social Sciences; Social Welfare; Sociology); **Veterinary Science** (Veterinary Science)

Graduate Schools
Agricultural Development (Rural Planning); **Business Administration** (Accountancy; Business Administration; Economics); **Education** (Education); **Environment Studies** (Environmental Engineering; Environmental Management; Environmental Studies); **Industrial Technology** (Chemical Engineering; Civil Engineering; Computer Engineering; Electrical Engineering; Electronic Engineering; Industrial Engineering; Information Sciences; Materials Engineering; Mechanical Engineering; Metallurgical Engineering; Mining Engineering; Textile Technology); **Occupational Health** (Occupational Health); **Public Administration** (Journalism; Public Administration; Public Relations)

Institutes
Automobile High-Technology Research (Automotive Engineering)

Schools
Dentistry; **Medicine** (Medicine)

Further Information: Also University Hospital and 27 Research Institutes and Centres
History: Founded 1947 under the programme for the decentralization of higher education.
Governing Bodies: University Council
Academic Year: March to February (March-August; September-February)
Admission Requirements: Graduation from high school or foreign equivalent, and entrance examination
Main Language(s) of Instruction: Korean
Degrees and Diplomas: *Bachelor's Degree*: 4 yrs; *Master's Degree*: a further 2 yrs; *Doctor's Degree*: 3 yrs following Master
Student Services: Academic counselling, Canteen, Cultural centre, Employment services, Health services, Language programs, Social counselling, Sports facilities
Student Residential Facilities: Yes
Special Facilities: University Museum. University Broadcasting Station (UBS). Health Clinic. University Hospital
Libraries: Central Library, c. 540,000 books, 1,900 periodicals; Libraries of each department
Publications: Annual Bulletins of Research Institutes
Last Updated: 02/01/09

CHONNAM NATIONAL UNIVERSITY (CNU)

300 Yongbong-dong, Puk-gu, Kwangju 500-757
Tel: +82(62) 530-1265
Fax: +82(62) 530-1269
EMail: cnupr@chonnam.ac.kr
Website: http://www.chonnam.ac.kr

President: Yoon Soo Kim
Tel: +82(62) 530-1001, Fax: +82(62) 530-1015
EMail: poffice@chonnam.ac.kr
Vice-President: Jong-Seok Seo
Tel: +82(62) 530-1009, Fax: +82(62) 530-1018
International Relations: Mijeong Park EMail: mjc@chonnam.ac.kr

Colleges
Agriculture and Life Sciences (Agricultural Economics; Agricultural Engineering; Agriculture; Animal Husbandry; Biotechnology; Botany; Forest Products; Forestry; Landscape Architecture; Zoology) *Principal*: Joon-Keun Park; **Arts** (Design; Fine Arts; Music) *Principal*: Sim-On Seong; **Business Administration** (Business Administration; Economics) *Principal*: Sung-Woo Hong; **Culture and Social Sciences** *(Yosu)* (Business Administration; Cultural Studies; Education; International Business; International Studies; Tourism; Transport Engineering) *Principal*: Jun-Ok Kim; **Education** (Business Education; Education; English; Ethics; Fine Arts; French; Home Economics; Korean; Mathematics Education; Music Education; Physical Education; Preschool Education; Science Education; Social Studies) *Principal*: Hee-Gyun Oh; **Engineering** *(Yosu)* (Applied Chemistry; Architecture; Automotive Engineering; Chemical Engineering; Civil Engineering; Computer Engineering; Earth Sciences; Electrical Engineering; Electronic Engineering; Engineering; Environmental Engineering; Industrial Engineering; Materials Engineering) *Principal*: Shang-Gyu Park; **Fisheries and Ocean Sciences** *(Yosu)* (Aquaculture; Fishery; Food Technology; Marine Science and Oceanography; Nutrition) *Principal*: Chang-Bum An; **Medicine** *Principal*: Hyun-Chul Lee; **Natural Sciences** (Biological and Life Sciences; Chemistry; Dentistry; Earth Sciences; Environmental Studies; Information Technology; Mathematics; Mathematics and Computer Science; Medicine; Natural Sciences; Physics; Statistics; Veterinary Science) *Principal*: Yong-Kook Choi; **Nursing** (Nursing) *Principal*: Sun-Hee Choi; **Pharmacy** (Pharmacy) *Principal*: Dong-Gu Lim; **Social Sciences** (Anthropology; Communication Studies; Geography; Information Sciences; International Relations; Library Science; Political Sciences; Psychology; Social Sciences; Sociology) *Principal*: Chae-Wan Lim; **Veterinary Science** (Veterinary Science) *Principal*: Dong-Ho Shin

Graduate Schools
Business Administration *Dean*: Tae-Koo Kang; **Culture** (Cultural Studies; Media Studies; Tourism) *Dean*: Gwang-Seo Park; **Dental Medicine** (Biochemistry; Microbiology; Oral Pathology; Pharmacology); **Dentistry** (Anaesthesiology; Dental Technology; Dentistry; Orthodontics) *Dean*: Won-Man Oh; **Education** *(Yosu)* (Education); **Educational and Industrial Cooperation** *(Yosu)* (Education; Industrial Arts Education) *Dean*: Hyun-Sik Shin; **Fisheries and Ocean Sciences** *(Yosu)* (Fishery; Marine Science and Oceanography) *Dean*: Chang-Bum An; **Human Ecology** *Principal*: Deok-Young Jeon; **Humanities** (Arts and Humanities; Chinese; English; French; German; History; Japanese; Korean; Philosophy) *Principal*: Pyung-Hyeon Yoon; **Industry and Technology** *Dean*: Byung-Teak Lee; **Law** (Law; Public Administration) *Principal*: Byung-Seok Jeong; **Medicine** *Head*: Duk-Ki Hong; **Public Administration** *Dean*: Byung-Teak Lee

Schools

Biological Science and Technology *Head*: Ho-Jun Chae; **Graduate Studies** *Dean*: Yoon-Su Kim

Further Information: Also 71 Research Centres and Research Institutes. Yosu campus

History: Founded 1909, acquired present status and title 1952.

Academic Year: March to February (March-June; September-February)

Admission Requirements: Graduation from high school or foreign equivalent, and entrance examination (for Korean citizens)

Fees: (Won): Undergraduate, 3,190,000-5,592,000 per annum; post-graduate, 3,406,000-9,942,000

Main Language(s) of Instruction: Korean

International Co-operation: Participates in DUO-Korea/ASEM-DUO Fellowship Programmes

Degrees and Diplomas: *Bachelor's Degree*: 4 yrs; *Master's Degree*: a further 1 1/2-2 yrs; *Doctor's Degree (PhD)*: a further 2-3 yrs

Student Services: Academic counselling, Cultural centre, Employment services, Foreign student adviser, Health services, Language programs, Social counselling, Sports facilities

Student Residential Facilities: For 2,000 students

Special Facilities: Equipment Management and maintenance Centre. Museum. Language Education Centre. Information Computing Institute. Press Centre. Industrial Laboratory. Agro-bioindustry Technical Support Centre. Animal Hospital

Libraries: Main Library, 1,126,458 vols

Publications: Chonnam National Journal *(bimonthly)*; Journal of Agricultural Science and Technology *(annually)*; Journal of Drug Development *(annually)*; Journal of Natural Science *(annually)*; Journal of Research Institute for Catalysis *(annually)*; Journal of Sciences for Better Living *(annually)*; Journal of Unification Studies *(annually)*; Review of American Studies *(annually)*; Rural Development Review *(annually)*

Press or Publishing House: The University Press

Last Updated: 23/03/09

CHUNCHEON NATIONAL UNIVERSITY OF EDUCATION (CNUE)

339 Seoksa-dong, Chuncheon-si, Gangwon-do 200-703
Tel: +82(33) 260-6000
Fax: +82(33) 261-4328
EMail: cnue-admin@cnue.ac.kr
Website: http://www.cnue.ac.kr

President: Woo-Youp Shim

Departments

Computer Education (Computer Education); **Education** (Education); **English Education** (English); **Ethics Education**; **Fine Arts Education** (Fine Arts); **Korean Education** (Korean; Teacher Training); **Mathematics Education**; **Music Education** (Music Education); **Physical Education** (Physical Education); **Practical Arts Education**; **Science Education**; **Social Studies Education** (Social Studies)

Further Information: Also Graduate School

History: Founded 1939.

Degrees and Diplomas: *Bachelor's Degree*; *Master's Degree*

Last Updated: 02/01/09

CHUNGBUK NATIONAL UNIVERSITY

48 Gaeshin-dong, Heungdeok-gu, Cheongju-si, Chungbuk-do 361-763
Tel: +82(43) 261-3293
Fax: +82(43) 326-2068
EMail: hrlee0420@chungbuk.ac.kr
Website: http://www.chungbuk.ac.kr

President: Dong Chol Lim

International Relations: Chul-am Whang
Tel: +82(43) 261-3299, Fax: +82(43) 268-2068

Colleges

Agriculture (Agricultural Economics; Agricultural Engineering; Agricultural Equipment; Agriculture; Agronomy; Animal Husbandry; Applied Chemistry; Biology; Chemistry; Food Science; Food Technology; Forest Products; Forestry; Horticulture); **Business Administration** (Business Administration); **Education** (Computer Education; Education; Mathematics Education; Pedagogy; Physical Education; Science Education); **Engineering** (Chemical Engineering; Civil Engineering; Computer Engineering; Electrical Engineering; Electronic Engineering; Engineering; Environmental Engineering; Industrial Engineering; Materials Engineering; Mechanical Engineering; Safety Engineering; Structural Architecture; Telecommunications Engineering; Town Planning); **Home Economics** (Home Economics); **Humanities** (Archaeology; Art History; Arts and Humanities; Chinese; English; French; German; History; Korean; Philosophy; Russian); **Law** (Law); **Medicine** (Medicine); **Natural Sciences** (Astronomy and Space Science; Biochemistry; Biology; Chemistry; Computer Science; Geology; Mathematics; Microbiology; Natural Sciences; Physics; Statistics); **Pharmacy** (Pharmacy); **Social Sciences** (Economics; International Relations; Political Sciences; Psychology; Public Administration; Social Sciences; Sociology); **Veterinary Science** (Veterinary Science)

Institutes

Agricultural Sciences and Technology (Agricultural Engineering; Agriculture); **Basic Sciences** (Natural Sciences); **Construction Technology** (Construction Engineering); **Social Sciences** (Social Sciences)

Schools

Business Administration (Business Administration); **Education** (Education); **Engineering** (Computer Engineering; Construction Engineering; Electrical Engineering; Engineering; Production Engineering); **Graduate**; **Law** (Law); **Public Administration** (Public Administration)

History: Founded 1951 as Junior Agricultural College, acquired present status and title 1977.

Governing Bodies: Board of Deans and Directors

Academic Year: March to December (March-June; September-December)

Admission Requirements: Graduation from high school and entrance examination

Main Language(s) of Instruction: Korean

Degrees and Diplomas: *Bachelor's Degree*: 4 yrs; *Master's Degree*: a further 2-3 yrs; *Doctor's Degree*: 3 yrs following Master

Student Services: Academic counselling, Canteen, Cultural centre, Employment services, Health services, Sports facilities

Student Residential Facilities: For c. 940 students

Special Facilities: University Museum

Libraries: Main Library, c. 520,000 vols

Publications: Chungbuk Times; Gaeshin Four Seasons

Press or Publishing House: University Press

Last Updated: 02/01/09

CHUNGJU NATIONAL UNIVERSITY

123 Geomdan-ri, Iryu-myeon, Chungju-si, Chungcheonbuk-do 380-702
Tel: +82(43) 841-5001
Fax: +82(43) 841-1236
Website: http://www.chungju.ac.kr

President: Byoung-Woo Ahn

International Relations: Gi-Bae Hong, Director, Academic and Planning Resources Fax: +82(43) 841-5109
EMail: gbhong@gukwon.chungju.ac.kr

Colleges

Construction and Applied Chemical Engineering (Chemical Engineering; Construction Engineering) *Dean*: Jae-Min Cho; **Electrical, Computer and Information Engineering** (Electrical Engineering; Electronic Engineering; Information Technology) *Dean*: Byung-Kuk Im; **Engineering** (Engineering; Industrial Engineering; Technology) *Dean*: Hong-Seo Lee; **Humanities and Social Science** (Arts and Humanities; Social Sciences) *Dean*: Jong-Hwa Byun

History: Founded 1962, acquired present status 1993.

Admission Requirements: High school certificate

Fees: (Won): 2m.

Main Language(s) of Instruction: Korean

International Co-operation: With universities in USA, United Kingdom, Australia, Japan, China, Philippines

Accrediting Agencies: Ministry of Education and Human Resources Development

Degrees and Diplomas: *Bachelor's Degree*: Administration; Engineering; Literature; Plans, 4 yrs; *Master's Degree*

Student Services: Academic counselling, Canteen, Cultural centre, Employment services, Foreign student adviser, Handicapped facilities, Health services, Nursery care, Social counselling, Sports facilities

Student Residential Facilities: Yes

Special Facilities: General Laboratory

Libraries: c. 196,230 vols

Last Updated: 02/01/09

CHUNGNAM NATIONAL UNIVERSITY (CNU)

220 Gung-dong, Yusong-gu, Daejeon, Chungnam-do 305-764
Tel: +82(42) 821-5114
Fax: +82(42) 823-8589
EMail: cnuint@cnu.ac.kr
Website: http://www.chungnam.ac.kr

President: Yong-ho Song

International Relations: Jong-Hyun Kim
Tel: +82(42) 821-5013, Fax: +82(42) 821-5125
EMail: ambigus@cnu.ac.kr

Centres

Industrial Education Research

Colleges

Agriculture (Agriculture; Animal Husbandry; Forestry; Horticulture; Veterinary Science); **Economics and Management** (Economics; Management); **Engineering** (Architecture; Engineering; Environmental Engineering; Industrial Engineering; Naval Architecture); **Fine Arts and Music** (Fine Arts; Music); **Home Economics** (Home Economics); **Humanities** (Arts and Humanities; Chinese; Education; English; French; German; History; Japanese; Korean; Philosophy); **Law** (Law); **Medicine** (Medicine); **Natural Sciences** (Natural Sciences); **Pharmacy** (Pharmacy); **Social Sciences** (International Relations; Library Science; Political Sciences; Psychology; Social Sciences)

Graduate Schools

Business Administration (Business Administration); **Education** (Education); **Industry** (Industrial Engineering); **Information Communications** (Telecommunications Services); **Public Administration** (Public Administration); **Public Health** (Public Health)

Institutes

Agricultural Science and Technology (Agricultural Engineering; Agriculture); **American Studies** (American Studies); **Arts** (Fine Arts); **Basic Science Research** (Natural Sciences); **Community Development Research** (Urban Studies); **Community Medicine** (Community Health); **Educational Research and Development** (Education); **Environment Science and Technology** (Environmental Studies; Technology); **Home Economics** (Home Economics); **Humanities Research** (Arts and Humanities); **Industrial Technology Research** (Industrial Engineering); **Language Research** (Linguistics); **Law and Public Administration** (Law; Public Administration); **Management and Economics** (Economics; Management); **Medicine Development** (Medicine); **Natural Sciences** (Natural Sciences); **Paekje Research**; **Physical Education and Sports Science** (Physical Education; Sports); **Research on Biological Engineering** (Bioengineering); **Unification Research**

Further Information: Also University Hospital

History: Founded 1952, a State Institution financed by the Government.

Academic Year: March to December (March-June; August-December)

Admission Requirements: Graduation from high school and entrance examination

Main Language(s) of Instruction: Korean

Degrees and Diplomas: *Bachelor's Degree*: 4 yrs; *Master's Degree*: a further 2 yrs; *Doctor's Degree*: 3 yrs following Master

Student Residential Facilities: Yes

Special Facilities: University Museum. Experimental Station. Arboretum

Libraries: Central Library, c. 305,000 vols; Medical College Library, c. 20,000

Publications: Papers of the Faculties

Press or Publishing House: The University Press

Last Updated: 02/01/09

DAEGU NATIONAL UNIVERSITY OF EDUCATION

1797-6 Daemyong2-8dong, Nam-gu, Daegu 705-715
Tel: +82(53) 620-1512
Fax: +82(53) 620-1510
EMail: abc@dnue.ac.kr
Website: http://www.dnue.ac.kr

President: Sohn Seokrak

Departments

Computer Education (Computer Education); **Education** (Education; Pedagogy; Preschool Education; Special Education); **English Education**; **Korean Language Education** (Korean); **Mathematics Education**; **Moral Education** (Ethics); **Music Education** (Music Education); **Physical Education**; **Practical Arts Education** (Agriculture; Computer Science; Home Economics; Technology); **School Art Education**; **Science Education** (Science Education); **Social Studies Education** (Social Studies)

Graduate Schools

Education (Education)

History: Founded 1950, acquired present status and title 1993.

Admission Requirements: Graduation from high school or equivalent, and entrance examination

Main Language(s) of Instruction: Korean

Degrees and Diplomas: *Bachelor's Degree*: 4 yrs; *Master's Degree*

Student Services: Academic counselling, Language programs, Nursery care, Sports facilities

Last Updated: 02/01/09

GONGJU NATIONAL UNIVERSITY OF EDUCATION

376 Pongwhang-dong, Gongju-si, Chungnam-do 314-711
Tel: +82(41) 850-1114
Fax: +82(41) 854-1578
EMail: jsha@gjue.ac.kr
Website: http://www.gjue.ac.kr

President: Ji-hyung Kang

Programmes

Education (Education)

History: Founded 1938.

GWANGJU INSTITUTE OF SCIENCE AND TECHNOLOGY (GIST)

261 Cheomdan-gwagiro (Oryong-dong), Buk-Gu, Gwangju-si, Gyeonggi-do 500-712
Tel: +82(62) 970-2003
Fax: +82(62) 970-2188
EMail: ciss@gist.ac.kr
Website: http://www.gist.ac.kr

President: Jung-Ho Sonu
Tel: +82(62) 970-2001 EMail: sijackie@gist.ac.kr

Dean of Planning: Won-Taek Han
Tel: +82(62) 970-2010 EMail: wthan@gist.ac.kr

International Relations: Soo-jung Park
Tel: +82(62) 970-2062, Fax: +82(62) 970-2069
EMail: soopark@gist.ac.kr

Departments

Environmental Science and Engineering *(Graduate School)*; **Information and Communications** *(Graduate School)* (Information Technology; Optics; Telecommunications Engineering); **Information and Mechatronics** *(Graduate School)* (Engineering; Information Sciences; Mechanical Engineering); **Life Science** *(Graduate School)*; **Materials Science and Engineering** *(Graduate School)* (Materials Engineering); **Nanobio Materials and Electronics** *(Graduate School)* (Biomedical Engineering; Electronic Engineering; Nanotechnology)

Programmes

Femto-Nano Science *(Graduate)*; **Medical System Engineering** *(Graduate)*; **Photon Science and Technology** *(Graduate)*

History: Founded 1993, an Institution of Graduate Studies. Acquired current title 2003

Governing Bodies: Board of Trustees

Academic Year: March to February (March-June; September-February)

Admission Requirements: Baccalaureate for admission to MS programmes and Master's Degree for PhD programmes

Fees: None

Main Language(s) of Instruction: English

Accrediting Agencies: Ministry of Education

Degrees and Diplomas: *Master's Degree*; *Doctor's Degree (PhD)*: 4 yrs following Master

Student Services: Academic counselling, Canteen, Foreign student adviser, Foreign Studies Centre, Health services, Language programs, Nursery care, Sports facilities

Student Residential Facilities: Yes

Libraries: LG Library; K-JIST on-line Library (http://library.kjist.ac.kr)

Last Updated: 08/10/09

GWANGJU NATIONAL UNIVERSITY OF EDUCATION (KNUE)

1-1 Punghyang-dong, Buk-gu, Gwangju-si, Gyeonggi-do 500-703
Tel: +82(62) 520-4084
Fax: +82(62) 520-4089
EMail: webmaster@gnue.ac.kr
Website: http://www.gnue.ac.kr

President: Nam Gi Park

Programmes

Computer Science (Computer Science); **Educational Studies** (Educational Sciences); **English** (English); **Ethics** (Ethics); **Fine Arts** (Fine Arts); **Korean Language** (Korean); **Mathematics** (Mathematics); **Music Education** (Music Education); **Physical Education** (Physical Education); **Practical Arts**; **Science Education** (Science Education); **Social Studies** (Social Studies)

History: Founded 1938 as School, became College of Teachers 1961, attached to Chonnam National University 1962 and acquired present status and title 1993. Graduate School established 1996.

Governing Bodies: Faculty Council

Academic Year: March to December (March-July; September-December)

Admission Requirements: Graduation from high school and entrance examination

Main Language(s) of Instruction: Korean

Accrediting Agencies: Ministry of Education

Degrees and Diplomas: *Bachelor's Degree*: Arts (BA), 4 yrs; *Master's Degree*: Education (MEd.), 3 yrs

Student Services: Academic counselling, Employment services, Foreign student adviser, Foreign Studies Centre, Language programs, Social counselling

Student Residential Facilities: For c. 175 students

Special Facilities: Education Museum. Educational Media Center

Last Updated: 02/01/09

GYEONGIN NATIONAL UNIVERSITY OF EDUCATION (GINUE)

Gyodae street 45, Kyeyang-gu, Incheon-si 407753
Tel: +82(32) 540-1114
Fax: +82(32) 541-0580
Website: http://www.ginue.ac.kr/

President: Sook Hur
Tel: +82(32) 540-1100, Fax: +82(32) 540-1199
EMail: hurs@ginue.ac.kr

Administrative Officer: Dae-hyuk Ko
Tel: +82(32) 540-1290, Fax: +82(32) 540-1294
EMail: koclass@ginue.ac.kr

International Relations: Sung-woong Park
Tel: +82(32) 540-1291, Fax: +82(32) 540-1294
EMail: swpark@ginue.ac.kr

Departments

Art Education *Head*: Joo-yeon Lee; **Computer Education** (Computer Science) *Head*: Seon-kwan Han; **Early Childhood Education** *Head*: Kyoung-min Lee; **English Education** *Head*: Ki-hwa Park; **Ethics Education** (Education; Ethics) *Head*: Jang-hee Lee; **Korean Education** *Dean*: Chang-deok Lee; **Mathematics Education** (Mathematics Education) *Head*: Jae-hoon Lim; **Music Education** (Music Education) *Head*: Doug-won Kwon; **Pedagogy** (Pedagogy) *Head*: Hae-sook Kim; **Physical Training Education** (Physical Education) *Head*: Saeng-ryul Yu; **Practical Arts Education** (Fine Arts) *Head*: Young-hee Kim; **Science** (Natural Sciences; Science Education) *Head*: Young-joon Shin; **Social Studies Education** (Social Studies) *Head*: Seon-joo Kang

Institutes

Elementary Education Research (Primary Education) *Head*: Young-hwan Choi; **Gyeonggi Cultural Studies** *Head*: Jin-soo Han; **Science Education Research** (Science Education) *Head*: Sang-heon Song

History: Founded 1946 as a normal school, acquired present status 1993 and name 2003.

Academic Year: March to December (March-June; August-December)

Admission Requirements: Graduation from high school or equivalent, and entrance examination

Fees: (US Dollars): 1,000 per semester

Main Language(s) of Instruction: Korean

Degrees and Diplomas: *Bachelor's Degree*: 4 yrs; *Master's Degree*: a further 2 1/2-3 yrs

Student Services: Academic counselling, Employment services, Foreign student adviser, Social counselling, Sports facilities

Special Facilities: GINUE Museum

Libraries: Digital Library, c. 220,000 vols

Publications: GINUE Culture Review of Kyouggi and Inchon Area; GINUE Education Research; GINUE Science Education Review

GYEONGNAM NATIONAL UNIVERSITY OF SCIENCE AND TECHNOLOGY

Dongjinro 33, Jinju-si, Gyeongnam-do 660-758
Tel: +82(55) 751-3100
Fax: +82(55) 751-3502
Website: http://www.gntech.ac.kr

President: Jo-won Kim

Colleges

Bio-science (Biomedical Engineering; Food Science); **Business Administration** (Accountancy; Business Administration; E-Business/Commerce; Economics; Engineering Management); **Construction and Environmental Engineering** (Civil Engineering; Construction Engineering; Environmental Engineering; Landscape Architecture; Materials Engineering); **Design** (Architecture; Textile Design); **Humanities and Social Science** (English; Family Studies; Linguistics; Welfare and Protective Services); **Integral Technology Engineering** (Automotive Engineering; Computer Engineering; Electronic Engineering; Mechanical Engineering); **Science and Natural Resources** (Agriculture; Forestry; Horticulture; Veterinary Science; Zoology)

Schools

Graduate Studies (Accountancy; Automation and Control Engineering; Business Administration; Civil Engineering; Computer Engineering; Construction Engineering; E-Business/Commerce; Economics; Electrical and Electronic Engineering; Food Technology; Forestry; Horticulture; Landscape Architecture; Materials Engineering; Mechanical Engineering; Microbiology; Natural Resources; Plant and Crop Protection; Social Welfare; Zoology)

History: Founded 1910. Previously known as Jinju National University, Acquired current title 2011,

Degrees and Diplomas: *Bachelor's Degree*; *Master's Degree*
Last Updated: 12/11/12

GYEONGSANG NATIONAL UNIVERSITY

900 Kajwa-dong, Jinju-si, Gyeongnam-do 660-701
Tel: +82(55) 751-6114
Fax: +82(55) 751-6134
EMail: belle@gshp.gsnu.ac.kr
Website: http://www.gsnu.ac.kr/english

President: Woo-Song Woo-Song Ha Tel: +82(55) 751-5000

Centres

Computer Science (Computer Science)

Colleges

Agriculture and Life Sciences (Agricultural Economics; Agricultural Engineering; Agriculture; Biological and Life Sciences; Food Science; Food Technology; Forestry; Veterinary Science) *Dean*: Ki-Hwan Sim; **Business** (Accountancy; Business Administration; Commercial Law; E-Business/Commerce; International Business) *Dean*: Jong-Soo Park; **Business Administration** *Dean*: Tae-Young Jeon; **Education** (Computer Education; Education; Ethics; Fine Arts; Home Economics; Korean; Mathematics Education; Music Education; Physical Education; Science Education; Social Studies) *Dean*: Byung-Tae Moon; **Engineering** *Dean*: Young-Jae Sim; **Humanities** (Arts and Humanities; Chinese; Dance; English; French; German; History; Korean; Literature; Modern Languages; Philosophy; Russian) *Dean*: Byung-Soon Hwang; **Industry** *Dean*: Young-Jae Sim; **Information Science** *Dean*: Jung-Sook Lee; **Law** (Law) *Dean*: Dae-Sung Kang; **Life and Environmental Sciences** (Biological and Life Sciences; Environmental Studies; Natural Sciences) *Dean*: Ki-Hwan Sim; **Marine Sciences** (Marine Science and Oceanography) *Dean*: Won-Chui Kim; **Medicine** (Medicine; Nursing) *Dean*: Won-Young Back; **Social Sciences** *Dean*: Jong-Su Park; **Veterinary Medicine** (Veterinary Science) *Dean*: Hyo-Jong Lee

Graduate Schools

Education (Education) *Dean*: Byung-Tae Moon; **Education** (Education); **General Studies** *Dean*: Soon-Bonk Kim; **Public Administration** (Public Administration) *Dean*: Tae-Young Jeon

Research Institutes

Agriculture and Life Sciences (Agriculture; Biological and Life Sciences) *Director*: Jong-Ryei Park; **Aircraft Technology** *Director*: Su-Gyen Lim; **Computer and Information Communication** *(RICIC)* (Computer Science; Information Sciences) *Director*: Young-Bong Tak; **Culture** *(Gyeong-Nam)* (Cultural Studies) *Director*: Jun-Hyung Kim; **Education** *(ERI)* (Education) *Director*: Gyu-Tae Cho; **Engineering** *Director*: Geun-Ki Lee; **Environmental and Regional Development** *Director*: Gyeong-Hwan Kim; **Global and Area Studies** *Director*: Young-Dae Kim; **Health Sciences** *Director*: Byung-Hun Lim; **Humanities** (Arts and Humanities) *Director*: Young-Suk Lee; **Law** *Director*: Dae-Sung Kang; **Life Sciences** *(RILS)* (Biotechnology; Social Sciences) *Director*: Hye-Gyu Kim; **Marine Industry** (Marine Engineering; Marine Science and Oceanography) *Director*: Jong-Duk Choi; **Natural Sciences** *(RINS)* (Biology; Chemistry; Earth Sciences; Mathematics; Natural Sciences; Physics) *Director*: Sin-Min Kang; **Plant Molecular Biology and Biotechnology** (Biotechnology; Molecular Biology; Plant and Crop Protection) *Director*: Gyu-Young Kang; **Social Sciences** (Social Sciences) *Director*: Jin-Sang Jung; **Veterinary Medicine** (Veterinary Science) *Director*: Ju-Hyen Kim

History: Founded 1948 as Junior Agricultural College. Became Provincial College 1953 and National Institution 1968. Graduate courses introduced 1975. Acquired present status and title 1980. Financially supported by the Government.

Academic Year: March to February (March-August; September-February)

Admission Requirements: Graduation from high school or equivalent and entrance examination

Fees: (Won) 1.6m. per semester

Main Language(s) of Instruction: Korean

Accrediting Agencies: Ministry of Education

Degrees and Diplomas: *Bachelor's Degree*; *Master's Degree*: a further 2 yrs; *Doctor's Degree*: a further 2 yrs. Also Teaching Certficate

Student Services: Academic counselling, Canteen, Cultural centre, Employment services, Foreign student adviser, Foreign Studies Centre, Health services, Language programs, Nursery care, Social counselling, Sports facilities

Student Residential Facilities: Yes

Special Facilities: University Museum

Libraries: Central Library, c. 730,000 vols

Press or Publishing House: GSNU University Press
Last Updated: 02/01/09

HANBAT NATIONAL UNIVERSITY

16-1 Deogmyeong-dong, Yuseong-gu, Daejeon, Chungnam-do 300-172
Tel: +82(42 821-1000
Fax: +82(42) 821-1013
EMail: lgtwins001@hotmail.com
Website: http://www.hanbat.ac.kr

President: Dong Ho Sul (2002-)

Director: Jong-Bong Hong

International Relations: Sang-Ho Lee
Tel: +82(42) 821-1033, Fax: +82(42) 821-1484

Colleges

Advanced Materials Engineering; **Architectural Engineering** (Architecture); **Chemical Engineering and Technology** (Chemical Engineering); **Civil, Environmental and Urban Engineering** (Civil Engineering; Construction Engineering; Environmental Engineering); **Cultural Studies** (Chinese; Cultural Studies; English; Japanese); **Economics and Business** (Accountancy; Business Administration; Economics); **Electrical, Electronic and Control Engineering** (Automation and Control Engineering; Electrical and Electronic Engineering); **Foreign Language Studies** (Modern Languages); **Industrial and Management Engineering**; **Industrial Design** (Industrial Design); **Information Communications and Computer Engineering** (Computer Engineering; Information Technology; Multimedia; Radio and Television Broadcasting); **Mechanical Engineering** (Engineering; Mechanical Engineering)

History: Founded 1927. Acquired present title 2001.

Main Language(s) of Instruction: Korean

Degrees and Diplomas: *Bachelor's Degree*; *Master's Degree*; *Doctor's Degree*
Last Updated: 02/01/09

HANKYONG NATIONAL UNIVERSITY (HNU)

67 Sokjong-dong, Anseong-si, Gyeonggi-do 456-749
Tel: +82(31) 670-5114
Fax: +82(31) 673-2704
Website: http://www.hankyong.ac.kr

President: Won Woo Lee (2001-)
Tel: +82(31) 670-5012 EMail: leww@hnu.hankyong.ac.kr

Administrative Officer: Won Hee Lee
Tel: +82(31) 670-5043 EMail: leewh@hnu.hankyong.ac.kr

International Relations: Won-hee Lee

Faculties

Agriculture and Life Sciences (Agriculture; Animal Husbandry; Dairy; Horticulture; Plant and Crop Protection; Rural Planning) *Dean*: Rye Pyo Chung; **Humanities and Social Sciences** (Arts and Humanities; Business Administration; English; Farm Management; Korean; Law; Literature; Media Studies; Public Administration; Science Education; Social Sciences) *Dean*: Heung Soo Cho; **Science and Engineering** (Chemical Engineering; Civil Engineering; Communication Studies; Computer Engineering; Construction Engineering; Ecology; Electrical Engineering; Engineering; Environmental Engineering; Landscape Architecture; Mathematics and Computer Science; Natural Sciences) *Dean*: In Bae Kim

Graduate Schools

Bio and Information Technology (Biotechnology; Information Technology; Multimedia; Plant and Crop Protection) *President*: Moon Won Lee; **Electronic Government** (Educational Administration; Labour and Industrial Relations; Law; Police Studies; Public Administration; Welfare and Protective Services) *President*: Young Man Kim; **Industry** (Architecture; Business Administration; Chemical Engineering; Child Care and Development; Civil Engineering; Communication Studies; Environmental Engineering; Family Studies; Food Science; Food Technology; Home Economics; Industrial Engineering; Landscape Architecture; Rural Studies; Safety Engineering) *President*: Young Man Kim

History: Founded 1939 as Ansung National University of Technology, Graduate School of Industry 1996, acquired present status 1993 and title 1999.

Academic Year: March to February (March-August; September-February)

Admission Requirements: Graduation from high school

Fees: (Won): 1,6m. per annum

Main Language(s) of Instruction: Korean

Degrees and Diplomas: *Bachelor's Degree*: 4 yrs; *Master's Degree*: a further 2 yrs; *Doctor's Degree*: 3 yrs

Student Services: Academic counselling, Canteen, Employment services, Foreign student adviser, Handicapped facilities, Health services, Language programs, Social counselling, Sports facilities

Student Residential Facilities: Yes

Libraries: Yes

JEONJU NATIONAL UNIVERSITY OF EDUCATION

128 Dongseohak-dong, Wansan-gu, Jeonju-si,
Jeollabuk-do 560-757
Tel: +82(63) 281-7114
Fax: +82(63) 281-0102
Website: http://www.jnue.ac.kr

President: Yong-suk Lee

Centres

Computer Science (Computer Science); **Educational Research** (Educational Research); **In-Service Teacher Training** (Teacher Training); **Science Education** (Science Education)

Departments

Education (Education; Primary Education); **English Language** (English); **Ethics** (Ethics); **Fine Arts** (Fine Arts); **Korean Language** (Korean); **Mathematics** (Mathematics); **Music** (Music); **Physical Education** (Physical Education); **Practical Arts**; **Science** (Natural Sciences); **Social Studies** (Social Studies)

History: Founded 1923 as Normal School, acquired present status and title 1983.

Academic Year: March to December (March-June; August-December)

Admission Requirements: Graduation from high school, Government qualifying examination and university entrance examination

Main Language(s) of Instruction: Korean

Degrees and Diplomas: *Bachelor's Degree*: 4 yrs; *Master's Degree*

Student Services: Academic counselling, Canteen, Cultural centre, Health services, Sports facilities

Student Residential Facilities: For c. 260 students

Special Facilities: University Museum

Libraries: University Library, c. 90,000 vols

Last Updated: 02/01/09

KANGNUNG NATIONAL UNIVERSITY

Gangneung-si, Gangwon-Do 210-702
Tel: +82(33) 640-2767
Fax: +82(33) 640-2768
EMail: ciec@kangnung.ac.kr
Website: http://www.kangnung.ac.kr

President: Song Han (2003-)
Tel: +82(33) 640-2001, Fax: +82(33) 640-2004
EMail: ceo@kangnung.ac.kr

Chief Secretary: Tae Yeol Moon
Tel: +82(33) 640-2001, Fax: +82(33) 640-2004
EMail: mtyol@kangnung.ac.kr

International Relations: Sung Pyo Chi
EMail: spchi@kangnung.ac.kr

Centres

Electronic Commerce Support (E-Business/Commerce) *Director*: Hyung Rae Park; **Small and Medium Enterprise Technology Support** *Director*: Deok-Su Jeon

Colleges

Arts and Physical Education *Dean*: Young Kyu Cha; **Cultural Industry** *Dean*: Byung Soo Hwang; **Dentistry** *Dean*: Deok-Young Park; **Engineering** *Dean*: Sang Min Lee; **Humanities** (Chinese; English; German; History; Japanese; Korean; Literature; Philosophy; Preschool Education) *Dean*: Gyung Sook Chung; **Life Sciences** (Bioengineering; Biological and Life Sciences; Horticulture; Landscape Architecture; Marine Biology; Marine Engineering; Marine Science and Oceanography; Natural Resources) *Dean*: Hyung Geun Kim; **Natural Sciences** *Dean*: Soon Kwi Kim; **Social Sciences** (Accountancy; Business Administration; Business and Commerce; Development Studies; Economics; Government; International Business; Law; Management; Public Administration; Regional Studies) *Dean*: Chung-Kon Cho

Graduate Schools

Education (Education); **Industrial Technology** *Dean*: Jin Sun Hong; **Management and Policy Science** *Dean*: Chung-Kon Cho; **Regular Studies** (Marine Science and Oceanography; Natural Resources; Natural Sciences) *Dean*: Chan Jung Park

Institutes

Education Programme for Future Forest Management *Director*: Gab Soo Han; **Gwangwon Advanced Materials Business Foundation** (Business and Commerce) *Director*: Byung-Hak Choe; **Marine Bio/Advanced Cluster Agency** (Marine Biology) *Director*: Sang Moo Kim; **Next Generation Marine Life Industry Human Resources Development Agency** (Human Resources; Marine Science and Oceanography) *Director*: In Hak Jeong

Research Centres

Dental Science *Director*: Bong Kuen Cha; **Disaster Prevention** (Safety Engineering) *Director*: Eun6lk Yang; **East Coast Marine Organisms and Resources** (Marine Biology; Natural Resources) *Director*: Heum Gi Park; **East Sea Rim** *Director*: Hong Gil Kim Kim; **East Sea Rim Bio Science** (Biological and Life Sciences) *Director*: Hakgi Kim; **Embedded Software Cooperative** (Software Engineering) *Director*: Tae-Yun Chung; **Engineering** *Director*: Hyung Jik Lee; **Environmental Issues** *Director*: Kyu Joong Kim; **Fine Arts/ Physical Education** (Fine Arts) *Director*: Han Kook Kim; **Geographic Information Systems Training** (Geography; Information Technology) *Director*: Chul Sohn; **Governmental Studies** (Government) *Director*: Hong Sik Park; **Humanities** (Arts and Humanities) *Director*: Chang Sub Choi; **Marine Censor Network System Technology** (Marine Science and Oceanography; Technology) *Director*: Chang Hwa Kim; **Natural Sciences** *Director*: Do Won Kim; **North Korea** (Asian Studies) *Director*: Kyong Ho Yoon; **Social Sciences** (Social Sciences) *Director*: Man Jae Kim; **Super Computing Super Speed** (Computer Science) *Director*: Il Ung Chung

History: Founded 1946 as Kangnung Teacher School. Acquired present status 1991.

Academic Year: March to February (March-August; September-February)

Admission Requirements: Graduation from high school or equivalent, and entrance examination

Fees: According to programme

Main Language(s) of Instruction: Korean

Degrees and Diplomas: *Bachelor's Degree*: 4 yrs; *Master's Degree*: 2 yrs; *Doctor's Degree*: 2 yrs

Student Services: Academic counselling, Canteen, Cultural centre, Employment services, Foreign student adviser, Foreign Studies Centre, Handicapped facilities, Health services, Language programs, Nursery care, Sports facilities

Student Residential Facilities: Yes

Libraries: Central Library, c. 530,097 vols

Press or Publishing House: Kangnung National University Press

Last Updated: 24/10/08

KANGWON NATIONAL UNIVERSITY (KNU)

192-1, Hyoja 2 dong, Chuncheon-si,
Gangwon-do 200-701
Tel: +82(33) 250-6114
Fax: +82(33) 251-9556
EMail: www.adm@www.kangwon.ac.kr
Website: http://www.kangwon.ac.kr

President: Kwon Yong Jung

Centres

Computer Science (Computer Science)

Colleges

Agriculture and Life Sciences (Agriculture); **Animal Husbandry** (Cattle Breeding); **Arts**; **Business Administration** (Business Administration); **Education** (Education); **Engineering** (Engineering); **Forestry** (Forestry); **Humanities**; **Law** (Law); **Medicine**; **Natural Sciences** (Natural Sciences; Pharmacy); **Pharmacy**; **Social Sciences** (Social Sciences)

Divisions

Physical Education

Graduate Schools

Business and Public Administration (Business and Commerce; Public Administration); **Education** (Education); **Industrial Technology**; **Information Sciences** (Information Sciences)

Schools

Bio-technology and Bio-engineering

History: Founded 1947 as Agricultural College, became university 1978. A State institution under the jurisdiction of the Ministry of Education.

Academic Year: March to December (March-June; September-December)

Admission Requirements: Graduation from high school or foreign equivalent, and entrance examination

Main Language(s) of Instruction: Korean

Degrees and Diplomas: *Bachelor's Degree*: All fields, 4 yrs; *Master's Degree*: a further 2 yrs; *Doctor's Degree*: 3 yrs following Master's

Student Services: Cultural centre, Employment services, Health services, Language programs, Sports facilities

Student Residential Facilities: Yes

Special Facilities: University Museum

Libraries: c. 100,000 vols

Publications: Journal of Social Sciences; Journal of the Humanities; Research Bulletin (Science and Technology)

Press or Publishing House: University Press

Last Updated: 02/01/09

KONGJU NATIONAL UNIVERSITY (KNU)

182 Singwan-dong, Gongju-si, Chungnam-do 314-701
Tel: +82(41) 850-8001
Fax: +82(41) 850-8000
EMail: bon303@knu.kongju.ac.kr
Website: http://www.kongju.ac.kr

President: Jae-Hyun Kim

Colleges

Education (Education; Secondary Education; Special Education; Vocational Education); **Engineering** (Chemical Engineering; Civil Engineering; Computer Engineering; Electrical and Electronic Engineering; Engineering; Environmental Engineering; Materials Engineering; Mechanical Engineering); **Humanities and Social Sciences** (Arts and Humanities; Business Administration; Business and Commerce; Economics; Geography; History; International Business; Law; Literature; Modern Languages; Social Sciences); **Industrial Sciences** (Agricultural Economics; Agriculture; Agronomy; Food Science; Forestry; Horticulture; Landscape Architecture); **Natural Sciences** (Biological and Life Sciences; Chemistry; Earth Sciences; Natural Sciences; Physics); **Visual Image and Health**

Graduate Schools

Business and Public Administration; **Education** (Education; Higher Education Teacher Training; Secondary Education; Special Education; Vocational Education); **Educational Information**; **Industrial Development** (Agricultural Economics; Agriculture; Food Science; Forestry; Landscape Architecture); **Special Education**

History: Founded 1948 as Kongju Provincial Teachers' College, acquired present status 1991. Under the jurisdiction of the Ministry of Education.

Academic Year: March to February (March-August; September-February)

Admission Requirements: Graduation from high school or foreign equivalent, and entrance examination

Main Language(s) of Instruction: Korean

Degrees and Diplomas: *Bachelor's Degree*: 4 yrs; *Master's Degree*: a further 2 yrs; *Doctor's Degree*: 2 1/2 yrs following Master

Student Services: Academic counselling, Canteen, Cultural centre, Employment services, Handicapped facilities, Language programs, Nursery care, Sports facilities

Student Residential Facilities: Yes

Special Facilities: University Museum

Libraries: c. 360,300 vols

Publications: Paekche Culture *(annually)*; Science Education *(annually)*; Thesis Collection *(annually)*

Press or Publishing House: University Press

Last Updated: 02/01/09

KOREA ADVANCED INSTITUTE OF SCIENCE AND TECHNOLOGY (KAIST)

373-1 Guseong-dong, Yuseong-gu, Daejeon,
Chungnam-do 305-701
Tel: +82(42) 869-2114
Fax: +82(42) 869-2110 +82(42) 869-2220
EMail: webadmin@kaist.ac.kr
Website: http://www.kaist.edu/

President: Nam Pyo Suh

Colleges

Engineering (Aeronautical and Aerospace Engineering; Chemical Engineering; Civil Engineering; Computer Science; Electrical Engineering; Engineering; Environmental Engineering; Industrial Design; Industrial Engineering; Materials Engineering; Mechanical Engineering; Mechanics; Molecular Biology; Nuclear Engineering; Optics); **Humanities and Social Sciences**; **Information Science and Technology**; **Interdisciplinary Studies**; **Life Science and Bioengineering** (Bioengineering; Biological and Life Sciences; Biotechnology); **Natural Sciences**

Graduate Schools

Management

History: Founded 1971 as Korea Advanced Institute of Science. Acquired present status and title 1980.

Degrees and Diplomas: *Bachelor's Degree*; *Master's Degree*; *Doctor's Degree*

Last Updated: 02/01/09

KOREA MARITIME UNIVERSITY

1 Dongsam-dong, Yeongdo-gu, Pusan 606-791
Tel: +82(51) 410-4114
Fax: +82(51) 405-2475
EMail: webmaster@hhu.ac.kr
Website: http://www.kmaritime.ac.kr/

International Relations: Si-Hwa Kim
Tel: +82(51) 410-4005, Fax: +82(51) 404-3984
EMail: shalom@hanara.kmaritime.ac.kr

Divisions

Applied Mathematics (Applied Mathematics); **Architecture Engineering** (Architecture; Engineering); **Automation and Information Engineering** (Automation and Control Engineering; Computer Engineering; Systems Analysis); **Business Administration and Economics** (Business Administration; Economics; International Business); **East Asian Studies** (East Asian Studies); **Electrical Engineering** (Electrical Engineering); **Electronics and Communication** (Communication Studies; Electronic Engineering); **English** (English); **Foreign Trade** (International Business); **Logistics Engineering** (Engineering); **Marine Civil Engineering** (Marine Engineering); **Marine Engineering** (Marine Engineering); **Marine Environmental Engineering** (Marine Engineering); **Marine Police Studies**; **Maritime Law** (Maritime Law); **Materials Engineering** (Materials Engineering); **Mechanical Engineering** (Heating and Refrigeration; Mechanical Engineering); **Naval Architecture and Maritime Engineering** (Marine Engineering; Naval Architecture); **Navigation** (Nautical Science); **Ocean Energy and Resources Engineering** (Marine Science and Oceanography); **Radio Sciences and Engineering** (Engineering); **Ship Operating System Engineering** (Engineering)

History: Founded 1945 at Chinhae, moved to Busan 1953.

Academic Year: March to December (March-June; August-December)

Admission Requirements: Graduation from high school

Main Language(s) of Instruction: Korean

Degrees and Diplomas: *Bachelor's Degree*: 4 yrs; *Master's Degree*: a further 2 yrs; *Doctor's Degree*: 3 yrs following Master

Student Services: Academic counselling, Canteen, Cultural centre, Health services, Sports facilities

Student Residential Facilities: For c. 1,400 students

Special Facilities: Maritime Museum

Libraries: Central Library, c. 100,500 vols

Publications: Journals *(annually)*

Press or Publishing House: Korea Maritime University Press

KOREA NATIONAL OPEN UNIVERSITY (KNOU)

169 Dongsung-dong, Jongno-gu, Seoul 110-791
Tel: +82(2) 3668-4323
Fax: +82(2) 747-7100
EMail: webmaster@knou.ac.kr
Website: http://www.knou.ac.kr

President: Kyoo-Hyang Cho

International Relations: Hye-soo Kim

Centres

Computer Science (Computer Science); **Educational Media Development** (Educational Research); **Student Guidance** (Educational and Student Counselling)

Departments

Agriculture (Agriculture); **Applied Statistics** (Statistics); **Business Administration** (Business Administration); **Chinese Language and Literature** (Chinese); **Computer Science and Statistics** (Computer Science; Statistics); **Early Childhood Education** (Preschool Education); **Economics** (Economics); **Education** (Education); **English Language and Literature** (English); **French Language and Literature** (French); **General Education** (Education); **Home Economics** (Home Economics); **Hygiene** (Hygiene); **Japanese Studies** (Japanese); **Korean Language and Literature** (Korean); **Law** (Law); **Media Arts and Sciences** (Media Studies); **Public Administration** (Public Administration); **Trade** (Business and Commerce)

Institutes

Distance Education

Further Information: Also 12 regional Study Centres, and 27 local Study Centres

History: Founded 1972 as junior college of Seoul National University. Reorganized as an independent university 1981. Instruction is given by radio, TV, computer network system, audio cassettes and correspondence, and students have to attend several face-to-face classes per semester. A State institution under the jurisdiction of the Ministry of Education.

Academic Year: March to February (March-August; September-February)

Admission Requirements: Graduation from high school or equivalent

Main Language(s) of Instruction: Korean

Degrees and Diplomas: *Bachelor's Degree*: 4 yrs

Student Services: Academic counselling, Canteen, Social counselling, Sports facilities

Student Residential Facilities: Yes

Libraries: University Library, c. 265,000 vols

Publications: Distance Education *(annually)*; KNOU Journal *(biannually)*

Press or Publishing House: KNOU Press

KOREA NATIONAL SPORT UNIVERSITY

88-15 Oryun-dong, Songpa-gu, Seoul 138-763
Tel: +82(2) 410-6700
Fax: +82(2) 418-1877
Website: http://www.knsu.ac.kr/eng/

President: Seung-Kuk Lee (2004-)

Departments

Community Sports Science; **Health Management** (Health Administration); **Physical Education** (Physical Education); **Safety Management**; **Sports Guidance** (Sports)

Institutes

Physical Education and Sports Science (Physical Education); **Physical Education Research**

Schools

Graduate *(Community Sports Science)*; **Graduate** (Measurement and Precision Engineering; Pacific Area Studies)

History: Founded 1976. A State institution under the jurisdiction of the Ministry of Education.

Academic Year: March to December (March-June; August-December)

Admission Requirements: Graduation from high school

Main Language(s) of Instruction: Korean

Degrees and Diplomas: *Bachelor's Degree*: 4 yrs; *Master's Degree*: a further 2 yrs; *Doctor's Degree*: 3 yrs following Master

Special Facilities: Central Sports Museum

Libraries: College Library, c. 110,000 vols; Science and Liberal Arts

Publications: Monographs of the Physical Education Institute; Monographs of the Research Institute of Physical Education and Sports Science

Last Updated: 02/01/09

KOREA NATIONAL UNIVERSITY OF EDUCATION (KNUE)

San 7 Darak-ri, Gangnae-myeon, Chungwon-kun, Chungcheongbukdo 363-791
Tel: +82(43) 230-3114
Fax: +82(43) 233-2960
Website: http://www.knue.ac.kr

President: Jaesool Kwon (2008-)
Tel: +82(43) 230-3200, Fax: +82(43) 232-7645
EMail: jskwon@knue.ac.kr

International Relations: Chul-woo Han, Provost
Tel: +82(43) 230-3202, Fax: +82(43) 232-7647
EMail: cwead@hanmail.net

International Relations: Hee Chan Lew, Dean of Planning and Budget
Tel: +82(43) 230-3204, Fax: +82(43) 233-2207
EMail: hclew@knue.ac.kr

Centres

Educational Research (Educational Research) *Director*: Don Hyung Choi; **In-service Education** (Teacher Training) *Director*: Sung Soo Park

Colleges

Education (Education; Preschool Education; Primary Education) *Dean*: Ki Yung Choi; **Humanities** (English; Ethics; French; Geography; German; History; Korean; Social Studies) *Dean*: Tae Hyeon Kim; **Music, Physical Education, Fine Arts** (Fine Arts; Music; Physical Education) *Dean*: Kil Jae Lee; **Science** (Biology; Chemistry; Computer Science; Earth Sciences; Environmental Studies; Home Economics; Mathematics; Mathematics and Computer Science; Physics; Technology) *Dean*: Myung Duk Joo

Graduate Schools

Education; **Educational Policy** (Educational Administration) *Dean*: Bum Ki Kim

Schools

Graduate (Art Education; Education; Humanities and Social Science Education; Music Education; Physical Education; Science Education) *Dean*: Bum Ki Kim

History: Founded 1984. Inception of Master's Degree courses, Opening of Center for Educational Research, In-service Center 1986. Inception of Doctoral courses, Opening of Affiliated elementary and middle school 1988. Opening of Affiliated High School 1994. Opening of Educational Graduate School 1997. Opening of Graduate School of Educational Policy and Administration 2001. International Symposium to found the first Asian Teachers Association 2006.

Academic Year: March to February (March-August; September-February)

Admission Requirements: Graduation from high school

Fees: (Won): c. 1,350,000 per semester

Main Language(s) of Instruction: Korean

Degrees and Diplomas: *Bachelor's Degree*: Education, 4 yrs; *Master's Degree*: a further 2-3 yrs; *Doctor's Degree*: Education, 3 yrs following Master

Student Services: Academic counselling, Canteen, Cultural centre, Employment services, Handicapped facilities, Health services, Language programs, Nursery care, Social counselling, Sports facilities

Student Residential Facilities: For c. 2,200 students (9 dormitory buildings)

Special Facilities: Educational Museum; Art Gallery; Astronomical Observatory; Biological Garden; Concert Hall; Earth Observatory

Libraries: University Library, c. 400,000 vols

Last Updated: 03/10/08

KUMOH NATIONAL INSTITUTE OF TECHNOLOGY

188 Shinpyung-dong, Gumi-si, Gyeongbuk-do 730-701
Tel: +82(54) 467-4114
Fax: +82(54) 467-4050
EMail: webmaster@kumoh.ac.kr
Website: http://www.kumoh.ac.kr

President: Choi Hwan

Centres

Computer Engineering (Computer Engineering); **Continuing Education**

Departments

Applied Mathematics (Applied Mathematics); **Architectural Engineering** (Architecture); **Civil Engineering** (Civil Engineering); **Electronic and Control Engineering** (Automation and Control Engineering; Electronic Engineering); **Electronic Engineering** (Electronic Engineering); **Electronics Communication** (Electronic Engineering); **Engineering Science and Mechanics** (Engineering; Mechanics); **Industrial Engineering** (Industrial Engineering); **Materials Science and Engineering** (Materials Engineering); **Mechanical and Precision Engineering** (Measurement and Precision Engineering; Mechanical Engineering); **Mechanical and Production Engineering** (Mechanical Engineering; Production Engineering); **Mechanical Engineering** (Mechanical Engineering); **Polymer Science and Engineering** (Polymer and Plastics Technology)

Institutes

Community Research; **Research on Manufacturing Productivity** (Production Engineering)

Schools

Industry *(Graduate)* (Industrial Engineering)

History: Founded 1980. A State institution under the jurisdiction of the Ministry of Education. Financially supported by the Government and tuition fees.

Academic Year: March to February (March-August; September-February)

Admission Requirements: Graduation from high school and entrance examination

Main Language(s) of Instruction: Korean

Degrees and Diplomas: *Bachelor's Degree*: 4 yrs; *Master's Degree*: a further 2 yrs

Student Residential Facilities: Yes

Libraries: c. 20,000 vols

Publications: Academic Journal *(annually)*

KUNSAN NATIONAL UNIVERSITY (KSNU)

68 Miryong-dong, Gunsan-si, Jeollabuk-do 573-701
Tel: +82(63) 469-4113 +82(63) 469-4114
Fax: +82(63) 469-4197
EMail: inter@kunsan.ac.kr
Website: http://www.kunsan.ac.kr

President: Hai-Jung Lim (2003-)
Tel: +82(63) 469-4101, Fax: +82(63) 466-2735
EMail: hjlim@kunsan.ac.kr

Director-General: Dae-Kyu Lee
Tel: +82(63) 469-4107, Fax: +82(63) 469-4833
EMail: dklee@kunsan.ac.kr

International Relations: Keum-Rok Yoo, Vice-President, Planning and Research Affairs
Tel: +82(63) 469-4101, Fax: +82(63) 469-4833
EMail: pire@kunsan.ac.kr

Centres

Environmental Research *(Saemankeum) Director*: Sang-Ho Lee; **Kunsan Automotive Technology Innovation** *Director*: Byong-Mu Heo; **Red Tide Research** *Director*: Hyun-Yong Choi; **Tidal Flat Research** (Coastal Studies) *Director*: Dong-Ki Ryu

Colleges

Arts and Music *Dean*: Byung-Ok Kim; **Engineering** (Automation and Control Engineering; Chemical Engineering; Civil Engineering; Construction Engineering; Electrical Engineering; Electronic Engineering; Engineering; Environmental Engineering; Materials Engineering; Mechanical Engineering; Telecommunications Engineering) *Dean*: Seung-Heun Lee; **Humanities** (Arts and Humanities; Chinese; English; European Studies; German; History; Japanese; Korean; Philosophy) *Dean*: Seok Park; **Natural Sciences** (Biology; Chemistry; Clothing and Sewing; Computer Science; Food Science; Health Administration; Household Management; Mathematics; Natural Sciences; Nutrition; Physics; Statistics) *Dean*: Ho-Soeb Choi; **Ocean Science and Technology** (Aquaculture; Biological and Life Sciences; Engineering; Environmental Engineering; Food Science; Food Technology; Marine Biology; Marine Engineering; Marine Science and Oceanography)

Dean: Keun-Woo Lee; **Social Sciences** (Accountancy; Business Administration; Business and Commerce; Economics; Government; Law; Public Administration; Social Sciences; Social Welfare) *Dean*: Jong-Sup Lee

Graduate Schools

Business and Public Administration *Dean*: Jong-Sup Lee; **Education** *Dean*: Hee-Seok Park; **Industry** *Dean*: Seung-Heum Lee

Institutes

Basic Sciences (Natural Sciences; Water Science) *Director*: Sun-Kun Bae; **Engineering** (Automation and Control Engineering; Automotive Engineering; Electronic Engineering; Engineering; Machine Building; Telecommunications Engineering) *Director*: Seung-Ki Koh; **Environmental Constructions** *Director*: Gyung-Soo Kim; **Fisheries Science** *Director*: Jeong-Yoi Lee; **Legal Studies** (Civil Law; Commercial Law; Human Rights; Labour Law) *Director*: Choong-Mook Kim; **Liberal Sciences** *Director*: Eun Jun; **Modern Art** *Director*: Hee-Sung Kim; **Modern Ideology** *Director*: Soon-Hong Kwon; **Ocean Development** *Dean*: Seung-Won Suh; **Regional Studies** *Director*: Soo-Kwan Kim; **Telecommunications Technology** *Director*: Jong-In Lee; **Yellow Sea Rim Research** *Director*: Min-Young Kim

Schools

Graduate *Director*: Young-Jae Kim

History: Founded 1979 as college, acquired present status 1991.

Academic Year: March to February (March-August; September-February)

Admission Requirements: Graduation from high school or equivalent, and entrance examination

Fees: (US Dollars): 1,600-1,800 per semester

Main Language(s) of Instruction: Korean

International Co-operation: With universities in USA, Japan, China, Germany, Russian Federation, Hungary, Thailand, Philippines, Australia. Also participates in HUMAP (Hyogo University Mobility in Asia and the Pacific) programme

Accrediting Agencies: Ministry of Education and Human Resources Development

Degrees and Diplomas: *Bachelor's Degree (BA)*: 4 yrs; *Master's Degree (MA)*: a further 2 yrs; *Doctor's Degree (PhD)*: a further 2 yrs. Honorary Doctor degrees. Certificates for course completion (Continuing Education Centre and Language Training Centre)

Student Services: Academic counselling, Canteen, Cultural centre, Employment services, Health services, Language programs, Nursery care, Sports facilities

Student Residential Facilities: Yes

Special Facilities: University Museum, Concert Hall. Training ships, Factories attached to the colleges (Engineering, Ocean Science & Technology)

Libraries: 283,121 vols

Press or Publishing House: University Press

KYUNGPOOK NATIONAL UNIVERSITY

1370 Sangyeok-dong, Buk-gu, Daegu 702-701
Tel: +82(53) 950-5114
Fax: +82(53) 950-5099
EMail: knuglobal@knu.ac.kr
Website: http://www.knu.ac.kr/

President: Dongil Noh

Colleges

Agriculture and Life Sciences (Agriculture; Agronomy; Forest Products; Forestry; Horticulture; Landscape Architecture); **Economics and Commerce** (Business and Commerce; Economics); **Education** (Education); **Engineering** (Architecture; Chemical Engineering; Civil Engineering; Computer Engineering; Electrical and Electronic Engineering; Engineering; Environmental Engineering; Industrial Chemistry; Materials Engineering; Mechanical Engineering; Metallurgical Engineering; Organic Chemistry; Polymer and Plastics Technology); **Human Ecology** (Clothing and Sewing; Ecology; Food Science; Home Economics; Nutrition; Textile Technology); **Humanities** (Anthropology; Archaeology; Arts and Humanities; Chinese; English; French; German; History; Japanese; Korean; Modern Languages; Philosophy; Russian); **Law** (Law; Public Administration); **Music and Visual Arts** (Music; Visual Arts); **Natural Sciences** (Astronomy and Space Science; Biochemistry; Biology; Chemistry; Computer Science; Genetics; Geology; Mathematics; Microbiology; Natural Sciences; Physics); **Social Sciences** (Geography; Information Sciences; International Relations; Journalism; Library Science; Political Sciences; Psychology; Social Sciences)

Graduate Schools

Agricultural Development (Agriculture); **Business Administration** (Business Administration); **Education** (Education); **Industry** (Industrial Engineering); **International Study** (International Studies); **Public Administration** (Public Administration); **Public Health** (Public Health)

Institutes

Agricultural Science and Technology (Agricultural Engineering); **Basic Sciences** (Natural Sciences); **Cancer Research** (Oncology); **Economics and Management Research** (Economics; Management); **Electronic Technology** (Electronic Engineering); **Environment and Open Space** (Environmental Studies); **Environmental Science** (Environmental Studies); **Genetic Engineering** (Genetics); **Humanities** (Arts and Humanities); **Industrial Technology Research** (Industrial Engineering); **Medical Research** (Medicine); **Nursing** (Nursing); **Pacific Rim Studies** (Pacific Area Studies); **Peace Research** (Peace and Disarmament); **Philosophy and Korean Studies** *(Toegye)* (Philosophy; Regional Studies); **Physical Education and Sports Science Research** (Physical Education; Sports); **Science Education Research** (Science Education); **Social Sciences Research** (Social Sciences); **Topology and Geometry Research** (Mathematics; Surveying and Mapping); **Veterinary Science** (Veterinary Science)

Schools

Dentistry (Dentistry); **Medicine** (Medicine; Nursing); **Veterinary Science** (Veterinary Science)

History: Founded as University 1946 incorporating 3 existing Institutions (Teachers, 1923; Medicine, 1933; Agriculture, 1944) and 2 newly established Colleges (Liberal Arts and Sciences). Main Campus at Sankyuk-dong and Medical Campus at Tongin-dong. Under the jurisdiction of the Ministry of Education.

Governing Bodies: Office of Academic Affairs; Office of Student Affairs; Office of General Affairs; Office of Planning and Research

Academic Year: March to February (March-June; September-February)

Admission Requirements: Graduation from high school or foreign equivalent, and competitive entrance examination

Main Language(s) of Instruction: Korean

Degrees and Diplomas: *Bachelor's Degree*: 4 yrs; *Master's Degree*: a further 1-2 yrs; *Doctor's Degree (PhD)*: 2-3 yrs following Master

Student Services: Academic counselling, Employment services, Foreign student adviser, Health services, Social counselling, Sports facilities

Student Residential Facilities: For c. 13,790 students

Special Facilities: University Museum (Antiques of Sill, Koryo, and Yi Dynasties). Auditorium. Veterinary Clinic

Libraries: Central Library, c. 1m. vols

Publications: Abstracts of Theses, Graduate School *(annually)*; Agricultural Research Bulletin of Kyungpook National University *(annually)*; Bulletin of the Institute for Industrial and Social Development *(annually)*; Electronic Technology Reports *(annually)*; History Education Review *(annually)*; Journal of English Language and Literature *(annually)*; Journal of Graduate School of Education *(annually)*; Journal of Humanities *(annually)*; Journal of Korean Language and Literature *(annually)*; Journal of Kyungpook Engineering *(annually)*; Journal of Language and Literature *(annually)*; Journal of Law and Political Science *(annually)*; Journal of Natural Sciences *(annually)*; Journal of Physical Education *(biannually)*; Journal of Science Education *(annually)*; Journal of Social Sciences *(annually)*; Journal of Student Guidance *(biannually)*; Kyungpook Education Forum *(annually)*; Kyungpook Historical Review *(annually)*; Kyungpook Mathematical Journal *(biannually)*; Kyungpook University Medical Journal *(biannually)*; Magazine of Geology *(annually)*; Nak-Dong Geography *(annually)*; Oriental Culture Research *(annually)*; Peace Research *(annually)*; Philosophy of

Korea *(annually)*; Research Review of Kyungpook University *(biannually)*; Review of Economics and Business *(annually)*; Saemaul Research Review *(annually)*; Thesis Collection of Korean Language and Literature *(annually)*; Zeitschrift für Germanistik *(annually)*

Press or Publishing House: The University Press
Last Updated: 05/01/09

MIRYANG NATIONAL UNIVERSITY

1025-1 Naei-dong, Miryang-si, Gyeongnam-do 627-702
Tel: +82(55) 354-3181
Fax: +82(55) 355-3186
EMail: sdlee@arang.miryang.ac.kr
Website: http://www.mnu.ac.kr/eng/01_about/03_his.php

President: Sang-hak Lee

International Relations: Ho-yeol Lee
Tel: +82(55) 350-5203, Fax: +82(55) 356-3307

Departments

Agriculture (Agriculture); **Arts and Humanities and Social Sciences** (Arts and Humanities; Social Sciences); **Natural Sciences and Engineering** (Engineering; Natural Sciences); **Technology and Industrial Engineering** (Industrial Engineering; Technology)

History: Founded 1923.

Main Language(s) of Instruction: Korean

Degrees and Diplomas: *Bachelor's Degree*; *Master's Degree*

MOKPO NATIONAL MARITIME UNIVERSITY

571-2 Chukyo-dong, Mokpo-si, Jeollanam-do 530-729
Tel: +82(61) 240-7157
Fax: +82(61) 240-7286
EMail: ryujb@mmu.ac.kr
Website: http://www.mmu.ac.kr

President: Byung-Joo Oh
Tel: +82(61) 240-7000, Fax: +82(61) 240-7290
EMail: bngjoo@mmu.ac.kr

Director of General Affairs: Maeng-Gyu Nah
Tel: +82(61) 240-7020 EMail: mgnah@mmu.ac.kr

International Relations: Shang-Hyon Shin
Tel: +82(61) 240-7159, Fax: +82(61) 240-7286
EMail: intercoop@mmu.ac.kr

Institutes

Maritime Industry (Marine Engineering) *Head*: Soon-Dong Yun; **Mechanics and Electronics** (Electronic Engineering; Marine Engineering; Mechanical Engineering) *Head*: Kyung-Ho Park

History: Founded 1950.

Academic Year: March to December (March-June; September-December)

Admission Requirements: Graduation from high school and entrance examination

Fees: (Won): 2.8m. per annum

Main Language(s) of Instruction: Korean

Degrees and Diplomas: *Bachelor's Degree*: 4 yrs; *Master's Degree*: a further 2 yrs; *Doctor's Degree*: a further 3 yrs

Libraries: 99,532 vols

MOKPO NATIONAL UNIVERSITY

61 Dorim-ri, Chungkye-myeon, Muan-gun, Jeollanam-do 534-729
Tel: +82(61) 450-2114
Fax: +82(61) 452-4793
EMail: yyy@chungkye.mokpo.ac.kr
Website: http://www.mokpo.ac.kr

President: Woong-Bae Kim

International Relations: Cheoul-jin Shin
Tel: +82(61) 450-2055, Fax: +82(61) 450-2051

Colleges

Engineering (Computer Engineering; Electrical Engineering; Electronic Engineering; Engineering; Food Technology; Mechanical Engineering; Naval Architecture); **Humanities** (Anthropology; Archaeology; Arts and Humanities; Business Education; Chinese; Education; English; Ethics; Fine Arts; History; Japanese; Korean; Music); **Natural Sciences** (Natural Sciences); **Social Sciences** (Business Administration; Economics; Finance; Insurance; International Business; Law; Public Administration; Regional Planning; Rural Planning; Social Sciences)

Institutes

Basic Sciences (Natural Sciences); **Littoral Management** (Environmental Management; Environmental Studies); **Unification Research**; **Welfare** (Welfare and Protective Services)

History: Founded 1946 as normal school. Acquired present status and title 1990.

Academic Year: March to February

Admission Requirements: Graduation from high school and entrance examination

Main Language(s) of Instruction: Korean

Degrees and Diplomas: *Bachelor's Degree*: 4 yrs; *Master's Degree*: a further 2 yrs

Student Residential Facilities: Yes

Special Facilities: Museum. Broadcasting System

Libraries: Central Library, c. 80,500 vols

Publications: Journals of Research Institutes *(annually)*

Press or Publishing House: University Press

PUKYONG NATIONAL UNIVERSITY (PKNU)

599-1 Daeyeon-dong 3, Nam-gu, Pusan 608-737
Tel: +82(51) 623-4555
Fax: +82(51) 628-6260
EMail: web@pknu.ac.kr
Website: http://www.pknu.ac.kr

President: Maeng Eon Park
Tel: +82(51) 620-6000, Fax: +82(51) 628-6260

Centres

Acoustics and Vibration Engineering; **Computer Science**; **Design**; **Euro Info**; **Fisheries Science and Technology**; **Foreign Language Education**; **Health Care**; **Ocean Industrial Development**

Colleges

Business Administration (Accountancy; Business Administration; International Business; Management Systems) *Dean*: Hong-Suk Choi; **Engineering** (Architecture; Automation and Control Engineering; Chemical Engineering; Computer Engineering; Construction Engineering; Electrical Engineering; Electronic Engineering; Heating and Refrigeration; Industrial Chemistry; Industrial Engineering; Information Technology; Instrument Making; Materials Engineering; Mechanical Engineering; Metallurgical Engineering; Multimedia; Polymer and Plastics Technology; Production Engineering; Safety Engineering; Structural Architecture; Telecommunications Engineering) *Dean*: Dong-Wook Lee; **Fisheries Sciences** (Bioengineering; Biological and Life Sciences; Biotechnology; Fishery; Food Technology; Marine Biology; Marine Engineering) *Dean*: Jae-Yoon Jo; **Humanities and Social Sciences** (Arts and Humanities; Asian Studies; Design; Economics; English; English Studies; European Studies; History; International Relations; International Studies; Japanese; Korean; Law; Mass Communication; Political Sciences; Preschool Education; Public Administration; Social Sciences) *Dean*: Jae-duk Bae; **Marine Sciences and Technology** (Marine Biology; Marine Engineering; Marine Science and Oceanography; Meteorology); **Natural Sciences** (Applied Mathematics; Chemistry; Microbiology; Natural Sciences; Physics; Sports; Statistics) *Dean*: Hyuk-dong Kwon

Institutes

Electronics and Telecommunications; **Environmental and Marine Sciences and Technology**; **Fisheries and Science**; **Humanities and Social Sciences**; **Industrial Science and Technology**; **Life Science and Biotechnology**; **Maritime Affairs**; **Mechanical Engineering and Technology**; **Ocean Sciences** *(Inter-University Institute)*; **Satellite Information Sciences**; **Seafood Science**; **Thermal and Fluids Engineering**

Research Centres

Dioxin; **Engineering**; **Nutrition**

Research Institutes
Basic Science; **Environmental Studies** *(Centre)*

Further Information: Also foreign student programme

History: Founded 1996, incorporating Pusan National University of Technology, now Yongdang Campus (founded 1924), and National Fisheries University of Pusan, now Daeyeon Campus (founded 1941).

Academic Year: March to December (March-June; August-December)

Admission Requirements: Graduation from high school and entrance examination

Fees: (Won): 1.2m.

Main Language(s) of Instruction: Korean, English

International Co-operation: With universities in Australia, America, China, Japan, Spain, Germany

Degrees and Diplomas: *Bachelor's Degree*: 4 yrs; *Master's Degree*: a further 2 yrs; *Doctor's Degree (PhD)*: a further 2-3 yrs

Student Services: Academic counselling, Employment services, Foreign student adviser, Health services, Language programs, Sports facilities

Student Residential Facilities: Yes

Special Facilities: University Museum

Libraries: Daeyeon Campus Library, Yongdang Campus Library

Publications: Pukyong Journal, In Korean *(quarterly)*

Last Updated: 05/01/09

PUSAN NATIONAL UNIVERSITY (PNU)

30 Jangjeon-dong, Geumjeong-gu, Pusan 609-735
Tel: +82(51) 510-3653
Fax: +82(51) 582-6980
EMail: pnuadmin@pusan.ac.kr
Website: http://www.pusan.ac.kr

President: Inn Se Kim (2003-)

International Relations: Young-In Chung
Tel: +82(51) 510-3652, Fax: +82(51) 582-6980
EMail: foreign@pusan.ac.kr

Centres
Computer (Computer Networks); **Dielectric and Advanced Matter Physics** (Electrical Engineering; Physics); **Dye Manufacturing**; **Korean Studies** (Korean)

Colleges
Art (Dance; Fine Arts; Music); **Business** (Accountancy; Business Administration; Business and Commerce; Economics; International Business; International Studies); **Dentistry** (Dentistry); **Education** (Education); **Engineering** (Aeronautical and Aerospace Engineering; Architecture; Automation and Control Engineering; Chemical Engineering; Civil Engineering; Computer Engineering; Electrical and Electronic Engineering; Engineering; Environmental Engineering; Industrial Engineering; Marine Engineering; Materials Engineering; Measurement and Precision Engineering; Mechanical Engineering; Metallurgical Engineering; Polymer and Plastics Technology; Production Engineering; Textile Technology; Town Planning; Urban Studies); **Human Ecology** (Ecology; Environmental Studies; Home Economics); **Humanities** (Archaeology; Arts and Humanities; Chinese; English; French; German; History; Japanese; Korean; Linguistics; Literature; Philosophy; Russian); **Law** (Law); **Medicine** (Medicine; Nursing); **Natural Sciences** (Biology; Chemistry; Computer Science; Earth Sciences; Geology; Marine Science and Oceanography; Mathematics; Microbiology; Molecular Biology; Natural Sciences; Physics; Statistics); **Pharmacy** (Pharmacy); **Social Sciences** (Archiving; Communication Studies; Information Sciences; International Relations; Library Science; Political Sciences; Psychology; Public Administration; Social Sciences; Social Welfare; Sociology)

Graduate Schools
Education (Education); **Environment** (Environmental Studies); **Industry** (Industrial Engineering); **International Studies** (International Studies); **Management** (Management); **Public Administration** (Public Administration; Social Policy; Urban Studies)

Institutes
Basic Sciences (Natural Sciences); **Computer and Information Communication** (Computer Science; Telecommunications Services); **Genetic Engineering** (Genetics); **Industrial Technology** (Industrial Engineering); **Mechanical Technology** (Mechanical Engineering); **Oral Biotechnology** (Biotechnology); **Technology and Industry** (Industrial Engineering; Technology)

Further Information: Also University Hospital

History: Founded 1946 as Pusan National College, acquired present status and title 1953.

Governing Bodies: Administration Committee; Planning Committee; Faculty Personnel Committee; Council of Deans

Academic Year: March to December (March-June; August-December)

Admission Requirements: Secondary school certificate and entrance examination

Main Language(s) of Instruction: Korean

Degrees and Diplomas: *Bachelor's Degree*: 4 yrs; *Master's Degree*: a further 2 yrs; *Doctor's Degree*: a further 2-3 yrs

Student Services: Academic counselling, Canteen, Cultural centre, Employment services, Foreign student adviser, Foreign Studies Centre, Health services, Language programs, Nursery care, Social counselling, Sports facilities

Special Facilities: University Museum

Libraries: c. 1m. vols

Press or Publishing House: PNU Press

PUSAN NATIONAL UNIVERSITY OF EDUCATION

263 Geoje-1-dong, Yeonje-gu, Pusan 611-736
Tel: +82(51) 500-7114
Fax: +82(51) 505-4908

President: Sung-Taek Park (2001-)

International Relations: Jae-Sik Kim
Tel: +82(51) 500-7117, Fax: +82(51) 500-7115
EMail: plan2@bnue.ac.kr

Graduate Schools
Education

Schools
Education (Computer Education; Education; English; Ethics; Fine Arts; Korean; Mathematics Education; Music Education; Physical Education; Preschool Education; Science Education; Social Studies)

History: Founded 1946.

Main Language(s) of Instruction: Korean

SAMCHEOK NATIONAL UNIVERSITY

San-253 Gyo-dong, Samcheok-si, Gangwon-do 245-711
Tel: +82(33) 572-8611 +82(33) 572-8619
Fax: +82(33) 572-8620
EMail: webadmin@samcheok.ac.kr
Website: http://www.samcheok.ac.kr

President: Dae Soo Kim

Programmes
Arts and Humanities (Arts and Humanities); **Design** (Design); **Engineering** (Engineering); **Fine Arts**; **Social Sciences**

History: Founded 1939.

SANGJU NATIONAL UNIVERSITY

386 Gajang-Dong, Sangju-si, Gyeongbuk-do 742-711
Tel: +82(54) 532-6000
Fax: +82(54) 532-6005
EMail: yscho@sangju.ac.kr
Website: http://www.sangju.ac.kr

President: Jong-ho Kim EMail: kjh@sangju.ac.kr

Graduate Schools
Graduate Studies

Programmes
Audiovisual Technology (Educational Technology); **Continuing Education**; **Electronic Commerce** (E-Business/Commerce)

History: Founded 1921.

SEOUL NATIONAL UNIVERSITY

San 56-1, Sillim-dong, Gwanak-gu, Seoul 151-742
Tel: +82(2) 880-5114
Fax: +82(2) 885-5272
EMail: webadmin@snu.ac.kr
Website: http://www.useoul.edu/

President: Un-chan Chung EMail: ucchung@snu.ac.kr

International Relations: Kyong-soo Lho

Centres
Advanced Materials Research (Materials Engineering); **Area Studies** (Cultural Studies; Regional Studies); **Inter-University Semiconductor**; **Medical Research** (Medicine)

Colleges
Agriculture and Life Sciences (Agricultural Economics; Agricultural Education; Agricultural Engineering; Agriculture; Agronomy; Applied Chemistry; Biological and Life Sciences; Biology; Chemistry; Economics; Food Technology; Forest Products; Home Economics; Horticulture; Landscape Architecture; Zoology); **Business Administration** (Business Administration); **Dentistry** (Dentistry); **Education** (Education); **Engineering** (Aeronautical and Aerospace Engineering; Architecture; Chemical Engineering; Civil Engineering; Computer Engineering; Electrical Engineering; Electronic Engineering; Engineering; Industrial Engineering; Marine Engineering; Mechanical Engineering; Metallurgical Engineering; Mining Engineering; Nuclear Engineering; Petroleum and Gas Engineering); **Fine Arts** (Crafts and Trades; Design; Fine Arts; Painting and Drawing; Sculpture); **Home Economics** (Home Economics); **Humanities** (Aesthetics; Archaeology; Art History; Arts and Humanities; Chinese; English; French; German; History; Korean; Linguistics; Philosophy; Religious Studies; Russian; Spanish); **Law** (Law); **Medicine** (Medicine); **Music** (Music); **Natural Sciences** (Astronomy and Space Science; Biology; Chemistry; Computer Science; Dentistry; Geology; Marine Science and Oceanography; Mathematics; Medicine; Meteorology; Microbiology; Molecular Biology; Natural Sciences; Physics; Statistics); **Nursing** (Nursing); **Pharmacy** (Pharmacy); **Social Sciences** (Anthropology; Communication Studies; Economics; Geography; International Economics; International Relations; Political Sciences; Psychology; Social Sciences; Social Welfare; Sociology); **Veterinary Science** (Veterinary Science)

Graduate Schools
Environmental Studies (Environmental Studies); **Public Administration** (Public Administration); **Public Health** (Public Health)

Institutes
Advanced Computer Technology Research (Computer Engineering); **Advanced Machinery and Design** (Industrial Design); **American Studies** (American Studies); **Automation and Systems Research** (Automation and Control Engineering); **Basic Sciences** (Natural Sciences); **Communication Sciences** (Telecommunications Engineering); **Economic Research** (Economics); **Engineering Science** (Engineering); **Environmental Science and Engineering** (Environmental Engineering); **Humanities** (Arts and Humanities); **Korean Studies** (Korean); **Language Research** (Linguistics); **Law Reseach** (Law); **Molecular Biology and Genetics** (Biological and Life Sciences); **Natural Products Research** (Natural Resources); **New Media and Communication** (Communication Studies; Media Studies); **Social Sciences** (Social Sciences)

Further Information: Also 61 Research Institutes of the Colleges. University Hospital

History: Founded 1946 in succession to former Keijo Imperial University. Reorganized 1975. A State Institution under the jurisdiction of the Ministry of Education.

Governing Bodies: University Council

Academic Year: March to February (March-June; September-February)

Admission Requirements: Graduation from high school or teachers' college, or equivalent qualification recognized by the Ministry of Education in Korea, and entrance examination

Main Language(s) of Instruction: Korean

Degrees and Diplomas: *Bachelor's Degree*: 4 yrs; *Master's Degree*: a further 2 yrs; *Doctor's Degree*: 3 yrs following Master

Student Residential Facilities: Yes

Special Facilities: University Museum

Libraries: Central Library and specialized libraries, c. 2m vols

Publications: Economic Review *(annually)*; Engineering Report *(annually)*; Home Economics Journal *(annually)*; Journal of Environmental Studies *(biannually)*; Journal of Humanities *(biannually)*; Journal of Pharmaceutical Sciences *(annually)*; Journal of the College of Education *(biannually)*; Korean Business Journal *(quarterly)*; Korean Development Policy Studies *(annually)*; Korean Economic Journal *(quarterly)*; Korean Journal of Public Administration *(biannually)*; Korean Journal of Public Health *(biannually)*; Law Journal *(quarterly)*; Proceedings of the College of Natural Sciences *(biannually)*; Publications of the Research Institutes; Seoul Journal of Medicine *(quarterly)*; Social Science Review *(quarterly)*; Social Sciences and Policy Studies *(quarterly)*

Press or Publishing House: Seoul University Press

SEOUL NATIONAL UNIVERSITY OF EDUCATION

1650 Seocho-dong, Seocho-gu, Seoul 137-742
Tel: +82(2) 3475-2114
Fax: +82(2) 581-7711
EMail: center@ns.snue.ac.kr
Website: http://www.snue.ac.kr

President: Ho Seong Kim
Tel: +82(2) 3475-2413, Fax: +82(2) 581-6555
EMail: khs@snue.ac.kr

International Relations: Hang-kyun Shin

Graduate Schools
Education (Education)

Schools
Education (Art Education; Computer Education; English; Ethics; Fine Arts; Foreign Languages Education; Korean; Mathematics Education; Music Education; Native Language Education; Physical Education; Primary Education; Science Education; Social Studies)

History: Founded 1946.

Main Language(s) of Instruction: Korean

Degrees and Diplomas: *Bachelor's Degree*; *Master's Degree*

Student Services: Academic counselling, Cultural centre, Employment services, Health services, Language programs, Social counselling, Sports facilities

Special Facilities: Museum, Art Gallery, Observatory

SEOUL NATIONAL UNIVERSITY OF TECHNOLOGY (SNUT)

172 Gongneung-dong 2, Nowon-gu, Seoul 139-743
Tel: +82(2) 970-6114 +82(2) 970-7114
Fax: +82(2) 970-6088
EMail: webmast@plaza.snut.ac.kr
Website: http://www.snut.ac.kr

President: Hyun-souk Cho

Centres
Computer Science (Computer Science)

Faculties
Cultural and Social Sciences (Arts and Humanities; Business Administration; Cultural Studies; English; Korean; Public Administration; Social Sciences; Sports); **Engineering I** (Automotive Engineering; Industrial Engineering; Materials Engineering; Mechanical Engineering; Safety Engineering); **Engineering II** (Architecture; Building Technologies; Civil Engineering; Engineering Drawing and Design; Structural Architecture); **Engineering III** (Automation and Control Engineering; Computer Science; Electrical Engineering; Electronic Engineering); **Engineering IV** (Chemical Engineering;

Environmental Engineering; Food Technology); **Plastic Arts** (Painting and Drawing)

Graduate Schools

Industry (Industrial Engineering)

Institutes

Technical Education Research

History: Founded 1910 as a technical school, became Open University 1982; acquired present status and title 1988.

Governing Bodies: Faculty Council; Academic Affairs Council

Academic Year: March to December (March-June; August-December)

Admission Requirements: Graduation from high school and entrance examination

Main Language(s) of Instruction: Korean, English

Degrees and Diplomas: *Bachelor's Degree*: 4 yrs; *Master's Degree*: a further 2 yrs

Student Services: Academic counselling, Canteen, Cultural centre, Employment services, Language programs, Nursery care, Social counselling, Sports facilities

Student Residential Facilities: Yes

Special Facilities: Broadcasting System

Libraries: c. 230,186 vols

Publications: Collegian Life Research *(annually)*; English Journal The Vision *(quarterly)*; Theses Collection *(annually)*; Vocational and Technical Education *(quarterly)*

Press or Publishing House: SNPU Times Publishing Centre

SUNCHON NATIONAL UNIVERSITY

315 Maegok-dong, Suncheon-si, Jeollanam-do 540-742
Tel: +82(61) 750-3001
Fax: +82(61) 750-3016
EMail: webmaster@sunchon.ac.kr
Website: http://www.sunchon.ac.kr

President: Jang-Man Chai EMail: president@sunchon.ac.kr

Colleges

Agricultural and Life Sciences (Agricultural Economics; Agricultural Equipment; Agriculture; Agronomy; Forestry; Horticulture; Landscape Architecture; Zoology); **Education** (Agricultural Education; Computer Education; Education; English; Environmental Studies; Korean; Mathematics; Social Studies); **Engineering** (Architecture; Automotive Engineering; Chemical Engineering; Civil Engineering; Computer Engineering; Electrical Engineering; Electronic Engineering; Engineering; Environmental Engineering; Materials Engineering; Mechanical Engineering; Metallurgical Engineering; Polymer and Plastics Technology); **Humanities and Social Sciences** (Accountancy; Arts and Humanities; Business Administration; Chinese; Economics; History; International Business; Japanese; Law; Literature; Painting and Drawing; Philosophy; Photography; Public Administration; Social Sciences); **Natural Sciences** (Biology; Chemistry; Clothing and Sewing; Computer Science; Cooking and Catering; Food Science; Home Economics; Natural Sciences; Nutrition; Physics; Textile Technology; Traditional Eastern Medicine)

Graduate Schools

Business and Public Administration; **Information Science**

Institutes

Agricultural Science Research (Agriculture; Marine Science and Oceanography); **Basic Sciences** (Applied Chemistry; Applied Mathematics; Applied Physics; Natural Sciences); **Engineering Research** (Engineering; Technology); **Language** (Chinese; English; Japanese; Linguistics); **Namdo Provincial Culture Research** (Cultural Studies; History); **Regional Development Research** (Regional Studies); **Science Education** (Science Education); **Smaller Business Management Research** (Small Business); **Social Sciences Research** (Social Sciences)

Schools

Education *(Graduate)* (Agriculture; Biology; Computer Education; Education; English; History; Korean; Mathematics); **Graduate** (Agriculture; Business Administration; Engineering; Humanities and Social Science Education; Law; Linguistics; Modern Languages; Natural Sciences); **Industry** *(Graduate)* (Construction Engineering; Electrical and Electronic Engineering; Industrial Engineering; Mechanical Engineering)

History: Founded 1935 as Agricultural School. Acquired present status and title 1982.

Academic Year: March to February (March-August; September-February)

Admission Requirements: Graduation from high school and entrance examination

Main Language(s) of Instruction: Korean

Degrees and Diplomas: *Bachelor's Degree*: 4 yrs; *Master's Degree*: a further 2 yrs; *Doctor's Degree*

Student Services: Canteen, Employment services, Foreign Studies Centre, Health services, Language programs

Student Residential Facilities: For c. 600 students

Special Facilities: Museum. Broadcasting Station. Farms

Libraries: Central Library, c. 210,825 vols (Oriental, c. 168,200; Western, c. 45,600)

Publications: Bulletin of Information of SNU *(annually)*; Statistical Yearbook of SNU *(biannually)*; Sunchon National University Bulletin *(annually)*

Press or Publishing House: University Press. English University Press

Last Updated: 05/01/09

UNIVERSITY OF INCHEON

177 Dowha-dong, Nam-gu, Incheon-si 402-749
Tel: +82(32) 770-8114
Fax: +82(32) 762-1548
EMail: sysop@incheon.ac.kwbadmin@incheon.ac.kr
Website: http://www.incheon.ac.kr

President: Ahn Kyung Soo Tel: +82(32) 770-8001

Centres

Computer Science (Computer Science); **Foreign Languages** (Modern Languages); **Physical Education Development** (Physical Education)

Colleges

Law

Research Institutes

Basic Sciences (Natural Sciences); **Engineering Development** (Engineering); **Industrial Development** (Industrial Management); **Local Community** (Regional Studies); **National Culture** (Cultural Studies); **Peace and Unification** (Peace and Disarmament); **Sports Science** (Sports)

Schools

Art and Physical Education (Art Therapy; Physical Education); **Economics and Business Administration** (Business Administration; Economics); **Engineering** (Architecture; Civil Engineering; Computer Science; Electrical Engineering; Electronic Engineering; Engineering; Industrial Engineering; Materials Engineering; Mechanical Engineering; Safety Engineering; Telecommunications Engineering); **Humanities** (Arts and Humanities; English; French; German; Japanese; Korean; Literature; Modern Languages); **Natural Sciences** (Biology; Chemistry; Clothing and Sewing; Home Economics; Mathematics; Natural Sciences; Physics; Textile Technology); **Social Sciences** (Ethics; International Relations; Law; Political Sciences; Public Administration; Social Sciences)

History: Founded 1979 as a private Institution supervised by Sunin Academic Foundation. Became Public Institution 1994.

Academic Year: March to December (March-June; September-December)

Admission Requirements: Graduation from high school or equivalent, and entrance examination

Main Language(s) of Instruction: Korean, English

Degrees and Diplomas: *Bachelor's Degree*; *Master's Degree*; *Doctor's Degree*

Libraries: Central Library c. 130,350 vols

Publications: Collection of Papers *(annually)*

Press or Publishing House: University Publishing Centre
Last Updated: 05/01/09

UNIVERSITY OF SEOUL

90 Jeonnong-dong, Dongdaemun-gu, Seoul 130-743
Tel: +82 (2) 2210-2114
Fax: +82 (2) 2243-2572
Website: http://www.uos.ac.kr

President: Sang-Bum Lee

Provost for Academic Affairs: Kyung-Hyo Park
Tel: +82(2) 2210-2739, Fax: +82(2) 2243-2572
EMail: wbear1974@uos.ac.kr

International Relations: Jeung An Kim
Tel: +82(2) 2210-2739, Fax: +82(2) 2243-2572
EMail: jagini@uos.ac.kr

Centres
Continuing Education

Colleges
Arts (Design; Industrial Design; Music; Sculpture); **Economics and Business Administration** (Accountancy; Business Administration; Economics; Information Management); **Engineering** (Chemical Engineering; Electrical and Electronic Engineering; Engineering; Materials Engineering; Mechanical Engineering); **Humanities, Arts and Natural Sciences** (Biological and Life Sciences; Computer Science; English; Environmental Studies; History; Horticulture; Industrial Design; Korean; Mathematics; Music; Philosophy; Physics; Statistics); **Law and Public Administration** (International Relations; Law; Public Administration); **Urban Sciences** (Architecture; Civil Engineering; Environmental Engineering; Landscape Architecture; Social Welfare; Town Planning; Transport Engineering; Urban Studies)

Divisions
Liberal Arts (Arts and Humanities)

Graduate Schools
Business Administration (Business Administration); **Education** (Education); **Industrial Engineering** (Industrial Engineering); **Taxation** (Taxation); **Urban Sciences** (Telecommunications Engineering; Urban Studies)

Institutes
Humanities (Arts and Humanities); **Industrial Technology** (Industrial Engineering); **Industry and Management** (Industrial Management) *Director*: Bong Ho Shin; **Law and Public Administration** (Industrial Management; Law; Public Administration); **Quantum Information Processing and Systems** (Information Sciences; Systems Analysis); **Seoul Studies** (Regional Studies)

Schools
Graduate

History: Founded 1918 as Seoul Public Agricultural College, became Seoul City University 1974, acquired present status 1987, changed name to University of Seoul 1997.

Governing Bodies: University Committee; Faculty Association; Directorate

Academic Year: March to February (March-August, September-February)

Admission Requirements: Graduation from high school and entrance examination

Main Language(s) of Instruction: Korean

Degrees and Diplomas: *Bachelor's Degree*: 4 yrs; *Master's Degree*: a further 2 yrs; *Doctor's Degree*: a further 2 yrs and dissertation

Student Services: Academic counselling, Canteen, Cultural centre, Employment services, Foreign student adviser, Foreign Studies Centre, Handicapped facilities, Health services, Language programs, Nursery care, Social counselling, Sports facilities

Special Facilities: University Museum; Movie Studio

Libraries: Central Library, 554,895 vols

Publications: International Journal of Urban Sciences *(biannually)*

Press or Publishing House: University of Seoul Press

PRIVATE INSTITUTIONS

AJOU UNIVERSITY

San-5 Woncheon-dong, Paldal-gu, Suwon-si, Gyeonggi-do 442-749
Tel: +82(31) 219-2921
Fax: +82(31) 213-5158
Website: http://www.ajou.ac.kr

President: Moon Ho Suh (2006-)

International Relations: Jay-ick Lim
Tel: +82(31) 219-2921, Fax: +82(31) 219-2924
EMail: inter@madang.ajou.ac.kr

Centres
Automotive Technology Innovation (Automotive Engineering); **Clinical Epidemiology** (Epidemiology); **Continuing Education**; **Counselling** (Educational Administration); **Genomic Research for Gastroenterology** (Gastroenterology); **Information and Electronics** (Electronic Engineering; Information Technology); **Korea-France Cooperation** (International Relations); **Language**; **Suwon Development**; **Women Leadership**

Colleges
Business Administration (Business Administration); **Engineering** (Biochemistry; Chemical Engineering; Electrical and Electronic Engineering; Engineering; Environmental Engineering; Industrial Engineering; Mechanical Engineering; Urban Studies); **Humanities** (Arts and Humanities); **Information and Computer Engineering** (Computer Engineering; Information Technology; Media Studies); **Medicine** (Medicine); **Natural Sciences** (Natural Sciences); **Social Sciences** (Social Sciences)

Institutes
Medical Sciences; **Science for Gifted Children** (Education of the Gifted)

Research Centres
Brain Disease (Neurology); **Energy System** (Energy Engineering); **Traffic** (Road Transport)

Research Institutes
Basic Sciences (Natural Sciences); **Cooperative Industry** (Industrial and Production Economics); **Engineering** (Engineering); **Environmental Science** (Environmental Studies); **Humanities** (Arts and Humanities); **Information and Communication** (Information Sciences; Telecommunications Engineering); **Information Display**; **Management** (Management); **Social Sciences** (Social Sciences)

Further Information: Also University Hospital

History: Founded 1973.

Academic Year: March to December (March-June; September-December)

Admission Requirements: Graduation from high school or foreign equivalent

Main Language(s) of Instruction: Korean, English

Degrees and Diplomas: *Bachelor's Degree*: 4 yrs; *Master's Degree*: a further 2 yrs; *Doctor's Degree*

Student Services: Academic counselling, Canteen, Employment services, Health services, Social counselling

Special Facilities: University Museum

Libraries: Central Library, c. 585,000 vols; Medical Library, c. 19,000 vols

Press or Publishing House: Ajou University Press
Last Updated: 02/01/09

ANYANG UNIVERSITY (AYU)

708-113 Anyang 5-dong, Manan-gu, Anyang-si,
Gyeonggi-do 430-714
Tel: +82(31) 467-0700
Fax: +82(31) 448-3870
EMail: webmaster@aycc.anyang.ac.kr
Website: http://www.anyang.ac.kr

President: Seung-Tae Kim

Colleges

Humanities and Art (Arts and Humanities; Chinese; English; Korean; Preschool Education; Russian); **Music** (Music); **Science and Engineering** (Computer Graphics; Computer Science; Engineering; Environmental Engineering; Natural Sciences; Statistics; Urban Studies); **Social Sciences** (Business Administration; Public Administration; Retailing and Wholesaling; Tourism); **Theology** (Pastoral Studies; Religious Education; Theology)

History: Founded 1948, acquired present status 1995.

Academic Year: March to December (March-June; August-December)

Main Language(s) of Instruction: Korean

Accrediting Agencies: Ministry of Education

Student Services: Academic counselling, Canteen, Employment services, Nursery care, Social counselling, Sports facilities

Press or Publishing House: The University Press

A-SHIN UNIVERSITY

San 151-1 Ashin-ri, Okchun-myun, Yangpyung-kun, Yangpyeong-gun, Kyunggi-do 476-751
Tel: +82(31) 770-7700
Fax: +82(31) 772-5479
EMail: donne@acts.ac.kr.
Website: http://www.acts.ac.kr

President: Se Jin Ko

International Relations: Dong-Il Kim Tel: +82(31) 770-7801

Graduate Schools

Theology

Schools

Theology (Christian Religious Studies; Missionary Studies; Theology)

History: Founded 1982.

Main Language(s) of Instruction: Korean

Degrees and Diplomas: *Bachelor's Degree*; *Master's Degree*; *Doctor's Degree*

ASIA UNIVERSITY

240-3 Yeocheon-dong, Gyeongsan-si, Gyeongbuk-do 712-220
Tel: +82(53) 819-8138
Fax: +82(53) 815-0194
Website: http://www.asiau.ac.kr

President: Jung-wi Kim

CALVIN UNIVERSITY

142-12, Mabuk-ri, Kusung-Myun, Yongin-si, Gyeonggi-do 449-910
Tel: +82(31) 284-4752
Fax: +82(31) 284-4588
EMail: calvin@calvin.ac.kr
Website: http://www.calvin.ac.kr

President: Eui-whan Kim

International Relations: Eui-whan Kim

Programmes

Child Care and Development; **Religious Music** (Religious Music); **Theology** (Theology)

History: Founded 1997.

CATHOLIC UNIVERSITY OF DAEGU

330 Geumnak 1-ri, Hayang-eup, Gyeongsan-si, Gyeongbuk-do 712-702
Tel: +82(53) 850-3114
Fax: +82(53) 852-8030
EMail: webmaster@cu.ac.kr
Website: http://www.cu.ac.kr

President: Kyung-Don Suh

International Relations: Sang-Wook Park
Tel: +82(53) 850-3039, Fax: +82(53) 850-3900
EMail: swpark@cuth.cataegu.ac.kr

Colleges

Economics and Commerce (Business Administration; Business and Commerce; Economics; International Business); **Education** (Education; Geology; History; Physical Education); **Engineering** (Automotive Engineering; Computer Engineering; Electronic Engineering; Engineering; Mechanical Engineering; Production Engineering); **Fine Arts** (Arts and Humanities; Communication Arts; Crafts and Trades; Fine Arts; Painting and Drawing; Sculpture); **Foreign Studies** (Chinese; English; French; German; Italian; Japanese; Russian; Spanish); **Home Economics** (Child Care and Development; Clothing and Sewing; Food Science; Home Economics; Nutrition; Textile Technology); **Humanities** (Arts and Humanities; Dance; History; Korean; Literature; Philosophy; Religious Studies); **Law and Politics** (International Relations; Political Sciences; Public Administration); **Music** (Music); **Natural Sciences** (Biology; Chemistry; Crop Production; Floriculture; Food Technology; Horticulture; Landscape Architecture; Mathematics; Natural Sciences; Occupational Health; Physics; Statistics); **Pharmacy** (Pharmacy); **Social Sciences** (Library Science; Psychology; Social Sciences; Social Welfare; Sociology)

Institutes

Applied Sciences (Natural Sciences); **Catholic Education** (Catholic Theology; Religious Education); **Catholic Thought** (Catholic Theology); **Korea Environmental Sanitation** (Sanitary Engineering); **Korean Traditional Culture** (Cultural Studies); **Korean Women's Problems** (Women's Studies)

Schools

Medicine (Medicine; Nursing); **Theology** (Theology)

Further Information: Also University Hospital

History: Founded 1914 as Hyosung Women's University. Taegu Catholic College founded 1982, and the two Institutions merged 1995 to create present university.

Governing Bodies: Sun-Mok Education Foundation; Board of Trustees

Academic Year: March to December (March-June; September-December)

Main Language(s) of Instruction: Korean

Degrees and Diplomas: *Bachelor's Degree*: Arts, 4 yrs; *Master's Degree*: a further 2 yrs; *Doctor's Degree (PhD)*: a further 3 yrs

Student Services: Academic counselling, Cultural centre, Employment services, Foreign student adviser, Handicapped facilities, Nursery care, Social counselling, Sports facilities

Student Residential Facilities: Yes

Special Facilities: Museum. University Farm. University Broadcasting System

Libraries: Central Library, c. 420,000 vols

Publications: Journal of the Research Center for Korean Women's Problems Institute *(annually)*; Research Bulletin of Catholic University of Taegu-Hyosung *(annually)*; The Research for Traditional Korean Culture *(annually)*

Press or Publishing House: University Press

Last Updated: 08/07/08

CATHOLIC UNIVERSITY OF PUSAN (CUP)

9 Bugok 3-dong, Geumjeong-gu, Pusan 609-757
Tel: +82(51) 515-5811
Fax: +82(51) 514-1576
EMail: skelhide@cup.ac.kr
Website: http://www.cup.ac.kr

President: Sam Seok Son (2001-) Tel: +82(51) 510-0500

Director: Young Chan No Tel: +82(51) 510-0690

International Relations: Eun Young Lee
EMail: monica-75@hanmail.net

Colleges

Health Sciences (Dental Technology; Health Administration; Laboratory Techniques; Physical Therapy; Radiology) *Director*:

Wha Gon Kim; **Nursing** (Nursing) *Director*: Yon Son Sin; **Theology** (Catholic Theology) *Director*: Man Su Kim

Departments

Business Administration (Business Administration; E-Business/ Commerce; Information Management) *Director*: Yong Ho Kim; **Environmental System Engineering and Industrial Health** (Environmental Engineering; Safety Engineering) *Director*: Jwa Kwan Kim; **Humanities and Sociology** (Social Welfare) *Director*: Mi Young Hwang; **Information Engineering** (Communication Studies; Computer Engineering; Information Technology) *Director*: Sang Kwan Lee

History: Founded 1964 as Pusan Catholic College, merged with Jisan College. Acquired present status and title 1999.

Academic Year: March to December (March-June; September-December)

Admission Requirements: Graduation from high school

Main Language(s) of Instruction: Korean

Degrees and Diplomas: *Associate Degree*: 2 yrs; *Bachelor's Degree*: 4 yrs

Student Services: Academic counselling, Canteen, Cultural centre, Employment services, Language programs, Nursery care, Sports facilities

CHEONAN UNIVERSITY

115 Anseo-dong, Cheonan-si, Chungnam-do 330-704
Tel: +82(41) 550-9114
Fax: +82(41) 550-9113
EMail: wonhlee@cheonan.ac.kr
Website: http://www.cheonan.ac.kr

President: Jong-hyun Chang

International Relations: Won-hyuk Lee

Programmes

Child and Special Education (Preschool Education; Special Education); **International Studies** (American Studies; Chinese; International Studies; Japanese); **Languages and Literature** (Literature; Modern Languages); **Music** (Music); **Social Welfare** (Social Welfare); **Theology** (Theology); **Welfare Studies and Social Work** (Child Care and Development; Social Welfare; Social Work)

History: Founded 1993.

CHODANG UNIVERSITY

419 Seongnam-ri, Muan-eup, Muan-gun, Jeollanam-do 534-701
Tel: +82(61) 453-4960
Fax: +82(61) 453-4969
EMail: president@chodang.ac.kr
Website: http://www.chodang.ac.kr

President: Jin-yeong Noh

Divisions

Business (Business and Commerce); **Engineering** (Engineering); **General Studies**; **Liberal Arts and Humanities** (Arts and Humanities)

History: Founded 1994.

CHONGJU UNIVERSITY

36 Naedok-dong, Sangdang-gu, Chongju-si, Chungbuk-do 360-764
Tel: +82(43) 229-8114
Fax: +82(43) 229-8110
EMail: INTL@chongju.ac.kr
Website: http://www.chongju.ac.kr/english

President: Yoon Bae Kim

International Relations: Man-Kun Yoon
Tel: +82(43) 229-8814, Fax: +82(43) 229-8944
EMail: spbae@chongju.ac.kr

Colleges

Arts (Fine Arts); **Economics and Business Administration** (Business Administration; Economics); **Education** (Education); **Humanities** (Arts and Humanities; Natural Sciences); **Law** (Law; Political Sciences); **Science and Engineering** (Engineering; Natural Sciences)

History: Founded 1946.

Academic Year: March to February (March-August; September-February)

Admission Requirements: Graduation from high school and entrance examination. Provision is made for the recognition of foreign qualifications

Degrees and Diplomas: *Bachelor's Degree*; *Master's Degree*; *Doctor's Degree*

Last Updated: 02/01/09

CHONGSHIN UNIVERSITY

San 31-3 Sadang-dong, Dongjak-gu, Seoul 156-763
Tel: +82(2) 3479-0200
Fax: +82(2) 536-2602
Website: http://www.chongshin.ac.kr

President: In Whan Kim
Tel: +82(2) 3479-0201, Fax: +82(2) 537-0752
EMail: iwkim@chongshin.ac.kr

Planning Director: Sung Tae Kim
Tel: +82(2) 3479-0206, Fax: +82(2) 593-6255

International Relations: Hoon Kwak
Tel: +82(2) 3479-0217, Fax: +82(2) 593-6256
EMail: hoonkwak@chongshin.ac.kr

Departments

Child Studies *Head*: Eun Joo Kang; **Christian Education** (Christian Religious Studies; Religious Education) *Head*: Chongsook Chung; **Church Music** *Head*: Soo Yeon Kim; **Early Childhood Education** *Head*: Dong Choon Kim; **English** *Head*: Sung Hee Lee; **History** *Head*: Tae Kyung Kweon; **Social Work** *Head*: Je Seo Lee; **Theology** *Head*: Kil Sung Kim

Graduate Schools

Arts (Arts and Humanities); **Education** (Education); **Music** (Music); **Philosophy** (Philosophy); **Social Work** (Social Work); **Theology** (Theology)

History: Founded 1901, acquired present status and title 1967.

Academic Year: March to December (March-June; September-December)

Admission Requirements: Graduation from High School or equivalent. For Department of Theology recommandation of a Presbytery of Hapdong denomination. Korean examination for foreign students

Fees: (Won): University, 2,144,000 per semester; Seminary, 1,760,000

Main Language(s) of Instruction: Korean

Accrediting Agencies: Asia Theological Association (ATA); ICHE

Degrees and Diplomas: *Bachelor's Degree*: Child Studies (BA); Christian Education (BA); Church Music (BA); Early Childhood Education (BA); English (BA); History (BA); Social Work (BA); Theology (BA), 4 yrs; *Master's Degree*: Arts (MA); Education (MEd); Music (MMus); Theology (ThM), a further 2 yrs; *Master's Degree*: Social Work (MSM), a further 2 1/2 yrs; *Doctor's Degree*: Minister (DMin); Philosophy (PhD), 3 yrs following Master's Degree

Student Services: Academic counselling, Canteen, Employment services, Language programs

Student Residential Facilities: None

Libraries: c. 200,000 vols

Publications: Chongshin Review, Collected theses of professors *(annually)*; Chongshin Theological Journal, Theological theses *(biannually)*

Press or Publishing House: Chongshin University Press; Chongshin Theological Seminary Press

CHOSUN UNIVERSITY

375 Seoseok-dong, Dong-gu, Gwangju-si, Gyeonggi-do 501-759
Tel: +82(62) 230-6493
Fax: +82(62) 232-7355
EMail: shajung@chosun.ac.kr
Website: http://www.chosun.ac.kr/eng

President: Ho-Jong Jeon

International Relations: Dong-suk Yang
Tel: +82(62) 230-6097, Fax: +82(62) 232-8977

Colleges

Commerce and Economics (Business and Commerce; Economics); **Dentistry** (Dentistry); **Design** (Design); **Education** (Education); **Engineering** (Architecture; Engineering); **Foreign Languages** (Modern Languages); **Law and Political Science** (Law; Political Sciences); **Liberal Arts and Science** (Arts and Humanities; Natural Sciences); **Medical Studies** (Medicine; Nursing); **Pharmacy** (Pharmacy); **Physical Education** (Physical Education)

History: Founded 1946.

Academic Year: March to February (March to August; September-February)

Admission Requirements: Graduation from high school and entrance examination

Main Language(s) of Instruction: Korean

Degrees and Diplomas: *Bachelor's Degree*: 4 yrs; *Bachelor's Degree*: Medicine, 6 yrs; *Master's Degree*: a further 2 yrs; *Doctor's Degree*: 3-4 yrs following Master

Student Residential Facilities: Yes

Libraries: c. 400,000 vols

Publications: Cho Dae Hag Bo; Cho Dae Shin Moon; Chong-Hap Theses Collection; Chosun World (English); Maek; Ye-dae Shin Moon

Last Updated: 02/01/09

CHUGYE UNIVERSITY FOR THE ARTS

190-1 Bukahyeon-dong, Seodaemun-gu, Seoul 120-763
Tel: +82(2) 362-7214
Fax: +82(2) 392-1777
EMail: chugye@chugye.ac.kr
Website: http://www.chugye.ac.kr

President: Sang-Hyok Yim

International Relations: H.S. Lyoo
Tel: +82(2) 362-5900, Fax: +82(2) 392-1777

Colleges

Fine Arts (Painting and Drawing; Printing and Printmaking); **Literature** (Writing); **Music** (Music; Music Theory and Composition; Musical Instruments; Singing)

Graduate Schools

Art Management (Art Management)

History: Founded 1973.

Degrees and Diplomas: *Bachelor's Degree*; *Master's Degree*

Last Updated: 02/01/09

CHUNG-ANG UNIVERSITY

221 Heukseok-dong, Dongjak-gu, Seoul 156-756
Tel: +82(2) 820-6124
Fax: +82(2) 813-8069
EMail: interedu@cau.ac.kr
Website: http://www.cau.ac.kr/english/

President: Bum-Hoon Park

International Relations: Young Chan Kim, Director, Office of External Cooperation
Tel: +82(2) 820-6122, Fax: +82(2) 813-8069
EMail: youngcha@cau.ac.kr

Centres

Chung-Ang Research; **Computer Science** (Computer Science); **Industrial and Academic Cooperation** *Head*: Kwee-Bo Sim

Colleges

Art (Acting; Cinema and Television; Dance; Handicrafts; Industrial Design; Painting and Drawing; Photography; Sculpture; Theatre; Writing) *Head*: Tea Joon Kam; **Business Administration** (Accountancy; Business Administration; International Business) *Head*: Jee Hin Kang; **Construction Engineering** (Architecture; Construction Engineering) *Head*: Sei Kwan Sohn; **Education** (Education; Home Economics; Physical Education) *Head*: Hyung Heo; **Engineering** (Chemical Engineering; Civil Engineering; Computer Science; Electrical Engineering; Electronic Engineering; Engineering; Mechanical Engineering) *Head*: Ho Jung Hwang; **Foreign Languages** (Chinese; English; French; German; Japanese; Modern Languages; Russian) *Head*: Jum Chool Lee; **Human Ecology** (Dietetics; Family Studies; Home Economics; Nutrition; Town Planning) *Head*: Sham Ho Chung; **Industrial Studies** (Animal Husbandry; Bioengineering; Food Technology; Horticulture; Industrial Management; Regional Planning) *Head*: Jae Wan Hur; **Korean Music** (Acting; Dance; Music; Music Theory and Composition; Musical Instruments; Musicology; Singing) *Head*: In Pyong Chun; **Law** (Law) *Head*: Joong Ho Lim; **Liberal Arts** (Arts and Humanities; English; French; German; History; Information Sciences; Japanese; Korean; Library Science; Philosophy; Psychology; Social Welfare) *Head*: Young Keun Park; **Medicine** (Medicine; Nursing) *Head*: Won Bok Lee; **Music** *Head*: Duk Sung Na; **Natural Sciences** (Biological and Life Sciences; Chemistry; Mathematics; Physics; Statistics) *Head*: Kyong Shine Koh; **Pharmacy** (Pharmacy) *Head*: Young Wook Choi; **Political Science and Economics** (Advertising and Publicity; Economics; Journalism; Political Sciences; Public Relations; Radio and Television Broadcasting; Statistics) *Head*: Dae Sik Kim; **Social Sciences** (Business Administration; Economics; International Business; Public Administration; Social Sciences) *Head*: Wan Kyu Park

Institutes

Advertising and Public Relations (Advertising and Publicity; Public Relations) *Head*: Myoung Chun Lee; **Arts** (Arts and Humanities) *Head*: Tae Joon Kam; **Australian Studies** (Pacific Area Studies) *Head*: Hoon Jaung; **Basic Sciences** (Natural Sciences) *Head*: In Hwan Choi; **Communication** (Communication Studies); **Cultural Studies of Korea and Japan** *(Chung-Ang) Head*: Jeon Yull Park; **Economics Research** (Economics) *Head*: Kyttack Hong; **Environmental Science and Construction** (Environmental Studies) *Head*: Kwoo Hong Park; **Family Life** (Family Studies) *Head*: Young Chun Lee; **Food Resource** (Food Science; Natural Resources) *Head*: Young Chun Lee; **Foreign Studies** (Literature; Modern Languages) *Head*: Jeoung Dong Bin; **Frontier Technology Innovation** (Mathematics and Computer Science; Technology) *Head*: Hong Sun Ryou; **Genetic Engineering** (Genetics) *Head*: Young Ho Yoon; **Humanities Ecology** *Head*: Kyong Hee Ree; **Humanities** (Arts and Humanities) *Head*: Chung Ho Chung; **Industrial Construction Technology** (Construction Engineering) *Head*: Chan Sik Park; **Industrial Design** *Head*: Jea Kook Ryu; **Industrial Management** (Industrial Management) *Head*: Kung Chun Jang; **Industrial Management Research** (Industrial Management) *Head*: Bong Han Yoon; **International Studies** *Head*: Yul Sohn; **Japanese Studies** (Japanese) *Head*: Jeon Yull Park; **Korean Cultural Heritage** (Folklore) *Head*: Sun Poong Kim; **Korean Education** *Dean*: Il Young Lee; **Korean Folklore** *Head*: Joong Dal Kwon; **Korean Germany Cultural Studies** *Head*: Young Uhn Chun; **Legal Research** (Law) *Head*: Hun Je Suh; **Medical Science** (Health Sciences) *Head*: Shin Yung Kang; **Music** *(Chung-Ang) Head*: In Sun Cho; **Nursing Science Research** (Music) *Head*: Hye Jin Kown; **Pharmaceutical Science** (Pharmacy) *Head*: Uy Dong Sohn; **Public Policy and Administration** (Public Administration) *Head*: Kyu Hwan Lee; **Social Sciences** *Head*: Young Sik Lim; **Sports Sciences Research** *Head*: Suk in Lee; **Statistical Studies** (Statistics) *Head*: Heayoung Shin; **Technology and Science** *Head*: Hyun Ryul Park; **Third World Studies** (Development Studies)

Research Institutes

Biomedical and Pharmaceutical Sciences (Biomedicine; Pharmacy) *Head*: Chul Bu Yim

Further Information: Also 2 Teaching Hospitals

History: Founded 1918 as Normal College for Women, became Chungoang (Central) Women's College 1945, co-educational 1948. Accredited with University status by Ministry of Education 1953 as private, non-denominational Institution. Financed by tuition fees and donations.

Governing Bodies: Board of Trustees

Academic Year: March to February (March-June; September-February)

Admission Requirements: Graduation from high school or foreign equivalent, and entrance examination

Main Language(s) of Instruction: Korean

Degrees and Diplomas: *Bachelor's Degree*: 4 yrs; *Bachelor's Degree*: Medicine, 6 yrs; *Master's Degree*: a further 2 yrs; *Doctor's Degree*: 3 yrs

Student Residential Facilities: For c. 2,080 students

Special Facilities: Theatre. Folk Art Museum. Experimental Farm

Libraries: Central Library c. 460,000 vols; Ansung Campus, c. 120,000

Publications: Journal (Arts) *(annually)*; Journal (Humanities) *(annually)*; Journal (Legal Studies) *(annually)*; Journal (Management Research) *(annually)*; Journal (Medical Science) *(annually)*; Journal (Technology and Science) *(annually)*

Press or Publishing House: The Publishing Department; Chung-Ang Research Centre

CHUNGWOON UNIVERSITY

San 29 Namjang-ri, Hongseong-eup, Hongseong-gun, Chungnam-do 350-701
Tel: +82(41) 630-3122
Fax: +82(41) 634-8760
EMail: admin@chungwoon.ac.kr
Website: http://www.chungwoon.ac.kr

President: Li Hyung Lee

Divisions

Broadcasting and Digital Imaging (Radio and Television Broadcasting); **Engineering and Natural Sciences** (Engineering; Natural Sciences); **Fine Arts**; **Humanities and Social Sciences** (Arts and Humanities; Social Sciences)

History: Founded 1994.

Degrees and Diplomas: *Bachelor's Degree*; *Master's Degree*
Last Updated: 02/01/09

COLLEGE OF MEDICINE, POCHON CHA UNIVERSITY

198-1 Donggyo-ri, Pochon-eup, Pocheon-si, Gyeonggi-do 487-800
Tel: +82(31) 543-2111
Fax: +82(31) 543-2716
Website: http://www.cha.ac.kr

President: Byung-su Kim (2002 -)
Tel: +82(31) 541-2151, Fax: +82(31) 725-8209
EMail: kbschadr@empal.com

Administrative Officer: Lee Yong-Ho
Tel: +82(31) 541-2151 EMail: Yhlee0219@cha.ac.kr

Colleges

Medicine (Medicine)

Divisions

Nursing (Nursing); **Public Health** (Public Health)

Graduate Schools

Alternative Complementary Medicine (Alternative Medicine); **Life Sciences** (Biological and Life Sciences); **Public Health** (Public Health)

History: Founded 1997.

Admission Requirements: Bachelor Degree

Main Language(s) of Instruction: Korean, English

International Co-operation: With universities in USA

Accrediting Agencies: Ministry of Education and Human Resources Development

Degrees and Diplomas: *Doctor's Degree*: Medicine (MD), 4 yrs

Student Services: Academic counselling, Employment services, Foreign student adviser, Handicapped facilities, Health services, Language programs, Social counselling, Sports facilities

Student Residential Facilities: Yes

Libraries: Yes

Publications: University and Hospital Journal *(monthly)*

DAEBUL UNIVERSITY

72 Sanho-ri, Samho-eup, Youngam-si, Chonnam-do 526-702
Tel: +82(61) 469-1114
Fax: +82(61) 469-2510
EMail: webmaster@mail.daebul.ac.kr
Website: http://www.daebul.ac.kr

President: Kyung-soo Lee

International Relations: Hyong-man Kim
Tel: +82(61) 469-1202, Fax: +82(61) 462-2510

Departments

Architecture (Architecture); **Business Administration** (Business Administration); **Chemical Engineering** (Chemical Engineering); **Computer Engineering** (Computer Engineering); **Computer Science** (Computer Science); **Electrical Engineering** (Electrical Engineering); **Electronic Engineering** (Electronic Engineering); **Industrial Design** (Industrial Design); **Industrial Engineering** (Industrial Engineering); **Physics** (Physics)

Institutes

Environmental Research (Environmental Studies); **Industrial Technology** (Industrial Engineering); **Regional Development** (Regional Planning); **Study on Korea and China Academic Exchanges**

History: Founded 1994.

DAEGU ARTS UNIVERSITY

117-6 Tabu-ri, Kasan-myeon, Chilgokgoon-si, Gyeongbuk-do 718-912
Tel: +82(54) 973-5311
Fax: +82(54) 973-5319
EMail: ssw09@news.tau.ac.kr
Website: http://www.tau.ac.kr

President: Seong-Keun Rhee
Tel: +82(54) 970-3101, Fax: +82(54) 973-5321
EMail: skrhee@news.tau.ac.kr

International Relations: Soon-Hyun Lee
Tel: +82(54) 970-3146 EMail: shlee3146@hanmail.net

Departments

Design; **Film and Acting** (Film; Photography; Radio and Television Broadcasting); **Fine Arts** (Fine Arts; Painting and Drawing); **Performing Music**; **Physical Education and Martial Arts**; **Social Affairs** (Business Administration; Social Policy; Tourism)

History: Founded 1997. Acquired present status 2006.

Admission Requirements: Secondary School Certificate

Fees: (Wons): 3.5m.

Main Language(s) of Instruction: Korean

Accrediting Agencies: Ministry of Education and Human Resources Development

Degrees and Diplomas: *Bachelor's Degree*: 4 yrs

Student Services: Academic counselling, Canteen, Health services, Nursery care, Sports facilities

Student Residential Facilities: Yes

Libraries: Yes

DAEGU HAANY UNIVERSITY

290 Yugok-dong, Gyeongsan-si, Gyeongbuk-do 712-715
Tel: +82(53) 813-5555
Fax: +82(53) 819-1258
EMail: webadmin@dhu.ac.kr
Website: http://www.dhu.ac.kr

President: Byung-chung Hwang

Colleges

Architecture and Design; **Business and Information**; **Cultural Sciences**; **Health and Welfare**; **Oriental Medicine** (Nursing; Traditional Eastern Medicine)

Faculties

Liberal Arts

History: Founded 1981 as Kyungsan University. Acquired present title 2004.

Degrees and Diplomas: *Bachelor's Degree*; *Master's Degree*; *Doctor's Degree*

DAEGU UNIVERSITY

Campus Jinryang, Gyeongsan-si, Gyeongbuk-do 712-714
Tel: +82(53) 850-5000
Fax: +82(53) 850-5009
EMail: dia@daegu.ac.kr
Website: http://www.daegu.ac.kr

President: Jae-Kyoo Lee EMail: president@daegu.ac.kr

International Relations: Doo-sub Cho
Tel: +82(53) 850-5682, Fax: +82(53) 850-5689

Colleges

Arts and Design (Design; Fashion Design; Fine Arts; House Arts and Environment; Interior Design); **Education** (Environmental Studies; Korean; Mathematics Education; Preschool Education; Science Education; Social Studies; Special Education); **Engineering** (Architecture; Automation and Control Engineering; Bioengineering; Chemical Engineering; Civil Engineering; Computer Engineering; Engineering; Environmental Engineering); **Humanities** (Arts and Humanities; Chinese; English; French; Health Sciences; Japanese; Korean; Literature; Physical Education; Russian; Sports); **Law**; **Natural Resources** (Biological and Life Sciences; Environmental Studies; Horticulture; Landscape Architecture; Natural Resources); **Public Administration** (Public Administration); **Rehabilitation Sciences** (Rehabilitation and Therapy)

Divisions

Public Health (Public Health)

Further Information: Also Graduate Schools and Research Institutes

History: Founded 1956.

Degrees and Diplomas: *Bachelor's Degree*; *Master's Degree*; *Doctor's Degree*

Last Updated: 02/01/09

DAEGU UNIVERSITY OF FOREIGN STUDIES (DUFS)

28-1 Hyeopsuk-ri Namcheon-myeon, Gyeongsan-si, Gyeongbuk-do 712-702
Tel: +82(53) 810-7000
Fax: +82(53) 810-7019
EMail: webmaster@dufs.ac.kr
Website: http://www.dufs.ac.kr/

DAEJEON UNIVERSITY

96-3 Yongun-dong, Dong-gu, Daejeon, Chungnam-do 300-716
Tel: +82(42) 280-2125
Fax: +82(42) 272-8533
EMail: contact@dju.ac.kr
Website: http://www.dju.ac.kr

President: Kuk-Bom Shin

International Relations: Hyon-kun Kwak
Tel: +82(42) 280-2125, Fax: +82(42) 272-8533

Colleges

Engineering (Architecture; Civil Engineering; Computer Engineering; Earth Sciences; Electronic Engineering; Environmental Engineering; Geology; Information Technology); **Law and Economics** (Accountancy; Business Administration; Business and Commerce; Economics; Industrial and Organizational Psychology; International Business; International Relations; Law; Political Sciences; Public Administration; Social Sciences; Social Welfare); **Liberal Arts** (Chinese; Communication Arts; English; Fine Arts; History; Japanese; Korean; Literature; Philosophy; Russian); **Natural Sciences** (Biological and Life Sciences; Chemistry; Dance; Fashion Design; Food Science; Leisure Studies; Mathematics; Natural Sciences; Nutrition; Physics; Sports; Statistics); **Oriental Medicine** (Acupuncture; Medicine; Nursing; Physical Therapy)

Graduate Schools

Graduate Studies; **Industrial Information**; **Public and Business Administration** (Business Administration; Social Welfare); **Public Health** (Health Administration; Public Health; Sports Medicine; Welfare and Protective Services)

History: Founded 1980.

Degrees and Diplomas: *Bachelor's Degree*; *Master's Degree*; *Doctor's Degree*

DAEJIN UNIVERSITY

San 11-1, Sundan-dong, Pocheon-si, Gyeonggi-do 487-711
Tel: +82(31) 539-1114
Fax: +82(31) 539-1115
EMail: kihyung@daejin.ac.kr
Website: http://www.daejin.ac.kr

President: Chunsoo Lee

Colleges

Arts; **Humanities** (English; History; Information Sciences; Korean; Library Science; Literature; Philosophy; Religious Studies; Writing); **Science and Engineering**; **Social Sciences**

Further Information: Also Graduate Schools and Research Institutes

History: Founded 1991.

Main Language(s) of Instruction: Korean

Degrees and Diplomas: *Bachelor's Degree*; *Master's Degree*; *Doctor's Degree*

Last Updated: 02/01/09

DANKOOK UNIVERSITY

San 8 Hannam-dong, Yongsan-gu, Seoul 140-714
Tel: +82(2) 709-2114
Fax: +82(2) 790-2782
Website: http://www.dankook.ac.kr

President: Hosung Chang

Divisions

Architectural Engineering; **Arts and Crafts** (Ceramic Art; Film; Industrial Design; Theatre; Visual Arts); **Business and Economics** (Business Administration; Economics); **Education** (Education; Mathematics Education; Physical Education; Science Education; Special Education); **Engineering** (Engineering); **Humanities** (Arts and Humanities; Chinese; English; German; History; Japanese; Korean); **Music**; **Natural Sciences**; **Social Sciences**

Graduate Schools

Drama (Theatre); **Education** (Agriculture; Biology; Business and Commerce; Chemistry; Chinese; Computer Education; Continuing Education; Education; Educational Administration; Electrical and Electronic Engineering; Ethics; Fine Arts; German; History; Japanese; Korean; Mathematics; Music; Physical Education; Physics; Preschool Education; Social Studies; Spanish); **Industrial Design**; **Industrial Information** (Production Engineering); **Industry and Business Management**; **Law and Public Administration** (Administration; Finance; Government; Health Administration; Insurance; International Relations; Labour Law; Law; Social Welfare); **Multimedia** (Computer Engineering; Data Processing; Multimedia; Radio and Television Broadcasting; Telecommunications Engineering); **Policy and Business Administration** (Business Administration; Economics; Health Administration; Law; Public Administration; Social Welfare); **Special Education** (Education; Special Education; Speech Therapy and Audiology); **Sports Science** (Sports)

Institutes

Biological Resources and Environment; **Biomedical Engineering** (Biomedical Engineering); **Ceramic Arts** (Ceramic Art); **Culture Behaviour and Economics** (Economics); **Curricula and Education** (Curriculum; Education); **Excavated Relics** (Archaeology); **Industrial Reseach**; **Industrial Technology** (Technology); **Law** (Law); **Medical Laser Technology** (Laser Engineering); **Multimedia and Industrial Technology**; **New Materials Technology**; **Oriental Studies** (Asian Studies; Middle Eastern Studies; Oriental Languages); **Public Policy and Science** (Public Administration); **Regional Development**

Research Centres

Gastroenterology; **Special Education**

Further Information: Also Cheonam Campus

History: Founded 1947.

Governing Bodies: Board of Trustees

Academic Year: March to February (March-August; September-February)

Admission Requirements: Graduation from high school and entrance examination

Main Language(s) of Instruction: Korean

Degrees and Diplomas: *Bachelor's Degree*: 4 yrs; *Master's Degree*: a further 2 1/2 yrs; *Doctor's Degree*: 3 yrs following Master

Special Facilities: Central Museum. Suk Ju-son Folk Arts Museum

Libraries: Central Library, c. 205,000 vols; Cheonan Campus library, c. 5,500; Oriental Studies library, c. 105

Publications: Business Studies; Commerce and Economics Review; Dongyang Hak; Essays on Korean Language and Literature; Historical Journal; Home Economic Studies; Journal of Industrial Studies; Law Review; The China Quarterly

Press or Publishing House: University Press

Last Updated: 02/01/09

DONG-A UNIVERSITY

Saha-gu Hadan 2-dong 840, Saha-gu, Pusan 604-714
Tel: +82(51) 200-6442
Fax: +82(51) 200-6445
EMail: President@donga.ac.kr
Website: http://www.donga.ac.kr

President: Kyoo-Hyang Cho

Centres

Population Research (Demography and Population)

Colleges

Agriculture (Agriculture); **Arts** (Arts and Humanities; Fine Arts; Industrial Design; Music; Sculpture); **Business Administration** (Accountancy; Business Administration; International Business; Management Systems; Statistics; Tourism); **Engineering** (Chemical Engineering; Civil Engineering; Computer Engineering; Electrical Engineering; Electronic Engineering; Engineering; Environmental Engineering; Industrial Engineering; Marine Engineering; Mechanical Engineering; Metallurgical Engineering; Mining Engineering; Structural Architecture; Town Planning); **Human Ecology** (Clothing and Sewing; Ecology; Food Science; Home Economics; Nutrition; Textile Technology); **Humanities** (Archaeology; Art History; Arts and Humanities; Chinese; Education; English; Ethics; French; German; History; Japanese; Korean; Modern Languages; Philosophy; Psychology); **Law** (Law); **Medicine** (Medicine); **Natural Sciences** (Natural Sciences); **Physical Education** (Physical Education); **Social Sciences** (Communication Studies; Economics; Public Administration; Social Sciences; Sociology)

Graduate Schools

Business Administration (Business Administration); **Education** (Education); **Industry** (Architecture; Chemical Engineering; Communication Studies; Computer Engineering; Construction Engineering; Electrical and Electronic Engineering; Environmental Engineering; Environmental Management; Industrial Engineering; Mechanical Engineering; Metallurgical Engineering; Telecommunications Engineering); **Mass Communication** (Mass Communication)

Institutes

Data Communication (Data Processing); **German Studies** (German); **Human Ecology** (Ecology); **Korean Resources Development**; **Study of Law** (Law)

Research Centres

Industrial Technology (Industrial Engineering)

Research Institutes

Agricultural Resources (Agriculture); **Basic Science** (Natural Sciences); **Business Management** (Management); **Clinical Medicine** (Medicine); **Environmental** (Environmental Studies); **Genetic Engineering** (Genetics); **Humanities** (Arts and Humanities); **Industrial Medicine** (Medicine); **Korean Culture** *(Sokdang)* (Cultural Studies); **Language** (Linguistics); **Life Sciences** (Biological and Life Sciences); **Ocean Resources** (Marine Science and Oceanography; Natural Resources); **Plastic Arts** (Fine Arts); **Social Sciences** (Social Sciences); **Sports Science** (Sports); **Tourism and Leisure** (Leisure Studies; Tourism)

Further Information: Also University Hospital

History: Founded as College 1946, became University 1959.

Governing Bodies: Board of Directors

Academic Year: March to February (March-August; September-February)

Admission Requirements: Graduation from high school or equivalent, and entrance examination

Main Language(s) of Instruction: Korean

Degrees and Diplomas: *Bachelor's Degree*: 4 yrs; *Master's Degree*: a further 2 yrs; *Doctor's Degree*: 2 yrs following Master

Student Residential Facilities: For c. 150 students

Special Facilities: University Museum (Collections from Chosan Dynasty); Broadcasting System

Libraries: Central Library, c. 590,130 vols

Publications: Journal of Agriculture; Journal of Engineering; Journal of Law and Economics

Press or Publishing House: University Press

Last Updated: 02/01/09

DONGDUK WOMEN'S UNIVERSITY

23-1 Wolgok-dong, Seongbuk-gu, Seoul 136-714
Tel: +82(2) 940-4062
Fax: +82(2) 940-4182
EMail: master@dongduk.ac.kr
Website: http://www.dongduk.ac.kr

President: Yang-hee Lee

Centres

Computer Science (Computer Science); **Environmental Health Research** (Health Sciences); **Industrial Design Research** (Industrial Design)

Colleges

Art (Arts and Humanities; Fine Arts; Industrial Design; Music); **Humanities** (Arts and Humanities; English; French; German; History; Japanese; Korean; Modern Languages); **Natural Sciences** (Child Care and Development; Computer Science; Food Science; Health Sciences; Home Economics; Natural Sciences; Nutrition; Pharmacy; Physical Education); **Pharmacy** (Pharmacy); **Social Sciences** (Business Administration; Economics; International Business; Library Science; Social Sciences)

Departments

General Studies and Teaching (Teacher Training)

Institutes

Business Administration (Business Administration); **Korean Studies** (Korean; Modern Languages); **Natural Drugs Research**

History: Founded 1950.

Governing Bodies: Board of Trustees

Academic Year: March to February (March-August; September-February)

Admission Requirements: Graduation from high school and entrance examination

Main Language(s) of Instruction: Korean

Degrees and Diplomas: *Bachelor's Degree*: 4 yrs; *Master's Degree*: a further 2 yrs; *Doctor's Degree*: a further 3 yrs

Special Facilities: Dongduck Women's Museum

Libraries: Choonkang Memorial Library, c. 110,000 vols

Publications: Journal of Korean Studies; Treaties *(annually)*

Press or Publishing House: Dongduk Women's University Press

DONG-EUI UNIVERSITY

995 Eomguangno, Pusanjin-ku, Pusan 614-714
Tel: +82(51) 890-1114
Fax: +82(51) 890-1234
Website: http://www.deu.ac.kr

President: Chang-Seok Kang EMail: cskang@deu.ac.kr

Centres

American Studies (American Studies); **Bio-Production Research**; **Local Government Research** (Government); **Medicine** (Medicine); **Unification Research**

Colleges

Commerce and Economics (Accountancy; Business Administration; Business and Commerce; Economics; International Business; Management); **Engineering** (Chemical Engineering; Civil Engineering; Communication Studies; Computer Science; Electrical and Electronic Engineering; Engineering; Industrial Engineering; Materials Engineering; Mechanical Engineering; Structural Architecture; Town Planning); **Human Ecology** (Clothing and Sewing; Ecology; Food Science; Household Management; Nutrition; Textile Technology); **Humanities** (Arts and Humanities; English; Ethnology; French; German; History; Information Sciences; Journalism; Korean; Library Science; Philosophy; Radio and Television Broadcasting); **Law and Political Science** (International Relations; Law; Political Sciences; Public Administration); **Natural Sciences** (Biology; Chemistry; Mathematics and Computer Science; Microbiology; Natural Sciences; Nursing; Physics; Statistics); **Oriental Medicine** (Traditional Eastern Medicine)

Graduate Schools

Arts (Fine Arts; Industrial Design; Music; Physical Education); **Industrial Technology** (Industrial Engineering); **Public Administration** (Government; Information Management; Law; Police Studies; Public Administration; Real Estate); **Small and Medium Business** (Business and Commerce; Small Business)

History: Founded 1976 by the Dong Eui Foundation. A private Institution financed by tuition fees (80%) and the Foundation.

Governing Bodies: Board of Trustees

Academic Year: March to February (March-July; September-December)

Admission Requirements: Graduation from high school or foreign equivalent, and entrance examination

Main Language(s) of Instruction: Korean

Degrees and Diplomas: *Bachelor's Degree*: 4 yrs; *Master's Degree*: a further 2-3 yrs; *Doctor's Degree (PhD)*: a further 3-4 yrs

Special Facilities: Museum. Broadcasting Station

Libraries: Central Library, c. 340,000 vols

Last Updated: 02/01/09

DONGGUK UNIVERSITY

3-26 Pil-dong, Jung-gu, Seoul 100-715
Tel: +82(2) 2260-3114
Fax: +82(2) 2277-1274
EMail: iie@dongguk.edu
Website: http://www.dongguk.edu/

President: Ki-sam Hong

Centres

Computer Science (Computer Science); **Dhyana** (Asian Religious Studies)

Colleges

Arts; **Buddhist Culture** *(Gyeongju)* (Asian Religious Studies); **Buddhist Studies** (Asian Religious Studies); **Business Administration** (Business Administration); **Economics and Commerce** *(Gyeongju)* (Business and Commerce; Economics); **Education** (Education); **Engineering** (Engineering); **Humanities** *(Gyeongju)*; **Law** (Law); **Law and Political Science** *(Gyeongju)* (Law; Political Sciences); **Liberal Arts** (Arts and Humanities); **Life Resource Science** (Biological and Life Sciences; Food Science; Forestry; Plant and Crop Protection); **Medicine** *(Gyeongju)*; **Natural Sciences** *(Gyeongju)* (Natural Sciences); **Oriental Medicine** *(Gyeongju)* (Acupuncture; Traditional Eastern Medicine); **Science**; **Social Sciences** (Social Sciences); **Tourism** *(Gyeongju)* (Tourism)

Graduate Schools

Business Administration (Business Administration); **Education** (Education); **Public Administration** (Public Administration)

Institutes

Buddhist Research (Asian Religious Studies); **National Security Research**

History: Founded 1906 as Myong Zin School, became Choong Ang Buddhist College 1930, Hye Wha College 1940, Dongguk College 1946. Acquired present title and status 1953.

Governing Bodies: Board of Trustees

Academic Year: March to February (March-July; September-December)

Admission Requirements: Graduation from high school or recognized foreign equivalent, and entrance examination

Main Language(s) of Instruction: Korean

Degrees and Diplomas: *Bachelor's Degree*: 4 yrs; *Master's Degree*: a further 2 yrs; *Doctor's Degree*: 3 yrs following Master

Student Residential Facilities: Yes

Special Facilities: University Museum

Libraries: Central Library, c. 360,000 vols

Publications: Bulgyo Hakpo (Buddhist Studies); Dongguk Munhak (Korean Literature); Dongguk Sasang (Buddhist Philosophy); Tripitaka Korean

DONGSEO UNIVERSITY

San 69-1, Churye-2 dong, Sasang-gu, Pusan 617-716
Tel: +82(51) 320-2092 +82(51) 320-2093
Fax: +82(51) 320-2094
EMail: anna1974@dongseo.ac.kr
Website: http://www.dongseo.ac.kr/en_dsull

President: Dong Soon Park

International Relations: Jeong-Hee Kim
Tel: +82(51) 320-2092, Fax: +82(51) 312-2094

Centres

Computer Science (Computer Science); **Continuing Education**

Colleges

Arts (Arts and Humanities); **Engineering** (Engineering); **Natural Sciences** (Natural Sciences)

Graduate Schools

Biotechnology (Biotechnology); **Fashion Design** (Fashion Design); **Management Information** (Management)

Institutes

Industry and Technology Development (Industrial Engineering; Technology)

History: Founded 1992.

Degrees and Diplomas: *Bachelor's Degree*; *Master's Degree*; *Doctor's Degree*

Last Updated: 02/01/09

DONGSHIN UNIVERSITY

252 Daeho-dong, Naju-si, Jeollanam-do 520-714
Tel: +82(61) 330-3018
Fax: +82(61) 330-3019
EMail: wow8001@daum.net
Website: http://www.dsu.ac.kr

President: Kyum-bum Lee

International Relations: Jung-chul Han
Tel: +82(61) 330-3010, Fax: +82(61) 330-3019

Colleges

Architecture (Architecture); **Chinese Language and Literature** (Chinese); **Civil Environmental Engineering** (Civil Engineering); **Clothing** (Clothing and Sewing; Textile Technology); **Communication** (Communication Studies); **Computer Science and Statistics** (Computer Science; Statistics); **Economics** (Economics); **Electrical and Electronic Engineering** (Electrical and Electronic Engineering); **English Language and Literature** (English; Modern Languages); **Environmental Engineering** (Environmental Engineering); **Food and Nutrition** (Food Science; Nutrition); **Industrial Engineering** (Industrial Engineering); **Information and Communication Engineering** (Information Technology; Telecommunications Engineering); **Inorganic Materials Engineering** (Materials Engineering); **Japanese Language and Literature** (Japanese; Modern Languages); **Korean Language and Literature** (Korean; Modern Languages); **Landscape Architecture** (Landscape Architecture); **Law** (Law); **Local Administration** (Administration);

Management Information Systems (Management Systems); **Mathematics** (Mathematics); **Oriental Medicine** (Traditional Eastern Medicine); **Physical Education** (Physical Education); **Physics** (Physics); **Preparatory Course for Oriental Medicine** (Traditional Eastern Medicine); **Social Welfare** (Social Welfare; Welfare and Protective Services); **Urban Planning** (Town Planning)

Institutes

Basic Sciences (Natural Sciences); **Humanities Research** (Arts and Humanities); **Industrial Research and Technology** (Technology); **Regional Development** (Regional Planning)

History: Founded 1987.

Academic Year: March to February (March-August; September-February)

Degrees and Diplomas: *Bachelor's Degree*: 4 yrs; *Master's Degree*: a further 2 yrs

Libraries: Central Library, c. 171,000 vols

Press or Publishing House: Dongshin University Press

DONGYANG UNIVERSITY

1 Kyochon-dong, Punggi-eup, Yeongju-si, Gyeongbuk-do 750-711
Tel: +82(54) 630-1248 +82(54) 6301029
Fax: +82(54) 636-1249 +82(54) 636-8523
EMail: wwwadmin@dyu.ac.kr
Website: http://www.dyu.ac.kr

President: Sung-Hae Choi

International Relations: Kyeong-Take Cheong
Tel: +82(54) 630-1248, Fax: +82(54) 630-1249
EMail: ktcheong@phenix.dyu.ac.kr

Colleges

Human and Social Sciences (Administration; Fashion Design; Graphic Design; Management); **Science and Engineering** (Architecture; Automation and Control Engineering; Chemical Engineering; Civil Engineering; Computer Engineering; Design; Electronic Engineering; Industrial Engineering; Information Technology; Interior Design; Mechanical Engineering; Systems Analysis)

Institutes

Computer Graphic Design (Computer Graphics); **Industrial Information Science and Technology** (Information Sciences; Technology); **Regional Development** (Regional Planning)

Schools

Public Administration (Public Administration)

History: Founded 1994.

Academic Year: March to December (March-June; July-December)

Main Language(s) of Instruction: Korean, English, Japanese

Degrees and Diplomas: *Bachelor's Degree*: 4 yrs

Student Services: Academic counselling, Canteen, Cultural centre, Employment services, Foreign student adviser, Handicapped facilities, Health services, Social counselling, Sports facilities

Student Residential Facilities: For c. 2,500 students

Libraries: Central Library

Publications: Dongyang University News

Press or Publishing House: Dongyang University Press

DUKSUNG WOMEN'S UNIVERSITY

419, Ssangmun-dong, Dobong-gu, Seoul 132-714
Tel: +82(2) 901-8114
Fax: +82(2) 901-8060
EMail: intl@duksung.ac.kr
Website: http://www.duksung.ac.kr

President: Eun Hee Chi

Colleges

Fine Arts (Fine Arts); **Humanities** (Arts and Humanities); **Natural Sciences** (Food Technology; Home Economics; Natural Sciences); **Pharmacy** (Pharmacy); **Social Sciences** (Business Administration; Library Science; Social Sciences)

History: Founded 1950.

Academic Year: March to February (March-August; September-February)

Admission Requirements: Graduation from high school or foreign equivalent, and entrance examination

Main Language(s) of Instruction: Korean

Degrees and Diplomas: *Bachelor's Degree*: 4 yrs; *Master's Degree*: a further 2 yrs; *Doctor's Degree*. Also Teaching Certificate

Libraries: c. 120,000 vols

Publications: Journal of Professors' Research *(annually)*

Last Updated: 02/01/09

EULJI UNIVERSITY

143-5 Yongdu-dong, Jung-gu, Daejeon, Chungnam-do 301-832
Tel: +82(42) 259-1701 +82(42) 259-1702
Fax: +82(42) 259-1047
Website: http://www.eulji.ac.kr

President: Joon-young Park

Programmes

Medicine (Endocrinology; Medicine; Neurology; Rheumatology; Surgery)

History: Founded 1997.

Degrees and Diplomas: *Bachelor's Degree*; *Master's Degree*

Last Updated: 02/01/09

EWHA WOMEN'S UNIVERSITY

11-1 Daehyun-dong, Seodaemun-gu, Seoul 120-750
Tel: +82(2) 3277-2114
Fax: +82(2) 393-5903
EMail: president@ewha.ac.kr
Website: http://www.ewha.ac.kr

President: Bae Yong Lee
Tel: +82(2) 3277-2746, Fax: +82(2) 364-6043

Colleges

Arts and Design (Ceramic Art; Design; Fashion Design; Fine Arts; Industrial Design; Painting and Drawing; Printing and Printmaking; Sculpture) *Dean*: Young-ki Kim; **Business Administration** *Dean*: Yoon-suk Suh; **Ecology** *(Human Ecology) Dean*: Seong-yeon Park; **Education** (Child Care and Development; Education; English Studies; Health Education; Mathematics Education; Primary Education; Social Studies; Special Education; Technology Education) *Dean*: Young-ju Ju; **Engineering** (Architecture; Computer Science; Electronic Engineering; Engineering; Environmental Engineering; Information Technology) *Dean*: Yeong-soo Shin; **Human Movement and Performance** (Dance; Leisure Studies; Sports) *Dean*: Young-ju Ju; **International Studies** *Dean*: Ki-suk Cho; **Law** (Law) *Dean*: Meong-cho Yang; **Liberal Arts** (Arts and Humanities; Chinese; Christian Religious Studies; English; French; German; History; Information Sciences; Korean; Library Science; Mass Communication; Modern Languages; Philosophy; Social Work; Sociology) *Dean*: Hyun-ja Kim; **Medicine** (Medicine) *Dean*: Wha-soon Chung; **Music** (Music; Musical Instruments) *Dean*: Kyu-do Lee; **Natural Sciences** (Biological and Life Sciences; Chemistry; Mathematics; Statistics) *Dean*: Nam-sook Lee; **Nursing** (Nursing) *Dean*: Young-soon Byun; **Pharmacy** (Pharmacy) *Dean*: Choon-mi Kim; **Social Sciences** *Dean*: Hong-sik Ahn

Graduate Schools

Business Administration (Business Administration) *Dean*: Yoon-suk Suh; **Clinical Dentistry** *Dean*: Myun-rae Kim; **Clinical Health Sciences** (Health Sciences) *Dean*: Choon-mi Kim; **Design** (Advertising and Publicity; Ceramic Art; Clothing and Sewing; Design; Photography; Textile Design; Visual Arts) *Dean*: Young-ki Kim; **Education** (Biology; Chemistry; Child Care and Development; Chinese; Computer Education; Earth Sciences; Education; Educational Administration; Educational Sciences; Environmental Studies; Ethnology; Family Studies; French; Geography; German; History; Korean; Mathematics; Music; Physical Education; Physics; Primary Education; Psychology; Social Studies; Special Education) *Dean*: Woun-sik Choi; **Graduate studies** *Dean*: Pil-wha Chang; **Information Sciences** (Architecture; Computer Science; Environmental Engineering; Information Sciences) *Dean*: Won Kim; **International Studies** (International Business; International Economics; International Law; International Relations; Political Sciences) *Dean*: Jang-hee Lee; **Policy Sciences** (Economics; Mass Communication; Public Law) *Dean*: Hong-sik Ahn; **Practical Music** (Music)

Dean: Kyu-do Lee; **Social Welfare** (Social Welfare; Welfare and Protective Services) *Dean*: Woun-sik Choi; **Theology** (Theology) *Dean*: Myung-su Yang; **Translation and Interpretation** (Chinese; English; French; German) *Dean*: Young Choi

Institutes

Career Development *Dean*: Ae-kyung Choi; **International Education** (International Studies) *Dean*: Eun-mee Kim; **Leadership Development** *(School for Leadership Development)* (Leadership) *Dean*: Hyooung Cho; **Multimedia Education** *Dean*: Young-ju Joo

Research Centres

Cell Signaling *(SRC) Director*: June-seung Lee; **Historical Studies** *Director*: So-ja Choi; **Management** *Director*: Seong-kook Kim; **Medical Studies**

Research Institutes

Asian Food and Nutrition; **Basic Science** *Director*: Gil-ja Jeon; **Biotechnology**; **Ceramic Art** *Director*: Suk-young Kang; **Colour and Design** *Director*: Gyoung-sil Choi; **Computer Graphics and Virtual Reality** *Director*: Myoung-hee Kim; **Curriculum** *Director*: Woun-sik Choi; **Ecology** *(Human Ecology)* (Ecology) *Director*: Seong-yeon Park; **Engineering** (Engineering); **English and American Studies** (American Studies; English Studies); **Environmental Studies** *Director*: Seok-soon Park; **Ewha Information Telecom** *(EITI) Director*: Ki-joon Chae; **Korean Culture** (Cultural Studies) *Dean*: Hyun-ja Kim; **Korean Women's Studies** (Women's Studies) *Dean*: Jung-wha Oh; **Language Education** *Dean*: Tae-kyeong Kang; **Legal Science** *(ELSI) Director*: Young-min Chang; **Mathematical Science** (Mathematics Education) *Director*: Yong-seung Cho; **Microelectronics** *(Hynix-Ewha Centre (HEMC))* (Microelectronics) *Director*: Hyung-soon Shin; **Movement Science** *Director*: Kee-woong Kim; **Music** (Music) *Director*: Bok-joo Jhong; **Natural History** (History) *Director*: In-sook Lee; **Neurosciences** (Neurosciences) *Director*: Won-ki Kim; **New Media Technology** (Media Studies) *Director*: Won-yong Kim; **Nursing** (Nursing) *Director*: Young-soon Byun; **Pharmacy** (Pharmacy) *Director*: Hea-young Park; **Science Education** *(RISE)* (Science Education) *Director*: Hee-jin Kim; **Semiotic Studies** *Director*: Min-suk Choi; **Social Sciences** (Social Sciences) *Director*: Young-ai Lee; **Special Education** (Special Education); **Textile and Fashion Design Centre** (Fashion Design; Textile Design); **Women's Theological Studies** *Director*: Kyung-sook Lee

Further Information: Also International Educational Institute (IEI). University Hospital

History: Founded 1886 as School by Mary Scranton (Methodist Missionary), became College 1910 and University 1945. A private Institution financed by tuition fees, Government grant, and donations.

Governing Bodies: University Council

Academic Year: March to February (March-August; September-February)

Admission Requirements: Graduation from high school or equivalent, and entrance examination

Main Language(s) of Instruction: Korean

International Co-operation: Partcipates in Isep, Asem and Duo programmes

Degrees and Diplomas: *Bachelor's Degree*: 4 yrs; *Bachelor's Degree*: Medicine, 6 yrs; *Master's Degree*: a further 2 yrs; *Doctor's Degree*

Student Services: Academic counselling, Canteen, Cultural centre, Employment services, Foreign student adviser, Foreign Studies Centre, Handicapped facilities, Health services, Language programs, Nursery care, Social counselling, Sports facilities

Student Residential Facilities: Yes

Special Facilities: University Museum. Natural History Museum. University Archives

Libraries: Ewha Centennial Library, c. 1,300,000 vols

Publications: Abstracts of Graduate School Theses *(annually)*; Academic Journal of Graduate School *(annually)*; Edae Hakbo *(weekly)*; Ewha Annual Report *(annually)*; Ewha Bulletin *(annually)*; Ewha Graduate School Bulletin *(annually)*; International Education Institute Bulletin *(annually)*; Journal of Korean Research Institute for Better Life *(biannually)*; Review of Women's Studies *(annually)*; University Museum Catalogue *(annually)*

Press or Publishing House: University Press

Last Updated: 02/01/09

FAR EAST UNIVERSITY

San 5 Wangjang-ri, Gamgok, Umsung, Chungbuk-do 369-851
Tel: +82(43) 879-3500
Fax: +82(43) 882-3310
EMail: webmaster@kdu.ac.kr
Website: http://www.kdu.ac.kr

President: Taek-hee Lyu

Programmes

Information (Communication Studies; Information Sciences)

History: Founded 1994. Acquired present status 1998.

Degrees and Diplomas: *Bachelor's Degree*; *Master's Degree*

Last Updated: 02/01/09

GACHON UNIVERSITY OF MEDICINE AND SCIENCE

534-2 Yeonsu3-dong, Yeonsu-gu, Incheon-si 406-799
Tel: +82(32) 820-4000
Fax: +82(32) 820-4059
Website: http://www.gachon.ac.kr

President: Suk-Yu Song

Departments

Business Administration (Business Administration)

Divisions

Biological Science; **Clinical Health Science** (Dental Hygiene; Food Science; Health Administration; Nutrition; Physical Therapy; Radiology); **Medical Engineering**; **Nursing** (Nursing); **Sports Science** (Physical Education)

History: Founded 1997. Acquired present status and title 2005.

Last Updated: 02/01/09

GEUMGANG UNIVERSITY

14-9 Daemyung-ri, Sangwoi-myeon, Nonsan-si,
Chungnam-do 320-931
Tel: +82(41) 580-2000
Fax: +82(41) 582-2117
EMail: admin@geumgang.ac.kr
Website: http://www.geumgang.ac.kr

President: Bong-sik Park

Schools

Buddhist Studies and Social Welfare (Asian Religious Studies; Social Welfare); **General Studies**; **International Trade and Public Administration** (International Business; Public Administration; Translation and Interpretation)

History: Founded 2003.

Degrees and Diplomas: *Bachelor's Degree*

Last Updated: 02/01/09

GWANGJU CATHOLIC UNIVERSITY

Nampyong-eup, Naju-si, Jeollanam-do 520-710
Tel: +82(61) 337-2181 +82(61) 337-2184
Fax: +82(61) 337-2185
EMail: samu12@hanmail.net
Website: http://www.kjcatholic.ac.kr

President: Young-heon Lee

International Relations: Young-jae Kim

Colleges

Theology and Philosophy (Philosophy; Theology)

History: Founded 1962.

Academic Year: March to February (March-August; September-February)

Admission Requirements: Graduation from high school and entrance examination

Main Language(s) of Instruction: Korean

Degrees and Diplomas: *Bachelor's Degree*: Theology, 4 yrs; *Master's Degree*: a further 2 yrs

Student Residential Facilities: For c. 250 students

Libraries: c. 60,000 vols

GWANGJU UNIVERSITY

52 Hydeok-ro, Nam-gu, Nam-gu, Gwangju-si, Gyeonggi-do 503-703
Tel: +82(62) 670-2151
Fax: +82(62) 670-2155
EMail: junni05@hosim.gwangju.ac.kr
Website: http://www.gwangju.ac.kr

International Relations: Se-Jin Cheon, Director
Tel: +82(62) 670-2151, Fax: +82(62) 670-2155
EMail: sjcheon@kwangju.ac.kr

International Relations: Hyuk-jong Kim

Centres

Business; **Design Support** (Design); **Electronic Commerce Research and Development**; **Foreign Languages** (Foreign Languages Education); **Industry**; **Lifelong Education**; **Optical Techniques Research and Development**; **Techno Park Support**

Colleges

Arts (Crafts and Trades; Fashion Design; Fine Arts; Graphic Arts; Industrial Design; Musical Instruments; Photography; Singing; Visual Arts; Writing); **Engineering** (Architectural and Environmental Design; Civil Engineering; Computer Engineering; Electronic Engineering; Engineering; Environmental Engineering; Industrial Engineering; Telecommunications Engineering; Town Planning); **Humanities and Social Sciences** (Administration; Advertising and Publicity; Art Education; Chinese; English; Humanities and Social Science Education; Information Sciences; Japanese; Law; Library Science; Mass Communication; Police Studies; Preschool Education; Public Relations; Social Sciences; Teacher Trainers Education; Welfare and Protective Services); **Management Commerce and Social Welfare** (Accountancy; Business Administration; Business and Commerce; Continuing Education; Economics; Education; Home Economics; Household Management; Service Trades; Social Sciences; Social Welfare; Tourism; Welfare and Protective Services)

Graduate Schools

Kyung-Sang (Accountancy; Administration; Architecture; Art Education; Banking; Business Administration; Business and Commerce; Civil Engineering; Computer Engineering; Computer Science; Economics; Electronic Engineering; Environmental Engineering; Fashion Design; Finance; Fine Arts; Graphic Arts; Humanities and Social Science Education; Industrial Design; Industrial Engineering; Law; Music; Photography; Preschool Education; Social Sciences; Social Welfare; Teacher Trainers Education; Telecommunications Engineering; Town Planning; Welfare and Protective Services; Writing); **Mass Communication** (Advertising and Publicity; Information Sciences; Mass Communication; Public Relations)

Institutes

Educational and Industrial Cooperation; **Humanities and Social Sciences** (Administration; Advertising and Publicity; Art Education; Chinese; English; Humanities and Social Science Education; Information Sciences; Japanese; Law; Library Science; Mass Communication; Police Studies; Preschool Education; Public Relations; Teacher Trainers Education); **Industrial Management** (Business Administration; Business and Commerce; Home Economics; Industrial Management; Service Trades; Social Sciences; Teacher Trainers Education); **Industrial Technology** (Architecture; Civil Engineering; Computer Engineering; Electronic Engineering; Engineering; Environmental Engineering; Industrial Engineering; Structural Architecture; Telecommunications Engineering; Town Planning); **Korean Culture and Art** (Crafts and Trades; Fashion Design; Fine Arts; Graphic Arts; Industrial Design; Music; Musical Instruments; Photography; Singing; Visual Arts; Writing)

Research Centres

21st Century Women's Information and Culture; **University Development** (Higher Education)

History: Founded 1981 as Kwangju Kyung-Sang Junior College. Acquired status of four year college in 1983 as Kwangju Open University and acquired present status and title in 1990.

Governing Bodies: Hoshim School Foundation

Academic Year: March to December (March-June; September-December)

Admission Requirements: Graduation from high school or equivalent

Main Language(s) of Instruction: Korean

Degrees and Diplomas: *Bachelor's Degree*: 4 yrs; *Master's Degree*: a further 2 yrs

Student Services: Academic counselling, Canteen, Cultural centre, Employment services, Foreign student adviser, Handicapped facilities, Health services, Language programs, Nursery care, Sports facilities

Student Residential Facilities: For c. 1,200 students

Special Facilities: Concert Hall; Broadcasting Station; Movie Studio

Libraries: Central Library, c. 350,000 vols

Publications: Collection of Research Papers and Statistics on Campus Life *(annually)*; Collection of Research Papers on Engineering *(annually)*; Collection of Research Papers on Fine & Applied Arts *(annually)*; Collection of Research Papers on Humanities *(annually)*; Collection of Research Papers on Industrial Management *(annually)*; Collection of Research Papers on Industrial Management *(annually)*; Collection of Research Papers on Social Sciences *(annually)*

Press or Publishing House: Kwangju University Press

GWANGJU WOMEN'S UNIVERSITY

165 Sanjeong-dong, Kwangsan-gu, Gwangju-si, Gyeonggi-do 506-713
Tel: +82(62) 950-3509
Fax: +82(62) 953-2218
EMail: id@mail.kwu.ac.kr
Website: http://www.kwu.ac.kr

President: Jang-won Oh

Divisions

Architectural Design; **Education**; **Health**; **Information Design** (Media Studies); **Medicine and Health**; **Performance Arts**; **Social Affairs and Welfare** (Gerontology; Law; Marketing; Police Studies; Social Welfare); **Teacher Training** (Preschool Education; Primary Education; Special Education)

History: Founded 1997.

Degrees and Diplomas: *Bachelor's Degree*; *Master's Degree*

Last Updated: 02/01/09

GYEONGJU UNIVERSITY

San 42-1 Hyohun-Dong, Gyeongju-si, Gyeongbuk-do 780-712
Tel: +82(561) 748-5551
Fax: +82(561) 746-3012
EMail: webmaster@gyeongju.ac.kr
Website: http://www.gju.ac.kr

President: Il Yun Kim

International Relations: Hoon-Suck Park
Tel: +82(561) 770-5041 EMail: Parkhs@tour.kyongju.ac.kr

Departments

Community Sports and Recreation (Sports); **Creative Writing**; **Cultural Assets**; **Visual Arts**

Graduate Schools

Graduate Studies (Business Administration; Landscape Architecture; Tourism); **Public and Business Administration** (Business Administration; Government; Hotel Management)

Schools

Business Administration and Advertising *(Evening)*; **Computer and Information Science**; **Construction and Environment System Public Engineering** (Architecture; Civil Engineering; Environmental Studies; Landscape Architecture; Urban Studies); **Foreign Languages and Tourism** (Chinese; English; Japanese; Modern Languages; Tourism); **Law and Public Administration** (Law; Public Administration; Real Estate); **Tourism Studies**

History: Founded 1988 as Korea Tourism University. Acuqired present status and title 1993.

Main Language(s) of Instruction: Korean

Degrees and Diplomas: *Bachelor's Degree*; *Master's Degree*

Special Facilities: University Museum

Libraries: Yes

Press or Publishing House: University Press Centre

Last Updated: 02/01/09

HALLA UNIVERSITY

San-66 Heungeop, Heungup-myeon, Wonju-si, Wonju-si, Gangwon-do 220-712
Tel: +82(33) 760-1114
Fax: +82(33) 766-6705
Website: http://www.halla.ac.kr

President: Zin-ho Kim

Programmes

Business and Economics; **Engineering** (Engineering)

History: Founded 1995.

HALLYM UNIVERSITY

39 Hallymdaehak-gil, Chuncheon-si, Gangwon-do 200-702
Tel: +82(33) 240-1323
Fax: +82(33) 255-3422
EMail: de1321@hallym.ac.kr
Website: http://www.hallym.ac.kr

President: Young Sun Lee

Colleges

Business (Business Administration; Economics; Finance); **Humanities** (Arts and Humanities; Chinese; English; History; Japanese; Korean; Literature; Philosophy; Russian); **Information and Electronic Engineering** (Computer Engineering; Electronic Engineering; Telecommunications Engineering); **Medicine** (Medicine; Nursing); **Natural Sciences** (Biological and Life Sciences; Biomedical Engineering; Biotechnology; Chemistry; Environmental Studies; Food Science; Mathematics; Natural Sciences; Nutrition; Physical Education; Physics; Speech Therapy and Audiology); **Social Sciences** (Communication Studies; Law; Political Sciences; Psychology; Social Sciences; Social Welfare; Sociology)

History: Founded 1982.

Degrees and Diplomas: *Bachelor's Degree*; *Master's Degree*; *Doctor's Degree*

Press or Publishing House: Hallym University Press

Last Updated: 02/01/09

HANBUK UNIVERSITY

233-1 Sangpae-dong, Dongducheon-si, Gyeonggi-do 483-120
Tel: +82(31) 860-1351 +82(31) 860-1359
Fax: +82(31) 860-1350
EMail: kimbc@hanbuk.ac.kr
Website: http://www.hanbuk.ac.kr

President: Byung-chul Kim (2003-)
Tel: +82(31) 860-1340, Fax: +82(31) 860-1345

Departments

Computer Engineering (Computer Engineering) *Head*: Dong-kyu Lee

History: Founded 2004.

Academic Year: March to December

Admission Requirements: Secondary School Certificate , Korean SAT

Fees: (Won): 3,500 per semester

Main Language(s) of Instruction: Korean

Degrees and Diplomas: *Bachelor's Degree*: Computer Engineering, 4 yrs

Student Residential Facilities: None

HANDONG GLOBAL UNIVERSITY

3 Namsong-ri, Heunghae-eup, Buk-gu, Pohang-si, Gyeongbuk 791-708
Tel: +82(54) 260-1763
Fax: +82(54) 260-1769
EMail: webmaster@handong.edu
Website: http://www.handong.edu

President: Kim Young-Gil (1995-) EMail: ygkim@handong.edu

International Relations: Abraham Lee EMail: alee@handong.edu

Schools

Bioscience and Food Technology (Biological and Life Sciences; Food Science; Food Technology) *Head*: Jin-Hwang Kwak; **Christian Culture and Mass Communication** (Cinema and Television; Mass Communication; Theatre) *Head*: Moon-Won Lee; **Computer Science and Electronic Engineering** (Computer Engineering; Computer Science; Electronic Engineering) *Head*: Youn-Sik Han; **Counselling and Social Welfare** (Social Work; Vocational Counselling) *Head*: Hye-Ree Hwang; **General Studies** (Chemistry; History; Linguistics; Mathematics; Physics; Psychology; Religious Studies; Sociology; Statistics; Theology) *Head*: Sung-Oek Kim; **Industrial and Media Design** (Art Management; Design; Industrial Design) *Head*: Won-Choi Cho; **International Studies, Languages and Literature** (Comparative Literature; History; Linguistics; Literature; Modern Languages; Writing) *Head*: Han-Woo Choi; **Law** (History of Law; International Law; Private Law; Public Law) *Head*: Kuk-Woon Lee; **Management and Economics** (Accountancy; Administration; Business and Commerce; Economics; Finance; Management; Marketing) *Head*: Sung-June Kang; **Mechanical and Control Systems Engineering** (Aeronautical and Aerospace Engineering; Automation and Control Engineering; Electrical and Electronic Engineering; Energy Engineering; Mechanical Engineering) *Head*: Yang-Gyu Jei; **Spatial Environmental Systems Engineering** (Architecture; Engineering Drawing and Design; Regional Planning; Rural Planning; Town Planning) *Head*: Dae-June Lee

History: Founded 1995.

Admission Requirements: High school certificate and National Entrance Examination

Fees: (Won): 3,064,000

Main Language(s) of Instruction: Korean and English

Accrediting Agencies: Ministry of Education

Degrees and Diplomas: *Bachelor's Degree*: 4 yrs; *Master's Degree*: 2-3 yrs

Student Services: Academic counselling, Canteen, Cultural centre, Employment services, Foreign student adviser, Foreign Studies Centre, Health services, Language programs, Social counselling, Sports facilities

Student Residential Facilities: Yes

Libraries: 119,220 vols; 3,801 periodical subscriptions

Press or Publishing House: Handong Press

Last Updated: 07/04/08

HANKUK AVIATION UNIVERSITY (HAU)

200-1 Hwajeon-dong, Deokyang-gu, Goyang-si, Gyeonggi-do 412-791
Tel: +82(2) 300-0114
Fax: +82(2) 3158-5769
Website: http://www.hau.ac.kr

President: Junku Yuh (2006-)
Tel: +82(2) 300-0001, Fax: +82(2) 3158-5770

Departments

Aeronautical Science and Flight Operation (Aeronautical and Aerospace Engineering) *Chair*: Hee-Bong Eun; **Air and Space Law** (Air and Space Law) *Chair*: Sun-Ihee Kim; **Business Administration** (Business Administration; Business and Commerce) *Chair*: Hee-Young Hurr; **English** *(Evening) Chair*: Suk-Jin Kang; **Materials Engineering** (Materials Engineering) *Head*: Kwang-Bae Kim

Institutes

Aerospace and Aviation Electronics *Director*: Young-Kil Kwag; **Aerospace Engineering and Technology** (Aeronautical and Aerospace Engineering) *Director*: Myoung-Shin Hwang; **Air Traffic Control Education** (Transport Management) *Director*: Maeng-Sun

Kim; **Aircraft Maintenance Technology** (Maintenance Technology) *Director*: Keun-Myung Lee; **Aircraft Safety and System Management** (Safety Engineering) *Director*: Hee-Bong Eun; **Aviation Industry, Policy and Law** (Air and Space Law; Transport Management) *Director*: Yeong-Heok Lee; **Business Studies** (Business and Commerce) *Director*: Yun-Cheol Lee; **Community Development Research** (Development Studies) *Director*: Suk-Hong Yoon; **Flight Training** *Director*: Chang-Yung Hwang; **Humanities and Natural Sciences** (Humanities and Social Science Education; Korean; Natural Sciences) *Director*: Seung-Hoe Choi; **Information Technology Research** (Information Technology) *Director*: Jong-Sou Park; **Internet Information Retrieval** *(Regional Research Centre) Director*: Sung-Joon Cho; **Transport and Logistics** (Air Transport; Transport Management) *Director*: Hun-Soo Lee

Schools

Aerospace and Mechanical Engineering (Aeronautical and Aerospace Engineering; Mechanical Engineering) *Head*: Hark-Bong Kim; **Air Transport, Transportation and Logistics** (Air Transport; Transport Management) *Head*: Han-Mo Yang; **Electronics, Telecommunications and Computer Engineering** (Computer Engineering; Electronic Engineering; Telecommunications Engineering) *Head*: Kang-Woong Lee; **General Studies** *Head*: Bong-Young Choi

History: Founded 1952 by the Ministry of Transport. Administrative control transferred to the Ministry of Education 1968. Transferred to Hanjin Group under Government plan for systematizing the aviation-related circles I978.

Governing Bodies: Jung-Seok Foundation

Academic Year: March to February (March-August; September-February)

Admission Requirements: Graduation from high school, or foreign equivalent, and entrance examination

Main Language(s) of Instruction: Korean

International Co-operation: With universities in USA, Russian Federation, China, Ukraine, United Kingdom, Philippines, Netherlands, Japan, New Zealand, Mongolia, Canada, Myanmar

Accrediting Agencies: Ministry of Education and Human Resources Development

Degrees and Diplomas: *Bachelor's Degree*: 4 yrs; *Master's Degree*: a further 2 yrs; *Doctor's Degree*: a further 2-3 yrs

Student Services: Academic counselling, Canteen, Employment services, Health services, Nursery care, Social counselling, Sports facilities

Special Facilities: Hankuk Aviation University Aerospace Museum

Libraries: Central Library, c. 270,000 vols

Publications: Journals of Aviation Industry, Policy and Law *(annually)*; Journals of Electronics, Information, and Telecommunication Engineering *(annually)*; Journals of Humanities and Natural Sciences *(annually)*

Press or Publishing House: Hankuk Aviation University Press

HANKUK UNIVERSITY OF FOREIGN STUDIES

270 Imun-dong, Dongdaemun-gu, Seoul 130-791
Tel: +82(2) 2173-2071
Fax: +82(2) 2173-3366
EMail: adms@hufs.ac.kr
Website: http://www.hufs.ac.kr

President: Park Chul

International Relations: Jeong-Woon Park Tel: +82(2) 2173-2051

Colleges

Business and Economics (Business Administration; Business and Commerce; Economics; International Business; International Economics; International Studies); **Central and East European Studies** *(Yong-in Campus)* (Central European Studies; Czech; Eastern European Studies; Hungarian; Polish; Romanian; Russian; Slavic Languages); **Economics and Business** *(Yong-in Campus)*; **Education** (Education; English; French; German; Korean); **English**; **Humanities** *(Yong-in Campus)* (Arts and Humanities; Cognitive Sciences; History; Linguistics; Philosophy); **Information and Industrial Engineering** *(Yong-in Campus)*; **Interpretation and Translation** *(Yong-in Campus)* (Arabic; Chinese; English; German; Italian; Japanese; Malay; Spanish; Thai Languages; Translation and Interpretation); **Language and Literature** *(Yong-in Campus)* (African Studies; Asian Studies; Bulgarian; French; Greek; Hindi; Literature; Modern Languages; Portuguese); **Law** (Law); **Natural Sciences** *(Yong-in Campus)* (Biological and Life Sciences; Biotechnology; Chemistry; Electronic Engineering; Environmental Studies; Mathematics; Natural Sciences; Physics; Statistics); **Occidental Languages** (Dutch; French; German; Italian; Portuguese; Russian; Scandinavian Languages; Spanish); **Oriental Languages** (Arabic; Chinese; Hindi; Japanese; Malay; Oriental Languages; Persian; Thai Languages; Turkish; Vietnamese); **Social Science** (Advertising and Publicity; Film; Journalism; Mass Communication; Media Studies; Political Sciences; Public Administration; Public Relations; Radio and Television Broadcasting; Social Sciences)

Graduate Schools

Business Administration; **Education** (Education); **International Area Studies** (International Studies); **Interpretation and Translation** (Translation and Interpretation); **Political Science, Government and Communication** (Communication Studies; Government; Political Sciences)

History: Founded 1954 with the approval of the Ministry of Education. Receives some financial support from the Government.

Governing Bodies: Board of Trustees

Academic Year: March to December (March-July; September-December)

Admission Requirements: Graduation from high school or equivalent, and entrance examination

Main Language(s) of Instruction: Korean

Degrees and Diplomas: *Bachelor's Degree (BA)*: 4 yrs; *Master's Degree (M.A., M.Ed)*: a further 2 yrs; *Doctor's Degree (PhD)*

Libraries: Central Library, c. 1,232,882 vols

Publications: Collections of articles *(annually)*

Press or Publishing House: University Press

Last Updated: 23/10/08

HANLYO UNIVERSITY

199-4 Duckrey-ri, Gwangyang-eup, Gwangyang-si, Jeollanam-do 545-704
Tel: +82(61) 760-1111 +82(61) 760-1112
Fax: +82(61) 761-6709
EMail: jhcho@hanlyo.ac.kr
Website: http://www.hanlyo.ac.kr

President: Tae-ho Kim

International Relations: Jun-ho Cho
Tel: +82(2) 760-1113, Fax: +82(2) 761-6709

Programmes

Multimedia (Multimedia; Telecommunications Engineering); **Physical Therapy** (Physical Therapy); **Physics** (Physics); **Police Administration** (Police Studies); **Social Welfare** (Social Welfare)

History: Founded 1994.

HANNAM UNIVERSITY

133 Ojeong-dong, Daedeok-gu, Daejeon, Chungnam-do 306-791
Tel: +82(42) 629-7114
Fax: +82(42) 625-5874
Website: http://www.hannam.ac.kr

President: Hyung-tae Kim
Tel: +82(42) 623-7100, Fax: +82(42) 627-6779

Colleges

Economics and Administration (Administration; Economics) *Head*: Sang-Jin Park; **Education** (Education) *Head*: Dong-Suk Kim; **Engineering** (Engineering) *Head*: Dae-Cheol Park; **Law** *Head*: Hong-Su Kim; **Liberal Arts** (Arts and Humanities) *Head*: Young-Dae Min; **Natural Sciences** (Natural Sciences) *Head*: Sang-Bae Kim; **Social Sciences** (Political Sciences; Social Sciences) *Head*: Bong-Cheol Lee

History: Founded in 1956 by a Presbyterian Missionary Foundation.

Academic Year: March to December (March-June; August-December)

Admission Requirements: Graduation from high school and entrance examination

Fees: (Won): c. 2.5m.

Main Language(s) of Instruction: Korean

Degrees and Diplomas: *Bachelor's Degree*: 4 yrs; *Master's Degree*: a further 1-2 yrs; *Doctor's Degree (PhD)*: 3-5 yrs following Master

Student Services: Academic counselling, Canteen, Employment services, Foreign student adviser, Foreign Studies Centre, Health services, Language programs, Nursery care

Student Residential Facilities: For c. 100 Men and c. 40 Women students

Special Facilities: University Museum. Natural History Museum. Broadcasting Station

Libraries: Central Library, c. 215,000 vols

Press or Publishing House: Han Nam University Press

Last Updated: 02/01/09

HANSEI UNIVERSITY

604-5 Dangjeung-dong, Gunpo-si, Gyeonggi-do 435-742
Tel: +82(31) 450-5114
Fax: +82(31) 457-6517
EMail: hansei@hansei.ac.kr
Website: http://www.hansei.ac.kr

President: Sung-hae Kim

Divisions

Communication Arts (Communication Arts); **E-Business** (E-Business/Commerce); **Industrial Design** (Industrial Design); **Information Technology** (Information Technology); **Music** (Music); **Police Administration and Social Welfare** (Police Studies; Social Welfare); **Theology** (Theology)

History: Founded 1953. Acquired present title 1997.

Degrees and Diplomas: *Bachelor's Degree*; *Master's Degree*; *Doctor's Degree*

Last Updated: 02/01/09

HANSEO UNIVERSITY

360 Daegok-ri, Haemi-myeon, Seosan-si, Chungnam-do 356-706
Tel: +82(41) 660-1197
Fax: +82(41) 660-1198
EMail: ring@hanseo.ac.kr
Website: http://www.hanseo.ac.kr

President: Kee Sun Ham (2000-)
Tel: +82(41) 660-1102, Fax: +82(41) 660-1109
EMail: ksham@hanseo.ac.kr

Secretary-General: Suang Rea Choi Tel: +82(41) 660-1140

International Relations: Byung-kook Lee

Colleges

Aeronautical Engineering (Aeronautical and Aerospace Engineering; Air Transport; Electronic Engineering; Transport Management); **Design and Graphics** (Design; Fashion Design; Graphic Arts; Industrial Design; Interior Design; Visual Arts); **Engineering** (Biotechnology; Chemical Engineering; Civil Engineering; Computer Engineering; Computer Networks; Electrical Engineering; Engineering; Environmental Engineering; Food Science; Materials Engineering; Metal Techniques; Structural Architecture); **Health Sciences** (Health Administration; Health Sciences; Medical Technology; Nursing; Occupational Therapy; Ophthalmology; Physical Therapy; Radiology); **Liberal Arts and Social Sciences** (Arts and Humanities; Chinese; English; Gerontology; International Business; International Relations; Japanese; Journalism; Literature; Mass Communication; Public Administration; Social Welfare; Sociology; Writing); **Multimedia, Music, and Fine Arts** (Art Education; Art Management; Cinema and Television; Fine Arts; Heritage Preservation; Multimedia; Music; Singing); **Sciences** (Applied Mathematics; Applied Physics; Biology; Chemistry; Civil Security; Computer Science; Engineering; Information Technology; Leisure Studies; Mathematics; Organic Chemistry; Physical Chemistry; Sports)

Institutes

International Humanitarian Studies (Social Sciences)

Research Institutes

Catalyst Technology *(RICT)* (Organic Chemistry); **Education-Industrial Cooperation**; **Humanities and Social Sciences** (Arts and Humanities; Social Sciences); **Student Guidance and Counselling** (Educational and Student Counselling)

Schools

Graduate Studies (Art Management; Education; Health Education; Information Management; Pedagogy)

History: Founded 1992.

Academic Year: March to September

Main Language(s) of Instruction: Korean

Degrees and Diplomas: *Bachelor's Degree*; *Master's Degree*; *Doctor's Degree*

Student Services: Academic counselling, Employment services, Foreign student adviser, Foreign Studies Centre, Handicapped facilities, Language programs, Nursery care, Social counselling, Sports facilities

Special Facilities: Museum. Art gallery. Movie Studio

Last Updated: 02/01/09

HANSHIN UNIVERSITY

411 Yangsandong, Osan-si, Gyeonggi-do 447-791
Tel: +82(339) 370-6524
Fax: +82(339) 370-6525
EMail: prco@hs.ac.kr
Website: http://www.hs.ac.kr

President: Eung-Jin Yun

Colleges

Humanities (Arts and Humanities; Chinese; Cultural Studies; English; German; History; Korean; Philosophy; Religious Studies; Writing); **Information Sciences**; **Management and Trade** (Advertising and Publicity; Business Administration; Business and Commerce; E-Business/Commerce; Economics; International Economics); **Social Sciences** (Chinese; Economics; International Studies; Japanese; Social Sciences; Social Welfare; Sociology); **Theology** (Christian Religious Studies; Theology)

History: Founded 1940.

Degrees and Diplomas: *Bachelor's Degree*; *Master's Degree*; *Doctor's Degree*

Last Updated: 02/01/09

HANSUNG UNIVERSITY (HU)

Samseon-dong 2-ga, Seongbuk-gu, Seoul 136-792
Tel: +82(2) 760-4261
Fax: +82(2) 762-9354
EMail: ilhwankim@hansung.ac.kr
Website: http://www.hansung.ac.kr

President: Kyung-Ro Yoon
Tel: +82(2) 760-4202, Fax: +82(2) 760-4203
EMail: ykr3041@hansung.ac.kr

Dean of Office of Planning and External Affairs: Jung-Soo Han
Tel: +82(2) 760-4260 EMail: jshan@hansung.ac.kr

International Relations: Il-Hwan Kim, Planning and External Affairs Officer Tel: +82(2) 760-4261

Colleges

Arts (Dance; Design; Fashion Design; Fine Arts; Media Studies; Painting and Drawing) *Dean*: Ju-Ja Kim; **Engineering** (Computer Engineering; Engineering; Industrial Engineering; Information Technology; Mechanical Engineering; Telecommunications Engineering) *Dean*: Yoon-Gee Hong; **Humanities** (Arts and Humanities; Cultural Studies; English; History; Information Sciences; Korean) *Dean*: Ho-Yung Park; **Social Sciences** (Economics; International Business; Public Administration; Real Estate; Social Sciences) *Dean*: Sung-Ky Min

Graduate Schools

Arts (Aesthetics; Design; Fashion Design) *Dean*: Ki-Hyang Lee; **Business Administration** (Business Administration; Hotel and Restaurant; Hotel Management; Tourism) *Dean*: Yong-Sik Hong; **Digital Small and Medium Business Management** *Division Head*: Jin-Taek Jung; **Education** *Dean*: Kyeong-Bae Kim; **General**

Studies (American Studies; Business Administration; Computer Engineering; Dance; Economics; Engineering; English Studies; Fashion Design; History; Industrial Engineering; Information Sciences; Information Technology; International Business; Korean; Library Science; Literature; Mechanical Engineering; Media Studies; Multimedia; Painting and Drawing; Public Administration; Telecommunications Engineering) *Dean*: Sang-Han Lee; **International Studies** *Dean*: Hyun-Sang You; **Public Administration** (Police Studies; Public Administration; Social Welfare; Toxicology) *Dean*: Seong-Uh Lee; **Real Estate** *Dean*: Young-Man Lee

History: Founded 1945, acquired present status and title 1972. Acquired ISO 9001 certification in July 2003

Governing Bodies: Office of Academic Affairs, Planning and External Affairs; Student Services, General Affairs, Admissions and Public Relations

Admission Requirements: Graduation from High School

Main Language(s) of Instruction: Korean

Degrees and Diplomas: *Bachelor's Degree*: 4 yrs; *Master's Degree*: 2 yrs; *Doctor's Degree*: 3 yrs

Student Services: Academic counselling, Canteen, Employment services, Foreign student adviser, Health services, Language programs, Sports facilities

Student Residential Facilities: Foreign student dormitory

Libraries: Digital library

Academic Staff *2008-2009*	MEN	WOMEN	TOTAL
FULL-TIME	69	45	**114**
STAFF WITH DOCTORATE FULL-TIME	3	–	**3**
Student Numbers *2008-2009*			
All (Foreign Included)	6,636	4,216	**10,852**
FOREIGN ONLY	28	52	**80**

Last Updated: 28/01/09

HANYANG UNIVERSITY

17 Haengdong-dong, Seongdong-gu, Seoul 133-791
Tel: +82(2) 2290-0114
Fax: +82(2) 2294-2442
Website: http://www.hanyang.ac.kr

President: Chong-yang Kim

Centres

Local Autonomy

Colleges

Commerce and Economics (Accountancy; Business Administration; Business and Commerce; Economics; International Business); **Education** (Education); **Engineering** (Architecture; Automotive Engineering; Chemical Engineering; Electrical Engineering; Electronic Engineering; Engineering; Industrial Engineering; Machine Building; Materials Engineering; Mechanical Engineering; Metallurgical Engineering; Mining Engineering; Nuclear Engineering); **Home Economics** (Home Economics); **Humanities** (Arts and Humanities; Cinema and Television; English; German; History; Korean; Philosophy; Theatre); **Law** (Law); **Medicine** (Medicine; Nursing); **Music** (Music); **Natural Sciences** (Biology; Chemistry; Mathematics; Natural Sciences; Physics); **Physical Education** (Physical Education); **Social Sciences** (International Relations; Journalism; Mass Communication; Political Sciences; Public Administration; Social Sciences; Sociology; Tourism)

Graduate Schools

Banking (Banking); **Business Administration** (Business Administration); **Education** (Education); **Environmental Sciences** (Environmental Studies); **Industry** (Industrial Engineering); **Public Administration** (Public Administration)

Institutes

Economics Research (Economics); **Industrial Science Research**

Further Information: Also 2 University Hospitals

History: Founded 1939 as Dong-Ah Polytechnic Academy, reorganized as Kunkuk College 1945 and Hanyang College of Engineering 1948. Acquired present title and status 1956. A private Institution financed by the Hanyang Educational Foundation.

Governing Bodies: Board of Trustees

Academic Year: March to February (March-June; September-February)

Admission Requirements: Graduation from high school and entrance examination

Main Language(s) of Instruction: Korean

Degrees and Diplomas: *Bachelor's Degree*: 4 yrs; *Bachelor's Degree*: Medicine, 6 yrs; *Master's Degree*: a further 2 yrs; *Doctor's Degree*: 3 yrs following Master

Student Residential Facilities: Yes

Special Facilities: Museum

Libraries: Central Library, c. 260,000 vols; College of Medicine library, c. 25,000; College of Engineering library, c. 35,000

Publications: Institute Research Publication *(biannually)*

Press or Publishing House: Hanyang University Press

HANZHONG UNIVERSITY

119 Jiheung-dong, Donghae-si, Gangwon-do 240-713
Tel: +82(33) 521-9900
Fax: +82(33) 521-9907
EMail: webmaster@mail.donghae.ac.kr
Website: http://www.donghae.ac.kr

President: Hee-pyo Hong

Colleges

Arts and Athletics (Industrial Design; Leisure Studies; Multimedia; Sports); **Engineering** (Automotive Engineering; Civil Engineering; Computer Engineering; Electrical and Electronic Engineering; Engineering; Environmental Engineering; Information Technology; Structural Architecture); **Industrial Food Service** (Food Technology); **Nursing** (Nursing)

History: Founded 1990.

HONAM THEOLOGICAL UNIVERSITY AND SEMINARY

108 Yangrim-dong, Nam-gu, Gwangju-si, Gyeonggi-do 503-756
Tel: +82(62) 650-1513
Fax: +82(62) 675-1552
EMail: cscha@htus.ac.kr
Website: http://www.htus.ac.kr

President: Chong-Soon Cha

Departments

Music (Music); **Social Welfare and Counselling** (Social Welfare); **Theology** (Theology)

History: Founded 1961.

Degrees and Diplomas: *Bachelor's Degree*; *Master's Degree*; *Doctor's Degree*

Last Updated: 02/01/09

HONAM UNIVERSITY

59-1 Seobong-dong Gwangsan-gu, Gwangju-si,
Gyeonggi-do 506-714
Tel: +82(62) 940-5114
Fax: +82(62) 940-5005
EMail: btoh@honam.honam.ac.kr
Website: http://www.honam.ac.kr

President: Byoung-wan Chang

Centres

Computer Science (Computer Science) *Director*: Hyun-Shik Na; **Honam Language** *Director*: Kwang-Ho Lee; **Industrial Technology** (Industrial Engineering) *Director*: Choon-Sik Yu; **Information Technology** (Information Sciences; Information Technology) *Director*: Joon-Seub Cha; **Tourism and Business** (Tourism) *Director*: Jong-Soo Ahn

Colleges

Arts and Physical Education (Fashion Design; Film; Fine Arts; Industrial Design; Multimedia; Physical Education; Theatre) *Dean*: Jae-Hyung Kim; **Economics and Business Administration** (Business Administration; Economics; Hotel Management; International Business; Tourism) *Dean*: Hwa-Jung Oh; **Engineering**

(Architecture; Civil Engineering; Computer Engineering; Electrical and Electronic Engineering; Engineering; Information Sciences; Landscape Architecture; Radio and Television Broadcasting; Software Engineering) *Dean*: Choon-Sik Yu; **Humanities** (Arts and Humanities; Chinese; East Asian Studies; English; History; Japanese; Korean; Literature; Modern Languages) *Dean*: Ki-Ju Kim; **Natural Sciences** (Biological and Life Sciences; Environmental Studies; Food Science; Horticulture; Household Management; Natural Sciences) *Dean*: Eun-Sung Ok; **Social Sciences** (Advertising and Publicity; Economics; International Relations; Journalism; Law; Political Sciences; Public Administration; Public Relations; Social Sciences; Social Welfare) *Dean*: Woom-Seon Paek

Institutes

Athletics (Physical Education; Sports) *Director*: Do-Hee Ahn; **Business and Economics** (Business and Commerce; Economics) *Director*: Dong-suk Kim

Schools

Business Administration (Banking; Business Administration; Insurance) *Director*: Hwa-Jung Oh; **Education** (English; Mathematics; Physical Education) *Director*: Yong-Hwa Kim; **Graduate Studies** (Business Administration; Civil Engineering; Computer Engineering; Economics; English; Fine Arts; Korean; Law; Mathematics; Public Administration) *Director*: Yong-Hwa Kim; **Industrial Technology** (Industrial Engineering) *Director*: Joon-Seub Cha; **Public Administration** (Justice Administration; Public Administration; Real Estate) *Director*: Woon-Seon Paek

History: Founded 1978 as Junior Commercial College, became 4-year College 1981, and acquired present status and title 1992.

Governing Bodies: Seong-In School Foundation

Academic Year: March to December (March-June; August-December)

Admission Requirements: Graduation from High school and entrance examination

Fees: (Won): Humanities and Social Sciences, 1,896,500 per semester; Engineering and Arts, 2,616,100 per semester; Natural Science and Physical Education, 2,332,600 per semester; Mathematics, 1,977,300 per semester

Main Language(s) of Instruction: Korean, English

Degrees and Diplomas: *Bachelor's Degree*: 4 yrs; *Master's Degree*: a further 4 semesters; *Doctor's Degree*: a further 6 semesters

Student Services: Academic counselling, Canteen, Cultural centre, Employment services, Foreign student adviser, Foreign Studies Centre, Handicapped facilities, Health services, Language programs, Nursery care, Social counselling, Sports facilities

Student Residential Facilities: For 200 students

Special Facilities: University museum. University farm. Educational broadcasting station. Satellite remote centre. Venture business centre. Venture inauguration centre

Libraries: Central Library, c. 420,251 vols

Publications: Honam University Bulletin *(biennially)*; Journal of Business and Economics *(annually)*; Journal of Computer and Communication Research *(annually)*; Journal of Industrial Technology *(annually)*; Journal of Research in Humanities and Social Sciences *(annually)*; Thesis Collection of Honam University *(annually)*

Press or Publishing House: Honam University Press

Last Updated: 02/01/09

HONGIK UNIVERSITY

72-1 Sangsu-dong, Mapo-gu, Seoul 121-791
Tel: +82(2) 320-1042
Fax: +82(2) 320-3339
EMail: int_rel@wow.hongik.ac.kr
Website: http://www.hongik.ac.kr

President: Myungkwang Kwon
Tel: +82(2) 320-1010, Fax: +82(2) 320-1019

Vice-President: Youngtae Chang
Tel: +82(2) 320-1016, Fax: +82(2) 320-1019

International Relations: Jaeyoung Chung

Centres

Color Design *(Jochiwon Campus)* (Design; Fine Arts) *Head*: Yonsuh Park

Colleges

Architecture *Dean*: Uk Kim; **Business Administration** (Business Administration) *Dean*: Donghun Kim; **Business Management** *(Jochiwon Campus)* (Business Administration) *Dean*: Yeon Choi; **Design and Arts** *(Jochiwon Campus)* (Visual Arts) *Dean*: Yonsun Park; **Education** (Education) *Dean*: Minjae Kim; **Engineering** (Engineering) *Dean*: Joonki Chung; **Fine Arts** (Fine Arts) *Dean*: Byunghoon Choi; **Law** (Law) *Dean*: Kyoungdo Min; **Law and Economics** (Economics; Law) *Dean*: Seunggwan Baek; **Liberal Arts** (Arts and Humanities) *Dean*: Hyungjoon Chin; **Science and Technology** *(Jochiwon Campus)* (Natural Sciences; Technology) *Dean*: Panseok Shin

Graduate Schools

Advertising and Public Relations (Advertising and Publicity; Public Relations) *Dean*: Dongryun Chang; **Architecture and Urban Design** *Dean*: Myungwon Chung; **Business Studies** (Business and Commerce) *Dean*: Kwangchul Lee; **Education** (Education) *Dean*: Sangok Park; **Education Management** (Educational Administration) *Dean*: Sangok Park; **Film and Digital Media** (Film; Media Studies) *Dean*: Jongdeok Kim; **Fine Arts** (Fine Arts) *Dean*: Taeho Kim; **General Studies** *Dean*: Wonpyo Chung; **Industrial Arts** (Industrial Design) *Dean*: Kunho Byun; **Industry** *(Jochiwon Campus) Dean*: Hosung Chang; **International Design** (Design) *Dean*: Chulho Kim

Institutes

East Asian Corporate Management (Management) *Head*: Taehong Jin; **Film, Video and Animation** (Film; Video) *Head*: Kwangmin Rho

Research Centres

Ceramic Art (Ceramic Art) *Head*: Kwanho Woo; **Creation and Law** (Law) *Head*: Seungjong Oh; **Design Information and Culture** (Design) *Head*: Dongsoo Suh; **Disaster Prevention and Safety Management** (Safety Engineering) *Head*: Kiyeon Hwang; **Electric Equipment** *(Jochiwon Campus)* (Electrical Engineering) *Head*: Panseok Shim; **Marine Systems** *(Jochiwon Campus)* (Marine Science and Oceanography) *Head*: Guenmoo Lee; **Mechatronics** *(Jochiwon Campus)* (Mechanical Engineering) *Head*: Dongmin Kim; **Northeast Asian Law** *Head*: Byungwoon Lyou; **Public Design** (Design) *Head*: Jooyun Kim; **Railway and Transportation** (Railway Transport) *Dean*: Jungsoo Kim; **Tribology** (Ethnology) *Head*: Chungkyun Kim

Research Institutes

Art and Design Technology (Design; Fine Arts; Technology) *Head*: Jooyun Kim; **Business Administration** (Business Administration) *Head*: Tonghun Kim; **East Asia Arts and Culture** (Cultural Studies; East Asian Studies) *Head*: Eankon Park; **Economics** (Economics) *Head*: Minjae Kim; **Environmental Arts** (Environmental Studies) *Head*: Junmo Kang; **Humanities** (Arts and Humanities) *Head*: Sungdo Hong; **Industrial Technology** (Industrial Engineering) *Head*: Iktai Kim; **Information and Communication** (Communication Studies; Information Sciences) *Head*: Bokgyu Joo; **Law** (Law) *Head*: Jonghoon Lim; **Science and Technology** (Natural Sciences; Technology) *Head*: Joonki Chung

History: Founded 1946 as a College, incorporated Soo-Do Engineering College and acquired University status 1971.

Governing Bodies: Board of Trustees

Academic Year: March to February (March-August; September-February)

Admission Requirements: Graduation from high school and entrance examination

Fees: (Won): Liberal Arts/Business/Education: 3,3m. per semester; Arts/Engineering: 4,5m.

Main Language(s) of Instruction: Korean

International Co-operation: With universities in USA, Japan, Finland, Australia, China, France, United Kingdom

Degrees and Diplomas: *Bachelor's Degree (BA, BS)*: 4 yrs; *Master's Degree (MA, MS)*: a further 2 yrs; *Doctor's Degree (PhD)*: 3 yrs following Master

Student Services: Academic counselling, Canteen, Cultural centre, Employment services, Foreign student adviser, Foreign Studies Centre, Handicapped facilities, Health services, Language programs, Social counselling, Sports facilities

Student Residential Facilities: Yes

Special Facilities: University Museum; Gallery of Modern Art

Libraries: Central Library, c. 1,712,000 vols

Publications: Art and Design Research Review; Bulletin of the Research Institute of Industrial Technology *(annually)*; Bulletin of the Research Institute of Science and Technology *(annually)*; Economic Review *(annually)*; Education Research Review *(annually)*; Environmental Development Institute *(annually)*; Hongik Faculty Journal *(annually)*; Humanities *(annually)*; Management Review *(annually)*; Studies on East-West Cultures *(annually)*

Press or Publishing House: University Press

Last Updated: 21/10/08

HOSEO UNIVERSITY

San 29-1 Sechul-ri, Baebang-myeon, Asan-si,
Chungnam-do 336-795
Tel: +82(41) 540-5114
Fax: +82(41) 548-1831
Website: http://www.hoseo.ac.kr

President: Il-kun Kang
Tel: +82(418) 540-5009, Fax: +82(418) 540-5000

Administrative Officer: Jungsuk Kim Tel: +82(418) 540-5006

International Relations: Mon-Bum Lee
Tel: +82(418) 540-5155, Fax: +82(418) 540-5294
EMail: curtis@office.hoseo.ac.kr

Colleges

Arts and Sports (Arts and Humanities; Sports); **Engineering** (Engineering); **Evening Courses**; **Human Sciences** (Arts and Humanities); **Natural Sciences** (Natural Sciences); **Social Sciences** (Social Sciences)

Graduate Schools

Industry and Management (Industrial Engineering; Management)

History: Founded 1978.

Fees: (US Dollars): 5,000 per annum

Main Language(s) of Instruction: Korean

Student Services: Academic counselling, Employment services, Foreign student adviser, Foreign Studies Centre, Health services, Language programs, Nursery care

HOWON UNIVERSITY

727 Wolha, Impi, Gunsan-si, Jeollabuk-do 573-718
Tel: +82(63) 450-7016
Fax: +82(63) 450-6171
EMail: gksk@sunny.howon.ac.kr
Website: http://www.howon.ac.kr

President: Hee-sung Kang

International Relations: Kwang-tae Goh

Departments

Accountancy (Accountancy); **Architectural Engineering** (Architecture; Structural Architecture); **Business Administration** (Business Administration); **Civil Engineering** (Civil Engineering); **Clothing and Textile** (Clothing and Sewing; Textile Technology); **Computer Engineering** (Computer Engineering); **Computer Science** (Computer Science); **Economics** (Economics); **Electrical Engineering** (Electrical Engineering); **Electronic Engineering** (Electronic Engineering); **Engineering Design** (Engineering Drawing and Design); **English** (English); **Food Engineering** (Food Technology); **Industrial Chemistry** (Industrial Chemistry); **Information and Telecommunications Engineering** (Information Technology; Telecommunications Engineering); **International Trade** (International Business); **Law** (Law); **Mechanical Engineering** (Mechanical Engineering); **Nursery and Kindergarden Education** (Preschool Education); **Public Administration** (Public Administration); **Recreation and Leisure Sports** (Leisure Studies; Parks and Recreation); **Tourism and Interpretation** (Tourism; Translation and Interpretation); **Tourism Management** (Tourism)

History: Founded 1977.

HYUPSUNG UNIVERSITY

14 Sang-Ri, Bongdam-eup, Hwaseong-si, Gyeonggi-do 445-745
Tel: +82(31) 299-0661
Fax: +82(31) 227-7501
Website: http://www.hyupsung.ac.kr

President: Sok-ghee Baek

International Relations: Won-suok Kim
Tel: +82(31) 299-0661, Fax: +82(31) 297-3131

Departments

Humanities and Arts (Arts and Humanities); **Theology** (Theology)

History: Founded 1977.

INCHEON CATHOLIC UNIVERSITY

495 Dojang-ri, Yangdo-myeon, Ganghwa-gun, Incheon-si 417-852
Tel: +82(32) 937-8111
Fax: +82(32) 937-8118
EMail: webmaster@iccu.ac.kr
Website: http://www.iccu.ac.kr

President: Bum-gi Hong

Programmes

Fine Arts (Fine Arts); **Theology** (Theology); **Traditional Religion** (Religious Studies)

History: Founded 1996.

INFORMATION AND COMMUNICATIONS UNIVERSITY (ICU)

PO Box 77, 58-4 Hwaam-dong, Yuseong-gu, Daejeon,
Chungnam-do 305-350
Tel: +82(42) 866-6114
Fax: +82(42) 866-6068
EMail: oga@icu.ac.kr
Website: http://www.icu.ac.kr

President: Unna Huh

Schools

Business; **Engineering**

History: Founded 2001 by the Ministry of Information and Communication, Electronics and Telecommunications Research Institute, and related industries. A University for Graduate Studies.

Academic Year: March to February

Admission Requirements: University Degree at Bachelor level; TOEFL test (Masters, at least 550; PhD, at least 600)

Main Language(s) of Instruction: English

Accrediting Agencies: Ministry of Education; Ministry of Information and Communication

Degrees and Diplomas: *Master's Degree*: $1\frac{1}{2}$-2 yrs; *Doctor's Degree (PhD)*: 3-5 yrs

Student Services: Academic counselling, Canteen, Employment services, Foreign student adviser, Handicapped facilities, Health services, Language programs, Nursery care, Social counselling, Sports facilities

Libraries: Yes

INHA UNIVERSITY

253 Yonghyun-dong, Nam-gu, Incheon-si 402-751
Tel: +82(32) 860-7114
Fax: +82(32) 967-1333
EMail: master@inha.ac.kr
Website: http://www.inha.ac.kr

President (Acting): Bon-Su Lee

Colleges

Arts and Sports; **Business Administration** (Business Administration); **Economics and International Trade** (Economics; International Business); **Education** (Education; English; Humanities and Social Science Education; Korean; Mathematics Education; Physical Education; Social Studies); **Engineering** (Aeronautical and Aerospace Engineering; Architecture; Bioengineering; Chemical Engineering; Civil Engineering; Computer Engineering; Electrical Engineering; Energy Engineering; Engineering; Environmental

Engineering; Geophysics; Industrial Engineering; Marine Engineering; Marine Science and Oceanography; Materials Engineering; Mathematics and Computer Science; Mechanical Engineering; Nanotechnology; Naval Architecture; Nuclear Engineering; Physics; Polymer and Plastics Technology; Textile Technology); **Human Ecology** (Child Care and Development; Clothing and Sewing; Consumer Studies; Family Studies; Fashion Design; Food Science; Nutrition; Textile Design); **Humanities** (Arts and Humanities; Chinese; Cultural Studies; English; French; French Studies; German; Germanic Studies; History; Japanese; Korean; Literature; Philosophy); **Information Technology and Engineering** (Computer Engineering; Electrical Engineering; Electronic Engineering; Engineering; Information Technology; Telecommunications Engineering); **Law** (Law); **Medicine** (Medicine; Nursing); **Natural Sciences** (Biology; Chemistry; Marine Science and Oceanography; Mathematics; Natural Sciences; Physics; Statistics); **Natural Sciences**; **Social Sciences**

Schools

Logistics *(Asia-Pacific)* (Transport Management)

Further Information: Also 31 Government-supported Research Centres and 62 Affiliated Research Centres

History: Founded 1954 as Institute of Technology, acquired present status and title 1972.

Governing Bodies: Board of Trustees; University Foundation

Academic Year: March to December (March-July; August-December)

Admission Requirements: Graduation from high school and entrance examination

Main Language(s) of Instruction: Korean, English

Degrees and Diplomas: *Bachelor's Degree*: 4 yrs; *Master's Degree*: a further 2 yrs; *Doctor's Degree*: 2 1/2 yrs or more

Student Services: Academic counselling, Canteen, Cultural centre, Employment services, Nursery care, Social counselling, Sports facilities

Student Residential Facilities: Yes

Libraries: c. 1,091,000 vols

Press or Publishing House: Inha University Press

Last Updated: 02/01/09

INJE UNIVERSITY

607 Obang-dong, Gimhae-si, Gyeongnam-do 621-749
Tel: +82(55) 334-7111 +82(55) 334-7118
Fax: +82(55) 334-0712
EMail: webmaste@inje.ac.kr
Website: http://www.inje.ac.kr

President: Kyeongho Lee

Colleges

Biomedical Science and Engineering (Biomedical Engineering; Biomedicine; Biotechnology; Food Science; Laboratory Techniques; Occupational Therapy; Physical Therapy; Safety Engineering); **Engineering** (Architecture; Automation and Control Engineering; Computer Engineering; Electronic Engineering; Engineering; Industrial Engineering; Materials Engineering; Mechanical Engineering; Optics; Telecommunications Engineering); **Humanities and Social Sciences** (Advertising and Publicity; Arts and Humanities; Business Administration; Chinese; Consumer Studies; Economics; English; English Studies; Health Administration; International Business; International Relations; Journalism; Korean; Law; Political Sciences; Social Sciences; Social Welfare); **Medicine** (Medicine; Nursing); **Natural Sciences** (Data Processing; Environmental Studies; Leisure Studies; Mathematics and Computer Science; Natural Sciences; Sports)

Schools

Design (Design)

Further Information: Also Research Institutes, Graduate Schools and 3 attached Hospitals

History: Founded as College 1979. Acquired present status and title 1989.

Governing Bodies: Inje Educational Foundation

Academic Year: March to February (March-August; September-February)

Admission Requirements: Graduation from high school and entrance examination

Main Language(s) of Instruction: Korean

Degrees and Diplomas: *Bachelor's Degree*: 4 yrs; *Bachelor's Degree*: Medicine, 6 yrs; *Master's Degree*: a further 2 yrs; *Doctor's Degree (PhD)*: 3-4 yrs following Master

Student Residential Facilities: Yes

Libraries: c. 130,000 vols

Publications: Bulletin *(monthly)*; In Je Journal *(biannually)*; In Je Medical Journal *(quarterly)*

Press or Publishing House: University Press

Last Updated: 02/01/09

INTERNATIONAL DESIGN SCHOOL FOR ADVANCED STUDIES

128-8 Yunkun-dong, Jongno-gu, Seoul 110-770
Tel: +82(2) 744-7700, Ext. 111
Fax: +82(2) 744-6866
Website: http://www.idas.ac.kr

Rector: Nahm-Sik Lee

International Relations: Hosun Nam EMail: info@idas.ac.kr

Programmes

Design

History: Founded 1996.

Degrees and Diplomas: *Master's Degree*; *Doctor's Degree*

JEONJU UNIVERSITY

1200 Hyoja-dong 3-ga, Wansan-gu, Jeonju-si,
Jeollabuk-do 560-759
Tel: +82(63) 220-2114
Fax: +82(63) 220-2404
EMail: drpark@jj.ac.kr
Website: http://www.jeonju.ac.kr

President: Nam-sik Lee

Colleges

Education (Chinese; Education; English; Home Economics; Korean; Mathematics Education)

Research Centres

Art and Culture (Cultural Studies; Fine Arts); **Christianity** (Christian Religious Studies); **Education** (Education; Educational Sciences); **Engineering and Technology** (Engineering; Technology); **History and Culture** (Cultural Studies; History); **Humanities** (Arts and Humanities); **Industrial Management** (Industrial Management); **Natural Sciences** (Architecture; Biological and Life Sciences; Chemistry; Civil Engineering; Electrical and Electronic Engineering; Environmental Engineering; Industrial Engineering; Materials Engineering; Mathematics and Computer Science; Mechanical Engineering; Natural Sciences; Urban Studies); **Politics and Development** (Development Studies; Political Sciences); **Regional Development** (Regional Planning); **Social Sciences** (Social Sciences)

Schools

Arts, Athletics and Visual Communication (Advertising and Publicity; Film; Fine Arts; Industrial Design; Music; Music Theory and Composition; Painting and Drawing; Photography; Physical Education; Sculpture; Theatre; Visual Arts); **Business Administration** (Accountancy; Advertising and Publicity; Business Administration; Business and Commerce; Finance; International Business; Taxation); **Christian Studies** (Christian Religious Studies; Music); **Culture and Tourism** (Cooking and Catering; Fashion Design; Hotel Management; Tourism); **Engineering** (Architecture; Civil Engineering; Electrical and Electronic Engineering; Environmental Engineering; Industrial Engineering; Mechanical Engineering; Town Planning); **Evening Studies** (Accountancy; Architecture; Business Administration; Christian Religious Studies; Civil Engineering; Computer Engineering; Electrical and Electronic Engineering; Environmental Engineering; Finance; Industrial Engineering; Information Technology; Insurance; International Business; International Relations; Law; Management; Mechanical Engineering; Real Estate; Statistics); **Finance and Real Estate** (Finance; Insurance; Real Estate); **Information Technology and Computer**

Engineering (Industrial Management; Information Management; Information Sciences; Information Technology; Multimedia; Statistics); **Language and Culture** (Asian Studies; Chinese; Cultural Studies; English; English Studies; European Studies; French; French Studies; German; Germanic Studies; Japanese; Korean; Literature); **Law and Politics** (Administration; International Relations; Law; Police Studies; Public Administration); **Management** (Accountancy; Advertising and Publicity; Banking; Finance; Information Management; International Business; Management; Management Systems; Public Relations; Small Business); **Mechanical and Industrial Engineering** (Industrial Engineering; Mechanical Engineering); **Natural Sciences** (Biological and Life Sciences; Chemistry; Environmental Management; Materials Engineering; Mathematics; Microbiology); **Social Sciences** (Information Sciences; Library Science; Public Administration; Real Estate; Social Sciences; Social Welfare); **Visual Arts** (Cinema and Television; Design; Film; Fine Arts; Theatre)

Further Information: Also Graduate Schools

History: Founded 1964, acquired present status 1978.

Academic Year: March to December (March-June; September-December)

Admission Requirements: Graduation from high school or equivalent

Main Language(s) of Instruction: Korean, English

Degrees and Diplomas: *Bachelor's Degree (BA)*: 4 yrs; *Master's Degree (MA/MS)*: a further 2 yrs; *Doctor's Degree (PhD)*: 3 yrs following Master's

Student Services: Academic counselling, Canteen, Cultural centre, Employment services, Foreign student adviser, Handicapped facilities, Health services, Language programs, Nursery care, Social counselling, Sports facilities

Student Residential Facilities: Yes

Special Facilities: University Museum. Multimedia Room. Language Education Center

Libraries: Central Library: c. 450,000 vols

Publications: Jeonju University Bulletin *(annually)*; Jeonju University Journal *(annually)*

Press or Publishing House: Jeonju University Press

JINJU INTERNATIONAL UNIVERSITY

San 270 Sangmoon-ri, Munsan-eup, Jinju-si,
Gyeongnam-do 660-845
Tel: +82(55) 751-8005
Fax: +82(55) 761-7407
EMail: parksw@jiu.ac.kr
Website: http://www.jiu.ac.kr

President: Kyung-mo Kang

Colleges

Arts and Sports (Fine Arts; Sports); **Engineering** (Engineering); **Humanities and Social Sciences** (Humanities and Social Science Education; Social Sciences); **Natural Sciences** (Natural Sciences)

JOONG-ANG SANGHA UNIVERSITY

159-1 Pungmu-dong, Gunpo-si, Gyeonggi-do 415-070
Tel: +82(31) 980-7777
Fax: +82(31) 980-7778
EMail: sangha@sangha.ac.kr
Website: http://www.sangha.ac.kr

President: Jong-beom Ven

Departments

Buddhism Studies (Asian Religious Studies); **Buddhist Scipture Translation**; **Social Welfare** (Social Welfare); **Sociology of Dissemination**

History: Founded 1996.

Degrees and Diplomas: *Bachelor's Degree*; *Master's Degree*
Last Updated: 02/01/09

JOONGBU UNIVERSITY

San 2-25 Daehang-ro, Chubu-myeon, Keumsan-gun,
Chungnam-do 312-702
Tel: +82(41) 750-6321
Fax: +82(41) 750-8748
EMail: international@joongbu.ac.kr
Website: http://www.joongbu.ac.kr

President: Ho-Il Lee (2001-)

International Relations: Jin-won Kim Tel: +82(41) 750-6522

Colleges

Arts and Physical Education; **Humanities and Social Sciences** (Arts and Humanities; Business Administration; Business and Commerce; Economics; Education of the Gifted; Law; Police Studies; Preschool Education; Social Sciences); **Information and Communication** (Computer Engineering; Graphic Arts; Information Technology); **Science and Engineering** (Acupuncture; Biological and Life Sciences; Construction Engineering; Engineering; Information Technology; Medicine; Technology)

Institutes

Arts and Sports (Fine Arts; Sports); **Humanities and Social Sciences** (Arts and Humanities; Social Sciences)

Research Institutes

Industry Technology (Technology); **Natural Sciences**

History: Founded 1983.

KANGNAM UNIVERSITY

San 6-2 Gugal-ri, Giheung-eup, Yongin-si, Gyeonggi-do 449-702
Tel: +82(31) 280-3424
Fax: +82(31) 281-3428
EMail: kimjh@kangnam.ac.kr
Website: http://sheep.kangnam.ac.kr/eng/

President: Shin-il Yoon

International Relations: Jin-hwack Kim

Colleges

Arts and Physical Education (Music; Painting and Drawing; Physical Education; Sports; Visual Arts); **Humanities** (Arts and Humanities; Chinese; Education; English; Japanese; Korean; Literature; Preschool Education; Special Education); **Management and Economics** (Business Administration; Economics; International Business; Management; Taxation); **Science and Engineering** (Architecture; Computer Engineering; Computer Science; Electronic Engineering; Engineering; Industrial Engineering; Mathematics; Natural Sciences; Urban Studies); **Social Sciences** (Law; Library Science; Public Administration; Real Estate; Social Sciences); **Social Welfare**; **Theology** (Philosophy; Religious Studies; Theology)

Research Institutes

Humanities; **Industrial Liaison** (Industrial Engineering; Science Education); **Social Sciences** (Social Sciences); **Woowon**

History: Founded 1946.

Degrees and Diplomas: *Bachelor's Degree*; *Master's Degree*; *Doctor's Degree*
Last Updated: 02/01/09

KAYA UNIVERSITY

San 120 Jisan-ri, Goryeong-eup, Goryeong-gun,
Gyeongbuk-do 717-802
Tel: +82(54) 950-5285
Fax: +82(54) 954-6094
Website: http://www.kaya.ac.kr

President: Sang-hee Lee

Colleges

Arts; **Engineering** (Ceramics and Glass Technology; Computer Engineering; Electronic Engineering; Materials Engineering); **Natural Sciences**; **Social Sciences**

History: Founded 1992 as Kaya Ceramic College. Acquired present title and status 1995.

Main Language(s) of Instruction: Korean
Last Updated: 02/01/09

KDI SCHOOL OF PUBLIC POLICY AND MANAGEMENT (KDI)

207-43 Chungnyangri 2-dong, Dongdaemun-gu, Seoul 130-868
Tel: +82(2) 3299-1259
Fax: +82(2) 968-5071
EMail: admissions@kdischool.ac.kr
Website: http://www.kdischool.ac.kr

Dean: Sang-Moon Hahm

Programmes

Economics and Public Policy; **Finance and Banking**; **Growth and Development**; **International Relations and Political Economy**; **Strategy and Global Management**

Further Information: Traditional and Open Learning Institution

History: Founded 1997.

Main Language(s) of Instruction: English

Degrees and Diplomas: *Master's Degree*: Asset Management (MAM); Business Administration (MBA), 1 1/2 yrs; *Master's Degree*: Foreign Direct Investment (MFDI), 11/2- 2 yrs (evening and weekend programme); *Master's Degree*: Public Policy (MPP), 11/2 yrs; *Doctor's Degree*: Public Policy; Management

Student Services: Academic counselling, Employment services, Foreign student adviser, Handicapped facilities, Health services, Language programs, Nursery care, Sports facilities

Student Residential Facilities: Yes

Last Updated: 02/01/09

KEIMYUNG UNIVERSITY (KU)

2800 Dalgubeoldaero, Dalseo-gu, Daegu 704-701
Tel: +82(53) 580-6022-8
Fax: +82(53) 580-6025
EMail: intl@kmu.ac.kr
Website: http://www.kmu.ac.kr

President: Synn Ilhi (2004-)
Tel: +82(53) 580-5000, Fax: +82(53) 580-5005
EMail: leechinu@kmu.ac.kr

Centres

Automotive Parts Technology (Automotive Engineering; Industrial Engineering; Mechanical Engineering) *Director*: Tae Kwon Kim; **Business Education** *(Keimyung University) Director*: Gwan Soo Hong; **Continuing Education** (Continuing Education) *Dean*: Won Hee Lee; **Engineering Education** (Engineering) *Head*: Seong Hoon Kim; **Fashion-Textile Design Research and Development** (Fashion Design; Textile Design) *Dean*: Geun Woo Ryu; **Secondary Education Teachers** *(In-Service Training)* (Teacher Training) *Dean*: Mun Jong Lee

Colleges

Business Administration (Accountancy; Business Administration; Information Management; Taxation; Tourism) *Dean*: Joong Hee Lee; **Business Economics and Commerce** (Consumer Studies; E-Business/Commerce; Economics; International Business) *Dean*: Jae Yool Lee; **Education** (Education; Literature; Preschool Education) *Dean*: Jong Mun Lee; **Engineering** (Architecture; Automotive Engineering; Chemical Engineering; Civil Engineering; Materials Engineering; Mechanical Engineering; Transport Engineering; Urban Studies) *Dean*: Seong Hark Chung; **Environmental Studies** (Environmental Engineering; Environmental Management; Environmental Studies) *Dean*: Sang Won Park; **Fashion** (Fashion Design; Textile Design) *Dean*: Ho-Jung Lee; **Fine Arts** (Fine Arts; Handicrafts; Industrial Design; Painting and Drawing; Photography) *Dean*: Won Hee Lee; **Foreign Language and Literature** (Chinese; English; French; German; Japanese; Korean; Russian; Writing) *Dean*: Il Woo Park; **Humanities** (Ethics; History; Korean; Philosophy; Theology; Writing) *Dean*: Chung Hee Han; **Information and Communication Engineering** *Dean*: Dae Wook Bang; **International Studies** (American Studies; Chinese; French Studies; Germanic Studies; Japanese) *Dean*: Byung Ohg Chang; **Law and Police Science** (Law; Police Studies) *Dean*: Shang Ho Choi; **Media and Visual Communication** (Advertising and Publicity; Journalism; Mass Communication; Media Studies; Public Relations) *Dean*: Jin Young Tak; **Media Art** (Music; Visual Arts) *Dean*: Keum Woo Nam; **Medicine** (Medicine) *Dean*: Man Bin Yim; **Music and Performing Arts** (Cinema and Television; Music; Music Theory and Composition; Musical Instruments; Performing Arts; Singing) *Dean*: Ho Uk Yu; **Natural Sciences** (Biology; Chemistry; Food Science; Mathematics; Microbiology; Physics; Public Health; Statistics) *Dean*: Jaesung Choi; **Nursing** (Nursing) *Dean*: Yeong Hee Shin; **Physical Education** (Dance; Leisure Studies; Physical Education; Sports) *Dean*: Jang Hwan Kim; **Social Sciences** (Advertising and Publicity; Library Science; Mass Communication; Psychology; Public Relations; Social Welfare; Sociology) *Dean*: Bong-Gi Choi

Faculties

Liberal Education (Arts and Humanities) *Dean*: Moo Jin Choi

Graduate Schools

Art and Design (Design; Fine Arts) *Dean*: Ho Uk Yu; **Business Administration** (Business Administration); **Early Childhood Education** (Preschool Education) *Dean*: Panhee Kim; **Education** (Education) *Dean*: Ah Chung Park; **Health Care Admininistration** *Dean*: Man Bin Yim; **Interpretation and Translation** (Translation and Interpretation) *Dean*: Jong Hwan Kim; **Policy Studies** (Political Sciences) *Dean*: Si Kyung Lee; **Sports Industry** (Sports) *Dean*: Sang Hong Kim; **Theology** (Theology) *Dean*: Joong Ho Chong; **Women's Studies** (Women's Studies) *Dean*: Ka Hyo Yoo

Research Institutes

Chronic Disease *Director*: Jong Wook Park; **Digital Art** *Dean*: Up Kwon; **Environmental** *(Nakdonggang) Dean*: Seong Woo Choi; **Small and Medium Business Technology Innovation** (Business Administration) *Director*: Cheol Soo Kim

Further Information: Also Dongsan Medical Centre; Student Exchange Programme

History: Founded 1954 by the Presbyterian Church in Korea as a small Christian Liberal Arts College. Received charter from the Government 1956 and became University 1978.

Governing Bodies: University Council

Academic Year: March to December (March-June; September-December)

Admission Requirements: Secondary school certificate or recognized equivalent

Fees: (Won): 2.8m. per semester

Main Language(s) of Instruction: Korean

International Co-operation: With universities in Japan, China, Thailand, USA, Russian Federation and Europe

Degrees and Diplomas: *Bachelor's Degree*: 4 yrs; *Master's Degree*: a further 2 yrs; *Doctor's Degree*: 3 yrs following Master

Student Services: Academic counselling, Canteen, Cultural centre, Employment services, Foreign student adviser, Foreign Studies Centre, Handicapped facilities, Health services, Language programs, Nursery care, Social counselling, Sports facilities

Student Residential Facilities: For 1,506 students

Special Facilities: University Museum (including Kaya Kingdom relics)

Libraries: Dong San Memorial Library, c. 1.3m. Vols

Publications: Accounting Information Review *(annually)*; Acta Koreana *(annually)*; Asian Journal of Business and Entrepreneurship *(annually)*; Business Management Review *(annually)*; Journal of Communication Research *(annually)*; Journal of Cross-Cultural Studies *(annually)*; Journal of International Studies *(annually)*; Journal of the Institute for Industrial Science *(annually)*; Keimyung Law Review *(annually)*; Keimyung Theology *(annually)*; Keimyung University Medical Journal *(quarterly)*; The Journal of Art and Culture *(annually)*; The Journal of Educational Research *(annually)*; The Journal of Social Sciences *(annually)*; The Journal of the Institute for International Studies *(annually)*; The Journal of the Institute of Natural Sciences *(biannually)*; The Proceedings of Mathematical Science *(annually)*

Press or Publishing House: The Keimyung University Press

Last Updated: 02/01/09

KKOTTONGNAE HYUNDO UNIVERSITY OF SOCIAL WELFARE

387 Sangsam-ri, Hyundo-myeon, Cheongwon-si, Chungbuk-do 363-823
Tel: +82(43) 270-0114
Fax: +82(43) 270-0120
Website: http://www.kkot.ac.kr

President: Dong-ho Lee

Programmes

Social Welfare

History: Founded 1998.

Main Language(s) of Instruction: Korean

KONKUK UNIVERSITY

1 Hwayang-dong, Gwangjin-gu, Seoul 143-701
Tel: +82(2) 450-3259
Fax: +82(2) 452-3257
EMail: imcim@konkuk.ac.kr
Website: http://www.konkuk.ac.kr

President: Kil-saeng Chung

International Relations: Il-min Chung

Colleges

Agriculture (Agriculture); **Animal Husbandry** (Animal Husbandry); **Arts and Home Economics** (Artificial Intelligence; Arts and Humanities; Home Economics); **Business Administration** (Business Administration); **Commerce and Economics** (Business and Commerce; Economics); **Education** (Education); **Engineering** (Aeronautical and Aerospace Engineering; Biotechnology; Chemical Engineering; Civil Engineering; Electrical and Electronic Engineering; Engineering; Environmental Engineering; Industrial Chemistry; Industrial Design; Mechanical Engineering; Structural Architecture; Textile Technology); **Law** (Law); **Liberal Arts** (Arts and Humanities; Chinese; English; German; History; Jewish Studies; Korean; Literature; Modern Languages; Philosophy); **Political Sciences** (Political Sciences); **Sciences** (Biology; Chemistry; Geography; Natural Sciences; Physics)

Graduate Schools

Agriculture (Agriculture); **Business Administration** (Business Administration); **Education** (Education); **Engineering** (Engineering); **Public Administration** (Public Administration)

Institutes

Agricultural Resources Development Research (Agriculture); **Arts and Design Research** (Design; Fine Arts); **Basic Sciences Research** (Natural Sciences); **Chinese Affairs** (International Relations); **Economics and Management** (Economics; Management); **Education Research** (Educational Research); **Environmental Science Research** (Environmental Studies); **Genetic Engineering** (Genetics); **Humanities Research** (Arts and Humanities); **Industrial Science and Technology** (Industrial Engineering); **Korean Reunification Studies**; **Life Culture** (Cultural Studies); **Medical Sciences Research** (Medicine); **Natural Sciences** (Natural Sciences); **Public Administration Research** (Public Administration); **Real Estate Policy** (Real Estate); **Social Development and Policy** (Development Studies); **Social Sciences Research** (Social Sciences)

History: Founded 1946 as Cho-Sun Political Science School, acquired present status and title 1959. A private Institution financed by the Konkuk University Foundation, but supervised by the Ministry of Education.

Academic Year: March to December (March-June; September-December)

Admission Requirements: Graduation from high school and entrance examination

Main Language(s) of Instruction: Korean

Degrees and Diplomas: *Bachelor's Degree*: Agriculture; Business Administration; Commerce; Economics; Engineering; Fine Arts; Home Economics; Law; Literature; Music; Physical Education; Political Science; Public Administration; Science; Veterinary Medicine, 4 yrs; *Bachelor's Degree*: Medicine, 6 yrs; *Master's Degree*: Agriculture; Business Administration; Economics; Education; Engineering; Fine Arts; Home Economics; Law; Literature; Medicine; Music; Physical Education; Political Science; Public Administration; Science; Veterinary Medicine, a further 2 yrs; *Doctor's Degree*: Agriculture; Business Administration; Economics; Education; Engineering; Law; Literature; Philosophy; Political Science; Public Administration; Science; Veterinary Medicine, a further 3 yrs

Student Residential Facilities: For c. 640 students

Special Facilities: University Museum

Libraries: Sang-Huh Memorial Library, c. 500,000 vols. Joongwon Library, c. 130,000 vols

Publications: Journals of the Research Institutes *(annually)*

Press or Publishing House: University Press

CHUNGJU CAMPUS

322 Danwol-dong, Chungju-si, Chungbuk-do 380-150
Tel: +82(441) 840-3114
Website: http://www.konkuk.ac.kr

Vice-President: Won Jai Maeng

Colleges

Art (Fine Arts); **Humanities** (Arts and Humanities); **Medicine** (Medicine); **Natural Sciences** (Natural Sciences); **Social Sciences** (Social Sciences)

History: Founded 1980.

KONYANG UNIVERSITY

26 Nae-dong, Nonsan-si, Chungnam-do 320-711
Tel: +82(41) 730-5114
Fax: +82(41) 733-2070
EMail: kyk8969@konyang.ac.kr
Website: http://www.konyang.ac.kr

President: Hee-Soo Kim

International Relations: Min-young Song

Centres

Computer Science (Computer Science)

Colleges

Business and Economics (Business and Commerce; Economics); **Commerce** (Business and Commerce); **Engineering** (Engineering); **Food Culture** (Food Science); **Humanities** (Arts and Humanities; English; Korean; Literature); **Industrial Technology** (Industrial Engineering); **Liberal Arts** (Arts and Humanities); **Natural Sciences** (Natural Sciences); **Science** (Natural Sciences)

Institutes

Research

History: Founded 1991.

KOOKMIN UNIVERSITY

861-1 Chongnung-dong, Songbuk-Gu, Seoul 136-702
Tel: +82(2) 910-4115 +82(2) 910-4118
Fax: +82(2) 910-4171
Website: http://www.kookmin.ac.kr

President: Sung Woo Lee

Colleges

Architecture Design (Design); **Art and Music** (Fine Arts; Music); **Economics and Business Administration** (Business Administration; Economics); **Education** (Education); **Engineering** (Engineering); **Forest Science** (Forestry); **Humanities** (Arts and Humanities); **Law** (Law); **Natural Sciences** (Natural Sciences); **Social Sciences** (Social Sciences)

Institutes

Economics Research (Economics); **Korean Studies** (Korean); **Language and Literature** (Literature; Modern Languages); **Legal Research** (Law)

History: Founded 1946 as night College, acquired present status and title 1981.

Academic Year: March to February (March-August; September-February)

Admission Requirements: Graduation from high school, or recognized equivalent, and entrance examination

Main Language(s) of Instruction: Korean

Degrees and Diplomas: *Bachelor's Degree*: 4 yrs; *Master's Degree*: a further 2 yrs; *Doctor's Degree (PhD)*: a further 6 yrs

Student Services: Academic counselling, Canteen, Employment services, Health services, Nursery care, Social counselling, Sports facilities

Student Residential Facilities: Yes

Libraries: Central Library, c. 450,000 vols

Publications: Design Review; Economics and Business Review; Journal of Language and Literature; Journal of Scientific Institute; Law and Political Review; Papers in Chinese Studies; Thesis of Engineering; Thesis of Korean Studies

Press or Publishing House: University Press

Last Updated: 02/01/09

KOREA BAPTIST THEOLOGICAL UNIVERSITY

San 14 Hagi-dong, Yuseong-gu, Daejeon, Chungnam-do 305-358
Tel: +82(42) 828-3114
Fax: +82(42) 825-1354
Website: http://www.kbtus.ac.kr

President: Han-ho Doh (2004-)
Tel: +82(42) 828-3112 EMail: dhh@kbtus.ac.kr

Dean, Academic Affairs: Sangki Moon
Tel: +82(42) 828-3130, Fax: +82(42) 828-3135
EMail: skmoon@kbtus.ac.kr

International Relations: Dae-Won Lee
Tel: +82(42) 825-3114, Fax: +82(42) 825-1354
EMail: Daewon@kbtus.ac.kr

Graduate Schools

Theology *Director*: Sunbae Kim

History: Founded 1953.

Admission Requirements: Bachelor of Arts (B.A.) for graduate programme (M.Div.); Master of Divinity (M.Div.) for postgraduate programmes (Th.M and Ph.D.)

Fees: (U.S. Dollars): 3,000 per semester

Main Language(s) of Instruction: Korean, English

Degrees and Diplomas: *Master's Degree (M.Th.)*: 2 yrs; *Master's Degree (M.Div.)*: 3 yrs; *Doctor's Degree (Ph.D.)*: 5 yrs

Student Services: Academic counselling, Employment services, Foreign student adviser, Handicapped facilities, Sports facilities

Publications: Gospel and Practice *(1-2 per annum)*

Press or Publishing House: University Publishing House

Last Updated: 16/10/08

KOREA NAZARENE UNIVERSITY (KNU)

456 Ssangyong-dong, Chonan-si, Chungnam-do 330-718
Tel: +82(41) 570-7831
Fax: +82(41) 570-7771
Website: http://www.kornu.ac.kr

President: Seung-an Im

Colleges

Theology *(Graduate)* (Theology)

Departments

Liberal Arts (Artificial Intelligence; Arts and Humanities)

Divisions

Computer Science (Computer Science); **English** (English); **Rehabilitation and Social Welfare** (Social Welfare; Welfare and Protective Services)

History: Founded 1954 as Bible College. Acquired Theological College status 1982, and present status and title 1994. Korea Nazarene University is one of 52 Nazarene Universities and Colleges around the world.

Governing Bodies: Nazarene Church

Academic Year: March to December (March-June; September-December)

Admission Requirements: Graduation from high school and SAT score

Main Language(s) of Instruction: Korean

International Co-operation: Student exchange with 8 major Nazarene universities/colleges in USA

Accrediting Agencies: Ministry of Education; Association of Universities in Korea

Degrees and Diplomas: *Bachelor's Degree*: 4 yrs; *Master's Degree*: a further 2 yrs

Student Services: Academic counselling, Canteen, Employment services, Foreign student adviser, Foreign Studies Centre, Handicapped facilities, Language programs, Sports facilities

Student Residential Facilities: Yes

Special Facilities: Rehabilitation Centre

Libraries: 2,297 vols; 59,771 periodicals

Publications: Jisung Kwa Changjo (Intelligence and Creation), Journal of Nazarene Academy; Nasaret Nonchong (Nazarene Review), Collected Research Papers *(annually)*

Press or Publishing House: Nasaret Daehakgyo Chulpansa (Nazarene University Press)

Last Updated: 05/01/09

KOREA POLYTECHNIC UNIVERSITY (KPU)

101 Jeongwang-dong 3-ga, Siheung-si, Gyeonggi-do 429-793
Tel: +82(31) 496-8000
Fax: +82(31) 496-8179
EMail: webmaster@kpu.ac.kr
Website: http://www.kpu.ac.kr

President: Jun Yeong Choi

Departments

Advanced Materials Engineering; **Chemical Engineering** (Chemical Engineering); **Computer Engineering** (Computer Engineering); **Control and Measurement Engineering** (Automation and Control Engineering; Measurement and Precision Engineering); **Game Engineering**; **Mechanical Design Engineering** (Design; Mechanical Engineering); **Mechanical Engineering** (Mechanical Engineering)

Further Information: Also Graduate Schools

History: Founded 1997.

Main Language(s) of Instruction: Korean

Degrees and Diplomas: *Bachelor's Degree*; *Master's Degree*; *Doctor's Degree*

Last Updated: 02/01/09

KOREA UNIVERSITY

Anam-dong, Seongbuk-gu, Seoul 136-701
Tel: +82(2) 3290-2951
Fax: +82(2) 921-5820
EMail: studyabroad@korea.ac.kr
Website: http://www.korea.edu

President: Ki-Su Lee (2008-) Tel: +82(2) 3290-1001

Colleges

Business Administration (Business Administration); **Education** (Computer Science; Education; English; Geography; History; Home Economics; Korean; Mathematics Education; Physical Education); **Engineering** (Architecture; Chemical Engineering; Civil Engineering; Electrical Engineering; Engineering; Industrial Engineering; Materials Engineering; Mechanical Engineering); **Law** (Law); **Liberal Arts** (Arts and Humanities; Asian Studies; Chinese; English; French; German; History; Japanese; Korean; Linguistics; Modern Languages; Philosophy; Psychology; Russian; Sociology; Spanish); **Life Sciences and Biotechnology** (Biological and Life Sciences; Biotechnology; Ecology; Environmental Studies; Food Science); **Medicine** (Medicine; Nursing); **Nursing** (Nursing); **Political Science and Economics** (Economics; International Relations; Mass Communication; Political Sciences; Public Administration; Statistics); **Sciences** (Biology; Chemistry; Computer Science; Earth Sciences; Environmental Studies; Mathematics; Natural Sciences; Physics)

Graduate Schools

Biotechnology (Biotechnology); **Business Administration** (Business Administration); **Computer Science and Technology** (Computer Science; Technology); **Education** (Educational Sciences); **Industrial Information Technology** (Information Technology); **International Studies** (International Studies); **Journalism and Mass Communication** (Journalism; Mass Communication); **Labour Studies** (Labour and Industrial Relations; Labour Law); **Legal Studies** (Law); **Management and Information** (Information Sciences; Management); **Natural Resources** (Natural Resources)

Research Centres

Advanced Materials Chemistry (Chemistry); **Asiatic Studies** (Asian Studies); **Behavioural Science** (Behavioural Sciences); **Disaster Prevention Science and Technology** (Safety Engineering); **European Union** (European Studies); **Korean Culture** (Cultural Studies); **Life Sciences** (Biological and Life Sciences); **Mineral Resources** (Mineralogy); **Public Administration** (Public Administration); **Semiconductor Technology** (Information Technology; Technology)

Research Institutes

Anglo-American Studies (American Studies; English Studies); **Economics Research** (Economics); **Energy Technology** (Energy Engineering); **Environmental Health** (Occupational Health); **Environmental Technology and Sustainable Development** (Development Studies; Environmental Engineering); **German Studies** (German; Modern Languages); **High Technology Materials and Devices** (Materials Engineering; Technology); **Industrial Technology** (Industrial Engineering); **Industry Development**; **Information and Communication Technology** (Communication Studies; Information Technology; Technology); **Labour Education**; **Language and Information** (Information Sciences); **Mass Communication** (Mass Communication); **Natural Resources and Environment** (Environmental Studies; Natural Resources); **Natural Sciences** (Natural Sciences); **Nutrition** (Nutrition); **Peace Studies** (Peace and Disarmament); **Philosophy Studies** (Philosophy); **Plastic Reconstructive and Special Surgery** (Plastic Surgery); **Russian Studies** (Russian); **Social Research** (Social Studies); **Tropical Epidemic Diseases** (Tropical Medicine); **Viral Diseases** (Virology)

Further Information: Also Teaching Hospitals (Anam, Guro, Yeoju, Ansan). Courses for Foreign Students. Language training programme (English, Japanese, Chinese). Students Exchange Programme

History: Founded 1905 as Posung College, acquired present status and title 1946. A private Institution operated by the Korea-Choongang Educational Foundation but supervised by the Ministry of Education.

Governing Bodies: University Council

Academic Year: March to December (March-June; September-December)

Admission Requirements: Graduation from high school or equivalent, and entrance examination

Main Language(s) of Instruction: Korean and English

Degrees and Diplomas: *Bachelor's Degree*: 4 yrs; *Bachelor's Degree*: Medicine, 6 yrs; *Master's Degree*: a further 2 yrs; *Doctor's Degree (PhD)*: a further 3 yrs. Also Teaching qualifications and Certificates in Education, Business Administration and Natural Resources

Student Services: Academic counselling, Cultural centre, Employment services, Foreign student adviser, Health services, Social counselling, Sports facilities

Student Residential Facilities: For c. 1,810 students

Special Facilities: Museum of Korean Antiquities

Libraries: Central Library, c. 1,501,000 vols; Medicine Library, c. 76,000; Science Library, c. 250,000; Seo Chang Library, c. 200,000

Publications: Business Administration Journal; Business Review; Journal of Asiatic Studies; Kodai Munwha (Culture); Korean Cultural Studies; Sa Chong (Historical Review)

Press or Publishing House: Korea University Press

Last Updated: 21/10/08

SEJONG CAMPUS

Chochiwon-uhp, Yonki-Kun, Chochiwon,
Chungcheongnam-do 339-800
Tel: +82(415) 860-1114
Fax: +82(415) 862-5182

Colleges

Economics and Commerce (Business and Commerce; Economics); **Humanities** (Archaeology; Art History; Arts and Humanities; Chinese; English; German; Korean; Sociology; Writing); **Information and Communications** (Computer Science; Radio and Television Broadcasting); **Journalism and Mass Communication** (Journalism; Mass Communication); **Science and Technology** (Automation and Control Engineering; Biomedical Engineering; Biotechnology; Chemistry; Environmental Engineering; Information Technology; Leisure Studies; Mathematics and Computer Science; Natural Sciences; Physics; Sports; Technology)

History: Founded 1980 as Seochang Campus. Acquired present title 2008.

KOREA UNIVERSITY OF TECHNOLOGY AND EDUCATION (KUT)

307 Gajeon-ri, Byeongcheon-myeon, Cheonan-si,
Chungnam-do 330-708
Tel: +82(41) 560-2527
Fax: +82(41) 560-2529
EMail: webmaster@kut.ac.kr
Website: http://www.kut.ac.kr

President: Hyung-Nam Moon

International Relations: Joo-sung Jang EMail: jjs1928@kut.ac.kr

Centres

Industrial Cooperative Research (Business Administration); **Semiconductor Equipment Technology Education** (Electronic Engineering; Technology Education)

Departments

Applied Chemical Engineering (Chemical Engineering); **Architectural Engineering** (Architecture; Construction Engineering); **Automatic Control and Systems Engineering** (Automation and Control Engineering); **New Materials Engineering** (Materials Engineering)

Institutes

Human Resources Development (Education; Human Resources; Technology Education)

Schools

Industrial Management (Industrial Management); **Information and Technology Engineering** (Computer Engineering; Electrical and Electronic Engineering; Information Technology); **Liberal Arts and Education** (Arts and Humanities; Education; Literature; Modern Languages); **Mechanical Engineering** (Mechanical Engineering); **Mechatronics Engineering** (Electrical Engineering; Industrial Design; Mechanical Engineering)

History: Founded 1992 with financial support from Ministry of Labour. Acquired present status and title 1995.

Admission Requirements: Graduation from high school and entrance examination

Main Language(s) of Instruction: Korean

Student Services: Academic counselling, Employment services, Health services, Language programs, Nursery care, Social counselling, Sports facilities

Student Residential Facilities: Yes

Libraries: Dasan Information Library

Publications: Journal of Technology and Education of Korea University *(annually)*

Press or Publishing House: KUT's Press

KOREAN BIBLE UNIVERSITY

205 Sanggye 7-dong, Nowon-Gu, Seoul 139-791
Tel: +82(2) 950-5436
Fax: +82(2) 950-5451
EMail: yesuwann2@bible.ac.kr
Website: http://www.bible.ac.kr

President: Uoo-Chung Kang
Tel: +82(2) 950-5426 EMail: uckang@bible.ac.kr

Planning Director: Tae-Kyu Kim
Tel: +82(2) 950-5481 EMail: tkkim@bible.ac.kr

International Relations: Seung-Ho Kim
Tel: +82(2) 950-5489 EMail: jshk@bible.ac.kr

Divisions

Arts and Humanities (Arts and Humanities; Education; Social Welfare); **Engineering** (Computer Engineering); **Religion** (Protestant Theology; Religion; Theology)

History: Founded 1952.

Admission Requirements: High school diploma

Main Language(s) of Instruction: Korean

Degrees and Diplomas: *Bachelor's Degree (BA)*: 4 yrs; *Master's Degree*; *Doctor's Degree*

Student Services: Academic counselling, Canteen, Foreign student adviser, Handicapped facilities, Language programs, Social counselling, Sports facilities

Student Residential Facilities: Yes

Libraries: Yes

Last Updated: 02/01/09

KOSIN UNIVERSITY

149-1, Dongsam-dong, Yeongdo-gu, Pusan 606-701
Tel: +82(51) 990-2114
Fax: +82(51) 911-2504
EMail: jhpark@kosin.ac.kr
Website: http://www.kosin.edu

President: Sung-soo Kim

Colleges

Art (Industrial Design; Music; Painting and Drawing); **Humanities and Social Sciences** (Advertising and Publicity; Arts and Humanities; Child Care and Development; Chinese; Computer Science; English; Health Administration; Literature; Social Welfare); **Medicine** (Health Sciences; Medicine; Nursing); **Natural Sciences** (Biology; Chemistry; Ecology; Environmental Studies; Food Science; Health Sciences; Mathematics and Computer Science; Natural Sciences; Nutrition); **Theology** (Christian Religious Studies; Missionary Studies; Theology)

Further Information: Also College Hospital

History: Founded 1946. A private Institution operated by the Presbyterian Church of Korea.

Academic Year: March to December (March-July; September-December)

Admission Requirements: Graduation from high school and entrance examination

Fees: (US Dollars): 5,000 per annum

Main Language(s) of Instruction: Korean

Degrees and Diplomas: *Bachelor's Degree*: 4 yrs; *Bachelor's Degree*: Medicine, 6 yrs; *Master's Degree*: a further 2 yrs; *Doctor's Degree*: Medicine, 3 yrs following Master

Student Services: Academic counselling, Employment services, Foreign student adviser, Health services, Language programs, Nursery care, Social counselling, Sports facilities

Student Residential Facilities: For 300 students

Special Facilities: Educational Broadcasting Station

Libraries: Total, 221,911 vols

KWANDONG UNIVERSITY (KDU)

522 Naegok-dong, Gangneung-si, Gangwon-do 210-701
Tel: +82(33) 649-7085 +82(33) 649-7086
Fax: +82(33) 649-7969
EMail: irc@kwandong.ac.kr
Website: http://www.kwandong.ac.kr

President: Dong-Gwan Han

Dean of Administrative Affairs: Sung-jung Mo
Tel: +82(33) 649-7110 EMail: sungjm@kwandong.ac.kr

International Relations: Yong-hoon Choi, Director, International Relations and Education Institute

Colleges

Arts and Design (Design; Fine Arts; Industrial Design; Music; Musical Instruments; Visual Arts) *Dean*: Seok-won Ryu; **Business Administration** (Advertising and Publicity; Business Administration; Economics; Finance; Health Administration; Information Technology; International Business) *Dean*: Joo-han Bae; **Education** (Computer Education; Education; English; Foreign Languages Education; Geography; Geography (Human); Home Economics; Korean; Mathematics Education; Physical Education; Science Education) *Dean*: Choong-woo Lee; **Engineering** (Architecture; Biomedical Engineering; Civil Engineering; Computer Science; Electronic Engineering; Environmental Engineering; Hygiene; Information Technology; Telecommunications Engineering) *Dean*: Jae-kug Jung; **Humanities** (Arts and Humanities; Chinese; Christian Religious Studies; Cultural Studies; East Asian Studies; English; History; Japanese; Literature) *Dean*: Choon-keun Yu; **Law and Politics** (Law; Police Studies; Public Administration; Social Welfare) *Dean*: Cheol-joo Kim; **Medicine** (Medicine; Nursing) *Dean*: Dong-su Yeon; **Tourism and Sports** (Health Administration; Health Sciences; Hotel Management; Leisure Studies; Sports; Sports Management; Tourism) *Dean*: Seung-dong Yoo

History: Founded 1954 as Junior College, acquired present status 1959. Acquired present title 1960. A Christian institution.

Governing Bodies: Myong-ji Educational Fundation

Academic Year: March to February (March-September; September-February)

Admission Requirements: Graduation from high school and entrance examination

Fees: (Won): 3,2 m.-4 m. per semester. 40% reduction on tuition fee for international students

Main Language(s) of Instruction: Korean

International Co-operation: With universities in Australia, China, Italy, Japan, USA, Switzerland, Vietnam, Russian Federation, Kazakhstan, Kyrgyzstan

Degrees and Diplomas: *Bachelor's Degree*: Architecture; Architecture Design, 5 yrs; *Bachelor's Degree*: Arts; Sinology; History; English Language and Literature; Japanese Language and Literature; Media Literature; Christian Studies; Korean Language Education; English Language Education; Geography Education; Business Administration; International Business; Management Information Technology; Advertising; Healthcare Management; Design; Interior Design; Economics and Finance; Engineering; Civil Engineering; Architecture Engineering; Electronic Information and Communication Engineering (Electronic, Information Communication); Computer Science; Biomedical Engineering; Health and Environmental Hygiene; Fine Arts; Visual Design; Home Economics; Home Economics Education; Law; Music (Winds, Strings, Percussions, Piano, Applied Music); Nursing Science; Physical Education; Sports and Leisure Studies (Sports & Leisure Studies, Sports Management, Sports and Health Management); Police Science; Police Administration; Public Administration; Science; Mathematics Education; Computer Education; Social Welfare; Tourism; Hotel and Tourism (Tourism Management, Hotel Management, Culinary Arts, Air & Travel Service), 4 yrs; *Bachelor's Degree*: Medicine; Medical Science, 6 yrs; *Master's Degree*: Arts; Korean Language and Literature; History; English Language and Literature; Business Administration; Business Management; International Trade; Management Accounting and Information Statistics; Design; Interior Design; Economics; Economics and Finance; Education; Engineering; Computer Science Engineering, Electronic Engineering, Civil Engineering, Environmental Engineering, Architecture Engineering, Transportation Engineering, Electronic Communication Engineering, Marine Engineering; Fine Arts; International Studies; Law; Medical Science; Missiology; Theology; Music; Nursing Science; Physical Education; Police Science; Police Administration; Public Administration; Science; Mathematics Information; Tourism; Tourism Management, 2 yrs; *Master's Degree*: Business Administration; Business Management, International Trade; Educational Administration, Psychology of Counselling, Educational Engineering, Christian Education, Korean Language Education, English Language Education, Geography Education, Home Economics Education, Mathematics Education, Computer Science Education; Engineering; Disaster Management (Coastal Disaster Management, Infrastructure Management, Disaster Prevention Policy); Physical Education, Music Education, Fine Arts Education, Infant Education, Nursing Education, Environment Education, French Language Education, Chinese Language Education, Social Studies Education, Technology Education; Police Science; Police Administration; Public Administration; Social Welfare; Tourism; Tourism Management, 2 1/2 yrs; *Doctor's Degree*: Arts; Korean Language and Literature; History; English Language and Literature; Business Administration; Business Management; International Trade; Economics and Finance; Education; Engineering; Computer Science Engineering; Electronic Engineering; Civil Engineering; Environmental Engineering; Architecture Engineering; Transportation Engineering; Electronic Communication Engineering;

International Studies; Law; Medicine; Science; Medical Science; Nursing Science; Physical Education; Police Science; Police Administration; Public Administration; Science; Mathematics Information; Tourism; Tourism Management, 3 yrs

Student Services: Academic counselling, Canteen, Employment services, Handicapped facilities, Health services, Language programs, Social counselling, Sports facilities

Student Residential Facilities: Yes

Special Facilities: Museum. Movie Studio

Libraries: Central Library, c. 700,000 vols

Publications: Journal of Humanities *(annually)*; Journal of Social Sciences *(annually)*; Journal of Student Life Research *(annually)*; Journal of Tourism Development *(annually)*

Academic Staff *2008-2009*	MEN	WOMEN	TOTAL
FULL-TIME	286	96	382
PART-TIME			237
STAFF WITH DOCTORATE			
FULL-TIME	–	–	281
Student Numbers *2008-2009*			
All (Foreign Included)	5,537	2,838	8,375

Last Updated: 27/01/09

KWANGSHIN UNIVERSITY

San-70 Bonchon-dong, Buk-gu, Gwangju-si, Gyeonggi-do 500-710
Tel: +82(62) 605-1111
Fax: +82(62) 572-0264
Website: http://www.kwangshin.ac.kr

President: Kyu-nam Jung

International Relations: Won-jun Jo EMail: jwj1015@korea.com

Programmes

Christian Childhood Education (Religious Education); **Church Music** (Religious Music); **Theology** (Theology)

History: Founded 1954.

KWANGWOON UNIVERSITY (KWU)

26 Kwangwoon-Gil, Wolgye-Dong, Nowon-gu, Seoul 139-701
Tel: +82(2) 940-5114
Fax: +82(2) 940-5506
EMail: webadmin@kw.ac.kr
Website: http://www.kw.ac.kr

President: Sang Chui Lee
Tel: +82(2) 940-5000, Fax: +82(2) 918-5682
EMail: pre-lsc@kw.ac.kr

Vice President: Sang Hoon Kim
Tel: +82(2) 940-5280, Fax: +82(2) 940-5278
EMail: shkim@kw.ac.kr

International Relations: Young Kyun Lim, Director
Tel: +82(2) 940-5013 EMail: lyk5316@kw.ac.kr

Colleges

Business Administration (Business Administration); **Engineering** (Architecture; Chemical Engineering; Civil Engineering; Engineering; Environmental Engineering; Structural Architecture); **Law** (International Law; Law); **Natural Sciences** (Chemistry; Computer Science; Electronic Engineering; Leisure Studies; Mathematics; Natural Sciences; Physics; Sports); **Northeast Asia Studies** (Business and Commerce; Chinese; Cultural Studies; East Asian Studies; International Relations; Japanese; Korean); **Social Sciences** (English; Industrial and Organizational Psychology; Journalism; Media Studies; Public Administration; Radio and Television Broadcasting; Social Sciences)

Departments

Electronics (Automation and Control Engineering; Computer Engineering; Computer Science; Electrical Engineering; Electronic Engineering; Information Technology; Telecommunications Engineering)

Divisions

Korean Language and Literature (Korean; Literature)

Graduate Schools

Business Administration (Business Administration; Business and Commerce; E-Business/Commerce); **Education** (Adult Education; Computer Education; Continuing Education; Education; Educational Administration; Educational and Student Counselling; Educational Psychology; English; Foreign Languages Education; Multimedia; Preschool Education); **Environmental Studies**; **Information and Communication**; **Information and Social Welfare** (Criminology; Information Sciences; Psychoanalysis; Social Welfare)

History: Founded 1934 as Institute of Technology, acquired present status and title 1988. A private Institution operated by the Kwangwoon Foundation but supervised by the Ministry of Education.

Academic Year: March to February (March-August; September-February)

Admission Requirements: Graduation from high school (vocational or training schools are not acceptable), language proficiency over TOPIK level 4 or equivalent and entrance examination (both written and spoken)

Fees: (Won): Admission fee, c. 950,000; tuition fee, an average 3,871,000 per semester

Main Language(s) of Instruction: Korean, English (for some programmes offered at the Graduate Schools)

Degrees and Diplomas: *Bachelor's Degree*: Architecture, 5 yrs; *Bachelor's Degree*: Business Administation; Engineering; Science; Physical Education; Arts; Trade; Cultural Industry Development; International Relations; Public Administration; Psychology; Law, 4 yrs; *Master's Degree*: Electronic Engineering, Electronics and Communications Engineering, Electrical Engineering, Electronic Materials Engineering, Computer Engineering, Chemical Engineering, Control and Instrumentation Engineering; Environmental Engineering, Architectural Engineering, Radio Science and Engineering, Computer Science, Electrophysics, Chemistry, Mathematics, Business Administration; International Trade, Public Administration, Law, Korean Language and Literature, English Language and Literature, Journalism and Communication Studies, Industrial Psychology, Management Information System, Information Display, Crime, 2 yrs following Bachelor's Degree; *Doctor's Degree*: Electronic Engineering, Electronics and Communications Engineering, Electrical Engineering, Electronic Materials Engineering, Computer Engineering, Chemical Engineering, Control and Instrumentation Engineering (PhD); Environmental Engineering, Architectural Engineering, Radio Science and Engineering, Computer Science, Electrophysics, Chemistry, Mathematics, Business Administration; International Trade, Public Administration, Law, Korean Language and Literature, English Language and Literature, Journalism and Communication Studies, Industrial Psychology, Management Information System, Information Display, Crime

Student Services: Academic counselling, Canteen, Cultural centre, Employment services, Foreign student adviser, Foreign Studies Centre, Handicapped facilities, Health services, Language programs, Nursery care, Social counselling, Sports facilities

Student Residential Facilities: International House for 96 students

Special Facilities: Theatres; Digial Studio

Libraries: Central Library, c. 508,139 vols

Publications: , 8,000 prints at a time distributed to alumni, current students, faculty members and staffs *(monthly)*; Kwangwoon University Newspaper; NEXT, 20,000 prints at a time distributed for nation-wide high-schoolers *(1-2 per annum)*

Press or Publishing House: and The Kwangwoon Annals

Last Updated: 23/10/08

KYONGGI UNIVERSITY

San 94-6 Yiui-dong, Paldal-gu, Suwon-si, Gyeonggi-do 443-760
Tel: +82(31) 249-8765
Fax: +82(31) 255-5915
EMail: oip@kyonggi.ac.kr
Website: http://www.kyonggi.ac.kr

President: Chong-kuk Son

International Relations: Jun-hyuk Lee

Departments

Accountancy (Accountancy); **Architecture** (Architecture); **Business Administration** (Business Administration); **Civil Engineering** (Civil Engineering); **English Language and Literature** (English);

Industrial Management (Industrial Management); **International Trade** (International Business); **Korean Language and Literature** (Korean); **Physical Education** (Physical Education); **Public Administration** (Public Administration); **Tourism Development** (Tourism); **Tourism** (Tourism)

Institutes

American Culture and Language (American Studies); **Chinese Studies** (Chinese); **Production Management** (Production Engineering); **Social Studies** (Social Studies); **Tourism Development** (Hotel Management; Tourism)

Further Information: Also Seoul Campus

History: Founded 1947 as Teacher Training College, acquired present status and title 1976. A private institution financed by tuition fees and Foundation support.

Academic Year: March to February (March-August; September-February)

Admission Requirements: Graduation from high school and entrance examination

Main Language(s) of Instruction: Korean

Degrees and Diplomas: *Bachelor's Degree*: 4 yrs

Student Residential Facilities: For c. 150 students

Libraries: c. 65,000 vols

Publications: Journal of Industrial Business Problems; Kyonggi Magazine; Research Journals *(annually)*; Study on Tourism

KYUNG HEE UNIVERSITY (KHU)

1 Hoeki-dong, Dongdaemoon-gu, Seoul 130-701
Tel: +82(2) 961-0031 +82(2) 961-0032
Fax: +82(2) 962-4343
EMail: cie@khu.ac.kr
Website: http://www.khu.ac.kr

President: Inwon Choue EMail: president@khu.ac.kr

Colleges

Arts and Design (Acting; Cinema and Television; Computer Graphics; Dance; Fashion Design; Film; Graphic Design; Industrial Design; Landscape Architecture; Textile Design); **Business Administration**; **Dentistry** (Dental Hygiene; Dental Technology; Dentistry; Oral Pathology; Orthodontics; Periodontics); **Human Ecology**; **Humanities**; **Law** (Administrative Law; Civil Law; Commercial Law; Comparative Law; Constitutional Law; Criminal Law; Fiscal Law; International Law; Labour Law; Law; Maritime Law; Public Administration; Public Law); **Medicine** (Anaesthesiology; Anatomy; Biochemistry; Biology; Biophysics; Cell Biology; Dermatology; Embryology and Reproduction Biology; Endocrinology; Gastroenterology; Genetics; Gynaecology and Obstetrics; Haematology; Health Administration; Histology; Immunology; Medical Parasitology; Medicine; Microbiology; Molecular Biology; Nephrology; Neurology; Nursing; Oncology; Ophthalmology; Otorhinolaryngology; Pathology; Pharmacology; Physiology; Plastic Surgery; Psychiatry and Mental Health; Radiology; Social and Preventive Medicine); **Music** (Music; Music Theory and Composition; Musical Instruments; Singing); **Oriental Medicine** (Acupuncture; Endocrinology; Gynaecology and Obstetrics; Hygiene; Otorhinolaryngology; Paediatrics; Pathology; Psychiatry and Mental Health; Rehabilitation and Therapy; Social and Preventive Medicine; Surgery; Traditional Eastern Medicine); **Pharmacy** (Pharmacy); **Political Science and Economics** (Accountancy; Administration; American Studies; Banking; Business Administration; Business and Commerce; Communication Studies; Comparative Politics; Comparative Sociology; East Asian Studies; Econometrics; Economic and Finance Policy; Economic History; European Studies; Finance; Government; Health Administration; History of Societies; Human Resources; Industrial and Production Economics; Industrial Management; International Business; International Economics; International Relations; International Studies; Journalism; Labour and Industrial Relations; Management; Management Systems; Marketing; Political Sciences; Public Administration; Social Policy; Social Studies; Sociology; Taxation); **Science** (Applied Chemistry; Applied Mathematics; Applied Physics; Atomic and Molecular Physics; Biology; Botany; Cell Biology; Chemistry; Geography; Inorganic Chemistry; Mathematics; Microbiology; Molecular Biology; Natural Sciences; Nuclear Physics; Optics; Organic Chemistry; Physical Chemistry; Physics; Solid State Physics; Statistics; Thermal Physics; Virology; Zoology); **Tourism and Hotel Management** (Cooking and Catering; English; Hotel Management; Japanese; Tourism; Translation and Interpretation)

Graduate Institutes

Peace Studies (Comparative Politics; East Asian Studies; Peace and Disarmament; Social Welfare)

Graduate Schools

Business Administration (Accountancy; Business Administration; Finance; Fiscal Law; International Economics; Management; Marketing; Retailing and Wholesaling; Taxation); **East-West Medicine** (Acupuncture; Health Administration; Immunology; Neurology; Nutrition; Oncology; Traditional Eastern Medicine); **Education** (Agricultural Education; Art Education; Business Education; Computer Education; Education; Educational Administration; Educational Psychology; Educational Technology; Ethics; Foreign Languages Education; Humanities and Social Science Education; Mathematics Education; Native Language Education; Preschool Education; Primary Education; Science Education); **Graduate Studies** (Accountancy; Agronomy; Architecture; Astronomy and Space Science; Biology; Ceramic Art; Chemical Engineering; Chemistry; Chinese; Civil Engineering; Clothing and Sewing; Computer Engineering; Dance; Economics; Electronic Engineering; English; Environmental Studies; Fine Arts; Food Science; Food Technology; Forestry; French; Genetics; Geography; History; Home Economics; Horticulture; Industrial Engineering; International Business; Japanese; Korean; Landscape Architecture; Law; Literature; Management; Mass Communication; Mathematics; Mechanical Engineering; Medicine; Music; Nuclear Engineering; Nursing; Nutrition; Pharmacy; Philosophy; Physics; Political Sciences; Public Administration; Sociology; Spanish; Textile Technology; Traditional Eastern Medicine); **Industry and Information Sciences** (Accountancy; Agriculture; Automation and Control Engineering; Automotive Engineering; Ceramic Art; Civil Engineering; Development Studies; Electronic Engineering; Food Science; Food Technology; Forestry; Horticulture; Industrial Design; Industrial Engineering; Information Management; Information Technology; International Business; Landscape Architecture; Materials Engineering; Mechanical Engineering; Software Engineering; Sports Management; Telecommunications Engineering); **International Legal Affairs** (Commercial Law; European Union Law; Fiscal Law; Insurance; International Law; Maritime Law); **Journalism and Mass Communication** (Communication Studies; Journalism; Mass Communication; Media Studies); **NGO Studies**; **Pan-Pacific International Studies** (Government; Information Technology; International Business; International Economics; Latin American Studies; Marketing); **Physical Education** (Physical Education; Sports); **Public Administration** (Information Management; Management; Public Administration; Urban Studies; Welfare and Protective Services); **Tourism** (Cooking and Catering; Hotel and Restaurant; Hotel Management; Leisure Studies; Tourism)

Schools

Civil and Architectural Engineering (Architectural Restoration; Architecture; Civil Engineering; Construction Engineering; Environmental Engineering; Landscape Architecture; Regional Planning; Town Planning); **Electronics and Information Technology** (Applied Mathematics; Applied Physics; Astronomy and Space Science; Computer Engineering; Electronic Engineering; Information Technology; Mathematics; Physics); **Environment and Applied Chemistry** (Chemical Engineering; Chemistry; Environmental Engineering; Materials Engineering; Textile Technology); **Foreign Languages** (Chinese; English; French; Japanese; Korean; Literature; Modern Languages; Russian; Spanish); **Life Sciences and Biotechnology** (Agronomy; Biotechnology; Food Science; Forestry; Genetics; Horticulture); **Management and International Relations** (Accountancy; American Studies; International Relations; Management; Marketing; Pacific Area Studies; Taxation); **Mechanical and Industrial System Engineering** (Engineering Management; Industrial Engineering; Materials Engineering; Mechanical Engineering; Nuclear Engineering); **Physical Education and Sports Sciences** (Physical Education; Sports Management; Sports Medicine)

Further Information: University and Dental Hospitals and Oriental Hospital. Seoul, Suwon and Kwangnung campuses

History: Founded 1949 as Shin Hung College, acquired present status and title 1951. A private institution financially supported by private business interests, and consisting of three campuses: Seoul, Suwon, and Kwangnung.

Governing Bodies: Board of Trustees

Academic Year: March to December (March-July; August-December)

Admission Requirements: Graduation from high school and entrance examination

Main Language(s) of Instruction: Korean, some English

International Co-operation: With 181 colleges/universities in 50 countries

Degrees and Diplomas: *Bachelor's Degree*: 4 yrs; *Master's Degree*: a further 2 1/2 yrs; *Doctor's Degree*: 3 yrs following Master

Student Services: Academic counselling, Cultural centre, Employment services, Foreign Studies Centre, Health services, Language programs, Nursery care, Social counselling, Sports facilities

Student Residential Facilities: Yes

Special Facilities: University Museum. Natural History Museum. Observatory. Experimental Nuclear Reactor

Libraries: Central Library and branch libraries, c. 1,2m. vols; Medical Library, c. 15,000 vols

Publications: College publications; Peace Forum *(biannually)*; Research Institutes' magazines

Press or Publishing House: Kyung Hee University Press

Last Updated: 05/01/09

KYUNGBUK FOREIGN LANGUAGE COLLEGE (KFLC)

220-1 Hyupsuk-li, Namchum-Myun, Kyungsangbuk-do
Tel: +82(53) 810 -0100
Fax: +82(53) 810 -0139
Website: http://www.kflc.ac.kr/

President: No Byung Su

Departments

Airline Service (Service Trades; Tourism); **Chinese** (Chinese); **Dental Hygiene** (Dental Hygiene); **English** (English); **Hotel Culinary and Bakery**; **Japanese**; **Medical Information System**; **Multi-images** (Advertising and Publicity; Computer Graphics; Graphic Arts; Video; Visual Arts); **Nursing**; **Occupational Therapy** (Occupational Therapy); **Oriental Martial Arts** (Philosophy; Physical Education); **Police and Security**; **Preschool Education** (Preschool Education); **Public Health Administration**; **Real Estate Finance Technology**; **Russian** (Russian); **Social Welfare** (Social Welfare); **Tourism**; **Wedding Coordination**

Research Institutes

Computing Information Centre; **Culture and Tourism Education Centre**; **Inauguration Incubation Centre**; **International Languages**

History: Founded 1988. Acquired present status and title 2005.

KYUNGDONG UNIVERSITY

San 91-1, Bongpo-ri, Tosung-myeon, Koseong-gun, Goseong-si, Gangwon-do 219-832
Tel: +82(33) 631-2000
Fax: +82(33) 631-9543
Website: http://www.kyungdong.ac.kr

President: Dong-Jin Shin

International Relations: Yung-Min Ko
EMail: ymk@kyungdong.ac.kr

Schools

Architectural Engineering; **Construction Engineering** (Civil Engineering; Construction Engineering); **Information Technology Engineering** (Computer Engineering; Computer Science; E-Business/Commerce); **Management** (Management; Marketing); **Tourism** (Hotel Management; Tourism; Translation and Interpretation)

History: Founded 1996.

Main Language(s) of Instruction: Korean

Degrees and Diplomas: *Bachelor's Degree*

Last Updated: 05/01/09

KYUNGIL UNIVERSITY

33 Buho-ri, Hayang-eup, Gyeongsan-si, Gyeongbuk-do 712-701
Tel: +82(53) 853-8001
Fax: +82(53) 853-8800
Website: http://www.kiu.ac.kr/

President: Nam-Kyo Lee (2008-)
Tel: +82(53) 850-7010, Fax: +82(53) 850-7970
EMail: lnk1000@kiu.ac.kr

Dean, Academic Affairs: Man-Woo Huh
Tel: +82(53) 850-7021, Fax: +82(53) 850-7972
EMail: mwhuh@kiu.ac.kr

International Relations: Sung-Ho Park, Dean, Planning and University Development
Tel: +82(53) 850-7024, Fax: +82(53) 850-8708
EMail: shpark@kiu.ac.kr

Centres

Continuing Education *Head*: Moo-Joon Chung; **International Relations and Foreign Language Education** *Executive Director*: Moo-Joo Chung; **Library and Computer Science** *Head*: Ki-Dong Bu; **Minor Enterprise Support** (Business Administration) *Head*: Ji-Hyeung Yoo; **Research Supporting** *Head*: Ji-Hyeung Yoo; **Teacher and Learning** *Head*: Hong-Kyu Choi

Colleges

Engineering (Engineering) *Head*: In-Sik Kim; **Formative Arts** *Head*: Bok-Sang Jung; **Humanities and Social Sciences** *Head*: In-Soo Moon

Graduate Schools

Design *Head*: Man-Woo Huh; **Industry** *Head*: Man-Woo Huh

Research Centres

Industrial Information Technology *Head*: In-Sik Kim; **Social Sciences** *Head*: In-Soo Moon

Research Institutes

Formative Arts *Head*: Kyung-Soon Choi

Schools

Graduate *Head*: Man-Woo Huh

History: Founded 1963 as Kyungpook San Up University. Acquired present title 1997.

Academic Year: March to December

Admission Requirements: SAT, Grade Point average of high school, and entrance examination

Fees: (US Dollars): c. 2,500-3,000

Main Language(s) of Instruction: Korean, English, Chinese

International Co-operation: With universities in USA, Japan, China, Russian Federation, Philippines, Mongolia

Accrediting Agencies: Ministry of Education, Science and Technology

Degrees and Diplomas: *Bachelor's Degree*: 4 yrs; *Master's Degree*: 2 yrs

Student Services: Academic counselling, Canteen, Employment services, Foreign student adviser, Foreign Studies Centre, Handicapped facilities, Health services, Language programs, Sports facilities

Student Residential Facilities: Yes

Special Facilities: Multi-Media Center; Laboratories

Libraries: Main Library

Last Updated: 06/11/08

KYUNGNAM UNIVERSITY (KU)

449 Wolyoung-dong, Masan-si, Gyeongnam-do 631-701
Tel: +82(55) 245-5000
Fax: +82(55) 247-9344
EMail: sfa0@kyungnam.ac.kr
Website: http://www.kyungnam.ac.kr

President: Jae-Kyu Park (2001-)

Vice-President: Soe Ki-Young
Tel: +82(55) 244-5833, Fax: +82(55) 245-8114
EMail: asam@kyungnam.ac.kr

International Relations: Sang-Bo Han, Executive Director
Tel: +82(55) 243-2821 EMail: sbhan@kyungnam.ac.kr

Colleges

Commerce and Economics (Business and Commerce; Economics); **Education** (Education); **Engineering** (Architecture; Engineering); **Law and Political Science** (Law; Political Sciences); **Liberal Arts** (Arts and Humanities); **Natural Sciences**

Graduate Schools

Business Administration (Business Administration); **Education** (Education)

Institutes

Environmental Research (Environmental Studies); **Far Eastern Studies** (Southeast Asian Studies); **Industrial Management** (Industrial Management); **International Education**

History: Founded 1946 as School in Seoul. Moved to Masan 1954 and acquired present status and title 1982.

Governing Bodies: Board of Trustees

Academic Year: March to February (March-August; September-February)

Admission Requirements: Graduation from high school and entrance examination

Main Language(s) of Instruction: Korean

Degrees and Diplomas: *Bachelor's Degree*: 4 yrs; *Master's Degree*: a further 2 yrs; *Doctor's Degree*: at least a further 3 yrs

Student Services: Academic counselling, Canteen, Employment services, Foreign student adviser, Handicapped facilities, Health services, Language programs, Social counselling, Sports facilities

Student Residential Facilities: Yes

Libraries: c. 170,000 vols

Press or Publishing House: University Printing Department

KYUNGSUNG UNIVERSITY

110-1 Daeyeon-dong, Nam-gu, Pusan 608-736
Tel: +82(51) 620-4114
Fax: +82(51) 623-7803
Website: http://ks.ac.kr/

President: Joong Shik Nah

Colleges

Arts (Arts and Humanities; Cinema and Television; Photography; Theatre); **Commerce and Economics** (Business and Commerce; Economics); **Engineering** (Engineering; Multimedia); **Law and Political Science** (Law; Political Sciences); **Liberal Arts** (Arts and Humanities); **Multimedia**; **Pharmacy** (Pharmacy); **Science** (Natural Sciences); **Theology**

Graduate Schools

Clinical Pharmacy; **Education** (Education); **Industry** (Industrial Engineering); **International Business** (International Business); **Multimedia**; **Social Welfare**

History: Founded 1955.

Main Language(s) of Instruction: Korean

Degrees and Diplomas: *Bachelor's Degree*; *Master's Degree*

Last Updated: 05/01/09

KYUNGWON UNIVERSITY

San-65 Bokjeong-dong, Sujeong-gu, Seongnam-si, Gyeonggi-do 461-701
Tel: +82(31) 750-5671 +82(31) 750-5672
Fax: +82(31) 750-5674
EMail: isk007@mail.kyungwon.ac.kr
Website: http://www.kyungwon.ac.kr

President: Gil Yeo Lee

International Relations: Son-koo Lee
Tel: +82(31) 750-5017, Fax: +82(31) 750-5076

Colleges

Arts (Design; Fine Arts; Industrial Design; Painting and Drawing; Photography; Sculpture; Visual Arts); **Business and Economics** (Accountancy; Business Administration; Business and Commerce; International Business); **Engineering**; **Human Ecology** (Child Care and Development; Clothing and Sewing; Food Science; Health Sciences; Nutrition; Sports); **Humanities**; **Law and Social Sciences**; **Natural Science**; **Oriental Medicine** (Anatomy; Medicine; Pathology; Pharmacology; Physiology); **Software**

Schools

Music (Music; Music Theory and Composition; Musical Instruments; Singing)

Further Information: Also Graduate School and Professional Graduate Schools

History: Founded 1982.

Main Language(s) of Instruction: Korean

Degrees and Diplomas: *Bachelor's Degree*; *Master's Degree*; *Doctor's Degree*

Last Updated: 05/01/09

KYUNGWOON UNIVERSITY

San 5-1, Indeong-ri, Sandong-myeon, Gumi-si, Gyeongbuk-do 730-850
Tel: +82(54) 479-1114
Fax: +82(54) 479-1029
EMail: master@ikw.ac.kr
Website: http://www.kyungwoon.ac.kr

President: Hyang-ja Kim

International Relations: Hong-Kug An
EMail: hKan@kyungwoon.ac.kr

Schools

Architectural Engineering; **Child Welfare** (Child Care and Development); **Computer Engineering** (Computer Engineering); **Electronics and Information Engineering** (Electronic Engineering; Information Technology); **Guarding**; **Health and Environment**; **Information and Communication Engineering** (Communication Studies; Information Technology); **Management** (Management); **Mass Communication and Advertising** (Advertising and Publicity; Mass Communication); **Multimedia Engineering** (Multimedia); **Multimedia Video and Photo** (Multimedia; Photography; Video); **Police Administration** (Police Studies); **Tourism** (Tourism); **Visual Image Design** (Visual Arts)

History: Founded 1997.

Main Language(s) of Instruction: Korean

Degrees and Diplomas: *Bachelor's Degree*; *Master's Degree*

Last Updated: 05/01/09

LUTHER UNIVERSITY (LTU)

17 Sanggal-ri, Kiheung-eup, Yongin-si, Gyeonggi-do 449-905
Tel: +82(31) 283-3593
Fax: +82(31) 283-1505
Website: http://www.ltu.ac.kr

President: Hilbert Riemer
Tel: +82(31) 283-6197, Fax: +82(31) 283-6197

International Relations: Il-young Park

Colleges

Social Welfare *Head*: Seon-Young Lee; **Theology** (Theology) *Head*: Il-Young Park

History: Founded 1966. Acquired present status 1997.

Governing Bodies: Board of Regents

Academic Year: March to December (March-June; August-December)

Admission Requirements: Graduation from high school

Fees: (Won): 2,4m. per semester

Main Language(s) of Instruction: Korean

International Co-operation: With universities in USA and Germany

Accrediting Agencies: Ministry of Education

Degrees and Diplomas: *Bachelor's Degree*: Social Welfare (BS); Theology (BTh), 4 yrs

Student Services: Academic counselling, Foreign student adviser, Language programs, Social counselling

Student Residential Facilities: For c. 100 students

Libraries: Central library c. 22,000 vols; Computer link access to other resources

Publications: Lutu Yunku (Luther Study), Journal of Luther and Reformation research published under auspices of LTU's Luther Study Institute *(annually)*; Shinhak Kwa Shinang (Theology and Faith), Theological journal written and edited by LTU Faculty *(annually)*

MARGARET PRITCHARD UNIVERSITY

168-1 Jungwasan 1-dong, Wasan-gu, Jeonju-si, Jeollabuk-do
Tel: +82(63) 230-7700
EMail: daniel@mail.mpu.ac.kr
Website: http://www.mpu.ac.kr

President: Kang Mi Ja Kim

Colleges

Nursing (Nursing); **Social Welfare**

History: Founded 1950.

MOKPO CATHOLIC UNIVERSITY

894-1 Seokhyeon-dong, Mokpo-si, Jeollanam-do 530-400
Tel: +82(61) 280-5000
Fax: +82(61) 280-5101
EMail: admin@mcu.ac.kr
Website: http://www.mcu.ac.kr

President: Joung-hee Lee

Departments

Early Childhood Education (Preschool Education); **Nursing**; **Social Welfare** (Social Welfare)

History: Founded 1966.

MOKWON UNIVERSITY

Doan-dong 800, Seo-gu, Daejeon, Chungnam-do 302-729
Tel: +82(42) 829-7114
Fax: +82(42) 829-5020
EMail: webmaster@mokwon.ac.kr
Website: http://www.mokwon.ac.kr

President: Yo-han Lee

Centres

Computer Science (Computer Science)

Colleges

Fine Arts (Fine Arts); **Humanities** (Arts and Humanities); **Liberal Arts and Science** (Arts and Humanities; Natural Sciences); **Music** (Music); **Science and Engineering** (Computer Science; Engineering; Natural Sciences); **Social Sciences** (Business Administration; Economics; Law; Social Sciences; Statistics)

Graduate Schools

Theology (Theology)

Institutes

Industrial Management (Industrial Management)

History: Founded 1954 as Seminary, acquired present status and title 1980.

Academic Year: March to February (March-August; September-February)

Admission Requirements: Graduation from high school or foreign equivalent, and entrance examination

Main Language(s) of Instruction: Korean

Degrees and Diplomas: *Bachelor's Degree*: 4 yrs; *Master's Degree*: a further 2 yrs

Student Residential Facilities: Yes

Libraries: c. 130,000 vols

Last Updated: 05/01/09

MYONGJI UNIVERSITY

San 38-2 Nam-dong, Yongin-si, Gyeonggi-do 449-728
Tel: +82(31) 330-6114
Fax: +82(31) 332-2459
EMail: shjoo@mju.ac.kr
Website: http://www.mju.ac.kr

President: Jung-ho Son
Tel: +82(31) 330-6121, Fax: +82(31) 330-6122

Colleges

Business Administration and Economics (Business Administration; Economics); **Electrical and Electronic Engineering** (Electrical and Electronic Engineering); **Humanities and Social Sciences** (Arts and Humanities; Social Sciences); **Humanities** (Arts and Humanities); **Law and Political Science** (Law; Political Sciences); **Science** (Natural Sciences)

Institutes

Humanities (Arts and Humanities); **Industrial Research** (Industrial Engineering); **Public Administration Research** (Public Administration); **Saemul**

Programmes

Civil and Transportation Engineering; **Information and Communication**

History: Founded 1948 as a private Institution of Higher Education for Women, reorganized 1962 as Seoul Moon-Lee College of Business and Technology, and achieved present status 1983.

Admission Requirements: Graduation from high school or equivalent and entrance examination

Main Language(s) of Instruction: Korean

Degrees and Diplomas: *Bachelor's Degree*: 4 yrs; *Master's Degree*: a further 2 yrs; *Doctor's Degree (PhD)*: 4 yrs

Libraries: Total, c. 200,500 vols

MYUNGSHIN UNIVERSITY

212-1 Gumchi-ri, Byollyang-myeon, Suncheon-si, Jeollanam-do 540-871
Tel: +82(61) 742-2351
Fax: +82(61) 742-2352
EMail: webmaster@myungshin.ac.kr
Website: http://www.myungshin.ac.kr

President: Jong-phil Lee

International Relations: Yoon-ju Lee

Colleges

Fine Arts; **Natural Sciences**; **Social Sciences** (Social Sciences)

History: Founded 2000.

NAMBU UNIVERSITY

864-1 Wolgye-dong, Gwangsan-gu, Gwangju-si, Gyeonggi-do 506-824
Tel: +86(62) 970-0001
Fax: +86(62) 970-0118
EMail: nambu@nambu.ac.kr
Website: http://www.nambu.ac.kr

President: Rim Yil-Nam Tel: +82(62) 970-0011

Schools

Automotive Engineering *Head*: Chi-Kyun Kim; **Computer Engineering** (Computer Engineering); **Electronic Engineering** (Electronic Engineering) *Head*: Hae-Am Park; **Mechanical Engineering**

History: Founded1998.

Fees: (US Dollars) 4,000 per annum

Main Language(s) of Instruction: Korean and English

Degrees and Diplomas: *Bachelor's Degree*: 4 yrs; *Master's Degree*; *Doctor's Degree*

Student Services: Academic counselling, Employment services, Foreign student adviser, Foreign Studies Centre, Health services, Language programs, Social counselling, Sports facilities

Last Updated: 02/04/09

NAMSEOUL UNIVERSITY

21 Maeju-ri, Seongwhan-eup, Cheonan-si, Chungnam-do 330-807
Tel: +82(41) 580-2000
Fax: +82(41) 582-2117
EMail: cscho@nsu.ac.kr
Website: http://www.nsu.ac.kr

President: Chung-ja Kong

Centres

Audiovisual (Media Studies); **Computer Science** (Computer Science)

Schools

Business and Management (Business and Commerce; Management); **Design** (Design); **Engineering** (Architecture; Communication Studies; Computer Science; Electronic Engineering; Engineering; Information Technology); **Humanities** (Arts and Humanities; Chinese; English; Japanese; Modern Languages)

History: Founded 1994.

Academic Year: March to December (March-June; August-December)

Admission Requirements: Graduation from high school

Main Language(s) of Instruction: Korean, English, Japanese, Chinese

Degrees and Diplomas: *Bachelor's Degree*: 4 yrs; *Master's Degree*

Libraries: Central Library, c. 20,500 vols

Publications: Namseoul Journal

Last Updated: 05/01/09

PAICHAI UNIVERSITY

439-6 Doma-dong, Seo-gu, Daejeon, Chungnam-do 306-735
Tel: +82(42) 520-5454
Fax: +82(42) 520-5799
EMail: inter@mail.pcu.ac.kr
Website: http://www.pcu.ac.kr

President: Soon-hoon Chung

International Relations: Jung-ik Hwang

Centres

Continuing Education (Continuing Education) *Director*: Mun Soo Lee; **Foreign Language Education** (Foreign Languages Education) *Director*: Chang In Lee; **Information Technology Education** (Information Technology) *Director*: Myung Yeol Cha; **Kindergarten** (Preschool Education) *Director*: Jung Ae Ohm; **Nursery** (Child Care and Development) *Director*: Young Shin Park; **Teacher Training** (Teacher Training) *Director*: Djeong Uk Seo

Colleges

Arts (Design; Fine Arts; Leisure Studies; Music; Performing Arts; Sports) *Dean*: Chee Joong Kim; **Engineering** (Architecture; Ceramics and Glass Technology; Environmental Engineering; Geological Engineering; Information Technology; Interior Design; Materials Engineering; Polymer and Plastics Technology; Telecommunications Engineering) *Dean*: Dae Young Lim; **Foreign Studies** *Dean*: Bong Lyong Jeon; **Humanities** (Home Economics; Korean; Literature; Philosophy; Preschool Education; Psychology; Theology) *Dean*: Kwang Soo Yoo; **Natural Sciences** (Biological and Life Sciences; Chemistry; Genetics; Horticulture; Landscape Architecture; Mathematics and Computer Science; Medicine; Natural Sciences; Physics) *Dean*: Hahn Shik Kwak; **Social Sciences** (Business and Commerce; International Business; International Relations; Law; Management; Political Sciences; Public Administration; Social Sciences) *Dean*: Kee Chae Lee; **Tourism and Fashion** (Clothing and Sewing; Hotel Management; Nutrition; Textile Technology; Tourism) *Dean*: Gang Hoan Jeong

Institutes

Korean Language (Korean) *Director*: Hee Im Pae

Research Centres

Biomedical Resources *(Regional)* (Biomedicine) *Director*: Ki Sung Lee

Research Institutes

Early Childhood Education *Director*: Young Shin Park; **Engineering** (Engineering) *Director*: Ho Woong Shon; **Humanities** (Humanities and Social Science Education) *Director*: Moun Kwon Jung; **Information and Communication Venture Business** (Business and Commerce) *Director*: Jong Whan Jang; **Korean-Siberian** *Director*: Jong Man Han; **Lacquer Craft** *Director*: Hae Cho Chung; **Life Sciences** (Biological and Life Sciences) *Director*: Chang Won Choi; **Natural Sciences** (Natural Sciences) *Director*: Sung Sook Kim; **Optical Control** (Optics) *Director*: Chil Min Kim; **Project Team for Brain Korea 21** *Director*: Jong Whan Jang; **Regional Technology Innovation for Biomedical Resources** *(Centre) Director*: Suhn Kee Chae; **Small and Medium-sized Enterprises Support** (Small Business) *Director*: Chae Hyun Lee; **Social Sciences** (Social Sciences) *Director*: Jeong Sik Ko; **Unification** *Director*: Hyuk Dong Kim

History: Founded 1885 as School, became Junior College 1978 and acquired present status and title 1980. A private Institution under the supervision of the Ministry of Education.

Governing Bodies: Pai Chai School (Juridical Foundation)

Academic Year: March to February (March-August; September-February)

Admission Requirements: Graduation from high school and entrance examination (KSAT)

Fees: (Won): 2.5m. per semester

Main Language(s) of Instruction: Korean

International Co-operation: Exchange students with China for 1 yr

Accrediting Agencies: KCUE (Korean Council for University Education)

Degrees and Diplomas: *Bachelor's Degree*: 4 yrs; *Master's Degree*: a further 2 yrs; *Doctor's Degree (PhD)*: 3 yrs

Student Services: Academic counselling, Canteen, Cultural centre, Employment services, Foreign student adviser, Foreign Studies Centre, Handicapped facilities, Health services, Language programs, Nursery care, Social counselling, Sports facilities

Student Residential Facilities: Yes

Special Facilities: University Museum. Multi-Media Centre. Digital Library

Libraries: Central Library, c. 1,400,000 vols

Press or Publishing House: Pai Chai University Press

POHANG UNIVERSITY OF SCIENCE AND TECHNOLOGY

77 Cheongam-Ro, Nam-Gu, Pohang-si, Gyeongbuk 790-784
Tel: +82(54) 279-0114
Fax: +82(54) 279-2099
EMail: choon@postech.ac.kr
Website: http://www.postech.ac.kr

President: Yongmin Kim EMail: president@postech.edu

Departments

Chemical Engineering (Chemical Engineering); **Chemistry** (Chemistry); **Computer Science and Engineering** (Computer Science; Engineering); **Electronic and Electrical Engineering** (Electrical and Electronic Engineering); **Industrial Engineering** (Industrial Engineering); **Life Sciences** (Biological and Life Sciences); **Materials Science and Engineering** (Engineering; Materials Engineering); **Mathematics** (Mathematics); **Mechanical Engineering** (Mechanical Engineering); **Physics** (Physics)

Divisions

Humanities and Social Sciences (Arts and Humanities; Social Sciences)

Graduate Schools

Environmental Science and Engineering (Environmental Engineering; Environmental Studies); **Ferrous Technology** (Metal Techniques; Metallurgical Engineering); **Information Technology** (Information Sciences; Information Technology)

Laboratories

Pohang Accelerator; **POSTECH Information Research**

Further Information: Also Research Centres

History: Founded 1986 by POSCO.

Governing Bodies: POSTECH Foundation

Academic Year: March to December (March-June; August-December)

Admission Requirements: Graduation from high school or equivalent, and competitive entrance examination

Main Language(s) of Instruction: Korean and English

International Co-operation: With universities in United States, United Kingdom, Canada, Australia, France, China, Japan

Degrees and Diplomas: *Bachelor's Degree*: Science; Engineering (BS), 4 yrs; *Master's Degree*: Science; Engineering (MS), a further 2 yrs; *Doctor's Degree (PhD)*: a further 3-4 yrs

Libraries: Tae-Joon Park Digital Library, c. 351,000 vols, 3,500 journal subscriptions, 20,000 e-books.

Last Updated: 07/04/08

PUSAN UNIVERSITY OF FOREIGN STUDIES

55-1 Uam-dong, Nam-gu, Pusan 608-738
Tel: +82(51) 640-5111
Fax: +82(51) 645-4525
EMail: thornbird@pufs.ac.kr
Website: http://www.pufs.ac.kr

President: Sun-Gyu You

Centres

Computer Science (Computer Science); **Cultural Studies** (Cultural Studies); **Linguistics Research** (Linguistics); **Social Sciences Research** (Social Sciences); **Trade and Management** (Business and Commerce; Management)

Faculties

Area Studies (Cultural Studies); **Economics and Trade** (Business and Commerce; Economics); **Foreign Studies** (International Studies); **Humanities and Social Sciences** (Arts and Humanities; Social Sciences); **Natural Sciences and Engineering** (Engineering; Natural Sciences)

Institutes

Audiovisual Education (Cinema and Television); **Foreign Language Training** (Foreign Languages Education); **International Studies** (International Studies); **Law** (Law)

Schools

Evening; **Graduate**

History: Founded 1982.

Degrees and Diplomas: *Bachelor's Degree*; *Master's Degree*; *Doctor's Degree*

Last Updated: 05/01/09

PYONGTAEK UNIVERSITY

111 Yongi-dong, Pyongtaek-si, Gyeonggi-do 450-701
Tel: +82(31) 659-8114
Fax: +82(31) 659-8004
EMail: master@ptu.ac.kr
Website: http://www.ptuniv.ac.kr

President: Ki Hung Cho
Tel: +82(31) 658-3121 EMail: chokh@ptuniv.ac.kr

Departments

Information Statistics (Statistics); **Korean Language and Literature** (Korean; Literature); **Music** (Music); **Theology** (Theology)

Divisions

Business Administration and E-Commerce; **General Education**; **Information Design**; **Information Sciences**; **International Relations**; **Social Sciences** (Public Administration; Social Sciences; Town Planning); **Social Welfare** (Social Welfare)

Further Information: Also Graduate Schools

History: Founded 1912 as Union Pierson Memorial Bible Institute. Acquired present name and status 1996.

Degrees and Diplomas: *Bachelor's Degree*; *Master's Degree*; *Doctor's Degree*

Last Updated: 05/01/09

SAHMYOOK UNIVERSITY

26-21 Gongneug-dong, Nohwon-gu, Seoul 139-742
Tel: +82(2) 3399-3636
Fax: +82(2) 3399-3398
EMail: info@syu.ac.kr
Website: http://www.syu.ac.kr

President: Dan-geuk Nam

International Relations: Ahn-duk Ki

Departments

Biology (Biology); **Business Administration** (Business Administration); **Chemistry** (Chemistry); **Dairy Farming Resources** (Dairy); **English Language and Literature** (English); **Horticulture** (Horticulture); **Industrial Education** (Industrial Arts Education); **Music** (Music); **Nursing** (Nursing); **Nutrition** (Nutrition); **Pharmacy** (Pharmacy); **Rehabilitation Therapy** (Rehabilitation and Therapy); **Theology** (Theology)

Research Institutes

Basic Sciences (Natural Sciences); **Behavioural Sciences** (Behavioural Sciences); **Christian Education** (Christian Religious Studies; Religious Education); **Evangelist** (Missionary Studies); **Language** (Linguistics; Modern Languages); **Life Sciences** (Biological and Life Sciences); **Theology** (Theology)

History: Founded 1906 as Seventh-day Adventist Denominational Training School, became College 1961 and University 1985. Graduate School established 1981, and Theological Seminary 1990.

Governing Bodies: Board of Management; Executive Board

Academic Year: March to February (March-July; August-February)

Admission Requirements: Graduation from high school and entrance examination

Main Language(s) of Instruction: Korean

Degrees and Diplomas: *Bachelor's Degree*: 4 yrs; *Master's Degree*: a further 2 yrs; *Doctor's Degree (PhD)*. Also junior college Diplomas, 2-3 yrs

Student Residential Facilities: Yes

Libraries: Central Library, c. 100,500 vols

Publications: Korean Sahmyook University Journal; Sahmyook Hag Bo *(monthly)*

SANGJI UNIVERSITY

660 Woosan-dong, Wonju-si, Gangwon-do 220-702
Tel: +82(33) 730-0181 +82(33) 730-0182
Fax: +82(33) 730-0128
EMail: kyholee@mail.sangji.ac.kr
Website: http://www.sangji.ac.kr

President: Jaecheon Yu

Colleges

Arts and Sports (Crafts and Trades; Food Science; Home Economics; Industrial Design; Nutrition; Physical Education; Sports); **Economics and Business Administration** (Accountancy; Business Administration; Economics; International Business; Tourism); **Health Sciences** (Bioengineering; Health Administration; Nursing); **Humanities and Social Sciences** (Arts and Humanities; Chinese; English; Korean; Law; Literature; Public Administration; Social Welfare); **Life Sciences and Natural Resources** (Agronomy; Biological and Life Sciences; Biotechnology; Botany; Forestry; Horticulture); **Oriental Medicine** (Medicine); **Science and Engineering**

Further Information: Also Graduate Schools

History: Founded 1962.

Degrees and Diplomas: *Bachelor's Degree*; *Master's Degree*; *Doctor's Degree*

Last Updated: 02/04/09

SANGMYUNG UNIVERSITY

7 Hongji-dong, Jongro-gu, Seoul 110-743
Tel: +82(2) 396-7465
Fax: +82(2) 3217-4744
EMail: webmaster@smu.ac.kr
Website: http://english.smu.ac.kr/

President: Myoung-duck Seo

International Relations: June-woo Park

Colleges

Arts (Cinema and Television; Display and Stage Design; Fine Arts; Graphic Arts; Photography; Theatre); **Arts and Physical Education** (Dance; Fine Arts; Graphic Arts; Handicrafts; Music; Music Theory and Composition; Musical Instruments; Painting and Drawing; Physical Education; Sculpture; Singing; Textile Design); **Design** (Ceramic Art; Design; Display and Stage Design; Fashion Design; Industrial Design; Interior Design; Textile Design); **Education** (Education; English; Foreign Languages Education; French; Japanese; Korean; Mathematics Education; Pedagogy); **Humanities and Social Sciences** (Arts and Humanities; Business Administration; Business and Commerce; Economics; Geography; History; Information Sciences; International Business; Library Science; Public Administration; Social Sciences); **Industry** *(Chonan)* (Agriculture; Architecture; Computer Engineering; Computer Science; Environmental Engineering; Finance; Health Administration; Horticulture; Industrial Engineering; Information Management; Information Sciences; Insurance; Landscape Architecture; Leisure Studies; Mathematics and Computer Science; Parks and Recreation; Sports; Sports Management; Telecommunications Engineering; Town Planning; Welfare and Protective Services); **Language and Literature** (American Studies; Chinese; English; English Studies; French; French Studies; Germanic Studies; Japanese; Korean; Literature; Modern Languages; Russian); **Natural Sciences** (Biological and Life Sciences; Biology; Chemistry; Clothing and Sewing; Computer Science; Consumer Studies; Engineering; Food Science; Home Economics; Household Management; Industrial Chemistry; Information Sciences; Information Technology; Natural Sciences; Nutrition; Software Engineering; Telecommunications Engineering; Telecommunications Services; Textile Technology; Transport and Communications)

Research Institutes

Advanced Information Technology; **Advancement**; **Basic Sciences** (Natural Sciences); **Computer Networks** (Computer Networks); **Cultural Studies** (Cultural Studies); **Design** (Design); **Economic Policy** (Economic and Finance Policy); **Formative Art and Music** (Art Education; Music Education); **Future Art**; **Industrial Science**; **Language and Literature** (Literature; Modern Languages); **Marketing Information**; **Natural Sciences** (Natural Sciences); **Photo-journalism** (Journalism; Photography); **Sino-Korean Culture and Information**; **Social Studies**; **Strategic Knowledge**; **Student Counselling Centre** (Educational and Student Counselling); **Technology** (Technology); **Unification**

Further Information: Also Study Abroad Programme

History: Founded 1965 as Sangmyung Girl's Handicraft High School, became Sangmyung Women's University, and acquired present title 1996.

Governing Bodies: Board of Trustees of Sangmyung Academic Foundation

Academic Year: March to December (March-August; September-December)

Admission Requirements: Graduation from high school or recognized equivalent, and entrance examination

Main Language(s) of Instruction: Korean

Degrees and Diplomas: *Bachelor's Degree*: 4 yrs; *Master's Degree*: 4-5 semesters; *Doctor's Degree*: 6 semesters

Student Services: Academic counselling, Canteen, Employment services, Foreign student adviser, Health services, Language programs, Social counselling, Sports facilities

Student Residential Facilities: For c. 320 students

Special Facilities: Folklore Museum. Art Gallery

Libraries: Central Library, c. 600,000 vols

SEJONG UNIVERSITY

98 Gunja-dong, Gwangjin-gu, Seoul 143-747
Tel: +82(2) 3408-3114
Fax: +82(2) 3408-3220
EMail: sjuoia@sejong.ac.kr
Website: http://www.sejong.ac.kr

President: Seung Kyu Yang
Tel: +82(2) 3408-3001, Fax: +82(2) 3408-3555

Departments

Applied Chemistry (Applied Chemistry) *Head*: Jong Min Kang; **Applied Mathematics** (Applied Mathematics) *Head*: Young Joon Cha; **Business Administration and Accountancy** (Accountancy; Business Administration) *Head*: Chaehwan Won; **Cartoon and Animation** (Painting and Drawing) *Head*: Sae Hoon Kim; **Communication Arts** (Communication Arts; Mass Communication) *Head*: Seung Hye Sohn; **Computer Science and Engineering** (Computer Science; Engineering) *Head*: Seungbin Moon; **Culinary and Food Service Management** (Cooking and Catering; Service Trades) *Head*: Yukyeong Chong; **Dance** (Dance) *Head*: Sun Hee Yang; **Earth and Environmental Sciences** (Earth Sciences; Environmental Studies) *Head*: Tae Woong Chun; **Economics and Trade** (Economics; International Business) *Head*: Han Gwang Choo; **Education** (Education) *Head*: Un Sunn Lee; **Electronic Engineering** (Electronic Engineering) *Head*: Seok Rim Choi; **English Language and Literature** (English) *Head*: Young Hee Chung; **Film Art** (Film) *Head*: Chul Park; **Fine Arts** (Fine Arts) *Head*: Hang Ryul Park; **Food Science and Technology** (Food Technology) *Head*: Hae Soo Kwak; **History** (History) *Head*: Moon Sik Ha; **Industrial Design** (Industrial Design) *Head*: Jin Sook Park; **Information and Communication Engineering** (Information Technology; Telecommunications Engineering) *Head*: Jong Ki Han; **Japanese Language and Literature** (Japanese) *Head*: Eung Soo Lee; **Korean Language and Literature** (Korean) *Head*: Kyung Hee Chu; **Music** (Music) *Head*: Jae Hee Hyun; **Physical Education** (Physical Education) *Head*: Yu Won Kang; **Physics** (Physics) *Head*: Yeong Duk Kim; **Public Administration** (Public Administration) *Head*: Young Shik Kim

Faculties

Architectural Engineering (Architecture) *Head*: Jae Hong Lee; **Civil and Environmental Engineering** (Civil Engineering; Environmental Engineering) *Head*: Soung Eock Kim; **Hospitality and Tourism Management** (Hotel Management; Tourism) *Head*: Hyung Ryong Lee

Institutes

Aerospace Industry Research (Aeronautical and Aerospace Engineering) *Head*: Kisang Lee; **Construction Technology** (Construction Engineering) *Head*: Seung Eock Kim; **Humanities and Social Sciences** (Arts and Humanities; Social Sciences) *Head*: Young Shik Kim; **International Economics Research** (International Economics) *Head*: Jong Eun Lee; **Language** (Linguistics; Modern Languages) *Head*: Eun Joo Kwak; **Science and Technology** (Natural Sciences; Technology) *Head*: Seungbin Moon; **Tourism Industry** (Tourism) *Head*: Soong Seop Kim; **Waterway Industry** (Water Management) *Head*: Deg Hyo Bae

History: Founded 1940. Acquired present status 1961.

Governing Bodies: Daeyang Educational Foundation

Academic Year: March to December (March-August; September-December)

Admission Requirements: Graduation from high school and entrance examination

Fees: (Won): 6.7m. per annum

Main Language(s) of Instruction: Korean, English

International Co-operation: With universities in USA

Degrees and Diplomas: *Bachelor's Degree*: 4 yrs; *Master's Degree*: a further 2 yrs; *Doctor's Degree (PhD)*: a further 3-4 yrs

Student Services: Academic counselling, Canteen, Employment services, Foreign student adviser, Health services, Nursery care, Social counselling, Sports facilities

Student Residential Facilities: Yes

Special Facilities: Sejong Museum. Daeyang Astronomical Observatory. Daeyang Concert Hall

Libraries: Sejong Central Library, c. 572,000 vols

Publications: Journal of Aerospace Industry *(quarterly)*; Journal of Economic Integration *(quarterly)*

Press or Publishing House: Sejong University Press

Last Updated: 05/01/09

SEMYUNG UNIVERSITY

San 21-1 Shinwol-dong, Jecheon-si, Chungbuk-do 390-711
Tel: +82(43) 649-1124
Fax: +82(43) 648-4178
Website: http://www.semyung.ac.kr

President: Gwang-lim Kim (2006-)

Centres

Human and Social Sciences Research (Social Sciences); **Industrial Technology Research** (Industrial Engineering); **Language Research** (Linguistics)

Colleges

Oriental Medicine (Medicine; Traditional Eastern Medicine)

Schools

Advertising and Tourism; **Business Administration and Trade** (Accountancy; Business Administration; International Business); **Computer Science and Information Science** (Computer Science; Software Engineering); **Design**; **Electrical and Electronic Engineering** (Electrical and Electronic Engineering); **Environmental and Safety System Engineering**; **Foreign Languages and Literature** (Chinese; English; Japanese; Literature; Modern Languages); **Internet Information**; **Law** (Law; Police Studies; Public Administration); **Media Literature** (Korean; Literature; Media Studies; Writing)

Further Information: Also Graduate Schools. Semyung Hospital of Oriental Medicine

History: Founded 1991.

Governing Bodies: Office of Student Affairs; Office of Planning

Academic Year: February to December (February-June; August-December)

Admission Requirements: Graduation from high school or equivalent

Main Language(s) of Instruction: Korean

Degrees and Diplomas: *Bachelor's Degree*: 4 yrs; *Master's Degree*: a further 3 yrs; *Doctor's Degree*

Libraries: Central Library, c. 130,000 vols

Publications: Senyung Annual Publication *(annually)*

Last Updated: 05/01/09

SEOKYEONG UNIVERSITY

16-1 Jungneung-dong, Sungbuk-gu, Seoul 136-704
Tel: +82(2) 940-7114
Fax: +82(2) 940-7009
EMail: webadmin@skuniv.ac.kr
Website: http://www.skuniv.ac.kr/

President: Young Choui Choi

Colleges

Arts (Arts and Humanities; Industrial Design); **Humanities** (Arts and Humanities; Chinese; English; French; Japanese; Korean; Philosophy; Russian); **Natural Sciences and Engineering** (Applied Mathematics; Bioengineering; Chemistry; Computer Engineering; Computer Science; Industrial Engineering; Statistics); **Social Sciences** (Accountancy; Business Administration; Computer Education; Economics; Information Management; International Business; Law; Public Administration; Social Sciences)

Institutes

Humanities (Arts and Humanities; History; Linguistics; Literature; Philosophy); **Industrial Technology** (Biochemistry; Computer Science; Industrial Engineering); **Industry and Business Administration** (Accountancy; Business and Commerce; Economics); **Social Sciences** (Business Administration; Economics; Law; Social Sciences)

Further Information: Also Social Education Centre

History: Founded 1947.

Academic Year: March to February (March-August; September-February)

Main Language(s) of Instruction: Korean

Degrees and Diplomas: *Bachelor's Degree*: 4 yrs; *Master's Degree*: a further 2 yrs; *Doctor's Degree*

Student Services: Academic counselling, Canteen, Employment services, Health services, Social counselling, Sports facilities

Student Residential Facilities: Yes

Libraries: Central Library

Publications: Seo Kyeong Dae Hak Bo

Press or Publishing House: Seo Kyeong University Press

Last Updated: 05/01/09

SEONAM UNIVERSITY

720 Kwangchi-dong, Namwon-si, Jeollabuk-do 590-711
Tel: +82(63) 620-0114
Fax: +82(63) 620-0013
EMail: pjr@seonam.ac.kr
Website: http://www.seonam.ac.kr

President: Won-young Lee

International Relations: Cheon-Gie Yun
Tel: +82(63) 620-0011, Fax: +82(63) 633-9306
EMail: cgyun@tiger.seonam.ac.kr

Departments

Architectural Engineering (Architecture); **Biology** (Biology); **Chemical Engineeering** (Chemical Engineering); **Chemistry** (Chemistry); **Civil Engineering** (Civil Engineering); **Computer Science and Information Science** (Computer Science; Information Sciences); **Computer Science and Statistics** (Computer Science; Statistics); **Computer Science** (Computer Science); **Electrical Engineering** (Electrical Engineering); **Electronic Engineering** (Electronic Engineering); **English Language and Literature** (English); **Industrial Design** (Industrial Design); **Korean Language and Literature** (Korean); **Law** (Law); **Management Information Systems** (Management Systems); **Management** (Management); **Mathematics** (Mathematics); **Physics** (Physics); **Public Administration** (Public Administration)

History: Founded 1991.

SEOUL CHRISTIAN UNIVERSITY

1-19 Sinsa-dong, Eunpyung-gu, Seoul 122-879
Tel: +82(2) 380-2525
Fax: +82(2) 380-2519
EMail: anjb@scu.ac.kr
Website: http://www.scu.ac.kr

President: Kang-Pyung Lee
Tel: +82(2) 380-2501 EMail: kplee@scu.ac.kr

Director for Administration: Ki-Bae Hong
Tel: +82(2) 380-2560 EMail: hp4953@hanmail.net

International Relations: Bu-Ja Kim
Tel: +82(2) 380-2597 EMail: kbj9512@dreamwiz.com

Departments

Dance (Dance) *Head*: Jung-Eun Song; **Global Business and Information** (Business Education; E-Business/Commerce) *Head*: Bu Ja Kim; **Music** (Music; Musical Instruments) *Head*: Eun-Jung Kim; **Social Welfare** (Social Policy; Social Welfare; Social Work) *Head*: Kug Hee Woo; **Theology** (New Testament; Theology) *Head*: Kung-Hee Woo

Graduate Schools

Healing and Counselling (Health Sciences); **Social Welfare** (Social Welfare) *Head*: Kug-Hee Woo; **Theology** *Head*: Chong-Ku Paek

History: Founded 1937. Acquired present status 1997. Acquired present title 1999.

Governing Bodies: Hwan Won School Foundation

Academic Year: March to December (March-June; September-December)

Admission Requirements: Graduation from senior high school

Fees: (Won) 2.9m. per semester

Main Language(s) of Instruction: Korean

International Co-operation: With universities in USA (dual degree programme with Hope International University)

Accrediting Agencies: Ministry of Education and Human Resources Development

Degrees and Diplomas: *Bachelor's Degree*: Arts; Music; Theology, 4 yrs; *Bachelor's Degree*: Business Administration; Dancing; *Master's Degree*: Arts; Divinity; Theology; Social Welfare; *Doctor's Degree (Ph.D; Th.D)*

Student Services: Academic counselling, Canteen, Foreign student adviser, Language programs, Sports facilities

Student Residential Facilities: Yes

Last Updated: 21/10/08

SEOUL JANGSIN UNIVERSITY (SJS)

219-1 Gyungan-dong, Gwangju-si, Gyeonggi-do 464-742
Tel: +82(31) 799-9000
Fax: +82(31) 765-1232
EMail: webmaster@sjs.ac.kr
Website: http://www.sjs.ac.kr

President: Sung-Mo Moon Tel: +82(31) 799-9001

Director of University Planning: In-Ki Choi
EMail: cik1370@unitel.co.kr

Departments

Religious Music *Director*: Jae-Hong Im; **Social Welfare** (Social Welfare) *Director*: Kim; **Theology** (Theology) *Director*: Inseol Song

History: Founded 1954. Acquired present status 1998.

Governing Bodies: Kwangmyung Hakwon

Academic Year: March to February (March-August; September-February)

Admission Requirements: Graduation from high school

Fees: (Won): 3,165,000 per semester; church music department, 4,530,000

Main Language(s) of Instruction: Korean

Accrediting Agencies: Ministry of Education and Human Resources Development

Degrees and Diplomas: *Bachelor's Degree*: Theology; Social Welfare; Church Music (BA), 4 yrs; *Master's Degree*: Theology; Social Welfare; Church Music; Divinity; Mission (MA), 2 1/2 yrs; *Doctor's Degree*: Theology; Christian Social Welfare; Music Theology (Ph.D.), 4 yrs

Student Services: Academic counselling, Canteen, Employment services, Foreign student adviser, Handicapped facilities, Health services, Language programs, Nursery care, Social counselling, Sports facilities

Student Residential Facilities: Yes

Special Facilities: Audio-Visual Studio

Libraries: c. 63,605 vols; 398 Journals; 150 Electronic Journals

Publications: Seoul Jangsin Non Dan, Academic Journal *(annually)*

Last Updated: 23/10/08

SEOUL SPORTS GRADUATE UNIVERSITY

134-2 Yongdungpo-dong 4-ga, Yongdungpo-gu, Seoul 150-034
Tel: 82(2) 835-5551
Fax: 82(2) 835-5554
EMail: admin@ssgu.ac.kr
Website: http://www.ssgu.ac.kr

President: Joong-Young Kim

Departments

Sports (Sports)

History: Founded 1999.

SEOUL WOMEN'S UNIVERSITY

126 Kongnung 2-dong, Nowon-gu, Seoul 139-774
Tel: +82(2) 970-5140
Fax: +82(2) 974-8487
EMail: webmaster@mail.swu.ac.kr
Website: http://www.swu.ac.kr

President: Kwan-gja Rhee

International Relations: Hyon-woo Seung

Centres

Continuing Education; **Nursery Teacher Training Education** (Preschool Education)

Colleges

Humanities (Arts and Humanities; Chinese; Christian Religious Studies; English; French; German; History; Korean); **Natural Sciences** (Biology; Chemistry; Clothing and Sewing; Computer Science; Food Technology; Horticulture; Mathematics; Microbiology; Natural Sciences; Nutrition; Physical Education); **Social Sciences** (Business Administration; Child Care and Development; Economics; Educational Psychology; Information Sciences; Library Science; Public Administration; Social Sciences; Social Work)

Institutes

Art and Design (Fine Arts); **Humanities Research** (Arts and Humanities); **Natural Sciences Research** (Natural Sciences); **Social Sciences Research** (Social Sciences); **Women's Studies** (Women's Studies)

History: Founded 1961 by Korean Presbyterian Church.

Academic Year: March to February (March-August; September-February)

Admission Requirements: Graduation from high school and entrance examination

Main Language(s) of Instruction: Korean

Degrees and Diplomas: *Bachelor's Degree*: 4 yrs; *Master's Degree*: a further 2 yrs; *Doctor's Degree*: 3-4 yrs following Master

Student Residential Facilities: Yes

Libraries: Central Libraries, c. 200,000 vols

Publications: Seoul Women's University Bulletin *(annually)*

Press or Publishing House: Seoul Women's University Press

SEOWON UNIVERSITY

231 Mochung-dong, Hungduk-gu, Cheongju-si,
Chungbuk-do 361-742
Tel: +82(43) 299-8114
Fax: +82(43) 283-8822
Website: http://www.seowon.ac.kr

President: Moon-ho Son

International Relations: Jin-kook Kim

Colleges

Arts; **Business Administration** (Accountancy; Business Administration; Economics; Insurance; International Business; Management); **Education** (Computer Education; Education; English; Ethics; Geography; History; Home Economics; Korean; Literature; Mathematics Education; Physical Education; Preschool Education; Science Education); **Liberal Arts and Social Sciences** (Advertising and Publicity; Arts and Humanities; Chinese; English; German; Korean; Law; Literature; Political Sciences; Public Administration; Public Relations; Social Sciences); **Natural Sciences and Technology** (Architecture; Clothing and Sewing; Communication Studies; Computer Science; Environmental Studies; Family Studies; Food Science; Health Education; Multimedia; Natural Sciences; Nutrition; Sports; Textile Design)

Further Information: Also Graduate Schools

History: Founded 1968.

Main Language(s) of Instruction: Korean

Degrees and Diplomas: *Bachelor's Degree*; *Master's Degree*

SHINGYEONG UNIVERSITY (SGU)

Hwaseong-si, Gyeonggi-do
Tel: +82(31) 369-9112
Fax: +82(31) 369-9116
Website: http://www.sgu.ac.kr/

SILLA UNIVERSITY

San1-1 Gwaebop-dong, Sasang-gu, Pusan 617-736
Tel: +82(51) 999-5480
Fax: +82(51) 999-5079
EMail: webadm@silla.ac.kr
Website: http://www.silla.ac.kr

President: Hong Sub Jung

Centres

Arts (Arts and Humanities); **Humanities** (Humanities and Social Science Education); **Natural Sciences** (Natural Sciences); **Social Sciences** (Social Sciences); **Women's Studies** (Women's Studies)

Colleges

Arts (Arts and Humanities); **Education** (Education); **Humanities and Social Sciences** (Arts and Humanities; Social Sciences); **Natural Sciences** (Natural Sciences)

Programmes

Computer and Information (Information Technology); **Engineering** (Engineering); **Tourism Management** (Tourism)

History: Founded 1964 as Women's College, acquired present status and title 1983.

Academic Year: March to February

Main Language(s) of Instruction: Korean

Degrees and Diplomas: *Bachelor's Degree*: 4 yrs; *Master's Degree*: a further 2 yrs; *Doctor's Degree*

Student Residential Facilities: Yes

Special Facilities: Museum

Libraries: 200,000 vols

Publications: Journal *(biannually)*; Women's Studies *(annually)*

Press or Publishing House: University Press

Last Updated: 05/01/09

SOGANG UNIVERSITY

1Shinsu-dong, Mapo-gu, Seoul 121-742
Tel: +82(2) 705-8118
Fax: +82(2) 705-8119
EMail: goabroad@sogang.ac.kr
Website: http://www.sogang.ac.kr

President: Byungdoo Sohn (2005-)
Tel: +82(2) 705-8200, Fax: +82(2) 705-8204
EMail: president@sogang.ac.kr

Vice-President for Academic Affairs: Chul An
Tel: +82(2) 705-8201 EMail: anchul@sogang.ac.kr

International Relations: Luke Jong-Hyeok Sim
EMail: jhsim@sogang.ac.kr

Colleges

Engineering (Biomedical Engineering; Chemical Engineering; Computer Science; Electronic Engineering; Mechanical Engineering) *Dean*: Hyung Sang Park; **Humanities** (American Studies; Chinese; English; English Studies; French Studies; German; History; Korean; Philosophy; Religious Studies) *Dean*: Doo Hee Chung; **Natural Sciences** (Biological and Life Sciences; Chemistry; Mathematics; Physics) *Dean*: Sung Ho Park; **Social Sciences** (Law; Political Sciences; Sociology) *Dean*: Ho Seong Park

Divisions

General Education (Education) *Dean*: Chung Mok Suh

Graduate Schools

International Studies *Dean*: Se Young Ahn

Institutes

Advanced Management and Accountancy (Accountancy; Management) *Director*: Soon Kee Kim; **Korean Language Education** (Korean) *Director*: Sang Woo Lim

Research Institutes

Applied Science and Technology (Natural Sciences; Technology); **Basic Sciences** (Natural Sciences) *Director*: Jong Bum Lee; **Business** *Director*: Sung Bin Chun; **East Asian Studies** (East Asian Studies) *Director*: Yoon Hwan Shin; **Economics** *Director*: Joon-Woo Namh; **Entrepreneurial Studies** *Director*: Yong Hee Chee; **Humanities** (Arts and Humanities) *Director*: Wan Yong Song; **Information and Technology** (Information Technology; Technology); **International and Area Studies** *Director*: Kyu Young Lee; **Language and Information** *Director*: Jong-Gou Park; **Legal Science** (Law); **Life and Culture** (Biological and Life Sciences; Cultural Studies) *Director*: Jae Myung Yang; **Philosophical Studies** (Philosophy) *Director*: Young Ahn Kang; **Religion** (Religion) *Director*: Chae Young Kim; **Social Sciences** (Social Sciences) *Director*: Ho Chul Sonn; **Study of Media Culture** *Director*: Dai Won Huyn; **Technology Management** (Management; Technology) *Director*: Byung-Yeon Kim; **Theology** (Theology)

Schools

Business Administration (Business Administration) *Director*: Joon Soo Jun; **Economics** (Economics) *Director*: Sung Il Nam; **Graduate** (Biological and Life Sciences; Business Administration; Business and Commerce; Chemical Engineering; Chemistry; Computer Science; Crafts and Trades; Economics; English; French; German; History; Korean; Law; Mass Communication; Mathematics; Philosophy; Physics; Religious Studies; Sociology) *Dean*: Young Han Kim; **Interdisciplinary Programmes** (Economics; Educational Sciences; Gender Studies; Japanese; Korean; Media Studies; Philosophy; Political Sciences; Sports Management)

History: Founded 1960 as College by the Society of Jesus, acquired University status 1970. A private institution financed by tuition fees (60%) and grants.

Governing Bodies: Board of Trustees

Academic Year: March to December (March-July; August-December)

Admission Requirements: Graduation from high school or equivalent, and entrance examination

Fees: (US Dollars): Undergraduate, 3,594-4,462 per semester; Graduate, 4,258-5,335

Main Language(s) of Instruction: Korean

International Co-operation: With universities in 20 countries such as China, Germany, USA, United Kingdom, Japan

Accrediting Agencies: Ministry of Education

Degrees and Diplomas: *Bachelor's Degree*: 4 yrs; *Master's Degree*: a further 2-3 yrs; *Doctor's Degree*: 3-4 yrs following Master

Student Services: Academic counselling, Canteen, Cultural centre, Employment services, Foreign student adviser, Handicapped facilities, Health services, Language programs, Social counselling, Sports facilities

Special Facilities: University Museum. Computer Centre; Media Communications Centre; Performance Hall

Libraries: Loyola Library, c. 720,000 vols

Publications: East Asian Studies *(biennially)*; Humanistic Studies *(annually)*; Humanities Journal *(biennially)*; Social Science Studies *(annually)*; Sogang Economics Papers *(biennially)*; Sogang Journal of Business *(biennially)*; Sogang Journal of Media and Culture *(annually)*; Sogang University General Bulletin *(biannually)*; Understanding People *(annually)*

Press or Publishing House: Sogang University Press

SOOKMYUNG WOMEN'S UNIVERSITY

53-12 Chungpa-dong 2 ka, Yongsan-gu, Seoul 140-742
Tel: +82(2) 710-9114
Fax: +82(2) 718-2337
EMail: webmaster@sookmyung.ac.kr
Website: http://www.sookmyung.ac.kr

President: Young Sil Han

Centres

Asia-Pacific Women's Information Network *(APWINC)* (Computer Networks); **Communication Development** (Communication Studies); **Cyber Education for Teaching and Learning** (Child Care and Development; Cosmetology; Gerontology; Nutrition; Pharmacy); **Leadership** (Leadership); **Linguaexpress (The International Institute of Languages Education)** (Chinese; English; Japanese; Korean)

Colleges

Economics and Commerce (Business and Commerce; Consumer Studies; Economics); **Fine Arts** (Architectural and Environmental Design; Design; Fine Arts; Graphic Design; Handicrafts; Industrial Design; Interior Design; Painting and Drawing); **Human Ecology** (Child Care and Development; Clothing and Sewing; Family Studies; Food Science; Home Economics; Nutrition; Textile Design; Textile Technology); **Liberal Arts** (Arts and Humanities; Chinese; Cultural Studies; Education; Educational Psychology; English; French; German; History; Information Sciences; Japanese; Korean;

Library Science; Tourism); **Music** (Music; Music Theory and Composition; Musical Instruments; Singing); **Pharmacy** (Pharmacy); **Political Science and Law** (Advertising and Publicity; International Relations; Law; Political Sciences; Public Administration; Public Relations; Telecommunications Engineering); **Science** (Biological and Life Sciences; Chemistry; Computer Science; Dance; Information Sciences; Mass Communication; Mathematics; Multimedia; Natural Sciences; Physical Education; Physics; Statistics)

Graduate Schools

Arts and Physical Education (Art History; Dance; Education; Handicrafts; Industrial Design; Music; Music Theory and Composition; Musical Instruments; Painting and Drawing; Physical Education; Singing); **Business** (Business Administration; Consumer Studies; Insurance; Management; Marketing); **Clinical Pharmacy** (Health Sciences; Pharmacy); **Computer-assisted Language Learning (TESOL)** (English); **Design** (Advertising and Publicity; Ceramic Art; Design; Fashion Design; Fine Arts; Industrial Design; Interior Design; Packaging Technology; Textile Design); **Distance Learning** (Business Administration; Child Care and Development; Cosmetology; Education; Preschool Education; Technology); **Education** (Art Education; Education; Home Economics; Modern Languages; Natural Sciences; Physical Education; Social Sciences); **Humanities and Social Sciences** (Arts and Humanities; Business Administration; Chinese; Consumer Studies; Economics; Education; Educational Psychology; English; French; German; History; Information Sciences; International Business; International Relations; Korean; Law; Library Science; Political Sciences; Public Administration; Social Sciences); **Information and Communication** (Communication Studies; E-Business/Commerce; Information Sciences); **International Services** (International Relations; International Studies; Social Studies); **Music Therapy** (Art Therapy; Rehabilitation and Therapy); **Natural Sciences** (Biology; Chemistry; Clothing and Sewing; Computer Science; Food Science; Home Economics; Household Management; Mathematics; Natural Sciences; Nutrition; Pharmacology; Pharmacy; Physics; Statistics; Textile Technology; Welfare and Protective Services); **Public Policy** (Public Administration; Social Sciences; Social Welfare); **Social Education**; **Traditional Culture and Arts** (Art History; Cultural Studies; Dance; Music)

Research Institutes

Asian Women (Social Sciences; Women's Studies); **Child Study** (Child Care and Development; Paediatrics); **Drug Information** (Toxicology); **Economics and Business Administration** (Business Administration; Economics); **Fine Arts** *(MOON SHIN)* (Fine Arts); **Industrial Design** (Industrial Design); **Natural Sciences** (Natural Sciences); **Pharmacy** (Pharmacy); **Regional Studies** (American Studies; Canadian Studies; Chinese; French Studies; Germanic Studies; Korean; Regional Studies; Translation and Interpretation); **Science for Health and Welfare** (Home Economics; Welfare and Protective Services); **Socio-educational Sciences** (Educational Sciences; Social Studies); **Unification** (Regional Studies)

Schools

Continuing Education (Child Care and Development; Cosmetology; Humanities and Social Science Education; Museum Studies; Paramedical Sciences; Performing Arts; Special Education)

History: Founded 1906, became College 1938, acquired University status 1955.

Governing Bodies: Board of Trustees

Academic Year: March to December (March-July; August-December)

Admission Requirements: Graduation from high school and entrance examination

Main Language(s) of Instruction: Korean

Degrees and Diplomas: *Bachelor's Degree*: 4 yrs; *Master's Degree*: a further 2-2½ yrs; *Doctor's Degree (PhD)*: 3-5 yrs

Student Services: Academic counselling, Canteen, Cultural centre, Employment services, Foreign student adviser, Foreign Studies Centre, Handicapped facilities, Health services, Language programs, Nursery care, Social counselling, Sports facilities

Student Residential Facilities: Yes

Special Facilities: Museum. MOON SHIN Art Gallery. Embroidery Museum

Libraries: c. 690,900 vols

Publications: Asian Women (English) *(annually)*; Chung-Pa (Korean) *(quarterly)*; Gentle Power to Change the World (English) *(3 per annum)*

Press or Publishing House: Sookdae Shinbo (Sookmyung Women's University Press)

Last Updated: 05/01/09

SOONCHUNHYANG UNIVERSITY

646 Eupnae-ri, Sinchang-myeon, Asan-si, Chungnam-do 336-745
Tel: +82(41) 530-1526
Fax: +82(41) 530-1381
EMail: ahnline@sch.ac.kr
Website: http://www.sch.ac.kr

President: Kyo Il Suh (2001-)
Tel: +82(41) 530-1001, Fax: +82(41) 530-1009
EMail: president@sch.ac.kr

Chief Administrative Officer: Duck-Hee Lee
Tel: +82(41) 530-1040, Fax: +82(41) 530-1067

International Relations: Seung-gyu Baek

Centres

Community Education *Director*: Kwang-Sun Suh; **Computer Education** *Director*: Yong-Hae Kong; **Foreign Language Education** *Director*: Gi-Pyo Park; **Integrated Circuit Design Education** *Director*: Kwangmin Park; **Software Education and Development** *Director*: Sung Geun Jang

Colleges

Engineering (Architecture; Chemical Engineering; Computer Science; Electrical Engineering; Electronic Engineering; Engineering; Information Sciences; Information Technology; Materials Engineering; Mechanical Engineering) *Dean*: Doo-Soon Park; **Humanities** (Arts and Humanities; Child Care and Development; Chinese; Cultural Studies; Dance; English; Film; German; International Studies; Korean; Special Education; Theatre) *Dean*: Hyuk-Tae Kwon; **Medicine** (Anatomy; Biochemistry; Medicine; Microbiology; Nursing; Parasitology; Pathology; Pharmacology; Physiology; Social and Preventive Medicine) *Dean*: Moo-Sik Jho; **Natural Sciences** (Biology; Biotechnology; Chemistry; Environmental Studies; Food Science; Genetics; Information Technology; Leisure Studies; Marine Science and Oceanography; Mathematics; Natural Sciences; Nutrition; Parks and Recreation; Physical Education; Physics; Sports Medicine) *Dean*: Jong-An Park; **Social Sciences** (Administration; Business Administration; Business and Commerce; Economics; Finance; Insurance; International Business; Journalism; Law; Social Sciences; Social Welfare; Tourism) *Dean*: Young-Soo Shim

Graduate Schools

Education *Dean*: Kyung-Ha Yoon; **Industrial Information** *Dean*: Byung-Soo Lee

Research Centres

Diagnosis of Electric Equipment in Bulk Power Systems *Director*: Suk Won Min; **Electronic Commerce Software** *Director*: Imyeong Lee; **RF and Microwave Component** *Director*: Dal Ahn

Research Institutes

Admiral Yi Sunshin *Director*: Hyuk-Tae Kwon; **Basic Sciences** *Director*: Jong-An Park; **Clinical Molecular Biology** *Director*: Hee Sook Park; **Gastroentorology** *Director*: Chan Sup Shim; **Group Occupational Health Management** *Director*: Kuck Hyeun Woo; **Humanities** *Director*: Hyuk-Tae Kwon; **Hyonam Kidney Laboratory** *Director*: Hi Bahl Lee; **Industrial Medicine** *Director*: Byung-Kook Lee; **Industrial Technology** *Director*: Doo-Soon Park; **Marine Research and Development** *Director*: Hyun Woong Shin; **Maternal and Child Health** *Director*: Dong Hwan Lee; **Social Sciences** *Director*: Young-Soo Shim; **Soonchunhyang Medical Science** *Director*: E-tay Ahn

Schools

Graduate *Dean*: Soo-Kyoon Rah

History: Founded 1978 as Medical College, acquired present status and title 1990.

Academic Year: March to December (March-June; August-December)

Admission Requirements: Graduation from high school and entrance examination

Main Language(s) of Instruction: Korean

Degrees and Diplomas: *Bachelor's Degree*: 4 yrs; *Master's Degree*: a further 2 yrs; *Doctor's Degree (PhD)*

Student Services: Academic counselling, Canteen, Employment services, Foreign student adviser, Health services, Language programs, Social counselling, Sports facilities

Student Residential Facilities: Yes

Libraries: Hyangseol Memorial Library c. 410,000 vols

Press or Publishing House: Soonchunhyang University Press

SOONGSIL UNIVERSITY

1-1 Sangdo 5-dong, Dongjak-ku, Seoul 156-743
Tel: +82(2) 820-0114
Fax: +82(2) 816-1513
EMail: webmaster@ssu.ac.kr
Website: http://www.ssu.ac.kr

President: Hyo-Gye Lee

Centres

Languages (Chinese; English; Japanese; Korean; Modern Languages)

Colleges

Engineering (Architecture; Chemical Engineering; Electrical and Electronic Engineering; Engineering; Industrial Engineering; Mechanical Engineering; Telecommunications Engineering; Textile Technology); **Humanities** (Arts and Humanities; Chinese; English; French; German; History; Korean; Literature; Philosophy); **Information Science** (Artificial Intelligence; Computer Science; Information Sciences; Software Engineering; Telecommunications Engineering); **Law** (Law); **Management and Commerce** (Accountancy; Business Administration; Economics; International Business; Small Business); **Natural Sciences** (Chemistry; Mathematics; Natural Sciences; Physics; Statistics); **Social Sciences** (International Relations; Japanese; Political Sciences; Public Administration; Social Sciences; Social Work)

Institutes

Adult and Continuing Education; **Business and Economic Strategies** (Business Administration; Finance); **Christian Social Studies** (Social Studies); **Humanities** (Arts and Humanities); **Industrial Technology** (Industrial Engineering); **Korean Christian Culture Research** (Cultural Studies); **Law** (Law); **Natural Sciences** (Natural Sciences); **Resource Recycling Research** (Ecology); **Social Sciences** (Social Sciences)

History: Founded 1897 by the Northern Presbyterian Church of the United States and became 4-year College 1905. Merged with Tae Jon College and became Soong Jun University 1971. Tae Jon College separated from the main campus 1983, and the School restored to its original name of Soong Sil 1987. A private institution.

Governing Bodies: University Council

Academic Year: March to February (March-June; August-February)

Admission Requirements: Graduation from high school or equivalent, and entrance examination

Main Language(s) of Instruction: Korean

Degrees and Diplomas: *Bachelor's Degree*: Business Administration; Economics; Engineering; Law; Literature; Natural Sciences; Political Science; Public Administration, 4 yrs; *Master's Degree*: a further 2-3 yrs; *Doctor's Degree*: Business Administration; Economics; Engineering; Law; Literature; Natural Sciences; Social Work, 3 yrs following Master

Student Residential Facilities: Yes

Special Facilities: Korean Christian Museum. Central Computer Centre; Audiovisual Education Institute. Theatre

Libraries: Central Library, c. 200,000 vols

Publications: Essays and Papers of the Graduate School; Joong Sil Sahak; Journal of Graduate School of Regional Development; Journal of Social Sciences; Soong Sil Law Review; Soong Sil University Essays and Papers, Natural Science, Humanities, Social Sciences

Press or Publishing House: Soong Sil University Press

Last Updated: 05/01/09

SUN MOON UNIVERSITY (SMU)

100 Kalsan-ri, Tangjeong-Myeon, Asan-si, Chungnam-do 336-708
Tel: +82(41) 530-2072
Fax: +82(41) 530-2075
EMail: oic@sunmoon.ac.kr
Website: http://www.sunmoon.ac.kr

President: Bong Tae Kim
Tel: +82(41) 530-2112, Fax: +82(41) 530-2109

Director of Planning: Chul-hee Han
Tel: +82(41) 530-2120, Fax: +82(41) 530-2988
EMail: chhan@sunmoon.ac.kr

International Relations: Lynne Kim
Tel: +82(41) 530-2070 EMail: lynnekim@sunmoon.ac.kr

Colleges

Engineering (Architecture; Biochemistry; Chemical Engineering; Civil Engineering; Electronic Engineering; Environmental Engineering; Materials Engineering; Measurement and Precision Engineering; Mechanical Engineering; Pharmacology); **Foreign Languages** (Chinese; English; Japanese; Latin American Studies; Russian; Spanish); **Humanities** (Arts and Humanities; History; Korean; Philosophy); **Natural Sciences** (Biological and Life Sciences; Biotechnology; Chemistry; Computer Science; Food Science; Leisure Studies; Marine Science and Oceanography; Materials Engineering; Mathematics; Natural Sciences; Physics; Sports); **Social Sciences** (Advertising and Publicity; Asian Studies; Business Administration; Industrial and Organizational Psychology; International Economics; International Studies; Journalism; Law; Mass Communication; Public Administration; Social Sciences; Social Welfare); **Theology** (Theology)

History: Founded 1986, acquired present status 1989.

Governing Bodies: Board of Directors

Academic Year: March to December (March-June; September-December)

Admission Requirements: Graduation from high school

Fees: (Won): 3m. per semester

Main Language(s) of Instruction: Korean

International Co-operation: With universities in USA; Canada; Australia; New Zealand; Philippines; China; Mexico; Russian Federation; Malaysia; Vietnam; Uzbekistan; Mongolia; Indonesia; Taiwan

Accrediting Agencies: Ministry of Education and Human Resource Development

Degrees and Diplomas: *Bachelor's Degree*: 4 yrs; *Master's Degree*: a further 2 yrs; *Doctor's Degree*: 5 yrs

Student Services: Academic counselling, Canteen, Cultural centre, Employment services, Foreign student adviser, Foreign Studies Centre, Handicapped facilities, Health services, Language programs, Social counselling, Sports facilities

Student Residential Facilities: Yes

Libraries: University Library c. 375,000 vols.

Press or Publishing House: The University Press

SUNGKONGHOE UNIVERSITY (SKHU)

1-1 Hang-dong, Kuro-gu, Seoul 152-716
Tel: +82(2) 2610-4129
Fax: +82(2) 2683-8858
Website: http://www.skhu.ac.kr

President: Soung-soo Kim Tel: +82(2) 2610-4102

Dean of Research: Chong-Koo Lee
Tel: +82(2) 2610-4133 EMail: cklee@mail.skhu.ac.kr

International Relations: Jinkyu Youn
EMail: jinkui@mail.skhu.ac.kr

Colleges

Humanities (Chinese; English; French; German; History; Japanese; Literature); **Social Sciences** (Business Administration;

Economics; Geography; International Relations; Law; Political Sciences; Psychology; Social Sciences)

Departments

Theology

Programmes

Computer and Information Science (Information Technology); **Media and Communication** (Media Studies)

History: Founded 1914. A university of the Anglican Church of Korea.

Main Language(s) of Instruction: Korean

Degrees and Diplomas: *Bachelor's Degree*; *Master's Degree*; *Doctor's Degree*

Student Services: Academic counselling, Cultural centre, Foreign student adviser, Sports facilities

Libraries: Central Library

Last Updated: 05/01/09

SUNGKYUL UNIVERSITY

147-2 Anyang 8-dong, Manan-gu, Anyang-si, Gyeonggi-do 430-742
Tel: +82(31) 467-8114
Fax: +82(31) 467-0529
EMail: webadm@sungkyul.edu
Website: http://www.sungkyul.ac.kr

President: Sung Young Kim (2002-)
Tel: +82(31) 467-8001, Fax: +82(31) 467-8006
EMail: ksy@sungkyul.edu

Administrative Officer: Sang Su Kim
Tel: +82(31) 467-8017 EMail: kimss@sungkyul.edu

International Relations: Seok-pal Cho

Colleges

Engineering (Computer Science; E-Business/Commerce; Engineering; Multimedia); **Humanities and Social Sciences** (Literature; Management; Preschool Education; Public Administration; Social and Community Services; Social Welfare); **Theology** (Christian Religious Studies; Missionary Studies; Theology) *Director*: Kook-Hwan Kim

Research Institutes

Humanities (Arts and Humanities) *Director*: Jong-Ki Jong; **Information Industry and Technology** (Information Technology) *Director*: Chang-Min Kim; **Social Sciences** (Social Sciences) *Director*: Kyung-Soo Lim; **Sung Kyul Theology** (Theology) *Director*: Suk-Won Sohn; **Young Am Theological Thought** (Theology) *Director*: Jung-jin Chun

History: Founded 1962 as Seminary, acquired present status 1991.

Governing Bodies: Sung Kyul Church Education Institute

Academic Year: March to December (March-June; September-December)

Admission Requirements: Graduation from high school

Fees: (Won): Tuition, 3.9m. per annum

Main Language(s) of Instruction: Korean

Accrediting Agencies: Asia Theological Association (ATA), Ministry of Education

Degrees and Diplomas: *Bachelor's Degree*: Administration; Arts; Business Administration; Divinity; Education; Engineering; Music; Science, 4 yrs; *Master's Degree*: Education (MEd); Social Development, a further 5 semesters; *Master's Degree*: Missiology; Theology (MTheol), a further 2 yrs; *Doctor's Degree*

Student Services: Academic counselling, Cultural centre, Employment services, Foreign student adviser, Foreign Studies Centre, Health services, Language programs, Nursery care, Social counselling, Sports facilities

Student Residential Facilities: For 89 students

Special Facilities: Educational Broadcasting Station

Libraries: 242,712 vols

Publications: Collection of Dissertations

Press or Publishing House: University Press

Last Updated: 05/01/09

SUNGKYUNKWAN UNIVERSITY (SKKU)

53 Myongnyun-dong 3-ga, Jongno-gu, Seoul 110-745
Tel: +82(2) 760-1152
Fax: +82(2) 744-1153
Website: http://www.skku.edu

President: Jung-Don Seo (2000-)
Tel: +82(2) 760-1012, Fax: +82(2) 763-6061
EMail: preskku@skku.edu

Vice-President: Jay-Young Chung
Tel: +82(2) 760-1003 EMail: c603jy@skku.edu

International Relations: Myeong-Ho Cheon, Supervisor
EMail: intl@skku.edu

Colleges

Education *(Humanities and Social Sciences Campus)* (Chinese; Computer Education; Education; Mathematics Education) *Dean*: Ok Ki Kang; **Engineering** *(Natural Sciences Campus) Dean*: Do Sung Lee; **Law** *(Humanities and Social Sciences Campus)* (Law) *Dean*: Kyu-Sang Chung; **Liberal Arts** *(Humanities and Social Sciences Campus)* (Chinese; English; French; German; History; Korean; Library Science; Literature; Philosophy; Russian) *Dean*: Dong Soon Kim; **Medicine** *(Natural Sciences Campus)* (Medicine) *Dean*: Dae-Yong Uhm

Schools

Art *(Humanities and Social Sciences Campus)* (Cinema and Television; Dance; Design; Film; Fine Arts; Multimedia) *Dean*: Myoun Kim; **Business Administration** *(Humanities and Social Sciences Campus)* (Business Administration) *Dean*: Young-Kwang Chang; **Confucian and Oriental Studies** *(Humanities and Social Sciences Campus)* (Arts and Humanities; Asian Religious Studies; Oriental Studies; Philosophical Schools; Philosophy) *Dean*: Suk Won Oh; **Economics** *(Humanities and Social Sciences Campus)* (Economics; Statistics) *Dean*: Kwansuck Lee; **Human Life Sciences** *(Humanities and Social Sciences Campus)* (Child Care and Development; Consumer Studies; Family Studies; Fashion Design; Home Economics; Household Management; Psychology) *Dean*: Hee Sun Cho; **Information and Communication Engineering** *(Natural Sciences Campus) Dean*: Dong Kyeol Shin; **Life Sciences and Natural Resources** *(Natural Sciences Campus)* (Biological and Life Sciences; Biotechnology; Genetics) *Dean*: Soo Won Lee; **Natural Sciences** *(Natural Sciences Campus)* (Biological and Life Sciences; Chemistry; Mathematics; Natural Sciences; Physics) *Dean*: Chong-Yun Park; **Pharmacy** *(Natural Sciences Campus)* (Pharmacy) *Dean*: Dong You Sun; **Social Sciences** *(Humanities and Social Sciences Campus)* (International Relations; Journalism; Mass Communication; Political Sciences; Psychology; Public Administration; Social Sciences; Social Welfare; Sociology) *Dean*: Dong-Woon Hahn; **Sport Science** *(Natural Sciences Campus)* (Leadership; Sports) *Dean*: Eue-Soo Awn; **Systems Management Engineering** *(Suwon)* (Computer Engineering; Engineering; Management Systems) *Dean*: Hoo-Gon Choi

History: Founded 992 as sole national institute of higher learning in Koryo Dynasty based on Confucian doctrine and principles. Reestablished 1398 on present site during Chosun Dynasty. Recognized by Government as College 1946 and private University 1953.

Governing Bodies: Board of Trustees

Academic Year: March to December (March-June; September-December)

Admission Requirements: Graduation from high school or equivalent recognized by the Ministry of Education, and entrance examination

Fees: (Won): Undergraduate, c. 3-5m per semester; graduate, c. 3.7-6 m per semester. Foreign students 30% and 50 % discount for undergraduates and graduates respectively

Main Language(s) of Instruction: Korean

International Co-operation: With 250 universities in USA, Europe, Asia, Oceania, Africa

Accrediting Agencies: Ministry of Education and Human Resources Development

Degrees and Diplomas: *Bachelor's Degree*: 4 yrs; *Master's Degree*: a further 2 yrs; *Doctor's Degree*: 3 yrs following Master

Student Services: Academic counselling, Canteen, Cultural centre, Employment services, Foreign student adviser, Handicapped facilities, Health services, Language programs, Nursery care, Social counselling, Sports facilities

Student Residential Facilities: Yes

Special Facilities: University Museum. Millennium Auditorium. Film Studio

Libraries: Central Library. Science Library. Medical Library. Law Library (Asian Studies Library). Jongyeonggak

Publications: Sungkyunkwan Journal of East Asian Studies *(quarterly)*

Press or Publishing House: Sungkyunkwan University Press

SUNGSAN HYODO GRADUATE SCHOOL

614 Kansuk 4-dong, Namdong-gu, Incheon-si 405-234
Tel: +82(32) 421-1996
Fax: +82(32) 421-4528
Website: http://www.hyo.ac.kr

International Relations: Young-Suk Oh

Programmes

Family Welfare (Family Studies; Social Welfare)

History: Founded 1966.

SUNGSHIN WOMEN'S UNIVERSITY

249-1 Dongseon-dong 3-ga, Seongbuk-gu, Seoul 136-742
Tel: +82(2) 920-7114
Fax: +82(2) 926-3120
EMail: inter@cc.sungshin.ac.kr
Website: http://www.sungshin.ac.kr

President: Hwa Jin Shim

Colleges

Education (Chinese; Education; Ethics; Preschool Education); **Fine Arts** (Crafts and Trades; Fine Arts; Industrial Design; Painting and Drawing; Sculpture); **Human Ecology** (Clothing and Sewing; Food Science; Home Economics; Nutrition; Textile Design); **Humanities**; **Music** (Music; Music Theory and Composition; Singing); **Natural Sciences**; **Social Sciences** (Business Administration; Economics; Geography; International Relations; Law; Political Sciences; Psychology; Social Sciences)

Further Information: Also Graduate Schools

History: Founded 1936.

Main Language(s) of Instruction: Korean

Degrees and Diplomas: *Bachelor's Degree*; *Master's Degree*; *Doctor's Degree*

Special Facilities: Museum

Libraries: Yes

Last Updated: 05/01/09

SUWON CATHOLIC UNIVERSITY

226 Wangrim-ri, Bongdam-eup, Hwasong-si, Gyeonggi-do 445-744
Tel: +82(33) 290-8800
Fax: +82(31) 227-4526
EMail: webmaster@suwoncatholic.ac.kr
Website: http://www.suwoncatholic.ac.kr

President: Kun-tai Kim

History: Founded 1983.

TAEJON CATHOLIC UNIVERSITY

263-3 Shinbang-ri, Jeonui-myeon, Yongi-si, Chungnam-do 339-854
Tel: +82(41) 867-8060
Fax: +82(41) 867-8069
EMail: dlwnrhks@dcatholic.ac.kr
Website: http://www.dcatholic.ac.kr

President: Chang-duk Lee

History: Founded 1992.

TAESHIN CHRISTIAN UNIVERSITY

137 Baekchun-dong, Gyeongsan-si, Gyeongbuk-do 712-713
Tel: +82(53) 810-0701 +82(53) 810-0703
Fax: +82(53) 813-0006
Website: http://www.taeshin.ac.kr

Departments

Literature (English; Literature) *Chairman*: Dae-Hae Choi; **Social Work** (Social Welfare; Social Work) *Chairman*: Jee-Hoon Lee

Divisions

Theology *Chairman*: Yoen-Hae Chung

History: Founded 1950, acquired present status 1997.

Admission Requirements: Graduation from high school

Fees: (US Dollars): c. 4,500 per annum

Main Language(s) of Instruction: Korean

Degrees and Diplomas: *Bachelor's Degree*

Student Services: Academic counselling, Language programs, Nursery care, Sports facilities

Libraries: Library 1,136 vols

TAMNA UNIVERSITY

San-70 Hawon-dong, Sogwipo-si, Cheju-do 697-340
Tel: +82(64) 735-2003
Fax: +82(64) 735-2005
EMail: webmaster@tnu.ac.kr
Website: http://www.tnu.ac.kr

President: Jang-gwon Koh

International Relations: Yeon-ju Im

Programmes

Commerce (Business and Commerce); **Engineering** (Civil Engineering; Construction Engineering; Information Technology); **International Studies** (International Studies); **Leisure and Gymnastics** (Leisure Studies; Sports); **Police Administration** (Police Studies); **Social Work** (Social Work); **Tourism** (Tourism)

History: Founded 1997.

Degrees and Diplomas: *Bachelor's Degree*

THE CATHOLIC UNIVERSITY OF KOREA

43-1 Yeokgok 2-dong, Wonmi-gu, Bucheon, Puchon-si, Gyeonggi-do 422-743
Tel: +82(32) 628-251
Fax: +82(32) 665-9798
Website: http://www.catholic.ac.kr

President: Byeng Hun Lim

Dean of Studies: Yoong Il Kim

Colleges

Humanities and Science *(Songsim)*; **Medicine and Nursing** *(Songeui)*; **Theology** *(Songsin)*

Departments

French Language and Culture; **Life Sciences**; **Music** (Music); **Religious Studies** (Religious Studies); **Special Education** (Special Education)

Graduate Schools

Business and Administration *(Songsim)*; **Church Music** *(Songsin)*; **Clinical Dental Science** *(Songeui)*; **Clinical Nursing Science** *(Songeui)*; **Counselling** *(Songsim)*; **Culture and Spirituality** *(Songsim)*; **Education** *(Songsim)*; **Healthcare and Policy** *(Songeui)*; **International Studies** *(Songsim)*; **Occupational Health** *(Songeui)*; **Public Administration** *(Songsim)*; **Social Welfare** *(Songsim)*

Schools

Business Administration (Accountancy; Business Administration); **Computer Science and Information Technology** (Computer Science; Information Sciences; Information Technology; Multimedia; Systems Analysis); **Foreign Languages and Cultures** (Cultural Studies; English; Japanese; Modern Languages); **Foreign Languages and Literatures** (Chinese; English; Literature; Modern Languages); **Human Ecology**; **Human Welfare** (Psychology; Social Welfare); **Humanities**; **Information, Communication and Electronic Engineering**; **International Studies**; **Law and Economics** (Economics; Law; Public Administration); **Life Sciences and Technology** (Biological and Life Sciences; Biotechnology;

Environmental Engineering); **Natural Sciences**; **Social Sciences** (Psychology; Social Sciences; Social Welfare; Sociology)

History: Founded 1855 as St. Joseph's Seminary. Merged with Songsim Women's University 1995 and acquired present status and title 1999.

Governing Bodies: Songsim School Corporation

Academic Year: March to December (March-July; September-December)

Admission Requirements: Graduation from high school and entrance examination

Main Language(s) of Instruction: Korean

Degrees and Diplomas: *Bachelor's Degree (BA)*: 4 yrs; *Master's Degree*: a further 2 yrs; *Doctor's Degree*: 3 yrs following Master

Student Residential Facilities: Yes

Special Facilities: University Museum

Libraries: Theology, c. 62,500 vols; Medicine, c. 31,500

Publications: Bulletin of Clinical Research Institute; Bulletin of the Catholic Medical; Catholic Theology and Thought *(biannually)*; Journal of Catholic Research Institute; Korean Journal of Occupational Health

Press or Publishing House: Catholic University Press

THE UNIVERSITY OF SUWON (USW)

San 2-2 Wau-ri, Bongdam-eup, Hwaseong-si, Gyeonggi-do 445-743
Tel: +82(31) 220-2562
Fax: +82(31) 222-1405
EMail: dhkim@suwon.ac.kr
Website: http://www.suwon.ac.kr

President: Chong-wook Lee

International Relations: In-hyung Lee EMail: ihlee@suwon.ac.kr

Colleges

Economics and Commerce (Business and Commerce; Economics); **Engineering** (Architecture; Chemical Engineering; Civil Engineering; Electrical and Electronic Engineering; Engineering; Environmental Engineering; Genetics; Industrial Engineering; Materials Engineering; Mechanical Engineering; Polymer and Plastics Technology; Town Planning); **Fine Arts** (Fine Arts); **Human Ecology** (Ecology); **Humanities** (Arts and Humanities; English; French; History; Japanese; Korean; Literature; Modern Languages); **Information Engineering**; **Law and Political Science** (Law; Political Sciences); **Music**; **Natural Sciences** (Natural Sciences); **Physical Education** (Physical Education)

Graduate Schools

Education (Education); **Industry and Business Administration**; **Public Administration** (Public Administration); **Studies**

Research Institutes

Business Administration (Business Administration); **Genetic Engineering** (Genetics); **Industry Administration**; **Kijon Culture** (Cultural Studies); **Local Society Development**; **Natural Sciences** (Natural Sciences); **Philosophy** (Philosophy); **Social Sciences** (Social Sciences)

Further Information: Also Suwon Industrial College

History: Founded 1982.

Governing Bodies: Board of Trustees

Academic Year: March to December (March-June; September-December)

Admission Requirements: Graduation from high school and entrance examination

Main Language(s) of Instruction: Korean, English

Degrees and Diplomas: *Bachelor's Degree*: 4 yrs; *Master's Degree*: a further 2-3 yrs; *Doctor's Degree*

Student Residential Facilities: Yes

Special Facilities: Museum

Libraries: Central Library, c. 255,000 vols

Last Updated: 05/01/09

TONGMYONG UNIVERSITY OF INFORMATION TECHNOLOGY (TIT)

535 Yongdang-dong, Nam-gu, Pusan 608-711
Tel: +82(51) 610-8000
Fax: +82(51) 610-8059
Website: http://www.tit.ac.kr

President: Seung-taik Yang

International Relations: Jao-ho Shin

Schools

Architecture; **Arts and Design** (Computer Graphics; Fashion Design); **Information Engineering** (Computer Engineering; Information Technology; Multimedia; Robotics); **Management and Social Sciences** (Management; Social Sciences; Tourism)

Further Information: Also Graduate Schools

History: Founded 1996.

Main Language(s) of Instruction: Korean

TRANSNATIONAL LAW AND BUSINESS UNIVERSITY (TLBU)

300 Naeyu-dong, Koyang-si, Gyeonggi-do 412-751
Tel: +82(31) 960-1002
Fax: +82(31) 964-7196
EMail: tlbu@tlbu.ac.kr
Website: http://www.tlbu.ac.kr

President: Byung-Hwa Lyou

Programmes

International Business (International Business); **International Law** (International Law)

History: Founded 2000. Acquired present status 2001.

Admission Requirements: Bachelor of Arts in Law, TOEFL score of 600 or above

Main Language(s) of Instruction: English

International Co-operation: With universities in France and China

Accrediting Agencies: Ministry of Education

Degrees and Diplomas: *Master's Degree*: International Law, 2 yrs

Student Services: Canteen, Health services, Language programs

Student Residential Facilities: Yes

Special Facilities: Art Gallery

Libraries: TLBU Law Library

Publications: TLBU Law Journal

UIDUK UNIVERSITY

San 50 Yugeom-ri, Gangdong-myeon, Gyeongju-si, Gyeongbuk-do 780-713
Tel: +82(54) 760-1114
Fax: +82(54) 760-1170
EMail: shkang@mail.uiduk.ac.kr
Website: http://www.uiduk.ac.kr

Head: Jae Souk Sohn
Tel: +82(54) 760-1009, Fax: +82(54) 760-1170
EMail: jssohn@mail.uiduk.ac.kr

International Relations: Ji-ho Choi

Colleges

Arts and Physical Sciences; **Engineering**; **Humanities** (Asian Religious Studies; Chinese; English; Japanese; Korean; Literature); **Natural Sciences**; **Social Sciences** (Business Administration; Economics; International Relations; Law; Social Welfare)

History: Founded 1996.

Degrees and Diplomas: *Bachelor's Degree*; *Master's Degree*; *Doctor's Degree*

Last Updated: 05/01/09

UNIVERSITY OF ULSAN (UOU)

San-29 Mungeo 2-dong, Nam-gu, Ulsan 680-749
Tel: +82(52) 277-3101
Fax: +82(52) 277-3419
EMail: webmaster@mail.ulsan.ac.kr
Website: http://www.ulsan.ac.kr

President: Doh-Yeon Kim

Schools

Architecture (Architecture); **Business Administration** (Business Administration); **Chemical Engineering** (Chemical Engineering); **Civil Engineering**; **Computer Engineering** (Computer Engineering); **Economics** (Economics); **Electronic Engineering** (Electronic Engineering); **Environmental Engineering** (Environmental Engineering); **Industrial Engineering** (Industrial Engineering); **Law** (Law); **Materials Science and Engineering** (Materials Engineering); **Mathematics** (Mathematics); **Medicine** (Medicine); **Political Science** (Political Sciences); **Sociology** (Sociology)

History: Founded 1970 with the aid of the Colombo Plan and Ulsan Foundation.

Academic Year: March to February (March-July; September-February)

Admission Requirements: Graduation from high school and entrance examination

Main Language(s) of Instruction: Korean

Degrees and Diplomas: *Bachelor's Degree*: 4 yrs; *Master's Degree*; *Doctor's Degree*

Student Services: Academic counselling, Canteen, Cultural centre, Employment services, Foreign student adviser, Foreign Studies Centre, Health services, Language programs, Social counselling, Sports facilities

Student Residential Facilities: Yes

Special Facilities: Museum, Art Gallery, Observatory, Movie Studio

Libraries: 641,946 vols
Last Updated: 05/01/09

WONKWANG UNIVERSITY

344-2 Sinyong-dong, Iksan-si, Jeollabuk-do 570-749
Tel: +82(63) 850-5221
Fax: +82(63) 850-5753
EMail: yemin@wonkwang.ac.kr
Website: http://www.wonkwang.ac.kr

President: Yong- Ho Nah

Colleges

Agriculture (Agriculture); **Commerce and Economics** (Business and Commerce; Economics); **Dentistry** (Dentistry); **Education** (Education); **Engineering** (Engineering); **Home Economics** (Home Economics); **Law and Political Science** (Law; Political Sciences); **Liberal Arts and Science** (Arts and Humanities; Natural Sciences); **Oriental Medicine** (Traditional Eastern Medicine); **Pharmacy** (Pharmacy); **Won Budddhism**

History: Founded 1946 as College.

Degrees and Diplomas: *Bachelor's Degree*; *Master's Degree*; *Doctor's Degree*
Last Updated: 05/01/09

WOOSONG UNIVERSITY

17-2 Jayang-dong, Dong-gu, Daejeon, Chungnam-do 300-178
Tel: +82(42) 630-9631
Fax: +82(42) 627-8636
EMail: hoya@itrc.woosong.ac.kr
Website: http://www.wsu.ac.kr

President: Sung-jong Kim

Colleges

Culinary Arts and Tourism (Cooking and Catering; Tourism); **Design and Information** (Architecture; Computer Graphics; Multimedia; Safety Engineering); **Health and Welfare**; **International Studies**; **Railroad Transportation** (Civil Engineering; Environmental Engineering; Railway Engineering)

Institutes

Languages
History: Founded 1995, acquired present status 1996.
Admission Requirements: Graduation from high school
Main Language(s) of Instruction: Korean
Degrees and Diplomas: *Bachelor's Degree*: Arts (BA), 4 yrs; *Master's Degree*: Arts (MA), a further 2 yrs
Student Services: Academic counselling, Canteen, Cultural centre, Employment services, Foreign student adviser, Foreign Studies Centre, Handicapped facilities, Health services, Language programs, Nursery care, Social counselling, Sports facilities
Student Residential Facilities: Yes
Special Facilities: Woosong Art Centre. Techno and Design Centre. Movie Studio
Press or Publishing House: Woosong University Press
Last Updated: 05/01/09

WOOSUK UNIVERSITY

490 Hujeong-ri, Samrye-eup, Wangju-si,
Jeollabuk-do 565-701
Tel: +82(63) 290-1078
Fax: +82(63) 290-1122
EMail: 2626bus@live.co.kr
Website: http://www.woosuk.ac.kr

President: Jong Yil Ra
Tel: +82(63) 290-1003, Fax: +82(63) 290-1004
EMail: zevo119@naver.com

International Relations: Suk Heung Oh, Dean of Global Relations
Tel: +82(63) 290-1250 EMail: shoh1573@yahoo.co.kr

Colleges

Culture and Social Sciences (Advertising and Publicity; Business Administration; Business and Commerce; Chinese; English; Fashion Design; Film; Hotel Management; Industrial Design; Japanese; Journalism; Korean; Landscape Architecture; Law; Leisure Studies; Mass Communication; Music; Public Administration; Social Sciences; Theatre; Tourism; Urban Studies; Writing); **Education** (Computer Education; Education; Humanities and Social Science Education; Mathematics Education; Modern Languages; Special Education); **Health and Welfare** (Alternative Medicine; Animal Husbandry; Child Care and Development; Cooking and Catering; Cosmetology; Fire Science; Food Science; Health Administration; Health Sciences; Information Management; Nutrition; Occupational Therapy; Pharmacy; Police Studies; Psychology; Rehabilitation and Therapy; Veterinary Science; Welfare and Protective Services); **Oriental Medicine** (Nursing; Traditional Eastern Medicine); **Pharmacy** (Pharmacy; Traditional Eastern Medicine); **Science and Technology**; **Sports Science** (Dance; Leisure Studies; Physical Education; Sports)

Further Information: Also Korean Language Education Centre

History: Founded 1979. Acquired present status 1992. Acquired present title 1995.

Academic Year: March to December (March-June; September-December)

Fees: (US Dollars): undergraduate, 3,000-4,000 per semester; graduate, 3,500-6,200 per semester. International students can be offered 50% of their tuition; Korean Language Education Centre, 1,700 for a 16-week course and 2,600 for a 24-week course.

Main Language(s) of Instruction: Korean

International Co-operation: With universities in the USA, Malaysia, Vietnam, Mongolia, Oman

Student Services: Academic counselling, Canteen, Cultural centre, Employment services, Foreign student adviser, Foreign Studies Centre, Handicapped facilities, Health services, Language programs, Nursery care, Social counselling, Sports facilities

Student Residential Facilities: Residence Hall for 2,086 students (1,124 male students and 962 female students)

Academic Staff *2008-2009*	MEN	WOMEN	TOTAL
FULL-TIME	88	23	**111**
Student Numbers *2008-2009*			
All (Foreign Included)	3,969	3,250	**7,219**
FOREIGN ONLY	435	463	**898**

Last Updated: 23/10/08

YEUNGNAM UNIVERSITY

214-1 Dae-dong, Gyeongsan-si, Gyeongbuk-do 712-749
Tel: +82(53) 810-2114
Fax: +82(53) 813-0188
EMail: webadmin@yu.ac.kr
Website: http://www.yu.ac.kr/

President: Tong Ki Woo

Colleges

Agriculture and Animal Husbandry (Agriculture; Animal Husbandry); **Arts and Design** (Design; Fine Arts); **Commerce and Economics** (Business and Commerce; Economics); **Education** (Education; Physical Education); **Engineering** (Engineering; Materials Engineering; Mechanical Engineering); **Evening**; **Fine Arts** (Fine Arts); **Home Economics** (Home Economics); **Law** (Law; Political Sciences); **Liberal Arts** (Arts and Humanities); **Medicine** (Medicine); **Music** (Music); **Natural Resources** (Natural Resources); **Pharmacy** (Pharmacy); **Political Science and Public Administration** (Political Sciences; Public Administration); **Science** (Natural Sciences)

Graduate Schools

Business Administration (Business Administration); **Education** (Education); **Environmental Studies** (Environmental Studies)

History: Founded 1947, incorporating Taegu College and Chonggu College founded 1947 and 1950 respectively.

Governing Bodies: Board of Trustees

Academic Year: March to February (March-August; September-February)

Admission Requirements: Graduation from high school or equivalent, and entrance examination

Main Language(s) of Instruction: Korean

Degrees and Diplomas: *Bachelor's Degree*: 4 yrs; *Master's Degree*: a further 2 yrs; *Doctor's Degree*

Student Residential Facilities: Yes

Special Facilities: University Museum

Libraries: Central Library, c. 250,000 vols

Publications: Business Administration Memoirs *(annually)*; Industrial Economy *(annually)*; Journal of Oriental Culture *(annually)*; Journal of Silla-Kaya Culture *(annually)*; Public Administration Review *(annually)*; Theses Collections (Humanities, Social and Natural Sciences); Yeungdae Shinmum

Press or Publishing House: University Press

Last Updated: 05/01/09

YEWON ARTS UNIVERSITY

271 Changin-ri, Sinpyeong-myeon, Imsil-si, Jeollabuk-do 566-822
Tel: +82(63) 640-7114
Fax: +82(63) 640-7773
EMail: mailto:gadmin@mail.yewon.ac.kr
Website: http://www.yewon.ac.kr

President: Sun-koo Lee

Departments

Animation (Cinema and Television); **Arts Management** (Art Management); **Comedy** (Theatre); **Cultural Product Design** (Design); **Cultural Property** (Heritage Preservation); **Dance** (Dance); **E-Business** (E-Business/Commerce); **Game Animation**; **Jewelry Art**; **Korea Painting** (Painting and Drawing); **Music** (Music); **Painting** (Painting and Drawing); **Sports Leisure**; **Visual Information Design** (Communication Studies)

History: Founded 2000.

Main Language(s) of Instruction: Korean

YONG-IN UNIVERSITY

470 Samga-dong, Yongin-si, Gyeonggi-do 449-714
Tel: +82(31) 330-2915
Fax: +82(31) 330-2957
EMail: webmaster@yongin.ac.kr
Website: http://www.yongin.ac.kr

President: Jung-haeng Kim

International Relations: Jun-oui Kang
Tel: +82(31) 330-2912, Fax: +82(31) 330-2957

Colleges

Arts (Dance; Film; Fine Arts; Heritage Preservation; Industrial Design; Multimedia; Music; Painting and Drawing; Theatre); **Management** (Business Administration; Chinese; Management; Police Studies; Tourism); **Martial Arts** (Sports); **Natural Sciences** (Biology; Computer Science; Environmental Studies; Food Science; Health Sciences; Natural Sciences; Nutrition; Physical Therapy; Statistics); **Sports Science** (Physical Education; Sports)

Further Information: Also Graduate Schools

History: Founded 1953.

Main Language(s) of Instruction: Korean

Degrees and Diplomas: *Bachelor's Degree*; *Master's Degree*; *Doctor's Degree*

Student Residential Facilities: Yes

Libraries: Yes

Last Updated: 05/01/09

YONSEI UNIVERSITY

134 Shinchon-dong, Seodaemun-gu, Seoul 120-740
Tel: +82(2) 361-2114
Fax: +82(2) 392-0618
EMail: webmaster@yonsei.ac.kr
Website: http://www.yonsei.ac.kr

President: Han-Joon Kim

International Relations: Chung Min Lee
Tel: +82(2) 2123-3490, Fax: +82(2) 393-7272
EMail: ysid@yonsei.ac.kr

Colleges

Business and Economics (Administration; Business and Commerce; Economics; Statistics); **Commerce and Law** (Business and Commerce; Economics; Information Management; International Relations; Law; Public Administration); **Dentistry** (Dentistry); **Educational Sciences** (Education); **Engineering** (Architecture; Engineering; Town Planning); **Health Sciences** (Biomedical Engineering; Environmental Engineering; Health Administration; Health Sciences; Medical Technology; Occupational Therapy; Physical Therapy); **Human Ecology** (Home Economics); **Law** (Law); **Liberal Arts** (Arts and Humanities; Linguistics); **Liberal Arts and Sciences** (Arts and Humanities; Computer Science; English Studies; Natural Sciences); **Medicine** *(Wonju)* (Medicine); **Medicine** (Medicine); **Music** (Music; Music Theory and Composition; Musical Instruments; Religious Music; Singing); **Nursing** (Nursing); **Science** (Astronomy and Space Science; Biochemistry; Biology; Chemistry; Earth Sciences; Mathematics; Natural Sciences; Physics); **Social Sciences** (International Relations; Journalism; Mass Communication; Political Sciences; Public Administration; Social Sciences; Social Welfare); **Theology** (Theology)

Graduate Schools

Administration (Administration); **Business Administration** (Business Administration); **Education**; **Engineering** (Engineering); **Health Sciences and Management** (Health Sciences; Management); **Intellectual Property and Law** (Civil Law); **International Studies** (International Studies; Korean; Regional Studies); **Law** (Criminal Law; Law); **Public Administration**; **Theology** (Christian Religious Studies; Theology)

Institutes

Automation Technology Research (Automation and Control Engineering); **Automotive Technology** (Automotive Engineering); **Communication Research** (Communication Studies); **Eastern and Western Studies** (American Studies; East Asian Studies; European Studies; International Studies); **Economics** (Economics); **Educational Research** (Educational Research); **Engineering**

Research (Engineering); **Food and Nutritional Sciences** (Food Science; Nutrition); **Groundwater and Soil Environment** (Natural Resources; Soil Conservation); **Human Environmental Sciences** (Environmental Studies); **Humanities** (Arts and Humanities); **Information and Telecommunication Research** (Information Sciences; Telecommunications Services); **Iron and Steel Technology** (Metal Techniques); **Korean Studies** (Korean); **Korean Unification Studies** (Korean); **Legal Research** (Law); **Life Sciences** (Biological and Life Sciences); **Mass Communication** (Mass Communication); **Mathematics Science** (Mathematics); **Medical Instruments Technology** (Medical Technology); **Natural Sciences Research** (Natural Sciences); **New Energy and Environmental Systems Research** (Energy Engineering; Environmental Studies); **Social Development Studies** (Social Policy); **Social Sciences Research** (Social Sciences); **Software Application Research** (Software Engineering); **Urban and Regional Planning** (Regional Planning; Town Planning)

Further Information: Also Centres and Research Centres

History: Founded 1885 as Severance Union Medical Clinic. Merged with Chosun Christian College, established 1915, to form present University 1957. The University is related to the United Board for Christian Higher Education in Asia. Recognized by the Government as a University entitled to award degrees. Subject to the educational law and ordinances of the Government.

Governing Bodies: Board of Directors, comprising representatives of Protestant churches in Korea and North America

Academic Year: March to February (March-August; September-February)

Admission Requirements: Graduation from high school, government qualifying examination and university entrance examination

Main Language(s) of Instruction: Korean

International Co-operation: With institutions worldwide

Degrees and Diplomas: *Bachelor's Degree*: Arts (BA); Health Sciences (BHS); Laws (LLB); Music (BM); Science (BS); Theology (BTh), 4 yrs; *Master's Degree*: a further 2-6 yrs; *Doctor's Degree (PhD)*

Student Services: Academic counselling, Canteen, Cultural centre, Employment services, Foreign student adviser, Foreign Studies Centre, Handicapped facilities, Health services, Language programs, Nursery care, Social counselling, Sports facilities

Student Residential Facilities: For c. 1,750 students in Seoul and c. 1,520 in Wonju

Special Facilities: University Museum. Observatory. Movie Studio

Libraries: Central Library, 1,345,757 vols

Publications: Etudes Franco-Coréennes; Journal of East and West Studies; Journal of Educational Science; Journal of Humanities; The Dong Bang Hak Chi (Journal of Far Eastern Studies); Yonsei Business Review; Yonsei Engineering Review; Yonsei Nonchong; Yonsei Social Science Review

Press or Publishing House: University Press

YOUNGDONG UNIVERSITY

12-1 Sulgye-ri, Youngdong-eup, Youngdong-si,
Chungbuk-do 370-701
Tel: +82(43) 740-1010
Fax: +82(43) 740-1019
Website: http://www.youngdong.ac.kr

President: Hun-gwan Chae

Programmes

Architecture (Architecture); **Computer Science** (Computer Science); **Engineering** (Chemical Engineering; Electronic Engineering; Engineering; Telecommunications Engineering); **Industrial and Production Economics** (Industrial and Production Economics); **Urban Studies** (Urban Studies)

History: Founded 1992.

YOUNGSAN UNIVERSITY (YSU)

150 Junam-ri, Ungsang-eup, Yangsan-si,
Pusan 626-847
Tel: +82(55) 380-9537
Fax: +82(55) 380-9109
EMail: grcho@ysu.ac.kr
Website: http://www.ysu.ac.kr

President: Gu-wuck Bu

International Relations: Gun-rae Cho

Schools

Architecture Engineering; **Commerce and Finance** (Business and Commerce; Finance; Information Management; Insurance; International Business); **Computer and Information Engineering**; **Design**; **Hotel and Tourism Management** (Food Science; Hotel Management; Leisure Studies; Tourism); **Information Management**; **International Studies** (Chinese; English; European Studies; International Studies; Japanese); **Law and Public Administration**; **Mass Communication**; **Multimedia Engineering**

History: Founded 1997.

Academic Year: March to February

Main Language(s) of Instruction: Korean

Degrees and Diplomas: *Bachelor's Degree (BA)*: 4 yrs; *Master's Degree (MA)*: a further 2 yrs

Student Services: Academic counselling, Employment services, Foreign student adviser, Foreign Studies Centre, Handicapped facilities, Health services, Language programs, Social counselling, Sports facilities

Special Facilities: Art Gallery

Publications: Youngsan Studies *(quarterly)*

YOUNGSAN WON BUDDHIST UNIVERSITY

20-2 Gillyong-ri, Baesku-eup, Younggwang-gun,
Jeollanam-do 513-902
Tel: +82(61) 350-6015
Fax: +82(61) 350-6040
Website: http://www.youngsan.ac.kr

President: Suk-hee Hwang

Colleges

Pharmacy (Pharmacy); **Religious Studies** (Asian Religious Studies)

History: Founded 1997.

Kuwait

STRUCTURE OF HIGHER EDUCATION SYSTEM

Description:

The Arab Open University, Kuwait and Kuwait University provide higher education in the country. It comprises 30 departments in the following colleges: Arts; Commerce, Economics and Political Science; Engineering and Petroleum; Law; Islamic Law (sharii 'a) and Islamic Studies; Medicine; Allied Health and Nursing; Science; Education; Graduate Studies; and the Women's College. There is also the Public Authority for Applied Education and Training, as well as the Higher Institute of Dramatic Arts and the Higher Institute of Musical Arts. Non university higher education is provided by several Colleges and a Cadet Academy (Military), as well as Training Centres.

Stages of studies:

University level first stage: *Undergraduate studies*

The University Colleges for Allied Health and Nursing, Arts, Education, Commerce, Economics and Political Science, Islamic Law and Islamic Science confer a Bachelor's degree at the end of four years of study. The same degree is conferred by the College of Engineering and Petroleum after five years of study.

University level second stage: *Graduate studies*

Kuwait University offers Master's degrees in Science, Engineering, Philosophy, and Medicine through the College of Graduate Studies. These programmes require one or two years' study beyond the Bachelor's degree.

ADMISSION TO HIGHER EDUCATION

Admission to university-level studies:

Name of secondary school credential required: Shahadat Al-Thanawiya-Al-A'ama

Minimum score/requirement: 65%

For entry to: All

Alternatives to credentials: Religious Secondary Education Certificate (only to enrol in the College of Arts and Education, the College of Law, or the College of Islamic Law and Islamic Studies). International Certificate of General Secondary Education; the Baccalauréat.

Foreign students admission:

Entrance exam requirements: A limited number of foreign students may be admitted, subject to availability of relevant resources and facilities. Selection is based on merit and national interest. Applicants should have a Bachelor's degree with a GPA of at least 2.67 on a scale of 4. For acceptance for scholarships, certificates must be either in Arabic, English or French or translated into one of these languages and authenticated. They must be attested by the Ministry of Education and the Ministry of External Affairs and the Embassy of Kuwait in the student's country. To obtain a scholarship students must be chosen to study in Kuwait by the students' government or by an institution, or a corporation accredited by the Government. The Kuwait National Commission for Education, Science and Culture is the only organ that has the right to consider each application and take a decision.

Entry regulations: Study visas are necessary for foreign students.

Language requirements: Students must have a good knowledge of Arabic or English. A minimum language score is necessary for admission to Master's degree programmes. Each applicant must satisfy one of the language proficiency requirements for the programme to which they are seeking application.

NATIONAL BODIES

Ministry of Higher Education

Minister: Nayif Falah al-Haj
PO Box 7
Safat 13001
Tel: +965 483 7890
Fax: +965 483 7601
WWW: http://www.mohe.edu.kw

Role of national body: Educational planning and policy; adoption of text books, curricula; supply of human/ material resources; coordination of education and development policies.

Private Universities Council

City Tower- Mezzanine
Sharq- Khalid Bin Waleed St.
Kuwait
Tel: +965 224 0591
Fax: +965 245 5326
EMail: info@puc.edu.kw
WWW: http://www.puc.edu.kw/

Public Authority for Applied Education and Training

PO Box 23167
Safat 13092
Tel: +965 2256 4690
Fax: +965 2252 8915
EMail: feedback@paaet.edu.kw
WWW: http://www.paaet.edu.kw

Role of national body: Supervises and plans programmes for applied education and training.

Data for academic year: 2008-2009

Source: IAU from Kuwait National Commission for UNESCO, 2008 (Bodies, 2012)

INSTITUTIONS

PUBLIC INSTITUTIONS

KUWAIT UNIVERSITY

Jami'at Al-Kuwait

PO Box 5969, Safat 13060
Tel: +965 481-1188
Fax: +965 484-8648
EMail: Prd@kuniv.edu.kw
Website: http://www.kuniv.edu.kw

President: Abdullatif Ahmad Al-Bader
Tel: +965 484-7559 EMail: president@ku.edu.kw

Secretary-General: Anwar Khalifa Al-Yatama
Tel: +965 481-1008, Fax: +965 483-2768
EMail: a.yatama@ku.edu.kw

Centres

Gulf and Arabian Peninsula Studies *(Shuwaikh Campus)* (Middle Eastern Studies); **Information System** *(Shuwaikh Campus)* (Computer Science; Information Management; Software Engineering); **Language** *(Shuwaikh Campus)* (Arabic; Modern Languages); **Strategic and Future Studies** *(Shuwaikh Campus)* (Development Studies)

Colleges

Allied Health Sciences and Nursing *(Shuwaikh Campus)* (Health Administration; Health Sciences; Information Management; Nursing; Physical Therapy; Radiology); **Arts** *(Kaifan Campus)* (Arabic; Arts and Humanities; English; History; Mass Communication; Philosophy); **Business Administration** *(Shuwaikh Campus)* (Accountancy; Administration; Business Administration; Economics; Finance; Information Management; Management; Marketing; Public Administration); **Dentistry** *(Jabriya Campus)* (Dental Hygiene; Dentistry; Surgery); **Education** *(Kaifan Campus)* (Curriculum; Education; Educational Administration; Educational Psychology; Pedagogy); **Engineering and Petroleum** *(Khaldiya Campus)* (Architecture; Chemical Engineering; Civil Engineering; Computer Engineering; Electrical Engineering; Industrial Engineering; Mechanical Engineering; Petroleum and Gas Engineering); **For Women** *(Adeliya Campus)* (Communication Studies; Design; Family Studies; Fine Arts; Information Sciences); **Graduate Studies**; **Law** *(Shuwaikh Campus)* (Criminal Law; International Law; Law; Private Law; Public Law); **Medicine** *(Jabriya Campus)* (Anatomy; Behavioural Sciences; Biochemistry; Community Health; Gynaecology and Obstetrics; Medicine; Microbiology; Paediatrics; Pathology; Pharmacology; Physiology; Psychiatry and Mental Health; Radiology; Surgery); **Pharmacy** *(Jabriya Campus)* (Chemistry; Pharmacology; Pharmacy); **Science** *(Khaldiya Campus)* (Biochemistry; Biological and Life Sciences; Chemistry; Computer Science; Earth Sciences; Environmental Studies; Geology;

Mathematics; Natural Sciences; Physics; Zoology); **Shari'a and Islamic Studies** *(Kaifan Campus)* (Comparative Law; Islamic Law; Islamic Studies; Koran; Law); **Social Sciences** *(Shuwaikh Campus)* (Geography; Information Sciences; Library Science; Political Sciences; Psychology; Social Sciences; Social Work; Sociology)

Further Information: A major public university with 14 colleges, 122 academic departments and numerous centres located in Khaldiya, Shuwaikh, Adeliya, Kheifan and Jabriya

History: Founded 1966. A State institution under the jurisdiction of the Ministry of Education.

Governing Bodies: University Council

Academic Year: September to August (September-January; February-June; July-August)

Admission Requirements: Secondary school certificate or equivalent and entrance examination

Main Language(s) of Instruction: Arabic, English

Degrees and Diplomas: *Bachelor's Degree*: Administration; Allied Health; Arts; Arts and Education; Basic Medical Sciences; Commerce; Education; Engineering; Law; Political Science; Science; Science and Education; Shari'a; Women's Studies, 4-5 yrs; *Bachelor's Degree*: Medicine and Surgery, 7 yrs; *Master's Degree*: Arts; Business Administration; Education; Engineering; Law; Library/Information; Science; Shari'a and Islamic Studies; Social Sciences, 2 yrs; *Master's Degree*: Medicine/Surgery, 2-3 yrs. Also PhD in Science and Medicine 2 yrs

Student Services: Academic counselling, Canteen, Cultural centre, Employment services, Foreign student adviser, Health services, Social counselling, Sports facilities

Student Residential Facilities: For c. 650 students

Special Facilities: Sabah Al-Salem Theatre; Abdullah Al-Jaber Theatre

Libraries: Total, c. 294,000 vols

Publications: Annals of Arts and Literature *(quarterly)*; Arab Journal for the Humanities (English and Arabic) *(quarterly)*; Arab Journal of Administrative Sciences *(quarterly)*; Journal of Education *(quarterly)*; Journal of Gulf and Arabian Peninsula Studies *(quarterly)*; Journal of Law *(quarterly)*; Journal of Shari'a and Islamic Studies *(quarterly)*; Journal of Social Sciences I (Arabic and English) *(quarterly)*; Kuwait Journal of Science and Engineering *(annually)*

Press or Publishing House: Kuwait University Press

Last Updated: 06/12/11

PRIVATE INSTITUTIONS

AMERICAN UNIVERSITY OF KUWAIT

P.O. Box 3323, Safat 13034
Tel: +965-2224-8399
EMail: hbouhatoum@auk.edu.kw
Website: http://www.auk.edu.kw/index.jsp

President: Winfred Thompson EMail: wthompson@auk.edu.kw

Colleges

Arts and Sciences (Accountancy; Behavioural Sciences; Business Administration; Communication Studies; Computer Engineering; Computer Science; Economics; English; Finance; Graphic Design; International Studies; Management; Marketing; Media Studies; Social Sciences)

History: Founded 2003.

Accrediting Agencies: Private Universities Council, Ministry of Higher Education

Degrees and Diplomas: *Bachelor's Degree*

Libraries: Yes

Last Updated: 07/12/11

AMERICAN UNIVERSITY OF THE MIDDLE EAST

P.O. Box 220, Dasman 15453
Tel: +965 2225 1400
EMail: info@aum.edu.kw
Website: http://www.aum.edu.kw

Colleges

Business (Accountancy; Business Administration; Finance; Human Resources; Management; Marketing); **Engineering** (Industrial Engineering)

Accrediting Agencies: Private Universities Council Ministry of Higher Education

Degrees and Diplomas: *Bachelor's Degree*; *Master's Degree*: Business Administration

Last Updated: 07/12/11

ARAB OPEN UNIVERSITY (AOU)

Kuwait Al-Khaitan - Block 2, P.O. Box 32004, Al-Jabria
Tel: +965 247-67291
Fax: +965 247-67286
EMail: Admission@aou.edu.kw
Website: http://www.aou.edu.kw/

Branch Director: Samir Qasim Fakhro

Faculties

Business Administration (Business Administration; Business and Commerce); **Computer Studies** (Computer Science; Information Technology); **Education** (Education); **Language Studies** (English)

Degrees and Diplomas: *Bachelor's Degree*

Last Updated: 06/12/11

GULF UNIVERSITY FOR SCIENCE AND TECHNOLOGY

P.O. Box 7207, Hawally 32093
Tel: +965 2530-7000
EMail: info@gust.edu.kw
Website: http://www.gust.edu.kw

President: Shuaib A. Shuaib (2009-)

Colleges

Arts and Sciences (Anthropology; Arabic; Art History; Chinese; Computer Science; English; French; History; Islamic Studies; Music; Philosophy; Political Sciences; Psychology; Sociology; Spanish; Theatre); **Business Administration** (Accountancy; Business Administration; Economics; Finance; Management; Marketing)

History: Founded 2000 by Private Universities Decree, No. 34, issued by the State of Kuwait.

Degrees and Diplomas: *Bachelor's Degree*

Last Updated: 07/12/11

Kyrgyzstan

STRUCTURE OF HIGHER EDUCATION SYSTEM

Description:

Higher education is provided by universities, academies, institutes and colleges, most of them state-run. According to the Higher Education Law of 1992, their structure was considerably changed. This Law was amended in 1997. New universities were founded in the central region and some specialized higher education institutions were reconstructed as multidisciplinary universities. Governmental and non-governmental institutions have equal status.There are also several private higher education institutions. The Ministry of Education is responsible for education in the country.

Stages of studies:

University level first stage: *Bakalavr, Diploma of Specialist*
The first stage of university studies leads to a Bachelor's degree after four to five years' study or to a Diploma of Specialist after five years' study.

University level second stage: *Master's degree, Kandidat Nauk*
The second stage leads to a Master's degree after a minimum of one year's further study or to a Kandidat Nauk after a further three years beyond the Diploma of Specialist and a thesis.

University level third stage: *PhD, Doktor Nauk*
A PhD degree is conferred after a further two to three years' study beyond the Master's degree and a Doktor Nauk is conferred after defence of a thesis.

Distance higher education:
Kyrgyz University offers correspondence courses.

ADMISSION TO HIGHER EDUCATION

Admission to university-level studies:

Name of secondary school credential required: Attestat o Srednem Obščem Obrazovanii

Entrance exam requirements: In 2002, national entrance exams were introduced (the Obšèepespyblikanskoe Testirovanie-Kyrgyz National Scholarship Test or the American SAT)

NATIONAL BODIES

Ministry of Education and Science

Minister: Kanat Sadykov
257 Tynystanov Street
Biškek 720040
Tel: +996(312) 662-442
Fax: +996(312) 228-604/ 228-786
WWW: http://edu.gov.kg/

Data for academic year: 2006-2007
Source: IAU from: Ministry of Education and Science, 2006 (Bodies, 2011)

INSTITUTIONS

PUBLIC INSTITUTIONS

ACADEMY OF MANAGEMENT UNDER THE PRESIDENT OF THE KYRGYZ REPUBLIC

Kyrgyz Respublikasynyn Prezidentinin aldyndagy Bashkaruu Akademiyasy

ul. Panfilov 237, 720040 Biškek
Tel: +996(312) 62-31-00 +996(312) 66-46-44
Fax: +996(312) 66-36-14
EMail: marketing.amp@gmail.com
Website: http://www.amp.kg/

Rector: Almazbek Akmataliev (2010-)
EMail: akmataliev@yahoo.com

International Relations: Chynara Ainekenova, Head of International Relations Office EMail: chynara_ainekenova@yahoo.com

Centres
Advanced Training and Retraining of Public and Municipal Servants (Government; Human Resources; Information Technology; Management; Public Administration)

Colleges
Finance and Economics *(Toktonaliev Bishkek Financial and Economic College)* (Accountancy; Banking; Economics; Finance; Insurance; Management; Marketing; Taxation)

Departments
International Relations and World Economy (Arts and Humanities; Civil Security; International Economics; International Relations; Modern Languages; Natural Sciences; Social Sciences)

Institutes
Distance Education (Accountancy; Banking; Business Administration; Finance; International Economics; International Relations; Law; Marketing; Taxation); **Finance and Accountancy** (Accountancy; Banking; Economics; Finance; Taxation); **Public Administration** (Government; Natural Resources; Political Sciences; Public Administration; Water Management); **Public Administration, Law and Business** (Business Administration; Economics; Information Management; Information Technology; Law; Management; Marketing; Mathematics; Native Language; Physical Education; Public Administration; Russian)

Programmes
Business and Management *(Master's programme)* (Business Administration; Economics; Finance; Management; Political Sciences)

History: Founded 1992 as Biškek International School of Management and Business. In 1997 the Academy of Management was founded to consolidate the International School.

Governing Bodies: Academic Council

Academic Year: September to June

Admission Requirements: Secondary school certificate

Fees: (Soms): Master, 20,000 per annum; Bachelor and Specialist, 16,400

Main Language(s) of Instruction: Russian, English

International Co-operation: With universities in USA and Kazakhstan

Accrediting Agencies: Ministry of Education, Science and Culture

Degrees and Diplomas: *Bakalavr*: Public Administration; Business Administration; Management, 4 yrs; *Diplom Specialista*: Finance and Accountancy, 5 yrs; *Magistr*: Management, a further 2 yrs. Also degree of Economist, 5 yrs full-time

Student Services: Academic counselling, Canteen, Language programs, Sports facilities

Student Residential Facilities: Yes

Libraries: Central Library, 18,667 vols

Publications: Vestnik Academii, Economics, Management, Public Administration, Civil Service Reforms, Political Processes, Local Self-government *(3 per annum)*

Last Updated: 21/06/11

ARABAEV KYRGYZ STATE UNIVERSITY

Arabaev atyndagy Kyrgyz Mamlekettik Universiteti (KSU)

ul. Razzakova 51, 720026 Biškek
Tel: +966(312) 66-03-47
Fax: +966(312) 66-05-88
EMail: akmpu@yandex.ru
Website: http://www.arunet.kg

Rector: Ablabek Asankanov EMail: rektorgu@mail.ru

Vice-Rector for Academic Affairs: Temirbek Choduraev
Tel: +966(312) 66-08-77 EMail: prorkgu.56@mail.ru

International Relations: Adina Boronov, Vice-Rector
Tel: +966(312) 66-07-66 EMail: a_boronov@hotmail.com

Centres
Humanities (Finance; Management; Philology)

Faculties
Artistic Culture and Education (Design; Fashion Design; Fine Arts; Music; Music Education; Native Language; Pedagogy)

Institutes
Developing Qualification in Further Training (Arts and Humanities; History; Natural Sciences; Psychology; Social Sciences; Teacher Training); **Ecology and Natural Resources** (Ecology; Natural Resources); **Economics and Management** *(International)* (Accountancy; Banking; Business Administration; Economics; Finance; Management); **Linguistics and European Civilisations** (International Economics; Political Sciences); **New Information Technology** (Computer Science; Mathematics; Physics); **Pedagogy and Psychology** (Pedagogy; Primary Education; Psychology); **Social and Oriental Studies** (Arts and Humanities; East Asian Studies; History; Information Sciences; International Relations; Journalism; Oriental Languages; Oriental Studies; Philology); **State Language and Culture** (Literature; Modern Languages; Native Language); **World Languages** (Philology)

Further Information: Also Branch in Talas

History: Founded 1952 as Kyrgyz State Pedagogical Institute. Acquired present status and title 1994, named after Išenaly Arabaev.

Governing Bodies: Rectorate, comprising the Rector, the First Vice-Rector and 5 Vice-Rectors; Academic Council

Admission Requirements: Secondary school certificate

Main Language(s) of Instruction: Kyrgyz, Russian

Accrediting Agencies: Ministry of Education, Science and Culture

Degrees and Diplomas: *Bakalavr*: 4 yrs; *Magistr*: a further 2 yrs. Also postgraduate studies in Higher Education, 5 yrs

Student Services: Academic counselling, Canteen, Cultural centre, Foreign student adviser, Foreign Studies Centre, Health services, Language programs, Nursery care, Sports facilities

Student Residential Facilities: 3 hostels

Special Facilities: Historical Museum. Language Laboratories; Computer Laboratories; Educational Laboratories

Libraries: University Library

BISHKEK HUMANITIES UNIVERSITY

Biškekskij Gumanitardyk Universiteti (BGU/BHU)

prosp. Tynchtyk 27, 720044 Biškek
Tel: +996(312) 54-88-00
Fax: +996(312) 54-14-05
EMail: rectorat@bgupub.freenet.bishkek.su
Website: http://bhu.kg

Rector: Mukanmedy Kerezovich Asanbekov
Tel: +996(312) 21-86-59

Vice-Rector for Academic Affairs: Mukhtar Duyshenovich Choguldurov Tel: +996(312) 21-88-76

International Relations: Suusar Iskenderovna Iskenderova, Vice-Rector for Science and International Relations
Tel: +996(312) 21-87-11

Departments

Ecology and Management (Advertising and Publicity; Ecology; Foreign Languages Education; Information Management; Management; Tourism; Water Management); **Postgraduate Studies** (Arts and Humanities; Ecology; Economics; History; Philology; Philosophy; Political Sciences; Psychology; Sociology); **Social Work and Psychology** (Psychology; Public Administration; Social Work)

Faculties

Economics and Finance (Accountancy; Business Administration; Economics; Finance; Management; Taxation); **European Civilization** (Economics; English; German; Literature; Modern Languages; Translation and Interpretation); **Journalism and Information Technology** (Computer Science; Information Sciences; Library Science; Pedagogy; Psychology; Social Work); **Kyrgyz Chinese** (Chinese; Economics; Literature); **Kyrgyz Philology** (Journalism; Linguistics; Native Language; Philology; Russian; Translation and Interpretation); **Oriental Studies and International Relations** (African Studies; Arabic; Asian Studies; Chinese; International Relations; Korean; Oriental Languages; Oriental Studies; Persian; Philology; Turkish); **Slavic Studies** (Literature; Modern Languages; Native Language; Philology; Turkish)

Institutes

Distance Education (Economics; Educational Sciences; Environmental Studies; International Economics; Journalism; Library Science; Modern Languages; Native Language; Philology; Political Sciences; Public Administration; Russian; Social Work; Sociology; Tourism)

History: Founded in 1979 from the Pedagogical Institute of Russian Language and Literature. A State institution.

Governing Bodies: Academic Board

Admission Requirements: Secondary school certificate (Attestat o srednem obrazovanii) and entrance examination

Fees: (US Dollars): 800-1,000 per annum

Main Language(s) of Instruction: Kyrgyz; Russian; English; Chinese; Korean; Turkish; Arabic; Italian

International Co-operation: With universities in Korea; China; Russia; Germany

Accrediting Agencies: Ministry of Education, Science and Culture

Degrees and Diplomas: *Bakalavr*: 4-5 yrs; *Diplom Specialista*: 4 yrs; *Kandidat Nauk*

Libraries: c. 300,000 vols

Press or Publishing House: Publishing Centre

Last Updated: 26/09/11

I.K AKHUNBAEV KYRGYZ STATE MEDICAL ACADEMY

Isa Akhunbaev atyndagy Kyrgyz Mamlekettik Medikalyk Akademiyasy

Ul. Akhunbaev 92, 720020 Biškek
Tel: +996(312) 54-58-81
Fax: +996(312) 54-58-59
EMail: akhunbaevksma@yandex.com
Website: http://www.kgma.aknet.kg

Rector: Zurdinov Ashirali Zurdinovich (2009-)

Vice-Rector: Ishenbek Satylganov

International Relations: Turnisa Yusupova

Faculties

Medicine (Biological and Life Sciences; Cardiology; Gynaecology and Obstetrics; Medicine; Oncology; Ophthalmology; Paediatrics; Surgery; Venereology) *Dean*: Ormonbek Djakypbaev; **Paediatrics and Nursing** (Nursing; Paediatrics) *Dean*: Stalbek Bakasov; **Pharmacy** (Pharmacy) *Dean*: Isabek Ismailov; **Post-Diploma Medical Education** (Medicine) *Dean*: Kuttubek Akynbekov; **Public Health** (Health Administration; Public Health) *Dean*: Jumabek Sydykov; **Stomatology** (Dentistry; Stomatology) *Dean*: Clara Kuttubaeva

Further Information: Also Faculty of General Medicine for Foreign Citizens

History: Founded 1939. Previously known as Kyrgyz Mamlekettik Medikalyk Akademiyasy (Kyrgyz State Medical Academy)

Academic Year: September to July

Admission Requirements: Secondary school certificate

Fees: (Soms): Local students (including Kazakhstan, Russia, Belarus, Tajikistan), 17,000-30,500 per annum; Foreign students, 78,100-110,200

Main Language(s) of Instruction: Russian and English (some courses in Kyrgyz)

Accrediting Agencies: Ministry of Health; Ministry of Education and Science

Degrees and Diplomas: *Bakalavr*: General Medicine; Paediatrics, 6 yrs; *Bakalavr*: Stomatology; Pharmacy; Public Health, 5 yrs; *Diplom Specialista*: Nursing, 5 yrs; *Magistr*: 6 yrs

Student Services: Academic counselling, Canteen, Cultural centre, Employment services, Foreign student adviser, Foreign Studies Centre, Handicapped facilities, Health services, Language programs, Nursery care, Social counselling, Sports facilities

Special Facilities: Museum; Training Centre for Clinical Skills; Medical Centre; Stomatologist Educational/Scientific Clinical Hospital

Publications: Vestnik KSMA *(quarterly)*

Press or Publishing House: KSMA Publishing Centre

Academic Staff *2011*	MEN	WOMEN	TOTAL
FULL-TIME	–	–	**837**
PART-TIME	–	–	**94**
STAFF WITH DOCTORATE			
FULL-TIME	38	14	**52**
PART-TIME	7	2	**9**
Student Numbers *2011*			
All (Foreign Included)	2,137	2,508	**4,645**
FOREIGN ONLY	697	140	**837**

Evening students, 117.

Last Updated: 07/11/11

INTERNATIONAL UNIVERSITY OF KYRGYZSTAN

Meždunarodnyj Universitet Kyrgyzstana (IUK)

prosp. Čui 255, 720001 Biškek
Tel: +996(312) 21-83-35
Fax: +996(312) 21-96-15
EMail: iuk@mail.elcat.kg
Website: http://www.iuk.kg

President: Asylbek Aidaraliev (1993-)
Tel: +996(312) 21-83-35, Fax: +996(312) 21-77-47

Vice-President, Academic Affairs: Amanbek Narkoziev
Tel: +996(312) 21-57-85

International Relations: Valentin Jantsen, Vice-President, International Relations and Planning
Tel: +996(312) 61-20-28 EMail: bms@iuk.kg

Colleges

Law, Business and Computer Technology *(Karakol)* (Banking; Business and Commerce; Finance; Information Technology; International Economics; International Law; International Relations; Law; Management; Management Systems; Public Administration) *Director*: Ryskul Kasimbekov; **Law, Business and Computer Technology** *(Djalal-Abad)* (Banking; Business and Commerce; Economics; Finance; Information Technology; International Economics; International Law; International Relations; Law; Management; Management Systems; Public Administration) *Director*: Makambai Darbanov; **Law, Business and Computer Technology** *(Osh)* (Accountancy; Banking; Economics; Finance; International Law; International Relations; Taxation) *Director*: Djumakan Omukeeva; **Management, Business and Tourism** (Hotel and Restaurant; Hotel Management; Tourism) *Director*: Bakyt Kenjebaer; **Mining Studies** *(International Institute)* (Ecology; Geology; Natural Sciences) *Director*: Valentin Mahnovski; **Multimedia Training** (Banking; Computer Science; Economics; Finance; Information Management; International Law; Law; Management; Multimedia)

Director: Valentin Jantsen; **Polytechnic** (Administration; Communication Studies; Computer Science; Economics; Engineering Management; Management) *Director*: Aman Tohlukov

Higher Schools

Diplomacy and International Law (International Law; International Relations) *Dean*: Tylek Asanaliev; **Ecology and Biotechnology** (Biotechnology; Ecology; Environmental Management; Environmental Studies) *Dean*: Margarita Prasolova; **Economics and Business** (Banking; Business and Commerce; Economics; International Economics; Management) *Dean*: Ainura Adieva; **Medicine** *(International)* (Medicine) *Director*: Shamil Chyngyshpaev; **New Information Technologies** (Computer Networks; Computer Science; Information Management; Information Technology; Public Administration) *Dean*: Leonid Mirkin

Institutes

Distance Education *(Kyrgyz-Russian Institute)* (Computer Science; Economics; Law; Management) *Rector*: Amanbek Narkoziev; **Distance Education** *(Kyrgyz-Indian Institute)* (Business Administration; Finance; Information Technology; Management; Marketing; Tourism) *Director*: Muratbek Baihodjoev; **Foreign Languages** (English; French; Modern Languages; Native Language; Russian) *Director*: Zinaida Karaeva; **International Business** (Economics; International Business; Management) *Director*: Rahat Bekboeva

Research Institutes

Economics and Science in Mountain Regions (Economics; Natural Sciences) *Director*: Shailoobek Musakojoev; **Ethnology** (Cultural Studies; Ethnology; Political Sciences; Psychology; Sociology; Turkish) *Director*: Ainura Elebaeva

Further Information: Also Branches at Osh, Karakol and Djalal-Abad

History: Founded 1993, acquired present status 1995.

Governing Bodies: Board of Trustees

Academic Year: September to June

Admission Requirements: Secondary school certificate

Fees: (US Dollars): 2,000 per annum

Main Language(s) of Instruction: Russian

International Co-operation: Participates in Tempus-Tacis programme

Accrediting Agencies: Ministry of Education, Science and Culture

Degrees and Diplomas: *Bakalavr*: Ecology (BA); Economics (BA); Foreign Langagues (BA); International Relations (BA); Jurisprudence (BA); Management (BA); Medicine (BA); Political Science (BA); Systems Analysis and Management (BA); Tourism (BA), 4 yrs; *Bakalavr*: New Information Technologies (BA), 4 yrs; *Magistr*: Economics (MBA); International Business (MBA); Jurisprudence (MBA); Political Science (MBA); State and Public Administration (MBA), a further 2 yrs

Student Services: Foreign student adviser, Foreign Studies Centre, Health services, Language programs, Sports facilities

Student Residential Facilities: Yes

Libraries: 100,000 vols

Publications: International University Link *(quarterly)*

JALALABAT STATE UNIVERSITY

Jalalabat Mamlekettik Universiteti (JASU)

Lenin Street 57, 715600 Jalal-Abad

Tel: +996(3722) 5-59-68

Fax: +996(3722) 5-03-33

EMail: interdepartment@mail.ru

Rector: Abdiumanatcadyr Ashiraliev EMail: mamat_a@rambler.ru

Colleges

Electrical Engineering and Technology (Electrical Engineering; Technology); **Pedagogy** (Pedagogy); **Technology** (Technology)

Faculties

Agriculture and Biology (Agriculture; Biology); **Computer Science** (Computer Science); **Economics** (Economics); **Engineering and Technology** (Engineering; Technology); **Foreign Languages** (Modern Languages); **Kyrgyz Language** (Native Language); **Medicine** (Medicine); **Pedagogy** (Biology; Business and Commerce; Computer Science; Economics; English; Mathematics; Modern Languages; Native Language); **Philology** (Philology); **Russian Language** (Russian); **Social Humanitarian** (Arts and Humanities; Social Sciences); **Technology** (Technology)

Further Information: Also Branches in Kara-Kul, Taš-Kumyr, Mailuu-Suu and Kočkor-Ata

History: Founded 1993 from former Jala-Abad Pedagogical School and Zoological-Veterinary Technical School.

Academic Year: September to June/July

Admission Requirements: Secondary school certificate

Main Language(s) of Instruction: Russian, Kyrgyz

Accrediting Agencies: Ministry of Education, Science and Culture

Degrees and Diplomas: *Diplom Specialista*: 5 yrs

Student Services: Academic counselling, Canteen, Cultural centre, Employment services, Foreign student adviser, Foreign Studies Centre, Handicapped facilities, Health services, Language programs, Nursery care, Social counselling, Sports facilities

Libraries: JASU Library, c. 58,000 vols

Publications: Vestnik *(bimonthly)*

KYRGYZ ECONOMICS UNIVERSITY

Kyrgyz Economicalyk Universiteti (KEU)

Ul. Togolok Moldo 58, 720033 Biškek

Tel: +996(312) 32-51-19 +996(312) 32-53-89

Fax: +996(312) 32-55-09

EMail: keu.edu.kg@gmail.com

Website: http://www.keu.edu.kg

Rector: Tolobek Kamchybekov (1995-)

Faculties

Economics and Trade (Business and Commerce; Economics); **Finance and Accounting** (Accountancy; Finance); **Management and Tourism** (Economics; International Economics; Management; Tourism)

History: Founded 1953. Formerly known as Bishkek Ekonomika jana Kommerziya Mamlekettik Universiteti (Bishkek State University of Economics and Commerce). Acquired current title and status 2008.

Degrees and Diplomas: *Diplom Specialista*; *Magistr*; *Kandidat Nauk*

Last Updated: 03/07/09

KYRGYZ NATIONAL UNIVERSITY NAMED AFTER JUSUP BALASAGYN

Jusup Balasagyn atyndagy Kyrgyz Uluttuk Universiteti (KSNU)

ul. Frunze 547, 720024 Biškek

Tel: +996(312) 323-394

Fax: +996(312) 323-221

Website: http://www.university.kg/

Rector: Aalybek Akunov

International Relations: Temir Djumakadyrov
Tel: +996(312) 313-226 EMail: temirk@gmail.com

Departments

Accounting and Commerce (Accountancy; Business and Commerce); **Biology** (Biology); **Chemistry and Technology** (Chemistry; Technology); **Economics and Management** (Economics; Management); **Foreign Languages** (Modern Languages); **Geography and Ecology** (Ecology; Geography); **History** (History); **Journalism** (Journalism); **Kyrgyz Philology** (Native Language; Philology); **Law** (Law); **Mathematics** (Mathematics); **Physics** (Physics); **Russian Philology** (Philology; Russian)

Faculties

Biology (Biology); **Business Administration** (Business Administration); **Chemistry** (Chemistry); **Economics** (Economics); **English Language and Literature** (English; English Studies); **Finance** (Finance); **Foreign Languages** (Modern Languages); **Geography** (Geography); **History** (History); **Law** (Law); **Marketing** (Marketing); **Mass Media** (Mass Communication; Media Studies); **Mathematics and Applied Mathematics** (Applied Mathematics; Mathematics); **Philology** (Philology); **Physics** (Physics)

History: Founded 1925. Acquired present status 1993.

Governing Bodies: Academic Council

Academic Year: September to July

Admission Requirements: Competitive entrance examination following general or special secondary school certificate

Fees: (US Dollars): c. 1,200 per annum

Degrees and Diplomas: *Diplom Specialista*: 5 yrs; *Kandidat Nauk*: a further 3 yrs and thesis; *Doktor Nauk*: by thesis after Kandidat

Student Services: Academic counselling, Canteen, Cultural centre, Employment services, Foreign student adviser, Foreign Studies Centre, Health services, Language programs, Sports facilities

Academic Staff *2011*	**TOTAL**
FULL-TIME	**1,072**
PART-TIME	**504**
Student Numbers *2011*	
All (Foreign Included)	**21,799**
FOREIGN ONLY	**760**

Part-time students, 6,538.

Last Updated: 01/08/11

KYRGYZ-RUSSIAN SLAVIC UNIVERSITY

Kyrgyz-Orus Slavyan Universiteti (KRSU)

ul. Kievskaja 44, 720000 Biškek

Tel: +996(312) 62-25-67

Fax: +996(312) 28-27-76

EMail: krsu@krsu.edu.kg

Website: http://www.krsu.edu.kg

Rector: Vladimir Nifadiev (1992-)

Departments

Distance Education; **Economics and Law** (Economics; Law); **Foreign Languages** (Modern Languages); **International Affairs** (International Relations); **Liberal Arts** (Arts and Humanities); **Medicine** (Medicine); **Natural and Technical Sciences** (Chemistry; Mathematics and Computer Science; Natural Sciences; Physics; Technology); **Sports** (Physical Education; Sports)

History: Founded 1992 on the basis of the Agreement on Friendship, Co-operation and Mutual Help between the Russian Federation and the Republic of Kyrgyzstan.

Main Language(s) of Instruction: Kyrgyz, Russian

KYRGYZ STATE INSTITUTE OF PHYSICAL EDUCATION AND SPORTS

Kyrgyz Mamlekettik Dene Tarbiya jana Sport Institutu

Ul. Ahunbaeva 97, 720064 Biškek

Tel: +996(312) 47-04-89

Fax: +996(312) 47-48-81

EMail: abakir@infotel.kg

Rector: Abakir Mamytovič Mamytov Fax: +996(312) 47-48-81

Departments

Military Science *(Pre-Military)* (Military Science); **Pedagogical Aspects of Physical Education** (Education; Pedagogy; Physical Education); **Pedagogy** (Education; Pedagogy); **Sport** (Education; Physical Education; Sports; Teacher Trainers Education)

History: Founded 1955.

Governing Bodies: Council comprising the Rector, 3 Vice-Rectors and 4 Deans of Faculty

Academic Year: September to June

Admission Requirements: Secondary school certificate

Main Language(s) of Instruction: Russian

Degrees and Diplomas: *Magistr*: Sport, 5 yrs; *Magistr*: Sport, 6 yrs (correspondence)

Student Services: Canteen, Cultural centre, Employment services, Health services, Language programs, Social counselling, Sports facilities

Student Residential Facilities: 2 hostels

Special Facilities: Museum. Art Gallery. Movie Studio

Publications: Theory and Practice of Physical Culture, Magazine *(weekly)*

KYRGYZ STATE UNIVERSITY OF CONSTRUCTION, TRANSPORT AND ARCHITECTURE

Kyrgyz Mamlekettit Kurulush, Transport jana Architectura Universiteti

ul. Maldybayeva 34, 720020 Biškek

Tel: +996(312) 54-35-61

Fax: +996(312) 54-51-36

EMail: ksucta@elcat.kg

Rector: Akymbek Abdykalykov (2005-)

Administrative Officer: Erkin Boronbaev Tel: +996(312) 56-14-86

International Relations: Saidulla Abdil Abylov
Tel: +996(312) 56-31-56

Centres

Distance Training; **International Relations** (International Relations)

Colleges

Architecture and Construction *(Biškek)* (Architecture; Construction Engineering); **Automobile and Road** (Automotive Engineering; Road Engineering); **Fine Arts** *(State)* (Fine Arts); **Industrial** *(Issyk-Kul)* (Industrial Engineering)

Departments

Military (Military Science)

Faculties

Humanities (Arts and Humanities); **Kyrgyz-Arabic** (Arabic; Slavic Languages)

Institutes

Architecture and Design (Architecture; Design); **Construction, Economy and Management** (Construction Engineering); **Ecology** (Ecology); **Economy and Management** (Economics; Management); **Innovative Professions**; **New Information Technology** (Information Technology); **Qualification Upgrading**; **Scientific Research** (Natural Sciences)

Further Information: Also Branches in Balykchy City and Talas City

History: The Kyrgyz State University of Construction, Transport and Architecture, named after N. Ilsanov was founded in 1992. Formerly known as Kyrgyz Architectural-Construction Institute and Architectural and Construction Faculties of the Frunze Polytechnic Institute.

Last Updated: 06/06/11

KYRGYZSTAN-TURKEY MANAS UNIVERSITY

Kyrgyz-Turk Manas Universiteti (KTMU)

Tynchtyk Avenue 56, 720044 Biškek

Tel: +996(312) 54-19-42

Fax: +996(312) 54-19-35

EMail: iro@manas.kg

Website: http://www.manas.kg

President: Sebahattin Balci (2010-2015)
Tel: +996(312) 54-19-40, Fax: +996(312) 54-19-04
EMail: ozelkalem@manas.kg

Co-President: Asylbek Kulmyrzaev (2011-)
Tel: +996(312) 54-20-04, Fax: +996(312) 54-19-04
EMail: kulmyrzaev@yandex.ru

Secretary-General: Mustafa Akdeniz
Tel: +996(312) 54-19-06, Fax: +996(312) 54-39-65
EMail: bilgi.gensek@manas.edu.kg

International Relations: Aiday Kasmalieva, Chief of International Relations Office
Tel: +996(312) 54-19-42, Fax: +996(312) 54-19-35
EMail: iro@manas.edu.kg

Conservatories

Music (Music; Performing Arts)

Faculties

Agriculture (Agriculture; Agronomy; Horticulture; Plant and Crop Protection; Zoology); **Communications** (Advertising and Publicity;

Cinema and Television; Communication Studies; Journalism; Public Relations; Radio and Television Broadcasting); **Economics and Administrative Sciences** (Economics; Finance; International Relations; Management); **Engineering** (Chemical Engineering; Computer Engineering; Ecology; Engineering; Environmental Engineering; Food Technology); **Fine Arts** (Fine Arts; Graphic Arts; Painting and Drawing); **Letters** (Arts and Humanities; Chinese; Educational Sciences; English; Eurasian and North Asian Languages; European Languages; European Studies; History; Literature; Philosophy; Russian; Slavic Languages; Sociology); **Science** (Biology; Mathematics; Natural Sciences); **Theology** (Theology); **Veterinary Medicine** (Veterinary Science)

Higher Schools

Foreign Languages (Foreign Languages Education; Modern Languages; Translation and Interpretation); **Tourism and Hotel Management** (Cooking and Catering; Hotel and Restaurant; Hotel Management; Tourism); **Vocational Education** *(Community College)* (Administration; Economics; Technology)

Institutes

Natural and Applied Sciences (Applied Chemistry; Applied Mathematics; Applied Physics; Chemical Engineering; Computer Engineering; Ecology; Environmental Engineering; Food Technology; Mathematics; Natural Sciences); **Social Sciences** (Communication Studies; Economics; Education; European Studies; Finance; History; Management; Social Sciences)

History: Founded 1995.

Governing Bodies: Board of Trustees, Administrative Board, Rectorate, Senate

Academic Year: September to June (September-December; April-June)

Admission Requirements: Secondary school certificate and entrance examination

Fees: None

Main Language(s) of Instruction: Turkish, Kyrgyz

International Co-operation: With universities in China, Japan,-Turkey, USA

Accrediting Agencies: Kyrgyz Ministry of Education and Science, Turkish Ministry of Education, Higher Education Council of Turkey

Degrees and Diplomas: *Bakalavr*: Economics; Finance; Management; Ecology; Computer Engineering (BSc); History; Turkish Studies; Language; Communications (BA), 4 yrs; *Magistr*: Economics; Finance; Management; History; Turkish Studies; Communications; *Kandidat Nauk*: Economics; Finance; Management; History; Turkish Studies (PhD)

Student Services: Academic counselling, Canteen, Cultural centre, Employment services, Foreign student adviser, Foreign Studies Centre, Health services, Language programs, Sports facilities

Special Facilities: Language Laboratory, Radio Station, Movie Studios

Libraries: Main library and Campus library, total 71,346 vols, 33 subscriptions to periodicals

Publications: Science Bulletin *(quarterly)*; Social Science Bulletin *(quarterly)*

Academic Staff *2011-2012*	MEN	WOMEN	**TOTAL**
FULL-TIME	216	160	**376**
PART-TIME	35	36	**71**
STAFF WITH DOCTORATE			
FULL-TIME	85	40	**125**
PART-TIME	22	14	**36**
Student Numbers *2011-2012*			
All (Foreign Included)	1,656	2,178	**3,834**
FOREIGN ONLY	470	128	**598**

Last Updated: 04/05/12

KYRGYZ-UZBEK UNIVERSITY

Kyrgyz-Ozbek Universiteti (KUU)

ul. Aitiev 27, 723500 Oš

Tel: +996(3222) 5-70-55

Fax: +996(3222) 2-54-73

EMail: kuu@ktnet.kg

Rector: Anvar Ismanjanov (2005-)

Vice-Rector: Aigul Navatova Tel: +996(3222) 2-34-73

International Relations: Muzaffar Kazakov, Director Department of International Relations and Investments EMail: kma_83@rambler.ru

Colleges

Medical (Midwifery; Nursing; Pharmacy) *Director*: Ravshan Jumaev; **Technological** (Automation and Control Engineering; Clothing and Sewing; Data Processing; Fashion Design)

Departments

Kyrgyz-Russian *(Branch of Kyrgyz-Russian Social University)* (Computer Science; Finance; History; Law; Management; Power Engineering) *Dean*: Rodimhan Toldieva

Faculties

Computer and Telecommunications Technologies (Automation and Control Engineering; Data Processing; Electrical and Electronic Engineering; Software Engineering; Telecommunications Engineering) *Dean*: Abdygany Satybaev; **Energy Engineering and Transport** (Civil Security; Electrical Engineering; Energy Engineering; Engineering Management; Environmental Engineering; Fire Science; Measurement and Precision Engineering; Natural Resources) *Dean*: Adylbek Kadyrkulov; **Finance and Economics** (Accountancy; Finance; Industrial and Production Economics; Industrial Management; Institutional Administration; International Economics; Taxation) *Dean*: Jasur Azimov; **Garment Design and Service Trades** (Fashion Design; Hotel and Restaurant; Tourism) *Dean*: Gulnara Maksytova; **History and Philology** (Foreign Languages Education; Humanities and Social Science Education; Journalism; Literature; Modern Languages; Native Language Education) *Dean*: Aida Baltabaeva; **Law and Customs** (Law; Taxation) *Dean*: Bakhtiyar Tolbaev; **Music and Pedagogy** (Educational Psychology; Music Education; Pedagogy; Preschool Education; Primary Education) *Dean*: Anvar Ismanjanov; **Natural Sciences and Geography** (Physical Education; Science Education) *Dean*: Bolot Murzurbaev; **Physics and Mathematics** (Computer Education; Mathematics Education; Science Education) *Dean*: Shhukhrat Tashkhodjaev; **World Languages and International Relations** (Foreign Languages Education; International Relations) *Dean*: Arstan Kulnazarov

Higher Schools

Vocational *(Kyrgyz-Uzbek)* (Clothing and Sewing; Cosmetology; Service Trades) *Director*: Karim Tillebaev

Institutes

Humanities and Economics *(Kyzylkia)* (Electrical Engineering; Finance; Humanities and Social Science Education; Industrial and Production Economics; Industrial Management; Law; Literature; Mathematics Education; Modern Languages; Physical Education; Preschool Education; Primary Education; Science Education) *Director*: Bakhtiyar Sulaimanov; **Humanities and Teacher Training** *(Alabuka)* (Finance; Foreign Languages Education; Humanities and Social Science Education; Literature; Mathematics Education; Native Language Education; Physical Education; Preschool Education; Primary Education; Science Education; Taxation) *Director*: Salima Rysbaeva

Schools

Postgraduate (Accountancy; Ecology; Economics; Educational Research; Energy Engineering; Finance; History; Linguistics; Literature; Management; Mathematics; Mechanical Engineering; Mining Engineering; Modern Languages; Native Language; Organic Chemistry; Philosophy; Statistics; Surveying and Mapping; Teacher Training)

History: Founded 1994. Acquired present status 1997.

Admission Requirements: Secondary school certificate (Attestat o Srednem Obrazovanii)

Fees: (Soms): Local students, 13,000-25,000 per annum; Foreign, 600-700 (US Dollars)

Main Language(s) of Instruction: Russian, Kyrgyz, Uzbek

International Co-operation: With universities in Greece, Italy, Germany, USA, Turkey and Saudi Ararbia. Also participates in Tempus Programme.

Accrediting Agencies: Ministry of Education, Science and Culture

Degrees and Diplomas: *Diplom Specialista*: 5-6 yrs; *Kandidat Nauk*: 3-4 yrs

Student Services: Canteen, Cultural centre, Foreign student adviser, Foreign Studies Centre, Health services, Language programs, Sports facilities

Student Residential Facilities: Yes

Special Facilities: "Granit" TV studio. Ethnographical and Historical Museum; Language and Cultural Centre (Arabic (Turkish,Korean); Slavic Centre; Scientific and Research Centres; Western Education Centre; Centre of State Language (Kyrgyz Language)

Libraries: Central Library; faculty libraries

Publications: Nauka, Obrazovanie, Tehnika, (Science, Education and Engineering) International scientific magazine *(quarterly)*; Planeta Drujby, (The Planet of Friendship) University newspaper *(biweekly)*

Press or Publishing House: Publishing Centre for Uzbek Schools

Last Updated: 19/08/08

NARYN STATE UNIVERSITY

Naryn Mamlekettik Universiteti (NSU)

ul. Sagynbay Orozbak Uulu 47, 722600 Naryn

Tel: +996(3522) 5-08-14

Fax: +996(3522) 5-08-14

EMail: nsu@ktnet.kg

Rector: Almaz Akmataliev (1999-)

Tel: +996(3522) 5-08-16 EMail: aakmataliev@ktnet.kg

Centres

American Studies (American Studies); **Arabic Language and Culture** (Arabic; Cultural Studies); **Korean Studies** (Korean); **Turkish Center** (Turkish)

Departments

Agriculture and Technology (Agriculture; Crop Production; Environmental Management; Environmental Studies; Natural Resources; Technology); **Linguistics** (English; Linguistics; Literature; Russian); **Natural Sciences and Humanities** (Arts and Humanities; Biology; Chemistry; Fine Arts; Music Education; Natural Sciences; Pedagogy; Physical Education; Primary Education); **New Information Technologies, Economy and Administration** (Computer Science; Economics; Information Technology; Mathematics; Political Sciences)

Divisions

Agricultural Technical School (Agriculture); **College of Pedagogy** (Pedagogy); **Training Center and Continuing Education**

History: Founded 1996.

Governing Bodies: Scholars Advisory Board

Admission Requirements: Attestat o Srednem Obrazovanii

Fees: (Soms): 7,500 per annum

Main Language(s) of Instruction: Kyrgyz, Russian

International Co-operation: With universities in USA and Europe

Accrediting Agencies: Ministry of Education, Science and Culture

Degrees and Diplomas: *Diplom Specialista*: 5 yrs

Student Services: Academic counselling, Canteen, Cultural centre, Employment services, Foreign student adviser, Foreign Studies Centre, Health services, Language programs, Social counselling, Sports facilities

Student Residential Facilities: Yes

Special Facilities: Internet Centre. Audio-Video Centre. Youth Centre. Youth Media Centre. Theatrical Club. Korean dancing troop. Driving School

Libraries: Central Library; Digital Library

Last Updated: 17/06/08

OSH STATE UNIVERSITY

Osskij Gosudarstvennyj Universiteti (OSHGU/OSU)

ul. Lenina 331, 723500 Oš

Tel: +996(3222) 2-22-73

Fax: +996(3222) 5-75-58

EMail: idosu@rambler.ru

Website: http://www.oshsu.kg/

Rector: Isakov Kanybek Abduvasitovich (2011-)

Fax: +996(3222) 2-40-66 EMail: Isakov_kanibek@mail.ru

Vice-Rector: Tajimamat Erkebaev

Tel: +996(3222) 2-04-38, Fax: +996(3222) 5-75-58

EMail: tajimamat-21@rambler.ru

International Relations: Taasilkan Zhumabaeva, Vice-Rector

Tel: +996(3222) 2-31-63 EMail: amanaiosh@rambler.ru

Colleges

Fiscal Studies and Law (Education; History; Law; Oriental Studies; Philosophy; Social Sciences) *Director*: Abdimalik Omaraliev; **Medical** (Anatomy; Health Sciences; Latin; Medicine) *Director*: Shamirbek Berkmamatov

Faculties

Business and Management (Business Administration; Business and Commerce; Economics; International Economics; Management; Mathematics; Social Studies) *Dean*: Avazbek Asanov; **Foreign Languages and International Studies** (American Studies; Chinese; English; French; German; History; International Law; International Relations; International Studies; Japanese; Korean; Persian; Regional Studies; Translation and Interpretation) *Dean*: Arap Anarbaev; **History and Law** (Business Administration; Education; History; Law; Oriental Studies; Philosophy; Public Administration; Social Sciences; Social Work) *Dean*: Cholpon Kuldysheva; **Kyrgyz Philology** (Arts and Humanities; Education; Foreign Languages Education; Information Sciences; Journalism; Literacy Education; Modern Languages; Native Language; Philology) *Dean*: Satkynbai Momunaliev; **Mathematics and Information Technology** (Applied Mathematics; Computer Science; Education; Information Sciences; Mathematics; Mathematics and Computer Science; Natural Sciences) *Dean*: Abdygany Abduvaliev; **Medicine** (Anatomy; Health Sciences; Latin; Medicine) *Dean*: Jolbors Jeenbaev; **Natural Sciences** (Agricultural Economics; Agriculture; Agronomy; Biology; Chemistry; Ecology; Education; Geography; Natural Sciences; Welfare and Protective Services; Zoology) *Dean*: Orunbek Kolanov; **Pedagogical Sciences and Art** (Design; English; Fine Arts; Industrial Arts Education; Industrial Design; Music; Painting and Drawing; Performing Arts) *Dean*: Tanavar Akmatova; **Pedagogy and Arts** (Arts and Humanities; Education; Pedagogy; Physical Education; Preschool Education; Primary Education; Psychology; Social Sciences) *Dean*: Tanavar Akmatova; **Physics and Technology** (Applied Physics; Computer Science; Education; English; History; Information Sciences; Mathematics; Physics) *Dean*: Islamidin Tashpolotov; **Russian Philology** (Arts and Humanities; Education; Foreign Languages Education; Literacy Education; Philology; Russian) *Dean*: Kapar Zulpukarov; **Theology** (Education; Religion; Theology) *Dean*: Asilbek Aliev

Institutes

Arashan *(Biškek)* (Education; Religion; Theology) *Director*: Rashat Shamilov

Further Information: Also Distance Education Centres and Regional Distance Education Centres

History: Founded 1951 as Oš State Pedagogical Institute, acquired present status and title 1992.

Governing Bodies: Academic Council

Academic Year: September to June (September-January; February-June)

Admission Requirements: Secondary school certificate (Atestat o srednem obrazovanii) or foreign equivalent

Fees: (Soms): Local students, 1,500-3,000 per annum; students of the CIS countries, 30,000-50,000; Foreign students, (US Dollars): 1,350 per annum

Main Language(s) of Instruction: Kyrgyz, Russian, English, German, French

International Co-operation: Participates in the DAAD, Logo, Ugrad, Actraccels and Muskie programmes (for students), and in the Carti, Reset and Tskuba programmes (for teachers)

Accrediting Agencies: Ministry of Education, Science and Culture

Degrees and Diplomas: *Diplom Specialista*: 5 yrs; *Magistr (MA; MBA)*: 2 yrs; *Kandidat Nauk*: All fields, a further 3 yrs by thesis; *Doktor Nauk*: All fields (PhD), a further 3 yrs by thesis

Student Services: Academic counselling, Canteen, Cultural centre, Foreign student adviser, Foreign Studies Centre, Health services, Language programs, Social counselling, Sports facilities

Student Residential Facilities: Yes

Special Facilities: Biological Garden. Museum. Movie Studio

Libraries: All Libraries, total, 767,000 vols

Publications: Trudy OshGu (OSU Works), Physics and Mathematics; Social; Philology and Pedagogy Series *(quarterly)*

Press or Publishing House: Publishing Centre, Bilim

Academic Staff *2011-2012*	MEN	WOMEN	TOTAL
FULL-TIME	593	802	**1,395**
STAFF WITH DOCTORATE			
FULL-TIME	33	7	**40**
Student Numbers *2011-2012*			
All (Foreign Included)	–	–	**25,000**
FOREIGN ONLY	–	–	**690**

Part-time students, 10,097. **Evening students**, 106.

Last Updated: 01/08/11

OSH TECHNOLOGICAL UNIVERSITY NAMED AFTER M.M. ADYSHEV

Adyshev atyndagy Osh Technologiya Universiteti (OSHTU)

ul. Isanova 81, 723503 Oš
Tel: +996(3222) 4-31-32
Fax: +996(3222) 5-29-07
EMail: oshtu2007@rambler.ru
Website: http:www.oshtu.kg

Rector: Abdykadyr Abidov

Vice-Rector: Kubanychbek Mansurov

International Relations: Bakytbek Shamshiev, Vice-Rector
EMail: Shamshiev@list.ru

Departments

Quality Technology (Technology) *Director*: Muratbek Adiev

Faculties

Civil Engineering (Civil Engineering; Engineering) *Dean*: Musa Shabdanov; **Cybernetics and Information Technology** (Automation and Control Engineering; Information Technology) *Dean*: Shairbek Saidamatov; **Economics** (Economics) *Dean*: Anipa Zulpuiva; **Energetics and New Energy Technology** (Electrical Engineering) *Dean*: Abdykapar Teshebaev; **Informatics** (Computer Science) *Dean*: Adilkan Sarimsakov; **International Relations** (International Relations) *Dean*: Murzabek Sagynaliev; **Technology and Nature Maintenance** (Ecology; Food Technology; Geology) *Dean*: Duishaan Jorokulov; **Training of Specialists** *Dean*: Ashim Zulpuiv

History: Founded 1993. Follows the Russian education standard system. Under supervision of the Ministry of Education and Science of Kyrgyzstan.

Governing Bodies: Rectorate, comprising the Rector and three Vice-Rectors

Academic Year: September to June

Admission Requirements: Secondary school certificate (Attestat o srednem obrazovanii) and entrance examination

Main Language(s) of Instruction: Russian, Kyrgyz

International Co-operation: Participates in Tempus-Tacis, Intas, Nato, Erasmus Mundus, IREX, PADOR and FFI programmes

Accrediting Agencies: Ministry of Education and Science

Degrees and Diplomas: *Bakalavr*: 4 yrs; *Diplom Specialista*: 5 yrs. Also Diploma, 3 yrs

Student Services: Academic counselling, Canteen, Employment services, Foreign student adviser, Foreign Studies Centre, Handicapped facilities, Health services, Language programs, Sports facilities

Student Residential Facilities: Yes (3 hostels for students; 2 hostels for teachers)

Special Facilities: Laboratories

Libraries: Central Library and faculty libraries

Press or Publishing House: yes

Last Updated: 11/07/11

RAZZAKOV KYRGYZ STATE TECHNICAL UNIVERSITY

Razzakov atyndagy Kyrgyz Mamlekettik Technikalyk Universiteti (KTU)

prosp. Mira 66, 720044 Biškek
Tel: +996(312) 54-51-25
Fax: +996(312) 54-51-62
EMail: rector@kstu.kg
Website: http://www.kstu.kg

Rector: Murataly Jamanbaev

Centres

Distance Education

Faculties

Information Technology (Automation and Control Engineering; Electronic Engineering; Software Engineering; Telecommunications Engineering); **Power Engineering** (Electrical Engineering; Engineering Management; Power Engineering; Safety Engineering; Thermal Engineering); **Technology** *(Kara-Balta)* (Food Technology; Textile Technology); **Transport and Machine Construction** (Automotive Engineering; Machine Building; Road Transport; Robotics; Transport Management)

Institutes

Business and Management (Accountancy; Banking; Business Computing; Industrial Management; Information Management; Journalism); **Mining Technology** (Mining Engineering)

Further Information: Also six-level intensive English programme at Higher College of English. Preliminary Training Centre and Lyceum

History: Founded 1954 as Frunse Polytechnical Institute. Acquired present status and title 1999.

Governing Bodies: Academic Council

Academic Year: September to July

Admission Requirements: Secondary school certificate and entrance examination

Main Language(s) of Instruction: Kyrgyz, Russian, English

Accrediting Agencies: Ministry of Education, Science and Culture

Degrees and Diplomas: *Bakalavr*: 4 yrs; *Diplom Specialista*: 5 yrs; *Magistr*: a further 2 yrs; *Doktor Nauk (PhD)*: 3-4 yrs

Student Services: Canteen, Cultural centre, Health services, Language programs, Sports facilities

Student Residential Facilities: No

Special Facilities: Museum

Publications: Polytechnic, Educational, political, cultural life of students *(monthly)*

Last Updated: 26/09/11

TALAS STATE UNIVERSITY

Talas Mamlekettit Universiteti (TSU)

ul. Karla Marksa 25, 722720 Talas
Tel: +996(3422) 52015 +996(3422) 53649
Fax: +996(3422) 52580
EMail: tsu@hotmail.kg

Rector: Torobek Omurbekov (2000-) EMail: tsu@ktnet.kg

International Relations: Aigul Nuralieva

Faculties

Ecology and Agronomy (Agronomy; Ecology); **Economics and Law** (Accountancy; Economics; Finance; Law; Public Administration; Social Work; Taxation); **Education** (Biology; Education; History; Information Technology; Mathematics; Secondary Education); **Modern Languages** (Arabic; English; French; German; Literature; Native Language; Russian); **Technology** (Design; Electrical Engineering; Radio and Television Broadcasting; Technology)

History: Founded 1996, acquired present status 2000.

Governing Bodies: Academic Council

Academic Year: September to June

Admission Requirements: Secondary school certificate (Attestat o srednem obrazovanii)

Fees: (US Dollars): 120-130 per annum. Foreign students, 250-300

Main Language(s) of Instruction: Kyrgyz, Russian, English

International Co-operation: Participates in IREX, ACCELS and DAAD programmes

Accrediting Agencies: Ministry of Education, Science and Culture

Degrees and Diplomas: *Diplom Specialista*: Mathematics; Biology; Ecology; Pedagogy; Modern Languages; History; Public Administration; Information Technology; Accountancy in Agriculture; Design; Economics; Electrical Engineering; Radio and Television Broadcasting; Taxation; Law; Social Work, 5 yrs

Student Services: Academic counselling, Canteen, Cultural centre, Foreign student adviser, Foreign Studies Centre, Handicapped facilities, Language programs, Nursery care, Social counselling, Sports facilities

Student Residential Facilities: Yes

Libraries: Central Library, 101,000 vols

Publications: Manas Urpagy

TYNYSTANOV ISSYK-KUL STATE UNIVERSITY

Tynystanov atyndagy Issyk-Kul Mamlekettik Universiteti

ul. Abdrahmanova 103, 722360 Karakol, Issyk-Kul
Tel: +996(3922) 5-01-23
Fax: +996(3922) 5-04-98
EMail: igu@issyk-kul.kg

Rector: Mustafa Musaevich Kidibaev

Centres

Distance Training (Education)

Faculties

Art and Modelling (Design; Fine Arts; Painting and Drawing; Textile Design); **Chemistry and Biology** (Biology; Chemistry); **Foreign Languages** (Chinese; English; French; German; Modern Languages; Philology); **Mathematics and Computer Science** (Accountancy; Applied Mathematics; Automation and Control Engineering; Management; Mathematics and Computer Science); **Medicine and Technology** (Medicine; Technology); **Natural Resources and Geography** (Geography; Geography (Human); Natural Resources); **Pedagogy and Physical Education** (Education; Pedagogy; Physical Education; Preschool Education; Psychology); **Philology** (Literature; Native Language; Philology; Russian); **Physics and Technology** (Applied Physics; Engineering; Materials Engineering; Mathematics; Optics; Physical Engineering; Physics; Technology)

Institutes

Economics, Management and Law (Accountancy; Economics; Engineering; Finance; Law; Management; Marketing; Mathematics; Physics; Public Administration); **Foreign Languages** (Modern Languages); **Tourism and Ecology** (Ecology; Forestry; Social Sciences; Tourism)

Further Information: Also Branch in Cholpon-Ata

History: Founded 1940 as Teachers' Institute, reorganized 1953 as Prjevalsk Pedagogical Institute. Attached to Kyrgyz State University 1988. Became independent institution 1992 and acquired present status and title, named after Kasym Tynystanov, the creator of the Kyrgyz Philosophy of the Kyrgyz Republic.

Governing Bodies: Academic Council

Admission Requirements: Secondary school certificate (Atestat o srednem obrazovanii)

Fees: (US Dollars): 130; Foreign students, 600

Main Language(s) of Instruction: Russian

International Co-operation: Participates in Irex, Accels, Daad, Soros, Iaeste and Tempus programmes

Accrediting Agencies: Ministry of Education, Science and Culture

Degrees and Diplomas: *Diplom Specialista*: 5 yrs; *Kandidat Nauk*; *Doktor Nauk*

Student Services: Cultural centre, Foreign student adviser, Social counselling

Special Facilities: Museum of Kyrgyz language; Art Gallery; Movie Studio

Libraries: c. 465,800 vols, 126 periodical subscriptions

PRIVATE INSTITUTIONS

AMERICAN UNIVERSITY IN CENTRAL ASIA

Borbordyk Aziyadagy Ameriki Universiteti (AUCA)

205 Abdumomunov Street, 720040 Biškek
Tel: +996(312) 66-33-09
Fax: +996(312) 66-32-01
EMail: niyazov_r@mail.auca.kg
Website: http://www.auca.kg

President: Andrew Wachtel
Tel: +996 (312) 66-33-09, Fax: +996 (312) 66-32-01
EMail: kasimova_s@mail.auca.kg

Programmes

American Studies (American Studies); **Anthropology** (American Studies; Anthropology; Archaeology; Asian Studies; Cultural Studies; East Asian Studies; Environmental Studies; History; Middle Eastern Studies; Modern Languages; Pacific Area Studies; Religion); **Business Administration** (Accountancy; Advertising and Publicity; Banking; Business Administration; Business and Commerce; Economics; Finance; Human Resources; Information Technology; Insurance; International Business; Leadership; Management; Marketing; Public Administration; Real Estate; Taxation); **Economics** (Economic and Finance Policy; Economics; Finance; Geography (Human); International Economics; Management; Statistics); **European Studies** (Economics; European Studies; European Union Law; French; Geography (Human); German; Government; History; Literature; Western European Studies); **International and Business Law** (Civil Law; Commercial Law; Constitutional Law; Criminal Law; Ethics; International Law; Labour Law; Private Law; Public Law); **International and Comparative Politics** (Comparative Politics; International Relations; Political Sciences); **Journalism and Mass Communications** (Advertising and Publicity; Cinema and Television; Journalism; Mass Communication; Media Studies; Public Relations; Radio and Television Broadcasting; Writing); **Languages** (English; Modern Languages; Native Language; Russian); **Psychology** (Anatomy; Industrial and Organizational Psychology; Pedagogy; Physiology; Psychoanalysis; Psychology; Social Psychology); **Sociology** (Applied Mathematics; Comparative Sociology; Gender Studies; Philosophy; Social Sciences; Sociology; Statistics); **Software Engineering** (Computer Graphics; Computer Networks; Mathematics and Computer Science; Software Engineering)

History: Founded 1997. In 1993, the Kyrgyz National State University Rector signed an order establishing the Kyrgyz-American Faculty (KAF) which was officially inaugurated and opened in December 1993. Acquired present name 1997.

Governing Bodies: Board of Trustees

Admission Requirements: Secondary school leaving certificate

Main Language(s) of Instruction: Russian and English

International Co-operation: Higher Education Support Programme of the Open Society Institute; Soros Foundation (Eastern Europe and CIS)

Accrediting Agencies: Ministry of Education and Science

Degrees and Diplomas: *Bakalavr (BA)*: 4 yrs; *Magistr*: Business Administration; Central Asian Studies; Environmental Sustainability; Economic Development, 2 yrs. Some dual degrees offerd with Bard College, NY, USA,

Student Services: Academic counselling, Canteen, Cultural centre, Employment services, Foreign student adviser, Health services, Language programs, Sports facilities

Special Facilities: Movie studio

Libraries: c. 59,000 vols.

Publications: Business Seminar Bulletin *(3 per annum)*

Academic Staff *2010*: Total: c. 130

Student Numbers *2010*: Total: c. 1,200

Last Updated: 12/04/11

INTERNATIONAL ATATÜRK ALATOO UNIVERSITY

El Aralyk Ataturk Alatoo Universiteti (ALATOO)
Gorky street, Tunguch, 720048 Biškek
Tel: +996(312) 63-14-23 +996(312) 63-14-25
Fax: +996(312) 63-04-09
EMail: info@iaau.edu.kg
Website: http://www.iaau.edu.kg

Rector: Ibrahim Hasgur (2001-)
EMail: ibrahimhasgur@iaau.edu.kg

Faculties

Economics and Administration (Administration; Banking; Economics; Finance; International Economics; International Relations; Management); **New Technologies** (Computer Engineering; Electrical and Electronic Engineering; Industrial Engineering; Mathematics and Computer Science); **Social Sciences** (Chinese; English; Native Language; Social Sciences; Translation and Interpretation; Turkish)

Programmes

Graduate Studies (Computer Engineering; Economics; International Relations; Management; Turkish)

History: Founded 1996 under agreement between Governments of Turkey and Kyrgyzstan. A private institution under the Ministry of Education of the Kyrgyz Republic

Governing Bodies: Rectorate

Academic Year: September to June

Admission Requirements: Identity Card; High School or Secondary school (11 yrs) certificate and fluency in English; Health Report

Main Language(s) of Instruction: English, Russian, Turkish; Kyrgyz

Accrediting Agencies: Ministry of Education, Science and Culture; International University Accrediting Association and Virtual University Accrediting Association; The South East Europe Education Cooperation Network, Education Network

Degrees and Diplomas: *Bakalavr*, *Diplom Specialista*; *Magistr*, *Doktor Nauk*. Also Certificates of English, Turkish and Computer Science

Student Services: Academic counselling, Canteen, Employment services, Foreign student adviser, Health services, Social counselling, Sports facilities

Student Residential Facilities: Yes

Publications: Alatoo Academic Studies, Academic journal (in English, Turkish, Russian, Kyrgyz) *(biannually)*

Last Updated: 27/09/11

Lao People's Democratic Republic

STRUCTURE OF HIGHER EDUCATION SYSTEM

Description:

Higher education is provided by universities, higher technical institutes and teacher training colleges. Higher education institutions are managed by the government. The universities are under the responsibility of the Ministry of Education.

Stages of studies:

University level first stage: *Bachelor's degree*

Universities offer a five to seven-year course leading to a Bachelor's degree. Students must spend one year at the School of Foundation Studies followed by specialized studies of four to six years. In Engineering, Teacher Training, Building and Construction and Agriculture, courses at university last for three to four years. In Dentistry, Medicine and Pharmacy, courses last for five to six years. Practical training is an important element. Each student must undergo a period of eight to ten weeks of practical training in an approved establishment, depending on the course of study. A practical training period is only considered as successfully completed after submission of a practical report, a log book and a training Certificate issued by the company or employer. Students who perform satisfactorily in the final examination obtain the Bachelor's degree of the university. An Honours Degree is conferred to students who have not less than an A grade in the final year project; not less than a B grade in each of the examinable subjects in the third and fourth years of study. The university also offers a three- to four-year course leading to a higher technical level.

University level second stage: *Master's degree*

Universities offer a 2- to 4-year course leading to a Master's degree. At present, it is only available in Medical Sciences; Economics; Forestry; Engineering; Education; Administration.

Distance higher education:

Bilateral cooperation: Lao-France; Lao-Belgium.

ADMISSION TO HIGHER EDUCATION

Admission to university-level studies:

Name of secondary school credential required: Upper Secondary School Diploma

Minimum score/requirement: 5/10 for each subject

For entry to: University

Alternatives to credentials: Special examination at national level for non-quota selection.

Entrance exam requirements: For access to some institutions, there is a national Entrance examination.

Other admission requirements: In addition, minimum requirements for admission to degree courses are at least five pass grades in Mathematics and Physics or Chemistry; Lao Litterature; Geography or History.

Foreign students admission:

Definition of foreign student: Students who do not have Lao nationality.

Quotas: There are quotas at the national level.

Entrance exam requirements: Students must hold a High School Certificate or equivalent.

Entry regulations: Entry is subject to bilateral agreements

Health requirements: Medical certificate.

Language requirements: French, English and Laotian

RECOGNITION OF STUDIES

Quality assurance system:

All programmes offered in universities are officially recognized and accredited by the Ministry of Education. Credit transfers are subject to direct agreement between institutes.

Special provisions for recognition:

Recognition for university level studies: University level studies are recognised by the Ministry of Education.

For exercising a profession: Under MOU between institutions and the industrial sector.

NATIONAL BODIES

Kaxouangsuksathikan (Ministry of Education and Sports)

Minister: Phankham Viphavanh
PO Box 67
Lanexang Vientiane Avenue
Vientiane
Tel: +856(21) 216 013 +856(21) 216 014
Fax: +856(21) 216 006
EMail: esitc@moe.gov.la
WWW: http://www.moe.gov.la/

Data for academic year: 2008-2009
Source: IAU from Lao National Commission for UNESCO, 2008 (Bodies, 2012).

INSTITUTIONS

PUBLIC INSTITUTIONS

CHAMPASACK UNIVERSITY

Champasack

Director-General: Sikhamtath Mitaray

Faculties

Agriculture (Agriculture); **Economics and Business Administration** (Business Administration; Economics); **Education** (Education)

History: Founded 2002.

NATIONAL UNIVERSITY OF LAOS

Mahavithagnalay Heang Xath Lao
PO Box 7322, Vientiane
Tel: +856(21) 770-720
Fax: +856(21) 770-069
EMail: somkotm@yahoo.com
Website: http://www.nuol.edu.la/

Rector: Soukkongseng Saignaleuth Tel: +856(21) 770-381

Centres

Teacher Development *(Dongdok Campus) Director*: Bountheung Chanmany

Faculties

Agriculture *(Nabong Campus)* (Agriculture; Agronomy; Animal Husbandry) *Dean*: Thongphanh Kousonsavath; **Architecture** (Architecture); **Economics and Business Administration** *(Dongdok Campus)* (Business Administration; Economics; Management) *Dean*: Khamlusa Nouansavanh; **Education** *(Dongdok Campus)* (Curriculum; Education; Pedagogy; Psychology) *Dean*: Kham Ane Sayasone; **Engineering** *(Sokpaluang Campus)* (Civil Engineering; Communication Studies; Electrical Engineering; Electronic Engineering; Engineering; Irrigation; Mechanical Engineering); **Forestry**; **Law and Political Science** *(Donenokkhoum Campus)* (Law; Political Sciences; Public Administration) *Dean*: Boun Oum Paphatsalang; **Letters** (Arts and Humanities); **Medical Science** *(Phiavat Campus)* (Dentistry; Health Sciences; Medicine; Pharmacy) *Dean*: Bounsay Thorvisouk; **Sciences** *(Dongkok Campus)* (Biology; Chemistry; Mathematics; Natural Sciences; Physics; Science Education) *Dean*: Bouakhaykhone Svengsuksa; **Social Sciences** *(Dongdok Campus)* (English; Foreign Languages Education; French; Geography; German; History; Literature; Political Sciences) *Dean*: Souphab Khouangvichith

Schools

Foundation Studies *(Dongkok Campus)* (Natural Sciences; Social Sciences) *Director*: Inpeng Khieovongphachanh

History: Founded 1995, incorporating ten existing Institutions and a Centre of Agriculture. Has six campuses: Dongdok Main Campus, Sokpaluang Campus, Phiavat Campus, Donenokkhoum Campus, Tatthong Campus, and Kilometre Five Campus.

Governing Bodies: University Council

Academic Year: September to June (September-January; February-June)

Admission Requirements: Upper secondary school Certificate or equivalent and entrance examination (for non-quota system)

Fees: (Kip): Tuition, 50,000-100,000 per annum; 320,000 for special courses

Main Language(s) of Instruction: Lao

Degrees and Diplomas: *Higher Diploma*; *Bachelor's Degree*: 5-7 yrs; *Master's Degree*

Student Services: Academic counselling, Canteen, Employment services, Foreign student adviser, Health services, Language programs, Nursery care, Sports facilities

Student Residential Facilities: Yes

Libraries: c. 120,000 vols

Publications: Mahavithagnalay Heang Xath Lao, Activities in the National University of Laos *(quarterly)*

Last Updated: 02/01/09

SOUPHANOUVONG UNIVERSITY

Mahavithayalay Souphanouvong

Ban Nasangveuy, Luang Prabang City

Tel: +856 (71) 212 127

Fax: +856 (71) 212 127

EMail: ssvanh@yahoo.com

Rector: Khamphay Sisavanh (2003-)

Vice-Rector for Academic Affairs: Vixay Chansavang EMail: cvixay@hotmail.com

International Relations: Som-Ock Phanthavong, Vice-Rector for Administration EMail: ptvong603@yahoo.com

Faculties

Agriculture (Agronomy; Animal Husbandry) *Dean*: Louis Vannamahaxay; **Architecture** (Architecture); **Economics and Business Administration** *Dean*: Soudthida Houngsengfa; **Education** (Education) *Dean*: Thongthiene Vatthanavong

History: Founded 2003.

Academic Year: October to July

Admission Requirements: Pakasaniyabath Chob Matthayom Somboun (Certificate of Completion of Complete Secondary Education)

Fees: (Kip): No fee for regular courses; special and evening courses, 700.00.

Main Language(s) of Instruction: Lao

Accrediting Agencies: Ministry of Education

Degrees and Diplomas: *Bachelor's Degree (Prin-Ya-Tree)*: 5 yrs

Student Residential Facilities: for c. 900 students

Libraries: c. 3,500 vols

Last Updated: 02/01/09

PRIVATE INSTITUTIONS

COMBIZ COLLEGE

Vithagnalay Combiz

Paksanh District, Bolykhamxay

Tel: +856(54) 212-895 +856(20) 233-7314

Website: http://www.mahasan.com/sponser/combiz/index.asp

Courses

Agriculture (Agriculture); **Business and Administration** (Administration; Business and Commerce); **Engineering**

Degrees and Diplomas: *Bachelor's Degree*

COMCENTER COLLEGE

Vithagnalay Comcenter

PO Box 2224, Khouvieng Road, Sisattanak District, Vientiane

Tel: +856(21) 216-532

Fax: +856(21) 222-433

EMail: comcenteruniversity@yahoo.com

Website: http://comcenterlao.com/index.php

Director: Xaiyonne Khammavong (1993-)

Centres

Computer Training Studies (Computer Science)

Colleges

Business (Business and Commerce)

History: Founded 1993.

Degrees and Diplomas: *Bachelor's Degree*

Last Updated: 29/08/08

LAO-AMERICA COLLEGE

Vithagnalay Lao-America

PO Box 327, Phonekheng Road, Vientiane

Tel: +856(21) 900-454

Fax: +856(21) 900-453

EMail: lac@etllao.com

Website: http://www.lac.edu.la/

Director: Thongsone Phoutsavat

Courses

Business Administration (Business Administration); **English Studies** (English; English Studies); **Hospitality** (Hotel Management; Tourism); **Information Technology** (Information Technology)

Degrees and Diplomas: *Higher Diploma*; *Bachelor's Degree*

Last Updated: 29/08/08

RATTANA BUSINESS ADMINISTRATION COLLEGE

Vithagnalay Rattana Borihane Thourakit

Saphanthong District, PO Box 977, Vientiane

Tel: +856(21) 413-871

Fax: +856(21) 413-280

EMail: rbac@laoskytelecom

Website: http://www.rbaclao.com

Director: Somphet Lattanasim

Programmes

Business Administration (Business Administration)

Degrees and Diplomas: *Bachelor's Degree*; *Master's Degree*

Last Updated: 29/08/08

SENGSAVANH COLLEGE

Vithagnalay Sengsavanh

124 Dongmieng Rd, Sisavath Village, Chanthabuli District, Vientiane

Tel: +856(21) 223-822

Fax: +856(21) 223-822

EMail: info@sengsavanh.net

Website: http://www.sengsavanh.net

Director: Khamsene Sisavong
Tel: +856-20 551-9127 EMail: ksisavong@hotmail.com

Colleges

Business Administration (Accountancy; Business Administration)

Degrees and Diplomas: *Bachelor's Degree*

Last Updated: 29/08/08

SOUTSAKA COLLEGE OF MANAGEMENT AND TECHNOLOGY

Sathabanh Soutsaka

Phosa arth Road, PO Box 390, Xaysetha District, Vientiane

Tel: +856(21) 900-337

EMail: info@simt.edu.la

Website: http://www.simt.edu.la

Director: Sousaka Boumanith

Programmes

Management (Management); **Technology** (Technology)

Degrees and Diplomas: *Higher Diploma*; *Bachelor's Degree*

Last Updated: 02/01/09

Latvia

STRUCTURE OF HIGHER EDUCATION SYSTEM

Description:

All state recognized higher education institutions in Latvia enjoy autonomy. Recognition of higher education institutions and programmes is based upon quality assessment, which is carried out as self-assessment followed by an evaluation visit with the participation of foreign experts. Higher education institutions confer academic degrees and professional higher education qualifications. Academic higher education programmes are based upon fundamental and/or applied science; they usually comprise a thesis at the end of each stage and lead to the degrees of Bakalaurs (Bachelor) and Maistrs (Master). The Bachelor degree is awarded after completion of the first stage of studies. Since 2001, professional Bakalaurs and Maistrs can also be awarded. The degree of Maistrs (or its equivalent) is required for admission to doctoral studies. According to the Law on Professional Education and the Law on Higher Education Establishments there are several types of higher professional education programmes in Latvia - first-level professional higher education programmes (also called college programmes) and second level professional higher education programmes which are considered as "completed" professional higher education and lead to the second-level professional higher education.

Stages of studies:

University level first stage: *Undergraduate*

The first cycle leads to the award of a Bakalaurs (Bachelor' degree), which in most cases includes the preparation of a thesis. The duration of studies varies from three to four years. Holders are eligible for further studies towards a Magistrs degree or higher professional education qualifications.

University level second stage: *Postgraduate*

The second cycle leads to the award of the Magistrs (Master's degree), a terminal higher education qualification awarded one to two years after the Bakalaurs. This degree also includes the presentation of a thesis. The total duration of the course of study is no less than five years. In Medicine and Dentistry, studies are not divided into two stages but the degrees Ārsta grāds (degree in Medicine) - six years - and Zobārsta grāds (degree in Dentistry) - five years - are considered equivalent to the Maistrs.

University level third stage: *Doctorate*

Doctoral studies are available at both higher education institutions and research institutes. A Doctor's degree is awarded three to four years after completion of the Master and following the public defense of a thesis.

ADMISSION TO HIGHER EDUCATION

Admission to university-level studies:

Name of secondary school credential required: Atestāts par visparējo vidējo izglītību

Name of secondary school credential required: Diploms par profesionālo vidējo izglītību

Numerus clausus/restrictions: At the level of the institution

Other admission requirements: Access is regulated by examinations, by ranking of secondary diplomas or by interview, or a combination of these. Institutions can define which of the elective secondary education courses have to be taken by the applicant to enter a particular programme.

Foreign students admission:

Definition of foreign student: A student who is resident of another country and pursues studies in Latvia.

Quotas: No

Entrance exam requirements: Foreign students must present a school-leaving certificate (original) with a transcript which can be recognized as being equivalent to the Latvian secondary education certificate.

Entry regulations: Students must hold a residence permit. Latvian diplomatic missions abroad provide all the necessary information to the applicants, make an initial recommendation and issue entry visas to candidates who have been accepted.

Health requirements: A health certificate is required.

Language requirements: Students must prove proficiency in Latvian for programmes offered in Latvian.

RECOGNITION OF STUDIES

Quality assurance system:

Accreditation of higher education institutions takes place according to the Law on Higher Education Establishments (LHE), adopted by Saeima on November 2, 1995; article 9 of which stipulates the general accreditation principles of higher education institutions (HEI). Only those higher education institutions that have been accredited and which offer state accredited study programmes have the right to issue higher education certificates recognised by the State to its graduates. The accreditation proceeds in accordance with the regulations on accreditation approved by the Cabinet of Ministers. Study programmes are accredited no less than once in six years. Credentials are awarded upon completion of studies in accredited programmes.

Bodies dealing with recognition:

Akadēmiskās informācijas centrs (Latvijas ENIC/NARIC) (Academic Information Centre (Latvian ENIC/ NARIC))

Director: Baiba Ramina
Valnu iela 2
Riga 1050
Tel: +371 6722 5155
Fax: +371 6722 1006
WWW: http://www.aic.lv/portal/en/

Special provisions for recognition:

Recognition for university level studies: ENIC/NARIC evaluates a credential and issues a statement which serves as a recommendation for universities and other higher education institutions which take the final decision upon recognition for further studies.

For access to advanced studies and research: ENIC/NARIC evaluates a credential and issues a statement which serves as a recommendation for universities and other higher education institutions which take the final decision upon recognition for further studies.

For exercising a profession: ENIC/NARIC evaluates a credential and issues a statement which serves as a recommendation for employers (in non-regulated professions) or competent professional bodies (in regulated professions) which take the final decision upon recognition for professional purposes.

NATIONAL BODIES

Izglītības un zinātnes ministrija (Ministry of Education and Science)

Minister: Roberts Ķīlis
Director, Higher Education: Gita Rēvalde
Valnu iela 2
Riga 1050
Tel: +371 6722 6209
Fax: +371 6722 3905
EMail: info@izm.gov.lv;pasts@izm.gov.lv
WWW: http://www.izm.gov.lv
Role of national body: Responsible for long-term planning of higher education, as well as for assessment, organization and administration and funds allocation

Augstākās Izglītības Padome (Council of Higher Education)

Chairman: Janis Vētra
Zigfrida Annas Meierovica bulv. 12

Riga 1050
Tel: +371(6) 722 3392
Fax: +371(6) 722 0423
EMail: aip@latnet.lv
WWW: http://www.aip.lv

Latvijas Rektoru Padome (Latvian Rectors' Council)
President: Arvīds Barševskis
Secretary-General: Andrejs Rauhvargers
Raina Bulv. 19
Riga 1586
Tel: +371 6703 4338
Fax: +371 66703 4368
EMail: rp@lanet.lv
WWW: http://www.aic.lv/rp

Augstakas izglītibas kvalitates novērtēšanas centrs (Higher Education Quality Evaluation Centre)
Valnu street 2
Riga 1050
Tel: +371 6721 3870
Fax: +371 6721 2558
EMail: aiknc@aiknc.lv
WWW: http://www.aiknc.lv

Valsts izglītibas attistības aentura- VIAA (State Education Development Agency)
Director: Dita Traidās
Vaļņu Street 1
Riga 1050
Tel: +371 6781 4322
Fax: +371 6781 4344
EMail: info@viaa.gov.lv
WWW: http://www.viaa.gov.lv
Role of national body: The task of the APA is to ensure the administrative, informative and financial support to the involvement of Latvian institutions in the EU-financed cooperation and assistance programmes and initiatives in education.

Data for academic year: 2011-2012
Source: IAU from the Latvian ENIC/NARIC, 2011. Bodies 2012.

INSTITUTIONS

PUBLIC INSTITUTIONS

ART ACADEMY OF LATVIA

Latvijas Mākslas Akadēmija (LMA)
Kalpaka bulvāris 13, LV-1867 Rīga
Tel: +371(67) 332-202
Fax: +371(67) 228-963
EMail: lma@latnet.lv
Website: http://www.lma.lv

Rector: Aleksejs Naumovs
Tel: +371(67) 326-068 EMail: aleksejs.naumovs@lma.lv

Pro-rector for Administrative Affairs: Kristaps Zariņš
Tel: +371(67) 332-202 EMail: kristaps.zarins@lma.lv

International Relations: Elina Gibiete, Head of the Department of International Relations and Exhibitions
Tel: +371(67) 332-202 EMail: elina.gibiete@lma.lv

Faculties
Audio-visual Media (Communication Arts; Display and Stage Design); **Design** (Architectural and Environmental Design; Design); **History and Theory of Art** (Art History; Arts and Humanities; Restoration of Works of Art); **Visual Arts (2D)** (Graphic Design; Painting and Drawing; Textile Design; Visual Arts); **Visual Plastic Arts (3D)** (Ceramic Art; Fashion Design; Glass Art; Sculpture; Visual Arts)

History: Founded 1921.

Governing Bodies: Senate, comprising no less than 75% of academic staff and no less than 10% of student body

Academic Year: October to May (October-January; February-May)

Admission Requirements: Secondary school certificate

Main Language(s) of Instruction: Latvian. Practical courses in Russian, English

Degrees and Diplomas: *Bakalaura diploms*; *Maistra diploms*; *Doktora diploms*

Libraries: c. 32,000 vols

Student Numbers *2010-2011*: Total: c. 600
Last Updated: 02/11/11

BA SCHOOL OF BUSINESS AND FINANCE

Banku Augstskola (BA)
K.Valdemāra 161, LV-1013 Rīga
Tel: +371(67) 360-133
Fax: +371(67) 320-620
EMail: info@ba.lv
Website: http://www.ba.lv

Rector: Andris Sarnovičs Tel: +371(67) 509-253

Assistant of Rector for Quality and Administration: Santa Bērziņa Tel: +371(67) 509-253

International Relations: Sandra Kraze
Tel: +371(67) 709-283 EMail: Sandra.kraze@lba.lv

Departments

Entrepreneurship and IT (Business Administration; Information Technology; Insurance; International Business; Management); **Finance** (Accountancy; Banking; Finance); **Foreign Languages** (English; German; Grammar; Modern Languages); **Information Sciences** (Information Sciences); **International Studies** (International Studies)

History: Founded 1992, acquired present title 1997.

Governing Bodies: Senate

Academic Year: September to June

Admission Requirements: Secondary school certificate

Fees: (Lats): 685 per annum

Main Language(s) of Instruction: Latvian, English

International Co-operation: With universities in Austria, Belgium, Czech Republic, Denmark, Finland, France, Germany, Hungary, Lithuania, the Netherlands, Norway, Poland, Portugal, Spain, Sweden and UK. Participates in the LLP-Erasmus programme.

Degrees and Diplomas: *Diploms par pirmā līmena augstāko profesionālo izglītību*; *Bakalaura diploms*; *Maistra diploms*; *Doktora diploms*

Student Services: Canteen, Employment services, Sports facilities

Student Residential Facilities: Yes

Libraries: Yes

Last Updated: 27/10/11

DAUGAVPILS UNIVERSITY

Daugavpils Universitāte (DU)
Vienības iela 13, LV-5400 Daugavpils
Tel: +371(654) 221-80 +371(654) 229-22
Fax: +371(654) 228-90
EMail: du@du.lv
Website: http://www.du.lv

Rector: Arvīds Barševkis
EMail: rektors@du.lv; arvids.barsevskis@du.lv

Direktor: Eduards Rapša
Tel: +371(54) 266-77 EMail: direktors@du.lv; eduards.rapsa@du.lv

International Relations: Inese Gaidule, ERASMUS Institutional Coordinator
Tel: +371(654) 216-06, Fax: +371(654) 216-06
EMail: ssad@du.lv; inese.gaidule@du.lv

Centres

Innovative Microscopy *(G. Liberts')* (Physics); **Oral History** (History; Regional Studies)

Faculties

Education and Management (Education; Educational Psychology; Management; Pedagogy; Physical Education; Preschool Education; Primary Education; Social Work; Vocational Counselling; Vocational Education); **Humanities** (Arts and Humanities; Baltic Languages; Cultural Studies; English; Foreign Languages Education; French; German; History; Humanities and Social Science Education; Linguistics; Literature; Philology; Polish; Russian; Secondary Education; Slavic Languages; Social Sciences; Spanish; Swedish; Translation and Interpretation); **Music and Arts** (Art Education; Art History; Art Management; Computer Graphics; Conducting; Design; Fine Arts; Graphic Arts; Music; Music Education; Musical Instruments; Secondary Education; Visual Arts); **Natural Sciences and Mathematics** (Anatomy; Chemistry; Computer Education; Computer Science; Environmental Studies; Geography; Information Technology; Mathematics; Mathematics Education; Natural Sciences; Physical Therapy; Physics; Physiology; Science Education; Secondary Education; Solid State Physics; Teacher Training); **Social Sciences** (Economics; Law; Psychology; Social Psychology; Social Sciences; Sociology)

Institutes

Comparative Studies (Arts and Humanities; Cultural Studies); **Ecology** (Ecology; Environmental Studies; Forest Biology); **Latgale Region Research** (Regional Studies); **Social Investigation** (Social Studies); **Sustainable Education** (Education); **Systematic Biology** (Biology)

Further Information: Also Centre for teaching Russian as a foreign language

History: Founded 1921 as Teachers' Institute, acquired present status and title of a second classical university in Latvia 2001. A public institution.

Governing Bodies: University Council

Academic Year: September to June (September-January; February-June)

Admission Requirements: Secondary school certificate, test in Latvian language, examination in a foreign language for students of foreign languages

Fees: None

Main Language(s) of Instruction: Latvian

International Co-operation: With institutions in Spain; Sweden; Germany; United Kingdom; Denmark

Degrees and Diplomas: *Diploms par pirmā līmena augstāko profesionālo izglītību*; *Bakalaura diploms*; *Maistra diploms*; *Doktora diploms*. Also 2nd level professional higher education programmes; Professional Master's degree.

Student Services: Canteen, Cultural centre, Foreign student adviser, Health services, Sports facilities

Student Residential Facilities: Yes

Special Facilities: Museum. Multimedia Centre. Summer Training Centre 'Ilgas'. Agrobiology Station

Libraries: Scientific Library, c. 400,000 vols; specialized libraries

Student Numbers *2009-2010*: Total: c. 4,200
Last Updated: 27/10/11

JĀZEPS VĪTOLS LATVIAN ACADEMY OF MUSIC

Jāzepa Vītola Latvijas Mūzikas akadēmija (JVLMA)
Kr. Barona iela 1, LV-1050 Rīga
Tel: +371(67) 228-684
Fax: +371(67) 820-271
EMail: academy@jvlma.lv
Website: http://www.jvlma.lv

Rector: Artis Sīmanis

Vice-Rector for Administrative Work: Armands Lapiņš
Tel: +371(67) 221-834 EMail: armands.lapins@jvlma.lv

International Relations: Maija Sīpola, Vice-rector for International Relations
Tel: +371(67) 223-522, Fax: +371(67) 820-271
EMail: maija.sipola@jvlma.lv

Departments

Accompanists (Music; Musical Instruments); **Chamber Ensemble and Piano Accompaniment** (Music; Musical Instruments); **Choir Conducting** (Conducting); **Choreography** (Dance); **Composition** (Music Theory and Composition); **Compulsory Piano** (Musical Instruments); **Early Music** (Music); **Humanities** (Arts and Humanities; English; Modern Languages); **Jazz Music** (Jazz and Popular

Music); **Music Education** (Music Education); **Music Technology** (Music; Technology); **Musicology** (Musicology); **Orchestra Conducting** (Conducting); **Piano** (Musical Instruments); **Science and Research** (Musicology); **Strings** (Musical Instruments); **Vocal Music** (Singing); **Wind, Brass and Percussions** (Musical Instruments)

History: Founded 1919 as Conservatoire, acquired present status and title 1991.

Governing Bodies: Senate

Main Language(s) of Instruction: Latvian

International Co-operation: With 86 partner institutions in almost all European countries. Participates in the Erasmus programme.

Degrees and Diplomas: *Bakalaura diploms*; *Maistra diploms*: Music; Choreography; *Doktora diploms*: Musicology

Libraries: c. 195,000 vols

Last Updated: 28/10/11

LATVIAN ACADEMY OF CULTURE

Latvijas Kulturas Akademija (LKA)
24, Ludzas Str., LV-1003 Rīga
Tel: +371(67) 140-175
Fax: +371(67) 141-012
EMail: admin@lka.edu.lv
Website: http://www.lka.edu.lv

Rector: Janis Siliņš (2004-)

Vice-Rector for Research and Academic Work: Daina Teters
Tel: +371(67) 114-810 EMail: daina.teters@lka.edu.lv

International Relations: Ilze Beimane, Head of International Exchange Programmes
Tel: +371(67) 114-807 EMail: beimane@lka.edu.lv

Departments

Cultural Theory and History (Cultural Studies; Folklore; Management); **Intercultural Communication and Foreign Languages** (Cultural Studies; Danish; English; French; German; History; International Relations; Italian; Literature; Modern Languages; Norwegian; Polish; Spanish; Swedish; Translation and Interpretation); **Sociology and Management of Culture** (Art Management; Cultural Studies; Museum Management; Museum Studies; Sociology); **Theatre and Audio-visual Arts** (Acting; Cinema and Television; Dance; Film; Theatre; Video)

History: Founded 1990. An autonomous Institution financed by the State.

Governing Bodies: Senate

Academic Year: September to June

Admission Requirements: Secondary education certificate and entrance examination

Fees: (Lats): c. 400 per term

Main Language(s) of Instruction: Latvian; German (Media and Culture Management programme)

International Co-operation: Participates in the Erasmus programme.

Accrediting Agencies: Latvian Accreditation Commission; Council of Higher Education of Latvia

Degrees and Diplomas: *Bakalaura diploms*; *Maistra diploms*; *Doktora diploms*

Student Services: Cultural centre

Student Residential Facilities: Yes

Special Facilities: Cinema, Ceramic Studio, Video Library, Computer Room

Libraries: Central Library

Publications: Kulturas telpa un laiks, Time and Space of Culture

Academic Staff *2010-2011*: Total 73

Student Numbers *2010-2011*: Total: c. 600

Last Updated: 02/11/11

LATVIAN ACADEMY OF SPORT EDUCATION

Latvijas Sporta pedagogijas akadēmija (LSPA)
Brīvibas gatve 333, LV-1006 Rīga
Tel: +371(67) 543-433
Fax: +371(67) 543-480
EMail: akademija@lspa.lv
Website: http://www.lspa.lv

Rector: Janis Židens (2009-)
Tel: +371(67) 543-410 EMail: rector@lspa.lanet.lv

Vice-Rector (Academic): Andra Fernate
Tel: +371(67) 543-373 EMail: andra.fernate@lspa.lv

Vice-Rector (Science): Juris Grants
Tel: +371(67) 543-412 EMail: juris.grants@lspa.lv

International Relations: Uldis Švinks, Vice-Rector (Sport, Erasmus Mobility) Tel: +371(7) 543-422 EMail: uldis.svinks@lspa.lv

Departments

Anatomy, Physiology and Biochemistry (Anatomy; Biochemistry; Physiology); **Gymnastics** (Sports); **Heavy Athletics, Boxing and Wrestling** (Sports); **Informatics, Biomechanics and Sports Facilities** (Biology; Computer Science; Mechanics; Sports); **Languages** (Modern Languages); **Medicine, Physiotherapy, Remedial Gymnastics and Massage** (Medicine; Physical Therapy; Rehabilitation and Therapy; Sports Medicine); **Skiing, Shooting, Orienteering and Tourism** (Sports; Tourism); **Social Sciences and Sport Management** (Social Sciences; Sports Management); **Sport and Training Theory, Pedagogy, Psychology and Pedagogical Practices** (Pedagogy; Physical Education; Psychology; Sports; Sports Medicine); **Sports Games** (Sports); **Swimming and Rowing** (Sports); **Track and Field Athletics** (Sports)

History: Founded 1921 as the Latvian Institute of Physical Education. Acquired present title 1991. Acquired present status 1998.

Degrees and Diplomas: *Bakalaura diploms*; *Augstakas profesionalas izglītibas diploms*; *Maistra diploms*; *Doktora diploms*

Last Updated: 05/09/11

LATVIAN MARITIME ACADEMY

Latvijas Juras Akademija (LJA/LMA)
Flotes iela 5B, LV-1016 Rīga
Tel: +371(67) 161-125
Fax: +371(67) 830-138
EMail: info@latja.lv
Website: http://www.latja.lv

Rector: Janis Berzins
Tel: +371(67) 321-259, Fax: +371(67) 830-138
EMail: janis.berzins@latja.lv

Pro-rector: Ilmars Lešinskis
Tel: +371(67) 161-122, Fax: +371(67) 830-138
EMail: lesinskis@yahoo.com

International Relations: Vija Kasakovska, Head, Foreign Relations Department
Tel: +371(67) 161-130, Fax: +371(67) 830-138
EMail: vija.kasakovska@latja.lv

Centres

LMA Research and Development (Business Administration; Marine Transport; Metal Techniques; Transport and Communications); **LMA Training** *(TC)* (Marine Transport)

Departments

Marine Engineering (Marine Engineering; Marine Transport); **Marine Transport** (Marine Transport; Transport and Communications; Transport Management); **Marine Transportation - Marine Electrical Automation** (Automation and Control Engineering; Electrical Engineering; Marine Transport); **Postgraduate Studies** (Human Resources; Marine Transport; Power Engineering; Transport Management)

Programmes

Practical Training (Electrical Engineering; Metal Techniques; Transport and Communications)

Schools

Marine Studies (Marine Engineering; Marine Science and Oceanography; Marine Transport)

History: Founded 1989 as department of Maritime Studies of Kaliningrad Technical Fishery Institute (Riga), acquired present status and title1993.
Governing Bodies: Senate; Academic Board
Academic Year: September to September
Admission Requirements: Secondary school certificate (Atestats par videjo izgliti bu) and entrance examination
Accrediting Agencies: Board of Higher Education
Degrees and Diplomas: *Bakalaura diploms*; *Maistra diploms*. Also 3rd level secondary professional education
Student Services: Academic counselling, Health services, Social counselling, Sports facilities
Student Residential Facilities: Yes
Libraries: 38,000 vols
Last Updated: 28/10/11

LATVIA UNIVERSITY OF AGRICULTURE

Latvijas Lauksaimniecības Universitāte (LLU)
Liela iela 2, LV-3001 Jelgava
Tel: +371(630) 225-84
Fax: +371(630) 272-38
EMail: rektors@llu.lv
Website: http://www.llu.lv

Rector: Juris Skujāns (2004-)
Tel: +371(630) 225-84 EMail: rector@llu.lv
Prorector of Science: Peteris Rivža
Tel: +371(630) 056-33, Fax: +371(630) 272-38
EMail: zinpror@llu.lv
International Relations: Ināra Melgalve, Head of Department of International Relations Tel: +371(630) 056-84 EMail: foreign@llu.lv

Faculties

Agriculture (Agricultural Business; Agricultural Management; Agriculture; Agronomy; Animal Husbandry; Crop Production; Horticulture; Plant and Crop Protection; Soil Management; Soil Science); **Economics** (Accountancy; Business Administration; Economics; Finance; Management; Marketing); **Engineering** (Agricultural Engineering; Art Education; Educational Technology; Engineering; Machine Building; Pedagogy; Technology; Vocational Counselling; Vocational Education); **Food Technology** (Cooking and Catering; Food Science; Food Technology; Hotel and Restaurant; Hotel Management; Nutrition); **Forestry** (Agricultural Engineering; Ecology; Forest Biology; Forest Economics; Forest Products; Forestry; Safety Engineering; Wood Technology); **Information Technology** (Automation and Control Engineering; Computer Science; Information Technology; Software Engineering); **Rural Engineering** (Architecture and Planning; Civil Engineering; Environmental Engineering; Environmental Studies; Landscape Architecture; Regional Planning; Surveying and Mapping; Water Management); **Social Sciences** (Management; Public Administration; Public Relations; Social Sciences; Sociology); **Veterinary Medicine** (Food Science; Hygiene; Veterinary Science)

Further Information: Also Veterinary Hospital; Branches in Laidze, Kandava, Limbazi, Smiltene and Sigulda; Training and research centers in Vecauce, Ozolnieki, Engure, Vaive and Peterlauki; Scientific institutes in Jelgava, Ulbroka, Sigulda and Skriveri.
History: Founded 1863 as Department of Riga Polytechnical Institute, became the Faculty of Agriculture and Forestry at the Latvia University 1919, Jelgava Agricultural Academy was founded on this basis 1939. Acquired present status and title 1991.
Governing Bodies: Convent; Senate
Academic Year: September to June (September-January; February-June)
Admission Requirements: Secondary school certificate
Fees: (Euro): Full-time, 800-1,800; Part-time, 553-1,100.
Main Language(s) of Instruction: Latvian. Separate courses are possible in Russian, English, German
International Co-operation: Participates in the LLP-Erasmus programme (Finland, Sweden, Denmark, Germany, Italy, France, Spain, Ireland, The Netherlands, Belgium)
Degrees and Diplomas: *Bakalaura diploms*; *Augstākas profesionālās izglītības diploms*; *Maistra diploms*; *Doktora diploms*
Student Services: Canteen, Cultural centre, Health services, Nursery care, Sports facilities
Student Residential Facilities: For 2,680 students
Special Facilities: Museum of the Jelgava Palace. Research and Training Farm. Forestry Centre
Libraries: The Fundamental Library, 509,173 vols
Publications: Proceedings of the Latvia University of Agriculture

Academic Staff *2010-2011*: Total 275
STAFF WITH DOCTORATE: Total 49
Student Numbers *2012-2013*: Total 4,820
Last Updated: 14/03/13

LIEPAJA UNIVERSITY

Liepājas Universitāte (LPA)
Liela iela 14, LV-3401 Liepaja
Tel: +371(63) 423-560
Fax: +371(63) 424-223
EMail: liepu@liepu.lv; info@liepu.lv
Website: http://www.liepu.lv

Rector: Janis Rimšane
Tel: +371(63) 423-568 EMail: liepu@liepu.lv
Vice Rector for Studies: Ilma Neimane
Tel: +371(63) 407-772 EMail: ilma.neimane@liepu.lv
International Relations: Agita Auza, Head of Foreign Relations Department
Tel: +371(63) 407-762, Fax: +371(63) 407-762
EMail: acentrs@liepu.lv

Departments

Adult Education (Adult Education; Education; Vocational Education)

Faculties

Arts and Humanities (Arts and Humanities; Baltic Languages; Communication Studies; Cultural Studies; Design; English; European Languages; European Studies; French; German; Linguistics; Media Studies; Philology; Russian; Translation and Interpretation; Writing); **Natural and Social Sciences** (Business Administration; Computer Science; Educational Administration; Educational Technology; Energy Engineering; Environmental Engineering; Information Technology; Management; Mathematics; Natural Sciences; Physics; Public Administration; Public Relations; Social Sciences; Software Engineering; Tourism); **Pedagogy and Social Work** (Art Therapy; Education; Pedagogy; Rehabilitation and Therapy; Secondary Education; Social Welfare; Social Work; Teacher Training)

History: Founded 1954. Acquired present title and status 1998.
Academic Year: September to June (September-December; February-June)
Admission Requirements: Secondary school certificate and entrance examination
Fees: (Lats): 300-350 per annum
Main Language(s) of Instruction: Latvian
International Co-operation: With universities in Belgium, Czech Republic, Denmark, Finland, France, Germany, Greece, Ireland, Italy, Lithuania, Netherlands, Norway, Poland, Portugal, Romania, Slovakia, Sweden, Switzerland, Turkey.
Degrees and Diplomas: *Diploms par pirmā līmeņa augstāko profesionālo izglītību*; *Bakalaura diploms*; *Augstākas profesionālās izglītības diploms*; *Maistra diploms*; *Doktora diploms*
Student Services: Canteen, Health services, Language programs, Social counselling, Sports facilities
Student Residential Facilities: For 582 students
Special Facilities: Computer Centre
Libraries: c. 80 000 vols; c. 10,000 periodical subscriptions
Publications: LPA Vestis, Bulletin of LPA *(monthly)*

Academic Staff *2009-2010*	**TOTAL**
FULL-TIME	**124**
STAFF WITH DOCTORATE FULL-TIME	**66**
Student Numbers *2009-2010*	
All (Foreign Included)	c. **2,659**

Part-time students, 1,078.
Last Updated: 02/11/11

NATIONAL DEFENCE ACADEMY OF LATVIA

Latvijas Nacionālā aizsardzības akadēmija (NAA)
Ezermalas iela 6/8, LV-1014 Rīga
Tel: +371(67) 076-883
Fax: +371(67) 076-888
EMail: post@mil.lv
Website: http://www.naa.mil.lv

Rector: Egils Leščinskis (2011-)
Tel: +371(67) 076-881, Fax: +371(67) 076-888
EMail: Egils.Lescinskis@mil.lv

International Relations: Jolanta Vilipsone
Tel: +371(67) 076-872 EMail: jolanta.vilipsone@mil.lv

Programmes

Military Science (Military Science)

History: Founded 1992.

Governing Bodies: Constituent Assembly; Senate; Teaching Council; Scientific Council

Degrees and Diplomas: *Bakalaura diploms*; *Augstākas profesionālas izglītības diploms*; *Maistra diploms*

Last Updated: 05/09/11

REZEKNE HIGHER EDUCATION INSTITUTION

Rēzeknes Augstskola (RA)
Atbrīvošanas aleja 90, LV-4601 Rezekne
Tel: +371(64) 623-709
Fax: +371(64) 625-901
EMail: ru@ru.lv
Website: http://www.ru.lv

Rector: Edmunds Teirumnieks EMail: Edmunds.Teirumnieks@ru.lv

Vice Rector for Studies: Angelika Juško-Štekele
Tel: +371(64) 624-533 EMail: promd@ru.lv

Faculties

Economics and Management (Accountancy; Business Administration; Business and Commerce; Commercial Law; Economics; Finance; Hotel Management; Management; Tourism); **Education and Design** (Architectural and Environmental Design; Business Education; Design; Education; Foreign Languages Education; Household Management; Humanities and Social Science Education; Interior Design; Pedagogy; Rehabilitation and Therapy; Science Education; Special Education; Teacher Training; Translation and Interpretation; Vocational Education); **Engineering** (Computer Engineering; Computer Science; Construction Engineering; E-Business/Commerce; Electronic Engineering; Engineering; Environmental Engineering; Environmental Studies; Mathematics; Mechanical Engineering; Natural Sciences); **Humanities and Law** (Archiving; Arts and Humanities; Baltic Languages; Geography; History; Literature; Philology; Religious Education; Social Sciences)

History: Founded 1993, incorporating the Latgalian Branch of Latvian University in Rezekne and the Rezekne Branch of Riga Technical University, founded 1970.

Governing Bodies: Satversme (Board); Senate; Dome, comprising representatives of the Faculties and students

Academic Year: September to June

Admission Requirements: Secondary school certificate

Fees: (Euro): Full-time, 600-900 per programme; Part-time, 630-1,350 per programme.

Main Language(s) of Instruction: Latvian

International Co-operation: With universities in Belgium; Finland; Germany; Sweden; Portugal; Greece. Also participates in the Erasmus programme

Degrees and Diplomas: *Diploms par pirmā līmeņa augstākō profesionālo izglītību*; *Bakalaura diploms*; *Augstākas profesionālas izglītības diploms*; *Maistra diploms*; *Doktora diploms*

Student Services: Canteen, Cultural centre, Foreign Studies Centre, Language programs, Sports facilities

Student Residential Facilities: Yes

Special Facilities: Video Centre.

Libraries: RA Library, 52,000 vols

Publications: Rezeknes Augstskolas Zinnesis *(monthly)*

Press or Publishing House: Rezeknes Augstskolas Izdevnieciba

Student Numbers *2010-2011*: Total: c. 520

Last Updated: 02/11/11

RIGA STRADIŅŠ UNIVERSITY

Rīgas Stradiņa Universitāte (RSU)
Dzirciema iela 16, LV-1007 Rīga
Tel: +371(67) 409-105
Fax: +371(67) 471-815
EMail: rsu@rsu.lv; infocentrs@rsu.lv
Website: http://www.rsu.lv

Rector: Jānis Gardovskis
Tel: +371 (67) 409-232 EMail: rector@rsu.lv

Vice-Rector for Education: Ilze Akota
Tel: +371(7) 409-115 EMail: ilze_akota@rsu.lv

International Relations: Juta Kroiča, Head of Department
Tel: +371(7) 409-170 EMail: juta.kroica@rsu.lv

Campuses

Liepaja (Medical Auxiliaries; Midwifery; Nursing)

Faculties

Communications (Anthropology; Communication Studies; English; French; German; Journalism; Management; Psychology; Public Relations; Sociology; Spanish); **Continuing Education** (Cardiology; Dentistry; Dermatology; Endocrinology; Forensic Medicine and Dentistry; Gastroenterology; Medicine; Ophthalmology; Orthopaedics; Paediatrics; Radiology; Surgery); **Dentistry** (Dental Hygiene; Dental Technology; Dentistry; Oral Pathology; Orthodontics; Surgery); **Doctoral Studies** (Law; Medicine; Pharmacy; Political Sciences; Sociology); **European Studies** (Advertising and Publicity; Business Administration; Communication Studies; Economics; European Studies; European Union Law; Government; International Relations; Management; Marketing; Political Sciences; Public Administration; Small Business); **Law** (European Union Law; International Law; Law); **Medicine** (Medicine); **Nursing** (Midwifery; Nursing); **Pharmacy** (Chemistry; Pharmacy); **Public Health** (Anatomy; Arts and Humanities; Biochemistry; Epidemiology; Ethics; Microbiology; Philosophy; Physiology; Psychology; Public Health); **Rehabilitation** (Art Therapy; Dental Technology; Nutrition; Occupational Therapy; Orthodontics; Physical Therapy; Rehabilitation and Therapy; Social Work; Speech Therapy and Audiology; Sports)

History: Founded 1950 as Riga Medical Institute. Became Latvian Academy of Medicine 1990. Acquired present status and title 2002. A public institution.

Governing Bodies: Constitutional assembly; Senate; Rector

Academic Year: September to June (September-January; February-June)

Admission Requirements: Secondary education or secondary medical education (Dokuments par vidéjo izglitibu)

Fees: (Euros): Faculty of Medicine, 6,000; Faculty of Stomatology, 10,000

Main Language(s) of Instruction: Latvian, English

International Co-operation: With universities in Denmark, France, Lithuania, Germany, United Kingdom, Portugal, Romania, Hungary, Belgium, Spain. Participates in the Erasmsus.

Accrediting Agencies: Higher Education Quality Evaluation Centre; Ministry of Education and Science

Degrees and Diplomas: *Diploms par pirmā līmeņa augstākō profesionālo izglītību*; *Bakalaura diploms*; *Ārsta diploms*; *Augstākas profesionālas izglītības diploms*; *Maistra diploms*; *Doktora diploms*

Student Services: Academic counselling, Canteen, Cultural centre, Foreign student adviser, Foreign Studies Centre, Handicapped facilities, Health services, Language programs, Nursery care, Social counselling, Sports facilities

Student Residential Facilities: Hostel

Special Facilities: Museums: Pharmacy; History of Medicine; Anatomy

Libraries: University Library, c. 320,000 vols

Publications: Ķirurija, Publiation dealing with surgical specialities *(biennially)*; Zinātniskie raksti, Publication dealing with Medicine Pharmacy, Dentistry *(annually)*

Press or Publishing House: University Publishing House

Academic Staff *2010-2011*	MEN	WOMEN	TOTAL
FULL-TIME	–	–	**367**
Student Numbers *2010-2011*			
All (Foreign Included)	1,288	4,847	**6,135**
FOREIGN ONLY		–	**368**

Last Updated: 03/11/11

RIGA TEACHER TRAINING AND EDUCATIONAL MANAGEMENT ACADEMY

Rīgas Pedagogijas un Izglītības Vadības Akademija (RPIVA)

Imantas 7 līnija 1, LV-1083 Rīga
Tel: +371(67) 808-010
Fax: +371(67) 808-034
EMail: rpiva@rpiva.lv; international@rpiva.lv
Website: http://www.rpiva.lv

Rector: Dace Markus
Tel: +371(67) 808-010 EMail: dace.markus@rpiva.lv

International Relations: Inga Ščerbinska
Tel: +371(7) 808-032 EMail: international@rpiva.lv

Faculties

Pedagogy (Art Education; Computer Education; Dance; Education; Humanities and Social Science Education; Mathematics Education; Music Education; Native Language Education; Pedagogy; Pre-school Education; Primary Education; Science Education; Secondary Education); **Social Sciences** (Business Administration; Business and Commerce; Computer Education; Computer Science; Educational Administration; Educational Psychology; Human Resources; Humanities and Social Science Education; Labour and Industrial Relations; Management; Marketing; Mathematics Education; Native Language Education; Primary Education; Psychology; Public Relations; Science Education; Secondary Education; Social Sciences; Welfare and Protective Services)

History: Founded 1946. Became Rīgas Pedagoijas un izglītības vadības augstskolas 1994. Acquired present status and title 2005.

Degrees and Diplomas: *Diploms par pirmā līmena augstāko profesionālo izglītību*; *Bakalaura diploms*; *Augstākās profesionālas izglītības diploms*; *Maistra diploms*; *Doktora diploms*. Also Professional Bachelor's and Master' degrees.

Last Updated: 06/09/11

RIGA TECHNICAL UNIVERSITY

Rīgas Tehniskā Universitāte (RTU)

Kaļķu iela 1, LV-1658 Rīga
Tel: +371(67) 089-333
Fax: +371(67) 089-302
EMail: info@rtu.lv
Website: http://www.rtu.lv

Rector: Leonids Ribickis (2011-)
Tel: +371(7) 089-300, Fax: +371(7) 820-094
EMail: Leonids.Ribickis@rtu.lv

Chancellor: Ingars Eriņš
Tel: +371(7) 089-440, Fax: +371(7) 820-094
EMail: kanclers@rtu.lv; ingars.erins@rtu.lv

International Relations: Igors Tipans, Director, Foreign Students Department
Tel: +371(67) 089-013, Fax: +371(67) 089-020
EMail: igors@latnet.lv; igors.tipans@rtu.lv

Campuses

Daugavpils (Automation and Control Engineering; Computer Science; Construction Engineering; Economics; Electrical Engineering; Electronic Engineering; Engineering; Heating and Refrigeration; Information Technology; Machine Building; Mechanics; Power Engineering; Railway Transport; Road Transport; Safety Engineering; Transport Economics); **Liepaja** (Computer Engineering; Construction Engineering; Electrical Engineering; Engineering; Heating and Refrigeration; Human Resources; Machine Building; Management; Mechanics; Metallurgical Engineering; Petroleum and Gas Engineering; Power Engineering; Production Engineering; Telecommunications Engineering; Transport Management; Waste Management); **Ventspils** (Automation and Control Engineering; Computer Engineering; Economics; Electrical Engineering; Electronic Engineering; Engineering; Information Sciences; Machine Building; Management; Mechanics; Power Engineering; Safety Engineering; Taxation; Telecommunications Engineering; Transport and Communications)

Centres

BALTECH Study (Natural Sciences; Technology); **Distance Education** (Air Transport; Automation and Control Engineering; Automotive Engineering; Construction Engineering; Electronic Engineering; Heating and Refrigeration; Hydraulic Engineering; Petroleum and Gas Engineering; Railway Engineering; Surveying and Mapping; Transport Engineering)

Faculties

Architecture and Town Planning *(FAUP)* (Architectural Restoration; Architecture; Electrical Engineering; Electronic Engineering; Energy Engineering; Fine Arts; Interior Design; Landscape Architecture; Textile Design; Town Planning); **Civil Engineering** *(FCE)* (Bridge Engineering; Civil Engineering; Construction Engineering; Geological Engineering; Heating and Refrigeration; Industrial Design; Materials Engineering; Petroleum and Gas Engineering; Road Engineering; Structural Architecture; Surveying and Mapping; Transport Engineering; Water Science); **Computer Science and Information Technology** *(FCSIT)* (Actuarial Science; Automation and Control Engineering; Business Computing; Computer Engineering; Computer Graphics; Computer Science; Information Management; Information Technology; Mathematics; Software Engineering; Statistics); **Electronics and Telecommunications** *(FET)* (Electronic Engineering; Telecommunications Engineering); **Engineering Economics and Management** *(FEEM)* (Banking; Business Administration; Economics; International Business; Management; Marketing; Occupational Health; Real Estate; Transport Management); **Materials Science and Applied Chemistry** *(FMSAC)* (Applied Chemistry; Chemical Engineering; Materials Engineering; Organic Chemistry; Physics; Polymer and Plastics Technology; Textile Design); **Power and Electrical Engineering** *(FPEE)* (Electrical and Electronic Engineering; Electrical Engineering; Energy Engineering; Environmental Engineering; Heating and Refrigeration; Power Engineering); **Transport and Mechanical Engineering** *(FTME)* (Aeronautical and Aerospace Engineering; Biomedical Engineering; Mechanical Engineering; Mechanics; Nanotechnology; Railway Transport; Road Transport; Safety Engineering; Transport Engineering)

Institutes

Humanities *(IH)* (Arts and Humanities; Pedagogy; Philosophy; Sociology; Sports; Teacher Training; Vocational Education); **Languages** *(IL)* (Baltic Languages; English; German; Modern Languages; Translation and Interpretation)

Schools

Business *(Riga - RBS)* (Business Administration)

Further Information: A traditional and distance education institution.

History: Founded 1862 as Riga Polytechnical Institute, became part of Latvia University 1919. Renamed Riga Polytechnical Institute 1958. Acquired present status and title 1990.

Governing Bodies: Academic Council, Senate

Academic Year: September to June

Admission Requirements: Centralized examinations when graduating from secondary education

Fees: (Lats): c. 780 per annum (most students are State supported)

Main Language(s) of Instruction: Latvian, Russian, English

International Co-operation: Participates in Socrates, Erasmus (Germany, Finland, Sweden, Denmark, Italy, Belgium) and Leonardo da Vinci (Germany, Finland)

Degrees and Diplomas: *Diploms par pirmā līmena augstāko profesionālo izglītību*; *Bakalaura diploms*; *Augstākās profesionālas izglītības diploms*; *Maistra diploms*; *Doktora diploms*

Student Services: Academic counselling, Canteen, Cultural centre, Foreign student adviser, Foreign Studies Centre, Language programs, Social counselling, Sports facilities

Student Residential Facilities: Yes

Special Facilities: RTU Museum

Libraries: c. 1,9m vols

Publications: Scientific Proceedings of RTU *(quarterly)*

Academic Staff *2010-2011*	TOTAL
FULL-TIME	764
STAFF WITH DOCTORATE FULL-TIME	135
Student Numbers *2010-2011*	
All (Foreign Included)	15,735
FOREIGN ONLY	3,980

Last Updated: 03/11/11

STOCKHOLM SCHOOL OF ECONOMICS IN RIGA

Rīgas Ekonomikas Augstskola (SSE RIGA)
Strēlnieku iela 4a, LV-1010 Rīga
Tel: +371(67) 015-800
Fax: +371(67) 830-249
EMail: office@sseriga.edu
Website: http://www.sseriga.edu.lv

Rector: Anders Paalzow (1999-)
Tel: +371(67) 015-801 EMail: anders.paalzow@sseriga.edu

Vice-Rector: Diāna Pauna
Tel: +371(67) 015-803 EMail: diana.pauna@sseriga.edu

International Relations: Evita Lukina, Manager, Exchange Programme Tel: +371(67) 015-804 EMail: evita.lukina@sseriga.edu

Departments

Business and Management (Accountancy; Anthropology; Business Administration; Commercial Law; Development Studies; Ethics; Leadership; Management; Mathematics; Philosophy; Taxation); **Economics** (Accountancy; Business Administration; Econometrics; Economics; Finance; International Economics); **Languages** (Baltic Languages; English; French; German; Russian; Spanish; Swedish)

History: Founded 1993 as a Branch of the Stockholm School of Economics, Stockholm, Sweden.

Governing Bodies: Board

Academic Year: August to June

Admission Requirements: Admission tests and interviews

Fees: (Euro): Undergraduate tuition, 3,500 per annum; Postgraduate tuition, 21,500-24,000 per annum.

Main Language(s) of Instruction: Latvian; English

International Co-operation: With universities in Sweden, France, Germany and Norway. Participates in the Erasmus programme.

Degrees and Diplomas: *Bakalaura diploms*; *Maistra diploms (Executive MBA)*

Student Services: Academic counselling, Canteen, Employment services, Social counselling

Student Residential Facilities: For c. 200 students

Libraries: c. 13,000 vols

Publications: SSE Riga Working Papers, Publication of the best BSc thesis *(annually)*

Last Updated: 02/11/11

UNIVERSITY OF LATVIA

Latvijas Universitāte (UL)
Raiņa bulvāris 19, LV-1586 Rīga
Tel: +371(67) 034-331
Fax: +371(67) 034-302
EMail: lu@lu.lv
Website: http://www.lu.lv

Rector: Mārcis Auziņš (2007-)
Tel: +371(67) 034-300 EMail: Marcis.Auzins@lu.lv

Administrative Director: Jānis Stonis
Tel: +371(7) 034-600, Fax: +371(7) 034-302
EMail: Janis.Stonis@lu.lv

International Relations: Alīna Gržibovska, Director, International Relations Department
Tel: +371(67) 034-334, Fax: +371(67) 243-091 EMail: ad@lu.lv

Centres

Baltic Studies (Baltic Languages); **Cognitive Sciences and Semantics** (Cognitive Sciences; Terminology); **Environmental Studies and Management** (Environmental Management; Environmental Studies); **European and Transition Studies** (European Studies); **Family Health Education** (Health Education); **Gender Studies** (Gender Studies); **Judaic Studies** (Judaic Religious Studies); **Language** (Baltic Languages; Chinese; English; French; German; Italian; Japanese; Russian; Spanish; Swedish); **Lithuanistics** (Baltic Languages; Cultural Studies); **Local-Government and Project Management State Trainings** (Government; Management; Public Administration); **North American Studies** (American Studies); **Pre-Studies Training**

Faculties

Biology (Biology; Biotechnology; Botany; Ecology; Microbiology; Molecular Biology; Physiology; Zoology); **Chemistry** (Analytical Chemistry; Chemistry; Environmental Studies; Food Technology; Inorganic Chemistry; Organic Chemistry; Physical Chemistry; Science Education); **Computing** (Computer Education; Computer Engineering; Computer Networks; Computer Science; Information Technology; Mathematics and Computer Science; Natural Sciences; Software Engineering); **Economics and Management** (Accountancy; Business Administration; Demography and Population; E-Business/Commerce; Economics; Environmental Management; European Studies; Finance; Insurance; International Business; International Economics; International Law; International Relations; Management; Marketing; Mathematics; Safety Engineering; Statistics; Tourism; Transport Management); **Education, Psychology and Art** (Adult Education; Art Education; Computer Education; Computer Networks; Computer Science; Education; Educational Administration; Educational Sciences; Foreign Languages Education; Handicrafts; Health Education; Home Economics; Humanities and Social Science Education; Literature; Native Language Education; Pedagogy; Preschool Education; Primary Education; Psychology; Special Education; Sports; Teacher Training); **Geography and Earth Sciences** (Earth Sciences; Environmental Studies; Geography; Geography (Human); Geology; Science Education); **History and Philosophy** (Archaeology; Contemporary History; History; Logic; Medieval Studies; Modern History; Philosophy); **Humanities** (Anthropology; Arts and Humanities; Asian Studies; Baltic Languages; Classical Languages; Cultural Studies; English; English Studies; Finnish; French; German; Hungarian; Linguistics; Oriental Languages; Philology; Romance Languages; Russian; Scandinavian Languages; Slavic Languages; Translation and Interpretation); **Law** (Civil Law; Constitutional Law; Criminal Law; European Union Law; History of Law; Human Rights; International Law; Law; Public Law); **Medicine** (Histology; Medicine; Nursing; Paediatrics; Pathology; Pharmacy; Social and Preventive Medicine; Surgery); **Physics and Mathematics** (Applied Mathematics; Astronomy and Space Science; Astrophysics; Atomic and Molecular Physics; Computer Science; Laser Engineering; Mathematics; Mechanics; Optics; Optometry; Physics; Polymer and Plastics Technology; Science Education; Statistics; Thermal Physics); **Social Sciences** (Cognitive Sciences; Communication Studies; Information Sciences; Library Science; Political Sciences; Social Sciences; Social Work; Sociology); **Theology** (Bible; Ethics; History of Religion; Religion; Religious Education; Religious Studies; Theology)

Research Institutes

Advanced Social and Political Sciences (Development Studies; Information Sciences; International Relations; Media Studies; Political Sciences; Regional Studies; Social Sciences); **Astronomy** (Astronomy and Space Science); **Atomic Physics and Spectroscopy** (Atomic and Molecular Physics; Optics; Physics); **Biology** (Biology; Botany; Ecology; Environmental Management; Environmental Studies; Natural Resources; Zoology); **Cardiology** (Cardiology; Epidemiology; Medicine); **Education** (Education; Educational Administration; Educational Sciences); **Experimental and Clinical Medicine** (Biology; Cell Biology; Diabetology; Endocrinology; Medicine; Oncology; Physiology); **Geodesy and Geo-informatics** (Computer Science; Earth Sciences; Geophysics); **History of Latvia** (Anthropology; Archaeology; Ethnology; History; Medieval Studies); **Latvian Language** (Grammar; Linguistics; Native Language; Terminology); **Literature, Folklore and Art** (Arts and Humanities; Comparative Literature; Folklore; Literature; Musicology; Theatre); **Mathematics and Computer Science** (Artificial Intelligence; Computer Engineering; Computer Networks; Mathematics and Computer Science; Systems Analysis); **Microbiology and Biotechnology** (Biotechnology; Cell Biology; Food Technology; Microbiology; Physiology); **Pedagogy** (Computer Education; Continuing Education; Distance Education; Pedagogy); **Philosophy and Sociology** (Philosophy; Sociology); **Physics** (Mechanics;

Physics); **Polymer Mechanics** (Materials Engineering; Mechanics; Physics); **Solid State Physics** (Materials Engineering; Optometry; Physics; Radiophysics)

History: Founded 1919. Acquired present status 1990.

Governing Bodies: Constituent Assembly; Senate

Academic Year: September to June (September-January; February-June)

Admission Requirements: Competitive entrance according to the results of the centralized examination following general or special secondary school certificate

Fees: (US Dollars): Foreign students, 3,000-4,500 per annum

Main Language(s) of Instruction: Latvian

International Co-operation: With 69 universities worldwide

Degrees and Diplomas: *Diploms par pirmā līmena augstāko profesionālo izglītību*; *Bakalaura diploms*: 3-4 yrs; *Augstākās profesionālās izglītības diploms*; *Maistra diploms*: a further 1-2 yrs; *Doktora diploms*: a further 3-4 yrs

Student Services: Academic counselling, Canteen, Cultural centre, Foreign student adviser, Language programs, Sports facilities

Student Residential Facilities: Yes

Special Facilities: University History Museum. Botanical Gardens

Libraries: c. 2m

Publications: Acta Universitatis Latviensis *(other/irregular)*; Automatic Control and Computer Science *(biennially)*; Journal of Baltic psychology *(annually)*; Journal of the Latvian Institute History *(quarterly)*; Latvian Human Rights Quarterly *(biannually)*; Latvijas Vēsture, History of Latvia *(quarterly)*; Likums un Tiesibas, Law and Human Rights *(monthly)*; Linguistica Lettica *(biannually)*; Magneto-hydro-dynamics *(quarterly)*; Mechanics of Composite Materials *(biennially)*; Terra *(monthly)*; Zvaigžņota Debess, The Starry Sky *(quarterly)*

Academic Staff *2010-2011*	**TOTAL**
FULL-TIME	**600**
PART-TIME	**130**
STAFF WITH DOCTORATE	
FULL-TIME	**390**
PART-TIME	c. **70**
Student Numbers *2010-2011*	
All (Foreign Included)	c. **17,000**
FOREIGN ONLY	**400**

Part-time students, 7,030.

Last Updated: 02/11/11

VENTSPILS UNIVERSITY COLLEGE

Ventspils Augstskola (VEA)

Inženieru 101a, LV-3601 Ventspils

Tel: +371(63) 629-657

Fax: +371(63) 629-660

EMail: venta@venta.lv

Website: http://www.venta.lv

Rector: Jānis Eglītis
Tel: +371(63) 628-303 EMail: janis.eglitis@venta.lv

Vice Rector for Administration and Finance: Aleksandrs Dupats
Tel: +371(63) 629-647 EMail: aleksandrs.dupats@venta.lv

International Relations: Liene Liepiņa, International Relations Officer Tel: +371(36) 283-02 EMail: international@venta.lv

Faculties

Economics and Business Administration *(FEBA)* (Accountancy; Business Administration; Economics; Finance; Management; Marketing; Social Sciences; Transport Management); **Information Technology** *(FIT)* (Computer Engineering; Computer Science; Electronic Engineering; Engineering; Information Technology; Mathematics; Telecommunications Engineering); **Translation Studies** (Baltic Languages; English; German; Linguistics; Russian; Translation and Interpretation)

History: Founded 1997 as the State higher education institution.

Academic Year: September to June

Fees: (Euro): 1,400-2,200 per annum

Main Language(s) of Instruction: Latvian

International Co-operation: With universities in Belgium, Estonia, Finland, France, Germany, Ireland, Italy, Norway. Participates in the Erasmus programme.

Accrediting Agencies: Latvian Board of Higher Education

Degrees and Diplomas: *Bakalaura diploms*; *Maistra diploms*; *Doktora diploms*

Student Services: Academic counselling, Canteen, Foreign student adviser, Handicapped facilities, Language programs, Sports facilities

Student Residential Facilities: Yes

Special Facilities: Language and Multimedia Laboratory

Libraries: Academic Library

Academic Staff *2011-2012*: Total 60

Student Numbers *2011-2012*: Total 890

Last Updated: 03/11/11

VIDZEME UNIVERSITY COLLEGE

Vidzemes Augstskola (VIA)

Cēsu Iela 4, LV-4200 Valmiera

Tel: +371(64) 207-230

Fax: +371(64) 207-229

EMail: info@va.lv

Website: http://www.va.lv

Rector: Vija Daukšte
Tel: +371(64) 250-841 EMail: vija.daukste@va.lv

Vice-Rector, Administrative Affairs: Ilgvars Ābols
Tel: +371(64) 250-841 EMail: ilgvars.abols@va.lv

International Relations: Iveta Putnina, Head of Study, Research and International Relations Department
Tel: +371(64) 250-853 EMail: iveta.putnina@va.lv

Centres

Language Study and Examination (Baltic Languages; English; French; German; Translation and Interpretation)

Faculties

Business Administration and Economics (Accountancy; Business Administration; Economics; Finance; Management; Marketing); **Engineering** (Computer Networks; Data Processing; Electronic Engineering; Engineering; Information Management; Information Technology; Mechanical Engineering); **Social Sciences** (Communication Studies; Government; Journalism; Media Studies; Political Sciences; Public Relations; Social Sciences); **Tourism and Hospitality Management** (Business Administration; Hotel Management; Management; Tourism)

Institutes

Socio-technical Systems Engineering (Engineering; Social Sciences)

History: Founded 1996, acquired present status 2001.

Governing Bodies: Senate

Academic Year: September to June

Admission Requirements: Secondary school certificate, English examination

Fees: (Lats): 560 per annum for paying students

Main Language(s) of Instruction: Latvian, English

International Co-operation: With universities in Belarus, Bulgaria, Denmark, Estonia, France, Finland, Germany, Italy, Ireland, Iceland, Kazakhstan, Kyrgyzstan, Lithuania, Norway, The Netherlands, Poland, Portugal, Russian Federation, Slovak Republic, Spain, Sweden, Ukraine, United Kingdom, USA. Also participates in Erasmus, Nordplus, HESP and Barons programmes.

Accrediting Agencies: AIKNC (Higher Education Quality Evaluation Centre of Latvia)

Degrees and Diplomas: *Diploms par pirmā līmena augstāko profesionālo izglītību*; *Bakalaura diploms*; *Augstākās profesionālās izglītības diploms*; *Maistra diploms*; *Doktora diploms*

Student Services: Academic counselling, Employment services, Foreign student adviser, Language programs

Student Residential Facilities: 3 Residence Halls

Special Facilities: Computer lab; Electronic lab; Free internet connection

Libraries: Main Library

Student Numbers *2010-2011*: Total 1,423

Part-time students, 499.

Last Updated: 03/11/11

PRIVATE INSTITUTIONS

BALTIC INTERNATIONAL ACADEMY

Baltijas Starptautiskā Akadēmija (BSA)
Lomonosova iela 4, LV-1003 Rīga
Tel: +371(67) 100-601 +371(67) 100-626
Fax: +371(67) 112-679 +371(67) 241-272
EMail: info@bsa.edu.lv
Website: http://bsa.edu.lv

Rector: Arkadijis Voicišs
Tel: +371(67) 100-554, Fax: +371(67) 100-554
EMail: vocish@bsa.edu.lv

Centres

Foreign Language Learning (English; French; German; Russian; Spanish; Swedish)

Programmes

Business Management and Administration *(Postgraduate Professional Education)* (Administration; Business Administration; English; Russian); **Computer Design** (Computer Graphics; Computer Science; Graphic Design); **Computer Science** (Computer Science; Microelectronics); **Cultural Management** (Cultural Studies; Management); **Design** *(Postgraduate Professional Education)* (Computer Graphics; Design); **Entrepreneurship** *(Professional Education)* (Business Administration; International Business; Management); **Environmental Design** *(Professional Education)* (Architectural and Environmental Design; Communication Arts; Interior Design; Visual Arts); **European Studies** *(Postgraduate)* (English; European Studies; Russian; Social Studies); **European Studies** (Baltic Languages; English; European Studies; International Relations; Political Sciences; Russian); **Financial Management** (Finance; Management); **Human Resources Management** *(Interuniversity Postgraduate Professional Education)* (Human Resources; Management); **Jurisprudence (Law)** *(Professional Education)* (Law); **Private Law** *(Postgraduate Professional Education)* (Private Law); **Public Relations** (Baltic Languages; Marketing; Public Relations; Russian); **Regional Economics and Economic Policy** *(International Doctoral Studies)* (Economic and Finance Policy; Economics; English; Russian); **Small and Medium Business Management** *(Professional Education)* (Business Administration; Management; Small Business; Tourism); **Tourism and Hospitality Management** (Hotel and Restaurant; Tourism); **Translation and Interpretation** (Baltic Languages; English; Russian; Translation and Interpretation)

Further Information: Also campuses in Daugavpils, Rezekne, Yekabpils, Yelgava, Liepaya, Ventspils, Smiltene. A traditional and distance education institution.

History: Founded 1992 as Baltijas Krievu Instituts (Baltic Russian Institute). Acquired present status 1999. Acquired present title 2006.

Fees: (US Dollar): 300-800 per semester. (Euro): for International students, 630-1,350 per semester.

Main Language(s) of Instruction: Latvian; English; Russian

International Co-operation: Participates in the Erasmus and Tempus programme.

Accrediting Agencies: Ministry of Education and Science

Degrees and Diplomas: *Diploms par pirmā līmena augstāko profesionālo izglītību*; *Bakalaura diploms*; *Maistra diploms*; *Doktora diploms*. Also Professional Bachelor's degree; 2nd level professional higher education diploma; MBA

Special Facilities: 17 reading rooms; "Media-bridge" system; 22 computer laboratories; Laboratory on investigation of small and medium business; Multidisciplinary Research Centre; Students' Advertising and PR Agency; Art Gallery "BIART"; Ceramics Studio; Drawing Studio

Academic Staff *2009-2010*	TOTAL
FULL-TIME	300
STAFF WITH DOCTORATE	
FULL-TIME	c. 100

Student Numbers *2009-2010*	
All (Foreign Included)	c. 7,500
FOREIGN ONLY	450

Last Updated: 27/10/11

BALTIC PSYCHOLOGY AND MANAGEMENT UNIVERSITY COLLEGE

Baltijas Psiholoijas un Menedžmenta Augstskola
Lomonosova iela 4, LV-1003 Rīga
Tel: +371(67) 100-608
Fax: +371(67) 100-218
EMail: psa@psy.lv
Website: http://www.psy.lv

Rector: Zhanna Caurkubule
Tel: 371(67) 100-628 EMail: rector@psy.lv

Programmes

European Economy and Business (Accountancy; Baltic Languages; Banking; Business Administration; Economics; English; European Union Law; Finance; International Business; International Economics; International Law; International Relations; Law; Marketing; Taxation); **Human Resources Management** (Human Resources); **Professional Work Psychology** *(Master)* (Industrial and Organizational Psychology; Psychology); **Psychologist Assistant** (Psychology); **Psychology** (Anatomy; Clinical Psychology; Cultural Studies; Educational Psychology; Gerontology; Logic; Modern Languages; Philosophy; Physiology; Psychology; Social Psychology); **Social Assistance Management** (Social Welfare; Social Work); **Social Work** (Social Work)

Further Information: Also branches in Liepaja and Daugavpils, Ekabpils, Elgava.

History: Founded 1995. Acquired present status 2004.

Governing Bodies: Constitutional Assembly; Senate

Main Language(s) of Instruction: Latvian

International Co-operation: Participates in the LPP-Erasmus programme.

Degrees and Diplomas: *Diploms par pirmā līmena augstāko profesionālo izglītību*: Social Assistance Management; *Bakalaura diploms*; *Maistra diploms*: Psychology; Human Resources Management

Libraries: c. 3,920 vols; c. 970 periodical subscriptions.

Last Updated: 02/11/11

HIGHER INSTITUTE OF SOCIAL TECHNOLOGY

Sociālo Tehnoloiju Augstskola (STA)
Bezdelīgu iela 12, LV-1048 Rīga
Tel: +371(67) 461-001 +371(67) 461-281
Fax: +371(67) 461-281
EMail: sta@sta-edu.lv
Website: http://www.sta-edu.lv

Rector: Juris Zaķis

Programmes

Entrepreneurial Economics and Administration (Accountancy; Business Administration; Economics; History; Labour and Industrial Relations; Management; Modern Languages; Philosophy; Political Sciences; Transport Management); **Entrepreneurial Management** *(Postgraduate)* (Accountancy; Business Administration; Economics; Finance; Management; Marketing; Pedagogy; Psychology; Social Work; Statistics); **Law** (Law; Real Estate; Small Business; Transport and Communications); **Translation and Interpretation** (Baltic Languages; Economics; English; German; Latin; Law; Psychology; Russian; Spanish; Translation and Interpretation)

History: Founded 1991, acquired present status 2000.

Degrees and Diplomas: *Bakalaura diploms*; *Maistra diploms*

Last Updated: 03/11/11

HIGHER SCHOOL OF MANAGEMENT AND SOCIAL WORK 'ATTISTIBA'

Vadības un Sociālā darba augstskola 'Attīstība' (HSMSW 'ATTISTIBA')

Eiženijas iela 1, LV-1007 Rīga
Tel: +371(67) 459-089
Fax: +371(67) 470-937
EMail: attistiba@attistiba.lv
Website: http://www.attistiba.lv

Deputy Rector: Aina Vilciņa

International Relations: Airita Brenča, Head of Centre of Public Relations and International Relations
Tel: +371(7) 470-917 EMail: sdspa@attistiba.lv; airita@attistiba.lv

Campuses

Daugavpils (Human Resources; Rehabilitation and Therapy; Social Problems; Social Work; Welfare and Protective Services); **Rezekne** (Human Resources; Rehabilitation and Therapy; Social Problems; Social Work; Welfare and Protective Services); **Smiltene** (Human Resources; Rehabilitation and Therapy; Social Problems; Social Work; Welfare and Protective Services)

Programmes

Human Resources *(Undergraduate)* (Human Resources); **Organising Social Assistance** *(Professional - 1st level)* (Social Welfare); **Social Care** *(Professional - 1st level)* (Social Welfare; Social Work); **Social Rehabilitation** *(Professional - 1st level)* (Rehabilitation and Therapy; Social Work); **Social Work** *(Postgraduate)* (Management; Social Policy; Social Welfare; Social Work); **Social Work** *(Professional - 2nd level)* (Human Rights; Social Policy; Social Problems; Social Work); **Social Work** *(Undergraduate)* (Development Studies; Human Rights; Social Policy; Social Problems; Social Studies; Social Welfare; Social Work; Welfare and Protective Services)

Degrees and Diplomas: *Diploms par pirmā līmena augstāko profesionālo izglītību*; *Bakalaura diploms*; *Augstākās profesionālās izglītības diploms*; *Maistra diploms*

Libraries: c. 8,000 vols; 70 professional dictionaries; 50 publications on Social Work written by faculty members.

Last Updated: 03/11/11

INFORMATION SYSTEMS MANAGEMENT INSTITUTE

Informācijas Sistēmu Menedžmenta Augstskola (ISMA)

Ludzas 91, LV-1019 Rīga
Tel: +371(67) 100-607 +371(67) 100-690
Fax: +371(67) 241-591
EMail: isma@isma.lv
Website: http://www.isma.lv

President: Romans Djakons
Tel: +371(67) 241-515 EMail: roman@isma.lv

Rector: Marga Živitere
Tel: +371(67) 100-589 EMail: marga@isma.lv

International Relations: Dennis Djakons, Vice Rector for External Relations Tel: +371(67) 708-9878 EMail: deniss.djakons@isma.lv

Departments

Business Communications Department (Communication Studies; English; German; Grammar; Spanish; Translation and Interpretation; Writing); **Computer Technologies and Natural Sciences** (Artificial Intelligence; Business Administration; Business Computing; Chemistry; Computer Engineering; Computer Graphics; Computer Networks; Computer Science; Data Processing; Design; E-Business/Commerce; Electronic Engineering; Information Management; Information Technology; Mathematics; Natural Sciences; Operations Research; Physics; Software Engineering; Statistics; Telecommunications Engineering; Transport and Communications; Transport Management); **Cultural Studies** (Architectural and Environmental Design; Art History; Computer Graphics; Cultural Studies; Ethics; Graphic Design; Interior Design; Marketing; Photography; Safety Engineering); **Law** (Administrative Law; Civil Law; Civil Security; Commercial Law; European Union Law; Fiscal Law; Information Technology; Insurance; Labour Law; Law; Marketing; Protective Services; Psychology; Real Estate; Sociology); **Management and Economics** (Accountancy; Banking; Business Administration; Commercial Law; Economics; Environmental Studies; Finance; Information Sciences; Management; Marketing; Transport Management); **Management and Marketing** (Human Resources; Management; Marketing; Safety Engineering; Tourism)

Further Information: Also Latgales Branch and Mission in Ulkraine. A traditional and distance education institution.

History: Founded 1996.

Main Language(s) of Instruction: Latvian

International Co-operation: Participates in the LLP-Erasmus programme.

Degrees and Diplomas: *Diploms par pirmā līmena augstāko profesionālo izglītību*; *Bakalaura diploms*; *Maistra diploms*; *Doktora diploms*

Last Updated: 28/10/11

INTERNATIONAL HIGHER SCHOOL OF PRACTICAL PSYCHOLOGY

Starptautiskā Praktiskās Psiholoijas Augstskola (SPPA)

Bruninieku 65, LV-1011 Rīga
Tel: +371(67) 803-919
EMail: sppa@sppa.lv
Website: http://www.sppa.lv

Rector: Dzidra Meikšane
Tel: +371(67) 506-257 EMail: rektors@sppa.lv

Departments

Advertising and Public Relations (Advertising and Publicity; Public Relations); **Business Administration** (Business Administration; Computer Science; Economics; Information Technology; Management; Mathematics); **Computer Design** (Computer Graphics; Design); **Directing** (Cinema and Television; Photography; Theatre; Writing); **Psychology** (Psychology); **Translation** (Baltic Languages; Chinese; English; French; German; Italian; Japanese; Polish; Russian; Spanish; Translation and Interpretation)

History: Founded 1988.

Main Language(s) of Instruction: Latvian, Russian

Degrees and Diplomas: *Bakalaura diploms*; *Augstākās profesionālās izglītības diploms*; *Maistra diploms*

Last Updated: 03/11/11

LATVIAN CHRISTIAN ACADEMY

Latvijas Kristīgā akadēmija (LKRA)

5.līnija 3, Bulduri, LV-2010 Jūrmala
Tel: +371(67) 753-360 +371 (67) 811-340
Fax: +371(67) 751-919
EMail: akademija@kra.lv
Website: http://www.kra.lv

Rector: Skaidrite Gūtmane Fax: +371(67) 751-919
EMail: rektore@kra.lv

Executive Secretary: Līva Fokrote

International Relations: Astra Pope, Pro-Rector
EMail: prorektore@kra.lv

Programmes

Biblical Arts (Religious Art); **Public Relations** (Public Relations); **Social Work** (Social Work); **Theology** (Theology)

History: Founded 1993, acquired present status 1997.

Fees: (Euro): 800-1,300 per programme.

Main Language(s) of Instruction: Latvian; English

International Co-operation: Participates in the Erasmus programme.

Degrees and Diplomas: *Bakalaura diploms*; *Maistra diploms*

Last Updated: 28/10/11

RIGA AERONAUTICAL INSTITUTE

Rīgas Aeronavigācijas Instituts (RAI)

Mezkalnu 9, LV-1058 Rīga
Tel: +371(67) 767-831
Fax: +371(67) 767-831
EMail: rai.lv@ml.lv
Website: http://www.rai.lv

Rector: Olafs Brinkmanis (1990-) EMail: Oladmi@ml.lv

Vice-President: Mikhail Karol

International Relations: Dmitrij Ulanov, First Prorector and Academic Secretary EMail: Ulanov@rai.lv

Departments

Aviation Engineering (Aeronautical and Aerospace Engineering; Air Transport; Computer Engineering; Electronic Engineering; Maintenance Technology; Power Engineering); **Economics** (Air Transport; Economics; International Business; Management; Psychology; Transport Management)

History: Founded 1942, acquired present status 1992.

Governing Bodies: Convent; Senate

Main Language(s) of Instruction: Latvian

Degrees and Diplomas: *Bakalaura diploms*; *Augstākas profesionālas izglītības diploms*; *Maistra diploms*

Last Updated: 02/11/11

RIGA GRADUATE SCHOOL OF LAW

Rīgas Juridiskā augstkola (RGSL)

Strēlnieku iela 4k-2, LV-1010 Rīga

Tel: +371(67) 039-230

Fax: +371(67) 039-240

EMail: office@rgsl.edu.lv

Website: http://www.rgsl.edu.lv

Rector: George Ulrich (2007-)
Tel: +371(67) 039-201, Fax: +371(67) 039-240
EMail: george.ulrich@rgsl.edu.lv

Director: Kitija Freija
Tel: +371 (67) 039-203 EMail: kitija@rgsl.edu.lv

Programmes

EU Law and Policy *(Graduate)* (Environmental Studies; European Studies; European Union Law; International Law; International Relations); **International and EU Law** *(Graduate)* (Commercial Law; European Union Law; Human Rights; International Law; Public Law); **Law and Business** (Administrative Law; Business Administration; Commercial Law; Comparative Law; Constitutional Law; Demography and Population; Economics; English; Ethics; Finance; French; German; Human Rights; Information Management; International Economics; International Law; Law; Marketing); **Law and Diplomacy** (Arts and Humanities; Business Administration; Comparative Politics; Economics; English; French; German; International Business; International Relations; Law; Psychology); **Law and Finance** *(Graduate)* (Accountancy; Commercial Law; Economics; Finance; International Law; Law; Taxation); **Legal Linguistics** *(Graduate)* (Comparative Law; European Union Law; Law; Linguistics; Philology; Terminology; Translation and Interpretation); **Public International Law and Human Rights** *(Graduate)* (Commercial Law; Criminal Law; Human Rights; International Law; Public Law); **Transborder Commercial Law** *(Graduate)* (Business Administration; Commercial Law; International Business; International Law)

History: Founded 1998 on the basis of a Swedish-Latvian agreement.

Governing Bodies: Board, Academic Council, Auditing Committee

Academic Year: August to June

Admission Requirements: Bachelor of Law or equivalent. TOEFL with minimum score of 550 points or 6.5 at IELTS

Fees: (Euro): 4,980-9,960 per programme.

Main Language(s) of Instruction: English

International Co-operation: With universities in Lithuania; Estonia; Germany; Sweden; Norway; Serbia. Participates in the Eramsus programme.

Accrediting Agencies: Ministry of Education and Science

Degrees and Diplomas: *Bakalaura diploms*; *Maistra diploms*

Student Residential Facilities: None

Libraries: Yes

Publications: RGSL Working Papers

Last Updated: 02/11/11

RIGA INTERNATIONAL SCHOOL OF ECONOMICS AND BUSINESS ADMINISTRATION

Rīgas Starptautiskā ekonomikas un biznesa administrācijas augstskola (RISEBA)

Meža iela 3, LV-1048 Rīga

Tel: +371(67) 500-265

Fax: +371(67) 500-252

EMail: riseba@riseba.lv

Website: http://www.riseba.lv/

Rector: Irina Sennikova (2010-)
Tel: +371(67) 500-251 EMail: irina.sennikova@riseba.lv

Vice-Rector: Ilmars Kreituss
Tel: +371(67) 500-253 EMail: ilmars.kreituss@riseba.lv

International Relations: Ella Kalnina, Head, External Relations
Tel: +371(67) 500-262, Fax: +371(67) 500-256
EMail: ella.kalnina@riseba.lv

Programmes

Architecture *(Undergraduate Studies)* (Architectural and Environmental Design; Architecture; Media Studies; Structural Architecture); **Audiovisual Media Arts** *(Postgraduate Studies)* (Cinema and Television; Communication Arts; Computer Graphics; Design; Leadership; Mass Communication; Music Theory and Composition; Photography; Visual Arts); **Audiovisual Media Arts** *(Undergraduate Studies)* (Aesthetics; Art History; Art Management; Cinema and Television; Communication Arts; English; Film; Journalism; Law; Philosophy; Psychology; Radio and Television Broadcasting); **Business Management** *(Postgraduate Studies)* (Accountancy; Business Administration; Commercial Law; Economics; Finance; Information Technology; Management; Marketing; Psychology); **Business Management and Administration of Organizations** *(Doctoral programme)* (Administration; Business Administration; Economics; English; Finance; Human Resources; Management; Marketing; Modern Languages; Operations Research; Safety Engineering); **Business Psychology** *(Undergraduate Studies)* (Industrial and Organizational Psychology); **Business Studies** *(Foundation Degree)* (Accountancy; Banking; Business Administration; Commercial Law; Economics; Finance; Human Resources; Information Technology; Labour Law; Management; Marketing; Statistics); **Business Studies** *(Undergraduate Studies)* (Accountancy; Banking; Business Administration; Civil Law; Commercial Law; Data Processing; English; European Union Law; Finance; Human Resources; Information Technology; International Business; International Economics; International Law; Labour Law; Management; Marketing; Social Psychology; Statistics; Transport Management); **E-Business** *(Undergraduate Studies)* (Business Administration; Business Computing; Computer Graphics; E-Business/Commerce; European Union Law; Information Technology; Marketing; Multimedia; Social Psychology; Statistics); **European Business Studies** *(Undergraduate Studies)* (Accountancy; Civil Law; Commercial Law; Communication Studies; Economics; European Studies; Finance; Information Technology; Law; Management; Marketing); **Human Resource Management** (Accountancy; Business Administration; Economics; European Union Law; Human Resources; Labour Law; Management; Occupational Health; Social Psychology); **International Business** *(Postgraduate Studies)* (E-Business/Commerce; Finance; International Business; International Law; Marketing); **Project Management** *(Postgraduate Studies)* (Accountancy; Economics; Finance; Human Resources; Information Sciences; Law; Leadership; Management; Marketing; Safety Engineering); **Public Relations and Advertising Management** *(Undergraduate Studies)* (Advertising and Publicity; Marketing; Mass Communication; Psychology; Public Relations); **Public Relations Management** *(Postgraduate Studies)* (Communication Studies; Journalism; Marketing; Political Sciences; Public Relations); **Real Estate Management** *(Foundation Degree)* (Accountancy; Commercial Law; Economics; European Union Law; Finance; Information Technology; Labour Law; Marketing; Real Estate; Statistics); **RISEBA MBA** *(Postgraduate Studies)* (Accountancy; Business Administration; Finance; Human Resources; Management; Marketing); **Work Safety** *(Foundation Degree)* (Occupational Health; Safety Engineering)

Further Information: Also Daugavpils Campus.

History: Founded 1992, acquired present status 2000.

Governing Bodies: Constitutional Assembly

Academic Year: September-mid-January; mid-January-mid-June

Admission Requirements: Depends on course

Fees: (Euro): Undergraduate Studies, 1,550-4,200 per annum; Postgraduate Studies, 2,800-6,840 per programme; Doctorate, 8,100 per programme.

Main Language(s) of Instruction: Latvian, Russian, English

International Co-operation: Wit universities in Austria, Belgium, Czech Republic, Denmark, France, Greece, Georgia, Estonia, Italy, Kazakhstan, Cyprus, Russia, Great Britain, Lithuania, Netherlands, Norway, Poland, Portugal, Romania, Slovakia, Finland, Spain, Switzerland, Turkey, Germany, Sweden. Participates in the Erasmus programme

Accrediting Agencies: Ministry of Education and Science

Degrees and Diplomas: *Diploms par pirmā līmena augstāko profesionālo izglītību*; *Bakalaura diploms*; *Maistra diploms*; *Doktora diploms*. Also MBA.

Student Services: Academic counselling, Canteen, Employment services, Foreign student adviser, Foreign Studies Centre, Handicapped facilities, Language programs, Sports facilities

Libraries: Yes

Last Updated: 03/11/11

SCHOOL OF BUSINESS ADMINISTRATION TURIBA

Biznesa Augstskola Turība (SBAT)
Graudu Str. 68, LV-1058 Rīga
Tel: +371(67) 622-551
Fax: +371(67) 619-152
EMail: turiba@turiba.lv
Website: http://www.turiba.lv

Rector: Antons Kiščenko
Tel: +371(67) 606-100 EMail: antons@turiba.lv

International Relations: Imants Bergs, Vice-Rector
Tel: +371(67) 607-661 EMail: imants.bergs@turiba.lv

Faculties

Business Administration (Accountancy; Advertising and Publicity; Business Administration; Economics; Finance); **International Tourism** *(Tourism and Hospitality Management)* (Hotel Management; Leisure Studies; Public Relations; Tourism); **Law** (Law; Public Administration); **Public Relations** (Public Relations)

History: Founded 1993.

Main Language(s) of Instruction: Latvian, Engish

Degrees and Diplomas: *Diploms par pirmā līmena augstāko profesionālo izglītību*; *Bakalaura diploms*: Business Administration; Law; Tourism and Hospitality Management; *Maistra diploms*: Business Administration; Law; Public Administration; Tourism Strategic Management; Public Relations; *Doktora diploms*: Business Administration; Law; Communication Management. Also MBA

Last Updated: 05/09/11

TRANSPORT AND TELECOMMUNICATION INSTITUTE

Transporta un Sakaru Institūts (TSI)
Lomonosova Street 1, LV-1019 Rīga
Tel: +371(67) 100-661
Fax: +371(67) 100-660
EMail: info@tsi.lv
Website: http://www.tsi.lv

Rector: Boriss Mishnev Tel: +371(67) 100-675 EMail: bfm@tsi.lv

Chancellor: Eugene Kopytov
Tel: +371(67) 100-669 EMail: kopitovj@tsi.lv

Academies

TTI IT (Computer Science; Information Technology)

Campuses

Latgalian (Computer Science; Economics; Information Management; Information Sciences; Management; Transport Management)

Centres

Academic and Professional Aviation Studies *(APAC)* (Air Transport)

Faculties

Computer Science and Electronics (Computer Science; Electronic Engineering; Mathematics; Physics; Software Engineering; Telecommunications Engineering); **Management and Economics** (Aesthetics; Civil Law; Cultural Studies; Economics; English; Ethics; International Law; Labour Law; Law; Linguistics; Management; Philosophy; Political Sciences; Psychology; Social Sciences; Sociology; Taxation)

Programmes

Telematics and Logistics (Telecommunications Engineering; Transport Management); **Transport and Logistics** (Air Transport; Maintenance Technology; Transport and Communications; Transport Management)

Further Information: Also Latgales branch (Daugavpils)

History: Founded 1919. Acquired present status 1999.

Governing Bodies: Senate

Academic Year: September to January; February to June

Admission Requirements: Secondary or Higher School Certificate

Fees: (Euros): 2,000 per annum

Main Language(s) of Instruction: Latvian, Russian, English

International Co-operation: Participates in the Erasmus, Leonardo da Vinci, INTERREG III and FP6 programmes

Accrediting Agencies: Ministry of Education and Science; International Civil Aviation Organization (ICAO), Erasmus University Charter

Degrees and Diplomas: *Diploms par pirmā līmena augstāko profesionālo izglītību*; *Bakalaura diploms*; *Augstākas profesionālas izglītības diploms*; *Maistra diploms*; *Doktora diploms*: Telematics and Logistics. Also Professional Diploma

Student Services: Academic counselling, Canteen, Cultural centre, Foreign student adviser, Health services, Language programs, Social counselling, Sports facilities

Student Residential Facilities: Student hotel

Special Facilities: Museum

Libraries: Yes

Publications: Computer Modelling and New Technologies *(quarterly)*; Transport and Telecommunication *(quarterly)*

Academic Staff *2010-2011*: Total 220

STAFF WITH DOCTORATE: Total 132

Student Numbers *2010-2011*: Total: c. 3,000

Last Updated: 03/11/11

UNIVERSITY COLLEGE OF ECONOMICS AND CULTURE

Ekonomikas un kultūras augstskola (UCEC)
Lomonosova 1, korp. 5, LV-1019 Rīga
Tel: +371 20-00-90-51
Fax: +371(67) 114-111
EMail: administracija@eka.edu.lv
Website: http://www.eka.edu.lv

Rector: Gunta Veismane EMail: gunta.veismane@eka.edu.lv

Vice Rector: Ineta Kristovska
Tel: +371 28-45-10-54 EMail: ineta.kristovska @ eka.edu.lv

International Relations: Zane Veidenberga, Erasmus Coordinator
Tel: +371 20-04-07-87 EMail: zane.veidenberga@eka.edu.lv

Departments

Cultural Management (Cultural Studies; Interior Design; Management; Marketing; Parks and Recreation; Sales Techniques); **Economics** (Accountancy; Administration; Business Administration; Economics; Management); **Foreign Languages** (Modern Languages; Translation and Interpretation)

History: Founded 1998.

International Co-operation: Participates in the Erasmus programme.

Accrediting Agencies: Ministry of Education and Science

Degrees and Diplomas: *Diploms par pirmā līmena augstāko profesionālo izglītību*; *Bakalaura diploms*; *Augstākas profesionālas izglītības diploms*; *Maistra diploms*

Last Updated: 28/10/11

Lebanon

STRUCTURE OF HIGHER EDUCATION SYSTEM

Description:

Higher education in Lebanon is provided by Technical and Vocational Institutes, University Colleges, University Institutes and Universities. Only one of them is a public institution: the Lebanese University. Both the private and public sectors are administrated by the Ministry of Education and Higher Education, Technical and Vocational Institutes are under the Directorate General of Technical and Vocational Education. University Colleges, University Institutes and Universities are under the responsibility of the Directorate General of Higher Education. Admission to higher education institutions is based on the Baccalauréat libanais or equivalent diplomas from other countries.

Stages of studies:

University level first stage:

Some institutions offer short courses (two to three years) leading to professional qualifications. Where longer studies are involved, the first stage leads, after three to five years' study, to the Licence, the Bachelor's degree or a Diploma, depending on the institution attended.

University level second stage:

The second stage involves more specialized work and leads, after one or two years' study beyond the first degree, to the Maîtrise in scientific subjects, the Master's degree at the American University, the Magistère, the Diplôme d'Etudes supérieures, and the Diplôme d'Etudes approfondies. In Medicine, the Medical Doctorate (MD) is awarded after seven years' study. It is a professional qualification.

University level third stage:

The third stage involves the writing of a thesis and leads to the award of a Doctorate. In French-speaking universities, a Doctorate is awarded after three years of study beyond the Diplôme d'Etudes approfondies which is equivalent to the PhDs awarded in the American system.

ADMISSION TO HIGHER EDUCATION

Admission to university-level studies:

Name of secondary school credential required: Baccalauréat général

For entry to: Universities.Minimum requirements: Average 10/20 minimum; Entrance Exam; Some universities like AUB ask for TOEFEL & SAT1 (American system)

Name of secondary school credential required: Baccalauréat technique

For entry to: Average 10/20 for entry to universities in specialties corresponding to those linked to the Baccalauréat technique

Entrance exam requirements: There is an entrance examination for access to some universities.

Foreign students admission:

Quotas: None

Entrance exam requirements: Foreign students are admitted to universities under the same conditions as Lebanese students, provided that they hold a qualification equivalent to the Lebanese Baccalauréat. They are not subject to any special quota system. Scholarships are granted within the framework of bilateral agreements concluded with other countries. In certain universities, students must sit for an entrance examination.

Entry regulations: A visa and resident permit are required.

RECOGNITION OF STUDIES

Quality assurance system:

Technical committee for licensing, starting up programmes and auditing HEIs; Equivalence committee for the recognition of degrees;
Engineering committee for Engineering qualifications; Examinations for all specialties in Health Sciences (MD, Dentistry, Physiotherapy, Nursing, etc.)

Special provisions for recognition:

Recognition for university level studies: Equivalence committee for higher education, MEHE – 6th floor
For access to advanced studies and research: Equivalence committee for higher education, MEHE – 6th floor
For exercising a profession: Equivalence committee for higher education; Examination committees in different sectors of Health Sciences (2 exams per year in July and December); Engineering qualification committee, MEHE – 6th floor

NATIONAL BODIES

Ministry of Education and Higher Education

Minister: Hassan Diab
Habib Abi-chahla Square
UNESCO Palace
Beirut
Tel: +961(1) 789-611
Fax: +961(1) 789-606
EMail: info@higher-edu.gov.lb
WWW: http://www.higher-edu.gov.lb/

Direction générale de l'Enseignement supérieur (Directorate General of Higher Education)

Director-General: Ahmad Jammal
Habib Abi Chahla Street
UNESCO Palace
Beirut
Tel: +961(1) 789 611
Fax: +961(1) 789 606
EMail: info@higher-edu.gov.lb
WWW: http://www.higher-edu.gov.lb
Role of national body: To supervise the activities of higher education institutions in Lebanon and coordinate the activities of:
- the Council of Higher Education;
- the Technical Committee for licensing, starting up & auditing;
- the Equivalence Committee for the recognition of degrees;
- the Colloquium Exams Committees;
- The Engineering qualification recognition Committee.

League of Lebanese Universities

President: Hassan Al Jalabi
Islamic University of Lebanon
Khaldeh, Aley
Role of national body: Association of HEIs

Data for academic year: 2010-2011
Source: IAU from Ministry of Education and Higher Education, Directorate General of Higher Education, Beirut (Lebanon), 2010. Bodies updated 2012.

INSTITUTIONS

PUBLIC INSTITUTION

LEBANESE UNIVERSITY

Al Jamiat Al-Lubnaniya (UL)
Place du Musée, Beirut 14/6573
Tel: +961(1) 612-830
Fax: +961(1) 612-815
EMail: rectorat@ul.edu.lb
Website: http://www.ul.edu.lb

Rector: Zouheir Ali Chokr (2006-)
Tel: +961(1) 612-624, Fax: +961(1) 612-572
EMail: recteur@ul.edu.lb

Senior Administrative Officer: Habib Charouk
Tel: +961(1) 612-577, Fax: +961(1) 612-577
EMail: maslaha@ul.edu.lb

Secretary-General: Mohammad El Baba
Tel: +961(1) 612-618, Fax: +961(1) 612-621
EMail: sgul@ul.edu.lb

International Relations: Bernadette Abi-Saleh
Tel: +961(1) 612-815, Fax: +961(1) 612-815 EMail: bre@ul.edu.lb

Faculties
Agronomy (Agronomy; Animal Husbandry; Food Science; Landscape Architecture; Plant and Crop Protection); **Arts and Humanities** (Ancient Civilizations; Ancient Languages; Applied Linguistics; Arabic; Archaeology; Arts and Humanities; Classical Languages; Comparative Literature; Contemporary History; Dutch; English; Ethics; French; Grammar; Greek; Hebrew; History; Italian; Latin; Logic; Medieval Studies; Metaphysics; Modern History; Modern Languages; Philology; Philosophical Schools; Philosophy; Phonetics; Prehistory; Psycholinguistics; Terminology; Translation and Interpretation; Turkish); **Economics and Business Administration** (Accountancy; Business Administration; Business Computing; Economics; Finance; Marketing); **Education** (Art Education; Education; Foreign Languages Education; Higher Education; Literacy Education; Music Education; Native Language; Pedagogy; Preschool Education; Primary Education; Science Education; Secondary Education; Teacher Trainers Education; Teacher Training); **Engineering** (Automation and Control Engineering; Bridge Engineering; Construction Engineering; Electrical Engineering; Electronic Engineering; Energy Engineering; Engineering; Geological Engineering; Hydraulic Engineering; Industrial Engineering; Laser Engineering; Machine Building; Measurement and Precision Engineering; Mechanical Engineering; Metallurgical Engineering; Microelectronics; Microwaves; Power Engineering; Production Engineering; Road Engineering; Safety Engineering; Telecommunications Engineering; Transport Engineering); **Information and Documentation** (Archiving; Communication Studies; Documentation Techniques; Information Management; Information Technology; Journalism; Library Science; Multimedia; Radio and Television Broadcasting); **Law, Political Science and Management** (Administration; Administrative Law; Air and Space Law; Civil Law; Commercial Law; Comparative Law; Constitutional Law; Criminal Law; Fiscal Law; History of Law; Human Rights; International Law; Islamic Law; Justice Administration; Labour Law; Law; Management; Maritime Law; Political Sciences; Private Law; Public Law); **Medicine** (Anaesthesiology; Cardiology; Diabetology; Endocrinology; Epidemiology; Gastroenterology; Gynaecology and Obstetrics; Medicine; Nephrology; Neurology; Oncology; Ophthalmology; Orthopaedics; Otorhinolaryngology; Paediatrics; Parasitology; Pathology; Plastic Surgery; Pneumology; Psychiatry and Mental Health; Radiology; Rheumatology; Surgery; Urology); **Pharmacy** (Pharmacy); **Public Health** (Community Health; Ergotherapy; Midwifery; Nursing; Occupational Therapy; Physical Therapy; Public Health; Social and Community Services; Social Welfare; Social Work; Speech Therapy and Audiology); **Science** (Analytical Chemistry; Anatomy; Biochemistry; Biological and Life Sciences; Biology; Botany; Chemistry; Computer Science; Crystallography; Earth Sciences; Embryology and Reproduction Biology; Entomology; Genetics; Geology; Histology; Immunology; Industrial Chemistry; Inorganic Chemistry; Marine Biology; Mathematical Physics; Mathematics; Mechanics; Microbiology; Mineralogy; Natural Sciences; Neurosciences; Optics; Organic Chemistry; Paleontology; Parasitology; Physical Chemistry; Physics; Plant Pathology; Statistics; Zoology); **Tourism and Hospitality Management** (Cooking and Catering; Hotel and Restaurant; Hotel Management; Sales Techniques; Tourism)

Institutes
Fine Arts (Acting; Architecture; Fine Arts; Interior Design; Painting and Drawing; Rural Planning; Theatre; Town Planning); **Social Sciences** (Social Sciences); **Technology** (Bridge Engineering; Civil Engineering; Computer Networks; Construction Engineering; Electrical and Electronic Engineering; Geological Engineering; Industrial Engineering; Road Engineering; Technology; Telecommunications Engineering; Transport Engineering)

Schools
Dentistry (Dental Hygiene; Dentistry; Oral Pathology; Orthodontics; Periodontics; Stomatology)

History: Founded 1951 as teacher training college, reorganized by decree as university 1953. An autonomous State institution under the responsibility of the Minister of Education. Financially supported by the State.

Governing Bodies: University Council

Academic Year: September to July

Admission Requirements: Secondary school certificate (baccalauréat) or recognized equivalent

Fees: (Lebanese Pounds): Registration: c. 250,000

Main Language(s) of Instruction: Arabic, French, English

International Co-operation: With universities in France, Italy; Belgium; Canada; Syria; Egypt

Degrees and Diplomas: *Licence*: 4 yrs; *Diplôme d'Etudes supérieures*: a further 2 yrs; *Diplôme d'Ingénieur*: 5 yrs; *Maîtrise*; *Diplôme d'Etudes approfondies*: a further 1 1/2-2 yrs; *Diplôme de Doctorat*: 3-5 yrs

Student Services: Canteen, Social counselling

Student Residential Facilities: Yes

Libraries: Central Library; libraries of the Faculties of Science, and Law, c. 20,000-30,000 vols each
Last Updated: 12/12/11

PRIVATE INSTITUTIONS

AL IMAM AL OUZAI UNIVERSITY

Jamiat Al-imam Al-Ouzai
PO Box 14-5355, Avenue al-Malaab Al Baladi, Beirut 2802 1105
Tel: +961(1) 704-454
Fax: +961(1) 704-453
EMail: islamic-studies@ouzai.org
Website: http://www.ouzai.org

President and Chairman, Board of Trustees: Toufic Al-Houri
Tel: +961(1) 311-831, Fax: +961(1) 704-449
EMail: houri@wakf.org

International Relations: Munir Saaddine, Director of International Relations
Tel: +961(3) 815-832, Fax: +961(1) 632-083
EMail: library@ouzai.org

Faculties
Islamic Business Administration (Business Administration); **Islamic Studies** (Arabic; Ethics; European Languages; History; Islamic Law; Islamic Studies; Koran)

Institutes
Supervision of Food Products (Food Science)

History: Founded 1979 as Al Imam Al Ouzai College for Islamic Studies. Acquired present status and title 1986.

Degrees and Diplomas: *Bachelor's Degree*; *Master's Degree*; *Doctorate*

Student Numbers *2008-2009*: Total 4,595
Last Updated: 21/10/09

AL-KAFAAT UNIVERSITY

Maahad al kafaat al jamee (AKI)

Ain Saade, Mount Lebanon
Tel: +961(1) 872-225
Fax: +961(1) 872-230
EMail: info@aku.edu.lb
Website: http://www.aku.edu.lb

President: Fathi Oueida

Faculties

Education (Community Health; Education; Gerontology; Preschool Education; Primary Education; Special Education); **Fine Arts and Advertising** (Advertising and Publicity; Cinema and Television; Interior Design; Marketing; Radio and Television Broadcasting; Theatre)

Institutes

Technology (Accountancy; Electronic Engineering; Food Technology; Hotel Management; Management; Mechanical Engineering)

History: Founded 1999.

Degrees and Diplomas: *Diplôme universitaire de Technologie*; *Licence*; *Maîtrise*

Student Residential Facilities: Yes

Libraries: Yes

Last Updated: 13/12/11

AL-MANAR UNIVERSITY OF TRIPOLI

Jamiat al-manar (MUT)

PO Box 676, Al-Manar Boulevard, Abou Samra, Tripoli, Abou Samra
Tel: +961(6) 426-800 +961(6) 426-801 +961(6) 426-802
Fax: +961(6) 426-803
EMail: info@mut.edu.lb
Website: http://www.mut.edu.lb

President: Sami Menkara EMail: s.menkara@mut.edu.lb

Faculties

Architecture and Design (Architecture; Fine Arts; Furniture Design; Graphic Design; Industrial Design; Interior Design; Photography); **Arts and Human Sciences** (Arabic; English; French; Literature; Philosophy; Primary Education; Psychology; Sociology; Translation and Interpretation); **Business Administration** (Accountancy; Banking; Economics; Finance; Information Management; Management; Marketing; Tourism); **Engineering and Information Technology** (Biomedical Engineering; Computer Engineering; Computer Networks; Computer Science; Electronic Engineering; Industrial Engineering; Information Technology; Telecommunications Engineering); **Public Health** (Nursing; Nutrition; Public Health; Speech Therapy and Audiology); **Science** (Biology; Chemistry; Mathematics; Physics)

Further Information: Also special programmes: Freshman programme; Intensive English Programme (IEP)

History: Founded 1990, courses started 2003.

Governing Bodies: Board of Trustees

Admission Requirements: Secondary school certificate (Lebanese Baccalaureate or equivalent); and TOFEL or SAT or MUT English entrance examination or equivalent; For Engineering Students, Mathematics and Physics entrance exams

Fees: (Lebanese Pounds): 6.6m. per annum (fall and spring semesters only)

Main Language(s) of Instruction: English

Degrees and Diplomas: *Bachelor's Degree*: Business Administration; Information Technology; Public Health; Design; Arts and Human Sciences; Science (BBA; BS; BFA; BA), 3 yrs; *Bachelor's Degree*: Engineering; Architecture; Agricultural Engineering (BE; B Arch), 5 yrs; *Master's Degree*: Business Administration

Student Services: Academic counselling, Employment services, Handicapped facilities, Language programs, Social counselling

Student Residential Facilities: None

Libraries: Main Library

Publications: MUT Quarterly

Last Updated: 20/10/09

AMERICAN UNIVERSITY OF BEIRUT (AUB)

PO Box 11-0236, Riad El Solh, Beirut 1107 2020
Tel: +961(1) 350-000
Fax: +961(1) 351-706
EMail: information@aub.edu.lb
Website: http://www.aub.edu.lb

President: Peter Dorman (2008-)
Tel: +961(1) 347-127, Fax: +961(1) 744-474
EMail: pdorman@aub.edu.lb

Provost: Ahmad Dallal Tel: +961(1) 340-619

Centres

Advanced Mathematical Sciences *(CAMS)* (Mathematics); **Agricultural Research and Education** *(AREC)* (Agriculture; Landscape Architecture); **Arab and Middle Eastern Studies** *(CAMES)* (Arabic; Middle Eastern Studies); **Behavioural Research** *(CBR)* (Arts and Humanities; Behavioural Sciences; Social Sciences); **Central Research Science Lab** *(Kamal A. Shair)*; **Research on Population and Health** *(CRPH)* (Demography and Population; Health Sciences); **Science and Mathematics Education** *(SMEC)* (Mathematics Education; Natural Sciences); **Teaching and Learning** *(CTL)*

Faculties

Agriculture and Food Science *(Beirut, Bekaa'a Valley)* (Agricultural Economics; Agriculture; Dietetics; Food Science; Irrigation; Landscape Architecture; Nutrition; Soil Science; Zoology); **Arts and Science** (Anthropology; Arabic; Archaeology; Art History; Arts and Humanities; Behavioural Sciences; Biology; Chemistry; Computer Science; Economics; Education; English; Fine Arts; Geology; History; Mathematics; Middle Eastern Studies; Philosophy; Physics; Political Sciences; Psychology; Public Administration; Social Sciences; Sociology); **Engineering and Architecture** (Architecture; Civil Engineering; Computer Engineering; Electrical Engineering; Engineering; Environmental Engineering; Graphic Design; Mechanical Engineering); **Health Sciences** (Demography and Population; Environmental Studies; Epidemiology; Health Administration; Health Education; Health Sciences; Laboratory Techniques; Public Health); **Medicine** (Anatomy; Biochemistry; Gynaecology and Obstetrics; Immunology; Medicine; Microbiology; Ophthalmology; Orthodontics; Paediatrics; Pathology; Pharmacology; Physiology; Psychiatry and Mental Health; Surgery)

Institutes

Financial Economics *(IFE)* (Economics; Finance)

Schools

Business *(Suleiman Olayan School)* (Business Administration); **Nursing** *(Rafic Hariri)* (Nursing)

Units

Environment and Sustainable Development *(ESDU)* (Environmental Studies)

History: Founded 1866 as Syrian Protestant College with School of Medicine added 1867 and Pharmacy 1871. Rechartered as American University of Beirut 1920. Institutional Accreditation granted 2004. A private non-denominational institution under charter from the educational authorities of the State of New York, USA, with a self-perpetuating Board of Trustees. Supported by fees, income from an endowment, and private gifts and donations. No organic relationship with any government, religious body, etc. [Mailing address: U.S. Office: 3 Dag Hammarskjold Plaza (8th Floor), New York, NY 10017-2303 Second Av. And 47th Str.USA].

Governing Bodies: Board of Trustees

Academic Year: September to June (September-February; February-June)

Admission Requirements: Graduation from high school, or secondary school certificate, recognized by the University, and entrance examination including SAT and English language proficiency test such as TOEFL

Fees: (US Dollars): 8,000-20,000 per annum depending on programme

Main Language(s) of Instruction: English

Accrediting Agencies: Middle States Commission on Higher Education.

Degrees and Diplomas: *Bachelor's Degree*: All fields, 4-6 yrs; *Professional Doctorate*: Medicine (MD), 8 yrs; *Master's Degree*: All fields, 1-3 yrs following Bachelor; *Doctorate (PhD)*. Also Teaching Diploma

Student Services: Academic counselling, Canteen, Cultural centre, Employment services, Foreign student adviser, Handicapped facilities, Health services, Language programs, Social counselling, Sports facilities

Special Facilities: Archaeology Museum; Geology Museum; Herbarium; Bird Collection

Libraries: University Libraries (includes the Jafet Memorial Library), Saab Memorial Medical Library.Total, c. 607,408 vols; about 21,228 e-journals in 107 databases. 2,457 periodical titles (207 in Arabic); 1,151,409 Audiovisual items (microforms, local and regional newspapers); Archives and Special Collections: 1,392 manuscripts, 13,300 vols of theses, projects and dissertations, 39,139 photographs, 5,858 posters, and 1,845 maps. The libraries are fully automated

Publications: Arab Political Documents *(annually)*; Berytus, Archaeological Studies *(annually)*

Press or Publishing House: Office of University Publications

Last Updated: 12/12/11

AMERICAN UNIVERSITY OF CULTURE AND EDUCATION

Badaro, Beirut
Tel: +961(5) 467-346
Fax: +961(5) 467-348
EMail: info@auce.edu.lb
Website: http://auce.edu.lb

President: Pierre Gedeon

Academies

Hospitality *(International)* (Cooking and Catering; Hotel Management; Human Resources; Tourism); **Information Technology** (Information Technology)

Faculties

Arts and Science (Computer Science; English; Literature; Translation and Interpretation); **Business** (Accountancy; Advertising and Publicity; Banking; Business Administration; Finance; Human Resources; Information Management; Marketing; Tourism; Transport Management); **Fine Arts** (Fine Arts; Graphic Design; Interior Design)

History: Founded 1983 as C&E College. Acquired present status and title 2000.

Degrees and Diplomas: *Bachelor's Degree*; *Master's Degree*

Last Updated: 12/12/11

AMERICAN UNIVERSITY OF SCIENCE AND TECHNOLOGY (AUST)

Ave. Alfred Naccache, Ashrafieh, Beirut
Tel: +961(1) 218-716
Fax: +961(1) 339-302
EMail: info@aust.edu.lb
Website: http://www.aust.edu.lb

President: Hiam Sakr (2005-)
Tel: +961(1) 666-384, Fax: +961(1) 203-921
EMail: hiamsakr@aust.edu.lb

Provost; Vice President for Institutional Advancement: Nabeel Haidar
Tel: +961(1) 698-688, Fax: +961(1) 203-921
EMail: nhaidar@aust.edu.lb

Schools

Arts and Science (Arts and Humanities; Biomedical Engineering; Communication Arts; Computer Engineering; Computer Science; Fine Arts; Graphic Design; Interior Design; Mathematics; Molecular Biology; Social Sciences; Toxicology; Translation and Interpretation); **Business and Economics** (Accountancy; Advertising and Publicity; Business Administration; Finance; Management; Marketing; Tourism); **Health Sciences** (Medical Technology; Molecular Biology; Optics; Optometry; Toxicology)

Further Information: Also Zahle and Sidon campuses

History: Founded 1989 as the American Universal College. Acquired present title and status 2007.

Main Language(s) of Instruction: English and French

Degrees and Diplomas: *Bachelor's Degree*; *Master's Degree*

Last Updated: 12/12/11

AMERICAN UNIVERSITY OF TECHNOLOGY (AUT)

Halat-Byblos Highway Fidar, Halat, Mount Lebanon
Tel: +961(9) 478-143
Fax: +961(9) 478-146
EMail: mail@aut.edu
Website: http://www.aut.edu.lb

President: Ghada Sakr Hinain (2000-)
Tel: +961(9) 478-144, Fax: +961(9) 478-310
EMail: ghada.hinain@aut.edu

Director, External Relations: Marcel Hinain
Tel: +961(3) 242-892 EMail: marcel.hinain@aut.edu

Faculties

Applied Sciences (Business Computing; Computer Science; Information Technology; Nutrition; Water Management); **Arts and Humanities** (Communication Arts; Graphic Design; Interior Design; Public Relations; Radio and Television Broadcasting); **Business Administration** (Accountancy; Advertising and Publicity; Banking; Business Administration; Economics; Finance; Hotel Management; Human Resources; Management; Marketing; Tourism)

History: Founded 2000.

Governing Bodies: Board of Trustees; Board of Directors

Academic Year: October to June

Admission Requirements: High school (G12) for Freshman; Baccalaureate for Sophomore admission

Fees: (US Dollars): 1,800 per semester

Main Language(s) of Instruction: English

International Co-operation: With universities in USA, Greece, Germany and Czech Republic

Accrediting Agencies: Ministry of Higher Education

Degrees and Diplomas: *Bachelor's Degree*: Business Administration; Graphic Design; Interior Design; Communication Arts; Computer Science; Computer Engineering (BBA; BA; BS), 3-4 yrs; *Master's Degree*: Business Administration; Computer Science; Marketing; Finance (MBA; MS), 2 yrs

Student Services: Academic counselling, Canteen, Employment services, Foreign student adviser, Language programs, Social counselling, Sports facilities

Student Residential Facilities: Yes (dormitories)

Special Facilities: Movie Studio; Computer Laboratory; Telecommunication Laboratory

Libraries: E-library access

Last Updated: 30/09/10

ANTONINE UNIVERSITY

Université Antonine (UPA)
Hadath - Baabda 40016
Tel: +961(5) 924-073 +961(5) 924-074
Fax: +961(5) 924-814 +961(5) 924-815
EMail: contact@upa.edu.lb
Website: http://www.upa.edu.lb

Rector: Germanos Germanos
Tel: +961(5) 924-076 EMail: recteur@upa.edu.lb

Secretary-General: Joe Abou Jaoud
Tel: +961(5) 924-073 EMail: sec.general@upa.edu.lb

Centres

Languages and Resources *(CLER)*

Faculties

Advertising and Media Studies *(Zahleh - Bekaa)* (Advertising and Publicity; Cinema and Television; Communication Studies; Graphic Design; Photography; Printing and Printmaking; Public Relations; Radio and Television Broadcasting); **Business Administration** (Accountancy; Banking; Finance; Information Management; Insurance; Management; Marketing; Tourism); **Engineering** *(Zahle-Bekaa)* (Computer Engineering; Computer Networks; Engineering; Multimedia; Telecommunications Engineering); **Public Health** (Nursing; Physical Therapy; Public Health); **Theological Science and Pastoral Studies** *(Other section in Zghorta-North)* (Pastoral Studies; Religion; Theology)

Higher Institutes

Music (Music)

Institutes

Dental Laboratory (Dental Technology; Laboratory Techniques)

Programmes

Continuing Education (Computer Networks; Dental Technology; Sports)

Schools

Music *(Antonine Fathers)* (Music)

Further Information: Also Campus in Zahlé-Békaa.

History: Founded 1996. A private institution under the supervision of the Antonin Maronite Order.

Governing Bodies: Board of Trustees; Antonine Council of the UPA; University Administration Council

Admission Requirements: Secondary school certificate (baccalauréat); Language Evaluation Test

Fees: (US Dollars): 1,000-5,000 per annum

Main Language(s) of Instruction: Arabic, French, English

International Co-operation: With universities in France, Belgium, Italy, Canada and USA

Accrediting Agencies: Lebanese Government

Degrees and Diplomas: *Bachelor's Degree*: Business Administration; Advertising; Computer Science; Telecommunication and Multimedia; Dental Prosthetics; Nursing, 3 yrs minimum; *Bachelor's Degree*: Physical Therapy, 4 yrs; *Licence*; *Diplôme d'Ingénieur*, *Maîtrise*; *Teaching Diploma*: Physical Education and Sports; Music; Theology, 4 yrs; *Master's Degree*: 5 yrs; *Master's Degree*: Theology, Ecumenical/Biblical and Religious Studies; Nursing; Advertising; Music; Physical Education and Sports, 2 yrs

Student Services: Academic counselling, Canteen, Cultural centre, Employment services, Foreign student adviser, Foreign Studies Centre, Handicapped facilities, Health services, Language programs, Nursery care, Social counselling, Sports facilities

Student Residential Facilities: Yes

Libraries: c. 100,000 vols; Internet; CD Roms

Press or Publishing House: Presses Universitaires Antonines

Last Updated: 12/12/11

ARAB OPEN UNIVERSITY - LEBANON BRANCH (AOU)

Omar Bayhoum street, Park Sector, Beirut
Tel: +961(1) 39-21-39
Fax: +961(1) 39-21-46
EMail: admin@aou.edu.lb
Website: http://www.aou.edu.lb

Branch Director: Fayrouz Farah Sarkis Tel: +961(3) 76-14-61

Faculties

Business Studies (Accountancy; Business Administration; Business Education; Economics; Marketing); **Computer Studies** (Business Computing; Computer Science; Information Technology); **Education** (Education; Primary Education); **English Studies** (English Studies)

History: Founded 2002. A private accredited Institution-subsidiary of Open University in Britain

Governing Bodies: Board of Trustees; University Council

Admission Requirements: Secondary school certificate or equivalent

Fees: (US Dollars): 1,500

Main Language(s) of Instruction: English; Arabic

International Co-operation: With Open University in United Kingdom

Accrediting Agencies: Lebanese Governement and OUVS (Open University Validating Services)

Degrees and Diplomas: *Bachelor's Degree*: Business Administration; Computer Science; English Language, 3 yrs; *Master's Degree*: Business Administration; English; Literature, 2 yrs. Also Postgraduate Diploma in Education

Student Services: Academic counselling, Cultural centre, Employment services, Foreign student adviser, Health services, Sports facilities

Special Facilities: Research centres; Cafeteria

Libraries: c. 100,000 vols; e-library, CD Roms

Last Updated: 12/12/11

ARTS, SCIENCE AND TECHNOLOGY UNIVERSITY LEBANON

University Building, Commodore Street, Hamra, Beirut
Tel: +961 (01) 34 32 22
Fax: +961 (01) 34 02 19
EMail: info@aul.edu.lb
Website: http://www.aul.edu.lb

President: Adnan Hamzeh

Faculties

Arts and Humanities (Anthropology; Communication Studies; Literature; Performing Arts; Religious Studies; Sociology); **Business Administration** (Accountancy; Advertising and Publicity; Banking; Business Administration; Finance; Management; Marketing); **Science and Fine Arts** (Biology; Chemistry; Computer Science; Environmental Studies; Graphic Design; Interior Design; Mathematics; Physics; Statistics)

History: Founded 2000 as Institute of Management and University Computer Science. Acquired present title and status 2007.

Main Language(s) of Instruction: English and French

Degrees and Diplomas: *Bachelor's Degree*; *Master's Degree*

Libraries: Yes

Last Updated: 30/09/10

BEIRUT ARAB UNIVERSITY

Jamiat Bâyrut Al-Arabiya (BAU)

PO Box 11-5020, Riad El Solh, Beirut 1107 2809
Tel: +961(1) 300-110
Fax: +961(1) 818-402
EMail: bau@bau.edu.lb
Website: http://www.bau.edu.lb

President: Amr Galal El-Adawi (2006-)
Tel: +961(1) 818-297 EMail: president@bau.edu.lb

Director, Head of Public Relations: Zina Ariss
Tel: +961(1) 300-110 ext 2445 EMail: public-relations@bau.edu.lb

International Relations: Mohamed Raslan, Dean, Scientific Research and International Relations
Tel: +961(1) 300-110 Ext. 2241 EMail: raslan@bau.edu.lb

Faculties

Architectural Engineering (Structural Architecture); **Arts** (Arabic; English; French; Geography; History; Literature; Mass Communication; Philosophy; Psychology; Sociology); **Commerce and Business Administration** (Accountancy; Banking; Economics; Finance; Management; Taxation); **Dentistry** (Dentistry; Oral Pathology; Orthodontics; Surgery); **Engineering** (Civil Engineering; Computer Engineering; Electrical Engineering; Electronic Engineering; Engineering; Environmental Engineering; Industrial Engineering; Industrial Management; Mechanical Engineering; Power Engineering); **Health Sciences** (Laboratory Techniques; Medical Technology; Nursing; Nutrition; Physical Therapy); **Law and Political Science** (Law; Political Sciences); **Medicine** (Medicine; Surgery); **Pharmacy** (Pharmacy); **Science** (Biology; Biotechnology; Chemistry; Computer Science; Environmental Studies; Information Technology; Mathematics; Physics)

History: Founded 1960 by the Lebanese El-Bir and El-Ihsan Society.

Governing Bodies: University Higher Council; University Council

Academic Year: Three semesters: Autumn, Spring, Summer

Admission Requirements: Secondary school certificate (baccalauréat) or equivalent; some faculties require entrance examinations.

Fees: (US Dollars): c. 2,000-11,000 per annum

Main Language(s) of Instruction: Arabic, English, French

International Co-operation: With local Lebanese Universities, also with universities in Egypt, France, Sweden, Italy, Turkey, Euro-Mediterranean area. Also cooperation with various international associations and organisations.

Degrees and Diplomas: *Bachelor's Degree*: Arts; Law and Political Science; Commerce and Business Administration; Sciences; Health Sciences, 4 yrs; *Bachelor's Degree*: Engineering; Architecture; Pharmacy; Dentistry, 5 yrs; *Bachelor's Degree*: Medicine, 6 yrs (plus 1yr residency); *Master's Degree*: a further 2-3 yrs; *Doctorate (PhD)*: a further 3 yrs

Student Services: Academic counselling, Canteen, Employment services, Foreign student adviser, Health services, Language programs, Social counselling, Sports facilities

Student Residential Facilities: Yes

Special Facilities: Architectural Museum Gallery; Medical Museum; Pharmacy Museum; Academic Development and Quality Assurance Center; Center for Consultation; Media Center; Human Rights Center; Language Center; Entrepreneurship Center

Libraries: Central Library, Faculty Libraries

Publications: Architecture and Planning Journal *(annually)*; Journal of Human Sciences *(biannually)*; Revue des Etudes Juridiques *(biannually)*

Student Numbers *2012-2013*: Total: c. 11,000

Last Updated: 11/03/13

BEIRUT ISLAMIC UNIVERSITY

Jamiat Bayrut al islamiyyah (BIU)

Dar El–Fatwa – Zyadyé, Beirut
Tel: +961(1) 797-602
Fax: +961(1) 790-667
EMail: info@biu.edu.lb
Website: http://www.biu.edu.lb

President: Mohamad Rachid Kabbani

Faculties

Islamic Sharia (Islamic Law; Islamic Studies)

History: Founded 1986 as Faculty of the Islamic Call. Acquired present status and title 1996.

Main Language(s) of Instruction: Arabic

Degrees and Diplomas: *Licence*; *Magistère*; *Doctorate*

Last Updated: 03/10/08

BUSINESS HIGHER SCHOOL

Ecole supérieure des Affaires (ESA)

Rue Clémenceau, Beirut
Tel: +961(1) 373-373
Fax: +961(1) 383-374
EMail: esainfo@esa.edu.lb
Website: http://www.esa.edu.lb

Directeur général: Stéphane Attali EMail: attali.s@esa.edu.lb

Institutes

Financial and Monetary Studies (Banking; Finance)

Programmes

Business Studies (Business and Commerce; Finance; Health Administration; Management)

History: Founded 1996 by the French and Lebanese Governments. Instituted by Decree no 9033.

Main Language(s) of Instruction: French

Degrees and Diplomas: *Master's Degree*: Business Administration; Executive Business Administration; Marketing; Finance; Hospital and Health Management. Also Master and Mastère de spécialisation

Last Updated: 20/10/09

DAAWA UNIVERSITY INSTITUTE FOR ISLAMIC STUDIES

Maahad al daawa al jamee lldrasat al islamih (DAAWA CIS)

Beirut
Tel: +961(1) 854-069
Fax: +961(1) 854-072

President: Abdel Naser Jabri (1999-)

International Relations: Majed Oueini, Secretary-General

Programmes

Arabic (Arabic); **Islamic Studies** (Islamic Studies)

History: Founded 1999. Affiliated to the Centre of Religion Endowment.

Admission Requirements: Lebanese Baccalauréat or equivalent

Main Language(s) of Instruction: Arabic

Accrediting Agencies: Ministry of Higher Education

Degrees and Diplomas: *Licence*; *Magistère*

Student Services: Canteen, Sports facilities

Libraries: Yes

Last Updated: 24/02/09

GLOBAL UNIVERSITY

Al Jamiaa Al Aalamia (GU)

Batrakieh Street, Beirut 15-5085
Tel: +961(1) 358-058
Fax: +961(1) 358-059
EMail: info@gu.edu.lb
Website: http://www.gu.edu.lb

President: Adnan Traboulsi (1992-)
Tel: +961(3) 725-680, Fax: +961(1) 358-059
EMail: atraboulsi@gu.edu.lb

Vice-President, Administrative and Financial Affairs: Ghaleb El Araissi
Tel: +961(1) 358-058 ext 4001, Fax: +961(1) 358-059
EMail: garaissi@gu.edu.lb

International Relations: Ahmad Shatila, International Relations Officer
Tel: +961(1) 358-058 ext 4045, Fax: +961(1) 358-059
EMail: ashatila@gu.edu.lb

Faculties

Administrative Sciences (Accountancy; Business Administration; Computer Science; Finance; Health Administration; Human Resources; Information Management; Information Sciences; Information Technology; Management; Marketing); **Health Sciences** (Dietetics; Health Sciences; Laboratory Techniques; Midwifery; Nursing; Nutrition; Physical Therapy); **Literature and Humanities** (Arabic; Communication Studies; Education; English; French; Geography; History; Islamic Studies; Linguistics; Literature; Media Studies; Political Sciences; Translation and Interpretation)

History: Created 1992. Acquired current status and title 1999.

Academic Year: October to September (autumn semester, 4 months, spring semester, 4 months, summer semester, 2 months)

Admission Requirements: Baccalauréat libanais (or equivalent secondary school diploma).

Fees: (Lebanese Pounds): 3m. per semester, autumn and spring; 1m. summer semester

Main Language(s) of Instruction: English, some Arabic

International Co-operation: With institutions in Lebanon, Egypt, Greece, Syria,Tunisia, Morocco

Accrediting Agencies: Association of Arab Universities (AARU); Ministry of Higher Education of Lebanon

Degrees and Diplomas: *Bachelor's Degree*: Business Management; Marketing; Accounting; Human Resource; Management Information Systems; Health Management Information Systems; Information Technology; Computer Science; Education, 3 yrs;

Bachelor's Degree: Translation and Linguistics; Press and Media, 4 yrs; *Master's Degree*: Business Administration; Arabic Language and Literature; Islamic Studies; 2-3 yrs; *Doctorate*: Education; Translation and Linguistics; Islamic Studies; Arabic Language and Literature (PhD), 3 yrs

Student Services: Academic counselling, Canteen, Cultural centre, Employment services, Foreign student adviser, Foreign Studies Centre, Handicapped facilities, Health services, Language programs, Nursery care, Social counselling, Sports facilities

Student Residential Facilities: Yes

Libraries: Two major libraries with electronic resources.
Last Updated: 06/08/09

HAIGAZIAN UNIVERSITY

Jamiat Haikazian (HU)
PO Box 11-1748, Riad el Sohl, Beirut 11072090
Tel: +961(1) 349-230 +961(1) 353-010
Fax: +961(1) 353-012
Website: http://www.haigazian.edu.lb

President: Paul Haidostian
Tel: +961(1) 739-412, Fax: +961(1) 350-926
EMail: president@haigazian.edu.lb

International Relations: Roubina Artinian, Registrar
EMail: rartinian@haigazian.edu.lb

Faculties

Business Administration and Economics (Accountancy; Advertising and Publicity; Business Administration; Economics; Finance; Hotel Management; Law; Management Systems); **Humanities** (Arabic; Armenian; English; History; Literature; Music; Philosophy; Religion); **Science** (Biology; Chemistry; Computer Science; Mathematics; Medical Technology; Physics); **Social and Behavioural Sciences** (Behavioural Sciences; Christian Religious Studies; Education; Political Sciences; Psychology; Social Sciences; Social Work)

History: Founded 1955, acquired present status 1996.

Governing Bodies: Board of Trustees; Faculty Assembly

Academic Year: October to June (October-February; February-June)

Admission Requirements: Secondary school certificate (baccalauréat). TOEFL test for all students

Fees: (Lebanese Pounds): 9,450,000 per annum (US Dollars, 6,300)

Main Language(s) of Instruction: English

International Co-operation: Member of the Association of American International Colleges and Universities (AAICU)

Accrediting Agencies: Lebanese Government

Degrees and Diplomas: *Bachelor's Degree*: Arabic (BA); Armenian Studies (BA); Biology (BS); Business Administration (BA); Chemistry (BS); *Bachelor's Degree*: Christian Education (Religion and Philosophy) (BA); Computer Science (BS); Economics (BA); Education (BA); English (BA); History (BA); Mathematics (BS); Medical Laboratory Sciences (BS); Music (BA); Physics (BS); Political Science (BA); Psychology (BA); Social Work (BA), 3-4 yrs; *Master's Degree*: Business Administration (MBA); Education (MA); Psychology (MA), 2 yrs. Normal Diploma

Student Services: Academic counselling, Cultural centre, Foreign student adviser, Health services, Social counselling, Sports facilities

Student Residential Facilities: None

Special Facilities: Art Gallery. Media Centre

Libraries: General English Library; Special Armenian Library
Last Updated: 13/12/11

HARIRI CANADIAN UNIVERSITY

Moujamaa al Hariri al Kanadi (HCU)
P.O. Box: 10 Damour – Chouf 2010, Al Mishrief
Tel: +961(5) 603-090
Fax: +961(5) 601-380
EMail: info@hcu.edu.lb
Website: http://www.hcu.edu.lb

President: Abdul Rahman Arkadan (2004-)

Colleges

Business Administration (Accountancy; Business Administration; Business Computing; Finance; Management; Marketing); **Engineering** (Civil Engineering; Computer Engineering; Electrical Engineering; Electronic Engineering; Environmental Engineering; Mechanical Engineering); **Science and Information Systems** (Computer Graphics; Computer Science; Software Engineering)

Departments

Languages and Humanities (English)

History: Founded 1999. Acquired present status 2006.

Degrees and Diplomas: *Bachelor's Degree*; *Master's Degree*

Libraries: Yes
Last Updated: 13/12/11

HOLY FAMILY UNIVERSITY INSTITUTE OF PHYSIOTHERAPY

Institut universitaire Sainte Famille de Physiothérapie
Batroun, North Lebanon
Tel: +961(6) 642-250
Fax: +961(6) 743-154
EMail: iussbat@inco.com.lb

President: Hilda Chlala

Programmes

Nursing (Nursing); **Physiotherapy** (Physical Therapy)

History: Founded 2000.

Main Language(s) of Instruction: French

Degrees and Diplomas: *Licence*: 4 yrs
Last Updated: 30/09/10

HOLY SPIRIT UNIVERSITY OF KASLIK

Université Saint-Esprit de Kaslik
PO Box 446, Jounieh
Tel: +961(9) 600-000
Fax: +961(9) 600-100
EMail: rectorat@usek.edu.lb; usek@usek.edu.lb
Website: http://www.usek.edu.lb

Recteur: P. Hady Mahfouz (2007-) EMail: rectorat@usek.edu.lb

Secretary General: Marwan Azar EMail: sgeneral@usek.edu.lb

International Relations: Youssef Tannous, Vice Recteur aux relations internationales et à la recherche
EMail: bri@usek.edu.lb; usek@usek.edu.lb

Centres

Research

Colleges

Doctoral Studies (Arts and Humanities; Business and Commerce; Fine Arts; Music; Philosophy; Theology)

Faculties

Agricultural Sciences (Agriculture; Dietetics; Food Science; Food Technology; Nutrition); **Business and Commercial Sciences** (Accountancy; Business Computing; Finance; Hotel and Restaurant; Hotel Management; Information Technology; International Business; Management; Marketing; Transport Management); **Engineering** (Chemical Engineering; Computer Engineering; Electrical Engineering; Electronic Engineering; Mechanical Engineering; Telecommunications Engineering); **Fine and Applied Arts** (Architecture; Fine Arts; Graphic Design; Interior Design; Performing Arts; Religious Art; Theatre; Visual Arts); **Law** (Commercial Law; International Law; Law; Private Law; Public Law); **Letters** (Arabic; Business and Commerce; Communication Studies; English; French; Journalism; Literature; Modern Languages; Translation and Interpretation); **Medicine and Medical Sciences** (Medicine); **Music** (Music; Music Education; Music Theory and Composition; Musicology; Religious Music; Singing); **Philosophy and Humanities** (Clinical Psychology; Education; Educational Psychology; Educational Technology; Industrial and Organizational Psychology; Philosophy; Psychology; Social Sciences); **Science** (Biological and Life Sciences; Chemistry; Computer Science; Mathematics; Technology); **Theology** *(Pontifical)* (Family Studies; Pastoral Studies; Religion; Religious Studies; Theology)

Institutes

History (Archaeology; Art History; History); **Liturgy** (Christian Religious Studies; Religion); **Nursing** (Nursing); **Political Science and Administration** (International Relations; Political Sciences; Public Administration)

History: Founded 1961 and run by the Lebanese Maronite Order.

Governing Bodies: University Council

Academic Year: September to July

Admission Requirements: Secondary school certificate (baccalauréat Part II) or foreign equivalent

Fees: (US Dollars): tuition, c. 120-220 (4,320-7,920 per annum)

Main Language(s) of Instruction: French; English; Arabic

International Co-operation: With universities in Belgium, Brazil, Canada, France, Jordan, Morocco, Syria, USA

Degrees and Diplomas: *Bachelor's Degree (BA; BS)*: 3 yrs + Teaching Diploma (1yr); *Bachelor's Degree (BA; BS)*: 3 yrs; *Master's Degree (MA; MS; MBA)*: 2 yrs after Bachelor's Degree; *Diplôme de Doctorat (PhD)*: 3-5 yrs after Master's Degree

Student Services: Academic counselling, Canteen, Cultural centre, Employment services, Health services, Language programs, Social counselling, Sports facilities

Student Residential Facilities: Yes

Special Facilities: Animal Sciences Laboratory; Archaeological Museum; Chemistry and Life Science Laboratories; Computer and Information Science Laboratories; Dealing Room (salle des marchés); Education Technology Laboratory; Experimental Plant Domain; Food Analysis Laboratory; Herbarium; Judicial Clinic; Psychology Laboratories; Photography Laboratory; Pilot Farm; Plant Biotechnology Laboratory; Plant Protection Laboratory; Sciences, Technology, Network and Telecommunication Laboratories; Soil and Environment Laboratory; Sound Recording Studio; Teleconferencing Auditorium; Translation and interpretation Laboratory

Libraries: Central Library, c. 250,000 vols; 3,500 manuscripts; 2,000 periodicals

Publications: Actes des colloques de l'Université Saint-Esprit de Kaslik; Annales de Philosophie et des Sciences Humaines; Collection de la bibliothèque de l'Université Saint-Esprit de Kalik; Maronite Encyclopaedia; Parole de l'Orient *(biannually)*; Revue des Lettres et de Traduction; Revue juridique; Revue Théologique de Kaslik - RThk; Sciences et Technologies

Press or Publishing House: Publications de l'Université Saint-Esprit de Kaslik (PUSEK)

Student Numbers *2012-2013*: Total 7,141
Last Updated: 11/03/13

INTERNATIONAL SCHOOL OF MANAGEMENT

Ecole supérieure internationale de Gestion

Aintoura, Mont-Liban
Tel: +96(9) 233183
EMail: admission@esig.edu.lb
Website: http://www.esig.edu.lb

Programmes

Management (Business Computing; Finance; Human Resources; Management; Marketing)

History: Founded 2000.

Main Language(s) of Instruction: English and French

Degrees and Diplomas: *Licence*; *Magistère*

Last Updated: 16/12/11

JINAN UNIVERSITY

Jamiat al-jinan (JU)

PO Box 818, Tripoli, Abou Samra
Tel: +961(6) 447-906
Fax: +961(6) 447-900
EMail: jinan@jinan.edu.lb
Website: http://www.jinan.edu.lb

President: Mona Haddad Yakan (1988-)
Tel: +961(6) 447-901, Fax: +961(6) 625-576
EMail: president@jinan.edu.lb

Faculties

Business Administration (Accountancy; Advertising and Publicity; Business Administration; Business Computing; Economics; Finance; International Business; Marketing; Taxation); **Information and Communication** (Communication Studies; Journalism; Radio and Television Broadcasting); **Literature and Humanities** (Arts and Humanities; Education; Islamic Studies; Literature; Translation and Interpretation); **Public Health** (Laboratory Techniques; Medical Technology; Nursing; Public Health; Social Work)

History: Founded 1988. Acquired present status 1999.

Governing Bodies: Jinan Association; Board of Trustees; University Council

Academic Year: September to June

Admission Requirements: Secondary school certificate, entrance exam for Bachelor's Degree

Fees: (US Dollars): 50-160 per credit

Main Language(s) of Instruction: Arabic, French, English

International Co-operation: With universities in France; Canada; Malaysia; United Arab Emirates; Sudan; United Kingdom; Yemen; Iran; Armenia; Egypt

Accrediting Agencies: Ministry of Higher Education; Association of Arab and European Universities; Association of Islamic Universities; Association of Arab Universities

Degrees and Diplomas: *Bachelor's Degree*: Business Administration; Communication; Public Health; Humanities and Literature (BA;BSc), 3 yrs; *Master's Degree*: Business Administration; Communication; Humanities and Literature (MBA; MA), a further 2 yrs; *Doctorate*: Business Administration; Communication; Humanities and Literature (PhD), a further 4 yrs. Also Honour's degree in Business Administration; Communication; Humanities and Literature (1 yr)

Student Services: Academic counselling, Canteen, Cultural centre, Employment services, Foreign student adviser, Foreign Studies Centre, Handicapped facilities, Health services, Language programs, Nursery care, Social counselling, Sports facilities

Student Residential Facilities: Yes

Special Facilities: Theatre; Editing Studio; Language; Science Laboratory

Libraries: Yes

Publications: Jinan Journal for Scientific Research

Press or Publishing House: Al-hasad

LA SAGESSE UNIVERSITY - UNIVERSITÉ LA SAGESSE

Furn El-Chebbak, Beirut 501-50
Tel: +961(1) 291-091
Fax: +961(1) 294-442
EMail: uls@uls.edu.lb
Website: http://www.uls.edu.lb

Rector: Camille Moubarak

Secretary-General: Antoine Saad EMail: ULS7@hotmail.com

Faculties

Canon Law (Canon Law; Law); **Ecclesiastical Science** (Religion; Theology); **Health Sciences** (Health Administration; Nursing); **Hospitality Management** (Hotel and Restaurant; Hotel Management; Tourism); **Law** (Law); **Management and Finance** (Business Administration; Economics; Finance; Management); **Political Science and International Relations** (International Relations; Political Sciences)

History: Founded 1875, acquired present status 1999.

Admission Requirements: Secondary school certificate (baccalauréat) or recognized equivalent

Fees: (US Dollars): 1,000-4,000

Main Language(s) of Instruction: Arabic, French, English

International Co-operation: With universities in France, Italy; Switzerland

Degrees and Diplomas: *Licence (BA)*: 3-4 yrs; *Diplôme d'Etudes supérieures spécialisées*; *Diplôme d'Etudes approfondies*; *Master's Degree*; *Doctorate (PhD)*: 3 yrs. Also Master and Mastère

Student Services: Academic counselling, Employment services, Foreign student adviser, Handicapped facilities, Health services, Language programs, Social counselling, Sports facilities

Student Residential Facilities: None

Special Facilities: Computer Centre, Language Laboratory, Movie Studio, Theatre

Libraries: Main Library

Publications: Canon Law; L'alliance de la Sagesse *(annually)*; Law and General Culture *(annually)*; Perspectives, Aba'ad *(annually)*
Last Updated: 12/12/11

LEBANESE AMERICAN UNIVERSITY (LAU)

PO Box 13-5053 Koritem, Beirut
Tel: +961(1) 867-620
Fax: +961(1) 867-098
EMail: relations@lau.edu.lb
Website: http://www.lau.edu.lb

President: Joseph G. Jabbra (2004-)
Tel: +961(1) 867-618, Fax: +961(1) 786-449
EMail: president@lau.edu.lb

Institutes

Banking and Finance *(IBAF)* (Banking; Finance); **Diplomacy and Conflict Transformation** (International Relations; Peace and Disarmament); **Family and Enterpreneurial Business** *(IFEB)* (Management); **Hospitality and Tourism Management** (Hotel and Restaurant; Hotel Management; Tourism); **Islamic Art and Architecture** (Architecture; Art Education); **Media Training and Research** *(Beirut)* (Media Studies) *Director*: Ramez Maluf; **Migration Studies** (Demography and Population); **Peace and Justice Education** *(IPJ)* (Peace and Disarmament); **Software** *(SI)* (Software Engineering); **Teacher Training** (Teacher Training); **Urban Planning** *(UPI)* (Town Planning); **Water Resources and Environmental Technology** *(IWRET)* (Environmental Studies; Water Science); **Women's Studies in the Arab World** (Women's Studies)

Schools

Architecture and Design (Architecture; Computer Graphics; Design; Fine Arts; Graphic Design; Interior Design); **Arts and Science** (Arts and Humanities; Chemistry; Computer Science; Education; Mathematics; Molecular Biology; Natural Sciences; Nutrition; Philosophy; Political Sciences; Psychology; Social Work); **Business** (Business Administration; Business and Commerce; Economics; Tourism); **Engineering** (Civil Engineering; Computer Engineering; Electrical Engineering; Environmental Engineering; Industrial Engineering; Mechanical Engineering); **Medicine** *(Gilbert and Rose-Marie Chagoury)* (Medicine); **Pharmacy** (Pharmacy)

History: Founded 1924 by the United Presbyterian Church, USA. Acquired present status 1994. Campuses in Beirut, Byblos, Sidon.

Governing Bodies: Board of Trustees

Academic Year: October to September (October-February; February-June). Also 2 summer sessions (July to September)

Admission Requirements: Graduation from high school with a minimum of 12 yrs study and entrance examination

Fees: (US Dollars): 385 per credit per annum, depending on majors

Main Language(s) of Instruction: English

International Co-operation: With universities in USA, Europe, Australia, Mexico

Accrediting Agencies: The University of the State of New York-Albany; American Council on Pharmaceutical Education; French Government; Arab Foundation of Engineering Organisations

Degrees and Diplomas: *Bachelor's Degree*: 4 yrs; *Bachelor's Degree*: Architecture (B Arch); Engineering (B.E.); Pharmacy; *Master's Degree*: a further 2 yrs; *Doctorate*: Pharmacy; Medicine, 6 yrs. Also Associate Degree, 2 yrs

Student Services: Academic counselling, Canteen, Cultural centre, Foreign student adviser, Handicapped facilities, Health services, Language programs, Nursery care, Social counselling, Sports facilities

Student Residential Facilities: For 340 students

Special Facilities: Theatres. Radio and TV studios

Libraries: Riyad Nassar Library and Byblos Library

Press or Publishing House: LAU Press
Last Updated: 30/09/10

LEBANESE CANADIAN UNIVERSITY

Université Libano-Canadienne (LCU)
PO Box 32 Zouk Mikael, Aintoura, Kesrouan
Tel: +961(9) 233-183 +961(9) 232-183 +961(9) 232-185
Fax: +961(9) 233-184
EMail: admission@esig.edu.lb
Website: http://www.esig.edu.lb

President: Rony Abi Nakhlé

Faculties

Arts and Humanities; **Arts and Science** (Computer Science; Geography; Graphic Design; Interior Design; Mathematics; Town Planning); **Management** (Accountancy; Business Administration; Business Computing; Economics; Human Resources; Management; Marketing; Tourism)

History: Founded 2000. Acquired present status 2008.

Main Language(s) of Instruction: English and French

Degrees and Diplomas: *Bachelor's Degree*; *Master's Degree*; *Doctorate*
Last Updated: 22/10/09

LEBANESE-GERMAN UNIVERSITY (HLIP)

Sahel Alma, Highway, P.O.Box 206, Jouneih, Kaserwan
Tel: +961(9) 938-938
Fax: +961(9) 938-933
EMail: info@lgu.edu.lb
Website: http://www.lgu.edu.lb

President: Marwan El Rassi

Centres

Business Training & Research (Business Administration); **Global Languages** (Modern Languages)

Faculties

Arts and Education (Film; Performing Arts; Preschool Education; Primary Education; Theatre); **Business and Insurance** (Accountancy; Banking; Finance; Hotel Management; Human Resources; Insurance; Management; Marketing); **Public Health** (Biomedical Engineering; Laboratory Techniques; Nursing; Nutrition; Physical Therapy)

Institutes

Chartered Insurance (Insurance); **Family Entrepreneurship** (Business Administration; Home Economics); **Healthcare Management and Quality** (Health Administration); **Media Professional Training** (Media Studies); **School Teacher Training** (Teacher Training)

History: Founded 1999 as Institut d'Enseignement supérieur de Physiothérapie. Acquired present title and status 2007.

Admission Requirements: Secondary school leaving certificate and entrance examination

Main Language(s) of Instruction: English and French

Degrees and Diplomas: *Licence*: 4 yrs; *Maîtrise*
Last Updated: 13/12/11

LEBANESE INTERNATIONAL UNIVERSITY

Beirut Campus, Po Box 146404, Beirut
Tel: +961(1) 706-881
Fax: +961(1) 306-044
EMail: info@liu.edu.lb
Website: http://www.liu.edu.lb

President: Abdel Rahim Mrad

Marketing and Career Director: Rana Sabra
Tel: +961(1) 706884, Ext. 1011 EMail: rana.sabra@liu.edu.lb

Schools

Arts and Science (Advertising and Publicity; Biochemistry; Biology; Biomedicine; Chemistry; Communication Arts; Computer Science; Dietetics; Economics; Food Science; Food Technology; Graphic Design; Information Technology; Interior Design; Journalism; Mathematics; Medical Technology; Nutrition; Physics; Public Relations; Radio and Television Broadcasting; Translation and Interpretation); **Business** (Accountancy; Banking; Business Administration; Finance; Hotel and Restaurant; Human Resources;

Information Management; Information Technology; International Business; Management; Marketing; Tourism); **Education** (Education); **Engineering** (Biomedical Engineering; Computer Engineering; Electrical Engineering; Electronic Engineering; Mechanical Engineering; Surveying and Mapping; Telecommunications Engineering); **Pharmacy** (Pharmacy)

Further Information: Also campuses in Bekaa, Tripoli, Nabatieh, Saida, JdeidehAden, Sanaa, Taiz, Mukalla, Nowakchott, Dakar, Casablanca

History: Founded 2001as Jamiat Al Bekaa (Al Bekaa University), acquired present name 2008. Operates six campuses in Lebanon, four campuses in Yemen, one in Senegal and one in Mauritania

Admission Requirements: Graduation from High School or equivalent secondary school certificate; entrance examination in English, Biology, Chemistry, Physics, Mathematics.

Main Language(s) of Instruction: English

Degrees and Diplomas: *Bachelor's Degree*; *Master's Degree*
Last Updated: 30/09/10

MAKASSED UNIVERSITY OF BEIRUT

Jamiat al-Makassed (MUB)
Uthman Bin Affan Street, Mseitbeh, Beirut 14-6179
Tel: +961(1) 377-533
Fax: +961(1) 377-285
EMail: makcier@cyberia.net.lb
Website: http://www.makassed.org.lb

President: Hisham Nashabe (1981-)
Tel: +961(1) 365-394, Fax: +961(1) 365-393
EMail: hinash@cyberia.net.lb

Secretary-General: Manal Mikdashi

International Relations: Manal Mikdashi
Tel: +961(1) 377-533, Fax: +961(1) 377-285

Faculties

Management and Information Technology (Information Technology; Management); **Nursing and Health Sciences** (Health Sciences; Nursing; Radiology; Respiratory Therapy)

History: Makassed Association established 1878. Founded 1981. Acquired present status and title 1986.

Governing Bodies: Board of Trustees, Board of Directors

Admission Requirements: Secondary school certificate (baccalauréat) or equivalent

Fees: (US Dollars): 2,500 per annum

Main Language(s) of Instruction: Arabic, English

Accrediting Agencies: Ministry of Higher Education

Degrees and Diplomas: *Bachelor's Degree*: Islamic Studies (BA); Nursing, 4 yrs; *Master's Degree*: Islamic Studies (MA), a further 2 yrs; *Doctorate*: Islamic Studies (PhD), 2 yrs following Master's Degree

Student Services: Academic counselling, Foreign student adviser, Social counselling

Student Residential Facilities: None

Libraries: Central Library

Publications: The Journal of the University *(biennially)*
Last Updated: 21/10/09

MIDDLE EAST UNIVERSITY

Kulliat Al-Sharq al-Awsat (MEU)
PO Box 1170, Beirut
Tel: +961(1) 883-065
Fax: +961(1) 684-800
EMail: meu@meu.edu.lb
Website: http://www.meu.edu.lb

President: L. Hongisto

Faculties

Arts and Science (Biology; Business Administration; Computer Science; English; History; Religion; Teacher Training); **Business Administration** (Accountancy; Banking; Business Administration; Computer Science; Finance; Hotel Management; Management; Marketing); **Education** (Education; Primary Education; Secondary Education); **Philosophy and Theology** (Philosophy; Theology)

History: Founded 1939 as The Adventist College of Beirut in Mouseitbeh. Renamed Middle East College 1946. Acquired present status and title 2001.

Accrediting Agencies: Lebanese Ministry of Education and Higher learning and Accrediting Association of Seventh-day Adventist Schools, Colleges, and Universities (AAA).

Degrees and Diplomas: *Bachelor's Degree*; *Master's Degree*

Libraries: George Arthur Keough Library
Last Updated: 13/12/11

MODERN UNIVERSITY FOR BUSINESS AND SCIENCE

Al Jamiaa Al Hadissa Lilidara wal Ouloum (MUBS)
Old Saida Road, Damour, Al-Chouf
Tel: +961(5) 601-801
Fax: +961(5) 601-667
EMail: info@mubs.edu.lb
Website: http://www.mubs.edu.lb

President: Ali Cheaib (2008-)
Tel: +961(3) 740-925, Fax: +961(3) 601-667
EMail: acheaib@mubs.edu.lb

Vice-President for Administrative Affairs: Sahira Moutaweh

International Relations: Nizam Najd, Vice-President for Academic Affairs (Acting)

Faculties

Business Administration (Accountancy; Banking; Business Administration; Finance; Human Resources; Information Sciences; Management; Marketing); **Computer and Applied Sciences** (Computer Science; Graphic Design; Information Sciences; Information Technology); **Education and Social Work** (Educational Administration; Preschool Education; Social Work; Teacher Training)

History: Founded 2000. Formerly known as MECAT (Al Mahaad Al Jamee Lilidara wal Ouloum). Acquired present status and title 2007.

Degrees and Diplomas: *Bachelor's Degree*: Business Administration; Computer Science; Computer and Communication Systems; Graphic Design; Education; Social Work, 3 yrs; *Master's Degree*: Business Administration; Management, a further 2 yrs

Libraries: c. 23,700 vols., 67 periodical subscriptions.

Academic Staff *2008-2009*	**TOTAL**
FULL-TIME	63
PART-TIME	46
STAFF WITH DOCTORATE	
FULL-TIME	51
Student Numbers *2008-2009*	
All (Foreign Included)	1,116
FOREIGN ONLY	51

Last Updated: 05/01/10

NOTRE DAME UNIVERSITY-LOUAIZÉ (NDU)

PO Box 72, Zouk Mikael, Zouk Mosbeh, Kaserwan
Tel: +961(9) 218-950
Fax: +961(9) 218-771
EMail: admission@ndu.edu.lb
Website: http://www.ndu.edu.lb

President: Walid Moussa (2005-)
Tel: +961(9) 218-772 +961(9) 208-888
EMail: president@ndu.edu.lb; ghosain@ndu.edu.lb

International Relations: Assaad Eid, Vice-President, Sponsored Research and Development
Tel: +961(9) 224-517, Fax: +961(9) 218-771
EMail: asaadeid@ndu.edu.lb

Divisions

Continuing Education (Business Administration; Computer Science; English; Hotel Management; Leadership; Management; Modern Languages; Music)

Faculties

Architecture, Art and Design (Architecture; Display and Stage Design; Fashion Design; Fine Arts; Graphic Design; Interior Design;

Landscape Architecture; Music Education; Musicology); **Business Administration and Economics** (Accountancy; Banking; Business Administration; Economics; Finance; Health Administration; Hotel and Restaurant; Hotel Management; Human Resources; International Business; Management; Marketing; Tourism; Transport Management); **Engineering** (Civil Engineering; Computer Engineering; Electrical Engineering; Engineering; Mechanical Engineering; Telecommunications Engineering); **Humanities** (Advertising and Publicity; Applied Linguistics; Arabic; Arts and Humanities; Clinical Psychology; Communication Arts; Education; Educational Psychology; English; Industrial and Organizational Psychology; Journalism; Marketing; Mass Communication; Media Studies; Radio and Television Broadcasting; Special Education; Translation and Interpretation); **Natural and Applied Sciences** (Actuarial Science; Biology; Biotechnology; Business Computing; Chemistry; Computer Graphics; Dietetics; Environmental Studies; Geography; Industrial Chemistry; Information Sciences; Information Technology; Insurance; Laboratory Techniques; Mathematics; Mathematics and Computer Science; Mathematics Education; Medical Technology; Natural Sciences; Nutrition; Pharmacology; Physics; Statistics); **Nursing and Health Sciences** (Health Sciences; Nursing); **Political Science, Public Administration and Diplomacy** (American Studies; Comparative Law; Criminal Law; European Studies; International Law; International Relations; Mediterranean Studies; Political Sciences; Public Administration)

Research Centres

Applied Research in Education *(CARE)* (Curriculum; Education; Educational Research); **Digitization and Preservation** *(CDP)* (Heritage Preservation); **Lebanese Emigration Research** *(LERC)* (Demography and Population); **Marian Studies** *(MSC)* (Religious Studies); **Societal Research** *(Lebanese Center for Societal Research (LCSR))* (Economics; Educational Sciences; Political Sciences; Social Studies); **Water, Energy and Environment Research** *(WEERC)* (Environmental Management; Environmental Studies; Water Management; Water Science)

Further Information: Also campuses in North Lebanon and in the Shouf, southeast of Beirut

History: Founded 1978 as Louaizé Centre for Higher Education, affiliated to Beirut University College. Acquired present status and title 1987.

Governing Bodies: Board of Trustees

Academic Year: October to August (October-February; February-June; July-August)

Admission Requirements: Secondary school certificate (baccalauréat) or equivalent

Fees: (Lebanese Pounds): 4.6m. per semester; Engineering and Architecture, 5.4m.; graduate studies, 4.8m

Main Language(s) of Instruction: English

International Co-operation: With universities in USA and Europe

Degrees and Diplomas: *Bachelor's Degree*: 7-13 sem; *Teaching Diploma*: 2 sem; *Master's Degree*: a further 4-5 sem

Student Services: Academic counselling, Employment services, Handicapped facilities, Health services, Language programs, Social counselling, Sports facilities

Special Facilities: Museum of Archeology

Libraries: c. 80,000 vols

Publications: NDU Chronicle (e-bulletin) *(quarterly)*

Student Numbers *2011-2012*: Total: c. 6,000

Last Updated: 30/09/10

SAINT-JOSEPH UNIVERSITY - UNIVERSITÉ SAINT-JOSEPH

BP 17-5208, Mar Mikhaël, Rue de Damas, Beirut 1104 2020
Tel: +961(1) 421-000
Fax: +961(1) 421-001
EMail: rectorat@usj.edu.lb
Website: http://www.usj.edu.lb

Recteur: Salim Daccache, s.j. (2012-)
Tel: +961(1) 421-101 EMail: recteur@usj.edu.lb

International Relations: Antoine Hokayem, Vice-Recteur, International Relations Tel: +961(1) 421-160 EMail: vrri@usj.edu.lb

Centres

Arabic Research and Studies (Arabic); **Banking** (Banking; Finance); **Euro-Lebanese Intercultural Studies** (Arts and Humanities; Cultural Studies); **Japanese** (Japanese); **Modern Languages** *(Branches in USJ regional centres: North Lebanon, South Lebanon, Bekaa)* (Modern Languages)

Faculties

Arts and Humanities *(French Literature branches in USJ regional centres: North Lebanon and South Lebanon)* (Anthropology; Archaeology; Arts and Humanities; Clinical Psychology; Communication Studies; Contemporary History; Educational Psychology; Environmental Studies; French; Geography; History; Human Resources; Industrial and Organizational Psychology; International Relations; Literature; Philosophy; Psychology; Public Relations; Sociology; Tourism); **Business Administration and Management** *(Branches in USJ regional centres: North Lebanon, South Lebanon and Bekaa)* (Accountancy; Banking; Business Administration; Finance; Health Administration; Management); **Dentistry** (Dentistry; Oral Pathology; Orthodontics); **Economics** (Banking; Economics; Finance); **Education** (Education; Educational Administration; Educational and Student Counselling; Educational Sciences); **Law and Political Science** (Commercial Law; Law; Political Sciences; Private Law; Public Law); **Medicine** (Biology; Medicine); **Nursing** *(Branches in USJ regional centres: North Lebanon, South Lebanon and Bekaa)* (Nursing); **Pharmacy** (Biology; Dietetics; Nutrition; Pharmacy); **Religious Sciences** (Religion; Religious Studies); **Science** (Biology; Chemistry; Earth Sciences; Mathematics; Natural Sciences; Physics)

Institutes

Business Administration (Advertising and Publicity; Business Computing; Hotel Management; Marketing); **Communication and Information** (Information Sciences; Telecommunications Services); **Confucius** (Chinese); **Health and Social Protection** (Health Administration; Public Health; Social Welfare); **Insurance Studies** (Insurance); **Islamic-Christian Studies** (Christian Religious Studies; Comparative Religion; Islamic Studies); **Oriental Literature** (Arabic; Education; History; Islamic Studies; Philosophy); **Physiotherapy** (Neurological Therapy; Osteopathy; Physical Therapy); **Political Science** (Political Sciences); **Psychomotricity** (Psychometrics; Rehabilitation and Therapy); **Religious Sciences** (Religious Studies); **Speech Therapy** (Speech Therapy and Audiology); **Teachers** *(Lebanese)* (Educational Sciences; Preschool Education; Primary Education; Special Education) *Division Head*: Zohrabian; **Theatre, Audiovisual and Film Studies** (Cinema and Television; Film; Theatre)

Laboratories

Biochemistry (Biochemistry); **Biostatical and Medical Epidemiology** (Epidemiology); **Cartography** (Surveying and Mapping); **E-learning Technologies** (Pedagogy); **Experimental Psychology** (Experimental Psychology); **Human Hispathology** (Histology; Pathology); **Medical Computer Science** (Computer Science); **Medical Genetics** (Genetics); **Mineralized Tissues** (Genetics); **Molecular Biology** (Molecular Biology); **Pharmacology** (Pharmacology); **Physiology** (Physiology); **Socio-economical Reality** (Economics); **Teaching Pedagogy** (Pedagogy; Teacher Training); **Teledetection** (Geography); **Tourism** (Tourism); **Toxicology** (Toxicology)

Research Centres

Arabic Terminology (Arabic; Terminology); **Archeology** *(Francis Hours)* (Archaeology; Prehistory); **Bioequivalence and Medicament Control** (Pharmacy); **Chemistry and Physics** (Chemistry; Physics); **Christian Arabs** (Religious Studies); **Construction** (Construction Engineering); **Economics** (Economics); **Electrical Industries and Telecommunications** (Telecommunications Engineering); **Ethics** (Ethics); **European Union Studies** (European Union Law; Law; Regional Studies); **Michel Henry** (French); **Middle East Markets** (Business and Commerce; Middle Eastern Studies); **Modelling and Information Technology** (Computer Networks; Data Processing; Information Sciences; Information Technology); **Modern Arab World Studies** (Middle Eastern Studies); **Religious Interpretation** (Religious Studies); **Rights of the Arab World** (Middle Eastern Studies); **Water and Environment** (Environmental Studies; Water Science)

Schools

Agro-industry *(Tanael, Bekaa)* (Agricultural Engineering); **Engineering** (Building Technologies; Civil Engineering; Computer Engineering; Construction Engineering; Electrical and Electronic Equipment and Maintenance; Electrical Engineering; Engineering; Environmental Engineering; Mechanical Engineering; Telecommunications Engineering); **Medical Laboratory Techniques** (Laboratory Techniques); **Mediterranean Agronomy** *(Tanael, Bekaa)* (Agronomy); **Midwifery** (Midwifery); **Social Work Training** *(USJ regional centre in North Lebanon)* (Social and Community Services; Social Work; Special Education); **Translation and Interpretation** (Modern Languages; Translation and Interpretation)

Units

Open University (Architecture; Art History; Economics; History; Hygiene; Law; Literature; Musicology; Painting and Drawing; Philosophy; Political Sciences; Religious Studies)

Further Information: Also Teaching Hospital; Speech Therapy Centre; Psychomotor Therapy Centre; Family and Community Health Centre; Dental Care Centres; Technological Pole 'Berytech'; Health Pole 'BerytechII'.

History: Founded 1875 by the Society of Jesus. Title of University confirmed by Pope Leo XIII 1881. Faculty of Medicine established 1883 by agreement with French Government. A private institution. Received some financial assistance from the French State until 1975 when the University became an autonomous institution financed by tuition fees and government subsidies. University Regional Centres at: Ras Maska (North Lebanon), Zahlé/Hazerta (Bekaa) and Saïda-Bramieh (South Lebanon). University Foreign Centres in Abudhabi (United Arab Emirates)

Governing Bodies: University Council

Academic Year: September to June (September-January; February-June)

Admission Requirements: Secondary school certificate (baccalauréat) or foreign equivalent; French language test; Entrance examination

Fees: (US Dollars): average 100 per credit; lowest, 75 per credit; highest, 201 per credit

Main Language(s) of Instruction: French; English obligatory in all majors, Arabic required in some majors

International Co-operation: With universities in Belgium, Canada, France, Italy, Japan, Portugal, Spain, Switzerland, Tunisia and USA

Degrees and Diplomas: *Diplôme d'Université*: Clinical Pharmacy; Clinical Pharmacology; Social Work; Prosthetics; Community Health; Child Health; Oncology; Nursery; Information Management (DU); Religious Studies; Cognitive Sciences and Comportmental Mental Illness; Digestive Surgery; Dentistry; Health Science Education; Pedagogy; Medical Ethics; Islamo-Christian Studies; Obstetrics; Occupational Medicine; Microsurgery; Health Sciences; Pathology (DU), 2-4 semesters concurrently with the 2nd or 3rd cycle; *Licence*: Clinical and Pathological Psychology; Educational and Training Psychology; Labour and Corporate Psychology; Psychomotricity; Advertising and Publicity; Religious Studies; Life and Biological Sciences - Biology; Laboratory Sciences; Insurance; Economics; Contemporary History and International Relations; Business Computing; Modern Languages - Translation; French Literature; Hostel Management and Tourism; Mathematics; Orthopedagogy; Philosophy; Physics; Nursing; Political and Administrative Sciences; Social Services; Corporate Sociology and Public Relations; Anthropology; Telecommunications; Theatre; Tourism and Cultural Studies; Social Work; Archaeology; Audiovisual; Chemistry; Dietetics and Nutrition; Pre-school and Primary Education; Special Education; Environmental and Regional Planning; Business Administration, 180 Credits; *Licence*: Law; Midwifery, 240 Credits; *Certificat d'Aptitude pédagogique de l'Enseignement secondaire*: Didactics (CAPES), 80 Credits following Licence; *Diplôme d'Etudes supérieures*: Oral Surgery; Pediatric Dentistry; Endotontics; Orthodontics; Parodontology; Oral Pathology; Prosthetics (CES), 37-55,5 Credits following Doctorat d'exercice in Dentistry; *Diplôme d'Ingénieur*: Agribusiness; Agronomy; Building and Corporate Engineering; Biomedicine; Water and Environment; Electrical and Mechanical Engineering; Engineering; Computer Science and Networks; Civil Engineering and Transports, 300 Credits; *Professional Doctorate*: Dentistry; Pharmacy, 300 credits; *Diplôme d'Etudes supérieures spécialisées*: Medical Biology, 8 semesters; *Maîtrise*: Biological and Medical Sciences; Laboratory Sciences; Telecommunications, 1 yr following Licence; *Maîtrise*: Health Administration; Tourism and Cultural Studies; Quality Control (Pharmacy, Cosmetics and Food); Pedagogical Counselling; Socio-Educative Counselling; Paediatric Dentistry; Community Development and Action; Distribution; Drama; Writing, 120 credits following Licence; *Diplôme d'Etudes approfondies*: Banking Law; Arbitration Law; Private Law; Public Law (DEA), 12 months; *Magistère*: Education; Arab history; Islamology; Arab Language and Literature; Arab Philosophy, 120 Credits following Licence d'enseignement; *Diplôme de Spécialité*: Medicine (Internal Medicine; Cardiology; Endocrinology; Pneumology; Hepato-gastro-enterology; Nephrology; Rhumatology; Dermatology; Neurology; Psychiatry; Oncology; Pediatrics; Family Medicine; Radiology; Pathological Anatomy; Nuclear Medicine; Genetics); Surgery (General Surgery; Plastical Surgery; Child Surgery; Vascular surgery; Orthopedic Surgery; Urology; Neurosurgery; Thoracic and Cardio-vascular Surgery; Gynecology and Obstetrics; Otorhinolaryngological Surgery; Ophtalmology; Anaesthesiology); *Master's Degree*: Health Administration; Business Administration; Financial Institutions Management (MBA); Professional (Film Direction; Actuarial Science and Finance; Insurance; Systems and Network Security; Sound; Industrial Engineering; Translation); Professional (Information & Communication; Business Computing; Sociocultural Eng.; Interpretation; Social Problems & Family Dynamics; Management of Infectious Risk at Hospital; Hostel Management & Tourism; Services Marketing; Directing; Orthopedagogy); Professional (Parodontology; Oral Pathology; Measurement/Precision Engineering; Advanced Obstetrics; Prosthetics; Clinical & Pathological Psychology; Education & Training Psychology; Labour & Corporate Psychology; Psychomotricity; Advertising & Publicity); Professional (Pre-school & Primary Education; Orthodontics; Entrepreneurship & New Technologies; Political Science; Mediation & Cooperation Training; Finance; Human Resources; School Management; Contemporary History & International Relations; Image); Research (Cinema; Cultural & Religious Diversity in the Mediterranean area; New Technologies, Information & Communication Economy); Research (Educational Sciences; Nursing; Religious Studies; Sociology; Genetics; Soil Science; Theatre; Toxicology; Translation); Research (Environmental and Regional Planning; Mathematics and Computer Science; Finance; Electrical Engineering; Interpretation; French Literature; Management; Microbiology; Nutrition; Orthopedagogy; Clinical and Experimental Pharmacology; Philosophy); Research (Physiology & Sports Nutrition; Economical Policy; Clinical & Pathological Psychology; Education & Training Psychology; Labour & Corporate Psychology; International Relations; Telecommunications Networks; Political Science; Water Studies); Research (Tourism & Cultural Studies; Anthropology; Archaeology; Banking & Finance; Biochemistry; Biology; Biomaterials; Food Chemistry), 120 Credits following Licence; *Master's Degree*: Professional (Physical Therapy; Neurological Rehabilitation; Therapy; Manual and Osteopathic Therapy), 60 credits following Physical Therapy Diploma; *Doctorate*: Anthropology; Archaeology; Chemistry; Law; Civil Engineering; Electrical Engineering; Geography; History; Modern Languages; French Literature; Mathematics; Philosophy; Physics; Psychology; Political Science; Health Sciences; Life and Biological Sciences; Educational Sciences; Sociology; Theatre, 180 Credits following Magistère; *Doctorate*: Education; Arab history; Islamology; Arab Language and Literature; Arab Philosophy, 240 Credits following Magistère; *Doctorate*: Medicine, 14 semesters. Also Licence d'enseignement in Arab Language and Literature, 180 Credits following Licence and in Educational Sciences, 30 Credits following Licence. Also Diplôme d'études supérieures appliquées (DESA) in Private and Public Contentious Law, 12 months. Diplôme d'éudes spécialisées de banques (DESB), 4 sem. following Licence in Business or Economics; Diplôme supérieur de gestion bancaire, 16 months following DESB.

Student Services: Academic counselling, Canteen, Handicapped facilities, Health services, Language programs, Nursery care, Social counselling, Sports facilities

Student Residential Facilities: Yes

Special Facilities: Prehistory Museum; Theatres (Beryte, Monnot)

Libraries: Libraries of the faculties; Oriental Library; Phares Zoghbi Library

Publications: ACES - Actualités cliniques et scientifiques, Revue de la Faculté de médecine dentaire de l' USJ *(biannually)*; Al-bayanat al-massihyia al-islamyia al mouchtaraka, Institu d'études islamo-chrétiennes; Annales de Géographie - Géosphères *(annually)*; Annales de la Faculté de droit *(other/irregular)*; Annales de lettres françaises- Acanthe *(annually)*; Annales de l'Institut de langues et de traduction - Al-Kimiya *(annually)*; Annales de l'Institut de lettres orientales *(annually)*; Annales de philosophie - Iris *(annually)*; Annales de psychologie et des sciences de l'éducation - Psy-écho, Faculté des Lettres et des sciences humaines *(annually)*; Annales de sociologie et d'anthropologie - Communautés et sociétés *(annually)*; Annales d'histoire - Tempora *(annually)*; Annuaire de l'Université de St.-Joseph *(annually)*; Attalkih al-istinahi al-moutajanes wa ghair al-moutajanes, Institut d'études islamo-chrétiennes; Bulletin annuel de la Faculté de médecine *(annually)*; Bulletin intérieur de l'Institut libanais d'éducateurs *(annually)*; CEMAM Reports, Centre d'études pour le monde arabe moderne *(other/irregular)*; Chroniques politiques *(annually)*; Chroniques sociales, Ecole libanaise de formation sociale *(annually)*; Chronologies du CEMAM, Centre d'études pour le monde arabe moderne *(annually)*; Conférences de l'ALDEC, Faculté des lettres et des sciences *(annually)*; Déclarations communes islamo-chrétiennes, Institut d'études islamo-chrétiennes; Dar el Mashrek; Enseignement continu post-universitaire, Faculté de pharmacie *(annually)*; Etudes de droit libanais, Faculté de droit et des sciences politiques *(other/irregular)*; Fondements théologiques du dialogue islamo-chrétien, Institut d'études islamo-chrétiennes; Hommes et sociétés du Proche-Orient - Nouvelle série, Faculté des lettres et des sciences humaines *(other/irregular)*; Journées d'études post-universitaires, Ecole de sages-femmes *(annually)*; La revue de l'Institut libanais d'éducateurs, Faculté des lettres et des sciences humaines *(annually)*; Livret Thèses et mémoires soutenus à l'Institut de lettres orientales(1968-2002), Collection Recherches; L'Orient des dieux *(annually)*; Mélanges de l'Université Saint-Joseph, Dar el Mashrek *(annually)*; Méthode rhétorique et herméneutique, Institut d'études Islamo-chrétiennes; Proche-Orient chrétien, Institut supérieur de sciences religieuses *(biannually)*; Proche-Orient Etudes économiques, Faculté des sciences économiques *(other/irregular)*; Proche-Orient Etudes en management, Faculté de gestion et de management *(other/irregular)*; Proche-Orient Etudes juridiques, Faculté de droit et des sciences politiques *(other/irregular)*; Publications techniques et scientifiques de l'ESIB *(other/irregular)*; Questions de bioéthique au regard de l'Islam et du Christianisme - Conférence à deux voix; Regards, Institut d'études scéniques audiovisuelles et cinématographiques *(annually)*; Rôle culturel des chrétiens dans le monde arabe- Cahiers de l'Orient chrétien, Centre de documentation et de recherches arabes chrétiennes; Tahadyiat attafahum lilmoutabadal, Institut d'études islamo-chrétiennes; Travaux et Jours *(biannually)*

Press or Publishing House: Presses de l'Université Saint-Joseph

Student Numbers *2012-2013*: Total 11,216
Last Updated: 11/03/13

SAINT PAUL'S INSTITUTE OF PHILOSOPHY AND THEOLOGY

Institut Saint-Paul de Philosophie et de Théologie
Harissa via Jounieh
Tel: +961(9) 903-920
Fax: +961(9) 903-818
EMail: g.khawam@inco.com.lb

Rector: Georges Khawam Tel: +961(9) 903-818

Secretary-General: Rita Daou Tel: +961(9)903-749

Faculties

Philosophy (Philosophy); **Theology** (Theology)

Research Centres

Muslim-Christian Dialogue

History: Founded 1939 as St Paul's School, acquired present statusand title 1972.

Governing Bodies: Board; Administration Board

Academic Year: October to May (October-January; February-May)

Admission Requirements: Secondary school certificate (baccalauréat) or foreign equivalent

Fees: (Lebanese Pounds): Tuition, c. 2.4m. per annum

Main Language(s) of Instruction: French

Degrees and Diplomas: *Licence*: Philosophy, 4 yrs; *Licence*: Theology, 4-6 yrs

Student Services: Academic counselling, Sports facilities

Student Residential Facilities: Residential facilities for20 students

Libraries:c. 70,000 vols
Last Updated: 24/02/09

THE ISLAMIC UNIVERSITY OF LEBANON

Al Jamiat Al Islamiah Fi Lobnan (IUL)
PO Box 30014, Khaldeh Highway, Khalde, Choueifat
Tel: +961(5) 807-711-16
Fax: +961(5) 807-719
EMail: iul@iul.edu.lb

President: Hassan Chalabi (1996-)
Tel: +961(5) 807-718 EMail: hassan.chalabi@iul.edu.lb

Director: Swidan Naser Tel: +961(5) 807-718

International Relations: Samiih Fayad, Secretary-General
Tel: +961(5) 807-717 EMail: samih.fayad@iul.edu.lb

Faculties

Economics and Business Administration (Accountancy; Banking; Business Administration; Business Computing; Economics; Finance; Health Administration; Industrial Management; Management; Marketing) *Director*: Anwar Tarhini; **Engineering** (Biomedical Engineering; Computer Engineering; Engineering; Surveying and Mapping; Telecommunications Engineering) *Director*: Abdel Mon'em Kobeissi; **Islamic Studies** (Islamic Law; Islamic Studies) *Dean*: Farah Moussa; **Law** (Commercial Law; Law; Private Law; Public Law) *Dean*: Hassan Chalabi; **Literature and Humanities** (Arabic; Arts and Humanities; English; French; Geography; History; Literature; Modern Languages; Philosophy; Psychology; Translation and Interpretation); **Nursing** (Nursing); **Political, Administrative and Diplomatic Sciences** (Administration; International Relations; Political Sciences); **Science and Arts** (Biochemistry; Biology; Chemistry; Computer Science; Graphic Design; Interior Design; Mathematics; Physics); **Tourism Sciences** (Hotel and Restaurant; Hotel Management; Tourism)

History: Founded 1994, sponsored by the Higher Islamic Shiite Council.

Governing Bodies: Board of Trustees

Admission Requirements: Secondary school certificate (baccalauréat) and entrance examination

Fees: (Lebanese Pounds): c. 3.8 m. per annum

Main Language(s) of Instruction: Arabic, English, French

International Co-operation: With universities in France; Russian Federation; Egypt; Germany; Iran; Iraq; Syria; Jordan; Netherlands

Accrediting Agencies: Association of Arab Universities (AARU); AUF and Association of Lebanon universities

Degrees and Diplomas: *Bachelor's Degree (BA)*: 3-4 yrs; *Master's Degree (MA)*: a further 2 yrs; *Doctorate*: Islamic Studies (PhD), 3-5 yrs

Student Services: Academic counselling, Canteen, Cultural centre, Employment services, Foreign student adviser, Foreign Studies Centre, Handicapped facilities, Health services, Language programs, Nursery care, Social counselling, Sports facilities

Special Facilities: Art Gallery; Movie Studio

Libraries: c. 35,000 vols

Publications: Islamic History Review *(annually)*; News of the University *(quarterly)*
Last Updated: 26/11/08

UNIVERSITY OF BALAMAND

Jamiat Al-Balamand (UOB)
PO Box 100, Tripoli, Abou Samra
Tel: +961(6) 93-0250
Fax: +961(6) 93-0278
EMail: info@balamand.edu.lb
Website: http://www.balamand.edu.lb

President: Elie A. Salem (1993-)
Tel: +961 322-9197 EMail: President@balamand.edu.lb

Dean, Admissions and Registration: Walid Moubayed

International Relations: Georges N. Nahas, Vice-President
Tel: +961(6) 93-0280, ext 141, Fax: +961(6) 93-0235
EMail: vp@balamand.edu.lb

Academies

Fine Arts *(Lebanese)* (Advertising and Publicity; Architecture; Cinema and Television; Fine Arts; Graphic Design; Interior Design; Town Planning)

Centres

Christian/Muslim Studies (Christian Religious Studies; Islamic Studies); **Computer** (Computer Science); **Engineering and Environmental Studies** (Engineering; Environmental Studies)

Faculties

Arts and Social Sciences (Arabic; Cultural Studies; Education; English; English Studies; French; French Studies; History; Mass Communication; Philosophy; Physical Education; Political Sciences; Psychology; Translation and Interpretation); **Business and Management** (Business Administration; Business and Commerce; Economics; Hotel Management; Management; Tourism); **Engineering** (Aeronautical and Aerospace Engineering; Civil Engineering; Computer Engineering; Electrical Engineering; Engineering; Mechanical Engineering); **Health Sciences** *(Ashrafich, Beirut)* (Health Education; Health Sciences; Laboratory Techniques; Nursing; Public Health); **Medicine** (Medicine); **Postgraduate Medical Education** *(Saint George Hospital, Beirut)* (Anaesthesiology; Cardiology; Gastroenterology; Gynaecology and Obstetrics; Medicine; Oncology; Orthopaedics; Paediatrics; Pneumology; Radiology; Surgery; Urology); **Science** (Computer Science; Mathematics; Natural Sciences; Physics)

Institutes

History, Archaeology, Near Eastern Heritage (Archaeology; Heritage Preservation; History); **Theology** *(St John of Damascus)* (Theology)

History: Founded 1936. Acquired present title and status 1988.

Governing Bodies: Board of Trustees

Academic Year: October to August (October-February; February-June;July-August)

Admission Requirements: Secondary school certificate (baccalauréat), or equivalent. Language tests, special tests based on major's needs

Fees: (Lebanese Pounds): Undergraduate, 280,000-370,000 (average 15 credits per semester); Graduate, 460,000-500,000 per credit (average 9 credits per semester)

Main Language(s) of Instruction: English, French, Arabic, Greek

International Co-operation: With universities in France, USA, Canada, Russia, Greece, Belgium, United Kingdom, Australia, Jordan

Degrees and Diplomas: *Bachelor's Degree*: Arts, Theology (BA); Business, Engineering (BBA), 3 yrs; *Bachelor's Degree*: Science, Health Sciences (BS), 3 yrs; *Licence*; *Professional Doctorate*: Medicine (MD), a further 4 yrs following Bachelor's Degree; *Diplôme d'Etudes supérieures spécialisées*: Fine Arts; *Teaching Diploma*: Education (TD), 1 further yr; *Master's Degree*: Architecture, Engineering (MBA); Arts, Theology (MA); Science (MS), a further 2 yrs; *Doctorate*: Education (PhD), 3 yrs after MA/MS

Student Services: Academic counselling, Canteen, Cultural centre, Employment services, Foreign student adviser, Handicapped facilities, Health services, Language programs, Sports facilities

Student Residential Facilities: Yes

Special Facilities: University hospital linked to the medical faculties

Libraries: Atef Danial Library, 100,000 vols. Theology Library, 25,000 vols

Publications: Al-Markab; Annals of the Faculty of Arts and Social Sciences *(biannually)*; Chronos *(annually)*

Press or Publishing House: PUB

Student Numbers *2012-2013*: Total 5,316

Last Updated: 14/02/13

UNIVERSITY OF TRIPOLI LEBANON (TUIS)

Abou-Samra, Tripoli, Abou Samra
Tel: +961(6) 441-756
Fax: +961(6) 447-202
Website: http://www.ut.edu.lb

President: Abdulsalam Ghaith Tel: +961(3) 211-742

Faculties

Educational Sciences (Education); **Shari'a and Islamic Studies** (Islamic Law; Islamic Studies); **The Holy Quran, Multi Readings and Science** (Islamic Theology; Koran)

History: Founded 1982 by the Islah Islamic Association as University Institute of Tripoli for Islamic Studies. Acquired present status and title 2009.

Admission Requirements: Secondary school certificate (baccalauréat) or equivalent

Main Language(s) of Instruction: Arabic

Accrediting Agencies: Ministry of Education and Higher Education

Degrees and Diplomas: *Licence*: 4 yrs; *Magistère*

Student Services: Academic counselling, Canteen, Cultural centre, Employment services, Foreign student adviser, Foreign Studies Centre, Health services, Language programs, Nursery care, Social counselling, Sports facilities

Student Residential Facilities: Yes

Special Facilities: Theatre. Observatory. Movie Studio

Libraries: Central Library

Publications: Al-Islah, Pamphlet *(monthly)*; Al-Islah Islamic Association *(annually)*; Islamic Conference on Shari'a and Law *(biennially)*; Islamic Educational Conference, Research papers *(biennially)*

Last Updated: 12/12/11

Lesotho

STRUCTURE OF HIGHER EDUCATION SYSTEM

Description:

Higher education in Lesotho includes all post-high school education with a minimum continuous duration of at least 2 academic years. It consists of several public and private institutions. The Lerotholi Polytechnic offers diplomas and certificates in technical fields, and should become a university of technology by 2015. The private institutions are relatively small in number.

Stages of studies:

University level first stage: *Diploma/ Certificate, Bachelor's degree*
Diplomas/ Certificates are usually conferred after two to three years' study. The Bachelor's degree is conferred after four years.

University level second stage: *Master's degree*
The Master's degree is conferred in Arts (MA) and Science (MSc) after two years' study beyond the Bachelor's degree.

University level third stage: *Doctorate*
The Doctorate is conferred after three years' study beyond the Master's degree. Candidates must submit a thesis and sit for an oral examination.

ADMISSION TO HIGHER EDUCATION

Admission to university-level studies:

Name of secondary school credential required: CGE O-level

Alternatives to credentials: Holders of the General Certificate of Education ('O' level) with at least four passes including English may also gain entrance to the university under certain conditions.

Foreign students admission:

Entrance exam requirements: Foreign students must hold qualifications equivalent to those required for entry to the university.

RECOGNITION OF STUDIES

Quality assurance system:

The CHE is in the process of implementing accreditation and quality assurance mechanisms and standards for both the public and private higher education sectors.

Bodies dealing with recognition:

Council on Higher Education (CHE)

P.O. BOx 14046
Maseru 100
Tel: +266 2231 3503
Fax: +266 2231 0070
WWW: http://www.che.ac.ls/

NATIONAL BODIES

Ministry of Education and Training

Minister: Makabelo Mosothoane
Chief Education Officer, Tertiary: Malerato Khoeli

Cnr Constitution and Pioneer Road
P.O. Box 47
Maseru 100
Tel: +266 2231 3045
Fax: +266 2231 0562
EMail: info@education.gov.ls
WWW: http://www.education.gov.ls
Role of national body: The Ministry of Education and Training is responsible for the management, provision and regulation of education and training in Lesotho.

Council on Higher Education (CHE)
Chairperson: Samuel T. Motlomelo
P.O. BOx 14046
Maseru 100
Tel: +266 2231 3503
Fax: +266 2231 0070
WWW: http://www.che.ac.ls/
Role of national body: Statutory corporate body established by Section 4 of the Higher Education Act of 2004. The overall mandate of CHE is to regulate the higher education sector and promote quality assurance in Lesotho.

Data for academic year: 2012-2013
Source: IAU from CHE website, Lesotho, 2012

INSTITUTIONS

PUBLIC INSTITUTIONS

LESOTHO INSTITUTE OF PUBLIC ADMINISTRATION AND MANAGEMENT (LIPAM)

Development House, LNDC Block A, Level 4, Kingsway, Maseru
Tel: +266 5885-4282

Director General: John Dzimba EMail: jdzimba@lipam.org.ls

Programmes
Human Resource Management (Human Resources); **Labour Laws** (Labour Law); **Leadership and Strategy** (Leadership)

Academic Year: From August to May

Degrees and Diplomas: *Diploma/ Certificate*; *Master's Degree*. Also Certificate in Human Resources Management and Post Graduate Diploma in Human ResourcesManagement and Labour Laws.

Last Updated: 29/10/12

IAU NATIONAL UNIVERSITY OF LESOTHO (NUL)

PO 180, Roma, 100 Maseru District
Tel: +266 2234-0601 +266 2221-3000
Fax: +266 2234-0000
EMail: info@nul.ls
Website: http://www.nul.ls

Vice-Chancellor: Sharon Siverts
Tel: +266 2234-0269, Fax: +266 2234-0702 EMail: vc@nul.ls

Registrar: A.M. Mphuthing

International Relations: Nthati Moorosi, Director for Marketing and Communications (Acting)
Tel: +226 2221-3796 EMail: ne.moorosi@nul.ls

Faculties
Agriculture (Agricultural Business; Agricultural Economics; Agricultural Engineering; Agricultural Equipment; Agricultural Management; Agriculture; Animal Husbandry; Biochemistry; Botany; Computer Science; Crop Production; Demography and Population; Ecology; Economics; Farm Management; Food Science; Food Technology; Genetics; Horticulture; Irrigation; Natural Resources; Rural Planning; Rural Studies; Soil Conservation; Soil Science; Water Management; Zoology); **Education** (Agricultural Education; Biology; Business Education; Chemistry; Curriculum; Development Studies; Education; Educational Administration; Educational and Student Counselling; Educational Psychology; Educational Research; Educational Sciences; Educational Technology; Educational Testing and Evaluation; English; Geography; Geography (Human); History; Humanities and Social Science Education; Mathematics Education; Natural Sciences; Physics; Religious Education; Science Education; Social Studies; Technology Education); **Health Sciences** (Health Sciences; Midwifery; Nursing; Nutrition; Pharmacy); **Humanities** (African Languages; Arts and Humanities; Development Studies; Education; English; French; Geography (Human); History; Philosophy; Religious Studies; Theology); **Law** (Law; Private Law; Public Law); **Postgraduate Studies** (Agriculture; Arts and Humanities; Economics; Education; Law; Mathematics and Computer Science; Natural Sciences; Social Sciences; Social Work; Sociology); **Science and Technology** (Applied Chemistry; Applied Mathematics; Applied Physics; Biology; Chemistry; Computer Science; Geography; Mathematics; Natural Sciences; Physics); **Social Sciences** (Administration; Anthropology; Business Administration; Demography and Population; Economics; Political Sciences; Social Sciences; Sociology; Statistics)

Institutes
Education (Curriculum; Education; Educational Research; Educational Testing and Evaluation; Human Resources); **Extra-Mural Studies** *(IEMS)* (Business Administration; Management; Media Studies); **Labour Studies** (Labour and Industrial Relations; Labour

Law); **Southern African Studies** *(ISAS)* (African Studies; Labour and Industrial Relations)

History: Founded 1945 as Pius XII College, became University of Basutoland, Bechuanaland Protectorate and Swaziland 1966; part of the trinational University of Botswana, Lesotho and Swaziland 1966. Acquired present status 1975.

Governing Bodies: Council; Senate

Academic Year: July to June (July -December; January-June)

Admission Requirements: Cambridge Overseas School Certificate or equivalent, with credit in English

Fees: (Loti): 2,000-3,400; foreign students, 2,000-10,500

Main Language(s) of Instruction: English

Accrediting Agencies: Council on Higher Education

Degrees and Diplomas: *Bachelor's Degree*: Arts (BA); Commerce (BCom); Education (BAEd); Law (LLB); Science (BSc); Science in Agriculture (BScAgric); Science in Education (BScEd), 4 yrs; *Master's Degree*: Arts (MA); Education (MEd); Law (LLM); Science, Economics, Agriculture, Sociology (MSc); Social Work (MSW), a further 1-2 yrs; *Doctorate (PhD)*: a further 2-3 yrs

Student Services: Canteen, Employment services, Handicapped facilities, Health services, Nursery care, Social counselling, Sports facilities

Student Residential Facilities: Yes

Special Facilities: Botanical Garden

Libraries: Thomas Mofolo Library, c. 180,000 vols, Roma Campus; IEMS Centre, Maseru, c. 6,000 vols

Publications: Lesotho Law Journal *(biannually)*; Lesotho Social Science Review *(annually)*; NUL Journal of Research *(other/irregular)*; NUL Student Law Review; Review of Southern African Studies *(biannually)*

Press or Publishing House: NUL Publishing House

Student Numbers *2008-2009*: Total 6,129

Last Updated: 03/07/12

PRIVATE INSTITUTION

LIMKOKWING UNIVERSITY OF CREATIVE TECHNOLOGY

PO Box 8971, Moshoeshoe Road, Maseru Central, Maseru, 101
Tel: +266 2231-5767
Fax: +266 2231-6260
Website: http://www.limkokwing.net/lesotho/

Academies

Lifestyle Design *(International)* (Design; Fashion Design; Marketing; Textile Design); **Sound and Music Design** (Music; Sound Engineering (Acoustics))

Faculties

Architecture and Built Environment (Architecture; Design; Interior Design); **Business Management and Globalization** (Business Administration; International Business; Marketing; Retailing and Wholesaling); **Communication, Media and Broadcasting** (Communication Studies; Journalism; Media Studies; Public Relations; Publishing and Book Trade; Writing); **Creativity in Tourism and Hospitality** (Hotel Management; Tourism); **Design Innovation** (Advertising and Publicity; Design; Fine Arts; Graphic Design; Photography); **Film, Television and Broadcasting** (Film; Radio and Television Broadcasting); **Information and Communication Technology** (Business Computing; Communication Studies; Computer Engineering; Information Technology; Multimedia; Software Engineering); **Multimedia Creativity** (Computer Graphics; Multimedia)

History: Founded 2008.

Accrediting Agencies: Council on Higher Education

Degrees and Diplomas: *Bachelor's Degree*. Also Associate Degree

Last Updated: 24/10/12

Liberia

STRUCTURE OF HIGHER EDUCATION SYSTEM

Description:

Higher education is provided by a number of public and private universities. The University of Liberia is the country's largest and oldest university.

Stages of studies:

University level first stage: *Bachelor's degree*

The first stage lasts for four years and leads to the award of the Bachelor's degree (3 years in Law; 5 years in Engineering). The curricular structure generally provides for the first two years to include basic and general courses. This is followed by courses in the student's area of specialization.

University level second stage: *Master's degree*

A second stage leads to the Master's degree after two years' graduate study.

University level third stage: *Doctorate in Medicine*

In Medicine, the Doctorate is conferred after seven years of study.

ADMISSION TO HIGHER EDUCATION

Admission to university-level studies:

Name of secondary school credential required: Liberia Senior High School Certificate

Entrance exam requirements: Entrance examination.

RECOGNITION OF STUDIES

Quality assurance system:

Recognition in Liberia implies obtaining a charter to operate from the National Legislature and to follow the policies as set by the National Commission on Higher Education.

NATIONAL BODIES

Ministry of Education

Minister: Etmonia David Tarpeh
EGV. King Plaza, Broad Street
Monrovia
Tel: +231 226 216/ 226 406
Fax: +231 226 144/ 226 216

National Commission on Higher Education

Director General: Michael P. Slawon
Ministry of Education
EWG. King Plaza
Broad Street
Monrovia
Tel: +231 226 216/ 226 406
Fax: +231 226 144/ 226 216
Role of national body: Supervises, coordinates, monitors, evaluates and accredits tertiary-level institutions.

Data for academic year: 2012-2013
Source: IAU from World Data on Education 2010/2011, UNESCO-IBE, 2012

INSTITUTIONS

PUBLIC INSTITUTION

UNIVERSITY OF LIBERIA (UL)

PO Box 9020, Capitol Hill, Monrovia, Montserrado County 231
Tel: +231(22) 6418 +231(22) 6418
EMail: alconteh@yahoo.com
Website: http://www.universityliberia.org

President: Emmet Dennis (2008-)
Tel: +231(6) 669-855
EMail: eadennis@ul.edu.lr; edennis@rci.rutgers.edu

Vice-President for Administration: Ansu Sonii
Tel: 231(6) 510-603 EMail: profdasoniisr@yahoo.com

Colleges
Agriculture and Forestry *(William R. Toblert, Jr.)* (Agriculture; Agronomy; Forestry; Home Economics; Primary Education; Secondary Education; Wood Technology); **Business and Public Administration** (Accountancy; Business and Commerce; Economics; Management; Public Administration); **General Studies** (Library Science); **Science and Technology** *(T. J. R. Faulkner)* (Biology; Botany; Chemistry; Civil Engineering; Electrical Engineering; Geology; Mathematics; Mining Engineering; Physics; Technology; Zoology); **Social Sciences and Humanities** (English; French; Geography; History; Mass Communication; Political Sciences; Sociology); **Teacher Training** *(William V. S. Tubman)* (Primary Education; Secondary Education; Teacher Training)

Graduate Schools
International Relations *(Ibrahim B. Babangida)* (International Relations)

Institutes
Population Studies (Demography and Population)

Programmes
Educational Administration and Supervision (MSED) (Educational Administration)

Schools
Law *(Louis Arthur-Grimes)* (Law); **Medicine** *(A. M. Dogliotti)* (Medicine; Public Health); **Pharmacy** (Pharmacy)

History: Founded 1851, opened as Liberia College1862. Became university 1951.

Governing Bodies: Faculty Senate; University Council

Academic Year: March to December (March-July; August-December)

Admission Requirements: Secondary school certificate and entrance examination

Main Language(s) of Instruction: English

Accrediting Agencies: National Commission on Higher Education

Degrees and Diplomas: *Bachelor's Degree*: Arts; Laws; Science, 4 yrs; *Master's Degree*

Student Residential Facilities: For c. 420 students

Libraries: c. 108,000 vols

Publications: Journal; Liberia Law Journal *(biannually)*; Science Magazine
Last Updated: 10/07/12

PRIVATE INSTITUTIONS

AFRICAN METHODIST EPISCOPAL UNIVERSITY (AMEU)

PO Box 3340, 34 Camp Johnson Road, Monrovia, Montserrado County 231
Tel: +231(377) 4751-6114
EMail: info@ameu.edu; barhsay@yahoo.com

President: Jean Bell Manning (2011-) Tel: +231-06-658-9075

Vice-President: Joseph N. Boakai

Colleges
Biyant Theological Seminary (Religious Education; Theology) *Dean*: E. Topo Johnson; **Business and Public Administration** (Accountancy; Business and Commerce; Economics; Management; Public Administration) *Dean*: Anselme B. Sao; **Liberal Arts and Social Sciences** (Arts and Humanities; Social Sciences) *Dean*: Dunalo B. G'dings

History: Founded 1995.

Governing Bodies: Board of Trustees, comprising 21 members

Academic Year: September to July

Admission Requirements: Secondary school certificate, present WAEC certificate and entrance examination

Fees: (Liberian Dollars): Tuition, 187,5 per credit; other fees, 1,8m. per annum. Foreign Students, US $5 per credit and US $76,5 per annum

Main Language(s) of Instruction: English

Accrediting Agencies: National Commission on Higher Education and University of Liberia

Degrees and Diplomas: *Bachelor's Degree*: English; Sociology; Political Science; Economics; Theology; Religious Education; Business Administration, 4 yrs

Student Services: Academic counselling, Health services, Language programs, Social counselling, Sports facilities

Special Facilities: Science Laboratory

Publications: Periodic Handbills, Information on current academic events of the university *(bimonthly)*
Last Updated: 18/09/09

CUTTINGTON UNIVERSITY (CU)

PO Box 10-0277, Suakoko, Monrovia 10,
Bong County 1000
Tel: +231-88-651-0952
Fax: +231-88-651-0301
EMail: cuttingtonuniversity@yahoo.com;
curegistraroffice@yahoo.com
Website: http://www.cuttington.org

President: Henrique F. Topka

Programmes
Agriculture and Rural Development (Agriculture; Rural Planning; Rural Studies); **Business Administration** (Accountancy; Business Administration; Economics; Finance; Management); **Education** (Education; Primary Education; Secondary Education); **Educational Administration** (Educational Administration); **Natural Sciences** (Biology; Chemistry; Mathematics; Natural Sciences); **Nursing** (Nursing); **Public Administration** (Public Administration); **Public Health** (Public Health); **Theology** (Theology)

History: Founded 1889 as Hoffman Institute. Renamed Cuttington College and Divinity School 1897. Closed 1929 to 1949. Acquired present title 1976. Administered by the Protestant Episcopal Church. Was closed for 9 years and reopened in 1998.

Governing Bodies: Board of Trustees, of which the Episcopal Bishop is President, and including the Minister of Education

Academic Year: September to July (September-February; March-July)

Admission Requirements: Secondary school certificate or recognized equivalent, and entrance examination

Main Language(s) of Instruction: English

Accrediting Agencies: National Commission on Higher Education; Association of Episcopal Colleges, USA; Association of African Universities

Degrees and Diplomas: *Bachelor's Degree*: Arts; Science; Nursing (BA; BSc; BSN), 4 yrs; *Master's Degree*: Education; Science; Arts; Business Administration; Public Health; Public Administration; Theology, a further 2 yrs. Also certificates in Peace Studies, Conflic Resolution and Microfinance

Student Services: Academic counselling, Canteen, Foreign student adviser, Health services, Social counselling, Sports facilities

Student Residential Facilities: Yes

Libraries: William V.S. Tubman Library

Publications: Cuttington Research Journal *(biannually)*

Student Numbers *2011-2012*: Total 2,787

Last Updated: 08/03/12

Libya

STRUCTURE OF HIGHER EDUCATION SYSTEM

Description:

Higher education is offered in universities, both general and specialized, technical colleges and higher vocational institutions. The study period lasts from 3 for some higher technical institutes to 6 years and more in universities.

Stages of studies:

University level first stage: *Bachelor's degree*
The Bachelor's degree is conferred after four years' study (five years in Architecture, Dentistry, Pharmacy, Veterinary Medicine, and Engineering; 6 years in Medicine and Surgery) in universities.

University level second stage: *Master's degree*
A Master's degree is conferred after two years' study following the Bachelor's degree.

University level third stage: *Doctorate*
A Doctorate may be awarded after three to four years' research. The award of this degree is conditional upon the submission of a thesis.

ADMISSION TO HIGHER EDUCATION

Admission to university-level studies:

Name of secondary school credential required: Secondary Education Certificate

Minimum score/requirement: A minimum of 65%, 75% for Medicine and Engineering

For entry to: Universities

Foreign students admission:

Entrance exam requirements: All foreign students should hold the Libyan Secondary Education Certificate or its equivalent, issued in the same or previous year of application. Grade averages required are the following: in scientific fields: Medicine 90%, Science 80%, Engineering and Veterinary Science 85%, Agriculture 80%, Economy 80%; in Liberal Arts: Law, Art and Information 85%, Languages 80%, Education 80%, Social Sciences, Physical Education and Sports 75%. The original certificate should be submitted. A coordinating committee is responsible for the placement of students admitted to the respective faculties in accordance with their total grades and percentage. Students have to pay the tuition fees fixed by the universities.
Language requirements: Language proficiency is required.

NATIONAL BODIES

Ministry of Higher Education and Scientific Research
Minister: Naeem Mohamed Abdurrahman al-Gheryani
Tripoli
WWW: http://www.higheredu.gov.ly/

Centre for Quality Assurance and Accreditation of Education Institutions
Tripoli
WWW: http://www.qaa.ly/

Data for academic year: 2012-2013
Source: IAU from Higher Education in Lybia, European Commission and documentation, 2012

INSTITUTIONS

PUBLIC INSTITUTIONS

AL ZAWIYA UNIVERSITY

Jamaa't Azzawia
PO Box 16418, Al-Zawia
Tel: +218(23) 626-882
Fax: +218(23) 626-882
EMail: president@zu.edu.ly
Website: http://zu.edu.ly

Rector: Mostafa Gomaa EMail: sahoub@zu.edu.ly

Faculties

Arts (Arts and Humanities); **Economics and Accountancy** (Accountancy; Administration; Economics; Political Sciences); **Engineering** (Engineering); **Law** (Law); **Medicine** (Medicine); **Science** (Natural Sciences); **Sports** (Sports)

History: Founded 1988 as Jamaa't Assaaba Men April (Seventh of April University). Acquired present title and status 2011.

Academic Year: September to July

Main Language(s) of Instruction: Arabic, English

Degrees and Diplomas: *Bachelor's Degree*: 4 yrs; *Master's Degree*: 3 yrs; *Doctorate*: 4 yrs

Student Services: Canteen, Foreign student adviser, Foreign Studies Centre, Health services, Social counselling, Sports facilities

Student Residential Facilities: Yes

Libraries: Yes
Last Updated: 02/10/12

AL-ARAB MEDICAL UNIVERSITY

PO Box 18251, Hawari Road, Benghazi
Tel: +218(61) 225-007
Fax: +218(61) 222-195

President: Amer Kahil (1999-)

Faculties

Dentistry (Dentistry; Surgery); **Medicine** (Gynaecology and Obstetrics; Medicine; Ophthalmology; Paediatrics; Pharmacology; Surgery); **Pharmacy** (Pharmacy)

Institutes

Medical Technology

Further Information: Also 8 Teaching Hospitals; 2 Medical Centres

History: Founded 1984.

Academic Year: September to May

Admission Requirements: Secondary school certificate or equivalent

Main Language(s) of Instruction: Arabic, English

Degrees and Diplomas: *Bachelor's Degree*: Dental Surgery; Medicine and Surgery, 5-7 yrs; *Master's Degree*: Anaesthesiology; Anatomy; Biochemistry; Dermatology; Histology; Laboratory Medicine; Pathology; Pharmacology; Physiology; Public Health, a further 2-3 yrs; *Master's Degree*: Community Medicine; Paediatrics; *Doctorate*: a further 2-3 yrs

Student Services: Academic counselling, Canteen, Cultural centre, Foreign student adviser, Health services, Sports facilities

Special Facilities: Anatomy Museum

Libraries: Central Library, c. 30,500 vols

Publications: Garyounis Medical Journal *(biannually)*

AL-JABAL AL GHARBI UNIVERSITY

PO Box 64101, Zawia, Gharian
Tel: +218(242) 630-263
Fax: +218(242) 635-316
EMail: engineeringgharyan@gmail.com
Website: http://jgu.edu.ly/

President: Ahmad Alwear Tel: +218(9) 1320-4412 (mobile)

Vice-President: Mehemed Al-Razzaghi
EMail: M_Razzaghi@yahoo.co.uk

Registrar: Mahmoud M. M. Bubakir
EMail: aljabalalgharabiregistrareng@gmail.com

Faculties

Accountancy (Accountancy; Economics); **Arts and Education** (Arts and Humanities; Education; Modern Languages); **Education** (Education); **Engineering** (Civil Engineering; Computer Engineering; Electrical Engineering; Engineering); **Law** (Law; Political Sciences); **Science** (Biology; Chemistry; Mathematics; Physics)

History: Founded 1991.

Academic Year: September to July

Main Language(s) of Instruction: Arabic, English

Degrees and Diplomas: *Bachelor's Degree*

ASMARYA UNIVERSITY FOR THE ISLAMIC SCIENCES

Aljamia Alasmariya Leloloum Aleslamiya
PO Box 471 / 495, Zliten,
Ashiekh District
Tel: +218(514) 627-039
Fax: +218(514) 620-040
EMail: asmarya@lttnt.net
Website: http://www.asmarya.edu.ly

Secretary of the Administration Committee: Mohmmed Kondi
Tel: +218 91 216-6164

General Director for the administrative and Financial Affairs: Abdu-Allah Azzerigani
Tel: +218 91 216-6158, Fax: +218(514) 627-039
EMail: abdoo195860@yahoo.com

International Relations: Emhemmed Alikisher, Director of the Cultural Cooperation Office
Tel: +218 91 358-9181, Fax: +218(514) 627-039

Faculties

Arabic and Islamic Studies (Arabic; History; Islamic Studies; Literature); **Preaching** *(Al-Emama Walkhataba)* (Religion; Religious Practice); **Shari'a and Law** *(Zliten)* (Islamic Law); **Theology** *(Asool Aldeen)* (Theology)

History: Founded 1995.

Academic Year: September to July

Admission Requirements: Secondary school certificate (Ashahada Athanawiya); Student should be a Social Science Secondary school graduate (specialization: shari'a or General Secondary); Student must know by heart the Holy Quran

Fees: (Libyan Dinars): Regular students: 20 per annum; 10 per semester; Part time students: 120 per annum; 60 per semester

Main Language(s) of Instruction: Arabic

International Co-operation: With Al-Ameer Abdulghader University of Islamic Studies/Qusantina (Algeria); Al-Azhar University, Cairo (Egypt); Holy Quran University for Islamic Studies (Sudan)

Accrediting Agencies: General People's Committee of Education and Scientific Research

Degrees and Diplomas: *Bachelor's Degree*: Islamic Law; Arabic; Islamic Studies; Historical Studies; Religion, 4 yrs; *Master's Degree*: Holy Quran; Islamic Studies; Literature; Religion; Philosophy, 36 months; *Doctorate*: Islamic Studies; Philosophie; Religion; Literature; Holy Quran, 48 months

Student Residential Facilities: Allowance of 70 US Dollars /month

Libraries: Central Library; Public Library; Graduate Studies Library

Publications: Aljamia University Publication, Scientific Publication *(annually)*

Last Updated: 19/06/09

HIGHER INSTITUTE OF COMPUTER TECHNOLOGY (HICT)

PO Box 6289, Tripoli
Tel: +218(21) 480-0413
Fax: +218(21) 480-0199
Website: http://www.hict.edu.ly/

President: Moftah Algurni

Departments

Computer Engineering (Computer Engineering; Computer Networks); **Software Engineering** (Software Engineering); **Training** (Computer Education; Computer Networks)

Admission Requirements: High school certificate

Fees: None

Main Language(s) of Instruction: Arabic, English

Degrees and Diplomas: *Bachelor's Degree*

Student Services: Academic counselling, Canteen, Employment services, Social counselling, Sports facilities

Libraries: Central Library, fully computerized with internet facilities

Last Updated: 31/10/12

IAU MISURATA UNIVERSITY

PO Box 2478, Misurata
Tel: +218(512) 627-203
Fax: +218(512) 627-350
EMail: info@7ou.edu.ly
Website: http://www.misuratau.edu.ly/

Acting President: Tahir bin Tahir (2011-)
Tel: +218(512) 610-659

Dean of Quality Assurance Office: Abdulwahab Sallabi
Tel: +218(512) 627-350 +218(92) 5509690,
Fax: +218(512) 627-350 EMail: qaao@7ou.edu.ly

International Relations: Ali Meftah Bakeer, Dean of International Office EMail: ico@7ou.edu.ly; ali.m.bakeer@gmail.com

Faculties

Agriculture *(Ben Walid)* (Agriculture; Animal Husbandry; Horticulture; Plant and Crop Protection; Soil Management; Soil Science; Water Management; Water Science); **Arts** *(Misurata)* (Arabic; Archaeology; Arts and Humanities; Education; English; French; Geography; History; Islamic Studies; Library Science; Media Studies; Philosophy; Psychology; Sociology; Tourism); **Arts** *(Ben Walid)* (Arabic; Archaeology; English; Geography; History; Islamic Studies; Media Studies; Philosophy; Psychology; Sociology); **Arts and Sciences** *(Zliten)* (Arabic; Archaeology; English; Geography; History; Islamic Studies; Media Studies; Philosophy; Psychology); **Arts and Sciences** *(Alkhomus)* (Arabic; Archaeology; English; Geography; History; Islamic Studies; Media Studies; Philosophy; Psychology; Sociology); **Dentistry** *(Zliten)* (Dentistry; Oral Pathology; Orthodontics); **Economics and Political Science** *(Misurata)* (Accountancy; Banking; Economics; Management; Political Sciences); **Economics and Trade** *(Alkhomus)* (Accountancy; Banking; Economics; Management); **Education** *(Alkhomus)* (Arabic; Art Education; Biology; Chemistry; Education; English; Geography; History; Islamic Studies; Mathematics; Physics; Psychology; Special Education); **Education** *(Misurata)* (Arabic; Art Education; Biology; Chemistry; Computer Education; Education; English; Geography; History; Islamic Studies; Mathematics; Music Education; Physical Education; Physics; Preschool Education; Psychology; Special Education); **Engineering** *(Alkhomus)* (Architecture; Civil Engineering; Electrical Engineering; Engineering; Industrial Engineering; Materials Engineering; Mechanical Engineering; Petroleum and Gas Engineering); **Engineering** *(Misurata)* (Architecture; Civil Engineering; Electrical Engineering; Engineering; Industrial Engineering; Materials Engineering; Mechanical Engineering; Petroleum and Gas Engineering); **Information Technology** *(Misurata)* (Communication Studies; Computer Networks; Computer Science; Information Technology; Software Engineering); **Law** *(Tarhunah)* (Law); **Law** *(Ben Walid)* (Criminal Law; Law; Private Law); **Medical Technology** *(Mslath)* (Dental Technology; Laboratory Techniques; Medical Technology); **Medical Technology** *(Ben Walid)* (Laboratory Techniques; Medical Technology); **Medicine** *(Misurata)* (Medicine); **Medicine** *(Alkhomus)* (Medicine); **Nursing** *(Misurata)* (Anaesthesiology; Gynaecology and Obstetrics; Nursing); **Pharmacy** *(Alkhomus)* (Pharmacy); **Pharmacy** *(Misurata)* (Pharmacy); **Science** *(Misurata)* (Biology; Botany; Chemistry; Mathematics; Physics; Zoology); **Science** *(Ben Walid)* (Biology; Botany; Chemistry; Computer Science; Mathematics; Physics; Zoology); **Veterinary Studies and Agriculture** (Agriculture; Veterinary Science)

History: Founded 1984. Previously known as Seventh of October University. Acquired current status 2010 after merger with the University of Elmergib (created 1986 as Nasser University).

Governing Bodies: People's Committee of the University

Academic Year: September to July

Admission Requirements: Specialized secondary school certificate.

Main Language(s) of Instruction: Arabic, English

Accrediting Agencies: Quality Assurance Agency

Degrees and Diplomas: *Bachelor's Degree*: Dentistry (BSc), 6 yrs; *Bachelor's Degree*: Engineering, 5 yrs; *Bachelor's Degree*: Islamic Studies (BSc), 4 yrs; *Bachelor's Degree*: Medicine, 7 yrs (6 yrs + 1 yr internship); *Master's Degree (MSc)*: 3 yrs; *Doctorate*. Also Licence (Lit. B): 4 yrs

Student Services: Academic counselling, Canteen, Cultural centre, Employment services, Foreign student adviser, Foreign Studies Centre, Handicapped facilities, Health services, Language programs, Nursery care, Social counselling, Sports facilities

Libraries: c. 100.000 vols; Sage online journals

Publications: Alsatil *(3 per annum)*

Academic Staff *2009-2010*	MEN	WOMEN	TOTAL
FULL-TIME	2,022	400	**2,422**
PART-TIME		–	**454**
STAFF WITH DOCTORATE			
FULL-TIME	393	20	**413**
PART-TIME	–	–	**8**
Student Numbers *2009-2010*			
All (Foreign Included)	24,466	37,222	**61,688**
FOREIGN ONLY	521	745	**1,266**

Part-time students, 810.

Last Updated: 06/01/11

OMAR-AL-MUKHTAR UNIVERSITY (OMU)

PO Box 919, El-Beida
Tel: +218(84) 632-946
Fax: +218(84) 637-052
EMail: admin@omu.edu.ly
Website: http://www.omu.edu.ly

President: Ibrahim Mohamed Ghariani

Faculties

Agriculture (Agriculture); **Arts** (Arts and Humanities; Education; Literature); **Arts and Science** *(Tobrak, Al-Quba and Derna)* (Arts and Humanities; Natural Sciences); **Economics** (Economics); **Engineering** (Engineering); **Law** (Law); **Medical Technology** (Medical Technology); **Medicine** (Medicine); **Natural Resources and Environmental Science** (Environmental Studies; Natural Resources); **Nursing** (Nursing); **Pharmacy** (Pharmacy); **Science** (Natural Sciences); **Teacher Training** *(Also in Derna, Tobrak and Al-Quba)* (Teacher Training); **Veterinary Medicine** (Veterinary Science)

History: Part of Garyounis University until 1984. Founded 1985.

Academic Year: October to July

Admission Requirements: High school certificate with a certain minimum percentage

Fees: Depends on faculty

Main Language(s) of Instruction: Arabic and English

International Co-operation: With Arab, American and European universities

Accrediting Agencies: Quality Assurance Agency

Degrees and Diplomas: *Bachelor's Degree*; *Master's Degree*

Student Services: Academic counselling, Canteen, Foreign student adviser, Health services, Language programs, Social counselling
Student Residential Facilities: Yes
Libraries: Main library and faculty libraries
Publications: Al-Mukhtar Journal of Humanities; Al-Mukhtar Journal of Science
Last Updated: 01/10/12

SEBHA UNIVERSITY

PO Box 18758, Sebha
Tel: +218(71) 621-575 +218(71) 632-960
Fax: +218(71) 629-201 +218(71) 627-019
EMail: cult-t-coop@sebhau.edu.ly
Website: http://www.sebhau.edu.ly

Chancellor: Mohamed Moftah Saleh
Tel: +218 91 218-8173 (mobile)

Registrar: Ali El Dakhil

Faculties

Agriculture (Agriculture); **Arts** (Arts and Humanities; English; Linguistics); **Arts and Science** (Arts and Humanities; Mathematics and Computer Science; Natural Sciences); **Economics and Accountancy** *(Merzig)* (Accountancy; Economics); **Engineering** *(Brak)*; **Law**; **Medicine** (Medicine); **Physical Education** (Physical Education); **Science** (Mathematics and Computer Science; Natural Sciences)

History: Founded 1983, incorporating the Faculty of Education of the University of Al-Fateh.
Academic Year: October to August
Admission Requirements: Secondary school certificate
Main Language(s) of Instruction: Arabic, English
Degrees and Diplomas: *Bachelor's Degree*: 3-4 yrs; *Master's Degree*
Student Residential Facilities: Yes
Libraries: Central Library, c. 110,000 vols

THE HIGHER INSTITUTE OF INDUSTRY (HII)

PO Box 841, Misurata
Tel: +218(51) 261-5312
Fax: +218(51) 261-5314
EMail: info@hii.edu.ly
Website: http://www.hii.edu.ly

Dean: Majdi Ashiban (2006-)
Tel: +218(51) 261-4109 EMail: mashibani@hii.edu.ly

Registrar: Ali Alfageeh
Tel: +218(51) 261-5313,Ext.132 EMail: aifeghi@hii.edu.ly

International Relations: Mohamed Shetwan
Tel: +218(51) 261-5313,Ext.112 EMail: shatwan57@hii.edu.ly

Departments

Electromechanical Engineering (Electronic Engineering; Mechanical Engineering; Power Engineering) *Head*: Mohamed Shetwan; **Electronic Engineering** (Computer Engineering; Electronic Engineering; Telecommunications Engineering) *Head*: Walid Algnaidi; **Industrial Engineering** (Industrial Engineering; Industrial Management; Production Engineering; Safety Engineering) *Head*: Mokhtar Albirgail

History: Founded 1989.
Academic Year: September to June
Admission Requirements: Secondary school certificate
Fees: (Libyan Dinars): 12 per semester
Main Language(s) of Instruction: Arabic
International Co-operation: With the University of Cape Town, South Africa; Nottingham Trent University, United Kingdom; University of Duisburg-Essen, Germany
Degrees and Diplomas: *Higher Technical Diploma*: Electronic Engineering; Industrial Engineering; Electromechanical Engineering (HD), 3 yrs; *Bachelor's Degree*: Engineering (Btech), 4 1/2 yrs; *Master's Degree*: Technology

Student Services: Academic counselling, Canteen, Language programs, Social counselling
Student Residential Facilities: Staff residence; Hotel
Libraries: Yes

Academic Staff *2009-2010*	MEN	WOMEN	**TOTAL**
FULL-TIME	36	7	**43**
PART-TIME	14	–	**14**
STAFF WITH DOCTORATE			
FULL-TIME	5	–	**5**
PART-TIME	–	–	**10**
Student Numbers *2009-2010*			
All (Foreign Included)	185	115	**300**
FOREIGN ONLY	5	–	**5**

Part-time students, 40.
Last Updated: 11/09/09

THE OPEN UNIVERSITY

PO Box 13375, Tripoli
Tel: +218(21) 487-4000
Fax: +218(21) 487-4000
EMail: info@libopenuniv-edu.org
Website: http://www.libopenuniv-edu.org/

President: Ibrahim Abu-Farwa EMail: iabufarwa@yahoo.com

Vice-President: Emhamed El-Harma
Tel: +218(21) 462-5501 EMail: info@libopenuniv.edu.org

Departments

Accountancy (Accountancy); **Administration** (Administration); **Arabic** (Arabic); **Economics** (Economics); **Education and Psychology** (Education; Psychology); **Geography** (Geography); **History** (History); **Islamic Studies** (Islamic Studies); **Law** (Law); **Political Science** (Political Sciences); **Sociology and Social Work** (Social Work; Sociology)

History: Founded 1987.
Academic Year: September to July
Admission Requirements: Secondary school certificate
Fees: (Libyan Dinars): 100 per annum + 10 per subject
Main Language(s) of Instruction: Arabic
Degrees and Diplomas: *Bachelor's Degree*: Law; Geography; History; Islamic Studies; Arabic; Sociology; Education; Economics; Administration; Accountancy; Political Science (BA, BSc), 4 yrs. Curricula and teaching programmes, both theoretical and applied, are via written and audiovisual material.
Student Services: Academic counselling, Handicapped facilities
Libraries: c. 6,300 books; 20 periodicals

Academic Staff *2008-2009*	MEN	WOMEN	**TOTAL**
FULL-TIME	12	3	**15**
PART-TIME	41	4	**45**
STAFF WITH DOCTORATE			
FULL-TIME	4	1	**5**
PART-TIME	18	–	**18**
Student Numbers *2008-2009*			
All (Foreign Included)	5,243	3,167	**8,410**
FOREIGN ONLY	147	84	**231**

Distance students, 8,410.
Last Updated: 13/05/09

UNIVERSITY OF BENGHAZI

PO Box 1308, Benghazi
Tel: +218(61) 222-0147 +218(61) 222-9021
Fax: +218(61) 223-0315 +218(61) 222-9022
Website: http://www.benghazi.edu.ly/

President: Mohammed Dghaim (2011-)

Faculties

Arts (Arabic; Archaeology; Educational Administration; Educational Sciences; English; French; Geography; History; Information Sciences; Islamic Studies; Italian; Library Science; Mass

Communication; Media Studies; Philosophy; Physical Education; Religion; Sociology); **Dentistry** (Dentistry; Oral Pathology; Orthodontics; Periodontics; Radiology); **Economics** (Accountancy; Banking; Business Administration; Economics; Finance; Political Sciences; Public Administration); **Education** *(Benghazi)* (Arabic; Art Education; Biology; Chemistry; Computer Science; English; Mathematics; Mathematics Education; Physical Education; Physics; Preschool Education; Teacher Training); **Engineering** (Architecture; Chemical Engineering; Civil Engineering; Electrical and Electronic Engineering; Engineering; Industrial Engineering; Mechanical Engineering; Petroleum and Gas Engineering; Structural Architecture; Town Planning); **Information Technology** (Computer Engineering; Computer Networks; Computer Science; Information Technology; Software Engineering; Telecommunications Engineering); **Law** (Commercial Law; Criminal Law; International Law; Islamic Law; Law; Private Law); **Media** (Journalism; Media Studies; Public Administration; Radio and Television Broadcasting); **Medicine** (Anaesthesiology; Anatomy; Biochemistry; Dermatology; Forensic Medicine and Dentistry; Gynaecology and Obstetrics; Histology; Laboratory Techniques; Medicine; Microbiology; Ophthalmology; Paediatrics; Parasitology; Pathology; Pharmacology; Physiology; Psychiatry and Mental Health; Radiology; Surgery); **Nursing** (Nursing); **Pharmacy** (Pharmacology; Pharmacy; Toxicology); **Public Health** (Environmental Engineering; Epidemiology; Health Administration; Health Education; Nutrition; Occupational Health; Tropical Medicine); **Science** (Botany; Chemistry; Earth Sciences; Geology; Mathematics; Physics; Statistics; Zoology)

Further Information: Also branches in Gmens, Solouq, El-Marj, Alabear, Tukheira, Ajdabia, El-Wahat, EL- Kufrah, AL- Agurea

History: Founded 1955 as University of Libya, reorganized as two separate Universities in Benghazi and Tripoli, 1974. Became Garyounis University, 1976. Acquired present title 2011.

Governing Bodies: University Council

Academic Year: October to June (October-January; February-June)

Admission Requirements: Secondary school certificate or equivalent

Fees: None

Main Language(s) of Instruction: Arabic, English

Degrees and Diplomas: *Bachelor's Degree*: 4 yrs; *Master's Degree*; *Doctorate*

Student Residential Facilities: Yes

Libraries: c. 295,000 vols

Publications: Arts *(annually)*; Economics *(annually)*; Law *(annually)*

Last Updated: 26/10/12

UNIVERSITY OF SIRTE

PO Box 674, Sirte
EMail: registrar@su.edu.ly
Website: http://su.edu.ly

Rector: Mousa Mohammed Musa

Vice-Chancellor: Ambark Mohamed Fari
EMail: chancellor@su.edu.ly

Colleges

Agriculture (Agriculture; Animal Husbandry; Plant and Crop Protection; Soil Science; Water Science); **Arts and Sciences** *(Jufrah)* (Arabic; Arts and Humanities; Chemistry; Computer Science; English; Geography; History; Mathematics; Natural Sciences; Physics; Psychology); **Business Administration** *(Jufrah)* (Accountancy; Business Administration); **Engineering** (Chemical Engineering; Civil Engineering; Electrical Engineering; Engineering; Mechanical Engineering; Petroleum and Gas Engineering); **Law** (Law; Public Law); **Medical Technology** *(Jufrah)* (Laboratory Techniques; Medical Technology; Physical Therapy); **Medicine, Oral and Dental Surgery** (Dentistry; Medicine; Oral Pathology; Stomatology); **Nursing** (Nursing)

Faculties

Arts and Education (Arabic; Arts and Humanities; English; French; Geography; History; Islamic Studies; Media Studies; Translation and Interpretation); **Economics** (Accountancy; Banking; Business Administration; Economics; Finance; Insurance; Statistics); **Education** *(Sirte)* (Arabic; Computer Education; Education; Educational Psychology; English; Koran; Mathematics; Physics); **Medicine** (Medicine; Surgery); **Science** (Botany; Chemistry; Computer Science; Mathematics; Natural Sciences; Physics; Zoology)

Degrees and Diplomas: *Bachelor's Degree*; *Master's Degree*: Arabic; Public Law; Economy; Electrical Engineering; *Doctorate*

Academic Staff *2010-211*: Total 201

STAFF WITH DOCTORATE: Total 100

Student Numbers *2010-211*: Total 10,593

Last Updated: 02/10/12

UNIVERSITY OF TRIPOLI

PO Box 13628, Tripoli, Sedi El-Masri
Tel: +218(21) 462-7910 +218(21) 462-7901
Fax: +218(21) 462-8839 +218(21) 462-7902
EMail: Info@registration.uot.edu.ly
Website: http://www.registration.uot.edu.ly

President: Madani A. Dakhil

Faculties

Agriculture (Agricultural Economics; Agricultural Engineering; Agriculture; Animal Husbandry; Aquaculture; Crop Production; Food Science; Forestry; Home Economics; Horticulture; Plant and Crop Protection; Soil Science; Water Science); **Arts** (Arabic; Arts and Humanities; Education; Educational Psychology; English; Geography; History; Islamic Studies; Library Science; Philosophy; Psychology; Psychotherapy; Social Sciences; Sociology; Tourism); **Economics and Political Science** (Accountancy; Banking; Economics; Electrical and Electronic Engineering; Finance; Management; Political Sciences; Statistics); **Education** *(Soak Ghoma)* (Arabic; Art Education; Biology; Chemistry; Computer Science; Education; English; Mathematics; Physics; Preschool Education; Primary Education; Special Education); **Education** *(Janzour)* (Arabic; Chemistry; Computer Education; Education; English; Mathematics; Physics; Preschool Education; Primary Education; Sociology; Special Education); **Education** *(Ghaser Ben Ghasir)* (Arabic; Biology; Chemistry; Computer Science; Education; English; Geography; Islamic Studies; Mathematics; Physics; Preschool Education; Primary Education; Social and Community Services); **Engineering** (Aeronautical and Aerospace Engineering; Architecture; Chemical Engineering; Civil Engineering; Computer Engineering; Electrical and Electronic Engineering; Engineering; Engineering Management; Geological Engineering; Materials Engineering; Mechanical Engineering; Mineralogy; Mining Engineering; Petroleum and Gas Engineering; Structural Architecture; Town Planning); **Fine Arts and Media** (Fine Arts; Information Sciences; Journalism; Music; Radio and Television Broadcasting; Theatre; Visual Arts); **Information Technology** (Computer Networks; Computer Science; Information Technology; Software Engineering); **Languages** (African Languages; Arabic; English; French; Italian; Spanish; Translation and Interpretation); **Law** (Criminal Law; Islamic Law; Law; Private Law; Public Law); **Medical Technology** (Anaesthesiology; Dental Technology; Medical Technology; Pathology; Physical Therapy; Public Health); **Medicine** (Medicine); **Nursing** (Anaesthesiology; Midwifery; Nursing; Surgery); **Oral Surgery and Dentistry** (Dentistry; Oral Pathology; Orthodontics; Stomatology); **Pharmacy** (Biochemistry; Microbiology; Pharmacology; Pharmacy); **Physical Education** (Physical Education; Physical Therapy; Teacher Training); **Science** (Botany; Chemistry; Computer Science; Geology; Geophysics; Mathematics; Meteorology; Natural Sciences; Physics; Statistics; Zoology); **Veterinary Medicine** (Microbiology; Parasitology; Surgery; Veterinary Science)

History: Founded 1957 as University of Libya, reorganized as two separate universities in Tripoli and Benghazi, 1973. Renamed Al Fateh University in 1976. Acquired former name of University of Tripoli in 2011.

Academic Year: September to July (September-January; February-July)

Admission Requirements: Secondary school certificate or equivalent

Fees: None

Main Language(s) of Instruction: Arabic, English

Degrees and Diplomas: *Bachelor's Degree (BS; BA)*: 4-6 yrs; *Master's Degree*: a further 2-3 yrs

Libraries: c. 10,000 vols

Last Updated: 11/07/12

PRIVATE INSTITUTIONS

ACADEMY OF GRADUATE STUDIES

Academiat Addirasat Alulia (AGS)
PO Box 79031, Janzour, Tripoli
Tel: +218(21) 487-2796
Fax: +218(21) 487-3075
EMail: info@alacademia.edu.ly
Website: http://www.alacademia.edu.ly/

Director-General: Saleh Ibrahim Almabruk (1998-)
Tel: +218(21) 487-3076

International Relations: Milad Saad Milad
Tel: +218(91) 218-1259

Schools

Administration and Finance (Accountancy; Administration; Banking; Business Administration; Economics; Educational Administration; Finance; Marketing) *Director*: Masoud Al-Barouni; **Art and Media** (Archaeology; Fine Arts; Media Studies; Theatre) *Director*: Ali Alrabiae; **Basic Sciences** (Biological and Life Sciences; Chemistry; Computer Science; Earth Sciences; Environmental Studies; Mathematics; Physics; Statistics) *Director*: Ali Benalashar; **Engineering Sciences** (Architecture; Biomedical Engineering; Chemical Engineering; Civil Engineering; Computer Engineering; Electrical and Electronic Engineering; Engineering; Environmental Engineering; Mechanical Engineering; Petroleum and Gas Engineering) *Director*: Mar'i Abu Setah; **Humanities** (Arabic; Arts and Humanities; Criminal Law; English; French; Geography; History; International Law; Italian; Law; Modern Languages; Philosophy; Political Sciences; Psychology; Social Sciences) *Director*: Bashir Abu Ghila; **International and Strategic Studies** (Economics; International Relations; Political Sciences) *Director*: Abdulhameed Al-Nami; **Languages** (African Languages; Arabic; English; French; German; Spanish; Translation and Interpretation) *Director*: Wedad Al-Aradi

History: Founded 1988 as Institute of Graduate Studies and Economic Sciences. Acquired present status and title 1994.

Governing Bodies: Council

Academic Year: September to February; February to June

Admission Requirements: First university degree with general average 'good'.

Main Language(s) of Instruction: Arabic and English

Degrees and Diplomas: *Master's Degree*: 2 yrs; *Doctorate*: 4 yrs. Also Postgraduate Diploma

Student Services: Academic counselling, Canteen, Cultural centre, Foreign student adviser, Foreign Studies Centre, Handicapped facilities, Language programs, Social counselling, Sports facilities

Libraries: 42,000 vols and 10,120 vols in Arabic and English. Also over 350 periodicals

Publications: The Academy Journal of Humanities and Social Sciences *(biennially)*; The Academy Journal of Pure and Applied Sciences *(biennially)*

Last Updated: 07/04/08

LIBYAN INTERNATIONAL MEDICAL UNIVERSITY (LIMU)

Kairawan St., AL-Fwaihat, Benghazi
Tel: +218(61) 470-6647
Fax: +218(61) 223-3909
EMail: aric@limu.edu.ly
Website: http://limu.edu.ly/ar/

President: Mohammed Saad Ambarak

Faculties

Basic Medical Sciences (Biology; Chemistry; Medicine; Microbiology; Parasitology; Physiology); **Dentistry** (Dentistry; Oral Pathology; Orthodontics); **Health Sciences** (Dental Hygiene; Dental Technology; Health Sciences; Medical Technology; Nursing; Physical Therapy; Radiology; Speech Therapy and Audiology); **Medicine** (Anaesthesiology; Forensic Medicine and Dentistry; Gynaecology and Obstetrics; Medicine; Ophthalmology; Paediatrics; Public Health; Radiology; Surgery); **Pharmacy** (Pharmacology; Pharmacy)

Degrees and Diplomas: *Bachelor's Degree*

Last Updated: 31/10/12

Liechtenstein

STRUCTURE OF HIGHER EDUCATION SYSTEM

Description:

Since the law governing higher education came into effect in 1992, Liechtenstein has a limited tertiary-education sector. In addition, Liechtenstein has contractual arrangements with Switzerland, Austria and Tübingen (Baden-Württemberg/Germany) allowing students free entry to university in these countries.

Stages of studies:

University level first stage: *Bachelor*

The final examination organized at the end of the first cycle of university studies, which lasts for at least 6 semesters, leads to the following degrees: Bachelor of Science (Bsc) or Bachelor of Arts (BA) + branch of study.

University level second stage: *Master*

The final examination organized at the end of second cycle university studies, which lasts for at least 4 semesters, leads to the following degrees: Master of Science (Msc) or Master of Arts (MA) + branch of study.

University level third stage: *Doctor*

On successful completion of doctoral studies (6 semesters) at the International Academy of Philosophy (IAP), students are awarded the following academic title: Doktor der Philosophie (Dr. Phil.). On successful completion of doctoral studies (6 semesters) at the Private University of the Principality of Liechtenstein (UFL), students are awarded the following academic title: Doctor of Scientific Medicine (Dr. scient. med.) and Doctor of Property Rights (Dr. jur.). Since 2008, the University of Liechtenstein offers doctoral programmes in Economics and Architecture leading to a doctoral degree (Dr.)

ADMISSION TO HIGHER EDUCATION

Admission to university-level studies:

Name of secondary school credential required: Maturazeugnis

Minimum score/requirement: 4

For entry to: All university-level institutions in Liechtenstein, Austria and Switzerland.

Name of secondary school credential required: Berufsmaturitätszeugnis

Minimum score/requirement: 4

For entry to: All university-level institutions and universities in Liechtenstein and Austria, universities of applied sciences in Switzerland.

Foreign students admission:

Entrance exam requirements: A short-stay permit can be granted for the duration of one semester or one academic year to students wishing to attend a recognised educational institution in Liechtenstein if: a) the educational institution confirms in writing that the student can take up or continue the studies concerned (confirmation of registration); b) the financial means are sufficient; c) proof of the required health insurance protection is provided; d) the student has the linguistic competences for the course concerned. A prolongation is possible according to the length of studies.

Language requirements: Good knowledge of German (written, oral).

RECOGNITION OF STUDIES

Quality assurance system:

Education is supervised by the State. All higher education institutions need to be authorized by the government on the basis of institutional and programme accreditations. Accreditation is done by a recognized quality assurance agency. There is no national quality assurance agency in Liechtenstein, but instead strong cooperation with foreign quality assurance agencies, especially from the neighboring countries (Switzerland, Austria and Germany) and the European Quality Assurance Register for Higher Education (EQAR). Liechtenstein is a full member of EQAR.

Bodies dealing with recognition:

Informationsstelle für Anerkennungsfragen - NARIC Liechtenstein (National Academic Recognition Information Centre)

Head: Helmut Konrad
Austrasse 79, Postfach 684
Vaduz 9490
Tel: +423 236 6758
Fax: +423 236 6771

Schulamt (Office of Education)

Austrasse 79
Vaduz 9490
Tel: +423 236 6770
Fax: +423 236 6771
EMail: info@sa.llv.li
WWW: http://www.sa.llv.li

Special provisions for recognition:

For exercising a profession: Only for regularised professions.

Recognition for university level studies: ENIC/NARIC Agency.

NATIONAL BODIES

Regierung, Ressort Bildung (Ministry of Education)

Minister: Hugo Quaderer
Regierungebäude, Peter-Kaiser-Platz 1
Vaduz FL-9490
Tel: +423 236 6011
Fax: +423 236 6184
WWW: http://www.regierung.li/index.php?id=689

Schulamt (Office of Education)

Austrasse 79
Vaduz 9490
Tel: +423 236 6770
Fax: +423 236 6771
EMail: info@sa.llv.li
WWW: http://www.sa.llv.li

Data for academic year: 2011-2012

Source: IAU from the Schulamt des Fürstentum Liechtenstein, 2011. Bodies 2012.

INSTITUTIONS

PUBLIC INSTITUTION

LIECHTENSTEIN UNIVERSITY

Universität Liechtenstein

Fürst-Franz-Josef-Strasse, 9490 Vaduz
Tel: +423 265-11-11
Fax: +423 265-11-12
EMail: info@uni.li
Website: http://www.uni.li/

Rector: Klaus Näscher (1985-) EMail: klaus.naescher@uni.li

International Relations: Trudi Ackermann
Tel: +423 265-11-03, Fax: +423 265-12-65
EMail: trudi.ackermann@uni.li

Centres

KMU (Management; Small Business)

Departments

Undergraduate Business Economics (Business Administration; Business Computing)

Institutes

Architecture and Planning (Architecture; Architecture and Planning; Design; Town Planning); **Entrepreneurship** (Finance; International Business; Management); **Financial Services** (Banking; Business Administration; Finance; International Business; International Law; Taxation); **Information Systems** (Business Administration; Information Management; Information Sciences; Production Engineering)

Research Centres

Liechtenstein Economic *(KOFL)* (Economics)

Schools

Graduate Studies (Architecture; Business Administration)

History: Founded 1961as Abendtechnikum Vaduz, acquired title of Hochschule Liechtenstein in 1992. Acquired current title and status 2011

Admission Requirements: Secondary school certificate (Matura)

Fees: (Swiss Francs): 750 per semester

Main Language(s) of Instruction: German, English

International Co-operation: Partcipates in EU mobility and research programmes.

Degrees and Diplomas: *Bachelor*: Architecture (BSc Arch); Business Administration (BSc); Information Systems (BSc), 3 yrs; *Master*: Architecture (MSc Arch); Business Process Management; Banking and Financial Management; Entrepreneurship (Major - Finance) (MSc), 2 yrs; *Doctorate*: Architecture and Planning (Dr. scient. / PhD); Business Economics (Dr. rer. oec. / PhD), 3-5 yrs. Also Executive MBA.

Student Services: Canteen, Foreign student adviser, Sports facilities

Student Residential Facilities: Yes

Academic Staff *2009-2010*	**TOTAL**
FULL-TIME	**30**
PART-TIME	c. **150**
Student Numbers *2009-2010*	
All (Foreign Included)	**660**

Last Updated: 19/05/11

PRIVATE INSTITUTIONS

INTERNATIONAL ACADEMY OF PHILOSOPHY IN THE PRINCIPALITY OF LIECHTENSTEIN

Internationale Akademie für Philosophie im Fürstentum Liechtenstein (IAP)

Im Schwibboga 7b, 9487 Bendern
Tel: +423 265-43-43
Fax: +423 265-43-41
EMail: admin@iap.li
Website: http://www.iap.li

President of Senate: Josef Seifert (1986-) EMail: jseifert@iap.li

Secretary-General: Hubertus Dessloch Tel: +423 265-43-02

International Relations: Doris Hager-Hämmerle, International Relations Officer Tel: +423 265-43-27, Fax: +423 265-43-47

Campuses

Main (Philosophy); **Offshore** *(: International Academy of Philosophy at Pontificia Universidad Católica de Chile (IAP-PUC))* (Philosophy)

Research Centres

Peace and Human Dignity at IAP *(Forschungszentrum für Frieden und Menschenwürde an der IAP)* (Philosophy); **Studies of Plato and the Platonic Roots of Western Philosophy at IAP** *(Internationalen Zentrum für Studien über Platon und die platonischen Wurzeln in der abendländischen Philosophie an der IAP)* (Philosophy)

History: Founded 1986.

Governing Bodies: Senate; Board of Trustees

Academic Year: September to June (September-January; March-June)

Admission Requirements: Master Programme: BA in Philosophy; Doctoral Programme: MA in Philosophy.

Fees: (Swiss Francs): 7,500 per semester; varies according to campus.

Main Language(s) of Instruction: German; English; Spanish

International Co-operation: Exchange and cooperation programmes in research and teaching with several European and other countries; additional cooperation programmes (student exchange) under development; an agreement has been signed integrating the Instituto de Filosofia Edith Stein (IFES) in Granada (www.if-edith-stein.org/) into the campus programme of the International Academy of Philosophy

Accrediting Agencies: Schulamt, Ressort Bildungswesen Fürstentum Liechtenstein http://www.llv.li/amtsstellen/llv-sa-home.htm (Office of Education, affiliated to Ministry of Education of the Principality of Liechtenstein)

Degrees and Diplomas: *Master*, *Doctorate*

Student Services: Academic counselling, Foreign student adviser, Language programs

Libraries: c. 14,500 vols on Philosophy (in the fields of Phenomenology, Ancient Greek philosophy, Philosophy of peace and intercultural dialogue, Philosophical Anthropology, Foundations of ethics and applied ethics, Philosophy of Science, Philosophy of Medicine, Metaphysics, etc.; and in more than 20 languages: German, English, French, Italian, Latin, Spain, Polish, (classical) Greek, Russian etc.). Online Library Catalogue Network (online catalogue: http://neptun.lbfl.li/);

Publications: Aletheia, International yearbook of philosophy on Western themes such as the nature and kinds of knowledge, the foundations of morality, the nature of substance, of causality, value, the person, beauty, and religion. *(other/irregular)*

Last Updated: 06/09/11

UNIVERSITY OF HUMAN SCIENCES

Private Universität im Fürstentum Liechtenstein (UFL)

Dorfstrasse 24, FL-9495 Triesen
Tel: +423 392-40-10
Fax: +423 392-40-11
EMail: info@ufl.li
Website: http://www.ufl.li

Rector: Karl Sudi EMail: karl.sudi@ufl.li

Head, Administration: Brigitte Alicke EMail: brigitte.alicke@ufl.li

Faculties

Law (Constitutional Law; European Union Law; International Law; Labour Law; Law; Private Law; Taxation); **Medical Science** (Medicine)

History: Founded 2000. Formerly known as Universität für Humanwissenschaften im Fürstentum Liechtenstein (University of Human Sciences).

Governing Bodies: University Council; Scientific Advisory Boards

Main Language(s) of Instruction: German

Degrees and Diplomas: *Doctorate*. Also MD-PhD programme jointly offered with the Medical University of Innsbruck.

Last Updated: 04/11/11

Lithuania

STRUCTURE OF HIGHER EDUCATION SYSTEM

Description:

Lithuania has a binary system of higher education consisting of college and university studies, which are organized in three cycles. College studies are only offered at the 1st cycle as undergraduate studies intended to prepare for professional activity on the basis of applied research activities. The studies require 180–240 ECTS credits to complete and lead to a degree of profesinis bakalauras (Professional Bachelor). Holders of the degree have the right to enter the 2nd cycle (Master) studies only after completion of additional requirements. University studies are organized in three cycles. The 1st cycle university studies require 210–240 ECTS credits to complete and lead to a degree of bakalauras (Bachelor), which gives direct access to the 2nd cycle studies. The 2nd cycle studies require 90–120 ECTS credits to complete and lead to a degree of magistras (Master), which gives access to the 3rd cycle studies. The 3rd cycle studies do not exceed 4 years and lead to a research degree of daktaras (Doctor). There are also vientisosios (integrated) university studies (combining studies of the 1st and 2nd cycle), which are usually offered in several fields of medicine, veterinary medicine, law, and religious studies. The studies require 300–360 ECTS credits to complete and lead to a degree of (magistras) Master. Higher education institutions can also offer non-degree programmes, which award additional professional qualification and/or prepare for independent practice in several professional activities. The workload of non-degree studies is 30–120 ECTS credits. Currently non-degree studies are offered in relation to training and education of teachers and doctors.

Stages of studies:

University level first stage: *University 1st cycle studies (universitetines pirmosios pakopos studijos)*
University 1st cycle studies are offered by university-level institutions called universities (universitetas), academies (akademija), or seminaries (seminarija). Studies last from 3.5 to 4 years (210 to 240 ECTS). The studies are research-oriented with subjects related to the field of study and to a certain extent a narrower specialization comprising most of the curriculum. The main standards and requirements irrespective of the field of study are nationally set. To complete the programme, students are expected to prepare and defend a final thesis or, in certain cases, to pass final examinations. Successful graduates are awarded a Bachelor's degree (bakalauro laipsnis) in the field of study. The Bachelor's degree (bakalauro laipsnis) gives access to the 2nd cycle (Master) programmes.

University level second stage: *University 2nd cycle studies (universitetines antrosios pakopos studijos)*
Master studies: University 2nd cycle studies are offered by university-level institutions called universities (universitetas), academies (akademija), or seminaries (seminarija) where research related to the subject area is conducted. The studies last from 1.5 to 2 years (90 to 120 ECTS). They prepare for independent research activities and activities which require scientific knowledge and analytical skills. The main standards and requirements irrespective of the field of study are nationally set. To complete the programme, students are expected to prepare and defend a final thesis, which should be analytical and based on independent research. Successful graduates are awarded a Master's degree (magistro laipsnis) in the field of study. Those who majored in Theology may be awarded a Licentiate degree in Theology (teologijos licenciato laipsnis). The Master's degree (magistro laipsnis) gives access to the 3rd cycle (Doctoral) programmes.
Integrated studies: Integrated (vientisosios) studies are long-cycle studies, which combine the 1st and 2nd university cycles. Holders of Maturity Certificate (Brandos atestatas) or a comparable qualification can be admitted.
The studies last from 5 to 6 years (300 to 360 ECTS). The first part of the studies (240 ECTS) is considered to be part of the 1st cycle, the rest of the studies belong to the 2nd cycle. The regulations for each of the cycles apply accordingly. Successful graduates are awarded a Master's degree (magistro laipsnis) in the field of study, which gives access to the 3rd cycle (Doctoral) programmes.

University level third stage: *University 3rd cycle studies (universitetines treciosios pakopos studijos)*
University 3rd cycle studies are offered by university-level institutions called universities (universitetas), academies (akademija), or seminaries (seminarija), which were granted the right to offer Doctoral studies by the Ministry of Education and Science as able to conduct advanced research activities. At times doctoral studies may

be jointly offered by university level higher education institutions and research institutes. Doctoral studies may be offered in the fields of science, humanities, and arts aimed at preparing for independent and/or experimental research. Doctoral studies last from 3 to 4 years (6 years part-time). They consist of doctoral courses (at least 30 ECTS), specific research activities, and preparation and public defence of a doctoral dissertation. Successful graduates are awarded a Degree of Doctor of Science (mokslo daktaro laipsnis) or a Degree of Doctor of Arts (meno daktaro laipsnis).

Distance higher education:

Currently, in Lithuania, there are no higher education institutions which would exclusively offer distance higher education. Usually, universities and colleges, in addition to the traditional learning paths, give an option to take a course or, less often, to complete an entire study programme through distance learning. Most higher education institutions have separate divisions, which are responsible for technical development, implementation, and coordination of distance learning courses or programmes. However, current legislation provisions that at least 5 to 10 percent of the programme, depending on the study cycle, should be carried out through direct classroom contact.

ADMISSION TO HIGHER EDUCATION

Admission to university-level studies:

Name of secondary school credential required: Brandos atestatas

For entry to: Bachelor's programmes and integrated programmes.

Alternatives to credentials: A comparable qualification.

Entrance exam requirements: Generally, maturity (school level and state level) examinations serve as graduation and admission requirement. However, for admission to certain programmes, especially in arts, an entrance examination may be held.

Numerus clausus/restrictions: There is a numerus clausus, which applies to state funded places, set by the Ministry of Education and Science according to the field of study. Institutions may set their own numerus clausus for fee paying students.

Foreign students admission:

Quotas: Study grants awarded to EU students with foreign qualifications, irrespective of their nationality (including Lithuanian citizens who have acquired their education abroad), should not exceed 10 percent of all state funded grants.

Entrance exam requirements: Foreign applicants should at least hold a level of education comparable to a Lithuanian qualification required for admission to the particular study programme. Information on the assessment and comparability of qualifications is provided by the Centre for Quality Assessment in Higher Education (Lithuanian ENIC/NARIC) (www.skvc.lt).

Entry regulations: Entry regulations may vary depending on the country of origin of a foreign student. Foreign nationals are encouraged to contact a Lithuanian embassy or check on the websites of the Ministry of Foreign Affairs (www.urm.lt) and Migration Department (www.migracija.lt) whether they need a visa and a temporary residence permit.

Health requirements: Health insurance is obligatory to all foreign students in Lithuania. EU citizens who have health insurance in their home country do not need additional insurance.

Language requirements: A student should be proficient in the language of instruction. Usually, the language of instruction is Lithuanian and an applicant has to pass the pass/fail test in Lithuanian language (www.flf.vu.lt/lsk/). In case the language of instruction is other than Lithuanian (English, German, or Russian), applicants must pass a test to demonstrate their proficiency in that language.

RECOGNITION OF STUDIES

Quality assurance system:

While higher education institutions are primarily responsible for the quality assurance and are setting up systems of internal quality assurance, the external quality assurance in higher education is carried out by the

Centre for Quality Assessment in Higher Education (www.skvc.lt). The Centre is an independent body, which carries out institutional and study programme assessment for the purposes of accreditation. The list of recognized higher education institutions and accredited study programmes is available at: www.aikos.smm.lt.

Bodies dealing with recognition:

Studijų kokybės vertinimo centras - SKVC (Centre for Quality Assessment in Higher Education (Lithuanian ENIC/NARIC))

Director: Artūras Grebliauskas
Deputy Director: Aurelija Valeikienė
A. Goštauto g. 12
Vilnius, 01108
Tel: +370(5) 210 4772
Fax: +370(5) 213 2553
EMail: enicnaric@skvc.lt;skvc@skvc.lt
WWW: http://www.skvc.lt/

Special provisions for recognition:

For exercising a profession: Information on recognition of foreign qualifications for the purposes of work for non-regulated professions can be provided by the Centre for Quality Assessment in Higher Education (www.skvc.lt).
Information on the recognition of regulated professions is available at www.profesijos.lt .

Recognition for university level studies: Information on recognition of foreign qualifications for the purposes of study can be provided by the Centre for Quality Assessment in Higher Education (www.skvc.lt).

For access to advanced studies and research: Information on recognition of foreign qualifications for the purposes of study can be provided by the Centre for Quality Assessment in Higher Education (www.skvc.lt).

NATIONAL BODIES

Švietimo ir mokslo ministerija (Ministry of Education and Science)

Minister: Gintaras Steponavičius
A. Volano g. 2/7
Vilnius 01516
Tel: +370(5) 219 1190
Fax: +370(5) 261 2077
EMail: smmin@smm.lt
WWW: http://www.smm.lt

Lietuvos mokslo taryba - LMT (Research Council of Lithuania)

Chairman: Eugenijus Butkus
Gedimino pr. 3
Vilnius 01103
Tel: +370(5) 2124 933
Fax: +370(5) 2618 535
EMail: lmt@ktl.mii.lt
WWW: http://www.lmt.lt/

Lietuvos universitetu rektorių konferencija (Lithuanian University Rectors' Conference)

President: Remigijus Žaliūnas
Secretary-General: Kęstutis Kriščiūnas
EMail: lurkbiuras@lurk.lt
WWW: http://www.lurk.lt

Lietuvos kolgiju direktoriu konferencija (Lithuanian College Directors' Conference)

Executive Director: Kristin Lakickaitė
J. Jasinskio g. 15
Vilnius 01111

Tel: +370(5) 219 1600
Fax: +370(5) 219 1622
WWW: http://www.kolegijos.lt

Data for academic year: 2011-2012
Source: IAU from the Lithuanian Centre for Quality Assessment in Higher Education, 2011. Bodies 2012.

INSTITUTIONS

PUBLIC INSTITUTIONS

ALEKSANDRAS STULGINSKIS UNIVERSITY

Aleksandro Stulginskio Universitetas (LŽŪU)
Studentų g. 11, Akademija, 53361 Kaunas
Tel: +370(37) 75-23-00
Fax: +370(37) 39-75-00
EMail: laa@lzuu.lt
Website: http://www.lzuu.lt/

Rector: Antanas Maziliauskas

Vice-Rector for Studies: Jonas Čaplikas
EMail: jonas.caplikas@lzuu.lt; studijos@lzuu.lt

International Relations: Minvydas Liegus
Tel: +370(37) 75-23-98 EMail: kontakt@lzuu.lt

Faculties
Agricultural Engineering (Agricultural Engineering; Agricultural Equipment; Energy Engineering; Mechanical Engineering); **Agronomy** (Agronomy; Animal Husbandry; Biology; Crop Production; Horticulture; Soil Science); **Economics and Management** (Accountancy; Business Administration; Economics; Finance; Management; Rural Planning); **Forestry and Ecology** (Ecology; Forest Management; Forestry); **Water and Land Management** (Agricultural Management; Hydraulic Engineering; Rural Planning; Surveying and Mapping; Water Management)

Institutes
Environment (Environmental Studies; Rural Planning) *Director*: Vida Rutkovienė; **Information Technology** (Computer Science; Information Technology; Mathematics) *Director*: Aleksandras Savilionis; **Rural Culture** (Cultural Studies; Modern Languages; Philosophy; Political Sciences; Psychology; Social Sciences) *Director*: Svetlana Statkevičienė

Further Information: Also Training Farm. Experimental Station. Innovation Centre. Caree Centre

History: Founded 1924 in Dotnuva (Kėdainiai district). Relocated to Kaunas, 1964. Under the resolution of Parliament on October 8th, 1996, the name of Lithuanian Academy of Agriculture was changed to Lithuanian University of Agriculture. Following the resolution of the LR Seimas on June 28th, 2011, it was granted the name of Aleksandras Stulginskis University.

Governing Bodies: Council, Senate

Academic Year: September to June (September-January; February-June)

Admission Requirements: Secondary school certificate (Vidurinės Mokyklos Baigimo Atestatas)

Main Language(s) of Instruction: Lithuanian

International Co-operation: With universities in Denmark, United Kingdom, Netherlands, France, Spain, Portugal, Italy, Austria, Germany, Sweden, Finland, Latvia, Estonia, Poland, Czech Republic, Slovak Republic

Accrediting Agencies: Lithuanian Centre for Quality Assessment in Higher Education

Degrees and Diplomas: *Bakalauro diplomas*: Agronomy; Forestry; Economics and Management; Agricultural Engineering; Water and Land Management; Applied Ecology (BSc), 4 yrs; *Magistro diplomas*: Agronomy; Forestry; Economics and Management; Agricultural Engineering; Water and Land Management; Applied Ecology (MSc), a further 2 yrs; *Daktaro diplomas*: Agronomy; Forestry; Economics and Management; Agricultural Engineering; Water and Land Management; Applied Ecology (PhD), a further 4 yrs

Student Services: Academic counselling, Canteen, Cultural centre, Foreign student adviser, Handicapped facilities, Health services, Language programs, Nursery care, Social counselling, Sports facilities

Student Residential Facilities: For 1,900 students

Special Facilities: Museum of the History of Lithuanian University of Agriculture; Ethnographical Museum; Museum of Hydraulic Engineering and Land Management

Libraries: Central Library, 580,000 vols

Publications: Science Reports, Yearbook *(annually)*

Press or Publishing House: Lietuvos Žemes Ukio Akademijos Leidybinis Centras

Last Updated: 28/10/11

KAUNAS UNIVERSITY OF TECHNOLOGY

Kauno Technologijos Universitetas (KTU)
K. Donelaičio g. 73, 44029 Kaunas
Tel: +370(37) 300-000 +370(37) 300-099 +370(37) 324-140
Fax: +370(37) 324-144
EMail: rastine@ktu.lt
Website: http://www.ktu.lt

Rector: Petras Baršauskas
Tel: +370(37) 300-001, Fax: +370(37) 324-054
EMail: rektorius@ktu.lt

Vice-Rector for Studies: Pranas Žiliukas
Tel: +370(37) 300-002 EMail: pranas.ziliukas@ktu.lt

International Relations: Sigitas Stanys, Vice-Rector
Tel: +370(37) 300-005, Fax: +370(37) 300-010
EMail: sigitas.stanys@ktu.lt

Centres
Computational Technologies (Computer Engineering; Mechanical Engineering; Systems Analysis) *Director*: Rimantas Barauskas; **International Studies** (Engineering Management; Mechanical Engineering) *Director*: Arvydas Palevičius; **Mechatronics Science, Studies and Information** *Director*: Ramutis Bansevičiuc; **Microsystems and Nanotechnology Research** (Nanotechnology) *Director*: Valentinas Snitka; **Physical Education and Health** (Health Education; Sports) *Director*: Vitas Linonis

Faculties
Chemical Technology (Applied Chemistry; Chemical Engineering; Chemistry; Environmental Engineering; Environmental Management; Food Science; Food Technology); **Civil Engineering and Architecture** (Architecture; Civil Engineering; Real Estate; Regional Planning; Town Planning); **Design and Technology** (Fashion Design; Furniture Design; Multimedia; Polymer and Plastics Technology; Printing and Printmaking; Textile Design; Textile Technology; Wood Technology); **Economics and Management** (Accountancy; Economics; Finance; International Business; Management; Marketing); **Electrical and Control Systems** (Automation and Control Engineering; Electrical Engineering; Electronic Engineering; Safety Engineering); **Fundamental Sciences** (Applied Mathematics; Applied Physics; Mathematics Education; Radiophysics); **Humanities** (Cultural Studies; Linguistics; Media Studies;

Philosophy; Translation and Interpretation); **Informatics** (Computer Engineering; Computer Science); **Management and Administration** *(Panevezys)* (Business Administration; Management); **Mechanical Engineering and Mechatronics** (Industrial Engineering; Materials Engineering; Mechanical Engineering; Packaging Technology; Production Engineering; Thermal Engineering; Transport Engineering); **Social Sciences** (Business Administration; Educational Sciences; Educational Technology; Pedagogy; Public Administration; Sociology); **Technology** *(Panevėžys)* (Automation and Control Engineering; Civil Engineering; Mechanical Engineering; Transport Engineering); **Telecommunications and Electronics** (Biomedical Engineering; Electronic Engineering; Engineering Management; Measurement and Precision Engineering; Telecommunications Engineering)

Institutes

Biomedical Engineering; **Defence Technologies**; **Energy Technologies** (Energy Engineering); **Environmental Engineering** (Environmental Engineering; Environmental Management; Natural Resources; Waste Management); **Europe** (European Studies); **Information Technology Development** (Computer Engineering; Information Technology); **Materials Science** (Materials Engineering); **Metrology**; **Synthetic Chemistry** (Chemistry); **Technological Systems Diagnostics**; **Ultrasound Research** *(Prof. K. Baršauskas)* (Sound Engineering (Acoustics))

History: Founded 1922, became University of Lithuania 1922 and University of Kaunas 1940. Technical Department detached and reorganized into Kaunas Polytechnic Institute 1950. Acquired university status 1990.

Governing Bodies: Senate and Board

Academic Year: September to June (September-January; February-June)

Admission Requirements: Maturity Certificate (Brandos atestatas) or equivalent

Main Language(s) of Instruction: Lithuanian, English, German, French, Russian

International Co-operation: With universities in Japan. Also participates in the Erasmus, Leonardo da Vinci, Vulcanus programmes

Degrees and Diplomas: *Bakalauro diplomas*: Science; Engineering (BSc), 4 yrs; *Magistro diplomas*: Science; Engineering (MSc), a further 1 1/2-2 yrs after BSc; *Daktaro diplomas*: Science, a further 4 yrs after MSc. Also Mokytojo diplomas in Teacher Training (a further 1 yr after BSc)

Student Services: Academic counselling, Canteen, Cultural centre, Employment services, Foreign student adviser, Health services, Language programs, Social counselling, Sports facilities

Student Residential Facilities: Yes

Special Facilities: University History Museum

Libraries: c. 2.2 m. vols (including a rare book collection of 30,000 foreign and Lithuanian vols which date back to the 15th century)

Publications: Chemical Technology *(quarterly)*; Electronics and Electrical Engineering *(other/irregular)*; Engineering Economics *(other/irregular)*; Environmental Research, Engineering and Management *(quarterly)*; Information Technology and Control *(other/irregular)*; Materials Science *(quarterly)*; Measurements *(quarterly)*; Mechanics *(biennially)*; Public Politics and Administration *(biennially)*; Social Sciences *(quarterly)*; Ultrasound *(quarterly)*

Press or Publishing House: Publishing Centre

Last Updated: 28/10/11

KLAIPĖDA UNIVERSITY

Klaipėdos Universitetas (KU)

Herkaus Manto g. 84, 92294 Klaipėda
Tel: +370(46) 39-89-00
Fax: +370(46) 39-89-99
EMail: rektorius@rekt.ku.lt
Website: http://www.ku.lt

Rector: Vaidutis Laurėnas EMail: vaidutis.laurenas@ku.lt

Vice-Rector for Research and Academic Affairs: Inga Dailidienė EMail: inga.dailidiene@ku.lt

International Relations: Inga Petrauskienė
Tel: +370(46) 39-89-51, Fax: +370(46) 39-89-52

Centres

American Studies (American Studies) *Head*: I. Sabaliauskaite; **Baltic Studies** (Baltic Languages) *Head*: A. Kaukienė; **English Language** (English); **Evangelical Theology** *(Study and Research Centre)* (Christian Religious Studies; Theology) *Director*: A. Baublys; **Oriental Studies** (Asian Studies; Middle Eastern Studies; Oriental Languages) *Head*: A. Čomičenkienė; **Scandinavian Languages and Cultures** (Scandinavian Languages) *Director*: K. Karčiauskienė; **Slavic Studies** *Head*: T. Vinogradova

Faculties

Arts (Fine Arts; Performing Arts); **Health Sciences** (Health Sciences); **Humanities** (Arts and Humanities); **Marine Engineering** (Marine Engineering); **Natural Sciences and Mathematics** (Mathematics; Natural Sciences); **Pedagogy** (Pedagogy); **Social Sciences** (Social Sciences)

Institutes

Coastal Research and Planning (Coastal Studies); **Continuing Studies** (Continuing Education); **History and Archaeology of the Baltic Region** (Archaeology; History); **Marine Seascape Science** (Marine Science and Oceanography); **Maritime** (Marine Science and Oceanography); **Mechatronics Science** (Electrical Engineering; Mechanical Engineering); **Regional Policy and Planning** (Regional Planning)

History: Founded 1991.

Governing Bodies: Senate; Faculty Council

Academic Year: September to June (September-January; February-June)

Admission Requirements: Secondary school certificate (Brandos Atestatas)

Main Language(s) of Instruction: Lithuanian

Degrees and Diplomas: *Bakalauro diplomas*: 4-5 yrs; *Magistro diplomas*: a further 2 yrs; *Daktaro diplomas (PhD)*: a further 4-5 yrs by thesis following Magistras

Student Services: Academic counselling, Canteen, Cultural centre, Handicapped facilities, Sports facilities

Student Residential Facilities: For 900 students

Special Facilities: Botanical Garden, 15 laboratories, 23 computer rooms

Libraries: Scientific library with 7 branches in faculties c. 500,000 vols

Publications: Acta Historica Universitatis Klaipedensis, Scientific Journal *(biannually)*; Archaeologica Baltica, Scientific Journal *(biannually)*; Jūra ir aplinka (Sea and Environment), Scientific Journal *(annually)*; Sociologija: mintis ir veiksmas (Sociology: Thought and Action), Scientific Journal *(annually)*; Tiltai (Bridges), Scientific Journal *(quarterly)*

Press or Publishing House: Klaipeda University Press

Last Updated: 27/02/12

LITHUANIAN ACADEMY OF MUSIC AND THEATRE

Lietuvos Muzikos ir Teatro Akademija (LMTA)

Gedimino pr. 42, 01110 Vilnius
Tel: +370(5) 261-26-91
Fax: +370(5) 212-69-82
EMail: rektoratas@lmta.lt
Website: http://www.lmta.lt

Rector: Zbignevas Ibelhauptas (2011-)

Vice-Rector for Studies: Vida Umbrasienė
Tel: +370(5) 261-81-40

Faculties

Music (Conducting; Music; Music Theory and Composition; Musical Instruments; Opera; Singing); **Theatre and Film** (Acting; Art Criticism; Art History; Art Management; Cinema and Television; Film; Theatre)

History: Founded 1933. Formerly Lietuvos Muzikos Akademija. In 1949 the Conservatoire of Kaunas and the Conservatoire of Vilnius (founded in 1945) were merged into the Lithuanian State Conservatoire. In 1992 the Conservatoire was renamed Lithuanian Academy of Music (LMA), and in 2004 Lithuanian Academy of Music and Theatre (LMTA).

Governing Bodies: Senate; College

Academic Year: September to June (September-January; February-June)

Admission Requirements: Certificate of secondary education and secondary musical education or equivalent

Main Language(s) of Instruction: Lithuanian, English, German, Russian

International Co-operation: Participates in the Socrates/Erasmus programme

Accrediting Agencies: Ministry of Education and Science; Lithuanian Centre for Quality Assessment in Higher Education

Degrees and Diplomas: *Bakalauro diplomas*: Music; Musicology; Music Education; Dramatic Art; Audivisual Art (BA), 4 yrs; *Magistro diplomas*: Music; Musicology; Dramatic Art; Audiovisual Art (MA; MMusEd), a further 2 yrs; *Daktaro diplomas*: Musicology; Ethnomusicology; History and Theory of Dramatic Art, 2 yrs (for musicologists) following Master's Degree

Student Services: Canteen, Foreign student adviser, Health services, Language programs, Nursery care, Sports facilities

Student Residential Facilities: For national students only

Special Facilities: Museum of LAM History.

Libraries: Central Library, 500,000 vols; Kaunas Faculty Library, 40,000 vols; Record Library, 50,000 records and tapes; Archives of Department of Ethno-Musicology, 86,000 items

Publications: Collection of Scientific Articles *(annually)*

Last Updated: 28/10/11

LITHUANIAN ACADEMY OF PHYSICAL EDUCATION

Lietuvos Kuno Kulturos Akademija (LKKA)

Sporto g. 6, 44221 Kaunas
Tel: +370(37) 30-26-21
Fax: +370(37) 20-45-15
EMail: lkka@lkka.lt
Website: http://www.lkka.lt/

Rector: Albertas Skurvydas (2001-)
Tel: +370(37) 30-26-21, Fax: +370(37) 20-45-15
EMail: rektorius@lkka.lt

Vice-Rector for Studies: Tomas Žalandauskas
EMail: studiju.prorektorius@lkka.lt

International Relations: Irena Cikotienė
Tel: +370(37) 30-26-72, Fax: +370(37) 30-26-72
EMail: i.cikotiene@lkka.lt

Faculties

Sports Biomedicine (Biomedicine; Education of the Handicapped; Health Education; Physical Therapy; Physiology); **Sports Education** (Dance; Education; Physical Education; Psychology; Social and Community Services; Sports) *Dean*: Juozas Kasiulis

History: Founded 1934 as Higher Courses of Physical Education; became Lithuanian National Institute of Physical Education 1945. Acquired present status and title 1999.

Governing Bodies: Senate

Academic Year: September to May (September-December; February-May)

Admission Requirements: High school certificate and entrance examination

Main Language(s) of Instruction: Lithuanian

International Co-operation: With universities in Austria, Belgium, Denmark, Finland, Germany, Greece, the Netherlands, Portugal and Spain. Also participates in the Socrates/Erasmus programme

Accrediting Agencies: Ministry of Education and Science

Degrees and Diplomas: *Bakalauro diplomas*: 4 yrs; *Magistro diplomas*: a further 2 yrs; *Daktaro diplomas*: 4 yrs

Student Services: Canteen, Foreign student adviser, Foreign Studies Centre, Handicapped facilities, Health services, Sports facilities

Student Residential Facilities: Yes

Special Facilities: Sports Museum

Libraries: Academy Library

Publications: Education, Physical Training, Sports, Scientific Journal *(quarterly)*; Physical Therapy, Journal *(biennially)*; Sports Science, Scientific Journal published together with Vilnius Pedagogical University *(quarterly)*

Last Updated: 28/10/11

LITHUANIAN UNIVERSITY OF EDUCATIONAL SCIENCES

Vilniaus Pedagoginis Universitetas (VPU)

Studentu g. 39, 08106 Vilnius
Tel: +370(5) 279-02-81
Fax: +370(5) 279-05-48
EMail: studsk@vpu.lt
Website: http://www.vpu.lt

Rector: Algirdas Gaižutis
Tel: +370(5) 279-02-81, Fax: +370(5) 279-05-48
EMail: rekt.vpu@vpu.lt

Vice-Rector for Research: Rimantas Želvys
EMail: rimantas.zelvys@vpu.lt

International Relations: Daiva Verikaitė, Head, International Relations Office
Tel: +370(5) 275-81-13, Fax: +370(5) 275-03-02
EMail: interdep@vpu.lt

Faculties

Education (Art Education; Dance; Education; Educational Psychology; Ethics; Music Education; Preschool Education; Primary Education; Psychology; Social Work; Theatre); **History** (Anthropology; Catholic Theology; History; History of Religion); **Lithuanian Philology** (Baltic Languages; Linguistics; Literature; Philology); **Mathematics and Information Technologies** (Information Technology; Mathematics; Mathematics and Computer Science); **Natural Sciences** (Biology; Chemistry; Geography; Natural Sciences; Technology Education); **Philology** (Applied Linguistics; Communication Studies; English; French; German; Modern Languages; Philology; Polish; Russian; Slavic Languages); **Physics and Technology** (Engineering; Information Technology; Physics; Technology); **Social Sciences** (Economics; Educational Administration; Philosophy; Social Sciences; Sociology); **Sports and Health** (Health Sciences; Physical Education; Sports)

History: Founded 1935, acquired present status 1992 and title 2012.

Governing Bodies: Senate

Academic Year: September to June

Admission Requirements: Secondary school certificate (Brandos Atestatas)

Fees: (Litai): 3,819-5,527 per semester

Main Language(s) of Instruction: Lithuanian (English, German, French, Russian, Polish, Belorussian in the Faculty of Philology)

International Co-operation: Lifelong Learning Programme (Erasmus Exchange Programme – over 100 Erasmus exchange agreements); bilateral agreements with universities in Germany, Poland, Belarus, Russia, the Ukraine, Kazakhstan, the USA, South Korea.

Degrees and Diplomas: *Bakalauro diplomas*; *Magistro diplomas*; *Daktaro diplomas*

Student Services: Canteen, Cultural centre, Handicapped facilities, Language programs, Sports facilities

Student Residential Facilities: Yes

Special Facilities: Scientific Laboratories

Libraries: University Library, 683,984 vols; 34 subscribed databases; 27,532 e-journals; over 51,000 e-books

Publications: Istorija (History), Scientific periodical on History *(quarterly)*; Pedagogika (Education), Scientific periodical on Education *(quarterly)*; Socialinis ugdymas (Social Education), Scientific periodical on Social Sciences *(3 per annum)*; Ugdymo psichologija (Developmental Psychology, Scientific periodical on Psychology and Education *(1-2 per annum)*; Žmogus ir žodis (Man and the Word), Scientific periodical on Philology (Linguistics), Philosophy and Education *(quarterly)*

Press or Publishing House: University Publishing House

Last Updated: 08/09/11

LITHUANIAN UNIVERSITY OF HEALTH SCIENCES

Lietuvos sveikatos mokslų universitetas (KMU)

A. Mickevičiaus g. 9, 44307 Kaunas
Tel: +370(37) 327-201
Fax: +370(37) 220-733
EMail: rektoratas@lsmuni.lt
Website: http://www.lsmuni.lt

Dean: Žilvinas Padaiga
Tel: +370(37) 327-200 EMail: zilvinas.padaiga@lsmuni.lt

Faculties

Medicine (Medicine); **Nursing** (Nursing); **Odontology** (Dentistry); **Pharmacy** (Pharmacy); **Public Health** (Public Health); **Veterinary Science** (Veterinary Science)

Institutes

Biomedical Research (Biomedicine) *Director*: Irena Misevičiene; **Cardiology** (Cardiology) *Director*: Rimantas Benetis; **Endocrinology** (Endocrinology) *Director*: Antanas Norkus; **Psycho-physiology and Rehabilitation** *(Palanga)* (Psychology; Rehabilitation and Therapy) *Director*: Robertas Bunevičius

Further Information: Teaching Hospital of Kaunas University of Medicine

History: Founded 1922 as a Faculty of Medicine of Kaunas University. Reorganized into a separate Kaunas Medical Institute 1950. Became Kaunas Medical Academy 1989. Acquired present title 2010 following merge with Lithuanian Veterinary Academy.

Governing Bodies: University Council; Senate

Academic Year: September to June (September-January; February-June)

Admission Requirements: Secondary school certificate (Brandos atestatas), and entrance examination

Main Language(s) of Instruction: Lithuanian. Also English for foreign students

International Co-operation: With universities in Finland, Sweden, Spain, Italy, France, Denmark, Belgium, United Kingdom, Netherlands, Portugal, Germany, Czech Republic, Poland, Latvia, Turkey, Norway

Degrees and Diplomas: *Bakalauro diplomas*: Nursing; Public Health, 4 yrs; *Magistro diplomas*: Nursing; Public Health, a further 2 yrs; *Magistro diplomas (integrated)*: Medicine, 6 yrs; *Magistro diplomas (integrated)*: Odontology; Pharmacy, 5 yrs; *Daktaro diplomas*. Also Certificate of Professional Qualification in Nursing (2 yrs)

Student Services: Academic counselling, Canteen, Cultural centre, Foreign student adviser, Foreign Studies Centre, Health services, Language programs, Sports facilities

Student Residential Facilities: For 908 students (5 dormitories)

Special Facilities: Museum of Medicine and Pharmacy. Anatomy Museum

Libraries: Central Library, 850,000 vols

Publications: Lithuanian Journal of Cardiology *(biennially)*; Medicina, Scientific journal *(monthly)*

Press or Publishing House: Publishing Office of Kaunas University of Medicine

Last Updated: 27/02/12

MYKOLAS ROMERIS UNIVERSITY

Mykolo Romerio Universitetas (MRU)

Ateities g. 20, 08303 Vilnius
Tel: +370(5) 271-46-25
Fax: +370(5) 267-60-00
EMail: roffice@mruni.eu
Website: http://www.mruni.eu/

Rector: Alvydas Pumputis (2010-2015) Tel: +370(5) 271-46-25

International Relations: Giedre Račienė, Head, International Relations
Tel: +370(5) 271-46-21 EMail: Inter@mruni.eu; giedre@mruni.eu

Faculties

Economics and Finance Management (Banking; Business Administration; Economics; Finance; International Business; Law; Management; Public Administration; Taxation); **Law** (Administrative Law; Civil Law; Commercial Law; Comparative Law; Constitutional Law; Criminal Law; European Union Law; History of Law; International Law; Labour Law; Law; Private Law; Public Law); **Politics and Management** (Business Administration; Environmental Management; Management; Political Sciences; Public Administration); **Public Security** (Arts and Humanities; Criminal Law; Criminology; Law; Physical Education; Police Studies; Protective Services; Public Administration); **Social Informatics** (Business Administration; Computer Science; E-Business/Commerce; Law; Mathematics; Mathematics and Computer Science; Public Administration; Software Engineering); **Social Policy** (Education; Educational Sciences; Law; Psychology; Social Policy; Social Work; Sociology)

Institutes

Humanities (Baltic Languages; Chinese; Danish; English; Finnish; French; German; Hebrew; Hindi; Italian; Japanese; Modern Languages; Norwegian; Philosophy; Portuguese; Russian; Spanish; Swedish; Turkish)

History: Founded 1990. Renamed Lietuvos Teisės Universitetas (Law University of Lithuania) 2000. Acquired present title and status 2004.

Governing Bodies: Senate; Council; Rectorate

Academic Year: September to June (September-January; February-June)

Admission Requirements: Certificate of Secondary Education (Brandos Atestatas). Students are admitted according to average marks in selected exams, plus the average of annual marks in relative subjects. Admission requirements for overseas students are to be found on the university website.

Fees: (Litai): National and EU students: Bachelor's degree, 3,840-5,220; Master's degree, 5,520-7,080. International Students: Bachelor's degree, 5,800-5,940; Master's degree 8,840-9,254.

Main Language(s) of Instruction: Lithuanian, some programmes are also offered in English and Russian

International Co-operation: Participates in: 7th Framework Programme, Asia-Link Programme, AGIS Programme, COST actions, Lifelong Learning Programme, NordPlus Programme; Mykolas Romeris University has 310 ERASMUS partnership agreements with 219 universities and 79 bilateral agreements with universities from 36 countries.

Accrediting Agencies: Lithuanian Centre for Quality Assessment in Higher Education

Degrees and Diplomas: *Bakalauro diplomas*: Economics; Informatics; Law; Psychology; Public Administration; Public Security; Social Work (Bacherlor's Degree); *Magistro diplomas*: Business; Economics; Education Sciences; Finance; Human Resource Management; Law; Management and Business Administration; Management; Politics; Project Management; Psychology; Public Administration; Social Work; Sociology (Master's Degree); *Daktaro diplomas*: Law; Management and Administration; Psychology

Student Services: Academic counselling, Canteen, Cultural centre, Employment services, Foreign student adviser, Foreign Studies Centre, Handicapped facilities, Health services, Language programs, Social counselling, Sports facilities

Student Residential Facilities: For c. 1,570 students

Special Facilities: Art Gallery; Distance Education Studio; Psychology Laboratory; Moot Court Hall

Libraries: Central Library. Specialized Library

Publications: Intellectual Economics, International scientific research journal *(biannually)*; Jurisprudence, Articles dealing with all branches of Law plus reviews of research monographs *(quarterly)*; Public Policy and Administration, Scientific research journal on public policy and administration issues *(quarterly)*; Social Sciences Studies, Analyzes social problems specific to the national situation and to global environment *(quarterly)*; Social Work, Articles on national and international social policy issues *(biannually)*

Academic Staff *2010-2011*	MEN	WOMEN	**TOTAL**
FULL-TIME	189	172	**361**
PART-TIME	271	301	**572**
STAFF WITH DOCTORATE			
FULL-TIME	227	148	**375**
Student Numbers *2012-2013*			
All (Foreign Included)	–	–	**19,425**

Last Updated: 11/03/13

SIAULIAI UNIVERSITY

Šiaulių Universitetas (ŠU)
Vilniaus g. 88, 76285 Šiauliai
Tel: +370(41) 59-58-00
Fax: +370(41) 59-58-09
EMail: all@cr.su.lt
Website: http://www.su.lt

Rector: Vidas Lauruska

Vice-Rector for Studies: Juozas Pabrėža EMail: studijos@cr.su.lt

International Relations: Teodoras Tamošiūnas, Vice-Rector, International Relations and Development
Tel: +370(41) 59-57-42, Fax: +370(41) 59-57-43
EMail: teodoras@cr.su.lt

Faculties

Arts (Design; Fine Arts; Graphic Arts; Interior Design; Music; Painting and Drawing; Technology; Theatre); **Education** (Educational Research; Physical Education; Preschool Education; Primary Education; Sports; Teacher Training); **Humanities** (Arts and Humanities; Classical Languages; Comparative Literature; Heritage Preservation; History; International and Comparative Education; International Studies; Linguistics; Literature; Mass Communication; Modern Languages; Philosophy; Translation and Interpretation); **Mathematics and Computer Science** (Computer Science; Mathematics and Computer Science; Statistics); **Natural Sciences** (Computer Science; Ecology; Environmental Studies; Optometry; Physics); **Social Sciences** (Business Administration; Economics; Management; Production Engineering; Public Administration; Teacher Training); **Social Welfare and Disability Studies** (Health Education; Physical Education; Physical Therapy; Special Education; Speech Therapy and Audiology); **Technology** (Construction Engineering; Electrical and Electronic Engineering; Electrical Engineering; Environmental Studies; Industrial Design; Information Technology; Mechanical Engineering; Power Engineering; Technology)

Institutes

Continuing Education (Computer Science; Educational Sciences; Ethics; Management; Modern Languages; Psychology; Public Administration; Social Work; Special Education; Teacher Training) *Director*: Lidija Ušeckienė; **European Studies** (European Studies); **Gender studies** (Gender Studies)

History: Founded 1948 as Teacher Training Institute. Acquired present status and title 1997 with the merging of Šiauliai Pedagogical Institute and Šiauliai Polytechnical Faculty of Kaunas Technological University.

Governing Bodies: Senate

Academic Year: September to June (September-December; February-June)

Admission Requirements: Secondary school certificate (Vidurines Mokyklos Baigimo Atestatas)

Main Language(s) of Instruction: Lithuanian

International Co-operation: with universities in United Kingdom, Belgium, France, Austria, Sweden, Denmark, Germany, Italy, Portugal, Spain, Norway, Netherlands, Finland, Switzerland, Latvia, Estonia, Poland, Hungary, Slovenia, Czech Republic, Bulgaria, Greece, Cyprus, Turkey, South Korea

Degrees and Diplomas: *Bakalauro diplomas*: Arts and Humanities; Business Administration; Education; Engineering; Fine Arts; Performing Arts; Mathematics and Computer Science; Natural Sciences; Social Sciences; Technology; Welfare and Protective Services; Agriculture (BSc; BA), 4-5 yrs; *Magistro diplomas*: Arts and Humanities; Business Administration; Education; Engineering; Fine Arts; Performing Arts; Social Sciences; Technology (MSc), a further 1 1/2-2 yrs; *Daktaro diplomas*: Education (PhD), a further 4 yrs

Student Services: Academic counselling, Canteen, Cultural centre, Employment services, Foreign student adviser, Foreign Studies Centre, Handicapped facilities, Language programs, Nursery care, Sports facilities

Student Residential Facilities: Yes

Special Facilities: University History Museum, Observatory, Botanical Garden, Zoological Museum, Art Gallery

Libraries: c. 390,000 vols

Publications: Šiaulių Universitetas *(bimonthly)*

Last Updated: 28/10/11

VILNIUS ACADEMY OF ARTS

Vilniaus Dailes Akademija (VDA)
Maironio g. 6, 01124 Vilnius
Tel: +370(5) 210-54-30
Fax: +370(5) 210-54-44
EMail: vda@vda.lt
Website: http://www.vda.lt

Rector (Acting): Audrius Klimas EMail: audrius.klimas@vda.lt

Vice-Rector forPersonnel and General Affair: Ruta Pilkauskienė
Tel: +370(5) 210-54-66 EMail: ruta.pilkauskiene@vda.lt

International Relations: Konstantinas Bogdanas
Tel: +370(5) 210-54-61

Chairs

Cultural Management and Cultural Policy *(UNESCO Chair)* (Cultural Studies; Heritage Preservation)

Faculties

Applied Arts (Architecture; Ceramic Art; Clothing and Sewing; Design; Fashion Design; Fine Arts; Textile Design) *Dean*: J. Palaima; **Architecture and Design** (Architecture; Design); **Arts** *(Kaunas)* (Architecture; Ceramic Art; Glass Art; Graphic Arts; Painting and Drawing; Sculpture; Textile Design); **Arts** *(Telsia)* (Clothing and Sewing; Design; Furniture Design; Jewelry Art; Sculpture); **Humanities and Social Sciences** (Art Education; Art History; Modern Languages); **Visual and Applied Arts** (Art History; Graphic Arts; Heritage Preservation; Painting and Drawing; Philosophy; Photography; Sculpture; Visual Arts)

Further Information: Branches in Telšiai, Kaunas and Klaipėda

History: Founded 1793 as Faculty of Architecture, of Vilnius University, reorganized 1941 and acquired present status and title 1990. A State institution.

Academic Year: September to May (September-December; February-May)

Admission Requirements: Secondary school certificate (Brandos Atestatas)

Main Language(s) of Instruction: Lithuanian

Degrees and Diplomas: *Bakalauro diplomas*: Arts (BA), 4 yrs; *Magistro diplomas*: Arts (MA), a further 2 yrs; *Daktaro diplomas (PhD)*: a further 4 yrs by thesis following Magistras

Student Services: Canteen, Cultural centre, Handicapped facilities, Sports facilities

Special Facilities: Museum. Gallery 'Academia'

Libraries: Central Library, 8,000 vols

Last Updated: 28/10/11

VILNIUS GEDIMINAS TECHNICAL UNIVERSITY

Vilniaus Gedimino Technikos Universitetas (VGTU)
Sauletekio al. 11, 10223 Vilnius
Tel: +370(5) 274-50-30
Fax: +370(5) 270-01-12
EMail: rastine@vgtu.lt
Website: http://www.vgtu.lt

Rector: Alfonsas Daniūnas
Tel: +370(5) 274-49-30, Fax: +370(5) 270-01-14

Chancellor: Arunas Komka
Tel: +370(5) 274-50-06 EMail: arunas.komka@vgtu.lt

International Relations: Asta Radzeviciene
Tel: +370(5) 237-05-57 EMail: asta.radzeviciene@vgtu.lt

Centres

International Studies (International Studies)

Faculties

Architecture (Architecture; Regional Planning; Structural Architecture; Town Planning); **Business Management** (Business Administration; Business Computing; Economics; Finance; International Business; International Economics; Law; Management); **Civil Engineering** (Bridge Engineering; Building Technologies; Civil Engineering; Construction Engineering; Economics; Fire Science; Geological Engineering; Materials Engineering; Mechanics; Real Estate; Safety Engineering; Structural Architecture); **Electronics** (Automation and Control Engineering; Computer Engineering; Electrical Engineering; Electronic Engineering; Telecommunications

Engineering); **Environmental Engineering** (Civil Engineering; Energy Engineering; Environmental Engineering; Environmental Studies; Hydraulic Engineering; Road Engineering; Surveying and Mapping; Urban Studies; Water Management); **Fundamental Sciences** (Bioengineering; Chemistry; Computer Graphics; Information Sciences; Information Technology; Materials Engineering; Mathematics; Mechanical Engineering; Physics; Statistics); **Mechanics** (Industrial Management; Machine Building; Mechanical Engineering; Mechanics; Metal Techniques; Printing and Printmaking); **Transport Engineering** (Management; Railway Transport; Road Transport; Transport and Communications; Transport Engineering; Transport Management)

Institutes

Aviation *(Antanas Gustaitis)* (Aeronautical and Aerospace Engineering; Air Transport; Mechanics); **Humanities** (Baltic Languages; English; Modern Languages; Philosophy; Physical Education; Political Sciences)

Research Centres

Property Valuation (Real Estate); **Science** (Natural Sciences); **Telecommunications** (Telecommunications Engineering)

Research Institutes

Architecture (Architecture); **Environmental Protection** (Environmental Studies); **Geodesy** (Geology); **Internet and Intelligent Technologies** (Information Technology); **Labour Safety** (Safety Engineering); **Open Source** (Information Sciences); **Special Structures** *(Kompozitas)* (Structural Architecture); **Territorial Planning** (Regional Planning); **Transport** (Transport and Communications); **Welding and Material Science** (Materials Engineering; Metal Techniques)

Research Laboratories

Aviation (Aeronautical and Aerospace Engineering); **Bioinformatics** (Biological and Life Sciences; Computer Science); **Building Physics** (Building Technologies; Physics); **Buildings** (Building Technologies); **Business Planning and Environment Economics** (Business Administration; Economics; Environmental Studies); **Calibration** (Measurement and Precision Engineering); **Construction Technology and Management** (Construction Engineering); **Constructions and Materials** (Construction Engineering; Materials Engineering); **Environmental Protection and Working Conditions** (Environmental Studies; Safety Engineering); **Geotechnical Engineering** (Geological Engineering); **High Magnetic Fields** (Physics); **Information Systems** (Information Sciences); **Material Physics** (Physics); **Nuclear Hydrophysics** (Nuclear Engineering); **Numerical Modeling** (Computer Graphics); **Parallel Computations** (Computer Science); **Roads** (Road Engineering); **Strength Mechanics** (Mechanics); **Urban Analysis** (Urban Studies); **Vibroacoustics and Diagnostics** (Sound Engineering (Acoustics))

History: Founded 1956 as Vilnius branch of Kaunas Polytechnic Institute, became Vilnius Civil Engineering Institute 1969, and acquired present status 1990 and title 1996.

Governing Bodies: University Council; Senate; Rectorate

Academic Year: September to June (September-February, February-June)

Admission Requirements: General or special secondary school certificate and entrance examination

Main Language(s) of Instruction: Lithuanian, English

International Co-operation: Participates in the Lifelong Learning Programme /Erasmus, Leonardo da Vinci, Phare, Eureka, Framework, Nato, Erasmus Mundus, Tempus, ALFA III programmes

Accrediting Agencies: Lithuanian Centre for Quality Assesment in Higher Education

Degrees and Diplomas: *Bakalauro diplomas*: Architecture; Physics; Social Sciences; Technological Science; *Magistro diplomas*: Arts; Biomedical Sciences; Physics; Social Sciences; *Daktaro diplomas*

Student Services: Academic counselling, Canteen, Employment services, Foreign student adviser, Foreign Studies Centre, Sports facilities

Student Residential Facilities: Yes

Libraries: 586,289 vols

Publications: Aviation, Text in English *(quarterly)*; Cultural regionalistics, Text in English; Abstracts in Lithuanian, English *(biannually)*; Gedimino universitetas *(bimonthly)*; Geodesy and Carthography, Text in German, Russian, Lithuanian, French, English *(quarterly)*; International Journal of Strategic Property Management, Text in English; Abstracts in Lithuanian, English *(quarterly)*; Inžinerija *(biweekly)*; Journal of Business Economics and Management, Text in English *(quarterly)*; Journal of Civil Engineering and Management, Reasearch journal, Text in English; Abstracts in Russian, Lithuanian *(quarterly)*; Journal of Environmental Engineering and Landscape Management, Text in German, Russian, Lithuanian, French, English; Abstracts in Russian, Lithuanian, English *(quarterly)*; Journal of Environmental Engineering and Landscape Management, Text in German, Russian, Lithuanian, French, English; Abstracts in Russian, Lithuanian, English *(quarterly)*; Mathematical Modelling and Analysis, Text in English; Abstracts in Lithuanian, English *(quarterly)*; Mokslas - Lietuvos ateitis, Text in Lithuanian, English *(bimonthly)*; Mokslo ir technikos raida, Text in German, Russian, Lithuanian, English *(quarterly)*; Santalka: Filologija, Edukologija, Text in Lithuanian, English *(quarterly)*; Santalka: Filosofija, Komunikacija, Text in Lithuanian, English *(quarterly)*; Statybinės konstrukcijos ir technologijos, Text in Lithuanian, English *(quarterly)*; Technological and Economic Development of Economy, Articles in Lithuanian, English, German, Russian *(quarterly)*; The Baltic Journal of Road and Bridge Engineering, Text in English *(quarterly)*; Transport, Text in English; Abstracts in Russian, Lithuanian *(quarterly)*; Urbanistika ir architektūra, Text in English, Lithuanian *(quarterly)*; Verslas teorija ir praktika, Text in Lithuanian, English *(quarterly)*; Verslas, vadyba ir studijos, Text in Lithuanian, English *(quarterly)*

Press or Publishing House: Publishing House 'Technika' and Taylor&Francis

Last Updated: 09/09/11

VILNIUS UNIVERSITY

Vilniaus Universitetas (VU)

Universiteto g.3, 01513 Vilnius

Tel: +370(5) 268-70-01

Fax: +370(5) 268-70-09

EMail: infor@cr.vu.lt

Website: http://www.vu.lt

Rector: Juras Banys (2012-)

Tel: +370(5) 268-70-10 EMail: rector@vu.lt

International Relations: Raimonda Markevičienė

Tel: +370(5) 268-71-82 EMail: raimonda.markeviciene@cr.vu.lt

Centres

Gender Studies (Gender Studies; Men Studies; Women's Studies); **Oriental Studies** (Arabic; Asian Studies; Chinese; Japanese; Middle Eastern Studies; Oriental Languages; Sanskrit); **Religious Studies and Research** (Religious Studies)

Faculties

Chemistry (Analytical Chemistry; Chemistry; Inorganic Chemistry; Organic Chemistry; Polymer and Plastics Technology); **Communication** (Archiving; Communication Studies; Information Management; Information Sciences; Journalism; Library Science; Public Relations); **Economics** (Accountancy; Business Administration; Business and Commerce; Business Computing; Economics; Finance; Insurance; International Business; Management); **History** (Archaeology; Contemporary History; History; Medieval Studies; Modern History); **Humanities** *(Kaunas)* (Business Administration; Computer Science; English; German; Management; Native Language; Philology); **Law** (Civil Law; Commercial Law; Criminal Law; International Law; Labour Law; Law; Public Law); **Mathematics and Informatics** (Applied Mathematics; Mathematics; Mathematics and Computer Science; Software Engineering; Statistics); **Medicine** (Dentistry; Ergotherapy; Hygiene; Medicine; Nursing; Occupational Therapy; Paediatrics; Public Health); **Natural Sciences** (Biophysics; Botany; Ecology; Environmental Management; Environmental Studies; Genetics; Geography; Geology; Meteorology; Microbiology; Molecular Biology; Natural Sciences; Zoology); **Philology** (Classical Languages; Dutch; English; Finnish; French; German; Greek; Latin; Native Language; Philology; Polish; Russian; Scandinavian Languages; Slavic Languages; Translation and Interpretation); **Philosophy** (Clinical Psychology; Educational Psychology; Educational Sciences; Industrial and Organizational Psychology; Philosophy; Psychology; Social Work; Sociology; Special Education); **Physics** (Applied Physics; Astrophysics; Biophysics; Physics; Radiophysics; Solid State Physics; Telecommunications Engineering)

Institutes
Applied Research (Materials Engineering); **Foreign Languages** (English; German; Romance Languages); **International Relations and Political Science** (International Relations; Political Sciences; Public Administration)

Schools
Business *(International)* (Finance; International Business; International Law; Marketing; Tourism)

History: Founded 1579 as Academica et Universitas Vilnensis with two Faculties: Philosophy and Theology. Reorganized 1781 and again 1803 as the Imperial University of Vilnius. Closed by Tsarist Government 1832 when Faculties of Medicine and Theology became separate Academies. Reopened 1919. Closed during German occupation 1943. A State Institution

Governing Bodies: Senate; Rectorate

Academic Year: September to July (September-January; February-July)

Admission Requirements: Secondary school certificate (Vidurines Mokyklos Baigimo Atestatas)

Main Language(s) of Instruction: Lithuanian

International Co-operation: With universities in all EU countries; Central and Eastern European countries; USA; Australia; Japan; Canada. Also participates in Tempus-Tacis; LLP; Socrates/Erasmus; Socrates/Lingua; Jean Monnet; Erasmus Mundus; Equal; eContentplus; Framework and other EU educational and scientific programmes. Member of several networks (11 Thematic networks under Erasmus; Utrecht: Maui; Aen; Bsrun, Crepuq; Unica). Member of EUA, IAU. Signatory of Magna Carta.

Accrediting Agencies: Lithuanian Centre for Quality Assessment in Higher Education

Degrees and Diplomas: *Bakalauro diplomas (Bachelor's Degree)*: 4 yrs; *Magistro diplomas (Master's Degree)*: a further 2 yrs; *Daktaro diplomas (Doctorate)*: a further 3-5 yrs

Student Services: Academic counselling, Canteen, Cultural centre, Employment services, Foreign student adviser, Foreign Studies Centre, Handicapped facilities, Health services, Language programs, Social counselling, Sports facilities

Student Residential Facilities: Yes

Special Facilities: 8 museums. Observatory. Botanical Garden. 3 university hospitals. Centre of Information Technology Development and St. John's Church.

Libraries: University Library and specialized departments Libraries, total, 5.5m. vols

Publications: Acta Orientalia Vilnensia *(annually)*; Acta Paedagogica Vilnensia *(biannually)*; Archaelogica Lituana *(annually)*; Baltistica *(3 per annum)*; Book Science *(biannually)*; Economics *(quarterly)*; Information Sciences *(quarterly)*; Journal of Political Science *(quarterly)*; Law *(quarterly)*; Linguistics, German and Romance Studies *(annually)*; Literature *(quarterly)*; Lithuanian Political Science Yearbook *(annually)*; Management *(biannually)*; Problems *(biannually)*; Psychology *(biannually)*; Respectus Philologicus *(biannually)*; Social Theory, Empirics, Policy and Practice *(biannually)*; Sociology, Thought and Action *(biannually)*; Studies of Lithuanian History *(biannually)*; Transformation in Business and Economics *(biannually)*

Press or Publishing House: Vilnius University Publishing House

Student Numbers *2012-2013*: Total 22,264
Last Updated: 11/03/13

VYTAUTAS MAGNUS UNIVERSITY

Vytauto Didžiojo Universitetas (VMU/VDU)
K. Donelaičio g. 58, 44248 Kaunas
Tel: +370(37) 22-27-39
Fax: +370(37) 20-38-58
EMail: info@adm.vdu.lt
Website: http://www.vdu.lt

Rector: Zigmas Lydeka (2006-)
Tel: +370(37) 20-67-53
EMail: rektorius@adm.vdu.lt; rektoratas@fc.vdu.lt

Administrative Officer: Nina Klebanskaja
Tel: +370(37) 228-696 EMail: Nina_Klebanskaja@fc.vdu.lt

Vice-Rector for Studies: Rimantas Laužackas
EMail: r.lauzackas@smf.vdu.lt; pror.st@adm.vdu.lt

International Relations: Kestutis Pukelis, Vice-Rector
Tel: +370(37) 32-31-75, Fax: +370(37) 22-56-62
EMail: pro.tr@adm.vdu.lt

Faculties
Arts (Art Criticism; Art History; Fine Arts; Theatre); **Catholic Theology** (Canon Law; Christian Religious Studies; Theology); **Economics and Management** (Economics; Finance; Management); **Humanities** (English; Ethnology; Folklore; French; German; History; Literature; Native Language; Philology; Philosophy); **Informatics** (Computer Science; Mathematics; Statistics); **Law** (Administrative Law; Commercial Law; International Law; Law); **Natural Sciences** (Biology; Chemistry; Environmental Studies; Physics); **Political Science and Diplomacy** (International Relations; Political Sciences); **Social Sciences** (Education; Psychology; Social Welfare; Sociology)

History: Founded 1922. Renamed Vytautas Magnus University 1930. Closed 1950, reopened 1989. A State Institution.

Governing Bodies: Rector's Council

Academic Year: September to June (September-December; February-June)

Admission Requirements: Secondary school certificate (Vidurinées Mokyklaos Baigimo Atestatas)

Main Language(s) of Instruction: Lithuanian (Also English, German and French)

International Co-operation: With universities in Germany, Sweden, France, Finland, Italy, Spain, Norway, Belarus, Russian Federation, Hungary and Romania. Also participates in Socrates, Erasmus, Cormenius, Tempus programmes.

Accrediting Agencies: Lithuanian Centre for Quality Assessment in Higher Education

Degrees and Diplomas: *Bakalauro diplomas*: Art Criticism; Political Science; Public Administration; Pedagogy; Sociology; Psychology; Social Work; Business Administration; Management; Physics; Environmental Sciences; Biology; German Philology; English Philology; Ethnology; Lithuanian Philology; French Philology; History; Philosophy; Mathematics; Computer Science; Catholic; Religious Sciences, 4 yrs; *Magistro diplomas*: Philosophy; Theology; Religious Sciences; Art Criticism; Lithuanian Philology; English Philology; German Philology; History; Ethnology; Law; Political Science; Management; Business Administration; Public Administration; Economics; Sociology; Social Work; Psychology; Pedagogy; Communication and Information; Mathematics; Chemistry; Computer Science; Biology; Environmental Sciences, a further 2 yrs; *Daktaro diplomas*: Biomedical Sciences; Physical Sciences; Humanities; Social Sciences, a further 3 yrs

Student Services: Academic counselling, Canteen, Foreign student adviser, Foreign Studies Centre, Handicapped facilities, Health services, Language programs, Sports facilities

Student Residential Facilities: Yes

Special Facilities: Botanical Gardens

Libraries: Central Library, 197,996 vols. Over 2,000 audio-visual materials. Over 400 periodicals. Over 4,700 manuscripts

Publications: Acta Baltica *(biannually)*; Aplinkos tyriami inginnerija ir vadyba *(quarterly)*; Darbai ir dienos, Humanistic Studies *(quarterly)*; Mintis ir veiksmas, Sociology Studies; Organizaciju Vadyba, Management Studies *(quarterly)*; Profesinis rengimas: tyrimai ir realijos, Vocational Training *(biannually)*; Soter, Religious Studies *(biannually)*; Teisės apzvalga *(quarterly)*

Last Updated: 28/10/11

PRIVATE INSTITUTIONS

EUROPEAN HUMANITIES UNIVERSITY

Europos Humanitarinis Universitetas
Tauro street, 12, 01114 Vilnius
Tel: +370(5) 263-9650
Fax: +370(5) 263-9651
EMail: office@ehu.lt
Website: http://www.ehu.lt/

Rector: Anatoli Mikhailov (2011-2016)
Tel: +370(5) 263-9655
EMail: rectorsoffice@ehu.lt; anatoli.mikhailov@ehu.lt

Communications Officer: Tatjana Rudzinskienė
EMail: Communications@ehu.lt; tajaana.rudzinskiene@ehu.lt

International Relations: Nico Rausch, International Relations Officer
Tel: +370(5) 263- 9652
EMail: international@ehu.lt; nico.rausch@ehu.lt

Centres

Business Studies (Business Administration)

Departments

Foreign Languages (English; French; German; Italian; Native Language); **History** (Anthropology; Cultural Studies; Heritage Preservation; History; Social Sciences; Tourism); **Law** (European Union Law; International Law; Law); **Media** (Cultural Studies; Design; Information Sciences; Journalism); **Social and Political Science** (European Studies; Philosophy; Political Sciences; Public Administration)

History: Founded in 1992 in Minsk, Belarusia. Closed down by authorities in 2004. Relaunched in Lithuania in 2005 and acquired current status 2006.

Governing Bodies: Governing Board; General Assembly of Part Owners; Rector; Senate; Rectorat

Academic Year: September to June (September-December; January-March; April-June)

Admission Requirements: Completed secondary education; required level of Russian and Belarusian language; foreign language at A2 on the scale of European Language Portfolio

Fees: (Euros): Undergraduate (high-residence programme), 1,200 for Belarusian students, 1,500 for non-Belarusian students; undergraduate (low-residence programme), 600 for Belarusian students, 1,200 for non-Belarusian students. Postgraduate programme, 600 for Belarusian students, 2,200 for non-Belarusian students. Fees per annum

Main Language(s) of Instruction: Russian, Belarusian, English

International Co-operation: with institutions in Finland, Germany, Luxembourg, Poland, Portugal, Serbia. Also Campus Europae, Erasmus, Baltic Region Philosophy Network

Accrediting Agencies: Centre for Quality Assessment in Higher Education (CQAHE)

Degrees and Diplomas: *Bakalauro diplomas*: Audio-Visual Arts; Arts; Philosophy; Political Science; Communication and Information; Law; Recreation and Tourism; History (Belarusian) (BA; LLB), 4 yrs; *Magistro diplomas*: History; Sociology; Political Science; Legal Studies; Philosophy (MA; LLM), a further 2 yrs

Student Services: Academic counselling, Canteen, Employment services, Foreign student adviser, Language programs, Sports facilities

Special Facilities: Radio and tv studio; photo and video media lab

Libraries: 10,904 vols; 15 periodical subscriptions; e-networks within the university

Publications: Crossroads *(biannually)*; Digest, Articles from Crossroads translated into English. *(annually)*; Historical Belarusian Review *(annually)*; Topos, Philosophical and cultural studies. *(3 per annum)*

Press or Publishing House: The EHU Press

Academic Staff *2009-2010*	**TOTAL**
FULL-TIME	**69**
PART-TIME	**130**
STAFF WITH DOCTORATE	
FULL-TIME	**72**
Student Numbers *2009-2010*	
All (Foreign Included)	**1,966**
FOREIGN ONLY	**67**

Part-time students, 1,101.
Last Updated: 28/10/11

ISM UNIVERSITY OF MANAGEMENT AND ECONOMICS

ISM Vadybos ir ekonomikos universitetas (ISM)

E. Ožeškienė g. 18, 44254 Kaunas
Tel: +370(37) 302-405
Fax: +370(37) 302-368
EMail: ism@ism.lt
Website: http://www.ism.lt

President: Nerijus Pačėsa

Vice-Dean, Academic Affairs: Ilona Bučiūnienė

International Relations: Tadas Šarapovas
Tel: +370(37) 30-23-66

Schools

Doctoral Studies; **Executive Studies**; **Graduate Studies**; **Undergraduate Studies** (Business Administration; Business Education; Economics; International Business; Political Sciences)

History: Founded 1999. Formerly International School of Management (ISM), Tarptautinė Auskštoji Mokykla (ISM).

Main Language(s) of Instruction: Lithuanian and English

Degrees and Diplomas: *Bakalauro diplomas*: Business Administration and Management (BBA); Economics (BE); *Magistro diplomas*: Business Administration and Management (MBA); International Management; Management (MSc; MM); *Daktaro diplomas*: Social Sciences

Last Updated: 28/10/11

LCC INTERNATIONAL UNIVERSITY

LCC Tarptautinis Universitetas (LCC)

Kretingos g. 36, LT-92307 Klaipėda
Tel: +370(46) 31-07-45
Fax: +370(46) 31-05-60
EMail: info@lcc.lt
Website: http://www.lcc.lt

President: Kyle B. Usrey (2010-)
Tel: +370(46) 31-07-45, Fax: +370(46) 31-05-60
EMail: president@lcc.lt

Programmes

Business Administration (Business Administration); **English and Literature** (English; Literature); **Intensive English Studies** (English); **Lithuanian Studies** (Baltic Languages; Cultural Studies); **Psychology** (Psychology); **Teaching English to Speakers of Other Languages** *(TESOL - Graduate)* (Foreign Languages Education); **Theology** (Theology)

History: Founded 1991 as Lietuvos Krikščioniškojo Fondo Aukštoji Mokykla. Relocated to the Baltic port city, Klaipėda 1992, and acquired present status and title 2000.

Governing Bodies: Board of Directors

Academic Year: September to May (September-December; January-May) plus June and July summer sessions.

Admission Requirements: High School Diploma (Brandos atestatas) or equivalent; English proficiency test

Main Language(s) of Instruction: English

International Co-operation: Participates in the Erasmus programme.

Accrediting Agencies: Ministry of Science and Education

Degrees and Diplomas: *Bakalauro diplomas*; *Magistro diplomas*

Student Services: Academic counselling, Canteen, Cultural centre, Employment services, Foreign student adviser, Foreign Studies Centre, Language programs, Social counselling, Sports facilities

Student Residential Facilities: Yes

Special Facilities: Computer Lab

Libraries: Central Library, 20,000 English vols

Publications: Transformations, Digital Newsletter *(monthly)*

Academic Staff *2010-2011*	MEN	WOMEN	**TOTAL**
FULL-TIME	–	30	**30**
PART-TIME	–	20	**20**
STAFF WITH DOCTORATE			
FULL-TIME	–	–	**15**
PART-TIME	–	–	c. **10**
Student Numbers *2010-2011*			
All (Foreign Included)	–	–	c. **650**
FOREIGN ONLY	–	–	**260**

Part-time students, 50.
Last Updated: 08/11/11

VILNIUS BUSINESS LAW ACADEMY

Vilniaus Verslo Teisės Akademija (VVTA)

Kauno g. 34, 03202 Vilnius
Tel: +370(5) 213-51-72
Fax: +370(5) 213-51-72
EMail: vvta@vvtakademija.lt
Website: http://www.vvtakademija.lt

Rector: Edmundas Trasauskas

Programmes

Commercial Law (Commercial Law)

History: Founded 2003.

Main Language(s) of Instruction: Lithuanian

Degrees and Diplomas: *Magistro diplomas*

Last Updated: 28/10/11

Luxembourg

STRUCTURE OF HIGHER EDUCATION SYSTEM

Description:

Since 2003, higher education has been offered at the University of Luxembourg in three faculties: Science, Technology and Communication; Law, Economics and Finance; Arts, Humanities and Education Sciences.

Stages of studies:

University level first stage: *Bachelor*
The Bachelor's degree requires 180 to 240 ECTS.

University level second stage: *Master*
The Master's degree requires 60 to 120 ECTS.

ADMISSION TO HIGHER EDUCATION

Admission to university-level studies:

Name of secondary school credential required: Diplôme de Fin d'Etudes secondaires

Name of secondary school credential required: Diplôme de Fin d'Etudes secondaires techniques

Name of secondary school credential required: Diplôme de Technicien

For entry to: Only for certain subjects

Alternatives to credentials: Work experience

Entrance exam requirements: Yes, for certain domains of study

Numerus clausus/restrictions: Yes, for certain domains of study

Foreign students admission:

Definition of foreign student: A student with a non Luxemburgish secondary school leaving diploma

Entrance exam requirements: Foreign students applying for admission to higher education institutions must hold a Secondary School Leaving Certificate recognized by the Ministère de l'Education nationale. Applications should be made to the individual institutions.
Those wishing to enrol at the Institut universitaire international must hold a postgraduate degree in Law, Political Economics or Political Science.

Entry regulations: A visa is required for non-European Union students.

Health requirements: A health visa is required.

Language requirements: A perfect command of French, German and English is necessary.

RECOGNITION OF STUDIES

Quality assurance system:

External and internal evaluations are compulsory (decree) for the University of Luxembourg.

NATIONAL BODIES

Ministère de la Culture, de l'Enseignement supérieur et de la Recherche (Ministry of Culture, Higher Education and Research)

Minister, Higher Education and Research: François Biltgen
20, Montée de la Pétrusse
Luxembourg L-2273

Tel: +352 2478 6619
Fax: +352 292186
EMail: info@mcesr.public.lu; guy.loos@mesr.etat.lu
WWW: http://www.mcesr.public.lu/

Data for academic year: 2008-2009
Source: IAU from Ministry for Culture, Higher Education and Research, Luxembourg, 2008. Bodies, 2012.

INSTITUTIONS

PUBLIC INSTITUTIONS

INTERNATIONAL UNIVERSITY INSTITUTE OF LUXEMBOURG

Institut Universitaire International de Luxembourg (IUIL)
Château de Munsbach, 31 rue du Parc, 5374 Munsbach
Tel: +352(26) 15-92-12
Fax: +352(26) 15-92-28
EMail: isabel.bozet@iuil.lu
Website: http://www.iuil.lu

Director: Pol Wagner
Tel: +352(26) 15-92-13, Fax: +352(26) 15-92-28
EMail: pol.wagner@iuil.lu

Centres
Entrepreneurship (International Business; Management); **European Law** (European Studies; European Union Law); **Media and Communication** (Mass Communication; Media Studies); **Public Health Management** (Health Administration; Management; Public Health)

History: Founded 1974.

Governing Bodies: Conseil universitaire

Admission Requirements: Licence

Main Language(s) of Instruction: French, English, German

International Co-operation: With universities in France, Germany, Belgium

Degrees and Diplomas: *Master*. Also postgraduate summer courses

Publications: Reports of Seminars, Colloquia

Last Updated: 20/10/08

UNIVERSITY OF LUXEMBOURG

Université du Luxembourg (UL)
Campus Limpertsberg, 162A, avenue de la Faïencerie, 1511 Luxembourg
Tel: +352(46) 66-44-6000
Fax: +352(46) 66-44-6567
Website: http://www.uni.lu

President: Rolf Tarrach (2010-2014)
Tel: +352(46) 66-44-6234, Fax: +352(46) 66-44-6506
EMail: rolf.tarrach@uni.lu

Head of PR Service: Britta Schlueter
Tel: +352 (46) 66-44-6563, Fax: +352 (46) 66-44-6961
EMail: britta.schlueter@uni.lu

International Relations: Jenny Hallen-Hedberg, Head of International Relations Service
Tel: +352(46) 66-44-6208, Fax: +352(46) 66-44-6313
EMail: jenny.hallen-hedberg@uni.lu

Faculties
Humanities, Arts and Education *(Campus Walferdange)* (Arts and Humanities; Education; European Studies; Psychology; Social Sciences); **Law, Economics and Finance** *(Campus Limpertsberg)* (Banking; Economics; European Union Law; Finance); **Science, Technology and Communication** *(Campus Kirchberg)* (Biological and Life Sciences; Engineering; Information Technology; Mathematics and Computer Science; Natural Sciences; Technology)

History: Founded 1848 as Cours supérieur. Centre Universitaire established 1968. Acquired present status and title 2003. A public autonomous institution.

Governing Bodies: Governing Board

Academic Year: September to June (September-January; February-June)

Admission Requirements: Secondary school certificate or foreign equivalent

Fees: (Euros): 100 per semester

Main Language(s) of Instruction: French, English, German

International Co-operation: With universities in France; Germany; Belgium, Portugal, USA, China

Degrees and Diplomas: *Bachelor*: 3 yrs; *Master*: 2 yrs; *Doctorat*: 3 yrs

Student Services: Academic counselling, Canteen, Cultural centre, Foreign student adviser, Foreign Studies Centre, Health services, Language programs, Sports facilities

Student Residential Facilities: Yes

Libraries: c. 215,000 vols

Academic Staff *2008-2009*	**TOTAL**
FULL-TIME	**158**
Student Numbers *2011-2012*	
All (Foreign Included)	**4,352**
FOREIGN ONLY	**2,151**

Part-time students, 658.

Last Updated: 17/02/10

Macedonia (former Yugoslav Republic of)

STRUCTURE OF HIGHER EDUCATION SYSTEM

Description:
Higher education is provided by universities and is undergoing reform in compliance with the Bologna Process.

Stages of studies:

University level first stage: *Bachelor/Diplomiran*
The first-level degree is obtained on completion of a four- to seven-year course in one of the universities. The exact duration of studies leading to higher level diplomas depends on the type of faculty.

University level second stage: *Master/Magister po, Specialization/Specijalizacija*
The Magister degree (Master of Science/Master of Arts) is awarded after one and a half years' study followed by research and the writing of a thesis which is defended in public and approved by a mentor. Each graduate student can specialize in relevant professional fields - e.g. Surgery, Obstetrics, Engineering. Such specialization requires one to five years of practical training.

University level third stage: *Doctorate/Doktor na nauki*
The title of Doctor of Science is conferred to candidates who have obtained the Master's degree and after an approved period of research and the defence of a doctoral dissertation.

ADMISSION TO HIGHER EDUCATION

Admission to university-level studies:

Name of secondary school credential required: Svidetelstvo za polo en maturski ispit

Minimum score/requirement: 40 points in secondary school results and 60 points in entrance examination

Alternatives to credentials: International Baccalaureate or special examinations

Entrance exam requirements: Entrance examination in two subjects depending on the educational programme of the institution (minimum 60 points).

Numerus clausus/restrictions: A numerus clausus is applied when there are more candidates than available places. Quotas are reserved for students from the minority groups.

Foreign students admission:
Entrance exam requirements: Foreign students with grants and scholarships from the Government of the Republic of Macedonia are not required to sit for the entrance examinations except for the Faculties of Architecture, Pedagogy, Physical Education and Art. Foreign students must have completed a four-year secondary school education and have passed the final examinations and meet the same enrolment requirements as national students.

Language requirements: A certificate of knowledge of Macedonian is compulsory.

RECOGNITION OF STUDIES

Quality assurance system:

The concept of accreditation refers to a process of evaluation and assessment of the quality of an institution or programme that leads to a recognized or accredited status. According to the new Law on Higher Education, a system of accreditation is prescribed for post-secondary institutions. There are procedures and regulations that provide ongoing assessment of the overall quality of an institution in terms of its objectives, processes and outcomes. Accreditation will foster institutional links by increasing the awareness of standard-setting processes and facilitating mobility between institutions at both the national and international levels. The Accreditation Board is also responsible for giving its opinion on the possibility for foreign higher education institutions to pursue activities in Macedonia.

The universities also deal with the recognition of foreign higher education degrees.

Bodies dealing with recognition:

Informativen Centar - Ministerstvo za Obrazovanie i Nauka (Informative Center - Ministry of Education and Science)

Head, Information Centre: Nadezda Uzelac
Dimitrie Cuposki 9
Skopje 1000
Tel: +389(2) 106 527
Fax: +389(2) 311 7631
WWW: http://www.mon.gov.mk/
Deals with credential recognition for entry to institution: Yes
Deals with credential recognition for entry to profession: Yes

NATIONAL BODIES

Ministry of Education and Science

Minister: Pance Kralev
ul. Mito Khatsivasilev-Jasmin 66
Skopje 1000
Tel: +389(2) 311 7896
Fax: +389(2) 311 8414
EMail: contact@mon.gov.mk
WWW: http://www.mon.gov.mk

Data for academic year: 2003-2004
Source: IAU from Ministry of Education and Science, Skopje, 2003. Bodies, 2012.

INSTITUTIONS

PUBLIC INSTITUTIONS

GOCE DELCHEV UNIVERSITY, STIP

Univerzitet 'Gotse Delchev' vo Štip
Krste Misirkov bb, PO Box 201, Štip
Tel: +389(32) 550-000
Fax: +389(32) 390-700
EMail: contact@ugd.edu.mk
Website: http://www.ugd.edu.mk/

Rector: Sasa Mitrev EMail: rektor@ugd.edu.mk

Faculties

Agriculture (Agriculture; Crop Production; Development Studies; Oenology; Viticulture); **Computer Science** (Business Computing; Computer Science); **Economics** (Accountancy; Banking; Economics; Finance; Health Administration; Insurance; International Economics; Management); **Education** (Archiving; Education; Educational Sciences; Library Science; Pedagogy; Philosophy of Education; Preschool Education; Primary Education; Sociology); **Electrical Engineering** (Automation and Control Engineering; Electrical Engineering); **Law** (European Union Law; International Relations; Journalism; Law; Public Administration; Public Relations); **Mechanical Engineering** (Machine Building; Mechanical Engineering; Production Engineering); **Medicine** (Dental Technology; Dentistry; Laboratory Techniques; Medicine; Nursing; Optometry; Pharmacy; Physical Therapy); **Music** (Jazz and Popular Music; Music; Music Education; Musical Instruments; Singing); **Natural and Technical Sciences** (Architecture; Civil Engineering; Computer Graphics; Furniture Design; Geography; Geological Engineering; Mineralogy; Mining Engineering; Petroleum and Gas Engineering; Technology; Textile Technology); **Philology** (Archaeology; English; French; German; History; Italian; Literature; Native Language; Philology; Slavic Languages; Turkish); **Tourism and Business** (Cooking and Catering; Dietetics; Nutrition; Tourism; Transport Management)

Institutes

Archaeology and History (Archaeology; History)

History: Created 2007.

Main Language(s) of Instruction: Macedonian

Accrediting Agencies: Ministry of Education and Science

Degrees and Diplomas: *Diplomiran (Bachelor of Science/Arts)*; *Magister (Master of Science/Arts)*; *Doktor na Nauki (Doctor of Philospohy)*

Libraries: Yes

Last Updated: 09/09/11

STATE UNIVERSITY OF TETOVA

Drzaven Univerzitet vo Tetovo
1200 Tetovo
Tel: +389(44) 330-807
Fax: +389(44) 330-815
EMail: international@unite.edu.mk
Website: http://www.unite.edu.mk

Rector: Agron Reka EMail: agron.reka@unite.edu.mk

Centres

Polytechnic Study (Architecture; Construction Engineering; Geological Engineering; Materials Engineering; Mechanics)

Faculties

Applied Sciences (Architecture; Construction Engineering; Electronic Engineering; Mechanical Engineering); **Art** (Aesthetics; Art History; Graphic Design; Music; Painting and Drawing; Sculpture; Theatre); **Economics** (Albanian; Economics; Finance; Marketing; Modern Languages; Public Administration; Tourism); **Food Technology and Nutrition** (Food Technology; Nutrition); **Law** (Administrative Law; Albanian; Civil Law; Constitutional Law; Criminal Law; Human Rights; Modern Languages); **Mathematics and Natural Sciences** (Biology; Chemistry; Ecology; Geography; Mathematics and Computer Science; Pharmacy; Physics); **Medicine** (Dentistry; Gynaecology and Obstetrics; Nursing; Pharmacy; Physical Therapy; Speech Therapy and Audiology); **Philology** (Albanian; English; French; German; Literature; Native Language); **Philosophy** (History; Pedagogy; Philosophy; Psychology; Sociology); **Physical Education** (Physical Education)

History: Founded in 1994. Obtained current status 2007.

Governing Bodies: University Senate

Main Language(s) of Instruction: Albanian; Macedonian

Accrediting Agencies: Ministry of Education and Science

Degrees and Diplomas: *Diplomiran*: Art; Music; Design; Theatre Arts; Physical Education; Modern Languages; Law; Economics; Biology; Chemistry; Physics; Mathematics; Mechatronics; Computer Science; Geography; Tourism; Ecology; History; Pedagogy; Pharmacy; Psychology; Philosophy; Sociology, 4 yrs; *Specijalizacija*: Computer Engineering. Also degree of Baccalaureus (3 yrs)

Libraries: c. 50,000 vols

Last Updated: 31/10/11

ST. KLIMENT OHRIDSKI UNIVERSITY, BITOLA

Univerzitet 'Sv. Kliment Ohridski' Bitola (UKLO)

Bulevar '1 Maj' bb, 7000 Bitola
Tel: +389(47) 223-788
Fax: +389(47) 223-594
EMail: rektorat@uklo.edu.mk
Website: http://www.uklo.edu.mk

Rector: Zlatko Zhoglev (2007-)
Tel: +389(47) 223-192 EMail: zlatko.zoglev@uklo.edu.mk

Secretary-General: Ofelija Hristovska
Tel: +389(47) 223-788 Ext. 116, Fax: +389(47) 223-594
EMail: ofelija.hristovska@uklo.edu.mk

International Relations: Kaliopa Stilinovic, Head, International Relations
Tel: +389(47) 242-278 Ext. 121
EMail: kaliopa.stilinovic@uklo.edu.mk

Faculties

Administration and Information Systems Management *(Bitola)* (Administration; Engineering Management; Information Management; Information Sciences; International Business; Public Administration; Software Engineering); **Biotechnical Sciences** *(Bitola)* (Animal Husbandry; Biotechnology; Farm Management); **Economics** *(Prilep)* (Accountancy; Business Administration; Business Computing; E-Business/Commerce; Economics; Finance; International Business; International Economics; Management; Marketing); **Education** *(Bitola)* (Computer Education; Education; English; Foreign Languages Education; French; German; Library Science; Preschool Education; Technology Education); **Law** *(Kichevo)* (Law); **Security** *(Skopje)* (Civil Security; Criminology; Finance; Protective Services); **Technical Sciences** *(Bitola)* (Computer Engineering; Computer Graphics; Environmental Engineering; Industrial Management; Information Technology; Mechanical Engineering; Power Engineering; Road Engineering; Transport Engineering); **Tourism and Hospitality** *(Ohrid)* (Cooking and Catering; Dietetics; Hotel and Restaurant; Insurance; Nutrition; Tourism; Transport Management)

Higher Schools

Medicine *(Bitola)* (Health Sciences; Laboratory Techniques; Medicine; Midwifery; Nursing; Physical Therapy; Radiology)

History: Founded 1979, incorporating previously existing institutions in the Southwest Macedonian Region founded between 1924 and 1979.

Governing Bodies: University Senate; Rector's Board

Academic Year: September to May (September-January; February-May)

Admission Requirements: Secondary school certificate and pass grades at the maturity exam (Diploma za polozhena matura).

Main Language(s) of Instruction: Macedonian

International Co-operation: Participates in the Tempus, Erasmus and Socrates programmes; Agreements with Germany, France, Slovenia and Poland – ERASMUS LLP bilateral agreements. General bilateral agreements signed with: Turkey, Bulgaria, Ukraine, Russia, Serbia, Croatia, Bosnia and Australia.

Accrediting Agencies: Accreditation and Evaluation Board

Degrees and Diplomas: *Diplomiran*; *Magister*; *Doktor na Nauki*

Student Services: Academic counselling, Canteen, Foreign student adviser, Handicapped facilities, Health services, Language programs, Sports facilities

Student Residential Facilities: For c. 360 students

Libraries: c. 160,000 vols; c. 500 periodicals; c. 1,000 microforms

Publications: Horizonti, Principal research journal. *(annually)*

Academic Staff *2010-2011*	MEN	WOMEN	TOTAL
FULL-TIME	–	–	**333**
PART-TIME	–	–	**121**
STAFF WITH DOCTORATE			
FULL-TIME	123	89	**212**
PART-TIME	66	30	**96**
Student Numbers *2010-2011*			
All (Foreign Included)	–	–	**11,671**
FOREIGN ONLY	–	–	**27**

Part-time students, 13,660.
Last Updated: 09/09/11

STS. CYRIL AND METHODIUS UNIVERSITY, SKOPJE

Univerzitet 'Sv. Kiril i Metódij' vo Skopje (UKIM)

Bul Goce Delcev, 9, 1000 Skopje
Tel: +389(2) 3293-293
Fax: +389(2) 3293-202
EMail: ukim@ukim.edu.mk
Website: http://www.ukim.edu.mk

Rector: Velimir Stojkovski (2008-)
Tel: +389(2) 3293-200 EMail: rector@ukim.edu.mk

Secretary-General: Ilija Piperkoski

International Relations: Meri Cvetkovska
Tel: +389(2) 3293-128 EMail: M.Cvetkovska@ukim.edu.mk

Faculties

Agricultural Science and Food (Agricultural Economics; Agricultural Engineering; Agricultural Equipment; Agriculture; Animal Husbandry; Botany; Cattle Breeding; Crop Production; Fruit Production; Genetics; Horticulture; Mechanical Engineering; Microbiology; Plant and Crop Protection; Soil Conservation; Soil Science; Vegetable Production); **Architecture** (Architectural and Environmental Design; Architecture; Building Technologies; Graphic Design; Mathematics; Town Planning); **Civil Engineering** (Building Technologies; Civil Engineering; Construction Engineering; Hydraulic Engineering; Irrigation; Mathematics; Power Engineering; Railway Engineering; Surveying and Mapping; Water Science); **Dentistry** (Dental Technology; Dentistry; Oral Pathology); **Dramatic Arts** (Acting; Cinema and Television; Film; Theatre; Writing); **Economics** (Accountancy; Business Administration; Computer Science; Economics; Finance; International Economics; Management; Marketing; Mathematics and Computer Science; Statistics); **Electrical Engineering and Information Technology** (Automation and Control Engineering; Computer Science; Electrical and Electronic Engineering; Information Technology; Physics; Power Engineering; Telecommunications Engineering); **Fine Arts** (Art Education; Fine Arts; Graphic Arts; Painting and Drawing; Sculpture; Visual Arts); **Forestry** (Environmental Management; Forestry; Wood Technology); **Furniture and Interior Design** (Furniture Design; Interior Design); **Law** *(Iustinianus Primus)* (Civil Law; Criminology; International Law; International Relations; Journalism; Law; Political Sciences); **Mechanical Engineering** (Hydraulic Engineering; Machine Building; Mathematics and Computer Science; Mechanical

Engineering; Mechanical Equipment and Maintenance; Metal Techniques; Power Engineering; Production Engineering; Thermal Engineering); **Medicine** (Anaesthesiology; Anatomy; Cardiology; Endocrinology; Epidemiology; Gynaecology and Obstetrics; Haematology; Health Sciences; Medicine; Nephrology; Neurology; Ophthalmology; Orthopaedics; Otorhinolaryngology; Physiology; Plastic Surgery; Psychology; Rheumatology; Surgery; Toxicology; Urology); **Music** (Conducting; Music; Music Theory and Composition; Musical Instruments; Musicology; Singing); **Natural Sciences and Mathematics** (Biology; Chemistry; Computer Science; Geography; Mathematics; Natural Sciences; Physics); **Pedagogy** *(St. Kliment Ohrid)* (Library Science; Pedagogy; Preschool Education; Primary Education); **Pharmacy** (Analytical Chemistry; Biochemistry; Botany; Computer Science; Immunology; Inorganic Chemistry; Molecular Biology; Organic Chemistry; Pharmacology; Pharmacy; Toxicology)); **Philology** *(Blaze Koneski)* (Albanian; Comparative Literature; English; German; Native Language; Philology; Romance Languages; Slavic Languages; Translation and Interpretation; Turkish); **Philosophy** (Archaeology; Art History; Classical Languages; History; Pedagogy; Philosophy; Protective Services; Psychology; Social Policy; Social Work; Sociology; Special Education); **Physical Education** (Physical Education; Sports); **Technology and Metallurgy** (Biotechnology; Industrial Design; Inorganic Chemistry; Metallurgical Engineering; Organic Chemistry; Technology; Textile Technology); **Veterinary Medicine** (Gender Studies; Microbiology; Pathology; Veterinary Science; Zoology)

Institutes

Agriculture *(Skopje)* (Agriculture; Chemistry; Fruit Production; Horticulture; Plant and Crop Protection; Viticulture); **Cattle Breeding** (Animal Husbandry; Cattle Breeding; Zoology); **Earthquake Engineering and Seismology** (Building Technologies; Computer Science; Engineering Management; Geology; Geophysics; Safety Engineering; Seismology); **Economics** (Business Administration; Business and Commerce; Development Studies; Economic and Finance Policy; Economics; Finance; International Economics; International Relations; Management; Marketing; Small Business; Taxation); **Folklore** *(Marko Cepenkov)* (Cultural Studies; Dance; Folklore; Music; Sociology); **Macedonian Language** *(Krste Misirkov)* (Cultural Studies; Literature; Native Language; Slavic Languages; Terminology); **Macedonian Literature** (Comparative Literature; Documentation Techniques; Literature; Native Language; Regional Studies); **National History** (Ancient Civilizations; Documentation Techniques; History; Library Science; Medieval Studies; Modern History; Publishing and Book Trade); **Sociology, Political Science and Law** (Communication Studies; Criminology; Cultural Studies; Demography and Population; Ethnology; Human Resources; Human Rights; International Relations; Law; Marketing; Media Studies; Political Sciences; Social Sciences; Sociology)

Research Institutes

Southern Crops *(Strumica)*

Further Information: Also branches in Štip and Strumica

History: Founded 1949, incorporating faculties of Letters (1946) and Agriculture and Medicine (1947). A State institution.

Governing Bodies: Senate, comprising 77 members; University Board, 40 members; Rector's Board, 5 members

Academic Year: October to June (October-January; February-June)

Admission Requirements: Secondary school leaving certificate (Matura), entrance examinations, depending on the faculty

Main Language(s) of Instruction: Macedonian, Faculty of Education: Albanian, Turkish

International Co-operation: With universities in Albania, Bulgaria, Croatia, Cyprus, Czech Republic, Denmark, Greece, Hungary, Italy, Poland, Romania, Russian Federation, Slovenia, Sweden, Turkey, Serbia and Montenegro.

Accrediting Agencies: Ministry of Education and Science

Degrees and Diplomas: *Diplomiran (BA, BSc)*: 4-6 yrs; *Specijalizacija*: 1-5 yrs; *Magister (MA, MSc)*: a further 2 yrs; *Doktor na Nauki (PhD)*: a further 5 yrs by thesis

Student Services: Cultural centre, Employment services, Foreign Studies Centre, Health services, Sports facilities

Student Residential Facilities: For 5,146 students

Libraries: Central Library

Press or Publishing House: University Press

Student Numbers *2012-2013*: Total 40,000
Last Updated: 25/02/13

PRIVATE INSTITUTIONS

BUSINESS ACADEMY SMILEVSKI

Biznis Akademija Smilevski (BAS)
bul. Avnoj 74a, 1000 Skopje
Tel: +389(2) 2455-754
Website: http://www.bas.edu.mk/

Director: Cvetko Smilevski

Programmes

Operational Management (Management); **Strategic Management** *(Postgraduate)* (Management)

History: Founded 2007.

Main Language(s) of Instruction: Macedonian

Degrees and Diplomas: *Diplomiran*; *Specijalizacija (MBA)*. Also undergraduate certificates.

Last Updated: 07/11/11

EUROPEAN UNIVERSITY OF MACEDONIA

Evropski Univerzitet vo Republika Makedonija
ul Anton Popov b.b., Skopje
Tel: +389(2) 2580-111 +389(2) 2580-112
Fax: +389(2) 2520-400
EMail: contact@eurm.edu.mk
Website: http://www.eurm.edu.mk

Vice-Chancellor: Aleksa Stamenkovski
EMail: Aleksa.stamenkovski@eurm.edu.mk

Secretary-General: Elizabeta Stamevska
EMail: elizabeta.stamevska@eurm.edu.mk

Faculties

Art and Design (Fashion Design; Graphic Arts; Interior Design); **Computer Science** (Computer Engineering; Computer Networks; Computer Science; Multimedia); **Detectives and Criminology** (Criminal Law; Criminology); **Economics** (Finance; Health Administration; Management; Marketing; Taxation); **Law** (Law); **Political Science** (International Relations; Political Sciences)

Further Information: Also Branch in Orhid

History: Created in 2001 as Faculty of Social Science. Obtained current status 2005

Governing Bodies: Board of Directors; Teaching Council

Academic Year: October to May (October-January; February-May)

Admission Requirements: Secondary School Certificate

Main Language(s) of Instruction: Macedonian; English

Accrediting Agencies: Ministry of Education and Science

Degrees and Diplomas: *Diplomiran*: 3/4 years; *Specijalizacija*: a further 1/2 yrs; *Magister*: a further 1/2 yrs; *Doktor na Nauki*

Student Services: Academic counselling, Canteen, Foreign Studies Centre, Language programs, Social counselling, Sports facilities

Libraries: Yes
Last Updated: 31/10/11

FACULTY OF BUSINESS STUDIES IN SKOPJE

Fakultet za delovni studii vo Skopje
Skopje

Faculties

Labour Economics (Business Administration; Economics; Labour and Industrial Relations)

Main Language(s) of Instruction: Macedonian

Accrediting Agencies: Ministry of Education and Science

Degrees and Diplomas: *Diplomiran*; *Magister*

Last Updated: 08/11/11

FON UNIVERSITY

FON Univerzitet

Str. Vojvodina b.b, 10000 Skopje
Tel: +389(2) 2445-555
EMail: info@fon.edu.mk
Website: http://www.fon.edu.mk

Chancellor: Aleksandar Nikolovskij

General Manager: Sefer Canoski

Faculties

Applied Foreign Languages (Albanian; European Languages; Foreign Languages Education; Linguistics; Slavic Languages; Translation and Interpretation; Turkish); **Communication and Information Technology** (Communication Studies; Computer Engineering; Computer Networks; Computer Science; Information Technology; Software Engineering); **Design and Multimedia** (Design; Multimedia); **Economics** (Banking; Economics; Finance; Management; Marketing); **Law** (Law); **Political Sciences, Diplomacy and Journalism** (International Relations; Journalism; Political Sciences); **Security and Detective Studies** (Criminology; Law; Police Studies); **Sport and Sport Management** (Sports; Sports Management)

Further Information: Branch in Struga

History: Previously part of European University of Macedonia (Evropskij Univerzitet Respublika Makedonija). Obtained current status 2003.

Academic Year: October to May (October-January; February-May)

Admission Requirements: Secondary School Leaving Certificate

Main Language(s) of Instruction: Macedonian; English; Albanian

Accrediting Agencies: Ministry of Education and Science

Degrees and Diplomas: *Diplomiran*: Law; Economics; Political Science; Detective and Security Studies; Environmental Management; Communication and Information Technology; Sport and Sports Management, 3/4 yrs; *Specijalizacija*: Law and European Law; Banking and Finance; International and International Politics and Diplomacy, a further year; *Magister*: Law and European Law; Banking and Finance; International and International Politics and Diplomacy, a further year after Specijalizacija

Student Services: Academic counselling, Canteen, Cultural centre, Employment services, Foreign student adviser, Language programs, Social counselling, Sports facilities

Student Residential Facilities: Yes

Special Facilities: Computer laboratories

Libraries: c. 2,000 vols

Last Updated: 31/10/11

HIGHER EDUCATION PROFESSIONAL INSTITUTION FOR BUSINESS STUDIES 'EURO COLLEGE KUMANOVO'

Visoka profesionalna ustanova za biznis studii Evro koledzh Kumanovo

Done Bozinov 41, 1300 Kumanovo
Tel: +389(31) 418-025
Fax: +389(31) 417-202
EMail: info@eurocollege.edu.mk
Website: http://www.eurocollege.edu.mk/

Dean: Ljubisa Petrusevski

Head, Administration: Oliver Mitevski

Programmes

Business Administration *(Macedonian degree)* (Accountancy; Advertising and Publicity; Business Administration; Commercial Law; Communication Studies; Computer Engineering; Finance; Human Resources; Information Technology; Management; Marketing; Software Engineering; Statistics); **Business Administration** *(Doctor - American Degree)* (Business Administration; Leadership; Management; Marketing); **Business Administration** *(Graduate - MBA - American Degree)* (Business Administration; Economics; Finance; Human Resources; Management; Marketing; Transport and Communications); **Business Administration** *(American Degree)* (Accountancy; Business Administration; Commercial Law; Communication Studies; Computer Engineering; Computer Networks; Ethics; Finance; Human Resources; Industrial and Organizational Psychology; Information Management; Information Technology; Insurance; Leadership; Management; Marketing; Statistics); **Business Administration** *(Graduate - Macedonian degree)* (Behavioural Sciences; Business Administration; Finance; Human Resources; Management; Marketing; Transport Management); **Computer Information** *(American Degree)* (Business Administration; Computer Engineering; Computer Graphics; Computer Science; Data Processing; Information Sciences; Management; Marketing; Software Engineering); **Film Studies** *(American Degree)* (Acting; Film; Media Studies)

History: Founded 2003.

International Co-operation: With universities in UK and USA.

Accrediting Agencies: Board of Accreditation of the Republic of Macedonia; Ministry of Education and Science

Degrees and Diplomas: *Diplomiran*; *Magister (MBA)*. Also American Bachelor's, Master's and Doctoral degrees.

Last Updated: 08/11/11

INSTITUTE FOR SOCIAL SCIENCES AND HUMANITIES 'EURO-BALKAN'

Institut za opštestveni i humanisticki istražuvanja 'Evro-Balkan' (EUBA)

ul. Partizanski odredi br. 63, 1000 Skopje
Tel: + 389(2) 3090-731
Fax: + 389(2) 3075-570
EMail: contact@euba.edu.mk
Website: http://www.euba.edu.mk/

Departments

Educational Activity *(Higher Education Studies of Second and Third cycle - School for Regional Studies; Adult Education Center)* (Ancient Civilizations; Anthropology; Cultural Studies; Eastern European Studies; European Studies; Gender Studies; Philosophy; Sociology); **Scientific Research and Policy** (Ancient Civilizations; Archiving; Cultural Studies; Gender Studies; Library Science; Political Sciences; Protective Services)

Fees: (Euro): 1,350-2,150 per annum

Main Language(s) of Instruction: Macedonian

Accrediting Agencies: Board for Accreditation of Higher Education

Degrees and Diplomas: *Magister*, *Doktor na Nauki*

Last Updated: 08/11/11

INTEGRATED BUSINESS FACULTY

Fakultet za Biznis Ekonomija (FBE)

Kosta Novakovic 8, 1000 Skopje
Tel: +389(2) 402-160 +389(2) 2402-161
Fax: +389(2) 2466-063
EMail: fbe@fbe.edu.mk
Website: http://www.fbe.edu.mk/

Director: Antonija Josifovska
EMail: antonija.josifovska@fbe.edu.mk

Courses

Business English (English); **Business English Written Communication** (Communication Studies; English); **Quantitative Methods for Business and Economics** *(Short)* (Business Administration; Economics)

Programmes

Banking (Banking); **Financial Management** (Finance; Management); **Marketing Management** (Management; Marketing); **Regional and Local Business Development** (Business Administration); **Sustainable Development - Environmental Economy** (Development Studies; Economics; Environmental Studies)

Fees: (Euro): 500-600 per annum

Main Language(s) of Instruction: Macedonian

Accrediting Agencies: Ministry of Education and Science

Degrees and Diplomas: *Diplomiran*; *Specijalizacija*

Libraries: c. 1,000 electronic vols

Last Updated: 07/11/11

INTERNATIONAL BALKAN UNIVERSITY

Megjunaroden Balkanski Univerzitet (IBU)
Samoilova 10, 1000 Skopje
Tel: +389(2) 3214-831
Fax: +389(2) 3214-832
EMail: info@ibu.edu.mk
Website: http://www.ibu.edu.mk/

Rector: Huner Sencan

Faculties

Communication (Communication Studies); **Economics and Administration Sciences** (Administration; Economics); **Fine Arts** (Design; Fine Arts); **Languages** (American Studies; English); **Social Sciences** *(New Balkan Faculty)* (International Economics; Public Administration); **Technical Sciences** (Industrial Engineering; Information Technology)

History: Founded in 2006 by the Foundation of Development for Education and Culture '(USKUP), Skopje through integration of the New Balkan Faculty and New Balkan Technical Sciences. Faculties received accreditation 2007.

Governing Bodies: Board of Trustees

Admission Requirements: Secondary School Leaving Certificate or equivalent.

Main Language(s) of Instruction: English

Accrediting Agencies: Ministry of Education and Science

Degrees and Diplomas: *Diplomiran*: Industrial Engineering; Management in Public Administration; International Economic Relations, 4 yrs; *Magister*

Last Updated: 31/10/11

INTERNATIONAL SLAVIC INSTITUTE GAVRIL ROMANOVICH DERZHAVIN, SVETI NIKOLE

Megjunaroden Slavjanski Institut 'Gavrilo Romanovic Deržavin', Sveti Nikole (PVU MSI "G.R.DERŽAVIN")
Maršal Tito 77, 2220 Sveti Nikole
Tel: +389(32) 440-330
Fax: +389(32) 440-201
EMail: info@slavinst.edu.mk
Website: http://www.slavinst.edu.mk/

Chairman: Dusan Nikolovski

Courses

Clinical and Counseling Psychology *(Postgraduate)* (Clinical Psychology; Psychology); **Human Resource Management in Small and Medium Enterprises** *(Postgraduate)* (Human Resources); **Marketing Management** *(Postgraduate)* (Marketing); **Psychology in Social Protection** *(Postgraduate)* (Psychology; Social Welfare); **Psychology of Social Security** *(Postgraduate)* (Psychology; Social Welfare)

Faculties

Economics and Organization of Entrepreneurship (Banking; Economics; Finance; Management); **Informatics** (Computer Science); **Psychology** (Psychology)

Institutes

Art and Culture (Cultural Studies; Fine Arts); **Engineering Economics** (Economics)

History: Founded 2004.

Degrees and Diplomas: *Diplomiran*; *Magister*

STAFF WITH DOCTORATE: Total 40

Last Updated: 07/11/11

INTERNATIONAL UNIVERSITY OF STRUGA

Megjunaroden Univerzitet Struga (IUST)
Ezerski Lozja N-1, 6330 Struga
Tel: +389(46) 786-160
EMail: info@eust.edu.mk
Website: http://www.eust.edu.mk/

Rector: Lisen Bashkurti EMail: l.bashkurti@eust.edu.mk

Faculties

Economics (Business Administration; Economics; Finance; Management; Marketing); **Information Technology** (Information Technology); **Law Science** (Criminology; Law); **Political Science** (Political Sciences)

History: Founded 2007.

Governing Bodies: Senate

Main Language(s) of Instruction: Macedonian

International Co-operation: With universities in USA, UK, Albania, Kosovo. Participates in the Erasmus progamme.

Accrediting Agencies: Ministry of Education and Science

Degrees and Diplomas: *Diplomiran*; *Magister*; *Doktor na Nauki*

Last Updated: 07/11/11

ITALIAN ACADEMY, SKOPJE

Akademija Italiana, Skopje
Saraj BB, 1066 Skopje
Tel: +389(2) 2034-629 +389(2) 2034-600
Fax: +389(2) 2034-629
Website: http://www.accademiaitaliana.com/balkans.html

Programmes

Fashion Design (Fashion Design); **Graphic Design and Visual Communications** (Communication Arts; Graphic Design); **Interior and Product Design** (Industrial Design; Interior Design)

History: Founded 2006. An affiliate centre to the Accademia Italiana in Firenze.

Main Language(s) of Instruction: English

Accrediting Agencies: Ministry o Higher Education and Science.

Degrees and Diplomas: *Diplomiran*

Last Updated: 07/11/11

MIT UNIVERSITY, SKOPJE

MIT Univerzitet, Skopje (MIT)
bul.Treta Makedonska Brigada BB, 1000 Skopje
Tel: +3892 2402373
EMail: contact@mit.edu.mk
Website: http://www.mit.edu.mk/

Rector: Gjorgji Gjorgjevski EMail: gjorgji.gjorgjevski@mit.edu.mk

Student Affairs Officer: Darko Daniloski
Tel: +389(2) 2402-373 EMail: darko.daniloski@mit.edu.mk

Faculties

Architecture (Architecture; Design; Engineering; Town Planning); **Computer Science and Technology** (Computer Engineering; Computer Science; E-Business/Commerce; Information Management; Information Technology; Software Engineering); **Ecological and Rural Tourism Management** (Ecology; Tourism); **Ecological Resources Management** (Agricultural Business; Ecology; Natural Resources); **Gastronomy** (Cooking and Catering); **Management** (Business Administration; Economics; Finance; Government; Health Administration; Management; Public Administration)

History: Founded 2007.

Main Language(s) of Instruction: Macedonian; English

Accrediting Agencies: Ministry of Education and Science

Degrees and Diplomas: *Diplomiran*; *Magister*

Last Updated: 07/11/11

NEW YORK UNIVERSITY SKOPJE

Njujork Univerzitet Skopje (NYUS)
Saraj BB, 1066 Skopje
Tel: +389(2) 2034-600
Fax: +389(2) 2034-630
EMail: info@nyus.edu.mk
Website: http://www.nyus.edu.mk/

Rector: Jane Miljovski (2006-) EMail: rector@nyus.edu.mk

Secretary-General: Marija Peseva EMail: mpeseva@nyus.edu.mk

International Relations: Zileska Lile, Academic Coordinator
EMail: lzileska@nyus.edu.mk

Faculties
Business Administration (Accountancy; Business and Commerce; Finance; Human Resources; Management; Marketing); **Business Law** (Banking; Commercial Law; Insurance; Labour Law; Law); **Communications and Media Studies** (Communication Studies; Media Studies; Multimedia; Public Relations); **Computer Science and Information Technology** (Computer Science; Information Technology); **English Language and Literature** (English; Literature); **International Relations, Politics and European Studies** (European Studies; International Relations; Political Sciences)

History: Created 2005

Governing Bodies: Board of Founders; Senate; Academic Council; Rector

Academic Year: September to June

Admission Requirements: High School Diploma (drzavna matura) or equivalent; English proficiency for English language programmes

Main Language(s) of Instruction: English, Macedonian

International Co-operation: With Staffordshire University, UK; State University New York, USA

Accrediting Agencies: Ministry of Education and Science

Degrees and Diplomas: *Diplomiran*: Business Studies; Human Resource Management; International Business Management; Marketing Management; Business Management & Entrepreneurship; Accounting & Finance; Accounting & Business; Finance (BA); Communications; Public Relations; New Media; English Language and Literature (BA); Computer Science; Software Engineering; Computer Systems (BSc); International Relations; Politics; European Studies (BA); Law (LLB), 3 yrs; *Magister (MA; MBA; MSc; LLm)*: a further 2 yrs

Student Services: Academic counselling, Canteen, Employment services, Foreign student adviser, Foreign Studies Centre, Language programs, Social counselling

Student Residential Facilities: Yes

Special Facilities: English Writing Centre

Libraries: 2,000 vols (all media)
Last Updated: 31/10/11

SCHOOL OF JOURNALISM AND PUBLIC RELATIONS, SKOPJE

Visokata škola za novinarstvo i odnosi so javnosta, Skpoje (VS)
ul. Jurij Gagarin 17/1-1, 1000 Skopje
Tel: +389(2) 3090-004
Fax: +389(2) 3090-104
EMail: info@vs.edu.mk
Website: http://vs.edu.mk/

Director: Zaneta Trajkoska

Programmes
Corporate Communications and Public Relations (Communication Studies; Public Relations); **Journalism and Production** (Journalism; Media Studies); **Media Management and Multimedia** *(Postgraduate)* (Management; Media Studies; Multimedia); **Strategic Communications Management** (Communication Studies; Management; Mass Communication)

Main Language(s) of Instruction: Macedonian

International Co-operation: Participates in the Erasmus programme.

Accrediting Agencies: Ministry of Education and Science

Degrees and Diplomas: *Diplomiran*; *Specijalizacija*
Last Updated: 08/11/11

SOUTH EAST EUROPEAN UNIVERSITY

Univerzitet na Jugoistocna Evropa
'Illindenska' p.n., 1200 Tetovo
Tel: +389(44) 356-000
EMail: z.tairi@seeu.edu.mk
Website: http://www.seeu.edu.mk

Rector: Zamir Dika
Tel: +389(44) 356-110, Fax: +389(44) 356-111
EMail: rectorate@seeu.edu.mk

Secretary-General: Dennis Farrington
Tel: +389(44) 356-040, Fax: +389(44) 356-111
EMail: d.farrington@seeu.edu.mk

International Relations: Ariana Kica EMail: a.kica@seeu.edu.mk

Faculties
Business and Economics (Accountancy; Agricultural Business; Business Administration; Economics; Finance; Health Administration; Management; Marketing; Tourism); **Contemporary Sciences and Technologies** (Business Computing; Computer Engineering; Computer Science; Information Technology; Software Engineering); **Languages, Cultures and Communications** (Albanian; Communication Studies; Cultural Studies; English; German; Literature; Media Studies); **Law** (Civil Law; Criminal Law; Criminology; Law); **Public Administration and Political Science** (Human Resources; International Business; Management; Political Sciences; Public Administration; Statistics)

History: Founded 2001.

Governing Bodies: University Board, Senate and Council

Academic Year: October to June

Admission Requirements: School certificate and entrance examination

Main Language(s) of Instruction: Albanian; Macedonian; English

International Co-operation: With universities in France, Switzerland, Austria, Albania, Kosovo, USA.

Accrediting Agencies: Ministry of Education and Science

Degrees and Diplomas: *Diplomiran (BA)*: 4 yrs; *Magister*. Diplomiran equivalent to Bachelor

Student Services: Academic counselling, Canteen, Employment services, Language programs, Sports facilities

Student Residential Facilities: 450 places

Libraries: Max van der Stoel library
Last Updated: 31/10/11

UNIVERSITY AMERICAN COLLEGE IN SKOPJE

Univerzitet Amerikan Koledz Skopje
Bul. Treta Makedonska Brigada b.b., 1000 Skopje
Tel: +389(2) 2463-156
Fax: +389(2) 2463-159
EMail: info@uacs.edu.com
Website: http://www.uacs.edu.mk/

Chancellor, Provost: Marjan Bojadziev
EMail: provost@uacs.edu.mk

Vice-Chancellor: Tome Nenenovski
EMail: nenovski@uacs.edu.mk

Schools
Architecture and Design (Architecture; Interior Design); **Business Administration** (Business Administration; Finance; Management; Marketing); **Computer Science and Information Technology** (Computer Networks; Software Engineering); **Foreign Languages** (Communication Studies; English; Foreign Languages Education; Translation and Interpretation); **Legal Studies** (Administrative Law; Law; Public Law); **Political Science** (Human Rights; International Relations; Political Sciences)

History: Created 2005. Obtained status 2006.

Governing Bodies: Business Council; Executive Board

Academic Year: September to June

Admission Requirements: Secondary School Leaving Certificate or equivalent; TOEFL score of at least 530 (written form) or 200 (computer form), for studies in English; High School GPA of 3.5 - 5.0

Main Language(s) of Instruction: English; Macedonian

Accrediting Agencies: Ministry of Education and Science

Degrees and Diplomas: *Magister*: Business Administration (MBA). Also Bachelor degree in 3 yrs in: Marketing; Finance; Management; International Relations and Diplomacy; Human Rights; English Language Teaching and Literature; Translation and Interpretation; Business Correspondence and Communication (English); Architecture; Interior Design; Computer Networks; Software Engineering.

Student Services: Academic counselling, Cultural centre, Employment services, Foreign Studies Centre, Language programs, Sports facilities

Libraries: Yes, also e-library
Last Updated: 09/09/11

UNIVERSITY OF AUDIOVISUAL ARTS - EUROPEAN FILM ACADEMY ESRA-SKOPJE PARIS-NEW YORK

Univerzitet za Audiovizuelni Umetnosti - Evropska Filmska Akademija ESRA Pariz-Skopje-Njujork (ESRA)
st.Nicholas Rusinski no. A, 1000 Skopje
Tel: +389(2) 3061-543
Fax: +389(2) 3067-609
EMail: info@esra.com.mk
Website: http://www.esra.com.mk/

Rector: Jordan Plevnesh

Faculties

Applied Music (Dance; Music; Music Theory and Composition); **Film** (Cinema and Television; Film; Radio and Television Broadcasting); **Stage Design** (Display and Stage Design; Visual Arts); **Theatre** (Acting; Multimedia; Theatre); **Tone Production** (Sound Engineering (Acoustics))

History: Founded 2007 on the model of the French ESRA Film School.

Fees: (Euro): 3,000-4,500 per annum

Degrees and Diplomas: *Diplomiran*; *Magister*
Last Updated: 07/11/11

UNIVERSITY OF TOURISM AND MANAGEMENT-SKOPJE

Univerzitet za Turizam i Menadzhment Skopje (UTMS)
Partizanski Odredi no. 99, 1000 Skopje
Tel: + 389(2) 3093-209 + 389(2) 3093-215
Fax: + 389(2) 3093-213
EMail: contact@utms.edu.mk
Website: http://www.utms.edu.mk/

Rector: Ace Milenkovski
Vice Chancellor for Teaching: Alexandra Stoilkovski
International Relations: Zoran Ivanovski, Vice Rector for International Cooperation

Faculties

Economics (Economics); **Entrepreneurial Business** (Business Administration; Management); **International Marketing and Management** (International Business; Management; Marketing); **Management of Human Resources** (Human Resources); **Public Relations** (Public Relations); **Sport Tourism** (Sports; Tourism); **Tourism** (Tourism)

Governing Bodies: University Council; University Senate

Main Language(s) of Instruction: Macedonian

International Co-operation: With universities in Croatia, Serbia, USA, Bulgaria, Montenegro and Turkey.

Degrees and Diplomas: *Diplomiran*; *Magister*; *Doktor na Nauki*
Last Updated: 07/11/11

Madagascar

STRUCTURE OF HIGHER EDUCATION SYSTEM

Description:

Higher education is provided by public and private universities and higher technical institutions. The universities are autonomous institutions. Each university is headed by a Rector and administered by a Conseil d'Administration. The three-tier system (Licence-Master-Doctorat) is to be fully implemented in the 2012/2013 academic year.

Stages of studies:

University level first stage: Licence

The first stage of higher education lasts three years and leads to the Licence.

University level second stage: Master

The Master is conferred after two years' further study beyond the Licence.

University level third stage: Doctorat

The Doctorat is awarded after two years' study following upon the Master degree. In Medicine, studies last 7 years.

ADMISSION TO HIGHER EDUCATION

Admission to university-level studies:

Name of secondary school credential required: Baccalauréat de l'Enseignement secondaire

Minimum score/requirement: 10/20

Name of secondary school credential required: Baccalauréat professionnel et technique

Minimum score/requirement: 10/20

Entrance exam requirements: Competitive examination in some cases.

Foreign students admission:

Entry regulations: Foreign students must hold a visa.

Language requirements: Good knowledge of French.

NATIONAL BODIES

Ministère de l'Enseignement Supérieur et de la Recherche Scientifique - MESUPRES (Ministry of Higher Education and Scientific Research)

Minister: Amette Etienne Hilaire Razafindehibe
Director, Higher Education: Armand Hubert Claude Aimé Rasoamiramanana
BP 4163
Antananarivo 101
Tel: +261 20 22271 85
Fax: +261 20 22238 97
WWW: http://www.mesupres.gov.mg/
Role of national body: Oversees the national education policy, including higher education policy.

Conférence des Présidents des Institutions de l'Enseignement supérieur - CoPRIES (Conference of the Presidents of Higher Education Institutions)

Antananarivo

Association des Établissements d'Enseignement supérieur privés homologués de Madagascar - AEESPHM (Association of Private Accredited Higher Education Institutions of Madagascar)

Antananarivo

Association des Etablissements de Formation professionnelle supérieure agréés - AEFPSA
(Association of Accredited Institutions of Vocational Training)
Antananarivo

Data for academic year: 2012-2013
Source: IAU from Fiche Curie Madagascar, Ministère des Affaires étrangères, France and MESUPRES website, 2012

INSTITUTIONS

PUBLIC INSTITUTIONS

NATIONAL INSTITUTE OF ACCOUNTANCY AND BUSINESS ADMINISTRATION

Institut national des Sciences comptables et de l'Administration d'Entreprises (INSCAE)
Maison des Produits 67 ha, Antananarivo 101
Tel: +261(20) 22-660-65
Fax: +261(20) 22-308-95
EMail: drinscae@inscae.mg
Website: http://www.inscae.mg

Directeur général: Victor Harison

Directeur administratif et financier: Fidelice Andrianandraina
Tel: +261(20) 22-660-66 EMail: daf-inscae@inscae.mg

Departments
Business Administration and Marketing (Business Administration; Marketing) *Head*: Felix Rasoloarijaona; **Finance and Accountancy** (Accountancy; Finance) *Head*: Felix Rasoloarijaoana

History: Founded 1983. Acquired present title 1986.

Governing Bodies: Dean; Academic Department; Administrative and Financial Affairs Department; Professional Training Department

Academic Year: Undergraduate Studies: January to December (January-May: Summer session; August-December: Spring Session); Master 1: November to September; Master 2: September to October; MBA: January to December

Admission Requirements: Undergraduate Studies: High School Diploma; Master : Bachelor; Master 2: Maîtrise/Master 1; MBA: Engineering Degree or equivalent with at least 3 years of professional experience.

Fees: (Ariary): Undergraduate Studies, 550,000-600,000 per annum; Master 1.5.; Master 2,600,000; MBA, 450,000 per module, Continuing Education: 75,000 per module

Main Language(s) of Instruction: French and English for some courses

International Co-operation: With universities in Canada (University of Trois-Rivières in Québec, University of Laval); France, (University of Poitiers, University of Lyon) ; Mauritius (University of Mauritius, French Institute of Entrepreneurship)

Degrees and Diplomas: *Master*: Marketing and Strategy; International Management; Finance and Banking; Management Contro and Operational Audit;International Trade; Accountancy, Control and Audit; Marketing Strategy; Research, 1 yr. Bachelor in Business Administration (3 yrs); Bachelor in Finance and Accountancy (3yrs) ; Business Administration (MBA): 2 yrs

Student Services: Cultural centre, Employment services

Academic Staff *2011-2012*	MEN	WOMEN	**TOTAL**
FULL-TIME	14	4	**18**
PART-TIME	32	8	**40**
STAFF WITH DOCTORATE			
FULL-TIME	8	4	**12**
PART-TIME	–	–	**3**
Student Numbers *2011-2012*			
All (Foreign Included)	489	670	**1,159**

Last Updated: 06/04/12

NATIONAL INSTITUTE OF NUCLEAR SCIENCES AND TECHNIQUES

Institut national des Sciences et Techniques nucléaires (MADAGASCAR-INSTN)
BP 4279, Antananarivo 101
Tel: +261(20) 24-714-03 +261(20) 22-355-84
Fax: +261(20) 22-355-83
EMail: instn@moov.mg
Website: http://www.madagascar-instn.org

Directeur général: Raoelina Andriambololona
Tel: +261(20) 22 356-96; +261 32-04-520-46,
Fax: +261(20) 22 355-83
EMail: Jacquelineraoelina@hotmail.com; raoelinasp@yahoo.fr

Directeur administratif et financier: Wilfrid Chrysante Solofoarisina
Tel: +261(20) 24-714-03, Fax: +261(20) 22-355-83
EMail: s.wilfridc@moov.mg

International Relations: Joël Rajaobelison, Directeur technique et du Développement
Tel: +261 32-07-022-84, Fax: +261 20-22-355-83
EMail: joelrajaobelison@yahoo.fr

Departments
Education (Education) *Head*: Gilbert Nirina Rasolofoson; **Informatics and Communication Technology** *Head*: Hanitriarivo Rakotoson; **Isotope Hydrology** *Head*: Voahirana Ramaroson; **Maintenance and Nuclear Instrumentation** (Maintenance Technology; Nuclear Engineering) *Head*: Hery Andrianiaina; **Nuclear Analysis and Techniques** (Nuclear Engineering) *Head*: Naivo Rabesiranana; **Radiation Protection and Dosimetry** (Safety Engineering) *Head*: Joseph Lucien Radaorolala Zafimanjato; **Theoretical Physics** (Physics) *Head*: Roland Raboanary; **XRF Techniques and Environment** (Environmental Engineering) *Head*: Lucienne Randriamanivo

History: Founded 1976 as Laboratory for Nuclear and Applied Physics (L.P.N.P.A.). Acquired present status and title 1992. A public autonomous institution.

Governing Bodies: Board of Governors

Academic Year: January to September

Admission Requirements: Baccalauréat scientifique for two-year cycle leading to technician in radiation protection; Maîtrise ès Sciences for postgraduate study

Fees: (Ariary): 1st yr: 650,000; 2nd yr: 700,000; 3rd yr: 720,000 per annum

Main Language(s) of Instruction: French

Accrediting Agencies: International Atomic Energy Agency, SADC

Degrees and Diplomas: *Licence*: Radiation Protection (LPRP), 3 yrs; *Master*: Nuclear Physics, 2 yrs; *Doctorat*: Nuclear Physics (DTC), 3-5 yrs

Student Services: Academic counselling, Employment services, Foreign student adviser, Sports facilities

Libraries: Raoelina Andriambololona Library

Publications: Journal des Sciences et Techniques Nucléaires; Raoelina Andriambololona Interdisciplinary Seminar

Press or Publishing House: Publishing Unit

Academic Staff 2012	MEN	WOMEN	TOTAL
FULL-TIME	9	1	10
STAFF WITH DOCTORATE			
FULL-TIME	6	1	7
PART-TIME	5	–	5
Student Numbers 2012			
All (Foreign Included)	32	25	57
FOREIGN ONLY	1	–	1

Last Updated: 21/06/12

NATIONAL SCHOOL OF ADMINISTRATION

Ecole nationale d'Administration (ENAM)

BP 1163 - Androhibe, Antananarivo
Tel: +261(20) 22-420-91
Fax: +261(20) 22-318-15
EMail: enam@enam.mg
Website: http://www.enam.mg/

Directeur Général: Théogène Rajaonarivelo
Tel: +261(20) 24-553-79 EMail: dg@enam.mg

Directeur de la Formation, des Recherches et des Stages: Hanitriniaina Liliane Ravaoharinirina EMail: dfrs@enam.mg

Departments

Administration (Administration; Public Administration)

History: Founded 1960, attached to the university until 1972, no activity 1972-1988, known as ENAM since 1988, acquired present status 1995.

Admission Requirements: Maîtrise and entrance examination

Fees: None

Main Language(s) of Instruction: French

International Co-operation: With institutions in Canada; France; Comoros

Degrees and Diplomas: Equivalent of Master's (professional), 2 yrs

Student Services: Health services, Language programs, Sports facilities

Last Updated: 28/09/12

UNIVERSITY OF ANTANANARIVO

Université d'Antananarivo (UA)

BP 566, Ambohitsaina, Antananarivo 101
Tel: +261(20) 22-326-39 +261(20) 22-241-14
Fax: +261(20) 22-279-26
EMail: presidence@univ-antananarivo.mg
Website: http://www.univ-antananarivo.mg

President: Panja Ramanoelina (2013-)

Vice-Présidente chargée de la Formation, de la Recherche et des Relations internationales: Bakolinirina Andriamihaja
Tel: +261 33-11-458-09
EMail: b.andriamihaja@moov.mg; vpfr@univ-antananarivo.mg

Vice Président, en charge du partenariat et des TIC: Jean Jules Harijaona
Tel: +261 34-43-713-43
EMail: jean-jules.harijaona@univ-montpellier3.fr

Faculties

Arts and Humanities (Anthropology; Archaeology; Arts and Humanities; Cultural Studies; English; French; Geography; German; History; Literature; Modern Languages; Philosophy); **Law, Economics, Administration and Sociology** *(DEGS)* (Administration; Economics; Law; Sociology); **Medicine** (Gynaecology and Obstetrics; Medicine; Paediatrics; Surgery); **Science** (Chemistry; Mathematics; Natural Sciences; Physics)

Institutes

Confucius (Chinese)

Schools

Agronomy *(ESSA)* (Agricultural Engineering; Agricultural Management; Agriculture; Agronomy; Animal Husbandry; Food Technology; Forestry; Water Management); **Education** *(ENS)* (Chemistry; Education; English; French; Geography; History; Modern Languages; Natural Sciences; Physical Education; Physics); **Polytechnics** *(ESPA)* (Engineering)

History: Founded 1955 as Institut des Hautes Etudes tracing origins to School of Medicine (1896) and School of Law (1941). Became Université de Madagascar 1960. Reorganized 1973 with six main divisions, and 1976 as a decentralized institution with six Regional Centres. Acquired present status as independent university 1988.

Governing Bodies: Administration Council

Academic Year: March-December

Admission Requirements: Secondary school certificate (baccalauréat) or equivalent, and entrance examination

Fees: (Euros): 12 for local students; 30 for foreign students

Main Language(s) of Instruction: French, Malagasy

International Co-operation: With AUF and institutions in Algeria, Belgium, Canada, France, Germany, Italy, La Réunion, Netherlands, South Africa, Switzerland, United Kingdom, Norway, Spain, China, Japan and USA

Degrees and Diplomas: *Licence*: Agronomy; Agriculture; Forestry; Agricultural Management; Animal Production; Food Technology; Technology; Arts and Humanities; Science; Mathematics, Computer Science; Physics; Chemistry; Technology; *Licence*: Law; Economics; Administration; Sociology; History; Literature; Modern Language; English; French; German; Spanish; Russian; Malagasy; Philosophy; Geography; Mathematics; Natural Sciences; Chemistry; Physics (L), 1 further yr; *Diplôme de Docteur en Médecine*: Medicine; Veterinary Medicine; Pharmacy, 7 yrs; *Master*: Economics; Management; Agriculture Management; Arts and Humanities;Geography; History; Communication Studies; Linguistics; Education; Pedagogy; Mathematics; Natural Sciences; Chemistry; Physics; Environmental Management; Law; Economics; Administration; Sociology; History; Literature; Modern Languages; English; French; German; Spanish; Russian; Malagasy; Philosophy; Geography; Mathematics; Natural Sciences; Chemistry; Physics; *Doctorat*: Education & Multilinguism, Pedagogy; Economics; Management; Agriculture Management; Arts & Humanities; Geography; History; Communication Studies; Mathematics; Natural Sciences; Chemistry; Physics; Water & Forestry; Development & Environment Studies

Student Services: Academic counselling, Foreign student adviser, Health services, Nursery care, Sports facilities

Student Residential Facilities: Yes

Special Facilities: Museum of Art and Archaeology; Institute of Civilizations; Institute and Observatory of Geophysics of Antananarivo

Libraries: c. 170,000 vols

Publications: Annales de la Faculté des Lettres et Sciences Humaines, Published by the Faculty of Arts and Humanities; Hiratra, Published by the Faculty of Arts and Humanities; Revue de Géographie, Related to Geography; Terre Malgache, Related to Agronomy

Academic Staff 2008-2009	MEN	WOMEN	TOTAL
FULL-TIME	–	–	697
STAFF WITH DOCTORATE			
FULL-TIME	–	–	515
Student Numbers 2008-2009			
All (Foreign Included)	–	–	21,564
FOREIGN ONLY	59	177	236

Last Updated: 11/02/13

GEOPHYSICAL INSTITUTE AND OBSERVATORY OF ANTANANARIVO

INSTITUT ET OBSERVATOIRE GEOPHYSIQUE D'ANTANANARIVO (IOGA)

BP 3843 Ambohidempona, Campus Universitaire, Antananarivo 101
Tel: +261(20) 22-253-53
Fax: +261(20) 22-253-53
EMail: ioga@syfed.refer.mg

Directeur: Jean-Bruno Ratsimbazafy EMail: jbratsim@wanadoo.mg

Departments

Geophysics (Geophysics)

History: Founded 1989.

INSTITUTE OF CIVILIZATIONS, MUSEUM OF ART AND ARCHAEOLOGY

INSTITUT DES CIVILISATIONS, MUSÉE D'ART ET D'ARCHÉOLOGIE (IC/MAA)

BP 564, 17 rue Docteur Villette, Isoraka, Antananarivo 101
EMail: musedar@gmail.com; vohitra@refer.mg

Directeur: Chantal Radimilahy
EMail: chradimi@refer.mg; radimilahych@gmail.com

Institutes

Civilizations, Museum of Art and Archaeology *(ICMAA)* (Anthropology; Archaeology; Arts and Humanities; Cultural Studies; Ethnology; Folklore; Geography; History; Musicology; Prehistory)

History: Founded 1964.

INSTITUTE OF ENERGY STUDIES

INSTITUT POUR LA MAÎTRISE DE L'ENERGIE (IME)

BP 566, Ambohitsaina, Antananarivo 101
Tel: +261(20) 22-311-91
Fax: +261(20) 22-279-96
EMail: ime@univ-antananarivo.mg

Directeur: Minoson Rakotomalala
EMail: minoson@univ-antananarivo.mg

Institutes

Energy and Thermal Engineering (Energy Engineering; Thermal Engineering)

History: Founded 1977.

RADIO-ISOTOPES LABORATORY

LABORATOIRE DE RADIO-ISOTOPES (LRI)

BP 3383, Antananarivo 101
Tel: +261(20) 24-161-03
EMail: lilia.rabeharisoa@ird.fr
Website: http://www.laboradioisotopes.com

Directeur: Lilia Rabeharisoa

Laboratories

Nuclear Medicine and Biology (Biology; Medical Technology)

History: Founded 1956.

Degrees and Diplomas: *Doctorat*. Also Master

UNIVERSITY OF ANTSIRANANA

Université d'Antsiranana (UNA)

BP 0, Antsiranana 201
Tel: +261(20) 82-925-96
EMail: presidence@univ-antsiranana.org
Website: http://www.univ-antsiranana.org

Présidente: Cécile Marie Ange Manorohanta (2001-)
Tel: +261-34-07-039-01 EMail: cmanoroh@moov.mg

Vice-Président: Charles Bernard Andrianirina
Tel: +261-34-07-039-00 EMail: niri_cha@yahoo.fr

Centres

Computer Studies (Computer Engineering; Electrical and Electronic Engineering; Systems Analysis; Telecommunications Engineering) *Head*: Charles Bernard Andrianirina; **Modern Languages and Communications Studies** *Head*: Cécile Marie Ange Manorohanta

Departments

Management *Head*: Gatien Horace

Faculties

Arts and Humanities (Arts and Humanities; Communication Studies; Modern Languages) *Dean*: Jean de Dieu Kalobotra; **Science** (Chemistry; Environmental Studies; Physics) *Director*: Hiviel Tsiresena Riziky

Institutes

Higher Education for Factory Administration *((ISAE))* *Director*: Claudia Razafintsalama

History: Founded 1975 as Regional Centre of the Université de Madagascar. Acquired present status as independent university 1992.

Governing Bodies: Board of Governors

Academic Year: March to December

Admission Requirements: Secondary school certificate (baccalauréat) or equivalent, and entrance examination

Main Language(s) of Instruction: French

International Co-operation: With universities in France and Switzerland

Accrediting Agencies: Ministry of National Education and Scientific Research

Degrees and Diplomas: *Licence*: Engineering; Language Studies; *Licence*: Physics, Chemistry, Environment, 3 yrs; *Master*: Physics, Chemistry, Environment; *Doctorat*: Physics, Chemistry, Engineering

Student Services: Academic counselling, Health services, Language programs, Sports facilities

Student Residential Facilities: For c. 1,200 students

Libraries: 8,000 vols. Virtual library (Madagascar Digital Library)

Academic Staff *2008-2009*	**TOTAL**
FULL-TIME	**72**
PART-TIME	**136**
STAFF WITH DOCTORATE	
FULL-TIME	**40**
PART-TIME	**21**

Student Numbers *2008-2009*	
All (Foreign Included)	**1,782**

Last Updated: 11/09/09

HIGHER POLYTECHNIC SCHOOL

ECOLE SUPÉRIEURE POLYTECHNIQUE (ESP)

BP 0, 201 Antsiranana
Tel: +261(20) 82-211-37, Ext. 49
Fax: +261(20) 82-214-93
EMail: chramino@yahoo.fr

Directeur: Chrysostôme Raminosoa (2002-)

Departments

Electronic Engineering (Electronic Engineering); **Hydraulic Engineering** (Hydraulic Engineering); **Industrial Engineering** (Computer Engineering; Industrial Engineering); **Mechanical Engineering** (Mechanical Engineering)

History: Founded 1977. Acquired present status 1994.

Degrees and Diplomas: *Master*: Mathematics

TEACHER TRAINING COLLEGE FOR TECHNICAL STUDIES

ECOLE NORMALE SUPÉRIEURE POUR L'ENSEIGNEMENT TECHNIQUE (ENSET)

BP 0, 201 Antsiranana
Tel: +261(20) 82-211-37, Ext. 50
Fax: +261(20) 82-294-09

Directeur: Jeannot (2006-)

Departments

Electrical Engineering (Electrical Engineering; Technology Education); **Mathematics and Computer Science** (Mathematics and Computer Science; Mathematics Education); **Mechanical Engineering** (Mechanical Engineering)

History: Founded 1991. Acquired present status 1994.

UNIVERSITY OF FIANARANTSOA

Université de Fianarantsoa (UF)

BP 1264, Campus Universitaire d'Andrainjato, Fianarantsoa 301
Tel: +261(20) 75-508-02
Fax: +261(20) 75-510-91
EMail: presidence@univ-fianar.mg
Website: http://www.univ-fianar.mg

Vice-Chancellor: Monique Rasoazananera (2010-)
Tel: +261 32-40-187-49 EMail: soanera@yahoo.fr

Directeur administratif et financier: Joseph Marie Andriamihaja
Tel: +261 34-60-070-86

International Relations: Josvah Paul Razafimandimby, Directeur d'appui à la recherche et au partenariat
Tel: +261 32-04-993-62 EMail: r_josvah@yahoo.fr

Centres

Professional Studies *(CUFP (Tanambao))* (Computer Engineering; Economics; Information Technology; Social Sciences) *Director*: Henri Rasamoelina

Faculties

Art and Human Sciences (Anthropology; Cultural Studies; English; French; History; Modern Languages; Spanish); **Law, Economy, Management and Social Sciences** *(DEGS)* (Economics; Law; Management; Private Law; Public Administration; Public Law; Social Sciences) *Dean*: Mamy Hary Jean Andriamitsiriniony; **Sciences** (Chemistry; Electrical and Electronic Equipment and Maintenance; Energy Engineering; Mathematics; Mathematics and Computer Science; Natural Sciences; Oenology; Physics) *Dean*: Benjamin Andrianirina

Institutes

Confucius (Chinese) *Director*: Patrice Goussot

History: Founded 1977 as Regional Centre of the Université de Madagascar. Acquired present status as independent University 1988.

Governing Bodies: Management Board

Academic Year: October to June

Admission Requirements: Secondary school certificate (baccalauréat) or equivalent, and entrance examination

Fees: (Ariary): 1st to 3rd year: 60,000-200,000; 4th and 5th: 70,000 to 300,000

Main Language(s) of Instruction: Malagasy and French

International Co-operation: With universities in France, USA, Indian Ocean, Canada and South Africa

Accrediting Agencies: Comité National d'habilitation (National Committee for Accreditation)

Degrees and Diplomas: *Licence*: Mathematics; Physics and Chemistry; Mathematics and Computing for Social Sciences; *Master*: Computer Science; Pedagogy; Adult Education; Physics; Environmental Sciences; Computer Science; *Master*: Mathematics; Physics and Chemistry; Mathematics and Computing for Social Sciences; Law, Economy and Management; Social Sciences, 4 yrs; *Doctorat*

Student Services: Cultural centre, Health services, Language programs, Sports facilities

Student Residential Facilities: Yes

Special Facilities: Museum

Libraries: Yes

Academic Staff *2011-2012*	MEN	WOMEN	**TOTAL**
FULL-TIME	53	48	**101**
PART-TIME	–	–	**120**
Student Numbers *2011-2012*			
All (Foreign Included)	3,518	2,935	**6,453**
FOREIGN ONLY	8	17	**25**

Distance students, 40.

Last Updated: 04/06/12

HIGHER PEDAGOGICAL SCHOOL

ECOLE NORMALE SUPÉRIEURE (ENS)

BP 1264, Fianarantsoa 301
Tel: +261(20) 75-508-12
Fax: +261(20) 75-506-19
EMail: ens@univ-fianar.mg

Directrice: Clarisse Rasoamampionona

Departments

Mathematics (Mathematics); **Physics** (Physics)

History: Founded 1981. Acquired present status 1983.

Admission Requirements: Entrance examination

INSTITUTE OF ENVIRONMENTAL TECHNIQUES AND SCIENCES

INSTITUT DES SCIENCES ET TECHNIQUES DE L'ENVIRONNEMENT (ISTE)

BP 1264, Ambalapaiso, Fianarantsoa 301
Tel: +261(20) 75-905-38
Fax: +261(20) 75-519-17
EMail: iste@univ-fianar.mg

Directeur: Edouard Rakoto (2010-)

Programmes

Environmental Studies (Agronomy; Ecology; Economics; Environmental Studies; Forestry; Management; Tourism; Water Management)

NATIONAL SCHOOL OF COMPUTER SCIENCE

ECOLE NATIONALE D'INFORMATIQUE (ENI)

BP 1487, Tanambao, Fianarantsoa 301
Tel: +261(20) 75-508-01
Fax: +261(20) 75-506-19
EMail: eni@univ-fianar.mg
Website: http://www.univ-fianar.mg

Head: Fontaine Rafamantanantsoa
Tel: +261 34-84-959-79 EMail: fontainerafamant@yahoo.fr

Departments

Doctoral Studies (Artificial Intelligence; Computer Science; Information Technology) *Chief of Department*: Josvah Paul Razafimandimby

Programmes

Computer Science *(Theorical Studies)* (Computer Engineering; Computer Networks; Computer Science; Software Engineering) *Chief of Department*: Venot Ratiarison; **Computer Science** *(Practical Studies and Internship))* (Computer Networks; Data Processing; Software Engineering; Systems Analysis) *Chief of Department*: Cyprien Rakotoasimbahoaka

History: Founded 1980. Acquired present status 1983.

Degrees and Diplomas: Diplôme universitaire de Technicien Superieur; Diplôme d'Ingénieur en Informatique

UNIVERSITY OF MAHAJANGA

Université de Mahajanga (IOSTM)

BP 652, Immeuble Kakal, 5 rue Georges V, Mahajanga 401
Tel: +261(20) 62-908-34
Fax: +261(20) 62-233-12
EMail: presidence@univ-mahajanga.mg
Website: http://www.univ-mahajanga.mg

Président: Antoine Rabesa Zafera

Directeur administratif: Jeanette Razafindralinina

Faculties

Medicine (Biology; Medicine; Natural Sciences; Public Health; Surgery); **Science** (Biochemistry; Biology; Botany; Chemistry; Earth Sciences; Environmental Studies; Natural Sciences)

History: Founded 1977 as Regional Centre of the Université de Madagascar. Acquired present status as independent University 1992.

Academic Year: November to July

Admission Requirements: Secondary school certificate (baccalauréat) or equivalent, and entrance examination

Main Language(s) of Instruction: French, Malagasy

Degrees and Diplomas: *Licence*: 1 further yr; *Diplôme de Docteur en Médecine*: 7 yrs; *Master*, *Doctorat*. Also teaching qualifications

INSTITUTE OF TROPICAL DENTISTRY

INSTITUT D'ODONTO-STOMATOLOGIE TROPICALE

BP 98, 7 rue Maréchal Joffre, Mahajanga 401
Tel: +261(20) 62-022-19
EMail: iostm@univ-mahajanga.mg

Directeur: Randrianodiasana

Institutes
Tropical Dentistry (Dentistry; Stomatology)

Degrees and Diplomas: Master en Santé publique; Diplôme d'Etudes Spécialisées en Chirurgie et en Médecine Buccale

UNIVERSITY OF TOAMASINA

Université de Toamasina
BP 591, Barikadimy, Toamasina 501
Tel: +261(20) 53-322-44
Fax: +261(20) 53-335-66
EMail: presidence@univ-toamasina.mg
Website: http://www.univ-toamasina.mg/

Président: Gatien Prudent Horace (2006-)
Tel: +261(20) 53-324-54

Directeur administratif: Rachelle Bienvenue Radifison

Centres
Applied Modern Language Studies (Modern Languages); **Computer-Aided Management** (Management); **Entrepreneurship Training** (Management); **Environment and Integrated Development** (Development Studies; Environmental Studies; French; Geography; History; Philosophy); **Foreign Languages** (Modern Languages)

Faculties
Arts and Humanities (Arts and Humanities); **Economics and Management** (Economics; Management)

Higher Schools
National Customs *(ENSD)* (Taxation)

History: Founded 1977 as Regional Centre of the Université de Madagascar. Acquired present status as independent University 1992.

Governing Bodies: Board of Trustees

Academic Year: October to June

Admission Requirements: Secondary school certificate (baccalauréat) or equivalent, and entrance examination

Fees: (Ariary): 5,000-6,000 per annum

Main Language(s) of Instruction: French, Malagasy

Degrees and Diplomas: *Licence*: 1 further yr; *Master*: 1 yr following Licence. Also: Diplome des Hautes Études Spécialisées en Administration des Douanes (DHESAD)

Special Facilities: Archaeological and Cultural Museum

Libraries: Management Library, 5,000 vols; Letters, 4,600 vols

UNIVERSITY OF TOLIARA

Université de Toliara (CEDRATOM)
BP 185, Maninday, Toliara 601
Tel: +261(20) 94-410-33
Fax: +261(20) 94-443-07
EMail: presidence@univ-toliara.mg
Website: http://www.univ-toliara.mg/

President: M. Theodoret (2003-)
Tel: +261(32) 07-602-54 EMail: soavelotheo@wanadoo.mg

Directeur administratif et financier: Ramahandrizo Kaludius
Tel: +261(32) 04-097-31

International Relations: Clément Sambo, Chef du Service des Relations extérieures et du Partenariat
Tel: +261(32) 40 930 06 EMail: samboclement@yahoo.fr

Faculties
Arts and Humanities (Arts and Humanities; French; Geography; History; Literature; Philosophy) *Dean*: Louis Mansare Marikandia; **Law and Management** *Dean*: A. Oelson Razafinjohany; **Natural Sciences** *Dean*: Alphonse Dina

Higher Schools
Philosophy *(Ecole normale supérieure) Director*: Charles Zeny

Institutes
Halieutics and Marine Science (Marine Science and Oceanography) *Director*: Man Wai Rabenevanana

History: Founded 1977 as Regional Centre of the Université de Madagascar. Acquired present status as independent University 1988.

Governing Bodies: President; Vice-President; Administration and Finance Director; Deans; Higher School Director; Institute Director

Academic Year: November to July

Admission Requirements: Secondary school certificate (baccalauréat) or equivalent, and entrance examination

Fees: (Ariary): 15,000-50,000 per annum

Main Language(s) of Instruction: French

International Co-operation: With universities in Norway; France; Belgium and Germany

Degrees and Diplomas: *Licence*: 3 yrs; *Master*: a further 2 yrs; *Doctorat*: at least 10 yrs

Student Services: Health services, Sports facilities

Student Residential Facilities: Yes

Special Facilities: Museum. Information Technology Centre

Libraries: Calvin Tsiebo Library

Publications: Talily *(other/irregular)*

Last Updated: 23/07/09

DOCUMENTATION AND RESEARCH CENTRE FOR ART AND ORAL TRADITIONS OF MADAGASCAR

CENTRE DE DOCUMENTATION ET DE RECHERCHE SUR L'ART ET LES TRADITIONS ORALES À MADAGASCAR

BP 185, Toliara 601

Directeur: M. Tsiazonera

Centres
Arts and Oral Traditions (Ethnology; Fine Arts)

History: Founded 1985.

HIGHER PEDAGOGICAL SCHOOL

ECOLE NORMALE SUPÉRIEURE (ENS)

BP 185, Maninday, Toliara 601
Tel: +261(20) 94-417-73
Fax: +261(20) 94-418-02

Directeur: Charles Zeny

Departments
Philosophy (Philosophy)

INSTITUTE OF MARINE SCIENCE

INSTITUT D'HALIEUTIQUE ET DES SCIENCES MARINES (IHSM)

BP 141, Toliara 601
Tel: +261(20) 94-435-52
Fax: +261(20) 94-435-52
EMail: manwaï@pop.wanadoo.mg

Directeur: Man Wai Rabenievanana Tel: +261(20) 94-419-89

Departments
Aquaculture (Aquaculture); **Fishery** (Fishery); **Safety Engineering** (Safety Engineering)

History: Founded 1986.

PRIVATE INSTITUTIONS

CATHOLIC UNIVERSITY OF MADAGASCAR

Université Catholique de Madagascar (UCM)
BP 6059, Ambatoroka, Antananarivo 101
Tel: +261(20) 22-340-09
Fax: +261(20) 22-340-13
EMail: contact@ucm.mg
Website: http://www.ucm.mg/

Recteur: Odilon Tiankavana

Secrétaire général: Hervé Rasamison

Departments

Philosophy (Philosophy); **Psychologie** (Psychology); **Theology** (Theology)

Faculties

Social Sciences (Economics; Law; Management; Political Sciences)

Schools

Management *(ESSVA)* (Communication Studies; Management; Tourism) *Director*: Jacques Vestalys

History: Founded 1960 as Institut Supérieur de Théologie et de Philosophie de Madagascar. Became Institut Supérieur de Théologie, 1973 then Institut Catholique de Madagascar, 1997. Acquired present status and title 2011.

Admission Requirements: Secondary school certificate (Baccalauréat) and entrance examination.

Fees: (Ariary): 780,000-1,2 m. per annum depending on degrees

Main Language(s) of Instruction: French

International Co-operation: With universities in France and USA

Degrees and Diplomas: *Licence*; *Master*

Student Services: Academic counselling, Canteen, Health services, Sports facilities

Student Residential Facilities: No

Libraries: Yes

Publications: Aspect du Christianisme à Madagascar, Theological review *(quarterly)*; Collection - ISTA - ICM Antananarivo, Studies in Anthropology, Social Sciences, Theology *(biannually)*

Last Updated: 22/09/09

SOCIAL SERVICE SCHOOL
ECOLE DE SERVICE SOCIAL

BP 7570, 133 Avenue Lénine, Antanimena, Antananarivo 101

Departments

Social Sciences (Social and Community Services; Social Sciences)

History: Founded 1960.

ST FRANÇOIS D'ASSISE SCHOOL OF NURSING
ECOLE D'INFIRMIERS(ÈRES) ST FRANÇOIS D'ASSISE

BP 7002, Antananarivo 101

Directrice: Angelina De Nobrega Baptista

Departments

Nursing

History: Founded 1993.

HIGHER CHRISTIAN STUDIES IN MANAGEMENT AND APPLIED MATHEMATICS
Hautes Etudes Chrétiennes du Management et de Mathématiques appliquées (HECMMA)

BP 7686, Lot II I, Alarobia Amboniloha, Antananarivo 101

Tel: +261(20) 26-393-17 +262 32-41-591-56

Fax: +261(20) 22-298-63

EMail: hecmma@yahoo.fr

Website: http://www.enduma.africa-web.org/hecmma/recherche.html

Président: Solonjatovo Rakotonirina

Departments

Economics and Political Science (Economics; Political Sciences); **Engineering** (Civil Engineering; Computer Science; Engineering; Telecommunications Engineering; Town Planning); **Management and Applied Mathematics in Economics** (Applied Mathematics; Economics; Management)

History: Founded 1997.

International Co-operation: With Prenslake InterContinental University (USA)

Degrees and Diplomas: DISMA (Diplôme supérieur en Management et Mathématiques appliquées); Bachelor (3 yrs); MMSI (Master en Management et Sciences de l'Ingénieur - 5 yrs)

Last Updated: 05/03/12

HIGHER INSTITUTE OF COMMUNICATION, BUSINESS AND MANAGEMENT
Institut supérieur de la Communication, des Affaires et du Management (ISCAM)

BP 8224, Lot IVN 68 A, Ankadifotsy, Antananarivo 101

Tel: +261(20) 22-224-88 +261(20) 22-256-27

Fax: +261(20) 22-255-43

EMail: contact@iscam.mg

Website: http://www.iscam-mada.com/

Directeur général: Jaona Ranaivoson

Programmes

Business Management and Development (Business Administration; Development Studies; Management); **Human Resource** (Tourism); **International Trade** (Business and Commerce; International Business); **Marketing and Communication** (Communication Studies; Marketing)

History: Founded in 1990. Acquired present status 1990.

International Co-operation: With Ecole EICD 3A, Lyon (France); IAE Savoie Mont-Blanc; Ecole superieure de Commerce (ESC) Grenoble; Institut d'Etudes Politiques de Toulouse

Degrees and Diplomas: *Licence*: Business Management and Development; International Trade; Marketing-Communication; Human Resources, 3 yrs. Master: Business Management and Development; International Trade; Marketing-Communication; Human Resources

Last Updated: 19/03/12

INSTITUTE OF SOCIAL WORK
Institut supérieur de Travail Social (ISTS)

BP 9103 Andoharanofotsy, Lot IAV 309 B Mandrimena Iavoloha, Antananarivo 102

Tel: +261(20) 22-460-34

EMail: estmadagascar@moov.mg; istmadagascar@moov.mg

Director: Olga Phan Van Hien

Programmes

Social Work (Social and Community Services; Social Welfare; Social Work; Special Education)

History: Founded as Ecole de service social, 1960. Acquired present title and status 2009.

Degrees and Diplomas: *Licence*; *Master*

Last Updated: 10/10/12

INSTITUTE OF TECHNICAL STUDIES
Institut de Formation Technique (IFT ANTANANARIVO)

Lot SIBE 5 Bis, Rue Andrianampoinimerina, Soarano, Antananarivo 101

EMail: iftmadagascar@moov.mg

Programmes

Engineering (Building Technologies; Computer Engineering; Construction Engineering); **Health Science** (Health Sciences); **Information, Communication and Journalism** (Communication Studies; Information Sciences; Journalism); **Law** (Law); **Management** (Management; Tourism)

Degrees and Diplomas: *Licence*; *Master*

Last Updated: 10/10/12

Malawi

STRUCTURE OF HIGHER EDUCATION SYSTEM

Description:

Higher education is provided by 3 public universities and a few private higher education institutions. The public universities are governed by a Council, most of whose members are appointed by the Government. The Senate, composed of academics, is responsible for academic matters. These universities are mainly supported by government grants and miscellaneous income. The private institutions have independant councils and senates appointed by the proprietors of the mission (who are mostly religious bodies).

Stages of studies:

University level first stage: *Bachelor's degree*
The Bachelor's degree is generally conferred after four to five years' study.

University level second stage: *Master's degree*
A Master's degree is conferred after one to two years' study beyond the Bachelor's degree.

University level third stage: *Doctor's degree*
The Doctor's degree is conferred after three to five years' study beyond the Master's degree. Candidates must submit a thesis.

ADMISSION TO HIGHER EDUCATION

Admission to university-level studies:

Name of secondary school credential required: Malawi School Certificate of Education
Minimum score/requirement: Excellent results in subjects the candidate wishes to study.
Entrance exam requirements: Entrance examination

Foreign students admission:

Entrance exam requirements: Foreign students should hold qualifications equivalent to the Malawi School Certificate of Education with two of the six credits in English and Mathematics.
Entry regulations: Foreign students must be in possession of a visa. Confirmation of admission to the university must be obtained prior to departure as well as an entry permit.
Language requirements: Good knowledge of English for regular university courses.

NATIONAL BODIES

Ministry of Education, Science and Technology

Minister: Eunice Kazembe
Private Bag 328, Capital Hill Circle
Lilongwe 3
Tel: +265(1) 789 422
Fax: +265(1) 788 064
EMail: education@education.gov.mw
Role of national body: Responsible for providing policy guidance and direction on all education, science and technology issues.

Data for academic year: 2012-2013
Source: IAU from The Education System in Malawi, World Bank Working Paper no 182 and desktop research, 2012

INSTITUTIONS

PUBLIC INSTITUTIONS

LILONGWE UNIVERSITY OF AGRICULTURE AND NATURAL RESOURCES (LUANAR)

PO Box 219, Lilongwe
Tel: +265(1) 277-222
Fax: +265(1) 277-364
EMail: bcaprincipal@bunda.luanar.mw
Website: http://www.bunda.luanar.mw/

Principal: Moses B. Kwapata (2008-)
Tel: +265(1) 277-260, Fax: +265(1) 277-251
EMail: bcaprincipal@bunda.unima.mw

Registrar: Martin Chimoyo

Colleges
Natural Resources (Natural Resources)

Departments
Agribusiness Management (Agricultural Business; Agricultural Management); **Agricultural Engineering** (Agricultural Engineering; Agricultural Equipment; Agriculture; Harvest Technology; Irrigation; Mechanical Engineering; Soil Science; Water Science); **Agricultural Extension** (Agricultural Management; Rural Planning); **Agriculture and Applied Economics** (Agricultural Economics); **Animal Science** (Animal Husbandry); **Aquaculture and Fisheries** (Aquaculture; Fishery); **Basic Sciences** (Natural Sciences); **Crop Science** (Crop Production); **Forestry and Horticulture** (Forestry; Horticulture); **Home Economics and Human Nutrition** (Home Economics; Nutrition); **Language and Development Communication** (Communication Studies; Modern Languages); **Natural Resources Management** (Natural Resources)

Research Centres
Agriculture *(ARET)* (Agriculture); **Chitedze**

History: Founded 1964 as Bunda College of Agriculture (a former constituent college of the University of Malawi). Acquired present status from the merging of Bunda College of Agriculture (Bunda), Natural Resources College (NRC) and Agricultural Research and Extension Trust (ARET), 2012.

Degrees and Diplomas: *Bachelor's Degree*; *Master's Degree*; *Doctor's Degree*

Academic Staff *2008-2009*	MEN	WOMEN	**TOTAL**
FULL-TIME	123	30	**153**
Student Numbers *2008-2009*			
All (Foreign Included)	681	292	**973**

Last Updated: 14/12/12

MZUZU UNIVERSITY

Private Bag 201, Luwinga, Mzuzu 2
Tel: +265(1) 333-575
Fax: +265(1) 333-497
EMail: registrar@mzuni.ac.mw
Website: http://www.mzuni.ac.mw

Vice-Chancellor (Acting): Orton Msiska (2011-)

Registrar: Reginald M. Mushani Fax: +265 333-568
EMail: rmushani@sdnp.org.mw

International Relations: Reginald M. Mushani

Faculties
Education (Biology; Chemistry; Continuing Education; Humanities and Social Science Education; Literature; Mathematics; Modern Languages; Natural Sciences; Physics; Science Education; Teacher Training); **Environmental Sciences** (Environmental Engineering; Environmental Management; Environmental Studies; Forestry); **Health Sciences** (Health Sciences); **Information Sciences and Communications** (Communication Studies; Information Management; Information Sciences; Information Technology)

History: Founded 1997.

Governing Bodies: Council

Academic Year: January to October (January-June; June-October)

Admission Requirements: Malawi Certificate of Education or equivalent

Fees: (Kwacha): Undergraduate, 43,200 per annum; foreign students, 92,500

Main Language(s) of Instruction: English

Degrees and Diplomas: *Bachelor's Degree*: Education; Forestry; Health Science Education; *Master's Degree*; *Doctor's Degree*

Student Services: Academic counselling, Canteen, Health services, Sports facilities

Student Residential Facilities: Yes

Libraries: University Library, 16,671 vols, 200 journals

Last Updated: 12/04/12

IAU UNIVERSITY OF MALAWI (UNIMA)

PO Box 278, Zomba
Tel: +265(1) 524-282
Fax: +265(1) 524-297
EMail: uniregistrar@unima.mw
Website: http://www.unima.mw/

Vice-Chancellor: Emmanuel Fabiano (2009-)
Tel: +265(1) 524-305, Fax: +265(1) 524-297
EMail: vc@unima.mw

International Relations: B.W. Malunga, Registrar
Tel: +265(1) 524-754, Fax: +265(1) 524-760

Centres
Agricultural Research and Development (Agronomy); **Commercial Technical Services** (Business and Commerce; Technology); **Continuing Education** (Business and Commerce; Technology); **Educational Research and Training** (Educational Research); **Language Studies** (Linguistics); **Management** (Management); **Natural Resources and Environmental Studies** (Environmental Studies; Natural Resources; Natural Sciences); **Nursing, Midwifery and Health Sciences** (Health Sciences; Midwifery; Nursing); **Social Sciences** (Social Studies); **Transport Technology Transfer** (Transport Engineering; Transport Management); **Water Sanitation, Health and Technology Development** (Health Sciences; Water Management; Water Science)

Faculties
Agriculture (Agricultural Business; Agricultural Economics; Agricultural Education; Agricultural Engineering; Agricultural Management; Agriculture; Aquaculture; Crop Production; Fishery; Food Science; Forestry; Rural Planning; Soil Science; Zoology); **Applied Sciences** (Computer Science; Environmental Engineering; Environmental Studies; Information Management; Information Technology; Mathematics Education; Statistics); **Built Environment** (Architecture; Rural Planning; Surveying and Mapping); **Commerce** (Accountancy; Business Administration; Business and Commerce; Management); **Development Studies** (Agricultural Business; Agricultural Economics; Agricultural Management; Development Studies; Rural Planning); **Education** (Curriculum; Education; Educational Administration; Educational Psychology; Educational Testing and Evaluation); **Education and Media Studies** (Education; Journalism; Media Studies; Technology Education); **Engineering** (Civil Engineering; Electrical Engineering; Engineering; Mechanical Engineering); **Environmental Sciences** (Aquaculture; Environmental Studies; Fishery; Forestry; Horticulture; Natural Resources); **Humanities** (African Languages; Arts and Humanities; Classical Languages; Communication Studies; English; Fine Arts; French; Linguistics; Literature; Music; Performing Arts; Philosophy; Religious Studies; Theatre; Theology); **Law** (Law); **Medicine** (Anaesthesiology; Anatomy; Biochemistry; Community Health; Gynaecology and Obstetrics; Haematology; Histology; Medicine; Microbiology; Ophthalmology; Orthopaedics; Paediatrics; Physiology; Psychiatry and Mental Health; Public Health; Surgery); **Nursing** (Community Health; Health Administration; Midwifery; Nursing); **Science** (Applied Physics; Biology; Chemistry; Computer Science; Demography and Population; Earth Sciences; Environmental Studies; Geography; Geology; Home Economics; Mathematics; Natural Sciences; Physics; Statistics); **Social Sciences**

(Administration; Economics; History; Political Sciences; Psychology; Social Sciences; Sociology)

History: Founded 1964, integrating all the country's facilities for further and higher education.

Governing Bodies: University Council

Academic Year: August to May (August-December; January-May)

Admission Requirements: Malawi School Certificate of Education or equivalent

Fees: (Kwacha): Residential students, 25,000 per annum; non-residential students, 100,000-115,000 per annum

Main Language(s) of Instruction: English

International Co-operation: With universities in Norway, United Kingdom and USA

Accrediting Agencies: Ministry of Education, Science and Technology

Degrees and Diplomas: *Bachelor's Degree*: Arts; Humanities; Science; Social Sciences (BA/BSc/BSoc), 4 yrs; *Bachelor's Degree*: Education (BEd(Hons)); History; English (BA(Hons)); Science (BSc(Hons)), Honours Degree, 1 further yr; *Bachelor's Degree*: Law (LLB), Honours Degree, 4 yrs; *Bachelor's Degree*: Medicine; Surgery (MBBS), 5 yrs; *Master's Degree*: Arts (Economics) (MA); Business Administration (MBA); Education (PPI; TME; Sociology) (MEd); Public Health (MPH); Science (Agriculture; Aquaculture; Fisheries; Agronomy; Forestry; Chemistry; Biology; Environmental Sciences; Mathematics; Midwifery) (MSc), a further 2 yrs; *Doctor's Degree*: Biology; Chemistry; Aquaculture; Fisheries Science (PhD); Theology (PhD(Theo)), a further 3-5 yrs

Student Services: Academic counselling, Canteen, Handicapped facilities, Health services, Language programs, Social counselling, Sports facilities

Student Residential Facilities: Yes

Libraries: Total, 582,514 vols; database of 1,700 online journals; 67 subscriptions to periodicals

Publications: Journal of Religious Education; Journal of Social Science; Malawi Journal of Science and Technology; Physical Scientist; Reports on Research Conferences

Press or Publishing House: Fattani Offset Printers

Academic Staff *2011-2012*	**TOTAL**
FULL-TIME	**700**
STAFF WITH DOCTORATE	
FULL-TIME	c. **140**
Student Numbers *2011-2012*	
All (Foreign Included)	c. **7,370**
FOREIGN ONLY	**20**

Last Updated: 06/07/12

CHANCELLOR COLLEGE (CHANCO)

PO Box 280, Zomba
Tel: +265(1) 524-222
Fax: +265(1) 524-046
EMail: registrar@chanco.unima.mw
Website: http://www.chanco.unima.mw

Principal: Christopher Kamlongera Tel: +265(1) 525-083

Registrar: Vyson Jedegwa

Departments

African Languages and Linguistics (African Languages; Linguistics; Phonetics; Translation and Interpretation); **Biology** (Biology); **Chemistry** (Chemistry); **Classics**; **Curriculum and Teaching Studies** *(CATS)* (Curriculum; Foreign Languages Education; Mathematics Education; Native Language Education; Social Studies); **Economics** (Economics); **Education** (Education; Educational Administration; Educational Psychology; Educational Testing and Evaluation); **English** (English; Linguistics; Literature); **Fine and Performing Arts** (Fine Arts; Music; Performing Arts; Theatre); **Foundation Law** (Law); **French** (French); **Geography and Earth Sciences** (Earth Sciences; Geography); **History**; **Home Economics** (Home Economics); **Language and Communication Skills** (Communication Studies); **Mathematical Sciences** (Mathematics); **Philosophy** (Philosophy); **Physics** (Physics); **Political and Administrative Studies** (Administration; Political Sciences); **Population Studies** (Demography and Population); **Practical Legal Studies** (Law); **Psychology** (Psychology); **Sociology** (Sociology); **Theology and Religious Studies** (Religious Studies; Theology)

History: Founded 1964.

Academic Staff *2008-2009*	MEN	WOMEN	**TOTAL**
FULL-TIME	164	38	**202**
Student Numbers *2008-2009*			
All (Foreign Included)	1,464	790	**2,254**

COLLEGE OF MEDICINE

Private Bag 360, Chichiri, Blantyre 3
Tel: +265(1) 871-911
EMail: registrar@medcol.mw
Website: http://www.medcol.mw

Principal: Mwapatsa Mipando
Tel: +265(1) 674-473 EMail: Principal@medcol.mw

Registrar: Chifundo Trigu

Departments

Anaesthesia (Anaesthesiology); **Anatomy** (Anatomy; Embryology and Reproduction Biology; Genetics); **Biochemistry** (Applied Chemistry; Biochemistry); **Community Health** (Community Health; Health Sciences; Public Health); **Gynaecology and Obstetrics**; **Haematology** (Haematology); **Histopathology** (Histology; Pathology); **Information and Communication** (Communication Studies; Information Technology); **Medicine** (Medicine); **Microbiology** (Biological and Life Sciences; Microbiology); **Paediatrics** (Paediatrics); **Pharmacy** (Pharmacy); **Physical Therapy** (Physical Therapy); **Physiology** (Physiology); **Surgery** (Surgery)

History: Founded 1991.

Academic Year: January to November

Admission Requirements: 'A' level passes in Biology, Chemistry, Mathematics or Physics

Fees: (Kwacha): 25,000

Main Language(s) of Instruction: English

Degrees and Diplomas: *Bachelor's Degree*: Medicine, Surgery, Medical Laboratory Technology, Pharmacy; *Master's Degree*: Public Health; Medicine, 5 yrs; *Doctor's Degree (PhD)*: by research

Student Services: Academic counselling, Social counselling, Sports facilities

Student Residential Facilities: Yes

Libraries: Yes

Academic Staff *2008-2009*	MEN	WOMEN	**TOTAL**
FULL-TIME	77	17	**94**
Student Numbers *2008-2009*			
All (Foreign Included)	306	133	**439**

KAMUZU COLLEGE OF NURSING

Private Bag 1, Lilongwe
Tel: +265(1) 751-622
Fax: +265(1) 756-424
EMail: principal@kcn.unima.mw
Website: http://www.kcn.unima.mw

Principal: Address Malata (2008-)

Registrar: Martin Chimoyo EMail: registrar@kcn.unima.mw

Departments

Basic Studies (Nursing; Psychiatry and Mental Health; Surgery) *Head*: M. Msiska; **Clinical** (Nursing) *Head*: M. Nyando; **Community and Mental Health Nursing** (Community Health; Nursing; Psychiatry and Mental Health) *Head*: W. Chilemba; **Maternal and Child Health Nursing** (Child Care and Development; Nursing) *Head*: I. Kumbani; **Medical/Surgical Nursing** *Head*: B. Gombachika

Faculties

Nursing (Child Care and Development; Community Health; Nursing; Psychiatry and Mental Health; Surgery) *Dean*: Regina Msolomba

History: Founded 1979.

Main Language(s) of Instruction: English

Degrees and Diplomas: *Bachelor's Degree*: 4 yrs; *Master's Degree*: Midwifery (BSc), 2 yrs following Bachelor's Degree. Also Diploma in Nursing

Academic Staff *2008-2009*	MEN	WOMEN	TOTAL
FULL-TIME	9	40	**49**
Student Numbers *2008-2009*			
All (Foreign Included)	102	367	**469**

THE MALAWI POLYTECHNIC (POLY)

Private Bag 303, Chichiri, Blantyre 3
Tel: +265(1) 870-411
Fax: +265(1) 870-578
EMail: principal@poly.ac.mw
Website: http://www.poly.ac.mw

Principal: G.K. Kululanga
Tel: +265(1) 671-637, Fax: +265(1) 670-578

Vice Principal: H. Gombachika EMail: hgombachika@poly.ac.mw

Departments

Accountancy (Accountancy; Management); **Architecture**; **Business Administration** (Business Administration; Finance; Human Resources; Management; Marketing); **Civil Engineering** (Civil Engineering); **Computing and Information Technology**; **Electrical and Electronic Engineering** (Electrical and Electronic Engineering); **Environmental Health** (Environmental Studies; Health Sciences); **Journalism** (Journalism; Media Studies); **Land and Quantity Surveying** (Surveying and Mapping); **Language and Communication** (Communication Studies; Modern Languages); **Management Studies** (Management); **Mathematics and Statistics** (Mathematics; Statistics); **Mechanical Engineering** (Mechanical Engineering); **Physical and Biochemical Sciences** (Biochemistry; Physics); **Technical Education** (Technology Education)

History: Founded 1964.

Academic Year: February to December

Admission Requirements: A minimum of 'O' levels with at least 6 credits including English or the equivalent from a recognized institution

Main Language(s) of Instruction: English

International Co-operation: With University of Strathclyde (UK) (exchange of technical staff)

Degrees and Diplomas: *Bachelor's Degree*: Accountancy (BAC); Arts; Business Administration (BBA); Science, 4 yrs; *Bachelor's Degree*: Engineering, Architecture, 5 yrs. 10 Diplomas in Technology and Business, 3-4 yrs

Student Services: Academic counselling, Canteen, Health services, Language programs, Social counselling, Sports facilities

Student Residential Facilities: Yes

Special Facilities: Audio Visual unit

Libraries: Central Library

Academic Staff *2008-2009*	MEN	WOMEN	TOTAL
FULL-TIME	159	43	**202**
Student Numbers *2008-2009*			
All (Foreign Included)	1,923	619	**2,542**

PRIVATE INSTITUTIONS

CATHOLIC UNIVERSITY OF MALAWI (CUNIMA)

Montfort Campus, P.O. Box 5452, Limbe
Tel: +265(1) 916-096
Fax: +256(1) 916-015
EMail: information@cunima.ac.mw
Website: http://www.cunima.ac.mw/

Vice-Chancellor: Anacklet Phiri (2001-)
Tel: +265(8) 553-751 EMail: anacklet@yahoo.com

Registrar: Nelson Mabvumbe
Tel: +265(1) 916-098 EMail: registrar@cunima.ac.mw

Centres

Legal Studies (Law)

Faculties

Education (Education; Geography; History; Linguistics; Literature; Mathematics; Religious Studies; Special Education); **Health Sciences** (Midwifery; Nursing); **Social Sciences** (Anthropology; Archaeology; Leadership; Social Sciences; Social Work)

Further Information: Campus in Montfort, Chiradzulu District (founded 2006).

History: Founded 2004. Acquired current status 2006.

Governing Bodies: The Episcopal Conference of Malawi; Board of Trustees; University Council

Academic Year: August to September

Fees: (Kwacha): 160,000 per semester

Main Language(s) of Instruction: English

International Co-operation: With universities in Norway and Netherlands

Accrediting Agencies: Government Accreditation Committee

Degrees and Diplomas: *Bachelor's Degree*: Education; Special Needs Education; Social Work; Anthropology; Political Leadership (BAEd; BScEd; BSNE; Bsoc), 4 yrs

Student Services: Academic counselling, Canteen, Handicapped facilities, Health services, Language programs, Social counselling, Sports facilities

Student Residential Facilities: For 540 students

Libraries: Yes
Last Updated: 12/04/12

UNIVERSITY OF LIVINGSTONIA (UNILIA)

P.O. Box 37, Livingstonia
Tel: +265(1) 368-234 +265(1) 333-111
Fax: +265(1) 368-731
EMail: info@ulivingstonia.com; unilia@malawi.net
Website: http://www.ulivingstonia.com

Registrar: Howard Matiya Nkhoma

International Relations: Jenny Sheldon Kirk, Director, University Relations

Colleges

Commerce *(Ekwendeni Campus)* (Business and Commerce); **Education** *(Livingstonia Campus)* (Education); **Nursing** *(Ekwendeni Campus)* (Nursing); **Technical Studies** *(Livingstonia Campus)* (Computer Science; Secretarial Studies); **Theology** *(Ekwendeni Campus)* (Theology)

History: Founded 1875 as Livingstonia Mission. Started offering Higher Education programmes 1895, acquired present title 2003.

Admission Requirements: Malawi School Certificate of Education (M.S.CE.) or equivalent, with an aggregate of not more than 36 points in the best 6 subjects. Applicants must have a credit in English; Admission tests and interview.

Fees: (Kwacha): 120,000 per annum. Application fee, 500

Degrees and Diplomas: *Bachelor's Degree*: Education; Theology. Also Certificates and Diplomas
Last Updated: 25/02/09

Malaysia

STRUCTURE OF HIGHER EDUCATION SYSTEM

Description:

Higher education is provided by universities, polytechnics, colleges and institutes. There are both public and a wide variety of private higher education institutions. The Ministry of Higher Education supervises higher education policy in the country.

Stages of studies:

University level first stage: *Bachelor's degree*

Courses leading to the award of the Bachelor's degree last for three years. They are awarded as First Class degrees, Second Class Upper with Honours, Second Class Lower with Honours, and General degrees. In Medicine, Dentistry, Veterinary Medicine and Architecture, the Bachelor's degree is awarded after five or six years.

University level second stage: *Master's degree*

The Master's degree is conferred after two years' further study. Students must hold a Bachelor's degree with Honours at least at Second Class level and be able to pursue in-depth study in a given field or a combination of fields as well as a project in the proposed field of study. For the Postgraduate Diploma, the entry requirements are a Bachelor's degree from the university or equivalent qualifications or other qualifications and experience acknowledged by the Senate.

University level third stage: *Doctor of Philosophy*

The Doctor of Philosophy degree is awarded after a minimum of two years' further study and research. The minimum entry requirements are a higher level Master's degree and the ability to pursue research in the proposed field. In addition, candidates must pass oral examinations and, in some cases, written examinations. Students must defend a thesis. There are also Higher Doctoral degrees for outstanding contributions to knowledge, e.g. Doctor of Science (DSc), Doctor of Letters (Dlitt) and Doctor of Laws (DLl). Some universities award a Doctoral Degree to known scholars on the basis of published work. An Honorary Doctoral Degree is awarded to those who have made an outstanding contribution to the field without pursuing typical academic careers.

ADMISSION TO HIGHER EDUCATION

Admission to university-level studies:

Name of secondary school credential required: Sijil Tinggi Pelajaran Malaysia

Other admission requirements: Students must hold credits in at least five subjects, Bahasa Melayu/Malay, Mathematics and two other subjects. These qualifications must be obtained in one examination.

Foreign students admission:

Definition of foreign student: Non resident and non citizen.

Entry regulations: Foreign students must hold a student pass and a visa. All applications for student passes are through Malaysia's educational institutions. International students are allowed to work part-time while studying full-time in Malaysia.

Health requirements: The student must be in good health.

Language requirements: The language of instruction is Bahasa Malaysia with some courses in English. Students must be proficient in the national language.

RECOGNITION OF STUDIES

Quality assurance system:

The Malaysian Qualifications Agency (MQA), which was created from the merger of the National Accreditation Board (LAN) and the Quality Assurance Division, Ministry of Higher Education (QAD), is responsible for quality

assurance of higher education for both the public and the private sectors.
MQA assures programmes through two distinct processes:
- Provisional Accreditation – this is initial process which will help higher education providers to achieve the accreditation by enhancing the standard and quality set in the provisional accreditation evaluation.
- Accreditation – this is a formal recognition that the certificates, diplomas and degrees awarded by higher education institutions are in accordance with the set standards.

Bodies dealing with recognition:

Malaysian Qualifications Agency - MQA (Agensi Kelayakan Malaysia)
Chairman: Mohamed Salleh Mohamed Yasin
Chief Executive Officer: Syed Ahmad Hussein
Tingkat 14B, Menara PKNS-PJ, 17 Jalan Yong Shook Lin
Petaling Jaya 46050
Tel: +603 7968 7002
Fax: +603 7956 9496
EMail: akreditasi@mqa.gov.my
WWW: http://www.mqa.gov.my

NATIONAL BODIES

Ministry of Higher Education
Minister: Mohamed Khaled Bin Nordin
Block E3, Parcel E Pusat Pentadbiran Kerajaan Persekutuan
Putrajaya 62505
Tel: +603 8883 5000
Fax: +603 8889 2476
EMail: pro@mohe.gov.my
WWW: http://www.mohe.gov.my

Malaysian Association of Private Colleges and Universities - MAPCU
President: Parmjit Singh
c/o International Medical University, No. 126 Jalan 19/155B, Bukit Jalil
Kuala Lumpur 57000
Tel: +60(3) 8656 9980
Fax: +60(3) 8656 9981
EMail: mapcu.my@tm.net.my
WWW: http://www.mapcu.com.my/

National Association of Private Educational Institutions - NAPEI
President: Elajsolan Mohan
C-M09, Suria Offices
Jalan JJU 10/4C, Damansara Damai
Petaling Jaya, Selangor 47830
Tel: +60(3) 6156-7100
Fax: +60(3) 6156-7100
EMail: enquiry@napei.org.my
WWW: http://www.napei.org.my/

Persatuan Kebangsaan Institusi Pengajian Tinggi Swasta Bumiputera Malaysia - PKIBM (National Association of Malaysian Bumiputera Institutions of Education)
President: Datin Hjh. Norayini Bt Ali
Urusetia PKIBM, d/a Kolej Teknologi Timur, Taman Kenanga, Bandar Baru Salak Tinggi
Sepang, Selangor 43900
Tel: +60(3) 8706 0181
Fax: +60(3) 8706 0180
WWW: http://www.pkibm.org

Role of national body: Association representing local indigenous private institutions with the aim of developing access to education and training for indigenous people (the Bumiputera).

Data for academic year: 2009-2010
Source: IAU from Ministry of Higher Education, Kuala Lumpur, 2007. Quality Assurance updated in 2009. Bodies, 2012.

INSTITUTIONS

PUBLIC INSTITUTIONS

INTERNATIONAL ISLAMIC UNIVERSITY MALAYSIA

Universiti Islam Antarabangsa Malaysia (IIUM)
P.O. Box 10, 50728 Kuala Lumpur
Tel: +60(3) 2056-4000
Fax: +60(3) 2056-4053
EMail: pro@iiu.edu.my
Website: http://www.iiu.edu.my

Rector: Zaleha Kamaruddin
Tel: +60(3) 2056-4001, Fax: +60(3) 2056-4858
EMail: rector@iiu.edu.my
Executive Director: Mohd. Hilmi Wan Kamal
Tel: +60(3) 2056-4966, Fax: +60(3) 2056-4967
EMail: wmhilmi@iiu.edu.my
International Relations: Shamsul Azhar Mohd. Yusof
Tel: +60(3) 2056-4010, Fax: +60(3) 2056-4053
EMail: shazhar@iiu.edu.my

Centres
Research *Dean*: Sahari Nordin

Faculties
Allied Health Sciences *(Kuantan Campus)* (Dietetics; Optometry; Radiology; Speech Therapy and Audiology) *Dean*: Mazidah Ahmad Mansur; **Architecture and Environmental Design** (Architecture; Building Technologies; Landscape Architecture; Regional Planning; Surveying and Mapping; Town Planning) *Dean*: Mansor Ibrahim; **Engineering** (Aeronautical and Aerospace Engineering; Automotive Engineering; Biotechnology; Computer Engineering; Electrical Engineering; Engineering; Materials Engineering; Mechanical Engineering; Production Engineering) *Dean*: Ahmad Faris Ismail; **Information and Communication Technology** (Information Sciences; Information Technology; Library Science; Telecommunications Engineering) *Dean*: Mohd. Adam Suhaimi; **Islamic Revealed Knowledge and Human Sciences** (Anthropology; Arabic; Communication Studies; English; History; Islamic Studies; Koran; Literature; Political Sciences; Psychology; Sociology) *Dean*: Hazizan Md. Noon; **Languages and Pre-University Academic Development** *(also Centre)* (Modern Languages) *Dean*: Isarji Hj. Sarudin; **Law** (Islamic Law; Law; Private Law; Public Law) *Dean*: Zaleha Kamaruddin; **Medicine** *(Kuantan Campus)* (Anaesthesiology; Community Health; Gynaecology and Obstetrics; Medicine; Ophthalmology; Orthopaedics; Paediatrics; Psychiatry and Mental Health; Radiology; Rehabilitation and Therapy) *Dean*: Md. Tahir Azhar; **Nursing** *(Kuantan Campus)* (Nursing) *Dean*: Kamaruzaman Wan Su; **Pharmacy** (Pharmacy) *Dean*: Tariq Abdul Razak; **Science** (Biomedical Engineering; Biotechnology; Computer Science; Mathematics and Computer Science) *Dean*: Ridzwan Hashim

Institutes
Education (Education) *Director*: Ahmad Mazrzuki Hj. Zainuddin; **Islamic Thought and Civilization** *(International)* (Ethics; Islamic Studies; Philosophy) *Dean*: Torla Hj. Hassan

History: Founded 1983 following a treaty between the Government of Malaysia and the Organization of the Islamic Conference for the Governments of Maldives, Bangladesh, Pakistan, Turkey, Libya, Egypt and Saudi Arabia to become co-sponsors.

Governing Bodies: Board of Governors; Council; Senate

Academic Year: September to June (September - January; February - June)

Admission Requirements: Malaysian Higher School Certificate (STPM)

Fees: (Ringgit): 500-2,200 per semester

Main Language(s) of Instruction: English

Degrees and Diplomas: *Bachelor's Degree*: 4 yrs; *Postgraduate Diploma*: Economics; Islamic Studies; Law, 1 yr; *Master's Degree*: a further 1-2 yrs; *Doctor's Degree (PhD)*: at least 3 yrs

Student Services: Academic counselling, Canteen, Cultural centre, Employment services, Foreign student adviser, Health services, Nursery care, Social counselling, Sports facilities

Student Residential Facilities: Yes

Libraries: Total, c. 95,350 vols

Publications: IIU Law Journal; Journal of Islamic Economics

Press or Publishing House: IIUM Press
Last Updated: 07/04/08

ISLAMIC SCIENCE UNIVERSITY OF MALAYSIA

Universiti Sains Islam Malaysia (USIM)
Bandar Baru Nilai, 71800 Nilai, Negeri Sembilan
Tel: +60(6) 798-8100
Fax: +60(6) 799-3843
EMail: su.pendaftar@usim.edu.my
Website: http://www.usim.edu.my

Vice-Chancellor: Abdul Shukor bin Haji Husin (1999-)
Tel: +60(6) 798-8013, Fax: +60(6) 794-1143
EMail: nc@usim.edu.my

Registrar: Addeban Abdul Rahman EMail: addenan@usim.edu.my

International Relations: Mohammad Haji Alias, Director, Centre for Strategic Development and Corporate
Tel: +60(6) 798-6001, Fax: +60(6) 798-8041
EMail: mohdhjalias@usim.edu.my; hjmohd_99@yahoo.co.uk

Centres
General Studies (Arabic; English) *Head*: Arif Fahmi Yusof; **Graduate Studies** *Head*: Bachok M. Taib; **Tamhidi/Matriculation** *Head*: Zanariah Ngah

Faculties
Dentistry *(Kuala Lumpur)* (Dentistry) *Head*: Mohamad Nasir Othman; **Economics and Muamalat** (Accountancy; Administration; Economics; Marketing) *Head*: Hajah Mustafa Mohd Hanefah; **Leadership and Management** (Communication Studies; Islamic Studies; Leadership; Management) *Head*: Hajjah Mizan Adiliah Ahmad Ibrahim; **Major Language Studies** *Head*: Rosni Samah; **Medicine and Health Studies** *(Kuala Lumpur)* (Health Sciences; Medicine; Surgery) *Head*: Mohd Nasri Ismail; **Quranic and Sunnah Studies** (Information Management; Islamic Theology; Koran; Multimedia) *Head*: Adnan Mohammed Yussof; **Science and Technology** (Actuarial Science; Applied Physics; Biotechnology; Computer Science; Finance; Food Science; Industrial Chemistry; Insurance; Mathematics) *Head*: Jalani Sukaimi; **Shariah and Law** *Head*: Abdul Samat Musa

Research Institutes
World Fatwa and Management

History: Founded 1997 as Kolej Universiti Islam Malaysia (KUIM). Started operating 2000. Acquired present title 2007.

Governing Bodies: Board of Directors; University Senate

Fees: (Ringgit): Registration fees, 325; Science programme, 1,360; Economics Programme, 1,270; Arts Programme, 1,270.

Main Language(s) of Instruction: Arabic and English

Accrediting Agencies: Malaysian Qualifications Agency

Degrees and Diplomas: *Bachelor's Degree*; *Master's Degree*; *Doctor's Degree*

Academic Staff *2008-2009*	MEN	WOMEN	**TOTAL**
FULL-TIME	537	531	**1,068**
PART-TIME	16	3	**19**
STAFF WITH DOCTORATE			
FULL-TIME	57	20	**77**
PART-TIME	–	–	**8**
Student Numbers *2008-2009*			
All (Foreign Included)	–	–	**4,611**

Last Updated: 06/11/08

MALAYSIA PERLIS UNIVERSITY

Universiti Malaysia Perlis (UNIMAP)
Taman JKKK, Kubang Gajah, 02600 Arau Perlis
Tel: +60(4) 979-8008
Fax: +60(4) 977-8011
EMail: pro@unimap.edu.my
Website: http://www.kukum.edu.my

Rector: Kamarudin b. Hussin

Schools

Bioprocess Engineering (Biotechnology); **Computer and Communication Engineering** (Communication Studies; Computer Engineering); **Electrical Systems Engineering** (Electrical Engineering; Industrial Engineering); **Environmental Engineering**; **Manufacturing Engineering** (Production Engineering); **Materials Engineering** (Materials Engineering; Metallurgical Engineering); **Mechatronic Engineering** (Electronic Engineering; Mechanical Engineering); **Microelectronic Engineering** (Electronic Engineering; Microelectronics)

History: Founded 2001 as Northern Malaysia University College of Engineering (KUKUM). Acquired present status and title 2007.

Degrees and Diplomas: *Bachelor's Degree*; *Master's Degree*; *Doctor's Degree*

NATIONAL UNIVERSITY OF MALAYSIA

Universiti Kebangsaan Malaysia (UKM)
43600 Bangi, Selangor Darul Ehsan
Tel: +60(3) 8921-5555
Fax: +60(3) 8925-6484
EMail: ncukm@ukm.my
Website: http://www.ukm.my

Vice-Chancellor: Sharifah Hapsah Syed Hasan Shahabudin (2006-) Tel: +60(3) 8921-5402

Registrar: Aziz Othman
Tel: +60(3) 8925-0144, Fax: +60(3) 8926-7950

International Relations: Imran Ho Abdullah, Director, Office of International Relations
Tel: +60(3) 8921-4188, Fax: +60(3) 8925-4890
EMail: oir@ukm.my

Centres

General Studies (Islamic Studies; Southeast Asian Studies) *Director*: Abdul Latiff Samian; **Graduate Studies** *Dean*: Laily Bin Din

Faculties

Allied Health Sciences (Biomedicine; Dietetics; Nutrition; Optometry; Pharmacy; Speech Therapy and Audiology) *Dean*: Norhani bt Mohidin; **Dentistry** (Dentistry; Oral Pathology; Periodontics) *Dean*: Ghazali Mat Nor; **Economics and Business** (Accountancy; Agricultural Economics; Business Administration; Development Studies; Econometrics; Economic and Finance Policy; Economics; Industrial and Production Economics) *Dean*: Mohd Fauzi Mohd Jani; **Education** (Education; Educational Sciences; Special Education; Teacher Training) *Dean*: Lilia Hamin; **Engineering** (Architecture; Chemical Engineering; Civil Engineering; Electrical and Electronic Engineering; Engineering; Materials Engineering; Mechanical Engineering) *Dean*: Mohd. Marzuki Mustafa; **Information Science and Technology** (Computer Science; Information Management; Information Sciences; Information Technology; Multimedia) *Dean*: Aziz Deraman; **Islamic Studies** (Arabic; Islamic Law; Islamic Studies; Islamic Theology; Koran; Middle Eastern Studies) *Dean*: Zakaria bin Stapa; **Law** (Civil Law; Islamic Law; Law) *Dean*: Kamal Halili bin Hassan; **Medicine** (Anaesthesiology; Anatomy; Biochemistry; Cardiology; Community Health; Dermatology; Diabetology; Endocrinology; Entomology; Epidemiology; Gastroenterology; Gynaecology and Obstetrics; Haematology; Health Sciences; Histology; Immunology; Medical Parasitology; Microbiology; Nephrology; Neurology; Nursing; Oncology; Ophthalmology; Orthopaedics; Otorhinolaryngology; Paediatrics; Parasitology; Pathology; Pharmacology; Physiology; Plastic Surgery; Pneumology; Psychiatry and Mental Health; Radiology; Rheumatology; Social and Preventive Medicine; Surgery; Urology; Venereology; Virology) *Dean*: Lokman Saim; **Science and Technology** (Actuarial Science; Biological and Life Sciences; Chemistry; Earth Sciences; Environmental Studies; Food Science; Food Technology; Marine Science and Oceanography; Physics; Statistics) *Dean*: Aminah bt Abdullah; **Social Sciences and Humanities** (Anthropology; Arts and Humanities; Cultural Studies; Demography and Population; Development Studies; English; Geography; History; International Studies; Linguistics; Literature; Mass Communication; Modern Languages; Political Sciences; Psychology; Social Sciences; Sociology; Translation and Interpretation; Writing) *Dean*: Sharifah Mastura Syed Abdullah

Institutes

Environment and Development (Biological and Life Sciences; Environmental Management; Environmental Studies) *Director*: Abdul Latiff Mohamed; **Genome** *(Malaysia)* (Biology); **Malay World and Civilization** (Cultural Studies; Southeast Asian Studies) *Director*: Shamsul Amri Baharudin; **Malaysian and International Studies** (International Studies; Southeast Asian Studies) *Director*: Ragayah Haji Mat Zin; **Medical Molecular Biology** (Molecular Biology) *Director*: A. Rahman A. Jamal; **Microengineering and Nano-electronics** (Engineering; Nanotechnology); **Occidental Studies** (American Studies; Latin American Studies; Nordic Studies; Western European Studies) *Director*: Shamsul Amri Baharuddin; **Space Sciences** (Aeronautical and Aerospace Engineering); **Systems Biology** (Biology)

Research Institutes

Fuel Cell; **Islam Hadhari** (Island Studies); **Solar Energy** (Energy Engineering)

History: Founded 1970.

Governing Bodies: Board of Directors; Senate

Academic Year: July to March (July-October; December-March)

Admission Requirements: Malaysian higher school certificate (STPM); Matriculation; Diploma

Fees: (Ringgit): Arts, 1,750; Science, 2,083; Medicine, 2,550 per annum

Main Language(s) of Instruction: Malay

Degrees and Diplomas: *Bachelor's Degree*: 3-5 yrs; *Postgraduate Diploma*; *Master's Degree*: a further 1-4 yrs; *Doctor's Degree*: at least 2 yrs

Student Services: Academic counselling, Canteen, Cultural centre, Employment services, Foreign student adviser, Foreign Studies Centre, Handicapped facilities, Health services, Language programs, Social counselling, Sports facilities

Student Residential Facilities: Yes

Libraries: 1,047,450 vols

Publications: Research Bulletin

Student Numbers *2012-2013*: Total 146,362

Last Updated: 08/04/13

NORTHERN UNIVERSITY OF MALAYSIA

Universiti Utara Malaysia (UUM)
06010 Sintok, Kedah
Tel: +60(4) 928-4000
Fax: +60(4) 928-3016
EMail: ukkuum@uum.edu.my
Website: http://www.uum.edu.my

Vice-Chancellor: Mohamed Mustafa Ishak
Tel: +60(4) 928-3000, Fax: +60(4) 928-5763

Registrar: Mohamad Aksuf hir Haji Yu
Tel: +60(4) 928-3020, Fax: +60(4) 928-3046

Faculties

Accountancy (Accountancy; Taxation) *Dean*: Zakaria Abas; **Business Administration** (Administration; Business Administration; Marketing; Transport and Communications) *Dean*: Juhary Ali; **Cognitive Sciences and Education** (Curriculum; Linguistics; Modern Languages; Pedagogy) *Dean*: Abdul Malek Abdul Karim; **Communication and Modern Languages** (Communication Studies; Media Studies; Modern Languages) *Dean*: Ahmad Affendi Shabdin; **Economics** (Banking; Economics; Environmental Management; Finance; International Business) *Dean*: Juzhar Jusoh; **Finance and Banking** *Dean*: Nor Hayati Ahmad; **Human and Social Development** (Communication Studies; International Studies; Management; Political Sciences; Public Administration; Social Studies; Social Work) *Dean*: Azmi Shaari; **Information Technology** (Artificial Intelligence; Computer Networks; Engineering Management; Information Technology; Multimedia) *Dean*: Suhaidi b. Hassan; **International Studies** (International Business; International Studies) *Dean*: Mohammed Mustafa Ishak; **Public Management and Law** (Development Studies; Law; Public Administration) *Dean*: Rusniah Ahmad; **Quantitative Sciences** *Dean*: Engku Muhammad Nazri Engku Abu Bakar; **Technology Management** *Dean*: Che Sobry Abdullah; **Tourism and Hospitality Management** *Dean*: Shaharuddin Tahir

Schools

Graduate Studies *Dean*: Juhary Ali

History: Founded 1984 by the University Utara Malaysia (Inc.) Order.

Governing Bodies: Board of Directors; Senate

Academic Year: May to May (May-October; November-March; April-May)

Admission Requirements: Malaysian Higher School Certificate (STPM) or equivalent

Fees: (Ringgit): Undergraduate 550-660 per semester; Graduate 1,200-2,000 per semester

Main Language(s) of Instruction: Malay, English

International Co-operation: Participates in UMAP, UMIOR, ACU, CUSAC, IMT-GT-UNINET, ASEAN UNINET, FUIW programmes

Degrees and Diplomas: *Bachelor's Degree*: 3-4 yrs; *Master's Degree*: 1-2 yrs; *Doctor's Degree*: Management; Information Technology; Education; Accountancy; Economics; Tourism; Decision Science (PhD), 3-4 yrs

Student Services: Academic counselling, Canteen, Cultural centre, Employment services, Foreign student adviser, Foreign Studies Centre, Handicapped facilities, Health services, Language programs, Nursery care, Social counselling, Sports facilities

Student Residential Facilities: Yes

Libraries: c. 150,000 vols

Publications: Malaysian Management Journal *(biennially)*

Press or Publishing House: UUM Press

Last Updated: 28/03/12

SULTAN IDRIS UNIVERSITY OF EDUCATION

Universiti Pendidikan Sultan Idris (UPSI)
Bangunan Canselori, 35900 Tanjong Malim, Perak
Tel: +60(5) 450-6000
Fax: +60(5) 468-2773
EMail: bhka@upsi.edu.my
Website: http://www.upsi.edu.my

Vice-Chancellor: Zakaria B, Kasa EMail: ncupsi@upsi.edu.my

Senior Assistant Register: Marini Binti Masdar (2000-)
Tel: (605) 450 6334, Fax: (605) 458 2776 EMail: tini@upsi.edu.my

International Relations: Mohammed Zin Nordin, Director of Corporate & International (2008-)
Tel: (605) 450 6334, Fax: (605) 458 2776
EMail: mohammedzin@gmail.com

Centres

Curriculum (Curriculum); **Educational Technology and Multimedia** (Educational Technology; Multimedia); **Global Studies** *(Amminudin Baki Centre)*; **Information and Communication Technology (ICT)** (Communication Studies; Information Technology); **Islamic** (Islamic Studies); **Modern Languages** (Arabic; Chinese; English; French; Japanese; Modern Languages; Spanish)

Faculties

Art and Music (Fine Arts; Music) *Dean*: Mohd Hassan Bin Abdullah; **Business and Economics** (Accountancy; Business Administration; Economics; Educational Administration) *Dean*: Norlia Bt Mat Norwani; **Cognitive Sciences and Human Development** (Cognitive Sciences; Curriculum; Development Studies; Educational and Student Counselling; Educational Psychology; Preschool Education; Primary Education; Special Education) *Dean*: Abdel Latif bin Gapor; **Information and Communications Technology** (Computer Science; Information Technology; Multimedia) *Dean*: Mohamad Bin Ibrahim; **Languages** (English; Literature; Malay; Modern Languages) *Dean*: Abdul Ghani Bin Abu; **Science and Technology** (Biology; Chemistry; Mathematics; Natural Sciences; Physics; Technology) *Dean*: Mustaffa bin Ahmad; **Social Sciences and Humanities** (Arts and Humanities; Geography; History; Islamic Studies; Social Studies; Social Sciences) *Dean*: Adnan Haji bin Nawang; **Sports Science** (Sports) *Dean*: Ahmad Bin Hashim

Institutes

Graduate Studies; **Malay Civilization** (Asian Studies)

Research Centres

Child Development *(National)* (Child Care and Development)

History: Founded 1922 as Sultan Indris Training College. Acquired present status and title 1997.

Governing Bodies: Board of Directors

Academic Year: May to March

Admission Requirements: Malaysian Higher School Certificate or equivalent

Fees: (Ringgit): 630 per semester

Main Language(s) of Instruction: Malay

International Co-operation: With universities in United Kingdom

Accrediting Agencies: Public Service Department

Degrees and Diplomas: *Bachelor's Degree*: Education (BEd), 3-4 yrs; *Master's Degree*: Education (M.Ed), 2 yrs; *Doctor's Degree*: Education (PhD), a minimum of 3 yrs

Student Services: Academic counselling, Canteen, Foreign student adviser, Foreign Studies Centre, Health services, Nursery care, Social counselling, Sports facilities

Student Residential Facilities: Yes

Special Facilities: Theatre. Music studio

Libraries: 82,946 vols

Last Updated: 28/07/09

TECHNICAL UNIVERSITY MALAYSIA MELAKA

Universiti Teknikal Malaysia Melaka (UTEM)
Karung Berkunci 1200, Hang Tuah Jaya, 76100 Durian Tunggal, Melaka
Tel: +60(6) 555-2000
Fax: +60(6) 331-6247
Website: http://www.utem.edu.my/

Vice-Chancellor: Datuk Ahmad Yusoff (2008-2013)
EMail: nc_utem@utem.edu.my

Director, Office of Corporate Planning and Communications: Mohd Rahimi EMail: rahimi@utem.edu.my

International Relations: Fazidah Ithnin, Head of Corporat Planning and Public Relations EMail: fazidah@utem.edu.my

Centres

Continuing Education; **Graduate Studies**; **Languages and Human Development** (Modern Languages); **Teaching and Learning**

Faculties

Electrical Engineering (Automation and Control Engineering; Electrical Engineering; Industrial Engineering; Power Engineering);

Electronics and Computer Engineering (Computer Engineering; Electronic Engineering; Telecommunications Engineering); **Information and Communication Engineering** (Artificial Intelligence; Computer Networks; Software Engineering); **Information and Communication Technology** (Artificial Intelligence; Engineering Management; Materials Engineering; Robotics); **Mechanical Engineering** (Automotive Engineering; Thermal Engineering); **Technology Management and Entrepreneurship** (Human Resources; Management; Technology)

History: Founded 2000.

Admission Requirements: Secondary School Certificate 'A' level for degree programmes.

Fees: (Ringgit): 11,770.00 to 13,368.00 per annum

Main Language(s) of Instruction: English

International Co-operation: with institutions in UK, Ireland, Japan, Australia, Somalia, Indonesia, France, China

Accrediting Agencies: Malaysian Qualifications Agency.

Degrees and Diplomas: *Diploma*; *Bachelor's Degree*: Engineering; Computer Science; Technology Management; *Master's Degree*; *Doctor's Degree*

Student Services: Academic counselling, Canteen, Cultural centre, Employment services, Foreign student adviser, Foreign Studies Centre, Handicapped facilities, Health services, Language programs, Nursery care, Social counselling, Sports facilities

Student Residential Facilities: 7 fully furnished residences.

Libraries: c. 40,000 vols.

Publications: Journal of Advanced Manufacturing Technology *(biannually)*; Journal of Engineering and Technology *(annually)*; Journal of Human Capital Development *(biannually)*; Journal of Mechanical Engineering and Technology *(biannually)*; Journal of Telecommunication, Electronics and Computer Engineering *(biannually)*

Press or Publishing House: NEWS@UTeM

Academic Staff *2011-2012*	MEN	WOMEN	TOTAL
FULL-TIME	1,156	703	**1,859**
PART-TIME	4	1	**5**
STAFF WITH DOCTORATE			
FULL-TIME	83	22	**105**
Student Numbers *2011-2012*			
All (Foreign Included)	4,347	2,702	**7,049**
FOREIGN ONLY	130	17	**147**

Evening students, 103.

Last Updated: 22/09/11

TUN HUSSEIN ONN UNIVERSITY OF MALAYSIA

Universiti Tun Hussein Onn Malaysia (UTHM)
Beg Berkunci 101, 86400 Parit Raja, Johor Darul Takzim
Tel: +60(7) 453-6000
Fax: +60(7) 453-2337
Website: http://www.uthm.edu.my/v2

Rector: MohdNoh DaliminTimbalan Naib

Centres

Graduate Studies (Engineering; Management; Real Estate; Technology); **Humanities and Communication Studies**

Faculties

Civil and Environmental Engineering; **Electrical and Electronic Engineering** (Automation and Control Engineering; Computer Engineering; Electrical Engineering; Electronic Engineering; Robotics); **Information Technology and Multimedia**; **Mechanical and Manufacturing Engineering**; **Technical Education** (Technology); **Technology Management** (Management; Real Estate; Technology)

History: Founded 1993 as Pusat Latihan Staf Politeknik. Acquired full university status 2000.

Degrees and Diplomas: *Bachelor's Degree*; *Master's Degree*; *Doctor's Degree*

Last Updated: 28/03/12

UNIVERSITI PUTRA MALAYSIA (UPM)

43400 UPM Serdang, Selangor
Tel: +60(3) 8946-6003 +60(3) 8946-6004
Fax: +60(3) 8656-3539 +60(3) 8948-7273
EMail: cco@putra.upm.edu.my; fnca@admin.upm.edu.my
Website: http://www.upm.edu.my

Vice-Chancellor: Fauzi Ramlan (2012-)
Tel: +60(3) 8946-6001/6002, Fax: +60(3) 8948-3244
EMail: nc@putra.upm.edu.my

Deputy Vice-Chancellor, Academic and International Affairs: Aini Ideris

International Relations: Shameem Rafik-Galea, Director, Office of Marketing and Communication
Tel: +60(3) 8946-6129, Fax: +60(3) 8948-8972
EMail: shameemgalea@gmail.com

Academies

Sports (Sports) *Division Head*: Muhammad Nazrul Hakim Abdullah

Centres

Extension, Entrepreneurship and Professional Advancement (Management) *Director*: Nordin Abd Rahman; **Foundation Studies for Agricultural Science** (Agricultural Education; Agriculture) *Director*: Mahiran Basri; **InfoComm Development** (Communication Studies; Information Technology) *Director*: Suhaimi Napis; **Islamic** (Islamic Studies) *Director*: Ghazali Ali Tuan Haji Mohamed

Faculties

Agriculture (Agricultural Business; Agricultural Engineering; Agriculture; Aquaculture; Crop Production; Horticulture; Plant and Crop Protection; Rural Planning; Soil Conservation; Zoology) *Dean*: Mad Nasir Shamsudin; **Agriculture and Food Sciences** *(Bintulu Campus)* (Agriculture; Animal Husbandry; Crop Production; Fishery; Food Science; Forestry) *Dean*: Japar Sidik Bujang; **Biotechnology and Biomolecular Sciences** (Biochemistry; Biotechnology; Cell Biology; Microbiology; Molecular Biology) *Dean*: Mohd Ali Hassan; **Computer Science and Information Technology** (Computer Networks; Computer Science; Information Technology; Multimedia; Telecommunications Engineering) *Dean*: Ramlan Mahmod; **Design and Architecture** (Architecture; Industrial Design; Landscape Architecture) *Dean*: Osman Mohd. Tahir; **Economics and Management** (Accountancy; Economics; Finance; Management; Marketing; Parks and Recreation; Tourism) *Dean*: Shamsher Mohamed Ramadili; **Educational Studies** (Arts and Humanities; Continuing Education; Education; Educational and Student Counselling; Educational Research; Educational Sciences; Modern Languages; Science Education; Sports) *Dean*: Rahim Bakar; **Engineering** (Aeronautical and Aerospace Engineering; Agricultural Engineering; Bioengineering; Chemical Engineering; Civil Engineering; Computer Engineering; Electrical Engineering; Electronic Engineering; Engineering; Engineering Management; Environmental Engineering; Food Technology; Mechanical Engineering; Production Engineering; Telecommunications Engineering) *Dean*: Fakhru'l Razi Ahmadun; **Environmental Studies** (Environmental Management; Environmental Studies) *Dean*: Ramdzani Abdullah; **Food Science and Technology** (Cooking and Catering; Food Science; Food Technology) *Dean*: Mohd Yazid Abdul Manap; **Forestry** (Forest Management; Forest Products; Forestry; Wood Technology) *Dean*: Faridah Hanum Ibrahim; **Human Ecology** (Consumer Studies; Development Studies; Family Studies; Government; Human Resources; Music; Natural Resources; Social Sciences) *Dean*: Zaid Ahmad; **Medicine and Health Sciences** (Anatomy; Biomedicine; Community Health; Development Studies; Dietetics; Gynaecology and Obstetrics; Health Sciences; Laboratory Techniques; Medicine; Nutrition; Orthopaedics; Pathology; Psychiatry and Mental Health; Surgery) *Dean*: Norlijah Othman; **Modern Languages and Communication** (Communication Studies; English; Malay; Modern Languages) *Dean*: Che Ibrahim Haji Salleh; **Science** (Biology; Chemistry; Mathematics; Microbiology; Petroleum and Gas Engineering; Physics; Statistics) *Dean*: Sidek Hj. Ab. Aziz; **Veterinary Medicine** (Microbiology; Pathology; Veterinary Science) *Dean*: Bashir Ahmad Fateh Mohamed

Graduate Schools

Management (Accountancy; Commercial Law; Finance; International Business; Management; Marketing) *Dean*: Arfah Salleh

Institutes

Advanced Technology *(R & D, ITMA)* (Engineering) *Director*: Borhanuddin Mohd Ali; **Agricultural and Food Policy Studies** (Agriculture; Food Science) *Director*: Fatimah Arshad; **Bioscience** *(IBS)* (Biological and Life Sciences; Biology) *Director*: Fatimah Md Yusoff; **Gerontology** (Gerontology) *Director*: Tengku Aizan Tengku Abdul Hamid; **Halal Product Research** (Food Science) *Director*: Yaakob Che Man; **Mathematical Research** (Mathematics) *Director*: Haji Kamel Ariffin Mohd. Atan; **Social Science Studies** (Social Sciences) *Director*: Md. Salleh Hj. Hassan; **Tropical Agriculture** (Tropical Agriculture) *Director*: Zulkifli Idrus; **Tropical Forestry and Forest Product** (Forest Products; Forestry; Tropical Agriculture) *Director*: Paridah Md Tahir

Schools

Graduate Studies (Agriculture; Applied Linguistics; Computer Science; Curriculum; Economics; Education; Educational Administration; Educational and Student Counselling; Educational Psychology; Educational Technology; Engineering Management; English; Environmental Engineering; Environmental Studies; Foreign Languages Education; Forest Management; Forest Products; Human Resources; Hydraulic Engineering; Landscape Architecture; Literature; Malay; Native Language Education; Natural Resources; Pathology; Pedagogy; Physical Education; Production Engineering; Road Engineering; Safety Engineering; Sports; Statistics; Structural Architecture; Surveying and Mapping; Technology Education; Transport Engineering; Veterinary Science; Water Management; Wood Technology) *Dean*: Hasanah Mohd Ghazali

Further Information: Also 7 Service Centres (University Business; Research Management; Alumni; Professional Advancement; Knowledge Management; Cultural Studies and Arts; Islamic Studies), University Agriculture Park, and Campus in Bintulu

History: Founded 1971 through merger with Faculty of Agriculture and Agriculture College in Serdang to form Universiti Pertanian Malaysia. Statutory body under the Ministry of Education. Acquired present status and title 1997.

Governing Bodies: Board of Directors; Senate

Academic Year: May to March (May-September; November-March)

Admission Requirements: Malaysian Higher School Certificate (STPM). Diploma: Malaysian Certificate of Education (MCE)/Sijil Tinggi Pelajaran Malaysia (SPM). Undergraduate: higher school certificate (HSC)/Sijil Tinggi Persekolahan (STPM)

Fees: (Ringgit): 950-3,150 per semester according to fields of study and degrees; International students, additional 1,000 per semester

Main Language(s) of Instruction: Malay, English

Accrediting Agencies: Ministry of Higher Education; Public Service Department

Degrees and Diplomas: *Diploma*: Human Development; Business Management; Forestry; Agriculture; Animal Health and Production; Food Estate Management, 3 yrs; *Bachelor's Degree*: Music Education; Accountancy; Engineering; Education; Science with Education; Landscape Architecture; Accountancy with Education; Science with Education (Hons), 4 yrs; *Bachelor's Degree*: Science (Hons); Science; Music; Economics; Business Administration; Food Science and Technology; Bio-industrial Science; English; Malay; Mandarin; Arabic; French; German; Communication; Design; Computer Science, 3 yrs; *Bachelor's Degree*: Medicine, 5 yrs; *Postgraduate Diploma*: Reproductive Medicine; *Master's Degree*: Agricultural Science; Arts and Humanities; Business Administration; Economics; Environmental Studies; Landscape Architecture; Management; Science; Veterinary Medicine; Veterinary Science, a further 1-3 yrs; *Doctor's Degree (PhD)*

Student Services: Academic counselling, Canteen, Cultural centre, Employment services, Foreign student adviser, Foreign Studies Centre, Handicapped facilities, Health services, Language programs, Nursery care, Social counselling, Sports facilities

Student Residential Facilities: Yes

Special Facilities: Putra Gallery. Sultan Salahuddin Abdul Aziz Shah Arts and Cultural Centre

Libraries: Total, c. 500,600 vols

Publications: Pertanika, Journal of Tropical Agricultural Science *(biennially)*; Pertanika, Journal of Science and Technology *(biennially)*; Pertanika, Journal of Social Science and Humanities *(biennially)*

Press or Publishing House: Universiti Putra Malaysia Press

Student Numbers *2010-2011*: Total 29,506

Last Updated: 26/03/13

UNIVERSITI SAINS MALAYSIA (USM)

USM Pulau, 11800 Minden, Penang
Tel: +60(4) 653-2770
Fax: +60(4) 653-2781
EMail: international@usm.com
Website: http://www.usm.my

Vice-Chancellor: Omar Osman
Tel: +60(4) 653-3101, Fax: +60(4) 656-5401 EMail: vc@usm.my

Registrar: Azman Abdullah
Tel: +60(4) 657-3989, Fax: +60(4) 657-5113
EMail: registrar@notes.usm.my

International Relations: Anees Janee Ali, Director of International Relations
Tel: +60(4) 653-2777, Fax: +60(4) 653-2781
EMail: aneesali@usm.my; aneesali15@yahoo.com

Centres

Archaeological Research (Archaeology) *Director*: Mohd. Mokhtar Saidin; **Drug Research** (Epidemiology; Toxicology) *Director*: Shariff Mashsufi Mansur; **Information Technology** (Computer Science; Information Technology) *Director*: Bahari Belaton; **Instructional Technology and Media** (Educational Technology; Media Studies) *Director*: Wan Mohd. Fanzy Wan Ismail; **Islamic Centre** (Islamic Studies) *Director*: Nasirun Hi Mohd. Saleh; **Marine and Coastal Studies** (Coastal Studies; Marine Science and Oceanography) *Director*: Khairun Yahya; **Policy Research and International Studies** (International Studies) *Director*: Azhari Karim; **Research in Molecular Medicine** (Medical Technology) *Director*: Asma Ismail; **Women's Studies and Youth Development** (Social Studies; Women's Studies) *Director*: Rashidah Shuib

Institutes

Higher Education Research (Higher Education) *Director*: Morshidi Sirat

Schools

Arts (Design; Fine Arts; Music; Performing Arts; Photography; Sculpture; Theatre) *Dean*: A. Rahman Hi Mohamed; **Biological Sciences** (Biotechnology; Botany; Entomology; Microbiology; Parasitology; Plant Pathology; Veterinary Science) *Dean*: Abu Hassan Ahmad; **Chemical Sciences** (Analytical Chemistry; Applied Chemistry; Industrial Chemistry; Inorganic Chemistry; Organic Chemistry; Physical Chemistry) *Dean*: Wan Ahmad Kamil Che Mahmood; **Communication** (Communication Arts; Communication Studies; Film; Journalism; Media Studies; Radio and Television Broadcasting) *Dean*: Adnam Hussein; **Computer Science** (Computer Engineering; Computer Science; Information Technology; Software Engineering) *Dean*: Rosni Abdullah; **Distance Education** (Accountancy; Anthropology; Biology; Chemistry; Economics; Finance; Geography; History; Human Resources; Literature; Management; Mathematics; Physics; Political Sciences; Sociology) *Dean*: Omar Majid; **Educational Studies** (Curriculum; Educational Administration; Educational Psychology; Educational Sciences; Preschool Education; Special Education) *Dean*: Abdul Rashid Mohamed; **Housing, Building and Planning** (Architecture; Building Technologies; Interior Design; Landscape Architecture; Regional Planning; Surveying and Mapping; Town Planning) *Dean*: Mahyuddin Ramli; **Humanities** (English; Geography (Human); History; Islamic Studies; Linguistics; Malay; Translation and Interpretation) *Dean*: Abu Talib Ahmad; **Industrial Technology** (Ecology; Food Technology; Paper Technology; Technology) *Dean*: Rozman Hi Din; **Languages, Literacies and Translation** (English Studies; Foreign Languages Education; Translation and Interpretation) *Dean*: Ambigapathy Pandian; **Management** (Development Studies; Finance; Industrial Management; International Business; Management; Marketing) *Dean*: Ishah Ismail; **Mathematical Sciences** (Applied Mathematics; Computer Science; Economics; Mathematics; Statistics) *Dean*: Ahmad Izani Md. Ismail; **Pharmaceutical Sciences** (Pharmacology; Pharmacy; Physiology) *Dean*: Syed Azhar Syed Sulaiman; **Physics** (Applied Physics; Geophysics; Physics) *Dean*: Haslan Abu Hassan; **Social Sciences** (Anthropology; Development Studies; Economics; Political

Sciences; Social Work; Sociology; Southeast Asian Studies) *Dean*: Baba Ismail

History: Founded 1979 as University of Penang. Acquired present title 1972.

Governing Bodies: Council; Senate

Academic Year: July to March (July-October; December-March)

Admission Requirements: Malaysian Higher School Certificate (STPM) or equivalent

Fees: (Ringgit): c. 725-915 per semester; Graduate, c. 50-135 per unit; Master's, Doctorate, c. 2,000-4,000 per session

Main Language(s) of Instruction: Malay, English

International Co-operation: With universities in Australia, United Kingdom, New Zealand, Canada, USA, Finland, Sweden, Netherlands, Switzerland, Fiji, South Africa, India, France, Germany, Hong Kong, Spain, Jamaica, Ireland, Thailand and Japan

Accrediting Agencies: Ministry of Higher Education

Degrees and Diplomas: *Bachelor's Degree*: Humanities; Social Sciences; Natural Sciences; Applied Sciences; Communication Studies; Computer Science; Management; Building and Urban Planning; Industrial Technology, 3 yrs; *Bachelor's Degree*: Pharmacy; Engineering; Education, 4 yrs; *Bachelor's Degree*: Medical Sciences (MD), 5 yrs; *Master's Degree*: a further 1-3 yrs; *Doctor's Degree*: a further 2-6 yrs

Student Services: Academic counselling, Canteen, Cultural centre, Employment services, Foreign student adviser, Health services, Language programs, Nursery care, Social counselling, Sports facilities

Student Residential Facilities: Yes (for 60% of full-time students)

Special Facilities: Museum and Gallery. Muka Head Research Station. Sheikh Tahir Astro-geophysical Centre; Islamic Centre

Libraries: Centralized Library, 800,667 vols. Medical Library, 111,959 vols; Engineering Library, 120,077 vols; Media and Educational Technology, 21,300 vols

Publications: USM Link *(biannually)*

Press or Publishing House: University Sains Malaysia Press

Student Numbers *2012-2013*: Total 29,000

Last Updated: 25/02/13

ENGINEERING CAMPUS

Seberang Perai Selatan, 14300 Nibong Tebal, Pulau Pinang
Tel: +60(4) 599-6401
Fax: +60(4) 594-1013
Website: http://www.eng.usm.my/v3/index.php?lang=en

Schools

Aerospace Engineering *Dean*: Zaidi Mohd Ripin; **Chemical Engineering** (Bioengineering; Chemical Engineering; Environmental Engineering) *Dean*: Abdul Latif Bin Ahmad; **Civil Engineering** (Civil Engineering; Engineering; Environmental Engineering; Industrial Engineering; Physical Engineering; Structural Architecture) *Dean*: Hamidi Abdul Aziz; **Electrical and Electronic Engineering** (Applied Mathematics; Electrical Engineering; Electronic Engineering; Industrial Engineering; Mechanics) *Dean*: Mohd. Zaid Abdullah; **Materials and Mineral Resources Engineering** (Engineering; Materials Engineering; Mineralogy; Mining Engineering; Polymer and Plastics Technology) *Dean*: Khairun Azizi Mohd. Azizli; **Mechanical Engineering** (Industrial Engineering; Mechanical Engineering; Production Engineering) *Dean*: Zaidi Mohd. Ripin

History: Founded 1986.

Degrees and Diplomas: *Bachelor's Degree*: 4 yrs; *Master's Degree*; *Doctor's Degree*

HEALTH CAMPUS

Kota Bharu, 16160 Kubang Kerian, Kelantan
Tel: +60(9) 766-3000
Fax: +60(9) 764-7884
Website: http://www.kck.usm.my

Director: Mohamad Mafauzy

Schools

Dental Sciences *Dean*: Abd. Rashid Hj Ismail; **Health Sciences** (Biomedicine; Dietetics; Environmental Studies; Forensic Medicine and Dentistry; Medical Technology; Nursing; Nutrition; Occupational Health; Pathology; Speech Therapy and Audiology; Sports Medicine) *Dean*: Ahmad Zakaria; **Medical Sciences** (Anaesthesiology; Anatomy; Applied Chemistry; Community Health; Gynaecology and Obstetrics; Haematology; Health Education; Immunology; Medicine; Microbiology; Neurosciences; Ophthalmology; Orthopaedics; Otorhinolaryngology; Paediatrics; Parasitology; Pathology; Pharmacology; Physiology; Psychiatry and Mental Health; Radiology; Social and Preventive Medicine; Surgery) *Dean*: Abdul Aziz Baba

Further Information: Also USM Hospital Centre

History: Founded 1979.

Degrees and Diplomas: *Bachelor's Degree*: 4 yrs; *Master's Degree*; *Doctor's Degree*

UNIVERSITY MALAYSIA TERENGGANU

Universiti Malaysia Terengganu (UMT)
21030 Kuala Terengganu
Tel: +60(9) 668-4100
Fax: +60(9) 669-7418
EMail: vc@umt.edu.my
Website: http://www.umt.edu.my

Vice-Chancellor: Sulaiman Md Yassin

Registrar: Mohd Suib Maulud
Tel: +60(9) 668-4470, Fax: +60(9) 669-6441
EMail: mdsuib@umt.edu.my

International Relations: Wan izzatul Asma Wan Talaat, Chief, Corporate Communciation an External Affairs Division
Tel: +60(9) 668-4391, Fax: +60(9) 668-4390
EMail: wia@umt.edu.my

Faculties

Agrotechnology and Food Science (Agriculture; Aquaculture; Fishery; Food Science; Technology); **Management and Economics** (Accountancy; Economics; Finance; Management; Marketing; Modern Languages; Psychology); **Maritime Studies and Marine Science**; **Science and Technology** (Biology; Chemistry; Computer Science; Engineering; Mathematics; Physics)

Institutes

Marine Biotechnology (Biotechnology; Marine Biology); **Oceanography** (Marine Science and Oceanography); **Tropical Aquaculture**

History: Founded 1979. Acquired present status and title 2007.

Degrees and Diplomas: *Diploma*; *Bachelor's Degree*; *Master's Degree*; *Doctor's Degree*

Student Services: Academic counselling, Canteen, Cultural centre, Employment services, Foreign student adviser, Foreign Studies Centre, Handicapped facilities, Health services, Language programs, Nursery care

Student Residential Facilities: Yes

Libraries: Yes

Academic Staff *2007-2008*	MEN	WOMEN	TOTAL
FULL-TIME	158	156	**314**
PART-TIME	18	5	**23**
Student Numbers *2007-2008*			
All (Foreign Included)	1,780	3,778	**5,558**
FOREIGN ONLY	6	10	**16**

Part-time students, 5,574.

Last Updated: 27/10/08

UNIVERSITY OF MALAYA

Universiti Malaya (UM)
Lembah Pantai, 50603 Kuala Lumpur
Tel: +60(3) 7967-7022
Fax: +60(3) 7956-0027
EMail: icr@um.edu.my
Website: http://www.um.edu.my

Vice-Chancellor: Ghauth Jasmon
Tel: +60(3) 7967-3510, Fax: +60(3) 7954-7551
EMail: vc@um.edu.my; ghauth@gmail.com

Deputy Vice-Chancellor (Academic & International): Mohd Jamil Maah
Tel: +60(3) 7967-3203, Fax: +60(3) 7957-2314
EMail: mjamil@um.edu.my

Registrar: Norilah Salam
Tel: +60(3) 7967-3510, Fax: +60(3) 7956-7551
EMail: registrar@um.edu.my

International Relations: Jagdish Kaur, Deputy Director, International and Corporate Relations Office (ICR)
Tel: +60(3) 7967-3423 / 3273, Fax: +60(3) 7967-7096

Academies

Islamic Studies (Development Studies; Economics; Human Resources; Islamic Law; Islamic Studies; Koran; Management; Philosophy; Political Sciences) *Dean*: Ahmad Hidayat Buang; **Malay Studies** (Cultural Studies; Fine Arts; Linguistics; Literature; Malay; Publishing and Book Trade) *Dean*: Zainal Abidin Borhan

Centres

Civilization Dialogue (Cultural Studies) *Director*: Azizan Baharuddin; **Culture** (Acting; Aesthetics; Art History; Art Management; Conducting; Cultural Studies; Dance; Display and Stage Design; Educational Technology; Ethnology; Human Resources; Marketing; Music; Music Education; Music Theory and Composition; Musicology; Opera; Performing Arts; Textile Design; Theatre; Visual Arts) *Dean*: Solehah Ishak; **Foundation Studies in Science** (Biology; Chemistry; Japanese; Natural Sciences; Physics) *Dean*: Zazli Chik; **Sports** (Sports; Sports Management) *Dean*: Ashril Yusof

Faculties

Arts and Social Sciences (Anthropology; Arts and Humanities; Chinese; Demography and Population; East Asian Studies; English; Geography; History; International Studies; Media Studies; Social Sciences; Social Studies; Sociology; Southeast Asian Studies) *Dean*: Mohamad Abu Bakar; **Built Environment** (Architecture; Real Estate; Surveying and Mapping) *Dean*: Hamzah Abdul Rahman; **Business and Accountancy** (Accountancy; Banking; Business and Commerce; Finance; International Business; Islamic Studies; Management; Management Systems; Marketing; Operations Research; Taxation) *Dean*: Ainin Sulaiman; **Computer Science and Information Technology** (Artificial Intelligence; Computer Science; Information Technology; Library Science; Software Engineering; Systems Analysis) *Dean*: Sapiyan Baba; **Dentistry** (Dental Hygiene; Dental Technology; Dentistry; Forensic Medicine and Dentistry; Oral Pathology; Orthodontics; Periodontics) *Dean*: Ishak Abdul Razak; **Economics and Administration** (Administration; Development Studies; Economics; Political Sciences; Statistics) *Dean*: Norma Mansor; **Education** (Curriculum; Education; Educational Administration; Educational and Student Counselling; Foreign Languages Education; Humanities and Social Science Education; Literacy Education; Mathematics Education; Pedagogy) *Dean*: Noraini Idris; **Engineering** (Biomedical Engineering; Chemical Engineering; Civil Engineering; Electrical and Electronic Engineering; Engineering; Materials Engineering; Mechanical Engineering; Production Engineering) *Dean*: Ghazaly Shaban; **Languages and Linguistics** (Arabic; European Languages; Foreign Languages Education; Linguistics; Modern Languages; Native Language; South and Southeast Asian Languages; Translation and Interpretation; Writing) *Dean*: Azirah Hashim; **Law** (Law) *Dean*: Cheong May Fong; **Medicine** (Anaesthesiology; Anatomy; Biochemistry; Gynaecology and Obstetrics; Medical Parasitology; Medicine; Microbiology; Nephrology; Neurology; Otorhinolaryngology; Paediatrics; Parasitology; Pharmacy; Physical Therapy; Physiology; Psychiatry and Mental Health; Social and Preventive Medicine; Surgery) *Dean*: Ikram Shah Ismail; **Science** (Biochemistry; Biological and Life Sciences; Biology; Biophysics; Biotechnology; Botany; Cell Biology; Chemistry; Embryology and Reproduction Biology; Genetics; Geology; Histology; Immunology; Marine Biology; Mathematics; Molecular Biology; Natural Sciences; Physics; Plant Pathology) *Dean*: Mohd Jamil Maah

Institutes

Asia-Europe (Asian Studies; European Studies) *Executive Director*: Roziah Omar; **China Studies** (Business Administration; Business and Commerce; Chinese; Cultural Studies; Economics; History; International Relations; Law; Philosophy; Political Sciences); **Graduate Studies** (Biotechnology; Development Studies; Developmental Psychology; Environmental Studies; Health Sciences; Industrial Engineering; Natural Resources; Philosophy; Technology) *Director*: Norhanom Abdul Wahab; **Principalship Studies** (Educational Administration; Leadership; Management; Secondary Education; Teacher Training) *Director*: Rahimah Hj Ahmad; **Public Policy and Management** *(International)* (Management; Public Administration) *Director*: Khadijah Md. Khalid; **Research Management and Consultancy** (Management; Technology) *Director*: Meriam Sulaiman

Further Information: University Hospital; Medical Centre

History: Founded 1905 as King Edward VII College of Medicine. Raffles College founded in 1929. Both merged in 1949 to form the University of Malaya. Rapid growth of the University resulted in the setting up of two autonomous Divisions in Singapore and Kuala Lumpur 1956. Acquired present status and title by Legislation 1962. Reorganized 1997 with new governance, administration and financial structures.

Governing Bodies: Board of Directors; Senate

Academic Year: July to July

Admission Requirements: Sijil Pelajaran Malaysia (SPM) or Malaysian Certificate of Education (MCE) or recognized equivalent; Sijil Tinggi Persekolahan (STP) or Higher School Certificate (HSC) or Sijil Tinggi Persekolahan Malaysia (STPM); equivalent recognized qualification

Fees: (Ringgit): 740-1,335 per semester; Postgraduate: 1,237-20,567 per semester for Malaysian candidates and 1,911-30,906 per semester for International candidates

Main Language(s) of Instruction: English, Malay

Accrediting Agencies: Ministry of Higher Education; Malaysian Public Services Department; National Professional Bodies

Degrees and Diplomas: *Bachelor's Degree*: 3-5 yrs; *Master's Degree*: a further 1-5 yrs; *Doctor's Degree (PhD)*: 2-8 yrs. Also Postgraduate Diplomas

Student Services: Academic counselling, Canteen, Cultural centre, Employment services, Foreign student adviser, Foreign Studies Centre, Handicapped facilities, Health services, Language programs, Nursery care, Social counselling, Sports facilities

Student Residential Facilities: 13 residential colleges

Special Facilities: Museum of Asian Art; Botanical Garden; Ulu Gombak Field Research Station

Libraries: Total, 1,275,868 vols. Non Book Items, 550,727 titles

Press or Publishing House: Jabatan Penerbitan Universiti Malaya (University of Malaya Press)

Student Numbers *2011-2012*: Total 26,018
Last Updated: 14/03/13

UNIVERSITY OF MALAYSIA KELANTAN

Universiti Malaysia Kelantan
Locked Bag 36, Pengkalan Chepa, 16100 Kelantan
Tel: +60(9) 771-7000
Fax: +60(9) 771-7006 09 - 7717006
Website: http://www.umk.edu.my

Vice-Chancellor: Zainai Bin Mohamed (2006-)
EMail: zainai@umk.edu.my

Registrar: Abdul Halim Bin Abdul Rahman
Tel: +60(9) 771-7050, Fax: +60(9) 771-7052
EMail: halim@umk.edu.my

International Relations: Wan Tik Sakinah Binti Wan Mohd Zain, Corporate Relations Director
Tel: +60(9) 771-7008, Fax: +60(9) 771-7022
EMail: wantik@umk.edu.my

Centres

Language Studies and Human Development (Development Studies; Modern Languages)

Faculties

Agro-Industry and Natural Resources (Agricultural Business; Agronomy; Natural Resources); **Entrepreneurship and Business**

(Business Administration); **Heritage and Creative Technology** (Heritage Preservation); **Veterinary Medicine** (Veterinary Science)

History: Founded 2006.

Admission Requirements: Diploma; Matriculation; Malaysian Higher School Certificate (Sijil Tinggi Persekolahan Malaysia; STPM) or Malaysian Higher Religious Certificate (Sijil Tinggi Agama Malaysia ; STAM)

Fees: (Ringgit): Bachelor's degree, 1,939-2,089; Master's degree, 2,800-3,200; Ph.D, 6,915-7,515.

Main Language(s) of Instruction: English

Accrediting Agencies: Malaysian Qualifications Agency (MQA)

Degrees and Diplomas: *Bachelor's Degree*; *Master's Degree*; *Doctor's Degree*

Student Services: Academic counselling, Canteen, Cultural centre, Health services, Language programs, Social counselling, Sports facilities

Student Residential Facilities: Student Hostel

Special Facilities: Wireless internet access; Student Entrepreneur Centre (SEC)

Libraries: Yes

Publications: Qoran, Fasa Infolik, Folio FTKW, Publication of the Centre for Corporate Relations *(monthly)*; Semasa, Publication of the Centre for Corporate Relations *(biweekly)*; Teraju, Publication of the Centre for Corporate Relations *(quarterly)*

Academic Staff *2010-2011*	MEN	WOMEN	**TOTAL**
FULL-TIME	80	83	**163**
PART-TIME	6	–	**6**
STAFF WITH DOCTORATE			
FULL-TIME	23	5	**28**
PART-TIME	3	2	**5**
Student Numbers *2010-2011*			
All (Foreign Included)	419	773	**1,192**
FOREIGN ONLY	–	1	**1**

Last Updated: 01/10/10

UNIVERSITY OF MALAYSIA PAHANG

Universiti Malaysia Pahang (UMP)

Lebuhraya Tun Razak, 26300 Gambang Kuantan, Pahang Darul Makmur
Tel: +60(09) 549-2501
Fax: +60(09) 549-2222
EMail: pro@ump.edu.my
Website: http://www.ump.edu.my

Vice Chancellor: Dain Mohd Nasir bin Daing Ibrahim
Tel: +60(09) 549-2002, Fax: +60(09) 549-2222
EMail: daing@ump.edu.my

Registrar: Mustafa bin Ibrahim
Tel: +60(09) 549-2006, Fax: +60 (09) 549-9181
EMail: mus@ump.edu.my

International Relations: Suhaida binti Sulaiman, Assistant Registrar Tel: +60 (09) 549-2619 EMail: suhaida@ump.edu.my

Centres

Modern Languages and Human Sciences *Head*: Nor Ashikin binti Abdul Aziz

Faculties

Chemical and Natural Resources Engineering (Chemical Engineering; Natural Resources) *Dean*: Zulkafli bin Hasan; **Civil and Environmental Engineering** *Dean*: Ideris bin Zakaria; **Computer Systems and Software Engineering** (Computer Science; Software Engineering) *Dean*: Jasni binti Mohamad Zain; **Electrical and Electronics Engineering** (Electrical and Electronic Engineering); **Manufacturing Engineering and Technology Management** *Dean*: Ahmad bin Othman; **Mechanical Engineering** *Dean*: Rosli bin Abu Bakar; **Science and Industrial Technology** (Industrial Chemistry; Industrial Engineering) *Dean*: Mashitah binti Mohd. Yusoff

History: Founded as Kolej Universiti Kejuruteraan dan Teknologi Malaysia.

Admission Requirements: Degree programme, Matriculation (under the Malaysian Ministry of Education) or equivalent (example: PASUM, Asasi UiTM, etc) with application obtaining at least a CGPA of 2.00 and passed with at least Grade C in the subjects of Mathematics, 2 form Chemistry/Physics/Biology; STPM or its equivalent passed with at least Grade C in the subjects of General Studies, Mathematic T/Advanced Mathematic T and 2 form Chemistry/Physics/Biology. Diplome programme, Passed in SPM or its equivalent qualification with at least 5 Credits including: Bahasa Melayu, Mathematics, additional Mathematics, Physics/Chemistry, 1 in Sciences/Technical Subject; English test.

Main Language(s) of Instruction: English, Malay

Accrediting Agencies: Engineering Accreditation Council (EAC)

Degrees and Diplomas: *Diploma*: in Chemical Engineering (Process Plant); Electrical Engineering (Industrial Electronics); Mechanical Engineering; Civil Engineering, 3-4 yrs; *Bachelor's Degree*: Chemical Engineering; Chemical Engineering(Gas Technology); Chemical Engineering (Biotechnology); Electrical Engineering (Electronics); Electrical Engineering (Power Systems); Mechanical Engineering; Mechanical Engineering with Manufacturing Engineering; Mechanical Engineering with Automotive Engineering; Civil Engineering; Civil Engineering with Environmental; Computer Science (Software Engineering); Computer Science (Computer Systems and Networks); Manufacturing Engineering; Project Management with Honours; Industrial Technology Management with Honours; Occupational Safety and Health with HonoursApplied Science (Honours) Industrial Chemistry, 4-6 yrs; *Master's Degree*: Engineering (Electric; Electronics; Instrumentation; Chemical; Bioprocess; Mechanical; Manufacturing; Automotive; Civil; Construction); Science (Computer; Software Engineering; Biotechnology; Industrial Chemistry); Technology Management (Industrial Safety & Health; Human Capital Resources; Project Management; Operation Management), 1-3 yrs (Part-time); 2-5 yrs (Full-time); *Doctor's Degree*: Engineering (Electrical; Electronics; Instrumentation; Bioprocess; Mechanical; Manufacturing; Automotive; Civil; Construction); Philosophy (Technology Management; Computer Science; Biotechnology; Industrial Chemistry), 3-5 yrs (Part-time); 4 yrs (Full-time)

Student Services: Academic counselling, Canteen, Cultural centre, Employment services, Foreign student adviser, Foreign Studies Centre, Handicapped facilities, Health services, Language programs, Nursery care, Social counselling, Sports facilities

Student Residential Facilities: Yes

Special Facilities: Entrepreneurship Unit; Integrity and Leadership Unit; Welfare and Finance Unit

Libraries: Yes. Electronic books; Electronic journal; online database; Media room; Computer Labs; OPAC Workstation

Academic Staff *2008-2009*	MEN	WOMEN	**TOTAL**
FULL-TIME	220	161	**381**
PART-TIME	10	12	**22**
STAFF WITH DOCTORATE			
FULL-TIME	20	10	**30**
Student Numbers *2008-2009*			
All (Foreign Included)	2,898	1,783	**4,681**
FOREIGN ONLY	18	8	**26**

Last Updated: 24/12/08

UNIVERSITY OF MALAYSIA SABAH

Universiti Malaysia Sabah (UMS)

Beg Berkunci 2073, Jalan Teluk Sepanggar, 88999 Kota Kinabalu, Sabah
Tel: +60(88) 320-000
Fax: +60(88) 320-223
EMail: crd@ums.edu.my
Website: http://www.ums.edu.my

Vice-Chancellor: Mohd Harun Abdullah
Tel: +60(88) 320-203, Fax: +60(88) 320-217

Registrar: Encik Abdullah Hj. Mohd. Said
Tel: +60(88) 320-123, Fax: +60(88) 320-243
EMail: penumshl@ums.edu.my

International Relations: Sanudin Hj. Tahir, Deputy Vice-Chancellor (Academic and International)
Tel: +60(88) 320-000 ext 1025, Fax: +60(88) 320-126

Centres
Materials and Minerals Studies (Mineralogy) *Head*: Yeo Kiam Beng; **Natural Disaster Studies** *Head*: Felix Tongkul

Colleges
Artificial Intelligence Studies (Artificial Intelligence) *Head*: Mohd. Yunus Hamid; **Promotion of Knowledge and Language Learning** (Modern Languages) *Dean*: Andreas Totu

Research Institutes
Biotechnology (Biotechnology; Environmental Studies; Microbiology; Molecular Biology; Pharmacology) *Director*: Ann Anton; **Borneo Marine Studies** (Aquaculture; Biotechnology; Marine Science and Oceanography) *Director*: Saleem Mustafa; **Tropical Biology and Conservation** (Biology; Ecology; Environmental Studies; Natural Resources; Tourism) *Director*: Abdul Hamid Ahmad

Schools
Art Studies (Fine Arts; Music; Visual Arts) *Dean*: Ridzwan Abdul Rahman; **Business and Economics** (Accountancy; Banking; Business Administration; Economics; Finance; Hotel Management; Human Resources; International Business) *Dean*: Kassim Mansur; **Education and Social Development** (Development Studies; Education; Sports) *Dean*: Zulkifli Bin Mohamed; **Engineering and Information Technology** (Civil Engineering; Computer Science; Electrical and Electronic Engineering; Engineering; Information Technology; Mechanical Engineering; Systems Analysis) *Dean*: Rosalam Hj. Sabartly; **Food Science and Nutrition** (Dietetics; Food Science; Food Technology; Nutrition) *Dean*: Mohd. Ismail bin Abdullah; **Informatic Sciences** *(Labuan)* (E-Business/Commerce; Multimedia) *Dean*: Rozaini Rosian; **International Business and Finance** *(Labuan)* (Banking; Finance; International Business; Marketing) *Dean*: Rosita Katherine Chong; **International Tropical Forestry** (Forestry; Parks and Recreation; Wood Technology) *Dean*: Mahmud Sudin; **Medicine** (Medicine) *Dean*: Osman Ali; **Psychology and Social Work** (Child Care and Development; Community Health; Family Studies; Industrial and Organizational Psychology; Psychology; Social Work) *Dean*: Shuaib Che Din; **Science and Technology** (Aquaculture; Biology; Biotechnology; Electronic Engineering; Environmental Studies; Geology; Industrial Chemistry; Natural Sciences; Physics; Technology) *Dean*: Harun Abdullah; **Social Sciences** (Anthropology; Communication Studies; Geography (Human); History; International Relations; Social Sciences; Sociology) *Dean*: Asmady Idris; **Sustainable Agriculture** (Cattle Breeding; Crop Production; Horticulture; Landscape Architecture) *Dean*: Ridzwan Abdul Rahman

Units
Ethnography and Social Development (Demography and Population; Ethnology) *Head*: Fadzilah Cooke; **Media and Education Technology** (Educational Technology; Media Studies) *Head (Acting)*: Effency Hadis

History: Founded 1994.

Degrees and Diplomas: *Bachelor's Degree*; *Master's Degree*; *Doctor's Degree*

Last Updated: 26/03/09

UNIVERSITY OF MALAYSIA SARAWAK

Universiti Malaysia Sarawak (UNIMAS)
94300 Kota Samarahan, Sarawk
Tel: +60(82) 581-388
Fax: +60(82) 665-088
EMail: enquiry@unimas.my
Website: http://www.unimas.my

Vice-Chancellor: Abdul Rashid Abdullah (2005-)
Tel: +60(82) 672-501, Fax: +60(82) 672-411

Registrar: Hamsawi Sani
Tel: +60(82) 672-404 EMail: registrar@unimas.my

International Relations: Henry Tenios, Public Relations Manager
Tel: +60(82) 671-000, Ext. 156 EMail: hts@unimas.my

Centres
Language Studies *(Also Sign Language and TESL)* (Arabic; Chinese; Communication Arts; Communication Studies; Japanese; Malay) *Dean*: Norsiah Fauzan; **Technology Transfer and Consultancy** (Technology) *Director*: Lee Nyanti

Faculties
Applied and Creative Arts (Art Management; Design; Film; Fine Arts; Music; Theatre) *Dean*: Mohd Fadzil Rahman; **Cognitive Sciences and Human Development** (Cognitive Sciences; Education; Educational Sciences; Human Resources) *Dean*: Ahmad Azean; **Computer Science and Information Technology** (Computer Networks; Computer Science; Information Technology; Software Engineering) *Dean*: Abdullah Johari; **Economics and Business** (Business and Commerce; Economics) *Dean*: Shazali Bin Abu Mansor; **Engineering** (Chemical Engineering; Civil Engineering; Electronic Engineering; Engineering; Mechanical Engineering) *Dean*: Azhaili Baharun; **Medicine and Health Sciences** (Dentistry; Health Sciences; Medicine; Nursing; Ophthalmology; Paediatrics; Paramedical Sciences; Radiology; Surgery) *Dean*: Mohamad Taha Arif; **Resource Science and Technology** (Biotechnology; Botany; Chemistry; Earth Sciences; Environmental Management; Marine Biology; Molecular Biology; Natural Resources; Wood Technology; Zoology) *Dean*: Wan Sulaiman Wan Harun; **Social Sciences** (Communication Studies; Government; Labour and Industrial Relations; Political Sciences; Social Sciences; Social Work) *Dean*: Abd. Mutalip Abdullah

Institutes
Biodiversity and Environmental Conservation (Biological and Life Sciences; Environmental Studies) *Director*: Andrew Alex Tuen; **East Asian Studies** (East Asian Studies) *Director*: James Chin Ung Ho; **Health and Community Medicine** (Community Health; Health Sciences) *Director*: Mary Jane Cardosa

Further Information: Also 4 Teaching Hospitals

History: Founded 1992.

Academic Year: July to June (July-October; November-March; April-June)

Admission Requirements: Malaysian Certificate of Education (SPM) or equivalent with a good pass in Bahasa Melayu, and a pass in Sijil Tinggi Persekolahan Malaysia (STPM) or equivalent, with passes in 2 subjects with grade E and 2 subjects with grade R or equivalent, or a pass in Matriculation Programme in local Malaysian Universities

Fees: (Ringgit): Tuition, 1,100-1,400 per annum

Main Language(s) of Instruction: Malay, English

Degrees and Diplomas: *Bachelor's Degree*: Applied Arts; Education ((TESL)); Engineering; Information Technology, 4 yrs; *Bachelor's Degree*: Medicine and Health Sciences, 5 yrs; *Bachelor's Degree*: Science; Social Sciences, 3 yrs; *Master's Degree*; *Doctor's Degree*. The Bachelor (Honours Degree) is awarded in the same fields of study as the Bachelor's Degree

Student Services: Academic counselling, Canteen, Cultural centre, Employment services, Health services, Social counselling, Sports facilities

Libraries: Central Library: Centre for Academic Information Service

UNIVERSITY OF TECHNOLOGY MALAYSIA

Universiti Teknologi Malaysia (UTM)
81310 UTM Skudai, 81310 Johor Bahru, Johor
Tel: +60(7) 553-3333
Fax: +60(7) 556-1722
EMail: webmaster@utm.my
Website: http://www.utm.my

Vice-Chancellor: Zaini Bin Ujang (2008-) Fax: +60(7) 557-9376
EMail: nc@utm.my; vicechancellor@utm.my

Registrar: Wan Mohd Zawawi bin Wan Abdul Rahman
Tel: +60(7) 550-2222, Fax: +60(7) 556-1722

International Relations: Mohd. Ismail Bin Abdul Aziz, Director, Office of International Affairs
Tel: +60(7) 553-8001, Fax: +60(7) 553-8003
EMail: mismail@utm.my; oia@utm.my

Centres
Advanced Software Engineering (Software Engineering); **Islamic Studies and Social Development** (Islamic Studies; Social Studies)

Colleges

Science and Technology *(City Campus)* (Civil Engineering; Computer Science; Electrical Engineering; Management; Mechanical Engineering; Science Education)

Faculties

Built Environment (Architecture; Landscape Architecture; Regional Planning; Surveying and Mapping; Town Planning); **Chemical and Natural Resources Engineering** (Bioengineering; Chemical Engineering; Petroleum and Gas Engineering; Polymer and Plastics Technology); **Civil Engineering** (Civil Engineering; Environmental Engineering; Geology; Hydraulic Engineering; Materials Engineering; Structural Architecture; Transport Engineering); **Computer Science and Information Systems** (Computer Networks; Computer Science; Information Technology; Multimedia; Software Engineering); **Education** (Education); **Electrical Engineering** (Biomedical Engineering; Electrical Engineering; Electronic Engineering; Telecommunications Engineering); **Geoinformation Science and Engineering** (Earth Sciences; Engineering; Geology); **Management and Human Resources Development** (Human Resources; Management); **Mechanical Engineering** (Aeronautical and Aerospace Engineering; Marine Engineering; Mechanical Engineering); **Science** (Biology; Chemistry; Mathematics; Natural Sciences; Physics)

Schools

Business *(International)* (Business Administration; Economics; Management); **Graduate Studies**

History: Founded 1925 as Technical School, became College 1946 and acquired present status and title 1972. Campus in Kuala Lumpur.

Governing Bodies: Court; Council; Senate

Academic Year: July to May

Admission Requirements: Malaysian School Certificate (SPM)

Main Language(s) of Instruction: Malay

Degrees and Diplomas: *Diploma*; *Bachelor's Degree*: 5 yrs; *Master's Degree*: a further 1-3 yrs; *Doctor's Degree (PhD)*: 3-7 yrs

Student Residential Facilities: Yes

Libraries: c. 245,000 vols

Student Numbers *2008-2009*: Total 22,468

Last Updated: 14/09/09

UNIVERSITY OF TECHNOLOGY MARA

Universiti Teknologi MARA

Shah Alam, 40450 Shah Alam, Selangor

Tel: +60(3) 5544-2000

Fax: +60(3) 5544-2223

Website: http://www.uitm.edu.my

Vice-Chancellor: Ibrahim bin Abu Shah
Tel: +60(3) 5544-2222 EMail: ibrahimshah@salam.uitm.edu.my

Registrar: Rabiah Latiff
Tel: +60(3) 5544-2266, Fax: +60(3) 5544-3001
EMail: rabiah@salam.uitm.edu.my

International Relations: Noraida Kasim
Tel: +60(3) 5544-2055 EMail: noraida@salam.uitm.edu.my

Academies

Language Studies (Modern Languages)

Centres

Islamic Thought and Understanding (Islamic Studies) *Director*: Musa Ahmad

Faculties

Accountancy (Accountancy) *Dean*: Ibrahim Kamal Abdul Rahman; **Administration and Policy Studies** (Law; Public Administration) *Dean*: Nooraini Mohamed Ismail; **Applied Sciences** (Applied Chemistry; Environmental Engineering; Food Technology; Furniture Design; Industrial Engineering; Medical Technology; Microbiology; Natural Sciences; Nursing; Occupational Therapy; Physical Therapy; Polymer and Plastics Technology; Textile Technology; Wood Technology) *Dean*: Mohamad Kamal Bin Hj. Harun; **Architecture, Planning and Surveying** (Architecture; Building Technologies; Interior Design; Landscape Architecture; Real Estate; Regional Planning; Surveying and Mapping; Town Planning) *Dean*: Mohamed Yusoff Abbas; **Art and Design** (Art Education; Ceramic Art; Design; Fashion Design; Fine Arts; Graphic Design; Industrial Design; Photography; Printing and Printmaking; Textile Design) *Dean*: Baharudin Ujang; **Business Administration** (Banking; Business and Commerce; Finance; Human Resources; Insurance; International Business; Management; Marketing; Retailing and Wholesaling; Transport Management) *Head*: Faridah Hassan; **Chemical Engineering** *Dean*: Sharifah Aishah Syed A.Kadir; **Civil Engineering** (Building Technologies; Civil Engineering; Construction Engineering) *Head*: Mohd Yusof Abd Rahman; **Communication and Media Studies** (Advertising and Publicity; Journalism; Mass Communication; Media Studies; Public Relations; Publishing and Book Trade; Radio and Television Broadcasting) *Dean*: Ilias Md. Salleh; **Education** (Art Education; Education; Health Education; Music Education; Physical Education) *Head*: Hazadiah Mohd Dahan; **Electrical Engineering** (Electrical Engineering; Electronic Engineering; Power Engineering) *Head*: Yusof Md. Salleh; **Hotel and Tourism Management** (Cooking and Catering; Hotel Management; Tourism) *Dean*: Abdul Azis Abdul Majid; **Information Studies** (Information Management; Library Science) *Dean*: Laili Hashim; **Information Technology and Quantitative Science** (Actuarial Science; Business Computing; Computer Networks; Computer Science; Data Processing; Information Technology; Statistics) *Dean*: Adnan Ahmad; **Mechanical Engineering** (Aeronautical and Aerospace Engineering; Automotive Engineering; Mechanical Engineering; Production Engineering) *Dean*: Abdul Rahman Omar; **Office Management and Technology** (Management; Management Systems; Secretarial Studies; Technology) *Dean*: Halimahton Khalid; **Performing Arts** (Acting; Art Management; Cinema and Television; Music; Music Theory and Composition; Performing Arts) *Dean*: Rushdi Kubon Mohd Shariff; **Pharmacy** (Pharmacy) *Dean*: Abu Bakar Abdul Majeed; **Sports Science and Recreation** (Leisure Studies; Parks and Recreation; Sports; Sports Management) *Head*: Anuar Suun

History: Founded 1957. Acquired present status 1999.

Governing Bodies: Board of Directors; Senate

Admission Requirements: Malaysian Certificate of Education (Sijil Pelajaran Malaysia) or 'O' Level with 5 credits including English and Mathematics

Fees: (Ringgit): 241.50-2,874.50

Main Language(s) of Instruction: Malay, English

International Co-operation: With universities in Germany and Thailand

Accrediting Agencies: Ministry of Higher Education; National Accreditation Board SIRIM (Standard Industrial Research Institute of Malaysia)

Degrees and Diplomas: *Diploma*: 3 yrs; *Bachelor's Degree*: 2-4 yrs; *Postgraduate Diploma*: Art Education, 3 yrs following Bachelor's; *Master's Degree*: a further 1-2 yrs; *Doctor's Degree*: at least 2 yrs following Master's

Student Services: Academic counselling, Canteen, Cultural centre, Employment services, Foreign student adviser, Health services, Language programs, Nursery care, Social counselling, Sports facilities

Student Residential Facilities: Yes

Special Facilities: Art gallery. Mosque

Libraries: 6 Libraries. Each branch has its own library

Publications: Journal of Administrative Science *(biennially)*; Journal of Bureau and Consultancy *(annually)*; Journal of International Business and Entrepreneurship (MEDEC) *(annually)*; UiTM Law Review *(biennially)*

JOHOR BRANCH

Km.12 Jln. Muar, 85200 Segamat, Johor

Tel: +60(7) 935-2000

Fax: +60(7) 935-2277

EMail: johor@johor.uitm.edu.my

Website: http://www.johor.uitm.edu.my

Director: Mohamed Hashim Bin Mohd Kamil

Faculties

Accountancy; **Business Management**; **Information Studies** (Information Sciences)

History: Founded 1983. Acquired present status 1990.

Degrees and Diplomas: *Diploma*: 3 yrs; *Bachelor's Degree*: 3 yrs

KEDAH BRANCH

Peti Surat 187, 08400 Merbok Kedah, Sungai Petani
Tel: +60(4) 456-2000
Fax: +60(4) 456-2223
EMail: pengarahkdh@kedah.uitm.edu.my
Website: http://www3.uitm.edu.my/kedah

Director: Zaliha Haji Hussin EMail: nasrudin@salam.itm.edu.my

Faculties

Accountancy; **Administration and Law**; **Business and Management**; **Information Studies**

History: Founded 1997.

Degrees and Diplomas: *Diploma*: 3 yrs

KELANTAN BRANCH

Bukit Ilmu, 18500 Machang, Kelantan
Tel: +60(9) 976-2000
Fax: +60(9) 976-2001
Website: http://www.kelantan.uitm.edu.my

Director: Hussin Mohammad Abdul Rahman
Tel: +60(9) 975-4300/302 EMail: hussin666@kelantan.itm.edu.my

Faculties

Accountancy (Accountancy); **Art and Design**; **Business and Management** (Banking; Business Administration; Finance; Management; Marketing); **Information Studies** (Information Sciences)

History: Founded 1985.

Degrees and Diplomas: *Diploma*: 3 yrs; *Bachelor's Degree*: 3-3 1/2 yrs. Also Certificate in Computer Programming, 1 yr

MELAKA BRANCH

KM 26, Jalan Lendu, 78000 Alor Gajah, Melaka
Tel: +60(6) 558-2003
Fax: +60(6) 558-2001
EMail: melaka@psmb.itm.edu.my

Director: Mohamed Kamal Haji Harun
Tel: +60(6) 559-1001
EMail: mohamadkamal@melaka.uitm.edu.my

Faculties

Accountancy (Accountancy); **Administration and Law** (Administration; Law); **Art and Design**; **Business Management** (Management); **Hotel and Tourism Management**

History: Founded 1984. Acquired present status 1993.

Degrees and Diplomas: *Diploma*: 3 yrs; *Bachelor's Degree*: 3-4 yrs

Publications: Discussion Paper in Economics *(biennially)*; Forum Academia *(annually)*; Penyelidik, UPP, UiTM research bulletin *(quarterly)*; UPP Annual Research *(annually)*

NEGERI SEMBILAN

Kampus Kuala Pilah, Kompleks IADP/NST, Jalan Melang, Lot 323, 787, 2002, 72000 Kuala Pilah, Negeri Sembilan
Tel: +60(6) 482-1202
Fax: +60(6) 484-1296

Director: Tengku Jamaluddin Tengku Mahmud Shah (1998-)
EMail: drtj@salam.itm.edu.my

Faculties

Accountancy (Accountancy); **Administration and Law** (Administration; Law); **Art and Design** (Design; Fine Arts); **Business Management** (Management); **Hotel and Tourism Management** (Hotel Management; Tourism)

History: Founded 1999.

Degrees and Diplomas: *Diploma*: 2 1/2-3 yrs

PAHANG BRANCH

Lintasan Semarak, 26400 Bandar Pusat Jengka, Pahang
Tel: +60(9) 466-3323
Fax: +60(9) 466-3343

Director: Abdullah Suhaimi Mohamad
EMail: provosphg@pahang.itm.edu.my

Faculties

Accountancy (Accountancy); **Applied Sciences** (Natural Sciences; Technology); **Business Management** (Business Administration); **Civil Engineering** (Civil Engineering); **Information Technology and Quantitative Science**; **Office Management and Technology**

History: Founded 1985. Acquired present status 1994.

Degrees and Diplomas: *Diploma*: 2 1/2-3 yrs; *Bachelor's Degree*: 3-4 yrs. Also Certificates in Information Technology, Computer Programming, 1 yr

PERAK BRANCH

Bandar Sri Iskandar, 32600 Bota, Perak
Tel: +60(5) 371-1800
Fax: +60(5) 371-2191

Director: Mohamed Yusoff Izzudin bin Mohamed Ali
Tel: +60(5) 371-2060 EMail: yusuf@salam.itm.edu.my

Faculties

Accountancy (Accountancy); **Architecture, Planning and Surveying** (Architecture and Planning; Surveying and Mapping); **Art and Design**; **Information Technology and Quantitative Science**; **Office Management and Technology**

History: Founded 1985.

Degrees and Diplomas: *Diploma*: 3-4 yrs; *Bachelor's Degree*: 3-4 yrs. Also Certificate in Town and Regional Planning, 2 yrs

PERLIS BRANCH

Peti Surat 41, 02600 Arau, Perlis
Tel: +60(4) 986-1299
Fax: +60(4) 986-2233

Director: Ahmad Redzuan Abd. Rahmanl Tel: +60(4) 986-1001

Faculties

Accountancy (Accountancy); **Administration and Law** (Administration; Law); **Applied Sciences** (Natural Sciences); **Architecture, Planning and Surveying**; **Business Management** (Business Administration; Management); **Civil Engineering**; **Electrical Engineering** (Electrical Engineering); **Information Technology and Quantitative Science**

History: Founded 1974.

Degrees and Diplomas: *Diploma*: 2 1/2-3 yrs; *Bachelor's Degree*: 3-4 yrs

PULAU PINANG BRANCH

Permatang Pasir, 13500 Permatang Pauh, Pulau Pinang
Tel: +60(4) 380-2332
Fax: +60(4) 380-2311
EMail: ppenang@uitm.edu.my

Director: Mohamed Nor bin Berhan

Faculties

Engineering

History: Founded 1996.

Degrees and Diplomas: *Diploma*: 3 yrs; *Bachelor's Degree*

SABAH BRANCH

Beg Berkunci 71, 88997 Sabah
Tel: +60(88) 492-746
Fax: +60(88) 492-900

Director: Abdullah Hj. Mohamad Said
EMail: drabdullah@sabah.itm.edu.my

Faculties

Accountancy (Accountancy); **Administration and Law** (Law; Public Administration); **Applied Sciences** (Computer Science; Natural Sciences; Technology); **Business and Management** (Banking; Business Administration; Management; Marketing); **Civil Engineering** (Civil Engineering); **Hotel and Tourism Management** (Hotel Management; Tourism)

History: Founded 1973.

Degrees and Diplomas: *Diploma*: 3 yrs; *Bachelor's Degree*: 3-3 1/2 yrs. Also Certificate in Travel Operations, 1 yr

SARAWAK BRANCH

Jalan Meranek, 94300 Kota Samarahan, Sarawak
Tel: +60(82) 672-153
Fax: +60(82) 672-155
EMail: sarawak@psmb.itm.edu.my
Website: http://sarawak.uitm.edu.my/

Director: Abdul Rahman Deen (1998-)
Tel: +60(82) 672-177 EMail: abdrahman@salam.itm.edu.my

Faculties

Accountancy (Accountancy); **Administration and Law**; **Applied Sciences** (Computer Science; Natural Sciences; Technology); **Business and Management** (Business Administration; Finance; Management); **Civil Engineering**; **Electrical Engineering** (Electrical Engineering); **Hotel and Tourism Management** (Hotel Management; Tourism); **Information Technology and Quantitative Science** (Information Technology; Mathematics); **Office Management and Technology**; **Sports Science and Recreation** (Parks and Recreation; Sports)

History: Founded 1973.

Degrees and Diplomas: *Diploma*: 2-3 yrs; *Bachelor's Degree*: 3-4 yrs. Also Certificate in Travel Operations, 1 yr

TERENGGANU BRANCH

Sura Hujung, 23000 Dungun, Terengganu
Tel: +60(9) 840-0400
Fax: +60(9) 840-0107

Director: Mustaff Mohamed Zain
Tel: +60(9) 840-101 EMail: dmustaff@tganu.itm.edu.my

Faculties

Accountancy (Accountancy); **Administration and Law** (Public Administration); **Business and Management** (Business Administration; Management); **Education** (Education); **Electrical Engineering** (Electrical Engineering); **Hotel and Tourism Management** (Food Science; Hotel Management; Tourism); **Information Technology and Quantitative Science**; **Office Management and Technology** (Secretarial Studies)

History: Founded 1975.

Degrees and Diplomas: *Diploma*: 2-3 yrs; *Bachelor's Degree*: 2-3 yrs

PRIVATE INSTITUTIONS

AL-MADINAH INTERNATIONAL UNIVERSITY (MEDIU)

40100 Selangor, Shah Alam
Tel: +60(3) 5511-3939
Fax: +60(3) 5511-3940
EMail: studentcare@mediu.edu.my
Website: http://www.mediu.edu.my/

Rector: Mohammad Khalifa Al-Tamimi
EMail: tamimi@mediu.edu.my

Manager Administrative Affairs: Khalid Mahamat Idriss Ahmat
EMail: khalid@mediu.edu.my

International Relations: Ahmed Al-Shiha, Deputy Rector for International Relations EMail: al-shiha@mediu.edu.my

Faculties

Computer and Information Technology (Computer Science; Information Technology); **Education** (Education); **Engineering** (Engineering); **Finance and Administrative Sciences** (Administration; Finance); **Islamic Sciences** (Islamic Studies); **Languages** (Arabic; English)

History: Created 2008.

Governing Bodies: University Council

Academic Year: Sep - Feb; Feb - Sep

Main Language(s) of Instruction: Arabic, English

International Co-operation: With institutions in Thailand.

Degrees and Diplomas: *Bachelor's Degree*; *Master's Degree*; *Doctor's Degree*

Student Services: Academic counselling, Canteen, Employment services, Foreign student adviser, Foreign Studies Centre, Health services, Language programs, Nursery care, Social counselling, Sports facilities

Academic Staff *2011-2012*	MEN	WOMEN	TOTAL
FULL-TIME	110	30	**140**
PART-TIME	12	10	**22**
STAFF WITH DOCTORATE			
FULL-TIME	18	4	**22**
PART-TIME	3	2	**5**
Student Numbers *2011-2012*			
All (Foreign Included)	3,240	839	**4,079**
FOREIGN ONLY	131	33	**164**

Part-time students, 290. **Distance students**, 2,030.

Last Updated: 25/10/11

ASIA E UNIVERSITY (AEU)

Tingkat Bawah, Blok Utama, Dataran Kewangan Darul Takaful, No.4, Jalan Sultan Sulaiman, 50000 Kuala Lumpur
Tel: +60(3) 2785-0000
Fax: +60(3) 2785-0001 +60(3) 2711-0436
EMail: enquiries@aeu.edu.my
Website: http://www.aeu.edu.my

President: Dato Ansary Ahmed

Schools

Education (Education; Foreign Languages Education; Higher Education); **Graduate Studies** (Business Administration; Education; Information Technology; Management); **Information and Communication Technology** (Information Management; Information Technology); **Management** (Business Administration; Management)

Accrediting Agencies: Malaysian Qualifications Agency

Degrees and Diplomas: *Bachelor's Degree*; *Master's Degree*; *Doctor's Degree*

Last Updated: 19/09/11

ASIA PACIFIC UNIVERSITY COLLEGE OF TECHNOLOGY AND INNOVATION (UCTI)

Technology Park Malaysia, Bukit Jalil, 57000 Kuala Lumpur
Tel: +60(3) 8996-1000
Fax: +60(3) 8996-1001
EMail: info@ucti.edu.my
Website: http://www.ucti.edu.my

Programmes

Business; **Computer Games Development and Web Technology** (Computer Engineering; Multimedia; Software Engineering); **Computing** (Artificial Intelligence; Computer Science; Multimedia; Software Engineering); **Engineering** (Electrical and Electronic Engineering; Electronic Engineering; Mechanical Engineering; Telecommunications Engineering); **Information Technology** (Business Computing; Computer Networks; Computer Science; Information Technology; Software Engineering); **Postgraduate Studies** (Business Administration; Computer Science; E-Business/Commerce; Information Management; Information Technology; Management; Multimedia; Software Engineering; Technology)

History: Founded 1993 as Asia Pacific Institute of Information Technolog (APIIT). Acquired present status and title 2005.

Admission Requirements: Completion of 'O' or 'A' levels or equivalent

Main Language(s) of Instruction: English

International Co-operation: With universities in United Kingdom and Australia

Accrediting Agencies: Malaysian Qualifications Agency

Degrees and Diplomas: *Diploma*: Information Technology; Business Administration, 2 yrs; *Bachelor's Degree*: Computer Science; Information Technology; Media Studies; Computer Games Development and Web Development; Engineering, 4-5 yrs; *Master's Degree*: Technology Management; Software Engineering; Information Technology Management; Multimedia; Mobile Computer; E-Business/Commerce; Computer Science, 1-5 yrs

Student Services: Academic counselling, Canteen, Cultural centre, Employment services, Foreign student adviser, Foreign Studies Centre, Health services, Language programs, Social counselling, Sports facilities

Student Residential Facilities: Yes

Special Facilities: ICT Labs; Engineering Labs; English Language Labs

Libraries: Comprehensive collection of books; journals; periodicals and on-line references (Proquet; ACM)

Last Updated: 07/11/08

ASIAN INSTITUTE OF MEDICINE, SCIENCE AND TECHNOLOGY

Institut Perubatan Sains Dan Teknologi Asia

Batu 31/2, Bukit Air Nasi, Jalan Bedong, Semeling, 08100 Bedong
Tel: +60(4) 459-8000
Fax: +60(4) 442-2881
EMail: contactus@aimst.edu.my
Website: http://www.aimst.edu.my

Vice-Chancellor: V.G. Kumar Das

Faculties

Applied Sciences (Biotechnology; Materials Engineering); **Engineering and Computer Technology** (Computer Science; Electrical and Electronic Engineering; Information Technology; Multimedia; Telecommunications Engineering); **Medicine and Health Sciences** (Dentistry; Medicine; Pharmacy; Surgery)

History: Founded 2001.

Degrees and Diplomas: *Bachelor's Degree*; *Master's Degree*

BINARY UNIVERSITY COLLEGE OF MANAGEMENT AND ENTREPRENEURSHIP (BUCME)

No 1, 101 Business Park, Persiaran Puchong Jaya Selatan, 47100 Puchong, Sengalor
Tel: +60(3) 8070-6590
Fax: +60(3) 8070-6594
EMail: info@binary.edu.my
Website: http://www.binary.edu.my

Vice-Chancellor and CEO: Joseph Adaikalam (1985-)
Tel: +60(3) 8070-6595, Fax: +60(3) 8070-6599
EMail: joseph@binary.edu.my

Deputy Vice Chancellor Administration and Finance: Rohini Devi Sinnadurai
Tel: +60(3) 8070-6601, Fax: +60(3) 8070-6601
EMail: rohinids@binary.edu.my

International Relations: Gilbert Alvin, Director of Business Development EMail: gilbert@binary.edu.my

Schools

Accountancy and Finance *Dean*: Cheng Ho Chung; **Business Administration** (Business Administration; Business and Commerce; Marketing) *Dean*: Karunanithi Murugiah; **Entrepreneurial Development** (Business Administration) *Dean*: Joseph Adaikalam; **Foundation Studies** *Dean*: Sudesh Prabakaran; **Postgraduate** *Dean*: Allen Lim; **Technology Management** (Computer Science; Information Technology) *Dean*: Amjad Hanesh

History: Founded 1984 as a learning centre. Became Binary Business School 1989. Became the first private insitution to offer MBA and MSc IT 1994. Acquired present status and title 2004.

Governing Bodies: University Senate; International Academic Advisory Panel

Academic Year: Starting in March and September

Admission Requirements: For undergraduate programmes, completed foundation Studies. For graduate programmes, a recognised Bachelor degree. For Postgraduate programmes, a reconised Master degree and five years experience.

Fees: (Ringgit): Foundation Studies, 9,600, Diploma, 6,300 per annum; Bachelor degree, 13,000 per annum; Masters, 13,500 per annum; Doctorate, 12,000 per annum

Main Language(s) of Instruction: English

International Co-operation: With universities in United Kingdom and Australia

Accrediting Agencies: Malaysian Qualifications Agency (MQA); Ministry of Higher Education

Degrees and Diplomas: *Diploma*: Business Administration; Marketing; Accountancy; Entrepreneurship and Information Technology, 2 1/2 yrs; *Bachelor's Degree*: Business Administration; Marketing; Accountancy; Computer Science; Management of Technology and Entrepreneurship (BA; BSc), 3 yrs; *Master's Degree*: Business Administration; Information Technology Management; Financial Planning (MBA:MSc), 1 yr and 4 months; *Doctor's Degree*: Business Administration (Specialising in Entrepreneurship; Human Resources Managment; Marketing; Logistic Management; E-commerce; Finance and Banking; Information Technology Management or Quality Management (DBA), 3 yrs. Also Foundation Programme in Business, Accountancy and IT, 1 yr.

Student Services: Academic counselling, Canteen, Cultural centre, Employment services, Foreign student adviser, Foreign Studies Centre, Health services, Language programs, Social counselling, Sports facilities

Student Residential Facilities: Yes

Special Facilities: Incubator; ISP Centre of Excellence; Reasearch and Development Centre; Jamming Studio

Libraries: Yes

Publications: International Journal of Management and Entrepreneurship, Refereed journal featuring contributions from researchers and scientists in the field of Managerial and Organisational Science, Entrepreneurship and Economics with strong theoretical and empirical analysis. *(1-2 per annum)*

Academic Staff *2008-2009*	MEN	WOMEN	TOTAL
FULL-TIME	36	17	**53**
PART-TIME	3	2	**5**
STAFF WITH DOCTORATE			
FULL-TIME	7	3	**10**
PART-TIME	2	1	**3**
Student Numbers *2008-2009*			
All (Foreign Included)	927	576	**1,503**
FOREIGN ONLY	282	34	**316**

Part-time students, 56.

Last Updated: 27/10/08

CYBERJAYA UNIVERSITY COLLEGE OF MEDICAL SCIENCES (CUCMS)

Unit N°2, Street Mall 2, 63000 Cyberjaya, Selangor
Tel: +60(3) 8319-1010
Fax: +60(3) 8319-1100
EMail: inquiry@cybermed.edu.my
Website: http://www.cybermed.edu.my/

President: Sulaiman Abdullah

Programmes

Medicine and Surgery (Medicine; Surgery); **Pharmacy**

History: Created in 2005.

Admission Requirements: Sijil Tinggi Pelajaran Malaysia or other secondary school leaving certificate.

Fees: (Ringgit): 50,000 per annum (Medicine and Surgery); 25,000 per annum (Pharmacy)

Degrees and Diplomas: *Bachelor's Degree*: Medicine and Surgery (MBBS), 5 yrs; *Bachelor's Degree*: Pharmacy (BPharm (Hons)), 4 yrs. Also Foundation courses in basic science, 1 year.

Student Services: Sports facilities

Last Updated: 28/03/12

HELP UNIVERSITY

Universiti HELP (HU)

BZ-2 Pusat Bandar Damansara, 50490 Kuala Lumpur

Tel: +60(3) 2094-2000

Fax: +60(3) 2095-7100

EMail: khong@help.edu.my

Website: http://www.help.edu.my

Vice-Chancellor, President: Paul Tuck Hoong Chan
Tel: +60(3) 2094-2000, Fax: +60(3) 2095-9554
EMail: paul@help.edu.my

Deputy Vice-Chancellor (Academic): Kim Hoong Khong
Tel: +60(3) 2094-2000, Fax: +60(3) 2093-1830

International Relations: Trille Siow, Senior Manager, International Marketing
Tel: +60(3) 2094-2000, Fax: +60(3) 2094-7495
EMail: siowty@help.edu.my

Centres

Psychology and Counseling (Clinical Psychology)

Faculties

Applied Sciences and Multimedia (Business Computing; Computer Graphics; Information Technology); **Behavioural Sciences** (Behavioural Sciences; Psychology); **Business, Economics and Accounting** (Accountancy; Administration; Banking; Business Administration; Economics; Finance; Human Resources; International Business; Management; Taxation); **Education** (Continuing Education; English; Literacy Education; Preschool Education; Teacher Training); **Humanities and Social Sciences** *(Also American degree programme in Arts)* (Advertising and Publicity; Journalism; Marketing; Mass Communication; Media Studies; Public Relations); **Law and Government** (Civil Law; Commercial Law; Law)

Graduate Schools

HELP Graduate School (Accountancy; Administration; Business Administration; Economics; Management)

Institutes

Crime and Criminology (Criminology)

Schools

Hospitality and Tourism (Hotel Management; Tourism)

History: Founded 1988. Previously known as Kolej Universiti HELP (HELP University College). Acquired current title 2010.

Governing Bodies: University Council; Senate

Academic Year: From Jan to Dec depending on programme

Admission Requirements: Bachelor programmes, recognized secondary school certificate(s); Postgraduate, an approved undergraduate degree or equivalent qualification.

Fees: (MYR): 54,000 - 60,000 per annum

Main Language(s) of Instruction: English

International Co-operation: With universities in Australia, New Zealand, United Kingdom, USA

Accrediting Agencies: Malaysian Qualifications Agency (MQA)

Degrees and Diplomas: *Bachelor's Degree*: Business; Economics; Management; Psychology; Education; Information Technology; Computer Science; *Master's Degree*: Business Administration; Psychology; Counselling; Management; Economics Crime Management; Accounting and Finance; *Doctor's Degree*: Business Administration

Student Services: Academic counselling, Canteen, Employment services, Foreign student adviser, Foreign Studies Centre, Health services, Language programs, Social counselling, Sports facilities

Student Residential Facilities: 432 rooms with 828 students capacity

Special Facilities: Wifi Access

Libraries: c. 45,000 vols; internet ready library system

Academic Staff *2012-2013*	MEN	WOMEN	TOTAL
FULL-TIME	97	92	**189**
PART-TIME	11	9	**20**
STAFF WITH DOCTORATE			
FULL-TIME	21	16	**37**
PART-TIME	4	–	**4**
Student Numbers *2012-2013*			
All (Foreign Included)	3,291	2,629	**5,920**
FOREIGN ONLY	494	446	**940**

Distance students, 650.

Last Updated: 31/01/13

INDUSTRIAL UNIVERSITY SELANGOR

Universiti Industri Selangor (UNISEL)

Jalan Zirkon A 7/A, Section 7, 40 000 Shah Alam, Selangor

Tel: +60(3) 552-23400

Website: http://www.unisel.edu.my

Vice-Chancellor: Adnan Alias

Faculties

Biotechnology and Life Science; **Engineering**; **Industrial Art and Design Technology** (Design; Industrial Arts Education); **Industrial Information Technology**; **Industrial Management**; **Medical Science** (Medicine); **Social Sciences and Industry Studies**

Graduate Schools

Management (Business Administration; Management)

Schools

Education (Education; Information Technology; Management; Natural Sciences)

Degrees and Diplomas: *Diploma*; *Bachelor's Degree*; *Master's Degree*

INTERNATIONAL MEDICAL UNIVERSITY

Universiti Perubatan Antarabangsa (IMU)

No 126, Jalan 19/155B, Bukit Jalil, 57000 Kuala Lumpur

Tel: +60(3) 8656-7228

Fax: +60(3) 8656-7229

EMail: enquiry@imu.edu.my

Website: http://www.imu.edu.my

Vice-Chancellor: Abu Bakar Suleiman (2001-)
Tel: +60(3) 8656-6229, Fax: +60(3) 8656-7232
EMail: abubakar_suleiman@imu.edu.my

Provost: Mei Ling Young
Tel: +60(3) 8656-7233, Fax: +60(3) 8656-7232
EMail: meiling_young@imu.edu.my

International Relations: Kok Hai Ong, Director, External Affairs
Tel: +60(3) 8656-7228 ext 5030 EMail: kokhai_ong@imu.edu.my

Faculties

Medicine and Health (Health Sciences; Medicine; Pharmacy) *Head*: Victor Lim

Schools

Clinical Studies *Head*: Kandasamy Palayan; **Dentistry** (Dentistry) *Head*: Chooi Gait Toh; **Medical Sciences** *Head*: Yasmin A. Malik; **Pharmacy and Health Sciences** (Dietetics; Nursing; Nutrition; Pharmacology; Pharmacy) *Head*: Peter Pook; **Postgraduate Studies and Research** *Head*: Joon Wah Mak

History: Founded 1992 as International Medical College. Acquired present name and status 1999.

Governing Bodies: Board of Directors; Board of Governors; Senate and Professional Bodies such as Malaysian Medical Council and Malaysian Dental Council.

Admission Requirements: School certificate (Sijil Tinggi Pelajaran Malaysia STPM) or equivalent

Fees: (Ringgit): vary from 9,000-40,000 per semester. Bachelor's degree, 28,600 (Phase I), 39,000 per semester (Phase II/Clinical Training); Pharmacy 16,200 per semester; Nursing, 9,000 per semester; Medical Sciences, 13,000 per semester; Biomedical Science, 13,000 per semester; Medical Biotechnology, 13,000 per semester; Pharmaceutical Chemistry, 13,000 per semester; Psychology, 12,800 per semester; Dentistry, 38,800 per semester (Phase I), 40,000 per semester (Phase II); Nutrition and Dietetics, 14,000 per semester

Main Language(s) of Instruction: English

International Co-operation: With universities in Australia, Canada, Ireland, United Kingdom and USA

Accrediting Agencies: Malaysian Qualifications Agency, Malaysian Medical Council, Malaysian Dental Council, Malaysian Pharmacy Board, Royal Pharmaceutical Society of Great Britain (RPSGB), Nursing Board Malaysian

Degrees and Diplomas: *Bachelor's Degree*: Biomedical Sciences; Medical Biotechnology; Psychology; Pharmaceutical Chemistry ((Hons)), 3 yrs; *Bachelor's Degree*: Medical Sciences (BMedSc), 3 1/2 yrs; *Bachelor's Degree*: Dental Surgery (BDS); Medicine (MBBS), 5 yrs; *Bachelor's Degree*: Nursing (Bnursing); Nutrition and Dietetics (BSc); Pharmacy (Bpharm), 4 yrs; *Master's Degree*: Medical Sciences and Community Health (MSc), 1-4 yrs (Full time); 2-6 yrs (Part time); *Doctor's Degree*: Medical Sciences and Community Health (by Research) (PhD), 2-6 yrs (Full time); 4-8 yrs (Part time)

Student Services: Academic counselling, Canteen, Foreign student adviser, Language programs, Social counselling, Sports facilities

Student Residential Facilities: yes (Off campus hostels)

Special Facilities: Digital Recording Studio (Theatre); Medical Museum; Auditorium; Multi Purpose Hall; Lecture Hall; Seminar Rooms; Multidisciplinary Laboratories; Skills Laboratory; Pathology Laboratory; Research Laboratory; Power Laboratory; Problem-Based Learning Rooms; E-learning Laboratories

Libraries: Yes

Academic Staff *2008-2009*	MEN	WOMEN	**TOTAL**
FULL-TIME	98	75	**173**
PART-TIME	24	17	**41**
STAFF WITH DOCTORATE			
FULL-TIME	78	73	**151**
PART-TIME	19	17	**36**
Student Numbers *2008-2009*			
All (Foreign Included)	780	1,337	**2,117**
FOREIGN ONLY	33	56	**89**

Last Updated: 19/11/08

INTERNATIONAL UNIVERSITY COLLEGE OF TECHNOLOGY TWINTECH (IUCTT)

Podium Plaza, Block E, Sri Damansara Business Park, Persiaran Industri, Bandar Sri Damansara, 52200 Kuala Lumpur
Tel: +60(3) 6275-1110 +60(3) 6286-1200
Fax: +60(3) 6277-1463
EMail: inquiry@iuctt.edu.my
Website: http://www.iuctt.edu.my/

Vice-Chancellor: Mohd Razali Agus

Centres

Foundation Studies (Business and Commerce; Computer Science; Engineering; Natural Sciences) *Director*: Salmi Idin

Faculties

Architecture and Built Environment (Architecture and Planning; Surveying and Mapping) *Dean*: Husin Hj Mohd Dini; **Biotechnology** (Biotechnology); **Business and Finance; Computer Science & Information Technology** *Dean*: Ruhi Hayati Abd. Rahman; **Engineering & Industrial Technology** (Civil Engineering; Electronic Engineering; Mechanical Engineering; Production Engineering) *Dean*: Shahrizal Shaik Ahmedullah; **Health Science & Medicine** *Dean*: Azrin Esmady Ariffin; **Multimedia and Creative Technology**

History: Created in 1994.

Governing Bodies: University Senate

Degrees and Diplomas: *Diploma*: Architectural Studies; Islamic Banking; Takaful; Accounting; Technology Management; Investment Analysis; Marketing; Multimedia; Biotechnology, 6 sem; *Bachelor's Degree*: Business Information Technology; Computer Science (BIT (Hons); BSc (Hons)); Industrial Biotechnology; Biotechnology (BSc (Hons)); International Business; Technology Management; Marketing; Accounting; Banking (BBA (Hons); Bacc (Hons)), 6 sem; *Bachelor's Degree*: Mechanical and Manufacturing Engineering; Electronic and Instrumentation Systems Engineering; Mechatronic Engineering (BEng (Hons)), 8 sem; *Bachelor's Degree*: Quantity Surveying (Bachelor (Hons)), 8 semesters; *Bachelor's Degree*: Architecture (BArch (Hons)), 10 sem; *Master's Degree*: Business Administration (MBA), 18 months full time; 24 months part time. Foundation courses (3 semesters) in Business, Computer Studies, Science, Engineering. Several other Diploma and Bachelor programmes run jointly with overseas institutions.

Last Updated: 28/03/12

INTI INTERNATIONAL UNIVERSITY COLLEGE

Kolej Universiti Antarabangsa Inti

Lot 12295, Jalan BBN 12/1, 17800 Nilai, Negeri Sembilan
Tel: +60(6) 798-2000
Fax: +60(6) 799-7531
EMail: excel@intimal.edu.my
Website: http://www.inti.edu.my

Programmes

Postgraduate (Information Sciences; Information Technology); **Undergraduate**

Further Information: Campuses in Subang Jaya, Sabah, Sarawak, Penang, Genting and Kuala Lumpur (Malaysia); Beijing (China); Jakarta (Indonesia)

History: Created 1986 as Inti College Malaysia. Acquired current title and status 2006.

Governing Bodies: Board of Governors

International Co-operation: With institutions in Australia, Canada, New Zealand, UK and USA

Degrees and Diplomas: *Diploma*: Accounting; Business Administration; Civil Engineering; Computer Engineering; Electrical and Electronic Engineering; Industrial Engineering; Information and Communication Technology; Mechanical Engineering; Mechatronics; Pharmacy; Quantity Surveying; *Bachelor's Degree*: Business Administration; Accounting; Business English; Business Information Technology; Finance; Marketing; Multimedia Computing; Biotechnology; Engineering; International Business; Mass Communication; Computer Science; Games Software; *Master's Degree*: Civil & Structural Engineering; Mechanical Engineering; E-Commerce; Management Information Systems; Personal, Mobile and Satellite Communications. Also Foundation courses. Some degree programmes offered in collaboration with overseas universities.

Student Services: Academic counselling, Canteen, Cultural centre, Foreign student adviser, Health services, Social counselling, Sports facilities

KUALA LUMPUR INFRASTRUCTURE UNIVERSITY COLLEGE

Kolej Universiti Infrastruktur Kuala Lumpur (KLIUC)

Corporate Block, IKRAM Park, Jalan Serdang, 43000 Kajang, Selangor
Tel: +60(3) 8926-6993
Fax: +60(3) 8925-9846
EMail: admin@kliuc.edu.my
Website: http://www.kliuc.edu.my

President: Zulkifli Bin Abd. Hamid

Centres

Continuing Education and Distance Learning *Director*: Suraya Amirrudin

Schools

Business Infrastructure (Accountancy; Business Administration) *Director*: Noor Saadah Zainal Abidin; **Engineering Infrastructure** (Automotive Engineering; Civil Engineering; Construction Engineering; Electrical and Electronic Engineering; Mechanical Engineering; Telecommunications Engineering) *Director*: Khairul Sallgh Baharuddin; **Information Technology Infrastructure** *Director*: Suhaila Sardi; **Linguistic Infrastructure and Liberal Studies** *Director*: Norzita Mohd. Yunus; **Material and Science** *Director*: Hock Ann Lim

History: Founded 1997. Acquired present status and name 2003.

Academic Year: 3 intakes: March, June, November.

Admission Requirements: Diploma, O level or equivalent; Bachelor's Degree, A level or equivalent; Master's degree, Bachelor's or equivalent

Fees: Diploma, 17,000; Bachelor's Degree, 35,000; Master's degree, 22,000

Main Language(s) of Instruction: English

Accrediting Agencies: Malaysian Qualifications Agency (MQA)

Degrees and Diplomas: *Diploma*: Accountancy; Business Administration; Information Technology; Corporate Communication; English for Professional Communication; Automotive Engineering; Electrical and Electronics Engineering; Mechanical Engineering; Civil Engineering; Geomatiç Engineering; Electrical and Communication Engineering, 2 1/2 yrs; *Bachelor's Degree*: Accountancy, 3 1/2 yrs; *Bachelor's Degree*: Civil Engineering; Electronic Engineering (Bach. (Hons)), 4 yrs; *Bachelor's Degree*: Construction Management; Business Administration; E-Commerce; Computer Science; Network Technology; Software Engineering; Corporate Communication; English for Professional Communication; Advertising; Applied Statistics; Material Technology (Bach. (Hons)); Mechanical Engineering (BSc), 3 yrs; *Master's Degree*: Business Administration, 1 1/2 yrs. Also certificates in English (in Intensive programme), Engineering and Business, 1 yr.

Student Services: Academic counselling, Canteen, Foreign student adviser, Foreign Studies Centre, Language programs, Sports facilities

Student Residential Facilities: Hostel Rooms

Libraries: 17,000 vols; e-library; Internet Services

Academic Staff *2007-2008*	MEN	WOMEN	TOTAL
FULL-TIME	45	61	**106**
PART-TIME	30	20	**50**
STAFF WITH DOCTORATE			
FULL-TIME	6	1	**7**
Student Numbers *2007-2008*			
All (Foreign Included)	1,776	624	**2,400**
FOREIGN ONLY	320	177	**497**

Part-time students, 10.

Last Updated: 28/03/12

LIMKOKWING UNIVERSITY OF CREATIVE TECHNOLOGY (LUCT)

Inovast 1-1, Jalan Teknokrat 1-1, 63000 Cyberjaya, Selangor
Tel: +60(3) 8317-8888
Fax: +60(3) 8317-8988
EMail: enquiry@limkokwing.edu.my
Website: http://www.limkokwing.net/

President: Kok Wing Lim (1991-)
EMail: tansrilim@limkokwing.edu.my

Vice-President, International Development: Jayles Ah Leong Yeoh Tel: +60(3) 8317-8708 EMail: jayles@limkokwing.edu.my

International Relations: Hamidah Binti Mohd Yusoff, Vice-President, International Relations
Tel: +60(3) 8317-8816 EMail: hamidahmy@limkokwing.edu.my

Centres

Postgraduate Studies (Banking; Business Administration; Communication Arts; Finance; Human Resources; Management; Multimedia; Public Relations; Sports Management; Tourism)

Faculties

Architecture and Built Environment (Architecture; Interior Design; Landscape Architecture; Town Planning); **Business Management and Globalisation**; **Communication Media and Broadcasting**; **Design Innovation** (Design; Fashion Design; Graphic Design; Industrial Design; Printing and Printmaking; Retailing and Wholesaling); **Information Communication and Technology**; **Multimedia Creativity**

History: Created 1988. Acquired status 2007.

Governing Bodies: Chancellery

Academic Year: February to December (February-June; July-December)

Admission Requirements: 3 credits SPM / O level or equivalent for diploma programme; 5 credits SPM / O level or equivalent for foundation and undergraduate degree programme; undergraduate degree for Master's programme; Master's degree for phd programme

Fees: (MYR): 9,750 - 19,550 per annum, undergraduate; postgraduate, 12,000 - 58,000 per course

Main Language(s) of Instruction: English

International Co-operation: With institutions in Australia and UK.

Accrediting Agencies: Malaysian Qualifications Agency (MQA)

Degrees and Diplomas: *Diploma*; *Bachelor's Degree (Bachelor's degree; Bachelor's (Hons) degree)*: 3 yrs; *Postgraduate Diploma*: 1 yr; *Master's Degree*: 1 1/2 yrs; *Doctor's Degree*: 3 yrs

Student Services: Academic counselling, Canteen, Cultural centre, Employment services, Foreign student adviser, Foreign Studies Centre, Handicapped facilities, Health services, Language programs, Social counselling, Sports facilities

Student Residential Facilities: Hostel

Special Facilities: Art gallery; sound and music studio; photography lab

Libraries: c. 18,000 vols; c. 2,500 print journal subscriptions; 37,700 e-books; 6,300 online journal subscriptions

Academic Staff *2009-2010*	MEN	WOMEN	TOTAL
FULL-TIME	429	368	**797**
PART-TIME	68	31	**99**
STAFF WITH DOCTORATE			
FULL-TIME	7	2	**9**
PART-TIME	8	1	**9**
Student Numbers *2009-2010*			
All (Foreign Included)	2,834	4,207	**7,041**
FOREIGN ONLY	2,828	1,540	**4,368**

Last Updated: 04/06/10

MALAYSIA UNIVERSITY OF SCIENCE AND TECHNOLOGY

Universiti Sains dan Teknologi Malaysia (MUST)

Unit GL33 (Ground Floor), Block C, Kelana Square, 17, Jalan SS7/ 26, 47301 Petaling Jaya, Sengalor
Tel: +60(3) 7880-1777
Fax: +60(3) 7880-1762
EMail: rizal@must.edu.my
Website: http://www.must.edu.my

Provost (Acting): Nor Adnan Yahya

Programmes

Biotechnology (Biotechnology); **Construction Engineering and Management**; **Energy and Environment** (Energy Engineering; Environmental Studies); **Information Technology** (Information Technology); **Materials Science and Engineering** (Materials Engineering); **Systems Engineering and Management**; **Transportation and Logistics** (Transport Management)

History: Founded 2000. A postgraduate institution established with the assistance of the Massachusetts Institute of Technology.

Degrees and Diplomas: *Master's Degree*; *Doctor's Degree (PhD)*

MANAGEMENT AND SCIENCE UNIVERSITY

Universiti Pengurusan Dan Sains (MSU)

Blok A, Jalan Equestrian 13/52, Off Jalan Persiaran Sukan, Seksyen 13, 40100 Shah Alam, Selangor
Tel: +60(3) 5510-6868
Fax: +60(3) 5510-8668
EMail: enquiry@msu.edu.my
Website: http://www.msu.edu.my

President and Vice-Chancellor: Mohd Shukri Ab Yajid
EMail: baya@msu.edu.my

Centres

Flexible Learning (Accountancy; Business Administration; Computer Science; E-Business/Commerce; Information Technology; Management); **Foundation Studies**

Faculties
Business Administration and Professional Studies; **Health Sciences** (Biomedicine; Food Science; Health Sciences; Laboratory Techniques; Nursing; Occupational Therapy; Physical Therapy; Radiology); **Information Sciences and Engineering**

Graduate Schools
Management (Business Administration; Management)

Schools
Graduate Studies (Business Administration; Health Sciences; Information Technology; International Business; Management); **Medicine** *(International)* (Dentistry; Medicine; Neurology; Nursing; Pharmacy; Physical Therapy; Rehabilitation and Therapy); **Pharmacy** (Chemistry; Medical Technology; Pharmacology; Pharmacy)

Further Information: Also Professional advancement Centre

History: Founded 2001. Formerly known as (Kolej Universiti Teknologi Dan Pengurusan Malaysia/ University College of Technology and Management of Malaysia).

International Co-operation: With universities in Australia, Czech Republic, India, Indonesia, Japan, New Zealand, Poland, South Africa, Switzerland, United Kingdom, USA

Degrees and Diplomas: *Diploma*; *Bachelor's Degree*; *Master's Degree*; *Doctor's Degree*
Last Updated: 02/10/08

MULTIMEDIA UNIVERSITY (MMU)

Jalan Multimedia, Cyberjaya, Selangor
Tel: +60(3) 8312 5012
Fax: +60(3) 8312 5115
EMail: mkt@mmu.edu.my
Website: http://www.mmu.edu.my

President: Ghauth Jasmon EMail: ghauth@mmu.edu.my

Faculties
Business and Law *(Melaka)* (Accountancy; Banking; Business Administration; Economics; Finance; Human Resources; International Business; Law; Management; Marketing) *Dean*: Goh Pek Chen; **Creative Multimedia** (Film; Media Studies; Multimedia) *Dean*: Harold M. Thwaites; **Engineering** (Computer Engineering; Electronic Engineering; Microwaves; Multimedia; Optical Technology; Telecommunications Engineering) *Dean*: Hean Chuah Teik; **Engineering and Technology** *(Melaka) Dean*: Peter von Brevern; **Information Science and Technology** *(Melaka)* (Artificial Intelligence; Information Technology; Software Engineering; Systems Analysis) *Dean*: Wong Eng Kiong; **Information Technology** *Dean*: Hong Tat Ewe; **Management** *Dean*: A. Seetharaman

Institutes
International Languages *(Melaka)* (English; Japanese)
History: Founded 1996.

Governing Bodies: Board of Directors

Admission Requirements: STPM at least 3 principals

Main Language(s) of Instruction: English

International Co-operation: With universities in Australia; China; Japan; France; Taiwan; Bangladesh; Germany; South Africa; UK; USA

Accrediting Agencies: Lembaga Akreditasi Negara

Degrees and Diplomas: *Diploma*; *Bachelor's Degree*; *Master's Degree*; *Doctor's Degree*

Student Services: Academic counselling, Canteen, Foreign student adviser, Foreign Studies Centre, Handicapped facilities, Health services, Language programs, Nursery care, Sports facilities

Press or Publishing House: MMU Press

OPEN UNIVERSITY MALAYSIA (UNITEM)

Jalan Tun Ismail, 50480 Kuala Lumpur
Tel: +60(3) 2773-2002
Fax: +60(3) 2697-8852
EMail: enquiries@oum.edu.my
Website: http://www.oum.edu.my

President and Vice-Chancellor: Anuwar Ali

Senior Vice-President: Mansor Bin Fadzil

Centres
Graduate Studies

Faculties
Applied Social Sciences (Communication Studies; Islamic Studies; Psychology); **Business and Management** (Accountancy; Business Administration; Human Resources; Management; Tourism); **Education and Languages** (Arabic; Chinese; Education; Educational Technology; English Studies; Islamic Studies; Malay; Physical Education; Preschool Education; Primary Education; Social Studies; South and Southeast Asian Languages; Special Education; Visual Arts); **Information Technology and Multimedia Communication** (Accountancy; Computer Networks; E-Business/Commerce; Information Sciences; Information Technology; Management; Multimedia; Software Engineering); **Science and Technology** (Civil Engineering; Electrical Engineering; Engineering; Environmental Studies; Industrial Management; Information Technology; Management; Mathematics; Mechanical Engineering; Occupational Health; Safety Engineering; Sports)

Institutes
Professional Development

Schools
Nursing and Allied Health Sciences (Health Sciences; Nursing)

History: Founded 2000.

Degrees and Diplomas: *Diploma*; *Bachelor's Degree*; *Master's Degree*; *Doctor's Degree*
Last Updated: 05/11/10

PETRONAS TECHNOLOGICAL UNIVERSITY

Universiti Teknologi Petronas (UTP)
Bandar Seri Iskandar, 31750 Perak
EMail: utp@petronas.com.my
Website: http://www.utp.edu.my

Rector: Zainal Abidin Kasim EMail: zainaks@petronas.com.my

Programmes
Engineering; **Technology**

History: Founded 1996.

Degrees and Diplomas: *Bachelor's Degree*; *Master's Degree*; *Doctor's Degree*

SUNWAY UNIVERSITY COLLEGE

N°5, Jalan Universiti, Bandar Sunway, 46150 Petaling Jaya, Selangor
Tel: +60(3) 7491-8622
Fax: +60(3) 5635-8630
EMail: info@sunway.edu.my
Website: http://www.sunway.edu.my/

Vice-Chancellor: Jarlath Ronayne (2003-)

Departments
Art and Design *Head*: Helena Chin; **Business** (Accountancy; Business Administration; Finance; Management) *Head*: Madelaine Cheah Hevera; **Law** *Head*: Paul Linus Andrews; **Performance and Media** (Performing Arts); **Psychology** *Head*: Teoh Hsien-Jin

Schools
Computer Technology (Computer Science; Information Sciences; Information Technology; Multimedia) *Head*: Wong Heng Hun; **Hospitality, Tourism and Leisure Management** *Head*: Baskaran Sabapathy

Further Information: Also Campuses in Ipoh and Johor Bahru.

History: Created in 1987 as Sunway College. Acquired current title and status in 2004.

Governing Bodies: Board of Trustees

Admission Requirements: Sijil Tinggi Pelajaran Malaysia or equivalent Secondary School Certificate.

International Co-operation: With institutions in Australia and United Kingdom

Degrees and Diplomas: *Diploma*: Business; Computer Technology; Hospitality; Performing Arts; Art and Design, 2 $\frac{1}{2}$ yrs; *Bachelor's Degree*: Accounting and Finance; Business Studies; Business Management; International Hospitality Management; International

Tourism Management (BSc (Hons)); Business Information Systems; Computer Science; Communication Systems; Interactive Multimedia; (BSc (Hons)); Law (LLB/BA (Hons)); Psychology (BPsychology (Hons)), 3 yrs; *Master's Degree*: Management and Law (LLM/MSc). Some degrees offered jointly with overseas universities - see website for more details. Also delivers MBA from Manchester Business School, University of Manchester, UK and Victoria University, Australia.

TAYLOR'S UNIVERSITY

N°1, Jalan Taylor's, 47500 Subang Jaya, Selangor
Tel: +60(3) 5629 5000
Fax: +60(3) 5629 5001
EMail: admissions@taylors.edu.my
Website: http://www.taylors.edu.my/

President: Dato' Hassan Said

Schools

Architecture, Building and Design (Architecture; Real Estate; Surveying and Mapping); **Bioscience** (Biomedicine; Biotechnology; Food Science; Nutrition); **Business** (Business Administration; Human Resources; International Business); **Communication** (Advertising and Publicity; Communication Studies; Mass Communication; Public Relations); **Computing and Information Technology** (Computer Science; Information Technology; Software Engineering); **Design** (Design; Interior Design; Multimedia); **Education** (Education); **Engineering** (Chemical Engineering; Electrical and Electronic Engineering; Engineering; Mechanical Engineering); **Hospitality, Tourism and Culinary Arts** (Cooking and Catering; Hotel Management; House Arts and Environment; Tourism); **Law** (Law); **Medicine** (Medicine; Surgery); **Pharmacy** (Pharmacy)

History: Created in 1969 as Taylor's College. Became University College in 2006. Acquired current title and status 2010.

Admission Requirements: Recognised secondary school certificate.

Degrees and Diplomas: *Diploma*; *Bachelor's Degree*; *Bachelor's Degree*; *Master's Degree*. Also joint degree programmes.
Last Updated: 27/01/12

TENAGA NATIONAL UNIVERSITY

Universiti Tenaga Nasional (UNITEN)
Km7, Jalan Kajang-Puchong, 43009 Kajang, Selangor
Tel: +60(3) 8921-2020
Fax: +60(3) 8928-7166
Website: http://www.uniten.edu.my

Vice-Chancellor: Mashkuri Yaacob (2007-)
Tel: +60(3) 8921-2020 Ext. 1002, Fax: +60(3) 8926-3507
EMail: mashkuri@uniten.edu.my

International Relations: Rusmala Mohd Daud, Director, Marketing and International Relations
Tel: +60(3) 8928-7106, Fax: +60(3) 8921-2113
EMail: rusmala@uniten.edu.my

Colleges

Business Administration and Accountancy (Accountancy; Business Administration; Finance; Human Resources; Management; Marketing); **Engineering** (Civil Engineering; Electrical and Electronic Engineering; Electrical Engineering; Mechanical Engineering; Power Engineering); **Graduate Studies** (Business Administration; Civil Engineering; Electrical Engineering; Engineering Management; Industrial Engineering; Information Technology; Mechanical Engineering; Telecommunications Engineering); **Information Technology** (Computer Engineering; Computer Graphics; Computer Networks; Computer Science; Information Technology; Multimedia; Software Engineering)

Institutes

Liberal Studies (Arts and Humanities; Communication Studies; Education; Modern Languages; Pedagogy; Social Sciences)

History: Founded 1976 as Institut Latihan Sultan Ahmad Shah (ILSAS). Renamed Institut Kejuruteraan Teknologi Tenaga Nasional (IKATAN) 1994. Acquired present status 1997.

Academic Year: July to June (July-November; December-April; April-June)

Admission Requirements: Local students: Passed foundation programme/ STPM/ A-level/ Matriculation/ Diploma or equivalent qualification and have been taking the Malaysian University English Test (MUET). International students: Passed 'A-Level' examinations or equivalent with good grades in Mathematics, Physics and Chemistry (depending on programme chosen) ; obtained minimum grade 'C' for English at 'O-level' examination; Applicants with IELTS (5;5-6;0) or TOEFL (550 and above) can be admitted directly in degree programme; otherwise students are required to pursue the Intensive English Programme in UNITEN.

Fees: (Ringgit): Bachelor's degree, 32,000-49,680 per programme; Master's degree by research, 1,300-2,500 per semester; Master's degree by coursework and research, 12,000 per programme; Master's degree by coursework and project, 10,000-22,470 per programme.

Main Language(s) of Instruction: English

Accrediting Agencies: Malaysian Qualifications Agency (MQA); Engineering Accreditation Council (EAC); Board of Engineers Malaysia (BEM); Institute of Engineering Malaysia (IEM)

Degrees and Diplomas: *Bachelor's Degree*; *Master's Degree*: Electrical Engineering; Mechanical Engineering; Civil Engineering; Industrial Science; Information Technology; Engineering Management; Business Administration; *Doctor's Degree*: Engineering; Industrial Science; Information and Communication Technology; Business Administration

Student Services: Academic counselling, Canteen, Cultural centre, Employment services, Foreign Studies Centre, Health services, Language programs, Nursery care, Sports facilities

Student Residential Facilities: Fully provided to first year students; Students from second year and above will be provided with accomodation subject to availability.

Special Facilities: Multipurpose Hall (3000-seat capacity)

Libraries: Yes. Online integrated computerised library system. Linked to 23 Perpun libraries, 75 international universities and academic libraries, 6 state libraries and 13 public libraries. Subscription to international journals such as Science Direct, Scopus, Emerald Insight, ProQuest.

Publications: Electronic Journal of Computer Science and Information Technology, Academic Journal published by the College of Information Technology that gathers papers by researchers and practitioners as well as case studies on issues in the area of Computer Science and Information Technology. *(biannually)*; Journal of Business and Management, Academic Journal published by the College of Business Administration and Accountancy in order to provide a platfrom for local and international researchers to have their work published. *(biannually)*; Journal of Energy and Environment, Papers on technological, theoretical, application and socio-economic aspects of energy and environment. All papers are reviewed by world renowned referees. The journal is dedicated to advancing knowledge and sharing ideas in the area of Energy/ Environment *(biannually)*

Academic Staff *2009-2010*	MEN	WOMEN	**TOTAL**
FULL-TIME	197	180	**377**
PART-TIME	28	13	**41**
STAFF WITH DOCTORATE			
FULL-TIME	82	31	**113**
PART-TIME	6	3	**9**
Student Numbers *2009-2010*			
All (Foreign Included)	4,940	3,325	**8,265**
FOREIGN ONLY	262	87	**349**

Last Updated: 05/11/10

TUN ABDUL RAZAK UNIVERSITY

Universiti Tun Abdul Razak (UNITAR)
Capital Square, Block C & D, No. 8, Jalan Munshi Abdullah, 50100 Kuala Lumpur
Tel: +60(3) 7627-7070
Fax: +60(3) 7627-7177
EMail: crm@unirazak.edu.my
Website: http://www.unirazak.edu.my/

President and Vice Chancellor: Md Zabid Abdul Rashid
Tel: +60(3) 7627-7201, Fax: +60(3) 7627-7377
EMail: zabid@unitar.edu.my

Deputy President: Mohamed Dahan
Tel: +60(3) 7809-2182, Fax: +60(3) 7627-7280
EMail: mahyuddin@unitar.edu.my

International Relations: Luffini Meela Kamaruzzaman, International Relations Executive
Tel: +60(3) 7627-7379, Fax: +60(3) 7627-7388
EMail: luffini@unitar.edu.my

Centres

Languages and General Studies (Business Administration; Communication Studies; English) *Head*: Lynne Catherine

Faculties

Business Administration *Dean*: Noor Raihan Ab Hamid; **Education and Social Sciences** *Dean*: Yousof MD Yasin; **Hospitality and Tourism Management** (Cooking and Catering; Hotel Management; Tourism) *Dean*: Nor Khomar Ishak; **Information Technology** (Information Management; Information Technology) *Dean*: Syed Malek Syed Mustapha

Schools

Entrepreneurship *Director*: Nazatul Shima Abd Rani; **Research and Graduate Studies** (Business Administration; Information Technology; Management) *Director*: Syed Raisudin Syed Hamzah

History: Founded 1997. Acquired present status 2000. First e-learning private university combining face-to-face classes with web-based courseware and online tutorials.

Admission Requirements: Foundation Programme, SPM/SPMV/'O' Levels with 5 credits including Mathematics or other equivalent qualification; for International students, minimum TOEFL score of 450 or IELTS band of 4. Diploma Programme, A pass in SPM / SPMV / 'O' Level with 3 credits and at least a pass in Mathematics and English Language or other equivalent. Bachelor Degree, A pass STPM with 3 principals and a pass in Mathematics at SPM/SPMV/'O' Level; or 'A' Levels, Matriculation, Foundation, Unified Examination Certificate (UEC) or Pre-university; or Diploma from a Public or Private Higher Education Institution with a minimum standard required by the Malaysian Qualifications Agency (MQA); or Certificate from a Polytechnic under the Ministry of Higher Education, Malaysia. Masters Degree, Bachelor degree (honours) or equivalent; For International Students, minimum TOEFL score of 550 or IELTS band of 6; Doctorate programme, A Masters degree in management or equivalent.

Fees: (Ringgit): Local students: Foundation programmes, 4,000; Diploma programme, 13,500-15,470; Bachelor degree, 30,250-36,300; Masters Degree, 12,504-16,875; Doctorate degree, 18,000. International Students: Foundation programmes, 5,000; Diploma programme, 13,356-15,530; Bachelor degree, 30,300-36,900; Masters Degree, 13,800-18,585; Doctorate degree, 19,824.

Main Language(s) of Instruction: English

International Co-operation: With Babson College (USA)

Accrediting Agencies: Malaysian Qualifications Agency (MQA)

Degrees and Diplomas: *Diploma*: Information Technology; Management; Accountancy; Hotel Management; Culinary Arts; Tourism Management; Food Service Management, 1-2 yrs; *Bachelor's Degree*: Information Technology; Information Systems; Business Administration; Management; Accountancy; English; Hospitality Management; Education; Software Engineering, 3 yrs; *Master's Degree*: Business Administration; Management; Information Technology; Scinece (Information Technology by Research); Science (Management by Research), 1-4 yrs; *Doctor's Degree*: Information Technology (by research); Management (by Research), 2-7 yrs. Also Foundation Programme in Information Technology, Business Administration, Management, 1-1 1/2 yrs.

Student Services: Academic counselling, Canteen, Employment services, Foreign student adviser, Foreign Studies Centre, Language programs

Libraries: Yes

Last Updated: 28/10/08

TUNKU ABDUL RAHMAN UNIVERSITY

Universiti Tunku Abdul Rahman (UTAR)

Petaling Jaya Campus, N°13, Section 13/6, 46200 Petaling Jaya, Selangor
Tel: +60(3) 7958-2628
Fax: +60(3) 7956-1923
EMail: info@mail.utar.edu.my
Website: http://www.utar.edu.my/

President: Ng Lay Swee

Faculties

Accountancy and Management; **Arts and Social Sciences**; **Engineering and Science** (Biochemistry; Biomedical Engineering; Biotechnology; Chemical Engineering; Chemistry; Civil Engineering; Electrical and Electronic Engineering; Electronic Engineering; Materials Engineering; Mechanical Engineering; Physics; Production Engineering; Surveying and Mapping; Telecommunications Engineering); **Information and Communication Technology** (Actuarial Science; Applied Mathematics; Computer Engineering; Computer Networks; Computer Science)

Institutes

Postgraduate Studies & Research (Accountancy; Business Administration; Chinese; Communication Studies; Computer Science; Engineering; Information Sciences)

History: Created in 1964 as Kolej Tunku Abdul Rahman. Acquired current title and status 2002.

Academic Year: May to April (May-September; October-December; January-April)

Admission Requirements: 2 'A' level passes (or equivalent secondary school certificate) in a relevant subject for undergraduate programmes; Honours Bachelor's degree for postgraduate programmes.

Fees: (Ringgit): 25,000 - 38,000 per undergraduate degree

Degrees and Diplomas: *Diploma*: 1 yr; *Bachelor's Degree*: Biochemistry; Biomedical Science; Biotechnology; Chemistry; Physics; Construction Management; Quantity Surveying (BSc (Hons)); Engineering (Biomedical; Chemical; Civil; Electrical & Electronic; Electronic; Electronic & Communications; Materials & Manufacturing; Mechanical; Mechatronics) (BEng (Hons)); Finance; Accounting; Business Administration; Entrepreneurship; Marketing; Economics; Banking and Finance (Bachelor's (Hons)); Graphic Design & Multimedia; Chinese Studies; English Language; Advertising; Broadcasting; Journalism; Public Relations; Psychology (BA (Hons); BComn (Hons); BSocSci (Hons)), 3-4 yrs; *Master's Degree*: Communication; Accounting; Applied Accounting; Business Administration; Computer Science; Information Systems; Chinese Studies; Science; Engineering Science, a further 1 1/2 yrs; *Doctor's Degree*: Science; Engineering (PhD), at least 2 yrs

UCSI UNIVERSITY

Kolej Universiti Antarabangsa Sedaya (UCSI)

No 1 Jalan Menara Gading, UCSI Heights, Cheras, 56000 Kuala Lumpur
Tel: +60(3) 9101-8880
Fax: +60(3) 9102-3606
EMail: admit@ucsi.edu.my
Website: http://www.ucsi.edu.my

President and Vice-Chancellor: Peter Tong Se Ng

Schools

Applied Sciences (Biotechnology; Food Science; Nutrition); **Architecture, Management and Surveying** (Architecture; Construction Engineering; Interior Design; Surveying and Mapping); **Creative Arts** (Design; Fashion Design); **Engineering**; **Graduate Studies**; **Management and Information Technology** (Accountancy; Business Administration; Computer Science; Finance; Information Technology; Management; Marketing); **Medicine**; **Music** (Music); **Nursing**; **Pharmacy** (Pharmacy); **Pre-University Studies**; **Social Science and Liberal Arts** (English; Mass Communication; Psychology; Social Sciences)

Further Information: Campuses also in Sarawak and Terengganu

History: Founded 1986 as Canadian Institute of Computer Science. Became Sedaya International College 1990. Acquired present status and title 2003.

Degrees and Diplomas: *Diploma*; *Bachelor's Degree*; *Master's Degree*

UNITAR INTERNATIONAL UNIVERSITY (UNITAR)

Block C, Leisure Commerce Square, No. 9, Jalan Pjs 8/9, 46150 Petaling Jaya, Selangor
Tel: +60(3) 7627-7200
Fax: +60(3) 7627-7447
Website: http://www.unitar.my/

Vice-Chancellor: Abdul Razak Habib (2012-)
Tel: +60(3) 7627-7202, Fax: +60(3) 7627-7377
EMail: abdrazak@unitar.my

Chief Executive Officer: Wan Ahmad Saifuddin Wan Ahmad Radzi
Tel: +60(3) 7627-7336, Fax: +60(3) 7627-7280
EMail: wansaifuddin@unitar.my

International Relations: Shahrul Annuar Abdul Halim, Sales and Marketing Executive
Tel: +60(3) 7627-7467, Fax: +60(3) 7627-7464
EMail: shahrul@unitar.my

Centres

Professional Development

Faculties

Business Administration (Business Administration); **Early Childhood Studies** (Child Care and Development; Preschool Education); **Education and Social Sciences** (Education; Social Sciences); **Hospitality and Tourism Management** (Hotel and Restaurant; Hotel Management; Tourism); **Information Technology** (Information Sciences; Information Technology; Mathematics and Computer Science)

Graduate Schools

Graduate Studies (Business Administration; Education; Home Economics; Information Sciences; Mathematics and Computer Science; Social Sciences)

Schools

Foundation and General Studies (Arts and Humanities; Business Administration; Education; Information Technology; Service Trades)

History: Created 2000 as University of Management and Technology (UMTECH). Acquired current status and name 2012.

Governing Bodies: EXCO, Senate, Board of Governance (BOG), Management Committee, University Curriculum Committee (UCC) and Academic Administration Committee (AAC)

Academic Year: Feb-June; June-Aug; and Sept-Jan

Admission Requirements: Secondary school diploma for undergraduate courses; undergrduate degree for postgraduate courses.

Fees: (MYR): c. 19,000 to 70,000 per annum.

Main Language(s) of Instruction: English

International Co-operation: with institutions in France

Accrediting Agencies: MQA

Degrees and Diplomas: *Diploma*: Management; Accountancy; Early Childhood Education; Culinary Art; Foodservice Management; Hotel Management; Tourism Management; Computer Security; Information Technology; *Bachelor's Degree*: Information Systems; Information Technology; Software Engineering; Accounting Information Systems; Computer Security (BA(Hons)); Management; Accounting; Business Administration; Education; English; Guidance and Counseling; Hospitality Management; Food Catering Management (BA(Hons)); *Master's Degree*: Information Technology; Computer Science; Early Childhood Education; Educational Leadership and Management; Curriculum and Instruction; English As a Second Language; Guidance and Counseling; Hospitality Management; Business Administration; Management; *Doctor's Degree*: Information Technology

Student Services: Academic counselling, Cultural centre, Foreign Studies Centre, Language programs, Social counselling

Student Residential Facilities: Yes

Libraries: c. 24,000 vols; A/V material; online databases

Academic Staff *2011-2012*	MEN	WOMEN	TOTAL
FULL-TIME	51	82	**133**
STAFF WITH DOCTORATE			
FULL-TIME	11	5	**16**
Student Numbers *2011-2012*			
All (Foreign Included)	418	880	**1,298**
FOREIGN ONLY	31	6	**37**

Last Updated: 10/08/12

UNIVERSITY OF KUALA LUMPUR

Universiti Kuala Lumpur
1016, Jalan Sultan Ismail, 50250 Kuala Lumpur
Tel: +60(3) 2175- 4000
EMail: drazemi@unikl.edu.my
Website: http://www.unikl.edu.my

President: Abdul Hakim Juri EMail: drhakim@unikl.edu.my

Colleges

Medicine *(Royal, Ipoh)* (Medicine)

Institutes

Aviation Technology; **British Malaysian** *(Gombak)*; **Chemical and Bioengineering Technology** *(Alor Gajah)* (Bioengineering; Chemical Engineering; Polymer and Plastics Technology); **Information Technology** *(Malaysian)* (Information Technology); **Malaysia-France** *(Bandar Baru Bangi)*; **Malaysian Spanish** *(Kulim)*; **Marine Engineering Technology** *(Sitiawan)*; **Product Design and Manufacturing**

History: Founded 2002.

Degrees and Diplomas: *Bachelor's Degree*; *Master's Degree*

WAWASAN OPEN UNIVERSITY

Universiti Terbuka Wawasan
54, Jalan Sultan Ahmad Shah, 10050 Georgetown,
Pulau Pinang
Tel: +60(4) 228-9323
Fax: +60(4) 226-9323
EMail: enquiry@wou.edu.my
Website: http://www.wou.edu.my

Vice-Chancellor and CEO: Gajaraj Dhanarajan (2004-)
Tel: +60(4) 229-3268 EMail: gdhan@wou.edu.my

Wong: Tat Meng Wong EMail: tmwong@wou.edu.my

International Relations: Agnes James, Director, Corporate Communications Fax: +60(4) 227-9214
EMail: agnesjames@wou.edu.my

Centres

Graduate Studies *Head*: Madhulika Kaushik

Schools

Business and Administration *Head*: Kim Loy Chee; **Foundation and Liberal Studies** *Head*: Mogana Dhamotharan; **Science and Technology** (Computer Engineering; Computer Networks; Electronic Engineering; Information Technology; Telecommunications Engineering) *Head*: Sinn Chye Ho

History: Founded 2006. Malaysia's first private non-for-profit university.

Governing Bodies: University Council; Senate

Admission Requirements: Undergraduate programmes: Regular entry, Minimum of 2 principals in Sijil Tinggi Pelajaran Malaysia (STPM)/HSC/A- levels or equivalent qualifications. For open entry, minimum age 21, minimum of 1 principal in STPM/HSC/A-levels or equivalent qualifications or PMR/SPM/MCE/UEC or equivalent qualifications with assessment of prior learning and work experience. For postgraduate programmes, Bachelor's degree with or without honours, with 2 years working experience at supervisory/managerial level; Minimum of STPM or equivalent qualifications and minimum of 2 years working experience at supervisory/managerial level and Commonwealth Management Aptitude Test (CEMAT)

Fees: (Ringgit): Bachelor's degree, 110.00 - 150.00 per credit unit (minimum of 120 credit units). Master's degree, 300.00 - 600.00 per credit unit (minimum of 48 credit units).

Main Language(s) of Instruction: English

International Co-operation: Postgraduate programmes with the Commonwealth of Learning

Accrediting Agencies: Malaysian Qualifications Agency, Ministry of Higher Education

Degrees and Diplomas: *Bachelor's Degree*: Accounting; Business Information Systems; Banking and Finance; Management; Sales and Marketing; Logistics and Supply Chain Management (BBus (Hons)); Computer Systems and Networks; Computing and

Intelligent Systems; Electronic Commerce; Electronics; Information and Communication Technology (BTech (Honours)), 5 yrs (102 credits); *Bachelor's Degree*: Liberal Arts (BA (Hons)), 5 yrs; *Master's Degree*: Business Administration (Commonwealth Executive Master) (CeMBA); Public Administration (Commonwealth Executive Master), 2 1/2 yrs

Student Services: Academic counselling, Canteen, Cultural centre, Handicapped facilities

Student Residential Facilities: None

Special Facilities: Theatrette

Libraries: Yes. Also digital resoures with off-campus access.

Press or Publishing House: In house publishing Department

Academic Staff *2007-2008*	MEN	WOMEN	**TOTAL**
FULL-TIME	12	8	**20**
PART-TIME	140	104	**244**
STAFF WITH DOCTORATE			
FULL-TIME	6	3	**9**
PART-TIME	11	6	**17**
Student Numbers *2007-2008*			
All (Foreign Included)	1,969	1,313	**3,282**

Last Updated: 07/11/08

Mali

STRUCTURE OF HIGHER EDUCATION SYSTEM

Description:

Higher education is provided by public universities and private higher education institutions. The Commission for the implementation of three-tier system (Licence-Master-Doctorat) will be created during the 2012-2013 academic year.

Stages of studies:

University level first stage:
The Diplôme d'Etudes universitaires générales is awarded after two years' study.

University level second stage:
The Licence is awarded after three years' study, the Maîtrise after four years' study.

University level third stage:
A Doctorat is conferred after a further three years and a thesis.

ADMISSION TO HIGHER EDUCATION

Admission to university-level studies:

Name of secondary school credential required: Baccalauréat
Name of secondary school credential required: Baccalauréat technique

NATIONAL BODIES

Ministère de l'Enseignement Supérieur et de la Recherche Scientifique (Ministry of Higher Education and Scientific Research)

Minister: Messaoud Ould Mohamed Lahbib
Bamako
Role of national body: Manages and administers higher education

Data for academic year: 2012-2013
Source: IAU from the website of the Ministry of Higher Education and World Data on Education 2010/2011, UNESCO-IBE, 2012

INSTITUTIONS

PUBLIC INSTITUTIONS

HIGHER INSTITUTE OF TRAINING AND APPLIED RESEARCH

Institut supérieur de Formation et de Recherche appliquée (ISFRA)
BPE 475, Bamako
Tel: +223-20-21-04-66
EMail: isframl@yahoo.fr

Head: Gaoussou Kanouté

Programmes
Teacher Training (Higher Education; Teacher Training)

Degrees and Diplomas: *Diplôme d'Etude supérieures spécialisées*; *Diplôme d'Etudes approfondies*; *Doctorat*
Last Updated: 22/10/12

NATIONAL SCHOOL OF ENGINEERING

Ecole nationale d'Ingenieur (ENI-ABT)
BP 242, Bamako
Website: http://eni-abt.edu.ml/

Directeur général: Sanata Diarra (2011-)

Programmes
Civil Engineering (Building Technologies; Civil Engineering; Construction Engineering; Hydraulic Engineering); **Geology** (Geology); **Industrial Engineering** (Electrical Engineering; Energy

Engineering; Industrial Engineering; Mechanical Engineering); **Surveying and Mapping** (Surveying and Mapping)

Degrees and Diplomas: *Diplôme d'Etudes universitaires générales; Licence; Diplôme d'Ingénieur.* Also Master
Last Updated: 19/10/12

RURAL POLYTECHNIC INSTITUTE FOR TRAINING AND APPLIED RESEARCH

Institut Polytechnique Rural de Formation et de Recherche Appliquée (IPR IFRA)
BP 06, Koulikoro
Tel: +223(226) 20-12
Fax: +223(226) 25-04
EMail: ipr-ifra@ipr-ifra.org
Website: http://www.ipr-ifra.org/

Director: Mahamoudou Famanta (2011-)

Programmes
Agriculture (Agricultural Business; Agriculture); **Agriculture Engineering** (Agricultural Engineering; Agricultural Equipment); **Agronomy** (Agronomy); **Animal Production** (Animal Husbandry; Zoology); **Forestry** (Environmental Studies; Forestry); **Water Science** (Water Science)

History: Founded 1897as a research centre, became Institut Polytechnique Rural (IPR) 1965, acquired present title and status 1996.

Fees: (CFA Franc): Local students: 5,000 per annum; Foreign students: 300,000 per annum

Degrees and Diplomas: *Diplôme de Technicien supérieur*; *Diplôme d'Ingénieur*; *Maîtrise*
Last Updated: 22/10/12

TEACHER TRAINING SCHOOL

Ecole normale supérieure (ENS)
BP 241, Bamako
Tel: +223(20) 22-21-89
EMail: info@ml.refer.org

Directeur général: Ibrahima Camara (2011-)

Programmes
Teacher Training (Teacher Training)

Admission Requirements: Licence
Last Updated: 22/10/12

UNIVERSITÉ DES LETTRES ET SCIENCES HUMAINES DE BAMAKO (ULSHB)

BP E2528, Bamako

Rectrice: Djeneba Traore

Faculties
Letters, Languages, and Linguistics *(FLLSL)* (Arts and Humanities; English; Linguistics; Modern Languages); **Social Sciences and Education** *(FSHSE)* (Anthropology; Education; Social Sciences)

Institutes
Technology *(IUT)* (Communication Studies; Library Science)
Last Updated: 16/04/12

UNIVERSITÉ DES SCIENCES JURIDIQUES ET POLITIQUES DE BAMAKO (USJPB)

BP E2528, Bamako

Recteur: Salif Berthe

Faculties
Political and Administrative Sciences (Administration; Political Sciences); **Private Law** (Private Law); **Public Law** (Public Law)
Last Updated: 16/04/12

UNIVERSITY OF BAMAKO

Université des Sciences, des Techniques et des Technologies de Bamako (USTTB)
BP E2528, Bamako
Tel: +223 222-32-44
Fax: +223 222-19-32
EMail: u-bamako@ml.refer.org
Website: http://www.ml.refer.org/u-bamako/

Recteur: Adama Diaman Keita (2011-)

Faculties
Dentistry and Stomatology (Dentistry; Stomatology); **Medicine** (Medicine); **Pharmacy** (Pharmacy); **Science and Technology** *(FAST)* (Applied Chemistry; Applied Mathematics; Applied Physics; Biochemistry; Bioengineering; Chemistry; Computer Engineering; Electrical Engineering; Geology; Mathematics; Microbiology; Natural Sciences; Physics; Technology)

Institutes
Agricultural Technology - Training and Applied Research *(IUSA)* (Agriculture; Agronomy; Forestry; Horticulture; Meat and Poultry; Water Management; Zoology); **Training and Applied Research** *(ISFRA)* (Anthropology; Applied Mathematics; Applied Physics; Chemistry; Civil Engineering; Demography and Population; Ecology; Educational Sciences; Environmental Studies; Mathematics; Microbiology; Nutrition; Physics)

History: Founded 1993 as Université du Mali. Renamed Université de Bamako 2002.

Governing Bodies: University Council

Academic Year: October to July

Admission Requirements: Secondary school certificate (Baccalauréat) or equivalent

Fees: (CFA Francs): 5,000-150,000 per annum; foreign students, 250,000-300,000

Main Language(s) of Instruction: French

Degrees and Diplomas: *Diplôme de Technicien supérieur*: 2 yrs; *Diplôme d'Etudes universitaires générales*; *Licence*; *Diplôme de Docteur*: Medicine; Pharmacy; *Diplôme d'Ingénieur*: Applied Sciences, 5 yrs; *Maîtrise*: 4 yrs; *Diplôme d'Etudes approfondies*: 1-2 further yrs following Maîtrise; *Doctorat*: a further 2-4 yrs
Last Updated: 25/06/09

UNIVERSITY OF SOCIAL SCIENCES AND MANAGEMENT

Université des Sciences Sociales et de Gestion (USSGB)
BP E2528, Bamako
Tel: +223 222-84-24

Recteur: Bani Touré

Faculties
Economics (Economics); **Geography** (Geography); **History** (History); **Management** (Management)

Institutes
Territorial Development Studies
Last Updated: 16/04/12

PRIVATE INSTITUTION

INSTITUTE OF POLITICAL SCIENCE, INTERNATIONAL RELATIONS AND COMMUNICATION

Institut des Sciences Politiques, des Relations internationales et de la Communication
BP 763, Bamako
Tel: +223 20-20-15-52
EMail: ispric@ispric.com
Website: http://www.ispric.com/

Directeur général: Mohamed Gakou (2006-)
Tel: +223 674-05-74 EMail: mohamedgakou@ispric.com

Departments
Communication Studies and Journalism (Communication Studies; Journalism); **Economics** (Economics); **International Relations** (International Relations); **Law** (Law); **Political Science** (Political Sciences)

History: Founded 1999.

Governing Bodies: Board

Admission Requirements: Secondary school certificate (baccalauréat) or Brevet de Technicien

Fees: (CFA Francs): 500,000-700,000

Main Language(s) of Instruction: French

International Co-operation: With universities in Senegal and France

Degrees and Diplomas: *Diplôme d'Etudes universitaires générales*: Economics; Law; Political Science; Internationational Relations; Journalism and Communication Studies, 2 yrs; *Licence*: 3 yrs; *Maîtrise*: a further yr. Also Master 2 in cooperation with l'Université Cheick Anta Diop (Senegal)

Student Services: Canteen, Foreign student adviser, Foreign Studies Centre, Social counselling

Libraries: Yes

Last Updated: 16/05/12

Malta

STRUCTURE OF HIGHER EDUCATION SYSTEM

Description:

Higher education in Malta is regulated by the Education Act of 1998 and subsequent amendments. Tertiary education is mainly provided by the University of Malta. But higher education is in the process of becoming a binary system following the foundation of the Malta College of Arts, Science and Technology (MCAST) which aims at providing ISCED 5 courses.

Stages of studies:

University level first stage: *Bachelor's degree*
The Bachelor's Degree is obtained in three to five years depending on the field of study.

University level second stage: *Master's degree/Postgraduate diploma*
The second stage leads to the award of a Master's Degree or a Postgraduate diploma after a period of one or two years of study.

University level third stage: *Doctor's degree*
The third stage leads, after at least three years of study following the award of a Master's Degree, to the Doctor's Degree. Candidates are required to submit a thesis after a period of research on an approved topic.

ADMISSION TO HIGHER EDUCATION

Admission to university-level studies:

Name of secondary school credential required: Matriculation Certificate

Minimum score/requirement: C

For entry to: All programmes except Medicine and Surgery.

Alternatives to credentials: Alternative qualifications are considered if comparable. In the case of students over 23, applicants are interviewed and assessed by the Faculty concerned.

Foreign students admission:

Definition of foreign student: A foreign student is a student who does not hold Maltese citizenship.

Quotas: In the case of Medical courses, thirty places are reserved for foreign applicants.

Entrance exam requirements: Foreign students must have qualifications equivalent to the Matriculation Certificate, such as the General Certificate of Education at Advanced (A) level, the International Baccalaureate and the American Advanced Placement System.

Entry regulations: Foreign students must have an entry permit and financial guarantees if they are staying for more than three months.

Language requirements: A good knowledge of English is essential. The University provides a Foundation Studies course and a Pre-Sessional Language course prior to entry to a regular course of study.

RECOGNITION OF STUDIES

Quality assurance system:

Articles 28(j) and 35(e) of the Education Act empower the University of Malta to evaluate degrees and academic distinctions.

Bodies dealing with recognition:

Kunsill Malti ghall-Kwalifiki (Malta Qualifications Council - MQC)

Chief Executive: Philip Von Brockdorff
Casa Leoni, 476, St Joseph High Road

St Venera
Tel: +356 2754 0051
Fax: +356 2180 8758
EMail: mqc@gov.mt
WWW: http://www.mqc.gov.mt
Deals with credential recognition for entry to institution: Yes
Deals with credential recognition for entry to profession: Yes

Special provisions for recognition:

Recognition for university level studies: Nationals and foreigners are given the same treatment.

NATIONAL BODIES

Ministry of Education and Employment

Minister: Dolores Cristina
201 Strait Street
Valletta 2000
Tel: +356 2568 9000
Fax: +356 2568 9148
WWW: https://www.education.gov.mt/

Data for academic year: 2006-2007
Source: IAU from NARIC Office, Malta, 2006 (Bodies, 2011)

INSTITUTIONS

IMO INTERNATIONAL MARITIME LAW INSTITUTE (IMLI)

P.O. Box 31, Msida, 1000 MSD
Tel: +356 21319343; +356 21310816
Fax: +356 21343092
EMail: info@imli.org
Website: http://www.imli.org

Director: David J. Attard EMail: director@imli.org

Programmes
International Maritime Law (International Law; Maritime Law)

History: Founded 1988.

Main Language(s) of Instruction: English

Degrees and Diplomas: *Master's Degree*; *Doctor's Degree (Ph.D.)*. Also Advanced Diploma for professionals

Student Services: Canteen

Student Residential Facilities: Yes

Libraries: Yes
Last Updated: 09/11/12

UNIVERSITY OF MALTA

L-Università ta' Malta (UOM)
Msida MSD 2080
Tel: +356(21) 2340-2340
Fax: +356(21) 2340-2342
EMail: comms@um.edu.mt
Website: http://www.um.edu.mt

Rector: Juanito Camilleri (2006-)
Tel: +356(21) 333-907, Fax: +356(21) 336-436
EMail: rector@um.edu.mt

Registrar: Veronica Grech
Tel: +356(21) 344-842 EMail: registrar@um.edu.mt

International Relations: Stefania Fabri, Director, International and European Union Office
Tel: +356(21) 2340-3182, Fax: +356(21) 347-813
EMail: int-eu@um.edu.mt

Academies
Diplomatic Studies (International Relations)

Campuses
Gozo (Arts and Humanities; Business and Commerce); **Valletta** *(Valletta - International Master's programme)*

Centres
Biomedical Cybernetics (Biomedical Engineering); **Education Resilience and Socio-Emotional Health** *(European)* (Educational Sciences; Health Sciences); **Educational Research** *(Euro-Mediterranean)* (International and Comparative Education; Mediterranean Studies); **European Documentation and Research** (European Studies; European Union Law); **Family Studies** (Family Studies); **Gerontology** *(European)* (Gerontology); **Labour Studies** (Labour and Industrial Relations); **Literacy Education** (Literacy Education)

Faculties
Arts (Archaeology; Art History; Arts and Humanities; Classical Languages; English; French; German; History; International Relations; Italian; Maltese; Oriental Studies; Philosophy; Sociology; Spanish; Translation and Interpretation); **Built Environment** (Architectural and Environmental Design; Architectural Restoration; Architecture; Civil Engineering; Construction Engineering; Heritage Preservation; Structural Architecture; Town Planning); **Dental Surgery** (Dentistry; Surgery); **Economics, Management and Accountancy** (Accountancy; Banking; Economics; Finance; Management; Marketing; Public Administration; Social Policy; Social Work); **Education** (Art Education; Education; Educational Sciences; Foreign Languages Education; Mathematics Education; Primary Education; Psychology; Science Education; Technology Education); **Engineering** (Automation and Control Engineering; Electrical

Engineering; Engineering; Industrial Engineering; Materials Engineering; Mechanical Engineering; Metallurgical Engineering; Power Engineering; Production Engineering); **Health Sciences** (Biomedicine; Food Science; Health Administration; Health Sciences; Midwifery; Nursing; Occupational Therapy; Physical Therapy; Podiatry; Radiology; Rehabilitation and Therapy); **Information and Communication Technology** (Artificial Intelligence; Computer Engineering; Computer Science; Information Technology; Microelectronics; Nanotechnology; Telecommunications Engineering); **Laws** (Civil Law; Commercial Law; Communication Studies; Comparative Law; Criminal Law; Environmental Studies; European Union Law; International Law; Law; Media Studies; Public Law); **Media and Knowledge Sciences** (Archiving; Cognitive Sciences; Communication Studies; Information Management; Information Sciences; Library Science; Mass Communication; Media Studies); **Medicine and Surgery** (Anatomy; Biochemistry; Community Health; Gynaecology and Obstetrics; Medicine; Paediatrics; Pathology; Pharmacology; Pharmacy; Physiology; Psychiatry and Mental Health; Public Health; Surgery); **Science** (Biology; Chemistry; Materials Engineering; Operations Research; Physics; Statistics); **Theology** (Canon Law; Greek (Classical); Hebrew; History of Religion; Holy Writings; Pastoral Studies; Philosophy; Religious Practice; Theology)

Institutes

Anglo-Italian Studies (Cultural Studies; English Studies; Italian; Literature); **Baroque Studies** (Architecture); **Confucius** (Asian Studies; Chinese); **Criminology** (Criminology); **Design and Development of Thinking** *(Edward de Bono)* (Cognitive Sciences); **Earth Systems** (Coastal Studies; Earth Sciences; Environmental Management; Food Science; Geography; Rural Studies); **Islands and Small States** (Geography (Human); Island Studies); **Linguistics** (Bilingual and Bicultural Education; Linguistics); **Maltese Studies** (Maltese; Mediterranean Studies); **Mediterranean** (Anthropology; Dance; Geography; History; Mediterranean Studies; Music; Theatre); **Physical Education and Sport** (Physical Education; Sports); **Public Administration and Management** (Management; Public Administration); **Sustainable Development** (Development Studies); **Sustainable Energy** (Energy Engineering); **Tourism, Travel and Culture** (Cultural Studies; Tourism)

Further Information: Also Teaching Hospital at Guardamangia

History: Founded 1592 by the Jesuits as Collegium Melitense. Reconstituted by Grandmaster Pinto 1769.

Governing Bodies: Council; Senate

Academic Year: October to July (October-January; February-June)

Admission Requirements: Matriculation Certificate, including 2 subjects taken at Advanced Level and 3 at Intermediate Level, together with Systems of Knowledge, or equivalent qualifications; passes in the Secondary Education Certificate at Grade 5 or better in Maltese, English Language and Mathematics. Enquiries to University Registrar or Director, International and EU Office.

Fees: All fees are available at the following link: http://www.um.edu.mt/finance/service/coursefees

Main Language(s) of Instruction: English, except for the study of a modern language or Maltese

International Co-operation: With universities in Europe, USA, Canada, Australia, China, South Korea and Japan. Also participates in the International Student Exchange Programme, and in the LLP (Lifelong Learning Programme) which comprises the following programmes: Erasmus, Grundtvig, Comenius, Leonardo da Vinci and Jean Monnet. Member of EUA, ACU, EUCEN, AUF, the European Access Network as well as of the Compostela, Santander and Utrecht networks.

Degrees and Diplomas: *Bachelor's Degree*; *Master's Degree*: a further 1-2 yrs; *Doctor's Degree*. Also Diplomas, 1-2 yrs (usually part-time evening courses); Honours Bachjelor's degrees, 3-4 yrs; Higher Diplomas (3 yrs part-time evening); Full-time day Diploma courses in various branches of Health Sciences (3 yrs).

Student Services: Academic counselling, Foreign student adviser, Health services, Social counselling, Sports facilities

Student Residential Facilities: Yes (University Residence, Lija)

Special Facilities: Argotti Botanical Gardens; Atmospheric Pollution Monitoring Station; Project Support Team

Libraries: c. 810,000 vols; 1,500 print journals; c. 24,000 online journals.

Publications: International Journal of Emotional Education; Journal of Anglo-Italian Studies; Journal of Baroque Studies; Journal of Economic and Social Studies; Journal of Education; Journal of Maltese Studies; Journal of Mediterranean Studies; Journal of the Malta University History Society; Lehen il-Malti; Malta Medical Journal; Malta Review of Educational Research; Mediterranean Journal of Educational Studies; Mediterranean Journal of Human Rights; Melita Theologica; Register of Graduates; Symposia Melitensia

Press or Publishing House: Malta University Press

Academic Staff *2010-2011*	**TOTAL**
Student Numbers *2010-2011*	
All (Foreign Included)	**10,000**
FOREIGN ONLY	**600**

Last Updated: 12/09/11

Mauritania

STRUCTURE OF HIGHER EDUCATION SYSTEM

Description:

Public higher education is provided by the University of Nouakchott and other higher education institutions. Private higher education institutions were allowed as from 2009. They have to be recognized by the Ministry of Education.

Stages of studies:

University level first stage: *Licence*

The first stage of higher education leads to the Licence after three years' university study.

University level second stage: *Master*

The Master is conferred after two years' study beyond the Licence.

ADMISSION TO HIGHER EDUCATION

Admission to university-level studies:

Name of secondary school credential required: Baccalauréat

Alternatives to credentials: Entrance examination.

NATIONAL BODIES

Ministère d'Etat à l'Education Nationale, à l'Enseignement Supérieur et la Recherche Scientifique (Ministry of National Education, Higher Education and Scientific Research)

Minister: Ahmed Ould Bahya

Nouakchott

WWW: http://www.education.gov.mr/MauritanieMen/Home.aspx

Data for academic year: 2012-2013

Source: IAU from World Data on Education 2010/2011, UNESCO-IBE, the World Bank's Restructuring Paper of the Higher Education Project and the website of the University of Nouakchott, 2012

INSTITUTIONS

PUBLIC INSTITUTIONS

ADVANCED TEACHERS' TRAINING COLLEGE

Ecole normale supérieure (ENS)

BP 990, Nouakchott

Tel: +222(525) 31-84

Fax: +222(525) 31-72

Website: http://www.ens.mr/index.php

Directeur: Mohamed Ould Abdelkader Ould Alada (2008-)
Tel: +222(525) 31-72 EMail: alada@univ.nkc.mr

Directeur adjoint: Taleb Sidi Ould Brahim

International Relations: Baba Ainina Moulaye Mohamed
Fax: +222(525) 13-61 EMail: ainina_3@hotmail.com

Departments

Educational Sciences (Educational Sciences); **Human Sciences** (Civics; Geography; History; Philosophy); **Modern Languages** (Arabic; English; French; Modern Languages); **Research**; **Science** (Mathematics; Natural Sciences; Physics)

History: Founded 1970, acquired present status and title 2001.

Governing Bodies: Board of Directors

Academic Year: October to July

Admission Requirements: School certificate for first year entry; Diploma of General University Studies (Second Year University Diploma) or Masters for Professor section depending on cycles. Assistant Inspector section is opened to primary school teacher with eight years of seniority. Inspector of the fundamental section is opened to primary school teacher with three year of seniority.

Main Language(s) of Instruction: Arabic, French

International Co-operation: With universities in Algeria, France, Morrocco, Senegal, South Africa. Also cooperates with ALECSO, AUF, ISESCO and UNESCO.

Degrees and Diplomas: *Licence*

Student Services: Academic counselling, Canteen, Cultural centre, Health services, Language programs, Sports facilities

Student Residential Facilities: Yes

Special Facilities: National Herbarium of Maurirania

Libraries:c. 10,000 vols.

Publications: Ettarbia; Radisma

Academic Staff *2011-2012*	**TOTAL**
FULL-TIME	**70**
PART-TIME	**50**
STAFF WITH DOCTORATE	
FULL-TIME	**50**
PART-TIME	c. **40**
Student Numbers *2011-2012*	
All (Foreign Included)	c. **500**

Last Updated: 24/08/12

NATIONAL SCHOOL OF ADMINISTRATION, JOURNALISM AND MAGISTRACY

Ecole nationale d'administration, de journalisme et de magistrature (ENAJM)

BP 252, Nouakchott
Tel: +222(525) 32-22 +222 66-5656
Fax: +222(525) 75-17 +222 66-5657
EMail: info@ena.mr; email@ena.mr
Website: http://www.ena.mr

Directeur général: Ismaïl Ould Sadegh

Programmes

Administration (Administration)

History: Founded 1969.

Degrees and Diplomas: *Master*

Last Updated: 09/07/12

UNIVERSITY OF NOUAKCHOTT

Université de Nouakchott

BP 5026, Nouakchott
Tel: +222(525) 39-77
Fax: +222(525) 32-77
EMail: webmaster@univ-nkc.mr; secrcentr@univ-nkc.mr
Website: http://www.univ-nkc.mr

Recteur: Isselkou Ould Ahmed Izid Bih (2007-)
Tel: +222(529) 32-77

Secrétaire général: Ibrahima Dia

International Relations: Ahmedou Ould Abdy, Director, International Cooperation

Faculties

Arts and Humanities (Arabic; Arts and Humanities; English; Geography (Human); History; Linguistics; Native Language; Philosophy; Tourism; Translation and Interpretation); **Law and Economics** (Economics; Law; Management; Private Law; Public Law); **Medicine** (Anatomy; Biochemistry; Biophysics; Cell Biology; Chemistry; Embryology and Reproduction Biology; Medicine; Physiology; Public Health); **Science and Technology** (Biology; Chemistry; Computer Science; Geology; Management; Mathematics; Natural Sciences; Physics; Technology; Technology Education)

Higher Institutes

Professional Studies (Business Administration; Economic and Finance Policy; Finance; Information Technology; Management; Marketing)

History: Founded 1981. Incorporated Institut supérieur scientifique (ISS) 2002.

Governing Bodies: Assemblée de l'Université

Main Language(s) of Instruction: French

Degrees and Diplomas: *Licence*; *Master*

Last Updated: 09/07/12

Mauritius

STRUCTURE OF HIGHER EDUCATION SYSTEM

Description:

The higher education system consists of universities, colleges and polytechnics operating in the public sector. Furthermore, private organizations, overseas and regional institutions deliver tertiary-level programmes. Most of these institutions are relatively small and are affiliated to an international institution in delivering tertiary-level courses using a mixed mode system, encompassing both distance learning and face-to-face tutorials.

Stages of studies:

University level first stage:
This stage consists in three- to four-year Bachelor (with Honours) degree programmes on a full-time basis.

University level second stage:
The third level relates to Master's programmes which are offered either in the form of taught (e.g. MSc, MBA, etc.) or research (i.e. M.Phil) programmes.

University level third stage:
This stage normally relates to Doctor in Philosophy (PhD) programmes that are undertaken through research. PhD students are required to complete their research/studies within a maximum of five years' full-time or seven years' part-time studies.

Distance higher education:
The University of Mauritius, the Mauritius College of the Air and the Mauritius Institute of Education, each have a Centre for Distance Learning.
The Government is working on the setting up of an Open University.

ADMISSION TO HIGHER EDUCATION

Admission to university-level studies:

Name of secondary school credential required: Cambridge Higher School Certificate

Minimum score/requirement: A pass in English Language or a pass in English Language and Credits in five other subjects or Credit in English Language and four other subjects

For entry to: Undergraduate degrees

Name of secondary school credential required: General Certificate of Education Advanced Level

Minimum score/requirement: Passes in three subjects at Advanced Level or at least two passes at Advanced level

For entry to: Undergraduate degrees

Alternatives to credentials: The French Baccalauréat; The IGCSE and the International Baccalaureate awarded by the International Baccalaureate Organisation, Switzerland; Qualifications awarded by other universities and institutions which have been approved by the governing body as satisfying the minimum requirements for admission; or Relevant subjects/combinations of related subjects included in any qualifications as may be approved by the governing body as being equivalent or comparable to an 'O' level or 'A' level may be accepted in lieu of equivalence.

Foreign students admission:

Definition of foreign student: Non-nationals of the Republic of Mauritius.

Entrance exam requirements: Higher degree students must hold a Bachelor Degree (at least 2nd class Honours) or a first degree; for degree courses they must hold GCE 'O' level passes in five subjects, two of which must also be at 'A' level; for diploma courses they must hold five GCE 'O' level passes including English and Mathematics; for certificate courses they must generally hold a Cambridge SC with passes in five subjects, including English language.

Entry regulations: Foreign students must hold a visa (http://passport.gov.mu) and a residence permit and present financial guarantees.

Health requirements: As established by the Ministry of Health and Quality of Life (http://health.gov.mu).

Language requirements: Students must have a good command of English.

RECOGNITION OF STUDIES

Quality assurance system:

The Mauritius Qualifications Authority (MQA) and the Tertiary Education Commission (TEC) are responsible for accreditation of institutions and programmes in respect of technical and vocational education and training and post-secondary education respectively.

Bodies dealing with recognition:

Quality Assurance and Accreditation Division - TEC

Quality Assurance and Accreditation Officer: V. G. Ramnarain
5 Floor, MCA building
Reduit
Tel: +230 467 8800
Fax: +230 467 6579
WWW: http://tec.intnet.mu/qaad.php

NATIONAL BODIES

Ministry of Tertiary Education, Science, Research and Technology

Permanent Secretary: Nirmala Devi
Cyber Tower 1, Wing A, Level 4
Ebene
Tel: +230 467 1450
Fax: +230 468 1446
EMail: nnababsingh@mail.gov.mu
WWW: http://www.gov.mu/portal/site/tertiary

Role of national body: To expand the tertiary education sector to further increase access and through the development of a research culture and the setting up of Science Parks improve linkages between Universities and the world of work.

Quality Assurance and Accreditation Division – Tertiary Education Commission

Executive Director:
Executive Director: Praveen Mohadeb
4th Floor, TEC Building
Reduit
Tel: +230 467 8800
Fax: +230 467 6579
EMail: director@tec.mu
WWW: http://tec.intnet.mu/qaad.php

Role of national body: The Tertiary Education Commission has as objects to promote, plan, develop and coordinate post-secondary education in Mauritius and to implement an overarching regulatory framework to achieve high international quality. It also has the responsibility to allocate government funds to the Tertiary Education Institutions under its purview and to ensure accountability and optimum use of resources.

Careers Guidance Services

Ministry of Education, Culture and Human Resources
2nd Floor, Social Security House,
Old Moka Road
Rose Hill
Tel: +230 466 8104
Fax: +230 466 8073

EMail: educare@intnet.mu
WWW: http://educare.intnet.mu/

Study Mauritius
Permanent Secretary: Nirmala Devi
Level 1, Cyber Tower 1
Ebene
Tel: +230 454 7105
Fax: +230 454 7112
EMail: http://www.studymauritius.info/
WWW: studymauritius@mail.gov.mu
Role of national body: To promote information on programmes offered by public and private Tertiary Education Institutions operating in Mauritius and overseas. The office links up with local Tertiary Institutions, local Recruiting agents and local Embassies to coordinate information on available programmes and better guide students in their choice. It also provides a window for prospective international students wishing to study locally to secure information on tertiary education programmes available in tertiary institutions in Mauritius.

Data for academic year: 2011-2012
Source: IAU from Mauritius Tertiary Education Commission, 2012.

INSTITUTIONS

PUBLIC INSTITUTIONS

MAURITIUS INSTITUTE OF EDUCATION (MIE)

Réduit, Moka
Tel: +230(401) 6555
Fax: +230(454) 1037
EMail: registrar@mieonline.org
Website: http://www.mieonline.org/home/

Director: Sheela Thamcamamootoo EMail: director@mieonline.org

Registrar: O. Cudian

Centres
Distance Education

Schools
Applied Sciences (Design; Economics; Home Economics; Physical Education; Technology); **Arts and Humanities** (Business Education; English; French; Social Studies; Visual Arts); **Education** (Computer Education; Curriculum; Educational Administration; Multimedia; Science Education); **Science and Mathematics** (Mathematics Education; Natural Sciences)

History: Founded 1974.

Main Language(s) of Instruction: English, French

Accrediting Agencies: Tertiary Education Commission, Ministry of Education, Culture and Human Resources

Degrees and Diplomas: *Bachelor's Degree*; *Master's Degree*. Also Postgraduate Certificate in Education, Advanced Certificate in Educational Administration

Student Services: Academic counselling

Libraries: Yes

Last Updated: 09/07/12

OPEN UNIVERSITY OF MAURITIUS

Réduit, Moka
Tel: +230(403) 8200
Fax: +230(464) 8854
EMail: openuniversity@open.ac.mu
Website: http://www.open.ac.mu

Director-General: Kaviraj Sukon (2005-)
Tel: +230(454) 7897 EMail: directorgeneral@open.ac.mu

Administrative Officer: Isswar Jheengut

Centres
Open Learning Resources *Head*: Christine Ah Fat

Divisions
Distance Education (Arts and Humanities; Business and Commerce; Computer Engineering; Management; Preschool Education; Teacher Trainers Education; Tourism; Transport Engineering) *Associate Professor*: Roshun Dhurbarrylall; **Media** (Media Studies)

Institutes
Confucius (Chinese); **Language** (Modern Languages)

History: Founded 2012. The Mauritius College of the Air (MCA), which was established in 1971 has integrated the Open University of Mauritius in July 2012.

Governing Bodies: Board of Directors

Main Language(s) of Instruction: English

Degrees and Diplomas: *Bachelor's Degree*; *Master's Degree (MA)*: 2 yrs; *Doctor of Philosophy*. Also Professional Diploma and Advanced Diploma with CILT (UK)

Student Services: Academic counselling

Special Facilities: Computer Lab with internet facilities

Libraries: Yes; Learning Resources Centre

Academic Staff *2011-2012*	MEN	WOMEN	TOTAL
FULL-TIME	1	3	**4**
PART-TIME	44	14	**58**
PART-TIME	3	6	**9**
Student Numbers *2011-2012*			
All (Foreign Included)	666	318	**984**

Part-time students, 47. **Distance students**, 809.
Note: On-line Students: 128
Last Updated: 22/06/12

UNIVERSITY OF MAURITIUS (UOM)

Réduit, Moka
Tel: +230(454) 1041
Fax: +230(454) 9642
EMail: centraladmin@uom.ac.mu
Website: http://www.uom.ac.mu

Vice-Chancellor: Harry C. S. Rughooputh
Tel: +230(403) 7400, ext 7415, Fax: +230(466) 7900
EMail: vc@uom.ac.mu

International Relations: S. Rekha Issur-Goorah, Registrar
Tel: +230(403) 7425, Fax: +230(454) 9642
EMail: registrar@uom.ac.mu

Centres

Applied Social Research (Social Studies) *Officer-in-Charge*: Nigel Richards; **Information Technology and Systems** (Information Management; Information Technology; Systems Analysis) *Director*: Roshan Halkhoree; **Innovative Learning Technologies** *(Virtual)* (Computer Engineering; Educational Technology; Information Technology; Multimedia) *Officer-in-Charge*: M. Santally; **Professional Development and Lifelong Learning** (Computer Education; Information Technology; Library Science; Marine Transport; Nursing; Police Studies; Textile Technology) *Officer-in-Charge*: R. Rampersad

Faculties

Agriculture (Agricultural Engineering; Agricultural Management; Agriculture; Food Science) *Dean*: A Jaufeerally-Fakim; **Engineering** (Chemical Engineering; Civil Engineering; Computer Science; Electrical and Electronic Engineering; Engineering; Environmental Engineering; Industrial Engineering; Mechanical Engineering; Production Engineering; Textile Technology) *Dean*: T Ramjeeawon; **Law and Management** (Accountancy; Business Administration; Business and Commerce; Finance; International Business; Law; Management) *Dean*: A Ramgutty-Wong; **Science** (Biology; Chemistry; Health Sciences; Mathematics; Medicine; Natural Sciences; Physics) *Dean*: A. H. Subratty; **Social Studies and Humanities** (Arts and Humanities; Economics; English; French; History; Social Studies; Statistics) *Dean*: J Chan Low

History: Founded 1965.

Governing Bodies: Council; Senate

Academic Year: August to May (August-November; January-May)

Admission Requirements: General Certificate of Education (GCE) with pass at Ordinary 'O' level or equivalent in English Language, and either passes in 5 other subjects with at least 2 passes at 'A' level or passes in 3 other subjects at 'A' level, or the French Baccalauréat, or the IGCSE and the International Baccalauréat

Fees: (Mauritius Rupees): Mauritian secondary school leavers on full-time programmes, general fees, 14,400 per annum (no tuition fees). Mauritian students on part-time postgraduate programmes, general fees 16,000. Foreign students, general fees for undergraduate programmes, 15,200 and for postgraduate programmes: 16,800 per annum.

Main Language(s) of Instruction: English

International Co-operation: With universities in South Africa; United Kingdom; France; Canada

Degrees and Diplomas: *Diploma*: 2 yrs full-time; 2-3 yrs part-time; *Bachelor's Degree (BA/BSc/B.Eng/BEd)*: 3-4 yrs; *Bachelor's Degree*: Medicine; Surgery (MBBS), 6 yrs; *Master's Degree (MA/MBA/MSc)*: 1yr full-time, 2-3 yrs part-time; *Master of Philosophy (MPhil)*: 2-3 yrs, 3-4 yrs part-time; *Doctor of Philosophy (PhD)*: 3-5 yrs, 5-7 yrs part-time. Also Certificates and Diplomas, 1-2 yrs

Student Services: Academic counselling, Canteen, Cultural centre, Employment services, Handicapped facilities, Health services, Sports facilities

Special Facilities: 21 acre University Farm. Crop Museum. Mauritius Radio Telescope (MRT)

Libraries: 167,000 vols (including student dissertations) and 30.000 bound periodicals

Publications: University of Mauritius Research Journal, Science and Technology; Law and Management; Social Sciences; Humanities *(3 per annum)*

Last Updated: 26/06/12

UNIVERSITY OF TECHNOLOGY, MAURITIUS (UTM)

La Tour Koenig, Pointe aux Sables, Port Louis
Tel: +230(234) 7624
Fax: +230(234) 1660
EMail: director@umail.utm.ac.mu
Website: http://www.utm.ac.mu

Director-General: Dharmanand Goopt Fokeer

Registrar: Mahendra ChutturdharryFax: +230(234) 6727
EMail: registrar@umail.utm.ac.mu

Schools

Business, Management and Finance *(SBMF)* (Business Administration; Economics; Finance; Management; Public Administration) *Head*: Deepika Faugoo; **Innovative Technologies and Engineering** *(SITE)* (Applied Mathematics; Computer Engineering; Industrial Engineering; Software Engineering; Systems Analysis) *Head*: Mohammad Sameer Sunhaloo; **Sustainable Development and Tourism** *(SSDT)* (Environmental Studies; Leisure Studies; Tourism) *Head*: Chandradeo Bokhoree

History: Founded 2000 following merger of Mauritius Institute of Public Administration and Management (MIPAM) and SITRAC.

Governing Bodies: Board of Governors

Academic Year: August to June

Admission Requirements: 5 'O' level (pass) including English + 2 'A' level/'O' level in English (pass) + 3 'A' level/ French baccalaureat/IGCSE + International Baccalaureat

Fees: (Mauritius rupees): Administrative Fees: 1,000-9,700 per annum; Tuition fees: 5,000-60,000 per semester, depending on degrees. MBA: 140,000; Executive MBA (EMBA): 160,000

Main Language(s) of Instruction: English

International Co-operation: With universities in India and United Kingdom

Degrees and Diplomas: *Diploma*: Administration, Management, 1 yr full-time; *Diploma*: Financial Management with specialization in Public Finance, 2 yrs full-time; *Diploma*: Fisheries; Human Resources Management (DHRM); Public Administration; Management (DPAM), 3 yrs part-time; *Diploma*: Graphics Design; Manufacturing Information Systems; Business Process Outsourcing Management; Information Technology (run by IVTB); Journalism; Public Sector Financial Management (DPSFM); Purchasing and Supply Management (DPSM), 2 yrs full-time; 3 yrs part-time; *Diploma*: Tourism, 2 yrs (in collaboration with Constance Hospitality); *Bachelor's Degree*: Accounting with Business (BSc (Hons)), 3 yrs full-time; *Bachelor's Degree*: Actuarial Science; Computer Aided Design (BSc (Hons)); Economics; Management (BSc (Hons)); Finance; Finance with Law; Finance with Global Business; Finance with Insurance; Management; Management with Marketing; Management with Law; Management with Finance (BSc (Hons)); Graphics Design; Management and Marketing (BSc (Hons)); Mathematics; Web Technologies (BSc (Hons)), 3 yrs full-time; 4 1/2 yrs part-time; *Bachelor's Degree*: Banking and International Finance (BBIF); Tourism and Hospitality Management (BSc (Hon)), 3 yrs full-time, 4 yrs part-time; *Bachelor's Degree*: Business Administration (Top Up) (Accounting; Finance; Banking; Marketing) (BA (Hons)), 1 yr- 1 1/2 yrs (in collaboration with Suami Dayanand Institute of Management; *Bachelor's Degree*: Communication (BA (Hons)), 4 1/2 yrs part-time; *Bachelor's Degree*: Computer Applications (Top Up) (BSc (Hons)), 1yr full-time, 1 1/2 yrs part-time (Top-up Programme); *Bachelor's Degree*: Computer Science; Information Systems (Top Up) (BSc (Hons)), 1 yr full-time; 1 1/2 yrs part-time (in collaboration with Swami Dayanand Institute of Management); *Bachelor's Degree*: Counselling (BA (Hons)); Entrepreneurial Management (BSc (Hons)), 3 yrs full-time; 4 yrs part-time; *Bachelor's Degree*: Financial Management with specialization in Public Finance (Top up) (BSc (Hons)); Human Resources Management (Top up) (BSc (Hons)); Occupational Safety and Health Management (Top Up), 1 1/2 yrs part-time; *Bachelor's Degree*: Graphics Design (Upgrade), 1 yr full-time; 1 1/2 yrs part-time; *Bachelor's Degree*: Human Resource Management, 3 yrs full-time; 4 yrs part time; *Bachelor's Degree*: Occupational Safety and Health Management, 3 yrs full time; 4 1/2 yrs; *Bachelor's Degree*: Public Administration and Management (BPAM), 3-4 yrs (full-time; part-time); *Bachelor's Degree*: Public Sector Financial Management (BPSFM), 1 1/2 yrs part-time (Top-up Programme); *Bachelor's Degree*: Purchasing and Supply Management, 4 1/2 yrs; *Bachelor's Degree*: Purchasing and Supply Management (Top up) (BCs (Hons)), 1 1/2 yrs (part-time); *Bachelor's Degree*: Software Engineering; Business Information Systems; Information Technology Enabled Services, Computer Science with Network Security (BSc (Hons)), 3 yrs full-time, 4 1/2 yrs part-time; *Bachelor's Degree*: Telecommunications; Electronic Engineering (BSc (Hons)), 4 yrs full-time; 6 yrs part-time; *Master's Degree*: Applied Mathematics with Computing (MSc); Computer

Science and Engineering (MSc); Information Systems (MSc), 1 yrs full-time, 2 yrs part-time; *Master's Degree*: Banking and Finance (MSc), 1-2 yrs; *Master's Degree*: Biometry, 1 yr full-time; 2 yrs part-time; *Master's Degree*: Business Administration with: Educational Administration; Health Care Services; Hospitality Management; Retail Management; Marketing; Corporate Governance and Corporate Social Responsibility; Freight and Operation Management; Corporate Governance and Corporate Social Responsibility; Project Management for Sustainable Development; Quality Management; Public Sector Management (MPM); Tourism and Marketing, 2 yrs part-time; *Master's Degree*: Business Administration; Financial Risk Management; Business Intelligence with Knowledge; E-Business; Human Resource with Knowledge Management; Marketing; Logistics and Supply Chain Management; Project Management; Finance and Investment (MBA); Business Administration; Marketing (Executive MBA); Educational Administration and Technology; Health Administration; International Business and Economics (MSc); Gender Studies; Woman Studies (MA), 2 yrs; *Master's Degree*: Counselling (MA), 1 1/2 yrs-2 yrs (full-time; part-time); *Master's Degree*: Software Engineering; Financial Engineering; Computer Networking; Computer Security and Forensics; Business Enterprise Systems; Multimedia (MSc), 1 yr full-time; 1 1/2 yrs part-time; *Master's Degree*: Sustainable Environmental Management, 2 yrs part-time (jointly offered by UoM and UTM. Also certificate in Industrial Relations (1 1/2 yrs); Post Graduate Diploma in Integrated Resort Management (1 yr part-time). Foundation Access Courses for Undergraduate Programmes (1 yr)

Student Services: Academic counselling, Canteen, Sports facilities

Libraries: yes

Academic Staff *2011-2012*	**TOTAL**
FULL-TIME	**50**
PART-TIME	**200**
STAFF WITH DOCTORATE	
FULL-TIME	**10**
PART-TIME	c. **20**

Student Numbers *2011-2012*	
All (Foreign Included)	c. **1,400**

Part-time students, 820.

Last Updated: 09/07/12

Mexico

STRUCTURE OF HIGHER EDUCATION SYSTEM

Description:

The higher education system has three basic pillars: free public education, laicism in both public and private institutions, and the autonomy of public universities. It is made up of over 6,000 institutions (approx. 3,500 are private; the remaining 2,500 public). Public higher education institutions are of three types: federal, state, and autonomous. Universities must offer a minimum of 5 academic programmes at Bachelor, Master and Ph.D levels in at least 3 areas of knowledge.

Stages of studies:

University level first stage: *Licenciatura*
The usual entrance qualification is the Bachillerato. In addition, students normally have to take an entrance examination. Courses leading to the Licenciatura normally last between three to five years. Four years in Education and Nursing, five in Dentistry, Medicine and Veterinary Medicine.

University level second stage: *Maestría or Especialización*
Students must hold a Licenciatura. Studies leading to the title of Especialista last 1 or 2 years and two years for the title of Maestro.

University level third stage: *Doctorado*
Students must hold a Maestría. Studies last between 2 and 4 years.

ADMISSION TO HIGHER EDUCATION

Admission to university-level studies:

Name of secondary school credential required: Bachillerato

Foreign students admission:

Entrance exam requirements: Students must be in possession of the Bachillerato or its equivalent. For certain universities, admission is based on an entrance examination.

Entry regulations: Foreign students must hold a visa which they can obtain from the Mexican consulates (those who have a scholarship from the Government are entitled to an official visa).

Language requirements: Students must have a good knowledge of Spanish.

RECOGNITION OF STUDIES

Quality assurance system:

CIEES: Inter-institutional Committees for the Assessment of Higher Education (in charge of programme assessments);
COPAES: Council for Higher Education Accreditation (in charge of registering and authorizing programme accreditation agencies).
CENEVAL: National Centre for the Assessment of Higher Education (in charge the higher education exams);
FIMPES: Federation of Mexican Private Higher Education Institutions (in charge of the institutional accreditation of private institutions);
PNCP : National Programme of Postgraduate Courses of Quality (in charge of the assessment of research-based programmes);
Each institution carries out evaluations.

NATIONAL BODIES

Secretaría de Educación Pública - SEP (Ministry of Public Education)

Minister: José Ángel Córdova Villalobos
Director, Accreditation and Certification: José Alberto Escamilla Martinez
Under-Secretary, Higher Education: Fernando Serrano Migallón
Argentina 28
Centro Histórico
México, D.F. 06029
Tel: +52(55) 3601 1000
WWW: http://www.sep.gob.mx

Comités Interinstitucionales para la Evaluación de la Educación Superior, A.C. - CIEES (Inter-institutional Committees for the Assessment of Higher Education)

General Coordinator: Javier de la Garza Aguilar
Av. San Jerónimo No. 120 Col. Jardines del Pedregal.
Delegación Álvaro Obregón
México 04500
Tel: +52(55) 5550 0530
EMail: comites@ciees.edu.mx
WWW: http://www.ciees.edu.mx/
Role of national body: The Committees for the Assessment of Higher Education (CIEES) are nine bodies composed of scholars from higher education institutions of different regions. They are responsible for evaluating higher education programmes of study.

Consejo Nacional de Ciencia y Tecnología - CONACYT (National Science and Technology Council)

Director: Enrique Cabrero Mendoza
Av. Insurgentes Sur 1582
Col. Crédito Constructor
México, D.F. 03940
Tel: +52(55) 5322 7700
WWW: http://www.conacyt.gob.mx/

Consejo para la Acreditación de la Educación Superior - COPAES (Commission for the Accreditation of Higher Education)

Director-General: Luis Eduardo Zedillo Ponce de León
Cádiz Norte No. 35
Col. Extremadura Insurgentes. Delegación Benito Juárez
México 03740
Tel: +52(55) 5615 7281
WWW: http://www.copaes.org.mx/
Role of national body: The COPAES provides formal recognition to organizations whose purpose is to accredit academic and professional programmes of study.

Centro Nacional de Evaluación para la Educación Superior - CENEVAL (National Center for the Assessment of Higher Education)

Director-General: Rafael Vidal Uribe
Av. Camino al Desierto de los Leones (Altavista) 19, Col. San Ángel, Deleg. Álvaro Obregón
México, D.F. 01000
Tel: +52(55) 3000 8700
WWW: http://www.ceneval.edu.mx/
Role of national body: The National Center for the Assessment of Higher Education (CENEVAL) is a private non-profit organization whose main activity is the design and implementation of assessment tools of learning outcomes.

Coordinación de Universidades Politécnicas (Coordination of Polytechnics)

Fernando de Alva Ixtlilxochitl # 185, 5° Piso Col. Tránsito, Del. Cuauhtémoc
México, D.F. 06820

Tel: +52(55) 3600 4250
WWW: http://politecnicas.sep.gob.mx/

Asociación Mexicana de Educación Continua y a Distancia, A.C. - AMECYD (Mexican Association of Distance Education)

President: Rafael López Castañares
Ignacio Manuel Altamirano#114
Col. Cuauhtémoc
Toluca, Estado de México 50130
Tel: +52 01(722) 215 8671
Fax: +52 01 (722) 215 8697
WWW: http://amecyd.uaemex.mx/

Asociación Nacional de Universidades e Institutos de Enseñanza Superior - ANUIES (National Association of Universities and Higher Education Institutions)

Executive Secretary-General: Rafael López Castañares
Director-General: Teresa Sánchez Becerril
Tenayuca 200,
Col. Santa Cruz Atoyac
México, D.F. 03310
Tel: +52(55) 5420 4900
WWW: http://www.anuies.mx

Role of national body: ANUIES is a non-governmental organization that brings together the main public and private higher education institutions. Its mission is to promote excellence in teaching, research and the extension of culture and services.

Asociación Nacional de Universidades Tecnológicas A.C. - ANUT (National Association of Technological Universities)

President: Jesús María Contreras Esparza
Blvd. Universidad Tecnológica #225 Col. San Carlos
Leon 37670
Tel: +52(477) 710 0020
Fax: +52(477) 772 5340
WWW: http://www.anut.org.mx/

Consorcio de Universidades Mexicanas - CUMex (Mexican University Consortium)

President: Heriberto Grijalva Monteverde
Coordinator: Francisco Javier Castillo Yáñez
Mexico
WWW: http://www.cumex.org.mx/

Federación de Institutiones Mexicanas Particulares de Educación Superior, A.C. - FIMPES (Federation of Mexican Private Higher Education Institutions)

President: Ángel Eliseo Cano Garza
Secretary-General: Rodrigo Guerra Botello
Río Guadalquivir #50, 4° Piso
Col. Cuauhtémoc
México, D.F. 06500
Tel: +52(55) 5514 5514
Fax: +52(55) 5207 0581
WWW: http://www.fimpes.org.mx/

Data for academic year: 2012-2013
Source: IAU from Ministry of Public Education, Mexico, 2012

INSTITUTIONS

PUBLIC INSTITUTIONS

ANTONIO NARRO AUTONOMOUS AGRICULTURAL UNIVERSITY

Universidad Autónoma Agraria Antonio Narro (UAAAN)
Buenavista, 25315 Saltillo, Coahuila
Tel: +52(844) 411-02-00 +52(844) 411-03-44
EMail: rector@uaaan.mx
Website: http://www.uaaan.mx/v2

Rector: Eladio Heriberto Cornejo Oviedo

Departments
Agricultural Economics (Agricultural Business; Agricultural Economics); **Agricultural Mechanics** (Agricultural Engineering); **Forestry** (Forestry); **Horticulture** (Horticulture); **Nutrition and Food** (Food Science; Nutrition); **Parasitology** (Parasitology); **Sociology** (Sociology); **Soil Sciences** (Agricultural Engineering; Environmental Engineering; Soil Science)

Divisions
Agronomy (Agrobiology; Agronomy); **Animal Husbandry** (Animal Husbandry; Dairy; Veterinary Science; Zoology); **Socio-economic Sciences** (Agricultural Management; Economics; Social Sciences)

Programmes
Irrigation (Irrigation)

Further Information: Also Laguna unit

History: Founded 1923. Acquired present status 2006.

Governing Bodies: Consejo Universitario

Academic Year: August to May (August-December; January-May)

Admission Requirements: Secondary school certificate (bachillerato)

Main Language(s) of Instruction: Spanish

Degrees and Diplomas: *Licenciatura*: 4 yrs; *Maestría*: a further 2 yrs; *Doctorado*: 3 yrs following Maestría

Student Services: Academic counselling, Canteen, Cultural centre, Employment services, Foreign student adviser, Health services, Language programs, Nursery care, Sports facilities

Student Residential Facilities: Yes

Special Facilities: Biological Garden. Observatory. Meteorological Station. Radio Station

Libraries: Biblioteca Egidio Rebonato; Depository of American and Canadian Agricultural Libraries

Publications: Avances de Investigación; Revista Agraria *(biennially)*

Last Updated: 03/09/12

APPLIED CHEMISTRY RESEARCH CENTRE

Centro de Investigación en Química Aplicada (CIQA)
Blvd. Enrique Reyna Hermosillo 140, 25253 Saltillo, Coahuila
Tel: +52(844) 438-98-30
Fax: +52(844) 438-98-39
EMail: posgrado@ciqa.mx; coordinacion_posgrado@ciqa.mx
Website: http://www.ciqa.mx/

Director: Juan Méndez Nonell

Departments
Advanced Materials (Materials Engineering); **Applied Chemistry** (Applied Chemistry); **Plasticulture** (Agriculture; Polymer and Plastics Technology); **Polymer Processing** (Polymer and Plastics Technology); **Polymer Synthesis** (Polymer and Plastics Technology)

History: Founded 1976 and acquired present status and title 2000.

Degrees and Diplomas: *Licenciatura*; *Especialización*; *Maestría*; *Doctorado*

Libraries: Yes

Last Updated: 12/07/12

AUTONOMOUS METROPOLITAN UNIVERSITY

Universidad Autónoma Metropolitana (UAM)
Prolongación Canal de Miramontes, 3855, Col. Ex-Hacienda de San Juan de Dios, Delegación Tlapán, 14387 México, D.F.
Tel: +52(55) 56-03-33-40 +52(55) 54-83-56-44
Fax: +52(55) 56-03-19-14
EMail: paga@correo.uam.mx
Website: http://www.uam.mx

Rector: Enrique P. A. Fernández Fassnacht (2009-2013)

Secretaria General: Iris Santacruz Fabila
EMail: sg@correo.uam.mx

Divisions
Basic Sciences and Engineering (Biomedical Engineering; Chemical Engineering; Chemistry; Civil Engineering; Engineering; Environmental Engineering; Industrial Engineering; Mathematics; Mechanical Engineering; Physics); **Biology and Health Sciences** (Biological and Life Sciences; Health Sciences); **Communication and Design Sciences** (Communication Studies; Graphic Design; Information Sciences; Information Technology); **Natural Sciences and Engineering** (Applied Mathematics; Computer Engineering; Molecular Biology); **Sciences and Arts for Design** (Architecture; Graphic Design; Industrial Design); **Social Sciences and Humanities** (Arts and Humanities; Social Sciences)

Further Information: Also Unidad Azcapotzalco, Unidad Cuajimalpa, Unidad Iztapalapa, Unidad Lerma and Unidad Xochimilco

History: Founded 1974.

Governing Bodies: Academic Council

Academic Year: September to July (September-December; January-April; May-July)

Admission Requirements: Secondary school certificate (bachillerato) and entrance examination

Main Language(s) of Instruction: Spanish

Degrees and Diplomas: *Licenciatura*: Architecture; Agronomy; Animal Production Studies; Applied Mathematics; Biology; Business Administration; Biomedical Engineering; Chemistry; Civil Engineering; Computing Engineering; Computer Sciences; Chemical Engineering; Communication Sciences; Computing Engineering; Electrical Engineering; Energy Engineering; Environmental Engineering; Economics; Experimental Biology; Food Engineering, 4 yrs; *Licenciatura*: Graphic and Communication Design; Graphic Design; Hydrologic Engineering; Hydrobiology; Human Geographic; History; Hispanic Language Studies; Humanistic Studies; Industrial Biochemical Engineering; Industrial Design; Industrial Engineering; Information Technology Systems; Land Use Planning; Law Studies; Linguistics; Mathematics; Mechanical Engineering; Metallurgical Engineering; Medicine; Nutrition; Nursing; Physics; Physical Engineering; Pharmaceutical Science and Biological Chemistry; Political Science; Philosophy; Politics and Social Administration; Psychology; Social Psychology; Social Communication; Stomatology; Social Anthropology; Socio-economic Studies for Land Use Planning; Sociology; Veterinary Medicine and Zootechnical Science; *Especialización*: Design; Sciences & Engineering; Acupuncture & Phytotherapy; Oral Medicine & Pathology; Social Medicine; 20th Century Mexican Literature; Sociology of Higher Education; Historiography; Anthropological Sciences; Rural Development; Women's Studies; *Maestría*: Agricultural Sciences; Pharmaceutical Sciences; Social Medicine; Neurologic Rehabilitation; Population & Health; Public Health Science; Economics; Metropolitan Management & Public Politics; Historiography; Public Politics; Design; Sciences & Arts for Design; Computing Science; Science & Engineering; Structural Engineering; Computer Sciences & Information Technology; Applied & Industrial Mathematics; Biology; Experimental Biology; Biotechnology; Sociology; Anthropological Sciences; Organizational Studies; Humanities; Social Studies; Rural Development; Education Development & Management; Economy & Management of Technical Change; Social Psychology; Women's Studies; Communication & Politics; *Doctorado*: Design; Sciences and Arts for Design; Sciences & Engineering; Structural Engineering; Experimental Biology; Biotechnology; Biological Sciences;

Collective Health Sciences; Historiography; Sociology; Economic Sciences; Anthropological Sciences; Organizational Studies; Humanities; Social Studies; Rural Development; Social Sciences; Economic Science

Student Services: Academic counselling, Canteen, Cultural centre, Employment services, Foreign student adviser, Foreign Studies Centre, Handicapped facilities, Health services, Language programs, Nursery care, Social counselling, Sports facilities

Special Facilities: Three academic and cultural extension centres: Casa del Tiempo, Casa de la Primera Imprenta de América and Casa Rafael Galván. 10 art galleries across the University Campuses and the Office of the Dean. Museo del Libro (Book Museum) in the Casa de la Primera Imprenta de América; Casa de la Paz Theater; Bookshops in every University Campus and in the metropolitan area.

Libraries: Campus libraries.

Publications: Casa Abierta al Tiempo *(monthly)*; Ciencia desde la UAM *(quarterly)*; Revista Casa del Tiempo *(monthly)*

Press or Publishing House: University Press

Last Updated: 07/09/12

AUTONOMOUS UNIVERSITY OF AGUASCALIENTES

Universidad Autónoma de Aguascalientes (UAA)

Ave.Universidad 940, Ciudad Universitaria, 20131 Aguascalientes, Aguascalientes
Tel: +52(449) 910-74-00
EMail: cvargas@correo.uaa.mx
Website: http://www.uaa.mx

Rector: Mario Andrade Cervantes (2011-)
EMail: mandrace@correo.uaa.mx

Secretario General: Francisco Javier Avelar González
EMail: fjavelar@correo.uaa.mx

Centres

Agricultural Sciences and Veterinary Medicine (Agricultural Engineering; Agriculture; Agronomy; Veterinary Science); **Agronomy** (Agricultural Engineering; Agronomy; Industrial Engineering; Veterinary Science; Zoology); **Arts and Culture** (Acting; Art History; Cultural Studies; Literature; Music; Theatre); **Basic Sciences** (Anatomy; Applied Mathematics; Biochemistry; Biology; Chemistry; Computer Engineering; Computer Science; Electronic Engineering; Engineering; Mathematics; Microbiology; Pharmacology; Physics; Physiology; Statistics; Telecommunications Engineering); **Design and Construction Sciences** (Architecture; Civil Engineering; Construction Engineering; Design; Graphic Design; Industrial Design; Interior Design; Textile Design; Town Planning); **Economics and Administration** (Accountancy; Administration; Business Administration; Economics; Finance; Labour and Industrial Relations; Marketing; Tourism); **Health Sciences** (Dentistry; Medicine; Nursing; Optometry; Physical Education; Physical Therapy; Public Health; Surgery); **Social Sciences and Humanities** (Education; Educational Psychology; Foreign Languages Education; History; Information Sciences; Law; Literature; Philosophy; Political Sciences; Psychology; Public Administration; Social Work; Sociology; Spanish)

Further Information: Also South campus

History: Founded 1871 as Instituto Autónomo de Ciencias y Tecnología, acquired present title and status 1973. An autonomous institution financially supported by the State and federal governments.

Governing Bodies: Consejo Universitario; Consejo de Representantes; Junta de Gobierno

Academic Year: August to June (August-December; January-June)

Admission Requirements: Secondary school certificate (bachillerato)

Main Language(s) of Instruction: Spanish

International Co-operation: With universities in Spain, USA, Canada, France, United Kingdom. Also participates in Alfa

Degrees and Diplomas: *Licenciatura*: 8-10 semesters; *Especialización*: 1-2 yrs; *Maestría*: a further 2-3 yrs; *Doctorado*: 2-4 yrs

Student Services: Academic counselling, Cultural centre, Employment services, Handicapped facilities, Health services, Language programs, Sports facilities

Special Facilities: Museum; Art Gallery

Libraries: Yes

Publications: Investigación y Ciencia, Research reports *(biannually)*; Scientiae Naturae, Sciences *(biannually)*

Last Updated: 03/09/12

AUTONOMOUS UNIVERSITY OF BAJA CALIFORNIA

Universidad Autónoma de Baja California (UABC)

Apartado postal 3-459, Avenida Obregón y Julián Carrillo s/n, 21100 Mexicali, Baja California
Tel: +52(686) 552-23-79
Fax: +52(686) 552-95-40
EMail: rector@uabc.mx
Website: http://www.uabc.mx

Rector: Gabriel Estrella Valenzuela
Tel: +52(686) 553-44-61, Fax: +52(686) 552-23-79
EMail: rector@info.rec.uabc.mx

Faculties

Accountancy and Administration *(Tijuana)* (Accountancy; Business Administration; Business Computing; International Business); **Administration** (Accountancy; Business Administration; International Business; Management; Marketing; Tourism); **Administration and Social Sciences** *(Ensenada)* (Accountancy; Administration; Business Administration; Communication Studies; Computer Science; Educational Sciences; Law; Social Sciences); **Architecture and Design** *(Mexicali)* (Architecture; Graphic Design; Industrial Design); **Arts** (Cinema and Television; Dance; Fine Arts); **Chemistry and Engineering** *(Tijuana)* (Chemistry; Computer Engineering; Electronic Engineering; Industrial Chemistry; Industrial Engineering); **Economics** *(Tijuana)* (Economics); **Engineering** (Aeronautical and Aerospace Engineering; Bioengineering; Civil Engineering; Computer Engineering; Electrical and Electronic Engineering; Energy Engineering; Engineering; Industrial Engineering; Mechanical Engineering; Microelectronics); **Engineering and Trade** *(San Quintín, Ensenada)* (Accountancy; Agricultural Engineering; Business Administration; Computer Engineering; Engineering); **Engineering, Architecture and Design** *(Ensenada)* (Architecture; Bioengineering; Civil Engineering; Computer Engineering; Electronic Engineering; Industrial Engineering; Nanotechnology); **Human Sciences** (Communication Studies; Educational Sciences; History; Psychology; Sociology); **Humanities** *(Tijuana)* (Arts and Humanities; Communication Studies; History; Literature; Pedagogy; Philosophy; Sociology); **Languages** (Modern Languages; Translation and Interpretation); **Languages** *(Ensenada)* (Translation and Interpretation); **Law** (Law); **Law** *(Tijuana)* (Law); **Marine Science** *(Ensenada)* (Aquaculture; Biotechnology; Environmental Studies; Marine Science and Oceanography); **Medicine** (Medicine); **Medicine and Psychology** *(Tijuana)* (Medicine; Psychology); **Nursing** (Nursing; Nutrition); **Odontology** *(Mexicali)* (Dentistry); **Odontology** *(Tijuana)* (Dentistry); **Science** *(Ensenada)* (Biology; Computer Science; Mathematics; Natural Sciences; Physics); **Social and Political Sciences** (Political Sciences; Social Sciences)

Institutes

Agricultural Sciences (Agriculture); **Educational Development and Research** *(Ensenada)* (Educational Research); **Engineering** (Engineering); **History Research** *(Tijuana)* (History); **Oceanology Research** *(Ensenada)* (Marine Science and Oceanography); **Social Research** (Social Studies); **Veterinary Science Research** (Veterinary Science)

Schools

Arts *(Ensenada)* (Fine Arts; Music); **Pedagogy** *(Mexicali)* (Pedagogy); **Tourism** *(Tijuana)* (Tourism)

History: Founded 1957. An autonomous institution financially supported by the State and Federal governments.

Governing Bodies: Junta de Gobierno comprising 11 honorary members; Consejo Universitario, including representatives of the academic and administrative staff and of the students

Academic Year: August to June (August-December; January-June)

Admission Requirements: Secondary school certificate (bachillerato)

Main Language(s) of Instruction: Spanish

Degrees and Diplomas: *Licenciatura*: 4-5 yrs; *Especialización*: Auditing; Finance; Financial Administration; Fiscal Control; Human Resources Administration; Teaching; Telecommunications, a further 1-2 yrs; *Especialización*: Endodontics; Paediatrics; Orthodontics, a further 2-3 yrs; *Especialización*: Law, a further 1-2 yrs; *Maestría*: Accounting; Administration; Agricultural Sciences; Public Administration, a further 2-3 yrs; *Maestría*: Animal Production; Architecture; Coastal Oceanography; Economics; Law; Management of Ecosystems in Arid Regions; Nutrition; Science and Engineering; Special Education; Teaching and Educational Management; Veterinary Sciences, a further 2-3 yrs; *Maestría*: Public Health, a further 3-4 yrs; *Doctorado*: Agricultural Sciences, a further 4-5 yrs; *Doctorado*: Coastal Oceanography; Economics; Science and Engineering, a further 4-5 yrs

Student Services: Academic counselling, Canteen, Cultural centre, Employment services, Health services, Nursery care, Social counselling, Sports facilities

Special Facilities: University Museum. Art Gallery. Theatre

Libraries: Central Library, Mexicali; Tijuana; Ensenada

Publications: Calafia *(quarterly)*; Ciencias Marinas *(quarterly)*; Estudios Fronterizos *(quarterly)*; Revista Universitaria, Composed of Yubai; Divulgare; Paradigma and Semillero de Ideas which merged into one *(bimonthly)*

Press or Publishing House: Editorial Department

Last Updated: 03/09/12

AUTONOMOUS UNIVERSITY OF CAMPECHE

Universidad Autónoma de Campeche (UACAM)

Avenida Agustín Melgar s/n, Ciudad Universitaria, Col. Buenavista, 24030 Campeche, Campeche
Tel: +52(981) 811-98-00
EMail: ennasandoval@mail.uacam.mx
Website: http://www.uacam.mx

Rectora: Adriana del Pilar Ortiz Lanz
EMail: adrianaortiz@uacam.mx

Faculties

Accountancy and Administration (Accountancy; Administration; Finance); **Chemistry and Biology** (Biochemistry; Biology; Chemistry; Food Technology; Pharmacology); **Dentistry** (Dentistry; Surgery); **Engineering** (Civil Engineering; Computer Engineering; Electrical Engineering; Electronic Engineering; Energy Engineering; Engineering; Mechanical Engineering; Metal Techniques); **Humanities** (Arts and Humanities; History; Latin American Studies; Literature; Psychology; Spanish); **Law** (Law); **Medicine** (Medicine; Nutrition; Surgery); **Nursing** (Gerontology; Nursing; Physical Therapy); **Social Sciences** (Economics; Political Sciences; Public Administration)

Institutes

Ecology, Fishery and Oceanography *(Golfo de México)* (Ecology; Fishery; Marine Science and Oceanography)

Schools

Agronomy (Agricultural Business; Veterinary Science; Zoology)

History: Founded 1965 as Universidad del Sudeste. Acquired present title 1989.

Admission Requirements: Secondary school certificate (bachillerato) and entrance examination

Main Language(s) of Instruction: Spanish

Degrees and Diplomas: *Licenciatura*: Accountancy (Contador público); Animal Husbandry (Técnico agropecuario); Civil Engineering; Dentistry (Cirujano dentista); Law; Topographical Engineering (Topógrafo geodesta); *Licenciatura*: Medicine, 6 yrs; *Especialización*; *Maestría*; *Doctorado*

Libraries: Biblioteca Central "Gral. José Ortiz Ávila"

Last Updated: 04/09/12

AUTONOMOUS UNIVERSITY OF CHAPINGO

Universidad Autónoma Chapingo (UACHA)

Km. 38.5 Carretera México-Texcoco, 56230 Chapingo, Estado de México
Tel: +52(595) 952-15-27
EMail: relacionespublicas@correo.chapingo.mx
Website: http://www.chapingo.mx

Rector: Carlos Alberto Villaseñor Perea
EMail: rectoria@correo.chapingo.mx

Director General Académico: Ramón Valdivia Alcala
EMail: diaca@correo.chapingo.mx

Departments

Agricultural Ecology (Agriculture; Ecology); **Agricultural Parasitology** (Parasitology); **Agro-industrial Engineering** (Agricultural Engineering; Industrial Engineering); **Irrigation** (Irrigation); **Mechanical and Agricultural Engineering** (Agricultural Engineering; Mechanical Engineering); **Phytotechnology** (Agriculture; Ecology; Floriculture; Fruit Production; Genetics; Plant and Crop Protection); **Rural Sociology** (Rural Studies); **Soil Science** (Natural Resources; Soil Science); **Zoology** (Zoology)

Divisions

Economics and Administration (Agricultural Business; Agricultural Economics; International Business); **Forestry Sciences** (Ecology; Forest Products; Forestry; Statistics)

Further Information: Also Regional Unit of the Arid Zones in Bermejillo and unit in Puyacatengo

History: Founded 1854 as School of Agriculture, became university 1978. An autonomous institution under the jurisdiction of the Ministry of Agriculture, and financially supported by the State and federal governments.

Governing Bodies: Consejo Universitario; Consejos Departamentales

Academic Year: August to June (August-December; February-June)

Admission Requirements: Secondary school certificate (bachillerato) and entrance examination

Main Language(s) of Instruction: Spanish

Degrees and Diplomas: *Licenciatura*: 4 yrs; *Maestría*: a further 2 yrs; *Doctorado*

Student Services: Academic counselling, Employment services, Foreign student adviser, Health services, Language programs, Social counselling, Sports facilities

Student Residential Facilities: Yes

Special Facilities: Museo Nacional de Agricultura.

Libraries: Central Library. Department libraries

Publications: Agriculture Geographic *(biannually)*; Mexican Journal of Underbrush Science *(biannually)*; Revista Chapingo, 3 series: Horticulture, Forestry, Agronomy (published in English and Spanish) *(biannually)*

Last Updated: 03/09/12

AUTONOMOUS UNIVERSITY OF CHIAPAS

Universidad Autónoma de Chiapas (UNACH)

Colina Universitaria s/n, Col. Centro, 29020 Tuxtla Gutiérrez, Chiapas
Tel: +52(961) 617-80-00
EMail: rectoria@unach.mx
Website: http://www.unach.mx

Rector: Jaime Valls Esponda

Centres

Agronomy *(Maya)* (Agricultural Engineering; Agronomy; Forestry; Rural Planning; Veterinary Science)

Faculties

Accountancy and Administration (Accountancy; Administration; Computer Engineering; Management; Tourism); **Administration** *(Tapachula)* (Administration; Agricultural Business; International Business); **Agriculture** *(Huehuetán)* (Agriculture; Forestry; Tropical Agriculture); **Agronomy** *(Villaflores)* (Agronomy); **Architecture**

(Architecture); **Chemistry** *(Tapachula)* (Chemistry); **Engineering** (Civil Engineering; Mathematics; Physics); **Humanities** (Arts and Humanities; Communication Studies; Latin American Studies; Library Science; Literature; Pedagogy; Philosophy); **Law** *(San Cristóbal de Las Casas)* (Law); **Medicine** (Medicine; Surgery); **Social Sciences** *(San Cristóbal de Las Casas)* (Anthropology; Economics; History; Sociology); **Veterinary Medicine** (Veterinary Science; Zoology)

Schools

Administration *(Arriaga)* (Accountancy; Administration; Agricultural Engineering; Business Administration; Computer Networks; International Business; Management)

History: Founded 1975, incorporating previously existing schools.

Governing Bodies: Junta de Gobierno; Consejo Universitario

Academic Year: September to June (September-January; February-June)

Admission Requirements: Secondary school certificate (bachillerato) and entrance examination

Main Language(s) of Instruction: Spanish

Degrees and Diplomas: *Licenciatura*: 5 yrs; *Especialización*: 1 yr; *Maestría*: a further 2 yrs; *Doctorado*

Student Services: Academic counselling, Cultural centre, Health services, Sports facilities

Libraries: Specialized libraries of the Departments

Last Updated: 04/09/12

AUTONOMOUS UNIVERSITY OF CHIHUAHUA

Universidad Autónoma de Chihuahua (UACH)

Avenida Escorza y Venustiano Carranza S/N, Col. Centro, 31000 Chihuahua, Chihuahua

Tel: +52(614) 439-15-00

EMail: transparencia@uach.mx

Website: http://www.uach.mx

Rector: Jesús Enrique Seañez Sáenz (2010-2016)

Secretario General: Saúl Arnulfo Martínez Campos

Faculties

Accountancy and Administration (Accountancy; Administration; Business Administration; Business Computing; Finance; Management); **Agricultural Engineering** (Agricultural Engineering; Fruit Production; Horticulture; Regional Planning); **Agriculture and Forestry** *(Ciudad Delicias)* (Agriculture; Forestry); **Chemistry** (Chemical Engineering; Chemistry; Parasitology); **Dentistry** (Dentistry); **Engineering** (Aeronautical and Aerospace Engineering; Civil Engineering; Geological Engineering; Mathematics; Metallurgical Engineering; Mining Engineering; Physical Engineering; Production Engineering; Software Engineering); **International Economics** (Economics); **Law** (Law); **Medicine** (Medicine; Surgery); **Nursing and Nutrition** (Nursing; Nutrition); **Philosophy and Letters** (Arts and Humanities; English; History; Journalism; Literature; Philosophy); **Physical Education and Sports** (Physical Education; Sports); **Political and Social Sciences** *(Ciudad Juárez)* (Political Sciences; Social Sciences); **Psychology** *(Sigmund Freud)* (Psychology); **Zoology and Ecology** (Ecology; Zoology)

History: Founded 1954.

Governing Bodies: Consejo Universitario

Academic Year: September to June (September-January; February-June)

Admission Requirements: High School diploma or equivalent (bachillerato)

Main Language(s) of Instruction: Spanish

Degrees and Diplomas: *Licenciatura*: 4-5 yrs; *Especialización*; *Maestría*: a further 2 yrs; *Doctorado*

Student Services: Academic counselling, Cultural centre, Employment services, Foreign student adviser, Handicapped facilities, Health services, Language programs, Nursery care, Social counselling, Sports facilities

Special Facilities: Museum; Art Gallery

Libraries: Yes

Last Updated: 04/09/12

AUTONOMOUS UNIVERSITY OF CIUDAD DEL CARMEN

Universidad Autónoma del Carmen (UNACAR)

Calle 56, 4, Esq. Avenida Concordia, Col. Benito Juárez, 24180 Ciudad del Carmen, Campeche

Tel: +52(938) 381-10-18 Ext. 1315

EMail: slopez@delfin.unacar.mx

Website: http://www.unacar.mx

Rector: Sergio Augusto López Peña (2012-2016)

Faculties

Chemistry and Petroleum Engineering (Chemical Engineering; Chemistry; Petroleum and Gas Engineering); **Economics and Administration** (Accountancy; Administration; Business Administration; Business and Commerce; International Business; Marketing; Tourism); **Education and Humanities** (Education; English); **Engineering and Technology** (Civil Engineering; Electrical and Electronic Engineering; Engineering; Mechanical Engineering); **Health Sciences** (Clinical Psychology; Health Sciences; Nursing; Nutrition; Physical Education; Physical Therapy); **Information Sciences** (Computer Engineering; Computer Science); **Law** (Law); **Natural Sciences** (Marine Biology; Natural Sciences)

History: Founded 1967.

Academic Year: September to June (September-February; March-June)

Admission Requirements: Secondary school certificate (bachillerato) and entrance examination

Main Language(s) of Instruction: Spanish

Degrees and Diplomas: *Licenciatura*; *Especialización*; *Maestría*; *Doctorado*

Libraries: Yes

Last Updated: 07/09/12

AUTONOMOUS UNIVERSITY OF CIUDAD JUÁREZ

Universidad Autónoma de Ciudad Juárez (UACJ)

Apartado postal 1594-D, Henry Dunant, 4016, Zona Circuito Pronaf, 32310 Ciudad Juárez, Chihuahua

Tel: +52(656) 688-21-00

EMail: rduarte@uacj.mx

Website: http://www.uacj.mx

Rector: Ricardo Duarte Jáquez (2012-2018)

Centres

Language *(In separate campus)*

Divisions

Scientific Research

Institutes

Architecture, Design and Art (Architecture; Graphic Design; Industrial Design; Interior Design; Music; Urban Studies; Visual Arts); **Biomedical Sciences** (Biology; Chemistry; Dentistry; Medicine; Nursing; Nutrition; Veterinary Science); **Engineering and Technology** (Aeronautical and Aerospace Engineering; Biomedical Engineering; Civil Engineering; Computer Engineering; Electrical Engineering; Electronic Engineering; Energy Engineering; Industrial Engineering; Mathematics; Mechanical Engineering; Physical Engineering; Software Engineering; Telecommunications Engineering); **Social Sciences and Administration** (Accountancy; Administration; Business Administration; Education; Law; Literature; Psychology; Social Sciences; Social Work; Sociology; Tourism)

Further Information: Campuses at Nuevo Casas Grandes, Campus Cuauhtémoc, Ciudad Universitaria

History: Founded 1973.

Governing Bodies: Consejo Universitario

Academic Year: January to December (January-June; August-December)

Admission Requirements: Secondary school certificate (bachillerato) and entrance examination. Secondary school or High School Diploma (bachillerato) for BA & BS, and BA & BS for graduate programmes

Fees: (US Dollars): 1,000 per semester except for Medicine and Dentistry

Main Language(s) of Instruction: Spanish

International Co-operation: With universities in USA, Latin America, Spain, Canada, United Kingdom

Accrediting Agencies: Medicine (AMFEM); CIEES; Secretaria de Educación Pública (SEP); Asociación Nacional de Universidades e Instituciones de Educación Superior (ANUIES)

Degrees and Diplomas: *Licenciatura*: 4-5 yrs; *Especialización*: Dentistry, Medicine, 2 yrs; *Maestría*: Social Sciences, Administration, Education, Economy, a further 2 yrs; *Doctorado*: Social Sciences, 3 yrs

Student Services: Academic counselling, Canteen, Cultural centre, Employment services, Foreign student adviser, Foreign Studies Centre, Handicapped facilities, Health services, Language programs, Nursery care, Social counselling, Sports facilities

Student Residential Facilities: No

Special Facilities: Theatre

Libraries: Main Library, and campus facilities. On-line services

Publications: Avances *(bimonthly)*

Last Updated: 04/09/12

AUTONOMOUS UNIVERSITY OF COAHUILA

Universidad Autónoma de Coahuila (UADEC)

Blvd. V. Carranza s/n, Col. República Oriente, 25280 Saltillo, Coahuila

Tel: +52(844) 438-16-20

EMail: mochoa@mail.uadec.mx

Website: http://www.uadec.mx

Rector: Mario Ochoa Rivera

Faculties

Administration and Accountancy (Accountancy; Administration; Business Administration; Human Resources; Taxation); **Chemistry** (Chemistry); **Civil Engineering** (Civil Engineering; Engineering); **Dentistry** (Dentistry); **Economics** (Economics); **Education and Human Sciences** (Arts and Humanities; Education; Social Sciences); **Law** (Law); **Marketing** (Marketing); **Mathematics and Physics** (Mathematics; Physics); **Medicine** (Medicine); **Systems** (Systems Analysis)

Higher Schools

Music (Music)

Schools

Architecture (Architecture); **Communication Sciences** (Communication Studies); **Nursing** (Nursing); **Plastic Arts** (Fine Arts; Painting and Drawing; Sculpture); **Political and Social Sciences** (Political Sciences; Public Administration; Regional Planning; Social Sciences; Sociology); **Psychology** (Psychology); **Social Work** (Social Work)

Further Information: Also campuses at Torreón and Monclova

History: Founded 1957.

Governing Bodies: Consejo Universitario

Academic Year: August to June (August-December; January-June)

Admission Requirements: Secondary school certificate (bachillerato) and entrance examination

Main Language(s) of Instruction: Spanish

International Co-operation: Participates in CONAHEC; CREPUQ; ANUIES; NAMP; CRUE; DAAD; IMHE

Degrees and Diplomas: *Licenciatura*; *Especialización*: Medicine; *Maestría*; *Doctorado*

Student Services: Academic counselling, Cultural centre, Foreign student adviser, Language programs, Nursery care, Social counselling, Sports facilities

Student Residential Facilities: for female students

Special Facilities: Museo 'Ateneo Fuente'. Museo Preparatorio 'Venustiano Carranza'

Libraries: Yes

Last Updated: 27/03/13

AUTONOMOUS UNIVERSITY OF GUERRERO

Universidad Autónoma de Guerrero (UAGRO)

Avenida Javier Méndez Aponte, 1, Col. Servidor Agrario, 39070 Chilpancingo de Los Bravo, Guerrero

Tel: +52(747) 471-93-10

EMail: rector@uagro.mx

Website: http://www.uagro.mx

Rector: Alberto Salgado Rodríguez

Faculties

Mathematics (Mathematics)

Units

Architecture and Town Planning (Architecture; Town Planning); **Communication Sciences and Marketing** (Communication Studies; Marketing); **Economics** (Economics; Finance); **Engineering** (Civil Engineering; Computer Engineering; Construction Engineering; Engineering; Surveying and Mapping); **Natural Sciences** (Biological and Life Sciences; Biology; Chemistry; Pharmacy); **Nursing 1** (Nursing); **Philosophy and Letters** (Arts and Humanities; Philosophy); **Social Anthropology** (Anthropology; Ethnology)

Further Information: Campuses at Acapulco (Zona Sur) and Iguala (Zona Norte)

History: Founded 1869, reorganized 1960.

Admission Requirements: Secondary school certificate (bachilletato) and entrance examination

Main Language(s) of Instruction: Spanish

Degrees and Diplomas: *Licenciatura*: Accountancy (Contador público); Agricultural Engineering (Agrónomo); Chemical Biology (Químico biólogo); Economics; History; Ibero-American Literature; Law; Philosophy; Sociology; Topography and Geology (Topógrafo y Geodesta); Tourism; *Licenciatura*: Medicine, 6 yrs; *Especialización*; *Maestría*; *Doctorado*

Libraries: Yes

Last Updated: 04/09/12

AUTONOMOUS UNIVERSITY OF NAYARIT

Universidad Autónoma de Nayarit (UAN)

Ciudad de la Cultura Amado Nervo, 63155 Tepic, Nayarit

Tel: +52(311) 211-88-00

EMail: contact@uan.edu.mx

Website: http://www.uan.edu.mx

Rector: Juan López Salasar EMail: rectoria@uan.edu.mx

Areas

Art (Music); **Basic Science and Engineering** (Automation and Control Engineering; Chemical Engineering; Computer Engineering; Electronic Engineering; Mathematics; Mechanical Engineering); **Biology and Fishery** (Agronomy; Biology; Fishery; Veterinary Science; Zoology); **Economics and Administration** (Accountancy; Administration; Business and Commerce; Economics; Marketing; Tourism); **Health Sciences** (Dentistry; Medicine; Nursing; Nutrition; Physical Education; Sports; Surgery); **Social Sciences and Humanities** (Applied Linguistics; Communication Studies; Educational Sciences; Law; Media Studies; Philosophy; Political Sciences; Psychology)

History: Founded 1962 as institute, became university 1969 and acquired present status and title 1985.

Academic Year: September to July (September-January; March-July)

Admission Requirements: Secondary school certificate (bachillerato) and entrance examination

Main Language(s) of Instruction: Spanish

Degrees and Diplomas: *Licenciatura*: Accountancy (Contador público); Law (Abogado); Nursing (Enfermera general); *Licenciatura*: Dentistry (Cirujano dentista); Economics; Engineering; Tourism; Veterinary Medicine and Animal Husbandry (Médico veterinario zootecnista), 5 yrs; *Licenciatura*: Medicine, 6 yrs; *Especialización*; *Maestría*; *Doctorado*

Libraries: Central Library; libraries of the schools

Publications: Revista Convergencia *(biannually)*

Last Updated: 05/09/12

AUTONOMOUS UNIVERSITY OF NUEVO LEÓN

Universidad Autónoma de Nuevo León (UANL)

Avenida Universidad s/n, Ciudad Universitaria, 66451 San Nicolás de los Garza, Nuevo León
Tel: +52(81) 83-29-40-00
EMail: jesus.ancer@uanl.mx
Website: http://www.uanl.mx

Rector: Jesus Ancer Rodríguez (2009-)

Faculties

Accountancy and Administration (Accountancy; Administration; Finance; Human Resources; Information Technology; International Business; Marketing); **Agronomy** (Agricultural Business; Agriculture; Agronomy; Biotechnology; Food Technology); **Architecture** (Architecture; Industrial Design); **Biology** (Biology; Biotechnology; Food Science; Immunology; Microbiology; Parasitology); **Chemistry** (Chemical Engineering; Chemistry; Industrial Chemistry); **Civil Engineering** (Civil Engineering; Construction Engineering; Environmental Engineering; Structural Architecture); **Communication Sciences** (Communication Studies); **Dentistry** (Dentistry; Orthodontics; Periodontics; Surgery); **Earth Sciences** (Earth Sciences; Geology; Mineralogy; Petroleum and Gas Engineering); **Economics** (Economics; Finance); **Forestry** (Forestry); **Law and Criminology** (Commercial Law; Constitutional Law; Criminology; Labour Law; Law); **Mathematics and Physics** (Computer Science; Mathematics; Multimedia; Physics); **Mechanical and Electrical Engineering** (Aeronautical and Aerospace Engineering; Automation and Control Engineering; Electrical Engineering; Electronic Engineering; Mechanical Engineering; Software Engineering; Telecommunications Engineering); **Medicine** (Anaesthesiology; Anatomy; Cardiology; Dermatology; Gynaecology and Obstetrics; Medicine; Ophthalmology; Radiology; Surgery); **Music** (Conducting; Music; Music Theory and Composition; Musical Instruments; Singing); **Nursing** (Nursing); **Philosophy and Letters** (Arts and Humanities; Bilingual and Bicultural Education; English; French; History; Library Science; Literature; Philosophy; Social Sciences; Sociology; Translation and Interpretation); **Political Science and Public Administration** (International Relations; Political Sciences; Public Administration); **Psychology** (Psychology); **Public Health and Nutrition** (Nutrition; Public Health); **Scenic Arts** (Dance; Performing Arts; Theatre); **Social Work and Human Development** (Development Studies; Social Work); **Sport** (Sports); **Veterinary Medicine and Animal Husbandry** (Animal Husbandry; Veterinary Science); **Visual Arts** (Cinema and Television; Painting and Drawing; Sculpture; Visual Arts)

History: Founded 1933 as Universidad de Nuevo León and acquired present status and title 1971.

Governing Bodies: Consejo Universitario

Academic Year: August to July (August-December; January-June)

Admission Requirements: Secondary school certificate (bachillerato)

Fees: (US Dollars): 300 per semester; foreign students, 1,100 per semester

Main Language(s) of Instruction: Spanish

International Co-operation: With universities in Spain, Germany, USA, France, Chile, Canada, Brazil

Degrees and Diplomas: *Licenciatura*: Agricultural Engineering; Environmental Agrobusiness Engineering; Food Industry Engineering; Computer Science; Physics; Economics; Mathematics; Political Science and Public Administration; International Relations; Visual Arts; Graphic Design; Audi-Visual Languages, 4 1/2 yrs; *Licenciatura*: Architecture; Industrial Design; Biology; Chemistry, Bacteriology and Parasitology; Food Science; Civil Engineering; Dentistry; Forest Engineering; Natural Resources Management Engineering; Genomic Biotechnology; Geophysical Engineering; Geological Engineering; Mineralogical and Geological Engineering; Industrial Administration Engineering; Chemical Engineering; Industrial Chemistry; Chemistry, Pharmacy and Biology; Public Accountancy; Administration; Administrative Informatics; International Business; Systems Administration Eng.; Electronics and Automation Eng.; Electronics and Communications Eng.; Manufacturing Eng.; Materials Eng.; Mechanical Administration Eng.; Mechanical and Electrical Eng.; Mechatronics Eng.; Veterinary Medicine and Animal Husbandry; *Licenciatura*: Clinical Chemistry and Biology; Communication Sciences; Criminology; Law; Library and Information Science; Philosophy and Humanities; History and Humanity Studies; Mexican Literature; Sociology; Education; Language Sciences; Music and Instruments; Music and Singing; Music and Writing; Music and Choir Director; Music Education; Nutrition; Psychology; Social Work & Human Development, 5 yrs; *Licenciatura*: Contemporary Dance, 2 yrs; *Licenciatura*: Nursing; Sports; Theatre Arts, 4 yrs; *Licenciatura*: Surgery and Obstetrics, 6 yrs; *Especialización*; *Maestría*: Agricultural and Animal Production; Construction Administration; Planning of Human Settlements; Architectural Design; Property Valuation; Arts; Comm. Science; Geology; Teleinformatics; Industrial Physics Eng.; Forestry; Public Policy and Management; Information Eng.; Veterinary Science; Dentistry; Dentistry Education; Advanced Dentistry; Restoring Dentistry; Exercise Sciences; Clinical Psychoanalysis; Labor and Organisational Psychology; Occupational Health; Public Health; Orientation and Social Work; International Business; Human Resources; Information Technology; Law; Fiscal Law; Constitutional Law and Government; Procedural Constitutional Law; Criminology; Alternative Methods of Dispute Resolution; Economics; Finance; Nursing; Higher Education; International Relations; Administration; Ceramics and Glass Tech.; Chemical Eng.; Industrial Microbiology; Science; Industrial Eng.; Auditing; International Accounting; Costs and Budget; Finance; Public Administration; Taxes and Fiscal Studies; Marketing; Science Teaching; English Teaching as a Second Language; Underground Hydrology; Environmental Eng.; Transit Eng.; Structural Eng.; Industrial Adm. and Business; Telecom. Eng.; Manufacturing Eng.; Electrical Eng.; Mechanical Eng.; System Eng.; Engineering; *Doctorado*: Agricultural Science; Science (Livestock); Architecture and Urban Affairs; Biological Science; Biotechnology; Microbiology; Geosciences; Physics Eng.; Natural Resources Management; Political Science; Ceramic Eng.; Chemistry; Administration; Law; Nursing (DSc.); Philosophy; Construction Materials and Structures; Systems Eng.; Materials Eng.; Electrical Eng.; Medicine; Veterinary Science; Psychology; Social Work and Social Welfare Compared Politics; Social Science (Sustainable Development)

Student Services: Academic counselling, Canteen, Cultural centre, Employment services, Foreign student adviser, Handicapped facilities, Health services, Language programs, Nursery care, Social counselling, Sports facilities

Libraries: Raúl Rangel Frias Central Library and 26 school libraries

Publications: Armas y Letras *(annually)*; Ciencia UANL *(quarterly)*; Humanitas *(annually)*; Ingenierías *(quarterly)*; Medicina Universitaria *(quarterly)*; Perspectivas Sociales *(biannually)*; Revista Salud Pública y Nutrición *(quarterly)*; Trayectorias *(quarterly)*

Last Updated: 05/09/12

AUTONOMOUS UNIVERSITY OF QUERÉTARO

Universidad Autónoma de Querétaro (UAQ)

Apartado postal 184, Edificio de Rectoría, Centro Universitario, Cerro de las Campanas, 76017 Querétaro, Querétaro
Tel: +52(442) 216-32-12 al 16 Ext. 101 y 102
Fax: +52(442) 216-76-59 +52(442) 216-85-15
EMail: rectoria@uaq.mx
Website: http://www.uaq.mx

Rector: Gilberto Herrera Ruiz (2012-)

Faculties

Accountancy and Administration (Accountancy; Business Administration; Finance; International Business); **Chemistry** (Agriculture; Applied Chemistry; Chemistry; Food Science; Pharmacy); **Computer Science** (Computer Science; Systems Analysis); **Engineering** (Applied Mathematics; Automation and Control Engineering; Civil Engineering; Engineering; Mechanical Engineering); **Fine Arts** (Cinema and Television; Fine Arts; Graphic Design; Music; Music Theory and Composition; Musical Instruments; Painting and Drawing; Sculpture; Visual Arts); **Languages and Letters** (Arts and Humanities; English; French; Literature; Modern Languages; Spanish); **Law** (Criminology; Law); **Medicine** (Medicine); **Natural Sciences** (Biology; Horticulture; Natural Sciences; Nutrition; Veterinary Science; Zoology); **Nursing** (Nursing; Physical Education; Physical Therapy; Public Health; Sports); **Philosophy** (Anthropology; History; Philosophy); **Political and Social Science** (Communication Studies; Journalism; Political Sciences; Public Administration; Sociology); **Psychology** (Psychology)

History: Founded as college 1625, became university 1951.

Governing Bodies: Consejo Universitario

Academic Year: August to June (August-December; January-June)

Admission Requirements: Secondary school certificate (bachillerato) or equivalent, and entrance examination

Main Language(s) of Instruction: Spanish

Degrees and Diplomas: *Licenciatura*: Accountancy (Contador público); Biology (Biólogo); Chemistry (Químico); Civil Engineering; Instrumentation and Control Processing Engineering; Medicine (Médico); Nursing (Enfermera general); Veterinary Medicine and Animal Husbandry (Médico veterinario zootecnista); *Licenciatura*: Business Administration; Law; Psychology; Sociology, 4-10 sem; *Especialización*; *Maestría*: Administration; Clinical Psychology; Construction; Education; Food Technology; Hydrology; Law; Mathematics; Philosophy; *Doctorado*

Student Services: Academic counselling, Cultural centre, Employment services, Foreign student adviser, Handicapped facilities, Health services, Social counselling, Sports facilities

Libraries: Central Library

Press or Publishing House: Imprenta Universitaria

Last Updated: 06/09/12

AUTONOMOUS UNIVERSITY OF SAN LUIS POTOSÍ

Universidad Autónoma de San Luis Potosí (UASLP)

Álvaro Obregón, 64, Col. Zona Centro, 78000 San Luis Potosí, San Luis Potosí

Tel: +52(444) 826-13-80

EMail: rectoria@uaslp.mx

Website: http://www.uaslp.mx

Rector: Manuel Fermin Villar Rubio EMail: villarm@uaslp.mx

Faculties

Accountancy and Administration (Accountancy; Administration; Agricultural Business; Public Administration); **Agronomy** (Agricultural Engineering; Agrobiology; Agronomy; Ecology; Veterinary Science; Zoology); **Architecture** (Architecture; Building Technologies; Construction Engineering; Graphic Design; Industrial Design; Restoration of Works of Art); **Chemistry** (Biochemistry; Chemical Engineering; Chemistry; Food Science; Pharmacy); **Economics** (Economics; International Business); **Engineering** (Agricultural Engineering; Arid Land Studies; Civil Engineering; Earth Sciences; Electrical Engineering; Engineering; Geology; Hydraulic Engineering; Industrial Engineering; Mechanical Engineering; Metallurgical Engineering; Surveying and Mapping); **Medicine** (Medicine; Surgery); **Nursing** (Nursing; Nutrition; Public Health); **Psychology** (Psychology); **Science** (Biology; Biomedicine; Electronic Engineering; Mathematics; Nanotechnology; Natural Sciences; Physical Engineering; Physics; Telecommunications Engineering); **Stomatology** (Dentistry; Stomatology)

Schools

Communication Studies (Communication Studies); **Information Sciences** (Archiving; Library Science); **Social Sciences and Humanities** (Anthropology; Archaeology; Arts and Humanities; Geography (Human); History; Social Sciences)

Units

Altiplano Region (Chemical Engineering; Electronic Engineering; Marketing; Mechanical Engineering; Nursing)

Further Information: Also campus Huasteca Sur

History: Founded 1624 as First School of Letters. Became First Guadalupano College 1826, First Institute of Science and Literature 1828. Acquired university status 1923, and became an autonomous institution 1934.

Governing Bodies: Junta de Gobierno

Academic Year: August to June

Admission Requirements: Secondary school certificate (bachillerato) and entrance examination

Fees: (Pesos): 2,000-4,000

Main Language(s) of Instruction: Spanish

International Co-operation: With universities in Spain, France,USA, Canada, Japan

Accrediting Agencies: Inter-Institutional Committee of Evaluation; Consejo par la Acreditación de la Educación Superior, A.C.

Degrees and Diplomas: *Licenciatura*: Agronomy; Engineering; Chemistry, 8-10 sems; *Licenciatura*: Library Sciences; Physics; Mathematics, 8 sem; *Licenciatura*: Medicine, 6 yrs; *Licenciatura*: Nursing; Business Administration; Accountancy; History; Geography; Anthropology, 9 sem; *Licenciatura*: Psychology; Law; Economics; Foreign Trade; Architecture; Graphic Design; Industrial Design, 10 sem; *Especialización*: Anatomy Pathology; Anaesthesiology; Surgery; Dermatology;Ophthalmology; Paediatrics; Medicine; Radiology; Nursing, 3 yrs; *Especialización*: Psychiatry; Gynaecology and Obstetrics, 4 yrs; *Maestría*: Education; Medicine; Architecture, 2 yrs; *Maestría*: Law and Research, 3 sem; *Maestría*: Physics; Applied Sciences; Chemistry; Engineering; Stomatology; Nursing, 4 sem; *Doctorado*

Student Services: Academic counselling, Canteen, Cultural centre, Employment services, Foreign student adviser, Foreign Studies Centre, Health services, Language programs, Nursery care, Sports facilities

Special Facilities: Minerals Museum. Botanical Garden. Art Gallery. Arts and Cultural Centre. Radio station

Libraries: Yes

Publications: Cuadrante *(bimonthly)*; Horizonte Contable *(bimonthly)*; Universitarios Potosinos *(bimonthly)*

Last Updated: 16/05/12

AUTONOMOUS UNIVERSITY OF SINALOA

Universidad Autónoma de Sinaloa (UAS)

Ángel Flores y Riva Palacio s/n, Edificio Central, Col. Centro, 80000 Culiacán, Sinaloa

Tel: +52(66) 7759-4529

Fax: +52(66) 7759-4529

EMail: americal@uas.edu.mx

Website: http://www.uas.edu.mx/

Rector: Víctor Antonio Corrales Burgueño (2009-)
EMail: rector@uas.uasnet.mx

Academic Secretary: Ismael García Castro

International Relations: América M. Lizárraga González, Director, International Relations and Outreach

Centres

Language Studies *(Culiacán)* (Modern Languages)

Faculties

Accountancy and Administration (Accountancy; Administration); **Agronomy** (Agricultural Business; Agricultural Economics; Agricultural Equipment; Agricultural Management; Agriculture); **Architecture** (Architectural and Environmental Design; Architecture; Regional Planning; Rural Planning; Structural Architecture; Town Planning); **Chemical and Biological Sciences** (Biomedicine; Food Science; Food Technology); **Computer Science** (Computer Science); **Dentistry** (Dentistry); **Economics and Social Sciences** (Accountancy; Administration; Business and Commerce; Economics; Finance; International Studies; Law; Marketing; Political Sciences; Psychology; Sociology); **Educational Sciences** (Educational Sciences); **Engineering** (Biomedical Engineering; Civil Engineering; Engineering; Industrial Engineering; Software Engineering); **History** (History); **International Studies and Public Policy** (American Studies; International Studies; Political Sciences); **Law** *(Culiacán)* (Law); **Medicine** (Medicine); **Medicine** *(Culiacán)* (Medicine); **Psychology** (Psychology); **Social Work** (Social Work)

Schools

Anthropology (Anthropology)

History: Founded 1873 as Liceo Rosales, became Universidad de Occidente 1918 and Universidad Socialista del Noroeste 1937, Universidad de Sinaloa 1941 and Universidad Autónoma 1965.

Governing Bodies: University Council

Academic Year: August to June (August-December; January-June)

Admission Requirements: Secondary school certificate (bachillerato)

Fees: (Euros): 100 per annum

Main Language(s) of Instruction: Spanish, English

International Co-operation: With institutions in Chile, Colombia, Brazil, Canada, Thailand and the Caribbean

Degrees and Diplomas: *Licenciatura*: 5 yrs; *Especialización*; *Maestría*: a further 2 yrs; *Doctorado*

Student Services: Academic counselling, Cultural centre, Employment services, Foreign student adviser, Handicapped facilities, Health services, Language programs, Nursery care, Social counselling, Sports facilities

Special Facilities: Cultural Centres; Computer Centres; Languages Centres; Cultural Extension and Services Coordination; Art Galleries; University Radio; Laboratory of Chemical Sciences; Accounting and Administration Research; Institute of Economic and Social Research

Libraries: Central Library, libraries of the schools

Press or Publishing House: University Press

Last Updated: 25/02/13

AUTONOMOUS UNIVERSITY OF SOUTH BAJA CALIFORNIA

Universidad Autónoma de Baja California Sur (UABCS)

Apartado postal 19-B, Carretera al Sur Km 5.5, 23080 La Paz, Baja California Sur

Tel: +52(612) 128-00-44

Fax: +52(612) 123-88-14

EMail: webmaster@uabcs.mx

Website: http://www.uabcs.mx

Rector: Gustavo Rodolfo Cruz Chávez EMail: gcruz@uabcs.mx

Areas

Agricultural Sciences (Agriculture; Animal Husbandry; Biotechnology); **Marine Science** (Aquaculture; Fishery; Geology; Marine Biology; Marine Science and Oceanography); **Social Sciences and Humanities** (Economics; English; Environmental Studies; French; German; History; International Business; Law; Literature; Modern Languages; Natural Resources; Political Sciences; Public Administration; Regional Studies; Social Sciences)

History: Founded 1975. An autonomous State university financially supported by the State and federal governments.

Governing Bodies: Consejo Universitario

Academic Year: January to December (January-June; August-December)

Admission Requirements: Secondary school certificate (bachillerato) and entrance examination

Main Language(s) of Instruction: Spanish, English, French, German

Degrees and Diplomas: *Licenciatura*: Agricultural Business; Computer Development Engineering; Economics; Foreign Commerce; Geology; History; Literature; Marine Biology; Philosophy, 8 sem; *Licenciatura*: Agricultural Engineering; Fisheries Engineering; Law, 10 sem; *Licenciatura*: Political Science and Public Administration; Zootechnical Engineering, 9 sem; *Especialización*: Computer Systems, 2 sem; *Maestría*: Science in Animal Husbandry; Science in Aquaculture; Science in Economics of the Environment and Natural Resources; Science in Regional History, a further 3-4 sem; *Doctorado*: 2 sem

Student Services: Academic counselling, Cultural centre, Health services, Sports facilities

Special Facilities: Natural History Museum. Video and Radio Studio

Libraries: Biblioteca Dr Rubén Cardoza Macías

Publications: Scientific Research in Agricultural Science magazine *(bimonthly)*; Scientific Research in Marine Sciences magazine *(bimonthly)*

Last Updated: 03/09/12

AUTONOMOUS UNIVERSITY OF TAMAULIPAS

Universidad Autónoma de Tamaulipas (UAT)

Matamoros 8 y 9, Colonia Centro, 87000 Ciudad Victoria, Tamaulipas

Tel: +52(834) 318-18-00

EMail: jlavin@uat.edu.mx

Website: http://www.uat.edu.mx

Rector: José María Leal Gutiérrez

Faculties

Architecture, Design and Urban Studies *(Tampico)* (Architecture; Graphic Design; Interior Design); **Commerce and Administration** (Accountancy; Administration; Business and Commerce; Computer Science); **Commerce, Administration and Social Sciences** *(Nuevo Laredo)* (Accountancy; Business Administration; Business and Commerce; Computer Science; International Business; Law; Social Sciences); **Dentistry** *(Tampico)* (Dental Technology; Dentistry); **Engineering** *(Tampico)* (Civil Engineering; Computer Engineering; Industrial Engineering); **Engineering and Science** (Agronomy; Ecology; Environmental Studies; Telecommunications Engineering); **Medicine** *(Tampico)* (Biomedicine; Medicine; Paramedical Sciences; Rehabilitation and Therapy; Surgery); **Medicine and Computer Engineering** *(Matamoros)* (Computer Engineering; Health Sciences; Medicine; Technology); **Music** *(Tampico)* (Art Education; Music); **Nursing** *(Tampico)* (Nursing); **Nursing** *(Nuevo Laredo)* (Midwifery; Nursing); **Nursing** (Nursing; Sports Management); **Veterinary Science and Zoology** (Public Health; Veterinary Science; Zoology)

Schools

Professional Studies *(Valle Hermoso)* (Marketing; Pedagogy)

Units

Law and Social Sciences *(Tampico)* (English; Family Studies; Law; Psychology; Public Administration; Social Sciences; Tourism); **Multidisciplinary** *(Reynosa-Aztlán)* (Biotechnology; Chemical Engineering; Criminology; Food Science; Industrial Chemistry; Industrial Engineering; Nutrition); **Multidisciplinary** *(Reynosa-Rodhe)* (Business and Commerce; Computer Science; Economics; Electronic Engineering; Environmental Engineering; Petroleum and Gas Engineering; Production Engineering); **Science, Education and Humanities** (Applied Linguistics; Arts and Humanities; Education; History; Pedagogy; Social Sciences; Sociology); **Social Work and Human Development Studies** (Clinical Psychology; Development Studies; Nutrition; Social Work)

History: Founded 1956, incorporating existing schools.

Academic Year: August to June (August-December; February-June)

Admission Requirements: Secondary school certificate (bachillerato)

Main Language(s) of Instruction: Spanish

Degrees and Diplomas: *Licenciatura*: Accountancy (Contador público); Accountancy and Informatics; Administration; Agricultural Engineering (Agrónomo); Architecture (Arquitecto); Banking and Finance; Business Administration; Chemical Biology (Químico farmacobiólogo); Civil Engineering; Commerce; Communication; Communication and Public Relations; Criminology; Dentistry (Cirujano dentista); Economics; Education Development; Graphic Design; Hotel Management and Tourism; Industrial Chemistry (Químico industrial); Informatics Applied to Administration; International Relations; International Trade; Law; Midwifery (Partera); Music; Nursing; Psychology; Social Work; Sociology; Teaching of Art; Veterinary Medicine and Animal Husbandry (Médico veterinario zootecnista); *Licenciatura*: Medicine, 6 yrs; *Especialización*; *Maestría*: Accountancy; Administration; Agriculture; Animal Husbandry; Foreign Commerce; Industrial Psychology; Information Systems; Law; Medical Sciences; Occupational Therapy; Public Health; *Doctorado*: Agricultural Sciences; Education; Law

Special Facilities: History Museum

Libraries: Central Library; 26 branch libraries

Last Updated: 06/09/12

AUTONOMOUS UNIVERSITY OF THE CITY OF MEXICO

Universidad Autónoma de la Ciudad de México (UACM)

División del Norte # 906, Col. Narvarte Pte., Del. Benito Juárez, 03100 México, D.F.

Tel: +52(5) 11-07-02-80

EMail: uacm.rectoria@uacm.edu.mx

Website: http://www.uacm.edu.mx

Rector (acting): Enrique Dussel Ambrossini

Colleges

Humanities and Social Sciences (Communication Studies; Contemporary History; Cultural Studies; Fine Arts; Heritage Preservation; Philosophy; Political Sciences; Social Sciences; Writing); **Science and Humanities** (Community Health; Environmental Studies; Genetics; Health Education); **Science and Technology** (Energy Engineering; Industrial Engineering; Software Engineering; Telecommunications Engineering; Transport Engineering)

Further Information: Planteles: Centro Histórico, del Valle, Casa Libertad (Iztapalapa), San Lorenzo Tezonco, Gustavo A. Madero, Vlady and Talavera

History: Founded 2001 by the Government of Mexico City.

Governing Bodies: Consejo Universitario (representatives of the social development area of the city's government and representatives of the academic body of the university); Advisory Council; Rector

Admission Requirements: Secondary school certificate or equivalent

Fees: None

Main Language(s) of Instruction: Spanish

International Co-operation: With Consejo Latinoamericano de Ciencias Sociales (CLACSO)

Degrees and Diplomas: *Bachillerato*; *Licenciatura*; *Maestría*; *Doctorado*

Student Services: Academic counselling, Canteen, Cultural centre, Health services, Language programs, Social counselling

Libraries: Yes

Last Updated: 26/03/13

AUTONOMOUS UNIVERSITY OF THE STATE OF HIDALGO

Universidad Autónoma del Estado de Hidalgo (UAEH)

Abasolo, 600, Col. Centro, 42000 Pachuca, Hidalgo
Tel: +52(771) 717-20-00 +52(771) 717-21-85
Fax: +52(771) 717-21-00
EMail: veras@uaeh.edu.mx
Website: http://www.uaeh.edu.mx/

Rector: Humberto Augusto Veras Godoy

Centres

Biological Research (Biology); **Chemical Research** (Chemistry); **Earth Sciences Research** (Earth Sciences); **Population Studies** (Demography and Population)

Institutes

Agronomy *(ICAP)* (Agronomy); **Arts**; **Economics and Administration** (Administration; Economics); **Exact Sciences** *(ICE)* (Mathematics and Computer Science; Natural Sciences); **Social Sciences** *(ICSO)* (Social Sciences)

Programmes

Mycology (Botany)

Schools

Dentistry (Dentistry); **Medicine** (Medicine); **Nursing** (Nursing); **Social Work** (Social Work)

Further Information: Campuses at Actopán, Sahagún and Tlahuelilpán

History: Founded 1869 as School, acquired present status and title 1961. An autonomous institution financially supported by the State and federal governments.

Governing Bodies: Consejo Universitario

Academic Year: January to December (January-June; July-December)

Admission Requirements: Secondary school certificate (bachillerato) and entrance examination

Main Language(s) of Instruction: Spanish

Degrees and Diplomas: *Licenciatura*: 9 sem; *Especialización*; *Maestría*: a further 2 yrs; *Doctorado*

Special Facilities: Mineralogy Museum. Galleries

Libraries: Central Library, c. 70,000 vols

Publications: Espacio Universitario *(monthly)*; Pancromo, Research Magazine *(biannually)*

Last Updated: 26/03/13

AUTONOMOUS UNIVERSITY OF THE STATE OF MEXICO

Universidad Autónoma del Estado de México (UAEMEX)

Avenida Instituto Literario, 100, Ote., Col. Centro, 50000 Toluca, Estado de México
Tel: +52(722) 213-47-32 +52(722) 215-95-89
Fax: +52(722) 214-92-19
EMail: rectoria@uaemex.mx
Website: http://www.uaemex.mx

Rector: Eduardo Gasca Pliego

Faculties

Accountancy and Administration (Accountancy; Administration; Business Computing; Marketing); **Agricultural Sciences** (Agriculture; Agronomy; Floriculture); **Anthropology** (Anthropology); **Architecture and Design** (Architecture; Design; Graphic Design; Town Planning); **Arts** (Art History; Fine Arts; Graphic Arts; Painting and Drawing; Performing Arts; Sculpture); **Behavioural Sciences** (Behavioural Sciences); **Chemistry** (Chemical Engineering; Chemistry); **Dentistry** (Dentistry; Surgery); **Economics** (Actuarial Science; Economics; International Business); **Engineering** (Civil Engineering; Computer Engineering; Electronic Engineering; Energy Engineering; Engineering; Mechanical Engineering); **Geography** (Geography); **Humanities** (Arts and Humanities; Documentation Techniques; History; Literature; Philosophy; Theatre); **Languages** (English; French; Modern Languages); **Law** (Law); **Medicine** (Biomedical Engineering; Medicine; Nutrition; Occupational Therapy; Physical Therapy; Surgery); **Obstetrics and Nursing** (Gynaecology and Obstetrics; Nursing); **Political and Social Sciences** (Communication Studies; Political Sciences; Public Administration; Sociology); **Science** (Biology; Biotechnology; Mathematics; Natural Sciences; Physics); **Tourism and Gastronomy** (Cooking and Catering; Tourism); **Town and Regional Planning** (Regional Planning; Town Planning); **Veterinary Science** (Veterinary Science; Zoology)

Further Information: Also professional units at Amecameca, Atlacomulco, Valle de México, Valle de Teotihuacán, Ecatepec, Temascaltepec, Tenancingo, Texcoco, Valle de Chalco and Zumpango

History: Founded 1828 as Institute of Science and Letters, acquired autonomous status 1943, and acquired present title 1956.

Governing Bodies: Consejo Universitario

Academic Year: September to August (September-February; March-August)

Admission Requirements: Secondary school certificate (bachillerato) or foreign equivalent, and entrance examination

Main Language(s) of Instruction: Spanish

Degrees and Diplomas: *Licenciatura*: 5 yrs; *Especialización*: 1-4 yrs; *Maestría*: 1-2 yrs; *Doctorado*: 3 yrs. Professional Titles are awarded in the same fields as Licenciatura

Student Services: Academic counselling, Canteen, Cultural centre, Employment services, Foreign student adviser, Foreign Studies Centre, Handicapped facilities, Health services, Language programs, Nursery care, Social counselling, Sports facilities

Special Facilities: Natural History Museum; University Museum; Meteorological Observatory; Camera Theatre; University Theatre.

Libraries: Yes

Publications: Collections: Sciences and Techniques; Futuro *(quarterly)*; La Colmena *(quarterly)*; Research *(quarterly)*

Last Updated: 07/09/12

AUTONOMOUS UNIVERSITY OF THE STATE OF MORELOS

Universidad Autónoma del Estado de Morelos (UAEMOR)

Avenida Universidad, 1001, Col. Chamilpa, 62210 Cuernavaca, Morelos
Tel: +52(777) 329-70-00
EMail: informacion@uaem.mx
Website: http://www.uaem.mx

Rector: Jesús Alejandro Vera Jiménez (2012-2018)

Areas

Agronomy (Animal Husbandry; Horticulture; Plant Pathology; Rural Planning; Vegetable Production); **Health Sciences** (Medicine; Nursing; Nutrition; Pharmacy; Psychology; Surgery); **Humanities and Arts** (Anthropology; Architecture; Arts and Humanities; Communication Studies; Design; Educational Sciences; History; Literature; Modern Languages; Pedagogy; Physical Education; Theatre); **Natural Sciences** (Biology; Environmental Studies); **Science and Engineering** (Chemical Engineering; Chemistry; Electrical Engineering; Engineering; Industrial Chemistry; Industrial Engineering; Mechanical Engineering); **Social Sciences** (Accountancy; Administration; Computer Science; Law; Public Administration; Public Relations; Sociology; Tourism)

Further Information: Also regional branches

History: Founded 1939 as a State higher education institution and tracing its history to a literary college founded 1872. Became university 1953. By decree of 1967 granted independence from federal and State governments as autonomous university.

Governing Bodies: Consejo Universitario; Junta de Gobierno

Academic Year: September to July

Admission Requirements: Secondary school certificate (bachillerato) and entrance examination

Main Language(s) of Instruction: Spanish

Degrees and Diplomas: *Licenciatura*; *Especialización*; *Maestría*; *Doctorado*

Student Services: Cultural centre, Foreign student adviser, Health services, Nursery care, Sports facilities

Special Facilities: Art Gallery. Botanical Garden

Libraries: Central Library; Science library; specialized libraries

Publications: Perspectiva Universitaria; Universidad Ciencia y Tecnología

Last Updated: 07/09/12

AUTONOMOUS UNIVERSITY OF TLAXCALA

Universidad Autónoma de Tlaxcala (UATX)

Apartado postal 19, Avenida Universidad, 1, Col. La Loma, 90070 Tlaxcala, Tlaxcala
Tel: +52(246) 462-11-67 +52(246) 462-42-28
Fax: +52(246) 462-11-67
EMail: rectoria@uatx.mx
Website: http://www.uatx.mx

Rector: Victor Job Paredes Cuahquentzi

Faculties

Agro-biology (Biology; Environmental Studies; Veterinary Science; Zoology); **Basic Science, Engineering and Technology** (Applied Mathematics; Chemical Engineering; Computer Engineering; Electronic Engineering; Engineering; Industrial Chemistry; Mechanical Engineering; Technology); **Dentistry** (Dentistry; Surgery); **Design, Art and Architecture** (Architecture; Textile Design; Visual Arts); **Economics and Administration** (Administration; Economics; International Business); **Education** (Education); **Health Sciences** (Gynaecology and Obstetrics; Nursing; Nutrition; Surgery); **Human Development Sciences** (Family Studies; Special Education); **Law, Political Science and Criminology** (Criminology; Law; Political Sciences; Public Administration); **Philosophy and Letters** (Anthropology; Arts and Humanities; History; Literature; Modern Languages; Philosophy); **Social Work, Sociology and Psychology** (Psychology; Social Sciences; Social Work; Sociology)

History: Founded as Universidad de Calpulalpan.

Governing Bodies: Consejo Universitario

Academic Year: September to June (September-January; February-June)

Admission Requirements: Secondary school certificate (bachillerato) and entrance examination

Main Language(s) of Instruction: Spanish

Degrees and Diplomas: *Licenciatura*: Accountancy; Administration; Law; Social Work, 4 1/2 yrs; *Licenciatura*: Biology; Economics; Education; Languages; Political Science and Public Administration, 5 yrs; *Licenciatura*: Dentistry; Engineering and Chemistry; Nursing; Veterinary Medicine and Animal Husbandry; *Licenciatura*: Special Education, 5-6 yrs; *Especialización*; *Maestría*: a further 2 yrs; *Doctorado*

Special Facilities: Botanical Garden and Herbarium

Libraries: Central Library

Last Updated: 06/09/12

AUTONOMOUS UNIVERSITY OF YUCATAN

Universidad Autónoma de Yucatán (UADY)

Calle 60 No. 491-A por 57 (Centro Histórico), Edificio Central Calle 60 y 57, 491-A, Centro, 97000 Mérida, Yucatán
Tel: +52(999) 930-09-00
EMail: gmontan@tunku.uady.mx
Website: http://www.uady.mx

Rector: Alfredo F. J. Dájer Abimerhi EMail: dabimer@uady.mx

Centres

Biomedical Research (Embryology and Reproduction Biology; Neurosciences; Parasitology); **Social Sciences Research** (Political Sciences; Regional Studies; Social Problems; Social Sciences; Women's Studies)

Faculties

Anthropology (Anthropology; Archaeology; History; Linguistics; Literature); **Architecture** (Architectural and Environmental Design; Architecture); **Business Administration and Accountancy** (Accountancy; Business Administration; Finance; Marketing); **Chemical and Industrial Engineering** (Chemical Engineering; Industrial Engineering); **Chemical Engineering** (Biotechnology; Chemical Engineering; Chemistry; Industrial Chemistry); **Dentistry** (Dental Technology; Dentistry; Orthodontics; Periodontics); **Economics** (Economics; Government); **Education** (Education; Educational Sciences; Higher Education); **Engineering** (Civil Engineering; Construction Engineering; Electronic Engineering; Engineering; Environmental Engineering; Hydraulic Engineering; Mechanical Engineering); **Law** (Civil Law; Criminal Law; Fiscal Law; Labour Law; Law); **Mathematics** (Actuarial Science; Computer Science; Mathematics; Statistics); **Medicine** (Anaesthesiology; Gynaecology and Obstetrics; Medicine; Nutrition; Orthopaedics; Paediatrics; Psychiatry and Mental Health; Radiology; Rehabilitation and Therapy; Sports Medicine; Surgery); **Nursing** (Nursing; Paediatrics; Public Health; Surgery); **Psychology** (Educational Psychology; Industrial and Organizational Psychology; Psychology); **Veterinary Science and Animal Husbandry** (Animal Husbandry; Apiculture; Biology; Tropical Agriculture; Veterinary Science; Zoology)

History: Founded 1922 as Universidad del Sureste. Acquired present status and title 1984.

Governing Bodies: Consejo Universitario

Academic Year: September to July (September-February; February-July)

Admission Requirements: Secondary school certificate (Bachillerato) and entrance examination

Main Language(s) of Instruction: Spanish

International Co-operation: With universities in United Kingdom, Germany, USA, Spain

Degrees and Diplomas: *Licenciatura*: 4-5 yrs; *Especialización*: 1-5 yrs; *Maestría*: a further 2-3 yrs; *Doctorado*: 4-5 yrs

Student Services: Academic counselling, Canteen, Cultural centre, Foreign student adviser, Health services, Language programs, Sports facilities

Special Facilities: Art Gallery. Biological Garden

Libraries: 124,036 vols. Central Library; libraries in each of the faculties

Publications: Revista de la Universidad de Yucatán

Last Updated: 26/03/13

AUTONOMOUS UNIVERSITY OF ZACATECAS

Universidad Autónoma de Zacatecas Francisco García Salinas (UAZ)

Jardín Juárez, 147, Col. Centro Historico, 98000 Zacatecas, Zacatecas
Tel: +52(492) 922-2001
EMail: rectoria@uaz.edu.mx
Website: http://www.uaz.edu.mx/

Rector: Armando Silva Chairez (2012-2016)

Areas
Agronomy (Agricultural Engineering; Agriculture; Agronomy; Animal Husbandry; Veterinary Science); **Art and Culture** (Cultural Studies; Music); **Basic Sciences** (Biology; Earth Sciences; Mathematics; Nuclear Physics; Physics); **Engineering and Technology** (Chemical Engineering; Civil Engineering; Computer Science; Electrical and Electronic Engineering; Energy Engineering; Engineering; Geological Engineering; Mechanical Engineering; Software Engineering; Surveying and Mapping; Water Science); **Health Sciences** (Anaesthesiology; Gynaecology and Obstetrics; Health Sciences; Medicine; Nursing; Nutrition; Paediatrics; Pharmacology; Surgery); **Humanities and Education** (Archaeology; Arts and Humanities; Development Studies; Education; History; Journalism; Literature; Philosophy; Tourism); **Political Science, Economics and Administration** (Accountancy; Administration; Demography and Population; Development Studies; Economics; Political Sciences; Social Sciences; Taxation); **Social Sciences and Administration** (Law; Psychology; Psychotherapy; Social Sciences)

Centres
Languages (Literature; Modern Languages)

History: Founded 1832 as State college, became Institute of Sciences 1920 and granted autonomy 1959. Acquired present title 1968.

Governing Bodies: Consejo Universitario

Academic Year: August to June (August-December; February-June)

Admission Requirements: Secondary school certificate (bachillerato)

Main Language(s) of Instruction: Spanish

Degrees and Diplomas: *Licenciatura*: Accountancy; Law; Mathematics; Nursing, 4 yrs; *Licenciatura*: Chemical Biology (Químico farmacobiólogo); Chemical Engineering (Químico); Engineering; Midwifery (Enfermera Obstetra); Veterinary Medicine and Animal Husbandry (Médico veterinario y zootecnista); *Licenciatura*: Dentistry (Dentista); Economics, 5 yrs; *Licenciatura*: Medicine, 6 yrs; *Especialización*; *Maestría*: a further 2 yrs; *Doctorado*

Special Facilities: Museo de Mineralogía

Libraries: Yes

Last Updated: 26/03/13

BENEMÉRITA AND CENTENARY NATIONAL SCHOOL OF TEACHERS

Benemérita y Centenaria Escuela Nacional de Maestros

Calzada México-Tacuba 75, Avenida de los Maestros, Col. Un Hogar Para Nosotros, 11330 México, D.F.

Tel: +52(55) 53-28-10-97

Fax: +52(55) 53-41-06-81

EMail: nacionaldemaestros@gmail.com

Programmes
Teacher Training (Primary Education; Teacher Training)

Degrees and Diplomas: *Licenciatura*

Last Updated: 10/07/12

BENEMÉRITA AND CENTENARY TEACHER TRAINING SCHOOL OF THE STATE OF DURANGO

Benemérita y Centenaria Escuela Normal del Estado de Durango

Apartado postal 309, Calzada Escuela Normal s/n, 34000 Durango, Durango

Tel: +52(618) 811-94-78 +52(618) 812-31-18

Fax: +52(618) 811-94-78

EMail: bycened@omanet.com.mx

Website: http://www.bycened.edu.mx

Directora: Luz María López Amaya

EMail: direccion@bycened.edu.mx

Programmes
Teacher Training (Teacher Training)

History: Founded 1916.

Main Language(s) of Instruction: Spanish

Degrees and Diplomas: *Licenciatura*

Last Updated: 10/07/12

BENEMÉRITA AUTONOMOUS UNIVERSITY OF PUEBLA

Benemérita Universidad Autónoma de Puebla (BUAP)

Calle 4 Sur, 104, Edificio Carolino, Planta Alta, Col. Centro, 72000 Puebla, Puebla

Tel: +52(222) 229-55-00

Fax: +52(222) 232-32-69

EMail: viep@correo.buap.mx

Website: http://www.buap.mx

Rector: Enrique Agüera Ibáñez

Tel: +52(222) 242-64-59 +52(222) 246-56-32

Vicerrector: Pedro Hugo Hernández Tejeda

Centres
Las Américas (Accountancy; Business Administration; Law)

Faculties
Accountancy (Accountancy); **Administration** (Business Administration; Cooking and Catering; Public Administration; Tourism); **Biology** (Biology); **Chemical Engineering** (Chemical Engineering; Chemistry; Environmental Engineering; Food Technology; Materials Engineering); **Chemistry** (Chemical Engineering; Pharmacy); **Communication Sciences** (Communication Studies); **Computer Science** (Computer Engineering; Computer Science; Information Technology); **Economics** (Economics; Finance); **Electronics** (Electronic Engineering); **Engineering** (Civil Engineering; Electrical Engineering; Industrial Engineering; Mechanical Engineering; Surveying and Mapping; Textile Technology); **Languages** (English; French; Modern Languages); **Law and Social Sciences** (Criminology; International Relations; Law; Social Sciences; Sociology); **Medicine** (Biomedicine; Medicine; Nutrition; Physical Therapy); **Nursing** (Nursing); **Philosophy** (Arts and Humanities; History; Linguistics; Philosophy; Social Sciences; Spanish); **Physics and Mathematics** (Applied Mathematics; Applied Physics; Mathematics; Physics); **Psychology** (Psychology) *Dean*: Alfredo Fernándo Mauleón Yunes; **Stomatology** (Stomatology); **Veterinary Science** (Veterinary Science)

Institutes
Judicial Sciences *(Puebla)* (International Relations; Law; Political Sciences; Psychology)

Schools
Agriculture and Hydrology Engineering (Agricultural Engineering; Agriculture; Soil Science; Water Science); **Arts** (Dance; Music; Theatre); **Communication Studies** (Communication Studies); **Physical Education** (Physical Education)

Further Information: Also 8 preparatory schools

History: Founded 1937 as Universidad de Puebla but tracing its origins to College of Holy Spirit 1578, subsequently State College 1825. Reorganized and granted present status 1956. An autonomous institution financed by State and federal governments.

Governing Bodies: Consejo Universitario, comprising 150 members

Academic Year: January to December (January-May; August-December). Summer courses, June to August

Admission Requirements: Secondary school certificate (bachillerato) and entrance examination (Prueba de Aptitud Académica)

Fees: Fees are waived in exchange agreements at BA level

Main Language(s) of Instruction: Spanish

International Co-operation: With universities in France, Canada, United Kingdom, Germany, Spain and USA

Accrediting Agencies: Comisión Nacional de Educación (CONAEVE); Consejo Interuniversitario para la Evaluación de la Educación Superior (CIEES)

Degrees and Diplomas: *Licenciatura*: all fields (BA), 4-7 yrs; *Especialización*: Chemical Sciences; Accountancy; Nursing; Stomatology; Engineering; Psychology; Medicine, 2-3 yrs; *Maestría*:

Electronic Sciences; Administration; Architecture; Computer Science; Physics; Mathematics; Chemical Sciences; Accountancy; Law; Social Sciences; Economics; Nursing; Stomatology; Arts and Humanities; Engineering; Chemical Engineering; Social Sciences; Medicine; Psychology; Environmental Science; Microbiology; Physiology; Language Sciences; History; Sociology; Science of Materials, 2 yrs following Licenciatura; *Doctorado*: Mathematics; Electronics; Chemical Sciences; Law; Environmental Sciences; Microbiology; Physiology; History; Sociology; Science of Materials; Physics (PhD), 3 yrs

Student Services: Academic counselling, Cultural centre, Employment services, Foreign student adviser, Health services, Language programs, Sports facilities

Student Residential Facilities: None

Special Facilities: Museo Universitario de Ciencia y Arte

Libraries: Central Library; 30 branch libraries

Publications: Cuaderno de Investigación; Dialéctica; Economía Internacional; Escritos; Foro Económico

Press or Publishing House: Ediciones BUAP

Last Updated: 10/07/12

BENEMERITA MANUEL AVILA CAMACHO TEACHER TRAINING SCHOOL OF ZACATECAS

Benemerita Escuela Normal de Zacatecas Manuel Avila Camacho

Elías Amador No. 302, Col. Sierra de Álica, 98000 Zacatecas, Zacatecas

Tel: +52(492) 922-0616

Fax: +52(492) 922-6857

EMail: direccion@normalavilacamacho.edu.mx

Website: http://www.normalavilacamacho.edu.mx/

Director: Ramiro Torres Bañuelos

Programmes

Education (Physical Education; Preschool Education; Primary Education; Secondary Education; Special Education)

Admission Requirements: Secondary school leaving certificate

Main Language(s) of Instruction: Spanish

Accrediting Agencies: Secretaría de Educación Pública

Degrees and Diplomas: *Especialización*

Student Services: Academic counselling, Canteen, Cultural centre, Employment services, Language programs, Social counselling, Sports facilities

Last Updated: 25/02/13

BENEMÉRITA PROFESOR JESÚS LUNA PRADO STATE TEACHER TRAINING SCHOOL OF ENSENADA

Benemérita Escuela Normal Estatal Profesor Jesús Luna Prado

Eucaliptos y de las Rosas s/n, Fracc. Valle Verde, 22810 Ensenada, Baja California

Tel: +52(646) 468-36-91 +52(646) 464-20-20

Fax: +52(646) 474-20-20

EMail: info@ene.edu.mx

Website: http://www.ene.edu.mx/

Directora: . María de la Paz Boni Acuña

Programmes

Teacher Training (Preschool Education; Primary Education; Secondary Education; Teacher Training)

History: Founded 1960 as Escuela Normal Estatal de Ensenada. Acquired present title 2009

Main Language(s) of Instruction: Spanish

Degrees and Diplomas: *Licenciatura*

Last Updated: 25/02/13

BENEMÉRITO GENERAL JUAN CRISOSTOMO BONILLA STATE TEACHER TRAINING INSTITUTE

Benemérito Instituto Normal del Estado General Juan Crisostomo Bonilla

Blvd. Hermanos Serdán, 203, Col. Valle del Rey, Puebla, Puebla

Tel: +52(22) 48-33-76

Fax: +52(22) 48-33-98

EMail: bine@bine.edu.mx

Website: http://www.bine.edu.mx/

Director: Juan Gabriel Macareno Flores

Programmes

Education (Education; Physical Education; Preschool Education; Primary Education; Secondary Education; Special Education; Teacher Training)

History: Founded 1879.

Main Language(s) of Instruction: Spanish

Degrees and Diplomas: *Licenciatura*; *Maestría*

Last Updated: 26/10/12

BENITO JUÁREZ AUTONOMOUS UNIVERSITY OF OAXACA

Universidad Autónoma Benito Juárez de Oaxaca (UABJO)

Avenida Universidad s/n, Ex-Hacienda de Cinco Señores, Ciudad Universitaria, 68120 Oaxaca, Oaxaca

Tel: +52(951) 502-07-00

EMail: fcauabjo@fca.uabjo.mx

Website: http://www.uabjo.mx

Rector: Eduardo Martínez Helmes (2012-2016)

EMail: rector@uabjo.mx

Faculties

Accountancy and Administration (Accountancy; Public Administration); **Architecture**; **Architecture** *(5 de Mayo)* (Architecture; Heritage Preservation); **Chemistry** (Chemistry); **Dentistry** (Dentistry; Surgery); **Languages** (Modern Languages; Translation and Interpretation); **Law** (Law); **Medicine and Surgery** (Biology; Medicine; Surgery)

Institutes

Educational Sciences (Education; Educational Psychology; Educational Sciences; Pedagogy); **Sociological Research** (Anthropology; Archaeology; Political Sciences; Regional Planning; Rural Planning; Social Sciences)

Schools

Fine Arts (Fine Arts; Graphic Arts; Painting and Drawing; Sculpture); **Nursing** (Midwifery; Nursing); **Science** (Biology; Computer Science; Mathematics; Physics); **Veterinary Medicine and Zoology** (Veterinary Science; Zoology)

History: Founded 1826 as an institute, became university 1955. An autonomous institution financially supported by the State and federal governments.

Governing Bodies: Consejo Universitario; Asamblea Universitaria (University Board); Consejo Técnico (Board of Schools)

Academic Year: February to November (February-June; July-November)

Admission Requirements: Secondary school certificate (bachillerato)

Main Language(s) of Instruction: Spanish

Degrees and Diplomas: *Licenciatura*: 5 yrs; *Especialización*; *Maestría*; *Doctorado*

Last Updated: 03/09/12

BENITO JUÁREZ REGIONAL TEACHER TRAINING CENTRE

Centro Regional de Educación Normal Benito Juárez

Gral. González y Dr. Agustín Torres Craviotto, s/n, Col. Doctores, 42090 Pachuca, Hidalgo

Tel: +52(771) 713-78-00 +52(771) 713-49-88

Website: http://www.paginasprodigy.com/crenbj

Director: José Cuatepotzo Costeira

Programmes

Education (Physical Education; Preschool Education; Primary Education; Special Education); **Teacher Training** (Teacher Training)

Main Language(s) of Instruction: Spanish

Degrees and Diplomas: *Licenciatura*

Last Updated: 13/03/08

BIOLOGICAL RESEARCH CENTRE OF THE NORTH-WEST

Centro de Investigaciones Biológicas del Noroeste, S.C. (CIBNOR)

nstituto Politécnico Nacional 195, Colonia Playa Palo de Santa Rita Sur, 23096 La Paz, Baja California Sur
Tel: +52(612) 123-8484
Fax: +52(612) 125-3625
Website: http://www.cibnor.gob.mx

Director General: Sergio Hernández Vázquez

Programmes

Agriculture in Arid Zones (Agriculture; Arid Land Studies); **Aquaculture** (Aquaculture); **Environmental Management** (Environmental Management; Environmental Studies); **Fishery** (Ecology; Fishery)

Further Information: Also units in Guerrero Negro, Hermosillo and Guaymas

History: Founded 1975.

Main Language(s) of Instruction: Spanish

Degrees and Diplomas: *Maestría*; *Doctorado*

Libraries: Biblioteca Daniel Lluch Belda

Last Updated: 18/07/12

CAMPECHE INSTITUTE

Instituto Campechano

Calle 10 No 357, Col. Centro V, 24000 Campeche, Campeche
Tel: +52(981) 816-22-92
Fax: +52(981) 816-29-75
Website: http://www.institutocampechano.edu.mx

Rector: Ramón Félix Santini Pech

Schools

Communication Studies (Communication Studies; Journalism); **Gastronomy** (Cooking and Catering); **Social Work** (Social Work); **Tourism** (Tourism)

History: Founded 1859.

Main Language(s) of Instruction: Spanish

Degrees and Diplomas: *Licenciatura*; *Maestría*

Last Updated: 22/02/08

CAP. DE ALT. ANTONIO GÓMEZ MAQUEO SCHOOL OF THE MERCHANT NAVY OF MAZATLAN

Escuela Náutica Mercante de Mazatlán 'Cap. de Alt. Antonio Gómez Maqueo'

Calzada Gabriel Leyva 2111, 82040 Mazatlán, Sinaloa
Tel: +52(69) 81-24-86
Fax: +52(69) 85-36-50 Ext. 50
EMail: direccion@nauticamztl.edu.mx

Director: Eugenio Soler Osuna

Programmes

Merchant Marine Engineering (Marine Engineering)

Degrees and Diplomas: *Licenciatura*; *Maestría*

Last Updated: 27/03/13

CAP. DE ALT. FERNANDO SILICEO Y TORRES MERCHANT NAVY SCHOOL

Escuela Náutica Mercante 'Cap de Alt. Fernando Siliceo y Torres'

Apartado postal 317, Blvd. Ávila Camacho s/n, 91700 Veracruz, Veracruz
Tel: +52(29) 31-33-36
Fax: +52(29) 31-08-73

Director: César Jesús Barradas Barbosa

Programmes

Hydraulic Engineering (Hydraulic Engineering); **Naval Engineering** (Marine Engineering; Naval Architecture)

History: Founded 1919.

Main Language(s) of Instruction: Spanish

Degrees and Diplomas: *Licenciatura*; *Especialización*; *Maestría*

Last Updated: 27/03/13

CENTRE FOR ADVANCED NAVAL STUDIES

Centro de Estudios Superiores Navales

Calzada de la Virgen #1800 Col. Ex- Ejido de San Pablo Tepetlapa, Delegación Coyoacán, 06056 México, D.F.
Tel: +52(55) 56-08-08-47
EMail: mmartinez@cesnav.edu.mx
Website: http://www.cesnav.edu.mx

Director: Carlos Federico Quinto Guillén
EMail: director-cesnav@semar.gob.mx

Programmes

Naval Studies (Nautical Science)

History: Founded 1970.

Main Language(s) of Instruction: Spanish

Degrees and Diplomas: *Especialización*; *Maestría*

Last Updated: 16/07/12

CENTRE FOR ADVANCED STUDIES IN EDUCATIONAL COMMUNICATION OF TLAXCALA

Centro de Estudios Superiores de Comunicación Educativa de Tlaxcala (CESCET)

Calle Ignacio Zaragoza, 3, Col. Zaragoza, 90160 Totolac, Tlaxcala
Tel: +52 (246) 46-2-74-00
EMail: cescet@cescet.com.mx
Website: http://www.actiweb.es/cescet/que_es_el_cescet.html

Director: Héctor Stevenson Carrasco

Programmes

Educational Communication (Educational Sciences; Educational Technology; Preschool Education; Primary Education; Secondary Education; Special Education)

History: Founded 1984.

Main Language(s) of Instruction: Spanish

Degrees and Diplomas: *Licenciatura*

Last Updated: 15/02/13

CENTRE FOR ADVANCED STUDIES IN HOMEOPATHY

Centro Superior de Estudios Homeopáticos

Pedro Moreno No. 668, Col. Centro, 44290 Guadalajara, Jalisco
Tel: +52(33) 38-54-14-49
EMail: informes@cesehom.com
Website: http://www.cesehom.com

Director: Gabriel Macias Muñiz
EMail: gamacias@cybercable.net.mx

Programmes

Homeopathy (Homeopathy)

History: Founded 2005.

Main Language(s) of Instruction: Spanish

Degrees and Diplomas: *Licenciatura*; *Especialización*

Last Updated: 27/03/13

CENTRE FOR ADVANCED STUDIES IN INFORMATION TECHNOLOGIES

Centro Superior en Tecnologías de Información

Avenida Federalismo Sur, 47, Col. Centro, 44100 Guadalajara, Jalisco
Tel: +52(33) 36-58-08-34
EMail: aolivares@era21.com.mx
Website: http://www.unisite.com.mx/

Director General: José Enrique Quiñonez Rodríguez
EMail: equinonez@era21.com.mx

Programmes
Administration; **Computer Science** (Computer Science); **Design and Web** (Software Engineering); **International Business** (International Business); **Marketing** (Marketing)

History: Founded 2004.

Main Language(s) of Instruction: Spanish

Degrees and Diplomas: *Licenciatura*. Also Diplomados

Last Updated: 23/07/12

CENTRE FOR ADVANCED STUDIES IN SPECIAL EDUCATION

Centro de Estudios Superiores de Educación Especializada (CESEE)

Avenida Tecnologico No. 308 s/n, Fraccionamiento Industrial Julian De Obregon, Agrícola el Pedregoso, 37290 León, Guanajuato
Tel: +52(477) 771-7164
Fax: +52(477) 711-4081
EMail: cesee@prodigy.net.mx

Director: Juan Carlos Solorzano Salinas

Programmes
Physical Education (Physical Education)

Main Language(s) of Instruction: Spanish

Degrees and Diplomas: *Licenciatura*

Last Updated: 15/02/13

CENTRE FOR ADVANCED STUDIES OF THE STATE OF SONORA

Centro de Estudios Superiores del Estado de Sonora (CESUES)

Rosales 189, Col. Centro, 83000 Hermosillo, Sonora
Tel: +52(662) 217-11-59
Fax: +52(662) 217-11-49
EMail: contacto@cesues.edu.mx
Website: http://www.cesues.edu.mx

Director General: Samuel Espinosa Guillén
Tel: +52(662) 217-11-50

Secretaria General: Ernestina Arabella Almada Ruiz

International Relations: Brenda María Vega Moreno, Coordinadora de Cooperación Académica y Asuntos Internacionales

Departments
Accountancy (Accountancy); **Business Administration** (Business Administration); **Ecology** (Ecology; Environmental Studies); **Geoscience** (Earth Sciences); **Horticulture** (Horticulture); **Industrial Engineering** (Industrial Engineering); **Nutrition** (Nutrition); **Sport Training** (Physical Education); **Tourism Management** (Management; Tourism)

Further Information: Also Academic Units at San Luis Río Colorado, Navojoa, Magdalena, Benito Juárez, and Nogales

History: Founded 1983.

Governing Bodies: Dirección General

Academic Year: August to June (August-January; February-June)

Admission Requirements: Secondary school certificate (bachillerato) and entrance examination

Fees: (Pesos): 1,160 per semester

Main Language(s) of Instruction: Spanish

International Co-operation: With universities in Canada, USA. Also exchange programmes with CONAHEC and IAESTE

Degrees and Diplomas: *Licenciatura*: Aquaculture; Business Administration; Ecology; Geoscience; Horticulture; Industrial Engineering; International Business; Management Computer Systems; Public Accountancy; Sport Training; Tourism, 5 yrs; *Maestría*: a further 2 yrs

Student Services: Academic counselling, Cultural centre, Employment services, Foreign student adviser, Handicapped facilities, Health services, Language programs, Nursery care, Sports facilities

Libraries: Yes

Last Updated: 16/07/12

CENTRE FOR APPLIED INNOVATION IN COMPETITIVE TECHNOLOGIES

Centro de Innovación Aplicada en Tecnologías Competitivas

Omega 201, Fracc. Delta, 37545 León, Guanajuato
Tel: +52(477) 710-0111
Fax: +52(477) 761-0913
Website: http://www.ciatec.mx

Director General: Luis Torreblanca Rivera
EMail: ltorreblanca@ciatec.mx

Courses
Automation (Automation and Control Engineering); **Biochemistry** (Biochemistry); **Design** (Design); **Engineering** (Engineering; Environmental Engineering); **Footwear** (Clothing and Sewing); **Leather and Tanning** (Leather Techniques)

History: Founded 1976.

Main Language(s) of Instruction: Spanish

Degrees and Diplomas: *Especialización*; *Maestría*; *Doctorado*

Last Updated: 12/07/12

CENTRE FOR FISCAL AND PUBLIC FINANCE STUDIES

Centro de Capacitación de Estudios Fiscales y Finanzas Públicas

Av. Milton Castellanos N° 1573 Conjunto Urbano Caliss, 21000 Mexicali, Baja California
Tel: +52(6) 554-76-96
Fax: +52(6) 554-76-95
EMail: cencafi@baja.gob.mx

Director: Francisco Javier Sanchez Vazquez

Programmes
Finance (Finance; Fiscal Law; Taxation)

History: Founded 1993.

Main Language(s) of Instruction: Spanish

Degrees and Diplomas: *Especialización*

Last Updated: 14/02/13

CENTRE FOR RESEARCH AND ADVANCED STUDIES IN SOCIAL ANTHROPOLOGY

Centro de Investigaciones y Estudios Superiores en Antropología Social (CIESAS)

Apdo. Postal N° 22-048, Calle Juárez N° 87, Col. Tlalpan, 14000 México, D.F.
Tel: +52(55) 54 87 36 00
EMail: dirgral@ciesas.edu.mx
Website: http://www.ciesas.edu.mx

Directora: Virginia García Acosta

Programmes
Anthropology (Anthropology); **History** (History); **Indian-American Linguistics** (Amerindian Languages); **Social Sciences** (Social Sciences)

Further Information: Also branches in Guadalajara, Merida, Xalapa, Oaxaca, and San Cristobal de las Casas

History: Founded 1980.

Main Language(s) of Instruction: Spanish

Degrees and Diplomas: *Maestría*; *Doctorado*

Libraries: 7 libraries

Last Updated: 18/07/12

CENTRE FOR RESEARCH AND ASSISTANCE IN TECHNOLOGY AND DESIGN OF THE STATE OF JALISCO

Centro de Investigación y Asistencia en Tecnología y Diseño del Estado de Jalisco (CIATEJ)

Av. Normalistas No. 800, Colinas de la Normal, 44680 Guadalajara, Jalisco
Tel: +52(3) 824-00-34
Fax: +52(3) 824-33-14
EMail: informes@ciatej.net.mx
Website: http://www.ciatej.net.mx

Director General: Gabriel Siade Barquet
EMail: gsiade@ciatej.net.mx

Programmes
Biotechnology (Biotechnology; Microbiology); **Environmental Technology** (Environmental Management); **Food Technology** (Food Technology)

History: Founded 1976.

Main Language(s) of Instruction: Spanish

Degrees and Diplomas: *Licenciatura*; *Maestría*; *Doctorado*
Last Updated: 27/03/13

CENTRE FOR RESEARCH AND TEACHING IN ECONOMICS

Centro de Investigación y Docencia Económicas, A.C. (CIDE)

Carretera México-Toluca, 3655, Col. Lomas de Santa Fe, Álvaro Obregón, Apartado postal 10-883, 01210 México, D.F.
Tel: +52(5) 55-27-98-00
Fax: +52(5) 57-27-98-74
EMail: enrique.cabrero@cide.edu
Website: http://www.cide.edu

Director General: Enrique Cabrero Mendoza

Divisions
Economics (Economics); **History** (History); **International Studies** (International Studies); **Legal Studies** (Law); **Political Studies** (Political Sciences); **Public Administration** (Government; Public Administration)

History: Founded 1975.

Main Language(s) of Instruction: Spanish

Degrees and Diplomas: *Licenciatura*; *Maestría*; *Doctorado*

Student Services: Employment services, Language programs, Nursery care, Sports facilities

Libraries: Yes

Publications: Economía Mexicana, Publication on Economics *(biennially)*; Gestion y Política Pública, Publication on Public Administration *(biennially)*; Istor, Publication on History *(biennially)*; Política y Gobierno, Publication on Political Science *(biennially)*
Last Updated: 18/07/12

CENTRE FOR RESEARCH AND TEACHING IN THE HUMANITIES OF THE STATE OF MORELOS

Centro de Investigación y Docencia en Humanidades del Estado de Morelos (CIDHEM)

Avenida Morelos Sur 154, Esq. Amates, Col. Las Palmas, 62050 Cuernavaca, Morelos
Tel: +52(777) 318-83-10 +52(777) 312-35-08
Fax: +52(777) 312-87-72
EMail: cidhem@prodigy.net.mx
Website: http://www.cidhem.edu.mx

Director General: Jesús Manuel Araiza Martínez
EMail: jaraiza@cidhem.edu.mx

Programmes
Anthropology (Anthropology); **Art History** (Art History); **Higher Education** (Higher Education); **History** (History); **Literature** (Literature); **Philosophy** (Philosophy); **Political and Social Sciences** (Political Sciences; Social Sciences)

History: Founded 1994.

Main Language(s) of Instruction: Spanish

Degrees and Diplomas: *Maestría*; *Doctorado*

Libraries: Yes
Last Updated: 18/07/12

CENTRE FOR RESEARCH AND TECHNOLOGICAL DEVELOPMENT IN ELECTROCHEMISTRY

Centro de Investigación y Desarrollo Tecnológico en Electroquímica, S.C. (CIDETEQ)

Parque Tecnológico Querétaro, Col. San Fandila, 76700 Pedro Escobedo, Querétaro
Tel: +52 (442) 211-60-00
Fax: +52 (442) 211-60-01
EMail: lgodinez@cideteq.mx
Website: http://www.cideteq.mx

Director General: Luis Arturo Godínez Mora Tovar

Programmes
Alternative Energies (Energy Engineering); **Biochemistry** (Biochemistry); **Corrosion** (Metal Techniques); **Electro-chemical Engineering** (Chemical Engineering; Electrical Engineering); **Electro-deposits** (Chemistry); **Nanotechnology** (Nanotechnology); **Soil Science** (Soil Science); **Water Science** (Water Science)

Further Information: Also branches in Corregidora and Tijuana

History: Founded 1991.

Main Language(s) of Instruction: Spanish

Degrees and Diplomas: *Maestría*; *Doctorado*
Last Updated: 18/07/12

CENTRE FOR SCIENTIFIC RESEARCH AND HIGHER EDUCATION OF ENSENADA

Centro de Investigación Científica y de Educación Superior de Ensenada (CICESE)

Apartado postal 360, Km. 107 Carretera Tijuana Ensenada, 22860 Ensenada, Baja California
Tel: +52(646) 174-50-50
Fax: +52(646) 174-47-29
EMail: dgeneral@cicese.mx
Website: http://www.cicese.mx

Director General: Federico Graef Ziehl (2005-)
EMail: fgraef@cicese.mx

Divisions
Information Sciences (Computer Science; Electronic Engineering; Telecommunications Engineering); **Life Sciences** (Aquaculture; Biology; Biotechnology; Ecology; Marine Science and Oceanography; Microbiology); **Physical Sciences** (Applied Physics; Optics; Physics); **Water and Earth Sciences** (Aquaculture; Ecology; Geology; Geophysics; Marine Biology; Marine Science and Oceanography)

History: Founded 1973.

Main Language(s) of Instruction: Spanish

Degrees and Diplomas: *Licenciatura*; *Maestría*; *Doctorado*

Student Services: Academic counselling, Employment services, Foreign student adviser

Libraries: CICESE library; Internet and Optic Disc formats

Publications: Anuario de Productividad *(annually)*
Last Updated: 12/07/12

CENTRE FOR TECHNICAL INDUSTRIAL STUDIES

Centro de Enseñanza Técnica Industrial (CETI)

Calle Nueva Escocia, 1885, Colonia Providencia 5a Sección, 44638 Guadalajara, Jalisco
Tel: +52(33) 36-41-32-50
EMail: direccion.general@ceti.mx
Website: http://www.ceti.mx

Director General: Celso Gabriel Espinosa Corona

Programmes
Chemical Engineering (Chemical Engineering); **Electronic Engineering** (Electronic Engineering); **Industrial Engineering** (Automation and Control Engineering; Industrial Engineering; Mechanical Engineering); **Mechanical and Electronic Engineering** (Automation and Control Engineering; Biomedicine; Production Engineering; Robotics)
Further Information: Also branches in Tonalá and Colomos
History: Founded 1968.
Main Language(s) of Instruction: Spanish
Degrees and Diplomas: *Licenciatura*
Libraries: Yes
Last Updated: 12/07/12

COLLEGE OF POSTGRADUATE STUDIES

Colegio de Postgraduados (COLPOS)
Km. 36.5 Carretera México-Texcoco, Montecillo, 56230 Texcoco de Mora, Estado de México
Tel: +52(595) 952-02-01 +52(55) 58-04-59-00
EMail: contacto@colpos.mx
Website: http://www.colpos.mx

Director General: Jesús María Moncada de la Fuente
EMail: dirgral@colpos.mx

Institutes
Genetics and Productivity Resources (Animal Husbandry; Crop Production; Fruit Production; Genetics; Physiology); **Natural Resources** (Botany; Forestry; Meteorology; Water Science); **Phytotherapy** (Alternative Medicine; Botany; Entomology); **Socio-economics, Statistics and Informatics** (Computer Science; Development Studies; Economics; Rural Studies; Statistics)
Further Information: Campuses in Veracruz, Tabasco, San Luis Potosi, Córdoba and Puebla
History: Founded 1959.
Governing Bodies: Board of Directors
Main Language(s) of Instruction: Spanish
Degrees and Diplomas: *Licenciatura*; *Maestría*; *Doctorado*
Student Services: Canteen, Language programs
Libraries: c. 60,000 vols
Last Updated: 27/07/12

COMMUNITY UNIVERSITY OF SAN LUIS POTOSÍ

Universidad Comunitaria de San Luis Potosí (UNICOM-S.L.P.)
Arista, 1000, Colonia Barrio del Tequis, 78230 San Luis Potosí, San Luis Potosí
Tel: +52(444) 813-30-70
Fax: +52(444) 813-30-70
EMail: salsilca@terra.com.mx; salsilca@hotmail.com

Rector: Salvador Silva-Carrillo (2002-)

Colleges
Higher Education (Anthropology; Archaeology; Arts and Humanities; Business Administration; Computer Science; Ethnology; History; Industrial Engineering; Law; Linguistics; Service Trades)
History: Founded 2001.
Governing Bodies: University Board
Academic Year: August to June
Admission Requirements: High school diploma (Bachillerato). Admission test and medical test
Fees: (US Dollars): 3,400 per annum
Main Language(s) of Instruction: Spanish
Accrediting Agencies: National and Federal Government Department of Education
Degrees and Diplomas: *Licenciatura*: Law (Lic), 4 1/2 yrs; *Licenciatura*: Service Trades; Business Administration; Social Sciences; Industrial Engineering; Anthropology; Arts and Humanities (Native Languages); Computer Science (Lic), 4 yrs
Student Services: Academic counselling, Language programs, Sports facilities
Student Residential Facilities: None
Libraries: Department Libraries

DR. ANDRÉS BUSTAMANTE GURRÍA NATIONAL INSTITUTE OF HUMAN COMMUNICATION

Instituto Nacional de la Comunicación Humana Dr. Andrés Bustamante Gurría
Calzada México Xochimilco 298, Col. Arenal de Guadalupe, Delegación Tlalpán, 14389 México, D.F.
Tel: +52(55) 5999-1000
EMail: padron@df1.telmex.net.mx

Director: Francisco Hernández Orozco

Programmes
Communication Therapy (Communication Studies); **Language and Audition** (Speech Therapy and Audiology); **Nursing** (Nursing); **Occupational Therapy** (Occupational Therapy); **Physiotherapy and Rehabilitation** (Physical Therapy; Rehabilitation and Therapy)
Main Language(s) of Instruction: Spanish
Degrees and Diplomas: *Licenciatura*; *Especialización*; *Maestría*
Last Updated: 07/03/13

DR. GONZALO AGUIRRE BELTRAN REGIONAL TEACHER TRAINING CENTRE

Centro Regional de Educación Normal Dr. Gonzalo Aguirre Beltran
Blvd.Manuel Maples Arce S/N, Ejido La Calzada, Tuxpán, Veracruz
Tel: +52(783) 834-33-24 +52(783) 834-33-76
EMail: crentux@prodigy.net.mx

Directora: Virginia Elizabeth Cobos Patiño

Programmes
Education and Teacher Training (Education; Teacher Training)
History: Founded 1978.
Main Language(s) of Instruction: Spanish
Degrees and Diplomas: *Licenciatura*
Last Updated: 23/07/12

DR. IGNACIO CHAVEZ NATIONAL INSTITUTE OF CARDIOLOGY

Instituto Nacional de Cardología Dr. Ignacio Chávez
Juan Badiano No. 1, Col. Sección XVI, Del. Tlalpan, 14080 Mexico, D.F.
Tel: +52(55) 5573-29-11
EMail: dirgral@cardiologia.org.mx
Website: https://www.cardiologia.org.mx

Director: Marco A. Martínez Ríos

Programmes
Cardiology (Cardiology)

Schools
Nursing (Gynaecology and Obstetrics; Nursing)
History: Founded 1944.
Main Language(s) of Instruction: Spanish
Degrees and Diplomas: *Licenciatura*; *Especialización*
Last Updated: 07/03/13

DR. JOSÉ MARIA LUIS MORA RESEARCH INSTITUTE

Instituto de Investigaciones Dr. José María Luis Mora
Plaza Valentín Gómez Farias No. 12, Col. San Juan Mixcoac, 03730 México, D.F.
Tel: +52(555) 5598-3777
Fax: +52(555) 5563-7162
EMail: udireccion@institutomora.edu.mx
Website: http://www.institutomora.edu.mx

Director: Luis Antonio Járegui Frías EMail: dgeneral@mora.edu.mx

Programmes

History (History; Modern History); **Political Sociology** (Political Sciences; Sociology); **Regional Studies** (Regional Studies)

History: Founded 1981.

Main Language(s) of Instruction: Spanish

Degrees and Diplomas: *Licenciatura*; *Maestría*; *Doctorado*

Libraries: Biblioteca Ernesto de la Torre Villar

Last Updated: 05/03/13

DR. MANUEL SUÁREZ TRUJILLO HIGHER TEACHER TRAINING SCHOOL OF VERACRUZ

Escuela Normal Superior Veracruzana Dr. Manuel Suárez Trujillo

Av. Revolución No. 255, Centro, 91000 Xalapa, Veracruz
Tel: +52(228) 814-72-18 +52(228) 814-27-61
Fax: +52(228) 814-76-32

Director: Pompilio Aguilar Schroeder

Programmes

Secondary Education (Secondary Education; Teacher Training)

Degrees and Diplomas: *Licenciatura*

Last Updated: 04/04/08

EMILIANO ZAPATA TECHNOLOGICAL UNIVERSITY OF THE STATE OF MORELOS

Universidad Tecnológica Emiliano Zapata del Estado de Morelos

Universidad Tecnológica No.1, Col. Palo Escrito, 62000 Emiliano Zapata, Morelos
Tel: +52(777) 368- 11-65
EMail: rectoria@utez.edu.mx
Website: http://www.utez.edu.mx

Rectora: Beatriz Ramírez Velázquez

Programmes

Business Administration (Business Administration); **Engineering** (Electronic Engineering; Engineering; Industrial Maintenance; Information Technology; Software Engineering); **Textile and Fashion Design** (Fashion Design; Textile Design)

History: Founded 2000.

Main Language(s) of Instruction: Spanish

Degrees and Diplomas: *Licenciatura*. Técnico Superior Universitario

Last Updated: 27/03/13

ENGINEERING AND INDUSTRIAL DEVELOPMENT CENTRE

Centro de Ingeniería y Desarrollo Industrial (CIDESI)

Avenida Playa Pie de la Cuesta 702, Desarrollo Habitacional San Pablo, 76130 Querétaro, Querétaro
Tel: +52(442) 211-98-00 +52(442) 220-64-26
Fax: +52(442) 211-98-37
EMail: vilomara@cidesi.mx
Website: http://cidesi.com

Director General: Felipe Alejandro Rubio Castillo
EMail: frubio@cidesi.mx

Programmes

Engineering and Technology (Automation and Control Engineering; Engineering; Industrial Engineering; Measurement and Precision Engineering; Mechanical Engineering; Technology)

Further Information: Also branches in Nuevo León, Baja California and Estado de México

History: Founded 1984. Acquired present status 1999.

Governing Bodies: Governing Board

Academic Year: September to August

Admission Requirements: Engineering undergraduate title

Fees: (US Dollars): 10,300 per 4 months term

Main Language(s) of Instruction: Spanish, English

International Co-operation: WIth universities in Germany

Accrediting Agencies: Secretaría de Educación Pública (SEP); CONACyT

Degrees and Diplomas: *Especialización*: Automation and Control Engineering, 4 months; *Maestría*: Mechanical Engineering; Mechatronics; Optical Technology; Measurement and Precision Engineering, 2 yrs; *Doctorado*: Mechanical Engineering; Automation and Control Engineering; Optical Technology, 4 yrs

Student Services: Academic counselling, Canteen, Foreign student adviser, Health services, Language programs, Social counselling

Student Residential Facilities: None

Special Facilities: Computer Centre

Libraries: Yes

Last Updated: 12/07/12

EXPERIMENTAL TEACHER TRAINING SCHOOL OF ACATLAN

Escuela Normal Experimental de Acatlán

Km. 3 carretera a San Juan Ixcaquixtla, Acatlán de Osorio, Puebla
EMail: nor_acatlan@hotmail.com

Director: Antonio Olivares Melo

Programmes

Teacher Training (Teacher Training)

History: Founded 1975.

Main Language(s) of Instruction: Spanish

Degrees and Diplomas: *Licenciatura*

Last Updated: 25/02/13

FEDERAL HIGHER TEACHER TRAINING SCHOOL OF VERACRUZ

Escuela Normal Superior Federal de Veracruz

Blvd. Adolfo Ruiz Cortines S/N, Fracc. Costa Verde, 94294 Boca del Río, Veracruz
Tel: +52 (299) 922-59-09
Fax: +52 (299) 922-59-09

Directora: Griselda Nava García

Programmes

Secondary Education (Secondary Education)

Degrees and Diplomas: *Licenciatura*: 8 sem.

Last Updated: 26/02/13

FEDERAL HIGHER TEACHER TRAINING SCHOOL OF HERMOSILLO

Escuela Normal Superior Federal de Hermosillo

Marruecos, s/n, Esq. Palma y Carbó, Col. el Choyal, 83079 Hermosillo, Sonora
Tel: +52(642) 262-05-88 +52(642) 262-05-96
Fax: +52(642) 262-05-88
EMail: ensh_correo@ifodes.edu.mx
Website: http://uva.ifodes.edu.mx/ensh/

Director: José Cipriano Andrade Zamora

Programmes

English (English); **History** (History); **Mathematics** (Mathematics); **Spanish** (Spanish); **Teacher Training** (Teacher Training)

History: Founded 1983.

Main Language(s) of Instruction: Spanish

Degrees and Diplomas: *Licenciatura*; *Maestría*

Libraries: Yes

Last Updated: 26/02/13

FELIPE CARRILLO PUERTO REGIONAL TEACHER TRAINING CENTRE

Centro Regional de Educación Normal Felipe Carrillo Puerto

Km. 1.5 Carretera Felipe Carrillo Puerto Valladolid, 77800 Felipe Carrillo Puerto, Quintana Roo
Tel: +52(983) 834-08-63 +52(983) 834-04-04
Fax: +52(983) 834-08-78

Directora: Bertha Cobos Villalobos

Programmes

Teacher Training (Education; Teacher Training)

Degrees and Diplomas: *Licenciatura*

FIDEL VELASQUEZ TECHNOLOGICAL UNIVERSITY

Universidad Tecnológica Fidel Velázquez (UTFV)

Ex-Hacienda La Encarnación, Emiliano Zapata s/n, Col. Tráfico, 54400 Nicolás Romero, Estado de México

Tel: +52(55) 58-21-50-84 al 87

Fax: +52(55) 58-21-29-02

EMail: contactoutfv@gmail.com

Website: http://www.utfv.edu.mx

Rector: Enrique Riva Palacio Galicia

Divisions

Accountancy (Accountancy); **Administration** (Administration); **Environmental Studies** (Environmental Management; Environmental Studies); **Industrial Maintenance** (Industrial Maintenance); **Informatics** (Computer Science); **Production Processes** (Graphic Design); **Telematics** (Information Technology; Telecommunications Engineering)

History: Founded 1994.

Main Language(s) of Instruction: Spanish

Degrees and Diplomas: *Licenciatura*

Libraries: Yes

Last Updated: 14/02/13

FRANCISCO MARTÍNEZ CABRERA STATE ACADEMY OF ARTS

Academia Estatal de Artes Francisco Martínez Cabrera

Niños Heroes 9, 82000 Mazatlán, Sinaloa

Tel: +52(69) 82-68-53

Director: Jesús Fernándo Martínez Cabréra

Programmes

Fine Arts (Fine Arts)

History: Founded 1995.

Main Language(s) of Instruction: Spanish

Degrees and Diplomas: *Licenciatura*

Last Updated: 05/03/08

FRAY MATÍAS ANTONIO DE CÓRDOBA Y ORDÓÑEZ FEDERAL EXPERIMENTAL SCHOOL OF PRIMARY EDUCATION TEACHER TRAINING

Escuela Normal Federal Experimental Primaria 'Fray Matías Antonio de Córdoba y Ordóñez'.

Km.1 Periférico Sur s/n, Col. Maria Auxiliadora, 29290 San Cristóbal de las Casas, Chiapas

Tel: +52(967) 678-26-62

EMail: admin@enfex.edu.mx

Website: http://enfex.edu.mx/

Director: José Luis Alcántara Reyes EMail: director@enfex.edu.mx

Programmes

Pre-School Education (Preschool Education); **Primary Education** (Primary Education; Teacher Training)

History: Founded 1977.

Main Language(s) of Instruction: Spanish

Degrees and Diplomas: *Licenciatura*

Last Updated: 25/02/13

FRONTERIZA URBAN FEDERAL TEACHER TRAINING SCHOOL

Escuela Normal Urbana Federal 'Fronteriza'

Calle de La Normal S/N, Ex-Ejido Coahuila, 21360 Mexicali, Baja California

Tel: +52(686) 666-44-35 +52(686) 666-49-60

Fax: +52(686) 666-44-35

Director: Eloy Jiménez Figueroa

Programmes

Primary Education (Primary Education); **Special Education** (Special Education; Teacher Training)

Degrees and Diplomas: *Licenciatura*: 8 sem.

Last Updated: 04/04/08

F.S.T.S.E. NATIONAL INSTITUTE OF TRADE UNION AND PUBLIC ADMINISTRATION STUDIES

Instituto Nacional de Estudios Sindicales y de Administración Pública F.S.T.S.E.

Antonio Caso 35, Col. Tabacalera, Delegación Cuauhtémoc, 06030 México, D.F.

Tel: +52(55) 55-25-65-34 +52(55) 55-92-85-59

Fax: +52(55) 57-05-11-80 +52(55) 55-07-34-89

EMail: inesap_fstse@yahoo.com.mx

Director General: Joel Ayala

Programmes

Labour and Industrial Relations (Labour and Industrial Relations)

Degrees and Diplomas: *Licenciatura*

Last Updated: 07/03/13

GABY BRIMMER REHABILITATION CENTRE OF THE ZAPATA FEDERAL DISTRICT

Centro de Rehabilitación del Dif. Zapata, Gaby Brimmer

Avenida Emiliano Zapata 300, Col. Santa Cruz Atoyac, 03300 Benito Juárez, D.F.

Tel: +52(55) 30-03-22-00 Ext. 6753

Fax: +52(55) 10-35-07-99

Directora: Martha Griselda del Valle Cabrera

Schools

Physical and Occupational Therapy

Degrees and Diplomas: *Licenciatura*: 8 sem.

Last Updated: 26/03/08

GENERAL IGNACIO M. BETETA TEACHER TRAINING SCHOOL IN PHYSICAL EDUCATION

Escuela Normal de Educación Física General Ignacio M. Beteta

Eduardo Monroy Cárdenas 100, Col. Cultural, 50110 Toluca, Estado de México

Tel: +52(722) 278-19-01 +52(722) 278-08-00

EMail: enefweb@gmail.com

Website: http://portal2.edomex.gob.mx/enef/index.htm

Director General: Félix Moisés Valdez Morales (1989-)

Programmes

Physical Education (Education; Physical Education)

History: Founded 1988.

Main Language(s) of Instruction: Spanish

Degrees and Diplomas: *Licenciatura*; *Especialización*

Last Updated: 22/02/13

GENERAL MARIANO ESCOBEDO TECHNOLOGICAL UNIVERSITY

Universidad Tecnológica General Mariano Escobedo

Km. 33.5 Libramiento Noreste, 66050 Ciudad General Escobedo, Nuevo León

Tel: +52 (81) 5000-4200

EMail: informes@ute.edu.mx

Website: http://www.ute.edu.mx

Rector: Lorenzo Vela Peña EMail: lvela@ute.edu.mx

Programmes

Business Administration (Business Administration; Economics; Finance; Sales Techniques); **Electronic and Mechanical Engineering** (Electronic Engineering; Mechanical Engineering); **Environmental Technology** (Environmental Engineering); **Industrial Maintenance** (Environmental Management; Industrial Maintenance; Labour and Industrial Relations); **Information Technology** (Information Technology)

History: Founded 1998.

Main Language(s) of Instruction: Spanish

Degrees and Diplomas: *Licenciatura*. Técnico Superior Universitario

Libraries: Yes

Last Updated: 31/01/13

GUADALAJARA COLLEGE OF PUBLIC ACCOUNTANTS

Colegio de Contadores Públicos de Guadalajara

Oscar Wilde, 5561, Jardines Vallarta, 45020 Zapopan, Jalisco

Tel: +52(33) 36-29-74-45

Fax: +52(33) 36-29-74-52

EMail: jorgenra@prodigy.net.mx

Website: http://www.ccpg.org.mx

Presidente: José Antonio Ramos Cárdenas

Programmes

Auditing, Finance and Taxation (Accountancy; Finance; Taxation)

History: Founded 1959. Acquired present status 1999.

Main Language(s) of Instruction: Spanish

Degrees and Diplomas: *Especialización*

Last Updated: 27/07/12

HEALTH SERVICES INSTITUTE OF THE FEDERAL DISTRICT

Instituto de Servicios de Salud del Distrito Federal

Av. Jardín N° 356, Col. del Gas, Delegación Azcapotzalco, 02950 México, D.F.

Tel: +52(555) 355-52-94

Website: http://www.hospitalsoup.com/listing/47997-instituto-de-servicios-de-salud-del-d-f-

Director: Manuel H. Ruiz de Chávez

Programmes

Health Services (Health Administration; Health Sciences)

Main Language(s) of Instruction: Spanish

Degrees and Diplomas: *Especialización*

Last Updated: 27/03/13

HIGHER COLLEGE OF STOCKBREEDING OF THE STATE OF GUERRERO

Colegio Superior Agropecuario del Estado de Guerrero

Av. Guerrero No. 81 Col. Centro, 40000 Iguala, Guerrero

Tel: +52(733) 332-62-55

EMail: contacto@csaegro.gob.mx

Website: http://www.csaegro.gob.mx

Director General: José Emilio Bueno Jaquez
EMail: emilio.bueno@csaegro.gob.mx

Centres

Professional Studies (Agriculture; Zoology); **Technical Studies** (Agriculture; Cattle Breeding)

Degrees and Diplomas: *Licenciatura*. Técnico Agropecuario

Libraries: Yes

Last Updated: 23/08/12

HIGHER TEACHER TRAINING SCHOOL IN PHYSICAL EDUCATION OF JALISCO

Escuela Normal Superior de Educación Física de Jalisco

Calle Nueva Escocia 1535, Col. Providencia, Unidad Deportiva Revolución, Zapopan, Jalisco

Tel: +52(33) 6-42-57-51

Fax: +52(33) 6-42-57-51

EMail: esfjal@mexico.com

Website: http://portalsej.jalisco.gob.mx/escuela-superior-educacion-fisica/node/43

Director: Antonio De Jesus Ibarra Medina

Programmes

Physical Education (Physical Education)

History: Founded 1977. Acquired present status 1984.

Main Language(s) of Instruction: Spanish

Degrees and Diplomas: *Licenciatura*

Last Updated: 25/02/13

HIGHER TEACHER TRAINING SCHOOL IN PHYSICAL EDUCATION OF THE EAST

Escuela Normal Superior de Educación Física de Oriente

Calle 16 x 47, s/n, Col. San Francisco, 97780 Valladolid, Yucatán

Tel: +52(995) 996-29-71

Director: Marcelino Aguilar Aguilar

Programmes

Physical Education (Physical Education; Teacher Training)

Main Language(s) of Instruction: Spanish

Degrees and Diplomas: *Licenciatura*

Last Updated: 04/04/08

HIGHER TEACHER TRAINING SCHOOL OF JALISCO

Escuela Normal Superior de Jalisco

Calle Lisboa, 488, Col. Sta. Elena Estadio, Guadalajara, Jalisco

Tel: +52(33) 38-24-54-01

EMail: ensj@hotmail.com

Website: http://www.ensj.edu.mx

Director: Víctor Manuel De la Torre Espinoza

Programmes

Secondary Education (Secondary Education); **Teacher Training** (Teacher Training)

History: Founded 1973.

Main Language(s) of Instruction: Spanish

Degrees and Diplomas: *Licenciatura*; *Maestría*

Last Updated: 25/02/13

HIGHER TEACHER TRAINING SCHOOL OF MEXICO

Escuela Normal Superior de México

Manuel Salazar, 201, Col. Ex-Hacienda El Rosario, Delegación Azcapotzalco, 02430 México, D.F.

Tel: +52(55) 53-94-33-93 +52(55) 53-94-33-79

Fax: +52(55) 53-82-60-45

Director: Héctor Cantú Lagunas

Programmes

Biology (Biology); **Chemistry** (Chemistry); **Civic Education and Ethics** (Civics; Ethics); **English** (English); **French** (French); **Geography** (Geography); **History** (History); **Mathematics** (Mathematics); **Pedagogy**; **Physics**; **Psychology** (Psychology); **Spanish**

History: Founded 1942.

Main Language(s) of Instruction: Spanish

Degrees and Diplomas: *Licenciatura*; *Especialización*; *Maestría*

Last Updated: 12/03/08

HIGHER TEACHER TRAINING SCHOOL OF NAYARIT

Escuela Normal Superior de Nayarit
Avenida 12 De Octubre s/n - s/n, Ciudad de la Cultura Amado Nervo, 63361 Tepic, Nayarit
Tel: +52(311) 213-31-74
Website: http://www.ensn.edu.mx

Director: David Corrales Zavalza

Programmes
Teacher Training (Teacher Training)

Main Language(s) of Instruction: Spanish

Degrees and Diplomas: *Licenciatura*; *Especialización*; *Maestría*
Last Updated: 25/02/13

HIGHER TEACHER TRAINING SCHOOL OF PHYSICAL EDUCATION

Escuela Normal Superior de Educación Física 'Profr. Luis Montaño Buis'
Chiapas S/N (UDA), Col. Progreso, 39350 Acapulco de Juárez, Guerrero
Tel: +52(74) 86-10-92
Fax: +52(74) 86-50-06
EMail: esefacapulco@prodigy.net.mx

Director: Octavio Augusto Pacheco Hernández

Programmes
Physical Education (Physical Education)
History: Founded 1983 as Escuela Normal Superior de Educación Física 'Profr. Luis Montaño Buis'. Acquired present title 1991.
Main Language(s) of Instruction: Spanish
Degrees and Diplomas: *Licenciatura*
Last Updated: 25/02/13

HIGHER TEACHER TRAINING SCHOOL OF QUERETARO

Escuela Normal Superior de Querétaro
Calle Colón No. 14, Col Centro Histórico, 76000 Querétaro, Querétaro
Tel: +52(442) 214-47-41
EMail: info@ensq.edu.mx
Website: http://www.ensq.edu.mx/

Directora: Rosa María Magallanes Moreno
EMail: rmagallanes@queretaro.gob.mx

Programmes
Education (Education; Secondary Education); **Teacher Training** (Teacher Training)

Main Language(s) of Instruction: Spanish

Degrees and Diplomas: *Licenciatura*; *Maestría*
Last Updated: 25/02/13

HIGHER TEACHER TRAINING SCHOOL OF SPECIALITIES OF GUADALAJARA

Escuela Normal Superior de Especialidades de Guadalajara
Francisco Siles, 1279, Jardines Plaza del Sol, 45000 Guadalajara, Jalisco
Tel: +52(33) 36-22-52-71
EMail: anav198@hotmail.com

Directora: Ana Vicenta Davila Chávez

Programmes
Special Education (Special Education); **Teacher Training** (Teacher Training)

Main Language(s) of Instruction: Spanish

Degrees and Diplomas: *Licenciatura*
Last Updated: 25/02/13

HIGHER TEACHER TRAINING SCHOOL OF THE STATE OF BAJA CALIFORNIA SUR

Escuela Normal Superior del Estado de Baja California Sur
Sierra las Vírgenes y Sierra San Javier, Col. 8 de Octubre, 23080 La Paz, Baja California Sur
Tel: +52(612) 221-20-95
Fax: +52(612) 221-04-90
EMail: ens@sepbcs.gob.mx
Website: http://www.normalsuperiorbcs.edu.mx

Director: Edgar León Alcántar

Programmes
Teacher Training (Teacher Training)

Further Information: Branches in Ciudad Constitución and San José del Cabo

Main Language(s) of Instruction: Spanish

Degrees and Diplomas: *Licenciatura*; *Maestría*

Libraries: Biblioteca Profr. Manuel Salgado Calderón
Last Updated: 26/02/13

HIGHER TEACHER TRAINING SCHOOL OF THE STATE OF CHIAPAS

Escuela Normal Superior del Estado de Chiapas
Av. 20 de Noviembre No. 2082, Albania Alta, 29800 Tuxtla Gutiérrez, Chiapas
Tel: +52(961) 618-19-18
Fax: +52(961) 618-19-18
Website: http://ensch-oficial.wix.com/ensch-oficial

Directora: Elizabeth Villalobos García

Programmes
Secondary Education (Secondary Education; Teacher Training)
History: Founded 1972.
Main Language(s) of Instruction: Spanish
Degrees and Diplomas: *Licenciatura*; *Maestría*
Last Updated: 26/02/13

HIGHER TEACHER TRAINING SCHOOL OF THE STATE OF COAHUILA

Escuela Normal Superior del Estado de Coahuila
Blvd. Nazario S. Ortíz Garza s/n, Col. Topochico, 25295 Saltillo, Coahuila
Tel: +52(844) 135-64-91
EMail: ense@galileo.educa.ws
Website: http://www.ense.sepc.edu.mx

Director: Carlos René Delgado de Jesús

Divisions
Graduate Studies (Teacher Training)

Programmes
Teacher Training (Biology; Civics; English; Ethics; History; Mathematics; Modern Languages; Spanish; Teacher Training)

History: Founded 1944.

Academic Year: August to June

Fees: (Pesos): 3,200 per annum

Main Language(s) of Instruction: Spanish

Accrediting Agencies: Secretaría de Educación Pública (SEP)

Degrees and Diplomas: *Maestría*: Biology; History; Mathematics; Modern Languages; English; Spanish; Civics; Ethics

Student Services: Handicapped facilities, Health services, Sports facilities

Student Residential Facilities: None
Last Updated: 26/02/13

HIGHER TEACHER TRAINING SCHOOL OF THE STATE OF MEXICO

Escuela Normal Superior del Estado de México
Apartado postal 48-D, Natalia Carrasco, 400, Col. Federal, 50120 Toluca, Estado de México
Tel: +52(722) 219-34-82 +52(722) 219-34-92
Fax: +52(722) 219-30-29
EMail: ensem@edomex.gob.mx
Website: http://www.ensem.edu.mx

Director: Maximino B. Ortiz Jiménez

Programmes
Biology (Biology); **Mathematics** (Mathematics); **Spanish** (Spanish)

History: Founded 1967.

Main Language(s) of Instruction: Spanish

Degrees and Diplomas: *Licenciatura*; *Maestria*
Last Updated: 26/02/13

HIGHER TEACHER TRAINING SCHOOL OF THE STATE OF PUEBLA

Escuela Normal Superior del Estado de Puebla
Calle 11 Sur No. 1102, Centro, 72000 Puebla, Puebla
Tel: +52(222) 243-84-73
Fax: +52(222) 243-84-73
Website: http://ensep.com.mx

Director: Jaime Marín Leal

Programmes
Secondary Education (Secondary Education; Teacher Training)

History: Founded 1984.

Main Language(s) of Instruction: Spanish

Degrees and Diplomas: *Licenciatura*
Last Updated: 26/02/13

HIGHER TECHNICAL INSTITUTE OF HUATUSCO

Instituto Tecnológico Superior de Huatusco
Avenida 25, pte., 100, Col. Reserva Territorial, 94100 Huatusco, Veracruz
Tel: +52 (273) 734-40-00
EMail: itsh@itshuatusco.edu.mx
Website: http://www.itshuatusco.edu.mx

Director: Tomás José Montalvo Aguilar

Programmes
Accountancy (Accountancy); **Business Administration** (Business Administration); **Engineering** (Computer Engineering; Electronic Engineering; Industrial Engineering; Mechanical Engineering); **Food Technology** (Food Technology)

History: Founded 2004.

Main Language(s) of Instruction: Spanish

Degrees and Diplomas: *Licenciatura*
Last Updated: 20/03/13

HIGHER TECHNOLOGICAL INSTITUTE OF ACATLÁN DE OSORIO

Instituto Tecnológico Superior de Acatlán de Osorio
Km. 5.5 Carretera Acatlán-San Juan Ixcaquixtla, 74949 Acatlán de Osorio, Puebla
Tel: +52(953) 5-34-18-77
EMail: buzon@itsao.edu.mx
Website: http://www.itsao.edu.mx/

Director: Luis Enrique Manzano Martinez (2001-)

Programmes
Computer Science (Computer Science); **Engineering**

History: Founded 1997.

Main Language(s) of Instruction: Spanish

Degrees and Diplomas: *Licenciatura*
Last Updated: 25/03/08

HIGHER TECHNOLOGICAL INSTITUTE OF ACAYUCÁN

Instituto Tecnológico Superior de Acayucán
Carretera Costera del Golfo Km. 216.4 Desviación a Monte Grande Col. Agrícola Michapan, Acayucán, Veracruz
Tel: +52(924) 925-62-39

Director: Juvencio Gerardo De León Olarte

Programmes
Biochemical Engineering (Bioengineering); **Computer Engineering** (Computer Engineering); **Computer Science** (Computer Science)

History: Founded 2000.

Main Language(s) of Instruction: Spanish

Degrees and Diplomas: *Licenciatura*
Last Updated: 20/03/13

HIGHER TECHNOLOGICAL INSTITUTE OF ÁLAMO-TEMAPACHE

Instituto Tecnológico Superior de Álamo-Temapache
Km. 6.5 Carretera Potrero del Llano, Tuxpán, 92750 Alamo-Temapache, Veracruz
Tel: +52(783) 844-00-38
EMail: itsalamo@itsalamo.edu.mx
Website: http://www.itsalamo.edu.mx

Director: Alejandro Villanueva Cerón

Programmes
Administration (Administration); **Computer Systems** (Computer Engineering); **Environmental Engineering** (Environmental Engineering); **Food Industries** (Food Technology); **Industrial Engineering** (Industrial Engineering); **Information Technology** (Information Technology)

History: Founded 2000.

Main Language(s) of Instruction: Spanish

Degrees and Diplomas: *Licenciatura*
Last Updated: 20/03/13

HIGHER TECHNOLOGICAL INSTITUTE OF ALVARADO

Instituto Tecnológico Superior de Alvarado
Escollera Norte S/N., Col. La Trocha, 95277 Alvarado, Veracruz
Tel: +52(297) 973-36-00
EMail: informacion@itsav.edu.mx
Website: http://www.itsav.edu.mx

Director: Ramses Alejandro Galindo Cota

Programmes
Accountancy (Accountancy); **Business Administration** (Business Administration); **Engineering** (Computer Engineering; Electronic Engineering; Industrial Engineering; Mechanical Engineering)

Further Information: Also Campus Tralixcoyan; Campus Lerdo and Campus Medellin

History: Founded 2003.

Main Language(s) of Instruction: Spanish

Degrees and Diplomas: *Licenciatura*
Last Updated: 26/03/13

HIGHER TECHNOLOGICAL INSTITUTE OF APATZINGÁN

Instituto Tecnológico Superior de Apatzingán
Km. 3.5 Carretera Apatzingán-Agulilla s/n, 60600 Apatzingán, Michoacán
Tel: +52(453) 534-03-71
EMail: direcciongeneral@itsa.edu.mx
Website: http://www.itsa.edu.mx

Director: José Luis Garibay Ibarra

Programmes
Accountancy (Accountancy); **Business Administration** (Business Administration); **Computer Science** (Computer Science);

Engineering (Biochemistry; Civil Engineering; Computer Engineering; Industrial Engineering)
History: Founded 1994.
Main Language(s) of Instruction: Spanish
Degrees and Diplomas: *Licenciatura*
Last Updated: 20/03/13

HIGHER TECHNOLOGICAL INSTITUTE OF ARANDAS

Instituto Tecnológico Superior de Arandas

Libramiento Sur. Km. 2.7, Arandas, 47180 Arandas, Jalisco
Tel: +52(1348) 783-20-20
EMail: direccion@tecarandas.edu.mx
Website: http://www.tecarandas.edu.mx

Director: Juan Pablo Cerrillo Hernández

Programmes
Administration (Administration; Business Administration); **Engineering** (Industrial Engineering); **Food Technology** (Food Technology)
History: Founded 2000.
Main Language(s) of Instruction: Spanish
Degrees and Diplomas: *Licenciatura*
Last Updated: 20/03/13

HIGHER TECHNOLOGICAL INSTITUTE OF ATLIXCO

Instituto Tecnológico Superior de Atlixco

Prolongación Heliotropo, 1201, Col. Vista Hermosa, 74218 Atlixco, Puebla
Tel: +52(244) 446-04-65 +52(244) 445-25-43
EMail: direccion@itsatlixco.edu.mx
Website: http://www.itsatlixco.edu.mx/v2

Director: José Guillermo Velázquez Gutiérrez
EMail: dgatlixco@gmail.com

Programmes
Biochemistry (Biochemistry); **Engineering** (Electronic Engineering; Industrial Engineering; Mechanical Engineering)
History: Founded 1998.
Main Language(s) of Instruction: Spanish
Degrees and Diplomas: *Licenciatura*
Last Updated: 20/03/13

HIGHER TECHNOLOGICAL INSTITUTE OF CAJEME

Instituto Tecnológico Superior de Cajeme (ITESCA)

Km. 2 Carretera Internacional a Nogales, 85010 Ciudad Obregón, Sonora
Tel: +52(644) 410-86-50
EMail: director@itesca.edu.mx
Website: http://www.itesca.edu.mx/

Director: Paulino Antonio Sánchez López

Programmes
Administration (Administration; Business Administration; International Business; Marketing); **Architecture** (Architecture); **Education** (Education); **Engineering** (Computer Engineering; Electronic Engineering; Environmental Engineering; Geological Engineering; Industrial Engineering; Mechanical Engineering)
History: Founded 1997.
Main Language(s) of Instruction: Spanish
Degrees and Diplomas: *Licenciatura*; *Maestría*
Last Updated: 20/03/13

HIGHER TECHNOLOGICAL INSTITUTE OF CALKINI IN THE STATE OF CAMPECHE

Instituto Tecnológico Superior de Calkini en el Estado de Campeche

Av. Ah Canul S/N por Carretera Federal, 24000 Calkini, Campeche
Tel: +52(996) 961-04-94
Fax: +52(996) 961-09-67
EMail: jmalcocer@itescam.edu.mx
Website: http://www.itescam.edu.mx

Director: Juan Manuel Alcocer Martínez

Programmes
Administration (Administration); **Computer Science** (Computer Science); **Engineering** (Bioengineering; Chemical Engineering; Computer Engineering; Food Technology; Industrial Engineering; Materials Engineering)
Further Information: Also branch in Hopelchén
History: Founded 2001.
Main Language(s) of Instruction: Spanish
Degrees and Diplomas: *Licenciatura*
Last Updated: 20/03/13

HIGHER TECHNOLOGICAL INSTITUTE OF CANANEA

Instituto Tecnológico Superior de Cananea

Km. 82.5 Carretera Cananea-Agua Prieta, Col. Agropecuaria, 84620 Cananea, Sonora
Tel: +52(645) 452-50-17
Fax: +52(645) 452-69-92
EMail: teccan@prodigy.net.mx
Website: http://www.teccan.edu.mx

Director: Pablo Andrade Gerardo
EMail: pablo.andrade@teccan.edu.mx

Programmes
Administration (Administration); **Engineering** (Computer Engineering; Electrical Engineering; Industrial Engineering; Mechanical Engineering)
History: Founded 1991.
Main Language(s) of Instruction: Spanish
Degrees and Diplomas: *Licenciatura*; *Maestría*
Last Updated: 20/03/13

HIGHER TECHNOLOGICAL INSTITUTE OF CENTLA

Instituto Tecnológico Superior de Centla

Calle Ejido S/N, Col. Siglo XXI, Frontera, 86751 Centla, Tabasco
Tel: +52(913) 332-13-81
EMail: itscentla@itscentla.edu.mx
Website: http://www.itscentla.edu.mx

Director: Carlos Alberto Ramón Güemes
EMail: direccion@itscentla.edu.mx

Programmes
Business Administration (Business Administration); **Engineering** (Chemical Engineering; Computer Engineering; Electronic Engineering; Environmental Engineering; Industrial Engineering; Information Technology; Mechanical Engineering)
History: Founded 2001.
Main Language(s) of Instruction: Spanish
Degrees and Diplomas: *Licenciatura*
Last Updated: 26/03/13

HIGHER TECHNOLOGICAL INSTITUTE OF CHAMPOTON

Instituto Tecnologico Superior de Champotón

Carretera Champotón - Isla Aguada Km. 2, Col. El Arenal, 24400 Champotón, Campeche
Tel: +52(982) 828–24-32
EMail: cinformacion@itescham.edu.mx
Website: http://www.itescham.com

Director: Edilberto Ramón Rosado Méndez

Programmes
Accountancy (Accountancy); **Administration** (Administration; Business Administration); **Engineering** (Computer Engineering; Electronic Engineering; Environmental Engineering; Mechanical Engineering; Software Engineering); **International Business** (International Business); **Tourism** (Tourism)

History: Founded 2007.

Main Language(s) of Instruction: Spanish

Degrees and Diplomas: *Licenciatura*; *Especialización*

Last Updated: 26/03/13

HIGHER TECHNOLOGICAL INSTITUTE OF CHAPALA

Instituto Tecnológico Superior de Chapala
Libramiento Chapala Ajijic #200, 45900 Chapala, Jalisco
Tel: +52(376) 76 - 6 -47- 58
EMail: planeacion@itschapala.com
Website: http://www.itschapala.com

Director: Morris Schwarzblat y Kat (2008-)

Programmes
Administration (Administration); **Engineering** (Computer Engineering; Electronic Engineering; Industrial Engineering)

History: Founded 2000.

Main Language(s) of Instruction: Spanish

Degrees and Diplomas: *Licenciatura*

Last Updated: 20/03/13

HIGHER TECHNOLOGICAL INSTITUTE OF CINTALAPA

Instituto Tecnológico Superior de Cintalapa
Carretera Panamericana Km. 995, 30400 Cintalapa de Figueroa, Chiapas
Tel: +52(968) 684-47-79
EMail: direccion@tecdecintalapa.edu.mx
Website: http://www.tecdecintalapa.edu.mx

Directora: María Magdalena Pérez Salgado

Programmes
Computer Science (Computer Science); **Engineering** (Energy Engineering; Food Technology; Industrial Engineering)

History: Founded 2001.

Main Language(s) of Instruction: Spanish

Degrees and Diplomas: *Licenciatura*

Last Updated: 20/03/13

HIGHER TECHNOLOGICAL INSTITUTE OF CIUDAD ACUÑA

Instituto Tecnológico Superior de Ciudad Acuña
Km. 9 Carretera a Presa la Amistad, 26200 Acuña, Coahuila
Tel: +52(877) 773-18-00
Fax: +52(877) 773-18-01
EMail: tsa@tecnologicodeacuna.edu.mx
Website: http://www.tecnologicodeacuna.edu.mx

Director: Raúl Sergio Farías Martínez

Programmes
Business Administration (Business Administration); **Engineering** (Computer Engineering; Electronic Engineering; Industrial Engineering; Mechanical Engineering)

History: Founded 1998.

Main Language(s) of Instruction: Spanish

Degrees and Diplomas: *Licenciatura*

Last Updated: 20/03/13

HIGHER TECHNOLOGICAL INSTITUTE OF CIUDAD CONSTITUCIÓN

Instituto Tecnológico Superior de Ciudad Constitución
Marcelo Ruiz, s/n, Col. Ampliación 4 de Marzo, Ciudad Constitución, 23080 Ciudad Constitución, Baja California Sur
Tel: +52(613) 132-53-57 +52(613) 132-54-50
Fax: +52(613) 132-53-66
EMail: itscc@.itscc.edu.mx
Website: http://www.itscc.edu.mx

Director: Edgar Guillermo Polanco Martínez

Programmes
Undergraduate and Professional (Administration; Architecture; Business Administration; Computer Engineering; Electrical Engineering; Engineering; Food Technology; Industrial Engineering; Mechanical Engineering)

History: Founded 1996.

Main Language(s) of Instruction: Spanish

Degrees and Diplomas: *Licenciatura*

Last Updated: 20/03/13

HIGHER TECHNOLOGICAL INSTITUTE OF CIUDAD HIDALGO

Instituto Tecnológico Superior de Ciudad Hidalgo
Av. Ing. Carlos Rojas Gutiérrez 2120. Fraccionamiento Valle de la Herradura, 61100 Ciudad Hidalgo, Michoacán
Tel: +52(786) 154-90-00
EMail: itschmich@gmail.com
Website: http://www.itsch.edu.mx

Director: Juan José Maldonado García

Programmes
Computer Science (Computer Science); **Engineering** (Bioengineering; Chemical Engineering; Computer Engineering; Electronic Engineering; Industrial Engineering; Mechanical Engineering)

History: Founded 2000.

Main Language(s) of Instruction: Spanish

Degrees and Diplomas: *Licenciatura*

Last Updated: 20/03/13

HIGHER TECHNOLOGICAL INSTITUTE OF CIUDAD SERDÁN

Instituto Tecnológico Superior de Ciudad Serdán
Avenida Instituto Tecnológico S/N Col. La Gloria, 75520 Ciudad Serdán, Puebla
Tel: +52(245) 452-18-34 +52(245) 452-18-35
EMail: mgglezgasca@hotmail.com

Director: José Pizano Calderón

Programmes
Engineering (Computer Engineering; Engineering; Industrial Engineering; Mechanical Engineering); **Food Technology** (Food Technology)

History: Founded 1999.

Main Language(s) of Instruction: Spanish

Degrees and Diplomas: *Licenciatura*

Last Updated: 20/03/13

HIGHER TECHNOLOGICAL INSTITUTE OF COATZACOALCOS

Instituto Tecnológico Superior de Coatzacoalcos
Carretera Antigua Minatitlan Coatzacoalcos Km 16.5, Col. Las Gaviotas, 96536 Coatzacoalcos, Veracruz
Tel: +52(921) 211-81-58
EMail: scruzr@itesco.edu.mx
Website: http://www.itesco.edu.mx

Director: Ricardo Orozco Alor

Programmes
Administration (Administration; Business Administration); **Computer Science** (Computer Science); **Engineering** (Biochemistry; Chemical Engineering; Electrical Engineering; Electronic

Engineering; Industrial Engineering; Mechanical Engineering; Petroleum and Gas Engineering)

History: Founded 1999.

Main Language(s) of Instruction: Spanish

Degrees and Diplomas: *Licenciatura*; *Maestría*

Last Updated: 20/03/13

HIGHER TECHNOLOGICAL INSTITUTE OF COMALCALCO

Instituto Tecnológico Superior de Comalcalco

Km. 2 Carretera Vecinal Comalcalco-Paraíso, Ranch. Occidente, 3ra Sección, 86650 Comalcalco, Tabasco

Tel: +52(933) 334-01-24

EMail: direcciongeneral@mail.itsc.edu.mx

Website: http://www.itsc.edu.mx/

Director: Carlos Mario Olán López EMail: tec@mail.itsc.edu.mx

Programmes

Accountancy (Accountancy); **Engineering** (Computer Engineering; Electronic Engineering; Industrial Engineering; Mechanical Engineering); **Food Technology** (Food Technology)

History: Founded 1994.

Main Language(s) of Instruction: Spanish

Degrees and Diplomas: *Licenciatura*; *Especialización*; *Maestría*

Last Updated: 20/03/13

HIGHER TECHNOLOGICAL INSTITUTE OF COSAMALOAPÁN

Instituto Tecnológico Superior de Cosamaloapán

Avenida Tecnológico s/n, Col. Los Ángeles, Cosamaloapan de Carpio, 95400 Cosamaloapán, Veracruz

Tel: +52(288) 882-31-00

EMail: itsco@hotmail.com

Website: http://www.itsco.edu.mx

Director: Ricardo Antonio Mondragón Ramos

Programmes

Accountancy (Accountancy); **Business Administration** (Business Administration); **Computer Science** (Computer Science); **Engineering** (Agricultural Engineering; Computer Engineering; Electronic Engineering; Industrial Engineering; Petroleum and Gas Engineering)

History: Founded 1998.

Main Language(s) of Instruction: Spanish

Degrees and Diplomas: *Licenciatura*

Last Updated: 20/03/13

HIGHER TECHNOLOGICAL INSTITUTE OF FELIPE CARRILLO PUERTO

Instituto Tecnológico Superior de Felipe Carrillo Puerto

Carretera Vigia Chico km. 1.5, 77200 Felipe Carrillo Puerto, Quintana Roo

Tel: +52(983) 834-00-51

EMail: co.hernandez@itscarrillopuerto.edu.mx

Website: http://www.itscarrillopuerto.edu.mx

Director: Sergio Efraín Chab

Programmes

Administration (Administration); **Business Administration** (Business Administration); **Engineering** (Computer Engineering; Industrial Engineering); **Food Technology** (Food Technology)

History: Founded 1997.

Main Language(s) of Instruction: Spanish

Degrees and Diplomas: *Licenciatura*

Last Updated: 20/03/13

HIGHER TECHNOLOGICAL INSTITUTE OF FRESNILLO

Instituto Tecnológico Superior de Fresnillo

Avenida Tecnológico, 2000, Col. Solidaridad, 99040 Fresnillo, Zacatecas

Tel: +52(493) 932-93-32 +52(493) 932-93-33

Fax: +52(493) 932-93-31

EMail: tecfres@itsf.edu.mx

Website: http://www.itsf.edu.mx/

Director: Hugo Jiménez Alvarez EMail: direccion@itsf.edu.mx

Programmes

Architecture (Architecture); **Business Administration** (Business Administration); **Computer Science** (Computer Science); **Engineering** (Computer Engineering; Electronic Engineering; Environmental Engineering; Industrial Engineering)

History: Founded 1994.

Main Language(s) of Instruction: Spanish

Degrees and Diplomas: *Licenciatura*

Last Updated: 20/03/13

HIGHER TECHNOLOGICAL INSTITUTE OF HUAUCHINANGO

Instituto Tecnológico Superior de Huauchinango

80 Lomas de Chapultepec, 73173 Huauchinango, Puebla

Tel: +52(776) 762-52-60

EMail: info@itsh.edu.mx

Head: Ulises Sánchez Morgado

Programmes

Computer Science (Computer Science); **Electrical Engineering** (Electrical Engineering); **Industrial Engineering** (Industrial Engineering); **Mechatronics** (Electronic Engineering; Mechanical Engineering)

History: Founded 2000.

Main Language(s) of Instruction: Spanish

Degrees and Diplomas: *Licenciatura*

Last Updated: 20/03/13

HIGHER TECHNOLOGICAL INSTITUTE OF HUETAMO

Instituto Tecnológico Superior de Huetamo

Carretera a Huetamo- Zitacuaro Kilómetro 1.5 Tenencia de Cutzeo, 61940 Huetamo, Michoacán de Ocampo

Tel: +52(435) 556-27-74

EMail: huetamo@ditd.gob.mx

Website: http://www.itshuetamo.edu.mx

Director: Flavio Luviano Juarez

Programmes

Business Administration (Business Administration); **Engineering** (Computer Engineering; Food Technology; Industrial Engineering; Software Engineering)

History: Founded 2001.

Main Language(s) of Instruction: Spanish

Degrees and Diplomas: *Licenciatura*

Last Updated: 27/03/13

HIGHER TECHNOLOGICAL INSTITUTE OF HUICHAPÁN

Instituto Tecnológico Superior de Huichapán

Domicilio Conocido s/n El Saucillo, 42400 Huichapán, Hidalgo

Tel: +52(761) 724-80-80

EMail: iteshu@iteshu.edu.mx

Website: http://www.iteshu.edu.mx

Directora: María Angélica Bravo Cadena

EMail: mabravo@iteshu.edu.mx

Programmes

Administration (Administration; Business Administration); **Engineering** (Computer Engineering; Electronic Engineering; Energy Engineering; Industrial Engineering; Mechanical Engineering)

History: Founded 1999.
Main Language(s) of Instruction: Spanish
Degrees and Diplomas: *Licenciatura*
Last Updated: 20/03/13

HIGHER TECHNOLOGICAL INSTITUTE OF IRAPUATO

Instituto Tecnológico Superior de Irapuato
Km. 12.5 Carretera Irapuato-Silao, 36800 Irapuato, Guanajuato
Tel: +52(462) 606-79-00
EMail: itesi@itesi.edu.mx
Website: http://www.itesi.edu.mx

Director: Rubén Lara Valdes EMail: direccion@itesi.edu.mx

Programmes
Biology (Biology); **Engineering** (Biochemistry; Computer Engineering; Electronic Engineering; Engineering; Industrial Engineering; Information Technology; Materials Engineering; Mechanical Engineering)
Further Information: Also branches in San Felipe; Abasolo; San Luis de la Paz; San José Iturbide; Purísima del Rincón; Tarimoro; and Cuerámaro
History: Founded 1996.
Main Language(s) of Instruction: Spanish
Degrees and Diplomas: *Licenciatura*; *Especialización*; *Maestría*
Last Updated: 20/03/13

HIGHER TECHNOLOGICAL INSTITUTE OF JEREZ

Instituto Tecnológico Superior de Jerez
Libramiento Fresnillo - Tepetongo s/n, Colonia Fracc. Los Cardos, 99360 Jerez de García, Salinas
Tel: +52(494) 945-12-26
EMail: tecjerez2003@yahoo.com.mx
Website: http://www.tecjerez.edu.mx

Director: Hebert Horacio Herrera Quezada

Programmes
Administration (Accountancy; Administration); **Engineering** (Computer Engineering; Electronic Engineering; Food Technology; Mechanical Engineering)
History: Founded 2003.
Main Language(s) of Instruction: Spanish
Degrees and Diplomas: *Licenciatura*
Last Updated: 27/03/13

HIGHER TECHNOLOGICAL INSTITUTE OF LAGOS DE MORENO

Instituto Tecnológico Superior de Lagos de Moreno
Libramiento Tecnológico No. 5000 Col. Portugalejo de los Romanes, 47480 Lagos de Moreno, Jalisco
Tel: +52(474) 741-24-74
EMail: director@teclagos.edu.mx
Website: http://www.teclagos.edu.mx

Director: David Avalos Cueva

Programmes
Civil Engineering (Civil Engineering); **Computer Engineering** (Computer Engineering); **Electrical and Mechanical Engineering** (Electrical Engineering; Mechanical Engineering); **Industrial Engineering** (Industrial Engineering)
History: Founded 2000.
Main Language(s) of Instruction: Spanish
Degrees and Diplomas: *Licenciatura*
Last Updated: 20/03/13

HIGHER TECHNOLOGICAL INSTITUTE OF LAS CHOAPAS

Instituto Tecnológico Superior de Las Choapas
Carretera Las Choapas-Cerro de Nanchital Km. 6, Col. J. Mario Rosado, 96980 Las Choapas, Veracruz
Tel: +52(923) 323-20-10
EMail: contacto@itschoapas.edu.mx
Website: http://www.itschoapas.edu.mx

Director: Alfredo Jaén García

Programmes
Engineering (Civil Engineering; Electronic Engineering; Food Technology; Industrial Engineering)
History: Founded 2000.
Main Language(s) of Instruction: Spanish
Degrees and Diplomas: *Licenciatura*
Last Updated: 20/03/13

HIGHER TECHNOLOGICAL INSTITUTE OF LERDO

Instituto Tecnológico Superior de Lerdo
Av. Tecnológico 1555 Sur, Periférico Lerdo, 35150 Ciudad Lerdo, Durango
Tel: +52(871) 725-23-71
EMail: direcciong@itslerdo.edu.mx
Website: http://www.itslerdo.edu.mx/

Director: Jaime Daniel González Reséndiz

Programmes
Computer Science (Computer Science); **Engineering** (Computer Engineering; Electronic Engineering; Environmental Engineering; Industrial Engineering; Mechanical Engineering)
History: Founded 1995.
Main Language(s) of Instruction: Spanish
Degrees and Diplomas: *Licenciatura*
Last Updated: 20/03/13

HIGHER TECHNOLOGICAL INSTITUTE OF LIBRES

Instituto Tecnológico Superior de Libres
Camino Real esquina Calle Cuauhtémoc, Barrio de Tetela, 73780 Libres, Puebla
Tel: +52(276) 473-08-28
EMail: direccion@itslibres.edu.mx
Website: http://www.itslibres.edu.mx/libres/

Director: Jair Nahúm Fierro Breton

Programmes
Business Administration (Business Administration); **Engineering** (Computer Engineering; Electronic Engineering; Industrial Engineering; Mechanical Engineering); **Food Technology** (Food Technology)
History: Founded 2000.
Main Language(s) of Instruction: Spanish
Degrees and Diplomas: *Licenciatura*
Last Updated: 20/03/13

HIGHER TECHNOLOGICAL INSTITUTE OF LORETO

Instituto Tecnológico Superior de Loreto
Carr. aTierra Blanca-Loreto Km. 22, 98800 Loreto, Zacatecas
Tel: +52(496) 962-51-51
EMail: tec_loreto@yahoo.com.mx
Website: http://www.itsloreto.edu.mx

Director: Salvador Lara Martínez

Programmes
Business Administration (Business Administration); **Engineering** (Computer Engineering; Electronic Engineering; Engineering; Industrial Engineering; Mechanical Engineering)
History: Founded 2002.

Main Language(s) of Instruction: Spanish
Degrees and Diplomas: *Licenciatura*
Last Updated: 20/03/13

HIGHER TECHNOLOGICAL INSTITUTE OF LOS REYES

Instituto Tecnológico Superior de Los Reyes
Carretera los Reyes Jacona 3 Libertad, 60330 Los Reyes de Salgado, Michoacán de Ocampo
Tel: +52(354) 542-51-70
EMail: itslr@prodigy.net.mx
Website: http://itslr.edu.mx

Director: Rigoberto Bartolo Mauricio

Programmes
Architecture (Architecture); **Business Administration** (Business Administration); **Engineering** (Agricultural Engineering; Computer Engineering; Electronic Engineering; Industrial Engineering; Mechanical Engineering)
History: Founded 2001.
Main Language(s) of Instruction: Spanish
Degrees and Diplomas: *Licenciatura*
Last Updated: 27/03/13

HIGHER TECHNOLOGICAL INSTITUTE OF LOS RÍOS

Instituto Tecnológico Superior de Los Ríos
Apartado postal 45, Km. 3 Carretera Balancán-Villahermosa, 86931 Balancán, Tabasco
Tel: +52(934) 344-90-00
EMail: itsr@inforedmx.com
Website: http://www.itsr.edu.mx/

Director: Emiliano Gutiérrez Carvarín

Programmes
Administration (Administration); **Engineering** (Biochemistry; Civil Engineering; Computer Engineering; Electronic Engineering; Industrial Engineering; Mechanical Engineering)
History: Founded 1996.
Main Language(s) of Instruction: Spanish
Degrees and Diplomas: *Licenciatura*
Last Updated: 20/03/13

HIGHER TECHNOLOGICAL INSTITUTE OF MACUSPANA

Instituto Tecnológico Superior de Macuspana
Avenida Tecnológico s/n, Lerdo de Tejada 1ra Secc., 86719 Macuspana, Tabasco
Tel: +52(936) 362-33-30
EMail: laguilar@itsmacuspana.edu.mx
Website: http://www.itsmacuspana.edu.mx

Director: Luis Felipe Aguilar Romero

Programmes
Business Administration (Administration; Business Administration); **Engineering** (Civil Engineering; Computer Engineering; Electrical Engineering; Electronic Engineering; Food Technology; Industrial Engineering; Mechanical Engineering)
History: Founded 2000.
Main Language(s) of Instruction: Spanish
Degrees and Diplomas: *Licenciatura*
Last Updated: 20/03/13

HIGHER TECHNOLOGICAL INSTITUTE OF MISANTLA

Instituto Tecnológico Superior de Misantla
Km. 1.8 Carretera a Loma del Cojolite, 93821 Misantla, Veracruz
Tel: +52(235) 323-60-03
EMail: itmis@itsm.edu.mx
Website: http://www.itsm.edu.mx

Director: José Alberto Gaytán (2001-)
EMail: albertogaytangarcia@hotmail.com

Programmes
Business Administration (Business Administration); **Computer Science** (Computer Science); **Engineering** (Biochemistry; Civil Engineering; Computer Engineering; Environmental Engineering; Industrial Engineering; Information Technology)
History: Founded 1994.
Main Language(s) of Instruction: Spanish
Degrees and Diplomas: *Licenciatura*; *Maestría*: Computer Science; Industrial Engineering
Last Updated: 20/03/13

HIGHER TECHNOLOGICAL INSTITUTE OF MONCLOVA

Instituto Tecnológico Superior de Monclova
Carretera 57 Km. 4.5, Lecho del Río Monclova, Unidad Tecnológica Universitaria, 25701 Monclova, Coahuila
Tel: +52(866) 639-12-10
Fax: +52(866) 639-12-09
EMail: jcg_itsm@hotmail.com
Website: http://www.itsmva.edu.mx/

Directora: Guillermina López Banda

Programmes
Business Administration (Business Administration); **Computer Science** (Computer Science); **Engineering** (Electronic Engineering; Industrial Engineering; Mechanical Engineering)
History: Founded 1996.
Main Language(s) of Instruction: Spanish
Degrees and Diplomas: *Licenciatura*
Last Updated: 20/03/13

HIGHER TECHNOLOGICAL INSTITUTE OF MOTUL

Instituto Tecnológico Superior de Motul
Carretera Mérida-Motul, Tablaje Catastral 383, 97430 Motul de Carrillo Puerto, Yucatán
Tel: +52(991) 9151632
EMail: motul@ditd.gob.mx
Website: http://www.itsmotul.edu.mx

Director: Luis Alberto García Domínguez

Programmes
Electrical and Mechanical Engineering (Electrical Engineering; Mechanical Engineering); **Industrial Engineering** (Industrial Engineering); **Systems Engineering** (Computer Engineering)
History: Founded 2000 as Instituto Tecnológico Superior Felipe Carrillo Puerto. Acquired present title 2003.
Main Language(s) of Instruction: Spanish
Degrees and Diplomas: *Licenciatura*
Last Updated: 20/03/13

HIGHER TECHNOLOGICAL INSTITUTE OF MULEGÉ

Instituto Tecnológico Superior de Mulegé
Loma de Los Frailes SN, Col. Centro, 23920 Santa Rosalia, Baja California Sur
Tel: +52(615) 152-16-73
EMail: itsmulege@prodigy.net.mx
Website: http://www.itesme.edu.mx

Director: Pedro G. Osuna López EMail: posuna@itesme.edu.mx

Programmes
Administration (Administration; Business Administration); **Engineering** (Electronic Engineering; Energy Engineering; Food Technology; Industrial Engineering; Mechanical Engineering; Mining Engineering)
History: Founded 2005.
Main Language(s) of Instruction: Spanish
Degrees and Diplomas: *Licenciatura*
Last Updated: 27/03/13

HIGHER TECHNOLOGICAL INSTITUTE OF NOCHISTLÁN

Instituto Tecnológico Superior de Nochistlán
Carretera a los Sandovales Km 2.8, 99900 Nochistlán, Zacatecas
Tel: +52(346) 713-18-05
EMail: itsnochistlan2000@yahoo.com.mx
Website: http://www.itsn.edu.mx

Director: Héctor Manuel Galindo Flores

Programmes
Administration (Administration); **Architecture** (Architecture); **Computer Science** (Computer Science; Systems Analysis); **Industrial Engineering**

History: Founded 2000.
Main Language(s) of Instruction: Spanish
Degrees and Diplomas: *Licenciatura*
Last Updated: 20/03/13

HIGHER TECHNOLOGICAL INSTITUTE OF NORTH ZACATECAS

Instituto Tecnológico Superior de Zacatecas Norte
Apartado postal 178, Km. 3 Carretera a González Arteaga, 98400 Río Grande, Zacatecas
Tel: +52(498) 882-23-90 +52(498) 882-04-66
Fax: +52(498) 882-00-00 +52(498) 882-02-36
EMail: direccion.general@mail.itszn.edu.mx
Website: http://www.itszn.edu.mx/

Director: José Manuel Peña Badillo

Programmes
Administration and Accountancy (Accountancy; Administration); **Computer Science** (Computer Science); **Engineering** (Computer Engineering; Electronic Engineering; Mechanical Engineering); **Food Technology** (Food Technology)

History: Founded 1991.
Main Language(s) of Instruction: Spanish
Degrees and Diplomas: *Licenciatura*
Last Updated: 21/03/13

HIGHER TECHNOLOGICAL INSTITUTE OF NUEVO CASAS GRANDES

Instituto Tecnológico Superior de Nuevo Casas Grandes
Av. Tecnológico No. 7100, 31789 Nuevo Casas Grandes, Chihuahua
Tel: +52(636) 692-95-00
EMail: informes@itsncg.edu.mx
Website: http://www.itsncg.edu.mx

Directora: Soraya Jaramillo Ontiveros

Programmes
Accountancy (Accountancy); **Administration** (Administration; Business Administration); **Engineering** (Computer Engineering; Electronic Engineering; Industrial Engineering)

History: Founded 1994.
Main Language(s) of Instruction: Spanish
Degrees and Diplomas: *Licenciatura*
Last Updated: 20/03/13

HIGHER TECHNOLOGICAL INSTITUTE OF PÁNUCO

Instituto Tecnológico Superior de Pánuco
Prolongación Avenida Artículo Tercero Constitucional s/n, Col. Solidaridad, 93997 Pánuco, Veracruz
Tel: +52(826) 266-28-98
EMail: comunicacionydifusion@itspanuco.edu.mx
Website: http://www.itspanuco.com/

Director: David Gerardo Velasco González

Programmes
Accountancy (Accountancy); **Business Administration** (Business Administration); **Computer Science** (Computer Science); **Engineering** (Electronic Engineering; Industrial Engineering)

History: Founded 1997.
Main Language(s) of Instruction: Spanish
Degrees and Diplomas: *Licenciatura*; *Maestría*
Last Updated: 21/03/13

HIGHER TECHNOLOGICAL INSTITUTE OF PATZCUARO

Instituto Tecnológico Superior de Pátzcuaro
Av. Tecnologico No. 1, Zurumutaro, Patzcuaro, Michoacan
Tel: +52(434) 542-50-49
EMail: gicopatzcuaro@gmail.com
Website: http://www.itspa.edu.mx

Director: Jaime Bulmaro Vázquez

Programmes
Administration (Administration; Biomedical Engineering; Business Administration; Information Technology); **Community Development** (Development Studies); **Engineering** (Environmental Engineering)

History: Founded 2005.
Main Language(s) of Instruction: Spanish
Degrees and Diplomas: *Licenciatura*
Last Updated: 27/03/13

HIGHER TECHNOLOGICAL INSTITUTE OF PEROTE

Instituto Tecnológico Superior de Perote
Km. 2.5 Carretera Federal Perote - México Col. Centro, 91270 Perote, Veracruz
Tel: +52(282) 825-31-50
EMail: itspe@tecperote.com
Website: http://www.tecperote.com

Director: Alfredo González Gutiérrez

Programmes
Business Administration (Business Administration); **Engineering** (Computer Engineering; Food Technology; Forest Management; Industrial Engineering)

History: Founded 2002.
Main Language(s) of Instruction: Spanish
Degrees and Diplomas: *Licenciatura*
Last Updated: 29/03/13

HIGHER TECHNOLOGICAL INSTITUTE OF PROGRESO

Instituto Tecnológico Superior de Progreso
Víctor Manuel Cervera Pacheco, S/N x 62, 97320 Progreso, Yucatán
Tel: +52(969) 934-30-23
EMail: lfrias@itsprogreso.edu.mx
Website: http://www.itsprogreso.edu.mx/

Directora: Lila Rosa Frías Castillo

Programmes
Administration (Administration; Business Administration); **Computer Science** (Computer Science; Systems Analysis); **Electrical and Mechanical Engineering** (Electrical Engineering; Energy Engineering; Mechanical Engineering)

History: Founded 2000.
Main Language(s) of Instruction: Spanish
Degrees and Diplomas: *Licenciatura*; *Maestría*: Business Administration
Last Updated: 21/03/13

HIGHER TECHNOLOGICAL INSTITUTE OF PUERTO PEÑASCO

Instituto Tecnológico Superior de Puerto Peñasco
Blvr. Tecnológico s/n, Col. Centro, 83550 Puerto Peñasco, Sonora
Tel: +52(638) 383-11-00
EMail: direccion@itspp.edu.mx
Website: http://www.itspp.edu.mx

Director: Rafael Lara Mungarro

Programmes
Administration (Administration); **Engineering** (Civil Engineering; Computer Engineering; Industrial Engineering)
History: Founded 2000.
Main Language(s) of Instruction: Spanish
Degrees and Diplomas: *Licenciatura*
Last Updated: 21/03/13

HIGHER TECHNOLOGICAL INSTITUTE OF PUERTO VALLARTA

Instituto Tecnológico Superior de Puerto Vallarta
Corea del Sur # 600, Col. El Mangal, El Pitiyal, 48290 Puerto Vallarta, Jalisco
Tel: +52(322) 226-56-00
EMail: informes@tecvallarta.edu.mx
Website: http://www.tecvallarta.edu.mx

Director: Emilio Contreras Reyes

Programmes
Administration (Administration; Business Administration); **Architecture** (Architecture); **Computer Science** (Computer Science); **Engineering** (Computer Engineering; Electronic Engineering; Engineering; Information Technology; Mechanical Engineering); **Gastronomy** (Cooking and Catering)
History: Founded 1999.
Main Language(s) of Instruction: Spanish
Degrees and Diplomas: *Licenciatura*; *Maestría*: Business Administration
Last Updated: 21/03/13

HIGHER TECHNOLOGICAL INSTITUTE OF RÍOVERDE

Instituto Tecnológico Superior de Rioverde
Carr. Rioverde-San Ciro de Acosta Km. 4.5, 79610 Ríoverde, San Luis Potosí
Tel: +52(487) 871-61-61
EMail: rioverde@ditd.gob.mx
Website: http://www.itsrv.edu.mx

Directora: Magdalena Guerrero Martínez

Programmes
Computer Science (Computer Science; Systems Analysis); **Industrial Engineering** (Agricultural Engineering; Engineering; Industrial Engineering)
History: Founded 1999.
Main Language(s) of Instruction: Spanish
Degrees and Diplomas: *Licenciatura*
Last Updated: 21/03/13

HIGHER TECHNOLOGICAL INSTITUTE OF SAN ANDRÉS TUXTLA

Instituto Tecnológico Superior de San Andrés Tuxtla
Km. 140 (+100) Carretera Costera del Golfo, Tramo Paso del Toro Acayucán-Matacapán, 95700 San Andrés Tuxtla, Veracruz
Tel: +52(294) 945-22-00
EMail: informacion@itssat.edu.mx
Website: http://www.itssat.edu.mx

Director: Jorge Alberto Alceda Ramón

Programmes
Administration (Administration; Business Administration); **Engineering** (Computer Engineering; Electronic Engineering; Environmental Engineering; Industrial Engineering; Mechanical Engineering)
History: Founded 1993.
Main Language(s) of Instruction: Spanish
Degrees and Diplomas: *Licenciatura*
Last Updated: 21/03/13

HIGHER TECHNOLOGICAL INSTITUTE OF SAN MARTÍN TEXMELUCAN

Instituto Tecnológico Superior de San Martín Texmelucan
Camino a Barranca de Pesos S/N, San Lucas Atoyatenco, 74120 San Martín Texmelucan, Puebla
Tel: +52(248) 111-11-32
EMail: itssmt@hotmail.com
Website: http://www.itssmt.edu.mx

Director: Fiacro Luis Torreblanca Coello
EMail: f_luis.torreblanca@hotmail.com

Programmes
Accountancy (Accountancy); **Engineering** (Computer Engineering; Electronic Engineering; Environmental Engineering; Industrial Engineering; Mechanical Engineering)
History: Founded 2002.
Main Language(s) of Instruction: Spanish
Degrees and Diplomas: *Licenciatura*
Last Updated: 29/03/13

HIGHER TECHNOLOGICAL INSTITUTE OF SAN PEDRO DE LAS COLONIAS

Instituto Tecnológico Superior de San Pedro de las Colonias
Calzada del Tecnológico San Pedro de las Colonias, San Pedro de las Colonias, Coahuila

Programmes
Computer Engineering (Computer Engineering); **Industrial Engineering** (Industrial Engineering)
History: Founded 2004.
Main Language(s) of Instruction: Spanish
Degrees and Diplomas: *Licenciatura*
Last Updated: 02/04/13

HIGHER TECHNOLOGICAL INSTITUTE OF SANTIAGO PAPASQUIARO

Instituto Tecnológico Superior de Santiago Papasquiaro
Carretera J. Guadalupe Aguilera-Guanacevi Km. 114, Francisco Javier Mina s/n, 34600 Santiago Papasquiaro, Durango
Tel: +52(186) 862-19-87
EMail: linces@itsantiago.edu.mx
Website: http://www.itsantiago.edu.mx

Directora: Analilia Lomas Aguirre

Programmes
Administration (Administration); **Environmental Engineering** (Environmental Engineering); **Food Engineering** (Food Technology); **Industrial Engineering** (Industrial Engineering); **Information Technology** (Information Technology); **Mechanical and Electronic Engineering** (Electronic Engineering; Mechanical Engineering); **Systems Engineering** (Computer Engineering)
History: Founded 1995.
Main Language(s) of Instruction: Spanish
Degrees and Diplomas: *Licenciatura*
Last Updated: 21/03/13

HIGHER TECHNOLOGICAL INSTITUTE OF SOUTH ZACATECAS

Instituto Tecnológico Superior de Zacatecas Sur
Av. Tecnológico #100, Col. Las moritas, 99700 Tlaltenango, Zacatecas
Tel: +52(437) 954-18-34
Fax: +52(437) 954-07-60
EMail: itszas@itszas.edu.mx
Website: http://www.itszas.edu.mx

Director: José Manuel Gaeta Carreón

Programmes
Accountancy (Accountancy); **Administration** (Administration; Business Administration); **Engineering** (Computer Engineering; Electronic Engineering; Mechanical Engineering)
History: Founded 1992.
Main Language(s) of Instruction: Spanish
Degrees and Diplomas: *Licenciatura*
Last Updated: 21/03/13

HIGHER TECHNOLOGICAL INSTITUTE OF TACÁMBARO

Instituto Tecnológico Superior de Tacámbaro
Av. Tecnológico # 201, Zona el Gigate, Tacámbaro, Michoacan
Tel: +52(459) 596-22-39
EMail: difusion@itstacambaro.edu.mx
Website: http://www.itstacambaro.edu.mx

Director: Luis Tapia Vargas EMail: direccion@itstacambaro.edu.mx

Programmes
Administration (Administration; Business Administration); **Engineering** (Computer Engineering; Earth Sciences; Food Technology)
History: Founded 2003.
Main Language(s) of Instruction: Spanish
Degrees and Diplomas: *Licenciatura*
Last Updated: 02/04/13

HIGHER TECHNOLOGICAL INSTITUTE OF TAMAZUNCHALE

Instituto Tecnológico Superior de Tamazunchale
Apartado postal 110, Km. 6.5 Carretera San Martín SLP, Chalchicuahutla, Ejido La Pitaya, 79960 Tamazunchale, San Luis Potosí
Tel: +52(483) 361-83-61
EMail: diracademica@tectamazunchale.edu.mx
Website: http://itstmz.edu.mx

Director: Ricardo Bárcenas Rivas

Programmes
Administration (Business Administration); **Engineering** (Computer Engineering; Industrial Engineering)
History: Founded 1997.
Main Language(s) of Instruction: Spanish
Degrees and Diplomas: *Licenciatura*
Last Updated: 21/03/13

HIGHER TECHNOLOGICAL INSTITUTE OF TANTOYUCA

Instituto Tecnológico Superior de Tantoyuca
Desv. Lindero Tametate S/N, Col. La Morita, 92100 Tantoyuca, Veracruz
Tel: +52(789) 893-16-80
EMail: contacto@itsta.edu.mx
Website: http://www.itsta.edu.mx
Director: Francisco Javier Hernadez Luna

Programmes
Accountancy (Accountancy); **Agronomy** (Agronomy); **Business Administration** (Business Administration); **Engineering** (Computer Engineering; Electronic Engineering; Environmental Engineering; Industrial Engineering; Petroleum and Gas Engineering)
History: Founded 1995.
Main Language(s) of Instruction: Spanish
Degrees and Diplomas: *Licenciatura*; *Maestría*: Industrial Engineering
Last Updated: 21/03/13

HIGHER TECHNOLOGICAL INSTITUTE OF TEPEACA

Instituto Tecnológico Superior de Tepeaca
Av. Tecnológico S/N, Ex-Hacienda Santa Ana, San Pablo Actipa, 75200 Tepeaca, Puebla
Tel: +52(223) 275-14-49
EMail: direccion.general@itstepeaca.edu.mx
Website: http://www.itstepeaca.edu.mx

Director: Luis Enrique Manzano Martínez

Programmes
Engineering (Computer Engineering; Food Technology; Industrial Engineering)
History: Founded 2000.
Main Language(s) of Instruction: Spanish
Degrees and Diplomas: *Licenciatura*
Last Updated: 21/03/13

HIGHER TECHNOLOGICAL INSTITUTE OF TEPEXI DE RODRÍGUEZ

Instituto Tecnológico Superior de Tepexi de Rodríguez
Avenida Tecnológico s/n, Col. Barrio San Sebastián, Tepexi de Rodríguez, 74690 Tepexi, Puebla
Tel: +52(224) 421-55-85
EMail: itstepexijaa@yahoo.com.mx
Director: Ismael Sánchez Huerta

Programmes
Administration (Administration); **Engineering** (Computer Engineering; Engineering; Industrial Engineering; Mechanical Engineering)
Degrees and Diplomas: *Licenciatura*
Last Updated: 21/03/13

HIGHER TECHNOLOGICAL INSTITUTE OF TEQUILA

Instituto Tecnológico Superior de Tequila
Dr. Joel Magallanes Rubio # 501, Col. Lomas del Paraíso, 46400 Tequila, Jalisco
Tel: +55(374) 742-18-88
EMail: informes@itstequila.edu.mx
Website: http://www.itstequila.edu.mx

Director: José Manuel Martínez Becerra
EMail: jmartinez@itstequila.edu.mx

Programmes
Administration (Administration; Business Administration); **Computer Science** (Computer Science); **Engineering** (Civil Engineering; Electronic Engineering; Industrial Engineering; Mechanical Engineering)
History: Founded 2001.
Main Language(s) of Instruction: Spanish
Degrees and Diplomas: *Licenciatura*
Last Updated: 21/03/13

HIGHER TECHNOLOGICAL INSTITUTE OF TEZIUTLÁN

Instituto Tecnológico Superior de Teziutlán
Fracc. 1 y 2 s/n, Predio Aire Libre, La Mina, 73960 Teziutlán, Puebla
Tel: +52(231) 312-05-09 +52(231) 313-33-83
Fax: +52(231) 313-33-82
EMail: itsteziutlan@hotmail.com
Website: http://www.itsteziutlan.edu.mx

Director: Gustavo Urbano Juárez
EMail: direccion@itsteziutlan.edu.mx

Programmes
Administration (Administration; Business Administration); **Engineering** (Computer Engineering; Electronic Engineering; Industrial Engineering; Mechanical Engineering); **Food Technology** (Food Technology)
History: Founded 1993.
Main Language(s) of Instruction: Spanish
Degrees and Diplomas: *Licenciatura*
Last Updated: 21/03/13

HIGHER TECHNOLOGICAL INSTITUTE OF THE COSTA CHICA

Instituto Tecnológico Superior de la Costa Chica
Apartado postal 9, Km. 1 Carretera Ometepec-Iguala, Barrio de Talapa, 41706 Ometepec, Guerrero
Tel: +52(741) 412-09-70
EMail: contacto@tscch.edu.mx

Director: Eloy Jiménez Molina

Programmes
Accountancy (Accountancy); **Civil Engineering** (Civil Engineering); **Computer Science** (Computer Science)
History: Founded 1990.
Main Language(s) of Instruction: Spanish
Degrees and Diplomas: *Licenciatura*
Last Updated: 20/03/13

HIGHER TECHNOLOGICAL INSTITUTE OF THE EAST OF THE STATE OF HIDALGO

Instituto Tecnológico Superior del Oriente del Estado de Hidalgo
Km. 3.5 Carretera Apán-Tepeapulco, Col. Las Peñitas, 43900 Apán, Hidalgo
Tel: +52(748) 912-34-89
EMail: direccion_general@itesa.edu.mx
Website: http://www.itesa.edu.mx

Director: José Antonio Zamora Guido

Programmes
Engineering (Civil Engineering; Computer Engineering; Electronic Engineering; Food Technology; Mechanical Engineering)
History: Founded 2000.
Main Language(s) of Instruction: Spanish
Degrees and Diplomas: *Licenciatura*
Last Updated: 20/03/13

HIGHER TECHNOLOGICAL INSTITUTE OF THE MOUNTAIN

Instituto Tecnológico Superior de la Montaña
Ampliación Ejido San Francisco s/n, 41304 Tlapa de Comonfort, Guerrero
Tel: +52(757) 476-02-67
EMail: itsm_tlapa@hotmail.com
Website: http://www.itsm-tlapa.edu.mx

Director: Uriel Hernández Galeana

Programmes
Accountancy (Accountancy); **Administration** (Administration); **Engineering** (Civil Engineering; Computer Engineering; Environmental Engineering)
History: Founded 1991.
Main Language(s) of Instruction: Spanish
Degrees and Diplomas: *Licenciatura*
Last Updated: 20/03/13

HIGHER TECHNOLOGICAL INSTITUTE OF THE REGION OF LOS LLANOS

Instituto Tecnológico Superior de la Región de los Llanos
Alberto M. Alvarado Lote 1 Manzana 258 Z II, Guadalupe Victoria, 34700 Ciudad Guadalupe Victoria, Durango
Tel: +52(676) 882-44-73
EMail: itsllanos@itsrll.edu.mx
Website: http://www.itsrll.edu.mx

Director: José Roberto Hernández Tinoco
EMail: direcciong@itsrll.edu.mx

Programmes
Administration (Administration); **Engineering** (Computer Engineering; Electronic Engineering; Food Technology; Industrial Engineering; Mechanical Engineering)
History: Founded 2002.
Main Language(s) of Instruction: Spanish
Degrees and Diplomas: *Licenciatura*
Last Updated: 27/03/13

HIGHER TECHNOLOGICAL INSTITUTE OF THE SIERRA NORTE OF PUEBLA

Instituto Tecnológico Superior de la Sierra Norte de Puebla
Avenida José Luis Martínez Vázquez, 200, 73310 Zacatlán, Puebla
Tel: +52(797) 975-16-94
EMail: informes@itssnp.edu.mx
Website: http://www.itssnp.edu.mx/

Director: Enrique Ignacio Sosa Toxqui
EMail: enriquetoxqui@gmail.com

Programmes
Accountancy (Accountancy); **Engineering** (Computer Engineering; Electronic Engineering; Forest Management; Mechanical Engineering); **Food Technology** (Food Technology)
History: Founded 1993.
Main Language(s) of Instruction: Spanish
Degrees and Diplomas: *Licenciatura*
Last Updated: 20/03/13

HIGHER TECHNOLOGICAL INSTITUTE OF THE SIERRA REGION

Instituto Tecnológico Superior de la Región Sierra
Km. 4.5 Carretera Teapa-Tacotalpa, Ej. Francisco Javier, Mina, 86801 Teapa, Tabasco
Tel: +52(932) 324-06-50
EMail: regionsierra@itss.edu.mx
Website: http://www.itss.edu.mx

Director: Lorenzo Mollinedo Aguilar

Programmes
Administration (Administration); **Agronomy** (Agronomy); **Biochemistry** (Biochemistry); **Computer Science** (Computer Science); **Electrical and Mechanical Engineering** (Electrical Engineering; Mechanical Engineering); **Energy Engineering** (Energy Engineering); **Industrial Engineering** (Industrial Engineering)
History: Founded 2000.
Main Language(s) of Instruction: Spanish
Degrees and Diplomas: *Licenciatura*
Last Updated: 20/03/13

HIGHER TECHNOLOGICAL INSTITUTE OF THE SOUTH OF GUANAJUATO

Instituto Tecnológico Superior del Sur de Guanajuato
Avenida Educación Superior, 2000, Col. Benito Juárez, Uriangato, 38980 Guanajuato, Guanajuato
Tel: +52(473) 737-74-68
Fax: +52(473) 737-74-69
EMail: direccion@itsur.edu.mx
Website: http://www.itsur.edu.mx

Director: Tarsicio Herrera Vega

Programmes
Computer Science (Computer Science); **Engineering** (Computer Engineering; Electronic Engineering; Environmental Engineering; Industrial Engineering)
History: Founded 1998.
Main Language(s) of Instruction: Spanish
Degrees and Diplomas: *Licenciatura*
Last Updated: 21/03/13

HIGHER TECHNOLOGICAL INSTITUTE OF THE SOUTH OF THE STATE OF YUCATAN

Instituto Tecnológico Superior del Sur del Estado de Yucatán

Km. 41 (+400) Carretera Muna-Felipe Carrillo-Puerto, Tramo Oxkutzcab-akil, Calle 51 x 70, 97880 Oxkutzcab, Yucatán
Tel: +52(999) 975-05-09
EMail: tecnologico@itsyucatan.edu.mx
Website: http://www.itsyucatan.edu.mx

Director: Juan Carlos Sánchez Vázquez

Programmes
Business Administration (Business Administration); **Community Development** (Development Studies); **Engineering** (Biochemistry; Computer Engineering; Industrial Engineering)
History: Founded 1998.
Main Language(s) of Instruction: Spanish
Degrees and Diplomas: *Licenciatura*
Last Updated: 21/03/13

HIGHER TECHNOLOGICAL INSTITUTE OF THE WEST OF THE STATE OF HIDALGO

Instituto Tecnológico Superior del Occidente del Estado de Hidalgo

Paseo del Agrarismo, 200, Km. 2.5 carretera Mixquiahuala - Tula, 42700 Mixquiahuala de Juárez, Hidalgo
Tel: +52(738) 725-3634
EMail: favila@itsoeh.edu.mx
Website: http://www.itsoeh.edu.mx

Director: Fernando Ávila Báez

Programmes
Computer Science (Computer Science); **Engineering** (Computer Engineering; Electronic Engineering; Food Technology; Industrial Engineering; Information Technology; Mechanical Engineering)
History: Founded 2000.
Main Language(s) of Instruction: Spanish
Degrees and Diplomas: *Licenciatura*
Last Updated: 21/03/13

HIGHER TECHNOLOGICAL INSTITUTE OF TIERRA BLANCA

Instituto Tecnológico Superior de Tierra Blanca

Av. Veracruz s/n esq. Héroes de Puebla, Col. PEMEX, 95110 Tierra Blanca, Veracruz
Tel: +52(274) 743-49-92
EMail: justiniana@itstb.edu.mx
Website: http://www.itstb.edu.mx

Directora: Justiniana Gutiérrez Lagunes (2007-)

Programmes
Engineering (Computer Engineering; Electronic Engineering; Food Technology; Industrial Engineering)
History: Founded 1999.
Main Language(s) of Instruction: Spanish
Degrees and Diplomas: *Licenciatura*
Last Updated: 21/03/13

HIGHER TECHNOLOGICAL INSTITUTE OF TLAXCO

Instituto Tecnológico Superior de Tlaxco

Predio Cristo Rey Ex-Hacienda de Xalostoc, Km. 16.8 Carretera Federal Apiztaco, 90250 Tlaxco, Tlaxcala
Tel: +52(241) 412- 31-15
EMail: informacion@itstlaxco.edu.mx
Website: http://www.itstlaxco.edu.mxhttp: // http://www.itstlaxco.e-du.mx

Director: Anibal George Haro

Programmes
Business Administration (Business Administration); **Engineering** (Chemical Engineering; Electronic Engineering; Materials Engineering; Mechanical Engineering; Production Engineering)
History: Founded 2004.
Main Language(s) of Instruction: Spanish
Degrees and Diplomas: *Licenciatura*
Last Updated: 02/04/13

HIGHER TECHNOLOGICAL INSTITUTE OF URUAPÁN

Instituto Tecnológico Superior de Uruapán

Carretera Uruapan-Carapan No. 5555 Col. La Basilia, 61100 Uruapán, Michoacán
Tel: +52(452) 527-50-50
EMail: itsu@prodigy.net.mx
Website: http://www.tecuruapan.edu.mx/

Director: Raúl Paz Álvarez

Programmes
Engineering (Computer Engineering; Electronic Engineering; Engineering; Food Technology; Industrial Engineering; Mechanical Engineering)
History: Founded 1999.
Main Language(s) of Instruction: Spanish
Degrees and Diplomas: *Licenciatura*
Last Updated: 21/03/13

HIGHER TECHNOLOGICAL INSTITUTE OF VALLADOLID

Instituto Tecnológico Superior de Valladolid

Km. 3.5 Carretera Valladolid-Tizimín, Tablaje Catastral 8850, 97780 Valladolid, Yucatán
Tel: +52(985) 856-63-00
Website: http://www.itsva.edu.mx

Director: Raúl Augusto Mendoza Alcocer

Programmes
Administration (Administration); **Computer Science** (Computer Science); **Industrial Engineering** (Civil Engineering; Environmental Engineering; Industrial Engineering)
History: Founded 2000.
Main Language(s) of Instruction: Spanish
Degrees and Diplomas: *Licenciatura*
Last Updated: 21/03/13

HIGHER TECHNOLOGICAL INSTITUTE OF VILLA LA VENTA

Instituto Tecnológico Superior de Villa la Venta

Circuito Tecnólogico No.1 - Col. El Cuatro, 86410 Huimanguillo, Tabasco
EMail: haleman@itslv.edu.mx

Director: Humberto Alemán Cruz

Programmes
Engineering (Computer Engineering; Food Technology; Industrial Engineering)
Main Language(s) of Instruction: Spanish
Degrees and Diplomas: *Licenciatura*
Last Updated: 02/04/13

HIGHER TECHNOLOGICAL INSTITUTE OF WESTERN ZACATECAS

Instituto Tecnológico Superior de Zacatecas Occidente

Avenida Tecnológico, 2000, Col. La Perla San Pedro s/n, 99000 Sombrerete, Zacatecas
Tel: +52(433) 935-14-99
EMail: itszo_som@hotmail.com
Website: http://www.itszo.edu.mx

Directora: Erica del Carmen Velázquez Vacío

Programmes
Business Administration (Business Administration); **Computer Engineering** (Computer Engineering); **Industrial Engineering** (Industrial Engineering); **Mining Techniques** (Mining Engineering); **Systems Engineering** (Systems Analysis)

History: Founded 2000.
Main Language(s) of Instruction: Spanish
Degrees and Diplomas: *Licenciatura*
Last Updated: 21/03/13

HIGHER TECHNOLOGICAL INSTITUTE OF XALAPA

Instituto Tecnológico Superior de Xalapa
Sección 5a. Reserva Territorial s/n, Col. Santa Bárbara, 91000 Xalapa, Veracruz
Tel: +52(228) 165-05-25
Website: http://www.itsx.edu.mx/

Director: Miguel Ángel Martínez Poceros

Programmes
Business Administration (Business Administration); **Engineering** (Biochemistry; Computer Engineering; Electronic Engineering; Engineering; Industrial Engineering; Mechanical Engineering); **Food Technology** (Food Technology)
History: Founded 1998.
Main Language(s) of Instruction: Spanish
Degrees and Diplomas: *Licenciatura*
Last Updated: 21/03/13

HIGHER TECHNOLOGICAL INSTITUTE OF ZACAPOAXTLA

Instituto Tecnológico Superior de Zacapoaxtla
Km. 8 Carretera Acuaco-Zacapoaxtla Col. Totoltepec, 73680 Zacapoaxtla, Puebla
Tel: +52(233) 317-50-00
EMail: tecnologico@itsz.edu.mx
Website: http://www.itsz.edu.mx

Directora: Arminda Juarez Arroyo

Programmes
Administration (Administration); **Biology** (Biology); **Computer Science** (Computer Science); **Engineering** (Forest Management; Industrial Engineering)
History: Founded 1997.
Main Language(s) of Instruction: Spanish
Degrees and Diplomas: *Licenciatura*
Last Updated: 21/03/13

HIGHER TECHNOLOGICAL INSTITUTE OF ZAPOPAN

Instituto Tecnológico Superior de Zapopan
Camino Arenero No.1101, Col. El bajío, 45019 Zapopan, Jalisco
Tel: +52(33) 36-82-11-80
EMail: itsdz@itszapopan.edu.mx
Website: http://www.itszapopan.edu.mx

Director: Alfonso Everardo Martín del Campo Gómez
EMail: amdelcampo@itszapopan.edu.mx

Programmes
Business Administration (Business Administration); **Engineering** (Computer Engineering; Electronic Engineering; Engineering; Industrial Engineering; Mechanical Engineering); **Gastronomy** (Cooking and Catering)
History: Founded 1999.
Main Language(s) of Instruction: Spanish
Degrees and Diplomas: *Licenciatura*; *Maestría*: Computer Systems
Last Updated: 21/03/13

HIGHER TECHNOLOGICAL INSTITUTE OF ZAPOTLANEJO

Instituto Tecnológico Superior de Zapotlanejo
Av. Tecnológico #300, Carretera Libre Zapotlanejo-Tepatitlán Km. 4.5, Predio Huejotitán, Zapotlanejo, Jalisco
Tel: +52(373) 735-60-60
EMail: instituto@itszapotlanejo.edu.mx
Website: http://www.itszapotlanejo.edu.mx

Director: Cruz Rivera Bravo

Programmes
Administration (Administration); **Engineering** (Computer Engineering; Industrial Engineering)
History: Founded 2004.
Main Language(s) of Instruction: Spanish
Degrees and Diplomas: *Licenciatura*
Last Updated: 02/04/13

HIM FEDERICO GOMEZ NATIONAL HEALTH INSTITUTE

Instituto Nacional de Salud 'HIM' 'Federico Gómez'
Dr. Márquez 162, Col. Doctores Cuauhtémoc, 06720 México, D.F.
Tel: +52(555) 761-02-70
Fax: +52(555) 761-03-33
EMail: jaranda@himfg.edu.mx
Website: http://www.himfg.edu.mx/interior/el_instituto.html

Director: José Alberto García Aranda

Programmes
Genetics (Genetics); **Paediatrics** (Paediatrics)
Main Language(s) of Instruction: Spanish
Degrees and Diplomas: *Especialización*
Last Updated: 07/03/13

HUMANIST CENTRE FOR STUDIES ON THE HUMAN BEING

Centro Humanístico del Ser
VidrioNo2055, Col. La Fayette Entre Marsella y Chapultepec, Guadalajara, Jalisco
Tel: +52(33)36-16-53-79
Website: http://www.cehus.edu.mx

Directora: Rosa Larios Novela

Programmes
Human Development and Group Support (Development Studies; Psychology)
History: Founded 1988.
Main Language(s) of Instruction: Spanish
Degrees and Diplomas: *Maestría*; *Doctorado*
Last Updated: 27/10/09

IMSS NURSING SCHOOL

Escuela de Enfermería del IMSS
C-58 Av 7 y 11A., Colonia Pensiones, Mérida, Yucatán
Tel: +52(999) 987-90-15
EMail: Leyser.padilla@imss.gob.mx
Website: http://www.imss.gob.mx/IMSS/IMSS_SITIOS/Regional/Yucatan/Escuela_Enfermeria/

Directora: Marlene Padilla Gómez

Programmes
Nursing (Nursing)
History: Founded 1972.
Main Language(s) of Instruction: Spanish
Degrees and Diplomas: *Licenciatura*
Last Updated: 21/02/13

INDIGENOUS AUTONOMOUS UNIVERSITY OF MEXICO

Universidad Autónoma Indígena de México
Benito Juárez, 39, Mochicahui, 81890 El Fuerte, Sinaloa
Tel: +52(698) 892-00-42 +52(698) 892-00-08
EMail: uaim@uaim.edu.mx
Website: http://www.uaim.edu.mx

Rector: Guadalupe Camargo Orduño
EMail: gcamargo@uaim.edu.mx

Programmes
Accountancy (Accountancy); **Computer Systems** (Computer Engineering; Software Engineering; Telecommunications Engineering); **Forestry and Silviculture** (Forestry); **Law**; **Production**

Engineering (Production Engineering); **Psychology** (Psychology); **Rural Sociology** (Rural Studies; Sociology); **Social Psychology** (Psychology); **Sustainable Development** (Environmental Engineering); **Tourism** (Tourism)

Further Information: Also campuses at Los Mochis (Sinaloa), Choix

History: Founded 2001.

Main Language(s) of Instruction: Spanish

Degrees and Diplomas: *Licenciatura*; *Maestría*; *Doctorado*

Publications: Revista Científica Ra-Ximhai

Last Updated: 07/09/12

INSTITUTE FOR SCIENTIFIC AND TECHNOLOGICAL RESEARCH OF SAN LUIS POTOSÍ

Instituto Potosino de Investigación Científica y Tecnológica A.C. (IPICYT)

Apartado postal 3-74, Camino a la Presa San José 2055, Col. Lomas 4 sección, Tangamanga, 78216 San Luis Potosí, San Luis Potosí

Tel: +52(444) 834-20-00

Fax: +52(444) 834-20-10

EMail: vladimir.escobar@ipicyt.edu.mx

Website: http://www.ipicyt.edu.mx

Director: David Ríos Jara

Divisions

Applied Geosciences (Earth Sciences; Geology); **Control Engineering** (Applied Mathematics; Automation and Control Engineering); **Environmental Sciences** (Environmental Studies); **Molecular Biology** (Biomedicine; Biotechnology; Molecular Biology; Neurosciences); **Nanoscience and Materials** (Materials Engineering; Nanotechnology)

Further Information: Also graduate programmes

History: Founded 2000.

Degrees and Diplomas: *Maestría*; *Doctorado*

Libraries: Yes

Last Updated: 07/03/13

INSTITUTE OF ADULT EDUCATION

Instituto de Educación Para Adultos

Carretera a San Luis Potosí Km. 2, 20190 Aguascalientes, Aguascalientes

Tel: 52(449) 741-868

Director: Eduardo Ramos Robles

Programmes

Adult Education

Main Language(s) of Instruction: Spanish

Degrees and Diplomas: *Doctorado*

Last Updated: 21/02/08

INSTITUTE OF ECOLOGY

Instituto de Ecología, A.C. (INECOL)

Km 2.5 Carretera Antigua a Coatepec 351, Congregación El Haya, 91070 Xalapa, Veracruz

Tel: +52(228) 842-18-00

Website: http://www.inecol.edu.mx

Director General: Martín Ramón Aluja Schuneman Hofer

Divisions

Ecology (Ecology; Environmental Studies; Plant and Crop Protection; Wildlife); **Natural Resources** (Biotechnology; Coastal Studies; Environmental Engineering; Management; Natural Resources; Wood Technology); **Systems** (Botany; Ecology; Entomology; Floriculture; Natural Sciences)

History: Founded 1975. Integrated into the Sistema Nacional de Centros SEP-CONACYT. Moved to Xalapa 1989.

Admission Requirements: Admission letter with field of interest and reason why; 2 letters of recommendation; Licenciatura or Maestría; Professional Studies certificate with minimum average of 8

Fees: (Pesos): 6,000 per semester

Main Language(s) of Instruction: Spanish

International Co-operation: With universities in Mexico, USA, Spain, Colombia, Argentina, Korea, France, Germany

Accrediting Agencies: CONACyT; Secretaría de Educación Pública (SEP); Gobiernos de los estados de Durango; Chihuahua; Veracruz; Distrito Federal; SHCP; SHCP; SEMARNAT; CONABIO; CICY; ECOSUR; CIBNOR

Degrees and Diplomas: *Maestría*: Ecology, Natural Resources Management, Wildlife Management; Systematics, 2 yrs (after Licenciatura); *Doctorado*: Ecology, Natural Resources Management, Taxonomy, a further 3 yrs (after Maestría); *Doctorado*: Ecology, Natural Resources Management, Taxonomy, a further 5 yrs (after Licenciatura)

Student Services: Academic counselling, Canteen

Special Facilities: Botanical Gardens

Libraries: Yes

Publications: Acta Botánica Mexicana, Botanical research *(quarterly)*; Acta Zoológica Mexicana, Zoological research in Ecology, Systematics, Zoography, Mexican and Latin American Fauna; Flora de Veracruz; Flora del Bajío y Regiones Adyacentes, Regional Plant Inventory; Madera y Bosques, Wood and Forests *(3 per annum)*

Last Updated: 28/02/13

INSTITUTE OF EDUCATIONAL SCIENCES OF THE STATE OF MEXICO

Instituto Superior de Ciencias de la Educación del Estado de México

Ex-Rancho Los Uribe, Santa Cruz Azcapotzaltongo, 50030 Toluca, Estado de México

Tel: +52(7) 272-70-22

EMail: isceem@edomex.gob.mx

Website: http://www.edomexico.gob.mx/isceem

Directora: Ada Esthela Rosales Morales

Programmes

Education (Education; Educational Administration; Educational Sciences)

History: Founded 1979.

Main Language(s) of Instruction: Spanish

Degrees and Diplomas: *Especialización*; *Maestría*; *Doctorado*

Libraries: Yes

Last Updated: 08/03/13

INSTITUTE OF FINE ARTS OF THE STATE OF BAJA CALIFORNIA

Instituto de Bellas Artes del Estado de Baja California

Avenida Obregón y Pedro F. Pérez y Ramírez s/n, Zona Centro de Mexicali, 21100 Mexicali, Baja California

Tel: +52(658) 552-88-92 +52(658) 552-28-13

EMail: ibaebc@prodigy.net.mx

Website: http://www.ibaebc.com/

Director: Carlos Alberto Carillo Uribe

Programmes

Fine Arts (Art History; Fine Arts)

History: Founded 1967.

Main Language(s) of Instruction: Spanish

Degrees and Diplomas: *Licenciatura*

Last Updated: 18/01/13

INSTITUTE OF HIGHER STUDIES OF THE STATE

Instituto de Estudios Superiores del Estado

Km.6.5 Carretera Federal Tehuacán- Orizaba s/n, Santa Ana, Nicolás Bravo, Puebla

Tel: +52(238) 37 204 29 - 01

Website: http://www.iese.edu.mx

Director: Francisco Martínez Galindo

Programmes

Accountancy and Finance (Accountancy; Finance); **Architecture** (Architecture); **Computer Engineering** (Computer Engineering);

Education (Education); **Graphic Design** (Graphic Design); **Information Technology** (Information Technology)

Main Language(s) of Instruction: Spanish

Degrees and Diplomas: *Licenciatura*; *Maestría*; *Doctorado*
Last Updated: 01/03/13

INSTITUTE OF POSTGRADUATE STUDIES

Instituto de Estudios de Posgrado
Avenida Jainá No.238, Esquina con Calle Tikal, Col. Maya, 29000 Tuxtla Gutiérrez, Chiapas
Tel: +52(961) 618-28-41
EMail: posgrado@iep.chiapas.gob.mx
Website: http://www.iep.chiapas.gob.mx

Directora: Verónica Rodríguez Montes
EMail: vrodriguez@iep.chiapa.gob.mx

Programmes
Pedagogy (Education; Pedagogy)

History: Founded 1994 as Institute de Posgrado en Educación de Chiapas.

Main Language(s) of Instruction: Spanish

Degrees and Diplomas: *Maestría*
Last Updated: 05/03/13

INSTITUTE OF PROFESSIONAL TRAINING OF THE GENERAL PROCTORSHIP OF MEXICO CITY

Instituto de Formación Profesional de la Procuraduría General de Justicia del Distrito Federal
4a y 5a Cerrada de Avenida Jardín s/n, Col. Ampliación Cosmopolita Azcapotzalco, México, D.F.
Tel: +52(555) 525-73-54
Fax: +52(555) 525-73-52
EMail: gisanchezr@pgjdf.gob.mx
Website: http://www.ifp.pgjdf.gob.mx

Coordinador General: Juan José Olea Valencia
EMail: joleav@pgjdf.gob.mx

Programmes
Law (Criminal Law; Criminology; Law); **Police Studies** (Police Studies)

Degrees and Diplomas: *Licenciatura*; *Maestría*
Last Updated: 04/03/13

INSTITUTE OF PUBLIC ADMINISTRATION OF THE STATE OF CHIAPAS

Instituto de Administración Pública del Estado de Chiapas
Libramiento Norte Poniente No 2718., Fraccionamiento Ladera de la Loma, Col. Centro, 29000 Chiapas
EMail: contacto@iapchiapas.org.mx
Website: http://www.iapchiapas.org.mx

Presidente: Adriana Camacho Pimienta
EMail: acamacho@iapchiapas.org.mx

Programmes
Public Administration (Finance; Public Administration)

History: Founded 1977.

Main Language(s) of Instruction: Spanish

Degrees and Diplomas: *Licenciatura*; *Especialización*; *Maestría*
Last Updated: 18/01/13

INSTITUTE OF PUBLIC ADMINISTRATION OF THE STATE OF GUANAJUATO

Instituto de Administración Pública del Estado de Guanajuato
Alonso 26 Planta Baja, Zona Centro, 36000 Guanajuato, Guanajuato
Fax: +52 (473) 732-2384
EMail: iapug99@prodigy.net.mx

Presidente: José Luis Romero Hicks

Programmes
Public Administration (Public Administration)

Degrees and Diplomas: *Especialización*; *Maestría*
Last Updated: 23/10/09

INSTITUTE OF PUBLIC ADMINISTRATION OF THE STATE OF HIDALGO

Instituto de Administración Pública del Estado de Hidalgo A.C.
Plaza Independencia, 106, Col. Centro, 42000 Pachuca, Hidalgo
Tel: +52(771) 715-0881
Fax: +52(771) 715-0882
EMail: informes@iaphidalgo.org
Website: http://www.iaphidalgo.org/

Presidente: Carlos Godínez Tellez

Secretario Ejecutivo: Gerardo Cruz González

Vicepresidente: Ramón Ramírez Valtierra

Programmes
Public Administration (Public Administration)

Main Language(s) of Instruction: Spanish

Degrees and Diplomas: *Especialización*; *Maestría*

Libraries: Yes
Last Updated: 18/01/13

INSTITUTE OF PUBLIC ADMINISTRATION OF THE STATE OF JALISCO

Instituto de Administración Pública del Estado de Jalisco
Calzada de Las Palmas, 89, Sector Reforma, 44460 Guadalajara, Jalisco
Tel: +52(33) 36-50-01-92
Fax: +52(33) 36-50-34-92
EMail: info@iapjalisco.org.mx
Website: http://www.iapjalisco.org.mx

Presidente: José Guillermo Vallarta Plata

Programmes
Public Administration (Public Administration)

History: Founded 1978.

Main Language(s) of Instruction: Spanish

Degrees and Diplomas: *Especialización*; *Maestría*

Libraries: Yes
Last Updated: 18/01/13

INSTITUTE OF PUBLIC ADMINISTRATION OF THE STATE OF MEXICO

Instituto de Administración Pública del Estado de México
Av. Hidalgo Pte. No. 503 Col. La Merced, 50080 Toluca, Estado de México
Tel: +52(722) 2-13-46-72
EMail: instituto@iapem.org.mx
Website: http://www.iapem.org.mx

Presidente: Mauricio Valdés Rodríguez

Secretario Ejecutivo: Román B. López Flores

Programmes
Public Administration (Public Administration)

Further Information: Also Delegaciones regionales Tlalnepantla, Valle de Chalco, Ixtlahuaca and Ixtapan de la Sal

History: Founded 1973.

Degrees and Diplomas: *Licenciatura*; *Maestría*
Last Updated: 18/01/13

INSTITUTE OF PUBLIC ADMINISTRATION OF THE STATE OF SINALOA

Instituto de Administración Pública del Estado de Sinaloa

Avenida Insurgentes Esq. Lázaro Cárdenas Planta Baja No. 2, Palácio de Gobierno, Col. Centro, 80129 Culiacán, Sinaloa
Tel: +52(667) 714-40-09
Fax: +52(667) 714-21-88
EMail: calixtoarellano@sinaloa.gob.mx
Website: http://www.iapsin.org.mx

Presidente: Luis Antonio Cárdenas Fonseca

Programmes
Public Administration (Public Administration)
Main Language(s) of Instruction: Spanish
Degrees and Diplomas: *Especialización*; *Maestría*
Libraries: Yes
Last Updated: 18/01/13

INSTITUTE OF PUBLIC ADMINISTRATION OF THE STATE OF TABASCO

Instituto de Administración Pública del Estado de Tabasco, A.C.

Venustiano Carranza 1209, Edif. D, Planta Baja, (Plaza Sur), Col. Centro, 86031 Villahermosa, Tabasco

Presidente: Juan Molina Becerra

Programmes
Public Administration (Public Administration)
Degrees and Diplomas: *Licenciatura*; *Especialización*; *Maestría*
Last Updated: 18/01/13

INSTITUTE OF PUBLIC ADMINISTRATION OF THE STATE OF VERACRUZ

Instituto de Administración Pública del Estado de Veracruz

Avenida Colmerillos 3, Col. Unidad Hab., 91097 Nuevo Xalapa, Veracruz
Tel: +52(228) 819-36-35
EMail: info@iap.edu.mx
Website: http://www.iap.edu.mx

Presidente: Ricardo García Guzmán

Programmes
Public Administration (Public Administration)
Main Language(s) of Instruction: Spanish
Degrees and Diplomas: *Maestría*; *Doctorado*
Last Updated: 18/01/13

INSTITUTE OF TELE-SECONDARY EDUCATION

Instituto Superior de Educación Telesecundaria

Km. 153 Carretera Internacional, Sur, 85890 Navojoa, Sonora
Tel: +52(642) 422-28-20

Director: José Manuel Durazo Fimbres

Programmes
Education (Education)
Degrees and Diplomas: *Licenciatura*

INSTITUTE OF VISUAL ARTS OF THE STATE OF PUEBLA

Instituto de Artes Visuales del Estado de Puebla

Blvd. 5 de Mayo, 208, Col. Xanenetla, 72290 Puebla, Puebla
Tel: +52(222) 232-24-94
EMail: informes@artesvisualespuebla.mx
Website: http://www.artesvisualespuebla.mx

Director: Roberto Rojas García (2002-)

Programmes
Advertising; **Graphic Design** (Graphic Design); **Plastic Arts** (Art History; Painting and Drawing; Sculpture)
History: Founded 1813 as Academia de Bellas Artes. Became Instituto de Artes Plásticas. Acquired present title 1979.
Main Language(s) of Instruction: Spanish
Degrees and Diplomas: *Licenciatura*
Last Updated: 18/01/13

INSTITUTO TECNOLÓGICO SUPERIOR DE POZA RICA

Luis Donaldo Colosio s/n, Col. Arroyo del Maíz, Poza Rica, 93230 Poza Rica, Veracruz
Tel: +52(782) 821-69-01
Fax: +52(782) 823-59-60
EMail: direccion@itspozarica.edu.mx
Website: http://www.itspozarica.edu.mx/

Director: Miguel Ángel Martínez Juárez (1998-)

Areas
Engineering (Computer Engineering; Electronic Engineering; Mechanical Engineering; Nanotechnology; Petroleum and Gas Engineering)

Programmes
Accountancy (Accountancy; Business Administration)
History: Founded 1998.
Main Language(s) of Instruction: Spanish
Degrees and Diplomas: *Licenciatura*; *Especialización*; *Maestría*
Libraries: Yes
Last Updated: 25/10/12

INSTITUTO TECNOLÓGICO SUPERIOR DE TAMAZULA DE GORDIANO

Carretera Tamazula-Santa Rosa No. 329, 49650 Tamazula de Gordiano, Jalisco
Tel: +52(358) 103-00-60
EMail: daniel.garza@tectamazula.edu.mx
Website: http://www.tectamazula.edu.mx

Director: Federico Daniel Garza García

Programmes
Engineering (Agricultural Engineering; Electronic Engineering; Food Technology; Mechanical Engineering)
History: Founded 2005.
Main Language(s) of Instruction: Spanish
Degrees and Diplomas: *Licenciatura*
Last Updated: 02/04/13

INTER-AMERICAN CENTRE FOR SOCIAL SECURITY STUDIES

Centro Interamericano de Estudios de Seguridad Social

Calle San Ramón s/n, Esq. Avenida San Jerónimo, Unidad Independencia Álvaro Obregón, 10100 México, D.F.
Tel: +52(55) 55-95-06-44
Fax: +52(55) 55-95-00-11
EMail: ciess@ciess.org.mx
Website: http://www.ciess.org.mx

Director: Miguel Ángel Fernández Pastor
EMail: mfernandezp@ciess.org.mx

Programmes
Social Security Studies (Social Welfare)
History: Founded 1960.
Main Language(s) of Instruction: Spanish
Degrees and Diplomas: *Especialización*; *Maestría*. Also Diplomados
Last Updated: 19/07/12

INTERCULTURAL UNIVERSITY OF CHIAPAS

Universidad Intercultural de Chiapas
Corral de Piedra No. 2, Ciudad Universitaria Intercultural, 29299 San Cristóbal de Las Casas, Chiapas
Tel: +52(967)631-6151
Fax: +52(967) 631-6152
EMail: rectoria@unich.edu.mx
Website: http://www.unich.edu.mx

Rector: Javier Alvarez Ramos

Programmes

Alternative Tourism (Tourism); **Intercultural Communication** (Communication Studies; Cultural Studies); **Languages and Cultures** (Cultural Studies; Modern Languages); **Sustainable Development** (Development Studies; Environmental Management; Environmental Studies)

Further Information: Also Oxchuc, Las Margaritas, Yajalón and Valle de Tulijà campuses

History: Founded 2004.

Main Language(s) of Instruction: Spanish

Degrees and Diplomas: *Licenciatura*
Last Updated: 10/10/12

INTERDISCIPLINARY CENTRE FOR RESEARCH AND TEACHING IN TECHNICAL EDUCATION

Centro Interdisciplinario de Investigación y Docencia en Educación Técnica (CIIDET)
Apartado postal 752, Avenida Universidad 282 Pte., 76000 Querétaro, Querétaro
Tel: +52(442) 216-37-45
Fax: +52(442) 216-35-40
EMail: subacade@ciidet.edu.mx
Website: http://www.ciidet.edu.mx

Directora: Maricela Castillo Leal EMail: director@ciidet.edu.mx

Programmes

Teaching and Educational Research (Education; Educational Research; Engineering; Teacher Training)

History: Founded 1976.

Degrees and Diplomas: *Especialización*
Last Updated: 19/07/12

ISIDRO ESPINOSA DE LOS REYES NATIONAL INSTITUTE OF PERINATAL STUDIES

Instituto Nacional de Perinatología Isidro Espinosa de los Reyes
Montes Urales 800, Lomas de Virreyes, 11000 México, D.F.
Tel: +52(555) 540-09-42
Fax: +52(555) 520-85-65
EMail: inperinf@servidor.inper.edu.mx
Website: http://www.inper.edu.mx

Director General: Javier Mancilla Ramírez

Programmes

Perinatal Studies (Gynaecology and Obstetrics; Paediatrics)

History: Founded 1977.

Main Language(s) of Instruction: Spanish

Degrees and Diplomas: *Especialización*; *Maestría*; *Doctorado*
Last Updated: 07/03/13

ISSTE DIETETICS AND NUTRITION SCHOOL

Escuela de Dietética y Nutrición del ISSTE
Callejón vía San Fernando y/o Sabino No. 12, Col. San Pedro Apóstol, Delegación Tlalpan, 14070 México, D.F.
Tel: +52(55) 56-06-05-32
EMail: ednisst@servidor.usnm.mx
Website: http://www.issste.gob.mx

Directora: Luz Elena Pale Montero (1998-)

Programmes

Dietetics and Nutrition (Dietetics; Nutrition)

History: Founded 1945.

Main Language(s) of Instruction: Spanish

Degrees and Diplomas: *Licenciatura*: 8 sem.; *Maestría*
Last Updated: 28/08/12

JESUS AQUINO JUAN SCHOOL OF SOCIAL WORK

Escuela Superior de Trabajo Social 'Jesus Aquino Juan'
Carretera Tuxtla-Chiapa de Corzo Km. 6.5, 29000 Tuxtla Gutiérrez, Chiapas
Tel: +52(961) 614-19-15
EMail: escuela_tsocial@hotmail.com
Website: http://www.trabajosocialchiapas.com.mx

Director: Jesús Aquino Juan

Programmes

Social Work (Social Work)

History: Founded 1994 as Escuela de Trabajo Social.

Main Language(s) of Instruction: Spanish

Degrees and Diplomas: *Licenciatura*: Social Work
Last Updated: 27/02/13

JOSÉ MARIA MORELOS INSTITUTE OF EDUCATIONAL SCIENCES OF MICHOACAN

Instituto Michoacano de Ciencias de la Educación José María Morelos
Calzada Juárez, 1600, Fracc. Villa Universidad, 58060 Morelia, Michoacán
Tel: +52(443) 316-75-15
Fax: +52(443) 316-75-93
EMail: cid@imced.edu.mx
Website: http://www.imced.edu.mx

Director: Maribel Ríos Granados

Programmes

Educational Sciences (Art Education; Educational Psychology; Educational Sciences; Pedagogy; Special Education)

Main Language(s) of Instruction: Spanish

Degrees and Diplomas: *Licenciatura*; *Maestría*
Last Updated: 06/03/13

JUAREZ AUTONOMOUS UNIVERSITY OF TABASCO

Universidad Juárez Autónoma de Tabasco (UJAT)
Avenida Universidad s/n, Zona de la Cultura, Col. Centro, 86040 Villahermosa, Tabasco
Tel: +52(993) 358-15-00
EMail: rectoria@ujat.mx
Website: http://www.ujat.mx

Rector: José Manuel Piña Gutiérrez (2012-)

Secretario de Servicios Académicos: Roberto Montes de Oca García Tel: +52(993) 312-29-69 EMail: academica@ujat.mx

International Relations: Laura Judith Quiñónez Díaz
Tel: +52(993) 312-72-10 EMail: investigacion.dip@ujat.mx

Divisions

Basic Sciences (Actuarial Science; Chemistry; Computer Science; Mathematics; Physics); **Biological Sciences** (Biological and Life Sciences; Biology; Ecology; Environmental Engineering); **Cattle Breeding** (Agricultural Engineering; Aquaculture; Food Science; Veterinary Science; Zoology); **Computer Science** (Business Computing; Computer Science; Information Technology; Telecommunications Engineering); **Economic and Administrative Sciences** (Accountancy; Administration; Business and Commerce; Economics); **Education and Arts** (Arts and Humanities; Communication Studies; Cultural Studies; Education; Modern Languages); **Engineering and Architecture** (Architecture; Chemical

Engineering; Civil Engineering; Electrical and Electronic Engineering; Mechanical Engineering); **Health Sciences** (Biomedicine; Dentistry; Dietetics; Health Sciences; Medicine; Nursing; Psychology); **Social Sciences and Humanities** (Arts and Humanities; History; Law; Social Sciences; Sociology)

History: Founded 1879 as Instituto Juárez. Acquired university status 1958.

Governing Bodies: Consejo Universitario

Academic Year: September to August (September-January; February-August)

Admission Requirements: Secondary school certificate (bachillerato) and entrance examination

Fees: (Pesos): Registration, 5,000

Main Language(s) of Instruction: Spanish

Degrees and Diplomas: *Licenciatura*: Administration; Administrative Computer Science; Agronomy Engineering; Aquaculture Engineering; Civil; Civil Engineering; Commercial Relations; Computer Systems; Economics; Electrico y Electronica, Electrical Engineering and Electronics; Environmental Engineering; Food Engineering; History; Law; Mecanico Electrico, Electromechanical Engineering; Modern Languages; Nursing; Public Accountancy; Químico, Chemical Engineering; Sociology, 5 yrs; *Licenciatura*: Architecture (Arquitecto); Nursing; Veterinary Medicine and Animal Husbandry (Médico veterinario zootecnista); *Licenciatura*: Biology; Chemistry; Communication; Computer Science; Ecology; Educational Sciences, 4 1/2 yrs; *Licenciatura*: Dentistry; Nutrition; Psychology, 6 yrs; *Licenciatura*: Mathematics; Physics, 4 yrs; *Licenciatura*: Medicine, 7 yrs; *Especialización*: 1-4 yrs; *Maestría*: a further 2-3 yrs; *Doctorado*: Law; Ecology

Student Services: Academic counselling, Canteen, Cultural centre, Foreign Studies Centre, Health services, Language programs, Sports facilities

Special Facilities: Zoology Museum. Art Gallery. Theatre. Herbarium. Botanical Garden

Libraries: Biblioteca Mario Melgar Pacchiano

Publications: Agrored, Agriculture Topics *(3 per annum)*; Hitos de Ciencias Económico-Admistrativas, Economics and Administration Topics *(3 per annum)*; Kuxulcab', Biological Sciences Topics *(biannually)*; Paradigmas Universitarios, Research and Academic Information *(bimonthly)*; Perspectivas Docentes, Education *(3 per annum)*; Revista de la Universidad, Social Sciences *(3 per annum)*; Universidad y Ciencia, Natural Science *(biannually)*

Last Updated: 11/10/12

CHONTALPA CAMPUS

UNIDAD CHONTALPA

Km. 1 Carretera Cunduacán-Jalpa de Méndez, Conduacán, Tabasco

Divisions

Basic Sciences (Chemistry; Computer Science; Mathematics; Natural Sciences; Physics); **Computer Science and Systems** (Computer Education); **Engineering and Architecture** (Architecture; Chemical Engineering; Civil Engineering; Electrical Engineering; Electronic Engineering; Engineering; Mechanical Engineering)

History: Founded 1985.

LOS RIOS BRANCH

EXTENSIÓN DE LOS RÍOS

Calle 28, Esq. Calle 19, Tenosique, Tabasco
Tel: +52(934) 342-21-10
Fax: +52(934) 342-14-10
EMail: coordinacion.eur@ujat.mx; e_pecero63@hotmail.com
Website: http://www.ujat.mx

Coordinador General: Enrique Pecero Covarrubias

Divisions

Aquaculture and Food Sciences (Aquaculture; Food Science)

History: Founded 1997.

SIERRA UNIT

UNIDAD SIERRA

Km. 25 Carretera Villahermosa-Teapa, 86000 Villahermosa, Tabasco
Tel: +52(993) 390-27-74

Divisions

Farming Sciences (Agronomy; Animal Husbandry; Aquaculture; Cattle Breeding; Food Science; Veterinary Science) *Head*: Jorge Arturo Díaz González

History: Founded 1985.

JUÁREZ UNIVERSITY OF THE STATE OF DURANGO

Universidad Juárez del Estado de Durango (UJED)

Constitución, 404, Sur, Zona Centro, 34000 Durango, Durango
Tel: +52(618) 812-00-44
EMail: ujed@ujed.mx
Website: http://www.ujed.mx

Rector: Oscar Erasmo Návar García

Faculties

Agriculture and Zoology *(Gómez Palacio)* (Agriculture; Fruit Production; Zoology); **Chemical Sciences** *(Durango and Gomez Palacio)* (Biochemistry; Cell Biology; Chemistry; Materials Engineering; Molecular Biology; Pharmacology); **Civil Engineering and Architecture** *(Gómez Palacio)* (Architecture; Civil Engineering); **Economics, Accountancy and Administration** (Accountancy; Administration; Economics); **Forestry** (Forestry); **Law** (Criminal Law; Human Rights; Law; Political Sciences); **Medicine** *(Gómez Palacio)* (Medicine); **Medicine and Nutrition** (Medicine; Nutrition); **Nursing and Midwifery** (Midwifery; Nursing); **Psychology** (Psychology); **Social Work** (Social Work); **Veterinary Medicine and Animal Husbandry** (Animal Husbandry; Veterinary Science)

Higher Schools

Biology *(Gómez Palacio)* (Biology)

Schools

Applied Mathematics (Applied Mathematics; Mathematics); **Dentistry** (Dentistry); **Food Technology** *(Gómez Palacio)* (Food Technology); **Music** (Music); **Painting, Sculpture and Handicraft** (Handicrafts; Painting and Drawing; Sculpture; Visual Arts); **Physical Education and Sport** (Physical Education; Sports); **Social Work** (Social Work)

Further Information: Also Campus Gomez Palacio

History: Founded 1856 as Colegio Civil, became Instituto Juárez 1872. Acquired present status and title 1957.

Governing Bodies: Consejo Universitario; Junta Directiva

Academic Year: February to November

Admission Requirements: Bachillerato

Main Language(s) of Instruction: Spanish

Degrees and Diplomas: *Licenciatura*: Accountancy (Contador público); Nursing (Enfermera); Veterinary Medicine (Médico veterinario); *Licenciatura*: Administration; Agricultural Engineering; Biology; Civil Engineering; Food Technology; Law, 9-10 semesters; *Licenciatura*: Dentistry, 5 yrs; *Licenciatura*: Medicine, 6 yrs; *Especialización*; *Maestría*; *Doctorado*

Libraries: Yes

Last Updated: 11/10/12

JUSTO SIERRA MÉNDEZ RURAL TEACHER TRAINING SCHOOL

Escuela Normal Rural Justo Sierra Méndez

Calle 20 s/n, Col. Emiliano Zapata, Hecelchakán, 24800 Hecelchakán, Campeche
Tel: +52(996) 827-01-22

Directora: Lourdes del C. Cambranis Pacheco

Programmes

Computer Science (Computer Science); **Education**

History: Founded 1930.

Main Language(s) of Instruction: Spanish

Degrees and Diplomas: *Licenciatura*
Last Updated: 20/03/08

JUSTO SIERRA MÉNDEZ RURAL TEACHER TRAINING SCHOOL

Escuela Normal Rural Justo Sierra Méndez
Emilio Rangel No. 208 Col. José Ma. Morelos y Pavón, 20320 Aguascalientes, Aguascalientes

Director: Raul Barcenas Ramirez

Programmes
Primary Education (Primary Education); **Teacher Training** (Teacher Training)

History: Founded 1984.

Main Language(s) of Instruction: Spanish

Degrees and Diplomas: *Licenciatura*
Last Updated: 25/02/13

LATIN AMERICAN FACULTY OF SOCIAL SCIENCES

Facultad Latinoamericana de Ciencias Sociales (FLACSO MEXICO)
Carretera al Ajusco, 377, Col. Héroes de Padierna Tlalpán, 14200 México, D.F.
Tel: +52(555) 300-00240
Fax: +52(555) 300-00284
EMail: flacso@flacso.edu.mx
Website: http://www.flacso.edu.mx

Director General: Francisco Valdés Ugalde
EMail: direccion@flacso.edu.mx

Programmes
Government and Public Administration (Government; Public Administration); **Population and Development** (Demography and Population; Development Studies); **Social Sciences** (Regional Studies; Social Sciences; Sociology)

Further Information: Branches in Argentina; Brazil; Chile; Costa Rica; Cuba; Ecuador; El Salvador; Guatemala; Dominican Republic.

History: Founded 1975. Acquired present status 1993.

Academic Year: September to July

Admission Requirements: Licenciatura

Main Language(s) of Instruction: Spanish, English, French

Degrees and Diplomas: *Maestría*: 2 further yrs; *Doctorado*: 3 further yrs

Libraries: Biblioteca Iberoamericana

Publications: Perfiles Latinoamericanos *(biennially)*

Last Updated: 30/08/12

LATIN AMERICAN INSTITUTE OF EDUCATIONAL COMMUNICATION

Instituto Latinoamericano de la Comunicación Educativa
Calle del Puente 45, Col. Ejidos de Huipulco Tlalpán, 14380 México, D.F.
Tel: +52(55) 57-28-65-00
EMail: contacto@ilce.edu.mx
Website: http://www.ilce.edu.mx

Director General: José Luis Espinosa Piña
EMail: jose.espinosa@ilce.edu.mx

Programmes
Educational Communication (Educational Sciences; Educational Technology)

History: Founded 1956 as Instituto Latinoamericano de la Cinematografía Educativa. Acquired present title 1969.

Main Language(s) of Instruction: Spanish

Degrees and Diplomas: *Maestría*
Last Updated: 06/03/13

LIC. ADOLFO LÓPEZ MATEOS REGIONAL TEACHER TRAINING CENTRE

Centro Regional de Educación Normal Lic. Adolfo López Mateos
Ignacio Maya, 85, 40000 Iguala, Guerrero
Tel: +52(733) 332-03-75 +52(733) 332-07-89

Director: Jorge Bello Bobadilla

Programmes
Preschool Education (Preschool Education); **Secondary Education** (Biology; Ethics; Secondary Education; Special Education)

Main Language(s) of Instruction: Spanish

Degrees and Diplomas: *Licenciatura*
Last Updated: 02/04/08

LIC. JAVIER ROJO GÓMEZ REGIONAL TEACHER TRAINING CENTRE

Centro Regional de Educación Normal Lic. Javier Rojo Gómez
Avenida Costera, s/n, Othón P. Blanco, 77930 Bacalar, Quintana Roo
Tel: +52(983) 421-85
Fax: +52(983) 421-85
EMail: lunachetumal@prodigy.net.mx

Director: Alfredo Ramón Vargas Maldonado

Programmes
Special Education (Primary Education; Special Education)

Degrees and Diplomas: *Licenciatura*
Last Updated: 27/03/08

LUIS HIDALGO MONROY CENTRE FOR HIGHER STUDIES IN RURAL EDUCATION

Centro de Estudios Superiores de Educación Rural 'Luis Hidalgo Monroy'
Carretera Estatal Libre 92108 Tramo Tantoyuca Platón Kilometro 12.5 s/n, Ranchería Acececa, Acececa, 92108 Tantoyuca, Veracruz
Tel: +52(789) 896-18-08
EMail: ceser_2001@hotmail.com

Director: Felix Hernandez Sanchez

Programmes
Rural Studies (Rural Studies)

History: Founded 1975.

Main Language(s) of Instruction: Spanish

Degrees and Diplomas: *Licenciatura*
Last Updated: 15/02/13

MAESTRO RAFAEL RAMÍREZ EXPERIMENTAL TEACHER TRAINING SCHOOL

Escuela Normal Experimental Maestro Rafael Ramírez
Blvd. Delta s/n, Ejido Nuevo León, 21705 Mexicali, Baja California
Tel: +52(686) 623-01-26
Fax: +52(686) 623-01-26
EMail: enerr@prodigy.net.mx
Website: http://www.normalrafaelramirez.com.mx

Director: José Isabel Barba Martínez (1997-)

Programmes
Teacher Training (Primary Education; Teacher Training)

History: Founded 1977.

Main Language(s) of Instruction: Spanish

Degrees and Diplomas: *Licenciatura*
Last Updated: 25/02/13

MARCELO RUBIO RUIZ REGIONAL TEACHER TRAINING CENTRE

Centro Regional de Educación Normal Marcelo Rubio Ruiz

Salvatierra, s/n, Col. Centro, 23880 Loreto, Baja California Sur
Tel: +52(613) 13 5 01 31
EMail: cren@prodigy.net.mx
Website: http://www.paginasprodigy.com/cren/default.htm

Director: José Martín Zapáta Flóres

Programmes
Preschool Education (Preschool Education); **Primary Education** (Primary Education); **Special Education** (Special Education)

History: Founded 1976.

Main Language(s) of Instruction: Spanish

Degrees and Diplomas: *Licenciatura*
Last Updated: 23/07/12

MATHEMATICS RESEARCH CENTRE

Centro de Investigación en Matemáticas, A.C. (CIMAT)

Jalisco s/n, Col. Valenciana, 36240 Guanajuato, Guanajuato
Tel: +52(473) 732-71-55
Fax: +52(473) 732-57-49
EMail: cimat@cimat.mx
Website: http://www.cimat.mx

Director General: José Antonio de la Peña Mena
EMail: jap@cimat.mx

Departments
Computer Science (Computer Science); **Probability and Statistics** (Statistics); **Pure and Applied Mathematics** (Applied Mathematics; Mathematics)

Main Language(s) of Instruction: Spanish

Degrees and Diplomas: *Licenciatura*; *Especialización*; *Maestría*; *Doctorado (PhD)*
Last Updated: 12/07/12

MATIAS ROMERO INSTITUTE

Instituto Matías Romero (IMR)

Ricardo Flores Magón, 2, Col. Guerrero, Delegación Cuauhtémoc, 06300 México, D.F.
Tel: +52(55) 36-86-51-00
Fax: +52(55) 36-86-50-41
EMail: imrinfo@sre.gob.mx
Website: http://www.sre.gob.mx/imr/

Director: Pablo Macedo Riba

Programmes
Diplomatic Studies (International Relations)

History: Founded 1974.

Main Language(s) of Instruction: Spanish

Degrees and Diplomas: *Especialización*; *Maestria*
Last Updated: 06/03/13

MERCHANT NAVY SCHOOL OF TAMPICO

Escuela Náutica Mercante de Tampico

Blvd. López Mateos y Blvd. Fidel Velázquez s/n, Col. Guadalupe Mainero, 89070 Tampico, Tamaulipas
Tel: +52(833) 12-88-82
Fax: +52(833) 19-05-59
EMail: fidenetm@tamnet.com.mx

Director: Gustavo Celis Olivera EMail: fidenatm@prodigy.net.mx

Programmes
Merchant Marine Engineering (Marine Engineering)

History: Founded 1945.

Main Language(s) of Instruction: Spanish

Degrees and Diplomas: *Licenciatura*
Last Updated: 18/03/08

METROPOLITAN TECHNOLOGICAL UNIVERSITY

Universidad Tecnológica Metropolitana

Calle 115, 404, Col. Santa Rosa, 97279 Mérida, Yucatán
Tel: +52(999) 929-16-66
Fax: +52(999) 929-27-46
EMail: helly.burgos@utmetropolitana.edu.mx
Website: http://www.utmetropolitana.edu.mx

Rector: Ricardo Bello Bolio
EMail: ricardo.bello@utmetropolitana.edu.mx

Divisions
Administration (Administration; Cooking and Catering; Hotel Management; Human Resources; Marketing; Tourism); **Information Technology** (Computer Science; Information Technology; Multimedia; Telecommunications Engineering); **Innovation and Strategic Development** (Computer Graphics; Design; Transport Management)

History: Founded 1999.

Main Language(s) of Instruction: Spanish

Degrees and Diplomas: *Licenciatura*. Técnico Superior Universitario
Last Updated: 01/02/13

MEXICAN PETROLEUM INSTITUTE

Instituto Mexicano del Petróleo

Eje Central Norte Lázaro Cárdenas, 152, San Bartolo Atepehuacán Gustavo A. Madero, 07730 México, D.F.
Tel: +52(555) 568-25-80
EMail: mmendoza@imp.mx
Website: http://www.imp.mx/

Director General: Viniciu Suro Pérez EMail: vsurop@imp.mx

Programmes
Petroleum and Gas Engineering (Environmental Engineering; Petroleum and Gas Engineering; Production Engineering; Safety Engineering)

History: Founded 1965.

Main Language(s) of Instruction: Spanish

Degrees and Diplomas: *Especialización*; *Maestría*; *Doctorado*
Last Updated: 06/03/13

MICHOACAN UNIVERSITY OF SAINT NICHOLAS OF HIDALGO

Universidad Michoacana de San Nicolás de Hidalgo (UMICH)

Avenida Francisco J. Mujica S/N Ciudad Universitaria, 58030 Morelia, Michoacán
Tel: +52(443) 322-35-00
EMail: rectoria@umich.mx
Website: http://www.umich.mx

Rector: Salvador Jara Guerrero (2011-)

Divisions
Administration and Social Sciences (Accountancy; Administration; Economics; Law; Social Sciences); **Agriculture** (Agricultural Business; Agrobiology; Veterinary Science; Zoology); **Engineering and Architecture** (Architecture; Chemical Engineering; Civil Engineering; Computer Engineering; Electrical and Electronic Engineering; Mechanical Engineering; Wood Technology); **Health Sciences** (Biology; Dentistry; Medicine; Nursing; Veterinary Science); **Humanities** (Dance; History; Literature; Music; Spanish; Theatre; Visual Arts)

Schools
Arts (Fine Arts)

History: Founded 1843 as Colegio de San Nicolás and traces its history back to the college originally established in 1542. Became University 1917. Reorganized 1939.

Academic Year: September to July (September-February; March-July)

Admission Requirements: Secondary school certificate (bachillerato) or equivalent, and entrance examination

Main Language(s) of Instruction: Spanish

Degrees and Diplomas: *Licenciatura*: 5 yrs; *Especialización*; *Maestría*; *Doctorado*

Special Facilities: Museo Michoacano

Libraries: Yes

Publications: Research Collection

Press or Publishing House: Editorial Universitaria

Last Updated: 15/10/12

MIGUEL HIDALGO RURAL TEACHER TRAINING SCHOOL

Escuela Normal Rural Miguel Hidalgo

Calzada Justo Sierra, 95, Ixtalhuacán de los Membrillos, 45860 Atequiza, Jalisco

Tel: +52(376) 767-00-02 +52(376) 767-09-43

Fax: +52(376) 767-10-02

Directora: Ma Del Refugio Lopez Martinez

Programmes

Teacher Training (Preschool Education; Primary Education; Special Education; Teacher Training)

Degrees and Diplomas: *Licenciatura*; *Especialización*

Last Updated: 25/02/13

MUSIC AND ARTS CONSERVATOIRE OF CELAYA

Conservatorio de Música y Artes de Celaya

Madero 110, Centro, Celaya, Guanajuato

EMail: schtocly@prodigy.net.mx.

Website: http://www.conservatoriocelaya.edu.mx

Director: Alejandro Montes Ávalos

Programmes

Music (Conducting; Music; Musical Instruments; Singing)

History: Founded 1991.

Main Language(s) of Instruction: Spanish

Degrees and Diplomas: *Licenciatura*

Last Updated: 24/08/12

MUSIC CONSERVATOIRE OF THE STATE OF MEXICO

Conservatorio de Música del Estado de México

José Ma. Morelos Pte. 816, Col. Centro, 50000 Toluca, Estado de México

Tel: +52(72) 15-68-48

Fax: +52(72) 15-68-63

EMail: comem.edomex@edomex.gob.mx

Website: http://www.edomex.gob.mx/comem

Programmes

Music (Music; Musical Instruments)

History: Founded 1991.

Main Language(s) of Instruction: Spanish

Degrees and Diplomas: *Licenciatura*

Last Updated: 24/08/12

MUSIC CONSERVATOIRE OF THE STATE OF PUEBLA

Conservatorio de Música del Estado de Puebla

Avenida Juárez 1301, Heroica Puebla de Zaragoza, 72000 Puebla, Puebla

Tel: +52(22) 32-30-74

EMail: angeles_nieto@hotmail.com

Website: http://www.consermuspue.edu.mx

Director: Cuauhtémoc Mario Cruz Abud

Programmes

Music (Music; Musical Instruments)

Further Information: Also campuses In San Francisco Mixtla, San Felipe Otlaltepec and Huauchinango

History: Founded 1917. Acquired present status 1998.

Main Language(s) of Instruction: Spanish

Degrees and Diplomas: *Licenciatura*

Last Updated: 20/02/13

NATIONAL AUTONOMOUS UNIVERSITY OF MEXICO

Universidad Nacional Autónoma de México (UNAM)

Ciudad Universitaria, Coyoacán, 04510 México, D.F.

Tel: +52(55) 56-22-12-80

Fax: +52(55) 56-16-00-30

Website: http://www.unam.mx/

Rector: José Narro Robles (2011-2015)
Tel: 52 55 5622 1280, Fax: 52 55 5550 8772
EMail: rectoria@servidor.unam.mx

International Relations: Martha Navarro-Albo, General Director for Cooperation and Internationalization
Tel: +52(55) 56-22-11-01, Fax: +52(55) 55-50-90-17
EMail: arlinan@unam.mx

Centres

Applied Physics and Advanced Technology (Applied Physics; Technology); **Applied Sciences and Technological Development** (Design; Electronic Engineering; Instrument Making; Measurement and Precision Engineering); **Astrophysics and Radioastronomy** (Astronomy and Space Science; Astrophysics); **Atmospheric Sciences** (Environmental Studies; Meteorology); **Ecosystems Research** (Ecology); **Energy Research** (Energy Engineering; Natural Resources); **Environmental Geography Research** (Environmental Studies; Geography); **Foreign Languages Teaching** (Arabic; Catalan; Chinese; English; Foreign Languages Education; French; German; Greek; Hebrew; Italian; Japanese; Korean; Linguistics; Portuguese; Russian; Swedish); **Foreign Students Education** (Hispanic American Studies; History; Literature; Native Language; Social Sciences; Spanish); **Genomic Sciences** (Genetics; Molecular Biology); **Geosciences** (Earth Sciences); **Humanities and Social Sciences** *(Peninsular)* (Arts and Humanities; Social Sciences); **Interdisciplinary Research on Science and Humanities** (Arts and Humanities; Development Studies; Social Sciences); **Latin America and Caribbean Research** (Caribbean Studies; Economics; History; Latin American Studies; Literature; Philosophy; Sociology); **Library Science Research** (Documentation Techniques; Information Technology; Library Science); **Nanotechnology and Nanosciences** (Nanotechnology; Physical Chemistry; Physics); **North America Research** (American Studies; Canadian Studies; International Relations); **Regional Multidisciplinary Research** (Regional Studies)

Programmes

Energy (Energy Engineering; Thermal Engineering); **Environment** (Environmental Studies); **Food** (Food Science); **Gender Studies** (Gender Studies); **Health Research** (Health Sciences); **Mexico - Multicultural Nation** (Cultural Studies); **Urban Studies** (Urban Studies)

Research Centres

Cinematographic Studies (Cinema and Television; Film; Sound Engineering (Acoustics); Writing); **Theatre Studies** (Acting; Display and Stage Design; Theatre)

Research Institutes

Aesthetical Research (Aesthetics); **Anthropological Research** (Anthropology); **Applied Mathematics and Systems** (Applied Mathematics; Computer Science; Systems Analysis); **Astronomy** (Astronomy and Space Science); **Bibliographic Research** (Library Science); **Biology** (Biology; Botany; Cell Biology; Ecology; Microbiology); **Biomedical Research** (Biomedicine; Biotechnology; Cell Biology; Immunology; Molecular Biology; Physiology; Toxicology); **Biotechnology** (Bioengineering; Biotechnology); **Cellular Physiology** (Biochemistry; Cell Biology; Physiology); **Chemistry** (Chemistry; Inorganic Chemistry; Organic Chemistry; Physical Chemistry); **Ecology** (Ecology; Natural Resources); **Economic Research** (Economics); **Engineering** (Automation and Control Engineering; Construction Engineering; Electronic Engineering; Engineering; Hydraulic Engineering; Mechanical Engineering); **Geography** (Geography; Geophysics; Surveying and Mapping); **Geology** (Geology; Geophysics; Paleontology; Petrology); **Geophysics** (Geophysics; Natural Resources; Seismology); **Historical**

Research (History); **Legal Research** (Law); **Materials Research** (Ceramics and Glass Technology; Heating and Refrigeration; Metal Techniques; Polymer and Plastics Technology; Solid State Physics); **Mathematics** (Mathematics); **Neurobiology** (Neurosciences); **Nuclear Science** (Energy Engineering; Nuclear Physics; Radiology); **Ocean Sciences and Limnology** (Coastal Studies; Limnology; Marine Science and Oceanography); **Philological Research** (Philology); **Philosophical Research** (Philosophy); **Physical Sciences** (Physics); **Physics** (Physical Chemistry; Physics; Solid State Physics); **Social Research** (Social Studies); **University and Educational Research** (Curriculum; Education; History; Pedagogy; Political Sciences; Social Sciences)

Schools

Accounting and Management (Accountancy; Business Administration; Management); **Architecture** (Architecture); **Chemistry** (Chemistry); **Dentistry** (Dentistry); **Economics** (Economics); **Engineering** (Civil Engineering; Computer Engineering; Engineering; Geological Engineering; Mechanical Engineering; Mining Engineering; Physical Engineering; Telecommunications Engineering); **Fine Arts** *(National School)* (Fine Arts); **Law** (Law); **Medicine** (Medicine); **Music** *(National School)* (Music); **Nursing and Obstetrics** *(National School)* (Gynaecology and Obstetrics; Nursing); **Philosophy and Literature** (Arts and Humanities; Classical Languages; English; French; Geography; German; History; Latin American Studies; Literature; Modern Languages; Pedagogy; Philosophy; Spanish; Theatre); **Political and Social Sciences** (Communication Studies; International Relations; Journalism; Political Sciences; Public Administration; Social Sciences; Sociology); **Psychology** (Psychology); **Science** (Actuarial Science; Astronomy and Space Science; Biology; Computer Science; Earth Sciences; Ecology; Marine Science and Oceanography; Materials Engineering; Mathematics; Natural Sciences; Physics; Water Science); **Social Work** *(National School)* (Social Work); **Veterinary Medicine and Zootechnology** (Animal Husbandry; Veterinary Science)

Further Information: Also Escuela de Enfermería María Elena Maza Brito; Project on Biodiversity

History: Founded 1551 with the creation of the founding document for the Royal and Pontifical University of Mexico. First classes delivered 1553 and it was the first to offer higher education in the Americas. The RPUM was organized along the lines of the European universities in the scholastic tradition, particularly Salamanca University. In 1910, it was established as the National University of Mexico, and finally in 1929 obtained its autonomy and current title and status.

Governing Bodies: Junta de Gobierno, Consejo Universitario, comprising the Rector, the Secretary-General and the directors of all faculties, schools and institutes, as well as members of the academic staff and student body

Academic Year: August to May (August-December; January-May)

Admission Requirements: Secondary school certificate (bachillerato) or recognized equivalent, and entrance examination

Main Language(s) of Instruction: Spanish

International Co-operation: Arrangements for exchanges of researchers, academic staff, and students with institutions worldwide. UNESCO Chair on Human Rights

Degrees and Diplomas: *Licenciatura*: 4-5 yrs; *Especialización*; *Maestría*: 1-2 yrs after Licenciatura or corresponding professional qualifications and thesis; *Doctorado*: by thesis. Also lower level technical qualifications

Student Services: Academic counselling, Cultural centre, Foreign student adviser, Health services, Nursery care, Sports facilities

Special Facilities: Arts and Science Museum; Geology Museum; El Chopo Museum; History and Philosophy of Medicine Museum; Palacio de Minería Museum; Science Museum 'Universum'. National Astronomy Observatory (San Pedro Mártir, B.C. and Tonantzintla, Puebla)

Libraries: 141 Libraries: 1 National Library, 1 Central Library, 139 specialized libraries of the Schools, Institutes and Centres

Publications: Los Universitarios; Publications of the Academic Divisions; Punto de Partida *(monthly)*; Voices of Mexico *(quarterly)*

Press or Publishing House: Dirección General de Publicaciones UNAM

Last Updated: 04/04/13

FACULTY OF ADVANCED STUDIES CUAUTITLÁN

FACULTAD DE ESTUDIOS SUPERIORES CUAUTITLÁN (FES-CUAUTITLÁN)

Apartado postal 25, Km. 2.5 Carretera Cuautitlán-Teoloyucán, San Sebastián Xhala, 54714 Cuautitlán Izcalli, Estado de México
Tel: +52(55) 56-23-19-61
Fax: +52(55) 58-70-56-71
EMail: montaraz@servidor.unam.mx
Website: http://www.cuautitlan2.unam.mx

Departments

Accountancy (Accountancy); **Administration** (Administration); **Agricultural Engineering** (Agricultural Engineering); **Chemical Engineering** (Chemical Engineering); **Chemistry** (Chemistry); **Computer Science** (Computer Science); **Electrical and Mechanical Engineering** (Electrical Engineering; Mechanical Engineering); **Food Processing** (Food Technology); **Industrial Chemistry** (Industrial Chemistry); **Pharmaceutical and Biological Chemistry** (Biochemistry; Chemistry; Pharmacy); **Veterinary Science and Animal Husbandry** (Animal Husbandry; Veterinary Science)

History: Founded 1974.

Main Language(s) of Instruction: Spanish

Degrees and Diplomas: *Licenciatura*; *Maestría*

FACULTY OF ADVANCED STUDIES IZTACALA

FACULTAD DE ESTUDIOS SUPERIORES IZTACALA (ENEP, IZTACALA)

Avenida los Barrios s/n, Unidad los Reyes Iztacala, 54090 Tlalnepantla, Estado de México
Tel: +52(55) 56-23-11-50
Fax: +52(55) 53-90-76-13
EMail: ramje@servidor.unam.mx
Website: http://www.iztacala.unam.mx

Departments

Biology (Biology); **Dentistry** (Dentistry); **Medicine** (Medicine); **Optics** (Optics); **Psychology** (Psychology)

History: Founded 1975. Formerly Escuela Nacional de Estudios Profesionales.

Main Language(s) of Instruction: Spanish

Degrees and Diplomas: *Licenciatura*; *Maestría*; *Doctorado*

FACULTY OF ADVANCED STUDIES ZARAGOZA

FACULTAD DE ESTUDIOS SUPERIORES ZARAGOZA (FES-ZARAGOZA)

Avenida Guelato 66, Col. Ejército de Oriente, 09230 México, D.F.
Tel: +52(55) 57-73-63-10 +52(55) 57-73-63-11
Fax: +52(55) 56-23-05-40
EMail: director@puma2.zaragoza.unam.mx
Website: http://www.zaragoza.unam.mx

Departments

Biological and Pharmaceutical Chemistry (Biochemistry; Pharmacy); **Biology** (Biology); **Chemical Engineering** (Chemical Engineering); **Dentistry** (Dentistry); **Medicine** (Medicine); **Nursing** (Nursing); **Psychology** (Psychology)

Main Language(s) of Instruction: Spanish

Degrees and Diplomas: *Especialización*; *Maestría*; *Doctorado*

NATIONAL SCHOOL OF PROFESSIONAL STUDIES ACATLÁN

ESCUELA NACIONAL DE ESTUDIOS PROFESIONALES ACATLÁN (ENEP, ACATLÁN)

Av. Alcanfores y San Juan Totoltepec s/n, 53150 Santa Cruz Acatlán, Estado de México
Tel: +52(55) 56-23-17-75
EMail: fesadireccion@apolo.acatlan.unam.mx
Website: http://www.acatlan.unam.mx

Departments
Actuarial Studies (Actuarial Science); **Applied Mathematics and Computer Science** (Applied Mathematics; Computer Science); **Architecture** (Architecture); **Civil Engineering** (Civil Engineering); **Economics** (Economics); **Education** (Education); **Graphic Design** (Graphic Design); **Hispanic Language and Literature** (Literature; Spanish); **International Relations** (International Relations); **Law** (Law); **Philosophy** (Philosophy); **Public Administration and Political Science** (Political Sciences; Public Administration); **Sociology** (Sociology); **Teaching of English Language** (Foreign Languages Education)

History: Founded 1975.

Degrees and Diplomas: *Licenciatura*; *Maestría*; *Doctorado*

NATIONAL SCHOOL OF PROFESSIONAL STUDIES ARAGÓN

ESCUELA NACIONAL DE ESTUDIOS PROFESIONALES ARAGÓN (ENEP, ARAGÓN)

Avenida Rancho Seco de Aragón s/n, 57170 Ciudad Nezahualcóyotl, Estado de México
Tel: +52(55) 56-23-08-30
Fax: +52(55) 56-23-08-56
EMail: turcott@servidor.unam.mx
Website: http://www.informatica.aragon.unam.mx

Departments
Agricultural Development Planning (Agricultural Economics); **Architecture** (Architecture); **Civil Engineering** (Civil Engineering); **Communication Studies and Journalism** (Communication Studies; Journalism); **Computer Engineering** (Computer Engineering); **Economics** (Economics); **Education** (Education); **Industrial Design** (Industrial Design); **International Relations** (International Relations); **Law** (Law); **Mechanical and Electrical Engineering** (Electrical Engineering; Mechanical Engineering); **Social Sciences** (Social Sciences); **Sociology** (Sociology)

History: Founded 1976.

Main Language(s) of Instruction: Spanish

Degrees and Diplomas: *Licenciatura*; *Maestría*; *Doctorado*

NATIONAL CENTRE FOR RESEARCH AND TECHNOLOGICAL DEVELOPMENT

Centro Nacional de Investigación y Desarrollo Tecnológico (CENIDET)

Interior Internado Palmira s/n, Col. Palmira, 62490 Cuernavaca, Morelos
Tel: +52(777) 314-06-37 Ext. 17
Fax: +52(777) 312-24-34
EMail: subacad@cenidet.edu.mx
Website: http://www.cenidet.edu.mx

Director: Víctor Hugo Olivares Peregrino
EMail: direccion@cenidet.edu.mx

Programmes
Computer Science (Computer Science); **Engineering** (Electrical Engineering; Electronic Engineering; Mechanical Engineering)

History: Founded 1987.

Main Language(s) of Instruction: Spanish

Degrees and Diplomas: *Maestría*; *Doctorado*

Last Updated: 19/07/12

NATIONAL INSTITUTE OF ANTHROPOLOGY AND HISTORY

Instituto Nacional de Antropología e Historia (INAH)

Córdoba 45, 1er Piso, Col. Roma, Delegación Cuauhtémoc, 06700 México, D.F.
Tel: +52(55) 55-33-20-15 al 18 +52(55) 55-25-91-78
Fax: +52(55) 55-25-22-13
EMail: direccion.dgeneral@inah.gob.mx
Website: http://www.inah.gob.mx

Director General: C. Alfonso de Maria y Campos Castelló

Programmes
Anthropology (Anthropology); **History** (History); **Museum Studies**

History: Founded 1939.

Main Language(s) of Instruction: Spanish

Degrees and Diplomas: *Licenciatura*; *Maestría*; *Doctorado*

Last Updated: 20/02/08

MANUEL DEL CASTILLO NEGRETE NATIONAL SCHOOL OF CONSERVATION, RESTORATION AND MUSEOGRAPHY

ESCUELA NACIONAL DE CONSERVACIÓN, RESTAURACIÓN Y MUSEOGRAFÍA 'MANUEL DEL CASTILLO NEGRETE'

Ex-Convento de Churubusco Xicotencatl y General Anaya, Col. San Diego Churubusco, Delegación Coyoacán, 04120 México, D.F.
Tel: +52(55) 56-04-51-88
Fax: +52(55) 56-04-51-63
EMail: inahmex@telecomm.net.mx
Website: http://www.encrym.edu.mx

Directora: Liliana Giorguli Chávez
EMail: liliana_giorguli@inah.gob.mx

Programmes
Conservation, Restoration and Museology (Heritage Preservation; Museum Studies; Restoration of Works of Art)

History: Founded 1968.

Main Language(s) of Instruction: Spanish

Degrees and Diplomas: *Licenciatura*; *Especialización*; *Maestría*

Libraries: Yes

NATIONAL SCHOOL OF ANTHROPOLOGY AND HISTORY

ESCUELA NACIONAL DE ANTROPOLOGÍA E HISTORIA

Periférico Sur y Calle Zapote, Col. Isidro Fabela Tlalpán, 14030 México, D.F.
Tel: +52(55) 56-06-03-30
Fax: +52(55) 56-65-92-28
EMail: direccion.enah@inah.gob.mx
Website: http://www.enah.edu.mx

Director: José Luis Vera Cortés

Programmes
Anthropology (Anthropology); **Archaeology** (Archaeology); **Ethnology** (Ethnology); **History** (History); **Linguistics** (Linguistics)

History: Founded 1938 as Department of Anthropology of the Instituto Politécnico Nacional, acquired present status and title 1946.

Governing Bodies: Consejo Técnico; Consejo Académico

Academic Year: January to December (January-June; June-December)

Admission Requirements: Secondary school certificate (bachillerato) and preparatory course

Fees: None

Main Language(s) of Instruction: Spanish

Degrees and Diplomas: *Licenciatura*: 4 yrs; *Maestría*: a further 2 yrs; *Doctorado*: 2 yrs

Student Services: Academic counselling, Cultural centre, Health services, Language programs, Nursery care, Social counselling, Sports facilities

Libraries: Specialized Library

Publications: Cuicuilco, Anthropology and History *(3 per annum)*

NATIONAL INSTITUTE OF ASTROPHYSICS, OPTICS AND ELECTRONICS

Instituto Nacional de Astrofísica, Óptica y Electrónica (INAOE)

Calle Luis Enrique Erro 1, Tonantzintla, 72840 Puebla, Puebla
Tel: +52(222) 266-31-00
EMail: grivera@inaoep.mx
Website: http://www.inaoep.mx

Director: Alberto Carramiñana Alonso EMail: alberto@inaoep.mx

Departments

Astrophysics (Astrophysics); **Computer Science** (Computer Science); **Electronics** (Electronic Engineering); **Optics** (Optics)

History: Founded 1971 integrating the National Observatory for Astrophysics, founded 1942 and reorganised 1950. A national postgraduate institution.

Governing Bodies: Government Committee

Academic Year: September to August

Admission Requirements: Bachelors Degree in Physics, Electronics, Engineering and Computer Sciences

Fees: (US Dollars): 5,000 per annum

Main Language(s) of Instruction: English, Spanish

Accrediting Agencies: Secretaría de Educación Pública

Degrees and Diplomas: *Maestría*: 2 yrs; *Doctorado*: 3 yrs

Student Services: Academic counselling, Foreign student adviser, Health services, Language programs, Sports facilities

Student Residential Facilities: Yes

Special Facilities: Observatory

Libraries: Central Library

Last Updated: 06/03/13

NATIONAL INSTITUTE OF FINE ARTS AND LITERATURE

Instituto Nacional de Bellas Artes y Literatura

Reforma y Campo Marte s/n, Polanco Chapultepec, Delegación Miguel Hidalgo, 11560 México, D.F.
Tel: +52(55) 52-80-54-74 +52(55) 52-80-70-97
Fax: +52(55) 52-80-48-65
Website: http://.bellasartes.gob.mx

Directora General: Teresa Vicencio Álvarez

Programmes

Fine Arts (Fine Arts); **Literature** (Literature)

History: Founded 1946.

Main Language(s) of Instruction: Spanish

Last Updated: 06/03/13

LA ESMERALDA NATIONAL SCHOOL OF PAINTING, SCULPTURE AND DRAWING OF THE INBA

ESCUELA NACIONAL DE PINTURA, ESCULTURA Y GRABADO 'LA ESMERALDA' DEL INBA

Calzada de Tlalpán y Río Churubusco No 79, Col. Contry Club Coyacán, 04220 México, D.F.
Tel: +52(55) 54-20-44-00

Programmes

Painting and Drawing (Painting and Drawing); **Sculpture** (Sculpture)

Main Language(s) of Instruction: Spanish

Degrees and Diplomas: *Licenciatura*

MONTERREY HIGHER SCHOOL OF MUSIC AND DANCE

ESCUELA SUPERIOR DE MÚSICA Y DANZA DE MONTERREY

Padre Mier, 1720, Pte., Col. Obispado, 64000 Monterrey, Nuevo León
Tel: +52(81) 348-42-65
Fax: +52(81) 347-17-78
EMail: lasuperior@esmdm.edu.mx
Website: http://esmdm.edu.mx

Directora: Elida Valdez Martínez EMail: evaldez@esmdm.edu.mx

Programmes

Dance (Dance); **Music** (Music; Musical Instruments; Singing)

History: Founded 1976.

Main Language(s) of Instruction: Spanish

Degrees and Diplomas: *Licenciatura*

NATIONAL CONSERVATORY OF MUSIC

CONSERVATORIO NACIONAL DE MÚSICA

Avenida Presidente Mazarik 582, Col. Polanco Reforma Miguel Hidalgo, 11560 México, D.F.
Tel: +52(55) 52-80-74-71
Fax: +52(55) 52-80-62-21

Programmes

Music (Music; Musical Instruments)

Degrees and Diplomas: *Licenciatura*

NATIONAL SCHOOL OF CLASSICAL AND CONTEMPORARY DANCE

ESCUELA NACIONAL DE DANZA CLÁSICA Y CONTEMPORÁNEA

Calzada de Tlalpán y Río Churubusco No. 79, Col. Contry Club Coyacán, 04220 México, D.F.
Tel: +52(55) 54-20-44-00

Directora: Ofelia Chávez

Programmes

Dance (Dance)

Main Language(s) of Instruction: Spanish

Degrees and Diplomas: *Licenciatura*

NELLY Y GLORIA CAMPOBELLO NATIONAL SCHOOL OF DANCE

ESCUELA NACIONAL DE DANZA NELLY Y GLORIA CAMPOBELLO

Campos Elíseos, 480, Col. Polanco Chapultepec, Delegación Miguel Hidalgo, 11000 México, D.F.
Tel: +52(55) 52-80-43-61
EMail: endngc.carrera@inba.gob.mx
Website: http://www.endngcampobello.bellasartes.gob.mx

Director: Fernando Aragón Monroy

Programmes

Dance (Dance)

History: Founded 1937.

Main Language(s) of Instruction: Spanish

Degrees and Diplomas: *Licenciatura*

SCHOOL OF DESIGN

ESCUELA DE DISEÑO

Xocongo 138, Col. Tránsito Cuauhtémoc, 06820 México, D.F.
Tel: +52(55) 55-22-57-61
EMail: edinba@inba.gob.mx
Website: http://www.edinba.bellasartes.gob.mx

Directora: Rosenda Berenice Miranda Vadillo

Programmes

Design (Design); **Painting and Drawing** (Painting and Drawing)

History: Founded 1949.

Main Language(s) of Instruction: Spanish

Degrees and Diplomas: *Licenciatura*; *Especialización*; *Maestría*

SCHOOL OF MUSIC

ESCUELA SUPERIOR DE MÚSICA

Fernández Leal, 31, Col. Del Carmen Coyoacán, 04000 México, D.F.
Tel: +52(55) 56-58-17-32
Fax: +52(55) 56-58-10-96
EMail: superiordemusica@gmail.com
Website: http://www.escuelasuperiordemusica.bellasartes.gob.mx

Director: Cuauhtémoc Rivera Guzmán

Programmes
Music (Music; Musical Instruments)

History: Founded 1922 as Conservatorio Nacional de Música. Acquired present title 1935.

Main Language(s) of Instruction: Spanish

SCHOOL OF THEATRE

ESCUELA DE ARTE TEATRAL

Calzada de Tlalpán y Río Churubusco, Col. Contry Club Coyacán, 04220 México, D.F.
Tel: +52(55) 54-20-44-00
Fax: +52(55) 54-20-44-60
Website: http://www.enat.bellasartes.gob.mx

Director: Gilberto Guerrero Vázquez

Programmes
Theatre (Theatre)

History: Founded 1946.

Main Language(s) of Instruction: Spanish

Degrees and Diplomas: *Licenciatura*; *Maestría*

NATIONAL INSTITUTE OF PENAL STUDIES

Instituto Nacional de Ciencias Penales (INACIPE)
Magisterio Nacional 113, Colonia San Fernando Tlalpán, 14000 México, D.F.
Tel: +52(55) 5487-15-00
EMail: inacipe@inacipe.gob.mx
Website: http://www.inacipe.gob.mx/

Director General: Gerardo Laveaga (2001-)
EMail: gerardo.laveaga@inacipe.gob.mx

Departments
Law (Criminal Law; Criminology; Law)

History: Founded 1976.

Governing Bodies: General Attorney Office

Academic Year: August to July

Admission Requirements: Licenciatura in Law (promedio minimo de 8)

Main Language(s) of Instruction: Spanish

Degrees and Diplomas: *Maestría*: Federal Justice; Penal Law; Victimology; Criminal Law, 2 yrs; *Doctorado*: Penal Law and Criminal Policy

Student Services: Academic counselling, Employment services, Social counselling

Libraries: Biblioteca '"Celestino Porte Petit"

Publications: Iter Criminis, Criminal Law Magazine *(biennially)*

Last Updated: 07/03/13

NATIONAL INSTITUTE OF PUBLIC ADMINISTRATION

Instituto Nacional de Administración Pública
Carretera Libre México-Toluca 2151 (Km. 14.5) Col. Palo Alto Deleg. Cuajimalpa de Morelos, 05110 México, D.F.
Tel: +52(555) 570-04-03
Fax: +52(555) 570-05-32
EMail: contacto@inap.org.mx
Website: http://www.inap.org.mx/

Presidente: José R. Castelazo EMail: jrcastelazo@inap.org.mx

Programmes
Public Administration (Finance; Public Administration)

Main Language(s) of Instruction: Spanish

Degrees and Diplomas: *Licenciatura*; *Especialización*; *Maestría*; *Doctorado*

Libraries: Yes

Last Updated: 06/03/13

NATIONAL INSTITUTE OF PUBLIC HEALTH

Instituto Nacional de Salud Pública (INSP)
Avenida Universidad 655, Col. Santa María Ahuacatitlán, 62508 Cuernavaca, Morelos
Tel: +52(777) 329-30-00
Website: http://www.insp.mx

Director General: Mauricio Hernández Ávila
EMail: director@insp.mx

Programmes
Health Sciences (Health Sciences; Nutrition); **Public Health** (Public Health)

Further Information: Also campus in Tapachula

History: Founded 1922.

Governing Bodies: Junta de Gobierno

Admission Requirements: Professional title with Grade 8 (minimum)

Main Language(s) of Instruction: Spanish

Degrees and Diplomas: *Especialización*: 1 yr; *Maestría*: 1 1/2-2 yrs; *Doctorado*: 2 yrs

Student Services: Academic counselling

Libraries: Central Library

Publications: Revista de Salud Pública de México *(bimonthly)*

Last Updated: 07/03/13

NATIONAL INSTITUTE OF REHABILITATION

Instituto Nacional de Rehabilitación
Calzada México Xochimilco No. 289, Col. Arenal de Guadalupe, Delegación Tlalpan, 14389 México, D.F.
Tel: +52(55) 59-99-10-00
EMail: webmaster@inr.gob.mx
Website: http://www.inr.gob.mx

Director General: Luis Guillermo Ibarra EMail: libarra@inr.gob.mx

Programmes
Anaesthesiology (Anaesthesiology); **Audiology and Speech Pathology** (Communication Disorders; Communication Studies; Speech Therapy and Audiology); **Diagnosis and Medical Treatment Auxiliary Services** (Medical Auxiliaries); **Ophthalmology** (Ophthalmology); **Orthopaedics** (Orthopaedics; Rheumatology; Sports Medicine; Surgery); **Otorhinolaryngology** (Otorhinolaryngology); **Rehabilitation Medicine** (Neurological Therapy; Neurology; Occupational Therapy; Physical Therapy; Rehabilitation and Therapy; Sports Medicine); **Sports Medicine** (Sports Medicine)

History: Founded 1997. Integrated part of the Centro Nacional de Rehabilitación 2001.

Main Language(s) of Instruction: Spanish

Degrees and Diplomas: *Licenciatura*; *Maestría*; *Doctorado*

Last Updated: 07/03/13

NATIONAL PAEDIATRICS INSTITUTE

Instituto Nacional de Pediatría
Insurgentes Sur 3700-C, Col. Insurgentes Cuicuilco Delegación Coyoacán Delegación Coyoacán, 04530 México, D.F.
Tel: +52(551) 1084-0900
EMail: ealvirezo@pediatra.gob.mx
Website: http://www.pediatria.gob.mx/

Director General: Alejandro Serrano Sierra
EMail: aserranos@pediatra.gob.mx

Programmes
Paediatrics (Paediatrics)

History: Founded 1970 as Hospital Infantil de la Institución Mexicana de Asistencia a la Niñez. Acquired present status and title 1983.

Main Language(s) of Instruction: Spanish

Degrees and Diplomas: *Licenciatura*; *Especialización*

Last Updated: 07/03/13

NATIONAL POLYTECHNIC INSTITUTE

Instituto Politécnico Nacional (IPN)
Unidad Profesional Adolfo López Mateos, Avenida Luis Enrique Erro s/n, Col. Zacatenco, Delegación Gustavo A. Madero, 07738 México, D.F.
Tel: +52(55) 57-29-60-03 +52(55) 57-54-45-32
Fax: +52(55) 57-29-60-01
Website: http://www.ipn.edu.mx

Directora General: Yoloxóchitl Bustamante Díez

Areas

Engineering , Physics and Mathematics (Aeronautical and Aerospace Engineering; Architecture; Automation and Control Engineering; Chemical Engineering; Civil Engineering; Computer Engineering; Electrical Engineering; Electronic Engineering; Geological Engineering; Geophysics; Industrial Engineering; Mathematics; Mechanical Engineering; Metallurgical Engineering; Petroleum and Gas Engineering; Physics; Robotics; Telecommunications Engineering; Textile Technology); **Medicine and Biological Sciences** (Biochemistry; Biology; Biomedical Engineering; Biotechnology; Dentistry; Environmental Engineering; Food Technology; Gynaecology and Obstetrics; Homeopathy; Nursing; Nutrition; Optometry; Parasitology; Psychology; Social Work; Surgery); **Social Sciences and Administration** (Accountancy; Business Administration; Business and Commerce; Economics; International Business; Tourism)

History: Founded 1936.

Governing Bodies: Consejo General Consultativo

Academic Year: August to July (August-February; February-July)

Admission Requirements: Secondary school certificate (bachillerato) and entrance examination

Main Language(s) of Instruction: Spanish

Degrees and Diplomas: *Licenciatura*; *Especialización*; *Maestría*: Science; *Doctorado*: Science

Student Services: Academic counselling, Cultural centre, Employment services, Health services, Language programs, Social counselling, Sports facilities

Libraries: Yes

Publications: Acta Médica *(quarterly)*; Acta Mexicana de Ciencia y Tecnología *(quarterly)*; Anales del Pestyc *(annually)*; Investigación Hoy *(monthly)*; Investigaciones Marinas *(biannually)*; IPN Arte, Ciencia y Cultura *(monthly)*; Revista Académica *(monthly)*

Press or Publishing House: Dirección de Publicaciones del IPN

Last Updated: 07/03/13

NATIONAL RESEARCH INSTITUTE IN FORESTRY, AGRICULTURE AND STOCKBREEDING

Instituto Nacional de Investigaciones Forestales, Agrícolas y Pecuarias (INIFAP)
Progreso No. 5 Barrio Santa Catarina, Coyoacán, 06740 México, D.F.
Website: http://www.inifap.gob.mx/.

Director: Pedro Brajcich Gallegos
EMail: brajcich.pedro@inifap.gob.mx

Programmes

Agriculture (Agriculture); **Cattle Breeding** (Cattle Breeding); **Fishery** (Fishery); **Forestry** (Forestry); **Rural Deevelopment** (Rural Planning)

Further Information: 8 Regional Research Centres and 38 experimental campuses

History: Founded 1985.

Main Language(s) of Instruction: Spanish

Degrees and Diplomas: *Maestría*; *Doctorado*

Last Updated: 07/03/13

NATIONAL SCHOOL FOR WOMEN KINDERGARTEN TEACHERS

Escuela Nacional para Maestras de Jardines de Niños
Gustavo E. Campa, 94, Col. Guadalupe Inn, Delegación Álvaro Obregón, 01020 México, D.F.
Tel: +52(55) 55-93-61-20 +52(55) 53-28-10-97
Fax: +52(55) 55-93-61-01 +52(55) 55-93-60-31
EMail: pezuela@sep.gob.mx

Directora: Georgina Quintanilla Cerda

Programmes

Education (Preschool Education; Primary Education); **Teacher Training** (Teacher Training)

History: Founded 1947.

Main Language(s) of Instruction: Spanish

Degrees and Diplomas: *Licenciatura*; *Especialización*; *Maestría*

Last Updated: 18/03/08

NATIONAL SCHOOL OF LIBRARY SCIENCE AND ARCHIVING

Escuela Nacional de Biblioteconomía y Archivonomía (ENBA)
Calzada Ticomán 645, Col. Santa María Ticomán Gustavo A. Madero, 07330 México, D.F.
Tel: +52(55) 57-52-75-75
Fax: +52(55) 57-52-74-55
EMail: buzon@sep.gob.mx
Website: http://www.enba.sep.gob.mx

Director: Joaquín Flores Méndez EMail: jfloresm@sep.gob.mx

Programmes

Archiving (Archiving); **Library Science** (Archiving; Library Science)

History: Founded 1945.

Main Language(s) of Instruction: Spanish

Degrees and Diplomas: *Licenciatura*

Libraries: Biblioteca "Francisco Orozco Muñoz"

Last Updated: 29/08/12

NATIONAL SCHOOL OF SPORTS TRAINERS

Escuela Nacional de Entrenadores Deportivos
Añil y Av. Rio Churubusco, Puerta "J" de la Ciudad Deportiva, de la Magdalena Mixihuca, Delegación Iztacalco, 08010 México, D.F.
Tel: +52(5) 56-49-19-51
Fax: +52(5) 56-49-18-00
EMail: ened@hotmail.com
Website: http://ened.conade.gob.mx

Director: William A. Maldonado Mauregui

Programmes

Sports (Sports)

History: Founded 1984.

Main Language(s) of Instruction: Spanish

Degrees and Diplomas: *Licenciatura*

Libraries: Yes

Last Updated: 10/01/13

NATIONAL UNIVERSITY OF EDUCATION SCIENCES

Universidad Pedagógica Nacional (UPN)
Carretera al Ajusco 24, Col. Héroes de Padierna, Delegación Tlalpán, 14200 México, D.F.
Tel: +52(555) 5630-9700
EMail: rectoria@ajusco.upn.mx
Website: http://www.upn.mx

Rectora: Sylvia Ortega Salazar (2007-)

Programmes

Education (Adult Education; Arts and Humanities; Computer Education; Education; Educational Administration; Educational Psychology; Educational Sciences; French; Natives Education; Pedagogy; Preschool Education; Primary Education; Special Education; Teacher Training)

Further Information: Also numerous 'Unidades UPN' throughout the country

History: Founded 1978.

Governing Bodies: Academic Council

Academic Year: September to July (September-February; March-July)

Admission Requirements: Secondary school certificate (bachillerato) with minimun average of 7 and entrance examination

Main Language(s) of Instruction: Spanish

International Co-operation: With universities in Colombia, Costa Rica, Dominican Republic, El Salvador, France, Honduras, Panama, Russian Federation and Spain

Degrees and Diplomas: *Licenciatura*: Adult Education; Educational Administration; Educational Psychology; Educational Sociology; Natives Education; Pedagogy, 4 yrs; *Licenciatura*: French Language Education, 3 yrs; *Especialización*: Computer Education; Environmental Education; Gender in Education, 1 yr; *Maestría*: Educational Development, 2 yrs; *Doctorado*: Educational Sciences, at least 5 yrs

Student Services: Academic counselling, Cultural centre, Employment services, Health services, Language programs, Nursery care, Sports facilities

Student Residential Facilities: None

Special Facilities: Languages Centre, Computer Centre, Videoconferences Hall, 5 auditoriums, Art Gallery

Libraries: 242,693 vols

Publications: Desarollo Académico, Magazine *(quarterly)*; Momento Pedagógico *(quarterly)*

Press or Publishing House: UPN Publishing House

Last Updated: 05/04/13

NAVY MEDICAL SCHOOL

Escuela Médico Naval de la Secretaría de Marina

Virgilio Uribe 1800, puerta 6, Alianza Popular Revolucionaria, Coyoacán, 01090 México, D.F.
Tel: +52(55) 56-84-48-92
EMail: digaden@semar.gob.mx
Website: http://www.semar.gob.mx/

Director: Ranulfo Martínez Mota

Programmes

Medicine (Medicine; Surgery)

Main Language(s) of Instruction: Spanish

Degrees and Diplomas: *Licenciatura*; *Especialización*

Last Updated: 22/02/13

NURSING SCHOOL OF THE NATIONAL MEDICAL CENTRE SIGLO XXI

Escuela de Enfermería Centro Médico Nacional Siglo XXI

Av. Periférico Sur No. 3400, Col. San Gerónimo Lídice, Magdalena Contreras, 10100 México, D.F.
Tel: +52(55) 56-81-08-36
Fax: +52(55) 56-81-08-36
EMail: alicia.garciaj@imss.gob.mx

Directora: Alicia García Juárez

Programmes

Nursing

History: Founded 1947.

Main Language(s) of Instruction: Spanish

Degrees and Diplomas: *Licenciatura*

Last Updated: 03/04/08

OFFICIAL HIGHER TEACHER TRAINING SCHOOL OF GUANAJUATO

Escuela Normal Superior Oficial de Guanajuato

Paseo de la Presa, 76, Km. 2.5 Carretera Guanajuato-Marfil, 36040 Guanajuato, Guanajuato
Tel: +52(473) 732-58-41

Directora: Elizabeth Torres Camacho
EMail: crstntrrs@ensog.edu.mx

Administrative Secretary: Margarita Escoto Alvarado
EMail: margarita@ensog.edu.mx

Programmes

Pedagogy *(Postgraduate)* (Pedagogy); **Secondary Education** (Secondary Education; Teacher Training)

History: Founded 1967.

Degrees and Diplomas: *Licenciatura*; *Maestría*

Last Updated: 04/04/08

OFFICIAL TEACHER TRAINING SCHOOL OF IRAPUATO

Escuela Normal Oficial de Irapuato

Calle Libra, 275, Col. Valle del Sol, 36590 Irapuato, Guanajuato
Tel: +52(462) 626-05-19
EMail: enoi@irapuato.vyd.com.mx
Website: http://home.enoi.edu.mx/

Director: Leonardo Julio Mendiola Martínez
EMail: ljmendiolam@enoi.edu.mx

Programmes

Education (Preschool Education; Primary Education; Special Education)

History: Founded 1951.

Main Language(s) of Instruction: Spanish

Degrees and Diplomas: *Licenciatura*; *Maestría*

Last Updated: 25/02/13

OPTICAL RESEARCH CENTRE

Centro de Investigaciones en Óptica (CIO)

Apdo. Postal N° 1 - 948, Loma del Bosque N° 115, Col. Lomas del Campestre, 3715 León, Guanajuato
Tel: +52(477) 441-42-00
Fax: +52(477) 441-42-09
EMail: dirac@cio.mx
Website: http://www.cio.mx/

Director General: Fernando Mendoza Santoyo

Programmes

Optical Engineering (Optical Technology); **Optical Metrology** (Optometry)

History: Founded 1980.

Main Language(s) of Instruction: Spanish

Degrees and Diplomas: *Maestría*; *Doctorado*

Libraries: Yes

Last Updated: 18/07/12

PABLO GARCÍA ÁVALOS TEACHER TRAINING SCHOOL IN PHYSICAL EDUCATION

Escuela Normal de Educación Física 'Pablo García Ávalos'

Velódromo de la Ciudad Deportiva s/n Col. Atasta, Villahermosa, Tabasco
Tel: +52(93) 13-02-98
Website: http://www.enef-tabasco.com.mx

Directora: Martina de TilaGoque Torruco

Programmes

Physical Education (Physical Education)

History: Founded 1984.

Main Language(s) of Instruction: Spanish

Degrees and Diplomas: *Licenciatura*

Last Updated: 22/02/13

PEDAGOGICAL UNIVERSITY OF DURANGO

Universidad Pedagógica de Durango
Avenida 16 de Septiembre, 132, Col. Silvestre Dorador, 34070 Durango, Durango
Tel: +52(618) 128-44-07
EMail: webmaster@www.upd.edu.mx
Website: http://www.upd.edu.mx

Director: Germán Lozano

Programmes

Education (Education; Pedagogy)

History: Founded 1997.

Main Language(s) of Instruction: Spanish

Degrees and Diplomas: *Licenciatura*; *Maestría*
Last Updated: 04/04/13

PEDAGOGICAL UNIVERSITY OF VERACRUZ

Universidad Pedagógica Veracruzana
Calle Museo 133, Col. Magisterial, 91010 Xalapa, Veracruz
Tel: +52(228) 840-18-48
Fax: +52(228) 814-00-36
EMail: rectoriaupv@hotmail.com
Website: http://www.secupv.org

Rector: Francisco Alfonso Avilés

Programmes

Education (Education; Higher Education Teacher Training); **Physical Education** (Physical Education)

History: Founded 1979.

Admission Requirements: Secondary school certificate (bachillerato)

Main Language(s) of Instruction: Spanish

Degrees and Diplomas: *Licenciatura*; *Maestría*

Student Services: Academic counselling

Publications: Universidad de Nuestro Siglo *(3 per annum)*
Last Updated: 05/04/13

PEOPLE'S UNIVERSITY OF LA CHONTALPA

Universidad Popular de la Chontalpa
Km. 2.0 de la Carretera Cárdenas - Huimanguillo, 86500 Cárdenas, Tabasco
Tel: +52(937) 372-7058
EMail: liliana.pelayo @ upch.edu.mx

Rector: Pedro Javier Muñoz Vergara

Programmes

Alternative Tourism (Tourism); **Chemistry, Pharmacy and Biology** (Biology; Chemistry; Pharmacy); **Engineering** (Agricultural Engineering; Chemical Engineering; Civil Engineering; Electrical Engineering; Engineering; Mechanical Engineering; Petroleum and Gas Engineering); **International Business and Finance** (Finance; International Business); **Marketing** (Marketing); **Political Science and Public Administration** (Political Sciences; Public Administration); **Psychology** (Psychology); **Zoology** (Zoology)

History: Founded 1995.

Main Language(s) of Instruction: Spanish

Degrees and Diplomas: *Licenciatura*; *Especialización*; *Maestría*

Libraries: Yes
Last Updated: 23/10/12

POLYTECHNIC UNIVERSITY OF AGUASCALIENTES

Universidad Politécnica de Aguascalientes
Calle Paseo San Gerardo No. 207. Fracc. San Gerardo., 20342 Aguascalientes, Aguascalientes
Tel: +52(449) 442-14-00
EMail: informes@upa.edu.mx
Website: http://www.upa.edu.mx

Rector: Eulogio Monreal Ávila (2012-)

Departments

Languages (Modern Languages); **Sports and Culture** (Dance; Music; Painting and Drawing; Sculpture; Sports; Theatre)

Programmes

Automation Engineering (Automotive Engineering); **Business Administration** (Administration; Business Administration; Business and Commerce; International Business; International Economics; Small Business); **Electronic Engineering** (Electronic Engineering); **Energy Engineering** (Energy Engineering); **Industrial Engineering** (Industrial Engineering); **Information Strategic Systems** (Computer Science); **Mechatronics** (Electronic Engineering)

History: Founded 2002.

Main Language(s) of Instruction: Spanish

Degrees and Diplomas: *Licenciatura*; *Maestría*
Last Updated: 05/04/13

POLYTECHNIC UNIVERSITY OF CHIAPAS

Universidad Politécnica de Chiapas
Calle Eduardo J.Selvas s/n entre Manuel de J.Cancino y Enriqueta Camarillo, Col. Magisterial, 29010 Tuxtla Gutiérrez, Chiapas
Tel: +52(961) 612-04-84
Fax: +52 (961) 612-04-99
EMail: rectoria@upchiapas.edu.mx
Website: http://www.upchiapas.edu.mx

Rector: Navor Francisco Ballinas Morales
EMail: rector@upchiapas.edu.mx

Programmes

Agroindustrial Engineering (Agricultural Engineering); **Biomedicine** (Biomedicine); **Energy Engineering** (Energy Engineering); **Environmental Engineering** (Environmental Engineering); **Mechatronics** (Electronic Engineering; Mechanical Engineering); **Software Engineering** (Software Engineering)

History: Founded 2005.

Main Language(s) of Instruction: Spanish

Degrees and Diplomas: *Licenciatura*; *Maestría*
Last Updated: 05/04/13

POLYTECHNIC UNIVERSITY OF PACHUCA

Universidad Politécnica de Pachuca
Carretera Pachuca-Cd. Sahagún, km 20, Ex-Hacienda de Santa Bárbara, 43830 Zempoala, Hidalgo
Tel: +52(771) 547-7510
EMail: upp@upp.edu.mx
Website: http://www.upp.edu.mx

Rector: Sergio Alejandro Arteaga Carreño

Secretario Académico: Sergio Alejandro Medina Moreno
EMail: samm67@upp.edu.mx

Programmes

Doctorado (Biotechnology); **Especialización** (Biotechnology; Computer Networks; Electrical Engineering; Environmental Engineering; Environmental Management; Environmental Studies); **Ingeniero** (Bioengineering; Biotechnology; Electrical Engineering; Engineering; Finance; Mechanical Engineering; Software Engineering; Telecommunications Engineering); **Licenciatura** (Physical Therapy); **Maestría** (Biotechnology; Information Technology; Mechanical Engineering)

History: Founded 2004.

Main Language(s) of Instruction: Spanish

Degrees and Diplomas: *Licenciatura*; *Especialización*; *Maestría*; *Doctorado*

Libraries: Yes
Last Updated: 22/10/12

POLYTECHNIC UNIVERSITY OF SAN LUIS POTOSÍ

Universidad Politécnica de San Luis Potosí
Urbano Villalón num 500, Col. La Ladrillera, 78000 San Luis Potosí, San Luis Potosí
Tel: +52(140) 812-65-19
EMail: politecnica@upslp.edu.mx
Website: http://www.upslp.edu.mx/

Rector: José Antonio Loyola Alarcón

Programmes
Business Administration (Administration; Business Administration; Marketing); **Engineering** (Industrial Engineering; Information Technology; Production Engineering; Telecommunications Engineering)

History: Founded 2001.

Main Language(s) of Instruction: Spanish

Degrees and Diplomas: *Licenciatura*
Last Updated: 05/04/13

POLYTECHNIC UNIVERSITY OF THE VALLEY OF MEXICO

Universidad Politécnica del Valle de México
Avenida Mexiquense s/n, Esquina Universidad Politécnica, Col. Villa Esmeralda, 54910 Tultitlán, Estado de México
Tel: +52(55) 50-62-64-60
EMail: informes@upvm.edu.mx
Website: http://www.upvm.edu.mx

Rector: F. Alberto Sánchez Flores (2012-)

Programmes
Administration (Administration; Business Administration; Communication Studies; Human Resources; Information Sciences; Information Technology; Small Business); **Computer Engineering** (Computer Engineering); **Industrial and Systems Engineering** (Industrial Engineering); **Mechanical and Electronic Engineering** (Electronic Engineering; Mechanical Engineering); **Nanotechnology** (Nanotechnology)

History: Founded 2004.

Main Language(s) of Instruction: Spanish

Degrees and Diplomas: *Licenciatura*; *Especialización*; *Maestría*
Last Updated: 05/04/13

POLYTECHNIC UNIVERSITY OF ZACATECAS

Universidad Politécnica de Zacatecas
Plan de Pardillo S/N, Parque Industrial Fresnillo, Fresnillo, 98600 Zacatecas, Zacatecas
Tel: +52(493) 935-71-06
EMail: upzac@upz.edu.mx
Website: http://www.upz.edu.mx/

Rector: Héctor Artemio Romo Moreno (2011-)

Programmes
Biotechnology (Biotechnology); **Business Administration** (Business Administration); **Engineering** (Computer Engineering; Electronic Engineering; Industrial Engineering; Mechanical Engineering); **International Business** (International Business)

History: Founded 2002.

Main Language(s) of Instruction: Spanish

Degrees and Diplomas: *Licenciatura*
Last Updated: 22/10/12

PROF. AMINA MADERA LAUTERIO REGIONAL TEACHER TRAINING CENTRE

Centro Regional de Educación Normal Profesora Amina Madera Lauterio
Manuel José Othón S/N, 78520 Cedral, San Luis Potosí
EMail: crenamina@msn.com

Director: Manuel García Ortiz

Programmes
Primary Education; **Teacher Training** (Teacher Training)

Main Language(s) of Instruction: Spanish

Degrees and Diplomas: *Licenciatura*
Last Updated: 13/03/08

PROF. AND LIC. FRANCISCO BENÍTEZ SILVA STATE TEACHER TRAINING INSTITUTE OF NAYARIT

Instituto Estatal de Educación Normal de Nayarit 'Profr. Y Lic. Francisco Benítez Silva'
Calle 12 De Octubre s/n, Colonia Menchaca, Abelardo Chaparro, Col. Menchaca, Tepic, Nayarit
Tel: +52(311) 13-31-73
EMail: ieenn@tepic.megared.net.mx

Directora General: Dora Evelia Bejar Fonseca

Programmes
Education (Education; Special Education)
Main Language(s) of Instruction: Spanish

Degrees and Diplomas: *Licenciatura*
Last Updated: 05/03/13

PROFESSOR ANTONIO BETANCOURT PÉREZ HIGHER TEACHER TRAINING SCHOOL OF YUCATAN

Escuela Normal Superior de Yucatán "Profesor Antonio Betancourt Pérez"
Calle 118, 318 s/n x 71-C, Fracc. Yucalpetén, 97248 Mérida, Yucatán
Tel: +52(999) 985-14-92
Fax: +52(999) 985-08-63
EMail: contacto@ensy.org
Website: http://www.ensy.org

Director: Fernando Pacheco Alcocer
EMail: fernandopacheco@hotmail.com

Programmes
Teacher Training (Art Education; English; Geography; Mathematics; Physical Education; Physics; Spanish; Teacher Training)
History: Founded 1971.

Main Language(s) of Instruction: Spanish

Degrees and Diplomas: *Licenciatura*; *Maestria*

Libraries: Biblioteca Pedagógica Humberto Lara y Lara
Last Updated: 26/02/13

PROF. GREGORIO TORRES QUINTERO EXPERIMENTAL TEACHER TRAINING SCHOOL

Escuela Normal Experimental 'Profr. Gregorio Torres Quintero'
Dom. Conocido, Ejido Raúl Sánchez Díaz, 22930 San Quintín, Baja California
Tel: +52(616) 165-2600 +52(616) 165-23-78
EMail: dirección_gtq@hotmail.com.mx

Director: Priciliano Viera Llamas

Programmes
Teacher Training (Primary Education; Teacher Training)

Main Language(s) of Instruction: Spanish

Degrees and Diplomas: *Licenciatura*
Last Updated: 25/02/13

PROF. JOSÉ SANTOS VALDÉS FEDERAL HIGHER TEACHER TRAINING SCHOOL OF AGUASCALIENTES

Escuela Normal Superior Federal de Aguascalientes Profr. José Santos Valdés
Blvd. Nazario Ortiz Garza s/n, Col. Santa Anita, 20170 Aguascalientes, Aguascalientes
Tel: +52(449) 975-2100
EMail: informacion@ensfa.edu.mx
Website: http://www.ensfa.edu.mx

Director: J. Jesús Lozano Torres

Programmes
Biology (Biology); **Chemistry** (Chemistry); **Civic Education and Ethics** (Civics; Ethics); **English** (English); **Geography** (Geography); **History** (History); **Mathematics** (Mathematics); **Physics** (Physics); **Spanish** (Spanish)
History: Founded 1977.
Main Language(s) of Instruction: Spanish
Degrees and Diplomas: *Licenciatura*; *Maestría*
Libraries: Yes
Last Updated: 26/02/13

PROF. MOISES SAENZ GARZA HIGHER TEACHER TRAINING SCHOOL

Escuela Normal Superior Profr. Moisés Sáenz Garza
Venustiano Carranza, 202, Esq. Ruperto Martínez, Centro, 64000 Monterrey, Nuevo León
Tel: +52(81) 83-43-83-69 +52(81) 83-44-68-20
Website: http://www.normalsuperior.com.mx/ens1/files/default/default.asp
Directora General: Leticia Rodríguez Arizpe (2006-)

Programmes
Teacher Training (Teacher Training)
History: Founded 1961.
Main Language(s) of Instruction: Spanish
Degrees and Diplomas: *Licenciatura*; *Maestría*; *Doctorado*
Last Updated: 26/02/13

PROF. RAFAEL RAMÍREZ CASTAÑEDA REGIONAL TEACHER TRAINING CENTRE

Centro Regional de Educación Normal Prof. Rafael Ramírez Castañeda
Carretera Internacional Km. 153 Sur Colonia Industrial, 85800 Navojoa, Sonora
Tel: +52(642) 2-28-20
EMail: crenrrc@prodigy.net.com
Director: Miguel Gonzálo Cota de la Crúz

Programmes
Teacher Training (Education; Teacher Training)
History: Founded 1972.
Main Language(s) of Instruction: Spanish
Degrees and Diplomas: *Licenciatura*
Last Updated: 10/03/08

PURHEPECHA HIGHER TECHNOLOGICAL INSTITUTE

Instituto Tecnológico Superior Purhepecha
Carr. Carapan-Uruapan Km 31.5, 60270 Cherán, Michoacán
Tel: +52(423) 594-20-97
Fax: +52(423) 594-20-97
EMail: its-purhepecha@its-purhepecha.edu.mx
Website: http://its-purhepecha.edu.mx
Director: Adán Avalos García

Programmes
Administration (Administration; Business Administration); **Engineering** (Agricultural Engineering; Biomedical Engineering; Computer Engineering; Industrial Engineering)
History: Founded 2000.
Main Language(s) of Instruction: Spanish
Degrees and Diplomas: *Licenciatura*
Last Updated: 21/03/13

QUETZALCOATL SCHOOL OF ART EDUCATION

Escuela Superior de Educación Artística Quetzalcoatl
Rafael Ramírez 64 Norte, 35168 Ciudad Lerdo, Durango
Tel: +52(17) 16-62-59
EMail: mrosgen58@hotmail.com
Directora: María del Rosario Eugenia Sepúlveda

Programmes
Art Education (Art Education)
Main Language(s) of Instruction: Spanish
Degrees and Diplomas: *Licenciatura*
Last Updated: 27/02/13

REGIONAL TEACHER TRAINING CENTRE OF AGUASCALIENTES

Centro Regional de Educación Normal de Aguascalientes
Avenida de los Maestros 3756, 20210 Aguascalientes, Aguascalientes
Tel: +52(449) 913-49-31
Fax: +52(449) 913-49-31
Director: Sabino TorresZamora

Programmes
Education (Preschool Education; Primary Education; Special Education; Teacher Training)
History: Founded 1973.
Main Language(s) of Instruction: Spanish
Degrees and Diplomas: *Licenciatura*
Last Updated: 23/07/12

REGIONAL TEACHER TRAINING CENTRE OF ARTEAGA

Centro Regional de Educación Normal de Arteaga
Calz. Gral. Enrique Ramírez S/N, 60920 Arteaga, Michoacán
Tel: +52(753) 541-07-02
Fax: +52(753) 541-07-03
Director: Herminio García Rueda

Programmes
Preschool Education (Preschool Education)
Degrees and Diplomas: *Licenciatura*: 8 sem.
Last Updated: 27/03/08

REGIONAL TEACHER TRAINING CENTRE OF CIUDAD GUZMÁN

Centro Regional de Educación Normal de Ciudad Guzmán
Calzada Madero y Carranza, s/n, Col. Ejidal, Mpio Zapotl'án el Grande, 49000 Ciudad Guzmán, Jalisco
Tel: +52(341) 413-28-29
Fax: +52(341) 413-47-55
EMail: crencgjal@latinmail.com
Director: Andrés Ruiz Mojica

Programmes
Teacher Training (Preschool Education; Primary Education; Special Education; Teacher Training)
History: Founded 1960.
Main Language(s) of Instruction: Spanish
Degrees and Diplomas: *Licenciatura*
Last Updated: 11/03/08

REGIONAL TEACHER TRAINING CENTRE OF OAXACA

Centro Regional de Educación Normal de Oaxaca
Calzada San Felipe del Agua, 208, 68020 Oaxaca, Oaxaca
Tel: +52(951) 513-40-14
Fax: +52(951) 515-94-66
EMail: crenoaxaca1@prodigy.net.mx

Director: Sergio Manuel Calleja Zorrilla

Programmes
Physical Education (Physical Education); **Primary Education** (Primary Education)
Main Language(s) of Instruction: Spanish
Degrees and Diplomas: *Licenciatura*
Last Updated: 11/03/08

REGIONAL TEACHER TRAINING CENTRE OF RÍO GRANDE

Centro Regional de Educación Normal de Río Grande
Km. 92 carretera Costera S/N, tramo Puerto Escondido Del Valle, 71830 Villa de Tututepec de Melchor Ocampo, Oaxaca
Tel: +52(954) 261-81
Fax: +52(954) 261-81
EMail: elhuanacastle@latinmail.com

Director: Crisoforo Carrillo Estrada

Programmes
Physical Education (Physical Education); **Primary Education**
Degrees and Diplomas: *Licenciatura*: 8 sem.
Last Updated: 27/03/08

REGIONAL TEACHER TRAINING SCHOOL IN SPECIALIZATION OF THE STATE OF COAHUILA

Escuela Normal Regional de Especialización del Estado de Coahuila
Blvd. Nazario Ortiz Garza s/n y Eugenio Aguirre Benavidez, 25280 Saltillo, Coahuila
Tel: +52(844) 414-96-27
EMail: contacto@enre.edu.mx
Website: http://www.enre.edu.mx

Director: Carlos Rodríguez Flores
EMail: carlos.rodriguez@enre.edu.mx

Programmes
Teacher Training (Special Education)
History: Founded 1976.
Main Language(s) of Instruction: Spanish
Degrees and Diplomas: *Licenciatura*; *Maestría*
Last Updated: 25/02/13

REHABILITATION AND SPECIAL EDUCATION CENTRE

Centro de Rehabilitación y Educación Especial
Velino M. Preza s/n, Col. Predio Canoas, 34079 Durango, Durango
Tel: +52(618) 11-57-37
Fax: +52(618) 11-57-37
EMail: creedgo@prodigy.net.mx

Director: Gerardo Quiñones Canales

Programmes
Rehabilitation and Therapy (Rehabilitation and Therapy)
Main Language(s) of Instruction: Spanish
Degrees and Diplomas: *Licenciatura*; *Especialización*
Last Updated: 20/03/08

REHABILITATION AND SPECIAL EDUCATION CENTRE

Centro de Rehabilitación y Educación Especial
Prolongación Carretera a la Calera s/n, Col. El Batán, 75240 Puebla, Puebla
Tel: +52(222) 44-24-03
Fax: +52(222) 16-00-28

Director: Marco Antonio Cubillo León

Schools
Education (Education; Special Education); **Physical and Occupational Therapy**
Degrees and Diplomas: *Licenciatura*; *Especialización*
Last Updated: 20/03/08

REHABILITATION CENTRE OF THE IZTAPALAPA FEDERAL DISTRICT

Centro de Rehabilitación del Dif. Iztapalapa
Guerra de Reforma s/n, Col. Leyes de Reforma 3a Sección, 09310 Iztapalapa, D.F.
Tel: +52(55) 56-94-98-86
Fax: +52(55) 56-94-99-46

Director: Jorge Hernández Wence (1987-)

Programmes
Physical and Occupational Therapy (Occupational Therapy; Physical Therapy)
History: Founded 1986.
Degrees and Diplomas: *Licenciatura*: 8 sem.
Last Updated: 26/03/08

RESEARCH AND ADVANCED STUDIES CENTRE OF THE IPN

Centro de Investigación y de Estudios Avanzados del IPN (CINVESTAV)
Apdo. Postal N° 14-740, Av. Instituto Politécnico Nacional 2508 Col. San Pedro Zacatenco, 07360 México, Distrito Federal
Tel: +52(555) 5747-3800
EMail: jruiz@cinvestav.mx
Website: http://www.cinvestav.mx

Director General: René Asomoza Palacio

Departments
Biological and Health Sciences (Biochemistry; Biomedicine; Biophysics; Cell Biology; Genetics; Molecular Biology; Neurosciences; Pathology; Pharmacology; Physiology; Toxicology); **Exact and Natural Sciences** (Applied Physics; Chemistry; Mathematics; Physics); **Humanities and Social Sciences** (Ecology; Educational Research; Educational Sciences; Mathematics); **Technology and Engineering** (Automation and Control Engineering; Biochemistry; Bioengineering; Biotechnology; Computer Engineering; Electrical Engineering; Electronic Engineering; Genetics; Materials Engineering; Mechanical Engineering; Metallurgical Engineering; Telecommunications Engineering)
Further Information: Also branches in Coahuila, Monterrey, Tamaupilas, Guanajuato, Jalisco, Merida, Zacatenco, Yucatan
History: Founded 1961.
Main Language(s) of Instruction: Spanish
Degrees and Diplomas: *Maestría*; *Doctorado*
Last Updated: 18/07/12

RESEARCH CENTRE IN ADVANCED MATERIALS

Centro de Investigación en Materiales Avanzados (CIMAV)
Miguel de Cervantes N° 120, Complejo Industrial I, 31110 Chihuahua, Chihuahua
Tel: +52(614) 439-11-61
Fax: +52(614) 439-11-58
EMail: info@cimav.edu.mx
Website: http://www.cimav.edu.mx

Director General: Jesús González Hernández
EMail: jesus.gonzalez@cimav.edu.mx

Programmes
Nanotechnology (Nanotechnology); **Renewable Energies** (Energy Engineering)
History: Founded 1994.
Main Language(s) of Instruction: Spanish
Degrees and Diplomas: *Maestría*; *Doctorado*
Last Updated: 12/07/12

RESEARCH CENTRE IN GEOGRAPHY AND GEOMATICS

Centro de Investigación en Geografía y Geomática
Contoy 137 Esq. Chemax, Col. Lomas de Padierna, Delegación Tlalpan, 14240 México, D.F.
Tel: +52(55) 26-15-22-24
EMail: cigget@centrogeo.org.mx
Website: http://www.centrogeo.org.mx

Directora General: Margarita Parás Fernández
EMail: direcciongeneral@CentroGeo.org.mx

Programmes
Geography (Geography)
History: Founded 1999.
Main Language(s) of Instruction: Spanish
Degrees and Diplomas: *Especialización*; *Maestría*; *Doctorado*
Last Updated: 12/07/12

SCHOOL OF EDUCATIONAL SCIENCES

Escuela de Ciencias de la Educación
Serafín Peña 130 Sur, 64010 Monterrey, Nuevo León
Tel: +52(8) 342-05-37
Fax: +52(8) 340-36-12
EMail: info@ece.edu.mx
Website: http://www.ece.edu.mx

Director: Domingo Castillo Moncada
EMail: casmon53@yahoo.com

Programmes
Education (Education); **Educational Administration** (Educational Administration); **Educational Psychology** (Educational Psychology)
History: Founded 1976.
Admission Requirements: Licenciatura
Fees: (US Dollars): 3,000 per semester
Main Language(s) of Instruction: Spanish
International Co-operation: With Hispanic Association of Colleges and Universities (HACU), USA and World Association for Educational Research (WAER), Canada
Degrees and Diplomas: *Maestría*: Educational Psychology, Educational Administration, 3 yrs; *Doctorado*
Student Services: Academic counselling, Canteen, Employment services, Foreign student adviser, Foreign Studies Centre, Handicapped facilities, Language programs, Social counselling, Sports facilities
Publications: Conciencias de la Educación *(monthly)*
Last Updated: 28/08/12

SCHOOL OF NAVAL AVIATION

Escuela de Aviación Naval
Campo Aéreo Las Bajadas, 91648 Veracruz, Veracruz
Tel: +52(29) 21-98-12

Director: Guillermo H. Ochoa

Programmes
Aeronautical and Aerospace Engineering (Aeronautical and Aerospace Engineering)
Main Language(s) of Instruction: Spanish
Degrees and Diplomas: *Licenciatura*
Last Updated: 20/02/13

SCHOOL OF NURSING OF THE ISSSTE

Escuela de Enfermería del Instituto de Seguridad y Servicios Sociales para los Trabajadores al Servicio del estado (ISSSTE)
Roberto Gayol 1421, Col. del Valle, Delegación Benito Juárez, 07760 México, D.F.
Tel: +52(55) 55-75-31-80
Fax: +52(55) 55-59-53-88
EMail: escenf@psi.net.mx
Website: http://www.issste.gob.mx/cnped/enfermeria/

Programmes
Nursing (Nursing); **Obstetrics** (Gynaecology and Obstetrics)
History: Founded 1965.
Degrees and Diplomas: *Licenciatura*
Last Updated: 27/05/09

SCHOOL OF PHYSICAL EDUCATION

Escuela Superior de Educación Física
Puerta No. 4, de Cd. Deportiva, Magdalena Mixhuca, Delegación Iztacalco, 08010 México, D.F.
Tel: +52(55) 55-19-50-60 +52(55) 55-19-50-61 Ext. 103
Fax: +52(55) 55-19-50-62

Director: Macario Molina Ramírez

Programmes
Physical Education (Physical Education)
History: Founded 1936.
Main Language(s) of Instruction: Spanish
Degrees and Diplomas: *Licenciatura*
Last Updated: 04/04/08

SCHOOL OF PHYSIOTHERAPY OF THE FEDERICO GOMEZ CHILDREN'S HOSPITAL OF MEXICO

Escuela Superior de Terapia Física del Hospital Infantil de México Federico Gómez
Dr. Márquez No. 162, Col. Doctores, Delegación Cuauhtémoc, 06720 México, D.F.
Tel: +52(55) 55-78-94-59
Fax: +52(55) 55-78-94-59
EMail: escuelatf@prodigy.net.mx

Directora: Laura Peñaloza Ochoa (1988-)
EMail: lapeo@prodigy.net.mx
Subdirectora: Ma. Antonia Monroy Maldonado

Programmes
Physiotherapy (Physical Therapy)
History: Founded 1943. Acquired present status 1988.
Admission Requirements: High school certificate with an average of 8. Maximum age, 25.
Fees: (Pesos): enrolment, 1,750 per annum and 1,500 every two months.
Accrediting Agencies: Secretaría de Educación Pública
Degrees and Diplomas: *Licenciatura*: 4 yrs
Student Services: Health services, Nursery care
Student Residential Facilities: None
Special Facilities: None
Libraries: Yes
Publications: Boletín del Hospital Infantil de México, Medical magazine *(quarterly)*

SCHOOL OF SOCIAL WORK OF THE STATE OF CHIHUAHUA

Escuela de Trabajo Social del Estado de Chihuahua
Calle Justiniani y 45, 31370 Chihuahua, Chihuahua
Tel: +52(614) 16-20-25
EMail: jbaca@etschihuahua.edu.mx
Website: http://etschihuahua.edu.mx/

Director: Jesús Javier Baca Gándara

Programmes
Gerontology (Gerontology); **Social Work** (Social Work)
Main Language(s) of Instruction: Spanish
Degrees and Diplomas: *Licenciatura*
Last Updated: 21/02/13

SCHOOL OF SOCIAL WORK OF ZACATECAS

Escuela de Trabajo Social de Zacatecas
Francisco E. García No. 129, Francisco de García, 98070 Zacatecas, Zacatecas
Tel: +52(49) 22-57-18
EMail: trabsocialzac@yahoo.com.mx

Directora: María del Socorro Becerra Nájera

Programmes
Social Work (Social Work)
History: Founded 1994.
Main Language(s) of Instruction: Spanish
Degrees and Diplomas: *Licenciatura*
Last Updated: 21/02/13

SCIENTIFIC RESEARCH CENTRE OF YUCATAN

Centro de Investigación Científica de Yucatán (CICY)
Calle 43 N° 130, Col. Chuburná de Hidalgo, 97200 Mérida, Yucatán
Tel: +52(999) 942-83-30
Fax: +52(999) 981-39-00
EMail: dirgen@cicy.mx
Website: http://www.cicy.mx/

Director General: Inocencio Higuera Ciapara

Programmes
Biotechnology (Biotechnology); **Materials** (Materials Engineering); **Natural Resources** (Ecology; Natural Resources); **Plant Biochemistry and Molecular Biology** (Biochemistry; Molecular Biology; Plant and Crop Protection); **Renewable Energy** (Energy Engineering); **Water Science** (Water Science)
History: Founded 1997.
Main Language(s) of Instruction: Spanish
Degrees and Diplomas: *Maestría*; *Doctorado*
Last Updated: 18/07/12

STATE DANCE SCHOOL

Escuela Estatal de Danza
Av. Constitución No. 400, 3er. piso, Centro, 78000 San Luis Potosí, San Luis Potosí
Tel: +52(48) 12-81-91

Directora: Graciela Alvarado Rosales

Programmes
Contemporary Dance (Dance)
History: Founded 1986.
Main Language(s) of Instruction: Spanish
Degrees and Diplomas: *Licenciatura*: 8 sem.
Last Updated: 22/02/13

STATE INSTITUTE FOR THE DEVELOPMENT OF WORK SAFETY

Instituto Estatal para el Desarrollo de la Seguridad en el Trabajo
Km. 4.5 Paseo Adolfo López Mateos, 51350 Zinacantepec, Estado de México
Tel: +52(7) 213-22-57

Director General: Sergio González Isunza

Programmes
Workplace Hygiene and Security (Hygiene; Safety Engineering)
Main Language(s) of Instruction: Spanish
Degrees and Diplomas: *Maestría*
Last Updated: 20/02/08

STATE INSTITUTE OF PENAL SCIENCES AND PUBLIC SECURITY

Instituto Estatal de Ciencias Penales y Seguridad Pública
Km. 12.5 Carretera a Navolato, 80000 Culiacán, Sinaloa
Tel: +52(667) 760-00-06
Website: http://institutodecienciaspenalessinaloa.gob.mx/

Director: Humberto López Favela

Programmes
Criminology (Criminology)
History: Founded 1969 as Escuela de Transito. Acquired present title 1993.
Main Language(s) of Instruction: Spanish
Degrees and Diplomas: *Licenciatura*
Libraries: Yes
Last Updated: 05/03/13

STATE MUSIC SCHOOL

Escuela Estatal de Música
Avenida Constitución 400, Centro, 78000 San Luis Potosí, San Luis Potosí
Tel: +52(48) 12-37-34

Director: José Guillermo González Fuentes

Programmes
Music (Music)
Degrees and Diplomas: *Licenciatura*
Last Updated: 03/04/08

STATE SCHOOL OF PLASTIC ARTS

Escuela Estatal de Artes Plásticas
Ignacio Comonfort 310, 78000 San Luis Potosí, San Luis Potosí
Tel: +52(444) 814-1095

Director: José I. Faz Ipiea

Programmes
Painting and Drawing (Painting and Drawing); **Sculpture** (Sculpture)
Main Language(s) of Instruction: Spanish
Degrees and Diplomas: *Licenciatura*: 8 sem.
Last Updated: 22/02/13

STATE THEATRE SCHOOL

Escuela Estatal de Teatro
Avenida Constitución 400, Centro, 78000 San Luis Potosí, San Luis Potosí
Tel: +52(48) 12-37-34

Directora: Yolanda Lagazpy Salinas

Programmes
Theatre (Theatre)
Main Language(s) of Instruction: Spanish
Degrees and Diplomas: *Licenciatura*
Last Updated: 03/04/08

STATE UNIVERSITY OF PEDAGOGICAL STUDIES

Universidad Estatal de Estudios Pedagógicos
Fresnillo y Cañitas No. 310, 21090 Mexicali, Baja California
Tel: +52(65) 554-959
EMail: ueep.@telnort.net
Website: http://ueep.com.mx

Rector: Alfonso Sepúlveda Ornelas

Programmes
Education and Pedagogy (Education; Pedagogy; Physical Education)
History: Founded 1982 as Centro de Capacitación y de Estudios Pedagógicos de Baja California. Acquired present status and title 1995.

Main Language(s) of Instruction: Spanish
Degrees and Diplomas: *Licenciatura*; *Maestría*
Last Updated: 03/04/13

STATE UNIVERSITY OF THE VALLEY OF ECATEPEC

Universidad Estatal del Valle de Ecatepec
Avenida Central s/n, Esq. Leona Vicario, Col. Valle de Anáhuac, 66120 Ecatepec de Morelos, Estado de México
Tel: +52(55) 55-69-37-02
EMail: uneve@uneve.edu.mx
Website: http://www.uneve.edu.mx

Rector: José Ángel Fernández García
EMail: rectoria_uneve@hotmail.com

Programmes
Acupuncture (Acupuncture); **Chiropractic** (Chiropractic); **Gerontology** (Gerontology); **Humanities-Business** (Accountancy; Administration; Anthropology; Classical Languages; Economics; Geography; History; Law; Marketing; Psychology); **Multimedia Communication** (Multimedia)
History: Founded 2000.
Main Language(s) of Instruction: Spanish
Degrees and Diplomas: *Licenciatura*
Libraries: Yes
Last Updated: 02/10/12

TAMAULIPAS INSTITUTE OF EDUCATIONAL RESEARCH AND PEDAGOGICAL DEVELOPMENT

Instituto Tamaulipeco de Investigación Educativa y de Desarrollo de la Docencia
Apartado postal 79, Blvd. Tamaulipas, 1355, Plaza Dorada, Victoria, 87050 Ciudad Victoria, Tamaulipas
Tel: +52(834) 314-11-22 +52(834) 314-12-37
Fax: +52(834) 314-11-33

Director: Alfredo Cuéllar Cuéllar

Programmes
Educational Research (Educational Research); **Pedagogy** (Pedagogy)
Main Language(s) of Instruction: Spanish
Degrees and Diplomas: *Licenciatura*
Last Updated: 04/04/08

TEACHER TRAINING INSTITUTE OF THE STATE OF MEXICO

Instituto de Capacitación Magisterial del Estado de México
Blvd. Isidro Fabela 601, Col. Doctores, 50060 Toluca, Estado de México
Tel: +52(72) 522-71

Director: José Luis Pérez Tovar

Programmes
Teacher Training (Teacher Training)
Degrees and Diplomas: *Licenciatura*
Last Updated: 04/04/08

TEACHER TRAINING SCHOOL FOR THE LICENCIATURA IN SPECIAL EDUCATION OF CALKINI

Escuela Normal de Licenciatura en Educación Especial de Calkini
Calle 22 s/n, Centro, 24900 Calkini, Campeche
Tel: +52(996) 961-03-52
Fax: +52(996) 961-03-52
EMail: enlee@prodigy.net.mx

Director: Carlos Alberto Rodríguez Sánchez (1991-)

Programmes
Special Education (Special Education)
History: Founded 1991.
Main Language(s) of Instruction: Spanish
Degrees and Diplomas: *Licenciatura*
Last Updated: 25/02/13

TEACHER TRAINING SCHOOL FOR THE LICENCIATURA IN PHYSICAL EDUCATION OF CALKINI

Escuela Normal de Licenciatura en Educación Física de Calkini
Calle 5, 108 o Calle 16 s/n, Col. Concepción, 24900 Calkini, Campeche
Tel: +52(996) 961-00-43
EMail: ENLEF_CALKI@hotmail.com

Director: Cecilio Chan Balán (1991-)

Programmes
Physical Education (Physical Education)
History: Founded 1991.
Main Language(s) of Instruction: Spanish
Degrees and Diplomas: *Licenciatura*
Last Updated: 31/03/08

TEACHER TRAINING SCHOOL FOR THE LICENCIATURA IN PRIMARY EDUCATION OF CALKINI

Escuela Normal de Licenciatura en Educación Primaria de Calkini
Calle 22 S/N, entre calles 15 y 13, Centro, 24900 Calkini, Campeche
Tel: +52(996) 961-02-28
Fax: +52(996) 961-02-28

Director: Miguel A. Flores Suárez

Programmes
Primary Education (Primary Education)
History: Founded 1967.
Main Language(s) of Instruction: Spanish
Degrees and Diplomas: *Licenciatura*
Last Updated: 25/02/13

TEACHER TRAINING SCHOOL IN HIGHER LAW STUDIES OF SAN LUIS POTOSI

Escuela Normal de Estudios Superiores del Magisterio Potosino
Av. San Carlos No. 345, Fracc. San Ángel, 2a Secc., 78129 San Luis Potosí, San Luis Potosí
Tel: +52(444) 823-08-88 +52(444) 823-08-89
Fax: +52(444) 823-08-89
EMail: direccióngeneral@enesmaposlp.edu.mx
Website: http://www.enesmaposlp.edu.mx

Director General: Emilio Pozos Correa

Programmes
Primary Education (Primary Education)
Further Information: Also branch in Ciudad Valles
Main Language(s) of Instruction: Spanish
Degrees and Diplomas: *Licenciatura*: 8 sem.
Libraries: Yes
Last Updated: 25/02/13

TEACHER TRAINING SCHOOL IN PHYSICAL EDUCATION OF AGUASCALIENTES

Escuela Normal de Educación Física de Aguascalientes
Rincón de Romos, Aguascalientes

Directora: Consuelo Méndez

Programmes
Physical Education (Physical Education)
History: Founded 1980.
Main Language(s) of Instruction: Spanish
Degrees and Diplomas: *Licenciatura*
Last Updated: 22/02/13

TEACHER TRAINING SCHOOL IN PRE-SCHOOL EDUCATION OF THE STATE OF COAHUILA

Escuela Normal de Educación Preescolar del Estado de Coahuila
Blvd. Nazario S. Ortiz Garza (entre David Berlanga y Eugenio Benavides), Centro de Escuelas Normales, Edificio B, 25000 Saltillo, Coahuila
Tel: +52(844) 135-07-52 +52(844) 135-07-53
Fax: +52(844) 135-07-54
EMail: enepsaltillo@galileo.educa.ws
Website: http://www.enep.sepc.edu.mx

Directora: Imelda Chavarria Valdes

Programmes
Preschool Education (Education; Preschool Education)
History: Founded 1973.
Academic Year: August to July
Admission Requirements: High school diploma and admission exams
Fees: (Pesos): 2,500 per annum
Main Language(s) of Instruction: Spanish
International Co-operation: None
Accrediting Agencies: Secretaría de Educación Pública
Degrees and Diplomas: *Licenciatura*: Preschool Education
Student Services: Academic counselling, Canteen, Employment services, Foreign student adviser, Handicapped facilities, Health services, Language programs, Nursery care, Social counselling
Student Residential Facilities: None
Libraries: Yes.
Last Updated: 22/02/13

TEACHER TRAINING SCHOOL OF AGUASCALIENTES

Escuela Normal de Aguascalientes
Av. Paseo de la Cruz N°904, Fracc. IV Centenario, 20260 Aguascalientes, Aguascalientes
Tel: +52(449) 915-15-74
Fax: +52(449) 918-29-20
EMail: ena@normal-de-aguascalientes.edu.mx

Directora: Georgina Sandoval Romo

Programmes
Initial Education (Education; Teacher Training); **Preschool Education** (Preschool Education); **Primary Education**
Degrees and Diplomas: *Licenciatura*
Last Updated: 22/02/13

TEACHER TRAINING SCHOOL OF SINALOA

Escuela Normal de Sinaloa
Blvd.Manuél J. Cloutier s/n, Col. Libertad, 80170 Culiacán, Sinaloa
Tel: +52(667) 714-01-94
Fax: +52(667) 714-08-08
EMail: aguillen@ens.edu.mx
Website: http://ens.edu.mx

Director: Abelino Guillén López
Coordinador Administrativo: Atanacio Cruz Higuera Contreras
EMail: ahiguera@ens.edu.mx

Programmes
Education (Education; Preschool Education; Primary Education; Secondary Education); **Human Development and Pedagogy** *(Postgraduate)* (Development Studies; Pedagogy; Preschool Education; Primary Education; Secondary Education)
History: Founded 1947.
Main Language(s) of Instruction: Spanish
Degrees and Diplomas: *Licenciatura*; *Maestría*; *Doctorado*
Last Updated: 25/02/13

TEACHER TRAINING SCHOOL OF TEOTIHUACÁN

Escuela Normal de Teotihuacán
Avenida Hank González y Eva Samano s/n, Col. Nueva Teotihuacán, Localidad Evangelista, 55816 Teotihuacán, Estado de México
Tel: +52(594) 956-29-33
Fax: +52(594) 956-29-33
EMail: norteot@hotmail.com

Director General: Mauricio Rivero Contreras

Programmes
Education (Primary Education; Secondary Education)
History: Founded 1974 as Escuela Normal No. 18.
Main Language(s) of Instruction: Spanish
Degrees and Diplomas: *Licenciatura*
Last Updated: 25/02/13

TEACHER TRAINING SCHOOL OF TEXCOCO

Escuela Normal de Texcoco
Km. 1.5 carretera Texcoco - Tepexpan, Tulantongo, 56200 Texcoco de Mora, Estado de México
Tel: +52(595) 954-20-73
Fax: +52(595) 954-20-73
Website: http://www.normaldetexcoco.edu.mx
Directora General: Romana Irma Morales González (1994-)

Programmes
Secondary Education (Geography; History; Secondary Education)
Degrees and Diplomas: *Licenciatura*: 8 sem.
Last Updated: 25/02/13

TEACHER TRAINING SPECIALIZATION SCHOOL OF THE FEDERAL DISTRICT

Escuela Normal de Especialización del Distrito Federal
Campos Elíseos, 467, Col. Polanco, Delegación Miguel Hidalgo, 11560 México, D.F.
Tel: +52(55) 52-80-27-35
Fax: +52(55) 52-80-84-68
EMail: ene@sep.gob.mx

Directora: Leonora Patricia Arias Lozano

Programmes
Education (Education; Teacher Training)
History: Founded 1943.
Main Language(s) of Instruction: Spanish
Degrees and Diplomas: *Licenciatura*; *Especialización*; *Maestría*
Last Updated: 22/02/13

TEACHER TRAINING SPECIALIZATION SCHOOL OF THE STATE OF SINALOA

Escuela Normal de Especialización del Estado de Sinaloa (ENEES)
Osa Menor s/n, Col.Cuauhtémoc, 80020 Culiacán, Culiacán
Tel: +52(667) 750-29-50
EMail: direccion@enees.edu.mx
Website: http://www.enees.edu.mx

Directora: Aurora Félix Delgado

Programmes
Special Education (Special Education)
History: Founded 1985.
Degrees and Diplomas: *Licenciatura*; *Maestría*; *Doctorado*
Last Updated: 14/04/09

TECHNOLOGICAL AND UNIVERSITY STUDIES CENTRE OF THE GULF

Centro de Estudios Tecnológicos y Universitarios del Golfo, A.C

Vícitmas del 25 de Junio 362, 91700 Veracruz, Veracruz
Tel: +52(229) 932-89-95
Fax: +52(229) 931-99-38
EMail: cetugmaestrias@hotmail.com

Rectora: Sirenia Domínguez Gámez

Programmes
Business Administration

History: Founded 1994.

Degrees and Diplomas: *Licenciatura*
Last Updated: 20/11/09

TECHNOLOGICAL INSTITUTE OF ACAPULCO

Instituto Tecnológico de Acapulco (ITACAP)

Avenida Instituto Tecnológico s/n, Crucero del Cayaco, 39905 Acapulco de Juárez, Guerrero
Tel: +52(744) 442-90-11
Fax: +52(744) 468-35-05
EMail: direccion@it-acapulco.edu.mx
Website: http://www.it-acapulco.edu.mx

Director: Antonio Enrique Leal Cruz

Programmes
Administration (Accountancy; Administration; Business Administration; Business and Commerce); **Architecture** (Architecture); **Biochemistry** (Biochemistry); **Electromechanical Engineering** (Electronic Engineering; Mechanical Engineering); **Regional Planning and Development** (Regional Planning); **Systems Engineering** (Computer Engineering)

History: Founded 1975.

Main Language(s) of Instruction: Spanish

Degrees and Diplomas: *Licenciatura*; *Maestría*
Last Updated: 12/03/13

TECHNOLOGICAL INSTITUTE OF ADVANCED STUDIES OF COACALCO

Tecnológico de Estudios Superiores de Coacalco

Avenida 16 de Septiembre, 54, Col. Cabecera Municipal, 55700 Coacalco de Berriozábal, Estado de México
Tel: +52(55) 2159-4324
EMail: dirgen@tesco.edu.mx
Website: http://www.tesco.edu.mx/

Director: Francisco José Plata Olvera

Programmes
Administration (Administration; Business Administration); **Computer Science** (Computer Science); **Engineering** (Automation and Control Engineering; Chemical Engineering; Electronic Engineering; Environmental Engineering; Industrial Engineering; Information Technology; Materials Engineering; Mechanical Engineering)

History: Founded 1996.

Main Language(s) of Instruction: Spanish

Degrees and Diplomas: *Licenciatura*; *Especialización*: Automation; *Maestría*
Last Updated: 22/03/13

TECHNOLOGICAL INSTITUTE OF ADVANCED STUDIES OF CHALCO

Tecnológico de Estudios Superiores de Chalco

Carretera Federal México-Cuautla s/n, La Candelaria, Tlapala, Chalco, Estado de México
Tel: +52(55) 59-82-10-89
EMail: demetrio.moreno@tesch.edu.mx
Website: http://tesch.edu.mx

Director: Demetrio Moreno Arcega

Programmes
Engineering (Computer Engineering; Electronic Engineering; Industrial Engineering; Mechanical Engineering)

History: Founded 1988.

Main Language(s) of Instruction: Spanish

Degrees and Diplomas: *Licenciatura*
Last Updated: 22/03/13

TECHNOLOGICAL INSTITUTE OF ADVANCED STUDIES OF CHIMALHUACÁN

Tecnológico de Estudios Superiores de Chimalhuacán

Primavera S/N, Santa María Nativitas, 56335 Chimalhuacán, Estado de México
Tel: +52(55) 50-44-41-31
EMail: direccion@teschi.edu.mx
Website: http://www.teschi.edu.mx

Director: Jorge Eleazar García Martínez

Programmes
Administration (Administration); **Engineering** (Chemical Engineering; Electronic Engineering; Industrial Engineering; Mechanical Engineering); **Gastronomy** (Cooking and Catering)

History: Founded 2000.

Main Language(s) of Instruction: Spanish

Degrees and Diplomas: *Licenciatura*; *Especialización*; *Maestría*
Last Updated: 22/03/13

TECHNOLOGICAL INSTITUTE OF ADVANCED STUDIES OF CUAUTITLÁN IZCALLI

Tecnológico de Estudios Superiores de Cuautitlán Izcalli

Avenida Nopaltepec s/n, Fracc. La Coyotera, Ejido de San Antonio, Cuamatla, 54748 Cuautitlán Izcalli, Estado de México
Tel: +52(55) 58-73-73-37
EMail: direccion@tesci.edu.mx
Website: http://tesci.edu.mx

Director: Salvador Herrera Toledano

Programmes
Accountancy (Accountancy); **Business Administration** (Business Administration); **Computer Science** (Computer Science); **Engineering** (Electronic Engineering; Transport Engineering)

History: Founded 1997.

Main Language(s) of Instruction: Spanish

Degrees and Diplomas: *Licenciatura*
Last Updated: 22/03/13

TECHNOLOGICAL INSTITUTE OF ADVANCED STUDIES OF ECATEPEC

Tecnológico de Estudios Superiores de Ecatepec (TESE) (TESE)

Avenida Tecnológico s/n, Col. Valle de Anáhuac, 55210 Ecatepec de Morelos, Estado de México
Tel: +52(55) 50-00-23-00
EMail: dirgral@tese.edu.mx
Website: http://www.tese.edu.mx

Director: Sergio Mancilla Guzman EMail: smancilla@tese.edu.mx

Programmes
Accountancy (Accountancy); **Computer Science** (Computer Science); **Engineering** (Biochemistry; Chemical Engineering; Electronic Engineering; Industrial Engineering; Mechanical Engineering)

History: Founded 1990.

Main Language(s) of Instruction: Spanish

Degrees and Diplomas: *Licenciatura*; *Maestría*
Last Updated: 25/03/13

TECHNOLOGICAL INSTITUTE OF ADVANCED STUDIES OF HUIXQUILUCÁN

Tecnológico de Estudios Superiores de Huixquilucán
Paraje el Río, Col. La Magdalena Chichicaspa, 52763 Huixquilucán, Estado de México
Tel: +52(55) 8288-1130
Website: http://www.tesh.edu.mx

Director: Miguel Ángel Pérez Carrillo

Programmes
Administration (Administration); **Biology** (Biology); **Engineering** (Civil Engineering; Computer Engineering; Industrial Engineering)
History: Founded 1997.
Main Language(s) of Instruction: Spanish
Degrees and Diplomas: *Licenciatura*
Last Updated: 25/03/13

TECHNOLOGICAL INSTITUTE OF ADVANCED STUDIES OF IXTAPALUCA

Tecnológico de Estudios Superiores de Ixtapaluca
Km. 7 de la carretera Ixtapaluca-Coatepec s/n San Juan, Distrito de Coatepec, 56580 Ixtapaluca, Estado de México
Tel: +52(55) 13-14-81-52
Website: http://qacontent.edomex.gob.mx/tesi/index.htm

Director: Jesús Martínez Perales

Programmes
Administration (Administration); **Architecture** (Architecture); **Engineering** (Computer Engineering; Electronic Engineering; Engineering; Environmental Engineering; Mechanical Engineering)
History: Founded 1999.
Main Language(s) of Instruction: Spanish
Degrees and Diplomas: *Licenciatura*
Last Updated: 25/03/13

TECHNOLOGICAL INSTITUTE OF ADVANCED STUDIES OF JILOTEPEC

Tecnológico de Estudios Superiores de Jilotepec
Km. 6.5 Carretera Jilotepec-Chapa de Mota, 54240 Jilotepec, Estado de México
Tel: +52(761) 734-22-83
EMail: tesjilotepec@edomex.gob.mx
Website: http://www1.edomexico.gob.mx/tesjilotepec

Director: Raymundo Bravo Godoy

Programmes
Business Administration (Business Administration); **Computer Science** (Computer Science); **Engineering** (Chemical Engineering; Civil Engineering; Computer Engineering; Electronic Engineering; Industrial Engineering; Mechanical Engineering)
History: Founded 1997.
Main Language(s) of Instruction: Spanish
Degrees and Diplomas: *Licenciatura*
Last Updated: 25/03/13

TECHNOLOGICAL INSTITUTE OF ADVANCED STUDIES OF JOCOTITLAN

Tecnológico de Estudios Superiores de Jocotitlán
Km. 44.8 Carretera Atlacomulco-Toluca, Ejido San Juan y San Agustín, Jocotitlán, 50700 Atlacomulco, Estado de México
Tel: +52(712) 123-13-13
EMail: tesjocotitlan@yahoo.com.mx
Website: http://qacontent.edomex.gob.mx/tesjo/index.htm

Director: José Luis Guillermo González Rodríguez

Programmes
Accountancy; **Architecture** (Architecture); **Business Administration** (Business Administration); **Engineering** (Chemical Engineering; Computer Engineering; Electronic Engineering; Materials Engineering; Mechanical Engineering)
History: Founded 1998.
Main Language(s) of Instruction: Spanish
Degrees and Diplomas: *Licenciatura*
Last Updated: 25/03/13

TECHNOLOGICAL INSTITUTE OF ADVANCED STUDIES OF LOS CABOS

Instituto Tecnológico de Estudios Superiores de los Cabos
Boulevard Tecnológico de Los Cabos y Gandhi, Col. Guaymitas, 23483 San José del Cabo, Baja California Sur
Tel: +52(624) 142-64-69
EMail: ites@prodigy.net.mx
Website: http://www.itesloscabos.edu.mx

Director: Adalberto Pérez Pérez

Programmes
Administration (Administration; Business Administration); **Computer Science**; **Engineering**
History: Founded 1999.
Main Language(s) of Instruction: Spanish
Degrees and Diplomas: *Licenciatura*
Last Updated: 07/03/08

TECHNOLOGICAL INSTITUTE OF ADVANCED STUDIES OF SAN FELIPE DEL PROGRESO

Tecnológico de Estudios Superiores de San Felipe del Progreso
Av. Instituto Tecnológico S/N Ejido de San Felipe del Progreso, 50640 San Felipe del Progreso, Estado de México
Tel: +52(712) 104-19-81
EMail: tessfp_dir@hotmail.com
Website: http://portal2.edomex.gob.mx/tessfp/index.htm

Directora: Amalia Cristina Gaytan Vargas

Programmes
Accountancy (Accountancy); **Engineering** (Chemical Engineering; Civil Engineering; Computer Engineering)
History: Founded 2001.
Main Language(s) of Instruction: Spanish
Degrees and Diplomas: *Licenciatura*
Last Updated: 25/03/13

TECHNOLOGICAL INSTITUTE OF ADVANCED STUDIES OF THE CARBONIFERA REGION

Instituto Tecnológico de Estudios Superiores de la Región Carbonífera
Km. 120 Carretera 57, Villa de Agujita, 26950 Sabinas, Coahuila
Tel: +52 (861) 613-36-07
EMail: itesrc@correo.itesrc.edu.mx
Website: http://www.itesrc.edu.mx

Director: Sergio Villarreal Cárdenas

Programmes
Administration (Administration); **Engineering** (Computer Engineering; Electronic Engineering; Mechanical Engineering)
History: Founded 1991.
Main Language(s) of Instruction: Spanish
Degrees and Diplomas: *Licenciatura*; *Maestría*
Last Updated: 12/03/13

TECHNOLOGICAL INSTITUTE OF ADVANCED STUDIES OF THE EAST OF THE STATE OF MEXICO

Tecnológico de Estudios Superiores del Oriente del Estado de México
Paraje San Isidro s/n, Barrio de Tecamachalco, 56400 La Paz, Estado de México
Tel: +52(55) 59-86-34-97
EMail: dir_tesoem@prodigy.net.mx
Website: http://qacontent.edomex.gob.mx/tesoem/index.htm

Directora: Ivette Topete García

Programmes
Accountancy (Accountancy); **Engineering** (Computer Engineering; Environmental Engineering; Industrial Engineering; Information Technology); **Gastronomy** (Cooking and Catering)

History: Founded 1997.

Main Language(s) of Instruction: Spanish

Degrees and Diplomas: *Licenciatura*; *Maestría*: Quality Systems
Last Updated: 25/03/13

TECHNOLOGICAL INSTITUTE OF ADVANCED STUDIES OF TIANGUISTENCO

Tecnológico de Estudios Superiores de Tianguistenco
Km. 22 Carretera Tenango-La Marquesa, Santiago Tilapa,
50139 Santiago Tianguistenco, Estado de México
Tel: +52(713) 131-09-34
EMail: tecnologico59@prodigy.net.mx
Website: http://www.edomexico.gob.mx/test/htm/html

Directora: Gabriela Nieto Cid del Prado

Programmes
Accountancy (Accountancy); **Engineering** (Computer Engineering; Environmental Engineering; Industrial Engineering; Mechanical Engineering)

History: Founded 1997.

Main Language(s) of Instruction: Spanish

Degrees and Diplomas: *Licenciatura*
Last Updated: 25/03/13

TECHNOLOGICAL INSTITUTE OF ADVANCED STUDIES OF VALLE DE BRAVO

Tecnológico de Estudios Superiores de Valle de Bravo
Km.30 de la Carretera Federal Monumento Valle de Bravo Ejido de San Antonio de la Laguna Valle de Bravo, 51200 Valle de Bravo, Estado de México
Tel: +52(726) 266-50-77
EMail: direcciontesvalle@gmail.com
Website: http://qacontent.edomex.gob.mx/tesvb/index.htm

Director: Roberto Laureles Solano

Programmes
Administration (Administration); **Architecture** (Architecture); **Engineering** (Computer Engineering; Electrical Engineering; Engineering; Forest Management; Industrial Engineering); **Gastronomy** (Cooking and Catering)

History: Founded 1999.

Main Language(s) of Instruction: Spanish

Degrees and Diplomas: *Licenciatura*
Last Updated: 25/03/13

TECHNOLOGICAL INSTITUTE OF ADVANCED STUDIES OF VILLA GUERRERO

Tecnológico de Estudios Superiores de Villa Guerrero
Carretera Federal Toluca - Ixtapan de la Sal, Km 64.5 La Finca, 51760 Villa Guerrero, Estado de México
Tel: +52(714) 146-14-87
EMail: tecvillaguerrero@yahoo.com.mx
Website: http://qacontent.edomex.gob.mx/tesvg/index.htm

Director: Rafael Adolfo Nuñez González

Programmes
Administration (Administration); **Architecture** (Architecture); **Engineering** (Agricultural Engineering; Computer Engineering; Electronic Engineering; Food Technology)

History: Founded 1999.

Main Language(s) of Instruction: Spanish

Degrees and Diplomas: *Licenciatura*
Last Updated: 25/03/13

TECHNOLOGICAL INSTITUTE OF ADVANCED STUDIES OF ZAMORA

Instituto Tecnológico de Estudios Superiores de Zamora
Km. 7 Carretera Zamora-La Piedad, El Sauz de Abajo,
59720 Zamora, Michoacán
Tel: +52(351) 520-02-19
EMail: dir_itzamora@dgest.gob.mx
Website: http://www.teczamora.edu.mx

Director: Carlos Alberto Cárdenas Vázquez (2000-)

Programmes
Accountancy (Accountancy); **Business Administration** (Business Administration); **Engineering** (Computer Engineering; Electronic Engineering; Industrial Engineering); **Food Technology** (Food Technology)

History: Founded 1994.

Main Language(s) of Instruction: Spanish

Degrees and Diplomas: *Licenciatura*
Last Updated: 13/03/13

TECHNOLOGICAL INSTITUTE OF AGUA PRIETA

Instituto Tecnológico de Agua Prieta
Carretera a Janos Chihuahua y Avenida Tecnológico s/n,
84268 Agua Prieta, Sonora
Tel: +52(633) 331-02-32
Fax: +52(633) 331-08-40
EMail: itap@mail.itap.edu.mx
Website: http://www.itap.edu.mx

Director: Víctor García Castellanos EMail: direc@mail.itap.edu.mx

Programmes
Accountancy (Accountancy); **Administration** (Administration); **Business Administration** (Business Administration); **Computer Science** (Computer Science); **Industrial Engineering** (Industrial Engineering); **Information Technology** (Information Technology); **Mechanical and Electronic Engineering** (Electronic Engineering; Mechanical Engineering)

History: Founded 1987.

Main Language(s) of Instruction: Spanish

Degrees and Diplomas: *Licenciatura*
Last Updated: 12/03/13

TECHNOLOGICAL INSTITUTE OF AGUASCALIENTES

Instituto Tecnológico de Aguascalientes
Apartado postal 263, Avenida Tecnólogico, Esq. Avenida A. López Mateos, 1801, Ote., 20256 Aguascalientes, Aguascalientes
Tel: +52(449) 970-07-40
Fax: +52(449) 970-04-23
EMail: allamas@seit.ita.mx; director@ita.mx
Website: http://www.ita.mx

Director: Carlos Aguilera Batista
Tel: +52(449) 970-07-40 Ext. 115 EMail: director@correo.ita.mx

International Relations: Gilberto Rodríguez Domínguez
Tel: +52(49) 10-50-02 Ext. 116, Fax: +52(49) 70-04-02
EMail: grodrigu@seit.ita.mx

Programmes
Business Administration (Business Administration); **Computer Science** (Computer Science); **Engineering** (Chemical Engineering; Electronic Engineering; Industrial Engineering; Mechanical Engineering)

Degrees and Diplomas: *Licenciatura*; *Especialización*; *Maestría*
Last Updated: 19/02/08

TECHNOLOGICAL INSTITUTE OF ALTAMIRA

Instituto Tecnológico de Altamira
Apartado postal 1, Km. 24.5 Carretera Tampico-Mante, 89600 Altamira, Tamaulipas
Tel: +52(833) 264-0545
EMail: ita4@acnet.net
Website: http://www.italtamira.edu.mx/

Director: Héctor Aguilar Ponce

Programmes
Administration (Administration); **Agronomy** (Agriculture; Agronomy); **Biology** (Biology); **Business Administration** (Business Administration); **Computer Science** (Computer Science); **Industrial Engineering** (Industrial Engineering)

History: Founded 1982 as Instituto Tecnológico agropecuario no. 4.

Main Language(s) of Instruction: Spanish

Degrees and Diplomas: *Licenciatura*

Last Updated: 11/03/13

TECHNOLOGICAL INSTITUTE OF ALTIPLANO DE TLAXCALA

Instituto Tecnológico del Altiplano de Tlaxcala (ITAT)
Km. 7.5 Carretera Federal San Martín-Tlaxcala, 90122 San Diego Xocoyucan, Tlaxcala
Tel: +52(248) 484-28-19
EMail: direccion@italtiplanotlaxcala.edu.mx
Website: http://www.italtiplanotlaxcala.edu.mx

Director: Francisco Javier Avalos Avalos

Programmes
Agronomy (Agronomy); **Food Industry** (Food Technology); **Information and Communication Technologies** (Communication Studies; Information Technology)

History: Founded 1982 as Instituto Tecnológico Agropecuario No. 29 de Xocoyucán. Acquired present status and title 2005.

Main Language(s) of Instruction: Spanish

Degrees and Diplomas: *Licenciatura*

Last Updated: 11/03/13

TECHNOLOGICAL INSTITUTE OF APIZACO

Instituto Tecnológico de Apizaco (ITAP)
Apartado postal 19, Avenida Instituto Tecnológico s/n, 90300 Apizaco, Tlaxcala
Tel: +52(241) 418-0306
EMail: direccion@itapizaco.edu.mx
Website: http://www.itapizaco.edu.mx

Director: Jesús Mario Flores Verduzco

Departments
Business Administration (Business Administration); **Engineering** (Civil Engineering; Electronic Engineering; Industrial Engineering; Mechanical Engineering); **Information Technology** (Computer Science; Information Technology)

History: Founded 1975.

Main Language(s) of Instruction: Spanish

Degrees and Diplomas: *Licenciatura*; *Maestría*

Last Updated: 12/03/13

TECHNOLOGICAL INSTITUTE OF BAHÍA DE BANDERAS

Instituto Tecnológico de Bahía de Banderas
Crucero a Punta de Mita s/n, Col. La Cruz de Huanacaxtle, Bahía de Banderas, Huanacaxtle, 63732 La Cruz de Huanacaxtle, Nayarit
Tel: +52(329) 295-58-88
EMail: informes@itbahiadebanderas.edu.mx
Website: http://www.itbahiadebanderas.edu.mx

Directora: Angélica Aguilar Beltrán

Programmes
Administration (Administration); **Biology** (Biology); **Environmental Engineering** (Environmental Engineering); **Tourism** (Tourism)

History: Founded 1993 as Extensión del Instituto Tecnológico del Mar No. 2 de Mazatlán, became Instituto Tecnológico del Mar No. 6 en Bahía de Banderas in 1997 and acquired present title 2005.

Main Language(s) of Instruction: Spanish

Degrees and Diplomas: *Licenciatura*

Last Updated: 12/03/13

TECHNOLOGICAL INSTITUTE OF BOCA DEL RÍO

Instituto Tecnológico de Boca del Río
Km. 12 Carretera Veracruz-Córdoba, 94290 Boca del Río, Veracruz
Tel: +52(229) 9-86-0189
Fax: +52(229) 9-86-1894
Website: http://www.itboca.edu.mx/

Director: José Manuel Rosado Pérez

Programmes
Administration (Administration); **Aquaculture** (Aquaculture; Marine Biology); **Biology** (Biology); **Business Administration** (Business Administration); **Engineering** (Civil Engineering; Mechanical Engineering; Naval Architecture); **Food Technology** (Food Technology)

History: Founded 1975 as Instituto Tecnológico del Mar en Boca del Río.

Main Language(s) of Instruction: Spanish

Degrees and Diplomas: *Licenciatura*; *Maestría*; *Doctorado*: Aquaculture

Last Updated: 12/03/13

TECHNOLOGICAL INSTITUTE OF CAMPECHE

Instituto Tecnológico de Campeche
Km. 9 Carretera Campeche-Escárcega, 24500 Campeche, Campeche
Tel: +52(981) 812-00-33
Fax: +52(981) 812-02-24
EMail: itescam@prodigy.net.mx
Website: http://www.itcampeche.edu.mx

Directora: Estela Rivero López

Programmes
Architecture (Architecture); **Business Administration** (Business Administration); **Computer Science** (Computer Science); **Engineering** (Chemical Engineering; Engineering; Industrial Engineering; Mechanical Engineering)

History: Founded 1976.

Main Language(s) of Instruction: Spanish

Degrees and Diplomas: *Licenciatura*

Last Updated: 12/03/13

TECHNOLOGICAL INSTITUTE OF CANCÚN

Instituto Tecnológico de Cancún
Avenida Kabah, km 3, Col. Centro, 77500 Cancún, Quintana Roo
Tel: +52(988) 880-74-32
Fax: +52(988) 880-74-33
EMail: direccion@itcancun.edu.mx
Website: http://www.itcancun.edu.mx

Director: Mario Vicente González Robles

Programmes
Business Administration (Accountancy; Administration; Business Administration); **Computer Science** (Computer Science); **Engineering** (Civil Engineering; Computer Engineering; Electronic Engineering; Environmental Engineering; Materials Engineering; Mechanical Engineering)

History: Founded 1984 as Instituto Tecnológico de Chetumal Q. Roo. Acquired present status and title 1986.

Main Language(s) of Instruction: Spanish

Degrees and Diplomas: *Licenciatura*; *Maestría*; *Doctorado*: Materials Engineering

Last Updated: 12/03/13

TECHNOLOGICAL INSTITUTE OF CELAYA

Instituto Tecnológico de Celaya (ITC)
Avenida Tecnológico y Antonio García Cubas s/n, Col. Alfredo V. Bonfil, 38020 Celaya, Guanajuato
Tel: +52(461) 611-75-75
EMail: direccion@itcelaya.edu.mx
Website: http://www.itc.mx

Director: Ignacio López Valdovinos EMail: aobo@itc.mx

Departments
Administration (Administration; Business Administration) *Head*: Julián Ferrer Guerra; **Biochemical Engineering** (Bioengineering) *Head*: Ma. De Los Angeles Vázquez Olvera; **Chemical Engineering** (Chemical Engineering) *Head*: Juan Francisco Javier Alvarado; **Computer Systems and Informatics** (Computer Engineering) *Head*: Francisco Gutiérrez Vera; **Electronic Engineering** (Electronic Engineering) *Head*: Justo Navarro Venegas; **Environmental Engineering** (Environmental Engineering); **Industrial Engineering** (Industrial Engineering) *Head*: Susana Goytia Acevedo; **Mechanical Engineering** (Mechanical Engineering) *Head*: Raúl Lesso Arroyo

History: Founded 1958.

Admission Requirements: School Certificate; Health Certificate

Main Language(s) of Instruction: Spanish

Degrees and Diplomas: *Licenciatura*; *Maestría*; *Doctorado*: Chemical Engineering; Biochemical Engineering

Student Services: Academic counselling, Canteen, Cultural centre, Employment services, Handicapped facilities, Health services, Language programs, Social counselling, Sports facilities

Student Residential Facilities: none

Publications: Ideas en Letras, General interest articles *(quarterly)*

Last Updated: 12/03/13

TECHNOLOGICAL INSTITUTE OF CERRO AZUL

Instituto Tecnológico de Cerro Azul (ITCA)
Km. 60 Carretera Tuxpán-Tampico, Lomas Verdes, 92519 Cerro Azul, Veracruz
Tel: +52(785) 852-07-03
EMail: direccion@itcerroazul.edu.mx
Website: http://www.itcerroazul.edu.mx

Directora: Yeyetzin Sandoval González

Programmes
Accountancy (Accountancy); **Administration** (Administration); **Computer Science** (Computer Science); **Engineering** (Civil Engineering; Electronic Engineering; Mechanical Engineering)

History: Founded 1982.

Main Language(s) of Instruction: Spanish

Degrees and Diplomas: *Licenciatura*

Last Updated: 12/03/13

TECHNOLOGICAL INSTITUTE OF CHETUMAL

Instituto Tecnológico de Chetumal (ITCHE)
Avenida Insurgentes 330, Col. David Gustavo Gutiérrez, Othón P. Blanco, 77013 Chetumal, Quintana Roo
Tel: +52(983) 832-10-19 +52(983) 832-84-20
Fax: +52(983) 832-23-30
EMail: direccion@correo.itchetumal.edu.mx
Website: http://www.itchetumal.edu.mx

Directora: Mirna A. Manzanilla Romero

Programmes
Architecture (Architecture); **Biology** (Biology); **Business Administration** (Accountancy; Business Administration); **Computer Science** (Computer Science); **Engineering** (Civil Engineering; Engineering; Industrial Engineering); **Information Technology** (Information Technology)

History: Founded 1975.

Main Language(s) of Instruction: Spanish

Degrees and Diplomas: *Licenciatura*; *Especialización*; *Maestría*

Last Updated: 12/03/13

TECHNOLOGICAL INSTITUTE OF CHIHUAHUA

Instituto Tecnológico de Chihuahua (ITCH)
Avenida Tecnológico, 2909, Col. Tecnológico, 31310 Chihuahua, Chihuahua
Tel: +52(614) 201- 20-00
EMail: direccion@itchihuahua.edu.mx
Website: http://www.itch.edu.mx

Director: Francisco Miguel Cabanillas Beltrán

Programmes
Business Administration *(Postgraduate)* (Business Administration); **Business and Commerce** *(Graduate)* (Business and Commerce); **Chemical Engineering** *(Graduate)* (Chemical Engineering); **Electrical Engineering** *(Graduate)* (Electrical Engineering); **Electromechanical Engineering** *(Graduate)* (Electronic Engineering; Mechanical Engineering); **Electronic Engineering** *(Graduate, Postgraduate and Doctorate)* (Electronic Engineering); **Industrial Engineering** *(Graduate)* (Industrial Engineering); **Manufacturing Systems** *(Postgraduate)* (Industrial Engineering); **Materials Engineering** *(Graduate)* (Materials Engineering); **Mechanical Engineering** *(Graduate)* (Mechanical Engineering)

History: Founded 1948.

Main Language(s) of Instruction: Spanish

Degrees and Diplomas: *Licenciatura (B.Sc.)*; *Maestría*: Electronic Engineering; Manufacturing System; Business Administration (M.Sc.); *Doctorado*: Electronic Engineering (Dr. Eng.)

Last Updated: 12/03/13

TECHNOLOGICAL INSTITUTE OF CHIHUAHUA II

Instituto Tecnológico de Chihuahua II (ITCH II)
Avenida de las Industrias, 11101, Complejo Industrial Chihuahua, 31000 Chihuahua, Chihuahua
Tel: +52(614) 442-50-00
Website: http://www.itchihuahuaii.edu.mx

Director: Gabriel Salazar Hernández

Programmes
Administration (Administration; Business Administration); **Architecture** (Architecture); **Computer Engineering** (Computer Engineering); **Industrial Engineering** (Industrial Engineering)

History: Founded 1987.

Degrees and Diplomas: *Licenciatura*

Last Updated: 12/03/13

TECHNOLOGICAL INSTITUTE OF CHILPANCINGO

Instituto Tecnológico de Chilpancingo
Avenida José Francisco Ruiz Massieu, 5, Col. Villa Moderna, 39090 Chilpancingo de los Bravo, Guerrero
Tel: +52(747) 472-71-52
EMail: macomaca@hotmail.com
Website: http://www.itchilpancingo.edu.mx/

Director: José Luis Morales Lucas EMail: jlml@prodigy.net.mx

Programmes
Business Administration (Accountancy; Business Administration); **Engineering** (Civil Engineering; Computer Engineering; Engineering)

History: Founded 1985.

Main Language(s) of Instruction: Spanish

Degrees and Diplomas: *Licenciatura*

Last Updated: 12/03/13

TECHNOLOGICAL INSTITUTE OF CHINÁ

Instituto Tecnológico de Chiná
Calle 11 s/n entre 22 y 28, 24520 Chiná, Campeche
Tel: +52(981) 8272082
EMail: itchina@hotmail.es
Website: http://www.itchina.edu.mx/

Director: Antonio Colli Misset

Programmes
Administration (Administration); **Agronomy** (Agronomy); **Biology** (Biology); **Business Administration** (Business Administration); **Forestry** (Forestry)
History: Founded 1975 as Instituto Tecnológico Agropecuario No. 5 de Campeche. Acquired present status and title 2005.
Main Language(s) of Instruction: Spanish
Degrees and Diplomas: *Licenciatura*
Special Facilities: Computer Centre
Libraries: Yes
Last Updated: 11/03/13

TECHNOLOGICAL INSTITUTE OF CIUDAD ALTAMIRANO

Instituto Tecnológico de Ciudad Altamirano
Ave. Pungarabato Poniente s/n, Col. Morelos, Pungarabato, 40660 Ciudad Altamirano, Guerrero
Tel: +52(767) 672-12-13
EMail: itagro@hotmail.com
Website: http://www.italtamirano.edu.mx

Director: Sergio Fernando Garibay Armenta

Programmes
Accountancy (Accountancy); **Administration** (Administration); **Agronomy** (Agronomy); **Biology** (Biology); **Computer Science** (Computer Science)
History: Founded 1982 as Instituto Tecnológico Agropecuario No. 25. Acquired present status and title 2005.
Main Language(s) of Instruction: Spanish
Degrees and Diplomas: *Licenciatura*
Last Updated: 11/03/13

TECHNOLOGICAL INSTITUTE OF CIUDAD CUAUHTÉMOC

Instituto Tecnológico de Ciudad Cuauhtémoc
Av. Tecnológico s/n, 31500 Ciudad Cuauhtémoc, Chihuahua
Tel: +52(625) 581-17-07
EMail: difusion@itcdcuauhtemoc.edu.mx
Website: http://www.itcdcuauhtemoc.edu.mx

Directora: Elizabeth Siqueiros Loera

Programmes
Accountancy (Accountancy); **Administration** (Administration; Business Administration); **Engineering** (Electronic Engineering; Industrial Engineering; Mechanical Engineering); **Food Technology** (Food Technology); **Information Technology** (Information Technology)
History: Founded 1984.
Main Language(s) of Instruction: Spanish
Degrees and Diplomas: *Licenciatura*; *Maestría*
Last Updated: 12/03/13

TECHNOLOGICAL INSTITUTE OF CIUDAD DELICIAS

Instituto Tecnológico de Delicias (ITDEL)
Paseo Tecnológico Km. 3.5, 33000 Ciudad Delicias, Chihuahua
Tel: +52(639) 474-50-83
EMail: direccion@itdelicias.edu.mx
Website: http://www.itdelicias.edu.mx

Directora: Flora Alicia González Jimenez

Programmes
Business Administration (Business Administration); **Computer Science** (Computer Science); **Engineering** (Electronic Engineering; Engineering; Industrial Engineering; Mechanical Engineering); **Information Technology** (Information Technology)
History: Founded 1986.
Main Language(s) of Instruction: Spanish
Degrees and Diplomas: *Licenciatura*
Last Updated: 12/03/13

TECHNOLOGICAL INSTITUTE OF CIUDAD GUZMAN

Instituto Tecnológico de Ciudad Guzmán (ITCG)
Avenida Tecnológico, 100, Zapotlán el Grande, 49100 Ciudad Guzmán, Jalisco
Tel: +52(341) 575-20-50
Fax: +52(341) 575-20-74
EMail: direccion@itcg.edu.mx
Website: http://www.itcdguzman.edu.mx

Director: José Roberto Gudiño Venegas

Programmes
Architecture (Architecture); **Basic Sciences** (Chemistry; Mathematics; Physics); **Business Administration** (Accountancy; Business Administration; Business and Commerce); **Computer Science** (Computer Science); **Engineering** (Computer Engineering; Electronic Engineering; Engineering; Environmental Engineering; Industrial Engineering; Mechanical Engineering)
History: Founded 1972.
Main Language(s) of Instruction: Spanish
Degrees and Diplomas: *Licenciatura*; *Maestría*
Last Updated: 12/03/13

TECHNOLOGICAL INSTITUTE OF CIUDAD JIMÉNEZ

Instituto Tecnológico de Ciudad Jiménez
Avenida Instituto Tecnológico s/n, Ejido Las Luisas, 33987 Ciudad Jiménez, Chihuahua
Tel: +52(629) 542-34-04
EMail: itcjimenez@yahoo.com.mx
Website: http://www.itcdjimenez.edu.mx

Directora: Verónica Espinoza Zapien

Programmes
Business Administration (Business Administration); **Engineering** (Computer Engineering; Electronic Engineering; Industrial Engineering; Mechanical Engineering)
History: Founded 1987.
Main Language(s) of Instruction: Spanish
Degrees and Diplomas: *Licenciatura*
Last Updated: 12/03/13

TECHNOLOGICAL INSTITUTE OF CIUDAD JUÁREZ

Instituto Tecnológico de Ciudad Juárez (ITCJ)
Ave. Tecnológico, 1340, Col. El Crucero, 32500 Ciudad Juárez, Chihuahua
Tel: +52(656) 688-25-00
Fax: +52(656) 688-25-01
EMail: direccion@itcj.edu.mx
Website: http://www.itcj.edu.mx

Director: Juan Armando Hurtado Corral

Departments
Business Administration (Accountancy; Business Administration) *Head*: Dulce Vargas; **Computer Engineering** (Computer Engineering) *Head*: Noe Rosales; **Electrical and Electronic Engineering** (Electrical and Electronic Engineering) *Head*: Efrain Herrera; **Industrial Engineering** (Industrial Engineering) *Head*: Isabel Torres; **Mechanical Engineering** (Mechanical Engineering) *Head*: Machelet Ruiz
History: Founded 1964.
Admission Requirements: High school certificate (bachillerato)
Main Language(s) of Instruction: Spanish
Degrees and Diplomas: *Licenciatura*; *Especialización*; *Maestría*; *Doctorado*: Industrial Engineering
Student Services: Academic counselling, Employment services, Foreign student adviser, Health services, Language programs, Social counselling, Sports facilities
Libraries: Yes
Last Updated: 12/03/13

TECHNOLOGICAL INSTITUTE OF CIUDAD MADERO

Instituto Tecnológico de Ciudad Madero (ITCM)
Ave 1o de Mayo y Sor Juana Inés de la Cruz, Col. Los Mangos, 89440 Ciudad Madero, Tamaulipas
Tel: +52(833) 357-48-20
EMail: direccion@itcm.edu.mx
Website: http://www.itcm.edu.mx

Director: Héctor Arnulfo Hernández Enríquez

Departments
Engineering (Chemical Engineering; Computer Engineering; Electrical Engineering; Electronic Engineering; Engineering; Geological Engineering; Industrial Engineering; Mechanical Engineering; Telecommunications Engineering); **Geosciences** (Earth Sciences; Geophysics)

History: Founded 1954.

Main Language(s) of Instruction: Spanish

Degrees and Diplomas: *Licenciatura*; *Maestría*; *Doctorado*
Last Updated: 12/03/13

TECHNOLOGICAL INSTITUTE OF CIUDAD VALLES

Instituto Tecnológico de Ciudad Valles (ITCVA)
Apartado postal 475, Km. 2 Carretera al Ingenio Ignacio, Plan de Ayala, 79000 Ciudad Valles, San Luis Potosí
Tel: +52(481) 811-46-05 +52(481) 811-21-63
Fax: +52(481) 811-20-44
Website: http://www.itcdvalles.edu.mx

Director: José Isaías Martínez Corona

Programmes
Business Administration (Administration; Business Administration); **Computer Science** (Computer Science); **Engineering** (Environmental Engineering; Industrial Engineering); **Food Technology** (Food Technology); **Information Technology** (Information Technology)

History: Founded 1982 as Instituto Tecnológico Agropecuario No.22.

Main Language(s) of Instruction: Spanish

Degrees and Diplomas: *Licenciatura*
Last Updated: 12/03/13

TECHNOLOGICAL INSTITUTE OF CIUDAD VICTORIA

Instituto Tecnológico de Ciudad Victoria (ITCV)
Blvd. Licenciado Emilio Portes Gil, 1301, Victoria, 87010 Ciudad Victoria, Tamaulipas
Tel: +52(834) 153-20-00
EMail: direccion@itvictoria.edu.mx
Website: http://www.itvictoria.edu.mx

Director: David Zepeda Sánchez

Programmes
Biology (Biology); **Business Administration** (Business Administration); **Computer Science** (Computer Science); **Engineering** (Civil Engineering; Electronic Engineering; Energy Engineering; Industrial Engineering; Mechanical Engineering)

History: Founded 1975.

Main Language(s) of Instruction: Spanish

Degrees and Diplomas: *Licenciatura*; *Maestría*; *Doctorado*: Biology
Last Updated: 12/03/13

TECHNOLOGICAL INSTITUTE OF COLIMA

Instituto Tecnológico de Colima (ITCOL)
Avenida Tecnológico 1, Villa de Álvarez, A.P. 10 y 128, 28976 Villa de Álvarez, Colima
Tel: +52(312) 312-99-20 +52(312) 314-09-33
EMail: informes@itcolima.edu.mx
Website: http://www.itcolima.edu.mx

Director: Saturnino Castro Reyes

Programmes
Accountancy (Accountancy); **Architecture** (Architecture); **Biochemistry** (Biochemistry); **Business Administration** (Business Administration); **Computer Science** (Computer Science); **Engineering** (Computer Engineering; Industrial Engineering)

History: Founded 1976.

Main Language(s) of Instruction: Spanish

Degrees and Diplomas: *Licenciatura*
Last Updated: 12/03/13

TECHNOLOGICAL INSTITUTE OF COMITÁN

Instituto Tecnológico de Comitán
Km. 3.5 Avenida Instituto Tecnológico s/n, Col. Yocnajab El Rosario, 30000 Comitán de Domínguez, Chiapas
Tel: +52(963) 225-17
EMail: itc@itcomitan.edu.mx
Website: http://www.itcomitan.edu.mx

Director: Jorge Márquez Juárez
EMail: direccion@itcomitan.edu.mx

Programmes
Engineering

History: Founded 1984 as instituto Tecnológico Agropecuario de Chiapas no. 31. Acquired present status and title 1992.

Main Language(s) of Instruction: Spanish

Degrees and Diplomas: *Licenciatura*
Last Updated: 12/03/13

TECHNOLOGICAL INSTITUTE OF COMITANCILLO

Instituto Tecnológico de Comitancillo
Carretera Ixtaltepec – Comitancillo Km. 7.5 San Pedro, 70750 Comitancillo, Oaxaca
Tel: +52(971) 711-21-09
EMail: itcomitancillo@yahoo.com.mx

Director: Antonio Versalles Sánchez

Programmes
Agronomy (Agronomy); **Business Administration** (Business Administration); **Computer Science** (Computer Science); **Food Technology** (Food Technology)

Main Language(s) of Instruction: Spanish

Degrees and Diplomas: *Licenciatura*
Last Updated: 12/03/13

TECHNOLOGICAL INSTITUTE OF CONKAL

Instituto Tecnológico de Conkal
Apartado postal 53-D, Km. 16.3 Carretera Antigua Mérida-Motul, Col. Itzimna, 93175 Conkal, Yucatán
Tel: +52(999) 912-41-29 +52(999) 912-41-30
EMail: msoria@mucuy.itaconkal.edu.mx
Website: http://www.itaconkal.edu.mx

Director: Pedro Alberto Haro Ramírez

Programmes
Administration (Administration); **Agronomy** (Agriculture; Agronomy; Horticulture; Tropical Agriculture); **Biology** (Biology); **Community Development** (Development Studies); **Information Technology** (Information Technology)

History: Founded 1974 as Instituto Tecnológico Agropecuario No 2 de Conkal.

Main Language(s) of Instruction: Spanish

Degrees and Diplomas: *Licenciatura*; *Maestría*; *Doctorado*
Last Updated: 11/03/13

TECHNOLOGICAL INSTITUTE OF CUAUTLA

Instituto Tecnológico de Cuautla
Libramiento a Cuautla-Oaxaca s/n Col. Juan Morales, 62745 Cuautla, Morelos
Tel: +52(735) 3-22-08 +52(735) 3-22-03
EMail: direccion@itcuautla.edu.mx
Website: http://www.itcuautla.edu.mx

Director: Gerardo Reyes Salgado

Programmes

Accountancy (Accountancy); **Business Administration** (Administration; Business Administration); **Engineering** (Computer Engineering; Electronic Engineering; Industrial Engineering; Mechanical Engineering)

History: Founded 1991.

Main Language(s) of Instruction: Spanish

Degrees and Diplomas: *Licenciatura*

Last Updated: 12/03/13

TECHNOLOGICAL INSTITUTE OF CUENCA DE PAPALOAPAN

Instituto Tecnológico de la Cuenca de Papaloapan

Av. Tecnológico 21, San Bartolo, 68446 Tuxtepec, Oaxaca

Tel: +52(287) 875-3926

EMail: itcuencadir@yahoo.com.mx

Website: http://itcuencadelpapaloapan.com

Director: Alejandro Cruz Galván

Programmes

Agronomy (Agronomy); **Biology** (Biology)

History: Founded 1975.

Main Language(s) of Instruction: Spanish

Degrees and Diplomas: *Licenciatura*

Last Updated: 12/03/13

TECHNOLOGICAL INSTITUTE OF CULIACÁN

Instituto Tecnológico de Culiacán

Av. Juan de Dios S/N, Col. Guadalupe, 80220 Culiacán, Sinaloa

Tel: +52(667) 713 -17-96

EMail: direccion@itculiacan.edu.mx

Website: http://itculiacan.edu.mx

Director: Francisco Rafael Saldaña Ibarra

Programmes

Biochemistry (Biochemistry); **Engineering** (Computer Engineering; Electrical Engineering; Electronic Engineering; Environmental Engineering; Industrial Engineering; Mechanical Engineering); **Information Technology** (Information Technology)

History: Founded 1968.

Main Language(s) of Instruction: Spanish

Degrees and Diplomas: *Licenciatura*; *Maestría*

Last Updated: 12/03/13

TECHNOLOGICAL INSTITUTE OF DURANGO

Instituto Tecnológico de Durango (ITD)

Felipe Pescador 1830, Ote. Col. Nueva Vizcaya, 34080 Durango, Durango

Tel: +52(618) 829-09-00

EMail: director@itdgo.mx

Website: http://www.itdurango.edu.mx

Director: Felipe Pascual Rosario Aguirre

Programmes

Administration (Administration); **Architecture** (Architecture); **Biochemistry** (Biochemistry); **Business Administration** (Business Administration); **Engineering** (Chemical Engineering; Civil Engineering; Electronic Engineering; Engineering; Industrial Engineering); **Information Technology** (Information Technology)

Main Language(s) of Instruction: Spanish

Degrees and Diplomas: *Licenciatura*; *Maestría*: Biochemical Engineering; Electronic Engineering; *Doctorado*: Biochemical Engineering

Last Updated: 12/03/13

TECHNOLOGICAL INSTITUTE OF EL LLANO AGUASCALIENTES

Instituto Tecnológico de El Llano Aguascalientes

Km. 18 Carretera Aguascalientes - San Luis Potosí El Llano, 20256 Aguascalientes, Aguascalientes

Tel: +52(449) 916-12-51

Fax: +52(449) 916-20-94

EMail: itllanoags@gmail.com

Website: http://www.itllano.edu.mx/

Director: Jose Guillermo Battista Ortiz

Programmes

Administration (Administration); **Agronomy** (Agronomy); **Business Administration** (Business Administration); **Computer Science** (Computer Science); **Sustainable Agricultural Innovation** (Agriculture)

History: Founded 1967 as Instituto Tecnológico Agropecuario No 20 de Aguascalientes.

Main Language(s) of Instruction: Spanish

Degrees and Diplomas: *Licenciatura*

Last Updated: 12/03/13

TECHNOLOGICAL INSTITUTE OF EL SALTO

Instituto Tecnológico de El Salto

Mesa del Tecnológico s/n, 34942 Pueblo Nuevo, Durango

Tel: +52(618) 876-02-39 +52(618) 876-07-83

EMail: direccion@itelsalto.edu.mx

Website: http://www.itelsalto.edu.mx

Director: Felipe Alanís González

Programmes

Business Administration (Business Administration); **Engineering** (Computer Engineering; Forestry)

History: Founded 1976 as Instituto Tecnológico Forestal No.1 de El Salto.

Main Language(s) of Instruction: Spanish

Degrees and Diplomas: *Licenciatura*; *Maestría*

Last Updated: 12/03/13

TECHNOLOGICAL INSTITUTE OF ENSENADA

Instituto Tecnológico de Ensenada

Apartado postal 1178, Km. 115 Carretera Transpeninsular El Ciprés, Col. Ex-Ejido Chapultepec, Ensenada, 22780 Tijuana, Baja California

Tel: +52(617) 177-56-80 +52(617) 177-56-82

Fax: +52(617) 177-56-78

EMail: direccion@itensenada.edu.mx

Website: http://www.itensenada.edu.mx

Director: Marcelino Bauzá Rosete

Programmes

Business Administration (Administration; Business Administration); **Engineering** (Computer Engineering; Electronic Engineering; Industrial Engineering; Mechanical Engineering)

History: Founded 1997.

Main Language(s) of Instruction: Spanish

Degrees and Diplomas: *Licenciatura*

Last Updated: 12/03/13

TECHNOLOGICAL INSTITUTE OF GUAYMAS

Instituto Tecnológico de Guaymas

Km. 4., Las Playitas, 85480 Guaymas, Sonora

Tel: +52(622) 22-153-67

Website: http://www.itg.edu.mx

Director: Juan Alfredo Moncayo López

Programmes

Administration (Administration; Economics); **Aquaculture** (Aquaculture); **Civil Engineering** (Civil Engineering); **Coastal Studies** (Coastal Studies); **Fishery** (Fishery)

History: Founded 1984 as Instituto Tecnológico del Mar. Acquired present status and title 2005.

Main Language(s) of Instruction: Spanish
Degrees and Diplomas: *Licenciatura*; *Maestría*: Coastal Studies
Last Updated: 13/03/13

TECHNOLOGICAL INSTITUTE OF HERMOSILLO

Instituto Tecnológico de Hermosillo (ITH)
Avenida Tecnológico y Periférico Poniente, Col. El Sahuaro, 83170 Hermosillo, Sonora
Tel: +52(662) 260-65-00
EMail: direccion@ith.mx
Website: http://www.ith.mx

Director: Adolfo Rivera Castillo

Programmes
Administration (Administration); **Computer Science** (Computer Science); **Engineering** (Electrical Engineering; Engineering; Industrial Engineering; Mechanical Engineering)
History: Founded 1975.
Main Language(s) of Instruction: Spanish
Degrees and Diplomas: *Licenciatura*; *Maestría*
Last Updated: 13/03/13

TECHNOLOGICAL INSTITUTE OF HUATABAMPO

Instituto Tecnológico de Huatabampo
Avenida Tecnológico s/n, Col. Unión, 85900 Huatabampo, Sonora
Tel: +52(647) 426-14-77
EMail: ithuatabampo@dgest.gob.mx
Website: http://www.ithua.edu.mx/

Director: Jesús David Estrada Ruiz
EMail: direccion@c.ithua.edu.max

Programmes
Business Administration (Accountancy; Administration; Business Administration); **Engineering** (Computer Engineering; Engineering; Industrial Engineering; Mechanical Engineering)
History: Founded 1987.
Main Language(s) of Instruction: Spanish
Degrees and Diplomas: *Licenciatura*
Last Updated: 13/03/13

TECHNOLOGICAL INSTITUTE OF HUEJUTLA

Instituto Tecnológico de Huejutla
Km. 5.5 Carretera Huejutla-Chalahuiyapa, Huejutla, 43000 Huejutla de Reyes, Hidalgo
Tel: +52(789) 896-06-48

Director: Quintín José Luis Mejía Ángeles

Programmes
Agronomy (Agriculture; Agronomy); **Biology** (Biology); **Computer Science** (Computer Science)
History: Founded 1975 as Instituto Tecnológico agropecuario N° 6. Acquired present status and title 2006.
Main Language(s) of Instruction: Spanish
Degrees and Diplomas: *Licenciatura*
Last Updated: 11/03/13

TECHNOLOGICAL INSTITUTE OF IGUALA

Instituto Tecnológico de Iguala
Carretera Nacional Iguala-Taxco, Esq. Periférico Norte, Colonia Adolfo López Mateos, 40030 Iguala, Guerrero
Tel: +52(733) 332-14-25
EMail: informacion@itiguala.edu.mx
Website: http://www.itiguala.edu.mx

Directora: Ana Alday Chávez

Programmes
Accountancy (Accountancy); **Computer Science** (Computer Science); **Engineering** (Computer Engineering; Industrial Engineering)
History: Founded 1989 as an extensión of the Instituto Tecnológico de Chilpancingo. Acquired present status and title 1991.
Main Language(s) of Instruction: Spanish
Degrees and Diplomas: *Licenciatura*
Last Updated: 13/03/13

TECHNOLOGICAL INSTITUTE OF JIQUILPÁN

Instituto Tecnológico de Jiquilpán
Km. 202 Carretera Nacional s/n, Parque Lázaro Cárdenas, 59510 Jiquilpán, Michoacán
Tel: +52(353) 533-02-37
EMail: director@mail.itjiquilpan.edu.mx
Website: http://www.itjiquilpan.edu.mx

Director: Jesús Zalapa Alemán

Programmes
Architecture (Architecture); **Biochemistry** (Biochemistry); **Business Administration** (Accountancy; Business Administration; Business and Commerce); **Computer Science** (Computer Science); **Industrial Engineering** (Industrial Engineering)
History: Founded 1977.
Main Language(s) of Instruction: Spanish
Degrees and Diplomas: *Licenciatura*
Last Updated: 13/03/13

TECHNOLOGICAL INSTITUTE OF LA LAGUNA

Instituto Tecnológico de La Laguna
Blvd. Revolución y Calzada Cuauhtémoc s/n, Col. Centro, 27000 Torreón, Coahuila
Tel: +52(871) 705-13-13
Fax: +52(871) 713-13-01
EMail: direccion@itlalaguna.edu.mx
Website: http://www.itlalaguna.edu.mx/

Director: Mario P. Valdés Garza

Programmes
Administration (Administration); **Engineering** (Computer Engineering; Electrical and Electronic Engineering; Engineering; Industrial Engineering; Mechanical Engineering)
History: Founded 1965.
Main Language(s) of Instruction: Spanish
Degrees and Diplomas: *Licenciatura*; *Maestría*; *Doctorado*
Last Updated: 13/03/13

TECHNOLOGICAL INSTITUTE OF LA PAZ

Instituto Tecnológico de La Paz
Blvd. Forjadores de Baja California Sur, 4720, Col. 8 de Octubre, 23080 La Paz, Baja California Sur
Tel: +52(612) 121-07-05
Fax: +52(612) 121-12-95
Website: http://www.itlp.edu.mx

Director: Oscar Báez Senties

Programmes
Architecture (Architecture); **Biochemistry** (Biochemistry); **Business Administration** (Accountancy; Business Administration); **Computer Science** (Computer Science); **Engineering** (Civil Engineering; Computer Engineering; Electronic Engineering; Engineering; Industrial Engineering; Mechanical Engineering)
History: Founded 1973.
Main Language(s) of Instruction: Spanish
Degrees and Diplomas: *Licenciatura*; *Maestría*
Last Updated: 13/03/13

TECHNOLOGICAL INSTITUTE OF LA PIEDAD

Instituto Tecnológico de La Piedad
Avenida Tecnológico, 2000, Meseta de los Laureles, 59370 La Piedad, Michoacán
Tel: +52(352) 526-06-80 +52(352) 526-22-94
Fax: +52(352) 526-23-69
EMail: admin@itlapiedad.edu.mx
Website: http://www.itlapiedad.edu.mx

Director: Oswaldo Padilla Gorosave

Programmes

Administration (Administration; Business Administration); **Biochemistry** (Biochemistry); **Engineering** (Computer Engineering; Electronic Engineering; Industrial Engineering); **Information Technology** (Information Technology)

History: Founded 1990.

Main Language(s) of Instruction: Spanish

Degrees and Diplomas: *Licenciatura*

Last Updated: 13/03/13

TECHNOLOGICAL INSTITUTE OF LA REGION MIXE

Instituto Tecnológico de la Región Mixe (ITRM)
9 Norte Coloia Cuauhtemoc 306, Santa Maria Tlahuitoltepec, Oaxaca
Tel: +52(951) 1321468
EMail: educaadistancia@hotmail.com
Website: http://www.itrm.edu.mx

Director: Rogelio Santiago Flores EMail: rogelio_itrm@hotmail.com

Programmes

Business Administration (Business Administration); **Community Development** (Social and Community Services); **Industry** (Industrial Engineering)

History: Founded 2000.

Main Language(s) of Instruction: Spanish

Degrees and Diplomas: *Licenciatura*

Last Updated: 12/03/13

TECHNOLOGICAL INSTITUTE OF LÁZARO CÁRDENAS

Instituto Tecnológico de Lázaro Cárdenas
Avenida Melchor Ocampo, Esq. Narciso Bassols s/n, 60950 Lázaro Cárdenas, Michoacán
Tel: +52(753) 526-06-80
EMail: difusion@itlazarocardenas.edu.mx

Director: José Ángel Esquivel Tovar

Programmes

Business Administration (Accountancy; Business Administration); **Engineering** (Chemical Engineering; Computer Engineering; Electronic Engineering; Engineering; Mechanical Engineering)

History: Founded 1987.

Main Language(s) of Instruction: Spanish

Degrees and Diplomas: *Licenciatura*

Last Updated: 13/03/13

TECHNOLOGICAL INSTITUTE OF LEÓN

Instituto Tecnológico de León (ITL)
Apartado postal 1-857, Avenida Tecnológico s/n, Fracc. Julián de Obregón, 37290 León, Guanajuato
Tel: +52(477) 710-52-00
Fax: +52(477) 711-20-72
Website: http://www.itleon.edu.mx

Director: Rafael Rodríguez Gallegos

Programmes

Business Administration (Business Administration); **Computer Science** (Computer Science); **Electromechanical Engineering** (Electrical Engineering; Mechanical Engineering); **Electronic Engineering** (Electronic Engineering); **Industrial Engineering** (Industrial Engineering); **Information Technology** (Information Technology)

History: Founded 1972.

Main Language(s) of Instruction: Spanish

Degrees and Diplomas: *Licenciatura*; *Maestría*: Computer Science; *Doctorado*: Computer Science

Last Updated: 13/03/13

TECHNOLOGICAL INSTITUTE OF LERMA

Instituto Tecnológico de Lerma
Km. 10 Carretera Campeche-Champotón, 24020 Lerma, Campeche
Tel: +52(981) 812-03-97
EMail: info@itlema.edu.mx
Website: http://www.itlerma.edu.mx

Director: Javier García González

Programmes

Administration (Administration); **Aquaculture** (Aquaculture); **Engineering** (Electronic Engineering; Mechanical Engineering)

History: Founded 1988 as Instituto Tecnológico del Mar. Acquired present status and title 2005.

Main Language(s) of Instruction: Spanish

Degrees and Diplomas: *Licenciatura*

Last Updated: 13/03/13

TECHNOLOGICAL INSTITUTE OF LINARES

Instituto Tecnológico de Linares
Carretera Nacional Km 157 tramo Linares Hualahuises, 67700 Linares, Nuevo León
Tel: +52(821) 212-68-05
Fax: +52(821) 212-67-05
Website: http://www.itlinares.edu.mx

Director: Luis Manuel Ferniza Pérez

Programmes

Business Administration (Business Administration); **Computer Science** (Computer Science); **Engineering** (Computer Engineering; Electrical Engineering; Industrial Engineering; Mechanical Engineering); **Food Technology** (Food Technology)

History: Founded 1977 as Instituto Tecnológico Agropecuario No 12. Acquired present status and title 1992.

Main Language(s) of Instruction: Spanish

Degrees and Diplomas: *Licenciatura*

Last Updated: 13/03/13

TECHNOLOGICAL INSTITUTE OF LOS MOCHIS

Instituto Tecnológico de Los Mochis (ITLM)
Apartado postal 766, Blvd. Juan de Dios Bátiz s/n y Prolongación 20 de Noviembre, Ahome, 81250 Los Mochis, Sinaloa
Tel: +54(668) 812-58-58 +54(668) 812-59-59
Fax: +54(668) 815-03-26
EMail: direccion@itmochis.edu.mx
Website: http://www.itmochis.edu.mx/

Director: Oscar Armando López González

Programmes

Aquaculture (Aquaculture); **Architecture** (Architecture); **Biochemistry** (Biochemistry); **Biology** (Biology); **Business Administration** (Accountancy; Business Administration); **Computer Science** (Computer Science); **Engineering** (Agricultural Engineering; Chemical Engineering; Electronic Engineering; Engineering; Industrial Engineering; Information Technology); **Food Technology** (Food Technology)

History: Founded 1976.

Main Language(s) of Instruction: Spanish

Degrees and Diplomas: *Licenciatura*

Last Updated: 13/03/13

TECHNOLOGICAL INSTITUTE OF MATAMOROS

Instituto Tecnológico de Matamoros
Apartado postal 339, Carretera Lauro Villar Km. 6.5, 87490 Matamoros, Tamaulipas
Tel: +52(868) 814-09-52 +52(868) 814-06-67
Fax: +52(868) 814-09-53
EMail: direccion@itmatamoros.edu.mx
Website: http://www.itmatamoros.edu.mx

Directora: Ana Isabel Lerma González

Programmes

Accountancy (Accountancy); **Administration** (Administration; Business Administration); **Computer Science** (Computer Science); **Engineering** (Chemical Engineering; Civil Engineering; Electronic Engineering; Engineering; Environmental Engineering; Industrial Engineering); **Industrial Management** (Industrial Management)

History: Founded 1972.

Main Language(s) of Instruction: Spanish

Degrees and Diplomas: *Licenciatura*
Last Updated: 13/03/13

TECHNOLOGICAL INSTITUTE OF MATEHUALA

Instituto Tecnológico de Matehuala

Km. 5 Carretera Matehuala-Saltillo, 78700 Matehuala, San Luis Potosí
Tel: +52(488) 882-38-77
EMail: itmdirecc@prodigy.net.mx
Website: http://www.itmatehuala.edu.mx

Director: Rogelio Chavarría Elizondo

Programmes

Accountancy (Accountancy); **Business Administration** (Business Administration); **Computer Science** (Computer Science); **Engineering** (Civil Engineering; Computer Engineering; Industrial Engineering)

History: Founded 1988.

Main Language(s) of Instruction: Spanish

Degrees and Diplomas: *Licenciatura*
Last Updated: 13/03/13

TECHNOLOGICAL INSTITUTE OF MAZATLÁN

Instituto Tecnológico de Mazatlán

Calle Corsario 1 No. 203 Col. Urias, 82070 Mazatlán, Sinaloa
Tel: +52(669) 983-84-00
Fax: +52(669) 984-72-09
EMail: ci@itmazatlan.edu.mx
Website: http://www.itmazatlan.edu.mx

Director: Manuel José Correa Pérez

Programmes

Administration (Administration); **Biochemistry** (Biochemistry); **Computer Engineering** (Computer Engineering); **Electrical and Electronic Engineering** (Electrical and Electronic Engineering); **Fishery** (Fishery); **Mechanical Engineering** (Mechanical Engineering); **Naval Engineering** (Naval Architecture)

History: Founded 1982.

Main Language(s) of Instruction: Spanish

Degrees and Diplomas: *Licenciatura*; *Maestría*
Last Updated: 15/03/13

TECHNOLOGICAL INSTITUTE OF MERIDA

Instituto Tecnológico de Mérida

Avenida Tecnológico km 4.5, 97118 Mérida, Yucatán
Tel: +52(999) 964-5000
Fax: +52(999) 944-81-81
EMail: direccion@itmerida.edu.mx
Website: http://www.itmerida.mx

Director: Abel Zapata Dittrich

Programmes

Business Administration (Business Administration); **Engineering** (Biomedical Engineering; Chemical Engineering; Civil Engineering; Computer Engineering; Electronic Engineering; Engineering; Environmental Engineering; Industrial Engineering; Mechanical Engineering); **Food Science and Biotechnology** (Biotechnology; Food Science)

History: Founded 1961.

Main Language(s) of Instruction: Spanish

Degrees and Diplomas: *Licenciatura*; *Maestría*; *Doctorado*: Fodd Science and Biotechnology
Last Updated: 15/03/13

TECHNOLOGICAL INSTITUTE OF MEXICALI

Instituto Tecnológico de Mexicali

Avenida Tecnolólogico s/n, Col. Elías Calles, 21396 Mexicali, Baja California
Tel: +52(686) 580-49-80
Fax: +52(686) 568-78-03
EMail: direccion@itmexicali.edu.mx
Website: http://www.itmexicali.edu.mx

Director: Francisco Javier Ortíz Serrano

Programmes

Accountancy (Accountancy); **Business Administration** (Business Administration); **Computer Science** (Computer Science); **Engineering** (Chemical Engineering; Electrical Engineering; Electronic Engineering; Energy Engineering; Industrial Engineering; Mechanical Engineering)

Main Language(s) of Instruction: Spanish

Degrees and Diplomas: *Licenciatura*; *Maestría*: Electronic Engineering. Also Inter-institutional Doctorado
Last Updated: 15/03/13

TECHNOLOGICAL INSTITUTE OF MINATITLÁN

Instituto Tecnológico de Minatitlán (ITMINA)

Blvd. Institutos Tecnológicos s/n, Col. Buenavista Norte, 96848 Minatitlán, Veracruz
Tel: +52(922) 222-43-45
Fax: +52(922) 222-43-36
EMail: direccion@itmina.edu.mx
Website: http://www.itmina.edu.mx

Director: José Carlos Diaz García

Programmes

Administration (Administration; Business Administration); **Engineering** (Chemical Engineering; Computer Engineering; Electronic Engineering; Environmental Engineering; Industrial Engineering; Mechanical Engineering)

History: Founded 1971.

Main Language(s) of Instruction: Spanish

Degrees and Diplomas: *Licenciatura*; *Maestría*: Electronic Engineering
Last Updated: 15/03/13

TECHNOLOGICAL INSTITUTE OF MORELIA

Instituto Tecnológico de Morelia (ITMO)

Apartado postal 262, Avenida Tecnológico, 1500, Col. Lomas de Santiaguito, 58120 Morelia, Michoacán
Tel: +52(443) 312-15-70
EMail: direccion@itmorelia.edu.mx
Website: http://www.tecmor.mx

Director: Paulino Alberto Rivas Martínez

Programmes

Administration (Administration); **Biochemistry** (Biochemistry); **Business Administration** (Business Administration); **Computer Engineering** (Computer Engineering); **Computer Science** (Computer Science); **Electronic Engineering** (Electronic Engineering); **Industrial Engineering** (Industrial Engineering); **Materials Engineering** (Materials Engineering); **Mechanical Engineering** (Mechanical Engineering)

History: Founded 1965.

Main Language(s) of Instruction: Spanish

Degrees and Diplomas: *Licenciatura*; *Maestría*; *Doctorado*: Electrical Engineering (Ph.D.)
Last Updated: 15/03/13

TECHNOLOGICAL INSTITUTE OF NOGALES

Instituto Tecnológico de Nogales (ITN)

Avenida Instituto Tecnológico, 911, Col. Granja, 84065 Nogales, Sonora
Tel: +52(631) 311-18-70
Fax: +52(631) 311-18-71
EMail: director@nogal.itn.mx
Website: http://www.itnogales.edu.mx/

Director: José Escárcega Castellanos

Programmes

Accountancy (Accountancy); **Administration** (Administration; Business Administration); **Engineering** (Civil Engineering; Electronic Engineering; Industrial Engineering; Materials Engineering; Mechanical Engineering); **Town Planning** (Town Planning)

History: Founded 1975.

Main Language(s) of Instruction: Spanish

Degrees and Diplomas: *Licenciatura*; *Maestría*: Computer Science; Materials Engineering; Town Planning
Last Updated: 15/03/13

TECHNOLOGICAL INSTITUTE OF NUEVO LAREDO

Instituto Tecnológico de Nuevo Laredo
Avenida Reforma, 2007 Sur, 88000 Nuevo Laredo, Tamaulipas
Tel: +52(867) 711-90-50
Fax: +52(867) 711-90-68
EMail: admin@itnuevolaredo.edu.mx
Website: http://www.itnuevolaredo.edu.mx

Director: Sergio Efraín Beltrán Beltrán

Programmes

Accountancy (Accountancy); **Administration** (Administration; Business Administration); **Architecture** (Architecture); **Engineering** (Civil Engineering; Computer Engineering; Electrical Engineering; Electronic Engineering; Industrial Engineering; Mechanical Engineering)

History: Founded 1964.

Main Language(s) of Instruction: Spanish

Degrees and Diplomas: *Licenciatura*
Last Updated: 15/03/13

TECHNOLOGICAL INSTITUTE OF NUEVO LEÓN

Instituto Tecnológico de Nuevo León (ITNL)
Avenida Eloy Cavazos 2001 Junto al Parque 'La Pastora', Col. Tolteca, 67170 Ciudad Guadalupe, Nuevo León
Tel: +52(81) 81-57-05-00
Website: http://www.itnl.edu.mx

Directora: María del Mar Cisneros Guerrero

Programmes

Business Administration (Business Administration); **Computer Engineering** (Computer Engineering; Computer Science); **Electricity and Electronics** (Electrical and Electronic Engineering); **Environmental Engineering** (Environmental Engineering); **Industrial Engineering** (Industrial Engineering); **Mechanical Engineering** (Mechanical Engineering)

History: Founded 1976.

Main Language(s) of Instruction: Spanish

Degrees and Diplomas: *Licenciatura*; *Especialización*: Mechanical and Electronic Engineering; *Maestría*: Mechanical and Electronic Engineering
Last Updated: 15/03/13

TECHNOLOGICAL INSTITUTE OF OAXACA

Instituto Tecnológico de Oaxaca (ITO)
Avenida Ing. Víctor Bravo Ahuja, 125 Esq. Calzada Tecnológico, 68030 Oaxaca, Oaxaca
Tel: +52(951) 501-50-16
EMail: tec_oax@itoaxaca.edu.mx
Website: http://www.itoaxaca.edu.mx

Director: Ángel Francisco Velasco Muñoz

Programmes

Administration (Administration; Business Administration); **Engineering** (Chemical Engineering; Civil Engineering; Computer Engineering; Electrical Engineering; Electronic Engineering; Industrial Engineering; Mechanical Engineering)

History: Founded 1968.

Main Language(s) of Instruction: Spanish

Degrees and Diplomas: *Licenciatura*; *Especialización*; *Maestría*; *Doctorado*
Last Updated: 18/03/13

TECHNOLOGICAL INSTITUTE OF OCOTLÁN

Instituto Tecnológico de Ocotlán
Avenida Tecnológico s/n, Fracc. La Primavera, 47829 Ocotlán, Jalisco
Tel: +52(392) 925-30-57
Fax: +52(392) 922-46-80
EMail: direccion@itocotlan.edu.mx
Website: http://www.itocotlan.edu.mx

Director: Juan Gerardo Muñoz Orozco

Programmes

Accountancy (Accountancy); **Business Administration** (Administration; Business Administration); **Computer Science** (Computer Science); **Engineering** (Electronic Engineering; Industrial Engineering; Mechanical Engineering)

History: Founded 1991.

Main Language(s) of Instruction: Spanish

Degrees and Diplomas: *Licenciatura*
Last Updated: 18/03/13

TECHNOLOGICAL INSTITUTE OF ORIZABA

Instituto Tecnológico de Orizaba (ITOR)
Avenida Instituto Tecnológico No. 852 Col. Emliano Zapata, 94320 Orizaba, Veracruz
Tel: +52(272) 724-40-96
Fax: +52(272) 725-17-28
EMail: direccion@itorizaba.edu.mx
Website: http://www.itorizaba.edu.mx

Director: Rogelio García Camacho

Programmes

Business Administration (Business Administration); **Engineering** (Chemical Engineering; Computer Engineering; Electronic Engineering; Industrial Engineering)

Main Language(s) of Instruction: Spanish

Degrees and Diplomas: *Licenciatura*; *Maestría*; *Doctorado*
Last Updated: 18/03/13

TECHNOLOGICAL INSTITUTE OF PACHUCA

Instituto Tecnológico de Pachuca (ITP)
Autopista México - Pachuca Km 87.5, 42080 Pachuca, Hidalgo
Tel: +52(771) 711-31-40
EMail: sii@itpachuca.edu.mx
Website: http://www.itpachuca.edu.mx

Directora: Gloria Edith Palacios Almont

Programmes

Administration (Administration; Business Administration); **Architecture** (Architecture); **Computer Science** (Computer Science); **Engineering** (Chemical Engineering; Civil Engineering; Computer Engineering; Electrical Engineering; Industrial Engineering)

History: Founded 1971.

Main Language(s) of Instruction: Spanish

Degrees and Diplomas: *Licenciatura*; *Maestría*
Last Updated: 18/03/13

TECHNOLOGICAL INSTITUTE OF PARRAL

Instituto Tecnológico de Parral (ITPARRAL)
Avenida Tecnológico, 57, Col. Tecnológico, 33850 Hidalgo del Parral, Chihuahua
Tel: +52(627) 523-02-12
Fax: +52(627) 523-07-52
EMail: direccion@mail.itparral.edu.mx
Website: http://www.itparral.edu.mx

Director: José Antonio Camaño Quevedo

Programmes

Accountancy (Accountancy); **Architecture** (Architecture); **Business Administration** (Business Administration); **Engineering**

(Chemical Engineering; Electrical and Electronic Engineering; Engineering; Industrial Engineering; Mechanical Engineering)

History: Founded 1975

Main Language(s) of Instruction: Spanish

Degrees and Diplomas: *Licenciatura*

Last Updated: 18/03/13

TECHNOLOGICAL INSTITUTE OF PIEDRAS NEGRAS

Instituto Tecnológico de Piedras Negras

Calle Instituto Tecnológico No. 310, Col. Tecnológico, 26080 Piedras Negras, Coahuila

Tel: +52(878) 783-07-13

Fax: +52(878) 783-07-13

EMail: direccion@itpiedrasnegras.edu.mx

Website: http://www.itpiedrasnegras.edu.mx

Director: José Claudio Tamez Sáenz

Programmes

Engineering (Computer Engineering; Industrial Engineering)

Main Language(s) of Instruction: Spanish

Degrees and Diplomas: *Licenciatura*

Last Updated: 18/03/13

TECHNOLOGICAL INSTITUTE OF PINOTEPA

Instituto Tecnológico de Pinotepa

Prolongación 10♀ Norte, Av. Tecnológico s/n., Pinotepa Nacional, Oaxaca., 71600 Pinotepa Nacional, Oaxaca

Tel: +52(954) 543-52-87

Website: http://www.itp.edu.mx

Director: René Javier Than Márquez

Programmes

Accountancy (Accountancy); **Administration** (Administration; Business Administration); **Agronomy** (Agronomy); **Computer Science** (Computer Science); **Engineering** (Computer Engineering; Industrial Engineering)

History: Founded as Instituto Tecnológico Agropecuario No. 13.

Main Language(s) of Instruction: Spanish

Degrees and Diplomas: *Licenciatura*

Last Updated: 18/03/13

TECHNOLOGICAL INSTITUTE OF PUEBLA

Instituto Tecnológico de Puebla

Avenida Tecnológico, 420, Col. Maravillas, 72220 Puebla, Puebla

Tel: +52(222) 229-88-10

EMail: fmedina10@hotmail.com

Director: José Luis Vigueras

Programmes

Administration (Administration; Business Administration); **Computer Science** (Computer Science); **Engineering** (Computer Engineering; Electrical and Electronic Engineering; Industrial Engineering); **Information Technology** (Information Technology)

History: Founded 1972.

Main Language(s) of Instruction: Spanish

Degrees and Diplomas: *Licenciatura*; *Especialización*; *Maestría*

Last Updated: 18/03/13

TECHNOLOGICAL INSTITUTE OF QUERÉTARO

Instituto Tecnológico de Querétaro (ITQ)

Avenida Tecnológico y General Mariano Escobedo s/n, Col. Centro, 76000 Querétaro, Querétaro

Tel: +52(442) 227-44-00

Fax: +52(442) 16-99-31

EMail: dir@mail.itq.edu.mx

Website: http://www.itq.edu.mx

Director: José Antonio Durán Mejía

Programmes

Administration (Administration; Business Administration); **Architecture** (Architecture); **Engineering** (Electrical and Electronic Engineering; Industrial Engineering; Materials Engineering; Mechanical Engineering)

History: Founded 1967.

Main Language(s) of Instruction: Spanish

Degrees and Diplomas: *Licenciatura*; *Especialización*; *Maestría*

Last Updated: 18/03/13

TECHNOLOGICAL INSTITUTE OF REYNOSA

Instituto Tecnológico de Reynosa (ITR)

Avenida Tecnológico s/n, Col. Lomas, Real de Jarachina Sur, 88730 Ciudad Reynosa, Tamaulipas

Tel: +52(899) 929-00-19

EMail: tecreynosa@hotmail.com

Website: http://www.tecreynosa.edu.mx

Director: Luis Manuel Ferniza Pérez

Programmes

Administration (Administration); **Architecture** (Architecture); **Computer Science** (Computer Science); **Engineering** (Civil Engineering; Electronic Engineering; Industrial Engineering; Mechanical Engineering); **Information Technology** (Information Technology)

History: Founded 1988.

Main Language(s) of Instruction: Spanish

Degrees and Diplomas: *Licenciatura*; *Maestría*

Last Updated: 18/03/13

TECHNOLOGICAL INSTITUTE OF ROQUE

Instituto Tecnológico de Roque

Km. 8 Carretera Celaya-Juventino Rosas, Col. Magisterial, Roque, 38110 Celaya, Guanajuato

Tel: +52(461) 611-59-03 +52(461) 611-63-61

Fax: +52(461) 611-52-58 +52(461) 611-63-62

EMail: itacelaya@webmail.dgit.gob.mx

Website: http://www.itroque.edu.mx

Director: David Rafael Trigueros Cázares

Programmes

Agricultural Innovation (Agriculture); **Agronomy** (Agronomy); **Business Administration** (Business Administration); **Food Technology** (Food Technology); **Hydrology** (Hydraulic Engineering); **Information Technology** (Information Technology)

History: Founded 1926 as Central Agrícola de Guanajuato. Became Instituto Tecnológico Agropecuario No. 33 1994. Acquired present title 2005.

Main Language(s) of Instruction: Spanish

Degrees and Diplomas: *Licenciatura*; *Maestría*

Last Updated: 19/03/13

TECHNOLOGICAL INSTITUTE OF SALINA CRUZ

Instituto Tecnológico de Salina Cruz

Carretera a San Antonio Monterrey, Col. Granadillo, 70680 Salina Cruz, Oaxaca

Tel: +52(971) 716-28-37

EMail: contacto@itsalinacruz.edu.mx

Website: http://www.itsalinacruz.edu.mx

Director: Juan Cruz Nieto

Programmes

Aquaculture (Aquaculture); **Business Administration** (Business Administration); **Engineering** (Electrical Engineering; Mechanical Engineering); **Information Technology** (Information Technology)

History: Founded 1993 as Instituto Tecnológico del Mar en Boca de Rio, Extensión Salina Cruz.

Main Language(s) of Instruction: Spanish

Degrees and Diplomas: *Licenciatura*

Last Updated: 19/03/13

TECHNOLOGICAL INSTITUTE OF SALTILLO

Instituto Tecnológico de Saltillo (ITS)
Blvd. Venustiano Carranza 2400, Col. Tecnológico, 25280 Saltillo, Coahuila
Tel: +52(844) 438-95-00
Fax: +52(844) 438-95-00
EMail: direccion@its.mx
Website: http://www.its.mx

Director: Jesús Contreras García (2001-)
Tel: +52(844) 415-48-77 EMail: jcontreras@its.mx

Programmes

Administration (Administration); **Computer Science** (Computer Science); **Engineering** (Computer Engineering; Electrical and Electronic Engineering; Industrial Engineering; Materials Engineering; Mechanical Engineering)

History: Founded 1951. Acquired present status and title 1981.

Main Language(s) of Instruction: Spanish

Degrees and Diplomas: *Licenciatura*; *Maestría*; *Doctorado*
Last Updated: 19/03/13

TECHNOLOGICAL INSTITUTE OF SAN JUAN DEL RÍO

Instituto Tecnológico de San Juan del Río
Apartado postal 49, Avenida Tecnológico, 2, Esq. Avenida Central, Centro, 76800 San Juan del Río, Querétaro
Tel: +52(427) 272-41-78 +52(427) 272-85-46
Fax: +52(427) 272-42-38
EMail: dirección@itsanjuan.edu.mx
Website: http://www.itsanjuan.edu.mx/

Director: Rafael Rodríguez Gallegos

Programmes

Computer Science (Computer Science); **Engineering**

History: Founded 1988.

Main Language(s) of Instruction: Spanish

Degrees and Diplomas: *Licenciatura*
Last Updated: 25/03/08

TECHNOLOGICAL INSTITUTE OF SAN LUIS POTOSÍ

Instituto Tecnológico de San Luis Potosí (ITSLP)
Unidad Ponciano Arriaga, Av. Tecnológico, S/N Col UPA, 78437 Soledad de Graciano Sánchez, San Luis Potosí
Tel: +52(444) 818-21-36
Fax: +52(444) 818-31-31
EMail: tecdir@itslp.edu.mx
Website: http://www.itslp.edu.mx/

Director: Javier Eliseo Muñoz de la Torre

Programmes

Administration (Administration); **Computer Science** (Computer Science); **Engineering** (Electrical and Electronic Engineering; Industrial Engineering; Mechanical Engineering; Metallurgical Engineering)

History: Founded 1970.

Main Language(s) of Instruction: Spanish

Degrees and Diplomas: *Licenciatura*; *Maestría*
Last Updated: 19/03/13

TECHNOLOGICAL INSTITUTE OF SONORA

Instituto Tecnológico de Sonora (ITSON)
5 de Febrero, 818, Sur, Col. Centro, Cajeme, 85000 Ciudad Obregón, Sonora
Tel: +52(644) 410-09-00
Fax: +52(644) 417-07-83
EMail: rectoria@itson.mx
Website: http://www.itson.mx

Rector: Isidro Roberto Cruz Medina

Programmes

Administration (Accountancy; Administration; Business Administration); **Agriculture** (Agriculture); **Art Management** (Art Management); **Biotechnology** (Biotechnology); **Chemistry** (Chemistry); **Civil Engineering** (Civil Engineering); **Economics and Finance** (Economics; Finance); **Education** (Education; Physical Education; Preschool Education); **Electrical Engineering** (Electrical Engineering); **Environmental Studies** (Environmental Studies); **Food Technology** (Food Technology); **Graphic Design** (Graphic Design); **Industrial Engineering** (Industrial Engineering); **Mechanical and Electronic Engineering** (Electronic Engineering; Mechanical Engineering); **Psychology** (Psychology); **Software Engineering** (Software Engineering); **Sports** (Sports); **Veterinary Medicine and Zoology** (Veterinary Science; Zoology)

Further Information: Campuses in Navojoa and Guaymas

History: Founded 1955 as preparatory school, acquired present status and title 1973. A State institution financed by the federal government.

Governing Bodies: Consejo Directivo, including the Rector, the Vice-Rectors, the Secretary of the Rector, the Directors of Academic Divisions, and Representatives of the academic staff and student body

Academic Year: August to July (August-December; January-May; June-July)

Admission Requirements: Secondary school certificate (bachillerato) and entrance examination

Main Language(s) of Instruction: Spanish

Degrees and Diplomas: *Licenciatura*: Accountancy (Contador público); Chemistry (Químico); Engineering; *Licenciatura*: Administration; Education; Psychology, 8 sem; *Licenciatura*: Veterinary Medicine and Animal Husbandry (Médico veterinario zootecnista), 10 sem; *Especialización*: Teaching of English as a Foreign Language; *Maestría*: Administration; Natural Resources; Production Systems; Water Resources, a further 2 yrs; *Doctorado*: Biotechnology, 2 yrs following Maestría

Student Services: Academic counselling, Cultural centre, Employment services, Health services, Sports facilities

Special Facilities: Art Gallery. Theatre

Libraries: c. 85,640 vols

Publications: ITSON-DIEP, Research reports *(biannually)*; Revista de la Sociedad Académica *(biannually)*

Press or Publishing House: Instituto Tecnológico de Sonora Press
Last Updated: 19/03/13

TECHNOLOGICAL INSTITUTE OF TAPACHULA

Instituto Tecnológico de Tapachula
Km. 2 Carretera a Puerto Madero, 30700 Tapachula, Chiapas
Tel: +52(962) 625-48-73
EMail: najera_trejo@hotmail.com
Website: http://www.ittapachula.edu.mx

Director: Miguel Cid Del Prado Martínez

Programmes

Business Administration (Business Administration); **Computer Science** (Computer Science); **Engineering** (Civil Engineering; Computer Engineering; Electrical and Electronic Engineering; Industrial Engineering; Mechanical Engineering)

History: Founded 1983.

Main Language(s) of Instruction: Spanish

Degrees and Diplomas: *Licenciatura*
Last Updated: 19/03/13

TECHNOLOGICAL INSTITUTE OF TECOMATLÁN

Instituto Tecnológico de Tecomatlán (ITT)
Km. 19.5, Carretera Palomas-Tlapa, 74870 Tecomatlán, Puebla
Tel: +52(275) 441-20-42
EMail: cc_ittecomatlan@dgest.gob.mx; depittecomatlan@hotmail.com
Website: http://www.itapuebla.edu.mx

Director: Gustavo Andrés Ortiz y Rivera

Programmes
Agronomy (Agriculture; Agronomy); **Business Administration** (Business Administration); **Computer Science** (Computer Science)
History: Founded 1987.
Main Language(s) of Instruction: Spanish
Degrees and Diplomas: *Licenciatura*
Last Updated: 12/03/13

TECHNOLOGICAL INSTITUTE OF TEHUÁCAN

Instituto Tecnológico de Tehuacán
Libramiento Instituto Tecnológico s/n, Col. Santo Domingo, 75770 Tehuacán, Puebla
Tel: +52(238) 382-24-48
EMail: dir@ittehuacan.edu.mx
Website: http://www.ittehuacan.edu.mx

Director: Felipe Martínez Vargas EMail: ittehuacan@dgest.gob.mx

Programmes
Accountancy (Accountancy); **Administration** (Administration; Business Administration); **Engineering** (Bioengineering; Civil Engineering; Computer Engineering; Electronic Engineering; Industrial Engineering; Mechanical Engineering)
History: Founded 1970.
Main Language(s) of Instruction: Spanish
Degrees and Diplomas: *Licenciatura*; *Maestría*: Administration; Industrial Engineering
Last Updated: 19/03/13

TECHNOLOGICAL INSTITUTE OF TEPIC

Instituto Tecnológico de Tepic
Avenida Tecnológico, 2595, Col. Lagos del Country, 63175 Tepic, Nayarit
Tel: +52(311) 211-94-00
Fax: +52(311) 211-94-01
EMail: direccion@ittepic.edu.mx
Website: http://www.ittepic.edu.mx
Director: Albino Rodríguez Díaz

Programmes
Administration (Administration; Business Administration); **Architecture** (Architecture); **Engineering** (Biochemistry; Chemical Engineering; Civil Engineering; Computer Engineering; Electrical Engineering; Industrial Engineering; Mechanical Engineering); **Food Technology** (Food Technology); **Information Technology** (Information Technology)
History: Founded 1975.
Main Language(s) of Instruction: Spanish
Degrees and Diplomas: *Licenciatura*; *Maestría*; *Doctorado*: Food Technology
Last Updated: 19/03/13

TECHNOLOGICAL INSTITUTE OF THE COSTA GRANDE

Instituto Tecnológico de la Costa Grande
Manzana, 30, Lote 1, Col. El Limón, 40030 Zihuatanejo, Guerrero
Tel: +52(755) 544-48-51
EMail: itcosta@prodigy.net.mx

Director: Gelasio Francisco Luna Conzuelo

Programmes
Accountancy (Accountancy); **Business Administration** (Accountancy; Business Administration); **Computer Science** (Computer Science); **Electronic and Mechanical Engineering** (Electronic Engineering; Mechanical Engineering)
History: Founded 1988.
Main Language(s) of Instruction: Spanish
Degrees and Diplomas: *Licenciatura*
Last Updated: 13/03/13

TECHNOLOGICAL INSTITUTE OF THE ISTHMUS

Instituto Tecnológico del Istmo (ITI)
Km. 821 Carretera Panamericana, Juchitán de Zaragoza, 70000 Juchitán de Zaragoza, Oaxaca
Tel: +52(971) 711-10-42 +52(971) 711-25-59
Fax: +52(971) 711-25-55
EMail: direccion@correo.itistmo.edu.mx
Website: http://www.itistmo.edu.mx

Director: Jesús Ramos Rodríguez
EMail: director@correo.itjuchitan.edu.mx

Programmes
Accountancy (Accountancy); **Architecture** (Architecture); **Computer Science** (Computer Science); **Engineering** (Civil Engineering; Electrical and Electronic Engineering; Engineering; Industrial Engineering; Mechanical Engineering)
History: Founded 1969.
Main Language(s) of Instruction: Spanish
Degrees and Diplomas: *Licenciatura*
Last Updated: 19/03/13

TECHNOLOGICAL INSTITUTE OF THE MAYA AREA

Instituto Tecnológico de la Zona Maya
Km. 21.5 Carretera Chetumal-Escárcega, Ejido Juan Sarabia, Othón P. Blanco, 77000 Chetumal, Quintana Roo
Tel: +52(983) 124-67-54
EMail: itzonamaya@dgest.gob.mx
Website: http://www.itzonamaya.edu.mx

Director: Manuel de Jesús Soria Fregoso
EMail: msoria@itzonamaya.edu.mx

Programmes
Administration (Administration); **Agronomy** (Agriculture; Agronomy; Animal Husbandry); **Business Administration** (Business Administration); **Forestry** (Forest Management; Forestry)
History: Founded 1976 as Instituto Tecnológico Agropecuario No. 16. Acquired present status and title 2006.
Main Language(s) of Instruction: Spanish
Degrees and Diplomas: *Licenciatura*
Last Updated: 11/03/13

TECHNOLOGICAL INSTITUTE OF THE MORELIA VALLEY

Instituto Tecnológico del Valle de Morelia
Km. 6.5 Carretera Morelia-Salamanca, Cap. Francisco Jiménez, 89, 58100 Morelia, Michoacán
Tel: +52(443) 321-12-12
Fax: +52(443) 321-12-13
EMail: it_vallemorelia@dgest.gob.mx
Website: http://www.itvallemorelia.edu.mx

Director: Roberto Hernández Hernández

Programmes
Administration (Administration); **Agronomy** (Agriculture; Agronomy); **Environmental Engineering** (Environmental Engineering); **Forestry** (Forestry)
History: Founded 1975 as Instituto Tecnológico Agropecuario No 7 de la Huerta, became Instituto Tecnológico Agropecuario de Michoacán 2004 and acquired present title 2005.
Main Language(s) of Instruction: Spanish
Degrees and Diplomas: *Licenciatura*
Last Updated: 11/03/13

TECHNOLOGICAL INSTITUTE OF THE OLMECA REGION

Instituto Tecnológico de la Zona Olmeca

Prolongación de Zaragoza s/n, Km. 20 Carretera Villahermosa-Frontera, Ocuiltzapotlán, 86270 Villahermosa, Tabasco
Tel: +52(993) 321-06-08
EMail: itao28@hotmail.com
Website: http://www.itzonaolmeca.edu.mx

Director: José Javier Peralta Cosgaya

Programmes
Agronomy (Agriculture; Agronomy); **Community Development** (Development Studies); **Computer Science** (Computer Science); **Forestry** (Forest Management; Forestry)

History: Founded 1982 as Instituto Tecnológico Agropecuario No. 28, became Instituto Tecnológico Agropecuario de Tabasco in 2005 and acquired present title 2006.

Main Language(s) of Instruction: Spanish

Degrees and Diplomas: *Licenciatura*
Last Updated: 11/03/13

TECHNOLOGICAL INSTITUTE OF THE VALLEY OF OAXACA

Instituto Tecnológico del Valle de Oaxaca

Ex-Hacienda de Nazareno s/n, 71230 Xoxocotlán, Oaxaca
Tel: +52(951) 517-04-44
EMail: itvalleoaxaca@gmail.com
Website: http://www.itvalleoaxaca.edu.mx

Directora: Rocío Castro González

Programmes
Agronomy (Agriculture; Agronomy); **Biology** (Biology); **Computer Science** (Computer Science); **Forestry** (Forest Management; Forestry); **Information Technology** (Information Technology)

History: Founded 1981 as Instituto Tecnológico Agropecuario No 23 de Santa Cruz Xoxocotlán.

Main Language(s) of Instruction: Spanish

Degrees and Diplomas: *Licenciatura*; *Maestría*
Last Updated: 11/03/13

TECHNOLOGICAL INSTITUTE OF THE VALLEY OF THE GUADIANA (VILLA MONTEMORELOS)

Instituto Tecnológico de Valle del Guadiana (Villa Montemorelos)

Km. 22 Carretera Durango-México, Ejido Villa Montemorelos, 34371 Montemorelos, Durango
Tel: +52(618) 817-47-48
Fax: +52(618) 817-47-87
EMail: dir_itvalleguadiana@dgest.gob.mx
Website: http://www.itvalledelguadiana.edu.mx

Director: Leoncio Ochoa Cervantes

Programmes
Accountancy (Accountancy); **Agriculture** (Agriculture; Animal Husbandry); **Agronomy** (Agronomy); **Biology** (Biology); **Computer Science** (Computer Science)

History: Founded 1972 as Instituto Tecnológico Agropecuario N° 1 de Durango. Acquired present status and title 2005.

Main Language(s) of Instruction: Spanish

Degrees and Diplomas: *Licenciatura*
Last Updated: 08/03/13

TECHNOLOGICAL INSTITUTE OF THE VALLEY OF YAQUI

Instituto Tecnológico del Valle de Yaqui

KM 25 Carretera a San Ignacio Río Muerto, 85201 Bácum, Sonora
Tel: +52(643) 435-71-00
Fax: +52(643) 435-71-01
EMail: ci@itvalledelyaqui.edu.mx
Website: http://www.itvalledelyaqui.edu.mx

Director: Rafael García Martínez
EMail: rgarciam@itvalledelyaqui.edu.mx

Programmes
Accountancy (Accountancy); **Administration** (Administration); **Agriculture** (Agriculture); **Biology** (Biology); **Business Administration** (Business Administration); **Computer Science** (Computer Science); **Food Industry** (Food Technology)

History: Founded 1977 as Instituto Tecnológico Agropecuario No. 21 de Ciudad Obregón.

Main Language(s) of Instruction: Spanish

Degrees and Diplomas: *Licenciatura*; *Especialización*
Last Updated: 08/03/13

TECHNOLOGICAL INSTITUTE OF TIJUANA

Instituto Tecnológico de Tijuana

Apartado postal 1166, Calzada del Tecnológico, s/n, Fracc. Tomás Aquino, 22379 Tijuana, Baja California
Tel: +52(664) 682-14-39 +52(664) 682-79-69
Fax: +52(664) 682-16-24
EMail: direccion@tectijuana.mx
Website: http://www.tectijuana.mx

Director: José Guerrero Guerrero

Programmes
Administration and Accountancy (Administration; Business Administration); **Architecture** (Architecture); **Bioengineering** (Biochemistry; Bioengineering); **Civil Engineering** (Civil Engineering); **Computer Engineering** (Computer Engineering); **Computer Science** (Computer Science); **Electronic Engineering** (Electronic Engineering); **Industrial Engineering** (Industrial Engineering)

History: Founded 1971.

Academic Year: August to June (August-December; January-June)

Admission Requirements: Secondary school certificate (bachillerato) and entrance examination

Main Language(s) of Instruction: Spanish

Degrees and Diplomas: *Licenciatura*: 9-12 sem; *Maestría*; *Doctorado*

Libraries: c. 20,550 vols

Publications: Tecamatl *(quarterly)*
Last Updated: 19/03/13

TECHNOLOGICAL INSTITUTE OF TIZIMIN

Instituto Tecnológico de Tizimín

Km. 3.5 Carretera Tizimín-Yucatán Final Aeropuerto Cupul, 97700 Tizimín, Yucatán
Tel: +52(986) 863-20-23 +52(986) 863-42-79
Website: http://www.ittizimin.edu.mx

Director: Carlos Durán Pérez

Programmes
Agronomy (Agronomy); **Biology** (Biology); **Business Administration** (Business Administration); **Computer Science** (Computer Science)

History: Founded 1976 as Instituto Tecnológico Agropecuario N° 19.

Main Language(s) of Instruction: Spanish

Degrees and Diplomas: *Licenciatura*
Last Updated: 11/03/13

TECHNOLOGICAL INSTITUTE OF TLAJOMULCO

Instituto Tecnológico de Tlajomulco

Km. 10 Carretera Tlajomulco–San Miguel Cuyutlán, 45640 Tlajomulco de Zúñiga, Jalisco
Tel: +52(379) 772-44-27
EMail: ittj@ittlajomulco.edu.mx
Website: http://www.ittlajomulco.edu.mx

Director: Alberto José Alarcón Menchaca

Programmes
Agro-biotechnology (Agriculture; Biotechnology); **Agronomy** (Agriculture; Agronomy); **Computer Science** (Computer Science); **Environmental Engineering** (Environmental Engineering); **Food Technology** (Food Technology)

History: Founded 1982 as Instituto Tecnológico Agropecuario No. 26.

Main Language(s) of Instruction: Spanish

Degrees and Diplomas: *Licenciatura*; *Maestría*; *Doctorado*: Agro-biotechnology

Libraries: Yes

Last Updated: 11/03/13

TECHNOLOGICAL INSTITUTE OF TLALNEPANTLA

Instituto Tecnológico de Tlalnepantla (ITTLA)
Avenida Instituto Tecnológico s/n, Col. La Comunidad, 54070 Tlalnepantla, Estado de México
Tel: +52(55) 53-90-02-09
EMail: ebernalittla@hotmail.com
Website: http://www.ittla.edu.mx

Director: Oscar Castellanos Hernandez

Programmes
Administration (Administration; Business Administration); **Computer Science** (Computer Science); **Engineering** (Electrical and Electronic Engineering; Industrial Engineering; Mechanical Engineering); **Information Technology** (Information Technology)

History: Founded 1971.

Main Language(s) of Instruction: Spanish

Degrees and Diplomas: *Licenciatura*; *Maestría*

Last Updated: 19/03/13

TECHNOLOGICAL INSTITUTE OF TLAXIACO

Instituto Tecnológico de Tlaxiaco
Km. 2.5 Carretera Tlaxiaco-Putla, Llano Yosovee, 69800 Tlaxiaco, Oaxaca
Tel: +52(953) 532-04-05 +52(953) 532-00-54
EMail: direccion@ittlaxiaco.edu.mx
Website: http://www.ittlaxiaco.edu.mx

Director: Pedro Ancheyta Bringas

Programmes
Administration (Administration; Business Administration); **Engineering** (Computer Engineering; Industrial Engineering)

History: Founded 1991.

Main Language(s) of Instruction: Spanish

Degrees and Diplomas: *Licenciatura*

Last Updated: 19/03/13

TECHNOLOGICAL INSTITUTE OF TOLUCA

Instituto Tecnológico de Toluca (ITTO)
Avenida Instituto Tecnológico s/n, Ex-Rancho La Virgen, 52140 Metepec, Estado de México
Tel: +52(722) 208-72-00
Fax: +52(722) 208-72-01
EMail: direccion@ittoluca.edu.mx
Website: http://www.ittoluca.edu.mx

Directora: Gloria Irene Carmona

Programmes
Business Administration (Business Administration); **Chemical Engineering** (Chemical Engineering); **Computer Systems** (Computer Science); **Electro-mechanical Engineering** (Electronic Engineering; Mechanical Engineering); **Environmental Studies** (Environmental Studies); **Industrial Engineering** (Industrial Engineering)

History: Founded 1972.

Admission Requirements: Certificado de Bachillerato

Main Language(s) of Instruction: Spanish

Degrees and Diplomas: *Licenciatura*: 4-6 yrs; *Maestría*: Environmental Studies; *Doctorado*: Environmental Studies

Student Services: Employment services, Health services, Language programs, Social counselling, Sports facilities

Libraries: Yes

Last Updated: 19/03/13

TECHNOLOGICAL INSTITUTE OF TORREON

Instituto Tecnológico de Torreón
Km. 7.5 Carretera Torreón-San Pedro, Ejido Ana, 27170 Torreón, Coahuila
Tel: +52(871) 750-71-98
EMail: dir.ittorreon@gmail.com
Website: http://www.ittorreon.edu.mx

Director: Nathanael Flores González

Programmes
Administration (Administration); **Agronomy** (Agronomy); **Business Administration** (Business Administration); **Computer Science** (Computer Science); **Food Industry** (Food Technology); **Irrigation** (Irrigation); **Soil Sciences** (Soil Science)

History: Founded 1976 as Instituto Tecnológico Agropecuario No. 10. Acquired present status and title 2005.

Main Language(s) of Instruction: Spanish

Degrees and Diplomas: *Licenciatura*; *Maestría*

Last Updated: 08/03/13

TECHNOLOGICAL INSTITUTE OF TUXTLA GUTIERREZ

Instituto Tecnológico de Tuxtla Gutiérrez (ITTG)
Km. 1080 Carretera Panamericana, 29050 Tuxtla Gutiérrez, Chiapas
Tel: +52(961) 615-04-61
Fax: +52(961) 615-16-87
EMail: director@ittg.edu.mx
Website: http://www.ittuxtlagutierrez.edu.mx

Director: José Luis Méndez Navarro

Programmes
Business Administration (Business Administration); **Engineering** (Biochemistry; Computer Engineering; Electrical Engineering; Electronic Engineering; Industrial Engineering; Mechanical Engineering)

History: Founded 1972.

Main Language(s) of Instruction: Spanish

Degrees and Diplomas: *Licenciatura*; *Maestría*

Last Updated: 19/03/13

TECHNOLOGICAL INSTITUTE OF ÚRSULO GALVÁN

Instituto Tecnológico de Úrsulo Galván
Km. 4.5 Carretera Federal Cardel-Chachalacas, 91680 Úrsulo Galván, Veracruz
Tel: +52(296) 962-05-33
Fax: +52(296) 961-04-30
Website: http://www.itursulogalvan.edu.mx

Director: Manuel de Jesús Soria Fregoso

Programmes
Agriculture (Agriculture; Animal Husbandry)

Degrees and Diplomas: *Licenciatura*

Last Updated: 19/03/13

TECHNOLOGICAL INSTITUTE OF VERACRUZ

Instituto Tecnológico de Veracruz (ITV)
Calzada Miguel Ángel de Quevedo, 2779, Col. Formando Hogar, 91860 Veracruz, Veracruz
Tel: +52(229) 934-15-00
EMail: dir_itv@itver.edu.mx
Website: http://www.itver.edu.mx

Directora: Maria Elena Rojas Rauda

Programmes
Administration (Administration); **Engineering** (Biochemistry; Chemical Engineering; Computer Engineering; Electrical and Electronic Engineering; Industrial Engineering; Mechanical Engineering)

History: Founded 1973.

Main Language(s) of Instruction: Spanish

Degrees and Diplomas: *Licenciatura*; *Maestría*; *Doctorado*

Last Updated: 19/03/13

TECHNOLOGICAL INSTITUTE OF VILLAHERMOSA

Instituto Tecnológico de Villahermosa (ITVH)

Carretera a Frontera Km. 3.5 Cd. Industrial, 86010 Villahermosa, Tabasco

Tel: +52(993) 353-02-59

EMail: direccion@itvillahermosa.edu.mx

Website: http://www.itvillahermosa.edu.mx

Director: Humberto José Cervera Brito

Programmes

Administration (Administration); **Computer Science** (Computer Science); **Engineering** (Biochemistry; Chemical Engineering; Civil Engineering; Environmental Engineering; Industrial Engineering); **Information Technology** (Information Technology)

History: Founded 1974.

Main Language(s) of Instruction: Spanish

Degrees and Diplomas: *Licenciatura*; *Maestría*

Last Updated: 19/03/13

TECHNOLOGICAL INSTITUTE OF ZACATECAS

Instituto Tecnológico de Zacatecas (ITZ)

Carretera Panamericana Entronque Guadalajara s/n, 'La Escondida', 98000 Zacatecas, Zacatecas

Tel: +52(492) 924-53-66 +52(492) 924-76-78

EMail: direcitz@mapaches.itz.edu.mx

Website: http://www.itz.edu.mx

Director: Rito Martín Herrera Flores

Programmes

Administration (Administration; Business Administration); **Architecture** (Architecture); **Computer Science** (Computer Science); **Engineering** (Electronic Engineering; Industrial Engineering; Materials Engineering; Mechanical Engineering)

History: Founded 1976.

Main Language(s) of Instruction: Spanish

Degrees and Diplomas: *Licenciatura*; *Maestría*: Administration; Architecture

Last Updated: 19/03/13

TECHNOLOGICAL INSTITUTE OF ZACATEPEC

Instituto Tecnológico de Zacatepec

Apartado Postal 45, Calzada Tecnológico, 27, 62780 Zacatepec, Morelos

Tel: +52(734) 343-07-23 +52(734) 343-21-10

Fax: +52(734) 343-41-41

Website: http://www.itzacatepec.edu.mx

Director: Roberto Ortiz Delgadillo

Programmes

Administration (Administration; Business Administration); **Engineering** (Biochemistry; Chemical Engineering; Civil Engineering; Computer Education; Electronic Engineering; Industrial Engineering; Materials Engineering; Mechanical Engineering; Polymer and Plastics Technology); **Information Technology** (Information Technology)

History: Founded 1961.

Main Language(s) of Instruction: Spanish

Degrees and Diplomas: *Licenciatura*; *Maestría*; *Doctorado*: Materials Engineering

Last Updated: 19/03/13

TECHNOLOGICAL INSTITUTE OF ZITÁCUARO

Instituto Tecnológico de Zitácuaro

Ex-Hacienda de Manzanillos s/n, Carretera Toluca-Morelia, 61500 Zitácuaro, Michoacán

Tel: +52(715) 153-44-45

Fax: +52(715) 153-39-00

EMail: dir_itzitacuaro@dgest.gob.mx.

Website: http://www.itzitacuaro.edu.mx

Director: Juan Manuel Padilla Hernández

Programmes

Accountancy (Accountancy); **Administration** (Administration; Business Administration); **Computer Science** (Computer Science); **Engineering** (Civil Engineering; Electronic Engineering; Industrial Engineering; Mechanical Engineering)

History: Founded 1991.

Main Language(s) of Instruction: Spanish

Degrees and Diplomas: *Licenciatura*

Last Updated: 19/03/13

TECHNOLOGICAL STOCKBREEDING INSTITUTE NO. 3 OF TUXTEPEC

Instituto Tecnológico de Tuxtepec

Av. Dr. Víctor Bravo Ahuja s/n, Col. 5 de Mayo, 68350 Tuxtepec, Oaxaca

Tel: +52(287) 875-10-44

EMail: direccion@ittux.edu.mx

Website: http://www.ittux.edu.mx

Director: Miguel Ángel Urrutia Salinas

Programmes

Accountancy (Accountancy); **Biochemistry** (Biochemistry); **Business Administration** (Business Administration); **Civil Engineering** (Civil Engineering); **Computer Science** (Computer Engineering; Computer Science); **Electrical and Mechanical Engineering** (Electrical Engineering; Mechanical Engineering); **Electronic Engineering** (Electronic Engineering)

History: Founded 1975 as Instituto Tecnológico Agropecuario No 3.

Main Language(s) of Instruction: Spanish

Degrees and Diplomas: *Licenciatura*

Last Updated: 11/03/13

TECHNOLOGICAL UNIVERSITY OF AGUASCALIENTES

Universidad Tecnológica de Aguascalientes

Blvd. Juan Pablo II, 1302, Ex-Hacienda La Cantera, 20206 Aguascalientes, Aguascalientes

Tel: +52(449) 910-50-00

EMail: raviles@utags.edu.mx

Website: http://www.utags.edu.mx

Rector: Jorge Armando Llamas Esparza

EMail: jllamas@utags.edu.mx

Programmes

Administration (Administration); **Civil Protection and Emergencies** (Safety Engineering); **Finance and Taxes** (Finance; Taxation); **Industrial Maintenance** (Industrial Maintenance); **Information Technology** (Information Technology); **Marketing** (Marketing); **Mechatronics** (Electronic Engineering; Mechanical Engineering)

History: Founded 1991.

Governing Bodies: Consejo Directivo; Consejo Electoral

Academic Year: September to August

Admission Requirements: Bachillerato and entrance examination

Main Language(s) of Instruction: Spanish

Degrees and Diplomas: *Licenciatura*

Student Services: Employment services, Foreign Studies Centre

Libraries: Biblioteca Central

Last Updated: 24/10/12

TECHNOLOGICAL UNIVERSITY OF CAMPECHE

Universidad Tecnológica de Campeche

Carretera Federal, 180, San Antonio Cárdenas, 24381 Campeche, Campeche

Tel: +52(981) 2-31-54

EMail: gordonez@utcam.edu.mx

Website: http://www.utcam.edu.mx

Rector: Manuel Jesús Cordero Rivera

EMail: mcordero@utcam.edu.mx

Programmes

Accountancy (Accountancy; Finance); **Industrial Maintenance** (Industrial Maintenance); **Mechanical and Electronic Engineering** (Electronic Engineering; Mechanical Engineering); **Metallurgical and Mechanical Engineering** (Mechanical Engineering; Metallurgical Engineering); **Renewable Energy** (Energy Engineering)

History: Founded 1997.

Main Language(s) of Instruction: Spanish

Degrees and Diplomas: *Licenciatura*. Técnico Superior Universitario

Libraries: Yes

Last Updated: 01/02/13

TECHNOLOGICAL UNIVERSITY OF CANCUN

Universidad Tecnológica de Cancún

Carretera Cancún-Aeropuerto, Km. 11.5, S.M. 299, Mz. 5, Lt, 77500 Cancún, Quintana Roo
Tel: +52(998) 881-19-00
Fax: +52(998) 886-20-75
EMail: jgonzalez@utcancun.edu.mx
Website: http://www.utcancun.edu.mx/

Rectora: Leslie Angelina Hendricks Rubio Ordaz Coral
EMail: lhendricks@utcancun.edu.mx

Programmes

Accountancy (Accountancy); **Administration** (Administration); **Business Development and Innovation** (Administration; Advertising and Publicity; Business Administration; Finance; Marketing); **Finance** (Finance; Fiscal Law); **Gastronomy** (Cooking and Catering); **Industrial Maintenance** (Industrial Maintenance); **Information Technology** (Information Technology); **Tourism Management** (Hotel Management; Tourism)

History: Founded 1998.

Main Language(s) of Instruction: Spanish

Degrees and Diplomas: *Licenciatura*. Técnico Superior Universitario

Libraries: Yes

Last Updated: 09/01/13

TECHNOLOGICAL UNIVERSITY OF CHIHUAHUA

Universidad Tecnológica de Chihuahua

Avenida Montes Americanos, 9501, Ejido La Haciendita, 31203 Chihuahua, Chihuahua
Tel: +52(614) 432-20-00
EMail: rectoria@utch.edu.mx
Website: http://www.utch.edu.mx

Rector: Pablo Espinoza Flores

Programmes

Business Administration (Business Administration); **Engineering** (Electronic Engineering; Energy Engineering; Engineering; Industrial Maintenance; Information Technology; Mechanical Engineering)

History: Founded 2000.

Main Language(s) of Instruction: Spanish

Degrees and Diplomas: *Licenciatura*. Técnico Superior Universitario

Last Updated: 09/01/13

TECHNOLOGICAL UNIVERSITY OF HERMOSILLO

Universidad Tecnológica de Hermosillo

Blvd. de los Seris Final Sur s/n, Col. Parque Industrial Hermosillo, 83290 Hermosillo, Sonora
Tel: +52(662) 251-11-00 al 04
EMail: administracion@uthermosillo.edu.mx
Website: http://www.uthermosillo.edu.mx

Rector: Miguel Ángel Salazar Candia
EMail: rectoria@uthermosillo.edu.mx

Secretario Académico: Antonio Quintal Berny
EMail: vinculacion@uthermosillo.edu.mx

Programmes

Business Administration (Business Administration); **Gastronomy** (Cooking and Catering); **Industrial Maintenance** (Industrial Maintenance); **Information Technology** (Information Technology); **Mechanics** (Mechanics)

Degrees and Diplomas: *Licenciatura*

Last Updated: 05/04/13

TECHNOLOGICAL UNIVERSITY OF IZÚCAR DE MATAMOROS

Universidad Tecnológica de Izúcar de Matamoros

Prolongación Reforma, 168, Barrio de Santiago Muhuacán, 74420 Izúcar de Matamoros, Puebla
Fax: +52(243) 436-26-13

Rector: José Antonio Velazquez Trejo

Programmes

Biotechnology (Biotechnology); **Business Development and Innovation** (Business Administration); **Finance** (Accountancy; Finance); **Food Processing** (Food Technology); **Information Technology** (Information Technology)

Further Information: Also branch in Tulcingo de Valle

History: Founded 1997.

Main Language(s) of Instruction: Spanish

Degrees and Diplomas: *Licenciatura*

Last Updated: 09/01/13

TECHNOLOGICAL UNIVERSITY OF LEON

Universidad Tecnológica de León

Blvd. Universidad Tecnológica, 225, Col. San Carlos, 37670 León, Guanajuato
Tel: +52(477) 710-00-20
Fax: +52(477) 772-53-40
EMail: rector@utleon.edu.mx
Website: http://www.utleon.edu.mx

Rector: Jesús María Contreras Esparza
EMail: jcontreras@utleon.edu.mx

Programmes

Business (Administration; Advertising and Publicity; Finance; Marketing; Sales Techniques); **Environmental Technology** (Environmental Engineering; Environmental Studies); **Industrial Maintenance** (Industrial Maintenance); **Information Technology** (Information Technology); **Mechanical and Electronic Engineering** (Electronic Engineering; Mechanical Engineering); **Organizational Planning** (Management); **Production Systems** (Production Engineering); **Tourism Development** (Hotel Management; Tourism)

History: Founded 1995.

Main Language(s) of Instruction: Spanish

Degrees and Diplomas: *Licenciatura*. Técnico Superior Universitario

Libraries: Yes

Last Updated: 10/01/13

TECHNOLOGICAL UNIVERSITY OF MATAMOROS

Universidad Tecnológica de Matamoros

Carr. a Reynosa Km. 8.5, Ej. Guadalupe, 87569 Matamoros, Tamaulipas
Tel: +52(868) 810-76-12
Website: http://www.utmatamoros.edu.mx

Rector: José Antonio Tovar Lara

Programmes

Industrial Maintenance (Industrial Maintenance); **Mechanical and Electronic Engineering** (Electronic Engineering; Mechanical Engineering); **Production Systems** (Production Engineering)

History: Founded 2001.

Main Language(s) of Instruction: Spanish

Degrees and Diplomas: *Licenciatura*

Libraries: Yes

Last Updated: 10/01/13

TECHNOLOGICAL UNIVERSITY OF MORELIA

Universidad Tecnológica de Morelia
Vicepresidente Pino Suárez 750, Ciudad Industrial, 58200 Morelia, Michoacán
Tel: +52(443) 317-72-77
Fax: +52(443) 317-62-76
EMail: contacto@utmorelia.edu.mx
Website: www.utmorelia.edu.mxhttp: //www.utmorelia.edu.mx

Rector: Alfredo Morales Morales

Programmes

Biotechnology (Biotechnology; Technology); **Gastronomy** (Cooking and Catering); **Industrial Design** (Industrial Design; Industrial Maintenance); **Information Technology** (Information Technology); **Renewable Energy**

History: Founded 2000.

Main Language(s) of Instruction: Spanish

Degrees and Diplomas: *Licenciatura*
Last Updated: 10/01/13

TECHNOLOGICAL UNIVERSITY OF NAYARIT

Universidad Tecnológica de Nayarit
Carretera Federal 200 Km. 9, Fracc. Ciudad del Valle, 63780 Xalisco, Nayarit
Tel: +52(311) 211-98-00
EMail: rectoria@utnay.edu.mx
Website: http://www.utnay.edu.mx/

Rector: Héctor Béjar Fonseca (2010-)

Programmes

Business Administration (Business Administration); **Engineering** (Electronic Engineering; Engineering; Food Technology; Industrial Maintenance; Information Technology; Mechanical Engineering); **Tourism** (Technology; Tourism)

History: Founded 2001.

Main Language(s) of Instruction: Spanish

Degrees and Diplomas: *Licenciatura*
Last Updated: 25/10/12

TECHNOLOGICAL UNIVERSITY OF NEZAHUALCÓYOTL

Universidad Tecnológica de Nezahualcóyotl
Circuito Universidad Tecnológica s/n, Col. Benito Juárez, 57000 Nezahualcóyotl, Estado de México
Tel: +52(55) 57-16-97-00
EMail: rector@utn.edu.mx
Website: http://www.utn.edu.mx

Rector: Noe Molina Rusiles

Divisions

Business Administration (Business Administration; Commercial Law; Economics; Sales Techniques); **Environment Technology** (Environmental Engineering; Environmental Studies); **Information Technology** (Information Technology); **Production Processing** (Production Engineering)

History: Founded 1991.

Main Language(s) of Instruction: Spanish

Degrees and Diplomas: *Licenciatura*
Last Updated: 10/01/13

TECHNOLOGICAL UNIVERSITY OF NOGALES

Universidad Tecnológica de Nogales
Avenida Universidad # 271, Col. Universitaria, 84000 Nogales, Sonora
Tel: +52(631) 315-90-01 +52(631) 315-90-02
Fax: +52(631) 315-90-32
EMail: rectoria@utnogales.edu.mx
Website: http://www.utnogales.edu.mx

Rector: Jesús Daniel Tavarez Valenzuela
EMail: jvalenzuelapaz@utnogales.edu.mx

Programmes

Industrial Maintenance (Industrial Maintenance); **Information Technology** (Information Technology); **Mechatronics** (Electronic Engineering; Mechanical Engineering)

History: Founded 1998.

Main Language(s) of Instruction: Spanish

Degrees and Diplomas: *Licenciatura.* Técnico Superior Universitario
Last Updated: 05/04/13

TECHNOLOGICAL UNIVERSITY OF NORTH TAMAULIPAS

Universidad Tecnológica de Tamaulipas Norte
Av. Universidad Tecnológica #1555 Col. La Escondida, 87300 Reynosa, Tamaulipas
Tel: +52(899) 920-12-16
EMail: uttn@prodigy.net.mx
Website: http://www.uttn.edu.mx

Rector: Sergio Humberto Zertuche Zuani

Programmes

Administration (Business Administration; Human Resources); **Industrial Maintenance** (Industrial Maintenance); **Industrial Processes** (Industrial Engineering; Polymer and Plastics Technology); **Information Technology** (Information Technology; Telecommunications Engineering); **Mechanical and Electronic Engineering** (Electronic Engineering; Engineering; Mechanical Engineering)

History: Founded 2000.

Main Language(s) of Instruction: Spanish

Degrees and Diplomas: *Licenciatura.* Tecnologico Superior Universitario
Last Updated: 21/01/13

TECHNOLOGICAL UNIVERSITY OF NUEVO LAREDO

Universidad Tecnológica de Nuevo Laredo
Héroe de Nacataz, 2447, Altos, despacho 4, Centro, Nuevo Laredo, Tamaulipas
Tel: +52(867) 713-28-68 +52(867) 713-69-87
EMail: rectoria@utnuevolaredo.edu.mx
Website: http://www.utnuevolaredo.edu.mx

Rector: Juan Leonardo Sánchez Cuellar

Programmes

Business Development and Innovation (Administration; Business Administration; Commercial Law; Economics; Finance; Sales Techniques); **Industrial Maintenance** (Industrial Maintenance); **International Logistics** (Business and Commerce; Finance; Labour and Industrial Relations; Marketing; Statistics; Transport Management); **Mechanical and Electronic Engineering** (Automation and Control Engineering; Computer Graphics; Electronic Engineering; Mechanical Engineering)

History: Founded 2004.

Main Language(s) of Instruction: Spanish

Degrees and Diplomas: *Licenciatura.* Técnico Superior Universitario
Last Updated: 10/01/13

TECHNOLOGICAL UNIVERSITY OF PUEBLA

Universidad Tecnológica de Puebla (UTP)
Antiguo Camino a la Resurrección, 1002-A, Zona Industrial, 72300 Puebla, Puebla
Tel: +52 (222) 309-88-87
EMail: info@utpuebla.edu.mx
Website: http://www.utpuebla.edu.mx
Rector: Jorge Alfredo Guillén Muñoz
EMail: rector@utpuebla.edu.mx

Director de Administración y Finanzas: Tomás E. Silva Limón
EMail: finanzas@utpuebla.edu.mx

Programmes

Automation Technology (Automation and Control Engineering); **Business Development and Innovation** (Business Administration; Commercial Law; Finance; Sales Techniques); **Environmental Engineering** (Environmental Engineering); **Food Processing** (Food Technology); **Industrial Engineering** (Industrial Engineering); **Industrial Maintenance** (Industrial Maintenance); **Information Technology** (Information Technology); **Mechanical and Electronic Engineering** (Electronic Engineering; Mechanical Engineering); **Renewable Energy** (Energy Engineering)

History: Founded 1994.

Main Language(s) of Instruction: Spanish

Degrees and Diplomas: *Licenciatura.* Técnico Superior Universitario

Last Updated: 10/01/13

TECHNOLOGICAL UNIVERSITY OF QUERETARO

Universidad Tecnológica de Querétaro
Avenida Pie de la Cuesta s/n, Col. San Pedrito Peñuelas, Centro, 76148 Querétaro, Querétaro
Tel: +52(442) 209-61-00 +52(442) 209-61-60
Fax: +52(442) 209-61-64
EMail: sacuna@uteq.edu.mx
Website: http://www.uteq.edu.mx

Rector: Salvador Lecona Uribe
EMail: salvador.lecona@uteq.edu.mx

Secretario Académico: Salvador Francisco Acuña Guzmán

Divisions

Automation and Information (Automation and Control Engineering); **Economics and Administration** (Business Administration; Business and Commerce); **Environmental Studies** (Environmental Engineering); **Industrial Maintenance** (Industrial Engineering; Industrial Maintenance)

History: Founded 1994.

Main Language(s) of Instruction: Spanish

Degrees and Diplomas: *Licenciatura.* Técnico Superior Universitario

Last Updated: 10/01/13

TECHNOLOGICAL UNIVERSITY OF SAN JUAN DEL RÍO

Universidad Tecnológica de San Juan del Río
Avenida La Palma, 125, Col. Vista Hermosa, 76800 San Juan del Río, Querétaro
Tel: +52(427) 129-20-00
EMail: rectoria@utsjr.edu.mx
Website: http://www.utsjr.edu.mx

Rector: Víctor Manuel Sánchez Cabrera
EMail: asarachol@utsjr.edu.mx

Programmes

Business; **Chemistry** (Chemistry); **Industrial Maintenance** (Industrial Maintenance); **Information Technology** (Information Technology); **Mechanical Engineering** (Electronic Engineering; Mechanical Engineering); **Production Processing** (Production Engineering); **Renewable Energy** (Energy Engineering)

History: Founded 1998.

Main Language(s) of Instruction: Spanish

Degrees and Diplomas: *Licenciatura.* Técnico Superior Universitario

Last Updated: 10/01/13

TECHNOLOGICAL UNIVERSITY OF SAN LUIS POTOSI

Universidad Tecnológica de San Luis Potosí
Prolongación Avenida de las Américas, 100, Rancho Nuevo, Soledad de Graciano Sánchez, 78430 San Luis Potosí, San Luis Potosí
Tel: +52(444) 431-10-00
Fax: +52(444) 434-81-12
EMail: vinculacion@utslp.edu.mx
Website: http://www.utslp.edu.mx

Rector: Carlos Alfredo Shiguetomi Villegas

Programmes

Automation (Automation and Control Engineering); **Business Administration** (Business Administration; Finance; Sales Techniques); **Industrial Maintenance** (Industrial Maintenance); **Mechanics** (Mechanical Engineering); **Production Processing** (Production Engineering)

History: Founded 1997.

Main Language(s) of Instruction: Spanish

Degrees and Diplomas: *Licenciatura.* Técnico Superior Universitario

Libraries: Yes

Last Updated: 21/01/13

TECHNOLOGICAL UNIVERSITY OF SANTA CATARINA

Universidad Tecnológica de Santa Catarina
Km. 61.5 Carretera Saltillo-Monterrey, 66359 Santa Catarina, Nuevo León
Tel: +52(81) 83-16-99-22 +52(83) 83-08-44-46
Fax: +52(81) 83-16-98-92
EMail: utsc@utsc.edu.mx
Website: http://www.utsc.edu.mx

Rector: José Cárdenas Cavazos

Programmes

Automation (Automation and Control Engineering); **Business Administration** (Business Administration); **Industrial Maintenance** (Industrial Maintenance); **Information Technology** (Information Technology); **Project Management** (Management)

History: Founded 1998.

Main Language(s) of Instruction: Spanish

Degrees and Diplomas: *Licenciatura.* Técnico Superior Universitario

Last Updated: 05/04/13

TECHNOLOGICAL UNIVERSITY OF SOUTHERN SONORA

Universidad Tecnológica del Sur de Sonora
Km. 14 Avenida Dr. Norman E. Borlaug, 85095 Ciudad Obregon, Sonora
Tel: +52(644) 414-86-87
EMail: rectoria@uts.edu.mx
Website: http://www.uts.edu.mx/

Rector: Hermenegildo Lagarda Leyva

Programmes

Automation (Automation and Control Engineering; Electrical Engineering); **Business Administration** (Business Administration; Commercial Law; Finance; Sales Techniques); **Information Technology** (Information Technology); **Production Engineering** (Production Engineering); **Software Engineering** (Software Engineering)

History: Founded 2003.

Main Language(s) of Instruction: Spanish

Degrees and Diplomas: *Licenciatura.* Técnico Superior Universitario

Libraries: Yes

Last Updated: 28/01/13

TECHNOLOGICAL UNIVERSITY OF TABASCO

Universidad Tecnológica de Tabasco
Km. 14.6 Carretera Villahermosa-Teapa, Fracc. Parrilla II, Parrilla Centro, 86280 Villahermosa, Tabasco
Tel: +52(993) 358-22-22
EMail: jfuentes@uttab.edu.mx
Website: http://www.uttab.edu.mx

Rectora: Saraí Aguilar Barojas

Programmes
Food Processing (Food Technology); **Environmental Technology** (Environmental Engineering; Environmental Studies); **Industrial Processes** (Industrial Engineering); **Information Technology** (Information Technology); **Mechanics** (Mechanical Engineering); **Project Management** (Business Administration; Management); **Tourism** (Tourism)

History: Founded 1996.

Main Language(s) of Instruction: Spanish

Degrees and Diplomas: *Licenciatura*. Técnico Superior Universitario

Last Updated: 05/04/13

TECHNOLOGICAL UNIVERSITY OF TECAMAC

Universidad Tecnológica de Tecámac
Carretera Federal México - Pachuca Km 37.5, CP 55740, Col. Sierra Hermosa, 55770 Tecámac, Estado de México
Tel: +52(55) 59-38-84-00
EMail: uttecamac@uttecamac.edu.mx
Website: http://www.uttecamac.edu.mx

Rector: Roberto Galván Peña
EMail: robertgalpena@uttecamac.edu.mx

Divisions
Biotechnology (Biotechnology; Microbiology; Molecular Biology); **Business Administration**; **Industrial Engineering** (Automation and Control Engineering; Industrial Engineering; Materials Engineering; Production Engineering; Statistics); **Industrial Maintenance** (Industrial Maintenance); **Information Technology** (Information Technology; Software Engineering); **Mechanical and Electronic Engineering** (Electronic Engineering; Mechanical Engineering)

History: Founded 1996.

Main Language(s) of Instruction: Spanish

Degrees and Diplomas: *Licenciatura*. Técnico Superior Universitario

Libraries: Yes

Last Updated: 21/01/13

TECHNOLOGICAL UNIVERSITY OF TECAMACHALCO

Universidad Tecnológica de Tecamachalco
Avenida Universidad Tecnológica, 1, Col. La Villita, 75482 Tecamachalco, Puebla
Tel: +52(249) 422-33-01
EMail: info@utt.mx
Website: http://www.uttecam.edu.mx

Rector: José Antonio Garrido Nataren

Programmes
Accountancy (Accountancy; Fiscal Law); **Business Administration** (Administration; Business Administration; Commercial Law; Finance; Sales Techniques); **Food Technology** (Food Technology); **Industrial Maintenance** (Industrial Maintenance); **Information Technology** (Information Technology); **Production Processing** (Production Engineering); **Project Administration** (Administration)

History: Founded 2001.

Main Language(s) of Instruction: Spanish

Degrees and Diplomas: *Licenciatura*. Técnico Superior Universitario

Libraries: Yes

Last Updated: 22/01/13

TECHNOLOGICAL UNIVERSITY OF THE CENTRAL REGION OF COAHUILA

Universidad Tecnológica de la Región Centro de Coahuila
Carretera 57 Norte Km. 14.5, Tramo Monclova Sabinas, 25720 Monclova, Coahuila
Tel: +52(866) 648-32-60
EMail: informacion@utrcc.edu.mx
Website: http://www.utrcc.edu.mx

Rector: Oscar Aguilar Salinas

Programmes
Business Development and Innovation (Administration; Business Administration; Economics; Finance); **Industrial Maintenance** (Industrial Maintenance); **Mechanical Engineering** (Mechanical Engineering); **Production Systems** (Production Engineering)

History: Founded 2001.

Main Language(s) of Instruction: Spanish

Degrees and Diplomas: *Licenciatura*

Last Updated: 09/01/13

TECHNOLOGICAL UNIVERSITY OF THE COAST

Universidad Tecnológica de la Costa
Carretera Santiago entronque internacional no. 15 km. 5, 32323 Santiago Ixcuintla, Nayarit
Tel: +52(323) 235-80-00
EMail: abogarin@utdelacosta.edu.mx
Website: http://www.utdelacosta.edu.mx

Rector: Francisco García Villela

Divisions
Administration (Administration; Advertising and Publicity; Business Administration; Finance; Marketing); **Science and Technology** (Agricultural Engineering; Aquaculture; Biotechnology; Food Technology; Information Technology)

History: Founded 2003.

Main Language(s) of Instruction: Spanish

Degrees and Diplomas: *Licenciatura*

Last Updated: 09/01/13

TECHNOLOGICAL UNIVERSITY OF THE COAST OF GUERRERO

Universidad Tecnológica de la Costa Grande de Guerrero
Km. 201 Carretera Nacional Acapulco-Zihuatanejo, Ejido El Cocotero, 40830 Petatlán, Guerrero
Tel: +52(758) 538-23-48 +52(758) 538-23-41
Fax: +52(758) 538-39-01
EMail: utcgg@yahoo.com.mx
Website: http://www.utcgg.edu.mx

Rector: Arturo Salgado Urióstegui

Programmes
Administration (Administration); **Business** (Business Administration); **Food Technology** (Food Technology); **Industrial Maintenance** (Industrial Maintenance); **Information Technology** (Information Technology); **Metal Techniques** (Metal Techniques); **Renewable Energy** (Energy Engineering); **Tourism Management** (Hotel Management; Tourism)

History: Founded 1997.

Main Language(s) of Instruction: Spanish

Degrees and Diplomas: *Licenciatura*. Técnico Superior Universitario

Last Updated: 09/01/13

TECHNOLOGICAL UNIVERSITY OF THE FOREST

Universidad Tecnológica de la Selva
Km. 0.5 Entronque Toniná Carretera Ocosingo-Altamirano, 29950 Ocosingo, Chiapas
Tel: +52(967) 9-09-70 +52(967) 9-09-72
Fax: +52(967) 9-09-70
EMail: rector@utselva.edu.mx
Website: http://www.utselva.edu.mx

Rector: Juan José Ortega Couttolenc

Directora de Administración y Finanzas: Rosa Elena Pulido Aguilar EMail: finanzas@utselva.edu.mx

Divisions
Administration (Administration); **Food Processing** (Biotechnology; Food Technology; Vegetable Production); **Information Technology** (Information Technology); **Tourism** (Tourism)

History: Founded 1997.

Main Language(s) of Instruction: Spanish

Degrees and Diplomas: *Licenciatura*. Técnico Superior Universitario

Last Updated: 09/01/13

TECHNOLOGICAL UNIVERSITY OF THE HIDALGO SIERRA

Universidad Tecnológica de la Sierra Hidalguense
Km. 100 Carretera México-Tampico, Cerrada Vargas Lugo s/n, 43200 Zacualtipán de los Ángeles, Hidalgo
Tel: +52(774) 742-01-23 +52(774) 742-11-21
Fax: +52(774) 742-00-67
EMail: utsh@utsh.edu.mx
Website: http://www.utsh.edu.mx

Rector: Eudaldo Rivas Gómez

Divisions
Economics and Administration (Accountancy; Administration; Business Administration; Economics; Finance; Fiscal Law); **Exact Sciences** (Design; Engineering; Fashion Design; Industrial Maintenance; Mechanical Engineering; Metal Techniques; Production Engineering); **Health Sciences** (Physical Therapy); **Information Technology** (Information Technology; Telecommunications Engineering); **Natural Sciences** (Environmental Studies; Forestry; Natural Resources)

History: Founded 1997.

Main Language(s) of Instruction: Spanish

Degrees and Diplomas: *Licenciatura*. Técnico Superior Universitario

Libraries: Yes
Last Updated: 09/01/13

TECHNOLOGICAL UNIVERSITY OF THE HUASTECA HIDALGUENSE

Universidad Tecnológica de la Huasteca Hidalguense
Carretera Huejutla a Chalahuiyapa S/N, Colonia Tepoxteco, 43000 Huejutla de Reyes, Hidalgo
Tel: +52(789) 896-20-88
EMail: rectoria@uthh.edu.mx
Website: http://www.uthh.edu.mx

Rector: Quintín José Luis Mejía Ángeles (2011-)

Programmes
Biotechnology (Biotechnology); **Finance** (Finance); **Food Technology** (Food Technology); **Information Technology** (Information Technology); **Metal Techniques** (Metal Techniques); **Project Management** (Management)

History: Founded 1997.

Main Language(s) of Instruction: Spanish

Degrees and Diplomas: Técnico Superior Universitario
Last Updated: 05/04/13

TECHNOLOGICAL UNIVERSITY OF THE METROPOLITAN ZONE OF GUADALAJARA

Universidad Tecnológica de la Zona Metropolitana de Guadalajara
Carretera Tlajomulco de Zúñiga-San Isidro Mazatepec., Km 4.7, Santa Cruz de las Flores, 45200 Tlajomulco de Zúñiga, Jalisco
Tel: +52 (33) 3770-1650
EMail: rectoria@utzmg.edu.mx
Website: http://www.utzmg.edu.mx

Rector: Braulio Vázquez Martínez
EMail: bvazquez@utzmg.edu.mx

Programmes
Business Administration (Business Administration; Finance; Marketing); **Information Technology** (Information Technology); **Mechanical and Electronic Engineering** (Electronic Engineering; Mechanical Engineering); **Paramedical Science** (Health Education); **Renewable Energy** (Energy Engineering); **Tourism** (Hotel Management; Tourism)

History: Founded 2003.

Main Language(s) of Instruction: Spanish

Degrees and Diplomas: *Licenciatura*. Técnico superior universitario
Last Updated: 17/01/13

TECHNOLOGICAL UNIVERSITY OF THE MIXTECA

Universidad Tecnológica de la Mixteca (UTM)
Km. 2.5 Carretera a Acatlima, Ciudad Universitaria, 69000 Huajuapán de León, Oaxaca
Tel: +52(953) 532-02-14
Fax: +52(953) 532-45-60
EMail: rortiz@mixteco.utm.mx
Website: http://www.utm.mx

Rector: Modesto Seara Vázquez (1990-)
EMail: msv@mixteco.utm.mx

Areas
Engineering (Computer Engineering; Electronic Engineering; Food Technology; Industrial Engineering; Mechanical Engineering)

Programmes
Applied Mathematics (Applied Mathematics); **Applied Physics** (Applied Physics); **Business Administration** (Business Administration); **Mexican Studies** (Latin American Studies)

History: Founded 1990.

Governing Bodies: Consejo Academico

Academic Year: October to July

Admission Requirements: Bachillerato

Main Language(s) of Instruction: Spanish

Degrees and Diplomas: *Licenciatura*: Applied Mathematics; Business Sciences; Computer Engineering; Design Engineering; Electronic Engineering; Food Technology; Industrial Engineering; Mechatronic Engineering, 10 semesters; *Maestría*: Computing; Electronics; *Doctorado*

Student Services: Employment services, Health services, Language programs, Nursery care, Social counselling, Sports facilities

Libraries: Biblioteca Central

Publications: Temas de Ciencia y Tecnología *(quarterly)*
Last Updated: 24/10/12

TECHNOLOGICAL UNIVERSITY OF THE NORTH OF COAHUILA

Universidad Tecnológica del Norte de Coahuila
Blvd. Fidel Villareal y Calle Nobel s/n, Col. Fovissste, 26080 Piedras Negras, Coahuila
Tel: +52(878) 783-47-97 +52(878) 783-60-77
Fax: +52(878) 783-48-57 +52(878) 783-42-69
EMail: info@utnc.edu.mx
Website: http://www.utnc.edu.mx

Rector: Anteo Ayala Garza

Programmes
Business Administration (Business Administration; Finance; Human Resources); **Mechanical and Electronic Engineering** (Electronic Engineering; Mechanical Engineering)
History: Founded 1998.
Main Language(s) of Instruction: Spanish
Degrees and Diplomas: *Licenciatura.* Técnico Superior Universitario
Libraries: Yes

TECHNOLOGICAL UNIVERSITY OF THE NORTH OF GUANAJUATO

Universidad Tecnológica del Norte de Guanajuato (UTNG)
Carretera Dolores Hidalgo-Río Laja, Avenida Educación Tecnológica, 37800 Dolores Hidalgo, Guanajuato
Tel: +52 (418) 182-55-00
EMail: utng@utng.edu.mx
Website: http://www.utng.edu.mx

Rectora: Sofía Ayala Rodríguez EMail: sayala@utng.edu.mx

Programmes
Business Administration (Business Administration; Business and Commerce; Finance); **Information Technology** (Information Technology); **Mechanics** (Electronic Engineering; Mechanical Engineering); **Production Engineering** (Production Engineering)
History: Founded 1994.
Main Language(s) of Instruction: Spanish
Degrees and Diplomas: *Licenciatura.* Técnico Superior Universitario
Libraries: Yes
Last Updated: 06/02/13

TECHNOLOGICAL UNIVERSITY OF THE SOUTH OF THE STATE OF MEXICO

Universidad Tecnológica del Sur del Estado de México
Km. 12 Carretera Tejupilco-Amatepec, Hacienda de San Miguel Ixtapán, 51400 Tejupilco, Estado de México
Tel: +52(724) 249-40-16
EMail: utsurrectoria@hotmail.com
Website: http://www.utsem.edu.mx

Rector: Hector Peña Campuzano

Programmes
Finance and Taxation (Finance; Taxation); **Food Processing** (Food Technology); **Information Technology** (Information Technology); **Mechanical and Electronic Engineering** (Electronic Engineering; Mechanical Engineering); **Project Management** (Management)
History: Founded 1997.
Main Language(s) of Instruction: Spanish
Degrees and Diplomas: *Licenciatura.* Técnico Superior Universitario
Last Updated: 28/01/13

TECHNOLOGICAL UNIVERSITY OF THE SOUTH WEST OF GUANAJUATO

Universidad Tecnológica del Suroeste de Guanajuato
Ecologista, 38400 Valle de Santiago, Guanajuato
Tel: +52(456) 563-71-80
EMail: jmendosa@utsoe.edu.mx
Website: http://www.utsoe.edu.mx

Rectora: Virginia Aguilera Santoyo EMail: vaguilera@utsoe.edu.mx

Programmes
Business Administration (Business Administration; Commercial Law; Finance; Sales Techniques); **Food Processing** (Food Technology); **Industrial Maintenance** (Industrial Maintenance); **Information Technology** (Information Technology); **Metal and Mechanical Engineering** (Mechanical Engineering; Metal Techniques); **Textile and Fashion Design** (Fashion Design; Textile Design)
History: Founded 1998.
Main Language(s) of Instruction: Spanish
Degrees and Diplomas: *Licenciatura.* Técnico Superior Universitario
Last Updated: 28/01/13

TECHNOLOGICAL UNIVERSITY OF THE STATE OF ZACATECAS

Universidad Tecnológica del Estado de Zacatecas
Km. 5 Carretera Guadalupe-Cd. Cuauhtémoc, Comunidad de Cieneguillas, 98000 Guadalupe, Zacatecas
Tel: +52(492) 927-61-80
EMail: aramirez@utzac.edu.mx
Website: http://www.utzac.edu.mx

Rector: Manuel Felipe Álvarez Calderón

Programmes
Business Administration (Business Administration; Commercial Law; Finance; International Business; Sales Techniques); **Industrial Maintenance** (Industrial Maintenance); **Industrial Processes** (Industrial Engineering); **Information Technology** (Information Technology; Multimedia); **Mechanical and Electronic Engineering** (Automation and Control Engineering; Electronic Engineering; Mechanical Engineering)
History: Founded 1998.
Main Language(s) of Instruction: Spanish
Degrees and Diplomas: *Licenciatura.* Técnico Superior Universitario
Libraries: Yes
Last Updated: 01/02/13

TECHNOLOGICAL UNIVERSITY OF THE VALLEY OF TOLUCA

Universidad Tecnológica del Valle de Toluca
Carretera del Departamento del D.F. km 7.5, Ejido de Santa María Atarasquillo, Lerma, Estado de México
Tel: +52(728) 285-9552
EMail: vinculacion@utvtol.edu.mx
Website: http://www.utvtol.edu.mx

Head: Martha Garciarivas Palmeros EMail: rectoria@utvtol.edu.mx

Programmes
Business Administration (Accountancy; Business Administration; Finance); **Environmental Technology** (Environmental Engineering; Environmental Management; Environmental Studies); **Industrial Maintenance** (Industrial Maintenance); **Information Technology** (Information Technology); **Mechanical and Electronic Engineering** (Electronic Engineering; Mechanical Engineering); **Production Systems** (Production Engineering)
History: Founded 2001.
Main Language(s) of Instruction: Spanish
Degrees and Diplomas: *Licenciatura.* Técnico Superior Universitario
Libraries: Yes
Last Updated: 29/01/13

TECHNOLOGICAL UNIVERSITY OF TIJUANA

Universidad Tecnológica de Tijuana
Km. 10 Carretera Libre Tijuana-Tecate, Fracc. El Refugio, 22685 Tijuana, Baja California
Tel: +52(664) 931-70-36 +52(664) 971-70-40
Fax: +52(664) 971-70-36
EMail: rectoria@uttij.edu.mx
Website: http://www.uttijuana.edu.mx

Rector: Miguel Ángel Mendoza González
EMail: mmendoza@uttijuana.edu.mx

Director de Administración y Finanzas: Victorl Octavio Soto Aguilar

Programmes
Business Administration (Business Administration); **Environmental Technology** (Environmental Engineering); **Finance and**

Taxation (Finance; Taxation); **Industrial Engineering** (Industrial Engineering); **Industrial Maintenance** (Industrial Maintenance); **Information Technology** (Information Technology); **Mechanical and Electronic Engineering** (Electronic Engineering; Mechanical Engineering); **Production Processing** (Production Engineering)

Further Information: Branches in Ensenada and San Quintin

History: Founded 1998.

Main Language(s) of Instruction: Spanish

Degrees and Diplomas: *Licenciatura*. Técnico Superior Universitario

Libraries: Yes

Last Updated: 22/01/13

TECHNOLOGICAL UNIVERSITY OF TLAXCALA

Universidad Tecnológica de Tlaxcala

Carretera a el Carmen Xalpatlahuaya s/n, Francisco I. Madero, 304, Fracc. El Calvario, 90500 Huamantla, Tlaxcala
Tel: +52(247) 472-53-00
EMail: omondragon@uttlaxcala.edu.mx
Website: http://www.uttlaxcala.edu.mx

Rector: José Luis González Cuéllar
EMail: j.l.gonzalez@uttlaxcala.edu.mx

Programmes

Business Administration (Business Administration); **Industrial Maintenance** (Industrial Maintenance); **Information Technology** (Information Technology); **Production Processing** (Production Engineering); **Technotronics** (Automation and Control Engineering; Mechanical Engineering); **Textile and Fashion Design** (Fashion Design; Textile Design; Textile Technology)

History: Founded 1996.

Main Language(s) of Instruction: Spanish

Degrees and Diplomas: *Licenciatura*. Técnico Superior Universitario

Libraries: Yes

Last Updated: 24/01/13

TECHNOLOGICAL UNIVERSITY OF TORREON

Universidad Tecnológica de Torreón

Km. 10 Carretera Torreón-Matamoros, Ejido El Águila, 27400 Torreón, Coahuila
Tel: +52(871) 729-74-00
Fax: +52(871) 729-71-22
EMail: utt@utt.edu.mx
Website: http://www.utt.edu.mx

Rector: Indalecio Medina Hernández

Programmes

Industrial Maintenance (Industrial Maintenance); **Mechanical and Electronic Engineering** (Electronic Engineering; Mechanical Engineering); **Metallurgical Engineering** (Metallurgical Engineering); **Production Processing** (Production Engineering)

History: Founded 1998.

Main Language(s) of Instruction: Spanish

Degrees and Diplomas: *Licenciatura*. Técnico Superior Universitario

Libraries: Yes

Last Updated: 24/01/13

TECHNOLOGICAL UNIVERSITY OF XICOTEPEC DE JUÁREZ

Universidad Tecnológica de Xicotepec de Juárez

Av. Universidad Tecnológica N° 1000. Col. Tierra Negra, Xicotepec de Juárez, Puebla
Tel: +52(764) 764-37-00
EMail: rectoriautxj@yahoo.com.mx
Website: http://www.utxj.edu.mx

Rector: Pedro Ramírez Legorreta

Programmes

Business Administration (Business Administration; Commercial Law; Economics; Finance; Sales Techniques; Statistics); **Food Processing** (Food Technology); **Industrial Maintenance** (Industrial Maintenance); **Information Technology** (Information Technology); **Mechanical and Electronic Engineering** (Electronic Engineering; Mechanical Engineering)

History: Founded 2003.

Main Language(s) of Instruction: Spanish

Degrees and Diplomas: *Licenciatura*. Técnico Superior Universitario

Last Updated: 25/01/13

THE COLLEGE OF JALISCO

El Colegio de Jalisco

Calle 5 de Mayo 321, Zona Centro, 45100 Zapopan, Jalisco
Tel: +52(33) 36-33-26-16
Fax: +52(33) 36-33-65-00
EMail: presidencia@coljal.edu.mx
Website: http://www.coljal.edu.mx

Presidente: José Luis Leal Sanabria

Programmes

Public Policy (Social Policy); **Regional Studies** (Anthropology; Economics; Fine Arts; Geography; History; Literature; Political Sciences; Regional Studies; Sociology); **Social Sciences** (Social Sciences)

History: Founded 1992.

Main Language(s) of Instruction: Spanish

Degrees and Diplomas: *Maestría*; *Doctorado*

Libraries: Yes

Last Updated: 24/08/12

THE COLLEGE OF MEXICO

El Colegio de México (COLMEX)

Apartado postal 20-671, Camino al Ajusco 20, Col. Pedregal de Santa Teresa, Delegación Tlalpán, 10740 México, D.F.
Tel: +52(55) 54-49-30-00
Fax: +52(55) 56-45-04-64
EMail: presidente@colmex.mx
Website: http://www.colmex.mx

Director: Javier Garciadiego Datán (2005-)
Tel: +52(55) 56-45-58-32

Secretario General: Manuel Ordorica Mellado
Tel: +52(55) 56-45-38-70

Centres

Asian and African Studies (African Studies; Asian Studies); **Demography and Urban Development** (Demography and Population; Town Planning); **Economics** (Economics); **History** (History); **International Studies** (International Relations; International Studies; Public Administration); **Linguistics and Literature** (Linguistics; Literature; Spanish); **Sociology** (Sociology)

History: Founded 1940.

Governing Bodies: Asamblea de Socios; Junta de Gobierno; Consejo Académico; Juntas de Profesores de los Centros

Academic Year: March to February (March-July; September-February)

Admission Requirements: Secondary school certificate (bachillerato) and entrance examination

Main Language(s) of Instruction: Spanish

International Co-operation: With universities in United Kingdom; France; Germany; Spain; Japan; Latin America

Degrees and Diplomas: *Licenciatura*: 3 yrs; *Maestría*: a further 2 yrs; *Doctorado*: 5 yrs

Student Services: Academic counselling, Canteen, Foreign student adviser, Health services, Language programs

Libraries: Bibliotecal Daniel Cosío Villegas

Publications: Boletín *(monthly)*; Estudios de Asia y Africa; Estudios Demográficos y Urbanos; Estudios Económicos; Estudios Sociológicos; Foro Internacional; Historia Mexicana; Nueva Revista de Filología Hispánica

Last Updated: 27/08/12

THE COLLEGE OF MICHOACAN

El Colegio de Michoacán, A.C (COLMICH)

Martínez de Navarrete 505, Col. las Fuentes, 59699 Zamora, Michoacán
Tel: +52(351) 515-71-00
EMail: presiden@colmich.edu.mx
Website: http://www.colmich.edu.mx

Presidente: Martín Sánchez. (2009-2015)

Centres

Anthropology (Anthropology); **Archaeology** (Archaeology); **History** (History); **Human Geography** (Geography; Social Sciences); **Rural Studies** (Rural Studies; Sociology); **Tradition Studies** (Cultural Studies; Ethnology)

History: Founded 1979 as part of initiative to decentralize education and research in Social Sciences and Humanities. A postgraduate institution.

Governing Bodies: Asamblea de Asociados; Junta de Gobierno

Academic Year: October to September

Admission Requirements: Degree of Licenciatura or Maestría with Grade 8 (minimum)

Fees: (US Dollars): Foreign students, 3,500 per semester

Main Language(s) of Instruction: Spanish

Degrees and Diplomas: *Maestría*; *Doctorado*: Anthropology, Ethnology; History; Humanities; Social Sciences, 5 yrs

Libraries: Biblioteca Luis González

Publications: Revista Relaciones, Anthropology, History, Economics of Mexican people *(quarterly)*

Last Updated: 27/08/12

THE COLLEGE OF PUEBLA

El Colegio de Puebla, A.C

Av Tehuacan Sur no. 91, Col. La Paz, 72160 Puebla, Puebla
Tel: +52(222) 226-5400
Fax: +52(222) 225-5401 ext 213
EMail: colpue@colpue.edu.mx
Website: http://www.colpue.edu.mx/

Presidente: Miguel Ángel Pérez Maldonado
EMail: miguel.maldonado@colpue.edu.mx

Director Academico: Armando Guillermo Guadarrama Luyando
EMail: armando.guadarrama@colpue.edu.mx

Programmes

Education Quality (Education); **Industrial Economics** (Economics); **Regional History** (History); **Regional Sustainable Development** (Development Studies; Environmental Studies)

History: Founded 1984.

Governing Bodies: Assembly of Associates

Academic Year: January to December

Admission Requirements: Licenciatura

Fees: (Pesos): 34,000 per annum

Main Language(s) of Instruction: Spanish

Degrees and Diplomas: *Maestría*: Regional Sustainable Development, 2 yrs

Libraries: Yes

Last Updated: 27/08/12

THE COLLEGE OF SAN LUIS

El Colegio de San Luis, A.C. (COLSAN)

Parque de Macul 155, Colinas del Parque, 78299 San Luis Potosí, San Luis Potosí
Tel: +52(444) 811-01-01
EMail: tcalvillo@colsan.edu.mx
Website: http://www.colsan.edu.mx

Presidente: María Isabel Monroy Castillo
EMail: imonroy@colsan.edu.mx

Programmes

Anthropology (Anthropology) *Director*: Isabel Mora Ledesma; **Hispanic Literature** (Literature); **History** (History) *Director*: Oresta López; **International Relations** (International Relations) *Director*: Cecilia Costero; **Political Science** (Political Sciences) *Director*: José Santos Zavala; **Public Administration** (Public Administration) *Director*: José Santos Zavala; **Water Management** (Water Management)

History: Founded 1997.

Governing Bodies: Junta Directiva; Junta Académica

Academic Year: January to December (January-July; September-December)

Main Language(s) of Instruction: Spanish, English

International Co-operation: With universities in Spain and USA.

Degrees and Diplomas: *Licenciatura (LRI)*: 4-5 yrs; *Maestría (MAP)*: a further 2 yrs1/2; *Doctorado*

Student Services: Academic counselling, Foreign student adviser, Language programs, Sports facilities

Libraries: Biblioteca Rafael Montejano y Aguiñaga

Publications: Vetas, Magazine for Social Sciences and Humanities *(quarterly)*

Last Updated: 27/08/12

THE COLLEGE OF SINALOA

El Colegio de Sinaloa

Calle A. Rosales 435, Pte. Centro, 80000 Culiacán, Sinaloa
Tel: +52(667) 716-10-46
Fax: +52(667) 716-10-50
EMail: coldesin@hotmail.com
Website: http://www.elcolegiodesinaloa.com

Presidente: José Ángel Pescador Osuna

Departments

Arts and Humanities (Arts and Humanities); **Education** (Education); **Information Sciences** (Information Sciences); **Law** (Law); **Performing Arts** (Performing Arts); **Religion** (Religion); **Social Sciences** (Social Sciences)

History: Founded 1990, acquired present status 1995.

Governing Bodies: Academic Council; Executive Council

Academic Year: January to December

Admission Requirements: Secondary school certificate

Fees: (Pesos): 12,500 per semester

Main Language(s) of Instruction: Spanish

Degrees and Diplomas: *Licenciatura*; *Especialización*: a further yr following Maestría; *Maestría*: 3 yrs

Student Services: Academic counselling, Cultural centre, Employment services

Special Facilities: Movie Studio. Museum. Art Gallery

Libraries: Yes

Last Updated: 27/08/12

THE COLLEGE OF SONORA

El Colegio de Sonora (COLSON)

Avenida Obregón 54, 83000 Hermosillo, Sonora
Tel: +52(662) 259-53-00
Fax: +52(662) 212-50-21
EMail: colson@colson.edu.mx
Website: http://www.colson.edu.mx/

Rectora: Gabriela Grijalva Monteverde

Secretaria General: Ma. Del Carmen Castro Vázquez
EMail: ccastro@colson.edu.mx

Centres

Development Studies (Development Studies; Economics; Regional Planning; Social Studies); **Health and Society** (Health Sciences; Social Sciences); **North American Studies** (American Studies); **Regional History** (History; Regional Studies)

Programmes

Political Studies and Public Management (Political Sciences; Public Administration)

History: Founded 1982 under the auspices of the Colegio de México and the Government of the State of Sonora. Acquired university status 1985.

Admission Requirements: Minimum average of 8.0 in degree studies, entrance examination, English

Main Language(s) of Instruction: Spanish

Accrediting Agencies: Padrón de Excelencia del Consejo Nacional de Ciencia y Tecnología, Programa Integral del Fortalecimiento al Posgrado

Degrees and Diplomas: *Maestría*: 2 yrs; *Doctorado*

Student Services: Academic counselling, Health services

Libraries: Yes

Publications: Región y Sociedad *(3 per annum)*

Last Updated: 20/02/13

THE COLLEGE OF THE NORTHERN FRONTIER, A.C.

El Colegio de la Frontera Norte, A.C.

Blvd. Abelardo L. Rodríguez No. 2925 Zona del Río, 22560 Tijuana, Baja California

Tel: +52(664) 631-63-00

Fax: +52(664) 631-63-05

EMail: publica@colef.mx

Website: http://www.colef.mx

Presidente: Tonatiuh Guillén López EMail: presidencia@colef.mx

Departments

Applied Economics (Economics) *Head*: Noé Arón Fuentes; **Cultural Studies** *Head*: José Manuel Valenzuela; **Environmental Studies** *Head*: José Luis Castro; **Population Studies** (Demography and Population; Social Studies) *Head*: Roberto Ham Chande; **Public Administration** *Head*: Vicente Sánchez; **Social Sciences** *Head*: Jorge Carrillo

Further Information: Branches in Monterrey, Ciudad Juarez, Mexicali, Nogales, Piedras Negras, Nuevo Laredo and Matamoros

History: Founded 1982.

Governing Bodies: Governing Committee

Admission Requirements: Licenciatura, interview and entrance examination

Fees: None

Main Language(s) of Instruction: Spanish

International Co-operation: With universities in USA and Canada

Degrees and Diplomas: *Maestría*; *Doctorado*: Social Sciences; Regional Planning

Student Services: Language programs, Nursery care, Sports facilities

Student Residential Facilities: None

Libraries: Yes

Publications: Migraciones Internacionales *(biannually)*

Last Updated: 27/08/12

THE COLLEGE OF THE SOUTHERN FRONTIER

El Colegio de la Frontera Sur (ECOSUR)

Carretera Panamericana y Periférico Sur s/n, Col. María Auxiliadora, 29290 San Cristóbal de las Casas, Chiapas

Tel: +52(967) 678-18-83

Fax: +52(967) 678-23-22

EMail: etunon@ecosur.mx

Website: http://www.ecosur.mx

Directora General: Esperanza Tuñón

Programmes

Development Studies (Development Studies); **Ecology** (Ecology); **Natural Resources** (Natural Resources); **Rural Studies** (Rural Studies)

Further Information: Also branches in Campeche; Chetumal; Tapachula and Villahermosa

History: Founded 1974 as Centro de Investigaciones Ecológicas del Sureste (CIES). Acquired present status and title 1994.

Main Language(s) of Instruction: Spanish

Degrees and Diplomas: *Maestría*; *Doctorado*

Last Updated: 27/08/12

THE COLLEGE OF THE STATE OF MEXICO

El Colegio Mexiquense, A.C.

Ex-Hacienda Santa Cruz de los Patos, 51350 Zinacantepec, Estado de México

Tel: +52(722) 279-99-08

Fax: +52(722) 279-99-08 Ext. 200

EMail: cdocen@cmq.edu.mx

Website: http://www.cmq.edu.mx

Presidente: José Alejandro Vargas Castro
EMail: avargas@cmq.edu.mx

Secretario General: José Antonio Alvarez Lobato
Tel: +52(722) 279-99-08 Ext. 105 EMail: jalvar@cmq.edu.mx

Centres

History (Ancient Civilizations; Arts and Humanities; Contemporary History; History); **Social Sciences** (Anthropology; Demography and Population; Social Sciences; Sociology); **Socio-spatial Studies and Public Policy** (Development Studies; Economics; Political Sciences; Urban Studies)

History: Founded 1986.

Governing Bodies: General Assembly; Council

Academic Year: September to July

Admission Requirements: Degree in Social Science; TOEFL

Main Language(s) of Instruction: Spanish

Degrees and Diplomas: *Maestría*: Social Sciences, 2 yrs; *Doctorado*: Social Sciences, 3-5 yrs

Student Services: Canteen

Libraries: "Fernando Rosenzweig" Library

Publications: Economía Sociedad y Territorio/Magazine: Economy, Society and Land, Scientific Magazine with emphasis on research in social sciences, economics, and urban studies *(biennially)*

Last Updated: 27/08/12

TRADE UNION CENTRE OF ADVANCED STUDIES OF THE CTM

Centro Sindical de Estudios Superiores de la CTM

Apartado postal 134-C, Calle Camelia 104, Fracc. Rancho Cortés, 62050 Cuernavaca, Morelos

Tel: +52(73) 13-07-00

Fax: +52(73) 17-39-11

EMail: cses@correoweb.com

Director: José Ramírez Gamero

Programmes

Administration (Administration); **Economics** (Administration; Economics); **Law** (Law)

History: Founded 1980.

Main Language(s) of Instruction: Spanish

Degrees and Diplomas: *Licenciatura*

Last Updated: 23/07/12

UNIVERSIDAD TECNOLÓGICA DE CIUDAD JUÁREZ

Ave. Universidad Tecnológica No. 3051, Col. Lote Bravo II, 32695 Ciudad Juárez, Chihuahua

Tel: +52(656) 649-06-00

Fax: +52(656) 649-06-18

EMail: candelario_villalobos@utcj.edu.mx

Website: http://www.utcj.edu.mx

Rector: Humberto Carlos Morales Moreno

Programmes

Business Administration (Business Administration); **Engineering** (Electronic Engineering; Energy Engineering; Engineering; Industrial Engineering; Information Technology; Mechanical Engineering; Nanotechnology; Production Engineering; Telecommunications Engineering)

History: Founded 1999.

Main Language(s) of Instruction: Spanish

Degrees and Diplomas: *Licenciatura*

Libraries: Yes
Last Updated: 25/10/12

UNIVERSIDAD TECNOLÓGICA DE COAHUILA

Apartado postal 160, Avenida Industria Metalúrgica, 2001, Parque Industrial Ramos Arizpe, 25900 Ramos Arizpe, Coahuila
Tel: +52(844) 488-38-00
EMail: utec2001@utc.edu.mx
Website: http://www.utc.edu.mx

Rector: Raúl Martínez Hernández

Programmes

Business (Business Administration); **Environmental Engineering** (Environmental Engineering); **Industrial Maintenance** (Industrial Maintenance); **Information Technology** (Information Technology); **Mechatronics** (Electronic Engineering; Mechanical Engineering)

History: Founded 1995.

Main Language(s) of Instruction: Spanish

Accrediting Agencies: Secretario de Educación

Degrees and Diplomas: *Licenciatura*

Libraries: Yes
Last Updated: 25/10/12

UNIVERSIDAD TECNOLÓGICA DE HUEJOTZINGO

Camino Real a San Mateo s/n, Col. Santa Ana, Yalmimilulco, 74169 Huejotzingo, Puebla
Tel: +52(227) 5-93-00
EMail: escolares@uth.edu.mx
Website: http://www.uth.edu.mx/

Rector: José Fabian Sandoval Carranza

Director de Administración y Finanzas: Enrique Capistrán Vázquez Tel: +52(227) 6-00-28

Programmes

Business Administration (Business Administration); **Food Technology** (Food Technology); **Industrial Processes** (Industrial Engineering); **Information Technology** (Information Technology); **Mechatronics** (Electronic Engineering; Mechanical Engineering); **Metal Techniques** (Metal Techniques); **Project Management** (Management); **Textile and Fashion Design** (Fashion Design; Textile Design)

History: Founded 1998.

Main Language(s) of Instruction: Spanish

Degrees and Diplomas: *Licenciatura*. Técnico Superior Universitario
Last Updated: 05/04/13

UNIVERSIDAD TECNOLÓGICA DE JALISCO

Luis J. Jiménez, 577, Esq. Juan Bautista Ceballos, Col. Primero de Mayo, 44100 Guadalajara, Jalisco
Tel: +52(33) 30-30-09-00
EMail: informes@utj.edu.mx
Website: http://www.utj.edu.mx/

Rector: José Antonio Herrera Lomelí

Programmes

Administration (Administration; Human Resources); **Environmental Engineering** (Environmental Engineering); **Industrial Maintenance** (Industrial Maintenance); **Information Technology** (Information Technology); **Mechatronics** (Electronic Engineering; Mechanical Engineering)

History: Founded 1999.

Main Language(s) of Instruction: Spanish

Degrees and Diplomas: *Licenciatura*. Técnico Superior Universitario
Last Updated: 09/01/13

UNIVERSIDAD TECNOLÓGICA DE TULANCINGO

Apartado postal 329, Camino a Ahuehuetitla, 301, Col. Las Presas, Ahuehuetitla, 43730 Tulancingo, Hidalgo
Tel: +52(775) 755-85-10
Fax: +52(775) 755-27-60
EMail: tellezjar@utec-tgo.edu.mx
Website: http://www.utec-tgo.edu.mx/

Rector: Gerardo M. Lara Orozco
EMail: gerardo.marcelino@utec-tgo.edu.mx

Programmes

Computer Science; **Marketing**; **Production Processing**

Degrees and Diplomas: Técnico Superior Universitario

UNIVERSIDAD TECNOLÓGICA DE TULA-TEPEJI (UTTT)

Av. Universidad Tecnológica No. 1000, Colonia El 61, El Carmen, 42800 Tula de Allende, Hidalgo
Tel: +52(773) 732-91-00
Fax: +52(773) 732-12-14
EMail: rectoria@uttt.edu.mx
Website: http://www.uttt.edu.mx

Rector: Leodan Portes Vargas

Programmes

Accountancy (Accountancy); **Business Administration** (Business Administration); **Environmental Technology** (Environmental Management; Environmental Studies); **Industrial Maintenance** (Industrial Maintenance); **Information Technology** (Information Technology); **Mechanical and Electronic Engineering** (Electronic Engineering; Mechanical Engineering); **Nanotechnology** (Nanotechnology); **Production Processing** (Production Engineering); **Renewable Energy** (Energy Engineering)

History: Founded 1991.

Main Language(s) of Instruction: Spanish

Degrees and Diplomas: *Licenciatura*. Técnico Superior Universitario

Libraries: Yes
Last Updated: 24/01/13

UNIVERSIDAD TECNOLÓGICA DEL NORTE DE AGUASCALIENTES

Avenida Universidad, 1001, Col. Estación Rincón, Rincón de Romos, 20420 Aguascalientes, Aguascalientes
Tel: +52(449) 910-32-60
Fax: +52(449) 910-32-61
EMail: jorgegm@utna.edu.mx
Website: http://www.utna.edu.mx

Rector: Fernando Macias Garnica
EMail: fernando.maciasg@utna.edu.mx

Programmes

Engineering

History: Founded 2000

Degrees and Diplomas: Técnico Superior Universitario

UNIVERSIDAD TECNOLÓGICA DEL VALLE DEL MEZQUITAL

Km. 4 Carretera Ixmiquilpán-Capula Nith, 42300 Ixmiquilpán, Hidalgo
Tel: +52(759) 723-27-90
Fax: +52(759) 723-27-29
EMail: utvm@esi.net.mx; sautvm@yahoo.com.mx
Website: http://www.utvm.edu.mx

Rector: Marco Antonio Ocadiz Cruz (2000-)

Programmes

Agro-industrial Processing; **Mechanics**; **Production Projects and Marketing**

Degrees and Diplomas: Técnico Superior Universitario

UNIVERSITY OF ARTS AND SCIENCE OF CHIAPAS

Universidad de Ciencias y Artes de Chiapas (UNICACH)
Apartado postal 782, 1a Avenida Sur Poniente, 1460, Zona Centro, 29000 Tuxtla Gutiérrez, Chiapas
Tel: +52(961) 602-89-85 +52(961) 602-85-23
Fax: +52(961) 602-89-90
EMail: rectoria@unicach.edu.mx
Website: http://www.unicach.edu.mx

Rector: Roberto Domínguez Castellanos (2012-2016)
Tel: +52(961) 602-89-86 EMail: rector@unicach.edu.mx

Faculties
Engineering (Energy Engineering; Environmental Engineering; Hydraulic Engineering; Surveying and Mapping)

Programmes
Marine Biology (Marine Biology)

Schools
Nutrition (Nutrition); **Psychology** (Psychology)

History: Founded 1982.

Main Language(s) of Instruction: Spanish

Degrees and Diplomas: *Licenciatura*; *Maestría*; *Doctorado*

Last Updated: 13/02/08

UNIVERSITY OF COLIMA

Universidad de Colima (UCOL)
Apartado postal 272, Avenida Universidad, 333, Col. Las Víboras, 28040 Colima, Colima
Tel: +52(312) 316-10-00
Fax: +52(312) 316-10-09
EMail: rector@ucol.mx
Website: http://www.ucol.mx

Rector: Miguel Ángel Aguayo Lopez (2005-)

Faculties
Accountancy and Administration (Accountancy; Administration); **Architecture and Design** (Architecture; Design; Graphic Design; Industrial Design); **Biological Sciences** (Agronomy; Biology); **Chemistry** (Chemistry); **Civil Engineering** (Civil Engineering); **Economics** (Economics); **Educational Sciences** (Mathematics Education; Physical Education; Special Education; Sports); **Foreign Languages** (Modern Languages); **Letters and Communication** (Arts and Humanities; Communication Studies; Journalism; Linguistics; Literature); **Marine Science** (Marine Engineering; Marine Science and Oceanography); **Mechanical and Electrical Engineering** (Electrical Engineering; Mechanical Engineering); **Medicine** (Medicine); **Nursing** (Nursing); **Pedagogy** (Education; Pedagogy); **Political and Social Sciences** (Political Sciences; Social Sciences); **Psychology** (Psychology); **Social Work** (Social Work); **Telematics** (Information Technology; Software Engineering; Telecommunications Engineering); **Tourism** (Tourism); **Veterinary Science and Animal Husbandry** (Animal Husbandry; Veterinary Science)

Institutes
Fine Arts (Art History; Dance; Fine Arts; Music; Music Theory and Composition; Musical Instruments; Visual Arts)

Further Information: Campuses at Manzanillo, Tecomán, Coquimatlán and Vila de Álvarez

History: Founded 1940 as Universidad Popular. Acquired present status and title 1960.

Academic Year: August to July (August-January; February-July)

Admission Requirements: Secondary school certificate (bachillerato) and entrance examination

Main Language(s) of Instruction: Spanish

Degrees and Diplomas: *Licenciatura*: Accountancy (Contador público); Architecture (Arquitecto); Biochemical Analyst (Químico farmacéutico biólogo); Veterinary Medicine and Animal Husbandry (Médico veterinario y zootecnista); *Licenciatura*: Business Administration; Engineering; Oceanology; Social Work, 5 yrs; *Licenciatura*: Economics; Education; Political Science; Public Administration; Sociology, 4 1/2 yrs; *Licenciatura*: Letters and Journalism; Nursing; Rural Communication, 4 yrs; *Licenciatura*: Medicine, 6 yrs; *Especialización*; *Maestría*; *Doctorado*

Student Services: Health services, Language programs, Sports facilities

Special Facilities: Art Museum. Archaeology Museum. Art Galleries

Libraries: Central Library; specialized libraries

Publications: Revistas

Last Updated: 18/09/12

UNIVERSITY OF GUADALAJARA

Universidad de Guadalajara (UDEG)
Avenida Juárez 975, Col. Centro, 44100 Guadalajara, Jalisco
Tel: +52(33) 36-30-98-90
Fax: +52(33) 36-30-95-92
EMail: jocelyne@cgci.udg.mx
Website: http://www.udg.mx

Rector: Marco Antonio Cortés Guardado (2008-)
EMail: mcortes@cencar.udg.mx

International Relations: Jocelyne Gacel-Ávila, Coordinadora General de Cooperación e Internacionalización (1987-)

Centres
Art, Architecture and Design *(CUAAD)* (Architecture; Arts and Humanities; Dance; Fine Arts; Graphic Design; Industrial Design; Interior Design; Music; Music Education; Music Theory and Composition; Production Engineering; Singing; Technology; Theatre; Town Planning; Urban Studies; Visual Arts); **Biology and Agronomy** *(CUCBA)* (Agronomy; Biology; Cattle Breeding; Environmental Studies; Forestry; Health Sciences; Veterinary Science); **Health Sciences** *(CUCS)* (Anaesthesiology; Anatomy; Cardiology; Clinical Psychology; Dentistry; Dermatology; Educational Psychology; Endocrinology; Epidemiology; Forensic Medicine and Dentistry; Genetics; Gerontology; Gynaecology and Obstetrics; Haematology; Health Administration; Health Sciences; Immunology; Medical Technology; Medicine; Midwifery; Molecular Biology; Nephrology; Neurology; Nursing; Nutrition; Oncology; Ophthalmology; Oral Pathology; Orthodontics; Orthopaedics; Otorhinolaryngology; Paediatrics; Pathology; Pharmacology; Physical Education; Plastic Surgery; Psychiatry and Mental Health; Psychology; Public Health; Radiology; Rehabilitation and Therapy; Rheumatology; Social and Preventive Medicine; Surgery; Urology); **La Ciénega** *(CUCIENEGA, Ocotlán, Jalisco)* (Accountancy; Chemical Engineering; Computer Engineering; Economics; Education; Industrial Engineering; Law; Management; Pharmacy; Social Studies); **La Costa** *(CUC, Puerto Vallart, Jalisco)* (Accountancy; Economics; Law; Management; Psychology; Social Studies; Social Welfare; Telecommunications Engineering; Tourism); **La Costa Sur** *(CUCSUR, Autlán de Navarro, Jalisco)* (Accountancy; Agricultural Engineering; Construction Engineering; Economics; Law; Management; Natural Resources; Regional Planning; Regional Studies; Social Studies; Tourism); **Los Altos** *(CUALTOS, Tepaitilán de Morelos, Jalisco)* (Accountancy; Cattle Breeding; Comparative Law; Economics; Engineering; Information Technology; International Relations; Law; Management; Social Studies; Taxation); **Los Lagos** *(CULAGOS, Lagos de Moreno, Jalisco)* (Accountancy; Agronomy; Business Administration; Computer Engineering; Computer Science; Electrical Engineering; Electronic Engineering; Industrial Engineering; Law; Management; Mechanical Engineering; Psychology; Technology; Telecommunications Engineering); **Los Valles** *(CUVALLES, Ameca, Jalisco)* (Accountancy; Agricultural Business; Agricultural Management; Computer Science; Education; Educational Technology; Law; Management; Tourism); **Management and Economics** *(CUCEA)* (Accountancy; Administration; Business Administration; Economics; Educational Administration; Finance; Human Resources; Information Technology; International Business; Management; Marketing; Taxation; Tourism); **Norte** *(CUNORTE, Colotlán, Jalisco)* (Accountancy; Agricultural Business; Agricultural Management; Computer Engineering; Computer Science; Electronic Engineering; Law; Management; Nursing; Nutrition; Psychology); **Science and Engineering** *(CUCEI)* (Biotechnology; Chemical Engineering; Chemistry; Civil Engineering; Computer Engineering; Computer Science; Earth Sciences; Electrical Engineering; Electronic Engineering; Engineering; Food Science; Forest Products; Industrial Engineering; Information Technology; Mathematics; Mathematics and Computer Science; Mathematics

Education; Mechanical Engineering; Natural Sciences; Pharmacology; Physics; Surveying and Mapping; Telecommunications Engineering); **Social Sciences and Humanities** *(CUCSH)* (Applied Linguistics; Arts and Humanities; Communication Studies; Cultural Studies; Education; English; Foreign Languages Education; French; Geography (Human); Government; History; International Relations; Law; Literature; Philosophy; Political Sciences; Regional Studies; Social Policy; Social Sciences; Social Studies; Social Work; Sociology; Spanish); **Sur** *(CUSUR, Zapotlán el Grande, Jalisco)* (Arts and Humanities; Biological and Life Sciences; Food Science; Law; Medicine; Psychology; Social Sciences; Veterinary Science)

Further Information: Also Centre of Studies for foreign students (including Spanish as a second Language); and Proulex Centres for English and French Studies

History: Founded 1792. First bylaws of the University of Guadalajara and first Rector named 1925. Academic departments grouped into divisions in the 1990s.

Governing Bodies: Consejo Universitario; Consejo Social; Consejo de Rectores

Academic Year: August to June

Admission Requirements: Secondary school certificate (bachillerato) or foreign equivalent, and entrance examination. Spanish proficiency for foreign students

Fees: (US Dollars): c. 1,100 per semester

Main Language(s) of Instruction: Spanish

International Co-operation: With institutions in Australia, Brazil , Canada, Cuba, Chile, France, Germany, Italy, Peru, Poland, Portugal, Spain, United Kingdom, USA

Accrediting Agencies: Secretaría de Educación Pública; CONACyT

Degrees and Diplomas: *Licenciatura*: 4 yrs; *Especialización*; *Maestría*: a further 2 yrs; *Doctorado*

Student Services: Academic counselling, Canteen, Cultural centre, Foreign student adviser, Foreign Studies Centre, Health services, Language programs, Social counselling, Sports facilities

Student Residential Facilities: No

Special Facilities: Art Museums, Art Galleries, Theatre Halls, Aula Magna, Cultural Centres, Concert Halls, Open Air Stages.

Libraries: Centre libraries

Publications: Carta Económica Regional; Ciencia Animal; Comunicación y Sociedad; Cuadernos; Dimensiones; Estudios Sociales; Función; Luvina, Literary articles *(quarterly)*; Palabra; Presencia Universitaria; Prometeo; Reforma y Utopia; Revista de la Universidad de Guadalajara, Scientific works of the University of Guadalajara *(quarterly)*; Sociedad y Estado; Tiempos de Arte; Tiempos de Ciencia; Vinculación Universidad-Sociedad

Last Updated: 18/09/12

UNIVERSITY OF GUANAJUATO

Universidad de Guanajuato (UGTO)

Lascuraín de Retana 5, Centro, 36000 Guanajuato, Guanajuato
Tel: +52(473) 732-00-06
EMail: enlacecgto@ugto.mx
Website: http://www.ugto.mx

Rector: José Manuel Cabrera Sixto (2011-2015)
EMail: rectoria@quijote.ugto.mx

Secretaria General: María Guadalupe Martínez Cadena
Tel: +52(473) 732-00-06, Ext.3021
EMail: margua@quijote.ugto.mx

International Relations: Sergio Arias Negrete
Tel: +52(473) 732-00-06, Ext. 1011, Fax: +52(473) 735-19-02
EMail: draii@quijote.ugto.mx

Divisions

Architecture, Arts and Design *(Campus Guanajuato)* (Architecture; Design; Graphic Design; Interior Design; Music; Visual Arts); **Economic and Administrative Science** *(Campus Guanajuato)* (Accountancy; Business Administration; Economics; Finance; Management); **Engineering** *(Campus Guanajuato)* (Civil Engineering; Geological Engineering; Geology; Hydraulic Engineering; Metallurgical Engineering; Mining Engineering); **Engineering** *(Campus Irapuato-Salamanca)* (Computer Graphics; Electrical Engineering; Electronic Engineering; Management; Mechanical Engineering); **Engineering and Health Sciences** *(Campus Celaya-Salvatierra)* (Agricultural Engineering; Clinical Psychology; Gynaecology and Obstetrics; Industrial Engineering; Nursing; Nutrition); **Engineering and Science** *(Campus León)* (Biomedical Engineering; Chemical Engineering; Electronic Engineering; Physical Engineering; Physics); **Health Sciences** *(Campus León)* (Gynaecology and Obstetrics; Health Sciences; Nursing; Nutrition; Psychology); **Life Sciences** *(Campus Irapuato-Salamanca)* (Agriculture; Agronomy; Environmental Studies; Food Science; Food Technology; Gynaecology and Obstetrics; Nursing); **Natural and Exact Science** *(Campus Guanajuato)* (Astronomy and Space Science; Biology; Chemical Engineering; Chemistry; Mathematics; Pharmacy); **Politics and Law** *(Campus Guanajuato)* (Law; Political Sciences; Public Administration); **Social Sciences and Administration** *(Campus Celaya-Salvatierra)* (Accountancy; Administration; Agricultural Business; Finance; Marketing; Regional Planning; Social Sciences); **Social Sciences and Humanities** *(Campus León)* (Cultural Studies; Development Studies; Social Studies); **Social Sciences and Humanities** *(Campus Guanajuato)* (Cultural Studies; English; History; Modern Languages; Philosophy; Spanish)

History: Founded 1732 as Colegio de la Santísima Trinidad. In 1828 became Colegio de la Purísima Concepción. In 1870 became a state institution, raised to University status in 1945. Acquired present status 2009.

Governing Bodies: Consejo Universitario; Consejo Académico de Área; Academia of each school; Colegio Directivo y Patronato

Academic Year: July to June (July-December; January-June)

Admission Requirements: Secondary school certificate (bachillerato) and entrance examination

Fees: (US Dollars): Undergraduate, 700 per semester, per course

Main Language(s) of Instruction: Spanish

International Co-operation: Participates in Intercampus Programme; Regional Academic Mobility Programme (RAMP); International Student Exchange Programme (ISEP); Hispanic Association of Colleges and Universities (HACU); Organización Universitaria Interamericana (OUI); Consortium for North American Higher Education Collaboration (CONAHEC); Organization for the Cooperation and Economic Development (OECD); Union of Universidades de America Latina (UDUAL); Asociación Nacional de Universidades e Instituciones de Educación Superior (ANUIES); Asociación Mexicana para la Educación Internacional (AMPEI)

Accrediting Agencies: Agencia Española de Cooperación Interuniversitaria (AECI); Servicio Alemán de Intercambio Académico (DAAD); The British Council; Japan International Cooperation Agency (JICA); Fundación Japón en México; Institute of International Education (IIE); Comisión México-Estados Unidos para el Intercambio Educativo y Cultural (COMEXUS); Embajada Americana en México; Consejo de Ciencia y Tecnología (CONACYT)

Degrees and Diplomas: *Licenciatura*: Architecture; Town Planning; Rural Planning; Regional Planning; Biological and Life Sciences; Chemistry; Applied Chemistry; Analytical Chemistry; Inorganic Chemistry; Organic Chemistry; Physical Chemistry; Industrial Chemistry; Civil Engineering (Lic); Arts and Humanities; Inorganic Chemistry; Social Sciences; Sociology; Demography and Population; Anthropology; Urban Studies; Rural Studies; Business and Commerce; International Business; Administration; Accountancy; Tourism; Marketing; Finance (Lic); Electrical and Electronic Engineering; Mechanical Engineering; Geophysics; Hydraulic Engineering; Management Systems; Human Resources; Labour and Industrial Relations; Business Administration; Public Administration; Law; Mathematics and Computer Science (Lic); Geology; Geological Engineering; Environmental Engineering; Metallurgical Engineering; Mining Engineering; Literature; History; Philosophy; Agronomy; Animal Husbandry; Horticulture; Statistics (Lic), 4-6 yrs; *Especialización*: Anaesthesiology; Surgery; Gynecology and Obstetrics; Pediatrics; Ophthalmology; Otorhinolaryngology; Psychiatry and Mental Health for Nurseries; Architecture and Planning; Notary Studies, $1\frac{1}{2}$-3 yrs; *Maestría*: Administration; Human Resources; Public Administration; Biological Sciences; Nursing; Mining Engineering; Medical Sciences; Optics; Health Sciences; Philosophy; Natural Resources (Water); Criminal Law; Medicine; Physics; Epidemiology, Statistics; Electrical Engineering; Mechanical Engineering; Chemical Engineering; Regional Planning; Labour and Industrial Relations; Restoration, a further 2-3 yrs; *Doctorado*:

Medical Sciences; Biology; Chemistry; Mechanical Engineering; Optics; Physics, 2-3 yrs following Maestría or 5 yrs following Licenciatura. Also Certificates in many Schools of the University and Continuous Education in almost all areas

Student Services: Academic counselling, Cultural centre, Foreign student adviser, Foreign Studies Centre, Language programs, Nursery care, Social counselling, Sports facilities

Student Residential Facilities: None

Special Facilities: Natural History Museum; Mineralogy Museum; Anatomy Museum; Observatory; Video Conference Rooms; Radio Station; Telecommunications Station; Art Collections; International Cervantes Festival

Libraries: 372,963 vols

Publications: Acta Universitaria, Results of scientific production of the University published by the Research Department and Graduate Affairs *(biennially)*; Centro, textos de historia guanajuatense, Guanajuato's city history essays *(1-2 per annum)*; Colmena Universitaria, Magazine with essays published by the School of Philosophy *(biennially)*; Gaceta Naturaleezza, Magazine about local, regional and national environment issues published by the Environmental Department *(biennially)*; Regiones, Humanities and Social Sciences magazine published by the Social Science Research Centre *(biennially)*; Revista Investigaciones Juridicas, Magazine published by the Law Research Department of the School of Law *(biennially)*; Voces, laboratorio de Historia Oral, History issues published by the Humanities Research Centre *(biennially)*

Press or Publishing House: Imprenta Universitaria

Last Updated: 19/09/12

UNIVERSITY OF QUINTANA ROO

Universidad de Quintana Roo (UQROO)

Apartado postal 10, Blvd. Bahía, Esq. Ignacio Comonfort s/n, Col. Del Bosque, Othón P. Blanco, 77019 Chetumal, Quintana Roo

Tel: +52(983) 835-03-00

Fax: +52(983) 832-96-56

EMail: lhmena@uqroo.mx

Website: http://www.uqroo.mx

Rectora: Elina Elfi Coral Castilla (2011-2016)
EMail: scastilla@uqroo.mx

Secretaria General: Lourdes Castillo Villanueva
EMail: loucasti@uqroo.mx

Divisions

International Studies and Humanities (Arts and Humanities; English; International Relations; International Studies); **Science and Engineering** (Energy Engineering; Engineering; Environmental Engineering; Mathematics; Tourism); **Social, Economic and Administrative Sciences** (Anthropology; Business Administration; Business and Commerce; Economics; Finance; Law; Social Sciences)

Units

Cozumel (Business and Commerce; Cooking and Catering; English; Hotel and Restaurant; Hotel Management; Marketing)

History: Founded 1991 as Universidad Estatal en el Estado de Quintana Roo.

Governing Bodies: Junta Directiva; Consejo Universitario; Consejo Divisional

Academic Year: January to December (January-March; August-December). Also summer session (June-July)

Admission Requirements: Secondary school certificate (bachillerato), entrance examination (CENEVAL) and preparatory summer course

Fees: (Pesos): 1,350 per semester

Accrediting Agencies: Secretaría de Educación Pública; Asociación Nacional de Universidades e Instituciones de Educación Superior (ANUIES)

Degrees and Diplomas: *Licenciatura*: Anthropology; Commercial Systems; Economics and Finance; Energy Systems Engineering; English Language; Environmental Engineering; International Relations; Law, 5 yrs; *Maestría*: a further 2 yrs; *Doctorado*

Student Services: Academic counselling, Canteen, Cultural centre, Foreign student adviser, Foreign Studies Centre, Health services, Language programs, Social counselling, Sports facilities

Libraries: Biblioteca Universitaria

Publications: Revista Mexicana del Caribe *(biannually)*

Last Updated: 12/09/11

UNIVERSITY OF SONORA

Universidad de Sonora (UNISON)

Calle Rosales y Blvd. Luis Encinas s/n Col. Centro, Edificio Principal, Planta Alta, 83000 Hermosillo, Sonora

Tel: +52(662) 259-21-36

Fax: +52(662) 259-21-35

EMail: rectoria@guaymas.uson.mx

Website: http://www.uson.mx

Rector: Heriberto Grijalva Monteverde
EMail: hgrijalv@guaymas.uson.mx

Secretaria General Administrativa: Rosa Elena Trujillo Llanes
EMail: rtrujillo@sociales.uson.mx

Divisions

Administration and Accountancy (Accountancy; Administration; Business Computing; International Business; Law); **Biological and Health Sciences** (Agronomy; Biology; Chemistry; Food Science; Medicine; Nursing; Nutrition; Physical Education; Sports); **Economics and Administration** (Accountancy; Administration; Business Computing; Economics; Finance; International Business; Marketing); **Economics and Social Sciences** (Accountancy; Administration; Business Computing; Economics; International Business; Law; Marketing); **Engineering** (Chemical Engineering; Civil Engineering; Computer Engineering; Electronic Engineering; Industrial Engineering; Materials Engineering; Mechanical Engineering; Metallurgical Engineering); **Exact and Natural Sciences** (Computer Science; Geology; Mathematics; Physics); **Humanities and Fine Arts** (Acting; Architecture; Dance; English; Fine Arts; Graphic Design; Linguistics; Literature; Music); **Social Sciences** (Communication Studies; History; Law; Psychology; Public Administration; Social Work; Sociology)

Further Information: Also Campuses at Carborca, Nogales, Santa Ana and Navojoa

History: Founded 1938, first students admitted 1942.

Governing Bodies: University Council; Board of Trustees

Academic Year: January to December (January-June; August-December)

Admission Requirements: Bachillerato and admission examination

Main Language(s) of Instruction: Spanish

International Co-operation: With universities in USA; Canada; Latin America; Spain and France

Degrees and Diplomas: *Licenciatura*: Accountancy; Agronomy; Administration; Biochemistry; Biology; Computer Science; Economics; Electrical and Electronic Engineering; Finance; Marketing; Foreign Language Education; Geology; History; Information Systems; Engineering; Industrial Engineering; Linguistics; Mass Communication; Mathematics; Mining Engineering; Psychology; Public Administration; Sociology; Chemical Engineering; Law, Civil Engineering, 4 1/2 yrs; *Licenciatura*: Architecture; Dance; Music; Theatre; Visual Art; Medicine, 5 yrs; *Licenciatura*: History; Literature; Management Systems; Nursing; Physics; Organizational Communication, 4 yrs; *Especialización*; *Maestría*; *Doctorado*

Student Services: Academic counselling, Cultural centre, Employment services, Foreign student adviser, Foreign Studies Centre, Handicapped facilities, Health services, Language programs, Nursery care, Social counselling, Sports facilities

Special Facilities: Anthropology and History Museum. Arts Centre. Radio Station and TV Studio

Libraries: Central Library and specialized school libraries

Publications: Revista Derecho Economico; Revista Universidad

Press or Publishing House: University of Sonora Press

Last Updated: 21/09/12

UNIVERSITY OF THE ARMED AND AIR FORCES

Universidad del Ejército y Fuerza Aérea

Calzada México-Tacuba y Felipe Carrillo Puerto s/n, Campo Militar 1-B, Col. Popotla Tacuba, Delegación Miguel Hidalgo, 11400 México, D.F.
Tel: +52(555) 396-90-99 +52(555) 3-96-95-80
Fax: +52(555) 341-58-68 +52(555) 3-96-95-82

Rector: Benito Medina Herrera

Programmes
Military Science (Military Science)

History: Founded 1975.

Main Language(s) of Instruction: Spanish

Degrees and Diplomas: *Licenciatura*; *Especialización*; *Maestría*
Last Updated: 02/04/13

UNIVERSITY OF THE CARIBBEAN

Universidad del Caribe

SM 78, Manzana 1, Lote 1, Fracc. Tabachines, 77528 Cancún, Quintana Roo
Tel: +52(998) 81-44-00 al 59
Fax: +52(998) 40-22-26
EMail: rectoria@ucaribe.edu.mx
Website: http://www.unicaribe.edu.mx

Rector: Arturo Escaip Manzur

Programmes
Economics and International Business (Economics; International Business); **Engineering** (Environmental Engineering; Industrial Engineering; Telecommunications Engineering); **Gastronomy** (Cooking and Catering); **Tourism and Hotel Management** (Hotel Management; Tourism)

History: Founded 2000.

Admission Requirements: Bachillerato and entrance examination

Main Language(s) of Instruction: Spanish

Degrees and Diplomas: *Licenciatura*; *Especialización*; *Maestría*

Libraries: Biblioteca Antonio Enríquez Savignac.

Last Updated: 24/09/12

UNIVERSITY OF THE CIÉNEGA OF THE STATE OF MICHOACAN DE OCAMPO

Universidad de La Ciénega del Estado de Michoacán de Ocampo (UCM)

Avenida Universidad 3000, Col. Lomas de la Universidad, 59000 Sahuayo, Michoacan
Tel: +52(353) 532-07-62
EMail: jesahagun@ucienegam.edu.mx
Website: http://www.ucienegam.edu.mx

Rector: José Eduardo Sahagún Sahagún (2013-)

Programmes
Educational Innovation (Education); **Engineering** (Energy Engineering; Nanotechnology); **Food Science** (Food Science); **Governance** (Government); **Multicultural Studies** (Cultural Studies; Journalism); **Town and Rural Planning** (Rural Planning; Town Planning)

History: Founded 2006.

Main Language(s) of Instruction: Spanish

Degrees and Diplomas: *Licenciatura*; *Maestría*; *Doctorado*

Libraries: Yes
Last Updated: 02/04/13

UNIVERSITY OF THE SEA

Universidad del Mar (UMAR)

Apartado postal 47, Km. 1.5 Carretera a Zipolite s/n, Ciudad Universitaria, San Pedro Pochutla, 70902 Puerto Ángel, Oaxaca
Tel: +52(958) 584-30-57
Fax: +52(958) 584-30-92
EMail: msv@angel.umar.mx
Website: http://www.umar.mx

Rector: Modesto Seara Vásquez (1992-)
EMail: msv@huatulco.umar.mx

Divisions
Marine Science (Aquaculture; Biology; Chemistry; Environmental Engineering; Food Technology; Marine Science and Oceanography; Physics)

Institutes
Ecology (Coastal Studies; Ecology); **Genetics** (Genetics); **Industry** (Industrial Arts Education); **International Studies** (International Studies); **Resources** (Natural Resources); **Tourism** (Tourism)

Further Information: Campuses in Puerto Escondido, Huatulco and Oaxaca

History: Founded 1991.

Governing Bodies: Consejo Académico

Academic Year: October to July (October-February; March-July)

Admission Requirements: Secondary school certificate (bachillerato) and entrance examination

Main Language(s) of Instruction: Spanish

Degrees and Diplomas: *Licenciatura*: 5 yrs; *Maestría*; *Doctorado*

Student Services: Academic counselling, Health services

Special Facilities: Botanical Gardens

Libraries: Biblioteca Central

Publications: Ciencia y Mar
Last Updated: 27/09/12

UNIVERSITY OF THE SIERRA

Universidad de la Sierra

Km. 2.5 Carretera Moctezuma-Cumpas, Moctezuma, 83000 Moctezuma, Sonora
Tel: +52(634) 342-9600
EMail: contacto@unisierra.edu.mx
Website: http://www.universidaddelasierra.edu.mx

Rector: Gabriel Amavizca Herrera

Divisions
Biology (Biology); **Economics and Administration** (Administration; Economics); **Engineering and Technology** (Industrial Engineering; Telecommunications Engineering)

History: Founded 2002.

Main Language(s) of Instruction: Spanish

Degrees and Diplomas: *Licenciatura*

Libraries: Yes
Last Updated: 19/09/12

UNIVERSITY OF THE WEST

Universidad de Occidente (UDO)

Apartado postal 936, Gabriel Leyva, 169, Sur, Col. Centro, 81200 Los Mochis, Sinaloa
Tel: +52(668) 816-10-50
EMail: hussein.munoz@udo.mx
Website: http://www.udo.mx

Rector: Guillermo Aarón Sánchez EMail: aaron.sanchez@udo.mx

Areas
Biology (Biology); **Economics** (Accountancy; Business Administration; Economics; Finance); **Engineering** (Civil Engineering; Engineering; Environmental Engineering; Industrial Engineering); **Social Sciences** (Communication Studies; Government; Law; Psychology; Public Administration; Social Sciences)

Institutes
Anthropological and Social Research (Anthropology; Sociology); **Aquacultural and Fishing Development Technology Research** (Aquaculture; Fishery; Technology)

Further Information: Also branches in Culiacán, Mazatlán, Guasave, Guamuchil and El Fuerte

History: Founded 1980. An autonomous institution under the jurisdiction of the State of Sinaloa and financially supported by the Centro de Estudios Superiores de Occidente.

Governing Bodies: Consejo Académico

Academic Year: August to July (August-November; January-April; May-July)

Admission Requirements: Secondary school certificate (bachillerato) and entrance examination

Main Language(s) of Instruction: Spanish

Degrees and Diplomas: *Licenciatura*: Agricultural Administration; Biology; Communication; Computer Systems Administration; Educational Administration; Financial Administration; Law; Marketing Administration; Psychology; Public Administration; Rural Sociology; Tourism Administration, 4 yrs; *Licenciatura*: Engineering, 5 yrs; *Maestría*; *Doctorado*

Special Facilities: Valley of Fuerte Regional Museum

Libraries: Central Library

Last Updated: 21/09/12

UNIVERSITY OF VERACRUZ

Universidad Veracruzana (UV)

Zona Universitaria, Lomas del Estadio s/n, Edificio A, 3er Piso, 91000 Xalapa, Veracruz
Tel: +52(228) 842-1763
Fax: +52(228) 817-6370
Website: http://www.uv.mx

Rector: Raúl Arias Lovillo (2009-2013) EMail: rarias@uv.mx

International Relations: Ángel Antonio Fernández Montiel
Tel: +52(228) 842-1700, Ext. 17665, Fax: +52(228) 817-3218
EMail: anfernandez@uv.mx

Faculties

Agronomy (Agriculture; Agronomy; Crop Production; Parasitology; Plant and Crop Protection) *Director*: Gustavo C. Ortíz Ceballos; **Anthropology** (Anthropology; Archaeology; History; Linguistics) *Director*: Jorge Francisco Javier Kuri Camacho; **Architecture** (Architectural Restoration; Architecture; Building Technologies; Design; Landscape Architecture; Structural Architecture; Town Planning) *Director*: Antonio Romero Cárcamo; **Bioanalysis** (Biochemistry; Chemistry; Microbiology; Pharmacology) *Director*: Francisco Solis Páez; **Biology** (Biology; Biotechnology; Botany; Cell Biology; Ecology; Marine Biology; Zoology) *Director*: Héctor Venancio Narave Flores; **Business Administration and Social Sciences** (Communication Studies; International Business; Labour and Industrial Relations; Marketing; Public Relations) *Dean*: Adelaida Rodríguez Arcos; **Business Administration, Tourism and Business Computing** (Accountancy; Business Administration; Business Computing; Management Systems; Tourism) *Director*: Martín Figueroa Escobar; **Chemical Engineering** (Agricultural Engineering; Applied Chemistry; Automation and Control Engineering; Chemical Engineering; Environmental Engineering; Industrial Engineering) *Director*: Miguel Ángel Fragoso López; **Civil Engineering** (Civil Engineering; Construction Engineering; Engineering Management; Hydraulic Engineering; Mechanical Engineering) *Director*: Arturo Ortiz Cedano; **Dance** (Dance) *Director*: Guadalupe Barrientos López; **Dentistry** (Dentistry) *Dean*: Guillermo Hernández Lira; **Economics** (Development Studies; Economic and Finance Policy; Economic History; Economics; Finance; International Economics; Political Sciences) *Director*: Rogelio Javier Rendón Hernández; **Education** (Education; Pedagogy; Teacher Training) *Dean*: Susano Malpica Ichante; **Electronic and Communications Engineering** (Electronic Engineering; Instrument Making; Meteorology; Telecommunications Engineering) *Dean*: Edmundo Leyva Jiménez; **Electronic Instrumentation** (Electronic Engineering; Engineering; Instrument Making) *Director*: Salvador Velasco Hernández; **Fine Arts** (Ceramic Art; Fine Arts; Graphic Design; Painting and Drawing; Photography; Sculpture) *Director*: Félix Andres Menier Villegas; **History** (Ancient Civilizations; Contemporary History; History; Modern History) *Director*: Julieta Arcos Chigo; **Languages** (English; French; Modern Languages) *Dean*: Rosalba Hess Moreno; **Law** (Administrative Law; Civil Law; Commercial Law; Constitutional Law; Criminal Law; Fiscal Law; International Law; Labour Law; Law; Public Law) *Dean*: Manlio Fabio Casarin León; **Mathematics** (Applied Mathematics; Computer Science; Mathematics; Physics; Statistics) *Director*: José Rigoberto Gabriel Argüelles; **Mechanical and Electrical Engineering** (Electrical Engineering; Mechanical Engineering) *Director*: Rafael Lozano González; **Medicine** (Medicine; Surgery) *Director*: Irma del Carmen Osorno Estrada; **Music** (Music; Music Education; Musical Instruments; Singing) *Director*: Guadalupe López Pérez; **Nursing** (Nursing) *Director*: Cristina H. Saavedra Vélez; **Nutrition** (Dietetics; Nutrition) *Director*: José Luis Castillo Hernández; **Pharmacy** (Analytical Chemistry; Biochemistry; Chemistry; Pharmacology; Pharmacy) *Director*: Rafael Díaz Sobac; **Philosophy** (Ethics; Logic; Philosophical Schools; Philosophy) *Director*: Alberto Conrado Ruiz Quiroz; **Physics** (Applied Physics; Physics) *Director*: Carlos Rubén de la Mora Basañez; **Psychology** (Psychology) *Director*: Agustín Aguirre Pitalúa; **Sociology** (Communication Studies; Cultural Studies; Public Health; Rural Studies; Social Policy; Sociology; Urban Studies) *Director*: Luis Antonio Magaña Cuellar; **Spanish Language and Literature** (Literature; Spanish) *Director*: Nidia Magdalena Vincent Ortega; **Statistics and Computer Science** (Computer Science; Design; Mathematics; Statistics) *Director*: Alma Rosa García Gaona; **Theatre** (Acting; Performing Arts; Theatre) *Director*: Domingo Adame Hernàndez; **Universidad Veracruzana Intercultural** (Agriculture; Cultural Studies; Development Studies; Ecology; Ethnology; Indigenous Studies; Native Language; Rural Studies; Social Studies; Soil Conservation; Water Management); **Universidad Veracruzana Virtual** (Art Education; Fine Arts; Sociology)

Further Information: Also University Hospital. 21 research Institutes. 4 Research Centres. School for foreign students. Distance education system with 5 regional videoconference centres. 4 advanced technology laboratories, 18 Foreign Languages Centres.

History: Founded 1944. Acquired present status 1997.

Governing Bodies: Consejo Universitario; Junta de Gobierno (Board of Trustees)

Academic Year: September to August (September-February; March-August)

Admission Requirements: Secondary school certificate (bachillerato) and entrance examination

Fees: (Pesos): Registration, 460; foreign students, 1,375; Tuition, 230 per semester; foreign students, Licenciatura, 2,000 per semester

Main Language(s) of Instruction: Spanish

International Co-operation: With universities in Canada, Cuba, Ecuador, Spain, USA

Degrees and Diplomas: *Licenciatura*: Agronomy; Biology; Farming and Agricultural Systems Engineering; Veterinary; Architecture; Atmospheric Science; Physics; Agrochemical Eng.; Environ. Eng.; Civil Eng.; Electronic and Comm. Eng.; Mech. and Electrical Eng.; Naval Eng.; Chem. Eng.; Electronic Instrument. Eng.; Math.; Agric. Chem.; Pharma.; Indus. Chem.; Earth Topo.; Fine Arts; Dance; Music Education; Music; Theatre; History and Anthropology; Linguistics and Anthropology; Social Anthropology; Archaeology; Communication Sciences; Law; Philosophy; History; French; English; Spanish Language and Literature; Education; Sociology; Social Assistance; Artistic Education; Internat. Business; Tourism Manag.; Bus. Admin.; Accountancy; Economics; Statistics; Geography; Comp. Sc.; Publicity and Public Relations; Industrial Relations; Business Computing; Physical Education; Sports and Recreation; Nursing; Medicine; Nutrition; Dentistry; Psychology; Clinical Chemistry; *Especialización*: Pasture Cattle Raising; Statistical Methods; Child Dentistry; Cattle Raising; Oral Restoration; Cattle Health Care; Foreign Trade Management; Tax Management; Farm Advisory; Financial Auditing; Building Industry; Quality Control; Groups Development; Environ. Diagnosis and Manag.; Financial Econ.; English Teaching; Sustainable Tropical Fruit Growing; *Maestría*: French Lang. Didactics; Ecology and Fisheries; Aplied Statistics; English Teaching as a Foreign Language; Genetics and Forestry; Quality Manag.; Sustainable Dev. Manag. and Promotion; Eng.; Software Eng.; Artificial Intel.; Clinic Research; Educ. Research; Health Systems Management; Foreign Agricultural Bus.; Comp. Archit. and Technol.; Animal Sciences; Admin. Sc.; Food Sc.; Env. Sc.; Phys. Activities Applied Sc.; Comp. Sc.; Comm.; Building Ind.; Acc. And Gov. Manag.; Regional Dev.; Law; Psychology and Education Research; Forest Resources Mang.; Sugar Cane Crops Manag.; Math. And Education; Forensic Medic.; Music; Neuroethology; Drugs Consumption Prevention; Dental Prosthesis; Distance Pscyhology and Community Development; Public Health; *Doctorado*: Ecology and Fisheries; Philosophy; Public Finances; Management and Control; History and Regional Research; Neuroethnology

Student Services: Academic counselling, Canteen, Cultural centre, Employment services, Foreign student adviser, Foreign Studies Centre, Handicapped facilities, Health services, Language programs, Nursery care, Social counselling, Sports facilities

Special Facilities: Anthropology Museum; Art Gallery, Forest Flora and Fauna Park, University Radio

Libraries: 5 Library and Information Services Units, 39 branches libraries, 15 Institute libraries, total, 559,500 vols; Virtual Library

Publications: Ciencia Administrativa, Administration and Business Articles *(biennially)*; La Ciencia y el Hombre, Science and Technology articles *(3 per annum)*; La Palabra y el Hombre, Literature and Humanities articles *(quarterly)*; Psicología y Salud, Psychology, Medicine and Health articles *(biennially)*; Revista Médica, Medicine and Health Science Articles *(biennially)*; Tramoya, Theatre Works, Critics, Analyses *(quarterly)*

Last Updated: 08/02/08

COATZACOALCOS-MINATITLÁN REGION

REGIÓN COATZACOALCOS-MINATITLÁN

Chihuahua 803, Esq. México, Col. Petrolera, Coatzacoalcos, Veracruz
Tel: +52(921) 213-63-00
Fax: +52(921) 215-09-79
Website: http://www.uv.mx

Vicerrector: Enrique Ramírez Nazariega (2000-)
Tel: +52(921) 214-85-93 EMail: enramirez@uv.mx

Faculties

Business Administration (Accountancy; Administration; Business Computing) *Director*: Javier Arenas Wagner; **Chemical Engineering** (Chemical Engineering; Chemistry; Industrial Chemistry) *Director*: Eruviel Flandez Alemán; **Civil Engineering** *Dean*: Ciro Castillo Pérez; **Dentistry** (Dental Hygiene; Dental Technology; Dentistry; Oral Pathology; Orthodontics; Periodontics) *Director*: Javier Gastón Pérez Ortíz; **Farming and Agriculture Sytems Engineering** (Agricultural Engineering; Agriculture; Aquaculture; Farm Management; Forestry) *Dean*: José Antonio Fernández Figueroa; **Mechanical and Electrical Engineering** *Dean*: Ciro Casillo Pérez; **Medicine** (Medicine; Surgery) *Director*: Francisco Ortíz Guerrero; **Nursing** (Nursing) *Director*: Morayma Kattz Ramírez; **Social Assistance** (Social and Community Services; Social and Preventive Medicine; Social Psychology; Social Welfare; Social Work) *Director*: Noemí Macedonio Toledo

History: Founded 1944.

ORIZABA-CÓRDOBA REGION

REGIÓN ORIZABA-CÓRDOBA

Poniente 7, 1383, Córdoba, Orizaba, Veracruz
Tel: +52(272) 725-94-17
Fax: +52(272) 725-45-96
Website: http://www.uv.mx

Vicerrector: Emilio Zilly Debernardi
Tel: +52(272) 726-12-99 EMail: ezilly@uv.mx

Faculties

Agronomy (Agriculture; Agronomy; Crop Production; Parasitology; Plant and Crop Protection) *Dean*: Joaquin Murguía González; **Architecture** *(Córdoba)* (Architecture) *Director*: Abel Colorado Saínz; **Biology** (Biology; Biotechnology; Botany; Cell Biology; Ecology; Marine Biology; Zoology) *Director*: Joaquín Murguía González; **Business Administration** (Accountancy; Business Administration; Business Computing; Marketing) *Dean*: Jorge Alberto Soto Huerta; **Chemical Engineering** (Agricultural Engineering; Automation and Control Engineering; Chemical Engineering; Environmental Engineering; Industrial Engineering) *Director*: Sofía Canales Chávez; **Dentistry** *(Río Blanco)* (Dentistry) *Director*: Guillermo Meraz Zuñiga; **Mechanical and Electrical Engineering** (Electrical Engineering; Mechanical Engineering) *Director*: Delfino Crescencio Hernández García; **Medicine** *(Ciudad Mendoza)* (Medicine) *Director*: José Ubaldo Trujillo García; **Nursing** (Nursing) *Director*: María Eugenia Valdez Altamirano; **Pharmacy** *Dean*: Sofía Canales Chávez; **Veterinary Science** *Dean*: Joaquín Murguía González

POZA RICA-TUXPÁN REGION

REGIÓN POZA RICA-TUXPÁN

Blvd. Adolfo Ruiz Cortines, 306, Col. Obrero Social, 93240 Poza Rica, Veracruz
Tel: +52(782) 824-15-40
Fax: +52(782) 823-45-70
Website: http://www.uv.mx

Vicerrectora: Clara Celina Medina Sagahún
EMail: cmedina@uv.mx

Faculties

Agronomy *(Tuxpán)* (Agriculture; Agronomy; Crop Production; Parasitology; Plant and Crop Protection) *Director*: Pablo Elorza Martínez; **Architecture** (Architecture) *Director*: Luis Manuel Villegas Salgado; **Biology** (Biology; Biotechnology; Botany; Cell Biology; Ecology; Marine Biology; Zoology) *Dean*: Pablo Elorza Martínez; **Business Administration** (Accountancy; Business Administration; Business Computing; Management) *Director*: Mario Soto Del Angel; **Chemical Engineering** (Agricultural Engineering; Automation and Control Engineering; Chemical Engineering; Chemistry; Environmental Engineering) *Director*: José Saúl Oseguera López; **Civil Engineering** (Civil Engineering) *Director*: Juan Pérez Hernández; **Dentistry** (Dental Hygiene; Dental Technology; Dentistry; Orthodontics; Periodontics; Surgery) *Director*: Javier Aguirre Bacerot; **Education** (Education) *Dean*: Ariel Rivera Torres; **Mechanical and Electrical Engineering** (Electrical Engineering; Mechanical Engineering) *Director*: Juan Carlos Anzelmetti Zaragoza; **Medicine** (Medicine; Surgery) *Director*: Jorge Constantino Villegas Patiño; **Nursing** (Nursing) *Director*: Nazaria Martínez Díaz; **Psychology** (Psychology) *Director*: Francisco Bermúdez Jiménez; **Social Assistance** (Labour and Industrial Relations; Social and Community Services; Social Psychology; Social Work) *Director*: Virginia Calleja Mateos; **Veterinary Science** (Immunology; Microbiology; Pathology; Toxicology; Veterinary Science; Virology; Wildlife) *Dean*: Pablo Elorza Martínez

History: Founded 1944. Acquired present status and title 1996.

VERACRUZ REGION

REGIÓN VERACRUZ

S.S. Juan Pablo II s/n, Esq. Calzada de los Deportes, Boca del Río, Veracruz
Tel: +52(229) 923-28-00
Fax: +52(229) 923-28-33
Website: http://www.uv.mx

Vicerrectora: Liliana Ivonne Betancourt
Tel: +52(229) 923-28-01 EMail: lbetancourt@uv.mx

Faculties

Bioanalysis (Analytical Chemistry; Chemistry; Health Sciences) *Director*: María del Refugio Salas Ortega; **Business Administration** (Accountancy; Business Administration; Management) *Director*: Celia del Pilar Garrido Vargas; **Chemical Engineering** *Dean*: Edmundo Leyva Jiménez; **Civil Engineering** (Civil Engineering; Construction Engineering; Engineering Management; Hydraulic Engineering; Mechanical Engineering) *Dean*: Edmundo Leyva Jiménez; **Communication Sciences** (Communication Studies; Design; Public Relations; Social Sciences) *Director*: Ma. del Rocio Ojedo Callado; **Dentistry** (Dentistry) *Director*: Leticia Tiburcio Morteo; **Education** (Education; Pedagogy; Teacher Training) *Dean*: Aurelio Vázquez Torres; **Engineering**; **Mechanical and Electrical Engineering** (Electrical Engineering; Mechanical Engineering) *Dean*: Edmundo Leyva Jiménez; **Medicine** (Medicine; Radiology; Surgery) *Director*: Alfonso Gerardo Pérez Morales; **Nursing** (Nursing) *Director*: Sofía Delfín Baduy; **Nutrition** (Dietetics; Health Sciences; Nutrition) *Director*: María de Lourdes Malpica Carlín; **Physical Education, Sports and Recreation** (Parks and Recreation; Physical Education; Sociology; Sports) *Director*: Sergio Hernández López; **Psychology** (Psychology) *Director*: Martha Elena Aguirre Serena; **Veterinary Science** (Immunology; Microbiology; Pathology; Toxicology; Veterinary Science; Virology; Wildlife) *Director*: Carlos Lamonthe Zavaleta

Institutes

Forensic Medicine *Director*: Ángel Augusto Aguirre Gutiérrez

History: Founded 1994. Acquired present status and title 1996.

URBAN EVENING SPECIALIZATION TEACHER TRAINING SCHOOL OF THE STATE OF BAJA CALIFORNIA

Escuela Normal Urbana Nocturna de Especialización del Estado de Baja California

Calle Río San Lorenzo y Avenida Juan Escutia, Col. Prohogar, 21240 Mexicali, Baja California
Tel: +52(686) 666-14-95
EMail: normal-nocturna@hotmail.co

Directora: Martha Irene Celaya Figueroa

Programmes
Teacher Training

History: Founded 1960.

Main Language(s) of Instruction: Spanish

Degrees and Diplomas: *Licenciatura*; *Maestría*

Last Updated: 25/02/08

PRIVATE INSTITUTIONS

20TH OF NOVEMBER SCHOOL OF ADMINISTRATIVE STUDIES

Escuela de Estudios Administrativos 20 de Noviembre

Avenida Ocotlán, 51, 90000 Ocotlán, Jalisco
Tel: +52(246) 2-18-11 +52(246) 2-16-89
Fax: +52(246) 2-44-92

Director: Eliseo Martínez Peralta

Programmes
Administration (Administration)

Degrees and Diplomas: *Bachillerato*; *Licenciatura*

Last Updated: 03/04/08

21ST CENTURY INTERNATIONAL CENTRE

Centro Internacional Siglo XXI

Independencia, 39, Col. Centro, Izúcar de Matamoros, 74400 Iztacala, Puebla
Tel: +52(243) 436-27-52

Director: César Arturo Vargas Delgado

Degrees and Diplomas: *Licenciatura*

Last Updated: 04/04/08

21ST CENTURY UNIVERSITY CENTRE

Centro Universitario Siglo XXI

Blvd. Felipe Ángeles, 403, 42080 Pachuca, Hidalgo
Tel: +52(771) 718-65-38
Fax: +52(771) 718-65-38
Website: http://www.cusigloxxi.com.mx

Rector: Francisco Javier Moreno Partido

Programmes
Accountancy; **Computer Systems** (Computer Engineering); **Gastronomy**; **International Business** (International Business); **Journalism** (Journalism); **Law**; **Marketing** (Marketing); **Mass Communication**; **Pedagogy** (Curriculum; Educational Administration; Pedagogy); **Tourism**

Further Information: Also campus in Zacualtipán

History: Founded 1997.

Main Language(s) of Instruction: Spanish

Degrees and Diplomas: *Licenciatura*; *Maestría*

Libraries: Yes

Last Updated: 27/07/12

ACADEMIC AND RESEARCH CENTRE IN TAXATION

Centro Académico y de Investigación de la Tributación Fiscal, A.C.

M.M. del Llano 1199 Pte., 64000 Monterrey, Nuevo León
Tel: +52(81) 83-43-61-35
Fax: +52(81) 83-43-61-35

Programmes
Business Administration (Business Administration); **Taxation** (Taxation)

Degrees and Diplomas: *Licenciatura*; *Maestría*

Last Updated: 10/07/12

ACADEMIC CENTRE OF ADVANCED STUDIES

Centro Académico de Estudios Superiores

Av Yucatán No 27, Col Roma, 06700 México, D.F.
Tel: +52(5) 511-64-48
Fax: +52(5) 514-49-09
EMail: informes@inace.net

Directora: Elisa Concepción Padilla Gómez (1999-)

Programmes
Education (Education; Educational Psychology; Pedagogy)

History: Founded 1999. Formerly known as Instituto Nacional Académico de Actualización y Capacitación Educativa.

Main Language(s) of Instruction: Spanish

Degrees and Diplomas: *Maestría*; *Doctorado*

Last Updated: 14/02/13

ADELE ANN YGLESIAS SCHOOL OF PHYSICAL MEDICINE AND REHABILITATION OF THE ABC MEDICAL CENTRE

Escuela de Medicina Física y Rehabilitación Adele Ann Yglesias del Centro Médico ABC

Rafael Rebollar 35, Col. San Miguel Chapultepec, Delegación Miguel Hidalgo, México, D.F.
Tel: +52(55) 5278 9911 Ext. 08802
Website: http://www.abchospital.com

Director: Juan Pedro Casales Quezada (1980-)

Programmes
Rehabilitation and Therapy (Physical Therapy; Rehabilitation and Therapy)

History: Founded 1954.

Main Language(s) of Instruction: Spanish

Degrees and Diplomas: *Licenciatura*

Last Updated: 21/02/13

ADOLFO LÓPEZ MATEOS CENTRE FOR ADVANCED STUDIES

Centro de Estudios Superiores Adolfo López Mateos

Avenida 9 No. 314, Colonia Centro, Córdoba, Veracruz
Tel: +52(271) 714-7155
EMail: lopez4diego@hotmail.com

Director General: Diego López Martínez

Programmes
Accountancy (Accountancy); **Business Computing** (Business Computing); **Social Work** (Social Work)

Main Language(s) of Instruction: Spanish

Degrees and Diplomas: *Licenciatura*

Last Updated: 17/07/12

ADOLFO LÓPEZ MATEOS UNIVERSITY STUDIES CENTRE

Centro de Estudios Universitarios Adolfo López Mateos
Ramón Corona, 820, Mascota, 47860 Ocotlán, Jalisco
Tel: +52(392) 922-32-73
Fax: +52(392) 922-21-25
EMail: ceudlm@yahoo.com.mx
Website: http://www.ceualm.com

Director: Jaime Ribera Varela (1991-)

Programmes
Business Computing (Business Computing)

History: Founded 1991.

Main Language(s) of Instruction: Spanish

Degrees and Diplomas: *Licenciatura*

ALBERT EINSTEIN UNIVERSITY

Universidad Albert Einstein (UAE)
Carr. Tlazala de Fabela- Santa Ana Jilotzingo Km. 23 Col. Isidro Fabela, 64000 Monterrey, Nuevo León
Tel: +52(81) 8996-91-43
EMail: informes@ualberteinstein.edu.mx
Website: http://www.ualberteinstein.edu.mx

Director General: Álvaro Guerra López

Programmes
Business Administration (Business Administration); **Design** (Design); **Human Development** (Development Studies); **Information Technology** (Information Technology); **Marketing** (Marketing); **Pedagogy** (Pedagogy); **Physics** (Physics); **Psychology** (Psychology)

History: Founded 1998 as Instituto Internacional de Ciencias Albert Einstein. Acquired present status and title 2000.

Main Language(s) of Instruction: Spanish

Degrees and Diplomas: *Licenciatura*; *Maestría*

Libraries: Yes

Last Updated: 30/08/12

ALFONSO CRAVIOTO INSTITUTE OF ADVANCED TEACHING

Instituto de Enseñanza Superior Alfonso Cravioto
Avenida 21 de Marzo Norte, 511, Col. Centro, 43600 Tulancingo, Hidalgo
Tel: +52(775) 755-11-70
EMail: iesac@prodigy.net

Directora: María Sofía Aguilar González

Programmes
Business Administration (Accountancy; Business Administration; Labour and Industrial Relations; Marketing)

History: Founded 1993.

Main Language(s) of Instruction: Spanish

Degrees and Diplomas: *Licenciatura*

Last Updated: 28/02/13

ALFONSO REYES UNIVERSITY

Universidad Alfonso Reyes, S.C.
Insurgentes, 1433, Col. Vicente Guerrero, 66437 San Nicolás de los Garza, Nuevo León
Tel: +52(81) 83-82-17-56 +52(81) 83-82-27-99
Fax: +52(81) 83-82-17-56
Website: http://www.uar.edu.mx

Rector: Gerardo Aguilera González

Faculties
Administration (Accountancy; Administration; Business Administration; Business Computing); **Architecture** (Architecture); **Communication Studies** (Communication Studies); **Engineering** (Computer Engineering; Industrial Engineering; Mechanical Engineering); **English** (English); **Law** (Law)

Programmes
Education (Education)

Further Information: Also Lindavista, La Fe, Monterrey units

History: Founded 1993.

Main Language(s) of Instruction: Spanish

Degrees and Diplomas: *Licenciatura*; *Maestría*

Last Updated: 25/03/13

ALFRED NOBEL UNIVERSITY OF MEXICO

Universidad Alfred Nobel de México
Maravillas 16 Nuevo Espíritu Santo, 76800 San Juan del Río, Querétaro
Tel: +52(427) 272-70-22
EMail: uninobel@hotmail.com
Website: www.uninobel.edu.mxhttp: //www.uninobel.edu.mx

Director General: Felipe Salinas Castillo (1997-)

Programmes
Accountancy (Accountancy); **Business Administration** (Administration; International Business); **Computer Networks** (Computer Networks); **Law** (Law); **Pedagogy** (Education; Pedagogy)

History: Founded 1997 as Colegio e Estudios Superiores de San Juan. Acquired present status and title 2000.

Main Language(s) of Instruction: Spanish

Degrees and Diplomas: *Licenciatura*

Last Updated: 31/08/12

ALLENDE CENTRE FOR ADVANCED STUDIES

Centro de Estudios Superiores Allende (CEESA)
Aurora no 30, Col. Guadalupe, 37710 San Miguel de Allende, Guanajuato
Tel: +52(415) 15-476-48
EMail: mortega73@hotmail.com
Website: http://ceesanet.edu.mx

Directora: María Isabel Vadillo Serrato (2001-)

Programmes
Administration (Public Administration); **Accountancy** (Accountancy); **Law** (Law)

History: Founded 2001.

Main Language(s) of Instruction: Spanish

Degrees and Diplomas: *Licenciatura*

Last Updated: 13/07/12

ALLENDE INSTITUTE

Instituto Allende
Ancha de San Antonio, 20, Centro, 37700 San Miguel de Allende, Guanajuato
Tel: +52(415) 152-01-90 +52(415) 152-02-26
Fax: +52(415) 152-45-38
EMail: fundacion@institutoallende.edu.mx
Website: http://www.instituto-allende.edu.mx

Director: Rodolfo Fernández Martínez Harris (1995-)

Schools
Fine Arts (Jewelry Art; Painting and Drawing; Photography; Sculpture; Visual Arts)

History: Founded 1937.

Main Language(s) of Instruction: Spanish

Degrees and Diplomas: *Licenciatura*

Last Updated: 30/08/12

ALLENDE UNIVERSITY CENTRE

Centro Universitario Allende
Avenida Vicente Guerrero, 419, Barrio Alto, 42800 Tula de Allende, Hidalgo
Tel: +52(773) 732-5934
EMail: informes@cenua.edu.mx
Website: http://www.upp.edu.mx

Rector: Alberto del Castillo del Valle

Programmes
Accountancy (Accountancy); **Business Administration** (Business Administration); **Business and Commerce** (Business and Commerce); **Gastronomy** (Cooking and Catering); **International Business** (International Business); **Law** (Law); **Marketing** (Marketing); **Psychology** (Psychology)

History: Founded 1997.

Main Language(s) of Instruction: Spanish

Degrees and Diplomas: *Licenciatura*; *Maestría*
Last Updated: 23/07/12

ALPHA AND OMEGA INSTITUTE OF HIGHER EDUCATION

Instituto de Educación Superior Alfa y Omega
Avenida 27 de Febrero, 1804 y, Paseo Usumacinta, 503, Col. Atasta, Centro, 86100 Villahermosa, Tabasco
Tel: +52(993) 315-34-29 +52(993) 315-89-58
Fax: +52(993) 315-03-16
EMail: iesao@prodigy.net.mx

Director: Josue Vera Granados

Programmes
Business Administration and Law (Accountancy; Administration; Law); **Pedagogy** (Education; Pedagogy)

History: Founded 1994.

Main Language(s) of Instruction: Spanish

Degrees and Diplomas: *Licenciatura*
Last Updated: 28/02/13

ALVA EDISON UNIVERSITY

Universidad Alva Edison
Avenida Reforma, 725, 72000 Puebla, Puebla
Tel: +52(222) 232-31-96
EMail: aedison@gemtel.com.mx
Website: http://www.unialvaedison.edu.mx

Presidente: Jorge León Vázquez

Programmes
Accountancy (Accountancy); **Administration** (Administration); **Architecture and Town Planning** (Architecture; Town Planning); **Business Computing** (Business Computing); **Communication Sciences** (Communication Studies); **Computer Science** (Computer Science); **Graphic Design** (Graphic Design); **Industrial Psychology** (Industrial and Organizational Psychology); **International Business** (International Business); **Law and Criminology** (Criminology; Law); **Marketing and Publicity** (Advertising and Publicity; Marketing)

History: Founded 1982 as Instituto de Computación. Acquired present status and title 1999.

Main Language(s) of Instruction: Spanish

Degrees and Diplomas: *Licenciatura*; *Maestría*

Libraries: Yes
Last Updated: 31/08/12

ALZATE UNIVERSITY OF OZUMBA

Universidad Alzate de Ozumba
Av. Alzate Norte # 4-A. Colonia Alzate, 56800 Ozumba, Estado de México
Tel: +52(597) 976-22-90
Fax: +52(597) 976-22-90
EMail: coalzate@prodigy.net.mx
Website: http://www.unicoalzate.com.mx

Rector: Víctor Rojas Adaya (2000-)

Programmes
Administration (Administration); **Architecture** (Architecture); **Law** (Law); **Pedagogy** (Pedagogy); **Psychology** (Psychology)

History: Founded 1977 as Colegio Alzate. Acquired present status and title 2000.

Main Language(s) of Instruction: Spanish

Degrees and Diplomas: *Licenciatura*
Last Updated: 12/04/11

AMAUTA UNIVERSITY

Universidad Amauta
Ricarte, 32, Col. Villa de Guadalupe, Delegación Gustavo A. Madero, 07020 México, D.F.
Tel: +52(55) 57-50-01-66
Fax: +52(55) 57-81-52-09
EMail: colegioamauta@hotmail.com
Website: http://www.universidad.amauta.edu.mx/

Director: Alberto Rivera Bendezu

Programmes
Accountancy (Accountancy); **Business Administration** (Business Administration); **Law** (Law)

History: Founded 1993.

Main Language(s) of Instruction: Spanish

Degrees and Diplomas: *Licenciatura*
Last Updated: 27/07/12

AMERICA INSTITUTE

Instituto América
Camino a Jesús Maria No. 1015, Fracc. de Alfaro, 37673 León, Guanajuato
Tel: +52(477) 741-80-20
EMail: informacion@institutoamerica.com.mx
Website: http://www.institutoamerica.com.mx

Directora: María Concepción Flores Montufar (1969-)
EMail: direcciongeneral@institutoamerica.com.mx

Programmes
Education (Education; Preschool Education; Primary Education; Secondary Education)

History: Founded 1955.

Main Language(s) of Instruction: Spanish

Degrees and Diplomas: *Licenciatura*
Last Updated: 26/02/08

AMERICAN CONTINENT UNIVERSITY

Universidad Continente Americano
Insurgentes, 150, Col. Centro, 38000 Celaya, Guanajuato
Tel: +52(461) 612-64-97
Fax: +52(461) 613-30-05
EMail: iamericano@prodigy.net.mx
Website: http://www.uca.edu.mx

Directora: Rebeca González Mejía (1977-)

Programmes
Accountancy (Accountancy); **Architecture** (Architecture); **Communication Studies** (Cinema and Television; Communication Studies; Journalism; Radio and Television Broadcasting); **Education** (Education; Primary Education; Secondary Education); **Engineering** (Civil Engineering; Computer Engineering; Industrial Engineering); **Gastronomy** (Cooking and Catering); **Law** (Law); **Physical Education and Sport** (Physical Education; Sports); **Psychology** (Psychology); **Stomatology** (Dentistry; Stomatology)

Further Information: Branches in Abasolo, Acámbaro, C orzar, Irapuato, León, San Luis de la Paz, San Miguel de Allende and Yuriria

History: Founded 1977 as Instituto Americano. Acquired present title 1993.

Main Language(s) of Instruction: Spanish

Degrees and Diplomas: *Licenciatura*; *Maestría*; *Doctorado*
Last Updated: 30/08/12

AMERICAN TECHNOLOGICAL UNIVERSITY

Universidad Tecnológica Americana (UTECA)
Viaducto Miguel Alemán, 255, Col. Roma Sur, Delegación Cuauhtémoc, 06760 México, D.F.
Tel: +52(555) 264-85-20
EMail: contacto@uteca.edu.mx
Website: http://www.uteca.mx

Rector: Gonzalo Antonio Vivanco Florido (1971-)

Programmes

Actuarial Science (Actuarial Science); **Business Administration** (Accountancy; Administration; Business Computing; Finance; Marketing); **Design** (Design); **Law** (Law); **Telematics** (Telecommunications Engineering); **Translation and Interpretation** (Modern Languages; Translation and Interpretation)

History: Founded 1971.

Admission Requirements: Secondary school certificate (bachillerato)

Main Language(s) of Instruction: Spanish

Degrees and Diplomas: *Licenciatura*; *Especialización*; *Maestría*
Last Updated: 05/04/13

AMERICAN UNIVERSITY

Universidad Americana
Avenida San Jerónimo, 111, Col. San Ángel, Delegación Álvaro Obregón, 01000 México, D.F.
Tel: +52(55) 56-16-14-52 +52(55) 56-16-14-66
Fax: +52(55) 55-50-33-89

Rector: Miguel Mandujano Contreras (1993-)

Programmes

Administration and Accountancy (Accountancy; Administration); **Communication Arts** (Communication Arts); **Computer Science** (Computer Science); **Economics** (Economics); **Education** (Education); **Graphic Design** (Graphic Design); **Law** (Law)

Further Information: Campuses: Teopanzolco, Acapantzingo and Desarrollo Laguna

History: Founded 1993

Main Language(s) of Instruction: Spanish

Degrees and Diplomas: *Bachillerato*; *Licenciatura*
Last Updated: 07/04/08

AMERICAN UNIVERSITY CENTRE OF THE STATE OF MORELOS

Centro Universitario Americano del Estado de Morelos
Avenida Domingo Diez 1898, Col. Chamilpa, Cuernavaca, Morelos
Tel: +52(777) 717-42-57
Fax: +52(777) 711-31-48
Website: http://www.cuadem.edu.mx

Programmes

Industrial Engineering (Industrial Engineering); **International Relations** (International Relations); **Journalism and Communication Studies** (Communication Studies; Journalism)

History: Founded 1997.

Main Language(s) of Instruction: Spanish

Degrees and Diplomas: *Licenciatura*
Last Updated: 23/07/12

AMERICAN UNIVERSITY OF ACAPULCO

Universidad Americana de Acapulco
Avenida Costera Miguel Alemán, 1756, Esq. Enrique El Navegante, Fracc. Magallanes, 39670 Acapulco de Juárez, Guerrero
Tel: +52(744) 469-17-00
EMail: rectoria@uaa.edu.mx
Website: http://www.uaa.edu.mx

Rector: Mario Mendoza Castañeda

Faculties

Accountancy (Accountancy); **Architecture** (Architecture); **Communication and Public Relations** (Communication Studies; Public Relations); **Computer Engineering** (Computer Engineering; Engineering); **Law** (Law); **Psychology** (Psychology); **Tourism** (Tourism)

Further Information: Also campus in Chilpancingo (Gro.)

History: Founded 1991.

Main Language(s) of Instruction: Spanish

Degrees and Diplomas: *Licenciatura*; *Maestría*; *Doctorado*: Administration; Law

Libraries: Biblioteca José Francisco Ruiz Massieu
Last Updated: 25/03/13

AMERICAN UNIVERSITY OF MORELOS

Universidad Americana de Morelos (UAM)
Calle del Ejido No 30 Col, Ejido de Acapatzingo, 62290 Cuernavaca, Morelos
Tel: +52(777) 310 - 66 - 66
EMail: informes@uam.edu.mx
Website: http://www.uam.edu.mx

Rector: Alejandro Román Robles (1986-) Fax: +52(777) 311-72-60 EMail: rectoria@uam.edu.mx

Campuses

Teopanzolco *(Teopanzolco and Loma del Águila)* (Accountancy; Administration; Business Administration; Computer Science; Economics; Education; Educational Psychology; Finance; Graphic Design; Higher Education; Human Resources; Marketing; Mass Communication; Media Studies)

Departments

Education *(Teopanzolco and Loma del Águila)* (Administration; Bilingual and Bicultural Education; Education; Higher Education; Pedagogy)

Divisions

Graphic Design and Communication Sciences *(Teopanzolco and Loma del Águila)* (Communication Studies; Graphic Design); **Law** *(Teopanzolco and Loma del Águila)* (Law); **Open Education System** *(Teopanzolco and Loma del Águila)* (Distance Education)

History: Founded 1986. Acquired present status 2000.

Governing Bodies: Junta de Gobierno (Governing Board); University and Academic Boards

Academic Year: August to June (August-January; February-June)

Admission Requirements: Secondary school certificate and entrance examination

Fees: (US Dollars): 85,000 per semester

Main Language(s) of Instruction: Spanish, English

International Co-operation: With universities in USA, Canada and Spain

Degrees and Diplomas: *Licenciatura*: 4 yrs; *Especialización*: a further yr; *Maestría*

Student Services: Academic counselling, Cultural centre, Employment services, Foreign student adviser, Handicapped facilities, Health services, Language programs, Social counselling, Sports facilities

Student Residential Facilities: None

Libraries: Yes; Traditional and Multimedia systems
Last Updated: 31/08/12

AMERICAN UNIVERSITY OF THE ISTHMUS

Universidad Istmo Americana
Avenida Universidad Km 8.5, Col. Santa Cecilia, 96420 Coatzacoalcos, Veracruz
Tel: +52(921) 214-37-14
Fax: +52(921) 214-96-18
EMail: direccion_academica_uia@live.com.mx
Website: http://www.istmoamericana.com.mx/

Rector: Juan Manuel Rodríguez Caamaño

Programmes

Administration (Accountancy; Administration; Commercial Law; Computer Science; Finance; Industrial and Organizational Psychology; Labour Law; Law; Management; Mathematics; Statistics); **Agricultural Business** (Agricultural Business); **Communication** (Advertising and Publicity; Communication Studies); **Computer Science** (Accountancy; Administration; Computer Science; Data Processing; Economics; Human Resources; Information Management; Information Sciences; Labour Law; Management; Mathematics; Operations Research; Software Engineering; Statistics); **Computer Systems** (Accountancy; Applied Mathematics; Chemistry; Computer Engineering; Computer Networks; Computer Science; Information Technology; Mathematics; Multimedia; Operations Research; Physics; Statistics; Systems Analysis); **Graphic Design** (Graphic Design); **Law** (Administrative Law; Civil Law; Commercial Law; Computer Science; Constitutional Law; Criminal Law; Economic and Finance Policy; History of Law; Labour Law;

Law; Political Sciences; Sociology); **Marketing** (Accountancy; Administration; Communication Studies; Development Studies; Ecology; Finance; Human Resources; Industrial and Organizational Psychology; Information Management; Marketing; Mathematics; Private Law; Public Law; Social Sciences); **Pedagogy** (Child Care and Development; Education; Educational Psychology; Educational Research; Educational Sciences; Pedagogy); **Psychology** (Computer Science; Industrial and Organizational Psychology; Mathematics; Neurology; Pathology; Psychology; Statistics); **Tourism** (Accountancy; Administration; Business Computing; Commercial Law; English; French; Labour Law; Tourism)

Further Information: Also campuses in Acayucan, Veracruz and Villahermosa, Tabasco

History: Founded 1999.

Main Language(s) of Instruction: Spanish

Degrees and Diplomas: *Licenciatura*; *Maestría*; *Doctorado*

Last Updated: 11/10/12

ANÁHUAC AMERICAN COLLEGE OF MONTERREY

Colegio Americano Anáhuac de Monterrey, S.C.

Prolongación Villa de Casas, 200, Villa de Anáhuac, 66420 San Nicolás de Los Garza, Nuevo León

Tel: +52(81) 83-76-33-37

EMail: sugerencia@americanoanahuac.edu.mx

Website: http://www.americanoanahuac.edu.mx

Directora: María Teresa Adel Blade (1999-)

Programmes

Education (Education)

History: Founded 1985.

Main Language(s) of Instruction: Spanish

Degrees and Diplomas: *Licenciatura*

Last Updated: 11/03/08

ANÁHUAC COLLEGE OF ADVANCED STUDIES

Colegio de Estudios Superiores Anáhuac

Nicolo Paganini, 303, Col. Jardines del Sur, 50377 Tulancingo, Hidalgo

Tel: +52(775) 753-61-00

Fax: +52(775) 753-61-00

EMail: colanahuac@prodigy.net.mx

Director General: Filiberto Herrera Mendoza (1995-)

Programmes

Accountancy (Accountancy; Taxation); **Administration** (Administration; Business Administration); **Law** (Law); **Marketing** (Marketing); **Psychology** (Psychology)

History: Founded 1995.

Main Language(s) of Instruction: Spanish

Degrees and Diplomas: *Licenciatura*; *Especialización*

Last Updated: 20/03/08

ANÁHUAC INCORPORATED PRIVATE TEACHER TRAINING SCHOOL

Escuela Normal Particular Incorporada Anáhuac

Isidro Huarte, 80, Col. Centro, 58000 Morelia, Michoacán

Tel: +52(443) 312-07-70

EMail: colegioanahuac@infosel.net.mx

Directora: Ma. Angelina Bello Camargo

Programmes

Education (Teacher Training)

History: Founded 1949.

Main Language(s) of Instruction: Spanish

Degrees and Diplomas: *Licenciatura*

Last Updated: 25/02/13

ANÁHUAC UNIVERSITY MAYAB

Universidad Anáhuac Mayab

Carretera Mérida Progreso Km. 15.5 AP. 96, Cordemex, 97310 Mérida, Yucatán

Tel: +52(999) 942-48-00

EMail: rectoria.anahuacmayab@anahuac.mx

Website: http://www.anahuacmayab.mx

Rector: Rafael Pardo Hervás

Divisions

Business Studies (Accountancy; Business Administration; Cooking and Catering; Finance; International Business; Management; Marketing); **Communication, Architecture and Design** (Architecture; Communication Studies; Graphic Design; Industrial Design; Multimedia); **Engineering and Exact Sciences** (Civil Engineering; Electrical Engineering; Industrial Engineering; Information Technology; Mechanical Engineering); **Health Sciences** (Dentistry; Medicine; Nutrition; Surgery); **Law and Social Sciences** (Law; Pedagogy; Psychology)

History: Founded 1984.

Admission Requirements: Bachillerato and entrance examination

Main Language(s) of Instruction: Spanish

Degrees and Diplomas: *Licenciatura*; *Especialización*; *Maestría*; *Doctorado*

Libraries: Yes

Last Updated: 25/03/13

ANÁHUAC UNIVERSITY OF CANCÚN

Universidad Anáhuac de Cancún (UAC)

Carretera Chetumal-Cancún Smza., 299 Mza 2, Zona 8, Lote 1, 77565 Cancún, Quintana Roo

Tel: +52(998) 881-44-50

Fax: +52(998) 881-44-50

EMail: promocion@anahuaccancun.edu.mx

Website: http://www.anahuaccancun.edu.mx

Rector: Miguel Pérez Gómez

Tel: +52(998) 881-44-50, Fax: +52(998) 881-77-50

Schools

Architecture (Architecture); **Business** (Accountancy; Administration; International Business; Marketing); **Communication Sciences** (Communication Studies; Graphic Design); **Design** (Graphic Design); **Engineering** (Industrial Engineering); **Gastronomy** (Cooking and Catering); **Law** (Law); **Psychology** (Psychology); **Tourism** (Hotel and Restaurant; Tourism)

History: Founded 1998.

Academic Year: August to June

Admission Requirements: Admission Exam and Psychology Test

Fees: (US Dollars): enrolment, 5,920 per semester; Credit fee, 527 per month

Main Language(s) of Instruction: Spanish

International Co-operation: With universities in Italy, Spain, USA and Chile

Accrediting Agencies: Secretaría de Educación Pública (SEP), Quintana Roo

Degrees and Diplomas: *Licenciatura*: $4\frac{1}{2}$ yrs; *Maestría*

Student Services: Academic counselling, Canteen, Cultural centre, Employment services, Foreign student adviser, Foreign Studies Centre, Language programs, Social counselling, Sports facilities

Student Residential Facilities: None

Special Facilities: Media Centre

Libraries: Yes

Last Updated: 31/08/12

ANÁHUAC UNIVERSITY OF NORTH MEXICO

Universidad Anáhuac México Norte

Av. Lomas Anáhuac s/n, Col. Lomas Anáhuac, 52786 Huixquilucán, Estado de México

Tel: +52(555) 627-02-10 +52(555) 328-80-06

Fax: +52(555) 596-19-38

EMail: anahuac@anahuac.mx

Website: http://www.anahuac.mx

Rector: Jesús Quirce Andrés (2002-) EMail: quirce@anahuac.mx

Secretario General: Abraham Cárdenas
EMail: abraham.cárdenas@anahuac.mx

International Relations: María Isabel Lozano
EMail: mlozano@anahuac.mx

Centres

Scientific and Technological Research on Tourism *(CIENTUR)* (Tourism); **Social Responsibility** *(Latin American)* (Social Studies)

Faculties

Bioethics (Ethics); **Communication Sciences** (Communication Studies); **Economics and Business Administration** (Business Administration; Economics; International Business; Management; Marketing); **Education** (Education; Educational Administration; Educational Psychology; Pedagogy); **Engineering** (Civil Engineering; Construction Engineering; Electronic Engineering; Engineering; Industrial Engineering; Information Technology; Mechanical Engineering); **Health Sciences** (Dentistry; Health Administration; Medicine; Nutrition); **Humanities** *(Graduate)* (Arts and Humanities; Cultural Studies; Philosophy; Religion); **Law** (International Relations; Law)

Schools

Actuarial Sciences (Actuarial Science; Insurance; Statistics); **Architecture** (Architectural and Environmental Design; Architecture; Interior Design; Landscape Architecture; Town Planning); **Design** (Design; Graphic Design; Industrial Design); **International Relations** (International Relations); **Languages** (Chinese; English; French; German; Italian; Translation and Interpretation); **Psychology** (Educational Psychology; Industrial and Organizational Psychology; Psychology); **Tourism Management** (Hotel and Restaurant; Hotel Management; Tourism)

Further Information: Also language courses, diploma courses and Study Abroad Undergraduate and Graduate Programmes.

History: Founded 1964.

Academic Year: January to December (January-June; August-December)

Admission Requirements: High school certificate and entrance examination

Fees: (Pesos): c. 55,000 per semester

Main Language(s) of Instruction: Spanish

Degrees and Diplomas: *Licenciatura*: 4 yrs; *Especialización*: 1 yr; *Maestría*: a further 1 1/2-2 yrs; *Doctorado*: a further 1 1/2-3 yrs

Student Services: Academic counselling, Cultural centre, Employment services, Foreign student adviser, Handicapped facilities, Health services, Language programs, Social counselling, Sports facilities

Libraries: Yes

Last Updated: 31/08/12

ANÁHUAC UNIVERSITY OF OAXACA

Universidad Anáhuac de Oaxaca
Blvd. Guadalupe Hinojosa de Murat 1100, Altos Centro, 68000 Oaxaca, Oaxaca
Tel: +52(951) 501-62-50
Fax: +52(951) 517-91-64
EMail: uao@anahuac.mx
Website: http://www.anahuacoaxaca.edu.mx

Rector: Rodrigo del Val Martín

Centres

Languages (Modern Languages; Special Education)

Schools

Communication (Communication Studies); **Economics and Trade** (Accountancy; Business Administration; Economics; Finance; International Business; Marketing); **Engineering** (Chemical Engineering; Civil Engineering; Electronic Engineering; Engineering; Mechanical Engineering; Telecommunications Engineering); **Law** (Law); **Psychology** (Psychology); **Tourism and Gastronomy** (Cooking and Catering; Tourism)

History: Founded 2000.

Academic Year: August to June

Admission Requirements: School certificate and College Board examination

Fees: (Pesos): 20,000 per semester

Main Language(s) of Instruction: Spanish

Degrees and Diplomas: *Licenciatura*; *Maestría*. Also Diplomados

Student Services: Academic counselling, Handicapped facilities, Language programs

Libraries: Yes

Last Updated: 25/03/13

ANAHUAC UNIVERSITY OF PUEBLA

Universidad Anáhuac de Puebla
Orión Norte s/n, Col. La Vista Country Club, 72810 San Andrés Cholula, Puebla
Tel: +52(222) 169-10-69
EMail: contacto@anahuacpuebla.org
Website: http://www.anahuacpuebla.org

Rector: José Gerardo Mata Temoltzin

Schools

Commerce (Business Administration; International Business; Marketing; Tourism); **Communication Studies** (Communication Studies); **Engineering** (Business and Commerce; Industrial Engineering); **Law** (Government; Law; Public Administration); **Psychology** (Psychology); **Tourism** (Hotel Management; Tourism)

Admission Requirements: Bachillerato and entrance examination

Degrees and Diplomas: *Licenciatura*; *Especialización*; *Maestría*

Libraries: Yes

Last Updated: 31/08/12

ANAHUAC UNIVERSITY OF QUERETARO

Universidad Anáhuac de Querétaro
Av. El Campanario #88, Fracc. El Campanario, Querétaro, Querétaro
Tel: +52 (442) 245-67-42
EMail: agonzalez@anahuacqro.com
Website: http://www.anahuacqro.edu.mx

Rector: Luis E. Alverde Montemayor

Schools

Economics and Commerce (Business Administration; Business and Commerce; Economics; International Business; Marketing); **Engineering** (Industrial Engineering); **Law** (Law); **Psychology** (Psychology); **Tourism** (Tourism)

History: Founded 2005.

Main Language(s) of Instruction: Spanish

Degrees and Diplomas: *Licenciatura*; *Maestría*

Last Updated: 25/03/13

ANÁHUAC UNIVERSITY OF XALAPA

Universidad Anáhuac de Xalapa
Circuito Arco Sur s/n Col. Lomas Verdes, 91180 Xalapa, Veracruz
Tel: +52(228) 819-15-15
EMail: dermot.mccluskey@uax.edu.mx
Website: http://www.uax.edu.mx

Rector: Dermot McCluskey

Schools

Communication and Graphic Design (Communication Studies; Graphic Design); **Economics and Business** (Accountancy; Administration; International Business; Marketing); **Engineering** (Engineering; Environmental Engineering; Industrial Engineering; Information Technology); **Law** (Law)

History: Founded 1993.

Main Language(s) of Instruction: Spanish

Degrees and Diplomas: *Licenciatura*; *Maestría*

Libraries: Yes

Last Updated: 31/08/12

ANÁHUAC UNIVERSITY SOUTH MEXICO

Universidad Anáhuac México Sur

Avenida de las Torres, 131, Col. Olivar de los Padres, Delegación Álvaro Obregón, 01780 México, D.F.
Tel: +52(55) 56-28-88-00
Fax: +52(55) 56-28-88-37
EMail: comunicacioninstitucional.uams@anahuac.mx
Website: http://www.uas.mx

Rector: Javier Vargas Diez Barroso

Secretario General: Vicente Cortina

International Relations: Nora Montiel Mancisidor

Centres

Language (Linguistics; Modern Languages)

Faculties

Engineering (Civil Engineering; Computer Engineering; Computer Science; Electronic Engineering; Engineering; Industrial Engineering; Mechanical Engineering); **Law** (Law)

Graduate Schools

Business (Business and Commerce); **Engineering** (Engineering)

Schools

Actuarial Sciences (Actuarial Science); **Administration** (Administration); **Architecture** (Architecture); **Communication Sciences** (Communication Studies); **Graphic Design** (Graphic Design); **International Studies** (International Relations; International Studies); **Tourism Management** (Tourism)

Further Information: Also four-week international programme entitled 'Introduction to the Mexican Legal System'. Other programmes are available in the areas of Language and Mexican Business

History: Founded 1981.

Admission Requirements: Secondary school certificate (bachillerato) and entrance examination

Main Language(s) of Instruction: Spanish

Degrees and Diplomas: *Licenciatura*; *Maestría*; *Doctorado*

Publications: Integración Anáhuac del Sur

Last Updated: 25/03/13

ANDAMAXEI UNIVERSITY CENTRE

Centro Universitario Andamaxei

16 de septiembre, 74 y 67 Ote., Centro, 76000 Querétaro, Querétaro
Tel: +52(442) 13-02-88
Fax: +52(442) 13-02-88

Directora: Martha Elvia Ortiz Espinoza (1999-)

Programmes

History (History); **International Business** (International Business)

History: Founded 1999.

Main Language(s) of Instruction: Spanish

Degrees and Diplomas: *Licenciatura*

Last Updated: 11/03/08

ANDRES INCORPORATED HIGHER TEACHER TRAINING SCHOOL OF QUINTANA ROO

Escuela Normal Superior Incorporada Andres Quintana Roo

Avenida Chac Mool Sm. 218 Mza 1 Lte. 2 entre Av. Talleres y Av. Leona Vicario, 77517 Cancún, Quintana Roo
Tel: +52(998) 132-76-93
Fax: +52(998) 132-76-94
EMail: contactanos@ensaqroo.edu.mx
Website: http://www.ensaqroo.edu.mx/

Director General: Gregorio Delgado Morales
EMail: direccion@ensaqroo.edu.mx

Director Administrativo: Jose I. Mena Madera
EMail: josem@ensaqroo.edu.mx

Programmes

Education (Education)

History: Founded 1997.

Main Language(s) of Instruction: Spanish

Degrees and Diplomas: *Licenciatura*

Last Updated: 26/02/13

ANGELÓPOLIS UNIVERSITY

Universidad Angelópolis

3 Ote. 1603, Col. Azcarate (Barrio de Analco), 72000 Puebla, Puebla
Tel: +52(222) 130-10-63
Fax: +52(222) 232-86-01
Website: http://www.uniangelopolis.edu.mx

Rector: Roberto Corvera Guzmán

Vicerrector: Martín Róman Núñez

Programmes

Architecture (Architecture); **Business Administration** (Accountancy; Administration; Business Administration; Economics; International Business); **Computer Science** (Computer Science); **Graphic Design** (Graphic Design); **Law** (Law); **Marketing and Advertising** (Advertising and Publicity; Marketing); **Public Relations and Communication** (Communication Studies; Public Relations)

History: Founded 1999 as Centro de Estudios Universitarios Angelópolis.

Main Language(s) of Instruction: Spanish

Degrees and Diplomas: *Licenciatura*; *Maestría*

Last Updated: 31/08/12

ANGLO-AMERICAN EDUCATION GROUP

Grupo Educativo Angloamericano

Eligio Villamar, 17 casi esquina División del Norte, Col. Churubusco, Delegación Coyoacán, 04210 México, D.F.
Tel: +52(55) 53-95-67-79
EMail: info@angloamericano.com.mx
Website: http://www.angloamericano.com.mx/

Director General: Jesús Hernández Ramos

Programmes

Interrnational Marketing (International Business; Marketing); **Modern Languages** (Linguistics; Modern Languages; Translation and Interpretation); **Nutrition** (Nutrition)

Further Information: Also Aguascalientes, Aragón, Cancún, Churubusco, Coacalco, Coyoacán, Cuernavaca, Cuautitlán, Diana Cazadora, Guadalajara, Gómez Palacio, Metepec, Monterrey, Morelia, Puebla, Puebla Triángulo, Querétaro, Roma, Santa Fe, Satélite, Toluca, Torreón and Veracruz centres

History: Founded 1972 as Centro de Idiomas.

Main Language(s) of Instruction: Spanish

Degrees and Diplomas: *Licenciatura*; *Especialización*; *Maestría*

Last Updated: 27/02/13

ANGLO-HISPANIC-MEXICAN UNIVERSITY

Universidad Anglohispanomexicana

15 Sur, 307, Col. Centro, Heroica Puebla de Zaragoza, 72000 Puebla, Puebla
Tel: +52(222) 232-07-98
Fax: +52(222) 246-21-43
EMail: informes@anglohispanomexicana.com
Website: http://www.anglohispanomexicana.com

Rector: Bernardo Mancillas Ruiz

Programmes

Accountancy (Accountancy); **Administration** (Administration); **Computer Science** (Computer Science); **Gastronomy and Restaurant Management** (Cooking and Catering; Hotel and Restaurant); **Law** (Law); **Psychology** (Psychology); **Tourism** (Tourism)

History: Founded 1992.

Main Language(s) of Instruction: Spanish

Degrees and Diplomas: *Licenciatura*; *Maestría*: Education

Last Updated: 25/03/13

ANGLO-SPANISH UNIVERSITY INSTITUTE

Instituto Universitario Anglo Español

Paseo del Condor, 100, Fracc. Real del Mezquital, Durango, Durango

Tel: +52(618) 811-78-11

EMail: iunaes@yahoo.com.mx

Website: http://www.iunaes.com.mx

Director: Arturo Barraza Macías

Programmes

Architecture (Architecture); **Industrial Design** (Industrial Design); **Industrial Management** (Industrial Management); **Information Systems and Technology** (Information Technology)

Further Information: Also campus in Victoria

Main Language(s) of Instruction: Spanish

Degrees and Diplomas: *Licenciatura*: 4 1/2 yrs; *Maestría*; *Doctorado*

Last Updated: 22/03/13

ANGLO ZACATLAN UNIVERSITY

Universidad Anglo Zacatlán

José Dolores Pérez, 4, Col. Centro, Zacatlán, Puebla

Tel: +52(797) 975-23-81

Website: http://www.angelfire.com/in4/pages/anglo/index.html

Rector: Joram Charolet Rodriguez

Programmes

Accountancy (Accountancy); **Banking and Finance** (Banking; Finance); **Business Administration** (Business Administration); **Computer Science** (Computer Science); **Law** (Law); **Psychology** (Psychology); **Tourism** (Tourism)

History: Founded 1996. Acquired present status and title 2002. Previously campus of the Universidad Hispanomexicana.

Main Language(s) of Instruction: Spanish

Degrees and Diplomas: *Licenciatura*; *Maestría*

Last Updated: 31/08/12

ANTHROPOLOGICAL UNIVERSITY OF GUADALAJARA

Universidad Antropológica de Guadalajara

José Guadalupe Zuno 1881, Col. Americana, 44150 Guadalajara, Jalisco

Tel: +52(33) 38-26-13-63

Fax: +52(33) 38-26-14-83

EMail: informes@unag.mx

Website: http://www.iseg.edu.mx/iseg/index.jsp

Director: José Garza Mora

Programmes

Family Studies (Education; Family Studies; Law; Philosophy; Psychology; Psychotherapy; Social Problems; Sociology); **Homeopathy** (Homeopathy); **Human Development and Bioenergy** (Development Studies; Social Sciences); **Human Sciences** (Pedagogy; Philosophy; Psychology; Sociology); **Management** (Administration; Human Resources; Management); **Nutrition** (Nutrition)

History: Founded 1985 as Instituto Superior de Especialidades de Guadalajara. Acquired present status and title 2000.

Main Language(s) of Instruction: Spanish

Degrees and Diplomas: *Licenciatura*; *Maestría*; *Doctorado*

Libraries: Yes

Last Updated: 08/03/13

ARKOS UNIVERSITY STUDIES CENTRE

Centro de Estudios Universitarios Arkos

Francisco I. Madero, 529, Col. Emiliano Zapata, 48380 Puerto Vallarta, Jalisco

Tel: +52(322) 222-05-88

Fax: +52(322) 222-35-38

EMail: ceuarkos@hotmail.com

Website: http://www.ceuarkos.com

Director: Eduardo Espinosa Herrera (1992-)

Programmes

Accountancy (Accountancy); **Business Administration** (Business Administration); **Communication Studies** (Communication Studies); **Law** (Law); **Marketing** (Marketing)

History: Founded 1992.

Main Language(s) of Instruction: Spanish

Degrees and Diplomas: *Licenciatura*

Last Updated: 07/03/08

ARMANDO OLIVARES CARRILLO INSTITUTE OF EDUCATION

Instituto de Educación Armando Olivares Carrillo

Avenida Villa Unión Norte No 110, Col. Ampliación Emiliano Zapata, Celaya, Guanajuato

Tel: +52(461) 608-73-72

Fax: +52(461) 608-73-73

EMail: omagr@prodigy.net.mx

Director: Octavio García Salgado

Programmes

Physical Education (Physical Education)

Main Language(s) of Instruction: Spanish

Degrees and Diplomas: *Licenciatura*

Last Updated: 28/02/13

ARTE AC TECHNOLOGICAL INSTITUTE OF MONTERREY

ARTE AC Tecnológico de Monterrey

Belisario Domínguez 2202 Pte. Col. Obispado, 64060 Monterrey, Nuevo León

Tel: +52(81) 8347-1128

EMail: info@arteac.edu.mx

Website: http://www.arteac.edu.mx

Programmes

Fashion Design (Fashion Design); **Graphic Design** (Graphic Design); **Interior Design** (Interior Design)

Main Language(s) of Instruction: Spanish

Degrees and Diplomas: *Licenciatura*

Last Updated: 10/01/13

ARTURO ROSENBLUETH FOUNDATION FOR SCIENTIFIC DEVELOPMENT

Fundación Arturo Rosenblueth para el Avance de la Ciencia

Horacio 124 piso 10, Col. Polanco, Del. Miguel Hidalgo, 03100 México, D.F.

Tel: +52(555) 5256-1256

EMail: info@rosenblueth.mx

Website: http://www.rosenblueth.mx

Director General: Enrique Calderón Alzati (1978-)
EMail: ecalderon@rosenblueth.org.mx

Programmes

Business Computing (Business Computing); **Computer Engineering** (Computer Engineering); **Computer Systems** (Computer Science)

Further Information: Branch in Xalapa

History: Founded 1978, acquired present status 1992.

Academic Year: January to December

Admission Requirements: Admission test and interview for postgraduates

Fees: (Pesos): 68,800 - 73,200 per semester

Main Language(s) of Instruction: Spanish

Degrees and Diplomas: *Licenciatura*: Computer Engineering; Information Technology; Information Management, 3 1/2 yrs; *Especialización*; *Maestría*: Sciences; Information Systems, 2 1/2 yrs

Student Services: Academic counselling, Employment services
Last Updated: 30/08/12

ATHENEUM OF TLALNEPANTLA

Ateneo de Tlalnepantla
Avenida de los Maestros, 34, San Andrés Atenco,
54040 Tlalnepantla, Estado de México
Tel: +52(55) 53-98-32-08 +52(55) 53-98-33-90
Fax: +52(55) 53-61-60-44
Website: http://www.ateneodetlalnepantla.edu.mx

Programmes

Accountancy (Accountancy); **Business Computing** (Business Computing); **International Business** (International Business); **Law** (Law)

History: Founded 1999.

Main Language(s) of Instruction: Spanish

Degrees and Diplomas: *Licenciatura*

Libraries: Yes

Last Updated: 10/07/12

ATHENEUM UNIVERSITY OF MONTERREY

Universidad Ateneo de Monterrey
Gonzalitos, 915-917, Sur, Col. Mitras, Sur, 64020 Monterrey, Nuevo León
Tel: +52(81) 83-46-92-65 +52(81) 83-46-92-25
Fax: +52(81) 83-33-94-97
EMail: rectoria@ateneo.edu.mx
Website: http://www.ateneo.edu.mx

Rectora: Lilia Estela Sandoval Garza
EMail: liliasandoval@ateneo.edu.mx

Programmes

Accountancy (Accountancy); **Administration** (Administration); **Business Computing** (Business Computing); **Communication** (Communication Studies); **Educational Sciences** (Educational Sciences); **Hotel Management and Tourism** (Hotel Management; Tourism); **Industrial Engineering** (Industrial Engineering); **International Business** (International Business); **Law** (Law); **Marketing** (Marketing); **Pedagogy** (Pedagogy)

History: Founded 1989 as Colegio Universitario Ateneo. Acquired present status 1995.

Main Language(s) of Instruction: Spanish

Degrees and Diplomas: *Licenciatura*; *Maestría*
Last Updated: 03/09/12

AURORA MEZA ANDRACA UNIVERSITY CENTRE

Centro Universitario Aurora Meza Andraca
Av. Revolución N° 502, Centro, 39200 Chilapa de Alvarez, Guerrero
Tel: +52(756) 475-06-15
EMail: cuamachilapa@hotmail.com

Director: José Díaz Navarro

Programmes

Accountancy (Accountancy); **Communication Studies**; **Computer Science** (Computer Science); **Dentistry** (Dentistry); **Economics** (Economics); **Law** (Law); **Psychology** (Psychology)

Main Language(s) of Instruction: Spanish

Degrees and Diplomas: *Licenciatura*
Last Updated: 18/03/08

AUTONOMOUS INSTITUTE OF EDUCATION OF TECOMÁN

Instituto Autónomo de Educación de Tecomán, A.C.
Km. 1 Carretera Costera, Col. Tecomán, Playa Azul,
28100 Tecomán, Colima
Tel: +52(313) 134-30-37 +52(313) 134-30-38
Fax: +52(313) 134-01-42
EMail: iaetac@cu.gdl.mx

Director: Oscar Armando Ávalos Verdugo (2001-)

Faculties

Administration, Accountancy and Computer Science (Accountancy; Administration; Computer Science); **Law** (Law)
History: Founded 1979.

Main Language(s) of Instruction: Spanish

Degrees and Diplomas: *Licenciatura*; *Maestría*
Last Updated: 22/02/08

AUTONOMOUS TECHNOLOGICAL INSTITUTE OF MEXICO

Instituto Tecnológico Autónomo de México (ITAM)
Río Hondo 1, Tizapán, San Ángel, Álvaro Obregón,
01000 México, D.F.
Tel: +52(555) 628-40-00
Fax: +52(555) 628-41-02
EMail: afernandez@itam.mx
Website: http://www.itam.mx

Rector: Arturo Manuel Fernández Pérez (1992-)

International Relations: Mary Ann Leenheer
Tel: +52(55) 56-28-41-59, Fax: +52(55) 56-28-41-77
EMail: leenheer@itam.mx

Centres

Competitiveness Studies (Marketing; Regional Studies); **Economic Research and Analysis** (Economics); **Extension** (Arts and Humanities; Business and Commerce; Computer Science; Economics; Finance; International Relations; Law); **International Business** (International Business); **Public Policy** (Public Administration)

Departments

Accountancy and Administration (Accountancy; Administration); **Applied Mathematics and Actuarial Sciences** (Actuarial Science; Applied Mathematics); **Computer Science** (Computer Science); **Economics** (Economics); **General Studies**; **Law** (Law); **Social Sciences** (Demography and Population; Political Sciences; Social Sciences)

History: Founded 1946. A private autonomous institution recognized by the State 1963.

Governing Bodies: Board of Governors

Academic Year: August to July (August-December; January-June; June-July)

Admission Requirements: Secondary school certificate and entrance examination

Fees: (Pesos): c. 6,060-16,160 per semester; graduate, c. 97,000 per term

Main Language(s) of Instruction: Spanish

Degrees and Diplomas: *Licenciatura*: 4 yrs; *Maestría*: Administration and International Business; Economics; Finance; Information Technologies; Insurance and Risk Management; Management; Public Policy, 2 yrs; *Doctorado*. Also Diplomado in Graduate Programmes

Student Services: Academic counselling, Canteen, Employment services, Foreign student adviser, Language programs, Sports facilities

Libraries: Manuel Gómez Marín Library. Raúl Bailleres Library

Publications: Estudios *(quarterly)*
Last Updated: 12/03/13

AUTONOMOUS UNIVERSITY OF DURANGO

Universidad Autónoma de Durango (UAD)
Ave. Universidad Autónoma de Durango y Orquidea s/n, Fracc. Jardines de Durango, 34200 Durango, Durango
Tel: +52(618) 129-5786 +52(618) 129-5901
Website: http://www.uad.mx

Rector: Martín Gerardo Soriano Sariñana (1992-)

Administrative Officer: Martha M. Gallegos Cuellar
EMail: totis6@hotmail.com

International Relations: Olga Catalina Santos Pérez
EMail: olgasantos28@hotmail.com

Departments

Accountancy (Accountancy); **Architecture** (Architecture; Architecture and Planning); **Communication Sciences and Techniques** (Communication Studies); **Computer Science** (Computer Science); **Education** (Education); **Fashion Design** (Fashion Design); **Graphic Design** (Graphic Design); **Hotel Management** (Hotel Management; Service Trades); **Interior Design** (Interior Design); **International Business** (Business Administration; International Business); **International Relations** (International Relations); **Law** (Criminology; Law); **Marketing** (Marketing); **Medicine** (Medicine); **Nutrition** (Nutrition); **Political Science** (Political Sciences); **Psychology** (Psychology)

Schools

Postgraduate (Accountancy; Clinical Psychology; Communication Studies; Education; Finance; Fiscal Law; Government; Information Sciences; Law; Marketing; Public Law; Taxation; Town Planning) *Director*: Luis Julían Barraza Mariscal

Further Information: Also campuses in Santiago Papasquiano (Dgo.), Mazatlán (Sin.), Los Mochis (Sin.), Culiacán (Sin.), Zacatecas (Zac.), Chihuahua (Chih), Cd. Juárez (Chih), Hermosillo (Son), Gómez Palacio (Dgo.)

History: Founded 1992.

Governing Bodies: Academic and Administrative Board

Academic Year: February to January (February-July; August-January)

Admission Requirements: Certificado de Preparatoria

Fees: (US Dollars): Registration 1,300; Tuition 1,200 per month

Main Language(s) of Instruction: Spanish

Degrees and Diplomas: *Licenciatura*: 41/2 yrs; *Maestría*: 2 yrs; *Doctorado*: 3 yrs

Student Services: Academic counselling, Employment services, Handicapped facilities, Language programs, Social counselling, Sports facilities

Special Facilities: FM Radio station, T.V. Laboratory

Libraries: Main Library

Last Updated: 26/03/13

AUTONOMOUS UNIVERSITY OF FRESNILLO

Universidad Autónoma de Fresnillo

Prolongación Av. Hidalgo S/N, Col. Centro, 99000 Fresnillo, Zacatecas

Tel: +52(493) 932-29-21 +52(493) 932-38-30

Fax: +52(493) 932-32-10

Website: www.uaf.mxhttp: //www.uaf.mx

Rectora: Giovanna Bañuelos

Centres

Research

Faculties

Business Administration (Business Administration); **Business and Systems Engineering** (Business and Commerce; Computer Engineering); **Computer Systems Engineering** (Computer Engineering); **Human Resources Administration** (Human Resources); **Public Accountancy** (Accountancy); **Tourism** (Tourism)

Further Information: Also Continuing Education

History: Founded 1985.

Governing Bodies: Board of Directors

Academic Year: January to December (January-June; August-December)

Admission Requirements: Secondary school certificate (bachillerato) and entrance examination

Main Language(s) of Instruction: Spanish

Degrees and Diplomas: *Licenciatura*: 4 yrs; *Maestría*: a further 2 yrs; *Doctorado*

Student Services: Academic counselling, Cultural centre, Employment services, Foreign student adviser, Handicapped facilities, Health services, Sports facilities

Special Facilities: Museums

Libraries: c. 7,200 vols

Last Updated: 26/03/13

AUTONOMOUS UNIVERSITY OF GUADALAJARA

Universidad Autónoma de Guadalajara (UAG)

Apartado postal 1-440, Avenida Patria, 1201, Lomas del Valle, 3a Sección, 44100 Guadalajara, Jalisco

Tel: +52(33) 36-48-88-24

EMail: leanoac@uag.mx

Website: http://www.uag.mx

Rector: Antonio Leaño Reyes EMail: aleano@uag.mx

Vicerrector Administrativo: Juan José Leaño Álvarez del Castillo

Secretario General: Humberto López Delgadillo

Areas

Architecture and Design (Architecture; Graphic Design; Industrial Design; Interior Design; Landscape Architecture); **Business** (Accountancy; Administration; Finance; International Business; Management; Marketing; Tourism); **Health Sciences** (Anatomy; Biochemistry; Cardiology; Cell Biology; Genetics; Health Sciences; Histology; Microbiology; Neurosciences; Nutrition; Ophthalmology; Paediatrics; Pathology; Pharmacology; Physiology; Public Health; Surgery; Virology); **Humanities and Social Sciences** (Communication Studies; Education; International Relations; Law; Political Sciences; Psychology; Public Administration); **Science and Technology** (Actuarial Science; Biology; Biomedical Engineering; Biotechnology; Chemical Engineering; Civil Engineering; Electrical Engineering; Electronic Engineering; Food Science; Industrial Engineering; Information Technology; Mechanical Engineering; Pharmacology; Software Engineering)

Schools

Medicine (Medicine)

Further Information: Branches in Colima, Nayarit and Tabasco

History: Founded 1935 as a private autonomous institution. Degrees recognized by the National University of Mexico. Independent of State and federal governments.

Governing Bodies: Consejo Universitario, comprising equal numbers of administrators, teaching staff and students

Academic Year: January to December (January-June; August-December)

Admission Requirements: Secondary school certificate (bachillerato) or foreign equivalent, and entrance examination

Main Language(s) of Instruction: Spanish

Degrees and Diplomas: *Licenciatura*: Accountancy; Anthropology; Archaeology; Architecture; Biology; Business Administration; Chemical Engineering; Chemistry; Computer Science; Dentistry; Economics; Education; Hispanic Languages and Literature; History; Industrial Design; Journalism; Law; Library Science; Mathematics; Nursing and Midwifery; Pharmacy; Psychology; Social Work; Tourism; Visual Arts, 3-5 yrs; *Licenciatura*: Agricultural Engineering; Civil Engineering; Computer Engineering; Electrical Engineering; *Licenciatura*: Medicine, 6 yrs; *Especialización*; *Especialización*: Medicine; *Maestría*: Administration and Economics; Architecture; Chemistry; Education; Languages; Law; Public Health; *Doctorado*: Chemistry; Education

Libraries: Central Library; Health Sciences

Publications: Actas de la Facultad de Medicina; Alma Mater; Docencia; Nexo Universitario; Ocho Columnas

Press or Publishing House: University Press

Last Updated: 04/09/12

AUTONOMOUS UNIVERSITY OF LA LAGUNA

Universidad Autónoma de La Laguna, A.C.

Apartado Postal 87, Avenida Universidad s/n, Col. El Tajito, 27100 Torreón, Coahuila

Tel: +52(871) 718-55-33 +52(871) 722-37-49

Fax: +52(871) 722-28-17

EMail: rector@ual.mx

Website: http://www.ual.mx

Rector: Jorge Yamil Darwich Ramírez (2007-)

Colleges

Administration (Accountancy; Business Administration; Human Resources; International Business; Marketing; Tourism); **Engineering** (Business Computing; Computer Engineering; Industrial Engineering); **Science and Humanities** (Architecture; Communication Studies; Graphic Design; Journalism; Law; Psychology; Visual Arts)

History: Founded 1988 as a private, independent, non-profit organization. Fully accredited by both State and federal governments.

Governing Bodies: Board of Trustees, comprising 20 members from the private sector

Academic Year: January to December (January-June; August-December)

Admission Requirements: Secondary school certificate (Bachillerato) and entrance examination (S.A.T)

Fees: (US Dollars): 2,500 per semester

Main Language(s) of Instruction: Spanish, English

Accrediting Agencies: Federación de Instituciones Mexicanas Particulares de Educación Superior (FIMPES); Asociación Nacional de Universidades e Instituciones de Educación Superior (ANUIES)

Degrees and Diplomas: *Licenciatura*: 4-5 yrs; *Especialización*; *Maestría*: a further 2 yrs

Student Services: Health services, Language programs, Social counselling, Sports facilities

Special Facilities: Museum

Libraries: Yes

Last Updated: 04/09/12

AUTONOMOUS UNIVERSITY OF PIEDRAS NEGRAS

Universidad Autónoma de Piedras Negras (UAPN)

Padre de Las Casas y Rayón, Centro, 26000 Piedras Negras, Coahuila
Tel: +52(878) 782-20-35
Fax: +52(878) 782-20-35
EMail: uapn@uapn.edu.mx
Website: http://www.uapn.edu.mx

Rector: Xavier N. Martínez Aguirre (1993-)

Secretario General: Rigoberto Losoya Reyes

International Relations: Azalia M. Ibarra Olguín

Faculties

Chemistry (Biochemistry; Botany; Chemistry; Histology; Hygiene; Physiology; Toxicology); **External Trade and Customs** (Accountancy; Economics; Fiscal Law; International Business; Marketing); **Law** (Civil Law; Commercial Law; Criminal Law; International Law; Law; Political Sciences); **Marketing** (Accountancy; Administration; Advertising and Publicity; Hotel Management; Labour Law; Marketing; Sales Techniques; Tourism); **Nursing and Midwifery** (Midwifery; Nursing); **Pharmacy** (Botany; Chemistry; Embryology and Reproduction Biology; Histology; Pharmacy; Physiology; Toxicology); **Social Work** (Anthropology; Ethics; Genetics; Nutrition; Psychiatry and Mental Health; Psychology; Social Work)

Laboratories

Pharmaco-biological Biochemistry (Biochemistry; Pharmacy)

History: Founded 1939 as Centro Universitario del Norte, acquired present status and title 1993.

Governing Bodies: Board of Councillors

Admission Requirements: Secondary school certificate (bachillerato)

Fees: (Pesos): c. 4,200-11,000 per semester. Technical courses, c. 3,900 per annum

Main Language(s) of Instruction: Spanish

Accrediting Agencies: Secretaría de Educación Pública; Secretaría de Educación Pública del Estado de Coahuila

Degrees and Diplomas: *Licenciatura*: 4 1/2-5 yrs; *Especialización*; *Maestría*: a further 2 yrs

Student Services: Academic counselling, Employment services, Health services, Social counselling, Sports facilities

Special Facilities: Movie Studio

Libraries: Central Library

Last Updated: 06/09/12

AUTONOMOUS UNIVERSITY OF THE NORTH EAST

Universidad Autónoma del Noreste

Calle Monclova, 1561, Col. República, 25180 Saltillo, Coahuila
Tel: +52(844) 416-46-77 +52(844) 416-30-33
Fax: +52(844) 416-31-53 +52(844) 415-33-79
Website: http://www.uane.edu.mx

Rector: Hilginio González Calserón

Programmes

Architecture (Architecture); **Business Administration** (Accountancy; Business Administration; Human Resources; Public Administration); **Computer Science** (Computer Science); **Development Studies** (Development Studies); **Educational Administration** (Educational Administration); **Engineering** (Computer Engineering; Industrial Engineering; Mechanical Engineering); **Graphic Design** (Graphic Design); **Law** (Law); **Political Science** (Political Sciences); **Psychology** (Psychology); **Tourism** (Tourism)

Further Information: Campuses: Saltillo, Torreón, Monclova, Piedras Negras, Sabinas (Coahuila); Ciudad Juarez (Chihuahua); Monterrey (Nuevo León); Matamoros, Reynosa (Tamaulipas)

History: Founded 1974.

Academic Year: August to June (August-December; January-June)

Admission Requirements: Secondary school certificate (bachillerato) and entrance examination

Main Language(s) of Instruction: Spanish

Degrees and Diplomas: *Licenciatura*: 4-4 1/2 yrs; *Especialización*: 1 yr; *Maestría*; *Doctorado*

Libraries: Central Library, c. 18,700 vols

Last Updated: 13/02/08

AUTONOMOUS UNIVERSITY OF THE PACIFIC

Universidad Autónoma del Pacífico

Primo de Verdad, 1090, 28000 Colima, Colima
Tel: +52(312) 122-80-10 +52(312) 122-62-16
Fax: +52(312) 122-80-10
EMail: academico@uap.edu.mx
Website: http://www.uap.edu.mx

Rector: Rafael Alfonso Acuña Cepeda EMail: rectoria@uap.edu.mx

Faculties

Engineering and Systems (Agricultural Engineering; Computer Engineering; Industrial Engineering; Systems Analysis)

Programmes

Administration (Accountancy; Business Administration); **Graphic Design** (Graphic Design); **Human Development** (Development Studies); **Law** (Law)

History: Founded 1990.

Admission Requirements: Secondary school certificate (bachillerato) and entrance examination

Main Language(s) of Instruction: Spanish

Degrees and Diplomas: *Licenciatura*: 8 semesters

Last Updated: 07/09/12

AZTEC UNIVERSITY

Universidad Azteca

Palma 61 y Calle 3 de Mayo s/n, Barrio de San Antonio, 56600 Chalco, Estado de México
Tel: +52(55) 59-75-21-61 +52(55) 59-73-08-65
Fax: +52(55) 59-73-08-65
EMail: international@universidadazteca.edu.mx
Website: http://www.universidadazteca.edu.mx

Director: Agustín López González Pacheco (1994-)

Programmes

Accounting (Accountancy); **Architecture** (Architecture); **Business Administration** (Business Administration); **Business Computing** (Business Computing); **Educational Sciences** (Educational Sciences); **International Business and Commerce** (International Business); **Law** (Criminal Law; Fiscal Law; Law); **Pedagogy** (Pedagogy); **Psychology** (Psychology)

Further Information: Also branches in Cancun, Los Reyes, Zaragoza and San Juan del Río

History: Founded 1994 as Centro de Estudios Superiores Azteca. Also previously known as Universidad Azteca de Chalco.

Main Language(s) of Instruction: Spanish

Degrees and Diplomas: *Licenciatura*: Social and Administrative Sciences; Science and Technology; Health Sciences; Humanities, 5 yrs; *Maestría*: Social and Administrative Sciences; Science and Technology; Health Sciences; Humanities, 1-2 yrs following Licenciatura; *Doctorado*: Education and Humanities
Last Updated: 07/09/12

AZTEC UNIVERSITY CENTRE

Centro Universitario Azteca
Garibaldi, 648, Centro, 44026 Guadalajara, Jalisco
Tel: +52(33) 13-40-94
Fax: +52(33) 13-40-94
EMail: info@cuazteca.edu.mx
Website: http://cuazteca.edu.mx

Rector: Rolando Romero y Romero

Programmes

Accountancy (Accountancy); **Administration** (Administration); **Computer Engineering** (Computer Engineering); **International Business** (International Business); **Law** (Law); **Marketing** (Marketing); **Nursing** (Nursing)

Main Language(s) of Instruction: Spanish

Degrees and Diplomas: *Licenciatura*; *Especialización*; *Maestría*
Last Updated: 23/07/12

BANKING AND COMMERCIAL INSTITUTE

Instituto Bancario y Comercial
Francisco Javier Mina, 1616, Mexicali, Baja California
Tel: +52(686) 634-19-90
Fax: +52(686) 623-13-88

Director: Ernesto Aello Arvizu

Programmes

Banking and Commerce (Banking; Business and Commerce)

Main Language(s) of Instruction: Spanish

Degrees and Diplomas: *Licenciatura*
Last Updated: 02/04/08

BANKING UNIVERSITY OF MEXICO

Universidad Bancaria de México
Avenida 5 de Mayo s/n, Barrio Tepanquiahuac, 54780 Teoloyucan, Estado de México
Tel: +52(593) 914-05- 01
EMail: informes@ubam.edu.mx
Website: http://www.ubam.edu.mx

Programmes

Accountancy (Accountancy); **Business Administration** (Business Administration; Tourism); **Computer Science** (Computer Engineering; Computer Science); **Gastronomy** (Cooking and Catering); **Governance and Public Administration** (Government; Public Administration); **Graphic Design** (Graphic Design); **Journalism** (Journalism); **Languages** (English; French; Translation and Interpretation); **Law** (Law); **Marketing and Advertising** (Advertising and Publicity; Marketing); **Mechanical Engineering and Automation** (Automation and Control Engineering; Mechanical Engineering); **Pedagogy** (Pedagogy); **Psychology** (Psychology); **Sports Management** (Sports Management)

History: Founded 1997 as Centro Universitario Teoloyucán.

Main Language(s) of Instruction: Spanish

Degrees and Diplomas: *Licenciatura*; *Especialización*; *Maestría*; *Doctorado*

Libraries: Yes
Last Updated: 07/09/12

BAUHAUS CENTRE OF TECHNICAL AND ADVANCED STUDIES

Centro de Estudios Técnicos y Superiores Bauhaus
Av. Salvador Díaz Mirón No.961 ESQ. Mina Col Centro, Centro, 91700 Veracruz, Veracruz
Tel: +52(229) 932-26-43
Fax: +52(229) 932-26-43
EMail: cets_bauhaus@hotmail.com

Director General: Enrique Ramírez Pacheco (1993-)

Programmes

Advertising and Publicity (Advertising and Publicity); **Fashion and Graphic Design** (Advertising and Publicity; Fashion Design; Graphic Design)

History: Founded 1993.

Main Language(s) of Instruction: Spanish

Degrees and Diplomas: *Licenciatura*
Last Updated: 17/07/12

BAUHAUS UNIVERSITY CENTRE

Universitario Bauhaus
11 Sur 1310, Centro Histórico, Puebla, Puebla
Tel: +52(22) 211-02-57
EMail: informes@bauhaus.edu.mx
Website: http://www.bauhaus.edu.mx

Rectora: Maruzka Zamynda Retif Altmann

Programmes

Design and Graphic Communication (Design; Graphic Design); **Interior Design** (Interior Design); **Plastic Arts** (Painting and Drawing; Sculpture)

History: Founded 1996 as Escuela Libre de Diseño y Arte Bauhaus.

Main Language(s) of Instruction: Spanish

Degrees and Diplomas: *Licenciatura*
Last Updated: 26/10/12

BEATRIZ GONZÁLEZ ORTEGA NURSING SCHOOL

Escuela de Enfermería Beatriz González Ortega
Prolongación Calle Plateros s/n, 99000 Zacatecas, Zacatecas
Tel: +52(492) 922-16-60
Fax: +52(492) 922-16-60
EMail: escenfbgo@prodigy.net.mx

Directora: Verónica Sosa Arredondo

Programmes

Nursing (Nursing)

Main Language(s) of Instruction: Spanish

Degrees and Diplomas: *Licenciatura*
Last Updated: 28/08/12

BENAVENTE HIGHER TEACHER TRAINING SCHOOL

Escuela Normal Superior Benavente
Avenida 25 Oriente, 9, Col. Del Carmen, 72530 Puebla, Puebla
Tel: +52(222) 243-63-00
Fax: +52(222) 237-24-32

Director: Enrique González Álvarez
EMail: enrique@benavente.edu.mx

Programmes
Educational Management (Educational Administration); **Higher Education** (Higher Education); **Teacher Training** (Educational Psychology; Preschool Education; Primary Education; Secondary Education; Teacher Training)

History: Founded 1956.

Main Language(s) of Instruction: Spanish

Degrees and Diplomas: *Licenciatura*; *Maestría*
Last Updated: 25/02/13

BENEMÉRITO CENTRE FOR ADVANCED STUDIES OF THE AMERICAS

Centro de Estudios Superiores Benemérito de Las Américas
Carr. Ocozocoautla - Ocuilapa, No. 1190 Barrio Cruz Blanca, Ocozocoautla de Espinosa, Chiapas
Tel: +52(968) 68- 8-31-61
Website: http://www.cesba.edu.mx

Director: Moisés Ulloa Solis (1999-)

Programmes
Accountancy (Accountancy); **Administration** (Administration); **Educational Sciences** (Educational Sciences); **Law** (Law)

Further Information: Campus in Tonala

History: Founded 2000.

Main Language(s) of Instruction: Spanish

Degrees and Diplomas: *Licenciatura*; *Maestría*
Last Updated: 15/02/13

BENITO JUÁREZ UNIVERSITY

Universidad Benito Juárez
36 Norte, 1609, Col. Cristóbal Colón, 72340 Puebla, Puebla
Tel: +52(222) 236-09-64 +52(222) 235-33-31
Fax: +52(222) 234-46-64
EMail: difusion@ubj.edu.mx
Website: http://www.ubj.edu.mx/

Rector: Jorge Sánchez Zacarias EMail: rectoria@ubj.edu.mx

Programmes
Accountancy (Accountancy); **Architecture** (Architecture; Graphic Design; Landscape Architecture; Town Planning); **Business Administration** (Business Administration; Hotel Management; Tourism); **Communication Studies** (Communication Studies; Journalism); **Electrical Engineering** (Electrical Engineering); **Gastronomy** (Cooking and Catering); **Law** (Fiscal Law; Law); **Psychology** (Psychology); **Stomatology** (Stomatology)

History: Founded 1995 as Centro de Estudios Universitarios Benito Juárez G. Acquired present title 1998.

Admission Requirements: Certificado de secundaria

Main Language(s) of Instruction: Spanish

Degrees and Diplomas: *Licenciatura*; *Maestría*

Libraries: Yes
Last Updated: 07/09/12

BONAMPAK INSTITUTE

Instituto Bonampak
Avenida del Riego, 151, Colonia Residencial Villa Coapa, Delegación Tlalpán, 14390 México, D.F.
Tel: +52(55) 55-94-55-70
Website: http://institutobonampak.edu.mx/

Directora: Yolanda Espino Carrera

Programmes
Business Administration *(Cuernavaca)* (Business Administration); **Gastronomy** *(Cuernavaca)* (Cooking and Catering); **Law** (Law); **Natural Resources** (Natural Resources); **Tourism** (Tourism)

Further Information: Also branch in Cuernavaca

History: Founded 1999.

Main Language(s) of Instruction: Spanish

Degrees and Diplomas: *Licenciatura*; *Maestría*
Last Updated: 27/02/13

BOSQUES DE ARAGON PATRIA INSTITUTE

Instituto Patria Bosques de Aragon A. C
Bosques de los Continentes s/n y Bosques de Irán, Bosques de Aragón, 57170 Nezahualcóyotl, Estado de México
Tel: +52(55) 57-94-28-74
Fax: +52(55) 57-99-56-91 +52(55) 57-94-80-98
EMail: info@institutopatria.com.mx
Website: http://www.institutopatria.com.mx

Director: José Alberto González Estrella (1983-)

Programmes
Business Administration and Law (Business Administration; Law); **Computer Science** (Computer Science)

History: Founded 1983.

Main Language(s) of Instruction: Spanish

Degrees and Diplomas: *Licenciatura*
Last Updated: 07/03/13

BRIBIESCA ART INSTITUTE

Instituto de Arte Bribiesca
Avenida Vallarta, 1543, Esquina con Marsella, Col. Americana, 44140 Guadalajara, Jalisco
Tel: +52(33) 36-15-01-29
Fax: +52(33) 36-16-80-23
EMail: info@bribiesca.edu.mx
Website: http://www.bribiesca.edu.mx

Director: Manuel Salvador Bribiesca Escalante

Programmes
Design (Advertising and Publicity; Design; Fashion Design; Graphic Design; Industrial Design; Jewelry Art)

History: Founded 1984.

Main Language(s) of Instruction: Spanish

Degrees and Diplomas: *Licenciatura*
Last Updated: 18/01/13

BRIMA INSTITUTE

Instituto Brima, S.C.
Independencia 411, 53000 Toluca, Estado de México
Tel: +52(722) 213-20-15
Website: http://www.brima.edu.mx

Director: Artemio Bringas Castañeda

Programmes
Accountancy (Accountancy); **Administration** (Administration); **Business Computing** (Business Computing); **Communication Studies** (Cinema and Television); **Educational Sciences** (Educational Sciences); **Law** (Law)

History: Founded 1996.

Main Language(s) of Instruction: Spanish

Degrees and Diplomas: *Licenciatura*; *Maestría*
Last Updated: 30/08/12

BRITISH INSTITUTE OF THE CITY OF PUEBLA

Instituto Británico de la Ciudad de Puebla, A.C.
Blvd. 5 de Mayo No. 117 Zona Dorada, Las Palmas, 72000 Puebla, Puebla
Tel: +52(222) 242-67-33
Fax: +52(222) 242-19-28
EMail: ibppuebla@yahoo.com

Director General: Marco Vinicio Arenas León (1986-)

Programmes
Tourism (Tourism)

Further Information: Also branch in Tlaxcala

History: Founded 1986.

Main Language(s) of Instruction: Spanish

Degrees and Diplomas: *Licenciatura*

Last Updated: 03/04/08

BUSINESS SCHOOL OF THE PACIFIC

Escuela de Negocios del Pacífico

Carretera a Mocorito Km 1.4, Col. Militar, 81440 Guamúchil, Sinaloa

Tel: +52(673) 732-45- 56

EMail: contacto@enepac.edu.mx

Website: http://www.anjor.com.mx

Directora General: María Dolores Castro Castro

Programmes

Business Administration (Business Administration); **Business Computing** (Business Computing); **Diplomacy and International Relations** (International Relations); **Industrial Engineering** (Industrial Engineering)

History: Founded 2001.

Main Language(s) of Instruction: Spanish

Degrees and Diplomas: *Licenciatura*

Last Updated: 28/08/12

ĆACATL MEXICAN FOLK DANCE SCHOOL

Escuela Superior de Danza Folklorica Mexicana ĆAcatl

Avenida 3 Poniente 1707, Centro Histórico, 72000 Puebla, Puebla

Tel: +52(222) 242-7051

EMail: informes@ceacatl.edu.mx

Website: http://www.ceacatl.edu.mx

Director: Vidal Calvario Tepox

Programmes

Folk Dance (Dance; Folklore)

History: Founded 1999.

Main Language(s) of Instruction: Spanish

Degrees and Diplomas: *Licenciatura*

Last Updated: 27/02/13

CALIFORNIA UNIVERSITY CENTRE

Centro Universitario de California

Calle Veracruz Sur, 115, Col. Centro, 63000 Tepic, Nayarit

Tel: +52(311) 240-93-98

Fax: +52(311) 211-11-17

EMail: univalifornia@hotmail.com

Director: Ezequiel Montiel Hernández (2001-)

History: Founded 2001.

Degrees and Diplomas: *Licenciatura*

Last Updated: 04/04/08

CANADIAN UNIVERSITY

Universidad Canadiense

Km. 1 Carretera Tula-Tepetitlán, Col. El Tesoro, Tula de Allende, Hidalgo

Tel: +52(773) 732-31-24

Fax: +52(773) 732-31-24

EMail: institutocanadienseac@hotmail.com

Website: http://www.icanadiense.org

Directora: Herlinda Maria del Carmen Hidalgo Herrera

Programmes

Accountancy (Accountancy); **Architecture** (Architecture); **Computer Science** (Computer Science); **Law** (Law); **Pedagogy** (Pedagogy)

Degrees and Diplomas: *Licenciatura*

Last Updated: 26/03/13

CARLOS A. CARRILLO CENTRE FOR ADVANCED STUDIES

Centro de Estudios Superiores Carlos A. Carrillo

Av. Revolucion No. 413, Col. Centro, Coatzacoalcos, Veracruz

Tel: +52(921) 212-6620

Programmes

Preschool Education (Preschool Education)

Main Language(s) of Instruction: Spanish

Degrees and Diplomas: *Licenciatura*

Last Updated: 17/07/12

CARLOS A. CARRILLO TEACHER TRAINING SCHOOL OF VERACRUZ

Escuela Normal de Veracruz Carlos A. Carrillo

Magnolia 27, Venustiano Carranza, 91070 Xalapa, Veracruz

Tel: +52(228) 841-42-60

Fax: +52(228) 817-79-73

Director General: Mario Antonio Chama Díaz

Programmes

Education; **Physical Education** (Physical Education)

History: Founded 2001.

Main Language(s) of Instruction: Spanish

Degrees and Diplomas: *Licenciatura*

Last Updated: 25/02/13

CARLOS SEPTIÉN GARCÍA SCHOOL OF JOURNALISM

Escuela de Periodismo Carlos Septién García

Basilio Badillo, 43, 1er Piso, Col. Tabacalera, Delegación Cuauhtémoc, 06030 México, D.F.

Tel: +52(55) 55-10-49-00 al 03

Fax: +52(55) 55-18-55-65

EMail: epcs@septien.edu.mx

Director: José Luis Vázquez Baeza EMail: jbaeza@septien.edu.mx

Programmes

Journalism (Journalism)

History: Founded 1949.

Main Language(s) of Instruction: Spanish

Degrees and Diplomas: *Licenciatura*; *Maestría*

Libraries: Biblioteca Fernando Díez de Urdanivia

Last Updated: 28/08/12

CASA BLANCA UNIVERSITY

Universidad Casa Blanca (UCB)

Rupert L. Paliza 694 Norte, Centro Histórico, 80200 Culiacán, Sinaloa

Tel: +52(667) 712-18-28

EMail: rectoria@ucb.edu.mx

Website: http://www.ucb.edu.mx

Rector: José Carlos Tarriba Urtuzuastegui

Programmes

Administration and Financial Planning (Administration; Finance); **Architecture** (Architecture); **Business Development**; **Fashion Design and Marketing** (Fashion Design; Marketing); **Graphic Design and Multimedia Arts** (Graphic Design; Multimedia); **Industrial Design** (Industrial Design); **Interior Architecture**; **International Commerce** (International Business); **Marketing** (Marketing)

History: Formerly known as Centro de Estudios Superiores Casa Blanca

Main Language(s) of Instruction: Spanish

Degrees and Diplomas: *Licenciatura*; *Especialización*; *Maestría*

Last Updated: 26/03/08

CASA LAMM CULTURAL CENTRE

Centro de Cultura Casa Lamm

Avenida Álvaro Obregón, 99, Col. Roma, Delegación Cuauhtémoc, 06700 México, D.F.
Tel: +52(55) 55-25-39-38
Fax: +52(55) 55-25-51-41
EMail: informes@casalamm.com.mx
Website: http://www.casalamm.com.mx

Directora Académica: Claudia Gómez Haro (1996-)

Programmes
History of Art (Art History); **Literature** (Literature); **Museology** (Museum Management; Museum Studies)

History: Founded 1996.

Main Language(s) of Instruction: Spanish

Degrees and Diplomas: *Licenciatura*; *Especialización*; *Maestría*; *Doctorado*
Last Updated: 12/07/12

CATHOLIC UNIVERSITY OF CULIACÁN

Universidad Católica de Culiacán, A.C. (UCC)

Catedráticos, 225, Oriente, Col. Tierra Blanca, 80030 Culiacán, Sinaloa
Tel: +52(667) 712-30-17
Fax: +52(667) 712-13-47
EMail: universidad-catolica@hotmail.com
Website: http://ucatolica.edu.mx

Rector: Javier Antuna García EMail: rectoria@ucatolica.edu.mx

Programmes
Professional Studies (Administration; Dietetics; Ecology; Education; Educational Psychology; Engineering; Family Studies; Home Economics; Nutrition)

History: Founded 1997, acquired present status 1998.

Admission Requirements: Secondary school certificate (bachillerato)

Fees: (Pesos): 15,575 per annum

Main Language(s) of Instruction: Spanish

Degrees and Diplomas: *Licenciatura*: 4 yrs; *Especialización*; *Maestría*; *Doctorado*: Education

Student Services: Academic counselling, Cultural centre, Employment services, Handicapped facilities, Health services, Language programs, Nursery care, Social counselling, Sports facilities

Libraries: Yes
Last Updated: 11/09/12

CELAYENSE INSTITUTE

Instituto Celayense, S.C.

Apdo. Postal N° 473, Paseo del Bajío y Magnolia Jardines de Celaya, 38080 Celaya, Guanajuato
Tel: +52(46) 13-43-85 +52(46) 12-48-37
Fax: +52(46) 13-44-59
EMail: inscel@ic.edu.mx

Director: Ramón Lemus Muñoz-Ledo

History: Founded 1997.

Degrees and Diplomas: *Licenciatura*; *Maestría*
Last Updated: 07/04/08

CENCALLI INSTITUTE OF FAMILY THERAPY

Instituto de Terapia Familiar Cencalli

Bajío 24, Col. Roma Sur, Entre Toluca y Av. Cuauhtémoc, 06760 México, D.F.
Tel: +52(555) 564-03-63 +52(555) 564-21-09
EMail: informacion@cencalli.edu.mx
Website: http://www.cencalli.edu.mx

Directora General: Luisa Velasco Campos

Programmes
Family Therapy (Family Studies; Psychotherapy)

History: Founded 1987.

Main Language(s) of Instruction: Spanish

Degrees and Diplomas: *Especialización*: 2 yrs; *Maestría*: 2 yrs
Last Updated: 05/03/13

CENTRAL UNIVERSITY OF MEXICO

Universidad Central de México

Francisco Javier Molina, Ote., 819, San Felipe Hueyotlipán, 72030 Puebla, Puebla
Tel: +52(224) 488-28-14 +52(224) 440-41-52
Website: http://www.ucm.mx

Rector: Luis Ignacio Rosas Soriano

Programmes
Business Administration (Accountancy; Business Administration; Finance); **Design and Visual Communication** (Advertising and Publicity; Communication Studies; Design); **Engineering** (Computer Engineering; Industrial Engineering); **Information Technology** (Information Technology); **Psychology** (Psychology)

History: Founded 2000 as Escuela de Ingeniería y Comunicación.

Main Language(s) of Instruction: Spanish

Degrees and Diplomas: *Licenciatura*
Last Updated: 11/09/12

CENTRE FOR ADVANCED STUDIES OF LOS TUXTLAS

Centro de Estudios Superiores de Los Tuxtlas

Calle Pino Suarez No. 7 Esq. Belisario Domínguez, Col. Centro, 95700 San Andrés Tuxtla, Veracruz
Tel: +52(294) 942-54-73
Fax: +52(294) 942-46-16
EMail: cest@prodigy.net.mx
Website: http://cestsatv.com/

Director General: Fernando Enríquez Jiménez (1998-)

Programmes
Accountancy (Accountancy); **Business Administration** (Business Administration); **Civil Engineering** (Civil Engineering); **Computer Engineering** (Computer Engineering); **Law** (Law); **Organizational Psychology** (Psychology); **Pedagogy** (Pedagogy)

History: Founded 1998.

Main Language(s) of Instruction: Spanish

Degrees and Diplomas: *Licenciatura*
Last Updated: 13/07/12

CENTRE FOR ADVANCED FAMILY STUDIES

Centro de Estudios Superiores y Atención a la Familia, A.C.

Tarascos, 3469-315, Fraccionamiento Monraz, 44670 Guadalajara, Jalisco
Tel: +52(33) 38-13-30-16
Fax: +52(33) 38-13-34-02
EMail: aegoldman@mexis.com.mx

Directora: Ana Elda Goldman Serafin

Programmes
Family Therapy (Family Studies; Social Problems)

History: Founded 2000.

Degrees and Diplomas: *Maestría*
Last Updated: 27/10/09

CENTRE FOR ADVANCED PEDAGOGICAL AND EDUCATIONAL STUDIES OF SAN LUIS POTOSÍ

Centro de Altos Estudios Pedagógicos y Educativos de San Luis Potosí

León García 1320, Col. San Juan de Guadalupe, 78359 San Luis Potosí, San Luis Potosí
Tel: +52(444) 820-96-13
EMail: caepe@slp1.telmex.net.mx
Website: http://www.caepe.edu.mx

Director General: Joel Cortés Valádez

Courses
Education (Education); **Pedagogy** (Pedagogy)
History: Founded 1993.
Admission Requirements: Licenciatura
Main Language(s) of Instruction: Spanish
Degrees and Diplomas: *Maestría*; *Doctorado*
Libraries: Yes
Last Updated: 12/07/12

CENTRE FOR ADVANCED STUDIES IN ADMINISTRATION

Centro de Estudios Avanzados en Administración
Manuel López Cotilla No. 864, Col. Del Valle, 03100 México, D.F.
Tel: +52(55) 55-59-76-15
EMail: armando@ceaa.edu.mx
Website: http://www.ceaa.edu.mx

Director: Armando Payno Fuentes (1990-)

Programmes
Business Administration (Administration; Business Administration); **Public Administration** (Public Administration)
History: Founded 1988.
Admission Requirements: Licenciatura
Main Language(s) of Instruction: Spanish
Degrees and Diplomas: *Especialización*; *Maestría*
Last Updated: 12/07/12

CENTRE FOR ADVANCED STUDIES IN ADMINISTRATION

Centro de Estudios de Administración Superior
Av. Presidente Masarik N° 25, 1er. Piso, Col. Polanco, 11560 México, D.F.
Tel: +52(55) 31-02-52 +52(55) 31-02-53

Director: Ubaldo Reyes López (1987-)

Programmes
Administration (Administration; Finance; Human Resources); **Fiscal Law** (Fiscal Law)
History: Founded 1987.
Main Language(s) of Instruction: Spanish
Degrees and Diplomas: *Especialización*
Last Updated: 12/07/12

CENTRE FOR ADVANCED STUDIES IN DESIGN OF MONTERREY

Centro de Estudios Superiores de Diseño de Monterrey (CEDIM)
Antiguo Camino a la Huasteca, (Acueducto) No.360, Col. Obispado, 64050 Santa Catarina, Nuevo León
Tel: +52(81) 82-62-22-00
EMail: info@cedim.edu.mx
Website: http://www.cedim.mx

Rector: Michael García Novak

Programmes
Architecture (Architecture); **Digital Arts** (Fine Arts; Multimedia); **Fashion Design** (Fashion Design); **Graphic Design** (Graphic Design); **Industrial Design** (Industrial Design); **Interior Design** (Interior Design); **Marketing** (Marketing)
History: Founded 1978. Acquired present status 2000.
Main Language(s) of Instruction: Spanish
Degrees and Diplomas: *Licenciatura*; *Maestría*
Publications: Neue
Last Updated: 13/07/12

CENTRE FOR ADVANCED STUDIES IN EDUCATION

Centro de Estudios Superiores en Educación (CESE)
Benito Juárez, 108, Col. Albert, Delegación Benito Juárez, 03560 México, D.F.
Tel: +52(55) 56-39-45-84
Fax: +52(55) 56-74-57-48
EMail: info@cese.edu.mx
Website: http://www.cese.edu.mx

Director: Rafael Lara Barragán Vargas (1990-)

Programmes
Educational Sciences (Educational Sciences)
History: Founded 1990.
Main Language(s) of Instruction: Spanish
Degrees and Diplomas: *Licenciatura*; *Especialización*; *Maestría*; *Doctorado*
Libraries: Yes
Last Updated: 16/07/12

CENTRE FOR ADVANCED STUDIES IN ORTHODONTICS

Centro de Estudios Superiores de Ortodoncia
Nicolás San Juan, 1628 entre Parroquia y Felix Cuevas, Col. del Valle, Benito Juárez, 03100 México, D.F.
Tel: +52(55) 55-34-40-16
Fax: +52(55) 55-34-13-19
EMail: ceso1984@hotmail.com; ceso1984@yahoo.com.mx; ceso1984@gmail.com
Website: http://www.ortodoncia.com.mx

Director General: Adán Alfredo Casasa Araújo
EMail: acasasa@hotmail.com

Programmes
Orthodontics (Orthodontics)
History: Founded 1984.
Main Language(s) of Instruction: Spanish
Degrees and Diplomas: *Maestría*
Last Updated: 13/07/12

CENTRE FOR ADVANCED STUDIES IN SCIENCE AND HUMANITIES

Centro de Estudios Superiores en Ciencias y Humanidades
Allende, 1990, Col. Vista Hermosa, Acuña, Coahuila
Tel: +52(877) 772-58-10
Fax: +52(877) 772-58-10

Director: Manyu A. Aparicio Sánchez

Programmes
Accountancy (Accountancy); **Business Computing** (Business Computing); **Law and Social Sciences** (Law; Social Sciences); **Psychology** (Psychology)
Main Language(s) of Instruction: Spanish
Degrees and Diplomas: *Licenciatura*
Last Updated: 16/07/12

CENTRE FOR ADVANCED STUDIES IN TOURISM

Centro de Estudios Superiores Turísticos, A.C.
Presidente Cárdenas, 651, 25000 Saltillo, Coahuila
Tel: +52(844) 412-63-73 +52(844) 412-23-68
Fax: +52(844) 414-67-40

Directora: Alicia E. Barajas Sosa

Programmes
Tourism (Tourism)
Main Language(s) of Instruction: Spanish
Degrees and Diplomas: *Licenciatura*
Last Updated: 10/03/08

CENTRE FOR ADVANCED STUDIES IN TOURISM OF XALAPA

Centro Superior de Estudios Turísticos de Xalapa
Avenida Miguel Alemán, 96, Col. Federal, 91140 Xalapa, Veracruz
Tel: +52(228) 14-20-05 +52(228) 14-83-38
Fax: +52(228) 14-49-52
EMail: informes@csetj.com
Website: http://www.csetj.com/

Director: Humberto Daniel Vicuña Beaumont (1992-)

Programmes
Gastronomy (Cooking and Catering); **Tourism** (Management; Tourism)

History: Founded 1983 as Instituto de Turismo Citlaltepetl. Acquired present title 1990.

Main Language(s) of Instruction: Spanish

Degrees and Diplomas: *Licenciatura*
Last Updated: 11/03/08

CENTRE FOR ADVANCED STUDIES OF CÓRDOBA

Centro de Estudios Superiores de Córdoba
Avenida 9, 1916, casi Esq. Calle 21, 94500 Córdoba, Veracruz
Tel: +52(271) 714-92-55
Fax: +52(271) 714-68-40
EMail: rjarviof@prodigy.net.mx
Website: http://www.cescocordoba.com.mx

Director: Raúl Jarvio Fernández (2000-)

Programmes
Accountancy (Accountancy); **Business Administration** (Business Administration; Management Systems); **Business Computing** (Business Computing); **International Trade** (International Business); **Law** (Law); **Pedagogy** (Pedagogy)

Degrees and Diplomas: *Licenciatura*
Last Updated: 13/07/12

CENTRE FOR ADVANCED STUDIES OF GUAMUCHIL

Centro de Estudios Superiores de Guamuchil, A.C.
Silverio Trueba y Fernando Amilpa, 720, Sur, Col. Cuauhtémoc, 81490 Guamúchil, Sinaloa
Tel: +52(673) 732-34-02
Fax: +52(673) 732-57-66
EMail: info@cesgac.edu.mx
Website: http://www.cesgac.edu.mx

Director General: Rafael Castro Juárez
EMail: rcastro@cesgac.edu.mx

Programmes
Criminology (Criminology); **Graphic Design** (Graphic Design); **Law** (Law); **Nursing** (Nursing); **Physical Education and Sport** (Physical Education; Sports)

Degrees and Diplomas: *Licenciatura*
Last Updated: 13/07/12

CENTRE FOR ADVANCED STUDIES OF HIDALGO

Centro Hidalguense de Estudios Superiores, S.C. (CENHIES)
Blvd. Luis Donaldo Colosio, 101, Col. Ampliación Santa Julia, Pachuca, 42080 San Cayetano, Hidalgo
Tel: +52(771) 718-64-74
EMail: contacto@cenhies.edu.mx
Website: http://www.cenhies.edu.mx

Rector: Leonardo Ramírez Álvarez (1994-)

Programmes
Business Administration and Law (Accountancy; Business Administration; Law); **Graphic Design** (Graphic Design); **Hotel Management** (Hotel Management); **Social Sciences** (Clinical Psychology; Communication Studies; Educational Psychology)

History: Founded 1993.

Main Language(s) of Instruction: Spanish

Degrees and Diplomas: *Licenciatura*; *Especialización*; *Maestría*
Last Updated: 07/03/08

CENTRE FOR ADVANCED STUDIES OF MARTÍNEZ DE LA TORRE

Centro de Estudios Superiores de Martínez de la Torre, S.C. (CESM)
Avenida Ignacio Zaragoza, 409, Col. Patria, Zona Centro, 93600 Martínez de La Torre, Veracruz
Tel: +52(232) 324-08-45
Fax: +52(232) 324-14-67
EMail: info@cesm.edu.mx
Website: http://www.cesm.mx

Directora General: Evelyn Dugas Salcedo

Programmes
Accountancy (Accountancy); **Business Administration** (Business Administration); **Business Computing** (Business Computing); **Educational Sciences** (Educational Sciences); **Law** (Law); **Marketing** (Marketing); **Organizational Psychology** (Psychology); **Pedagogy** (Pedagogy); **Physical Education and Sport** (Physical Education; Sports); **Pre-school Education** (Preschool Education)

History: Founded 1996 as Centro Universitario Salvador Díaz Mirón.

Main Language(s) of Instruction: Spanish

Degrees and Diplomas: *Licenciatura*; *Maestría*
Last Updated: 13/07/12

CENTRE FOR ADVANCED STUDIES OF SAN ÁNGEL

Centro de Estudios Superiores de San Ángel
Morelos, 7, Col. Tizapán-San Ángel, Delegación Álvaro Obregón, 01090 México, D.F.
Tel: +52(55) 8503 - 8810
EMail: informes@cessa.edu.mx
Website: http://www.cessa.edu.mx

Directora General: Luz María Arteaga de Guerrero (1976-)

Programmes
Gastronomy and Culinary Arts (Cooking and Catering); **Hotel and Restaurant Management** (Hotel and Restaurant; Hotel Management)

Further Information: Also Campus Estado de México

History: Founded 1976.

Main Language(s) of Instruction: Spanish

Degrees and Diplomas: *Licenciatura*; *Especialización*; *Maestría*
Last Updated: 13/07/12

CENTRE FOR ADVANCED STUDIES OF TAMAULIPAS

Centro de Estudios Superiores de Tamaulipas, A.C.
Av. Gral. Manuel González No. 262, Zona Industrial, Centro, Heroica Matamoros, Matamoros, 87130 Matamoros, Tamaulipas
Tel: +52(834) 312-67-02 +52(834) 312-43-05

Director: Francisco Lerma Alvarado

Programmes
Accountancy (Accountancy); **Business Administration** (Business Administration); **Industrial Engineering** (Industrial Engineering); **Law** (Law); **Marketing** (Marketing)

History: Founded 1970.

Degrees and Diplomas: *Licenciatura*
Last Updated: 15/02/13

CENTRE FOR ADVANCED STUDIES OF TAPACHULA

Centro de Estudios Superiores de Tapachula, S.C.
Apartado postal 257, Monte Lago Eureka s/n, Col. Guadalupe, 30700 Tapachula, Chiapas
Tel: +52(962) 625-03-20
Fax: +52(962) 625-11-39
EMail: dircest@prodigy.net.mx

Schools
Law (Law); **Psychology** (Psychology)
History: Founded 1995.
Main Language(s) of Instruction: Spanish
Degrees and Diplomas: *Licenciatura*
Last Updated: 13/07/12

CENTRE FOR ADVANCED STUDIES OF TEPEACA

Centro de Estudios Superiores de Tepeaca, A.C.
9 Poniente, 202, Col. Hermosa Provincia, 72000 Tepeaca, Puebla
Tel: +55(223) 275-3268
Website: http://www.ces-tepeaca.edu.mx

Programmes
Administration (Administration); **Computer Science** (Computer Science); **Dentistry** (Dentistry); **Law** (Law); **Surgery** (Surgery)
History: Founded 1996.
Admission Requirements: Bachillerato or equivalent
Main Language(s) of Instruction: Spanish
Degrees and Diplomas: *Licenciatura*
Last Updated: 13/07/12

CENTRE FOR ADVANCED STUDIES OF THE EAST OF MICHOACÁN

Centro de Estudios Superiores del Oriente de Michoacán
Carretera Maravatío-Ciudad Hidalgo s/n, Col. San Miguel Curahuango, 61250 Maravatío de Ocampo, Michoacán
Tel: +52(447) 478-48-94
EMail: universidadcesom@yahoo.com.mx
Website: http://www.cesom.edu.mx
Director: Juan Manuel Almanza Bedolla

Programmes
Accountancy (Accountancy); **Administration** (Administration); **Computer Science** (Computer Science); **International Business** (International Business); **Law** (Law); **Psychology** (Psychology)
Further Information: Also campus in Zitácuaro
History: Founded 2000.
Main Language(s) of Instruction: Spanish
Degrees and Diplomas: *Licenciatura*; *Maestría*
Last Updated: 16/07/12

CENTRE FOR ADVANCED STUDIES OF THE FRONTIER

Centro de Estudios Superiores de la Frontera (UNIFRONT)
Paseo de los Héroes, 17, Zona del Río, 22320 Tijuana, Baja California
Tel: +52(666) 634-70-91
Fax: +52(666) 634-75-09
EMail: unifronttijuana@hotmail.com
Director General: Guillermo Gutiérrez Apocada (1999-)

Programmes
Graphic Design (Graphic Design); **Psychology**
History: Founded 1999.
Main Language(s) of Instruction: Spanish
Degrees and Diplomas: *Licenciatura*
Last Updated: 15/02/13

CENTRE FOR ADVANCED STUDIES OF THE GULF

Centro de Estudios Superiores del Golfo
Anesagasti, 196, Col. Centro, 45400 Tonalá, Jalisco
Tel: +52(33) 36-83-60-11
EMail: cesgpalacios@prodigy.net.mx
Website: http://www.cesg.edu.mx/
Directora: Noemí Rodríguez Torres

Programmes
Education (Education; Educational Administration; Pedagogy)
History: Founded 2003.
Main Language(s) of Instruction: Spanish
Degrees and Diplomas: *Maestría*
Last Updated: 16/07/12

CENTRE FOR ADVANCED STUDIES OF THE ISTHMUS

Centro de Estudios Superiores del Istmo
Km. 8 Avenida Universidad Veracruzana, 18 de Marzo, 211, Col. Santa Cecilia, 96537 Coatzacoalcos, Veracruz
Tel: +52(921) 922-02-54 +52(921) 922-01-75
Fax: +52(921) 928-50-05
EMail: cesiuav@moomsa.com.mx
Director: Leonardo Gómez Navas Chapa

Programmes
Industrial Relations and Computer Networks (Computer Networks; Industrial Management)
History: Founded 1996.
Main Language(s) of Instruction: Spanish
Degrees and Diplomas: *Licenciatura*
Last Updated: 05/03/08

CENTRE FOR ADVANCED STUDIES OF THE NORTH

Centro de Estudios Superiores del Norte
Aldama No. 805 Altos, Col. Centro, Col. Margaritas, 31000 Chihuahua, Chihuahua
Tel: +52(614) 416-26-16
EMail: info@cesno.edu.mx
Website: http://www.cesno.edu.mx

Programmes
Accountancy (Accountancy); **Business Administration** (Business Administration); **Law** (Commercial Law; Constitutional Law; Law); **Psychology** (Psychology)
Further Information: Also campus in Ciudad Juarez
History: Founded 1998
Main Language(s) of Instruction: Spanish
Degrees and Diplomas: *Licenciatura*; *Maestría*
Last Updated: 16/07/12

CENTRE FOR ADVANCED STUDIES OF THE NORTH WEST

Centro de Estudios Superiores del Noroeste (CESUN)
Blvd. Cucapah Sur #20100 Fracc. El Lago, 22400 Tijuana, Baja California
Tel: +52(666) 886-16-01 al 04
EMail: informacion@cesun.edu.mx
Website: http://www.cesun.edu.mx
Director General: Ernesto Aello Arvizu (1992-)
EMail: aello@cesun.edu.mx

Programmes
Administration (Administration; Business Administration; International Business); **Education** (Education)
Further Information: Also Centre in Cucapah
History: Founded 1992.
Main Language(s) of Instruction: Spanish
Degrees and Diplomas: *Licenciatura*; *Especialización*; *Maestría*
Last Updated: 16/07/12

CENTRE FOR ADVANCED STUDIES OF THE SOUTH EAST

Centro de Estudios Superiores del Sureste
Calle 51, 506 x 60 y 62, Col. Centro, 97000 Mérida, Yucatán
Tel: +52(999) 924-63-91
Fax: +52(999) 924-60-68
EMail: info@cess.edu.mx
Website: http://www.cess.edu.mx

Director: Francisco Arrañaga Ramírez

Programmes
Educational Sciences (Educational Sciences); **International Business and Taxation** (International Business; Taxation); **Psychopedagogy** (Child Care and Development; Pedagogy; Psychology)

Further Information: Also campus in Campeche

History: Founded 1986.

Main Language(s) of Instruction: Spanish

Degrees and Diplomas: *Licenciatura*; *Maestría*. Also Diplomados

Last Updated: 16/07/12

CENTRE FOR ADVANCED STUDIES OF THE SOUTH OF SINALOA

Centro de Estudios Superiores del Sur de Sinaloa
Morelos No. 87 - Col. Centro, 82800 El Rosario, Sinaloa
Tel: +52(69) 52-10-29
EMail: rlhli@hotmail.com

Directora: María Belen López López

Programmes
Business Computing (Business Computing); **Computer Science** (Computer Science); **Digital Graphic Design** (Computer Graphics); **Law** (Law); **Public Accountancy** (Accountancy); **Teleinformatics** (Computer Science)

Further Information: Also Campus Escuinapa

Main Language(s) of Instruction: Spanish

Degrees and Diplomas: *Licenciatura*

Last Updated: 16/07/12

CENTRE FOR ADVANCED STUDIES OF THE STATE OF AGUASCALIENTES

Centro de Estudios Superiores del Estado de Aguascalientes
Av. Las Américas No. 502 - Fracc. Las Américas, Aguascalientes, Aguascalientes

Programmes
Business Administration (Business Administration); **Communication Studies** (Communication Studies); **Law** (Law); **Public Administration** (Public Administration)

Main Language(s) of Instruction: Spanish

Degrees and Diplomas: *Licenciatura*

Last Updated: 18/07/12

CENTRE FOR ADVANCED STUDIES OF THE VALLEY

Centro de Estudios Superiores del Valle
Ajusco y Citlaltepetl, Manzana 632, Lote 25, 3a Sección, Ciudad Azteca, 66120 Ecatepec de Morelos, Estado de México
Tel: +52(55) 57-77-18-07 +52(55) 57-77-78-16

Director: José Luis Morales Cárdenas

Degrees and Diplomas: *Licenciatura*

Last Updated: 04/04/08

CENTRE FOR ADVANCED STUDIES OF THE VALLEY OF IGUALA

Centro de Estudios Superiores del Valle de Iguala (CESVI)
Zaragoza, 101, Col. Centro, 40000 Iguala, Guerrero
Tel: +52(733) 333-49-85
Fax: +52(733) 332-57-21
EMail: cesvidireccion@hotmail.com
Website: http://cesviuniversidad.edu.mx

Director: Carlos C. Acosta-Viquez Ortiz (1997-)

Programmes
Business Administration and Law (Accountancy; Administration; Law); **Graphic Design** (Graphic Design); **Psychology** (Psychology)

History: Founded 1992.

Main Language(s) of Instruction: Spanish

Degrees and Diplomas: *Licenciatura*

Last Updated: 16/07/12

CENTRE FOR ADVANCED STUDIES OF TLAXCALA

Centro de Estudios Superiores de Tlaxcala
Calle Josefa Ortiz de Domínguez No. 4, 3ra Sección, Col. Guardia, 90740 Zacatelco, Tlaxcala
Tel: +52(246) 497-33-38
EMail: admisiones@unitlaxcala.com
Website: http://www.unitlaxcala.com

Director General: Felipe de los Angeles Vargas

Programmes
Accountancy (Accountancy); **Law** (Law); **Marketing and Publicity** (Advertising and Publicity; Marketing)

History: Founded 1996.

Main Language(s) of Instruction: Spanish

Degrees and Diplomas: *Licenciatura*; *Maestría*

Last Updated: 16/07/12

CENTRE FOR ADVANCED STUDIES OF TUXTEPEC

Centro de Estudios Superiores de Tuxtepec
Jazmines, 58, Col. Las Flores, San Juan Bautista Tuxtepec, 68354 Tuxtepec, Oaxaca
Tel: +52(287) 875-26-95
Fax: +52(287) 875-39-28
EMail: cest-tuxtepec@hotmail.com
Website: http://cestuxtepec.edu.mx

Directora: María del Refugio Román Salgado (1993-)

Programmes
Accountancy (Accountancy); **Business Computing** (Business Computing); **Pedagogy** (Pedagogy); **Physical Education** (Physical Education); **Psychology** (Psychology); **Sports** (Sports)

History: Founded 1992.

Main Language(s) of Instruction: Spanish

Degrees and Diplomas: *Licenciatura*; *Especialización*; *Maestría*

Last Updated: 16/07/12

CENTRE FOR ADVANCED STUDIES OF VERACRUZ

Centro de Estudios Superiores de Veracruz (CESVER)
Serafín Olarte # 43, Col. Mártires de Chicago, Xalapa, Veracruz
Tel: +52(229) 818-20-38
Fax: +52(229) 818-20-39
EMail: cesverites@hotmail.com
Website: http://www.cesver.edu.mx

Rector: Nicodemus Santos Luck

Programmes
Accountancy (Accountancy); **Business Administration** (Business Administration); **Communication Studies** (Communication Studies); **Computer Science**; **Education** (Education; Educational

Administration; Pedagogy); **Industrial Relations** (Industrial Arts Education); **Information Sciences** (Information Sciences); **Trade and Commerce** (Business and Commerce)
History: Founded 1998.
Admission Requirements: Certificado de Bachillerato, Certificado de Secundaria
Fees: (Pesos): 1,600 per month
Main Language(s) of Instruction: Spanish
Degrees and Diplomas: *Licenciatura*: 4 yrs; *Especialización*; *Maestría*: a further 2 yrs; *Doctorado*
Student Services: Academic counselling, Canteen
Student Residential Facilities: None
Special Facilities: None
Libraries: Yes
Last Updated: 16/07/12

CENTRE FOR ADVANCED STUDIES OF XALAPA

Centro de Estudios Superiores de Xalapa
Lucio Blanco No. 2, Colonia Obrera Campesina, 91020 Xalapa, Veracruz
Tel: +52(2) 814-26-24
Fax: +52(2) 814-26-24

Directora General: Marisa I. Fernández y Pérez

Programmes
Psychology
History: Founded 1996.
Main Language(s) of Instruction: Spanish
Degrees and Diplomas: *Maestría*
Last Updated: 03/03/08

CENTRE FOR ADVANCED UNIVERSITY STUDIES

Centro de Estudios Superiores Universitarios
Ave. Constituyentes 600, Tianguistenco de Galeana, 52600 Santiago Tianguistenco, Estado de México
Tel: +52(713) 133-61-08
Website: http://www.cesu.com.mx

Director: Jaime Ilpas Arriaga

Programmes
Accountancy (Accountancy); **Administration** (Administration); **Business Computing** (Business Computing); **Computer Engineering** (Computer Engineering); **Law** (Civil Law; Criminal Law; Law; Taxation); **Psychology** (Psychology)
History: Founded 1993.
Main Language(s) of Instruction: Spanish
Degrees and Diplomas: *Licenciatura*; *Maestría*
Libraries: Yes
Last Updated: 17/07/12

CENTRE FOR APPLIED STUDIES IN ORTHODONTICS

Centro de Estudios de Ortodoncia Aplicada
Calle José Eguiara y Eguren, 30-A, Col. Viaducto Piedad, Delegación Iztacalco, 08200 México, D.F.
Tel: +52(55) 55-53-03-02

Director: Teófilo Ricardo Miranda Téllez

Programmes
Orthodontics (Orthodontics)
Degrees and Diplomas: *Licenciatura*

CENTRE FOR AUDIOVISUAL TECHNIQUES

Centro de Medios Audiovisuales (CAAV)
Lerdo de Tejada 2071, Col. Americana, 44150 Guadalajara, Jalisco
Tel: +52(133) 3615-6603
EMail: info@centroaudiovisual.com
Website: http://www.centroaudiovisual.com

Director general: Daniel Varela
EMail: d.varela@centroaudiovisual.com
Directora: Margarita Sierra EMail: m.sierra@centroaudiovisual.com

Programmes
Audiovisual Techniques (Advertising and Publicity; Cinema and Television; Communication Arts; Media Studies; Multimedia; Music; Painting and Drawing; Photography; Radio and Television Broadcasting; Speech Studies)
History: Founded 1995. Acquired present status 2003.
Main Language(s) of Instruction: Spanish
Degrees and Diplomas: *Licenciatura*. Also Diplomados
Last Updated: 27/10/09

CENTRE FOR DESIGN AND VISUAL COMMUNICATION

Centro de Diseño y Comunicación Visual
General Cepeda, 542, Sur, Col. Centro, 25000 Saltillo, Coahuila
Tel: +52(844) 410-39-84
Fax: +52(844) 417-48-56

Director: Juan Manuel Rodríguez Rodríguez

Programmes
Design (Design; Interior Design; Visual Arts)
Degrees and Diplomas: *Licenciatura*
Last Updated: 14/02/13

CENTRE FOR EDUCATION IN HEALTH AND SEXUALITY STUDIES

Centro de Educación y Atención en la Salud y la Sexualidad, A. C.
José Guadalupe Montenegro No. 2361, 44150 Guadalajara, Jalisco
Tel: +52(33) 38-26-98-61
Fax: +52(33) 38-26-12-02
EMail: ceass_mesh@yahoo.com.mx
Website: http://portalsej.jalisco.gob.mx/sites/portalsej.jalisco.gob.mx.posgrado/files/pdf/ceass.pdf

Directora: Matilde Isabel Corrales Carvajal

Programmes
Health and Sexuality Studies (Health Sciences)
History: Founded 1998.
Main Language(s) of Instruction: Spanish
Degrees and Diplomas: *Especialización*; *Maestría*. Also Diplomado
Last Updated: 14/02/13

CENTRE FOR GESTALT STUDIES AND RESEARCH

Centro de Estudios e Investigación Guestalticos
Estanzuela N°110, Fracc. Pomona, 91040 Xalapa, Veracruz
Tel: +52(128) 817-51-99
Fax: +52(128) 812-29-55
EMail: cesigue.gestalt@gmail.com
Website: http://www.cesigue.edu.mx

Directora: Guadalupe Amezcua Villela
EMail: direccion@cesigue.edu.mx

Programmes
Education (Education); **Gestalt Psychotherapy** (Psychotherapy)
Further Information: Also branches in Villahermosa
History: Founded 1991.
Main Language(s) of Instruction: Spanish
Degrees and Diplomas: *Especialización*; *Maestría*; *Doctorado*. Also Diplomado
Libraries: Yes
Last Updated: 13/07/12

CENTRE FOR GESTALT STUDIES FOR DESIGN

Centro de Estudios Gestalt Para el Diseño
S.S. Juan Pablo II, 1390, Fracc. Costa Verde, 94294 Boca del Río, Veracruz
Tel: +52(229) 921-31-08 +52(229) 922-07-86
EMail: informes@cegestalt.com.mx
Website: http://www.cegestalt.com.mx

Directora General: Aurora Susana Malpica Mancera (1995-)
EMail: auroramalpica@cegestalt.com.mx

Centres
Language (English; French; German; Italian)

Programmes
Fashion Design (Fashion Design); **Foreign Trade** (International Business); **Graphic Design** (Graphic Design); **Interior Design** (Interior Design); **Typography**

Further Information: Also Campus Cancún
History: Founded 1987.
Admission Requirements: Bachillerato
Main Language(s) of Instruction: Spanish
Degrees and Diplomas: *Licenciatura*; *Maestría*. Also Diplomados
Libraries: Yes
Last Updated: 13/07/12

CENTRE FOR HISTORICAL AND CULTURAL RESEARCH OF THE AMPARA MUSEUM

Centro de Investigaciones Históricas y Culturales Museo Ampara
2 Sur N° 708, 72000 Puebla, Puebla
Tel: +52(2) 246-42-00 +52(2) 246-42-07
Fax: +52(2) 246-63-33

Directora: Ángeles Espinosa Iglesias

Programmes
History and Cultural Studies
Degrees and Diplomas: *Especialización*

CENTRE FOR HUMAN AND FAMILY DEVELOPMENT

Centro de Desarrollo Humano y Familiar
Avenida Chapultepec 67 Interior 23, Col. Americana, 44600 Guadalajara, Jalisco
Tel: +52(133) 36-15-69-29
EMail: enlacejalisco@yahoo.com.mx

Directora: Alejandra Cortina Campero

Programmes
Family Development Studies (Family Studies)

History: Founded 2003.
Admission Requirements: Licenciatura
Main Language(s) of Instruction: Spanish
Degrees and Diplomas: *Maestría*
Last Updated: 27/10/09

CENTRE FOR HUMAN DEVELOPMENT AND GESTALT PSYCHOTHERAPY

Centro de Desarrollo Humano y Psicoterapia 'Gestalt'
Jazmines No. 104, Col. Reforma, 68000 Oaxaca, Oaxaca
Tel: +52(951) 516-69-29
EMail: gestaltoax@infosel.net.mx
Website: http://www.gestaltoaxaca.com

Directora General: Pilar Ocampo Pizano (1995-)

Divisions
Bach Flowers Remedies; **Clinical Psychology** (Clinical Psychology); **Gestalt Psychotherapy** (Psychotherapy)

History: Founded 1995.
Main Language(s) of Instruction: Spanish
Degrees and Diplomas: *Especialización*. Also Diplomados
Last Updated: 29/10/12

CENTRE FOR HUMAN ORIENTATION AND PROMOTION

Centro de Orientación y Promoción Humana
Vía Lactea 45, Col. Prado, Churubusco, 04230 México, D.F.
Tel: +52(55) 56-97-86-33
Fax: +52(55) 56-97-85-08
EMail: cophac@cophac.com

Directora: María Sánchez Quintanar (1992-)

Programmes
Applied Psychology (Psychology)
Degrees and Diplomas: *Especialización*; *Maestría*
Last Updated: 29/02/08

CENTRE FOR ODONTOLOGICAL STUDIES OF QUERÉTARO

Centro de Estudios Odontológicos de Querétaro
Av. Ejercito Republicano N° 119 2° Piso, Col. Carretas (Centro Historico), 76050 Querétaro, Querétaro
Tel: +52(4) 253-72-70
EMail: ceoqro@aol.com

Director: Luis Felipe Cámara Chejín (1997-)

Programmes
Dentistry (Dentistry)
History: Founded 1997.
Main Language(s) of Instruction: Spanish
Degrees and Diplomas: *Especialización*
Last Updated: 14/02/13

CENTRE FOR PERSONAL AND FAMILY DEVELOPMENT STUDIES

Centro de Crecimiento Personal y Familiar, S.C.
20 de Noviembre 857 Sur, Col. Obispado, 64060 Monterrey, Nuevo León
Tel: +52(81) 83-43-51-02
Fax: +52(81) 83-43-51-03
EMail: informes@centrodecrecimiento.com
Website: http://www.centrodecrecimiento.com

Director: Ruperto Charles Torres

Programmes
Psychology (Clinical Psychology; Industrial and Organizational Psychology; Psychology)

Further Information: Also Institute in Jalisco
Main Language(s) of Instruction: Spanish
Degrees and Diplomas: *Licenciatura*; *Especialización*; *Maestría*; *Doctorado*
Last Updated: 12/07/12

CENTRE FOR POSTGRADUATE STUDIES

Centro de Estudios de Posgrado
Mariano Escobedo 373, 2do Piso, Chapultepec, 11580 Mexico, DF
Tel: +52(3) 830-44
EMail: informes@cposgrado.edu.mx
Website: http://www.cposgrado.edu.mx

Rector: Simón Pablo Herrera Bazán

Programmes
Criminology (Criminology); **Labour Law** (Labour Law); **Penal Law** (Criminal Law)

Further Information: Campuses nationwide
History: Founded 2007.
Main Language(s) of Instruction: Spanish
Degrees and Diplomas: *Especialización*; *Maestría*; *Doctorado*
Last Updated: 14/02/13

CENTRE FOR POSTGRADUATE STUDIES IN ADMINISTRATION AND COMPUTER SCIENCE

Centro de Posgrado en Administración e Informática, A.C.
Calle Nayarit, 300, Col. Unidad Nacional, Ciudad Madero, 10152 Ciudad Madero, Tamaulipas
Tel: +52(833) 200-01-52 +52(833) 216-75-81
EMail: info@cpai.edu.mx

Director: Javier Chávez Melendez

Programmes

Administration (Administration); **Computer Studies**

History: Founded 1998.

Main Language(s) of Instruction: Spanish

Degrees and Diplomas: *Licenciatura*; *Maestría*; *Doctorado*
Last Updated: 29/02/08

CENTRE FOR POSTGRADUATE STUDIES IN DENTISTRY

Centro de Estudios de Posgrado en Odontología
Calle Ley 2639, Col. Circunvalación Vallarta, 44680 Guadalajara, Jalisco
Tel: +52(33) 3616-0248
EMail: admon@cepomexico.com.mx

Director General: Manuel Navarro Herrera

Courses

Dentistry (Dentistry; Orthodontics)

History: Founded 1994.

Main Language(s) of Instruction: Spanish

Degrees and Diplomas: *Especialización*
Last Updated: 13/07/12

CENTRE FOR POSTGRADUATE STUDIES IN LAW

Centro de Estudios de Posgrado en Derecho
Augusto Rodín 499, Col. Insurgentes Mixcoac, Benito Juárez, 03910 México, D.F.
Tel: +52(55) 56-15-24-54
EMail: direccion@ueped.com
Website: http://www.eped.edu.mx

Director: Othon Pérez Fernández del Castillo

Courses

Law (Law)

Further Information: Also campuses in Satelite, Cuernavaca

Main Language(s) of Instruction: Spanish

Degrees and Diplomas: *Licenciatura*; *Maestría*; *Doctorado*
Last Updated: 13/07/12

CENTRE FOR POSTGRADUATE STUDIES IN ORTHODONTICS OF THE VALLEY OF ANÁHUAC

Centro de Estudios de Posgrado en Ortodoncia Valle de Anáhuac
Calzada de Tlalpan No. 2287, Col. Cd. Jardín, Desp. 602 Coyoacán, 04370 México, D.F.
Tel: +52(55) 34-11-92
Fax: +52(55) 336-95-45
EMail: cepova@att.net.mx

Director: Octavio Hiram Navarro Robles (1992-)

Courses

Orthodontics (Orthodontics)

History: Founded 1986.

Main Language(s) of Instruction: Spanish

Degrees and Diplomas: *Especialización*
Last Updated: 13/07/12

CENTRE FOR POSTGRADUATE STUDIES OF THE MEXICAN PSYCHOANALYTICAL ASSOCIATION

Centro de Estudios de Posgrado de la Asociación Psicoanalítica Mexicana
Bosque de Caobas 67 Fracc. Bosques de las Lomas Miguel Hidalgo, 11700 México, D.F.
Tel: +52(55) 596-00-09
Fax: +52(55) 596-74-27
EMail: cepapm@prodigy.net.mx
Website: http://www.apm.org.mx/Portal%20APM/centro%20estudios%20postgrado/CEP.html

Director: David López Garza
EMail: davidlopezgarza@prodigy.net.mx

Centres

Postgraduate Studies (Psychotherapy)

Institutes

Psychoanalysis (Psychoanalysis; Psychotherapy)

History: Founded 1988.

Admission Requirements: Licenciatura

Main Language(s) of Instruction: Spanish

Degrees and Diplomas: *Especialización*; *Maestría*; *Doctorado*. Also Diplomado Internacional

Libraries: Yes
Last Updated: 14/02/13

CENTRE FOR PROFESSIONAL DEVELOPMENT (UNIVERSITY DIVISION)

Centro de Desarrollo Profesional (División Universitaria)
21 Oriente, 4004, 2° Piso, Col. El Carmen, 72000 Puebla, Puebla
Tel: +52(222) 240-49-83 +52(222) 237-35-47

Rector: Bernardo Reyes Guerra

Programmes

Computer Science (Computer Science); **Electronics and Telecommunications** (Electronic Engineering; Telecommunications Engineering)

Main Language(s) of Instruction: Spanish

Degrees and Diplomas: *Licenciatura*
Last Updated: 05/03/08

CENTRE FOR PROFESSIONAL STUDIES OF SALAMANCA

Centro de Estudios Profesionales de Salamanca, S.C.
Blvd. Las Reynas, 100, Fracc. Las Reynas, 36720 Salamanca, Guanajuato
Tel: +52(464) 1-05-75
Fax: +52(464) 1-05-78
EMail: informes@cepsa.edu.mx

Director: Miguel López Rodríguez (1993-)
EMail: miguel.lopez@cepsa.edu.mx

Programmes

Business Computing and Management Systems (Accountancy; Administration; Applied Mathematics; Business Computing; Civil Law; Computer Engineering; Economics; Human Resources; Industrial and Organizational Psychology; Labour Law; Management Systems; Marketing; Statistics)

History: Founded 1993.

Main Language(s) of Instruction: Spanish

Degrees and Diplomas: *Licenciatura*
Last Updated: 14/02/13

CENTRE FOR PROFESSIONAL STUDIES OF THE GULF

Centro de Estudios Profesionales del Golfo
Víctimas del 25 de Junio, 362, Col. Centro, 91700 Veracruz, Veracruz
Tel: +52(229) 932-89-95
Fax: +52(229) 932-89-95
EMail: cetug@hotmail.com

Rectora: Sirenia Domínguez Gámez (2001-)

Director General Académico: Víctor M. García Contreras

Programmes
Accountancy (Accountancy); **Business Administration** (Business Administration; Business and Commerce); **Computer Science** (Computer Science); **Industrial Management** (Industrial Management); **Pedagogy** (Pedagogy)

Further Information: Also Piedras Negras campus

History: Founded 2001.

Main Language(s) of Instruction: Spanish

Degrees and Diplomas: *Licenciatura*; *Especialización*; *Maestría*

Last Updated: 13/07/12

CENTRE FOR PSYCHOLOGICAL ASSISTANCE TO THE FAMILY

Centro de Atención Psicológica a la Familia
Privada Juan de la Barrera No. 30, Col. Obreros Textiles, 91060 Xalapa, Veracruz
Tel: +52(288) 8-17-41-05
EMail: martacam2000@yahoo.com.mx
Website: http://www.capaf.com.mx

Programmes
Family Studies (Family Studies); **Psychology** (Psychology)

History: Founded 1990.

Main Language(s) of Instruction: Spanish

Degrees and Diplomas: *Especialización*; *Maestría*

Last Updated: 29/10/12

CENTRE FOR RESEARCH AND STUDIES IN PSYCHOANALYSIS

Centro de Investigaciones y Estudios Psicoanalíticos (CIEP)
Tecoyotitla N° 154, Col. Florida, 01030 México, D.F.
Tel: +52(555) 662-22-22
Fax: +52(555) 661-77-84
EMail: fmpiap@prodigy.net.mx

Director: Nestor Alberto Braunstein

Programmes
Psychoanalysis (Psychoanalysis)

Main Language(s) of Instruction: Spanish

Degrees and Diplomas: *Maestría*

CENTRE FOR SPECIALIZATION IN DEVELOPMENT AND EDUCATION

Centro de Especialidades en Desarrollo y Educación
Ernesto Talavera, 1612, Col. Linss, 31020 Chihuahua, Chihuahua
Tel: +52(614) 433-23-74
EMail: direccion.general@cede.edu.mx
Website: http://www.cede.edu.mx/

Directora: Yolanda Manquero

Programmes
Education (Education; Educational Psychology; Educational Technology; Special Education)

History: Founded 1990.

Degrees and Diplomas: *Licenciatura*; *Maestría*

Last Updated: 14/02/13

CENTRE FOR SPECIALIZATION IN ODONTOPAEDIATRICS

Centro de Especialización en Odontopediatría
Avenida Constituyentes 385-501, Col. América, Delegación Miguel Hidalgo, 11820 México, D.F.

Director: Samuel Rajunov Sarafanov

Programmes
Dentistry (Dentistry); **Paediatrics** (Paediatrics)

Degrees and Diplomas: *Maestría*

Last Updated: 07/02/08

CENTRE FOR STUDIES AND RESEARCH IN BIOETHICS

Centro de Estudios e Investigaciones de Bioética
Av. España N° 1840, Col. Moderna, 44100 Guadalajara, Jalisco
Tel: +52(3) 611-74-14

Director: Miguel Ayala Fuentes

Programmes
Bioethics (Biology; Ethics)

History: Founded 1995.

Main Language(s) of Instruction: Spanish

Degrees and Diplomas: *Especialización*; *Maestría*

Last Updated: 13/07/12

CENTRE FOR STUDIES AND RESEARCH IN ORTHODENTICS

Centro de Estudios e Investigación en Ortodoncia
Canal de Miramontes No. 15, Col. San Bartolo El Chico Tlalpan, 14350 México, D.F.
Tel: +52(555) 673-65-15 +52(555) 673-97-99
Fax: +52(555) 673-66-01
EMail: allen@adg.net.mx

Director: Juan Morales Pacheco

Courses
Orthodontics (Orthodontics)

History: Founded 1997.

Main Language(s) of Instruction: Spanish

Degrees and Diplomas: *Especialización*

Last Updated: 03/03/08

CENTRE FOR STUDIES IN COMMUNICATION SCIENCES

Centro de Estudios en Ciencias de la Comunicación
Valle #12, Col. Jardines del Pedregal, 03020 México, D.F.
Tel: +52(555) 565-21593
EMail: informes@cecc.edu.mx
Website: http://www.cecc.edu.mx

Director General: Jesús Cuevas Sánchez
EMail: jesus.cuevas@cecc.edu.mx

Programmes
Advertising (Advertising and Publicity); **Cinema and Television** (Cinema and Television); **Communication Studies** (Communication Studies); **Fashion Design and Marketing** (Fashion Design; Marketing); **Graphic Design** (Graphic Design); **Journalism** (Journalism); **Marketing** (Marketing); **Public Relations** (Public Relations)

History: Founded 1974.

Admission Requirements: Bachillerato

Main Language(s) of Instruction: Spanish

Degrees and Diplomas: *Licenciatura*; *Especialización*; *Maestría*

Libraries: Yes

Last Updated: 13/07/12

CENTRE FOR STUDIES IN RURAL DEVELOPMENT

Centro de Estudios para el Desarrollo Rural
Rancho Capolihtic, Zautla, 73740 Zautla, Puebla
Tel: +52(233) 33-15-045
EMail: direccion@cesder-prodes.org
Website: http://www.cesder-prodes.org

Director: Feliciano Aguilar Hernández

Programmes
Rural Studies (Rural Planning; Rural Studies)

History: Founded 1982.

Main Language(s) of Instruction: Spanish

Degrees and Diplomas: *Licenciatura*; *Maestría*
Last Updated: 14/02/13

CENTRE FOR STUDIES IN STOMATOLOGY

Centro de Actualización y Superación Académica en Estomatología
Ruperto Martínez, 1142, Poniente, Colonia Centro, 64000 Monterrey, Nuevo León
Tel: +01 (81) 8340-2500
EMail: casaeamm@hotmail.com
Website: http://casae.edu.mx

Director: Antonio Medellín Morales

Programmes
Endodontics (Dentistry); **Orthodontics** (Orthodontics)
Admission Requirements: Título de Cirujano Dentista.
Main Language(s) of Instruction: Spanish

Degrees and Diplomas: *Especialización*; *Maestría*
Last Updated: 12/07/12

CENTRE FOR STUDIES, CLINIC AND PSYCHOLOGICAL RESEARCH

Centro de Estudios, Clínica e Investigación Psicológica
Calle Justo Sierra No. 5 entre 14 y 16 Col. Pensiones Barrio de San Román, 24040 San Francisco de Campeche, Campeche
Tel: +52(981) 816-62-17
EMail: escolarescampeche@cecip.edu.mx
Website: http://www.cecip.edu.mx

Courses
Psychology (Child Care and Development; Clinical Psychology; Pedagogy; Psychotherapy)

Further Information: Also campus in Merida
Admission Requirements: Licenciatura
Main Language(s) of Instruction: Spanish
Degrees and Diplomas: *Maestría*; *Doctorado*
Publications: Revista de Estudios Clinicos e investigacion psicologica
Last Updated: 30/10/12

CENTRE FOR THE STUDY OF SOCIAL COMMUNICATION

Centro de Estudios de la Comunicación Social
Tepic, 43, Col. Roma Sur, Delegación Cuauhtémoc, 06760 México, D.F.
Tel: +52(5) 55-64-98-43 +52(5) 55-74-33-09
Fax: +52(5) 55-64-79-76
EMail: cecs1910@prodigy.net.mx
Website: http://www.cecs.com.mx

Director General: Luis Alonso Sordo Murguía (1980-)

Programmes
Accountancy (Accountancy); **Administration** (Administration); **Social Communication** (Communication Studies)
History: Founded 1980.
Main Language(s) of Instruction: Spanish
Degrees and Diplomas: *Licenciatura*

CENTRE FOR THE STUDY OF ENDODONTICS OF THE WEST

Centro de Estudios Endodónticos de Occidente
Manuel M. Diéguez 124-11 Sector Hidalgo, 44600 Guadalajara, Jalisco
Tel: +52(33) 3615-9144
Fax: +52(33) 3615-1968

Director: José G. Flores Gutiérrez

Programmes
Dentistry (Dentistry)

History: Founded 1989.

Main Language(s) of Instruction: Spanish
Degrees and Diplomas: *Especialización*
Last Updated: 14/02/13

CENTRE FOR THE STUDY OF ORTHODONTICS OF THE BAJÍO

Centro de Estudios de Ortodoncia del Bajío
Blvd. Lázaro Cárdenas 1477, Prolongación Col. Moderna, 36690 Irapuato, Guanajuato
Tel: +52(141) 5-36-77
EMail: ceob@prodigy.net.mx
Website: http://www.ceob.com.mx

Director: Alejandro Rocha

Programmes
Orthodontics (Dentistry; Orthodontics)
History: Founded 1994.
Main Language(s) of Instruction: Spanish
Degrees and Diplomas: *Especialización*
Last Updated: 30/10/12

CENTRE FOR THE STUDY OF THE AMERICAS

Centro de Estudios de Las Américas, A.C. (CELA)
Calle 21-A No. 357-A x 26 San Pedro Cholul, 97118 Mérida, Yucatán
Tel: +52(999) 943-5629
Website: http://www.cela.edu.mx

Director General: Enrique Santacruz Polanco B.

Programmes
Business Administration (Business Administration); **Graphic Design and Publicity** (Advertising and Publicity; Graphic Design); **Interior Design** (Interior Design); **Psychology** (Psychology); **Website Design** (Computer Science)
History: Founded 1984.
Main Language(s) of Instruction: Spanish
Degrees and Diplomas: *Licenciatura*; *Especialización*
Last Updated: 12/07/12

CENTRE FOR TOURISM STUDIES OF GUADALAJARA

Centro de Estudios de Turismo de Guadalajara
Avenida Hidalgo, 1402 y Ladrón de Guevara, Sector Hidalgo, 44600 Guadalajara, Jalisco
Tel: +52(33) 38-26-17-81 +52(33) 38-25-59-68

Directora: Araceli Celaya Quintana

Programmes
Tourism (Tourism)

Main Language(s) of Instruction: Spanish

Degrees and Diplomas: *Licenciatura*

CENTRE FOR UNIVERSITY STUDIES IN JOURNALISM, RADIO AND TELEVISION

Centro de Estudios Universitarios de Periodismo y Arte en Radio y Televisión (PART)

Antonio Caso, 53, Col. Tabacalera, Delegación Cuauhtémoc, 06030 México, D.F.
Tel: +52(55) 55-91-04-23 +52(55) 55-91-06-38
Fax: +52(55) 55-91-17-02
EMail: part@ri.redint.com
Website: http://www.part.edu.mx.

Director General: Francisco Fortuño

Programmes

Journalism (Journalism); **Radio and Television Broadcasting** (Radio and Television Broadcasting)

Further Information: Campus Zacatecas

History: Founded 1985.

Main Language(s) of Instruction: Spanish

Degrees and Diplomas: *Licenciatura*; *Maestría*
Last Updated: 17/07/12

CENTRE OF ADVANCED STUDIES OF THE NORTHWEST OF VERACRUZ

Centro de Estudios Superiores del Noroeste de Veracruz

Calle Mariano Arista No. 123 Col. Tajín, Poza Rica
Tel: +52(782) 822- 10-45
EMail: contacto@cesunv.edu.mx
Website: http://www.cesunv.edu.mx

Directora: Norma Aide Blanco Ornelas

Programmes

Accountancy (Accountancy); **Business Administration** (Business Administration); **Computer Science** (Computer Science); **Industrial Engineering** (Industrial Engineering); **Law** (Law); **Pedagogy** (Pedagogy); **Petroleum Engineering** (Petroleum and Gas Engineering); **Psychopedagogy** (Pedagogy; Psychology)

Further Information: Also branches in Tantoyuca, Chalma

Admission Requirements: Bachillerato

Main Language(s) of Instruction: Spanish

Degrees and Diplomas: *Licenciatura*; *Maestría*
Last Updated: 16/07/12

CENTRE OF VALUES

Centro de Valores, S.C.

Avenida Normalistas, 564, Col. Colinas de la Normal, 44270 Guadalajara, Jalisco
Tel: +52(33) 38-54-54-63
Fax: +52(33) 38-54-10-03
Website: http://www.centrodevalores.com

Director: Rosalio Barajas Cervantes

Programmes

Personal and Rural Property Studies (Finance; Real Estate)

Degrees and Diplomas: *Especialización*; *Maestría*
Last Updated: 27/10/09

CERVANTINE LYCEUM UNIVERSITY

Universidad Liceo Cervantino

Allende, 199, Centro, 36500 Irapuato, Guanajuato
Tel: +52(461) 616-54-49
EMail: univliceo@infosel.net.com
Website: http://www.ulc.edu.mx

Rectora: Consuelo Camarena Gómez

Programmes

Business Administration (Administration; Industrial and Organizational Psychology; Marketing; Public Administration); **Education** (Preschool Education; Primary Education; Secondary Education); **Law** (Law)

History: Founded 1977.

Main Language(s) of Instruction: Spanish

Accrediting Agencies: FIMPES

Degrees and Diplomas: *Licenciatura*; *Maestría*
Last Updated: 12/10/12

CERVANTINE UNIVERSITY

Universidad Cervantina, A.C.

Padre Mier, 1430, Pte, Entre Bravo y Ángela Peralta, 64080 Monterrey, Nuevo León
Tel: +52(81) 83-45-86-20
Fax: +52(81) 83-45-86-80

Rector: Eduardo Macías Santos

Programmes

Business Administration (Business Administration); **English Studies** (Business Administration; English Studies)

History: Founded 1985.

Main Language(s) of Instruction: Spanish

Degrees and Diplomas: *Licenciatura*
Last Updated: 02/04/08

CÉSAR RITZ INSTITUTE

Instituto César Ritz

Huatabampo, 76, Col. Roma Sur, Delegación Cuauhtémoc, 06760 México, D.F.
Tel: +52(55) 55-64-12-63 +52(55) 55-64-14-67
Fax: +52(55) 55-84-69-45
EMail: cosuth@cosuth.edu.mx
Website: http://www.cosuth.edu.mx

Director General: J. Emigdio Herrera Calderón (1984-)

Programmes

Gastronomy (Cooking and Catering); **Tourism**

History: Founded 1984.

Degrees and Diplomas: *Licenciatura*
Last Updated: 04/04/08

CETYS UNIVERSITY

CETYS Universidad

Apartado postal 3-797, Calzada CETYS s/n, Col. Rivera, 21259 Mexicali, Baja California
Tel: +52(686) 567-37-30 +52(686) 567-37-72
Fax: +52(686) 565-02-41 +52(686) 565-02-41
EMail: infocetys@cetys.mx
Website: http://www.cetys.mx

Rector: Fernando León García (2010-)
Tel: +52(686) 567-37-72, Fax: +52(686) 565-03-00
EMail: fernando.leongarcia@cetys.mx

Areas

Engineering (Computer Engineering; Electronic Engineering; Engineering; Industrial Engineering; Mechanical Engineering; Software Engineering)

Programmes

Accountancy (Accountancy); **Administration** (Administration; Business Administration; Marketing); **Graphic Design** (Graphic Design); **International Business** (International Business); **Law** (Law); **Psychology** (Clinical Psychology; Educational Psychology; Psychology)

Further Information: Campuses also in Tijuana and Ensenada.

History: Founded 1961, a private institution and authorized by the Secretary for Education to award degrees including doctorates.

Governing Bodies: Board of Trustees

Academic Year: August to June (August-December; January-June)

Admission Requirements: Secondary school certificate or equivalent and minimum SAT score of 1160

Main Language(s) of Instruction: Spanish

International Co-operation: Exchanges with some 40 universities in North America, South America and Europe

Degrees and Diplomas: *Licenciatura*: 8 sem; *Especialización*; *Maestría*; *Doctorado*

Special Facilities: Access to electronic/virtual libraries. Videoconferencing

Libraries: Mexicali, c. 38,000 vols; Tijuana, c. 20,000 vols; Ensenada, c. 8,000 vols

Last Updated: 27/07/12

CEUNICO UNIVERSITY

Universidad CEUNICO

Av. Corregidora #900 esq. Madero. Col. Centro, 96400 Coatzacoalcos, Veracruz

Tel: +52(921) 212-68-03

Fax: +52(921) 212-50-04

Website: http://www.ceunico.edu.mx

Rectora: Alba Elena Arenas Cruz

Areas

Economics and Administration (Accountancy; Business Administration; International Business); **Exact Sciences** (Business Computing; Computer Engineering; Electronic Engineering; Graphic Design); **Social Sciences** (Communication Studies; Educational Sciences; Law)

Further Information: Campuses in Minatitlán and Acayucan

History: Founded 1990 as Instituto Galileo. Acquired present title and status 2008.

Admission Requirements: Bachillerato

Main Language(s) of Instruction: Spanish

Degrees and Diplomas: *Licenciatura*; *Maestría*

Last Updated: 26/03/13

CHAMPAGNAT UNIVERSITY

Universidad Champagnat

Venustiano Carranza, 1003, Col. Moderna, 78230 San Luis Potosí, San Luis Potosí

Tel: +52(444) 413-44-06

Fax: +52(444) 413-44-06

Rector: Ignacio Algara Cossio EMail: ialgara@champagnat.edu.mx

Areas

Administration (Accountancy; Administration; Business Administration; Finance; International Business); **Education** (Education); **Engineering and Architecture** (Archaeology; Electronic Engineering; Engineering; Industrial Design; Industrial Engineering); **Social Studies** (Social Studies; Social Work)

Degrees and Diplomas: *Licenciatura*; *Maestria*

Last Updated: 29/03/13

CHAPULTEPEC UNIVERSITY

Universidad Chapultepec

Ave Eugenia, 1010, Col. Del Valle, Delegación Benito Juárez, 03100 México, D.F.

Tel: +52(55) 11-67-57-73

EMail: fpaez@univchapultepec.edu.mx

Website: http://www.univchapultepec.edu.mx

Rector: Francisco Lejarza Gallegos (1992-)
EMail: flejarza@univchapultepec.edu.mx

Programmes

Business Administration (Accountancy; Administration; Business and Commerce; Business Computing; Finance; Human Resources; Marketing); **Graphic Design** (Graphic Design); **Information Technology** (Engineering; Information Technology; Systems Analysis); **Law** (Law); **Psychology** (Psychology)

History: Founded 1977.

Academic Year: January to December (January-April; May-August; September-December)

Admission Requirements: Secondary school certificate (bachillerato)

Main Language(s) of Instruction: Spanish

Degrees and Diplomas: *Licenciatura*: 3 yrs; *Especialización*; *Maestría*: a further 2 1/2 yrs; *Doctorado*

Libraries: Yes

Last Updated: 11/09/12

CHAYITO GARZÓN SCHOOL OF FINE ARTS

Escuela superior de Las Bellas Artes Chayito Garzón

Genáro Estráda 204, 82000 Mazatlán, Mazatlán

Tel: +52(669) 981-01-75

EMail: esba_academico@hotmail.com

Website: http://www.esbachayitogarzon.edu.mx/

Directora: María del Rosario Garzón Zúñiga

Programmes

Architecture (Architecture); **Art Education** (Dance; Music; Painting and Drawing; Theatre); **Child Care** (Child Care and Development); **Human Nutrition** (Dietetics; Food Science; Food Technology; Nutrition); **Psychopedagogy** (Pedagogy; Psychology); **Public Relations and Marketing** (Advertising and Publicity; Communication Studies; Marketing; Mass Communication; Photography; Public Relations)

History: Founded 1984.

Main Language(s) of Instruction: Spanish

Degrees and Diplomas: *Licenciatura*; *Maestría*; *Doctorado*

Libraries: Yes

Last Updated: 28/08/12

CHIHUAHUA CENTRE FOR POSTGRADUATE STUDIES

Centro Chihuahuense de Estudios de Posgrado

División del Norte 3705, Col. Alta Vista, 31330 Chihuahua, Chihuahua

Tel: +52(14) 371-74 +52(14) 207-84

Fax: +52(14) 14-26-76

EMail: direccion@cchep.edu.mx

Website: http://www.cchep.edu.mx/

Director: Mario Jesús Franco García (1999-)

Programmes

Educational Development (Educational Sciences)

History: Founded 1990.

Admission Requirements: Licenciatura en educación

Main Language(s) of Instruction: Spanish

Degrees and Diplomas: *Maestría*

Publications: Rumbo Educativo

Last Updated: 10/07/12

CHRISTOPHER COLUMBUS UNIVERSITY

Universidad Cristóbal Colón (UCC)

Apartado postal 167, Km. 1.5 Carretera Boticaria-Mocambo, Col. Militar Cristóbal Colón, 91930 Veracruz, Veracruz

Tel: +52(229) 923-29-50

EMail: informes@ucc.mx

Website: http://www.ver.ucc.mx

Rector: Juan Jaime Escobar Valencia

Areas

Economics and Administration (Accountancy; Administration; Business Administration; Economics; International Business; Management; Marketing); **Exact Sciences** (Architecture; Industrial Engineering; Telecommunications Engineering); **Health Sciences** (Food Science; Nutrition; Surgery); **Humanities** (Art Education; Communication Studies; Education; Educational Sciences; English; Ethics; Graphic Design; Human Rights; Information Sciences; Journalism; Law; Mass Communication; Modern Languages; Psychology; Public Relations; Radio and Television Broadcasting; Translation and Interpretation)

History: Founded 1969, inspired by San José de Calansanz's philosophy and run by Escolapios religious Order. The first Catholic Institution created in the southern part of Mexico.

Governing Bodies: Consejo de Gobierno; Consejo Académico

Academic Year: February to January

Admission Requirements: Secondary school certificate (bachillerato) and entrance examination

Main Language(s) of Instruction: Spanish

Accrediting Agencies: Federación de Instituciones Mexicanas Particulares de Educación Superior (FIMPES); Asociación Nacional de Universidades e Instituciones de Educación Superior (ANUIES); Organización Universitaria Interamericana (OUI); Asociación Mexicana de Instituciones de Educación Superior de Inspiración Cristiana

Degrees and Diplomas: *Licenciatura*: 4 yrs; *Especialización*: Higher Education, 1 yr; *Maestría*: Administration; Communication; Education; Finance; International Business; Law; Marketing; Networks and Communication; Taxation, a further 2 yrs; *Doctorado*

Student Services: Academic counselling, Canteen, Employment services, Health services, Language programs, Social counselling, Sports facilities

Student Residential Facilities: For 2,500 students

Special Facilities: Art Gallery 'Xanatl'. Radio and Television Set Laboratories. Food and Beverage Laboratory. Photography Laboratory. Computer Laboratory. Computer Centre. Languages Centre

Libraries: Biblioteca 'Segismundo Balagué'

Publications: Revista de la Universidad Cristóbal Colón *(biannually)*

Last Updated: 13/09/12

CHRISTOPHER COLUMBUS UNIVERSITY CENTRE OF CUERNAVACA

Centro Universitario Cristóbal Colón de Cuernavaca

Avenida Morelos, 345, Calvario E., Col. Centro, 62000 Cuernavaca, Morelos

Tel: +52(777) 718-57-07 +52(777) 718-14-56

Fax: +52(777) 712-43-73

Director: Ovidio Noval Nicolau (1992-)

Programmes

Communication Studies (Communication Studies); **Computer Networks** (Computer Networks); **Journalism** (Journalism); **Labour and Industrial Relations** (Labour and Industrial Relations)

History: Founded 1992.

Main Language(s) of Instruction: Spanish

Degrees and Diplomas: *Licenciatura*

Last Updated: 11/03/08

CIRCLE OF PSYCHOLOGY STUDIES

Círculo de Estudios de Psicología Profunda, A.C.

Avenida Guanajuato 139, Col. Jardines del Moral, 37160 León, Guanajuato

Tel: +52(477) 17-72-08

Fax: +52(477) 17-72-08

EMail: ceppac@hotmail.com

Directora: Ana María Chávez Hernández

Programmes

Psychology (Psychology)

Main Language(s) of Instruction: Spanish

Degrees and Diplomas: *Maestría*

COLLEGE OF ADVANCED STUDIES IN ADMINISTRATION

Colegio de Estudios en Administración Superior

Orizaba 93-Casa C, Col. Roma Sur, Cuauhtémoc, 06700 México, D.F.

Tel: +52(55) 55-11-07-10

Fax: +52(55) 55-11-92-69

Rector: Víctor Manuel del Castillo Pérez Tejada

Programmes

Administration (Administration)

Degrees and Diplomas: *Maestría*

Last Updated: 28/02/08

COLLEGE OF ADVANCED STUDIES IN BUSINESS ADMINISTRATION

Colegio en Alta Dirección Empresarial

Boulevard Adolfo López Mateos 45, Colonia Ignacio López Rayón, 53100 Atizapán de Zaragoza, Estado de México

Tel: +52(55) 5236-4580

EMail: info@cade.edu.mx

Website: http://www.cade.edu.mx

Director General: Juan Bosco Villaseñor Córdova

EMail: direcciongeneral@cade.edu.mx

Programmes

Accountancy (Accountancy); **Business Administration** (Business Administration); **International Business** (International Business); **Law** (Law)

History: Founded 1989.

Main Language(s) of Instruction: Spanish

Degrees and Diplomas: *Licenciatura*; *Maestría*

Last Updated: 27/07/12

COLLEGE OF ADVANCED STUDIES IN SOCIAL SCIENCES OF NUEVO LEÓN A.C.

Colegio Superior de Ciencias Sociales de Nuevo León, A.C.

Vía Triunfo No. 407, Fuentes del Valle, San Pedro, Garza Garcia, Nuevo León

Programmes

Social Sciences (Social Sciences)

Degrees and Diplomas: *Maestría*

Last Updated: 28/02/08

COLLEGE OF ADVANCED STUDIES OF THE CONTINENT

Colegio de Estudios Superiores del Continente

Avenida Azcapotzalco, 214, Col. Clavería, Delegación Azcapotzalco, 02480 México, D.F.

Tel: +52(55) 53-99-00-42 +52(55) 55-27-07-36

Directora General: Graciela Pérez Uribe

Degrees and Diplomas: *Licenciatura*

Last Updated: 04/04/08

COLLEGE OF BUSINESS MANAGEMENT

Colegio de Alta Dirección de Empresas, A.C.

Río Jamapa 5721 Col. Jardines de San Manuel, 72160 Puebla, Puebla

Tel: +52(222) 298-20-30

Fax: +52(222) 298-20-40

EMail: academi@cadem.edu.mx

Website: http://www.cadem.edu.mx

Director: Luis Fernando Jimenez y Flores

Programmes

Business Administration (Accountancy; Business Administration; Commercial Law; Economics; Finance)

Main Language(s) of Instruction: Spanish

Degrees and Diplomas: *Licenciatura*. Also Diplomados

Last Updated: 27/07/12

COLLEGE OF CONSULTANTS IN PUBLIC IMAGE

Colegio de Consultores en Imagen Pública

Colima 56, Col. Roma, 06700 México, D.F.

Tel: +52(55) 50-80-88-00, Ext. 2

EMail: info@imagenpublica.com.mx

Website: http://www.imagenpublica.com.mx

Rector: Victor Gordoa

Vicepresidente y Director de Desarrollo: Álvaro Gordoa Fernández

Programmes

Public Image (Communication Studies; Design; Graphic Design; Psychology; Sociology)

Main Language(s) of Instruction: Spanish

Degrees and Diplomas: *Licenciatura*; *Especialización*; *Maestría*
Last Updated: 27/07/12

COLLEGE OF GASTRONOMY

Colegio Superior de Gastronomía

Sonora No. 189, Hipódromo Condesa, Delegación Cuauhtémoc, 6170 México, D.F.
Tel: +52(55) 55-84-38-00
Website: http://www.csgastronomia.edu.mx

Rectora: Esmeralda Chalita Kaim
EMail: echalita@csgastronomia.edu.mx

Programmes

Gastronomy (Cooking and Catering)

Further Information: Also Campus Lomas Verdes

History: Founded 1992.

Main Language(s) of Instruction: Spanish

Degrees and Diplomas: *Licenciatura*; *Especialización*
Last Updated: 23/08/12

COLLEGE OF HIGHER EDUCATION OF TUXTEPEC

Colegio de Educación Superior de Tuxtepec

Calle Jazmines, 58, Col. Las Flores, San Juan Bautista Tuxtepec, 68354 Tuxtepec, Oaxaca
Tel: +52(287) 875-26-95
EMail: cest-tuxtepec@hotmail.com
Website: http://cestuxtepec.edu.mx

Directora: María del Refugio Román Salgado (1999-)

Programmes

Accountancy (Accountancy); **Business Computing** (Business Computing); **Law** (Law); **Pedagogy** (Pedagogy); **Physical Education** (Physical Education); **Psychology** (Psychology); **Sports** (Sports)

History: Founded 1992.

Main Language(s) of Instruction: Spanish

Degrees and Diplomas: *Licenciatura*; *Maestría*
Last Updated: 27/07/12

COLLEGE OF NEURO-LINGUISTICS AND PSYCHO-PEDAGOGY

Colegio Superior de Neurolingüística y Psicopedagogía

Leonardo de Vinci, 56-58, Col. Mixcoac, Delegación Benito Juárez, 03910 México, D.F.
Tel: +52(55) 55-98-06-94
Fax: +52(55) 55-63-39-91
EMail: info@colsup.edu.mx
Website: http://www.colsup.com.mx

Directora General: Rosa María García Arana (1979-)

Programmes

Educational Psychology (Educational Psychology); **Neurolinguistics** (Linguistics; Neurosciences)

History: Founded 1979.

Main Language(s) of Instruction: Spanish

Degrees and Diplomas: *Licenciatura*; *Especialización*; *Maestría*
Last Updated: 23/08/12

COLLEGE OF POSTGRADUATE STUDIES OF THE CITY OF MEXICO

Colegio de Estudios de Posgrado de la Ciudad de México (CEPCM)

Andador Sur No. 4 Local 13, Col. Centro Urbano, 54700 Cuautitlán Izcalli, Estado de México
Tel: +52(555) 868-38-89
Fax: +52(555) 868-37-78
EMail: colposgrado@colposgrado.edu.mx
Website: http://www.colposgrado.edu.mx

Director General: Valentin Sosa Lora
EMail: director_general@colposgrado.edu.mx

Director, Administration and Finance: Valentín Sosa Hernández
EMail: valentin_sosa@colposgrado.edu.mx

International Relations: Filiberto Hernández Perea, Operative Director, Public Relations EMail: d_operativa@colposgrado.edu.mx

Campuses

Acolman (Computer Science); **Atlacomulco** *Director General*: Valentin Sosa Lora; **Cuautitlán Izcalli** (Business Administration; Computer Science; Education; Educational Administration; Fiscal Law; Higher Education; International Business; Public Administration; Taxation); **Cuernavaca** (Education; Educational Administration; Fiscal Law; Higher Education; Taxation); **Ixtlahuaca** (Business Administration; Education; Educational Administration; Fiscal Law; Higher Education; International Business; Law; Public Administration; Taxation) *Director General*: Valentin Sosa Lora

Colleges

Postgraduate Studies (Administration; Education; Law; Social Sciences); **Temascalingo** (Accountancy; Advertising and Publicity; Business Administration; Computer Engineering; Educational Administration; Educational Sciences; Finance; Fiscal Law; International Business; Law; Marketing; Public Administration)

History: Founded 1999.

Main Language(s) of Instruction: English (Master); French and English (Doctorado)

International Co-operation: None

Degrees and Diplomas: *Maestría*: 2 yrs; *Doctorado*

Student Services: Academic counselling, Employment services, Health services

Student Residential Facilities: None

Special Facilities: None

Libraries: Yes

Publications: Revista Conocimiento y Espíritu, Articles on Education issues *(biennially)*; Revista la Nueva Gestión Organizacional, International Review (implying Universidad Autónoma del Estado de Hidalgo, Universidad Autónoma del Estado de Tlaxcala, Universidad de Camagüey Cuba y el Colegio de Estudios de Posgrado de la Ciudad de México) *(biennially)*
Last Updated: 28/02/08

COLLEGE OF SPECIALIZATIONS OF THE WEST

Colegio de Especialidades de Occidente

Avenida Vallarta 6503 Local E40 Y 41, Ciudad Granja, 45010 Zapopan, Jalisco
Tel: +52(33) 31-10-21-96
Fax: +52(33) 31-10-21-97
EMail: ceomexico@ceomexico.com

Directora: Carlota Aznar Rivadeneyra

Programmes

Taxation (Taxation)

History: Founded 2002.

Main Language(s) of Instruction: Spanish

Degrees and Diplomas: *Especialización*; *Maestría*
Last Updated: 28/10/09

COLUMBIA UNIVERSITY CENTRE

Centro Universitario Columbia

Xochicalco, 195, Col. Narvarte, Delegación Benito Juárez, 03020 México, D.F.

Tel: +52(55) 5519-6287 +52(55) 55-19-52-79

EMail: mgarate@unicolumbia.com.mx; midaz3000@unicolumbia.com.mx

Website: http://centrouniversitariocolumbia.com

Director: Raymundo Ampudia Malacara (1999-)

Programmes

Accountancy (Accountancy); **Administration** (Administration); **Computer Science** (Computer Science); **Law**; **Marketing** (Marketing)

History: Founded 1953 as Columbia College Panamericano de México.

Main Language(s) of Instruction: Spanish

Degrees and Diplomas: *Licenciatura*; *Maestría*

Last Updated: 23/07/12

COLUMBIA UNIVERSITY STUDIES CENTRE

Centro de Estudios Universitarios Columbia

Pedro Moreno, 633, 1er. Piso, Centro, 44100 Guadalajara, Jalisco

Tel: +52(33) 36-13-69-69

Fax: +52(33) 36-14-94-14

EMail: columbi@jal1.telmex.net

Director: Ignacio Méndez Garavito

Programmes

Accountancy

Main Language(s) of Instruction: Spanish

Degrees and Diplomas: *Licenciatura*

Last Updated: 07/03/08

COMMERCIAL BANKING INSTITUTE

Instituto Comercial Bancario, A.C.

Calle 62, 373 x 45, Col. Centro, 97000 Mérida, Yucatán

Tel: +52(999) 924-77-96

Fax: +52(999) 924-72-56

EMail: info@institutobancario.edu.mx

Website: http://www.institutobancario.edu.mx

Director: Arsenio Rosado Lope (1987-)

Programmes

Accountancy (Accountancy); **Business Administration** (Business Administration); **Computer Science** (Computer Science); **International Business** (International Business); **Law** (Law); **Marketing** (Marketing); **Psychology** (Psychology)

History: Founded 1952.

Main Language(s) of Instruction: Spanish

Degrees and Diplomas: *Licenciatura*

Last Updated: 27/02/13

COMPREHENSIVE ORTHODONTIC INSTITUTE IN MÉXICO, A.C.

Comprehensive Orthodontic Institute en México, A.C.

Calle 17 Sur N° 1308, 2° Piso, Col. Santiago, 72000 Puebla, Puebla

Tel: +52(2) 24-14-48

Director: Víctor Hugo Toledo Minutti

Programmes

Orthodontics (Orthodontics)

Main Language(s) of Instruction: Spanish

Degrees and Diplomas: *Especialización*

Last Updated: 24/08/12

COMPUTRADE

Lerdo de Tejada, 2100, Col. Americana, 44160 Guadalajara, Jalisco

Tel: +52(33) 36-16-15-40

EMail: informes@computrade.com.mx

Director General: Daniel Castellanos Reynoso

Programmes

Computer Engineering (Computer Engineering); **Computer Science** (Computer Science)

History: Founded 1994.

Main Language(s) of Instruction: Spanish

Degrees and Diplomas: *Licenciatura*

Last Updated: 24/08/12

CONTEMPORARY UNIVERSITY

Universidad Contemporánea

Ignacio Pérez, 54, Sur, Col. Centro, 76000 Querétaro, Querétaro

Tel: +52(442) 196-14-00

EMail: admisiones@contemporanea.edu.mx

Website: http://www.contemporanea.edu.mx

Rector: Darío Malpica B

Programmes

Accountancy and Finance (Accountancy; Finance); **Administration** (Administration); **Advertising and Communication** (Advertising and Publicity; Communication Studies); **Gastronomy** (Cooking and Catering); **Graphic Design and Multimedia** (Graphic Design; Multimedia); **International Business** (International Business); **Law** (Law); **Marketing** (Marketing); **Psychology** (Psychology)

History: Founded 1993 as CUDEC. Acquired present status 2000.

Admission Requirements: Bachillerato

Fees: (Pesos): 55,200 per annum

Main Language(s) of Instruction: Spanish. Some courses in English

International Co-operation: With universities in Canada, USA, France, Germany, Australia

Accrediting Agencies: Federación de Instituciones Mexicanas Particulares de Educación Superior (FIMPES)

Degrees and Diplomas: *Licenciatura*: 3 yrs; *Especialización*: 1 yr; *Maestría*

Student Services: Academic counselling, Employment services, Foreign student adviser, Foreign Studies Centre, Language programs, Sports facilities

Libraries: Biblioteca Viktor Frankl

Last Updated: 11/09/12

CONTINENTAL VALLEY UNIVERSITY

Universidad Valle Continental

Calle México 703 Sur, Col. Obispado, 64060 Monterrey, Nuevo León

Tel: +52(81) 8123-13-50

EMail: info@vallecontinental.com

Website: http://www.vallecontinental.com

Director general: Carlos Quiroga

Areas

Commerce (Accountancy; Business and Commerce; International Business; Marketing); **Education** (Educational Administration; Educational and Student Counselling; Pedagogy); **Imagery** (Communication Studies; Fashion Design; Graphic Arts; Graphic Design); **Law** (Law); **Psychology** (Psychology)

Further Information: Also Las Torres and Los Leones units

History: Founded 1994. Formerly known as Instituto Universitario Valle Continental.

Main Language(s) of Instruction: Spanish

Degrees and Diplomas: *Licenciatura*; *Maestría*

Last Updated: 29/10/12

COPHAC INSTITUTE OF HIGHER EDUCATION

Cophac Institución de Enseñanza Superior
Vía Lactea, 45, Prado Churubusco, Delegación Coyoacán, 4230 México, D.F.
Tel: +52(55) 56-97-82-58
Fax: +52(55) 56-46-44-53
EMail: cophac@cophac.com

Programmes

Family Studies (Family Studies; Psychology)

Degrees and Diplomas: *Especialización*; *Maestría*
Last Updated: 20/02/13

COYOACÁN ANGLO-MEXICAN COLLEGE, DIVISION OF ADVANCED STUDIES

Colegio Anglo Mexicano de Coyoacán, División de Estudios Superiores
H. Escuela Naval Militar, 42, Col. San Francisco, Culhuacán, Delegación Coyoacán, 04430 México, D.F.
Tel: +52(55) 56-07-07-41
Fax: +52(55) 56-07-73-16

Directora General: Elisa Carolina Armendariz del Valle
Degrees and Diplomas: *Licenciatura*
Last Updated: 04/04/08

CRISOL CENTRE FOR POSTGRADUATE STUDIES IN FAMILY THERAPY

Centro de Posgrado en Terapía Familiar - CRISOL
Paseo del Conquistador No. 611, Col. Lomas de Cortés, Cuernavaca, Morelos
Tel: +52(777) 311-71-95
EMail: contacto@institutocrisol.org
Website: http://www.institutocrisol.org

Director: Javier Vicencio EMail: vicenciojavier@yahoo.com

Programmes

Family Therapy (Family Studies; Social Psychology); **Rehabilitation and Therapy** (Rehabilitation and Therapy)

Further Information: Branch in México, D. F.
History: Founded 1991.
Main Language(s) of Instruction: Spanish
Degrees and Diplomas: *Maestría*. Also Diplomado
Last Updated: 29/02/08

CUAUHNÁHUAC UNIVERSITY

Universidad Cuauhnáhuac
Jacarandas 333, Fraccionamiento Lomas de Cuernavaca, Temixco, Morelos
Tel: +52(777) 312-51-35 +52(777) 312-61-45
EMail: unic@unic.edu.mx
Website: http://www.unic.edu.mx

Rector: Alfonso Rodriguez Najera (1995-)

Programmes

Accountancy and Finance (Accountancy; Finance); **Communication Studies** (Advertising and Publicity; Communication Studies; Journalism; Public Relations); **Education** (Education; Pedagogy; Special Education); **Human Resources** (Human Resources); **Industrial Engineering** (Industrial Engineering); **International Business** (Accountancy; Commercial Law; Finance; Fiscal Law; International Business); **Law** (Administrative Law; Civil Law; Constitutional Law; Fiscal Law; Labour Law); **Marketing and Publicity** (Advertising and Publicity; Marketing; Staff Development)

History: Founded 1987.
Admission Requirements: Certificado de Preparatoria and entrance examination
Main Language(s) of Instruction: Spanish
Degrees and Diplomas: *Licenciatura*
Last Updated: 13/09/12

CUAUHTÉMOC UNIVERSITY

Universidad Cuauhtémoc
Oriental, 38, Col. La Paz, 72160 Puebla, Puebla
Tel: +52(222) 248-20-44
EMail: rector@cuauhtemoc.edu.mx
Website: http://www.cuauhtemoc.edu.mx

Rector: Francisco Martínez Briones Tel: +52(222) 248-22-18

Programmes

Accountancy (Accountancy); **Architecture** (Architecture; Design; Structural Architecture); **Business Administration** (Accountancy; Administration; Business and Commerce; Economics; Statistics); **Communication Sciences** (Communication Studies; Photography; Radio and Television Broadcasting); **Dentistry** (Dental Hygiene; Dentistry); **Graphic Design** (Graphic Design); **International Business** (International Business); **Law** (Administrative Law; Civil Law; Commercial Law; Constitutional Law; Fiscal Law; Labour Law; Law); **Tourism** (Tourism)

Further Information: Branches in Aguascalientes, Guadalajara, Querétaro and San Luis Potosí
History: Founded 1977.
Academic Year: August to July (August-January; February-July)
Admission Requirements: Secondary school certificate (bachillerato) or recognized foreign equivalent
Main Language(s) of Instruction: Spanish
Degrees and Diplomas: *Licenciatura*; *Especialización*; *Maestría*
Special Facilities: Radio Stations
Libraries: Yes
Publications: Themis *(monthly)*
Last Updated: 13/09/12

CUAUTLA SCHOOL OF ADVANCED STUDIES IN PHYSICAL EDUCATION

Escuela Superior de Educación Física de Cuautla
Calle del fresnal S/N col. Amp Francisco I. Madero, 06274 Cuautla, Morelos
Tel: +52(735) 308-90-21
EMail: contacto@esefcuautla.mx
Website: http://esefcuautla.mx

Director: Jesús Alberto Martínez Barrón

Programmes

Physical Education (Physical Education; Sports)

History: Founded 2005.
Degrees and Diplomas: *Licenciatura*; *Maestría*
Last Updated: 27/02/13

CULTURAL INSTITUTE OF HUMAN RIGHTS

Instituto Cultural Derechos Humanos
Emilio N. Acosta, 62, Col. Ampliación Santa Martha, Acatitla, Delegación Iztapalapa, 09510 México, D.F.
Tel: +52(55) 57-44-37-70 +52(55) 57-44-20-68
EMail: informes@derhum.edu.mx
Website: http://www.icdh.edu.mx

Director: Bautista Bautista Evangelina

Programmes

Education (Educational Sciences; Preschool Education; Primary Education); **Law** (Law)

History: Founded 1966. Acquired present status 1989.
Main Language(s) of Instruction: Spanish
Degrees and Diplomas: *Licenciatura*
Libraries: Yes
Last Updated: 27/02/13

DESAFÍO INSTITUTE

Instituto Desafío, A.C.

Calle cerezos #705 Col. Jardines de Celaya Tercera Sección, 38080 Celaya, Guanajuato

Tel: +52(461) 159-00-19

EMail: desafio97@yahoo.com.mx

Website: http://www.institutodesafio.com

Director: Luis G. Velazco Lafarga EMail: luisvel@pormexico.com

Programmes

Personal Development (Development Studies)

Further Information: Also branch in Leon

History: Founded 1997.

Main Language(s) of Instruction: Spanish

Degrees and Diplomas: *Maestría*

Last Updated: 05/03/13

DIDASKALOS UNIVERSITY CENTRE

Centro Universitario Didaskalos

Vicente Guerrero, 277, 52140 Metepec, Estado de México

Tel: +52(722) 32-31-41

Fax: +52(722) 31-41-44

EMail: didaskalos@prodigy.net

Website: http://www.cudidaskalos.com.mx

Director: Naim Libien Tella

Programmes

Administration and Law (Accountancy; Administration; Law)

History: Founded 1994.

Main Language(s) of Instruction: Spanish

Degrees and Diplomas: *Licenciatura*

Last Updated: 24/07/12

DIDAXIS INSTITUTE OF HIGHER STUDIES

Instituto Didaxis de Estudios Superiores

Av. Ocampo 225 Pte., Zona Centro, 27000 Torreón, Coahuila

Tel: +52(871) 712-48-54

Fax: +52(871) 712-48-55

EMail: didaxis@megared.net.mx

Website: http://www.institutodidaxis.com

Director: Carlos Zarzar Charur (1989-)
EMail: czcharur@hotmail.com

Programmes

Education (Education)

History: Founded 1989. Formerly known as Instituto Didaxis de Formación y Capacitación S.C.

Main Language(s) of Instruction: Spanish

Degrees and Diplomas: *Especialización*; *Maestría*; *Doctorado*

Last Updated: 05/03/13

DIVISION OF ADVANCED STUDIES OF THE 18TH MARCH INSTITUTE

División de Estudios Superiores del Instituto 18 de Marzo

Antigua Casa Redonda del FFCC s/n, Col. Felipe Carrillo Puerto, 35010 Gómez Palacio, Durango

Tel: +52(871) 15-19-49

Fax: +52(871) 15-19-49

EMail: divest98@prodigy.net.mx

Website: http://www.instituto18demarzo.edu.mx

Programmes

Accountancy (Accountancy); **Industrial Administration** (Administration; Industrial Management); **Law** (Law)

History: Founded 1997.

Main Language(s) of Instruction: Spanish

Degrees and Diplomas: *Licenciatura*; *Maestría*

Last Updated: 24/08/12

DON VASCO UNIVERSITY

Universidad Don Vasco, A.C.

Km. 1100 Entronque Carretera a Pátzcuaro, Col. Residencial Don Vasco, 60110 Uruapán, Michoacán

Tel: +52(452) 524-25-26

EMail: rectoria@udv.edu.mx

Website: http://www.udv.edu.mx

Rector: Rafael Anaya González

Programmes

Accountancy (Accountancy); **Architecture** (Architecture); **Pedagogy** (Education; Pedagogy); **Psychology** (Psychology)

Schools

Administration (Administration; Business Administration; Finance; Marketing); **Civil Engineering** (Civil Engineering); **Design** (Art History; Design; Graphic Design; Painting and Drawing; Photography); **Law** (Law); **Social Work** (Social Work)

History: Founded 1972.

Academic Year: March to February (March-August; September-February)

Admission Requirements: Secondary school certificate (bachillerato) and entrance examination

Main Language(s) of Instruction: Spanish

Degrees and Diplomas: *Licenciatura*. Also Diplomados

Libraries: Yes

Last Updated: 02/10/12

DORADOS UNIVERSITY

Universidad Dorados

Km. 2.5 Carretera Cocoyoc-Oaxtepec, Yautepec, Oaxtepec, Morelos

Tel: +52(735) 356-48-19 +52(735) 356-50-55

Fax: +52(735) 356-02-12

EMail: contacto@universidaddorados.edu.mx

Website: http://www.universidaddorados.edu.mx

Rector: Pedro Pacheco Cuevas

Programmes

Accountancy and Finance (Accountancy; Finance); **Business Administration and Marketing** (Business Administration; Marketing); **Communication** (Communication Studies); **Computer Engineering** (Computer Engineering); **Educational Sciences** (Educational Sciences); **Graphic Design** (Graphic Design); **Hotel Management and Gastronomy** (Cooking and Catering; Hotel Management); **Law** (Law); **Tourism** (Tourism)

Main Language(s) of Instruction: Spanish

Degrees and Diplomas: *Licenciatura*

Last Updated: 12/02/08

DR. ALFONSO TOHEN ZAMUDIO SCHOOL OF PHYSIOTHERAPY

Escuela de Terapia Física Dr. Alfonso Tohen Zamudio

Avenida Insurgentes, 480, 77000 Chetumal, Quintana Roo

Tel: +52(983) 832-04-08

Fax: +52(983) 832-04-08

Director: Roberto Gutiérrez Betancourt

Programmes

Physiotherapy (Physical Therapy)

Main Language(s) of Instruction: Spanish

Degrees and Diplomas: *Licenciatura*

Last Updated: 19/03/08

DR. PORFIRIO PARRA HIGHER TEACHER TRAINING SCHOOL

Escuela Normal Superior Dr. Porfirio Parra

Calle 24a Esq. con 10 de Mayo, 1803 y 1805, Col. De Santa Rita, 31020 Chihuahua, Chihuahua

Tel: +52(614) 10-10-37

Director: Jesús M. Ramírez Lara

Programmes
Teacher Training (Teacher Training)

Degrees and Diplomas: *Licenciatura*
Last Updated: 04/04/08

DR. YURI KUTTLER INSTITUTE OF ADVANCED STUDIES IN ODONTOLOGY

Instituto de Estudios Avanzados en Odontología Dr. Yuri Kuttler
Magdalena 37-303 y 304, Col. Del Valle, Benito Juárez, 03100 México, D.F.
Tel: +52(55) 55-23-93-92
Fax: +52(55) 55-23-98-55
EMail: institutokuttler@gmail.com
Website: http://www.institutokuttler.edu.mx

Director: David Samuel Gutverg Rosenblum

Programmes
Dentistry (Dentistry; Surgery)

Main Language(s) of Instruction: Spanish

Degrees and Diplomas: *Maestría*
Last Updated: 01/03/13

DUXX GRADUATE SCHOOL OF BUSINESS LEADERSHIP

Duxx Escuela de Graduados en Liderazgo Empresarial
Rio Sena No 500 Pte Col. Del Valle, 62220 San Pedro Garza García, Nuevo León
Tel: +52(81) 8173-5530
EMail: zvallado@duxx.mx
Website: http://www.duxx.mx

Rector: Mateo Mazal Beja

Programmes
Business and Commerce (Business and Commerce)

History: Founded 1995.

Main Language(s) of Instruction: Spanish

Degrees and Diplomas: *Maestría*

Libraries: Yes
Last Updated: 20/02/13

E UNIVERSITY OF PROFESSIONAL STUDIES OF ATLIXCO

Universidad E de Estudios Profesionales de Atlixco
4 Sur, 103, 72340 Atlixco, Puebla
Tel: +52(244) 446 -21-27
EMail: ueep@ueep.edu.mx
Website: http://www.ueep.edu.mx

Rector: Fernando Machorro Martínez

Programmes
Accountancy (Accountancy); **Business Administration** (Business Administration); **Chemical Engineering** (Chemical Engineering); **Computer Science** (Computer Science); **Graphic Design** (Graphic Design); **Industrial Engineering** (Industrial Engineering); **Law and Social Sciences** (Law; Social Sciences)

History: Founded 1996.

Main Language(s) of Instruction: Spanish

Degrees and Diplomas: *Licenciatura*
Last Updated: 21/02/13

EASTERN UNIVERSITY CENTRE OF MEXICO

Centro Universitario Oriente de México
José Rojo Gómez, 375, Col. Agrícola Oriental, Delegación Iztacalco, 08500 México, D.F.
Tel: +52(55) 57-01-26-50
Fax: +52(55) 57-01-22-84
Website: http://www.cuom.com.mx

Directora: Guadalupe Constantino Durzo (2002-)

Programmes
Accountancy (Accountancy); **Administration** (Administration); **Law** (Law); **Marketing** (Marketing); **Pedagogy** (Pedagogy)

History: Founded 2002.

Main Language(s) of Instruction: Spanish

Degrees and Diplomas: *Licenciatura*
Last Updated: 19/03/08

EDGAR MORÍN REAL WORLD MULTIVERSITY

Multiversidad Mundo Real Edgar Morín
Israel Gonzalez 292, Col. Mision del Real, 83145 Hermosillo, Sonora
Tel: +52(662) 147-06-00
Fax: +52(662) 210-51-50
EMail: contactomultiversidad@multiversidadreal.org
Website: http://www.multiversidadreal.org

Rector: Rubén Reynaga Valdez
EMail: rubenreynaga@multiversidad.org

Programmes
Art Appreciation (Art Education); **Education** (Education; Educational Sciences; Educational Technology); **Global Bioethics** (Biology; Ethics); **Government and Public Policy** (Cultural Studies; Economics; Information Technology; Logic); **Organizational Information** (Anthropology; Art History; Communication Studies; Cultural Studies; Information Technology; Logic)

History: Founded 2006.

Main Language(s) of Instruction: Spanish

Degrees and Diplomas: *Especialización*; *Maestría*; *Doctorado*
Last Updated: 22/03/13

EDUCATION AND CULTURAL DEVELOPMENT OF MONTERREY

Educación y Desarrollo Cultural de Monterrey
Avenida Revoluciónn # 850 Sur, Col. Jardín Español, Monterrey, Nuevo León
Tel: +52(81) 8387-6833
EMail: info@edecdemonterrey.edu.mx
Website: http://www.edecdemonterrey.edu.mx

Rector: Jesús Ramiro Del Bosque García

Programmes
Accountancy (Accountancy); **Business Administration** (Business Administration); **Computer Science** (Computer Science); **Law** (Law)

History: Founded 1996. Acquired present status 2002.

Main Language(s) of Instruction: Spanish

Degrees and Diplomas: *Licenciatura*; *Maestría*
Last Updated: 24/08/12

EDUCATIONAL ATHENEUM OF INTEGRAL TRAINING

Ateneo Educativo de Formación Integral
Calle Margarita, 801, Col. Vallehermoso, 38010 Celaya, Guanajuato
Tel: +52(461) 611-52-44
Fax: +52(461) 611-52-44
EMail: rectoria@adsumus.edu.mx
Website: http://www.seminariodecelaya.com/

Director: Wilfrido Mancera Mendoza

Courses
Humanities (Arts and Humanities); **Philosophy** (Philosophy)

History: Founded 1999.

Main Language(s) of Instruction: Spanish

Degrees and Diplomas: *Licenciatura*
Last Updated: 10/07/12

ELEIA CENTRE OF PSYCHOLOGICAL ACTIVITIES

Centro Eleia Actividades Psicológicas
Insurgentes Sur 1971, 3er. Piso. Nivel Terraza, Plaza Inn, Col.Guadalupe Inn, 11560 México, D.F.
Tel: +55(555) 661-21-77
EMail: informes@centroeleia.com.mx
Website: http://www.centroeleia.com.mx

Director: Norberto Mario Bleichmar (1998-)

Programmes
Psychology (Psychology)
History: Founded 1990.
Main Language(s) of Instruction: Spanish
Degrees and Diplomas: *Licenciatura*; *Maestría*; *Doctorado*
Last Updated: 29/02/08

ELIZABETH SETON CENTRE FOR ADVANCED STUDIES

Centro de Estudios Superiores Elizabeth Setón
Retorno Haciendas Del Valle No. 6721, Fracc.Mosaico Lomas Del Valle, 31238 Chihuahua, Chihuahua
Tel: +52(614) 423-25-30
Fax: +52(614) 423-20-70
EMail: cesesch@gmail.com

Directora: Blanca Magrassi Scano
History: Founded 1998.
Main Language(s) of Instruction: Spanish
Degrees and Diplomas: *Licenciatura*
Last Updated: 16/07/12

ELOISA PATRÓN DE ROSADO INSTITUTE

Instituto Eloisa Patrón de Rosado
Calle 17 n° 101-E, entre calles 20 y 22, Col. Itzimná, 97100 Mérida, Yucatán
Tel: +52(999) 927-00-73
Fax: +52(999) 927-00-73
EMail: informacion@iuepr.edu.mx
Website: http://www.iuepr.edu.mx

Directora: Gabriela Medina Rosado de Isaac

Programmes
Agricultural Administration (Administration); **Special Education** (Special Education); **Tourism** (Tourism)
History: Founded 1929.
Main Language(s) of Instruction: Spanish
Degrees and Diplomas: *Licenciatura*
Last Updated: 05/03/13

EMILIO CÁRDENAS UNIVERSITY

Universidad Emilio Cárdenas
Avenida Atlacomulco, 193 y 191, Col. La Loma, 54060 Tlalnepantla, Estado de México
Tel: +52(55) 55-65-10-20
EMail: contacto@udec.com.mx
Website: http://www.udec.com.mx

Rector: Alfonso Malpica EMail: alfonso.malpica@udec.com.mx

Programmes
Accountancy (Accountancy); **Administration** (Administration); **Advertising** (Advertising and Publicity); **Computer Engineering** (Computer Engineering); **Graphic Design** (Graphic Design); **International Business** (International Business); **Law** (Law); **Marketing** (Marketing); **Pedagogy** (Pedagogy); **Psychology** (Psychology)
History: Founded 1983.
Admission Requirements: Bachillerato
Main Language(s) of Instruction: Spanish
Accrediting Agencies: FIMPES
Degrees and Diplomas: *Licenciatura*; *Especialización*; *Maestría*
Libraries: Yes
Last Updated: 02/10/12

EMMANUEL KANT UNIVERSITY CENTRE

Centro Universitario Emmanuel Kant
Calle Sevilla, 110, Col. Portales, Delegación Benito Juárez, 03300 México, D.F.
Tel: +52(55) 56-72-08-11
Fax: +52(55) 56-72-06-13
EMail: difusion@cuek.edu.mx
Website: http://www.cuek.edu.mx

Programmes
Administration (Business Administration; Public Administration); **Law** (Labour Law; Law); **Psychology** (Psychology)
History: Founded 1996.
Main Language(s) of Instruction: Spanish
Degrees and Diplomas: *Licenciatura*; *Maestría*; *Doctorado*
Last Updated: 25/07/12

ENRIQUE DÍAZ DE LEÓN UNIVERSITY

Universidad Enrique Díaz de León
Av. Enrique Díaz de León Norte No. 90, 44100 Guadalajara, Jalisco
Tel: +52(33) 38-27-09-06
EMail: rectoria@unedl.edu.mx
Website: http://unedl.edu.mx

Director: Héctor Manuel Roble Ibarra

Programmes
Accountancy (Accountancy); **Administration** (Administration); **Communication Studies** (Communication Studies); **Finance** (Finance; Taxation); **International Business** (International Business); **Law** (Law); **Marketing** (Marketing); **Tourism** (Tourism)
History: Founded 1969.
Main Language(s) of Instruction: Spanish
Degrees and Diplomas: *Licenciatura*; *Maestría*
Last Updated: 03/04/13

ENRIQUE REBSAMEN INSTITUTE

Instituto Enrique Rebsamen
Francisco I Madero 411 A, Sector Juarez, 44100 Guadalajara, Jalisco
Tel: +52(33) 35-62-03-57
EMail: angelica_rebsamen@hotmail.com
Website: http://www.enriquerebsamen.com

Director: Eddilberto Toledo Muñoz

Programmes
Criminology (Criminology); **Education** (Education); **Human Resources** (Human Resources); **Law** (Law); **Marketing and Publicity** (Advertising and Publicity; Marketing); **Pedagogy** (Pedagogy); **Psychopedagogy** (Educational Psychology)
History: Founded 1998.
Degrees and Diplomas: *Licenciatura*; *Maestría*
Last Updated: 05/03/13

ERICH FROMM MEXICAN INSTITUTE OF HIGHER EDUCATION

Instituto Mexicano de Educación Superior Erich Fromm
Calle Guelatao, 129, Col. Las Palmas, Cuernavaca, Morelos
Tel: +52(777) 318-18-15

Director: Ludgar Melling Paredes Hernández
Degrees and Diplomas: *Licenciatura*
Last Updated: 07/04/08

ESPAÑA DE DURANGO AUTONOMOUS UNIVERSITY

Universidad Autónoma España de Durango (UAED)
Av. Universidad España #7, Fracc. Jardines de Durango, 34200 Durango, Durango
Tel: +52(618) 818-33-22 +52(618) 817-59-59
Fax: +52(618) 817-23-49
EMail: unes@unes.edu.mx
Website: http://www.unes.edu.mx

Rector: Juan Manuel Rodríguez y Rodríguez (1994-)
EMail: unesryr@unes.edu.mx

Schools

Architecture (Architecture); **Business** (Accountancy; Business Administration; Cooking and Catering; Hotel Management; Marketing; Tourism); **Communication Studies** (Advertising and Publicity; Journalism; Public Relations); **Design** (Graphic Design; Industrial Design); **Education** (Bilingual and Bicultural Education; Education; Physical Education; Special Education; Sports); **Engineering** (Automotive Engineering; Electrical Engineering; Information Technology; Mechanical Engineering); **Law and Social Sciences** (Criminal Law; Criminology; International Relations; Law; Political Sciences; Public Administration); **Medical Sciences** (Medicine; Nutrition; Surgery); **Psychology** (Clinical Psychology; Educational Psychology)

Further Information: Also Guadalupe Victoria, Durango, Vicente Guerrero, Durango.Calle Octavio Paz s/nentre la Calle Aldama y Calle Ignacio ZaragozaCol. Escritores, C.P. 34890Ciudad Vicente Guerrero, Dgo, Parral, Chihuahua andInstituto Universitario España de Coahuila (Saltillo, Coah.)

History: Founded 1977 as Colegio España. Acquired present status and title 1994.

Governing Bodies: Board of Owners, Board of Directors, Board of Planning, Board of Academics

Academic Year: August to June

Admission Requirements: Secondary school certificate (bachillerato) and entrance examination

Fees: (Pesos): 10,500 per semester for College (9 semesters); 48,000 per term for Master's degree; 90,000 per term for Doctors degree

Main Language(s) of Instruction: Spanish

International Co-operation: With universities in Spain, USA and Cuba

Accrediting Agencies: Federación de Instituciones Mexicanas Particulares de Educación Superior (FIMPES), Future SACS

Degrees and Diplomas: *Licenciatura (Lic.)*: 4 1/2 yrs; *Maestría (Mtro.)*: 2 yrs; *Doctorado (Dr.)*: 3 yrs

Student Services: Sports facilities

Special Facilities: Radio Station; Theatre

Libraries: Yes

Publications: Espacio Científico, Postgraduate investigation publication *(quarterly)*; Fundación Editorial UAED, Teachers academic research, monographs, texts and books *(other/irregular)*

Last Updated: 07/09/12

ETAC UNIVERSITY

Universidad ETAC
Viveros de Asís, 96, Col. Viveros de la Loma, 54680 Tlalnepantla, Estado de México
Tel: +52(55) 30-67-68-00
EMail: alfajason_2000@yahoo.com
Website: http://www.etac.edu.mx

Rector: Jesús Nájera Martínez (2000-)

Programmes

Accountancy (Accountancy); **Business Administration** (Business Administration); **Business Computing** (Business Computing); **Computer Networks** (Computer Networks); **Education** (Education); **Graphic Design** (Graphic Design); **Journalism and Advertising** (Advertising and Publicity; Journalism); **Law** (Law); **Marketing** (Marketing); **Organizational and Social Psychology** (Psychology)

Further Information: Also campuses in Coacalco, Tulancingo and Chalco

History: Founded 1966.

Main Language(s) of Instruction: Spanish

Degrees and Diplomas: *Licenciatura*; *Especialización*; *Maestría*

Libraries: Yes

Last Updated: 02/10/12

EULALIO FERRER CENTRE FOR ADVANCED STUDIES IN COMMUNICATION

Centro Avanzado de Comunicación Eulalio Ferrer
Comunal # 7, Col. Chimalistac, 01050 México, D.F.
Tel: +52(555) 662-28-53 +52(555) 661-60-20
Fax: +52(555) 661-74-17
EMail: cadec@prodigy.net.mx
Website: http://www.cadec.edu.mx

Directora: Ana Sara Ferrer Bohorques (1987-)

Programmes

Advertising (Advertising and Publicity); **Communication Studies** (Communication Studies)

Further Information: Also branch in Vera Cruz

History: Founded 1987.

Main Language(s) of Instruction: Spanish

Degrees and Diplomas: *Licenciatura*; *Especialización*; *Maestría*; *Doctorado*. Also Diplomados

Last Updated: 10/07/12

EURO-AMERICAN UNIVERSITY

Universidad Euroamericana, S.C. (UEA)
Avenida José Garci-Crespo, 2421, Col. San Nicolás, 75710 Tetitzintla, Puebla
Tel: +52(238) 382-04-85 +52(238) 383-39-06
Fax: +52(238) 382-01-90

Director: René Velázquez Herrera

Programmes

Business Administration (Accountancy; Business Administration; Finance; International Business); **Fashion Design** (Fashion Design); **Graphic Design** (Graphic Design); **International Relations** (International Relations); **Law** (Law); **Tourism** (Tourism)

History: Founded 1991.

Main Language(s) of Instruction: Spanish

Degrees and Diplomas: *Licenciatura*

Last Updated: 11/02/08

EUROMAR TECHNOLOGICAL INSTITUTE OF HOTEL MANAGEMENT AND GASTRONOMY

Instituto Tecnológico de Alta Hotelería y Gastronomía Euromar
Coyotepec, 5, Col. Lomas de Cortes, 62240 Cuernavaca, Morelos
Tel: +52(777) 313-96-36
Fax: +52(777) 310-96-36
EMail: direccion@euromar.edu.mx

Directora: Norma Patricia Guerrero Pliego

Programmes

Gastronomy (Cooking and Catering); **Hotel Management** (Hotel and Restaurant; Hotel Management)

History: Founded 1996.

Main Language(s) of Instruction: Spanish

Degrees and Diplomas: *Licenciatura*

Last Updated: 25/03/08

EUROPEAN UNIVERSITY

Universidad Europea, A.C.
Blvd. Valsequillo N° 1035 Col. Bugambilias, 72550 Puebla, Puebla
Tel: +52(222) 244-90-00
EMail: universidadeuropea@yahoo.com
Website: http://www.universidadeuropeapuebla.edu.mx

Directora: María Cristina Said Elías (1997-)

Programmes
Accountancy (Accountancy); **Banking and Finance** (Banking; Finance); **Communication** (Communication Studies); **International Business** (International Business); **Law and Criminology** (Criminology; Law); **Marketing** (Marketing); **Modern Languages** (English; French; German; Italian; Translation and Interpretation); **Psychology** (Psychology)

History: Founded in 1994.

Admission Requirements: Secondary school certificate and entrance examination

Degrees and Diplomas: *Licenciatura*

Student Services: Academic counselling, Foreign student adviser, Handicapped facilities, Health services, Language programs, Social counselling, Sports facilities

Special Facilities: Computer laboratory

Last Updated: 03/04/13

EXCELLENTIA FERVIC BUSINESS COLLEGE

Colegio de Empresarios Excellentia FERVIC

Paseo de Tamarindos No. 400-A 5to. piso, Col. Bosques de las Lomas, Cuajimalpa de Morelos, 05120 México, D.F.
Tel: +52(55) 2457-0120
EMail: dir_academica@colegiodeempresarios.edu.mx
Website: http://www.colegiodeempresarios.edu.mx/

Rector: Fernando Jiménez Chávez

Programmes
Business Administration (Business Administration); **Business and Commerce** (Administration; Business Administration; Business and Commerce); **Marketing** (Marketing)

Degrees and Diplomas: *Licenciatura*; *Maestría*

Last Updated: 27/07/12

FACULTY OF DESIGN AND GRAPHIC COMMUNICATION

Facultad de Diseño y Comunicación Gráfica

Avenida División del Norte, 3102, Col. Altavista, 31320 Chihuahua, Chihuahua
Tel: +52(614) 413-65-05 +52(614) 414-14-54
Fax: +52(614) 414-72-66 +52(614) 414-76-78
EMail: contacto@escograf.com
Website: http://www.escograf.com

Director: Juan E. Ruiz Trujillo (1980-)

Programmes
Graphic Communication (Communication Arts; Graphic Arts); **Graphic Design** (Graphic Design)

History: Founded 1980 as Escuela Superior de Comunicación Gráfica.

Main Language(s) of Instruction: Spanish

Degrees and Diplomas: *Licenciatura*; *Maestría*

Last Updated: 26/02/13

FACULTY OF LAW OF THE NATIONAL BAR OF LAWYERS

Facultad de Derecho de la Barra Nacional de Abogados

Calzada de los leones No. 144, Col. Los Alpes (Las Águilas), Delegación Álvaro Obregón, Juárez, 01010 México, D.F.
Tel: +52(55) 55-36-68-69
EMail: ingresos@bna.edu.mx
Website: http://www.bna.edu.mx

Rector: Armando Quirasco Hernández

Programmes
Law (Law)

History: Founded 1998.

Main Language(s) of Instruction: Spanish

Degrees and Diplomas: *Licenciatura*; *Especialización*; *Maestría*; *Doctorado*

Libraries: Yes

Last Updated: 30/08/12

FASHION DESIGN CENTRE

Centro de Diseño de Modas

Buenos Aires, 2998, Colonia Providencia, 44630 Guadalajara, Jalisco
Tel: +52(33) 36-42-25-59
Fax: +52(33) 36-42-69-14
EMail: info@cdmmexico.com.mx
Website: http://www.cdmmexico.com.mx

Directora: Marbel Rodríguez

Programmes
Fashion Design (Fashion Design)

History: Founded 1983.

Main Language(s) of Instruction: Spanish

Degrees and Diplomas: *Licenciatura*

Last Updated: 10/01/13

FELIPE CARRILLO PUERTO SCHOOL CENTRE

Centro Escolar Felipe Carrillo Puerto

Calle 65 No. 583-B x calle 72, Centro, 97000 Mérida, Yucatán
Tel: +52(999) 928-85-45 +52(999) 923-94-72 Ext. 114
EMail: consulto@prodigy.net.com
Website: http://www.ceccuniversidad.com

Director: Andrés Bazán Aguilar

Programmes
Administration and Business Administration (Administration; Business Administration); **Computer Science** (Computer Science); **Law** (Law); **Marketing** (Marketing); **Public Accountancy** (Accountancy); **Tourism** (Tourism)

Degrees and Diplomas: *Licenciatura*: 8-10 sem.

Last Updated: 27/03/08

FEP HIGHER TEACHER TRAINING SCHOOL

Escuela Normal Superior FEP (Federación de Escuelas Particulares)

Sadi Carnot 44, Col. San Rafael, 06470 México, D.F.
Tel: +52(55) 55-46-89-64 +52(55) 55-46-38-08
Fax: +52(55) 55-46-89-64
EMail: aletseia_00@yahoo.com.mx

Directora: Estela Iñiguez Amézquita

Programmes
Teacher Training (Secondary Education; Teacher Training)

History: Founded 1947.

Degrees and Diplomas: *Licenciatura*

Last Updated: 04/04/08

FEP TEACHER TRAINING SCHOOL

Escuela Normal 'FEP' (Federación de Escuelas Particulares)

Sadi Carnot No. 13, Col. San Rafael, Delegación Cuauhtémoc, 06470 México, D.F.
Tel: +52(55) 55-46-93-78
Fax: +52(55) 55-35-08-15

Directora General: Guadalupe Rubio Cervantes

Programmes
Preschool Education (Preschool Education); **Primary Education** (Primary Education)

Degrees and Diplomas: *Licenciatura*: 8 sem.

Last Updated: 03/04/08

FILADELFIA UNIVERSITY OF MEXICO

Universidad Filadelfia de México

Carretera Antigua a Coatepec Km 2.5 Fraccionamiento Briones, 91020 Xalapa, Veracruz
Tel: +52(28) 833-40-03
EMail: cuv@hotmail.com
Website: http://www.filadelfia.mx

Rector: Candelario Miranda Amador (1994-)

Programmes
Accountancy (Accountancy); **Biblical Theology** (Bible; Theology); **Business Administration** (Business Administration); **Business Computing** (Business Computing); **Communication Studies** (Advertising and Publicity; Cinema and Television; Communication Studies; Photography; Radio and Television Broadcasting); **Computer Engineering** (Computer Engineering); **Graphic Design** (Graphic Design); **International Business** (International Business); **Law** (Civil Law; Commercial Law; Criminal Law; Fiscal Law; Labour Law; Law; Private Law); **Pedagogy** (Pedagogy)

Further Information: Also campuses in Papantla, Perote, and Cuenca

History: Founded as Centro Cultural Universitario Veracruzano. Acquired present name and status 2003.

Admission Requirements: Bachillerato

Main Language(s) of Instruction: Spanish

Degrees and Diplomas: *Licenciatura*; *Maestría*. Also Diplomado

Last Updated: 03/09/12

FRANCES HIDALGO UNIVERSITY CENTRE

Centro Universitario Francés Hidalgo
Calle Huitzilihuitl, 30, Col. Sta. Isabel Tola, Delegación Tlalpán, 07010 México, D.F.
Tel: +52(55) 57-81-50-44
EMail: rpublica@cfh.edu.mx

Rector: Eduardo Luis Tapia Soto (1993-)

Programmes
Accountancy (Accountancy); **Business Administration** (Business Administration); **Business Computing** (Business Computing); **Law** (Law); **Marketing** (Marketing)

History: Founded 1993.

Main Language(s) of Instruction: Spanish

Degrees and Diplomas: *Licenciatura*

Last Updated: 13/03/08

FRANCISCO DE MONTEJO CENTRE FOR ADVANCED STUDIES

Centro de Estudios Superiores Francisco de Montejo, A.C.
Calle 49, 142-A, Col. San Francisco, 97780 Valladolid, Yucatán
Tel: +52(985) 986-12-95
Fax: +52(985) 986-12-95

Directora: Verónica Guadalupe Villanueva Badillo
EMail: cuv98@yahoo.com.mx

Programmes
Advertising; **Graphic Design** (Graphic Design)

Main Language(s) of Instruction: Spanish

Degrees and Diplomas: *Licenciatura*

Last Updated: 12/03/08

FRANCISCO DE VITORIA CENTRE FOR ADVANCED STUDIES

Centro de Estudios Superiores Francisco de Vitoria
Av. Orizaba no. 622, Colonia Obrera Campesina, 91020 Xalapa
Tel: +52(228) 890-11-60
EMail: ifvxal@xal.megared.net.mx

Programmes
Computer Science (Computer Science); **Law** (Law)

Main Language(s) of Instruction: Spanish

Degrees and Diplomas: *Licenciatura*

Last Updated: 17/07/12

FRANCISCO FERREIRA Y ARREOLA UNIVERSITY CENTRE OF TEXCOCO

Centro Universitario de Texcoco Francisco Ferreira y Arreola
Allende, 723, Barrio San Sebastián, 56170 Texcoco de Mora, Estado de México
Tel: +52(595) 954-04-84
Fax: +52(595) 955-19-85

Rector: Ángel López Vergara (1993-)

Programmes
Administrative Informatics (Business Computing); **Business Administration** (Business Administration); **Educational Sciences** (Educational Sciences); **International Business** (International Business); **Law** (Law); **Psychology** (Psychology); **Public Accountancy** (Accountancy)

History: Founded 1993.

Main Language(s) of Instruction: Spanish

Degrees and Diplomas: *Licenciatura*: 9-10 sem.

Last Updated: 27/03/08

FRANCISCO GONZÁLEZ DE LA VEGA INSTITUTE OF HIGHER EDUCATION

Instituto de Educación Superior Francisco González de la Vega
Calle Dr. Fleming No.439 Sur, 35000 Gómez Palacio, Durango
Tel: +52(871) 614-54-09
EMail: fagoveccz@hotmail.com

Directora: Blanca Patricia Reyes Martínez

Programmes
Law (Law)

Degrees and Diplomas: *Licenciatura*

Last Updated: 28/02/13

FRANCISCO LARROYO UNIVERSITY CENTRE

Centro Universitario Francisco Larroyo
Avenida Tlahuac 7367, Col. Santa Cecilia, Delegación Tlahuac, 13010 México, D.F.
Tel: +52(5) 58-42-12-61
Website: http://www.cufla.edu.mx

Director: José Luis Martínez Galicia (2000-)

Programmes
Accountancy (Accountancy); **Administration** (Administration); **Computer Science** (Computer Science); **Law** (Law)

History: Founded 2000.

Admission Requirements: Secondary school certificate

Degrees and Diplomas: *Licenciatura*

Last Updated: 25/07/12

FRANCO-MEXICAN UNIVERSITY

Universidad Franco Mexicana (UFRAM)
Álamo Plateado, 45, Fracc. Los Álamos, 53230 Naucalpán de Juárez, Estado de México
Tel: +52(55) 53-43-46-12 +52(55) 53-43-61-21
Fax: +52(55) 53-44-07-89
EMail: ufram@ufram.edu.mx
Website: http://www.ufram.edu.mx

Rector: Hector A. Esquer Gallardo EMail: hesquerg@ufram.edu.mx

Programmes
Communication (Communication Studies; Journalism; Media Studies); **Graphic Design and Advertising** (Advertising and Publicity; Graphic Design); **International Business** (International Business); **Law** (Law); **Marketing** (Marketing); **Psychology** (Psychology)

Further Information: Also Plantel Norte at Cuautitlán Izcalli

History: Founded 1981.

Academic Year: August to July

Admission Requirements: Secondary school certificate (bachillerato) and entrance examination

Main Language(s) of Instruction: Spanish

Degrees and Diplomas: *Licenciatura.* Also Diplomados
Last Updated: 03/10/12

FRANKLIN D. ROOSEVELT INSTITUTE

Instituto Franklin D. Roosevelt, A.C.
Avenida 15 de Mayo número 2939-7, fraccionamiento Las Hadas, 72000 Puebla, Puebla
Tel: +52(222) 246-91-34

Directora: Catalina Ocelotl Tlaxcalteca

Programmes
Tourism Administration (Hotel Management; Tourism)

Degrees and Diplomas: *Licenciatura*
Last Updated: 05/03/13

FRAY ANDRÉS DE URDANETA CENTRE OF AUGUSTINIAN STUDIES

Centro de Estudios Agustinianos Fray Andrés de Urdaneta
Calle Juárez, 5, Col. Zacautitla, 55700 Coacalco de Berriozábal, Estado de México
Tel: +52(55) 1542-03-64
EMail: cea@fadu.edu.mx

Director: Miguel Ángel Hernández Montero

Programmes
Psychology (Clinical Psychology; Educational Psychology; Industrial and Organizational Psychology; Psychology)

History: Founded 1970.

Main Language(s) of Instruction: Spanish

Degrees and Diplomas: *Licenciatura*
Last Updated: 14/02/13

FRAY BARTOLOMÉ DE LAS CASAS CENTRE FOR PROFESSIONAL STUDIES OF CHIAPAS

Centro de Estudios Profesionales de Chiapas Fray Bartolomé de Las Casas
Blvd. Belisario Domínguez, 1030, 29000 Tuxtla Gutiérrez, Chiapas
Tel: +52(961) 602-68-66 +52(961) 602-68-72
EMail: fbc@fbc.edu.mx
Website: http://www.fbc.edu.mx

Rector: Gilberto de la Peña Figueredo

Programmes
Accountancy (Accountancy); **Administration** (Administration; Business Administration); **Graphic Design** (Graphic Design); **Hotel Management** (Hotel Management); **Industrial and Educational Psychology** (Educational Psychology; Industrial and Organizational Psychology); **Institutional Management** (Institutional Administration); **International Relations** (International Relations); **International Trade** (International Business); **Journalism and Communication** (Communication Studies; Journalism); **Law** (Law)

History: Founded 1991

Governing Bodies: Rectoría

Academic Year: January to December. Two modalities: Semester (January-June;August-December) or Quatrimester (January-April;-June-August;September-December)

Admission Requirements: High School Certificate

Fees: (Pesos): 7,900 for four months

Main Language(s) of Instruction: Spanish

Degrees and Diplomas: *Licenciatura*; *Especialización*; *Maestría*

Student Services: Academic counselling, Employment services, Sports facilities

Special Facilities: Audiovisual room; Photography Laboratory; T.V. Studio

Libraries: Yes
Last Updated: 13/07/12

FRENCH-ENGLISH UNIVERSITY INSTITUTE OF MEXICO

Instituto Universitario Franco Inglés de México, S.C
Avenida Árbol de la Vida, 10, Col. Bellavista, 52172 Metepec, Estado de México
Tel: +52(722)- 271-1318
EMail: diracademica@iufim.com.mx
Website: http://www.iufim.com.mx

Directora: María de la Luz Aurea García García

Programmes
Accountancy (Accountancy; Administration; Commercial Law; Finance; Labour Law; Management; Marketing; Mathematics; Statistics); **Business Administration** (Advertising and Publicity; Applied Mathematics; Business Administration; Business Computing; Commercial Law; Economics; English; Environmental Management; Finance; Human Resources; Labour Law; Management; Marketing; Psychology); **Communication Studies** (Communication Studies); **Dentistry** (Dental Technology; Dentistry; Orthodontics; Radiology; Surgery); **Education** (Education); **Languages** (Communication Studies; Cultural Studies; English; English Studies; French; Linguistics; Modern Languages; Phonetics; Spanish); **Law** (Administrative Law; Civil Law; Constitutional Law; Criminal Law; Fiscal Law; International Law; Law; Private Law; Public Law)

Main Language(s) of Instruction: Spanish

Degrees and Diplomas: *Licenciatura*: 8-10 sem.; *Especialización*; *Maestría*: Educational Management
Last Updated: 22/03/13

FRENCH-MEXICAN CENTRE FOR ADVANCED STUDIES

Centro de Estudios Superiores Francés Mexicano
Manuel Carpio No. 109, Col. Santa Maria la Ribera, Delegación Cuauhtémoc, 6400 México, D.F.
Website: http://www.centrolefranc.net/

Rector: José Manuel Carrada Lefranc

Programmes
Business Administration (Business Administration); **International Business** (International Business); **Law** (Law); **Marketing** (Marketing)

Degrees and Diplomas: *Licenciatura*
Last Updated: 16/07/12

FRITZ PERLS TRAINING AND RESEARCH INSTITUTE IN GESTALT PSYCHOTHERAPY

Centro de Investigación y Entrenamiento en Psicoterapia Gestalt Fritz Perls, S.C.
Avenida Lázaro Cárdenas 1111 Ote, Plazas Las Brisas, Col. Las Brisas, 64780 Monterrey, Nuevo León
Tel: +52(81) 83-57-82-29
Fax: +52(81) 83-49-99-20
EMail: escolar@cgestalt.com
Website: http://www.gestalt-mty.com/

Rector: Fernando García Licea

Programmes
Education (Education; Educational Psychology); **Psychotherapy** (Development Studies; Family Studies; Psychotherapy)

History: Founded 1991.

Main Language(s) of Instruction: Spanish

Degrees and Diplomas: *Maestría*; *Doctorado*
Last Updated: 18/07/12

FROEBEL COLLEGE

Colegio Froebel
3 Norte 1000, Col. Tehuacan Centro, 75700 Tehuacán, Puebla
Tel: +52(238) 382-06-87

Director: Norberto Vázquez Rodríguez

Programmes
Foreign Languages; **Psychology** (Psychology)

Degrees and Diplomas: *Licenciatura*; *Maestría*
Last Updated: 10/11/09

GABRIEL MÉNDEZ PLANCARTE INSTITUTE OF THEOLOGY AND PHILOSOPHY

Instituto de Ciencias Teológicas y Filosóficas Gabriel Méndez Plancarte

Javier Mina, 39, Col. Centro, 59800 Jacona de Plancarte, Michoacán
Tel: +52(351) 35-16-01-67
EMail: inicitefi@yahoo.com.mx

Programmes
Philosophy (Philosophy); **Theology** (Theology)

History: Founded 2000.

Main Language(s) of Instruction: Spanish

Degrees and Diplomas: *Licenciatura*

Libraries: Yes

Last Updated: 28/02/13

GALILEA UNIVERSITY

Universidad Galilea

Avenida Esfuerzo Nacional, 612, Fracc. Ojo Caliente, 4, Delegación de Jesús Terán, 20197 Aguascalientes, Aguascalientes
Tel: +52(449) 975-19-99
Fax: +52(449) 975-19-96
EMail: universidadgalilea@live.com.mx
Website:http: //www.universidadgalilea.com.mx

Rector: Alfonso María Alva Martínez (1982-)
EMail: dr_alva@hotmail.com

Secretario General: Mauricio Alva Moreno

International Relations: Mauricio Alva Moreno
EMail: tampis@hotmail.com

Faculties
Accountancy (Accountancy); **Law** (Law)

Schools
Psychology

History: Founded 1982. Acquired present status 1989.

Governing Bodies: University Council; Board of Directors

Academic Year: September to June (September-January; February-June)

Admission Requirements: Secondary school leaving Certificate (Bachillerato)

Main Language(s) of Instruction: Spanish

International Co-operation: With universities in El Salvador, Peru, United Kingdom

Accrediting Agencies: Secretaría de Educación Pública

Degrees and Diplomas: *Licenciatura*

Student Services: Academic counselling, Canteen, Social counselling

Student Residential Facilities: None

Libraries: Yes

Last Updated: 03/10/12

GAUSS JORDAN SPECIALIZED INSTITUTE IN COMPUTER SCIENCE AND ADMINISTRATION

Instituto Especializado en Computación y Administración Gauss Jordan

Dvorak, 59, Col. Vallejo, Delegación Gustavo A. Madero, 07870 México, D.F.
Tel: +52(55) 55-37-44-00 +52(55) 55-17-52-60
Fax: +52(55) 55-37-22-20
EMail: contacto@gaussjordan.edu.mx
Website: http://www.gaussjordan.edu.mx

Director: Maximiliano Burillo Velzaco
EMail: mburillo@gaussjordan.edu.mx

Programmes
Accountancy (Accountancy); **Administration** (Administration); **Communication Sciences** (Communication Studies); **Computer Science** (Computer Science); **Law** (Law); **Tourism** (Tourism)

History: Founded 1994.

Main Language(s) of Instruction: Spanish

Degrees and Diplomas: *Licenciatura*

Last Updated: 05/03/13

GENERAL EMILIANO ZAPATA UNIVERSITY CENTRE

Centro Universitario General Emiliano Zapata

Avenida Progreso, 449, Col. Plan de Ayala, Cuautla, Coquimatlán, Morelos
Tel: +52(735) 352-38-50
Fax: +52(735) 352-38-50
EMail: mendeznet.@yupimail.com

Director: Javier Sánchez Rubio

Programmes
Accountancy and Finance (Accountancy; Finance); **Administration and International Business** (Administration; International Business); **Administration and Marketing** (Administration; Marketing); **Law** (Law)

Admission Requirements: Secondary school certificate

Main Language(s) of Instruction: Spanish

Degrees and Diplomas: *Licenciatura*

Last Updated: 25/07/12

GENERAL HERMENEGILDO GALEANA SCHOOL CENTRE

Centro Escolar General Hermenegildo Galeana

Galileo, 4, Fracc. Ajuquiac, Tecpán de Galeana, 40911 Galeana, Guerrero
Tel: +52(744) 425-02-95
Fax: +52(744) 425-03-54

Directora: María Celia Armenta de León

Programmes
Accountancy (Accountancy); **Biology** (Biology); **Computer Science** (Computer Science); **History** (History); **Law** (Law); **Secondary Education** (Secondary Education)

Degrees and Diplomas: *Licenciatura*

Last Updated: 27/03/08

GEO UNIVERSITY CENTRE

Centro Universitario Geo

Avenida Poniente 7, 459, Col. Centro, 94300 Orizaba, Veracruz
Tel: +52(272) 727-17-49 +52(272) 727-55-96
Fax: +52(272) 725-57-22

Director General: Fidel Saavedra Uribe (1997-)

Programmes
Business Administration and Accountancy

History: Founded 1997.

Degrees and Diplomas: *Licenciatura*

Last Updated: 04/04/08

GESTALT CENTRE OF HUMANISTIC TRAINING AND PSYCHOTHERAPY

Centro de Formación Humanística y Psicoterapía 'Gestalt'

Calzada Héroes de Chapultepec, 321, Col. Xochimilco, 68000 Oaxaca, Oaxaca
Tel: +52(951) 513-11-18
EMail: cidh@telnor.net

Director: Alfredo Zetina Moguel

Programmes
Human Sciences (Social Sciences); **Psychotherapy** (Psychotherapy)

Main Language(s) of Instruction: Spanish

Degrees and Diplomas: *Licenciatura*; *Maestría*

Last Updated: 29/02/08

GESTALT INSTITUTE

Instituto de Gestalt

Mesalina 8-A Col. Delicias, Cuernavaca, Morelos
Tel: +52(7) 316-07-29
Fax: +52(7) 316-07-29
EMail: info@institutodegestalt.edu.mx
Website: http://www.institutodegestalt.edu.mx

Directora: Jenny Roldán Hayen

Programmes

Education (Education); **Human Development** (Development Studies; Psychotherapy); **Psychotherapy** (Psychotherapy)

History: Founded 1991.

Main Language(s) of Instruction: Spanish

Degrees and Diplomas: *Licenciatura*; *Especialización*; *Maestría*
Last Updated: 04/03/13

GESTALT INSTITUTE OF GUADALAJARA

Instituto Gestalt de Guadalajara

Mexicaltzingo 1949 entre Av.Chapultepec y Calle Progreso, Sec. Juarez, 44150 Guadalajara, Jalisco
Tel: +52(33) 38-25-66-36
EMail: institutogestalt@gestaltguadalajara.com
Website: http://www.gestaltguadalajara.com.mx

Director: Luis Manuel Preciado Medina (2003-)
EMail: luispreciado@gestaltguadalajara.com

Programmes

Psychology and Psychotherapy (Psychology; Psychotherapy)

History: Founded 1992. Acquired present status 1997.

Admission Requirements: Licenciatura in Psychology or equivalent

Main Language(s) of Instruction: Spanish

Degrees and Diplomas: *Especialización*

Student Services: Academic counselling

Special Facilities: Video studio

Libraries: Yes
Last Updated: 05/03/13

GESTALT SCHOOL OF ART AND DESIGN OF TUXTLA GUTIÉRREZ

Escuela Gestalt de Arte y Diseño de Tuxtla Gutiérrez

Quinta Poniente Nte, 1443, 29000 Tuxtla Gutiérrez, Chiapas
Tel: +52(961) 618-09-11
EMail: ivangestalt@hotmail.com
Website: http://www.escuelagestalt.edu.mex

Directora: Paola Sánchez

Programmes

Architecture (Architecture); **Graphic Design** (Graphic Design)

Degrees and Diplomas: *Licenciatura*: 8-9 sem.
Last Updated: 29/08/12

GESTALT UNIVERSITY

Universidad Gestalt

Eucken 19, Col. Nueva Anzures, 11590 México, D.F.
Tel: +52(55) 52-03-20-08
EMail: unigea@mundogestalt.com
Website: http://www.mundogestalt.com

Rector: Héctor Salama Penhos (1983-)

Programmes

Accountancy (Accountancy); **Business Administration** (Accountancy; Business Administration; Marketing); **Pedagogy** (Education; Pedagogy); **Psychology** (Psychology); **Psychotherapy** (Psychotherapy)

History: Founded 1983. Acquired present status 1991. Formerly known as Instituto Mexicano de Psicoterapía Gestalt

Admission Requirements: High school certificate

Main Language(s) of Instruction: Spanish

Degrees and Diplomas: *Licenciatura*: 4 yrs; *Maestría*: 2 1/2 yrs; *Doctorado*: 2 1/2 yrs

Student Services: Academic counselling, Employment services, Health services, Social counselling

Student Residential Facilities: None

Libraries: Yes

Publications: Mundo Gestalt *(bimonthly)*
Last Updated: 03/10/12

GESTALT UNIVERSITY OF DESIGN

Universidad Gestalt de Diseño

Av. 1o de Mayo No. 113. Col. Obrero campesina, 91020 Xalapa, Veracruz
Tel: +52(228) 815-63-92
EMail: informes@ugd.edu.mx
Website: http://ugd.edu.mx

Rector: Joel Olivares Ruiz (1988-) EMail: jor@ugd.edu.mx

Programmes

Architecture (Architecture); **Graphic Design** (Graphic Design); **Industrial Design** (Industrial Design); **Interior Design** (Interior Design)

History: Founded 1987 as Escuela Gestalt de Diseño. Acquired present status 1992.

Main Language(s) of Instruction: Spanish

Degrees and Diplomas: *Licenciatura*; *Especialización*; *Maestría*
Last Updated: 29/08/12

GLORIA CAMPOBELLO DANCE SCHOOL

Escuela de Danza Gloria Campobello

Blvd. Fundadores, 312 Col. Juárez, Tijuana, Baja California
EMail: informes@gloriacampobello.com
Website: http://www.gloriacampobello.com

Directora: Margarita Robles Regalado

Programmes

Dance (Dance)

History: Founded 1964.

Main Language(s) of Instruction: Spanish

Degrees and Diplomas: *Licenciatura*
Last Updated: 20/02/13

GRUPO SOL UNIVERSITY CENTRE

Centro Universitario Grupo Sol (EPCA)

Av. Cuauhtémoc No. 60, Col. Doctores, 06050 México, D.F.
Tel: +52(55) 55-78-78-15
EMail: rectoria@cugs.edu.mx

Rector: Heriberto Solís Torres

Programmes

Administration and Accountancy (Accountancy; Administration)

Further Information: Also Santo Tomas Branch

Degrees and Diplomas: *Licenciatura*; *Maestría*
Last Updated: 28/02/08

GUADALAJARA LAMAR UNIVERSITY

Universidad Guadalajara Lamar

José Guadalupe Zuno Hernández 1994, Col. Americana, Esq. con Chapultepec, 44100 Guadalajara, Jalisco
Tel: +52(33) 38-25-09-90
Website: http://www.lamar.edu.mx

Rector: Ricardo Ramírez Ángulo (1978-)

Areas

Art, Architecture and Design (Architecture; Design; Interior Design); **Economics, Administration and Gastronomy** (Accountancy; Business Administration; Cooking and Catering; International Business; Marketing; Tourism); **Exact Sciences and Engineering** (Civil Engineering; Computer Engineering; Electronic Engineering; Industrial Engineering; Telecommunications Engineering); **Health Sciences** (Dentistry; Medicine; Nutrition; Psychology; Surgery);

Social Sciences and Humanities (Communication Studies; Education; Educational Administration; Journalism; Law)

Further Information: Also Hidalgo I, Hidalgo II, Vallarta, Guadalupe Zona and Palomar campuses

History: Founded 1978.

Admission Requirements: Certificado de Secundaria

Main Language(s) of Instruction: Spanish

Degrees and Diplomas: *Licenciatura*; *Especialización*; *Maestría*: Education; Law; Clinical Psychology

Last Updated: 03/04/13

GUADALUPE NURSING SCHOOL

Escuela de Enfermeras de Guadalupe, A.C.

Plaza San Lorenzo, 13, Col. Tepeyac Insurgentes, Delegación Gustavo A. Madero, 07020 México, D.F.

Tel: +52(55) 57-48-01-37

Fax: +52(55) 57-81-14-04

EMail: escenter@prodigy.net.mx

Directora: Concepción Pucheta Ovil

Programmes

Nursing and Obstetrics (Gynaecology and Obstetrics; Nursing)

Degrees and Diplomas: *Licenciatura*: 8 sem.

Last Updated: 28/08/12

HAHNEMANN HOMEOPATHY

Homeopatas Hahnemann

Calle Pedro Moreno, 935, 44140 Guadalajara, Jalisco

Tel: +52(33) 38-25-79-17

EMail: homeopatash@yahoo.com.mx

Directora: Maria Audelia Avedoy Delgado

EMail: jorgeolvera1818@hotmail.com

Programmes

Homeopathy (Homeopathy)

History: Founded 1988.

Main Language(s) of Instruction: Spanish

Degrees and Diplomas: *Licenciatura*; *Maestría*

Last Updated: 28/10/09

HEALTH EDUCATION COMPLEX

Complejo Educativo de la Salud

Río Grijalva, 1003, León, Guanajuato

Director: Mario Martínez Rangel

Programmes

Health Sciences (Health Sciences)

Main Language(s) of Instruction: Spanish

Degrees and Diplomas: *Licenciatura*

Last Updated: 24/08/12

HEBREW UNIVERSITY

Universidad Hebraica (UH)

Prol. Av. De los Bosques no. 292A, 5° piso Colonia lomas del Chamizal, 05129 México, Distrito Federal

Tel: +52(5) 245-8600

EMail: comunicacion@universidadhebraica.edu.mx

Website: http://www.universidadhebraica.edu.mx/

Rector: Daniel Fainstein (2002-)

Programmes

Educational Sciences (Educational Sciences); **Educational Sciences and Techniques** (Education; Educational Sciences; Educational Technology); **Jewish Studies** (Aesthetics; Art History; Jewish Studies); **Pedagogy** (Pedagogy)

History: Founded 1992, acquired present status 1996.

Admission Requirements: Secondary school certificate, and practice of Spanish, English, and Hebrew

Main Language(s) of Instruction: Spanish, English and Hebrew

Degrees and Diplomas: *Licenciatura*: Educational Science; Pedagogy, 4 yrs; *Licenciatura*: Educational Science and Techniques, 3 yrs; *Maestría*: Educational Science; Jewish Studies, a further 2 yrs

Student Services: Academic counselling, Cultural centre, Employment services, Language programs, Nursery care

Publications: Revista Universidad Hebraica, Academic Journal *(biennially)*

Last Updated: 03/04/13

HERMANN HESSE COLLEGE

Colegio Hermann Hesse

Cedro, 219, Col. Santa María la Ribera, Delegación Cuauhtémoc, 06400 México, D.F.

Tel: +52(55) 52-47-15-54

Website: http://colegiohermannhesse.edu.mx

Director: Vianney Arturo Vergara Mariño (1998-)

History: Founded 1998.

Degrees and Diplomas: *Licenciatura*

Last Updated: 04/04/08

HERNÁN CORTÉS UNIVERSITY

Universidad Hernán Cortés

Angel Nuñez Beltrán No. 149, Col. Emiliano Zapata, 91000 Xalapa, Veracruz

Tel: +52(228) 812-20-24

EMail: informes@uhc.edu.mx

Website: http://uhc.com.mx

Rectora: Irma Rodríguez Pérez

Programmes

Accountancy (Accountancy); **Advertising and Public Relations** (Advertising and Publicity; Public Relations); **Business Administration** (Business Administration); **Business Computing** (Business Computing); **Communication** (Communication Studies; Journalism; Photography; Public Relations; Radio and Television Broadcasting); **Educational Sciences** (Educational Sciences); **Law** (Administrative Law; Civil Law; International Law; Labour Law; Private Law); **Marketing** (Marketing); **Physical Education and Sports** (Physical Education; Sports); **Tourism** (Tourism)

History: Founded 1997.

Main Language(s) of Instruction: Spanish

Degrees and Diplomas: *Licenciatura*; *Maestría*

Libraries: Yes

Last Updated: 03/10/12

HIDALGO INSTITUTE OF HIGHER STUDIES

Instituto de Estudios Superiores Hidalgo

Avenida Texcoco, 51, Los Reyes Acaquilpán, 56400 Los Reyes La Paz, Estado de México

Tel: +52(55) 58-55-12-91

Fax: +52(55) 58-55-05-47

EMail: iesh2001@yahoo.com.mx

Director: Luis Manuel Ceja García

Programmes

Accountancy (Accountancy); **Law**

Main Language(s) of Instruction: Spanish

Degrees and Diplomas: *Licenciatura*

Last Updated: 04/03/13

HIGHER COLLEGE OF MEXICO

Colegio Superior de México

Las Rosas, 106, Esq. Eucaliptos, Col. Reforma, 68000 Oaxaca, Oaxaca

Tel: +52(951) 519-96-63

Website: http://www.angelfire.com/de/cosumex/

Director: Gerardo Valentin Zavaleta Ruíz

Programmes

Accountancy and Business Administration (Accountancy; Business Administration); **Computer Networks** (Computer Networks); **Family Psychology** (Social Psychology)

Main Language(s) of Instruction: Spanish

Degrees and Diplomas: *Licenciatura*
Last Updated: 23/08/12

HIGHER COLLEGE OF SAN CARLOS

Colegio Mayor de San Carlos

Campus Pacífico, Avenida Lázaro Cárdenas, 21, Col. La Haciendita, 03900 Chilpancingo de los Bravo, Guerrero
Tel: +52(747) 471-5121
Fax: +52(747) 471-5121
EMail: admi_educ@hotmail.com; posgrados2004@yahoo.com.mx
Website: http://colegiomayor.edu.mx/

Directora: Sandra Sánchez Álvarez

Programmes
Administration (Administration; Commercial Law; E-Business/Commerce; Economics; Finance; Human Resources; Marketing; Taxation); **Education** (Education); **Fiscal Law** (Economics; Finance; Fiscal Law; International Business; Law; Taxation)

History: Founded 1999.

Degrees and Diplomas: *Licenciatura*; *Maestría*; *Doctorado*
Last Updated: 23/08/12

HIGHER EDUCATION CENTRE

Centro Educativo de Estudios Superiores

Colón 90, 44100 Guadalajara, Jalisco
Tel: +52(33) 36-13-56-28
Fax: +52(33) 36-13-27-41

Director: José Luis Gallegos Escobedo

Programmes
Business Computing (Business Computing); **Communication Sciences** (Communication Studies); **Psychology** (Psychology)

History: Founded 2002.

Main Language(s) of Instruction: Spanish

Degrees and Diplomas: *Licenciatura*
Last Updated: 27/10/09

HIGHER INSTITUTE OF INTERNATIONAL BUSINESS EDUCATION AND RESEARCH

Instituto de Enseñanza e Investigación Superior en Comercio Internacional

Cafetal, 537, Col. Granjas, Delegación, Itzcalco, 08400 México, D.F.
Tel: +52(55) 56-57-12-66
Fax: +52(55) 56-57-12-66
EMail: iesci@fc.camoapa.com.mx

Director General: Juan Manuel Ávila García (1979-)

Programmes
International Business (International Business)

History: Founded 1979.

Main Language(s) of Instruction: Spanish

Degrees and Diplomas: *Licenciatura*
Last Updated: 28/02/13

HIGHER TEACHER TRAINING SCHOOL OF CIUDAD MADERO, A.C.

Escuela Normal Superior de Ciudad Madero, A.C.

Díaz Mirón y 5 de Mayo, 306, Col. Felipe Carrillo Puerto, 89430 Ciudad Madero, Tamaulipas
Tel: +52(833) 215-21-92 +52(833) 216-37-45
Fax: +52(833) 216-35-38
EMail: informes@enscm.com.mx
Website: http://www.enscm.com.mx

Director: Oscar Hernández Gutiérrez

Programmes
Biology; **Chemistry**; **Civics and Ethics** (Civics; Ethics); **Foreign Languages** (Modern Languages); **Geography** (Geography); **History**; **Mathematics** (Mathematics; Mathematics Education); **Physical Education** (Physical Education); **Physics** (Physics); **Preschool Education**; **Spanish** (Spanish)

History: Founded 1979.

Main Language(s) of Instruction: Spanish

Degrees and Diplomas: *Licenciatura*
Last Updated: 27/02/13

HIGHER TEACHER TRAINING SCHOOL OF DURANGO

Escuela Normal Superior de Durango

Calle Francisco de Ibarra, 1000-A, Col. Nueva Viscaya, 34080 Durango, Durango

Director: Jorge Aguilar Moncada

Programmes
Teacher Training (Teacher Training)

Main Language(s) of Instruction: Spanish

Degrees and Diplomas: *Licenciatura*; *Maestría*
Last Updated: 25/02/13

HIGHER TEACHER TRAINING SCHOOL OF LA LAGUNA

Escuela Normal Superior de La Laguna

Blvd. Guadalupe Victoria s/n, Col. Sacramento, 27050 Gómez Palacio, Durango
EMail: cide_difusion@normalsuperiordelalagunamm.edu.mx
Website: http://www.normalsuperiordelalagunamm.edu.mx

Director: J. Ángel Ibarra López

Programmes
Education (Secondary Education)

History: Founded 1974.

Main Language(s) of Instruction: Spanish

Degrees and Diplomas: *Licenciatura*
Last Updated: 25/02/13

HIGHER TEACHER TRAINING SCHOOL OF TAMAULIPAS

Escuela Normal Superior de Tamaulipas, A.C.

Apartado Postal 328, Km. 2 Carretera a Soto la Marina, Col. Horacio Terán, 87130 Ciudad Victoria, Tamaulipas
Tel: +52(834) 412-43-57
Fax: +52(834) 412-67-01
EMail: enstam@prodigy.net.mx

Directora: Josefina Flores Vázque

Programmes
Teacher Training (Teacher Training)

History: Founded 1969.

Main Language(s) of Instruction: Spanish

Degrees and Diplomas: *Maestría*
Last Updated: 26/02/13

HIGHER TEACHER TRAINING SCHOOL OF THE SOUTH OF TAMAULIPAS

Escuela Normal Superior del Sur de Tamaulipas

Calle México, 415, Col. Guadalupe, 89120 Tampico, Tamaulipas
Tel: +52(833) 213-62-70
Fax: +52(833) 213-41-27
EMail: info@ensst.com

Directora: Esperanza Garza Rodríguez

Programmes
Secondary Education (Art Education; Biology; Chemistry; English; Ethics; Geography; History; Mathematics; Physical Education; Physics; Secondary Education; Spanish; Technology)

History: Founded 1975.

Main Language(s) of Instruction: Spanish

Degrees and Diplomas: *Licenciatura*
Last Updated: 31/03/08

HIGHER TECHNOLOGICAL INSTITUTE OF EL GRULLO

Instituto Tecnológico Superior de El Grullo
Km 5. Carretera El Grullo - Ejutla S/N Puerta de Barro, El Grullo, Jalisco
Tel: +52(321) 387-34-35
EMail: jonas.michel@itselgrullo.edu.mx
Website: http://itselgrullo.edu.mx

Director: Pedro Agustin Duran Leal
EMail: pduran@itselgrullo.edu.mx

Programmes
Architecture (Architecture); **Business Administration** (Business Administration); **Engineering** (Computer Engineering; Electronic Engineering; Engineering; Industrial Engineering; Mechanical Engineering)
History: Founded 2003.
Main Language(s) of Instruction: Spanish
Degrees and Diplomas: *Licenciatura*
Last Updated: 26/03/13

HIGHER TECHNOLOGICAL INSTITUTE OF LOS MOCHIS

Instituto Tecnológico Superior de Los Mochis, S.C.
Marcial Ordóñez, 71, Ote., 81280 Los Mochis, Sinaloa
Tel: +52(668) 812-92-50
EMail: mayala@itesum.edu.mx
Website: http://www.itesum.edu.mx
Director: Manuel Alonso Ayala Castro

Programmes
Computer Science (Business Computing; Computer Science); **Engineering** (Electronic Engineering; Engineering; Telecommunications Engineering); **Graphic Design** (Graphic Design); **Music** (Music); **Pedagogy** (Pedagogy); **Physical Education and Sport** (Physical Education; Sports)
History: Founded 1985.
Main Language(s) of Instruction: Spanish
Degrees and Diplomas: *Licenciatura*; *Maestría*: Telecommunications; Pedagogy
Last Updated: 20/03/13

HIGHER TECHNOLOGICAL INSTITUTE OF SAN MIGUEL EL GRANDE

Instituto Tecnológico Superior de San Miguel el Grande

Melchor Ocampo S/N, San Miguel el Grande, Oaxaca
Tel: +52(953) 503-91-34
EMail: tecnologico@itsmigra.edu.mx
Website: http://itsmigra.edu.mx
Director: Jaime Chávez Flores

Programmes
Community Development (Development Studies); **Engineering** (Forest Management; Information Technology)
History: Founded 2004.
Main Language(s) of Instruction: Spanish
Degrees and Diplomas: *Licenciatura*
Last Updated: 29/03/13

HIGHER TECHNOLOGICAL INSTITUTE OF SINAOLA

Instituto Tecnológico Superior de Sinaloa
Calle Aquiles Serdan No.2443 1er. Piso, 82010 Mazatlán, Sinaloa
Tel: +52(669) 981-74-46
EMail: halcones@itesus.edu.mx
Website: http://www.itesus.edu.mx/
Director: Gerardo López del Río

Programmes
Business Computing (Business Computing); **Criminology** (Criminology); **Engineering** (Computer Engineering; Electronic Engineering; Telecommunications Engineering); **Graphic Design** (Graphic Design); **Law** (Law); **Marketing** (Marketing); **Physical Education and Sports** (Physical Education; Sports); **Physiotherapy** (Physical Therapy); **Psychology** (Clinical Psychology; Educational Psychology)
History: Founded 1989.
Main Language(s) of Instruction: Spanish
Degrees and Diplomas: *Licenciatura*; *Maestría*
Last Updated: 21/03/13

HIPPOCRATES UNIVERSITY OF ACAPULCO

Universidad Hipócrates de Acapulco
Av. Andrés de Urdaneta No. 360, y M. López de Legazpi No. 15, Fracc. Hornos, 39350 Acapulco de Juárez, Guerrero
Tel: +52(744) 485-79-91
Fax: +52(744) 485-33-67
EMail: contacto@uhipocrates.edu.mx
Website: http://www.uhipocrates.edu.mx
Rector: Armando Hernández Torres (1986-)

Programmes
Architecture (Architecture); **Business Administration and Law** (Accountancy; Advertising and Publicity; Business Administration; Law); **Computer Engineering**; **Social Sciences** (Communication Studies; Educational Psychology; Psychology; Social Sciences)
History: Founded 1986 as Intituto Hipocrates
Degrees and Diplomas: *Bachillerato*; *Licenciatura*; *Maestría*
Last Updated: 26/03/09

HISPANIC UNIVERSITY

Universidad Hispana
31 Poniente, 118, Colonia Chulavista, 72420 Puebla, Puebla
Tel: +52(222) 266-30-10
EMail: uhispana@puebla.megared.net.mx
Website: http://www.uhispana.net
Rector: Adolfo G. Figueroa Martínez
International Relations: Andrea Estupinán Villanueva

Programmes
Administration (Accountancy; Administration; Business Administration; Economics); **Architecture** (Architecture); **Engineering** (Computer Engineering; Electronic Engineering); **Graphic Communication and Advertising** (Advertising and Publicity; Graphic Design); **Graphic Design** (Graphic Design); **Law** (Law); **Psychology** (Psychology)
History: Founded 1985.
Academic Year: August to June
Admission Requirements: Bachillerato, Preparatoria or equivalent
Main Language(s) of Instruction: Spanish
Degrees and Diplomas: *Licenciatura*: 4 yrs
Student Services: Academic counselling, Cultural centre, Employment services, Handicapped facilities, Language programs, Sports facilities
Last Updated: 04/10/12

HISPANIC-AMERICAN EDUCATIONAL COMPLEX

Complejo Educativo Hispanoamericano, A.C
Felipe B. Martínez Chapa s/n, Col. Real del Campestre, 37120 León, Guanajuato
Tel: +52(477) 781-06-21
Fax: +52(477) 781-06-22
EMail: hispano@cehispano.edu.mx
Website: http://www.cehispano.edu.mx
Directora General: Patricia Aranda Orozco (1997-)

Programmes
Psychology (Psychology); **Secondary Education** (Secondary Education)
History: Founded 1980.
Main Language(s) of Instruction: Spanish

Degrees and Diplomas: *Licenciatura*
Last Updated: 24/08/12

HISPANIC-ANGLO-FRENCH CENTRE FOR ADVANCED STUDIES OF XALAPA

Centro de Estudios Superiores Hispano Anglo Francés de Xalapa

Cerrada de Panuco, 45, Col. Obreros Textiles, 91060 Xalapa, Veracruz
Tel: +52(228) 818-44-23
Fax: +52(228) 818-65-77
EMail: ceshaf@yahoo.com.mx

Directora: María del Pilar Landeros López (1993-)

Programmes
Accountancy (Accountancy); **Dietetics and Nutrition** (Dietetics; Nutrition); **Law** (Law)

History: Founded 1993.
Main Language(s) of Instruction: Spanish
Degrees and Diplomas: *Licenciatura*
Last Updated: 16/07/12

HISPANIC-MEXICAN POLYTECHNIC UNIVERSITY

Universidad Politécnica Hispano Mexicana

25 Poniente, 503, Col. Chulavista, 72420 Puebla, Puebla
Tel: +52(222) 240-65-73 +52(222) 240-05-85
Fax: +52(222) 237-53-64
EMail: uphm2000@hotmail.com
Website: http://www.uphm.edu.mx

Rector: Fausto Díaz Guttiérez EMail: fdiaz@uphm.edu.mx

Programmes
Accountancy (Accountancy); **Gastronomy** (Cooking and Catering); **Industrial Engineering** (Industrial Engineering); **International Business** (International Business); **Law** (Law); **Marketing and Advertising** (Advertising and Publicity; Marketing); **Tourism** (Tourism)

History: Founded 1993.
Main Language(s) of Instruction: Spanish
Degrees and Diplomas: *Licenciatura*
Last Updated: 05/04/13

HISPANIC-MEXICAN UNIVERSITY

Universidad Hispano Mexicana

El Huizache No. 16, 53520 Naucalpán de Juárez, Estado de México
Tel: +52(555) 343-88-14
Fax: +52(555) 343-85-93
EMail: informes@uhm.edu.mx

Rector: Luis L. Calzado Rodríguez (1985-)

Programmes
International Business (International Business)

History: Founded 1985. A private institution. Degrees recognized by the National University of Mexico.
Admission Requirements: Secondary school certificate (bachillerato)
Main Language(s) of Instruction: Spanish
Degrees and Diplomas: *Licenciatura*; *Especialización*; *Maestría*
Last Updated: 11/02/08

HISPANIC-MEXICAN UNIVERSITY CENTRE

Centro Universitario Hispano Mexicano

Ing. Ernesto Domínguez, 111, Fracc. Reforma, 91919 Veracruz, Veracruz
Tel: +52(229) 935-68-22
Fax: +52(229) 937-39-19 +52(229) 937-27-20
EMail: info@cuhm.mx
Website: http://www.cuhm.mx

Rectora: Mercedes Ramírez Llaca (2000-)
EMail: mramirez@cuhm.mx

Programmes
Communication and Advertising (Advertising and Publicity; Communication Studies); **Industrial Engineering** (Industrial Engineering); **International Business** (International Business); **Marketing** (Marketing)

History: Founded 1993.
Admission Requirements: Bachillerato
Main Language(s) of Instruction: Spanish
Degrees and Diplomas: *Licenciatura*; *Especialización*; *Maestría*
Last Updated: 25/07/12

HISPANIC UNIVERSITY CENTRE OF TEXMELUCAN

Centro Universitario Hispánico de Texmelucán

Francisco I Madero Norte, 102, Col. Domingo Arenas, 74050 San Martín Texmelucán, Puebla
Tel: +52(248) 484-42-22
Fax: +52(248) 484-42-22
EMail: cuht@cumpu-redes.mx

Directora: María Violeta Martínez Ahuatzi

Programmes
Computer Engineering (Computer Engineering)

Degrees and Diplomas: *Licenciatura*: 8 sem.
Last Updated: 27/03/08

HOMEOPATHY OF GUADALAJARA

Homeopatía de Guadalajara, A. C.

Galileo Galilei, 4131, Fraccionamiento Arboledas, 45070 Zapopan, Jalisco
Tel: +52(33) 36-32-90-65
EMail: info@hdeg.com.mx
Website: http://www.hdeg.com.mx/

Director: José Antonio Rafael Ugartechea Marrón
EMail: director@hdeg.com.mx

Programmes
Homeopathy (Homeopathy)

History: Founded 1976.
Admission Requirements: Título y Cédula Profesional de Médico
Main Language(s) of Instruction: Spanish
Degrees and Diplomas: *Especialización*
Last Updated: 30/08/12

HORACIO ZUÑIGA UNIVERSITY STUDIES CENTRE

Centro de Estudios Universitarios Horacio Zuñiga

Av. Toluca Num. 300, 52080 Villa Cuauhtémoc, Estado de México
Tel: +52(719) 249-6251
Website: http://www.ceuhz.com

Director: Juan Antonio Colín Ortiz

Programmes
Administration and Social Sciences (Accountancy; Administration; Business Computing; International Business; Law; Management; Public Administration)

Main Language(s) of Instruction: Spanish
Degrees and Diplomas: *Licenciatura*: 9-10 sem.
Last Updated: 17/07/12

HOUSE OF FRANCE INSTITUTE FOR HIGHER STUDIES IN FASHION

Instituto de Estudios Superiores de Moda Casa de Francia

Calle Amberes 70, Col. Benito Juárez, Delegación Cuauhtémoc, 06600 México, D.F.
Tel: +52(55) 55-14-25-94
Fax: +52(55) 52-07-85-77
EMail: informes@iesmoda.edu.mx
Website: http://www.iesmoda.edu.mx

Directora: C. Emmanuele M.M. de Román (1998-)

Programmes
Fashion Design (Fashion Design)

Degrees and Diplomas: *Licenciatura*
Last Updated: 01/03/13

HUMANIST INSTITUTE OF GESTALT THERAPY

Instituto Humanista de Psicoterapia Gestalt, A.C.
Africa 6, Col. La Concepción, Delegación Coyoacán, 04020 México, D.F.
Tel: +52(55) 55-54-47-97
Fax: +52(55) 55-54-45-82
EMail: coyoacan@gestalthumanista.com
Website: http://www.gestalthumanista.com

Rectora: Myriam Muñoz Polit

Programmes
Human Development (Development Studies; Educational and Student Counselling; Educational Psychology; Leadership; Pedagogy; Psychology; Psychotherapy)

Further Information: Also branches in Cancun; Tuxtla Gutiérrez; Naucalpan; Morelia; Puebla; Saltillo; Tijuana; and Vera Cruz

History: Founded 1985.

Degrees and Diplomas: *Especialización*; *Maestría*
Last Updated: 05/03/13

HUMANIST INSTITUTE OF GESTALT THERAPY OF QUERETARO

Instituto Humanista de Psicoterapia Gestalt de Querétaro
Colombia, 3, Col. Lomas de Querétaro, 76190 Querétaro, Querétaro
Tel: +52(442) 216-02-85
EMail: informes@utopiagestalt.com
Website: http://www.utopiagestalt.com

Directora: María de Lourdes Zozaya y Rubio

Programmes
Family Therapy (Family Studies); **Psychotherapy** (Psychotherapy)

Main Language(s) of Instruction: Spanish

Degrees and Diplomas: *Especialización*; *Maestría*
Last Updated: 05/03/13

HUMANIST UNIVERSITY OF THE AMERICAS

Universidad Humanista de las Américas
Martín de Zavala no 510 Sur Esquina 15 de Mayo, Centro, 64000 Monterrey, Nuevo León
Tel: +52(81) 83-40-57-00
EMail: escolar@uha.edu.mx
Website: http://uha.edu.mx

Rector: Bernardo Martínez Raposú (1989-)
EMail: bernardom@upmty.edu.mx.

Programmes
Accountancy (Accountancy); **Anthropology** (Anthropology); **Archaeology** (Archaeology); **Art and Design** (Fine Arts; Graphic Design); **Business Administration** (Business Administration); **Communication** (Communication Studies; Mass Communication); **Economics** (Economics); **Education** (Education); **Hotel and Tourism** (Hotel Management; Tourism); **International Commerce** (International Business); **Law** (Law); **Marketing** (Marketing); **Nutrition** (Nutrition); **Paleontology** (Paleontology); **Philosophy** (Philosophy); **Psychology** (Psychology); **Sociology** (Sociology)

History: Founded 1989 as Centro Educativo Universitario Panamericano.

Main Language(s) of Instruction: Spanish

Degrees and Diplomas: *Licenciatura*; *Maestría*; *Doctorado*

Special Facilities: Museum
Last Updated: 04/10/12

HUMANITAS UNIVERSITY

Universidad Humanitas
California, 212, Col. del Valle, Delegación Benito Juárez, 03100 México, D.F.
Tel: +52(55) 55-59-82-84 +52(55) 55-59-38-88
Fax: +52(55) 55-59-23-36
EMail: humanitas@hotmail.com
Website: http://www.universidadhumanitas.com

Rector: Juan Luis González Alcántara Carrancá

Programmes
Administration and Accountancy (Accountancy; Administration; Business Administration); **Education** (Education); **Law** (Law); **Political Science** (Political Sciences); **Psychology** (Psychology)

Further Information: Also branches in Cancun, Tijuana, Guadalajara and Cuernavaca

History: Founded 1979.

Main Language(s) of Instruction: Spanish

Degrees and Diplomas: *Licenciatura*; *Maestría*; *Doctorado*
Last Updated: 03/04/13

IAMP TECHNOLOGICAL AND UNIVERSITY STUDIES CENTRE

Centro de Estudios Tecnológicos y Universitarios IAMP
Guillermo Prieto, 2, Col. San Rafael, Delegación Cuauhtémoc, 06470 México, D.F.
Tel: +52(55) 55-35-66-03
Fax: +52(55) 55-92-62-25
EMail: iamp@prodigy.net.mx
Website: http://www.cetuiamp.edu.mx

Director: Jaime Garduño Garfias (1971-)

Programmes
Accountancy (Accountancy); **Administration** (Administration); **Computer Science** (Computer Science); **Law** (Law); **Marketing** (Marketing)

History: Founded 1971 as Instituto Activo de Mercadotecnia y Publicidad.

Main Language(s) of Instruction: Spanish

Degrees and Diplomas: *Licenciatura*; *Especialización*; *Maestría*
Last Updated: 17/07/12

IBERO-AMERICAN CENTRE OF TECHNOLOGICAL STUDIES, MANTE

Centro de Estudios Tecnológicos Iberoamericana Mante
Pedro José Méndez, 903, Ote., 89800 Ciudad Mante, Tamaulipas
Tel: +52(831) 122-51-70 +52(831) 122-09-50

Directora: Elizabeth Robbins Williams (1991-)

Programmes
Pedagogy (Pedagogy); **Social Work** (Social Work)

History: Founded 1991.

Main Language(s) of Instruction: Spanish

Degrees and Diplomas: *Licenciatura*
Last Updated: 10/03/08

IBERO-AMERICAN INSTITUTE OF COMPUTER SCIENCE

Instituto Iberoamericano de Informática, S.C.
Calzada de Tlalpán, 1064, Col. Nativitas, Delegación Benito Juárez, 03500 México, D.F.
Tel: +52(55) 55-32-11-67 +52(55) 55-39-92-64
Fax: +52(55) 55-32-18-15

Directora: Laura Rodríguez Shomar

Programmes
Computer Science (Computer Science)

Main Language(s) of Instruction: Spanish

Degrees and Diplomas: *Licenciatura*

IBERO-AMERICAN INSTITUTE OF TECHNOLOGY OF ARAGÓN

Tecnológico Iberoamericano Aragón

Avenida Yang-Tse, 288, Col. Valle de Aragón, 1era. Sección, 57100 Nezahualcóyotl, Estado de México
Tel: +52(55) 57-12-57-05
EMail: tecaragon@yahoo.com
Website: http://www.tecaragon.edu.mx

Director: Alfredo Baños Martínez (1999-)

Programmes
Accountancy (Accountancy); **Business Administration** (Business Administration); **Computer Science** (Computer Science); **Law** (Law); **Psychology** (Psychology)

History: Founded 1999.

Main Language(s) of Instruction: Spanish

Degrees and Diplomas: *Licenciatura*

Last Updated: 25/03/13

IBERO-AMERICAN TECHNOLOGICAL UNIVERSITY

Universidad Tecnológica Iberoamericana

Carretera Tenango-La Marquesa km 20.05, 52600 Santiago Tianguistenco, Estado de México
Tel: +52(713) 135-46-16
EMail: uniteciberoamericana@prodigy.net.mx
Website: http://uteci.com.mx

Director: Alejandro Saldívar Arellano (1997-)

Programmes
Accountancy (Accountancy); **Administration** (Administration; Business Administration; Business Computing; Tourism); **Communication** (Communication Studies); **Computer Science** (Computer Science); **Criminology** (Criminology); **Dentistry** (Dentistry); **Education** (Education); **Gastronomy** (Cooking and Catering); **Marketing** (Marketing); **Psychology** (Psychology)

History: Founded 1997.

Main Language(s) of Instruction: Spanish

Degrees and Diplomas: *Licenciatura*

Last Updated: 05/04/13

IBERO-AMERICAN TECHNOLOGICAL UNIVERSITY INSTIUTE OF POZA RICA

Tecnológico Universitario Iberoamericano de Poza Rica, S.C.

Guadalupe Victoria, 106, Col. 27 de Septiembre, 93320 Poza Rica, Veracruz
Tel: +52(782) 822-18-14 +52(782) 823-40-49

Directora: Rosario Priego Martínez

Programmes
Engineering (Engineering); **Technology** (Technology)

Main Language(s) of Instruction: Spanish

Degrees and Diplomas: *Licenciatura*

Last Updated: 24/04/08

IAU IBERO-AMERICAN UNIVERSITY, MEXICO CITY

Universidad Iberoamericana, Ciudad de México (UIA)

Prolongación Paseo de la Reforma, 880, Col. Lomas de Santa Fé, Delegación Álvaro Obregón, 01219 México, D.F.
Tel: +52(55) 5950-4000
Fax: +52(55) 5292-2133
EMail: javier.prado@uia.mx
Website: http://www.uia.mx

Rector: José Morales Orozco, S.J. (2004-)
EMail: jose.morales@ibero.mx

Vicerrector Académico: Javier Prado Galán

International Relations: Luis Núñez Gornés, Director of Academic Cooperation EMail: luis.nunez@ ibero.mx

Divisions
Humanities and Communication (Arts and Humanities; Communication Studies; Development Studies; Education; Educational Research; Fine Arts; History; Literature; Philosophy; Religion; Social Welfare); **Science, Art and Technology** (Architecture; Chemistry; Design; Engineering; Mathematics; Physics; Town Planning); **Social Studies** (Business Administration; Economics; Health Sciences; International Studies; Law; Political Sciences; Psychology; Social Sciences)

Further Information: Also Study Abroad programme. Courses for foreign students. Centro de Extensión Saltillo

History: Founded 1943 as university cultural centre with faculty of Philosophy, became university 1952. Degrees recognized by the Ministry of Education.

Governing Bodies: Senado Universitario; Consejo Universitario; Comités Académicos

Academic Year: January to December (January-May; August-December). Intensive Summer Term (May-July)

Admission Requirements: Secondary school certificate (bachillerato) or recognized foreign equivalent, and entrance examination

Main Language(s) of Instruction: Spanish

International Co-operation: With universities in Canada, Latin America, USA, Europe and Asia

Degrees and Diplomas: *Licenciatura*: Accountancy; Biomedical Engineering; Business Administration; Chemical Engineering; Civil Engineering; Communication Studies; Computer Science and Electronics; Digital Design; Economics; Electronic and Telecommunication Engineering; Food Engineering; Graphic Design; History; History of Art; Hospitality Management; Human Resources; Industrial Design; Industrial Engineering; International Business Administration; International Relations; Latin American Literature; Law; Marketing; Mechanical and Electrical Engineering; Mechatronic Engineering; Philosophy; Physics Engineering; Psychology; Religious Sciences; Sociology; Software Engineering; Textile Design, 4 yrs; *Licenciatura*: Architecture, 5 yrs; *Especialización*: Special Education, 1 1/2 yrs; *Maestría*: Art Studies; Business Administration; Chemical Sciences Engineering; Communication; Community Counselling; Construction Management; Engineering in Enterprise Systems Engineering; History; Human Development; Human Rights; Humanist Education; International Business Law; Management in Information Technology Services; Philosophy; Projects for Urban Development; Quality Engineering; Research and Development; Social Anthropology; Sociology; Strategic Design and Innovation; Theology and Modern Society, 2 yrs; *Doctorado*: Education; History; Modern Literature; Philosophy; Psychology; Social and Political Sciences; Social Anthropology, 3 yrs

Student Services: Cultural centre, Employment services, Foreign student adviser, Handicapped facilities, Health services, Language programs, Nursery care, Sports facilities

Special Facilities: Movie Studio; TV Studio; Radio Studio and Station; Observatory, Engineering Laboratories

Libraries: 'Francisco Xavier Clavigero' Library

Publications: Arqui Tectónica, Publication of the Department of Architecture, Urbanism and Design. *(biennially)*; Boletín de Relaciones Industriales, Publication on Administration and Public Accountancy *(biennially)*; Comunidad Ibero; Cuadernos de Filosofía; Documentos de Investigación, Department of Economics *(biennially)*; Historia y Geografía, Publication of the Department of History *(biannually)*; Human Resources Online; Psychología Iberoamericana; Revista de Filosofía, Publication of the Department of Philosophy. *(quarterly)*; Revista Didac, Electronic Version *(biennially)*; Revista Iberoamericana de Comunicación, Department of Communication. Electronic Version. *(biennially)*; Revista Jurídica: Anuario de Derecho de la Ibero; Revista Psicología Iberoamericana *(quarterly)*

Student Numbers *2012-2013*: Total 10,549

Last Updated: 04/10/12

IBERO-AMERICAN UNIVERSITY LEÓN

UNIVERSIDAD IBEROAMERICANA LEÓN (UIA/LEON)

Apartado postal 1-26, Blvd. Jorge Bertiz Campero, 1640, Cañada de Alfaro, 37238 León, Guanajuato
Tel: +52(477) 710-06-06
Fax: +52(477) 711-54-77
EMail: antonio.cruz@leon.uia.mx
Website: http://www.leon.uia.mx

Rector: Marco Antonio Bran Flores (2012-)

Departments

Art and Design (Architecture; Design; Graphic Design; Interior Design; Landscape Architecture; Photography); **Basic Sciences** (Biotechnology; Environmental Studies; Food Science; Nanotechnology; Nutrition; Safety Engineering; Statistics); **Economics and Administrative Sciences** (Accountancy; Business Administration; International Business; Marketing; Tourism); **Education** (Education); **Engineering** (Civil Engineering; Computer Engineering; Electrical Engineering; Electronic Engineering; Industrial Engineering; Mechanical Engineering; Telecommunications Engineering); **Human and Social Sciences** (Communication Studies; Psychology; Psychotherapy); **Law** (Constitutional Law; Criminal Law; International Relations; Law; Political Sciences; Public Administration)

History: Founded 1978.

Governing Bodies: Senado Universitario

Academic Year: August to May (August-December;January-May); also summer session May to July

Admission Requirements: Certificado de Bachillerato o Preparatoria o Constancia con promedio global.

Fees: (Pesos): exam fee, 500; 5,540, per semester

Main Language(s) of Instruction: Spanish

International Co-operation: With universities in Spain, France, Canada, Italy, Brazil and South America

Degrees and Diplomas: *Licenciatura*: 4 yrs; *Maestría*; *Doctorado*

Student Services: Academic counselling, Cultural centre, Employment services, Foreign student adviser, Handicapped facilities, Health services, Language programs, Nursery care, Social counselling, Sports facilities

Student Residential Facilities: Yes

Special Facilities: Art Gallery

Libraries: Yes

Publications: Cuadernos de la Equidad, Publication of the university programme on poverty *(biennially)*

IBERO-AMERICAN UNIVERSITY PUEBLA

UNIVERSIDAD IBEROAMERICANA PUEBLA (UIA PUEBLA)

Apartado postal 1436, Blvd. del Niño Poblano, 2901, Unidad Territorial Atlixcayotl, 72430 Puebla, Puebla
Tel: +52(222) 229-07-00 +52(222) 372-30-00
Fax: +52(222) 229-07-36
Website: http://www.iberopuebla.edu.mx

Rector: Juan Luis Hernández Avendaño
Tel: +52 (222) 229-07-31, Fax: +52 (222) 231-01-80

Director General de Promoción y Desarrollo Institucional: Javier Sanchez-Diaz de Rivera
EMail: javier.sanchez@iberopuebla.edu.mx

International Relations: Alberto Fischer-Garcia, Director de Relaciones Externas e Incambios
Tel: +52 (222) 229-07-28, Fax: +52 (222) 229-07-36
EMail: alberto.fischer@iberopuebla.edu.mx

Departments

Art, Design and Architecture (Architecture; Fine Arts; Graphic Arts; Graphic Design; Textile Design; Textile Technology) *Head*: José Valderrama-Izquierdo; **Business and Economic Sciences** (Accountancy; Banking; Business Administration; Business and Commerce; Finance; International Business; Labour and Industrial Relations; Marketing; Taxation) *Head*: Jorge Enrique Rodríguez-Torres; **Education and Psychology** (Clinical Psychology; Education; Philosophy of Education; Psychology; Science Education) *Head*: Guillermo Hinojosa-Rivero; **Engineering and Sciences** *Head*: Luis Enrique Fernández-Lomelín; **Social Sciences and Humanities** *Head*: Noe Castillo-Alarcon

History: Founded 1983.

Governing Bodies: Senate; Academic Committee

Academic Year: August to May (August-December;January-May)

Main Language(s) of Instruction: Spanish

International Co-operation: With universities United States, Europe and Latin America

Student Services: Academic counselling, Employment services, Foreign student adviser, Foreign Studies Centre, Health services, Language programs, Sports facilities

Student Residential Facilities: Dormitories

Special Facilities: Computer Lab

Libraries: Yes; also access to Electronic Databases

IBERO-AMERICAN UNIVERSITY TIJUANA

UNIVERSIDAD IBEROAMERICANA TIJUANA

Apartado postal 185 (1723 Zona Centro), Avenida Centro Universitario, 2501, Playas de Tijuana, 22200 Tijuana, Baja California
Tel: +52(664) 630-15-77
Fax: +52(664) 630-15-91
Website: http://www.tij.uia.mx

Rector: Rubén Arceo López (2012-)

Programmes

Architecture (Architecture); **Business Administration** (Accountancy; Administration; Business Administration; Commercial Law; Fiscal Law; International Business; Labour Law; Marketing); **Communication** (Advertising and Publicity; Communication Studies; Journalism; Photography); **Education** (Education); **Electronics and Telecommunications** (Electronic Engineering; Telecommunications Engineering); **Graphic Design** (Graphic Design; Photography); **Industrial Engineering** (Industrial Engineering); **Law** (Administrative Law; Civil Law; Commercial Law; Constitutional Law; Criminal Law; International Law; Law); **Mechanical and Electrical Engineering** (Electrical Engineering; Mechanical Engineering); **Nursing** (Nursing); **Nutrition and Food Science** (Food Science; Nutrition); **Psychology** (Psychology)

Further Information: Also Mexicali Campus

History: Founded 1982.

Main Language(s) of Instruction: Spanish

Degrees and Diplomas: *Licenciatura*; *Maestría*; *Doctorado*

Libraries: Biblioteca Loyola

IBERO-AMERICAN UNIVERSITY TORREÓN

UNIVERSIDAD IBEROAMERICANA LAGUNA (UIA TORREÓN)

UNIVERSIDAD IBEROAMERICANA TORREÓN

Apartado postal 28-D, Calzada Iberoamericana, 2255, Suc. Abastos, 27020 Torreón, Coahuila
Tel: +52(871) 705-10-10
Fax: +52(871) 705-10-80
EMail: webmaster@lag.uia.mx
Website: http://sitio.lag.uia.mx/publico/uia_laguna2007.html

Rector: Héctor Acuña Nogueira S.J. Tel: +52(871) 705-10-11

Departments

Architecture and Design; **Economics and Administration** (Accountancy; Business Administration; International Business; Labour and Industrial Relations; Taxation); **Engineering**; **Humanities** (Communication Studies; Education; Law; Psychology); **Master's Degree**

IBERO-MEXICAN UNIVERSITY

Universidad Iberomexicana

Calz. Arenal, 651, Col. Tepepan, Delegación Xochimilco, 16020 México, D.F.
Tel: +52(555) 641-20-00
Fax: +52(555) 555-84-87
EMail: lsixto@uim.edu.mx
Website: http://www.uim.edu.mx

Areas

Arts and Humanities (Art History; Cultural Studies; Economics; Philosophy; Social Sciences); **Biological and Health Sciences**

(Biological and Life Sciences; Chemistry; Health Sciences; Physics); **Physics, Mathematics and Engineering** (Construction Engineering; Engineering; Mathematics; Physics); **Social Sciences** (Social Sciences; Social Studies; Statistics)

Further Information: Also Campus Querétaro

History: Founded 1997.

Main Language(s) of Instruction: Spanish

Last Updated: 11/02/08

ICEL UNIVERSITY

Universidad ICEL

Calle Iglesia No. 2 Torre E Piso 3, Col. Tizapán San Ángel, Delegación Coyoacán, 07060 México, D.F.
Tel: +52(55) 54-81-02-00
Fax: +52(55) 54-81-02-05
EMail: informesicel@icel.edu.mx
Website: http://www.icel.edu.mx

Director General: Alfonso Nacer Gobera
EMail: alfonsonacer@icel.edu.mx

Programmes
Accountancy (Accountancy); **Architecture** (Architecture); **Business Administration** (Business Administration); **Communication** (Communication Studies); **Computer Engineering** (Computer Engineering; Computer Networks; Electrical and Electronic Engineering; Engineering); **Economics** (Economics); **Graphic Design** (Advertising and Publicity; Graphic Design; Industrial Design); **Law** (Law); **Pedagogy** (Pedagogy); **Psychology** (Educational Psychology; Psychology); **Tourism** (Tourism)

History: Founded 1996.

Main Language(s) of Instruction: Spanish

Degrees and Diplomas: *Licenciatura*; *Especialización*; *Maestría*

Last Updated: 03/04/13

IFAC CENTRE FOR FAMILY STUDIES AND RESEARCH

Centro de Estudios e Investigación Sobre la Familia IFAC

Jalisco N° 8, Col. Progreso Tizapan San Ángel Delegación Álvaro Obregón, 01080 México, D.F.
Tel: +52(555) 550-05-46
Fax: +52(555) 550-47-57
EMail: ensenanza_ifac@yahoo.com.mx
Website: http://www.ifac.org.mx

Presidenta: María Alejandra Esquivel Camacho

Programmes
Family Studies (Family Studies; Psychotherapy; Social Problems)

History: Founded 1972.

Admission Requirements: Licenciatura

Main Language(s) of Instruction: Spanish

Degrees and Diplomas: *Especialización*; *Maestría*. Also Diplomados

Last Updated: 13/07/12

IGNACIO COMONFORT SCHOOL OF SOCIAL WORK

Escuela de Trabajo Social Ignacio Comonfort

Francisco E. García No. 129, 97000 Mérida, Yucatán
Tel: +52(999) 923-5573

Directora: Leticia Ramos C.

Programmes
Social Work (Social Work)

Main Language(s) of Instruction: Spanish

Degrees and Diplomas: *Licenciatura*: 8 sem.

Last Updated: 03/04/08

IGNACIO MANUEL ALTAMIRANO CENTRE OF UNIVERSITY STUDIES

Centro de Estudios Universitarios Ignacio Manuel Altamirano

Carretera La Boticaria Km. 3.5, Prolongación Díaz Mirón, Colonia Antillas, 91320 Veracruz, Veracruz
Tel: +52(229) 922-77-19
Fax: +52(229) 922-77-19
EMail: tecerca_chicon@hotmail.com

Rector: Manuel Francisco Martínez Martínez (2001-)
EMail: rector@ceu-mexico.edu.mx

Programmes
Accountancy (Accountancy); **Business Administration** (Business Administration); **Computer Science** (Computer Science); **Education** (Education); **Law** (Law); **Pedagogy**; **Postgraduate Studies** (Education)

Further Information: Also Poza Rica, Chicontepec, Huasteca Veracruzana and Tlacolula campuses.

History: Founded 2000.

Degrees and Diplomas: *Licenciatura*; *Maestría*: Education

Last Updated: 26/03/08

ILEF INSTITUTE OF FAMILY STUDIES

Instituto Superior de Estudios de la Familia ILEF

Avenida Mexico 191, Col. Del Carmen, Delegación Coyacán, 04100 México, D.F.
Tel: +52(55) 56-59-05-04

Directora: Diana S. Rubni Posner de Bronfman

Programmes
Family Studies (Family Studies; Psychotherapy)

History: Founded 1997.

Main Language(s) of Instruction: Spanish

Degrees and Diplomas: *Maestría*

Last Updated: 08/03/13

INCARNATE WORD UNIVERSITY CENTRE

Centro Universitario Incarnate Word (CIW)

Tlacoquemécatl 433, Col. Del Valle, 03100 México, D.F.
Tel: +52(55) 55-75-03-77
EMail: admisiones@ciw.edu.mx
Website: http://www.ciw.edu.mx

Rector: Matthew Whitehouse EMail: direccion@ciw.edu.mx

Programmes
Administration and Finance (Administration; Business Administration; Finance); **Business Administration** (Business Administration); **International Business** (International Business); **Law** (Law); **Marketing** (Marketing); **Nutrition** (Nutrition); **Psychology** (Psychology)

History: Founded 2002.

Main Language(s) of Instruction: Spanish

Degrees and Diplomas: *Licenciatura*; *Maestría*. Also double degrees

Last Updated: 25/07/12

INDO-AMERICAN UNIVERSITY CENTRE

Centro Universitario Indoamericano, S.C.

Cumbres de Aculcingo, 3, Col. Los Pirules, 54040 Tlalnepantla, Estado de México
Tel: +52(55) 53-70-54-33
Fax: +52(55) 53-70-38-96
EMail: cuia@indoamericano.edu

Director: Arturo Nuñez Cortes

Programmes
Business Administration and Tourism (Business Administration; Tourism)

History: Founded 1975.

Main Language(s) of Instruction: Spanish

Degrees and Diplomas: *Licenciatura*

Last Updated: 21/03/08

INSTITUTE FOR ADVANCED STUDIES IN COMMUNICATION

Instituto de Estudios Superiores de la Comunicación
Revillagigedo, 331, 58000 Morelia, Michoacán
Tel: +52(443) 312-02-87
Fax: +52(443) 312-02-87
EMail: iescac@terra.com

Director: Alfredo Patiño Ferrer

Programmes
Communication Studies
Main Language(s) of Instruction: Spanish
Degrees and Diplomas: *Licenciatura*
Last Updated: 01/03/13

INSTITUTE FOR HUMAN DEVELOPMENT AND RESEARCH

Instituto de Desarrollo Humano e Investigación, S.C.
Blvd. Sinaloa 730, Local 9, Col. Las Quintas, 60060 Culiacán, Sinaloa
Tel: +52(667) 716-59-96
Fax: +52(667) 715-74-04
EMail: idehi2007@yahoo.com.mx

Director: Jorge Guadalúpe Aros Rodríguez

Programmes
Human Sciences (Development Studies)
Main Language(s) of Instruction: Spanish
Degrees and Diplomas: *Maestría*; *Doctorado*
Last Updated: 21/02/08

INSTITUTE FOR SPECIAL EDUCATION TEACHERS

Instituto Superior de Docentes en Educación Especial
Playa Regatas 473, Col. Marte, Iztacalco, 08830 México, D.F.
Tel: +52(55) 56-33-03-96
Fax: +52(55) 56-33-57-56

Director General: Salvador Valdés Cárdenas

Programmes
Teacher Training - for the Disabled (Special Education; Teacher Training)
Main Language(s) of Instruction: Spanish
Degrees and Diplomas: *Licenciatura*

INSTITUTE FOR THE DEVELOPMENT AND UPGRADING OF PROFESSIONALS

Instituto para el Desarrollo y Actualización de Profesionales, S.C.
Progreso, 227, Col. Escandón, Delegación Miguel Hidalgo, 11800 México, D.F.
Tel: +52(5) 55-15-16-56
Fax: +52(5) 55-16-01-32
EMail: df@idap.com.mx
Website: http://www.idap.com.mx

Director General: Luis Alfonso Ruiz Martínez (1983-)

Programmes
Dentistry (Dentistry; Orthodontics; Paediatrics)
Further Information: Also campuses in Tijuana, Culiacán, Monterrey, Guadalajara, Morelia, Puebla, Tehuacán, Oaxaca, Tuxtla Gtz and Merida
History: Founded 1983.
Main Language(s) of Instruction: Spanish
Degrees and Diplomas: *Especialización*
Last Updated: 07/03/13

INSTITUTE FOR TOURISM AND TRAVEL STUDIES

Instituto de Turismo Studio Viajes, A.C.
Blvd. Aarón Merino Fernández, 8-C, Col. Amor, 72140 Puebla, Puebla
Tel: +52(222) 230-44-25
Fax: +52(222) 230-50-39
EMail: ucap@prodigy.net.mx

Director: Álvaro de Cosio Hernández

Programmes
Tourism and Travel (Tourism)
Main Language(s) of Instruction: Spanish
Degrees and Diplomas: *Licenciatura*
Last Updated: 07/04/08

INSTITUTE IN FISCAL AND FINANCIAL SPECIALITIES

Instituto de Especialidades Fiscales y Financieras
Avenida Circunvalación División del Norte, 1217, 44220 Guadalajara, Jalisco

Directora: Alma Araceli Chávez Cuevas

Programmes
Finance (Finance); **Taxation** (Taxation)
Main Language(s) of Instruction: Spanish
Degrees and Diplomas: *Licenciatura*; *Maestría*
Last Updated: 03/04/08

INSTITUTE OF ACADEMIC, TEACHING AND BUSINESS UPGRADING OF PUEBLA

Instituto de Superación Académica, Docente y Empresarial de Puebla
9 Sur N° 2914, 7200 Puebla, Puebla
Director: José Antonio Fernández Aparicio

Programmes
Law (Law)
Main Language(s) of Instruction: Spanish
Degrees and Diplomas: *Especialización*; *Maestría*
Last Updated: 20/02/08

INSTITUTE OF ADVANCED AND UPGRADING STUDIES

Instituto de Estudios Avanzados y de Actualización
Venustiano Carranza, 500, Norte, 64000 Monterrey, Nuevo León
Tel: +52(81) 346-56-00
EMail: informes@idesaa.edu.mx
Website: http://www.idesaa.edu.mx

Director: José René Mena Seifert

Schools
Leadership (Leadership); **Sales** (Marketing; Sales Techniques)
Further Information: Also branch in Mexico City
History: Founded 1992.
Main Language(s) of Instruction: Spanish
Degrees and Diplomas: *Especialización*; *Maestría*
Last Updated: 01/03/13

INSTITUTE OF ADVANCED STUDIES OF TEXMELUCAN

Instituto de Estudios Superiores de Texmelucán
Avenida Libertad Norte, 303, Altos, Centros, 74100 San Martín Texmelucán, Puebla
Tel: +52(248) 484-29-91 +52(248) 484-51-45
EMail: iest@compuredes.net.mx

Director: Rodolfo Salamanca Llanos (1995-)
History: Founded 1995.
Degrees and Diplomas: *Licenciatura*
Last Updated: 07/04/08

INSTITUTE OF ADVANCED STUDIES OF THE EAST

Instituto de Estudios Avanzados de Oriente
Avenida Poniente 5, No. 454, Col. Centro, 94300 Oribaza, Veracruz
Tel: +52(272) 725-00-07
EMail: informes@ideadeoriente.edu.mx
Website: http://www.ideadeoriente.edu.mx

Director: Leandro Flores Rasenzweig (1990-)

Programmes

Accountancy (Accountancy); **Business Administration** (Business Administration); **Business Computing** (Business Computing); **International Business** (International Business); **Law** (Law); **Tourism** (Tourism)

History: Founded 1990.

Main Language(s) of Instruction: Spanish

Degrees and Diplomas: *Licenciatura*; *Maestría*: Business Administration; Private Law

Libraries: Yes
Last Updated: 28/02/13

INSTITUTE OF ADVANCED TEACHING IN ACCOUNTANCY AND ADMINISTRATION

Instituto de Enseñanza Superior en Contaduría y Administración
Calzada de Tlalpán, 393, Col. Alamos, Delegación Benito Juárez, 03400 México, D.F.
Tel: +52(55) 55-38-19-93 +52(55) 55-19-24-43
EMail: informes@iesca.edu.mx
Website: http://www.iesca.edu.mx

Director: Jesús Cendejas Contreras

Programmes

Accountancy (Accountancy); **Business Administration** (Administration; Business Administration); **Computer Science** (Computer Science); **Law** (Law)

History: Founded 1995.

Main Language(s) of Instruction: Spanish

Degrees and Diplomas: *Licenciatura*; *Especialización*; *Maestría*
Last Updated: 28/02/13

INSTITUTE OF ARCHITECTURE AND DESIGN

Instituto Superior de Arquitectura y Diseño
Avenida Misión del Bosque, 10701, Col. Valle Escondido, Centro, 31054 Chihuahua, Chihuahua
Tel: +52(614) 410-07-94
EMail: isad@isad.edu.mx
Website: http://www.isad.edu.mx/

Director: Miguel Corral EMail: mcorral@isad.edu.mx

Divisions

Architecture (Architecture); **Design** (Design)

History: Founded 1992.

Main Language(s) of Instruction: Spanish

Degrees and Diplomas: *Licenciatura*; *Especialización*; *Maestría*
Last Updated: 08/03/13

INSTITUTE OF ART AND DESIGN

Instituto de Arte y Diseño, A.C.
Avenida los Reyes 914 . Col. Monclova, 25710 Monclova, Coahuila
Tel: +52(866) 635-75-24
EMail: marcelarivero_59@hotmail.com

Directora: Marcela Ivón Rivero Lumbreras

Programmes

Fine Arts (Fine Arts); **Painting and Drawing** (Painting and Drawing)

Main Language(s) of Instruction: Spanish

Degrees and Diplomas: *Licenciatura*; *Maestría*
Last Updated: 27/02/13

INSTITUTE OF BIOPROGRESSIVE ORTHODONTICS

Instituto de Ortodoncía Bioprogresiva
Coyotepec Manzana 8, Lote 10, Altavilla, 55390 Ecatepec de Morelos, Estado de México
Tel: +52(55) 57-14-83-28
EMail: ortoibo@prodigy.net.mx
Website: http://www.ortoibo.com.mx

Director: Gustavo Altamirano Hernández

Programmes

Orthodontics (Dentistry; Orthodontics; Surgery)

Degrees and Diplomas: *Especialización*
Last Updated: 05/03/13

INSTITUTE OF BUSINESS COMPUTING SYSTEMS OF MONTERREY

Instituto de Sistemas Administrativos Computacionales de Monterrey, A.C.
Modesto Arreola 406, Poniente, 64000 Monterrey, Nuevo León
Tel: +52(81) 83-40-21-15
Fax: +52(81) 83-40-21-15
EMail: al_valdez@isac.edu.mx
Website: http://www.isac.edu.mx

Directora: Silvia González Vázquez

Programmes

Business Administration (Business Administration); **Commerce** (Accountancy; Business and Commerce; Labour Law); **Computer Science** (Computer Science); **Educational Intervention** (Education; Educational Administration); **Marketing** (Marketing); **Psychology** (Psychology)

Further Information: Also branch in San Nicolas de los Garza

History: Founded 1980.

Main Language(s) of Instruction: Spanish

Degrees and Diplomas: *Licenciatura*
Last Updated: 05/03/13

INSTITUTE OF CLINICAL AND CORRECTIVE ORTHODONTICS

Instituto de Ortodoncia Clínica y Correctiva
Diego de Ordaz, 207, Fracc. Viraenia, Boca del Río, 95263 Veracruz, Veracruz
Tel: +52(297) 937-23-00

Director: Teofilo Ricardo Miranda Téllez

Programmes

Dentistry (Dentistry; Orthodontics)

Main Language(s) of Instruction: Spanish

Degrees and Diplomas: *Licenciatura*; *Especialización*
Last Updated: 20/02/08

INSTITUTE OF COGNITIVE AND BEHAVIOURAL PSYCHOTHERAPY

Instituto de Psicoterapia Cognitivo Conductual
Gabriel Mancera, 111, Bénito Juarez, Colonía del Valle, 06600 México, D.F.
Tel: +52(555) 511-82-09 +52(555) 264-14-01
Fax: +52(555) 514-91-06
EMail: administracion@tcognitiva.org
Website: http://www.tcognitiva.org

Directora: Ma. Guadalupe Hasbach Soto
EMail: direccion@tcognitiva.org

Programmes

Cognitive and Behavioural Psychotherapy (Psychotherapy)

History: Founded 1999.

Main Language(s) of Instruction: Spanish

Degrees and Diplomas: *Maestría*
Last Updated: 05/03/13

INSTITUTE OF COMMUNICATION STUDIES AND PHILOSOPHY

Instituto de Comunicación y Filosofía, A.C.
Avenida Taxqueña, 1792, Col. Paseos de Taxqueña, Delegación Coyoacán, 04250 México, D.F.
Tel: +52(55) 55-44-83-91
Fax: +52(55) 55-82-92-14
EMail: comfil@sanpablo.com.mx
Website: http://www.comfil.edu.mx

Director General: Rafael González Beltrán (1993-)

Programmes
Communication Studies (Communication Studies); **Philosophy** (Linguistics; Philosophy)
History: Founded 1993.
Main Language(s) of Instruction: Spanish
Degrees and Diplomas: *Licenciatura*
Last Updated: 28/02/13

INSTITUTE OF COMMUNICATION STUDIES OF YUCATAN

Instituto de Estudios de la Comunicación de Yucatán, A.C.
56, 330 entre 25 y 29, Col. Itzimna, Fracc. Jardines de Mérida, 97100 Mérida, Yucatán
Tel: +52(999) 926-61-66

Directora General: Rebeca Elisa Rodríguez Arceo

Programmes
Hispanic-American Languages and Literature (Hispanic American Studies; Literature); **Journalism** (Journalism); **Public Relations** (Public Relations)
Main Language(s) of Instruction: Spanish
Degrees and Diplomas: *Licenciatura*
Last Updated: 01/03/13

INSTITUTE OF COMMUNICATION STUDIES, ARTS AND HUMANITIES OF MONTERREY

Instituto de Comunicación, Artes y Humanidades de Monterrey, A.C.
Villagrán #630 cruz con Matamoros, 64060 Monterrey, Nuevo León
Tel: +52(81) 83-42-20-50
EMail: info@icahm.edu.mx
Website: http://www.icahm.edu.mx

Director: Guillermo Sánchez Garay

Programmes
Arts and Humanities (Arts and Humanities; Literature; Philosophy); **Communication Studies** (Communication Studies)
History: Founded 1988.
Main Language(s) of Instruction: Spanish
Degrees and Diplomas: *Licenciatura*
Last Updated: 28/02/13

INSTITUTE OF COMPUTER SCIENCE OF THE NORTH EAST IN MATAMOROS

Instituto de Computación del Noreste en Matamoros, A.C.
Avenida Quinta y Juárez S/N esquina, Col. Heroíca Matamoros, 87300 Matamoros, Tamaulipas
Tel: +52(868) 813-38-49

Director: José Luis Lucio Botello

Programmes
Computer Science; **Electronic Engineering** (Electronic Engineering)
History: Founded 1981.
Main Language(s) of Instruction: Spanish
Degrees and Diplomas: *Licenciatura*; *Maestría*; *Doctorado*
Last Updated: 31/03/08

INSTITUTE OF COMPUTING AND COUNSELLING IN COMPUTER SCIENCE

Instituto de Computación y Asesoría en Informática, A.C.
Calle 39, 177-F x 24 y 26, Col. Santa Ana, 97780 Valladolid, Yucatán
Tel: +52(985) 986-31-78
Director: Raúl Mendoza Alcocer

Programmes
Computer Science (Computer Science)
Main Language(s) of Instruction: Spanish
Degrees and Diplomas: *Licenciatura*
Last Updated: 03/04/08

INSTITUTE OF CULTURE AND ART OF MONTERREY

Instituto Superior de Cultura y Arte de Monterrey
Avenida San Jerónimo, 201, Pte., 64640 Monterrey, Nuevo León
Tel: +52(81) 83-47-19-17

Directora General: Rosalía M. Manzano Sevilla

Programmes
Cultural Studies (Cultural Studies); **Fine Arts** (Fine Arts)
Main Language(s) of Instruction: Spanish
Degrees and Diplomas: *Licenciatura*

INSTITUTE OF DENTAL STUDIES OF MATAMOROS

Instituto Odontológico de Matamoros
Calle Primera y Nardos, 253, Col. Jardín, 87330 Matamoros, Tamaulipas
Tel: +52(868) 812-38-34
Fax: +52(868) 813-31-07
EMail: lom_educa@hotmail.com
Website: http://iomeduca.com

Director: Ernesto F. Morales Lozano

Programmes
Dentistry (Dentistry; Surgery)
History: Founded 1972.
Main Language(s) of Instruction: Spanish
Degrees and Diplomas: *Licenciatura*
Last Updated: 07/03/13

INSTITUTE OF DENTAL STUDIES OF THE SOUTH OF THE STATE OF CHIHUAHUA

Instituto de Estudios Odontológicos del Sur del Estado de Chihuahua
Calle 7a Poniente, 27, Delicias, 33000 Cárdenas, Chihuahua
Tel: +52(639) 392-80-09

Director: Alfredo Rojas Zapata

Programmes
Dentistry and Odonthology (Dentistry)
Main Language(s) of Instruction: Spanish
Degrees and Diplomas: *Licenciatura*
Last Updated: 04/04/08

INSTITUTE OF ECCLESIASTICAL STUDIES

Instituto Superior de Estudios Eclesiásticos
Gral. Victoria, 133, Col. Tlalpán, Delegación Tlalpán, 14000 México, D.F.
Tel: +52(55) 55-73-22-22
Fax: +52(55) 56-73-22-47
EMail: isee@prodigy.net.mx
Website: http://www.isee.edu.mx/

Director General: Federico Altbach Núnez

Programmes
Philosophy; **Theology** (Pastoral Studies; Theology)

Main Language(s) of Instruction: Spanish
Degrees and Diplomas: *Licenciatura*; *Maestria*
Last Updated: 08/03/13

INSTITUTE OF ENGINEERING

Instituto Superior de Ingeniería
Instituto Literario, Ote., 309 y 311, Col. Centro, 50000 Toluca, Estado de México
Tel: +52(722) 214-81-86
Fax: +52(722) 214-81-86
EMail: isima@toluca.podernet.com.mx
Website: http://isima.com.mx

Director General: Edgar Raúl Romero Granados (2002-)

Programmes
Engineering (Automotive Engineering; Computer Engineering)
History: Founded 2002.
Main Language(s) of Instruction: Spanish
Degrees and Diplomas: *Licenciatura*
Last Updated: 28/03/08

INSTITUTE OF FAMILY STUDIES

Instituto Superior de Estudios para la Familia (ISEF)
Avenida Anáhuac s/n, Col. Lomas Anáhuac, 52760 Huixquilucán, Estado de México
Tel: +52(55) 56-27-02-10
EMail: acastell@anahuac.mx
Website: http://www.isef.edu.mx//

Director: Alberto Castellanos Franco

Programmes
Family Studies
Further Information: Campuses in Mexico Norte, Mexico Sur, Guadalajara, Monterrey, Mérida,Puebla, León and Queretajo
History: Founded 1992.
Main Language(s) of Instruction: Spanish
Degrees and Diplomas: *Licenciatura*; *Maestria*

INSTITUTE OF FISCAL AND ADMINISTRATION STUDIES

Instituto de Estudios Fiscales y Administrativos, A.C.
Sinaloa N° 115, Col. Roma, Delegación Cuauhtémoc, México, D.F.
EMail: cursos@iefa.com.mx
Website: http://www.iefa.com.mx

Director: Jesús Patiño

Programmes
Corporate Finance and Administration
History: Founded 1979.
Main Language(s) of Instruction: Spanish
Degrees and Diplomas: *Especialización*
Last Updated: 01/03/13

INSTITUTE OF FORENSIC AND EXPERTISE SCIENCES OF THE STATE OF PUEBLA

Instituto de Ciencias Forenses y Periciales del Estado de Puebla, S.C.
17 Sur 4721, Col Reforma Agua Azul, 72430 Puebla, Puebla
Tel: +52(222) 500-38-94
EMail: informes@cfp.edu.mx
Website: http://www.cfp.edu.mx

Directora: Elia Cristina Quiterio Montiel

Programmes
Criminal Law (Criminal Law); **Criminology** (Criminology); **Forensic Medicine and Dentistry** (Forensic Medicine and Dentistry)
History: Founded 1998.
Main Language(s) of Instruction: Spanish
Degrees and Diplomas: *Licenciatura*; *Especialización*; *Maestria*
Last Updated: 18/01/13

INSTITUTE OF GESTALT THERAPY OF THE WESTERN REGION

Instituto de Terapia Gestalt Región Occidente (INTEGRO)
8 de julio N° 320, Sector Juárez, 44100 Guadalajara, Jalisco
Tel: +52(3) 613-27-06
Fax: +52(3) 614-88-99
EMail: integro@mail.udg.mx

Programmes
Therapy (Family Studies; Linguistics; Neurological Therapy; Speech Therapy and Audiology)
History: Founded 1993.
Main Language(s) of Instruction: Spanish
Degrees and Diplomas: *Especialización*; *Maestría*
Last Updated: 05/03/13

INSTITUTE OF GRAPHIC COMMUNICATION OF THE NORTH

Instituto de Comunicación Gráfica del Norte
Emiliio Carranza No.900 esquina con Ramón Corona, Centro, 25000 Saltillo, Coahuila
Tel: +52(844) 412-11-66
EMail: contacto@icnsaltillo.com
Website: http://icnsaltillo.edu.mx

Directora: Ana Isabel Arrellano Lara

Programmes
Adverting and Graphics (Advertising and Publicity; Graphic Design); **Business and Commerce** (Business and Commerce); **Public Relations** (Public Relations)
History: Founded 1991.
Main Language(s) of Instruction: Spanish
Degrees and Diplomas: *Licenciatura*
Last Updated: 28/02/13

INSTITUTE OF HELLENIC CULTURE

Instituto Cultural Helénico
Avenida Revolución, 1500, Col. Guadalupe Inn, Delegación Álvaro Obregón, 01020 México, D.F.
Tel: +52(555) 662-57-93
Fax: +52(555) 662-97-92
EMail: informes@helenico.edu.mx
Website: http://www.helenico.edu.mx

Director: Francisco Javier Gaxiola Ochoa
EMail: gaxgaxjr@prodigy.net.mx

Programmes
Arts and Humanities (Arts and Humanities; Cultural Studies); **Fine Arts** (Painting and Drawing; Sculpture); **History and Art** (Fine Arts; Heritage Preservation; History); **Religion and Philosophy** (Philosophy; Religion); **World Cultures** (Cultural Studies)
History: Founded 1973.
Main Language(s) of Instruction: Spanish
Degrees and Diplomas: *Licenciatura*; *Maestria*
Last Updated: 30/08/12

INSTITUTE OF HIGHER CULTURE

Instituto de Cultura Superior
Avenida Prado Norte, 664, Col. Lomas de Chapultepec, Delegación Miguel Hidalgo, 11000 México, D.F.
Tel: +52(55) 52-02-02-12
Fax: +52(55) 55-40-27-92
EMail: iculturasuperior@prodigy.net
Website: http://www.institutodeculturasuperior.edu.mx

Director General: Ricardo Mena Penna (1964-)

Programmes
Art History (Art History)
History: Founded 1964.
Main Language(s) of Instruction: Spanish
Degrees and Diplomas: *Licenciatura*
Last Updated: 28/02/13

INSTITUTE OF HIGHER STUDIES IN ACCOUNTANCY AND ADMINISTRATION OF THE SOUTH-EAST

Instituto de Estudios Superiores Contables y Administrativos del Sureste
4a Calle Oriente Sur, 354 y 2° Sur Oriente, 379, Centro, 29000 Tuxtla Gutiérrez, Chiapas
Tel: +52(961) 612-13-22 +52(961) 613-07-58

Directora General: Brenda Patricia Leal Herrera (1996-)

Programmes
Accountancy (Accountancy); **Administration** (Administration)
History: Founded 1996
Main Language(s) of Instruction: Spanish
Degrees and Diplomas: *Licenciatura*
Last Updated: 03/04/08

INSTITUTE OF HIGHER STUDIES IN ARCHITECTURE AND DESIGN

Instituto de Estudios Superiores en Arquitectura y Diseño, A.C.
7 Oriente, 2402, Azcárate, 72501 Puebla, Puebla
Tel: +52(222) 236-04-38
EMail: iesxh@prodigy.net.mx

Director: Alejandro Pérez Robledo

Programmes
Architecture (Architecture); **Computer Science** (Computer Science); **Graphic Design and Publicity** (Advertising and Publicity; Graphic Design); **Telecommunications Engineering** (Telecommunications Engineering)
History: Founded 1995.
Main Language(s) of Instruction: Spanish
Degrees and Diplomas: *Licenciatura*: 10 sem.
Last Updated: 07/04/08

INSTITUTE OF HIGHER STUDIES IN ENGINEERING

Instituto de Estudios Superiores en Ingeniería
Reforma, 3521, Col. La Paz, 72160 Puebla, Puebla
Tel: +52(222) 249-84-51
Fax: +52(222) 231-38-25
EMail: guziesi@pue.telmex.net.mx

Rector: Jorge Guzmán Arciniega (1997-)

Programmes
Engineering
History: Founded 1997.
Degrees and Diplomas: *Licenciatura*; *Especialización*; *Maestría*
Last Updated: 26/02/08

INSTITUTE OF HIGHER STUDIES IN FASHION AND DESIGN

Instituto de Estudios Superiores en Moda y Diseño, A.C.
Isauro Martínez, 246 Pte., Col. Ampliación Los Ángeles, 27140 Torreón, Coahuila
Tel: +52(871) 116-68-23

Directora: María Guadalupe Adame Hernández

Programmes
Fashion Design (Fashion Design; Marketing)
Degrees and Diplomas: *Licenciatura*
Last Updated: 07/04/08

INSTITUTE OF HIGHER STUDIES IN HEALTH SCIENCES

Instituto de Estudios Superiores en Ciencias de la Salud
Circuito Interior, San Francisco, 332, Industrial Norte Zapopán, 45130 Zapopan, Jalisco
Tel: +52(33) 834-07-43

Director: Francisco Javier Ramos Arias

Programmes
Health Sciences (Health Sciences)
Degrees and Diplomas: *Licenciatura*
Last Updated: 07/04/08

INSTITUTE OF HIGHER STUDIES IN NEUROSCIENCES, PSYCHOANALYSIS AND MENTAL HEALTH

Instituto de Estudios Superiores en Neurociencias, Psicoanálisis y Salud Mental
Av. México 194, Col. Hipódromo, Condesa, Delegación Cuauhtémoc, 06100 México, D.F.
EMail: info@psicoanalisis.org.mx
Website: http://www.psicoanalisis.org.mx

Presidente: Alberto Montes de Oca Tamez
EMail: neuro_psique@yahoo.com.mx

Programmes
Neurosciences (Neurosciences); **Psychoanalysis** (Psychoanalysis)
History: Founded 1991.
Main Language(s) of Instruction: Spanish
Degrees and Diplomas: *Licenciatura*; *Maestria*; *Doctorado*
Last Updated: 04/03/13

INSTITUTE OF HIGHER STUDIES IN PUBLIC ADMINISTRATION

Instituto de Estudios Superiores en Administración Pública
Chihuahua N° 167, Esq. Jalapa y Tonalá, Col. Roma, Cuauhtémoc, 06700 México, D.F.
Tel: +52(555) 5584-3157
EMail: direccion@iesap.edu.mx
Website: http://www.iesap.edu.mx

Director: Enrique Peña Nieto (1994-)

Programmes
Administration (Private Administration; Public Administration)
History: Founded 1976.
Main Language(s) of Instruction: Spanish
Degrees and Diplomas: *Maestría*; *Maestría*; *Doctorado*
Libraries: Yes
Last Updated: 04/03/13

INSTITUTE OF HIGHER STUDIES IN REHABILITATION

Instituto de Estudios Superiores en Rehabilitación
2 Sur, 4913, Col. Las Palmas, 72000 Puebla, Puebla
Tel: +52(222) 240-03-27

Programmes
Rehabilitation and Therapy (Rehabilitation and Therapy)
Main Language(s) of Instruction: Spanish
Degrees and Diplomas: *Licenciatura*
Last Updated: 07/04/08

INSTITUTE OF HIGHER STUDIES IN TOURISM

Instituto de Estudios Superiores de Turismo
Privada de Lago No. 38, Col. Américas Unidas, Delegación Benito Juárez, 03610 México, D.F.
Tel: +52(55) 55-32-32-24
EMail: iestur@prodigy.net.mx
Website: http://www.iestur.edu.mx

Directora General: Nadia Rocío Cedillo González (1994-)

Programmes
Gastronomy (Cooking and Catering); **Tourism** (Tourism)
History: Founded 1978.
Main Language(s) of Instruction: Spanish

Degrees and Diplomas: *Licenciatura*; *Maestría*
Last Updated: 01/03/13

INSTITUTE OF HIGHER STUDIES OF AUTLAN

Instituto de Estudios Superiores de Autlán
Ignacio López Rayón, 699, Col. La Granja, Autlán, 48900 Antotonilco el Alto, Jalisco
Tel: +52(317) 172-31-57

Director: Santiago Rubio Clemente

Programmes
Education (Education); **Law** (Law); **Philosophy** (Philosophy); **Political and Social Sciences** (Political Sciences; Social Sciences); **Psychology** (Psychology)
History: Founded 2000.
Main Language(s) of Instruction: Spanish
Degrees and Diplomas: *Licenciatura*
Last Updated: 01/03/13

INSTITUTE OF HIGHER STUDIES OF CAMPECHE

Instituto de Estudios Superiores de Campeche, S.C.
Calle 35 No.67, Nueva Jerusalem, 24400 Champotón, Campeche
Tel: +52(981) 5-03-22
EMail: contacto@iescampeche.edu.mx
Website: http://www.iescampeche.edu.mx

Director: Miguel Ángel Apolinar Herrera (1999-)

Programmes
Accountancy (Accountancy); **Administration** (Administration; Human Resources); **Computer Science** (Computer Science; Information Technology); **Law** (Civil Law; Criminal Law; Law); **Tourism** (Tourism)
History: Founded 1999
Main Language(s) of Instruction: Spanish
Degrees and Diplomas: *Licenciatura*; *Maestría*
Last Updated: 01/03/13

INSTITUTE OF HIGHER STUDIES OF CHIAPAS

Instituto de Estudios Superiores de Chiapas
Blvd. Paso Limón, 244, Col. Paso Limón, 29045 Tuxtla Gutiérrez, Chiapas
Tel: +52(961) 4-08-18 +52(961) 4-04-18
Fax: +52(961) 4-16-21
EMail: info@iesch.edu.mx
Website: http://www.iesch.edu.mx

Rector: Emilio Enrique Salazar Narváez (1999-)
EMail: rector@iesch.edu.mx

Programmes
Animal Husbandry (Animal Husbandry); **Architecture** (Architecture); **Business Administration** (Accountancy; Business Administration; Tourism); **Business Computing** (Business Computing); **Chemistry, Pharmacy and Biology** (Biology; Chemistry; Pharmacy); **Communication Sciences** (Communication Studies); **Dentistry** (Dentistry); **Educational Sciences** (Educational Sciences); **Engineering** (Civil Engineering; Computer Engineering; Construction Engineering; Data Processing); **Gastronomy** (Cooking and Catering); **Graphic Design** (Graphic Design); **Law** (Law); **Marketing** (Marketing); **Medicine** (Medicine); **Nursing** (Nursing); **Physical Education and Sports** (Physical Education; Sports); **Psychology** (Psychology)
Further Information: Also Cintalapa de Comitán, Figueroa, Palenque, Tapachula de Córdova y Ordóñez, Pichucalco, San Cristobal and Tonala campuses
History: Founded 1982.
Main Language(s) of Instruction: Spanish
Degrees and Diplomas: *Licenciatura*; *Especialización*; *Maestría*; *Doctorado*
Libraries: Yes
Last Updated: 01/03/13

INSTITUTE OF HIGHER STUDIES OF CHIHUAHUA

Instituto de Estudios Superiores de Chihuahua, A.C.
Blas Cano De los Rios N° 703, Col. San Felipe, 31240 Chihuahua, Chihuahua
Tel: +52(614) 413-29-82
EMail: iesch583@yahoo.com
Website: http://claudiag41.wordpress.com

Rectora: Pura C. Orozco Armendáriz (1991-)
EMail: profesoraorozco@hotmail.com.mx.

Programmes
Accountancy (Accountancy); **Business Administration** (Business Administration); **Computer Science** (Computer Science); **Industrial Relations** (Labour and Industrial Relations)
History: Founded 1987.
Main Language(s) of Instruction: Spanish
Degrees and Diplomas: *Licenciatura*
Last Updated: 01/03/13

INSTITUTE OF HIGHER STUDIES OF COAHUILA

Instituto de Estudios Superiores de Coahuila
Bogotá, 35, Col. Guadalupe, 25750 Monclova, Coahuila
Tel: +52(866) 632-00-28
Fax: +52(866) 632-11-01
EMail: informacion@iesc.edu.mx
Website: http://www.iesc.edu.mx

Director: José Luis Garzón Valdés (1993-)

Programmes
Business Administration (Business Administration); **International Business** (International Business)
History: Founded 1993.
Main Language(s) of Instruction: Spanish
Degrees and Diplomas: *Licenciatura*
Last Updated: 01/03/13

INSTITUTE OF HIGHER STUDIES OF GUASAVE

Instituto de Estudios Superiores de Guasave
Blvd. 16 de Septiembre #1742, 81000 Guasave, Sinaloa
Tel: +52(687) 871 08-86
EMail: ies_g@yahoo.com.mx
Website: http://www.iesg.edu.mx

Director: Martín de Jesús Espinóza Gaxíola

Programmes
Accountancy (Accountancy); **Administration** (Administration); **Computer Science** (Computer Science); **Criminology** (Criminology); **Food Processing** (Food Technology); **Graphic Design** (Graphic Design)
History: Founded 2003 as Colegio Guasave.
Degrees and Diplomas: *Licenciatura*
Last Updated: 01/03/13

INSTITUTE OF HIGHER STUDIES OF LA SIERRA

Instituto de Estudios Superiores de la Sierra
Circuito Profra. Margarita Cardoso Ramirez 7, Junta Auxiliar de San Diego, 73800 Teziutlán, Puebla
Tel: +52(231) 311-31- 67
Website: http://www.ties.com.mx/

Director: Arturo Abraham Becerra Castillo

Campuses
Cuetzálan (Computer Science; Cooking and Catering; Hotel and Restaurant; Law; Tourism); **Hueyapan** (Agricultural Business; Business Administration; Law); **Libres** (Administration; Business Administration; Communication Studies; International Business; Law); **Teziutlán** (Accountancy; Administration; Automation and Control Engineering; Communication Studies; Computer Science; Cooking and Catering; Criminology; Graphic Design; Gynaecology and Obstetrics; Industrial Engineering; Law; Mechanical Engineering; Nursing; Veterinary Science; Zoology); **Tlatlauquitepec**

(Computer Science; Cooking and Catering; Graphic Design; Hotel and Restaurant; Tourism); **Zacapoaxtla** (Accountancy; Architecture; Graphic Design; Gynaecology and Obstetrics; Law; Nursing; Veterinary Science; Zoology); **Zaragoza**
Main Language(s) of Instruction: Spanish
Degrees and Diplomas: *Licenciatura*; *Maestría*; *Doctorado*
Last Updated: 18/01/13

INSTITUTE OF HIGHER STUDIES OF MERIDA

Instituto de Estudios Superiores de Mérida
Calle 62 No. 619A por 79 y 85, Col. Centro, 97000 Mérida, Yucatán
EMail: info@iesmer.edu.mx
Website: http://www.iesmer.edu.mx

Director General: Arturo Jesús Laflor Hernández

Programmes
Accountancy (Accountancy); **Educational Sciences** (Educational Sciences); **Marketing** (Marketing); **Nursing** (Nursing); **Nutrition** (Nutrition)
Further Information: Also branch in Tuxtla Gutiérrez
History: Founded 1999.
Main Language(s) of Instruction: Spanish
Degrees and Diplomas: *Licenciatura*
Last Updated: 01/04/08

INSTITUTE OF HIGHER STUDIES OF OAXACA

Instituto de Estudios Superiores de Oaxaca, A.C.
Camino Nacional, 704, Santa Rosa, Panzacola, 68039 Oaxaca, Oaxaca
Tel: +52(951) 512-69-59
EMail: comunica@ieso.edu.mx
Website: http://www.ieso.edu.mx

Director General: Luis Cortés Osorio
EMail: recepcion@ieso.edu.mx

Programmes
Accountancy and Business Administration (Accountancy; Business Administration); **Communication Sciences** (Communication Studies); **Computer Engineering** (Computer Engineering); **History** (History); **Pedagogy** (Pedagogy); **Political Science and Public Administration** (Political Sciences; Public Administration); **Psychology** (Psychology)
History: Founded 1985.
Main Language(s) of Instruction: Spanish
Degrees and Diplomas: *Licenciatura*; *Maestría*
Last Updated: 01/03/13

INSTITUTE OF HIGHER STUDIES OF POZA RICA

Instituto de Estudios Superiores de Poza Rica
Calle General O'Highins s/n, Col. Morelos, Poza Rica de Hidalgo, 93340 Poza Rica, Veracruz
Tel: +52(782) 824-08-31
EMail: iespr@prodigy.net.mx
Website: http://www.iespr.com.mx

Rectora: Erika del Carmen Cruz Espinosa

Programmes
Business Administration (Business Administration); **Computer Engineering** (Computer Engineering); **Graphic Design** (Graphic Design); **Journalism** (Journalism)
History: Founded 1985.
Main Language(s) of Instruction: Spanish
Degrees and Diplomas: *Licenciatura*; *Especialización*; *Maestría*
Last Updated: 01/03/13

INSTITUTE OF HIGHER STUDIES OF TAMAULIPAS

Instituto de Estudios Superiores de Tamaulipas, A.C. (IEST)
Apartado postal 257, Av. Dr. Burton E. Grossman, 501, Pte. Col. Tampico - Altamira Sector 1, 89605 Altamira, Tamaulipas
Tel: +52(833) 230-25-50
Fax: +52(833) 230-25-75
EMail: david.gomez@iest.edu.mx
Website: http://www.iest.edu.mx

Rector: David Efrain Gómez Fuentes (2000-)

Areas
Business Administration (Accountancy; Administration; Advertising and Publicity; Business Administration; Cooking and Catering; Finance; Human Resources; International Business; Marketing; Sales Techniques; Tourism); **Educational Sciences** (Music Education; Pedagogy; Preschool Education; Primary Education); **Engineering and Science** (Agronomy; Architecture; Civil Engineering; Computer Science; Environmental Studies; Industrial Design; Mechanical Engineering; Petroleum and Gas Engineering; Robotics; Telecommunications Engineering); **Health Sciences** (Gynaecology and Obstetrics; Nursing; Nutrition; Psychology; Radiology; Rehabilitation and Therapy; Social Work; Surgery; Veterinary Science); **Humanities and Social Sciences** (Communication Studies; Criminology; Finance; Graphic Design; History; Journalism; Law; Media Studies; Modern Languages; Philosophy; Political Sciences; Public Administration; Sociology; Spanish; Theatre)
Further Information: Also campuses in Nuevo León, Vera Cruz, San Luis Potosí, Hidalgo, Michoacan, Ciudad de México
History: Founded 1974.
Main Language(s) of Instruction: Spanish
Degrees and Diplomas: *Licenciatura*; *Especialización*; *Maestría*
Libraries: Yes
Last Updated: 18/01/13

INSTITUTE OF HIGHER STUDIES OF THE BAJIO

Instituto de Estudios Superiores del Bajío
Joaquín García Icazbalceta, 110, Zona Comercial, Col. Ciudad Industrial, 38010 Celaya, Guanajuato
Tel: +52(461) 611-74-54

Rector: Joel Othón Aguirre Rodríguez (1984-)

Programmes
Engineering; **Gastronomy** (Cooking and Catering); **Law** (Law); **Management** (Management); **Marketing** (Marketing); **Tourism**
History: Founded 1983.
Main Language(s) of Instruction: Spanish
Degrees and Diplomas: *Licenciatura*
Last Updated: 01/03/13

INSTITUTE OF HIGHER STUDIES OF THE CENTRE

Instituto de Estudios Superiores del Centro
Mariano J. García 355, San Miguelito, 36559 Irapuato, Guanajuato
Tel: +52(462) 623-59-69
EMail: fomeduc@prodigy.net.mx

Rector: Jesús Contreras Esparza (1991-)

Programmes
Agricultural Engineering; **Industrial Engineering** (Industrial Engineering)
History: Founded 1991.
Degrees and Diplomas: *Licenciatura*: 8 sem.
Last Updated: 01/03/13

INSTITUTE OF HIGHER STUDIES OF THE CENTRE OF CHIAPAS

Instituto de Estudios Superiores del Centro de Chiapas
Calle Cuarta Norte Poniente No.728, 29000 Tuxtla Gutiérrez, Chiapas

Director: Iran Molina Alegria

Programmes

Accountancy (Accountancy); **Computer Engineering** (Computer Engineering; Computer Science); **Mathematics** (Mathematics); **Pedagogy** (Pedagogy)

Main Language(s) of Instruction: Spanish

Degrees and Diplomas: *Licenciatura*; *Maestría*
Last Updated: 01/03/13

INSTITUTE OF HIGHER STUDIES OF THE DUTCH COLLEGE

Instituto de Estudios Superiores del Colegio Holandés
Marsella, 43, Col. Juárez, Delegación Cuauhtémoc, 06600 México, D.F.
Tel: +52(55) 55-11-68-41
EMail: isabel.godoy@colegioholandes.edu.mx

Rector: Rodolfo G. Del Monte Sánchez (1998-)

Programmes

Accountancy; **Business Administration**; **Communication Studies** (Communication Studies); **Customs and International Business** (International Business; Taxation); **International Relations** (International Relations); **Law** (Law); **Marketing** (Marketing)

Further Information: Also Benito Baruch Espinoza, Lafontaine and Marsella campuses

History: Founded 1990.

Degrees and Diplomas: *Licenciatura*
Last Updated: 07/04/08

INSTITUTE OF HIGHER STUDIES OF THE GULF

Instituto de Estudios Superiores del Golfo
Revillagigedo, 3166, Esq. Echeven, Col. Centro, 91700 Heroica Veracruz, Veracruz
Tel: +52(229) 934-34-42 +52(229) 931-75-24

Director: Luis Antonio Cruz Martínez

History: Founded 1994.

Degrees and Diplomas: *Licenciatura*
Last Updated: 07/04/08

INSTITUTE OF HIGHER STUDIES OF THE SOUTH-EAST

Instituto de Estudios Superiores del Sureste, S.C.
2a. Avenida Sur y 7 a. Poniente, Col. Barrio San Martín, 30470 Villaflores, Chiapas
Tel: +52(965) 652-00-39
Fax: +52(965) 652-25-70
EMail: info@iessuniversidad.edu.mx
Website: http://www.iessuniversidad.edu.mx

Directora: Elena Osorio Coutiño (1990-)

Programmes

Accountancy (Accountancy); **Business Administration** (Business Administration; Finance); **Computer Science** (Computer Science); **Law** (Law); **Pedagogy**; **Psychology** (Psychology)

Further Information: Also campus in Chiapas

History: Founded 1990.

Main Language(s) of Instruction: Spanish

Degrees and Diplomas: *Licenciatura*: 8 sem.; *Maestría*; *Doctorado*: Education

Libraries: Yes
Last Updated: 01/03/13

INSTITUTE OF HIGHER STUDIES OF THE VALLEY OF PARRAS

Instituto de Estudios Superiores del Valle de Parras, A.C.
Avenida Cinco de Mayo, 102, Centro, 27980 Parras de La Fuente, Coahuila
Tel: +52(842) 422-01-93 +52(842) 222-01-15
Fax: +52(842) 222-01-15

Director: José Antonio Bárcena Gama (1998-)

Programmes

Accountancy (Accountancy); **Business Administration** (Business Administration); **Computer Systems** (Computer Science); **Psychology** (Psychology)

History: Founded 1998.

Main Language(s) of Instruction: Spanish

Degrees and Diplomas: *Licenciatura*
Last Updated: 04/03/13

INSTITUTE OF HIGHER STUDIES OF THE VIZCAYA PACIFIC REGION

Instituto de Estudios Superiores Vizcaya Pacífico, A.C.
Carretera Internacional Norte Km. 11.5, 80020 Culiacán, Sinaloa
Tel: +52(667) 750-00-81
EMail: boanerges74@hotmail.com

Director: Edmigdio Duarte Figueroa

Programmes

Philosophy (Philosophy)

History: Founded 1995.

Degrees and Diplomas: *Licenciatura*
Last Updated: 04/03/13

INSTITUTE OF HIGHER STUDIES OF TUXTLA

Instituto de Estudios Superiores de Tuxtla
Palma Comedor, 209, Col. Las Palmas, 29000 Tuxtla Gutiérrez, Chiapas
Tel: +52(961) 4-03-29

Director: Jesús Arturo Yáñez Zúñiga

Programmes

Law (Law)

Degrees and Diplomas: *Licenciatura*
Last Updated: 07/04/08

INSTITUTE OF HIGHER STUDIES OF XALAPA

Instituto de Estudios Superiores de Xalapa, A.C.
Melchor Ocampo, 52-54, Esq. J. Azueta, Col. Centro, 91000 Xalapa, Veracruz
Tel: +52(228) 815-50-59
Fax: +52(228) 815-98-10
EMail: iesxalapa@aol.com

Director: Ramón de Jesús Francisco Castilla Segovia (1998-)

Programmes

Architecture (Architecture); **Business Computing** (Business Computing); **Public Relations** (Public Relations)

History: Founded 1998.

Main Language(s) of Instruction: Spanish

Degrees and Diplomas: *Licenciatura*
Last Updated: 01/03/13

INSTITUTE OF HOMEOPATHIC MEDICINE, TEACHING AND RESEARCH

Instituto Superior de Medicina Homeopática de la Enseñanza e Investigación
Humbolt No. 717, Centro, Monterrey, Nuevo León
Website: http://www.ismhei.com.mx

Director: Guillermo Montfort Ulloa

Programmes
Homeopathic Medicine (Homeopathy)
History: Founded 1988.
Main Language(s) of Instruction: Spanish
Degrees and Diplomas: *Especialización*
Last Updated: 08/03/13

INSTITUTE OF INTERPRETERS AND TRANSLATORS

Instituto Superior de Intérpretes y Traductores
Calle Río Rhin, 40, Col. Cuauhtémoc, Delegación Cuauhtémoc, 06500 México, D.F.
Tel: +52(55) 55-66-77-22
Fax: +52(55) 55-66-83-12
EMail: isit@isit.edu.mx
Website: http://www.isit.edu.mx/

Director General: Jacob Chencinsky Veksler

Programmes
Modern Languages (Cultural Studies; English; French; Spanish); **Translation and Interpretation** (Translation and Interpretation)
History: Founded 1980.
Main Language(s) of Instruction: Spanish
Degrees and Diplomas: *Licenciatura*; *Especialización*
Last Updated: 08/03/13

INSTITUTE OF MARKETING AND ADVERTISING

Instituto de Mercadotecnia y Publicidad
Guanajuato 228, Col. Roma, Delegación Cuauhtémoc, 06700 México, D.F.
Tel: +52(555) 5584-0824
EMail: informes@improma.com
Website: http://www.improma.com

Director General: Reynaldo Ampudia Carrillo (1986-)

Programmes
Advertising (Advertising and Publicity); **Design** (Design; Graphic Design); **Marketing** (Marketing)
History: Founded 1963.
Main Language(s) of Instruction: Spanish
Degrees and Diplomas: *Licenciatura*
Last Updated: 05/03/13

INSTITUTE OF MARKETING AND PUBLICITY OF NAUCALPAN

Instituto de Mercadotécnia y Publicidad Naucalpán
Calle 16 de Septiembre 4, Casi Esq. Periférico, Col. El Parque Naucalpán, 53560 Naucalpán de Juárez, Estado de México
Tel: +52(5) 53-58-08-55
Fax: +52(5) 53-76-34-30

Director General: Adolfo Malo Pérez

Programmes
Marketing, Advertising and Publicity (Advertising and Publicity; Marketing)
History: Founded 1988.
Main Language(s) of Instruction: Spanish
Degrees and Diplomas: *Licenciatura*

INSTITUTE OF MEDIATION OF MEXICO

Instituto de Mediación de México
Guadalupe Victoria, 39, Esq. Tamaulipas, Col. San Benito, 83190 Hermosillo, Sonora
Tel: +52(662) 210-59-89

Directora: Luz de Lourdes Ángulo López

Programmes
Conflict Resolution (Law; Peace and Disarmament)
History: Founded 1999.
Main Language(s) of Instruction: Spanish
Degrees and Diplomas: *Especialización*
Last Updated: 05/03/13

INSTITUTE OF MENTAL HEALTH OF NUEVO LEÓN

Instituto de Salud Mental de Nuevo León
Rayón No. 438 Sur, 64000 Monterrey, Nuevo León
Tel: +52(8) 344-34-44
EMail: ismnl@enlace.net

Director: Javier Falcón Morales

Programmes
Mental Health (Psychiatry and Mental Health)
Main Language(s) of Instruction: Spanish
Degrees and Diplomas: *Especialización*
Last Updated: 05/03/13

INSTITUTE OF MENTAL HEALTH STUDIES

Instituto Superior de Estudios para la Salud Mental
Insurgentes Sur N° 550 2° Piso, Col. Roma Sur, Cuauhtémoc, 06760 México, D.F.
Tel: +52(555) 574-86-53
Fax: +52(555) 574-87-66

Directora: Angela Ibarrola Díaz Barriga

Programmes
Mental Health Studies
Degrees and Diplomas: *Especialización*

INSTITUTE OF MONTSERRAT

Instituto de Montserrat
Ignacio M. Altamirano, 48, Centro, 39000 Chilpancingo de los Bravo, Guerrero
Tel: +52(747) 471-52-96
EMail: info@indemont.edu.mx
Website: http://www.indemont.edu.mx

Director General: Miguel Quevedo Reyes

Programmes
Administration (Administration); **Law** (Criminal Law; Law); **Psychology** (Psychology)
History: Founded 1999.
Main Language(s) of Instruction: Spanish
Degrees and Diplomas: *Licenciatura*; *Maestría*
Last Updated: 05/03/13

INSTITUTE OF PHILOSOPHY

Instituto de Filosofía
Camino Real a Colima 5160, Col. Balcones de Santa María, 45606 Tlaquepaque, Jalisco
Tel: +52(33) 36-31-09-34
EMail: administracion@if.edu.mx
Website: http://www.if.edu.mx

Rector: Luis Fernando Falcón Pliego (2000-)
EMail: rector@if.edu.mx

Programmes
Philosophy (Philosophy)
Degrees and Diplomas: *Licenciatura*
Libraries: Yes
Last Updated: 04/03/13

INSTITUTE OF PHILOSOPHY

Instituto Superior de Filosofía
Avenida Madero, 2000, Centro, 21100 Mexicali, Baja California
Tel: +52(686) 554-44-78
Fax: +52(686) 554-10-60
EMail: seminario@server.diocesismxl.org.mx

Rector: David Cortés Rivera

Programmes
Philosophy (Philosophy)
History: Founded 1992 as Seminario Diocesano de Mexicali.
Main Language(s) of Instruction: Spanish
Degrees and Diplomas: *Licenciatura*
Last Updated: 28/03/08

INSTITUTE OF POSTGRADUATE STUDIES IN PSYCHOANALYSIS AND PSYCHOTHERAPY

Instituto de Estudios de Posgrado en Psicoanálisis y Psicoterapia
Av. México N° 37 403-404, Col. Condesa, Delegación Cuauhtémoc, 06100 México, D.F.
Tel: +52(555) 553-35-99
Fax: +52(555) 286-75-99
EMail: spm@spm.org.mx
Website: http://www.spm.org.mx/

Director: Roberto Gaitán-González (1994-)

Programmes
Psychoanalysis and Psychotherapy (Psychoanalysis; Psychotherapy)
History: Founded 1982.
Governing Bodies: Comisión de Enseñanza y Director Académico
Admission Requirements: College degree or Licenciatura
Fees: (Pesos): c. 60,000 per annum
Main Language(s) of Instruction: Spanish
Accrediting Agencies: Secretaría de Educación Pública
Degrees and Diplomas: *Especialización*: Psychoanalysis, 2 yrs postgraduate study; *Maestría*: Psychoanalysis, 2 yrs postgraduate study; *Doctorado*: Psychoanalysis, 2 yrs
Student Services: Academic counselling, Canteen, Foreign student adviser
Libraries: Specialised library
Last Updated: 01/03/13

INSTITUTE OF POSTGRADUATE STUDIES IN SCIENCE AND HUMANITIES

Instituto de Estudios de Posgrado en Ciencias y Humanidades
Avenida Insurgentes Sur 933, 8o piso, Col. Nápoles, Benito Juárez, 03810 México, D.F.
Tel: +52(55) 55-43-18-66
Fax: +52(55) 55-43-08-90
EMail: inespo@df1.telmex.net.mx
Website: http://www.inespo.com

Director: Darvelio Alberto Castaño Asmitia (1993-)

Programmes
Organisational Development (Development Studies)
History: Founded 1993.
Main Language(s) of Instruction: Spanish
Degrees and Diplomas: *Maestría*
Last Updated: 01/03/13

INSTITUTE OF POTOSÍ

Instituto del Potosí
Agustín de Iturbide 330, Esq. Morelos, Centro Histórico, 78000 San Luis Potosí, San Luis Potosí
Tel: +52(44) 812-80-20
EMail: institutodelpotosi@hotmail.com
Website: http://institutodelpotosi.edu.mx

Director: Agustín Lanuza Araujo

Programmes
Business Administration (Business Administration; Commercial Law; Economic and Finance Policy; Economics; Finance; International Business; International Law); **Engineering** (Engineering; Industrial Engineering; Production Engineering)
History: Founded 1997.
Main Language(s) of Instruction: Spanish
Degrees and Diplomas: *Licenciatura*; *Maestría*
Last Updated: 05/03/13

INSTITUTE OF PROFESSIONAL EVALUATION

Instituto de Asesoramiento Profesional
Manuel Merino, 16, Col. Centro, 33800 Hidalgo del Parral, Chihuahua
Tel: +52(627) 272-70-73
Fax: +52(627) 272-34-13

Programmes
Computer Systems (Computer Science); **Psychology** (Psychology)
History: Founded 1989.
Main Language(s) of Instruction: Spanish
Degrees and Diplomas: *Licenciatura*; *Maestría*
Last Updated: 22/02/08

INSTITUTE OF PROFESSIONAL STUDIES OF CIUDAD MANTE

Instituto Mantense de Estudios Profesionales
Melchor Ocampo, 212, Sur, Col. Centro, Mante, 89800 Ciudad Mante, Tamaulipas
Tel: +52(831) 232-17-78
Website: http://www.imep.com.mx

Director: Arturo Eduardo Millan Ortíz

Programmes
Accountancy (Accountancy); **Business Administration** (Business Administration); **Business Computing** (Business Computing); **Communication Sciences** (Communication Studies; Journalism; Photography; Radio and Television Broadcasting); **Law** (Law); **Pedagogy** (Pedagogy); **Social Work** (Social Work)
Main Language(s) of Instruction: Spanish
Degrees and Diplomas: *Licenciatura*
Last Updated: 06/03/13

INSTITUTE OF PROFESSIONAL STUDIES OF SALTILLO

Instituto de Estudios Profesionales de Saltillo
Villa de Santiago No 4813, Colonia Villas de San Lorenzo, 25000 Saltillo, Coahuila
Tel: +52(844) 414-03-20
EMail: ieps@ieps.edu.mx
Website: http://www.ieps.edu.mx

Coordinador General: Jesús Arnoldo Sánchez González

Programmes
Business Administration (Business Administration); **Law**; **Public Accountancy** (Accountancy)
History: Founded 1966.
Main Language(s) of Instruction: Spanish
Degrees and Diplomas: *Licenciatura*
Last Updated: 01/03/13

INSTITUTE OF PROFESSIONAL STUDIES, CITLALLI COLLEGE

Instituto de Estudios Profesionales, Colegio Citlalli
Colina del Manantial, 3, Col. Residencial Boulevares, 53140 Naucalpán de Juárez, Estado de México
Tel: +52(55) 53-93-29-71
Fax: +52(55) 55-62-73-72
EMail: eitlalsc@df.telmex.net.mx

Director: Roberto Gálvez Rodríguez

Programmes
Law (Law)
Main Language(s) of Instruction: Spanish
Degrees and Diplomas: *Licenciatura*
Last Updated: 01/03/13

INSTITUTE OF PROSPECTIVE STUDIES

Instituto Superior de Estudios Prospectivos
Plaza de la República 48, 5o piso, Col. Tabacalera, Cuauhtémoc, 03060 México, D.F.
Tel: +52(555) 535-43-40
Fax: +52(555) 535-99-48
EMail: informacion@isep.edu.mx
Website: http://isep.edu.mx

Director General: Adip Sabag (1998-)

Programmes
Prospective Studies (Development Studies)
History: Founded 1998.
Main Language(s) of Instruction: Spanish
Degrees and Diplomas: *Especialización*; *Maestría*
Last Updated: 08/03/13

INSTITUTE OF PSYCHOANALYTICAL PSYCHOTHERAPY OF CHILDREN AND ADOLESCENTS

Instituto de Psicoterapia Psicoanalítica de la Infancia y Adolescencia
Patriotismo N° 8 Piso 12, Col. Hipódromo Condesa, 06100 México, D.F.
Tel: +52(555) 516-51-58

Directora: Maria Luisa Rodríguez Hurtado

Programmes
Psychotherapy (Psychoanalysis; Psychotherapy)
Main Language(s) of Instruction: Spanish
Degrees and Diplomas: *Especialización*; *Maestría*; *Doctorado*
Last Updated: 20/02/08

INSTITUTE OF PSYCHOTHERAPY

Instituto de Psicoterapia
Prolongación Vasconcelos 115, 66230 San Pedro Garza García, Nuevo León
Tel: +52(818) 338-28-72
EMail: idepsicoterapia@prodigy.net.mx
Website: http://psicoterapia.edu.mx

Directora General: Nora Adriana Hinojosa Ayala

Programmes
Psychotherapy (Psychoanalysis; Psychotherapy)
History: Founded 1973.
Main Language(s) of Instruction: Spanish
Degrees and Diplomas: *Especialización*; *Maestría*; *Doctorado*
Last Updated: 05/03/13

INSTITUTE OF PUBLIC ADMINISTRATION OF THE STATE OF PUEBLA

Instituto de Administración Pública del Estado de Puebla, A.C.
22 Oriente 1409, Col. Xonaca, 72280 Puebla, Puebla
Tel: +52(222) 236-00-17
Fax: +52(222) 236-57-92
EMail: teresa_espino@iappuebla.edu.mx
Website: http://iappuebla.edu.mx

Presidente: Eukid Castañón Herrera
EMail: eukid_castanon@iappuebla.edu.mx

Programmes
Finance (Finance); **Public Administration** (Public Administration; Regional Planning; Regional Studies); **Public Finance** (Economic and Finance Policy; Finance); **Taxation** (Taxation)
History: Founded 1978.
Main Language(s) of Instruction: Spanish
Degrees and Diplomas: *Licenciatura*; *Maestría*; *Doctorado*
Last Updated: 18/01/13

INSTITUTE OF PUEBLA

Instituto de Puebla
3 Sur, 3309, Col. Chulavista, 72420 Puebla, Puebla
Tel: +52(222) 240-58-76
Director: Juan Manuel Reyes Cardoso
Degrees and Diplomas: *Licenciatura*
Last Updated: 07/04/08

INSTITUTE OF RATIONAL EMOTIONAL BEHAVIOUR THERAPY

Instituto de Terapia Racional Emotiva
Calle Chiclayo 720, Miraflores, 11560 México, D.F.
Tel: +52(555) 447-43-86
Fax: +52(555) 241-24-79
EMail: administracion@itrec.org
Website: http://www.itrec.org

Director General: Pedro Reyes Mispereta

Programmes
Therapy (Psychotherapy)
History: Founded 1989.
Main Language(s) of Instruction: Spanish
Degrees and Diplomas: *Maestría*
Last Updated: 05/03/13

INSTITUTE OF SCIENCE AND CULTURE

Instituto de Ciencia y Cultura, A.C
Salazar Sur 896, 25000 Saltillo, Coahuila
Tel: +52(844) 410-15-15
EMail: iccac70@hotmail.com
Website: http://www.iccac.edu.mx

Directora: Griselda Cuevas Flores

Programmes
Biology (Biology); **Business Administration** (Business Administration); **Labour and Industrial Relations** (Labour and Industrial Relations)
Main Language(s) of Instruction: Spanish
Degrees and Diplomas: *Licenciatura*
Last Updated: 18/01/13

INSTITUTE OF SCIENCE AND HIGHER EDUCATION

Instituto de Ciencias y Educación Superior, A.C.
Iturbide, 63, Col. 5 de Mayo, 83010 Hermosillo, Sonora
Tel: +52(662) 214-60-77
Fax: +52(662) 214-60-77
EMail: informes@ices.edu.mx
Website: http://www.ices.edu.mx

Rector: René Llamas Rembao EMail: rectoria@ices.edu.mx

Areas
Administration (Marketing; Public Administration); **Arts and Humanities** (Arts and Humanities; Fashion Design; Interior Design; Philosophy)
History: Founded 1999.
Main Language(s) of Instruction: Spanish
Degrees and Diplomas: *Licenciatura*; *Maestría*
Last Updated: 18/01/13

INSTITUTE OF SCIENCE AND HIGHER STUDIES OF TAMAULIPAS

Instituto de Ciencias y Estudios Superiores de Tamaulipas, A.C.
Prol. Agua Dulce No. 1014, Ave. Universidad y R. Bustamante, Tampico, Tamaulipas
Tel: +52(833) 217-46-10
EMail: evaluacion@icest.edu.mx
Website: http://www.icest.edu.mx

Directora: Virginia Ruth Rodríguez Muro

Areas

Administration and Commerce (Accountancy; Administration; Advertising and Publicity; Business Administration; Cooking and Catering; Finance; Information Technology; International Business; Marketing; Public Relations; Sales Techniques; Tourism); **Education** *(Ciudad Madero)* (Music Education; Pedagogy; Preschool Education; Primary Education); **Engineering and Science** (Agricultural Engineering; Agronomy; Architecture; Chemical Engineering; Civil Engineering; Computer Science; Environmental Studies; Industrial Design; Mechanical Engineering; Petroleum and Gas Engineering; Robotics; Telecommunications Engineering); **Health Sciences** (Dentistry; Gynaecology and Obstetrics; Nursing; Nutrition; Physical Therapy; Psychology; Radiology; Rehabilitation and Therapy; Social Work; Surgery; Veterinary Science); **Humanities and Social Sciences** (Communication Studies; Criminology; Graphic Design; Hispanic American Studies; History; Journalism; Law; Library Science; Media Studies; Modern Languages; Philosophy; Political Sciences; Public Administration; Sociology; Theatre)

Further Information: Also campuses in Nuevo León; Vera Cruz; San Luis Potosí; Hidalgo; Michoacan and Mexico City

History: Founded 1980.

Main Language(s) of Instruction: Spanish

Degrees and Diplomas: *Licenciatura*; *Maestría*; *Doctorado*

Libraries: Yes

Last Updated: 28/02/13

INSTITUTE OF SCIENCE, HUMANITIES AND TECHNOLOGY OF GUANAJUATO

Instituto de Ciencias, Humanidades y Tecnologías de Guanajuato, A.C.

Francisco Sarabia No. 1 Col. La Moderna, 36690 Irapuato, Guanajuato

Tel: +52(462) 625-88-97

Fax: +52(461) 625-57-12

EMail: informes@icyteg.com.mx

Website: http://www.icyteg.com.mx/

Director: Francisco Javier Ladino Hernández

Programmes

Automation and Control Engineering (Automation and Control Engineering; Robotics); **Economics** (Economics); **Educational Sciences** (Educational Sciences; Sociology); **Information Technology** (Information Technology); **Philology and Literature** (Literature; Philology); **Robotics** (Robotics); **Sociology** (Sociology)

Further Information: Also branch in Mexico City and Zacatecas

History: Founded 1988.

Main Language(s) of Instruction: Spanish

Degrees and Diplomas: *Licenciatura*; *Especialización*; *Maestría*; *Doctorado*

Last Updated: 28/02/13

INSTITUTE OF SOCIAL SCIENCES OF MERIDA

Instituto de Ciencias Sociales de Mérida, A.C.

Km 24 Periférico Norte Tablaje Catastral 14067 Chichí Díaz, 97000 Mérida, Yucatán

Tel: +52(999) 943-81-37

Director General: Jorge Barquet Chel

EMail: direccion@icsmac.com

Programmes

Communication Studies (Communication Studies); **Educational Sciences** (Educational Sciences); **Labour Psychology** (Psychology); **Political Science and Public Administration** (Political Sciences; Public Administration); **Sociology** (Sociology)

History: Founded 1982.

Main Language(s) of Instruction: Spanish

Degrees and Diplomas: *Licenciatura*

Last Updated: 27/02/13

INSTITUTE OF SOCIAL SCIENCES, ECONOMICS AND ADMINISTRATION

Instituto de Ciencias Sociales, Económicas y Administrativas

Balderas, 138, Col. Centro, Delegación Cuauhtémoc, 06700 México, D.F.

Tel: +52(555) 709-12-21

Rector: Alberto Ponce de León López

Programmes

Administration (Administration; Business Administration); **Communication Studies** (Communication Studies); **Criminology** (Criminology); **Economics** (Economics); **Law** (Law); **Pedagogy** (Pedagogy); **Psychopedagogy** (Pedagogy; Psychology); **Social Sciences** (Social Sciences)

History: Founded 1937.

Main Language(s) of Instruction: Spanish

Degrees and Diplomas: *Licenciatura*; *Maestría*

Last Updated: 27/02/13

INSTITUTE OF SPECIALIZED STUDIES FOR EXECUTIVES

Instituto de Especialización para Ejecutivos, S.C.

Protasio Tagle, 95, Col. San Miguel Chapultepec, 11850 México, D.F.

Tel: +52(55) 52-77-45-88

Fax: +52(55) 55-15-28-40

EMail: direccioniee@iee.com.mx

Website: http://www.iee.com.mx

Rector: Salvador Leaños Flores

EMail: salvador.leanos@iee.com.mx

Programmes

Business Administration (Business Administration); **Finance** (Finance); **Fiscality** (Fiscal Law); **Taxation** (Taxation)

Further Information: Campuses in Guadalajara, Mérida, and Monterrey

History: Founded 1969.

Main Language(s) of Instruction: Spanish

Degrees and Diplomas: *Especialización*; *Maestría*; *Doctorado*

Last Updated: 28/02/13

INSTITUTE OF TECHNOLOGICAL AND ADVANCED STUDIES OF MATATIPAC

Instituto de Estudios Tecnológicos y Superiores de Matatipac, A.C.

Bugambilias, 124, Jardines del Valle, 63038 Tepic, Nayarit

Tel: +52(311) 216-74-74

Fax: +52(311) 216-90-00

EMail: informes@institutomatatipac.edu.mx

Website: http://institutomatatipac.edu.mx

Directora: Soledad Rubio Torres

Programmes

Accountancy (Accountancy); **Administration** (Administration); **Computer Science** (Computer Science; Technology); **Homeopathy** (Homeopathy); **Law** (Criminology; Law); **Natural Sciences** (Natural Sciences); **Psychology** (Psychology); **Security** (Protective Services)

History: Founded 1986.

Main Language(s) of Instruction: Spanish

Degrees and Diplomas: *Licenciatura*; *Especialización*; *Maestría*; *Doctorado*

Last Updated: 04/03/13

INSTITUTE OF TECHNOLOGY AND HIGHER STUDIES OF NAYARIT

Instituto Tecnológico y de Estudios Superiores de Nayarit

Abasolo, 25 Ote., 63000 Tepic, Nayarit
Tel: +52(311) 591-10-19
EMail: itesnay@gmail.com
Website: http://www.itesnay.edu.mx/tepic

Director: Andrés Muñoz Velazco

Programmes
Education Sciences (Educational Sciences); **Law** (Law); **Psychology** (Psychology); **Social Work** (Social Work)

History: Founded 1992.
Main Language(s) of Instruction: Spanish
Degrees and Diplomas: *Licenciatura*
Last Updated: 21/03/13

INSTITUTE OF TOURISM STUDIES OF CHIHUAHUA

Instituto Superior de Turismo de Chihuahua

Calle 24A y 1o de Mayo, 1809, Santa Rita, 31020 Chihuahua, Chihuahua
Tel: +52(614) 416-40-14

Director: Daniel García Coello

Programmes
Tourism (Tourism)

History: Founded 1989
Main Language(s) of Instruction: Spanish
Degrees and Diplomas: *Licenciatura*
Last Updated: 04/04/08

INSTITUTE OF UNIVERSITY STUDIES

Instituto de Estudios Universitarios, A.C.

4 poniente 1919, Col. San Matias Heroica Puebla de Zaragoza, 72150 Puebla, Puebla
Tel: +52(222) 141-75-75
Fax: +52(222) 141-75-75
EMail: puebla@sistemaieu.edu.mx
Website: http://www.sistemaieu.edu.mx

Rectora: Lourdes Montaño
EMail: direccionpuebla@sistemaieu.edu.mx

Programmes
Accountancy and Finance (Accountancy; Finance); **Administration** (Administration); **Educational Sciences** (Education; Educational Sciences); **Gastronomy** (Cooking and Catering); **Graphic Design** (Graphic Design); **Law** (Law); **Marketing and Advertising** (Advertising and Publicity; Marketing); **Psychology**; **Systems Engineering and Information Technology** (Engineering Management; Information Technology); **Tourism** (Tourism)

Further Information: Also campuses in Acapulco, Campeche, Cancún, Cd. del Carmen, Chilpancingo, Coatzacoalcos, Iguala, Oaxaca, Poza Rica, Salamanca, Tehuacán, Teziutlán,Tuxtla Gutierrez, Veracruz, Villahermosa and Xalapa
History: Founded 1976.
Main Language(s) of Instruction: Spanish
Degrees and Diplomas: *Licenciatura*; *Maestría*; *Doctorado*
Last Updated: 04/03/13

INSTITUTE OF UNIVERSITY STUDIES OF LEÓN

Instituto de Estudios Universitarios de León

Avenida Hernández Álvarez, 341, Col. Centro, 37000 León, Guanajuato
Tel: +52(477) 713-55-24
EMail: universitariosdeleon@gmail.com

Director: Héctor Delgado Castillo

Programmes
Law (Law); **Public Accounting** (Accountancy)

History: Founded 1990.
Main Language(s) of Instruction: Spanish
Degrees and Diplomas: *Licenciatura*
Last Updated: 04/03/13

INSTITUTO SUPERIOR DE ESTUDIOS EMPRESARIALES

Mérida, 20, Col. Roma, Delegación Cuauhtémoc, 06700 México, D.F.

Rector: Manuel Cervera Medel

Programmes
Business Studies (Business Administration; Management)

History: Founded 1996.
Main Language(s) of Instruction: Spanish
Degrees and Diplomas: *Licenciatura*
Last Updated: 18/01/13

INSTITUTO TECNOLÓGICO DE ESTUDIOS SUPERIORES DEL SURESTE

5 de Mayo Num. 21 (Lerdo y Pino Suárez), 96700 Minatitlán, Veracruz de Ignacio de la Llave

Programmes
Higher Education (Higher Education)

Main Language(s) of Instruction: Spanish
Degrees and Diplomas: *Licenciatura*
Last Updated: 13/03/13

INSTITUTO TECNOLÓGICO DE PEROTE

Last Updated: 29/03/13

INSTITUTO TECNOLÓGICO SUPERIOR DE SAN LUIS POTOSÍ, CAPITAL

Carr.57 México-Piedras Negras Km. 189 + 100 Tram Qro. - San Luis No. 6501, Delegacion Mpal. de Villa de Pozos, 78421 San Luis Potosí, San Luis Potosí
Tel: +52(444) 804-12-20
Website: http://www.tecsuperiorslp.edu.mx

Programmes
Administration (Administration); **Engineering** (Computer Engineering; Electronic Engineering; Industrial Engineering; Mechanical Engineering)

Main Language(s) of Instruction: Spanish
Degrees and Diplomas: *Licenciatura*
Last Updated: 29/03/13

INSTITUTO TECNOLÓGICO SUPERIOR DE VILLA LA VENTA

Last Updated: 02/04/13

INSURGENTES UNIVERSITY

Universidad Insurgentes (U.I.)

Calzada de Tlalpán, 390, Col. Viaducto Piedad, Delegación Iztacalco, 08200 México, D.F.
Tel: +52(55) 55-38-45-14 AL 16
Fax: +52(55) 55-38-15-29
EMail: rectoria@universidadinsurgentes.edu.mx
Website: http://www.universidadinsurgentes.edu.mx

Rectora: Argelia Hernandez Espinoza

Areas
Business Studies (Accountancy; Administration; International Business; Marketing); **Engineering and Technology** (Architecture; Computer Science; Design; Graphic Design; Industrial Engineering); **Humanities** (Pedagogy)

Further Information: Also Plantel Álamos, Plantel Tlalpán, Plantel Norte, Plantel Sur I, Plantel Sur II, Plantel Tláhuac, Plantel Vía Moleros, Plantel Centro, Plantel Ecatepec, Plantel Toreo, Plantel Viaducto, Plantel Xola, Plantel León, Plantel Tlalnepantla, Plantel Cd. Azteca and Plantel San Ángel.

History: Founded 1976.
Main Language(s) of Instruction: Spanish
Degrees and Diplomas: *Licenciatura*; *Especialización*; *Maestría*
Last Updated: 10/10/12

INTEC ADVANCED STUDIES IN COMPUTER SCIENCE

INTEC Estudios Superiores en Informática
11 Sur, 3308, Chulavista, 72420 Puebla, Puebla
Tel: +52(222) 243-62-66
EMail: informes@admisionesdasc.com
Website: http://www.dasc.com.mx

Director: Alejandro Gerardo García Sainos

Programmes
Business Administration (Business Administration); **Computer Science** (Computer Science); **Engineering** (Engineering; Industrial Engineering; Software Engineering); **Graphic Design** (Graphic Design); **Information Systems**; **Marketing** (Marketing)
History: Founded 1991.
Main Language(s) of Instruction: Spanish
Degrees and Diplomas: *Licenciatura*
Last Updated: 22/03/13

INTEGRAL CENTRE FOR FASHION AND DESIGN

Centro Integral de Moda y Estilo (CIME)
Avenida Vallarta, 1044-2 Planta Alta, (Entre Prado y Enrique Díaz de León), Col. Americana, 44100 Guadalajara, Jalisco
Tel: +52(33) 38-25-59-17
EMail: informes@cimemoda.edu.mx
Website: http://www.cimemoda.edu.mx

Directora General: Martha Patricia Trujillo Sepúlveda

Programmes
Fashion Design (Fashion Design; Textile Design)
History: Founded 2004.
Main Language(s) of Instruction: Spanish
Degrees and Diplomas: *Licenciatura*; *Maestría*
Last Updated: 27/10/09

INTEGRAL UNIVERSITY CENTRE OF ZACATLÁN

Centro Universitario Integral de Zacatlán
Matamoros, Esq. con Balderas, Zacatlán, Puebla
EMail: informes@cuiza.ed.mx; cuiza@hotmail.com

Director: Ángel Hernández Corta

Programmes
Business Computing (Business Computing); **Computer Engineering** (Computer Engineering)
Main Language(s) of Instruction: Spanish
Degrees and Diplomas: *Licenciatura*; *Maestría*
Last Updated: 12/03/08

INTERACTIVE AND DISTANCE UNIVERSITY OF THE STATE OF GUANAJUATO

Universidad Interactiva y a Distancia del Estado de Guanajuato
Carretera Acámbaro-Parácuaro Km.12., 37234 Acámbaro, Guanajuato
Tel: +52(428) 471-04-03
EMail: unideg_acambaro@hotmail.com
Website: http://unidegacambaro.netii.net

Directora General: Alma Verónica López López
EMail: direccion_general@sabes.edu.mx

Programmes
Business Administration (Business Administration); **Industrial Engineering** (Industrial Engineering); **Information Technology** (Information Technology); **Marketing** (Marketing)
Further Information: Also campuses in Acámbaro, Apaseo el Grande, Celaya, Comonfort, Irapuato, Juventino Rosas, Pénjamo, Salvatierra, San Felipe, San José I., San Luis de la Paz and Villagrán
History: Founded 2000.
Main Language(s) of Instruction: Spanish
Degrees and Diplomas: *Licenciatura*
Last Updated: 03/04/13

INTER-AMERICAN UNIVERSITY

Universidad Interamericana
Lateral Sur de la Vía Atilxcayolt #7007, 72000 San Andrés Cholula, Puebla
Tel: +52(222) 246-50-05
EMail: info@lainter.edu.mx
Website: http://www.lainter.edu.mx

Rector: Jesús Ángel Ortega Zamora (1986-)

Schools
Communication and Design (Advertising and Publicity; Design; Media Studies); **Economics and Administration** (Accountancy; Business Administration; International Business; Marketing); **Engineering** (Computer Engineering; Electronic Engineering; Industrial Engineering; Telecommunications Engineering); **Nutrition and Biotechnology** (Biotechnology; Food Technology; Nutrition); **Social Sciences and Humanities** (Advertising and Publicity; International Relations; Law; Modern Languages); **Tourism and Gastronomy** (Cooking and Catering; Hotel and Restaurant; Tourism)
History: Founded 1986.
Main Language(s) of Instruction: Spanish
Degrees and Diplomas: *Licenciatura*; *Maestría*
Last Updated: 10/10/12

INTER-AMERICAN UNIVERSITY CENTRE

Centro Universitario Interamericano
Tablaje Catastral 13940, Polígono Chuburná 1634, 97070 Mérida, Yucatán
Tel: +52(999) 987-03-41 +52(999) 941-20-18
Fax: +52(999) 941-20-30
EMail: inter@interamericano.edu.mx
Website: http://www.interamericano.edu.mx/mid

Director: Marco de la Rosa (1994-)
EMail: marco@interamericano.edu.mx

Programmes
Interior Design (Interior Design); **Marketing** (Marketing); **Photography** (Photography); **Publicity** (Advertising and Publicity)
History: Founded 1994.
Degrees and Diplomas: *Licenciatura*; *Maestría*
Libraries: Yes
Last Updated: 25/07/12

INTER-AMERICAN UNIVERSITY FOR DEVELOPMENT, TLALNEPANTLA

Universidad Interamericana para el Desarrollo
Av. Dr. Gustavo Baz, 2160, Acceso 4, Esq. Mario Colín, Col. La Loma, 54060 Tlalnepantla, Estado de México
Tel: +52(55) 52-36-30-38
Fax: +52(55) 26-28-03-34
EMail: contacto@uid.com.mx
Website: http://www.unid.edu.mx

Rector: Carlos Güereca Lozano

Programmes
Accountancy and Finance (Accountancy; Finance); **Administration** (Accountancy; Administration; Business Administration; Marketing; Tourism); **Communication Studies** (Communication Studies); **Education** (Education; Educational Technology; Physical Education; Preschool Education; Primary Education); **Fashion Design** (Fashion Design); **Gastronomy** (Cooking and Catering); **Information Systems** (Information Management; Information Technology); **Law** (Law); **Nursing** (Nursing)

Further Information: Campuses: Aguascalientes (Aguascalientes); Ensenada, Tijuana (Baja California); Campeche, Ciudad del Carmen (Campeche); Tapachula (Chiapas); Saltillo (Coahuila); Tejupilco, Tlalnepantla, Toluca, Valle de Chalco, Taxqueña (Distrito Federal y Estado de México); Durango, Gómez Palacio (Durango); Acapulco (Guerrero); Pachuca, Tula (Hidalgo); Guadalajara, Ocotlán, Tepatitlán (Jalisco); Cotija, Morelia, Sahuayo, Uruapan (Michoacán); Cuernavaca (Morelos); Monterrey (Nuevo León); Juchitán, Tuxtepec (Oaxaca); Atlixco, Tehuacán (Puebla); Cancún, Chetumal, Cozumel, Playa del Carmen (Quintana Roo); San Luis Potosí (San Luis Potosí); Hermosillo, Ciudad Obregón (Sonora); Villahermosa (Tabasco); Reynosa, Tampico (Tamaulipas); Coatzacoalcos, Tuxpan, Veracruz (Veracruz); Mérida Vista Alegre, Mérida Fco. de Montejo, Tizimín (Yucatán); Fresnillo, Zacatecas (Zacatecas)

History: Founded 2000.

Main Language(s) of Instruction: Spanish

Degrees and Diplomas: *Licenciatura*; *Maestría*
Last Updated: 10/10/12

INTER-AMERICAN UNIVERSITY OF CUERNAVACA

Universidad Interamericana Cuernavaca

Campus Chapultepec, Calle de la Luz No 8, Col. Chapultepec, Cuernavaca, Morelos
Tel: +52(777) 315-80-01
Website: http://www.unit.edu.mx

Rector: José Alberto Pérez Apáez

Programmes
Accountancy (Accountancy); **Administration** (Administration; Marketing); **Computer Science** (Computer Science; Software Engineering); **Human Resources** (Human Resources; Staff Development); **Industrial Engineering Management** (Industrial Engineering; Industrial Management); **Law** (Administrative Law; Commercial Law; Criminal Law; Labour Law; Law)

History: Founded 1999.

Main Language(s) of Instruction: Spanish

Degrees and Diplomas: *Licenciatura*; *Especialización*
Last Updated: 10/10/12

INTER-AMERICAN UNIVERSITY OF THE NORTH AND OF TECHNOLOGY OF THE SIERRA MADRE

Universidad Interamericana del Norte y Tecnológico Sierra Madre

Carretera Nacional Km. 967, Hacienda La Estanzuela, 64988 Monterrey, Nuevo León
Tel: +52(181) 83-17-94-90
EMail: rectoria@uin.com.mx
Website: http://www.uin.com.mx

Rector: Marco Antonio Rendón Sandoval (2003-)

Programmes
Accountancy (Accountancy); **Administration** (Administration); **Cinema** (Cinema and Television; Film); **Communication Studies** (Communication Studies); **Dentistry** (Dentistry); **Fashion Design** (Fashion Design); **Gastronomy** (Cooking and Catering); **Graphic Design** (Graphic Design); **Hotel Management and Tourism** (Hotel Management; Tourism); **Industrial Engineering** (Industrial Engineering); **Interior Design** (Interior Design); **International Business** (International Business); **Law and International Affairs** (International Relations; Law); **Marketing** (Marketing); **Nutrition** (Nutrition)

Further Information: Campuses: Tampico, Ciudad Juárez, Eloy Cavazos, La Fe, Montemorelos, Reynosa, San Nicolás, San Nicolás Oriente (Plaza Conductores), and Guadalupe Centro (Palacio Federal)

History: Founded 1989. Acquired present status 1997.

Admission Requirements: Bachillerato.

Main Language(s) of Instruction: Spanish

International Co-operation: With universities in Guatemala

Degrees and Diplomas: *Licenciatura*: 3 yrs; *Maestría*

Student Services: Employment services, Foreign student adviser, Handicapped facilities, Health services, Language programs, Sports facilities

Student Residential Facilities: None

Special Facilities: Yes

Libraries: Yes
Last Updated: 10/10/12

INTERCONTINENTAL CENTRE FOR ADVANCED STUDIES

Centro de Estudios Superiores Intercontinental

5 de Mayo, 8, Centro, 36100 Silao, Guanajuato
Tel: +52(472) 722-10-99
Fax: +52(472) 549-63-39
EMail: cesi100@hotmail.com

Director: Marcos Alba Rodríguez

Programmes
Administration (Administration); **Industrial Engineering** (Industrial Engineering); **Law** (Law)

History: Founded 1997.

Main Language(s) of Instruction: Spanish

Degrees and Diplomas: *Licenciatura*
Last Updated: 16/07/12

INTERCONTINENTAL UNIVERSITY

Universidad Intercontinental (UIC)

Avenida Insurgentes Sur, 4303, Col. Santa Úrsula Xitle, Delegación Tlalpan, 14420 México, D.F.
Tel: +52(555) 487-13-00 +52(555) 487-14-00
EMail: buzon@uic.edu.mx
Website: http://www.uic.edu.mx

Rector: Juan José Corona López EMail: rectoria@uic.edu.mx

Areas
Business (Accountancy; Finance; Industrial Engineering; International Business; Management; Marketing; Tourism); **Communication and Architecture** (Advertising and Publicity; Architecture; Communication Studies; Graphic Design; Media Studies; Photography; Radio and Television Broadcasting; Translation and Interpretation; Video); **Health** (Dentistry; Nutrition; Psychology); **Humanities** (Commercial Law; Criminal Law; Labour Law; Law; Pedagogy; Philosophy; Theology)

History: Founded 1976 as International Institute of Philosophy, AC. Acquired present status and title 2010.Degrees recognized by the Secretaria de Educación Pública.

Governing Bodies: Consejo de Gobierno; Claustro Universitario

Academic Year: August to May (August-December; January-May)

Admission Requirements: Secondary school certificate (bachillerato)

Main Language(s) of Instruction: Spanish

International Co-operation: With universities in USA, Canada, Spain

Accrediting Agencies: Federación de Instituciones Mexicanas Particulares de Educación Superior (FIMPES), Asociación Nacional de Universidades e Instituciones de Educación Superior (ANUIES)

Degrees and Diplomas: *Licenciatura*: 4-4 1/2 yrs; *Especialización*: Commercial Law; Electoral Law; Visual Arts (Diseño de Imagen Corporativa); Typography, 1 yr; *Especialización*: Periodoncy; Prostodoncy, 2 yrs; *Maestría*: Education; Administration; Tourism; Philosophy; Journalism; Orthodontics, 2 yrs; *Maestría*: Special Education; Psychoanalysis; Finance, 2 1/2 yrs; *Doctorado*: Psychoanalysis; Administration; Education

Student Services: Academic counselling, Canteen, Cultural centre, Handicapped facilities, Health services, Language programs, Social counselling, Sports facilities

Student Residential Facilities: Not on campus

Special Facilities: TV Studio; Radio Studio; Labs (Mass Media, Design, Architecture, Cooking, Psychology)

Libraries: Yes

Publications: Ducit et Docet, International Research Review *(biennially)*; Estudios Jurídicos *(biennially)*; Intersticios (Filosofía, Religión y Arte) *(biennially)*; Psicología y Educación *(biennially)*; Unidad y Diversidad, Revista Interdisciplinaria *(biennially)*; Voces (Teologia Misionera) *(biennially)*
Last Updated: 10/10/12

INTERCONTINENTAL UNIVERSITY, MONTERREY

Universidad Intercontinental, Monterrey
General Santiago Tapia, 818, 828, Ote., 64000 Monterrey, Nuevo León
Tel: +52(81) 83-75-54-60

Director: Jesús Homero Sandoval Garza (1997-)

Programmes
Administration (Administration; Banking; Finance; Marketing; Public Administration); **Business Computing** (Business Computing); **International Relations** (International Relations)
Main Language(s) of Instruction: Spanish
Degrees and Diplomas: *Licenciatura*
Last Updated: 03/04/13

INTERCULTURAL UNIVERSITY OF THE STATE OF MEXICO

Universidad Intercultural del Estado de México
Libramiento Francisco Villa, S/N, Col. Centro, 50640 San Felipe del Progreso, Estado de México
EMail: correo@uiem.edu.mx
Website: http://www.uiem.edu.mx

Rector: José Francisco Monroy Gaytan
Director, Administration and Finance: Fanny Nelia Terron Botello
EMail: adyfinanzas_uiem@yahoo.com.mx

Programmes
Intercultural Communication (Communication Studies; Cultural Studies; Information Technology; Multimedia); **Intercultural Health** (Health Education); **Languages and Culture** (Cultural Studies; Modern Languages); **Sustainable Development** (Development Studies)
History: Founded 2004.
Main Language(s) of Instruction: Spanish
Degrees and Diplomas: *Licenciatura*
Libraries: Yes
Last Updated: 10/10/12

INTERNATIONAL CENTRE OF ADVANCED STUDIES

Centro Internacional de Educación Avanzada, A. C.
Calle Juárez, 626, 87000 Ciudad Victoria, Tamaulipas
Tel: +52(834) 345-36-76
Fax: +52(834) 345-36-76
EMail: unida2000@hotmail.com

Director: Marcelino Magaña

Programmes
Law (Law); **Public Administration** (Public Administration)
Main Language(s) of Instruction: Spanish
Degrees and Diplomas: *Maestría*; *Doctorado*
Last Updated: 19/07/12

INTERNATIONAL CENTRE OF ADVANCED STUDIES

Centro Internacional de Estudios Superiores, A.C.
Blvd. Federico Benítez, 5, Fracc. Los Españoles, 22450 Tijuana, Baja California
Tel: +52(666) 622-15-50
Fax: +52(666) 622-15-52
EMail: cieseduca@ciudadtijuana.info

Director: Carlos Serrano Torres

Programmes
Accountancy (Accountancy); **Business Administration** (Business Administration); **International Business** (International Business); **Marketing** (Marketing)
History: Founded 2000.
Main Language(s) of Instruction: Spanish
Degrees and Diplomas: *Licenciatura*; *Maestría*
Last Updated: 29/02/08

INTERNATIONAL CENTRE OF ADVANCED STUDIES OF MORELOS

Centro Internacional de Estudios Superiores de Morelos
Humboldt No. 46, Col. Centro, 62000 Cuernavaca, Morelos
Tel: +52(777) 318-25-13
EMail: aruelas@cies.com.mx
Website: http://www.cies.com.mx

Rector: Ramón Haces Álvarez

Programmes
Accountancy (Accountancy); **Business Administration** (Business Administration; Tourism); **Education** (Education; Educational Sciences); **Gastronomy** (Cooking and Catering); **International Business** (International Business); **Law** (Criminal Law; Law)
History: Founded 1997.
Main Language(s) of Instruction: Spanish
Degrees and Diplomas: *Licenciatura*; *Maestría*
Last Updated: 19/07/12

INTERNATIONAL CENTRE OF RESEARCH AND POSTGRADUATE STUDIES

Centro Internacional de Investigaciones y de Estudios de Posgrado
Av. de los Maestros No. 203, Col. el Vergel, Cuernavaca, Morelos
Tel: +52(7) 314-13-03 +52(7) 312-85-03
Fax: +52(7) 314-13-03
EMail: ceujova@prodigy.net.mx

Director: Emilio Ricardo Peña Rangel
Degrees and Diplomas: *Doctorado*

INTERNATIONAL COLLEGE OF GASTRONOMY

Colegio Gastronómico Internacional
Lopez Cotilla, 1854, Col. Americana, Lafayette, 44160 Guadalajara, Jalisco
Tel: +52(33) 36-30-07-95
Fax: +52(33) 36-30-07-94
Website: http://www.colegiogastronomico.com

Director: Juan José Tamayo Dávalos

Programmes
Gastronomy (Cooking and Catering; Hotel and Restaurant)
History: Founded 2006.
Main Language(s) of Instruction: Spanish
Degrees and Diplomas: *Licenciatura*; *Especialización*
Last Updated: 28/10/09

INTERNATIONAL COLLEGE OF HIGHER EDUCATION

Colegio Internacional de Educación Superior (CIES)
Rómulo O'Farril, 351, Col. Olivar de los Padres, Delegación Álvaro Obregón, 01780 México, D.F.
Tel: +52(55) 56-81-47-02
Fax: +52(55) 56-81-76-17
EMail: cies@cies-mex.com
Website: http://www.cies-mex.edu.mx

Director General: Jaime F. Ayala Villarreal (1998-)
EMail: jfayalav@mexis.com
Directora Académica: María de la I. Concepción Rabadán
EMail: conchitarabadan@hotmail.com; diracademica@cies-mex.-com

Programmes
Psychology (Psychology)

History: Founded 1998.

Admission Requirements: High school diploma

Fees: (Pesos): 3,100 per month

Main Language(s) of Instruction: Spanish, English

Degrees and Diplomas: *Licenciatura*: 4 yrs; *Maestría*: 2 1/2-3 yrs; *Doctorado*. Also Diplomados

Student Services: Academic counselling, Employment services, Foreign student adviser, Handicapped facilities, Health services, Language programs

Student Residential Facilities: None

Libraries: Yes

Last Updated: 27/07/12

INTERNATIONAL FACULTY OF EDUCATIONAL SCIENCES

Facultad Internacional de Ciencias de la Educación (FICED)

Calle Salvador Novo. No. 1050-C (Segundo Nivel) Entre calzada Paseo del Centenario y Via Rapida Poniente Zona Rio, 22320 Tijuana, Baja California

Tel: +52(664) 684-00-04

Fax: +52(664) 684-15-87

EMail: informes@ficed.org

Website: http://www.ficed.org

Directora General: María Esther Uriegas (2000-)

Director de Desarollo Institucional: Eduardo Cooley Lugo

Units
Educational Sciences (Education; Educational Sciences)

History: Founded 1995.

Academic Year: August to June

Admission Requirements: Secondary school certificate

Fees: (Pesos): c. 35,000-40,000 per annum

Main Language(s) of Instruction: Spanish

Accrediting Agencies: Secretaría de Educación Pública (SEP)

Degrees and Diplomas: *Maestría*: a further 2 yrs; *Doctorado*: 2 yrs

Last Updated: 30/08/12

INTERNATIONAL FOUNDATION FOR HOLISTIC EDUCATION

Fundación Internacional para la Educación Holista

Jalisco, 305, 49000 Zapopan, Jalisco

Tel: +52(33) 32-80-23-18

EMail: fundacion@ramongallegos.com

Website: http://www.ramongallegos.com

Director: Ramón Gallegos Nava

Programmes
Holistic Education (Education)

History: Founded 2005.

Main Language(s) of Instruction: Spanish

Degrees and Diplomas: *Maestría*; *Doctorado*

Libraries: Yes

Last Updated: 30/08/12

INTERNATIONAL INSTITUTE OF HIGHER STUDIES

Instituto Internacional de Estudios Superiores

Avenida San Jerónimo, 137, Col. San Ángel, Delegación Álvaro Obregón, 01000 México, D.F.

Tel: +52(555) 616-37-42

Fax: +52(555) 550-38-22

Rector: Sergio Ulloa Castellanos (1992-)

Degrees and Diplomas: *Licenciatura*; *Maestría*

INTERNATIONAL INSTITUTE OF HIGHER STUDIES, TAMAULIPAS

Instituto Internacional de Estudios Superiores, Tamaulipas (IIES)

Avenida Tiburcio Garza Zamora, 1700, Col. El Círculo, 88640 Reynosa, Tamaulipas

Tel: +52(899) 261-44-00

EMail: admisiones@iies.edu.mx

Website: http://www.iies.edu.mx

Director: Juan Rosendo Martínez Gómez (1997-)
EMail: rmartinez@iies.edu.mx

Programmes
Administration and Commerce (Administration; Business and Commerce); **Engineering** (Computer Engineering; Electrical Engineering; Electronic Engineering; Industrial Engineering; Mechanical Engineering)

Further Information: Also Campus Vista Hermosa

History: Founded 1993.

Main Language(s) of Instruction: Spanish

Degrees and Diplomas: *Licenciatura*; *Maestría*

Last Updated: 20/02/08

INTERNATIONAL PROFESSIONAL DEVELOPMENT CENTRE

Centro Internacional de Desarrollo Profesional (CIDEP)

Antonio de Mendoza 261, Washington y Martí, Fracc. Reforma, 91700 Veracruz, Veracruz

Tel: +52(229) 931-20-62

Fax: +52(229) 931-20-62

EMail: fucaver@hotmail.com.mx

Director: Francisco Blanco Calderón

Programmes
Education (Education)

Degrees and Diplomas: *Licenciatura*

Last Updated: 04/04/08

INTERNATIONAL SCHOOL OF TOURISM/ INTERNATIONAL PROFESSIONS UNIVERSITY

Escuela Internacional de Turismo/ Universidad Internacional de Profesiones (EIT/UNIPRO)

Amores, 314, Col. Del Valle, Delegación Benito Juárez, 03100 México, D.F.

Tel: +52(55) 56-87-21-11

Fax: +52(55) 56-23-40-12

EMail: correo@unipro.edu.mx

Website: http://www.unipro.edu.mx

Director General: Álvaro Jorge Becker Cuellar

Programmes
Fashion and Textile Design (Fashion Design; Textile Design); **Gastronomy** (Cooking and Catering); **Tourism Management** (Hotel Management; Tourism)

Further Information: Also campuses in León and Toluca

History: Founded 1993.

Main Language(s) of Instruction: Spanish

Degrees and Diplomas: *Licenciatura*

Last Updated: 06/03/13

INTERNATIONAL TECHNOLOGICAL UNIVERSITY

Universidad Tecnológica Internacional

16 de Septiembre, Esq. Narciso Mendoza s/n, San Pedro Atzompa, 55770 Tecámac, Estado de México

Tel: +52(55) 59-32-15-22

EMail: unitecinter@prodigy.net

Website: http://www.uti.edu.mx

Rector: Alberto García Velázquez (1994-)

Programmes

Accountancy (Accountancy); **Administration** (Administration); **Communication** (Communication Studies); **Computer Engineering** (Computer Engineering); **International Business** (International Business); **Law** (Law); **Marketing** (Marketing); **Pedagogy** (Pedagogy); **Tourism** (Tourism)

History: Founded 1944 as Centro Universitario Tecamac. Acquired present title and status 1996.

Main Language(s) of Instruction: Spanish

Degrees and Diplomas: *Licenciatura*; *Maestría*

Last Updated: 05/04/13

INTERNATIONAL UNIVERSITY

Universidad Internacional

Avenida General Anaya, 313, Col. del Carmen Coyoacán, Delegación Coyoacán, 04100 México, D.F.

Tel: +52(55) 56-58-64-21

Fax: +52(55) 56-58-62-46

EMail: informes@internacional.edu.mx

Website: http://www.internacional.edu.mx

Rectora: Illiana Barocio de las Fuentes (1994-)

Programmes

Accountancy (Accountancy); **Business Administration** (Business Administration); **Computer Science** (Computer Science); **Law** (Law); **Pedagogy** (Pedagogy)

History: Founded 1994.

Main Language(s) of Instruction: Spanish

Degrees and Diplomas: *Licenciatura*: 5 yrs

Student Services: Academic counselling, Foreign student adviser, Health services, Language programs, Social counselling, Sports facilities

Last Updated: 18/03/08

INTERNATIONAL UNIVERSITY

Universidad Internacional, S.C.

Avenida 5 de Mayo, 212, Pte., Centro, Monterrey, Nuevo León

Tel: +52(81) 834-07-755

EMail: universidadinternacional@internacional.net

Website: http://www.universidadinternacional.com.mx

Rector: Jaime Rafael Paz Fernández (1974-)

Programmes

Accountancy; **Business Administration** (Business Administration; International Business); **Engineering** (Automation and Control Engineering; Computer Engineering; Industrial Engineering; Industrial Maintenance); **English** (English); **Modern Languages** (Modern Languages); **Theology** (Theology); **Town Planning and Ecology** (Ecology; Town Planning)

History: Founded 1974 as Centro de Idiomas Extranjeros y de Enseñanza Superior, CEIEYES.

Main Language(s) of Instruction: Spanish

Degrees and Diplomas: *Licenciatura*; *Maestría*

Last Updated: 04/04/13

INTERNATIONAL UNIVERSITY CENTRE

Centro Universitario Internacional

Av. Revolución 595, Colonia San Pedro de los Pinos, Del. Benito Juárez, México, D.F.

Tel: +52(55) 56-51-76-73

EMail: informes@cuin.edu.mx

Website: http://cuin.edu.mx

Programmes

Administration and Marketing (Administration; Marketing); **Business and Marketing** (Business Administration; Business and Commerce; Marketing); **Law** (Law); **Social Sciences** (Social Sciences)

Main Language(s) of Instruction: Spanish

Degrees and Diplomas: *Licenciatura*; *Maestría*. Also Diplomados

Libraries: Yes

Last Updated: 25/07/12

INTERNATIONAL UNIVERSITY FOR DEVELOPMENT

Universidad Internacional para el Desarrollo, S.A. de C.V. (UNIDES)

Augusto Rodín, 128, Col. Mixcoac, Delegación Benito Juárez, 03910 México, D.F.

Tel: +52(555) 598-45-39

Fax: +52(555) 598-45-39

EMail: unides@data.net.mx

Directora: Elsy Méndez Baeza Tel: +52(555) 598-43-53

Faculties

Science, Administration and Law (Administration; Law; Natural Sciences)

History: Founded 1990.

Governing Bodies: Consejo

Admission Requirements: Secondary school certificate (bachillerato)

Main Language(s) of Instruction: Spanish, English

Accrediting Agencies: Secretaría de Educación Pública (SEP)

Degrees and Diplomas: *Licenciatura*; *Maestría*; *Doctorado*

Student Services: Academic counselling, Foreign student adviser, Foreign Studies Centre, Handicapped facilities, Social counselling

Student Residential Facilities: Yes

Libraries: Library

Publications: Memories and Statistics *(annually)*

Last Updated: 04/04/13

INTERNATIONAL UNIVERSITY OF ADVANCED INTERNATIONAL STUDIES

Universidad Internacional de Estudios Superiores Internacionales

Avenida Avila Camacho 2095, Col. Chapultepec, 44210 Guadalajara, Jalisco

Tel: +52(33) 38-25-02-22

Fax: +52(33) 38-25-02-22

Website: http://www.ui.com.mx/

Director: Francisco Javier Castellanos Silva

Faculties

Economics/Administration (Accountancy; Business Administration; International Business; Marketing); **Law** (Law); **Psychology and Communication Studies** (Communication Studies; Psychology)

Further Information: Branches: Vidrio, Avenida América and '16 de Septiembre'

History: Founded 1991.

Degrees and Diplomas: *Licenciatura*

Last Updated: 05/11/09

INTERNATIONAL UNIVERSITY OF ADVANCED STUDIES

Universidad Internacional de Estudios Superiores

Avenida Américas 459, Col. Ladrón de Guevara, 44600 Guadalajara, Jalisco

Tel: +52(33) 36-16-24-09

Fax: +52(33) 36-16-24-09

EMail: americas-coord@hotmail.com

Director: Francisco Javier Castellanos Silva

Programmes

Business Administration; **Communication Studies** (Communication Studies); **Human Development**; **Law** (Law)

Further Information: Also '16 de Septiembre' Branch

History: Founded 2002.

Degrees and Diplomas: *Licenciatura*; *Especialización*; *Maestría*

Last Updated: 04/11/09

INTERNATIONAL UNIVERSITY OF AMERICA

Universidad Internacional de América

Calle Pino Suarez No. 153 entre Hidalgo y Juárez, Zona Centro, 87000 Ciudad Victoria, Tamaulipas
Tel: 52+(834)134-18-25

Rector: Marcelino Magaña

Divisions

Education (Education; Preschool Education; Primary Education; Special Education; Teacher Training); **Law** (Law; Political Sciences)

History: Founded 1995. Acquired present title 2000.

Main Language(s) of Instruction: Spanish

Degrees and Diplomas: *Licenciatura*; *Maestría*; *Doctorado*

Last Updated: 14/04/09

INTERNATIONAL UNIVERSITY OF LA PAZ

Universidad Internacional de La Paz (UNIPAZ)

Km. 11 Carretera al Norte, Ejido Chametla-El Centenario, 23201 La Paz, Baja California Sur
Tel: +52 (612) 12-46851
EMail: info@unipaz.edu.mx
Website: http://www.unipaz.edu.mx

Rector: Miguel Albáñez Espinoza (1999-)

Directora de Asuntos Académicos: María del Carmen Rodríguez
EMail: unipaz@hotmail.com

Areas

Economics and Administration (Accountancy; Business Administration; Hotel Management; International Business; Marketing; Tourism); **Health Sciences** (Nursing; Psychology; Social Work); **Social Sciences and Humanities** (Communication Studies; Education; Graphic Design; Law)

History: Founded 1997.

Admission Requirements: Secondary school certificate (bachillerato)

Fees: (Pesos): 2,000 per month

Main Language(s) of Instruction: Spanish

Accrediting Agencies: Secretaría de Educación Pública

Degrees and Diplomas: *Licenciatura*; *Maestría*

Student Services: Academic counselling, Cultural centre, Foreign student adviser, Foreign Studies Centre, Health services, Language programs, Social counselling, Sports facilities

Special Facilities: TV Station, Radio studio, Graphic Design workshop

Libraries: Main Library

Last Updated: 11/10/12

INTERNATIONAL UNIVERSITY OF THE PROFESSIONS/ INTERNATIONAL SCHOOL OF STUDIES IN TOURISM

Universidad Internacional de Profesiones / Escuela Internacional de Turismo A.C.

Amores, 314, Col. del Valle, Delegación Benito Juárez, 03100 México, D.F.
Tel: +52(55) 56-87-21-11 +52(55) 56-87-82-20
Fax: +52(55) 55-23-62-69
EMail: correo@eit.edu.mx
Website: http://www.unipro.edu.mx

Director: Álvaro Jorge Becker Cuéllar (1976-)

Programmes

Fashion Design and Textiles (Fashion Design; Textile Design); **Gastronomy** (Cooking and Catering); **Tourism** (Tourism)

Further Information: Also campuses in León and Toluca

History: Founded 1976.

Admission Requirements: Certificado de secundaria and bachillerato

Main Language(s) of Instruction: Spanish

Degrees and Diplomas: *Licenciatura*

Last Updated: 11/10/12

IN-VIA SCHOOL OF SOCIAL WORK

Escuela de Licenciatura en Trabajo Social In-Via

35 Poniente No. 115, Col. Chulavista, 72420 Puebla, Puebla
Tel: +52(222) 237-42-71
EMail: invia@net.mx

Directora: Josefina Rodriguez Tapia

Programmes

Social Work (Social Work)

History: Founded 1987.

Main Language(s) of Instruction: Spanish

Degrees and Diplomas: *Licenciatura*

Last Updated: 28/08/12

IRISH UNIVERSITY CENTRE

Centro Universitario Irlandés, A.C.

43 Oriente No. 2422, Fracc. Campestre del Real, 72543 Puebla, Puebla
Tel: +52(222) 130-96-97
EMail: irishuniversity@hotmail.com
Website: http://www.centrouniversitarioirlandes.edu.mx

Rector: José María Sánchez Reche

Programmes

Accountancy (Accountancy); **Banking**; **Business Administration**; **Commercial Law**; **Computer Engineering** (Computer Engineering); **Finance** (Finance); **Information Systems** (Information Management; Information Sciences); **International Business** (International Business); **Law** (Commercial Law; Law); **Marketing**; **Modern Languages** (Modern Languages)

Main Language(s) of Instruction: Spanish

Degrees and Diplomas: *Licenciatura*: 3-4 yrs; *Maestría*: a further 2 yrs

Last Updated: 25/07/12

ISEC UNIVERSITY OF BUSINESS STUDIES

Universidad de Negocios ISEC

Mier y Pesado, 227, Col. del Valle, Delegación Benito Juárez, 03100 México, D.F.
Tel: +52(555) 5687-9000
Website: http://uneg.edu.mx

Rector: Rodrigo Mora Fernández

Vicerrector: Adrián Mora Fernández
Tel: +52(55) 56-82-76-88 EMail: amorafer@mail.internet.com.mx

Programmes

Accountancy (Accountancy); **Business Administration** (Business Administration) *Division Head*: Cuandón Vieyra; **Computer Science** (Computer Science); **Finance** (Finance); **Law** (Civil Law; Law); **Marketing** (Marketing); **Pedagogy** (Pedagogy); **Psychology** (Psychology); **Tourism** (Tourism)

History: Founded 1954 as Instituto Superior de Estudios Comerciales.

Admission Requirements: Secondary school certificate, TOEFL test for foreign students

Main Language(s) of Instruction: Spanish

Degrees and Diplomas: *Licenciatura*: 4 yrs; *Maestría*: 2 yrs; *Doctorado*: 3 yrs

Student Services: Academic counselling, Employment services, Foreign student adviser, Handicapped facilities, Health services, Language programs, Social counselling, Sports facilities

Libraries: Central Library

Publications: Comunica *(monthly)*

Last Updated: 21/09/12

ISIDRO FABELA UNIVERSITY CENTRE

Centro Universitario Isidro Fabela

Huerto Oriente, 400, Fracc. Santa María, Cuautitlán Izcalli, 54820 Cuautitlán Izcalli, Estado de México
Tel: +52(55) 58-72-77-06
Fax: +52(55) 58-72-00-48 +52(55) 58-72-77-06

Director General: Abel Miguel Palma Mondragón (1988-)

Programmes

Architecture and Civil Engineering; **Business Administration**; **Law** (Law)

History: Founded 1988.

Main Language(s) of Instruction: Spanish

Degrees and Diplomas: *Licenciatura*

Last Updated: 10/03/08

ISIDRO FABELA UNIVERSITY OF TOLUCA

Universidad Isidro Fabela de Toluca, S.C

González y Pichardo, 1219, Col. Granjas, 50120 Toluca, Estado de México

Tel: +52(722) 217-41-08

EMail: uift@hotmail.com

Website: http://www.uift.com.mx/

Director: Ricardo Mercado Galan

Programmes

Administration and Accountancy (Accountancy; Administration); **Business Computing** (Business Computing); **Computer Engineering** (Computer Engineering; Computer Science); **Dental Surgery** (Dentistry; Surgery); **Law** (Law); **Psychology** (Psychology)

History: Founded 1970.

Main Language(s) of Instruction: Spanish

Degrees and Diplomas: *Licenciatura*

Last Updated: 11/10/12

ITACA UNIVERSITY

Universidad Itaca

Calle Morelos, 12, Col. Barrio del Niño Jesús, 14080 México, D.F.

Tel: +52(5) 55-73-24-40

Fax: +52(5) 55-73-54-21

EMail: info@i.edu.mx

Website: http://www.i.edu.mx

Directora: Magdalena Lorenzo Rio EMail: magdalena@i.edu.mx

Programmes

Accountancy (Accountancy); **Administration** (Administration; Business Administration); **Education** (Education; Teacher Training); **Human Development** (Development Studies)

History: Founded 1991.

Main Language(s) of Instruction: Spanish

Degrees and Diplomas: *Licenciatura*; *Maestría*

Last Updated: 04/04/13

ITIAN UNIVERSITY

Universidad ITIAN

Calle 8, Nte. s/n, Esq. 6 Ote. 1er. Piso, Col. Obrera, 93260 Poza Rica, Veracruz

Tel: +52(782) 822-79-78

Fax: +52(782) 822-17-71

EMail: info@itiam.com.mx

Website: http://www.itian.edu.mx

Director: César Lugo Barrera EMail: cesar@itian.com.mx

Programmes

Accountancy (Accountancy); **Business Administration and Finance** (Administration; Business Administration; Finance); **Computer Science** (Computer Science); **Education** (Education); **Industrial Engineering** (Industrial Engineering); **International Business** (International Business)

History: Founded 1990 as Instituto Tecnológico de Informática y Administración. Acuqired present status and title 2007.

Main Language(s) of Instruction: Spanish

Degrees and Diplomas: *Licenciatura*

Last Updated: 13/03/13

JAIME TORRES BODET INSTITUTE OF HIGHER EDUCATION

Instituto de Educación Superior Jaime Torres Bodet

Avenida La Suiza, 160 y Privada Farallón, 18, Fracc. Las Playas, 39390 Acapulco de Juárez, Guerrero

Tel: +52(744) 482-37-77 +52(744) 483-81-84

Fax: +52(744) 482-61-21

EMail: iesjtb@terra.com

Director General: Euripides Astudillo Ávila (1996-)

Programmes

Accountancy (Accountancy); **Business Administration** (Business Administration); **Business Computing** (Business Computing); **International Business** (International Business); **Law** (Law); **Physical Education** (Physical Education); **Pre-school Education** (Preschool Education)

History: Founded 1963.

Main Language(s) of Instruction: Spanish

Last Updated: 28/02/13

JALISCO INSTITUTE OF PSYCHOANALYSIS AND PSYCHOTHERAPY

Instituto Jalisciense de Psicoanálisis y Psicoterapia

Alfredo R. Plascencia 896, Col. Santa Teresita, 44600 Guadalajara, Jalisco

Tel: +52(33) 36-42-58-34

EMail: apjal@gmail.com

Website: http://www.apj.org.mx

Coordinadora Académica: Ignacio Mendoza Gutiérrez.

Programmes

Psychoanalysis and Psychotherapy (Psychoanalysis; Psychotherapy)

History: Founded 1979.

Main Language(s) of Instruction: Spanish

Degrees and Diplomas: *Maestría*

Last Updated: 06/03/13

JAVIER BARROS SIERRA FOUNDATION

Fundación Javier Barros Sierra, A.C.

Camino al Ajusco N° 203, Col. Héroes de Padierna, 14200 Tlalpan, D.F.

Tel: +52(555) 544-69009, +52(555) 544-69864

Fax: +52(555) 308-94762

EMail: fundbarros@fundacionbarrossierra.org.mx

Website: http://www.fundacionbarrossierra.org.mx/FJBS

Director: Carlos Alfonso Lara Esparza (1993-)
EMail: carlaresp@prodigy.net.mx

Degrees and Diplomas: *Maestría*

JEAN PIAGET UNIVERSITY STUDIES CENTRE

Centro de Estudios Universitarios Jean Piaget

Miguel Lerdo, 630, 645, Nicolás Bravo, 400, Col. Centro, 91700 Veracruz, Veracruz

Tel: +52(229) 931-63-63

Fax: +52(229) 932-78-98

EMail: informes@universidadjeanpiaget.com

Website: http://www.universidadjeanpiaget.com

Rectora: María de la Paz Delfín Vargas (2000-)

Programmes

Accountancy (Accountancy); **Computer Engineering** (Computer Engineering); **Education** (Education); **International Business** (International Business); **Law** (Law)

History: Founded 2000.

Main Language(s) of Instruction: Spanish

Degrees and Diplomas: *Licenciatura*; *Especialización*; *Maestría*

Last Updated: 17/07/12

JESUS HOSPITAL NURSING SCHOOL

Escuela de Enfermería del Hospital de Jesús
Avenida 20 de Noviembre, 82, Col. Centro, Delegación Cuauhtémoc, 06090 México, D.F.
Tel: +52(55) 55-42-65-01
Fax: +52(55) 55-42-24-08
EMail: mabello@servidor.unam.mx

Directora: Marina Bello Pérez (1978-)

Programmes
Nursing and Obstetrics
History: Founded 1978.
Main Language(s) of Instruction: Spanish
Degrees and Diplomas: *Licenciatura*
Last Updated: 21/02/13

JOSÉ MARÍA MORELOS Y PAVÓN INSTITUTE OF ADVANCED TRAINING

Instituto de Educación Superior José María Morelos y Pavón
José María Morelos, 137, Celaya, Guanajuato
Tel: +52(461) 461-38-77
Fax: +52(461) 461-38-77

Director: Raúl Flores Guzmán
Degrees and Diplomas: *Licenciatura*
Last Updated: 04/04/08

JOSÉ VASCONCELOS TECHNOLOGICAL UNIVERSITY

Universidad Tecnológica José Vasconcelos
Calle Guadalupe, 312 Norte, Zona Centro, 34000 Durango, Durango
Tel: +52(618) 813-37-51
Fax: +52(618) 811-31-61
EMail: uni_jv@yahoo.com.mx

Departments
Communications (Communication Studies); **Graphic Design** (Design; Graphic Design); **Psychology** (Psychology)
Academic Year: January to December (January-June; August-December)
Admission Requirements: Secondary school certificate (bachillerato) and entrance examination
Main Language(s) of Instruction: Spanish
Degrees and Diplomas: *Licenciatura*; *Maestría*
Libraries: c. 1,000 vols
Last Updated: 05/04/13

JOSÉ VASCONCELOS UNIVERSITY CENTRE

Centro Universitario José Vasconcelos
Av. Chapultepec 133 Piso 4, Colonia Juárez, 06600 México, DF
Tel: +52(55) 5591-0909
EMail: conoce@cujv.edu.mx
Website: http://www.cujv.edu.mx

Director: Uriel Carmona Sánchez (1999-)

Programmes
Pedagogy (Pedagogy)
Further Information: Section in Cuauhtemoc
History: Founded 1999.
Main Language(s) of Instruction: Spanish
Degrees and Diplomas: *Licenciatura*; *Especialización*; *Maestría*
Last Updated: 25/07/12

JOSÉ VASCONCELOS UNIVERSITY OF OAXACA

Universidad José Vasconcelos de Oaxaca (UJVO)
Crespo, 601, Centro, Oaxaca, Oaxaca
Tel: +52(951) 514-80-47
EMail: univas@univas.edu.mx
Website: http://www.univas.mx

Rector: Carlos Spíndola Pérez Guerrero

Areas
Communication and Media (Communication Studies; Graphic Arts; Media Studies); **Economics and Business** (Accountancy; Business Administration; Economics; International Business; Marketing); **Government and Social Sciences** (Government; International Relations; Political Sciences; Public Administration); **Humanities** (Educational Sciences; Psychology); **Law** (Commercial Law; Constitutional Law; Criminal Law)
History: Founded 1993.
Governing Bodies: Board of Directors; Academic Council
Academic Year: August to June (August-December; February to June)
Admission Requirements: Secondary school certificate (Certificado de Bachillerato) and admissions examination
Fees: (Pesos): 1,200-1,500 per semester
Main Language(s) of Instruction: Spanish
Accrediting Agencies: Secretaría de Educación Pública (SEP)
Degrees and Diplomas: *Licenciatura*: 4 yrs; *Maestría*
Student Services: Academic counselling, Canteen, Cultural centre, Foreign student adviser, Language programs, Sports facilities
Special Facilities: Computer centre. Video and audio studio
Libraries: Yes
Last Updated: 11/10/12

JUAN BAUTISTA UNIVERSITY STUDIES CENTRE

Centro de Estudios Universitarios Juan Bautista
Avenida Revolución, 59, Col. Hogares Marla, 55030 Ecatepec de Morelos, Estado de México
Tel: +52(55) 57-87-59-35 +52(55) 57-87-03-74
Fax: +52(55) 57-70-12-82

Director Académico: Rubén Ángeles Mercado (1994-)

Programmes
Business Administration; **Computer Science** (Computer Science)
History: Founded 1994.
Main Language(s) of Instruction: Spanish
Degrees and Diplomas: *Licenciatura*
Last Updated: 18/03/08

JUAN RUIZ DE ALARCÓN INSTITUTE OF HIGHER STUDIES

Instituto de Estudios Superiores Juan Ruiz de Alarcón
Aguacatitlán s/n., Barrio de Casallas, 40220 Taxco de Alarcón, Guerrero
Tel: +52(762) 622-77-00
Fax: +52(762) 622-77-00
EMail: iesjra@prodigy.net.mx
Website: http://www.iesjra.edu.mx

Programmes
Accountancy (Accountancy); **Administration** (Administration); **Computer Science** (Computer Science); **Law** (Fiscal Law; Law); **Psychology** (Psychology)
Further Information: Campuses in Cancún and Iguala
History: Founded 1992.
Main Language(s) of Instruction: Spanish
Degrees and Diplomas: *Licenciatura*; *Maestría*
Libraries: Yes
Last Updated: 04/03/13

JUANA DE ASBAJE UNIVERSITY CENTRE

Centro Universitario Juana de Asbaje
Dr. Verdusco, 380 Sur, Zona Centro, 59600 Zamora, Michoacán
Tel: +52(351) 512-07-14
Fax: +52(351) 512-45-68
EMail: patria00@prodigy.net.mx

Directora: Maria de Lourdes Méndez Alfaro

Programmes

Education (Educational Administration; Preschool Education; Primary Education; Secondary Education)

History: Founded 1957.

Degrees and Diplomas: *Licenciatura*; *Maestría*
Last Updated: 04/04/08

JUSTO SIERRA CONTINENTAL UNIVERSITY

Universidad Continental Justo Sierra
Calle Palma Real, 15, Fracc. La Palma, Col. Tlahuapán, 62550 Jiutepec, Morelos
Tel: +52(777) 321-83-68 +52(777) 321-83-70
EMail: informes@unicon.edu.mx
Website: http://www.unicon.edu.mx

Rector: Sergio E. Aguilar Sánchez (2001-)

Programmes

Accountancy and Finance (Accountancy; Finance); **Business Administration** (Business Administration); **Computer Engineering** (Computer Engineering); **Education** (Education; Pedagogy); **International Relations** (International Relations); **Law** (Law); **Psychology** (Psychology)

History: Founded 2001.

Admission Requirements: Certificado de Preparatoria or equivalent

Main Language(s) of Instruction: Spanish

Degrees and Diplomas: *Licenciatura*; *Maestría*
Last Updated: 11/09/12

JUSTO SIERRA HISPANIC-AMERICAN UNIVERSITY

Universidad Hispano Americana Justo Sierra
Prolongación avenida del Duque esquina con calle Jade s/n, Colonia Vicente Guerrero, 64000 San Francisco de Campeche, Campeche
Website: http://universidadhispanoamericana.edu.mx
Rector: Alejandro Baqueiro

Programmes

Administration (Administration); **Business Administration** (Business Administration); **Computer Science** (Computer Science); **Educational Technology** (Educational Technology); **Environmental Law** (Law); **Law** (Law); **Modern Languages** (English; French; Linguistics; Literature); **Nutrition** (Nutrition)

History: Founded 2001. Acquired present status 2009.

Main Language(s) of Instruction: Spanish

Degrees and Diplomas: *Licenciatura*; *Maestría*; *Doctorado*
Last Updated: 03/04/13

JUSTO SIERRA INSTITUTE OF HIGHER STUDIES

Instituto de Estudios Superiores Justo Sierra
Hidalgo, 8, Altos, Centro, 79610 San Luis Potosí, San Luis Potosí
Tel: +52(444) 442-53-99
Fax: +52(444) 442-53-99

Director: Fransisco Javier Bazaldua

Degrees and Diplomas: *Licenciatura*
Last Updated: 07/04/08

JUSTO SIERRA MÉNDEZ SCHOOL OF TOURISM

Escuela Superior de Turismo Justo Sierra Méndez
Calle 24, No. 47, Centro, 24100 Ciudad del Carmen, Campeche
Tel: +52(981) 2-00-44
Fax: +52(981) 2-06-44

Directora: María Teresa Romero Brown

Programmes

Tourism (Tourism)

History: Founded 1996.

Main Language(s) of Instruction: Spanish

Degrees and Diplomas: *Licenciatura*
Last Updated: 31/03/08

JUSTO SIERRA O'REILLY CTM CENTRE FOR ADVANCED STUDIES

Centro de Estudios Superiores CTM Justo Sierra Oreilly
Calle 59 No. 849, Fracc. del Parque, 97160 Mérida, Yucatán
Tel: +52(999) 982-29-44
Fax: +52(999) 982-29-19
EMail: luis_echeverria@hotmail.com
Website: http://www.cesctm.edu.mx/

Director General: Luis Alberto Echeverria Navarro (1998-)

Programmes

Accountancy and Administration (Accountancy; Administration); **Computer Science** (Computer Science); **Education** (Education); **Information Technology** (Information Technology); **Law** (Law); **Psychology** (Psychology)

History: Founded 1987.

Main Language(s) of Instruction: Spanish

Degrees and Diplomas: *Licenciatura*; *Maestría*
Last Updated: 13/07/12

JUSTO SIERRA UNIVERSITY

Universidad Justo Sierra
Acueducto Num. 914-B, Col. Laguna Ticomán, Deleg. Gustavo A. Madero, 07340 México, D.F.
Tel: +52(55) 57-54-69-29
Fax: +52(55) 57-62-34-35
Website: http://www.universidad-justosierra.edu.mx

Rector: Francisco Javier Bazaldua Cardenas

Programmes

Accountancy and Finance (Accountancy; Finance); **Administration** *(Acueducto, San Mateo)* (Administration); **Architecture** *(Cien Metros Campus)* (Architecture); **Business Computing** *(Cien Metros Campus)* (Business Computing); **Communication Studies** *(San Mateo Campus)* (Communication Studies); **Communication Studies** *(Cien Metros Campus)* (Communication Studies); **Computer Systems** *(San Mateo, Cien Metros)* (Systems Analysis); **Design and Visual Communication** *(San Mateo, Cien Metros)* (Advertising and Publicity; Design); **Gastronomy** (Cooking and Catering); **Law** *(San Mateo Campus)* (Law); **Law** *(Cien Metros)* (Law); **Marketing** *(Acueducto Campus)* (Marketing); **Marketing and Publicity** *(San Mateo Campus)* (Advertising and Publicity; Marketing); **Nutrition** (Nutrition); **Pedagogy** *(San Mateo campus)* (Pedagogy); **Psychology** *(Cien Metros Campus)* (Psychology); **Psychology** *(San Mateo Campus)* (Psychology); **Stomatology** *(Acueducto Campus)* (Stomatology); **Surgery** *(Ticomán Campus)* (Surgery); **Systems and Telematics** *(Cien Metros Campus)* (Systems Analysis; Telecommunications Engineering)

History: Founded 1994. Formerly known as Centro Cultural Universitario Justo Sierra.

Main Language(s) of Instruction: Spanish

Degrees and Diplomas: *Licenciatura*; *Maestría*
Last Updated: 11/10/12

KINO UNIVERSITY

Universidad Kino, A.C.
Calzada Pbro. Pedro Villegas Ramírez final Ote, Col. Casa Blanca, 83079 Hermosillo, Sonora
Tel: +52(662) 259-08-08
Fax: +52(662) 213-50-66
EMail: germanvaldez@unikino.mx
Website: http://www.unikino.mx

Rector: José Rentería Torres (2013-)

Programmes

Business Administration (Accountancy; Administration; Business Administration; Human Resources; International Business; Marketing); **Education** (Education); **Engineering** (Computer Engineering; Electronic Engineering; Engineering; Information Technology); **Graphic Design** (Graphic Design); **Journalism and Social Communication** (Communication Studies; Journalism)

History: Founded 1985.
Academic Year: September to June (September-January; February-June)
Admission Requirements: Bachillerato
Main Language(s) of Instruction: Spanish
Degrees and Diplomas: *Licenciatura*: 4 yrs; *Maestría*; *Doctorado*: Education
Libraries: c. 10,000 vols
Last Updated: 04/04/13

LA ANTIGUA UNIVERSITY STUDIES CENTRE, VERACRUZ

Centro de Estudios Universitarios La Antigua Veracruz
Chalchihuecán, 39, entre Colón y Rafael Freyre, Fracc. Reforma, 91919 Veracruz, Veracruz
Tel: +52(229) 937-93-38
Fax: +52(229) 937-93-65

Rector: Agustín Carmona Rascón (1994-)

Programmes
Business Relations; **Industrial Relations**
History: Founded 1994.
Main Language(s) of Instruction: Spanish
Degrees and Diplomas: *Licenciatura*
Last Updated: 10/03/08

LA CIÉNEGA UNIVERSITY

Universidad de la Ciénega (UC)
Plantel Poncitlán, Km. 62 Carretera Guadalajara-La Barca, Col. Santa Elena de la Cruz, 45950 Poncitlán, Jalisco
Tel: +52(391) 921-2058
Fax: +52(391) 921-0303
EMail: info@ucienega.edu.mx
Website: http://www.ucienega.edu.mx

Director: Juán António Martínez García

Programmes
Business Administration (Business Administration); **Computer Science** (Computer Science); **Gastronomy** (Cooking and Catering); **Law** (Law); **Pedagogy** (Education; Pedagogy); **Taxation** (Taxation)
Further Information: Also branches in Guadalajara and Zapopan
History: Founded 2003.
Admission Requirements: Bachillerato
Main Language(s) of Instruction: Spanish
Degrees and Diplomas: *Licenciatura*; *Especialización*
Last Updated: 19/09/12

LA CIÉNEGA UNIVERSITY CENTRE

Centro Universitario de la Ciénega
Av. Universidad Núm. 1115, 47840 Ocotlán, Jalisco
Tel: +52(392) 925-29-82
Fax: +52(392) 925-13-01
EMail: rmc@cuci.udg.mx
Website: http://cuci.udg.mx

Rector: Raúl Medina Centeno

Divisions
Engineering (Biotechnology; Chemical Engineering; Computer Engineering; Computer Science; Engineering; Industrial Engineering); **Social Studies and Economics** (Accountancy; Administration; Economics; Human Resources; Journalism; Law; Social Studies)
Main Language(s) of Instruction: Spanish
Degrees and Diplomas: *Licenciatura*; *Maestría*; *Doctorado*
Libraries: Yes
Last Updated: 24/07/12

LA SALLE COLLEGE OF LA MONTAÑA

Colegio La Salle de la Montaña
Pradera y Montaña s/n - Fracc. Jardines de la Victoria, 36100 Silao, Guanajuato
Tel: +52(472) 722-02-31
Director: Edmundo Araujo Vázquez

Programmes
Education (Education)
Main Language(s) of Instruction: Spanish
Degrees and Diplomas: *Licenciatura*
Last Updated: 23/08/12

LA SALLE LAGUNA UNIVERSITY

Universidad La Salle Laguna
Canatlán, 150, Parque Industrial Lagunero, 35078 Gómez Palacio, Durango
Tel: +52(87)150-21-77
Fax: +52(87) 150-20-49
EMail: promocion@ulsalaguna.edu.mx
Website: http://www.ulsalaguna.edu.mx

Rector: Luis Arturo Dávila de León
EMail: luisarturo@ulsalaguna.edu.mx

Programmes
Accountancy (Accountancy); **Administration** (Administration; Finance; Hotel Management); **Architecture** (Architecture); **Communication Studies** (Communication Studies; Media Studies; Public Relations; Radio and Television Broadcasting); **Design** (Graphic Design; Industrial Design); **Educational Innovation** (Education; Educational Administration); **Engineering** (Civil Engineering; Electrical Engineering; Electronic Engineering; Mechanical Engineering; Mining Engineering); **Family Studies** (Family Studies); **Gastronomy and Nutrition** (Cooking and Catering; Nutrition); **International Business** (International Business); **Marketing** (Marketing); **Modern Languages and Public Relations** (Cultural Studies; English; French; German; Italian; Literature; Public Relations; Spanish); **Psychology** (Psychology)
History: Founded 1974 as Instituto Superior de Ciencia y Tecnología de la Laguna. Acquired present status and title 2003.
Main Language(s) of Instruction: Spanish
Degrees and Diplomas: *Licenciatura*; *Maestría*
Libraries: Yes
Last Updated: 08/03/13

LA SALLE UNIVERSITY

Universidad La Salle (ULSA)
Avenida Benjamín Franklin, 47, Col. Condesa, Delegación Cuauntémoc, 06140 México, D.F.
Tel: +52(55) 5278-9500
EMail: jrbi@ulsa.mx
Website: http://www.ulsa.edu.mx

Rector: Enrique Alejandro González Alvarez (2011-)
EMail: enrique.gonzalez@ulsa.mx

Administrative and Financial Director: José Ramon Barreiro Iglesias

International Relations: Joan M.W. de Landeros, Director, Centre for International Education EMail: jmwl@ulsa.mx

Centres
Continuing Education *Coordinator*: Eva Pantoja Arenas; **Cultural Formation** *Coordinator*: Raquel Elias Hernandez; **Distance Education** *Director*: Maria del Carmen de Urquijo; **Human and Professional Development** *Coordinator*: Ana Marcela Castellanos Guzman; **Language Centre** *Coordinator*: Maria del Rosario Escalada Ruiz; **Library** *Coordinator*: Maria Asuncion Mendoza Becerra; **Physical Education and Sports** *Coordinator*: Jose Alexandro Colin Rivera; **Social and Community Development** *Coordinator*: Salvador Flores Vega; **Student Life and Welfare** *Coordinator*: Haide Negretti Rodriguez; **Teacher Formation** *Coordinator*: Jennie Brand Barajas

Institutes
Bioethics (Ethics) *Director*: Manuel Alarcón Vázquez

Schools

Architecture, Graphic Design and Communication (Architecture; Communication Studies; Graphic Design) *Director*: Jorge Iturbe Bermejo; **Business** (Accountancy; Actuarial Science; Administration; Business Administration; Business and Commerce; Business Computing; International Business; Marketing) *Director*: Adolfo Cervantes Ruiz; **Chemical Sciences** (Chemical Engineering; Chemistry; Environmental Engineering; Food Science; Pharmacy) *Director*: José Elias Garcia Zahoul; **Engineering** (Biomedical Engineering; Civil Engineering; Computer Engineering; Industrial Engineering; Mechanical Engineering; Robotics) *Director*: Eduardo Gomez Ramirez; **Graduate Studies and Research** (Administration; Business Administration; Computer Engineering; Economics; Education; Finance; Health Administration; International Business; Law; Management) *Director*: María Teresa Estrada Alvarado; **Humanities and Social Sciences** (Education; Philosophy; Primary Education; Psychology) *Director*: José Ignacio Rivero Calderón; **Law** (International Relations; Law) *Director*: German Martinez Cazares; **Medicine** (Medicine) *Director*: Jorge Arguelles Domenzain; **Religious Sciences** (Religious Studies) *Director*: Manuel Alarcón Vázquez

Further Information: Campuses: Ciudad Obregón; Chihuahua; Laguna; Monterrey; Ciudad Victoria; Bajio; Morelia; Pachuca; Nezahualcóyotl; Ciudad de México; Cuernavaca; Puebla; Cancún and Saltillo. For information on campuses, please consult: http://www.ulsa.edu.mx/conocenos/?pagina=mexico. Also Study Abroad programmes. Special programmes for foreign students. Spanish courses for non-native speakers

History: Founded 1962 as a school by the Jean Baptiste de la Salle Congregation, officially recognized as an autonomous private institution 1987.

Governing Bodies: Board of Governors; University Council

Academic Year: August to June (August-December; January-June)

Admission Requirements: Secondary school certificate (bachillerato), or recognized foreign equivalent, and entrance examination

Fees: (Pesos): 7,000-50,000 per semester

Main Language(s) of Instruction: Spanish

International Co-operation: With Canadian universities through the Conference of Rectors and Principals of Québec Universities and with USA and Canadian universities through Regional Academic Mobility Program (Consortium RAMP)

Accrediting Agencies: Federación de Instituciones Mexicanas Particulares de Educación Superior (FIMPES)

Degrees and Diplomas: *Bachillerato*; *Licenciatura*: 4-5 yrs; *Licenciatura*: Medicine, 6 yrs; *Maestría*: a further 2 yrs; *Doctorado*: a further 2 yrs

Student Services: Academic counselling, Canteen, Cultural centre, Employment services, Foreign student adviser, Foreign Studies Centre, Handicapped facilities, Health services, Language programs, Social counselling, Sports facilities

Libraries: Central Library, 300,000 vols; Medicine Library, 20,000 vols

Publications: Desde el CIEL *(biennially)*; Logos *(quarterly)*; Revista de Investigación *(biannually)*; Revista Médica *(quarterly)*; Vera Humanitas *(quarterly)*

Academic Staff *2008-2009*	MEN	WOMEN	TOTAL
FULL-TIME	40	32	**72**
PART-TIME	621	295	**916**
Student Numbers *2012-2013*			
All (Foreign Included)	–	–	**5,336**

Last Updated: 23/08/11

LA SILLA INSTITUTE

Instituto Superior La Silla, A.C.

Tamaulipas, 2827, Col. Vivienda Popular, Guadalupe, Nuevo León

Programmes

Accountancy (Accountancy); **Business Administration** (Business Administration); **Law** (Law); **Marketing** (Marketing); **Psychology** (Psychology)

History: Founded 2001.

Main Language(s) of Instruction: Spanish

Degrees and Diplomas: *Licenciatura*

Last Updated: 07/04/08

LABASTIDA COLLEGE

Colegio Labastida, A.C.

José Vasconcelos 110 Ote., Col. del Valle, 66220 San Pedro Garza García, Nuevo León
Tel: +52(81) 335-45-30
Website: http://www.colegiolabastida.edu.mx

Directora: Guadalupe Uribe Beltrán

Programmes

Education (Educational Psychology; Pedagogy; Preschool Education; Primary Education)

Main Language(s) of Instruction: Spanish

Degrees and Diplomas: *Licenciatura*

Last Updated: 23/08/12

LAGRANGE INSTITUTE OF HIGHER STUDIES

Instituto de Estudios Superiores Lagrange

José María Vasconcelos, 169, Col. San Miguel Chapultepec, Delegación Miguel Hidalgo, 11850 México, D.F.
Tel: +52(55) 55-53-37-81

Director General: Juventino Muñoz Velázquez

Programmes

Accountancy (Accountancy); **Administration and Finance** (Administration; Finance); **Law** (Law)

History: Founded 1987.

Main Language(s) of Instruction: Spanish

Degrees and Diplomas: *Licenciatura*; *Especialización*

Last Updated: 04/03/13

LANSPIAC STUDIES CENTRE

Centro de Estudios Lanspiac

Avenida Vallarta, 1168, Sector Juárez, Col. Americana, 44100 Guadalajara, Jalisco
Tel: +52(33) 18-26-14-30

Rectora: María Lambertina Ugalde Domínguez (1993-)

Programmes

Business Administration (Business Administration)

History: Founded 1993.

Main Language(s) of Instruction: Spanish

Degrees and Diplomas: *Licenciatura*

Last Updated: 14/02/13

LASALLE BENAVENTE UNIVERSITY

Universidad Lasallista Benavente

Avenida Universidad s/n, Col. La Favorita, 38030 Celaya, Guanajuato
Tel: +52(461) 612-52-52
EMail: ulsab@ulsab.edu.mx

Rector: Héctor Aguilar Tamayo (1997-)
EMail: haguilar@ulsab.edu.mx

Vicerrectora Administrativa: María Carmen Jamaica Arreguín
EMail: mjamaica@ulsab.edu.mx

International Relations: Rosa Elia Montoya de Nieto, Director, Language and International Exchange
EMail: rmontoya@ulsab.edu.mx

Faculties

Business Administration (Accountancy) *Dean*: Elba Aguilar Rendón; **Communication Studies** (Communication Studies) *Dean*: Jorge de la Rocha Ledezma; **Engineering** (Computer Engineering) *Dean*: Miguel Angel Jamaica Arreguín; **International Relations** (International Relations) *Dean*: Graciela Jiménez Larios; **Law** (Law) *Dean*: Juan José Muñoz Ledo Rabago

History: Founded 1969 as Colegio Benavente, acquired present status and title 1978.

Governing Bodies: President; Board of Directors

Academic Year: September to June (September-January; February-June)

Admission Requirements: High school certificate

Main Language(s) of Instruction: Spanish

International Co-operation: With universities in USA, China

Degrees and Diplomas: *Licenciatura*: Accountancy; Computer Engineering; Law, 5 yrs; *Licenciatura*: Communication Sciences; International Relations, 4 yrs; *Maestría*: Law, a further 2 yrs; *Doctorado*: Law, 2 yrs

Student Services: Academic counselling, Cultural centre, Employment services, Foreign student adviser, Health services, Nursery care, Social counselling, Sports facilities

Special Facilities: Radio, TV, Movie Studio, Audiovisual Equipment, Internet, Laboratory, Satillite Programme, Computers

Libraries: Main Library

Press or Publishing House: Editorial ULSAB

Last Updated: 04/04/13

LATIN AMERICA UNIVERSITY

Universidad América Latina

Avenida Patria 1286, Col. Villa Universitaria, 45110 Zapopan, Jalisco

EMail: informes@ual.edu.mx

Website: http://www.ual.edu.mx/

Rector: José de Jesús Ruiz Ángel EMail: rectoria@ual.edu.mx

Vicerrector Administrativo: Erick Ruiz Tovar EMail: eruiz@ual.edu.mx

Programmes

Accountancy (Accountancy); **Business Administration** (Business Administration); **Business Computing** (Business Computing); **Communication Studies** (Communication Studies; Journalism); **Economics** (Economics); **Educational Sciences** (Education; Educational Administration; Educational Sciences); **History** (History); **Hotel Management and Tourism** (Hotel Management; Tourism); **International Business** (International Business); **Law** (Law); **Marketing** (Marketing); **Philosophy** (Philosophy); **Political Science and Public Administration** (Political Sciences; Public Administration); **Sociology** (Sociology)

Further Information: Planteles: Patria, Centro, Circunvalación, Cubilete, Vallarta y Unión, Paseos del Sol, Tonala and Ciudad Granja, San Luis Potosí and Acapulco.

History: Founded 2000.

Main Language(s) of Instruction: Spanish

Degrees and Diplomas: *Licenciatura*; *Maestría*

Last Updated: 31/08/12

LATIN AMERICAN CENTRE FOR ADVANCED AND INTERMEDIATE STUDIES

Centro Latinoamericano de Estudios Superiores y Medio Superior

Diego Leño, 51-201, Centro, 91000 Xalapa, Veracruz

Tel: +52(228) 817-55-66

Fax: +52(228) 818-31-33

EMail: claes@.gorsa.net.mx

Director: Elías Galicia Bravo (1993-)

Further Information: Also branch in Boca del Río

Degrees and Diplomas: *Licenciatura*; *Especialización*; *Maestría*

Last Updated: 15/02/08

LATIN AMERICAN CENTRE OF ORTHODONTIC STUDIES

Centro Latinoamericano de Estudios Ortodónticos

Porfirio Díaz N° 85, Col. Del Valle, Benito Juárez, 03100 México, D.F.

Tel: +52(555) 575-92-06 +52(555) 575-89-48

EMail: rmomex@compuserve.com

Website: http://cleo.mx

Directora: Gloria López Velarde Zapata (1993-)

Programmes

Orthodontics (Orthodontics)

Further Information: Also branch in Morelia

History: Founded 1993.

Main Language(s) of Instruction: Spanish

Degrees and Diplomas: *Especialización*

Libraries: Yes

Last Updated: 19/07/12

LATIN AMERICAN EDUCATIONAL CENTRE

Centro Educacional Latinoamericano

Montevideo, 303, Col. Lindavista, Delegación Gustavo A. Madero, 07300 México, D.F.

Tel: +52(55) 55-86-07-09 +52(55) 55-86-95-08

Director: Jorge Zárate González (1994-)

Degrees and Diplomas: *Licenciatura*

Last Updated: 04/04/08

LATIN AMERICAN INSTITUTE FOR EDUCATIONAL TECHNOLOGY AND COMMUNICATION

Instituto Latinoamericano de Tecnología Educativa y Comunicación

3 Sur, Esq. 41, Pte., Puebla, Puebla

Director: Óscar Daniel Ceballos

Programmes

Communication Studies (Communication Studies); **Educational Technology** (Educational Technology)

Main Language(s) of Instruction: Spanish

Degrees and Diplomas: *Bachillerato*; *Licenciatura*

Last Updated: 07/04/08

LATIN AMERICAN INSTITUTE OF SCIENCE AND HUMANITIES

Instituto Latinoamericano de Ciencias y Humanidades

Calle Londres, 203, Col. Andrade, Centro, 37000 León, Guanajuato

Tel: +52(477) 713-34-83

EMail: gabyruchis14@hotmail.com

Website: http://www.ilaleon.com/

Director: Pedro Ardines Limonchi

Programmes

Dentistry (Dental Technology; Dentistry; Surgery)

Main Language(s) of Instruction: Spanish

Degrees and Diplomas: *Licenciatura*; *Especialización*

Last Updated: 06/03/13

LATIN AMERICAN SCIENTIFIC UNIVERSITY OF HIDALGO

Universidad Científica Latinoamericana de Hidalgo

Avenida del Roble, 402, Fracc. Villas del Álamo, 42000 Pachuca de Soto, Hidalgo

Tel: +52(771) 716-09-46

Fax: +52(771) 716-09-36

EMail: informes@uclah.edu.mx

Website: http://www.uclah.edu.mx

Rectora: Begoña Márquez Camacho EMail: buzon@uclah.edu.mx

Programmes

Accountancy (Accountancy); **Administration** (Administration); **Education** (Education; Educational Administration; Pedagogy); **Gastronomy** (Cooking and Catering); **Law** (Law); **Marketing** (Marketing); **Public Administration and Political Science** (Political Sciences; Public Administration); **Tourism** (Tourism)

History: Founded 1987 as Colegio Londres de Pachuca. Acquired present status and title 1993.

Admission Requirements: Bachillerato

Main Language(s) of Instruction: Spanish

Degrees and Diplomas: *Licenciatura*; *Especialización*; *Maestría*

Last Updated: 11/09/12

LATIN AMERICAN TECHNOLOGICAL INSTITUTE

Instituto Tecnológico Latinoamericano (ITLA)
Carretera Pachuca-Ciudad Sahagún km 7 Rancho San José
Buenavista, Col. El Venado, 42083 Mineral de la Reforma, Hidalgo
Tel: +52(771) 718-10-20 +52(771) 718-10-30
EMail: rectoria@itla.edu.mx
Website: http://www.itla.edu.mx

Rector: Andres Acosta EMail: andresacostac@itla.mx

Programmes
Accountancy (Accountancy); **Administration** (Administration); **Architecture** (Architecture); **Computer Science** (Computer Science); **Education** (Education); **Graphic Design** (Graphic Design); **Political Science** (Political Sciences)

History: Founded 1992

Admission Requirements: Bachillerato

Fees: (Pesos): 1,500 per month

Main Language(s) of Instruction: Spanish

Accrediting Agencies: CALMECAC; Secretaría de Educación Pública (SEP)

Degrees and Diplomas: *Licenciatura*; *Especialización*; *Maestría*

Student Services: Academic counselling, Canteen, Employment services, Handicapped facilities, Health services, Language programs, Nursery care, Sports facilities

Last Updated: 19/03/13

LATIN AMERICAN UNIVERSITY

Universidad Latinoamericana
Gabriel Mancera, 1402, Col. del Valle, Delegación Benito Juárez,
03100 México, D.F.
Tel: +52(555) 800-81-00
EMail: info@ula.edu.mx
Website: http://www.ula.edu.mx

Rector: Eric A. Pearse Hughes (2011-)

Programmes
Administration and Accountancy (Accountancy; Administration); **Architecture** (Architecture; Interior Design); **Commerce and Finance** (Business and Commerce; Finance; International Business); **Communications and Public Relations** (Communication Studies; Public Relations); **Dental Surgery** (Dentistry; Surgery); **Fashion Design** (Fashion Design); **Graphic Design**; **Informatics** (Computer Science); **Law** (Law); **Nutrition** (Nutrition); **Psychology** (Psychology)

Further Information: Also Norte, Cuernavaca, Florida, and Reforma campuses

History: Founded 1976.

Governing Bodies: Consejo de Administración

Academic Year: September to June (September-January; February-June)

Admission Requirements: Secondary school certificate (bachillerato) and entrance examination

Main Language(s) of Instruction: Spanish

Degrees and Diplomas: *Licenciatura*: Accountancy; Informatics; Law; Public Relations, 4 yrs; *Licenciatura*: Business Administration, 4 1/2 yrs; *Licenciatura*: Dentistry (Cirujano Dentista); *Especialización*; *Maestría*: Dentistry, a further 2 yrs

Libraries: c. 9,000 vols

Last Updated: 04/04/13

LATIN AMERICAN UNIVERSITY CENTRE OF MORELOS

Centro Universitario Latinoamericano de Morelos
2a cerrada de Chapultepec No. 3. Colonia Chapultepec,
Cuernavaca, Morelos
Tel: +52(777) 315-15-30 +52(777) 316-17-27
Fax: +52(777) 316-27-37
EMail: ceulam@ceulam.com
Website: http://ceulam.com

Director: Héctor Ordóñez Lomelí

Degrees and Diplomas: *Licenciatura*

Last Updated: 04/04/08

LATIN EDUCATIONAL CENTRE

Centro Educativo Latino, A.C.
Calle 16 # 473 x 47 Diagonal Petcanche, 97145 Mérida, Yucatán
Tel: +52(999) 986-11-94 +52(999) 986-23-66
EMail: informes@centroeducativolatino.edu.mx
Website: http://www.centroeducativolatino.edu.mx

Presidente: Jorge Tenreiro

Programmes
Administration (Administration); **Computer Science** (Computer Science); **International Business** (International Business)

History: Founded 1972.

Degrees and Diplomas: *Licenciatura*; *Maestría*

Last Updated: 10/03/08

LATIN UNIVERSITY

Universidad Latina, S.C. (UNILA)
Chihuahua, 202, Col. Roma, Delegación Cuauhtémoc,
06700 México, D.F.
Tel: +52(555) 364-00-870
Website: http://www.unila.edu.mx

Rector: Angel Eliseo Cano Garza

Programmes
Accountancy and Finance (Accountancy; Finance); **Administration** (Administration; Business Administration); **Communication and Journalism** (Communication Studies; Journalism); **Computer Science** (Computer Science); **Law** (Law); **Marketing and Publicity** (Advertising and Publicity; Marketing)

Further Information: Also campus Sur, and campuses in Cuernavaca and Cuautla

History: Founded 1996.

Academic Year: August to July (August-December; January-July)

Admission Requirements: Secondary school certificate (bachillerato)

Main Language(s) of Instruction: Spanish

Degrees and Diplomas: *Licenciatura*: 4 yrs; *Especialización*; *Maestría*

Libraries: Yes

Last Updated: 11/10/12

LATIN UNIVERSITY OF AMERICA

Universidad Latina de América (UNLA)
Manantial Cointzio Norte, 355, Fracc. Los Manantiales,
58170 Morelia, Michoacán
Tel: +52(443) 322-1500
EMail: informes@unla.edu.mx
Website: http://unla.mx

Rector: Luis Roberto Mantilla Sahagún
EMail: rectoria@mail.unla.edu.mx

Programmes
Accountancy (Accountancy) *Head*: Maria Teresa Montaño Espinosa; **Business Administration** (Business Administration); **Civil Engineering** (Civil Engineering; Engineering); **Communication Studies** (Communication Studies); **Computer Systems** (Computer Engineering); **Graphic Design** (Graphic Design); **International Commercial Relations** (International Business; International Relations); **Law** (Law); **Marketing** (Marketing); **Psychology** (Psychology); **Tourism** (Tourism)

Further Information: Also campus in Uruapan

History: Founded 1991.

Governing Bodies: Board of Trustees (General Assembly of Associates); University Council; General Academic Committee;

Academic Year: August to July (August-December; January-May; Summer semester: June-July)

Admission Requirements: Bachillerato

Main Language(s) of Instruction: Spanish

International Co-operation: With universities in Canada, France, Spain and USA. Member of CONAHEC, AMPEI, Academic University Mobility System (SUMA). Also agreement with Centro Avanzado en Comunicacion (CADEC), ITESO, Fundación Arturo Rosemblueth and various NGOs.

Accrediting Agencies: Federación de Instituciones Mexicanas Particulares de Educación Superior (FIMPES)

Degrees and Diplomas: *Licenciatura*: 4 1/2 yrs; *Maestría*: a further 2 yrs

Student Services: Academic counselling, Canteen, Cultural centre, Employment services, Foreign student adviser, Foreign Studies Centre, Handicapped facilities, Health services, Language programs, Social counselling, Sports facilities

Libraries: Central Library

Last Updated: 11/10/12

LATIN UNIVERSITY OF MEXICO

Universidad Latina de México (ULM)

Paseo del Bajío y Magnolias, Col. Jardines de Celaya, 38080 Celaya, Guanajuato

Tel: +52(461) 612-48-37

Fax: +52(461) 613-44-59

EMail: info@ulm.edu.mx

Website: http://www.ulm.edu.mx

Rector: Ramón Y. Lemus Muñoz-Ledo (1975-)

Programmes

Accountancy (Accountancy); **Architecture** (Architecture); **Dental Surgery** (Dentistry; Surgery); **Graphic Design** (Design; Graphic Design); **Interior Design** (Interior Design); **International Business** (International Business); **Law** (Law); **Nutrition** (Nutrition); **Psychology** (Psychology)

History: Founded 1975.

Main Language(s) of Instruction: Spanish

Degrees and Diplomas: *Licenciatura*; *Especialización*; *Maestría*

Last Updated: 11/10/12

LAURA ARCE SCHOOL OF EDUCATORS

Escuela de Educadoras Laura Arce

Avenida Hidalgo 1540 Pte y Avenida Constitución 1525, Col. Obispado, 64000 Monterrey, Nuevo León

Tel: +52(81) 83-43-52-90

Fax: +52(81) 83-44-48-61

Website: http://www.lauraarce.edu.mx/

Programmes

Preschool Education (Preschool Education)

History: Founded 1948.

Main Language(s) of Instruction: Spanish

Degrees and Diplomas: *Licenciatura*

Last Updated: 28/08/12

LAURENS INSTITUTE

Instituto Laurens, A.C.

Insurgentes, 1515, Pte., Colinas de San Jerónimo, 64630 Monterrey, Nuevo León

Tel: +52(81) 83-46-77-01

EMail: informacion@laurens.edu.mx

Directora General: Elva Miriam Peña Martinez

Programmes

Bilingual Education (Bilingual and Bicultural Education)

Further Information: Santiago (Nuevo León)

History: Founded 1885 as Colegio Fronterizo

Main Language(s) of Instruction: Spanish

Degrees and Diplomas: *Licenciatura*

Last Updated: 06/03/13

LAW SCHOOL OF ATLACOMULCO

Escuela de Derecho de Atlacomulco

Calle 12 de Octubre No.3, Col. San Jerónimo Chicahualco, 52140 Metepec, Estado de México

Tel: +52(722) 244-05-27

Director: Jaime Fernando Calzada Rodríguez

Programmes

Law (Law)

Main Language(s) of Instruction: Spanish

Degrees and Diplomas: *Licenciatura*

Last Updated: 20/02/13

LEONA VICARIO CENTRE FOR ADVANCED STUDIES

Centro de Estudios Superiores Leona Vicario

Niños Héroes, 1407, Col. Guadalupe Victoria, 96520 Coatzacoalcos, Veracruz

Tel: +52(921) 213-56-31

Fax: +52(921) 213-56-78

EMail: direcciongeneral@escleonavicario.com

Directora: Ada Aurora Puig May (1993-)

Programmes

Accountancy (Accountancy); **Educational Sciences** (Educational Sciences)

History: Founded 1993.

Main Language(s) of Instruction: Spanish

Degrees and Diplomas: *Licenciatura*; *Maestría*

Last Updated: 16/07/12

LEONARDO BRAVO INSTITUTE

Instituto Leonardo Bravo

Ezequiel Montes, 115 y 116, Col. Tabacalera, Delegación Cuauhtémoc, 06030 México, D.F.

Tel: +52(55) 57-05-67-43

EMail: ilbcentro@ilb.edu.mx

Website: http://ilb.mx

Director General: Hugo Francisco Bravo Malpica (1999-)

Programmes

Accountancy (Accountancy); **Business Administration** (Business Administration); **Computer Science** (Computer Science); **Industrial Management** (Industrial Management); **International Business** (International Business); **Law** (Law); **Tourism** (Tourism)

Further Information: Also Tlalnepantla De Baz, Vera Cruz and Acapulco campuses

History: Founded 1961.

Main Language(s) of Instruction: Spanish

Degrees and Diplomas: *Licenciatura*; *Maestría*

Last Updated: 06/03/13

LERDO UNIVERSITY UNIT

Unidad Universitaria de Lerdo, A.C.

Avenida Zaragoza, 443 Norte, 35150 Ciudad Lerdo, Durango

Tel: +52(871) 25-16-02

Fax: +52(871) 25-16-02

Rector: Juan José Vargas Meraz

Programmes

Accountancy (Accountancy); **Business Administration** (Business Administration); **Law** (Law); **Social Work** (Social Work)

Main Language(s) of Instruction: Spanish

Degrees and Diplomas: *Licenciatura*

Last Updated: 25/03/13

LIBERTAD SCHOOL OF HIGHER EDUCATION

Escuela de Educación Superior Libertad
Hidalgo 508, Zona Centro, 37000 Salamanca, Guanajuato
Tel: +52(464) 647-41-06
Fax: +52(464) 648-50-58.
EMail: universidadlibertad@hotmail.com
Website: http://universidad-libertad.tripod.com/index.html

Director: Jaime Víctor Prieto Ortega

Programmes
Business Administration (Business Administration); **International Business** (International Business); **Law** (Law); **Public Accountancy** (Accountancy)

History: Founded 2002.

Main Language(s) of Instruction: Spanish

Degrees and Diplomas: *Licenciatura*
Last Updated: 21/02/13

LIC. JESÚS ROJAS VILLAVICENCIO LAW SCHOOL

Escuela de Derecho Lic. Jesús Rojas Villavicencio
Jiménez 9, Col. Centro, Huajuapán de León, Oaxaca
Tel: +52(953) 532-16-85
Fax: +52(953) 532-01-65

Directora: Roxana Ambrosio Hernández

Programmes
Law (Law)

History: Founded 1998.

Main Language(s) of Instruction: Spanish

Degrees and Diplomas: *Licenciatura*
Last Updated: 20/02/13

LIC. MIGUEL ALEMÁN SCHOOL TLAXCALA

Escuela Superior Lic. Miguel Alemán Valdés de Tlaxcala
Km. 5 Carretera Tlaxcala-Puebla, Palacio de Cortés, 90110 Acuitlapilco, Tlaxcala
Tel: +52(246) 248-02-65
Fax: +52(246) 468-03-92
EMail: esmav@prodigy.net.mx
Website: http://www.esmav.com.mx

Director: Juan Carlos Hernández Wahibe

Programmes
Tourism Management (Hotel Management; Tourism)

Main Language(s) of Instruction: Spanish

Degrees and Diplomas: *Licenciatura*
Last Updated: 27/02/13

LICEO LONDRES COLLEGE OF ADVANCED STUDIES

Colegio de Estudios Superiores Liceo Londres
Av. Nicolás Bravo, 183, Col. Jardínes de Morelos, 55070 Ecatepec de Morelos, Estado de México
Tel: +52(55) 58-54-10-98
Fax: +52(55) 58-54-10-98

Programmes
Psychology (Psychology)

Degrees and Diplomas: *Licenciatura*
Last Updated: 22/10/09

LIPRO EDUCATIONAL CENTRE

Centro Educativo Lipro
Contreras Medellín, 16, Centro, 44200 Guadalajara, Jalisco
Tel: +52(33) 36-14-52-14
Fax: +52(33) 36-13-38-59

Director: Marco Antonio Robles Morales

Programmes
Architecture (Architecture); **Computer Science** (Computer Science); **Design**; **Psychology** (Psychology)

Main Language(s) of Instruction: Spanish

Degrees and Diplomas: *Licenciatura*

LIVERPOOL TRAINING INSTITUTE

Instituto de Formación Liverpool, A.C.
Hesiodo 540, Col. Chapultepec Morales, Miguel Hidalgo, México, D.F.
Tel: +52(55) 52-62-35-33
EMail: uvlcorporativo@liverpool.com.mx
Website: http://www.uvl.com.mx

Programmes
Business Administration; **Optometry** (Optometry)

History: Created 2000.

Degrees and Diplomas: *Licenciatura*; *Especialización*; *Maestría*
Last Updated: 27/05/09

LOMA CENTRE OF FAMILY STUDIES

Centro de Ciencias Para la Familia Loma
Amargura # 74, San Angel, México, D.F.
EMail: contacto@loma.org.mx
Website: http://www.loma.org.mx/contacto.htm

Director: José Antonio López Ortega Müller

Programmes
Family Studies (Family Studies)

Further Information: Toluca, Guadalajara, Hermosillo, Guanajuato, León, Culiacán, Chihuahua, Monterrey, Cuernavaca, Querétaro, Puebla, Mexicali, Ensenada, Tijuana, Tecate, Pachuca, Mazatlán, Aguascalientes, San Juan del Río, Cancún, Tuxtla Gutiérrez, Tepic, Durango, Chetumal, Guanajuato, Silao, Celaya, Acámbaro, Dolores hIdalgo.

Main Language(s) of Instruction: Spanish

International Co-operation: With institutions in Argentina, Brazil, Chile, Colombia, El Salvador, United States, Honduras, Peru, Dominican Republic and Venezuela

Degrees and Diplomas: *Maestría*
Last Updated: 12/07/12

LONDRES UNIVERSITY

Universidad de Londres
Plaza Luis Cabrera, 9, Col. Roma, entre Zacatecas y Guanajuato, Delegación Cuauhtémoc, 06700 México, D.F.
Tel: +52(55) 55-74-65-02 +52(55) 52-86-22-46
Fax: +52(55) 52-64-34-54
Website: http://www.udlondres.com/

Rectora: Ma. Cristina Gabriela de la Vega y Vega

Programmes
Accountancy (Accountancy); **Business Administration** (Business Administration); **Communication and Multimedia** (Communication Studies; Multimedia); **Computer Science** (Computer Science); **Fashion Design** (Fashion Design); **Finance** (Finance); **Gastronomy** (Cooking and Catering); **Graphic Design** (Graphic Design); **Law** (Law); **Marketing** (Marketing); **Psychology** (Psychology); **Tourism** (Tourism)

Further Information: Also campuses in Guanajuato, Luis Cabrera, Hamburgo, Tabasco,Medellín, San Luis Potosí, Orizaba, Querétaro and Vertiz

History: Founded 1980 as Centro de Estudios Universitarios Londres.

Degrees and Diplomas: *Licenciatura*; *Especialización*; *Maestría*
Last Updated: 15/02/08

LOS ALTOS DE CHIAPAS UNIVERSITY

Universidad de Los Altos de Chiapas (UACH)
Periférico Sur 1016, Barrio de María Auxiliadora, 29290 San Cristóbal de Las Casas, Chiapas
Tel: +52(967) 678-56-57
Fax: +52(967) 678-56-57
EMail: uach@uach.edu.mx
Website: http://www.uach.edu.mx

Rectora: Norma Angelica Molina Zuñiga

Programmes

Accountancy (Accountancy); **Advertising and Public Relations** (Advertising and Publicity; Public Relations); **Architecture** (Architecture); **Business Administration** (Business Administration; Business Computing); **Civil Engineering** (Civil Engineering); **Communication** (Communication Studies); **Computer Engineering** (Computer Engineering); **Gastronomy** (Cooking and Catering); **Graphic Design** (Graphic Design); **Law** (Law); **Tourism** (Tourism)

History: Founded 1993 as Centro de Estudios Superiores de Contaduría y Administración. Acquired present status and title 1998.

Main Language(s) of Instruction: Spanish

Degrees and Diplomas: *Licenciatura*; *Maestría*

Libraries: Yes

Last Updated: 19/09/12

LOYOLA UNIVERSITY OF AMERICA

Universidad Loyola de América

Galeana 157, Col. Las Palmas, 62050 Cuernavaca, Morelos

Tel: +52(777) 318-13-17

EMail: uniloyola@morelos.com

Website: http://www.universidadloyola.edu.mx

Rector: Carlos Hernández Adán

Programmes

Administration and Accountancy (Accountancy; Administration); **Computer Science** (Computer Science); **Economics** (Economics); **Law** (Law); **Political Science** (Political Sciences)

History: Founded 1997.

Main Language(s) of Instruction: Spanish

Degrees and Diplomas: *Licenciatura*

Last Updated: 04/03/08

LOYOLA UNIVERSITY OF THE PACIFIC

Universidad Loyola del Pacífico

Avenida Heroico Colegio Militar s/n, Fracc. Cumbres del Llano Largo, 39820 Acapulco de Juárez, Guerrero

Tel: +52(744) 446-52-25

EMail: jguzman@loyola.edu.mx

Website: http://www.loyola.edu.mx

Rector: Enrique Pasta EMail: enrique.pasta@loyola.edu.mx

Programmes

Architecture (Architecture; Interior Design); **Business Administration** (Accountancy; Administration; Business Administration; Finance); **Communication Studies** (Communication Studies); **Environmental Studies and Sustainable Development** (Development Studies; Environmental Studies); **Graphic Design** (Graphic Design); **Industrial Engineering** (Industrial Engineering); **Information Technology** (Information Technology); **Law** (Law)

History: Founded 1993.

Main Language(s) of Instruction: Spanish

Degrees and Diplomas: *Licenciatura*

Libraries: Yes

Last Updated: 12/10/12

LUCERNA UNIVERSITY

Universidad Lucerna

Vía José López Portillo, 123, Col. Coacalco, 55700 Coacalco de Berriozábal, Estado de México

Tel: +52(555) 874-27-82 +52(555) 874-83-69

Fax: +52(555) 879-22-66

EMail: rectoria@lucerna.edu.mx

Website: http://www.lucerna.edu.mx

Directora: Miriam Ivonne Trejo Rodríguez

Programmes

Accountancy (Accountancy); **Business Administration** (Business Administration; International Business; Marketing); **Computer Science** (Computer Science); **Education** (Education); **Gastronomy** (Cooking and Catering); **Graphic Design** (Graphic Design); **Journalism and Social Communication** (Communication Studies; Journalism); **Law** (Criminal Law; Fiscal Law; International Law; Law; Private Law; Public Law); **Psychology** (Psychology)

History: Founded 1991, acquired present status 1995.

Governing Bodies: Consejo General del Sistema Lucerna, Consejo Técnico, Rectoría

Admission Requirements: Certificado de Bachillerato

Fees: (Pesos): 9,000 per semester

Main Language(s) of Instruction: Spanish

Degrees and Diplomas: *Licenciatura*: Accountancy, Administration, Pedagogy, Computer Science, Computer Engineering, Marketing,Law; *Maestría*

Student Services: Academic counselling, Language programs, Nursery care, Sports facilities

Special Facilities: Theatre, Audio-Visual facilities

Libraries: 2 Libraries

Last Updated: 04/04/13

LUIS DONALDO COLOSIO MURRIETA UNIVERSITY CENTRE

Centro Universitario Luis Donaldo Colosio Murrieta

Azucenas 14, Col. Jardines del Sur, Centro, 69000 Huajuapán de León, Oaxaca

Tel: +52(953) 532-25-77

EMail: dirgral@cucolosio.edu.mx

Website: http://cucolosio.edu.mx

Directora: Esther Ochoa Rios

Programmes

Accountancy (Accountancy); **Law** (Law)

Main Language(s) of Instruction: Spanish

Degrees and Diplomas: *Licenciatura*

Last Updated: 10/03/08

LYCEUM OF ADVANCED STUDIES

Liceo Estudios Superiores

Calle Allende 81 Norte, Esquina Avenida Universidad, Col. Centro, Querétaro, Querétaro

Tel: +52(442) 251-87-00

EMail: liceol@att.net.mx

Website: http://www.de-paseo.com/liceo/liceo.htm

Director: Enrique Jímenez Hernández

Programmes

Architecture; **Business Administration**; **Communication Studies** (Communication Studies); **Law** (Law); **Marketing** (Marketing); **Tourism** (Tourism)

Main Language(s) of Instruction: Spanish

Degrees and Diplomas: *Licenciatura*; *Maestría*: Business Administration

Last Updated: 22/03/13

MACUL XOCHITL INSTITUTE

Instituto Macul Xochitl

2 Ote. No. 2603, 72000 Puebla, Puebla

Director: Ildefonso Hernández Jiménez

Degrees and Diplomas: *Licenciatura*

Last Updated: 07/04/08

MADERO UNIVERSITY

Universidad Madero (UMAD)

Camino Real a Cholula, 4212, San Andrés Cholula, 72150 Puebla, Puebla

Tel: +52(222) 284-59-59

EMail: rectoria@umad.edu.mx

Website: http://www.umad.edu.mx

Rector: Job César Romero Reyes (1985-)

Administrative Officer: Donaciano Alvarado Hernández
EMail: donal@umad.edu.mx

International Relations: Noé Chirino Hernández
EMail: cnoe@umad.edu.mx

Programmes
Accountancy and International Finance (Accountancy; Administration; Banking; Computer Science; English; Finance; Labour Law; Mathematics); **Administration and Innovative Commerce** (Accountancy; Business Administration; Business and Commerce; Finance; International Business); **Business Law** (Labour Law); **Communication and Multimedia** (Communication Studies; Media Studies; Multimedia); **Education** (Bilingual and Bicultural Education; English; French; German; Pedagogy; Phonetics; Psychology); **Fashion Design** (Fashion Design); **Foreign Languages** (English; Ethics; French; German; Modern Languages; Phonetics); **Foreign Trade** (International Business); **Graphic Design, Art and Media** (Design; Graphic Design; Painting and Drawing; Photography; Visual Arts); **Images and Public Relations** (Cinema and Television; Photography; Public Relations; Video); **Industrial Engineering** (Engineering; Engineering Management; Industrial Engineering; Production Engineering); **Information Technology and Internet** (Information Technology); **Marketing** (Banking; Business Administration; Finance; Management; Marketing); **Psychology** (Psychology); **Software Engineering** (Software Engineering); **Systems Engineering** (Computer Engineering; Systems Analysis); **Tourism** (Tourism)

History: Founded 1982, acquired present status 1986. The first University of the Methodist Church in Mexico.

Governing Bodies: Administrative Council

Academic Year: January to December (January-May; August-December)

Admission Requirements: Secondary school certificate (bachillerato) or equivalent, and entrance examination

Main Language(s) of Instruction: Spanish, English

International Co-operation: With universities in Brazil; USA; Australia; Germany; Canada; Argentina; Peru; Chile

Accrediting Agencies: Federación de Instituciones Mexicanas Particulares de Educación Superior (FIMPES)

Degrees and Diplomas: *Licenciatura*: 5 yrs; *Especialización*; *Maestría*; *Doctorado*

Student Services: Academic counselling, Canteen, Employment services, Foreign student adviser, Health services, Language programs, Nursery care, Social counselling, Sports facilities

Libraries: Biblioteca 'Gabriel Alarcón Chargoy'

Last Updated: 12/10/12

MANAGEMENT STUDIES CENTRE

Centro de Estudios en Alta Dirección

Calle Agua Caliente No. 205, Col. Lomas Hipodromo, 53900 Naucalpán de Juárez, Estado de México
Tel: +52(55) 55-62-26-17
Fax: +52(55) 55-62-06-98
EMail: altadir@prodigy.net.mx
Website: http://alta-direccion.edu.mx

Director General: Alfredo Farias Arias

Programmes
Business Administration (Business Administration); **Law** (Law); **Pedagogy** (Pedagogy); **Teleinformatics** (Computer Science)

History: Founded 1989.

Main Language(s) of Instruction: Spanish

Degrees and Diplomas: *Licenciatura*; *Maestría*

Libraries: Yes

Last Updated: 13/07/12

MANUEL JOSÉ DE ROJAS INSTITUTE OF HIGHER STUDIES

Instituto de Estudios Superiores Manuel José de Rojas

Avenida Río Verde s/n y Calle del Molino, 18, Col. La Isla, 29200 San Cristóbal de Las Casas, Chiapas
Tel: +52(967) 678-56-69
Fax: +52(967) 678-56-69
EMail: contacto@iesderecho.zzn.com
Website: http://www.ies.edu.mx

Rector: Gabriel I. Sarmiento Robles

Programmes
Law (Constitutional Law; Criminal Law; Law)

History: Founded 1996.

Main Language(s) of Instruction: Spanish

Degrees and Diplomas: *Licenciatura*; *Maestría*; *Doctorado*

Last Updated: 04/03/13

MARÍA ESTHER ZUNO DE ECHEVERRIA INSTITUTE OF PSYCHOLOGY

Instituto de Psicología María Esther Zuno de Echeverria, A.C.

Calzada Ávila Camacho, 3750, Ote., 27040 Torreón, Coahuila
Tel: +52(871) 121-63-55
Website: http://www.meze.com.mx

Director: Raymundo Ramón Peña

Programmes
Accountancy (Accountancy); **Industrial Hygiene and Safety** (Hygiene; Safety Engineering); **Nursing** (Nursing); **Psychology** (Psychology)

History: Founded 1975.

Main Language(s) of Instruction: Spanish

Degrees and Diplomas: *Licenciatura*

Last Updated: 05/03/13

MARÍA TERESA ZAZUETA Y ZAZUETA SCHOOL OF SOCIAL COMMUNICATION

Escuela de Comunicación Social María Teresa Zazueta y Zazueta

Riva Palacio, 684, Nte., Col. Centro, 80000 Culiacán, Sinaloa
Tel: +52(667) 713-58-29
Fax: +52(667) 713-58-29
EMail: ecs@cln.megared.net.mx

Directora: María Teresa Zazueta y Zazueta (1964-)

Programmes
Social Communication (Communication Studies)

History: Founded 1964.

Main Language(s) of Instruction: Spanish

Degrees and Diplomas: *Licenciatura*

Last Updated: 20/02/13

MARILLAC INSTITUTE

Instituto Marillac

Frontera, 60, Col. Tizapan, San Ángel, Delegación Álvaro Obregón, 01090 México, D.F.
Tel: +52(555) 616-1314
Website: http://www.institutomarillac.edu.mx

Programmes
Nursing (Anatomy; Ecology; Gynaecology and Obstetrics; Health Administration; Health Education; Health Sciences; Nursing; Nutrition; Pharmacology; Physiology; Psychology)

Main Language(s) of Instruction: Spanish

Degrees and Diplomas: *Licenciatura*: 4 yrs

Last Updated: 06/03/13

MARIST UNIVERSITY

Universidad Marista (UMG)

Av. Gral. Leandro Valle # 928, Col. del Mar, Del. Tláhuac, 13270 México, DF
EMail: informes@umarista.edu.mx
Website: http://www.uma.maristas.edu.mx

Rector: José Antonio Espinoza Medina

Areas
Applied Science and Technology (Actuarial Science; Electronic Engineering; Industrial Engineering; Mechanical Engineering); **Arts and Humanities** (Architecture; Graphic Design); **Business and Finance** (Accountancy; Administration; International Business; Marketing; Sports Management); **Social Sciences and Education** (Communication Studies; Education; Law; Psychology)

Further Information: Also Campuses in Mérida, Monterrey, Querétaro, and San Luis Potosí

History: Founded 1993 as Centro Universitario México, División Estudios Superiores. Acquired present status and title 2002.

Governing Bodies: Junta de Gobierno; Consejo Académico

Academic Year: August to June

Admission Requirements: Secondary school certificate (bachillerato)

Main Language(s) of Instruction: Spanish

Degrees and Diplomas: *Licenciatura*; *Especialización*: Education, 1 1/2 yrs; *Maestría*: Research and Education (MIE), 2 yrs; *Doctorado*: Educational Research (D.E), 2 1/2 yrs

Student Services: Academic counselling, Canteen, Cultural centre, Employment services, Language programs, Social counselling, Sports facilities

Student Residential Facilities: Yes

Libraries: 2 libraries

Last Updated: 12/10/12

MATER INSTITUTE OF THE HOLY HEART

Instituto Mater Sagrado Corazón

Avenida Gómez Morín 1000 Sur, Col. Carrizalejo, 66254 Garza García, Nuevo León

Tel: +52(81) 50-00-46-22

Fax: +52(81) 50-00-46-98

EMail: comunicacion@imac.edu.mx

Website: http://www.imac.edu.mx

Directora General: Marcela Cantú de la Garza

Programmes

Human Development (Art Education; Communication Studies; Development Studies; Education; Educational Sciences; Native Language Education; Preschool Education; Primary Education; Secondary Education); **Literature** (Literature); **Plastic Arts** (Painting and Drawing; Photography)

History: Founded 2000.

Main Language(s) of Instruction: Spanish

Degrees and Diplomas: *Licenciatura*; *Maestría*

Last Updated: 06/03/13

MAYA INTERNATIONAL UNIVERSITY OF CANCUN

Universidad Internacional Maya Cancún

Av. Kabah Lote, 5 Manzana 72, Supermanzana 51, 77533 Cancún, Querétaro

Tel: +52(998) 80-80-70

Fax: +52(998) 88-07-41

EMail: edudocbazan@yahoo.com.mx

Director: Carlos Alberto Bazán Castro (1999-)

Programmes

International Business (International Business); **International Relations** (International Relations); **Law** (Law); **Public Relations and Marketing** (Marketing; Public Relations)

History: Founded 1993.

Main Language(s) of Instruction: Spanish

Degrees and Diplomas: *Licenciatura*

Last Updated: 06/03/08

MAYA UNIVERSITY

Universidad Maya

Prolongación Insurgentes No. 100 e Ignacio Ramírez No. 6, Barrio de San Diego, 29200 San Cristóbal de Las Casas, Chiapas

Tel: +52(967) 678-81-91

Fax: +52(967) 678-81-91

EMail: umaya.rectoria@seccionamarilla.com.mx

Rector: Francisco Javier Hernández Domínguez (1998-)

Programmes

Education (Educational Administration; Educational Psychology); **Pedagogy** (Pedagogy); **Psychology of Adolescents** (Psychology); **Social Psychology** (Psychology; Social Psychology)

History: Founded 1998

Main Language(s) of Instruction: Spanish

Accrediting Agencies: Secretaria de Educación

Degrees and Diplomas: *Licenciatura*: Psychology; Pedagogy; Educational Administration

Last Updated: 04/03/08

MAYA UNIVERSITY OF THE AMERICAS

Universidad Maya de las Américas

Avenida Francisco I. Madero, 23, Lote 15, Manzana 6, Super Manzana 65 entre Bonampak y Tulum, 77500 Cancún, Quintana Roo

Tel: +52(998) 884-10-03

EMail: contacto-uma@uma.edu.mx

Website: http://uma.edu.mx

Rector: Rubén Hernández López

Programmes

Accountancy (Accountancy); **Business Administration** (Business Administration); **Business Computing** (Business Computing); **Communication** (Communication Studies); **Law** (Law); **Marketing** (Marketing); **Tourism Management**

History: Founded 2000.

Main Language(s) of Instruction: Spanish

Degrees and Diplomas: *Licenciatura*

Last Updated: 12/10/12

MAYA WORLD UNIVERSITY

Universidad Mundo Maya (UMMA)

Km 4.5 Carretera Villahermosa-Buenavista, Col. Miguel Hidalgo, 86126 Villahermosa, Tabasco

Tel: +52(993) 350-30-37

EMail: difusion@umma.com.mx

Website: http://www.umma.com.mx

Rector: Rosendo C. García Martínez (1989-)

EMail: garciarosendo@umma.com.mx

Divisions

Architecture and Graphic Design (Architecture; Graphic Design); **Business Administration and Service Trades** (Accountancy; Administration; Marketing; Tourism); **Computer Science and Engineering** (Computer Engineering; Computer Science; Electronic Engineering); **Humanities and Information Sciences** (Communication Studies; Law; Philosophy)

Further Information: Also campus in Campeche, Cd. del Carmen, Oaxaca and Cardenas

History: Founded 1989 as Centro de Estudios Universitarios de Villahermosa, acquired present name and status 2000.

Admission Requirements: High school certificate

Fees: (US Dollars): Registration: 2,000; Tuition, 1,662 per month (6 installments)

Main Language(s) of Instruction: Spanish

Accrediting Agencies: Secretaría de Educación Pública

Degrees and Diplomas: *Licenciatura*: Accountancy; Architecture; Administration; Communication; Graphic Design; Law; Philosophy; Computer Science; Electronic Engineering; Computer Engineering; Tourism; Marketing, 4 yrs; *Especialización*: Finance; Commercial Law; Corporative Law, a further yr; *Maestría*: Finance; Commercial Law; High Business Management, a further 2 yrs

Student Services: Academic counselling, Employment services, Foreign Studies Centre, Language programs, Nursery care, Sports facilities

Special Facilities: Art and Design laboratory; Communication laboratory; Computer laboratory

Libraries: Total, c. 66,000 vols

Last Updated: 04/04/13

MESO-AMERICAN INSTITUTE

Instituto Mesoamérica
Portal de Mercaderes, Esq. Plateros, Col. Metropolitana,
57730 Nezahualcóyotl, Estado de México
Tel: +52(55) 57-93-66-41
Fax: +52(55) 57-93-66-41

Directora: Abigail Salcedo Solís (2000-)

Programmes
Accountancy (Accountancy); **Educational Sciences** (Educational Sciences); **Law** (Law)
History: Founded 2000.
Main Language(s) of Instruction: Spanish
Degrees and Diplomas: *Licenciatura*
Last Updated: 06/03/13

MESO-AMERICAN TECHNOLOGICAL UNIVERSITY

Universidad Tecnológica Mesoamericana, S.C.
Centenario, 67, Col. Centro, 91000 Minatitlán, Veracruz
Tel: +52(922) 3-19-97
EMail: informes@utm.com.mx

Programmes
Commercial Relations (Business and Commerce); **Computer Science** (Computer Science); **Industrial Management** (Industrial Management); **Tourism** (Tourism)
Main Language(s) of Instruction: Spanish
Degrees and Diplomas: *Licenciatura*
Last Updated: 05/04/13

MESO-AMERICAN UNIVERSITY

Universidad Mesoamericana
García Vigil, 202, Centro Histórico, Oaxaca de Juárez,
68000 Oaxaca, Oaxaca
Tel: +52(951) 514-13-83
EMail: unimeso@prodigy.net.mx
Website: http://www.universidadmesoamericana.edu.mx

Rector: Marco Antonio Moreno Nishisaki (1989-)

Programmes
Accountancy (Accountancy); **Administration** (Administration; Tourism); **Architecture** (Architecture); **Communication Studies** (Communication Studies); **Computer Science** (Computer Science); **Graphic Design** (Graphic Design); **Law** (Law); **Pedagogy** (Pedagogy); **Psychology** (Psychology)
Further Information: Campuses in San Luis Potosí and San Juan del Río
History: Founded 1989.
Admission Requirements: Bachillerato and entrance examination
Main Language(s) of Instruction: Spanish
Degrees and Diplomas: *Licenciatura*; *Maestría*
Last Updated: 12/10/12

MESO-AMERICAN UNIVERSITY OF SAN AGUSTÍN

Universidad Mesoamericana de San Agustín, A.C. (UMSA)
Calle 47 Núm. 536 por 72 Av. Reforma, 97000 Mérida, Yucatán
Tel: +52(999) 928-45-46
Fax: +52(999) 928-74-11
EMail: preguntas@umsa.edu.mx
Website: http://www.umsa.edu.mx

Rectora: María Eugenia Sansores Ruz

Programmes
Administration (Accountancy; Administration; Business Administration; International Relations; Public Relations; Tourism); **Design and Visual Communication** (Design; Visual Arts); **Gastronomy** (Cooking and Catering); **Gerontology** (Gerontology); **Humanities and Philosophy** (Arts and Humanities; History; Philosophy); **Industrial Engineering** (Industrial Engineering); **Information Technology** (Information Technology); **Law** (Law); **Marketing and Advertising** (Advertising and Publicity; Marketing); **Psychology** (Psychology); **Psychopedagogy** (Pedagogy; Psychology); **Tourism** (Tourism)
History: Founded 1995 following merger of the Colegio San Agustín and the Instituto de Estudios Superiores de Yucatán.
Governing Bodies: Consejo Directivo; Consejo Académico
Academic Year: September to July
Admission Requirements: Secondary school certificate (bachillerato)
Fees: (US Dollars): 1,000 per semester
Main Language(s) of Instruction: Spanish
Degrees and Diplomas: *Licenciatura*: 4-5 yrs; *Maestría*
Student Services: Academic counselling, Employment services, Social counselling, Sports facilities
Libraries: Main Library
Press or Publishing House: UMSA Consejo Editorial
Last Updated: 12/10/12

MESO-AMERICAN UNIVERSITY, PUEBLA

Universidad Mesoamericana, Puebla
Blvd. Valsequillo y 24 "A" Sur, 72595 Puebla, Puebla
Tel: +52(222) 409-93-01
EMail: admisiones@umaweb.com.mx
Website: http://www.umaweb.edu.mx

Rector: Salvador Calva Morales

Areas
Economics and Administration (Accountancy; Administration; Business Administration; Economics; International Business; Marketing); **Engineering** (Automotive Engineering; Electronic Engineering; Mechanical Engineering); **Health Sciences** (Cosmetology; Dietetics; Nutrition); **Humanities** (Cooking and Catering; Modern Languages; Special Education; Tourism); **Law** (Criminology; Law); **Scenic Arts** (Theatre); **Veterinary Science and Animal Husbandry** (Agricultural Engineering; Animal Husbandry; Veterinary Science; Zoology)
Further Information: Also campuses in Tehuacán and Morelos
History: Founded 1982.
Admission Requirements: Bachillerato
Main Language(s) of Instruction: Spanish
Degrees and Diplomas: *Licenciatura*; *Especialización*; *Maestría*
Last Updated: 12/10/12

METROPOLITAN CENTRE OF ADVANCED STUDIES IN ORTHODONTICS

Centro Metropolitano de Estudios Superiores en Ortodoncia
Avenida Emilio Carranza 23, 55000 San Cristóbal Ecatepec, Estado de México
Tel: +52(5) 770-30-49

Director: Marcial Jorge A. Chirinos Fano

Programmes
Orthodontics (Orthodontics)
Main Language(s) of Instruction: Spanish
Degrees and Diplomas: *Maestría*
Last Updated: 28/02/08

METROPOLITAN INSTITUTE OF APPLIED SCIENCES

Instituto Metropolitano de Ciencias Aplicadas
Av. Juárez 12, 7000 Juchitán de Zaragoza, Oaxaca
Tel: +52(971) 20-083
Fax: +52(971) 20-083
EMail: imes199@yahoo.com.mx

Director: Rodrigo Salomón Flores Peñaloza

Programmes
Administration (Accountancy; Administration; Business Administration; Business Computing); **Computer Science** (Computer Science); **Law** (Law)
History: Founded 1999.
Main Language(s) of Instruction: Spanish
Degrees and Diplomas: *Licenciatura*
Last Updated: 06/03/13

METROPOLITAN UNIVERSITY CENTRE OF GUADALAJARA

Centro Universitario Metropolitano de Guadalajara
Mezquital, 302, Sector Hidalgo, 44000 Guadalajara, Jalisco
Tel: +52(33) 613-40-94 +52(33) 613-01-32

Director: Rolando Marino y Romero
Degrees and Diplomas: *Licenciatura*
Last Updated: 04/04/08

METROPOLITAN UNIVERSITY OF COAHUILA

Universidad Metropolitana de Coahuila
Calle Venustiano Carranza, Zona Centro, 25700 Monclova, Coahuila
Tel: +52(866) 632-02-00
EMail: metropolitana1@prodigy.net.mx

Rector: Sergio Camacho Huerta

Programmes
Accountancy (Accountancy); **Business Administration** (Business Administration); **Business Computing** (Business Computing); **Communication** (Communication Studies); **International Business** (International Business); **Law** (Law); **Psychology** (Psychology)
Further Information: Nueva Rosita, Monclova and Acuña Units
History: Founded 1997
Main Language(s) of Instruction: Spanish
Degrees and Diplomas: *Licenciatura*
Last Updated: 04/04/13

METROPOLITAN UNIVERSITY OF MONTERREY

Universidad Metropolitana de Monterrey (UMM)
Washington 424-A ote. Centro, 64000 Monterrey, Nuevo León
Tel: +52(81) 81-30-79-00
EMail: comunicaciones@umm.edu.mx
Website: http://www.umm.edu.mx

Rector: Héctor Sepúlveda Prieto
EMail: comunica.rectoria@umm.edu.mx

Programmes
Accountancy (Accountancy); **Architecture** (Architecture); **Business Administration** (Business Administration; Business Computing; International Business; Marketing); **Communication** (Communication Studies); **Criminology** (Criminology); **Dental Surgery** (Dentistry; Surgery); **Education** (Education; Educational Administration); **Graphic Design** (Graphic Design); **Law** (Law); **Psychology** (Psychology); **Sports** (Sports)
History: Founded 1991.
Main Language(s) of Instruction: Spanish
Degrees and Diplomas: *Licenciatura*; *Maestría*
Last Updated: 04/04/13

METROPOLITAN UNIVERSITY OF PUEBLA

Universidad Metropolitana de Puebla
Blvd. Carmen Serdán, 19, 72050 Puebla, Puebla
Tel: +52(222) 220-30-20
Fax: +52(222) 220-23-53
EMail: unimetropue@hotmail.com

Rector: Carlos Cid Pérez

Programmes
Architecture (Architecture); **Civil Engineering** (Civil Engineering); **Environmental Engineering** (Environmental Engineering); **Finance and Marketing** (Finance; Marketing); **Graphic Communication** (Communication Studies); **Industrial Engineering** (Industrial Engineering); **Town Planning** (Town Planning)
Further Information: Also Teziutlan Branch
Main Language(s) of Instruction: Spanish
Degrees and Diplomas: *Licenciatura*
Last Updated: 04/04/13

METROPOLITAN UNIVERSITY OF THE CENTRE

Universidad Metropolitana del Centro
Libramiento Poniente Esq. Insurgentes s/n Col. la Joya, Jerez de García Salinas, Zacatecas
EMail: umc@yahoo.com.mx
Website: http://www.umcentro.edu.mx

Programmes
Business Administration (Business Administration; E-Business/Commerce; Marketing); **Nutrition** (Nutrition); **Psychology and Social Communication** (Communication Studies; Psychology; Social Studies)
Degrees and Diplomas: *Licenciatura*
Last Updated: 04/04/13

METROPOLITAN UNIVERSITY UNIVERSIDAD METROPOLITANA LATIN CAMPUS

Universidad Metropolitana Latin Campus
San Uriel 690-6 esquina Avenida Guadalupe, Col. Chapalita, Guadalajara, Jalisco
Tel: +52(33) 31-22-42-22
EMail: rectoria@umla.edu.mx
Website: http://www.umla.edu.mx

Programmes
Accountancy (Accountancy); **Administration** (Administration; Business Administration); **Communication Studies** (Communication Studies); **International Business** (International Business); **Law** (Administrative Law; Civil Law; Commercial Law; Criminal Law)
Main Language(s) of Instruction: Spanish
Degrees and Diplomas: *Licenciatura*. Also Diplomados
Last Updated: 12/10/12

MEXICAN ACADEMY OF FISCAL RESEARCH

Academia Mexicana de Investigación Fiscal (AMIF)
Av. Centenario No. 478, PA despachos B y C, Mixcoac, Delegación Álvaro Obregón C.P. 1600, México, D.F.
Tel: +52(55) 1285-6272
EMail: academia@amif.edu.mx

Director: Mariano Latapí Ramírez (1999-)

Programmes
Finance (Finance); **Human Resources** (Human Resources); **International Studies** (International Studies); **Law** (Fiscal Law; International Law; Law); **Public Administration** (Public Administration)
History: Founded 1996.
Main Language(s) of Instruction: Spanish
Degrees and Diplomas: *Licenciatura*; *Especialización*; *Maestría*; *Doctorado*
Last Updated: 10/07/12

MEXICAN AMERICAN SCHOOL, HIGHER EDUCATION DIVISION

Escuela Mexicana Americana, División de Estudios Superiores
Gabriel Mancera, 1604-1616 y Aniceto Ortega, Col. Del Valle, Delegación Benito Juárez, 03100 México, D.F.
Tel: +52(55) 55-34-96-35

Rector: Daniel López Flores (1997-)
History: Founded 1997.

Main Language(s) of Instruction: Spanish
Degrees and Diplomas: *Bachillerato*; *Licenciatura*
Last Updated: 03/04/08

MEXICAN ART CENTRE

Centro de Arte Mexicano

Cascada 180, Jardines del Pedregal San Ángel, Delegación Álvaro Obregón, 01900 México, D.F.
Tel: +52(55) 5535-3684
Fax: +52(55) 5652-4352
EMail: contacto@centrodeartemexicano.edu.mx
Website: http://www.centrodeartemexicano.edu.mx

Directora: Lourdes Turrent Díaz (1992-)

Courses
Art History (Art History); **Fine Arts** (Art History; Painting and Drawing; Sculpture); **Museology** (Museum Studies)
History: Founded 1972.
Main Language(s) of Instruction: Spanish
Degrees and Diplomas: *Licenciatura*; *Maestría*
Last Updated: 12/07/12

MEXICAN ASSOCIATION FOR PRACTICE, RESEARCH AND TEACHING OF PSYCHOANALYSIS

Asociación Méxicana Para la Práctica, Investigación y Enseñanza del Psicoanalisis, A.C

Arquímedes No. 3 - Piso 6, Col. Bosque de Chapultepec, Del. Miguel Hidalgo, 11580 México, D.F.
Tel: +52(5) 5280-3809
EMail: info@ampiep.org
Website: http://www.ampiep.org

Institutes
Sigmund Freud (Psychoanalysis)

Programmes
Psychotherapy (Psychoanalysis; Psychotherapy)
History: Founded 1965.
Main Language(s) of Instruction: Spanish
Degrees and Diplomas: *Maestria*
Last Updated: 26/10/12

MEXICAN CENTRE FOR NEURO-LINGUISTIC PROGRAMMING

Centro Mexicano de Programación Neurolingüística

Av. Hidalgo No. 1681, Col. Ladrón de Guevara, 44600 Guadalajara, Jalisco
Tel: +52(33) 615-84-47
EMail: informes@cmpnl.edu.mx
Website: http://www.cmpnl.edu.mx

Director: Juan Francisco Ramírez Martínez
EMail: juan_francisco@cmpnl.edu.mx

Programmes
Clinical Psychology (Clinical Psychology); **Neurolinguistics** (Linguistics; Neurology)
Further Information: Also branches in México City and Cuautitlán Izcalli
History: Founded 1988.
Main Language(s) of Instruction: Spanish
Degrees and Diplomas: *Licenciatura*; *Especialización*; *Maestría*
Last Updated: 19/07/12

MEXICAN CENTRE IN STOMATOLOGY

Centro Mexicano en Estomatología

17 Sur No. 1308, Col. Huexotitla, 72000 Puebla, Puebla
Tel: +52(2) 240-14-48
Fax: +52(2) 240-14-48
EMail: informes@cme.edu.mx
Website: http://www.cme.edu.mx

Director: Víctor Hugo Toledo Minutti

Programmes
Dentistry (Dentistry; Orthodontics; Stomatology; Surgery)
Further Information: Also campus in Veracruz
History: Founded 1990.
Main Language(s) of Instruction: Spanish
Degrees and Diplomas: *Licenciatura*; *Especialización*
Last Updated: 28/02/08

MEXICAN CORPORATION FOR MATERIALS RESEARCH

Corporación Mexicana de Investigación en Materiales, S.A. de C.V.

Ciencia y Tecnología No 790 Col. Saltillo, 25290 Saltillo, Coahuila
Tel: +52(844) 411-21-00 +52(844) 416-77-98
Fax: +52(844) 416-77-38
Website: http://www.comimsa.com.mx

Director General: José Antonio Lazcano Ponce

Programmes
Engineering (Civil Engineering; Electrical Engineering; Engineering; Environmental Engineering; Materials Engineering; Production Engineering)
History: Founded 1991.
Main Language(s) of Instruction: Spanish
Degrees and Diplomas: *Especialización*; *Maestría*; *Doctorado*
Last Updated: 24/08/12

MEXICAN COUNCIL OF GERIATRICS AND GERONTOLOGY

Consejo Mexicano de Geriatria y Gerontologia

Calle 21 Oriente No. 3205, colonia Miguel Negrete, Puebla, Puebla
Tel: +52(222) 235-2400
EMail: onti33@hotmail.com
Website: http://www.geriatriapuebla.com/

Director: Guillermo Oltiveros Martínez

Programmes
Geriatrics and Gerontology (Gerontology; Podiatry); **Podology** (Podiatry)
Main Language(s) of Instruction: Spanish
Degrees and Diplomas: *Especialización*
Last Updated: 24/08/12

MEXICAN DENTISTRY ASSOCIATION FOR TEACHING AND RESEARCH

Asociación Odontológica Mexicana para la Enseñanza y la Investigación (AOMEI)

Tlaxcala N° 177, Deptos. 301 y 304, Col. Hipódromo Condesa, Delegación Cuauhtémoc, 06170 México, D.F.
Tel: +52(5) 553-09-00
Fax: +52(5) 553-05-87
EMail: aodontologica02@prodigy.net.mx

Director: José Antonio Villavicencio Limón (1995-)

Programmes
Dentistry (Dentistry)
History: Founded 1995.
Main Language(s) of Instruction: Spanish
Degrees and Diplomas: *Licenciatura*; *Especialización*
Last Updated: 10/07/12

MEXICAN HEARING AND LANGUAGE INSTITUTE

Instituto Mexicano de la Audición y el Lenguaje

Avenida Progreso, 141-A, Col. Escandón, Delegación Miguel Hidalgo, 11800 México, D.F.
Tel: +52(55) 52-77-64-44 +52(55) 52-77-65-20
EMail: imal@imal.org.mx
Website: http://www.imal.org.mx

Directora General: María Paz Berruecos Villalobos (1985-)

Programmes
Speech Therapy and Language (Linguistics; Speech Therapy and Audiology)
History: Founded 1951.
Main Language(s) of Instruction: Spanish
Degrees and Diplomas: *Licenciatura*; *Especialización*; *Maestría*
Libraries: Yes
Last Updated: 06/03/13

MEXICAN INSTITUTE OF HIGHER EDUCATION

Instituto Mexicano de Educación Superior
San Jerónimo y Avenida Revolución San Ángel Inn, Álvaro Obregón, 01000 México, D.F.
Director: Pedro González Olvera
Degrees and Diplomas: *Maestría*

MEXICAN INSTITUTE OF HIGHER STUDIES

Instituto Mexicano de Estudios Superiores
Av. Ocampo y Rayón No 245, Col. Centro, 27000 Torreón, Coahuila
Tel: +52(871) 716-68-82
Fax: +52(871) 716-68-82
EMail: ime@lagnet.com.mx
Website: http://imes.edu.mx

Directora: Mayela Carmona Núñez

Programmes
Nutrition (Nutrition)
History: Founded 1964.
Main Language(s) of Instruction: Spanish
Degrees and Diplomas: *Licenciatura*
Last Updated: 06/03/13

MEXICAN INSTITUTE OF MATRIMONIAL STUDIES

Instituto Mexicano de la Pareja
Paseo de la Reforma 2693, Torre A, 4o piso, Col. Lomas Bezares, Delegación Miguel Hidalgo, 11910 México, D.F.
Tel: +52(55) 52-57-40-13
EMail: ametep@aol.com
Website: http://www.ametep.com.mx

Director: Mariano Barragán Gutiérrez

Programmes
Psychology (Psychology); **Psychotherapy** (Psychotherapy)
History: Founded 1987.
Main Language(s) of Instruction: Spanish
Degrees and Diplomas: *Licenciatura*; *Maestría*; *Doctorado*
Last Updated: 06/03/13

MEXICAN INSTITUTE OF PROFESSIONAL EDUCATION

Instituto Mexicano de Educación Profesional
Calzada Ignacio Zaragoza, 3001, Col. Santa Martha Acatitla, 09510 México, D.F.
Tel: +52(5) 57-32-43-62
Website: http://www.imeprofesional.com.mx

Directora General: Ana Erika Hernández Mayén

Divisions
Gastronomy (Cooking and Catering)

Programmes
Accountancy (Accountancy); **Computer Science** (Computer Science); **Tourism** (Tourism)
Further Information: Also Iztapalapa Campus
History: Founded 1997.
Main Language(s) of Instruction: Spanish
Degrees and Diplomas: *Licenciatura*
Last Updated: 06/03/13

MEXICAN INSTITUTE OF PSYCHOPEDAGOGY

Instituto Mexicano de Psicopedagogía, A.C. (IMPAC)
Insurgentes Sur, 429, 2° Piso, Col. Condesa, Delegación Cuauhtémoc, 06100 México, D.F.
Tel: +52(55) 55-53-03-13
EMail: impacdf@yahoo.com.mx

Presidente: Joaquín Alberto Montes de Oca Támez

Programmes
Neurosciences (Neurosciences); **Psychoanalysis** (Psychoanalysis); **Psychotherapy** (Psychotherapy)
History: Founded 1991.
Main Language(s) of Instruction: Spanish
Degrees and Diplomas: *Licenciatura*; *Especialización*; *Maestría*
Last Updated: 06/03/13

MEXICAN INSTITUTE OF SEXOLOGY

Instituto Mexicano de Sexología, A.C.
Calzada de Las Águilas 657, Col. Ampliación Águilas, Del. Álvaro Obregón, 01710 México, D.F.
Tel: +52(555) 574-90-70
EMail: diracad@imesex.edu.mx
Website: http://www.imesex.edu.mx

Director: Juan Luis Álvarez-Gayou Jurgenson
EMail: gayou@imesex.edu.mx

Programmes
Sexology (Embryology and Reproduction Biology)
Further Information: Also Instituto de Enseñanza Superior e Investigación Sexologica IMESEX
History: Founded 1979.
Main Language(s) of Instruction: Spanish
Degrees and Diplomas: *Especialización*; *Maestría*
Last Updated: 06/03/13

MEXICAN INSTITUTE OF TOURISM STUDIES

Instituto Mexicano de Turismo (IMT)
Venustiano Carranza # 999 nte, Col. Centro, 64000 Monterrey, Nuevo León
Tel: +52(81) 83-45-20-75
EMail: aarongonzalez@inmextur.com.mx
Website: http://www.inmextur.com.mx

Director: Iván González González (2001-)

Programmes
Tourism (Tourism)
History: Founded 1979.
Main Language(s) of Instruction: Spanish
Degrees and Diplomas: *Licenciatura*
Last Updated: 06/03/13

MEXICAN SCHOOL OF TOURISM

Escuela Mexicana de Turismo, A.C.
Barcelona, 28, Col. Juárez, Delegación Cuauhtémoc, 06600 México, D.F.
Tel: +52(55) 55-35-56-20 +52(55) 55-35-56-59
Fax: +52(55) 55-35-64-61
EMail: emt2003@prodigy.net.mx
Website: http://www.emt2003.net/

Director General: Jaime Alfonso Barcelo Infante (1998-)

Programmes
Gastronomy (Cooking and Catering); **Hotel and Restaurant** (Hotel and Restaurant; Hotel Management); **Tourism** (Hotel and Restaurant; Tourism)
History: Founded 1947. Acquired present status and title 1962.
Main Language(s) of Instruction: Spanish
Degrees and Diplomas: *Licenciatura*
Libraries: Yes
Last Updated: 10/01/13

MEXICAN TECHNOLOGICAL INSTITUTE

Instituto Tecnológico Mexicano
5 de Febrero, 283, Esq. Gutiérrez Nájera, Col. Obrera, Delegación Cuauhtémoc, 06800 México, D.F.
Tel: +52(55) 57-40-39-99
Fax: +52(55) 57-40-34-99

Directora General: Joaquina Gallardo Peña (1998-)

Programmes

Business Administration (Accountancy; Business Administration)

Degrees and Diplomas: *Licenciatura*; *Especialización*
Last Updated: 27/02/08

MEXICAN UNIVERSITY

Universidad Mexicana (UNIMEX)
Río Duero, 37, Col. Cuauhtémoc, Delegación Cuauhtémoc, 06500 México, D.F.
Tel: +52(55) 52-82-04-77 +52(55) 91-38-00-60
Fax: +52(55) 52-07-53-64 +52(55) 52-81-29-85
EMail: umrec_rectorasist@unimex.edu.mx
Website: http://www.unimex.edu.mx

Rector: Ángel Mattiello Canales (1995-) EMail: umret@mx.inter.net

Faculties

Business Administration (Business Administration); **Education** (Education); **Fine Arts** (Fine Arts); **Law** (Law); **Mathematics and Computer Science** (Mathematics and Computer Science); **Service Trades** (Tourism); **Social Sciences** (Social Sciences)

Further Information: Also branch in Veracruz

History: Founded 1553 as Institute of Higher Education. Became Hispanic Mexican University 1939. Merged with Mexican University 1980.

Academic Year: September to August

Admission Requirements: High school certificate (bachillerato)

Main Language(s) of Instruction: Spanish, English

Degrees and Diplomas: *Licenciatura*: 3 1/2 yrs; *Especialización*: 1 yr; *Maestría*: 1 1/2 yr

Student Services: Academic counselling, Employment services, Foreign student adviser, Language programs, Nursery care, Social counselling, Sports facilities

Special Facilities: Radio and TV Studio

Libraries: Central Library
Last Updated: 04/04/13

MEXICAN UNIVERSITY OF DISTANCE EDUCATION

Universidad Mexicana de Educación a Distancia (UMED)
Copa de Oro no 28, Col.Santa María Ahuacatitlan, 62100 Cuernavaca, Morelos
Tel: +52(777) 317-62-04
EMail: umed@umed.edu.mx
Website: http://www.umed.edu.mx

Rector: José Fausto Gutiérrez Aragón EMail: rector@umed.edu.mx

Programmes

Accountancy (Accountancy); **Administration** (Administration; Business Administration); **Business Computing** (Business Computing); **Law** (Law); **Psychology** (Psychology)

Further Information: Centres in Acapulco, Toluca, Morelia, Cuautla, León.

History: Founded 1988.

Main Language(s) of Instruction: Spanish

Degrees and Diplomas: *Licenciatura*: Administration; Law; Accountancy; Computer Science; Psychology; *Maestría*

Libraries: Yes
Last Updated: 12/10/12

MEXICAN UNIVERSITY OF THE NORTH-EAST

Universidad Mexicana del Noreste
Quinta Zona 409, Col. Caracol, 64810 Monterrey, Nuevo León
Tel: +52(181) 8343-70-03
EMail: josefinadse@umne.edu.mx

Rector: Juan Antonio González Aréchiga y de la Cueva (1976-)
Tel: +52(81) 81-90-05-91 +52(81) 81-90-11-04
EMail: jagzza@giga.com

Secretaria Administrativa: Josefina Espinoza Jara

International Relations: Eugenia Mireya Martínez
Tel: +52(81) 81-90-17-27

Departments

Administration and Social Sciences (Accountancy; Administration; Banking; Business Administration; Finance; Management; Social Sciences); **Engineering and Science** (Automation and Control Engineering; Construction Engineering; Electrical Engineering; Engineering; Engineering Drawing and Design; Industrial Design; Industrial Engineering; Mathematics and Computer Science; Mechanical Engineering; Natural Sciences; Systems Analysis)

History: Founded 1976. A private institution recognized by the Nuevo León State government.

Governing Bodies: Board of Directors, comprising 13 members

Academic Year: January to December (January-April; May-August; September-December)

Admission Requirements: Secondary school certificate (bachillerato)

Main Language(s) of Instruction: Spanish

Accrediting Agencies: FIMPES

Degrees and Diplomas: *Licenciatura*: 4-4 1/2 yrs; *Maestría*: a further 2-3 yrs

Libraries: 2 Department libraries

Publications: Ánimo *(quarterly)*; Aprender a Ser *(quarterly)*
Last Updated: 04/04/13

MEXICO-AMERICAN UNIVERSITY INSTITUTE

Instituto Universitario México-Americano
Digital 3801 Col. 13 de Mayo, Guadalupe, Nuevo León
Website: http://www.iuma.edu.mx

Directora: Thelma González Rojas

Programmes

Administration (Administration); **Linguistics** (Linguistics); **Music** (Music); **Pastoral Theology** (Pastoral Studies); **Pedagogy** (Pedagogy); **Theological Studies** (Theology)

Main Language(s) of Instruction: Spanish

Degrees and Diplomas: *Licenciatura*; *Maestría*
Last Updated: 22/03/13

MEXICO-AMERICAN UNIVERSITY OF THE NORTH

Universidad México Americana del Norte (UMAN)
Calle Primera S/N, Col. Círculo, 88560 Ciudad Reynosa, Tamaulipas
Tel: +52(899) 922-20-02
Fax: +52(899) 922-85-68
Website: http://www.uman.edu.mx

Rectora: Edith Cantú de Morett (1982-)

Divisions

Economics and Administration (Accountancy; Business Administration; International Business; Marketing); **Exact Sciences** (Architecture; Civil Engineering; Computer Science; Design; Electronic Engineering; Telecommunications Engineering); **Health Sciences** (Dentistry; Nursing; Surgery); **Humanities and Social Sciences** (Communication Studies; Law; Primary Education; Psychology)

Further Information: Also Teaching Affiliated Hospital, Dental Clinic, and Preparatory School

History: Founded 1982, acquired present status 1983.

Governing Bodies: Patronato (Board of Trustees)

Academic Year: August to June (August-December; January-June); four months programmes, September to August (September-December; January-April; May-August)

Admission Requirements: Bachillerato, or 12 years of general studies

Main Language(s) of Instruction: Spanish

International Co-operation: With universities in USA, Brazil, France

Accrediting Agencies: Secretaría de Educación Pública (SEP); Tamaulipas State Department of Education

Degrees and Diplomas: *Licenciatura*: Dentistry; Electronic Engineering, Industrial & Computer Systems Engineering, Architecture; Medicine; *Licenciatura*: Marketing, International Commerce, Psychology, Accounting, Business Administration, Communication, Computer Systems, Design, Industrial Relations, Education, Law, 32-40 months; *Maestría*: Business Administration, Information Systems, Higher Education, Taxation (MA), a further 2 1/2 yrs; *Doctorado*

Student Services: Academic counselling, Employment services, Foreign student adviser, Language programs, Social counselling, Sports facilities

Special Facilities: Agricultural Experimental Station. FM Radio Station (Xhrya)

Libraries: Central Library and Branch Libraries

Press or Publishing House: Editorial UMAN

Last Updated: 12/10/12

MEXICO CENTRE FOR ADVANCED STUDIES

Centro de Estudios Superiores México

20 de Noviembre, 399, Centro, 91700 Heroica Veracruz, Veracruz

Tel: +52(229) 932-55-44 +52(229) 932-67-52

Fax: +52(229) 932-58-38

Director General: Rafael Contreras Fernández (1997-)

Programmes

Accountancy; **International Commercial Law** *(Postgraduate)* (Commercial Law; International Law); **Law**

History: Founded 1997.

Degrees and Diplomas: *Licenciatura*: 10 sem.; *Licenciatura*: 8 sem.; *Maestría*: 4 sem.

Last Updated: 26/03/08

MEXICO CENTRE FOR ADVANCED STUDIES, CUERNAVACA

Centro de Estudios Superiores México, Cuernavaca

Calle Teopanzolco No. 102-B, Col. Vista Hermosa, Cuernavaca, Morelos

Tel: +52(777) 318-05-02

Director: Guillermo Agustín Pantoja Maldonado

MEXICO CULINARY INSTITUTE

Instituto Culinario de México, A.C.

Teziutlán Norte, 43, Col. la Paz, 72000 Puebla, Puebla

Tel: +52(222) 266-16-90

Website: http://www.icum.edu.mx

Directora: Giovanna Medina Brozafferri

Programmes

Gastronomy (Cooking and Catering); **Management of the Food and Drink Industry** (Food Science; Management)

Further Information: Also campus in Monterrey

History: Founded 1994.

Main Language(s) of Instruction: Spanish

Degrees and Diplomas: *Licenciatura*; *Maestría*

Last Updated: 27/02/13

MEXICO-VALLE UNIVERSITY CENTRE

Centro Universitario México-Valle

Capitán Aguilar, 606, Sur, Col. Obispado, 64040 Monterrey, Nuevo León

Tel: +52(81) 83-47-60-54

EMail: cumv@prodigy.net.mx

Rector: Rubén Luna Villarreal

Programmes

Accountancy (Accountancy); **Business Administration** (Business Administration); **Business Computing** (Business Computing); **Communication** (Communication Studies); **Industrial Engineering** (Industrial Engineering); **Law** (Law); **Marketing** (Marketing)

Degrees and Diplomas: *Licenciatura*; *Maestría*

Last Updated: 21/03/08

MEXIQUENSE UNIVERSITY

Universidad Mexiquense

Avenida Miguel Hidalgo, Ote., 1329, Col. Ferrocarriles, 50070 Toluca, Estado de México

Tel: +52(722) 217-22-46

EMail: aginfante@umex.edu.mx

Website: http://umex.edu.mx

Director: Antonio García Infante

Programmes

Business Administration (Accountancy; Business Administration; Business Computing; Economics); **Graphic Design** (Graphic Design); **Law** (Law); **Psychology** (Psychology)

Further Information: Also branch in Metepec

History: Founded 1978.

Governing Bodies: Academic Counselling

Academic Year: September to August

Admission Requirements: Certificado de Estudios de Preparatoria

Main Language(s) of Instruction: Spanish

International Co-operation: With universities in Canada

Degrees and Diplomas: *Licenciatura*; *Maestría*

Student Services: Academic counselling, Health services, Sports facilities

Last Updated: 04/04/13

MICHOACAN UNIVERSITY OF THE EAST

Universidad Michoacana de Oriente

Hidalgo, Esq. Venustiano Carranza, Col. La Cuesta, 61512 Zitácuaro, Michoacán

Tel: +52(715) 153-89-90

Fax: +52(715) 153-89-90

EMail: info@umo.edu.mx

Website: http://www.umo.edu.mx/

Rector: Luis Carlos Chávez Santacruz

EMail: luisc@evonet.com.mx

Programmes

Accountancy (Accountancy); **Administration** (Administration); **Architecture** (Architecture); **Communication Studies** (Communication Studies); **Law** (Law); **Psychology** (Psychology)

History: Founded 2000.

Governing Bodies: Governing Board

Admission Requirements: Bachillerato

Main Language(s) of Instruction: Spanish

Degrees and Diplomas: *Licenciatura*

Student Services: Academic counselling, Employment services, Language programs

Student Residential Facilities: None

Libraries: Yes

Last Updated: 15/10/12

MIGUEL ALEMÁN UNIVERSITY

Universidad Miguel Alemán

Calle 12 y Calixto Ayala # 324, Col. Buena Vista, Ciudad Miguel Alemán, Tamaulipas

Tel: +52(897) 972-15-35 +52(897) 972-15-77

EMail: uma_matamoros@hotmail.com

Website: http://www.unimiguelaleman.edu.mx

Rector: Roberto Ramírez Ramírez

Faculties

Commerce (Accountancy; Administration; Business Administration; Business Computing); **Education** (Educational Administration; Educational Psychology; Pedagogy); **Law a** (Civil Law; Constitutional Law; Criminal Law; Law)

Main Language(s) of Instruction: Spanish

Degrees and Diplomas: *Licenciatura*

Last Updated: 04/04/13

MIGUEL ALEMÁN VALDÉS SCHOOL CENTRE

Centro Escolar Miguel Alemán Valdés, A.C.

A.C. Calle 27 No. 150 con 14, Fracc. San Miguel, 97140 Mérida, Yucatán

Tel: +52(999) 927-05-98 +52(999) 927-37-10 +52(999) 927-37-71

Fax: +52(999) 927-76-97

EMail: contacto@cema.edu.mx

Website: http://www.cema.edu.mx

Director General: Carlos Ruben Ávila González

Programmes

Accountancy (Accountancy); **Computer Engineering** (Computer Engineering)

Degrees and Diplomas: *Licenciatura*: 9-10 sem.

Last Updated: 27/03/08

MIGUEL CÁSTULO ALATRISTE TEACHER TRAINING SCHOOL

Escuela Normal Miguel Cástulo Alatriste

Corregidora, 5, Col. Centro, Izúcar de Matamoros, 74400 Iztacala, Puebla

Tel: +52(243) 436-04-30 +52(243) 436-08-48

Fax: +52(243) 436-09-30

EMail: uep@hotmail.com

Director: Juan Miguel Bagatella Bermúdez

Programmes

Accountancy; **Education** (Education; Physical Education; Teacher Trainers Education)

Main Language(s) of Instruction: Spanish

Degrees and Diplomas: *Licenciatura*

Last Updated: 20/03/08

MIGUEL HIDALGO COLLEGE

Colegio Miguel Hidalgo

9, Sur, 3104, Col. Chulavista, 72420 Puebla, Puebla

Tel: +52(222) 243-10-33

Fax: +52(222) 243-05-10

EMail: admpa@colegiomiguelhidalgo.edu.mx

Website: http://www.colegiomiguelhidalgo.edu.mx

Directora: Ma. Gudela Sánchez Vélez

Programmes

Educational Innovation (Education); **Preschool Education** (Preschool Education); **Primary Education** (Primary Education)

Main Language(s) of Instruction: Spanish

Degrees and Diplomas: *Licenciatura*; *Maestría*

Last Updated: 23/08/12

MIGUEL HIDALGO REGIONAL UNIVERSITY

Universidad Regional Miguel Hidalgo (URMH)

16 de Septiembre, 102, Ote, Col. Árbol Grande, 89490 Ciudad Madero, Tamaulipas

Tel: +52(833) 215-90-99

EMail: rectoria@urmh.edu.mx

Website: http://www.urmh.edu.mx

Rectora: Lillia Torres Reyes

Programmes

Administration and Commerce (Administration; Business and Commerce); **Nursing** (Nursing); **Nutrition** (Nutrition); **Physical Education** (Physical Education); **Social Work** (Social Sciences; Social Work)

History: Founded 1982.

Main Language(s) of Instruction: Spanish

Degrees and Diplomas: *Licenciatura*; *Especialización*; *Maestría*

Last Updated: 23/10/12

MILLENNIUM UNIVERSITY OF MEXICO

Universidad de Mexico Milenio

Abasolo 29, Col. Centro, 45750 Zacoalco de Torres, Jalisco

Tel: +52(32) 42-32-350

Fax: +52(32) 42-32-405

EMail: udmzacoalco@yahoo.com.mx

Director: Mario Artúro Ortiz Sevilla

Programmes

Business Administration (Accountancy; Business Administration; Business Computing; Marketing); **Law** (Law)

History: Founded 2005.

Degrees and Diplomas: *Licenciatura*; *Especialización*

Last Updated: 04/11/09

MIXTEC INSTITUTE OF INTEGRAL EDUCATION

Instituto Mixteco de Educación Integral, A.C.

Aquiles Serdán, 11, Col. Centro, 74400 Izúcar de Matamoros, Puebla

Tel: +52(243) 436-22-50 +52(243) 436-27-52

Fax: +52(243) 436-23-68

EMail: institutomixteco@hotmail.com

Director General: César Arturo Vargas Salgado (1996-)

Programmes

Education (Education)

History: Founded 1996.

Main Language(s) of Instruction: Spanish

Degrees and Diplomas: *Licenciatura*

MODELO UNIVERSITY

Universidad Modelo

Carretera antigua a Cholul, 200 mts del Periférico, 97000 Mérida, Yucatán

Tel: +52(999) 930-19-00

EMail: unimo@modelo.edu.mx

Website: http://www.unimodelo.edu.mx/univ/

Rector: Carlos Sauri Duch (1997-)

Programmes

Accountancy (Accountancy); **Administration** (Administration; Business Administration; Marketing); **Architecture** (Architecture); **Communication** (Communication Studies); **Dental Surgery** (Dentistry; Surgery); **Design** (Design; Fashion Design; Graphic Design); **Law** (Law); **Modern Languages and Literature** (Literature; Modern Languages); **Nutrition** (Nutrition); **Physical Education** (Physical Education; Sports); **Poiltical Science** (International Relations; Political Sciences; Public Administration); **Psychology** (Psychology); **Tourism** (Tourism)

Further Information: Also campus Valladolid and campus Chetumal

History: Founded 1910 as Escuela Moderno. Acquired present status and title 1997.

Main Language(s) of Instruction: Spanish

Degrees and Diplomas: *Licenciatura*; *Maestría*

Last Updated: 04/04/13

MODELO UNIVERSITY AND TECHNOLOGICAL INSTITUTE

Instituto Universitario y Tecnológico Modelo

Cerrada Vía López Portillo, 3, Col. Villa de las Flores, 55710 Coacalco de Berriozábal, Estado de México

Tel: +52(55) 5875-3999

EMail: info@universidadmodelo.edu.mx

Website: http://www.universitariomodelo.edu.mx

Directora General: Magda Aurora Britto Serna (1996-)

Programmes

Business Administration (Accountancy; Administration; Business Administration); **Communication Studies**; **Computer Engineering and Computer Networks** (Computer Engineering; Computer Networks); **Graphic Design** (Graphic Design); **Law** (Law); **Pedagogy** (Education; Pedagogy); **Tourism** (Tourism)

History: Founded 1983.

Main Language(s) of Instruction: Spanish

Degrees and Diplomas: *Licenciatura*; *Especialización*; *Maestría*

Last Updated: 22/03/13

MODERN UNIVERSITY COLLEGE

Colegio Universitario Moderno

Avenida Guerrero Oriente, 265, La Venta, 54240 Jilotepec, Estado de México

Tel: +52(761) 734-06-78

Directora: Nora Maldonado Garrido (2000-)

Programmes

Accountancy (Accountancy); **Administration** (Administration); **Business Administration** (Business Administration); **Civil Law** (Civil Law); **Communication Studies** (Communication Studies); **Criminalistics and Criminology** (Criminology); **Education for Persons with Trisomy 21** (Special Education); **Finance** (Finance); **International Commerce** (International Business); **Law** (Criminal Law; Law); **Marketing** (Marketing); **Taxation** (Taxation); **Tourism** (Tourism)

History: Founded 2000.

Main Language(s) of Instruction: Spanish

Degrees and Diplomas: *Licenciatura*: 8-10 sem.; *Especialización*

Last Updated: 24/08/12

MONTE FENIX CENTRE FOR ADVANCED STUDIES

Centro de Estudios Superiores Monte Fenix

Las Flores N° 439, Col. San Ángel Inn, Delegación Álvaro Obregón, 01060 México, D.F.

Tel: +52(555) 681-30-11

Fax: +52(555) 95-33-49

EMail: difusion@cesmf.edu.mx

Website: http://www.cesmf.edu.mx

Director: Carlos Enrique Acuña Escobar

Programmes

Family Studies (Family Studies); **Toxicology** (Toxicology)

History: Founded 1994.

Main Language(s) of Instruction: Spanish

Degrees and Diplomas: *Especialización*

Last Updated: 03/03/08

MONTECRISTO COLLEGE

Colegio Montecristo

2 de Abril 37, Col. Centro, 86080 Villahermosa, Tabasco

Tel: +52(934) 343-07-49

EMail: normontecristo@hotmail.com

Programmes

Accountancy (Accountancy); **Primary Education** (Primary Education)

Main Language(s) of Instruction: Spanish

Degrees and Diplomas: *Licenciatura*

Last Updated: 23/08/12

MONTECRISTO COLLEGE

Colegio de Montecristo, S.C.

2 de Abril, 37, Centro, 86980 Emiliano Zapata, Sonora

Tel: +52(934) 343-07-49

EMail: normontecristo@hotmail.com

Directora: Dalia Margarita Margalli Aguilar (2000-)

Programmes

Accountancy (Accountancy)

History: Founded 1984.

Main Language(s) of Instruction: Spanish

Degrees and Diplomas: *Licenciatura*

Last Updated: 04/04/08

MONTERREY INSTITUTE OF TECHNOLOGY

Tecnológico de Monterrey (ITESM)

Campus Monterrey, Avenida Eugenio Garza Sada 2501, Col. Tecnológico, 64849 Monterrey, Nuevo León

Tel: +52(818) 358-20-00

Fax: +52(818) 359-59-19

EMail: contacto@itesm.mx

Website: http://www.itesm.edu

Rector: David Noel Ramírez Padilla Tel: +52(818) 358-28-24

International Relations: Enrique Alejandro Zepeda Bustos Tel: +52(818) 328-43-68 EMail: eazepeda@itesm.mx

Centres

Artificial Intelligence Studies (Artificial Intelligence); **Automation and Industrial Process Control** (Automation and Control Engineering); **Biotechnology** (Biotechnology); **Economic Politics for Sustainable Development** (Development Studies; Economic and Finance Policy); **Electronics and Telecommunications** (Electronic Engineering; Telecommunications Engineering); **Environmental Quality Research** (Environmental Management; Environmental Studies); **Information Research** (Information Sciences); **Integrated Systems of Manufacture Studies** (Production Engineering); **Knowledge Systems**; **Optics** (Optics); **Quality Research**; **Solar Energy Technology** (Energy Engineering); **Strategic Studies** (Military Science; Peace and Disarmament); **Sustainable Development** (Development Studies); **Technology, Education and Science Supercomputing** (Computer Science; Technology)

Departments

Project and Industrial Security Studies (Safety Engineering)

Faculties

Administration and Social Sciences (Administration; Social Sciences); **Agriculture and Marine Sciences** (Agriculture; Marine Science and Oceanography); **Engineering and Architecture** (Architecture; Engineering); **Graduate Studies and Research** (Agriculture; Communication Studies; Computer Science; Engineering; Technology); **Health Sciences** (Health Sciences); **Science and Humanities** (Arts and Humanities; Natural Sciences)

Schools

Architecture, Art and Design *(Puebla)* (Architecture; Design; Fine Arts); **Business Administration** *(EGADE)* (Business Administration); **Medicine** *('Ignacio A. Santos')* (Medicine)

Further Information: Also Virtual University. Campuses: Zona Metropolitana de Monterrey: Monterrey, Cumbres, Eugenio Garza Lagüera, Eugenio Garza Sada, Santa Catarina, Valle Alto. Zona

Metropolitana de la Ciudad de México: Ciudad de México, Santa Fe. Zona Norte: Aguascalientes, Chihuahua, Ciudad Juárez, Laguna, Saltillo, San Luis Potosí, Tampico, Zacatecas. Zona Centro: Estado de México, Querétaro, Toluca. Zona Sur: Central de Veracruz, Chiapas, Cuernavaca, Hidalgo, Morelia, Puebla. Zona Occidente: Ciudad Obregón, Colima, Guadalajara, Irapuato, León, Mazatlán, Sinaloa, Sonora Norte

History: Founded 1943 as Enseñanza e Investigación Superior, A.C. (EISAC). Renamed Instituto Tecnológico y de Estudios Superiores de Monterrey 1958.

Academic Year: January to December (January-June; August-December)

Fees: (Pesos): 36,100 per annum

Main Language(s) of Instruction: Spanish, English

Degrees and Diplomas: *Licenciatura*: 4-5 yrs; *Maestría*: 1-2 yrs; *Doctorado*: 4-5 yrs

Student Services: Academic counselling, Canteen, Cultural centre, Employment services, Foreign student adviser, Health services, Sports facilities

Libraries: Central Library, 289,654 vols

Last Updated: 15/02/08

MORELOS INSTITUTE OF HIGHER STUDIES

Instituto de Estudios Superiores Morelos

Obreros Textiles Esq. Juan de la Barrera, Col. Marco Antonio Muñoz, 91060 Xalapa, Veracruz
Tel: +52(228) 817-45-28
EMail: iesmorelos@yahoo.com.mx
Website: http://www.escuelamorelos.edu.mx/instituto.html

Director General: Juan Beristain de los Santos
EMail: juanberistain9@hotmail.com

Programmes

Information and Social Communication (Communication Studies; Information Sciences); **Psychology** (Clinical Psychology; Educational Psychology; Neurology; Psychology; Psychotherapy; Social Psychology)

History: Founded 2001.

Main Language(s) of Instruction: Spanish

Degrees and Diplomas: *Licenciatura*

Last Updated: 04/03/13

MORELOS UNIVERSITY OF CUERNAVACA

Universidad Morelos de Cuernavaca (UMC)

Avenida Teopanzolco, 1000, Col. Recursos Hidráulicos, 62260 Cuernavaca, Morelos
Tel: +52(777) 101-01-98
Fax: +52(777) 313-07-22
EMail: claudiam@umc.edu.mx

Directora: Verónica E. Palmerín López
EMail: vpalmerin@umc.edu.mx

Departments

Engineering (Computer Engineering; Industrial Engineering; Telecommunications Engineering) *Director*: Héctor José Duarte-Ochoa; **Humanities** (Educational Sciences; Law) *Director*: Carlos F. de J. González-Sánchez; **Management** *Director*: Salvador Cuevas-Estrada

History: Opened as University Centre September 1997 inside Colegio Morelos, as an integral professional programme which goes from kindergarden to university, in order to fulfil the needs of the firms of the region. Acquired present status and title 2001.

Governing Bodies: Government Committee

Admission Requirements: High school certificate (certificado de preparatoria)

Fees: (Pesos): 51,000 per annum

Main Language(s) of Instruction: Spanish

Accrediting Agencies: CENEVAL

Degrees and Diplomas: *Licenciatura*. Also Diplomados

Student Services: Academic counselling, Canteen, Health services, Sports facilities

Special Facilities: Two Auditoriums. Two Computing Laboratories and Engineering Laboratories.

Libraries: University Library

Last Updated: 04/04/13

MOTOLINÍA UNIVERSITY OF THE PEDEGRAL

Universidad Motolinía del Pedegral

Avenida de las Fuentes, 525, Jardines del Pedregall, 01900 México, D.F.
Tel: +52(55) 55-68-05-59
Fax: +52(55) 55-68-83-24
EMail: promocion@ump.edu.mx
Website: http://www.universidadmotolinia.edu.mx

Rector: Jorge Arturo Sibaja López.

Programmes

Architecture and Interior Design (Architecture; Interior Design); **Business Administration** (Administration; Business Administration); **Law** (Law); **Marketing** (Marketing); **Modern Languages** (Modern Languages)

Further Information: Also campuses in Guanajuato, Nuevo León, Oaxaca, Veracruz and Tabasco

History: Founded 1943. Acquired present status and title 1965.

Admission Requirements: Bachillerato

Main Language(s) of Instruction: Spanish

Degrees and Diplomas: *Licenciatura*; *Especialización*; *Maestría*

Libraries: Biblioteca Dolores Echeverría Esparza

Last Updated: 04/04/13

MUKILA MAZO SCHOOL OF ART

Escuela Superior de Arte Mukila Mazo

Rafael Buelna s/n, Col. Centro, 80200 Culiacán, Sinaloa
Tel: +52(667) 717-04-77
Fax: +52(667) 717-04-77
EMail: mukilamazo@hotmail.com

Director: Rubén Efrén Benítez Aguilar

Programmes

Fine Arts (Dance; Fine Arts)

Main Language(s) of Instruction: Spanish

Degrees and Diplomas: *Licenciatura*

Last Updated: 26/02/13

MULTICULTURAL INTERNATIONAL UNIVERSITY

Universidad Multicultural Internacional, A.C.

Olmos No. 413, 89000 Tampico, Tamaulipas

Programmes

Business Administration (Accountancy; Banking; Business Administration; Finance; International Business); **Law** (Law); **Pedagogy** (Pedagogy)

History: Founded 1998.

Main Language(s) of Instruction: Spanish

Degrees and Diplomas: *Licenciatura*

Last Updated: 04/04/13

MULTIDISCIPLINARY SPECIALIZATION INSTITUTE

Instituto Multidisciplinario de Especialización

Calzada Porfirio Diaz No. 112 Colonia Reforma, 72000 Oaxaca, Oaxaca
Tel: +52(951) 51-85-112
EMail: informes@ime.edu.mx
Website: http://www.ime.edu.mx

Directora: María Eugenia Pena Arvizu

Programmes

Administration (Administration); **Education** (Education; Pedagogy)

Main Language(s) of Instruction: Spanish

Degrees and Diplomas: *Especialización*; *Maestría*; *Doctorado*
Last Updated: 06/03/13

MULTITECHNICAL PROFESSIONAL INSTITUTE

Instituto Multitécnico Profesional, S.C.
Río Marabasco #449, 28050 Colima, Colima
Tel: +52(312) 123-39-38
EMail: mail@institutomultitecnico.edu.mx
Website: http://www.institutomultitecnico.edu.mx

Director: Francisco Javier Valdés Mejía

Programmes

Administration and Finance (Administration; Finance); **Computer Engineering** (Computer Engineering); **International Business** (International Business); **Law** (Law); **Marketing** (Marketing); **Pedagogy** (Pedagogy); **Psychology** (Psychology)

Main Language(s) of Instruction: Spanish

Degrees and Diplomas: *Licenciatura*
Last Updated: 06/03/13

MUNICIPAL SCHOOL OF ENGINEERING

Escuela de Ingeniería Municipal
Calzada de Tlalpan No. 810, Colonia Iztaccihuatl, Delegación Benito Juárez, 04620 México, D.F.
Tel: +52(55) 5445-5401

Director General: Carlos Becker Perdomo (1986-)

Programmes

Engineering (Engineering)
History: Founded 1936.
Main Language(s) of Instruction: Spanish

Degrees and Diplomas: *Licenciatura*; *Especialización*; *Maestría*
Last Updated: 21/02/13

NARVARTE UNIVERSITY CENTRE

Centro Universitario Narvarte
Tajín, 295, Col. Narvarte, 03020 México, D.F.
Tel: +52(55) 55-43-60-07 +52(55) 56-82-79-29
Fax: +52(55) 55-36-53-06
EMail: cunavarte@prodigy.net.mx
Website: http://www.cunarvarte.edu.mx

Director General: Gilberto Morett Valeriano (1970-)
EMail: gilbertomorett@prodigy.net.mx

Programmes

Accountancy (Accountancy); **Administration** (Administration); **Criminology**; **Law** (Law); **Legal Clinical Psychology** (Clinical Psychology); **Marketing and Publicity** (Advertising and Publicity; Marketing); **Tourism**

History: Founded 1982.

Main Language(s) of Instruction: Spanish

Degrees and Diplomas: *Licenciatura*; *Maestría*
Last Updated: 27/07/12

NATION INSTITUTE OF HUMANITIES

Instituto Patria de Humanidades, A.C.
Misión de Santiago, 6, Col. Francisco Misiones, 53140 Naucalpán de Juárez, Estado de México
Tel: +52(55) 343-42-30 +52(55) 343-83-40

Directora: Aída Grijalva Yeruz

Programmes

Arts and Humanities (Arts and Humanities)

Degrees and Diplomas: *Licenciatura*

NATION UNIVERSITY CENTRE

Centro Universitario Patria
Carlota, 68, Col. Guadalupe Tepeyrac, Delegación Gustavo A. Madero, 07840 México, D.F.
Tel: +52(55) 55-37-18-42 +52(55) 55-17-71-83
EMail: informe@cup.edu.mx
Website: http://www.cup.edu.mx

Director General: José Lavalle Montalvo

Programmes

Accountancy (Accountancy); **Law** (Law); **Organization Management** (Management); **Pedagogy** (Pedagogy)

Main Language(s) of Instruction: Spanish

Degrees and Diplomas: *Licenciatura*; *Maestría*
Last Updated: 17/03/08

NATIONAL COLLEGE OF CONTEMPORARY DANCE

Colegio Nacional de Danza Contemporánea
Sierra de Tilaco, 201, Ote., Col. Villas del Sol, 76046 Querétaro, Querétaro
Tel: +52(442) 213-72-55
Fax: +52(442) 213-72-56
EMail: informes@conadaco.org
Website: http://www.conadaco.org.mx

Director: Orlando de Jesús Scheker Román (1991-)

Programmes

Contemporary Dance (Dance)
History: Founded 1991.
Admission Requirements: Secondary school certificate
Main Language(s) of Instruction: Spanish

Degrees and Diplomas: *Licenciatura*
Last Updated: 23/08/12

NATIONAL INSTITUTE OF HIGHER STUDIES IN PENAL LAW

Instituto Nacional de Estudios Superiores en Derecho Penal
California No. 103, Col. del Parque San Andrés, Coyoacán, 04040 México, D.F.
Tel: +52(555) 549-39-88
Fax: +52(555) 549-15-63
EMail: indepac@prodigy.net.mx
Website: http://www.indepac.edu.mx

Director: Alfredo Delgadillo Aguirre

Programmes

Criminal Law (Constitutional Law; Criminal Law); **Human Rights** (Human Rights)

Research Institutes

Law (Criminal Law; Law)
Further Information: Campuses nationwide
History: Founded 1997.
Main Language(s) of Instruction: Spanish

Degrees and Diplomas: *Especialización*; *Maestría*; *Doctorado*
Last Updated: 07/03/13

NATIONAL INSTITUTE OF ORTHODONCY AND MAXILLARY ORTHOPEDICS

Instituto Nacional de Ortodoncia y Ortopedia Maxilar
Avenida Vallarta 1191, Segundo Piso Entre Robles Gil y Atenas Colonia Americana, 44160 Guadalajara, Jalisco
Tel: +52(33) 3825-18-76
EMail: informes@inoom.com
Website: http://www.inoom.com

Director: Alfonso Alberto Argote Sahagún

Programmes

Dentistry (Dentistry); **Orthodontics** (Orthodontics)
History: Founded 1992.

Main Language(s) of Instruction: Spanish

Degrees and Diplomas: *Especialización*

Last Updated: 07/03/13

NAYARIT SCHOOL FOR THE LICENCIATURA IN SOCIAL WORK

Escuela de Licenciatura en Trabajo Social. Nayarit

Abasolo, 25 Ote., Col. Centro, 63000 Tepic, Nayarit

Tel: +52(311) 212-09-63

Director: Andrés Muñoz Velasco

Programmes

Social Work (Social Work)

Main Language(s) of Instruction: Spanish

Degrees and Diplomas: *Licenciatura*

Last Updated: 03/04/08

NEW ENGLAND INSTITUTE OF HIGHER STUDIES

Instituto de Estudios Superiores Nueva Inglaterra

San Juan de Dios, 11, Col. Huipulco, Delegación Tlalpán, 14370 México, D.F.

Tel: +52(55) 56-55-28-57 +52(55) 5655-92-93

EMail: dirgral@institutonuevainglaterra.edu.mx

Website: http://www.institutonuevainglaterra.edu.mx

Director General: Luis Tapia Islas (1995-)

Programmes

Accountancy (Accountancy); **Administration** (Administration); **Computer Science** (Computer Science); **Law** (Law)

History: Founded 1995.

Main Language(s) of Instruction: Spanish

Degrees and Diplomas: *Licenciatura*

Last Updated: 04/03/13

NEW MILLENNIUM EDUCATION

Educación Nuevo Milenio

Plantel Celaya, Avenida Hidalgo, 305, Zona Centro, 38000 Celaya, Guanajuato

Tel: +52(461) 612-6950

Fax: +52(461) 612-9663

EMail: nuevomilenio@enm.edu.mx

Website: http://www.enm.edu.mx

Rector: Fernándo Eugenio Ramírez Vera

Programmes

Human Resources (Business Administration; Human Resources); **Law** (Law)

Further Information: Also Irapuato and San Francisco del Rincón branches

Main Language(s) of Instruction: Spanish

Degrees and Diplomas: *Licenciatura*; *Especialización*

Last Updated: 24/08/12

NEW WORLD UNIVERSITY

Universidad Nuevo Mundo

Bosque de Moctezuma, 124, Fracc. La Herradura, 53920 Huixquilucán, Estado de México

Tel: +52(55) 55-89-15

EMail: infounum@unum.edu.mx

Rector: Rodrigo Amat Martínez

Programmes

Accountancy (Accountancy); **Business Administration** (Business Administration); **Graphic Design** (Graphic Design); **Industrial Design** (Industrial Design); **Law** (Law); **Mass Communication** (Mass Communication); **Mechanical Engineering** (Mechanical Engineering); **Philosophy** (Philosophy); **Psychology** (Psychology)

History: A private institution attached to the National Autonomous University of Mexico.

Academic Year: September to June (September-January; February-June)

Admission Requirements: Secondary school certificate (bachillerato)

Main Language(s) of Instruction: Spanish

Degrees and Diplomas: *Licenciatura*: 4-5 yrs

Last Updated: 04/04/13

NICOLÁS GUILLÉN CULTURAL INSTITUTE

Instituto Cultural Nicolás Guillén, S.C.

Avenida Córdoba, 490, Valle Dorado, 54020 Tlalnepantla, Estado de México

Tel: +52(55) 53-70-02-95

Fax: +52(55) 53-70-04-83

EMail: info@nicolasguillen.edu.mx

Website: http://www.nicolasguillen.edu.mx/

Director General: Porfirio Arizmendi Labat

Programmes

Accountancy (Accountancy; Business Administration); **Gastronomy** (Cooking and Catering); **Marketing** (Marketing)

History: Founded 1979.

Main Language(s) of Instruction: Spanish

Degrees and Diplomas: *Licenciatura*

Last Updated: 27/02/13

NORMAN ROCKWELL SCHOOL OF ILLUSTRATION

Escuela de Ilustración Norman Rockwell, A.C.

Sixto Verduzco No. 302, San Felipe de Tlalmilopan, 50250 Toluca, Estado de México

Tel: +52(722) 198-04-92

Fax: +52(722) 217-64-02

EMail: normanrockwell@terra.com.mx

Website: http://norman_rockwell.mx.tripod.com

Directora: Victoria Evelia Flores Pardo

Programmes

Architecture (Architecture); **Graphic Illustration** (Graphic Design)

Main Language(s) of Instruction: Spanish

Degrees and Diplomas: *Licenciatura*: 8 sem.

Last Updated: 21/02/13

NORTH OF HIDALGO CENTRE FOR ADVANCED STUDIES

Centro de Estudios Superiores del Norte de Hidalgo

Cuauhtémoc, 18, Col. Antonio Reyes, 43000 Huejutla de Reyes, Hidalgo

Tel: +52(789) 6-01-92

Fax: +52(789) 6-13-50

Director: Narciso Flores Antonio

Programmes

Law (Law)

Main Language(s) of Instruction: Spanish

Degrees and Diplomas: *Licenciatura*

Last Updated: 04/04/08

NOVARE IUVENTA PRIVATE UNIVERSITY

Novare Iuventa Universidad Privada

Sitio Grande, 101, Fracc. Carrizal, 86100 Villahermosa, Tabasco

Tel: +52(993) 316-90-16

Fax: +52(993) 316-90-17

NUESTRA SEÑORA DE LA SALUD HOSPITAL NURSING SCHOOL

Escuela de Enfermería del Hospital de Nuestra Señora de la Salud

Eduardo Ruiz 152, Col. Centro, 05800 Morelia, Michoacán
Tel: +52(443) 317-40-57
Fax: +52(443) 312-24-25
EMail: escenfsrasalud@hotmail.com

Directora: Avelina Ramírez Izquierdo

Programmes
Nursing (Nursing); **Obstetrics** (Gynaecology and Obstetrics)

History: Founded 1964.
Main Language(s) of Instruction: Spanish
Degrees and Diplomas: *Licenciatura*
Last Updated: 21/02/13

NUEVO LEÓN COLLEGE OF BIOETHICS

Colegio de Bioética de Nuevo León, A.C.

Calle Venustiano Carranza No. 556 Sur, Monterrey, Nuevo León
Tel: +52(8) 318-07-74
Website: http://colegiodebioetica.org.mx/

Programmes
Bioethics (Biology; Ethics)

Degrees and Diplomas: *Especialización*; *Maestría*

NÚÑEZ FRAGOSO INSTITUTE OF HIGHER STUDIES

Instituto de Estudios Superiores Núñez Fragoso

Calzada de Tlalpán, 1621, Col. Portales, Delegación Benito Juárez, 03300 México, D.F.
Tel: +52(55) 56-74-37-11

Director: Ernesto Núñez Revilla (1999-)

Programmes
Accountancy (Accountancy); **Administration** (Administration); **Business Computing** (Business Computing); **Computer Science** (Computer Science); **Graphic Design** (Graphic Design); **Law** (Law); **Marketing** (Marketing); **Pedagogy** (Pedagogy); **Public Relations** (Public Relations)

History: Founded 1918.
Main Language(s) of Instruction: Spanish
Degrees and Diplomas: *Licenciatura*
Last Updated: 04/03/13

NURSING SCHOOL OF MEXICALI

Escuela de Enfermería de Mexicali

Calle del Hospital s/n, Col. Centro Cívico, 21100 Mexicali, Baja California
Tel: +52(686) 556-11-23 al 29

Directora: María Dolores Martínez Trigueros

Programmes
Nursing (Nursing)

Main Language(s) of Instruction: Spanish
Degrees and Diplomas: *Licenciatura*
Last Updated: 19/03/08

NURSING SCHOOL OF THE RED CROSS OF SAN LUIS POTOSI

Escuela de Enfermería de la Cruz Roja Mexicana de San Luis Potosí

Calzada de Guadalupe, 540, Barrio de San Miguelito, 78330 San Luis Potosí, San Luis Potosí
Tel: +52(444) 820-39-02
Fax: +52(444) 815-05-19

Directora: Matilde Hernández Nava (1970-)

Programmes
Nursing and Obstetrics (Gynaecology and Obstetrics; Nursing)

History: Founded 1970.
Main Language(s) of Instruction: Spanish
Degrees and Diplomas: *Licenciatura*

NURSING SCHOOL OF TUXTLA GUTIÉRREZ

Escuela de Enfermería de Tuxtla Gutiérrez

Blvd. Belisario Domínguez, 1030, 29000 Tuxtla Gutiérrez, Chiapas
Tel: +52(961) 3-75-15
EMail: fbc@siicsa.com.mx

Director: Arturo Morales Urioste

Programmes
Nursing (Nursing)

Main Language(s) of Instruction: Spanish
Degrees and Diplomas: *Licenciatura*
Last Updated: 20/03/08

NURSING SCHOOL OF ZAMORA

Escuela de Enfermería de Zamora, A.C.

Martínez de Navarrete 611, Fracc. Las Fuentes, 59699 Zamora, Michoacán
Tel: +52(351) 512-07-60
Fax: +52(351) 515-22-51
EMail: contacto@escueladeenfermeriadezamora.org
Website: http://www.escueladeenfermeriadezamora.org

Directora: Marisol Sánchez Arnosi

Programmes
Nursing (Nursing); **Obstetrics** (Gynaecology and Obstetrics)

History: Founded 1962.
Main Language(s) of Instruction: Spanish
Degrees and Diplomas: *Licenciatura*
Last Updated: 21/02/13

OAXACA UNIVERSITY INSTITUTE

Instituto Universitario de Oaxaca

Victoriano González 266, Col. de Maestro, 68010 Oaxaca, Oaxaca
Tel: +52(951) 132-02-40
Fax: +52(951) 132-02-40
EMail: info@iuo.edu.mx
Website: http://iuo.edu.mx

Director: Jesús Pérez Altamirano

Programmes
Gastronomy; **Modern Languages** (Cultural Studies; English; French; Spanish)

History: Founded 2004.
Main Language(s) of Instruction: Spanish
Degrees and Diplomas: *Licenciatura*; *Especialización*
Last Updated: 22/03/13

OLIMPO CENTRE FOR ADVANCED STUDIES

Centro de Estudios Superiores Olimpo

Rinconada de Pino Suárez, 111, Centro, 50000 Toluca, Estado de México
Tel: +52(722) 215-82-68
Fax: +52(722) 214-14-37
EMail: contacto@olimpo.edu.mx
Website: http://www.olimpo.edu.mx

Director: Miguel Roberto Silva García (2000-)

Programmes
Accountancy (Accountancy); **Business Administration** (Administration; Business Administration); **Gastronomy** (Cooking and Catering); **International Business** (International Business); **Law** (Law); **Marketing** (Marketing); **Tourism** (Tourism)

History: Founded 2000.
Main Language(s) of Instruction: Spanish
Degrees and Diplomas: *Licenciatura*; *Maestría*. Also Diplomados
Last Updated: 16/07/12

OLMEC UNIVERSITY

Universidad Olmeca (UO)

Km. 14.5 Carretera Villahermosa-, Macuspana Dos Montes, 86280 Villahermosa, Tabasco
Tel: +52(993) 356-01-09 +52(993) 356-01-11
Fax: +52(993) 356-01-13
EMail: rector@olmeca.edu.mx
Website: http://www.olmeca.edu.mx

Rector: Lácides García Detjen (2002-)

Centres

University Extension (Business Education; Dance; English; French; German; Music; Portuguese; Spanish; Theatre)

Departments

Architecture and Landscape Architecture (Architecture; Landscape Architecture); **Economics and Business Administration** (Accountancy; Business Administration; Finance; International Business; Taxation); **Engineering and Computer Systems** (Computer Engineering; Computer Networks; Electronic Engineering; Petroleum and Gas Engineering); **Humanities and Social Sciences** (Arts and Humanities; Commercial Law; Communication Studies; Law)

Programmes

Surgery (Medicine; Surgery)

History: Founded 1991.

Governing Bodies: Board of Directors

Academic Year: January to December (January-May; May-July; August-December)

Admission Requirements: Bachillerato

Main Language(s) of Instruction: Spanish

International Co-operation: With universities in Canada, Germany and USA (Texas)

Accrediting Agencies: Secretaría de Educación Pública (SEP); Federación de Instituciones Mexicanas Particulares de Educación Superior (FIMPES)

Degrees and Diplomas: *Licenciatura*: Accountancy and Finances; Business Administration; International Business and Customs; Law; Corporate Law; Communication Studies; Architecture; Graphic Design; Humanities; Computer Engineering; Electronic and Computer Networks Eng.; Oil and Nature Eng. (Lic. (BA)), 4 1/2 yrs; *Maestría*: Business Administration; Law; Labour Law; Computer Engineering; International Business and Customs; Health Administration, a further 2 yrs; *Doctorado*: Law

Student Services: Academic counselling, Employment services, Foreign student adviser, Health services, Language programs, Sports facilities

Libraries: Main Library

Last Updated: 16/10/12

OPARIN UNIVERSITY

Universidad Oparín, S.C.

Isabel la Católica, 29, San Cristóbal, 55000 Ecatepec de Morelos, Estado de México
Tel: +52(55) 57-87-05-62
Fax: +52(55) 57-70-06-68
EMail: oparinet_mx@yahoo.com.mx

Programmes

Psychology, Administration and Law (Administration; Law; Psychology)

History: Founded 1973 as Colegio Oparín.

Degrees and Diplomas: *Licenciatura*; *Maestría*

Last Updated: 04/04/13

OPEN UNIVERSITY

Universidad Abierta

Jiménez 315, Barrio el Montecillo, 78000 San Luis Potosí, San Luis Potosí
Tel: +52 (444) 812-56-10
EMail: recepcion@universidadabierta.edu.mx; informacion@universidadabierta.edu.mx
Website: http://www.universidadabierta.edu.mx

Rector: Santiago Alfredo Salas de León
EMail: rectoria@universidadabierta.edu.mx

Programmes

Accountancy (Accountancy); **Business Administration** (Business Administration); **Communication Studies** (Cinema and Television; Communication Studies; Linguistics; Radio and Television Broadcasting); **Economics** (Economics; Finance; Statistics); **Law** (Civil Law; Commercial Law; Constitutional Law; Criminal Law; Fiscal Law; Law); **Philosophy** (Philosophy); **Public Administration** (Public Administration); **Sociology** (Demography and Population; Sociology)

History: Founded 1994.

Admission Requirements: Bachillerato or equivalent

Main Language(s) of Instruction: Spanish

Degrees and Diplomas: *Licenciatura*; *Maestría*; *Doctorado*

Libraries: Yes

Last Updated: 30/08/12

OXFORD EDUCATIONAL CONSORTIUM

Consorcio Educativo Oxford

Hidalgo 1745 Poniente, Colonia Obispado, 64000 Monterrey, Nuevo León
Tel: +52(81) 80-47-00-00
Website: http://www.ceox.edu.mx

Directora: Hilda Guerrero Alanís

Programmes

Business Computing (Business Computing)

History: Founded 1990 as Instituto Universitario Oxford. Acquired present title 2006.

Main Language(s) of Instruction: Spanish

Degrees and Diplomas: *Licenciatura*

Last Updated: 22/03/13

PABLO GUARDADO CHÁVEZ UNIVERSITY

Universidad Pablo Guardado Chávez

Libramiento Norte-Oriente, 3450, Fracc. Resicencial, Las Palmas, 29040 Tuxtla Gutiérrez, Chiapas
Tel: +52(961) 614-11-12
Fax: +52(961) 614-11-13
EMail: upgch@upgch.edu.mx
Website: http://www.upgch.edu.mx

Director: José Ramón Velázquez Moreno (1990-)

Areas

Business Studies (Accountancy; Business Administration; Business Computing; Finance; Marketing); **Engineering and Exact Sciences** (Computer Engineering; Electronic Engineering); **Health Sciences** (Medicine; Nursing; Psychology; Social Work; Surgery); **Law** (Law); **Social Sciences and Education** (English; Pedagogy; Physical Education; Sports)

History: Founded 1990.

Admission Requirements: Bachillerato

Main Language(s) of Instruction: Spanish

Degrees and Diplomas: *Licenciatura*; *Maestría*; *Doctorado*: Education

Last Updated: 04/04/13

PACCIOLI UNIVERSITY OF CÓRDOBA

Universidad Paccioli de Córdoba

Autopista Córdoba-Fortín, Km. 290, 94540 Córdoba, Veracruz
Tel: +52(271) 716-07-70 +52(271) 716-46-30
Fax: +52(271) 716-07-70
EMail: informes@universidadpaccioli.edu.mx
Website: http://www.universidadpaccioli.edu.mx

Rectora: Teresita Monlui Fernández (1990-)
EMail: rectoria@universidadpaccioli.edu.mx

Programmes

Business Administration (Business Administration); **Business Computing** (Business Computing); **Law** (Law); **Pedagogy** (Pedagogy); **Public Accountancy** (Accountancy)

History: Founded 1990 as Instituto de Estudios Superiores Paccioli. Acquired present status and title 2000.

Admission Requirements: Secondary School Certificate (Certificado de Secundaria) and Junior High School Certificate (Certificado de Bachillerato)

Main Language(s) of Instruction: Spanish

Degrees and Diplomas: *Licenciatura*; *Especialización*; *Maestría*

Student Services: Employment services, Health services, Nursery care, Sports facilities

Libraries: Yes

Last Updated: 16/10/12

PACCIOLI UNIVERSITY OF XALAPA

Universidad Paccioli Xalapa

Teotihuacan 91y 22, Col. Sebastián Lerdo de Tejada, 91180 Xalapa, Veracruz
Tel: +52(228) 814-69-10
EMail: universidadpacciolixalapa@hotmail.com
Website: http://www.upx.edu.mx

Rector: Basilio Cobis Ponceano

Programmes

Business Administration (Business Administration); **Business Computing** (Accountancy; Administration; Applied Mathematics; Civil Law; Commercial Law; Computer Networks; Computer Science; Data Processing; Economics; Finance; Human Resources; Information Technology; Labour Law; Mathematics; Operations Research; Software Engineering; Statistics); **Law** (Human Rights; Law); **Pedagogy** (Pedagogy); **Public Accountancy** (Accountancy; Administration; Administrative Law; Banking; Civil Law; Economics; Finance; Mathematics)

History: Founded 2002.

Main Language(s) of Instruction: Spanish

Degrees and Diplomas: *Licenciatura*

Last Updated: 16/10/12

PACELLI SCHOOL OF MUSIC

Escuela Superior de Música Pacelli

Avenida Guadalupe Victoria, 2, Col. La Paz, 72160 Puebla, Puebla
Tel: +52(222) 248-18-65
Fax: +52(222) 248-36-87
EMail: pacellilive@hotmail.com

Directora: María Petra Ignacia Burgos Barranco

Programmes

Music (Music; Music Education; Music Theory and Composition; Musical Instruments)

Main Language(s) of Instruction: Spanish

Degrees and Diplomas: *Licenciatura*; *Maestría*

Last Updated: 27/02/13

PAIDEIA CULTURAL INSTITUTE

Instituto Cultural Paideia, S.C.

Andrés Benavides, 205, Col. Residencial Colón, 50120 Toluca, Estado de México
Tel: +52(722) 217-98-63
Fax: +52(722) 212-36-23
Website: http://paideia.mx

Director: Melchor Dávila Maldonado

Programmes

Educational Sciences (Educational Sciences); **Law** (Law)

Degrees and Diplomas: *Licenciatura*; *Maestría*

Last Updated: 30/08/12

PALMORE REGIONAL CENTRE OF ADVANCED STUDIES

Centro Regional de Estudios Superiores Palmore

Gómez Farias 9 col.Centro, 31000 Chihuahua, Chihuahua
Tel: +52(614) 410-25-92
Fax: +52(614) 410-25-92
EMail: universidad@palmore.edu.mx
Website: http://www.palmore.edu.mx

Director: Edgar Pacheco González
EMail: edgarpachecog@hotmail.com

Programmes

Accountancy (Accountancy); **Administration** (Administration); **Computer Science** (Computer Science); **Multimedia** (Multimedia); **Taxation** (Taxation); **Visual Arts** (Visual Arts)

History: Founded 2000.

Main Language(s) of Instruction: Spanish

Degrees and Diplomas: *Licenciatura*

Last Updated: 23/07/12

PANAMERICAN COLLEGE, DIVISION OF ADVANCED STUDIES

Colegio Panamericano, División de Estudios Superiores

Calle Camino a San José de Guanajuato, 202, Zona de Oro 1, 38020 Celaya, Guanajuato
Tel: +52(461) 614-59-68 +52(461) 614-59-69

Director: Fernando Motas Espadas

Degrees and Diplomas: *Licenciatura*

Last Updated: 04/04/08

PANAMERICAN INSTITUTE (CENTRE FOR ADVANCED STUDIES)

Instituto Panamericano (Centro de Estudios Superiores)

Arista, 646 y Zaragoza, 91700 Heroica Veracruz, Veracruz
Tel: +52(229) 932-30-67

Directora: Catalina Dosel del Valle

Degrees and Diplomas: *Licenciatura*

Last Updated: 07/04/08

PANAMERICAN UNIVERSITY

Universidad Panamericana (UP)

Augusto Rodín 498, Col. Insurgentes Mixcoac, 03920 México, D.F.
Tel: +52(55) 5482-16-00
EMail: contacto@up.edu.mx
Website: http://www.up.edu.mx

Rector: José Manuel Núñez Pliego

Secretario General: Claudio Manuel Rivas Cuevas
Tel: +52(55) 5482-16-00, Ext 6042,
Fax: +52(55) 5482-17-00, Ext 6048
EMail: crivas@mixcoac.upmx.mx

International Relations: Liliana Álvarez Tostado Penella
Tel: +52(55) 5482-16-00, 5,920/5021
EMail: lalvarez@mixcoac.upmx.mx

Programmes

Administration (Accountancy; Administration; Finance; Marketing); **Economics** (Economics); **Education** (Education); **Engineering** (Computer Engineering; Hydraulic Engineering; Industrial Engineering; Information Technology); **Law** (Law); **Medicine** (Medicine); **Nursing** (Nursing); **Pedagogy** (Pedagogy); **Philosophy** (Philosophy); **Psychology** (Psychology)

Further Information: Also Teaching Hospitals. Spanish Courses for foreign students. History of Thought. Campuses in Aguascalientes and Guadalajara

History: Founded 1968 as institute, became University 1978. A private institution attached to the National Autonomous University of Mexico.

Governing Bodies: Junta de Gobierno

Academic Year: August to June (August-December; January-June)

Admission Requirements: Secondary school certificate (bachillerato)

Fees: (Pesos): c. 49,000 per semester, except Medicine which is 14% higher

Main Language(s) of Instruction: Spanish

Degrees and Diplomas: *Licenciatura*: 4-5 yrs; *Especialización*; *Maestría*: Law, a further 2 yrs; *Doctorado*: 3-4 yrs

Student Services: Academic counselling, Cultural centre, Employment services, Foreign student adviser, Handicapped facilities, Social counselling, Sports facilities

Libraries: c. 45,000 vols

Publications: Ars Iuris *(quarterly)*; Revista Istmo *(bimonthly)*; Tópicos (Philosophical Review) *(annually)*

Last Updated: 14/04/09

IPADE BUSINESS SCHOOL

INSTITUTO PANAMERICANO DE ALTA DIRECCIÓN DE EMPRESAS (IPADE)

Floresta 20, Col. Clavería, Delegación Azcapotzalco, 02080 México, D.F.
Tel: +52(55) 55-54-18-00
Fax: +52(55) 55-27-31-79
Website: http://www.ipade.mx/IPADE

Director General: Rafael Gómez Nava

Departments

Business Administration (Banking; Business Administration; Business and Commerce; Finance; Marketing); **Business Management** (Business Administration; Management); **Executive Business Administration** (Business Administration)

Further Information: Also continuing education for graduate students. Also campuses at Monterrey and Guadalajara

History: Founded 1967 by Mexican entrepreneurs.

Governing Bodies: Board of Directors

Admission Requirements: University degree at Bachelor level

Main Language(s) of Instruction: Spanish

Degrees and Diplomas: *Licenciatura*: Business Administration; Business Management; *Maestría*

Student Services: Academic counselling, Employment services, Foreign student adviser, Health services, Language programs, Social counselling

Libraries: Business Library

PANAMERICAN UNIVERSITY OF NUEVO LAREDO

Universidad Panamericana de Nuevo Laredo

Avenida Morelos, 2311, Col. Juárez, 88000 Nuevo Laredo, Tamaulipas
Tel: +52(867) 715-27-31
EMail: info@unipanam.edu.mx
Website: http://www.unipanam.edu.mx

Rectora: Guadalupe Jasso Juárez

Programmes

Law, Accountancy and Administration (Accountancy; Administration; Law); **Medicine** (Medicine); **Pedagogy** (Pedagogy); **Preschool Education** (Preschool Education); **Psychology** (Psychology); **Secondary Education** (Secondary Education); **Veterinary Science** (Veterinary Science; Zoology)

Further Information: Also branch in Reynosa

History: Founded 1980.

Academic Year: September to July

Main Language(s) of Instruction: Spanish

Degrees and Diplomas: *Licenciatura*

Last Updated: 04/04/13

PARTHENON COLLEGE

Colegio Partenón

Playa Manzanillo, 360, Col. Reforma, Iztaccíhuatl, Delegación Iztacalco, 08810 México, D.F.
Tel: +52(55) 56-33-66-55 +52(55) 56-33-11-45
EMail: informes@colegio-partenon.edu.mx
Website: http://www.colegio-partenon.edu.mx

Directora: Lucila Sosa Viderique (1986-)

Programmes

Administration; **Law**; **Psychology** (Psychology)

History: Founded 1986.

Main Language(s) of Instruction: Spanish

Degrees and Diplomas: *Licenciatura*

Last Updated: 19/03/08

PARTHENON UNIVERSITY OF COZUMEL

Universidad Partenón de Cozumel (UPC)

11 Av. Sur entre 90 y 95 Colonia Cuzamil, 77642 Cozumel, Quintana Roo
Tel: +52(987) 869-38-74
Fax: +52(987) 869-38-74
EMail: universidad@upc.edu.mx
Website: http://www.upc.edu.mx

Directora General: Armonia Valasis

Programmes

Accountancy (Accountancy); **Administration** (Administration); **Law** (Law)

History: Founded 1996.

Admission Requirements: Secondary school certificate

Main Language(s) of Instruction: Spanish

Accrediting Agencies: Universidad Nacional Autónoma de México

Degrees and Diplomas: *Licenciatura*

Student Services: Academic counselling, Canteen, Employment services, Foreign student adviser, Handicapped facilities, Health services, Language programs, Nursery care, Social counselling, Sports facilities

Libraries: Yes

Last Updated: 04/04/13

PEDAGOGICAL INSTITUTE OF POSTGRADUATE STUDIES

Instituto Pedagógico de Estudios de Posgrado (IPEP)

Calle Hidalgo 30, Col. Rancho Seco, 38140 Celaya, Guanajuato
Tel: +52(461) 616-47-53
EMail: posgrados@ipep.edu.mx
Website: http://www.ipep.edu.mx

Directora General: Natalia Mendoza Flores
EMail: natalia@ipep.edu.mx

Programmes

Education (Education; Educational Administration; Educational Sciences; Pedagogy; Preschool Education)

Degrees and Diplomas: *Maestría*; *Doctorado*

Last Updated: 07/03/13

PEDAGOGICAL INSTITUTE OF POSTGRADUATE STUDIES OF SONORA

Instituto Pedagógico de Posgrado en Sonora, A.C. (IPPSON)

Arzobispo Emérito Carlos Quintero Arce 85, Col. El Llano, 83210 Hermosillo, Sonora
Tel: +52(662) 260-60-85
Fax: +52(662) 260-60-85
EMail: ippson@hotmail.com
Website: http://www.ippson.com

Director General: Rubén Ríos Enríquez

Programmes
Education - Social Sciences (Administrative Law; Anthropology; Archaeology; Constitutional Law; Curriculum; Education; Educational Administration; Educational Psychology; Educational Research; Educational Sciences; English; Environmental Studies; History; Information Technology; International Relations; Linguistics; Pedagogy; Public Administration; Social Problems; Social Sciences; Social Studies; Sociology; Statistics; Teacher Trainers Education; Teacher Training; Writing); **Education - Spanish and Literature** (Communication Studies; Cultural Studies; Curriculum; Education; Educational Psychology; Educational Research; Educational Sciences; Educational Technology; English; Environmental Studies; Linguistics; Literature; Pedagogy; Science Education; Social Sciences; Social Studies; Spanish; Statistics; Teacher Trainers Education; Teacher Training; Writing)

Further Information: Campuses in Obregón and Navojoa

History: Founded 2003.

Main Language(s) of Instruction: Spanish

Degrees and Diplomas: *Licenciatura*; *Maestría*; *Doctorado*
Last Updated: 07/03/13

PEDRO DE GANTE LYCEUM UNIVERSITY

Liceo Universidad Pedro de Gante (LICEO UPG)

Km. 1 Carretera Molino de Flores, Col. Xocotlán, Texcoco de Mora, 56130 Texcoco, Estado de México
Tel: +52(595) 954-22-12 +52(595) 954-97-20
EMail: rectoria@liceoupg.edu.mx
Website: http://www.liceoupg.edu.mx

Rector: Miguel Reyes Ramírez

Programmes
Accountancy (Accountancy); **Business Administration** (Business Administration); **Commerce** (Business and Commerce); **Computer Science and Engineering** (Computer Engineering; Computer Science); **Gastronomy** (Cooking and Catering); **Graphic Design** (Graphic Design); **Law** (Law); **Pedagogy** (Pedagogy); **Psychology** (Psychology)

Further Information: Also Campus Tepotzotlán

History: Founded 1989, acquired present status 1990.

Governing Bodies: Consejo Universitario

Admission Requirements: Certificado de Preparatoria

Fees: (Pesos): 8,000 per quarter

Main Language(s) of Instruction: Spanish

Degrees and Diplomas: *Licenciatura*: 3 yrs; *Licenciatura*: Law, 3-4 yrs; *Maestría*

Student Services: Academic counselling, Employment services, Handicapped facilities, Health services, Language programs, Sports facilities

Libraries: Main Library
Last Updated: 22/03/13

PENITENCIARY RESEARCH INSTITUTE

Instituto de Prevención del Delito e Investigación Penitenciara

Calzada de Los Misterios, 534, Col. Industrial, Delegación Gustavo A. Madero, 07800 México, D.F.
Tel: +52(555) 537-05-12
Fax: +52(555) 537-77-97
EMail: ipip_edu@Yahoo.com.mx
Website: http://prevenimpip.blogspot.fr

Directora: Ruth Villanueva Castilleja (1997-)

Programmes
Law (Criminal Law; Law)

History: Founded 1997.

Main Language(s) of Instruction: Spanish

Degrees and Diplomas: *Licenciatura*; *Especialización*; *Maestría*
Last Updated: 05/03/13

PEOPLE'S AUTONOMOUS UNIVERSITY OF THE STATE OF PUEBLA

Universidad Popular Autónoma del Estado de Puebla (UPAEP)

21, Sur, 1103, Colonia Santiago, 72160 Puebla, Puebla
Tel: +52(222) 229-94-00 Ext. 401 a la 403
Fax: +52(222) 232-04-53 +52(222) 232-52-51
EMail: admisiones@upaep.mx
Website: http://www.upaep.mx

Rector: José Alfredo Miranda López (2005-)
EMail: rector@upaep.mx

Departments
Arts and Humanities (Advertising and Publicity; Architecture; Arts and Humanities; Cinema and Television; Graphic Design; Pedagogy; Philosophy; Psychology); **Computer Engineering and Information Technology** (Computer Engineering; Electronic Engineering; Industrial Engineering; Information Technology; Mechanical Engineering; Production Engineering; Software Engineering); **Economics and Administration** (Accountancy; Banking; Business Administration; Economics; Finance; International Business; Marketing); **Engineering** (Agricultural Engineering; Biotechnology; Chemical Engineering; Civil Engineering; Environmental Engineering; Veterinary Science; Zoology); **Health Sciences** (Dentistry; Medicine; Nursing; Physical Therapy); **Social Sciences** (Communication Studies; International Relations; Journalism; Law; Political Sciences)

History: Founded 1973.

Academic Year: January to December (January-May; June-July; August-December)

Admission Requirements: Secondary school certificate (bachillerato) and entrance examination

Main Language(s) of Instruction: Spanish

Degrees and Diplomas: *Licenciatura*: 8-10 sem; *Especialización*: 1-2 yrs; *Maestría*: a further 1-2 yrs; *Doctorado*

Student Services: Academic counselling, Canteen, Cultural centre, Employment services, Foreign student adviser, Health services, Social counselling, Sports facilities

Special Facilities: Museo OPAEP de Arte Poblano

Libraries: Total, c. 281,000 vols
Last Updated: 05/04/13

PERSONAL INFORMATICS EDUCATIONAL AND DEVELOPMENT CENTRE

Centro Educacional y Desarrollo en Informática Personal

Blvd. Loma Real, 301, Entre 2a. y 3a., 89160 Tampico, Tamaulipas
EMail: gcedip@tamnet.com.mx

Director: Antonio Andrés Pascual García

Programmes
Administration and Accountancy (Accountancy; Administration); **Computer Science** (Computer Science); **Industrial Engineering** (Industrial Engineering); **Marketing** (Marketing)

Main Language(s) of Instruction: Spanish

Degrees and Diplomas: *Licenciatura*
Last Updated: 18/07/12

PITMAN CENTRE FOR PROFESSIONAL STUDIES

Centro de Estudios Profesionales Pitman

Velázquez de la Cadena, 649, Col. Centro, 91700 Veracruz, Veracruz
Tel: +52(229) 939-32-81
Fax: +52(229) 938-40-88
EMail: info@pitman.com.mx
Website: http://www.pitman.com.mx

Director: Humberto Manuel Gómez Manzano (1997-)

Programmes
Accountancy (Accountancy); **Business Administration** (Business Administration)

History: Founded 1997.
Main Language(s) of Instruction: Spanish
Degrees and Diplomas: *Licenciatura*
Last Updated: 15/02/13

PONTIFICAL UNIVERSITY OF MÉXICO

Universidad Pontificia de México

Calle Seminario No. 26, Col. Santa Ursula Xitla, Tlalpán, 14000 México, D.F.
Tel: +52(555) 573-06-00
Fax: +52(555) 573-05-71
EMail: universidad@pontificia.edu.mx
Website: http://www.pontificia.edu.mx

Rector: Mario Ángel Flores Ramos EMail: rector@pontificia.edu.mx

Faculties
Canon Law (Canon Law); **Law** (Law); **Philosophy** (Philosophy); **Theology** (Pastoral Studies; Theology)

Institutes
Religious Science (Religious Studies)

History: Founded 1982.
Main Language(s) of Instruction: Spanish
Degrees and Diplomas: *Licenciatura*; *Maestría*; *Doctorado*
Last Updated: 23/10/12

POSTGRADUATE SCHOOL OF HOMEOPATHY OF MEXICO

Escuela de Posgrado de Homeopatía de México

Tlaxcala 58, Col. Roma, Delegación Cuauhtémoc, 06700 México, D.F.
Tel: +52(55 5) 584-50-22
Fax: +52(5 55) 584-25-60 +52(5 55) 564-50-08
EMail: contacto@homeopatiademexico.org.mx

Director General: Antonio Sánchez Caballero

Programmes
Homeopathy (Homeopathy)

History: Founded 1960.
Main Language(s) of Instruction: Spanish
Degrees and Diplomas: *Especialización*
Last Updated: 27/02/08

PRISCILIANO SÁNCHEZ INSTITUTE

Instituto Prisciliano Sánchez

López Cotilla 1527, Col. Americana, 44140 Guadalajara, Jalisco
Tel: +52(33) 30-01-71-00
EMail: telectoral@megaret.net.mx
Website: http://www.triejal.gob.mx

Director: Benjamín Robles Suárez

Programmes
Law

History: Founded 2001.
Main Language(s) of Instruction: Spanish
Degrees and Diplomas: *Maestría*; *Doctorado*
Libraries: Yes
Last Updated: 07/03/13

PRIVATE COLLEGE OF UNIVERSITY STUDIES

Colegio Libre de Estudios Universitarios (CLEU)

Camino Real a San Andrés Cholula 4406 "A" Emiliano Zapata, 72000 Puebla, Puebla
Tel: +52(222) 285-62-13
Fax: +52(222) 285-62-40
Website: http://www.cleu.com.mx

Rector: José Luis Pérez Ángeles

Programmes
Criminology (Criminology)

Further Information: Branches in Mérida, Mexico D.F., Guadalajara, Oaxaca, Puebla, Veracruz
History: Founded 1992.
Main Language(s) of Instruction: Spanish
Degrees and Diplomas: *Licenciatura*; *Especialización*; *Maestría*
Last Updated: 23/08/12

PRIVATE FACULTY OF LAW OF MONTERREY

Facultad Libre de Derecho de Monterrey, A.C

Ave. Morones Prieto, 1000 Pte, 64010 Santa Catarina, Nuevo León
Tel: +52(81) 8048-2500
Fax: +52(81) 8048-2510
EMail: contacto@fldm.edu.mx
Website: http://www.fldm.edu.mx

Director: José Roble Flores Fernández
EMail: jrflores@fldm.edu.mx

Programmes
Law (Law)

History: Founded 1988.
Admission Requirements: Secondary school certificate and entrance examination
Main Language(s) of Instruction: Spanish
Degrees and Diplomas: *Licenciatura*; *Maestría*
Libraries: Biblioteca "Dr. Arturo Salinas Martínez"
Publications: Revista Derecho en Libertad
Last Updated: 30/08/12

PRIVATE LAW SCHOOL

Escuela Libre de Derecho (ELD)

Dr. Vértiz, 12, Esq. Arcos de Belén, Col. Doctores, Delegación Cuauhtémoc, 06720 México, D.F.
Tel: +52(55) 55-88-02-11
EMail: libredederecho@eld.edu.mx
Website: http://www.eld.edu.mx

Rector: Fauzi Hamdan Amad EMail: rectoria@eld.edu.mx

Programmes
Law (Law)

History: Founded 1912.
Main Language(s) of Instruction: Spanish
Degrees and Diplomas: *Licenciatura*; *Especialización*; *Maestría*
Libraries: Yes
Last Updated: 29/08/12

PRIVATE LAW SCHOOL OF PUEBLA

Escuela Libre de Derecho de Puebla, A.C. (ELDP)

Avenida 13, Ote., 5, Col. El Carmen, 72000 Puebla, Puebla
Tel: +52(222) 246-25-13 +52(222) 246-42-42
Fax: +52(222) 232-23-67
EMail: info@eldp.edu.mx
Website: http://www.eldp.edu.mx/

Presidente: Gerardo Tejeda Foncerrada
Vicepresidente: Alberto Jiménez Morales

Programmes
Law (Civil Law; Commercial Law; Criminal Law; Fiscal Law; International Law; Law; Political Sciences)

History: Founded 1983.
Main Language(s) of Instruction: Spanish
Degrees and Diplomas: *Licenciatura*; *Maestría*; *Doctorado*
Libraries: Yes
Last Updated: 29/08/12

PRIVATE LAW SCHOOL OF SINALOA

Escuela Libre de Derecho de Sinaloa

A. Rosales, 266, Pte., Col. Centro, 80000 Culiacán, Sinaloa
Tel: +52(667) 712-71-68
EMail: elibrederecho@hotmail.com
Website: http://libresinaloa.com

Rector: Rodolfo Campoy de la Vega

Programmes
Law (Administrative Law; Commercial Law; Constitutional Law; Fiscal Law; Law)

Main Language(s) of Instruction: Spanish

Degrees and Diplomas: *Licenciatura*; *Maestría*; *Doctorado*

Libraries: Yes
Last Updated: 29/08/12

PRIVATE LAW SCHOOL OF VERACRUZ

Escuela Libre de Derecho de la Ciudad de Veracruz, A.C.

Calle Benito Juarez Esquina Vicente Guerrero 747, Veracruz, Veracruz
Tel: +52(229) 939-38-12
EMail: libredederechoveracruz@yahoo.com.mx
Website: http://www.libredederechoveracruz.edu.mx

Director: Pedro Olea Breton

Programmes
Law (Commercial Law; Law)
History: Founded 2001.
Main Language(s) of Instruction: Spanish
Degrees and Diplomas: *Licenciatura*; *Maestría*
Last Updated: 29/08/12

PRIVATE SCHOOL OF HOMEOPATHY OF MEXICO

Escuela Libre de Homeopatía de México

Calle Santa Lucía, 6, Col. Morelos, Delegación Cuauhtémoc, 06200 México, D.F.
Tel: +52(55) 55-26-09-49
Fax: +52(55) 55-26-09-49
EMail: ellmiap@prodigy.net.mx
Website: http://www.homeopatia.com.mx/escuelalibre

Director General: Pedro Fernando Infante Leonides (1994-)

Programmes
Homeopathy (Gynaecology and Obstetrics; Homeopathy; Paediatrics; Surgery)
History: Founded 1912.
Main Language(s) of Instruction: Spanish
Degrees and Diplomas: *Licenciatura*
Last Updated: 22/02/13

PRIVATE SCHOOL OF POLITICAL SCIENCES OF PUEBLA

Escuela Libre de Ciencias Políticas de Puebla, A.C.

Privada 14-B Sur, 1310, Col. Los Ángeles, 72440 Puebla, Puebla
Tel: +52(222) 237-85-68

Director: José Bustos Jiménez

Programmes
Political Science (Political Sciences)
Main Language(s) of Instruction: Spanish
Degrees and Diplomas: *Licenciatura*
Last Updated: 03/04/08

PRIVATE SCHOOL OF PSYCHOLOGY

Escuela Libre de Psicología

3 Oriente, 1601, Col. Azcárate, 72000 Puebla, Puebla
Tel: +52(222) 236-67-70
EMail: librepsicologia@gmail.com
Website: http://www.libredepsicologia.com

Director: Germán Molina Carrillo

Programmes
Psychology (Psychoanalysis; Psychology)
History: Founded 1996.
Main Language(s) of Instruction: Spanish
Degrees and Diplomas: *Licenciatura*; *Maestría*
Last Updated: 29/08/12

PRIVATE SCHOOL OF PSYCHOLOGY

Escuela Libre de Psicología, A.C. (ELPAC)

Calle Ccamino a Universidad la Salle No. 8805, Col. Labor de Terrazas, Atrás del Parque Relix, Frente a la CANACO, 31010 Chihuahua, Chihuahua
Tel: +52(614) 410-23-66 Ext. 20
EMail: direcciongeneral@elpac.edu.mx
Website: http://www.elpac.edu.mx

Directora: Rosario Valdés Caraveo

Programmes
Psychology (Clinical Psychology; Family Studies; Industrial and Organizational Psychology; Psychology; Social Psychology)
History: Founded 1972.
Main Language(s) of Instruction: Spanish
Degrees and Diplomas: *Licenciatura*; *Especialización*; *Maestría*
Last Updated: 22/02/13

PRIVATE UNIVERSITY OF IRAPUATO

Universidad Privada de Irapuato

Camino al Carrizal, 225, Col. Las Delicias, 36680 Irapuato, Guanajuato
Tel: +52(462) 626-22-09
EMail: irapuato@upi.edu.mx
Website: http://www.upi.edu.mx

Rector: Arturo Solís Torres EMail: rectoria@upi.edu.mx

Programmes
Accountancy (Accountancy); **Business Administration** (Business Administration); **Dentistry** (Dentistry); **Education** (Education); **Graphic Design** (Graphic Design); **Law** (Law); **Marketing** (Marketing); **Nutrition** (Nutrition); **Psychology** (Psychology)
Further Information: Also branches in Salamanca, León and Mexico City
History: Founded 1995.
Main Language(s) of Instruction: Spanish
Degrees and Diplomas: *Licenciatura*; *Especialización*; *Maestría*; *Doctorado*
Last Updated: 23/10/12

PRIVATE UNIVERSITY OF THE SOUTH OF MEXICO

Universidad Privada del Sur de Mexico

Carretera Chicoasén No. 4166, Blvd. Los Laguitos, San Isidro Buenavista, 29026 Tuxtla Gutiérrez, Chiapas
Tel: +52(961) 615-68-04
Website: http://www.upsum.edu.mx

Rector: Jorge A. Pola Figueroa

Programmes
Accountancy (Accountancy); **Advertising** (Advertising and Publicity); **Business Administration** (Business Administration); **Business Computing** (Business Computing); **Computer Engineering** (Computer Engineering); **Education** (Education); **Law** (Civil Law; Commercial Law; Law); **Marketing** (Marketing); **Political Science** (Political Sciences); **Psychology** (Psychology); **Telecommunications** (Telecommunications Engineering)
Further Information: Also campus in Tapachula
History: Founded 1999 as Instituto Privado del Sur de México.
Main Language(s) of Instruction: Spanish
Degrees and Diplomas: *Licenciatura*; *Maestría*; *Doctorado*
Libraries: Yes
Last Updated: 07/03/13

PRIVATE UNIVERSITY OF THE STATE OF MEXICO

Universidad Privada del Estado de México
Avenida Revolución, 46, Col. San Cristóbal, Centro, 55000 Ecatepec de Morelos, Estado de México
Tel: +52(55) 57-60-64-31
Fax: +52(55) 57-70-42-18
EMail: admisiones@upemex.edu.mx
Website: http://www.upemex.edu.mx

Rectora: Jose Antonio Herrera Aguilar
EMail: rectoria@upemex.edu.mx

Programmes
Accountancy (Accountancy); **Business Administration** (Business Administration); **Communication Sciences** (Communication Studies); **Computer Engineering** (Computer Engineering; Systems Analysis); **Computer Science** (Computer Science); **Criminology** (Criminology); **Fashion Design** (Fashion Design); **Gastronomy** (Cooking and Catering); **Graphic Design** (Graphic Design); **Industrial Engineering** (Industrial Engineering); **Law** (Law); **Marketing** (Marketing); **Nutrition** (Nutrition); **Pedagogy** (Pedagogy); **Psychology** (Psychology); **Tourism** (Tourism)

Further Information: Branches in Tecámac, Texcoco, Pachuca, Merida and Ixtapaluca

History: Founded 2000.

Main Language(s) of Instruction: Spanish

Degrees and Diplomas: *Licenciatura*; *Especialización*; *Maestría*

Last Updated: 05/04/13

PRIVATE UNIVERSITY OF THE STATE OF MORELOS

Universidad Privada del Estado de Morelos, S.C. (UPEM)
Avenida Alvaro Obregón, 624, Col. Centro, 62740 Cuernavaca, Morelos
Tel: +52(777) 314-50-00
EMail: coor-academica@upem.edu.mx
Website: http://www.upem.edu.mx

Rector: Ovidio Nobal Nicolau (1997-)

Programmes
Accountancy (Accountancy); **Administration** (Administration); **Law** (Law); **Organizational Psychology** (Psychology)

Further Information: Also campus in Cuautla

History: Founded 1997.

Main Language(s) of Instruction: Spanish

Degrees and Diplomas: *Licenciatura*

Libraries: Yes

Last Updated: 23/10/12

PROCIENCIA

Prociencia, A.C.
Edificio CINERMEX local No. 31, Planta Baja, Av. fundidora No. 501, Col. Obrera, Monterrey, Nuevo León
Tel: +52(8) 369-67-45

Programmes
Environmental Studies (Environmental Studies)

Degrees and Diplomas: *Maestría*

PROF. ANTONIO ESTOPIER ESTOPIER TEACHER TRAINING SCHOOL FOR THE LICENCIATURA IN PHYSICAL EDUCATION

Escuela Normal de Licenciatura en Educación Física Profr. Antonio Estopier Estopier
Avenida Calmecac y Calle Enrique Rebsamen, Col. Magisterial, 35150 Ciudad Lerdo, Durango
Tel: +52(871) 23-01-66
Fax: +52(871) 23-01-66
EMail: elefestopier@infosel.net.mx

Directora: Rosa Elena Ríos Ortega

Programmes
Physical Education (Physical Education)

Main Language(s) of Instruction: Spanish

Degrees and Diplomas: *Licenciatura*

Last Updated: 25/02/13

PROFESSIONAL DEVELOPMENT COLLEGE

Colegio de Desarrollo Profesional
9 Norte, 1603, Col. Centro, 72000 Puebla, Puebla
Tel: +52(222) 232-41-18
Fax: +52(222) 232-41-18

Director: Carlos Islas y Gamboa

Degrees and Diplomas: *Licenciatura*

Last Updated: 04/04/08

PROFESSIONAL INSTITUTE OF ART AND DESIGN

Instituto Profesional de Arte y Diseño, A.C.
Modesto Arreola, 1015, Pte., 64000 Monterrey, Nuevo León
Tel: +52(81) 83-42-50-15
Fax: +52(81) 83-42-64-51
EMail: ipadac@hotmail.com
Website: http://ipadac.edu.mx

Directora General: Emma Bertha López Rodríguez (1991-)

Programmes
Architecture and Interior Design (Architecture; Interior Design); **Graphic Design and Advertising** (Advertising and Publicity; Graphic Design); **International Fashion Design** (Fashion Design); **Mechanical and Industrial Design** (Industrial Design)

Degrees and Diplomas: *Licenciatura*

Last Updated: 07/03/13

PROFESSIONAL LYCEUM OF COMMERCE AND ADMINISTRATION

Liceo Profesional de Comercio y Administración
Bravo y 7 No. 1501, Col. Heroíca Matamoros, Col. Centro, 87300 Matamoros, Tamaulipas
Tel: +52(868) 816-71-71
EMail: gonneto@prodigy.net.mx
Website: http://www.liceoprofesional.edu.mx

Director: Alfredo Aldrete Herrera (1982-)

Programmes
Accountancy (Accountancy); **Business Administration** (Administration; Business Administration)

History: Founded 1982.

Main Language(s) of Instruction: Spanish

Degrees and Diplomas: *Licenciatura*

Last Updated: 22/03/13

PROFESSIONAL SCHOOL OF FASHION DESIGN, PUEBLA

Escuela Profesional de Diseño de Modas, Puebla
Avenida Reforma 105 Tercer Piso, Col. Centro Historico, 72000 Puebla, Puebla
Tel: +52(222) 232-96-46 +52(222) 242-06-98
EMail: escumoda@modapuebla.edu.m
Website: http://www.modapuebla.edu.mx

Directora: Elizabeth González Hermosillo

Programmes
Fashion Design (Fashion Design; Textile Design)

Main Language(s) of Instruction: Spanish

Degrees and Diplomas: *Licenciatura*; *Especialización*

Last Updated: 29/08/12

PROFESSIONAL SCHOOL OF INTEGRAL DEVELOPMENT

Escuela Profesional De Desarrollo Integral

Avenida Federalismo Norte, 560, Col. Centro, 44100 Guadalajara, Jalisco
Tel: +52(33) 36-58-51-10
Fax: +52(33) 36-58-39-81

Director: Carlos Ernesto Salazar Carrillo

Programmes
Business Administration (Business Administration); **Computer Systems Administration** (Business Computing; Computer Engineering); **Computer Systems Engineering** (Computer Engineering); **Law** (Administrative Law; Law); **Public Accountancy** (Accountancy)

History: Founded 2003.

Main Language(s) of Instruction: Spanish

Degrees and Diplomas: *Licenciatura*

Last Updated: 28/10/09

PROF. JOSÉ E. MEDRANO R. HIGHER TEACHER TRAINING SCHOOL

Escuela Normal Superior "Profr. José E. Medrano R."

Calle 4 y Ramírez #2600 Col. Centro, 03100 Chihuahua, Chihuahua
Tel: +52(614) 410-09-40
EMail: informatica@ensech.edu.mx
Website: http://www.ensech.edu.mx

Director: Arturo Vázquez Marín

Programmes
Teacher Training (Secondary Education; Teacher Training)

History: Founded 1960.

Main Language(s) of Instruction: Spanish

Degrees and Diplomas: *Licenciatura*

Last Updated: 25/02/13

PROMEDAC UNIVERSITY CENTRE

Centro Universitario Promedac

Cartagena, 116, Fracc. Guadalupe, 34220 Durango, Durango
Tel: +52(618) 818-05-11
EMail: promedac@prodigy.net.mx

Director General: Joel Bautista Sandoval (1972-)

Programmes
Accountancy (Accountancy); **Administration** (Administration); **Law** (Law); **Psychology** (Psychology)

History: Founded 1972 as Colegio de Ciencias y Humanidades Promedac. Acquired present title 1996.

Main Language(s) of Instruction: Spanish

Degrees and Diplomas: *Licenciatura*

Last Updated: 10/03/08

PUEBLA INSTITUTE OF HIGHER STUDIES

Instituto Poblano de Estudios Superiores

Avenida Juárez, 1302, Col. La Paz, 72000 Puebla, Puebla
Tel: +52(222) 246-80-84 +52(222) 232-71-55
Website: http://www.ipes.edu.mx

Director: Emiliano Urbina Rosas

Programmes
Accountancy (Accountancy); **Business Administration** (Business Administration); **Computer Science** (Computer Science); **Law** (Law)

History: Founded 1994.

Main Language(s) of Instruction: Spanish

Degrees and Diplomas: *Licenciatura*

Libraries: Yes

Last Updated: 07/03/13

PUEBLA SPECIALIZATION INSTITUTE IN PSYCHOLOGY

Instituto Poblano de Especialidades en Psicología

5 Poniente 1309 y 1316 Col. Centro Histórico, 72000 Puebla, Puebla
EMail: capacita@ipep-jpc.com
Website: http://www.ipep-pjc.com

Directora: María Teresa Arellano Díaz

Programmes
Child Development (Child Care and Development); **Psychology** (Psychology)

History: Founded 1997.

Main Language(s) of Instruction: Spanish

Degrees and Diplomas: *Especialización*

Last Updated: 07/03/13

PUEBLA UNIVERSITY INSTITUTE

Instituto Universitario Puebla, S.C.

Av. 27 Oriente No. 1 Int. 201 Col. El Carmen, 72500 Puebla, Puebla
Tel: +52(222) 40-15-40
EMail: rectoria@iup.mx
Website: http://www.iup.mx/

Rectora: Ines Ruiz Salinas

Programmes
Accountancy (Accountancy); **Administration** (Administration); **Engineering** (Civil Engineering; Computer Engineering; Industrial Engineering); **Foreign Languages** (English; French; German; Linguistics); **Law** (Law)

Further Information: Also branches in Cordoba,Rojano and Xalapa

History: Founded 1993.

Main Language(s) of Instruction: Spanish

Degrees and Diplomas: *Licenciatura*; *Maestría*; *Doctorado*

Last Updated: 22/03/13

QUETZALCOATL INSTITUTE

Instituto Quetzalcoatl

11 Poniente, 112, Heroica Puebla de Zaragoza, 72000 Puebla, Puebla
Tel: +52(222) 246-60-80

Director: Ignacio Bravo Cid de León

Programmes
Accountancy (Accountancy); **Business Administration** (Business Administration)

Main Language(s) of Instruction: Spanish

Degrees and Diplomas: *Licenciatura*

Last Updated: 07/03/13

QUETZALCOATL UNIVERSITY IN IRAPUATO

Universidad Quetzalcóatl en Irapuato

Blvd. Arandas, 975, Fracc. Tabachines, 36615 Irapuato, Guanajuato
Tel: +52(462) 624-50-95
EMail: uqi@uqi.edu.mx
Website: http://www.uqi.edu.mx

Rector: Agustín Gasca Chávez (1982-)
EMail: agasca@uqi.edu.mx

Programmes
Accountancy (Accountancy); **Architecture** (Architecture); **Business Administration** (Business Administration; Finance); **Communication Studies** (Communication Studies); **Dentistry** (Dentistry); **Engineering** (Civil Engineering; Electronic Engineering); **Law** (Law); **Psychology** (Psychology)

History: Founded 1982.

Main Language(s) of Instruction: Spanish

Degrees and Diplomas: *Licenciatura*; *Especialización*; *Maestría*

Libraries: Yes

Last Updated: 23/10/12

RAFAEL GUIZAR VALENCIA INSTITUTE OF HIGHER STUDIES

Instituto de Estudios Superiores Rafael Guizar Valencia
Prolongación Diamante s/n, Unidad Fovissste, 91070 Xalapa, Veracruz
Tel: +52(228) 840-79-59
EMail: iesraguiv@hotmail.com

Director General: José Benigno Zilli Manica

Programmes

Philosophy (Philosophy)

History: Founded 1999.

Main Language(s) of Instruction: Spanish

Degrees and Diplomas: *Licenciatura*

Last Updated: 04/03/13

RAFAEL HALLER INSTITUTE

Instituto Rafael Haller
Enrique Trejo, 11, Col. Bo. San Martín, 54600 Tepozotlán, Estado de México
Tel: +52(55) 58-76-44-30
EMail: instituto_haller@live.com.mx
Website: http://www.institutohaller.edu.mx/

Director: Roberto López Rosas (2001-)
EMail: rlopez@haller.edu.mx

Programmes

Business Administration (Business Administration); **Business Computing** (Business Computing); **Education** (Education); **Gastronomy** (Cooking and Catering); **International Business and Customs** (International Business); **Law** (Law); **Marketing** (Marketing); **Tourism** (Tourism)

Further Information: Also Plantel Izcalli

History: Founded 1986. Incorporated Centro Universitario Haller 2001.

Main Language(s) of Instruction: Spanish

Degrees and Diplomas: *Licenciatura*: 8 sem.; *Especialización*. Also Diplomados

Last Updated: 07/03/13

REALÍSTICA UNIVERSITY OF MEXICO

Universidad Realística de México (URM)
Privada 2-C Sur No. 5914 Colonia Bugambilias, 72580 Puebla, Puebla
Tel: +52(222) 755-29-80
EMail: informes@urm.edu.mx
Website: http://www.urm.edu.mx

Rectora: Ana Cabrera Montaño EMail: ana@urm.edu.mx

Programmes

Dental Surgery (Dentistry; Surgery); **Fashion Design** (Fashion Design); **Law** (Administrative Law; Civil Law; Commercial Law; Constitutional Law; Criminal Law; Labour Law); **Veterinary Science and Zoology** (Veterinary Science; Zoology)

History: Founded 1985.

Admission Requirements: Bachillerato

Main Language(s) of Instruction: Spanish

Degrees and Diplomas: *Licenciatura*: 4-5 yrs

Student Services: Academic counselling, Employment services, Language programs, Social counselling

Libraries: Yes

Publications: Realidades *(bimonthly)*

Last Updated: 23/10/12

REGIOMONTANA UNIVERSITY

Universidad Regiomontana, A.C. (UR)
Apartado postal 243, Villagrán, 238, Sur, 2° Piso, entre Washington y Modesto Arreola, Col. Centro, 64000 Monterrey, Nuevo León
Tel: +52(81) 8220-46-11
EMail: informes@mail.ur.mx
Website: http://www.ur.mx

Rector: Ángel Casán Marcos (2012-)

Faculties

Administration and Economics (Business Administration; Economics); **Engineering and Architecture** (Architecture; Chemical Engineering; Civil Engineering; Computer Engineering; Electronic Engineering; Engineering; Mechanical Engineering); **Humanities and Social Sciences** (Arts and Humanities; Communication Studies; Education; Law; Psychology; Social Sciences)

History: Founded 1951 as Instituto Modelo de Enseñanza, became university 1969.

Governing Bodies: Board of Trustees; Academic Council

Academic Year: September to August (September-December; January-April; May-August)

Admission Requirements: Bachillerato and entrance examination

Main Language(s) of Instruction: Spanish

Degrees and Diplomas: *Licenciatura*: 3-4 yrs

Libraries: Yes

Publications: Veritas, Annual research book *(annually)*

Last Updated: 23/10/12

REGIOMONTANO INSTITUTE

Instituto Regiomontano, A.C.
Calle Francisco Garza Sada No. 432, Col. Chepevera, 64000 Monterrey, Nuevo León
Tel: +52(81) 80-48-84-70
EMail: info@ir.edu.mx
Website: http://www.ir.edu.mx

Director: Tarsicio Larios Félix

Programmes

Education (Education; Educational Psychology; Preschool Education; Primary Education)

History: Founded 1948.

Main Language(s) of Instruction: Spanish

Degrees and Diplomas: *Licenciatura*; *Maestría*

Libraries: Yes

Last Updated: 07/03/13

REGIOMONTANO INSTITUTE OF HOTEL MANAGEMENT

Instituto Regiomontano de Hotelería
Argentina 3937, Col. Desarrollo Las Torres, 64760 Monterrey, Nuevo León
EMail: irh@irh.edu.mx
Website: http://www.irh.edu.mx

Director: Arturo Sierra Barrera (1978-) EMail: asierra@irh.edu.mx

Programmes

Gastronomy (Cooking and Catering); **Nutrition** (Nutrition); **Tourism** (Management; Tourism)

History: Founded 1978.

Main Language(s) of Instruction: Spanish

Degrees and Diplomas: *Licenciatura*: Tourism Business Administration; Alimentary Services Administration; *Maestría*: Hotel Management

Last Updated: 07/03/13

REGIONAL INSTITUTE OF FAMILY STUDIES

Instituto Regional de Estudios de la Familia
Río de Janeiro 911, 31200 Chihuahua, Chihuahua
Tel: +52(614) 13-29-33
Fax: +52(614) 14-66-14
EMail: contacto@irefam.edu.mx
Website: http://www.irefam.edu.mx

Directora: Flora Aurón Zaltzman

Programmes

Family Studies (Family Studies; Psychotherapy)

Further Information: Also Campus Juarez

History: Founded 1995.

Main Language(s) of Instruction: Spanish

Degrees and Diplomas: *Especialización*; *Maestría*; *Doctorado*

Last Updated: 07/03/13

REGIONAL UNIVERSITY CENTRE OF THE TOTONACAPÁN

Centro Universitario Regional del Totonacapán

Olivo, 204, Altos, Col. Centro, 93400 Papantla, Veracruz

Tel: +52(784) 842-44-94

Fax: +52(784) 842-44-94

EMail: curt_papantla@hotmail.com

Rectora: PatriciaOdet Belin

Programmes

Accountancy (Accountancy); **Administration** (Administration); **Law** (Law); **Pedagogy** (Pedagogy)

Degrees and Diplomas: *Licenciatura*

Last Updated: 14/03/08

REGIONAL UNIVERSITY OF THE NORTH

Universidad Regional del Norte (URN)

Avenida Allende, 2628, Col. Zarco, 31020 Chihuahua, Chihuahua

Tel: +52(614) 411-14-51

EMail: rector@urn.edu.mx

Website: http://www.urn.edu.mx

Rector: Daniel García Coello (1991-)

Secretario General: Carlos González Montijo
EMail: cgonzalezm@urn.edu.mx

International Relations: Edmundo Treviño Fernández
EMail: internacional@urn.edu.mx

Courses

Accountancy (Accountancy); **Business Administration** (Business Administration); **Communication Studies** (Communication Studies); **Finance** (Finance); **Graphic Design** (Graphic Design); **International Business and Foreign Trade** (International Business); **Law** (Law); **Tourism** (Tourism)

Further Information: Also campuses at Ciudad Juárez, Cuauhtémoc, and Parral

History: Founded 1991.

Academic Year: February to December (February-July; August-December)

Admission Requirements: Bachillerato and entrance examination

Main Language(s) of Instruction: Spanish

Degrees and Diplomas: *Licenciatura*: 4 1/2-5 yrs; *Maestría*

Student Services: Academic counselling, Employment services, Foreign student adviser, Handicapped facilities, Health services, Language programs, Social counselling

Libraries: Yes

Last Updated: 23/10/12

REGIONAL UNIVERSITY OF THE SOUTH-EAST

Universidad Regional del Sureste

Eulalio Gutiérrez 1002 Col. Miguel Alemán, Oaxaca de Juárez, 68120 Oaxaca, Oaxaca

Tel: +52(951) 514-14-10

EMail: rectoria@urse.edu.mx

Website: http://www.urse.edu.mx

Rector: Benjamín Alonso Smith Arango

Faculties

Administration and Accountancy *(El Rosario Campus)* (Accountancy; Administration); **Law and Social Sciences** *(El Rosario Campus)* (Law; Social Sciences); **Medicine and Surgery** (Medicine; Surgery); **Psychology** *(El Rosario Campus)* (Psychology)

Schools

Architecture *(El Rosario Campus)* (Architecture); **Dentistry** (Dentistry); **Modern Languages** (English; Linguistics; Literature; Modern Languages); **Nursing** (Nursing); **Nutrition** *(El Rosario Campus)* (Nutrition)

History: Founded 1977.

Academic Year: August to June (August-December; January-June)

Admission Requirements: Bachillerato

Main Language(s) of Instruction: Spanish

Degrees and Diplomas: *Licenciatura*; *Especialización*; *Maestría*; *Doctorado*

Libraries: Yes

Last Updated: 23/10/12

RENÉ DESCARTES INSTITUTE OF TECHNOLOGY AND HIGHER STUDIES

Instituto Tecnológico y de Estudios Superiores René Descartes

J. Barragán, 430, Col. Ricardo Flores Magón, Centro, 91700 Veracruz, Veracruz

Tel: +52(229) 931-07-96

EMail: ites_descartes_ver @ hotmail.comites_descartes_ver @ hotmail.com

Website: http://www.itesrenedescartes.edu.mx

Programmes

Business Administration (Accountancy; Business Administration; Business Computing; Management Systems); **Pedagogy** (Education; Pedagogy)

Further Information: Also campuses in Campeche, Coatzacoalcos and Tampico

Degrees and Diplomas: *Licenciatura*

Last Updated: 21/03/13

RESEARCH AND TEACHING CENTRE

Centro de Investigación y Docencia

Lucio Cabañas 27, Col. Pablo Gómez, 31100 Chihuahua, Chihuahua

Tel: +52(61) 144-23-78

EMail: contacto@cid.edu.mx

Website: http://cid.edu.mx

Directora General: Ana María González Ortiz
EMail: ana.gonzalez@cid.edu.mx

Programmes

Educational Research (Educational Psychology; Sociology)

Main Language(s) of Instruction: Spanish

Degrees and Diplomas: *Maestría*

Libraries: Yes

Last Updated: 18/07/12

RESEARCH CENTRE IN VIRTUAL EDUCATION

Centro de Investigación en Educación Virtual, S.C.

Nayarit 288-D entre Arizona y Gándara, Col. San Benito, 83190 Hermosillo, Sonora

Tel: +52(662)210-20-67

EMail: direcciongeneral@ciev.edu.mx

Website: http://www.ciev.edu.mx

Directora General: Dora Luz López

Jefe del Departamento de Administración y Cobranza: Rosaura Velasco García EMail: posgrado@ciev.edu.mx

Areas

Administration (Administration; Business Administration); **Communication** (Communication Studies; Journalism; Public Relations; Social Studies); **Computer Systems** (Computer Engineering); **Education**; **Mediation**

History: Founded 2001.

Degrees and Diplomas: *Licenciatura*; *Especialización*; *Maestría*

Last Updated: 19/11/09

RESEARCH CENTRE ON EDUCATIONAL ADMINISTRATION

Centro de Investigación para la Administración Educativa
Calle Independencia 1100 Esq. con Inturbide, Zona Centro, San Luis Potosí, San Luis Potosí
Tel: +52(444) 814-01-54
Fax: +52(444) 128-69-67
EMail: cinade@cinade.com.mx
Website: http://www.cinade.edu.mx/

Director: Joel Ramos Leyva

Programmes
Educational Administration (Educational Administration); **Higher Education** (Higher Education)

Further Information: Campuses in Rio Verde, Matehuala, Ciudad Valles and Tamazunchale

History: Founded 2002.

Main Language(s) of Instruction: Spanish

Degrees and Diplomas: *Especialización*; *Maestría*; *Doctorado*

Last Updated: 12/07/12

RESEARCH CENTRE ON FOOD AND DEVELOPMENT

Centro de Investigación en Alimentación y Desarrollo, A.C. (CIAD)
Carretera a La Victoria Km. 0.6, 83000 Hermosillo, Sonora
Tel: +52(662) 289-24-00
EMail: rpacheco@ciad.mx
Website: http://www.ciad.mx

Director General: Ramón Pacheco Aguilar

Programmes
Food Science (Food Science); **Food Technology**; **Nutrition** (Nutrition); **Regional Development** (Regional Planning)

Further Information: Also units in Guaymas, Cuauhtémoc, Delicias, Mazatlán and Culiacán

History: Founded 1982.

Main Language(s) of Instruction: Spanish

Degrees and Diplomas: *Maestría*; *Doctorado*

Libraries: Yes

Last Updated: 12/07/12

RESEARCH CENTRE ON HUMAN DEVELOPMENT, CIDH UNIVERSITY

Centro de Investigación para el Desarrollo Humano, CIDH Universidad
Paseo Playas 501 Secc. Jardines Playas de Tijuana, Tijuana, Baja California
Tel: +52(664) 680-9293
Fax: +52(664) 631-8173
EMail: rectoria@cidhuniversidad.edu.mx
Website: http://www.cidhuniversidad.edu.mx

Directora General: Lucia Sotelo Guerrero
EMail: direccion@cidhuniversidad.edu.mx

Programmes
Business Administration (Business Administration); **Family Psychology** (Family Studies; Psychology); **Hotel Management** (Hotel Management); **Law** (Law)

Main Language(s) of Instruction: Spanish

Degrees and Diplomas: *Licenciatura*; *Maestría*. Also Diplomados

Last Updated: 12/07/12

RESEARCH INSTITUTE IN CLINICAL AND SOCIAL PSYCHOLOGY

Instituto de Investigación en Psicología Clínica y Social
Minerva N° 83, Col. Crédito Constructor, Benito Juarez, 03940 México, D.F.
Tel: +52(555) 661-39-65
Fax: +52(555) 661-39-65
EMail: informes@iipcs.edu.mx
Website: http://www.iipcs.edu.mx/

Presidenta: Jael Alatriste Garcia

Programmes
Clinical and Social Psychology (Clinical Psychology; Psychoanalysis; Psychotherapy; Social Psychology)

History: Founded 1979.

Main Language(s) of Instruction: Spanish

Degrees and Diplomas: *Licenciatura*; *Maestría*; *Doctorado*

Last Updated: 04/03/13

REYNA SCHOOL CENTRE

Centro Escolar Reyna
Mar de Akaba, 8, Ote., Fracc. Las Anclas, 39630 Acapulco de Juárez, Guerrero
Tel: +52(744) 486-98-55
Fax: +52(744) 485-35-87
EMail: centroescolarreina@yahoo.com

Directora: Patricia Reyna Soto Aoyama

Programmes
Modern Languages (Modern Languages)

Degrees and Diplomas: *Licenciatura*

Last Updated: 04/04/08

RICARDO FLORES MAGÓN EDUCATION CENTRE

Centro Educativo Ricardo Flores Magón
Corregidoras, 1419, Centro, 36500 Irapuato, Guanajuato
Tel: +52(462) 627-04-11

Director: Ezequiel Soto Martínez

Degrees and Diplomas: *Licenciatura*

Last Updated: 04/04/08

ROBERTO CAÑEDO MARTÍNEZ SCHOOL OF TOURISM

Escuela Superior de Turismo Roberto Cañedo Martínez
Avenida 9 Poniente, 911, Centro Historico, 72000 Puebla, Puebla
Tel: +52(222) 232-50-35
Fax: +52(222) 246-14-77
EMail: esuperturismo@yahoo.com.mx
Website: http://www.est.edu.mx

Directora: Aurora Mendoza Moreno

Programmes
Child Development (Child Care and Development); **Gastronomy** (Cooking and Catering); **Hostelry and Gastronomy** (Cooking and Catering; Hotel Management)

Main Language(s) of Instruction: Spanish

Degrees and Diplomas: *Licenciatura*; *Especialización*

Last Updated: 27/02/13

RUDOLPH DIESEL SCHOOL OF AUTOMATION ENGINEERING

Escuela de Ingeniería Automotriz Rudolph Diesel
3 Sur 1505, Col. El Carmen, 72000 Puebla, Puebla
Tel: +52(222) 240-57-41
EMail: rudolph_diesel@hotmail.com
Website: http://rudolphdiesel.mx

Directora: Lourdes Granados Marín

Programmes
Accountancy (Accountancy); **Administration** (Administration); **Engineering** (Automotive Engineering; Engineering; Mechanical Engineering)

Further Information: Branches in Toluca, Acapulco and Chilpancingo

Main Language(s) of Instruction: Spanish

Degrees and Diplomas: *Licenciatura*; *Maestría*
Last Updated: 29/08/12

SAHAGÚN CENTRE FOR ADVANCED STUDIES

Centro de Estudios Superiores Sahagún
Xochiatipán, 25, Col. Javier Rojo Gómez, Tepeapulco, 43990 Ciudad Sahagún, Hidalgo
Tel: +52(791) 913-28-65
Fax: +52(791) 913-28-65
EMail: velarde28@yahoo.com

Director: Enrique Castañeda Paredes (1995-)

Programmes
Accountancy (Accountancy); **Architecture** (Architecture); **Business Computing** (Business Computing); **Law** (Law); **Tourism** (Administration; Tourism)

Further Information: Also campus in Tula de Allende

History: Founded 1995.

Main Language(s) of Instruction: Spanish

Degrees and Diplomas: *Licenciatura*
Last Updated: 17/07/12

SAINT TERESA CENTRE OF ADVANCED STUDIES

Centro Teresiano de Estudios Superiores
Plutarco Elías Calles, 651 y Avenida De La Raza, 32341 Ciudad Juárez, Chihuahua
Tel: +52(656) 613-38-20
Fax: +52(656) 613-38-20
EMail: cert@infolink.net

Director: Rúben Acosta Estrada

Programmes
Educational Sciences (Educational Sciences); **Psychology** (Psychology)

History: Founded 1997.
Main Language(s) of Instruction: Spanish

Degrees and Diplomas: *Licenciatura*

SAINT THOMAS AQUINAS INSTITUTE OF HIGHER STUDIES

Instituto de Estudios Superiores Tomás de Aquino
Avenida Perú, 300, Col. El Retiro, 29000 Tuxtla Gutiérrez, Chiapas
Tel: +52(961) 614-15-59
EMail: sdtgar@invitados.itesm.mx
Website: http://iestafil.wordpress.com

Director: José Luis Madrigal F

Programmes
Philosophy (Philosophy)

History: Founded 2000.

Main Language(s) of Instruction: Spanish

Degrees and Diplomas: *Licenciatura*
Last Updated: 04/03/13

SAINT VINCENT HOSPITAL NURSING SCHOOL

Escuela de Enfermería del Hospital San Vicente
Serafín Peña 119 Norte, Col.Centro, 64000 Monterrey, Nuevo León
Tel: +52(81) 83-45-77-77
Fax: +52(81) 83-45-87-76
EMail: escuelasanvicente@prodigy.net.mx

Directora: María Esperanza Hernández Garza

Programmes
Nursing and Obstetrics (Gynaecology and Obstetrics; Nursing)

History: Founded 1961.

Main Language(s) of Instruction: Spanish

Degrees and Diplomas: *Licenciatura*
Last Updated: 21/02/13

SALESIAN INSTITUTE OF HIGHER STUDIES

Instituto Salesiano de Estudios Superiores
San Juan Bosco, 24, Col. Lázaro Cárdenas Tlalpan, 14370 México, D.F.
Tel: +52(55) 56-71-10-87
EMail: comunicacion@ises.edu.mx
Website: http://institutosalesiano.edu.mx

Director General: Carmelo Reyes G.
EMail: direccion@institutosalesiano.edu.mx

Programmes
Education (Education; Educational Administration; Educational Sciences; Teacher Training); **Philosophy** (Philosophy)

History: Founded 1993.

Main Language(s) of Instruction: Spanish

Degrees and Diplomas: *Licenciatura*; *Especialización*; *Maestría*

Libraries: Yes
Last Updated: 07/03/13

SALESIAN UNIVERSITY MEXICO CITY

Universidad Salesiana México
Laguna de Tamiahua No. 97, Col. Anáhuac, Del. Miguel Hidalgo, 11320 México, D.F.
Tel: +52(55) 53-96-33-51
EMail: contacto@universidadsalesiana.edu.mx
Website: http://www.universidadsalesiana.edu.mx

Rector: Luis Rolando Valerdi Sánchez

Programmes
Accountancy (Accountancy); **Administration** (Administration); **Communication Studies** (Communication Studies); **Law** (Law); **Pedagogy** (Pedagogy); **Psychology** (Psychology)

History: Founded 1972.

Main Language(s) of Instruction: Spanish

Degrees and Diplomas: *Licenciatura*; *Especialización*
Last Updated: 23/10/12

SÄMANN UNIVERSITY OF JALISCO

Universidad Sämann de Jalisco
Avenida Hidalgo 1717, Col. Ladrón de Guevara, 44600 Guadalajara, Jalisco
Tel: +52(33) 33-43-35-14
EMail: contacto@usj.edu.mx
Website: http://www.usj.edu.mx

Rectora: Adalid Pedraza Silva

Programmes
Business Administration (Business Administration); **Communication Studies** (Communication Studies); **Graphic Design** (Graphic Design); **Information Technology** (Information Technology); **Law** (Law); **Pedagogy** (Education; Pedagogy)

History: Founded 2003.

Admission Requirements: Bachillerato

Main Language(s) of Instruction: Spanish

Degrees and Diplomas: *Licenciatura*. Also Diplomados

Libraries: Yes
Last Updated: 23/10/12

SAMUEL HAHNEMANN INSTITUTE OF HIGHER STUDIES

Instituto de Estudios Superiores Samuel Hahnemann

Jalisco, 305, Col. Centro, 49000 Zapotlan, Jalisco

Tel: +52(33) 14-12-49-90

EMail: contacto@iessh.com

Website: http://www.iessh.com

Director: Jorge Enrique Olvera Ruiz

Programmes

Homeopathy (Anatomy; Development Studies; Embryology and Reproduction Biology; Homeopathy; Nutrition; Pathology; Pharmacology; Physiology; Public Health)

History: Founded 2000.

Main Language(s) of Instruction: Spanish

Degrees and Diplomas: *Licenciatura*

Last Updated: 28/10/09

SAN CARLOS UNIVERSITY

Universidad San Carlos

Vía Morelos, 182 y 208, Col. Nuevo Laredo, 55080 Ecatepec de Morelos, Estado de México

Tel: +52(55) 57-70-08-24

EMail: contactousc@universidadsancarlos.edu.mx

Website: http://www.universidadsancarlos.edu.mx

Director: Victor Hugo Mendieta Reyes

Programmes

Accountancy (Accountancy); **Business Administration** (Business Administration); **Law** (Law); **Marketing** (Marketing); **Pedagogy** (Pedagogy); **Telematics** (Telecommunications Engineering)

History: Founded 1972 as Instituto Técnico y Bancario San Carlos.

Main Language(s) of Instruction: Spanish

Degrees and Diplomas: *Licenciatura*; *Especialización*; *Maestría*

Last Updated: 11/03/13

SAN JUAN DEL RÍO COLLEGE OF ADVANCED STUDIES

Colegio de Estudios Superiores de San Juan del Río

Blvd. Hidalgo, 37, Col. La Viña, 76800 San Juan del Río, Querétaro

Tel: +52(427) 272-70-22

Fax: +52(427) 272-70-22

Director: Felipe Salinas Castillo

Degrees and Diplomas: *Licenciatura*

Last Updated: 04/04/08

SAN LUIS POTOSÍ UNIVERSITY

Universidad Potosina

Ignacio Comonfort No. 135, San Sebastián, 78000 San Luis Potosí, San Luis Potosí

Tel: +52(444) 818-34-01

EMail: informes@campusup.edu.mx

Website: http://www.universidadpotosina.edu.mx

Rector: José Arturo Segoviano García

Programmes

Accountancy (Accountancy); **Communication Studies** (Communication Studies); **Gastronomy** (Cooking and Catering); **International Business** (International Business); **Law** (Law); **Marketing** (Marketing); **Mechatronics** (Electronic Engineering; Mechanical Engineering); **Protected Crops** (Crop Production); **Social Work** (Social Work); **Stomatology** (Stomatology)

History: Founded 2000.

Main Language(s) of Instruction: Spanish

Degrees and Diplomas: *Licenciatura*

Last Updated: 23/10/12

SAN MARCOS UNIVERSITY

Universidad San Marcos (USAM)

4a Norte Oriente, 2284, Col. El Brasilito, 29040 Tuxtla Gutiérrez, Chiapas

Tel: +52(961) 614-27-29

EMail: rectoria@usam.edu.mx

Website: http://www.usam.edu.mx

Rector: José Guadalupe Méndez Toscano (1992-)

Vicerrectora: Guadalupe Méndez Lau

EMail: usam_92@hotmail.com

Programmes

Accountancy (Accountancy); **Architecture** (Architecture); **Business Administration** (Business Administration); **Computer Science** (Computer Science); **Computer Systems** (Computer Engineering); **e-Commerce** (E-Business/Commerce); **Education** (Education; Pedagogy); **International Business and Customs** (International Business); **Law** (Civil Law; Criminal Law; Fiscal Law; Law)

Further Information: Campuses in San Cristóbal de las Casas and Tapachula

History: Founded 1992.

Academic Year: August to June (August-December; February-June)

Admission Requirements: Secondary school certificate (bachillerato)

Main Language(s) of Instruction: Spanish

Degrees and Diplomas: *Licenciatura*: 5 yrs; *Maestría*; *Doctorado*

Student Services: Academic counselling, Employment services, Foreign student adviser, Sports facilities

Last Updated: 05/04/13

SAN MIGUEL UNIVERSITY

Universidad de San Miguel

Blvd. Alfonso Zaragoza Maytorena 1800 Nte, Desarrollo Urbano Tres Ríos, 80000 Culiacán, Sinaloa

Tel: +52(667) 758 - 08 - 00

EMail: info@usm.edu.mx

Website: http://www.usm.edu.mx

Rector: Jorge René Meléndrez Quezada (2000-)

EMail: pvillegas@usm.edu.mx

Areas

Business Administration (Accountancy; Administration; Agricultural Business; Finance; International Business; Tourism)

History: Founded 1990.

Main Language(s) of Instruction: Spanish

Degrees and Diplomas: *Licenciatura*; *Especialización*; *Maestría*

Last Updated: 21/09/12

SAN PABLO UNIVERSITY

Universidad San Pablo

Prol. Mariano Jiménez 2500, José Alfredo Jiménez 450, 78359 San Luis Potosí, San Luis Potosí

Tel: +52(444) 815-99-93

EMail: jcca4@hotmail.com

Website: http://www.univsanpablo.edu.mx

Rector: José Homero Garza Rodarte

EMail: rectoria@univsanpablo.edu.mx

Directora Académica: María Alicia González Galarza

Programmes

Accountancy (Accountancy; Finance); **Business Administration** (Business Administration); **Family Studies** (Family Studies); **International Business** (International Business); **Law** (Law); **Psychology** (Psychology)

History: Founded 2003.

Main Language(s) of Instruction: Spanish

Degrees and Diplomas: *Licenciatura*. Also Diplomados

Last Updated: 21/04/11

SANTA FE INSTITUTE OF HIGHER EDUCATION

Instituto de Educación Superior Santa Fe

Km. 0.750 Carretera San José Cervera, Col. Puentecillas, 36262 Guanajuato, Guanajuato
Tel: +52(473) 733-17-92 +52(473) 732-49-26
Fax: +52(473) 733-16-29

Rector: Gerardo Alfonso Jiménez Cabrera

Programmes
Tourism (Tourism)

History: Founded 1993.

Main Language(s) of Instruction: Spanish

Degrees and Diplomas: *Licenciatura*; *Maestría*
Last Updated: 03/04/08

SANTA FE UNIVERSITY

Universidad Santa Fe

Km. 0.75 Carretera a San José Puentecillas, 36250 Guanajuato, Guanajuato
Tel: +52(473) 734-50-00
EMail: usf.educacion@usf.com.mx
Website: http://usf.com.mx

Rector: Rodrigo Enrique Martínez Nieto EMail: rector@usf.com.mx

Schools
Communication and Public Relations (Communication Studies; Public Relations); **Economics and Administration** (Business Administration; International Business; Tourism); **Law** (Law)

History: Founded 1990.

Main Language(s) of Instruction: Spanish

Degrees and Diplomas: *Licenciatura*
Last Updated: 05/04/13

SAPIENTIA INSTITUTE

Instituto Sapientia

Callejón del Arrastradero, 314, 62260 Cuernavaca, Morelos
Tel: +52(777) 313-55-83

Director: Juan Alvarado López

Programmes
Philosophy (Philosophy); **Theology** (Theology)
Main Language(s) of Instruction: Spanish

Degrees and Diplomas: *Licenciatura*
Last Updated: 08/03/13

SCHOOL OF ACCOUNTANCY OF TLAXCALANCINGO

Escuela de Contaduría de Tlaxcalancingo

Km. 6 Carretera Federal Puebla-Atlixco, Tlaxcalcingo, 72000 San Andrés Cholula, Puebla

Programmes
Accountancy (Accountancy)
Main Language(s) of Instruction: Spanish

Degrees and Diplomas: *Licenciatura*
Last Updated: 03/04/08

SCHOOL OF ACCOUNTANCY AND ADMINISTRATION

Escuela Superior de Contaduría y Administración

Avenida Monterrey S/N, Col. Chapultepec, 26890 Nueva Rosita, Coahuila
Tel: +52(861) 614-37-45
EMail: informacion@esca.edu.mx
Website: http://www.esca.edu.mx

Director: Carlos Ángel Garza Ramírez
EMail: garzaca@esca.edu.mx

Programmes
Accountancy (Accountancy); **Business Administration**

Degrees and Diplomas: *Licenciatura*: 9-10 sem.
Last Updated: 04/04/08

SCHOOL OF ADMINISTRATION AND PUBLIC ACCOUNTANCY OF SINALOA

Escuela de Administración y Contaduría Pública de Sinaloa

Mariano Escobedo, 361, Ote., Col. Centro, o, Niños Héroes, 602, Ote., 80000 Culiacán, Sinaloa
Tel: +52(667) 713-49-17

Director: Ramiro Cervantes Castro

Programmes
Accountancy (Accountancy); **Administration** (Administration)

Degrees and Diplomas: *Licenciatura*
Last Updated: 31/03/08

SCHOOL OF AGRICULTURE AND VETERINARY SCIENCE

Escuela Superior de Agricultura y Veterinaria

Km. 25 Carretera 30, Fracc. San Andrés, 25500 San Buenaventura, Coahuila
Tel: +52(869) 69-60-93

Director: Héctor Menchaca Campos

Programmes
Agriculture (Agriculture); **Veterinary Science** (Veterinary Science)

History: Founded 1974.

Main Language(s) of Instruction: Spanish

Degrees and Diplomas: *Licenciatura*
Last Updated: 26/02/13

SCHOOL OF ALTERNATIVE MEDICINE

Escuela de Medicina Alternativa

3a Norte Poniente, No. 1415, Col. Moctezuma, 29000 Tuxtla Gutiérrez, Chiapas
EMail: info@ema.edu.mx
Website: http://ema.edu.mx

Directora: Fabiola Davis Lucas

Programmes
Alternative Medicine (Acupuncture; Homeopathy)
History: Founded 1994.

Main Language(s) of Instruction: Spanish
Degrees and Diplomas: *Licenciatura*; *Maestría*
Last Updated: 28/08/12

SCHOOL OF ARCHITECTURE

Escuela Superior de Arquitectura

Av. Libertad #1745, Col. Americana, 44160 Guadalajara, Jalisco
Tel: +52(33) 36-16-76-06
Fax: +52(33) 36-16-76-05
EMail: informes@esarq.edu.mx
Website: http://esarq.edu.mx

Directora: Lilliane Ponce

Programmes
Architecture (Architecture)

History: Founded 1997.

Main Language(s) of Instruction: Spanish

Degrees and Diplomas: *Licenciatura*
Last Updated: 26/02/13

SCHOOL OF ARCHITECTURE OF CHIHUAHUA

Escuela de Arquitectura de Chihuahua, A.C.

Avenida Instituto Politécnico Nacional, 2710, Col. Quintas del Sol, 31250 Chihuahua, Chihuahua
Tel: +52(614) 411-09-19
Fax: +52(614) 411-09-19
EMail: each@sercor.net.mx
Website: http://www.each.itgo.com

Director Académico: Fernando Hiram Gallegos Lozano (1998-)

Programmes
Architecture (Architecture; Construction Engineering; Design; Graphic Design; Structural Architecture; Town Planning)
History: Founded 1970.
Main Language(s) of Instruction: Spanish
Degrees and Diplomas: *Licenciatura*
Last Updated: 27/08/12

SCHOOL OF AUTOMOTIVE ENGINEERING

Escuela Superior de Ingeniería Automotriz
Avenida Toltecas, 231, 402, Aculco, 234 y Aztecas, 219, Col. La Romana, 54030 Tlalnepantla, Estado de México
Tel: +52(55) 53-90-48-49 +52(55) 55-65-82-70
Fax: +52(55) 55-65-82-70
EMail: cedva@hotmail.com

Director: Miguel Ángel López Vega (1998-)

Programmes
Automotive Engineering (Automotive Engineering; Electronic Engineering; Mechanical Engineering)
Further Information: Also branches in Morelia and San Luis Potosí
History: Founded 1998.
Main Language(s) of Instruction: Spanish
Degrees and Diplomas: *Licenciatura*; *Maestría*
Last Updated: 27/02/13

SCHOOL OF BANKING AND COMMERCE

Escuela Bancaria y Comercial (EBC)
Paseo de la Reforma, 202, Col. Juárez, Delegación Cuauhtémoc, 06600 México, D.F.
Tel: +52(55) 57-26-99-33 +52(55) 55-46-03-26
Fax: +52(55) 57-03-36-06 +52(55) 55-46-03-26
EMail: jprieto@ebc.mx
Website: http://www.ebc.mx

Presidente: Javier Prieto Sierra (1990-)

Programmes
Accountancy (Accountancy); **Administration** (Administration); **Business Computing** (Business Computing); **Economics** (Economics); **Finance and Banking** (Banking; Finance); **International Business and Commerce** (International Business); **Marketing** (Marketing); **Tourism**
Further Information: Campuses: Tlalnepantla, Toluca, Chiapas, Dinamarca and Querétaro. Also virtual campus
History: Founded 1929.
Main Language(s) of Instruction: Spanish
Degrees and Diplomas: *Licenciatura*; *Especialización*; *Maestría*
Special Facilities: EBC Museum
Last Updated: 27/08/12

SCHOOL OF COMMERCE

Escuela Superior de Comercio
Paseo de la Reforma, 51-4, Delegación Cuauhtémoc, 06600 México, D.F.

Director: Marcos Pérez Arenas

Programmes
Business and Commerce (Business and Commerce)
Degrees and Diplomas: *Licenciatura*
Last Updated: 04/04/08

SCHOOL OF COMMERCE OF THE CHAMBER OF COMMERCE

Escuela Comercial Cámara de Comercio
Querétaro 34, Col. Roma, Delegación Cuauhtémoc, 06700 México, D.F.
Tel: +52(55) 55-84-13-70 +52(55) 55-84-15-80
Fax: +52(55) 55-84-08-72 +52(55) 55-84-16-52
EMail: ov@eccc.com.mx
Website: http://www.eccc.com.mx

Presidente: Raymundo Solís Rodríguez

Directora General: Ana María Zorrilla Hernández

Programmes
Business (Accountancy; Business Administration; Business and Commerce; Business Computing; International Business; Management; Marketing); **Hotel Management and Tourism** (Hotel Management; Tourism); **Law** (Law); **Psychology** (Psychology)
History: Founded 1923.
Main Language(s) of Instruction: Spanish
Degrees and Diplomas: *Licenciatura*; *Maestría*
Last Updated: 27/08/12

SCHOOL OF COMMUNICATION AND HUMANITIES

Escuela de Comunicación y Ciencias Humanas (ECCH)
7 Sur, 1108, Col. Centro, 72000 Puebla, Puebla
Tel: +52(222) 242-37-41
EMail: ecch@ecch.edu.mx; direccion@ecch.edu.mx
Website: http://www.ecch.edu.mx

Programmes
Communication and Human Sciences (Communication Studies; Graphic Design; Photography; Public Relations; Radio and Television Broadcasting)
History: Founded 1987.
Main Language(s) of Instruction: Spanish
Degrees and Diplomas: *Licenciatura*
Libraries: Yes
Last Updated: 28/08/12

SCHOOL OF ENTREPRENEURSHIP

Escuela Superior de Emprendedores
Padre Mier, 1002, Pte. Esq. Miguel Nieto, Centro, Monterrey, Nuevo León

Programmes
Entrepreneurship (Business Administration; Management)
History: Founded 2001.
Main Language(s) of Instruction: Spanish
Degrees and Diplomas: *Licenciatura*
Last Updated: 04/04/08

SCHOOL OF FOREIGN TRADE

Escuela Superior de Comercio Exterior, A.C.
Blvd. López Mateos 1622, Col. Zactecas, 21100 Mexicali, Baja California
Tel: +52(686) 553-41-34
Fax: +52(686) 553-41-34
EMail: direcciongeneral@escomex.com.mx
Website: http://www.escomex.com.mx

Director General: José Gerardo Aguíñiga Montes

Programmes
International Business (Business Administration; International Business; Marketing)
Further Information: Campuses: Mesa de Otay and Zaragoza
History: Founded 1995.
Main Language(s) of Instruction: Spanish
Degrees and Diplomas: *Licenciatura*; *Maestría*
Last Updated: 26/02/13

SCHOOL OF HIGHER EDUCATION IN HISTORY AND ANTHROPOLOGY

Escuela de Educación Superior en Ciencias Históricas y Antropológicas
General Mariano Arista, 920, Col. Tequisquiapán, 78250 San Luis Potosí, San Luis Potosí
Tel: +52(444) 813-44-74
Fax: +52(444) 811-72-48
EMail: fundacioneduardoseler@yahoo.com.mx
Website: http://fundacioneduardseler.4mg.com/fundacion_eduard_seler.htm

Director General: Joaquin Muñoz Mendoza (2002-)
EMail: joaquinmunoz@fundacioneduardseler.org

Academic and Administrative Coordinator: Urbano Flores Romero EMail: urbanof@fundacioneduardseler.org

International Relations: Nicola Kuehne Heyder
Tel: +52(444) 835-05-09 EMail: nicola@fundacioneduardseler.org

Areas
Anthropology (Anthropology); **Cultural Anthropology** (Anthropology; Cultural Studies); **History** (Ancient Civilizations; Art History; History)

History: Founded 1994.

Academic Year: August to June (August-December; January-June)

Fees: (U.S. Dollars): 1,400 per annum

Main Language(s) of Instruction: Spanish

Degrees and Diplomas: *Licenciatura*; *Especialización*; *Maestría*; *Doctorado*

Student Services: Academic counselling, Employment services, Foreign student adviser, Language programs, Nursery care, Sports facilities

Special Facilities: Museo Universitario 'Lariab' de Historia Antigua de la Huaxteca; Area de Vestigios Arqueológicos 'El Consuelo-Tamuín

Libraries: Biblioteca Herman Beyer

Publications: De Historia y Antropología, Bulletin *(bimonthly)*; Huaxteca: El Hombre y su Pasado, History and Anthropology *(biennially)*

Last Updated: 28/08/12

SCHOOL OF HIGHER STUDIES IN REHABILITATION

Escuela de Estudios Superiores en Rehabilitación

Calle 39 Pte. no. 903, Gabriel Pastor, 72550 Puebla, Puebla
Tel: +52(222) 237-59-20
Fax: +52(222) 243-81-52
EMail: eesrehab@pue1.telmex.net.mx

Directora: Silvia Dolores Salomón Ramos

Programmes
Occupational Therapy (Occupational Therapy); **Physical Therapy** (Physical Therapy); **Speech Therapy and Audiology** (Speech Therapy and Audiology)

Main Language(s) of Instruction: Spanish

Degrees and Diplomas: *Licenciatura*: 9 sem.

Last Updated: 03/04/08

SCHOOL OF HOMEOPATHY

Escuela Homeopatas Puros

Avenida López Mateos Sur, 2199, Col. Ciudad del Sol, 45050 Zapopan, Jalisco
Tel: +52(33) 38-70-02-66
EMail: hompuros@prodigy.net.mx
Website: http://homeopataspuros.com/index.html

Director: Javier Vidales Gurrola

Programmes
Homeopathy (Anatomy; Homeopathy; Nutrition; Pharmacology)

History: Founded 1983. Acquired present status 2006.

Main Language(s) of Instruction: Spanish

Degrees and Diplomas: *Licenciatura*

Last Updated: 29/08/12

SCHOOL OF HOMEOPATHY

Escuela Superior de Homeopatía

Héctor Berlioz, 4783, A Residencial Cordilleras, Entre Av. Manuel J. Clouthier y Av. Patria, 45030 Zapopan, Jalisco
Tel: +52(33) 35-60-49-29
Fax: +52(33) 35-60-53-06
EMail: informacion@esh.edu.mx
Website: http://www.esh.edu.mx/

Director: José Cruz Rubalcava Ornelas

Programmes
Homeopathy (Homeopathy)

History: Founded 2004. Acquired present status 2009.

Main Language(s) of Instruction: Spanish

Degrees and Diplomas: *Licenciatura*

Last Updated: 28/10/09

SCHOOL OF HUMANITIES

Escuela Superior de Estudios Humanísticos

Ixtlememelixtle, 40, 55700 Coacalco de Berriozábal, Estado de México
Tel: +52(55) 58-79-68-77 +52(55) 58-74-20-15
Fax: +52(55) 58-74-20-15
EMail: corporativo@cum-coacalco.edu.mx

Rector: Arturo Méndez y García (1994-)

Programmes
Accountancy (Accountancy); **Business Administration** (Business Administration); **Business Computing** (Business Computing); **Communication Studies** (Communication Studies); **Journalism** (Journalism); **Law** (Criminal Law; Fiscal Law; Law); **Marketing** (Marketing); **Psychology** (Psychology)

History: Founded 1994.

Main Language(s) of Instruction: Spanish

Degrees and Diplomas: *Licenciatura*

Last Updated: 27/02/13

SCHOOL OF INTERNATIONAL BUSINESS

Escuela Superior de Comercio Internacional, S.C.

Fray Servando Teresa de Mier, 839, 3er Piso, Col. Jardín Balbuena, Delegación Venustiano Carranza, 15900 México, D.F.
Tel: +52(55) 55-12-13-04 +52(55) 55-52-74-37
Fax: +52(55) 55-52-74-56
EMail: escia@correoweb.com
Website: http://www.esci.edu.mx

Director General: Salvador Gómez Moreno (1970-)

Programmes
International Business (International Business)

Further Information: Also branches in Coacalco, Guadalajara, Veracruz and Tampico

History: Founded 1970.

Main Language(s) of Instruction: Spanish

Degrees and Diplomas: *Licenciatura*; *Especialización*

Last Updated: 26/02/13

SCHOOL OF JOURNALISM AND COMMUNICATION

Escuela Superior de Periodismo y Comunicación

Parque Magdaleno Varela s/n, Col. Buenos Aires, 98056 Zacatecas, Zacatecas
Tel: +52(492) 925-13-84
Fax: +52(492) 925-16-15
EMail: espczacatecas@hotmail.com
Website: http://www.espc.edu.mx/

Directora General: María de Lourdes González Huerta

Programmes
Administration (Administration); **Communication and Journalism** (Communication Studies; Journalism); **Graphic Design** (Advertising and Publicity; Communication Studies; Graphic Arts; Graphic Design; History; Management; Multimedia; Painting and Drawing; Photography; Public Relations; Sociology); **Marketing** (Administration; Advertising and Publicity; Business Administration; Labour Law; Management; Marketing; Modern Languages; Statistics); **Organizational Communication** (Accountancy; Communication Studies; Graphic Design; History; Literature; Marketing; Multimedia; Photography; Public Relations; Social Psychology); **Psychology** (Accountancy; Administration; Clinical Psychology; Communication Studies; Ethics; Family Studies; History; Human Resources; Labour Law; Literature; Management; Modern Languages; Neurology; Pedagogy; Psychology; Psychotherapy; Social Psychology; Sociology; Statistics)

History: Founded 2004.

Main Language(s) of Instruction: Spanish

Degrees and Diplomas: *Licenciatura*; *Especialización*

Last Updated: 27/02/13

SCHOOL OF JURIDICAL SCIENCES

Escuela Superior de Ciencias Jurídicas, S.C.

Colina del Manantial, 3, Fracc. Boulevares, Naucalpán de Juárez, 53140 Naucalpán de Juárez, Estado de México

Tel: +52(55) 53-93-29-71

Fax: +52(55) 562-73-72

Director: Armando López Salinas (1991-)

Programmes

Law (Law)

History: Founded 1991.

Main Language(s) of Instruction: Spanish

Degrees and Diplomas: *Licenciatura*

Last Updated: 26/02/13

SCHOOL OF JURISPRUDENCE AND HUMANITIES OF PUEBLA

Escuela de Jurisprudencia y Humanidades de Puebla

Avenida 15 de Mayo, 2939-3, Fracc. Las Hadas, 72070 Puebla, Puebla

Tel: +52(222) 248-80-88

Fax: +52(222) 248-99-99

EMail: ejh@gemtel.com.mx

Website: http://pueblauniversitaria.mx/index.php/instituciones/item/escuela-de-jurisprudencia-y-humanidades-de-puebla

Rector: Luis Enrique Crispín Campos Ramírez (1996-)

Programmes

Administration (Administration); **Communication** (Communication Studies); **Criminology and Criminal Law** (Criminal Law; Criminology); **Gastronomy** (Cooking and Catering); **Law** (Constitutional Law; Fiscal Law; Law)

History: Founded 1996.

Main Language(s) of Instruction: Spanish

Degrees and Diplomas: *Licenciatura*; *Maestría*

Last Updated: 21/02/13

SCHOOL OF MARKETING, SALES AND PUBLICITY

Escuela de Mercadotecnia, Ventas y Publicidad

Calzada de Tlalpán, 1947, Col. Parque San Andrés, Delegación Coyoacán, 04040 México, D.F.

Tel: +52(55) 56-89-83-31 +52(55) 56-89-63-23

Director General: Guillermo Schwartau Salorio (1997-)

Programmes

Advertising and Publicity (Advertising and Publicity); **Marketing** (Marketing); **Sales Techniques** (Sales Techniques)

History: Founded 1997.

Main Language(s) of Instruction: Spanish

Degrees and Diplomas: *Licenciatura*

Last Updated: 21/02/13

SCHOOL OF NATURAL RESOURCE STUDIES

Escuela Superior de Recursos Naturales

Blvd. Ortiz Mena y Prolongación Sonora, Centro, 33800 Hidalgo del Parral, Chihuahua

Tel: +52(627) 272-12-09

Director: Carlos Enrique García Orozco (1989-)

Programmes

Natural Resources (Natural Resources)

History: Founded 1989

Main Language(s) of Instruction: Spanish

Degrees and Diplomas: *Licenciatura*

Last Updated: 04/04/08

SCHOOL OF NURSING OF THE HEALTH DEPARTMENT

Escuela de Enfermería de la Secretaría de la Salud

Av. Instituto Politécnico Nacional 5160, Col. Magdalena de las Salinas, Delegación Gustavo A. Madero, 07760 México, D.F.

Tel: +52(55) 57-47-76-25

Fax: +52(55) 57-47-76-27

Directora: Pascuala Olguín Tavera

Programmes

Nursing (Nursing)

Further Information: Branch in Miguel Hidalgo, Popotla

History: Founded 1968.

Degrees and Diplomas: *Licenciatura*

Last Updated: 27/05/09

SCHOOL OF PHYSICAL EDUCATION OF ORIZABA

Escuela Superior de Educación Física de Orizaba

Prolongación de Calle Jalapilla s/n, Benito Juárez, 94390 Orizaba, Veracruz

Tel: +52(272) 724-41-20 +52(272) 724-65-88

Fax: +52(272) 724-41-20

Website: http://eseforizaba.edu.mx

Director: Víctor Manuel Contreras Cuburu

Programmes

Physical Education (Physical Education)

History: Founded 1980.

Main Language(s) of Instruction: Spanish

Degrees and Diplomas: *Licenciatura*

Last Updated: 27/02/13

SCHOOL OF PHYSIOTHERAPY AND REHABILITATION

Escuela en Terapia Física y Rehabilitación

Felipe Lardizabal no. 1706, Col. San Martín, 90300 Apizaco, Tlaxcala

Tel: +52(241) 417-70-34

EMail: cri_apizaco@hotmail.com

Website: http://www.criescuela.org.mx

Directora General: Maria Antonieta Ordoñez Carrera

Programmes

Physiotherapy; **Rehabilitation and Therapy**

History: Founded 1995 as Escuela de Terapia Física y Rehabilitación Catalina Lima. Acquired present status and title 1999.

Main Language(s) of Instruction: Spanish

Degrees and Diplomas: *Licenciatura*

Last Updated: 22/02/13

SCHOOL OF POSTGRADUATE STUDIES IN INTEGRAL EDUCATION

Escuela de Estudios de Posgrado en Educación Integral

Enrique C. Rebsamen 1808, 2a Sección de Ciudad Satélite, 72320 Puebla, Puebla

Tel: +52(222) 243-0982

Fax: +52(222) 243-0982

EMail: escueladeposgrados@hotmail.com

Directora: Lucía del Carmen Bustos Aguilera (1999-)

Coordinador de Servicios Externos: Gabriel Osio Rodriguez Tel: +52(222) 287-1604

International Relations: Luz Raquel Sandoval Martínez, Coordinador de relaciones internacionales Tel: +52(222) 287-1604

Programmes

Organization Management (Management); **Sociology** (Sociology); **University Teaching** (Higher Education)

History: Founded 1997. Acquired present status 1998.

Admission Requirements: Licenciatura and good knowledge of English
Fees: (Pesos): 2,000 per semester; 1,500 per month
Main Language(s) of Instruction: Spanish
Degrees and Diplomas: *Maestría*
Student Services: Health services, Language programs, Sports facilities
Publications: El Renacimiento, Cultural Studies *(annually)*
Last Updated: 21/02/13

SCHOOL OF PSYCHOLOGY OF CIUDAD JUÁREZ

Escuela Superior de Psicología de Ciudad Juárez
Demián Carmona, 676 Sur, Col. El Barreal, 32040 Ciudad Juárez, Chihuahua
Tel: +52(656) 614-58-54
Fax: +52(656) 612-18-78
EMail: informacion@superiordepsicologia.com
Website: http://www.superiordepsicologia.com

Directora: Martha E. Cabada S.

Programmes
Psychology (Clinical Psychology; Psychology)
History: Founded 1982.
Main Language(s) of Instruction: Spanish
Degrees and Diplomas: *Licenciatura*; *Especialización*; *Maestría*
Last Updated: 27/02/13

SCHOOL OF SOCIAL WORK OF TIJUANA

Escuela de Trabajo Social de Tijuana
Apartado postal 885, Calzada de Guadalupe, 6, Fracc. La Villa, La Mesa, 22630 Tijuana, Baja California
Tel: +52(666) 686-89-11
Fax: +52(666) 686-89-11

Director: Roberto Barbara Camacho

Programmes
Social Work (Social Work)
Degrees and Diplomas: *Licenciatura*

SCHOOL OF THE GULF OF MEXICO

Escuela Superior del Golfo de México
2° Norte 251, Col. Centro, 75700 Tehuacán, Puebla
Tel: +52(238) 2-02-56
Fax: +52(238) 2-15-94
EMail: rreyes@mailorgam.educ.mx

Director General: Roberto Reyes Larios

Programmes
Business Administration (Business Administration); **Computer Science** (Computer Science); **Law** (Law); **Psychology** (Psychology); **Tourism Administration** (Administration; Tourism)
Main Language(s) of Instruction: Spanish
Degrees and Diplomas: *Licenciatura*
Last Updated: 27/02/13

SCHOOL OF THE PACIFIC

Escuela del Pacífico
Paseo del Centenario 9211, Pueblo Amigo, Zona del Rio, Tijuana, Baja California

Director: Jesús Alfonso León López

Programmes
Accountancy and Finance (Accountancy; Finance); **Business Administration** (Administration; Business Administration)
History: Founded 1983.
Main Language(s) of Instruction: Spanish
Degrees and Diplomas: *Licenciatura*; *Maestría*
Last Updated: 22/02/13

SCHOOL OF TOURISM OF THE REPUBLIC OF MEXICO

Escuela de Turismo de la República de México
Calle 72 No 453, esq. con Avenida Reforma, 97000 Mérida, Yucatán
Tel: +52(999) 923-06-01

Director: Felipe Hernández Rendón

Programmes
Tourism (Tourism)
Main Language(s) of Instruction: Spanish
Degrees and Diplomas: *Licenciatura*
Last Updated: 22/02/13

SCHOOL OF VETERINARY MEDICINE AND ZOOTECHNOLOGY, A.C.

Escuela Superior de Medicina Veterinaria y Zootecnia, A.C.
Calle Guadalupe Victoria #31, San Gregorio Atzompa, Cholula, Puebla
Tel: +52(222) 647-11-03
EMail: //supervet@prodigy.com.mx

Director General: Jesús Mario Labastida Gómez

Programmes
Veterinary Science (Animal Husbandry; Veterinary Science; Zoology)
History: Founded 1984.
Main Language(s) of Instruction: Spanish
Degrees and Diplomas: *Licenciatura*; *Especialización*
Last Updated: 27/02/13

SCIENTIFIC TECHNICAL AND EDUCATIONAL INSTITUTE

Instituto Científico Técnico y Educativo
San Francisco, 1526, Col. del Valle, Delegación Benito Juárez, 03100 México, D.F.
Tel: +52(55) 55-75-17-90
Fax: +52(55) 55-59-50-48
EMail: info@universidadicte.edu.mx
Website: http://www.universidadicte.edu.mx

Directora General: María Antonia Muñiz Escobedo (1992-)

Programmes
Accountancy (Accountancy); **Interior Design** (Interior Design); **Philosophy** (Philosophy)
History: Founded 1990.
Main Language(s) of Instruction: Spanish
Degrees and Diplomas: *Licenciatura*
Last Updated: 27/02/13

SIGLO XXI CENTRE FOR ADVANCED STUDIES

Centro de Estudios Superiores Siglo XXI, A.C.
Blvd. Agua Caliente, 12027, Entrada por Club Hípico, Tijuana, Baja California
Tel: +52(666) 634-10-51
Fax: +52(666) 634-10-51
EMail: sergiomonzon@hotmail.com

Directora: Yolanda Madrid Gómez Tagle
Degrees and Diplomas: *Licenciatura*
Last Updated: 04/04/08

SIGLO XXI INSTITUTE OF ADVANCED STUDIES

Instituto de Estudios Avanzados Siglo XXI
7 Poniente # 303, Centro Histórico, 72000 Puebla, Puebla
Tel: +52(222) 246-15-23
EMail: admisionbuap@sigloxxi.edu.mx
Website: http://www.sigloxxi.edu.mx/secciones/?se=55

Directora: Maria de Lourdes Nares Rodriguez
EMail: lourdes.nares@sigloxxi.edu.mx

Programmes
Communication Studies (Communication Studies); **Criminology** (Criminology); **International Relations** (International Relations); **Law** (Law); **Teaching of English** (English)

Degrees and Diplomas: *Licenciatura*

Libraries: Yes

Last Updated: 01/03/13

SIMÓN BOLÍVAR UNIVERSITY

Universidad Simón Bolívar (USB)

Avenida Río Mixcoac, 48, Col. Insurgentes, Mixcoac, Delegación Benito Juárez, 03920 México, D.F.
Tel: +52 (55) 5629-97-00
EMail: promocio@bolivar.usb.mx
Website: http://www.usb.edu.mx

Rectora: Clotilde Montoya Juárez (1990-)
EMail: rector@bolivar.usb.mx

Directora Académica: Laura Uribe Solís
EMail: luribe@bolivar.usb.mx

International Relations: Laura Uribe Solís, Academic Exchange Director

Faculties
Economics and Administration (Accountancy; Business Administration; Economics; International Business; Marketing); **Humanities** (Communication Studies; Multimedia); **Science and Technology** (Biology; Biotechnology; Chemistry; Computer Engineering; Electronic Engineering; Food Technology; Pharmacology)

History: Founded 1990.

Admission Requirements: Bachillerato

Main Language(s) of Instruction: Spanish

International Co-operation: With universities in Spain, Canada, Argentina

Degrees and Diplomas: *Licenciatura*: 4 yrs; *Especialización*; *Maestría*: 2 yrs

Student Services: Academic counselling, Cultural centre, Foreign student adviser, Foreign Studies Centre, Health services, Language programs, Nursery care, Social counselling, Sports facilities

Student Residential Facilities: Yes

Libraries: Biblioteca "Lic. Clotilde Montoya Juárez"

Last Updated: 23/10/12

SONORA INSTITUTE OF PUBLIC ADMINISTRATION

Instituto Sonorense de Administración Pública

Nicolás Bravo No. 29, Col. Centenario, 83260 Hermosillo, Sonora
Tel: +52(6) 217-36-02
EMail: isap_ac@hotmail.com
Website: http://www.isapac.org

Director: Edmundo Chávez Méndez

Programmes
Health Administration (Health Administration); **Public Administration** (Public Administration)

History: Founded 1990.

Main Language(s) of Instruction: Spanish

Degrees and Diplomas: *Maestría*; *Doctorado*

Libraries: Yes

Last Updated: 08/03/13

SOR JUANA INÉS DE LA CRUZ INSTITUTE OF HIGHER STUDIES

Instituto de Estudios Superiores Sor Juana Inés de la Cruz

17a. Oriente Sur, 890, Centro, 29000 Tuxtla Gutiérrez, Chiapas
Tel: +52(961) 613-79-26

Programmes
Business Computing (Business Computing); **Business Development** (Business Administration); **Computer Science** (Computer Science); **Economics** (Economics); **Nursing** (Nursing); **Tourism** (Tourism)

Degrees and Diplomas: *Licenciatura*
Last Updated: 04/03/13

SOR JUANA INÉS UNIVERSITY STUDIES CENTRE

Centro de Estudios Universitarios Sor Juana Inés

Libramiento, 4129, 38190 Morelia, Michoacán
Tel: +52(443) 26-27-37

Directora: Reynalda Herrejón López (1999-)

Programmes
Accountancy (Accountancy); **Business Computing** (Business Computing); **Pedagogy** (Pedagogy)

Further Information: Also branch in Uruapan

History: Founded 1999.

Main Language(s) of Instruction: Spanish

Degrees and Diplomas: *Licenciatura*
Last Updated: 14/03/08

SOUTHERN FRONTIER INSTITUTE OF HIGHER STUDIES

Instituto de Estudios Superiores Frontera Sur

2a. Oriente Norte, 169, Frontera Comalapa, 30140 Tuxtla Gutiérrez, Chiapas

Director: Arnoldo Hernández Mérida

Programmes
Administration (Administration); **Business Computing** (Business Computing); **Law** (Law)

Main Language(s) of Instruction: Spanish

Degrees and Diplomas: *Licenciatura*; *Maestría*
Last Updated: 04/03/13

SPANISH UNIVERSITY CENTRE

Centro Universitario Español

Calle Durango 121, Esq. Michoacán, Col. Progreso, 39350 Acapulco de Juárez, Guerrero
Tel: +52(744) 486-02-23
Fax: +52(744) 486-72-35
EMail: informes@cue.edu.mx
Website: http://www.cue.edu.mx

Director: Víctor M. Jorrin Lozano EMail: vjorrin@cue.edu.mx

Programmes
Accountancy (Accountancy); **Administration** (Administration; International Business); **Communication and Public Relations** (Communication Studies; Public Relations); **Computer Systems** (Software Engineering); **Design** (Graphic Design; Interior Design); **Journalism** (Journalism); **Law** (Criminology; Law); **Psychology** (Psychology)

History: Founded 1991.

Main Language(s) of Instruction: Spanish

Degrees and Diplomas: *Licenciatura*; *Maestría*
Last Updated: 25/07/12

SPECIALIZED INSTITUTE IN ADVERTISING

Instituto Especializado en Publicidad

Blvd. Adolfo López Mateos, 1139, 2° Piso, 37260 León, Guanajuato
Tel: +52(477) 713-82-44
Fax: +52(477) 713-82-44

Director: Francisco Javier Hernández Lozano

Programmes
Advertising and Publicity (Advertising and Publicity)
Degrees and Diplomas: *Licenciatura*
Last Updated: 04/04/08

SPECIALIZED INSTITUTE IN INTERNATIONAL BUSINESS

Instituto de Especialización en Comercio Exterior
Avenida Juárez, 3245, Ote., 27000 Torreón, Coahuila
Director: José Francisco Marcos Ávila

Programmes
International Business (International Business)
Main Language(s) of Instruction: Spanish
Degrees and Diplomas: *Licenciatura*
Last Updated: 21/02/08

TAJÍN UNIVERSITY

Universidad Tajín
Rafael Ramírez 4 Altos, Col. Unidad Veracruzana, 91030 Xalapa, Veracruz
Tel: +52(228) 820-33-36
Fax: +52(228) 820-33-36
EMail: info@utajin.edu.mx
Website: http://www.utajin.edu.mx/
Rector: René Garruña Sánchez EMail: rectoria@utajin.edu.mx

Programmes
Advertising and Public Relations (Advertising and Publicity; Business Administration); **Computer Science** (Computer Science); **Education** (Curriculum; Education; Educational Administration; Educational Psychology; Educational Research; Ethics; Philosophy; Philosophy of Education; Psychology; Statistics); **International Business Administration** (Accountancy; Business Administration; Civil Law; Commercial Law; Communication Studies; Computer Science; Cultural Studies; Fiscal Law; Human Resources; International Business; Marketing; Mathematics; Political Sciences; Public Relations; Small Business; Transport Management); **Law** (Administrative Law; Civil Law; Commercial Law; Constitutional Law; Criminal Law; Ecology; Economics; Environmental Management; Fiscal Law; Forensic Medicine and Dentistry; International Law; Law; Political Sciences; Private Law); **Tourism** (Accountancy; Administration; Business Administration; Commercial Law; Cooking and Catering; Finance; Food Science; Hotel and Restaurant; Human Resources; International Business; Labour Law; Law; Leisure Studies; Marketing; Parks and Recreation; Public Relations; Small Business; Tourism; Transport Management; Viticulture)
History: Founded 2003.
Main Language(s) of Instruction: Spanish
Degrees and Diplomas: *Licenciatura*
Libraries: Yes
Last Updated: 05/04/13

TAMAZUNCHALE UNIVERSITY

Universidad Tamazunchale
Boulevard 20 de Noviembre esq. con Belisario Domínguez, Barrio del Carmen, 79960 Tamazunchale, San Luis Potosí
Tel: +52(483) 362-21-07
EMail: unitam.tmz@live.com.mx
Website: http://www.unitam.edu.mx/
Rector: Cirilo Quintana Alvarado

Programmes
Accountancy (Accountancy); **Administration** (Administration); **Computer Systems** (Computer Science); **Higher Education Sciences** (Higher Education); **Law** (Law); **Social Work** (Social Work)
History: Founded 2004.
Main Language(s) of Instruction: Spanish
Degrees and Diplomas: *Licenciatura*
Last Updated: 24/10/12

TANGAMANGA UNIVERSITY

Universidad Tangamanga, S.C.
Avenida Fray Diego de la Magdalena, 42, Col. El Saucito, 78110 San Luis Potosí, San Luis Potosí
Tel: +52(444) 823-4900
Fax: +52(444) 823-4901
EMail: sanluis@utan.edu.mx
Website: http://www.universidadtangamanga.edu.mx/
Rector: Guillermo Arturo Casto Pérez EMail: rectoria@utan.edu.mx

Programmes
Accountancy (Accountancy); **Administration** (Administration; Business Administration); **Communication** (Communication Studies; Phonetics); **Law** (Administrative Law; Civil Law; Constitutional Law; Criminal Law; Labour Law; Law); **Nursing** (Nursing); **Pedagogy** (Pedagogy); **Physical Education and Sports** (Physical Education; Sports); **Psychology** (Psychology); **Social Work** (Social Work); **Teaching of Foreign Languages** (Modern Languages)
Further Information: Also Plantel Huasteca, Plantel Tequis, and Plantel Av. Industrias
History: Founded 1997.
Main Language(s) of Instruction: Spanish
Accrediting Agencies: FIMPES
Degrees and Diplomas: *Licenciatura*; *Maestría*
Libraries: Yes
Last Updated: 24/10/12

TBC UNIVERSITY

TBC Universidad
Blvd. Federico Benitez 500, (esq. con calle Ermita), El Pedregal, 22104 Tijuana, Baja California
Tel: +52(664) 621-71-11
EMail: vicerectoria@tbcuniversidad.net
Website: http://www.tecbc.mx

Programmes
Accountancy (Accountancy); **Business Administration** (Business Administration); **Commerce** (Business and Commerce); **Computer and Telecommunications Engineering** (Computer Engineering; Telecommunications Engineering); **Information Technology** (Information Technology); **Law** (Law); **Marketing** (Marketing); **Psychology** (Psychology); **Tourism, Hotel and Restaurant** (Hotel and Restaurant; Tourism)
Further Information: Campuses: Ensenada and Mexicali
History: Founded 1993 in Tecate. Moved to Tijuana 1995.
Main Language(s) of Instruction: Spanish
Degrees and Diplomas: *Licenciatura*; *Especialización*; *Maestría*
Last Updated: 22/03/13

TEC UNIVERSITY OF THE EAST

Universidad Tec de Oriente
Avenida 14 Poniente 517, Col. Centro, Puebla, Puebla
EMail: unitec.promocion@gmail.com
Website: http://www.unitecdeoriente.edu.mx
Rector: Rafael Arronte Vicario EMail: unitec.rectoria@gmail.com

Programmes
Architecture (Architecture); **Criminal Law** (Criminal Law); **Criminology** (Criminology); **Graphic Design** (Graphic Design); **Law** (Law); **Tourism** (Hotel Management; Tourism)
History: Founded 1994.
Main Language(s) of Instruction: Spanish
Degrees and Diplomas: *Licenciatura*
Last Updated: 24/10/12

TECHNOLOGICAL AND UNIVERSITY COLLEGE OF THE NORTH EAST

Colegio Universitario y Tecnológico del Noreste
Avenida Venustiano Carranza 614, Norte, Col. Centro, 64000 Monterrey, Nuevo León
Tel: +52(81) 88-64-00-99
Fax: +52(81) 88-64-08-64
EMail: amedellin@cutn.edu
Website: http://www.cutn.edu.mx

Rector: César Luis Peña Martínez EMail: cesarluis@cutn.edu.mx
General Adviser: Ruth Prado Rodríguez
EMail: rprado@cutn.edu.mx

Programmes

Administrative Computer Systems (Business Computing); **Communication** (Communication Studies); **Educational Psychology and School Administration** (Educational Administration; Educational Psychology); **Graphic Design** (Graphic Design); **Hotel and Tourism** (Hotel and Restaurant; Hotel Management; Tourism); **International Business** (International Business); **International Marketing** (Marketing); **Law** (Law); **Psychology** (Educational Psychology; Psychology); **Public Accountancy** (Accountancy)

History: Founded 1999. Acquired present status 2002.

Main Language(s) of Instruction: Spanish

Degrees and Diplomas: *Licenciatura*; *Maestría*

Libraries: 750 vols; 2 subscriptions to periodicals

Last Updated: 24/08/12

TECHNOLOGICAL INSTITUTE OF CONSTRUCTION STUDIES

Instituto Tecnológico de la Construcción
Avenida Rómulo O Farril, 480, Col. Olivar de los Padres, Delegación Álvaro Obregón, 01780 México, D.F.
Tel: +52(55) 56-68-16-76 +52(55) 56-68-14-99
Fax: +52(55) 56-68-11-06
EMail: admisionitc@itc-ac.edu.mx
Website: http://www.itc.org.mx

Director General: Gilberto Enrique Caballero Gutiérrez
EMail: gcaballero@itc-ac.edu.mx

Programmes

Architecture (Architecture); **Business Administration** (Business Administration); **Construction Engineering** (Construction Engineering; Road Engineering)

Further Information: Campuses in Tabasco and Oaxaca

History: Founded 1983.

Main Language(s) of Instruction: Spanish

Degrees and Diplomas: *Licenciatura*; *Maestría*

Last Updated: 13/03/13

TECHNOLOGICAL INSTITUTE OF FASHION DESIGN

Instituto Tecnológico de Diseño de Modas, A.C.
Juventino Rosas, 551, 36580 Irapuato, Guanajuato
Tel: +52(462) 626-13-92
Fax: +52(462) 626-13-92

Directora: María de la A. Padilla Hernández

Programmes

Fashion Design (Fashion Design)

Main Language(s) of Instruction: Spanish

Degrees and Diplomas: *Licenciatura*

Last Updated: 23/04/08

TECHNOLOGICAL INSTITUTE OF TELEPHONES OF MEXICO

Instituto Tecnológico de Teléfonos de México
Tepepán, 31, Col. Toriello Guerra Tlalpán, 14050 México, D.F.
Tel: +52(555) 665-19-19
Fax: +52(555) 666-00-38
EMail: inttelmex@telmex.com

Rector: Javier A. Elaguea Solís

Programmes

Telecommunications Engineering (Telecommunications Engineering)

Degrees and Diplomas: *Maestría*

Last Updated: 18/02/08

TECHNOLOGICAL INSTITUTE OF THE SOUTH EAST

Universidad Tecnológica del Sureste, S.C.
Avenida Gobernadores, 135, Esq. Calle 105-A, Col. Santa Lucía, 24000 Campeche, Campeche
Tel: +52(981) 5-04-98
EMail: cucsa29@hotmail.com
Website: http://www.unitsur.edu.mx

Rectora: Asucena Cuevas Fragoso

Programmes

Accountancy (Accountancy); **Computer Science** (Computer Science; Systems Analysis); **International Business** (International Business)

Further Information: Also campus in Coatzacoalcos

History: Founded 1995.

Main Language(s) of Instruction: Spanish

Degrees and Diplomas: *Licenciatura*

Last Updated: 07/04/08

TECHNOLOGICAL UNIVERSITY OF MEXICO

Universidad Tecnológica de México (UNITEC)
Av. Marina Nacional No. 162, Col. Anáhuac, 11320 México, D.F.
Website: http://www.unitec.mx

Rector: Manuel Campuzano Treviño

Areas

Administration and Economics (Administration; Business Administration; Finance; Fiscal Law; Human Resources; Management; Marketing; Service Trades; Social Sciences); **Arts for Design** (Architecture; Graphic Design); **Engineering** (Civil Engineering; Computer Engineering; Electronic Engineering; Environmental Engineering; Industrial Engineering; Mechanical Engineering; Robotics; Telecommunications Engineering); **Health Sciences** (Dentistry; Nursing; Nutrition; Physical Therapy; Psychology; Surgery); **Hospitality and Tourism** (Hotel and Restaurant; Tourism); **Social Sciences** (Advertising and Publicity; Law; Pedagogy; Social Sciences)

Further Information: Campuses in Atizapán, Cuitláhuac, Ecatepec, Toluca, Marina and Sur.

History: Founded 1966.

Governing Bodies: Junta de Gobierno

Academic Year: September to August (September-December; January-April; May-August)

Admission Requirements: Secondary school certificate (bachillerato) and entrance examination

Main Language(s) of Instruction: Spanish

Accrediting Agencies: Secretaria de Educación Pública; Federación de Instituciones Mexicanas Particulares de Educación Superior FIMPES)

Degrees and Diplomas: *Licenciatura (Lic)*: 3-4 yrs; *Especialización*; *Maestria*: a further 2 yrs

Student Services: Academic counselling, Canteen, Cultural centre, Employment services, Handicapped facilities, Health services, Language programs, Nursery care, Social counselling

Libraries: 4 libraries. Total, c. 60,000 vols

Publications: Enlace *(monthly)*

Press or Publishing House: Comunitec

Last Updated: 05/04/13

TECHNOLOGICAL UNIVERSITY OF SINALOA

Universidad Tecnológica de Sinaloa

Antonio Rosales, 373, 80000 Culiacán, Sinaloa
Tel: +52(667) 715-27-85
EMail: dif_cultural@unitesin.com
Website: http://www.unitesin.com

Rector: Carlos Héctor Camacho Robledo

Programmes
Design (Design; Graphic Arts; Graphic Design; Interior Design); **International Relations** (International Relations); **Tourism** (Tourism)

History: Founded 1986 as Universidad Femenina de Sinaloa. Acquired present title 1996.

Admission Requirements: Bachillerato

Main Language(s) of Instruction: Spanish

Degrees and Diplomas: *Licenciatura*

Last Updated: 05/04/13

TECHNOLOGICAL UNIVERSITY OF THE CENTRE OF MEXICO

Universidad Tecnológica del Centro de México, S.C.

Gaspar de Almanza, 100, Fracc. Exelaris, 38010 Celaya, Guanajuato
Tel: +52(461) 613-36-66
Fax: +52(461) 613-83-87
EMail: derecho@utec.edu.mx
Website: http://www.utec-celaya.edu.mx

Rector: Elidier Sánchez Aguilar

Programmes
Accountancy (Accountancy; Commercial Law; Labour Law); **Computer Science** (Business Computing; Computer Networks; Computer Science); **Industrial Administration** (Accountancy; Industrial Management; Labour and Industrial Relations; Taxation); **Industrial Design** (Industrial Design; Photography); **Law** (Administrative Law; Civil Law; Commercial Law; Constitutional Law; Criminal Law); **Marketing and International Trade** (International Business; Marketing)

History: Founded 1997.

Main Language(s) of Instruction: Spanish

Degrees and Diplomas: *Licenciatura*; *Maestría*

TECHNOLOGICAL UNIVERSITY OF VERACRUZ

Universidad Tecnológica de Veracruz

Hidalgo, 471, 91700 Heroica Veracruz, Veracruz
Tel: +52(229) 931-30-75

Director: Jesús Moctezuma Estefa

Degrees and Diplomas: *Licenciatura*

TECMILENIO UNIVERSITY

Universidad TecMilenio

Carretera a Puerto Madero Km. 4.5, Esquina Libramiento Sur, 30790 Tapachula, Chiapas
Tel: +52(962) 628-16-22
Website: http://www.tecmilenio.edu.mx

Rector: Héctor Mauricio Escamilla Santana

Programmes
Business (Administration; Business Administration; Cooking and Catering; Finance; Hotel Management; International Business; Marketing; Tourism); **Engineering** (Business Administration; Computer Engineering; Electronic Engineering; Engineering; Finance; Industrial Engineering; International Business); **Health Sciences** (Nursing; Nutrition; Psychology); **Humanities and Social Sciences** (Law); **Information Technology**

Further Information: 40 campuses in 21 states and online campus

History: Founded 2002.

Main Language(s) of Instruction: Spanish

Degrees and Diplomas: *Licenciatura*; *Maestría*

Last Updated: 24/10/12

TECNOLÓGICO UNIVERSITARIO DE MÉXICO - UNIVERSIDAD

Avenida Azcapotzalco, 308, Col. Clavería, Delegación Azcapotzalco, 02090 México, D.F.
Tel: +52(55) 55-61-86-46 +52(55) 53-52-47-80
Fax: +52(55) 53-53-43-60
EMail: informes@tum.edu.mx
Website: http://www.tum.edu.mx

Director General: Salvador Rocha Segura

Programmes
Accountancy (Accountancy); **Administration** (Administration; Business Administration); **Computer Science** (Computer Science); **Law** (Law); **Psychology** (Psychology)

History: Founded 1959.

Degrees and Diplomas: *Licenciatura*

Last Updated: 25/10/12

TECOMÁN INSTITUTE OF HIGHER EDUCATION

Instituto de Educación Superior de Tecomán

Km. 1 Carretera Costera Tecomán-Playa Azul, 28100 Tecomán, Colima
Tel: +52(313) 134-30-37
EMail: ieatac@cu.gdl.mx

Director: Jesús Murguía

Programmes
Accountancy (Accountancy); **Business Administration** (Business Administration); **Computer Science** (Computer Science); **Law** (Law)

Degrees and Diplomas: *Licenciatura*

Last Updated: 28/02/13

TECPATL CENTRE OF ADVANCED STUDIES

Tecpatl Centro de Estudios Superiores

Galana 168, 47600 Tepatitlán de Morelos, Jalisco
Tel: +52(378) 781-41-61
Fax: +52(378) 781-41-61
EMail: berthadeanda3@hotmail.com

Directora: Bertha Josefina de Anda Gómez

Courses
Industrial Design (Graphic Design; Industrial Design); **Interior Design** (Interior Design)

History: Founded 2004.

Main Language(s) of Instruction: Spanish

Degrees and Diplomas: *Licenciatura*

Last Updated: 25/03/13

TEHUACÁN SCHOOL OF HIGHER EDUCATION

Escuela de Estudios Superiores de Tehuacán, A.C.

Priv. Dr. Bentazo, 27, Col. Centro, 75700 Tehuacán, Puebla
Tel: +52(238) 383-54-60
Fax: +52(238) 383-37-70
EMail: ceut@cath.com.mx

Director General: Clemente Cid Pérez (1990-)

Programmes
Computer Science (Computer Science)

Degrees and Diplomas: *Bachillerato*; *Licenciatura*

Last Updated: 03/04/08

TELEDDES FOUNDATION (TELECOMMUNICATIONS FOR EDUCATION AND DEVELOPMENT)

Fundación Teleddes (Telecomunicación para Educación y Desarrollo)

Av. Punta Banda 141, Fracc. Chapultepec, 22870 Ensenada, Baja California
EMail: info@fundacionteleddes.org
Website: http://www.fundacionteleddes.org

Director Ejecutivo: Arturo Serrano Santoyo

Directora Administrativa: Patricia Ramonetti Chávez

Programmes
Telecommunications and Information Networks (Computer Networks; Telecommunications Engineering)

History: Founded 1998.

Main Language(s) of Instruction: Spanish

Degrees and Diplomas: *Licenciatura*; *Maestría*

Last Updated: 30/08/12

TEPEYAC INSTITUTE

Instituto Tepeyac

Tres Guerras, 113 y 115, Zona Centro, 37000 León, Guanajuato
Tel: +52(477) 716-99-14
Fax: +52(477) 716-62-69
EMail: itac-leon@hotmail.com
Website: http://www.ites.edu.mx

Directora General: Margarita Morales Manrique (1990-)

Programmes
Education (Education)

Degrees and Diplomas: *Licenciatura*

TEPEYAC INSTITUTE OF HIGHER STUDIES - CUAUTITLÁN CAMPUS

Instituto Tepeyac de Estudios Superiores - Campus Cuautitlán

Manuel Ávila Camacho s/n, Santiago Tepalcapa, 54769 Cuautitlán Izcalli, Estado de México
Tel: +52(55) 58-81-25-80 +52(55) 58-81-25-82
Website: http://www.itc.edu.mx

Director: Guillermo Manzo Mercado (1991-)

Programmes
Business Administration and Law; **Computer Science** (Computer Science)

Degrees and Diplomas: *Licenciatura*

TERRANOVA UNIVERSITY

Universidad Terranova

Mariano Matamoros, 820, Col. Francisco Murguía, 50130 Toluca, Estado de México
Tel: +52(722) 22-12-34-86
Fax: +52(722) 22-12-28-20
EMail: uniterr@hotmail.com

Rector: Jorge Sánchez Mondragón

Programmes
Accountancy (Accountancy); **Business Administration** (Business Administration); **Business Computing** (Business Computing); **Law** (Law)

History: Founded 1999.

Main Language(s) of Instruction: Spanish

Degrees and Diplomas: *Licenciatura*

Last Updated: 05/04/13

THE AMERICAS INSTITUTE OF HIGHER STUDIES

Instituto de Estudios Superiores Las Américas, A.C.

Calle 71, 539 x 52 y 78, Col. Centro, 97000 Mérida, Yucatán
Tel: +52(999) 924-41-28

Director: Gabriel de Jesús León Carrillo

Programmes
Accountancy (Accountancy); **Business Administration** (Administration; Business Administration; Tourism); **Journalism** (Journalism)

Main Language(s) of Instruction: Spanish

Degrees and Diplomas: *Licenciatura*

Last Updated: 04/03/13

THE AMERICAS INSTITUTE OF NAYARIT

Instituto Las Américas de Nayarit

Mar Rojo No. 45, Col. Pedregal, 63164 Tepic, Nayarit
Tel: +52(311) 213-01-00
EMail: ilan.edu@gmail.com
Website: http://www.ilan.com.mx/

Directora: Rodelina Mendoza Velazquez.

Programmes
Education (Education; Educational Psychology; Educational Sciences; Educational Technology; Pedagogy; Physical Education; Sports); **Engineering** (Computer Engineering; Electronic Engineering; Engineering; Industrial Engineering; Telecommunications Engineering); **Humanities** (Psychology); **Social Sciences and Administration** (Accountancy; Communication Studies; International Business; Law; Physical Education; Political Sciences; Public Administration)

History: Founded 1985.

Main Language(s) of Instruction: Spanish

Degrees and Diplomas: *Licenciatura*; *Maestría*; *Doctorado*

Last Updated: 06/03/13

THE COLLEGE OF LEON

El Colegio de León, A.C.

Avenida Guanajuato, 139, Jardines del Moral, 37160 León, Guanajuato
Tel: +52(477) 718-07-23
Fax: +52(477) 717-72-08
EMail: info@colegiodeleon.edu.mx
Website: http://www.colegiodeleon.edu.mx

Director: Juan Jauregui Jiménez

Programmes
Accountancy (Accountancy); **Business Administration** (Administration; Business Administration; Finance; International Business); **International Business** (International Business); **Marketing** (Marketing); **Philosophy** (Philosophy); **Social Sciences** (Political Sciences; Psychology)

Degrees and Diplomas: *Licenciatura*; *Maestría*; *Doctorado*

Last Updated: 27/08/12

THIRD MILLENNIUM INSTITUTE OF TECHNICAL BASIC, INTERMEDIATE AND HIGHER EDUCATION

Instituto de Enseñanza Basica Tecnica Media y Superior Tercer Milenio

Av. México No 4982 A - Col. Juan Manuel Vallarta, 44120 Zapopan, Jalisco
Tel: +52(33) 31-21-71-73
EMail: itemac@hotmail.com

Director: Rúben Orendain Guerra

Programmes
Education (Curriculum; Education; Educational Research; Pedagogy)

History: Founded 1999.

Main Language(s) of Instruction: Spanish

Degrees and Diplomas: *Maestría*

Last Updated: 28/02/13

THOMAS AQUINAS CENTRE FOR STUDIES IN PHILOSOPHY

Centro de Estudios Filosóficos Tomás de Aquino
Avenida Palmas y Chiapas s/n, Col. Arbide, 37360 León, Guanajuato
Tel: +52(477) 713-34-10
Fax: +52(477) 714-58-29
EMail: centrocefta@prodigy.net.mx
Website: http://www.filosofiacefta.com

Director: Jesús García Álvarez (2001-)

Programmes
Philosophy (Philosophy)

History: Founded 1992. Acquired present status 1996.

Main Language(s) of Instruction: Spanish

Degrees and Diplomas: *Licenciatura*. Also Diplomados

Libraries: Yes

Publications: Revista Filosófica

Last Updated: 13/07/12

TLAMATINI INSTITUTE

Instituto Tlamatini
Cantador, 9, Centro, 36000 Guanajuato, Guanajuato
Tel: +52(473) 732-21-96
Fax: +52(473) 732-21-96

Director General: Fidencio Váldez Alvarado (2002-)

History: Founded 1997.

Main Language(s) of Instruction: Spanish

Degrees and Diplomas: *Licenciatura*

TOMINAGA NAKAMOTO UNIVERSITY

Universidad Tominaga Nakamoto
Luis Freg, 12, Lomas de Sotelo, 53390 Naucalpán de Juárez, Estado de México
Tel: +52(55) 53-59-12-54
Fax: +52(55) 53-58-15-06
EMail: cleliamarquezcanales@yahoo.com.mx
Website: http://utominaga.edu.mx/utominaga

Rectora: Clelia Márquez Canales (1999-)

Programmes
Accountancy (Accountancy); **Business Administration** (Business Administration); **Computer Science** (Computer Science); **Educational Sciences** (Educational Sciences); **Gastronomy** (Cooking and Catering); **Law** (Law); **Medicine** (Medicine; Surgery)

History: Founded 1999 as Escuela de Medicina Tominaga Nakamoto. Acquired present status 2008.

Main Language(s) of Instruction: Spanish

Degrees and Diplomas: *Licenciatura*

Last Updated: 21/02/13

TORRES ANDRADE UNIVERSITY CENTRE

Centro Universitario Torres Andrade, A.C.
Mariano Bárcenas, 168, Col. Centro, 44150 Guadalajara, Jalisco
Tel: +52(33) 36-13-21-74
Fax: +52(33) 36-13-53-90

Director General: Luis Alberto Preciado Montero

Degrees and Diplomas: *Licenciatura*

Last Updated: 04/04/08

TOTAL TOURISM TECHNOLOGY

Tecnología Turística Total, A.C.
Calle 57 No 492, entre 56 y 58, Col. Centro, 97000 Mérida, Yucatán
Tel: +52(999) 928-35-15
Fax: +52(999) 923-24-29
EMail: infotttac@prodigy.net.mx
Website: http://www.tttac.com

Director: Jorge Carlos Rosado Baeza

Programmes
Business Administration (Business Administration); **Modern Languages** (English; French; Modern Languages; Spanish); **Multimedia** (Multimedia); **Tourism** (Tourism)

History: Founded 1990.

Main Language(s) of Instruction: Spanish

Degrees and Diplomas: *Licenciatura*

Last Updated: 28/08/12

TRAINING AND RESEARCH INSTITUTE IN PSYCHOTHERAPY

Instituto de Entrenamiento e Investigación en Psicoterapia
Capuchinas No. 10-104, Colonia San Jose Insurgentes Benito Juárez, 03310 México, D.F.
EMail: informes@institutopersonas.org
Website: http://www.institutopersonas.org

Directora: Lina Martinez Negrete Cornejo

Programmes
Psychotherapy (Psychotherapy)

History: Founded 1997.

Main Language(s) of Instruction: Spanish

Degrees and Diplomas: *Especialización*

Last Updated: 28/02/13

TRAINING INSTITUTE IN PSYCHOTHERAPY

Instituto de Entrenamiento en Psicoterapias, A.C.
Delfino Valenzuela s/n, Veracruz, Veracruz
Tel: +52(229) 937-10-73

Director: Camerino Vázquez Martínez

Programmes
Psychotherapy (Family Studies; Psychotherapy)

Main Language(s) of Instruction: Spanish

Degrees and Diplomas: *Especialización*

Last Updated: 28/02/13

TUXTLA UNIVERSITY OF ADVANCED STUDIES

Universidad de Estudios Superiores deTuxtla
Palma Camedor, 509, Col. Las Palmas, 29000 Tuxtla Gutiérrez, Chiapas
Tel: +52(961) 614-03-29
Fax: +52(961) 614-03-29

Rector: Jesús Arturo Yañez Reyes

Programmes
Communication Studies (Communication Studies); **Criminology** (Criminology); **Law** (Civil Law; Constitutional Law; Criminal Law; Law); **Psychology** (Clinical Psychology; Educational Psychology; Industrial and Organizational Psychology); **Tourism** (Tourism)

Main Language(s) of Instruction: Spanish

Degrees and Diplomas: *Licenciatura*; *Maestría*; *Doctorado*

Last Updated: 28/08/12

UNIVER UNIVERSITY

Universidad UNIVER
Avenida de las Rosas, 171, Col. Chapalita, 45000 Guadalajara, Jalisco
Tel: +52(33) 3540-16-45
Fax: +52(33) 3540-16-19
EMail: jramirez@universidad-niver.edu.mx
Website: http://www.univer.com.mx

Rector: Pedro Ernesto Gómez Limón y González

Divisions
Business Administration (Business Administration; Cooking and Catering; International Business; Tourism); **Communication, Design and Merchandising** (Communication Studies; Design; Fashion Design; Marketing); **Engineering** (Industrial Engineering; Structural Architecture); **Informatics and Computer Systems** (Computer Engineering; Information Technology); **Law and**

Accounting (Accountancy; Law); **Psychology and Education** (Child Care and Development; Education; Pedagogy; Psychology)

Further Information: Also branches in Tonalá; Tlaquepaque; Zapopan

History: Founded 1955 as Escuela de Decoración Veracruz de Guadalajara. Acquired present status 1987. Formerly known as Centro de Estudios Universitarios Veracruz 'UNIVER'.

Governing Bodies: Regent's Board

Admission Requirements: Bachillerato

Main Language(s) of Instruction: Spanish

Accrediting Agencies: Secretaría de Educación Pública

Degrees and Diplomas: *Licenciatura*: Business Administration; International Business and Taxation; Tourism; Gastronomy; Communication Studies; Graphic Design; Marketing; Administrative Computing; Structural Architecture; Psychology; Pedagogy; Law; Public Accountancy, 3 yrs; *Licenciatura*: Computer Systems; Industrial Engineering; Preschool Education;, 4 yrs; *Especialización*: Strategic Business Planning; Business Consulting; Quality Management; Programming; Networks and Internet; Creativity Development; Teaching Methodology; Commercial Law; Penal Law; Taxation; International Business; Small Business Administration, 1 yr; *Maestría*: Leadership; Business Administration; Organisational Psychology, 2 yrs

Student Services: Academic counselling, Employment services, Handicapped facilities, Social counselling

Special Facilities: Movie Labs; Computer Labs; Radio Broadcasting Labs

Libraries: One in every campus

Last Updated: 16/11/12

UNIVERSITY AND OPEN EDUCATION SYSTEMS OF IRAPUATO

Universidad y Sistemas Educativos Abiertos de Irapuato

Avenida San Miguel 573, Vasco de Quiroga, 36666 Irapuato, Guanajuato

Tel: +52(462) 625-45-31

Fax: +52(462) 625-45-31

EMail: palacios_adventista@hotmail.com

Directora: Laura Lares Quinto

Programmes

Accountancy (Accountancy); **Business Administration** (Business Administration); **Law** (Law)

Main Language(s) of Instruction: Spanish

Degrees and Diplomas: *Licenciatura*

Last Updated: 15/04/11

UNIVERSITY CENTRE CORAL REEF-CARIBE

Avenida Kuklcaán Km 12.5 Zona Hotelera, Col. Centro Empresarial, 75500 Cancún, Quintana Roo

Programmes

Gastronomy (Cooking and Catering); **Hotel Management**; **International Relations**; **Psychology**; **Tourism**

Degrees and Diplomas: *Licenciatura*

Last Updated: 10/11/09

UNIVERSITY CENTRE FOR COMMERCE AND DIPLOMACY OF ZACATECAS

Centro Universitario de Negocios y Diplomacia de Zacatecas

Ledesma, 210, Col. Centro, 98000 Zacatecas, Zacatecas

Tel: +52(492) 924-34-41

Fax: +52(492) 924-34-41

EMail: cundzac@prodigy.net.mx

Presidenta: Martha Elvia Ortiz Espinoza (1999-)

Programmes

History (History); **International Business** (International Business); **Private Law** (Private Law)

History: Founded 1999.

Degrees and Diplomas: *Licenciatura*: 8 sem.; *Especialización*: 2 sem.

Last Updated: 27/03/08

UNIVERSITY CENTRE FOR EDUCATION AND CULTURE

Centro Universitario Educativo y Cultural (CUEC)

Hidalgo 205 c/Padre Mier, Zona Centro, San Nicolás de Los Garza, Nuevo León

Tel: +52(81) 81-34-54-01 +52(81) 81-30-07-73

Fax: +52(81) 81-34-54-01

EMail: informacion@cuec.edu.mx

Website: http://www.unicuec.com

Programmes

Business Administration (Business Administration); **Marketing** (Marketing)

History: Founded 2001.

Admission Requirements: Secondary school certificate

Main Language(s) of Instruction: Spanish

Degrees and Diplomas: *Licenciatura*

Last Updated: 25/07/12

UNIVERSITY CENTRE FOR JOURNALISM AND ADVERTISING STUDIES

Centro Universitario en Periodismo y Publicidad

Avenida Chapultepec, 133, 1°Piso, Col. Juárez, Delegación Cuauhtémoc, 06600 México, D.F.

Tel: +52(55) 55-35-99-40

Website: http://www.cupp.edu.mx

Director General: C. Alejandro Tovar Urbina (1992-)

Programmes

Business Administration (Business Administration); **Journalism** (Journalism); **Marketing and Publicity** (Advertising and Publicity; Marketing)

History: Founded 1992.

Main Language(s) of Instruction: Spanish

Degrees and Diplomas: *Licenciatura*; *Especialización*

Last Updated: 13/03/08

UNIVERSITY CENTRE FOR STUDIES IN LANGUAGES, TOURISM AND SERVICES

Centro Universitario en Lenguas, Turismo y Empresas de Servicio

Calle Vulcano, 10, Fracc. Parque América, Col. Delicias, 62330 Cuernavaca, Morelos

Tel: +52(777) 322-29-50

Fax: +52(777) 322-59-57

EMail: director@cultures.com.mx

Website: http://www.cultures.edu.mx

Director General: Fernando Ariño Oliveros

Programmes

Hotel and Restaurant; **Modern Languages** (Modern Languages); **Tourism**

History: Founded 1992.

Main Language(s) of Instruction: Spanish

Degrees and Diplomas: *Licenciatura*. Also Diplomados

Last Updated: 25/07/12

UNIVERSITY CENTRE IN MARKETING AND ADVERTISING STUDIES

Centro Universitario de Mercadotecnia y Publicidad

Cerrada de la Florecita No. 1, Col. Santa Cruz del Monte, Col. Lomas Verdes, 53120 Naucalpán de Juárez, Estado de México

Tel: +52(55) 53-93-30-50

Website: http://www.cump.edu.mx

Directora General: Claudia Ruiz Mogel (2000-)

EMail: claudia@cump.edu.mx

Programmes
Advertising (Advertising and Publicity); **Communication** (Communication Studies); **Design** (Graphic Design); **Marketing** (Marketing)
History: Founded 1999.
Main Language(s) of Instruction: Spanish
Degrees and Diplomas: *Licenciatura*; *Maestría*. Also Diplomados
Libraries: Yes
Last Updated: 24/07/12

UNIVERSITY CENTRE OF ART EDUCATION

Centro Universitario de Educación Artística
Calle Cupil s/n, Centro, 39170 Tixtla de Guerrero, Guerrero
Tel: +52(754) 544-11-90
Fax: +52(754) 544-11-90

Director: Lorenzo Urzúa Rodríguez

Programmes
Art Education (Art Education)
Main Language(s) of Instruction: Spanish
Degrees and Diplomas: *Licenciatura*
Last Updated: 01/04/08

UNIVERSITY CENTRE OF ART, TECHNOLOGY AND EDUCATION

Centro Universitario de Arte, Tecnología y Educación
36, Pte., 519, Santa María, Puebla, Puebla

Directora: Lidia Victoria Ruiz Escobar

Programmes
Art (Fine Arts); **Education** (Education); **Technology** (Technology)
Degrees and Diplomas: *Licenciatura*
Last Updated: 04/04/08

UNIVERSITY CENTRE OF BUSINESS MANAGEMENT

Centro Universitario de Dirección Empresarial y de Negocios (CUDEN)
Calle del Prado, 119, Col. Jardines del Moral, León, Guanajuato
Tel: +52(477) 718-1887
Fax: +52(477) 717-0562
Website: http://cuden.edu.mx

Director General: Noé Mosqueda Martínez

Programmes
Business Administration, Accountancy, Finance and Human Resources (Accountancy; Administration; Business Administration; Business Computing; Commercial Law; Communication Studies; Computer Science; Constitutional Law; Finance; Fiscal Law; Human Resources; International Business; Labour Law; Law; Marketing; Mathematics; Social Studies; Statistics; Taxation)
History: Founded 1995.
Degrees and Diplomas: *Licenciatura*: 8-9 sem.; *Maestría*
Last Updated: 23/10/09

UNIVERSITY CENTRE OF CHIHUAHUA

Centro Universitario de Chihuahua
Sor Juana Inés de la Cruz, 2306, Col. Altavista, 31030 Chihuahua, Chihuahua
Tel: +52(614) 413-93-67
Fax: +52(614) 413-93-67
EMail: centrounivchih@yahoo.com.mx

Directora: Olga Graciela Ríos Ríos

Programmes
Accountancy (Accountancy); **Business Administration**; **Marketing**
Main Language(s) of Instruction: Spanish
Degrees and Diplomas: *Licenciatura*
Last Updated: 11/03/08

UNIVERSITY CENTRE OF CIUDAD JUÁREZ

Centro Universitario de Ciudad Juárez
Avena 8611 Colonia El Granjero, 32690 Ciudad Juárez, Chihuahua
Tel: +52(614) 623-03-67
Website: http://www.cucj.com

Director: Rodolfo Acosta Benavides

Programmes
Business Administration (Business Administration); **Customs Administration** (Administration; Taxation); **Environmental Engineerng** (Environmental Engineering); **Law** (Law); **Production Engineering** (Production Engineering)
Further Information: Also campuses in Chihuahua and Vila Ahumada
History: Founded 1996.
Main Language(s) of Instruction: Spanish
Degrees and Diplomas: *Licenciatura*
Libraries: Yes
Last Updated: 24/07/12

UNIVERSITY CENTRE OF EASTERN HIDALGO

Centro Universitario del Oriente de Hidalgo
Avenida Juárez Sur, 101-B, 43600 Tulancingo, Hidalgo
Tel: +52(775) 755-48-05
Website: http://www.cuoh.edu.mx

Director: Francisco Javier Fragoso Silva

Programmes
Business Computing (Business Computing); **Landscape and Sustainable Tourism** (Landscape Architecture; Tourism); **Law** (Law); **Pedagogy** (Pedagogy)
History: Founded 1997.
Main Language(s) of Instruction: Spanish
Degrees and Diplomas: *Licenciatura*; *Maestría*
Last Updated: 24/07/12

UNIVERSITY CENTRE OF HIDALGO

Centro Universitario Hidalguense
Boulevard del Minero No 305, Col. Rojo Gómez, Pachuca, Hidalgo
Website: http://www.cuh.edu.mx

Programmes
Accountancy (Accountancy); **Administration** (Administration); **Law** (Law); **Psychology** (Psychology)
Main Language(s) of Instruction: Spanish
Degrees and Diplomas: *Licenciatura*
Last Updated: 24/07/12

UNIVERSITY CENTRE OF HUMAN INTEGRATION

Centro Universitario de Integración Humanística
Colibrí, 6, Lomas Verdes, 1a Sección Naucalpán, 53120 Naucalpán de Juárez, Estado de México
Tel: +52(555) 343-2496
EMail: contacto@cuih.edu.mx
Website: http://www.cuih.org

Rectora: María del Pilar Galindo López Portillo de Cordero (1969-)

Programmes
Human Sciences (Art Education; Art History; History; Literature; Philosophy; Sociology)
History: Founded 1969 as Asociación Satélite de Estudios Culturales, (ASEC). Became Centro Universitario ASEC Sor Juana. Acquired present title 1995.
Main Language(s) of Instruction: Spanish
Degrees and Diplomas: *Licenciatura*; *Maestría*. Also Diplomados
Last Updated: 24/07/12

UNIVERSITY CENTRE OF IXTLAHUACA

Centro Universitario de Ixtlahuaca, A.C.
Km. 1 Carretera Ixtlahuaca-Jiquipilco, 50740 Ixtlahuaca, Estado de México
Tel: +52(712) 123-03-65
Fax: +52(712) 123-03-65
EMail: contacto.cui@gmail.com
Website: http://www.ceui.com.mx

Director: Margarito Ortega Ballesteros

Programmes
Accountancy; **Administration** (Administration); **Architecture** (Architecture); **Communication** (Communication Studies); **Computer Science** (Computer Science); **Dental Surgery** (Dentistry; Surgery); **Graphic Design** (Graphic Design); **Law** (Law); **Psychology** (Psychology)

History: Founded 1993 as Centro Universitario"Químico José Donaciano Morales" A. C.

Main Language(s) of Instruction: Spanish

Degrees and Diplomas: *Licenciatura*; *Maestría*
Last Updated: 24/07/12

UNIVERSITY CENTRE OF MAZATLAN

Centro Universitario de Mazatlán
Apartado postal 275, Calle Cruz, 2, Paseo Olas Altas, Centro, 82000 Mazatlán, Sinaloa
Tel: +52(669) 982-69-88
Fax: +52(669) 981-73-04

Director General: Ernesto Magaña Velarde (1991-)

Programmes
Accountancy and Administration (Accountancy; Administration); **Law** (Law)

History: Founded 1991.

Main Language(s) of Instruction: Spanish

Degrees and Diplomas: *Licenciatura*
Last Updated: 11/03/08

UNIVERSITY CENTRE OF PHYSICAL EDUCATION

Centro Universitario de Educación Física
Sufragio Efectivo, 171, Col. Emiliano Zapata, Cuautla, 62744 Coquimatlán, Morelos
Tel: +52(735) 358-02-37
Fax: +52(735) 358-02-37

Director: Roberto M. Botello Monroy (1999-)

Programmes
Physical Education (Physical Education)

History: Founded 1999.

Main Language(s) of Instruction: Spanish

Degrees and Diplomas: *Licenciatura*
Last Updated: 31/03/08

UNIVERSITY CENTRE OF PUEBLA

Centro Universitario de Puebla, A.C.
5-A Sur, 4717, Col. Gabriel Pastor, 72420 Puebla, Puebla
Tel: +52(222) 242-01-82
Fax: +52(222) 243-85-79

Directora: Eugenia Escamilla Navarro

Programmes
Psychology (Psychology)

Degrees and Diplomas: *Licenciatura*
Last Updated: 04/04/08

UNIVERSITY CENTRE OF SALINA CRUZ

Centro Universitario Salina Cruz
Guaymas, 35, Col. Centro, 70600 Salina Cruz, Oaxaca
Tel: +52(971) 513-12-09 +52(971) 515-08-23
EMail: slunava@hotmail.com

Rector: Ricardo Maravilla Méndez (1997-)

Programmes
Business Administration and Law (Business Administration; Law); **Computer Science** (Computer Science); **Industrial Engineering** (Industrial Engineering)

History: Founded 1997.

Main Language(s) of Instruction: Spanish

Degrees and Diplomas: *Licenciatura*
Last Updated: 14/03/08

UNIVERSITY CENTRE OF TENANGO DEL VALLE

Centro Universitario Tenango del Valle
Patriotismo, 107, Centro, Tenango de Arista, 52300 Tenango del Valle, Estado de México
Tel: +52(717) 174-03-13
EMail: cutvac@prodigy.net.mx
Website: http://www.cutvac.edu.mx

Director: Alfredo Rosales García

Programmes
Accountancy (Accountancy); **Administration** (Administration); **Business Computing** (Business Computing); **Computer Engineering** (Computer Engineering); **Law** (Law)

Main Language(s) of Instruction: Spanish

Degrees and Diplomas: *Licenciatura*. Also Diplomado in Criminology

Libraries: Yes
Last Updated: 27/07/12

UNIVERSITY CENTRE OF THE CITY OF MEXICO

Centro Universitario de la Ciudad de México
Tula N° 66, Col. Condesa, Cuauhtémoc, 06140 México, D.F.
Tel: +52(555) 553-08-86
Fax: +52(555) 211-82-33
EMail: ucime@prodigy.net.mx

Rector: María de la Luz García Alonso (1979-)

Administrative Vice-Chancellor: Sergio Humana García

International Relations: Sergio Humana García

Programmes
Education (Education); **Humanities** (Arts and Humanities); **Philosophy** (Arts and Humanities; Philosophy)

History: Founded 1978, as second division of the Ateneo Filosófico, A.C. foundation. Acquired present status 1997.

Academic Year: February to December (February-June; August-December)

Admission Requirements: Certificado de Licenciatura

Fees: (Pesos): 5,000; 30,000 per semester

Main Language(s) of Instruction: Spanish

International Co-operation: With universities in Greece, Spain, Canada and Liechtenstein

Accrediting Agencies: Secretaría de Educación Pública

Degrees and Diplomas: *Especialización*: 1 yr; *Maestría*: 3 sem; *Doctorado*: 3 yrs

Student Services: Academic counselling
Last Updated: 28/02/08

UNIVERSITY CENTRE OF THE NORTH-EAST

Centro Universitario del Noreste, A.C. (CUN)
Roberto F. García N°116 Con Ocampo y Canales. Col. Modelo, 87360 Matamoros, Tamaulipas
Tel: +52(868) 816-15-80
EMail: cun@cun.com.mx
Website: http://www.cun.com.mx

Rector: Ricardo Díaz Garza

Programmes
Accountancy (Accountancy); **Architecture** (Architecture); **Business Administration** (Business Administration); **Clinical Chemistry** (Chemistry); **Law** (Law); **Psychology** (Psychology)

History: Founded 1982.

Main Language(s) of Instruction: Spanish

Degrees and Diplomas: *Licenciatura*
Last Updated: 17/03/08

UNIVERSITY CENTRE OF THE SOUTH PACIFIC

Centro Universitario del Pacifico Sur
Avenida Acapulco, 303-B casi Esq. Calle 8, Col. Cuauhtémoc, 39550 Acapulco de Juárez, Guerrero
Tel: +52(744) 483-38-62
Fax: +52(744) 82-95-06

Rector: Francisco Mosso Orcasitas (1993-)

Programmes
Business Administration and Law (Accountancy; Business Administration; Business Computing; Law)

History: Founded 1993.

Main Language(s) of Instruction: Spanish

Degrees and Diplomas: *Licenciatura*
Last Updated: 17/03/08

UNIVERSITY CENTRE OF THE STATE OF MEXICO

Centro Universitario del Estado de México
Vicente Guerrero, Lote 8 y 10, Col. San José Jajalpa, Ecatepec de Morelos, 55000 Ecatepec de Morelos, Estado de México
Tel: +52(55) 787-02-97 +52(55) 787-35-36

Director: Rodolfo Gómez Tous (1999-)

Programmes
Accountancy (Accountancy); **Business Computing** (Business Computing); **Communication and Journalism** (Communication Studies; Journalism); **Computer Science**; **Digital Systems Engineering** (Engineering); **Electronic and Computer Engineering** (Computer Engineering; Electronic Engineering); **Graphic Design**; **Law**; **Nursing** (Nursing); **Pedagogy**

History: Founded 1999.

Degrees and Diplomas: *Licenciatura*: 9-10 sem.
Last Updated: 27/03/08

UNIVERSITY CENTRE OF THE VALLEY OF TEOTIHUACAN

Centro Universitario del Valle de Teotihuacán
Palma, 13-A, Col. Purificación, 55800 Teotihuacán, Estado de México
Tel: +52(594) 956-10-35 +52(594) 456-04-97
Fax: +52(594) 456-04-97
EMail: gee@g-educempresarios.edu.mx
Website: http://cuvate.edu.mx

Director: Hugo Pedro La Torre Díez (1997-)

Programmes
Accountancy; **Administration**; **Law** (Law); **Marketing** (Marketing)

History: Founded 1997.

Degrees and Diplomas: *Licenciatura*; *Especialización*; *Maestría*
Last Updated: 24/07/12

UNIVERSITY CENTRE OF THE VALLEY OF ZACAPU

Centro Universitario del Valle de Zacapu, A.C.
Avenida Universidad, 1000, Col. Antigua La Soledad, Ajolotes, 58677 Zacapu, Michoacán
Tel: +52(436) 363-28-39 +52(436) 363-01-50
Fax: +52(436) 363-44-46
EMail: cubz_zacapu@yahoo.com

Directora: Felicitas A. Flores Fuentes (1991-)

Programmes
Agricultural Development (Rural Planning; Rural Studies); **Industrial Engineering** (Industrial Engineering)

History: Founded 1984.

Main Language(s) of Instruction: Spanish

Degrees and Diplomas: *Licenciatura*
Last Updated: 24/07/12

UNIVERSITY CENTRE OF THE WEST

Centro Universitario de Occidente
Avenida Hidalgo, 1583, Col. Americana, 44602 Guadalajara, Jalisco
Tel: +52(33) 36-15-80-20

Director: Cayetano Mercado Pérez (1999-)

Programmes
Law (Law)

History: Founded 1999.

Main Language(s) of Instruction: Spanish

Degrees and Diplomas: *Licenciatura*: 8 sem.
Last Updated: 27/03/08

UNIVERSITY CENTRE SPECIALIZED IN BUSINESS STUDIES

Centro Universitario Especializado en Negocios
Oxo, 14, Planta Baja, Col. Industrial, Delegación Gustavo A. Madero, 07800 México, D.F.
Tel: +52(5) 55-77-57-82
Fax: +52(5) 57-81-10-96

Director: Octavio Escalante Guadarrama (2001-)

Programmes
Business Administration (Business Administration)

Degrees and Diplomas: *Licenciatura*; *Especialización*
Last Updated: 04/04/08

UNIVERSITY COLLEGE OF BUSINESS STUDIES

Colegio Universitario de Formación Empresarial
República de Panamá, 124, Col. Américas, 50130 Toluca, Estado de México
Tel: +52(722) 12-09-00 +52(722) 17-60-75
Fax: +52(722) 17-62-04
EMail: cufemtol@cufem.com
Website: http://www.cufem.com

Programmes
International Business (International Business)

History: Founded 2002.

Main Language(s) of Instruction: Spanish

Degrees and Diplomas: *Licenciatura*
Last Updated: 23/08/12

UNIVERSITY COLLEGE OF PUEBLA

Colegio Universitario de Puebla, A.C. (UNICUP)
5 Poniente, 1310, Centro, 72000 Puebla, Puebla
Tel: +52(222) 409-75-55
Fax: +52(222) 246-69-01
EMail: cup@prodigy.net.mx
Website: http://www.unicup.edu.mx

Director General: Mario Ernesto Mundo (2006-)

Programmes

Administration and Commerce *(Postgraduate)* (Administration; Business and Commerce); **Business Administration** (Business Administration); **Law** (Law); **Podology** (Podiatry); **Public Accountancy** (Accountancy)

History: Founded 1994.

Degrees and Diplomas: *Licenciatura*; *Maestría*

Last Updated: 24/08/12

UNIVERSITY COLLEGE OF THE AMERICAS

Colegio Universitario de las Américas

Avenida Plan de Ayala, 999, Col. Chapultepec, Cuernavaca, Morelos

Tel: +52(777) 316-38-55

Fax: +52(777) 316-38-55

EMail: coua@mail.com.mx

Director: Jesús Jaime Rivera Ugalde

Programmes

Business Computing (Business Computing); **Business Relations** (Business and Commerce; Business Education); **Economic Development** (Economics); **Law** (Law)

Degrees and Diplomas: *Licenciatura*

Last Updated: 24/08/12

UNIVERSITY CULTURAL CENTRE OF CIUDAD JUÁREZ

Centro Cultural Universitario de Ciudad Juárez

Fracc Villahermosa, Ciudad Juárez, Chihuahua

Tel: +52(656) 617-00-70

EMail: info@ccu.mx

Website: http://www.ccu.com.mx

Director: Jorge Agustín Rojas López

Programmes

Accountancy (Accountancy); **Business Administration** (Business Administration); **Computer Science** (Computer Science); **Criminology** (Criminology); **Gastronomy** (Cooking and Catering); **Industrial Engineering** (Industrial Engineering); **Law** (Law); **Pedagogy** (Pedagogy); **Psychology** (Psychology)

History: Founded as Colegio de Psicología, Cultural, A.C.

Admission Requirements: Certificado de Secundaria

Fees: (Pesos) 1,450

Main Language(s) of Instruction: Spanish

Degrees and Diplomas: *Licenciatura*; *Maestría*

Last Updated: 10/07/12

UNIVERSITY FOR FOOTBALL AND SPORTS SCIENCE

Universidad del Fútbol y Ciencias del Deporte

Km. 2 Libramiento Circuito de la Ex-Hacienda de la Concepción s/n, San Agustín Tlaxiaca, San Agustín Tlaxcala, Hidalgo

Tel: +52(771) 711-88-11

Fax: +52(771) 717-04-00

EMail: informes@ufd.mx

Website: http://www.ufd.mx

Directora: Yesenia Lara Mayorga

Programmes

Administration (Business Administration; Sports Management); **Communication** (Communication Studies); **Nutrition** (Nutrition); **Physical Education** (Physical Education); **Physiotherapy** (Physical Therapy); **Psychology** (Psychology); **Sports** (Sports)

History: Founded 2001.

Admission Requirements: Bachillerato and entrance examination

Main Language(s) of Instruction: Spanish

Degrees and Diplomas: *Licenciatura*; *Maestría*: Sports Science; *Doctorado*

Last Updated: 25/09/12

UNIVERSITY FOR PROFESSIONAL DEVELOPMENT

Universidad del Desarrollo Profesional

Blv. José Maria Chavez No.1323 entre Av. Aguacalientes Sur y Av Convención de 1914, Col. Agricultura, 20234 Aguascalientes, Aguascalientes

Tel: +52 (449) 913-20-23

EMail: infoagc@unidep.edu.mx

Website: http://www.unidep.edu.mx

Rectora: María Luisa Valdez Ibarra

Director General: Jose López Padilla

Director Regional Centro: Fernando Elías Meléndrez

Directora, Aguascalientes: Claudia Padilla González

Programmes

Accountancy (Accountancy); **Advertising and Marketing** (Advertising and Publicity; Marketing); **Business Administration** (Accountancy; Advertising and Publicity; Business Administration; International Business; Marketing; Public Relations); **Communication Studies** (Communication Studies; Public Relations); **Design and Interior Design** (Graphic Design; Interior Design; Multimedia); **Graphic Design and Multimedia** (Graphic Design; Multimedia); **Industrial Psychology** (Industrial and Organizational Psychology); **Information Technology** (Information Technology); **Law** (Commercial Law; Education; Law); **Nursing** (Nursing); **Systems Engineering** (Computer Engineering); **Teaching of English** (English; Teacher Training)

Further Information: Campuses: CENTRO: Aguascalientes, Querétaro, Saltillo, Torreón, Zacatecas; GOLFO: Altamira, Ciudad Mante, Ciudad del Carmen, Tuxpan; NOROESTE: Cabo San Lucas, Ensenada, La Paz, Mexicali, San José Del Cabo, San Luis Río Colorado, Tijuana; PACIFICO: Culiacán, Escuinapa, Guasave, Lázaro Cárdenas, Los Mochis, Manzanillo, Mazatlán, Zihuatanejo; SONORA NORTE: Aguaprieta, Caborca, Cananea, Ciudad Juárez, Chihuahua, Magdalena, Nogales, Presidentes, Puerto Peñasco; SONORA SUR: Ciudad Obregón, Empalme, Guaymas, Hermosillo, Navojoa

History: Founded 2003.

Main Language(s) of Instruction: Spanish

Degrees and Diplomas: *Licenciatura*; *Especialización*; *Maestría*

Last Updated: 25/09/12

UNIVERSITY FOR THE DEVELOPMENT OF THE STATE OF PUEBLA

Universidad del Desarrollo del Estado de Puebla

13 Poniente 2904 - Col. La Paz, 72000 Puebla, Puebla

Tel: +52(222) 620-03-00

EMail: informes@unides.edu.mx

Website: http://www.unides.edu.mx/

Rector: José Ojeda Bustamante

Areas

Education and Humanities (Aesthetics; Art Education; English; History; Literature; Philosophy; Psychology; Sociology; Spanish); **Engineering** (Agricultural Engineering; Architecture; Automotive Engineering; Civil Engineering; Computer Engineering; Ecology; Electrical Engineering; Electronic Engineering; Industrial Engineering; Mechanical Engineering; Telecommunications Engineering); **Health Sciences** (Nutrition; Pharmacology); **Natural and Exact Sciences** (Mathematics; Physics); **Social Sciences and Administration** (Accountancy; Business Administration; Business Computing; Communication Studies; Economics; Environmental Management; Geography; Graphic Design; International Business; Journalism; Law; Marketing; Political Sciences; Regional Planning; Social Work; Tourism)

History: Founded 1997.

Admission Requirements: Bachillerato

Main Language(s) of Instruction: Spanish

Degrees and Diplomas: *Licenciatura*; *Maestría*; *Doctorado*

Last Updated: 25/09/12

UNIVERSITY FRAY LUCA PACCIOLI

Universidad Fray Luca Paccioli (UFLP)
Francisco Zarco, 8, Col. Centro, 62000 Cuernavaca, Morelos
Tel: +52(777) 312-10-54
EMail: informes@uflp.edu.mx
Website: http://www.uflp.edu.mx/

Rector: Christian Domínguez Guzmán

Programmes

Postgraduate (Administration; Education; Film; Justice Administration; Multimedia); **Professional** (Computer Science; Mechanical Engineering; Telecommunications Engineering); **Undergraduate** (Architecture; Business Administration; Communication Arts; Graphic Design; Nutrition; Psychology; Tourism)

Further Information: Also Azteca Tejalpa, Olmeca Temixco, Iguala and Cuautla campuses

History: Founded 1979 as Centro de Estudios Universitarios.

Admission Requirements: High School Certificate.

Main Language(s) of Instruction: Spanish

International Co-operation: With institutions in France and Spain

Accrediting Agencies: FIMPES

Degrees and Diplomas: *Licenciatura*: Business Administration (Tourism); Graphic Design; Communication Sciences; Architecture; Psychology; Nutricion, 3 yrs; *Licenciatura*: Computer Systems; Mechatronics; Communications and Electronics; Telematics (Ingeniería); *Maestría*: Administration; E-learning; Multimedia; Justice Administration; Film-making, 2 yrs

Student Services: Academic counselling, Canteen, Cultural centre, Employment services, Foreign student adviser, Foreign Studies Centre, Handicapped facilities, Health services, Language programs, Nursery care, Social counselling, Sports facilities

Special Facilities: Specialized laboratories for study fields; tv and radio studios

Libraries: Individual campus libraries.

Last Updated: 03/10/12

UNIVERSITY INSTITUTE IN ADMINISTRATION SYSTEMS OF MONTERREY

Instituto Universitario en Sistemas Administrativos de Monterrey
M. M. Del Llano, 141, Ote., Entre Juárez y Guerrero, Centro, 64000 Monterrey, Nuevo León
Tel: +52(81) 83-44-96-36 +52(81) 83-52-77-33
Website: http://www.tuscreen.com/iusam

Director: Alfonso Montemayor Martínez

Programmes

Accountancy (Accountancy); **Applied Computer Science** (Computer Engineering; Computer Science); **Business Administration** (Administration; Business Administration); **Education** (Education); **Marketing** (Marketing)

History: Founded 1995.

Main Language(s) of Instruction: Spanish

Degrees and Diplomas: *Licenciatura*; *Maestría*: Education

Last Updated: 22/03/13

UNIVERSITY INSTITUTE OF NEZAHUALCÓYOTL

Instituto Universitario Nezahualcoyotl
Avenida Nezahualcoyotl, 418, Col. Agua Azul, Neza II, 57500 Nezahualcóyotl, Estado de México
Tel: +52(55) 57-92-19-43
Fax: +52(55) 57-65-31-41
EMail: unineza@prodigy.net.mx
Website: http://www.univerneza.com/home.html

Director: Rodolfo Calvillo Popoca

Programmes

Business Administration and Law; **Computer Science** (Computer Science)

History: Founded 1997.

Main Language(s) of Instruction: Spanish

Degrees and Diplomas: *Licenciatura*

Last Updated: 22/03/13

UNIVERSITY INSTITUTE OF TECHNOLOGY AND HUMANITIES

Instituto Universitario de Tecnologia y Humanidades
0 Oriente 402, frente al IMSS San José por la 4 Norte, Col. San Francisco, 72000 Puebla, Puebla
Tel: +52(222) 232-68-05
EMail: iuth1 @ yahoo.com
Website: http://iunivertech.com.mx

Director: Nicolás Arrioja Landa Cosío

Programmes

Computer Science (Computer Engineering; Computer Networks; Engineering; Software Engineering); **International Business** (International Business); **Psychology** (Psychology)

History: Founded 2002.

Main Language(s) of Instruction: Spanish

Degrees and Diplomas: *Licenciatura*; *Maestría*

Last Updated: 22/03/13

UNIVERSITY INSTITUTE OF THE EAST

Instituto Universitario de Oriente
Calle 40 s/n, Col. Santa Lucia, 97780 Valladolid, Yucatán
Tel: +52(985) 856-21-11

Director: Rodrigo Ariel Pérez Cervera

Programmes

Accountancy (Accountancy)

Main Language(s) of Instruction: Spanish

Degrees and Diplomas: *Licenciatura*

Last Updated: 10/01/13

UNIVERSITY INSTITUTE OF THE LAKE AND SUN

Instituto Universitario del Lago y del Sol
Carretera Valle de Bravo-Amanalco, 62.5, Santa María Pipioltepec, 51200 Valle de Bravo, Estado de México
Tel: +52(726) 262-5826

Director: Norberto Martínez Colin

Programmes

Administration (Accountancy; Administration); **Law** (Law); **Modern Languages** (Modern Languages)

Degrees and Diplomas: *Licenciatura*: 4-10 sem.

Last Updated: 22/03/13

UNIVERSITY INSTITUTE OF THE STATE OF MEXICO

Instituto Universitario del Estado de México
Boulevard Toluca-Metepec, No 814 Norte, Col. Hípico, 52140 Metepec, Estado de México
Tel: +52(722) 262-48-36
EMail: iuem@universidad.uiem.com
Website: http://www.universidadiuem.edu.mx

Rector: Mario Luis Pérez Méndez (1994-)
EMail: rectoria@universidadiuem.edu.mx

Programmes

Accountancy (Accountancy); **Administration** (Administration; Business Administration; Management Systems); **Architecture** (Architecture); **Communication Studies** (Communication Studies); **Dentistry** (Dentistry); **Engineering** (Computer Engineering; Industrial Engineering); **Graphic Design** (Graphic Design); **International Business** (International Business); **Law** (Law); **Marketing** (Marketing); **Pedagogy** (Pedagogy); **Psychology** (Psychology)

History: Founded 1994.

Main Language(s) of Instruction: Spanish

Degrees and Diplomas: *Licenciatura*; *Maestría*

Last Updated: 22/03/13

UNIVERSITY INSTITUTE OF THE VALLEY OF SANTIAGO

Instituto Universitario Valle de Santiago (IUNIVAS)
Calle Manuel Acuña Sur, 368, Centro, 25000 Saltillo, Coahuila
Tel: +52(844) 414-96-27
Fax: +52(844) 410-54-34
EMail: contacto@iunivas.edu.mx
Website: http://www.iunivas.edu.mx/

Director: Efraín Zúñiga Castañeda (1998-)

Programmes
Accountancy (Accountancy); **Business Administration** (Business Administration); **Engineering** (Computer Engineering; Industrial Engineering; Production Engineering); **Law** (Law); **Psychology** (Psychology)

History: Founded 1992.

Main Language(s) of Instruction: Spanish

Degrees and Diplomas: *Licenciatura*
Last Updated: 22/03/13

UNIVERSITY INSTITUTE OF TOURISM AND GASTRONOMY

Instituto Universitario Turístico y Gastronómico
Fuente Bella, 132, Col. Rincón del Pedregal, Delegación Tlalpan, 14140 México, D.F.
Tel: +52(5) 56-52-04-18
Fax: +52(5) 56-52-02-66

Director: Mauricio Becker Ávila (2000-)

Programmes
Business Administration (Business Administration; Tourism); **Gastronomy**

History: Founded 2000.

Main Language(s) of Instruction: Spanish

Degrees and Diplomas: *Licenciatura*
Last Updated: 23/04/08

UNIVERSITY OF ACADEMIC STUDIES OF THE AMERICAS

Universidad de Estudios Académicos Américas
Avenida Américas, 459, 44650 Guadalajara, Jalisco
Tel: +52(33) 36-16-24-09
Fax: +52(33) 36-16-24-09

Rector: Arturo Martínez Tel: +52(33) 36-16-24-09

Programmes
American Studies (American Studies)

Main Language(s) of Instruction: Spanish

Degrees and Diplomas: *Licenciatura*

UNIVERSITY OF ACAYUCÁN

Universidad de Acayucán
Km 1.2 Carretera Acayucán-Oluta, Col. Olmeca, 96160 Villa Oluta, Veracruz
Tel: +52(924) 106-41-97
EMail: informacion@universidaddeacayucan.edu.mx

Rector: Juan C. Muñoz Ortiz (1997-)

Programmes
Accountancy (Accountancy); **Law** (Law); **Pedagogy** (Educational Sciences; Pedagogy)

History: Founded 1994 as Colegio de Altos Estudios de Acayucán.

Main Language(s) of Instruction: Spanish

Degrees and Diplomas: *Licenciatura*; *Maestria*
Last Updated: 29/03/13

UNIVERSITY OF ADVANCED COMMUNICATION

Universidad de Comunicación Avanzada
Matamoros No 552, Col. Centro, 64000 Monterrey, Nuevo León
Tel: +52(81) 83-44-05-06
EMail: info@unica.edu.mx
Website: http://www.unica.edu.mx

Rectora: Marla Estrada

Programmes
Communication Studies (Communication Studies; Media Studies; Multimedia)

History: Founded 1999.

Admission Requirements: Certificado de Secundaria

Main Language(s) of Instruction: Spanish

Degrees and Diplomas: *Licenciatura*; *Maestría*

Libraries: Yes
Last Updated: 18/09/12

UNIVERSITY OF BUSINESS AND PEDAGOGICAL DEVELOPMENT

Universidad del Desarrollo Empresarial y Pedagógico
Miguel Laurent, 719, Col. del Valle, Delegación Benito Juárez, 03100 México, D.F.
Tel: +52(55) 56-88-83-15 +52(55) 56-04-21-78
Fax: +52(55) 56-88-35-12
EMail: rangelesl@univdep.edu.mx
Website: http://www.univdep.edu.mx

Rector: Roberto Ángeles Lemus (2004-)

Areas
Business Studies (Accountancy; Business Administration; Business Computing; Computer Engineering; Cooking and Catering; Design; Finance; International Business; Marketing; Tourism); **Humanities** (Law; Pedagogy; Psychology)

History: Founded 1994. Acquired present status 2005. Formerly known as Centro Universitario de Desarrollo Empresarial y Pedagógico (University Centre of Business and Pedagogical Development).

Admission Requirements: Certificado de Preparatoria; Certificado de Licenciatura

Main Language(s) of Instruction: Spanish

Degrees and Diplomas: *Licenciatura*: 3 yrs; *Especialización*; *Maestría*: a further 2 yrs

Student Services: Employment services, Language programs, Nursery care

Libraries: Yes
Last Updated: 25/09/12

UNIVERSITY OF CELAYA

Universidad de Celaya (UDEC)
Km. 269 Carretera Panamericana, Col. Rancho Pinto, 38080 Celaya, Guanajuato
Tel: +52(461) 613-90-99
EMail: cesponda@udec.educ.mx
Website: http://www.udec.edu.mx

Rector: Carlos Fernandez Collado (2003-)
EMail: cfernan@udec.edu.mx

Vicerrectora Academica: Martha Aguilar
EMail: m.aguilar@udec.edu.mx

International Relations: María Ordoñez, Directora de Idíomas

Programmes
Architecture (Architecture); **Business Administration** (Business Administration; Business and Commerce); **Communication Studies** (Communication Studies); **Digital Design** (Design); **Engineering** (Biomedical Engineering; Industrial Design; Industrial Engineering); **Gastronomy** (Cooking and Catering); **Interior Design** (Interior Design); **International Business** (International Business); **Law** (Private Law; Public Administration; Public Law); **Marketing** (Advertising and Publicity; Marketing); **Nutrition**

(Nutrition); **Psychology** (Psychology); **Surgery** (Surgery); **Tourism** (Tourism)

History: Founded 1988. Recognized by the federal government through the Secretariat of Public Education and financed by a civil association.

Academic Year: August to June (August-December; January-June)

Admission Requirements: Secondary school certificate (Bachillerato) and entrance examination

Fees: (US Dollars): 22,120 per semester

Main Language(s) of Instruction: Spanish

International Co-operation: With universities in Spain and Canada

Accrediting Agencies: Federación de Instituciones Mexicanas Particulares de Educación Superior (FIMPES)

Degrees and Diplomas: *Licenciatura*: Architecture (ARQ); Business Administration (LAE); Communication (LCC); Computer System Administration (ISC); Industrial Administrative Engineering (IIA); International Business (LCI); Law (LD); Marketing (MKT); Public Accountancy (CPF), 8-10 sem; *Especialización*: Organizational Communication (ECO), 11 months; *Maestría*: Administration (MA); Fiscal Law (MDF); International Business (Commercio Exterior) (MCE), a further 4 sem; *Doctorado*: Administration, 2 yrs. Also Postgraduate Diploma in 4 yrs (Mtro.)

Student Services: Academic counselling, Canteen, Cultural centre, Employment services, Handicapped facilities, Health services, Language programs, Sports facilities

Libraries: Yes

Publications: Pensando Juntos *(bimonthly)*

Last Updated: 18/09/12

UNIVERSITY OF CENTRAL BAJÍO

Universidad del Centro del Bajío (UCB)

Antonio García Cubas, 704, Col. Fovissste, 38010 Celaya, Guanajuato
Tel: +52(461) 612-98-32 +52(461) 611-74-70
Fax: +52(461) 612-98-32
Website: http://www.uniceba.edu.mx

Directora Académica: Silvia Macias Salinas

Programmes

Accountancy (Accountancy); **Administration** (Administration); **Computer Science** (Computer Science); **International Business** (International Business); **Law** (Law); **Pedagogy** (Pedagogy)

History: Founded 1993 as Centro de Estudios Superiores del Bajío. Acquired present status and title 2000.

Main Language(s) of Instruction: Spanish

Degrees and Diplomas: *Licenciatura*; *Maestría*; *Doctorado*

Last Updated: 24/09/12

UNIVERSITY OF COMMUNICATION

Universidad de la Comunicación

Zacatecas, 120, Col. Roma, Delegación Cuauhtémoc, 06700 México, D.F.
Tel: +52(55) 52-64-40-45 +52(55) 52-64-43-06
Fax: +52(55) 52-64-21-40 +52(55) 55-53-33-28
EMail: comunicacion@uc.edu.mx
Website: http://www.uc.edu.mx

Rector: Salvador Corrales Ayala (1976-) EMail: rector@uc.edu.mx

Programmes

Advertising (Advertising and Publicity); **Cinema** (Aesthetics; Cinema and Television); **Communication Studies** (Communication Studies); **Cultural and Art Management** (Anthropology; Art Education; Cultural Studies; Heritage Preservation; Philosophy); **Education and Environmental Communication** (Ecology; Education); **Marketing** (Marketing)

History: Founded 1976.

Governing Bodies: Junta Directiva

Academic Year: February to January (February-July; August-January)

Admission Requirements: Secondary school certificate (bachillerato) and entrance examination

Main Language(s) of Instruction: Spanish

Degrees and Diplomas: *Licenciatura*: Accountancy and Administration; Marketing; Publicity; Social Communication; Visual and Organizational Communication, 4 yrs; *Especialización*: 1 yr; *Maestría*

Student Services: Cultural centre, Foreign student adviser, Language programs

Special Facilities: TV Studio. Computer Centre

Last Updated: 19/09/12

UNIVERSITY OF COMMUNICATION SCIENCES OF PUEBLA

Universidad de Ciencias de la Comunicación de Puebla, S.C.

27 Sur, 708, Col. La Paz, 72160 Puebla, Puebla
Tel: +52(222) 248-35-41
EMail: informes@ucic.edu.mx
Website: http://www.ucic.edu.mx

Rectora: Ana María Fernández Aparicio
EMail: anafernandez@ucic.edu.mx

Programmes

Advertising and Digital Design (Advertising and Publicity; Design); **Interior Design** (Interior Design)

History: Founded 1992.

Admission Requirements: Certificado de preparatoria

Main Language(s) of Instruction: Spanish

Degrees and Diplomas: *Licenciatura*; *Especialización*; *Maestría*

Last Updated: 18/09/12

UNIVERSITY OF CONTEMPORARY MEXICO

Universidad del México Contemporáneo

Calle 18 de Marzo, 10-Bis, Ciudad Zoquiapán, 56530 Ixtapaluca, Estado de México
Tel: +52(55) 59-72-05-84
Fax: +52(55) 59-72-05-83
EMail: unimec@unimec.com.mx
Website: http://unimec.com.mx

Director General: Juan Antonio Soberanes Lara (1998-)

Programmes

Administration (Administration); **Applied Pedagogy** (Pedagogy); **Family Studies** (Family Studies); **Law** (Law); **Psychology** (Psychology)

History: Founded 1998.

Main Language(s) of Instruction: Spanish

Degrees and Diplomas: *Bachillerato*; *Licenciatura*; *Especialización*; *Maestría*

Last Updated: 02/04/13

UNIVERSITY OF CUAUTITLÁN IZCALLI

Universidad de Cuautitlán Izcalli

Avenida Nopaltepec, 100, Santa Rosa de Lima, 54760 Cuautitlán Izcalli, Estado de México
Tel: +52(55) 58-71-71-65
EMail: informes@uci.com.mx
Website: http://www.udeci.edu.mx

Rector: Juan Manuel Gutierrez Pilloni EMail: jmpilloni@uci.edu.mx

Programmes

Accountancy (Accountancy); **Administration** (Administration); **Architecture** (Architecture); **Communication Studies** (Communication Studies); **Computer Engineering** (Computer Engineering); **Dentistry** (Dentistry); **Gastronomy** (Cooking and Catering); **Graphic Design** (Graphic Design); **Information Technology** (Information Technology); **Law** (Law); **Marketing** (Marketing); **Pedagogy** (Pedagogy); **Psychology** (Psychology)

Further Information: Also Plantel Balcones del Valle and Plantel Chopos

History: Founded 1991.

Admission Requirements: Secondary school certificate (bachillerato) and entrance examination

Main Language(s) of Instruction: Spanish

Degrees and Diplomas: *Licenciatura*; *Especialización*; *Maestría*; *Doctorado*

Libraries: Yes

Last Updated: 18/09/12

UNIVERSITY OF ECATEPEC

Universidad de Ecatepec

Agricultura num. 16 San Cristóbal Ecatepec, 55000 Ecatepec de Morelos, Estado de México

Tel: +52(55) 57-70-06-33

EMail: informes@universidaddeecatepec.edu.mx

Website: http://www.uecatepec.edu.mx

Rectora: Gloria Rangel Ortega

Programmes

Accountancy (Accountancy); **Administration** (Administration; Business Administration); **Architecture** (Architecture); **Business Computing** (Business Computing); **Communication Studies** (Communication Studies; Photography; Radio and Television Broadcasting); **Graphic Design** (Graphic Design); **Law** (Criminal Law; Fiscal Law; Law); **Pedagogy** (Pedagogy); **Psychology** (Psychology); **Tourism** (Tourism)

History: Founded 1995.

Main Language(s) of Instruction: Spanish

Degrees and Diplomas: *Licenciatura*; *Especialización*; *Maestría*

Special Facilities: Museo Soumaya

Libraries: Yes

Last Updated: 18/09/12

UNIVERSITY OF HERMOSILLO

Universidad de Hermosillo

Félix Soria 38-B esq. Tamaulipas, Col. San Benito, 83190 Hermosillo, Sonora

Tel: +52(662) 210-66-48

EMail: rectoria@udeh.us

Website: http://www.udeh.us/

Rector: Federico Saviñón Plaza

Schools

Administration (Accountancy; Administration; Finance; International Business; Taxation); **Languages** (English; Modern Languages; Native Language); **Law** (Law; Private Law; Public Law); **Music** (Music; Music Education); **Political Science** (Political Sciences)

Further Information: Campus in Nogales

History: Founded 1986.

Main Language(s) of Instruction: Spanish

Degrees and Diplomas: *Licenciatura*

Libraries: Yes

Last Updated: 19/09/12

UNIVERSITY OF HUMANISTIC INTEGRATION

Universidad de Integración Humanística

Durango, 15, Col. Unidad Hogar, 87360 Matamoros, Tamaulipas

Tel: +52(868) 816-12-01

EMail: univerih@hotmail.com

Directora: Doris Berrones Espericueta (1998-)

Programmes

Psychology (Clinical Psychology; Psychotherapy)

History: Founded 1995.

Main Language(s) of Instruction: Spanish

Degrees and Diplomas: *Licenciatura*; *Maestría*

UNIVERSITY OF INTERNATIONAL RELATIONS AND STUDIES

Universidad de Relaciones y Estudios Internacionales, A.C. (UREI)

Avenidad Chariel, 208, Col. Ex-Country Club, 89250 Tampico, Tamaulipas

Tel: +52(833) 219-24-98

Fax: +52(833) 219-12-76

EMail: universidad@urei.org.mx

Website: http://www.urei.org.mx

Rector: Jorge Rivera Chávez (1990-) EMail: rectoria@urei.org.mx

General Director of Management: Manuel Enrique Ferrer Rivera Tel: +52(833) 219-22-69 EMail: rectoria@urei.org.mx

International Relations: Rafael Humberto Luengas Piñero Tel: +52(833) 219-96-56, Fax: +52(833) 219-12-76

Schools

Foreign Languages (English; French; German; International Business; International Relations; Italian; Tourism; Translation and Interpretation)

History: Founded 1990. Acquired present status 1991.

Academic Year: August to May (August-December; January-May)

Admission Requirements: Secondary school certificate (Bachillerato)

Fees: (US Dollars): 8,500 per annum

Main Language(s) of Instruction: Spanish, French, German, Italian

International Co-operation: With universities in Italy, France, Canada, Spain, Germany, Switzerland and Malta

Accrediting Agencies: Alianza Francesa; Sociedad Dante Aliguieri; Asociación Mexicana de Estudios Internacionales; Asociación Nacional de Instituciones de Relaciones Internacionales; Academia Mexicana de Protocolo

Degrees and Diplomas: *Licenciatura*: Foreign languages, 4 1/2 yrs

Student Services: Academic counselling, Employment services, Foreign student adviser, Language programs, Nursery care, Social counselling

Student Residential Facilities: None

Special Facilities: Audiovisual Department

Libraries: Yes

Publications: Interurei *(monthly)*

Last Updated: 02/04/13

UNIVERSITY OF LATIN AMERICA

Universidad de América Latina

17 Poniente No. 309, Col. El Carmen, 72000 Puebla, Puebla

Tel: +52(222) 298-84-38

EMail: puebla@udal.edu.mx

Website: http://www.udal.edu.mx

Rector: Jesús López Chargoy EMail: jesuslopezch@udal.edu.mx

Programmes

Architecture (Architecture); **Business Administration** (Accountancy; Administration; Business Administration; Finance; International Business; Marketing); **Civil Engineering** (Civil Engineering); **Communication Studies** (Communication Studies; Computer Science); **Gastronomy** (Cooking and Catering); **Graphic Design** (Advertising and Publicity; Graphic Design); **Law** (Civil Law; Commercial Law; Constitutional Law; Criminal Law; Human Rights; Labour Law; Law); **Modern Languages** (English; French; German; Modern Languages; Translation and Interpretation); **Psychology** (Psychology)

Further Information: Also branches in Xalapa and Teziutlán

History: Founded 1996 as Escuela Superior de Administración y Ciencias Sociales. Acquired present status and title 2003.

Admission Requirements: Bachiller

Main Language(s) of Instruction: Spanish

Degrees and Diplomas: *Licenciatura*; *Maestría*

Libraries: Yes

Last Updated: 13/09/12

UNIVERSITY OF LEÓN

Universidad de León (UDL)

Avenida Juárez, 224, Zona Centro, 37000 León, Guanajuato
Tel: +52(477) 714-42-00
Fax: +52(477) 714-78-94
EMail: calidadacademica@universidaddeleon.edu.mx
Website: http://www.universidaddeleon.edu.mx

Rector: Fernando Arturo Calderón Gama (1989-)
EMail: acalderon@universidaddeleon.edu.mx

Vicerrector Académico: Fernando Arturo Calderón Espinosa

International Relations: Olga Noemi Cabrera Treviño
EMail: edualternativa_udl@hotmail.com

Programmes
Accountancy (Accountancy); **Architecture** (Architecture); **Business Administration** (Business Administration); **Communication** (Communication Studies); **Fashion Design** (Fashion Design); **Finance** (Finance); **Gastronomy** (Cooking and Catering); **Graphic Design** (Graphic Design); **International Business** (International Business); **Law** (Law); **Plastic Arts** (Fine Arts); **Scenic Arts** (Theatre)

Further Information: Also campuses in Aguacalientes, Celaya, Irapuato, Los Paraisos, Moroleón, Salamanca, San Francisco del Rincón, San Luis de La Paz, San Miguel de Allende, Santa Ana Pacueco, and Silao

History: Founded 1989.

Governing Bodies: Rector; Vice Rectors; Campus and Faculties Directors

Academic Year: September to August (September-December;-January-April;May-August)

Admission Requirements: Secondary education completion certificate ("Secundaria" or "Bachillerato"); Admission exam

Fees: (Pesos): 21,000 per annum

Main Language(s) of Instruction: Spanish; English as second language; French as third language

Accrediting Agencies: Secretaria de Educación Pública (SEP); Secretaria de Educación de Guanajuato (SEG); Centro Nacional de Evaluación (CENEVAL); Asociación Nacional de Facultades y Escuelas en Contaduria y Administración (ANFECA); Asociación Nacional de Instituciones de Educación en Informática (ANIEI).

Degrees and Diplomas: *Licenciatura*: Business Administration; Architecture; Fine Arts; International Business; Communication Studies; Accountancy; Law; Graphic Design; Finance; Administrative Informatics; Civil Eng.; Industrial Eng.; Computer Eng.; Marketing; Psychology; Tourism (Lic.), 4 1/2 yrs; *Especialización*: Strategic Administration; Organisational Development; Architectural Design; Web Design; Advertising Design; Urban Design; University Teaching; Finance; Quality Management; International Business; Human Resources; Computer Networks; Public Relations (Esp.), 1 furhter yr; *Maestría*: Administration; Organisational Development; Forensic Sciences; Communication; Higher and Intermediate Education; Finance; Taxation; Quality Management; International Business; Advertising; Computer Networks; Public Relations, a further 1 1/2 yr

Student Services: Academic counselling, Canteen, Employment services, Foreign student adviser, Foreign Studies Centre, Language programs, Social counselling, Sports facilities

Student Residential Facilities: None

Special Facilities: Auditorium; Art Gallery (San Miguel de Allende Campus)

Libraries: Yes

Publications: Investigacción, Publication of Research Work by Alumni of UDL *(3 per annum)*; Nosotros (Revista), Internal information publication for the University community of UDL *(3 per annum)*; Revista Diversidades, Articles and academic essays written by deans of UDL *(3 per annum)*

Last Updated: 19/09/12

UNIVERSITY OF MATAMOROS

Universidad de Matamoros, A.C. (UDM)

1a. y Av. Manuel Cavazos Lerma # 2, Col. Encantada, 87389 Matamoros, Tamaulipas
Tel: +52(868) 817-40-55
Fax: +52(868) 817-40-55
EMail: univdmat@gmail.com

Rector: Enrique G. Sánchez de la Barquera R. (1998-)
Tel: +52(868) 819-3750

Secretario General: Goracio García G.
EMail: horaciogarciagalvan@yahoo.com.mx

International Relations: Alfredo Lopéz Z.
Tel: +52(868) 813-32-27, Fax: +52(868) 813-32-27
EMail: alopezzu@yahoo.com

Faculties
Accountancy and Administration (Accountancy; Administration); **Communication Sciences** (Communication Studies); **Computer Science** (Computer Science); **Engineering and Automation Systems** (Automation and Control Engineering; Engineering); **Law** (Law); **Odontology** (Dentistry)

History: Founded 1982.

Admission Requirements: Secondary school certificate and Preparatory year certificate

Fees: (Pesos): 900 per month

Main Language(s) of Instruction: Spanish

Degrees and Diplomas: *Licenciatura*

Student Services: Health services

Student Residential Facilities: None

Special Facilities: Auditorium

Libraries: Main Library

Last Updated: 06/03/08

UNIVERSITY OF MATEHUALA

Universidad de Matehuala

Xicotencatl, 607, 78700 Matehuala, San Luis Potosí
Tel: +52(488) 882-37-77
Fax: +52(488) 882-04-69
Website: http://www.unimatehuala.edu.mx

Rector: Alfonso Nava Díaz

Schools
Accountancy (Accountancy); **Business Administration** (Business Administration); **Business Computing** (Business Computing); **Communication Studies** (Communication Studies); **Law** (Law); **Paediatrics** (Paediatrics); **Social Work** (Social Work)

History: Founded 1996.

Main Language(s) of Instruction: Spanish

Degrees and Diplomas: *Licenciatura*; *Especialización*; *Maestría*

Last Updated: 02/04/13

UNIVERSITY OF MAZATLÁN

Universidad de Mazatlán

Venustiano Carranza N° 11 Sur, Col. Centro, 82000 Mazatlán, Sinaloa
Tel: +52(669) 981-56-20
Fax: +52(667) 982-52-55

Rector: Fernando A. Orrantia Arellano (1986-)

Programmes
Business Computing (Business Computing); **Marketing** (Marketing)

Degrees and Diplomas: *Licenciatura*

UNIVERSITY OF MONTEMORELOS

Universidad de Montemorelos (UM)

Apartado postal 16-5, Libertad No 1300 Pte., Col. Montemorelos No 16-5, 67500 Montemorelos, Nuevo León
Tel: +52(826) 263-09-00 +52(826) 263-31-67
Fax: +52(826) 263-09-01
EMail: promocion@um.edu.mx
Website: http://www.um.edu.mx

Rector: Ismael Castillo Osuna (2001-)

Faculties
Administration (Accountancy; Administration; Business Administration); **Education** (Curriculum; Education; Educational Administration); **Engineering and Technology** (Computer Engineering; Electronic Engineering; Industrial Engineering; Information Technology; Telecommunications Engineering); **Health Sciences** (Dental Technology; Dentistry; Medicine; Nursing; Nutrition;

Ophthalmology; Public Health; Surgery); **Theology** (Pastoral Studies; Theology)

Schools

Arts and Communication (Communication Studies; Fine Arts; Visual Arts); **Music** (Music)

History: Founded 1942 as college. Later attached to the Autonomous University of Nuevo León. Acquired present status and title 1973.

Academic Year: September to June (September-November; December-March; March-June)

Admission Requirements: Secondary school certificate (Bachillerato)

Main Language(s) of Instruction: Spanish

Degrees and Diplomas: *Licenciatura*: Education, Administration, Theology; Music, Graphic Design; Nursing, Chemistry, Dietetics, 4 yrs; *Licenciatura*: Medicine, 6 yrs; *Especialización*: Ophthalmology, Reconstructive Dentistry; *Maestría*: Education, Public Health, Theology, Family Studies; *Doctorado*: Education

Student Services: Academic counselling, Canteen, Employment services, Foreign student adviser, Health services, Language programs, Nursery care, Sports facilities

Student Residential Facilities: Yes

Libraries: c. 32,980 vols

Last Updated: 02/04/13

UNIVERSITY OF MONTERREY

Universidad de Monterrey (UDEM)

Ignacio Morones Prieto, 4500, Pte., Col. Jesús M. Garza, 66238 San Pedro Garza García, Nuevo León

Tel: +52(81) 81-24-10-00 +52(81) 81-24-15-02

Fax: +52(81) 81-24-11-03

EMail: rectoria@udem.edu.mx

Website: http://www.udem.edu.mx

Rector: Antonio José Dieck-Assad (2009-)
Tel: +52(81) 81-24-11-06, Fax: +52(81) 81-24-15-04

Vicerrector Administrativo: Ricardo Montemayor Cantú
Tel: +52(81) 81-24-15-05 EMail: rmontemayor@udem.edu.mx

International Relations: Thomas Buntru Wezler, Director de Programas Internacionales EMail: tbuntru@udem.edu.mx

Schools

Art, Architecture, and Design (Architecture; Design; Fashion Design; Fine Arts; Graphic Design; Industrial Design; Interior Design; Textile Design); **Business** (Accountancy; Business Administration; Economics; Finance; Human Resources; International Business; International Economics; Safety Engineering; Social Sciences; Tourism); **Education and Humanities** (Communication Studies; Education; Educational Psychology; Humanities and Social Science Education; Information Sciences; Literature; Philosophy; Sociology); **Engineering and Technology** (Automotive Engineering; Civil Engineering; Computer Engineering; Electronic Engineering; Industrial Engineering; Mechanical Engineering; Robotics); **Health Sciences** (Anaesthesiology; Biomedical Engineering; Dentistry; Gynaecology and Obstetrics; Health Sciences; Medicine; Orthopaedics; Paediatrics; Pathology; Psychology; Radiology; Surgery); **Law and Social Sciences** (International Relations; International Studies; Law; Political Sciences; Public Administration; Social Sciences)

History: Founded 1969. A private autonomous institution accredited by the State of Nuevo León.

Governing Bodies: Board of Trustees

Academic Year: August to May (August-December; January-May); summer sessions June-July

Admission Requirements: Secondary school certificate (bachillerato) or foreign equivalent; entrance examination (SAT)

Fees: (Pesos): 35,000 per semester

Main Language(s) of Instruction: Spanish

International Co-operation: With universities in Argentina, Brazil, Canada, Chile, Cuba, France, Germany, Hungary, Norway, Spain, USA. Also participates in the ISEP programme

Accrediting Agencies: Ministry of Education of the State of Nuevo León; Federación de Instituciones Mexicanas Particulares de Educación Superior (FIMPES); Asociación Nacional de Universidades e Instituciones de Educación Superior (ANUIES); Southern Association of Colleges and Schools (USA:SACS)

Degrees and Diplomas: *Licenciatura*: Accounting (Contador Público y Auditor); Architecture (Arquitecto); Industrial, Mechanical & Computer Engineering (Ingeniero); Medicine (Médico Cirujano y Partero); *Especialización*; *Maestría*: Business Administration, International Commerce, Integral Quality Control, Organizational Development, Education, Humanities, 2-3 yrs

Student Services: Academic counselling, Canteen, Cultural centre, Employment services, Foreign student adviser, Foreign Studies Centre, Health services, Language programs, Social counselling, Sports facilities

Special Facilities: Theatre

Libraries: Central Library

Publications: Diálogo (Cultural magazine), Cultural Magazine *(biannually)*

Press or Publishing House: Imprenta UDEM

Last Updated: 21/09/12

UNIVERSITY OF MORELIA

Universidad de Morelia (UDEM)

Fray Antonio de Lisboa, 22, Col. 5 de Mayo, 58230 Morelia, Michoacán

Tel: +52(443) 317-7771

EMail: contacto@udemorelia.edu.mx

Website: http://www.udemorelia.edu.mx

Rector: Pedro Chávez Villa (2002-)
EMail: rector@udemorelia.edu.mx

International Relations: Theresa Marie Cadena, English Coordinator EMail: deptoingles@udemorelia.edu.mx

Programmes

Accountancy (Accountancy); **Administration** (Administration); **Art History** (Art History); **Cultural Tourism** (Tourism); **Information Technology** (Information Technology); **International Business** (International Business); **Journalism** (Journalism); **Nutrition** (Nutrition); **Psychology** (Psychology)

History: Founded 1994.

Admission Requirements: Certificado de Preparatoria or equivalent and Entrance Examination

Main Language(s) of Instruction: Spanish

Accrediting Agencies: Secretaria de Educación Pública

Degrees and Diplomas: *Licenciatura*: 4 yrs; *Especialización*; *Maestría*

Student Services: Canteen, Employment services

Special Facilities: Photography Laboratory, Audio-Visual processing Laboratory

Libraries: Yes

Last Updated: 21/09/12

UNIVERSITY OF NAVOJOA

Universidad de Navojoa, A.C

Km. 13 carretera Navojoa-Huatabampo, 85800 Navojoa, Sonora

Tel: +52(642) 423-30-50

Fax: +52(642) 423-30-55

EMail: unav@unav.edu.mx

Website: http://www.unavojoa.net/

Rector: Orley Sánchez Jiménez

Institutes

Languages (English)

Programmes

Accountancy and Finance (Accountancy; Finance); **Business Administration** (Business Administration); **Computer Systems** (Computer Engineering; Telecommunications Engineering); **Education** (Education; Educational Psychology; Literature; Mathematics; Modern Languages; Physics; Social Sciences); **Graphic Design** (Graphic Design); **Nutrition** (Nutrition); **Theology** *(Montemorelos)* (Theology)

History: Founded 2001.

Main Language(s) of Instruction: Spanish

Degrees and Diplomas: *Licenciatura*; *Maestría*

Libraries: Yes

Last Updated: 21/09/12

UNIVERSITY OF NORTH AMERICA

Universidad de Norteamérica

Avenida Lomas Verdes, 64, Esq. Paseo de Tabaquitos, Lomas Verdes, 53120 Naucalpán de Juárez, Estado de México

Tel: +52(55) 53-43-87-79

EMail: nbtello@cel.edu.mx

Website: http://www.un.mx

Rectora: Teutila Bárbara West de Lerdo de Tejada (1993-) EMail: barbarawest@cel.edu.mx

Vicerrector: Patricio Lerdo de Tejada EMail: pltw@cel.edu.mx

Programmes

Cooking and Catering (Cooking and Catering); **Pedagogy** (Pedagogy)

History: Founded 1993.

Academic Year: February to December (February-June; August-December)

Admission Requirements: Secondary school certificate (bachillerato)

Fees: (US Dollars): 6,500 per annum

Main Language(s) of Instruction: Spanish, English, French

International Co-operation: With universities in Canada, France

Degrees and Diplomas: *Licenciatura*: Administration; Cooking and Catering; Management Systems; Marketing; Pedagogy; Tourism, 4 yrs

Student Services: Academic counselling, Employment services, Language programs

UNIVERSITY OF OPEN AND DISTANCE EDUCATION

Universidad de Educación Abierta y a Distancia

Blvd. Lázaro Cárdenas, 1651-14, Centro Comercial Carlota, Col. Hidalgo, 21389 Mexicali, Baja California

Tel: +52(686) 562-60-23

Fax: +52(686) 562-60-23

EMail: udead@telnor.net

Director General: Jesús Ortiz Figueroa (1994-)

Programmes

Business Administration (Business Administration); **Educational Sciences** (Educational Sciences); **Food Technology** (Food Technology); **History** (History); **International Business** (International Business)

History: Founded 1994.

Main Language(s) of Instruction: Spanish

Degrees and Diplomas: *Licenciatura*

Last Updated: 02/04/08

UNIVERSITY OF PROFESSIONAL STUDIES IN SCIENCE AND ARTS

Universidad de Estudios Profesionales de Ciencias y Artes

Independencia, 1706, Col. San Miguel, 37190 León, Guanajuato

Tel: +52(477) 712-09-38

EMail: info@epca.edu.mx

Website: http://www.epca.edu.mx

Rector: José de Jesús Zúñiga Morales

Programmes

Accountancy (Accountancy); **Administration** (Administration); **Architecture** (Architecture); **Graphic Design** (Graphic Design); **International Business** (International Business); **Law** (Law); **Marketing** (Marketing); **Nutrition** (Nutrition); **Pedagogy** (Pedagogy); **Psychology** (Psychology)

Further Information: Also Plantel Hidalgo

History: Founded 1960 as Escuela Profesional de Comercio y Administración.

Admission Requirements: Certificado de Secundaria

Main Language(s) of Instruction: Spanish

Degrees and Diplomas: *Licenciatura*; *Maestría*

Last Updated: 18/09/12

UNIVERSITY OF PUEBLA

Universidad de Puebla

Prolongación de la 11 sur y Av. Cuauhtemóc, Col. Guadalupe Hidalgo, 72490 Puebla, Puebla

Tel: +52(222) 241-71-23

Website: http://www.unipuebla.com.mx

Rector: Juan Manuel Reyes Cardoso

Programmes

Architecture (Architecture); **Business Administration** (Business Administration); **Business Computing** (Business Computing); **Chemical Engineering** (Chemical Engineering); **Communication** (Communication Studies); **Computer Engineering** (Computer Engineering); **Environmental Engineering** (Environmental Engineering); **Foreign Languages** (English); **Gastronomy** (Cooking and Catering); **Graphic Design** (Graphic Design); **International Business** (International Business); **Law** (Law); **Marketing** (Marketing); **Nursing and Obstetrics** (Gynaecology and Obstetrics; Nursing); **Pharmaco-biological Chemistry** (Biology; Chemistry; Pharmacology); **Special Education** (Special Education); **Sports** (Sports); **Stomatology** (Stomatology)

Further Information: Also Teziutlán, Libres, Zaragoza, Zacapoaxtla,Cuetzalan, Tlatlauquitepec and San Martin Texmelucan branches

Admission Requirements: Bachillerato

Main Language(s) of Instruction: Spanish

Degrees and Diplomas: *Licenciatura*; *Maestría*

Libraries: Yes

Last Updated: 21/09/12

UNIVERSITY OF SAHAGÚN

Universidad de Sahagún

Calzada de Guadalupe, 300, Col. Vallejo, Delegación Gustavo A. Madero, 07870 México, D.F.

Tel: +52(55) 55-17-25-73

Fax: +52(55) 55-17-29-41

EMail: univdes@prodigy.net.mx

Rector: Marcelo Campos Ortega (1992-)

Programmes

Law (Law)

History: Founded 1992.

Main Language(s) of Instruction: Spanish

Degrees and Diplomas: *Licenciatura*

Last Updated: 06/03/08

UNIVERSITY OF SCIENCE AND HUMANITIES OF VERACRUZ QUETZALCOATL

Universidad de Ciencias y Humanidades de Veracruz Quetzalcoatl (UEES)

Dr. Horacio Díaz, 311, Esq. 23 de Noviembre, Col. Zaragoza, 91910 Veracruz, Veracruz

Tel: +52(229) 935-16-65

EMail: quetzalcoatl@ver.megared.net.mx

Rector: Rubén Quiroz Cabrera

Programmes

Accountancy (Accountancy); **Law** (Law)

Degrees and Diplomas: *Licenciatura*

Last Updated: 13/02/08

UNIVERSITY OF SOTAVENTO

Universidad de Sotavento

Martires de Chicago #205, Col. El Tesoro, 96420 Coatzacoalcos, Veracruz
Tel: +52(921) 218-23-11
Website: http://www.us.edu.mx

Rector: Juan Manuel Rodríguez García (1994-)

Programmes

Accountancy (Accountancy); **Architecture** (Architecture); **Business Administration**; **Communication Studies** (Communication Studies); **Computer Engineering** (Computer Engineering); **Law** (Law); **Pedagogy** (Pedagogy); **Psychology** (Psychology)

Further Information: Also campuses in Orizaba and Villahermosa

History: Founded 1994.

Admission Requirements: Bachillerato

Main Language(s) of Instruction: Spanish

Degrees and Diplomas: *Licenciatura*; *Maestría*

Last Updated: 21/09/12

UNIVERSITY OF SPECIALITIES

Universidad de Especialidades (UNE)

Avenida López Mateos, 4175, Col. La Giralda, Zapopan, 45088 Guadalajara, Jalisco
Tel: +52(33) 36-32-40-95
EMail: informes@universidad-une.com
Website: http://www.universidad-une.com

Director: José Luis Gallegos Escobedo

Centres

Languages (English; French; Modern Languages)

Programmes

Administration (Accountancy; Administration; Business Computing; International Business; Marketing); **Architecture** (Architecture); **Communication Studies** (Communication Studies); **Computer Engineering** (Computer Engineering); **Graphic Design** (Graphic Design); **Industrial Engineering** (Industrial Engineering); **Law** (Law); **Nursing** (Nursing); **Psychology** (Psychology); **Tourism** (Tourism)

Further Information: Campuses: UNE Condoplaza del Sol; Centro; Acacias; Plaza del Sol; Plaza Milenium; López Mateos; Vallarta; Américas; Centro Médico; Torre Quetzal; Puerto Vallarta; Tepic; Escuela de Idiomas; Torre Milenio and Las Juntas Puerto Vallarta

History: Founded 2002.

Main Language(s) of Instruction: Spanish

Degrees and Diplomas: *Licenciatura*

Last Updated: 27/07/12

UNIVERSITY OF SPECIALIZATIONS

Universidad de Especialidades, A.C. (UNE)

Chmalhuacán, 6, Esq. López Mateos, Ciudad del Sol, 45050 Guadalajara, Jalisco
Tel: +52(33) 31-22-18-34 +52(33) 31-22-18-27
Fax: +52(33) 36-47-82-83
EMail: mgestrada_une@hotmail.com

Director General Académico: José Luis Gallegos Escobedo (1995-)

International Relations: María Guadalupe Estrada De Rio

Programmes

Accountancy; **Administration** (Business Administration); **Architecture** (Architecture); **Communication Studies** (Communication Studies); **Computer Engineering** (Computer Engineering); **Computer Science** (Computer Science); **Graphic Design** (Graphic Design); **Industrial Engineering** (Industrial Design); **Information Technology** (Information Technology); **International Business** (International Business); **Marketing** (Marketing); **Psychology** (Psychology); **Tourism** (Tourism)

Further Information: Acacias Centre; Américas Centre; Centro Centre; Centro Médico Centre; Condoplaza Centre; López Mateos Centre; Millenium Centre; Plaza del Sol Centre; Vallarta Centre; Puerto Vallarta Centre

History: Founded 1995 by its owner Andres Contreras Sobrino.

Governing Bodies: Academic Board

Academic Year: Some fields of study begin in January and August and others in January, May and September

Admission Requirements: Certificado de Secundaria; Certificado de Preparatoria

Fees: (US Dollars): 7,202 per semester; 4,330 per term

Main Language(s) of Instruction: Spanish

Degrees and Diplomas: *Licenciatura*: 3-4 yrs

Student Services: Handicapped facilities, Sports facilities

Last Updated: 02/04/08

UNIVERSITY OF TAMAULIPECA

Universidad Tamaulipeca

Mariano Escobedo No. 390 Esq. Colón, Zona Centro, 88560 Reynosa, Tamaulipas
Tel: +52(899) 930 0606
EMail: guadalupe.martinez@universidadtamaulipeca.edu.mx
Website: http://www.universidadtamaulipeca.edu.mx

Rector: Oscar W. Aguilera Rodríguez
EMail: oscar.aguilera@universidadtamaulipeca.edu.mx

Faculties

Accountancy and Administration (Accountancy; Advertising and Publicity; Business Administration; Business Computing; Economics; Finance; Interior Design; Landscape Architecture; Marketing; Tourism); **Engineering** (Computer Engineering; Electronic Engineering; Industrial Engineering; Systems Analysis); **Law** (Law); **Psychology and Psychopedagagy** (Educational Psychology; Pedagogy; Psychology)

Further Information: Also Rio Bravo and Matamoros campuses

Main Language(s) of Instruction: Spanish

Degrees and Diplomas: *Licenciatura*; *Maestría*

Libraries: Yes

Last Updated: 05/04/13

UNIVERSITY OF TEPEYAC

Universidad del Tepeyac, A.C.

Avenida Callao, 802, Col. Lindavista, Delegación Gustavo A. Madero, 07300 México, D.F.
Tel: +52(55) 57-81-40-33
EMail: rectoría@tepeyac.edu.mx
Website: http://www.tepeyac.edu.mx

Rector: Rodrigo Valle Sánchez (1993-)

Programmes

Administration (Administration); **Architecture** (Architecture); **Communication Science and Techniques** (Communication Studies); **Graphic Design** (Graphic Design); **Humanities** (Anthropology; Education); **Industrial Engineering** (Industrial Engineering); **Law** (Law); **Psychology** (Psychology); **Tourism** (Tourism)

History: Founded 1975.

Academic Year: February to January (February-June; August-January)

Admission Requirements: High school diploma or equivalent, and entrance examination

Main Language(s) of Instruction: Spanish

Accrediting Agencies: Federación de Instituciones Mexicanas Particulares de Educación Superior, A.C. (FIMPES).

Degrees and Diplomas: *Licenciatura*: Administration; Marketing; Accounting and Finance; Graphic Design; Science and Techniques of Communication; Industrial Engineering; Tourism, 8 sem; *Licenciatura*: Architecture; Psychology, 9 sem; *Licenciatura*: Law, 10 sem; *Especialización*: Philosophic Anthropology; Religious Anthropology; Educational Anthropology; Business Communication; Management Models; Organisational Development; Image and Publicity; Corporative Publicity; *Maestría*: Arts and Humanities; Business Administration; Publicity and Advertising

Special Facilities: Movie and T.V. Studios. Radio Station

Libraries: Yes

Publications: Boletín Tepeyac *(monthly)*; Horizontes *(3 per annum)*
Last Updated: 28/09/12

UNIVERSITY OF THE ÁLICA

Universidad del Álica
Dresde, 101, Col. Nueva Alemania, 63140 Tepic, Nayarit
Tel: +52(311) 214-03-07
EMail: udelatepic@hotmail.com
Website: http://www.universidaddelalica.edu.mx

Rector: Manuel Palomar (2012-)

Programmes

Accountancy (Accountancy); **Business Administration** (Business Administration); **Communication Studies** (Communication Studies); **Educational Psychology** (Educational Psychology); **Graphic Design** (Graphic Design); **Law** (Law); **Marketing** (Marketing); **Nutrition** (Nutrition); **Physical Education** (Physical Education)

History: Founded 1988.

Main Language(s) of Instruction: Spanish

Degrees and Diplomas: *Licenciatura*; *Maestría*
Last Updated: 02/04/13

UNIVERSITY OF THE ALTIPLANO

Universidad del Altiplano
Eucalipto No. 1, Col. El Sabinal, 90000 Tlaxcala, Tlaxcala
Tel: +52(246) 462-14-58
EMail: vicerrectoria@universidaddelaltiplano.com
Website: http://www.universidaddelaltiplano.com

Rectora: Susana Fernández Ordóñez
EMail: rectoria@uda-normatividad.com

Programmes

Business and Administration (Accountancy; Administration; Finance; Hotel Management; Marketing); **Communication** (Advertising and Publicity; Multimedia; Public Relations); **Gastronomy** (Cooking and Catering); **Graphic Design** (Graphic Design); **Languages** (English); **Nutrition** (Nutrition); **Social Sciences** (Communication Studies; Industrial and Production Economics)

History: Founded 1988.

Main Language(s) of Instruction: Spanish

Degrees and Diplomas: *Licenciatura*; *Maestría*

Libraries: Yes
Last Updated: 24/09/12

UNIVERSITY OF THE AMERICAS OF MEXICO CITY

Universidad de las Américas de la Ciudad de México
Puebla 223, Col. Roma, Delegación Cuauhtémoc, 06700 México, D.F.
Tel: +52(55) 52-09-98-00
EMail: rectoria@udla.mx
Website: http://www.udladf.mx

Rector: Alejandro Gertz Manero (1995-)

Centres

Languages (Literature; Modern Languages)

Programmes

Business Administration (Accountancy; Business Administration; Computer Science; Finance; Human Resources; Management; Marketing); **Communication** (Communication Studies); **Education** (Education; Education of the Gifted; Education of the Handicapped; Speech Therapy and Audiology); **Information Technology** (Information Technology); **International Relations** (International Relations; International Studies); **Law** (Law); **Psychology** (Psychology)

Further Information: Also Clinic for Human Communication Disorders

History: Founded 1940 as junior college, acquired present title 1963. Moved to Cholula, Puebla, 1970, returned to present site 1985. A private bilingual institution recognized by the Mexican Ministry of Education.

Governing Bodies: Board of Trustees, comprising 29 members

Academic Year: September to August (September-December; January-April; May-August)

Admission Requirements: Secondary school certificate (bachillerato) or equivalent and entrance examination

Main Language(s) of Instruction: Spanish, English

Accrediting Agencies: Southern Association of Colleges and Schools, USA.

Degrees and Diplomas: *Licenciatura*: Arts, 4-4 1/2 yrs; *Maestría*: Arts; *Doctorado*

Libraries: Yes
Last Updated: 19/09/12

UNIVERSITY OF THE AMERICAS PUEBLA

Universidad de las Américas Puebla (UDLAP)
Santa Catarina Mártir, 72820 Cholula, Puebla
Tel: +52(222) 229-20-00
Fax: +52(222) 229-20-96
EMail: jwelti@mail.udlap.mx
Website: http://www.udlap.mx

Rector: Luis Ernesto Derbez Bautista (2008-2013)
EMail: claudia.olivares@udlap.mx

Vicerrector Académico: Jorge Welti Chanes

Centres

Regional Development *(Cholula Project)* (Development Studies; Regional Planning)

Institutes

Public Policy and Development Studies (Development Studies; Political Sciences); **Research and Graduate Studies** (Accountancy; American Studies; Anthropology; Applied Linguistics; Business Administration; Chemical Engineering; Computer Engineering; Construction Engineering; Design; Economics; Education; Electronic Engineering; Food Science; Industrial Engineering; Laboratory Techniques; Literature; Modern Languages; Natural Sciences; Psychology)

Schools

Arts and Humanities (Architecture; Arts and Humanities; Dance; Fine Arts; Graphic Design; Literature; Music; Painting and Drawing; Philosophy; Sculpture; Theatre); **Business Administration** (Accountancy; Business Administration; Finance; Hotel Management; International Business); **Engineering** (Chemical Engineering; Civil Engineering; Computer Engineering; Computer Science; Electrical and Electronic Engineering; Engineering; Environmental Engineering; Food Technology; Industrial Engineering; Mechanical Engineering; Telecommunications Engineering; Textile Technology); **Science** (Actuarial Science; Biology; Chemistry; Mathematics; Natural Sciences; Pharmacy; Physics); **Social Sciences** (Anthropology; Communication Studies; Economics; Education; History; International Relations; Law; Psychology; Social Sciences)

Further Information: Special courses for foreign students (Spanish Language, Mexican Literature, Mexican Culture)

History: Founded 1940 as Mexico City College, acquired present title 1963, and present status 1968.

Governing Bodies: Board of Trustees; Governing Board

Academic Year: August to May

Admission Requirements: Secondary school certificate (bachillerato) and entrance examination

Main Language(s) of Instruction: Spanish, English

International Co-operation: With universities in 29 countries (coopint@mail.udlap.mx)

Accrediting Agencies: Southern Association of Colleges and Schools

Degrees and Diplomas: *Licenciatura*: 8-10 sem; *Especialización*; *Maestría*; *Doctorado*: Computer Science; Economics. Also Diploma in Art History, Dance, History, Humanities, Literature, Music, Philosophy and Theatre, 1-2 yrs

Student Residential Facilities: For 1,600 students

Special Facilities: Art Exhibition Centre. Computer Centres

Libraries: Yes
Last Updated: 19/09/12

UNIVERSITY OF THE ATLANTIC

Universidad del Atlántico

Carretera Matamoros-Victoria km 4.5 Frente a la gasolinera "Ragoz", 87393 Matamoros, Tamaulipas

Tel: +52(868) 824-00-70

EMail: informes@uda.edu.mx

Website: http://www.uda.edu.mx

Rector: Jesús Pedraza Chaverrí EMail: rector@uda.edu.mx

Programmes

Accountancy (Accountancy; Finance); **Business Administration** (Business Administration); **Communication Studies** (Communication Studies); **Computer Engineering** (Computer Engineering); **Educational Sciences** (Education; Educational Sciences); **Electronic Engineering** (Electronic Engineering); **Graphic Design** (Graphic Design); **Industrial Engineering** (Industrial Engineering); **Law** (Law); **Marketing** (Marketing); **Organizational Psychology** (Psychology); **Petroleum Engineering** (Petroleum and Gas Engineering)

Further Information: Campuses in Reynosa, Río Bravo and San Fernando

History: Founded 1992.

Main Language(s) of Instruction: Spanish

Degrees and Diplomas: *Licenciatura*

Last Updated: 24/09/12

UNIVERSITY OF THE CALIFORNIAS INTERNATIONAL

Universidad de las Californias Internacional

Blvd. Federico Benitez No 460, Fracc. Los Españoles, 22104 Tijuana, Baja California

Tel: +52(666) 686-27-44

Fax: +52(666) 686-54-79

EMail: info@udc.com.mx

Website: http://www.udc.com.mx

Rector: Antonio Carrillo Rodríguez

Programmes

Accountancy (Accountancy); **Architecture** (Architecture); **Business Administration** (Administration; Business Administration; Finance; Human Resources; Marketing); **Business Computing** (Business Computing); **Cinema** (Cinema and Television; Film); **Civil Engineering** (Civil Engineering; Hydraulic Engineering); **Educational Sciences** (Educational Sciences); **Fashion Design** (Fashion Design); **Graphic Design** (Graphic Design); **Law** (Law); **Psychology** (Psychology)

History: Founded 1992.

Admission Requirements: Certificado de secundaria

Main Language(s) of Instruction: Spanish

Degrees and Diplomas: *Licenciatura*; *Maestría*

Last Updated: 19/09/12

UNIVERSITY OF THE CENTRE OF MEXICO

Universidad del Centro de México (UCEM)

Capitán Caldera, 75, Col. Tequisquiapán, 78250 San Luis Potosí, San Luis Potosí

Tel: +52(444) 813-19-23

Fax: +52(444) 817-25-39

EMail: relacionespublicas@ucem.edu.mx

Website: http://www.ucem.edu.mx

Rector: Gerardo Maya González EMail: rectoria@ucem.edu.mx

Programmes

Administration (Administration; Finance; Human Resources; Public Administration); **Communication** (Communication Studies); **Engineering** (Engineering; Industrial Engineering; Production Engineering; Safety Engineering); **Law** (Law); **Marketing** (Marketing); **Nutrition** (Nutrition); **Philosophy** (Philosophy); **Political Science and Public Administration** (Political Sciences; Public Administration)

History: Founded 1995.

Main Language(s) of Instruction: Spanish

Degrees and Diplomas: *Licenciatura*; *Especialización*; *Maestría*

Last Updated: 28/02/08

UNIVERSITY OF THE CLOISTER OF SOR JUANA

Universidad del Claustro de Sor Juana (UCSJ)

Izazaga, 92, Centro Histórico, Delegación Cuauhtémoc, 06080 México, D.F.

Tel: +52(55) 51-30-33-03

Fax: +52(55) 57-09-38-14

EMail: rectoria@elclaustro.edu.mx

Website: http://elclaustro.edu.mx

Rectora: Carmen Beatriz López Portillo (1979-)

Colleges

Art (Fine Arts); **Communication** (Communication Studies); **Creative Writing and Literature** (Literature; Writing); **Cultural Studies and Management** (Cultural Studies; Management); **Gastronomy** (Cooking and Catering); **Human Rights and Peace Studies** (Human Rights; Peace and Disarmament); **Philosophy** (Arts and Humanities; Literature; Philosophy); **Psychology** (Psychology)

History: Founded 1975 as Centro Universitario de Ciencias Humanas, acquired present status 1991.

Governing Bodies: Asamblea General de Asociados

Admission Requirements: Secondary school certificate and preparatory course

Fees: (US Dollar): 3,500 per semester

Main Language(s) of Instruction: Spanish

Accrediting Agencies: Federación de Instituciones Mexicanas Particulares de Educación Superior (FIMPES)

Degrees and Diplomas: *Licenciatura*: Fine Arts; Cultural Sciences; Humanities; Gastronomy; Literature & Linguistics; Audiovisual Communication; Philosophy; Psychology, 5 yrs; *Maestría*: Colonial Culture; Psychoanalysis (M.A.)

Student Services: Academic counselling, Canteen, Cultural centre, Employment services, Handicapped facilities, Health services, Language programs, Nursery care, Social counselling

Student Residential Facilities: Yes

Special Facilities: Art gallery; Radio station and television labs

Libraries: Central Library

Last Updated: 25/09/12

UNIVERSITY OF THE EAST

Universidad de Oriente

21 Oriente 1816, Col. Azcárate, 725 Puebla, Puebla

Tel: +52(222) 211-16-99

Fax: +52(222) 211-16-99

EMail: un@un.edu.mx

Website: http://www.uo.edu.mx

Directora General: Martha P. Agüera Ibañez

Director Admistrativo: Juan Manuel Agüera Castro

International Relations: Jorge David Cortés Moreno

Departments

Academic Studies (Accountancy; Administration; Architecture and Planning; Arts and Humanities; Banking; Business Administration; Engineering; English; Fine Arts; French; German; Graphic Design; Information Sciences; International Business; Law; Management; Marketing; Mass Communication; Modern Languages; Private Law; Public Law; Service Trades; Software Engineering; Tourism); **International Relations and Research** (Business Administration; Marketing; Small Business; Social Sciences)

Further Information: Also campus in Veracruz

History: Founded 1996. Acquired present status 1997.

Governing Bodies: Administrative Board

Academic Year: August to July

Admission Requirements: Secondary school certificate

Main Language(s) of Instruction: Spanish, English

Degrees and Diplomas: *Licenciatura*: Business Administration; Marketing; Publicity, 4 yrs; *Maestría*: Social Sciences, a further 2 yrs

Student Services: Academic counselling, Foreign student adviser, Language programs, Social counselling, Sports facilities

Student Residential Facilities: no

Special Facilities: Gallery; TV studio

Libraries: yes

Publications: Universciencia *(bimonthly)*

Press or Publishing House: Universidad de Oriente Press

UNIVERSITY OF THE FEDERAL DISTRICT

Universidad del Distrito Federal
Cedro No.16, Colonia Santa María la Ribera, Delegación Cuauhtémoc, Delegación Cuauhtémoc, 06400 México, D.F.
Tel: +52(55) 36-11-00-30
EMail: relacionespublicas@udf.edu.mx
Website: http://www.udf.edu.mx

Rector: Eduardo Bermejo Quezada (2000-)

Programmes

Accountancy (Accountancy); **Administration** (Administration); **Business Computing** (Business Computing); **Communication** (Communication Studies); **International Commerce** (International Business); **Law** (Law); **Psychology** (Psychology)

History: Founded 1984.

Admission Requirements: Bachillerato or equivalent

Main Language(s) of Instruction: Spanish

Degrees and Diplomas: *Licenciatura*; *Especialización*; *Maestría*

Last Updated: 25/09/12

UNIVERSITY OF THE GULF

Universidad del Golfo
Obregón, 203, Pte., Zona Centro, 89000 Tampico, Tamaulipas
Tel: +52(833) 212-97-25 +52(833) 212-58-82
Fax: +52(833) 212-92-22
EMail: rectoria@unigolfo.edu.mx
Website: http://www.unigolfo.edu.mx

Rector: Heriberto Florencia Menéndez (1980-)
Tel: +52(833) 212-05-30

Vicerrector: Hilario Zúñiga Menchaca Tel: +52(833) 216-56-84

International Relations: Rosa Amalia Velázquez del Angel

Programmes

Business Administration (Accountancy; Administration; Business Computing; Economics; Marketing); **Engineering**; **Graphic Design**; **Industrial Engineering** (Industrial Engineering); **Law**; **Nursing** (Nursing); **Nutrition** (Nutrition); **Pedagogy** (Educational Psychology; Educational Sciences; Pedagogy); **Psychology** (Psychology); **Tourism** (Tourism)

History: Founded 1971.

Academic Year: August to June (August-September; January-June)

Fees: (Pesos): 4,800 per semester

Main Language(s) of Instruction: Spanish

Degrees and Diplomas: *Licenciatura*: Accountancy; Administration; Computer Science; Computer Systems; Economics; Industrial and System Engineering; Law; Pedagogy; Psychology; Systems; *Especialización*; *Maestría*: Administrative Sciences; Education; Penal Studies

Student Services: Academic counselling, Employment services, Foreign student adviser, Social counselling, Sports facilities

Libraries: Yes

Last Updated: 25/09/12

UNIVERSITY OF THE GULF OF MEXICO

Universidad del Golfo de México (UGM)
Oriente 17 No. 1625, 94300 Orizaba, Veracruz
Tel: +52(272) 724-14-44 +52(272) 724-15-55
Website: http://www.ugm.edu.mx

Rectora: Ana María Ramírez Vazquez

Programmes

Architecture (Architecture); **Business Administration** (Business Administration; Business and Commerce); **Communication Studies and Psychology** (Communication Studies; Psychology); **Computer Science** (Computer Science); **Hotel Management** (Hotel Management); **Industrial Engineering** (Industrial Engineering); **Law** (Law); **Pedagogy** (Pedagogy)

Further Information: Also campuses at Ciudad Mendoza, Coatzacoalcos, Córdoba, Cosamaloapán, Coscomatepec, Martínez de la Torre, Minatitlán, Oaxaca, Poza Rica, San Andrés Tuxtla, Tehuacán, Tierra Blanca and Tuxpán.

History: Founded 1989.

Main Language(s) of Instruction: Spanish

Degrees and Diplomas: *Licenciatura*: Architecture; Accountancy; Business Administration; Commerce; Law; Tourism; Communication; Computer Science; Industrial Engineering; Pedagogy, Psychology; *Especialización*

Last Updated: 06/03/08

UNIVERSITY OF THE NATIONS

Universidad de las Naciones
Av. 16 de Septiembre No. 1498, casi esq. José Azueta. Col. Centro, 91700 Veracruz, Veracruz
Tel: +52(229) 932-31-10
Fax: +52(229) 931-67-07
EMail: rectoria@uninaciones.com
Website: http://www.uninaciones.com

Rector: Arturo Mattiello Canales

Director Académico: Jeremías Zúñiga Mezano
EMail: dacademica@uninaciones.com

Areas

Administration (Accountancy; Business Administration; Finance; Marketing; Public Administration); **Law and Social Sciences** (Civil Law; Commercial Law; Constitutional Law; Criminal Law; International Relations; Labour Law; Law)

History: Founded 1993.

Main Language(s) of Instruction: Spanish

Degrees and Diplomas: *Licenciatura*; *Maestría*; *Doctorado*

Last Updated: 20/11/09

UNIVERSITY OF THE NORTH

Universidad del Norte, A.C.
Venustiano Carranza, 1350, Nte., Centro, 64000 Monterrey, Nuevo León
Tel: +52(81) 83-48-97-83
EMail: un@un.edu.mx
Website: http://www.un.edu.mx

Rector: Marcelo J. González Villarreal

Divisions

Computer Science (Computer Science; Information Sciences); **Engineering** (Electrical Engineering; Electronic Engineering; Engineering; Industrial Engineering; Mechanical Engineering); **Humanities and Social Sciences** (Accountancy; Banking; Business Administration; Communication Studies; Finance; Marketing); **Law** (Law); **Psychology** (Psychology)

History: Founded 1973. A private institution recognized by the State.

Academic Year: January to December (January-April; May-August; September-December)

Admission Requirements: Secondary school certificate (Bachillerato)

Main Language(s) of Instruction: Spanish

Degrees and Diplomas: *Licenciatura*: 4 yrs; *Licenciatura*: Engineering, 5 yrs; *Maestría*: 1-3 yrs. Also Preparatoria, 2 yrs

Student Services: Academic counselling, Employment services, Handicapped facilities, Social counselling, Sports facilities

Libraries: Yes

Last Updated: 27/09/12

UNIVERSITY OF THE NORTHEAST

Universidad del Noreste, A.C. (UNE)
Prolongación Avenida Hidalgo 6315, Colonia Nuevo Aeropuerto, 89337 Tampico, Tamaulipas
Tel: +52(833) 230-38-30
Fax: +52(833) 230-38-30
EMail: informes@une.edu.mx
Website: http://www.une.edu.mx

Rector: Fernando Rubén Chung Hernández

Divisions

Arts and Humanities (Advertising and Publicity; Arts and Humanities; Communication Studies; Graphic Design; Interior Design; Marketing); **Behavioural Sciences and Education** (Preschool Education; Psychology; Special Education); **Chemistry and Biology** (Biology; Chemistry; Environmental Studies; Industrial Chemistry); **Economics and Administration** (Accountancy; Business Administration; Computer Engineering; Economics; Electronic Engineering; Industrial Engineering; Information Technology); **Health Sciences** (Medicine; Nursing; Nutrition; Surgery)

Further Information: Also University Hospital

History: Founded as Instituto de Ciencias Biológicas del Noreste 1970. Acquired present status and title 1977.

Governing Bodies: Consejo Universitario

Academic Year: August to June (August-December; January-June)

Admission Requirements: Certificado de Preparatoria

Fees: (Pesos): 4,705-30,155 per semester

Main Language(s) of Instruction: Spanish

Accrediting Agencies: Federación de Instituciones Mexicanas Particulares de Educación Superior (FIMPES); Asociación Nacional de Universidades e Instituciones de Educación Superior (ANUIES); Unión de Universidades de América Latina (UDUAL); Consejo Tamaulipeco de Ciencia y Tecnología (COTACYL); Consorcio para la Colaboración en la Educación Superior de América Latina (CONAHEC); Consejo Mexicano para la Acreditación de la Educación Médica (COMAEM); Asociación Mexicana de Facultades y Escuelas de Medicina (AMFEM); Consejo Nacional para la Eneñanza e Investigación en Psicología (CNEIP); Asociación de Escuelas de Diseño Gráfico (ENCUADRE); Consejo Nacional para la Enseñanza y la Investigación en Ciencias de la Comunicación (CONEICC); Asociación Mexicana de Bioquímica Clínica, A.C. (AMBC); Asociación Nacional de Facultades y Escuelas de Contaduría y Administración (ANFECA); Consejo de Acreditación en la Enseñanza de la Contaduría y Administración (CACECA); Tribunal Examinador de Médicos de Puerto Rico

Degrees and Diplomas: *Licenciatura*: 4-4 1/2 yrs; *Especialización*; *Maestría*: 2 yrs; *Doctorado*

Student Services: Academic counselling, Canteen, Cultural centre, Employment services, Foreign student adviser, Foreign Studies Centre, Handicapped facilities, Health services, Language programs, Social counselling, Sports facilities

Libraries: Biblioteca Don Rodolfo Sandoval Álvarez

Publications: Gaceta de Medicina *(biennially)*; Jaguar *(biennially)*

Last Updated: 03/04/13

UNIVERSITY OF THE NORTHEAST OF MEXICO

Universidad del Noreste de México, A.C.
Av. Las Palmas S/N (entre Morelos y Av. Las Americas)., Fraccionamiento Rio Bravo, 88900 Rio Bravo, Tamaulipas
Tel: +52(899) 934-0092
EMail: contacto@unm.edu.mx
Website: http://www.unm.edu.mx

Rector: Eduardo González Oropeza (2012-)

Faculties

Economics and Administration (Accountancy; Administration; Business Administration; Business Computing; Economics; Marketing); **Educational Sciences** (Education; Educational Administration); **Engineering** (Computer Engineering; Electrical Engineering; Mechanical Engineering; Production Engineering); **Law** (Law)

History: Founded 1996.

Main Language(s) of Instruction: Spanish

Degrees and Diplomas: *Licenciatura*

Last Updated: 27/09/12

UNIVERSITY OF THE NORTHWEST

Universidad del Noroeste, S.C. (UNO)
Blvd. Enrique Mazón No. 617, Colonia Cafe Combate, 83169 Hermosillo, Sonora
Tel: +52(662) 212-59-10
EMail: antonio.quintal@uvmnet.edu

Rector: Antonio Quintal Berny Fax: +52(622) 280-03-05
EMail: rector@villa1.uno.mx

Directora Administrativa: Ana Bertha Salazar
Tel: +52(662) 280-03-03, Fax: +52(662) 280-03-05
EMail: asalazar@villa1.uno.mx

International Relations: Beatriz López Moreno
Tel: +52(662) 280-03-03, Fax: +52(662) 280-03-85
EMail: beatrizl@villa1.uno.mx

Departments

Administration (Accountancy; Administration; Business Administration; Human Resources; International Business; Marketing; Tourism); **Social Sciences** (Accountancy; Business Administration; Communication Studies; Education; Graphic Design; Law; Psychology)

History: Founded 1979.

Governing Bodies: Junta Directiva

Academic Year: January to December (January-May; June-July; August-December)

Admission Requirements: Secondary school certificate (bachillerato) and entrance examination

Fees: (Pesos): 2,768 per subject

Main Language(s) of Instruction: Spanish

International Co-operation: Participates in SUMA, ANUIES, CONASEP, CREPUQ programmes

Accrediting Agencies: Federación de Instituciones Mexicanas Particulares de Educación Superior (FIMPES), Asociación Nacional de Universidades e Instituciones de Educación Superior (ANUIES)

Degrees and Diplomas: *Licenciatura*: 4 yrs; *Especialización*; *Maestría*: 2 1/2 yrs

Student Services: Academic counselling, Cultural centre, Employment services, Foreign student adviser, Handicapped facilities, Language programs, Nursery care, Social counselling, Sports facilities

Libraries: Total, 14,784 vols

Publications: Tiempo y Espiritú *(quarterly)*

Last Updated: 03/04/13

UNIVERSITY OF THE PACIFIC OF CHIAPAS

Universidad del Pacífico de Chiapas
6a. Avenida Poniente No. 7, Centro, 30450 Arriaga, Chiapas
Tel: +52(966) 66- 07-57
EMail: upach_eca@hotmail.com
Website: http://www.upach-eca.edu.mx

Rector: Neftali Castilejos Toledo (1994-)

Programmes

Accountancy (Accountancy); **Business Administration** (Business Administration; Finance; Marketing); **Business Computing** (Business Computing); **International Business** (International Business); **Law** (Law); **Psychology** (Psychology)

Further Information: Also campus in Tonala

History: Founded 1994.

Main Language(s) of Instruction: Spanish

Degrees and Diplomas: *Licenciatura*; *Especialización*; *Maestría*

Last Updated: 27/09/12

UNIVERSITY OF THE PEDREGAL

Universidad del Pedregal
Avenida Transmisiones, 51, Col. Ex-Hacienda de San Juan, Delegación Tlalpán, 14370 México, D.F.
Tel: +52(555) 603-50-49 +52(555) 6-03-16-40
Fax: +52(555) 603-33-44
EMail: sriarectoria@upedregal.edu.mx
Website: http://www.upedregal.edu.mx

Rector: Armando Martínez Gómez

Directora académica: Yolanda Nava Borrayo
EMail: yolandanava@upedregal.edu.mx

Schools

Accountancy (Accountancy; Finance); **Administration** (Business Administration); **Computer Engineering** (Computer Engineering); **Graphic Design** (Art Management; Graphic Design); **Industrial Relations** (Labour and Industrial Relations); **International Marketing** (Advertising and Publicity; International Business; Marketing); **Law** (Law); **Psychology** (Psychology)

History: Founded 1990.

Governing Bodies: Governing Board

Academic Year: August to June (August-December; January-June)

Admission Requirements: Certificado de preparatoria.

Main Language(s) of Instruction: Spanish

Accrediting Agencies: Secretaría de Educación Pública; Federación de Instituciones Mexicanas Particulares de Educación Superior (FIMPES)

Degrees and Diplomas: *Licenciatura*: 4 yrs; *Especialización*: 1 yr; *Maestría*: 2 yrs

Student Services: Academic counselling, Canteen, Cultural centre, Employment services, Foreign student adviser, Handicapped facilities, Health services, Language programs, Social counselling, Sports facilities

Student Residential Facilities: None

Libraries: Biblioteca San Juan Bautista de La Salle

Publications: Cybernews *(quarterly)*; Impulso *(bimonthly)*
Last Updated: 27/09/12

UNIVERSITY OF THE SIERRA

Universidad de la Sierra, A. C. (USAC)

Apartado postal 90, Avenida de los Técnicos s/n, Fracc. El Paraíso, 73160 Huauchinango, Puebla
Tel: +52(776) 712-04-91 +52(776) 712-20-34
Fax: +52(776) 762-25-99
EMail: usac@usac.edu.mx
Website: http://www.usac.edu.mx

Rector: Hugo Jiménez Arroyo EMail: rectoria@usac.edu.mx

Vicerrector académico: Juan Carlos Rangel De Con
EMail: vicerrectoria_pue@usac.edu.mx

Departments

Languages (English)

Faculties

Accountancy and Administration (Accountancy; Administration; Business Computing); **Law** (Law)

Programmes

Gastronomy (Cooking and Catering); **Marketing** (Marketing); **Nursing** (Nursing); **Pedagogy** (Pedagogy); **Psychology** (Psychology)

Schools

Engineering and Architecture (Architecture; Civil Engineering; Computer Engineering; Engineering)

Further Information: Also Campus in Puebla

History: Founded 1980 as Instituto Poblano de Estudios Superiores A. C. Acquired present title 1984 and present status 1997.

Academic Year: January to December (January-May; August-December)

Admission Requirements: Secondary school certificate (bachillerato)

Fees: (Pesos): c. 4,000 per semester

Main Language(s) of Instruction: Spanish, English

Degrees and Diplomas: *Licenciatura*: 5 yrs; *Maestría*: a further 1-2 yrs

Student Services: Academic counselling, Employment services, Foreign student adviser, Health services, Sports facilities

Student Residential Facilities: For c. 300 students
Last Updated: 19/09/12

UNIVERSITY OF THE SOCONUSCO REGION

Universidad del Soconusco

Cuarta Norte, 6, Col. Centro, 30700 Tapachula, Chiapas
Tel: +52(962) 625-67-67
EMail: cucs@acnet.net
Website: http://www.cucs.edu.mx

Rector: Sergio Agustín Cruz Maldonado
EMail: cucsdireccion@hotmail.com

Programmes

Business Administration (Business Administration); **Business Computing** (Business Computing); **Communication** (Communication Studies); **Educational Innovation** (Education); **International Relations** (International Relations); **Law** (Law); **Marketing** (Marketing); **Organizational Psychology** (Industrial and Organizational Psychology); **Social Work** (Social Work)

History: Created 1998. Formerly known as Centro Universitario Cultural del Soconusco (Cultural University Centre of the Soconusco Region).

Main Language(s) of Instruction: Spanish

Degrees and Diplomas: *Licenciatura*; *Maestría*; *Doctorado*
Last Updated: 27/09/12

UNIVERSITY OF THE SUN

Universidad del Sol (UNISOL)

Blvd del Lago, 7, Col. Villas del Lago, 62270 Cuernavaca, Morelos
Tel: +52(777) 100-72-65
Fax: +52(777) 362-02-10
EMail: info@unisol.edu.mx
Website: http://www.unisol.edu.mx

Rectora: Leonor S. Figueroa Ojeda

Courses

Administration (Administration; Business and Commerce); **Engineering** (Automation and Control Engineering; Computer Engineering; Mechanical Engineering)

History: Founded 1986.

Governing Bodies: Administration Council; Board of Trustees

Academic Year: September to August (September-January; February-June; July-August)

Admission Requirements: Secondary school certificate

Main Language(s) of Instruction: Spanish, English, French

Accrediting Agencies: Federación de Instituciones Mexicanas Particulares de Educación Superior (FIMPES)

Degrees and Diplomas: *Licenciatura*: 4 yrs; *Maestría*

Student Services: Academic counselling, Employment services, Foreign student adviser, Language programs, Sports facilities

Special Facilities: Cinema and Radio Studio

Libraries: Central Library, c. 15,000 vols

Publications: Expresate *(monthly)*
Last Updated: 03/04/13

UNIVERSITY OF THE TACANA

Universidad del Tacana

8a. Avenida Sur 54 Col. Centro, 30700 Tapachula, Chiapas
Tel: +52(962) 625-74-92
EMail: utac@tap.com.mx
Website: http://www.utac.edu.mx/

Programmes

Accountancy (Accountancy); **Architecture** (Architecture); **Computer Science** (Computer Science); **Education** (Education); **Law** (Law)

History: Founded 1996. Formerly known as Instituto de Estudios Superiores Tacana.

Main Language(s) of Instruction: Spanish

Degrees and Diplomas: *Licenciatura*; *Maestría*; *Doctorado*
Last Updated: 03/04/13

UNIVERSITY OF THE VALLEY OF ATEMAJAC

Universidad del Valle de Atemajac (UNIVA)

Avenida Tepeyac 4800, Prados Tepeyac, 45050 Zapopan, Jalisco
Tel: +52(33) 31-34-08-00
EMail: informacion.univa@univa.mx
Website: http://www.univa.mx

Rector: Francisco Ramírez Yáñez (2012-)

Centres
Humanities and Health Sciences (Arts and Humanities; Cultural Studies; Nutrition; Psychology); **Innovation Enterprise** (Business Administration); **Language** *(CELE)* (Linguistics; Modern Languages); **Lifelong Education** (Arts and Humanities)

Departments
Distance Education *(UNADIS)* (Distance Education)

Faculties
Economics and Administration (Administration; Economics); **Engineering** (Architecture; Computer Engineering; Electronic Engineering; Engineering; Graphic Design; Industrial Design; Industrial Engineering; Information Technology); **Social and Health Sciences** (Communication Studies; Law; Nutrition; Psychology); **Well-being and Development** (Development Studies; Philosophy; Religious Studies)

Further Information: Also Campuses in La Piedad; Zamora; Lagos de Moreno; Puerto Vallarta; León; Tepic; Colima; Colima - San Fernando; Manzanillo; Querétaro; Aguascalientes and Uruapan

History: Founded 1962 as Instituto Pío XII, became Instituto Superior del Valle de Atemajac 1977 and university 1979. Acquired present status 2005.

Governing Bodies: Consejo Universitario; Consejo de Directores; Equipo de Rectoría; Consejo Académico; Consejos de Facultad; Consejos de Departamento

Academic Year: January to December (January-April; May-August; September-December)

Admission Requirements: Secondary school certificate; Postgraduate, Professional Certificate

Main Language(s) of Instruction: Spanish

Degrees and Diplomas: *Licenciatura*: 3 yrs; *Especialización*: 1 yr; *Maestría*: a further 2-3 yrs

Libraries: Document Information Centre, c. 76,000 vols; 23,331 magazines; 1,924 video titles; 9 databases. The system is completely computerized with connections to the internet

Publications: Encuentro Internal Magazine *(quarterly)*; Religion Science Book *(quarterly)*; UNIVA Research Magazine *(quarterly)*

Last Updated: 28/09/12

UNIVERSITY OF THE VALLEY OF CUERNAVACA

Universidad del Valle de Cuernavaca

Calle Chimalpa, 13 y 15, Esq. Madero, Col. Miraval, 62240 Cuernavaca, Morelos
Tel: +52(777) 312-49-31
Fax: +52(777) 318-45-72
EMail: contacto@univac.edu.mx
Website: http://www.univac.edu.mx

Rector: Jorge Arizmendi García (1995-)

Programmes
Accountancy and Finance (Accountancy; Finance); **Business Administration** (Accountancy; Business Administration; Business and Commerce; Human Resources; Labour Law; Marketing); **Computer Science** (Computer Engineering; Computer Science); **Graphic Design** (Graphic Design); **Industrial Relations** (Industrial Arts Education); **Journalism** (Journalism); **Law** (Administrative Law; Commercial Law; Constitutional Law; Criminal Law; Fiscal Law; International Law; Law; Private Law; Public Law); **Nutrition** (Nutrition); **Pedagogy** (Pedagogy); **Psychology** (Psychology)

History: Founded 1998.

Admission Requirements: Certificado de Secundaria.

Main Language(s) of Instruction: Spanish

Degrees and Diplomas: *Licenciatura*; *Maestría*

Last Updated: 28/09/12

UNIVERSITY OF THE VALLEY OF GUADIANA

Universidad del Valle de Guadiana (UVG)

Francisco I. Madero 614 Norte, Centro Histórico, 34000 Durango, Durango
Tel: +52(618) 812-28-07
EMail: kbn@uvguad.edu.mx
Website: http://www.uvguad.edu.mx

Rector: Sergio Arturo Aldaba Carreón (1993-)
EMail: aldaba.uvg@gmail.com

Administrador General: Gerardo Chávez
EMail: gerardoch@starmedia.com

International Relations: Carla Borrego
EMail: cborrego@logicnet.com.mx

Divisions
Human Resources Management (Human Resources); **Modern Languages** (English; French; Linguistics; Modern Languages); **Postgraduate Studies** (Education; Psychology; Social Sciences); **Psychology** (Psychology)

History: Founded 1993, acquired present status 1995.

Governing Bodies: Consejo Técnico Administrativo y Académico

Admission Requirements: Secondary school certificate (bachillerato) and entrance examination

Main Language(s) of Instruction: Spanish

Accrediting Agencies: Secretaría de Educación Pública

Degrees and Diplomas: *Licenciatura*: Administration; Psychology, 4 1/2 yrs; *Maestría*: Psychology; Education, a further 2 yrs

Student Services: Academic counselling, Language programs, Social counselling

Libraries: Central Library

Press or Publishing House: Editorial Nahui Ollin

Last Updated: 28/09/12

UNIVERSITY OF THE VALLEY OF MATATIPAC

Universidad del Valle de Matatipac (UNIVAM)

Avenida de la Cultura, 30, Fracc. Ciudad del Valle, 63175 Tepic, Nayarit
Tel: +52(311) 214-21-45
EMail: vallarta@univam.edu.mx,
Website: http://www.univam.edu.mx

Rectora: Rosalba del Carmen Brambila Moreno

Programmes
Accountancy (Accountancy); **Administration** (Business Administration); **Architecture** (Architecture); **Graphic and Visual Design** (Advertising and Publicity; Graphic Design; Photography); **Law** (Civil Law; Criminal Law; Law); **Marketing** (Marketing); **Pedagogy** (Pedagogy); **Psychology** (Psychology)

Further Information: Also Campus Nuevo Vallarte

History: Founded 1992.

Academic Year: August to June

Admission Requirements: Bachillerato

Main Language(s) of Instruction: Spanish

Accrediting Agencies: Universidad Nacional Autonóma de México; Secretaría de Educación Pública

Degrees and Diplomas: *Licenciatura*: 5 yrs

Student Services: Academic counselling, Language programs, Sports facilities

Last Updated: 03/04/13

UNIVERSITY OF THE VALLEY OF MEXICO

Universidad del Valle de México
Tehuantepec 250, Col. Roma Sur, 06760 México, D.F.
Tel: +52(55) 52-65-99-14
Fax: +52(55) 52-64-05-08 52(55) 55-84-94-25
Website: http://www.uvmnet.edu

Rector: César Morales Hernández EMail: cmorales@uvmnet.edu

Divisions

Business Studies (Accountancy; Administration; Business Administration; Economics; Finance; International Business; Labour and Industrial Relations; Marketing; Sports Management; Tourism); **Design, Art and Architecture** (Architecture; Fashion Design; Graphic Design; Industrial Design); **Engineering** (Civil Engineering; Computer Engineering; Construction Engineering; Electronic Engineering; Environmental Engineering; Industrial Engineering; Mechanical Engineering; Production Engineering; Telecommunications Engineering); **Hospitality, Gastronomy and Tourism** (Cooking and Catering; Hotel Management; Tourism); **Social Sciences** (Communication Studies; Education; International Relations; Law; Pedagogy; Public Relations; Social Sciences)

Schools

Health Sciences (Dentistry; Medicine; Nutrition; Pharmacology; Physical Therapy; Psychology; Speech Therapy and Audiology; Surgery; Veterinary Science)

Further Information: 37 campuses throughout the country

History: Founded 1960 as Institución Harvard, became University 1968.

Governing Bodies: Junta de Gobierno

Academic Year: August to July

Admission Requirements: Bachillerato and entrance examination

Main Language(s) of Instruction: Spanish

Degrees and Diplomas: *Licenciatura*: 2 1/2 yrs; *Especialización*; *Maestría*: a further 2 yrs

Student Services: Academic counselling, Canteen, Cultural centre, Employment services, Foreign student adviser, Health services, Social counselling, Sports facilities

Libraries: Yes

Press or Publishing House: Editorial Universidad del Valle de México
Last Updated: 28/09/12

UNIVERSITY OF THE VALLEY OF ORIZABA

Universidad del Valle de Orizaba (UNIVO)
Prolongación Avenida 20 de Noviembre, 1, Esq. Calle de los Censos, Col. El Espinal, 94330 Orizaba, Veracruz
Tel: +52(272) 726-14-36
Fax: +52(272) 725-20-22
EMail: univ2000@prodigy.net.mx
Website: http://www.univo.edu.mx

Rector: Antonio Gutiérrez Hernández

Centres

Modern Languages (English; French; German; Japanese)

Faculties

Economics and Administration (Accountancy; Administration; Economics; Marketing; Taxation); **Engineering** (Computer Science; Engineering; Systems Analysis); **Humanities** (Arts and Humanities; Communication Studies; Education)

Further Information: Branch in Cordoba

History: Founded 1988 as Instituto des Estudios Superiores del Valle de Orizaba, acquired present status and title 1992.
Admission Requirements: Bachillerato

Main Language(s) of Instruction: Spanish

Accrediting Agencies: Secretaría de Educación Pública

Degrees and Diplomas: *Licenciatura*; *Especialización*: 1 yr; *Maestría*: 1 1/2 yr

Student Services: Academic counselling, Canteen, Employment services, Foreign student adviser, Foreign Studies Centre, Handicapped facilities, Health services, Language programs, Nursery care, Social counselling, Sports facilities

Libraries: Biblioteca 'Dr Othón Arróniz Báez'
Last Updated: 28/09/12

UNIVERSITY OF THE VALLEY OF PUEBLA

Universidad del Valle de Puebla, A.C. (UVP)
3 Sur, 5759, Col. El Cerrito, 72440 Puebla, Puebla
Tel: +52(222) 240-26-00
Fax: +52(222) 243-04-94
EMail: uvpcontacto@uvp.edu.mx
Website: http://www.uvp.edu.mx

Rector: Jaime Illescas López (1981-) EMail: rectoria@uvp.mx

Divisions

Economics and Social Sciences (Accountancy; Administration; Business Administration; Communication Studies; Economics; International Business); **Engineering** (Computer Engineering; Electronic Engineering; Engineering; Industrial Engineering; Mechanical Engineering); **Hospitality and Humanities** (Cooking and Catering; Modern Languages; Tourism)

Further Information: Also Plantel Tehuacán

History: Founded 1991.

Admission Requirements: Bachillerato and entrance examination

Main Language(s) of Instruction: Spanish

Accrediting Agencies: Federación de Instituciones Mexicanas Particulares de Educación Superior

Degrees and Diplomas: *Licenciatura*; *Maestría*
Last Updated: 03/04/13

UNIVERSITY OF THE VALLEY OF THE GRIJALVA

Universidad Valle del Grijalva
Boulevard Dr. Belisario Dominguez No. 1755, Fracc. Bugambilias, 29020 Tuxtla Gutiérrez, Chiapas
Tel: +52(961) 617 10 90
EMail: rectoria@uvg.edu.mx
Website: http://www.uvg.edu.mx

Rector: Mario Alberto González González EMail: uvg@uvg.edu.mx

Schools

Computer Science (Computer Science; Electronic Engineering; Systems Analysis; Telecommunications Engineering); **Economics and Administration** (Accountancy; Business Administration; International Business; Marketing; Tourism); **Education and Humanities** (Education; Pedagogy); **Exact Sciences** (Architecture; Civil Engineering; Graphic Design); **Social Sciences** (Economics; Law; Political Sciences; Public Administration)

Further Information: Campuses in Cintalapa, Coatzacoalcos, Comitán, Campeche, Pichucalco, Merida and Tapachula

History: Founded 1989 as Centro de Estudios Profesionales del Grijalva. Acquired current status 1993.

Admission Requirements: Secondary school certificate (Bachillerato)

Main Language(s) of Instruction: Spanish

International Co-operation: With the University of the Incarnate Word, in San Antonio,Texas (USA)

Degrees and Diplomas: *Licenciatura*: 4 yrs; *Especialización*; *Maestría*; *Doctorado*

Student Services: Language programs
Last Updated: 26/10/12

UNIVERSITY OF THE VALLEY OF TLAXCALA

Universidad del Valle de Tlaxcala (UVT)
Av. Universidad s/n, San Andrés Ahuashuatepec, 90300 Tzompantepec, Tlaxcala
Tel: +52(241) 417-70-56 +52(241) 417-17-93
Fax: +52(241) 417-73-77
EMail: rectoria@univalletlax.edu.mx
Website: http://www.univalletlax.edu.mx/

Rector: Miguel García Méndez Salazar (2007-)

Areas

Economics and Administration (Accountancy; Business Administration; Finance; International Business); **Social Sciences** (Criminology; Law)

Departments

Design and Technology (Architecture; Computer Science; Design); **Humanities** (Education; English; German; Literature; Psychology)

History: Founded 1993.

Admission Requirements: Secondary school certificate (bachillerato)

Main Language(s) of Instruction: Spanish

Degrees and Diplomas: *Licenciatura*: 4 yrs; *Maestría*: 2 yrs following Licenciatura

Student Services: Academic counselling, Canteen, Handicapped facilities, Language programs, Sports facilities

Libraries: Yes

Publications: Gaceta Universidad del Valle de Tlaxcala *(monthly)*

Last Updated: 24/10/12

UNIVERSITY OF THE VALLEY OF TOLUCA

Universidad del Valle de Toluca, S.C. (UVT)

Mariano Matamoros Sur, 1069, Col. Universidad, 50130 Toluca, Estado de México

Tel: +52(722) 270-32-80

Fax: +52(722) 212-02-94

EMail: uvtrectoria@uvt.edu.mx

Website: http://www.uvt.edu.mx

Rector: Alejandro Barrera Villar

Areas

Arts (Architecture; Graphic Design; Town Planning); **Economics and Administration** (Accountancy; Administration; Finance; International Business; Marketing); **Health Sciences** (Dentistry; Dietetics; Nutrition); **Law** (Constitutional Law; Criminal Law; International Law; Law; Private Law)

Further Information: Also Ixtapan de la sal campus

History: Founded 1978.

Academic Year: August to July (August-January; February-July)

Admission Requirements: Bachillerato

Main Language(s) of Instruction: Spanish

Degrees and Diplomas: *Licenciatura*: 4-5 yrs; *Maestría*

Last Updated: 24/10/12

UNIVERSITY OF TIJUANA

Universidad de Tijuana

Avenida J.Lucrecia Torriz 1010, Colonia Altamira, 22054 Tijuana, Baja California

Tel: +52(664) 68-94-54

EMail: rectoria@udetijuana.edu.mx

Website: http://cut.edu.mx

Rector: Jesús J. Ruíz Barraza (1994-)

Vicerrectora: Nélida Ruíz Uribe

Programmes

Accountancy (Accountancy); **Administration** (Administration); **Architecture** (Architecture); **Communication Studies** (Communication Studies); **Computer Science** (Computer Science); **Graphic Design** (Graphic Design); **International Business** (International Business); **International Relations** (International Relations); **Law** (Law); **Psychology** (Psychology); **Tourism** (Tourism)

Further Information: Campuses: Ensenada, Los Cabos, La Paz, San Luis Río Colorado, San Quintin and Mexicali

History: Founded 1993 as Centro Universitario de Tijuana. Acquired present status 1999.

Governing Bodies: Consejo universitario

Admission Requirements: Secondary school certificate (bachillerato)

Main Language(s) of Instruction: Spanish

Degrees and Diplomas: *Licenciatura*: 4 yrs; *Maestría*: a further 2 yrs; *Doctorado*: 2 yrs

Student Services: Academic counselling, Canteen, Employment services, Language programs, Sports facilities

Libraries: Yes

Last Updated: 21/09/12

UNIVERSITY OF TOLOSA

Universidad de Tolosa

Calzada Universidad, 230, Fracc. La Loma, 98000 Zacatecas, Zacatecas

Tel: +52(492) 925-09-33

Fax: +52(492) 925-09-33

EMail: direccion@udetolosa.com

Rector: Erick Alonso Ramirez Aguilera

Programmes

Architecture (Architecture); **Finance** (Finance); **Graphic Design** (Graphic Design); **Marketing** (Marketing); **Political Science and Public Administration** (Political Sciences; Public Administration); **Psychopedagogy** (Pedagogy; Psychology); **Tourism** (Tourism)

History: Founded 2001.

Main Language(s) of Instruction: Spanish

Degrees and Diplomas: *Licenciatura*

Last Updated: 05/03/08

UNIVERSITY OF TOURISM AND ADMINISTRATION

Universidad de Turismo y Ciencias Administrativas

Prolongación Martín Mendalde, 1795, Col. del Valle, Delegación Benito Juárez, 03100 México, D.F.

Tel: +52(555) 534-84-21

Fax: +52(555) 524-62-44

EMail: dirrelacionespublicas@eph-utca.edu.mx

Website: http://www.eph-utca.edu.mx

Rector: Miguel Torrruco Marqués EMail: migueltorruco@gmail.com

Vicerrector: David E. Freyer Manjárrez
EMail: vicerrector@eph-utca.edu.mx

Programmes

Administration (Administration; Hotel Management); **Gastronomy** (Cooking and Catering); **Tourism** (Tourism)

History: Founded 1976.

Main Language(s) of Instruction: Spanish

Degrees and Diplomas: *Licenciatura*; *Especialización*

Last Updated: 21/09/12

UNIVERSITY OF TULANCINGO

Universidad Tulancingo

Jesús Morales, 109, Ex-Hacienda de Ahuehuetitla, Col. Plan de Ayala, Tulancingo de Bravo, 43690 Tulancingo, Hidalgo

Tel: +52(775) 753-39-74

Fax: +52(775) 753-39-74

EMail: tollancingo@uol.com.mx

Rector: José Rubén Velázquez Vargas (1998-)

Programmes

Architecture (Architecture); **Business Administration** (Accountancy; Business Administration); **Computer Science** (Computer Science); **Law** (Law); **Pedagogy** (Pedagogy); **Psychology** (Psychology)

History: Founded 1992.

Main Language(s) of Instruction: Spanish

Degrees and Diplomas: *Licenciatura*

Last Updated: 18/03/08

UNIVERSITY OF VALLE DEL FUERTE

Universidad del Valle del Fuerte
Río Presidio No. 1955 Nte, Col. Tepeca, 81200 Los Mochis, Sinaloa
Tel: +52(668) 880-73-74
Website: http://www.univafu.edu.mx

Rector: Miguel Ángel Bojorquez Valdez

Programmes
Business Administration (Business Administration; Hotel Management; International Business); **Computer Engineering** (Computer Engineering; Industrial Engineering); **Gastronomy and Tourism** (Cooking and Catering; Tourism); **Graphic Design** (Graphic Design); **Nutrition** (Nutrition); **Pedagogy** (Pedagogy); **Physiotherapy and Rehabilitation** (Physical Therapy; Rehabilitation and Therapy); **Speech Therapy** (Speech Therapy and Audiology); **Sports** (Sports); **Tourism** (Tourism)

History: Founded 1999 as Centro de Estudios Superiores del Valle del Fuerte.

Main Language(s) of Instruction: Spanish

Degrees and Diplomas: *Licenciatura*; *Maestría*

Last Updated: 02/10/12

UNIVERSITY OF XALAPA

Universidad de Xalapa (UX)
Km. 2 Carretera Xalapa-Veracruz, Col. Ánimas, 91190 Xalapa, Veracruz
Tel: +52(228) 812-81-92
Fax: +52(228) 812-57-87
EMail: informes@ux.edu.mx
Website: http://www.ux.edu.mx

Rector: Carlos García Méndez

Centres
Foreign Languages (English; French; Japanese)

Programmes
Accountancy (Accountancy); **Business Administration** (Administration; Business Administration; Business Computing; Management); **Communication Sciences** (Advertising and Publicity; Communication Studies; Information Sciences; Mass Communication; Radio and Television Broadcasting); **Educational Sciences** (Education; Educational Administration; Educational and Student Counselling; Educational Research; Educational Sciences; Educational Testing and Evaluation; Pedagogy); **International Business** (International Business); **Journalism** (Journalism); **Law** (Civil Law; Commercial Law; Constitutional Law; Fiscal Law; Human Rights; International Law; Labour Law; Law)

History: Founded 1992.

Governing Bodies: Board of Directors

Academic Year: August to June

Admission Requirements: Secondary school certificate (bachillerato)

Fees: (Pesos): 11,185 per semester

Main Language(s) of Instruction: Spanish

International Co-operation: With universities in Spain

Accrediting Agencies: Secretaría de Educación Pública

Degrees and Diplomas: *Licenciatura*: Accountancy; Business Administration; Communication Science and Techniques; Educational Sciences; Law; International Business, 4 yrs; *Licenciatura*: Electronic Engineering; Management Systems, 5 yrs; *Especialización*; *Maestría*: Finance; Education; Law, 2 yrs; *Doctorado*: Law; Education; Environmental Studies; Economics and Business Administration, 2 yrs

Student Services: Canteen, Employment services, Health services, Language programs, Social counselling, Sports facilities

Student Residential Facilities: None

Special Facilities: TV and Radio Studio

Libraries: Yes

Last Updated: 02/04/13

UNIVERSITY OF XICOTEPETL

Universidad Xicotepetl, A.C.
Av. Universidad s/n Col. Montanejos, 73080 Xicotepec de Juárez, Puebla
Tel: +52(776) 764-13-10 +52(776) 764-06-44
Fax: +52(776) 764-11-32
EMail: info@uxac.edu.mx
Website: http://www.uxac.edu.mx

Rectora: Grabriela Fonseca Marín

Programmes
Accountancy (Accountancy); **Business Administration** (Business Administration); **Engineering** (Agricultural Engineering; Computer Engineering; Electrical Engineering; Engineering; Mechanical Engineering); **Law** (Law); **Marketing** (Marketing); **Veterinary Science** (Veterinary Science)

History: Founded 1983.

Academic Year: September to June (September-January; February-June)

Admission Requirements: Bachillerato or equivalent

Main Language(s) of Instruction: Spanish

Degrees and Diplomas: *Licenciatura*: 5 yrs; *Maestría*

Libraries: 'Juventino Fosado Paredes' Library

Last Updated: 29/10/12

UNIVERSITY OF ZAMORA

Universidad de Zamora
Hidalgo Sur, 149, Col. Centro, 59600 Zamora, Michoacán
Tel: +52(351) 512-00-09
EMail: direccionacademica@universidaddezamora.edu.mx
Website: http://universidaddezamora.edu.mx

Rectora: Alejandra Cerda González
EMail: rectoria@universidaddezamora.edu.mx

Programmes
Accountancy (Accountancy); **Communication** (Communication Studies; Journalism); **Law** (Civil Law; Commercial Law; Human Rights; Labour Law; Law); **Psychology** (Psychology); **Social Work** (Social Work)

History: Founded 1993 as Instituto de Estudios Universitarios del Valle de Zamora. Acquired present status and title 1999.

Main Language(s) of Instruction: Spanish

Degrees and Diplomas: *Licenciatura*

Last Updated: 21/09/12

UNIVERSITY STUDIES CENTRE

Centro de Estudios Universitarios (CEU)
América, 214, Parque San Andrés Coyoacán, Delegación Coyoacán, 04040 México, D.F.
Tel: +52(55) 55-89-27-58 +52(55) 55-78-11-04
Fax: +52(55) 55-49-28-58
EMail: ceu2000@infosel.com; cenestuni@mns.com

Directora General: Jenny Stoopen Rometti (1980-)

Programmes
Law (Law)

History: Founded 1980.

Main Language(s) of Instruction: Spanish

Degrees and Diplomas: *Licenciatura*: 10 sem.

Last Updated: 27/03/08

UNIVERSITY STUDIES CENTRE OF ACUÑA

Centro de Estudios Universitarios de Acuña, A.C.
Km. 4 Carretera Presa la Amistad, 26200 Ciudad Acuña, Coahuila
Tel: +52(877) 72-14-97
EMail: jmendez@ciqa.mx

Rector: Misael López Reyes

Degrees and Diplomas: *Licenciatura*

Last Updated: 04/04/08

UNIVERSITY STUDIES CENTRE OF MONTERREY

Centro de Estudios Universitarios Monterrey (CEUM)

Hidalgo, 531, Pte., Col. Centro, 64000 Monterrey, Nuevo León
Tel: +52(81) 82-62-72-00
Fax: +52(81) 83-44-39-60
EMail: rectoria@ceu.edu.mx
Website: http://www.ceu.edu.mx

Rector: Ramón de la Peña Manrique

Directora Administrativa: San Juana Castro
EMail: sanjuanac@ceu.edu.mx

Vicerrector: Juan Roberto Martínez EMail: juanm@ceu.edu.mx

Divisions

Administration (Administration; Business Administration; Economics; Human Resources; International Business; International Economics; International Relations; Marketing); **Engineering and Computer Science** (Electrical and Electronic Engineering; Electrical Engineering; Engineering; Industrial Management; Mechanical Engineering; Systems Analysis); **Humanities and Social Sciences** (Administrative Law; Advertising and Publicity; Arts and Humanities; Cinema and Television; Civil Law; Communication Studies; Constitutional Law; Criminal Law; Design; Development Studies; Documentation Techniques; Educational Psychology; Fiscal Law; Graphic Design; International Law; Journalism; Labour Law; Law; Mass Communication; Pedagogy; Photography; Private Law; Psychology; Psychotherapy; Public Relations; Radio and Television Broadcasting; Social Psychology; Social Sciences; Social Studies; Special Education; Vocational Education); **Sports and Physical Education** (Physical Education; Sports; Sports Management)

Programmes

Veterinary Medicine (Veterinary Science)

Further Information: Units: Monterrey, Guadalupe, América, Loma Larga and Victoria

History: Founded 1970.

Academic Year: January to December (January-April; May-August; September-December)

Admission Requirements: Secondary school certificate (bachillerato)

Fees: (Pesos): Registration, 1,620; tuition, 1,830 per quarter

Main Language(s) of Instruction: Spanish, English

Accrediting Agencies: Asociación Nacional de Universidades e Instituciones de Educación Superior (ANUIES); Federación de Instituciones Mexicanas Particulares de Educación Superior (FIMPES)

Degrees and Diplomas: *Licenciatura*: 4 yrs; *Maestría*: a further 2 yrs

Student Services: Academic counselling, Cultural centre, Employment services, Foreign student adviser, Handicapped facilities, Language programs, Nursery care, Sports facilities

Libraries: Central Library

Press or Publishing House: CEU Press

Last Updated: 18/07/12

UNIVERSITY STUDIES CENTRE OF THE CRISTÓBAL COLÓN INSTITUTE

Centro de Estudios Universitarios del Instituto Cristóbal Colón

5 de Mayo, 5210, Diagonal Defensores de la República, Col. Adolfo López Mateos, 72240 Puebla, Puebla
Tel: +52(222) 220-11-17
Fax: +52(222) 220-11-17

Director: Luis Mirón Terrón

Degrees and Diplomas: *Licenciatura*

Last Updated: 04/04/08

UNIVERSITY STUDIES CENTRE OF THE GULF

Centro de Estudios Universitarios del Golfo

Mérida, 6, Col. Progreso, Macuiltepetl, 91130 Xalapa, Veracruz
Tel: +52(228) 815-28-16
Fax: +52(228) 815-28-16

Director: Daniel Apolos Flores Salazar

Degrees and Diplomas: *Licenciatura*

Last Updated: 04/04/08

UNIVERSITY STUDIES CENTRE OF THE NORTH

Centro de Estudios Universitarios del Norte (CEUN)

Avenida 3era. Norte, 107, Ciudad Delicias, Chihuahua
Tel: +52(614) 474-44-66
Website: http://www.ceun.com.mx

Director: Humberto Licón Mendoza

Programmes

Business Computing (Business Computing); **Communication Studies** (Communication Studies); **Computer Science** (Computer Science); **Law** (Law); **Psychology** (Psychology)

History: Founded 1992.

Main Language(s) of Instruction: Spanish

Degrees and Diplomas: *Licenciatura*

Last Updated: 10/03/08

UREG UNIVERSITY CENTRE

El Centro Universitario UTEG

Héroes Ferrocarrileros 1325, Col. La Aurora, 44460 Guadalajara, Jalisco
Tel: +52(33) 10-78-80-00
Website: http://www.uteg.edu.mx

Rector: José Roque Albin Huerta

Programmes

Accountancy (Accountancy); **Administration** (Administration); **Architecture** (Architecture); **Business and Commerce**; **Business Computing** (Business Computing); **Chemistry** (Biology; Chemistry; Pharmacy); **Engineering** (Civil Engineering; Computer Engineering; Electronic Engineering; Industrial Engineering); **Gastronomy** (Cooking and Catering); **Graphic Design** (Graphic Design); **Interior Design** (Interior Design); **International Business** (International Business); **Law** (Law); **Marketing** (Marketing); **Nutrition** (Nutrition); **Physical Education and Sports** (Physical Education; Sports); **Psychology** (Psychology); **Social Work** (Social Work)

Further Information: Also branch in Zapopan, Cruz del Sur, Pedro Moreno

History: Founded 1968 as Instituto Superior de Comercio y Administración. Acquired present status and title 2008.

Main Language(s) of Instruction: Spanish

Degrees and Diplomas: *Licenciatura*; *Maestría*

Last Updated: 08/03/13

VALLE DEL BRAVO UNIVERSITY

Universidad Valle del Bravo (UVB)

Calle Laredo #1107, Esq. Laguna del Carpintero, Col. La Laguna, 88760 Ciudad Reynosa, Tamaulipas
Tel: +52(889) 920-04-71 +52(889) 920-03-95
Fax: +52(889) 920-17-50 Ext.1215
EMail: lng_gastelum@mail.uvb.edu.mx

President: Juan Gastélum Castro

Executive President: Bertha de Lourdes Gastélum
Tel: +52(889) 920-20-65 Ext.1207/1217
EMail: bgastelum@mail.uvb.edu.mx

International Relations: Yadira Maribel Corona Silva
Tel: +52(899) 920-20-65 Ext. 1229
EMail: yarida-corona@mail.uvb.edu.mx

Divisions

Economic and Administration (Accountancy; Administration; Economics; International Business; Labour and Industrial Relations; Marketing; Psychology); **Engineering and Technology** (Civil Engineering; Computer Engineering; Electronic Engineering; Environmental Engineering; Industrial Engineering; Information Technology; Mechanical Engineering); **Health Sciences** (Dentistry;

Medicine; Nursing); **Social Sciences** (Communication Studies; Fiscal Law; Graphic Design; International Law; Law; Tourism)

History: Founded 1976. A private institution recognized by the State.

Academic Year: September to August (September-December; January-April; May-August) and January to December (January-June; August-December)

Admission Requirements: Secondary school certificate (Certificado de Secundaria), High School Certificate (Certificado de Preparatoria)

Fees: (US Dollars): 10,500-18,200 per semester

Main Language(s) of Instruction: Spanish

Degrees and Diplomas: *Licenciatura*: 3-5 yrs; *Maestría*: a further 2-3 yrs

Student Services: Academic counselling, Employment services, Foreign student adviser, Handicapped facilities, Health services, Social counselling, Sports facilities

Special Facilities: Laboratories; Dental Clinic

Libraries: Library with access to Internet and databases

CIUDAD VICTORIA UNIT

UNIDAD CIUDAD VICTORIA

Ocho Matamoros y Guerrero, 306, Col. Centro, 87000 Ciudad Victoria, Tamaulipas
Tel: +52(834) 312-13-92 +52(834) 312-01-80
Fax: +52(834) 312-79-02
EMail: leticia.ortiz@victoria.uvb.edu.mx

Vicerrectora: Leticia Ortíz Luna Tel: +52(834) 312-01-80 Ext. 102

Divisions

Economics and Administration (Accountancy; Administration; Psychology) *Director*: Daniel Eduardo Sánchez; **Health Sciences** (Dentistry) *Director*: José Luis Hernández; **Health Sciences** (Medicine) *Director*: Daniel Eduardo Sánchez; **Social Sciences** *Director*: Sara Carolina Sánchez

History: Founded 1981.

Degrees and Diplomas: *Licenciatura*

CULIACÁN UNIT

UNIDAD CULIACÁN

Plaza Palassio, No. 750, Col. Lázaro Cárdenas, 80000 Culiacán, Sinaloa
Tel: +52(667) 715-2888
Fax: +52(667) 715-28-88
EMail: raul.carrillo@culiacan.uvb.edu.mx

Vicerrectora: Susana Cota Guajardo
Tel: +52(667) 715-28-99 Ext. 103

Divisions

Economics and Administration *Director*: Ismael Ortiz; **Engineering and Technology** (Computer Engineering; Industrial Engineering; Mechanical Engineering) *Director*: Ismael Ortiz; **Social Sciences** (Communication Studies; Graphic Design; Law; Tourism) *Director*: Ismael Ortiz

History: Founded 1999.

MANTE UNIT

UNIDAD MANTE

Ocampo Sur, 509, Zona Centro, 89800 El Mante, Tamaulipas
Tel: +52(831) 232-52-68
Fax: +52(831) 232-26-18
EMail: david.rodriguez@mante.uvb.edu.mx

Vicerrector: David Rodríguez Alvarado (2001-)
Tel: +52(831) 232-52-68 Ext.225/226

Divisions

Economics and Administration (Accountancy; Administration; Marketing; Psychology) *Director*: Laura Edith Barrios; **Engineering and Technology** (Industrial Engineering; Information Technology) *Director*: Linda Lamarka; **Social Sciences** *Director*: Claudia Echagaray

History: Founded 1981.

Degrees and Diplomas: *Licenciatura*; *Maestría*

MATAMOROS UNIT

UNIDAD MATAMOROS

Km 2.7 Carretera Matamoros-Reynosa, 87560 Matamoros, Tamaulipas
Tel: +52(868) 810-39-40 al 44
Fax: +52(868) 816-39-38
EMail: magarita.delgado@matamoros.uvb.edu.mx

Vicerrectora: Bertha Margarita Delgado
Tel: +52(868) 815-39-40 al 44 Ext. 102

Divisions

Economics and Administration (Accountancy; Administration; International Business; Labour and Industrial Relations; Marketing; Psychology) *Director*: José Angel Ramírez; **Engineering and Technology** (Computer Engineering; Industrial Engineering; Mechanical Engineering) *Director*: Carlos Joaquín Peña; **Social Sciences** *Director*: José Angel Ramírez

History: Founded 1980.

Degrees and Diplomas: *Licenciatura*; *Maestría*

MOCHIS UNIT

UNIDAD MOCHIS

Blvd. Rosendo G., Castro 119 ote., Entre Zapata y Niños Héroes, 81200 Los Mochis, Sinaloa
Tel: +52(889) 817-36-71
Fax: +52(889) 817-36-72

Vicerrectora: Susana Cota Guajardo

Programmes

Administration - Industrial Relations *(Postgraduate)*; **Administration - Informatics** *(Postgraduate)*; **Business Administration** (Business Administration); **Civil Engineering** *(Preparatoria)* (Civil Engineering); **Communication Sciences** (Communication Studies); **Computer Systems** *(Preparatoria)* (Computer Engineering; Computer Science); **Computer Systems** *(Postgraduate)* (Computer Engineering; Computer Science); **Continuing Education**; **Economics**; **Electrical Mechanism** *(Preparatoria)* (Electrical Engineering); **Electronic Systems** *(Preparatoria)* (Electronic Engineering); **Environmental Engineering** *(Preparatoria)* (Environmental Engineering); **Fiscal Law**; **Graphic Design**; **Higher Education** *(Postgraduate)* (Higher Education); **Industrial Design** *(Postgraduate)* (Industrial Design); **Industrial Management** *(Preparatoria)* (Industrial Management); **Industrial Relations** *(Postgraduate)*; **Informatics** *(Postgraduate)* (Computer Science); **International Business** (International Business); **International Business** *(Postgraduate)* (International Business); **International Law**; **International Marketing** *(Postgraduate)* (International Business; Marketing); **International Relations** *(Postgraduate)* (International Relations); **Law**; **Organisational Development** *(Postgraduate)*; **Political Science** (Political Sciences); **Psychology** *(Postgraduate)* (Psychology); **Public Administration** (Public Administration); **Security and Industrial Hygiene** *(Preparatoria)* (Hygiene; Safety Engineering); **Social Work** *(Postgraduate)* (Social Work); **Taxation** *(Postgraduate)*; **Total Quality** *(Postgraduate)* (Safety Engineering); **Tourism** *(Postgraduate)* (Tourism)

History: Founded 2003.

Degrees and Diplomas: *Licenciatura*: 4 yrs; *Maestría*: a further 2 yrs following Licenciatura

NUEVO LAREDO UNIT

UNIDAD NUEVO LAREDO

Calle Emiliano Zapata, 6150 entre Ave. Monterrey Blvd. Las Torres Col. La Concordia, 88280 Nuevo Laredo, Tamaulipas
Tel: +52(867) 718-70-31 +52(867) 718-70-33
Fax: +52(867) 718-66-26
EMail: jorge.lopez@laredo.uvb.edu.mx

Director: Jorge Luis López Vargas
Tel: +52(867) 718-70-31 Ext. 105 +52(867) 718-70-33 Ext. 105

Divisions

Economics and Administration (International Economics; Marketing; Psychology) *Director*: Mayra Elena García; **Engineering and Technology** *Director*: Noe Aarón Benavides; **Health Sciences** (Dentistry) *Director*: Adolfo Benavides; **Social Sciences** (Communication Studies; Graphic Design; Law) *Director*: Juan Manuel Elizondo

History: Founded 1980.

Degrees and Diplomas: *Licenciatura*; *Maestría*

REYNOSA UNIT

UNIDAD REYNOSA

Calle Laredo 1107, entre Américo Villarreal, y Laguna del Carpintero, Col. La Laguna, 88760 Ciudad Reynosa, Tamaulipas
Tel: +52(899) 920-17-50 +52(899) 920-17-65
Fax: +52(899) 920-03-95
EMail: luciano@mail.uvb.edu.mx

Rector: Efraín Flores Alba

Divisions

Economics and Administration *Director*: María Lina Martínez; **Engineering and Technology** (Computer Engineering; Industrial Engineering; Mechanical Engineering) *Director*: Fabiola Reyes; **Health Sciences** (Medicine; Nursing) *Director*: Raúl Cavazos; **Health Sciences** (Dentistry) *Director*: Eduardo Cano; **Social Sciences** (Communication Studies; Fiscal Law; Graphic Design; International Law; Law; Tourism) *Director*: Antonio Espinoza

History: Founded 1976.

Degrees and Diplomas: *Licenciatura*; *Maestría*

SAN FERNANDO UNIT

UNIDAD SAN FERNANDO

Avenida 2do Centenario s/n, 887600 San Fernando, Tamaulipas
Tel: +52(841) 944-20-96
Fax: +52(841) 844-04-82
EMail: magarita.delgado@matamoros.uvb.edu.mx

Directora: Elena Flores Montalvo
EMail: maria.floresmo@uvb.edu.mx

Divisions

Economics and Administration (Accountancy; Administration) *Director*: josé Luis Flores; **Engineering and Technology** *Director*: José Luis Flores; **Health Sciences** *Director*: José Luis Flores; **Social Sciences** (Social Sciences) *Director*: José Luis Flores

History: Founded 1991.

Main Language(s) of Instruction: Spanish

Degrees and Diplomas: *Licenciatura*; *Maestría*

TAMPICO UNIT

UNIDAD TAMPICO

Prolongación Calle Diez No. 106, Entre Ave. Universidad y Wisconsin, Col. Gustavo Díaz Ordaz, 89108 Tampico, Tamaulipas
Tel: +52(833) 230-25-00
EMail: lourdes.garcia@tampico.uvb.edu.mx

Directora: María de Lourdes García Guerrero (1981-)

Divisions

Economics and Administration (Accountancy; Administration; Labour and Industrial Relations; Marketing) *Director*: Alejandra Sandoval; **Engineering and Technology** (Computer Engineering; Industrial Engineering) *Director*: Alejandro Calderón; **Social Sciences** (Fiscal Law; International Law; Tourism) *Director*: Ricardo Salmón

Degrees and Diplomas: *Licenciatura*; *Maestría*

VASCO DE QUIROGA SCHOOL OF SOCIAL WORK

Escuela de Trabajo Social Vasco de Quiroga
KM. 6 Carretera Colima-Comala, 28450 Comala, Colima
Tel: 52(312)315-54-00
EMail: direccion@etsvascodequiroga.edu.mx
Website: http://www.etsvascodequiroga.edu.mx/

Directora: Clara Alcántar

Programmes

Social Work (Social Work)

History: Founded 1962.

Main Language(s) of Instruction: Spanish

Degrees and Diplomas: *Licenciatura*

Last Updated: 14/02/13

VASCO DE QUIROGA UNIVERSITY

Universidad Vasco de Quiroga (UVAQ)
Avenida Juan Pablo II No. 555, Col. Santa María de Guido, 58090 Morelia, Michoacán
Tel: +52(443) 323-51-71
EMail: informacion@uvaq.edu.mx
Website: http://www.uvaq.edu.mx

Rector: Raúl Martínez Rubio EMail: rectoria@uvaq.edu.mx

Programmes

Administration (Business Administration; Business and Commerce; International Business; Marketing); **Architecture** (Architecture; Design; Interior Design; Regional Planning; Town Planning); **Graphic Design** (Communication Studies; Graphic Design; Interior Design); **Industrial Engineering** (Electrical Engineering; Electronic Engineering; Human Resources); **International Commerce** (International Business; Law; Marketing); **Law** (Law); **Nutrition** (Nutrition); **Philosophy** (Philosophy); **Physical Education and Sports** (Physical Education; Sports); **Psychology** (Clinical Psychology; Experimental Psychology; Psychology; Rehabilitation and Therapy; Social Psychology); **Public Accountancy** (Accountancy)

History: Founded 1980. Acquired present status 1991.

Governing Bodies: Board of Trustees

Academic Year: August to June (August-December; January-June)

Admission Requirements: Secondary school certificate (bachillerato)

Fees: (Pesos): c. 16,500 per annum

Main Language(s) of Instruction: Spanish

International Co-operation: With universities in USA and Spain

Accrediting Agencies: Secretaría de Educación Pública

Degrees and Diplomas: *Licenciatura*: 4-5 yrs; *Especialización*; *Maestría*: 2-2 1/2 yrs

Student Services: Academic counselling, Cultural centre, Employment services, Foreign student adviser, Health services, Language programs, Social counselling, Sports facilities

Special Facilities: Movie studio

Libraries: Yes

Last Updated: 26/10/12

VASCO DE QUIROGA UNIVERSITY CENTRE OF HUEJUTLA

Centro Universitario Vasco de Quiroga de Huejutla
Calle Juárez, 73, Col. Juárez, Huejutla, 43000 Huejutla de Reyes, Hidalgo
Tel: +52(789) 896-01-18
Fax: +52(789) 896-01-18
EMail: cuvaqh@prodigy.net.com
Website: http://cuvaqhstj.edu.mx

Directora: Josefina Matesanz Íbañez

Programmes

Education (Education); **Psychology** (Psychology); **Social Work** (Social Work)

History: Founded 1997.
Main Language(s) of Instruction: Spanish
Degrees and Diplomas: *Licenciatura*
Last Updated: 27/07/12

VERACRUZ CENTRE FOR ADVANCED STUDIES

Centro Superior de Estudios Veracruzano
Av. V. Gómez Farias #722, (E. Zapata y M. Doblado), Col. Centro, 91700 Veracruz, Veracruz
EMail: mkt.univ@cesuver.edu.mx
Website: http://www.cesuver.edu.mx/web2/

Rector: Armando Notario Iparrea

Programmes

Accountancy (Accountancy); **Business Administration** (Business Administration); **Computer Systems** (Computer Science); **Foreign Trade** (Business and Commerce); **International Business** (Business Administration; International Business); **Law** (Law); **Marketing and Advertising** (Advertising and Publicity; Marketing); **Mechanical and Electronic Engineering** (Electronic Engineering; Mechanical Engineering); **Pedagogy** (Pedagogy)

History: Founded 1988.
Main Language(s) of Instruction: Spanish
Degrees and Diplomas: *Licenciatura*; *Maestría*; *Doctorado*
Libraries: Yes
Last Updated: 23/07/12

VERACRUZ INSTITUTE OF HIGHER EDUCATION

Instituto Veracruzano de Educación Superior
Azueta #34, Zona Centro, 91000 Xalapa, Veracruz
Tel: +52(228) 817-20-26
EMail: informes@ives.edu.mx
Website: http://www.ives.edu.mx

Rector: Carlos Arturo Luna Escudero (2001-)
EMail: rectoria@ives.edu.mx

Faculties

Administration and Social Sciences (Accountancy; Business Administration; Marketing); **Engineering** (Architecture; Civil Engineering; Computer Engineering; Graphic Design; Industrial Engineering; Mechanical Engineering); **Humanities** (Communication Studies; Law; Pedagogy; Psychology)

History: Founded 1995.
Main Language(s) of Instruction: Spanish
Degrees and Diplomas: *Licenciatura*; *Especialización*; *Maestría*; *Doctorado*: Education
Last Updated: 22/03/13

VERACRUZ STUDIES CENTRE

Centro de Estudios Veracruz
Ursulo Galvan #383, Col. Adalberto Tejeda, 91910 Boca del Río, Veracruz
Tel: +52(229) 921-68-86
EMail: cev_2003@hotmail.com
Website: http://www.cev.edu.mx
Rector: Carlos Raúl Velázquez Hernández (1999-)

Programmes

Accountancy (Accountancy); **Business Administration** (Business Administration); **Law** (Law); **Marketing and Advertising** (Advertising and Publicity; Marketing); **Psychology** (Psychology)

History: Founded 1999.
Main Language(s) of Instruction: Spanish
Degrees and Diplomas: *Licenciatura*; *Maestría*
Last Updated: 18/07/12

VILLA DEL ESPIRITU SANTO INSTITUTE

Instituto Villa del Espiritu Santo
Nuevo León, Esq. Sinaloa s/n, Col. Petrolera, 96500 Coatzacoalcos, Veracruz
Tel: +52(2) 114-77-05
EMail: ivescoat@prodigy.net

Director: Manuel Alcocer Barrera

Programmes

Education (Education; Preschool Education; Primary Education)

History: Founded 1993.
Main Language(s) of Instruction: Spanish
Degrees and Diplomas: *Licenciatura*; *Especialización*
Last Updated: 22/03/13

VILLANUEVA MONTAÑO SCHOOL OF ACCOUNTANCY AND ADMINISTRATION

Escuela Superior de Contaduría y Administración Villanueva Montaño, S.C.
Calzada de Tlalpán, 2441, Col. Xotepingo, Delegación Coyoacán, 04610 México, D.F.
Tel: +52(55) 55-49-56-61
Fax: +52(55) 55-49-68-77
EMail: informes@villanuevamontano.edu.mx; villamontano@infosel.net.mx
Website: http://www.villanuevamontano.edu.mx

Rector: Eduardo Villanueva Montaño (1993-)

Programmes

Accountancy (Accountancy); **Administration** (Administration); **Business Computing** (Business Computing; Computer Science); **Law** (Law)

History: Founded 1992.
Main Language(s) of Instruction: Spanish
Degrees and Diplomas: *Licenciatura*; *Maestría*
Last Updated: 26/02/13

VILLA RICA UNIVERSITY

Universidad Villa Rica
Avenida Urano, Esq. Progreso, Fracc. Jardines de Mocambo, 92299 Boca del Río, Veracruz
Tel: +52(229) 921-20-01 +52(229) 922-21-47
Fax: +52(229) 921-54-40
EMail: contacto@univillarica.mx
Website: http://www.univillarica.mx

Rector: Héctor Irón Ariza García EMail: rectoria@univillarica.mx

Divisions

Business (Accountancy; Business Administration; Economics; Finance; Marketing); **Design** (Architecture; Graphic Design; Industrial Design); **Engineering** (Civil Engineering; Computer Engineering; Electronic Engineering; Environmental Engineering; Industrial Engineering; Information Technology; Mechanical Engineering; Telecommunications Engineering); **Hospitality, Gastronomy and Tourism** (Cooking and Catering; Hotel Management; Tourism); **Social Sciences** (Communication Studies; Law)

Schools

Health Sciences (Dentistry; Medicine; Nutrition; Physical Therapy; Psychology; Surgery)

Further Information: Also campus in Coatzacoalcos.
History: Founded 1972. Reached an alliance with the Universidad del Valle de México 2011.
Academic Year: September to July (September-January; February-July)
Admission Requirements: Bachillerato
Main Language(s) of Instruction: Spanish
Degrees and Diplomas: *Licenciatura*: 4-5 yrs; *Especialización*; *Maestría*
Last Updated: 29/10/12

VILLASUNCIÓN UNIVERSITY

Universidad Villasunción

Avenida Las Américas, 601 esq. Brasilia, Fracc.
Las Fuentes, 20239 Aguascalientes,
Aguascalientes
Tel: +52(449) 918-08-66
Fax: +52(449) 918-51-12
EMail: uni_villasuncion@hotmail.com
Website: http://www.uvas.edu.mx

Rector: José de Jesús López Muñoz (2008-)
EMail: jesus.lopez@uvas.edu.mx

Programmes

Criminology (Criminology); **Engineering** (Automation and Control Engineering; Computer Engineering; Industrial Engineering); **Law** (Law); **Nursing** (Nursing); **Philosophy** (Philosophy)

Further Information: Also Campus Villa Hidalgo and Campus Encarnación de Díaz

History: Founded in 2000.

Admission Requirements: Certificado de Preparatoria, Certificado de Secundaria

Fees: (Pesos): 9,700 per semester

Main Language(s) of Instruction: Spanish

Degrees and Diplomas: *Licenciatura*

Student Services: Academic counselling, Canteen, Health services, Social counselling, Sports facilities

Last Updated: 15/04/11

VIZCAYA UNIVERSITY OF THE AMERICAS

Universidad Vizcaya de las Américas

Miñón No. 7 Col. Centro, 63000 Tepic, Nayarit
Tel: +52(311) 210-08-00
EMail: contacto@uva.edu.mx
Website: http://www.uva.edu.mx

Director: Ismael Lechuga Rodríguez
EMail: ismael_lechuga@uva.edu.mx

Programmes

Accountancy (Accountancy); **Architecture** (Architecture); **Business Administration** (Business Administration); **Business Computing** (Business Computing); **Communication Sciences and Techniques** (Communication Studies); **Criminology** (Criminology); **Education** (Education); **Fashion Design** (Fashion Design); **Gastronomy** (Cooking and Catering); **Graphic Design** (Graphic Design); **Law** (Criminal Law; Criminology; Law); **Marketing** (Marketing); **Psychology** (Psychology)

Further Information: Also campuses in Ciudad Delicias (Chihuahua); Ciudad Obregón, Sonora; Ciudad Victoria (Tamaulipas); Colima (Colima); Manzanillo (Colima); Piedras Negras (Coahuila) and Uruapan (Michoacán)

History: Founded 2000.

Main Language(s) of Instruction: Spanish

Degrees and Diplomas: *Licenciatura*; *Especialización*; *Maestría*; *Doctorado*: Law

Last Updated: 15/04/11

WESTERN INSTITUTE OF TECHNOLOGY AND HIGHER STUDIES

Instituto Tecnológico y de Estudios Superiores de Occidente (ITESO)

Periférico Sur Manuel Gómez Morin 8585, 45090 Tlaquepaque,
Jalisco
Tel: +52(333) 669-34-34
Fax: +52(333) 669-34-85
EMail: rectoria@iteso.mx
Website: http://www.iteso.mx

Rector: Juan Luis Orozco Hernández

Centres

Social Research and Education (Development Studies; Educational Research; Political Sciences; Social Sciences)

Departments

Architecture and Urban Development (Architectural and Environmental Design; Architecture and Planning; Civil Engineering); **Commerce and Exchange Processes** (Business and Commerce; International Business; Marketing); **Economics, Administration and Finance** (Accountancy; Administration; Economics; Finance; Labour and Industrial Relations); **Education and Values** (Education); **Electronics, Systems Engineering and Informatics** (Computer Engineering; Computer Science; Electronic Engineering); **Health, Psychology and Community Studies** (Development Studies; Health Sciences; Psychology; Social and Community Services); **Social and Culture Studies** (Communication Studies; Education; Social Studies); **Socio-politics and Law** (International Relations; Law; Political Sciences); **Technological and Industrial Processes** (Chemistry; Environmental Engineering; Industrial Engineering; Mechanical Engineering; Safety Engineering)

History: Founded 1957. Recognized by the State 1975.

Governing Bodies: Junta de Gobierno, comprising members of the Instituto Tecnológico y de Estudios Superiores de Occidente (ITESO) Civil Association and members of the Jesuit Congregation; Consejo Universitario; Consejo Académico

Academic Year: August to May (August-November; January-May)

Admission Requirements: Secondary school certificate (bachillerato) and entrance examination (College Board)

Main Language(s) of Instruction: Spanish

Degrees and Diplomas: *Licenciatura*: Administration; Social Sciences, 4 yrs; *Licenciatura*: Architecture (Arquitecto); Engineering; *Especialización*; *Maestría*: a further 2 yrs; *Doctorado*

Student Services: Academic counselling, Canteen, Cultural centre, Employment services, Foreign student adviser, Health services, Nursery care, Social counselling, Sports facilities

Libraries: 'Jorge Villalobos Padilla, S.J.' Library, c. 87,000 vols, c. 1,400 video tapes, c. 22,000 slides; History Library, c. 17,000 vols; Psychology Library, c. 7,000

Publications: Revista Huella *(quarterly)*; Revista Renglones *(quarterly)*; Revista Sinéctica *(quarterly)*

Press or Publishing House: ITESO Press

Last Updated: 21/03/13

WESTHILL UNIVERSITY

Universidad Westhill

Domingo García Ramos, 56, Col. Prados de la Montaña,
Delegación Cuajimalpa De Morelos, 01210 México, D.F.
Tel: +52(555) 292-23-77 al 80
Fax: +52(555) 292-11-21
EMail: admisiones@uw.edu.mx
Website: http://www.westhill.edu.mx

Rector: José María Rioboo Martín

Departments

Languages (Modern Languages)

Faculties

Medicine (Dentistry; Medicine)

Programmes

Architecture (Architecture); **Business Administration** (Business Administration; Marketing); **Dental Surgery** (Dentistry); **Interior Design** (Interior Design); **International Relations** (International Relations); **Law** (Law); **Pedagogy** (Pedagogy); **Psychology** (Psychology)

History: Founded 1992 as Westhill Institute. Acquired present status and title 2001.

Admission Requirements: Certificado de Secundaria and entrance examination

Main Language(s) of Instruction: Spanish

Degrees and Diplomas: *Licenciatura*; *Maestría*

Libraries: Yes

Last Updated: 17/07/12

WINDSOR INSTITUTE OF PROFESSIONAL STUDIES

Instituto Superior de Estudios Profesionales Windsor

Sofía Tena, 1, Col. Viguri, 39060 Chilpancingo de los Bravo, Guerrero
Tel: +52(747) 472-24-66
Fax: +52(747) 472-24-66
EMail: inswind@prodigy.net.mx

Director General: Tony Banden Harden Atkinson

Programmes

English (English); **Marketing and Public Relations** (Marketing; Public Relations); **Tourism** (Management; Tourism)

History: Founded 1995.

Main Language(s) of Instruction: Spanish

Degrees and Diplomas: *Licenciatura*
Last Updated: 07/04/08

WOMEN'S UNIVERSITY OF VERACRUZ-LLAVE

Universidad Femenina de Veracruz-Llave

Vasco Nunez de Balboa, 524, Fracc. Reforma, 91910 Veracruz, Veracruz
Tel: +52(229) 937-14-60

Rectora: Gemma Odila Garzón Arcos

Programmes

Social Work (Social Work)

History: A private institution attached to the Universidad de Veracruz.

Academic Year: March to February (March-August; September-February)

Admission Requirements: Secondary school certificate (bachillerato)

Main Language(s) of Instruction: Spanish

Degrees and Diplomas: *Licenciatura*: 4 yrs

WORLD SCHOOL

Escuela Mundial

Clavel Norte, 6, Col. San Pedro Mártir, Delegación Tlalpán, 14650 México, D.F.
Tel: +52(55) 55-73-11-52
Fax: +52(55) 55-73-28-43
EMail: direccion@escuelamundial.edu.mx
Website: http://www.escuelamundial.edu.mx

Directora: Gabriela Islas Pascual (1993-)

Programmes

Gastronomy (Cooking and Catering); **International Business** (International Business); **Tourism** (Tourism)

History: Founded 1993.

Main Language(s) of Instruction: Spanish

Degrees and Diplomas: *Licenciatura*
Last Updated: 10/01/13

WORLD UNIVERSITY

Universidad Mundial

Abasolo s/n, Entre Colima y Luis Donaldo Colosio, Col. Pueblo Nuevo, 23000 La Paz, Baja California Sur
Tel: +52(612) 125-89-55
Fax: +52(612) 125-89-60
EMail: gallardo@unimundo.edu.mx
Website: http://www.universidadmundial.edu.mx

Rector: Ignacio Gallardo Ballacey (1999-)

Programmes

Accountancy (Accountancy); **Administration** (Administration; Business Administration); **Communication Studies** (Communication Studies); **Criminology** (Criminal Law); **Environmental Engineering** (Environmental Engineering); **Fashion Design** (Fashion Design); **Gastronomy** (Cooking and Catering); **Graphic and Interior Design** (Graphic Design; Interior Design); **Industrial Design** (Industrial Design); **Law** (Law); **Marketing** (Marketing); **Nutrition** (Nutrition); **Psychology** (Psychology); **Tourism** (Tourism); **Visual Arts** (Visual Arts)

Further Information: Also Los Cabos Campus

History: Founded 1999.

Governing Bodies: Asamblea General

Academic Year: September to August

Admission Requirements: Bachillerato

Fees: (Pesos): 24,000 per annum

Main Language(s) of Instruction: Spanish

International Co-operation: With universities in Chile

Accrediting Agencies: Secretaría de Educación Pública

Degrees and Diplomas: *Licenciatura*: 31/2 yrs; *Maestría*; *Doctorado*

Student Services: Academic counselling, Cultural centre, Handicapped facilities, Language programs, Social counselling, Sports facilities

Student Residential Facilities: None

Libraries: Yes
Last Updated: 16/10/12

XOCHICALCO UNIVERSITY

Universidad Xochicalco (CEUX)

Avenida San Francisco, 1139, Fracc. Misión, 22830 Ensenada, Baja California
Tel: +52(646) 174-39-80
EMail: info@xochicalco.edu.mx
Website: http://www.xochicalco.edu.mx

Rector: René Martínez Zabatdeny

Programmes

Accountancy (Accountancy); **Administration** (Administration); **Architecture** (Architecture); **Communication** (Communication Studies); **Criminal Law** (Criminal Law); **Design** (Design); **International Business** (International Business); **International Business and Customs** (International Business); **Law** (Law); **Marketing** (Marketing); **Optometrics** (Optometry); **Psychology** (Psychology)

Schools

Medicine (Medicine)

Further Information: Also branches in Tijuana, La Paz, Hermosillo and Mexicali

History: Founded 1974.

Admission Requirements: Bachillerato

Main Language(s) of Instruction: Spanish

Accrediting Agencies: Secretaría de Educación Pública (SEP); FIMPES

Degrees and Diplomas: *Licenciatura*; *Maestría*

Libraries: Yes
Last Updated: 29/10/12

YMCA UNIVERSITY

Universidad YMCA

Lago Alberto, No 337, Col. Anáhuac, Delegación Miguel Hidalgo, 11320 México, D.F.
Tel: +52(555) 531-05-74 +52(555) 255-47-19
Fax: +52(555) 531-05-74
EMail: uniymca@terra.com
Website: http://www.uniymca.edu.mx

Rector: Juan Baqué González EMail: juanbaque@uniymca.edu.mx

Programmes

Accountancy (Accountancy); **Administration** (Administration); **Computer Engineering** (Computer Engineering); **Education** (Education); **International Marketing** (Marketing); **Law** (Law); **Leisure Administration** (Administration; Leisure Studies); **Psychology** (Psychology); **Sports Science** (Sports)

History: Founded 1993 as Instituto de Estudios Profesionales para la Administración del Tiempo Libre. Acquired present status 2000.

Admission Requirements: College certificate

Main Language(s) of Instruction: Spanish

Degrees and Diplomas: *Licenciatura*: 3 yrs; *Especialización*: 1 yr; *Maestría*: 2 yrs

Student Services: Academic counselling, Employment services, Health services, Language programs, Sports facilities

Libraries: Yes

Last Updated: 17/07/12

ZACI CENTRE FOR ADVANCED STUDIES

Centro de Estudios Superiores Zaci

Calle 40 n°157, Jardines de Santa Lucía, Valladolid, Yucatán

Directora General: Lucila Aguilar

Programmes

Accountancy (Accountancy); **Architecture** (Architecture)

Main Language(s) of Instruction: Spanish

Degrees and Diplomas: *Licenciatura*

Last Updated: 17/07/12

ZAPOPAN INSTITUTE

Instituto Zapopan

Plaza de los Caudillos No 110, 45150 Zapopan, Jalisco

Tel: +52(33) 3342-25-89

EMail: info@instituto-zapopan.com.mx

Website: http://www.instituto-zapopan.com.mx

Directora: Petra Tayde Leal de la Mora

Programmes

Accountancy (Accountancy); **Law** (Law)

History: Founded 2005.

Main Language(s) of Instruction: Spanish

Degrees and Diplomas: *Licenciatura*

Last Updated: 22/03/13

Moldova (Republic of)

STRUCTURE OF HIGHER EDUCATION SYSTEM

Description:

Higher education in Moldova is provided by private and public universities, academies and institutes.The first diploma can be obtained after 4 years for students entering higher education with the Diploma de Bacalaureat, 5 for those with the Atestat de Studi medii de Cultura Generala. Two types of first diplomas are available: the diploma de Licenþã or the diploma de studii superioare universitare. Only the first gives access to higher studies (Master or Doctorate).

Stages of studies:

University level first stage: *Undergraduate studies*
Higher education institutions offer full-time courses in all fields of study, and extramural courses for some of them. Full-time courses last for four to six years, depending on the field of study, external courses require one additional year of study. Two kinds of diplomas are awarded: The Diploma de Licenþã or Diploma de Studii superioare. Only the first gives access to higher studies and research, the second doesn't require any research activity or defence of a thesis.

University level second stage: *Master studies*
Master degree studies aim at consolidating the competences acquired before. The programme lasts from 1 to 2 years after the Diplomã de Licenþã. The admission to this programme is at the institution level. It requires the presentation and defence of a research thesis (Teza de Master).

University level third stage: *Doctoral studies*
This level of higher education in the Republic of Moldova comprises two stages: Doctor of Science and Doctor Habilitat. Admission to doctoral studies is submitted to a competitive examination. Only students with a Master or Licence Degree can participate. The National Council for Certification and Accreditation in collaboration with the Ministry of Education and the Academy of Science establishes the admission criteria and procedures. The title of Doctor of Science is awarded after three to four years of study and research. The public defence of an original research work (Teza de Doctor) is required. Doctor Habilitat is the highest scientific degree conferred in all fields. Candidates must normally hold a Doctor of Science Diploma to be able to apply to the programme. The degree is conferred after the public defence of a doctoral thesis presenting an original contribution in a particular field (Teza de Doctor Habilitat).

ADMISSION TO HIGHER EDUCATION

Admission to university-level studies:

Name of secondary school credential required: Atestat de Studii Medii de Cultura Generală

Name of secondary school credential required: Diploma de Bacalaureat

For entry to: Higher education institutions

Entrance exam requirements: There is a competitive entrance examination in some institutions.

Foreign students admission:

Definition of foreign student: A foreign student is a person enrolled at a higher education institution in a country of which he/she is not a permanent resident.

Entrance exam requirements: Foreign students must present a Secondary School Leaving Certificate. For access to doctoral studies, they must pass a competitive entrance examination.

Entry regulations: Visas may be obtained at the Moldovan Embassies or at border check points.

Health requirements: Medical certificate.

Language requirements: Students must have a good knowledge of Romanian or Russian.

RECOGNITION OF STUDIES

Quality assurance system:

Recognition of studies, diplomas, and academic degrees as well as the confirmation of doctoral or academic degrees fall under the responsibility of the Higher Commission for Diplomas and Degrees (Comisia Superioarã de Atestare).

Bodies dealing with recognition:

Information and Qualification Recognition Office, Ministry of Education

Senior Education Adviser: Rodica Isac
1, Piata Marii Adunari Nationale
Chisinau 2033
Tel: +373(22) 234 570
Fax: +373(22) 233 315
EMail: international@edu.md
WWW: http://www.edu.md/?lng=ro&MenuItem=5&SubMenu0=5

NATIONAL BODIES

Ministerul Educaţiei (Ministry of Education)

Minister: Maia Sandu
Piaţa Marii Adunări Naţionale nr. 1
Chisinau 2033
Tel: +373(22) 233 348
Fax: +373(22) 233 515
EMail: consilier@edu.md
WWW: http://www.edu.md
Role of national body: Governs and finances institutions of higher education.

Consiliul Naţional pentru Acreditare şi Atestare - CNAA (National Council on Accreditation and Attestation)

President: Valeriu Canter
Ştefan cel Mare bd., 180
Chisinau 2004
Tel: +373(22) 296 271
Fax: +373(22) 296 271
EMail: info@cnaa.md
WWW: http://www.cnaa.acad.md/

Data for academic year: 2005-2006
Source: IAU from Division for European Integration, Ministry of Education, 2005, updated by AUF-Chisinau, 2006. Bodies, 2012.

INSTITUTIONS

PUBLIC INSTITUTIONS

ACADEMY OF ECONOMIC STUDIES OF MOLDOVA

Academia de Studii Economice a Moldovei (ASEM)

Strada Banulescu-Bodoni, 51, 2005 Chişinău
Tel: +373(22) 22-41-28
Fax: +373(22) 22-19-68
EMail: anticamera@ase.md
Website: http://www.ase.md

Rector: Grigore Belostecinic (2001-) Tel: +373(22) 40-27-09

Vice Rector, Scientific Research and Foreign Relations: Vadim Cojocaru
Tel: +373(22) 40-27-05, Fax: +373(22) 27-34-91
EMail: aesm@mail.md

International Relations: Victor Grebenscikov, Head of Office, International Relations
Tel: +373(22) 40-27-43, Fax: +373(22) 27-34-91
EMail: grebenscikov@ase.md

Faculties

Accounting (Accountancy; Banking; Finance; Taxation); **Business Management and Administration** (Business Administration;

Human Resources; International Business; Management; Marketing; Public Administration; Public Relations; Retailing and Wholesaling; Technology; Tourism; Transport Management); **Economic Cybernetics, Statistics and Informatics** (Computer Science; Economic and Finance Policy; Information Technology; Mathematics and Computer Science; Statistics; Systems Analysis); **Economics and Law** (Commercial Law; Economic and Finance Policy; Economics; Environmental Management; Geography (Human); Human Resources; Law; Private Law; Public Administration; Public Law); **Finance** (Banking; Finance; Insurance; Philosophy; Political Sciences); **International Economic Relations** (Economic and Finance Policy; International Economics; International Relations)

History: Founded 1991.

Governing Bodies: Senate; Rector

Academic Year: September to December; January to May

Admission Requirements: Diploma de Bacalaureat (or equivalent secondary school certificate)

Fees: (Moldovan Leu): 7,000 for home students; (Euro): 1,000 for international students, per annum

Main Language(s) of Instruction: Romanian, Russian, English, French

International Co-operation: With institutions in Poland, Sweden, Latvia, Bulgaria, France, Ukraine, Romania, Turkey

Accrediting Agencies: National Council of Accreditation and Attestation

Degrees and Diplomas: *Diplomă de Licență*; *Diploma de Studii Superioare Universitare*; *Diploma de Magistru*; *Diploma de Doctor în Științe*; *Diploma de Doctor Habilitat*

Student Services: Academic counselling, Canteen, Cultural centre, Foreign student adviser, Foreign Studies Centre, Health services, Language programs, Social counselling, Sports facilities

Student Residential Facilities: 7 student hostels

Publications: Drept, Economie si Informatica *(quarterly)*; Economica, Scientific and educational journal. *(quarterly)*

Press or Publishing House: AESM Editing; AESM Publishing

Last Updated: 28/02/12

ACADEMY OF MUSIC, THEATRE AND FINE ARTS

Academia de Muzică, Teatru și Arte Plastice (AMTAP)

Strada A. Mateevici, 111, 2014 Chișinău
Tel: +373(22) 24-15-21
Fax: +373(22) 23-40-60
EMail: amtap@mdl.net
Website: http://www.amtap.md

Rector: Victoria Melnic
Tel: +373(22) 22-19-49, Fax: +373(22) 22-19-49

Vice-rector for Economy and Administration: Ion Butucea
Tel: +373(2) 23-81-38

International Relations: Victoria Tcacenco, Head, International Relations and European Integration Department
EMail: amtap2003@yahoo.com

Departments

Modern Languages (Modern Languages); **Philosophy** (Philosophy); **Physical Education** (Physical Education)

Faculties

Fine Arts (Ceramic Art; Fashion Design; Fine Arts; Graphic Arts; Interior Design; Painting and Drawing; Sculpture); **Instrumental Art, Composition and Musicology** (Jazz and Popular Music; Music; Music Theory and Composition; Musical Instruments; Musicology); **Theatre and Arts Management** (Acting; Art Management; Dance; Film; Theatre); **Vocal Art, Conducting and Musical Pedagogy** (Conducting; Music; Music Education; Opera; Religious Music; Singing)

History: Founded 1940. Reorganised into Institute of Arts 1964. Reorganised into Moldova State University of Arts 1998. Acquired present status and title 2002.

Academic Year: September to June

Admission Requirements: Secondary school certificate in Romanian and entrance examination. For the applicants to the Music and Fine Arts, diploma or certificate of vocational school

Fees: (Lei): c. 10,000 per annum; (Euros): foreign students, c. 1,500

Main Language(s) of Instruction: Romanian, Russian

Degrees and Diplomas: *Diplomă de Licență*; *Diploma de Magistru*; *Diploma de Doctor în Științe (PhD)*

Student Residential Facilities: For 160 students

Special Facilities: 2 Concert Halls. Art Gallery

Libraries: Yes

Last Updated: 28/02/12

ALECU RUSSO BALTI STATE UNIVERSITY

Universitatea de Stat Alecu Russo din Bălți (ARUB)

Strada Pușkin, 38, 2131 Bălți
Tel: +373(231) 2-30-66
Fax: +373(231) 2-30-39
EMail: rectorat.usb@gmail.com
Website: http://www.usb.md

Rector: Gheorghe Popa

First Vice-Rector: Alexandru Balanici
EMail: Alexandru.Balanici@usb.md

International Relations: Valentina Pritcan
EMail: Valentina.Pritcan@usb.md

Centres

British Culture (Cultural Studies; Education; Teacher Training) *Director*: Elena Varzari; **Continuing Education** (Education; Educational Technology; Staff Development; Teacher Training) *Director*: Valeriu Guțan; **Documentation** (Economics; Education; European Studies; Health Sciences; Law; Public Health; Social Sciences; Sociology) *Director*: Elena Harconita; **Francosphere** *Director*: Tatiana Grosu; **Information Technology** (Information Management; Information Sciences; Information Technology) *Head*: Mihail Pascaru; **Polish Culture** *Division Head*: Danuta Kopecka; **Regional Depitory Fund of World Bank** *Director*: Elena Harconita; **Resource** *(Regional) Director*: Dina Puiu

Colleges

"Amadeus" Art Lycee (Dance; Education; Painting and Drawing; Teacher Training; Theatre) *Director*: Petru Roman; **"Ion Creangă" Theoretical Lycee** (Education; Native Language Education; Pedagogy; Teacher Training; Technology) *Head*: Petru Roman; **Ion Crengă Pedagogical College** (Education; Pedagogy; Preschool Education; Primary Education; Teacher Training) *Head*: Petru Roman

Departments

Agricultural Technology *Head*: Boris Boincean; **Applied Informatics and Information Technology** (Computer Engineering; Computer Networks; Data Processing; Systems Analysis) *Head*: Eugeniu Plohotniuc; **Biology, Chemistry and Geography** (Analytical Chemistry; Biochemistry; Biological and Life Sciences; Chemistry; Geography; Histology; Inorganic Chemistry; Mathematics; Meteorology; Mineralogy; Natural Resources; Natural Sciences; Organic Chemistry; Petrology; Physiology; Surveying and Mapping) *Head*: Maria Nicorici; **Economics and Management** (Business Administration; Business and Commerce; Management; Management Systems; Marketing; Private Administration; Public Administration; Public Relations; Secretarial Studies; Small Business) *Head*: Ala Trusevici; **Electronics and Informatics** *Head*: Nicolae Filip; **English Language** *Head*: Liubovi Tomailî; **English Philology** (Arts and Humanities; Education; Linguistics; Literature; Teacher Training; Writing) *Head*: Lulia Ignatiuc; **Finance and Accountancy** (Accountancy; Administration; Banking; Business Administration; Business and Commerce; Business Computing; Finance; Human Resources; Insurance; Taxation) *Head*: Nelli Amarfii-Raileanu; **French Language** *Head*: Ludmila Cabac; **French Philology** (Arts and Humanities; Education; Literature; Teacher Training; Translation and Interpretation; Writing) *Head*: Angela Cosciug; **German Philology** (Arts and Humanities; Education; Linguistics; Literature; Teacher Training; Writing) *Head*: Ana Pomelnicova; **Information Technology** (Information Management; Information Sciences; Information Technology) *Head*: Mihail Pascaru; **Mathematics** (Education; Mathematics; Mathematics Education; Teacher Trainers Education) *Head*: Natalia Gasitoi; **Military** (Military Science; Peace and Disarmament) *Head*: Stefan Grosu; **Musical Instruments** *Head*: Marina Morari; **Pedagogy, Primary Education and Pre-school Education** (Educational Sciences; Pedagogy;

Preschool Education; Primary Education; Teacher Trainers Education) *Head*: Maria Pereteatcu; **Physical Training** (Physical Education; Sports) *Head*: Alexandru Moraru; **Physics** *Head*: Mihail Popa; **Private Law** (Administrative Law; Canon Law; Civil Law; Commercial Law; Constitutional Law; Criminal Law; Fiscal Law; International Law; Justice Administration; Labour Law; Law; Notary Studies) *Head*: Veaceslav Pînzari; **Psychology and Social Assistance** (Clinical Psychology; Communication Studies; Educational Psychology; Educational Sciences; Psychology; Social Problems; Social Psychology; Social Sciences; Sociology) *Head*: Galina Petcu; **Public Law** (Administrative Law; Constitutional Law; Criminal Law; Fiscal Law; Human Rights; International Law; Public Law) *Head*: Elena Botnari; **Romanian and Universal Literature** (Arts and Humanities; Comparative Literature; Education; Ethnology; Folklore; Journalism; Literacy Education; Teacher Training) *Head*: Nicolae Leahu; **Romanian Language** (Ethnology; Folklore; Grammar; Native Language; Philology; Phonetics; Teacher Training; Terminology) *Head*: Gheorghe Popa; **Russian Language and Literature** *Head*: Elena Sirota; **Social Subjects and the Humanities** *Head*: Nicolae Enciu; **Techniques and Technology** (Maintenance Technology; Mechanical Equipment and Maintenance; Metal Techniques; Technology Education) *Head*: Pavel Topala; **Theory and Conducting** (Acting; Conducting; Music Education; Music Theory and Composition; Performing Arts; Singing; Theatre) *Head*: Vlmadimir Babii; **Ukrainian Language and Literature** *Head*: Valeriu Vorobceno

Faculties

Economics (Business Administration; Economics; Management; Marketing; Social Sciences) *Dean*: Ala Trusevici; **Foreign Languages and Literatures** (Arts and Humanities; English; French; German; Linguistics; Literature; Modern Languages; Spanish; Teacher Training; Translation and Interpretation; Writing) *Dean*: Elena Dragan; **Law** (Criminology; Law; Private Law; Public Law; Welfare and Protective Services) *Dean*: Gheorghe Neagu; **Music and Music Pedagogy** (Arts and Humanities; Conducting; Music; Music Education; Musical Instruments; Musicology; Singing; Teacher Training; Theatre) *Dean*: Margareta Tetelea; **Natural Sciences and Agro-ecology** (Agriculture; Agronomy; Biology; Geography; Natural Sciences; Soil Science) *Dean*: Stanislav Stadnic; **Pedagogy, Psychology and Social Assistance** (Pedagogy; Preschool Education; Primary Education; Psychology; Social Problems; Social Psychology; Social Work; Teacher Training) *Dean*: Valentina Pritcan; **Philology** (Arts and Humanities; Classical Languages; English; French; German; Journalism; Linguistics; Literature; Romanian; Russian; Spanish; Teacher Training) *Dean*: Maria Şleahtiţchi; **Techniques, Physics, Mathematics and Informatics** (Computer Science; Mathematics; Metal Techniques; Physics; Radiophysics; Solid State Physics; Teacher Training; Technology) *Dean*: Alexandru Balanici

History: Founded 1945 and became Pedagogical Institute 1953. Acquired present status and title 1992.

Governing Bodies: Senate

Academic Year: September to June (September-January; February-June)

Admission Requirements: Secondary school certificate

Fees: (Lei): c. 6,500 per annum

Main Language(s) of Instruction: Romanian, Russian; Ukrainian; English; French; German

International Co-operation: With universities in Germany; France; Russian Federation; Ukraine; Romania; Netherlands; Greece; Norway; USA; Belarus; Malta; Bulgaria and Spain

Accrediting Agencies: Ministry of Education

Degrees and Diplomas: *Diploma de Studii Superioare Universitare*: Philology; Law; Modern Languages and Literatures; Psychology; Pedagogy; Mathematics and Informatics; Management; Music Choregraphy; Acting; Translation and Interpretation; Physics; Social Work; Economy; Computer Science; Physics; *Diploma de Magistru*: Education; Linguistics; Literatures; Modern and Classical Languages; Philology; Pedagogy; Computer Science; Physics; Mathematics

Student Services: Academic counselling, Canteen, Cultural centre, Employment services, Foreign student adviser, Foreign Studies Centre, Handicapped facilities, Health services, Language programs, Social counselling, Sports facilities

Student Residential Facilities: For c. 2,200 students

Libraries: Scientific Library, c. 1.2 m. vols

Publications: Scientific Papers, Physics and Technology; Artistic Education *(biannually)*

Last Updated: 22/01/10

'B.P.HAŞDEU' CAHUL STATE UNIVERSITY

Universitatea de Stat din Cahul 'B.P.Haşdeu'
Piata Independentei, 1, 3901 Cahul
Tel: +373(299) 2-24-81
Fax: +373(299) 2-47-52
EMail: rectorat@usch.md
Website: http://www.usch.md

Rector: Andrei Popa
Tel: +373(299) 2-24-82, Fax: +373(299) 2-24-82

Faculties

Economics, Mathematics and Computer Science (Accountancy; Applied Mathematics; Business Administration; Economics; Engineering; Finance; Management; Mathematics and Computer Science); **Law and Public Administration** (Law; Public Administration); **Philology and History** (Classical Languages; Educational Psychology; English; French; History; Literature; Modern Languages; Pedagogy; Philology; Primary Education; Psychology; Romanian)

History: Founded 1999.

Degrees and Diplomas: *Diplomă de Licenţă*; *Diploma de Magistru*

Last Updated: 23/02/12

COMRAT STATE UNIVERSITY

Universitatea de Stat din Comrat
Strada Galatsana 17, 3800 Comrat
Tel: +373(298) 2-43-45
Fax: +373(298) 2-34-81
EMail: kdu_91@mail.ru
Website: http://www.kdu.md

Rector: Zinaida Arikova
Tel: +373(298) 2-34-81, Fax: +373(298) 2-34-81

Faculties

Agricultural Technology (Agricultural Engineering; Agronomy; Zoology); **Economics** (Accountancy; Economics; Management; Marketing); **Law** (Law); **National Culture** (Bulgarian; Cultural Studies; English; History; Pedagogy; Primary Education; Romance Languages; Romanian; Turkish)

History: Founded 1991 as Gagauz National University. Acquired present status and title 2002.

Academic Year: September to June (September-December; January-June)

Fees: (Lei): 2,500-5,500 per annum

Main Language(s) of Instruction: Romanian, Caucasian, Russian, Bulgarian

Degrees and Diplomas: *Diploma de Studii Superioare Universitare*: Law; Economics; Agriculture; Philology; Pedagogy; Culture, 4-5 yrs; *Diploma de Magistru*: Law; Economics; Turkish Philology, 1 yr; *Diploma de Doctor în Ştiinţe*: Economics; Turkish Philology, 4 yrs

Student Services: Academic counselling, Canteen, Cultural centre, Employment services, Foreign student adviser, Foreign Studies Centre, Health services, Language programs, Social counselling, Sports facilities

Libraries: Central Library, c. 55,000 vols

Press or Publishing House: University Press

Last Updated: 28/02/12

ION CREANGĂ PEDAGOGICAL STATE UNIVERSITY

Universitatea Pedagogică de Stat Ion Creangă (UPS)
Strada Ion Creangă, 1, 2069 Chişinău
Tel: +373(22) 74-54-14
Fax: +373(22) 74-99-14
EMail: upsc_studii@yahoo.com
Website: http://www.upsc.md

Rector: Nicolae Chicuş

First Vice-Rector: Mihail Grosu
Tel: +373(22) 74-33-64 EMail: grosump@yahoo.com

Vice-Rector, Administration: Tudor Rotaru
Tel: +373(22) 74-33-58 EMail: rotaru_t@yahoo.com

Faculties

Computer Science and Information Technology in Education (Educational Technology; Information Technology; Mathematics and Computer Science); **Continuing Education in K-12 Institutional Management and Pre-School Educators** (Educational Administration; Preschool Education); **Fine Arts and Design** (Design; Educational Technology; Fashion Design; Fine Arts; Graphic Arts; Graphic Design; Painting and Drawing; Sculpture); **Foreign Languages and Literatures** (Bulgarian; Comparative Literature; English; French; German; Italian; Modern Languages; Philology); **History and Ethno-Pedagogy** (Civics; English Studies; Ethnology; French Studies; Geography (Human); History); **Pedagogy** (Dance; Educational Technology; Pedagogy; Preschool Education; Primary Education; Social Sciences); **Philology** (Bulgarian; Cultural Studies; English; Italian; Linguistics; Literature; Philology; Romanian; Russian; Turkish); **Psychology and Special Psycho-Pedagogy** (Educational Psychology; Psychology; Social Work; Special Education)

History: Founded 1940, acquired present status 1992. A public institution.

Governing Bodies: Senate comprising 35 members

Academic Year: September to June

Admission Requirements: Secondary school certificate (Diplom de bacalaureat), Atestat de Studii Medii (11-12 clase)

Fees: (US Dollars): 800 per annum; preparatory pre-university course, 500

Main Language(s) of Instruction: Romanian, Russian, English, German, French, Italian

International Co-operation: With universities in Germany. Also participates in DAAD; Arbeitskreis Beldrussisch-Deutsche Begegnungen; Soros Foundation and ECTS programmes.

Degrees and Diplomas: *Diplomă de Licenţă*: Psychology; History; Pedagogy; Philology; *Diploma de Studii Superioare Universitare*: Psychology; History; Pedagogy; Philology; *Diploma de Magistru*: Philology; History; Pedagogy; Psychology; Fine Arts (MA)

Student Services: Academic counselling, Canteen, Cultural centre, Employment services, Foreign student adviser, Health services, Language programs, Social counselling, Sports facilities

Student Residential Facilities: Yes

Special Facilities: "Ion Creangă" Museum

Libraries: University Scientific Library

Press or Publishing House: University Publishing House

Last Updated: 01/03/12

MOLDOVA INTERNATIONAL RELATIONS INSTITUTE

Institutul de Stat de Relaţii Internaţionale din Modova (IRIM)

Puşkin, 54, Chişinău
Tel: +373(22) 22-83-20
Fax: +373(22) 21-09-62
EMail: irim_lawdepartment@mail.md
Website: http://www.irim.md

Rector: Vasile Guţu

Faculties

Law (Law); **Modern Languages** (Modern Languages; Translation and Interpretation); **World Economics and International Economic Relations** (Administration; Business Education; Economics; Marketing; Tourism)

History: Founded in 2003.

Degrees and Diplomas: *Diplomă de Licenţă*

Last Updated: 28/02/12

MOLDOVA STATE UNIVERSITY

Universitatea de Stat din Moldova (USM)

Str. A. Mateevici, 60, 2009 Chişinău
Tel: +373(22) 57-74-01
Fax: +373(22) 24-42-48
EMail: rectorat@usm.md; international@usm.md
Website: http://www.usm.md

Rector: Gheorghe Ciocanu (2007-)
Tel: +373(22) 57-74-01, Fax: +373(22) 24-42-48
EMail: rector@usm.md

Vice-Rector: Igor Enicov
Tel: +373(22) 57-78-32 EMail: enicov@usm.md

International Relations: Angela Niculita, Head of International Relations
Tel: +373(22) 57-78-08, Fax: +373(22) 24-42-48
EMail: angela.niculitsa@yahoo.com

Faculties

Biology and Soil Science (Biology; Biotechnology; Ecology; Environmental Studies; Forestry; Geography; Geology; Industrial Chemistry; Molecular Biology; Parks and Recreation; Soil Science) *Dean*: Maria Duca; **Chemistry and Chemical Technology** (Analytical Chemistry; Ceramics and Glass Technology; Chemistry; Cosmetology; Environmental Engineering; Industrial Chemistry; Inorganic Chemistry; Medical Technology; Organic Chemistry; Physical Chemistry) *Dean*: Viorica Gladchih; **Economics** (Accountancy; Banking; Economics; Finance; International Economics; Management; Marketing) *Dean*: Galina Ulian; **Foreign Languages and Literatures** (Arabic; English; French; German; Greek; Italian; Japanese; Modern Languages; Polish; Portuguese; Spanish; Swedish; Turkish) *Dean*: Ludmila Zbant; **History and Psychology** (Archaeology; Ethnology; History; Museum Studies; Philosophy; Psychology) *Dean*: Constantin Solomon; **International Relations, Political and Administrative Sciences** (International Relations; Political Sciences; Public Administration) *Dean*: Vasile Cujba; **Journalism and Communication Sciences** (Archiving; Communication Studies; Documentation Techniques; Information Management; Journalism; Library Science; Publishing and Book Trade) *Dean*: Constantin Marin; **Law** (Administrative Law; Civil Law; Commercial Law; Constitutional Law; Criminal Law; International Law; Law) *Dean*: Gheorghe Avornic; **Mathematics and Computer Science** (Applied Mathematics; Automation and Control Engineering; Computer Science; Information Management; Mathematics; Modern Languages) *Dean*: Andrei Perjan; **Philology** (English; French; Greek; Latin; Philology; Romance Languages; Romanian; Russian) *Dean*: Irina Condrea; **Physics** (Computer Science; Information Technology; Measurement and Precision Engineering; Meteorology; Physics; Power Engineering) *Dean*: Petru Gaşin; **Psychology and Educational Sciences** *Dean*: Vladimir Gutu; **Sociology and Social Work** (Demography and Population; Philosophy; Social Work; Sociology) *Dean*: Maria Bulgaru

Further Information: Also preparatory courses for foreign students

History: Founded 1946. Under the authority of the Ministry of Education. Financed by the State.

Governing Bodies: Senate; Administrative Council

Academic Year: September to June (September-December; January-June)

Admission Requirements: Competitive entrance examination; Baccalaureat Diploma required or Secondary School Certificate or equivalent certificate

Fees: (Lei): 2,000-7,000 per annum, depending on Faculty; Extramural (correspondence) courses, 800-3,500

Main Language(s) of Instruction: Romanian, Russian

International Co-operation: With universities in Belgium; Bulgaria; Finland; France; Greece; Germany; Italy; Poland; Romania; Russian Federation; Spain; Sweden; Turkey; Ukraine and USA. Also participates in Tempus, Erasmus Mundus, FP-7, CRDF and DAAD programmes

Accrediting Agencies: Ministry of Education

Degrees and Diplomas: *Diplomă de Licenţă*: 3-4 yrs; *Diploma de Magistru*: 1 1/2-2 yrs after Licenţa; *Diploma de Doctor în Ştiinţe*: a further 3 yrs and thesis; *Diploma de Doctor Habilitat*: by thesis

Student Services: Academic counselling, Canteen, Cultural centre, Foreign student adviser, Health services, Language programs, Social counselling, Sports facilities

Special Facilities: Natural History Museum; Astrophysical Observatory

Libraries: c. 2m. vols

Publications: Analele Stiintifice ale Universitatii de Stat Din Moldova, Scientific Annals (Exact and Natural Sciences; Social

Sciences and Humanisties) *(annually)*; Studia Universitatis, University Studies (since 2007); Series: Natural Sciences; Exact and Economic Sciences; Social Sciences; Humanities; Educational Sciences *(biannually)*; Universitatea de Stat din Moldova, Newspaper *(monthly)*

Press or Publishing House: Centrul Editorial al USM (MSU Publishing Centre)

Last Updated: 22/01/10

NICOLAE TESTEMIŢANU MOLDOVA STATE UNIVERSITY OF MEDICINE AND PHARMACY

Universitatea de Stat de Medicină şi Farmacie Nicolae Testemiţanu (USMF)

Bulevardul Ştefan cel Mare, 165, 2004 Chişinău
Tel: +373(22) 24-34-08
Fax: +373(22) 24-23-44
EMail: rector@usmf.md
Website: http://www.usmf.md

Rector: Ion Ababii (2008-)
Tel: +373(22) 24-34-08, Fax: +373(22) 24-23-44

Vice-Rector for Quality and Integration in Education: Olga Cernetchi Tel: +373(22) 24-27-54 EMail: ocernetchi@yahoo.com

International Relations: Rodica Gramma, Director, Department of External Relations and European Integration
Tel: +373(22) 20-03-40, Fax: +373(22) 20-03-40
EMail: relatiiexterne@usmf.md

Faculties

Continuous Medical Education (Medicine); **Dentistry** (Dentistry; Stomatology); **Medicine I** *(National students)* (Anaesthesiology; Anatomy; Epidemiology; Medicine; Orthopaedics; Paediatrics; Parasitology; Surgery; Tropical Medicine); **Medicine II** *(Overseas students)* (Dermatology; Ethics; Genetics; Modern Languages; Molecular Biology; Neurology; Otorhinolaryngology; Paediatrics; Philosophy; Public Health; Romanian; Social and Preventive Medicine; Surgery; Venereology); **Pharmacy** (Pharmacology; Pharmacy); **Residency and Fellowship Studies**

History: Founded 1945, acquired present status 1991. A State institution.

Governing Bodies: Senate, Senate Bureau, Scientific Council, Administration Council, Rectorate

Academic Year: September-January; February-June

Admission Requirements: Diploma de Bacalaureat, Diploma de studii medii de specialitate de medicină – for local students

Fees: (MDL): 17,400 (Faculty of Medicine); 20,300 (Faculty of Dentistry); 18,200 (Faculty of Pharmacy). Most local students studies are financed by the state, and there are limited places for fee-paying students.

Main Language(s) of Instruction: Romanian, Russian, English, French

International Co-operation: with institutions in Romania, France, Poland, Germany, Belgium.

Accrediting Agencies: National Council of Evaluation and Accreditation of Educational Institutions.

Degrees and Diplomas: *Diplomă de Licenţă*: Medicine; Public Health; Pharmacy; Stomatology, 3 - 5 yrs; *Diploma de Studii Superioare Universitare*: Medicine; Public Health; Pharmacy; Stomatology, 5 - 6 yrs; *Diploma de Magistru*: Medicine; Public Health; Pharmacy; Stomatology, 2 yrs; *Diploma de Doctor în Ştiinţe*: Medicine; Public Health; Pharmacy; Stomatology

Student Services: Academic counselling, Canteen, Cultural centre, Employment services, Foreign student adviser, Foreign Studies Centre, Handicapped facilities, Health services, Language programs, Social counselling, Sports facilities

Student Residential Facilities: Yes

Special Facilities: Anatomy Museum

Libraries: Central Library, c. 1,000,000 vols

Publications: Curierul Medical (Medical Courier), Medical journal published 6 times per year *(bimonthly)*

Academic Staff *2012-2013*	**TOTAL**
FULL-TIME	**698**
PART-TIME	**143**
STAFF WITH DOCTORATE	
FULL-TIME	**698**
Student Numbers *2012-2013*	
All (Foreign Included)	**5,595**
FOREIGN ONLY	**1,401**

Last Updated: 07/02/13

STATE AGRARIAN UNIVERSITY OF MOLDOVA

Universitatea Agrară de Stat din Moldova (UASM)

Strada Mirceşti, 44, 2049 Chişinău
Tel: +373(22) 31-22-58
Fax: +373(22) 31-22-76
EMail: info@uasm.md
Website: http://www.uasm.md

Rector: Gheorghe Pavel Cimpoieş (1998-)
Tel: +373(22) 43-24-90 EMail: cimpoies@uasm.md

Vice-Rector: Vasile Vrancean

Faculties

Accountancy (Accountancy); **Agricultural Engineering and Auto Transportation** (Agricultural Engineering; Automotive Engineering); **Agronomy** (Agricultural Engineering; Agricultural Management; Agronomy; Biochemistry; Botany; Natural Sciences); **Animal Husbandry and Biotechnologies** (Animal Husbandry; Biotechnology; Physical Education); **Cadastre and Law** (Environmental Engineering; Law; Physics; Private Law; Public Law; Real Estate; Rural Planning; Surveying and Mapping); **Economics** (Banking; Business Administration; Business and Commerce; Crop Production; Economics; Finance; International Economics; Marketing; Tourism; Transport Management); **Horticulture** (Forestry; Horticulture; Viticulture); **Veterinary Medicine** (Animal Husbandry; Parasitology; Veterinary Science; Zoology); **Zootechnics and Biotechnology** (Biotechnology; Zoology)

Further Information: Also Pre-University Training of International Students

History: Founded 1940. A State institution.

Governing Bodies: Senate

Academic Year: September to July (September-January; February-July)

Admission Requirements: Secondary school certificate or equivalent

Fees: (US Dollars): c. 800-1,000 per annum

Main Language(s) of Instruction: Romanian, Russian, English

Degrees and Diplomas: *Diplomă de Licenţă*; *Diploma de Studii Superioare Universitare*; *Diploma de Magistru*; *Diploma de Doctor în Ştiinţe*

Student Services: Academic counselling, Canteen, Cultural centre, Foreign student adviser, Health services, Social counselling, Sports facilities

Student Residential Facilities: Yes

Special Facilities: University Museum

Libraries: c. 80,000 vols

Publications: 'Scientific Works' (Vol. I, II, III)

Last Updated: 28/02/12

STATE UNIVERSITY OF PHYSICAL EDUCATION AND SPORTS

Universitatea de Stat de Educaţie Fizică şi Sport

Strada A. Doga, 24/1, 2024 Chişinău
Tel: +373(22) 49-40-81
Fax: +373(22) 49-76-71
EMail: inefs@mdl.net
Website: http://www.usefs.md

Rector: Veaceslav Manolachi (1996-) Tel: +373(22) 49-41-82

First Vice-Rector: Victor Lupaşcu Tel: +373(2) 49-41-22

International Relations: Boris Rîşneac Tel: +373(2) 49-74-33

Faculties
Pedagogy (Pedagogy); **Physiotherapy** (Physical Therapy); **Protection, Guard and Security** (Safety Engineering); **Sports** (Physical Education; Sports; Sports Management)

History: Founded 1991. A State institution.

Main Language(s) of Instruction: Russian and Romanian

Degrees and Diplomas: *Diplomă de Licenţă*; *Diploma de Magistru*; *Diploma de Doctor în Ştiinţe*

Last Updated: 02/03/12

TECHNICAL UNIVERSITY OF MOLDOVA

Universitatea Tehnică a Moldovei (UTM)
Bulervardul Ştefan cel Mare, 168, 2012 Chişinău
Tel: +373(22) 23-78-61
Fax: +373(22) 23-22-52
EMail: utm@adm.utm.md
Website: http://www.utm.md

Rector: Ion Bostan (1998-)
Tel: +373(22) 23-54-26 EMail: bostan@mail.utm.md

First Vice-Rector: Petru Todos

International Relations: Valentin Amariei, Vice-Rector for Continuing Education and International Relations
EMail: tiginyanu@yahoo.com

Faculties
Cadastre, Geodesy and Civil Engineering (Building Technologies; Civil Engineering; Construction Engineering; Geological Engineering; Real Estate; Surveying and Mapping; Wood Technology); **Computers, Informatics and Microelectronics** (Business Computing; Computer Engineering; Computer Graphics; Computer Networks; Computer Science; Data Processing; Information Sciences; Information Technology; Mathematics and Computer Science; Microelectronics; Software Engineering; Translation and Interpretation); **Economic Engineering and Business** (Accountancy; Civil Engineering; Economics; Finance; Industrial Management; Marketing); **Engineering and Management in Machine Buiding** (Agricultural Equipment; Agriculture; Engineering; Engineering Management; Industrial Design; Machine Building); **Engineering and Management in Mechanics** (Automation and Control Engineering; Engineering Management; Hydraulic Engineering; Management; Mechanical Engineering; Road Transport; Transport and Communications; Transport Economics; Transport Engineering; Transport Management); **Food Industry Technology and Management** (Agriculture; Brewing; Cooking and Catering; Dairy; Food Science; Food Technology; Meat and Poultry; Nutrition; Oenology; Service Trades); **Power Engineering** (Electrical and Electronic Engineering; Electrical Engineering; Energy Engineering; Engineering Management; Measurement and Precision Engineering; Power Engineering; Thermal Engineering); **Radio-Electronics and Telecommunications** (Electrical and Electronic Engineering; Electronic Engineering; Engineering; Telecommunications Engineering); **Textile Industry** (Art Management; Design; Leather Techniques; Textile Design; Textile Technology); **Urban Planning and Architecture** (Architectural Restoration; Architecture; Architecture and Planning; Bridge Engineering; Ceramics and Glass Technology; Environmental Engineering; Environmental Management; Interior Design; Landscape Architecture; Road Engineering; Rural Planning; Town Planning; Waste Management; Water Management)

History: Founded 1964 as Polytechnic Institute, acquired present status 1993.

Governing Bodies: Senate; Council of Administration

Academic Year: September to June (September-January; February-June)

Admission Requirements: Secondary school certificate (Diploma de bacalaureate) and entrance examination

Fees: (Lei): c. 2,000-4,500 per annum; foreign students, (US Dollars): c. 1,200-1,500

Main Language(s) of Instruction: Romanian and Russian

Degrees and Diplomas: *Diploma de Studii Superioare Universitare*: 5 yrs; *Diploma de Magistru*; *Diploma de Doctor în Ştiinţe*: 3-4 yrs; *Diploma de Doctor Habilitat*

Student Services: Academic counselling, Canteen, Cultural centre, Employment services, Foreign student adviser, Health services, Social counselling, Sports facilities

Libraries: c. 1m. vols

Publications: Meridian Ingineresc *(quarterly)*

Press or Publishing House: Technica Publishing House

Last Updated: 01/03/12

TIRASPOL STATE UNIVERSITY

Universitatea de Stat din Tiraspol (UST)
Strada Iablocikin, 5, 2069 Chişinău
Tel: +373(22) 75-49-24
Fax: +373(22) 75-49-42
EMail: info@ust.md
Website: http://www.ust.md

Rector: Laurenţiu Calmuţchi

Vice-Rector: Donţoi Petru Tel: +373(2) 74-49-42

International Relations: Lora Mosanu-Supac
EMail: moshanu_ssust@yahoo.com

Faculties
Biology and Chemistry (Biology; Chemistry; Ecology; Physics); **Geography** (Biology; Computer Science; English; Geography; Geography (Human); International Economics; Meteorology; Tourism; Water Science); **Pedagogy** (Educational Psychology; English; Pedagogy; Preschool Education; Primary Education; Psychology); **Philology** (Classical Languages; English; French; Literature; Modern Languages; Philology; Romanian; Russian); **Physics, Mathematics and Information Technology** (Computer Science; Information Technology; Mathematics; Modern Languages; Physics)

History: Founded 1930. Reorganized 1932. Acquired present status 1992. A State institution.

Governing Bodies: Senate

Academic Year: September to July

Admission Requirements: Diploma de Bacalaureat or Atestat

Main Language(s) of Instruction: Romanian and Russian

International Co-operation: With universities in Romania, Russian Federation, Spain, Bulgaria

Degrees and Diplomas: *Diplomă de Licenţă*: Mathematics; Physics; Biology; Chemistry; Romanian; French; English; Russian; Pedagogy; Psychology; Primary Education Pedagogy, 4 1/2 yrs; *Diploma de Magistru*: Mathematics; Physics; Biology; Geography; Pedagogy and Psychology, 1 yr; *Diploma de Doctor în Ştiinţe*: Mathematics; Physics; Biology; Geography; Pedagogy and Psychology, 3-4 yrs. Also 1-year Postdoctoral degrees in Mathematics, Physics, Biology, Geography and Pedagogy and Psychology

Student Services: Academic counselling, Canteen, Cultural centre, Employment services, Foreign student adviser, Handicapped facilities, Health services, Nursery care, Social counselling, Sports facilities

Student Residential Facilities: Yes

Libraries: Yes

Publications: Aeta et Commentationes

Last Updated: 29/02/12

UNIVERSITY OF THE ACADEMY OF SCIENCES OF MOLDOVA

Universitatea Academiei de Ştiinţe a Moldovei
3/2, Academiei Street, Chişinău
Tel: +373(22) 738016
EMail: personal.univer@asm.md
Website: http://www.mrda.md

Rector: Maria Duca EMail: mduca2000@yahoo.com

Faculties
Exact Sciences (Chemistry; Mathematics and Computer Science; Physics); **Humanities** (Anthropology; English; Ethics; French; History; Linguistics; Modern Languages; Philosophy; Romanian);

Natural Sciences (Biology; Ecology; Environmental Studies; Geography; Soil Science)

History: Founded 2007.

Degrees and Diplomas: *Diplomă de Licență*; *Diploma de Magistru*

Last Updated: 02/03/12

PRIVATE INSTITUTIONS

CONSTANTIN STERE UNIVERSITY OF EUROPEAN POLITICAL AND ECONOMIC STUDIES

Universitatea de Studii Politice și Economice Europene Constantin Stere

200 Stefan cel Mare Blvd, Chișinău
Tel: +373(22) 756427
EMail: uspee@mail.md
Website: http://www.uspee.md/

Rector: Gheorghe Avornic

Faculties

Ecology and Protection of the Environment (Ecology; Environmental Studies; Forestry); **International Relations and Political Science** (International Relations; Political Sciences); **Law** (Civil Law; Commercial Law; Criminal Law; International Law; Public Law)

History: Successor of the Institute of Political Studies and International Relations (I.S.P.R.I.), founded in June 1997.

Main Language(s) of Instruction: Romanian and Russian

Degrees and Diplomas: *Diplomă de Licență*; *Diploma de Magistru*

Last Updated: 06/03/12

COOPERATIVE TRADE UNIVERSITY OF MOLDOVA

Universitatea Cooperatist Comercială din Moldovei (UCCM)

Bulevardul Iu Gagarin, 8, MD-2001 Chișinău
Tel: +373(22) 27-02-03
Fax: +373(22) 54-12-10
EMail: rectorat@uccm.md
Website: http://www.uccm.md/

Rector: Larisa Șavga Tel: +373(222) 54-49-22

Centres

Didactics-Science Studies (Accountancy; Business and Commerce; Commercial Law; Computer Education; Consumer Studies; Economic and Finance Policy; Economics; Law; Management; Marketing; Public Relations; Sociology) *Head*: Larisa Șavga

Colleges

Co-operative Studies (Accountancy; Applied Physics; Arts and Humanities; Banking; Biochemistry; Biology; Business Administration; Business and Commerce; Chemistry; Civil Law; Commercial Law; Computer Education; Computer Science; Constitutional Law; Cooking and Catering; Crafts and Trades; Demography and Population; Economics; English; Finance; Food Science; Food Technology; French; Geography; German; Health Education; History; Information Sciences; Information Technology; Insurance; Labour and Industrial Relations; Labour Law; Latin; Law; Leisure Studies; Linguistics; Literature; Management; Marketing; Mathematics; Mathematics and Computer Science; Microbiology; Modern Languages; Native Language; Natural Sciences; Nutrition; Physical Education; Physics; Public Law; Religious Education; Retailing and Wholesaling; Romanian; Russian; Sales Techniques; Secretarial Studies; Service Trades; Social Sciences; Spanish; Statistics; Taxation; Technology; Technology Education) *Director*: Eleonora Cogălniceanu

Faculties

Accountancy and Business Computing (Accountancy; Actuarial Science; Banking; Business and Commerce; Business Computing; Economics; Finance; Insurance; Law; Management; Marketing; Systems Analysis); **Management and Law** (Accountancy; Administration; Administrative Law; Business and Commerce; Commercial Law; Constitutional Law; Criminal Law; Cultural Studies; Economics; English; Finance; Fiscal Law; French; German; History; History of Law; Human Resources; Industrial Management; Insurance; International Law; Labour and Industrial Relations; Labour Law; Leadership; Logic; Management; Management Systems; Marketing; Philosophy; Political Sciences; Psychology; Romanian; Secretarial Studies; Sociology; Taxation); **Marketing and Commodities Science** (Accountancy; Business and Commerce; Chemistry; Consumer Studies; Demography and Population; Economics; English; Finance; Food Technology; French; Hotel and Restaurant; Hotel Management; International Business; International Economics; International Relations; Labour and Industrial Relations; Management; Marketing; Modern Languages; Secretarial Studies; Service Trades; Technology; Tourism; Translation and Interpretation)

Further Information: Also Branch in Soroca

History: Founded 1993. A collective form of organization belonging to the Consumer Co-operation of Moldova.

Governing Bodies: Administrative Council comprising 11 members; Scientific Senate comprising 35 members

Academic Year: September to June (September-December; February-June)

Admission Requirements: Secondary school certificate (Atestat) or incomplete secondary school certificate and entrance examination to college

Fees: (Lei MD): 2,200-5,000 per annum

Main Language(s) of Instruction: Romanian, Russian, English, French

International Co-operation: With universities in Romania, Russian Federation, Belarus, Ukraine, Georgia, Kazakhstan, Uzbekistan, Lithuania and Poland

Accrediting Agencies: National Council of Academic Estimate and Accreditation and Attestation; Ministry of Education

Degrees and Diplomas: *Diplomă de Licență*: Cybernetics; Economic Informatics; Economic Law; Taxation; Modern Languages; Tourism; Hotel and Restaurant Services; Metrology; Quality Control; Management; Marketing; Consumer Studies; International Economics; Finance; Insurance; Accountancy; Banking; Economics; Business and Commerce, 4-5 yrs; *Diploma de Magistru*; *Diploma de Doctor în Științe*

Student Services: Academic counselling, Canteen, Cultural centre, Employment services, Foreign student adviser, Health services, Language programs, Social counselling, Sports facilities

Student Residential Facilities: For 3,000 students

Special Facilities: University Museum; The Consumer Co-operation of Moldova Museum. Cultural Centre

Libraries: Central Library, c. 100,000 vols

Publications: Scientific-Didactic Staff Research Work, Research Reports *(annually)*

Press or Publishing House: Publishing Minicentre

Last Updated: 28/02/12

FREE INTERNATIONAL UNIVERSITY OF MOLDOVA

Universitatea Liberă Internațională din Moldova (ULIM)

Strada Vlaicu Pârcalab, 52, 2012 Chișinău
Tel: +373(22) 22-00-29
Fax: +373(22) 22-00-28
EMail: office@ulim.md
Website: http://www.ulim.md

Rector: Andrei Galben (1992-) EMail: agalben@ulim.md

International Relations: Ana Gutu, First Vice-Rector
Tel: +373(22) 22-55-05, Fax: +373(22) 22-55-05
EMail: agutu@ulim.md

Departments

Library Science (Library Science)

Faculties

Biomedicine and Ecology (Anatomy; Biochemistry; Botany; Chemistry; Cosmetology; Environmental Management; Ergotherapy; Forestry; Hygiene; Inorganic Chemistry; Medicine; Molecular Biology; Organic Chemistry; Parasitology; Pathology; Pharmacology; Pharmacy; Physiology; Psychology; Public Health; Toxicology); **Computer Science and Engineering** (Bioengineering; Computer

Engineering; Computer Science; Electronic Engineering; Engineering; Fashion Design; Information Management; Information Technology; Interior Design); **Economics** (Accountancy; Banking; Business Administration; Economics; Finance; International Economics; Management; Marketing; Statistics; Tourism); **Foreign Languages and Communication Sciences** (English; French; German; Journalism; Linguistics; Modern Languages; Public Relations; Spanish; Translation and Interpretation); **History and International Relations** (Anthropology; Archaeology; Ethnology; History; International Relations; Museum Studies; Political Sciences); **Law** (Civil Law; Criminal Law; International Law; Law); **Psychology and Social Assistance** (Pedagogy; Psychoanalysis; Psychology; Social and Community Services; Social Psychology; Sociology)

Research Institutes

Ecology and Biomedicine; **Economics** (Economics); **History** (History); **Human Rights Protection**; **Mass Media** (Journalism; Mass Communication); **Philology and Intercultural Studies**; **Social Formation and Research**

History: Founded 1992 by Government Decision.

Governing Bodies: Senate; Board of Directors

Academic Year: September to July (September-January; February-July)

Admission Requirements: Secondary school certificate

Fees: (Lei): 3,000-7,000 per annum

Main Language(s) of Instruction: Romanian, Russian, English, French

Accrediting Agencies: National Council of Accreditation and Attestation

Degrees and Diplomas: *Diplomă de Licență*: Law; Economics; Medicine; Engineering; Foreign Languages; Journalism and Public Communication; History; International Relations; Psychology and Social Assistance (DL), 3 yrs; *Diploma de Magistru*: Law; Engineering; Economics; Medicine; Modern Languages; Journalism and Public Communication; History; European Studies; International Relations; Psychology (DM), 1 1/2 - 2 yrs; *Diploma de Doctor în Științe*: Law, Economics, Modern Languages, History (DD), 3-4 yrs; *Diploma de Doctor Habilitat*: Law, Economics, Modern Languages, History (DDH). Also Adeverinta de Conferentiar, and Adeverinta de Profesor Universitate titles

Student Services: Academic counselling, Canteen, Foreign student adviser, Foreign Studies Centre, Health services, Language programs, Social counselling, Sports facilities

Student Residential Facilities: For c. 650 students

Special Facilities: Art Gallery, Media Centre

Libraries: c. 250,000 vols; electronic catalogue Internet

Publications: Anale, Scientific articles in the fields of law, medicine, economy, philology, history and engineering *(annually)*; Symposia Professorum, Scientific reports from the annual professors' symposium in the fields of law, medicine, economy, history, philology *(annually)*; Symposia Studentium, Scientific reports from the annual student symposium in the fields of law, medicine, economy, history and philology *(annually)*; Universitas *(bimonthly)*

Press or Publishing House: ULIM

Last Updated: 01/03/12

INTERNATIONAL MANAGEMENT INSTITUTE

Institutul Internațional de Management
Strada Hristo Botev, 9/1, 2043 Chișinău
Tel: +373(22) 56-85-36
EMail: info@imi-nova.md
Website: http://www.imi-nova.md

Rector: Valentin Răilean (1995-)

First Vice-Rector: Corina Studeonov Tel: +373(2) 78-07-14

International Relations: Vilena Borș Tel: +373(2) 58-07-14

Faculties

Business and Economics (Accountancy; Banking; Economics; Finance; International Business; International Economics; Management; Marketing; Tourism); **Law** (Law)

History: Founded 1995, a private institution.

Degrees and Diplomas: *Diplomă de Licență*; *Diploma de Magistru*

MOLDOVA UNIVERSITY OF EUROPEAN STUDIES

Universitatea de Studii Europene din Moldova
2/1, Iablocikin str, 2069 Chișinău
Tel: +373(22) 509-122
Website: http://www.usem.md

Rector: Iurie Sedlețchi (1995-)
Tel: +373(22) 24-50-40, Fax: +373(2) 24-31-15

Faculties

Economics and Computer Science (Banking; Computer Science; Economics; Finance; Management; Tourism); **Foreign Languages** (English; French; German; Modern Languages; Spanish; Translation and Interpretation; Turkish); **Journalism and Public Communication** (Communication Studies; Journalism); **Law** (Administrative Law; Commercial Law; Constitutional Law; Criminal Law; International Law; Law)

History: Founded 1992 as Academiei de Drept din Moldova. Acquired present status and title 2006.

Degrees and Diplomas: *Diplomă de Licență*; *Diploma de Magistru*; *Diploma de Doctor Habilitat*

Last Updated: 28/02/12

PERSPECTIVA UNIVERSITY-INT

Universitatea "Perspectiva"-INT
Strada Alba-Iulia, 75, 2071 Chișinău
Tel: +373(22) 75-35-83
EMail: university@perspectiva.md
Website: http://www.perspectiva.md

Rector: Rodica Odineț (1995-) Tel: +373(22) 74-79-58

First Vice-Rector: Tudor Caraijdan Tel: +373(2) 74-66-31

International Relations: Arina Craijdan Tel: +373(2) 74-66-31

Faculties

Arts and Design (Design; Fashion Design; Fine Arts; Interior Design); **Economics and Law** (Business and Commerce; Commercial Law; Economics; Hotel and Restaurant; International Economics; International Relations; Law; Tourism)

History: Founded 1995 as International Relations Institute "Perspectiva". Acquired present status and title 2004.

Main Language(s) of Instruction: Romanian and Russian.

Degrees and Diplomas: *Diplomă de Licență*; *Diploma de Magistru*

Last Updated: 01/03/12

SLAVONE UNIVERSITY

Universitatea Slavonă
Strada Florilor, 28/1, 2068 Chișinău
Tel: +373(22) 43-03-81
Fax: +373(22) 43-03-80
EMail: olesea@meganet.md
Website: http://www.surm.md

Rector: Victor Kostețky (2001-) Tel: +373(2) 43-03-80

Faculties

Business and Economics (Accountancy; Banking; Economics; Management); **Humanities** (Arts and Humanities; Modern Languages; Psychology; Russian); **Law** (Commercial Law; International Law; Law)

History: Founded 1997, a private institution.

TRANSPORTS, INFORMATICS AND COMMUNICATIONS ACADEMY

Academia de Transporturi, Informatică și Comunicații
șos. Muncești, 121 A, sectorul Botanica, Chișinău
Tel: +373(22) 73-84-63
Fax: +373(22) 72-95-27
EMail: dsolomon@softhome.net
Website: http://www.aticmd.md

Rector: Dumitru Solomon Tel: +373(22) 78-50-29

Faculties

Economics and Computer Science (Accountancy; Economics; Finance; Management; Mathematics and Computer Science);

Engineering and Transport (Engineering; Transport Engineering; Transport Management); **Television and Radio Communication** (Automation and Control Engineering; Computer Science; Electronic Engineering; Radio and Television Broadcasting)

History: Founded 1999.

Degrees and Diplomas: *Diplomă de Licenţă*; *Diploma de Magistru*

Libraries: Yes

Last Updated: 28/02/12

UNIVERSITY OF APPLIED SCIENCES OF MOLDOVA

Universitatea de Ştiinţe Aplicative din Moldova (UŞAM)

Strada Iablocikin, 2, 2069 Chişinău
Tel: +373(22) 50-85-18
Fax: +373(22) 29-53-57
EMail: edu@usam.md
Website: http://www.usam.md

Rector: Nicolae Pelin (1994-) Tel: +373(2) 48-47-04

Prorector: Mihail Rotaru

International Relations: Vera Pelin, Staff Administrator
Tel: +373(2) 50-85-18

Centres

Scientific Production *(Sisteme expert)* (Industrial Engineering; Management Systems; Production Engineering) *Director*: Nadejda Cotov

Faculties

Economics and Law (Accountancy; Commercial Law; Economics; Finance; Industrial and Production Economics; International Economics; Law; Management) *Dean*: Anatol Radevici; **Modern Technologies** (Automation and Control Engineering; Computer Engineering; Computer Science; Information Technology; Software Engineering) *Dean*: Nicolae Pelin; **Postgraduate Education** *Dean*: Serghei Pelin

History: Founded 1992, acquired present status 1994. A private institution.

Governing Bodies: Senate

Academic Year: September to July (September-December; February-July)

Admission Requirements: Secondary school certificate (Atestat, or Bacalaureat), entrance examinations, and health certificate

Fees: (US Dollars): Tuition, foreign students, 1,800 per anum; part-time foreign students, 900; postgraduate, 600

Main Language(s) of Instruction: Romanian, Russian, English

Accrediting Agencies: Certification Commitee of the Republic of Moldova; Ministry of Education

Degrees and Diplomas: *Diplomă de Licenţă*: Commercial Engineering; Economics-Accountancy; Law, 4 yrs; *Diploma de Magistru*: Science, a further 1 1/2 yrs. Also Certificate in Programming, 3 weeks

Student Services: Academic counselling, Cultural centre, Foreign student adviser, Health services, Sports facilities

Student Residential Facilities: For 500-600 students

Special Facilities: Distance Education Studio. Computer Centre

Libraries: c. 7,000 vols

Publications: Applied Sciences Journal *(biennially)*

UNIVERSITY OF INTEGRATED APPLIED STUDIES

Universitatea de Studii Aplicative Integrate

Strada Grenoble, 147 b, 2012 Chişinău
Tel: +373(22) 72-35-14
EMail: usum@mdl.net

Rector: Teodosie Pasecinic Tel: +373(22) 22-65-95

Faculties

Cosmetics and Scents (Cosmetology); **Economics** (Economics); **Law** (Law); **Modern and Classic Languages** (Classical Languages; Modern Languages); **Political History and Political Science** (History; Political Sciences)

History: Founded 1993. Formerly Universitatea de Studii Umanistice din Moldova.

UNIVERSITY SCHOOL OF ANTHROPOLOGY

Universitatea Scoala Antropologica Superiora

Strada Zimbrului, 10 a, 2004 Chişinău
Tel: +373(22) 43-83-42
Fax: +373(22) 44-59-78
EMail: has@anthropology.moldline.net
Website: http://www.ant.md/

Rector: Nicolai Russev

Academic Vice-Rector: Igor Manzura

Faculties

Humanitarian Technologies (Administration; Anthropology; Communication Studies; European Studies; Information Technology; Linguistics; Sociology)

History: Founded 1998, a private institution.

Degrees and Diplomas: State diploma with qualification "Licensed Anthropologist".

Publications: Stratum Plus

UNIVERS-MOLDOVA UNIVERSITY

Universitatea Univers-Moldova

Bulevardul Moscova, 4/2, 2068 Chişinău
Tel: +373(22) 43-47-42
Fax: +373(22) 32-42-11
EMail: info@univers.net.md
Website: http://www.univers.md

Rector: Iurie Crotenco Tel: +373(22) 43-47-33

Administrative Officer: Eduard Melnic
Tel: +373(2) 43-80-34 EMail: emelnic@yahoo.com

International Relations: Petru Dăscălescu, Head
Tel: +3732(2) 49-92-94

Faculties

Design (Design) *Dean*: Ion Tigulea; **Economics** (Economics) *Dean*: Iurii Krotenko; **Information Technology** (Information Technology) *Division Head*: Sergiu Tutunaru; **Modern Languages** (English; German; Modern Languages) *Dean*: Vera Goncearenco; **Psychology** (Psychology) *Dean*: Carolina Perjan

History: Founded 1998, a private institution.

Governing Bodies: Academic Council

Academic Year: Septermber to June

Admission Requirements: Secondary school certificate (Bacalaureat), and admission test

Fees: (US Dollars): 500 per annum

Main Language(s) of Instruction: Russian, Romanian, English

International Co-operation: With Holborn College, London (United Kingdom)

Accrediting Agencies: Ministry of Education

Degrees and Diplomas: *Diplomă de Licenţă*: Language Studies; Information Technology; Economics; Tourism, 4 yrs

Student Services: Canteen, Cultural centre, Foreign student adviser, Language programs

Monaco

INSTITUTIONS

PUBLIC INSTITUTION

ÉCOLE SUPÉRIEURE D'ARTS PLASTIQUES DE LA VILLE DE MONACO (PAVILLON BOSIO) (ESAP)

1, Avenue des Pins, MC 98000 Monaco
Tel: +377(93) 30-18-39
Fax: +377(93) 30-34-36
EMail: contact@pavillonbosio.com
Website: http://www.pavillonbosio.com/

Directrice: Isabelle Lombardot

Administratrice: Marie Hélène Savigneux
EMail: savigneux@pavillonbosio.com

International Relations: Ivana Milovic La Fata, Responsable des Relations internationales EMail: lafata@pavillonbosio.com

Programmes

Fine Arts and Scenography *(Undergraduate)* (Display and Stage Design; Fine Arts); **Stage Design and Scenography** *(Postgraduate)* (Display and Stage Design; Fine Arts)

Degrees and Diplomas: Diplôme National d'Arts Plastiques (DNAP), 3 yrs; Diplôme National Supérieur d'Expression Plastique (DNSEP), 5 yrs, which is equivalent to a Master's degree and recognised by the French government.

Special Facilities: Studios

Last Updated: 04/11/11

PRIVATE INSTITUTION

INTERNATIONAL UNIVERSITY OF MONACO (IUM)

2, avenue Albert II, 98000 Monaco
Tel: +377 (97) 986-986
Fax: +377 (92) 052-830
EMail: info@monaco.edu
Website: http://www.monaco.edu

Dean: Antonella Patras
Tel: +377(97) 986-992, Fax: +377(97) 778-418
EMail: apatras@monaco.edu

Vice-President: Sandrine Ricard
Tel: +377(97) 986-997, Fax: +377(92) 052-830
EMail: sricard@monaco.edu

Schools

Business *(Monaco)* (Business Administration; Economics; Finance; International Business; Management)

Further Information: Campuses in Paris and London

History: Founded 1986 as University of Southern Europe (Monaco Business School). An independent University fully accredited by the Ministry of Education in Monaco, by ACICS in the USA and by AMBA. Acquired present title 2002.

Academic Year: September to June; also summer sessions

Admission Requirements: Secondary school certificate for undergraduate programmes. English proficiency required for all students

Main Language(s) of Instruction: English

International Co-operation: With universities in Europe, China, Mexico, Norway, Thailand, USA

Accrediting Agencies: Accrediting Council for Independent Colleges and Schools (ACICS). Government of the Principality of Monaco, Association of MBAs

Degrees and Diplomas: *Bachelor*: Business Administration (BS; BA), 3-4 yrs; *Master*: Business Administration; Finance; Hedge Funds; Marketing; Luxury Brands (MBA), 1 yr (intensive); *Master*: Executive Business (EMBA), 18 months; *Master*: Financial Engineering, Luxury Goods and Services, 12 months. Also Doctorate in Business Administration

Student Services: Academic counselling, Social counselling, Employment services, Foreign student adviser, Sports facilities, Handicapped facilities, Canteen, Foreign Studies Centre

Student Residential Facilities: For c. 300 students

Libraries: Central Library

Last Updated: 31/10/11

Mongolia

STRUCTURE OF HIGHER EDUCATION SYSTEM

Description:

Higher education is provided by universities, colleges, institutes and private higher education institutions. The Ministry of Science, Technology, Education and Culture (MOSTEC) is responsible for higher education matters. Since 1991, following the reform of higher education, the former Polytechnic, the Russian Language Institute, the State Pedagogical Institute, the Pedagogical Institute, the Agricultural Institute, the Medical Institute, the Management Institute and the Military Institute have been upgraded to university status. BA, MA and PhD degrees were introduced in 1992. Public higher education institutions are funded by the central or local governments. There are also private higher education institutions. The Ministry approves these institutions and sets their standards.

Stages of studies:

University level first stage: *Bachelor's degree*

Students follow three- to five-year programmes leading to a Bachelor's degree. Professional qualifications in Medicine are conferred after six years of study and in Dentistry, Pharmacy and Veterinary Medicine after five years.

University level second stage: *Master's degree*

The Master's degree is conferred after one-and-a-half to two years' study following upon the Bachelor's degree.

University level third stage: *Doctor of Philosophy*

The Doctor of Philosophy is awarded to those who have obtained a Master's degree and have studied at postgraduate level for several years and submitted a dissertation.

Distance higher education:

Distance education is provided by the Distance Education unit of the Mongolian Technical University.

ADMISSION TO HIGHER EDUCATION

Admission to university-level studies:

Name of secondary school credential required: Gerchilgee

Entrance exam requirements: Entrance Examination in relevant subjects.

Foreign students admission:

Entrance exam requirements: Students must hold a secondary school leaving certificate which gives access to higher education institutions. They must also sit for an entrance examination.

Language requirements: Mongolian is the language of instruction but theses and dissertations may be submitted in another language.

RECOGNITION OF STUDIES

Quality assurance system:

The National Council of Higher Education Accreditation (http://www.accmon.mn) accredits HE institutions and programmes.

NATIONAL BODIES

Ministry of Education, Culture and Science

Minister: Luvsannyam Gantmur

Government Building III - Baga toiruu 44

Ulaanbataar 44
Tel: +976(11) 322480
Fax: +976(11) 323158
EMail: mecs@mecs.gov.mn;info@mecs.gov.mn
WWW: http://www.mecs.gov.mn/
Role of national body: Responsible for the reform of higher education, international relations, student activities.

National Council for Education Accreditation - NCEA
CEO: V Alzakhgui
The Teacher Development Palace Unit 401, Peace Avenue 10, Sukhbaatar District
Ulaanbaatar 38
Tel: +976 70109391
Fax: +976 70104507
EMail: accmon@mongolnet.mn
WWW: http://www.accmon.mn

Consortium of Mongolian Universities and Colleges - CMUC
President: Acad B. Jadambaa
Peace Avenue Baga toiruu-14,
(Mongolian State University of Education, building A203)
Ulaanbaatar 210648
Tel: +976(11) 9668 5877/9995 7907
Fax: +976(11) 322 705
EMail: info@cmuc.edu.mn
WWW: http://www.cmuc.edu.mn
Role of national body: Responsible for the reform of higher education, international relations, student activities.

Data for academic year: 2006-2007
Source: IAU from National Commission for UNESCO, Ulaanbataar, 2006. Bodies updated 2012..

INSTITUTIONS

PUBLIC INSTITUTIONS

ACADEMY OF MANAGEMENT

Knan-Uul Duureg, Ulaanbaatar 210636
Tel: +976(11) 341754-2757
Fax: +976(11) 343037
EMail: aom@aom.edu.mn
Website: http://www.aom.url.mn/

Rector: Togoosh Lkhagvaa

Centres
Management Development and Consulting (Management)

Research Institutes
Management and Policy Studies (Management)

Schools
Governance and Management (Business Administration; Economics; Law; Management; Public Administration); **Public Affairs and Management** (Business Administration; Public Administration)

History: Created 1924. Acquired status 1999.

Academic Year: September to June

Main Language(s) of Instruction: Mongolian

Accrediting Agencies: National Council for Higher Education Accreditation

Degrees and Diplomas: *Bachelor's Degree*; *Master's Degree*; *Doctor of Philosophy*. Also Diploma and Postgraduate diplomas.
Last Updated: 03/12/09

HEALTH SCIENCES UNIVERSITY OF MONGOLIA

Eruul mendiin Shinjlekh Ukhaanii Ikh Surguuli (NMUM)
PO Box 48/111, Choidog Street 4, Ulaanbaatar UB-976-11
Tel: +976(11) 328-670 +976(11) 321-249
Fax: +976(11) 321-249
EMail: Tsetselkh@yahoo.com
Website: http://www.hsum.edu.mn

President: Tserenkhuu Lkhagvasuren (1995-)
EMail: lkhagvasuren@nmum.edu.mn

Vice-Director for Educational Affairs: Desnmaa Dungedorj
Tel: +976(11) 328-924

International Relations: S. Narantuya

Departments
Biology and Genetics (Biology; Genetics); **Cardiology** (Cardiology); **Dermatology** (Dermatology); **Diagnosis and Rehabilitation** (Rehabilitation and Therapy); **Endocrinology and Haematology** (Endocrinology; Haematology); **Family Medicine** (Family Studies; Medicine); **Foreign Languages** (Modern Languages); **Gastroenterology** (Gastroenterology); **Medical Chemistry** (Chemistry); **Medical Physics and Informatics** (Computer Science; Physics); **Microbiology and Immunology** (Immunology; Microbiology); **Morphology** (Anatomy); **Nephrology** (Nephrology); **Neurology and Psychiatry** (Neurology; Psychiatry and Mental Health); **Obstetrics and Gynaecology** (Gynaecology and Obstetrics); **Ophthalmology** (Ophthalmology); **Otorhinolaryngology** (Otorhinolaryngology); **Paediatrics** (Paediatrics); **Pathological Anatomy and Forensic Medicine** (Anatomy; Forensic Medicine and

Dentistry; Pathology); **Pathophysiology** (Pathology); **Pharmacology** (Pharmacology); **Pharmacy** (Pharmacy); **Physiology** (Physiology); **Pneumonology** (Pneumology); **Radiology** (Radiology); **Surgery I** (Surgery); **Surgery II** (Surgery); **Tuberculosis**

Faculties

Dentistry (Dentistry) *Dean*: B. Oyunbat; **Medicine** (Medicine) *Dean*: T. Altantsetseg; **Pharmacy** (Pharmacy) *Dean*: S. Tsetsegmaa; **Public Health** *Dean*: Ch. Tsolmon; **Traditional Medicine** (Traditional Eastern Medicine) *Dean*: N. Tumurbaatar

Institutes

Public Health (Public Health) *Dean*: L. Narantuya

Schools

Dentistry (Dentistry; Orthodontics; Stomatology) *Director*: B. Oyunbat; **Mongolian Traditional Medicine** (Traditional Eastern Medicine) *Director*: N. Tumurbaatar; **Nursing** (Nursing) *Director*: P. Haidav; **Public Health** (Anatomy; Biology; Cardiology; Dermatology; Endocrinology; Epidemiology; Foreign Languages Education; Forensic Medicine and Dentistry; Gastroenterology; Genetics; Gynaecology and Obstetrics; Haematology; Health Administration; Hygiene; Immunology; Microbiology; Nephrology; Neurology; Ophthalmology; Otorhinolaryngology; Paediatrics; Pathology; Pharmacology; Pharmacy; Physiology; Psychiatry and Mental Health; Public Health; Radiology; Rehabilitation and Therapy; Surgery) *Director*: Ch. Tsolmon

Further Information: Also University Central Clinical Hospital, and 4 medical colleges (Ulaanbaatar, Gobi-Altai Province, Dorno-Gobi Province, Darkhan-Uul Province)

History: Founded 1942 as Medical Faculty of the Mongolian State University. Separated in 1941 and renamed Mongolian State Medical Institute. Acquired present status and title 1995.

Governing Bodies: Administration Council; Academic Council

Academic Year: September to July (September-January; February-July)

Admission Requirements: Secondary school certificate (Gerchilgee) and entrance examination

Fees: (US Dollars): 2,000 per annum

Main Language(s) of Instruction: Mongolian and Russian

International Co-operation: With universities in Korea. Also participates in Tempus TACIS

Accrediting Agencies: National Council for Higher Education Accreditation

Degrees and Diplomas: *Bachelor's Degree*: Medicine, 5-6 yrs; *Master's Degree*: Medicine, 2 yrs; *Doctor of Philosophy*: Medicine, Science, 3-31/2 yrs

Student Services: Academic counselling, Canteen, Cultural centre, Health services, Language programs, Nursery care, Sports facilities

Student Residential Facilities: Yes

Special Facilities: Anatomy Museum

Libraries: Medical Central Library, 210,000 vols; Yonsei Memorial Library

Last Updated: 03/12/09

INSTITUTE OF COMMERCE AND BUSINESS

PO Box 404, Office 48, Sukhbaatar District, Ulaanbaatar 210648
Tel: +976(11) 326-748
Fax: +976(11) 326-748

Rector: M. Batsaikhan

Departments

Accountancy (Accountancy); **Advanced Training**; **Economic Theory and Management** (Economics; Management); **Humanities** (Arts and Humanities); **Marketing**; **Mathematics and Informatics**

History: Founded 1924.

Main Language(s) of Instruction: Mongolian

Accrediting Agencies: National Council for Higher Education Accreditation

Degrees and Diplomas: *Bachelor's Degree*; *Master's Degree*

Last Updated: 16/12/09

INSTITUTE OF FINANCE AND ECONOMICS

Sankhuu Ediin Zasgiin Deed Surguuli

12 Peace Avenue, Ulaanbaatar
Tel: +976(11) 458-378
Fax: +976(11) 458-378
EMail: tomco@ife.edu.mn
Website: http://www.ife.edu.mn

President: Batjargal

Departments

Accountancy (Accountancy); **Banking and Finance**; **Business Studies** (Business Administration); **Foreign Languages**; **Informatics** (Computer Science; Information Technology)

History: Founded 1924. Acquired present status 1996.

Accrediting Agencies: National Council for Higher Education Accreditation

Degrees and Diplomas: *Bachelor's Degree*; *Master's Degree*; *Doctor of Philosophy*

Last Updated: 17/12/09

MONGOLIAN STATE PEDAGOGICAL UNIVERSITY

Mongol Ulsyn Bolovsroliin Ikh Surguuli

Baga Toiruu-14, Yiii Khoroo, Sukhbaatar District, Ulaanbaatar 210648
Tel: +976(11) 326010-179
Fax: +976(11) 322705

Rector: Badrakh Jadamba EMail: jadamba@mspu.edu.mn

Faculties

Computers and Information Technology; **Creative Art Techniques** (Design; Fine Arts; Handicrafts; Painting and Drawing; Sculpture; Weaving); **Foreign Languages** (Chinese; English; German; Japanese; Russian; Translation and Interpretation; Writing); **Mathematics** (Actuarial Science; Applied Mathematics; Mathematics; Statistics); **Mongolian Language and Literature** (Applied Linguistics; Comparative Literature; Grammar; Linguistics; Literature; Mongolian; Philology; Phonetics; Psycholinguistics; Terminology; Writing); **Natural Sciences** (Analytical Chemistry; Anatomy; Biology; Biotechnology; Botany; Chemistry; Genetics; Geochemistry; Geography; Geology; Immunology; Industrial Chemistry; Inorganic Chemistry; Meteorology; Microbiology; Mineralogy; Molecular Biology; Organic Chemistry; Paleontology; Parasitology; Physical Chemistry; Zoology); **Physics** (Applied Physics; Astronomy and Space Science; Astrophysics; Atomic and Molecular Physics; Nuclear Physics; Optics; Physics; Solid State Physics; Thermal Physics); **Social Sciences** (American Studies; Asian Studies; European Studies; History; History of Societies; Philosophy; Political Sciences; Social Policy; Social Studies)

Further Information: Also Mongolian Language Courses for foreign students

History: Founded 1951 as Teacher Training Institute, renamed Pedagogical University 1991. Formerly known as National Pedagogical University, Ulaanbaatar.

Governing Bodies: Governing Board

Academic Year: September to June (September-January; February-June)

Admission Requirements: Secondary school certificate and entrance examination

Fees: (Tughriks): c. 200,000 to 250,000 per annum

Main Language(s) of Instruction: Mongolian

Accrediting Agencies: National Council for Higher Education Accreditation

Degrees and Diplomas: *Bachelor's Degree*; *Master's Degree*; *Doctor of Philosophy*. Also Diploma 3-4 yrs.

Student Services: Academic counselling, Canteen, Foreign student adviser, Language programs, Sports facilities

Student Residential Facilities: Yes

Libraries: Central Library, c. 145,600 vols; college libraries, total, c. 256,000 vols

Publications: Research Papers; Tavan ukhaan

Last Updated: 16/12/09

MONGOLIAN STATE UNIVERSITY OF AGRICULTURE

Khodoo Aj Akhuin Ikh Surguuli (MSUA)

Zaisan, P.O. Box 53/1, Khan-Uul district, Ulaanbaatar 210153
Tel: +976(11) 341-770 +976(11) 341-153
Fax: +976(11) 341-770
EMail: infotech@magicnet.mn
Website: http://www.msua.edu.mn

President: Badarch Byambaa (2006-) EMail: haaint@magicnet.mn

Schools

Agrobiology (Agronomy; Biotechnology; Crop Production; Forestry; Horticulture; Soil Science; Water Management; Water Science); **Biological Resources and Management**; **Ecology and Technology Development** (Ecology; Technology); **Economics and Business**; **Engineering** (Agricultural Equipment; Machine Building; Technology); **Natural Sciences** (Biological and Life Sciences; Chemistry; Computer Science; Korean; Mathematics; Modern Languages; Physical Education; Physics; Social Sciences; Tourism); **Veterinary Medicine and Biotechnology** (Gynaecology and Obstetrics; Hygiene; Microbiology; Pharmacology; Physiology; Sanitary Engineering; Surgery; Veterinary Science)

History: Founded 1958 as it became an independent Institute. Acquired present status and title 1993.

Academic Year: September to June

Admission Requirements: Secondary school certificate (gerchilgee) or equivalent, entrance examination

Fees: (Tughriks): 396,500 to 436,500 per annum at undergraduate level; foreign students (US Dollars) 450 per annum; 600 master level

Main Language(s) of Instruction: Mongolian

International Co-operation: With universities in Russian Federation, Japan, Canada, EU, USA, Republic of Korea, China, Vietnam. Also participates in Tempus, TACIS CD and TRAMAL programmes.

Accrediting Agencies: National Council for Higher Education Accreditation

Degrees and Diplomas: *Bachelor's Degree*; *Master's Degree*; *Doctor of Philosophy*

Student Services: Academic counselling, Canteen, Cultural centre, Employment services, Foreign student adviser, Handicapped facilities, Health services, Language programs, Nursery care, Social counselling, Sports facilities

Special Facilities: Mongolian Nomadic Civilization Museum

Libraries: Agricultural Central Library, together with the Library of Economics and Business School: more than 190,000 vols

Publications: Research Bulletins for Animal Husbandry, Veterinary Science, Crop Science, Plant Protection, 4 volumes *(annually)*; Rural Newspaper *(monthly)*; University Research Bulletins *(annually)*

Press or Publishing House: University Press

Last Updated: 16/12/09

MONGOLIAN UNIVERSITY OF SCIENCE AND TECHNOLOGY

Mongol Ulsyn Shinkleh Ukhaan Tekhnologiin Ikh Surguuli (MUST)

PO Box 46/520, Ulaanbaatar 216046
Tel: +976(11) 329-081 +96(11) 324-709
Fax: +976(11) 324-121
EMail: intrel@must.edu.mn; admissn@must.edu.mn
Website: http://www.mtu.edu.mn/

President: Damsinsuren Bayanduuren (2006-)
Tel: +976(11) 329-746

Schools

Civil Engineering (Architectural and Environmental Design; Architecture; Bridge Engineering; Building Technologies; Civil Engineering; Construction Engineering; Ecology; Heating and Refrigeration; Hydraulic Engineering; Natural Resources; Road Engineering; Sanitary Engineering; Soil Science; Town Planning; Water Management); **Computer Science and Management** (Business Administration; Computer Networks; Computer Science; Higher Education; Human Resources; Industrial and Production Economics; Information Management; Information Technology; International Business; International Studies; Management; Marketing; Public Administration; Small Business; Software Engineering; Systems Analysis); **Food and Technology** (Biotechnology; Brewing; Cooking and Catering; Dairy; Food Science; Food Technology; Hygiene; Meat and Poultry; Microbiology; Nutrition); **Foreign Languages** (English; Japanese; Korean; Modern Languages; Russian); **Geology** (Geochemistry; Geology; Geophysics; Petroleum and Gas Engineering; Petrology; Surveying and Mapping); **Humanities** (Cultural Studies; Economics; History; Management; Philosophy; Social Work; Tourism); **Industrial Technology and Design** (Art Management; Clothing and Sewing; Computer Graphics; Design; Fashion Design; Forestry; Furniture Design; Graphic Design; Industrial Design; Industrial Engineering; Interior Design; Printing and Printmaking; Textile Design; Textile Technology; Wood Technology); **Materials Science** (Analytical Chemistry; Applied Physics; Chemical Engineering; Ecology; Environmental Engineering; Industrial Engineering; Materials Engineering; Organic Chemistry; Petroleum and Gas Engineering; Physical Engineering; Physics; Technology; Textile Technology); **Mathematics** (Engineering; Mathematics; Mathematics Education); **Mechanical Engineering** (Air Transport; Electronic Engineering; Mechanical Engineering; Metal Techniques; Metallurgical Engineering; Road Transport; Transport Economics; Transport Management); **Mining Engineering** (Astronomy and Space Science; Electrical Engineering; Management; Mechanical Engineering; Mining Engineering; Surveying and Mapping); **Power Engineering** (Computer Science; Electrical Engineering; Electronic Engineering; Energy Engineering; Heating and Refrigeration; Maintenance Technology; Medical Technology; Natural Resources; Power Engineering; Thermal Engineering); **Technology I** *(Darkhan City, Darkhan-Uul aimag)*; **Technology II** *(Erdenet City)* (Electrical Engineering; Metal Techniques; Mineralogy; Mining Engineering; Road Transport); **Technology III** *(Sukhbaatar aimag)* (Computer Engineering; Production Engineering; Software Engineering); **Technology IV** *(Uvurkhangai aimag)* (Clothing and Sewing; Finance; Food Technology; Industrial and Production Economics; Mechanical Engineering; Production Engineering; Public Administration; Road Engineering; Road Transport); **Telecommunications and Information Technology** (Computer Networks; Electrical and Electronic Engineering; Information Technology; Library Science; Postal Services; Radio and Television Broadcasting; Telecommunications Engineering; Telecommunications Services)

History: Founded 1969 as part of National University of Mongolia. Became an independent institution 1983, acquired present status 2001 and present title 2003.

Governing Bodies: Governing Board; President's Council; Academic Council; Faculty Senate

Academic Year: September to June (September-January; February-June)

Admission Requirements: Secondary school certificate (Gerchilgee)

Main Language(s) of Instruction: Mongolian

International Co-operation: With more than 100 foreign universities and colleges. Also participates in International Association of Exchange of Students for Technical Experiences

Accrediting Agencies: National Council for Higher Education Accreditation

Degrees and Diplomas: *Bachelor's Degree*; *Master's Degree*; *Doctor of Philosophy*. Also Diploma, 3 yrs

Student Services: Academic counselling, Canteen, Cultural centre, Foreign student adviser, Foreign Studies Centre, Health services, Language programs, Social counselling, Sports facilities

Student Residential Facilities: For 2,100 students (9 dormitories in Ulaanbaatar City)

Special Facilities: University History Museum; Mineralogical Museum; "Wonders of Science" Museum; TV Studio; FM Studio

Libraries: Educational and Research Library, c. 265,000 vols

Publications: Bileg, News in Telecommunications and Information Technology *(monthly)*; Food *(monthly)*; Geology *(monthly)*; Light Industry *(monthly)*; Mining *(monthly)*; MUST News *(monthly)*; Power Engineering *(monthly)*; Science and Technology *(quarterly)*; Scientific Transactions of MUST *(quarterly)*

Press or Publishing House: MUST Publishing House

Last Updated: 17/12/09

NATIONAL UNIVERSITY OF ARTS AND CULTURE

Mongol Ulsyn Soyel Urlagyn Ikh Surguuli

PO Box 46, Baga Toyruu 22, Ulaanbaatar 210646
Tel: +976(11) 372-881
Fax: +976(11) 325-205

Rector: Tsedev Dojoo (1997-)

Faculties

Music (Music; Singing); **Social Sciences** (International Studies); **Theatrical Art** (Acting; Theatre)

Institutes

Arts and Design (Design; Fine Arts); **Fine Arts** (Fine Arts; Graphic Arts; Handicrafts); **Radio and Television** *(Ulaanbaatar, Darkhan, Khenty Province)* (Cultural Studies; Fine Arts; Radio and Television Broadcasting)

History: Founded 1946, acquired present status and title1990.

Accrediting Agencies: National Council for Higher Education Accreditation

Degrees and Diplomas: *Bachelor's Degree*; *Master's Degree*; *Doctor of Philosophy*

Last Updated: 17/12/09

NATIONAL UNIVERSITY OF MONGOLIA

Mongol Ulsyn Ikh Surguuli (NUM)

Ikh Surguuliin gudamj 1, PO Box 46A/523, Ulaanbaatar 210646
Tel: +976(11) 320-159 +976(11) 320-668
Fax: +976(11) 320-159 +976(11) 320-668
EMail: num@num.edu.mn
Website: http://num.edu.mn

President: Suren Davaa (2009-2014)
Tel: +976(11) 320-160, Fax: +976(11) 320-668
EMail: davaa@num.edu.mn

Media Officer: Dashzend Ariunaa
Tel: +976(11) 317-050 EMail: ariuna78@yahoo.com

International Relations: Shuurai Mendbayar, Head, Office for International Affairs EMail: mendbayar_oia@num.edu.mn

Faculties

Biology (Biochemistry; Biology; Biophysics; Biotechnology; Botany; Ecology; Forestry; Gender Studies; Microbiology; Zoology); **Chemistry** (Chemistry; Inorganic Chemistry; Organic Chemistry); **Earth Sciences**

Schools

Economics Sciences (Accountancy; Economics; Finance; Human Resources; Management; Marketing; Taxation); **Foreign Languages and Cultures** (American Studies; Chinese; Cultural Studies; English; French; German; Italian; Japanese; Korean; Russian; Slavic Languages; Spanish); **Foreign Services**; **Information Technology** (Computer Engineering; Computer Networks; Electronic Engineering; Information Technology); **Law** (Civil Law; Criminal Law; Human Rights; International Law; Law; Private Law; Public Law); **Mathematics and Computer Science** (Computer Science; Mathematical Physics; Mathematics; Statistics); **Mongol Studies** (Applied Linguistics; Art Education; Chinese; Cultural Studies; Ethnology; Folklore; Journalism; Linguistics; Literature; Mongolian; Native Language; Phonetics; Terminology; Tibetan; Turkish); **Physics and Electronics** (Applied Physics; Ecology; Electronic Engineering; Energy Engineering; Hydraulic Engineering; Meteorology; Nuclear Engineering; Physics); **Social Sciences** (Anthropology; Archaeology; Banking; Business Administration; Demography and Population; Economics; Ethnology; Finance; Fine Arts; History; Journalism; Philosophy; Political Sciences; Psychology; Social Sciences; Sociology; Theology; Tourism)

Further Information: Also Colleges in Zavkhan and Orkhon.

History: Founded 1942 as a State institution.

Governing Bodies: Senate

Academic Year: September to June (September-January; February-June)

Admission Requirements: Secondary school certificate (gerchilgee)

Fees: (Tughriks): 378,000 to 1.2m. per annum

Main Language(s) of Instruction: Mongolian

International Co-operation: With 103 foreign universities

Accrediting Agencies: National Council for Higher Education Accreditation

Degrees and Diplomas: *Bachelor's Degree*; *Master's Degree*; *Doctor of Philosophy*

Student Services: Academic counselling, Canteen, Cultural centre, Foreign student adviser, Foreign Studies Centre, Health services, Language programs, Sports facilities

Student Residential Facilities: For c. 1,000 students

Special Facilities: Zoology Museum; Botany Museum; Archaeology and Anthropology Museum; Ethnography Museum

Libraries: Educational and Scientific Library, c. 350,000 vols

Publications: NUM Scientific Journal *(quarterly)*

Last Updated: 05/01/10

ULAANBAATAR UNIVERSITY

PO Box 167/ 51, Bayan-Zurkh District, Ulaanbaatar 210651
Tel: +976(11) 358-327
Fax: +976(11) 458-327
EMail: utu@magicnet.mn
Website: http://www.ulaanbaatar.edu.mn

Rector: Kh. Baigalsiakhan

Faculties

Business Management (Business Administration); **Linguistics and Literature**; **Social Sciences**; **Technology**

History: Founded 1992 as Technological Institute. Acquired present status 1995.

Main Language(s) of Instruction: Mongolian

International Co-operation: With universities in Russian Federation; Kazakhstan; USA; Japan; France; China

Accrediting Agencies: National Council for Higher Education Accreditation

Degrees and Diplomas: *Bachelor's Degree*; *Master's Degree*; *Doctor of Philosophy*

Last Updated: 17/12/09

UNIVERSITY OF THE HUMANITIES

Humuunlegiin Uhaanii Ih Surguuli

Sukhbaatar Square, 20/4, Baga Toiruu, Sukhbaatar District, Ulaanbaatar 210646
Tel: +976(11) 318 524
Fax: +976(11) 322 702
EMail: uh@humanities.mn
Website: http://www.humanities.mn

President: Chuluundorj Begz EMail: chukab@hotmail.com

Secretary: Enkhsaruul Tsebaljir EMail: jumna7555@yahoo.com

International Relations: Uuriintuya Batjargal, Foreign Affairs Assistant Tel: +976 8807 8800 EMail: b.uuriintuya@yahoo.com

Programmes

Graduate Studies (Business Administration; Chinese; Comparative Literature; Cultural Studies; Education; English; Environmental Management; Foreign Languages Education; French; German; Industrial Management; International Economics; International Relations; Japanese; Journalism; Korean; Linguistics; Mongolian; Russian; Sociology; Translation and Interpretation)

Research Centres

Language Policy

Schools

Business (Accountancy; Business Administration; Economics; Environmental Management; Human Resources; International Business; International Economics; Management; Marketing; Tourism); **Information and Communication Management** (Computer Education; Computer Graphics; Computer Networks; Computer Science; Journalism; Mass Communication); **Languages and Culture** (American Studies; Behavioural Sciences; Chinese; English Studies; Foreign Languages Education; French; German; History; International Economics; International Relations; Japanese;

Journalism; Korean; Modern Languages; Russian; Translation and Interpretation)

History: Founded 1979 as the Institute of Liberal Arts (Russian Language).

Governing Bodies: Board of Trustees

Academic Year: Sept - Dec; Jan - June

Admission Requirements: High school certificate.

Fees: (Tughriks): 1,296,000 to 1,944,000 per annum.

Main Language(s) of Instruction: Mongolian

International Co-operation: with institutions in China, Japan, and Korea.

Accrediting Agencies: National Council for Higher Education Accreditation

Degrees and Diplomas: *Bachelor's Degree*: Computer Graphics and Design; Information System Management; Computer Programming; Computer Education; International Relations; Behavioural Sciences; Education; Linguistics and Translation; Civilization Studies; History; Economics; Environmental and Ecological Management; Business Administration; Accounting; International Business; Tourism; Financial Management; Marketing; Mining Management, 4 yrs; *Master's Degree*: Education; Education Administration; Foreign Languages; Cultural Studies; Literature; Journalism; Ecology Management; Mongolian Studies; Information Systems Management; Business Administration; Sociology;Producation Management, a further 2 yrs; *Doctor of Philosophy*: Linguistics and Foreign Languages; Comparative Literature and Translation; Education and Education Administration; Business Management; Cultural Studies; Journalism and Mass Communication, 3 yrs

Student Services: Academic counselling, Canteen, Employment services, Foreign student adviser, Language programs, Social counselling, Sports facilities

Special Facilities: Laboratory of Ecology; Institute of Knowledge Management and Technology; Research Centre for Language Policy

Libraries: 130,051 vols including electronic library

Publications: Research Journal *(biannually)*

Academic Staff *2010-2011*	MEN	WOMEN	**TOTAL**
FULL-TIME	35	56	**91**
PART-TIME	8	11	**19**
STAFF WITH DOCTORATE			
FULL-TIME	8	11	**19**
PART-TIME	3	6	**9**
Student Numbers *2010-2011*			
All (Foreign Included)	1,900	2,328	**4,228**
FOREIGN ONLY	–	–	**20**

Part-time students, 1,016. **Distance students**, 30.

Last Updated: 08/07/11

PRIVATE INSTITUTIONS

KHAN-UUL INSTITUTE

Khan-Uul Deed Surguuli

PO Box 419, Ulaanbaatar 46

Tel: +976(11) 342-888

Rector: Demberel Tserengiin EMail: han_uul@mongol.net

Faculties

Economics (Economics); **Mathematics** (Mathematics)

History: Created 1994

Academic Year: September to June (September-January; February-June)

Admission Requirements: Certificate of basic education (over 10 years)

Main Language(s) of Instruction: Mongolian, English

Accrediting Agencies: National Council for Higher Education Accreditation

Degrees and Diplomas: *Bachelor's Degree*; *Master's Degree*

Publications: 'Applied Mathematics' magazine *(quarterly)*

Press or Publishing House: 'Sukhbator' Publishing House

Last Updated: 17/12/09

OTGONTENGER UNIVERSITY

PO Box 51/35, Jucov Street, Ulaanbaatar 325205

Tel: +976(11) 458-635

Fax: +976(11) 463-547

EMail: info@otgontenger.edu.mn

Website: http://www.otgontenger.edu.mn

President: Naranchimeg Davaasuren

Departments

European Languages (American Studies; English; English Studies; German; Germanic Studies; History; Literature); **Oriental Languages and Culture and Linguistics** (Chinese; Japanese; Korean; Linguistics); **Social Sciences** (History; Journalism; Philosophy; Physical Education; Social Sciences)

Schools

Economic and Business Administration; **Humanities**; **Law**

History: Founded 1991.

Governing Bodies: Board of Directors

Admission Requirements: Secondary School Certificate and score of general examination

Fees: (Tughriks): 480,000 per annum

Main Language(s) of Instruction: Mongolian

International Co-operation: With universities in Japan and Germany

Accrediting Agencies: National Council for Higher Education Accreditation

Degrees and Diplomas: *Bachelor's Degree*; *Master's Degree*; *Doctor of Philosophy*

Student Services: Academic counselling, Canteen, Cultural centre, Employment services, Health services, Language programs, Nursery care, Social counselling, Sports facilities

Student Residential Facilities: None

Special Facilities: Museum; Movie Studio

Libraries: 3 Libraries: 50,000 vols

Last Updated: 17/12/09

ULAANBAATAR COLLEGE

PO Box 658, Bayangol District, Ulaanbaatar 210644

Tel: +976(11) 312-271

Fax: +976(11) 311-080

EMail: ubinev@magicnet.mn

Director: Yun Sunje

Divisions

Business Administration (Business Administration); **Computer Science**; **Korean Language** (Korean)

History: Founded 1993.

Accrediting Agencies: National Council for Higher Education Accreditation

Degrees and Diplomas: *Bachelor's Degree*; *Master's Degree*

Last Updated: 17/12/09

ZASAGT KHAN INSTITUTE

Zasagt Khan Deed Surguuli

p/b-510, Baynzurkh District, Ulaanbaatar 13381

Tel: +976(1) 146-1880

Fax: +976(1) 146-1880

EMail: zasagtkhan99@yahoo.com

Website: http://www.zasagtkhan.edu.mn/

Rector: Altangerel Sambuu
EMail: zasagtkhan_khan_1999@yahoo.com

Director: Yunden Yadamjav EMail: ya_yunden@yahoo.com

International Relations: Enkhnasan Namjiljav, International Relations Officer EMail: enhee_4188@yahoo.com

Divisions

Business Administration (Business Administration); **Government** (Government); **Human and Social Sciences**; **Information Science**

History: Created 1999.

Governing Bodies: University Council

Academic Year: September - January; February - June

Admission Requirements: Successful completion of secondary school; entrance exam (min score 400)

Main Language(s) of Instruction: Mongolian

International Co-operation: With institutions in China, Korea, Russian Federation

Accrediting Agencies: National Council for Higher Education Accreditation

Degrees and Diplomas: *Bachelor's Degree*; *Master's Degree*

Student Services: Canteen, Cultural centre, Employment services, Handicapped facilities, Health services, Language programs, Nursery care, Sports facilities

Libraries: 12,000 vols

Academic Staff *2009-2010*	MEN	WOMEN	**TOTAL**
FULL-TIME	6	19	**25**
PART-TIME	2	3	**5**
STAFF WITH DOCTORATE			
FULL-TIME	3	–	**3**
PART-TIME	2	1	**3**
Student Numbers *2009-2010*			
All (Foreign Included)	355	145	**500**

Part-time students, 250. **Distance students**, 750.

Last Updated: 22/01/10

Montenegro

STRUCTURE OF HIGHER EDUCATION SYSTEM

Description:

On 22 October 2003, the Assembly of Montenegro adopted the new Law on Higher Education. The Law was drafted according to the objectives of the Bologna Declaration. Its overall goal is to give higher education institutions maximum autonomy in their activities, particularly in the academic field, with minimal mediation from the State, except when requested to protect the public interest. The mission of the university becomes to educate young people to be qualified citizens in a democratic society and a qualified workforce in the European labour market. Degrees and diplomas are delivered according to the Bologna standards. The first generation of students under this system was enrolled in the academic year 2004/2005. Higher education is provided by the universities and higher education institutions that are licensed and accredited in accordance to the rules set in the new Law. The University of Montenegro is the only public university in Montenegro. It was officially founded in 1974 and is now comprised of 19 faculties and 3 scientific research institutes offering undergraduate, graduate and doctoral studies. The first private Faculty of Tourism and Hotel Management opened in September 2004 in Bar, Montenegro, enrolling 50 students. At the moment, there are 2 private universities and 5 private faculties in Montenegro. The implementation of the Bologna process is overseen by a National Team of Bologna experts. Working groups are set up within the team to advise higher education institutions on the three Bologna priorities: 1) quality assurance, 2) three cycle system and 3) recognition, the quality assurance issue having been defined as the highest priority in the area of higher education development policy. The language of studies is the Montenegrin language.

Stages of studies:

University level first stage: Undergraduate studies
Students are eligible to attend higher study courses in public institutions on a competitive basis. Depending on the institution, the competition is based on the results achieved at secondary school; the results at the matriculation exam; or upon completion of secondary education or its equivalent.
Additional conditions may be introduced for admission to some specific programmes.
The enrolment process is explained in the Guidelines for Enrollment. The names of enrolled students are publicly announced. The tests and their results are public and can be consulted. In case a student would consider that the process had not been regularly performed, he is entitled to appeal to the Central Enrolment Commission.
After completion of the undergraduate study programme, the student is awarded a diploma of undergraduate applied/academic studies and a Bachelor degree.
Undergraduate studies at most faculties of the University of Montenegro last for three years.

University level second stage: Graduate studies
Students are eligible for graduate study courses in public institutions on a competitive basis, according to their results in undergraduate studies.
After the defense of his/her master's thesis in public, the student obtains the academic title of Master of science or Master of arts in a particular field.

University level third stage: Doctoral degree
Doctoral degrees last for three academic years (180 ECTS). Students with the academic title of Master can enrol in doctoral studies. They are the compilation of taught courses (one third) and independent research (two third of studies' duration). The type of courses and the ratio between compulsory and selected courses are defined by the HEI's regulations. The supervisory and assessment procedures for doctoral studies have recently been revised by the University of Montenegro (UOM). The new regulations deal with the supervision of studies in an extensive manner through the clear division of responsibilities between the adviser (mentor), the respective department authority and the Senate. Scientists from institutions outside the University of Montenegro also take part in the procedure of independent thesis assessment. There is a possibility of interdisciplinary training in the first year of studies. Doctoral candidates can be, at early stages, both full time students and researchers.
After defending his/her doctoral thesis in public, a student obtains the academic title of PhD. Applied studies, due to their nature, do not give access to the third cycle.

ADMISSION TO HIGHER EDUCATION

Admission to university-level studies:

Name of secondary school credential required: Secondary school leaving certificate

For entry to: University. The minimum score/requirement is based on a competitive basis. Conditions are prescribed by the Guidelines for Enrolment to the First Study Year.

RECOGNITION OF STUDIES

Quality assurance system:

The Council for Higher Education is the national body responsible for higher education. It is nominated by the Government. The Council analyzes the state and achievements of the higher education sector and advices the Government on possible ways forwards to improve the sector. Montenegro does not have a national QA agency. Information sources on quality assurance: the University of Montenegro's Quality Assurance Centre, the link to the ENIC Centre on the website of the Ministry of Education and Science.

Bodies dealing with recognition:

ENIC Centar Crne Gore (ENIC Centre of Montenegro)

Manager: Vanja Srdanovic
Officer: Mubera Kurpejovic
Advisor: Ranko Lazović
Rimski trg bb
Podgorica 81000
Tel: +382 20 405 301
Fax: +382 20 405 334
EMail: mpin@gov.me
WWW: http://www.mpin.gov.me/rubrike/enic-centar

Special provisions for recognition:

Recognition for university level studies: The recognition procedure is prescribed by the Law on the Recognition and Assessment of Educational Certificates.

For exercising a profession: A Law on Regulated Professions is being prepared. At the moment, some professional bodies grant working licenses to enable people to exercise their professions in the field of regulated professions.

NATIONAL BODIES

Ministarstvo prosvjete i sporta (Ministry of Education and Sport)

Minister: Slavoljub Stijepović
Adviser: Jelena Abramović
Director, International Relations: Tanja Ostojic
Vaka Djurovica b.b.
Podgorica 81000
Tel: +382(20) 410 100
Fax: +382(20) 410 101
EMail: mps@mps.gov.me
WWW: http://www.mpin.gov.me
Role of national body: Elaborates the overall education policy.

Data for academic year: 2010-2011
Source: IAU from Ministry of Education and Science of Montenegro, 2010. Bodies, 2012.

INSTITUTIONS

PUBLIC INSTITUTIONS

UNIVERSITY OF MONTENEGRO

Univerzitet Crne Gore
Dzordza Vasingtona bb, 81000 Podgorica
Tel: +381(81) 241-777 +381(81) 241-888
Fax: +381(81) 242-301
EMail: ucg@cis.cg.ac.yu
Website: http://www.ucg.ac.me/cg/

Rektor: Predrag Miranovic EMail: rektor@ac.me

Secretary-General: Dragiša Ivanović EMail: ivanovic@cg.ac.yu

International Relations: Mira Vukčević, Vice-Rector for International and Inter-institutional Relations Tel: +381(81) 225-984

Academies
Music (Conducting; Music; Music Theory and Composition; Musical Instruments)

Colleges
Physiotherapy *(Igalo, Herceg Novi)* (Physical Therapy)

Faculties
Civil Engineering (Architecture; Civil Engineering; Construction Engineering; Road Engineering; Town Planning); **Drama** *(Cetinje)* (Theatre); **Economics** (Business Administration; Economics; Finance; International Business; Management; Marketing); **Electrical Engineering** (Electrical Engineering); **Fine Arts** *(Cetinje)* (Fine Arts; Graphic Design; Painting and Drawing; Sculpture); **Law** (Law; Political Sciences); **Marine Studies** *(Kotor)* (Marine Engineering; Marine Science and Oceanography; Marine Transport; Nautical Science); **Mechanical Engineering** (Automotive Engineering; Mechanical Engineering; Thermal Engineering); **Medicine** (Medicine); **Metallurgy and Technology** (Metal Techniques; Metallurgical Engineering; Technology); **Natural Sciences and Mathematics** (Biology; Mathematics; Mathematics and Computer Science; Natural Sciences; Physics); **Philosophy** *(Nikšić)* (Philosophy); **Tourism and Hotel Management** *(Kotor)* (Cooking and Catering; Hotel and Restaurant; Hotel Management; Tourism)

Institutes
Biotechnology (Agriculture; Agrobiology; Biotechnology); **Foreign Languages** (Modern Languages); **History** (History); **Marine Biology** *(Kotor)* (Marine Biology; Marine Science and Oceanography)

Further Information: Campuses: Podgorica, Nikšic, Cetinje, Kotor and Herceg Novi

History: Founded 1974 incorporating faculties formerly attached to University of Belgrade. An independent self-governing Institution financed by the State. Acquired present title 1992.

Governing Bodies: Senate, comprising 39 members; University Assembly, comprising 28 members

Academic Year: October to July (October-January; February-July)

Admission Requirements: Secondary school certificate or recognized equivalent

Accrediting Agencies: Ministarstvo prosvjete i nauke (Ministry of Education and Science)

Degrees and Diplomas: *Bachelor, Master, Doctorate*

Student Services: Academic counselling, Canteen, Cultural centre, Foreign Studies Centre, Health services, Social counselling, Sports facilities

Student Residential Facilities: Yes

Libraries: University Library. Specialized libraries

Publications: Bilten *(quarterly)*

Last Updated: 04/10/11

PRIVATE INSTITUTIONS

DONJA GORICA UNIVERSITY

Univerzitet Donja Gorica
Donja Gorica bb, 81000 Podgorica
Tel: +382-(20) 410-777
Fax: +382-(20) 410-766
EMail: udg@t-com.me; ps@udg.edu.me
Website: http://www.udg.edu.me/

Rector: Veselin Vukotic

Centres
Foreign Languages (Albanian; Arabic; English; German; Italian; Modern Languages)

Faculties
Arts (Fine Arts); **Humanities** (Arts and Humanities; International Relations); **Information Systems and Technology** (Information Management; Information Sciences; Information Technology); **International Economics, Finance and Business** (Business Administration; Business and Commerce; Finance; International Economics); **Law** (Law)

History: Created 2010 incorporating Fakultet pravnih nauka (Faculty of Law), Fakultet za humanističke studije (Faculty of Humanities), Fakultet za međunarodnu ekonomiju, finansije i biznis (Faculty of International Economics, Finance and Business) and Fakultet za informacione sisteme i tehnologije (Faculty of Information Systems and Technologies).

Accrediting Agencies: Ministarstvo prosvjete i nauke (Ministry of Education and Science)

Degrees and Diplomas: *Bachelor, Master*

Last Updated: 30/11/10

FACULTY FOR BUSINESS MANAGEMENT

Fakultet za poslovni menadžment
Maršala Tita 7, 85000 Bar
Tel: +38 (85) 312-233
EMail: fpm@t-com.me
Website: http://www.fpm.me

Dean: Milenko Radoman

Programmes
Business Management (Business Administration; Commercial Law; Economics; Management; Marketing; Psychology); **Criminal Law** (Criminal Law; Criminology)

History: Created 2006.

Accrediting Agencies: Ministarstvo prosvjete i nauke

Degrees and Diplomas: *Bachelor, Specialist Diploma*

Last Updated: 04/10/11

FACULTY FOR STATE AND EUROPEAN STUDIES

Fakultet za državne i evropske studije
Jovana Tomaševića bb, 81000 Podgorica
Tel: +382(20) 244-828 +382(20) 244-909
Fax: +382(20) 244-929
EMail: info@fdes.me
Website: http://www.fdes.me/

Dean: Sonja Bjeletić EMail: dekanat@fdes.me

Programmes
Administrative and European Studies *(Undergraduate)* (Economics; English; European Studies; European Union Law; Finance; International Law; Political Sciences; Public Administration; Public Law; Sociology); **Administrative Studies** *(Postgraduate)* (European Union Law; Government; Law; Political Sciences; Public Administration; Social Sciences); **European Studies** *(Postgraduate)* (Economics; European Studies; European Union Law; Finance; International Relations)

History: Created 2005. Acquired current status 2006.

Accrediting Agencies: Ministarstvo prosvjete i nauke (Ministry of Education and Science)

Degrees and Diplomas: *Bachelor*: Administrative and European Studies, 3 yrs or 180 ECTs; *Master*: Administrative Studies; European Studies, 2 yrs or 120 ECTs

Last Updated: 04/10/11

FACULTY OF INTERNATIONAL CATERING AND TOURIST MANAGEMENT

Fakultet za internacionalni hotelski i turistički menadžment

Sveti Stefan, 85310 Miločer
Tel: +382(33) 468-246
Fax: +382(33) 468-503
EMail: algonquinfakultet@t-com.me
Website: http://www.algonquinfakultet.com/

Dean: Rade Ratković EMail: njasa@cg.yu

Programmes

Hotel and Tourism Management (Hotel and Restaurant; Hotel Management; Tourism)

History: Created 2008.

Accrediting Agencies: Ministarstvo prosvjete i nauke

Degrees and Diplomas: *Bachelor*, *Master*. Also offers Canadian Bachelor's degree.

Last Updated: 04/11/09

FACULTY OF TRAFFIC AND COMMUNICATION MANAGEMENT

Fakultet za menadžment u saobraćaju i komunikacijama

Donje Luge bb, 84300 Berane
Tel: +382(5) 238-100
EMail: fmsk-ba@t-com.me
Website: http://www.fmsk.me

Dean: Vujadin Vešović EMail: dekan@fmsk.me

Departments

E-Communications (Telecommunications Engineering); **Logistics** (Transport Management); **Transport** (Transport Management)

History: Created 2008.

Accrediting Agencies: Ministarstvo prosvjete i nauke

Degrees and Diplomas: *Bachelor*, *Master*

Last Updated: 21/02/12

KRALJICA JELENA HIGHER NURSING SCHOOL

Visoka škola sestrinstva 'Kraljica Jelena'

Sava Ilica 1, 85347 Igalo
Tel: +382(88) 330-020
Fax: +382(88) 658-869

Dean: Milan Obradović

Programmes

Nursing (Nursing)

History: Created 2005.

Accrediting Agencies: Ministarstvo prosvjete i nauke

Degrees and Diplomas: *Bachelor*, *Master*

Last Updated: 04/11/09

MEDITERRANEAN UNIVERSITY

Univerzitet Mediteran

Vaka Đurovića b.b., 81 000 Podgorica
Tel: +382(20) 409-200
Fax: +381(20) 409-232
EMail: office@unimediteran.net
Website: http://www.unimediteran.net

Rector: Stevan Popović EMail: stevan.popovic@unimediteran.net

International Relations: Janko Radulović, Vice-Rector for International Cooperation
Tel: +382(20) 409-202 EMail: janko.radulovic@unimediteran.net

Faculties

Business Studies *(Montenegro Business School)* (Business Administration; Finance; Marketing); **Foreign Languages** (American Studies; English; Italian); **Information Technologies** (Information Technology); **Law** (Commercial Law; Law); **Tourism and Hospitality Management** *(Montenegro Tourism School)* (Hotel Management; Tourism); **Visual Arts** (Cinema and Television; Communication Arts; Visual Arts)

History: Created 2006. Montenegro's first private university.

Accrediting Agencies: Ministarstvo prosvjete i nauke (Ministry of Education and Science)

Degrees and Diplomas: *Bachelor*: 3 yrs; *Master*: 1 yr; *Doctorate*

Libraries: c. 300,000 vols; 10 periodical subscriptions; access to electronic networks

Last Updated: 04/10/11

Morocco

STRUCTURE OF HIGHER EDUCATION SYSTEM

Description:

Higher education is provided by universities, grandes écoles, institutes, teacher-training schools and centres. A characteristic feature of training is the existence, besides the traditional system of higher education, of higher education institutions (Etablissements de Formation des Cadres) which provide specialized training for high-level personnel in Science/Technology; Law/Economics/Administration/Social Sciences and Teacher Training. Both public and private higher education institutions are under the supervision of the Ministry of Higher Education. Some Grandes Ecoles and Institutes are under the supervision of their specific ministries. University councils rule on important questions related to university life. Universities are institutions with budgetary autonomy.

Stages of studies:

University level first stage: *Licence*
The first stage at university lasts for three years (six semesters) leading to the Licence.

University level second stage: *Master*
The second stage is a phase of in-depth training which lasts for two years and leads to the Master.

University level third stage: *Doctorat*
The third stage leads to the Doctorat which is conferred after three years' further study beyond the Master.

ADMISSION TO HIGHER EDUCATION

Admission to university-level studies:

Name of secondary school credential required: Baccalauréat

Other admission requirements: There is an entrance examination for some institutions and some subjects (Medicine, Pharmacy, Dentistry, Translation and Interpreting, for example).

Foreign students admission:

Entrance exam requirements: Foreign students must hold the Baccalaureat or an equivalent qualification.

Language requirements: Good knowledge of Arabic or French

NATIONAL BODIES

Ministère de l'Enseignement supérieur, de la Recherche scientifique et de la Formation des Cadres (Ministry of Higher Education and Research)

Minister: Lahcen Daoudi
Secretary-General: Abdelhafid Debbarh
Director, Higher Education: El bachir Kouhlani
rue Idrissi Al Akbar - Hassan
BP 4500
Rabat
Tel: +212 05 3721 7501
Fax: +212 05 3721 7547
EMail: enssup@enssup.gov.ma
WWW: http://www.enssup.gov.ma/

Conférence des Présidents des Universités marocaines (Conference of Moroccan University Presidents)

President: Taïeb Chkili
Université Mohammed V
Rabat

Data for academic year: 2012-2013
Source: IAU from the website of the Ministry of Higher Education, 2012

INSTITUTIONS

PUBLIC INSTITUTIONS

ABDELMALEK ESSAÂDI UNIVERSITY

Université Abdelmalek Essaâdi

Mhannech 2, Avenue Palestine, B.P. 2117, 93030 Tétouan
Tel: +212(539) 97-93-16
Fax: +212(539) 97-91-51
EMail: president@uae.ma
Website: http://www.uae.ma

President: Houdaifa Ameziane (2010-) Tel: +212(539) 97-90-95

Secrétaire général: Lahcen Dassar
Tel: +212(539) 68-99-16, Fax: +212(539) 68-99-16
EMail: sg@uae.ma

International Relations: Ahmed El Moussaoui, Vice President
Tel: +212(539) 68-87-27
EMail: vp-cr@uae.ma; elmoussaoui@uae.ma

Faculties

Arts and Humanities *(Martil, Tétouan)* (Arabic; Arts and Humanities; Cinema and Television; Development Studies; French; Geography; History; Islamic Studies; Social and Community Services; Sociology; Spanish; Tourism); **Law, Economics and Social Sciences** *(Tanger)* (Economics; Law; Social Sciences); **Polydisciplinary** *(Larache)* (Business Computing; Computer Science; Hotel Management; Tourism); **Polydisciplinary** *(Tétouan)* (Economics; Law; Management); **Science** *(Tétouan)* (Biology; Chemistry; Geology; Mathematics; Natural Sciences; Physics); **Science and Technology** *(Tangiers)* (Bioengineering; Biology; Chemical Engineering; Civil Engineering; Computer Engineering; Electrical Engineering; Industrial Engineering; Maintenance Technology; Mathematics and Computer Science; Mechanical Engineering; Natural Sciences; Statistics; Technology)

Schools

Applied Sciences *(ENSA Tangiers)* (Computer Engineering; Computer Networks; Systems Analysis); **Applied Sciences** *(ENSA Tétouan)* (Computer Engineering; Computer Networks; Telecommunications Engineering); **Commerce and Management** *(ENCGT)* (Accountancy; Advertising and Publicity; Business Administration; Business and Commerce; Business Computing; Finance; International Business; Management; Marketing; Transport Management); **Translation** *(Tangiers)* (Arabic; English; Spanish; Translation and Interpretation)

History: Founded 1989. Incorporation of ENS Tétouan.

Governing Bodies: Conseil de l'Université

Academic Year: September to July (September-December; January-March; April-July)

Admission Requirements: Secondary school certificate (baccalauréat). Entrance examination for Schools; national selection for Faculty of Sciences and Technolgy

Fees: None

Main Language(s) of Instruction: Arabic, French

International Co-operation: With Universities in France, Spain, Italy, Germany, Tunisia and Algeria

Degrees and Diplomas: *Diplôme universitaire de Technologie*; *Licence d'Etudes fondamentales*: 3 yrs; *Licence en Sciences et Techniques*; *Licence professionnelle*; *Diplôme de Commerce et de Gestion*; *Diplôme d'Ingénieur*, *Master Sciences et Techniques*; *Master spécialisé*: 2 yrs; *Master*: 2 yrs; *Doctorat*: 3-4 yrs

Student Services: Handicapped facilities, Sports facilities

Student Residential Facilities: 3 residences

Libraries: Libraries of the Faculties and Schools

Publications: Cahier de la Recherche de l'Université, Publication on Scientific Research conducted at University *(1-2 per annum)*; Tourjouman, Journal of the School of Translation

Academic Staff *2011-2012*: Total 1,320
STAFF WITH DOCTORATE: Total 760

Student Numbers *2011-2012*: Total 36,000

Last Updated: 14/05/12

ADVANCED TEACHER TRAINING COLLEGE OF TETOUAN

Université Abdelmalek Essaâdi Tétouan (ENS-TÉTOUAN)

ECOLE NORMALE SUPÉRIEURE, TÉTOUAN

Avenue Moulay Hassan, BP 209, Martil, Tétouan
Tel: +212(539) 97-91-75
Fax: +212(539) 97-91-80
EMail: ens@uae.ma
Website: http://www.ens.uae.ma/

Directeur: Abdelaziz Mimet
Tel: +212(539) 97-91-75, Fax: +212(539) 97-91-80
EMail: abdelaziz.mimet@uae.ma

Secrétaire général: Choukri Barbara
Tel: +212(539) 68-81-02
EMail: barbara.choukri@gmail.com; choukri@uae.ma

International Relations: Zouhaire Lamrani, Directeur Adjoint
Tel: +212(539) 68-81-02 EMail: zh.amrani@yahoo.fr

Departments

Computer Science and Management (Computer Networks; Computer Science; Management; Multimedia; Software Engineering); **Environmental Studies** (Environmental Management; Environmental Studies; Town Planning); **Modern Languages** (Modern Languages); **Sciences** (Biology; Chemistry; Mathematics Education; Natural Sciences; Physics; Science Education)

History: Founded 1987. Integrated into University Abdelmalek Essaadi.

Governing Bodies: Conseil d'établissement

Admission Requirements: Baccalauréat

Main Language(s) of Instruction: Arabic; French

International Co-operation: With European Union countries

Accrediting Agencies: Commission Nationale de Coordination de l'Enseignement Supérieure (CNCES); Ministère de l'Enseignement

Supérieur de la Formation des Cadres et de la Recherche Scientifique

Degrees and Diplomas: *Licence professionnelle*: Arabic; Geography; History; Natural Science, Earth Science; Physics, Chemistry; French; Computer Engineering; Sport Administration; *Master spécialisé*: Computer Science; Natural Science and Earth Science; Islamic Studies

Student Services: Academic counselling, Canteen, Foreign student adviser, Language programs, Social counselling, Sports facilities

Student Residential Facilities: Yes

Libraries: Yes

Academic Staff *2011-2012*	MEN	WOMEN	TOTAL
FULL-TIME	57	6	**63**
STAFF WITH DOCTORATE FULL-TIME	40	3	**43**
Student Numbers *2011-2012*			
All (Foreign Included)	427	413	**840**
FOREIGN ONLY	3	3	**6**

AL AKHAWAYN UNIVERSITY

Université Al Akhawayn (ENS-TÉTOUAN)

BP 104, Avenue Hassan II, 53000 Ifrane
Tel: +212(535) 86-20-00
Fax: +212(535) 56-71-50
EMail: info@aui.ma
Website: http://www.aui.ma

President: Driss Ouaouicha (2008-)
Tel: +212(535) 86-2-0-01, Fax: +212(535) 56-7-1-42
EMail: president@aui.ma

Admissions and Outreach Coordinator: Smail Mojahid
EMail: admissions@aui.ma

Institutes

Leadership Development Studies (Leadership)

Schools

Business Administration *(SBA)* (Business Administration); **Humanities and Social Sciences** *(SHSS)* (Arts and Humanities; Social Sciences); **Science and Engineering** *(SSE)* (Computer Science; Engineering)

History: Founded 1993 as an English-language institution based on the American higher education model.

Governing Bodies: Board of Trustees, President and Vice-Presidents, Associate Vice-President, Directors

Academic Year: September to May (September-December; January-May). Also optional Summer Session (June-July)

Admission Requirements: Bachelor's Degree: Secondary school certificate (baccalaurèat) with excellent academic credentials, written aptitude test and an interview. Masters degree: Bachelor degree

Fees: (Dirhams): National students, 27,000; foreign students, 40,500

Main Language(s) of Instruction: English (Also Arabic course for foreign students and Business English for executives)

International Co-operation: With universities in USA, France, Japan, Germany, Finland, Korea, Spain, Australia. Also participates in Erasmus Mundus - Tempus programmes.

Accrediting Agencies: Ministère de l'Education nationale, de l'Enseignement supérieur, de la Formation des Cadres et de la Recherche scientifique

Degrees and Diplomas: *Licence d'Etudes fondamentales*; *Master*

Student Services: Academic counselling, Canteen, Employment services, Foreign student adviser, Health services, Language programs, Social counselling, Sports facilities

Student Residential Facilities: For c. 1,547 students, Off-campus residences for staff and faculty

Special Facilities: Shuttle Services, Laundry, Computer Labs, Bookstore, Post Office and ATM, Copy Center

Libraries: Mohammed VI Library. 92,000 vols. in addition to over 355 national and international academic journals, magazines and newspapers

Publications: Al Hayat Al Jamiiya (Arabic); AUI Bridge; Avant-Garde (French); Conferences' Proceedings *(annually)*; Faculty of Applied Research *(annually)*; Outstanding Graduate Students' Culminating Projects *(annually)*

Academic Staff *2012*	TOTAL
FULL-TIME	**44**
PART-TIME	**14**
STAFF WITH DOCTORATE FULL-TIME	**81**
Student Numbers *2011*	
All (Foreign Included)	**1,772**

Last Updated: 11/04/12

CADI AYYAD UNIVERSITY

Université Cadi Ayyad (ENS-MARRAKECH)

BP 511, Avenue Prince Abdellah,
Marrakech
Tel: +212(524) 43-48-14
Fax: +212(524) 43-44-94
EMail: rectorat@ucam.ac.ma
Website: http://www.ucam.ac.ma

Président: Abdellatif Miraoui EMail: Presidence@ucam.ac.ma

Secrétaire général: Imane Kerkeb

Faculties

Arts and Humanities *(FLSH)* (Arabic; Arts and Humanities; English; French; Geography; History; Islamic Studies); **Law, Economics, and Social Sciences** *(FSJES Marrakech)* (Economics; Law; Social Sciences); **Medicine and Pharmacy** (Medicine; Pharmacology); **Polydisciplinary** *(Safi)* (Arts and Humanities; Computer Engineering; Economics; Geography; Law; Literature; Mathematics; Natural Sciences; Social Sciences); **Science** *(Semlalia, FSSM)* (Biology; Chemistry; Computer Science; Geology; Mathematics; Natural Sciences; Physics); **Science and Technology** *(Marrakech)* (Biology; Chemistry; Geology; Mathematics; Natural Sciences; Physics; Technology)

Schools

Applied Sciences *(ENSA Safi)* (Computer Engineering; Electrical Engineering; Telecommunications Engineering); **Applied Sciences** *(ENSA Marrakech)* (Computer Engineering; Computer Networks; Electrical Engineering); **Business Studies and Management** *(ENCG)* (Business and Commerce; Management); **Technology** *(EST Safi)* (Industrial Maintenance; Management Systems; Production Engineering; Technology); **Technology** *(EST Essaouira)* (Computer Engineering; Technology; Tourism)

History: Founded 1978.

Academic Year: September to June (September-December; January-April; May-June)

Admission Requirements: Secondary school certificate (baccalauréat) or equivalent

Fees: None

Main Language(s) of Instruction: French

International Co-operation: With universities in Spain; Italy; France; Tunisia; Belgium; USA; Germany

Degrees and Diplomas: *Diplôme universitaire de Technologie*; *Licence d'Etudes fondamentales*; *Licence en Sciences et Techniques*; *Licence professionnelle*; *Diplôme d'Ingénieur*; *Master spécialisé*; *Master*; *Doctorat*

Student Services: Canteen, Health services, Sports facilities

Student Numbers *2010-2011*: Total 29,703

Last Updated: 04/07/12

ADVANCED TEACHER TRAINING COLLEGE OF MARRAKECH
ECOLE NORMALE SUPÉRIEURE, MARRAKECH

BP 2400, Route d'Essaouira, 40000 Marrakech
Tel: +212(544) 34-01-25
Fax: +212(544) 34-22-87
Website: http://www.ens-marrakech.ac.ma/newsite/index.php

Directeur: Mohamed Fliyou

Programmes

Teacher Training (Biology; Business Education; Chemistry; Computer Education; Economics; Geology; Humanities and Social Science Education; Mathematics Education; Philosophy; Physics; Science Education)

History: Founded 1979.

Degrees and Diplomas: *Licence professionnelle*: Biology; Computer Education; Geology; Mathematics; Philosophy; *Master*: Chemistry; Mathematics; Physics

CHOUAÏB DOUKKALI UNIVERSITY

Université Chouaïb Doukkali

B.P.299, 2, avenue Mohamed Ben Larbi Alaoui, 24000 El Jadida
Tel: +212(523) 34-44-47
Fax: +212(523) 34-44-49
EMail: contact@ucd.ac.ma
Website: http://www.ucd.ac.ma

Président: Boumediene Tanouti (2011-)

Faculties

Arts and Humanities (Arabic; Arts and Humanities; Communication Studies; English; French; Geography; History; Islamic Studies; Literature); **Polydisciplinary** (Banking; Economics; Finance; Human Resources; Management; Marketing; Tourism; Transport Management); **Science** (Biology; Chemistry; Geology; Mathematics; Natural Sciences; Physics)

Schools

Applied Science *(ENSA)* (Computer Engineering; Industrial Engineering; Telecommunications Engineering); **Commerce and Management** *(ENCG)* (Business and Commerce; Management)

History: Founded 1989.

Academic Year: September to July

Admission Requirements: Secondary school certificate (baccalauréat)

Fees: None

Main Language(s) of Instruction: Arabic, French, English

Degrees and Diplomas: *Licence d'Etudes fondamentales*; *Licence professionnelle*; *Diplôme de Commerce et de Gestion*; *Diplôme d'Ingénieur*; *Master spécialisé*; *Master*; *Doctorat*

Student Services: Cultural centre, Health services, Sports facilities

Student Residential Facilities: For c. 10,000 students

Libraries: Faculty Libraries, total, 14,460 vols

Publications: Revue de la Faculté des Lettres

Last Updated: 04/07/12

DAR-AL-HADITH AL-HASSANIA

BP: 6549 Al Irfane, 465 Bd. Azzaitoun - Hay Ryad, Rabat
Tel: +212(537) 72-25-87
Fax: +212(537) 72-62-01
EMail: darhadit@menara.ma
Website: http://www.darhadit.ac.ma

Directeur: Ahmed El Khamlichi
Tel: +212(537) 20-08-82, Fax: +212(537) 76-16-16

Secrétaire général: Mohamed El Yaalaoui

International Relations: Hamid Achak

Programmes

Islamic Studies (Islamic Studies; Koran); **Languages** (Arabic); **Law** (Law); **Religious Studies** (Religious Studies)

History: Founded 1968. Acquired present status 2005.

Admission Requirements: High school certificate

Main Language(s) of Instruction: Arabic

Degrees and Diplomas: *Licence d'Etudes fondamentales*: Islamic Studies, 4 yrs; *Doctorat*: Advanced Islamic Studies, 3 yrs. Ta'heel in Advanced Islamic Studies 2 yrs

Student Residential Facilities: Yes

Libraries: Yes

Publications: Al Wachiha *(biennially)*

Student Numbers *2011-2012*	MEN	WOMEN	**TOTAL**
All (Foreign Included)	–	–	c. **200**
FOREIGN ONLY	–	10	**10**

Last Updated: 13/07/12

HASSAN I UNIVERSITY

Université Hassan 1er (UH1)

BP. 539, Route de Casablanca, km3, 26000 Settat
Tel: +212(523) 72-12-75 +212(523) 72-12-76
Fax: +212(523) 72-12-74
Website: http://www.uh1.ac.ma

Président: Ahmed Nejmeddine (2010-)
EMail: nejmeddine@uh1.ac.ma

Secrétaire Général: Mouloudi Zaidi EMail: m.zaidi@uh1.ac.ma

Faculties

Law, Economics and Social Sciences *(Settat)* (Economics; Law; Social Sciences) *Dean*: Rachid Essaid; **Polydisciplinary** *(Khouribga)* (Arabic; Automation and Control Engineering; Biological and Life Sciences; Business Administration; Chemistry; Economics; Electronic Engineering; Geography; Industrial Engineering; Mathematics; Physics; Telecommunications Engineering) *Dean*: Ali Baja; **Sciences and Techniques** *(Settat)* (Automation and Control Engineering; Biochemistry; Biological and Life Sciences; Biomedical Engineering; Chemical Engineering; Civil Engineering; Computer Engineering; Computer Networks; Construction Engineering; Electrical and Electronic Engineering; Environmental Engineering; Industrial Engineering; Information Technology; Mathematics and Computer Science; Mechanical Engineering; Microbiology; Multimedia; Natural Sciences; Production Engineering; Systems Analysis; Telecommunications Engineering)

Schools

Applied Sciences *(ENSA Khouribga)* (Computer Engineering; Computer Networks; Electrical Engineering; Energy Engineering; Environmental Engineering; Telecommunications Engineering); **Commerce and Management** *(ENCG Settat)* (Accountancy; Business Administration; Business and Commerce; Communication Studies; Finance; Human Resources; Information Technology; Management; Marketing; Secretarial Studies); **Technology** *(EST Berrechid)* (Computer Engineering; Electrical Engineering; Energy Engineering; Industrial Engineering; Transport Management) *Directeur*: El Mostafa Walim

History: Founded 1997. The National School of Trade and Management and the Faculty of Sciences and Techniques already existed since 1994.

Governing Bodies: Conseil de l'Université, Conseil de Gestion; Commissions

Academic Year: September to July

Admission Requirements: Secondary school Certificate (Baccalauréat). For Faculty of Sciences and Techniques: Baccalauréat with scientific specialisation. For National School of Trade and Management: Baccalauréat with specialisation in Experimental Science, Mathematics, Economics, Accountancy or Administration Techniques; preselection based on average grade obtained at the Baccalauréat; written and oral examinations. For the National School of Applied Sciences, Baccaluréat with scientific specialisation; written and oral examinations. For the Higher School of Technology: Baccalauréat with specialisation in Experimental Science, Mathematics, Economics, Accountancy or Administration Techniques; preselection based on average grade obtained at the Baccalauréat.

Fees: None

Main Language(s) of Instruction: French and Arabic

International Co-operation: With universities in France, Spain, Italy, Portugal, Germany, United Kingdom, Canada, USA, Switzerland, Senegal, Tunisia

Accrediting Agencies: National Commission

Degrees and Diplomas: *Diplôme universitaire de Technologie*; *Licence d'Etudes fondamentales*; *Licence professionnelle*; *Diplôme de Commerce et de Gestion*; *Diplôme d'Ingénieur*; *Master Sciences et Techniques*; *Master spécialisé*; *Master*; *Doctorat*

Student Services: Academic counselling, Cultural centre, Handicapped facilities, Health services, Nursery care, Sports facilities

Student Residential Facilities: Yes
Libraries: Yes

Academic Staff *2011-2012*: Total 330
Student Numbers *2011-2012*: Total 13,085
Last Updated: 17/07/12

HASSAN II INSTITUTE OF AGRONOMY AND VETERINARY MEDICINE

Institut agronomique et vétérinaire Hassan II (IAV HASSAN II)

BP 6202 Rabat-Instituts, Rabat
Tel: +212(537) 77-17-58
Fax: +212(537) 77-81-35
EMail: sg@iav.ac.ma
Website: http://www.iav.ac.ma

Directeur: Mohammed Sadiki
Tel: +212(537) 77-09-35, Fax: +212(537) 77-58-45
EMail: dg@iav.ac.ma

Secrétaire général: Mostafa Agbani
Tel: +212(537) 77-17-59, Fax: +212(537) 77-58-45

Areas

Agronomy (Agronomy; Analytical Chemistry; Animal Husbandry; Biochemistry; Biotechnology; Ecology; Fishery; Forestry; Horticulture; Modern Languages; Plant Pathology; Soil Science; Zoology); **Food Processing Technology** (Food Technology); **Horticulture** (Architectural and Environmental Design; Horticulture; Plant and Crop Protection); **Rural Engineering** (Agricultural Engineering; Environmental Engineering; Water Management); **Veterinary Science** (Anatomy; Parasitology; Pathology; Pharmacy; Physiology; Veterinary Science)

History: Founded 1966.

Main Language(s) of Instruction: French

International Co-operation: With universities in Africa, Asia, Middle East, USA, Canada, Europe, Japan. Also cooperation agreements with the following organisations: FAO, OMS, UNESCO, USAID, UE, FIS, AUF, ACCT, GTZ, AGCD, ACDI, CRDI, CIHEAM

Degrees and Diplomas: *Diplôme universitaire de Technologie*: Horticulture; *Diplôme d'Ingénieur*; *Master*: Irrigation; Biotechnology; Plant Protection, Water Management; *Doctorat*: Veterinary Science, Agriculture Engineering, Agronomy

Special Facilities: 70 laboratories; Agricultural Documentation Centre; Pilot Plant; Veterinary Health Centre; Plant Clinic; Training Centre for Agricultural Mechanization ; Computer Centres

Libraries: Yes

Publications: Actes de l'Institut Agronomique et Vétérinaire Hassan II *(quarterly)*; Rapport d'activités *(annually)*

Academic Staff *2011-2012*: Total 600
STAFF WITH DOCTORATE: Total 330
Student Numbers *2011-2012*: Total: c. 1,800
Last Updated: 07/08/12

HASSAN II UNIVERSITY - CASABLANCA

Université Hassan II - Casablanca

BP 9167, 19, rue Tarik Bnou Ziad, Mers Sultan, 21100 Casablanca
Tel: +212(522) 43-30-30
Fax: +212(522) 27-61-50
EMail: presidence@uh2c.ac.ma
Website: http://www.uh2c.ac.ma

Président: Jaafer Khalid Naciri EMail: naciri@uh2c.ac.ma

Secrétaire Général: Abdelhadi Moslih
Tel: +212(522) 43-30-55, Fax: +212(522) 27-61-50
EMail: moslih@uh2c.ac.ma

Faculties

Arts and Humanities (Arabic; Arts and Humanities; English; French; Geography; German; History; Islamic Studies; Spanish); **Dentistry** (Dental Technology; Dentistry); **Law, Economics, and Social Sciences** (Economics; Law; Political Sciences; Social Sciences); **Medicine and Pharmacy** (Anaesthesiology; Anatomy; Biology; Cardiology; Dermatology; Epidemiology; Gastroenterology; Gynaecology and Obstetrics; Haematology; Medical Technology; Medicine; Nephrology; Neurology; Neurosciences; Oncology; Ophthalmology; Orthopaedics; Otorhinolaryngology; Paediatrics; Pharmacy; Pneumology; Psychiatry and Mental Health; Rheumatology; Surgery; Urology); **Science** (Biology; Chemistry; Computer Science; Electrical Engineering; Engineering; Environmental Management; Geology; Mathematics; Mechanical Engineering; Natural Sciences; Physics)

Schools

Education *(ENS Casablanca)* (Chemistry; Education; Mathematics Education; Natural Sciences; Physical Education; Physics; Science Education); **Electrical and Mechanical Engineering** *(ENSEM)* (Electrical Engineering; Mechanical Engineering); **Technology** *(EST)* (Electrical Engineering; Engineering Management; Mechanical Engineering; Technology)

History: Founded 1962. Acquired present status 1975.

Governing Bodies: University Council

Academic Year: September to July

Admission Requirements: Secondary school certificate (baccalauréat) and entrance examination

Fees: None

Main Language(s) of Instruction: Arabic, French

International Co-operation: With universities in Belgium, Canada, Egypt, Spain, France, Iraq, Italy, Mali, Senegal, Switzerland, Tunisia, USA

Degrees and Diplomas: *Diplôme universitaire de Technologie*: Electrical Engineering; Mechanical Engineering; Materials Engineering; Management, 2 yrs; *Licence d'Etudes fondamentales*: History and Geography; Physics; Electrical Engineering; Mechanical Engineering; Chemistry; Computer Science; Biology; Engineering; Environment Management; Private Law; Public Law; Economics; Management; Commerce; Insurance; Business Law; Arabic Language and Literature; French Language and Literature; Spanish Language and Literature; German Language and Literature; English Language and Literature, 4 yrs; *Diplôme d'Ingénieur*: Electrical Engineering; Mechanical Engineering, 5 yrs; *Master spécialisé*: Economics; Public Law; Private Law; Engineering; Physics, 2 yrs following Licence; *Master*: Engineering; Public Law; Geography; Islamic Studies; Biology; Physics; Chemistry; Environment Sciences; Medicine, a further 2 yrs; *Doctorat*: Dentistry, 5 yrs; *Doctorat*: Economics; Literature; Geography; *Doctorat*: Medicine, 7 yrs; *Doctorat*: Public Law; Private Law; Engineering; Geology; Physics; Mathematics; Chemistry, 4 yrs

Student Services: Academic counselling, Canteen, Cultural centre, Foreign Studies Centre, Handicapped facilities, Sports facilities

Student Residential Facilities: Yes

Libraries: Libraries of the Faculties and Schools, total, c. 150,320 vols

Publications: Annales de la Faculté de Lettres Aïn Chok; Cahiers de Recherche de l'Université Hassan II; Revue marocaine de Droit et de l'Economie de Développement

Academic Staff *2011-2012*: Total 1,160
Student Numbers *2011-2012*: Total 28,725
Last Updated: 04/07/12

HASSAN II UNIVERSITY - MOHAMMEDIA

Université Hassan II - Mohammedia (ENSET-MOHAMMEDIA)

BP 150, 279 Cité Yassmina, Mohammedia
Tel: +212(523) 31-46-35
Fax: +212(523) 31-46-34
EMail: presidence@univh2m.ac.ma
Website: http://www.univh2m.ac.ma/

Président: Saâd Charif d'Ouazzane

Secrétaire général: Mohammed Sabbani
Tel: +212(523) 31-46-35 EMail: m.sabbani@univh2m.ac.ma

Faculties

Arts and Humanities *(Mohammedia)* (Arabic; Arts and Humanities; English; French; Geography; History; Islamic Studies); **Arts and Humanities** *(Ben M'sick)* (Communication Studies; Cultural Studies; English; French; Literature); **Law, Economics and Social**

Sciences *(Mohammedia)* (Economics; Law; Social Studies); **Law, Economics and Social Sciences** *(Ain Sebâa)* (Economics; Law; Social Sciences); **Science** *(Ben M'sik)* (Natural Sciences); **Science and Technology** *(Mohammedia)* (Biological and Life Sciences; Chemistry; Communication Studies; Electrical Engineering; Environmental Studies; Natural Sciences; Physics; Technology)

Schools

Arts and Crafts *(ENSAM Casablanca)* (Civil Engineering; Computer Engineering; Electrical Engineering; Industrial Engineering; Mechanical Engineering); **Commerce and Management Studies** *(ENCG)* (Business Administration; Business and Commerce; Management); **Technology Education** *(ENSET Mohammedia)* (Computer Engineering; Computer Networks; Economics; Human Resources; Management; Mechanical Engineering; Technology Education)

History: Founded 1992.

Governing Bodies: University Council

Main Language(s) of Instruction: Arabic, French, English

Degrees and Diplomas: *Diplôme universitaire de Technologie*; *Licence d'Etudes fondamentales*; *Licence professionnelle*: 4 yrs; *Diplôme d'Ingénieur*; *Master spécialisé*; *Master*; *Doctorat*

Libraries: c. 100,000 vols

Publications: Aqlam al-Jamia; Bahuth; Basamat

Academic Staff *2011-2012*: Total 913

Student Numbers *2011-2012*: Total 31,244

Last Updated: 04/07/12

ADVANCED TECHNICAL TEACHER TRAINING COLLEGE OF MOHAMMEDIA

ECOLE NORMALE SUPÉRIEURE DE L'ENSEIGNEMENT TECHNIQUE DE MOHAMMEDIA

BP 159, Bd Hassan II, Mohammedia
Tel: +212(523) 32-22-20
Fax: +212(523) 32-25-46
EMail: enset-media@enset-media.ac.ma
Website: http://www.enset-media.ac.ma

Directeur: Bachir Salhi

Departments

Economics and Management (Business and Commerce; Economics; Human Resources; Management); **Electrical Engineering** (Electrical Engineering; Electronic Engineering); **Languages, Communication and Educational Sciences** (Communication Studies; Educational Sciences; French; Modern Languages); **Mathematics and Computer Science** (Computer Networks; Computer Science; Mathematics; Multimedia; Software Engineering); **Mechanical Engineering** (Mechanical Engineering)

History: Founded 1985.

International Co-operation: With Institutions in France

Degrees and Diplomas: *Diplôme universitaire de Technologie*; *Licence professionnelle*; *Master*

HASSANIA SCHOOL OF CIVIL ENGINEERING

Ecole Hassania des Travaux publics (EHTP)

Km 7, Route d'El Jadida, BP 8108 Oasis, 20230 Casablanca
Tel: +212(522) 99- 87-30
Fax: +212(522) 42-05-26
EMail: info@ehtp.ac.ma
Website: http://www.ehtp.ac.ma

Directeur général: Adnane Boukamel EMail: ehtpdg@menara.ma

Secrétaire général: Hicham Ourzik
Tel: +212(522) 42-05-13, Fax: +212(522) 23-07-37
EMail: ourzik@ehtp.ac.ma

Departments

Civil Engineering (Civil Engineering; Engineering; Industrial Engineering; Road Engineering; Transport Engineering); **Computer Engineering** (Computer Engineering); **Electrical Engineering** (Electrical Engineering; Engineering); **Information Technology and Geography** (Geography; Information Technology; Telecommunications Engineering); **Meteorology** (Meteorology); **Town Planning, Hydraulic and Environmental Engineering** (Environmental Engineering; Hydraulic Engineering; Town Planning)

History: Founded 1971.

Admission Requirements: DEUG

Accrediting Agencies: Ministère de l'Equipement et des Transports

Degrees and Diplomas: *Diplôme de Commerce et de Gestion*; *Diplôme d'Ingénieur*; *Master*. MBA

Last Updated: 16/07/12

HIGHER MAGISTRACY INSTITUTE

Institut supérieur de la Magistrature (ISM)

PO Box 1007, Boulevard Mehdi Ben Berka, Souissi, Rabat
Tel: +212(537) 75-19-92 +212(537) 75-39-16
Fax: +212(537) 75-49-02
EMail: ism@ism.ma
Website: http://www.ism.ma/

Directeur général: Mohamed Said Bennani

Secrétaire général: Amine Serghini Fax: +212(537) 63-97-70

International Relations: Latifa Kham
Tel: +212(537) 63-02-52, Fax: +212(537) 63-97-99

Institutes

Legal Studies *(National)* (Law)

History: Founded 1970 as Institut national d'Etudes judiciaires. Acquired present status and title 2002. Reform of training and diplomas of the Institute in progress.

Fees: None

Main Language(s) of Instruction: Arabic

Accrediting Agencies: International Agency of Cooperation

Student Services: Canteen, Cultural centre, Foreign student adviser, Health services, Language programs, Nursery care, Sports facilities

Student Residential Facilities: Yes

Libraries: Central Library

Publications: The Judicial Attaché

Last Updated: 20/08/12

IBN TOFAIL UNIVERSITY

Université Ibn Tofail

BP 242, 14000 Kénitra
Tel: +212(537) 37-92-00
Fax: +212(537) 37-40-52
EMail: abderrahmantenkoul@yahoo.fr; ruitk@menara.ma
Website: http://www.univ-ibntofail.ac.ma/

Président: Abderrahman Tenkoul (2010-)

Secrétaire général: Al Mustapha Mehdi

International Relations: Karima Selmaoui
EMail: karima_selmaoui@yahoo.fr

Faculties

Arts and Humanities (Arabic; Arts and Humanities; English; French; Geography; History; Islamic Studies; Literature); **Law, Economics and Social Sciences** (Economics; Law; Management); **Science** (Biology; Chemistry; Geology; Mathematics; Natural Sciences; Physics)

Schools

Applied Sciences *(ENSA)* (Engineering; Microelectronics); **Commerce and Management** *(ENCG)* (Business and Commerce; Management)

History: Founded 1989.

Governing Bodies: University Council

Academic Year: September to July

Admission Requirements: Secondary school certificate (baccalauréat)

Fees: None

Main Language(s) of Instruction: Arabic, French

International Co-operation: With universities in France; Italy; USA; Canada; Belgium; Tunisia; Sweden; Germany; Spain; Egypt; Portugal; China; Malaysia; Romania; Yemen; Turkey

Degrees and Diplomas: *Licence d'Etudes fondamentales*: 3 yrs; *Licence professionnelle*; *Master spécialisé*; *Master*: 2 yrs; *Doctorat*: 3 yrs

Student Services: Academic counselling, Cultural centre, Health services, Language programs, Nursery care, Sports facilities

Student Residential Facilities: Yes

Libraries: 51,291 vols.

Academic Staff *2011-2012*	MEN	WOMEN	**TOTAL**
FULL-TIME	334	144	**478**
STAFF WITH DOCTORATE			
FULL-TIME	327	134	**461**
Student Numbers *2011-2012*			
All (Foreign Included)	11,724	10,546	**22,270**
FOREIGN ONLY	422	168	**590**

Last Updated: 10/04/12

IBN ZOHR UNIVERSITY

Université Ibn Zohr (UIZ)
BP 32/S, 80000 Agadir
Tel: +212(528) 22-70-17
Fax: +212(528) 22-72-60
EMail: puiz@univ-ibnzohr.ac.ma
Website: http://www.univ-ibnzohr.ac.ma

Président: Omar Halli (2011-)

Faculties

Arts and Humanities (Arabic; Arts and Humanities; English; French; Geography; History; Islamic Studies; Literature; Modern Languages; Sociology; Spanish); **Law, Social and Economic sciences** (Economics; Law; Management); **Polydisciplinary** *(Ouarzazate)* (Business Computing; Computer Science; Modern Languages; Sound Engineering (Acoustics); Tourism); **Polydisciplinary** *(Taroudant)* (Computer Science; Management); **Science** (Biology; Chemistry; Geology; Mathematics; Mathematics and Computer Science; Natural Sciences; Physics)

Schools

Applied Science *(ENSA)* (Agricultural Business; Agricultural Engineering; Electrical Engineering; Industrial Engineering; Telecommunications Engineering); **Commerce and Management** *(ENCG)* (Business and Commerce; Communication Studies; Management; Marketing; Transport Management); **Technology** *(EST)* (Computer Engineering; Electrical Engineering; Engineering Management; Environmental Engineering; Food Technology; Maintenance Technology; Marketing; Statistics; Technology)

Further Information: The university is located on 3 sites: Agadir; Ouarzazate,and Taroudant

History: Founded 1989.

Academic Year: September to July (September-December; January-March; April-July)

Admission Requirements: Secondary school certificate (baccalauréat)

Fees: None

Main Language(s) of Instruction: Arabic, French

Accrediting Agencies: Ministère de l'Education nationale, de l'Enseignement supérieur, de la Formation des Cadres et de la Recherche scientifique

Degrees and Diplomas: *Diplôme universitaire de Technologie*; *Licence d'Etudes fondamentales*; *Licence professionnelle (LP)*; *Diplôme de Commerce et de Gestion*; *Diplôme d'Ingénieur*; *Master spécialisé*: 5 yrs; *Master*: 5 yrs; *Doctorat*: 8 yrs

Student Services: Academic counselling, Cultural centre, Health services, Language programs, Nursery care, Social counselling, Sports facilities

Student Residential Facilities: Yes

Special Facilities: Theatre. Photography workshop. Exhibition Centre

Libraries: Yes

Publications: Dirassat, Journal of the College of Arts and Human Sciences *(annually)*; Revue Economique du Sud, A journal related to economics *(annually)*

Academic Staff *2011-2012*	MEN	WOMEN	**TOTAL**
FULL-TIME	–	–	**677**
STAFF WITH DOCTORATE			
FULL-TIME	–	–	**546**
Student Numbers *2011-2012*			
All (Foreign Included)	–	–	**54,000**
FOREIGN ONLY	158	25	**183**

Last Updated: 12/07/12

INSTITUTE OF COMMERCIAL STUDIES AND BUSINESS ADMINISTRATION

Institut supérieur de Commerce et d'Administration des Entreprises (ISCAE)
BP 8114, Km 95 route de Nouasseur, Oasis, Casablanca
Tel: +212(522) 33-54-82
Fax: +212(522) 33-54-96
Website: http://www.groupeiscae.ma/

Directeur Général: Mohamed El Moueffak
EMail: elmoueffak58@yahoo.fr

Departments

Economics and Law (Commercial Law; Economics; Law); **Finance and Accountancy** (Accountancy; Finance); **Management** (Human Resources; International Business; Management; Sports Management); **Marketing and Communication** (Communication Studies; Marketing); **Organization and General Policy** (Business Administration; Business and Commerce; International Business; Marketing)

Further Information: Also branch in Rabat and Guinea

History: Founded 1971.

Main Language(s) of Instruction: French, Arabic, English

International Co-operation: With universities in France, Spain, USA, Guinea, Netherlands, Canada

Degrees and Diplomas: *Master*: 1 yr; *Doctorat*. Diplôme du cycle normal (4 yrs), Diplôme national d'expert comptable (3 yrs), Executive MBA (2 yrs)

Student Services: Academic counselling, Canteen, Cultural centre, Employment services, Foreign student adviser, Health services, Sports facilities

Last Updated: 14/08/12

INSTITUTE OF DRAMA AND CULTURAL STUDIES

Institut supérieur d'Art dramatique et d'Animation culturelle (ISADAC)
BP 6834, Avenue Allal Fassi, Madinat Al Irfane, Rabat
Tel: +212 (537) 77-28-62/46
Fax: +212 (537) 77-28-60
EMail: isadac2008@hotmail.fr

Directeur: Salama El Ghiam (2011-)

Directeur adjoint: Naoual Benbrahim

Institutes

Cultural Studies (Art History; Cultural Studies; Psychology; Sociology)

Programmes

Cultural Mediation (Cultural Studies; Management; Museum Studies; Musicology); **Performing Arts** (Cinema and Television; Display and Stage Design; Music; Performing Arts; Radio and Television Broadcasting; Singing; Theatre); **Scenography** (Display and Stage Design)

History: Founded 1986.

Admission Requirements: Baccalauréat; Entrance examination

Main Language(s) of Instruction: Arabic and French

International Co-operation: With institutions in Belgium, France, Spain

Degrees and Diplomas: Diplome de l'établissement (4 yrs)

Libraries: Yes

Publications: Revue ISADAC *(annually)*

Last Updated: 14/08/12

INSTITUTE OF INFORMATION AND COMMUNICATION

Institut supérieur de l'Information et de la Communication (ISIC)

BP 6205, Madinat Al Irfane, Avenue Allal Al Fassi, Rabat
Tel: +212(537) 77-33-40
Fax: +212(537) 77-27-89
EMail: contact@isic.ma
Website: http://www.isic.ma

Directeur: Aârab Issiali (2010-)

Directeur des Etudes: Mimoun Ibrahimi

Departments

Audio-Visual Studies (Radio and Television Broadcasting); **Communication Studies** (Communication Studies); **Journalism** (Journalism)

Admission Requirements: Secondary school certificate (baccalauréat)

Main Language(s) of Instruction: Arabic, French

Degrees and Diplomas: *Diplôme de Commerce et de Gestion*: 4 yrs. Diplôme du cycle normal (4 yrs)

Last Updated: 18/07/12

INSTITUTE OF MARINE STUDIES

Institut supérieur des Etudes maritimes (ISEM)

Km 7, Route d'El Jadida, Casablanca
Tel: +212(522) 23-07-44
Fax: +212(522) 23-15-68
EMail: isem@isem.ac.ma
Website: http://www.isem.ac.ma/

Directeur: Abdelaziz Benhaida

Programmes

Marine Science and Oceanography (Marine Science and Oceanography)

History: Founded 1957.

Admission Requirements: Secondary school certificate (baccalauréat); Entrance examination

International Co-operation: With institutions in France and Belgium

Degrees and Diplomas: Diplôme du cycle normal (4 yrs), Diplôme du cycle supérieur (1-2 yrs)

Last Updated: 21/08/12

INTERNATIONAL HIGHER INSTITUTE FOR TOURISM OF TANGIERS

Institut supérieur international du Tourisme de Tanger

BP 1651, Baie de Tanger, Tanger
Tel: +212(539) 30-10-53
Fax: +212(539) 94-59-05
EMail: isittconcours@isitt.ma
Website: http://www.isitt.ma/

Directeur: Abdelhaq Mouhtaj

Programmes

Hotel Management (Hotel Management); **Production and Sales Techniques** (Production Engineering; Sales Techniques); **Tourism** (Business Administration; Hotel and Restaurant; Hotel Management; Tourism)

History: Founded 1972.

Admission Requirements: Secondary school certificate (baccalauréat) and entrance examination

Accrediting Agencies: Ministry of Tourism

Degrees and Diplomas: Diplôme du cycle normal (3 yrs): Tourism, Hotel Management); Diplôme du cycle supérieur (5 yrs): (Tourism, Hotel and Restauration Management)

Last Updated: 15/05/12

MEKNES NATIONAL SCHOOL OF AGRICULTURE

Ecole nationale d'Agriculture de Meknès

km. 10, Route Haj Kaddour, BP S/40, 50001 Meknès
Tel: +212(555) 30-02-39
Fax: +212(555) 30-02-38
EMail: ena@enameknes.ac.ma
Website: http://www.enameknes.ma/

Directeur: El Hadi Boumahdi (2011-)

Departments

Agricultural Equipment (Agricultural Equipment); **Agronomy and Plants** (Agriculture; Pedagogy); **Animal Production** (Animal Husbandry); **Basic Sciences** (Natural Sciences); **Development Engineering** (Development Studies); **Food Technology** (Food Technology); **Fruit Growing and Viticulture** (Fruit Production; Viticulture); **Plant Protection** (Plant and Crop Protection); **Rural Economics** (Agricultural Economics); **Soil Science** (Soil Science); **Vegetal Ecology** (Ecology)

History: Founded 1942 as Ecole Marocaine d'Agriculture. Acquired present title 1957.

Degrees and Diplomas: *Diplôme d'Ingénieur*: 6 yrs

Last Updated: 16/07/12

MOHAMMED I UNIVERSITY - OUJDA

Université Mohammed Premier - Oujda

BP 524, 60000 Oujda
Tel: +212(536) 50-06-12/14
Fax: +212(536) 50-06-09
EMail: presidence@ump.ma

Président: Abdelazizd Sadok Tel: +212(536) 50-06-13

Centres

Migration Studies (Demography and Population); **Water Science and Technology** (Water Science)

Faculties

Arts and Humanities (Arts and Humanities; English; French; Geography; History; Islamic Studies); **Law, Economics and Social Sciences** (Economics; Law; Political Sciences; Social Sciences); **Medicine and Pharmacy** (Anatomy; Applied Chemistry; Biochemistry; Biophysics; Chemistry; Embryology and Reproduction Biology; Histology; Medicine; Microbiology; Parasitology; Pathology; Pharmacology; Pharmacy; Physiology); **Polydisciplinary** *(Nador)*; **Science** (Natural Sciences)

Schools

Applied Sciences (Chemistry; Earth Sciences; Electrical Engineering; Mathematics; Mechanical Engineering); **Applied Sciences** *(ENSA Al Hoceima)*; **Commerce and Management** *(ENCG)* (Business and Commerce; Management); **Technology** *(EST)* (Accountancy; Business Administration; Computer Science; Electrical Engineering; Electronic Engineering; Engineering; Technology)

History: Founded 1978.

Governing Bodies: Conseil de l'Université

Academic Year: October to June

Admission Requirements: Secondary school certificate (baccalauréat) or equivalent

Fees: None

Main Language(s) of Instruction: Arabic, French

International Co-operation: With universities in France, Belgium, Italy, Spain, Netherlands, Germany, United Kingdom, Iraq, Algeria, Tunisia and Romania

Degrees and Diplomas: *Licence d'Etudes fondamentales*; *Licence professionnelle*; *Diplôme de Commerce et de Gestion*; *Diplôme d'Ingénieur*, *Master spécialisé*; *Master*, *Doctorat*

Student Residential Facilities: Yes

Libraries: Faculty libraries, total, 128,612 vols

Publications: Journal of Administrative Studies *(annually)*; Journal of Juridical, Economic and Social Studies *(annually)*; Moroccan Journal of International Relations *(annually)*

Last Updated: 22/11/12

MOHAMMED V UNIVERSITY-AGDAL

Université Mohammed V-Agdal

BP 554, Rabat-Chellah, Avenue des Nations Unies, Agdal, Rabat
Tel: +212(537) 27-27-50
Fax: +212(537) 67-14-01
EMail: presidence@um5a.ac.ma
Website: http://www.um5a.ac.ma

Président: Wail Benjelloun (2010-2014) Tel: +212(537) 27-27-55

Secrétaire général: Mohammed Khalfaoui

International Relations: Driss Aboutajdine, Vice-Président (2010-2014) Tel: +212(537) 27-27-76 EMail: aboutaj@um5a.ac.ma

Faculties

Arts and Humanities (Arabic; Arts and Humanities; English; French; Geography; German; History; Islamic Studies; Island Studies; Italian; Library Science; Literature; Modern Languages; Portuguese; Psychology; Sociology; Spanish); **Law, Economics and Social Sciences** (Accountancy; Banking; Economics; Finance; Law; Management; Political Sciences; Public Law; Social Sciences); **Science** (Biology; Chemistry; Computer Networks; Computer Science; Earth Sciences; Mathematics; Natural Sciences; Physics)

Institutes

Scientific Research (Botany; Earth Sciences; Ecology; Geography; Geology; Natural Sciences; Physics; Surveying and Mapping; Zoology); **Spanish/Portuguese Studies** (Portuguese; Spanish)

Schools

Education *(ENS)* (Biological and Life Sciences; Chemistry; Earth Sciences; Education; English; French; French Studies; Geography; History; Physics); **Engineering** *(EMI)* (Civil Engineering; Computer Engineering; Computer Networks; Electrical Engineering; Engineering; Engineering Management; Industrial Engineering; Mechanical Engineering; Mining Engineering; Software Engineering); **Technology** *(EST Salé)* (Banking; Civil Engineering; Computer Engineering; Computer Networks; Construction Engineering; Energy Engineering; Environmental Studies; Finance; Industrial Design; Industrial Maintenance; Maintenance Technology; Technology; Town Planning; Water Science)

History: Founded 1957 incorporating former Institutes of Letters (1912), Law (1920), and Science (1940) of the Mohammed V University. Reorganized 1975 and 1993. ENS Rabat became part of the University early 2011.

Governing Bodies: Conseil de l'Université

Academic Year: September to June (September-December; January-March; April-June)

Admission Requirements: Secondary school certificate (baccalauréat) or equivalent. Entrance EMI: Bac+2 class preparatory + DEUG or equivalent, entrance examination for Engineering with a DEUG certificate

Fees: None

Main Language(s) of Instruction: Arabic, French

International Co-operation: With universities in Belgium; Canada; France; Germany; Iraq; Tunisia; Mauritania; USA; Russian Federation; Syria; Italy; Spain; Algeria; Egypt; United Arab Emirates; Senegal; Argentina; Brazil; China; Republic of Korea; Japan; Bulgaria; Finland; United Kingdom; Poland; Romania and Switzerland

Degrees and Diplomas: *Diplôme universitaire de Technologie*: Engineering; Technology, 2 yrs; *Licence d'Etudes fondamentales*: Economics; Arts and Humanities; Private Law; Public Law; Science; Engineering, 3 yrs; *Master spécialisé*: Engineering; Arts and Humanities; Science, a further 2 yrs; *Master*: Economics; Engineering; Law; Arts and Humanities; Science, a further 2 yrs; *Doctorat*: Economics; Engineering; Arts and Humanities; Private Law; Public Law; Science, a further 4 yrs

Student Services: Academic counselling, Canteen, Foreign student adviser, Foreign Studies Centre, Health services, Language programs, Social counselling, Sports facilities

Student Residential Facilities: Yes

Special Facilities: Scientific Research Institute Museum

Libraries: Presidence, c. 98,106 vols, review 400; Faculty libraries, 303,344 vols, 19,001+3 vulgarisation periodicals and review

Publications: Annales du Centre des Etudes stratégiques de Rabat; Bulletin de l'Institut scientifique; Bulletin séismologique; Bulletins du Département de Physique du globe; Hespéris Tamuda *(annually)*; Journal marocain d'Automatisation, d'Informatique et de Traitement de Signal; La Recherche scientifique; Langues et Littérature *(annually)*; Revue Attadriss; Revue de la Faculté des Lettres et des Sciences humaines *(annually)*; Revue juridique, politique, économique du Maroc; Travaux de l'Institut scientifique

Academic Staff *2011-2012*	MEN	WOMEN	**TOTAL**
FULL-TIME	777	351	**1,128**
STAFF WITH DOCTORATE			
FULL-TIME	–	–	**695**
Student Numbers *2011-2012*			
All (Foreign Included)	11,856	9,662	**21,518**
FOREIGN ONLY	672	199	**871**

Last Updated: 19/09/12

MOHAMMED V UNIVERSITY-SOUISSI

Université Mohammed V-Souissi

Angle avenue Allal El Fassi et Mfadel Cherkaoui, Al Irfane, 8007. N.U, Rabat
Tel: +212(537) 68-11-60
Fax: +212(537) 68-11-63
EMail: presidence@um5s.ac.ma
Website: http://www.um5s.ac.ma

Président: Radouane Mrabet

Secrétaire général: Rachid Agaddou

Faculties

Dentistry (Dentistry); **Educational Sciences** (Education; Educational Sciences); **Law, Economics and Social Sciences** *(Salé)* (Economics; Law; Social Sciences); **Law, Economics and Social Sciences** *(Souissi)* (Economics; Law; Social Sciences); **Medicine and Pharmacy** (Medicine; Pharmacy)

Institutes

African Studies (African Studies); **Scientific Research**; **Studies and Research on Arabisation** (Arabic)

Schools

Computer Science and Systems Analysis *(ENSIAS)* (Computer Engineering; Systems Analysis); **Teacher Training and Technical Studies** *(ENSET)* (Automation and Control Engineering; Communication Studies; Economics; Educational Technology; Electrical Engineering; Electronic Engineering; Energy Engineering; Environmental Engineering; Industrial Engineering; Management; Mathematics and Computer Science; Mechanical Engineering; Modern Languages; Production Engineering; Teacher Trainers Education; Telecommunications Engineering)

History: Founded 1992 incorporating faculties which were originally part of the Mohammed V University after division of this institution into two universities: Mohammed V Souissi and Mohammed V Agdal.

Governing Bodies: Conseil de l'Université

Fees: None

Main Language(s) of Instruction: Arabic, French

International Co-operation: With universities in Italy, Belgium, Germany, Egypt, Senegal

Degrees and Diplomas: *Licence d'Etudes fondamentales*; *Diplôme d'Ingénieur*: Computer Science, Systems Analysis; *Master spécialisé*: 2 yrs following Licence; *Master*: 2 yrs following Licence; *Doctorat (PhD)*; *Doctorat*: Medicine, 7 yrs; *Doctorat*: Pharmacy, 5 yrs

Student Services: Academic counselling, Canteen, Cultural centre, Foreign student adviser, Foreign Studies Centre, Health services, Language programs, Social counselling, Sports facilities

Student Residential Facilities: Yes

Libraries: Faculty libraries

Publications: Al Ifrane; Al Maghrin Al Ifriqi, African Studies Institute *(annually)*; Bulletin d' Information, Scientific Research Institute *(biennially)*; Linguistic Research, Studies and Research on Arabization *(monthly)*

Last Updated: 04/07/12

MOHAMMED VI INTERNATIONAL ACADEMY OF CIVIL AVIATION

Académie internationale Mohammed VI de l'Aviation civile (AIAC)
Technopole de l'aéroport Mohammed V, Nouasser, Casablanca
Tel: +212(22) 538-380
EMail: academie@onda.ma
Website: http://www.aviation.ma

Institutes

Air Security Systems (Transport Engineering); **Air Traffic Services** (Aeronautical and Aerospace Engineering); **Aviation Management** (Aeronautical and Aerospace Engineering); **Civil Aviation Security**

History: Founded 2000.

Admission Requirements: Secondary school certificate (Baccalauréat) and entrance examination

Degrees and Diplomas: *Diplôme d'Ingénieur*

MOULAY ISMAIL UNIVERSITY

Université Moulay Ismail
Marjane II BP 298, 5003 Meknès
Tel: +212(535) 46-73-06
Fax: +212(535) 46-73-05
EMail: presidence@umi.ac.ma
Website: http://www.umi.ac.ma

Président: Ahmed El Brihi (2010-)
Tel: +212(535) 46-73-20 EMail: president@umi.ac.ma

Secrétaire général: Houssine Mejdoul
Tel: +212(535) 46-73-19 EMail: mejdoul@umi.ac.ma

International Relations: Hajji Abdelmajid EMail: hajji@yahoo.com

Faculties

Arts and Humanities (Arabic; Arts and Humanities; Communication Studies; English; French; Geography; History; Islamic Studies; Literature; Modern Languages); **Law, Economics and Social Sciences** (Economic and Finance Policy; Economics; Law; Social Sciences); **Polydisciplinary** *(Errachidia)* (Arabic; Arts and Humanities; French; Literature; Modern Languages); **Science** (Biology; Biotechnology; Chemistry; Environmental Studies; Geology; Mathematics and Computer Science; Mining Engineering; Natural Sciences; Physics; Urban Studies); **Science and Technology** *(Errachidia)* (Natural Sciences; Technology)

Schools

Arts and Crafts *(Meknès)* (Computer Engineering; Electrical and Electronic Engineering; Industrial Engineering; Mechanical Engineering; Production Engineering); **Education** *(ENS Meknes)* (Arabic; French; Philosophy; Teacher Training; Translation and Interpretation); **Technology** *(EST Meknès)* (Engineering; Management; Sales Techniques; Social and Community Services)

History: Founded 1982, acquired present status 1989. Integration of ENS Meknes since July 2010.

Governing Bodies: University Council

Academic Year: September to July (September-December; January-March; April-July)

Admission Requirements: Secondary school certificate (baccalauréat). Competitive examination for Technology and Engineering Schools

Main Language(s) of Instruction: Arabic, French, English

International Co-operation: With universities in France; Belgium; Spain; Italy; Romania; Poland; USA; Senegal

Degrees and Diplomas: *Diplôme universitaire de Technologie*; *Licence d'Etudes fondamentales*; *Licence professionnelle*; *Diplôme d'Ingénieur*: 5 yrs; *Master spécialisé*: a further 2 yrs; *Master*: a further 2 yrs; *Doctorat*

Student Services: Academic counselling, Cultural centre, Handicapped facilities, Language programs, Sports facilities

Student Residential Facilities: Yes

Libraries: Each Institute has its own Library

Publications: Azzaitouna; Maknasat, Revue de la Faculté des Lettres *(annually)*; Minbar Al Jamia

Last Updated: 12/07/12

NATIONAL INSTITUTE OF ARCHAEOLOGY AND CULTURAL HERITAGE

Institut national des Sciences de l'Archéologie et du Patrimoine (INSAP)
Madinat al Irfane-Hay Riyad, 10 000 Rabat
Tel: +212(537) 77-77-16
Fax: +212(537) 77-27-99
EMail: insap@menara.ma
Website: http://www.minculture.gov.ma/fr/index.php?option=com_content&view=article&id=413&Itemid=148&lang=fr

Directeur: Aomar Akerraz (2008-) EMail: akerraz@menara.ma

Directeur adjoint: Abdelouahed Ben-Ncer
EMail: a.benncer@minculture.gov.ma

International Relations: El Hassan Mazouzi, Secrétaire général

Departments

Anthropology (Anthropology) *Head*: Khalid El Aroussi; **Islamic Archaeology** (Archaeology); **Museum Studies** (Museum Studies); **Prehistory** (Prehistory); **Pre-Islamic Archaeology** (Archaeology); **Sites and Historical Monument Studies** (History)

History: Founded 1985.

Admission Requirements: Secondary school certificate (baccalauréat), entrance examination

Fees: None

Main Language(s) of Instruction: Arabic, French

International Co-operation: With universities in France; Germany; Spain; Italy; United Kingdom; Belgium and more

Accrediting Agencies: Ministère de la Culture

Degrees and Diplomas: *Doctorat*. Diplôme de 1er, 2eme et 3eme cycles

Student Services: Foreign Studies Centre, Health services

Libraries: Central Library

Publications: Bulletin d'Archéologie Marocaine *(annually)*

Last Updated: 13/08/12

NATIONAL INSTITUTE OF ARTS

Institut national des Beaux-Arts (INBA)
BP 89, Av. Mohamed V, Tétouan
Tel: +212(539) 96-15-45
Fax: +212(539) 96-42-92
EMail: inba1945@yahoo.fr

Directeur: Abdelkrim Ouazzani

Departments

Cartoons (Film); **Design** (Design; Industrial Design; Interior Design); **Fine Arts** (Engraving; Fine Arts; Painting and Drawing; Sculpture)

History: Founded 1947 as Ecole Nationale des Beaux-Arts. Acquired present status and title 1993.

Admission Requirements: Secondary school certificate (baccalauréat) or equivalent

Main Language(s) of Instruction: Arabic, French, Spanish

International Co-operation: With universities in France and Belgium

Degrees and Diplomas: Diplôme du 1er Cycle (2 yrs), Diplôme du 2eme Cycle (2 yrs)

Last Updated: 27/07/09

NATIONAL INSTITUTE OF HEALTH ADMINISTRATION

Institut national d'Administration sanitaire (INAS)
Rue Lamfadel Cherkaoui. Madinat Al Irfane, 6329 Rabat
Tel: +212(537) 68-31-61/62
Fax: +212(537) 68-31-61
EMail: inas@sante.gov.ma; direction.inas@gmail.com
Website: http://www.sante.gov.ma/Departements/inas/index.asp

Director: Abderrahmane Maarouffi
Tel: +212(537) 68-31-61 EMail: inasmaaroufi@gmail.com

Administrative Officer: Ahmed Ait Malek
EMail: aaitmalek2006@yahoo.fr

International Relations: Ahmed Agyo EMail: aagyo@yahoo.fr

Programmes

Health Sciences (Epidemiology; Health Administration; Health Sciences; Public Health)

History: Founded 1994.

Main Language(s) of Instruction: French

Degrees and Diplomas: *Master*: Health Administration and Public Health, 2 yrs

Libraries: Yes

Last Updated: 18/06/12

NATIONAL INSTITUTE OF POST AND TELECOMMUNICATIONS

Institut national des Postes et Télécommunications (INPT)

2 Avenue Allal El Fasse, Madinat Al Irfane, Rabat
Tel: +212(537) 77-30-79
Fax: +212(537) 77-30-44
EMail: riouch@inpt.ac.ma
Website: http://www.inpt.ac.ma

Directeur: Mohamed Abdelfattah Charif Chefchaouni EMail: charifm@inpt.ac.ma

Secrétaire général: Abderrahman Rafi EMail: rafi@inpt.ac.ma

Programmes

Telecommunications Engineering (Accountancy; Applied Mathematics; Business Administration; Computer Networks; Economics; English; Multimedia; Software Engineering; Statistics; Telecommunications Engineering)

History: Founded 1971.

Degrees and Diplomas: *Diplôme d'Ingénieur*, *Master*, *Doctorat*. Also Doctoral programme in cooperation with other Universities

Last Updated: 13/08/12

NATIONAL INSTITUTE OF REGIONAL AND TOWN PLANNING

Institut national d'Aménagement et d'Urbanisme (INAU)

BP 6215, Avenue Allal El Fassi, Rabat
Tel: +212(537) 77-16-24
Fax: +212(537) 77-50-09
EMail: inau@inau.ac.ma
Website: http://www.inau.ac.ma

Directeur: Abdelaziz Adidi

Secrétaire général: Hafid Hafdaoui

Programmes

Regional and Town Planning (Economics; Environmental Studies; Law; Regional Planning; Rural Planning; Town Planning; Urban Studies)

Research Centres

Town and Regional Planning

History: Founded 1981.

Admission Requirements: Diplôme d'Ingénieur urbaniste or equivalent and entrance examination

Degrees and Diplomas: *Licence professionnelle*; *Master*, *Doctorat*

Last Updated: 10/08/12

NATIONAL INSTITUTE OF STATISTICS AND APPLIED ECONOMICS

Institut national de Statistique et d'Economie appliquée

BP 6217, Madinat El Irfane, 10100 Rabat
Tel: +212(537) 77-48-59
Fax: +212(537) 77-94-57
EMail: webmaster@insea.ac.ma
Website: http://www.insea.ac.ma

Directeur: Abdelaziz Chaoubi

Secrétaire général: Mustapha Berrouyne

Departments

Accountancy and Finance (Accountancy; Finance); **Computer Studies** (Artificial Intelligence; Computer Engineering; Computer Networks; Computer Science); **Demography and Humanities** (Applied Mathematics; Arts and Humanities; Demography and Population; English; Statistics); **Economics** (Applied Mathematics; Business Administration; Economics; English; Finance; Statistics); **Mathematics and Operational Research** (Mathematics); **Statistics** (Banking; Economics; English; Finance; Mathematics; Statistics)

History: Founded 1961.

Admission Requirements: First year: University Certificate of Advanced Studies in Mathematics - Physics (CUES-MP) or university degree in general Mathematics - Physics (DEUG-MP)

Main Language(s) of Instruction: French

Degrees and Diplomas: *Diplôme d'Ingénieur*

Academic Staff *2011-2012*	**TOTAL**
FULL-TIME	**40**
PART-TIME	c. **30**
Student Numbers *2011-2012*	
All (Foreign Included)	c. **600**
FOREIGN ONLY	**20**

Last Updated: 10/08/12

NATIONAL SCHOOL OF ADMINISTRATION - RABAT

Ecole nationale d'Administration de Rabat (ENA)

BP 165, 1, avenue de la Victoire, 10000 Rabat
Tel: +212(537) 72-44-00
Fax: +212(537) 73-09-29
EMail: direction@ena.ac.ma
Website: http://w3.ena.ac.ma

Directeur: Mustapha Taimi

Programmes

Public Administration (Accountancy; Economics; Finance; Human Resources; Law; Modern Languages; Public Administration)

History: Founded 1948. Acquired present status 2000.

Degrees and Diplomas: Diplôme du Cycle supérieur en Gestion administrative

Last Updated: 16/07/12

NATIONAL SCHOOL OF ARCHITECTURE

Ecole nationale d'Architecture (ENA)

BP 6372, Avenue Allal El Fassi, Rabat
Tel: +212(537) 67-84 51
Fax: +212(537) 77-52-76
EMail: ena@archi.ac.ma
Website: http://www.archi.ac.ma/

Directeur général: El Montacir Bensaïd Tel: +212(537) 67-84-51, Fax: +212(537) 77-52-76

Departments

Architecture (Architecture); **Arts and Humanities** (Arts and Humanities); **Patrimoinial Studies** (Architectural Restoration; Real Estate); **Regional and Town Planning, Environmental Design** (Architectural and Environmental Design; Architecture and Planning; House Arts and Environment; Regional Planning; Town Planning)

History: Founded 1980.

Admission Requirements: Secondary school certificate (baccalauréat) and entrance examination

Main Language(s) of Instruction: French

International Co-operation: With institutions in France, Italy, Spain

Accrediting Agencies: Ministère de l'Aménagement du Territoire, de l'Urbanisme et de l'Habitat

Degrees and Diplomas: *Master spécialisé*. Diplôme d'Architecte (6yrs)

Student Services: Language programs, Sports facilities

Student Residential Facilities: None

Libraries: Documentation Centre

Last Updated: 16/07/12

NATIONAL SCHOOL OF FORESTRY ENGINEERING

Ecole nationale forestière d'Ingénieurs (ENFI)
BP 511, Avenue Moulay Youssef, 11000 Salé
Tel: +212(537) 86-37-04
Fax: +212(537) 86-11-49
EMail: eauxetforets@iam.net.ma
Website: http://www.enfi.ac.ma

Directeur: Mohamed Sabir (2003-)
EMail: sabirenfi@wanadoo.net.ma

Secretary-General: Mohamed Qarro
EMail: qarro@wanadoopro.net.ma

International Relations: Abdenbi Zine El Abidine
Tel: +212(06) 277-3594 EMail: abdenbi_zine@hotmail.com

Schools

Forestry (Botany; Environmental Engineering; Environmental Management; Environmental Studies; Forest Biology; Forest Economics; Forest Management; Forest Products; Forestry; Natural Resources; Soil Conservation; Tourism; Wood Technology)

History: Founded 1968.

Academic Year: September to July

Admission Requirements: Secondary school certificate (baccalauréat) + 2 years

Fees: None

Main Language(s) of Instruction: French

International Co-operation: With universities in France; Belgium; Spain and Canada

Degrees and Diplomas: *Diplôme d'Ingénieur*: 6 yrs. Also Diplôme de Foresterie Générale, (4yrs)

Student Services: Health services

Student Residential Facilities: Yes

Last Updated: 17/07/12

NATIONAL SCHOOL OF THE MINERAL INDUSTRY

Ecole nationale de l'Industrie minérale (ENIM)
BP 753, Avenue Hadj Ahmed, Cherkaoui, Agdal, Rabat
Tel: +212(537) 77-00-81
Fax: +212(537) 77-10-55
EMail: info@enim.ac.ma
Website: http://www.enim.ac.ma

Directeur: Omar Debbaj EMail: debbaj@enim.ac.ma

Secrétaire général: Abdelhaq Sibari
EMail: abdelhaqsibari@hotmail.com

Departments

Computer Science (Computer Science); **Earth Sciences** (Earth Sciences; Geological Engineering); **Electromechanical Engineering** (Electronic Engineering; Mechanical Engineering); **General Studies** (Communication Studies; Economics; Engineering; Mathematics; Modern Languages; Social Sciences); **Materials Engineering** (Materials Engineering); **Mining** (Mineralogy; Mining Engineering); **Process Engineering** (Energy Engineering; Production Engineering)

History: Founded 1972. Acquired present status 1983.

Accrediting Agencies: Ministère de l'Energie et des Mines

Degrees and Diplomas: *Diplôme d'Ingénieur*, *Master spécialisé*; *Master*, *Doctorat*

Last Updated: 17/07/12

QUARAOUIYINE UNIVERSITY

Université Quaraouiyine
BP 2509, Fès
Tel: +212(535) 64-10-06
Fax: +212(535) 64-10-13
EMail: facharag@iam.net.ma

Recteur: Abdelwahab Tazi Saoud

Centres

Islamic Studies and Research (Islamic Studies)

Faculties

Arabic and Arab Literature *(Marrakech)* (Arabic; Literature); **Islamic Law** *(Fes)* (Islamic Law); **Islamic Law** *(Agadir)* (Islamic Law); **Theology and Philosophy** *(Tétouan)* (Philosophy; Theology)

History: Founded 859, reorganized 1788-89 by Mohammed III. Became State institution 1947.

Academic Year: November to June (November-December; January-March; April-June)

Admission Requirements: Secondary school certificate (baccalauréat) or equivalent

Fees: None

Main Language(s) of Instruction: Arabic

Degrees and Diplomas: *Licence d'Etudes fondamentales*: 4 yrs; *Master*: a further 2 yrs; *Doctorat*: 4 yrs

Student Residential Facilities: Yes

Libraries: Central Library; faculty libraries

Last Updated: 22/11/12

ROYAL INSTITUTE OF TERRITORIAL ADMINISTRATION

Institut royal de l'Administration territoriale (IRAT)
3ème Base Militaire, Kénitra
Tel: +212(537) 37-13-66
Fax: +212(537) 37-13-66

Directeur: Amine Mzouri

Departments

Public Administration (International Relations; Public Administration)

History: Founded 1964. Acquired present title 2007.

Admission Requirements: Licence and entrance examination

Accrediting Agencies: Ministère de l'Intérieur

Degrees and Diplomas: Diplôme du cycle normal

Last Updated: 14/08/12

ROYAL NAVAL SCHOOL

Ecole royale navale (ERN)
PB 16303, Boulevard Sour Jdid, Casablanca
Tel: +212(522) 27-22-96
Fax: +212(522) 22-16-72
EMail: ernmr@yahoo.com; ern@yahoo.com
Website: http://www.ern.ac.ma

Programmes

Marine Engineering (Marine Engineering); **Mathematics** (Mathematics); **Navigation** (Nautical Science); **Physics** (Physics)

History: Founded 1967.

Degrees and Diplomas: *Diplôme d'Ingénieur*

Last Updated: 19/12/12

ROYAL SCHOOL OF AERONAUTICS

Ecole royale de l'Air (ERA)
BEFRA/ERA, 4000 Marrakech
Tel: +212(524) 44-79-17
Fax: +212(524) 76-44-01
EMail: diremi@emi.ac.ma

Programmes

Mechanical Engineering (Aeronautical and Aerospace Engineering; Mechanical Engineering); **Piloting** (Air Transport)

History: Founded 1970.

Degrees and Diplomas: *Diplôme d'Ingénieur*: 5 yrs

ROYAL TRAINING INSTITUTE OF YOUTH AND SPORTS TRAINERS

Institut royal de Formation des Cadres de la Jeunesse et des Sports

Institut National des Sports Moulay Rachid, Km 12, Route de Meknès, Salé
Tel: +212(537) 67-42-81
Fax: +212(537) 67-42-81
EMail: contact@irfc.ma
Website: http://www.irfc.ma

Directeur: El Mostafa Aouchar

Programmes

Sports Management (Physical Education; Sports; Sports Management)

History: Founded 1980.

Degrees and Diplomas: *Licence professionnelle*; *Master*; *Doctorat*. Also Diplôme Universitaire

Last Updated: 13/08/12

SCHOOL OF INFORMATION SCIENCES

Ecole des Sciences de l'Information (ESI)

BP 6204, Avenue Allal El Fassi, cité Al Irfane, 10000 Rabat
Tel: +212(537) 77-49-13
Fax: +212(537) 77-02-32
EMail: esi@esi.ac.ma
Website: http://www.esi.ac.ma

Directeur: El Hassan Lemallem (2009-)
EMail: hlemallem@esi.ac.ma; haslem.esi@gmail.com

Secrétaire général: Ahmed El Khamlichi
EMail: aelkhamlichi@esi.ac.ma

International Relations: Nazha Hachad
EMail: nhachad@esi.ac.ma; n_hachad@yahoo.com

Programmes

Information Sciences (Archiving; Documentation Techniques; Information Management; Information Sciences)

History: Founded 1974 to meet the needs of the country for professionnals by ensuring their training in the areas of Documentation Techniques, Information Sciences, Science and Librarianship.

Governing Bodies: Conseil de l'Etablissement

Academic Year: September to July

Admission Requirements: Secondary school certificate (baccalauréat)

Fees: None

Main Language(s) of Instruction: French

International Co-operation: With: PNUD, UNESCO, USIA (USA) and IFLA (International Federation of Library Associations and Institutions)

Accrediting Agencies: Haut Commissariat au Plan

Degrees and Diplomas: *Diplôme de Commerce et de Gestion (Diplôme d'Informatiste Spécialisé)*: 3-4 yrs; *Master spécialisé*: a further 2 yrs; *Master*: a further 2 yrs; *Doctorat*

Student Services: Academic counselling, Canteen, Employment services, Health services, Language programs, Social counselling, Sports facilities

Student Residential Facilities: Yes

Libraries: Central Library

Publications: Revue de la Science de l'information *(biannually)*

Academic Staff *2011-2012*	**TOTAL**
FULL-TIME	**20**
PART-TIME	**50**
STAFF WITH DOCTORATE	
FULL-TIME	c. **10**
Student Numbers *2011-2012*	
All (Foreign Included)	c. **350**
FOREIGN ONLY	**20**

Last Updated: 16/07/12

SCHOOL OF TEXTILE AND CLOTHING INDUSTRIES

Ecole supérieure des Industries du Textile et de l'Habillement (ESITH)

BP 7731, Km 8, Route d'El Jadida, Oulfa, 20000 Casablanca
Tel: +212(522) 23-41-24
Fax: +212(522) 23-15-85
EMail: esith@esith.ac.ma
Website: http://www.esith.ac.ma

President of the Board: Mohamed Lahlou

Director General: Abderrahmane Farhate
EMail: farhate@esith.ac.ma

Programmes

Clothing and Fashion (Clothing and Sewing; Fashion Design); **Commercial Management** (Business and Commerce; Management; Marketing; Sales Techniques); **Industrial Management** (Industrial Management; Information Sciences; Management; Transport Management); **Textiles** (Clothing and Sewing; Textile Technology)

History: Founded 1996.

Academic Year: September to June (September-January; February-June)

Admission Requirements: Secondary school certificate; Preparatory classes graduation

Fees: (Dirhams): 20,000 per annum (accommodation and food are not included)

Main Language(s) of Instruction: French

International Co-operation: With institutions in France (ENSAIT, in Roubaix; MOD'SPE, in Paris) and in Canada (Laval University)

Accrediting Agencies: Ministry of Labour and Vocational Education

Degrees and Diplomas: *Licence professionnelle*: 3 yrs; *Diplôme d'Ingénieur*: 3 yrs; *Master spécialisé*: 2 yrs

Student Services: Academic counselling, Canteen, Employment services, Foreign student adviser, Health services, Language programs, Sports facilities

Student Residential Facilities: Yes

Academic Staff *2011-2012*	**TOTAL**
FULL-TIME	**46**
PART-TIME	**120**
Student Numbers *2011-2012*	
All (Foreign Included)	**960**

Last Updated: 23/07/12

SIDI MOHAMMED BEN ABDELLAH UNIVERSITY - FEZ

Université Sidi Mohammed Ben Abdellah-Fès (ENS-FÈS)

BP 2626, Route d'Imouzzer, 30000 Fès
Tel: +212(535) 60-96-60
Fax: +212(535) 60-96-50
EMail: usmba@menara.ma
Website: http://www.usmba.ac.ma

Président: Esserrhini Farissi Tel: +212(55) 65-04-52

Faculties

Arts and Humanities *(Dhar El Mehraz)* (Arabic; Arts and Humanities; English; French; Geography; German; History; Islamic Studies; Literature; Modern Languages; Philosophy; Psychology; Sociology; Spanish); **Arts and Humanities** *(Saïs)* (Arts and Humanities; Geography; History; Islamic Studies; Literature; Modern Languages); **Law, Economics and Social Sciences** (Economics; Law; Social Sciences); **Medicine and Pharmacy** (Medicine; Pharmacology; Pharmacy); **Polydisciplinary** *(Taza)* (Arabic; Chemistry; Earth Sciences; Economics; Geography; History; Law; Management; Mathematics; Natural Sciences; Physics); **Science** *(Dhar El Mehraz)* (Biological and Life Sciences; Chemistry; Geology; Mathematics; Mathematics and Computer Science; Natural Sciences; Physics); **Science and Techniques** *(Saïs)* (Biology; Chemistry; Geology; Mathematics; Natural Sciences; Physics; Technology)

Institutes
Medicinal and Aromatic Plants *(National)*

Schools
Advanced Technology *(Saïs)* (Electrical Engineering; Engineering Management; Industrial Engineering; Management; Mechanical Engineering; Production Engineering); **Applied Science**; **Business and Management** (Business Administration; Business and Commerce; Management)

History: Founded 1975.

Governing Bodies: Conseil de l'Université

Academic Year: September to June (September-February; February-June)

Admission Requirements: Secondary school certificate (baccalauréat) or equivalent

Fees: None

Main Language(s) of Instruction: Arabic, French

Degrees and Diplomas: *Diplôme universitaire de Technologie*: 2 yrs; *Licence d'Etudes fondamentales*: 3 yrs; *Licence en Sciences et Techniques*; *Licence professionnelle*; *Diplôme de Commerce et de Gestion*; *Diplôme d'Ingénieur*; *Master Sciences et Techniques*; *Master spécialisé*; *Master*: a further 2 yrs; *Doctorat*: a further 3 yrs

Student Services: Canteen, Cultural centre, Employment services, Health services, Social counselling, Sports facilities

Student Residential Facilities: For c. 5,000 students

Libraries: c. 170,000 vols

Student Numbers *2010-2011*: Total 61,021
Last Updated: 05/07/12

ADVANCED TEACHER TRAINING COLLEGE OF FEZ
ECOLE NORMALE SUPÉRIEURE, FÈS
BP 2206, Kariat Ben Souda Ahouaz-Oued, Fès
Tel: +212(535) 65-50-83
Fax: +212(535) 65-50-69

Programmes
Teacher Training (Arabic; Chemistry; Computer Science; Geography; History; Humanities and Social Science Education; Islamic Studies; Mathematics; Mathematics Education; Native Language Education; Philosophy; Physics; Psychology; Science Education)

History: Founded 1978.

Degrees and Diplomas: *Licence professionnelle*; *Master*

PRIVATE INSTITUTIONS

BUSINESS SCHOOL OF MARRAKECH
Ecole supérieure de Commerce de Marrakech (ESC)
BP 595, Boulevard Prince Moulay Abdellah, Guéliz, 40000 Marrakech
Tel: +212(544) 43-33-93
Fax: +212(544) 43-60-67
EMail: contact@supdeco.ma
Website: http://www.supdeco.ma/

Head: Ahmed Bennis

Programmes
Accountancy (Accountancy); **Business Administration** (Business Administration; Human Resources; International Business; Management; Marketing); **Data Processing** (Data Processing); **Economics and Law** (Commercial Law; Economics; International Economics; Law); **Management and Finance** (Banking; Finance; Management); **Modern Languages** (Arabic; Communication Studies; English; French; Spanish); **Statistics** (Mathematics and Computer Science; Secretarial Studies; Statistics)

Further Information: Also ESC Casablanca (2011)

History: Founded 1987.

Admission Requirements: Secondary school certificate (baccalauréat), entrance examination and interview

Main Language(s) of Instruction: French

Degrees and Diplomas: *Master*: 5 yrs

Student Services: Academic counselling, Canteen, Cultural centre, Employment services, Foreign student adviser, Foreign Studies Centre, Health services, Language programs, Nursery care, Social counselling, Sports facilities

Student Residential Facilities: Yes

Libraries: Central Library, c. 3,000 vols
Last Updated: 20/07/12

CASABLANCA SCHOOL OF ARCHITECTURE
Ecole supérieure d'Architecture de Casablanca (EAC)
Angle Avenue A &Tarik AlKhayr Sidi Bernoussi, Casablanca
Tel: +212(522) 75-03-75
Fax: +212(522) 75-27-37
EMail: ecole_archi_casa@menara.ma
Website: http://www.ecole-archi-casa.com

Directeur général: Abdelmoumen Benabdeljalil

Directeur Pédagogique: Abderrafih Lahbabi

Programmes
Architecture (Architecture; Building Technologies; Communication Studies; Computer Science; Fine Arts; History; Modern Languages; Social Sciences)

History: Founded 2005.

Admission Requirements: Scientific baccalauréat or equivalent recognized by the Ministry of Education and competitive examination

Degrees and Diplomas: *Licence professionnelle*; *Master*
Last Updated: 19/07/12

CNCD - SCHOOL OF ADVANCED MANAGEMENT AND INTERNATIONAL TRADE STUDIES - CASABLANCA
CNCD - Hautes Etudes de Gestion et de Commerce International - Casablanca (CNCD-HEGCI)
3, rue Lavoisier, Casablanca
Tel: +212(522) 86-02-13
Fax: +212(522) 86-01-65
EMail: webmaster@cncd.ac

Directeur: Mohamed Aoune

Programmes
Finance and Accounting (Accountancy; Finance); **International Business** (International Business; Management)

History: Founded 1992.

Degrees and Diplomas: Diplôme du cycle normal (2-4 yrs); Diplôme du cycle supérieur
Last Updated: 27/03/13

FREE UNIVERSTITY OF FÈZ - TECHNOLOGIA
Université libre de Fès - Technologia
Lotissement Quaraouiyine - Route d'Ain Chkef, 30000 Fès
Tel: +212(535) 61-03-20
Fax: +212(535) 60-18-73
EMail: info@technologia.ma
Website: http://www.technologia.ma/

Institutes
Law and Social Studies (Commercial Law; Law)

Schools
Engineering (Civil Engineering; Computer Engineering; Computer Networks; Engineering; Industrial Engineering; Software Engineering); **Management** (Banking; Finance; Hotel Management; Human Resources; Management); **Tourism** (Tourism)

History: Founded 2006.

Admission Requirements: Secondary school certificate (Baccalauréat)

Degrees and Diplomas: Diplôme du cycle normal (3yrs), Diplôme du cycle spécialisé (4-5yrs)
Last Updated: 08/10/12

GRADUATE SCHOOL OF MANAGEMENT

Groupe Ecole supérieur de gestion (ESG)

32, rue El Bakri (ex Dumont D'urville), Casablanca
Tel: +212(522) 44-40-01
Fax: +212(522) 31-56-26
EMail: infoesg@esg.ma
Website: http://www.esg.ma/

Président, Directeur général: Jacques Knafo

Registrar: Najat Mgharfaoui EMail: dakirnajat@yahoo.fr

Programmes

Computing and Information Technology (Business Computing; Computer Science; Management); **Finance and Accountancy** (Accountancy; Banking; Business and Commerce; Finance; Management); **Management and Marketing** (Advertising and Publicity; Business and Commerce; Communication Studies; Finance; International Business; Management; Marketing)

Further Information: Also branch in Marrakech and Agadir

History: Founded 1985.

Academic Year: September to July

Admission Requirements: Secondary school certificate (Baccalauréat), entrance examination and interview

Main Language(s) of Instruction: French

Accrediting Agencies: Ministère de l'Education nationale, de l'Enseignement supérieur, de la Formation des Cadres et de la Recherche scientifique

Degrees and Diplomas: *Diplôme universitaire de Technologie*; *Licence professionnelle*; *Master spécialisé*; *Master*

Student Services: Academic counselling, Canteen, Cultural centre, Employment services, Foreign student adviser, Handicapped facilities, Health services, Language programs, Sports facilities

Libraries: Yes

Academic Staff *2011-2012*	**TOTAL**
FULL-TIME	**20**
PART-TIME	**100**
STAFF WITH DOCTORATE	
FULL-TIME	**10**
PART-TIME	c. **50**
Student Numbers *2011-2012*	
All (Foreign Included)	c. **800**

Evening students, 350.

Last Updated: 07/08/12

HECC BUSINESS SCHOOL

Hautes Etudes citoyennes commerciales (HECC)

37 Avenue De France Agdal, Rabat
Tel: +212(537) 68-23-48
Fax: +212(537) 68-21-48
EMail: contact@hecc.ma

Programmes

Finance (Finance); **Human Resource** (Human Resources); **Marketing** (Marketing)

Admission Requirements: Secondary school certificate (baccalauréat)

Degrees and Diplomas: Diplôme de l'établissement (3 yrs and 5 yrs)

Last Updated: 21/09/12

HEM BUSINESS SCHOOL

HEM - Institut des hautes Etudes de Management

Avenue El Qods - Quartier Californie, 20150 Casablanca
Tel: +212(522) 52-52-52
Fax: +212(522) 21-55-30
EMail: hem@hem.ac.ma
Website: http://www.hem.ac.ma

Président: Abdelali Benamour EMail: a.benamour@hem.ac.ma

Board Director: Yasmine Benamour
EMail: y.benamour@hem.ac.ma

Director of Studies and Deputy General Manager: Hassan Sayarh EMail: hassan.sayarh@hem.ac.ma

International Relations: Ali El Quammah, Co-Director of Academic Affairs in charge of International Affairs

Programmes

Accounting, Control and Audit (Accountancy); **Business Administration** (Business Administration); **Finance** (Finance); **Human Resources** (Human Resources); **Industrial Management** (Industrial Management); **Information Systems Management** (Information Management; Information Technology); **International Management** (International Business; Transport Management); **Marketing** (Marketing); **Political Sciences and Management Organizations** (Management; Political Sciences); **Tourism** (Hotel Management; Tourism); **Town Planning** (Town Planning)

Further Information: Also campuses in Rabat (1993) - Marrakech (2004) - Tanger (2007); Fès (2010)

History: Founded 1988.

Governing Bodies: Board of Directors

Academic Year: September to July

Admission Requirements: Secondary school certificate (baccalauréat), and entrance examination

Fees: (Dirhams): 60.000 per annum

Main Language(s) of Instruction: French

International Co-operation: With universities in France, Canada, the Netherlands, Belgium and in UK

Accrediting Agencies: Ministry of Higher Education, Training Managers and Scientific Research

Degrees and Diplomas: *Master*. 5 yrs. Also MBA (2 yrs)

Student Services: Academic counselling, Canteen, Employment services, Health services, Language programs, Social counselling, Sports facilities

Libraries: Library in each campus (books and reviews) / e-library

Academic Staff *2011-2012*	MEN	WOMEN	**TOTAL**
FULL-TIME	21	16	**37**
PART-TIME	–	–	**300**
STAFF WITH DOCTORATE			
FULL-TIME	6	3	**9**
PART-TIME	–	–	**100**
Student Numbers *2011-2012*			
All (Foreign Included)	924	1,190	**2,114**
FOREIGN ONLY	–	–	**4**

Evening students, 46.

Last Updated: 19/06/12

HESTIM SCHOOL

Ecole des hautes Etudes des Sciences et Techniques de l'Ingénierie et du Management. (HESTIM)

34, Boulevard Chefchaouni, Lotissement Angel, Ain Sebaa, Casablanca
Tel: +212(522) 34-17-23/24
Fax: +212(522) 34-17-25
EMail: contact@hestim.ma
Website: http://www.hestim.ma

President: Abdelilah Bennis

Programmes

Engineering (Civil Engineering; Engineering; Industrial Engineering; Safety Engineering; Transport Engineering)

History: Founded 2008.

Admission Requirements: Secondary school certificate (Baccalauréat), entrance examination

Degrees and Diplomas: *Licence professionnelle*; *Master spécialisé*; *Master*. Also School Diploma (3 yrs)

Student Services: Sports facilities

Special Facilities: Wifi

Libraries: Yes

Last Updated: 11/10/12

HIGH TECHNOLOGY SCHOOL IN MOROCCO (HIGH-TECH)

34, rueJabal Al Ayachi, Agdal, Rabat
Tel: +212(537) 67-09-99
Fax: +212(537) 67-09-86
EMail: contact@hightech.edu
Website: http://www.hightech.edu

President: Zouhair Benfaida
Tel: +212(537) 67-09-71/72 EMail: benfaida@hightech.edu

Director General: Awatif Sayeh EMail: sayeh@hightech.edu

International Relations: Imane Belmeki

Institutes

Continuing Education (Engineering; Management; Technology)

Programmes

Aeronautical Engineering (Aeronautical and Aerospace Engineering); **Computer Engineering** (Computer Engineering; Computer Networks; Software Engineering; Telecommunications Engineering); **Management** (Accountancy; Business Administration; Finance; Human Resources; Information Technology; Management; Marketing)

Further Information: Also 3 other campuses in Fès (2010), Rabat (2007) and Casablanca (2011)

History: Founded 1986.

Admission Requirements: Secondary school-leaving certificate, portfolio and interview

Fees: (Dirhams): 9,300-10,500 per semester

Main Language(s) of Instruction: French

International Co-operation: With institutions in France (ESC de Dijon, Université d'Orléans, Université Leonard de Vinci-Paris)

Degrees and Diplomas: *Diplôme d'Ingénieur*; *Master (MBA)*. Also Bachelor

Student Services: Handicapped facilities, Sports facilities

Student Residential Facilities: Yes

Libraries: Yes

Academic Staff *2011-2012*	MEN	WOMEN	**TOTAL**
FULL-TIME	–	–	**20**
PART-TIME	–	–	**120**
STAFF WITH DOCTORATE			
FULL-TIME	–	–	**30**
PART-TIME	–	–	c. **50**
Student Numbers *2011-2012*			
All (Foreign Included)	600	400	c. **1,000**

Distance students, 340. **Evening students**, 300.
Last Updated: 07/08/12

HIGHER INSTITUTIONS OF SCIENCES AND TECHNOLOGY (SIST)

87 Bd Nador Polo, Casablanca
Tel: +212(522) 21-16-80
Fax: +212(522) 21-36-33
EMail: info@sunderland.ac.ma
Website: http://www.sunderland.ac.ma

President: Tarik Obaid

Vice-President: Abdellatif Mazouz

Programmes

Business Administration (Banking; Business Administration; Economics; Finance; Human Resources; Information Management; Management; Marketing); **Computer Science** (Business Computing; Information Technology; Software Engineering); **Education** (Education); **Tourism** (Tourism)

Further Information: Also a branch in Rabat

History: Founded 2001, in Morocco as an off-campus centre for University of Sunderland, a public British university established in the UK.

Admission Requirements: Secondary School Certificate (Baccalauréat)

Degrees and Diplomas: *Master*. Also Bachelors and MBA

Libraries: Yes
Last Updated: 03/10/12

HIGHER INSTITUTE OF ELECTRONICS AND TELECOMMUNICATIONS NETWORKS

Institut supérieur d'Electronique et des Réseaux de Télécommunications (ISERT)
30, rue Kamal Mohammed, 20000 Casablanca
Tel: +212(522) 45-08-45
Fax: +212(522) 45-08-47
EMail: scolarité@isert.ma
Website: http://www.isert.ma

Executive Director: Boujemâa Charoub EMail: bcharoub@isert.ma

International Relations: Abdellah Charoub, Director of studies
EMail: acharoub@isert.ma

Programmes

Computer Engineering (Computer Engineering; Systems Analysis); **Electronic Engineering** (Electronic Engineering); **Telecommunications Networks** (Telecommunications Engineering)

History: Founded 1996.

Admission Requirements: Secondary School certificate, scientific or technological (baccalauréat)

Main Language(s) of Instruction: French, English

International Co-operation: With institutions in France

Accrediting Agencies: Ministère de l'Education nationale, de l'Enseignement supérieur, de la Formation des Cadres et de la Recherche scientifique

Degrees and Diplomas: *Diplôme d'Ingénieur*: Telecommunications; Networks; Computing; Electronic Engineering, 5 yrs. Also Diploma in Business Computing (MIAGE): 3 yrs

Student Services: Academic counselling, Cultural centre, Employment services, Foreign student adviser, Health services, Language programs, Nursery care, Social counselling, Sports facilities

Student Residential Facilities: Yes

Libraries: Yes

Academic Staff *2008-2009*	MEN	WOMEN	**TOTAL**
FULL-TIME	8	6	**14**
Student Numbers *2008-2009*			
All (Foreign Included)	184	39	**223**

Last Updated: 21/08/12

HIGHER INSTITUTE OF FOOD SCIENCES

Institut supérieur de Formation en Technologie alimentaire (ISFORT)
94, rue Allal Ben Abdellah, 20000 Casablanca
Tel: +212(522) 44-88-28
Fax: +212(522) 44-88-26
EMail: isfort.direction@gmail.com
Website: http://www.isfort-maroc.com/

President: Hicham Lahlou EMail: isfort@menara.ma

Counsellor: Abdelouahhab Tazi EMail: atazi81@yahoo.fr

Programmes

Bioengineering (Bioengineering); **Bio-Pharmaceutical Sciences**; **Chemical Processes** (Chemical Engineering); **Food Technology** (Food Technology); **Quality Management** (Safety Engineering)

History: Founded 1995.

Fees: (Dirhams): 25,000-40,000 per annum

Main Language(s) of Instruction: French

International Co-operation: With universities in France; Canada; Germany

Degrees and Diplomas: Diplôme du cycle normal (3-4yrs), Diplôme du cycle supérieur (5yrs)

Student Services: Academic counselling, Canteen, Employment services, Foreign student adviser, Social counselling

Student Residential Facilities: None

Special Facilities: Computer Centre

Libraries: Yes
Last Updated: 14/08/12

INSTITUTE FOR LANGUAGE AND COMMUNICATION STUDIES (ILCS)

29 Rue Oukaimeden Agdal, 10080 Rabat
Tel: +212(537) 67-59-68
Fax: +212(537) 67-59-65
EMail: ilcs.adm@ilcs.ac.ma
Website: http://www.ilcs.ac.ma/

Schools

Communication Studies (Advertising and Publicity; Communication Studies; Marketing; Public Relations); **Interpreting, Translation and Languages** (English; French; Modern Languages; Spanish; Translation and Interpretation); **Jounalism** (Journalism); **Management and Leadership** (Business and Commerce; Finance; International Business; Leadership; Management)

Admission Requirements: Secondary school certificate or equivalent

Degrees and Diplomas: Diploma of the Institute (3 and 5 yrs)
Last Updated: 26/09/12

INSTITUTE FOR LEADERSHIP AND COMMUNICATION STUDIES GROUP (ILCS RABAT)

29 rue Oukaimeden, Agdal, 10080 Rabat
Tel: +212(537) 67-59-68
Fax: +212(537) 67-59-65
EMail: ilcs.info@ilcs.ac.ma
Website: http://www.ilcs.ac.ma

Directeur: Abderrafi Benhallam EMail: abenhallam@gmail.com

International Relations: Aïcha Lemtouni
EMail: ilcs.adm@ilcs.ac.ma

Schools

Communication (Advertising and Publicity; Communication Studies; Marketing; Public Relations); **Journalism** (Journalism; Media Studies); **Leadership and Management**; **Translation and Interpretation** (Modern Languages; Translation and Interpretation)

History: Founded 1996 to offer training in the fields of Business Communication and Languages. Formerly known as Institute for Language and Communication Studies.

Governing Bodies: Board of Advisers

Academic Year: September to June (September-December; January-June)

Admission Requirements: Secondary school certificate (baccalauréat), TOEFL and DALF

Fees: (Dirhams): 18,000-21,000 per semester

Main Language(s) of Instruction: English, French

Degrees and Diplomas: *Master*. Bachelor (3-4 yrs)

Student Services: Academic counselling, Canteen, Employment services, Foreign student adviser, Language programs

Student Residential Facilities: None

Libraries: Central Library
Last Updated: 24/07/09

INSTITUTE FOR MANAGEMENT TECHNIQUES STUDIES

Institut supérieur de Formation aux Techniques de Gestion (ISFOTEG)

47, boulevard Pasteur, 90000 Tanger
Tel: +212(539) 93-71-01
Fax: +212(539) 37-17-71
EMail: isfoteg@menara.ma
Website: http://www.isfoteg.net.ma

General Manager: Abassi Chraibi Mounir
EMail: isfoteg.chraibi@gmail.com

Programmes

Management (Accountancy; Advertising and Publicity; Arabic; Business Administration; Civil Law; Commercial Law; Communication Studies; Economics; English; Finance; Fiscal Law; French; Human Resources; Industrial Management; Management; Marketing; Software Engineering; Spanish; Transport Management)

History: Founded 1988.

Governing Bodies: Professors' Council; General Manager

Academic Year: October to June

Admission Requirements: Baccalaureat

Fees: (Dirhams): 30,000 per annum

Main Language(s) of Instruction: French; Arabic; English; Spanish

International Co-operation: With WESFORD in Grenoble (France), UNIMAN (Paris)

Degrees and Diplomas: *Master*. Diplôme du cycle normal: Management (3 yrs); Diplôme du cycle spécialisé: Marketing-Management, Logistics, Finance (2 yrs)

Student Services: Academic counselling, Foreign student adviser

Special Facilities: Multimedia; Internet room

Libraries: Yes
Publications: Partenaires *(biannually)*

Academic Staff *2010-2011*	MEN	WOMEN	TOTAL
FULL-TIME	4	3	**7**
PART-TIME	22	4	**26**
STAFF WITH DOCTORATE			
FULL-TIME	–	–	**1**
PART-TIME	–	–	**10**
Student Numbers *2010-2011*			
All (Foreign Included)	44	61	**105**
FOREIGN ONLY	–	–	**7**

Last Updated: 19/03/12

INSTITUTE OF ACCOUNTANCY, AUDIT AND FINANCE

Institut supérieur de Comptabilité, Audit et Finance (ISCAF)

21, rue de l'Olympe, Quartier des Hôpitaux, Casablanca
Tel: +212(522) 86-20-40
Fax: +212(522) 86-24-40
EMail: iscaf@iscaf.ma
Website: http://www.iscaf.net/

Directeur: Mohamed Douch

Programmes

Accountancy (Accountancy); **Business Administration** (Business Administration); **Finance** (Finance)

History: Founded 1996.

International Co-operation: With Université Montesquieu Bordeaux (France)

Degrees and Diplomas: *Diplôme universitaire de Technologie*; *Licence professionnelle*; *Master spécialisé*; *Master*
Last Updated: 14/08/12

INSTITUTE OF ADVANCED BANKING AND FINANCIAL STUDIES

Institut des hautes Etudes bancaires et financières, Oujda (HBF OUJDA)

Rue Al Khalil, Quartier El Qods, Oujda
Tel: +212(536) 74-60-60
EMail: hbf.ro@iam.net.ma
Website: http://www.hbf.ma

Directeur: Moulay Abdelhamid Smaili

Programmes

Banking and Finance

History: Founded 1998.

Degrees and Diplomas: Diplôme de l'établissement, 4 yrs; Diplôme du cycle de perfectionnement de l'établissement, 15 mths

INSTITUTE OF ADVANCED BANKING, FINANCE AND MANAGEMENT STUDIES - CASABLANCA

Institut des hautes Etudes en Banque, Finance et Assurances - Casablanca (HBFA)

4, rue Van Zeeland angle 113 Bd
Abdelmoumen Quartier des Hôpitaux,
Casablanca
Tel: +212(522) 47-65-54
Fax: +212(522) 47-65-57
EMail: sarah.belacheheb@hbfa.ma
Website: http://www.hbfa.ma

Directeur général: Driss Rhafes EMail: driss.rhafes@hbfa.ma

Programmes

Finance and Banking (Banking; Finance); **Insurance** (Insurance); **Management** (Communication Studies; Human Resources; Management; Marketing)

History: Founded 1995.

Admission Requirements: Secondary school-leaving certificate (baccalauréat); Entrance examination, interview

Degrees and Diplomas: *Licence professionnelle*: 3 yrs; *Master*: 5 yrs
Last Updated: 09/08/12

INSTITUTE OF ADVANCED ECONOMIC AND SOCIAL STUDIES

Institut des hautes Etudes économiques et sociales (IHEES)

3 rue Taieb Abdelkrim, Anfa,
Casablanca
Tel: +212(522) 30-24-20
Fax: +212(522) 54-33-63
EMail: rachid.elabboubi@groupe-ihees.com
Website: http://www.groupe-ihees.com

Président: Abdelhamid Lazrak EMail: a.lazrak@groupe-ihees.com

Directeur Pédagogique: Rachid EL Abboubi

Programmes

Computer Networks (Computer Networks); **Finance** (Finance); **Human Resources** (Human Resources); **International Business** (International Business); **Management** (Management); **Marketing** (Marketing); **Tourism and Hotel Management** (Hotel Management; Tourism)

History: Founded 1984.

Degrees and Diplomas: *Master*. Diplôme du cycle normal (3 yrs), Diplôme du cycle supérieur et spécialisé (2 yrs)
Last Updated: 09/08/12

INSTITUTE OF ADVANCED STUDIES IN SUSTAINABLE DEVELOPMENT

Institut supérieur des Hautes Etudes en développement durable (ISHEDD)

15 Bis, Rue Darâa,
Agdal, Rabat
Tel: +212(537) 77-99-76
EMail: info@ishedd.com
Website: http://www.ishedd.com

President: Kamal El Haji

Programmes

Energy and Materials Engineering (Energy Engineering; Materials Engineering); **Management** (Management); **Water Science and Environmental Studies** (Environmental Studies; Water Science)

Degrees and Diplomas: *Licence professionnelle*; *Master*
Last Updated: 15/10/12

INSTITUTE OF ADVANCED STUDIES IN TELECOMMUNICATIONS AND MANAGEMENT

Institut des hautes Etudes en Télécommunications et Management - Casablanca (IN.SUP)

3, rue Brahim Ibnou Adham, Maârif, Casablanca
Tel: +212(522) 98-25-25
Fax: +212(522) 25-24-15
EMail: insup@casanet.net.ma

Programmes

Engineering (Computer Engineering; Telecommunications Engineering); **Management** (Management)

Admission Requirements: Baccalauréat; Entrance examination

Degrees and Diplomas: *Diplôme de Commerce et de Gestion*: 4 yrs

INSTITUTE OF APPLIED COMPUTER STUDIES AND MANAGEMENT

Institut supérieur d'Informatique appliquée et de Management (ISIAM)

BP 805, Boulevard Hassan 1er, Agadir
Tel: +212(528) 22-32-10
Fax: +212(528) 22-33-68
EMail: isiam@menara.ma
Website: http://www.isiam.ma

Président: Aziz Bouslikhane

Programmes

Computer Science (Business Computing; Computer Networks; Computer Science); **Management** (Accountancy; Banking; Business Administration; Business and Commerce; Commercial Law; Communication Studies; Economics; English; Finance; Hotel Management; Human Resources; Management; Marketing; Social Sciences; Statistics; Tourism)

History: Founded 1989.

International Co-operation: With Institutions in France and Canada

Degrees and Diplomas: *Master*. Also Diplôme de l'établissement (3-5 yrs)
Last Updated: 21/08/12

INSTITUTE OF APPLIED ENGINEERING - RABAT

Institut supérieur du Génie appliqué - Rabat (IGA RABAT)

27, rue Oqba, Angle rue Al Battani et Ibnou Al Haitam, Agdal, Rabat
Tel: +212(537) 77-14-68
Fax: +212(537) 77-14-72
EMail: iga@iga.ma

Président: Mohammed Diouri

Directeur: Rachid Chakib

Schools

Business Administration (Business Administration; Business and Commerce; Finance; Management; Marketing); **Engineering** (Computer Engineering; Computer Networks; Software Engineering; Systems Analysis; Telecommunications Engineering)

Further Information: IGA has 7 other centres: IGA Casablanca (IGA Belvédère, IGA Maârif et IGA 2Mars), IGA Marrakech, IGA Fès, IGA Settat et IGA El Jadida.

History: Founded 1996.

Admission Requirements: Secondary school certificate (baccalauréat) and entrance examination

Degrees and Diplomas: *Licence professionnelle*; *Master*. Diplôme du cycle général (3-4 yrs), Diplôme du cycle supérieur (5 yrs)
Last Updated: 27/07/09

INSTITUTE OF BUSINESS ADMINISTRATION

Institut d'Administration des Entreprises (IAE)

56, rue Al Fourat Maarif, Casablanca
Tel: +212(522) 23-45-08
Fax: +212(522) 23-45-56
Website: http://www.iaemaroc.com

President: Atif Boucif

Programmes

Business Administration (Banking; Business Administration; Communication Studies; Finance; Marketing)

History: Founded 1997.

Degrees and Diplomas: *Licence professionnelle*; *Master*
Last Updated: 18/09/12

INSTITUTE OF COMMERCE AND MANAGEMENT

Institut supérieur de Gestion et de Commerce (ISGC)
23, rue Hafid Ibrahim, Quartier Gauthier, Casablanca
Tel: +212(522) 26-63-12
Fax: +212(522) 47-46-43
EMail: info@isg.ma
Website: http://www.isg.ma

General Manager: Driss Skalli-Housseini
EMail: d.skalli@isg.ma; driss.skalli@gmail.com

Studies Manager: Hassan Skalli-Hosseini EMail: h.skalli@isg.ma
International Relations: Driss Skalli-Housseini
EMail: d.skalli@isg.ma

Programmes

Accountancy and Marketing; **Commerce** (Business and Commerce); **Computer Science** (Computer Science); **Management** (Management)

History: Founded 1989.

Academic Year: October to June

Admission Requirements: Entrance examination

Fees: Depending on programmes

International Co-operation: With universities in France

Degrees and Diplomas: *Master*: 5 yrs. Diplôme de l'établissement, 5 yrs (Auditing; Accounting; Marketing)

Student Services: Academic counselling, Cultural centre, Employment services, Foreign student adviser, Language programs, Social counselling, Sports facilities

Student Residential Facilities: Yes

Libraries: Yes

Academic Staff *2011-2012*	**TOTAL**
FULL-TIME	**30**
STAFF WITH DOCTORATE	
FULL-TIME	c. **10**
Student Numbers *2011-2012*	
All (Foreign Included)	c. **200**
FOREIGN ONLY	**5**

Last Updated: 19/06/12

INSTITUTE OF COMMERCE, MANAGEMENT AND COMPUTER SCIENCE

Institut supérieur de l'Entreprise en Commerce, Gestion et Informatique (ISE)
30, rue Mohamed Kamal, 2ème étage, Casablanca
Tel: +212(522) 44-96-76
Fax: +212(522) 44-91-74
EMail: info@ISEmaroc.com
Website: http://www.isemaroc.com

Directeur Adjoint: Ahmed Driouech

Programmes

Business Administration (Accountancy; Business Administration; Business and Commerce; Finance; Hotel Management; International Business; Management; Marketing; Tourism); **Computer Engineering** (Computer Engineering)

History: Founded 1999.

Degrees and Diplomas: *Diplôme universitaire de Technologie*; *Licence professionnelle*; *Master*
Last Updated: 03/10/12

INSTITUTE OF JOURNALISM AND COMMUNICATION

Institut supérieur du Journalisme et de Communication (ISJC)
47, bd Rahal Al Maskini 1er étage, Casablanca
Tel: +212(522) 44-13-23
Fax: +212(522) 54-06-20

Programmes

Communication Studies (Communication Studies); **Journalism** (Journalism; Media Studies)

History: Founded 2001.

Admission Requirements: Secondary School Certificate (Baccalauréat)

Degrees and Diplomas: Diplôma of the Institute (4yrs)
Last Updated: 03/10/12

INSTITUTE OF JOURNALISM AND INFORMATION

Institut supérieur du Journalisme et de l'Information (IF-JSUP)
97, avenue Hassan SGHR- Derb Omar, Casablanca
Tel: +212(522) 49-29-94
Fax: +212(522) 44-06-89

Programmes

Information (Media Studies; Radio and Television Broadcasting); **Journalism** (Journalism)

History: Founded 2003.

Degrees and Diplomas: Diploma of the Institute (3 and 5 yrs)
Last Updated: 27/09/12

INSTITUTE OF MANAGEMENT SCIENCES

Institut libre des Sciences de Gestion (ILSG)
22, Rue Mohamed Diouri, V.N, Fès
Tel: +212(535) 94-33-56
Fax: +212(535) 93-00-28
EMail: ilsg@menara.ma
Website: http://www.ilsg.ma/

Directeur général: Hassan Drissi
Directrice pédagogique: Laïla Berrada

Programmes

Management (Accountancy; Business Administration; Business and Commerce; E-Business/Commerce; Management; Marketing)

History: Founded 2004.

Admission Requirements: Secondary school certificate (Baccalauréat), interview

International Co-operation: With universities in Canada

Degrees and Diplomas: Diplôme cycle normal (3yrs), Diplôme cycle supérieur (5yrs)
Last Updated: 05/10/12

INSTITUTE OF TRANSPORT AND LOGISTICS

Institut supérieur du Transport et de la Logistique (ISTL)
30, Rue d'Avesne - Immeuble B, 20300 Casablanca
Tel: +212(522) 24-64-64
Fax: +212(522) 40-62-04
Website: http://www.istl.ma/

Fondateur: Abdelilah Hifdi

Programmes

Logistics (Transport Management)

History: Founded 2007.

Degrees and Diplomas: *Licence professionnelle*; *Master*. Diplôme de Directeur Logistique (4yrs); Joint Licence Professionnelle with Cnam (France) ; Joint Master with Sorbone Université, Panthéon Assas - Paris 2
Last Updated: 11/10/12

INTERNATIONAL INSTITUTE FOR HIGHER EDUCATION IN MOROCCO (IIHEM)

Avenue Mohamed VI, Km 42 (Route des Zaërs), Souissi, Rabat
Tel: +212(537) 75-19-20
Fax: +212(537) 65-97-70
EMail: info@iihem.ac.ma
Website: http://www.iihem.ac.ma/

President: Saâd Kabbaj

Schools

Business Administration (Banking; Business Administration; Communication Studies; Finance; Information Management; Management; Marketing; Transport Management); **Engineering** (Civil Engineering; Computer Engineering; Computer Networks; Industrial Engineering; Information Technology; Software Engineering)

History: Founded 1988.

Admission Requirements: Secondary school certificate (baccalauréat) and entrance examination

Main Language(s) of Instruction: English, French

Degrees and Diplomas: *Master.* Diplôme cycle normal (3 yrs), Diplôme cycle spécialisé (5yrs)
Last Updated: 22/08/12

INTERNATIONAL SCHOOL OF MANAGEMENT - CASABLANCA CAMPUS

Ecole supérieure internationale de Gestion - Campus Casablanca (ESIG CASABLANCA)

Route de Nouasseur, Sidi Maârouf, Casablanca
Tel: +212(522) 33-50-78
Fax: +212(522) 33-56-72
EMail: esigcasa@esigmaroc.com
Website: http://www.esigmaroc.com

Président: Azzeddine Bennani

Directrice générale, Groupe ESIG: Saloua Hajji

Directrice: Nadia El Bouaamri

Programmes

Business Administration (Business Administration; Business Computing; E-Business/Commerce); **Finance** (Finance); **Human Resources** *(Certificate)* (Human Resources); **International Business** (International Business); **Management** (Communication Studies; Management); **Marketing** (Marketing); **Organisations Management** (Management); **Project Management** (Management)

Further Information: Also a branch in Marrakech, Rabat and Fès

History: Founded 1985.

Academic Year: September to June (September-January; February-June)

Admission Requirements: High school diploma; Entrance examination

Main Language(s) of Instruction: French and English

International Co-operation: With universities in Canada

Accrediting Agencies: Ministère de l'Education nationale, de l'Enseignement supérieur, de la Formation des Cadres et de la Recherche scientifique

Degrees and Diplomas: *Diplôme de Commerce et de Gestion*; *Master.* Also Executive MBA (2 yrs); Certificates in Business Administration, Human Resources Management and Marketing (12 mths)

Student Services: Academic counselling, Canteen, Employment services, Foreign student adviser, Language programs, Nursery care, Social counselling, Sports facilities
Last Updated: 08/06/09

KENITRA BUSINESS SCHOOL

Ecole supérieure de Commerce de Kénitra (ESCK)

34 Rue Ghandi - Ville Haute, 14000 Kénitra
Tel: +212(537) 36-77-77
Fax: +212(537) 36-42-42
EMail: contact@esck.ma
Website: http://www.esck.ma/

Co-Fondateur: Mohammed Aboutahir

Co-Fondateur: Mustapha Bachiri

Programmes

Business Administration (Accountancy; Business Administration; Communication Studies; Computer Science; Finance; Human Resources; Information Technology; Management; Marketing)

Admission Requirements: Secondary school certificate (Baccalauréat) and interview

Degrees and Diplomas: Diplôme du cycle normal (3yrs), Diplôme du cycle spécialisé (5yrs)
Last Updated: 23/08/12

KNOWLEDGE COMPUTER AND BUSINESS INSTITUTE (KCBI)

4, rue Moulay Ali Cherif Hassan, Rabat
Tel: + 212(537) 66-06-47
Fax: + 212(537) 66-06-50
EMail: admin@kcbi.ma
Website: http://www.kcbi.ma/

Director of Educational and International Affairs: Jihad Pharaon

Programmes

Business Administration (Banking; Business Administration; Communication Studies; E-Business/Commerce; Finance; Human Resources; Information Management; Marketing)

History: Founded 2001.

Degrees and Diplomas: *Master*; *Doctorat.* Also Bachelor
Last Updated: 03/10/12

MANAGEMENT AND TECHNOLOGICAL INSTITUTE

Institut supérieur de Management et de Technologie (MATCI)

3, rue Tarablous, Casablanca
Tel: +212(522) 22-09-09
Fax: +212(522) 22-43-50
Website: http://www.matci.ac.ma/

President: Saloua Zraida

Programmes

Business Administration (Business Administration; Business and Commerce; Finance; Human Resources; Information Technology; Management; Marketing); **Computer Science** (Computer Engineering; Multimedia); **Sustainable Development** (Development Studies; Ethics; Government)

History: Founded 2008 as a branch of Management and Technological Canadian Institute.

Degrees and Diplomas: Joint diploma with MATCI Canada (DEC, Bachelor, Master); Diplome du cycle supérieur (5yrs)
Last Updated: 18/10/12

MARRAKECH PRIVATE BUSINESS SCHOOL

Ecole de Management Marrakech Privée (EMMARRAKECH)

km 13, route d'Amzmiz, Marrakech

Programmes

Business and Commerce (Agricultural Management; Business Administration; Management; Marketing; Tourism; Transport Management)

Degrees and Diplomas: Diplôme du cycle normal 3yrs, Diplôme du cycle supérieur (5yrs)
Last Updated: 30/10/12

MEDSUP MANAGEMENT SCHOOL

Ecole MedSup Management (MEDSUP MANAGEMENT)

BP 1208, Avenue Moulay Rachid, Lotissement Ritchard, villa 72, Tanger
Tel: +212(539) 38-16-38
Fax: +212(539) 33-82-81
EMail: medsup@menara.ma
Website: http://www.med-sup.org

Président: Amine Abdelmajid

Directeur: Said Mssassi

Programmes

Management (Finance; Human Resources; Management; Marketing; Transport Management)

History: Founded 2008.

Degrees and Diplomas: *Master*
Last Updated: 30/10/12

MOROCCAN BUSINESS SCHOOL

Ecole supérieure de Management Hôtelier et Gestion de l'Entreprise (MOBS ESMHTG)
16 rue Zallagh- Agdal, Rabat
Tel: +212(537) 67-33-57
Fax: +212(537) 67-33-58
EMail: info@mobs.ma
Website: http://www.mobs.ma/

Directeur pédagogique: Mbarek Belmerhnia

Programmes

Management (Accountancy; Business Administration; Finance; Hotel Management; Management; Marketing; Tourism)

History: Founded 2007.

Degrees and Diplomas: Diplôme de Management (3yrs); Diplôme en gestion et administration de l'entreprise (3yrs); Diplôme du cycle Supérieur de Management (5yrs); Diplôme d'études supérieures spécialisées (5yrs): Joint Degree programms with institutions in France (IEA, UPEC, Université Paris Est Créteil, ESC Toulouse)
Last Updated: 11/10/12

MOROCCAN INSTITUTE OF MANAGEMENT

Institut Marocain de Management (IMM)
Angle Bd Mohammed V, Rue Chaouia, Casablanca
Tel: +212(522) 20-22-88
Fax: +212(522) 20-26-39
EMail: imm@imm.ac.ma
Website: http://www.imm.ac.ma

Directeur général: Khalid Idrissi Kaitouni
EMail: idrissikhalid@imm.ac.ma

Directeur des Programmes: Adil Benchekroun
EMail: a.benchekroun@imm.ac.ma

Programmes

Accountancy (Accountancy); **Business Administration** (Business Administration); **Finance** (Finance); **Human Resources Management**; **International Business** (International Business); **Management** (Information Technology; Management); **Marketing** (Marketing); **Tourism Management** (Tourism)

History: Founded 1989.

Degrees and Diplomas: *Licence professionnelle*: Management, 3 yrs; *Master*: Management, 5 yrs
Last Updated: 10/08/12

MOROCCAN SCHOOL FOR HIGHER STUDIES IN BUSINESS AND COMPUTER SCIENCE (MSHS)

45 avenue 2 Mars, 20000 Casablanca
Tel: +212(522) 26-34-02
Fax: +212(522) 26-34-12
EMail: mshs@menara.ma
Website: http://www.mshs.ma

President: Najib K. Bennani

Programmes

Business Administration (Business Administration; E-Business/Commerce; Information Technology; International Business; Management; Marketing); **Engineering** (Computer Engineering; Computer Networks; Industrial Engineering; Software Engineering; Telecommunications Engineering)

History: Founded 2004.

Admission Requirements: Secondary School Certificate (Baccalauréat), Admission test, interview, TOEFL

Degrees and Diplomas: Graduate Diploma (4yrs and 5 yrs)
Last Updated: 04/10/12

MOROCCAN SCHOOL OF BANKING AND INTERNATIONAL TRADE

Ecole marocaine de Banque et de Commerce international - Rabat (MBCI)
26 bis Avenue du Souss, Souissi, Rabat
Tel: +212(537) 63-12-12
Fax: +212(537) 75-37-19
EMail: mbci@menara.ma
Website: http://www.mbci.ma/

Directeur: Tahar Daoudi

Directeur: Mohamed Kettani

Programmes

Banking (Banking); **International Trade** (International Business)

History: Founded 1998.

Admission Requirements: Baccalauréat

Degrees and Diplomas: *Diplôme de Commerce et de Gestion*: 4 yrs. Also Diplôme du cycle supérieur (12-15 mths)
Last Updated: 13/07/12

MOROCCAN SCHOOL OF ENGINEERING

Ecole marocaine d'Ingénierie (EMG)
BP 23550 Casa - Lissasfa, Km 9, Route d'El Jadida, Casablanca
Tel: +212(522) 65-08-08
Fax: +212(522) 65-03-03
EMail: info@emg.ac.ma
Website: http://www.emg.ac.ma/

Directeur Général: M. Rejdali

Programmes

Civil Engineering (Civil Engineering); **Industrial Engineering** (Industrial Engineering)

Further Information: Also a branch in Rabat

History: Founded 2008.

Admission Requirements: Secondary school certificate (Baccalauréat)

Fees: (Dirhams): 21.000 semestre

Degrees and Diplomas: *Diplôme d'Ingénieur*
Last Updated: 12/10/12

MORROCAN SCHOOL OF ENGINEERING

Ecole marocaine des Sciences de l'Ingénieur, Casablanca (EMSI)
154, Rue El Bakri, Casablanca
Tel: +212(522) 54-31-70
Fax: +212(522) 99-26-26
EMail: info.casa@emsi.ma
Website: http://www.emsi.ma

President: Kamal Daissaoui

Programmes

Civil and Construction Engineering (Civil Engineering; Construction Engineering); **Computer Engineering and Networks** (Computer Engineering; Computer Networks); **Industrial Engineering** (Industrial Engineering); **Industrial Engineering and Telecommunications** (Automation and Control Engineering; Industrial Engineering; Telecommunications Engineering)

Further Information: Also branches in Rabat and Marrakech.

History: Founded 1986.

Admission Requirements: Baccalauréat

Degrees and Diplomas: *Master*. Diplôme du cycle superieur (5 yrs). Joint Master with Universities in France
Last Updated: 13/07/12

MORROCAN SCHOOL OF TRANSLATION AND INTERPRETATION

Ecole supérieure marocaine de Traduction et d'Interpretariat (ESMTI)

39 boulevard Mohammed V, Casablanca
Tel: +212(522) 29-81-34
Fax: +212(522) 29-81-34
EMail: contact@esmtimaroc.com
Website: http://www.esmtimaroc.com/

President: Mohammed Bourkadi

Programmes

Journalism and Communication (Communication Studies; Journalism); **Translation and Interpretation** (Translation and Interpretation)

Further Information: Also a branch in Fès

History: Founded 2007.

Admission Requirements: Secondary school certificate (Baccalauréat), entrance examination, interview

Degrees and Diplomas: *Licence professionnelle*; *Master*
Last Updated: 05/10/12

MUNDIAPOLIS UNIVERSITY

Université Mundiapolis (MUNDIAPOLIS)

Aéropole de formation, 52 Nouacer, 20180 Casablanca
Tel: +212(529) 01-37-07
EMail: accueil@lemiae.ma
Website: http://www.lemiae.ma

Directeur: Amine Bensaid

Institutes

Social and Political Sciences and Law (Commercial Law; Economics; International Studies; Law; Political Sciences; Public Administration; Social Sciences)

Programmes

Engineering (Automation and Control Engineering; Computer Networks; Computer Science; Electronic Engineering; Engineering; Mathematics; Physics; Software Engineering)

Schools

Business (Accountancy; Business Administration; Finance; Insurance; Management; Marketing; Transport Economics; Transport Management)

Further Information: Also Branch at : Bd d'Anfa, 77, Casablanca

History: Founded 2002 as Ecole marocaine d'Informatique automatique et électronique, became Université Mundiapolis after merging of Polyfinance, IMADE and EMIAE, 2009.

Admission Requirements: Baccalauréat and entrance examination

Degrees and Diplomas: *Licence professionnelle*; *Diplôme d'Ingénieur*; *Master*
Last Updated: 16/07/12

POLY MANAGEMENT SCHOOL

Ecole des hautes Etudes Poly Management (HEP MANAGEMENT)

9 rue Essakhra - Hay Alquods, Oujda
Tel: +212(536) 50-54-10
Fax: +212(536) 50-54-10
EMail: hepoudja@gmail.com
Website: http://hep.ma/

Programmes

Management (Commercial Law; Finance; International Business; Marketing)

History: Founded 2005.

Degrees and Diplomas: Diplôme du cycle normal (3yrs), Diplôme du cycle spécialisé (5yrs)
Last Updated: 05/10/12

POLYVALENT SCHOOL OF COMPUTER SCIENCE AND ELECTRONICS

Ecole polyvalente supérieure d'Informatique et d'Electronique (EPSIEL)

4, avenue Allal Ben Abdellah, 30000 Fès
Tel: +212(535) 65-25-54
Fax: +212(535) 94-32-45
EMail: epsiel@epsiel.net
Website: http://www.epsiel.net

Président: Berrada Sad

Programmes

Computer Science (Business Computing; Computer Science); **Electronic Engineering** (Electronic Engineering); **Industrial Computing** (Computer Science); **Telecommunications Engineering** (Computer Networks; Telecommunications Engineering)

History: Founded 1989.

Fees: (Dirhams): 25,800

Degrees and Diplomas: Diplôme supérieur d'informatique et d' électronique (4yrs)
Last Updated: 18/07/12

PRIVATE INTERNATIONAL INSTITUTE OF MANAGEMENT AND TECHNOLOGY (PIIMT)

13, Rue Qadi Ben Said El Filali, Av. John Kennedy, Souissi, Rabat
Tel: +212(537) 75-67-11
Fax: +212(537) 75-62-95
EMail: webmaster@piimt.us
Website: http://www.piimt.us

President and CEO: Anass Lahlou

Programmes

Computer Science (Computer Science)

Schools

Business (Communication Studies; Finance; Human Resources; Information Management; Management; Marketing); **Health Management** (Health Administration)

Further Information: Also campuses in Casablanca and Marrakech

History: Founded 2006. A subsidiary of "American University of Leadership " offering double Moroccan and American degrees.

Admission Requirements: Secondary school certificate (Baccalauréat), entrance examination

Degrees and Diplomas: *Master*, *Doctorat*. Also Bachelor
Last Updated: 08/10/12

PRIVATE POLYTECHNIC INSTITUTE OF CASABLANCA

Institut polytechnique privé de Casablanca

Rue 10, No. 2 Lotissement Allaimoun 1, Route d'El Jadida, Casablanca
Tel: +212(522) 93-65-50
Fax: +212(522) 93-65-59
EMail: info@polytechnique.ma
Website: http://www.polytechnique.info

Directeur général: Mouhsine Berrada

Schools

Business (Business Administration; Business Computing; Finance; Management; Marketing); **Engineering** (Computer Engineering; Electrical Engineering; Engineering; Mechanical Engineering; Mining Engineering)

International Co-operation: WithUniversities in Canada (Université Laval, UQAT)

Degrees and Diplomas: Diploma of the Institute (3 and 5 yrs). Diplome d'ingénieur canadien (5yrs) with Université Laval and UQAT
Last Updated: 24/09/12

PRIVATE SCHOOL OF ACCONTANCY, AUDIT AND MANAGEMENT

Haute Ecole de Comptabilite d'Audit et Management (HECAM)

Lotissement le château n°29, El Jadida
Tel: +212(523) 39-46-54
Fax: +212(532) 39-46-71
EMail: contact@hecam.ma
Website: http://www.hecam.ma/

Programmes

Management (Accountancy; Human Resources; Management; Marketing)

History: Founded 2006.

Degrees and Diplomas: School Diploma (3 yrs) and Joint Degrees with Univérsite du Littoral Côte d'Opale (France) (5yrs)
Last Updated: 10/10/12

PRIVATE SCHOOL OF ENGINEERING OF AGADIR

Ecole polytechnique privée d'Agadir

BP 805, Avenue Hassan II, Quartier Dakhla, Agadir
Tel: +212(528) 23-34-34
Fax: +212(528) 21-00-05
EMail: direction@e-polytechnique.ma
Website: http://www.e-polytechnique.ma

Président: Aziz Bouslikhane

Directeur: Ilias Majdouline EMail: ilias@e-polytechnique.ma

International Relations: Loubna Boujlaleb
EMail: loubna@e-polytechnique.ma

Programmes

Computer Engineering (Computer Engineering); **Electrical Engineering** (Electrical Engineering); **Industrial Engineering** (Industrial Engineering); **Mechanical Engineering** (Mechanical Engineering)

History: Founded 2005. Being part of Universiapolis-Groupe ISIAM.

Degrees and Diplomas: Diplôme du premier cycle de l'etablissement (3 yrs); Diplôme du deuxieme cycle de l'etablissement (2 yrs)

Student Services: Canteen, Foreign student adviser, Foreign Studies Centre, Health services, Language programs, Social counselling, Sports facilities

Academic Staff *2009*	MEN	WOMEN	TOTAL
FULL-TIME	7	4	**11**
PART-TIME	–	–	**19**
STAFF WITH DOCTORATE			
FULL-TIME	–	–	**2**
PART-TIME	–	–	**9**
Student Numbers *2009*			
All (Foreign Included)	154	59	**213**
FOREIGN ONLY	25	7	**32**

Evening students, 4.
Last Updated: 11/04/12

PRIVATE SCHOOL OF HOTEL MANAGEMENT, MARRAKECH

Ecole supérieure d'Hôtellerie Marrakech Privée (SUPHOTELLERIE)

Km 13, route d'Amezmiz, 42312 Marrakech
Tel: +212(524) 48-70-01
Fax: +212(524) 48-38-49
EMail:
contact@campusmarrakech.comcontact@campusmarrakech.com

Programmes

Hotel Management (Hotel and Restaurant; Hotel Management)

Degrees and Diplomas: Diplôme du cycle supérieur (5yrs)
Last Updated: 30/10/12

PRIVATE SCHOOL OF TOURISM AND HOTEL MANAGEMENT

Ecole supérieure de Tourisme et Technologie Hôtelière Privée (ESTTH)

BP 805, Campus ISIAM, Av. Hassan 1er. Quartier Dakhla, Agadir
Tel: +212(528) 23-66-50
Fax: +212(528) 23-06-55
EMail: info@e-tourisme.ma
Website: http://www.e-tourisme.ma/

President: Aziz Bouslikhane

Programmes

Tourism (Hotel Management; Tourism)

History: Founded 2006. Being part of Universiapolis-Groupe ISIAM.

International Co-operation: With universities in France and Canada

Degrees and Diplomas: Diplôme 1er Cycle (3yrs); Diplôme 2e cycle (5yrs)
Last Updated: 23/08/12

SCHOOL OF ACCOUNTANCY AND FINANCE

Ecole des hautes Etudes comptables et financières (HECF)

Rue Abou Hamid El Ghazali, n°6, Commune Agdal - Ville nouvelle, Fès
Tel: +212(535) 93-14-44
Fax: +212(535) 94-21-89
EMail: hecf@hecfsup.com; moussa@hecfsup.com
Website: http://www.hecfsup.com/

Président: Abdelkarim Moussa

Programmes

Management (Accountancy; Banking; Finance; Human Resources; Management)

Further Information: Also a Branch in Meknès

History: Founded 2004.

Admission Requirements: Secondary School Certificate (Baccalauréat); Admission test

Degrees and Diplomas: Diplôme du cycle normal (3 yrs); Diplôme du cycle supérieur (5yrs); Joint Bachelor program with ESC Pau (France)
Last Updated: 05/10/12

SCHOOL OF ADMINISTRATION AND BUSINESS MANAGEMENT

Ecole d'Administration et Direction des Affaires (EAD)

2, avenue Moulay Youssef, 1000 Rabat
Tel: +212(537) 70-19-23 +212(537) 73-78-95
Fax: +212(537) 70-81-36
EMail: eadber@iam.net.ma

Head: Ahmed Berrelel

Programmes

Business, Finance and Management (Business Administration; Finance; International Business; Management)

History: Founded 1984.

Academic Year: September to June

Admission Requirements: Secondary school certificate (baccalauréat)

Main Language(s) of Instruction: French, English

Degrees and Diplomas: *Diplôme de Commerce et de Gestion*

Student Services: Academic counselling, Canteen, Cultural centre, Employment services, Foreign student adviser, Foreign Studies Centre, Language programs, Nursery care, Sports facilities

Student Residential Facilities: Yes

Libraries: Central Library

Publications: La Vie Economique; Le Matin; L'Economiste; L'Opinion; Radio-T.V.
Last Updated: 04/06/09

SCHOOL OF ADVANCED BUSINESS AND COMPUTER STUDIES

Ecole des hautes Etudes commerciales et informatiques (HECI)

66, boulevard de l'Atlantide, Polo n°1, Casablanca
Tel: +212(522) 50-02-02
Fax: +212(522) 21-00-30
EMail: contact@groupeheci.net
Website: http://www.groupeheci.ac.ma

Head: Fayçal Ghissassi

Departments

Business and Commerce (Banking; Business and Commerce; Finance; Human Resources; Insurance; International Business; Marketing; Transport Management); **Computer Science** (Computer Science)

Further Information: Also branches in Agadir; Fès; Kenitra; Marrakech Meknes; Mohammadia; Tanger, Tetouan, Oujda and Rabat.

History: Founded 1986.

Admission Requirements: Secondary school certificate (Baccalauréat) and competitive examination

Degrees and Diplomas: *Licence professionnelle*; *Master*; *Doctorat*
Last Updated: 19/12/12

SCHOOL OF ADVANCED BUSINESS TECHNOLOGY AND COMPUTER SCIENCE - TANGIERS

Ecole des hautes Etudes commerciales techniques et informatiques - Tanger (EHECT-TANGER)

Demeure Allal Elfassi, rue Passadena, Tanger
Tel: +212(531) 06-06-39
Fax: +212(531) 06-06-38
EMail: ehect@ehect.ac.ma
Website: http://www.ehect.net/

Directeur: Y. Mensoum

Schools

Computer Engineering (Business Computing; Computer Engineering; Computer Networks; Multimedia; Software Engineering; Telecommunications Engineering); **Management** (Accountancy; Business Administration; Business and Commerce; Finance; Management; Marketing; Transport Management)

Further Information: Also a branch in Tétouan

History: Founded 2000.

Admission Requirements: Secondary school certificate (Baccalauréat)

Degrees and Diplomas: *Licence professionnelle*: 3 yrs; *Master*: 5 yrs
Last Updated: 13/07/12

SCHOOL OF ADVANCED COMMERCIAL STUDIES

Ecole des hautes Etudes commerciales (HEC)

1, rue Jaber Ansari Bouremmana, Fès
Tel: +212(535) 64-33-28
Fax: +212(535) 64-05-07
EMail: hecfes@menara.ma
Website: http://www.hec.ac.ma/

Directeur général: Ilham Skalli Housseini

Directeur pédagogique: Azzeddine Khamlichi Idrissi
Tel: 212 (535) 64-33-28 EMail: az.khamlichi@gmail.com

Programmes

Business Administration (Business Administration)

Further Information: Also centre in Rabat

History: Founded 1988.

Admission Requirements: Secondary school certificate (Baccalauréat)

Fees: (Dirhams): 40,000

Degrees and Diplomas: Diplôme du cycle normal (3yrs), Diplôme du cycle supérieur (5yrs)
Last Updated: 19/03/12

SCHOOL OF ADVANCED STUDIES IN BIOTECHNOLOGY

Ecole des hautes Etudes de Biotechnologie (EHEB)

N° 380 Av Ghandi, Casablanca
Tel: +212(522) 99-67-58
Fax: +212(522) 99-67-92
EMail: eheb@menara.ma
Website: http://www.eheb.ma

Président: Mhammed Chaoui Roqai EMail: direction@eheb.ma

Deputy Director: Nadia El Jaouhari
Tel: +212(22) 27-66-36 EMail: contact@eheb.ma

Departments

Bio-engineering (Bioengineering; Biology; Biotechnology; Forest Management; Management); **Health Sciences** (Paramedical Sciences)

History: Founded 1996.

Admission Requirements: Baccalauréat

Degrees and Diplomas: *Diplôme d'Ingénieur*, *Master*
Last Updated: 13/07/12

SCHOOL OF ADVANCED STUDIES IN ECONOMICS AND BUSINESS

Ecole des hautes Etudes économiques et commerciales (HEEC)

BP 1514, Avenue Allal Fassi, Rue Abou Oubaïda, Hay Mohammadi, Marrakech
Tel: +212(524) 31-44-10
Fax: +212(524) 31-44-20
EMail: ecoleheec.ma@gmail.com
Website: http://www.ecoleheec.ac.ma

Président: My Ahmed Lamrani

Programmes

Business Administration (Business Administration; Commercial Law; Finance; Information Management; Marketing)

History: Founded 1997.

Admission Requirements: Secondary School certificate (Baccalauréat)

Degrees and Diplomas: *Master*. School Diploma (3 yrs and 5 yrs); Also Master in cooperation with Université Montpellier and Université de Bourgogne
Last Updated: 13/07/12

SCHOOL OF ADVANCED STUDIES IN INFORMATION SYSTEMS COMPUTING

Ecole des hautes Etudes en Ingénierie des Systèmes d'Information (HEISI)

14 rue Malouiya, Avenue Hassan II, Casablanca
Tel: +212(522) 202-766
EMail: info@heisi.ma
Website: http://www.heisi.ma

Directeur général: Raouf Mohammed Guessous

Programmes

Computer Systems and Networks; **Software Engineering**

History: Founded 2003.

Admission Requirements: Baccalauréat

Degrees and Diplomas: *Licence d'Etudes fondamentales*; *Diplôme d'Ingénieur*
Last Updated: 20/07/09

SCHOOL OF ADVANCED STUDIES IN MANAGEMENT, COMPUTER SCIENCE AND COMMUNICATION - CASABLANCA

Ecole des hautes Etudes de Gestion Informatique et Communication de Casablanca (EDHEC)
23, rue Ibn Majid Al Bahar, 20000 Casablanca
Tel: +212(522) 44-98-51
Fax: +212(522) 44-98-52
EMail: edhec@edhec.ac.ma
Website: http://www.edhec.ac.ma

Programmes
Computer Science (Computer Networks; Computer Science; Systems Analysis); **Management** (Accountancy; Banking; Business Computing; Finance; International Business; Management; Marketing)

History: Founded 1995.

Governing Bodies: Scientific and Pedagogical Council

Admission Requirements: Baccalauréat

Degrees and Diplomas: *Licence d'Etudes fondamentales*; *Master spécialisé*; *Master*
Last Updated: 13/07/12

SCHOOL OF APPLIED COMPUTER SCIENCE

Ecole supérieure d'Informatique appliquée (ESIA)
Avenue de la Résistance, Angle Rue Puissesseau, Casablanca
Tel: +212(522) 30-63-32 +212(522) 30-64-24
Fax: +212(522) 30-32-86
EMail: esia@menara.ma
Website: http://www.esia.ma

Directeur: Tayeb Louafa EMail: touafa@hotmail.com

Programmes
Computer Engineering (Business Computing; Computer Engineering; Computer Networks; Computer Science; Electronic Engineering; Information Technology; Mathematics; Software Engineering; Statistics; Systems Analysis; Telecommunications Engineering)

History: Founded 1993.

Admission Requirements: Secondary school certificate (Baccalauréat)

Degrees and Diplomas: Diplôme de l'établissement (2 yrs); Diplôme du cycle normal (3yrs), Diplôme du cycle spécialisé (5yrs)
Last Updated: 11/04/12

SCHOOL OF ARCHITECTURE AND INTERIOR DESIGN

Ecole supérieure des Arts et Métiers d'Architecture de Rabat (ESAMA/ESAI)
N° 7, Avenue Ahmed Belafrej, Souissi, Rabat
Tel: +212(537) 65-41-20
Fax: +212(537) 63-96-94
EMail: esai_architecture@menara.ma
Website: http://www.esama.ma

Programmes
Architecture (Architecture); **Civil Engineering** (Civil Engineering); **Interior Design** (Design; Interior Design)

History: Founded 1998 as Ecole supérieure d'Architecture d'Intérieur.
Degrees and Diplomas: *Master*
Last Updated: 19/12/12

SCHOOL OF COMMERCE AND BUSINESS - CASABLANCA

Ecole supérieure de Commerce et des Affaires (ESCA)
7, rue Abou Youssef El Kindy, Bd Moulay Youssef, Casablanca
Tel: +212(522) 20-91-20
Fax: +212(522) 20-91-15
EMail: h.hdidou@esca.ma
Website: http://www.esca.ma/index.php

Président: Thami Ghorfi

Departments
Finance (Banking; Business Administration; E-Business/Commerce; Finance; Management); **Geopolitics** (Economic and Finance Policy; Political Sciences); **Information Technology** (Information Technology); **International Business** (International Business); **Leadership** (Leadership); **Management** (Human Resources; Management; Transport Management); **Marketing** (E-Business/Commerce; Marketing)
History: Founded 1992.

Degrees and Diplomas: *Master*

Academic Staff *2011-2012*: Total: c. 90

Student Numbers *2011-2012*: Total: c. 1,050
Last Updated: 20/07/12

SCHOOL OF COMMERCE AND MANAGEMENT

Ecole supérieure de Commerce et de Gestion (ESCG)
Route de Tétouan, Rue Ahmed Attadili, 90000 Tanger
Tel: +212(539) 95-43-10
Fax: +212(539) 95-43-20
EMail: escg@escg-a.com
Website: http://www.escg-a.com

Directeur: A. Chraibi

Departments
Commerce (Business and Commerce; International and Comparative Education; Marketing; Transport Management); **Management** (Accountancy; Finance; Human Resources; Management)
History: Founded 2008.

Admission Requirements: Secondary school certificate (Baccalauréat)

Degrees and Diplomas: Diplôme du Cycle Normal (3yrs), Diplôme du Cycle Supérieur (5yrs)
Last Updated: 11/10/12

SCHOOL OF COMMERCE AND MANAGEMENT

Ecole supérieure de Commerce et de Management (ESCM)
270 bd Zerktouni, Casablanca
Tel: +212(522) 22-04-33
Fax: +212(522) 20-97-38
Website: http://www.escm.ma/

Directeur Général: Mohamed Tazi

Programmes
Business Administration (Business Administration; Finance; Hotel Management; Management; Marketing); **Hotel Management** (Hotel Management)

History: Founded 2003.

Admission Requirements: Secondary School Certificate (Baccalauréat), entrance test and interview

Degrees and Diplomas: School Diploma (3 to 5yrs), Joint Bachelor and Master with ESC Saint-Etienne (France)
Last Updated: 03/10/12

SCHOOL OF COMMERCE, MANAGEMENT AND COMPUTER SCIENCE

Ecole des Métiers de Commerce, de Gestion et d'Informatique
KSAIBI, Rue E, Lot n°3, Tanger
Tel: +212(539) 37-34-34
EMail: emcgi@emcgi.ma
Website: http://www.emcgi.ma/

Programmes
Business Administration (Business Administration; Finance; Marketing); **Computer Engineering** (Computer Engineering); **Mathematics and Business Computing** (Business Computing; Mathematics and Computer Science); **Transport Management** (Transport Management)

History: Founded 2008.

Degrees and Diplomas: Diplôme du cycle normale (3yrs); Diplôme du cycle supérieur (5yrs); Also joint Licence and Master in

"Sciences et Techniques du Génie Logistique" with Universite de Versailles Saint-Quentin-en-Yvelines (France); Bachelors and Masters with Fédération Européenne Des Ecoles (FEDE)
Last Updated: 15/10/12

SCHOOL OF COMMERCIAL ENGINEERING - MEKNÈS

Ecole supérieure des Sciences de l'Ingénierie Commerciale - Meknès (ESSIC)
132, avenue des FAR, 50000 Meknès
Tel: +212(535) 51-41-65
Fax: +212(535) 51-41-63
EMail: essic@essic.ma
Website: http://www.essic.ma

Président Directeur général: Fouad Benchekroune
EMail: benchekroune@essic.ma

Directeur Pédagogique: Abdelaziz Badaoui

Programmes

Business Administration (Accountancy; Business Administration; Business and Commerce; Computer Science; Finance; Information Technology; International Business; Management)

Further Information: Also branches in Kénitra (1999) , Rabat, Fès

History: Founded 1990 as Ecole supérieure de Secrétariat, d' Informatique et de Comptabilité.

Admission Requirements: Secondary school certificate (baccalauréat)

Main Language(s) of Instruction: French, English

Degrees and Diplomas: *Master spécialisé*; *Master*

Student Services: Cultural centre, Foreign student adviser, Foreign Studies Centre, Language programs, Nursery care, Sports facilities

Student Residential Facilities: Yes (free of charge)

Libraries: Central Library; Photographic library

Last Updated: 24/07/12

SCHOOL OF COMMUNICATION AND ADVERTISING

Ecole supérieure de Communication et de Publicité (COM' SUP)
18, rue Bachir Al Ibrahimi, Quartier Bel Air, Casablanca
Tel: +212(522) 47-30-67
Fax: +212(522) 48-07-79
EMail: comsup@ecolecomsup.com
Website: http://www.ecolecomsup.com

Directeur pédagogique: Azzeddine Lazrak

Directrice d'étude: Dalila Chaouky

Departments

Communication of Organizations (Advertising and Publicity; Communication Studies; Human Resources; Public Relations); **Culture, Tourism and Communication** (Communication Studies; Cultural Studies; Tourism); **Media and Multimedia** (Mass Communication; Media Studies; Multimedia)

History: Founded 1996.

Admission Requirements: Baccalauréat and interview

Main Language(s) of Instruction: French

Degrees and Diplomas: *Master*: 5 yrs. Diplôme du 1er cycle de l'Ecole; Diplôme du 2éme cycle de l'Ecole. Also joint Master with Université de Versailles Saint Quentin en Yvelines; Université de Paris II Panthéon Assas – Institut Francais de Presse and Université de Nice Sophia Antipolis

Student Services: Academic counselling, Canteen, Employment services, Foreign student adviser, Health services, Language programs, Social counselling

Libraries: Yes

Last Updated: 20/07/12

SCHOOL OF COMPUTER ENGINEERING

Ecole d'Ingénierie informatique (E2I)
14 avenue Ibn Khaldoun, Agdal, Rabat
Tel: +212(537) 77-46-36
Fax: +212(537) 77-89-99
EMail: e2i@e2i.ma

Programmes

Computer Engineering (Computer Engineering; Computer Networks; Software Engineering; Telecommunications Engineering)

History: Founded 2002.

Admission Requirements: Secondary school certificate (Baccalauréat)

Degrees and Diplomas: Diplôme de l'Etablissement (5yrs)

Last Updated: 13/07/12

SCHOOL OF COMPUTER NETWORKS AND MANAGEMENT

Ecole supérieure des Réseaux Informatiques et de Management (ESRIM)
BP 573, 46, avenue Mohammed V, Settat
Tel: +212(523) 40-27-05
Fax: +212(523) 40-47-28
EMail: esrim@menara.ma
Website: http://www.esrim.ma

Directeur: Abdelaly Guissi

Programmes

Computer Engineering (Computer Engineering; Computer Networks; Software Engineering; Systems Analysis); **Management** (Accountancy; Business and Commerce; Finance; Human Resources; Management; Marketing)

History: Founded 1996.

Admission Requirements: Secondary school certificate (baccalauréat)

Degrees and Diplomas: *Licence professionnelle*; *Diplôme de Commerce et de Gestion*; *Master*

Last Updated: 23/07/12

SCHOOL OF COMPUTER SCIENCE AND BUSINESS MANAGEMENT

Ecole supérieure d'Informatique et de Management des Affaires (ESIMA)
Place Hansali, Immeuble Mounia, 1er étage Appt 1 et 2, El Jadida, 24000
Tel: +212(523) 34-04-04
Fax: +212(523) 34-06-61
EMail: esima@esima-egc.com
Website: http://www.esima-egc.com/

Président: Abdelwabi Azzam EMail: esima@menara.ma

Directeur Pédagogique: Meriem Lattaoui
EMail: esima@menara.ma

International Relations: Abdelkader Bousfika
Fax: +212(523) 34-34-06

Programmes

Business and Management (Business Administration; Commercial Law; Management; Marketing); **Computer Science** (Business Computing; Computer Engineering; Computer Science; Information Technology); **Finance; Accountancy** (Accountancy; Finance; International Business)

History: Founded 1998. Part of the French EGC network.

Admission Requirements: Baccalauréat and entrace examination, interview

Main Language(s) of Instruction: French

Degrees and Diplomas: *Licence professionnelle*; *Diplôme de Commerce et de Gestion*: 3 yrs; *Master*: 5 yrs

Student Services: Canteen, Employment services, Language programs

Last Updated: 04/08/09

SCHOOL OF COMPUTER SCIENCE, TELECOMMUNICATION AND ECONOMICS - ENITE

Ecole nouvelle d'Informatique des Télécommunications et d'Economie (ENITE)

16, Rue Chasseur Jules Gros Oasis Route d'El Jadida, Casablanca
EMail: y.tidli@enite.ma
Website: http://www.enite.ma/

Président, Directeur Général: Anass Berrada
EMail: a-berrada@enite.ma

Directeur Pédagogique: Youssef Tidli

Programmes
Computer Engineering (Computer Engineering; Computer Networks; Information Technology; Telecommunications Engineering); **Finance** (Accountancy; Finance)

History: Founded 2004.

Admission Requirements: Secondary School Certificate (Baccalauréat)

Degrees and Diplomas: Graduate Diploma (3-5 yrs). Also Master professionnel - MIAGE with Université de Nancy (France)
Last Updated: 04/10/12

SCHOOL OF DESIGN

Ecole supérieure de Design (ART COM-SUP)

18 rue Bachir Al Ibrahim - quartier Belair, Casablanca
Tel: +212(522) 26-18-54
Fax: +212(522) 27-46-02
Website: http://www.ecole-artcom.com/

Directeur: Abdelmoumen Benabdeljalil

Programmes
Architecture (Architecture; Graphic Design; Interior Design; Multimedia)

History: Founded 2005.

Admission Requirements: Secondary school certificate (Baccalauréat), entrance examination, interview

Degrees and Diplomas: Diplôme du cycle normal (3yrs), Diplôme du cycle spécialisé (5yrs)
Last Updated: 05/10/12

SCHOOL OF DESIGN AND VISUAL ARTS

Ecole supérieure de Design et des Arts Visuels

Angle Avenue Tantan / Rue Bengurir, Hay El Manar Anfa, Casablanca
Tel: +212 (522) 368-001
Fax: +212 (522) 368-923
EMail: contact@ecole-design.com
Website: http://www.ecole-design.com

Directeur: Abderrahim Jabrani

Programmes
Graphic Design (Graphic Design); **Interior Design** (Interior Design)

History: Founded 2006.

Admission Requirements: Baccalauréat and interview

Degrees and Diplomas: *Licence d'Etudes fondamentales*; *Master*
Last Updated: 13/03/12

SCHOOL OF ENGINEERING IN APPLIED SCIENCES

Ecole supérieure d'Ingénierie en Sciences Appliquées (ESISA)

29 bis Av Ibn Khatib Route d'Immouzzer, Fès
Tel: +212(535) 65-70-95
Fax: +212(535) 65-97-90
EMail: info@esisa.ma
Website: http://esisa.ac.ma/

Président: Khalid Mekouar EMail: k.mekouar@esisa.ma

Administrative Officer: Ali Ouazzani Touhami

Programmes
Computer Engineering (Computer Engineering; Information Technology; Systems Analysis)

History: Founded 1999.

Degrees and Diplomas: *Master*
Last Updated: 21/09/12

SCHOOL OF FOOD INDUSTRY

Ecole supérieure de l'Agro-Alimentaire (SUP AGRO)

22, rue le Câtelet (niveau 227Bd Emile Zola) Belvédère, 20300 Casablanca
Tel: +212(522) 24-54-05
Fax: +212(522) 24-53-99
EMail: supagro@casanet.net.ma
Website: http://www.supagro.ma/news.html

Président: Abdelrhafour Tantaoui El Araki

Schools
Food Industry (Food Science; Food Technology)

History: Founded 1997

Governing Bodies: Administrative Board

Academic Year: October to July

Admission Requirements: Secondary school certificate (baccalauréat)

Main Language(s) of Instruction: French

Degrees and Diplomas: *Master spécialisé*: Quality, 5 yrs; *Master*: Food Technology, 4 yrs. Also preparing Diplôma in Food Technology (2-3 yrs)

Student Services: Canteen, Language programs, Social counselling

Libraries: Central Library
Last Updated: 24/07/09

SCHOOL OF HUMAN SCIENCES AND COMMUNICATION

Ecole supérieure des Sciences Humaines et de Communication (SUPH'COM)

BP 805, Campus ISIAM, Bd Hassan 1er, Quartier Dahkla, Agadir
Tel: +212(528) 23-33-51
Fax: +212(528) 22-33-68
EMail: info@suphcom.ma
Website: http://www.suphcom.ma

Programmes
Communication Studies (Communication Studies)

History: Part of Universiapolis-Groupe ISIAM.

Degrees and Diplomas: Diplôme 1er cycle (3 yrs); Diplme cycle spécialisé (5 yrs)
Last Updated: 23/08/12

SCHOOL OF INDUSTRIAL SYSTEMS ENGINEERING

Ecole d'Ingénierie en Génie des Systèmes Industriels (EIGSICA)

Centre des Affaires Allal Ben Abdellah, 6ème étage, Angle rue Allal Ben Abdellah et rue Fakir Mohamed, Casablanca
Tel: +212(522) 47-56-03
Fax: +212(522) 47-59-38
EMail: admission@eigsica.ma
Website: http://www.eigsica.ma/

Programmes
Engineering (Computer Engineering; Electrical Engineering; Engineering; Industrial Engineering; Mechanical Engineering)

History: Founded 2008 as a branch of EIGSI La Rochelle.

Degrees and Diplomas: Diplôme du cycle normal (3 yrs); Diplôme d'ingénieur avec EIGSI La Rochelle (5 yrs)
Last Updated: 10/10/12

SCHOOL OF INFORMATION TECHNOLOGY, TELECOMMUNICATION AND MANAGEMENT

Ecole supérieure en Ingénierie de l'Information,Télécommunication et de Management (ESTEM)

BP 20060, 4-6, Rue Moussa Bnou Nouceir Bd Moulay Youssef, Quartier Gautier, Casablanca
Tel: +212(522) 26-02-60
Fax: +212(522) 26-26-62
EMail: information@estem.ma
Website: http://www.etud-estem.ma

Directrice: Wafaâ Bouab Bennani

Programmes

Engineering (Business Computing; Computer Engineering; Computer Networks; Multimedia); **Management** (Communication Studies; Finance; Hotel Management; Human Resources; International Business; Management; Marketing; Tourism)

History: Founded 2001.

Admission Requirements: Secondary school certificate (baccalauréat)

International Co-operation: With universities in France

Degrees and Diplomas: *Master spécialisé*; *Master*. Joint Master with Université de Bretagne occidentale and Université de Savoie; Joint diplôme d'ingénieur with private schools in France

Last Updated: 24/09/12

SCHOOL OF INTERIOR ARCHITECTURE

Ecole supérieure d'Architecture d'intérieur (ESAI)

7, avenue Ahmed Balafrej, Rabat
Tel: +212(537) 65-23-10
Fax: +212(537) 65-41-20
EMail: info@ecole-esai.com
Website: http://www.ecole-esai.com

Programmes

Architecture (Architecture; Interior Design)

Further Information: Also branch in Marrakech

History: Founded 1988.

Degrees and Diplomas: School Diploma (4yrs)

Last Updated: 21/09/12

SCHOOL OF JOURNALISM AND COMMUNICATION

Ecole supérieure de Journalisme et de Communication (ESJC)

37, rue Tata, Casablanca
Tel: +212(522) 26-40-10
Fax: +212(522) 26-20-60
Website: http://www.esjc.ma

Head: A. Dilami

Programmes

Communication Studies (Communication Studies); **Journalism** (Journalism)

Degrees and Diplomas: *Master*. School Diploma (3-5 yrs)

Last Updated: 26/09/12

SCHOOL OF LAW AND ECONOMICS

Ecole supérieure des Etudes Juridiques et Economiques (ESEJE)

BP 1214, 146, Nice 1 - Près de Marjane, Mohammedia
Tel: +212(523) 30-44-44
Fax: +212(523) 32-50-24
EMail: contact@eseje.ma
Website: http://www.eseje.ma/

Directeur: Mostafa Brahimi

Programmes

Law (Commercial Law); **Management** (Banking; Business Administration; Finance; Human Resources; Management; Sales Techniques)

History: Founded 2004.

Admission Requirements: Secondary school certificate, entrance examination

Degrees and Diplomas: Diplôme du cycle normal (3yrs); Diplôme du cycle supérieur (5yrs)

Last Updated: 05/10/12

SCHOOL OF LEADERSHIP AND MANAGEMENT

Ecole supérieure de Direction et de Gestion (ESDG)

BP 774, 8, rue Oued Souss-Agdal, Rabat
Tel: +212(537) 77-01-83
Fax: +212(537) 77-67-60
EMail: info@esdg.ma
Website: http://www.esdg.ma/

Programmes

Management (Accountancy; Finance; International Business; Management)

History: Founded 2007.

Degrees and Diplomas: *Licence professionnelle*; *Master spécialisé*; *Master*. Also School Diploma (3-5 yrs); Joint Master with Université de Rennes (France)

Last Updated: 11/10/12

SCHOOL OF MANAGEMENT

Ecole supérieure de Management (ESM)

Bd. de la Résistance, Angle rue Puissesseau, Casablanca
Tel: +212(522) 30-81-30
Fax: +212(522) 30-32-86
EMail: esm1@menara.ma
Website: http://www.esm.ma/

Programmes

Management (Communication Studies; Finance; International Business; Management; Marketing)

History: Founded 1992.

Admission Requirements: Secondary school certificate (baccalauréat)

Degrees and Diplomas: School Diploma (4 yrs); Postgraduate diploma (3 yrs)

SCHOOL OF MANAGEMENT AND APPLIED COMPUTER ENGINEERING

Ecole supérieure de Management et d'Ingénierie Informatique Appliqués (ESMA)

1, Avenue Prince My Abdellah, Immeuble Berrada, Rouidate II, Gueliz, Marrakech
Tel: +212(524) 33-02-23 +212(524) 33-11-25
Fax: +212(524) 33-02-23
EMail: esma@menara.ma
Website: http://www.esmamaroc.com/

Directeur général: Mohamed Berrada

Departments

Engineering (Computer Engineering; Industrial Management); **Management** (Business Administration; Tourism)

History: Founded 1996 as Ecole supérieure de Management appliqué. Acquired present title 2011.

Admission Requirements: Secondary school certificate (baccalauréat)

International Co-operation: With Univeristé Paris13 and Univeristé du Littoral Côte d'Opale ULCO (France)

Degrees and Diplomas: *Licence professionnelle*; *Master*

Last Updated: 24/07/09

SCHOOL OF MANAGEMENT AND BUSINESS ADMINISTRATION

Ecole de Management et d'Administration des Affaires (EMAA)

Cité Dakhla - Av, Hassan 1er, mmeuble Ennour 105, Agadir
EMail: contact@emaa.ma
Website: http://www.emaa.ma/

Président: Tarik Lafou

Programmes
Management (Accountancy; Business Administration; Finance; Management; Marketing)
Admission Requirements: Secondary school cerfiticate and entrance examination
Degrees and Diplomas: Diplôme de l'établissement (3 to 5 yrs)
Last Updated: 22/08/12

SCHOOL OF MANAGEMENT AND COMMUNICATION

Ecole supérieure de Management et de Communication (ESMC)
57 boulevard Abdelmoumen Résidence Al Hadi, Rabat

Programmes
Management (Management; Marketing; Media Studies; Tourism)
History: Founded 2007.
Degrees and Diplomas: School Diploma (3- 5 yrs)
Last Updated: 11/10/12

SCHOOL OF MANAGEMENT AND COMPUTER SCIENCES

Ecole supérieure de Gestion et des Sciences de l'Informatique (EGICO)
2, rue Chouaib Doukkali, les Orangers, Rabat
Tel: +212(537) 73-25-64
Fax: +212(537) 73-25-70
EMail: Egicosup@menara.ma
Website: http://www.egicosup.ac.ma

Présidente: Fouzia Tarik

Programmes
Computer Sciences (Business Computing; Computer Science; Telecommunications Engineering); **Management** (Accountancy; Business and Commerce; E-Business/Commerce; Finance; Management; Marketing)
Further Information: Also branch in Tangiers
History: Founded 1994.
Admission Requirements: Secondary school certificate (baccalauréat)
Degrees and Diplomas: School Diploma (2 to 4 yrs); Postgraduate diploma (1 to 3 yrs)
Last Updated: 28/07/09

SCHOOL OF MANAGEMENT AND HUMAN RESOURCE MANAGEMENT

Ecole supérieure de Management et de Gestion des Ressources Humaines (SUP'RH)
20, Rue Mohamed Kamal, Immeuble Semiramis, Casablanca, 20000
Tel: +212 (522) 27-46-27
Fax: +212 (522) 27-08-08
EMail: contact@suprh.com
Website: http://www.suprh.com

Head: Abdelhak Moutawakkil

Programmes
Human Resource (Business Administration; Human Resources; Management)
History: Founded 2008.
Academic Year: October to June
Admission Requirements: Secondary school certificate (Baccalauréat)
Degrees and Diplomas: Diplôme du cycle Bachelor (3yrs); Diplôme du cycle Master (5yrs)
Last Updated: 18/10/12

SCHOOL OF MANAGEMENT COMPUTING

Ecole supérieure d'Informatique appliquée à la Gestion (ESIAG)
Villa Thérèse 1, Quartier Saâdia, Guéliz, Marrakech
Tel: +212(524) 43-72-95
Fax: +212(524) 43-91-53
EMail: esiag@iam.net.ma

Programmes
Computing (Business Computing; Computer Engineering; Information Technology); **Management** (Data Processing; Finance; Hotel Management; International Business; Marketing; Tourism)
History: Founded 1987.
Admission Requirements: Baccalauréat
Degrees and Diplomas: Diplôme du cycle normal (3yrs), Diplôme du cycle spécialisé (5yrs)
Last Updated: 28/07/09

SCHOOL OF MANAGEMENT, COMMERCE AND COMPUTER SCIENCE - FÈS

Ecole supérieure de Management du Commerce et d'Informatique - Fès (GROUPE SUP' MANAGEMENT)
28 place du 11 Janvier et rue Patrice Lumumba, Ville Nouvelle, Fès
Tel: +212(535) 65-34-31 +212(55) 94-00-39
Fax: +212(535) 65-27-32
EMail: supmgt@menara.ma

Président: Abdesselam Erkik (1985-) Tel: +212 (661) 21-64-72
Sécretaire génerale: Rachida Erkik
International Relations: Sanae Khlifi

Academies
NTIC and Offshore

Schools
Business Administration (Business and Commerce; Environmental Management; Finance; Human Resources; International Business; Management; Marketing); **Computer Engineering** (Computer Networks; Engineering; Telecommunications Engineering); **Tourism** (Hotel Management; Leisure Studies; Tourism)
History: Founded 1995.
Governing Bodies: Conseil d'Administration
Academic Year: October to June
Admission Requirements: Secondary school certificate (baccalauréat) for professional cycle; bac +3 for advanced cycle
Fees: (Dirhams): undergraduate: 28,000-35,000 per annum; postgraduate: 32,000-70,000
Main Language(s) of Instruction: French, English
International Co-operation: With universities in France, Switzerland, Belgium, USA, Spain and Canada
Accrediting Agencies: EREDU (Europe)
Degrees and Diplomas: *Licence d'Etudes fondamentales*: Computer Engineering, Finance and Management, International, Marketing and Communication, Computer Science, Computer Networks, Tourism, Hotel Management, 3 yrs; *Master spécialisé*: Commercial Engineering, Financial Engineering, International Management, Computer Engineering, Computer Networks, Telecommunication Engineering,Tourism, Hotel Management, 5 yrs; *Master*: Computer Engineering, Finance Management, Management and Commerce, 3-4 yrs. Certificats de formation continue (CFC). Certificats de Cycles Spéciaux (CCS). Certificats NTIC. Certificats Offshoring
Student Services: Academic counselling, Cultural centre, Employment services, Foreign student adviser, Foreign Studies Centre, Language programs, Social counselling, Sports facilities
Student Residential Facilities: Yes
Special Facilities: Computer facilities
Libraries: Yes
Publications: Flash Managers, Cultural Studies, Management, Economics and Leisure *(3 per annum)*; International Eview of Management Science and Engineering Management, Research in Management and Engineering *(biannually)*

Academic Staff 2011-2012	MEN	WOMEN	TOTAL
FULL-TIME	21	23	44
PART-TIME	66	17	83
STAFF WITH DOCTORATE			
FULL-TIME	7	1	8
PART-TIME	43	10	53
Student Numbers 2011-2012			
All (Foreign Included)	609	396	1,005
FOREIGN ONLY	368	221	589

Last Updated: 20/03/12

SCHOOL OF MANAGEMENT, COMPUTER SCIENCE AND TELECOMMUNICATION

Ecole supérieure de Management d'Informatique et de Télécommunication (SUP MTI)

23, avenue Chellah, Hassan, Rabat
Tel: +212(537) 70-89-89
Fax: +212(537) 70-89-73
EMail: mit@mit.ma
Website: http://www.mit.ma/

Schools

Engineering (Computer Engineering; Engineering); **Management** (Management)

Further Information: Also a branch in Ouja and Beni Mellal

History: Founded 2006.

Degrees and Diplomas: Diplôme Management des Entreprises (3yrs); Diplôme d'ingénieur en Systemes Informatiques (3 yrs); Diplôme d'ingénieur en Systemes d'Information (5yrs); Diplome Management des Systemes et Technologies de l'Information et de Communication (5 yrs);

Last Updated: 10/10/12

SCHOOL OF MULTIMEDIA, COMPUTER SCIENCE AND NETWORKS

Ecole supérieure des Multimedia, Informatique et Réseaux (SUPEMIR)

15 rue Barrii Debbass, Avenue Constantinople - Mers Sultan, Casablanca
Tel: +212(522) 473-481
Fax: +212(522) 473-482
EMail: info@supemir.com
Website: http://www.supemir.com

Président: Khalid Rifi EMail: rifi@email.com

Director: Abderrahim Medbouhi

Programmes

Business Computing (Business Computing); **Computer Networks and Multimedia** (Computer Networks; Multimedia)

History: Founded 2004.

Admission Requirements: Baccalauréat

Fees: (Dirhams): 28,000 per annum

Main Language(s) of Instruction: French

Degrees and Diplomas: *Diplôme de Commerce et de Gestion*: Engineering, 5 yrs; *Master*. School Diploma (3yrs)

Student Services: Foreign student adviser

Last Updated: 18/06/12

SCHOOL OF PSYCHOLOGY

Ecole supérieure de Psychologie (ESP)

88 Avenue Ibn Sina, Hay Hassani, Casablanca
Tel: +212(522) 95-16-66
Fax: +212(522) 95-06-62
EMail: psychosup@menara.ma
Website: http://www.psychosup.net

Directrice: Assia Akesbi Msefer

Programmes

Psychology (Biology; Clinical Psychology; Educational Psychology; Neurology; Psychiatry and Mental Health; Psychoanalysis; Psychology; Statistics)

History: Founded 2003.

Admission Requirements: Secondary school certificate (baccalauréat), interview and written examination

Degrees and Diplomas: *Diplôme de Commerce et de Gestion*: 5 yrs

Last Updated: 23/07/12

SCHOOL OF QUALITY MANAGEMENT

Ecole supérieure de Management de la Qualité (ESIMAQ)

56, rue Ibnou Hamdis, Casablanca
Tel: +212(522) 36-92-27
Fax: +212(522) 94-00-37
EMail: esimaq2008@gmail.com
Website: http://www.esimaq.ma

Programmes

Quality Management (Industrial Management)

History: Founded 1997.

Admission Requirements: Secondary school certificate (baccalauréat)

Degrees and Diplomas: *Diplôme d'Ingénieur*

Last Updated: 23/07/12

SCHOOL OF TECHNOLOGY AND MANAGEMENT

Ecole supérieure des Sciences Techniques et de Management (SUPTEM)

6, rue Mohamed Tazi, Quartier Marshan, 90000 Tanger
Tel: +212(539) 93-10-06
Fax: +212(539) 93-78-86
EMail: info@groupebmhs.com
Website: http://www.suptem.ac.ma

Head: Abdellah Aboussoror

Programmes

Computer Engineering (Computer Engineering; Computer Networks; Multimedia); **Management** (Banking; Business Computing; Finance; Information Technology; Management; Marketing; Transport Management)

Further Information: Also a campus in Safi

History: Founded 2001. Being part of Groupe BMHS.

Degrees and Diplomas: Diplôme 1er cycle (3 yrs); Diplôme cycle spécialisé (5 yrs)

Last Updated: 26/09/12

SCHOOL OF TELECOMMUNICATION AND MANAGEMENT

École supérieure de Télécommunications et Management (SUPTEMA)

N°67, Rue Khalid ibn Oualid Bouramana, Fès
Tel: +212(535) 64-12-30
Fax: +212(535) 64-12-21
EMail: suptema@yahoo.fr
Website: http://www.suptema.com/

Directeur général: Jamal Kohen

Directeur pédagogique: Mohamed Chater
EMail: chatereco@yahoo.com

Programmes

Management (Finance; Human Resources; Management; Marketing); **Telecommunication Engineering** (Computer Engineering; Computer Networks; Telecommunications Engineering)

Degrees and Diplomas: School Diploma (3-5 yrs)

Last Updated: 05/10/12

SCHOOL OF TELECOMMUNICATIONS STUDIES

Ecole supérieure des Télécommunications (SUP-TELECOM)

BP 8977, 51 rue 16 Novembre, Agdal, Rabat
Tel: +212(537) 67-37-37
Fax: +212(537) 67-47-99
EMail: suptelecom@menara.ma
Website: http://www.suptelecom.ma

Programmes

Computer Engineering (Computer Engineering); **Telecommunications Engineering** (Computer Networks; Telecommunications Engineering)

History: Founded 1999.

Degrees and Diplomas: Diplôme 1er cycle (3 yrs); Diplôme cycle spécialisé (5 yrs)

Last Updated: 24/07/09

SCHOOL OF VISUAL ARTS

Ecole supérieure des Arts Visuels Privée (ESAV)

BP 4006-400002, 7-9 rue Lakhdar, Marrakech-Amerchich
Tel: +212(524) 44-30-26 +212(80) 200-2006
Fax: +212(524) 29-15-75
EMail: contact@esavmarrakech.com
Website: http://www.esavmarrakech.com/

Directeur: Vincent Melilli

Departments

Cinema (Cinema and Television; Communication Arts; Film; Multimedia; Sound Engineering (Acoustics)); **Graphisme** (Graphic Arts; Graphic Design; Visual Arts)

History: Founded 2008.

Admission Requirements: Secondary school certificate (baccalauréat)

Fees: (Dirhams): 55.000 (5,000 euros) per annum

International Co-operation: With Université Cadi Ayyad (Marrakech), and universities in France, Belgium, Canada and Switzerland

Degrees and Diplomas: Diploma in Media Design and Graphic Design (4-5 yrs)

Academic Staff *2011-2012*: Total 90

Student Numbers *2011-2012*: Total 200

Last Updated: 11/10/12

SULTAN MOULAY SLIMANE UNIVERSITY - BENI-MELLAL

Université Sultan Moulay Slimane - Beni-Mellal (USMS)

BP. 523, 23000 Béni Mellal
Tel: +212(523) 48-02-18
Fax: +212(523) 48-13-51
EMail: sgpusms@usms.ma
Website: http://www.usms.ma/

Président: Bouchaib Mernari

Vice President of Academiv Affairs: Mohamed Taki

Faculties

Arts and Humanities (Arts and Humanities; English; French); **Polydisciplinary** (Economics; Management; Physics); **Science and Technology** (Applied Mathematics; Bioengineering; Biology; Chemical Engineering; Computer Engineering; Electronic Engineering; Environmental Engineering; Food Technology; Materials Engineering; Mathematics and Computer Science; Mechanical Engineering; Natural Resources; Technology; Telecommunications Engineering)

History: Founded 2007, incorporated Faculté des Lettres et des Sciences Humaines (1987), Faculté des Sciences et Techniques (1994), and Faculté Polydisciplinaire (2003-2004).

International Co-operation: With universities in Canada, France, Germany, and South Africa

Degrees and Diplomas: *Licence d'Etudes fondamentales*; *Licence professionnelle*; *Diplôme d'Ingénieur*; *Master Sciences et Techniques*; *Master spécialisé*; *Master*; *Doctorat*

Student Residential Facilities: Yes

Academic Staff *2011-2012*: Total 267

Student Numbers *2011-2012*: Total 7,467

Last Updated: 12/07/12

SUP TECHNOLOGY SCHOOL

Ecole supérieure des Hautes Etudes en Technologies de l'Information et de la Communication (SUP TECHNOLOGY)

4 Avenue Cadi Iass, Maarif, 20333 Casablanca
Tel: +212(522) 99-65-66
Fax: +212(522) 99-65-96
EMail: infos-casa@suptechnology.ma
Website: http://www.suptechnology.ma/

Président: Abdelaziz S. Doukali
EMail: doukkali@suptechnology.com

Directeur pédagogique: Mohamed Belam
EMail: belam@suptechnology.ma

Programmes

Computer Engineering (Computer Engineering; Computer Networks; Management Systems; Software Engineering)

Further Information: Also a branch in El Jadida

Degrees and Diplomas: *Licence d'Etudes fondamentales*; *Master*. Diplôme du cycle normal (3yrs); Diplôme du cycle spécialisé (5yrs); Joint Licence and Master with Univesrité du littoral côte d'Opale

Last Updated: 08/10/12

VINCI INSTITUTE OF COMPUTER ENGINEERING AND TELECOMMUNICATIONS NETWORKS

Ecole supérieure Vinci

10 Bis, Rue El Yamama, Rabat
Tel: +212(537) 70-69-05
Fax: +212(537) 70-69-06
EMail: vinci@vinci.ac.ma
Website: http://www.vinci.ma

Président: Amin Rachdi

Programmes

Computer Engineering (Computer Engineering; Computer Networks; Information Technology); **Telecommunications Engineering** (Telecommunications Engineering)

History: Founded 2003.

Degrees and Diplomas: *Diplôme de Commerce et de Gestion*: 5 yrs

Last Updated: 19/06/12

Mozambique

STRUCTURE OF HIGHER EDUCATION SYSTEM

Description:

Higher education is provided by public and private institutions classified by universities, higher institutes, higher polytechnics institutes, higher schools and academies. Higher education is under the responsibility of the Ministry of Education through the Directorate for the Coordination of Higher Education (previously it was under the former Ministry of Higher Education, Science and Technology - MESCT). The Strategic Plan of Higher Education in Mozambique 2012-2020 was approved in 2012. Higher education is funded by the State but universities have a high degree of autonomy (in the administrative, juridical, pedagogical and financial fields) and they coordinate their activities with the Directorate for the Coordination of Higher Education (Direcção de Coordenação do Ensino Superior).

Stages of studies:

University level first stage: *University degree (Licenciatura)*
The licenciatura is awarded after three or four years' study, 4 years in Veterinary Science, 5 years in Medicine.

University level second stage: *Master of Arts or Master of Sciences (Mestrado)*
Studies last for at least two years after the first degree.

University level third stage: *Doctoral degree*
A Doctoral degree conferred three to five years after the Mestrado is catered for in the new law.

Distance higher education:
The National Institute of Distance Education (INED) is the entity responsible for the coordination and regulation of distance and open education in Mozambique. There are seven institutions providing distance education at higher level with a total number of around 5,000 students. Amongst them 4 are private and 3 are public.

ADMISSION TO HIGHER EDUCATION

Admission to university-level studies:

Name of secondary school credential required: Certificado de Habilitações

Alternatives to credentials: Completion of middle level technical courses may also qualify a student for undergraduate entry.

Entrance exam requirements: Access to universities is based on the Secondary School Leaving Certificate and an entrance examination.

Other admission requirements: Professional experience and document evaluation upon approval by the Ministry supervising higher education

Foreign students admission:

Quotas: Quotas fixed according to SADC protocol

Entrance exam requirements: Access to university-level education is based on the Secondary School Leaving Certificate, an entrance examination and a good score.

Entry regulations: Law 27/2009

Health requirements: Medical certificate

Language requirements: Fluency in Portuguese

NATIONAL BODIES

Ministério da Educação (Ministry of Education)

Minister: Zeferino Martins

Permanent Secretary: Maria de Fatima Zacarias Zacarias

Director: Manuel Rego
Av. 24 de Julho, n° 167
C.P. 34
Maputo
Tel: +258(21) 490 677
Fax: +258(21) 492 196
WWW: http://www.mined.gov.mz/

Ministério da Ciência e Tecnologia (Ministry of Science and Technology)
Minister: Venâncio Massingue
Av. Patrice Lumumba, 770
Maputo
Tel: +258(21) 352 800
WWW: http://www.mct.gov.mz

Data for academic year: 2011-2012
Source: IAU from the Ministry of Education, Maputo, 2012.

INSTITUTIONS

PUBLIC INSTITUTIONS

ACADEMY OF POLICE SCIENCES
Academia de Ciências Policiais (ACIPOL)
Estrada Nacional 1, Michafutene, Maputo
Tel: +258(21) 470319
Fax: +258(21) 470542
Website: http://www.acipol.ac.mz

Reitor: José Nhantave (2010-)

Programmes
Police Studies (Police Studies)

History: Founded 1999.
Degrees and Diplomas: *Licenciatura*
Last Updated: 15/06/12

EDUARDO MONDLANE UNIVERSITY
Universidade Eduardo Mondlane (UEM)
Caixa postal 257, Praça 25 de Junho, Maputo
Tel: +258(21) 430239 +258(21) 428-198
Fax: +258(21) 304405
EMail: luis.muchanga@uem.mz
Website: http://www.uem.mz

Reitor: Orlando Antonio Quilambo (2012-)
Tel: +258(21) 428-196, Fax: +258(21) 428-128

Vice-Reitor Académica: Ana Monjane
Tel: +258(21) 307-271/76, Fax: +258(21) 307-272
EMail: angelomc@uem.mz

International Relations: Antonio Bernardo, Director
Tel: +258(21) 428-411, Fax: +258(21) 313-846
EMail: antonio.bernardo@uem.mz

Centres
African Studies (African Studies) *Director*: Armindo Ngunga; **Biotechnology** (Biotechnology) *Director*: Luis Gil das Neves; **Computer Science** (Computer Science) *Director*: Francisco Mabila; **Engineering Studies** *(UP)* (Engineering) *Director*: J. Diniz; **Habitat Studies and Development** *(CEDH)* (Town Planning) *Director*: Júlio Carrilho; **Industrial Studies, Safety and Environment** (Environmental Engineering; Industrial Engineering; Safety Engineering) *Director*: Gabriel Amós; **Population Studies** *(CEP)* (Demography and Population) *Director*: Manuel de Araújo

Faculties
Agronomy and Forest Engineering (Agricultural Economics; Agronomy; Forestry) *Dean*: Falcáo Mário; **Architecture** (Architecture and Planning) *Dean*: Manuel Lage; **Economics** (Economics); **Education** (Education) *Dean*: Inocente Vasco; **Engineering** (Chemical Engineering; Civil Engineering; Electrical Engineering; Engineering; Hydraulic Engineering; Mechanical Engineering) *Dean*: Jorge Nhambiu; **Law** (Law) *Dean*: Armando Dimande; **Letters and Social Sciences** (Arts and Humanities; Geography; History; Linguistics; Social Sciences; Translation and Interpretation) *Dean*: Armando Jorge; **Medicine** (Medicine) *Dean*: Mamudo Ismail; **Science** (Biology; Chemistry; Computer Science; Geology; Natural Sciences; Physics) *Dean*: Amália Uamusse; **Veterinary Science** (Veterinary Science) *Dean*: Dácia Correia

Schools
Business and Enterprise (Business Administration; Management) *Head*: Sylvestre Mandella; **Communication and Arts** (Fine Arts; Journalism; Public Relations) *Dean*: Abdulssatar N. Saubhai; **Marine and Coastal Sciences** (Marine Biology) *Dean*: António Hoguane; **Tourism** *(Inhambane)* (Hotel Management; Tourism) *Dean*: Mário Jessen

History: Founded 1962 as Estudios Gerais Universitários, became Universidade de Lourenço Marques 1968, acquired present title 1976. A State institution responsible to the Ministry of Higher Education.

Governing Bodies: Conselho Universitário (University Council)

Academic Year: February to December (February-June; August-December)

Admission Requirements: Secondary school certificate or equivalent, and entrance examination

Fees: (Metical): Home students: Tourism, 400, enrolment fee plus 420 per subject per semester and 840 per annual subject; other courses, 100, enrolment fee plus 105 per subject per semester and 210 per annual subject. International students, 1,000, enrolment fee plus 350 per subject per semester and 700 per annual subject

Main Language(s) of Instruction: Portuguese

International Co-operation: With universities in South Africa; Italy; Portugal; United Kingdom; USA; Brazil; Netherlands; Norway; Sweden; Germany; France; Canada and other countries.

Degrees and Diplomas: *Licenciatura*: Anthropology; Biology; Business and Enterprise; Chemistry; Economics; Finance and Accounting; Geography; Geology; History; Law; Linguistics and Literature; Management; Mathematics; Meteorology; Oceanography; Physics; Psychology; Public Administration; Sociology;

Tourism; Translation and Interpretation (Portuguese-English; Portuguese-French), 4 yrs; *Licenciatura*: Architecture; Medicine, 6 yrs; *Licenciatura*: Engineering; Informatics, 4 1/2 yrs; *Licenciatura*: Veterinary Medicine, 5 yrs; *Mestrado*: Administration and Management of Education; Agrarian Development; Adult Education; Curriculum Development; Natural Sciences and Mathematics Education; Information Systems; Law (Juridical Sciences; International Trade Law; International Law; Juridico-Political Sciences); Linguistics; Population and Development; Public Health; Software Engineering, 2 yrs; *Doutoramento*: Linguistics

Student Services: Canteen, Cultural centre, Health services, Nursery care, Social counselling, Sports facilities

Student Residential Facilities: For c. 1,067 students

Special Facilities: Natural History Museum; Historic Archive of Mozambique

Libraries: 12,660 books; 1,893 journals; faculty libraries; special collections: World Bank publications, Mozambican fiction

Publications: Boletim informativo *(monthly)*; Estudos Moçambicanos *(biannually)*

Press or Publishing House: UEM Press

Academic Staff *2011-2012*	**TOTAL**
FULL-TIME	c. **1,200**
Student Numbers *2011-2012*	
All (Foreign Included)	c. **11,600**
FOREIGN ONLY	**120**

Last Updated: 29/03/12

GAZA POLYTECHNIC INSTITUTE

Instituto Superior Politécnico de Gaza (ISPG)
Recinto da Escola Agrária, Chokwe, Gaza 1
Tel: +258(82) 3047056
EMail: polgaza@tdm.co.mz
Website: http://www.ispg.ac.mz/

Director: Hortêncio Pedro Comissal

Courses

Accountancy (Accountancy); **Agricultural Engineering** (Agricultural Engineering; Earth Sciences; Water Management); **Zoology** (Zoology)

History: Founded 2005.

Degrees and Diplomas: *Licenciatura*

Last Updated: 24/08/12

INSTITUTE OF ART AND CULTURE

Instituto Superior de Artes e Cultura
Avenida das Indústrias, Machava, Maputo
Website: http://www.isarc.edu.mz/

Director: Filimone Meigos

Courses

Art and Culture (Cultural Studies; Design; Fine Arts; Visual Arts)

History: Founded 2008.

Degrees and Diplomas: *Licenciatura*

Last Updated: 15/06/12

INSTITUTE OF HEALTH SCIENCES

Instituto Superior de Ciências de Saúde (ISCISA)
Avenida Tomás Nduda, 977, Maputo
Fax: +258(21) 496083
EMail: iscisamz@tvcabo.co.mz
Website: http://www.iscisa.ac.mz

Director Geral: Aurélio Amândio Zilhão

Director Adjunto para Area Administrativa: Eugénia Vasco Mabunda

Courses

Biomedical and Laboratory Technology (Biomedical Engineering; Laboratory Techniques); **Clinical Psychology** (Clinical Psychology); **Gynaecology and Obstetrics Nursing** (Gynaecology and Obstetrics); **Hospital Administration and Management** (Health Administration); **Nursing** (Nursing); **Nutrition** (Nutrition); **Occupational Therapy** (Occupational Therapy); **Paediatric Nursing** (Nursing; Paediatrics); **Pathological Anatomy** (Anatomy); **Physical Therapy** (Physical Therapy); **Public Health** (Public Health); **Surgery** (Surgery)

History: Founded 2004.

Degrees and Diplomas: *Licenciatura*

Last Updated: 15/06/12

INSTITUTE OF INTERNATIONAL RELATIONS

Instituto Superior de Relações Internacionais (ISRI)
Rua Damião de Góis, 100, Sommerchield, Maputo
Tel: +258(21) 491233
Fax: +258(21) 493213
EMail: secretaria@isri.academi.imoz.com
Website: http://www.isri.ac.mz

Reitor: Patrício José EMail: patricio@tdm.co.mz

Administrador: Odete da Luz Chirindza
Tel: +258(21) 491-800, Fax: +258(21) 491-506

Academies

Languages and Literature (Literature; Modern Languages) *Division Head*: Cumbana

Centres

Strategic Studies (Development Studies; International Relations)

Departments

Administration and Finance (Administration; Finance; Human Resources; Public Administration); **Communication and Community Relations** (Communication Studies); **Economics and Applied Science** (Economics); **International Relations** (International Relations); **Law and Public Administration** (Law; Public Administration); **Social Sciences and Languages** (Modern Languages; Social Sciences)

History: Founded 1986 to train diplomats and those concerned with international relations, acquired present status 1997.

Academic Year: February to December (February -June; Augustus-December)

Admission Requirements: Secondary school certificate and entrance examination

Main Language(s) of Instruction: Portuguese

Degrees and Diplomas: *Licenciatura*: International Relations; Public Administration; *Mestrado*

Student Services: Academic counselling, Canteen, Handicapped facilities, Language programs

Student Residential Facilities: Yes

Libraries: c. 5,000 vols

Last Updated: 20/06/12

INSTITUTE OF PUBLIC ADMINISTRATION

Instituto Superior de Administração Pública (ISAP)
Avenida Vladeimir Lenine, 1985, Maputo
Tel: +258(21) 417549
Fax: +258(21) 417551
Website: http://www.isap.gov.mz/

Director Geral: Almiro Lobo EMail: almirolobo@hotmail.com

Courses

Public Administration (Administrative Law; Communication Studies; Cultural Studies; Economics; Finance; Government; History; Human Resources; Information Management; Management; Political Sciences; Public Administration)

History: Founded 2005.

Degrees and Diplomas: *Licenciatura*. Also Diploma

Last Updated: 15/06/12

LURIO UNIVERSITY

Universidade Lúrio
Avenida Eduardo Mondlane, 39, Nampula
Tel: +258(26) 218365
EMail: greitor@unilurio.ac.mz
Website: http://www.unilurio.ac.mz

Reitor: Luis Jorge Ferrão

Centres

Computer Science (Computer Science)

Faculties

Agrarian Sciences *(Niassa)* (Agriculture); **Architecture and Physical Planning** *(Nampula)*; **Engineering and Natural Sciences** *(Cabo Delgado)* (Biology; Computer Engineering; Environmental Engineering); **Health Sciences** (Dentistry; Health Sciences; Medicine; Nutrition; Optometry; Pharmacy)

History: Founded 2006.

Main Language(s) of Instruction: Portuguese

Degrees and Diplomas: *Licenciatura*

Last Updated: 20/06/12

MANICA POLYTECHNIC INSTITUTE

Instituto Superior Politécnico de Manica (ISPM)

Campus de Matsinho, Estrada Nacional n°6, desvio nas Antenas
Km 45, Gondola, Manica
Tel: +258(23) 910101
Fax: +258(23) 910043
EMail: info@ispm.ac.mz
Website: http://www.ispm.ac.mz

Director: Rafael Massinga

Courses

Accountancy and Auditing (Accountancy); **Agriculture** (Agricultural Engineering; Forestry; Zoology); **Economics, Management and Tourism** (Economics; Management; Tourism)

Further Information: Also Matsinho Campus

History: Founded 2005.

Degrees and Diplomas: *Licenciatura*

Last Updated: 20/06/12

MOZAMBIQUE INSTITUTE OF ACCOUNTANCY AND AUDITING

Instituto Superior de Contabilidade e Auditoria de Moçambique

Avenida Vlademir Lenine, Maputo
Website: http://www.iscam.ac.mz

Director General: Joao Moreno

Courses

Accountancy (Accountancy)

History: Founded 2005.

Degrees and Diplomas: *Licenciatura*

Last Updated: 22/06/12

PEDAGOGICAL UNIVERSITY

Universidade Pedagógica

BP 3276, Com. Augusto Cardoso 135, Maputo
Tel: +258 (21) 320861
Fax: +258 (21) 322113
EMail: grupsede@zebra.uem.mz
Website: http://www.up.ac.mz/

Reitor: Rogério José Uthui

International Relations: Ana Paula Manso
EMail: apmanso@up.ac.mz

Faculties

Languages (English; French; Modern Languages; Portuguese); **Natural Sciences and Mathematics** (Biology; Chemistry; Mathematics; Natural Sciences; Physics); **Pedagogy** (Educational Sciences; Pedagogy; Psychology; Special Education); **Physical Education and Sports** (Physical Education; Sports); **Social Sciences** (Anthropology; Geography; History; Philosophy; Social Sciences)

Schools

Engineering (Agricultural Engineering; Civil Engineering; Construction Engineering; Design)

History: Founded 1986.

Academic Year: August to June (August-December; January-June)

Admission Requirements: Secondary school certificate or equivalent, and entrance examination

Main Language(s) of Instruction: Portuguese

Degrees and Diplomas: *Licenciatura*: 5 yrs; *Mestrado*; *Doutoramento*. Also post-doctorate

Student Services: Canteen, Health services, Sports facilities

Special Facilities: Natural History Museum

Last Updated: 26/06/12

SCHOOL OF JOURNALISM

Escola Superior de Jornalismo (ESJ)

Avenida Ho Chi Min, 103, Maputo MPM- 001
Tel: +258(21) 302726
Fax: +258(21) 302727
EMail: esj.ac@tdm.co.mz

General-Director: Tomás Jane

Administrative-Director: Moises Ernesto
Tel: +258(21) 305613 EMail: mangumo@hotmail.com

International Relations: Leonel Simila, Lecturer
Tel: +258(21) 299530 EMail: leonelsimila@gmail.com

Programmes

Information Sciences (Information Sciences; Library Science); **Journalism** (Advertising and Publicity; Journalism; Marketing; Public Relations); **Marketing and Public Relations** (Communication Studies; Marketing; Public Relations)

History: Founded 2008.

Governing Bodies: ESJ Board; General-Director; Scientific Board

Main Language(s) of Instruction: Portuguese

International Co-operation: With universities in Brazil, Portugal and South Africa

Accrediting Agencies: Ministry of Education

Degrees and Diplomas: *Licenciatura*; *Mestrado*: Communication Sciences

Student Services: Academic counselling, Foreign student adviser, Language programs, Social counselling, Sports facilities

Libraries: Yes

Academic Staff *2012*	MEN	WOMEN	**TOTAL**
FULL-TIME	18	8	**26**
PART-TIME	23	10	**33**
STAFF WITH DOCTORATE			
FULL-TIME	–	–	**1**
PART-TIME	–	–	**3**
Student Numbers *2012*			
All (Foreign Included)	245	119	**364**

Last Updated: 14/05/12

SCHOOL OF NAUTICAL SCIENCES

Escola Superior de Ciências Náuticas

Caixa postal 637, Avenida 10 de Novembro, 1, Maputo
Tel: +258(21) 320164
Fax: +258(21) 320164
Website: http://www.enautica.ac.mz

Director Geral: Guides Raúl Gote Cossa

Director Adjunto: José Simão

Courses

Electronic and Telecommunications Engineering (Electronic Engineering; Telecommunications Engineering); **Marine Engineering** (Marine Engineering); **Marine Transport** (Marine Transport); **Maritime Law** (Maritime Law)

History: Founded 2004.

Degrees and Diplomas: *Licenciatura*

Last Updated: 15/06/12

SONGO POLYTECHNIC INSTITUTE

Instituto Superior Politécnico de Songo
Songo, Tete

Director: Francisco Vieira

Programmes

Engineering (Civil Engineering; Construction Engineering; Electronic Engineering; Engineering; Mechanical Engineering)

History: Founded 2008.

Degrees and Diplomas: *Licenciatura*

Last Updated: 20/06/12

TETE POLYTECHNIC INSTITUTE

Instituto Superior Politécnico de Tete (ISPT)
Tete, Tete

Director: Bernardo Bene EMail: bernardo.bene@uem.mz

Courses

Technology (Engineering; Technology)

History: Founded 2005.

Degrees and Diplomas: *Licenciatura*

Last Updated: 20/06/12

ZAMBEZE UNIVERSITY

Universidade Zambeze (UNIZAMBEZE)
Rua Alfredo Lawley, 1018, Matacuane, Beira, Sofala
Tel: +258(23) 362487
EMail: reitoria.informacao@unizambeze.ac.mz
Website: http://www.unizambeze.ac.mz

Reitor: Bangy Cassy

Courses

Agricultural Engineering (Agricultural Engineering; Agronomy; Floriculture; Forestry); **Civil Engineering** (Civil Engineering); **Computer Engineering** (Computer Engineering); **Dentistry** (Dentistry); **Economics** (Economics); **Environmental Engineering** (Environmental Engineering; Natural Resources); **Finance and Accountancy** (Accountancy; Finance); **Law** (Law); **Management** (Management); **Mechatronics** (Electronic Engineering; Mechanical Engineering); **Medicine** (Medicine); **Pharmacy** (Pharmacy)

History: Founded 2006.

Degrees and Diplomas: *Licenciatura*; *Mestrado*

Last Updated: 27/06/12

PRIVATE INSTITUTIONS

ALBERTO CHIPANDE INSTITUTE OF SCIENCE AND TECHNOLOGY

Instituto Superior de Ciências e Tecnologia Alberto Chipande
Av. Correia de Brito, n° 1259 - Ponta-Gea, Beira, Sofala
Tel: +258(233) 20794
EMail: isctac@isctac.org
Website: http://www.isctac.org/

Director Geral: Rizuane Mubarak

Schools

Economics (Accountancy; Agricultural Economics; Economics; Human Resources; Management); **Engineering and Technology** (Engineering; Technology); **Health Science** (Health Education; Medicine; Pharmacy); **Juridical Studies** (Law; Private Law; Public Law); **Political Sciences** (International Relations; Political Sciences; Psychology; Sociology)

History: Founded 2009.

Degrees and Diplomas: *Licenciatura*; *Mestrado*

Last Updated: 25/06/12

CATHOLIC UNIVERSITY OF MOZAMBIQUE

Universidade Católica de Moçambique (UCM)
Caixa Postal 821, Rua Marquês de Soveral, 960, Beira, Sofala
Tel: +258(23) 313077
Fax: +258(23) 311520
EMail: reitoria@ucm.ac.mz
Website: http://www.ucm.ac.mz

Reitor: Alberto Ferreira (2006-) EMail: aferreira@ucm.ac.mz

Vice-Reitor: Francisco Ponsi
Tel: +258(23) 311-493, Fax: +258(23) 311-520
EMail: fponsi@ucm.ac.mz

Centres

Distance Education *(CDE)* (Biology; Chemistry; Geography; History; Information Technology; Mathematics; Physical Education; Physics; Portuguese; Public Administration; Sports) *director*: Wisdom Machacha; **Geography** (Environmental Management; Geography; Regional Planning; Town Planning; Urban Studies) *Director*: António dos Anjos Luís

Faculties

Agriculture *(Cuamba)* (Agricultural Business; Agriculture; Animal Husbandry; Botany; Earth Sciences; Environmental Management; Forestry; Harvest Technology; Natural Resources; Plant and Crop Protection; Public Administration; Rural Studies) *Dean*: José Savanguana; **Economics and Management** *(Beira)* (Development Studies; Economics; English; Geography (Human); History; Management; Regional Studies; Sociology) *Dean*: Alfandega Monjoro; **Education and Communication Studies** (Accountancy; Adult Education; Advertising and Publicity; Anthropology; Communication Studies; Economics; Education; Educational Administration; Educational Psychology; Human Resources; Marketing; Public Relations; Social and Community Services) *Dean*: Martins Vilanculos; **Engineering** (Accountancy; Business Administration; Civil Engineering; Engineering; Food Science; Food Technology; Public Administration) *Director*: João Luís Ferrão; **Health Sciences** *(Beira)* (Clinical Psychology; Health Administration; Laboratory Techniques; Medicine; Nursing) *Dean*: Josefo Ferro; **Law** *(Nampula)* (Law) *Dean*: Fernao Magalhaes; **Social Sciences and Political Sciences** *(Nampula)* (Accountancy; Business Administration; Cinema and Television; Communication Studies; Development Studies; Ethics; Human Resources; International Relations; Journalism; Law; Leadership; Marketing; Philosophy; Public Administration; Public Relations; Social Sciences; Sociology); **Tourism and Computer Science** *(Pemba)* (Accountancy; Computer Networks; Economics; Hotel and Restaurant; Hotel Management; Information Management; Information Sciences; Information Technology; Leisure Studies; Management; Software Engineering; Tourism) *Director*: Lino Marques Samuel

History: Founded 1996.

Admission Requirements: Secondary school certificate or equivalent

Main Language(s) of Instruction: Portuguese, English

Degrees and Diplomas: *Licenciatura*: 2 yrs; *Mestrado*: 2 yrs following Bacharelato; *Doutoramento*

Libraries: Yes

Publications: Voz da UCM *(1-2 per annum)*

Academic Staff *2011-2012*: Total: c. 500

Student Numbers *2011-2012*: Total: c. 3,100

Distance students, 4,497.

Last Updated: 24/08/12

DON BOSCO INSTITUTE OF SCIENCE AND MANAGEMENT

Instituto Superior Dom Bosco (ISDB)
Maputo, Maputo
Tel: +25(21) 405631
Fax: +25(21) 405634

Director Geral: Jose Angel Rajoy

Programmes
Agriculture (Agriculture; Animal Husbandry); **Engineering** (Electrical Engineering; Mechanical Engineering; Technology); **Management** (Accountancy; Management; Tourism)
Further Information: Also Distance Education
Degrees and Diplomas: *Licenciatura*
Last Updated: 25/06/12

INDICO UNIVERSITY

Universidade do Indico
Maputo

Reitor: António Saraiva
History: Founded 2008.
Degrees and Diplomas: *Licenciatura*
Last Updated: 03/11/09

INSTITUTE OF COMMUNICATION AND IMAGE STUDIES

Instituto Superior de Comunicação e Imagem (ISCIM)
Avenida Zedequias Manganhela, 267, Maputo
EMail: lider@iscim.ac.mz

Directora: Fernanda Maria Correia Lisboa de Almeida Cavacas

Programmes
Communication and Image Studies (Communication Studies; Visual Arts)
History: Founded 2008.
Degrees and Diplomas: *Licenciatura*
Last Updated: 22/06/12

INSTITUTE OF MANAGEMENT, BUSINESS AND FINANCE

Instituto Superior de Gestão, Comércio e Finanças (ISGECOF)
Avenida Eduardo Mondlane, 245, Maputo
Tel: +258(21) 497891
EMail: isgecof@ymail.com
Director Geral: Julio Gonçalves Cunela

Courses
Business (Business Administration; Business and Commerce); **Finance** (Finance); **Management** (Management)
History: Founded 2009.
Degrees and Diplomas: *Licenciatura*
Last Updated: 25/06/12

INSTITUTE OF SCIENCE AND MANAGEMENT

Instituto Superior de Ciência e Gestão (INSCIG)
Nacala, Nampula

Director: Vasco Lino

Courses
Management (Management); **Science** (Mathematics and Computer Science; Natural Sciences)
History: Founded 2009.
Degrees and Diplomas: *Licenciatura*
Last Updated: 22/06/12

INSTITUTE OF TECHNOLOGY AND MANAGEMENT

Instituto Superior de Tecnologia e Gestão (ISTEG)
Estrada Nacional, 4, Boane-Belo Horizonte, Maputo
Tel: +258 (21) 777160
Fax: +258 (21) 777161
EMail: isteg@isteg.ac.mz
Website: http://www.isteg.ac.mz
Reitor: Samaria Tovela

Programmes
Management (Accountancy; Advertising and Publicity; Banking; Business Administration; Communication Studies; Economics; Finance; Human Resources; Information Management; Law; Management; Marketing; Social Psychology; Tourism); **Technology** (Construction Engineering; Environmental Management; Technology)
History: Founded 2008.
Degrees and Diplomas: *Licenciatura*
Last Updated: 25/06/12

INSTITUTE OF TECHNOLOGY EDUCATION

Instituto Superior de Educação Tecnológica (ISET)
Changalane-Namaacha
Director Geral: Thomas Jensen

Courses
Technology (Technology)
History: Founded 2005.
Degrees and Diplomas: *Licenciatura*
Last Updated: 22/06/12

INSTITUTE OF TRAINING, RESEARCH AND SCIENCE

Instituto Superior de Formação, Investigação e Ciência (ISFIC)
Estrada Nacional, 4, Boane-Belo Horizonte, Maputo

Programmes
Training, Research and Science (Mathematics and Computer Science; Natural Sciences)
History: Founded 2005.
Degrees and Diplomas: *Licenciatura*
Last Updated: 22/06/12

INSTITUTE OF TRANSPORT AND COMMUNICATIONS

Instituto Superior de Transportes e Comunicações (ISUTC)
Caixa Postal 2088, Prolong. da Av. Kim Il Sung (IFT/TDM) - Edifício D1, Maputo
Tel: +258(21) 488795
Fax: +258(21) 488794
EMail: isutc@isutc.transcom.co.mz
Website: http://www.transcom.co.mz/isutc/

Reitor: Fernando Leite (2010-)

Departments
Basic Sciences (Chemistry; Mathematics; Natural Sciences; Physics); **Construction Engineering** (Building Technologies; Civil Engineering; Construction Engineering; Hydraulic Engineering; Surveying and Mapping); **Information Technology** (Computer Engineering; Information Technology; Telecommunications Engineering); **Management and Finance** (Accountancy; Banking; Business Administration; Commercial Law; Computer Science; Economic and Finance Policy; Economics; English; Finance; Human Resources; International Economics; Labour Law; Management; Marketing; Operations Research; Statistics; Taxation); **Mechanical Engineering** (Heating and Refrigeration; Materials Engineering; Mechanical Engineering; Transport Engineering; Transport Management); **Transport Engineering and Logistics** (Transport Engineering; Transport Management)
History: Founded 1999.
International Co-operation: With universities in Cuba and Portugal
Degrees and Diplomas: *Licenciatura*: 4-5 yrs
Last Updated: 25/06/12

JEAN PIAGET UNIVERSITY OF MOZAMBIQUE

Universidade Jean Piaget de Moçambique (UJPM)
Campus Universitário da Beira, Inhamízua, Maputo
Tel: +258(23) 346200
Fax: +258(23) 346201
EMail: mozambique@funiber.org
Website: http://unipiaget.ac.mz

Rector: Rui Cumbana

Programmes

Arts and Humanities (Architecture; Arts and Humanities; Linguistics); **Education** (Education; Primary Education); **Engineering** (Agricultural Engineering; Civil Engineering; Computer Engineering; Engineering; Environmental Engineering; Food Technology; Mechanical Engineering; Telecommunications Engineering); **Health SicIences** (Dentistry; Health Administration; Medicine; Nursing; Pharmacy; Physical Therapy); **Social Sciences** (Accountancy; Administration; Advertising and Publicity; Banking; Business Administration; Economics; Hotel Management; Human Resources; Hygiene; International Relations; Law; Marketing; Political Sciences; Social Sciences; Sociology; Tourism)

History: Founded 2004.

Degrees and Diplomas: *Licenciatura*; *Mestrado*; *Doutoramento*
Last Updated: 28/06/12

MONITOR INSTITUTE

Instituto Superior Monitor (ISM)
Avenida Samora Machel, 202, Maputo
Tel: +258(21) 300447
Fax: +258(21) 323432
EMail: ismonitor@ismonitor.info
Website: http://www.monitor.co.mz

Director Geral: Augusto Duane

Programmes

Accountancy (Accountancy; Finance; Taxation); **Business Administration** (Business Administration; Communication Studies; Hotel Management; Management; Tourism); **Computer Science** (Computer Science); **Economics** (Development Studies; Economics; International Economics); **Environemental Studies** (Environmental Studies); **Human Resources** (Human Resources); **Law** (Law); **Marketing and Public Relations** (Marketing; Public Relations); **Psychology** (Educational Psychology; Psychology)

History: Founded 2008.

Degrees and Diplomas: *Licenciatura*
Last Updated: 27/06/12

MOTHER MARY AFRICA INSTITUTE

Instituto Superior Maria Mãe de África (ISMMA)
Caixa Postal 3661, Avenida Vlademir Lenine, 3621, Maputo
Tel: +258(21) 419772
Fax: +258(21) 419771
EMail: ismma@tropical.co.mz

Director Geral: Altamiro Tenório da Paz

Programmes

Education (Civics; Curriculum; Education; Educational Technology; Pedagogy; Primary Education; Religious Studies; Secondary Education; Teacher Training)

History: Founded 2008.

Degrees and Diplomas: *Licenciatura*
Last Updated: 03/11/09

MOZAMBIQUE INSTITUTE OF SCIENCE AND TECHNOLOGY

Instituto Superior de Ciências e Tecnologia de Moçambique (ISCTEM)
Rua 1394, Zona da Facim 322, Maputo
Tel: +258(21) 312014
Fax: +258(21) 312993
EMail: ibs@isctem.ac.mz; info@isctem.ac.mz
Website: http://www.isctem.ac.mz

Reitor: João Leopoldo da Costa
Tel: +258(21) 312-015 EMail: reitoria@isctem.ac.mz

Administrator: Rumina Fareally EMail: rfareally@isctem.ac.mz

International Relations: Craig Young
Tel: +258(21) 315-521, Fax: +258(21) 315-521
EMail: cyoung@isctem.ac.mz

Schools

Architecture (Architecture; Town Planning); **Business Studies** (Accountancy; Business Administration; Management); **Computer Engineering** (Computer Engineering); **Health Sciences** (Dentistry; Medicine; Pharmacy); **Law** (Law); **Social Sciences** (Public Administration; Social Sciences; Sociology)

History: Founded 1996.

Governing Bodies: Conselho Directivo

Main Language(s) of Instruction: Portuguese

Degrees and Diplomas: *Licenciatura*: Dentistry; Computer Engineering; Management; Accountancy; Law; Architecture; Urban Planning; Public Administration; Pharmacy, 4 yrs; *Mestrado*: Law; Sociology; Development Studies; Public Health, 2 yrs; *Doutoramento*: Law, 4 yrs

Student Services: Academic counselling, Canteen, Health services, Language programs, Social counselling

Special Facilities: Theatre

Libraries: Yes

Academic Staff *2011-2012*	**TOTAL**
FULL-TIME	**160**
PART-TIME	**170**
STAFF WITH DOCTORATE	
FULL-TIME	**5**
PART-TIME	c. **10**
Student Numbers *2011-2012*	
All (Foreign Included)	c. **1,300**
FOREIGN ONLY	**40**

Part-time students, 350. **Evening students**, 890.
Last Updated: 22/06/12

MUSSA BIN BIQUE UNIVERSITY

Universidade Mussa Bin Bique (UMB)
Rua Cidade de Moçambique, 10, Nampula
Tel: +258(26) 215919
Fax: +258(26) 215903

Reitor: Francisco Alar

Vice-Reitor: Hamim Hussen Hassam

Courses

Agriculture (Agriculture); **Management** (Accountancy; Management)

History: Founded 1998.

Degrees and Diplomas: *Licenciatura*
Last Updated: 30/10/09

POLYTECHNIC UNIVERSITY

Universidade Politécnica
Avenida Paulo Samuel Kankhomba, 1011, Maputo
Tel: +258(21) 352700
Fax: +258(21) 352701
EMail: de@apolitecnica.ac.mz
Website: http://www.apolitecnica.ac.mz/

Reitor: Lourenço Joaquim da Costa Rosário

Campuses

Nampula *(ESEUNA)* (Accountancy; Business Administration; Civil Engineering; Development Studies; Information Management; Management); **Tete** *(ISUTE)*

Institutes

Humanities and Technology *(Quelimane)* (Accountancy; Business Administration; Business Computing; Civil Engineering; Communication Studies; Electrical Engineering; Law; Psychology); **Polytechnic** *(IMEP)* (Accountancy; Civil Engineering; Computer

Science; Hotel Management; Management; Primary Education; Secretarial Studies; Tourism)

Schools

Business *(ESAEN)* (Business Administration; Fiscal Law; Human Resources; Marketing; Public Administration); **Management, Science and Technology** *(ESGCT)* (Management; Natural Sciences; Technology)

Further Information: Also Distance Education

History: Founded 1995 as Instituto Superior Politécnico e Universitário. Acquired present status and title 2007.

Governing Bodies: Rector; Heads of Departments

Academic Year: February to December

Admission Requirements: High school certificate and entrance examination

Fees: (US Dollars): Admission Fee, 225; Tuition, 2,400 per annum

Main Language(s) of Instruction: Portuguese

International Co-operation: With universities in Portugal and Brazil

Degrees and Diplomas: *Licenciatura*: Accountancy (CA); Business Administration (AGE); Civil Engineering (EC); Educational Sciences (CE); Law (CJ); Psychology (PS); Secretarial Studies (AD); Social Communications (CC); Tourism (TR), 4 1/2 yrs; *Licenciatura*: Informatic Systems Management (IG), 5 yrs; *Mestrado*; *Doutoramento*

Student Services: Academic counselling, Canteen, Cultural centre, Foreign Studies Centre, Sports facilities

Student Residential Facilities: Dormitory

Libraries: 5 Libraries

Last Updated: 24/08/12

SAINT THOMAS UNIVERSITY OF MOZAMBIQUE

Universidade São Tomás de Moçambique

Avenida Ahmed Sekou Torré, 610, Maputo

Tel: +258(21) 304946

Fax: +258(21) 305054

EMail: ustm@ustm.ac.mz

Website: http://www.ustm.ac.mz/

Reitor: Joseph Wamala

Faculties

Agriculture (Agricultural Economics; Agricultural Engineering; Agriculture; Agronomy; Development Studies; Rural Planning; Rural Studies; Zoology); **Economics and Business Administration** (Accountancy; Business Administration; Economics; Finance; Management); **Information Technology** (Computer Science; Information Technology; Software Engineering); **Philosophy and Arts and Humanities** (Arts and Humanities; Law; Philosophy; Sociology)

History: Founded 2004.

Degrees and Diplomas: *Licenciatura*; *Mestrado*. Also Joint African Master in Comparative Local Development, in collaboration with the Polytechnic of Namibia (Namibia), the University of Trento (Italy), Tshwane University of Technology (South Africa) and the University of Botswana (Botswana)

Last Updated: 28/06/12

SCHOOL OF ECONOMICS AND MANAGEMENT

Escola Superior de Economia e Gestão

Avenida Zedequias Manganhela, 309, Maputo

Tel: +258(21) 327144

Fax: +258(21) 309310

Website: http://www.eseg.ac.mz

Director: Guilande

Courses

Accountancy and Auditing (Accountancy; Commercial Law; English; Finance; Human Resources; International Economics; Law; Marketing; Mathematics; Statistics; Taxation); **Business Administration and Management**; **Civil Engineering** (Civil Engineering); **Economics** (Accountancy; Commercial Law; Economic and Finance Policy; Economic History; Economics; English; Finance; International Economics; Law; Management; Mathematics; Statistics); **Educational Administration**; **Law** (Administrative Law; Civil Law; Constitutional Law; Criminal Law; Criminology; Economic and Finance Policy; Economics; Finance; Fiscal Law; Forensic Medicine and Dentistry; International Law; Labour Law; Law; Political Sciences; Private Law; Public Law); **Tourism** (Accountancy; Communication Studies; Economic and Finance Policy; English; Hotel and Restaurant; Hotel Management; International Economics; Law; Management; Marketing; Mathematics; Statistics; Tourism)

History: Founded 2004.

Degrees and Diplomas: *Licenciatura*

Last Updated: 03/11/09

TECHNICAL UNIVERSITY OF MOZAMBIQUE

Universidade Técnica de Moçambique

Avenida Albert Lithuli, 418/38, Maputo

Tel: +258(21) 302102

Fax: +258(21) 302107

Website: http://www.udm.ac.mz/

Reitor: José Luis de Oliveira Cabaço

Courses

Business Administration and Management (Business Administration; Management); **Energy Engineering** (Energy Engineering; Petroleum and Gas Engineering); **Enviromental Engineering** (Environmental Engineering); **Industrial Engineering** (Industrial Engineering); **Information Technology and Communication Studies** (Computer Engineering; Information Technology; Technology); **Law** (Government; Human Rights; Political Sciences)

History: Founded 2002.

Degrees and Diplomas: *Licenciatura*; *Mestrado*. Master in Human Rights, Democracy and Good Governance in partnership with the Federal University of Para(UFPara) and the Open Society of South Africa (OSISA),

Last Updated: 28/06/12

Myanmar

STRUCTURE OF HIGHER EDUCATION SYSTEM

Description:

Higher education is provided by universities and specialized institutions (teacher training schools and colleges, technical and professional institutes and an Institute for Foreign Languages). They are all state institutions. Most of them are under the control of the Departments of Higher Education (one for lower Myanmar in Yangon and one for upper Myanmar in Mandalay) of the Ministry of Education.They are independent units. Each university has an academic and an administrative board. National policies are established by the Universities' Central Council and the Council of University Academic Bodies which are chaired by the Minister of Education. All universities and colleges are state-financed. A nominal fee is charged for studies.

Stages of studies:

University level first stage: *Bachelor's degree*

The Bachelor (pass degree) is obtained on successful completion of a three-year course (four in law) and the Bachelor (honours) degree after an additional year. The Bachelor's degrees in Engineering, Architecture and Forestry require five to six years' study. In Dentistry, Medicine and Veterinary Sciences studies last for six to six-and-a-half years. In Law, the Bachelor's degree is obtained after two years' study following upon a Bachelor's degree in Arts, Science or Social Science, which is a prerequisite.

University level second stage: *Master's degree, Postgraduate Diploma*

Master's degrees (MA, MSc, MEd, MDSc, MAgrSc, MPhil, etc.) are conferred after two years' study beyond the Bachelor's degree. Postgraduate Diplomas are also offered in some institutions following one or two years' study.

University level third stage: *Doctorate*

A PhD is conferred by certain universities after at least four years' further study and research.

Distance higher education:

Yangon University of Distance Education and Mandalay University of Distance Education provide distance education at e-learning centres located all over the country.

ADMISSION TO HIGHER EDUCATION

Admission to university-level studies:

Name of secondary school credential required: Basic Education Standard Examination (Matriculation)

Other admission requirements: Entrance examination at some universities.

Foreign students admission:

Entry regulations: Foreign students are admitted to Myanmar higher educational institutions only under officially sponsored programmes.

Language requirements: A good knowledge of Burmese is essential.

NATIONAL BODIES

Ministry of Education

Minister: Chan Nyein
Theinbyu Street
Yangon
Tel: +95(1) 286704
Fax: +95(1) 285480
WWW: http://www.myanmar-education.edu.mm/

Data for academic year: 2004-2005

Source: IAU from IBE website, 2003 and MOE website, 2005 (Bodies, 2012)

INSTITUTIONS

PUBLIC INSTITUTIONS

DAGON UNIVERSITY

North Dagon Township, Yangon
Tel: +95(1) 585-001
Fax: +95(1) 585-171

Pro-Rector: U Sann

Programmes

Arts and Humanities (Arts and Humanities); **Mathematics and Computer Science** (Mathematics and Computer Science); **Natural Sciences** (Natural Sciences)

History: Founded 1993.

Academic Year: July to March (July-December; January-March)

Admission Requirements: Secondary school certificate

Main Language(s) of Instruction: Myanmar

INSTITUTE OF DENTAL MEDICINE, YANGON

Thingangyun, Yangon 11071
Tel: +95(1) 571-270
Fax: +95(1) 571-269

Rector: Myo Win

Programmes

Dentistry (Dental Technology; Dentistry; Nursing; Surgery)

History: Founded 1964, acquired present status 1974. A State institution responsible to the Ministry of Health.

Governing Bodies: Academic and administrative boards under the Directorate of Medical Sciences, Ministry of Health

Academic Year: November to September (November-March; April-September)

Admission Requirements: Matriculation (Basic Education High School) and entrance examination

Main Language(s) of Instruction: English

Degrees and Diplomas: *Bachelor's Degree*; *Postgraduate Diploma*; *Master's Degree*. Also Certificate in Dental Nursing 3 yrs following Matriculation

Student Services: Academic counselling, Canteen, Cultural centre, Health services, Social counselling, Sports facilities

Special Facilities: Pathology Museum

Publications: Myanmar Dental Journal *(annually)*

MAGWAY UNIVERSITY

Myinkin Road, Soekawmin Quarter, Magway
Tel: +95(63) 231-92
Fax: +95(63) 233-41
EMail: recmg@dheum-edu.gov.mm

Rector: Htay Maung

History: Founded 1958.

MANDALAY TECHNOLOGICAL UNIVERSITY (MTU)

Patheingyi Township, Mandalay
Tel: +95(2) 887-27 +95(2) 887-56
Fax: +95(2) 887-02
EMail: mtu01@mtu.gov.mm
Website: http://www.most.gov.mm/mtu

Rector: Aung Kyaw Myat Tel: +95(2) 887-12, Fax: +95(2) 887-02

Registrar: Aung Moe Khaing
Tel: +95(2) 887-56, Fax: +95(2) 887-02
EMail: mtu04@mtu.gov.mm

Departments

Architecture (Architecture); **Chemical Engineering** (Chemical Engineering); **Civil Engineering** (Civil Engineering); **Electrical Engineering** (Electrical Engineering); **Electronics** (Electronic Engineering); **Mechanical Engineering** (Mechanical Engineering); **Technology** (Technology)

History: Founded as Institute of Technology 1991. Acquired present status 1993 and title 1998.

Governing Bodies: University Administration Board; University Senat

Academic Year: December to September

Admission Requirements: Candidates must pass the Matriculation Examination

Fees: (Kyats): 48,000 per annum

Main Language(s) of Instruction: English; Myanmar

Accrediting Agencies: National Education Committee

Degrees and Diplomas: *Bachelor's Degree (BE)*: 5 yrs; *Master's Degree (ME; MS)*: a further 2 yrs; *Doctorate (PhD)*: 3 yrs

Student Services: Canteen, Health services, Language programs, Sports facilities

Student Residential Facilities: Yes

Libraries: E. Library and Internet Application Facilities

Last Updated: 28/03/13

MANDALAY UNIVERSITY

University Quarter, Mahar Aungmyay Township, Mandalay
Tel: +95(2) 344-20
Fax: +95(2) 366-29
EMail: drn1@dheum-edu.gov.mm

Pro-Rector: Mya Aye

Programmes

Arts and Humanities (Arts and Humanities); **Oriental Languages, Asian and Oriental Studies** (Asian Studies; Oriental Languages; Oriental Studies); **Philosophy** (Philosophy); **Science** (Mathematics and Computer Science; Natural Sciences)

History: Founded 1958 as separate university. Formerly a college of the University of Rangoon, originated as an intermediate college 1923, and an Agricultural College 1938. Recognized 1964 and Faculties of Medicine and Agriculture detached as separate institutions. Financed by the Central Government and responsible to the Ministry of Education.

Academic Year: July to March (July-December; January-March)

Admission Requirements: Secondary school certificate

Main Language(s) of Instruction: Myanmar

Degrees and Diplomas: *Bachelor's Degree*: Arts; Science, 4 yrs; *Bachelor's Degree (Honours)*: Arts; Science, 5 yrs; *Master's Degree*: Arts or Science, at least 1 yr following Bachelor (Honours); *Doctorate*

Libraries: c. 175,000 vols

MAWLAMYING UNIVERSITY

Taung Waing Road, Mawlamying
Tel: +95(32) 211-80
EMail: recmlm@dhelm-edu.gov.mm

Rector: San Tint

Faculties

Botany (Botany); **Chemistry** (Chemistry); **English** (English); **Geography** (Geography); **Geology** (Geology); **History** (History); **Marine Science** (Marine Science and Oceanography); **Mathematics** (Mathematics); **Myanmar Studies** (Cultural Studies); **Oriental Studies** (Asian Studies; Oriental Languages; Oriental Studies); **Philosophy** (Philosophy); **Physics** (Physics); **Zoology** (Zoology)

Research Centres

Aquaculture (Aquaculture; Marine Biology); **Zoology** (Zoology)

History: Founded 1953 as Mawlamein University, acquired present status and title 1986.

Admission Requirements: Secondary school certificate, List 'A'

Main Language(s) of Instruction: Myanmar, English

Degrees and Diplomas: *Bachelor's Degree*: 4 yrs; *Bachelor's Degree (Honours)*: 1 further yr; *Master's Degree*: Philosophy, a further 2-3 yrs

Student Residential Facilities: For c. 3,420 students

Special Facilities: Geological and Zoological Museums. Botanical Garden

Libraries: c. 78,000 vols (36,000 in Myanmar, c. 42,000 in English)

MONYWA UNIVERSITY (MYA)

Thanlar New Extension, North of Kyaukhar Road, Monywa
Tel: +95(71) 211-65
Fax: +95(71) 227-47
EMail: recmya@dheum-edu.mm

Rector: Maung Htoo

Programmes

Arts and Humanities (Arts and Humanities); **Natural Sciences, Mathematics and Computer Science** (Mathematics and Computer Science; Natural Sciences)

History: Founded 1996.

Degrees and Diplomas: *Bachelor's Degree*; *Master's Degree*

MYITKYINA UNIVERSITY (MKN)

Sitapu Quarter, Myitkyina, Kachin State
Tel: +95(74) 223-53
Fax: +95(74) 224-02

Rector: U Soe

Departments

Arts and Humanities (Arts and Humanities); **Natural Sciences, Mathematics and Computer Science** (Mathematics and Computer Science; Natural Sciences)

History: Founded 1963. Acquired present status 1997.

NATIONAL UNIVERSITY OF ARTS AND CULTURE, YANGON (YIE)

Yangon 11431
Tel: +95(1) 590-250
Fax: +95(1) 590-251
EMail: ygnuoc@mptmail.net.mm

Rector: U Tin Soe (1999-)

Head of the Department of Administration and Finance: Myat Thura Tel: +95(1) 590-264

International Relations: Nanda Hmun
EMail: nandahmun21683@gmail.com

Departments

Academic (Arts and Humanities; Computer Networks; Educational Sciences; Geography; Geography (Human); Literature; Mathematics) *Pro-Rector*: Nanda Hmun; **Cinematography** (Acting; Cinema and Television; Film) *Head*: Ko Ko Lay; **Dramatic Arts** (Acting; Dance; Performing Arts; Theatre) *Head*: Thein Thein Khin; **Music** (Conducting; Music Education; Musical Instruments; Performing Arts; Singing) *Head*: Aung Kein; **Painting** (Graphic Design; Painting and Drawing) *Head*: Tin Maung Lwin; **Sculpture** (Sculpture) *Head*: Myint San

Faculties

Arts (Art History; Art Management; Design; Fine Arts; Visual Arts) *Pro-Rector*: Nanda Hmun

History: Founded 1993 as University of Culture. Acquired present title 2008.

Governing Bodies: Board of Academic and Administration

Academic Year: November to September (November-March; May-September)

Admission Requirements: High school certificate with 'A' level

Fees: (Kyats): 1,200 per annum

Main Language(s) of Instruction: English

International Co-operation: Hasebe Asean Scholarship Foundation, Japan

Accrediting Agencies: Ministry of Culture; Cultural University Council

Degrees and Diplomas: *Diploma*: Computer Graphics (Dip: CA), 1 yr; *Bachelor's Degree*: Music; Dramatic Arts; Painting; Sculpture (BA), 3 yrs; *Bachelor's Degree (Honours)*: Music; Dramatic Arts; Painting; Sculpture (BA (Hons)), 3 yrs; *Postgraduate Diploma*: Musicology (P.G: D.M), 1 yr

Student Services: Academic counselling, Canteen, Cultural centre, Employment services, Foreign student adviser, Foreign Studies Centre, Health services, Language programs, Social counselling, Sports facilities

Student Residential Facilities: None

Special Facilities: Movie studio; Museum; Art Gallery

Libraries: Yes
Last Updated: 09/09/08

PATHEIN UNIVERSITY

Ayeyarwady Division, Pathein
Tel: +95(42) 24953
Fax: +95(42) 24118
EMail: recpt@dhelm-edu.gov.mm

Pro-Rector: U Hla Tint

Director Administration and Finance: U Tin Myint

Departments

Botany (Biochemistry; Biology; Botany; Cell Biology; Ecology; Floriculture; Horticulture; Microbiology; Plant and Crop Protection) *Head*: Aye Pwa; **Chemistry** (Analytical Chemistry; Chemistry; Organic Chemistry) *Head*: Khin Ohn Kyi; **English** (Applied Linguistics; English; Grammar; Literature; Phonetics) *Head*: Daw Than Than Nyunt; **Geography** (Earth Sciences; Geography) *Head*: Saw Paiklay; **Geology** (Crystallography; Earth Sciences; Geological Engineering; Geology; Mineralogy) *Head*: Daw Kyu Kyu Win; **History** (History) *Head*: U Myint Saw; **Law** (Criminal Law; International Law; Labour Law; Law) *Head*: Daw Marlar Nay Win; **Marine Sciences** (Aquaculture; Coastal Studies; Marine Science and Oceanography) *Head*: U Khin Maung Cho; **Mathematics** (Applied Mathematics; Mathematics; Statistics) *Head*: U Myint Ohn; **Myanmar Language** (Applied Linguistics; Linguistics; Native Language) *Head*: Daw Ahmar Ni; **Oriental Studies** (Cultural Studies; Literature; Oriental Languages; Oriental Studies; Philosophy) *Head*: Daw Yu Yu Saw; **Philosophy** (Aesthetics; Logic; Philosophy) *Head*: Daw Nwe New Win; **Physics** (Nuclear Physics; Physics) *Head*: U Thet Tun Aung; **Psychology** (Behavioural Sciences; Cognitive Sciences; Psychology) *Head*: Daw Myint Myint Swe; **Zoology** (Fishery; Genetics; Zoology) *Head*: Daw Myint Myint Kyi

History: Founded 1958 as college. Acquired present status 1996.

Governing Bodies: University Senate

Main Language(s) of Instruction: Myanmar, English

Accrediting Agencies: Government of the Union of Myanmar

Degrees and Diplomas: *Bachelor's Degree*: 3 yrs; *Bachelor's Degree (Honours)*: 4 yrs; *Master's Degree*: 6 yrs

Student Services: Academic counselling, Canteen, Health services, Language programs, Social counselling, Sports facilities

Student Residential Facilities: Yes

Libraries: Pathein University Library
Last Updated: 31/07/08

SITTWAY UNIVERSITY

Sittway, Rakhine State

Rector: Sein Moe Moe Fax: +95(1) 246-704
EMail: hivdog@undp.org

Programmes

Arts and Humanities (Arts and Humanities); **Natural Sciences, Mathematics and Computer Science** (Mathematics and Computer Science; Natural Sciences)

History: Founded 1996.

TAUNGGYI UNIVERSITY (TU)

Between Hopone and Naung Motor road, Taunggyi, 06011 Shan State
Tel: +95(81) 22649
Fax: +95(81) 21160
EMail: rector@tgu.dheu.moe.mm; rectg@dheum-edu.gov.mm

Rector: Maung Kyaw (1999-)

Director General: Thein Myint (1997-)
Tel: +95(02) 39315, Fax: +95 2000206
EMail: drtmyint@dheum-edu.gov.mm

International Relations: Thein Myint, Director General
EMail: drtmyint@dheum-edu.gov.mm

Faculties

Humanities (Arts and Humanities); **Law** (Law); **Life Science** (Biological and Life Sciences); **Science** (Forest Biology; Forestry; Mathematics and Computer Science; Natural Sciences); **Social Sciences** (Social Sciences)

History: Founded 1961. Became Taunggyi College 1986. Acquired present title 1992.

Governing Bodies: Administrative Board

Admission Requirements: Certificate of matriculation examination

Main Language(s) of Instruction: Myanmar & English

International Co-operation: None

Degrees and Diplomas: *Diploma*: English Language Teaching (ELT), 2 yrs; *Bachelor's Degree*: Chemistry; Physics; Mathematics; Zoology; Botany; Geology; Environmental Studies; Biotechnology (B.Sc.); Law (LL.B); Myanmar; English; History; Geography; Oriental Studies; Philosophy; Psychology; South East Asia and Pacific Studies (B.A.), 3 yrs; *Master's Degree*: Chemistry; Physics; Mathematics; Zoology; Botany; Geology; Environmental Studies; Biotechnology (M.Sc.); *Master's Degree*: Law (LL.M.), 3 yrs; *Master's Degree*: Myanmar; English; History; Geography; Oriental Studies; Philosophy; Psychology; South East Asia and Pacific Studies (M.A.), 3. Also Master of Research (M.Sc., a further 1 yr) in Chemistry; Physics; Mathematics; Zoology; Botany; Geology; Environmental Studies; Biotechnology; Myanmar; English; History; Geography; Oriental Studies; Philosophy; Psychology; South East Asia and Pacific Studies

Student Services: Academic counselling, Canteen, Health services, Language programs, Social counselling, Sports facilities

Student Residential Facilities: None

Special Facilities: Computer Training Centre; Multimedia Lecture Theatre; Language Lab; e-Resource Centre; e-Education Learning Centre; Museum; Internet Access

Libraries: University Library, c. 33,000 vols; E-Library software offering e-catalogue

Publications: Research Papers of Academic Departments *(annually)*

Press or Publishing House: Universities Press

UNIVERSITY OF COMPUTER STUDIES, MANDALAY (UCSM)

Mandalay

Departments

Chemistry (Chemistry); **Computational Mathematics** (Mathematics and Computer Science); **English** (English); **Hardware Technology** (Computer Engineering; Computer Science); **Information Science** (Information Sciences); **Myanmar Studies** (South and Southeast Asian Languages; South Asian Studies; Southeast Asian Studies); **Physics** (Physics); **Software Technology** (Software Engineering)

History: Founded 1997.

Main Language(s) of Instruction: English

Degrees and Diplomas: *Diploma*: Computer Studies; Computer Maintenance; *Bachelor's Degree*: Computer Science; Computer Technology; *Bachelor's Degree (Honours)*: Computer Science; Computer Technology; *Postgraduate Diploma*: Computer Science; *Master's Degree*: Computer Science; Computer Technology; Information Science; Applied Science; *Doctorate*: Information Technology; Hardware Technology

Last Updated: 20/03/08

UNIVERSITY OF COMPUTER STUDIES, YANGON

Thamaing Campus, Hlaing Township, Yangon
Tel: +95(1) 610-655
Fax: +95(1) 610-633
EMail: ucsy23@most.gov.mm; ucsystaff@mptmail.net.mm
Website: http://www.ucsy.edu.mm/

Departments

Application (Computer Science); **Computational Mathematics** (Mathematics and Computer Science); **English** (Communication Studies; English); **Hardware Technology** (Computer Engineering; Computer Science); **Information Science** (Information Sciences); **Myanmar Language** (Cultural Studies; Native Language; South and Southeast Asian Languages; South Asian Studies; Southeast Asian Studies); **Physics** (Physics); **Research and Development**; **Software Technology** (Software Engineering)

History: Founded 1971 as University Computer Center of the University of Rangoon. Acquired present status and title 1998.

Academic Year: June to March

Admission Requirements: Secondary school certificate and entrance examination

Main Language(s) of Instruction: English

Degrees and Diplomas: *Bachelor's Degree*: Computer Science; Computer Technology, 3 yrs; *Bachelor's Degree (Honours)*: Computer Science; Computer Technology, 4 yrs; *Master's Degree*: Computer Science; Computer Technology; Information Science; Applied Science, a further 2-3 yrs; *Doctorate*: Information Technology; Hardware Technology

Special Facilities: Computer rooms with 300 PCs

Libraries: ICST Library, c. 11,000 vols

Last Updated: 27/09/11

UNIVERSITY OF FORESTRY

Nay Pyi Taw, Yezin
Tel: +95(67) 405-009
Fax: +95(67) 405-012

Rector: Myint Oo (2010-)

Departments

Forest Products (Forest Products; Forestry); **Forestry** (Environmental Studies; Forest Biology; Forest Economics; Forest Management; Forestry; Parks and Recreation; Wildlife); **Support Subjects** (Biological and Life Sciences; English; Oriental Languages)

History: Founded 1992 as Institute of Forestry, acquired present title ans status 2002.

Governing Bodies: Administrative Affairs Committee; Academic Affairs Committee

Academic Year: November to September (November-April; May-September)

Admission Requirements: Secondary school certificate or equivalent

Main Language(s) of Instruction: English

Degrees and Diplomas: *Diploma*: Forestry, I yr; *Bachelor's Degree*: Science, Forestry, 5 yrs; *Postgraduate Diploma*: Forestry, Science, I yr following first degree; *Master's Degree*: Science, Forestry, A further 3 yrs

Student Residential Facilities: For c. 300 students

Special Facilities: Museum (Forestry, Forest Products)

Libraries: Institute Library, c. 10,000 vols

Last Updated: 31/10/12

UNIVERSITY OF MEDICINE 1, YANGON

PO 11131, 245 Myoma Road, Lanmadow, Yangon
Tel: +95(1) 226-086
Website: http://www.um1ygn.edu.mm

Rector: Myo Myint

Departments

Biomedical Sciences (Botany; Chemistry; Mathematics; Physics; Statistics; Zoology); **Family and Communication Medicine**

(Medicine); **Haematology**; **Human Anatomy, Physiology and Biochemistry** (Anatomy; Biochemistry; Physiology); **Languages** (English; Native Language); **Medicine** (Medicine); **Microbiology** (Microbiology); **Pathology** (Pathology); **Personal Professional Development** (Behavioural Sciences); **Pharmacology** (Pharmacology)

Further Information: Also Teaching Hospitals. Courses for foreign students. 13 Study Abroad programmes

History: Founded 1923. Formerly part of the University of Rangoon.

Admission Requirements: Secondary school certificate and entrance examination

Main Language(s) of Instruction: English, Myanmar

Degrees and Diplomas: *Bachelor's Degree*; *Postgraduate Diploma*; *Master's Degree*

Special Facilities: Pathological Museum; Microbiological Museum; Parasitological Museum

Libraries: Total, c. 52,000 vols

Publications: Scientific Paper Reports

Last Updated: 27/09/11

UNIVERSITY OF MEDICINE 2, YANGON

Khaemarthi Road, North Okkalapa, Yangon 11031
Tel: +95(1) 690-127
Fax: +95(1) 690-265
EMail: iomnoka@mptmail.net.mm

Rector: Tha Hla Shwe (12 years)
Tel: +95(1) 699-851 EMail: thahs@iomnoka.com.mm

Pro-Rector: Aung Gyi
Tel: +95(1) 699-143 EMail: aung@iomnoka.com.mm

International Relations: Aye Aye Nu, Head of Administration and Finance Tel: +95(1) 699-589

Departments

Anatomy (Anatomy; Biological and Life Sciences; Embryology and Reproduction Biology; Genetics; Histology); **Biochemistry** (Biochemistry; Biological and Life Sciences; Chemistry; Molecular Biology; Nutrition); **Botany** (Biological and Life Sciences; Botany; Genetics; Plant Pathology); **Chemistry** (Chemistry; Inorganic Chemistry; Natural Sciences; Organic Chemistry); **English** (Arts and Humanities; English); **Forensic Medicine** (Ethics; Forensic Medicine and Dentistry; Pathology; Toxicology); **Medicine** (Cardiology; Gastroenterology; Medicine; Nephrology; Neurology; Psychiatry and Mental Health; Urology); **Microbiology** (Biological and Life Sciences; Medical Parasitology; Microbiology; Virology); **Myanmar Studies** (Cultural Studies); **Obstetrics and Gynaecology** (Gynaecology and Obstetrics); **Orthopaedics** (Orthopaedics); **Paediatrics** (Paediatrics); **Pathology** (Haematology; Immunology; Pathology); **Pharmacology** (Biological and Life Sciences; Pharmacology; Pharmacy); **Physics** (Applied Mathematics; Natural Sciences; Physics); **Physiology** (Embryology and Reproduction Biology; Endocrinology; Haematology; Nutrition; Physiology); **Preventive and Social Medicine** (Epidemiology; Public Administration; Public Health; Social and Preventive Medicine); **Surgery** (Anaesthesiology; Ophthalmology; Otorhinolaryngology; Radiology; Surgery); **Zoology** (Anatomy; Biological and Life Sciences; Ecology; Entomology; Medical Parasitology; Physiology; Zoology)

Further Information: Also Teaching Hospitals

History: Founded 1962. Formerly part of the University of Rangoon.

Governing Bodies: Administrative Board, comprising 12 members; Academic Board, comprising 25 members

Academic Year: November to July

Admission Requirements: Secondary school certificate or General Certificate of Education with Ordinary ('O') level. Direct entrance to second year for General Certificate of Education holders with Advanced ('A') level, or equivalent foreign qualification, and entrance examination (IMAT)

Main Language(s) of Instruction: Myanmar, English

Degrees and Diplomas: *Bachelor's Degree*: Medicine (MB); Surgery (BS), 6 yrs; *Postgraduate Diploma*: Medicine (Dip.Med.Sc), 1 yr; *Master's Degree*: Medicine (M.Med.Sc), 2 yrs; *Doctorate*: Anatomy (PhD); Biochemistry (PhD); Microbiology (PhD); Pathology (PhD); Pharmacology (PhD); Physiology (PhD); Public Health (PhD), 3-5 yrs; *Doctorate*: Medicine (Dr.Med.Sc), 3 yrs

Student Services: Academic counselling, Canteen, Health services, Social counselling, Sports facilities

Student Residential Facilities: For c. 410 women students and c. 410 men students. Also for c. 50 interns

Libraries: Institute Library, c. 24,000 vols

Publications: Annual Magazine *(annually)*; Medical Education Report *(quarterly)*

UNIVERSITY OF MEDICINE, MANDALAY

30th Street, Between 73rd & 74th Street, Chan Aye Thar Zan Township, Mandalay
Tel: +95(2) 366-34
EMail: IMMMDYREC@mptmail.net.mm

Rector: Win Myat Aye

Departments

Anaesthesiology (Anaesthesiology); **Anatomy** (Anatomy); **Biochemistry** (Biochemistry); **Biology** (Biology); **Chemistry** (Chemistry; Physiology); **English** (English); **Forensic Medicine** (Forensic Medicine and Dentistry); **Medicine** (Medicine); **Microbiology** (Microbiology); **Myanmar** (Native Language; South and Southeast Asian Languages; South Asian Studies; Southeast Asian Studies); **Obstetrics and Gynaecology** (Gynaecology and Obstetrics); **Orthopaedic and Traumatology** (Orthopaedics; Surgery); **Paediatrics** (Paediatrics); **Pathology** (Pathology); **Pharmacology** (Pharmacology); **Physics and Mathematics** (Mathematics; Physics); **Physiology** (Physiology); **Preventive and Social Medicine** (Medicine; Social and Preventive Medicine); **Surgery** (Surgery)

History: Founded 1954 as branch faculty, became faculty of University of Mandalay 1958 and acquired present title and status 1964. A State institution.

Academic Year: September to August (September-December; January-April; May-August)

Admission Requirements: Secondary school certificate

Main Language(s) of Instruction: Myanmar, English

Degrees and Diplomas: *Bachelor's Degree (MBBS)*: 6 1/2 yrs; *Postgraduate Diploma*; *Master's Degree*: a further 2 yrs; *Doctorate*

Student Residential Facilities: Yes

Libraries: c. 18,000 vols

Last Updated: 27/09/11

UNIVERSITY OF VETERINARY SCIENCE, YEZIN (UVS)

Yezin, Pyinmana, 05282 Mandalay
Tel: 95(2) 671-596

Rector: Min Soe

Programmes

Animal Husbandry and Fishery (Animal Husbandry; Fishery); **Veterinary Science** (Veterinary Science)

History: Founded 1957 as Veterinary College of the University of Rangoon. Acquired present status and title 1999.

Admission Requirements: Basic Education High School Certificate ('A') level

Main Language(s) of Instruction: English, Myanmar

Accrediting Agencies: Ministry of Livestock and Fisheries

Degrees and Diplomas: *Bachelor's Degree*: Animal Husbandry; Veterinary Science, 5 yrs; *Master's Degree*: Animal Husbandry; Veterinary Science (M.Phil, M.V.Sc; M.Sc), 3 yrs

Student Services: Academic counselling, Canteen, Cultural centre, Employment services, Foreign student adviser, Foreign Studies Centre, Handicapped facilities, Health services, Language programs, Nursery care, Social counselling, Sports facilities

Student Residential Facilities: Yes

UNIVERSITY OF YANGON (YU)

University Avenue Road, Kamayut, Yangon
Tel: +95(1) 514-908
Fax: +95(1) 510-721
EMail: uylibrary@gmail.com; recyu@dhelm-edu.gov.mm

Pro-Rector: Ko Ko Kyaw Soe EMail: uylibrary@gmail.com

Departments
Botany (Botany); **Chemistry** (Chemistry); **English** (English); **Geology** (Geology); **History** (History); **Industrial Chemistry**; **Information Technology**; **International Relations** (International Relations); **Law** (Law); **Mathematics** (Mathematics); **Myanmar Studies** (Cultural Studies; Native Language); **Physics** (Geology; Physics); **Zoology** (Zoology)

Further Information: Also Multidisciplinary Research Laboratory

History: Founded 1878 as Rangoon College incorporating Government College, Rangoon, and Judson College, both established in the late 19th century and formerly affiliated to the University of Calcutta. Closed during the Japanese occupation of Burma and reopened as University of Rangoon 1946. Reorganized and acquired current title and status 1964.

Governing Bodies: Administrative and Academic Board

Academic Year: July to March (July-December; January-March)

Admission Requirements: Secondary school certificate

Main Language(s) of Instruction: Myanmar

Degrees and Diplomas: *Bachelor's Degree*; *Bachelor's Degree (Honours)*; *Postgraduate Diploma*; *Master's Degree*: Arts; Law; Science; *Doctorate*: Arts; Law; Science (Ph.D)

Student Residential Facilities: Limited accommodation in male and female hostels

Libraries: Main Library and Institute Libraries
Last Updated: 20/03/08

WORKERS' COLLEGE, YANGON

Botahtaung PO, 273 Konthe Lan, Yangon
Tel: +95(1) 292-825

Pro-Rector: Soe Ko Ko Kyaw

Departments
Botany (Botany); **Chemistry** (Chemistry); **English** (English); **Geography** (Geography); **History** (History); **Mathematics** (Mathematics); **Myanmar** (Cultural Studies; Native Language); **Philosophy** (Philosophy); **Physics** (Physics); **Psychology** (Psychology); **Zoology** (Zoology)

History: Founded 1964. Formerly University for Adult Education founded 1947. Acquired current title 1974.

Degrees and Diplomas: *Bachelor's Degree*

YADANABON UNIVERSITY (YDP)

near Taungthaman Village and Htantaw Village, Amarapura, Mandalay
Tel: +95(2) 548-43
Fax: +95(2) 538-95
EMail: recydp@dheum-edu.gov.mm

Rector: U Win Maung

Faculties
Arts (Arts and Humanities); **Science** (Mathematics and Computer Science; Natural Sciences)

History: Created in 1977 as Yadanapon College. Acquired current title and status 2003.

Degrees and Diplomas: *Bachelor's Degree*: Arts; Science, 3 yrs; *Bachelor's Degree (Honours)*: Arts; Science, 4 yrs; *Master's Degree*: Arts; Science, a further 2 yrs
Last Updated: 27/10/09

YANGON INSTITUTE OF ECONOMICS (YECO)

Yangon 11041
Tel: +95(1) 536-761
Fax: +95(1) 534-376
EMail: iey@mptmail.net.mm

Rector: Kan Zaw Tel: +95(1) 585-068

Departments
Applied Economics (Agricultural Economics; Economics; Public Administration; Transport Economics) *Head*: Htau Htay Lwin; **Commerce** (Accountancy; Banking; Business Administration; Business and Commerce; Data Processing; Finance; Human Resources) *Head*: Yee Yee Than; **Economics** (Economics; Institutional Administration; Public Administration; Social Sciences) *Head*: Yee Aye; **English** (Cultural Studies; English) *Head*: Yee Yee Maw; **Geography** (Geography) *Head*: Cho Win Kyaw; **Management Studies** (Business Administration; Human Resources; Industrial Management; Management; Marketing) *Head*: Nu Nu Yin; **Mathematics** (Applied Mathematics; Mathematics) *Head*: Soe Soe Hlaing; **Myanmar Studies** (Asian Studies; Cultural Studies) *Head*: San San New; **Statistics** (Demography and Population; Mathematics and Computer Science; Social Sciences; Statistics; Systems Analysis) *Head*: Lay Kyi

History: Founded 1964. Formerly part of the University of Yangon. Under the jurisdiction of the Ministry of Education.

Academic Year: December to September (December-March; June-September)

Admission Requirements: Matriculation Certificate & Grading

Fees: (Kyats): 8,000 (undergraduate)-15,000 (postgraduate)

Main Language(s) of Instruction: Myanmar, English

International Co-operation: With universities in China, Japan, Germany, Malaysia

Accrediting Agencies: Department of Higher Education, Ministry of Education (Lower Myanmar)

Degrees and Diplomas: *Diploma*: Economics (DES); Management and Administration (DMA); Statistics, 2 yrs part-time; *Bachelor's Degree*: Accountancy; Business Administration; Commerce; Public Administration; Statistics (B.Econ), 3 yrs; *Bachelor's Degree*: Economics; *Master's Degree*: Business Administration (M.B.A); Commerce (M.Com); Economics, Statistics (M. Econ); Public Administration (MPA), a further 2 yrs; *Doctorate (PhD)*

Student Services: Academic counselling, Canteen, Health services, Social counselling, Sports facilities

Student Residential Facilities: Yes

Special Facilities: Language laboratories. E-Resource Centre; IT Learning Centre; Computer Training Centre

Libraries: c. 80,000 vols
Last Updated: 01/08/08

YANGON INSTITUTE OF EDUCATION (YIOE)

Pyay Road, University PO, Kamayut Township, Yangon
Tel: +95(1) 504-771
Fax: +95(1) 504-773
EMail: rectoryioe@mptmail.net.mm

Rector: Khin Zaw (1998-)

Pro-Rector: Htoo Htoo Aung

Departments
Biology (Biology); **Chemistry** (Chemistry); **Economics** (Economics); **Educational Psychology** (Educational Psychology; Educational Testing and Evaluation); **Educational Theory** (Educational Administration; Philosophy of Education); **English** (English; Linguistics; Teacher Training); **Geography** (Geography); **History** (History); **Mathematics** (Mathematics); **Methodology** (Educational Technology; Pedagogy); **Myanmar** (Linguistics; Native Language); **Physical Education and School Health** (Health Education; Physical Education); **Physics** (Physics)

History: Founded 1931. The Teacher's Training College (TTC) Yangon, a constituent college of former University of Yangon, became Yangon Institute of Education 1964. Financed by the Government of the Union of Myanmar and responsible to the Ministry of Education, the Universities Central Council and the Council of Universities Academic Bodies.

Governing Bodies: Academic Body; Administrative Body

Academic Year: June to March (June-September; December-March)

Admission Requirements: Matriculation

Fees: (Kyats): 7,500 per annum

Main Language(s) of Instruction: Myanmar, English

Degrees and Diplomas: *Bachelor of Education*: Education (BEd), 4 yrs; *Master's Degree*: Education (MEd), a further 2 yrs; *Doctorate*: Education (PhD), a further 5 yrs. Postgraduate Diploma in Teaching-PGDT; Postgraduate Diploma in Multimedia Arts (Education);-PGDMA (Education), Diploma in English Language Teaching Methodology -Dip (ELTM); Master of Arts (Teaching of English as a foreign Language) -MA(TEFL) under Human Resource Development (HRD) Programme

Student Services: Academic counselling, Canteen, Cultural centre, Health services, Language programs, Social counselling, Sports facilities

Student Residential Facilities: Yes

Special Facilities: Computer Training Centre, e-Education Resource Centre, e-Education Learning Centre, Language Laboratory

Libraries: Institute Library

Press or Publishing House: University Press

YANGON TECHNOLOGICAL UNIVERSITY (YTU)

Insein Township, Yangon 11011
Tel: +95(1) 651-717 +95(1) 663-357
EMail: yit.yangon@pemail.net
Website: http://www.most.gov.mm/ytu/

Departments

Architecture (Architecture; Architecture and Planning; Regional Planning; Structural Architecture; Town Planning); **Chemical Engineering** (Chemical Engineering); **Civil Engineering** (Civil Engineering; Environmental Engineering; Hydraulic Engineering; Structural Architecture); **Electric Power Engineering** (Electrical Engineering; Energy Engineering; Power Engineering); **Electronic Engineering and Information Technology** (Electronic Engineering; Information Technology); **Engineering Chemistry** (Chemical Engineering; Chemistry; Engineering); **Engineering Mathematics** (Applied Mathematics; Mathematics); **Engineering Physics** (Applied Physics; Electronic Engineering); **English** (English); **Geological Engineering** (Geological Engineering; Geology; Geophysics; Metallurgical Engineering; Mineralogy; Mining Engineering; Petroleum and Gas Engineering; Surveying and Mapping); **Mechanical Engineering** (Mechanical Engineering); **Metallurgical Engineering** (Materials Engineering; Metallurgical Engineering); **Mining Engineering** (Environmental Engineering; Geological Engineering; Mining Engineering); **Petroleum Engineering** (Petroleum and Gas Engineering); **Textile Engineering** (Textile Technology)

History: Founded 1924 as department of the former University of Rangoon. Became faculty 1947. Detached as independent institute following reorganization of university education and renamed Yangon Institute of Technology 1964. Acquired present status and title 1998. Financed by the Central Government and responsible to the Ministry of Education.

Governing Bodies: Senate; Administrative Board

Academic Year: October to July (October-March; May-July)

Admission Requirements: Secondary school certificate

Main Language(s) of Instruction: Myanmar, English

Degrees and Diplomas: *Bachelor's Degree*: 6 yrs; *Postgraduate Diploma*: 1 yr; *Master's Degree*: 3 yrs; *Doctorate*

Student Residential Facilities: Hostels for c. 2,500 students

Libraries: c. 48,000 vols.

Last Updated: 27/09/11

YANGON UNIVERSITY OF DISTANCE EDUCATION (YUDE)

47(A) Inya Road, Kamaryut Township, Yangon 11041
Tel: +95(1) 525-138
Fax: +95(1) 512-865
EMail: udey@mptmail.net.mm

Rector: Mya Oo (2001-) Tel: +95(1) 536-555

Pro-Rector: Mg Mg Aye Tel: +95(1) 535-137

International Relations: Ngwe Soe Tel: +95(1) 534-546

Programmes

Distance Education (Economics; Law)

History: Founded 1975. Acquired present status 1992.

Academic Year: December to October

Admission Requirements: Basic Education Standard (Matriculation)

Fees: (Kyats): 8,000 per annum

Main Language(s) of Instruction: English

Accrediting Agencies: Department of Higher Education, Ministry of Education

Degrees and Diplomas: *Bachelor's Degree*: Arts; Science (B.A; B.Sc), 3 yrs; *Bachelor's Degree*: Law (LLB), 4 yrs. Also Diploma in Information Technology

Student Services: Academic counselling, Canteen

Special Facilities: Broadcasting Studio

Libraries: Yes

YANGON UNIVERSITY OF FOREIGN LANGUAGES

119-131 University Avenue, Kamaryut Township, Yangon
Tel: +95(1) 531-713

Programmes

Foreign Languages (Chinese; French; German; Japanese; Korean; Modern Languages; Russian; Thai Languages)

History: Founded 1964 as Institute of Foreign Languages. Acquired present status 1996.

YEZIN UNIVERSITY OF AGRICULTURE, PYINMANA

University Campus, Yezin, Pyinmana, 05282 Mandalay
Tel: +95(2) 671-098
Fax: +95(2) 671-437
EMail: dg.fd@mptmail.net.mm

Director: Tin Aye Aye Naing
Tel: +95(1) 664-457, Fax: +95(1) 664-336

Administrative Officer: Soe Soe Thein

Departments

Agricultural Botany (Agriculture; Botany); **Agricultural Chemistry** (Agriculture; Applied Chemistry); **Agricultural Engineering** (Agricultural Engineering); **Agronomy** (Agronomy); **Animal Science** (Animal Husbandry; Zoology); **Economics** (Agricultural Economics); **English** (English); **Entomology** (Entomology); **Horticulture** (Horticulture); **Mathematics** (Mathematics); **Myanmar Studies** (Cultural Studies); **Physics** (Physics); **Plant Pathology** (Plant Pathology)

History: Founded 1924 as Agricultural College and Research Institute of Mandalay. Reorganized 1937 as college of former University of Rangoon. Became Faculty of University of Rangoon 1946 and Faculty of University of Mandalay on its establishment in 1958. Detached as independent institute following reorganization of university education 1964. Transferred from the Ministry of Education to the Ministry of Agriculture 1993. Acquired present title and status 1998.

Governing Bodies: Academic Board; Administrative Board

Academic Year: November to September (November-March; May-September)

Admission Requirements: Secondary school certificate or equivalent

Main Language(s) of Instruction: Myanmar, English

Degrees and Diplomas: *Bachelor's Degree*: Agriculture (BAgrSc), 5 yrs; *Master's Degree*: Agricultural Science (MAgrSc)

Student Residential Facilities: Yes

Libraries: c. 23,000 vols

Namibia

STRUCTURE OF HIGHER EDUCATION SYSTEM

Description:

Higher education is provided by universities, a polytechnic, colleges of education, colleges of agriculture, and vocational education training centres.

Stages of studies:

University level first stage: *Bachelor's degree*
Bachelor's degrees are awarded after four years' study in most fields (5 1/2 in Engineering)

University level second stage: *Master's degree*
Master's degrees are conferred after two years' full-time study following upon the Bachelor's degree by course or research work in an approved topic.

University level third stage: *Doctorate*
Doctorates are conferred after three years' full-time research work. Students must present a dissertation.

ADMISSION TO HIGHER EDUCATION

Admission to university-level studies:

Name of secondary school credential required: Namibia Senior Secondary Certificate
Entrance exam requirements: Entrance examination or interview
Other admission requirements: English is compulsory.

Foreign students admission:

Entrance exam requirements: Foreign students must hold a similar qualification to the one required of Namibian students. Applications should be made to the university Registrar.

Language requirements: Students whose language is not English may be required to pass an approved test in English.

NATIONAL BODIES

Ministry of Education

Minister: Abraham Iyambo
Government Office Park (Luther Street)
Private Bag 13186
Windhoek
Tel: +264(61) 293 3358
Fax: +264(61) 293 3368
EMail: info@moe.gov.na
WWW: http://www.moe.gov.na/

National Council for Higher Education

Executive Director: Mocks Shikalepo Shivute
PO Box 90890
Klein
Windhoek
Tel: +264(61) 307 012
Fax: +264(61) 307 014
EMail: info@nche.org.na
WWW: http://www.nche.org.na/

Role of national body: The NCHE has as objects to promote the establishment of a co-ordinated higher education system, the access of students to higher education institutions, and quality assurance in higher education; as well as to advise on the allocation of funds to public higher education institutions.

Data for academic year: 2012-2013
Source: IAU from NCHE and World Data on Education 2010/2011, UNESCO-IBE, 2012

INSTITUTIONS

PUBLIC INSTITUTIONS

POLYTECHNIC OF NAMIBIA

13 Storch Street, Private Bag 13388,
Windhoek
Tel: +264(61) 207-9111
Fax: +264(61) 207-2100
EMail: registrar@polytechnic.edu.na
Website: http://www.polytechnic.edu.na

Rector: Tjama Tjivikua (1995-)
Tel: +264(61) 207-2001/2, Fax: +264(61) 207-2100
EMail: rector@polytechnic.edu.na

Registrar: Corneels Jafta
Tel: +264(61) 207-2008, Fax: +264(61) 207-2113

Schools
Economics and Finance (Accountancy; Economics; Finance; Marketing); **Engineering** (Architecture; Civil Engineering; Electronic Engineering; Engineering; Mechanical Engineering; Mining Engineering; Power Engineering; Technology Education; Vocational Education); **Humanities** (Communication Studies; Criminal Law; English; Journalism; Media Studies; Modern Languages; Police Studies); **Information Technology** (Business Computing; Computer Engineering; Computer Networks; Information Technology; Software Engineering); **Management** (Business Administration; Criminal Law; Human Resources; Management; Public Administration; Technology); **Natural Resources and Tourism** (Agriculture; Ecology; Tourism)

History: Founded 1985 as Technikon Namibia. Reorganized 1994, incorporating the Technikon Namibia and College for Out-of-School Training. Acquired present status 1994.

Governing Bodies: Council

Academic Year: February to November (February-June; July-November)

Admission Requirements: Senior certificate

Fees: (Namibian Dollars): 1st year: 13,200-23,650; 2nd year: 13,000-26,300; National Diploma: 11,300-26,000 per annum; Bachelor : 13,500-27,500 per annum; Master: 25,500-75,000 per annum

Main Language(s) of Instruction: English

Accrediting Agencies: Higher Educational Council of Southern Africa (HEQC); Foundation for International Business and Accreditation (FIBAA); Namibia Qualification Authority (NQA)

Degrees and Diplomas: *Bachelor's Degree*; *Master's Degree*: 2 yrs. Also National Higher Certificate, 2 yrs

Student Services: Academic counselling, Canteen, Cultural centre, Employment services, Health services, Social counselling, Sports facilities

Student Residential Facilities: For 400 students

Libraries: Central Library

Publications: Echoes *(quarterly)*
Last Updated: 06/04/12

UNIVERSITY OF NAMIBIA (UNAM)

Private Bag 13303, 340 Mandume
Ndemufayo Avenue, Pioneerspark,
Windhoek
Tel: +264(61) 206-3111
Fax: +264(61) 206-3866
Website: http://www.unam.na

Vice-Chancellor: Lazarus Hangula (2003-)
Tel: +264(61) 206-3937 +264(61) 206-3933,
Fax: +264(61) 206-3320 EMail: lhangula@unam.na

Registrar: Alois Fledersbacher

International Relations: Kenneth Kamwi Matengu
Tel: +264(61) 206-3944 EMail: kmatengu@unam.na

Centres
External Studies; **Human Rights and Documentation** (Human Rights); **Justice Training** (Law); **Language** (Modern Languages); **Multidisciplinary Research and Consultancy**; **Public Service Training** *(CPST)* (Public Administration)

Colleges
Agriculture *(Ongongo)* (Agriculture) *Principal*: M.M. Mushabati

Faculties
Agriculture and Natural Resources *(Neudamm)* (Agricultural Economics; Agriculture; Animal Husbandry; Aquaculture; Crop Production; Fishery; Food Science; Food Technology); **Agriculture and Natural Resources** (Agriculture; Crop Production; Food Science; Food Technology; Natural Resources); **Economics and Management Sciences** (Accountancy; Administration; Business Administration; Business and Commerce; Economics; Management; Public Administration; Taxation); **Education** (Adult Education; Curriculum; Education; Educational Administration; Educational Psychology; Mathematics Education; Physical Education; Science Education; Special Education); **Engineering and Information Technology** (Electrical Engineering; Engineering; Industrial Engineering; Information Technology; Mechanical Engineering; Metallurgical Engineering; Mining Engineering; Telecommunications Engineering); **Health Sciences** (Anaesthesiology; Community Health; Gynaecology and Obstetrics; Health Sciences; Medicine; Midwifery; Nursing; Psychiatry and Mental Health; Radiology; Surgery); **Humanities and Social Sciences** (Arts and Humanities; Christian Religious Studies; Clinical Psychology; Environmental Studies; Geography; History; Media Studies; Performing Arts; Social Sciences; Social Work; Sociology; Theology; Visual Arts); **Law** (Commercial Law; Justice Administration; Law; Public Law); **Science** (Biology; Chemistry; Engineering; Mathematics; Natural Sciences; Physics; Statistics)

Institutes
Ecumenical *(Namibia)* (Religion)

Laboratories
Spatial Analysis

Research Centres
Marine and Coastal Resource *(Sam Nujoma Henties Bay)* (Coastal Studies; Marine Science and Oceanography)

Research Units

Oral Tradition

History: Founded 1992 to provide a University responsive to the needs, culture and values of Namibia through highest quality education and research for students who may benefit from them, regardless of race, colour, gender, ethnic origin, religion, creed, social and economic status or physical condition.

Governing Bodies: University Council; Senate

Academic Year: January to November

Admission Requirements: International General Certificate of Secondary Education, with 5 subjects passed normally in not more than 3 examination sittings, and with a minimum of 25 points on the UNAM evaluation scale. English IGCSE (English as First, or Second, Language) compulsory. Entrance examination and/or interview

Fees: (Namibian Dollars): Registration, c. 215; Tuition fees, 3,250 per annum

Main Language(s) of Instruction: English

Accrediting Agencies: Ministry of Education

Degrees and Diplomas: *Bachelor's Degree*: Accountancy; Adult Education; Business Administration; Education; Science (BSc); Science (Population and Development), 4-6 yrs; *Bachelor's Degree*: Administration; Arts (BA); Arts (Library Science and Archiving); Arts (Media Studies); Arts (Social Work); Arts (Theology); Arts (Tourism); Commerce; Economics; Natural Resources, 4 yrs; *Bachelor's Degree*: Agriculture, 4 yrs; *Bachelor's Degree*: Law; *Bachelor's Degree*: Science (Engineering), 5 yrs; *Master's Degree*: 1-2 yrs following Bachelor; *Doctorate*: 2-3 yrs following Master

Student Residential Facilities: Yes (4 hostels)

Libraries: Central Library, 95,694 vols; 11,978 UNIN books and documents; 270 periodical subscriptions

Last Updated: 06/07/12

PRIVATE INSTITUTION

INTERNATIONAL UNIVERSITY OF MANAGEMENT

PO Box 14005, Windhoek Campus, 59 Banhof Street, Bachbrecht
Tel: +264(61) 245-150
Fax: +264(61) 248-112
EMail: ium@ium.edu.na
Website: http://www.ium.edu.na

Vice-Chancellor: V. Namwandi (2010-)

Pro-Vice Chancellor Academic Affairs and Research: Fred Opali

Faculties

HIV and AIDS (Health Administration; Health Education; Health Sciences); **Information Technology** (Business Computing; Computer Science; Information Technology); **Small Business and Entrepreneurial Studies**; **Strategic Management**; **Tourism and Hospitality** (Hotel Management; Tourism)

Further Information: Branches in Swakopmund, Ongwediva and Walvis-Bay

History: Founded 1993 as Institute of Higher Education (IHE). Acquired present status and title 2002.

Fees: (Namibian Dollars): 13,529.75-16,257.78 per annum depending on programmes

International Co-operation: With universities in the UK, Malaysia and Malawi

Accrediting Agencies: Namibia Qualifications Authority

Degrees and Diplomas: *Bachelor's Degree*; *Postgraduate Diploma*; *Master's Degree*. Also Higher Diplomas and Higher Certificates

Last Updated: 24/08/12

Nepal

STRUCTURE OF HIGHER EDUCATION SYSTEM

Description:

Higher education is provided by both public and private universities and colleges. The Ministry of Education is the authority responsible for policy formulation at national level. The budget allocated for development is disbursed to the universities by the Ministry of Education and the budget for the operation of the universities of the public sector is allocated through the University Grants Commission. Each university has a University Council, an Academic Council, an Executive Council and a University Service Commission. Universities are autonomous.

Stages of studies:

University level first stage: *Bachelor's degree*

Courses leading to the Bachelor's degree last between three and four years.

University level second stage: *Master's degree*

The Master's degree may be taken after a further two years' study.

University level third stage: *Doctor of Philosophy*

A Doctor of Philosophy degree may be taken after a further three years' study following upon the Master's degree.

Distance higher education:

The creation of an Open University is planned.

ADMISSION TO HIGHER EDUCATION

Admission to university-level studies:

Name of secondary school credential required: Higher Secondary Certificate

For entry to: Bachelor studies

Alternatives to credentials: Proficiency Certificate (two years' training offered by universities to students entering with a School Leaving Certificate or an Uttar Madhyama Certificate)

Entrance exam requirements: There is an entrance examination (Prabeshika Parikshya Ra Prabesh Parikshya) to be admitted to Tribhuvan University

Foreign students admission:

Entrance exam requirements: Students must have qualifications equivalent to the Higher secondary school leaving certificate.

Entry regulations: Foreign students must hold a visa.

Language requirements: Students must be proficient in English, Nepali and Sanskrit.

RECOGNITION OF STUDIES

Quality assurance system:

The institutions responsible for quality assurance are : UGC (though its Quality Assurance and Accreditation Council); higher education institutions; professional councils/societies.

NATIONAL BODIES

Ministry of Education

Minister: Gangalal Tuladhar
Singhadurbar
Kathmandu

Tel: +977(1) 441 2804
Fax: +977(1) 442 3252
EMail: infomoe@moe.gov.np
WWW: http://www.moe.gov.np/
Role of national body: To develop and implement policies regarding higher education; to decide and manage the directions about the rules and regulations of higher education; to coordinate higher education; to manage financial supports from the government to universities; to coordinate with donors on supporting the development of higher education; to evaluate the educational system in comparison with international standards; to prepare long term and short term plans for higher education.

University Grants Commission
Chairman: Ganesh Man Gurung
Sanothimi, Bhaktapur
P.O. Box: 10796
Kathmandu
Tel: +977 663 8548
Fax: +977 663 8552
EMail: ugc@ugcnepal.edu.np
WWW: http://www.ugcnepal.edu.np/
Role of national body: Responsible for allocation and disbursement of grants to the universities, regulating their activities and formulating policies and programmes for the establishment of new universities.

Data for academic year: 2010-2011
Source: IAU from Tribhuvan University, 2001, updated from documentation, 2010. Bodies updated 2012.

INSTITUTIONS

B.P. KOIRALA INSTITUTE OF HEALTH SCIENCES (BPKIHS)

PO Box 7053, Dharan
Tel: +977(25) 525555
Fax: +977(25) 520251
EMail: bpkihs@bpkihs.edu
Website: http://www.bpkihs.edu/

Vice-Chancellor: Purna Chandra Karmacharya
Tel: +977(25) 520802 EMail: vc@bpkihs.edu

Colleges
Dental Surgery (Dentistry; Forensic Medicine and Dentistry; Oral Pathology; Orthodontics; Periodontics); **Nursing**

Faculties
Medicine (Anaesthesiology; Anatomy; Biochemistry; Community Health; Dermatology; Forensic Medicine and Dentistry; Gynaecology and Obstetrics; Medicine; Microbiology; Ophthalmology; Orthopaedics; Otorhinolaryngology; Paediatrics; Pathology; Pharmacology; Physiology; Psychiatry and Mental Health; Radiology; Surgery)

Schools
Public Health (Public Health)

Degrees and Diplomas: *Bachelor's Degree*: Nursing; *Master's Degree*. Also MBBS, BDS and postgraduate degree MD/MS

KATHMANDU UNIVERSITY
Kathmandu Vishwavidalaya (KU)

PO Box 6250, Dhulikhel, Kabhre
Tel: +977(11) 61511 +977(11) 61399
Fax: +977(11) 61443
EMail: info@ku.edu.np
Website: http://www.ku.edu.np

Vice-Chancellor: Suresh Raj Sharma (1991-)
Tel: +977(11) 61390 EMail: vc@ku.edu.np

Registrar: Bhadra Man Tuladhar EMail: registrar@ku.edu.np

Schools
Arts (Arts and Humanities; Design; Fine Arts; Human Resources; Mass Communication; Modern Languages; Music; Natural Resources) *Dean*: Mahesh Banskota; **Education** (Curriculum; Education; Pedagogy) *Dean*: Man Prasad Wagley; **Engineering** (Computer Engineering; Computer Science; Electrical and Electronic Engineering; Engineering; Mechanical Engineering) *Dean*: Bhola Thapa; **Management** *(Lalitpur)* (Finance; Management; Marketing) *Dean*: K.C. Subas; **Medical Sciences** (Health Sciences; Medical Auxiliaries; Nursing; Orthopaedics) *Dean*: Narendra Bahadur. Rana; **Science** (Chemistry; Environmental Studies; Mathematics; Natural Sciences; Pharmacy; Physics) *Dean*: Panna Thapa

Further Information: Also Affiliated Colleges

History: Founded 1991.

Governing Bodies: Senate; Board of Trustees

Academic Year: August to June

Admission Requirements: 12-year secondary studies with minimum score of 50% for undergraduate level admission. 16 years for graduate level admission

Fees: (Nepalese Rupees): Tuition, undergraduate, 375,000-445,000 for Engineering and Science. For SAARC students 11/2 times; Foreign students, double

Main Language(s) of Instruction: English

International Co-operation: With 70 universities in Austria, Australia, Bangladesh, Canada, China, Finland, Germany, Netherlands, Hungary, India, Japan, Korea, Lithuania, Norway, Philippines, Russia, Sri Lanka, Switzerland, Thailand, United Kingdom and USA

Degrees and Diplomas: *Bachelor's Degree*: Management, Science, Engineering, Arts, Medicine, 4 yrs; *Master's Degree*: Pharmacy; Environmental Science, Science, Engineering,

Medicine, Management, 2 yrs; *Master of Philosophy*: Education, Physics, Chemistry, Mathematics, 1 1/2-2 yrs; *Doctor of Philosophy*: Education, Science, Engineering, Human and Natural Resources. Also Certificate in Health Sciences 3 yrs and Postgradutae Diploma in Education 1 yr

Student Services: Academic counselling, Canteen, Foreign student adviser, Foreign Studies Centre, Health services, Sports facilities

Student Residential Facilities: Yes

Libraries: 45,000 vols; 130 journals and newsletters; 1,200 CD Roms; 200 video cassettes; 75 audio cassettes

Publications: Business Vision *(biannually)*; Essence *(annually)*; Journal of Education; Kathmandu University Medical Journal; Nepalese Journal of Management; Prelude; Spectrum

Last Updated: 15/09/08

MAHENDRA SANSKRIT UNIVERSITY

Mahendra Sanskrit Vishwavidalaya (MSU)

Kathmandu 5003
Tel: +977(1) 221510 (Kathmandu) +977(82) 29019 (Dang)
Fax: +977(1) 221510 (Kathmandu) +977(82) 29019 (Dang)
Website: http://www.msu.edu.np

Vice-Chancellor: Purna Chandra Dhungel Tel: +977(82) 29019

Departments

Ayurveda Sahitya (Ayurveda); **Darshna, Buddhist Philosophy and Tantra** (Asian Religious Studies; Philosophy); **Dernashast**; **Economics** (Economics); **English** (English); **Hindi and Maithali** (Indic Languages); **Itihasa Purana**; **Karmakanda**; **Mathematics** (Mathematics); **Nepali**; **Nyaya (Logic)**; **Political Science** (Political Sciences); **Purva Mamamsa**; **Veda** (Asian Religious Studies); **Vedanta** (Asian Religious Studies); **Vyakarana**; **Yoga**

Further Information: The University has 13 affiliated campuses situated in different parts of the country

History: Founded 1986.

Governing Bodies: University Council

Academic Year: July to May

Admission Requirements: Secondary school certificate

Main Language(s) of Instruction: Sanskrit, Nepali, English

Degrees and Diplomas: *Bachelor's Degree*: 3 yrs; *Master's Degree*: 2 yrs; *Doctor of Philosophy (PhD)*: 2 yrs. Also Diploma in Sanskrit for foreign students

Publications: Maryada, In Sanskrit and Nepali; Ritambhara, Research Journal in Sanskrit, Nepali and English

POKHARA UNIVERSITY

Pokhara Vishwovidhyalaya

PO Box 427, Pokhara, Gandaki
Tel: +977(61) 560639
Fax: +977(61) 560392
EMail: info@pu.edu.np
Website: http://www.pu.edu.np

Chief Executive Officer: Keshar J. Baral
EMail: vice-chancellor@pu.edu.np

Registrar: Om Prakash Sharma EMail: registrar@pu.edu.np

Faculties

Science and Technology (Natural Sciences; Technology)

Schools

Business Administration (Business Administration); **Development and Social Engineering** (Demography and Population; Development Studies; Gender Studies); **Engineering** (Civil Engineering; Electrical and Electronic Engineering; Engineering); **Health and Allied Sciences** (Health Sciences; Laboratory Techniques; Medical Technology; Nursing; Pharmacy; Public Health)

History: Founded 1997.

Governing Bodies: University Council

Admission Requirements: Undergraduate studies: Secondary school certificate. Postgraduate studies: Bachelor certificate.

Main Language(s) of Instruction: English

International Co-operation: With universities in Japan, Korea, U.S.A., India, Norway, Thailand, Nepal.

Degrees and Diplomas: *Bachelor's Degree*; *Master's Degree*; *Master of Philosophy*; *Doctor of Philosophy*. Also Postgraduate Diplomas

Student Services: Academic counselling, Canteen, Employment services, Health services, Social counselling, Sports facilities

Student Residential Facilities: None

Libraries: Yes

Publications: Journal of Pharmaceutical and Biomedical Sciences *(annually)*; PACE *(annually)*

Last Updated: 05/11/10

PURBANCHAL UNIVERSITY

Purbanchal Vishwavidalaya

Biratnagar, Morang Koshi
Tel: +977(21) 21204
Fax: +977(21) 21204
Website: http://purbuniv.edu.np/

Vice-Chancellor: Toran B. Karki Tel: +977(21) 22165

Registrar: Krishna P. Shrama

Colleges

Social Work

Faculties

Arts (Anthropology; Arts and Humanities; Demography and Population; Development Studies; Gender Studies; Interior Design; Journalism; Mass Communication; Media Studies; Peace and Disarmament; Social Work; Sociology); **Education** (Education); **Law**; **Management** (Business and Commerce; Fashion Design; Hotel Management; Management; Public Administration; Tourism) *Dean*: Durganand Chaudhary; **Medical and Allied Sciences**; **Science and Technology** (Agricultural Management; Agriculture; Animal Husbandry; Architecture; Biochemistry; Biological and Life Sciences; Biotechnology; Civil Engineering; Computer Science; Engineering; Engineering Management; Food Technology; Information Technology; Natural Sciences; Technology; Veterinary Science) *Dean*: Pradeep Raj Pradhan

History: Founded 1995.

Governing Bodies: Academic Council

Academic Year: July to June

Admission Requirements: 12th year senior or intermediate examination or equivalent

Fees: (Nepalese Rupees): Registration, 800; tuition, 6,000-36,000

Main Language(s) of Instruction: English, Nepalese

Accrediting Agencies: University Grants Commission

Degrees and Diplomas: *Bachelor's Degree*: Architecture; Veterinary Science & Animal Husbandry; Law, 5 yrs; *Bachelor's Degree*: Business Administration; Hospitality & Catering Management; Pharmacy; Nursing; Information Technology; Computer Engineering; Civil Engineering; Electronic & Communication Engineering; Biomedical Engineering; Geomatic & Land Resources Management; Agriculture; Biotechnology; Biochemistry; Food Technology; Dairy Technology, 4 yrs; *Bachelor's Degree*: Commercial Studies; Travel & Tourism Studies; Hotel Management; Fashion Design; Computer Applications; Public Health; Education; Media Technology; Journalism & Mass Communication; Liberal Arts & Science; Interior Design; Social Work, 3 yrs; *Bachelor's Degree*: Homeopathic Medicine & Surgery; Medicine & Surgery (BHMS; MBBS), 5 1/2 yrs; *Master's Degree*: Business Administration; Tourism Studies; Public Administration; Hotel & Hospitality Management; Nursing; Education; Law; Computer Applications; Life Sciences; Meat Technology; Dairy Technology; Environment & Resource Management; Information System Engineering; Engineering Management; Urban Design & Conservation; Engineering (Earthquake); Agricultural Business Management; Sociology & Anthropology; Population Management & Rural Development; Mass Communication & Journalism; Rural Development Planning & Gender Studies; Regional Development Planning & Management; Development Communication; Social Work; Development Studies, a further 2 yrs; *Master's Degree*: Human Rights; Conflict and International Humanitarian Law, a further 1 yr. Also Executive Master of Business Administration; Postgraduate Diploma: Computer Applications;

Peace & Conflict Journalism; Psycho-Social Intervention; Conflict Management & Peace Building; Rural Economics; Development & Planning Studies, 1 year

Student Services: Academic counselling, Canteen, Employment services, Foreign student adviser, Social counselling

Publications: Business Horizon; Expressions; Purbanchal University Bulletin *(monthly)*

TRIBHUVAN UNIVERSITY

Tribhuvan Vishwavidalaya (TU)

Central Administrative Building, PO Box. 8212, Kirtipur, Kathmandu, Bagmati

Tel: +977(1) 4330842

Fax: +977(1) 4331964

Website: http://www.tribhuvan-university.edu.np

Vice-Chancellor: Hira Bahadur Maharjan
Tel: +977(1) 4330433 EMail: vcoffice@tribhuvan-university.edu.np

Registrar: Geeta Bhakta Joshi Tel: +977(1) 4330436

International Relations: Mukunda Gajurel, Executive Director, Centre for International Relations
Tel: +977(1)4 330840, Fax: +977(1) 4332500
EMail: tucir@ntc.net.np

Faculties

Education (Education; Educational Technology; English; Indic Languages; Social Studies; Vocational Education); **Humanities and Social Sciences** (Anthropology; Arts and Humanities; Cultural Studies; Dance; Demography and Population; Economics; English; Fine Arts; Geography; Hindi; History; Home Economics; Indic Languages; Journalism; Linguistics; Mathematics; Military Science; Music; Peace and Disarmament; Philosophy; Political Sciences; Psychology; Rural Planning; Sanskrit; Social Sciences; Social Work; Sociology; Statistics; Urdu; Women's Studies); **Law** *(Kathmandu)* (Law); **Management** (Business and Commerce; Hotel Management; Management; Public Administration; Tourism)

Institutes

Agriculture and Animal Science *(Rampur, Chitwan)* (Agriculture; Animal Husbandry; Horticulture; Veterinary Science); **Engineering** *(Pulchowk, Lalitpur)* (Architecture; Civil Engineering; Construction Engineering; Electrical and Electronic Engineering; Engineering; Environmental Engineering; Heating and Refrigeration; Mechanical Engineering; Town Planning); **Forestry** *(Pokhara, Gandaki Zone)* (Forest Biology; Forest Management; Forest Products; Forestry; Soil Conservation; Water Management; Wildlife); **Medicine** *(Maharajgunj, Kathmandu)* (Medicine; Nursing; Ophthalmology; Paediatrics; Pathology; Pharmacy; Psychiatry and Mental Health; Radiology; Surgery); **Science and Technology** (Biology; Botany; Chemistry; Computer Science; Environmental Studies; Food Technology; Geology; Mathematics; Meteorology; Microbiology; Natural Sciences; Physics; Statistics; Technology; Zoology)

Research Centres

Applied Science and Technology *(RECAST)* (Natural Sciences; Technology); **Economic Development and Administration** *(CEDA)* (Administration; Economics); **Educational Innovation and Development** *(CERID)* (Development Studies; Educational Research); **Nepalese and Asian Studies** *(CNAS)* (Asian Studies; Cultural Studies)

Further Information: Also T.U. Teaching Hospitals. Kirtipur Health Centre. Veterinary Teaching Hospital. Zero Energy House Laboratory

History: Founded 1958 as a teaching and affiliated University with a National Institute of Higher Education. Reorganized 1971 and 1993. An autonomous Institution financed by the State.

Governing Bodies: T.U. Council

Academic Year: July to July

Admission Requirements: Secondary school certificate and entrance examination (Prabeshika Parikshya Ra Prabesh Parikshya)

Main Language(s) of Instruction: English, Nepali

Degrees and Diplomas: *Bachelor's Degree*: 3-4-51/2 yrs; *Master's Degree*: a further 1-3 yrs; *Doctor of Philosophy (PhD)*: a further 3 yrs

Student Services: Canteen, Handicapped facilities, Health services, Nursery care, Sports facilities

Student Residential Facilities: Yes

Special Facilities: Natural History Museum. IOM-Health Learning Material Centre

Libraries: Central Library, c. 260,000 vols, 18,000 microforms

Publications: T.U. Journal

Press or Publishing House: T.U. Press

Last Updated: 27/02/08

Netherlands (The)

STRUCTURE OF HIGHER EDUCATION SYSTEM

Description:

The Netherlands higher education system is a binary system, composed of Wetenschappelijk Onderwijs (WO which is more research-oriented and traditionally offered by universities) and Hoger Beroepsonderwijs (HBO - professional higher education, traditionally offered by hogescholen). WO programmes provide education and research in a wide range of disciplines: language and culture, behaviour and society, economics, law, medical and health sciences, natural sciences, engineering and agriculture. In addition, there is the Open Universiteit (OU - Open University) which offers fully recognized university degree programmes through distance education. Since September 2002, the higher education system in the Netherlands has been organized around a three-cycle degree system consisting of Bachelor, Master and PhD degrees. At the same time, the ECTS system (European Credit Transfer System) was implemented as a means to quantify all higher education study programmes.

Stages of studies:

University level first stage:

The focus of degree programmes (research-oriented, WO or the Applied Arts and Sciences, HBO) determines both the number of ECTS credits required to complete the programme and the degree which is awarded. A WO Bachelor's programme requires the completion of 180 credits (3 years) and graduates obtain the degree Bachelor of Arts or Bachelor of Science (BA/BSc), depending on the discipline. The WO Bachelor's programme provides a thorough introduction to the major discipline and primarily prepares students for admission to graduate education. A Bachelor's thesis is usually required. An HBO Bachelor's programme requires the completion of 240 credits (4 years) and graduates obtain a degree indicating the field of study. The HBO titles in use before the higher education system was restructured (bc., ing.) may still be used. A major component of every HBO programme is the stage (internship), typically offered in the third year, as well as a scriptie or major paper in the last year.

University level second stage:

A WO Master's programme requires the completion of 60, 90 or 120 credits (1, 1.5 or 2 years). In engineering, agriculture, maths and the natural sciences, 120 credits are always required. A Master's thesis is a major component of the programme and graduates obtain the degree of Master of Arts or Master of Science (MA/MSc). The WO Master's programme requires the completion of 60 to 120 credits and graduates obtain a degree indicating the field of study. An HBO Master's programme requires the completion of 60, 90 or 120 credits (1, 1.5 or 2 years), and graduates obtain a degree indicating the field of study (for example: Master of Social Work).

University level third stage: *Doctoraat*

The Dutch Doctoraat is obtained through the 'Promotie'. It is a research degree which entitles the holder to the title of Doctor (dr.), the highest university degree in the Netherlands. After the Master's degree, it can be obtained in two ways: 1. by serving as 'Assistent in Opleiding' (AIO) or 'Onderzoeker in Opleiding' (OIO), i.e. assistant researchers. The former also does some teaching. Candidates are required to carry out the necessary research and to write and publicly defend a doctoral dissertation over a period of four years. They are paid a small salary which increases every year. Competition for these positions is fierce. 2. By researching and writing a doctoral dissertation under the supervision of a full professor. The dissertation must be defended in public. University level third stage programmes in medical professions require a total of 360 credits (Dentistry, Medicine, Veterinary Medicine) to complete.

ADMISSION TO HIGHER EDUCATION

Admission to university-level studies:

Name of secondary school credential required: HAVO Diploma (Hoger Algemeen Vormend Onderwijs)

For entry to: HBO Bachelor's programmes

Name of secondary school credential required: MBO Diploma

For entry to: HBO Bachelor's programmes

Entrance exam requirements: Potential students older than 21 years of age who do not possess one of the qualifications mentioned above can qualify for access to higher education on the basis of an entrance examination and assessment.

Numerus clausus/restrictions: Numerus clausus for specific Bachelor's programmes are determined by the Ministry of Education and vary from year to year. A numerus clausus still applies for programmes in fields such as medicine; dentistry; pharmacy; and veterinary medicine.

Other admission requirements: For access to many WO Bachelor's programmes, pupils are required to have completed a specific subject cluster at the secondary level, providing sufficient preparation for the higher education programme in question. For admission to programmes in medicine for example the Science and Health cluster is required.

Foreign students admission:

Definition of foreign student: For the purpose of evaluation: a student admitted to an institution of higher education on the basis of a foreign diploma, whether he has Dutch nationality or not. For the purpose of statistics, scholarships: any student who does not hold a Dutch passport.

Entrance exam requirements: Foreign students in the Netherlands must have reached in their home country a level of education considered at least equivalent to that required for entry into the proposed programme. In addition, certain programmes require sufficient preparation in subjects at the secondary level.

Entry regulations: Every foreign student needs a residence permit. To be eligible for this permit one must: hold a valid passport, be registered in a full-time course of study, have enough money to cover study and living expenses, have medical insurance, have enough money to pay for a return ticket. Nationals of some countries may apply and obtain a residence permit after their arrival in the Netherlands; others must obtain an authorization of temporary residence (MVV) from the Netherlands embassy or consulate of their country. Non EU students need a visa.

Language requirements: A language test is usually required. Most universities organize Dutch language courses.

RECOGNITION OF STUDIES

Quality assurance system:

A guaranteed standard of higher education is maintained through a national system of legal regulation and quality assurance. The Ministry of Education, Culture and Science is responsible for legislation pertaining to education. The agriculture and public health ministries play an important role in monitoring the content of study programmes in their respective fields. Since 2002, responsibility for accreditation lies with the Accreditation Organization of the Netherlands and Flanders (NVAO). According to the section of the Dutch Higher Education Act dealing with the accreditation of higher education (2002), all degree programmes offered by research universities and universities of professional education must be evaluated according to established criteria, and programmes that meet those criteria will be accredited: i.e. recognized for a period of six years. Only accredited programmes are eligible for government funding, and students can receive financial aid and graduate with a recognized degree only when enrolled in, or after having completed, an accredited degree programme. Accredited programmes are listed in the Central Register of Higher Education Study Programmes (CROHO) and the information is available to the public. Besides the accreditation of degree programmes, the Netherlands has a system whereby the Ministry of Education, Culture and Science recognizes higher education institutions by conferring on them the status of either bekostigd (funded) or aangewezen (approved). Bekostigd indicates that the institution is fully financed by the government. Aangewezen indicates that the institution does not receive funds from the government and has to rely on its own sources of funding. Whether a degree programme is offered by a 'funded' or an 'approved' institution, it must be accredited and registered in CROHO to be considered recognized. If a bachelor or master programme is not registered in the CROHO, the quality is not assured by the Dutch quality assurance system. The quality might however be assured by another system.

Special provisions for recognition:

Recognition for university level studies: HBO and WO: For holders of foreign qualifications regardless of nationality there are no special provisions or practices. The institution decides and the applicants should contact the Hogeschool or university of their choice.

For access to advanced studies and research: Institutions are empowered by law to make their own decisions.

For exercising a profession: As EU member state, the Netherlands adheres to the regulations prescribed by the EU Directives for Professional Recognition. In most cases, admission to regulated professions based on qualifications obtained in non-EU countries, involves evaluation of the credential and formal recognition by the competent authority.

NATIONAL BODIES

Ministerie van Onderwijs, Cultuur en Wetenschap (Ministry of Education, Culture and Science)

Minister: Marja van Bijsterveldt-Vliegenthart
PO Box 16375
The Hague 2500 BJ
Tel: +31(70) 412 3456
Fax: +31(70) 412 3450
WWW: http://www.rijksoverheid.nl/ministeries/ocw
Role of national body: Principal authority responsible for administration, financing and coordination of higher education.

HBO-Raad, Verenigin van Hogescholen (Netherlands Association of Universities of Applied Sciences)

President: Thomas Carolus de Graaf
Postbus 123
The Hague 2501 CC
Tel: +31(70) 312 2121
Fax: +31(70) 312 2100
WWW: http://www.hbo-raad.nl
Role of national body: The HBO-raad focuses on strengthening the social position of Universities of Professional Education and to this end maintains contacts with a broad range of people and organisations.

Vereniging van Universiteiten (Association of Universities in the Netherlands - VSNU)

President: Sijbolt Noorda
Senior Adviser: Charlotte van Heese
Postbus 13739
The Hague 2501
Tel: +31(70) 302 1400
Fax: +31(70) 302 1495
EMail: post@vsnu.nl
WWW: http://www.vsnu.nl
Role of national body: Drawing-up a common policy of long-term development of education and research; promoting inter-university co-operation, and co-operation between universities and the Ministry.

European Consortium of Innovative Universities - ECIU

Secretary-General: Katrin Dirksen
c/o Katrin Dircksen,
University of Twente
PO Box 217
Enschede 7500 AE
Tel: +31(53) 489 2684
EMail: k.dircksen@utwente.nl
WWW: http://eciu.web.ua.pt/
Role of national body: Network of universities with its base in Europe, but building on the experience and insights of institutions in other parts of the world.

Data for academic year: 2008-2009

Source: IAU from International Recognition Department, Nuffic, the Hague, 2008 (Bodies, 2012)

INSTITUTIONS

AMSTERDAM SCHOOL OF THE ARTS

Amsterdamse Hogeschool voor de Kunsten
Postbus 15079, Jodenbreestraat 3, 1001 MB Amsterdam
Tel: +31(20) 527-7710
Fax: +31(20) 527-7712
EMail: info@ahk.nl
Website: http://www.ahk.nl

President, Board of Directors: Olchert Brouwer
Tel: +31(20) 527-7811 EMail: college.van.bestuur@ahk.nl

Faculties

Architecture (Architecture; Landscape Architecture; Regional Planning); **Cultural Heritage** *(The Reinwardt Academy of Cultural Heritage)* (Cultural Studies; Heritage Preservation; Museum Management; Museum Studies); **Dance** (Dance); **Film and Television** (Film; Radio and Television Broadcasting; Sound Engineering (Acoustics); Visual Arts); **Fine Arts** (Art Education); **Music** *(Conservatorium van Amsterdam)* (Jazz and Popular Music; Music; Music Education; Opera); **Theatre** (Theatre)

History: Founded 1987, through a merger of the Academy of Fine Arts, the Amsterdam Academy of Architecture, the Netherlands Film and Television Academy, and the Reinwardt Academy. The Theatre School and the Hilversum Conservatory joined in 1988. A merger with the Sweelinck Conservatory in 1994 resulted in the establishment of the Conservatorium van Amsterdam. The postgraduate DasArts Institute was set up 1994, followed by the BINGER Institute 1995.

Fees: (Euros): c. 1,700 per annum for EEC students.

Accrediting Agencies: Netherlands and Flemish Accreditation Organisation (NVAO)

Degrees and Diplomas: *HBO Bachelor*, *HBO Master*

Student Services: Academic counselling, Canteen, Foreign student adviser, Nursery care

Special Facilities: Radio and Television Studios

Libraries: Yes

Last Updated: 14/02/11

ARTEZ INSTITUTE OF THE ARTS

ArtEZ Hogeschool voor de Kunsten
PO Box 49, 6800 AA Arnhem, Gelderland
Tel: +31(26) 353-5600
Fax: +31(26) 353-5677
EMail: communicatie@artez.nl; internationaloffice@artez.nl
Website: http://www.artez.nl

Chairman, Board of Governors: Dingeman Kuilman

Academies

Art and Design (Art Education; Fashion Design; Fine Arts; Graphic Design; Interior Design; Visual Arts); **Theatre** (Acting; Art Education; Dance; Theatre; Writing)

Institutes

Architecture (Architecture; Interior Design)

Schools

Dance (Dance); **Music** (Conducting; Jazz and Popular Music; Music; Music Education; Music Theory and Composition; Musical Instruments; Singing)

Further Information: Branches also in Enschede and Zwolle.

History: Founded 1987 as the Arnhem Institute of the Arts. Merged with AKI, Academie voor Beeldende Kunst en Vormgeving/ AKI (AKI Academy of Visual Arts, Enschede) and Christelijke Hogeschool voor de Kunsten 'Constantijn Huijgens' ('Constantijn Huijgens' Christian School of Fine and Performing Arts, Kampen) and acquired present title 2001.

Admission Requirements: Senior secondary education/university preparatory education and entrance examination

Main Language(s) of Instruction: Dutch; English

International Co-operation: With universities in Belgium, Austria, Germany, Denmark, Spain, France, Hungary, Romania and the United Kingdom.

Accrediting Agencies: Netherlands-Flemish Accreditation Organization (NVAO)

Degrees and Diplomas: *HBO Bachelor*, *HBO Master*. Also Associate Degree and Advanced Courses 1-2 yrs

Student Services: Canteen, Foreign student adviser, Language programs, Social counselling

Special Facilities: Yes

Libraries: Main Library

Last Updated: 14/02/11

AVANS UNIVERSITY OF APPLIED SCIENCE

Avans Hogeschool
Postbus 90116, 4800 RA Breda, Noord-Brabant
Tel: +31(76) 523-8001
EMail: cic@avans.nl; internationaloffice@avans.nl
Website:http: //www.avans.nl

President: F.J.M. van Kalmthout

Faculties

Arts (Design; Fine Arts; Visual Arts); **Economics** (Accountancy; Administration; Business and Commerce; Economic History; Human Resources; International Business; Law; Management; Marketing; Retailing and Wholesaling; Safety Engineering); **Education** (Teacher Training); **Healthcare** (Health Sciences; Medical Auxiliaries; Medical Technology; Nursing; Physical Therapy; Social Work); **Information and Communication Technology** (Communication Studies; Computer Science; Information Sciences; Information Technology; Multimedia); **Law** (Law); **Technology** (Architecture; Biology; Business Administration; Chemical Engineering; Chemistry; Civil Engineering; Electrical Engineering; Environmental Studies; Laboratory Techniques; Materials Engineering; Mechanical Engineering)

Further Information: Also branches in Tilburg and s' Hertogenbosch

History: Founded 2004 following merger of Hogeschool Brabant and Hogeschool 's Hertogenbosch.

Degrees and Diplomas: *HBO Bachelor*, *HBO Master*. Fine Arts; Graphic Design; Photography

Last Updated: 15/02/11

BUSINESS SCHOOL NETHERLANDS

Business School Nederland
Herenstraat 25, Postbus 709, 4116ZJ Buren
Tel: +31(34) 4579-030
Fax: +31(34) 4579-050
EMail: international@bsn.eu; info@bsn.eu
Website: http://www.bsn.eu

President: D.J. Gerdzen EMail: ikolmus@bsn.eu

Programmes

Management (Business Administration; Finance; Human Resources; Insurance; Management; Marketing)

History: Founded 1988, acquired status of University of Applied Sciences by the gouvernement 2006.

Admission Requirements: Bachelor's Degree, 3 yrs relevant working/managerial experience, Fluent English

Main Language(s) of Instruction: Dutch, English

Accrediting Agencies: Dutch Validation Council (DVC); Netherlands Flanders Accreditation Organisation (NVAO)

Degrees and Diplomas: *WO Master*. Business Adminstration (MBA); *Doctor's Graad*: Business Administration (DBA). Also International MBA programmes, Executive MBA

Libraries: Yes

Last Updated: 15/02/11

BUSINESS SCHOOL NOTENBOOM

Postbus 307, 5600 AH Eindhoven
Tel: +31(40) 252-0620
EMail: hogeschool@notenboom.nl
Website: http://www.notenboom.nl

Dean: Dewanand Mahadew

Programmes

Business (Business Administration; Business and Commerce; International Business; Management; Marketing; Sports Management); **Events, Travel and Leisure Management** (Leisure Studies; Sports Management; Tourism); **Hotel Management** (Hotel Management)

Degrees and Diplomas: *HBO Bachelor*, *HBO Master*
Last Updated: 07/03/11

CODARTS UNIVERSITY FOR THE ARTS

Codarts, Hogeschool voor de Kunsten
Kruisplein 26, 3012 CC Rotterdam
Tel: +31(10) 217-1100
Fax: +31(10) 217-1101
EMail: codarts@codarts.nl
Website: http://www.codarts.nl/

President: Carey Eykelen Burg

Academies

Dance *(Rotterdam Dance Academy)* (Dance)

Conservatories

Music *(Rotterdam Conservatory)* (Conducting; Jazz and Popular Music; Music; Music Theory and Composition; Musical Instruments; Singing)

Schools

Circus Arts (Performing Arts)

History: Founded 1980 as Hogeschool voor Muziek en Dans/University of Professional Education for Music and Dance. Acquired present status and title 2005.

Admission Requirements: Entrance audition

Fees: (Euros): 1,476 per annum; Institutional Fee (non EU-members and/or

Main Language(s) of Instruction: Dutch, English

Degrees and Diplomas: *HBO Bachelor*, *HBO Master*

Student Services: Academic counselling, Canteen, Foreign student adviser, Handicapped facilities, Health services, Social counselling

Special Facilities: Theatre, Concert Hall, Recording Studio

Libraries: Yes, Multimedia Center

Publications: Codarts Magazine *(bimonthly)*
Last Updated: 15/02/11

DELFT UNIVERSITY OF TECHNOLOGY

Technische Universiteit Delft
Postbus 5, 2600 AA Delft, Zuid-Holland
Tel: +31 (15) 278-9111
EMail: info@tudelft.nl
Website: http://www.tudelft.nl

President: D.J. van den Berg EMail: D.J.vandenBerg@tudelft.nl

Rector Magnificus and Vice-President: Karel Ch.A.M. Luyben EMail: K.C.A.M.Luyben@tudelft.nl

Faculties

Aerospace Engineering (Aeronautical and Aerospace Engineering; Astronomy and Space Science); **Applied Sciences** (Applied Physics; Biochemistry; Biological and Life Sciences; Chemical Engineering; Materials Engineering; Nuclear Engineering; Optics; Solid State Physics; Sound Engineering (Acoustics)); **Architecture** (Architecture; Town Planning); **Civil Engineering and Geosciences** (Building Technologies; Civil Engineering; Earth Sciences; Engineering Drawing and Design; Engineering Management; Geological Engineering; Hydraulic Engineering; Mechanical Engineering; Petroleum and Gas Engineering; Railway Engineering; Road Engineering; Sanitary Engineering; Surveying and Mapping; Transport Engineering; Water Management); **Electrical Engineering, Mathematics and Computer Sciences** (Architecture; Automation and Control Engineering; Computer Networks; Electrical Engineering; Electronic Engineering; Information Sciences; Mathematics and Computer Science; Telecommunications Engineering); **Industrial Design Engineering** (Engineering; Industrial Design; Industrial Engineering; Marine Engineering; Mechanical Engineering); **Mechanical, Maritime and Materials Engineering** (Marine Engineering; Materials Engineering; Mechanical Engineering); **Technology, Policy and Management** (Automation and Control Engineering; Computer Engineering; Economic and Finance Policy; Energy Engineering; Hydraulic Engineering; Industrial Engineering; Management; Marine Engineering; Mechanics; Social Policy; Technology; Transport and Communications)

Research Centres

Telecommunications and Radar (Telecommunications Engineering; Telecommunications Services)

Research Institutes

Housing, Urban and Mobility Studies (Urban Studies); **Reactor**

Research Schools

Biotechnological Sciences (Biotechnology); **Computing and Imaging** (Computer Graphics; Computer Science); **Information Technology, Micro-Electronics and Submicron Physics** (Electronic Engineering; Information Technology; Nanotechnology); **Integral Design of Structures** (Structural Architecture); **Systems and Control** *(Dutch Institute)* (Automation and Control Engineering); **Technical Geosciences** *(CTG)* (Surveying and Mapping); **Transport, Infrastructure and Logistics** (Transport Engineering; Transport Management)

Further Information: Also other small Research Institutes and Affiliate Research Schools.

History: Founded 1842 as 'Royal Academy' for the Education of Engineers. Acquired present status and title 1986. A State institution financed by the government.

Governing Bodies: Executive Board; Supervisory Board, from outside the University appointed by the government

Academic Year: September to August (September-January; February-June; July-August)

Admission Requirements: Secondary school certificate (Voorbereidend Wetenschappelijk Onderwijs, VWO)

Main Language(s) of Instruction: Dutch

International Co-operation: Participates in the 'European Leuven-network' with institutions in Germany, Belgium, France, United Kingdom, Norway

Degrees and Diplomas: *HBO Bachelor*, *HBO Bachelor*, *Doctor's Graad*: by thesis or experimental work

Special Facilities: History of Technology Museum

Libraries: Central Library, c. 990,000 vols

Publications: Departmental publications; International Shipbuilding Progress (in English) *(quarterly)*; The Netherlands Journal of Housing and the Built Environment

Press or Publishing House: Delft University Press (Delftse Universitaire Pers)
Last Updated: 02/03/11

DESIGN ACADEMY EINDHOVEN

Postbus 2125, 5611 AZ Eindhoven
Tel: +31(40) 239-3939
Fax: +31(40) 239-3940
EMail: info@designacademy.nl
Website: http://www.designacademy.nl

President: Lidewij Edelkoort

Programmes

Industrial Design (Design; Industrial Design; Interior Design)

History: Founded 1980.

Main Language(s) of Instruction: English, Dutch

Degrees and Diplomas: *WO Bachelor*, *WO Master*

Special Facilities: Digital workshop, mechanichal workshop, auditorium, Exhibition spaces

Libraries: Yes
Last Updated: 15/02/11

DRIESTAR UNIVERSITY FOR TEACHER EDUCATION

Driestar Hogeschool
Postbus 368, 2800 AJ Gouda
Tel: +31(182) 540-333
Fax: +31(182) 538-449
EMail: internationaloffice@driestar-educatief.nl
Website: http://www.driestar-hogeschool.nl

Programmes

Education (Education; Educational Administration; Pedagogy; Special Education)

Degrees and Diplomas: *HBO Bachelor*, *HBO Master*
Last Updated: 07/03/11

DRONTEN UNIVERSITY OF APPLIED SCIENCES

CAH Dronten - Christelijke Agrarische Hogeschool (CAH)
De Drieslag 1, 8251 JZ Dronten, Flevoland
Tel: +31(321) 386-100
Fax: +31(321) 313-040
EMail: info@cah.nl
Website: http://www.cah.nl

President: H.E. Verweij EMail: veh@cah.nl

Departments

Agricultural Business and Management (Agricultural Management; Business Administration); **Agriculture** (Agriculture); **Biotechnology and Culture** (Biotechnology); **Horticulture** (Horticulture); **Technology and Automatisation** (Technology)

History: Founded 1965, acquired present status 1986.

Governing Bodies: Board of Governors; Ministry of Agriculture

Academic Year: September to July

Admission Requirements: Degree Programmes: 3 yrs completed university studies or equivalent. Recognized certificate of English

Fees: (Euros): Tuition, 1,538 per annum for european students; others, 3,750

Main Language(s) of Instruction: Dutch, English

International Co-operation: With Poland, Hungary, France, Portugal, Latvia and Slovenia. Also participates in Socrates and Erasmus programmes

Accrediting Agencies: The Netherlands Validation Authority

Degrees and Diplomas: *HBO Bachelor*: 4 yrs; *HBO Master*

Student Services: Academic counselling, Canteen, Employment services, Foreign student adviser, Foreign Studies Centre, Language programs, Social counselling, Sports facilities

Student Residential Facilities: "De Drieslag " guesthouse can host 29 persons

Special Facilities: University Farm; Student Enterprises; Agribusiness Park; Consultancy Unit

Libraries: Open Learning Centre; Multimedia Library
Last Updated: 15/02/11

EDE CHRISTIAN UNIVERSITY

Christelijke Hogeschool Ede
Postbus 80, Oude Kerkweg 100, 6717 BB Ede
Tel: +31(318) 696-300
Fax: +31(318) 696-396
EMail: info@che.nl
Website: http://www.che.nl

President: M. Burggraaf

Programmes

Business Administration (Business Administration); **Communication Studies** (Communication Studies); **Human resources Management** (Human Resources); **Journalism** (Journalism); **Nursing** (Nursing); **Social Work** (Social Work); **Teacher Education for Primary Schools** (Primary Education); **Theology and Religion**

History: Created 1980.

Main Language(s) of Instruction: Dutch, English

Degrees and Diplomas: *HBO Bachelor*: 4 yrs; *HBO Master*: 1 or 2 yrs
Last Updated: 15/02/11

EINDHOVEN UNIVERSITY OF TECHNOLOGY

Technische Universiteit Eindhoven
Postbus 513, 5600 MB Eindhoven
Tel: +31(40) 247-9111 +31(40) 247-2296
EMail: csc@tue.nl
Website: http://www.tue.nl

Rector Magnificus: Hans van Duijn EMail: c.j.v.duijn@tue.nl

Secretary: H.P.J.M. Roumen
Tel: +31(40) 247-4534 EMail: H.P.J.M.Roumen@tue.nl

Faculties

Applied Physics (Applied Physics; Nuclear Physics; Physics; Solid State Physics; Thermal Physics); **Architecture, Building and Planning** (Architecture; Architecture and Planning; Building Technologies; Construction Engineering; Engineering Drawing and Design; Town Planning); **Biomedical Engineering** (Biomedical Engineering); **Chemical Engineering and Chemistry** (Analytical Chemistry; Chemical Engineering; Industrial Chemistry; Inorganic Chemistry; Organic Chemistry; Physical Chemistry; Polymer and Plastics Technology); **Electrical Engineering** (Computer Engineering; Electrical Engineering; Measurement and Precision Engineering; Power Engineering; Telecommunications Engineering); **Industrial Design** (Industrial Design); **Industrial Engineering and Innovation Sciences** (Human Resources; Industrial and Organizational Psychology; Industrial Engineering; Labour and Industrial Relations); **Mathematics and Computer Science** (Computer Science; Mathematics); **Mechanical Engineering** (Materials Engineering; Measurement and Precision Engineering; Mechanical Engineering)

Research Institutes

Centre for Innovation Studies (Industrial and Organizational Psychology; Management); **Centre for Wireless Technology** (Radiophysics; Telecommunications Engineering; Telecommunications Services); **Embedded Systems Institute** (Electrical and Electronic Engineering; Measurement and Precision Engineering); **European Institute for Statistics, Probability, Stochastic Operations Research and its Applications** (Finance; Statistics); **Institute for Complex Molecular Systems** (Applied Mathematics; Chemistry; Statistics)

History: Founded 1956 as Technische Hogeschool. Acquired present status 1986. A State institution mainly financed by the government.

Governing Bodies: Universiteitsraad (University Council); College van Bestuur (Executive Board)

Academic Year: September to August (September-December; December-March; March-August)

Admission Requirements: Secondary school (VWO) certificate in appropriate subjects (profile N+T; N+G; or combinatieprofiel van beiden N+T/N+G), or recognized equivalent

Main Language(s) of Instruction: Dutch; English (Master)

International Co-operation: With universities in Belgium and Singapore. Also participates in Erasmus, Sefi, Delta, Comett, Brite-Euram, Esprit-II programmes. Member of Cluster, Santander group, Cesar Foundation

Degrees and Diplomas: *WO Bachelor*, *WO Master*, *Doctor's Graad*

Student Services: Academic counselling, Canteen, Cultural centre, Employment services, Foreign student adviser, Handicapped facilities, Health services, Nursery care, Social counselling, Sports facilities

Student Residential Facilities: Yes

Libraries: Central Library, c. 500,000 vols

Publications: Wetenschappelijk Verslag *(annually)*
Last Updated: 02/03/11

ERASMUS UNIVERSITY ROTTERDAM

Erasmus Universiteit Rotterdam
Postbus 1738, 3000 DR Rotterdam
Tel: +31(10) 408-1111
Fax: +31(10) 408-9008
Website: http://www.eur.nl/

Rector Magnificus: Henk Schmidt (2009-)

Centres

Medical (Biological and Life Sciences; Health Sciences; Medicine)

Faculties

Philosophy (Philosophy); **Social Sciences** (Psychology; Public Administration; Sociology)

Institutes

Health Policy and Management (Health Administration; Public Health); **Social Studies** *(International)* (Social Studies)

Schools

Economics (Econometrics; Economics); **History, Culture and Communication** (Communication Studies; Cultural Studies; History; History of Societies; Journalism; Media Studies); **Law** (Law); **Management** (Management)

History: Founded 1973, incorporating the former Netherlands School of Economics, founded 1913, and the Medical School, Rotterdam, founded 1965. Merged with Institute of Sociel Studies 2009.

Governing Bodies: Universiteitsraad (University Council); College van Bestuur (Executive Board)

Academic Year: September to August

Admission Requirements: Secondary school certificate (diploma eindexamen Gymnasium A or B, or Atheneum A or B), or recognized equivalent

Main Language(s) of Instruction: Dutch, English

Degrees and Diplomas: *WO Bachelor*; *WO Master*: 1-2 yrs; *Doctor's Graad*

Student Services: Academic counselling, Canteen, Cultural centre, Employment services, Language programs, Sports facilities

Student Residential Facilities: Yes

Libraries: Library, c. 723,500 vols; 'Rotterdamsch Leeskabinet', 191,500 vols

Last Updated: 15/02/11

EUROPORT BUSINESS SCHOOL

Postbus 21510, 3001 AM Rotterdam
Tel: +31(10) 201-2320
Fax: +31(10) 201-2321
EMail: info@epbs.nl
Website: http://www.epbs.nl

Programmes

Business Administration (Business Administration)

Further Information: Also branch in Amsterdam and Beijing

Degrees and Diplomas: *HBO Bachelor*, *HBO Master*

Last Updated: 02/03/11

FONTYS UNIVERSITY OF APPLIED SCIENCES

Fontys Hogescholen
Postbus 347, 5600 AH Eindhoven
Tel: +31(877) 877-877
Fax: +31(877) 876-233
EMail: info@fontys.nl
Website: http://www.fontys.nl

President, Chairman of Executive Board: Marcel Wintels (2008-)
EMail: m.wintels@fontys.nl

Programmes

Arts (Dance; Design; Fine Arts; Music; Music Education; Performing Arts); **Business Management and Logistics** (Business Administration; Management; Transport Management); **Economics, Marketing and Law** (Accountancy; Economics; Law; Marketing; Real Estate; Retailing and Wholesaling; Taxation); **Engineering** (Automotive Engineering; Electrical Engineering; Engineering; Industrial Design; Industrial Engineering; Mechanical Engineering; Physics); **Healthcare** (Gerontology; Health Administration; Medical Parasitology; Nursing; Physical Therapy; Podiatry; Speech Therapy and Audiology; Sports); **ICT** (Business Computing; Information Management; Information Sciences; Information Technology); **Media and Communications** (Communication Studies; Journalism; Media Studies); **Teacher Training** (Business Education; Educational Technology; Foreign Languages Education; Humanities and Social Science Education; Science Education; Teacher Training; Technology Education)

History: Founded 1986. Acquired present name 2006. Former name Fontys University of Professional Education.

Main Language(s) of Instruction: Dutch, German, English

Degrees and Diplomas: *HBO Bachelor*, *HBO Master*

Last Updated: 17/02/11

GEREFORMEERDE HOGESCHOOL

Postbus 10030, 8000 GA Zwolle
Tel: +31(38) 425-5542
Fax: +31(38) 423-0785
EMail: info@gh-gpc.nl; internationaloffice@gh-gpc.nl
Website: http://www.gh.nl

President: J.D. Schaap

Programmes

Educational Leadership *(Postgraduate)* (Educational Administration); **Nursing** (Nursing); **Primary Education** (Primary Education; Teacher Training); **Social Educational Care** (Social Work); **Social Work and Social Services** (Social Work); **Theology** (Pastoral Studies; Theology)

Degrees and Diplomas: *HBO Bachelor*, *HBO Master*: Special Educational Needs; Educational Leadership

Last Updated: 03/03/11

GERRIT RIETVELD ACADEMY

Gerrit Rietveld Academie
Fred. Roeskestraat 96, 1076 ED Amsterdam
Tel: +31(20) 571-1600
Fax: +31(20) 571-1654
EMail: info@grac.nl
Website: http://www.rietveldacademie.nl

President: Tijmen van Grootheest

Programmes

Design (Design; Graphic Design); **Fine Arts** (Ceramic Art; Fashion Design; Fine Arts; Glass Art; Jewelry Art; Photography); **Visual Arts** (Visual Arts)

History: Founded 1925.

Governing Bodies: Board of Directors

Academic Year: September to August

Admission Requirements: Entrance examinations

Fees: (Euros) c. 1,500 per annum

Main Language(s) of Instruction: Dutch and English

Degrees and Diplomas: *WO Bachelor*, *WO Master*

Student Services: Academic counselling, Canteen, Foreign student adviser, Language programs, Social counselling

Student Residential Facilities: None

Libraries: Yes

Last Updated: 17/02/11

HAS DEN BOSCH UNIVERSITY OF APPLIED SCIENCES

HAS Den Bosch
Postbus 90108, 5200 MA 's-Hertogenbosch, Noord Brabant
Tel: +31(73) 692-3600
Fax: +31(73) 692-3699
EMail: hasdb@hasdb.nl
Website: http://www.hasdenbosch.nl

CEO: D.J. Pouwels

Faculties

Agribusiness Management (Agricultural Business; Finance); **Animal Production and Animal Care** (Animal Husbandry; Cattle Breeding; Farm Management; Meat and Poultry; Natural Resources; Technology; Veterinary Science; Wildlife; Zoology); **Environmental Technology** (Environmental Management; Environmental Studies; Technology); **Food Design** (Agricultural Business; Food Technology); **Food Science and Technology** (Food Science; Food Technology); **Garden and Landscape Management** (Landscape Architecture); **Horticulture** (Horticulture); **Rural Development and Innovation** (Agricultural Engineering; Development Studies; Rural Studies)

History: Founded 1948 through the merger of the School of Dairy Production in 's-Hertogenbosch and the Horticulture School in Roermond, Netherlands. Acquired present status and title in 1983.

Governing Bodies: Board of Directors

Academic Year: September to August

Admission Requirements: Secondary school certificate in subjects appropriate to the faculty requirements (diploma eindexamen Gymnasium A or B, Atheneum A or B) or foreign equivalent

Fees: (Euros): Bachelor, 2,000 per annum; Master, 5,500 (for EU students), 10,130 (for non-EU students)

Main Language(s) of Instruction: English; Dutch

International Co-operation: Participates in the Erasmus/ Socrates and Leonardo programmes (Austria, Belgium, Finland, France, Germany, Greece, Hungary, Italy, Latvia, Poland, Portugal, Spain and United Kingdom)

Degrees and Diplomas: *HBO Bachelor*: Horticulture; Agribusiness (BSc); *HBO Master*: International Horticulture; Agribusiness; Food Technology; Environmental Technology; Animal Biology and Welfare

Student Services: Academic counselling, Canteen, Employment services, Foreign student adviser, Foreign Studies Centre, Nursery care, Social counselling, Sports facilities

Student Residential Facilities: Yes

Special Facilities: Environment Technology Centre, Food Technology and Food Design Centres, Landscape Design Studio

Libraries: yes

Last Updated: 17/02/11

HAN UNIVERSITY OF APPLIED SCIENCES

Hogeschool van Arnhem en Nijmegen (HAN)

Postbus 5375, 6802 EJ Arnhem, Gelderland
Tel: +31(26) 369-1555
Fax: +31(26) 369-1515
EMail: info@han.nl
Website: http://www.han.nl

President: Ron Bormans (2008-)

Faculties

Business, Management and Law (Communication Studies; Human Resources; International Business; Transport Management); **Education** (Education); **Engineering and Life Sciences** (Automotive Engineering; Biological and Life Sciences)

Programmes

Information Technology, Media and Communication (Communication Studies; Computer Science); **Sports and Exercise** (Health Education; Physical Education; Sports; Sports Management)

History: Founded 1996 following merger of four Hogescholen in Arnhem and Nijmegen. Incorporated Hogeschool Diedenoort, 2005.

Governing Bodies: Board of Trustees, Executive Board

Academic Year: September to August

Admission Requirements: HAVO or VWO diploma or equivalent

Fees: (Euros): 1,500 per annum (for students from EU)

Main Language(s) of Instruction: Dutch

International Co-operation: With universities in USA; Australia; Chile; Mexico; Canada; Taiwan; South Africa. Participates in Erasmus and Leonardo programmes

Accrediting Agencies: Dutch Flemish Accreditation Organization

Degrees and Diplomas: *HBO Bachelor*: 4 yrs; *HBO Master*: a further 1-2 yrs

Student Services: Academic counselling, Employment services, Foreign student adviser, Language programs, Social counselling, Sports facilities

Last Updated: 18/02/11

HANZE UNIVERSITY GRONINGEN, UNIVERSITY OF APPLIED SCIENCES

Hanzehogeschool Groningen

Zernikeplein 11, 9747 AS Groningen
Tel: +31(50) 595-7115
Fax: +31(50) 595-7115
EMail: iso@org.hanze.nl
Website: http://www.hanze.nl

President: Henk J. Pijlman

Academies

Arts *(Academy Minerva, School for Fine Arts and Design)* (Art Education; Design; Fine Arts); **Dance** *(Dansacademie Noord-Nederland)* (Dance); **Pop Culture** (Cultural Studies; Jazz and Popular Music; Music)

Conservatories

Music *(Prince Claus)* (Music)

Institutes

Technology *(Hanze)* (Agriculture; Energy Engineering; Health Administration; Transport Engineering)

Schools

Architecture, Built Environment and Civil Engineering (Architecture; Civil Engineering; Construction Engineering; Engineering Management); **Business Management** (Business and Commerce; Human Resources; Labour and Industrial Relations; Law; Real Estate); **Communication and Media** (Communication Studies; Journalism); **Computer Science** (Business Computing; Computer Science; Technology); **Education** (Primary Education); **Engineering** (Biomedical Engineering; Electrical Engineering; Power Engineering); **Facility Management** (Management); **Financial and Economic Management** (Accountancy; Economics; Finance; Management); **Health Care Studies** (Dietetics; Health Administration; Medical Technology; Nutrition; Oral Pathology; Physical Therapy; Radiology; Speech Therapy and Audiology); **International Business** (Accountancy; Business Administration; Finance; International Business; Management; Marketing; Tourism); **Law** (Law; Private Law; Public Law; Social Work); **Life Sciences and Technology** (Chemical Engineering; Chemistry; Medical Auxiliaries; Medical Technology); **Marketing Management** (International Business; Marketing; Retailing and Wholesaling; Small Business); **Nursing** (Nursing; Public Health); **Social Studies** (Psychology; Social Work); **Sports Studies** (Physical Education; Sports; Sports Management)

History: Founded 1986, acquired present status 1993.

Governing Bodies: Executive Board

Academic Year: September to July

Admission Requirements: Secondary School Certificate

Main Language(s) of Instruction: Dutch, English

International Co-operation: With universities in Europe, North and South America, South East Asia, Australia

Degrees and Diplomas: *HBO Bachelor*, *HBO Master*. Also Executive MBA

Student Services: Academic counselling, Canteen, Employment services, Foreign student adviser, Foreign Studies Centre, Handicapped facilities, Language programs, Social counselling, Sports facilities

Student Residential Facilities: For foreign students

Special Facilities: Recording Studio

Libraries: Multi-media Library

Last Updated: 17/02/11

HOGESCHOOL EDITH STEIN - OCT UNIVERSITY OF PROFESSIONAL TEACHER EDUCATION

Hogeschool Edith Stein - OCT
Postbus 568, M.A. de Ruyterstraat 3, 7550 AN Hengelo
Tel: +31(74) 851-6100
Fax: +31(74) 851-6161
EMail: info@edith.nl
Website: http://www.edith.nl

President, Administration Board: Henk Mulders

Programmes

Education (Education; Primary Education; Teacher Trainers Education)

History: Founded 1980.

Degrees and Diplomas: *HBO Bachelor*

Last Updated: 17/02/11

HOGESCHOOL LEIDEN - UNIVERSITY OF APPLIED SCIENCES

Hogeschool Leiden
Postbus 382, 2300 AJ Leiden, Zuid-Holland
Tel: +31(71) 518-8800
Fax: +31(71) 518-8801
EMail: infohl@hsleiden.nl
Website: http://www.hsleiden.nl

President: Paul van Maanen

Faculties

Education (Education; Primary Education; Teacher Training); **Health Sciences** (Art Therapy; Nursing; Physical Therapy; Rehabilitation and Therapy); **Management and Business Studies** (Communication Studies; Human Resources; Labour and Industrial Relations; Law; Management); **Social Work and Applied Psychology** (Cultural Studies; Psychology; Social Work); **Technology** (Biomedicine; Chemistry; Information Technology; Laboratory Techniques)

History: Founded 1987.

Governing Bodies: Executive Board; Board of Governors

Admission Requirements: Secondary school diploma on HAVO level, NT 2 course (for Dutch courses)

Main Language(s) of Instruction: Dutch

International Co-operation: With universities in the United Kingdom, Germany, Spain, Finland, Norway, Belgium, France, Costa Rica, China, South Africa.

Degrees and Diplomas: *HBO Bachelor*: 4 yrs; *HBO Master*

Student Services: Academic counselling, Canteen, Cultural centre, Employment services, Foreign student adviser, Foreign Studies Centre, Handicapped facilities, Language programs, Social counselling, Sports facilities

Student Residential Facilities: Yes

Libraries: Main Library

Publications: Hogeschool Leiden Krant *(quarterly)*

Last Updated: 18/02/11

HOGESCHOOL UTRECHT - UNIVERSITY OF APPLIED SCIENCES

Hogeschool Utrecht
Postbus 13102, 3507 LC Utrecht
Tel: +31(88) 481-89-28
Fax: +31(88) 481-64-48
EMail: info@hu.nl
Website: http://www.hu.nl

President: G.T.C. Bonhof

Institutes

Social Work *(De Hosrt (Amersfoort))* (Social Work)

Programmes

Communication and Journalism (Communication Studies; Journalism); **Economics, Business and Commerce** (Business and Commerce; Economics); **Health Sciences** (Health Sciences); **Law and Social Studies** (Law; Social Studies); **Nautical Science** (Nautical Science); **Pedagogy** (Education; Pedagogy); **Technology** (Technology)

History: Founded 1987. Integrated Hogeschool de Horst in September 2005, Hogeschool Domstad 2010.

Degrees and Diplomas: *HBO Bachelor*, *HBO Master*

Last Updated: 18/02/11

HOGESCHOOL ZEELAND - UNIVERSITY OF APPLIED SCIENCES

Hogeschool Zeeland (HZ)
Postbus 364, 4380 AJ Vlissingen
Tel: +31(118) 489-000
Fax: +31(118) 489-200
EMail: info@hz.nl
Website: http://www.hz.nl

President: P. C. A. van Dongen

Departments

Business Administration (Business and Commerce; Business Computing; Commercial Law; Computer Science; Economics; International Business; Management; Modern Languages); **Education** (Education); **Engineering** (Chemical Engineering; Civil Engineering; Construction Engineering; Machine Building; Marine Engineering; Technology); **Environment Studies and Applied Sciences** (Biological and Life Sciences; Environmental Studies); **Health Care and Social Welfare** (Health Sciences; Nursing; Teacher Training); **Information and Communication** (Communication Studies; Computer Science); **Maritime Technology** (Marine Transport)

History: Created 1987.

Main Language(s) of Instruction: Dutch; English

Degrees and Diplomas: *HBO Bachelor*: 4 yrs; *HBO Master*: a further 1-2 yrs

Student Services: Academic counselling, Canteen, Cultural centre, Employment services, Foreign student adviser, Foreign Studies Centre, Handicapped facilities, Health services, Language programs, Nursery care, Social counselling, Sports facilities

Student Residential Facilities: Yes

Libraries: yes

Last Updated: 21/02/11

HOTEL SCHOOL THE HAGUE - INTERNATIONAL INSTITUTE FOR HOSPITALITY MANAGEMENT

Hotelschool Den Haag
Brusselselaan 2, 2587 AH Den Haag, Zuid Holland
Tel: +31(70) 351-2481
Fax: +31(70) 351-2155
EMail: info@hdh.nl
Website: http://www.hotelschool.nl

President: W. Dooge

Programmes

Hotel Management (Hotel Management)

Further Information: Branch in Amsterdam

History: Founded 1929.

Admission Requirements: International Baccalaureate, European Baccalaureate, Abitur, Cou, Artium, High School with certain conditions

Fees: (Euros): first year 5,080 per annum; second year 656; third year 435; Fourth year, 656. 1,476 per annum payment to the Dutch government

Main Language(s) of Instruction: English

Accrediting Agencies: EFAH (European Foundation for Accreditation of Hotel Schools)

Degrees and Diplomas: *HBO Bachelor*: Hospitality Management, 4 yrs; *HBO Master*: Hospitality Management, 1 yr (full time)-2 yrs (part time)

Student Services: Academic counselling, Canteen, Foreign student adviser, Sports facilities

Student Residential Facilities: Yes
Libraries: Media Centre
Last Updated: 21/02/11

INHOLLAND UNIVERSITY OF APPLIED SCIENCES

Hogeschool INHOLLAND
Postbus 558, 2003 RN Haarlem
Tel: +31(23) 522-3275
Fax: +31(23) 541-2235
EMail: Info@inholland.nl
Website: http://www.inholland.com

Dean: Geert Dales

Faculties

Communication, Media and Music (Communication Studies; Information Sciences; Media Studies; Music); **Education, Learning and Philosophy** (Education; Philosophy); **Engineering, Design and Computing** (Aeronautical and Aerospace Engineering; Computer Science; Design; Engineering); **Health, Sports and Social Work** (Social Work; Sports); **Management, Finance and Law** (Finance; Law; Management); **Marketing, Tourism and Leisure** (Leisure Studies; Marketing; Tourism)

Units

Agriculture (Agricultural Business; Agricultural Engineering; Agriculture)

Further Information: Campus sites in Alkmaar, Amsterdam/Diemen, Delft, Den Haag, Haarlem and Rotterdam. Degree programmes are also offered in Dordrecht and Hoofddorp.

Academic Year: September to June

Admission Requirements: Secondary school certificate.

Main Language(s) of Instruction: Dutch, English

Degrees and Diplomas: *HBO Bachelor*: 3-4 yrs; *HBO Master*: 1-2 yrs

Student Services: Academic counselling, Canteen, Foreign student adviser, Foreign Studies Centre, Handicapped facilities, Social counselling

Student Residential Facilities: Yes

Libraries: Yes
Last Updated: 17/02/11

INSTITUTE FOR HOUSING AND URBAN DEVELOPMENT STUDIES (IHS)

Postbus 1935, 3000 BX Rotterdam
Tel: +31(10) 408-9825
Fax: +31(10) 408-9826
EMail: admission@ihs.nl
Website: http://www.ihs.nl

Director: Kees van Rooijen

Programmes

Management of Competitive Urban Regions (Development Studies; Town Planning; Urban Studies); **Urban Management and Development** (Regional Planning; Regional Studies; Town Planning; Urban Studies)

History: Created 1948 as Bouwcentrum. Acquired current title 1991.

Degrees and Diplomas: *WO Master*: Urban Management and Development; Management of Competitive Urban Regions; *Doctor's Graad*
Last Updated: 02/03/11

LEIDEN UNIVERSITY

Universiteit Leiden
Postbus 9500, 2300 RA Leiden
Tel: +31 71-527-2727
Fax: +31 71-527-3118
EMail: info@leidenuniv.nl
Website: http://www.leiden.edu

Rector Magnificus and President: C.J.J.M. (Carel) Stolker (2007-)
Tel: +31 71-527-3982, Fax: +31 71-527-3052

Vice-President: H.W. te Beest Tel: +31 71-527-3127

International Relations: Robert Coelen, Vice-President International
Tel: +31(71) 527-3105, Fax: +31(71) 527-7298
EMail: j.coelen@leidenuniv.nl; a.petit@io.leidenuniv.nl

Faculties

Archaeology (Archaeology); **Humanities** (African Languages; African Studies; Ancient Civilizations; Art History; Chinese; Classical Languages; Dutch; English; Film; French; German; Hebrew; Hispanic American Studies; History; Indic Languages; Indonesian; Islamic Theology; Italian; Japanese; Jewish Studies; Korean; Latin American Studies; Linguistics; Literature; Mediterranean Studies; Middle Eastern Studies; Philosophy; Religion; Russian; Slavic Languages; South and Southeast Asian Languages; Spanish; Theology; Tibetan); **Law** (Criminal Law; Criminology; Law; Private Law; Public Law); **Medicine** *(Leiden University Medical Centre)* (Medicine; Nursing); **Science** (Astronomy and Space Science; Biology; Botany; Chemistry; Computer Science; Mathematics; Physics); **Social and Behavioural Sciences** (Anthropology; Behavioural Sciences; Education; Pedagogy; Political Sciences; Psychology; Public Administration; Social Sciences; Women's Studies)

Graduate Schools

Education *(ICLON)* (Educational Sciences; Teacher Trainers Education)

Institutes

Public Administration (Public Administration)

Further Information: Also University Hospital and Clinics. Campus at The Hague.

History: Founded 1575 by William the Silent, Prince of Orange, reorganized as Rijksuniversiteit Leiden, a State institution in the 19th century, acquired present status and title 1999.

Governing Bodies: Raad van Toezicht (Board of Governors); College van Bestuur (Executive Board); the members of the Board of Governors are appointed by the Minister of Education, Culture and Science; the Board of Governors appoints the members of the Executive Board

Academic Year: September to August

Admission Requirements: Secondary school certificate in subjects appropriate to faculty requirements or equivalent

Fees: (Euros): Home fee, 1,520 per annum; c. 11,000-17,000 for international programmes

Main Language(s) of Instruction: Dutch, English

Degrees and Diplomas: *WO Bachelor (BA, BSc)*: 3 yrs; *WO Master (MA, MSc)*: 1-2 yrs; *Doctor's Graad (Dr.,PhD)*: a further 4 yrs. Postgraduate, 1-2 yrs. International Programmes. MA, MSc, Advanced LL.M, Mphil

Student Services: Academic counselling, Canteen, Cultural centre, Foreign student adviser, Social counselling, Sports facilities

Student Residential Facilities: For 5,500 students

Special Facilities: Natural History Museum; Archaeology Museum; Geology and Mineralogy Museum; Ethnology Museum; Natural Sciences Museum; Historical Museum. Botanical Garden (16th century)

Libraries: University Library, c. 3m. vols; Faculty and Institute Libraries
Last Updated: 28/03/13

MAASTRICHT SCHOOL OF MANAGEMENT (MSM)

Endepolsdomein 150, 6229 EP Maastricht
Tel: +31(43) 387-0808
Fax: +31(43) 387 0800
EMail: info@msm.nl
Website: http://www.msm.nl/

Dean, Director: Peter P. de Gijsel
Tel: +31(43) 387-0820 EMail: Gijsel@msm.nl

Manager Quality Control and Accreditations: Katalin Kovacs
Tel: +31(43) 387-0833 EMail: kovacs@msm.nl

International Relations: Helmy Koolen, Senior Manager Outreach Education Operations
Tel: +31(43) 387-0851 EMail: koolen@msm.nl

Programmes

Business Administration (Accountancy; Business Administration; Business Computing; Economic and Finance Policy; Finance; International Business; Management)

History: Created 1952 as the Research Instituut voor Bedrijfswetenschappen (RVB) at the Delft University of Technology. Acquired status 1993.

Governing Bodies: Board of Trustees; Board of Directors

Academic Year: September to September

Admission Requirements: Bachelor's degree from a recognized university, preferably with a foundation in economics and management, or equivalent; GMAT test score of at least 500; TOEFL, 88 internet-based test, 230 computer-based test, 570 paper-based test or IELTS score of 6.5

Fees: (Euro): MBA/MSc, 12,900 per degree; Doctoral programme, 28,585 (four years).

Main Language(s) of Instruction: English

International Co-operation: with institutions in China, Indonesia, Kazakhstan, Vietnam, Peru, Suriname, Kuwait, Saudi Arabia, Yemen, Egypt, Ghana, Kenya, Malawi, Namibia, Rwanda, Tanzania, Uganda, Zambia, Zambia, Zimbabwe, Romania

Accrediting Agencies: Nederlands-Vlaamse Accreditatieorganisatie (NVAO); Association of MBAs (AMBA); The Accreditation Council for Business Schools and Programs (ACBSP); International Assembly for Collegiate Business Education (IACBE)

Degrees and Diplomas: *WO Master*: Management; Business; International Business (MBA; MSc), 1-2 yrs; *Doctor's Graad*: Management; Business Administration (DBA), 4-6 yrs. Also Executive Master programmes and other short executive programmes.

Student Services: Academic counselling, Canteen, Cultural centre, Employment services, Foreign student adviser, Foreign Studies Centre, Handicapped facilities, Health services, Social counselling, Sports facilities

Student Residential Facilities: Yes

Libraries: c. 10,000 vols

Academic Staff *2010-2011*	MEN	WOMEN	TOTAL
FULL-TIME	12	3	**15**
PART-TIME	47	5	**52**
STAFF WITH DOCTORATE			
FULL-TIME	8	2	**10**
PART-TIME	31	1	**32**
Student Numbers *2010-2011*			
All (Foreign Included)	1,264	682	**1,946**
FOREIGN ONLY	1,258	679	**1,937**

Part-time students, 16. **Distance students**, 4.

Last Updated: 19/01/11

MAASTRICHT UNIVERSITY

Universiteit Maastricht (UM)

Postbus 616, 6200 MD Maastricht
Tel: +31(43) 388-2222
Fax: +31(43) 388-4898
EMail: study@maastrichtuniversity.nl
Website: http://www.maastrichtuniversity.nl/

Rector Magnificus: G.P.M.F. Mols

President: Martin Paul (2011-)

Vice-President: A. Postema

Academies

Teaching (Education; Teacher Training)

Centres

Integrated Assessment and Sustainable Development *(International)* (Environmental Management; Environmental Studies; Public Administration)

Colleges

Science (Biology; Chemistry; Mathematics; Neurosciences; Physics)

Departments

Architecture (Architecture); **Knowledge Engineering** (Artificial Intelligence)

Faculties

Arts and Social Sciences (Arts and Humanities; Cultural Studies; European Studies; Fine Arts); **Health, Medicine and Life Sciences** (Biomedicine; Health Sciences; Medicine; Public Health); **Law** (Law); **Psychology and Neuroscience** (Neurosciences; Psychology)

Graduate Schools

Cognitive and Clinical Neuroscience (Cognitive Sciences; Neurosciences); **Governance** (Administration; Leadership); **Law**

Schools

Business and Economics (Business Administration; Economics; International Business; International Economics; Management); **Health Professions Education** (Health Administration; Health Education; Health Sciences)

Further Information: Centre for European Studies

History: Founded 1974 as Medische Faculteit te Maastricht, acquired present title 1976.

Governing Bodies: Universiteitsraad (University Council); College van Bestuur (Executive Board); Raad van Toezicht (Supervisory Board)

Academic Year: Differs for each Faculty. Divided into blocks of 7 weeks

Admission Requirements: Secondary school certificate. If over 21 years of age, diploma eindexamen VWO, Gymnasium, Atheneum, or HBO

Fees: (Euros): Tuition, 1,519 per annum

Main Language(s) of Instruction: Dutch, English

International Co-operation: Participates in the Alma, Socrates, Tempus programmes

Degrees and Diplomas: *WO Bachelor*: 3 yrs; *WO Master*: a further 1-2 yrs; *Doctor's Graad (PhD)*: a further 4 yrs. Also Post-graduate degrees

Student Services: Academic counselling, Canteen, Cultural centre, Employment services, Foreign student adviser, Handicapped facilities, Health services, Language programs, Nursery care, Social counselling, Sports facilities

Student Residential Facilities: Yes

Special Facilities: Jezuïeten Collection

Libraries: University Library, c. 550,000 vols, 4,750 journals

Publications: ContinuUM *(biennially)*; Maastricht Journal of European and Comparative Law, Transnational Legal Research *(quarterly)*

Last Updated: 02/03/11

MARNIX ACADEMY - UNIVERSITY FOR TEACHER TRAINING

Marnix Academie

Postbus 85002, Vogelsanglaan 1, 3571 ZM Utrecht
Tel: +31(30) 275-3400
Fax: +31(30) 271-1324
EMail: marnix.academie@hsmarnix.nl
Website: http://www.hsmarnix.nl

Director: K. Aardse
Tel: +31(30) 275-3482 EMail: k.aardse@hsmarnix.nl

Head of Communications and Publications: A. Zegers
Tel: +31(30) 275-472

International Relations: J. K. Verheij, Head Internationalisering
Tel: +31(30) 275-3515 EMail: j.verheij@hsmarnix.nl

Programmes

Teacher Training (Education; Primary Education; Teacher Training)

Main Language(s) of Instruction: Dutch

Degrees and Diplomas: *HBO Bachelor*

Student Services: Academic counselling, Canteen, Foreign student adviser, Foreign Studies Centre, Handicapped facilities, Language programs, Social counselling, Sports facilities

Student Residential Facilities: No

Libraries: Yes

NHL UNIVERSITY OF APPLIED SCIENCES

NHL Hogeschool
PO Box 1080, 8900 CB Leeuwarden
Tel: +31(58) 251-2345
Fax: +31(58) 251-1950
EMail: infocentrum@nhl.nl
Website: http://www.nhl.nl

President: F. Kuipers

Institutes

Business and Management (Business Administration; Business Computing; Communication Studies; Economics; European Studies; Finance; Human Resources; International Business; Law; Management; Marketing; Public Administration); **Education and Communication Studies** (Art Education; Communication Studies; Design; Education; Modern Languages; Natural Sciences; Social Sciences; Theatre); **Health Care and Welfare** (Health Sciences; Pedagogy; Social Welfare; Social Work); **Technology** (Biological and Life Sciences; Building Technologies; Chemical Engineering; Civil Engineering; Engineering; Environmental Engineering; European Studies; Marine Transport; Rural Planning; Technology; Town Planning; Transport and Communications; Transport Engineering; Transport Management)

History: Founded 1987.

Fees: (Euros): 3,700 per annum for students from outside EU, 1,538 for students from EU

Main Language(s) of Instruction: Dutch and English

Degrees and Diplomas: *HBO Bachelor*: 4 yrs; *HBO Master*

Student Services: Academic counselling, Canteen, Foreign student adviser, Foreign Studies Centre, Handicapped facilities, Social counselling, Sports facilities

Student Residential Facilities: None

Libraries: Yes

Last Updated: 21/02/11

NHTV BREDA UNIVERSITY OF APPLIED SCIENCES

NHTV Internationale Hogeschool Breda
Postbus 3917, 4800 DX Breda,
Noord-Brabant
Tel: +31(76) 533-2203
Fax: +31(76) 533-2205
EMail: international.office@nhtv.nl; communicatie@nhtv.nl
Website: http://www.nhtv.nl

Rector Magnificus: Jaap Lengkeek

President, Board of Governors: Hans Uijterwijk

Programmes

Facility Management (Management; Real Estate); **Games and Media** (Computer Graphics; Multimedia); **Hotel Management** (Hotel Management); **Leisure** (Leisure Studies; Sports Management); **Tourism** (Tourism); **Urban Development, Logistics and Mobility** (Transport Management)

History: Founded 1967, acquired present status 1987.

Academic Year: September to July

Admission Requirements: Completed secondary education or equivalent

Main Language(s) of Instruction: Dutch, English

International Co-operation: With universities in Germany, France, Spain, United Kingdom, Portugal, Italy, Greece, Sweden, Finland, USA, China, Hungary.

Degrees and Diplomas: *HBO Bachelor*: 4 yrs; *HBO Master*: a further 1 1/2 yrs

Student Services: Academic counselling, Canteen, Foreign Studies Centre, Handicapped facilities, Language programs, Social counselling

Last Updated: 21/02/11

NYENRODE BUSINESS UNIVERSITY

Nyenrode Business Universiteit
Postbus 130, 3620 AC Breukelen
Tel: +31(34) 6291-211
Fax: +31(34) 6264-204
EMail: info@nyenrode.nl
Website: http://www.nyenrode.nl

CEO, Rector Magnificus: Maurits van Rooijen

Centres

Accounting, Auditing and Control (Accountancy; Management); **Business Ethics** (Business Administration; Ethics); **Entrepreneurship** (Management); **Executive and Management Development** (Business Administration; Management); **Finance** (Finance); **Human Resources, Organisations and Management Effectiveness** (Human Resources; Management); **Law** (Law); **Leadership and Personal Development** (Human Resources; Leadership); **Marketing and Supply Chain Management** (Marketing; Transport Management); **Strategy**; **Sustainability** (Development Studies); **Talent Management** (Human Resources; Management); **Tax Management** (Management; Taxation)

Institutes

Competition; **Cooperative Entrepreneurship**; **Europe China**

Schools

NIVRA-Nyenrode (Accountancy)

History: Founded 1946, acquired present title and status in 1982.

Main Language(s) of Instruction: Dutch, English

Accrediting Agencies: EQUIS; Association of MBAs; Nederlands-Vlaamse Accreditatieorganisatie (NVAO

Degrees and Diplomas: *HBO Bachelor*, *WO Master*. Also offers International MBA

Student Services: Academic counselling, Employment services, Sports facilities

Student Residential Facilities: Yes

Special Facilities: Auditorium and lecture rooms; Coach House

Libraries: C. 25,000 vols

Last Updated: 23/02/11

OPEN UNIVERSITY OF THE NETHERLANDS

Open Universiteit Nederland (OUNL)
Postbus 2960, 6401 DL Heerlen
Tel: +31(45) 576-2888 +31(45) 576-2897
Fax: +31(45) 576-2908
EMail: info@ou.nl
Website: http://www.ou.nl

Rector Magnificus: Anja Oskamp

Institutes

Education and Training (Education; Educational Sciences)

Schools

Computer Science (Artificial Intelligence; Computer Science; Information Technology); **Cultural Sciences** (Cultural Studies; Fine Arts; Museum Management; Museum Studies); **Law** (Administrative Law; Constitutional Law; Criminal Law; European Union Law; International Law; Law; Private Law); **Management** (Administration; Business Computing; Management); **Psychology** (Clinical Psychology; Industrial and Organizational Psychology; Psycholinguistics); **Science** (Environmental Management; Environmental Studies; Natural Sciences; Surveying and Mapping)

History: Founded 1982, admitted first students 1984. A State institution for distance education.

Governing Bodies: College van Bestuur (Board of Governors); Raad van Toezicht (Supervisory Board)

Academic Year: September to August (September-January; February-August)

Admission Requirements: No qualifications required. Minimum age, 18

Main Language(s) of Instruction: Dutch, English

International Co-operation: With universities in Belgium

Degrees and Diplomas: *WO Bachelor (BA)*: 3 yrs; *WO Master (MA)*: 1 yr; *Doctor's Graad (PhD)*: with dissertation. Also Course Certificates and Higher Vocational Education Diploma (168 credits, 5,600 hours)

Student Services: Academic counselling, Handicapped facilities

Libraries: Central Library Heerlen Libraries in Study Centres

Publications: Modulair *(other/irregular)*; Onderwijsjinnovatie *(quarterly)*

Last Updated: 23/02/11

PROTESTANT THEOLOGICAL UNIVERSITY

Protestantse Theologische Universiteit (PTHU)
Postbus 5021, 8260 GA Kampen
Tel: +31(38) 337-1600
Fax: +31(38) 337-1613
EMail: info@pthu.nl
Website: http://www.pthu.nl

Rector: F.G. Imminck EMail: fgimmink@pthu.nl

Programmes

Theology (Christian Religious Studies; Missionary Studies; Pastoral Studies; Theology)

Further Information: Branches in Utrecht and Leiden. Continuing Education in Doorn.

History: Founded 2007, of the merging of three institutions: the Theological Academic Institute (TAI) of the Protestant Church of the Netherlands, the Theological University Kampen (ThUK), and the Evangelical Lutheran Seminary (ELS).

Governing Bodies: Protestant Church in The Netherland

Academic Year: September to August

Admission Requirements: Bachelor's degree in Theology or an equivalent diploma, a good command of English

Main Language(s) of Instruction: Dutch, English

International Co-operation: With universities in Germany; Indonesia; Hungary; South Africa; Suriname; USA

Accrediting Agencies: NVAO and Nuffic.

Degrees and Diplomas: *WO Bachelor*, *WO Master*. 1 yr; *Doctor's Graad*

Student Services: Academic counselling, Canteen, Cultural centre, Employment services, Foreign student adviser, Handicapped facilities, Social counselling, Sports facilities

Student Residential Facilities: Yes

Libraries: Yes

Last Updated: 23/02/11

RADBOUD UNIVERSITY NIJMEGEN

Radboud Universiteit Nijmegen (KUN)
Postbus 9102, Comeniuslaan 4, 6500 HC Nijmegen
Tel: +31(24) 361-6161
Fax: +31(24) 356-4606
EMail: info@communicatie.ru.nl
Website: http://www.ru.nl

Rector Magnificus: S.C.J.J. Kortmann (2007-)
Tel: +31(24) 361-3082 EMail: h.klerkx@cvb.ru.nl

International Relations: Marian L.M. Janssen, Director, International Relations
Tel: +31(24) 361-6055, Fax: +31(24) 361-2757
EMail: m.janssen@io.ru.nl

Faculties

Arts (Art History; Cultural Studies; Dutch; English; Fine Arts; German; Greek; History; Information Sciences; Latin; Literature; Romance Languages); **Law** (European Union Law; International Law; Law; Management); **Management** (Business Administration; Economics; Environmental Studies; Geography (Human); Management; Political Sciences; Public Administration; Social Studies); **Medical Sciences** (Biomedicine; Dentistry; Medicine; Nursing); **Philosophy, Theology and Religious Studies** (Philosophy; Religious Studies; Theology); **Science and Computer Science** (Astronomy and Space Science; Biology; Computer Science; Environmental Studies; Information Sciences; Mathematics; Physics); **Social Sciences** (Anthropology; Artificial Intelligence; Cognitive Sciences; Communication Studies; Development Studies; Educational Sciences; Pedagogy; Psychology; Social Sciences; Sociology)

Further Information: Also 22 research institutes.

History: Founded 1923 as Katholieke Universiteit Nijmegen (Catholic University of Nijmegen) by decree of the Sacred Congregation of Studies and by Royal Decree. The University is based on the principles of the Roman Catholic Church. Although a private institution, it receives financial support from the State, and its degrees are recognized as equivalent to and as affording the same rights as those of the State Universities. Acquired present title 2004.

Governing Bodies: College van Bestuur (University Board); Universitaire Gezamenlijke Vergaderirg (University Council)

Academic Year: September to June (September-January; February-June)

Admission Requirements: Secondary school certificate in subjects appropriate to Faculty requirements (diploma eindexamen Gymnasium A or B, Atheneum A or B, or HBS. A or B), or equivalent. VWO (Voorbereidend Wetenschappelijk Onderwijs)

Fees: (Euros): Registration, 1,538 per annum for students from European countries, 2,655 for others

Main Language(s) of Instruction: Dutch, English

International Co-operation: Participates in Erasmus and International Student Exchange Programme (ISEP) USA.

Degrees and Diplomas: *WO Bachelor*, *WO Master*, *Doctor's Graad*

Student Services: Academic counselling, Canteen, Cultural centre, Foreign student adviser, Foreign Studies Centre, Handicapped facilities, Language programs, Nursery care, Social counselling, Sports facilities

Student Residential Facilities: Yes

Special Facilities: Anatomy Museum; Cultural Anthropology Museum. Biological Garden; Audiovisual Centres

Libraries: Central Library, c. 1.2m. vols; Scientific journals, 7,166

Student Numbers *2011-2012*: Total 18,624

Last Updated: 23/02/11

ROTTERDAM UNIVERSITY (OF APPLIED SCIENCES)

Hogeschool Rotterdam
Postbus 25035, 3001 HA Rotterdam
Tel: +31(10) 794-9494
EMail: studievoorlichting@hro.nl
Website: http://www.hogeschool-rotterdam.nl

President: J.A.C.F. Tuytel EMail: J.A.C.F.tuytel@hro.nl

Programmes

Arts (Art Education; Design; Fine Arts); **Behaviour and Society** (Cultural Studies; Labour and Industrial Relations; Pedagogy; Social Studies; Social Work); **Economics** (Accountancy; Business Administration; Communication Studies; International Business; Management; Modern Languages; Retailing and Wholesaling; Small Business; Sports Management; Taxation; Transport Management); **Education** (Education; Foreign Languages Education; Humanities and Social Science Education; Mathematics Education; Science Education; Secondary Education; Technology Education); **Healthcare** (Gynaecology and Obstetrics; Nursing; Occupational Therapy; Physical Therapy; Speech Therapy and Audiology); **Media and ICT** (Business Computing; Information Sciences; Information Technology; Multimedia); **Technology** (Automotive Engineering; Biology; Chemical Engineering; Chemistry; Civil Engineering; Electrical Engineering; Engineering; Industrial Design; Industrial Engineering; Laboratory Techniques; Marine Transport; Mechanical Engineering; Medical Technology; Transport Management)

History: Founded 1988.

Degrees and Diplomas: *HBO Master*

Last Updated: 18/02/11

ROYAL TROPICAL INSTITUTE

Koninklijk Instituut voor de Tropen (KIT)
Postbus 95001, 1090 HA Amsterdam
Tel: +31(20) 568-8711
Fax: +31(20) 668-4579
EMail: communication@kit.nl
Website: http://www.kit.nl

President: Jan Donner

Programmes

Health Development (Health Administration; Health Education; Public Health; Tropical Medicine)

History: Created 1910 as the 'Colonial Institute' to study the tropics and to promote trade and industry in the (at that time) colonial territories of the Netherlands. Acquired current title 1950.

Degrees and Diplomas: *WO Master*: Public Health; International Health. Also short courses and postgraduate specialities for Doctors.

Last Updated: 02/03/11

SAXION UNIVERSITIES OF APPLIED SCIENCES

Saxion Hogescholen
Postbus 501, 7400 KM Deventer
Tel: +31(570) 603-789
Fax: +31(570) 603-628
EMail: internationaloffice@saxion.nl
Website: http://www.saxion.edu

President: W. Boomkamp

Schools

Applied Arts and Technology (Fashion Design; Graphic Arts; Graphic Design); **Business Engineering and Entrepreneurship** (Business and Commerce; Management); **Communication, Information Technology and Information Management** (Computer Engineering; Information Management; Information Technology; Software Engineering); **Education** (Education); **Environmental Planning and Building** (Architecture and Planning; Environmental Management); **Finance and Accounting** (Accountancy; Finance); **Governance and Law** (Law; Private Law; Public Law); **Hospitality** (Hotel Management; Tourism); **Human Resources Management** (Human Resources); **Life Sciences, Engineering and Design** (Biological and Life Sciences; Design; Engineering); **Marketing and International Management** (International Business; Marketing); **Social Work** (Social Work; Sociology)

Further Information: Also campuses in Enschede and Apeldoorn

History: Founded 1989. Acquired present title and status 1998 following merger of Saxion Hogeschool Enschede and Saxion Hogeschool Ijselland.

Admission Requirements: Secondary school certificate

Fees: (Euros): 1st yr, 3,500; Master, 8,650

Main Language(s) of Instruction: Dutch, English

International Co-operation: Participates in the Erasmus/Socrates programmes

Degrees and Diplomas: *HBO Bachelor*: 4 yrs; *HBO Master*: 1 yr

Student Services: Academic counselling, Canteen, Foreign student adviser, Handicapped facilities, Health services, Language programs, Nursery care, Social counselling, Sports facilities

Student Residential Facilities: Yes

Libraries: Yes

Publications: Saxion, Magazine *(other/irregular)*

Last Updated: 23/02/11

STENDEN UNIVERSITY OF APPLIED SCIENCES

Stenden Hogeschool
Postbus 1298, 8900 CG Leeuwarden
Tel: +31(58) 244-1441
Fax: +31(58) 244-1401
EMail: info@stendon.com
Website: http://www.stenden.com

President: Leendert Klaassen

Programmes

Postgraduate (Leisure Studies; Tourism); **Undergraduate** (Business Administration; Hotel and Restaurant; Hotel Management; Information Management; International Business; Leisure Studies; Management; Modern Languages; Tourism)

Further Information: Campus sites in Leeuwarden, Emmen, Groningen, Meppel, Assen (all Netherlands), Doha (Qatar), Bangkok (Thailand), Port Alfred (South Africa) and Bali (Indonesia).

History: Founded 1987 as Christelijke Hogeschool Nederland. Acquired current status and name when merged with Hogeschool Drenthe in 2008.

Main Language(s) of Instruction: Dutch, English

Degrees and Diplomas: *WO Bachelor*; *WO Master*

Student Services: Academic counselling, Canteen, Employment services, Foreign student adviser, Foreign Studies Centre, Language programs, Social counselling, Sports facilities

Last Updated: 15/02/11

STOAS UNIVERSITY OF APPLIED SCIENCES AND TEACHER EDUCATION

Stoas Hogeschool
Agripark Oost 2, 8251 KH Dronten
Tel: +31(321) 386-123
Fax: +31(321) 313-500
EMail: mail@stoashogeschool.nl
Website: http://www.stoashogeschool.nl

Programmes

Agriculture (Agricultural Business; Agriculture); **Animal Husbandry** (Animal Husbandry); **Food Technology** (Food Technology); **Horticulture** (Horticulture; Landscape Architecture)

History: Created 1981.

Degrees and Diplomas: *WO Bachelor*

Last Updated: 03/03/11

THE HAGUE UNIVERSITY OF APPLIED SCIENCES

Haagse Hogeschool
Stamkartplein 40, 2521 ED Den Haag
Tel: +31(70) 445-8888
Fax: +31(70) 445-8825
EMail: info@hhs.nl
Website: http://www.haagsehogeschool.nl

President of the Executive Board: Pim Breebaart

Programmes

European Studies (European Studies); **Food Technology** (Food Technology); **Industrial Design Engineering** (Engineering; Industrial Engineering); **International and European Law** (European Union Law; International Law); **International Business and Management** (International Business; Management); **International Communications Management** (Communication Studies); **Public Management** (Management; Public Administration)

History: Founded 1987. Merged with Technische Hogeschool Rijswijk 2002.

Governing Bodies: Board of Governors; Executive Board

Academic Year: September to July

Fees: (Euros): EU students, 1,538; Non-EU students, 3,500

Main Language(s) of Instruction: Dutch and English

International Co-operation: With universities in Europe, USA, Asia, Australia

Accrediting Agencies: Ministry of Education; NVAO (Nederlands Vlaamse Accreditatie Organisatie)

Degrees and Diplomas: *HBO Bachelor*; *HBO Master*

Student Services: Academic counselling, Canteen, Cultural centre, Employment services, Foreign student adviser, Handicapped facilities, Language programs, Social counselling, Sports facilities

Student Residential Facilities: Yes

Libraries: Yes

Last Updated: 17/02/11

TIASNIMBAS BUSINESS SCHOOL

Postbus 2040, 3500 GA Utrecht
Tel: +31(30) 230-3050
Fax: +31(30) 236-7320
EMail: information@tiasnimbas.edu
Website: http://www.tiasnimbas.edu/

Dean: Ramon O'Callaghan

Managing Director: Jan Henk van der Werff

Programmes

Accounting (Accountancy); **Business Law** (Commercial Law); **Finance** (Finance); **Information Management** (Information Management); **Management and Organisation Strategy** (Management); **Marketing** (Marketing); **Operations Management and Research Methods** (Management); **Public and Non-Profit Management** (Management)

Further Information: Also campuses in Eindhoven and Tilburg

History: Founded 2006, a merger of Tias Business School and Universiteit Nimbas.

Main Language(s) of Instruction: Dutch, English

Accrediting Agencies: AMBA (Association of MBAs); NVAO (Dutch Flemish Accreditation Organisation), RICS (Royal Institution of Chartered Surveyors)

Degrees and Diplomas: *WO Master*; *Doctor's Graad*: Business Administration (DBA)

Last Updated: 02/03/11

TILBURG UNIVERSITY

Universiteit van Tilburg (UVT)

Postbus 90153, 5000 LE Tilburg
Tel: +31(13) 466-2236
Fax: +31(13) 466-2921
EMail: info@tilburguniversity.edu
Website: http://www.tilburguniversity.edu/

President of the Executive Board: K.M. Becking (2012-)
Tel: +31(13) 466-2327, Fax: +31(13) 466-8068
EMail: m.g.s.westerburgen@tilburguniversity.edu

International Relations: Roos Hogenkamp, Director International Office
Tel: +31(13) 466-3051
EMail: r.j.e.hogenkamp@tilburguniversity.edu

Centres

Applied Research; **Bilingual Studies in the Bilingual Society** *(Babylon)* (Communication Studies; Cultural Studies); **Cooperational Universities from Brabant** *(SOBU)* (Law); **Data**; **Innovation for Electronic Resources (Ticer)** *(Tilburg ICT)*; **Language Studies** *(CLS)* (Modern Languages); **Meditation** *(CWL)*; **Nature Conservation** *(European (ECNC))* (Law; Natural Resources); **Organization for Strategic Labour Market Research** *(OSA)*; **Research Group on Information and Communication Technology** *(Infolab)* (Communication Studies; Information Technology); **Social Entrepreneurship** (Philosophy); **Sustainability Problems** *(Brabant (TELOS))* (Economics; Social Studies)

Faculties

Arts and Humanities (Arts and Humanities; Communication Studies; Cultural Studies; Grammar; Information Sciences; Linguistics; Literature; Philosophy; Religion); **Catholic Theology** (Catholic Theology); **Economics and Business Administration** (Business Administration; Business and Commerce; Econometrics; Economic and Finance Policy; Economics; Information Management; International Business; International Economics; Taxation); **Law** (Administrative Law; Constitutional Law; Criminal Law; European Union Law; Fiscal Law; History of Law; International Law; Labour Law; Law; Private Law; Public Administration; Social Policy); **Social and Behavioural Sciences** (Behavioural Sciences; Human Resources; Institutional Administration; Leisure Studies; Psychology; Social Sciences; Social Welfare; Sociology)

Graduate Schools

Philosophy (Philosophy)

Institutes

Centre of Finance *(Tilburg)* (Finance); **Development Research** *(IVO)* (Development Studies); **Fiscal Law** *((FIT) Tilburg)* (Fiscal Law); **Globalization and Sustainable Development** *(Globus)* (Development Studies; Environmental Studies); **Jurisprudence and Comparative Law** *(Schoordijk)* (Law); **Liturgy** (Religion); **Nexus** (Cultural Studies; Philosophy); **Research of Intercultural Cooperation** *(IRIC)* (Cultural Studies); **Social and Socio-Economic Research (Tisser)** *(Tilburg)* (Economics; Social Studies); **Social Policy Research and Consultancy** *(Tilburg (IVA))* (Social Studies); **Tilburg Law and Economics Center** *(TILEC)* (Economics; Law)

Research Institutes

Oldendorff

Research Schools

Legislation Studies

Schools

Business *(TIAS)* (Business Administration; Business and Commerce)

History: Founded 1927 as a private but government accredited Catholic University of Economics. In the 1950s and 1960s other faculties developed. Became a government financed university 1963.

Governing Bodies: Board of the Foundation; Board of Governors

Academic Year: September to June (September-January; February-June)

Admission Requirements: Secondary school certificate in subjects appropriate to faculty requirements (diploma eindexamen Gymnasium or Atheneum), or equivalent

Fees: (Euros): EU/EEA students: 1,565 per annum for Bachelor and Master programmes; non-EU/EEA students 5,964 for Bachelor programmes; 9,768 for Master programmes

Main Language(s) of Instruction: Dutch, English

International Co-operation: Participates in the International Student Exchange Programme (ISEP). Every year c. 300 outgoing students for study abroad (student exchange). Exchanges with over 30 countries.

Degrees and Diplomas: *WO Bachelor*: Arts and Language; Economics; Law; Philosophy; Social Sciences (BA; BSc), 3 yrs; *WO Master*: Arts and Language; Economics; Law; Philosophy; Social Sciences (MA; MSc; LLM), a further yr; *Doctor's Graad*. Also Certificate of Advanced Studies (not leading to a formal degree) for progammes in TIAS Business School; Master of Philosophy in Arts and Language; Economics; Law; Philosophy; Social Sciences 2 yrs

Student Services: Academic counselling, Canteen, Cultural centre, Foreign student adviser, Handicapped facilities, Health services, Language programs, Social counselling, Sports facilities

Libraries: c. 800,000 vols, more than 11,000 electronic periodicals and 130 databases

Student Numbers *2012-2013*: Total: c. 12,000

Last Updated: 14/03/13

TIO UNIVERSITY OF APPLIED SCIENCES

Hogeschool TIO

Julianalaan 9, 7553 AB Hengelo
Tel: +31(742) 550-610
Fax: +31(742) 550-611
EMail: info@tio.nl
Website: http://www.tio.nl

Programmes

Hotel and Even Management (Hotel Management); **International Tourism Management** (Tourism)

Further Information: Branches in Utrecht, Amsterdam, Rotterdam and Eindhoven.

Degrees and Diplomas: *HBO Bachelor*, *HBO Master*

Last Updated: 07/03/11

UNESCO-IHE INSTITUTE FOR WATER EDUCATION

PO Box 3015, 2601 AX Delft, Zuid-Holland
Tel: +31(15) 215-1715
Fax: +31(15) 212-2921
EMail: info@unesco-ihe.org
Website: http://www.unesco-ihe.org/

Rector: András Szöllösi-Nagy (2009-)
Tel: +31(15) 215-1701 EMail: a.szollosi-nagy@unesco-ihe.org

Acting Deputy Director: Joop de Schutter
EMail: j.deschutter@unesco-ihe.org

Departments

Environmental Resources (Environmental Management; Environmental Studies; Water Science); **Hydroinformatics and Knowledge Management** (Hydraulic Engineering); **Management and Institutions** (Water Management); **Urban Water and Sanitation** (Waste Management; Water Management); **Water Engineering** (Hydraulic Engineering; Water Management; Water Science)

History: Created in 1957. Acquired current status and title 2003. A postgraduate institution.

Governing Bodies: Governing Board

Academic Year: October to September

Admission Requirements: (for Masters programme): Undergraduate degree in related field, 2-3 years' practical or research experience; (PhD programme): UNESCO-IHE MSc or equivalent. English proficiency for all courses (IELTS: min 6.0; TOEFL paper-based: min 550; TOEFL computer-based test: min 213; TOEFL internet-based: min 79)

Fees: (Euros): 16,500 per Masters (18 months); PhD fee on demand; Short courses, 1,360 - 2,900. Online courses, 550 - 950

Main Language(s) of Instruction: English

International Co-operation: With institutions in Austria, China, Indonesia, India, UK

Accrediting Agencies: NVAO Dutch National Accrediting Agency for Universities

Degrees and Diplomas: *WO Master*: Environmental Science; Municipal Water and Infrastructure; Water Management; Water Science and Engineering (MSc), 18 months; *Doctor's Graad (PhD)*: 4 yrs. Also short professsional courses and online courses.

Student Services: Academic counselling, Canteen, Foreign student adviser, Foreign Studies Centre, Health services, Language programs, Social counselling, Sports facilities

Student Residential Facilities: Yes.

Special Facilities: Distance Learning Centre

Libraries: 22,000 titles plus connection to international network of libraries.

Last Updated: 02/03/11

UNIVERSITY OF AMSTERDAM

Universiteit van Amsterdam (UVA)
Postbus 19268, 1012 WX Amsterdam
Tel: +31(20) 525-9111
Fax: +31(20) 525-2136
Website: http://www.uva.nl

Rector Magnificus: Dymph van den Boom
EMail: rectormagnificus@uva.nl

President: K. van der Toor EMail: voorzittercvb@uva.nl

Faculties

Dentistry (Dentistry); **Economics and Business** (Business Administration; Econometrics; Economics); **Humanities** (Anthropology; Arabic; Archaeology; Art History; Arts and Humanities; Cultural Studies; Dutch; Educational Sciences; English; European Studies; French; Greek; Greek (Classical); Hebrew; History; Italian; Latin; Literature; Media Studies; Modern Languages; Musicology; Philosophy; Religious Studies; Romanian; Scandinavian Languages; Slavic Languages; Sociology; Spanish; Theatre); **Law** (Law); **Medicine** (Medicine); **Science** (Artificial Intelligence; Astronomy and Space Science; Biology; Chemistry; Computer Science; Earth Sciences; Information Sciences; Mathematics; Natural Sciences; Physics); **Social and Behavioural Sciences** (Behavioural Sciences; Child Care and Development; Communication Studies; Geography (Human); Political Sciences; Preschool Education; Psychology; Social Sciences)

History: Founded 1632 as 'Athenaeum Illustre', became university 1877. Responsible to municipal authorities until 1961, now independent. Financially supported by the State.

Governing Bodies: College van Bestuur (Executive Board); Raad van Toezicht (Board of Overseers)

Academic Year: September to July (September-January; February-July)

Admission Requirements: Secondary school certificate in subjects appropriate to faculty requirements (diploma eindexamen Gymnasium A or B, or Atheneum A or B) or equivalent

Fees: (Euros): NL/EU students, 1,445 per annum; non-EU students, varies according to courses

Main Language(s) of Instruction: Dutch, English

International Co-operation: With several Dutch Institutes abroad: Rome, Florence, Cairo, Tokyo, Athens, St Petersburg. With universities in United Kingdom, Germany and USA. Also participates in the Erasmus/Socrates and Tempus programmes.

Accrediting Agencies: Nederlands-Vlaamse Accreditatie Organisatie

Degrees and Diplomas: *WO Bachelor (BA/BSc)*: 3 yrs; *WO Master*; *Doctor's Graad (dr.)*: by thesis

Student Services: Academic counselling, Canteen, Cultural centre, Employment services, Foreign student adviser, Handicapped facilities, Health services, Language programs, Nursery care, Social counselling, Sports facilities

Student Residential Facilities: Yes

Special Facilities: Allard Pierson Museum (Archaeology); Zoology Museum; University Museum (History of the University); Central Library special collections

Libraries: Central Library, c. 3m.; libraries of faculties and institutes

Press or Publishing House: Amsterdam University Press (AUP)

Last Updated: 02/03/11

UNIVERSITY OF AMSTERDAM - UNIVERSITY OF APPLIED SCIENCES

Hogeschool van Amsterdam (HVA)
Postbus 1025, 1000 BA Amsterdam
Tel: +31(20) 595-3200
Fax: +31(20) 570-2510
EMail: studievoorlichting@hva.nl
Website: http://www.hva.nl

Chairman, Executive Board: K. Toor EMail: voorzittercvb@uva.nl

Programmes

Economics and Management (Accountancy; Business Administration; Business and Commerce; Communication Studies; Economics; Human Resources; International Business; Management; Sports Management; Taxation; Transport Management); **Education** (Business Education; Education; Foreign Languages Education; Humanities and Social Science Education; Mathematics Education; Science Education; Teacher Training; Technology Education); **Exercise, Sports and Nutrition** (Dietetics; Nutrition; Physical Education; Sports; Sports Management); **Healthcare** (Nursing; Occupational Health; Physical Therapy); **Media and Information Science** (Computer Graphics; Design; Information Sciences; Multimedia); **Social Work and Law** (Administration; Law; Psychology; Social Work); **Technology** (Civil Engineering; Engineering; Engineering Management; Industrial Engineering; Technology; Transport Management)

History: Founded 1993. Integrated Hogeschool voor Economische Studies Amsterdam/HES Amsterdam School of Business 2005.

Academic Year: September to September

Admission Requirements: MBO; HAVO; VWO

Main Language(s) of Instruction: Dutch; English

International Co-operation: With universities in all European countries

Accrediting Agencies: NVAO

Degrees and Diplomas: *HBO Bachelor*: 4 yrs; *HBO Master*: 1 yr

Student Services: Academic counselling, Canteen, Foreign student adviser, Foreign Studies Centre, Sports facilities

Last Updated: 18/02/11

UNIVERSITY OF GRONINGEN

Rijksuniversiteit Groningen
Postbus 72, 9700 AB Groningen
Tel: +31(50) 363-9111
Fax: +31(50) 363-5380
EMail: communicatie@rug.nl
Website: http://www.rug.nl

President: Sibrand Poppema EMail: s.poppema@rug.nl

Rector Magnificus: Frans Zwarts EMail: f.zwarts@rug.nl

Faculties

Arts (American Studies; Arabic; Archaeology; Art History; Arts and Humanities; Classical Languages; Communication Studies; Computer Science; Dutch; European Languages; Fine Arts; Hebrew; History; International Studies; Slavic Languages); **Behavioural and Social Sciences** (Behavioural Sciences; Cognitive Sciences; Educational Sciences; Pedagogy; Psychology; Social Sciences); **Economics and Business** (Accountancy; Eastern European Studies; Econometrics; Economics; International Business; Labour and Industrial Relations; Taxation; Transport Management); **Law** (Law); **Mathematics and Natural Sciences** (Astronomy and Space Science; Biology; Chemical Engineering; Chemistry; Computer Science; Environmental Studies; Mathematics; Mechanics; Natural Sciences; Pharmacology; Pharmacy; Physical Engineering; Physics); **Medical Sciences** (Dentistry; Medicine; Nursing); **Philosophy** (Ethics; Philosophy); **Spatial Sciences** (Demography and Population; Geography (Human)); **Theology and Religious Studies** (Religious Studies; Theology)

History: Founded 1614 as an Academy by the Province of Groningen. In 1811, during the Napoleonic invasion, the University was attached to the Université impériale. Became a State institution 1876.

Governing Bodies: Universiteitsraad (University Council); College van Bestuur (Executive Board)

Academic Year: September to July (September-December; December-March; March-July)

Admission Requirements: Secondary school certificate in subjects appropriate to faculty requirements (diploma eindexamen Gymnasium A or B, Atheneum A or B) or foreign equivalent

Main Language(s) of Instruction: Dutch, English

International Co-operation: Participates in the Erasmus, Lingua, Tempus, Comett, and Isep (USA) programmes. Member of the Coimbra Group

Degrees and Diplomas: *WO Bachelor*: 4 yrs; *WO Master*, *Doctor's Graad*: by thesis

Student Services: Academic counselling, Canteen, Cultural centre, Employment services, Foreign student adviser, Handicapped facilities, Language programs, Social counselling, Sports facilities

Special Facilities: University Museum; Gerardus van der Leeuwmuseum (Ethnographic Museum); Netherlands Institute, Rome

Libraries: University Library, including faculty and institute libraries, c. 3m. Vols

Last Updated: 23/02/11

UNIVERSITY OF PROFESSIONAL TEACHER EDUCATION PABO ZWOLLE

Katholieke PABO Zwolle (KPZ)
Ten Oeverstraat 68, 8012 EW Zwolle
Tel: +31(38) 421-7425
Fax: +31(38) 421-0914
EMail: info@kpz.nl
Website: http://www.kpz.nl

Programmes

Primary Education (Physical Education; Primary Education; Teacher Training)

Main Language(s) of Instruction: Dutch

Degrees and Diplomas: *HBO Bachelor*: Primary Teaching; *HBO Master*: Primary Teaching

Last Updated: 03/03/11

UNIVERSITY OF THE ARTS, THE HAGUE

Hogeschool der Kunsten Den Haag
Juliana van Stolberglaan 1, 2595 CA Den Haag
Tel: +31(70) 315-1515
Fax: +31(70) 315-1518
EMail: info@koncon.nl
Website: http://www.kabk.nl

Director: Henk van der Meulen

Faculties

Fine Arts and Design *(The Royal Academy of Fine Arts)* (Design; Fine Arts; Graphic Design; Industrial Design; Interior Design; Textile Design); **Music and Dance** *(The Royal Conservatory)* (Dance; Jazz and Popular Music; Music; Music Education; Music Theory and Composition; Musical Instruments; Musicology)

History: Founded 1990 as the Academy of Fine Arts, Music and Dance out of the merger between the Royal Conservatory and the Royal Academy of Fine Arts. Acquired current title and status 2010.

Admission Requirements: Secondary school certificate or equivalent

Main Language(s) of Instruction: Dutch and English

International Co-operation: Participates in Socrates, Erasmus (United Kingdom, France, Germany, Spain, Finland, Denmark, Switzerland, Hungary, Greece, Poland, Czech Republic)

Degrees and Diplomas: *HBO Bachelor*, *HBO Master*. Also PhD with Leiden University.

Student Services: Academic counselling, Canteen, Foreign student adviser, Foreign Studies Centre, Handicapped facilities, Language programs, Social counselling

Special Facilities: Art gallery, Multi-media center, Video and Photography studios. Music studios

Last Updated: 14/02/11

UNIVERSITY OF TWENTE

Universiteit Twente (UT)
Postbus 217, Drienerlolaan 5, 7500 AE Enschede, Overijsel
Tel: +31(53) 489-9111
Fax: +31(53) 489-2000
EMail: info@utwente.nl
Website: http://www.utwente.nl

Rector Magnificus: H. Brinksma (2009-)
Tel: +31(53) 489-2009, Fax: +31(53) 489-2191
EMail: h.brinksma@utwente.nl

International Relations: Karin Paardenkooper, Head, International Relations Office

Centres

Conflict, Risk and Safety Perception *(iCRiSP)*; **E-government Studies** *(CFES)*; **eHealth Research** *(CEHRS)*; **European Studies** *(CES)*; **Examinering en certificering** *(RCEC)*; **Healthcare Operations Improvement and Research** *(CHOIR)*; **Higher Education Policy Studies** *(CHEPS)*; **Integrale ProductieVernieuwing** *(CIPV)*; **Philosophy of Technology and Engineering Science** *(CEPTES)*; **Studies of Science, Technology and Society** *(CSSTS)*; **The Study of Democracy** *(CSD)*; **Transport Studies** *(CTS)*; **Twente Center for Career Research** *(TCCR)*; **Twente Centre for Studies in Technology and Sustainable Development** *(CSTM)*; **Twente Embedded Systems Initiative** *(TESI)*; **Twente Water Centre** *(TWC)*; **Virtual Reality Initiative Twente** *(VRINT)*

Faculties

Behavioural Sciences (Communication Studies; Educational Sciences; Educational Technology; Ethics; Philosophy; Psychology; Science Education) *Dean*: H.W.A.M. Coonen; **Electrical Engineering, Mathematics and Computer Science** (Applied Mathematics; Artificial Intelligence; Computer Networks; Computer Science; Electrical Engineering; Software Engineering; Systems Analysis; Telecommunications Engineering) *Dean*: A.J. Mouthaan; **Engineering Technology** (Civil Engineering; Construction Engineering; Energy Engineering; Engineering Management; Environmental Engineering; Industrial Design; Industrial Engineering; Mechanical Engineering) *Dean*: F. Eising; **Geo-Information Science and Earth Observation** (Geography) *Dean*: M. Molenaar;

Science and Technology (Applied Physics; Biomedical Engineering; Chemical Engineering; Medical Technology; Nanotechnology) *Dean*: G. van der Steenhoven

Graduate Schools

Behavioural Research; **Biomedical Technology and Technical Medicine**; **Energy and Resources**; **Geo Information Science and Earth Observation**; **Innovation and Governance Studies**; **Nanotechnology**; **Telematics and Information Technologies**

Institutes

Dutch Institute for Knowledge Intensive Entrepreneurship *(Nikos)*; **Maatschappelijke veiligheidsvraagstukken** *(IPIT)*; **Mechatronics** *(Drebbel)*; **Sports and Leisure**; **Technical Medicine** *(ITM)*

Research Centres

ThermoPlastic Composite Research Centre *(TPRC)*

Research Institutes

Biomedical Technology and Technical Medicine *(MIRA) Managing Director*: M. Kuit; **Governance Studies** *(IGS) Executive Director*: S. van Tongeren; **Mechanics, Processes and Control** *(IMPACT)* (Applied Physics; Chemical Engineering; Civil Engineering; Electrical Engineering; Mathematics; Mechanical Engineering) *Managing Director*: J.P. Emmerzaal; **Nanotechnology** *(MESA+)* (Nanotechnology) *Technical Commercial Director*: M. Luizink; **Social Sciences and Technology** *(IBR) Managing Director*: O. Peters; **Telematics and Information Technology** *(CTIT)* (Behavioural Sciences; Business Administration; Computer Science; Electrical Engineering; Engineering Management; Mathematics; Public Administration) *Managing Director*: Iddo Bante

Schools

Management and Governance (Business Administration; Economics; European Union Law; Health Administration; Human Resources; Industrial Management; Information Management; Information Technology; International Business; International Law; Political Sciences; Public Administration; Public Law; Sociology) *Dean*: P.J.J.M. van Loon

History: Founded 1961 as Technische Hogeschool Twente. Acquired present title and status 1986. It is now an Institute for Research and Education at University level, focussing on technological development and its social contExt. In January 2010 merged with the International Institute for Geo-Information Science and Earth Observation.

Governing Bodies: Executive Board and Supervisory Board

Academic Year: September to July

Admission Requirements: Dutch VWO or equivalent

Fees: (Euros): EU citizens 1,713 per annum; Non-EU citizens (non-technical studies) 10,000 per annum;Non-EU citizens (technical studies) 12,500 per annum.

Main Language(s) of Instruction: English; Dutch

International Co-operation: Participates in Erasmus and other exchange programmes with universities in many European countries, Indonesia, China, India,etc .

Accrediting Agencies: Netherlands-Flemish Accreditation Organisation; European Association for Public Administration Accreditation

Degrees and Diplomas: *WO Bachelor*: (Taught in Dutch) Business and IT; Business Administration; Public Administration; Biomedical Technology; Civil Engineering and Management; Communication Studies; Electrical Engineering; Health Sciences; Industrial Design Engineering (BSc); (Taught in Dutch) Educational Science; Psychology; Chemical Engineering; Industrial Engineering and Management; Technical Medicine; Computer Science; Applied Physics; Applied Mathematics; Mechanical Engineering (BSc); (Taught in English) Advanced Technology; Creative Technology; Public Administration – track European Studies; International Business Administration (BSc), 3 yrs; *WO Master*: Civil Engineering and Management; Construction Management and Engineering; Industrial Design Engineering; Mechanical Engineering; Sustainable Energy Technology; Business Information Technology (MSc); Industrial Engineering and Management; Applied Physics; Biomedical Engineering; Chemical Engineering; Nanotechnology (MSc); Philosophy of Science, Technology and Society; Science Education and Communication; Applied Mathematics; Computer Science; Electrical Engineering; Embedded Systems; Human Media Interaction; Systems and Control; Telematics (MSc), 2 yrs; *WO Master*: Communication Studies; Educational Science and Technology; Business Administration; Public Administration; Environmental and Energy Management; European Studies; Health Sciences (MSc), 1 yr; *WO Master*: Geo-Information Science and Earth Observation (MSc), 1 1/2 yrs

Student Services: Academic counselling, Canteen, Cultural centre, Foreign student adviser, Foreign Studies Centre, Handicapped facilities, Health services, Language programs, Nursery care, Social counselling, Sports facilities

Student Residential Facilities: Dormitories and apartments

Special Facilities: Museum; Art Gallery; Campus with wireless network; Movie and Sound Studio; Theatres; Praying Rooms; Restaurant; Cinema

Libraries: Yes

Publications: Research Group Periodicals

Press or Publishing House: Twente University Press

Student Numbers *2012-2013*: Total 6,600

Last Updated: 05/05/11

UTRECHT SCHOOL OF THE ARTS

Hogeschool voor de Kunsten Utrecht (HKU)

Postbus 1520, 3500 BM Utrecht
Tel: +31(30) 234-9440
Fax: +31(30) 234-9484
EMail: info@ssc.hku.nl
Website: http://www.hku.nl

Chairman, Board of Trustees: Piet Klaver

Faculties

Art and Economics (Art Management; Fine Arts; Management; Theatre); **Art, Media and Technology** (Computer Graphics; Multimedia; Music; Sound Engineering (Acoustics); Technology; Video); **Fine Arts and Design** (Art Management; Design; Fashion Design; Graphic Design; Interior Design; Photography; Visual Arts); **Music** *(The Utrecht Conservatory)* (Music; Music Education); **Theatre** (Acting; Art Education; Theatre)

History: Founded 1987.

Main Language(s) of Instruction: Dutch, English

Degrees and Diplomas: *HBO Bachelor*; *HBO Master*

Student Services: Foreign student adviser

Last Updated: 21/02/11

UTRECHT UNIVERSITY

Universiteit Utrecht (UU)

P.O Box 80125, 3508 TC Utrecht
Tel: +31(30) 253-9111
Fax: +31(30) 253-3388
Website: http://www.uu.nl

Rector Magnificus and Vice-President: Bert van der Zwaan
Tel: +31(30) 253-5131, Fax: +31(30) 253-7745
EMail: G.J.vanderZwaan@uu.nl

President: Yvonne C.M.T. van Rooy
Tel: +31(30) 253 5150 EMail: y.vanrooy@uu.nl

Director, Academic Affairs: Erwin Vermeulen

Faculties

Arts and Humanities (Cultural Studies; Dutch; Fine Arts; History; Media Studies; Modern Languages; Philosophy; Theology); **Geosciences** (Earth Sciences; Environmental Studies; Geography; Geography (Human); Regional Planning; Town Planning); **Law, Economics and Governance** (Economics; Law; Management); **Medicine** *(University Medical Centre, Utrecht)*; **Science** (Natural Sciences); **Social and Behavioural Sciences** (Behavioural Sciences; Social Sciences); **Veterinary Medicine** (Veterinary Science)

Graduate Schools

Arts and Humanities *(Utrecht)* (Arts and Humanities); **Geosciences** *(Utrecht)* (Earth Sciences; Geography); **Law, Economics and Governance** *(Utrecht)* (Economics; Government; Law); **Life Sciences** *(Utrecht)* (Biological and Life Sciences; Biology;

Chemistry; Physical Therapy); **Natural Sciences** *(Utrecht)* (Natural Sciences); **Social and Behavioural Sciences** *(Utrecht)*

Institutes

Education *(IVLOS)* (Education); **Ethics** (Ethics)

Further Information: Also two teaching hospitals; Interfaculty research and educational institutes: University College (UCU); Academic Biomedical Centre

History: Founded 1636 and established as State University. The status of the Universitiy is defined in the Higher Education and Scientific Research Act of 1992, and it is financially supported by the State.

Governing Bodies: University Board; University Council; Supervisory Board

Academic Year: September to July

Admission Requirements: Secondary school certificate in subjects appropriate to faculty requirements (eindexamen Gymnasuim A or B, or Atheneum)

Fees: (Euros): 1,565 per annum for students from European/European Economic Area (EU/EEA) countries; 5,500-10,000 per annum for non EU/EEA students.

Main Language(s) of Instruction: Dutch, English

Degrees and Diplomas: *WO Bachelor*: 3 yrs; *WO Master*, *Doctor's Graad (PhD)*: 4 yrs, by thesis

Student Services: Academic counselling, Canteen, Cultural centre, Foreign student adviser, Health services, Language programs, Social counselling, Sports facilities

Special Facilities: University Museum. Botanical Gardens. Central laboratory Animal Facilities (GDL), James Boswell Institute, Utrecht Summer School

Libraries: Utrecht University Library, c. 4,5m. vols. Catalogues avalaible online

Publications: Ontwikkelingsplan *(biennially)*

Last Updated: 29/03/11

VAN HALL LARENSTEIN UNIVERSITY OF APPLIED SCIENCES

Hogeschool Van Hall Larenstein
PO Box 1528, 8901 BV Leeuwarden
Tel: +31(58) 284-6100
Fax: +31(58) 284-1964 +31(58) 284-1923
EMail: info@vanhall-larenstein.nl
Website: http://www.vanhall-larenstein.nl

Chairman: Ellen Marks EMail: ellen.marks@wur.nl

Programmes

Agriculture (Agriculture); **Animal Management** (Animal Husbandry); **Bioengineering** (Biochemistry; Bioengineering); **Business and Agribusiness** (Agricultural Business; Business Administration); **Environmental Sciences** (Coastal Studies; Environmental Studies; Forestry; Horticulture; Landscape Architecture; Water Management); **Food Technology** (Food Technology)

History: Founded 1992. Previously known as Van Hall Institute.

Governing Bodies: Wageningen Agricultural University / Ministry of Agriculture

Academic Year: September to July

Main Language(s) of Instruction: Dutch, English

Degrees and Diplomas: *Propedeuse HBO*; *HBO Master*

Last Updated: 02/03/11

VRIJE UNIVERSITY AMSTERDAM

Vrije Universiteit Amsterdam (VU)
De Boelelaan 1105, 1081 HV Amsterdam
Tel: +31(20) 598-9898
Fax: +31(20) 598-9899
EMail: international@dienst.vu.nl
Website: http://www.vu.nl

President: René Smit
Tel: +31(20) 598-5305, Fax: +31(20) 598-5300
EMail: rm.smit@dienst.vu.nl

Secretary of the Executive Board: Roeleke Vunderink
Tel: +31(20) 598-5333, Fax: +31(20) 598-5300
EMail: r.vunderink@dienst.vu.nl

International Relations: Kees Kouwenaar, International Capacity Building Support Officer
Tel: +31(20) 598-9097, Fax: +31(20) 598-9095
EMail: k.kouwenaar@dienst.vu.nl

International Relations: Harriet van Daal, International Office
Tel: +31(20) 598-5000, Fax: +31(20) 598-5059

Faculties

Arts (Ancient Civilizations; Applied Linguistics; Arabic; Archaeology; Art Education; Art History; Arts and Humanities; Comparative Literature; Dutch; English; French; German; Greek (Classical); Hebrew; History; Islamic Studies; Jewish Studies; Latin; Linguistics; Literature; Terminology); **Dentistry** (Dentistry); **Earth and Life Sciences** (Biological and Life Sciences; Biology; Biomedicine; Earth Sciences; Environmental Studies; Geography; Geology); **Economics and Business Administration** (Accountancy; Business Administration; Econometrics; Economics; Finance; Marketing); **Human Movement Sciences** (Demography and Population); **Law** (Law); **Medicine** (Medicine); **Philosophy** (Philosophy); **Psychology and Education** (Education; Psychology); **Science** (Astronomy and Space Science; Chemistry; Computer Science; Environmental Studies; Mathematics; Pharmacology; Physics); **Social Sciences** (Anthropology; Cultural Studies; Gerontology; Political Sciences; Public Administration; Social Studies; Sociology); **Theology** (Theology)

Graduate Schools

Neurosciences *(Amsterdam)* (Neurosciences); **Oncology** *(Amsterdam)* (Oncology)

Further Information: Interdisciplinary Research Centers: CAMeRA, CLUE, MOVE, NCA, NI, VISOR, AZIRE, EMGO+, IVM+, CCA/V-ICI, ICaR-VU, Phoolan Devi

History: Founded 1880 by the Society for Higher Education as independent institution of higher education based on the principles of Calvinism. Officially recognized 1905.

Governing Bodies: College van Bestuur (Executive Board); Ondernemingsraad en Universitaire Studentenraad (University Council); College van Decanen (Board of Deans)

Academic Year: September to July (September-February; February-July)

Admission Requirements: For Bachelor's: Secondary school certificate in subjects appropriate to faculty requirements (diploma eindexamen Gymnasium A or B, Atheneum A or B) or equivalent.For Master's programmes: Academic Bachelor's diploma closely related tot the Master's programme. Additional language requirements.

Main Language(s) of Instruction: Dutch and English. 2 Bachelor's programme's in English; 89 Master's programmes in English

Accrediting Agencies: NVAO

Degrees and Diplomas: *WO Bachelor (BA, BSc)*: 3 yrs; *WO Master (MA, MSc, Mphil)*: 1-2 yrs; *WO Master*: Medicine and Natural Sciences, 3 yrs; *Doctor's Graad*: by thesis

Student Services: Academic counselling, Canteen, Cultural centre, Employment services, Foreign student adviser, Foreign Studies Centre, Handicapped facilities, Health services, Language programs, Nursery care, Social counselling, Sports facilities

Student Residential Facilities: Yes

Libraries: University Library of the VU (UBVU), consisting of Central Library and libraries of the institutes of the various faculties, about 1,022,151 vols (incl. 9.100 periodicals).

Last Updated: 02/03/11

WAGENINGEN UNIVERSITY AND RESEARCH CENTRE

Wageningen Universiteit en Researchcentrum
Postbus 9101, 6700 HB Wageningen
Tel: +31 (317) 480-100
Fax: +31 (317) 484-884
EMail: info@wur.nl
Website: http://www.wur.nl

Rector Magnificus: Martin J. Kropff EMail: martin.kropff@wur.nl

Departments

Agro-technology and Food Sciences (Agricultural Engineering; Biochemistry; Biophysics; Environmental Engineering; Food Science; Food Technology; Microbiology; Nutrition; Organic Chemistry; Physical Chemistry; Physics; Production Engineering; Safety Engineering; Toxicology); **Animal Sciences** (Animal Husbandry; Cell Biology; Epidemiology; Fishery; Genetics; Immunology; Nutrition; Physiology; Production Engineering; Veterinary Science; Zoology); **Environmental Sciences** (Ecology; Environmental Studies; Forest Management; Geology; Hydraulic Engineering; Information Sciences; Irrigation; Landscape Architecture; Meteorology; Natural Resources; Soil Management; Soil Science; Surveying and Mapping; Water Management; Water Science); **Plant Sciences** (Bioengineering; Biotechnology; Botany; Cell Biology; Crop Production; Ecology; Entomology; Genetics; Horticulture; Mathematics; Molecular Biology; Physiology; Plant and Crop Protection; Plant Pathology; Production Engineering; Statistics; Virology); **Social Sciences** (Agricultural Economics; Agriculture; Business and Commerce; Communication Studies; Development Studies; Economics; Education; Environmental Management; Environmental Studies; Gender Studies; Government; History; Household Management; Information Technology; Law; Management; Marketing; Natural Resources; Philosophy; Rural Planning; Rural Studies; Social Sciences; Sociology; Technology; Transport Management)

Institutes

Agro-technology and Food Innovations (Agronomy); **Animal Disease Control** *(CIDC-Lelystad (Central))*; **Food Safety** *(RIKILT)* (Food Science; Safety Engineering); **International Agricultural Centre** *(IAC)* (Agriculture); **Plant Research** *(International)* (Plant and Crop Protection)

Research Institutes

Agricultural Economics *(LEI)* (Agricultural Economics); **Applied Plant Research** *(PPO)*; **Green World** *(ALTERRA)* (Ecology)

Schools

Business *(Wageningen)* (Business Administration; Business and Commerce)

Further Information: Also international courses

History: Founded 1876 as National Agricultural College, granted university status 1918.Wageningen UR is a collaboration between Wageningen University, Van Hall Larenstein School of Higher Professional Education and the specialised institute (DLO) from the Dutch Ministry of Agriculture

Governing Bodies: Executive Board; University Council; Works Council; Students Council

Academic Year: September to July (September-October; October-December; January-February; March-April; May-July)

Admission Requirements: Secondary school certificate in appropriate subjects (diploma VWO) or equivalent

Main Language(s) of Instruction: Dutch, English

International Co-operation: Projects in Africa (Benin, Mozambique, Zambia, Zimbabwe, Burkina Faso, South Africa), South America (Costa Rica, Nicaragua, Bolivia), and Asia (India, Bangladesh, Indonesia, Viet Nam). On the initiative of Wageningen, a network of European agricultural faculties has been set up, known as Natura

Degrees and Diplomas: *WO Bachelor*: 3 yrs; *WO Master*: 2 yrs; *Doctor's Graad*: a further 3-4 yrs

Student Services: Academic counselling, Canteen, Cultural centre, Employment services, Foreign student adviser, Handicapped facilities, Health services, Social counselling, Sports facilities

Student Residential Facilities: For c. 4,600 students

Special Facilities: Arboretum De Dreijen; Arboretum Belmonte; Herbarium Vadense

Libraries: Central Library, c. 1m. vols

Publications: Wageningen Economic Studies *(other/irregular)*; Wageningen Social Studies *(other/irregular)*; Wageningen University Papers

Last Updated: 02/03/11

WEBSTER UNIVERSITY

Boommarkt 1, 2311 EA Leiden
Tel: +31(71) 516-8000
Fax: +31(71) 516-8001
EMail: info@webster.nl
Website: http://www.webster.nl

Director: Jean Paul van Marissing EMail: marissing@webster.nl

Programmes

Applied Behavioral and Social Sciences (Behavioural Sciences; Psychology; Sociology); **Business and Management** (Business Administration; Business and Commerce; Management); **European Studies** (European Studies); **International Business and Management Studies** (International Business); **International Relations** (International Relations); **Media Communications** (Media Studies); **Psychology and Social Sciences**

Further Information: Also Amsterdam Graduate Studies Center

History: Created 1983. Acquired status 2008.

Accrediting Agencies: Netherlands-Flemish Accreditation Agency (NVAO)

Degrees and Diplomas: *HBO Bachelor*. Also International MA/MBA recognized by The Higher Learning Commission and is a member of theNorth Central Association, USA.

Last Updated: 03/03/11

WINDESHEIM UNIVERSITY OF APPLIED SCIENCES

Hogeschool Windesheim

Postbus 10090, Campus 2-6, 8017 CA Zwolle
Tel: +31(38) 469-9911 +31(38) 469-9699
Fax: +31(38) 468-8970 +31(38) 468-8970
EMail: info@windesheim.nl
Website: http://www.windesheim.nl

President: A Cornelissen

Schools

Built Environment and Transport (Architecture and Planning; Civil Engineering; Construction Engineering; Road Engineering; Transport and Communications; Transport Engineering); **Business and Economics** (Business and Commerce; Economics); **Education** (Education); **Engineering and Design** (Electrical Engineering; Industrial Design; Industrial Management; Management; Mechanical Engineering; Technology); **Health Care** (Nursing; Speech Therapy and Audiology); **Human Movements and Sports** (Physical Education; Physical Therapy; Sports; Teacher Training); **Information Sciences** (Business Computing; Information Management; Information Sciences; Information Technology); **Management and Law** (Human Resources; Labour and Industrial Relations; Law; Management); **Media** (Media Studies); **Social Work** (Social Work)

History: Founded 1986. Previously known as Christelijke Hogeschool Windesheim.

Main Language(s) of Instruction: Dutch, English

Degrees and Diplomas: *HBO Bachelor*, *HBO Master*

Last Updated: 15/02/11

WITTENBORG UNIVERSITY OF APPLIED SCIENCES

Hogeschool Wittenborg

Laan van de Mensenrechten 500, 7331 VZ Apeldoorn
Tel: +31(88) 667-2688
Fax: +31(88) 667-2699
Website: http://www.wittenborg.nl/

Chief Executive: Peter Birdsall

Programmes

Business Administration (Business Administration; Hotel Management; Information Management; Management; Marketing; Real Estate; Small Business; Transport Management); **International Business and Management** *(Postgraduate)* (International Business; Management)

History: Created 1987. Acquired status 2006.

Main Language(s) of Instruction: English, Dutch

Accrediting Agencies: NVAO (Nederlands-vlaamse accreditatieorganisatie)

Degrees and Diplomas: *HBO Bachelor*, *HBO Master*

Last Updated: 02/03/11

ZUYD UNIVERSITY

Hogeschool Zuyd

Postbus 550, 6400 AN Heerlen
Tel: +31(45) 400-6060
Fax: +31(45) 400-6069
EMail: info@hszuyd.nl
Website: http://www.hszuyd.nl

Chairman, Executive Board: Karel van Rosmalen

Programmes

Arts (Design; Fine Arts; Jazz and Popular Music; Music; Theatre; Visual Arts); **Business** (Accountancy; Business Administration; Business and Commerce; Economics; European Studies; Hotel Management; Human Resources; Information Management; International Business; Law; Management; Oriental Languages; Translation and Interpretation); **Education** (Art Education; Education; Music Education; Primary Education); **Healthcare** (Midwifery; Nursing; Occupational Therapy; Physical Therapy; Speech Therapy and Audiology); **Social Work** (Art Therapy; Rehabilitation and Therapy; Social Work); **Technology and Science** (Architecture; Biological and Life Sciences; Chemical Engineering; Chemistry; Civil Engineering; Computer Networks; Computer Science; Electrical Engineering; Engineering; Industrial Engineering; Laboratory Techniques; Mechanical Engineering; Medical Technology; Multimedia; Technology)

Further Information: Campuses in Sittard and Maastricht.

History: Founded 1987.

Main Language(s) of Instruction: Dutch, English

Degrees and Diplomas: *HBO Bachelor*, *HBO Master*

Last Updated: 21/02/11

New Zealand

STRUCTURE OF HIGHER EDUCATION SYSTEM

Description:

Higher education is provided by three kinds of state tertiary institutions, each defined in legislation. They are: universities, institutes of technology and polytechnics, and wãnanga (Mãori centres of higher learning). Governance and funding are also defined by legislation. Each institution is governed by its own council, and is accountable to public sector accounting processes. Each institution determines its own programmes. In addition, there are several thousand private training establishments in New Zealand. More than 700 are registered with the New Zealand Qualifications Authority. They offer a wide range of courses. A small number are accredited by the New Zealand Qualifications Authority to offer degrees. Private training establishments may be considered for government funding on a per student basis, although the total amount available is capped. There are also Government Training Establishments. These include institutions such as the NZ Police Training Service Centre, Army Qual, Prison Services GTE and Child Youth and Family.

Stages of studies:

University level first stage: *Bachelor's degree/ Graduate Certificate/ Graduate Diploma (Levels 7-8)*
The first stage of tertiary education leads to the award of certificates, diplomas or Bachelor's degrees. All three are available in all universities, some institutes of technology and polytechnics, wananga, and private training establishments. A Bachelor's degree course is normally of three years' duration for Arts, Commerce, Science, Agriculture and Horticulture, four years for Engineering, Law, Pharmacy, Medical Laboratory Science, Optometry and Physiotherapy, five years for Architecture, Dentistry and Veterinary Science, and six years for Medicine. Entry to a Bachelor's degree with Honours is usually after the award of a first degree. In some Honours programmes selection may take place during the first degree programme on the basis of merit.

University level second stage: *Master's degree/ Postgraduate Certificate/ Postgraduate Diploma (Levels 8-9)*
The second stage of tertiary education is available in universities and some institutes of technology and polytechnics and leads to a Master's degree. A prerequisite is a Bachelor's degree (sometimes with Honours) and the course of study is sometimes one year, more frequently two years, and may be as long as four years. A Master's degree is typically awarded on the results of a piece of research through the presentation of a thesis. Becoming more common are Master's degrees by coursework (often including a substantial research component) or by coursework combined with a thesis.

University level third stage: *Doctor's degree (Level 10)*
The third stage is where specialization becomes more focused and properly-directed research is crucial. After a minimum of two years' study (generally four years or longer) and the presentation of a thesis, for which a viva voce examination is normal, a student may be awarded the degree of Doctor of Philosophy (PhD). This degree is available at all universities in most subjects, and in one institute of technology and one wananga in a limited range of subjects. A Master of Philosophy (MPhil) is available at some universities. This may be completed in one year of full-time research, but typically requires longer. Candidates for the PhD or the MPhil must previously have completed at least a Bachelor's degree with first-or second-class Honours.

University level fourth stage: *Higher Doctorate (Level 10)*
A range of Higher Doctorates is also available in Law, Letters, etc. These are normally awarded on the basis of published work. No graduate may apply for the award of a Higher Doctorate until at least five years after his/her first graduation from the institution.

Distance higher education:
Most universities and institutes of technology and polytechnics offer some form of distance education, including via the Internet, in a range of subjects. Some examples are:
- The Open Polytechnic provides a full range of distance learning packages from certificate to degree levels by correspondence or online tuition;
- Massey University offers a range of degree and diploma courses by correspondence;
- The University of Otago complements the Massey University extramural programme by offering a number of

courses through its 'teaching at a distance' teleconference network;
- The University of Waikato offers off-campus certificates at first-year undergraduate level in association with regional institutes of technology and polytechnics.

ADMISSION TO HIGHER EDUCATION

Admission to university-level studies:

Name of secondary school credential required: National Certificate of Educational Achievement

Minimum score/requirement: A minimum of 42 credits at level 3 or higher on the National Qualifications Framework including specific achievements.

For entry to: Universities.Minimum mark: A minimum of 42 credits at level 3 or higher on the New Zealand Qualifications Framework including specific achievements.

Alternatives to credentials: Students who can demonstrate in other ways that they are adequately prepared may be admitted.

Numerus clausus/restrictions: The Education Act 1989 states in s224(5): "Where the Council of an institution is satisfied that it is necessary to do so because of insufficiency of staff, accommodation or equipment, the Council may determine a maximum number of students who may be enrolled in a particular course of study or training at the institution in a particular year".

Foreign students admission:

Definition of foreign student: Education Act 1989, s159:" 'Foreign student', at any time, means a person who is not then a domestic student".

Entrance exam requirements: Foreign students should apply directly to the university of their choice. Students seeking first-year places must have acceptable university entrance qualifications, eg. Australia Year 12 and acceptable Tertiary Entrance Score; Malaysia STPM; UK any combination of 'A', 'AS' and GCSE which is acceptable for admission to a British university; USA High School Diploma and acceptable score in SAT; International Baccalaureate acceptable providing the diploma has been awarded (minimum 24 points); countries offering University of Cambridge International Examinations 3 passes at Advanced level (not including General Studies) including at least one C grade or better.

Entry regulations: Foreign students intending to study in New Zealand should contact the nearest New Zealand embassy or high commission to obtain information on visa regulations. Alternatively, information on visas for New Zealand is available at www.immigration.govt.nz.

Language requirements: Unless student's mother tongue is English, evidence of competence in English is required. Requirements are: TOEFL iBT 80 and IELTS (Min: 6.0-6.5),

RECOGNITION OF STUDIES

Quality assurance system:

The primary responsibility for the quality of education delivered rests with the organisation that provides those services. However, quality assurance processes are in place to ensure government and individuals are investing time and money in quality education and training.

Quality assurance focuses on the quality of learning outcomes recognised through qualifications as a whole. It also examines the systems and processes that support delivery of quality by providers.

The New Zealand Qualifications Framework (NZQF) is a comprehensive list of all quality assured qualifications in New Zealand. This includes NCEA (National Certificates of Educational Achievement) which are the national qualifications for senior secondary school students.

Quality assurance bodies are responsible for approving qualifications in New Zealand and for the quality that underpins the delivery of those qualifications. The bodies are:

• the New Zealand Qualifications Authority (NZQA), which approves all qualifications outside of universities. This includes national qualifications delivered by schools, institutes of technology and polytechnics, private training establishments, wānanga and government training establishments, as well as all degrees outside universities

• the Committee on University Academic Programmes (CUAP) of the New Zealand Vice-Chancellors' Committee (branded as Universities New Zealand) which approves all university qualifications.
Only those tertiary qualifications and providers that are quality assured by a quality assurance body (QAB) can receive government financial assistance. QABs decide if providers and qualification developers meet the required standards.
Quality Assurance Framework: NZQA has developed an Evaluative Approach to Quality Assurance - Policy Framework (PDF, 61KB). This document outlines the policy requirements for the quality assurance framework applying to private training establishments, institutes of technology and polytechnics, wānanga, government training establishments and industry training organisations. The policies reflect government policy and have been approved by the Board of NZQA.
Quality assurance processes: Education providers, qualifications and courses are quality assured in the following ways.
Registration of private training establishments: Registration ensures that a private training establishment (PTE) is able to provide a sound and stable learning environment. NZQA is responsible for the registration of PTEs. Schools, institutes of technology and polytechnics, universities and wānanga do not need to be registered, as they are set up by the Government under legislation.
Course approval and accreditation: Course approval confirms that a course is based on clear and consistent aims, content, outcomes and assessment practices, which meet the necessary criteria and requirements. Course accreditation confirms that a provider is deemed capable of delivering an approved course. A provider may seek accreditation to deliver their own or another organisation's approved course.
All quality assurance bodies in New Zealand use the same criteria for course approval and accreditation. See New Zealand Gazette.
Moderation: Moderation normally involves selection of a sample of assessment materials and learner evidence, to ensure that assessments are fair and valid and assessors are making consistent judgments about student or candidate performance.
External evaluation and review: External evaluation and review is a periodic evaluation of a tertiary education organisation, to provide an independent judgment of their educational performance and capability in self-assessment.

Bodies dealing with recognition:

New Zealand Qualification Authority - NZQA (Mana Tohu Mātauranga o Aotearoa)

PO Box 160
Wellington 6140
Tel: +64(4) 463 3000
Fax: +64(4) 463 3112
EMail: helpdesk@nzqa.govt.nz
WWW: http://www.nzqa.govt.nz
Deals with credential recognition for entry to institution: Yes
Deals with credential recognition for entry to profession: Yes

Universities New Zealand - Te Pōkai Tara

PO Box 11915
Wellington 6142
Tel: +64(4) 381 8500
Fax: +64(4) 381 8501
WWW: http://www.universitiesnz.ac.nz/

NATIONAL BODIES

Ministry of Education (Te Tāhuhu o te Matauraugа)

Minister of Education: Hekia Parata
Minister for Tertiary Education: Steven Joyce
PO Box 1666
Wellington 6140
Tel: +64(4) 463 8000

Fax: +64(4) 463 8001
EMail: tertiary.strategy@minedu.govt.nz
WWW: http://www.minedu.govt.nz
Role of national body: The Ministry of Education is the Government's lead adviser on the education system, shaping direction for education agencies and providers and contributing to the Government's goals for education.

Tertiary Education Commission - TEC (Te Amorangi Mātauranga Matua)
Chief Executive: Belinda Clark
1 Ash Road, Wiri
Private Bag 76928
Manukau City 2241
Tel: +64(9) 263 1735
Fax: +64(9) 262 2150
EMail: servicecentre@tec.govt.nz
WWW: http://www.tec.govt.nz
Role of national body: Responsible for funding all post-compulsory education and training offered by universities, institutes of technology and polytechnics, wananga, private training establishments, foundation education agencies, industry training organisations and adult and community education providers.

New Zealand Qualification Authority - NZQA (Mana Tohu Mātauranga o Aotearoa)
Board Chairperson: Sue Suckling
Chief Executive: Karen Poutasi
PO Box 160
Wellington 6140
Tel: +64(4) 463 3000
Fax: +64(4) 463 3112
EMail: helpdesk@nzqa.govt.nz
WWW: http://www.nzqa.govt.nz
Role of national body: Quality assures secondary and tertiary qualifications and education providers, evaluates overseas qualifications and administers the New Zealand Register of Quality Assured Qualifications and the National Qualifications Framework.

New Zealand Council for Educational Research - NZCER (Te Rūnanga o Aotearoa Mō te Rangahau I Te Māta)
Director: Robyn Baker
PO Box 3237
Wellington 6140
Tel: +64(4) 384 7939
Fax: +64(4) 384 7933
WWW: http://www.nzcer.org.nz
Role of national body: Fosters educational research of a high standard and disseminates its results; provides information, advice and assistance to those involved in education.

Universities New Zealand - Te Pōkai Tara
Chairperson: Pat Walsh
Executive Director: Penny Fenwick
PO Box 11915
Wellington 6142
Tel: +64(4) 381 8500
Fax: +64(4) 381 8501
WWW: http://www.universitiesnz.ac.nz/
Role of national body: On behalf of the universities, the NZVCC gives policy advice, undertakes course approval, administers scholarships, and fosters links between the New Zealand system and those overseas.

Data for academic year: 2011-2012
Source: IAU from the National Education Information Centre (NEIC), New Zealand Qualifications Authority (NZQA), 2011. Bodies 2012.

INSTITUTIONS

PUBLIC INSTITUTIONS

AUCKLAND UNIVERSITY OF TECHNOLOGY / TE WANANGA ARONUI O TAMAKI MAKAU RAU (AUT)

Private Bag 92006, Auckland 1142
Tel: +64(9) 921-9999
Fax: +64(9) 921-9968
EMail: courseinfo@aut.ac.nz
Website: http://www.aut.ac.nz

Vice-Chancellor: Derek McCormack (2004-)
Tel: +64(9) 921-9828, Fax: +64(9) 921-9983
EMail: derek.mccormack@aut.ac.nz

General Manager, Services and Operations: John Williams
Tel: +64(9) 921-9850, Fax: +64(9) 921-9983
EMail: john.williams@aut.ac.nz

International Relations: Des Graydon, Pro-Vice-Chancellor
Tel: +64(9) 921-9870, Fax: +64(9) 921-9983
EMail: Des.Graydon@aut.ac.nz

Faculties
Applied Humanities (Education; Linguistics; Social Sciences) *Dean*: Robert Allen; **Design and Creative Technologies** *Dean*: Kathryn Garden; **Health and Environmental Services** (Community Health; Midwifery; Nursing; Occupational Therapy; Paramedical Sciences; Psychoanalysis; Psychology; Public Health; Rehabilitation and Therapy; Social Studies) *Dean*: Max Abbot; **Te Ara Poutama (Maori Education)** (Indigenous Studies)

Schools
Business (Accountancy; Business and Commerce; Economics; Finance; International Business; Marketing; Taxation); **Law** (Law)

History: Founded 1895 as Auckland Technical School. Changed its name to Seddon Memorial Technical College 1913. Became Auckland Institute of Technology 1989. Acquired present status and title 2000.

Governing Bodies: University Council

Academic Year: February to November; Summer School December to January

Admission Requirements: Secondary school certificate or equivalent, entrance examination

Fees: (NZ Dollars): c. 4,500 per annum per full-time domestic student

Main Language(s) of Instruction: English

International Co-operation: With over 160 institutions

Accrediting Agencies: New-Zealand Vice-Chancellors' Committee

Degrees and Diplomas: *Diploma*: 1-2 yrs; *Graduate Diploma*: 1yr; *Bachelor's Degree*: 3-4 yrs; *Bachelor's Degree with Honours*: 1 yr following Bachelor's or 4 yrs; *Postgraduate Diploma*: 2 yrs; *Master's Degree*: a further 1-2 yrs; *Doctoral Degree*: 3 yrs following Master's Degree

Student Services: Academic counselling, Canteen, Cultural centre, Employment services, Foreign student adviser, Foreign Studies Centre, Handicapped facilities, Health services, Language programs, Nursery care, Social counselling, Sports facilities

Student Residential Facilities: Yes

Special Facilities: TV Studio. Radio Station

Libraries: University Library
Last Updated: 12/11/08

CENTRE FOR HIGHER LEARNING OF NGATI RAUKAWA, NGATITOA AND TE ATIAWA TRIBES / TE WANANGA O RAUKAWA

P.O. Box 119, 144 Tasman Road, Otaki
Tel: +64(6) 364-7820
Fax: +64(6) 364-7822
EMail: tetomonga@twor-otaki.ac.nz
Website: http://www.twor.ac.nz

Tumuaki (Principal): Mereana Selby
EMail: whatarangi.winiata@twor-otaki.ac.nz

Departments
Administration (Administration); **Art and Design** (Design; Fine Arts); **Environmental Studies** (Environmental Studies); **Hapu Development**; **Health Studies** (Health Sciences); **Language Studies** (Modern Languages); **Law and Philosophy** (Law; Philosophy); **Matauranga Maori**

History: Founded 1981. A State Institution.

Degrees and Diplomas: *Diploma*; *Bachelor's Degree*; *Postgraduate Diploma*; *Master's Degree*
Last Updated: 15/12/08

CHRISTCHURCH POLYTECHNIC INSTITUTE OF TECHNOLOGY / TE WANANGA O OTAUTAHI (CPIT)

P.O. Box 540, 130 Madras Street, Christchurch 8032
Tel: +64(3) 940-8000
Fax: +64(3) 366-6544
EMail: info@cpit.ac.nz
Website: http://www.cpit.ac.nz

Chief Executive: Kay Giles (2010-) EMail: kay.giles@cpit.ac.nz

International Relations: Elizabeth Knowles, International Director
EMail: beth.knowles@cpit.ac.nz

Faculties
Commerce (Business Administration; Business and Commerce; Computer Science; Food Science; Tourism); **Creative Industries** (Building Technologies; Computer Engineering; Cosmetology; Design; Electrical Engineering; Engineering; Fine Arts; Interior Design; Performing Arts; Radio and Television Broadcasting; Technology); **Health, Humanities and Science** (Community Health; Health Sciences; Horticulture; Mathematics; Midwifery; Nursing; Radiology); **Maori** (Natives Education); **Trades and Engineering** (Automotive Engineering; Computer Engineering; Engineering; Furniture Design; Metal Techniques)

History: Founded 1906, acquired present status and title 1990. A State Institution.

Main Language(s) of Instruction: English

Degrees and Diplomas: *Certificate*; *Diploma*; *Graduate Diploma*; *Bachelor's Degree*

Libraries: Yes
Last Updated: 15/12/08

EASTERN INSTITUTE OF TECHNOLOGY/TE WHARE TAKIURA O KOHUNGUNU (EIT HAWKE'S BAY)

501 Gloucester Street, Taradale, Hawke's Bay
Tel: +64(6) 974-8000
Fax: +64(6) 974-8910
EMail: info@eit.ac.nz
Website: http://www.eit.ac.nz

Chief Executive: Chris Collins

Corporate Services Manager: Kerry Marshall
EMail: kmarshall@eit.ac.nz

International Relations: Helen Kemp, International Marketing Manager EMail: hkemp@eit.ac.nz

Faculties
Applied Science, Business and Computing (Agriculture; Automotive Engineering; Business Administration; Electrical Engineering; Horticulture; Maintenance Technology; Mechanical Engineering; Natural Sciences; Oenology; Technology; Viticulture); **Health and Sports Science** (Cosmetology; Health Sciences; Nursing; Sports); **Humanities, Arts and Trades** (Arts and Humanities; Clothing and Sewing; Cooking and Catering; Design; English; Fashion Design; Performing Arts; Preschool Education; Social and

Community Services; Social Sciences; Textile Design; Theatre; Tourism; Video; Visual Arts); **Maori Studies** (Indigenous Studies)

History: Founded 1975 as Hawke's Bay Community College. Acquired present status and title 1996.

Main Language(s) of Instruction: English

Degrees and Diplomas: *Certificate*; *Diploma*; *Graduate Certificate*; *Graduate Diploma*; *Bachelor's Degree*; *Master's Degree*

Student Residential Facilities: Residential Village

Special Facilities: Audio-visual Centre

Libraries: Twist Library

Last Updated: 31/08/11

HOUSE FOR HIGHER LEARNING OF AWANUIARANGI / TE WHARE WANANGA O AWANUIARANGI

Private Bag 1006, Francis Street, Whakatane
Tel: +64(7) 307-1467
Fax: +64(7) 307-1475
EMail: reception@wananga.ac.nz
Website: http://www.wananga.ac.nz

Chief Executive: Graham Smith (1992-)
EMail: gary.hook@wananga.ac.nz

Schools

Indiginous Graduate Studies (Education; Environmental Studies; Indigenous Studies); **Iwi Development** (Indigenous Studies); **Undergraduate Studies**

History: Founded 1992. A State Institution.

Degrees and Diplomas: *Certificate*; *Diploma*; *Bachelor's Degree*; *Master's Degree*; *Doctoral Degree*

Last Updated: 31/08/11

LINCOLN UNIVERSITY / TE WHARE WANAKA O AORAKI

P.O. Box 94, Lincoln University, Canterbury 7647
Tel: +64(3) 325-2811
Fax: +64(3) 325-2965
EMail: info@lincoln.ac.nz
Website: http://www.lincoln.ac.nz

Vice-Chancellor: Andrew West (2012-)
EMail: andrew.west@lincoln.ac.nz

Finance Director: John Clark EMail: john.clark@lincoln.ac.nz

International Relations: Melanie O'Toole, Director International
EMail: otoolem@lincoln.ac.nz

Faculties

Agriculture and Life Sciences (Agriculture; Cell Biology; Food Science; Oenology; Physics; Soil Science); **Commerce** (Accountancy; Agricultural Business; Business Administration; Business and Commerce; Economics; Finance; Marketing); **Environment, Society and Design** (Arts and Humanities; Communication Studies; Environmental Management; Indigenous Studies; Landscape Architecture; Leisure Studies; Natural Resources; Parks and Recreation; Social Sciences; Tourism; Transport Management)

Research Centres

Accountancy, Education and Research *(CAER) Director*: C. Wright; **Advanced Bio-Protection Technologies** *Director*: Alison Stewart; **Advanced Computational Solutions** (Computer Science) *Head*: Don Kulasiri; **Environmental Toxicology** *Manager*: Ravi Gooneratne; **Mountain Studies** *Director*: Kenneth F.D. Hughey; **Natural Resources Engineering**; **Nature Conservation** *(Isaac)* (Environmental Studies) *Director*: Ian Spellerberg; **Soil and Environmental Quality** *Head*: Keith C. Cameron; **Soil and Physical Sciences** (Environmental Studies; Soil Science) *Director*: Keith Cameron; **Tourism, Recreation Research and Education** *(TRREC)*; **Viticulture and Oenology** (Oenology; Viticulture) *Head*: Roland Harrison

Research Units

Agribusiness and Economics *(AERU)* (Agricultural Business; Business Administration; Economics)

History: Founded 1878 as Lincoln School of Agriculture, 1961 became Lincoln College and was Constituent College of University of Canterbury. Acquired present status and title 1990.

Governing Bodies: University Council

Academic Year: February to November (February-May; May-August; September-November). Summer schools November to February

Admission Requirements: Acceptable grades in the National Certificate of Education Achievement Level 3 or equivalent

Main Language(s) of Instruction: English

Degrees and Diplomas: *Graduate Certificate*; *Graduate Diploma*; *Bachelor's Degree*: Agricultural Science (BAgrSc); Horticulture Science (Bhor.Sc); Landscape Architecture (BLA), 4 yrs; *Bachelor's Degree*: Applied Computing (BApplComp); Commerce (Agriculture) (Bcom(Ag)); Commerce (Food Industry) (BCom(Food Industry)); Commerce (Hotel and Institutional Management) (BCom(H&IM)); Commerce (Transport and Logistics) (BCom(T&L)); Commerce (Valuation and Property Management) (BCom(VPM)); Commerce and Management (Bcom); Environmental Management (BEM); Maori Planning and Development (BMPD); Recreation Management (Parks) (BRM (Parks)); Science (Biological Sciences, Environmental Sciences, Computing and Mathematical Sciences, Food Science) (BSc); Social Science (BSocSc); Software and Information Technology (BSIT); Tourism Management (BTourMgt); Viticulture and Oenology (BV&O), 3 yrs; *Postgraduate Certificate*; *Postgraduate Diploma*: 1 yr; *Master's Degree*: a further 1-2 yrs; *Doctoral Degree (PhD)*: 2-4 yrs; *Higher Doctorate*: Science; Commerce; Natural Resources (DSc, Dcomm, DNatRes)

Student Services: Academic counselling, Canteen, Cultural centre, Employment services, Foreign student adviser, Foreign Studies Centre, Handicapped facilities, Health services, Language programs, Nursery care, Social counselling, Sports facilities

Student Residential Facilities: For c. 600 students

Libraries: c. 210,000 vols

Publications: Agribusiness and Economic Research Unit publications

Last Updated: 13/09/12

MASSEY UNIVERSITY / TE KUNENGA KI PUREHUROA

Private Bag 11-222, Palmerston North
Tel: +64(6) 350-5799
Fax: +64(6) 350-5630
EMail: contact@massey.ac.nz
Website: http://www.massey.ac.nz

Vice-Chancellor and President: Steve Maharey (2008-)
Tel: +64(6) 350-5096 EMail: S.Maharey@massey.ac.nz

University Registrar: Stuart Morriss
Tel: +64(6) 350-5799 Ext.7172, Fax: +64(6) 350-5666
EMail: S.D.Morriss@massey.ac.nz

International Relations: John Raine, Deputy Vice-Chancellor
Tel: +64(6) 414-0800 Ext. 9517, Fax: +64(6) 414-0841
EMail: J.Raine@massey.ac.nz

Colleges

Business (Accountancy; Air Transport; Banking; Business and Commerce; Business Computing; Commercial Law; Economics; Finance; Human Resources; Institutional Administration; International Business; International Economics; Management; Management Systems; Marketing; Public Administration; Real Estate; Sports Management; Systems Analysis); **Creative Arts** (Dance; Design; Fashion Design; Fine Arts; Industrial Design; Music; Performing Arts; Photography; Textile Design; Theatre; Visual Arts); **Education** (Adult Education; Bilingual and Bicultural Education; Continuing Education; Educational Research; Educational Sciences; Mathematics; Native Language Education; Preschool Education; Primary Education; Science Education; Secondary Education; Teacher Trainers Education; Vocational Education); **Humanities and Social Sciences** (Anthropology; Chinese; Cultural Studies; English; Environmental Management; European Studies; French; Geography; German; Greek (Classical); Health Administration; Heritage Preservation; History; International Studies; Japanese; Linguistics; Literature; Media Studies; Museum Studies; Native Language; Natural Resources; Nursing; Pacific Area Studies;

Philosophy; Police Studies; Political Sciences; Psychology; Regional Planning; Religious Studies; Social Policy; Sociology; Spanish; Women's Studies; Writing); **Science** (Agricultural Engineering; Agronomy; Anatomy; Animal Husbandry; Applied Mathematics; Biochemistry; Biology; Biomedicine; Biophysics; Botany; Chemistry; Consumer Studies; Ecology; Engineering; Farm Management; Food Science; Food Technology; Health Sciences; Horticulture; Information Sciences; Information Technology; Mathematics; Mathematics and Computer Science; Microbiology; Molecular Biology; Natural Resources; Natural Sciences; Nutrition; Packaging Technology; Physics; Physiology; Production Engineering; Soil Science; Statistics; Technology; Veterinary Science; Water Science; Zoology)

Further Information: Also Research Centres http://research.massey.ac.nz/massey/research/research-centres.cfm

History: Founded 1963 as Massey University College of Manawatu, incorporating Massey College (1926) and Palmerston North Branch of Victoria University of Wellington (1960). Acquired present status 1964. Established Albany Campus 1993. Merged with Palmerston North College of Education 1996. Merged with Wellington Polytechnic 1999.

Governing Bodies: Council; Academic Board

Academic Year: January to December

Admission Requirements: Acceptable grades in the National Certificate of Educational Achievement Level 3, or by applied Discretionary Entrance following National Certificate of Educational Achievement Level 2

Fees: (NZ Dollars): Undergraduate, c. 3,175-7,110 per annum; postgraduate taught, c. 3,964-7,271 per annum; postgraduate research: 1,635-2,810; foreign students: undergraduate, c. 16,000-28,750; postgraduate taught 17,600-30,200

Main Language(s) of Instruction: English

Accrediting Agencies: Committee for University Academic Programmes; New Zealand Qualification Authority

Degrees and Diplomas: *Bachelor's Degree*; *Bachelor's Degree*: Accountancy (Bacc); Agri-Commerce (BAgriCom); Agri-Science (BAgriSc); Applied Economics (BAppEcon); Arts (BA); Business Studies (BBS); Communication (BC); Defence Studies (BDefStuds); Education (BEd); Education (Teaching) (BEd(Tchg)); Engineering Technology (BEngTech); Environmental Management (BEnvMgmt); Health Science (BHlthSc); Information Sciences (BInfSc); Music (Bmus); Science (BSc); Sports and Exercise (BSpEx), 3 yrs; *Bachelor's Degree*: Aviation (BAv); Aviation Management (BAvMan); Construction (BC); Design (BDes); Engineering (BE (Hons)); Fine Arts (BFA); Maori Visual Arts (MVA); Medical Laboratory Science (MLS); Midwifery (BN); Nursing (BN); Performance Design (BPerfDes); Resource and Environmental Planning (BRP); Social Work (BSW); Speech and Language Therapy (BSpchLangTher); Technology (Btech (Hons)), 4 yrs; *Bachelor's Degree*: Veterinary Science (BVSc), 5 yrs; *Bachelor's Degree with Honours*: Applied Economics with Honours (BapplEcon(Hons)); Applied Science with Honours (BapplSc(Hons)); Arts with Honours (BA(Hons)); Aviation Management with Honours (BAvMan (Hons)); Aviation with Honours (Bav (Hons)); Business Studies with Honours (BBS(Hons)); Education (Teaching) with Honours (Bed(Tchg) (Hons)); Education with Honours (BEd(Hons)); Information Science with Honours (BInfSc(Hons)); Music with Honours (Bmus (Hons)); Science with Honours (BSc(Hons)), 1 yr; *Master's Degree*: Applied Economics (MapplEcon); Applied Science (MapplSc); Applied Statistics (MapplStats); Arts (MA); Aviation (MAv); Business Administration (MBS); Business Studies (MBS); Counselling (MCouns); Development Administration (MDA); Education (MEd); Educational Administration (MEdAdmin); Educational Psychology (MEDPsych); Educational Studies (MEdStud); Ergonomics (MErg); Fine Arts (MFA); Information Sciences (MInfSc); Information Systems (MInfSyst); Literacy Education (MLitEd); Maori Visual Art (MMVA); Midwifery (Mmid); Music (MMus); Music Therapy (MMusTher); Nursing (MNurs); Public Health (MPH); Public Policy (MPP); Resource and Environmental Planning (MRP); Science (MSc); Social Work (MSW); Technology (MTech); Veterinary Science (MVSc); Veterinary Studies (MVS), 2 yrs; *Master's Degree*: Dairy Science and Technology (MDairyScTech); Design (MDesign); Engineering (ME); Management (MMgt); Veterinary Medicine (MVM), 1 yr; *Master's Degree*: Philosophy (MPhil), a further 2 yrs; *Doctoral Degree*: Business and Administration (DBA); Clinical Psychology (DClinPsych); Education (EdD), 3 yrs; *Doctoral Degree*: Literature (DLitt); Science (DSc); *Doctoral Degree*: Philosophy (PhD), 4 yrs. Also undergraduate and postgraduate Diplomas

Student Services: Academic counselling, Canteen, Cultural centre, Employment services, Foreign student adviser, Foreign Studies Centre, Handicapped facilities, Health services, Language programs, Nursery care, Social counselling, Sports facilities

Student Residential Facilities: For c. 1,300 students

Special Facilities: 2000 ha of farmlands

Libraries: Total: c. 800,000 vols. of books, videos, microfilms and subscriptions to c. 9,000 journals

Publications: Massey University Charter; Reports of Research Centres *(annually)*

Last Updated: 31/08/11

ALBANY CAMPUS

Private Bag 102-904, North Shore, North Shore City
Tel: +64(9) 443-9517
Fax: +64(9) 443-9414
EMail: J.Raine@massey.ac.nz
Website: http://www.massey.ac.nz

Deputy Vice-Chancellor Auckland: John Raine (2004-)
Tel: +64(9) 443-9517, Fax: +64(9) 443-9414

History: Founded 1963. Acquired present status and title 1993.

PALMERSTON NORTH CAMPUS

Private Bag 11-222, Palmerston North
Tel: +64(6) 356-9099
Fax: +64(6) 350-5630
EMail: contact@massey.ac.nz
Website: http://www.massey.ac.nz/massey/student-life/manawatu-campus/palmerston-north_home.cfm

Campus Registrar: Sandi Shillington

Programmes

Agriculture (Agriculture); **Horticulture** (Horticulture); **Life Sciences** (Biological and Life Sciences); **Veterinary Science** (Veterinary Science)

History: Founded 1963. Acquired present status and title 1964.

Degrees and Diplomas: *Bachelor's Degree*; *Postgraduate Diploma*; *Master's Degree*; *Doctoral Degree*

WELLINGTON CAMPUS

Private Bag 756, Wallace Street, Wellington
Tel: 64(4) 801-5799
Fax: 64(4) 801-2779
EMail: contact@massey.ac.nz
Website: http://www.massey.ac.nz/massey/contact/wellington-campus/en/wellington-campus_home.cfm

Principal: Andrea McIlroy (2006-)
Tel: +64(4) 801 5799 Ext. 62302, Fax: +64(4) 801-2790
EMail: A.McIlroy@massey.ac.nz

Centres

Public Health Research (Public Health); **Sleep/Wake Research** (Behavioural Sciences)

Departments

Educational Development (Educational Sciences)

Institutes

Food, Nutrition and Human Health (Food Science; Health Sciences; Nutrition); **Information Sciences and Technology** (Information Sciences; Information Technology); **Technology and Engineering** (Engineering; Technology)

Schools

Business and Information Systems (Business Administration); **Design** (Design); **Engineering and Construction** (Construction Engineering; Engineering); **Health Sciences** (Health Sciences); **Language Studies** (Modern Languages); **Maori Studies** (Indigenous Studies); **Psychology** (Psychology); **Social Work and Social Policy** (Social Policy; Social Work)

History: Founded 1963. Acquired present status and title 1998.

NELSON MARLBOROUGH INSTITUTE OF TECHNOLOGY / TE WHARE WANANGA O TE TAU IMU (NMIT)

Private Bag 19, Nelson 7042
Tel: +64(3) 546-9175
Fax: +64(3) 546-3325
EMail: info@nmit.ac.nz; international@nmit.ac.nz
Website: http://www.nmit.ac.nz

Chief Executive: Tony Gray (2006-)
EMail: tony.gray@nmit.ac.nz

Senior Executive Assistant: Linnea Brown
Tel: +64(3) 546-2479 EMail: Linnea.Brown@nmit.ac.nz

International Relations: Joanna Hannaford, International Business Development Manager
Tel: +64(3) 546-9175 ext 611, Fax: +64(3) 546-3325
EMail: Joanna.Hannaford@nmit.ac.nz

Programmes

Applied Business (Accountancy; Business and Commerce; Management; Tourism); **Aviation** (Aeronautical and Aerospace Engineering; Air Transport); **Business Services** (Business Administration; Computer Science; Information Technology); **Creative Industries** (Fine Arts; Media Studies; Music; Writing); **Health** (Nursing; Social Welfare; Social Work); **Hospitality and Wellbeing** (Cooking and Catering; Cosmetology; Sports); **Maritime** (Aquaculture; Marine Biology; Marine Science and Oceanography; Marine Transport); **Primary Industries** (Horticulture; Viticulture); **Trades** (Automotive Engineering; Construction Engineering; Mechanical Equipment and Maintenance)

History: Founded 1905. Nelson Marlborough Institute of Technology (NMIT) has provided high quality innovative applied and vocational education courses in the Nelson Marlborough region for over 105 years. NMIT welcomes 5000 students including 500 international students from more than 35 countries.

Governing Bodies: NMIT Council

Academic Year: Semester One, February to June; Semester Two, July to November; Summer School, December to February,

Admission Requirements: Secondary school certificate or recognized equivalent; IELTS 5.5 - 6.5 for non-native English speakers,

Fees: (NZ$): 17,000 per annum (international students)

Main Language(s) of Instruction: English

International Co-operation: with institutions in Sweded, Germany, Austria, Japan, China.

Accrediting Agencies: New Zealand Qualifications Authority (NZQA)

Degrees and Diplomas: *Graduate Diploma*: Accounting; Management; Marketing; Information Technology; *Bachelor's Degree*: Arts and Media; Commerce; Information Technology; *Bachelor's Degree with Honours*

Student Services: Academic counselling, Canteen, Cultural centre, Employment services, Foreign student adviser, Handicapped facilities, Health services, Language programs, Nursery care, Social counselling, Sports facilities

Student Residential Facilities: Yes

Special Facilities: Arts and Media Building; Tourism, Hospitality and Wellbeing Building; Student Centre;

Libraries: c. 59,000 vols; 279 periodical subscriptions; 33 database subscriptions

Academic Staff *2012-2013*	MEN	WOMEN	**TOTAL**
FULL-TIME	57	32	**89**
PART-TIME	46	74	**120**
STAFF WITH DOCTORATE			
FULL-TIME	–	3	**3**
PART-TIME	2	1	**3**
Student Numbers *2012-2013*			
All (Foreign Included)	2,963	3,318	**6,281**
FOREIGN ONLY	310	184	**494**

Part-time students, 3,235. **Distance students**, 399. **Evening students**, 1,402.

Last Updated: 14/12/12

OTAGO POLYTECHNIC

Private Bag 1910, Forth Street, Dunedin
Tel: +64(3) 477-3014
Fax: +64(3) 477-6870
EMail: info@tekotago.ac.nz
Website: http://www.otagopolytechnic.ac.nz

Chief Executive: Phil Ker (2004-)
Tel: +64(3) 479-6001, Fax: +64(3) 477-5185
EMail: pker@tekotago.ac.nz

Centres

Educational Development (Education)

Institutes

Sport and Adventure (Mountain Studies; Physical Education; Sports)

Schools

Applied Business (Accountancy; Business Administration; Management; Marketing; Tourism); **Architecture, Building and Engineering** (Architecture; Building Technologies; Civil Engineering; Electrical Engineering; Engineering; Fine Arts; Information Technology); **Art** *(Dunedin)* (Ceramic Art; Fine Arts; Visual Arts); **Design** (Design; Fashion Design; Interior Design); **Hospitality** (Cooking and Catering; Food Science; Hotel Management); **Information Technology** (Information Technology); **Midwifery** (Midwifery); **Natural Resources** (Forestry; Horticulture; Landscape Architecture; Viticulture); **Nursing** (Nursing); **Occupational Therapy** (Occupational Therapy); **Social Services** (Social and Community Services); **Veterinary Nursing** (Veterinary Science)

History: Founded 1966.

Main Language(s) of Instruction: English

Degrees and Diplomas: *Certificate*; *Diploma*; *Bachelor's Degree*; *Postgraduate Certificate*; *Postgraduate Diploma*; *Master's Degree*

Student Residential Facilities: Yes

Libraries: Yes

Last Updated: 31/08/11

SOUTHERN INSTITUTE OF TECHNOLOGY / TE WHARE WANANGA O MURIHIKU (SIT)

Private Bag 90114, Invercargill 9840
Tel: +64(3) 211-2699
Fax: +64(3) 211-4977
EMail: info@sit.ac.nz
Website: http://www.sit.ac.nz

Chief Executive Officer: Penny Simmonds (1997-)
Tel: +64(3) 211-2600, Fax: +64(3) 211-2620
EMail: penny.simmonds@sit.ac.nz

Deputy Chief Executive Officer, Academic Manager: Julian Galt
Tel: +64(3) 211-2602, Fax: +64(3) 211-2620
EMail: julian.galt@sit.ac.nz

International Relations: Bharat Guha, Business Services Manager
Tel: +64(3) 211-2603, Fax: +64(3) 211-4977
EMail: bharat.guha@sit.ac.nz

Divisions

SIT2LRN *(Flexible Mixed Mode Division (distance education))* (Agriculture; Arts and Humanities; Business Administration; Education; Information Sciences; Service Trades; Welfare and Protective Services)

Faculties

Health, Humanities and Computing (Computer Science; English; Health Sciences; Leisure Studies; Nursing; Parks and Recreation; Social Welfare); **New Media, Arts and Business** (Business and Commerce; Cinema and Television; Design; Hotel and Restaurant; Journalism; Media Studies; Music; Native Language; Radio and Television Broadcasting; Theatre; Tourism; Visual Arts); **Trades and Technology** (Architecture; Automotive Engineering; Biological and Life Sciences; Building Technologies; Cosmetology; Electrical Engineering; Engineering; Mechanical Engineering; Pharmacy; Veterinary Science; Wood Technology)

Further Information: SIT also operates sites in Queenstown, Gore and Christchurch.

History: Founded 1971. Provides applied vocational education in flexible learning methods.

Governing Bodies: SIT Council

Academic Year: January to December

Admission Requirements: Subject to level or degree of qualification.

Fees: Subject to programme type and duration.

Main Language(s) of Instruction: English

International Co-operation: With institutions in Australia, China, Czech Republic, Japan, UK.

Accrediting Agencies: NZQA

Degrees and Diplomas: *Bachelor's Degree*: Media Arts (Dramatic Arts, Journalism, Visual Media); Audio Production; Contemporary Music; Digital Media; Environmental Management; Hotel Management; Information Technology; Nursing; Sport and Recreation; Therapeutic and Sports Massage, 3 yrs; *Postgraduate Diploma*: Business Enterprise; Health Science, 1 yr - 18 months

Student Services: Academic counselling, Canteen, Cultural centre, Employment services, Foreign student adviser, Foreign Studies Centre, Handicapped facilities, Health services, Language programs, Nursery care, Social counselling, Sports facilities

Academic Staff *2010*	TOTAL
FULL-TIME	161
STAFF WITH DOCTORATE FULL-TIME	7

Student Numbers *2010*	
All (Foreign Included)	4,843
FOREIGN ONLY	362

Distance students, 1,201.

Last Updated: 31/08/11

THE UNIVERSITY OF AUCKLAND / TE WHARE WANANGA O TAMAKI MAKAURAU (UOA)

Private Bag 92019, Auckland 1142
Tel: +64(9) 308-2386
Fax: +64(9) 373-7507
EMail: studentinfo@auckland.ac.nz
Website: http://www.auckland.ac.nz

Vice-Chancellor: Stuart N. McCutcheon (2004-)
Tel: +64(9) 373-7518, Fax: +64(9) 373-7407

Registrar and General Counsel: Timothy P. Greville
Tel: +64(9) 303-5963 EMail: t.greville@auckland.ac.nz

International Relations: Christopher Tremewan
Tel: +64(9) 373-7599, Ext.84799, Fax: +64(9) 373-7646
EMail: int-questions@auckland.ac.nz

Faculties

Arts and Humanities (Ancient Civilizations; Anthropology; Archaeology; Art History; Arts and Humanities; Asian Studies; Chinese; Classical Languages; Comparative Literature; Computer Science; Continuing Education; Criminology; Development Studies; Economics; Education; English; Ethics; European Languages; European Studies; Film; French; Geography; German; Greek; Hebrew; History; Human Rights; International Relations; Italian; Japanese; Korean; Labour and Industrial Relations; Latin; Latin American Studies; Linguistics; Literature; Media Studies; Medieval Studies; Modern Languages; Museum Studies; Music; Native Language; Pacific Area Studies; Philosophy; Polish; Political Sciences; Public Health; Radio and Television Broadcasting; Russian; Slavic Languages; Social Sciences; Sociology; Spanish; Theatre; Theology; Translation and Interpretation; Women's Studies; Writing); **Creative Arts and Industries** (Architecture and Planning; Dance; Fine Arts; Music; Performing Arts; Visual Arts); **Education** (Education); **Engineering** (Bioengineering; Chemical Engineering; Civil Engineering; Computer Engineering; Electrical and Electronic Engineering; Environmental Engineering; Materials Engineering; Mechanical Engineering); **Law** (Commercial Law; Comparative Law; Criminal Law; International Law; Law; Private Law; Public Law); **Medical and Health Sciences** (Anaesthesiology; Anatomy; Community Health; Epidemiology; Gynaecology and Obstetrics; Health Sciences; Medicine; Nursing; Nutrition; Ophthalmology; Paediatrics; Pathology; Pharmacology; Pharmacy; Physiology; Psychology; Radiology; Speech Therapy and Audiology; Surgery); **Science** (Biological and Life Sciences; Chemistry; Computer Science; Environmental Studies; Geography; Geology; Marine Science and Oceanography; Mathematics; Optometry; Physics; Psychology; Sports; Statistics)

Institutes

Liggins (Child Care and Development)

Schools

Business (Accountancy; Business and Commerce; Commercial Law; Economics; Finance; International Business; Management; Marketing; Real Estate); **Psychology** (Psychology); **Theology** (Theology) *Head*: Elaine Wainwright

History: Founded 1883 as Auckland University College, acquired present title and became Constituent Institution of University of New Zealand 1957. Became autonomous 1961. Incorporated the former Auckland College of Education 2004.

Governing Bodies: Council; Senate

Academic Year: February to November (Semester One: February-June; Semester Two: July-November). Summer school, January-February

Admission Requirements: International students who have attained University Entrance (the minimum standard for admission to New Zealand universities) must fulfil additional requirements for certain Auckland degree programmes with higher entry standards. Applications will be assessed on a case-by-case basis. If English is not the first language students will be required to submit proof of English language proficiency.

Fees: (NZ Dollars): Domestic students: 4,784-12,274; international students: 20,040-60,720 per annum

Main Language(s) of Instruction: English

Degrees and Diplomas: *Bachelor's Degree*: 3-5 yrs; *Master's Degree*: 1-2 yrs; *Doctoral Degree (PhD)*: approximately 3-4 yrs

Student Services: Academic counselling, Canteen, Cultural centre, Employment services, Foreign student adviser, Foreign Studies Centre, Handicapped facilities, Health services, Language programs, Nursery care, Social counselling, Sports facilities

Student Residential Facilities: Yes

Special Facilities: Gus Fisher Gallery. George Fraser Gallery. Maidment Theatre.

Libraries: c. 2.2 m. print, multimedia and microtext collections; access to more than 850 databases, 100,000 electronic journals and 420,000 electronic books

Press or Publishing House: Auckland University Press

Academic Staff *2010*	MEN	WOMEN	TOTAL
FULL-TIME	–	–	2,036
Student Numbers *2010*			
All (Foreign Included)	17,588	23,389	40,977
FOREIGN ONLY	–	–	4,709

Last Updated: 31/08/11

THE UNIVERSITY OF WAIKATO / TE WHARE WANANGA O WAIKATO

Private Bag 3105, Hamilton
Tel: +64(7) 856-2889
Fax: +64(7) 838-4545
EMail: info@waikato.ac.nz
Website: http://www.waikato.ac.nz

Vice-Chancellor: Roy Crawford
Tel: +64(7) 838-4006, Fax: +64(7) 838-4443

Assistant Vice-Chancellor (Executive): Helen Pridmore
EMail: hmp@waikato.ac.nz

International Relations: Ed Weymes, Pro-Vice-Chancellor International
Tel: +64(7) 838-4842, Fax: +64(7) 838-4063
EMail: weymesed@waikato.ac.nz

Centres

Animal Behaviour and Welfare Research (Zoology) *Director*: R.J. Wilkins; **Coastal Oceanography and Marine Geology** (Coastal Studies; Marine Science and Oceanography) *Director*: K. P. Black; **Executive Education** (Business Education) *Director*: E. Weynes;

Labour and Trade Union Studies (Labour and Industrial Relations) *Director*: D. Neilson; **Maori Studies and Research** (Indigenous Studies) *Senior Research Fellow*: B. Harrison; **Science, Mathematics and Technology, Education Research** (Educational Research; Mathematics; Natural Sciences; Technology) *Director*: A.T. Jones

Faculties

Arts and Social Sciences (Fine Arts; Psychology; Social Sciences); **Computing and Mathematical Science** (Computer Science; Mathematics; Statistics); **Education** (Education; Leisure Studies; Sports); **Law** (Law)

Institutes

Language *(Second Language Research and English for foreign students)* (Linguistics; Modern Languages) *Director*: L. Finch; **Teaching and Learning Development** (Pedagogy) *Director*: N. Haigh

Schools

Computing and Mathematical Sciences (Computer Science; Mathematics; Statistics) *Dean*: Mark Apperley; **Education** (Art Education; Austronesian and Oceanic Languages; Bilingual and Bicultural Education; Child Care and Development; Communication Studies; Education; Health Education; Leisure Studies; Mathematics; Modern Languages; Native Language Education; Natural Sciences; Physical Education; Preschool Education; Science Education; Social Studies; Technology Education) *Dean*: N. Alcorn; **Law** (Law); **Management** (Accountancy; Communication Studies; Economics; Finance; International Business; Leadership; Management; Management Systems; Marketing) *Dean*: M.J. Pratt; **Maori and Pacific Development** *(Te Timatanga Hou Programme)* (Austronesian and Oceanic Languages; Demography and Population; Development Studies); **Science and Technology** (Biological and Life Sciences; Chemistry; Earth Sciences; Electronic Engineering; Engineering Management; Materials Engineering; Natural Sciences; Physics; Technology; Zoology) *Dean*: R. Price

Units

Antarctic Research (Regional Studies) *Director*: C.H. Hendy; **Carbon Dating** *Senior Research Officer*: A.G. Hogg; **Co-operative Education** (Education) *Director*: R.K. Coll; **Geo-chronology Research** *Director*: C.S. Nelson; **Honey Research** (Apiculture) *Director*: P.C. Molan; **Thermophile and Microbial Biochemistry and Biotechnology** (Biochemistry; Biotechnology) *Director*: R.M. Daniel; **Waikato Stable Isotope** *Director*: W.B. Silvester; **Water Research** (Water Science) *Director*: W.E. Bardsley

History: Founded 1964. Branch Campus, Tauranga University College, Bongard Centre, Tauranga.

Governing Bodies: Council; Academic Board; Boards of Studies

Academic Year: January to November

Admission Requirements: New Zealand Universities entrance, Bursaries and Scholarship Examination, or recognized foreign equivalent

Fees: A schedule of the University's tuition fees is available on request

Main Language(s) of Instruction: English. Immersion degree in Maori also available.

Degrees and Diplomas: *Bachelor's Degree*: Arts; Communication Studies (BCS); Computer Graphic Design (BCGD); Laws and Arts (BA/LLB); Laws and Management Studies (BMS/LLB); Laws and Science (BSc/LLB); Laws and Social Sciences (BSocSc/LLB); Science (BSc); Social Sciences (BSocSc); Teaching (BTchg), 3-4 yrs; *Bachelor's Degree*: Computing and Mathematical Sciences (BCMS); Engineering (BE); Laws (LLB); Management Studies (BMS); Science (Technology) (BSc(Tech)), 4 yrs; *Bachelor's Degree*: Electronic Commerce (BECom); Liberal Studies (BLibS); Maori and Pacific Development (BMPD); Music (BMus); Sport and Leisure (BSpLs); Tourism (BTour), 3 yrs; *Bachelor's Degree with Honours*: Arts (BA(Hons)); Computer Graphic Design (BCGD(Hons)); Electronic Commerce (BECom(Hons)); Music (BMus(Hons)); Science (BSc(Hons)); Social Sciences (BSocSc(Hons)); Sport and Leisure Studies (BSpLs(Hons)), 1 yr; *Bachelor's Degree with Honours*: Communications Studies (BCS(Hons)), At least 1 yr; *Bachelor's Degree with Honours*: Engineering (BE(Hons)); Laws (LLB(Hons)), 4 yrs; *Bachelor's Degree with Honours*: Management Studies (BMS(Hons)), 4 1/2 yrs; *Bachelor's Degree with Honours*: Teaching (BTChg(Hons)), 1 further yr; *Master's Degree*: Applied Arts (MA (Applied)); Applied Psychology (MAppPsy); Arts (MA); Business Administration (MBA); Computing and Mathematical Sciences (MCMS); Laws (LLM); Management Studies (MMS); Philosophy (MPhil); Social Sciences (MSocSc), a further 1-2 yrs; *Master's Degree*: Computer Graphic Design (MCGD); Environmental Planning (MEP); Maori and Pacific Development (MMPD); Music (MMus), at least 1 yr; *Master's Degree*: Counselling (MCouns); Education (MEd); Educational Leadership (MEdLeadership); Science (MSc); Science (Technology) (MSc (Tech)); Special Education (MSpEd); Sport and Leisure Studies (MSpLs), at least 2 yrs; *Master's Degree*: Electronic Commerce (MECom), at least 1 yr; *Master's Degree*: Engineering (ME), at least 15 months; *Master's Degree*: Innovation and Technology (MTM), 3-4 yrs (part-time); *Master's Degree*: Laws in Maori/Pacific and Indigenous Peoples' Law (LLM (Maori/Pacific and Indigenous Peoples)), at least 1 yr; *Doctoral Degree*: Education (EdD); Philosophy (PhD), at least 2 yrs; *Doctoral Degree*: Literature (DLit); Science (DSc), Published work. Also Graduate, Postgraduate and Higher Diplomas

Student Residential Facilities: Yes

Special Facilities: Microscope Unit. Carbon Dating Unit

Libraries: Central, Education and Law Libraries; total, c. 840,500 vols

Last Updated: 15/12/08

UNITEC INSTITUTE OF TECHNOLOGY / TE WHARE WANANGA O WAIRAKA

Private Bag 92025, Auckland
Tel: +64(9) 849-4180
EMail: ceo@unitec.ac.nz
Website: http://www.unitec.ac.nz

President and Chief Executive: Rick Ede (2008-)
Tel: +64(9) 815-4321, ext 7794 EMail: rede@unitec.ac.nz

International Relations: Ray Meldrum, Executive Dean, Academic
Tel: +64(9) 815-4321, ext 7792 EMail: acodling@unitec.ac.nz

Faculties

Creative Industries and Business (Accountancy; Architecture; Business Administration; Communication Studies; Computer Science; Design; Finance; Information Technology; Landscape Architecture; Law; Management; Marketing; Performing Arts; Tourism; Visual Arts); **Social and Health Sciences** (Community Health; Education; Health Sciences; Medical Technology; Modern Languages; Natural Sciences; Nursing; Osteopathy; Sports); **Technology and Built Environment** (Automotive Engineering; Building Technologies; Civil Engineering; Construction Engineering; Electronic Engineering; Surveying and Mapping; Technology; Transport Engineering)

History: Founded 1976 as Carrington Technical Institute. Acquired present status 1994.

Governing Bodies: Unitec Council

Academic Year: February to November

Main Language(s) of Instruction: English

Accrediting Agencies: New Zealand Qualifications Authority

Degrees and Diplomas: *Certificate*: 12 weeks-1 yr; *Diploma*: 2 yrs; *Bachelor's Degree*: 3-4 yrs; *Postgraduate Certificate*; *Postgraduate Diploma*; *Master's Degree*: 2 yrs; *Doctoral Degree*: Computer Science (DComp); Education (PhD), 3 yrs

Student Services: Academic counselling, Canteen, Cultural centre, Employment services, Foreign student adviser, Foreign Studies Centre, Handicapped facilities, Health services, Language programs, Nursery care, Social counselling, Sports facilities

Student Residential Facilities: For 300 students

Libraries: c. 105,000 vols; periodicals, 785 hard copies and 7,220 electronic items

Publications: Annual Research Report *(annually)*

Student Numbers *2011-2012*: Total 23,000

Last Updated: 31/08/11

UNIVERSAL COLLEGE OF LEARNING/KARETI A IWI

Private Bag 3020, 57 Campbell Street, Wanganui
Tel: +64(6) 965-3800
Fax: +64(6) 965-3838
EMail: enquiry@ucol.ac.nz
Website: http://www.ucol.ac.nz

Chief Executive: Paul McElroy Tel: +64(6) 952-7000

International Relations: Bruce Osborne Tel: +64(6) 965-3845

Faculties

Health Science (Health Sciences; Nursing); **Humanities and Business** (Business Administration; Management)

Further Information: Also campuses in Palmerston North/Masterton

History: Founded 1994 as Wanganui Regional Community Polytechnic. Acquired present status and title 2002

Degrees and Diplomas: *Diploma*; *Bachelor's Degree*; *Postgraduate Diploma*; *Master's Degree*

Last Updated: 15/12/08

UNIVERSITY OF CANTERBURY / TE WHARE WANANGA O WAITAHA

Private Bag 4800, Christchurch
Tel: +64(3) 366-7001
Fax: +64(3) 364-2999
EMail: info@canterbury.ac.nz
Website: http://www.canterbury.ac.nz

Vice-Chancellor: Rod Carr (2009-) Tel: +64(3) 364-8858

Registrar/Director of University Services: Alan Hayward
Tel: +64(3) 364-2854 EMail: alan.hayward@canterbury.ac.nz

International Relations: Bob Kirk, Deputy Vice-Chancellor
Tel: +64(3) 364-2893, Fax: +64(3) 364-2856
EMail: bob.kirk@canterbury.ac.nz

Colleges

Arts (American Studies; Anthropology; Austronesian and Oceanic Languages; Chinese; Classical Languages; Cultural Studies; Education; English; Film; Fine Arts; French; Gender Studies; German; Health Sciences; History; Japanese; Journalism; Linguistics; Mass Communication; Music; Philosophy; Political Sciences; Religious Studies; Russian; Social Work; Sociology; Spanish; Theatre); **Business and Economics** (Accountancy; Economics; Finance; Information Technology; Management); **Education** (Education); **Engineering** (Chemical Engineering; Civil Engineering; Computer Engineering; Computer Science; Electrical Engineering; Engineering; Engineering Management; Forestry; Mathematics; Mechanical Engineering; Statistics); **Science** (Astronomy and Space Science; Biology; Chemistry; Communication Disorders; Geography; Geology; Physics; Psychology)

Schools

Forestry (Forestry); **Law** (Law); **Music** (Fine Arts; Music)

History: Founded 1873 as Canterbury College, became Canterbury University College 1933 and acquired present title 1957. Incorporated Christchurch College of Education 2007.

Governing Bodies: University Council; Academic Board

Academic Year: March to November (March-June; July-November)

Admission Requirements: New Zealand citizens, acceptable grades in the National Certificate of Educational Achievement (NCEA); international students, equivalent or by admission ad eundem statum (by equivalent qualification)

Fees: (NZ Dollars): 3,400-4,200 per annum; international fees, 14,700-22,700, depending on course and level of study

Main Language(s) of Instruction: English

International Co-operation: With universities in Australia, Canada, China, Denmark, France, Germany, Italy, Japan, Korea, Malaysia, Nigeria, Norway, Papua New Guinea, Singapore, Sweden, United Kingdom and USA

Degrees and Diplomas: *Bachelor's Degree*: 3 yrs; *Bachelor's Degree with Honours*: 4 yrs; *Master's Degree*: a further 1-2 yrs; *Doctoral Degree (PhD)*: a further 2-3 yrs. Postgraduate qualifications (including B(Hons) degrees) require an undergraduate degree with a major in the same field of study

Student Services: Academic counselling, Canteen, Cultural centre, Employment services, Foreign student adviser, Foreign Studies Centre, Handicapped facilities, Health services, Language programs, Nursery care, Social counselling, Sports facilities

Student Residential Facilities: Yes

Special Facilities: 5 field stations (observatory, marine biology, biological and geological sciences)

Libraries: c. 1.3m. items including books, periodicals and microfilms. Macmillan Brown Collection, c. 57,000 vols specializing in Pacific Ocean Studies, Anthropology, and Ethnology; Specialist libraries in Law, Engineering, Physical Sciences

Publications: Canterbury French Monographs; Canterbury Law Review; History Today; New Zealand Natural Sciences Review; Research Report, Department of Mathematics; Sound Ideas (Journal of the School of Music)

Press or Publishing House: Canterbury University Press

Last Updated: 31/08/11

IAU UNIVERSITY OF OTAGO / TE WHARE WANANGA O OTAGO

P.O. Box 56, Dunedin
Tel: +64(3) 479-8344
Fax: +64(3) 479-8367
EMail: university@otago.ac.nz
Website: http://www.otago.ac.nz

Vice-Chancellor: Harlene Hayne (2011-)
Tel: +64(3) 479-8253, Fax: +64(3) 479-8544
EMail: vice-chancellor@otago.ac.nz

International Relations: Sarah Todd, Pro-Vice-Chancellor, International EMail: pvc.international@otago.ac.nz

Divisions

Commerce (Accountancy; Business Administration; Business and Commerce; Economic and Finance Policy; Economics; Finance; Information Sciences; International Business; Management; Marketing; Mathematics; Tourism) *Pro-Vice-Chancellor*: G. L. Benwell; **Health Sciences** (Anaesthesiology; Anatomy; Biochemistry; Biomedicine; Dentistry; Gynaecology and Obstetrics; Health Administration; Health Sciences; Immunology; Medical Technology; Medicine; Microbiology; Nursing; Orthopaedics; Paediatrics; Pathology; Pharmacology; Pharmacy; Physical Therapy; Physiology; Psychology; Public Health; Radiology; Surgery; Toxicology) *Pro-Vice-Chancellor*: D. M. Roberton; **Humanities** (Anthropology; Archaeology; Art History; Arts and Humanities; Asian Studies; Chinese; Classical Languages; Communication Studies; Design; Education; Educational Sciences; English; Environmental Studies; Film; French; Gender Studies; Geography; German; Graphic Arts; Hebrew; History; Home Economics; Indigenous Studies; International Studies; Japanese; Law; Linguistics; Modern Languages; Music; Pacific Area Studies; Philosophy; Political Sciences; Regional Planning; Religion; Religious Studies; Social Sciences; Social Work; Sociology; Spanish; Special Education; Teacher Training; Theatre; Theology; Visual Arts) *Pro-Vice-Chancellor*: M. M. Franzmann; **Science** (Agriculture; Anatomy; Applied Physics; Astronomy and Space Science; Biochemistry; Biology; Biotechnology; Botany; Chemistry; Clothing and Sewing; Cognitive Sciences; Computer Science; Design; Ecology; Electronic Engineering; Energy Engineering; Environmental Management; Environmental Studies; Fishery; Food Science; Geography; Geology; Geophysics; Immunology; Information Sciences; Leisure Studies; Marine Science and Oceanography; Mathematics; Mathematics and Computer Science; Microbiology; Microelectronics; Molecular Biology; Natural Resources; Natural Sciences; Neurosciences; Nutrition; Pharmacology; Physical Education; Physics; Physiology; Psychology; Rural Planning; Software Engineering; Sports; Sports Management; Statistics; Surveying and Mapping; Telecommunications Engineering; Textile Design; Toxicology; Wildlife; Zoology) *Pro-Vice-Chancellor*: V. Squire

Further Information: Division of Health Sciences includes a Medical School with branches in Dunedin, Christchurch and Wellington.

History: Founded 1869. New Zealand's oldest University. Incorporated Dunedin College of Education 2007.

Governing Bodies: University Council

Academic Year: February to November (February-June; July-November)

Admission Requirements: Acceptable grades in the New Zealand National Certificate of Educational Achievement; University of Otago Foundation Studies Certificate or recognized foreign equivalents

Fees: (NZ Dollars): 3,952 - 26,500 per annum; foreign students fees, available on request. All fees subject to annual review

Main Language(s) of Instruction: English

Degrees and Diplomas: *Bachelor's Degree*: Applied Sciences (BAppSc); Laws (LLB); Medical Laboratory Science (BMLSc); Pharmacy (BPharm); Physical Education (BPhEd); Physiotherapy (BPhty); Social and Community Work (BSCW); Surveying (BSurv), 4 yrs; *Bachelor's Degree*: Arts (BA); Biomedical Sciences (BBiomedSc); Commerce (BCom); Consumer and Applied Science (BCApSc); Dental Technology (BDent Tech); Education Sciences; Health Sciences (BHealSci); Music (MusB); Oral Health (BOH); Science (BSc); Teacher Education (Secondary) (BTchg(Sec)); Teaching (BTchg); Theology (BTheol); Tourism (Btour), 3 yrs; *Bachelor's Degree*: Dental Surgery (BDS), 5 yrs; *Bachelor's Degree*: Medicine and Surgery (MBChB), 6 yrs; *Bachelor's Degree with Honours*: 1 further yr; *Bachelor's Degree with Honours*: Law (LLB(Hons)); Pharmacy (BPharm(Hons)); Physical Education (BPhEd(Hons)), 4 yrs; *Postgraduate Diploma (PgDip)*: 1-2 yrs; *Master's Degree (MPharm)*: a further 1-2 yrs; *Master's Degree*: Applied Sciences (MAppSc); Business Studies (MBus); Education (MEd); International Studies (MIntSt); Ministry (MMin); Planning; Primary Health Care (MPHC); Science Communication (MSciComm); Social and Community Work (MSCW); Social Welfare (MSW); Tourism (MTour); *Master's Degree*: Arts (MA); Bioethics and Health Law (MBHL); Business Administration (MBA); Clinical Pharmacy (MClinPharm); Commerce (MCom); Community Dentistry (MComDent); Consumer and Applied Sciences (MCApSc); Dental Surgery (MDS); General Practice (MGP); Health Science (MHealSc); Law (LLM); Literature (Mlitt); Manipulative Physiotherapy (MMPhty); Medical Laboratory Science (MMLSc); Medical Sciences (MMedSc); Music (MMus); Pharmacy (MPharm); Physical Education (MPhEd); Public Health (MPH); Regional and Resource Planning (MRRP); Science (MSc); Surveying (MSurv); Theology (MTheol), a further 1-2 yrs; *Doctoral Degree (PhD)*: a further 3 yrs by thesis

Student Services: Academic counselling, Canteen, Cultural centre, Employment services, Foreign student adviser, Foreign Studies Centre, Handicapped facilities, Health services, Language programs, Nursery care, Social counselling, Sports facilities

Student Residential Facilities: Yes

Special Facilities: Anatomy Museum; Pathology Museum; Geology Museum. Hocken Gallery. Marine Aquarium. Aquatics and Controlled Environment Centre. Language Learning Centre. Allen Hall Theatre. Marama Hall (Recital Hall)

Libraries: Total, c. 3m. vols. Central Library, 600,000 vols; Hocken Library (New Zealand and Pacific Material), c. 1.4m. vols; Dental library, 100,000 vols; Medical library, 100,000 vols; Law library,100,000 vols; Science library, 200,000 vols

Publications: A History of the University of Otago (1869-1919); Annals of Otago Medical School; He Kitenga, Research Highlights *(annually)*; Quality Portfolio (2000); Research Management Plan (2000); The University of Otago: a Centennial History; University of Otago Charter

Press or Publishing House: University of Otago Press

Last Updated: 04/07/11

VICTORIA UNIVERSITY OF WELLINGTON / TE WHARE WANANGA O TE UPOKO O TE IKA A MAUI

P.O. Box 600, Wellington
Tel: +64(4) 472-1000
Fax: +64(4) 499-4601
EMail: info-desk@vuw.ac.nz
Website: http://www.vuw.ac.nz

Vice-Chancellor: Pat Walsh (2005-)
Tel: +64(4) 463-5301, Fax: +64(4) 463-5240
EMail: Pat.Walsh@vuw.ac.nz

Deputy Vice-Chancellor: Penny Boumelha
Tel: +64(4) 463-5201 EMail: Penny.Boumelha@vuw.ac.nz

International Relations: Rob Rabel, Pro-Vice-Chancellor (International) EMail: Rob.Rabel@vuw.ac.nz

Faculties

Architecture and Design (Architecture; Building Technologies; Design; Interior Design; Landscape Architecture); **Commerce and Administration** (Administration; Business and Commerce; Communication Studies; Economics; Finance; Government; Information Management; Public Administration); **Education** (Education; Teacher Training); **Humanities and Social Sciences** (Anthropology; Art History; Arts and Humanities; Asian Studies; Classical Languages; Criminology; Education; English; History; International Relations; Leisure Studies; Linguistics; Midwifery; Music; Nursing; Pacific Area Studies; Philosophy; Political Sciences; Religious Studies; Social Policy; Sociology; Theatre; Women's Studies); **Law** (Law) *Dean*: Tony Smith; **Science** (Biological and Life Sciences; Biology; Biomedicine; Biotechnology; Cell Biology; Chemistry; Computer Science; Earth Sciences; Ecology; Electronic Engineering; Environmental Studies; Geography; Geology; Geophysics; Marine Biology; Mathematics; Molecular Biology; Natural Sciences; Petroleum and Gas Engineering; Physics; Psychology; Statistics)

Graduate Schools

Nursing, Midwifery and Health (Midwifery; Nursing) *Head*: Jo Walton

Schools

Te Kawa a Maui; **Te Kura Maori** (Teacher Training)

History: Founded 1897 as Victoria University College, became autonomous 1962. Merged with the Wellington College of Education, founded in 1880, on 1 January 2005.

Governing Bodies: Council; Academic Board

Academic Year: (March-June; July-October; November-February

Admission Requirements: Acceptable credits in the National Certificate of Educational Achievement or approved alternative

Main Language(s) of Instruction: English

Degrees and Diplomas: *Graduate Certificate*; *Graduate Diploma*; *Bachelor's Degree*: 3-4 yrs; *Bachelor's Degree with Honours*: a further 1-2 yrs; *Postgraduate Certificate*; *Postgraduate Diploma*; *Master's Degree*: 1-2 yrs following Bachelor Degree; *Doctoral Degree (PhD)*: a further 2-4 yrs

Student Residential Facilities: Yes

Libraries: Victoria University of Wellington Library, c. 1,500,000 vols; 70,000 periodicals

Publications: Victoria University of Wellington Law Review *(quarterly)*

Press or Publishing House: Victoria University Press

Last Updated: 01/09/11

WAIKATO INSTITUTE OF TECHNOLOGY / TE KURATINI O WAIKATO (WINTEC)

Private Bag 3036, Tristram Street, Hamilton
Tel: +64(7) 834-8888
Fax: +64(7) 834-8814
EMail: info@twp.ac.nz.
Website: http://www.twp.ac.nz

Chief Executive: Mark Flowers
Tel: +64(7) 834-8899 EMail: mark.flowers@wintec.ac.nz

Group Manager, Academic Services: Terry Barnett
Tel: +64(7) 834-8800 Ext. 8947

International Relations: Irene Robb
Tel: +64(7) 834-8888 Ext. 8013, Fax: +64(7) 834-8895
EMail: icimr@twp.ac.nz

Schools

Business (Business Administration; Business Computing; Management); **Education** (Education; Teacher Training); **Engineering, Science and Primary Industries** (Agriculture; Animal Husbandry; Architecture; Civil Engineering; Construction Engineering; Dairy; Electrical Engineering; Engineering; Floriculture; Horticulture; Landscape Architecture; Mechanical Engineering; Technology;

Veterinary Science); **Health** (Midwifery; Nursing; Occupational Therapy); **Information Technology** (Information Technology); **International Tourism, Hospitality and Events** (Cooking and Catering; Cosmetology; Hotel Management; Tourism); **Media Arts** (Communication Studies; Fashion Design; Journalism; Media Studies; Radio and Television Broadcasting); **Social Development** (Psychiatry and Mental Health; Social and Community Services; Social Sciences); **Sport and Exercise Science** (Physical Education; Sports); **Trades** (Electrical Engineering; Mechanical Engineering; Metal Techniques; Technology)

History: Founded 1968 as The Waikato Polytechnic. Acquired present title 2001. A State Institution.

Main Language(s) of Instruction: English

Degrees and Diplomas: *Certificate*; *Diploma*; *Graduate Certificate*; *Graduate Diploma*; *Bachelor's Degree*; *Postgraduate Certificate*; *Postgraduate Diploma*; *Master's Degree*. Also Advanced Cerificates and Diplomas

Last Updated: 31/08/11

PRIVATE INSTITUTIONS

AIS ST HELENS

28a Linwoood Avenue, Mt Albert, Auckland 1015
Tel: +64(9) 815-1717
Fax: +64(9) 815-1802
EMail: enquiry@ais.ac.nz
Website: http://www.ais.ac.nz

President: Richard Goodall
Tel: +64(9) 815-3771 EMail: rgoodall@ais.ac.nz

Academic Registrar: Richard Smith
Tel: +64(9) 815-3772 EMail: richards@ais.ac.nz

International Relations: Anatole Bogatski
Tel: +64(9) 815-3763 EMail: anatoleb@ais.ac.nz

Centres

Research in International Education (Education)

Programmes

English Language Centre (English); **Hospitality, Tourism, Arts** (Asian Studies; Cultural Studies; Modern Languages; Pacific Area Studies; Tourism); **Information Technology** (Information Technology); **International Business** (International Business); **Master of Business Administration** (Business Administration; International Business)

History: Founded 1990.

Admission Requirements: Undergraduate degree/Graduate diploma: New Zealand Bursary or Tertiary Study or NCEA equivalent or New Zealand sixth form equivalent, IELTS 6,0/TOEFL 550; Postgraduate degree/diploma: undergraduate degree, IELTS 6,5/ TOEFL 575; two years recognised experience in relevant position

Fees: (NZ Dollars): Domestic students, undergraduate, 575 per course, graduate, 19,940; International students, undergraduate, 2,250 per course, graduate, 29,990

Main Language(s) of Instruction: English

International Co-operation: With Korea, China, Japan, Tonga

Accrediting Agencies: New Zealand Qualifications Authority, Tertiary Education Commission, New Zealand Ministry of Education

Degrees and Diplomas: *Certificate*: Hospitality; Information Technology; Teaching English to Speakers of Other Languages; General English; Business English; English for Academic Purposes; *Diploma*: International Business; Language and Culture; Tourism Management; Computing and Information Technology; *Graduate Diploma*: Information Technology; International Business; Tourism Management; *Bachelor's Degree*: International Business; Arts; Tourism Management; *Postgraduate Certificate*: International Business; *Postgraduate Diploma*: International Business; *Master's Degree*: Business Administration (MBA)

Student Services: Academic counselling, Canteen, Employment services, Foreign student adviser, Language programs, Sports facilities

Student Residential Facilities: Yes

Libraries: Yes

Student Numbers *2010*	MEN	WOMEN	TOTAL
All (Foreign Included)	690	327	**1,017**
FOREIGN ONLY	552	262	**814**

Last Updated: 30/08/11

BIBLE COLLEGE OF NEW ZEALAND / TE KARETI PAIPERA O AOTEAROA

Private Bag 93104, 221 Lincoln Road, Henderson, Auckland
Tel: +64(9) 836-7800
Fax: +64(9) 836-7801
EMail: admin@bcnz.ac.nz
Website: http://www.bcnz.ac.nz

National Principal: Mark Strom (2005-)
Tel: +64(9) 836-7819 EMail: mstrom@bcnz.ac.nz

Director, Finance and Administration: Allan Officer
Tel: +64(9) 836-7817 EMail: finance@bcnz.ac.nz

International Relations: Derek Martin, Academic Registrar
Tel: +64(9) 836-7832 EMail: derekm@.bcnz.ac.nz

Centres

Distance Learning *Director*: Charles Erlam

Graduate Schools

Theology *(Tyndale)* (Theology) *Dean*: Tim Meadowcroft

Schools

Contemporary Christian Studies (Christian Religious Studies) *Director*: Martien Kelderman; **English Language Studies** *Head*: Alison Matai'a; **Global Mission** (Religion) *Director*: Cathy Ross

History: Founded 1922, acquired present status and title 1990.

Main Language(s) of Instruction: English

Accrediting Agencies: New Zealand Qualifications Authority (NZQA)

Degrees and Diplomas: *Certificate*; *Diploma*; *Graduate Diploma*; *Bachelor's Degree*; *Master's Degree*; *Doctoral Degree*

Student Services: Academic counselling, Canteen, Cultural centre, Foreign student adviser, Foreign Studies Centre, Handicapped facilities, Health services, Language programs, Nursery care, Social counselling, Sports facilities

Student Residential Facilities: Yes

Libraries: Yes

Publications: Reality *(bimonthly)*

INTERNATIONAL PACIFIC COLLEGE (IPC)

Private Bag 11-021, Palmerston North
Tel: +64(6) 354-0922
Fax: +64(6) 354-0935
EMail: info@ipc.ac.nz
Website: http://www.ipc.ac.nz

President: Ken Cunningham
Tel: +64(6) 350-2821, Fax: +64(6) 350-2849
EMail: kcunningham@ipc.ac.nz

Chief Executive Officer: Minoru Kasuya
Tel: +64(6) 350-2838, Fax: +64(6) 350-2849
EMail: mkasuya@ipc.ac.nz

Programmes

International Studies (Business Administration; Environmental Studies; International Relations; International Studies); **Japanese** (Japanese); **Sports** (Sports)

History: Founded 1990. A private tertiary institution.

Governing Bodies: Board of Trustees

Academic Year: April to March

Main Language(s) of Instruction: English

Degrees and Diplomas: *Certificate*: 1 yr; *Diploma*: 4 yrs; *Bachelor's Degree*: 3 yrs; *Postgraduate Diploma*: 1 yr; *Master's Degree*: 2 yrs

Student Services: Academic counselling, Canteen, Employment services, Foreign student adviser, Foreign Studies Centre, Health services, Language programs, Social counselling, Sports facilities

Student Residential Facilities: Yes

Libraries: Yes

Last Updated: 31/08/11

NEW ZEALAND DRAMA SCHOOL / TE KURA TOI WHAKAARI O AOTEAROA

P.O. Box 7146, 11 Hutchison Road, Newton, Wellington South 6242
Tel: +64(4) 381-9250
Fax: +64(4) 389-4996
EMail: drama@toiwhakaari.ac.nz
Website: http://www.toiwhakaari.ac.nz

Director: Christian Penny
Tel: +64(4) 381-9228 EMail: christian.penny@toiwhakaari.ac.nz

Divisions

Drama (Acting; Art Management; Design; Display and Stage Design; Theatre)

History: Founded 1970.

Academic Year: February to December

Main Language(s) of Instruction: English

Degrees and Diplomas: *Diploma*: Entertainment Technology; Costume Construction (Film, Theatre and Allied Arts); *Bachelor's Degree*: Performing Arts (Acting); Performing Arts Management; Design (Stage and Screen); *Master's Degree*: Theatre Arts (Directing)

Special Facilities: Theatres

Libraries: Nola Miller Library

Last Updated: 31/08/11

PACIFIC INTERNATIONAL HOTEL MANAGEMENT SCHOOL (PIHMS)

Henwood Road, Bell Block, Private Bag 2062, New Plymouth
Tel: +64(6) 755-0030
Fax: +64(6) 755-0030
EMail: marketing@pihms.ac.nz
Website: http://www.pihms.ac.nz

Principal: Flora Gilkinson
Tel: +64(6) 755-0025 Ext. 8007, Fax: +64(6) 755-2919

Courses

Hotel Management (Hotel Management)

History: Founded 1995.

Main Language(s) of Instruction: English

Degrees and Diplomas: *Diploma*: Hotel Management; *Bachelor's Degree*: Applied Hospitality and Tourism Management; *Postgraduate Diploma*: Hotel Management. Also Advanced Diploma in Hotel Management

Student Services: Academic counselling, Canteen, Foreign student adviser, Language programs, Social counselling, Sports facilities

Student Residential Facilities: Yes

Libraries: Yes

Last Updated: 31/08/11

WHITECLIFFE COLLEGE OF ARTS AND DESIGN / TE WHARE TAKIURA O WIKIRIWHI

P.O. Box 8192, Symonds Street, 136 Grafton Road, Auckland
Tel: +64(9) 309-5970
Fax: +64(9) 302-2957
EMail: info@whitecliffe.ac.nz
Website: http://www.whitecliffe.ac.nz

President: Michelle Whitecliffe (1982-)
Tel: +64(9) 89 00 57 EMail: michelew@wcad.ac.nz

Dean of College and Registrar: Fionna Scott-Milligan
EMail: fionnas@whitecliff.ac.nz

Departments

Art Therapy (Art Management; Art Therapy); **Arts Management** (Art Management); **Fine Arts** (Fashion Design; Fine Arts; Graphic Design; Photography)

History: Founded 1982.

Main Language(s) of Instruction: English

Degrees and Diplomas: *Certificate*; *Bachelor's Degree*: 4 yrs; *Master's Degree*

Special Facilities: Gallery. Studios

Libraries: Parkyn Library

Last Updated: 01/09/11

Nicaragua

STRUCTURE OF HIGHER EDUCATION SYSTEM

Description:

Higher education is provided by universities and centros de educación técnica superiores (polytechnics and technological institutions). There are both state and private universities. All universities enjoy academic, financial and administrative autonomy. The Consejo Nacional de Universidades (CNU) is responsible for higher education planning.

Stages of studies:

University level first stage: *Licenciatura*
The Licenciatura is awarded after four to six years' study, depending on the subject. A professional qualification is awarded after studies lasting five years in Engineering (Ingeniero) and Architecture (Arquitecto) and six years in Medicine (Doctor).

University level second stage: *Maestría, Especialización*
A Maestría is conferred after studies lasting for two years beyond the Licenciatura. Students must present a thesis. There are also postgraduate courses in various specialities in Medicine, Law, Psychology etc.

ADMISSION TO HIGHER EDUCATION

Admission to university-level studies:

Name of secondary school credential required: Bachillerato

Foreign students admission:

Entrance exam requirements: Foreign students should hold the same School Leaving Certificates as nationals.

Entry regulations: Applications are through the diplomatic missions in their respective country.

Language requirements: Students must be proficient in Spanish.

NATIONAL BODIES

Consejo Nacional de Universidades - CNU (National Council of Universities)

President: Telémaco Talavera Siles
Apartado postal: EC-44
Managua
Tel: +505 278 5072
Fax: +505 278 3385
WWW: http://www.cnu.edu.ni

Data for academic year: 2010-2011
Source: IAU from IBE website, 2003 and CNU website, 2010. Bodies 2012.

INSTITUTIONS

ADVENTIST UNIVERSITY OF NICARAGUA

Universidad Adventista de Nicaragua (UNADENIC)
Carretera Vieja a León, Km 12, 1500 Metros al Sur, Managua
Rectora: Adelina Simpson EMail: adesimpson@msn.com

Programmes
Business Administration (Business Administration); **Primary Education**; **Systems Engineering** (Systems Analysis); **Theology** (Theology)

Degrees and Diplomas: *Licenciatura*: 5 yrs; *Licenciatura*: Engineering, 5 yrs

AMERICAN COLLEGE UNIVERSITY

Universidad American College
Plaza España, De la Rotonda el Gueguense 2c. al Oeste 1c al Norte, Managua
Tel: +505 2268-7555
EMail: info@americancollege.edu.ni
Website: http://www.americancollege.edu.ni/

Rector: Eduardo Chamorro Coronel

Faculties

Economics and Administration (Administration; Business Administration; Economics); **Engineering** (Industrial Engineering; Systems Analysis); **Law and Humanities** (Communication Studies; International Relations; Law; Public Relations); **Tourism** (Tourism)

Main Language(s) of Instruction: Spanish

Degrees and Diplomas: *Licenciatura*. Also Ingeniero
Last Updated: 17/12/09

AMERICAN UNIVERSITY

Universidad Americana (UAM)
Campus Universitario, Costado Noroeste Camino de Oriente, Managua
Tel: +505(2) 783-800
EMail: correo@uam.edu.ni
Website: http://www.uam.edu.ni

Rector: Ernesto Medina Sandino

Faculties

Architecture (Architecture); **Business Administration**; **Dentistry** (Dentistry); **Diplomacy and International Relations** (International Relations); **Economics and Administration** (Administration; Advertising and Publicity; Business Administration; Economics; Hotel Management; Marketing; Tourism); **Engineering** (Engineering; Industrial Engineering; Systems Analysis); **Law and Social Sciences** (Law); **Medicine** (Dentistry; Medicine)

History: Founded 1992.

Main Language(s) of Instruction: Spanish, English

Degrees and Diplomas: *Licenciatura*; *Especialización*; *Maestría*. Also Posgrados and Diplomados
Last Updated: 16/12/09

AUTONOMOUS UNIVERSITY OF CHINANDEGA

Universidad Autónoma de Chinandega (UACH)
Club Eden 1/2 c. abajo, Chinandega
Tel: +505 341-2188
EMail: uach@alfa.com.ni

Rector: Álvaro Alberto Fajardo Salgado

Faculties

Administration and Accountancy (Accountancy; Administration); **Agronomy** (Agronomy); **Building Technology** (Building Technologies); **Law and Social Sciences** (Law; Social Sciences); **Science**

Further Information: Also branch in Managua

History: Founded 1995.

Main Language(s) of Instruction: Spanish
Last Updated: 16/12/09

BLUEFIELDS INDIAN AND CARIBBEAN UNIVERSITY (BICU)

Apartado postal 88, Avenida Universitaria, Barrio San Pedro, Bluefields
Tel: +505 572-1910
Fax: +505 572-1277
EMail: bicu@ibw.com.ni
Website: http://www.bicu.edu.ni

Rector: Faran Dometz Hebbert

Secretaria General: Carroll Ray Harrison

International Relations: Carroll Ray Harrison

Faculties

Agricultural Engineering and Forestry (Agricultural Engineering; Forestry); **Economics and Administration** (Accountancy; Administration; Economics; Hotel Management); **Educational Sciences** (Educational Sciences); **Law and Social Sciences** (Law; Social Sciences); **Natural Resources and Environment** (Environmental Studies; Natural Resources)

Institutes

Biodiversity and Environment (Biological and Life Sciences; Environmental Studies); **Development** (Development Studies); **Socio-economic Research** (Economics; Social Sciences)

Research Centres

Aquatic Research (Aquaculture)

Schools

Accountancy and Finance (Accountancy; Finance); **Business Administration** (Business Administration); **Civil Engineering** (Civil Engineering); **Computer Science**; **Hotel Management and Tourism** (Hotel Management; Tourism); **Marine Biology** (Marine Biology)

History: Founded 1990. Acquired present status 1992.

Main Language(s) of Instruction: Spanish

Degrees and Diplomas: *Técnico Superior*, *Licenciatura*: 5 yrs; *Licenciatura*: Engineering, 5 yrs; *Maestría*
Last Updated: 16/12/09

CATHOLIC UNIVERSITY OF STOCKBREEDING OF THE DRY TROPICS

Universidad Católica Agropecuaria del Trópico Seco (UCATSE)
Km 166 1/2carretera Panamericana, Estelí
Tel: +505(71) 361-86
Fax: +505(71) 323-47
EMail: ucatse@ucatse.edu.ni
Website: http://www.ucatse.edu.ni

Rector: Juan Abelardo Mata

Faculties

Medicine *(San Lucas)* (Dentistry; Medicine; Nursing); **Stockbreeding** (Animal Husbandry; Management; Rural Studies; Sociology); **Theology** (Theology)

History: Founded 1968 as Escuela de Agricultura y Ganadería. Acquired present status and title 2004.

Main Language(s) of Instruction: Spanish

Degrees and Diplomas: *Técnico Superior*, *Licenciatura*: Engineering, 5 yrs; *Especialización*; *Maestría*

CENTRAL AMERICAN UNIVERSITY

Universidad Centroamericana (UCA)
Apartado postal 69, Rotonda Rubén Darío 150 mts al oeste, Managua
Tel: +505(2) 278-3923
Fax: +505(2) 267-0106
EMail: comsj@ns.uca.edu.ni
Website: http://www.uca.edu.ni

Rectora: Mayra Luz Pérez Díaz (2005-)
Tel: +505(2) 673-3990 EMail: asrector@ns.uca.edu.ni

Secretaria General: Vera Amanda Solís Reyes
EMail: nancym@ns.uca.edu.ni

International Relations: Kathe Welles, Directora de Relaciones Internacionales
Tel: +505(2) 278-6505
EMail: riuca@ns.uca.edu.ni; kathe@ns.uca.edu.ni

Faculties

Economics and Business Administration (Accountancy; Banking; Business Administration; Economics; Finance; Marketing; Tourism); **Humanities and Communication** (Arts and Humanities; Communication Studies; Cultural Studies; Development Studies; English; Foreign Languages Education; Psychology; Social Work; Women's Studies); **Law** (Commercial Law; Constitutional Law; Criminal Law; Law; Private Law; Public Law); **Science, Technology and Environment** (Animal Husbandry; Architecture; Civil Engineering; Computer Engineering; Environmental Studies; Graphic Design; Industrial Engineering; Natural Sciences; Systems Analysis)

Institutes

History of Nicaragua and Central America *(IHNCA)* (History; Latin American Studies; Regional Studies); **Institute of Education 'Xabier Gorostiaga, S.J.'** *(IDEUCA)* (Educational Sciences); **Research and Development** *(Nitlapán)* (Economics) *Director*: Arturo Grigsby; **Social Work** *(Juan XXIII)* (Social and Community Services) *Director*: Edwin Novoa

Programmes

Interdisciplinary Gender Studies *(PIEG)* (Gender Studies) *Coordinator*: Ligia Arana

History: Founded 1960 as a private autonomous university by the Society of Jesus. Mainly financed by student fees and grants, but receives some support from the State and international cooperation.

Governing Bodies: Junta de Directores; Consejo Universitario

Academic Year: February to December (February-April; May-August; September-December)

Admission Requirements: Secondary school certificate (bachillerato); Entrance examination required for some majors.

Fees: (US Dollars): 60-100 per subject per term, depending on each subject.

Main Language(s) of Instruction: Spanish

International Co-operation: With institutions in Austria, Mexico, Spain, USA.

Degrees and Diplomas: *Técnico Superior*: Religious Studies, 3 yrs; *Licenciatura*: Accountancy; Applied Economics; Law; Psychology, 41/2 yrs; *Licenciatura*: Architecture; Environmental Quality; Industrial Engineering; Information and Communication Systems and Technologies; Social Work; Development Management; Sociology, 5 yrs; *Licenciatura*: Business Administration; Tourism Management; Finance; Civil Engineering; Communication Studies; Humanities; Teaching English as a Foreign Language, 4 yrs; *Maestría*: Business Management; Economics; Development Studies; Gender Studies; Business Law, 2 yrs. Also Diplomado superior

Student Services: Academic counselling, Canteen, Cultural centre, Employment services, Foreign student adviser, Language programs, Nursery care, Social counselling, Sports facilities

Special Facilities: Collection of Nicaraguan fauna, National Herbarium.

Libraries: Central Library 'José Coronel Urtecho' - 106,966 vols. Instituto de Historia de Nicaragua y Centroamérica - IHNCA-UCA - 40,000 vols.

Publications: Revista de Derecho, Legal issues *(3 per annum)*; Revista de Historia, Historical studies *(biennially)*; Revista Encuentro, Research publication of the university community *(quarterly)*; Revista Envío, Political reviews and analyses of Nicaragua and Central America *(monthly)*; Revista WANI *(quarterly)*

Press or Publishing House: Editorial UCA

Last Updated: 17/12/09

CENTRAL AMERICAN UNIVERSITY OF BUSINESS STUDIES

Universidad Centroamericana de Ciencias Empresariales (UCEM)

De la Embajada americana 1 c. arriba 1 c. al lago, Managua

Tel: +505(2) 266-9374

Fax: +505(2) 266-9441

EMail: info@ucem.edu.ni

Website: http://www.ucem.edu.ni

Rector: Álvaro Banchs Fabregas EMail: rectoria@ucem.edu.ni

Vicerrector: Oscar Gómez Jiménez

Programmes

Bilingual Preschool Education; **Business Administration**; **Computer Science**; **Industrial Engineering**; **Interior Design**; **International Relations**; **Law**; **Medicine**; **Microbiology**; **Pharmacy**; **Photography**; **Systems Engineering** (Systems Analysis); **Tourism**

History: Created 1991.

Degrees and Diplomas: *Licenciatura*; *Especialización*; *Maestría*

CENTRAL UNIVERSITY OF NICARAGUA

Universidad Central de Nicaragua (UCN)

Reparto el Carmen Frente a la Radio 580, Managua

Tel: +505(22) 687-144 +505(22) 663-364

Fax: +505(22) 686-603

EMail: dirrelpub@ucn.edu.ni

Website: http://www.ucn.edu.ni

Rector: Gilberto Cuadra Solórzano (1998-)
EMail: sria.vicerrectoria@ucn.edu.ni

Vice-Rector: Francisco López Pérez
EMail: vicerrectoria@ucn.edu.ni

International Relations: Doris Saldamando Díaz, Direcor of Public and International Affairs

Faculties

Business Administration (Accountancy; Banking; Business Administration; Hotel Management; Marketing; Tourism); **Engineering** (Computer Engineering; Computer Science); **Health Science** (Medicine; Pharmacy; Surgery); **Law and Social Sciences** (International Business; International Relations; Law; Psychology); **Veterinary Medicine** (Veterinary Science)

History: Founded 1997. Acquired present status 1998.

Governing Bodies: Rectorat, Academic Council

Academic Year: January - June; July - December

Admission Requirements: High School Diploma or equivalent.

Fees: (US Dollars): 900.00 per semester

Main Language(s) of Instruction: Spanish

Accrediting Agencies: Consejo Nacional de Universidades (CNU)

Degrees and Diplomas: *Licenciatura*: Accounting and Auditing; Business Administration; Marketing; Banking; Tourism and Hotel Management; Pharmacy; Psychology; International Relations and Foreign Trade; Law (Bachelor's degree); Systems Engineering (Ingenerio), 4-5 yrs; *Especialización*: Medicine; Veterinary Medicine (Doctor), 6 yrs; *Maestría*: Business Administration; Law; Health Sciences; Human Resources; Engineering; Pharmacy; Marketing, a further 2-3 yrs. Also Doctoral degrees (PhD) and Double Degrees

Student Services: Academic counselling, Canteen, Cultural centre, Foreign student adviser, Handicapped facilities, Language programs, Social counselling, Sports facilities

Academic Staff *2011-2012*	MEN	WOMEN	TOTAL
FULL-TIME	–	–	**104**
PART-TIME	–	–	**164**
STAFF WITH DOCTORATE			
FULL-TIME	4	1	**5**
Student Numbers *2011-2012*			
All (Foreign Included)	–	–	**3,306**
FOREIGN ONLY	–	–	**70**

Distance students, 67.

Last Updated: 24/01/12

CHRISTIAN AUTONOMOUS UNIVERSITY OF NICARAGUA

Universidad Cristiana Autónoma de Nicaragua (UCAN)

Iglesia La Merced, 21/2 c.al Norte, León

Tel: +505(2) 311-0353

Fax: +505(2) 311-0360

EMail: ucanleon@cablenet.com.ni

Website: http://www.ucan.edu.ni

Rectora: Jeannette Bonilla de García Tel: +502(2) 311-1287

International Relations: Juanita Bravo

Faculties

Business Administration; **Engineering** (Animal Husbandry; Civil Engineering; Environmental Engineering; Industrial Engineering; Mechanical Engineering; Systems Analysis)

Schools

Agriculture (Animal Husbandry; Tropical Agriculture); **Law, Diplomacy and International Relations**; **Veterinary Medicine and Zoology**

Further Information: Also branches in Chontales, Chinandega, Masaya and Matagalpa

History: Founded 1995.

Governing Bodies: Board of trustees

Admission Requirements: Graduation from high school

Fees: (US Dollars): School of Medicine, 2,000 per annum

Main Language(s) of Instruction: Spanish

International Co-operation: Participates in the Central American Cooperation Programme

Accrediting Agencies: National Agency of Nicaraguan Universities; Consejo Nacional de Universidades

Degrees and Diplomas: *Licenciatura (Lic)*

Student Services: Academic counselling, Canteen, Employment services, Foreign student adviser, Health services, Social counselling, Sports facilities

Student Residential Facilities: Yes (in Leon City)

Last Updated: 17/12/09

HISPANIC-AMERICAN UNIVERSITY

Universidad Hispanoamericana (UHISPAM)

Apartado Postal No. 531, Reparto Bolonia, Canal 2 de TV, 2 cuadras al Oeste, Managua

Website: http://www.uhispam.edu.ni

Rector: Leonardo Torres Céspedes

Tel: +505(2) 681-918 EMail: ltc@uhispam.edu.ni

Faculties

Administration and Economics; **Communication**; **Engineering and Computer Science**; **Law and Social Sciences**; **Tourism and Hotel Management**

History: Founded 1999.

Main Language(s) of Instruction: Spanish

Degrees and Diplomas: *Licenciatura*; *Maestría (MPA; LLM)*. Also Postgrados and Diplomas

Last Updated: 17/12/09

IBERO-AMERICAN UNIVERSITY OF SCIENCE AND TECHNOLOGY

Universidad Iberoamericana de Ciencia y Tecnología (UNICIT)

Avenida Bolívar, Rotonda Universitaria 100 mts al Sur, Managua

Fax: +505(2) 278-7423

EMail: unicit@unicit.edu.ni

Website: http://www.unicit.edu.ni

Rector: Dagoberto Mejía EMail: dmejia@unicit.edu.ni

Faculties

Economics; **Electronics and Computer Science**; **Engineering and Architecture**; **Health Sciences** (Optics; Optometry; Pharmacy); **Law**

History: Founded 1996.

Admission Requirements: Diploma de Bachiller

Main Language(s) of Instruction: Spanish

Degrees and Diplomas: *Licenciatura*; *Maestría*

Last Updated: 17/12/09

INTERNATIONAL SCHOOL OF AGRICULTURE AND STOCKBREEDING

Escuela Internacional de Agricultura y Ganadería

Apartado 5, De la Iglesia Bautista 1 Calle al Oeste, Rivas

Tel: +505(45) 335-51

Fax: +505(45) 339-57

EMail: eiag@tmx.com.ni

Website: http://www.eiag.edu.ni

Rector: Gregorio Barreales

Programmes

Agricultural Engineering (Agriculture); **Veterinary Science** (Veterinary Science); **Zootechnology** (Zoology)

Main Language(s) of Instruction: Spanish

Degrees and Diplomas: *Licenciatura*: Engineering, 5 yrs. Also Ingeniero

Last Updated: 16/12/09

INTERNATIONAL UNIVERSITY FOR SUSTAINABLE DEVELOPMENT

Universidad Internacional para el Desarrollo Sostenible

Km. 9 1/2 Carretera a Masaya, Managua

EMail: informacion@unides.edu.ni

Website: http://www.unides.edu.ni

Rector: Roberto García Boza

Programmes

Business Administration (Business Administration); **Business Economics**; **Strategic Management of Human Resources** (Human Resources)

Degrees and Diplomas: *Licenciatura*; *Maestría*

Last Updated: 16/12/09

INTERNATIONAL UNIVERSITY OF INTEGRATION OF LATIN AMERICA

Universidad Internacional de la Integración de América Latina (UNIVAL)

Reparto San Juan Calle El Carmen, No. 529, Managua 945

Fax: +505(2) 781-417

EMail: unival@unival.edu.ni

Website: http://www.unival.edu.ni

Rector: Sergio Bonilla Delgado (1995-)

EMail: rectoria@unival.edu.ni

Secretary-General: Ileana Jérez Navarro

EMail: secretariageneral@unival.edu.ni

International Relations: Alan González Miller

Centres

Postgraduate

Faculties

Administration and Economics (Administration); **International Science** (Natural Sciences); **Law** (Law)

History: Founded 1995.

Governing Bodies: Academic Council, Rector, Vice-Rectors, Secretary-General, Directors and Owners

Admission Requirements: Diploma de Bachiller

Main Language(s) of Instruction: Spanish

Degrees and Diplomas: *Licenciatura*: 5 yrs; *Maestría*: a further 2 yrs

Student Services: Academic counselling, Language programs, Social counselling, Sports facilities

Student Residential Facilities: No.

Last Updated: 17/12/09

JEAN-JACQUES ROUSSEAU UNIVERSITY

Universidad Jean-Jacques Rousseau (UNIJJAR)

Del Edificio Armando Guido 1 c. arriba, 31/2 c. al sur Barrio San Luis, Managua

Tel: +505(2) 248-3411

EMail: unijjar@cablenet.com.ni

Website: http://www.unijjar.edu.ni/home.htm

Rector: Anibal Lanuza

Faculties

Economics (Economics); **Law** (Law); **Medical Sciences** (Medicine)

History: Founded 2000.

Main Language(s) of Instruction: Spanish

Degrees and Diplomas: *Técnico Superior*, *Licenciatura*: 4 yrs. Also professional title

Last Updated: 17/12/09

JOHN PAUL II UNIVERSITY

Universidad Juan Pablo II
Costado Norte del Polideportivo España, 2 cuadras al lago., Managua
Tel: +505(2) 787-546
Fax: +505(2) 787-547
EMail: univjuanpablo2@turbonett.com.ni
Website: http://www.univjuanpablo2.com

Rectora: Natalia Rosa Barillas de Montiel

Programmes
Humanities (Arts and Humanities; Theology); **Social and Human Promotion** (Social Studies)

History: Founded 1996. Acquired present status 2002.

Main Language(s) of Instruction: Spanish

Degrees and Diplomas: *Licenciatura*. Also Diplomado
Last Updated: 17/12/09

LA ANUNCIATA UNIVERSITY

Universidad La Anunciata
Frente al Estadio Yamil Ríos Ugarte, Rivas
Tel: +505 563-3320
EMail: cfstima@ibw.com.ni

Rectora: Ana María Exposito

Programmes
Business Administration (Business Administration); **Systems Engineering**; **Tourism and Hotel Management**

Main Language(s) of Instruction: Spanish

Degrees and Diplomas: *Licenciatura*
Last Updated: 17/12/09

LA SALLE TECHNOLOGICAL UNIVERSITY

Universidad Tecnológica La Salle
Km. 4 Carretera a Poneloya, León
Tel: +505 2311-2032
EMail: rectoria@ulsa.edu.ni
Website: http://www.ulsa.edu.ni

Rector: Manuel Estrada Carpintero

Programmes
Electronic Cybernetics (Electronic Engineering); **Industrial Management**; **Mechanical Engineering and Renewable Energy** (Energy Engineering; Mechanical Engineering); **Mechatronics and Control Systems** (Automation and Control Engineering; Electronic Engineering; Mechanical Engineering)

Main Language(s) of Instruction: Spanish

Degrees and Diplomas: Ingeniero
Last Updated: 17/12/09

LATIN AMERICAN INSTITUTE OF COMPUTER SCIENCE

Instituto Latinoamericano de Computación
Semáforos del Colonial 1 1/2c al Norte, Managua
Tel: +505 2249-3716
EMail: ilcomp@ilcomp.edu.ni
Website: http://www.ilcomp.edu.ni

Rector: Héctor Antonio Lacayo Hernández

Faculties
Economics and Administration (Administration; Economics); **Engineering** (Engineering)

History: Founded 1991. Acquired present status 2002.

Main Language(s) of Instruction: Spanish

Degrees and Diplomas: *Licenciatura*. Also Ingeniero
Last Updated: 18/12/09

MARTIN LUTHER KING JR PROTESTANT NICARAGUAN UNIVERSITY

Universidad Evangélica Nicaragüense, Martin Luther King JR (UENIC-MLK)
Contiguo Shell Plaza el Sol., Managua
Tel: +505(2) 701-600
Fax: +505(2) 770-157
EMail: info@uenicmlk.edu.ni
Website: http://www.uenicmlk.edu.ni

Rector: Benjamín Cortés Marchena (1994-)
Tel: +505(2) 701-599 EMail: rector@uenicmlk.edu.ni

Vicerrector Académico: Omar Antonio Castro
Tel: +505(2) 701-600 EMail: vra@uenicmlk.edu.ni

Schools
Computer Science; **Economics and Administration**; **Education** (Education; Educational Administration; Pedagogy; Psychology); **Law and Social Sciences**; **Theology**

History: Founded 1994. Acquired present status 1999.

Governing Bodies: Board of Directors

Academic Year: February to December

Admission Requirements: Secondary school certificate

Fees: (US Dollars): 507 per annum

Main Language(s) of Instruction: Spanish

International Co-operation: With universities in Mexico, Cuba, Germany, France, USA and Central American Countries

Accrediting Agencies: Central American Association of Private Universities

Degrees and Diplomas: *Licenciatura*: 5 yrs; *Especialización*; *Maestría*
Student Services: Academic counselling, Canteen, Cultural centre, Employment services, Language programs, Nursery care, Social counselling
Student Residential Facilities: None
Libraries: "Georges Cacaus" Library, 40,000 vols
Publications: Sacuanjoche Journal *(quarterly)*
Last Updated: 17/12/09

MARTIN LUTHER UNIVERSITY "A MINISTRY OF THE ASSEMBLIES OF GOD"

Universidad Martín Lutero "Un Ministerio de las Asambleas de Dios
Km 101/2 Carretera Vieja à León, 100 mts al norte, Managua
Tel: +505(2) 652-650
Fax: +505(2) 653-587
EMail: ucdn@ibw.com.ni
Website: http://www.uml.edu.ni

Rector: José Moisés Rojas Talavera

Programmes
Accountancy (Accountancy); **Banking and Finance** (Banking; Finance); **Business Administration**; **Clinical Psychology** (Clinical Psychology); **Computer Science** (Computer Science); **Educational Sciences** (Educational Sciences; English); **Law**; **Pedagogy** (Pedagogy); **Theology**

History: Founded 2002.

Main Language(s) of Instruction: Spanish

Degrees and Diplomas: *Técnico Superior*, *Licenciatura*. Also Ingeniero
Last Updated: 17/12/09

METROPOLITAN UNIVERSITY

Universidad Metropolitana (UNIMET)
Altamira d'Este, De la Vicky 21/2 Cuadras al Sur, Managua
Tel: +505(2) 770-705
EMail: unimet@ibw.com.ni

Rector: Oscar Moreira Araica

Programmes
Accountancy and Finance (Accountancy; Finance); **Business Administration**; **Civil Engineering** (Civil Engineering); **Computer**

Engineering (Computer Engineering); **Industrial Engineering** (Industrial Engineering); **Law**; **Systems Engineering**; **Tourism and Hotel Management** (Hotel Management; Tourism)

Main Language(s) of Instruction: Spanish

Degrees and Diplomas: *Licenciatura*; *Licenciatura*: Engineering, 5 yrs

NATIONAL AUTONOMOUS UNIVERSITY OF NICARAGUA-LEÓN

Universidad Nacional Autónoma de Nicaragua-León (UNAN-LEÓN)

Edificio Central, Contiguo a Iglesia La Merced, León
Tel: +505(311) 5013 +505(311) 5035 +505(311) 2614 +505(311) 5091
Fax: +505(311) 4970
EMail: rectoria@unanleon.edu.ni
Website: http://www.unanleon.edu.ni

Rector: Rigoberto Sampson Granera

Faculties

Business (Accountancy; Business Administration; Economics; Marketing; Tourism); **Chemical Sciences** (Food Science; Pharmacy); **Dentistry** (Dentistry); **Education Sciences and Humanities** (Educational Sciences; English; Mathematics Education; Natural Sciences; Social Work); **Law** (Law); **Medical Sciences**; **Science and Technology**

Programmes

Veterinary Medicine (Veterinary Science)

History: Founded 1812.

Governing Bodies: Junta Universitaria

Academic Year: February to December (February-July; August-December)

Admission Requirements: Secondary school certificate (bachillerato) or recognized equivalent, and entrance examination

Main Language(s) of Instruction: Spanish

Degrees and Diplomas: *Licenciatura*; *Maestría*

Last Updated: 23/03/09

NATIONAL AUTONOMOUS UNIVERSITY OF NICARAGUA-MANAGUA

Universidad Nacional Autónoma de Nicaragua-Managua

Apartado postal 663, De Enel Central 21/2 Km al Sur, Villa Fontana, Managua
Tel: +505 2786779 +505 2675071
Fax: +505 2774943
EMail: unanread@ns.tmx.com.ni
Website: http://www.unan.edu.ni

Rector: Francisco Guzmán Pasos EMail: rectoria@unan.edu.ni

Vice-Rector: Elmer Cisneros Moreira
EMail: vrgeneral@unan.edu.ni

Secretary-General: Nívea González Rojas
EMail: secgeneral@unan.edu.ni

Faculties

Economics (Accountancy; Administration; Agricultural Economics; Economics); **Education and Humanities** (Education); **Law** (Law); **Medicine** (Medicine); **Science** (Biology; Chemistry; Computer Science; Mathematics; Natural Sciences; Physics)

Institutes

Health *(Polytechnic)* (Health Sciences)

Research Centres

Economics and Technology; **Geoscience** *(CIGEO)* (Geography; Science Education); **Health** *(CIES)*; **Social Studies** (Social Studies); **Socio-educational Sciences** (Educational Sciences; Social Sciences); **Water Resources** *(CIRA)*

Further Information: Also regional centres in Carazo, Estelí, Matagalpa and Chontales

History: Founded 1812 as Universidad de León in succession to a 17th century seminary. Retained characteristics of Spanish colonial university until reorganization at end of 19th century. Granted autonomous status 1958 and reforms initiated. Financially supported by the State through the Ministry of Finance (72.3%), tuition fees (25.2%), and other sources (2.5%).

Governing Bodies: Junta Universitaria

Academic Year: February to December (February-July; August-December)

Admission Requirements: Secondary school certificate (bachillerato) or recognized equivalent, and entrance examination

Fees: None

Main Language(s) of Instruction: Spanish

Degrees and Diplomas: *Técnico Superior*; *Licenciatura*: Biology; Chemistry; Dentistry; Education Sciences; Food Sciences; Law and Social Sciences; Mathematics; Pharmacy; Statistics, 5 yrs; *Licenciatura*: Medicine; Surgery, 6 yrs; *Maestría*. Also specializations

Student Residential Facilities: Yes

Special Facilities: Museo Entomológico; Museo Archivo 'Rubén Darío'

Libraries: Central Library, c. 32,000 vols; Law library, c. 12,000; Medicine library, c. 23,500; Education Sciences library, c. 8,000; Social Sciences library, c. 26,000; Health Sciences library, c. 14,000

Publications: Cuadernos Universitariàs *(quarterly)*; Revista Médica *(biennially)*

Last Updated: 07/04/08

NATIONAL UNIVERSITY OF AGRICULTURE

Universidad Nacional Agraria (UNA)

Apartado postal 453, Kilometro 125, Carretera Norte, Managua
Tel: +505(2) 331-619
Fax: +505(2) 331-950
EMail: info@una.edu.ni
Website: http://www.una.edu.ni

Rector: Francisco Telémaco Talavera Siles

Secretario General: Ronald Quiroz Ocampo

Vicerrector: Alberto Sediles Jaen

Faculties

Agronomy (Agricultural Engineering; Agronomy; Forestry; Horticulture; Plant and Crop Protection); **Animal Sciences** (Animal Husbandry; Aquaculture; Veterinary Science); **Natural Resources and Environment** (Environmental Studies; Forestry; Irrigation; Natural Resources; Soil Science; Water Science); **Rural Development** (Rural Studies)

History: Founded 1929 as secondary level institute, acquired present status 1951.

Governing Bodies: University Council

Academic Year: March to November (March-July; August-November)

Admission Requirements: Secondary school certificate (bachillerato)

Main Language(s) of Instruction: Spanish

Degrees and Diplomas: *Técnico Superior*: 5 yrs; *Licenciatura*: 5 yrs; *Licenciatura*: Engineering, 5 yrs; *Maestría*

Student Residential Facilities: Yes

Special Facilities: Botanical Garden. Seed Resources

Libraries: Centro National de Información; Documentación Agro (CENIDA)

Last Updated: 17/12/09

NATIONAL UNIVERSITY OF ENGINEERING

Universidad Nacional de Ingeniería (UNI)

Apartado postal 5595, Avenidad Universitaria, Frente a la Escuela de Danza, Managua
Tel: +505(2) 771-650
EMail: rector@uni.edu.ni
Website: http://www.uni.edu.ni

Rector: Aldo José Urbina Villalta (2002-) Fax: +505(2) 673-709

Vicerrector: Victor Emilio Arcia Gómez
Tel: +505(2) 781-465 EMail: Victor.Arcia@uni.edu.ni

Faculties

Architecture *(Simón Bolívar Campus)* (Architecture); **Chemical Engineering** *(Simón Bolívar Campus)* (Chemical Engineering); **Construction Engineering** *(Pedro Arauz Palacios Campus)* (Agricultural Engineering; Construction Engineering; Transport Engineering); **Electronics and Computer Science** *(Simón Bolívar Campus)* (Architecture; Computer Science; Electrical and Electronic Engineering; Telecommunications Engineering); **Industrial Engineering** *(Pedro Arauz P. Campus)* (Energy Engineering; Engineering; Industrial Engineering; Mechanical Engineering; Production Engineering); **Science and Systems** *(Pedro Arauz Palacios Campus)* (Mathematics; Physics; Social Sciences)

Programmes

Environmental Research *(CIEMA)* (Environmental Studies) *Director*: Sergio Gánez Gurerrero

History: Founded 1983. A State institution.

Governing Bodies: Consejo Universitario

Academic Year: March to August

Admission Requirements: Secondary school certificate (bachillerato)

Main Language(s) of Instruction: Spanish

International Co-operation: Participates in AECI, ICI, SAREC

Degrees and Diplomas: *Técnico Superior*: Architecture (Arquitecto); Engineering (Ingeniero), 5-6 yrs; *Maestría*: 2 yrs. Also Ingeniero

Student Services: Canteen, Cultural centre, Health services, Sports facilities

Libraries: Biblioteca 'Esman Marin', 15,000 vols; Julio Buitrago, 8,000 vols

Publications: Nexo *(quarterly)*

Last Updated: 17/12/09

NICARAGUAN TECHNOLOGICAL UNIVERSITY

Universidad Tecnológica Nicaragüense (UTN)

Rotonda Metrocentro 150vs al Oeste, Managua

Tel: +505 278-0889

Fax: +505 278-7366

EMail: utn@ibw.com.ni

Rector: Horacio Bermúdez Cuadra (1996-)

General Dean: Alejandro Quintana Nájera
Tel: +505 278-1400 EMail: aquintananajera@yahoo.es

International Relations: Rosario Verónica Sotelo Contreras, Secretary-General
Tel: +505 278-1400 EMail: rsotelo2005@yahoo.com

Faculties

Law and Administration (Accountancy; Administration; Business Administration; Economics; Finance; Hotel Management; Law; Tourism) *Dean*: Diego Aragón Ruiz; **Technical Sciences** *Dean*: Keitelle Campos; **Technology Transfer** *Dean*: Ricardo Fajardo

History: Founded 1994.

Governing Bodies: University Council

Admission Requirements: High School Certificate

Fees: (US Dollars): 475 per annum

Main Language(s) of Instruction: Spanish

International Co-operation: With universities in Mexico, Germany and Spain

Degrees and Diplomas: *Técnico Superior*: Electrical Engineering; Civil Engineering, 3 yrs; *Técnico Superior*: Interior Design and Decoration; Surveying and Mapping; Mechanical Engineering, 2 1/2 yrs; *Licenciatura*: Architecture (Arq.); Electromechanical Engineering; Telecommunication Engineering; Electronic Engineering; Computer Engineering; Systems; Industrial Engineering (Ing.); Financial Law; International Commerce, 4 1/2 yrs; *Licenciatura*: Business Administration; Tourism and Hotel Management; Customs Administration; Economics; Accounting; Industrial Engineering; Civil Engineering, 4 yrs

Student Services: Academic counselling, Canteen, Health services, Social counselling, Sports facilities

Libraries: Central Campus Library "Alfredo Solózano Lacayo"; Sub-regional Library "Rubén Dario"

Last Updated: 27/02/08

NICARAGUAN UNIVERSITY OF HUMANIST STUDIES

Universidad Nicaragüense de Estudios Humanisticos

Reparto Nueva Reforma, Iglesia El Carmen, 2c norte 1/2 c oeste, Frente al Parque, Managua

EMail: universidaduneh@gmail.com

Website: http://www.uneh.es.tl/Inicio.htm

Rector: Fanor Ángel Avendaño Soza

Faculties

Economics, Administration and Finance (Accountancy; Administration; Business Administration; Economics; Finance); **Humanities, Law and Social Sciences**; **Technology and Systems**

History: Founded 2008.

Main Language(s) of Instruction: Spanish

Degrees and Diplomas: *Licenciatura*; *Especialización*; *Maestría*

Last Updated: 17/12/09

NICARAGUAN UNIVERSITY OF SCIENCE AND TECHNOLOGY

Universidad Nicaragüense de Ciencia y Tecnología (UCYT)

Semáfaros de Rubenia 700 mts. al Norte, Managua

EMail: rector@ucyt.edu.ni

Website: http://www.ucyt.edu.ni

Rector: Fernando Robleto Lang

Programmes

Accountancy (Accountancy); **Business Administration**; **Computer Science** (Computer Science); **International Relations**; **Law** (Law); **Psychology** (Psychology); **Systems Engineering** (Systems Analysis); **Tourism and Hotel Management** (Hotel Management; Tourism)

Degrees and Diplomas: *Licenciatura*

Last Updated: 17/12/09

PAULO FREIRE UNIVERSITY

Universidad Paulo Freire

De Semáforos de Linda Vista 6 1/2 c. al Sur, Managua

Tel: +505(2) 250-5380

Fax: +505(2) 250-5380

EMail: upf@upfni.com

Website: http://www.upf.edu.ni

Rector: Adrián Meza Soza (1998-)
Tel: +505(2) 250-5380, Ext. 20, Fax: +505(2) 250-5380, Ext. 26
EMail: ameza@cablenet.com.ni

Vicerrectora: Susy Duriez
Tel: +505 (2) 250-3849, Fax: +505 (2) 266-5939
EMail: sduriez@cablenet.com.ni

Faculties

Computer Science (Computer Science); **Economics** (Accountancy; Business Administration; Human Resources; Marketing; Tourism); **Education** (Education; Psychology; Sociology) *Dean*: Rosa Argentina Granados; **Law and Political Science** (Law; Political Sciences) *Dean*: René Cruz; **Psychology** (Psychology)

Institutes

Juan Bautista Arrien *(Instituto de Secundaria) Principal*: Edwin Cuadra Alemán

Further Information: Also branches in Carazo, Río San Juan, Matagalpa

History: Founded 1998 as Instituto Universitario "Paulo Freire" (IPF). Acquired present status and title 2002.

Governing Bodies: Rector, Vice-Rectors, Secretary-General, Executive Director, Rector Delegates

Academic Year: January to December

Admission Requirements: High school certificate (Bachillerato)

Fees: (US Dollars): 25 per month; (Cordoblas): Administration fees, 400 per annum

Main Language(s) of Instruction: Spanish

International Co-operation: With universities in Italy, Spain, Germany, Central America and Venezuela

Degrees and Diplomas: *Licenciatura (Ing)*; *Especialización*; *Maestría (MSc)*

Student Services: Academic counselling, Cultural centre, Employment services, Foreign Studies Centre, Handicapped facilities, Language programs, Nursery care, Sports facilities

Libraries: Yes.

Last Updated: 17/12/09

PEOPLE'S UNIVERSITY OF NICARAGUA

Universidad Popular de Nicaragua (UPONIC)

Delicias del Volga 1/2 c. al este. Frente a Mántica Repuestos, Managua

Tel: +505 268-0058

Fax: +505 266-2659

EMail: uponic@tmx.com.ni

Website: http://www.uponic.edu.ni

Rectora: Olga Soza Bravo

Faculties

Agriculture (Agriculture); **Computer Science** (Computer Science); **Economics** (Accountancy; Business Administration; Economics; Finance); **Education** (Education); **Engineering** (Engineering); **Law and Political Science** (Law; Political Sciences); **Natural Medicine** (Medicine)

History: Founded 1991.

Main Language(s) of Instruction: Spanish

Degrees and Diplomas: *Licenciatura*; *Maestría*

Last Updated: 28/03/13

POLYTECHNIC UNIVERSITY OF NICARAGUA

Universidad Politécnica de Nicaragua (UPOLI)

Apartado postal 3595, Costado Sur Villa 'Ruben Darío', Managua

Tel: +505(2) 897-740

Fax: +505(2) 499-232

EMail: rpublicas@upoli.edu.ni

Website: http://www.upoli.edu.ni

Rector: Emerson Pérez Sandoval

Tel: +505(2) 289-7740 EMail: rectoria@upoli.edu.ni

Vicerrector Administrativo Financiero: Douglas Prado López

EMail: vradmonfinan@upoli.edu.ni

International Relations: Tomás Téllez Ruiz, Secretario General

EMail: uporein@upoli.edu.ni

Academies

Homeopathic Medicine (Homeopathy) *Director*: Javier Lacayo

Centres

Latin American and Caribbean Studies *(CIELAC, Interuniversity)* *Director*: Guillermo Gómez Santibáñez

Institutes

Gender Studies *Director*: Brenda Consuelo Ruíz; **Humanistic Research and Development** *(IDEHU)* (Cultural Studies; Education; Justice Administration; Latin American Studies; Theology) *Director*: Jerjes Ruiz; **Research in Integral Rural Development** *(ICIDRI)* *Director*: Hugo Silva; **Social Research and Action** *(Martin Luther King)* (Human Rights; International Relations; Peace and Disarmament; Theology) *Director*: Denis Torres

Schools

Administration, Commerce, and Finance (Administration; Business and Commerce; Finance) *Director*: Miguel Murillo; **Design** (Design) *Director*: Eduardo Vanegas; **Economics** (Economics) *Director*: Eyra Reyes; **Engineering** (Computer Networks; Computer Science; Engineering; Information Management) *Director*: Gladys Aguilar; **Law** (Law) *Director*: Oscar L. Castillo Guido; **Nursing** (Nursing) *Director*: Margarita Guevara; **Tourism** (Tourism) *Director*: Cecilia Paredes

Further Information: Also Regional Branches in Boaco, Esteli and Rivas

History: Founded 1967 by the Nicaraguan Baptist Convention with the aid of the American Baptist Home Mission Society. Became university 1976. A private university receiving government subsidy for operating expenses. Relies on outside contributions for the other costs.

Governing Bodies: Board of Trustees

Academic Year: February to November (February-July; August-November)

Admission Requirements: Secondary school certificate (bachillerato)

Fees: None

Main Language(s) of Instruction: Spanish

Degrees and Diplomas: *Técnico Superior*: Administration; Banking and Finance; Marketing; Nursing; Professional Design, 2 1/2-3 yrs; *Licenciatura*: Banking and Finance; Business Administration; Computer Science; Industrial Design; Nursing; *Licenciatura*: Economic Management; Foreign Trade; Law; Public Accountancy and Finance; Systems Engineering; Tourism and Hotel Industry, 4 1/2 yrs; *Maestría*: Social Qualititative Research; Homeopathy; Ecosustainable Rural Development; Economic Law; Business Administration; Advanced Clinical Nursing; Procedural and Penal Law; Entrepreneurial Law; Auditing; Health Services Management. Also Postgrado

Libraries: c. 11,000 vols

REDEMPTORIS MATER CATHOLIC UNIVERSITY

Universidad Católica 'Redemptoris Mater' (UNICA)

Carretera a Masaya, Km 91/2, 500 vrs al suroeste, Managua

Tel: +505(2) 760-004

EMail: info@unica.edu.ni

Website: http://www.unica.edu.ni

Rectora: Michelle Rivas de Molina

Vicerrector Académico: Roberto Rivas Reyes

Faculties

Economics and Administration (Administration; Banking; Economics; Finance; Hotel Management; Marketing; Tourism); **Engineering and Architecture** (Architecture; Civil Engineering; Engineering; Industrial Engineering; Systems Analysis); **Humanities** (Arts and Humanities; Education; Educational Administration; Educational Psychology; Mathematics; Pedagogy; Philosophy; Preschool Education; Religious Studies; Spanish); **Law and Social Sciences** (International Relations; Law; Social Sciences); **Medicine**

History: Founded 1992.

Admission Requirements: Diploma de Bachiller

Main Language(s) of Instruction: Spanish

Degrees and Diplomas: *Licenciatura*; *Especialización*

Last Updated: 16/12/09

SANTO TOMÁS UNIVERSITY OF ORIENTE Y MEDIO DÍA

Universidad Santo Tomás de Oriente y Medio Día (USTOM)

Calle El Consuldado. De la Iglesia La Merced 1c. Al norte, 1c. Al oeste, Granada

Tel: +505(552) 2545

Fax: +505(552) 2545

EMail: ustom@cablenet.com.ni

Rector: Roberto Ferrey EMail: rferreye@gmail.com

Administrative Director: Mary Lara Tel: +505 889-2856

International Relations: Roberto Ferrey

Programmes

Accountancy (Accountancy) *Director*: Miguel López; **Commercial Engineering** *Director*: Francisco Lozano; **Design and Construction** *Director*: Harvin Cabezas; **Law** *Director*: Ernesto Zambrana

Admission Requirements: High School Diploma (Diploma de Bachiller)

Main Language(s) of Instruction: Spanish

Degrees and Diplomas: *Técnico Superior*: Tourism; *Licenciatura*: Accounting; Law; Commercial Engineering; Engineering; Design and Contruction Engineering, 5 yrs. Also Degrees in Secretarial Studies

Student Services: Employment services, Foreign student adviser

Libraries: Yes

Last Updated: 28/02/08

TECHNICAL UNIVERSITY OF COMMERCE

Universidad Técnica de Comercio (EPC)

Antiguo Cine Salinas 5c abajo, 2c al lago Bo. Campo bruce, Managua

Tel: +505(2) 490-880

Fax: +505(2) 497-416

EMail: unitco@utc.edu.ni

Website: http://www.utc.edu.ni

Rectora: Gladys Bonilla Muñoz

Programmes

Accountancy; **Business Administration** (Business Administration); **Computer Science** (Computer Science); **Marketing and Publicity**; **Systems Engineering** (Systems Analysis)

History: Founded 1966 as Escuela Politécnica de Comercio. Acquired present status and title 2006.

Main Language(s) of Instruction: Spanish

Degrees and Diplomas: *Licenciatura*; *Especialización*

Last Updated: 18/12/09

THOMAS MORE UNIVERSITY

Universidad Thomas More (UTM)

Semáforos Club Villa Fontana 150 vrs al Sur, Managua

EMail: informacion@unithomasmore.edu.ni

Website: http://www.unithomasmore.edu.ni

Rectora: Irene D'Franco

Programmes

Economics (Economics); **Industrial and Systems Engineering** (Industrial Engineering); **Management** (Management); **Political Science** (Police Studies); **Tourism** (Tourism)

Degrees and Diplomas: *Licenciatura*. Also Ingeniero

Last Updated: 17/12/09

UNIVERSITY OF COMMERCIAL SCIENCE

Universidad de Ciencias Comerciales (UCC)

Apartado Postal, 84 Frente al Polideportivo España, Bosques de Altamira, Managua

Tel: +505(2) 277-1931

EMail: ucc@ucc.edu.ni

Website: http://www.ucc.edu.ni

Rector: Gilberto Bergman Padilla
EMail: gilberto.bergman@ucc.edu.ni

Secretario General: Jorge Quintana
EMail: jorge.quintana@ucc.edu.ni

Faculties

Agriculture (Agriculture; Food Science; Food Technology; Management; Rural Planning; Veterinary Science; Zoology); **Commercial Law** (Commercial Law; Law); **Economics and Business Studies** (Accountancy; Advertising and Publicity; Banking; Business Administration; Finance; Graphic Design; International Business; Marketing; Public Relations); **Engineering and Computer Science** (Civil Engineering; Computer Engineering; Computer Science; Industrial Engineering; Systems Analysis; Telecommunications Engineering); **Tourism and Hotel Management**

Schools

Photography

Further Information: Also branch in León

History: Founded 1964. Acquired present status 1997.

Admission Requirements: Diploma de Bachiller

Main Language(s) of Instruction: Spanish

Degrees and Diplomas: *Licenciatura*; *Licenciatura*: Engineering, 5 yrs; *Especialización*; *Maestría*. Also Diplomado

Last Updated: 17/12/09

UNIVERSITY OF MANAGUA

Universidad de Managua (U DE M)

Hospital Vélez Paiz 1 c. al Este, Reparto Belmonte, Managua

Tel: +505(2) 652-632

Fax: +505(2) 265-2608

EMail: udm@ibw.com.ni

Website: http://www.udem.edu.ni

Rectora: Doris Meza Cornavaca EMail: rectoria@udem.edu.ni

Faculties

Economics (Accountancy; Business Administration; Economics; Hotel Management; Tourism); **Engineering**; **Law** (Journalism; Law)

Further Information: Also branch in León

History: Founded 1998.

Main Language(s) of Instruction: Spanish

Degrees and Diplomas: *Licenciatura*; *Maestría*

Last Updated: 17/12/09

UNIVERSITY OF TECHNOLOGY AND COMMERCE

Universidad de Tecnología y Comercio

Miguel Gutierrez, Semaforos 150 mts al Norte, Managua

Tel: +505 2249-7617

Website: http://www.unitec.edu.ni

Rector: José Jorge Mojica Mejia

Faculties

Administration and Commerce (Accountancy; Administration; Business and Commerce; Human Resources); **Engineering** (Computer Engineering; Engineering; Systems Analysis; Telecommunications Engineering)

Main Language(s) of Instruction: Spanish

Degrees and Diplomas: *Licenciatura*. Also Ingeniero and Diplomado

Last Updated: 18/12/09

UNIVERSITY OF WEST-LEÓN

Universidad de Occidente-León (UDO)

Apartado Postal 615 Parque San Juan $\frac{1}{2}$ c. al oeste, León

EMail: udoleon@yahoo.es

Rector: Armando Gutiérrez

Programmes

Agricultural Engineering (Agricultural Engineering); **Civil Engineering** (Civil Engineering); **Systems Engineering**

UNIVERSITY OF THE AMERICAS

Universidad de las Américas (ULAM)

Antigua Pepsi, Km. 3 Carretera Norte 1 c. al Sur, 1 c. abajo., Managua

Tel: +505(2) 483-122

Fax: +505(2) 248-3082

EMail: ulam@ulam.edu.ni

Website: http://www.ulam.edu.ni/

Rector: Evenor Estrada García EMail: estrada@ulam.edu.ni

Secretario General: Ariel José Otero Castañeda
Tel: +505(2) 442-645, Fax: +505(2) 442-645
EMail: otero@ulam.edu.ni

International Relations: Eduardo Julio Martínez Rizo
Tel: +505(2) 442-645, Fax: +505(2) 483-081
EMail: rpublicas@ulam.edu.ni

Faculties

Economics and Administration; **Tourism**

History: Founded 1995. Acquired present status 1998.

Governing Bodies: Board of Directors; Academic Council; Control Council

Academic Year: March to February

Admission Requirements: High School Diploma (Diploma de Bachiller)

Fees: (Córdobas): 560 per month

Main Language(s) of Instruction: Spanish

International Co-operation: With universities in El Salvador

Accrediting Agencies: Consejo Nacional de Universidades

Degrees and Diplomas: *Licenciatura*. Also Posgrados

Student Services: Academic counselling, Cultural centre, Employment services, Social counselling

Student Residential Facilities: None

Libraries: Yes

Last Updated: 17/12/09

UNIVERSITY OF THE AUTONOMOUS REGIONS OF THE CARIBBEAN COAST OF NICARAGUA

Universidad de las Regiones Autónomas de la Costa Caribe Nicaragüense (URACCAN)

Apartado postal 891, Puerto Cabezas

EMail: rectoria@uraccan.edu.ni

Website: http://www.uraccan.edu.ni

Rectora: Alta Suzanne Hooker Blandford

Institutes

Language and Cultural Heritage (IPILC); **Natural Resources, Environment and Sustainable Development (IREMADES)**; **Study and Promotion of Autonomy (IEPA)**; **Traditional Medicine and Community Development (IMTRADEC)**

Research Centres

Multiethnic Women

Further Information: Also branches in Bluefields, Managua, Las Minas

History: Founded 1993.

Main Language(s) of Instruction: Spanish

Degrees and Diplomas: *Técnico Superior*, *Licenciatura*; *Maestría*

Last Updated: 17/12/09

UNIVERSITY OF THE NORTH OF NICARAGUA

Universidad del Norte de Nicaragua (UNN)

Antiguas Oficinas de Enabas, Estelí

EMail: unn@ibw.com.ni

Rector: Noel Ponce

Programmes

Accountancy; **Administration** (Business Administration; Hotel Management; Tourism); **Animal Husbandry**; **Banking and Finance** (Banking; Finance); **Computer Science**; **Ecology and Natural Resources** (Ecology; Natural Resources); **Journalism**; **Law**; **Psychology**; **Sociology** (Social Work; Sociology)

Main Language(s) of Instruction: Spanish

Degrees and Diplomas: *Licenciatura*; *Licenciatura*: Engineering, 5 yrs

UNIVERSITY OF THE VALLEY

Universidad del Valle

Rotonda del Periodista, 25 varas al Sur, Managua

Tel: +505(2) 278-8634

Fax: +505(2) 278-8729

EMail: admisiones@univalle.edu.ni

Website: http://www.univalle.edu.ni

Rectora: Socorro Bonilla Castellón EMail: rectoria@univalle.edu.ni

Gerente General: Arnoldo Arreaga Carrera
EMail: :arreaga@univalle.edu.ni

Faculties

Architecture and Design (Architecture; Design; Fashion Design; Interior Design); **Business Administration** (Administration; Advertising and Publicity; Banking; Business Administration; Finance; Hotel Management; Marketing; Tourism); **Communication**; **Engineering** (Computer Engineering; Systems Analysis); **Law**

History: Founded 1997.

Admission Requirements: Diploma de Bachiller

Main Language(s) of Instruction: Spanish

Degrees and Diplomas: *Técnico Superior*, *Licenciatura*. Also Ingeniero

Last Updated: 17/12/09

Niger

STRUCTURE OF HIGHER EDUCATION SYSTEM

Description:

Post-secondary-level education takes place at public universities under the jurisdiction of the Ministry of Secondary and Higher Education and other public institutes under the jurisdiction of their corresponding Ministries. It also takes place at several private institutions.

Stages of studies:

University level first stage: *Licence*
The first cycle is a three-year period of general university studies. It leads to the Licence.

University level second stage: *Master*
The second cycle lasts for a further two years, leading to the Master.

University level third stage: *Doctorat*
The third cycle leads to the Doctorat, conferred after three years' study. Candidates must carry out original research and defend their thesis in front of a jury. The Docteur en Médecine is conferred after eight years' study.

ADMISSION TO HIGHER EDUCATION

Admission to university-level studies:

Name of secondary school credential required: Baccalauréat

For entry to: University

Alternatives to credentials: An entrance exam can be taken by non-holders of the Baccalauréat.

Foreign students admission:

Entrance exam requirements: Foreign students should hold a Baccalauréat or an equivalent qualification.

Language requirements: Good knowledge of French is required.

RECOGNITION OF STUDIES

Quality assurance system:

Standards are set by the Ministry.

Bodies dealing with recognition:

Office national des Equivalences, des Examens et Concours du Supérieur (ONEECS)
Niamey

NATIONAL BODIES

Ministère de l'Enseignement secondaire, supérieur et de la Recherche scientifique - MESSRS (Ministry of Secondary and Higher Education and Research)
Minister: Mamadou Youba Diallo
Niamey
Tel: +227 2072 3635
WWW: http://www.messrs.ne/

Data for academic year: 2012-2013
Source: IAU from the website of the Ministry of Higher Education and World Data on Education 2010/2011, UNESCO-IBE, 2012

INSTITUTIONS

PUBLIC INSTITUTIONS

ABDOU MOUMOUNI UNIVERSITY OF NIAMEY

Université Abdou Moumouni de Niamey
BP 10896, 10896 Niamey
Tel: +227(20) 73-27-13
Fax: +227(20) 73-38-62
EMail: scre_uam@gmail.com
Website: http://uam.refer.ne

Recteur: Abarchi Habibou

Vice-Recteur chargé des Affaires académiques: Amadou Boureima

International Relations: Moussa Baragé, Vice-Recteur chargé de la Recherche et des relations extérieures

Centres
Agriculture *(CRESA)* (Agriculture); **Documentation and Distance Training** *(Campus Numérique Francophone, CNF)*

Faculties
Agronomy (Agronomy; Animal Husbandry; Soil Science); **Arts and Humanities** (Arts and Humanities; English; Geography; Geography (Human); History; Linguistics; Literature; Philosophy; Psychology; Sociology); **Health Sciences** (Health Sciences; Public Health); **Law and Economics** (Economics; Law); **Science and Technology** (Biology; Chemistry; Geography; Geology; Mathematics; Natural Sciences; Physics; Soil Science)

Institutes
Radio-Isotopes *(IRI)*

Programmes
Distance Learning *(Université Virtuelle Africaine, UVA)*

Research Institutes
Humanities *(IRSH)* (Arts and Humanities; Social Sciences); **Mathematics Education** *(IREM)* (Mathematics Education)

Schools
Education *(Ecole normale supérieure)* (Education; Pedagogy; Teacher Training)

History: Founded 1971 as Centre d'Enseignement supérieur. Renamed University of Niamey 1973. Under the jurisdiction of the Ministry of Secondary and Higher Education, Research and Technology.

Governing Bodies: Conseil, composed of the Rector, Deans and Directors of the faculties and institutes, representatives of the academic staff and student body, and government representatives

Academic Year: October to June (October-December; January-March; April-June)

Admission Requirements: Secondary school certificate (baccalauréat) or special entrance examination

Main Language(s) of Instruction: French

International Co-operation: With universities in Africa, Europe and USA

Accrediting Agencies: Ministère de l'enseignement secondaire, supérieur et de la recherche scientifique

Degrees and Diplomas: *Licence*: Agronomy, Biology, Geology; Economics, Law; English, Geography, History, Modern Languages, Linguistics, Philosophy, Psychology, Sociology; Mathematics, Chemistry, Natural sciences, Physics; *Docteur en Médecine*: Medicine; *Master*: Agricultural Engineering; Agronomy, Chemistry, Mathematics, Natural Sciences, Physics; *Doctorat*

Student Residential Facilities: Yes

Libraries: c. 62,000 vols

Publications: Les Annales de l'Université Abdou Moumouni *(annually)*

Press or Publishing House: RESADEP

Last Updated: 10/07/12

AFRICAN SCHOOL OF METEOROLOGY AND CIVIL AVIATION

École africaine de la Météorologie et de l'Aviation civile (EAMAC)
BP 746, Niamey
Tel: +227(20) 72-36-62
Fax: +227(20) 72-22-36
EMail: eamacsec@asecna.org
Website: http://www.eamac.ne/

Directeur: Sadamba Tchagbele

Divisions
Air Navigation (Air Transport); **Air Transport** (Air Transport); **Electronics and Computer Science** (Computer Science; Electronic Engineering); **Meteorology** (Meteorology)

History: Founded 1963.

Governing Bodies: ASECNA

Accrediting Agencies: CAMES

Degrees and Diplomas: *Master*

Last Updated: 10/07/12

AGRHYMET REGIONAL CENTRE

Centre régional Agrhymet (CRA/ARC)
BP 11011, Niamey
Tel: +227(20) 31-54-48
Fax: +227(20) 31-54-35
EMail: admin@agrhymet.ne
Website: http://www.agrhymet.ne

Director-General: Mohamed Yahya Ould Mahmoud
EMail: m.yahya@agrhymet.ne

Head, Training and Research Department: Etienne Sarr
EMail: E.Sarr@agrhymet.ne

Programmes
Agrometeorology *(IRD)* (Agricultural Equipment; Agricultural Management; Meteorology); **Computer Engineering** (Computer Engineering; Computer Science; Information Technology; Software Engineering); **Hydrology** (Hydraulic Engineering); **Plant Protection** (Plant and Crop Protection)

History: Founded 1974 as specialized Institute of the Permanent Interstate Committee for drought control in the Sahel (CILSS). Offers training and information in the fields of food security and sustainable natural resources management.

Governing Bodies: Technical and Management Committee; Scientific and Pedagogic Committee

Academic Year: October to June

Admission Requirements: Secondary school certificate (baccalaureat, Science option) or equivalent for the higher diploma; and higher diploma or equivalent for the diploma of Ingénieur

Main Language(s) of Instruction: French

Accrediting Agencies: Conseil Africain et Malgache pour l' Enseignement Supérieur (CAMES)

Degrees and Diplomas: *Master*: Agrometeorology; Hydrology, Computer Engineering; Crop Protection; Management of Natural Resources

Student Services: Academic counselling, Cultural centre, Health services, Language programs, Sports facilities

Student Residential Facilities: 130-Room Residence Halls

Special Facilities: Specialized Laboratories (Entomology, Phytopathology, Phytopharmacy, Electronics, Hydrology, Geographic Information Systems and Remote Sensing); WIFI

Libraries: Central Library, 32,000 references completely computerized and connected to Internet

Publications: Bulletin du Département Formation et Recherche, Liaison Bulletin specially designed for former students *(biennially)*

Academic Staff *2011-2012*	TOTAL
FULL-TIME	20
PART-TIME	20
STAFF WITH DOCTORATE	
FULL-TIME	5
PART-TIME	c. 5

Student Numbers *2011-2012*	
All (Foreign Included)	c. 80

Note: In addition to long-term students, the Centre trains more than 200 trainees annually through short-term programmes
Last Updated: 10/07/12

NATIONAL SCHOOL OF ADMINISTRATION AND MAGISTRACY

École nationale d'Administration et de Magistrature (ENAM)

BP 542, Rue Martin Luther King Jr, Niamey
Tel: +227(20) 72-31-83
Fax: +227(20) 72-43-83
EMail: enaniger@intnet.ne
Website: http://enam.refer.ne

Directeur Général: Boukar Abba Kaka (2011-)

Programmes
Administration (Accountancy; Administration; Finance; Management; Public Administration; Secretarial Studies; Social Welfare; Taxation); **Law** (Law)

History: Founded 1963.

Admission Requirements: DUEL, DEUG or equivalent

Main Language(s) of Instruction: French

Academic Staff *2011-2012*	TOTAL
FULL-TIME	30
PART-TIME	c. 120

Student Numbers *2011-2012*	
All (Foreign Included)	c. 1,000

Last Updated: 10/07/12

SCHOOL OF MINING ENGINEERING, INDUSTRY AND GEOLOGY

École des Mines, de l'Industrie et de la Géologie (EMIG)

BP 732, Niamey
Tel: +227(20) 31-51-00
Fax: +227(20) 31-57-97
EMail: emig@intnet.ne
Website: http://www.emig-niger.org

Directeur Général: Iliassou Alzouma B

Departments
Computer Engineering (Computer Education); **Electrical Engineering** (Electrical Engineering); **General Studies** (Accountancy; Applied Mathematics; Business Administration; Communication Studies; Economics; English; Labour Law; Law; Mathematics; Operations Research; Optics; Physical Education; Sociology; Statistics); **Mechanical Engineering** (Electronic Engineering; Mechanical Engineering; Mechanics); **Mining and Environment** (Environmental Engineering; Mining Engineering); **Mining and Geology** (Geology; Mining Engineering)

History: Founded 1990.

Governing Bodies: CEAO

Main Language(s) of Instruction: French

Accrediting Agencies: Ministère des Mines et de l'Energie

Degrees and Diplomas: *Master*
Last Updated: 10/07/12

UNIVERSITY OF MARADI

Université de Maradi

Maradi

Rector: Saadou Mahamane

Faculties
Agronomy (Agronomy); **Arts and Humanity** (Arts and Humanities); **Economics and Law** (Economics; Law); **Education** (Education); **Health Sciences** (Health Sciences); **Science and Technology** (Biology; Chemistry; Geology; Mathematics; Natural Sciences; Physics; Technology)

Institutes
Technology *(IUT)* (Civil Engineering; Electrical Engineering; Mechanical Engineering)

History: Formerly integrated as part of University Abdou Moumouni de Niamey. Acquired present status 2010.

Accrediting Agencies: Ministère de l'enseignement secondaire, supérieur et de la recherche scientifique

Degrees and Diplomas: *Licence*; *Master*. Also Diplôme universitaire de Technologie (DUT)
Last Updated: 02/10/12

UNIVERSITY OF TAHOUA

Universté de Tahoua

Tahoua

Rector: Jean Marie Ambouta Karimou

Faculties
Agronomy; **Arts and Humanity** (Arts and Humanities; Modern Languages); **Economics and Law** (Economics; Law; Management); **Educational Sciences** (Education; Educational Sciences); **Health Sciences** (Health Sciences); **Science and Technology** (Accountancy; Finance; Hotel Management; Sales Techniques; Tourism)

History: Formerly integrated as part of University Abdou Moumouni de Niamey. Acquired present status 2010.

Accrediting Agencies: Ministère de l'enseignement secondaire, supérieur et de la recherche scientifique

Degrees and Diplomas: *Licence*; *Master*, *Doctorat*
Last Updated: 02/10/12

UNIVERSITY OF ZINDER

Université de Zinder

Zinder

Rector: Henri Kokou Motcho

Faculties
Agronomy (Agronomy); **Arts and Humanity** (Arts and Humanities; English; Geography; Sociology); **Economics and Law** (Economics; Law); **Educational Sciences** (Educational Sciences); **Health Sciences** (Health Sciences); **Science and Technology** (Natural Sciences; Technology)

Institutes
Technology *(IUT)* (Secretarial Studies; Surveying and Mapping; Transport Management; Urban Studies)

History: Formerly integrated as part of University Abdou Moumouni de Niamey. Acquired present status 2010.

Accrediting Agencies: Ministère de l'enseignement secondaire, supérieur et de la recherche scientifique

Degrees and Diplomas: *Licence*; *Master*. Also Diplôme universitaire de Technologie (DUT)
Last Updated: 02/10/12

PRIVATE INSTITUTION

ISLAMIC UNIVERSITY OF NIGER

Université Islamique du Niger

BP 11507, 11507 Niamey
Tel: +227(20) 72-39-03
Fax: +227(20) 73-37-96
EMail: unislam@intnet.ne; unislamsay@gmail.com
Website: http://www.universite-say.ne/

Rector: Abdeljaouad Sekkat (2009-)

Secretary-General: Abu Boubacar Turay

International Relations: Inwa Maman

Faculties
Arabic Language and Arts Studies (Arabic; Fine Arts; Literature); **Economics and Administration** (Administration; Economics); **Islamic and Arabic Studies** *(For Women)* (Arabic; Islamic Studies); **Sharia and Islamic Studies** (Islamic Law; Law)

Institutes
Pedagogy and Teacher Training (Education; Educational and Student Counselling; Pedagogy; Teacher Training)

Further Information: Also Campus in Say

History: Founded 1974. Acquired present status 1986.

Academic Year: September to June

Admission Requirements: High school leaving certificate or equivalent

Main Language(s) of Instruction: Arabic

International Co-operation: With universities in 21 West African countries

Degrees and Diplomas: *Licence*; *Master*

Student Services: Health services, Language programs, Sports facilities

Student Residential Facilities: Yes

Libraries: Central library

Publications: University Journal *(annually)*

Academic Staff *2011-2012*	**TOTAL**
FULL-TIME	**60**
PART-TIME	**10**
STAFF WITH DOCTORATE	
FULL-TIME	c. **20**

Student Numbers *2011-2012*	
All (Foreign Included)	c. **1,100**
FOREIGN ONLY	**760**

Last Updated: 10/07/12

Nigeria

STRUCTURE OF HIGHER EDUCATION SYSTEM

Description:

Higher education is provided by universities, polytechnics, colleges of education, and innovative entreprise institutions. The Federal Ministry of Education (FME) is the organ of Government charged with policy formulation, monitoring of implementation and setting and maintenance of standards within the nation's education sector. The Nigerian Universities Commission (NUC), the National Board for Technical Education (NBTE), and the National Commission for Colleges of Education (NCCE) are the supervisory bodies which coordinate the activities of the institutions of each sub-sector. The tertiary institutions draw a significant part of their funds from the proprietors (Federal government, State governments and private proprietors) while the remaining part is internally generated from levies/charges/fees (for private institutions), international development partners, support from alumni associations, and linkages with industries in Nigeria and abroad.

Stages of studies:

University level first stage: *Bachelor's degree*
First degree courses in Arts, Social Sciences and Pure Sciences are usually of four years' duration, whilst professional degrees last between four and six years (Medicine, Dentistry). The Bachelor's degree may be awarded as an Honours degree.

University level second stage: *Master's degree*
Master's degree courses last between one and two years after the Bachelor's degree.

University level third stage: *Doctorate*
The Doctorate degree is usually conferred at least two years after the Master's degree.

ADMISSION TO HIGHER EDUCATION

Admission to university-level studies:

Name of secondary school credential required: Senior School Certificate Examination

For entry to: Bachelor's degree

Alternatives to credentials: National Certificate of Education passes at Credit or Merit levels or Ordinary National Diploma at upper credit level.

Entrance exam requirements: Universities Matriculation Examination (UME) for all first Degrees. Good GCE 'A' level results give direct access to universities.

Numerus clausus/restrictions: For most fields as determined by the National Universities Commission and conditioned by availability of instructional facilities available in different programmes at the level of institution.

Foreign students admission:

Definition of foreign student: A student who is not a citizen of Nigeria, where citizenship is defined in terms of being born in Nigeria after 1960, or both parents being Nigerian and not being a citizen of another country.

Entrance exam requirements: Foreign students should have qualifications equivalent to the General Certificate of Education in at least 5 subjects, after 6 years of secondary school. At postgraduate level, foreign students must have an appropriate first degree with upper second class honours. Those with a lower grade have to take admission exams.

Entry regulations: Resident permits required of ECOWAS Nationals. Visas and resident permits required of Nationals of other countries.

Health requirements: Certificate of medical fitness at Medical Centre of Institution.

RECOGNITION OF STUDIES

Quality assurance system:

NUC is responsible for programme and institutional accreditation. Its work comprises pre-accreditation, accreditation and post-accreditation activities.

Bodies dealing with recognition:

National Universities Commission (NUC)

Aja Nwachukwu House, no 26
Aguiyi-Ironsi St., Maitama District P.M.B. 237 Garki G.P.O
Abuja
Tel: +234 080 2745 5412
Fax: +234 070 8202 4412
WWW: http://www.nuc.edu.ng

NATIONAL BODIES

Federal Ministry of Education

Minister: Raqayyatu Ahmed Rufa'i
Director, Tertiary Education: Jamila Shu'ara
Federal Secretariat
Central Business District
Abuja
Tel: +234(9) 523 7487
EMail: inquiries@fme.gov.ng
WWW: http://www.fme.gov.ng/
Role of national body: The Federal Ministry of Education has been vested with the overall responsibility for laying down national policies and guidelines for uniform standards for all levels of education in Nigeria.

Federal Ministry of Science and Technology (FSMT)

Minister: Ita Okon Bassey Ewa
Federal Secretariat
Phase II, Block D
Shehu Shagari Way,Central Area,
P.M.B. 331, Garki
Abuja
Tel: +234(9) 523 3397
Fax: +234(9) 523 5204
WWW: http://www.fmst.gov.ng/

National Universities Commission (NUC)

Aja Nwachukwu House, no 26
Aguiyi-Ironsi St., Maitama District P.M.B. 237 Garki G.P.O
Abuja
Tel: +234 080 2745 5412
Fax: +234 070 8202 4412
WWW: http://www.nuc.edu.ng
Role of national body: Parastatal entity under the Ministry of Education. It allocates funds to Federal universities; examines the curriculum so that it corresponds to professional requirements; accredits academic programmes; processes applications for the establishment of private universities; and, more generally, develops university education.

National Board for Technical Education (NBTE)

Executive Secretary: Masa'udu Adamu Kazaure
P.M.B 2239
Plot "B" Bida Road

Kaduna
Tel: +234 062 246554
Fax: +234 062 247507
EMail: enquiries@nbte.gov.ng
WWW: http://www.nbte.gov.ng/
Role of national body: The National Board for Technical Education is a principal organ of the Federal Ministry of Education specifically created to handle all aspects of technical and vocational education falling outside university education.

National Commission for Colleges of Education (NCCE)
Executive Secretary: I. Junaid
Plot 829 Cadastral Zone A01, Ralph Shodeinde Street,
Opposite Akwa Ibom House, Off Ahmadu Bello Way,
P.M.B. 0394, Garki
Abuja
Tel: +234 9234 6531
EMail: info@ncceonline.org
WWW: http://www.ncceonline.org/
Role of national body: The National Commission for Colleges of Education was established in 1989 for the supervision of teacher education in the country.

Joint Admissions and Matriculation Board (JAMB)
Suleja Road, Bwari,
P.M.B. 189, Garki
Abuja
Tel: +234(9) 850 1756/7
Fax: +234(9) 850 1284
EMail: enquiries@jambng.com
WWW: http://www.jamb.org.ng/

IAU Committee of Vice-Chancellors of Nigerian Federal Universities (CVC)
Secretary-General: M.O. Faborode
Deputy Secretary-General: Ayodele Adigun
No 4, Parakou Street,
Wuse II,
P.M.B. 5286, Wuse G.P.O.
Abuja
Tel: +234(90) 780 5338
EMail: cvc@cvcnigeria.org
WWW: http://www.cvcnigeria.org/
Role of national body: Provides a platform for discussion of issues common to Nigerian universities; improves the visibility of Nigerian universities; acts as a bureau of information on Nigerian universities; facilitates communication amongst Nigerian universities; and serves as a forum for concerned parties.

Association of West African Universities - AWAU
President: Nana Jane Okoku Agyemang
Acting CEO, Coordinator: Is-haq Oloyede
19 Ukpabi Asika Street
Ilorin
Tel: +234 803 608 7987
EMail: info@awau.org
WWW: http://www.awau.org
Role of national body: Provides coordination and networking for universities in West Africa.

Data for academic year: 2012-2013
Source: IAU from Federal Ministry of Education and National Universities Commission websites, Education Reform Act, Nigeria, World Data on Education 2010/2011, UNESCO-IBE, 2012

INSTITUTIONS

PUBLIC INSTITUTIONS

ABIA STATE UNIVERSITY (ABSU)

P.M.B. 2000, Uturu, Abia State
Tel: +234(803) 6811-454
Fax: +234(805) 2610-681
EMail: absu@infoweb.abs.net
Website: http://www.absuu.net/

Vice-Chancellor: Chibuzo B. Ogbuagu (2010-)
EMail: vc@absu.edu.ng

Registrar: O. E. Onuoha

Deputy Vice Chancellor, Administration: E.A. Udensi

Faculties

Agriculture (Agricultural Economics; Agriculture; Animal Husbandry; Crop Production; Fishery; Food Science; Food Technology; Plant and Crop Protection; Soil Science); **Biological and Physical Sciences** (Applied Physics; Biochemistry; Biological and Life Sciences; Biology; Biotechnology; Botany; Environmental Studies; Industrial Chemistry; Mathematics; Microbiology; Physics; Statistics; Zoology); **Business Administration** (Accountancy; Banking; Business Administration; Economics; Finance; Management; Marketing; Public Administration); **Education** (Accountancy; Agricultural Education; Art Education; Biology; Business Education; Chemistry; Economics; Education; Educational and Student Counselling; English; Fine Arts; Foreign Languages Education; Geography; Government; History; Home Economics Education; Human Rights; International Relations; Library Science; Literature; Management; Mathematics; Native Language Education; Physics; Political Sciences; Psychology; Religion; Science Education; Social Studies); **Environmental Sciences** (Architecture; Building Technologies; Environmental Management; Environmental Studies; Geography; Natural Resources; Real Estate; Regional Planning; Rural Planning; Town Planning); **Humanities and Social Sciences** (Arts and Humanities; Communication Studies; English; French; Government; History; Information Sciences; International Relations; Library Science; Linguistics; Literature; Mass Communication; Modern Languages; Native Language; Philosophy; Political Sciences; Public Administration; Religious Studies; Social Sciences; Sociology; Translation and Interpretation); **Law** (Civil Law; Commercial Law; Constitutional Law; International Law; Law; Private Law; Public Law); **Medicine** (Dentistry; Medicine; Nursing; Optometry; Surgery)

Schools

Postgraduate Studies (Architecture; Arts and Humanities; Biological and Life Sciences; Business Administration; Education; Environmental Studies; Law; Social Sciences)

Further Information: Also campus in Umuahia.

History: Founded 1981. The University operates a collegiate system with related disciplines clustered into Schools and Schools grouped into Colleges. Interdisciplinary in structure and mission, each school is flexible in function.

Governing Bodies: Governing Council; Senate

Academic Year: October to July (October-March; April-July)

Admission Requirements: Universities Matriculation Examination (UME) following secondary school education

Main Language(s) of Instruction: English

Degrees and Diplomas: *Bachelor's Degree*: 5 yrs; *Bachelor's Degree*: 4 yrs; *Postgraduate Diploma*; *Master's Degree*; *Doctor of Philosophy (PhD)*. Also Executive MBA; Undergraduate Diplomas in French, Law.

Student Residential Facilities: Yes

Libraries: 27,000 vols, 35 periodical subscriptions

Student Numbers *2011-2012*: Total: c. 20,400
Last Updated: 04/07/12

ABUBAKAR TAFAWA BALEWA UNIVERSITY (ATBU)

Tafawa Balewa Way, PMB 0248, Bauchi, Bauchi State
Tel: +234(77) 542-464 +234(77) 543-500
Fax: +234(77) 542-065
EMail: amdanlami@atbu.edu.ng
Website: http://www.atbu.edu.ng

Vice-Chancellor: Hamisu Muhammad (1995-)
Tel: +234(77) 542-065 EMail: vc@atbu.edu.ng

Deputy Vice Chancellor, Administration: A. M. Gani
EMail: dvcadm@atbu.edu.ng

Registrar: Ibrahim Musa
Tel: +234(77) 542-092 EMail: registrar@registry.atbu.edu.ng

Schools

Agriculture and Agricultural Technology (Agricultural Economics; Agricultural Engineering; Agriculture; Agronomy; Animal Husbandry; Chemical Engineering; Crop Production; Farm Management); **Engineering and Engineering Technology** (Agricultural Engineering; Chemical Engineering; Civil Engineering; Electrical and Electronic Engineering; Electrical Engineering; Electronic Engineering; Engineering; Mechanical Engineering; Production Engineering); **Environmental Technology** (Architectural and Environmental Design; Architecture; Building Technologies; Environmental Engineering; Environmental Management; Industrial Design; Real Estate; Regional Planning; Safety Engineering; Surveying and Mapping; Town Planning); **Management Technology** (Accountancy; Banking; Business Administration; Finance; Information Technology; Insurance; Management; Technology; Transport and Communications; Transport Management); **Postgraduate Studies**; **Science** (Botany; Chemistry; Computer Science; Ecology; Geology; Geophysics; Industrial Chemistry; Mathematics; Mathematics and Computer Science; Microbiology; Nuclear Physics; Physics; Statistics; Zoology); **Technology Education** (Agricultural Education; Automotive Engineering; Biology; Building Technologies; Business Education; Chemistry; Computer Education; Education; Electrical and Electronic Engineering; Information Technology; Library Science; Mathematics Education; Metal Techniques; Physics; Science Education; Technology Education; Vocational Education; Wood Technology)

Further Information: Three sites: Yelwa Campus, Gubi campus and a residential estate along Kari-Maiduguri Road (Kari Road Housing Estate).

History: Founded 1980 as the Federal University of Technology, Bauchi. Acquired present status 1988.

Governing Bodies: University Council

Academic Year: October to August (October-April; April-August)

Admission Requirements: Senior Secondary Certificate of Education (SSCE) or General Certificate of Education (GCE) 'O' levels with at least 5 credits

Main Language(s) of Instruction: English

International Co-operation: With universities in USA and Chad

Degrees and Diplomas: *National Diploma*; *Higher National Diploma*; *Bachelor's Degree (BTech)*: 5 yrs; *Postgraduate Diploma*: Education; *Master's Degree*; *Doctor of Philosophy (PhD)*

Student Services: Academic counselling, Employment services, Health services, Nursery care, Social counselling, Sports facilities

Student Residential Facilities: Students' Halls of Residence for c. 1,500 students; Staff Quarters and Guest Houses

Special Facilities: Information and Telecommunication Cenre; entre for Industrial Studies (CIS); Zero Emission Research Institute (ZERI); Computer Centre; Lecture Theatres; Laboratories; Assembly Hall/Auditorium; Staff Primary School; International secondary school; University Poultry and Research Farm; Information Communication Technology Centre with V-sat Facilities

Libraries: University Library, 45,000 vols

Press or Publishing House: ATBU Printing Press
Last Updated: 04/07/12

ADAMAWA STATE POLYTECHNIC

P.M.B. 2146, Yola, Adamawa State
Website: http://www.adamawastatepoly.edu.ng/

Departments

Accountancy (Accountancy; Banking; Finance; Taxation); **Administrative and Business Studies** (Business Administration; Management; Marketing); **Consultancy Unit** (Accountancy; Computer Science; Finance; Management); **General Studies** (Secretarial Studies); **Local Governement/Social Services** (Development Studies; Government; Social and Community Services; Social Welfare); **Office Technology and Management** (Secretarial Studies); **Public Administration** (Public Administration)

History: Founded 1991 trhough the merger of the College of Preliminary Studies Yola and the Staff Development Institute Numan.

Governing Bodies: Academic Board

Main Language(s) of Instruction: English

Accrediting Agencies: National Board for Technical Education (NBTE)

Degrees and Diplomas: *National Diploma*; *Higher National Diploma*; *Postgraduate Diploma*. Also Certificates, Intermediate Certificates, Advanced Diplomas, Pre-National Diplomas, Typist Grades.

Last Updated: 05/10/12

ADAMAWA STATE UNIVERSITY (ADSU)

PMB 25, Mubi, Adamawa State 650001
Tel: +234(75) 883-620 +234 8058421126
EMail: info@adsu.edu.ng
Website: http://www.adsu.edu.ng

Vice-Chancellor: Alkasum Abba (2007-)
Tel: +234(80) 3701-5774
EMail: vc@adsu.edu.ng; alkasumabba@yahoo.com

Registrar: Jinatu Medina Garnvwa
EMail: regadsu@yahoo.com; regadsu@adsu.edu.ng

Faculties

Agriculture (Agricultural Economics; Agriculture; Animal Husbandry; Aquaculture; Crop Production; Fishery; Forestry; Wildlife); **Science** (Biological and Life Sciences; Botany; Chemistry; Computer Science; Geography; Mathematics; Mathematics and Computer Science; Physics; Science Education; Zoology); **Social and Management Sciences** (Accountancy; Business Administration; Economics; Management; Political Sciences; Public Administration; Social Sciences)

Schools

Postgraduate

History: Founded 2002.

Governing Bodies: Governing Council

Admission Requirements: Five(5) Credit in O'Level including English and Mathematics and at least not less than 170 points in UME

Fees: (Naira): Tuition fee, free for Adamawa state students, 20,000 per session for other Nigerian students; 30,000 per session for Foreign students.

Main Language(s) of Instruction: English

International Co-operation: With universities in Nigeria (Obafemi Awolowo University; Ahmadu Bello University); India (Bombay University; Banaras Hindu University; Amity University); Thailand; Malaysia; Ghana

Accrediting Agencies: National Universities Commission (NUC)

Degrees and Diplomas: *Bachelor's Degree*: 4-5 yrs; *Postgraduate Diploma*; *Postgraduate Diploma*; *Master's Degree*; *Doctor of Philosophy*. Also MBA; MPA

Student Services: Academic counselling, Canteen, Cultural centre, Employment services, Health services, Language programs, Social counselling, Sports facilities

Student Residential Facilities: 87 houses

Libraries: 33,500 Text books; 2,000 International Journals; 5,000 online books

Publications: ADSU Journal of Social Economic Structure *(biannually)*

Last Updated: 05/07/12

ADEKUNLE AJASIN UNIVERSITY (AAU)

PMB 001, Akungba-Akoko, Ondo State
Tel: +234(705) 789-0597 +234(816) 165-1123 +234(708) 910-5452
EMail: info@adekunleajasinuniversity.edu.ng; webmaster@adekunleajasinuniversity.edu.ng
Website: http://www.adekunleajasinuniversity.edu.ng/

Vice-Chancellor: N. Oluwafemi Mimiko (2010-)
Tel: +234(802) 345-2987, Fax: +234(805) 420-1214
EMail: femi.mimiko@yahoo.com; vc@adekunleajasinuniversity.edu.ng

Registrar: R.B. Olotu
Tel: +234(805) 607-3890
EMail: registrar@adekunleajasinuniversity.edu.ng

Centres

Diploma and Pre-Degree Studies; **Entrepreneurial Studies** (Management); **Information and Communication Technology Application** (Information Technology); **Research and Development**; **Women Studies and Development** (Development Studies; Women's Studies)

Faculties

Arts (Advertising and Publicity; African Studies; Arts and Humanities; English; English Studies; Ethics; History; International Studies; Journalism; Linguistics; Literature; Logic; Mass Communication; Metaphysics; Modern Languages; Native Language; Philosophy; Public Relations; Radio and Television Broadcasting; Religion); **Education** (Adult Education; Art Education; Education; Educational Administration; Educational and Student Counselling; English; Foreign Languages Education; History; Humanities and Social Science Education; Native Language Education; Religious Education; Religious Studies; Science Education; Technology Education); **Law** (Commercial Law; International Law; Law; Private Law; Public Law); **Science** (Biochemistry; Biology; Biotechnology; Botany; Chemistry; Computer Science; Electronic Engineering; Environmental Studies; Fishery; Geology; Geophysics; Industrial Chemistry; Mathematics; Microbiology; Physics); **Social and Management Sciences** (Accountancy; Banking; Business Administration; Economics; Finance; Geography; Management; Political Sciences; Psychology; Public Administration; Social Sciences; Sociology)

Institutes

Education (Education; Primary Education; Secondary Education; Teacher Training); **Part Time Programmes** (Accountancy; Banking; Business Administration; Environmental Management; Finance; Management; Public Administration; Social Sciences); **Public Policy and Sustainable Development** *(Leadership)* (Development Studies)

Research Centres

Space, Energy and Environmental (Aeronautical and Aerospace Engineering; Energy Engineering; Environmental Engineering)

History: Founded 1982 as Obafemi Awolowo University, Ado-Ekiti. 1985, renamed Ondo State Universty, Ado-Ekiti. 1996, when Ekiti State created from the former Ondo State, the two States jointly owned the University until December 1999. 2002, relocated to Akungba-Akoko and was renamed Adekunle Ajasin University, Akungba-Akoko.

Governing Bodies: University Governing Council

Admission Requirements: Universities Matriculation Examination. Secondary School Certificate of Education (SSCE), NECO, GCE 'O' Level, or equivalent with credits in 5 relevant subjects including English, obtained at no more than 2 sittings. For Master's Degree, in addition to the basic requirements, applicants must hold either a Postgraduate Diploma with an overall minimum average score of 60%, or a First or Second Class Division obtained from University recognized by Senate. For Ph.D. Degree Programmes: a minimum of aggregate grade of 60% (B) or a GPA of at least 2.8 on a 4-point scale at Master's or equivalent obtained from University recognized by Senate.

Fees: (Naira): 28,100 ($210) per session; Fresh students: 18,100 ($150) per session

Accrediting Agencies: National Universities Commission, Abuja, Nigeria; Accounting Professional Body (ICAN); Nigeria Mining & Geological Science Professional Body; Council of Legal Education of Nigeria

Degrees and Diplomas: *National Diploma*; *Bachelor's Degree (BA(Ed.); BSc (Ed); BEd)*: 3-4 yrs; *Postgraduate Diploma (PGDE; PGDFM)*; *Master's Degree (Med; MSc; MBA)*: 1-2 yrs; *Doctor of Philosophy (PhD)*: 3 yrs (Full time); 5 yrs (Part-time)

Student Services: Academic counselling, Handicapped facilities, Nursery care

Student Residential Facilities: Halls of residence for 30% of the student population

Special Facilities: Ajasin Varsity Theatre

Libraries: 40,000 vols; over 50 foreign and 150 local journals; Internet Connectivity; E-library

Last Updated: 05/07/12

AHMADU BELLO UNIVERSITY (ABU)

PMB 1045, Zaria
Tel: +234(69) 550-691
EMail: vc@abu.edu.ng
Website: http://www.abu.edu.ng

Vice-Chancellor: Abdullahi Mustapha (2010-)
Tel: +234(69) 550-691

Registrar: Isah Abbas EMail: registrar@abu.edu.ng

Deputy Vice-Chancellor, Administration: I. Funtua

Centres

Computer *(Iya Abubakar)* (Computer Science); **Disaster Risk Management and Development Studies** (Development Studies; Safety Engineering); **Energy Research and Training** (Energy Engineering); **Equipment Maintenance and Development** (Maintenance Technology); **Islamic Legal Studies** (Islamic Law)

Faculties

Administration (Accountancy; Administration; Banking; Business Administration; Development Studies; Finance; Government; Management; Public Administration); **Agriculture** (Agricultural Economics; Agriculture; Agronomy; Animal Husbandry; Botany; Crop Production; Physiology; Plant and Crop Protection; Rural Studies; Sociology; Soil Science); **Arts** (African Languages; Arabic; Archaeology; Arts and Humanities; Communication Studies; English; French; History; Linguistics; Literature; Modern Languages; Museum Management; Performing Arts; Theatre; Video); **Education** (Administration; African Languages; Agricultural Education; Arabic; Art Education; Biology; Business Education; Chemistry; Child Care and Development; Christian Religious Studies; Clothing and Sewing; Curriculum; Economics; Education; Educational Administration; Educational and Student Counselling; Educational Psychology; Educational Technology; English; Family Studies; Fine Arts; Foreign Languages Education; Health Education; Home Economics Education; Humanities and Social Science Education; Information Management; Information Sciences; Islamic Studies; Library Science; Mathematics Education; Native Language Education; Physical Education; Physics; Psychology; Religious Education; Science Education; Social Studies; Sports; Sports Management; Technology Education; Textile Technology; Vocational Education); **Engineering** (Agricultural Engineering; Agricultural Equipment; Chemical Engineering; Civil Engineering; Electrical Engineering; Energy Engineering; Engineering; Environmental Engineering; Geological Engineering; Mechanical Engineering; Metallurgical Engineering; Power Engineering; Road Engineering; Water Science); **Environmental Design** (Architectural and Environmental Design; Architecture; Building Technologies; Fine Arts; Industrial Design; Surveying and Mapping); **Law** (Civil Law; Commercial Law; International Law; International Relations; Islamic Law; Law; Private Law; Public Law; Real Estate); **Medicine** (Anatomy; Chemistry; Epidemiology; Immunology; Medicine; Nursing; Pathology; Physiology; Public Health); **Pharmaceutical Science** (Chemistry; Microbiology; Pharmacology; Pharmacy); **Science** (Analytical Chemistry; Biochemistry; Biological and Life Sciences; Biology; Biophysics; Botany; Chemistry; Computer Science; Development Studies; Fishery; Geography; Geology; Geophysics; Information Technology; Inorganic Chemistry; Mathematics; Mathematics and Computer Science; Microbiology; Nutrition; Organic Chemistry; Physical Chemistry; Physics; Polymer and Plastics Technology; Radiophysics; Rural Planning; Statistics; Textile Technology; Zoology); **Social Science** (Administration; Criminal Law; Development Studies; Economics; International Relations; International Studies; Justice Administration; Mass Communication; Police Studies; Political Sciences; Protective Services; Social Sciences; Social Work; Sociology); **Veterinary Medicine** (Anatomy; Embryology and Reproduction Biology; Entomology; Histology; Microbiology; Neurology; Parasitology; Pharmacology; Physiology; Public Health; Surgery; Toxicology; Tropical Medicine; Veterinary Science)

Institutes

Administration (Administration); **Agricultural Research** (Agriculture); **Development Research**; **Education** (Education)

Programmes

Biotechnology Research and Training (Biotechnology)

Research Institutes

National Animal Production *(NAPRI)* (Animal Husbandry)

Schools

Postgraduate (Accountancy; Administration; African Languages; African Studies; Agricultural Economics; Agricultural Education; Agriculture; Agronomy; Animal Husbandry; Arabic; Archaeology; Botany; Business Administration; Business Education; Child Care and Development; Clothing and Sewing; Crop Production; Curriculum; Development Studies; Education; Educational Administration; Educational and Student Counselling; Educational Psychology; English; Family Studies; Finance; Foreign Languages Education; French; Government; Health Education; History; Home Economics; Home Economics Education; Humanities and Social Science Education; Information Sciences; Library Science; Literature; Management; Mathematics Education; Performing Arts; Physical Education; Physiology; Plant and Crop Protection; Public Administration; Religious Education; Rural Studies; Science Education; Sociology; Soil Science; Sports; Sports Management; Technology Education; Theatre; Vocational Education)

Sections

National Agricultural Extension and Research Liaison Services *(NAERLS)* (Agriculture)

Further Information: Also Teaching Hospitals and Veterinary Teaching Hospital

History: Founded 1962, acquired present status and title 1975.

Governing Bodies: Governing Council; Senate

Academic Year: October to July

Admission Requirements: Direct entry for holders of the Higher School Certificate (General Certificate of Education, Advanced ('A') level). Evidence of minimum standard in English

Main Language(s) of Instruction: English

International Co-operation: With universities in USA; United Kingdom; India; Canada; Italy; Israel

Accrediting Agencies: National Universities Commission (NUC)

Degrees and Diplomas: *National Diploma*; *Bachelor's Degree*: 4 yrs; *Bachelor's Degree*: 5 yrs; *Postgraduate Diploma*: 1 yr; *Master's Degree (MA/MSc)*: 1-2 yrs following Bachelor; *Doctor of Philosophy (PhD)*: 3-5 yrs. Also Advanced Diploma (Accounting and Finance, Local Government Studies, Public Admin, Sharia and Civil Law), 1-2 yrs; Undergraduate Diploma (Accounting, Banking, Insurance, Local Government Studies, Public Admin, Civil Law, Sharia and Civil Law, Computer Science & Diploma in Computer Engineering, Computer Application Packages, Hardware Mentainance) and Higher Diploma (Local Government Studies) 2 yrs; Doctor of Verterinary Medicine and Surgery, 6 yrs; MBA; and MPA (Public Administration)

Student Services: Academic counselling, Canteen, Foreign student adviser, Foreign Studies Centre, Health services, Language programs, Social counselling, Sports facilities

Student Residential Facilities: Yes

Special Facilities: Museums. Art Gallery. Biological Garden. Drama Village

Libraries: Kashim Ibrahim Library (the main Library) and 11 other satellite libraries located in different campuses of the University: over 1.2 m. vols and 66,000 periodical titles.

Publications: Nigerian Journal of Pharmaceutical Sciences

Press or Publishing House: Ahmadu Bello University Press Ltd

Academic Staff *2011-2012*: Total: c. 1,400
Student Numbers *2011-2012*: Total: c. 35,000
Last Updated: 05/07/12

AIR-FORCE INSTITUTE OF TECHNOLOGY (AFIT)

Nigerian Air Force Base, Kaduna
Tel: +234(702) 930-6014
Website: http://www.afit.edu.ng/

Commander: John Olusola Oshoniyi

Provost: Emmanuel Ezugwu

Departments

General Academics (Natural Sciences; Technology; Transport Management)

Schools

Air Engineering *(SAE)* (Aeronautical and Aerospace Engineering; Maintenance Technology; Mechanical Engineering); **Ground Engineering and Management Studies** *(SGEMS)* (Civil Engineering; Electrical and Electronic Engineering; Environmental Engineering; Management); **Postgraduate Programmes** *(SPS)* (Aeronautical and Aerospace Engineering; Construction Engineering; Electronic Engineering; Management; Telecommunications Engineering; Thermal Engineering)

History: Founded 1977 as NAF Technical and Supply School (TSS) in Kaduna. Renamed Technical Training Wing in 1979 under the Ground Training Group (GTG). Transformed into the 320 Technical Training Group (320 TTG) 2000. Upgraded to a National Diplomas awarding institution 2004. Acquired institute of Technology status and current title 2008.

Fees: (Naira): For Nigerian students 52,990-197,190 per session for National Diplomas; 64,345-239,445 per session for Higher diplomas; 519,750 per session for Postgraduate Diplomas. (US Dollar): For International Students, 1,743-4,325 per session for National Diplomas; 2,625-5,251 per session for Higher National Diplomas.

Main Language(s) of Instruction: English

Accrediting Agencies: National Board for Technical Education (NBTE); Nigerian Civil Aviation Authority (NCAA)

Degrees and Diplomas: *National Diploma*; *Higher National Diploma*; *Postgraduate Diploma*. The PGD programme is specially designed to prepare candidates for the one year MSc in Aerospace Engineering programme at Cranfield University, United Kingdom. Also Pre-National Diploma (Pre-ND), Pre-Higher National Diploma (Pre-HND)

Student Residential Facilities: Yes

Libraries: Library; E-Library

Last Updated: 09/10/12

AKWA IBOM STATE UNIVERSITY (AKSU)

P.M.B. 1167, Uyo, Akwa Ibom State
EMail: info@akutech.edu.ng
Website: http://www.aksu.edu.ng/

Vice-Chancellor (Acting): Sunday Petters
EMail: sundaypetters_2006@yahoo.com

Deputy Vice-Chancellor: Akpan Ibanga Akpan

Faculties

Agriculture *(Obio Akpa Campus)* (Agricultural Economics; Agriculture; Animal Husbandry; Crop Production; Soil Science); **Engineering** (Agricultural Economics; Agricultural Engineering; Chemical Engineering; Civil Engineering; Electrical and Electronic Engineering; Engineering; Information Technology; Mechanical Engineering; Petroleum and Gas Engineering; Telecommunications Engineering); **Natural and Applied Sciences** (Biological and Life Sciences; Biotechnology; Botany; Chemistry; Computer Science; Earth Sciences; Genetics; Mathematics; Microbiology; Natural Sciences; Physics; Statistics; Zoology); **Ocean Science and Technology** (Environmental Studies; Marine Biology; Marine Science and Oceanography; Marine Transport; Naval Architecture); **Social and Management Sciences** (Accountancy; Business Administration; Economics; Management; Marketing; Public Administration; Social Sciences)

Further Information: Also Obio Akpa Campus

History: Founded 2005. Acquired present title 2009. Formerly known as Akwa Ibom State University of Technology (AKUTECH). Relocated to Ikot Akpaden 2011.

Governing Bodies: Governing Council

Fees: (Naira): Tuition fee 30,000 per session; First year students are also expected to pay non-refundable acceptance fee of 5,000.

Main Language(s) of Instruction: English

Accrediting Agencies: National Universities Commission (NUC); National Board for Technical Education (NBTE)

Degrees and Diplomas: *Bachelor's Degree*: 4-5 yrs

Student Numbers *2010-2011*: Total: c. 300
Last Updated: 05/07/12

AMBROSE ALLI UNIVERSITY (AAU)

PMB 14, Ekpoma
Tel: +234(54) 340-719
Fax: +234(54) 340-719
EMail: info@aauekpoma.edu.ng
Website: http://www.aauekpoma.edu.ng/

Vice-Chancellor (Acting): C.A. Agbebaku

Registrar: L.I. Edopkayi EMail: registrar@aauekpoma.edu.ng

Deputy Vice-Chancellor, Administration: A. U. Omoregie

Centres

Strategic and Development Studies *(CSDS)* (Development Studies)

Colleges

Medicine (Laboratory Techniques; Medicine; Physiology; Public Health)

Faculties

Agriculture (Agricultural Economics; Agriculture; Agronomy; Animal Husbandry; Botany; Chemistry; Crop Production; Home Economics; Irrigation; Microbiology; Plant and Crop Protection; Rural Studies; Sociology; Soil Conservation; Soil Science; Surveying and Mapping); **Arts** (Cultural Studies; Economics; English; Fine Arts; French; History; International Studies; Literature; Media Studies; Modern Languages; Philosophy; Political Sciences; Religion; Religious Studies; Theatre); **Basic Medical Sciences** (Anatomy; Biochemistry; Medicine; Physiology); **Clinical Sciences** (Anatomy; Community Health; Gynaecology and Obstetrics; Haematology; Health Sciences; Medicine; Microbiology; Paediatrics; Pathology; Pharmacology; Surgery; Toxicology); **Education** (Accountancy; Agricultural Education; Biology; Business Education; Chemistry; Computer Education; Curriculum; Economics; Education; Educational Administration; Educational and Student Counselling; English; Foreign Languages Education; French; Geography; Geography (Human); Health Education; History; Home Economics Education; Humanities and Social Science Education; Mathematics; Mathematics Education; Pedagogy; Physical Education; Physics; Political Sciences; Religious Education; Religious Studies; Science Education; Secretarial Studies; Social Studies; Technology Education; Vocational Education); **Engineering and Technology** (Civil Engineering; Computer Engineering; Electrical and Electronic Engineering; Electrical Engineering; Electronic Engineering; Engineering; Materials Engineering; Mechanical Engineering; Production Engineering; Technology); **Environmental Studies** (Architecture; Building Technologies; Ceramic Art; Environmental Studies; Fine Arts; Geography; Graphic Arts; Handicrafts; Metal Techniques; Painting and Drawing; Regional Planning; Sculpture; Textile Design; Visual Arts); **Law** (Civil Law; Commercial Law; International Law; Labour Law; Law; Public Law); **Natural Sciences** (Analytical Chemistry; Applied Mathematics; Applied Physics; Biochemistry; Botany; Chemistry; Computer Science; Data Processing; Design; Ecology; Environmental Studies; Fishery; Food Science; Genetics; Geophysics; Immunology; Industrial Chemistry; Inorganic Chemistry; Mathematics; Microbiology; Molecular Biology; Natural Sciences; Organic Chemistry; Parasitology; Physics; Physiology; Plant and Crop Protection; Polymer and Plastics Technology; Safety Engineering; Software Engineering; Soil Science; Statistics;

Systems Analysis; Zoology); **Social Sciences** (Accountancy; Banking; Business Administration; Economics; Finance; Information Sciences; Library Science; Political Sciences; Psychology; Public Administration; Social Sciences; Sociology)

Institutes

Education (Adult Education; Communication Arts; Development Studies; Education; Labour and Industrial Relations; Social Welfare); **Governance and Development** (Development Studies; Government)

Schools

Postgraduate Studies (Agricultural Economics; Animal Husbandry; Architecture; Biochemistry; Botany; Chemistry; Civil Engineering; Commercial Law; Crop Production; Cultural Studies; Curriculum; Education; Electrical and Electronic Engineering; English; Geography; Health Education; History; International Law; International Studies; Laboratory Techniques; Materials Engineering; Mathematics; Mechanical Engineering; Microbiology; Modern Languages; Philosophy; Physical Education; Physics; Physiology; Political Sciences; Private Law; Production Engineering; Public Administration; Public Law; Regional Planning; Religious Studies; Sociology; Soil Science; Zoology)

Further Information: Abraka campus

History: Founded 1981 as Bendel State University, later known as Edo State University. Acquired present status 1991.

Governing Bodies: Council; Senate

Academic Year: October to June

Admission Requirements: Universities Matriculation Examination (UME) following secondary school education, or direct entry for holders of the Higher School Certificate (General Certificate of Education, Advanced ('A') level)

Fees: (Naira): Undergraduate programmes, (full-time) 49,500-80,000 per session full-time; (Part-time) 60,000 per session. Ph.D., for 199,000 Indigene students; 219,000 for non-indigene students; (Dollars): 5,000 for Foreign Students. Master's degree, for 110,000 Indigene students; 130,000 for non-indigene students; (Dollars): 2,500 for Foreign Students. Postgraduate diploma, for 89,000 Indigene students; 109,000 for non-indigene students; (Dollars): 1,500 for Foreign Students.

Main Language(s) of Instruction: English

Accrediting Agencies: National Universities Commission (NUC)

Degrees and Diplomas: *Bachelor's Degree*: 3-4 yrs; *Bachelor's Degree*: Medicine and Bachelor of Surgery, 5-6 yrs; *Postgraduate Diploma*; *Master's Degree*: a further 2 yrs; *Doctor of Philosophy (PhD)*

Student Services: Canteen, Health services

Libraries: Central Library, 14,000 items; Abraka campus library, 80,000 vols

Publications: Faculty Journals *(annually)*

Press or Publishing House: University Press

Last Updated: 06/07/12

ANAMBRA STATE UNIVERSITY (ANSU)

PMB 02, Uli, Anambra State
Tel: +234(48) 582-042
EMail: oyeka@rbow.net
Website: http://ansu.edu.ng/

Vice-Chancellor: Fidelis Okafor (2011-)

Deputy Vice Chancellor Administration: O.S.A. Obikeze

Registrar: S.E. Ofoegbu

Faculties

Agricultural Science (Agricultural Business; Agricultural Economics; Agricultural Management; Agriculture; Animal Husbandry; Biochemistry; Biology; Crop Production; Environmental Management; Farm Management; Horticulture; Irrigation; Management; Marketing; Plant and Crop Protection; Rural Studies; Sociology; Soil Conservation; Soil Science; Surveying and Mapping; Water Management); **Arts and Social Sciences** (African Languages; Arts and Humanities; Economics; English; Mass Communication; Political Sciences; Public Administration; Social Sciences); **Basic Medical Sciences** (Medicine); **Education** (Adult Education; Education; Science Education; Technology Education); **Engineering** (Chemical Engineering; Civil Engineering; Electrical and Electronic Engineering; Engineering; Mechanical Engineering); **Environmental Sciences** (Architecture; Environmental Management; Environmental Studies; Regional Planning); **Law** (Law); **Management** (Accountancy; Banking; Business Administration; Finance; Management; Marketing); **Science** (Applied Physics; Biochemistry; Biological and Life Sciences; Computer Science; Geology; Industrial Chemistry; Mathematics; Microbiology; Statistics)

Further Information: Also Igbariam and Alor Campuses.

History: Founded 2000 as Anambra State University of Science and Technology. Acquired present title 2006.

Governing Bodies: Governing Council

Main Language(s) of Instruction: English

Degrees and Diplomas: *Bachelor's Degree*; *Bachelor's Degree*: English; *Postgraduate Diploma*: Farm Management and Production Economics; Agribusiness Marketing; Agricultural Cooperatives; Farm Resources and Environmental Economics; Organizational Management of Extension Services; Agricultural Policy and Planning; Rural Sociology; Crop Science; Statistics; *Master's Degree*: Farm Management and Production Economics; Agribusiness Marketing; Agricultural Cooperatives; Farm Resources and Environmental Economics; Organizational Management of Extension Services; Agricultural Policy and Planning; Rural Sociology; Crop Science; *Doctor of Philosophy*: Farm Management and Production Economics; Agribusiness Marketing; Agricultural Cooperatives; Farm Resources and Environmental Economics; Organizational Management of Extension Services; Agricultural Policy and Planning; Rural Sociology; Crop Science (Ph.D.)

Last Updated: 06/07/12

AUCHI POLYTECHNIC, AUCHI (AUCHIPOLY)

PMB 13, Okene Road, Auchi, Edo State
Tel: +234(57) 200-159
Fax: +234(57) 200-148
EMail: support@auchipoly.edu.ng
Website: http://auchipoly.edu.ng

Rector: Philipa O. Idogho EMail: Rector@auchipoly.edu.ng

Registrar: M. Aashikpelokha EMail: Registrar@auchipoly.edu.ng

Deputy Rector Administration: S. G. Eshoitse

Schools

Applied Science and Technology (Food Technology; Hotel and Restaurant; Laboratory Techniques; Polymer and Plastics Technology); **Art and Design** (Ceramic Art; Design; Fine Arts; Graphic Design; Painting and Drawing; Sculpture; Textile Design); **Business Studies** (Accountancy; Banking; Business Administration; Finance; Management; Marketing; Public Administration); **Engineering Technology** (Agricultural Engineering; Chemical Engineering; Civil Engineering; Electrical and Electronic Engineering; Engineering; Mechanical Engineering; Mining Engineering); **Environmental Studies** (Building Technologies; Computer Science; Environmental Studies; Geology; Real Estate; Regional Planning; Structural Architecture; Surveying and Mapping; Town Planning); **General Studies**; **Information and Communication Technology** (Business Computing; Computer Science; Information Technology; Mass Communication; Statistics); **Post Graduate Studies** (Building Technologies; Civil Engineering; Electrical Engineering; Mechanical Engineering; Polymer and Plastics Technology; Power Engineering; Production Engineering; Regional Planning; Town Planning)

History: Founded 1963 as a technical college. Transformed into a Polytechnic 1973.

Governing Bodies: Governing Council

Admission Requirements: 5 credit passes at a sitting or 6 credit passes at two sittings in the relevant subjects

Fees: (Naira): 33,000 for post HND; 5,400 for HND II; 14,550 for HND I; 5,400 for ND II; 14,550 for ND I; 23,850 for Pre-ND

Main Language(s) of Instruction: English

Accrediting Agencies: National Board for Technical Education (NBTE)

Degrees and Diplomas: *National Diploma*; *Higher National Diploma*. Also Pre-national Diploma, 1 yr; Post-Higher National Diploma (POST-HND), postgraduate professional degree in 4 semesters.

Student Services: Academic counselling, Health services, Social counselling, Sports facilities

Student Numbers *2011-2012*: Total: c. 8,000
Last Updated: 11/07/12

BAYERO UNIVERSITY, KANO (BUK)

PMB 3011, Kano, Kano State
Tel: +234(64) 666-023
EMail: vc@buk.edu.ng
Website: http://buk.edu.ng/

Vice-Chancellor: Abubakar Rasheed EMail: bukvc@yahoo.com

Registrar: Habiba Adieza

Deputy Vice Chancellor, Academics: Muhammad Yahuza Bello

Faculties

Agriculture (Agricultural Economics; Agriculture; Agronomy; Animal Husbandry; Plant and Crop Protection; Soil Science); **Arts and Islamic Studies** (African Languages; Arabic; English; French; History; Islamic Studies; Literature); **Education** (Adult Education; Education; Educational and Student Counselling; Health Education; Information Management; Library Science; Parks and Recreation; Physical Education; Science Education; Special Education; Technology Education; Tourism); **Law** (Commercial Law; Islamic Law; Law; Private Law; Public Law); **Medicine** (Anaesthesiology; Anatomy; Community Health; Dentistry; Gynaecology and Obstetrics; Haematology; Laboratory Techniques; Medicine; Microbiology; Nursing; Ophthalmology; Otorhinolaryngology; Paediatrics; Parasitology; Pathology; Pharmacology; Physical Therapy; Physiology; Psychiatry and Mental Health; Radiology; Surgery); **Science** (Biochemistry; Biological and Life Sciences; Biology; Botany; Chemistry; Computer Science; Electronic Engineering; Geography; Industrial Chemistry; Mathematics; Microbiology; Natural Sciences; Physics; Zoology); **Social and Management Sciences** (Accountancy; Banking; Business Administration; Economics; Environmental Management; Finance; Geography; Management; Mass Communication; Police Studies; Political Sciences; Public Administration; Social Policy; Social Sciences; Sociology); **Technology** (Agricultural Engineering; Civil Engineering; Computer Engineering; Electrical Engineering; Energy Engineering; Hydraulic Engineering; Materials Engineering; Mechanical Engineering; Metallurgical Engineering; Production Engineering; Technology; Water Management)

Institutes

Islamic Banking and Finance *(International)* (Banking; Finance; Islamic Studies)

Further Information: A traditional and distance learning institution. Also Aminu Kano Teaching Hospital

History: Founded 1960 as Ahmadu Bello College, renamed Abdullahi Bayero College 1962. Acquired present status 1975 and title 1977.

Governing Bodies: Universities Governing Council

Academic Year: October to July (October-February; March-July)

Admission Requirements: Universities Matriculation Examination (UME) following secondary school education, or direct entry for holders of the Higher School Certificate (General Certificate of Education, Advanced ('A') level)

Fees: (Niara): Tuition fees for Ordinary and Advanced Diplomas, 20,000-25,000 per annum for Nigerian students and 40,000-50,000 per annum for foreign students; Undergraduate programmes, none for Nigerian students; 30,000-60,000 per annum for non-Nigerian students. For Ph.D., 80,000-100,000 for Nigerian students and 160,000-200,000 for foreign students. Master's degree, 40,000-100,000 for Nigerian students and 80,000-200,000 for foreign students. For Postgraduate diploma, 80,000 for Nigerian students and 100,000 for foreign students.

Main Language(s) of Instruction: English

International Co-operation: With Libya, WARDA, Italy, USA, Germany, UK, Canada, SAFE, Poland

Accrediting Agencies: National Universities Commission (NUC); Nigerian Medical and Dental Council, COREN, ICAN

Degrees and Diplomas: *Bachelor's Degree*; *Postgraduate Diploma*; *Master's Degree*; *Doctor of Philosophy*. Also Undergraduate Certificates and Diplomas; Advanced Diplomas; Professional Master's degree, including MBA.

Student Services: Academic counselling, Canteen, Employment services, Health services, Language programs, Nursery care, Social counselling, Sports facilities

Student Residential Facilities: Yes

Libraries: Central Library, c. 200,000 vols; 2,000 periodicals

Publications: Bayero Journal of Interdisciplinary Studies, Academic Journal *(1-2 per annum)*

Last Updated: 06/07/12

BENUE STATE UNIVERSITY (BSU)

PMB 102119, Km 1, Gboko Road, Makurdi, Benue State
Tel: +234(703) 332-6160
EMail: info@bsum.edu.ng
Website: http://www.bsum.edu.ng/

Vice-Chancellor: Charity Angya
Tel: +234 808-235-8053 EMail: vicechancellor@bsum.edu.ng

Deputy Vice Chancellor, Administration: Nicolas A. Ada

Registrar: Timoty I. Utile
Tel: +234(706) 690-7871 EMail: registrar@bsum.edu.ng

International Relations: Shima Gyoh, Director, Development Linkages Tel: +234 802-453-4700 EMail: shimagyoh@yahoo.com

Centres

Peace and Development Studies (Development Studies; Peace and Disarmament)

Colleges

Health Sciences (Health Sciences; Medicine; Surgery)

Faculties

Arts (Arts and Humanities; Christian Religious Studies; Cultural Studies; English; French; History; Linguistics; Philosophy; Religion; Religious Studies; Theatre); **Education** (Agricultural Equipment; Biology; Building Technologies; Chemistry; Curriculum; Economics; Education; Electronic Engineering; English; Foreign Languages Education; French; Health Education; Heating and Refrigeration; History; Humanities and Social Science Education; Mathematics; Mathematics Education; Mechanics; Metal Techniques; Philosophy; Physical Education; Physics; Preschool Education; Primary Education; Religious Education; Science Education; Social Studies; Teacher Training; Technology Education; Vocational Education; Wood Technology); **Law** (Commercial Law; Law; Private Law; Public Law); **Management Sicences** (Accountancy; Banking; Business Administration; Finance; Management); **Science** (Biology; Botany; Chemistry; Computer Science; Mathematics; Mathematics and Computer Science; Microbiology; Natural Sciences; Physics; Zoology); **Social Sciences** (Economics; Geography; Mass Communication; Meteorology; Political Sciences; Psychology; Regional Planning; Social Sciences; Sociology; Town Planning)

Schools

Postgraduate Studies (Accountancy; Analytical Chemistry; Arts and Humanities; Botany; Business Administration; Clinical Psychology; Curriculum; Development Studies; Economics; Education; Educational Administration; Educational and Student Counselling; English; Finance; Foreign Languages Education; French; Gender Studies; Geography; Health Administration; Health Education; History; Humanities and Social Science Education; Industrial and Organizational Psychology; Inorganic Chemistry; International Relations; Law; Linguistics; Literature; Management; Mass Communication; Mathematics Education; Organic Chemistry; Physical Chemistry; Physical Education; Physics; Political Sciences; Psychology; Public Administration; Regional Planning; Religious Studies; Science Education; Social Studies; Sociology; Sports; Sports Management; Theatre; Town Planning; Zoology)

History: Founded 1992.

Governing Bodies: University Council

Academic Year: September to August

Admission Requirements: General Certificate of Education (Ordinary level) with minimum of 5 credits at single sitting

Fees: (Naira): c. 20,000 per session; Postgraduate tuition fees, 33,500-48,500 per semester for indigene students and 40,000-81,000 per semester for foreign students.

Main Language(s) of Instruction: English

International Co-operation: With universities in United Kingdom

Accrediting Agencies: National Universities Commission

Degrees and Diplomas: *National Diploma*; *Bachelor's Degree*: 4-5 yrs; *Postgraduate Diploma*; *Master's Degree*; *Doctor of Philosophy (PhD)*: 3 yrs

Student Services: Academic counselling, Health services, Nursery care, Sports facilities

Student Residential Facilities: Yes

Publications: Departmental Journal of Economic and social Research (JESR), Publication of the Faculty of Social Sciences; Monograph Series: Social Science Study Group (SSSG), Publication of the Faculty of Social Sciences; National fellowship of Economics Christian Students (NAFECS) BSU Chapter Magazine, Publication of the Faculty of Social Sciences; Nigeria Economic Students association (NESA) Magazine, Publication of the Faculty of Social Sciences; Sundry Periodicals *(quarterly)*

Last Updated: 10/07/12

BUKAR ABBA IBRAHIM UNIVERSITY

PMB 1144, KM 7, Sir Kashim Ibrahim Way, Damaturu, Yobe State
EMail: info@baiu.edu.ng; admissions@baiu.edu.ng
Website: http://www.baiu.edu.ng/

Vice-Chancellor: Musa Alabe

Registrar: Alhaji Ibrahim Jaji Maude

Faculties

General Studies; **Science** (Biology; Chemistry; Computer Science; Mathematics; Physics); **Social and Management Science** (African Languages; Arabic; Business Administration; Economics; Geography; Islamic Studies; Management; Political Sciences; Public Administration; Social Sciences; Sociology)

Schools

Law (Law); **Pre-Degree Studies**

History: Founded 2006.

Main Language(s) of Instruction: English

Accrediting Agencies: National Universities Commission (NUC)

Degrees and Diplomas: *Bachelor's Degree*. Also Pre-Degree programmes.

Special Facilities: ICT Centre

Last Updated: 10/07/12

CROSS RIVER UNIVERSITY OF TECHNOLOGY (CRUTECH)

PMB 1123, Calabar, Cross River State
Tel: +234(87) 232-303
Website: http://crutech-nig.net/

Vice-Chancellor: Effiom Ene-Obong (2009-2013)
Tel: +234(80) 63920168 EMail: eeneobong_pr@yahoo.com

Faculties

Agriculture and Forestry *(Obubra)* (Agricultural Economics; Agriculture; Agronomy; Animal Husbandry; Aquaculture; Fishery; Forest Products; Forestry; Wildlife); **Basic Medical Sciences** *(Okuku)* (Anatomy; Biochemistry; Medicine; Physiology); **Communication Technology** (Mass Communication); **Education** (Curriculum; Education; Educational Administration; Educational Technology); **Engineering** (Civil Engineering; Electrical and Electronic Engineering; Engineering; Mechanical Engineering; Wood Technology); **Environmental Sciences** (Architecture; Environmental Studies; Real Estate; Regional Planning; Town Planning; Visual Arts); **Management Science** *(Ogoja)* (Accountancy; Business Administration; Management; Tourism); **Science** (Biological and Life Sciences; Chemistry; Computer Science; Mathematics; Physics; Statistics)

Further Information: Also Obubra, Ogoja and Okuku campuses.

History: Founded 1973 as College of Technology. Acquired present status 2002.

Governing Bodies: University Council; Senate

Academic Year: October to July

Admission Requirements: School Certificate; English, Mathematics and any other three subjects relevant to the course at credit level

Fees: (Naira): 23,600 (Local students); 35,600 (Foreign students)

Main Language(s) of Instruction: English

Accrediting Agencies: National Universities Commission (NUC)

Degrees and Diplomas: *Bachelor's Degree (BSc; Bagric)*: 4 yrs; *Bachelor's Degree (BTech; Beng)*: 5 yrs; *Bachelor's Degree*: Medicine, 6 yrs; *Postgraduate Diploma (PGD)*; *Master's Degree*; *Doctor of Philosophy (Ph. D.)*

Student Services: Academic counselling, Health services, Sports facilities

Student Residential Facilities: Residential quarters for staff and hostel for students

Special Facilities: Art Gallery

Libraries: Link with Questia online library

Last Updated: 10/07/12

DELTA STATE UNIVERSITY (DELSU)

PMB 1, Abraka, Delta State 330106
EMail: delsu03@yahoo.com
Website: http://www.delsunigeria.net

Vice-Chancellor: E. A. Arubayi (2011-2013)
Tel: +234(806) 440-2503 EMail: Arubayi@yahoo.com

Registrar: Ejiro Udjo
Tel: +234(803) 387-3228 EMail: ejirogheneudjo@yahoo.com

International Relations: Peter Eruotor, Director of Research and International Centre

Faculties

Agriculture (Agricultural Economics; Agriculture; Agronomy; Animal Husbandry; Fishery; Food Science; Food Technology; Forestry; Wildlife); **Art** (Arts and Humanities; English; Fine Arts; French; History; International Studies; Linguistics; Literature; Modern Languages; Music; Native Language; Religious Studies; Theatre); **Education** (Agricultural Education; Art Education; Business Education; Education; Educational Administration; Educational and Student Counselling; Health Education; Home Economics Education; Humanities and Social Science Education; Information Sciences; Library Science; Mathematics Education; Music Education; Nursing; Physical Education; Primary Education; Religious Education; Science Education; Technology Education); **Engineering** (Ceramics and Glass Technology; Chemical Engineering; Civil Engineering; Computer Engineering; Electrical and Electronic Engineering; Engineering; Mechanical Engineering; Metallurgical Engineering; Petroleum and Gas Engineering; Production Engineering); **Law** (Commercial Law; International Law; Law; Private Law; Public Law); **Management Sciences** (Accountancy; Banking; Business Administration; Finance; Management; Marketing); **Medical Sciences** (Anaesthesiology; Anatomy; Biochemistry; Community Health; Gynaecology and Obstetrics; Haematology; Medicine; Microbiology; Nursing; Paediatrics; Parasitology; Pathology; Pharmacology; Physiology; Psychiatry and Mental Health; Radiology; Surgery); **Pharmacy** (Alternative Medicine; Pharmacology; Pharmacy); **Science** (Biochemistry; Biology; Botany; Chemistry; Geology; Mathematics and Computer Science; Microbiology; Natural Sciences; Physics; Zoology); **Social Sciences** (Accountancy; Business Administration; Economics; Finance; Geography (Human); Mass Communication; Political Sciences; Regional Planning; Social Sciences; Sociology)

Further Information: Also Anwai and Oleh campuses.

History: Founded 1992.

Governing Bodies: University Council

Admission Requirements: Five 'O' Level Credit Passes in relevant subjects (Credit Pass in English Language Compulsory)

Fees: (Naira): c. 19,000 per session

Main Language(s) of Instruction: English

International Co-operation: With Universities in UK and USA

Accrediting Agencies: National Universities Commission (NUC)

Degrees and Diplomas: *Bachelor's Degree (B.A.)*: 4 yrs; *Bachelor's Degree*: Agriculture; Engineering; Law (B.Agric; B.Eng.; L.L.B.), 5 yrs; *Bachelor's Degree*: Medicine; Surgery (M.B.B.S.),

6 yrs; *Postgraduate Diploma (P.G.D)*: 1 yr; *Master's Degree*: 1- 1 1/2 yrs; *Doctor of Philosophy (Ph.D.)*

Student Services: Academic counselling, Handicapped facilities, Health services, Language programs, Nursery care, Social counselling, Sports facilities

Special Facilities: Music Studio; Fine Art Studio; Theatre Arts Studio; Languages Studio; E-learning Centre

Libraries: E-library; Textbooks; Periodicals (Newspaper, Bulletins, Magazines, etc.), Journals, Reference Section

Publications: Convocation Lecture Series *(annually)*; Faculty Journals *(annually)*; University Inaugural Lecture Series *(quarterly)*

Last Updated: 10/07/12

EBONYI STATE UNIVERSITY (EBSU)

PMB 053, Abakaliki, Ebonyi State
Tel: +234 803-572-7788
EMail: registrar@ebsu-edu.net
Website: http://www.ebsu-edu.net

Vice-Chancellor: Francis Idike (2008-)
Tel: +234 803-572-7788 EMail: vc@ebsu-edu.net

Registrar: Samuel Nte Egwu Tel: +234 803-549-4406

International Relations: Johnny O. Ogunji, Coordinator International Linkage/Collaboration
Tel: +234 806-755-8863 EMail: ogunjijo@yahoo.com

Faculties

Agriculture (Agricultural Economics; Agriculture; Animal Husbandry; Aquaculture; Crop Production; Fishery; Food Science; Food Technology; Soil Science); **Arts and Humanities** (Arts and Humanities; English; French; History; International Relations; Linguistics; Literature; Mass Communication; Philosophy; Religion); **Basic Medical Sciences** (Anatomy; Biochemistry; Medicine; Physiology); **Biological Sciences** (Biochemistry; Biological and Life Sciences; Biology; Biotechnology; Microbiology); **Clinical Medicine** (Anatomy; Community Health; Gynaecology and Obstetrics; Haematology; Health Sciences; Histology; Immunology; Medicine; Microbiology; Ophthalmology; Pathology; Pharmacology; Psychiatry and Mental Health; Surgery); **Education** (Agricultural Education; Business Education; Computer Education; Education; Educational Administration; Educational Sciences; Educational Technology; Health Education; Home Economics Education; Humanities and Social Science Education; Physical Education; Science Education; Technology Education; Vocational Education); **Health Science and Technology** (Laboratory Techniques; Nursing); **Law** (Commercial Law; International Law; Labour Law; Law; Private Law; Public Law); **Management and Sciences** (Accountancy; Banking; Business Administration; Finance; Management; Marketing; Public Administration); **Physical Sciences** (Computer Education; Geology; Industrial Chemistry; Mathematics; Statistics); **Social Sciences** (Anthropology; Mass Communication; Political Sciences; Psychology; Social Sciences; Sociology)

History: Founded 1999 through the upgrade of the Ebonyi State University College, that itself resulted from the upgrade of the Abakaliki campus of the Enugu State University of Science and Technology (ESUT) 1998. Acquired autonomous status 2000.

Governing Bodies: Council Members

Admission Requirements: University Matriculation Examination UME/DE. Credit passes in English Language, Mathematics and other three (3) courses, relevant in the area of study in not more than two (2) sittings

Main Language(s) of Instruction: English

Accrediting Agencies: National University Commission (NUC); National Institution of Legal Education (ILE); Dental and Medical Council of Nigeria (DMCN); Nursing Council of Nigeria (NCN)

Degrees and Diplomas: *Bachelor's Degree*: Agriculture and Natural Resources Management; Health Science and Technology; Law;, 5 yrs; *Bachelor's Degree*: Arts and Humanities; Basic Medical Sciences; Biological Sciences; Education; Management Sciences; Physical Sciences; Social Sciences, 4 yrs; *Bachelor's Degree*: Clinical Medicine, 6 yrs. Also MBBS (6 yrs)

Student Services: Academic counselling, Canteen, Health services, Language programs, Nursery care, Sports facilities

Student Residential Facilities: Yes

Libraries: E-Library

Publications: EBSU Journal of Nature, National Academic Journal *(quarterly)*; EBSU Journal of Society, National Academic Journal *(quarterly)*; EBSU Research Bulletin, Internal Research News Publication *(monthly)*

Academic Staff *2011-2012*	MEN	WOMEN	**TOTAL**
FULL-TIME	418	109	**527**
PART-TIME	226	52	**278**
Student Numbers *2011-2012*			
All (Foreign Included)	9,232	10,521	**19,753**

Part-time students, 1,966.

Last Updated: 29/06/12

EKITI STATE UNIVERSITY, ADO-EKITI (EKSU)

PMB 5363, Ado-Ekiti, Ekiti State
Tel: +234(30) 250-026
Website: http://eksu.edu.ng/

Vice-Chancellor: Patrick Oladipo Aina
Tel: +234(30) 250-997 EMail: vca@unadportal.com

Registrar: Omojola Awosusi EMail: registrar@unad.edu.ng

Colleges

Medicine (Anatomy; Biochemistry; Community Health; Epidemiology; Gynaecology and Obstetrics; Medicine; Pathology; Physiology; Surgery)

Faculties

Agricultural Sciences (Agricultural Economics; Agriculture; Animal Husbandry; Crop Production; Environmental Studies; Fishery; Forestry; Soil Science; Wildlife); **Arts** (African Languages; Arts and Humanities; English; French; History; International Studies; Linguistics; Literature; Philosophy; Religious Studies); **Education** (Accountancy; Adult Education; African American Studies; Agricultural Education; Biology; Business Education; Chemistry; Computer Science; Economics; Education; Educational Administration; Educational and Student Counselling; Educational Testing and Evaluation; English; Foreign Languages Education; French; Geography; Health Education; History; Humanities and Social Science Education; Mathematics; Philosophy of Education; Physical Education; Physics; Political Sciences; Preschool Education; Primary Education; Religious Studies; Science Education; Social Studies; Technology Education; Vocational Education); **Engineering** (Civil Engineering; Electrical and Electronic Engineering; Mechanical Engineering); **Law** (Law; Private Law; Public Law); **Management Science** (Accountancy; Banking; Business Administration; Finance; Management); **Science** (Biochemistry; Botany; Chemistry; Geology; Laboratory Techniques; Mathematics; Microbiology; Natural Sciences; Physics; Zoology); **Social Sciences** (Economics; Geography; Political Sciences; Psychology; Regional Planning; Social Sciences; Sociology)

Institutes

Science Laboratory Technology (Biochemistry; Botany; Chemistry; Geology; Laboratory Techniques; Microbiology; Physics; Zoology)

Schools

Postgraduate Studies

Further Information: Campuses in Ondo, Ikole, Okitipupa, Ikere, Akure, Owo, Ikare, Ijero.

History: Founded 2011 as a result of merger between the University of Ado-Ekiti (former Ondo State University), the University of Education, Ikere-Ekiti and University of Science and Technology, Ifaki-Ekiti.

Governing Bodies: Governing Council; Senate

Academic Year: October to July (October-March; April-July)

Admission Requirements: Senior School Certificate (SSC) or General Certificate of Education (GCE) 'O' levels, with credits in 5 relevant subjects, obtained at no more than 2 sittings; and University Matriculation Examination (UME). Some courses have additional requirements. International applicants: equivalent qualifications and UME

Main Language(s) of Instruction: English

Accrediting Agencies: National Universities Commission (NUC)

Degrees and Diplomas: *Bachelor's Degree (BA, BEd, BSc)*; *Postgraduate Diploma*; *Master's Degree*; *Doctor of Philosophy (PhD)*

Student Services: Academic counselling, Health services, Social counselling, Sports facilities

Student Residential Facilities: Yes

Libraries: 150,000 vols

Last Updated: 17/07/12

ENUGU STATE UNIVERSITY OF SCIENCE AND TECHNOLOGY (ESUST)

PMB 01660, Independence Layout, Enugu, Enugu State
Tel: +234(803) 452-3866
EMail: info@esut.edu.ng
Website: http://www.esut.edu.ng/

Vice-Chancellor: Ogbonna Cyprain Onyeji (2010-)
Tel: +234(42) 451-244, Fax: +234(42) 455-765

Registrar: Chris Igbokwe

Faculties

Agriculture (Agricultural Economics; Agriculture; Agronomy; Animal Husbandry; Crop Production; Ecology; Environmental Management; Fishery; Food Science; Food Technology; Natural Resources; Soil Science; Zoology); **Applied Natural Sciences** (Applied Mathematics; Biochemistry; Biology; Demography and Population; Geology; Industrial Chemistry; Mathematics; Microbiology; Mining Engineering; Physics; Statistics); **Education** (Adult Education; Agricultural Education; Agriculture; Biology; Building Technologies; Chemistry; Computer Education; Education; Educational Administration; Educational and Student Counselling; Electrical and Electronic Engineering; Health Education; Information Sciences; Library Science; Mathematics; Parks and Recreation; Physical Education; Physics; Science Education; Technology; Technology Education; Vocational Education; Wood Technology); **Engineering** (Agricultural Engineering; Chemical Engineering; Civil Engineering; Computer Engineering; Electrical and Electronic Engineering; Engineering; Materials Engineering; Mechanical Engineering; Metallurgical Engineering; Production Engineering); **Environmental Sciences** (Architecture; Building Technologies; Environmental Studies; Geography; Meteorology; Real Estate; Regional Planning; Surveying and Mapping; Town Planning); **Law** (Civil Law; Commercial Law; International Law; Law; Private Law; Public Law); **Management** (Accountancy; Banking; Business Administration; Finance; Insurance; Management; Marketing; Mass Communication; Public Administration; Rural Planning); **Medical and Health Sciences** (Anaesthesiology; Anatomy; Biochemistry; Community Health; Gynaecology and Obstetrics; Haematology; Health Sciences; Histology; Medicine; Microbiology; Ophthalmology; Paediatrics; Pathology; Pharmacology; Radiology; Surgery); **Social Sciences** (Anthropology; Economics; Political Sciences; Psychology; Social Sciences; Sociology)

Institutes

Education *(Sandwich)* (Education)

Programmes

Mature Students

Schools

Business *(EBS)* (Business Administration); **Postgraduate Studies** (Accountancy; Adult Education; Agricultural Economics; Agricultural Engineering; Agriculture; Animal Husbandry; Anthropology; Applied Physics; Architecture; Banking; Biology; Business Administration; Chemical Engineering; Civil Engineering; Computer Engineering; Development Studies; Economics; Educational Administration; Educational and Student Counselling; Electrical and Electronic Engineering; Environmental Management; Finance; Food Science; Food Technology; Geology; Health Education; Industrial Chemistry; Insurance; Mass Communication; Materials Engineering; Mechanical Engineering; Metallurgical Engineering; Microbiology; Mining Engineering; Physical Education; Political Sciences; Production Engineering; Psychology; Public Administration; Regional Planning; Sociology; Soil Science; Technology Education; Town Planning); **Pre Degree**

History: Founded 1991, following creation of new States in Nigeria, and incorporating the Enugu and Abakaliki campuses of the former Anambra State University of Technology, founded 1982.

Governing Bodies: University Council

Academic Year: September to August (September-March; April-August)

Admission Requirements: Universities Matriculation Examination (UME) following secondary school education, or direct entry for holders of the Higher School Certificate (General Certificate of Education, Advanced Level); or pre-science internal examination (science examination only).

Fees: (US Dollars): Foreign students, c. 5,000

Main Language(s) of Instruction: English

Accrediting Agencies: National Universities Commission (NUC)

Degrees and Diplomas: *Bachelor's Degree*: 5 yrs; *Bachelor's Degree*: Engineering; *Postgraduate Diploma*: Agriculture (PGD); *Master's Degree*: a further 1-1 1/2 yrs; *Doctor of Philosophy (PhD)*. Also MBA.

Student Services: Canteen, Health services, Sports facilities

Special Facilities: ICT Center; Software Engineering Laboratory; Engineering Laboratories

Libraries: 35,000 vols; 1,200 periodicals; 50,000 electronic books; Academia Virtual Library System

Last Updated: 11/07/12

FEDERAL COLLEGE OF FISHERIES AND MARINE TECHNOLOGY (FCF&MT)

PMB 80063, Wilmot point road, Victoria Island, Lagos
EMail: info@fcfmt.edu.ng
Website: http://www.marinecollege-edu.org/

Provost: S.A.A. Zelibe

Registrar: I.I. Y. Ohiokpehai

Departments

Fisheries Technology (Fishery); **General Studies** (Biology; Chemistry; Engineering Drawing and Design; Geography; Mathematics; Natural Sciences; Physics); **Marine Engineering** (Marine Engineering); **Nautical Science** (Nautical Science)

History: Founded 1969 as Federal School of Fisheries. Acquired present status 1992.

Governing Bodies: Governing Board

Main Language(s) of Instruction: English

Accrediting Agencies: National Board for Technical Education (NBTE)

Degrees and Diplomas: *National Diploma*; *Higher National Diploma*; *Postgraduate Diploma*: Maritime Technology Management. Also Preliminary National Diploma

Student Services: Health services

Student Residential Facilities: 2 blocks of hostels for c. 420 students

Libraries: Yes

Last Updated: 08/10/12

IAU FEDERAL POLYTECHNIC, OKO (FEDPOLY, OKO)

PMB 21, Aguata, Anambra State 423121
Tel: +234(48) 911-144 +234(803) 408-9994
EMail: info@federalpolyoko.edu.ng; rector@federalpolyoko.edu.ng
Website: http://federalpolyoko.edu.ng/

Rector: Godwin Onu (2010-)
Tel: +234 8034 089994 EMail: rectoroko2010@gmail.com

Registrar: Olih Nwokolobia

International Relations: Maurice Umeakuka, Liaison Officer
Tel: +234 8063 328580
EMail: hodofurp@gmail.com; umeakukamaurice@yahoo.com

Schools

Applied Science Technology (Computer Science; Cooking and Catering; Food Technology; Home Economics; Hotel and Restaurant; Hotel Management; Laboratory Techniques; Mathematics; Statistics); **Art Design and Printing Technology** (Clothing and Sewing; Fashion Design; Fine Arts; Printing and Printmaking); **Business** (Business Administration; Marketing; Public Administration; Secretarial Studies); **Engineering and Technology**

(Agricultural Engineering; Civil Engineering; Computer Engineering; Electrical and Electronic Engineering; Mechanical Engineering); **Environmental Design and Technology** (Architecture; Building Technologies; Computer Science; Earth Sciences; Real Estate; Regional Planning; Surveying and Mapping; Town Planning); **Financial Studies** (Accountancy; Banking; Finance; Insurance); **General Studies** (Modern Languages; Natural Sciences; Social Sciences); **Information and Technology** (Information Sciences; Library Science; Mass Communication)

Further Information: Campuses in Atani and Ufuma.

History: Founded 1979 as a College of Arts and Science. Upgraded to a College of Arts, Science and Technology in 1980. Became Anambra State Polytechnic, Oko in 1985, and becamce Federal Polytechnic, Oko in 1993.

Academic Year: September to July

Admission Requirements: Through the Joint Admissions and Matriculation Board. The prospective candidate must however obtain five credits including English and maths in O'level

Fees: (Naira): 25,000 per annum

Main Language(s) of Instruction: English

International Co-operation: With Sharda University Noida, India

Accrediting Agencies: National Board for Technical Education (NBTE)

Degrees and Diplomas: *National Diploma (N.D.)*: 2 yrs; *Higher National Diploma (H.N.D.)*: 2 yrs

Student Services: Canteen, Health services, Sports facilities

Student Residential Facilities: Yes

Special Facilities: Mass communication studio; Mechanical Engineering Workshop; Laboratories and workshop equipment

Libraries: Over 200,000 vols; 127 journal subscriptions.

Press or Publishing House: Polytechnic Printing Press

Academic Staff *2010-2011*	**TOTAL**
FULL-TIME	**523**
PART-TIME	**12**
STAFF WITH DOCTORATE	
FULL-TIME	**51**
Student Numbers *2010-2011*	
All (Foreign Included)	**2,953**

Part-time students, 857. **Evening students**, 1,025.

Last Updated: 17/01/13

FEDERAL UNIVERSITY OF AGRICULTURE, ABEOKUTA (FUNAAB)

PMB 2240, Abeokuta, Ogun State
Tel: +234(806) 888-8660 +234 (803) 332-0972
Fax: +234(39) 243-045
EMail: unaab@unaab.edu.ng; registrar@unaab.edu.ng
Website: http://www.unaab.edu.ng

Vice-Chancellor: Olusola Bandele Oyewole (2011-)
Tel: +234(803) 335-1814
EMail: oyewole@aau.org; vcunaab@unaab.edu.ng

Registrar: Mathew Odunlade Ayoola
EMail: registrar@unaab.edu.ng

International Relations: Olasunkanmi Peter Somoye, Assistant Director, Public Relations
Tel: +234(803) 344-6044, Fax: +234(39) 243-045
EMail: lasunsop@yahoo.com

Colleges

Agricultural Management and Rural Development *(COLAMRUD)* (Agricultural Economics; Agricultural Management; Communication Studies; English; Farm Management; Philosophy; Political Sciences; Rural Planning; Sociology); **Animal Science and Livestock Production** *(COLANIM)* (Animal Husbandry; Cattle Breeding; Farm Management; Food Technology; Genetics; Nutrition; Rural Planning); **Engineering** *(COLENG)* (Agricultural Engineering; Civil Engineering; Electrical and Electronic Engineering; Engineering; Mechanical Engineering); **Environmental Resources Management** *(COLERM)* (Aquaculture; Biochemistry; Crop Production; Ecology; Environmental Management; Environmental Studies; Fishery; Forest Management; Forestry; Meteorology; Toxicology; Water Management; Water Science; Wildlife); **Food Science and Human Ecology** *(COLFHEC)* (Dietetics; Food Science; Food Technology; Home Economics; Nutrition; Tourism); **Natural Sciences** *(COLNAS)* (Biochemistry; Biological and Life Sciences; Botany; Chemistry; Computer Science; Mathematics; Microbiology; Natural Sciences; Physics; Statistics; Zoology); **Plant Science and Crop Production** *(COLPLANT)* (Botany; Crop Production; Horticulture; Physiology; Plant and Crop Protection; Plant Pathology; Rural Planning; Soil Science); **Veterinary Medicine** *(COLVET)* (Anatomy; Embryology and Reproduction Biology; Microbiology; Parasitology; Pathology; Pharmacology; Physiology; Public Health; Surgery; Veterinary Science)

Schools

Postgraduate Studies (Agricultural Business; Agricultural Economics; Agricultural Engineering; Agriculture; Analytical Chemistry; Anatomy; Animal Husbandry; Aquaculture; Biochemistry; Biological and Life Sciences; Biotechnology; Botany; Cattle Breeding; Civil Engineering; Communication Studies; Computer Science; Crop Production; Dairy; Dietetics; Ecology; Electrical and Electronic Engineering; Entomology; Environmental Engineering; Environmental Management; Farm Management; Fishery; Food Technology; Forest Economics; Forest Products; Forestry; Genetics; Geophysics; Horticulture; Industrial Chemistry; Industrial Engineering; Information Technology; Inorganic Chemistry; Materials Engineering; Mathematics; Meat and Poultry; Mechanical Engineering; Metallurgical Engineering; Microbiology; Nutrition; Organic Chemistry; Paper Technology; Pathology; Physical Chemistry; Physics; Physiology; Plant and Crop Protection; Power Engineering; Production Engineering; Public Health; Rural Planning; Soil Science; Solid State Physics; Statistics; Textile Technology; Toxicology; Veterinary Science; Virology; Water Management; Wildlife; Wood Technology; Zoology)

Further Information: Also Veterinary Teaching Hospital

History: Founded 1983 as Federal University of Technology, Abeokuta, merged with University of Lagos 1984, and acquired present status 1988.

Governing Bodies: Governing Council; Senate

Academic Year: October to July (October-February; March-July)

Admission Requirements: Universities Matriculation Examination (UME) following secondary school education, or direct entry for holders of the General Certificate of Education, Advanced ('A') level) or Diploma in relevant programmes

Fees: (Naira): 25,805 per session

Main Language(s) of Instruction: English

International Co-operation: Participates in the British Council-sponsored Academic Programme: University of Sao Paulo (Brazil); Sokoine University (Tanzania); Clark Atlanta University, Cornell University, Spelman College, Turkesgee University (USA); etc.

Accrediting Agencies: National Universities Commission (NUC); Council of Registered Engineers (COREN) and Veterinary Council of Nigerian (VCN)

Degrees and Diplomas: *Bachelor's Degree*; *Postgraduate Diploma*; *Master's Degree*; *Doctor of Philosophy (PhD)*. Also Doctor of Veterinary Medicine; MBA in Agribusiness and Professional Master programmes in Environmental Management (MEM) and Information and Communication Technology (MICT).

Student Services: Academic counselling, Canteen, Employment services, Health services, Sports facilities

Student Residential Facilities: Hostel with beds for 416 male and 678 female students.

Special Facilities: Teaching/Research farms; Agricultural Media Resources & Extension Centre (AMREC); Research and Development Centre (RESDEC)

Libraries: 50,622 vols; 150 foreign journals electronic and print), 35 local journals titles

Publications: ASSET Journal, Series A: Agricultural Science and Environment; B: Natural Sciences, Engineering & Technology; C: Humanities and Social Sciences *(quarterly)*; UNAAB Inaugural Lectures Series, Inaugural lectures of Professors *(quarterly)*

Last Updated: 18/07/12

FEDERAL UNIVERSITY OF AGRICULTURE, MAKURDI (UAM)

PMB 2373, Makurdi, Benue State
Tel: +234(44) 533-204 +234(44) 533-577
Fax: +234(44) 531-455
EMail: ro-uam@yahoo.com
Website: http://uamkd.com/

Vice-Chancellor: Daniel V. Uza (2007-) EMail: vc@fuam.edu.ng

Registrar: Samuel A. Edeh Tel: 08,032-188-082

Faculties

Agricultural and Science Education (Agricultural Education; Education; Educational Administration; Educational and Student Counselling; English; Environmental Management; Foreign Languages Education; Preschool Education; Science Education; Technology Education; Vocational Education); **Agricultural Economics, Extension and Management** (Agricultural Economics; Agricultural Management; Agriculture); **Agronomy** (Agronomy; Botany; Crop Production; Environmental Management; Plant and Crop Protection; Soil Conservation; Soil Science; Water Management); **Animal Science** (Animal Husbandry; Genetics; Nutrition; Physiology; Zoology); **Engineering** (Agricultural Education; Civil Engineering; Electrical and Electronic Engineering; Engineering; Environmental Engineering; Mechanical Engineering); **Food Technology** (Food Science; Food Technology; Home Economics; Household Management); **Forestry and Fisheries** (Aquaculture; Fishery; Forest Management; Forest Products; Forestry; Wildlife); **Management Sciences** (Management); **Science** (Biological and Life Sciences; Chemistry; Computer Science; Mathematics; Mathematics and Computer Science; Natural Sciences; Physics; Statistics); **Veterinary Medicine** (Anatomy; Animal Husbandry; Biochemistry; Entomology; Microbiology; Parasitology; Pathology; Pharmacology; Physiology; Public Health; Social and Preventive Medicine; Veterinary Science)

History: Founded 1988 as a specialized University of Agriculture.

Governing Bodies: University Council; Senate

Academic Year: October to September (March-June; June-September)

Admission Requirements: 5 credits in Senior Secondary School Certificate (SSSC) or West African School Certificate (WASC) or General Certificate of Education (GCE) ('O') level or equivalent, and English Language and University Matriculation Examination (UME)

Fees: (Naira): Undergraduate fees, 11,000-39,150 per semester depending on level; Fresh Postgraduate Diploma, 50,000; Master of Science, 60,000; Doctor of Philosophy, 70,000.

Main Language(s) of Instruction: English

Accrediting Agencies: National Universities Commission (NUC)

Degrees and Diplomas: *Bachelor's Degree*; *Postgraduate Diploma*; *Master's Degree*; *Doctor of Philosophy*. Also MBA (Full-time or Part-time)

Student Services: Academic counselling, Canteen, Employment services, Health services, Social counselling, Sports facilities

Student Residential Facilities: Yes

Special Facilities: Information Technology Centre (ICT)

Libraries: c. 30,000 vols; 700 periodicals; Nigerian/Canadian soil science documents

Publications: Journal of Agriculture, Science and Technology *(biannually)*

Press or Publishing House: Onaivi Printing Press, Makurdi

Last Updated: 11/07/12

FEDERAL UNIVERSITY OF PETROLEUM RESOURCES (FUPRE)

PMB 1221, Effurun, Delta State
EMail: inforeg@mail.fupre.edu.ng
Website: http://www.fupre.edu.ng/

Vice-Chancellor: Babatunde Alabi

Registrar: Linda Ogugua Onwuka

Colleges

Management Sciences (Actuarial Science; Business Administration; Economics; Management); **Science** (Chemistry; Computer Science; Earth Sciences; Environmental Studies; Geology; Geophysics; Industrial Chemistry; Mathematics; Physics); **Technology** (Chemical Engineering; Electrical and Electronic Engineering; Electronic Engineering; Marine Engineering; Mechanical Engineering; Petroleum and Gas Engineering; Technology)

History: Founded 2007.

Admission Requirements: Admissions through the Joint Admissions and Matriculations Board (JAMB); For admission to 100 level, candidates must possess five (5) credit passes at Senior Secondary School Certificate Examination (SSSCE) or equivalent in relevant subjects in only one sittings; and obtain a minimum of 200 points in University Matriculation Examination. All candidates who score above 200 UME and choose FUPRE as either first or second choice are further invited to a Post University Matriculation Examination (PUME) of the Federal University of Petroleum Resources Effurun. FUPRE Post University Matriculation Examination (PUME) is a two stage (written and oral) assessment process.

Main Language(s) of Instruction: English

Accrediting Agencies: National Universities Commission (NUC)

Degrees and Diplomas: *Bachelor's Degree*

Last Updated: 11/07/12

FEDERAL UNIVERSITY OF TECHNOLOGY, AKURE (FUTA)

PMB 704, Ilesha-Akure Expressway, Akure, Ondo State
Tel: +234(34) 243-490
EMail: info@futa.edu.ng; administration@futa.edu.ng
Website: http://futa.edu.ng/

Vice-Chancellor: Adebiyi Gregory Daramola (2012-)
Tel: +234(34) 243-060 EMail: vc@futa.edu.ng

Registrar: Modupe Olayinka
Tel: +234(803) 4016-340
EMail: modupe_ajayi@yahoo.com; registry@futa.edu.ng

Centres

Computer Resource *(CRC)* (Computer Science; Information Technology); **Continuing Education** *(CCE)*; **Research and Development** *(CERAD)*

Schools

Agriculture and Agricultural Technology *(SAAT)* (Agricultural Economics; Agriculture; Animal Husbandry; Aquaculture; Crop Production; Fishery; Food Science; Food Technology; Forestry; Soil Management; Tourism; Wildlife; Wood Technology); **Earth and Mineral Sciences** *(SEMS)* (Computer Science; Earth Sciences; Geology; Geophysics; Marine Engineering; Marine Science and Oceanography; Meteorology; Surveying and Mapping); **Engineering and Engineering Technology** *(SEET)* (Agricultural Engineering; Civil Engineering; Electrical and Electronic Engineering; Engineering; Materials Engineering; Mechanical Engineering; Metallurgical Engineering; Mining Engineering); **Environmental Technology** *(SET)* (Architecture; Industrial Design; Real Estate; Regional Planning; Surveying and Mapping; Town Planning); **Management Technology** *(SMAT)* (Information Management; Library Science; Management; Management Systems; Transport Management); **Postgraduate Studies** *(SPGS)* (Agricultural Engineering; Architecture; Engineering; Technology); **Sciences** *(SOS)* (Biochemistry; Biology; Chemistry; Computer Science; Mathematics; Microbiology; Physics)

History: Founded 1981. Acquired present status 1982.

Governing Bodies: Council, comprising 17 members; Senate

Academic Year: October to July

Admission Requirements: For undergraduate programmes, Minimum 5 credits at GCE (General Certificate of Education), Ordinary ('O') level. Admission through Universities Matriculation Examinations conducted by Joint Admissions and Matriculation Board (JAMB) and qualification through the University Pre-degree Programme. For Postgraduate programmes, All candidates must possess five (5) 'O' level credits as required in relevant disciplines but must include English Language and Mathematics.

Fees: (US Dollars): tuition fee, 1,500 per session for foreign students

Main Language(s) of Instruction: English

Accrediting Agencies: National Universities Commission (NUC) and various professional bodies

Degrees and Diplomas: *Bachelor's Degree (B.Tech)*: 5 yrs; *Bachelor's Degree*: Architecture, 6 yrs; *Postgraduate Diploma (PGD)*; *Master's Degree*; *Doctor of Philosophy (Ph.D)*: a further 3 yrs (minimum). Also Pre-degree diplomas; University diplomas; Certificate and Executive Certificates; Professional training programmes;

Student Services: Academic counselling, Canteen, Health services, Nursery care, Social counselling, Sports facilities

Student Residential Facilities: Yes. All foreign students are accomodated on-campus

Special Facilities: Meteorological Observatory, Industrial Design Studio

Libraries: c. 55,000 vols; 237 periodicals. Special collection: UN Food and Agricultural Organization's depositary library.

Publications: Foundation Day Lecture Series; Inaugural Lecture Series

Last Updated: 11/07/12

FEDERAL UNIVERSITY OF TECHNOLOGY, MINNA (FUTM)

PMB 65, Gidan Kwano, Minna, Niger State
Tel: +234(803) 821-2228
Fax: +234(66) 224-422
EMail: info@futminna.edu.ng; registrar@futminna.edu.ng
Website: http://www.futminna.edu.ng

Vice-Chancellor: Muhammed Salihu Audu (2007-2012)
Tel: +234(66) 222-887, Fax: +234(66) 625-426

Registrar: Victoria Nnawo Kolo Fax: +234(66) 224-305

Deputy Vice-Chancellor, Administration: Mohammed A.T. Suleiman

Schools

Agriculture and Agricultural Technology *(SAAT)* (Agricultural Economics; Agricultural Engineering; Agriculture; Animal Husbandry; Aquaculture; Crop Production; Fishery; Soil Science; Water Management); **Engineering and Engineering Technology** *(SEET)* (Agricultural Engineering; Automation and Control Engineering; Automotive Engineering; Biotechnology; Chemical Engineering; Civil Engineering; Electrical and Electronic Engineering; Electronic Engineering; Energy Engineering; Engineering; Environmental Engineering; Geological Engineering; Industrial Engineering; Mechanical Engineering; Mechanics; Metallurgical Engineering; Petroleum and Gas Engineering; Polymer and Plastics Technology; Power Engineering; Production Engineering; Soil Science; Structural Architecture; Telecommunications Engineering; Transport Engineering; Water Management; Water Science); **Environmental Technology** *(SET)* (Architecture; Building Technologies; Real Estate; Regional Planning; Surveying and Mapping; Town Planning); **Information and Communication Technology** *(SICT)* (Computer Engineering; Computer Science; Information Technology; Library Science; Media Studies; Telecommunications Engineering); **Postgraduate Studies** *(PG)* (Agricultural Engineering; Animal Husbandry; Chemical Engineering; Computer Science; Crop Production; Educational Technology; Environmental Engineering; Fishery; Landscape Architecture; Management; Mechanical Engineering; Soil Science); **Science and Science Education** *(SSSE)* (Automotive Engineering; Biochemistry; Biology; Building Technologies; Chemistry; Computer Science; Educational Technology; Electrical and Electronic Engineering; Electronic Engineering; Geography; Geology; Mathematics; Mathematics Education; Metal Techniques; Metallurgical Engineering; Meteorology; Microbiology; Physics; Polymer and Plastics Technology; Power Engineering; Science Education; Statistics; Surveying and Mapping; Technology Education; Telecommunications Engineering; Wood Technology)

Further Information: Also Bosso Campus. A traditional, open and distance learning institution.

History: Founded 1983.

Governing Bodies: Governing Council; Senate

Admission Requirements: Universities Matriculation Examination (UME) following secondary school education

Fees: (Naira): Nationals, c. 4,000-18,000; foreign students, 18,000-28,000; postgraduates, 12,000-21,000

Main Language(s) of Instruction: English

Accrediting Agencies: National Universities Commission (NUC)

Degrees and Diplomas: *Bachelor's Degree*: 5 yrs; *Master's Degree*: a further 2 yrs; *Doctor of Philosophy (PhD)*: 3 yrs

Student Residential Facilities: Yes

Libraries: c. 20,000 vols

Academic Staff *2011-2012*: Total 795

Student Numbers *2011-2012*: Total: c. 15,000

Last Updated: 11/07/12

FEDERAL UNIVERSITY OF TECHNOLOGY, OWERRI (FUTO)

PMB 1526, Owerri, Imo State
Tel: +234(83) 426-0769
Fax: +234(83) 230-969
EMail: admissions@futo.edu.ng
Website: http://www.futo.edu.ng/

Vice-Chancellor: Chigozie Cyril Asiabaka (2011-)
Tel: +234(83) 722-5385 EMail: vc6@futo.edu.ng

Registrar: Orje Ishegh-Nor
Tel: +234(83) 547-1310 EMail: registrar@futo.edu.ng

Deputy Vice-Chancellor, Administration: R.N. Nwabueze
EMail: dvcadmin6@futo.edu.ng

International Relations: R.M. Aguta, Director of International Association for Exchange of Students for Technical Experience (IAESTE) Tel: +234(83) 332-1129 EMail: muiloeje@yahoo.com

Centres

Agricultural Research *(CAR)* (Agriculture); **Energy and Power Systems Research** *(CEPSR)* (Energy Engineering; Power Engineering)

Institutes

Erosion Studies *(IES)* (Earth Sciences)

Schools

Agriculture and Agricultural Sciences *(SAAT)* (Agricultural Economics; Agriculture; Animal Husbandry; Aquaculture; Crop Production; Fishery; Forestry; Soil Science; Wildlife); **Engineering and Engineering Technology** *(SEET)* (Agricultural Engineering; Chemical Engineering; Civil Engineering; Electrical and Electronic Engineering; Food Technology; Materials Engineering; Mechanical Engineering; Metallurgical Engineering; Petroleum and Gas Engineering; Textile Technology); **Environmental Science and Technology** *(SOET)* (Building Technologies; Computer Science; Earth Sciences; Environmental Studies; Regional Planning; Surveying and Mapping; Town Planning); **Health** *(SOHT)* (Biomedical Engineering; Biomedicine; Dental Technology; Dentistry; Health Sciences; Optometry; Orthopaedics; Physical Therapy; Public Health); **Management and Management Technology** *(SMAT)* (Finance; Information Management; Management; Marine Transport; Philosophy; Transport and Communications; Transport Management); **Science** *(SOSC)* (Biochemistry; Biology; Biotechnology; Chemistry; Computer Science; Geology; Laboratory Techniques; Mathematics; Microbiology; Physics; Statistics)

Further Information: Also Directorate of General Studies (DGS); Directorate of Information and Communication Technology (ICT) and International Association for the Exchange of Students for Technological Experience (IAESTE)

History: Established 1980.

Governing Bodies: Governing Council; Senate; Convocation and Congregation

Academic Year: October to July (October-February; March-July)

Admission Requirements: 5 O'level credit passes in General Certificate of Education (GCE), or Senior School Certificate (SSC), or National Examination Council (NECO), or National Board for Technical Education (NABTEB) in relevant subjects including English Language and Mathematics

Fees: Tuition free

Main Language(s) of Instruction: English

International Co-operation: With higher education institutions in Canada; China; Germany; Ghana; Hong Kong; Sweden; United Kingdom and USA

Accrediting Agencies: National University Commission(NUC); Council for the Regulation of Engineering in Nigeria (COREN)

Degrees and Diplomas: *Bachelor's Degree*: 5 yrs; *Postgraduate Diploma (PGD)*: 1 yr; *Master's Degree*; *Doctor of Philosophy (PhD)*. Also MBA.

Student Services: Academic counselling, Canteen, Cultural centre, Employment services, Foreign student adviser, Foreign Studies Centre, Handicapped facilities, Health services, Language programs, Nursery care, Social counselling, Sports facilities

Student Residential Facilities: For c. 1,950 students

Special Facilities: Engineering workshop; Afrihub-Zinox Digital Centre; Expansive university farm for crop and animal production; fisheries and aquaculture; soil laboratory

Libraries: 95,000 vols; 200 Journal titles; over 3,500 technical documents; 1,000 maps; Virtual Library

Press or Publishing House: FUTO Press Ltd

Academic Staff *2010-2011*: Total 926

STAFF WITH DOCTORATE: Total 156

Student Numbers *2010-2011*: Total 21,039

Last Updated: 11/07/12

GOMBE STATE UNIVERSITY (GSU)

PMB 127, Tudun Wada, Gombe, Gombe State
Tel: +234(72) 222-091
Fax: +234(72) 221-097
EMail: vcgsu2004@yahoo.com; admin@gsu.edu.ng
Website: http://gsu.edu.ng

Vice-Chancellor: Abdullahi Mahadi (2004-)
EMail: abdullahimahadi@yahoo.com

Registrar: Aliyu Kamara
EMail: aliyukamara@gomsu.org; registra@gsu.edu.ng

International Relations: Ahmed Garba Musa, Secretary to Vice-Chancellor EMail: ahmedgarbamusa10@yahoo.com

Faculties

Arts (Arts and Humanities; Political Sciences; Public Administration; Religious Studies; Sociology); **Education** (Biology; Chemistry; Christian Religious Studies; Education; English; Foreign Languages Education; Geography; History; Humanities and Social Science Education; Islamic Theology; Mathematics Education; Physics; Religious Studies; Science Education); **Medicine** (Medicine); **Other**; **Pharmacy** (Pharmacy); **Postgraduate**; **Science** (Biology; Chemistry; Geography; Geology; Mathematics; Natural Sciences; Physics); **Social Sciences** (Social Sciences)

History: Founded 2005.

Governing Bodies: University Council.

Admission Requirements: Senior Secondary School Certificate (SSSC) with credits in English and Mathematics; Other admission requirements set out by each facultty, which should be obtained at not more than two sittings of the SSSC.

Fees: (Naira): 19,000 - 75,000 per annum

Main Language(s) of Instruction: English

International Co-operation: With University of Canterbury (New Zealand); University of Cape Coast (Ghana)

Accrediting Agencies: National Universities Commission (NUC)

Degrees and Diplomas: *Bachelor's Degree*: Science; Education; Arts and Social Sciences (BA; BSc; BA(Ed); BSc (Ed)), 4 yrs

Student Services: Academic counselling, Canteen, Cultural centre, Employment services, Foreign student adviser, Foreign Studies Centre, Handicapped facilities, Health services, Language programs, Nursery care, Social counselling, Sports facilities

Student Residential Facilities: Staff quarters and University Guest House

Special Facilities: Zoo; Botanical Gardens

Libraries: Yes.

Publications: Gombe State University Journal, Academic affairs *(annually)*

Last Updated: 11/07/12

IBRAHIM BADAMASI BABANGIDA UNIVERSITY, LAPAI (IBBUL)

P.M.B. 11, Lapai, Niger 920001-911001
Tel: +234(80) 280-15151
EMail: info@ibbu.edu.ng
Website: http://www.ibbu.edu.ng

Vice-Chancellor: Ibrahim Adamu Kolo (2010-)
Fax: +234(80) 274-31026 EMail: iakolo@ibbu.edu.ng

Registrar: Samaila Muhammad
Tel: +234(80) 370-01284 EMail: smohd@ibbu.edu.ng

International Relations: Godwin Ashituabe, Director, Development Office Tel: +234(80) 359-92855 EMail: godashi2003@yahoo.com

Faculties

Agriculture (Agricultural Economics; Agriculture; Animal Husbandry; Crop Production); **Applied Science and Technology** (Food Science; Food Technology; Geology; Mining Engineering; Technology); **Education and Arts** (Education; Educational and Student Counselling; Educational Psychology; Health Education; History; Sports); **Language and Communication** (Arabic; English; French; Modern Languages); **Management and Social Sciences** (Business Administration; Economics; Mass Communication; Political Sciences; Public Administration; Sociology); **Natural Science** (Biochemistry; Biology; Chemistry; Computer Science; Geography; Mathematics; Microbiology; Natural Sciences; Physics)

History: Founded 2005.

Governing Bodies: Governing Council

Admission Requirements: I - Minimum of five (5) credits (including Maths and English) in SSCE; II - Minimum of 200 points Jamb score.

Fees: (Naira): 64,000 (£400) per session.

Main Language(s) of Instruction: English

International Co-operation: With University of Arkansas Pine Bluff, USA.

Degrees and Diplomas: *Bachelor's Degree*: Animal Production; Agricultural Economics; Crop Production (B. Agriculture); Food Science and Technology (B.Sc. Food Science), 5 yrs; *Bachelor's Degree*: Arabic; English; French (B.A.); Continuing Education; History; Sport Science and Health Education (B.Ed.); Counselling Psychology (B.Sc. (ED) Counselling Psychology); Geology and Mining; Business Administration; Economics; Mass Communication; Public Administration; Political Science; Sociology; Biology; Biochemistry; Chemistry; Computer Science; Geography; Mathematics; Microbiology; Physics (B.Sc.), 4 yrs

Student Services: Academic counselling, Canteen, Health services, Social counselling, Sports facilities

Student Residential Facilities: Students Hostels and Staff Housing

Special Facilities: Mass Communication Studio; Language Lab/ Studio

Libraries: E-Library

Publications: Haskenmu, Publication of the Faculty of Education and Arts; IBBUL News *(biweekly)*; IBBUL Trumpet, Training Publication of the Department of Mass Communication; Jolae, Journal of Arts and Education, Publication of the Faculty of Education and Arts; Journal of Education and Applied Psychology, Publication of the Faculty of Education and Arts *(annually)*

Press or Publishing House: IBBUL News

Academic Staff *2011-2012*	MEN	WOMEN	TOTAL
FULL-TIME	646	113	**759**
PART-TIME	40	24	**64**
STAFF WITH DOCTORATE			
FULL-TIME	52	7	**59**
PART-TIME	26	1	**27**
Student Numbers *2011-2012*			
All (Foreign Included)	3,170	1,582	**4,752**

Last Updated: 04/06/12

IMO STATE UNIVERSITY (IMSU)

PMB 2000, Owerri, Imo State
Tel: +234(705) 869-3138
Website: http://imsuonline.edu.ng/

Vice-Chancellor: B.E. Nwoke
Tel: +234(705) 869-3138
EMail: bebnwoke@imsuonline.edu.ng; Vcoffice@imsuonline.e-du.ng; bebndie@yahoo.com

Registrar: Ifeanyichukwu Godfrey Aniche

Faculties

Agriculture and Veterinary Medicine (Agricultural Economics; Agriculture; Animal Husbandry; Biotechnology; Crop Production; Dietetics; Fishery; Food Science; Food Technology; Nutrition; Rural Studies; Soil Science; Veterinary Science); **Business Administration** (Accountancy; Actuarial Science; Banking; Business Administration; Finance; Hotel and Restaurant; Insurance; Management; Marketing; Tourism); **Education** (Curriculum; Education; Educational Administration; Educational and Student Counselling; Educational Psychology; Educational Technology; Educational Testing and Evaluation); **Engineering** (Agricultural Engineering; Civil Engineering; Electrical and Electronic Engineering; Engineering; Mechanical Engineering); **Environmental Science** (Architecture; Building Technologies; Computer Science; Environmental Management; Environmental Studies; Fine Arts; Geography; Real Estate; Regional Planning; Surveying and Mapping; Town Planning); **Health Sciences** (Health Sciences; Laboratory Techniques; Nursing; Optometry); **Humanities** (African Languages; Arts and Humanities; English; French; History; International Studies; Linguistics; Literature; Philosophy; Religion; Theatre); **Law** (Commercial Law; International Law; Law; Private Law; Public Law); **Medicine** (Anatomy; Biochemistry; Community Health; Gynaecology and Obstetrics; Laboratory Techniques; Medicine; Nursing; Optometry; Paediatrics; Pathology; Pharmacology; Physiology; Surgery); **Science** (Applied Physics; Biochemistry; Biology; Biotechnology; Botany; Chemistry; Computer Science; Environmental Studies; Industrial Chemistry; Mathematics; Microbiology; Natural Sciences; Physics; Statistics; Zoology); **Social Sciences** (Anthropology; Economics; Government; Information Sciences; Library Science; Mass Communication; Psychology; Public Administration; Social Sciences; Sociology)

Institutes

Continuing Education Programme *(ICEP)* (Accountancy; Administration; Banking; Economics; Finance; Government; Management; Marketing; Mass Communication; Nursing; Public Administration)

Schools

Postgraduate Studies (Business Administration)

History: Founded 1981. Acquired present status 1992.

Governing Bodies: Council; Senate

Admission Requirements: Minimum of 5 'O' level passes, including English and Mathematics and University Matriculation Examination (UME)

Main Language(s) of Instruction: English

Accrediting Agencies: National Universities Commission (NUC); Ministry of Education, Imo State; Council

Degrees and Diplomas: *Bachelor's Degree*; *Bachelor's Degree*: Social Sciences; *Postgraduate Diploma*; *Master's Degree*; *Doctor of Philosophy*. Also Diplomas in various fields; MBA.

Student Services: Academic counselling, Canteen, Cultural centre, Health services, Language programs, Nursery care, Social counselling, Sports facilities

Student Residential Facilities: Off-campus residence

Special Facilities: Art Gallery

Libraries: 30,000 vols in main University Library and Faculty, College and Department Libraries
Last Updated: 12/07/12

KADUNA POLYTECHNIC

PMB 2021, Kaduna, Kaduna State
Tel: +234(62) 419-503 +234(62) 414-493
Fax: +234(62) 416-055
EMail: ca@kadpoly.com
Website: http://www.kadunapolytechnic.edu.ng

Acting Rector: Aliyu Mamman (2012-)

Deputy Rector, Administration: Alhaji Bello Ahmed

Acting Registrar: Zayyana Ibrahim Kukasheka

Colleges

Administrative Studies and Social Sciences *(CASSS)* (Administration; Arabic; Criminology; Development Studies; Government; Information Sciences; International Relations; Law; Library Science; Mass Communication; Modern Languages; Public Administration; Rehabilitation and Therapy; Social Sciences); **Business and Management Studies** *(CBMS)* (Accountancy; Banking; Business Administration; Finance; Management; Marketing; Secretarial Studies); **Engineering** *(COE)* (Agricultural Engineering; Chemical Engineering; Civil Engineering; Computer Engineering; Electrical and Electronic Engineering; Engineering; Geological Engineering; Industrial Engineering; Mechanical Engineering; Mining Engineering; Natural Resources; Structural Architecture; Transport Engineering); **Environmental Studies** *(CES)* (Architecture; Building Technologies; Computer Science; Earth Sciences; Environmental Studies; Real Estate; Regional Planning; Safety Engineering; Surveying and Mapping; Town Planning); **Science and Technology** *(CST)* (Biological and Life Sciences; Biology; Biotechnology; Chemistry; Computer Science; Cooking and Catering; Education; Fashion Design; Food Technology; Health Education; Hotel Management; Laboratory Techniques; Mathematics; Mathematics and Computer Science; Metal Techniques; Microbiology; Nursing; Printing and Printmaking; Statistics; Technology; Technology Education; Textile Technology; Wood Technology)

History: Founded 1956 as Kaduna Technical Institute. Became Kaduna Polytechnic 1968. Acquired present status 1991.

Governing Bodies: Governing Council

Main Language(s) of Instruction: English

Accrediting Agencies: National Board of Technical Education (NBTE)

Degrees and Diplomas: *National Diploma*; *Higher National Diploma*; *Bachelor's Degree (B.Tech)*; *Postgraduate Diploma*. Also Certificates; Diplomas; Post Higher National Diploma (Post-HND) in Urban and Regional Planning, Land Surveying, Building Technology, Electronics and Communication Engineering; The B.Tech is run in affiliation with the Federal University of Technology, Minna.

Student Numbers *2011-2012*: Total: c. 20,000
Last Updated: 12/07/12

KADUNA STATE UNIVERSITY

PMB 2339, Tafawa Balewa Way, Kaduna, Kaduna State
Tel: +234(62) 211-799
EMail: info@kasu.edu.ng
Website: http://www.kasuportal.net

Vice-Chancellor: Ezzeldin Mukhtar Abdurahman

Registrar: Saidu Goje

Colleges

Basic and Remedial Studies

Faculties

Arts (African Languages; Arabic; Arts and Humanities; Christian Religious Studies; English; French; History; Islamic Studies; Linguistics; Theatre); **Medicine** (Anatomy; Medicine; Pharmacology; Physiology; Public Health); **Science** (Biochemistry; Biological and Life Sciences; Chemistry; Geography; Mathematics; Microbiology; Natural Sciences; Physics)

Units

Arabic-French Preliminary Studies (Arabic; French); **General Studies**

Further Information: Also College of Basic and Remedial Studies

History: Founded 2004.

Governing Bodies: Council; Senate; Management Committee; Congregation; Convocation; University Consultative Committee

Main Language(s) of Instruction: English

Degrees and Diplomas: *Bachelor's Degree*

Special Facilities: Computer/ICT Centre

Libraries: Yes
Last Updated: 12/07/12

KANO UNIVERSITY OF SCIENCE AND TECHNOLOGY, WUDIL (KUST)

PMB 3244, Wudil, Kano State
Tel: +234(64) 241-149
Fax: +234(64) 241-175
EMail: info@kustportal.edu.ng
Website: http://kustportal.edu.ng/

Vice-Chancellor: Ibrahim Diso EMail: vc@kustportal.edu.ng

Faculties

Agricultural Technology (Agriculture; Food Science; Food Technology); **Engineering** (Civil Engineering; Electrical Engineering; Food Science; Food Technology; Mechanical Engineering); **Environmental Sciences** (Architecture; Geography); **Science and Science Education** (Biology; Chemistry; Computer Science; Mathematics; Physics; Science Education; Statistics); **Social Sciences** (Social Sciences)

History: Founded 2000. Formerly Bagauda University of Science and Technology.

Accrediting Agencies: National Universities Commission (NUC)

Degrees and Diplomas: *Bachelor's Degree*: Agriculture; Food Science and Technology; Civil Engineering; Mechanical Engineering; Electrical Engineering; Geography; Microbiology; Urban and Regional Planning; Biochemistry; Geology (B.Tech; B.Eng.;B.Sc.); Biology; Mathematics; Statistics; Computer Science; Physics; Architecture; Physics Education; Biology Education; Chemistry Education; Mathematics Education; Geography Education (B.Sc Ed.)

Last Updated: 31/05/12

KEBBI STATE UNIVERSITY OF SCIENCE AND TECHNOLOGY (KSUSTA)

PMB 1144, Aliero, Aliero, Nigeria
EMail: admin@ksusta.edu.ng; kebbistateuni@yahoo.com
Website: http://www.ksusta.com/

Vice-Chancellor: Abdullahi Abu Zuru (2011-2016)
Tel: +234(80) 350-51784 EMail: zurupeni@yahoo.com

Registrar: Ibrahim Abubakar Mungadi
Tel: +234(80) 272-06701 EMail: ibmungadi@yahoo.com

International Relations: Habiba Lami Musa, Principal Assistant Registrar

Faculties

Agriculture (Agricultural Economics; Agriculture; Animal Husbandry; Crop Production; Fishery; Forestry; Soil Science); **Science** (Applied Chemistry; Biochemistry; Botany; Chemistry; Computer Science; Information Technology; Mathematics; Microbiology; Natural Sciences; Physics; Statistics; Zoology)

History: Founded 2006 as a science and Technology-focused Institution. Academic activities started 2007-2008 with two faculties: Faculty of Science and Faculty of Agriculture (Departements of Forestry and Fisheries added to the latter 2008-2009).

Governing Bodies: Council, Senate, Faculty Boards, Depatmental Boards and Committees.

Admission Requirements: Undergraduate admissions through Tertiary Matriculation Examination (UTME) or Direct Entry (DE). UTME Candidates must hold one of the following qualifications: General Certificate of Eduction (GCE) ordinary level, Senior Secondary Certificate Examination (SSCE), National Business and Technical Examination Board Certificate (NABTEB), National Examination Council Certificate (NECO), Teachers Grade II Certificate; passed with at least five credits, which must include English Language and Mathematics, passed at one or two sittings. DE candidates should possess one of the following qualifications which must also be acceptable to the University: Higher National Diploma (HND), National Certificate in Education (NCE), Ordinary National Diploma (OND; obtained from any recognized institution in at least credit level.

Main Language(s) of Instruction: English

International Co-operation: With Niger Republic

Accrediting Agencies: National Universities Commission (NUC), Abuja, Nigeria

Degrees and Diplomas: *Bachelor's Degree*: Agricultural Science; Forestry; Fisheries (B. Agriculture), 5 yrs; *Bachelor's Degree*: Biochemistry; Botany; Microbiology; Zoology; Computer Science; Information Technology; Mathematics; Pure Chemistry; Applied Chemistry; Physics (B.Sc.), 4 yrs

Student Services: Academic counselling, Canteen, Cultural centre, Employment services, Foreign student adviser, Handicapped facilities, Health services, Language programs, Nursery care, Social counselling, Sports facilities

Student Residential Facilities: Staff Quarters

Special Facilities: Museum

Libraries: Books, Journals, Periodicals and e-Library

Publications: KSUSTA Bulletin *(quarterly)*

Academic Staff *2011-2012*	MEN	WOMEN	TOTAL
FULL-TIME	120	18	**138**
PART-TIME	32	–	**32**
STAFF WITH DOCTORATE			
FULL-TIME	11	2	**13**
PART-TIME	32	–	**32**
Student Numbers *2011-2012*			
All (Foreign Included)	1,483	347	**1,830**
FOREIGN ONLY	–	–	**5**

Last Updated: 04/06/12

KOGI STATE UNIVERSITY (KSU)

PMB 1008, Anyigba, Kogi State
Tel: +234(803) 358-4418
EMail: fsiaya@skannet.com; info@ksuportal.edu.ng
Website: http://www.kogistateuniversity.edu.ng/

Vice-Chancellor: Hassan Salihu Isah (2008-)
EMail: ksuanyigba@yahoo.com

Deputy Vice Chancellor Administration: Stephen Metiboba

Registrar: Joseph Audu Zhizhi EMail: jazhizhi@yahoo.com

Faculties

Agriculture (Agricultural Economics; Agriculture; Animal Husbandry; Crop Production; Food Science; Food Technology; Home Economics; Nutrition; Soil Science); **Arts and Humanities** (Arabic; Arts and Humanities; Christian Religious Studies; English; History; International Studies; Islamic Studies; Philosophy; Religious Studies; Theatre); **Law** (International Law; Islamic Law; Law; Private Law; Public Law); **Management Sciences** (Banking; Business Administration; Finance; Management; Public Administration); **Medicine** (Anatomy; Dentistry; Medicine; Pharmacy; Physiology); **Natural Sciences** (Biochemistry; Biological and Life Sciences; Chemistry; Computer Science; Geology; Mathematics; Mathematics and Computer Science; Microbiology; Natural Sciences; Physics); **Social Sciences** (Economics; Geography; Mass Communication; Political Sciences; Social Sciences; Sociology)

History: Founded 2000.

Governing Bodies: Council

Admission Requirements: Five 'O' level credits including English and/or Mathematics

Fees: (Naira): 22,000 per annum

Main Language(s) of Instruction: English

Accrediting Agencies: National Universities Commission (NUC)

Degrees and Diplomas: *Bachelor's Degree*: Accounting; Business Administration (Management); Business Administration (Banking and Finance); Public Administration; Agricultural Economics and Extension; Animal Production; Crop Production; Soil Sciences; Food Sciences; Home Sciences; Food Science Technology; Arabic Studies; Islamic Studies; History and International Studies; English; Christian Religious Studies; Philosophy; Philosophy and Religious Studies; Theatre Arts; Biochemistry; Biological Sciences (Botany); Biological Sciences (Zoology); Chemistry; Geology; Mathematical Sciences (Computer); Mathematical Sciences (Mathematics); Mathematical Sciences (Statistics); Microbiology; Physics; Economics; Geography and Planning; Mass Communication; Political Science; Sociology; Private and Sharia Law; Public and International Law; *Postgraduate Diploma*: Accounting; Banking and Finance; Management; Public Administration; Arabic and Islamic Studies; Theatre Arts; Christian Religious Studies; Biochemistry; Chemistry; Botany; Computer Science; Zoology; Crop Production; Food, Nutrition and Home Sciences; Soil and Environmental

Management; Agricultural Economics and Extension; Animal Production; Development and Rural Sociology; Industrial and Labour Relations; Economics; Environmental Resources Management; Remote Sensing and Geographical Information System; Cartography; Rural Development; Transport Management; Urban and Regional Planning; Broadcast Journalism; Public Relations and Advertising; Social Work; Industrial and Labour Relations; Community Health; Criminal Justice and Corrections; Law; *Master's Degree*; *Master's Degree*: (Professional): Public Administration; Environmental Management; Transport Management; Animal Production; Crop Production; Food Science and Technology; Home Science; Agriculture; Agricultural Economics; Agricultural Extension; Arabic Language and Literature; Islamic Studies; English Language; Literature in English; History and International Studies; Philosophy; Christian Religious Studies; Theatre Arts; Law; Law and Diplomacy; Biochemistry/Biotechnology; Botany; Zoology; Chemistry; Microbiology; Geology; Computer Science; Mathematics; Statistics; Physics; Economics; Geography; Urban and Regional Planning; Mass Communication; Political Science; Sociology; Public Administration; *Doctor of Philosophy*; *Doctor of Philosophy*: Animal Science; Crop Production; Food Science and Technology; Agriculture; Agricultural Economics; Agricultural Extension; Arabic Language and Literature; Islamic Studies; English Language; Literature in English; History and International Studies; Philosophy; Christian Religious Studies; Theatre Arts; Biochemistry/Biotechnology; Botany; Zoology; Chemistry; Microbiology; Geology; Physics; Geography; Urban and Regional Planning; Mass Communication; Political Science; Sociology; Law; Public Administration

Student Services: Academic counselling, Canteen, Health services, Language programs, Nursery care

Student Residential Facilities: Yes

Libraries: Yes

Publications: Anyigba Journal of Arts and Humanities; Journal of Health and Drug Law; Kogi Journal of Management; Kogi State University Law Journal; Savannah Journal of Science and Agriculture

Last Updated: 13/07/12

KWARA STATE POLYTECHNIC (KWARAPOLY)

PMB 1375, Ilorin, Kwara State
Tel: +234(31) 221-441
Website: http://www.kwarapolytechnic.com/

Rector: Alh. Mashood Akanbi-Elelu
EMail: yahayabdulkareem@yahoo.com

Registrar: M.O. Salami
Tel: +234(80) 3573-0013 +234(80) 5302-7119

Centres

Post Graduate Studies (Agricultural Engineering; Business Administration; Computer Science; Demography and Population; Electrical and Electronic Engineering; Mathematics; Mechanical Engineering; Public Administration; Public Relations; Rural Planning; Social Policy; Statistics; Water Science)

Institutes

Basic and Applied Sciences (Biology; Chemistry; Computer Science; Geography; Hotel and Restaurant; Laboratory Techniques; Mathematics; Physics; Rural Studies; Statistics); **Environmental Sciences** (Building Technologies; Environmental Studies; Real Estate; Rural Planning; Structural Architecture; Surveying and Mapping; Town Planning); **Finance and Management Studies** (Accountancy; Banking; Business Administration; Finance; Management; Marketing); **Information and Communication Technology** (Business Computing; Computer Science; Information Technology); **Technology** (Agricultural Engineering; Civil Engineering; Electrical and Electronic Engineering; Harvest Technology; Mechanical Engineering; Metallurgical Engineering; Mining Engineering; Power Engineering; Production Engineering; Soil Science; Technology; Telecommunications Engineering; Transport Engineering)

History: Founded in 1972.

Governing Bodies: Governing Council

Academic Year: July to September

Admission Requirements: Minimum of 4 credits in relevant subject (including English & Mathematics)

Fees: (Naira): 18,500 per annum

Accrediting Agencies: NBTE Professional Bodies (ICAN) NIEVS, CIBN, NIMN, Ministry of Architects; Governing Council, Ministry of Education, National Board for Technichal Education (NBTE)

Degrees and Diplomas: *National Diploma*; *Higher National Diploma*; *Postgraduate Diploma (PGD)*. Also Pre-National Diploma (Pre-ND)

Student Services: Sports facilities

Special Facilities: Mini Museum, Laboratory

Libraries: Yes

Last Updated: 13/07/12

KWARA STATE UNIVERSITY (KWASU)

PMB 1530, Ilorin, Kwara State
Tel: +234(803) 191-5699 +234(703) 234-0536 +234(807) 983-0799
EMail: kwasu@kwasu.edu.ng
Website: http://www.kwasu.edu.ng

Vice-Chancellor: Abdul-Rasheed Na-Allah

Registrar: Modupe Oluyinka Akinrinmade

Centres

Community Development (Development Studies); **Ecological and Environmental Research, Management and Studies** (Environmental Studies; Health Sciences); **Entrepreneurship** (Management); **Innovation and International Studies** (International Studies); **Innovation in Teaching and Research** *(CITR)* (Chinese; Literature; Spanish)

Colleges

Agriculture and Veterinary Sciences (Agricultural Economics; Agriculture; Animal Husbandry; Aquaculture; Crop Production; Fishery; Veterinary Science); **Education** (Business Education; Education; Health Education; Physical Education; Preschool Education; Primary Education; Special Education; Teacher Training); **Engineering and Technology** *(CET)* (Aeronautical and Aerospace Engineering; Bioengineering; Chemical Engineering; Civil Engineering; Computer Engineering; Electrical and Electronic Engineering; Engineering; Environmental Engineering; Food Technology; Materials Engineering; Mechanical Engineering; Technology); **Humanities, Management and Social Sciences** (Accountancy; African Languages; Applied Linguistics; Arabic; Arts and Humanities; Banking; Business Administration; Christian Religious Studies; Economics; English; Finance; Hotel and Restaurant; Islamic Studies; Linguistics; Literature; Management; Social Sciences; Tourism); **Information and Communication Technology** (Computer Science; Information Technology; Library Science; Mass Communication); **Pure and Applied Sciences** (Biochemistry; Biological and Life Sciences; Biology; Biotechnology; Botany; Chemistry; Geology; Industrial Chemistry; Materials Engineering; Mathematics; Microbiology; Mineralogy; Physics; Statistics)

Schools

Visual and Performing Arts (Art Management; Cinema and Television; Dance; Film; Fine Arts; Music; Performing Arts; Theatre; Tourism; Visual Arts; Writing)

History: Founded 2009.

Governing Bodies: Governing Council; Senate

Main Language(s) of Instruction: English

Degrees and Diplomas: *Bachelor's Degree*; *Postgraduate Diploma*: Environmental Health; *Master's Degree*: Aeronautics and Astronautics Engineering; *Doctor of Philosophy*: Aeronautics and Astronautics Engineering. Also Diploma in Visual and Performing Arts, 18 months; Pre-Degree programmes.

Student Residential Facilities: Hostels

Special Facilities: Counselling and Career Services

Libraries: Yes

Last Updated: 13/07/12

LADOKE AKINTOLA UNIVERSITY OF TECHNOLOGY (LAUTECH)

P.M.B. 4000, Ogbomoso, Oyo State
Tel: +234(806) 762-4977 +234(806) 762-4952
EMail: contact@lautech.edu.ng
Website: http://www.lautech.edu.ng

Vice-Chancellor: A.S. Gbadegesin EMail: vc@lautech.edu.ng

Registrar: J. A. Agboola EMail: registrar@lautech.edu.ng

International Relations: Akintunde Yomi, Deputy Registrar

Colleges

Health Sciences (Anaesthesiology; Anatomy; Biochemistry; Gynaecology and Obstetrics; Haematology; Health Sciences; Histology; Laboratory Techniques; Medicine; Microbiology; Nursing; Ophthalmology; Otorhinolaryngology; Paediatrics; Pathology; Physiology; Psychiatry and Mental Health; Radiology; Surgery)

Faculties

Agricultural Sciences (Agricultural Economics; Agriculture; Animal Husbandry; Biotechnology; Crop Production; Environmental Management; Nutrition; Plant and Crop Protection; Rural Studies; Soil Science); **Engineering and Technology** (Agricultural Engineering; Chemical Engineering; Civil Engineering; Computer Engineering; Computer Science; Electrical and Electronic Engineering; Engineering; Food Science; Food Technology; Mechanical Engineering; Technology); **Environment Sciences** (Architecture; Fine Arts; Regional Planning; Town Planning); **Management Sciences** (Accountancy; Management; Transport Management); **Pure and Applied Science** (Applied Chemistry; Applied Mathematics; Applied Physics; Biological and Life Sciences; Biology; Chemistry; Earth Sciences; Laboratory Techniques; Mathematics; Physics)

Schools

Post-Graduate Studies (Agricultural Economics; Agronomy; Animal Husbandry; Biology; Computer Science; Crop Production; Engineering; Soil Science; Transport Management)

Further Information: Also Osogbo campus. A traditional and distance learning institution.

History: Founded 1990 as Oyo State University of Technology, acquired present title 1991.

Governing Bodies: Governing Council; Senate; Congregation

Academic Year: October to September

Admission Requirements: 5 '0' level credits including Mathematics, English Language, Biology, Chemistry, Physics

Fees: (Naira): Undergraduate tuition fee for indigenous students, 65,000 per session; For non-indigenous students, 72,500 per session. Postgraduate tuition fee for indigenous students, 65,000 per session; For non-indigenous students, 72,500 per session.

Main Language(s) of Instruction: English

International Co-operation: With universities in Sweden, Malaysia, China, Thailand, India, Japan, Vietnam

Accrediting Agencies: National Universities Commission (NUC) and Professional Bodies

Degrees and Diplomas: *Bachelor's Degree*; *Postgraduate Diploma*; *Master's Degree*; *Doctor of Philosophy*. Also Pre-Degree Programmes; Professional Diploma

Student Services: Academic counselling, Canteen, Employment services, Health services, Nursery care, Social counselling, Sports facilities

Student Residential Facilities: None

Special Facilities: Central Research Laboratory; Biotechnology Centre; Teaching/Research Farm; Earth Science Museum; Lipid Research Laboratory; Drawing Studio; Molecular Biology Laboratory; Engineering Workshops; Information and Technology Facilities

Libraries: 58,124 vols; 778 periodicals; e-library

Publications: International Journal of African Culture and Indigenous Studies *(quarterly)*; International Journal of Applied Agricultural and Apicultural Research, Journal published by the Faculty of Agricultural Sciences *(biannually)*; LAUTECH Journal of Computer Science and Engineering, Official publication of the department of Computer Science and Engineering made up of submissions from scholars and experts. *(biennially)*; Science Focus, International Journal of Biological and Physical Sciences *(quarterly)*

Press or Publishing House: LAUTECH Press

Last Updated: 13/07/12

LAGOS STATE UNIVERSITY (LASU)

PMB 01, Ojo, Lagos State
Tel: +234(1) 854-7000
EMail: info@lasunigeria.org
Website: http://www.lasu.edu.ng/

Vice-Chancellor: John Oladapo Obafunwa (2011-)
EMail: vicechancellor@lasunigeria.org

Registrar and Secretary: Oluwatoyin Gladstone Oshun
Tel: +234 803-304-8984
EMail: oshun_oluwatoyin@yahoo.com; oshuntoyin@hotmail.com

International Relations: Ibilola Ibiyemi Olatunji-Bello, Vice-Chancellor Tel: +234 803-4004-236 EMail: yemi2bello@yahoo.com

Centres

Environment and Science Education (Environmental Studies; Science Education)

Faculties

Arts (African Languages; Arabic; Arts and Humanities; Christian Religious Studies; Communication Arts; English; French; History; International Relations; Islamic Studies; Literature; Modern Languages; Music; Philosophy; Religious Studies; Theatre); **Education** (Curriculum; Education; Educational Administration; Health Education; Physical Education); **Engineering** (Chemical Engineering; Computer Engineering; Electronic Engineering; Engineering; Mechanical Engineering; Polymer and Plastics Technology); **Law** (Law); **Management Sciences** (Accountancy; Business Administration; Finance; Human Resources; Labour and Industrial Relations; Management; Public Administration); **Medicine** (Medicine; Surgery); **Science** (Aquaculture; Biochemistry; Biology; Botany; Chemistry; Computer Science; Fishery; Mathematics; Microbiology; Physics; Zoology); **Social Science** (Economics; Geography; Political Sciences; Sociology)

Schools

Communication (Communication Studies; Mass Communication); **Postgraduate Studies** (Administrative Law; Advertising and Publicity; African Languages; Anatomy; Applied Mathematics; Arabic; Biochemistry; Botany; Business Administration; Chemical Engineering; Chemistry; Christian Religious Studies; Commercial Law; Communication Studies; Community Health; Computer Education; Computer Engineering; Curriculum; Economics; Education; Educational Administration; Educational and Student Counselling; Educational Psychology; Educational Technology; Electronic Engineering; English; Environmental Management; Environmental Studies; Fishery; Foreign Languages Education; Forensic Medicine and Dentistry; Geography; Health Administration; Health Education; History; Human Resources; International Business; International Law; International Relations; International Studies; Islamic Law; Journalism; Labour and Industrial Relations; Labour Law; Management; Maritime Law; Marketing; Mass Communication; Mathematics; Mathematics Education; Mechanical Engineering; Microbiology; Natural Resources; Occupational Health; Parks and Recreation; Pathology; Physical Education; Physics; Physiology; Polymer and Plastics Technology; Public Administration; Public Health; Public Relations; Radio and Television Broadcasting; Regional Planning; Science Education; Social Work; Sociology; Statistics; Technology Education; Tourism; Town Planning; Transport and Communications; Zoology)

History: Founded 1983, acquired present status and title 1984.

Governing Bodies: Council; Senate

Academic Year: September to July

Admission Requirements: Universities Matriculation Examination (UME) following secondary school education, or direct entry for holders of the Higher School Certificate (General Certificate of Education, Advanced ('A') Level)

Main Language(s) of Instruction: English

International Co-operation: With universities in Ghana; USA; United Kingdom

Accrediting Agencies: National Universities Commission; Council for Legal Education in Nigeria; Medical and Dental Council in Nigeria; Council for Regulation of Engineering in Nigeria

Degrees and Diplomas: *Bachelor's Degree (BSs; BA)*: 3-5 yrs; *Postgraduate Diploma (PGD)*: 1-2 yrs; *Master's Degree*; *Master of Philosophy (MPhil)*: a further 1-2 yrs; *Doctor of Philosophy (PhD)*: 2-3 yrs. Also Diplomas; MBA; Professional Masters

Student Services: Academic counselling, Canteen, Cultural centre, Foreign Studies Centre, Health services, Nursery care, Social counselling, Sports facilities

Special Facilities: Language Laboratory; Radio Station; Museum; Radiation Monitoring Laboratory

Libraries: c. 60,000 vols; 3,000 academic journal subscriptions; 200 local journal and newspapers subscriptions. Special collection: railway archives

Publications: Compendium of Academic Publications *(annually)*

Press or Publishing House: Lasu Press

Last Updated: 13/07/12

MARITIME ACADEMY OF NIGERIA, ORON

4, College Road, Oron
Tel: +234(703) 005-2564 +234(807) 203-4148 +234(1) 738-4132
EMail: maritimeacademysupport@fleettechltd.com
Website: http://www.maritimeacademyportal.org/

Programmes

Boat/Shipbuilding Technology (Marine Transport); **Electrical and Electronic Engineering** (Electrical and Electronic Engineering); **Marine Engineering** (Marine Engineering); **Marine Transport** *(Post Graduate Diploma)*; **Marine Transport and Business Studies** (Business Administration; Marine Transport); **Nautical Science** (Nautical Science); **Shipping Transport Management** *(Post Graduate)* (Transport Management)

History: Founded 1979. Acquired present status 1988. Formerly known and addressed as the Nautical College of Nigeria.

Main Language(s) of Instruction: English

Accrediting Agencies: National Board for Technical Education (NBTE)

Degrees and Diplomas: *National Diploma*; *Higher National Diploma*; *Postgraduate Diploma*

Student Residential Facilities: Yes

Last Updated: 09/10/12

MICHAEL OKPARA UNIVERSITY OF AGRICULTURE UMUDIKE (MOUAU)

PMB 7267, Umuahia, Umudike, Abia State
Tel: +234(82) 440-555
Fax: +234(82) 441-595
EMail: info@mouau.edu.ng
Website: http://www.mouau.edu.ng/

Vice-Chancellor: Hilary O. Edeoga (2011-)
EMail: vicechancellor@mouau.org

Registrar: A. C. Nwokocha EMail: registrar@mouau.org

Centres

Continuing Education *(CEC)*

Colleges

Agribusiness and Financial Management *(CABFM)* (Agricultural Business; Finance; Management); **Agricultural Economics, Rural Sociology and Extension** *(CAERSE)* (Agricultural Economics; Rural Studies; Sociology); **Animal Science and Animal Production** *(CASAP)* (Animal Husbandry); **Applied Food Science and Tourism** *(CAFST)* (Dietetics; Food Science; Nutrition; Tourism); **Crop and Soil Science** *(CCSS)* (Crop Production; Soil Science); **Engineering and Engineering Technology** *(CEET)* (Engineering; Technology); **Natural and Applied Science** *(CNAS)* (Natural Sciences); **Natural Resources and Environmental Management** *(CNREM)* (Environmental Management; Natural Resources); **Veterinary Medicine** *(CVM)* (Veterinary Science)

Schools

Post Graduate Studies *(PGS)*

History: Founded 1993.

Governing Bodies: Governing Council

Academic Year: January to October

Admission Requirements: Universities Matriculation Examination (UME) following secondary school education, or direct entry.

Main Language(s) of Instruction: English

Accrediting Agencies: National Universities Commission

Degrees and Diplomas: *Bachelor's Degree*; *Master's Degree*; *Doctor of Philosophy (PhD)*

Student Services: Academic counselling, Canteen, Health services, Language programs, Social counselling, Sports facilities

Student Residential Facilities: Yes

Libraries: c. 17,000 vols, c. 360 periodical subscriptions

Publications: Journal of Sustainable Agriculture and the Environment (JSAE), International journal which publishes results of original research and special reviews *(biannually)*

Last Updated: 13/07/12

MODIBBO ADAMA UNIVERSITY OF TECHNOLOGY, YOLA (MAUTECH, YOLA)

PMB 2076, Yola, Adamawa State 640001
Tel: +234 (80) 659-80380 +234 (80) 361-62740
EMail: vc@mautech.edu.ng
Website: http://www.mautech.edu.ng/

Vice-Chancellor: Bashir Haruna Usman (2009-2014)
Tel: +234(80) 342-26485, Fax: +234(75) 625-176

Registrar, Chief Aministrative Officer: Ahmed Usman Wurochekke
Tel: +234 (80) 342-26485 EMail: registrar@mautech.edu.ng

International Relations: Mustafa Usman Migawa, Information and Public Relation Officer
Tel: +234(80) 240-40140 EMail: mustafamigawa@yahoo.co.uk

Schools

Agriculture and Agricultural Technology *(SAAT)* (Agricultural Economics; Agriculture; Animal Husbandry; Crop Production; Fishery; Food Science; Food Technology; Forestry; Horticulture; Plant and Crop Protection; Soil Science; Wildlife; Zoology); **Engineering and Engineering Technology** *(SEET)* (Agricultural Engineering; Chemical Engineering; Civil Engineering; Electrical and Electronic Engineering; Electrical Engineering; Electronic Engineering; Environmental Engineering; Mechanical Engineering); **Environmental Sciences** *(SES)* (Architecture; Building Technologies; Geography; Industrial Design; Regional Planning; Surveying and Mapping; Town Planning); **Management and Information Technology** *(SMIT)* (Accountancy; Economics; Information Sciences; Information Technology; Library Science; Management); **Post Graduate Studies** *(SPGS)* (Agricultural Economics; Agricultural Education; Agricultural Engineering; Agricultural Equipment; Agronomy; Analytical Chemistry; Animal Husbandry; Aquaculture; Architecture; Architecture and Planning; Biochemistry; Biological and Life Sciences; Biology; Botany; Business Administration; Ceramics and Glass Technology; Chemical Engineering; Chemistry; Computer Science; Construction Engineering; Crop Production; Educational Administration; Electrical and Electronic Engineering; Electrical Engineering; Electronic Engineering; Engineering Management; English; Entomology; Environmental Engineering; Environmental Management; Fishery; Food Science; Food Technology; Forest Management; Forest Products; Forestry; Genetics; Geography; Geology; Geophysics; Harvest Technology; Horticulture; Humanities and Social Science Education; Industrial Chemistry; Industrial Engineering; Information Management; Information Technology; Management; Mathematics; Mathematics and Computer Science; Mathematics Education; Mechanical Engineering; Microbiology; Mineralogy; Natural Resources; Operations Research; Organic Chemistry; Parasitology; Peace and Disarmament; Physical Chemistry; Physics; Physiology; Plant and Crop Protection; Plant Pathology; Polymer and Plastics Technology; Power Engineering; Public Administration; Public Health; Regional Planning; Rural Planning; Science Education; Soil Science; Surveying and Mapping; Technology; Technology Education; Town Planning; Water Science; Wildlife; Zoology); **Pure and Applied Sciences** *(SPAS)* (Biochemistry; Biological and Life Sciences; Botany; Chemistry; Computer Science; Geology; Industrial Chemistry; Mathematics; Mathematics and Computer Science; Microbiology; Natural Sciences; Operations Research; Physics; Statistics; Zoology); **Technology and Science Education** *(STSE)* (Agriculture; Automotive Engineering; Biology; Building Technologies; Chemistry; Computer Education; Design; Electrical and Electronic Engineering; Fine Arts; Geography; Heating and Refrigeration; Home Economics; Library Science; Mathematics Education; Physics; Printing and Printmaking; Science Education; Statistics; Technology Education; Vocational Education; Wood Technology)

Further Information: A traditional and Distance Learning institution.

History: Founded 1981. First set of 214 students admitted 1982. Merged with the University of Maiduguri and became Modibbo Adama College Campus of University of Maiduguri 1984. Separated and granted full autonomy with the name reverted to Federal University of Technology, Yola 1988. Acquired present title 2011.

Governing Bodies: Governing Council; Senate

Academic Year: October to July

Admission Requirements: University Tertiary Matriculation Examination (UTME) with minimum of five (5) 'O" level credits in WAEC, NECO, NABTECH or Direct Entry and Advance A' Level results for holders of Diploma and National Certificate of Education (NCE) certificates.

Fees: (Naira): Undergraduate programmes, 29,240-37,990 per annum for national students and 54,490-62,990 per annum for foreign students; Postgraduate Diplomas, 56,200 per annum for national students and 81,200 per annum for foreign students; Master's degrees, 66,200-71,200 per annum for national students and 91,200-106,200 per annum for foreign students; MBA, 156,200 per annum for national students and 256,200 per annum for foreign students; MPA, 126,000 per annum for national students and 206,000 per annum for foreign students; Ph.D., 106,200 per annum for national students and 156,200 per annum for foreign students.

Main Language(s) of Instruction: English

International Co-operation: Collaborations with institutions in Israel, Poland, USA, Turkey, United Kingdom; World Bank's Science and Technology Post Basic (STEP-B) Projects and German Consulate in Nigeria

Accrediting Agencies: National Universities Commission (NUC)

Degrees and Diplomas: *National Diploma*: 2 yrs; *Bachelor's Degree (B.Sc.)*: 4-6 yrs; *Bachelor's Degree (B.Tech.)*: 5-8 yrs; *Postgraduate Diploma (P.G.D.)*: 1-2 yrs; *Master's Degree (M.Tech; M.Sc.)*: 1-2 yrs; *Doctor of Philosophy (Ph.D.)*: 3-5 yrs

Student Services: Academic counselling, Canteen, Foreign Studies Centre, Health services, Nursery care, Social counselling, Sports facilities

Student Residential Facilities: Junior and Senior Staff Quarters; Professors Staff Quarter; University Lodges

Libraries: 34,529 vols; 1,516 e-journals; E-resources

Publications: Journal of Technology, Academic Journal *(annually)*; MAUTECH News, Magazine publication produced by the Information and Publicity Unit in the office of the Vice Chancellor. It reports the events and activities of the university to the outside world *(quarterly)*

Academic Staff *2011-2012*	MEN	WOMEN	**TOTAL**
FULL-TIME	410	25	**435**
PART-TIME	859	142	**1,001**
STAFF WITH DOCTORATE			
FULL-TIME	134	9	**143**
Student Numbers *2011-2012*			
All (Foreign Included)	10,266	3,422	**13,688**
FOREIGN ONLY	1,076	195	**1,271**

Last Updated: 05/06/12

NASARAWA STATE UNIVERSITY (NSUK)

PMB 1022, Keffi, Nasarawa State
EMail: nsukeffi@yahoo.co.uk
Website: http://www.nsukonline.com/big_index.php

Vice-Chancellor: Shamsudeen O. O. Amali
EMail: vcnsuk@nsuk.edu.ng

Registrar: Dalhatu Odoga Mamman Ficen
EMail: registrar@nsuk.edu.ng; dalhatuodoga@yahoo.co.uk

International Relations: James Otuka
EMail: jimotuka@yahoo.com

Faculties

Administration (Accountancy; Administration; Banking; Business Administration; Finance; Management; Public Administration); **Agriculture** (Agricultural Economics; Agriculture; Agronomy; Animal Husbandry; Fishery; Forestry; Home Economics; Management; Wildlife); **Arts** (African Languages; Arts and Humanities; Cultural Studies; English; History; Linguistics; Mass Communication; Modern Languages; Religious Studies; Theatre); **Education** (Art Education; Education; Humanities and Social Science Education; Mathematics Education; Science Education; Technology Education); **Law** (Civil Law; Law); **Natural Sciences** (Biochemistry; Biological and Life Sciences; Chemistry; Geology; Mathematics; Mining Engineering; Molecular Biology; Natural Sciences; Physics); **Social Sciences** (Economics; Geography; Political Sciences; Psychology; Social Sciences; Sociology)

Schools

Postgraduate Studies (Accountancy; Actuarial Science; Agricultural Economics; Agriculture; Agronomy; Animal Husbandry; Arabic; Biotechnology; Botany; Business Administration; Clinical Psychology; Education; Educational Administration; Educational Psychology; Educational Testing and Evaluation; English; Environmental Management; Farm Management; Finance; Geography; Geology; History; Human Resources; Industrial and Organizational Psychology; Industrial Chemistry; Insurance; International Studies; Law; Linguistics; Management; Marketing; Mathematics; Mathematics Education; Meteorology; Mining Engineering; Modern Languages; Natural Resources; Petroleum and Gas Engineering; Physics; Plant and Crop Protection; Political Sciences; Psychology; Public Administration; Science Education; Sociology; Soil Management; Water Management)

Units

Remedial Studies (Biology; Chemistry; French; Geography; Mathematics; Physics)

Further Information: Also Lafia and Pyanku Campuses. A traditional, open and distance learning insitution.

History: Founded 2002.

Governing Bodies: Council, Senate, Faculty Boards

Admission Requirements: Five credits in the Senior Secondary Certificate Examination or equivalent in addition to acceptable score in the Joint Matriculation Examination

Fees: (Naira): 18,000-27,000 per annum

Main Language(s) of Instruction: English

Accrediting Agencies: National Universities Commission

Degrees and Diplomas: *Bachelor's Degree*: 4-5 yrs; *Postgraduate Diploma*: 1 yr; *Master's Degree*: 1-2 yrs; *Doctor of Philosophy*: 2 yrs. Also Certificate and Advanced Certificate Programme in IT and Applications; MBA

Student Services: Academic counselling, Canteen, Health services, Language programs, Nursery care, Sports facilities

Student Residential Facilities: Yes

Libraries: Yes

Publications: Keffi Journal of Educational Studies; Nasara Journal of Humanities; Nasara Scientific; Nasarawa State University Law Journal; Nasarawa University Journal of Administration *(quarterly)*; Production Agriculture and Technology; The Nigerian Journal of Social Research

Academic Staff *2010-2011*	MEN	WOMEN	**TOTAL**
FULL-TIME			**250**
STAFF WITH DOCTORATE			
FULL-TIME	–	–	**50**
PART-TIME	–	–	c. **10**
Student Numbers *2010-2011*			
All (Foreign Included)	6,330	3,670	c. **10,000**

Last Updated: 13/07/12

NATIONAL OPEN UNIVERSITY OF NIGERIA (NOUN)

14/16 Ahmadu Bello Way, Victoria Island, Lagos, Lagos State
Tel: +234(807) 507-491 +234(1) 818-8849 +234(1) 482-0720
Fax: +234(1) 271-2665
EMail: registrar@nou.edu.ng; centralinfo@nou.edu.ng
Website: http://www.nou.edu.ng/

Vice-Chancellor: Vincent A. Tenebe
Tel: +234(80)23-53-38-17
EMail: vc@nou.edu.ng; vtenebe@nou.edu.ng

Registrar: Josephine Olasumbo Akinyemi
Tel: +234(1) 818-8849, Fax: +234(1) 267-1098
EMail: registrar@nou.edu.ng

International Relations: Fatai Lawal, Senior Legal Officer
EMail: fatailawal2001@yahoo.com

Centres

Access and General Studies (Biology; Chemistry; English; Literature; Mathematics; Physics); **Lifelong Learning and Workplace Training**

Research Institutes

Regional Training for Open and Distance Learning *(RETRIDAL)* (Distance Education; Educational Sciences)

Schools

Arts and Social Sciences (Arts and Humanities; Christian Religious Studies; Criminology; English; French; International Studies; Islamic Studies; Journalism; Peace and Disarmament; Political Sciences; Protective Services; Social Sciences; Theology); **Education** (Agricultural Education; Business Education; Chemistry; Computer Education; Education; English; Foreign Languages Education; French; Mathematics Education; Physics; Preschool Education; Primary Education; Science Education); **Law** (Law); **Management Sciences** (Accountancy; Banking; Business Administration; Cooking and Catering; Finance; Government; Hotel and Restaurant; Human Resources; Management; Public Administration; Tourism); **Science and Technology** (Agricultural Management; Community Health; Computer Science; Data Processing; Environmental Management; Environmental Studies; Information Technology; Mathematics; Natural Resources; Nursing; Physics; Technology)

Further Information: A traditional, open and distance education institution.

History: Founded 2002.

Governing Bodies: Governing Council

Main Language(s) of Instruction: English

Accrediting Agencies: National Universities Commission (NUC) and Professional Organisations

Degrees and Diplomas: *Bachelor's Degree*; *Postgraduate Diploma*; *Master's Degree*; *Doctor of Philosophy*: Education. Also Certificates and Diplomas.

Student Services: Academic counselling

Libraries: E-Library

Last Updated: 13/07/12

NIGER DELTA UNIVERSITY (NDU)

PMB 071, Wilberforce Island, Amassoma, Bayelsa State
Tel: +234(703) 652-4826
EMail: info@ndu.edu.ng
Website: http://www.ndu.edu.ng

Vice-Chancellor: Chris Ikporukpo EMail: vc@ndu.edu.ng

Registrar: Tonbra Morris-odubo

Colleges

Health Sciences (Health Sciences; Laboratory Techniques; Medicine; Nursing; Pharmacy)

Faculties

Agricultural Technology (Agricultural Economics; Animal Husbandry; Aquaculture; Crop Production; Environmental Management; Fishery; Genetics; Physiology; Rural Studies; Sociology; Soil Science); **Arts** (Arts and Humanities; Christian Religious Studies; English; Fine Arts; History; International Relations; Linguistics; Literature; Philosophy; Theatre); **Education** (Adult Education; Art Education; Business Education; Curriculum; Education; English; Foreign Languages Education; French; Health Education; Industrial Arts Education; Mathematics Education; Physical Education; Political Sciences; Technology Education; Vocational Education); **Engineering** (Agricultural Engineering; Chemical Engineering; Civil Engineering; Electrical and Electronic Engineering; Engineering; Environmental Engineering; Marine Engineering; Mechanical Engineering; Petroleum and Gas Engineering; Water Science); **Law** (Civil Law); **Management Sciences** (Accountancy; Banking; Business Administration; Finance; Insurance; Management; Marketing); **Sciences** (Analytical Chemistry; Applied Chemistry; Biochemistry; Biological and Life Sciences; Biology; Chemistry; Computer Science; Geology; Geophysics; Industrial Chemistry; Inorganic Chemistry; Mathematics; Microbiology; Parasitology; Physical Chemistry; Physics); **Social Sciences** (Economics; Environmental Management; Food Science; Geography; Meteorology; Political Sciences; Social Sciences; Sociology; Transport and Communications; Waste Management; Water Management; Water Science)

Further Information: Also Centre for Niger Delta Studies

History: Founded 2000.

Governing Bodies: Governing Council; Senate

Fees: (Naira): Tuition fee, 20,000 per session

Main Language(s) of Instruction: English

Accrediting Agencies: National Universities Commission (NUC)

Degrees and Diplomas: *Bachelor's Degree*; *Postgraduate Diploma*: Aquaculture; Fisheries Biology and Management; Aquatic Environmental Management; Animal Science; *Master's Degree*; *Doctor of Philosophy (PhD)*

Last Updated: 16/07/12

NIGERIAN DEFENCE ACADEMY, KADUNA (NDA)

Kaduna, Kaduna State
Tel: +234(819) 193-3775
EMail: info@nda.edu.ng
Website: http://www.nda.edu.ng/

Commandant: Emeka Onwumaegbu

Registrar: H.E. Ayamasaowei

Departments

Military Training (Military Science)

Faculties

Art and Social Sciences (Accountancy; Arabic; Arts and Humanities; Demography and Population; Economics; Environmental Management; French; Geography; Geography (Human); History; International Studies; Management; Meteorology; Military Science; Modern Languages; Social Sciences; Surveying and Mapping); **Engineering** (Civil Engineering; Electrical Engineering; Electronic Engineering; Engineering; Mechanical Engineering; Power Engineering; Production Engineering; Telecommunications Engineering; Thermal Engineering); **Sciences** (Analytical Chemistry; Biological and Life Sciences; Botany; Chemistry; Computer Science; Environmental Management; Inorganic Chemistry; Marine Biology; Materials Engineering; Mathematics; Natural Sciences; Nuclear Physics; Operations Research; Organic Chemistry; Parasitology; Physical Chemistry; Physics; Solid State Physics; Zoology)

Further Information: A traditional and distance learning institution.

History: Founded 1964.

Main Language(s) of Instruction: English

Accrediting Agencies: National Universities Commission (NUC)

Degrees and Diplomas: *Bachelor's Degree*; *Master's Degree*; *Doctor of Philosophy*

Last Updated: 04/10/12

IAU NNAMDI AZIKIWE UNIVERSITY

PMB 5025, Along Enugu - Onitsha Express Way, Awka, Anambra State
Tel: +234(4) 55-0018
Fax: +234(4) 55-3061
EMail: info@unizik.edu.ng
Website: http://www.unizik.edu.ng/

Vice-Chancellor: Boniface Egboka (2009-)
Tel: +234(48) 550-018, Fax: +234(48) 553-061
EMail: vc@unizik.edu.ng

Deputy Vice Chancellor (Administration): Benchucks Okeke
EMail: dvc_admin@unizik.edu.ng

Registrar: C. C. Okeke EMail: registrar@unizik.edu.ng

International Relations: Francis Chukwuemeka Ezeonu, Director, International Cooperation
Tel: 234 803 6686 326 EMail: dir_ic@unizik.edu.ng

Faculties

Agriculture (Agricultural Economics; Agriculture; Animal Husbandry; Crop Production; Food Science; Horticulture); **Arts** (African Studies; Asian Studies; English; European Languages; Fine Arts; History; International Studies; Linguistics; Modern Languages; Music; Philosophy; Religion; Theatre); **Basic Medical Sciences** (Anatomy; Biochemistry; Physiology); **Biosciences** (Biochemistry; Biological and Life Sciences; Botany; Entomology; Microbiology; Parasitology; Zoology); **Education** (Adult Education; Business Education; Education; Educational Administration; Health Education; Information Sciences; Library Science; Physical Education; Preschool Education; Primary Education; Science Education; Vocational Education); **Engineering** (Agricultural Engineering; Chemical Engineering; Civil Engineering; Computer Engineering; Electrical Engineering; Electronic Engineering; Engineering; Industrial Engineering; Materials Engineering; Mechanical Engineering; Metallurgical Engineering; Polymer and Plastics Technology; Production Engineering; Textile Technology); **Environmental Sciences** (Architecture; Building Technologies; Computer Science; Earth Sciences; Environmental Management; Environmental Studies; Fine Arts; Geography; Meteorology; Real Estate; Surveying and Mapping); **Health Sciences/Technology** (Health Sciences; Laboratory Techniques; Nursing; Physical Therapy; Radiology; Technology); **Law** (Law); **Management Sciences** (Accountancy; Banking; Business Administration; Economics; Finance; Management; Marketing; Public Administration); **Medicine** (Medicine); **Pharmaceutical Sciences** (Pharmacy); **Physical Sciences** (Applied Physics; Chemistry; Computer Science; Geology; Industrial Chemistry; Mathematics; Physics; Statistics); **Social Sciences** (Anthropology; Economics; Mass Communication; Political Sciences; Psychology; Social Sciences; Sociology)

Further Information: Also Teaching Hospital, Nnewi

History: Founded 1980 as Anambra State University of Technology. Acquired present status 1991.

Governing Bodies: Council

Academic Year: November to August (November-March; April-August)

Admission Requirements: Five credits in West African School Certificate (WASC), Senior Secondary Certificate Examination (SSCE) or General Certificate of Education (GCE) 'O' level, with minimum grade C and including English language. For direct entry, candidates must possess a higher qualification from an accredited university or polytechnic

Fees: (Naira): Tuition, undergraduate, 5,000-9,400 per annum

Main Language(s) of Instruction: English

Degrees and Diplomas: *Bachelor's Degree*: Arts, Science, Education, 4 yrs; *Bachelor's Degree*: Engineering, Law, 5 yrs; *Bachelor's Degree*: Medicine, Surgery, 6 yrs; *Postgraduate Diploma*: 1 1/2 yrs; *Master's Degree*: a further 1 1/2-2 yrs; *Doctor of Philosophy (PhD)*: minimum 3 yrs. Also Diplomas and Certificates

Student Services: Academic counselling, Canteen, Health services, Sports facilities

Libraries: Main Library, c. 70,000 vols; 73 periodicals

Last Updated: 16/07/12

OBAFEMI AWOLOWO UNIVERSITY (OAU)

Ile-Ife, Osun State
Tel: +234(36) 231-822
EMail: registra@oauife.edu.ng
Website: http://www.oauife.edu.ng

Vice-Chancellor: Idowu Bamitale Omole (2011-2016)
Tel: +234(36) 233-128

Deputy Vice-Chancellor, Administration: Jimi Adesanya

Registrar: Ayorinde Olurinde Ogunruku

Colleges

Health Sciences (Anatomy; Community Health; Dentistry; Medicine; Nursing; Pathology; Physical Therapy; Physiology; Psychiatry and Mental Health; Rehabilitation and Therapy); **Postgraduate** (Administration; Agriculture; Architecture; Arts and Humanities; Dentistry; Environmental Studies; Fine Arts; Health Sciences; Law; Medicine; Pharmacy; Social Sciences)

Faculties

Administration (Accountancy; Government; International Relations; Management; Public Administration); **Agriculture** (Agricultural Economics; Agriculture; Animal Husbandry; Food Science; Food Technology; Nutrition; Rural Studies; Soil Science; Zoology); **Arts** (African Languages; Archaeology; Arts and Humanities; English; Fine Arts; French; German; History; Linguistics; Literature; Music; Philosophy; Portuguese; Religious Studies; Theatre); **Basic Medical Sciences** (Anatomy; Community Health; Dermatology; Epidemiology; Forensic Medicine and Dentistry; Gynaecology and Obstetrics; Haematology; Immunology; Microbiology; Nursing; Nutrition; Paediatrics; Parasitology; Pathology; Physiology; Psychiatry and Mental Health; Rehabilitation and Therapy; Venereology); **Clinical Sciences** (Medicine; Radiology; Surgery); **Dentistry** (Dentistry; Oral Pathology; Social and Preventive Medicine; Surgery); **Education** (African Languages; Art Education; Biology; Botany; Chemistry; Continuing Education; Curriculum; Economics; Education; Educational Administration; Educational and Student Counselling; Educational Technology; English; Fine Arts; Foreign Languages Education; French; Geography; Geography (Human); Health Education; History; Humanities and Social Science Education; Mathematics; Mathematics Education; Music; Music Education; Native Language Education; Physical Education; Physics; Political Sciences; Preschool Education; Religious Studies; Social Studies; Special Education); **Environmental Design and Management** (Architectural and Environmental Design; Architecture; Building Technologies; Fine Arts; Real Estate; Regional Planning; Rural Planning; Surveying and Mapping; Town Planning); **Law** (Commercial Law; International Law; Law; Private Law; Public Law); **Pharmacy** (Alternative Medicine; Biochemistry; Inorganic Chemistry; Organic Chemistry; Pathology; Pharmacology; Pharmacy; Physical Chemistry; Toxicology); **Science** (Biochemistry; Botany; Chemistry; Computer Science; Geology; Geophysics; Mathematics; Microbiology; Natural Sciences; Physics; Statistics; Zoology); **Social Sciences** (Anthropology; Demography and Population; Economics; Geography (Human); International Relations; Philosophy; Political Sciences; Psychology; Social Sciences; Sociology; Statistics); **Technology** (Agricultural Engineering; Chemical Engineering; Civil Engineering; Computer Engineering; Computer Science; Electrical and Electronic Engineering; Food Science; Food Technology; Materials Engineering; Mechanical Engineering; Metallurgical Engineering; Technology)

Further Information: A traditional and distance education institution.

History: Founded 1961 as University of Ife, acquired present title 1987.

Governing Bodies: Council; Senate

Academic Year: January to December (January-June; July-December)

Admission Requirements: Universities Matriculation Examination (UME), or five credits passes in relevant subjects at Senior Secondary Certificate (SSC) level, or at School Certificate/General Certificate of Education 'O' level in no more than two sittings.

Fees: (US Dollars): Foreign students, c. 1,000-2,000 per annum

Main Language(s) of Instruction: English

Degrees and Diplomas: *Bachelor's Degree*: 4 yrs; *Bachelor's Degree*: Health Sciences; Pharmacy; Engineering, 5 yrs; *Bachelor's Degree*: Medicine (MBBS), 6 yrs; *Master's Degree*: a further 1 1/2-2 yrs; *Master of Philosophy*; *Doctor of Philosophy (PhD)*: a further 2 yrs

Student Services: Sports facilities

Student Residential Facilities: 10 undergraduate hostels and 1 postgraduate hall of residence

Special Facilities: Power station; Dam; Water treatment plant; Obafemi Awolowo University Staff School; Obafemi Awolowo University International School

Libraries: Central Library (The Hezekiah Oluwasanmi Library): 645,553 vols; c. 7,000 periodicals; Africana collection; audio-visual materials; government documents

Publications: African Journal of Philosophy *(biannually)*; Ife Journal of Science; Ife Journal of Technology; Ife Studies in African Literature and the Arts; Ife Studies in English Language; Obafemi Awolowo University Law Reports *(quarterly)*; Odu: a Journal of West African Studies *(biannually)*; Quarterly Journal of Administration

Press or Publishing House: University Press

Student Numbers *2011-2012*: Total: c. 35,000
Last Updated: 16/07/12

OLABISI ONABANJO UNIVERSITY (OOU)

PMB 2002, Ago-Iwoye, Ogun State
Tel: +234(37) 432-384 +234(8) 0586-96202
EMail: anujah@yahoo.com; femioyewole4@yahoo.com
Website: http://www.oouagoiwoye.edu.ng/

Deputy Vice-Chancellor: Wale Are Olaitan
Tel: +234(805) 869-6203 EMail: aujah@yahoo.com

Registar: Oyewole Emmanuel Olufemi Tel: +234(8) 058-696-216

Colleges

Agricultural Sciences *(Aiyetoro Campus)* (Agricultural Business; Agricultural Economics; Agricultural Management; Agriculture; Crop Production; Farm Management; Fishery; Forestry; Home Economics; Hotel Management; Rural Studies; Sociology; Soil Science); **Engineering and Environmental Studies** *(Ibogun Campus)* (Agricultural Engineering; Architectural Restoration; Architecture; Computer Engineering; Design; Electrical and Electronic Engineering; Fine Arts; Mechanical Engineering; Regional Planning; Town Planning); **Health Sciences** *(Obefami Alowolo)* (Anaesthesiology; Anatomy; Biochemistry; Community Health; Gynaecology and Obstetrics; Haematology; Health Sciences; Histology; Medicine; Microbiology; Ophthalmology; Orthopaedics; Paediatrics; Pathology; Pharmacology; Physiology; Public Health; Radiology; Surgery)

Faculties

Arts *(Ago-Iwoye Campus)* (African Languages; Arts and Humanities; Christian Religious Studies; English; French; History; International Relations; Islamic Studies; Mass Communication; Modern Languages; Native Language; Performing Arts; Philosophy; Religious Studies); **Basic Medical Sciences** *(Ikenne/Shagamu Campus)* (Anatomy; Biochemistry; Haematology; Histology; Microbiology; Parasitology; Pathology; Pharmacology; Physiology); **Clinical Sciences** *(Ikenne/Shagamu Campus)* (Anaesthesiology; Community Health; Gynaecology and Obstetrics; Medicine; Paediatrics; Radiology; Surgery); **Education** *(Ago-Iwoye Campus)* (Biology; Business Education; Chemistry; Curriculum; Education; Educational Administration; Educational Technology; English; Foreign Languages Education; French; Health Education; Humanities and Social Science Education; Mathematics Education; Native Language Education; Physical Education; Physics; Political Sciences; Preschool Education; Primary Education; Religious Education; Science Education; Secretarial Studies; Social Studies); **Law** *(Ago-Iwoye Campus)* (Commercial Law; International Law; Law; Private Law; Public Law); **Management** (Accountancy; Banking; Business Administration; Economics; Finance; Management); **Pharmacy** *(Ikenne/Shagamu Campus)* (Biological and Life Sciences; Microbiology; Pharmacology; Pharmacy); **Science** *(Ago-Iwoye Campus)* (Biochemistry; Botany; Chemistry; Computer Science; Earth Sciences; Geography; Geology; Geophysics; Industrial Chemistry; Mathematics; Mathematics and Computer Science; Microbiology; Physics; Regional Planning; Statistics; Zoology); **Social Sciences and Management Sciences** *(Ago-Iwoye Campus)* (Accountancy; Banking; Business Administration; Economics; Geography; Geography (Human); Labour and Industrial Relations; Mass Communication; Political Sciences; Psychology; Public Administration; Regional Planning; Social Sciences; Sociology; Transport Management)

Institutes

Education (Education)

Schools

Postgraduate Studies (Agricultural Business; Agricultural Economics; Analytical Chemistry; Animal Husbandry; Applied Chemistry; Biochemistry; Business Administration; Business and Commerce; Christian Religious Studies; Crop Production; Curriculum; Economics; Education; Educational Administration; Educational and Student Counselling; Farm Management; Health Education; Industrial Chemistry; International Relations; Islamic Theology; Labour and Industrial Relations; Management; Microbiology; Pathology; Physical Education; Psychology; Public Administration; Public Relations; Rural Studies; Soil Science; Sports Management; Transport and Communications; Zoology)

Further Information: Also Teaching Hospital. Campuses in Aiyetoro, Ibogun, Shagamu, Ijebu-Igbo, Ikenne. A traditional and distance learning institution.

History: Founded 1982 as Ogun State University. Acquired present status and title 2001. One of the University's distinctive characteristics is the adoption of an innovative programme of compulsory credit-earning courses on modern agricultural and rural life, Nigerian life and culture for all students in their first 2 years of study.

Governing Bodies: Council

Academic Year: October to July (October-March; March-July)

Admission Requirements: Universities Matriculation Examination (UME) following secondary school education, or direct entry for holders of the Higher School Certificate (General Certificate of Education, Advanced 'A' Level)

Fees: Varies by Programme/per year

Main Language(s) of Instruction: English

International Co-operation: North-Western University, Evanston, Illinois USA; University of Jyvaskyja, Finland; University of Winneba, Ghana; University of Antigua, West Indies; University of South Africa

Accrediting Agencies: National Universities Commission

Degrees and Diplomas: *Bachelor's Degree*: Agriculture (Bagric); Science; Social Sciences; Management (BSc), 3-5 yrs; *Bachelor's Degree*: Arts (BA), 3-4 yrs; *Bachelor's Degree*: Medicine; Surgery (MB; ChB), 5-6 yrs; *Bachelor's Degree*: Pharmacy (Bpharm), 4-5 yrs; *Postgraduate Diploma*; *Master's Degree*; *Master of Philosophy*: 1 further yr; *Doctor of Philosophy (PhD)*

Student Services: Academic counselling, Health services, Nursery care, Sports facilities

Student Residential Facilities: Yes (off campus)

Special Facilities: Language Laboratory, Audio Visual Centre

Libraries: Main Library, c. 30,000 vols
Last Updated: 16/07/12

ONDO STATE UNIVERSITY OF SCIENCE AND TECHNOLOGY (OSUSTECH)

PMB 353, Km. 6 Okitipupa-Igbokoda Road, Okitipupa, Ondo State
Tel: +234(709) 880-9476 +234(703) 227-0305
EMail: info@osustech.edu.ng
Website: http://www.osustech.edu.ng

Vice-Chancellor: Tolu Odugbemi (2011-)

Schools

Engineering and Engineering Technology (Engineering; Technology); **Information and Communications Technology** (Communication Studies; Computer Engineering; Computer Science; Information Technology; Library Science; Software Engineering); **Science** (Biochemistry; Biological and Life Sciences; Chemistry; Mathematics; Physics; Veterinary Science)

Further Information: Also Okitipupa Campus

History: Founded 2008.

Governing Bodies: Governing Council

Main Language(s) of Instruction: English

Accrediting Agencies: National Universities Commission (NUC)

Degrees and Diplomas: *Bachelor's Degree*: 5 yrs

Student Residential Facilities: On-campus hostel
Last Updated: 16/07/12

OSUN STATE UNIVERSITY (UNIOSUN)

Room 228, Admission Office, Administrative building, Osun State University main Campus, Osogbo, Osun State
Tel: +234 03520-6440 +234(706) 537-2579
EMail: registrar@uniosun.edu.ng; admission@uniosun.edu.ng
Website: http://uniosun.edu.ng/

Vice-Chancellor: Sola Akinrinade EMail: vc@uniosun.edu.ng

Registrar: J.O. Faniran
EMail: registrar@uniosun.edu.ng; olusakinfaniran@yahoo.com

Colleges

Agriculture *(Ejigbo Campus)* (Agricultural Economics; Agriculture; Agronomy; Environmental Management; Fishery; Wildlife; Zoology);

Education *(Ipetu-Jesa Campus)* (Art Education; Education; Humanities and Social Science Education; Mathematics Education; Science Education; Technology Education); **Health Sciences** (Health Sciences; Medicine; Surgery); **Humanities and Culture** *(Ikire Campus)* (Arts and Humanities; Communication Studies; Cultural Studies; English; French; History; International Studies; Linguistics; Modern Languages); **Law** (Law); **Management and Social Sciences** *(Okuku Campus)* (Accountancy; Anthropology; Banking; Business Administration; Demography and Population; Economics; Environmental Studies; Finance; Geography; Geography (Human); Hotel Management; Human Resources; International Relations; Political Sciences; Public Administration; Social Sciences; Sociology; Statistics; Tourism); **Science, Engineering and Technology** (Architecture; Biochemistry; Biological and Life Sciences; Chemical Engineering; Chemistry; Civil Engineering; Computer Science; Electrical and Electronic Engineering; Engineering; Environmental Studies; Geological Engineering; Geology; Industrial Chemistry; Information Technology; Mathematics; Microbiology; Physics; Real Estate; Regional Planning; Town Planning)

History: Founded 2006. Enrolment of the first set of students September 2007.

Governing Bodies: Governing Council

Fees: (Naira): 75,000-100,000 per session.

Main Language(s) of Instruction: English

Accrediting Agencies: National Universities Commission (NUC)

Degrees and Diplomas: *Bachelor's Degree*; *Bachelor's Degree*: Geography

Publications: African Nebula, Official peer-reviewed journal of the College of Humanities and Culture *(1-2 per annum)*

Last Updated: 16/07/12

PLATEAU STATE UNIVERSITY (PLASU)

P.M.B. 2012, Bokkos, Plateau State
EMail: enquiries@plasu.edu.ng
Website: http://www.plasu.edu.ng/

Vice-Chancellor: Nenfort E. Gomwalk EMail: vc@plasu.edu.ng

Divisions

General Studies (Anthropology; English; History; Information Technology; Philosophy; Political Sciences; Sociology)

Schools

Agriculture and Agricultural Technology (Agriculture); **Environmental Sciences**; **Management Sciences** (Accountancy; Economics; Management); **Science and Foundation Studies** (Biology; Chemistry; Mathematics and Computer Science; Physics)

History: Founded 2005.

Main Language(s) of Instruction: English

Accrediting Agencies: National Universities Commission (NUC)

Degrees and Diplomas: *Bachelor's Degree*

Student Numbers *2010-2011*: Total: c. 350

Last Updated: 17/07/12

RIVERS STATE UNIVERSITY OF SCIENCE AND TECHNOLOGY (RSUST)

P.M.B. 5080, Nkpolu - Oroworukwo, Port Harcourt, Rivers State
Tel: +234(709) 541-5002
EMail: info@ust.edu.ng
Website: http://www.ust.edu.ng/

Vice-Chancellor: Barineme B. Fakae Tel: +234(84) 233-288

Registrar: D. C. Odimabo

Centres

Continuing Education

Faculties

Agriculture (Agricultural Economics; Agriculture; Animal Husbandry; Crop Production; Environmental Studies; Fishery; Food Science; Food Technology; Forestry; Home Economics; Management; Soil Science); **Engineering** (Agricultural Engineering; Chemical Engineering; Civil Engineering; Computer Engineering; Electrical Engineering; Engineering; Environmental Engineering; Marine Engineering; Mechanical Engineering; Petroleum and Gas Engineering); **Environmental Science** (Architecture; Real Estate; Regional Planning; Surveying and Mapping; Town Planning); **Law** (Civil Law; Commercial Law; International Law; Law; Private Law); **Management Sciences** (Accountancy; Banking; Finance; Information Management; Management; Marketing; Mass Communication; Secretarial Studies); **Sciences** (Biological and Life Sciences; Biology; Chemistry; Laboratory Techniques; Mathematics and Computer Science; Natural Sciences; Physics); **Technical and Science Education** (Accountancy; Business Administration; Business Education; Management; Marketing; Science Education; Secretarial Studies; Technology; Technology Education)

Institutes

Education (Education); **Foundation Studies** (Education); **Geosciences and Space Technology** (Astronomy and Space Science; Earth Sciences); **Pollution Studies** (Environmental Studies); **RIART**

Schools

Postgraduate Studies

History: Founded 1980 from the Rivers State College of Science and Technology which was established in 1972.

Governing Bodies: Council; Senate

Academic Year: October to July (October-February; March-July)

Admission Requirements: Universities Matriculation Examination (UME) following secondary school education, or direct entry for holders of the Higher School Certificate (General Certificate of Education, Advanced ('A') Level)

Main Language(s) of Instruction: English

Degrees and Diplomas: *Bachelor's Degree*: 4-6 yrs; *Postgraduate Diploma*; *Master's Degree*: a further 11/2-2 yrs; *Master of Philosophy*; *Doctor of Philosophy (PhD)*: a further 2 yrs. Also Certificates; MBA and Executive MBA.

Student Residential Facilities: Hostels

Special Facilities: Information and Communications Technology (ICT) Centre

Libraries: 125,900 vols, 220 periodical subscriptions

Press or Publishing House: Rivers State University Press

Academic Staff *2011-2012*: Total 1,870

Student Numbers *2011-2012*: Total 29,939

Last Updated: 17/07/12

SHEHU IDRIS COLLEGE OF HEALTH SCIENCES AND TECHNOLOGY (SICHST)

P.M.B. 1050, Makarfi, Kaduna State
Website: http://sichstmakarfi.edu.ng/

Schools

Community Health Sciences (Community Health; Development Studies; Health Sciences; Physical Therapy; Rehabilitation and Therapy); **Dental Therapy** (Dental Hygiene; Dental Technology; Dentistry; Medical Auxiliaries); **Environmental Health Sciences** (Dietetics; Environmental Studies; Health Education; Health Sciences; Medical Auxiliaries; Nutrition); **General Health Sciences** (Health Administration; Information Management; Information Technology; Laboratory Techniques; Medical Technology; Pharmacy; Statistics); **Public Health, Nursing and Midwifery** (Midwifery; Nursing; Public Health)

Further Information: Also Campuses in Kaduna and Pambeguwa.

History: Founded 1954 as Centre for Training Community Nurses (CNTC) in what is now called Family Health Unit {FHU) Tudun Wada Kaduna. Renamed Kaduna State School of Health Technology 1998. Renamed Shehu Idris School of Health Technology 2003. Acquired present status and title 2005.

Governing Bodies: Governing Council

Main Language(s) of Instruction: English

Accrediting Agencies: National Board for Technical Education (NBTE)

Degrees and Diplomas: *National Diploma*; *Higher National Diploma*; *Postgraduate Diploma*. Pre-Higher National Diploma (Pre-HND); Undergraduate dIplomas and Certificates.

Last Updated: 09/10/12

TAI SOLARIN UNIVERSITY OF EDUCATION (TASUED)

PMB 2118, Ijebu Ode, Ogun State
EMail: info@tasu.edu.ng; enquiry@tasu.edu.ng
Website: http://www.tasu.edu.ng/

Vice-Chancellor: Segun Awonusi (2010-)
Tel: +234 806-322-7788 EMail: vc@tasu.edu.ng

Registrar: Emmanuel Olufemi Kayode J.P.
Tel: +234(803) 410-6497
EMail: registrar@tasu.edu.ng; efemkay@yahoo.com

International Relations: Temitope Ekundayo, Administrative Officer Tel: +234(803) 380-6539 EMail: topegold08@gmail.com

Centres
Continuous Education; **E-Learning**; **Human Rights and Gender Education**; **Part-Time and External Programmes**; **Vocational Skills, Entrepreurship and External Studies**; **Vocational Training in Research and Agriculture**

Colleges
Applied Education and Vocational Technology (Business Education; Educational Administration; Educational and Student Counselling; Home Economics; Hotel Management; Information Management; Library Science; Preschool Education; Secretarial Studies; Technology Education); **Humanities** (African Languages; Arts and Humanities; Christian Religious Studies; English; Fine Arts; French; History; International Relations; Islamic Studies); **Science and Information Technology** (Agriculture; Biology; Chemistry; Computer Science; Health Education; Industrial Chemistry; Information Technology; Mathematics; Petroleum and Gas Engineering; Physical Therapy; Physics; Sports); **Social and Management Sciences** (Accountancy; Business Administration; Economics; Environmental Management; Geography; Labour and Industrial Relations; Management; Mass Communication; Political Sciences; Social Studies; Social Work; Sociology; Transport and Communications; Transport Management)

Units
Science and Pre-Degree Foundation

History: Founded 1978 as Ogun State College of Education. Acquired present status and title 2005.

Governing Bodies: Ministries of Education (Federal and State)

Admission Requirements: 5 'O' Level credits at a sitting or 6 at not more than 2 sittings

Accrediting Agencies: National Universities Commission (NUC)

Degrees and Diplomas: *Bachelor's Degree*

Student Services: Academic counselling, Canteen, Employment services, Health services, Language programs, Social counselling, Sports facilities

Student Residential Facilities: Hostel Accommodation

Special Facilities: Art Gallery

Libraries: E-Library

Last Updated: 17/07/12

TARABA STATE UNIVERSITY (TSU)

PMB 1167, Jalingo, Taraba State
Tel: +234(803) 636-3172
EMail: tsuijal@gmail.com
Website: http://tsujalingo.com/index.php/en/

Deputy Vice Chancellor, Administration: Catherine Asashim

Registrar: John Danjuma

Faculties
Agriculture (Agricultural Economics; Agriculture; Agronomy; Animal Husbandry); **Arts and Social Sciences** (Archaeology; Arts and Humanities; Economics; Geography (Human); History; International Relations; Linguistics; Mass Communication; Modern Languages; Political Sciences; Religious Studies; Social Sciences; Sociology); **Education** (African Languages; Biology; Chemistry; Economics; Education; Educational Administration; English; Foreign Languages Education; Geography; Humanities and Social Science Education; Native Language Education; Physics; Political Sciences; Science Education); **Science** (Biological and Life Sciences; Biology; Botany; Chemistry; Computer Science; Geology; Mathematics; Mathematics and Computer Science; Physics; Statistics; Zoology)

Research Centres
Peace Studies (Peace and Disarmament)

Research Institutes
Animal Breading and Dairy (Animal Husbandry; Dairy); **Fresh Water Biology and Fisheries**; **Solid Minerals** (Mineralogy)

Schools
Post Graduate Studies

Further Information: A traditional and distance learning institutions.

History: Founded 2008.

Governing Bodies: Governing Council; Senate

Main Language(s) of Instruction: English

Accrediting Agencies: National Universities Commission (NUC)

Degrees and Diplomas: *Bachelor's Degree*

Student Services: Sports facilities

Student Residential Facilities: Hostels

Special Facilities: ICT Center

Last Updated: 17/07/12

THE POLYTECHNIC, IBADAN (POLY IBADAN)

PMB 22, U.I. Post Office, Ibadan, Oyo State
Tel: +234(22) 810-0154 +234(22) 751-7470
Fax: +234(2) 810-1122
EMail: info@polyibadan.edu.ng
Website: http://www.polyibadan.edu.ng/

Rector: Olusegun Odunola EMail: rector@polyibadan.edu.ng

Registrar: H.A. Ededokun EMail: HadjiBobby@yahoo.com

Faculties
Business Administration and Management *(FBCS)* (Business and Commerce; Management); **Engineering** *(FENG)* (Engineering); **Environmental Studies** *(FFMS)* (Environmental Studies); **Financial and Management Studies** *(FFMS)* (Accountancy; Finance; Insurance); **Science** *(FSC)* (Natural Sciences)

History: Founded 1960, acquired present status and title 1970.

Governing Bodies: Governing Council, Board of Studies, Management Board

Admission Requirements: Four credits including English Language and Mathematics at WASCE

Fees: (Naira): 12,000 per annum

Main Language(s) of Instruction: English

Accrediting Agencies: National Board of Technical Education

Degrees and Diplomas: *National Diploma*: 2 yrs; *Higher National Diploma*: 2 yrs; *Postgraduate Diploma*

Student Services: Academic counselling, Canteen, Health services, Nursery care, Social counselling, Sports facilities

Student Residential Facilities: Yes (for staff and students)

Special Facilities: Art gallery; TV and radio studio

Libraries: Main (Central) Library and branch libraries: c. 60,000 vols; c. 2,300 periodical subscriptions.

Publications: Engineers, Engineering and scientific journal *(annually)*; Journal of Science and Technology *(quarterly)*; POLYCOM, Behavioural Sciences journal *(quarterly)*; The Environs, Environmental studies journal *(quarterly)*

Last Updated: 17/07/12

UMARU MUSA YAR'ADUA UNIVERSITY (UMYU KATSINA)

PMB 2218, Dutsinma Road, Katsina, Katsina State
Tel: +234(9) 783-0054
EMail: info@katsu.edu.ng; webmaster@umyu.edu.ng
Website: http://www.katsu.edu.ng/

Vice-Chancellor: Mu'uta Ibrahim (2010-)

Registrar: Abdu Halliru Abdullahi
Tel: +234(9) 783-0,054; +234 803-3973-570
EMail: abduabdullahi@yahoo.com; registrar@katsu.edu.ng

Deputy Vice Chancellor, Administration: Ibrahim Sada

International Relations: Muhammad Yusufu Abubakar, Academic Secretary
Tel: +234 803-6920864 EMail: myusufuabubakar@yahoo.com

Faculties

Education (Arabic; Art Education; Biology; Chemistry; Economics; Education; Educational Sciences; English; Foreign Languages Education; Geology; Humanities and Social Science Education; Information Sciences; Islamic Studies; Library Science; Mathematics Education; Physical Therapy; Physics; Religious Education; Science Education); **Humanities** (Arabic; Arts and Humanities; Economics; English; French; History; Islamic Studies); **Natural and Applied Sciences** (Biological and Life Sciences; Chemistry; Computer Science; Geology; Mathematics; Natural Sciences; Physics)

Research Centres

Renewable Energy *(CeRER)* (Energy Engineering)

Schools

Postgraduate Studies (Arabic; Arts and Humanities; Chemistry; Computer Science; Curriculum; Education; Educational Psychology; Geography; Islamic Studies; Mathematics; Natural Resources; Natural Sciences)

History: Founded 2006. Previously known as Katsina State University.

Governing Bodies: Governing Council; Senate; Congregation; Convocation

Academic Year: October to September: October-February; March-July; July-September

Admission Requirements: Senior secondary school certificate (WAEC, NECO, GCE) or equivalent with credit passes in five subjetcs in not more than two sittings. An acceptable score in the universities matriculation examination (UME) is required. Credit pass in English is required for all programmes. A credit pass in Mathematics is required for all science-based and a selected arts-based programmes.

Fees: (US Dollars): 4,000 per annum (c.600,000 Naira)

Main Language(s) of Instruction: English

International Co-operation: With International Islamic University (Malaysia); Valparaiso University, Indiana (USA)

Accrediting Agencies: National Universities Commission (NUC)

Degrees and Diplomas: *Bachelor's Degree*; *Postgraduate Diploma*; *Master's Degree*; *Doctor of Philosophy*

Student Services: Academic counselling, Canteen, Cultural centre, Health services, Language programs, Social counselling, Sports facilities

Student Residential Facilities: 2 hostels accommodating 576 female students; Private hostel accommodation for 200 male students

Special Facilities: Wireless

Libraries: A total of 10,899 vols; 199 journal titles and 250 CDs. The e-Library has access to 13 databases

Publications: Katsina Journal of Pure and Applied Sciences *(annually)*; Taguwa, Journal of Humanities *(3 per annum)*

Academic Staff *2011-2012*	**TOTAL**
FULL-TIME	**200**
PART-TIME	**50**
STAFF WITH DOCTORATE	
FULL-TIME	**60**
PART-TIME	c. **30**

Student Numbers *2011-2012*	
All (Foreign Included)	c. **2,900**

Last Updated: 17/07/12

UNIVERSITY OF ABUJA (UNIBUJA)

PMB 117, Abuja, Federal Capital Territory
Tel: +234(9) 882-1393 +234(9) 882-1380 +234(9) 882-1972
EMail: info@uniabuja.edu.ng
Website: http://www.uniabuja.edu.ng/

Vice-Chancellor: James Sunday Adebowale Adelabu
EMail: vc@mailu.unibuja.edu.ng

Centres

Distance Learning and Continuing Education

Colleges

Health Sciences (Anaesthesiology; Anatomy; Biochemistry; Community Health; Gynaecology and Obstetrics; Haematology; Health Sciences; Medical Technology; Microbiology; Nursing; Ophthalmology; Paediatrics; Pathology; Pharmacy; Physiology; Psychiatry and Mental Health; Radiology; Surgery)

Faculties

Agriculture (Agricultural Economics; Agriculture; Animal Husbandry; Aquaculture; Crop Production; Fishery; Food Science; Nutrition; Soil Science); **Arts** (African Languages; Arts and Humanities; Chinese; English; French; German; History; Linguistics; Literature; Philosophy; Portuguese; Religion; Spanish; Theatre); **Education** (Education); **Engineering** (Agricultural Engineering; Chemical Engineering; Civil Engineering; Computer Engineering; Electrical and Electronic Engineering; Engineering; Mechanical Engineering); **Law** (Law); **Management Sciences** (Management); **Science** (Biological and Life Sciences; Chemistry; Computer Science; Mathematics; Mathematics and Computer Science; Physics; Statistics); **Social Sciences** (Banking; Criminology; Demography and Population; Development Studies; Economics; Environmental Management; Finance; Gender Studies; Geography; International Relations; Political Sciences; Public Administration; Social Sciences; Sociology); **Veterinary Medicine** (Veterinary Science)

Institutes

Education (Biology; Chemistry; Christian Religious Studies; Economics; Education; Educational and Student Counselling; English; Foreign Languages Education; Geography; History; Humanities and Social Science Education; Islamic Studies; Mathematics Education; Physics; Primary Education; Religious Education; Science Education)

Schools

Post Graduate Studies (Analytical Chemistry; Banking; Biology; Botany; Business Administration; Demography and Population; Economics; Education; Educational Administration; Educational and Student Counselling; Educational Psychology; English Studies; Environmental Engineering; Finance; Gender Studies; Geography; Geophysics; History; Inorganic Chemistry; International Economics; International Relations; Islamic Law; Law; Media Studies; Microbiology; Natural Resources; Organic Chemistry; Physical Chemistry; Political Sciences; Public Administration; Science Education; Sociology; Solid State Physics; Theatre; Zoology)

Further Information: Also Mini-Campus in Gwagwalada.

History: Founded 1988.

Governing Bodies: Council; Senate

Academic Year: October to September

Admission Requirements: Senior School Certificate (SSC) with credits in 5 relevant subjects obtained at no more than 2 sittings, or General Certificate of Education (GCE) O level in 5 subjects, or equivalent qualification; and University Matriculation Examination (UME) in 3 relevant subjects and knowledge of English

Main Language(s) of Instruction: English

Degrees and Diplomas: *Bachelor's Degree*; *Postgraduate Diploma*; *Master's Degree*; *Master of Philosophy*; *Doctor of Philosophy (PhD)*

Special Facilities: Open Air Theatre; Information and Communication Technology (ICT) Centre

Libraries: 19,866 vols; 540 periodical subscriptions

Publications: Abuja Journal of Education *(annually)*; Abuja Journal of Humanities *(annually)*

Last Updated: 17/07/12

UNIVERSITY OF BENIN (UNIBEN)

PMB 1154, Benin City, Edo State
Tel: +234(52) 600-366
EMail: pro@uniben.edu
Website: http://www.uniben.edu/

Vice-Chancellor: Osayuki Godwin Oshodin
Tel: +234(52) 600-366, Fax: +234(52) 602-370

Registrar: Gladys Osebun Ogboghodo
EMail: registrar@uniben.edu

International Relations: Anthony Benjamin Ebeigbe, Chairman, Exchange and Linkages

Colleges

Medicine (Anaesthesiology; Community Health; Medicine; Nephrology; Public Health)

Faculties

Agriculture (Agricultural Economics; Agriculture; Animal Husbandry; Biochemistry; Crop Production; Environmental Management; Fishery; Forest Products; Forestry; Nutrition; Soil Science; Wildlife; Wood Technology); **Arts** (Advertising and Publicity; African Languages; Arts and Humanities; Ceramic Art; English; Fashion Design; Fine Arts; History; International Relations; Linguistics; Literature; Mass Communication; Modern Languages; Painting and Drawing; Philosophy; Printing and Printmaking; Religion; Sculpture; Textile Design; Theatre); **Dentistry** (Dentistry); **Education** (Adult Education; Agricultural Education; Biology; Business Education; Chemistry; Computer Science; Curriculum; Economics; Education; Educational Administration; Educational and Student Counselling; Educational Psychology; Educational Sciences; Electrical and Electronic Equipment and Maintenance; English; Environmental Studies; Fine Arts; Foreign Languages Education; French; Geography; Health Education; History; Home Economics; Home Economics Education; Humanities and Social Science Education; Industrial Arts Education; Leisure Studies; Literature; Mathematics; Mathematics Education; Native Language; Natural Sciences; Parks and Recreation; Physical Education; Physics; Political Sciences; Religion; Science Education; Social Studies; Sports; Technology Education; Tourism; Vocational Education); **Engineering** (Chemical Engineering; Civil Engineering; Electrical and Electronic Engineering; Electrical Engineering; Electronic Engineering; Energy Engineering; Engineering; Engineering Drawing and Design; Engineering Management; Environmental Engineering; Heating and Refrigeration; Industrial Engineering; Mechanical Engineering; Petroleum and Gas Engineering; Power Engineering; Production Engineering; Sound Engineering (Acoustics); Structural Architecture; Telecommunications Engineering; Thermal Engineering); **Law** (Law); **Life Sciences** (Biochemistry; Biological and Life Sciences; Biology; Biotechnology; Botany; Environmental Management; Environmental Studies; Laboratory Techniques; Microbiology; Natural Resources; Optometry; Zoology); **Management Sciences** (Accountancy; Banking; Business Administration; Finance; Management); **Pharmacy** (Chemistry; Immunology; Microbiology; Pharmacology; Pharmacy; Toxicology); **Physical Sciences** (Applied Mathematics; Chemistry; Computer Science; Geology; Industrial Chemistry; Mathematics; Physics); **Social Sciences** (Administration; Anthropology; Economics; Geography (Human); Government; Political Sciences; Public Administration; Regional Planning; Social Sciences; Social Work; Sociology; Statistics; Town Planning)

Institutes

Education *(Postgraduate)* (Education; Technology Education); **Public Administration** *(IPAES)* (Health Administration; Management; Nursing; Public Administration)

Schools

Basic Medical Sciences (Anatomy; Biochemistry; Laboratory Techniques; Medicine; Nursing; Physiology)

Further Information: Also Ugbowo Campus; Teaching Hospital

History: Founded 1970 as the Institute of Technology, Benin City, acquired present title 1972 and status 1975.

Governing Bodies: Council; Senate

Academic Year: October to June

Admission Requirements: Unified Tertiary Matriculation Examination (UTME) plus 5 General Certificate of Education (GCE) 'O' level passes or 2 A/Level passes plus appropriate diploma/certificate

Main Language(s) of Instruction: English

Degrees and Diplomas: *Bachelor's Degree*: 4-6 yrs; *Postgraduate Diploma*: 2 yrs; *Master's Degree*: a further 1 1/2-2 yrs; *Doctor of Philosophy (PhD)*: at least 3 yrs following Master's Degree

Student Residential Facilities: Yes

Libraries: 204,329 vols; 145 periodical subscriptions; 3,130 bound periodicals

Publications: Bini Journal of Educational Studies; Faculty of Arts Journal *(quarterly)*; Faculty of Education Journal *(biennially)*; Nigerian Bulletin of Contemporary Law; Nigerian Journal of Educational Research Association; Physical Health Education and Recreational Journal; University Report *(biannually)*

Last Updated: 27/06/12

UNIVERSITY OF CALABAR (UNICAL)

PMB 1115, Calabar, Cross River State
Tel: +234(87) 233-969
EMail: asubaok@unical.anpa.net.org
Website: http://www.unical.edu.ng

Vice-Chancellor: James Epoke (2010-)
Tel: +234(87) 232-790, Fax: +234(87) 231-766
EMail: vcunical@yahoo.com

Acting Registrar: Julia D. Omang
Tel: +234(87) 233-989 EMail: registrar@unical.edu.ng

International Relations: Julia D. Omang, Registrar

Faculties

Agriculture (Agricultural Economics; Agriculture; Animal Husbandry; Crop Production; Environmental Studies; Forestry; Natural Resources; Soil Science; Wildlife); **Allied Health Sciences** (Health Sciences); **Arts** (Arts and Humanities; Communication Arts; English; French; History; International Studies; Linguistics; Literature; Modern Languages; Philosophy; Religious Studies; Theatre; Translation and Interpretation); **Basic Medical Sciences** (Anatomy; Applied Chemistry; Biochemistry; Biological and Life Sciences; Food Science; Nutrition; Pharmacology; Physiology); **Clinical Sciences**; **Education** (Adult Education; Biology; Chemistry; Continuing Education; Economics; Education; Educational Administration; Educational and Student Counselling; English; Geography (Human); Health Education; History; Humanities and Social Science Education; Information Sciences; Library Science; Mathematics; Mathematics Education; Physical Education; Physics; Political Sciences; Religion; Science Education; Special Education; Technology Education; Vocational Education); **Law** (International Law; Law; Private Law; Public Law); **Management Sciences** (Accountancy; Banking; Business Administration; Finance; Management; Marketing); **Science** (Applied Chemistry; Aquaculture; Biology; Biotechnology; Botany; Chemistry; Computer Science; Electronic Engineering; Fishery; Genetics; Geology; Geophysics; Marine Biology; Marine Science and Oceanography; Mathematics; Microbiology; Physics; Statistics; Zoology); **Social Sciences** (Administration; Economics; Environmental Management; Environmental Studies; Geography (Human); Political Sciences; Public Administration; Regional Planning; Social Sciences; Social Work; Sociology)

Institutes

Education (Education); **Oceanography** (Marine Science and Oceanography; Social and Community Services); **Public Policy and Administration** (Public Administration)

Further Information: Also campus at Ogoja

History: Founded as a Federal University 1975.

Governing Bodies: University Council; Senate; Committee of Deans; Management Committee

Academic Year: October to July

Admission Requirements: Senior School Certificate (SSCE) or equivalent, with 5 passes at credit level, taken at no more than 2 sittings, and either University Matriculation Examination UTME or (for direct entry) General Certificate of Education (GCE) 'A' level in 3 subjects or equivalent. For a Master's degree, candidates must possess either a First or Second Class Honours Degree of the University of Calabar or an equivalent degree from another recognised University with a Cumulative Grade Point Average of 2.75 on 4 grading point system or 3.44 on 5 grading point system. Candidate for Ph.D degree shall be required to hold good Master's degree in the relevant field of the University of Calabar or any recognised University.

Fees: (Naira): Undergraduate Fresh Students, 31,950 per annum; Undergraduate Returning Students, 24,550 per annum; Undergraduate Final Year Students, 25,050 per annum. Graduate School Fees: Master programmes, Local Students, 65,800-74,300

(part-time); 75,800-84,300 (full-time); MBA programmes, 106,800-109,300; MPA/MPAS programmes, 91,800-94,300; Postgraduate Diplomas: 81,300-81,800. For foreign Students: 166,800-175,8,000 (African students), 293,300-349,300 (Non-African students); MBA programmes, 256,800-259,300 (African Students), 406,800-409,300 (Non-African students); MPA/MPAS, 226,800-229,300 (African Students), 471,800-474,300 (Non-African Students); Post-graduate programmes, 231,300 (African Students), 476,300 (Non-African).

Main Language(s) of Instruction: English

International Co-operation: With universities in United Kingdom, China, Ghana, South Africa, Canada, USA, Germany. Also programmes with One Sky (a Canadian N.G.O.), the Cross River National Park (National Park Service), the Cross River Forestry Commission and Leventis Foundation, the Council of Renewable Energy in Nigeria, the European Project Funding and Management Academy (Knowledge Factory International Ltd.), the Natural resources Institute, University of Greenwich, the Amercian Council of Learned Societies (ACLS), New York, USAID for Assistance in Collaboration activities with some US universities.

Accrediting Agencies: National Universities Commission

Degrees and Diplomas: *Bachelor's Degree*: 4-5 yrs; *Master's Degree*: a further 1-2 yrs; *Doctor of Philosophy (PhD)*: 2-3 yrs following Master's Degree

Student Services: Academic counselling, Canteen, Handicapped facilities, Health services, Language programs, Social counselling, Sports facilities

Student Residential Facilities: For 3,599 students and 254 staff members.

Special Facilities: Cartographical Studio; Meteorological Stations; Biological Garden; Audiovisual Studio

Libraries: 150,625 vols; 9,193 bound journals; 14,745 current journals; 14,456 magazines; 4,139 monographs; virtual library

Press or Publishing House: University of Calabar Press

Academic Staff *2011-2012*	MEN	WOMEN	**TOTAL**
FULL-TIME	881	227	**1,108**
PART-TIME	46	6	**52**
STAFF WITH DOCTORATE			
FULL-TIME	341	53	**394**
PART-TIME	58	11	**69**
Student Numbers *2011-2012*			
All (Foreign Included)	14,000	10,000	**24,000**
FOREIGN ONLY	8	2	**10**

Last Updated: 27/06/12

UNIVERSITY OF IBADAN (UI)

Ibadan, Oyo State
Tel: +234(2) 810-3380 +234(2) 810-3168
Fax: +234(2) 810-3043
EMail: inforeg@mail.ui.edu.ng
Website: http://www.ui.edu.ng

Vice-Chancellor: I.F. Adewole
Tel: +234(2) 810-3168 EMail: vc@mail.ui.edu.ng

Registrar: O.I. Olukoya
Tel: +234(2) 8032188996 EMail: registrar@mail.ui.edu.ng

Deputy Vice-Chancellor, Administration: Arinola Sanya
EMail: dvcadmin@mail.ui.edu.ng

International Relations: I. Bola Udegbe, Director, Office of International Programmes

Centres

Computing (Computer Science); **Entrepreneurship and Innovation** *(CEI)* (Management); **Industrial Training Coordinating** *(ITCC)*; **Information Science** *(ARCIS - Africa Regional)* (Information Sciences); **Literacy Training and Development Programme in Africa** *(CLTDPA)* (Literacy Education); **Media** *(University)* (Media Studies); **Media Resource** *(Abadina)* (Media Studies); **Peace and Conflict Studies** *(CEPACS)* (Peace and Disarmament); **Petroleum, Energy Economics and Law** (Economics; Finance; Law; Petroleum and Gas Engineering); **Social Orientation** (Social Sciences); **Sustainable Development** (Development Studies; Environmental Management; Government; Leadership; Natural Resources; Tourism); **Yoruba Language** (African Languages; Native Language Education)

Colleges

Medicine (Anaesthesiology; Anatomy; Biochemistry; Community Health; Dentistry; Epidemiology; Gynaecology and Obstetrics; Haematology; Health Administration; Health Sciences; Medicine; Microbiology; Nursing; Nutrition; Ophthalmology; Otorhinolaryngology; Paediatrics; Pathology; Pharmacology; Physical Therapy; Physiology; Psychiatry and Mental Health; Public Health; Radiology; Social and Community Services; Statistics; Surgery; Treatment Techniques; Virology)

Faculties

Agriculture and Forestry (Agricultural Economics; Agricultural Management; Agriculture; Agronomy; Animal Husbandry; Biochemistry; Crop Production; Fishery; Forest Management; Forestry; Horticulture; Nutrition; Plant and Crop Protection; Rural Planning; Wildlife); **Arts** (African Languages; Arabic; Arts and Humanities; Classical Languages; Communication Studies; English; European Studies; History; Islamic Studies; Linguistics; Modern Languages; Philosophy; Religious Studies; Theatre); **Education** (Adult Education; Education; Educational Administration; Educational and Student Counselling; Health Education; Information Sciences; Library Science; Media Studies; Physical Education; Social Work; Special Education; Teacher Training); **Law** (Commercial Law; International Law; Law; Private Law; Public Law); **Pharmacy** (Administration; Chemistry; Microbiology; Pharmacology; Pharmacy); **Sciences** (Anthropology; Archaeology; Botany; Chemistry; Computer Science; Geology; Mathematics; Microbiology; Natural Sciences; Physics; Statistics; Zoology); **Technology** (Agricultural Engineering; Civil Engineering; Electrical and Electronic Engineering; Environmental Engineering; Food Technology; Industrial Engineering; Mechanical Engineering; Petroleum and Gas Engineering; Production Engineering; Structural Architecture; Wood Technology); **The Social Science** (Economics; Geography (Human); Political Sciences; Psycholinguistics; Regional Planning; Social Sciences; Sociology; Town Planning); **Veterinary Medicine** (Veterinary Science)

Institutes

African Studies (African Studies); **Child Health** (Child Care and Development; Health Sciences); **Education** (Education; Teacher Training); **Life and Earth Sciences** (Biological and Life Sciences; Botany; Earth Sciences; Embryology and Reproduction Biology; Environmental Engineering; Geology; Health Sciences; Mineralogy; Petroleum and Gas Engineering)

Programmes

Health Policy Training and Research (Health Administration; Health Education)

Research Laboratories

Multidisciplinary *(MCRL - Central)*

Schools

Postgraduate Studies

Further Information: Also Teaching Hospital. A traditional and distance learning institution.

History: Founded 1948 as a college of the University of London. Acquired present status and title 1962.

Governing Bodies: University Council; University Senate

Academic Year: September to June

Admission Requirements: Universities Matriculation Examination (UME). Secondary School Certificate of Education (SSCE) with 5 credits, including English

Main Language(s) of Instruction: English

International Co-operation: With universities in USA, Canada, Europe, Asia

Accrediting Agencies: National Universities Commission (NUC)

Degrees and Diplomas: *Bachelor's Degree*; *Postgraduate Diploma*; *Master's Degree*; *Master of Philosophy (M.Phil)*; *Doctor of Philosophy (PhD)*

Student Services: Academic counselling, Canteen, Cultural centre, Employment services, Foreign student adviser, Foreign Studies Centre, Handicapped facilities, Health services, Language programs, Social counselling, Sports facilities

Student Residential Facilities: Yes

Special Facilities: Abadina Media Resource Centre; Basel Convention Regional Centre; Industrial Training Coordinating Centre and University Media Centre. Botanical and Zoological gardens. Community Radio Station

Libraries: Main Library, c. 56,000 vols; c. 6,000 journals and other serials

Publications: African Journal for the Psychological study of Social Issues; African Journal of Biomedical Research; African Journal of Education Management; African Journal of Education Research; African Journal of Labour Studies; African Journal of Medicine & Medical Sciences; African Journal of Peace and Conflict; African Notes *(3 per annum)*; Al-Fikir: Annual Journal of the Department of Arabic and Islamic Studies; Archives of Ibadan Medicine; Ibadan Journal of Agricultural Research; Ibadan Journal of Education; Ibadan Journal of English Studies; Ibadan Journal of Humanistic Studies; Ibadan Journal of the Social Sciences; Ibadan University Law Review; International Journal of Continuing and Non-Formal Education; International Journal of Literacy Education; ISESE: Ibadan Journal of Folklore; Journal of Applied Science, Engineering and Technology; Journal of Clinical And Counselling Psychology; Journal of Communication and Language Arts; Journal of Educational Theory and Practice; Journal of Environment and Culture; Journal of Historical Society of Nigeria; Journal of Science Research; Journal of Sociology and Education in Africa; Journal of Special Education; Journal of the Nigerian Association for Physical Health Education, Recreation, Sports and Dance (OYO-JPNAPHER); Journal of the Nigerian English Students Association; Journal of Tropical Forest Resources; Nigerian Education Law Journal; Nigerian Geographical Journal; Nigerian Journal of Applied Psychology; Nigerian Journal of Clinical Practice; Nigerian Journal of Computer Literacy (NJCL); Nigerian Journal of Economic and Social Studies; Nigerian Journal of Health, Education and Welfare of Special People; Nigerian Journal of Physiological Sciences; Nigerian journal of Physiological Sciences; Nigerian Journal of Science; Nigerian Journal of Social Work Education; Nigerian Journals of Paediatrics; Nigerian School Health Journal (NSHA); Orita; Review of Leadership in Africa (RoLA); The Nigerian Journal of Industrial and Labour Relations; The Nigerian Journal of Sociology and Anthropology; The Statesman (Student Publication); Tropical Journal of Obstetrics and Gynaecology; Tropical Veterinarian; University of Ibadan Journal of Private and Business Law; University of Ibadan Public and International Law Journal; West African Journal of Archaelogy; West African Journal of Education; West African Journal of Medicine; West African Journal of Physical And Health Education (WAJOPHE)

Press or Publishing House: Ibadan University Press
Last Updated: 18/07/12

IAU UNIVERSITY OF ILORIN (UNILORIN)

PMB 1515, Ilorin, Kwara State 234031
Tel: +234(31) 741058 +234(31) 221-911 +234(31) 221691
Fax: +234(31) 222561
EMail: vc@unilorin.edu.ng
Website: http://www.unilorin.edu.ng/

Vice-Chancellor: Abdul Ganiyu Ambali (2012-)
EMail: aambali076@yahoo.com

Deputy Vice-Chancellor, Academic: Bayo Lawal
Tel: +234(80) 3376-8610 EMail: dvcacad@unilorin.edu.ng

Registrar: Olufolake O. Oyeyemi
Tel: +234(80) 3405-7082 EMail: registrar@unilorin.edu.ng

International Relations: Yisa Moronfola Fakunle, Deputy Vice-Chancellor, Management Services
Tel: +234(80) 3371-2849
EMail: dvcadmin@unilorin.edu.ng; acadplan@unilorin.edu.ng; bolayemi_2005@yahoo.com

Centres

Peace and Strategic Studies (Peace and Disarmament)

Colleges

Health Sciences (Anatomy; Behavioural Sciences; Biochemistry; Community Health; Epidemiology; Haematology; Medicine; Microbiology; Ophthalmology; Pathology; Pharmacology; Pharmacy; Physiology; Public Health; Surgery; Virology)

Faculties

Agriculture (Agricultural Economics; Agriculture; Animal Husbandry; Cattle Breeding; Farm Management; Food Science; Forest Management; Forestry; Home Economics; Plant and Crop Protection; Rural Planning; Wildlife); **Arts** (African Languages; Arabic; Arts and Humanities; Christian Religious Studies; Comparative Religion; English; French; History; Islamic Studies; Linguistics; Native Language; Performing Arts; Social Sciences); **Basic Medical Sciences** (Anatomy; Haematology; Medicine; Microbiology; Pathology; Pharmacology; Physiology); **Business and Social Sciences** (Accountancy; Business Administration; Economics; Finance; Geography; Political Sciences; Social Sciences; Sociology); **Clinical Sciences** (Behavioural Sciences; Community Health; Epidemiology; Ophthalmology); **Communication and Information Sciences** (Communication Studies; Computer Science; Information Sciences; Library Science; Mass Communication; Telecommunications Engineering); **Education** (Curriculum; Education; Educational Administration; Educational and Student Counselling; Educational Technology; Foreign Languages Education; Health Education; Humanities and Social Science Education; Native Language Education; Physical Education; Preschool Education; Primary Education; Religious Education; Science Education; Teacher Training); **Engineering and Technology** (Agricultural Engineering; Bioengineering; Biomedical Engineering; Chemical Engineering; Civil Engineering; Electrical Engineering; Materials Engineering; Mechanical Engineering; Metallurgical Engineering); **Law** (Commercial Law; International Law; Islamic Law; Law; Private Law; Public Law); **Science** (Biochemistry; Biological and Life Sciences; Botany; Chemistry; Computer Science; Geology; Industrial Chemistry; Mathematics; Microbiology; Mineralogy; Natural Sciences; Physics; Statistics; Zoology)

Schools

Postgraduate Studies (Accountancy; African Languages; Agricultural Economics; Agricultural Engineering; Agronomy; Anatomy; Ancient Religions; Animal Husbandry; Arabic; Arts and Humanities; Biochemistry; Biology; Business Administration; Chemistry; Civil Engineering; Commercial Law; Community Health; Computer Science; Crop Production; Economics; Educational Administration; Electrical Engineering; English; Epidemiology; Farm Management; Finance; French; Geography; Geology; Health Education; History; International Law; Islamic Law; Law; Linguistics; Mathematics; Mechanical Engineering; Microbiology; Mineralogy; Parasitology; Peace and Disarmament; Performing Arts; Physical Education; Physics; Physiology; Plant and Crop Protection; Political Sciences; Private Law; Psychology; Public Administration; Public Law; Radiology; Religion; Religious Studies; Rural Planning; Science Education; Social Sciences; Sociology; Statistics; Zoology)

History: Founded 1975 as University College of Ilorin - initially affiliated to the University of Ibadan. Acquired present status and title 1977. Under the jurisdiction of the Federal Government.

Governing Bodies: University Council

Academic Year: October to July (October-January; March-July)

Admission Requirements: Universities Matriculation Examination (UME) following secondary school education, or direct entry for holders of the Higher School Certificate (General Certificate of Education, Advanced ('A') level)

Fees: (Naira): c. 750-1,200; postgraduate, c. 500-700; foreign students, US $ 2,000-3,000

Main Language(s) of Instruction: English

Accrediting Agencies: National Universities Commission (NUC); Nigeria Legal Council; Medical and Dental Council of Nigeria; Institute of Chartered Accountants of Nigeria; Council for Regulation of Engineers

Degrees and Diplomas: *Bachelor's Degree*: 4-5 yrs; *Bachelor's Degree*: Medicine and Surgery; *Postgraduate Diploma (PGD)*; *Master's Degree*; *Master of Philosophy (M.Phil)*; *Doctor of Philosophy (PhD)*. Also MBA and Executive MBA.

Student Services: Academic counselling, Canteen, Employment services, Foreign student adviser, Foreign Studies Centre, Handicapped facilities, Health services, Language programs, Social counselling, Sports facilities

Student Residential Facilities: Hostels for c. 3,610 students; Guest Houses

Special Facilities: Computer Centre; Central Workshop and Stores; Biological Garden; Multipurpose auditorium (2,000 seats)

Libraries: University Library, 374,604 vols; 39,851 periodicals
Publications: Ilorin Lectures *(annually)*
Press or Publishing House: University Press
Last Updated: 18/07/12

UNIVERSITY OF JOS (UNIJOS)

PMB 2084, Jos, Plateau State
Tel: +234(73) 610-936
Fax: +234(73) 610-514
EMail: vc@unijos.edu.ng
Website: http://www.unijos.edu.ng/

Vice-Chancellor: Hayward B. Mafuyai
Tel: +234(73) 453-724 +234(73) 612-513, Fax: +234(73) 611-928

Deputy Vice-Chancellor, Administration: Musa Andrew Ibrahim

Registrar: Danjuma Jilli-Dandam
Tel: +234(73) 610-514, Fax: +234(73) 610-514
EMail: registrar@unijos.edu.ng

Deputy Vice-Chancellor, Academic: Benjamin Tagbo Ugwu

Centres

Conflict Management and Peace Studies *(CECOMPS)* (Peace and Disarmament); **Continuing Education** (Continuing Education); **General Studies**

Faculties

Arts (Arabic; Arts and Humanities; English; Film; French; Islamic Studies; Linguistics; Mass Communication; Religious Studies; Theatre); **Education** (Art Education; Curriculum; Education; Educational and Student Counselling; Educational Psychology; Humanities and Social Science Education; Philosophy of Education; Science Education; Social Studies; Special Education; Technology Education); **Environmental Sciences** (Architecture; Building Technologies; Environmental Studies; Geography; Real Estate; Regional Planning; Surveying and Mapping; Town Planning); **Law** (Civil Law; Commercial Law; International Law; Law; Private Law; Public Law); **Medical Sciences** (Anaesthesiology; Anatomy; Biochemistry; Community Health; Gynaecology and Obstetrics; Haematology; Health Sciences; Laboratory Techniques; Medical Technology; Medicine; Microbiology; Nursing; Ophthalmology; Paediatrics; Pathology; Physiology; Psychiatry and Mental Health; Radiology; Surgery); **Natural Sciences** (Applied Chemistry; Botany; Chemistry; Computer Science; Geology; Industrial Chemistry; Laboratory Techniques; Mathematics; Microbiology; Mineralogy; Natural Sciences; Physics; Statistics; Zoology); **Pharmaceutical Sciences** (Administration; Chemistry; Pharmacology; Pharmacy; Technology; Toxicology); **Social Sciences** (Accountancy; Economics; Management; Political Sciences; Psychology; Sociology)

Institutes

Education *(Part-time and Sandwich programmes)* (Education); **Nomadic Education**; **Ornithological Research** *(A.P. Leventis - APLORI)* (Zoology)

Schools

Postgraduate Studies (Arts and Humanities; Education; Environmental Studies; Law; Medicine; Natural Sciences; Pharmacy)

Further Information: Also Teaching Hospital. A traditional and distance learning institution.

History: Founded 1971 as a campus of the University of Ibadan, acquired present status and title 1975.

Governing Bodies: Council; Senate; Congregation; Convocation

Academic Year: March to December (March-July; August-December)

Admission Requirements: Universities Matriculation Examination (UME) following Secondary School education, i.e for holders of the Senior Secondary School Certificate (SSSC) or General Certificate of Education (GCE) with ('O') levels with at least 5 credits, or direct entry for IJMB, Diploma, NCE and A'Level holders with appropriate O'level credits

Fees: (Naira): 7,600 - 11,600 per session (returning students); 24,350 - 30,350 (New Students); 27,600 - 31,600 per session for foreign students (returning); and 144,350 -150,350 for foreign students (new)

Main Language(s) of Instruction: English

International Co-operation: With universities in Canada, United Kingdom, Poland. Also cooperates with the Japanese International Cooperation Agency and Harvard School of Public Health (HSPH).

Accrediting Agencies: National Universities Commission

Degrees and Diplomas: *Bachelor's Degree*; *Postgraduate Diploma*; *Master's Degree*; *Master of Philosophy*; *Doctor of Philosophy (PhD)*

Student Services: Academic counselling, Employment services, Handicapped facilities, Health services, Nursery care, Social counselling, Sports facilities

Student Residential Facilities: Yes

Special Facilities: Anatomy Museum. Geography Observatory. House of Animal Pharmacology. Botanical and Zoological gardens

Libraries: 165,741 vols; 6,796 periodicals

Press or Publishing House: Jos University Press Ltd, Unijos Consultancy Ltd Press

Last Updated: 18/07/12

UNIVERSITY OF LAGOS (UNILAG)

Akoka, Yaba, Lagos, Lagos State
Tel: +234(1) 8033-028995
EMail: dsa@unilag.edu.ng
Website: http://www.unilag.edu.ng

Acting Vice-Chancellor: R.A. Bello Fax: +234(1) 774-1872
EMail: vc@unilag.edu.ng

Registrar: Oluwarotimi O.A. Shodimu
Tel: +234(1) 805536-9863 EMail: registrar@unilag.edu.ng

International Relations: Akin Oyebode, Head, Office of International Relations, Partnership and Prospects
EMail: akinoyebode@unilag.edu.ng; akin.oyebode@gmail.com; inter-rel@unilag.edu.ng

Centres

Information Technology and Systems (Computer Engineering; Computer Networks; Computer Science; Data Processing; Graphic Design; Information Technology; Management)

Colleges

Medicine *(Idi-Araba)* (Dental Technology; Dentistry; Medicine; Paediatrics; Pharmacy; Physical Therapy; Physiology; Surgery)

Faculties

Arts (African Languages; Arts and Humanities; English; Fine Arts; French; History; International Relations; Islamic Studies; Linguistics; Modern Languages; Music; Performing Arts; Philosophy; Russian; Theatre; Visual Arts); **Business Administration** (Accountancy; Actuarial Science; Banking; Business Administration; Finance; Human Resources; Insurance; Labour and Industrial Relations); **Education** (Accountancy; Adult Education; Art Education; Biology; Business and Commerce; Business Education; Chemistry; Christian Religious Studies; Curriculum; Economics; Education; Educational Administration; Educational and Student Counselling; Educational Technology; English; Foreign Languages Education; French; Geography; Health Education; History; Home Economics; Humanities and Social Science Education; Islamic Studies; Islamic Theology; Mathematics; Mathematics Education; Native Language Education; Nursing; Physical Education; Physics; Political Sciences; Religious Education; Science Education; Social Studies; Technology Education); **Engineering** (Chemical Engineering; Civil Engineering; Computer Engineering; Computer Science; Electrical and Electronic Engineering; Engineering; Environmental Engineering; Materials Engineering; Mechanical Engineering; Metallurgical Engineering; Surveying and Mapping; Systems Analysis); **Environmental Sciences** (Architecture; Building Technologies; Real Estate; Regional Planning; Town Planning); **Law** (Commercial Law; International Law; Labour Law; Law; Private Law; Public Law); **Pharmacy** (Biological and Life Sciences; Pharmacology; Pharmacy; Technology); **Science** (Applied Physics; Biochemistry; Botany; Cell Biology; Chemistry; Computer Science; Earth Sciences; Genetics; Geography; Geology; Geophysics; Industrial Chemistry; Marine Science and Oceanography; Mathematics; Mathematics and Computer Science; Microbiology; Physics; Statistics; Zoology); **Social Sciences and Management Sciences** *(Ago-Iwoye Campus)* (Accountancy; Banking; Business Administration; Economics;

Geography; Labour and Industrial Relations; Management; Mass Communication; Political Sciences; Psychology; Public Administration; Regional Planning; Social Sciences; Sociology; Transport Management)

Institutes

Distance Learning (Accountancy; Business Administration; Communication Studies; Educational Sciences; Information Technology; Library Science)

Schools

Postgraduate Studies (Accountancy; Actuarial Science; Adult Education; African Languages; Anaesthesiology; Analytical Chemistry; Anatomy; Architectural and Environmental Design; Architecture; Art Education; Biochemistry; Biology; Biomedical Engineering; Botany; Building Technologies; Business Administration; Cell Biology; Chemical Engineering; Civil Engineering; Computer Science; Criminology; Economics; Education; Educational Administration; Electrical and Electronic Engineering; Engineering Management; English; Environmental Engineering; Environmental Management; Finance; Fishery; Foreign Languages Education; French; Genetics; Geography; Geology; Geophysics; Haematology; Health Education; History; Humanities and Social Science Education; Industrial and Organizational Psychology; Information Sciences; Information Technology; Insurance; International Law; International Relations; Labour and Industrial Relations; Landscape Architecture; Law; Management; Marine Biology; Marine Science and Oceanography; Marketing; Mass Communication; Materials Engineering; Mathematics; Mechanical Engineering; Metallurgical Engineering; Microbiology; Modern Languages; Music; Natural Resources; Operations Research; Parasitology; Pathology; Pharmacology; Philosophy; Physical Education; Physical Therapy; Political Sciences; Psychology; Public Administration; Public Health; Real Estate; Regional Planning; Sociology; Statistics; Surveying and Mapping; Technology Education; Theatre; Town Planning; Toxicology; Translation and Interpretation; Transport Management; Visual Arts)

Further Information: Also Teaching Hospital. A traditional and distance learning institution.

History: Founded 1962.

Governing Bodies: Governing Council headed by a Pro-Chancellor

Academic Year: October to July (October-February; March-July)

Admission Requirements: Universities Matriculation Examination (UME) following secondary school education, or direct entry for holders of the Higher School Certificate (General Certificate of Education, GCE, Advanced ('A') level)

Fees: (Naira): New students: 31,500 (Science); 29,500 (Non-Science) per session; Returning Students: 5,500-6,000 -per session - Undergraduate programme

Main Language(s) of Instruction: English

International Co-operation: With universities in United Kingdom and USA

Accrediting Agencies: National Universities Commission (NUC); Variuous Professional Bodies i.e COREN, Pharmacy Board etc.

Degrees and Diplomas: *Bachelor's Degree*; *Postgraduate Diploma (PGD)*; *Master's Degree*; *Master of Philosophy (M.Phil)*; *Doctor of Philosophy (PhD)*. Also MBA and Executive MBA.

Student Services: Academic counselling, Canteen, Cultural centre, Employment services, Foreign Studies Centre, Health services, Language programs, Nursery care, Social counselling, Sports facilities

Student Residential Facilities: Yes

Special Facilities: Biological Garden; Arts Gallery; Guest House; Conference Centre

Libraries: A total of 460,317 books; 4,690 journal titles; 622,922 vols of journals and on-line journal subscriptions

Press or Publishing House: University of Lagos Press

Academic Staff *2011-2012*	**TOTAL**
FULL-TIME	**810**
PART-TIME	c. **2,620**
Student Numbers *2011-2012*	
All (Foreign Included)	c. **40,000**

Part-time students, 6,000. **Distance students**, 7,200.

Last Updated: 18/07/12

UNIVERSITY OF MAIDUGURI (UNIMAID)

PMB 1069, Maiduguri, Borno State
Tel: +234(76) 231-730
EMail: info@unimaid.edu.ng; uni_maid@hotmail.com
Website: http://www.unimaid.org

Vice-Chancellor: M.M. Daura

Registrar: Baba Gana M. Aji

Deputy Vice-Chancellor, Central Administration: Yaganami Karta

Centres

Arid Zone Studies (Arid Land Studies); **Disaster and Risk** (Safety Engineering); **Distance Learning**; **ICT** (Information Technology); **Normadic Education** (Education); **Peace and Development** (Development Studies; Peace and Disarmament); **Trans-Saharan Studies** (Arid Land Studies)

Colleges

Medical Sciences (Anatomy; Dentistry; Laboratory Techniques; Medicine; Nursing; Physical Therapy; Radiology; Surgery)

Faculties

Agriculture (Agricultural Economics; Agriculture; Animal Husbandry; Crop Production; Fishery; Forestry; Plant and Crop Protection; Soil Science; Wildlife); **Arts** (African Languages; Arabic; Arts and Humanities; English; Fine Arts; History; Islamic Studies; Linguistics; Modern Languages); **Education** (Adult Education; Art Education; Education; Health Education; Library Science; Physical Education; Science Education); **Engineering** (Agricultural Engineering; Chemical Engineering; Civil Engineering; Computer Engineering; Electrical and Electronic Engineering; Engineering; Food Science; Food Technology; Mechanical Engineering; Water Science); **Law** (Islamic Law; Law; Private Law; Public Law); **Management Sciences** (Accountancy; Business Administration; Economics; Management; Public Administration); **Pharmacy** (Pharmacy); **Science** (Biochemistry; Biological and Life Sciences; Chemistry; Geology; Mathematics; Microbiology; Physics; Statistics); **Social Sciences** (Anthropology; Geography; Mass Communication; Political Sciences; Sociology); **Veterinary Science** (Anatomy; Biochemistry; Medicine; Microbiology; Parasitology; Pathology; Pharmacology; Physiology; Public Health; Social and Preventive Medicine; Surgery; Veterinary Science)

Schools

Postgraduate Studies

Further Information: Also Teaching Hospital. A traditional and distance learning institution.

History: Founded 1975.

Governing Bodies: Governing Council; Senate

Academic Year: October to June (October-February/March; March-June)

Admission Requirements: Either Senior School Leaving Certificate (SSLC) or General Certificate of Education (GCE) 'O' level with at least 5 credits in relevant subjects and good scores in the University Matriculation Examination; or GCE 'A' level with minimum C grade in at least 3 relevant subjects. Application is through Joint Admission and Matriculation Board (JAMB).

Main Language(s) of Instruction: English

Degrees and Diplomas: *Bachelor's Degree*; *Postgraduate Diploma (PGD)*; *Master's Degree (MA)*; *Master of Philosophy (MPhil)*; *Doctor of Philosophy (PhD)*

Student Services: Academic counselling, Cultural centre, Foreign Studies Centre, Health services, Nursery care, Social counselling, Sports facilities

Student Residential Facilities: Yes

Libraries: Main Library, c. 116,500 vols

Publications: The Annals of Borno (Multidisciplinary Yearbook of Research) *(annually)*

Press or Publishing House: University of Maiduguri Printing Press

Last Updated: 18/07/12

UNIVERSITY OF NIGERIA NSUKKA (UNN)

Nsukka, Enugu State
Tel: +234(42) 771-500
Fax: +234(42) 770-644
EMail: misunn@aol.com
Website: http://www.unn.edu.ng/

Vice-Chancellor: Bartholomew N. Okolo
Tel: +234(708) 861-7000, Fax: +234(42) 770-644
EMail: batho.okolo@unn.edu.ng

Registrar: Anthony I. Okonta
Tel: +234(805) 0259-490 EMail: anthony.okonta@unn.edu.ng

Deputy Vice-Chancellor, Administration: Malachy Ike Okwueze
Tel: +234(803) 775-9549 EMail: okwueze.malachy@unn.edu.ng

Centres

American Studies (American Studies); **Basic Space Science** (Astronomy and Space Science); **Curriculum Development and Instructional Materials** (Curriculum; Educational Technology); **Energy Research and Development** (Energy Engineering; Environmental Engineering); **Entreprenarial and Development Research** (Management); **Rural Development and Cooperatives** (Rural Studies)

Faculties

Agriculture (Agricultural Economics; Agriculture; Animal Husbandry; Crop Production; Dietetics; Food Science; Food Technology; Home Economics; Nutrition; Soil Science); **Arts** (African Languages; Archaeology; Arts and Humanities; English; Film; Fine Arts; French; German; History; International Studies; Linguistics; Literature; Mass Communication; Modern Languages; Music; Performing Arts; Philosophy; Religion; Russian; Theatre; Tourism); **Biological Sciences** (Biochemistry; Biological and Life Sciences; Botany; Microbiology; Zoology); **Business Administration** (Accountancy; Banking; Business Administration; Finance; Management; Marketing); **Education** (Adult Education; Art Education; Education; Health Education; Humanities and Social Science Education; Information Sciences; Library Science; Native Language Education; Physical Education; Religious Education; Science Education; Teacher Training; Vocational Education); **Engineering** (Agricultural Engineering; Civil Engineering; Electrical and Electronic Engineering; Engineering; Mechanical Engineering); **Environmental Studies** (Architecture; Real Estate; Rural Planning; Surveying and Mapping; Town Planning); **Health Sciences and Technology** (Health Administration; Laboratory Techniques; Nursing; Radiology; Rehabilitation and Therapy); **Law** (Commercial Law; International Law; Law; Private Law; Public Law); **Medical Sciences and Dentistry** (Anaesthesiology; Anatomy; Biochemistry; Clinical Psychology; Community Health; Dentistry; Dermatology; Forensic Medicine and Dentistry; Gynaecology and Obstetrics; Haematology; Immunology; Medicine; Microbiology; Nursing; Ophthalmology; Otorhinolaryngology; Paediatrics; Pathology; Pharmacology; Physiology; Radiology; Surgery); **Pharmaceutical Sciences** (Chemistry; Pharmacology; Pharmacy; Technology; Toxicology); **Physical Sciences** (Astronomy and Space Science; Chemistry; Computer Science; Geology; Industrial Chemistry; Mathematics; Physics; Statistics); **Social Sciences** (Anthropology; Economics; Geography (Human); Government; Philosophy; Political Sciences; Psychology; Public Administration; Religion; Social Sciences; Social Work; Sociology); **Veterinary Science** (Anatomy; Animal Husbandry; Embryology and Reproduction Biology; Entomology; Parasitology; Pathology; Pharmacology; Physiology; Public Health; Social and Preventive Medicine; Surgery; Veterinary Science)

Institutes

African Studies (African Studies; Museum Studies); **Development Studies** (Development Studies); **Education** (Adult Education; Curriculum; Distance Education; Education; Gender Studies; Health Education; Humanities and Social Science Education; Information Technology; Library Science; Physical Education; Science Education; Teacher Training; Vocational Education; Women's Studies)

Schools

General Studies (African Languages; African Studies; Archaeology; Arts and Humanities; Cultural Studies; Economic History; Economics; English; Fine Arts; Graphic Arts; Handicrafts; Human Rights; Islamic Studies; Leadership; Linguistics; Modern Languages; Natural Sciences; Peace and Disarmament; Philosophy; Phonetics; Tourism); **Postgraduate Studies** (Agriculture; Archaeology; Architecture; Arts and Humanities; Business Administration; Development Studies; Education; Engineering; Environmental Studies; Fine Arts; Health Sciences; Humanities and Social Science Education; Information Sciences; Library Science; Medicine; Music; Pharmacy; Public Administration; Public Health; Social Sciences; Surgery; Veterinary Science; Vocational Education)

Further Information: Also Enugu and Aba Campuses; Teaching Hospital; Management Information Systems Unit; Medical Centre; Works Services Department; Computing Centre; ICT and Innovation Centre and Centre for Technical Vocational Education, Training and Research.

History: Founded 1960. The former Nigerian College of Arts, Science and Technology, Enugu, was incorporated into the University 1961 and its buildings now form the Enugu campus of the University.

Governing Bodies: Governing Council, comprising 21 members; Senate

Academic Year: October to September

Admission Requirements: Universities Matriculation Examination (UME) following secondary school education, or direct entry for holders of the Higher School Certificate (General Certificate of Education, Advanced ('A') level)

Fees: (Naira): Tuition, undergraduate, free; postgraduate, c. 6,000-8,000 per annum; foreign students, African students, c. 8,000-16,000; students from Europe and North America, US$ c. 500-750

Main Language(s) of Instruction: English

Accrediting Agencies: National Universities Commission

Degrees and Diplomas: *Bachelor's Degree*; *Postgraduate Diploma*; *Master's Degree*; *Doctor of Philosophy (PhD)*. Also MBA.

Student Services: Academic counselling, Canteen, Foreign Studies Centre, Health services, Nursery care, Sports facilities

Student Residential Facilities: for c. 11,230 students

Special Facilities: Zoological Garden

Libraries: Nnamdi Azikiwe Library, 735,157 vols; c. 99,760 bound volumes of journals.

Press or Publishing House: University of Nigeria Press Ltd

Academic Staff *2011-2012*: Total: c. 1,700

Student Numbers *2011-2012*: Total: c. 36,000

Last Updated: 19/07/12

UNIVERSITY OF PORT HARCOURT (UNIPORT)

PMB 5323, Choba, Port Harcourt, Rivers State
Tel: +234(84) 817-941
EMail: registrar@uniport.edu.ng
Website: http://www.uniport.edu.ng

Vice-Chancellor: Joseph A. Ajienka
Tel: +234(84) 817-940 EMail: vc@uniport.edu.ng

Registrar: Matilda Nnodim

International Relations: Ngozi Ordu
Tel: +234(80) 64-34-19-44 EMail: uac@uniport.edu.ng

Centres

Continuing Education

Colleges

Health Sciences (Anaesthesiology; Anatomy; Gynaecology and Obstetrics; Haematology; Health Sciences; Medicine; Microbiology; Paediatrics; Pathology; Pharmacology; Physiology; Psychiatry and Mental Health; Social and Preventive Medicine; Surgery)

Faculties

Agriculture (Agriculture); **Basic Medical Sciences** (Medicine); **Clinical Sciences** (Medicine); **Dentistry** (Dentistry); **Education** (Accountancy; Adult Education; Continuing Education; Cultural Studies; Curriculum; Education; Educational Administration; Educational and Student Counselling; Educational Psychology; English; French; Health Education; History; Humanities and Social Science Education; International Relations; Religious Studies; Sports; Theatre; Visual Arts); **Engineering** (Chemical Engineering; Civil Engineering; Electrical and Electronic Engineering; Engineering; Environmental Engineering; Mechanical Engineering; Petroleum and Gas Engineering); **Humanities** (African Languages; Arts and Humanities; Communication Studies; English; Fine Arts; French; History; International Relations; Linguistics; Literature; Modern Languages; Philosophy; Religious Studies; Theatre); **Management Sciences** (Accountancy; Banking; Business Administration;

Finance; Management; Marketing); **Pharmacy** (Pharmacy); **Science** (Biochemistry; Biotechnology; Botany; Chemistry; Computer Science; Geology; Industrial Chemistry; Mathematics; Natural Sciences; Physics; Statistics; Zoology); **Social Sciences** (Administration; Economics; Environmental Management; Environmental Studies; Geography (Human); Political Sciences; Social Sciences; Sociology)

Institutes

Agricultural Research and Development (Agriculture); **Education** (Education); **Maternal and Child Care** (Child Care and Development); **Petroleum Studies** (Petroleum and Gas Engineering)

Schools

Graduate Studies

History: Founded 1975 as University College, acquired present status 1977.

Governing Bodies: Governing Council; Senate; Congregation; Convocation

Academic Year: October to July (October-February; April-July)

Admission Requirements: University Matriculation Examination (UME) following secondary school education

Fees: (Naira): Returning students and first year students: 2,700-9,750 per annum

Main Language(s) of Instruction: English

International Co-operation: With universities in USA, Canada and South Africa

Accrediting Agencies: National Universities Commission (NUC)

Degrees and Diplomas: *Bachelor's Degree (BA; BSc; BED)*: 4-6 yrs; *Postgraduate Diploma*: Education (PGDE), 1 yr following Bachelor's Degree; *Master's Degree (MA; MSc; MEd)*: a further 1-2 yrs; *Doctor of Philosophy (PhD)*: 3 yrs following Master's Degree

Student Services: Academic counselling, Canteen, Foreign student adviser, Health services, Language programs, Nursery care, Social counselling, Sports facilities

Student Residential Facilities: Yes

Libraries: c. 940,713 vols

Publications: JASEM, Journal of Applied Science and Environmental Management *(biannually)*; Kiabara: A Journal of the Humanities *(biannually)*

Press or Publishing House: University of Port Harcourt Press Limited

Last Updated: 04/06/12

UNIVERSITY OF UYO (UNIUYO)

PMB 1017, 1, Ikpa Road, Uyo, Akwa Ibom State
Tel: +234(85) 201-111
Fax: +234(85) 202-694
EMail: root@uniuyo.edu.ng
Website: http://www.uniuyo.edu.ng

Vice-Chancellor: Comfort Memfin Ekpo (2010-)
Tel: +234(85) 202-693, Fax: +234(85) 202-694
EMail: vc@uniuyo.edu.ng

Registrar: Edak Umondak
Tel: +234(0) 7068014231 EMail: uniuyo@yahoo.com

International Relations: Eno Etim Ituen, Director, International Pogrammes
Tel: +234(80) 65-213-967 EMail: enoituenus@gmail.com

Faculties

Agriculture (Agricultural Economics; Agriculture; Agronomy; Animal Husbandry; Aquaculture; Crop Production; Fishery; Food Science; Food Technology; Forestry; Home Economics; Soil Science; Wildlife; Zoology); **Arts and Humanities** (Advertising and Publicity; African Languages; Arts and Humanities; Communication Arts; English; French; History; International Studies; Journalism; Linguistics; Mass Communication; Modern Languages; Music; Philosophy; Public Relations; Radio and Television Broadcasting; Religion; Religious Studies; Theatre); **Basic Medical Sciences** (Anatomy; Biochemistry; Physiology); **Business Administration** (Accountancy; Banking; Business Administration; Finance; Insurance; Marketing); **Clinical Sciences** (Anaesthesiology; Community Health; Gynaecology and Obstetrics; Haematology; Medicine; Microbiology; Ophthalmology; Orthopaedics; Paediatrics; Parasitology; Pathology; Psychiatry and Mental Health; Radiology; Surgery); **Education** (Accountancy; African Languages; Agricultural Education; Agriculture; Art Education; Biology; Botany; Building Technologies; Business Education; Chemistry; Child Care and Development; Community Health; Computer Education; Curriculum; Economics; Education; Educational Administration; Educational and Student Counselling; Educational Psychology; Educational Technology; Electrical and Electronic Engineering; English; Fine Arts; French; Geography; Health Education; History; Home Economics; Home Economics Education; Humanities and Social Science Education; Information Sciences; Library Science; Mathematics; Mathematics Education; Music; Physical Education; Physics; Political Sciences; Preschool Education; Primary Education; Religion; Religious Studies; Science Education; Secretarial Studies; Social Studies; Special Education; Sports Management; Technology Education; Vocational Education; Wood Technology); **Engineering** (Agricultural Engineering; Chemical Engineering; Civil Engineering; Computer Engineering; Electrical Engineering; Electronic Engineering; Food Technology; Mechanical Engineering; Petroleum and Gas Engineering); **Environmental Studies** (Architecture; Building Technologies; Ceramic Art; Fine Arts; Graphic Arts; Industrial Design; Painting and Drawing; Real Estate; Regional Planning; Rural Planning; Sculpture; Surveying and Mapping; Textile Design; Textile Technology; Town Planning); **Law** (International Law; Law; Private Law; Public Law); **Pharmacy** (Alternative Medicine; Chemistry; Pharmacology; Pharmacy; Toxicology); **Science** (Analytical Chemistry; Applied Chemistry; Botany; Chemistry; Computer Science; Environmental Management; Geology; Mathematics; Microbiology; Physics; Statistics; Zoology); **Social Sciences** (Anthropology; Demography and Population; Development Studies; Economic History; Economics; Environmental Management; Geography (Human); International Relations; Management; Meteorology; Natural Resources; Political Sciences; Psychology; Public Administration; Regional Planning; Regional Studies; Social Sciences; Sociology; Urban Studies)

Schools

Continuing Education *(Diploma and Certificate programmes)* (Economic and Finance Policy; Environmental Studies; Finance; Fine Arts; French; Government; Human Resources; Insurance; International Relations; Library Science; Music; Public Administration; Religious Studies; Rural Planning; Theatre); **Postgraduate** (Accountancy; Advertising and Publicity; African Languages; Agricultural Economics; Agricultural Education; Analytical Chemistry; Anthropology; Applied Chemistry; Banking; Biology; Botany; Business Education; Ceramic Art; Chemistry; Child Care and Development; Community Health; Computer Education; Crop Production; Curriculum; Demography and Population; Development Studies; Economic History; Economics; Education; Educational Administration; Educational and Student Counselling; Educational Technology; English; Environmental Studies; Finance; Fine Arts; Forestry; French; Geography (Human); History; Home Economics; Home Economics Education; Information Sciences; International Relations; International Studies; Journalism; Library Science; Linguistics; Management; Marketing; Mass Communication; Mathematics; Mathematics Education; Meteorology; Microbiology; Native Language; Natural Resources; Painting and Drawing; Pharmacology; Pharmacy; Physical Education; Physics; Preschool Education; Public Administration; Public Relations; Radio and Television Broadcasting; Regional Planning; Regional Studies; Religion; Rural Planning; Science Education; Sculpture; Sociology; Soil Science; Sports Management; Technology Education; Textile Design; Town Planning; Urban Studies; Wildlife; Zoology)

Further Information: Also Commercial Farm; Educational Technology Unit; Science laboratory Technology Training Unit; Centre for Skills Development and Rural Development; Centre for Wetlands and Waste Management Studies.

History: Founded 1983 as University of Cross River State. Acquired present status of national university and title of University of Uyo in 1991.

Governing Bodies: Council; Senate

Academic Year: October to September

Admission Requirements: Senior Secondary Certificate/West African School Certificate/General Certificate of Education (GCE),

Ordinary ('O') level, or equivalent, with credit passes in at least 5 subjects, including English Language. Credit pass in Mathematics is required for Science-based and Social Science courses.

Fees: None

Main Language(s) of Instruction: English

International Co-operation: With universities in United Kingdom, USA, Germany, Namibia, Republic of Korea, Brazil, Ukraine

Accrediting Agencies: NUC; COREN; Council for Legal Education; Pharmacy Council of Nigeria; Dental and Medical Council of Nigeria.

Degrees and Diplomas: *Bachelor's Degree*: 3-7 yrs; *Postgraduate Diploma*: 1 further yr; *Master's Degree (M. A.)*: a further 1-2 yrs; *Doctor of Philosophy (PhD)*: a further 3-5 yrs; *Doctor of Philosophy*: (Collaborative) (Ph.D), a further 3-5 yrs. Also Certificates, 1 yr; Diplomas, 2 yrs; MBA and Executive MBA 1-2 yrs.

Student Services: Academic counselling, Canteen, Cultural centre, Employment services, Health services, Language programs, Nursery care, Sports facilities

Student Residential Facilities: 16 Hostels

Special Facilities: 9 Lecture Theatres/Auditoriums; 53 Laboratories; 16 Workshops/Studios/Gymnasia

Libraries: 4 Main Libraries; 12 Faculty Libraries; 50 Departmental Libraries. c. 64,000 vols, 1,420 journal titles

Publications: UNIUYO News Bulletin *(biannually)*

Academic Staff *2011-2012*	MEN	WOMEN	TOTAL
FULL-TIME	760	211	**971**
PART-TIME	197	17	**214**
STAFF WITH DOCTORATE			
FULL-TIME	557	111	**668**
PART-TIME	83	17	**100**
Student Numbers *2011-2012*			
All (Foreign Included)	9,578	7,459	**17,037**

Part-time students, 1,880. **Evening students**, 1,950.

Last Updated: 22/06/12

USMANU DANFODIYO UNIVERSITY, SOKOTO (UDUS)

PMB 2346, Sokoto
Tel: +234(60) 232-134
Fax: +234(60) 236-688
EMail: info@udusok.edu.ng

Vice-Chancellor: Shehu Arabu Riskuwa
Tel: +234(80) 3504-2256
EMail: rashehu@udusok.edu.ng; vc@udusok.edu.ng

Registrar: Umar U. Bunza
Tel: +234(80) 3579-5551
EMail: uubunza@udusok.edu.ng; registrar@udusok.edu.ng

International Relations: Lawal S. Bilbis, Director, Development Office Tel: +234(80) 33422-7001 EMail: bilbis360@hotmail.com

Colleges

Health Sciences (Anatomy; Community Health; Gynaecology and Obstetrics; Health Sciences; Medicine; Microbiology; Paediatrics; Pathology; Surgery)

Faculties

Agriculture (Agricultural Economics; Agricultural Engineering; Agriculture; Animal Husbandry; Crop Production; Fishery; Forestry; Soil Science; Zoology); **Law** (Commercial Law; Islamic Law; Law; Private Law); **Management** (Accountancy; Administration; Business Administration; Management; Public Administration); **Science** (Applied Chemistry; Biochemistry; Biology; Botany; Chemistry; Computer Science; Mathematics; Microbiology; Natural Sciences; Physics; Statistics; Zoology); **Social Sciences** (Social Sciences); **Veterinary Sciences** (Microbiology; Parasitology; Pathology; Pharmacology; Physiology; Surgery; Veterinary Science)

Further Information: Also Teaching Hospital.

History: Founded 1975 as University of Sokoto, acquired present title 1985.

Governing Bodies: Council; Senate

Academic Year: September to June (September-December; January-March; April-June)

Admission Requirements: Universities Matriculation Examination (UME) following secondary school education, or direct entry for holders of the Higher School Certificate (General Certificate of Education, Advanced ('A') level)

Fees: (Naira): Nigerians, 11,500-35,000; Non-Nigerians, 41,500-65,000. Postgraduate: Nigerians, 39,000-70,000; Non-Nigerians, 54,000-111,000

Main Language(s) of Instruction: English, Hausa, Arabic

Accrediting Agencies: National Universities Commission (NUC)

Degrees and Diplomas: *Bachelor's Degree*: Science; Arts; Law; Education; Veterinary Sciences; Agriculture; Forestry; Fishery; Medical Laboratory Science, 3-5 yrs; *Postgraduate Diploma*: Public Administration; Management; Education (PGD), 1-2 yrs; *Master's Degree*: Public Administration; Business Administration; International Affairs and Diplomacy; International Studies; Science; Arts; Education; Veterinary Science, 1-2 yrs; *Doctor of Philosophy*: Science; Arts; Agriculture; Forestry; Fisheries; Education; Veterinary Sciences; Health Sciences (PhD), 3-5 yrs

Student Services: Academic counselling, Canteen, Cultural centre, Health services, Language programs, Sports facilities

Libraries: 280,000 vols; 55,000 periodicals

Publications: Annals of African Medicine *(quarterly)*; Degel *(annually)*; Journal of Agriculture and Environment *(annually)*; Journal of Basic and Applied Sciences *(annually)*; Mallam, Journal of Hausa Research *(annually)*; Sahel Medical Journal, Basic and Clinical Medicine Journal *(quarterly)*; Sokoto Education Review *(annually)*; Sokoto Journal of Veterinary Medicine *(annually)*

Press or Publishing House: University Press

Last Updated: 06/11/12

WAZIRI UMARU FEDERAL POLYTECHNIC (WUFPBK)

34, Arugugun Road, Birnin Kebbi, Kebbi 1034
Tel: +234(68) 320-597 +234(68) 320-693 +234(68) 322-720
Fax: +234(68) 320-597
EMail: info@wufpbk.com; admissions@wufpbk.com
Website: http://wufpbk.com/

Rector: Mohammed Kabir Nabade

Colleges

Administration (Accountancy; Banking; Business Administration; Finance; Government; Marketing; Public Administration); **Engineering** (Agricultural Engineering; Civil Engineering; Electrical Engineering; Mechanical Engineering; Metallurgical Engineering; Power Engineering; Soil Science; Water Science); **Environmental Sciences** (Architecture; Building Technologies; Real Estate; Regional Planning; Surveying and Mapping; Town Planning); **Science and Technology** (Accountancy; Business Education; Computer Science; Laboratory Techniques; Mathematics; Metal Techniques; Secretarial Studies; Statistics; Technology; Technology Education; Vocational Education; Wood Technology)

Schools

Postgraduate Studies (Accountancy; Administration; Agricultural Engineering; Business Administration; Construction Engineering; Education; Environmental Engineering; Public Administration; Structural Architecture; Water Management)

History: Founded 1976 as Waziri Umaru Polytechnic. Became The Polytechnic, Birnin Kebbi 1991, with the creation of Kebbi State. Acquired present status and title 2006.

Governing Bodies: Governing Council

Fees: (Naira): 27,300-29,300 per session.

Main Language(s) of Instruction: English

Degrees and Diplomas: *National Diploma*; *Higher National Diploma*; *Postgraduate Diploma*. Also Certificates.

Special Facilities: Workshop; Centre for Information Technology

Libraries: Yes

Student Numbers *2011-2012*: Total: c. 8,000

Last Updated: 19/07/12

YABA COLLEGE OF TECHNOLOGY (YABATECH)

PMB 2011, Yaba, Lagos State
Tel: +234(1) 800-160
Fax: +234(1) 860-211
EMail: registrar@yabatech.edu.ng
Website: http://portal.yabatech.edu.ng/

Rector: M. K. Ladipo (2001-) EMail: rector@yabatech.edu.ng

Deputy Rector, Administration: H. A. Akubuiro

Registrar: Biekoroma C. Amapakabo Tel: 234(1) 794-9077

Centres

Entrepreneurship Development (Business Administration; Commercial Law; Insurance; Management; Marketing)

Schools

Art, Design and Printing (Ceramic Art; Design; Fashion Design; Fine Arts; Graphic Arts; Graphic Design; Industrial Design; Painting and Drawing; Photography; Printing and Printmaking; Sculpture; Textile Design); **Engineering** (Automotive Engineering; Building Technologies; Civil Engineering; Computer Engineering; Electrical and Electronic Engineering; Electrical Engineering; Engineering; Industrial Engineering; Industrial Maintenance; Maintenance Technology; Mechanical Engineering; Metallurgical Engineering; Power Engineering; Production Engineering; Structural Architecture; Transport Engineering); **Environmental Studies** (Architecture; Building Technologies; Civil Engineering; Real Estate; Regional Planning; Surveying and Mapping; Town Planning); **Liberal Studies** *(SLS)* (Mass Communication; Modern Languages; Social Sciences); **Management and Business Studies** *(SMBS)* (Accountancy; Banking; Business Administration; Finance; Management; Marketing; Secretarial Studies); **Science** (Biological and Life Sciences; Biology; Chemistry; Laboratory Techniques; Mathematics; Physics; Statistics); **Technical Education** (Art Education; Computer Education; Home Economics; Mathematics Education; Primary Education; Science Education; Secondary Education; Teacher Training; Technology Education; Vocational Education); **Technology** (Computer Science; Cooking and Catering; Food Science; Mathematics; Polymer and Plastics Technology; Technology; Textile Technology)

Units

Applied Research and Technology Innovation *(ARTI)* (Technology)

History: Founded as Yaba Technical Institute 1947 and renamed Yaba College of Technology 1963. Became an autonomous Federal Government owned institution with the promulgation of Yaba College of Technology Decree N° 23 of 1969. Presently the College is governed under the Federal Polytechnics Act [CAP, 139] of the Laws of the Federation 1990, and the Federal Polytechnics (Amendment) Decree 1993.

Governing Bodies: College Governing Council; College Management comprising principal officers [Rector, Deputy Rector (Academics and Administration), Polytechnic librarian, Registar and Business], Heads of Service Units, Deans of Schools and Heads of Departments

Academic Year: September to December

Admission Requirements: For National Diploma (ND): 5 credit passes, including English Language and Mathematics at Senior school Certificate Examination (SSCE), General Certificate Examination (GCE) or approved equivalent. For Higher National Diploma (HND) and BSc (Ed.): 5 credit passes as indicated for ND and a Minimum of Lower Credit at ND level in addition to one year compulsory industrial training or minimum of National Certificate Examination (NCE) at merit level.

Fees: (Naira): 32,000 per session.

Main Language(s) of Instruction: English

Accrediting Agencies: National Board for Technical Education (NBTE)

Degrees and Diplomas: *National Diploma (ND)*: 2 yrs; *Higher National Diploma (HND)*; *Bachelor's Degree*; *Postgraduate Diploma*: Urban and Regional Planning (PGD). Also Certificates; Post-Higher National Diploma (Post-HND). The Bachelor's degree is run in affiliation with the University of Nigeria, Nsukka.

Student Services: Academic counselling, Canteen, Health services, Language programs, Social counselling, Sports facilities

Student Residential Facilities: Staff Quarters, Students' Hostels

Special Facilities: Art Gallery

Libraries: c. 73,000 vols; E-Library

Academic Staff *2011-2012*: Total: c. 1,600

Student Numbers *2011-2012*: Total 15,000

Last Updated: 19/07/12

PRIVATE INSTITUTIONS

ACHIEVERS UNIVERSITY

PMB 1030, Km 1, Idasen/Ute Road, Owo, Ondo State
Tel: +234(803) 374-6527 +234(803) 370-8660 +234(803) 219-7040
EMail: info@achievers.edu.ng
Website: http://achievers.edu.ng

Vice-Chancellor: Johnson A. Odebiyi EMail: vc@achievers.edu.ng

Registrar: T.E. Ojo

Colleges

Natural and Applied Sciences (Biochemistry; Biological and Life Sciences; Biology; Biotechnology; Chemistry; Computer Science; Electronic Engineering; Genetics; Geology; Industrial Chemistry; Information Sciences; Laboratory Techniques; Mathematics; Medical Technology; Microbiology; Natural Sciences; Physics; Statistics); **Social and Management Sciences** (Actuarial Science; Banking; Business Administration; Economics; Finance; Geography; Human Resources; Insurance; International Business; International Relations; Management; Marketing; Political Sciences; Social Sciences)

History: Founded 2007.

Governing Bodies: Senate; Governing Council

Fees: (Naira): 200,000-320,000 per session.

Main Language(s) of Instruction: English

Degrees and Diplomas: *Bachelor's Degree*

Special Facilities: Information and Communication Technology Center

Last Updated: 04/07/12

AFRICAN UNIVERSITY OF SCIENCE AND TECHNOLOGY (AUST)

PMB 681, Garki, (Street address: Km 10 Airport Road, Galadimawa), Abuja, Federal Capital Territory
Tel: +234(9) 780-0680
EMail: studentaffairs@aust.edu.ng
Website: http://aust-abuja.org/

President: Wale Soboyejo

Chief Academic Officer: Charles Chidume

Programmes

Computer Science (Computer Engineering; Computer Science; Software Engineering); **Materials Science and Engineering** (Materials Engineering); **Petroleum Engineering** (Petroleum and Gas Engineering); **Pure and Applied Mathematics** (Applied Mathematics; Mathematics; Statistics); **Theoretical Physics** (Astronomy and Space Science; Physics)

History: Founded 2007.

Governing Bodies: Board of Trustees; Nelson Mandela Institution (NMI, Inc.) Board of Directors; Independent Scientific Advisory Board; African Scientific Committee

Admission Requirements: BSc Honours Degree in Mathematics, Computer Science, Engineering or Science from a recognized university with a minimum of Second Class Upper or a G.P.A. of at least 3.5

Fees: (U.S. Dollars): 10,000 per annum

Degrees and Diplomas: *Master's Degree (MSc)*; *Doctor of Philosophy*: Petroleum Engineering (PhD)

Last Updated: 05/07/12

AJAYI CROWTHER UNIVERSITY

PMB 1066, Ibadan, Oyo State
EMail: info.ajayicrowtheruniversityoyo@gmail.com
Website: http://www.acu.edu.ng

Vice-Chancellor: Kolawole Timothy Jaiyeoba (2010-)

Registrar: Josephine Oyebanji

Faculties

Humanities (Arts and Humanities; Christian Religious Studies; Comparative Religion; English; History; International Relations; Modern Languages; Religion; Theology); **Natural Sciences** (Biological and Life Sciences; Biology; Chemistry; Computer Science; Earth Sciences; Electronic Engineering; Geology; Industrial Chemistry; Information Technology; Mineralogy; Natural Sciences; Physics); **Social and Management Sciences** (Accountancy; Actuarial Science; Advertising and Publicity; Banking; Business Administration; Communication Studies; Economics; Finance; Insurance; Journalism; Management; Marketing; Mass Communication; Media Studies; Public Relations; Radio and Television Broadcasting; Social Sciences; Sociology)

Further Information: A Faculty of Law is to be set up in the 2,010-2,015 period.

History: Founded 2005.

Governing Bodies: Board of Trustees; Governing Council

Main Language(s) of Instruction: English

Degrees and Diplomas: *Bachelor's Degree*: 4-5 yrs

Student Services: Health services, Sports facilities

Student Residential Facilities: Halls of residence (3,000 beds capacity)

Special Facilities: Career placement and counselling unit; Lecture rooms and Theatres; Language laboratory; Television and one radio broadcast studio; Printing studio; Photo studio; 20 laboratories/workshops; 3 entrepreneurial education workshops

Libraries: Over 20,000 vols

Last Updated: 05/07/12

AL-HIKMAH UNIVERSITY

P.M.B. 1601, Adeta Road, Adewole Housing Estate, Ilorin, Kwara State
Tel: +234 7065 446931
EMail: info@alhikmah.edu.ng; admissions@alhikmah.edu.ng; dynmo2002@yahoo.com; dynmo2002@hotmail.com
Website: http://www.alhikmahuniversity.com/index.php

Vice-Chancellor: Suleman Age Abdul Kareem (2010-)
EMail: sakareem54@yahoo.com; vcalhikmah@yahoo.com

Registrar: Rasheedat Modupe Oladimeji
Tel: +234 8039 170445 EMail: rashdupe@yahoo.com

International Relations: R.K. Omoloso, Academic Planning Unit
Tel: +234 8035 061088 EMail: gbolaloso@yahoo.com

Colleges

Education (Accountancy; Agricultural Education; Arabic; Biology; Business Education; Chemistry; Computer Education; Economics; Education; Educational Administration; Educational and Student Counselling; English; Foreign Languages Education; Humanities and Social Science Education; Islamic Studies; Mathematics Education; Physics; Political Sciences; Preschool Education; Primary Education; Science Education; Secondary Education; Social Studies); **Humanities** (Arabic; English; History; International Studies; Islamic Studies; Mass Communication; Peace and Disarmament; Political Sciences); **Management Sciences** (Accountancy; Banking; Business Administration; Economics; Finance; Marketing); **Natural Sciences** (Biochemistry; Biology; Computer Science; Geology; Industrial Chemistry; Mathematics; Microbiology; Mineralogy; Physics; Statistics)

Further Information: Also Igbaja campus.

History: Founded 2005.

Main Language(s) of Instruction: English

Accrediting Agencies: National Universities Commission (NUC)

Degrees and Diplomas: *Bachelor's Degree*. Also Sub-degree Diploma in Arabic and Islamic Studies, English Language, International Relations, Accountancy, Business Administration, Marketing, Computer Science.

Student Services: Health services, Sports facilities

Student Residential Facilities: Hall of Residence

Libraries: c. 7,000 vols; 500 periodical subscriptions

Student Numbers *2012-2013*: Total 3,200
Last Updated: 14/03/13

AMERICAN UNIVERSITY OF NIGERIA (AUN)

PMB 2250, Lamido Zubairu Way, Yola Township By-Pas, Yola, Adamawa State
Tel: +234(805) 200-0703
Fax: +234(805) 200-2962
EMail: admissions@aun.edu.ng
Website: http://www.americanuniversitynigeria.org/

President: Margee M. Ensign
Tel: +234(805) 502-7774
EMail: margee.ensign@aun.edu.ng; president@aun.edu.ng

Vice President, Enrollment Management and Dean of Student Life: Byron Bullock EMail: byron.bullock@aun.edu.ng

Registrar: Monique Davis
Tel: +234(805) 824-5008 EMail: registrar@aun.edu.ng

International Relations: Conrad Festa, Academic Vice-President
Tel: +234(805) 720-2980 EMail: conrad.festa@aun.edu.ng

Programmes

Graduate Studies (Information Technology; Telecommunications Engineering)

Schools

Arts and Science (Biology; Chemistry; Comparative Politics; Economics; English; Environmental Studies; Health Sciences; International Relations; Literature; Natural Sciences; Petroleum and Gas Engineering); **Business and Entrepreneurship** (Accountancy; Business Administration; Economics; Finance; Management; Marketing); **Information Technology and Communications** (Computer Engineering; Computer Networks; Computer Science; Data Processing; Information Technology; Software Engineering; Telecommunications Engineering)

History: Founded 2003. Acquired present status 2007.

Governing Bodies: Board of Trustees

Academic Year: September to May

Admission Requirements: JAMB with 160 points and above; 5 academic credits including mathematics and English; or equivalent from other countries; excellent transcript and recommendation from last school attended

Fees: (Naira): Tuition 53,000 per credit; 1,590,000 per annum

Main Language(s) of Instruction: English

International Co-operation: Consultancy agreement with American University (AU) in Washington D.C. (USA)

Degrees and Diplomas: *Bachelor's Degree*; *Postgraduate Diploma*: Telecommunications Systems; *Master's Degree*: Information Technology; Telecommunications Systems, 1 1/2-3 yrs; *Doctor of Philosophy*: Telecommunications Systems (PhD), 3-5 yrs

Student Services: Academic counselling, Canteen, Employment services, Foreign student adviser, Health services, Language programs, Social counselling, Sports facilities

Student Residential Facilities: Yes

Last Updated: 06/07/12

BABCOCK UNIVERSITY (BU)

Campus, Ilishan-Remo, Ogun State
Tel: +234(803) 402-3361 +234(805) 829-9014
EMail: registrar@babcock.edu.ng
Website: http://www.babcock.edu.ng/

President / Vice-Chancellor: James Kayode Makinde (2006-)
Tel: +234(803) 402-3356

EMail: president@babcock.edu.ng; babcokuniversity.vc@gmail.com; makindej@babcock.edu.ng

Associate Vice-President, Enrolment and Records/Registrar: Pastor Hakeem Smith

Director, Academic Planning: James Ogunji
EMail: ogunjija@yahoo.com

Senior Vice President/Deputy Vice Chancellor: Iheanyichukwu Okoro

Vice President Student Development: Janet Ola

Vice President, Financial Affairs: Luke Onuoha
EMail: registrar@babcockuni.edu.ng

International Relations: Olukunle Iyanda, Vice-President, Development and Strategy
Tel: +234(803) 978-8027 EMail: vpds@babcock.edu.ng

Schools

Business *(Babcock)* (Accountancy; Banking; Business Administration; Economics; Finance; Information Management; Marketing; Mass Communication; Political Sciences; Public Administration); **Education and Humanities** (Arts and Humanities; Education; English; French; History; International Studies; Religious Studies); **Graduate**; **Law and Security Studies** (Criminology; International Law; International Relations; Law); **Medicine** *(Benjamin S. Carson)* (Anatomy; Biochemistry; Medicine; Microbiology; Physiology); **Nursing** (Nursing); **Postgraduate** (Agricultural Economics; Agronomy; Biochemistry; Business Administration; Computer Science; Finance; History; Information Management; International Relations; Literature; Marketing; Mass Communication; Modern Languages; Pastoral Studies; Political Sciences; Public Administration; Public Health; Zoology); **Public Health** (Laboratory Techniques; Public Health; Social Work); **Science and Technology** (Agricultural Engineering; Biological and Life Sciences; Biotechnology; Computer Engineering; Computer Science; Industrial Engineering; Mathematics; Technology)

History: Founded 1959 as Adventist College of West Africa (ACWA). Acquired present status 1999.

Degrees and Diplomas: *Bachelor's Degree*: Agriculture; Crop Production; Animal Husbandry; Agriculture Economics, Nutrition and Dietetics; Nursing; Medical Laboratory, 5 yrs; *Bachelor's Degree*: Information Resources Management; Public Health; Microbiology; Biochemistry; Computer Science; Economics; Marketing; Banking and Finance; Accounting; Political Science; Public Administration; International Law and Diplomacy; Law; Social Works, 4 yrs; *Bachelor's Degree*: Medicine, 6 yrs; *Bachelor's Degree*: Religion Studies; History and International Studies; English Studies; Mass Communication; French Studies; *Postgraduate Diploma*: Education; Finance; Mass Communication; *Master's Degree*: Finance; Political Science; Public Management; Agronomy, Animal Science; Biochemistry; Microbiology; Environmental Management Science; Computer Science; Public Health; Mass Communication; Marketing; Pastoral Ministry; Information Resource Management; Education (Counseling Psychology); Diplomatic Studies; History; English (English Language and English Literature); Accounting; Business Administration (MA, MSc, M.Ed, MIRM, MPM, MBA, MILD, MDS, MPH); *Doctor of Philosophy*: Agronomy, Animal Science; Biochemistry; Microbiology; Environmental Management Science; Computer Science; Public Health; Mass Communication; Marketing; Information Resource Management; Education (Counseling Psychology); Diplomatic Studies; History; English (English Language & English Literature); Accounting; Business Administration; Finance; Political Science; Public Management (Ph.D.)

Publications: ACTA SATECH, Journal of the School of Science and Technology; Babcock Journal of Economics, Banking and Finance, Publication of the School of Management and Social Sciences; Babcock Journal of Management and Social Science (BJMASS), Publication of the School of Management and Social Sciences; Babcock Journal of Mass Communication, Publication of the Dept. of Mass Communication; Beyond Babel, Journal of Language and Literary Studies; BU Journal of History and International Studies, Publication of the School of Law and Security Studies; BU Social-Legal Journal; Contemporary Humanities, Produced by the School of Education and Humanities; Insight, Journal of Religious Studies Department; International Review of Politics and Development, Publication of the School of Management and Social Sciences

Press or Publishing House: Babcock University Press

Academic Staff *2011-2012*	MEN	WOMEN	**TOTAL**
FULL-TIME	231	95	**326**
PART-TIME	11	6	**17**
STAFF WITH DOCTORATE			
FULL-TIME	100	21	**121**
Student Numbers *2011-2012*			
All (Foreign Included)	3,584	3,876	**7,460**

Last Updated: 27/06/12

BELLS UNIVERSITY OF TECHNOLOGY

PMB 1015, Km. 8, Idiroko Road, Benja Village, Ota, Ogun State
Tel: +234(1) 794-9215
EMail: info@bellsuniversity.org
Website: http://www.bellsuniversity.org/

Vice-Chancellor: Isaac Adebayo Adeyemi (2006-)
EMail: adeagiri@bellsuniversity.org

Registrar: Oluyemisi O. Gbadebo
EMail: registrar@bellsuniversity.org

Colleges

Engineering (Biomedical Engineering; Computer Engineering; Electrical and Electronic Engineering; Electronic Engineering; Engineering; Mechanical Engineering; Telecommunications Engineering); **Environmental Sciences** (Building Technologies; Computer Science; Earth Sciences; Environmental Studies; Real Estate; Regional Planning; Surveying and Mapping; Town Planning); **Food Science** (Biotechnology; Business Administration; Cooking and Catering; Dietetics; Food Science; Food Technology; Home Economics; Hotel and Restaurant; Nutrition); **Information and Communications Technology** (Computer Engineering; Computer Science; Information Technology); **Management Sciences** (Accountancy; Banking; Business Computing; Economics; Finance; Human Resources; International Business; Management; Marketing; Transport Management); **Natural and Applied Sciences** (Applied Mathematics; Biochemistry; Industrial Chemistry; Microbiology; Natural Sciences; Physics; Statistics)

Further Information: Also Badagry Campus

History: Founded 2005.

Governing Bodies: Board of Trustees; Council; Senate

Admission Requirements: Candidates must have sat for the current year's Unified Tertiary Matriculation Examination (UTME) or obtained the UTME Direct Entry Form where applicable. Candidates applying for admission into any undergraduate Programme must possess a minimum of five (5) O' Level Credit passes at one sitting or two sittings in SSCE / GCE / NECO / NABTEB or equivalents which must include Credit passes in English Language and Mathematics, and other subjects relevant to the proposed course of study

Main Language(s) of Instruction: English

Degrees and Diplomas: *Bachelor's Degree*: 4-5 yrs. Also Predegree Programmes.

Last Updated: 06/07/12

BENSON IDAHOSA UNIVERSITY (BIU)

PMB 1100, University Way, Off Upper Adesuwa Grammar School Rd, Benin City, Edo State
Tel: +234(807) 976-1091 +234(807) 330-7885
EMail: info@biu.edu.ng
Website: http://www.biu.edu.ng/

Vice-Chancellor: Idu MacDonald

Registrar: Timothy M.E. Dogun II

Colleges

Law (Civil Law; Law; Private Law; Public Law)

Faculties

Agriculture and Agricultural Technology (Agricultural Economics; Agriculture; Animal Husbandry; Crop Production; Fishery; Forestry; Soil Science); **Arts and Education** (Business Education; Christian Religious Studies; Computer Education; Economics; Education; English; Foreign Languages Education; French; Humanities and Social Science Education; Information Sciences; International Relations; International Studies; Library Science; Mathematics; Mathematics Education; Political Sciences; Religious Studies; Science Education; Theology); **Basic and Applied**

Sciences (Agriculture; Applied Physics; Biochemistry; Biological and Life Sciences; Botany; Chemistry; Computer Engineering; Computer Science; Economics; Fishery; Forestry; Geophysics; Information Technology; Mathematics; Microbiology; Physics; Zoology); **Social and Management Sciences** (Accountancy; Anthropology; Banking; Business Administration; Economics; Finance; International Relations; Mass Communication; Political Sciences; Public Administration; Sociology)

Schools

Basic Studies *(SBS)*; **Postgraduate Studies**

History: Founded 2002.

Governing Bodies: Governing Council

Main Language(s) of Instruction: English

Degrees and Diplomas: *Bachelor's Degree*; *Postgraduate Diploma*; *Master's Degree*; *Doctor of Philosophy*

Libraries: 42,014 vols; 317 current journal titles (204 foreign and 113 local titles).

Last Updated: 06/07/12

BINGHAM UNIVERSITY

P.M.B 005, KM 26 Abuja-Keffi Expressway Kodope, Karu, Nasarawa State
Tel: +234(9) 670-0785
EMail: registrar@binghamuni.edu.ng
Website: http://www.binghamuni.edu.ng/

Vice-Chancellor: Felix Anjorin EMail: vc@binghamuni.edu.ng

Registrar: S. S. Sule

Colleges

Medical Science (Anatomy; Medicine; Physiology; Surgery)

Faculties

Humanities, Social and Management Sciences (Accountancy; Arts and Humanities; Business Administration; Economics; English; Geography; Management; Mass Communication; Political Sciences; Social Sciences; Sociology); **Science and Technology** (Biochemistry; Biological and Life Sciences; Biology; Botany; Chemistry; Computer Science; Industrial Chemistry; Mathematics; Microbiology; Physics; Statistics; Zoology)

History: Founded 2005.

Fees: (Naira): Tuition fee, 390,000-590,000

Degrees and Diplomas: *Bachelor's Degree*

Last Updated: 10/07/12

BOWEN UNIVERSITY

P.M.B. 284, Iwo, Osun State 232001
Tel: +234(803) 376-7903 +234(803) 546-9130
EMail: registrar_info@bowenuniversity-edu.org; timolag@yahoo.com
Website: http://www.bowenuniversity-edu.org

Vice-Chancellor: Timothy Oyebode Olagbemiro (2003-)
EMail: timolag@yahoo.com

International Relations: Elvis Abiodun Lawale, Registrar
EMail: registrar_infobowen@yahoo.com; lawale_biodun@yahoo.com

Colleges

Health Sciences (Anatomy; Arts and Humanities; Christian Religious Studies; Commercial Law; Communication Arts; English; Health Sciences; History; International Law; International Studies; Law; Medicine; Music; Philosophy; Physiology; Private Law; Public Law; Religious Studies; Surgery; Theatre)

Faculties

Agriculture (Agricultural Economics; Agriculture; Animal Husbandry; Crop Production; Environmental Management; Farm Management; Fishery; Food Science; Food Technology; Forestry; Rural Planning; Soil Management); **Science and Science Education** (Biochemistry; Biology; Chemistry; Computer Science; Energy Engineering; Industrial Chemistry; Information Technology; Mathematics; Microbiology; Physics; Plant Pathology; Statistics; Zoology); **Social and Management Sciences** (Accountancy; Banking; Business Administration; Economics; Finance; Mass Communication; Sociology)

Graduate Schools

Postgraduate Studies (Accountancy; Agricultural Economics; Agriculture; Animal Husbandry; Chemistry; Crop Production; Environmental Management; Management; Mathematics; Microbiology; Natural Sciences; Physics; Science Education; Social Sciences)

History: Founded 2001.

Governing Bodies: Governing Council; Senate

Academic Year: September to June

Admission Requirements: Minimum 5 passes at GCE 'O' level, including English and Mathematics.

Fees: (Naira): 450,000 and 750,000 per annum, depending on the programme

Main Language(s) of Instruction: English

International Co-operation: with institutions in USA, UK, Nigeria.

Accrediting Agencies: National Universities Commission

Degrees and Diplomas: *Bachelor's Degree*: Accounting; Banking and Finance; Business Administration; Economics; Mass Communication; Sociology (BSc); Agricultural Economics and Farm Management; Agricultural Extension and Rural Development; Animal Science and Fisheries Management; Crop Production and Soil Management; Forestry and Environmental Technology; Food Science and Technology (B.Agric; BSc); Microbiology; Plant Biology; Zoology; Biochemistry; Chemistry; Industrial Chemistry; Computer Science; Mathematics; Statistics; Physics and Solar Energy (BSc); Public and International Law; Private and Commercial Law (LLB), 4-5 yrs; *Bachelor's Degree*: Anatomy; Physiology (B.Sc.); Communication Arts; Music; Theatre Arts; English; History; History and International Studies; Philosophy; Religious Studies; Christian Religious Studies (B.A.), 3-4 yrs; *Bachelor's Degree*: Medicine; Surgery (MBBS), 5-6 yrs

Student Services: Academic counselling, Canteen, Employment services, Health services, Nursery care, Social counselling, Sports facilities

Student Residential Facilities: Fully residential for students

Special Facilities: Cow Ranch; Worship Centre; ICT Training and Service Centres

Libraries: c. 20,000 vols; 400 periodical subscriptions

Academic Staff *2010-2011*	MEN	WOMEN	TOTAL
FULL-TIME	175	42	**217**
PART-TIME	80	4	**84**
STAFF WITH DOCTORATE			
FULL-TIME	90	16	**106**
PART-TIME	60	3	**63**
Student Numbers *2009-2010*			
All (Foreign Included)	1,958	2,566	**4,524**

Last Updated: 01/06/12

CALEB UNIVERSITY

PMB 21238, Imota, Lagos, Lagos State
Tel: +234 (01) 291-0684 +234 (01) 291-0685
EMail: info@calebuniversity.edu.ng
Website: http://www.calebuniversity.edu.ng

Vice-Chancellor: Ayodeji O. Olukoju

Registrar: Bamidele Adetutu Awere

Colleges

Environmental Sciences and Management *(COLENSMA)* (Architecture; Building Technologies; Computer Science; Earth Sciences; Environmental Management; Environmental Studies; Real Estate; Regional Planning; Surveying and Mapping; Town Planning); **Pure and Applied Sciences** *(COPAS)* (Applied Physics; Biochemistry; Biological and Life Sciences; Biotechnology; Botany; Chemistry; Computer Science; Industrial Chemistry; Mathematics; Physics; Statistics; Zoology); **Social and Management Sciences** *(COSOMAS)* (Accountancy; Anthropology; Business Administration; Economics; Finance; International Relations; Journalism; Management; Mass Communication; Philosophy; Political Sciences; Social Sciences; Sociology)

History: Founded 2007.

Governing Bodies: Board of Trustees; Council; Senate

Main Language(s) of Instruction: English

Accrediting Agencies: National Universities Commission (NUC)

Degrees and Diplomas: *Bachelor's Degree*: 4-5 yrs

Special Facilities: Information and Communication Technology Unit (ICT Unit)

Libraries: c. 5,000 vols; 430 vols of reference materials; Collection of foreign and local Journals

Last Updated: 10/07/12

CARITAS UNIVERSITY

PMB 01784, Amorji Nike, Enugu State
Tel: +234(42) 306-788
EMail: caritasuniv@yahoo.com; info@caritasuni.edu.ng; enquiries@caritasuni.edu.ng
Website: http://www.caritasuni.edu.ng/

Vice-Chancellor: Lawrence Onukwube

Registrar: Thomas Ochang

Academies

Education (Biology; Business Education; Computer Education; Education; Foreign Languages Education; Geography; Science Education)

Faculties

Engineering (Chemical Engineering; Computer Engineering; Electrical Engineering; Engineering; Mechanical Engineering); **Environmental Sciences** (Architecture; Building Technologies; Environmental Studies; Real Estate; Regional Planning; Town Planning); **Management Sciences** (African Languages; Business Administration; Cultural Studies; English; Human Resources; Labour and Industrial Relations; Management; Public Administration); **Natural Sciences and Technology** (Biochemistry; Biological and Life Sciences; Biotechnology; Computer Science; Industrial Chemistry; Information Technology; Mathematics; Microbiology; Natural Sciences; Statistics; Technology); **Social Sciences** (Accountancy; Banking; Economics; Finance; Marketing; Mass Communication; Philosophy; Political Sciences; Psychology; Social Sciences; Sociology)

History: Founded 2005.

Admission Requirements: Senior Secondary School Certificate (SSCE) or the General Certificate of Education (G.C.E) Ordinary Level or its equivalent with Credit passes in five relevant subjects. Holders of the Higher School Certificate (GCE) Advanced Level will be considered for admission to Direct Entry provided that they also meet the minimum entry requirement stated above (this category of students will be admitted into the 100 level). Holders of the National Diploma (ND) in Estate Management with a minimum of Upper Credit (ie 60% mark and above) will be considered for admission by Direct Entry into the 200 level provided they meet requirements initially mentionned.

Main Language(s) of Instruction: English

Accrediting Agencies: National Universities Commission (NUC)

Degrees and Diplomas: *Bachelor's Degree*: 3-4 yrs; *Bachelor's Degree*: Engineering (B.Eng), 5 yrs; *Bachelor's Degree*: Industrial Relations and Personnel Management; Psychology; Sociology and Anthropology; *Master's Degree*: Architecture

Last Updated: 10/07/12

COVENANT UNIVERSITY (CU)

KM. 10 Idioko Road, Canaan Land, Ota, Ogun State
Tel: 234(1) 790-0724
EMail: contact@covenantuniversity.com
Website: http://www.covenantuniversity.com

Vice-Chancellor: Charles Korede Ayo (2012-)
Tel: +234(803) 406-8057, Fax: +234(806) 067-2018
EMail: vc@covenantuniversity.com

Acting Registrar: Ojo Emmanuel Olatunde
Tel: +234(803) 720-9306 EMail: registrar@covenantuniversity.com

International Relations: Nnamdi T. Ekeanyanwu, Director, International Office and Linkages
Tel: +234(803) 830-6772 EMail: nnamdiekeanyanwu@yahoo.com

Colleges

Development Studies *(CBS)* (Accountancy; Banking; Business Administration; Development Studies; Economics; English; Finance; French; Human Resources; International Relations; Mass Communication; Modern Languages; Political Sciences; Psychology; Social Sciences; Sociology); **Science and Technology** *(CST)* (Architecture; Biological and Life Sciences; Building Technologies; Chemical Engineering; Chemistry; Civil Engineering; Computer Science; Electrical and Electronic Engineering; Engineering; Environmental Studies; Information Sciences; Information Technology; Mathematics; Mechanical Engineering; Natural Sciences; Petroleum and Gas Engineering; Physics; Real Estate; Technology)

Schools

Postgraduate Studies (Accountancy; Architecture; Banking; Biochemistry; Building Technologies; Business Administration; Chemical Engineering; Chemistry; Civil Engineering; Computer Science; Development Studies; Economics; Energy Engineering; English; Finance; Human Resources; Industrial Engineering; Information Sciences; Information Technology; International Relations; Management; Mass Communication; Materials Engineering; Mechanical Engineering; Metallurgical Engineering; Microbiology; Physics; Political Sciences; Production Engineering; Psychology; Sociology)

History: Founded 2002.

Governing Bodies: Board of Trustees, Board of Regents

Academic Year: September to June

Admission Requirements: Passes in 5 subjects at SSCE/GCE 'O' level or equivalent and UME examination of the Joint Admissions and Matriculations Board (JAMB)

Fees: (Naira): 334,000-394,000 depending on field of studies

Main Language(s) of Instruction: English

International Co-operation: With universities in USA (Oral Roberts University; Fayetteville University; Texas A&M University) and Ukraine (Donetsk Technical University)

Accrediting Agencies: National Universities Commission (NUC)

Degrees and Diplomas: *Bachelor's Degree*; *Postgraduate Diploma*; *Master's Degree*: 2 yrs; *Doctor of Philosophy*: 3-4 yrs. Also MBA and Executive MBA

Student Services: Academic counselling, Canteen, Employment services, Foreign student adviser, Foreign Studies Centre, Health services, Language programs, Social counselling, Sports facilities

Student Residential Facilities: 10 Residential Halls (5 male and 5 female Halls) that can accommodate 9,150 students.

Special Facilities: Internet; Multimedia

Libraries: 70,000 vols; 1,515 electronic book titles, over 40,000 e-journal titles and 791 hardcopy titles

Publications: Covenant Journal of Business and Social Sciences *(biannually)*

Last Updated: 26/03/13

CRAWFORD UNIVERSITY

PMB 2001, Faith City, Kilometer 8, Atan - Agbara Road, Igbesa, Ogun State
Tel: +234(1) 813-4785 +234(1) 850-2828 +234(1) 5543-4412
EMail: info@crawforduniversity.edu.ng; registry@crawforduniversity.edu.ng
Website: http://www.crawforduniversity.edu.ng/

Vice-Chancellor: Samson Ayanlaja
EMail: vc@crawforduniversity.edu.ng

Colleges

Agriculture (Agricultural Economics; Agricultural Equipment; Agriculture; Animal Husbandry; Crop Production; Development Studies; Environmental Management; Farm Management; Fishery; Food Science; Food Technology; Plant and Crop Protection; Rural Studies; Soil Science); **Business and Social Sciences** (Accountancy; Actuarial Science; Administration; Banking; Business Administration; Economics; Finance; Geography; Labour and Industrial Relations; Marketing; Political Sciences; Public Administration; Regional Planning; Secretarial Studies; Social Sciences; Sociology; Town Planning); **Natural and Applied Sciences** (Biological and Life Sciences; Botany; Chemistry; Computer Science; Electronic Engineering; Geology; Industrial Chemistry; Information Technology; Mathematics; Mathematics and Computer Science; Microbiology; Mineralogy; Natural Sciences; Physics; Statistics; Zoology)

History: Founded 2005.

Governing Bodies: Governing Council

Admission Requirements: 100 Level students must have sat for the Unified Tertiary Matriculation Examination (UTME) and attained the cut-off marks as prescribed by the University Senate. In addition, candidates applying for admission into any undergraduate programme of Crawford University must possess a minimum of 5 O'Level Credit passes at not more than two sittings in SSCE, GCE, NECO or their equivalent, which must include Credit passes in English Language and Mathematics while the candidates must in addition satisfy the specific requirements for each programme. Direct Entry Candidates Candidates who seek direct entry admission into 200 Level of a degree programme must have any of the following:: B. Sc degree of a recognized university in a related field; 3 A'Level passes in the relevant courses acceptable to the University; O.N.D upper credit or H.N.D. in relevant courses.

Fees: (Naira): 295,000 per session

Main Language(s) of Instruction: English

Degrees and Diplomas: *Bachelor's Degree*: 4-5 yrs

Student Services: Canteen, Sports facilities

Libraries: Capacity of over 2 m. vols and over 1 m. vols of references/serial materials; Also 2 E-libraries with 60 and 25 computer units facilities.

Last Updated: 10/07/12

CRESCENT UNIVERSITY

PMB 2104, Sapon, Km 5 Ayetoro Road, Lafenwa, Abeokuta, Ogun State

Tel: +234(80) 306-44731

EMail: info@crescentuniversityng.com

Website: http://www.crescent-university.edu.ng

Vice-Chancellor: Kehinde Okeleye (2010-)
Tel: +234(80) 345-41894 EMail: professorokeleye@yahoo.co.uk

Registrar: Zakariyau Ajibola
Tel: +234(80) 381-71727 EMail: zakademda@yahoo.co.uk

International Relations: Idris Katib, Public Relations Officer
Tel: +234(80) 966-29914 EMail: idriskatib@yahoo.com

Colleges

Environmental Sciences (Architecture; Environmental Management; Environmental Studies; Natural Resources; Real Estate; Water Management); **Information and Communication Technology** (Computer Science; Economics; Information Technology; Statistics); **Law** (Commercial Law; International Law; Islamic Law; Law; Private Law); **Natural and Applied Sciences** (Analytical Chemistry; Applied Mathematics; Applied Physics; Aquaculture; Biochemistry; Biology; Chemistry; Fishery; Industrial Chemistry; Mathematics; Microbiology; Physics; Statistics); **Social and Management Sciences** (Accountancy; Actuarial Science; Banking; Business Administration; Demography and Population; Economics; Finance; Geography (Human); Human Resources; International Relations; Islamic Studies; Labour and Industrial Relations; Marketing; Mass Communication; Operations Research; Political Sciences; Sociology)

History: Founded 2005.

Governing Bodies: Council

Academic Year: September to July

Admission Requirements: Five 'O' Level credit passes including English language, Mathematics and other three relevant subjects at no more than two sittings in SSCE/WASC/GCE and NECO.

Fees: (Naira): 480,000 per session

Main Language(s) of Instruction: English

Accrediting Agencies: National Universities Commission (NUC); Council of Legal Education; Institute of Architecture; Chartered Institute of Bankers of Nigeria; Institute of Chartered Accountants of Nigeria.

Degrees and Diplomas: *Bachelor's Degree (B.Sc.)*

Student Services: Academic counselling, Canteen, Health services, Language programs, Social counselling, Sports facilities

Student Residential Facilities: Yes

Libraries: Yes

Publications: Crescent Voice

Press or Publishing House: Crescent University Press

Academic Staff *2011-2012*	MEN	WOMEN	TOTAL
FULL-TIME	65	17	**82**
PART-TIME	37	2	**39**
STAFF WITH DOCTORATE			
FULL-TIME	17	1	**18**
PART-TIME	22	1	**23**
Student Numbers *2011-2012*			
All (Foreign Included)	535	465	**1,000**

Part-time students, 12.

Last Updated: 04/06/12

FOUNTAIN UNIVERSITY

PMB 4491, Oke-Osun, Osogbo, Osun State

Website: http://www.fountainuniversity.edu.ng/

Vice-Chancellor: Hussain Oloyede

Registrar: Hakeem Bola Adekola

Colleges

Management Sciences (Accountancy; Administration; Banking; Business Administration; Economics; Finance; Human Resources; Labour and Industrial Relations; Management; Political Sciences; Psychology; Social Work; Sociology); **Natural and Applied Sciences** (Aquaculture; Biochemistry; Biological and Life Sciences; Biotechnology; Botany; Chemistry; Computer Science; Earth Sciences; Electronic Engineering; Environmental Management; Fishery; Genetics; Geology; Geophysics; Industrial Chemistry; Mathematics; Mathematics and Computer Science; Natural Resources; Natural Sciences; Nutrition; Physics; Statistics; Wood Technology; Zoology)

History: Founded 2007.

Fees: (Naira): School fee, 341,500 per degree programme; Acceptance fee, 25,000.

Main Language(s) of Instruction: English

Degrees and Diplomas: *Bachelor's Degree*

Last Updated: 11/07/12

IGBINEDION UNIVERSITY, OKADA (IUO)

PMB 0006, Okada, Benin City, Edo State

Tel: +234(52) 260-005 +234(52) 260-017

EMail: infor@iuokada.edu.ng; admission@iuokada.edu.ng

Website: http://www.iuokada.edu.ng/

Vice-Chancellor: Egosha Emmanuel Osaghae
EMail: e.e.osaghae@iuokada.edu.ng; vc@iuokada.edu.ng

Deputy Vice-Chancellor: Tonye. G. Okori
EMail: t.g.okori@iuokada.edu.ng; dvc@iuokada.edu.ng

Registrar: Edwin. O. Okoro
EMail: e.o.okoro@iuokada.edu.ng; registrar@iuokada.edu.ng

Colleges

Arts and Social Sciences (Advertising and Publicity; African Languages; Agricultural Economics; Anthropology; Arts and Humanities; Development Studies; Economics; English; French; Geography; International Relations; Mass Communication; Modern Languages; Public Administration; Public Relations; Regional Planning; Social Sciences; Sociology; Theatre); **Business Administration** (Accountancy; Banking; Business Administration; Finance); **Engineering** (Engineering); **Law** (Law); **Medicine** (Anatomy; Laboratory Techniques; Medicine; Nursing; Physiology); **Natural and Applied Sciences** (Biological and Life Sciences; Biology; Chemistry; Computer Science; Environmental Studies; Food Science; Information Technology; Microbiology; Natural Sciences; Physics); **Pharmacy** (Pharmacy)

Further Information: Also Igbinedion University Teaching Hospital campus and Crown Estate campus.

History: Founded 1999.

Governing Bodies: Board of Regents; Governing Council; Senate

Academic Year: September to June

Admission Requirements: School certificate SSCE/GCE/NECO with Credit Passes in 5 subjects

Fees: (Naira): 364,320-493,350 per annum

Main Language(s) of Instruction: English

International Co-operation: Participates in ICAN, CIBN, NMDC, NUC programmes.

Accrediting Agencies: National Universities Commission (NUC); Medical and Dental Council of Nigeria (MDCN)

Degrees and Diplomas: *Bachelor's Degree*: 4 yrs; *Bachelor's Degree*: Law; Engineering, 5 yrs; *Bachelor's Degree*: Medicine (MBBS), 6 yrs; *Master's Degree*: Accountancy; Business and Management, Sociology and Anthropology; Political Science; Medical Laboratory Sciences. Also Doctorates

Student Services: Academic counselling, Canteen, Health services, Social counselling, Sports facilities

Student Residential Facilities: For students and staff; Also Guest house

Special Facilities: Teaching Hospital

Libraries: c. 28,000 vols; Online Public Access Catalogue (OPAC) software (over 3,000 records); Strategic Library Automation Management (SLAM)

Academic Staff *2011-2012*	MEN	WOMEN	TOTAL
FULL-TIME	–	–	c. **400**
Student Numbers *2011-2012*			
All (Foreign Included)	2,340	2,860	c. **5,200**

Last Updated: 12/07/12

KATSINA UNIVERSITY (KUK)

PMB 2137, Dustinma Road, Katsina, Katsina State
EMail: info@kuk.edu.ng; registry@kuk.edu.ng
Website: http://www.kukportal.com/

Vice Chancellor: Nasiru Musa Yauri (2012-)

Colleges

Humanities (Arabic; Arts and Humanities; English; Islamic Studies); **Natural and Applied Sciences** (Computer Science; Natural Sciences)

History: Founded 2005.

Governing Bodies: University Board; Senate

Main Language(s) of Instruction: English

Degrees and Diplomas: *Bachelor's Degree*

Libraries: Central Library; Virtual Library

Last Updated: 12/07/12

KWARARAFA UNIVERSITY WUKARI

PMB 1019, Wukari, Taraba State
EMail: wukari_jubilee@yahoo.com
Website: http://kwararafauniversity.edu.ng/

Vice-Chancellor: Yakubu Ochefu (2012-)
Tel: +234(802) 305-8509

Colleges

Natural and Applied Sciences (Biochemistry; Biology; Biotechnology; Botany; Chemistry; Computer Science; Fishery; Geography; Industrial Chemistry; Mathematics; Microbiology; Natural Sciences; Physics; Statistics; Zoology)

Research Institutes

Conflict Management and Resolution (Peace and Disarmament); **Food Science and Technology** (Food Science; Food Technology); **Gender Issues** (Gender Studies); **Peace and Conflict Resolution** (Peace and Disarmament); **Science Education** (Science Education)

History: Founded 2005 as Wukari Jubilee University.

Governing Bodies: Board of Trustees; Governing Council; Management committee

Main Language(s) of Instruction: English

Accrediting Agencies: National Universities Commission (NUC)

Degrees and Diplomas: *Bachelor's Degree*

Student Services: Health services, Sports facilities

Special Facilities: Computer laboratory; ICT Centre; Clinic

Libraries: Yes

Last Updated: 19/07/12

NOVENA UNIVERSITY

PMB 2, Kwale, Ogume, Delta State
Tel: + 234(803) 330-2376 + 234(806) 241-1131
EMail: registrar@novenauniversity.edu.ng
Website: http://www.novenauniversity.edu.ng/

Vice-Chancellor: E.O. Adedeji
Tel: +234(803) 572-483 EMail: vc@novenauniversity.edu.ng

Registrar and Secretary to Council: Linus Ilogho
Tel: +234(803) 716-7418

Colleges

Food Science and Technology (Agriculture; Dietetics; Food Science; Food Technology; Home Economics; Microbiology; Nutrition; Tourism); **Information and Communication Technology** (Information Management; Information Technology; Telecommunications Engineering); **Management and Social Sciences** (Accountancy; Arts and Humanities; Business Administration; Economics; Management; Mass Communication; Political Sciences; Psychology; Social Sciences; Sociology); **Natural and Applied Sciences** (Biological and Life Sciences; Chemistry; Mathematics; Natural Sciences; Physics)

Further Information: Also campuses in Amai, Abbi and Kwale.

History: Founded 2005.

Governing Bodies: Board of Trustees; Governing Council; Senate.

Main Language(s) of Instruction: English

International Co-operation: With universities in USA, Belgium, United Kingdom, Israel and Australia.

Accrediting Agencies: Federal Ministry of Education; National Universities Commission (NUC)

Degrees and Diplomas: *Bachelor's Degree*

Libraries: Central Library; E-Library

Academic Staff *2011-2012*: Total 112
STAFF WITH DOCTORATE: Total 15
Student Numbers *2011-2012*: Total 1,258
Last Updated: 16/07/12

PAN-AFRICAN UNIVERSITY (PAU)

P.O. Box 73668, 2, Ahmed Onibudo St, Off Adeola Hopewell St, Victoria Island, Lagos, Lagos State 101003
Tel: +234(1) 461-6170 +234(1) 461-6171 +234(1) 461-6172
Fax: +234(1) 461-6173
EMail: info@pau.edu.ng
Website: http://www.pau.edu.ng/

Vice-Chancellor: Juan Manuel Elegido (2010-)
EMail: jelegido@pau.edu.ng

Registrar: John Cay Ihejieto EMail: jlhejieto@pau.edu.ng

Centres

Enterprise Development *(EDC)* (Management; Small Business)

Schools

Business *(Lagos Business School)* (Business Administration; Business and Commerce; Management); **Media and Communication** *(SMC)* (Communication Studies; Film; Journalism; Leadership; Media Studies; Radio and Television Broadcasting; Writing)

Further Information: Also Enterprise Development Services (EDS); Ajah Campus

History: Founded 1991 as Lagos Business School. Acquired present status and title 2002.

Governing Bodies: Governing Council; Managing Council

Main Language(s) of Instruction: English

Accrediting Agencies: National Universities Commission

Degrees and Diplomas: *Postgraduate Diploma (PGD)*; *Master's Degree*; *Doctor of Philosophy*: Business Administration, 4 yrs. Also Certificates; MBA and Executive MBA.

Student Services: Academic counselling, Canteen, Employment services, Handicapped facilities, Social counselling, Sports facilities

Student Residential Facilities: None

Special Facilities: Virtual Museum of Modern Nigerian Art; Video editing studio

Libraries: Two libraries
Last Updated: 17/07/12

REDEEMER'S UNIVERSITY (RUN)

PMB 3005, Redemption Camp, Mowe, Ogun State 7914
Tel: +234(1) 793-1780 +234(1) 850-2921
EMail: info@run.edu.ng; vc@run.edu.ng
Website: http://www.run.edu.ng

Vice-Chancellor: Zachariah Debo Adeyewa (2011-)
Tel: +234 815 551 1135 EMail: vc@run.edu.ng

Acting Registrar: Mojisola O. Oje
Tel: +234(1) 850-2921 EMail: registrar@run.edu.ng

International Relations: Bukola Oladipo, Strategic Communications and Linkages Officer
Tel: +234 808-758-3561
EMail: oladipoe@run.edu.ng; bukoladipo@gmail.com

Colleges

Humanities (English; History; International Relations; Modern Languages; Philosophy; Theatre); **Management Science** (Accountancy; Actuarial Science; Banking; Business Administration; Economics; Finance; Insurance; Management; Marketing; Mass Communication; Political Sciences; Psychology; Public Administration; Social Work; Sociology; Tourism; Transport and Communications; Transport Management); **Natural Sciences** (Biochemistry; Biological and Life Sciences; Biology; Chemistry; Computer Science; Industrial Chemistry; Mathematics; Microbiology; Natural Sciences; Physics; Statistics; Zoology)

History: Founded 2005.

Governing Bodies: The Governing Council and the University Senate

Academic Year: September to June

Admission Requirements: 5 credits at SSCE (or equivalent) in relevant subjects including English Language in not more than 2 sittings. A minimum of 200 points in University Matriculation Examination (UME) in relevant subjets for the degree programme and should attain the prescribed cut off marks as set by the Joint Admissions & Matriculation Board (JAMB)

Fees: (Naira): 300,000-350,000 per annum

Main Language(s) of Instruction: English

International Co-operation: With Trent University (Canada); Regent University (USA)

Accrediting Agencies: National Universities Commission (NUC)

Degrees and Diplomas: *Bachelor's Degree*

Student Services: Academic counselling, Canteen, Cultural centre, Employment services, Foreign student adviser, Handicapped facilities, Health services, Language programs, Nursery care, Social counselling, Sports facilities

Student Residential Facilities: Hostels

Special Facilities: Art Theatre; Dance Studio; Music Studio; Language Laboratory; Psychology Laboratory; Mass Communication Studio; Science Laboratories; Computer Science Laboratory; Information and Communication Technology Unit

Libraries: 20,122 vols; 980 Titles/20,000 Vols; 12 online and networked databases; 267 CD-ROMS; Coursework papers; Subscription to Nigerian newspapers (Guardian, Punch, Tribune, The Nation, Tell Magazine, Times Magazine and Four Four Two).

Publications: Run Pearl & Run Chronicle, Publication of the Department of Mass Communications *(biannually)*

Student Numbers *2012-2013*: Total 2,565
Last Updated: 11/03/13

RENAISSANCE UNIVERSITY (RNU)

PMB 01610, Enugu, Enugu State
Tel: +234(42) 304-4400
EMail: info@rnu.edu.ng; studentaffairs@rnu.edu.ng
Website: http://www.rnu.edu.ng

Vice-Chancellor: Emeka Okpara (2009-)

Colleges

Arts (Arts and Humanities; History; International Relations; Mass Communication); **Information and Communication** (Computer Engineering; Computer Science; Economics; Information Management; Information Sciences; Information Technology; Software Engineering); **Management and Social Sciences** (Accountancy; Business Administration; Economics; Finance; History; Insurance; International Relations; Management; Marketing; Mass Communication; Political Sciences; Psychology; Social Sciences; Sociology); **Natural and Applied Sciences** (Applied Physics; Aquaculture; Biochemistry; Earth Sciences; Environmental Management; Fishery; Geology; Geophysics; Industrial Chemistry; Mathematics; Microbiology; Natural Sciences; Statistics; Zoology)

History: Founded 2005.

Governing Bodies: Senate

Main Language(s) of Instruction: English

International Co-operation: With universities in Ukraine.

Accrediting Agencies: National Universities Commission (NUC)

Degrees and Diplomas: *Bachelor's Degree*
Last Updated: 17/07/12

SALEM UNIVERSITY

PMB 1060, Lokoja, Kogi State
Tel: +234(80) 733-41658 +234(80) 783-75358
EMail: registrar@salemuniversity.edu.ng
Website: http://www.salemuniversity.edu.ng

Vice-Chancellor: Paul Omaji (2008-)
Tel: +234(80) 706-20605
EMail: vicechancellor@salemuniversity.edu.ng

Registrar: Daniel Itodo

Colleges

Information and Communication Technology (Computer Science; Information Technology; Telecommunications Engineering); **Natural and Applied Sciences** (Animal Husbandry; Aquaculture; Biochemistry; Biology; Biotechnology; Chemistry; Crop Production; Earth Sciences; Energy Engineering; Fishery; Geology; Mathematics; Microbiology; Natural Resources; Natural Sciences; Physics; Soil Science; Statistics); **Peace and Social Sciences** (Accountancy; Banking; Business Administration; Criminology; Development Studies; Economics; Finance; International Relations; Marketing; Peace and Disarmament; Public Administration; Social Sciences)

History: Founded 2007.

Governing Bodies: Board of Trustees; Governing Council; Senate

Admission Requirements: SSCE (WAEC, NECO, NABTEB) or equivalent; Unified Tertiary Matriculation Examination (UTME) or Direct Entry (DE),

Fees: (Nairas): 400,000 with accomodation

Main Language(s) of Instruction: English

Accrediting Agencies: National Universities Commission (NUC)

Degrees and Diplomas: *Bachelor's Degree*: Management; Social Sciences; ICT

Student Services: Academic counselling, Canteen, Foreign student adviser, Health services, Social counselling, Sports facilities

Student Residential Facilities: Yes

Libraries: Physical and e-liberary

Publications: Global Leaders' Voice, History, programmes and testimonies of global leaders

Press or Publishing House: Aslove Publications, Lagos

Academic Staff *2011-2012*	MEN	WOMEN	TOTAL
FULL-TIME	194	71	**265**
PART-TIME	33	1	**34**
STAFF WITH DOCTORATE			
FULL-TIME	25	4	**29**
PART-TIME	21	–	c. **21**
Student Numbers *2011-2012*			
All (Foreign Included)	390	367	c. **757**

Last Updated: 04/06/12

UNIVERSITY OF MKAR (UMM)

Hospital Road, Mkar, Gboko, Benue State
Tel: +234(44) 6257-9802
Fax: +234(44) 6257-6377
EMail: info@unimkar.edu.ng
Website: http://unimkar.edu.ng/

Vice-Chancellor: Emmanuel H. Agba EMail: vc@unimkar.edu.ng

Registrar: Timothy Terpase Mkena

Faculties

Food Science and Technology (Food Science; Food Technology); **Natural and Applied Sciences** (Applied Physics; Biochemistry; Biology; Chemistry; Computer Education; Computer Science; Industrial Chemistry; Mathematics; Mathematics Education; Microbiology; Natural Sciences; Physics; Science Education); **Social and Management Sciences** (Accountancy; Business Administration; Economics; Management; Mass Communication; Political Sciences; Public Administration; Sociology)

History: Founded 1993 as Hilltop University. Acquired present title 2005.

Governing Bodies: Governing Council

Main Language(s) of Instruction: English

Degrees and Diplomas: *Bachelor's Degree*

Special Facilities: Laboratories; Internet access.

Libraries: c. 5,000 vols; 150 journal tiles; Over 1m. e-books/e journals.

Last Updated: 18/07/12

VERITAS UNIVERSITY (VUNA)

PMB 5171, Wuse GPO, Plot 1, Block 1,
By Urban Planning Way, Gwarinpa Abuja, Abuja, Federal Capital Territory
Tel: +234(806) 423-7983
EMail: info@veritas.edu.ng; admissions@veritas.edu.ng
Website: http://www.veritas.edu.ng

Vice-Chancellor: David Iyornongu Ker (2010-)

Registrar: Mojisola O. Ladipo

Colleges

Management and Social Sciences, Arts and Theology Studies *(MSAT)* (Accountancy; Advertising and Publicity; Arts and Humanities; Economics; English; History; International Relations; Literature; Marketing; Political Sciences; Social Sciences; Theology); **Natural and Applied Sciences** *(NAS)* (Applied Chemistry; Applied Physics; Biochemistry; Biological and Life Sciences; Chemistry; Industrial Chemistry; Microbiology; Natural Sciences; Physics)

Further Information: Also Obehie Campus.

History: Founded 2007.

Fees: (Naira): 250,000 per session.

Main Language(s) of Instruction: English

Accrediting Agencies: National Universities Commission (NUC)

Degrees and Diplomas: *Bachelor's Degree (BA; BTh; BSc)*

Last Updated: 19/07/12

WESLEY UNIVERSITY OF SCIENCE AND TECHNOLOGY (WUSTO)

PMB 507, Ondo, Ondo State
Website: http://82.206.239.12/wusto/index.php

Vice-Chancellor: Tola Badejo

Registrar: Ukamaka P. Atulomah

Colleges

Chemical Engineering (Chemical Engineering; Civil Engineering; Computer Engineering; Computer Science; Earth Sciences; Electrical and Electronic Engineering; Engineering; Environmental Engineering; Marine Engineering; Mechanical Engineering; Metallurgical Engineering; Petroleum and Gas Engineering; Robotics; Surveying and Mapping); **Environmental Sciences** (Architectural and Environmental Design; Architecture; Building Technologies; Geography; Real Estate; Regional Planning; Rural Planning; Surveying and Mapping; Town Planning); **Food Science and Technology** (Dietetics; Food Science; Food Technology; Home Economics; Hotel Management; Nutrition; Tourism); **Natural and Applied Sciences** (Biochemistry; Biological and Life Sciences; Biology; Biotechnology; Chemistry; Computer Engineering; Computer Networks; Computer Science; Earth Sciences; Environmental Studies; Fishery; Geology; Geophysics; Industrial Chemistry; Information Technology; Marine Biology; Mathematics; Microbiology; Natural Sciences; Physics; Software Engineering; Statistics); **Social and Management Sciences** (Actuarial Science; Banking; Business Administration; Economics; Finance; Insurance; Management; Mass Communication; Political Sciences; Social Sciences)

History: Founded 2007.

Degrees and Diplomas: *Bachelor's Degree*

Last Updated: 19/07/12

WESTERN DELTA UNIVERSITY (WDU)

PMB 10, Oghara, Delta State
EMail: info@wduniversity.net
Website: http://www.wduniversity.net/

Vice-Chancellor: Peter Gbewa Hugbo
EMail: peterhugbo@yahoo.com

Registrar: Godwin O. Egbri EMail: g.egbri@yahoo.com

Colleges

Art (Arts and Humanities); **Management and Social Sciences** (Accountancy; Banking; Business Administration; Economics; Film; Finance; Hotel Management; Human Resources; Marketing; Mass Communication; Media Studies; Political Sciences; Public Administration; Social Sciences; Sociology; Tourism; Video); **Natural and Applied Sciences** (Applied Mathematics; Biochemistry; Computer Science; Environmental Studies; Geography; Geology; Industrial Chemistry; Mathematics; Natural Sciences; Petroleum and Gas Engineering; Physics)

History: Founded 2007.

Governing Bodies: Board of Trustees; Governing Council

Fees: (Naira): 180,000-230,000 per annum

Main Language(s) of Instruction: English

Degrees and Diplomas: *Bachelor's Degree*

Last Updated: 19/07/12

Norway

STRUCTURE OF HIGHER EDUCATION SYSTEM

Description:

All higher education institutions are subject to the authority of the Ministry of Education and Research. Higher education in Norway is mainly offered at state institutions, notably universities, specialized university colleges, university colleges and art colleges. All accredited institutions, including private institutions, are covered by the same Act which entered into force on 1 August 2005. The degrees and titles that each institution can award and their professional and educational programmes, as well as the duration and specific requirements concerning breadth and depth are all laid down in the Royal Decree of 11 October 2002 (last revision 21 December 2005). In June 2001, the Norwegian Parliament (Storting) passed an extensive reform of higher education, the so-called Quality Reform. The main points include a new degree structure: Bachelor, of 3 years' duration; Master of 2 years' duration, and PhD of 3 years' duration; a credit system based on ECTS was introduced with 60 credits (studiepoeng) being equivalent to 1 year's full-time study; the possibility for some types of colleges to become universities; the redefinition of governing bodies and management of the institutions; an increase in student loans/grants; priority is given to the improvement of teaching and assessment; and the introduction of mutual and formalized agreements between students and institutions. Priority is given to participation in international programmes and exchange agreements. Higher education institutions strive to offer students a period of study abroad as a component of their degree programme. Institutions are encouraged to cooperate with public institutions in developing countries. More programmes in English have been introduced. Institutions have been given greater autonomy in academic and financial matters. They have the main responsibility for the quality assurance of their own provisions and for the follow up of quality development strategies and use of available resources. The Norwegian Agency for Quality Assurance in Education (NOKUT) was established on 1 January 2003. Its purpose is to make decisions on general recognition of foreign education, to oversee the quality of Norwegian higher education by means of evaluation, accreditation and approval of quality systems, institutions, and course programmes. These tasks should be carried out in such a way that the institutions can use the results to develop their own quality system. NOKUT represents Norway in the ENIC-NARIC network and is the information agency described in the Lisbon Convention on Recognition.

Stages of studies:

University level first stage: Høgskolekandidat, Bachelor
The Høgskolekandidat (College candidate) degree is obtained after two years of study (120 ECTS credits). This degree may be built upon to obtain a Bachelor's degree. The degree is offered at state university colleges and a few private institutions.
The Bachelor's degree is awarded by all institutions subject to the Universities and University Colleges Act. It is obtained after a minimum of three years' study (180 ECTS credits). Academies of Arts offer a Bachelor's degree of four years' duration.

University level second stage: Master; Candidata/Candidatus
The Master's degree is a degree created by the 2001 reform. Normally, it requires two years of study (120 ECTS credits) beyond the Bachelor's degree, and it includes an independent research project/thesis. In some fields of study the Master's degree is awarded after a five-year one-tier programme. Some institutions offer an experience-based Master's degree after one-and-a-half to two years' study (90-120 ECTS credits). Admission is based on a Bachelor' degree and two years of work experience. The degrees of Candidata/Candidatus medicinae/ psychologiae/theologiae have been retained from the old system. Studies last for six years.

University level third stage: Ph.D, Dr. Philos.
The Ph.D degree programmes generally consist of three years of study (180 ECTS credits) following completion of a Master's degree or a six-year professional degree and are essentially research programmes. The main part of the programme is independent research and writing a dissertation. Doctoral degree programmes are offered by universities, specialized university institutions and some university colleges. The title Doctor Philosophiae (dr. philos.) is more general and can be obtained in all fields without a specific study programme.

Distance higher education:
There are several distance education institutions offering more than 3500 courses. All courses must be approved by the Ministry of Education and Research. Most courses are vocational or lead to formal qualifications. Several schools are now cooperating with higher education institutions in setting up courses in e.g. Media Studies, Economics and Administration.

ADMISSION TO HIGHER EDUCATION

Admission to university-level studies:

Name of secondary school credential required: Vitnemål Fra Videregående Skole

Minimum score/requirement: Completed and Passed ("Fullført og bestått")

For entry to: All higher education programmes

Alternatives to credentials: Applicants who do not have a secondary school leaving certificate but who: 1) are 23 or more 2) can prove 5 years of work experience and education 3) have passed the required 6 basic subjects (Norwegian; English; civics; modern history; natural sciences and mathematics), are eligible for admission to higher education. It is also possible to be admitted to specific programmes based on assessment of prior learning(realkompetanse).

Numerus clausus/restrictions: Medicine, Dentistry, Pharmacy, Psychology.

Other admission requirements: Admission may also be gained with other qualifications recognized as being on par with the general matriculation standard. Some fields of study have additional entrance requirements.

Foreign students admission:

Definition of foreign student: Foreign citizens who do not have a permanent residence permit in Norway.

Entrance exam requirements: Foreign students should have qualifications equivalent at least to a completed general education at the upper secondary level. For some countries, there may be additional requirements. For more information, refer to the Universities and Colleges Admission Service (UCAS) at http://www.samordnaopptak.no/english/ or the Norwegian Centre for International Cooperation in Higher Education (SIU) or NOKUT at http://www.nokut.no/sw14437.asp.

Entry regulations: Students should inquire about visa regulations at Norwegian embassies or consulates. They should apply for a residence permit before arrival in Norway. A residence permit will often require a financial guarantee.

Language requirements: Students should have good knowledge of English assessed by TOEFL or IELTS (Minimum score of 500 in TOEFL and 5.0 points in IELTS). For programmes taught in Norwegian also a good command of Norwegian (minimum mark: 3.0 / Norsk for utlendinger, trinn 3. Minimum mark: 450 / Bergenstesten, høyere nivå) For more information, see http://siu.no/en/programoversikt/kvoteordningen/admission_requirements

RECOGNITION OF STUDIES

Quality assurance system:

Through evaluation, accreditation and recognition of quality systems, institutions and course provisions the Norwegian Agency for Quality Assurance in Education (NOKUT) supervises and helps to develop the quality of higher education in Norway. http://www.nokut.no

Special provisions for recognition:

For exercising a profession: Access to a profession is subject to the Ministry responsible for the practice of that profession.

Recognition for university level studies: Academic recogntition is divided between NOKUT (Norwegian ENIC-NARIC)and the higher education institutions. NOKUT is responsible for general recognition while the institutions are responsible for subject spesific recognition.

NATIONAL BODIES

Kunnskapsdepartementet (Ministry of Education and Research)

Minister: Kristin Halvorsen
Secretary-General: Trond Fevolden
Postboks 8119 Dep
Oslo 0032
Tel: +47(22) 249 090
Fax: +47(22) 249 544
EMail: postmottak@kd.dep.no
WWW: http://www.regjeringen.no/en/dep/kd
Role of national body: Responsible for all higher education institutions

Nasjonalt organ for kvalitet i utdanningen - NOKUT (Norwegian Agency for Quality Assurance in Education)

Director-General: Terje Mørland
PO Box 1708 Vika
Oslo 0121
Tel: +47 2102 1800
Fax: +47 2102 1801
EMail: postmottak@nokut.no
WWW: http://www.nokut.no
Role of national body: Through evaluation, accreditation and recognition of quality systems, institutions and course provisions, the purpose of NOKUT is to supervise and help to develop the quality of higher education in Norway.

Universitets-og Høgskolerådet - UHR (The Norwegian Association of Higher Education Institutions)

Chairman: Jan I. Haaland
Secretary-General: Ola Stave
Pilestredet 46
Oslo 0167
Tel: +47 2245 3950
Fax: +47 2245 3951
EMail: postmottak@uhr.no
WWW: http://www.uhr.no/
Role of national body: To develop strategies for the Norwegian system of higher education institutions, to promote coordination and division of labour within the higher education sector and to serve as a common instrument for the member institutions in their international cooperation.

Senter for internasjonalisering av utdanning - SIU (Norwegian Centre for International Cooperation in Education)

Director General: Alf Rasmussen
P.O. Box 1093
Bergen 5809
Tel: +47 55 30 38 00
Fax: +47 55 30 38 01
EMail: siu@siu.no
WWW: http://www.siu.no/
Role of national body: SIU is a knowledge and service organization with the mission of promoting and facilitating cooperation, standardization, mobility, and the overcoming of cultural barriers to communication and exchange within the realm of higher education on an international level. The Centre is charged with the important task of coordinating national measures according to official Norwegian policy within the field of internationalisation. The Centre is Norway's official agency for international programmes and measures related to higher education. It is commissioned by several national and international public organizations to administer programmes within all levels of education. In addition to programme administration, SIU is responsible for

promoting Norway as an education and research nation, as well as providing information and advisory services within the field of internationalisation in education.

Data for academic year: 2007-2008

Source: IAU from Norwegian Agency for Quality Assurance in Education (NOKUT), Oslo, 2007. Bodies, 2012.

INSTITUTIONS

PUBLIC INSTITUTIONS

ÅLESUND UNIVERSITY COLLEGE

Høgskolen i Ålesund (HIÅ)
Larsgårdsvegen 2, 6025 Ålesund
Tel: +47 70-16-12-00
Fax: +47 70-16-13-00
EMail: postmottak@hials.no
Website: http://www.hials.no

Rector: Geirmund Oltedal (2007-)
Tel: +47 70-16-13-90 EMail: go@hials.no

International Relations: Åse Mørkeset
Tel: +47 70-16-13-10 EMail: am@hials.no

Faculties
Engineering and Natural Sciences (Automation and Control Engineering; Civil Engineering; Computer Engineering; Mechanical Engineering); **Health Sciences** (Biomedical Engineering; Laboratory Techniques; Nursing); **International Marketing** (Business Administration; International Business; Management; Marketing; Transport Management); **Life Sciences** (Aquaculture; Biotechnology; Fishery; Food Technology; Marine Biology); **Maritime Technology and Operations** (Marine Engineering; Nautical Science)

History: Founded 1994 through merger of former Aalesund Colleges of Marine Studies, Engineering and Nursing.

Governing Bodies: College Board

Academic Year: August to June (August-December; January-June)

Fees: None

Main Language(s) of Instruction: Norwegian

International Co-operation: With universities in USA and Thailand. Also participates in Socrates/Erasmus (Spain, Germany, Portugal, Finland, Sweden, Denmark, Hungary, Lithuania, Latvia); Leonardo da Vinci (Germany) and Nordplus (Sweden, Denmark, Finland).

Degrees and Diplomas: *Bachelor*: 3 yrs; *Master*

Student Services: Academic counselling, Canteen, Cultural centre, Foreign student adviser, Health services, Social counselling, Sports facilities

Student Residential Facilities: Yes

Special Facilities: Ship manoeuvering simulator

Last Updated: 25/10/11

BERGEN NATIONAL ACADEMY OF THE ARTS

Kunsthøgskolen i Bergen (KHIB)
Strømg. 1, 5015 Bergen
Tel: +47 55-58-73-00
Fax: +47 55-58-73-10
EMail: khib@khib.no
Website: http://www.khib.no

Rector: Paula Crabtree (2011-)
Tel: +47 55-58-73-01 EMail: paula.crabtree@khib.no

Director: Cecilie Ohm
Tel: +47 55-58-73-02 EMail: cecilie.ohm@khib.no

International Relations: Ingjald Selland
Tel: +47 55-58-73-21 EMail: ingjald.selland@khib.no

Departments
Design (Furniture Design; Interior Design; Visual Arts); **Fine Arts** (Ceramic Art; Design; Fine Arts; Furniture Design; Photography; Printing and Printmaking); **Specialized Arts** (Ceramic Art; Fine Arts; Printing and Printmaking; Textile Design)

History: Founded 1909. Acquired present status 1996.

Governing Bodies: Department Boards

Admission Requirements: Entrance examination

Main Language(s) of Instruction: Norwegian

International Co-operation: Participates in Nordplus and Erasmus programmes.

Degrees and Diplomas: *Bachelor*, *Master*

Student Services: Academic counselling, Canteen, Employment services, Foreign student adviser, Health services, Nursery care, Social counselling, Sports facilities

Student Residential Facilities: Yes

Special Facilities: Fisk Galleri, Rom 8

Libraries: 1 library

Last Updated: 22/09/11

BERGEN UNIVERSITY COLLEGE

Høgskolen i Bergen (HIB)
Postboks 7030, 5020 Bergen
Tel: +47 55-58-75-00
Fax: +47 55-32-64-07
EMail: post@hib.no
Website: http://www.hib.no

Rector: Ole-Gunnar Søgnen
Tel: +47 55-58-75-13 EMail: ole-gunnar.sognen@hib.no

Faculties
Education (Education; History; Music Education; Teacher Training; Theatre); **Engineering** (Business Administration; Chemical Engineering; Civil Engineering; Computer Engineering; Electrical Engineering; Engineering; Environmental Studies; Mechanical Engineering; Surveying and Mapping); **Health and Social Sciences** (Health Sciences; Midwifery; Nursing; Occupational Therapy; Physical Therapy; Psychiatry and Mental Health; Public Health; Radiology; Social Sciences; Social Work)

History: Founded 1994 by the merging of six former independent colleges in Bergen.

Admission Requirements: General Study Competence and Bergen test (Norwegian language)

Main Language(s) of Instruction: Norwegian

International Co-operation: Participates in Erasmus; Nordplus; Leonardo da Vincil; Norad

Degrees and Diplomas: *Bachelor*: 3 yrs; *Master*

Student Services: Academic counselling, Canteen, Cultural centre, Employment services, Foreign student adviser, Handicapped facilities, Social counselling, Sports facilities

Special Facilities: Media Centre

Libraries: 5 libraries.

Last Updated: 25/10/11

BUSKERUD UNIVERSITY COLLEGE

Høgskolen i Buskerud (HIBU)
Postboks 235, 3601 Kongsberg
Tel: +47 32-86-95-00
Fax: +47 32-86-98-83
EMail: postmottak@hibu.no
Website: http://www.hibu.no

Rector: Kristin Ørmen Johnsen (1997-)
Tel: +47 32-86-98-80 EMail: kristin.ormen.johnsen@hibu.no

Administrative Director: Kai Mjøsund Tel: +47 32-86-98-51

International Relations: Julie-Ann Svenkerud
Tel: +47 32-11-71-97 EMail: julie-ann.svenkerud@hibu.no

Schools

Business and Social Sciences (Business Administration; Economics; International Business; Law; Management; Marketing; Political Sciences; Tourism); **Education** (Education); **Engineering** (Computer Engineering; Electronic Engineering; Engineering; Mechanical Engineering); **Health Studies** (Health Sciences; Nursing; Radiology); **Optometry and Visual Sciences** (Optometry)

Further Information: Also campuses in Drammen and Hønefoss.

History: Founded 1994.

Main Language(s) of Instruction: Norwegian and English

Degrees and Diplomas: *Bachelor*; *Master*

Libraries: Yes
Last Updated: 27/10/11

FINNMARK UNIVERSITY COLLEGE

Høgskolen i Finnmark (HIF)
Follums vei 31, 9509 Alta
Tel: +47 78-45-05-00
Fax: +47 78-43-44-38
EMail: postmottak@hifm.no
Website: http://www.hifm.no

Rector: Sveinung Eikeland
Tel: +47 78-45-04-14 EMail: Sveinung.eikeland@hifm.no

Director: Pål Markusson
Tel: +47 78-45-02-15 EMail: paal.markusson@hifm.no

Faculties

Business and Social Work *(Alta)* (Aquaculture; Business Administration; Hotel Management; Information Technology; Mathematics; Natural Sciences; Public Administration; Social Work; Tourism); **Education and Liberal Arts** *(Alta)* (Communication Studies; Education; Fine Arts; Literature; Modern Languages; Physical Education; Religion; Social Sciences; Sports; Teacher Training); **Nursing** *(Hammerfest)*

History: Founded 1994.

Main Language(s) of Instruction: Norwegian and English

International Co-operation: Participates in Erasmus, Nordplus, Barentsplus and Norreg programmes.

Degrees and Diplomas: *Bachelor*: 3 yrs; *Master*: a further 2 yrs

Student Services: Academic counselling, Canteen, Cultural centre, Employment services, Foreign student adviser, Foreign Studies Centre, Handicapped facilities, Health services, Nursery care, Social counselling, Sports facilities

Libraries: Main Library
Last Updated: 27/10/11

GJØVIK UNIVERSITY COLLEGE

Høgskolen i Gjøvik (HIG)
Postboks 191, Teknologivn. 22, 2802 Gjøvik
Tel: +47 61-13-51-00
Fax: +47 61-13-51-70
EMail: postmottak@hig.no
Website: http://www.hig.no

Rector: Joern Wroldsen
Tel: +47 61-13-51-01 EMail: joern.wroldsen@hig.no

International Relations: Bente Gaalaas Rønningen
Tel: +47 61-13-51-20 EMail: inger.hjelle@hig.no

Faculties

Computer Science and Media Technology (Computer Science; Media Studies); **Health, Care and Nursing** (Community Health; Health Sciences; Nursing); **Technology, Economy and Management** (Economics; Engineering; Management; Technology)

Academic Year: August to June (August-December; January-June)

Admission Requirements: Higher education entrance qualification

Fees: (Norwegian Kroner): 750 per semester

Main Language(s) of Instruction: Norwegian

International Co-operation: Participates in the Erasmus, Erasmus Mundus and Nordplus programme

Accrediting Agencies: NOKUT

Degrees and Diplomas: *Bachelor*; *Master*; *Ph.D.*

Student Services: Academic counselling, Canteen, Foreign student adviser, Foreign Studies Centre, Handicapped facilities, Nursery care, Social counselling, Sports facilities

Libraries: Central Library
Last Updated: 27/10/11

HARSTAD UNIVERSITY COLLEGE

Høgskolen i Harstad (HUC)
Havnegata 5, 9480 Harstad
Tel: +47 77-05-81-00
Fax: +47 77-05-81-04
EMail: postmottak@hih.no
Website: http://www.hih.no

Rector: Bodil Olsvik (2011-2015)
Tel: +47 77-05-81-05 EMail: bodil.olsvik@hih.no

Managing Director: Karl Erik Arnesen
Tel: +47 77-05-81-10 EMail: karl.arnesen@hih.no

Departments

Business Administration and Social Sciences (Accountancy; Business Administration; E-Business/Commerce; English; Health Administration; International Business; Management; Marketing; Political Sciences; Social Sciences; Tourism); **Health and Social Studies** (Food Science; Health Sciences; Nutrition; Rehabilitation and Therapy; Social Work)

History: Founded 1983. Acquired present status 1994.

Degrees and Diplomas: *Bachelor*; *Master*

Student Residential Facilities: Yes

Libraries: Yes
Last Updated: 27/10/11

HEDMARK UNIVERSITY COLLEGE

Høgskolen i Hedmark (HH)
Laererskolealléen 1, 2418 Elverum
Tel: +47 62-43-00-00
Fax: +47 62-43-00-01
EMail: hogskolen.hedmark@hihm.no
Website: http://www.hihm.no

Rector: Lise Iversen Kulbrandstad
Tel: +47 62-43-00-73 EMail: lise.kulbrandstad@hihm.no

Managing Director: Paul E. Dietrichs
Tel: +47 62-43-00-04 EMail: pal.dietrichs@hihm.no

International Relations: Harald S. Smedstad
Tel: +47 62-43-01-23 EMail: harald.smedstad@hihm.no

Faculties

Applied Ecology and Agricultural Sciences *(Evenstad)* (Agricultural Engineering; Agriculture; Agronomy; Ecology; Forestry; Wildlife); **Business Administration** (Business Administration; Social Sciences); **Education and Natural Sciences** *(Hamar)* (Arts and Humanities; Biotechnology; Computer Science; Fine Arts; Social Sciences; Teacher Trainers Education); **Health and Sport Science** (Nursing; Psychiatry and Mental Health; Sports)

History: Founded 1994.

Main Language(s) of Instruction: Norwegian

Degrees and Diplomas: *Bachelor*; *Master*

Libraries: Yes
Last Updated: 27/10/11

LILLEHAMMER UNIVERSITY COLLEGE

Høgskolen i Lillehammer (HIL)
Postboks 952, 2626 Lillehammer
Tel: +47 61-28-80-00
Fax: +47 61-26-07-50
EMail: post@hil.no
Website: http://www.hil.no

Rector: Bente Ohnstad
Tel: +47 61-28-83-90 EMail: bente.ohnstad@hil.no

Director: Kari Kjenndalen
Tel: +47 61-28-83-89, Fax: +47 61-26-07-50
EMail: kari.kjenndalen@hil.no

Faculties

Economy and Organization Science (Economics; Management); **Health and Social Work** (Health Sciences; Social Work); **Social Sciences** (Business Administration; Educational Sciences; Management; Social Sciences; Sports; Tourism); **Television Production and Film Science** (Media Studies; Radio and Television Broadcasting; Video)

Schools

Film *(Norwegian)* (Cinema and Television; Film)

History: Founded 1971 as Oppland College. Acquired present status 1994.

Governing Bodies: Senate

Academic Year: August - June

Admission Requirements: Studiekompetanse or Realkompetanse

Fees: (Norwegian Kroner): c. 1,200 per term

Main Language(s) of Instruction: Norwegian

International Co-operation: With universities in Scandinavian countries, the Netherlands, Belgium, Austria, Germany, Spain, Greece, With universities in Europe, USA, Australia, Namibia and South Africa. Also participates in Erasmus and Nordplus

Accrediting Agencies: Norwegian Agency for Quality Assurance in Education

Degrees and Diplomas: *Bachelor*: 3 yrs; *Master*: 5 yrs

Student Services: Academic counselling, Canteen, Cultural centre, Employment services, Foreign student adviser, Handicapped facilities, Health services, Nursery care, Social counselling, Sports facilities

Student Residential Facilities: Yes

Libraries: Yes

Last Updated: 27/10/11

MOLDE UNIVERSITY COLLEGE

Høgskolen i Molde
Postboks 2110, 6402 Molde
Tel: +47 71-21-40-00
Fax: +47 71-21-41-00
EMail: post@himolde.no
Website: http://www.himolde.no

Rector: Solfrid Vatne
Tel: +47 71-21-40-26 EMail: solfrid.vatne@himolde.no

Executive Director: Paul S. Valle
Tel: +47 71-21-41-48 EMail: paul.s.valle@himolde.no

International Relations: Ragnhild Oddrun Brakstad
Tel: +47 71-21-41-05 EMail: ragnhild.o.brakstad@himolde.no

Faculties

Economics, Informatics and Social Sciences (Accountancy; Computer Science; E-Business/Commerce; Economics; Political Sciences; Public Administration; Social Sciences; Sports; Sports Management; Transport Economics; Transport Management); **Health Sciences and Social Care** (Health Sciences; Nursing; Social and Preventive Medicine)

History: Founded 1994.

Main Language(s) of Instruction: Norwegian; English

Degrees and Diplomas: *Bachelor*, *Master*, *Ph.D.*

Student Numbers *2010-2011*	**TOTAL**
All (Foreign Included)	c. **1,800**
FOREIGN ONLY	**160**

Last Updated: 20/09/11

NARVIK UNIVERSITY COLLEGE

Høgskolen i Narvik (HIN)
Lodve Langes gate 2, Serviceboks 385, 8505 Narvik
Tel: +47 76-96-60-00
Fax: +47 76-96-68-10
EMail: postmottak@hin.no
Website: http://www.hin.no

Rector: Arne Erik Holdø
Tel: +47 76-96-64-64 EMail: arnhol@hin.no

Administrative Director: Bjørnar Storeng
Tel: +47 76-96-61-60 EMail: bjornar.storeng@hin.no

International Relations: Tor-Arne Jenssen, International Coordinator Tel: +47 76-96-61-59 EMail: taj@hin.no

Faculties

Health and Society *(AHS)* (Educational and Student Counselling; Health Sciences; Nursing; Psychiatry and Mental Health; Public Health; Toxicology); **Technology** *(AT)* (Building Technologies; Business Administration; Civil Engineering; Computer Engineering; Computer Science; Construction Engineering; Electronic Engineering; Energy Engineering; Engineering Management; Finance; Industrial Engineering; Information Technology; Mechanical Engineering; Technology; Telecommunications Engineering)

History: Founded 1969, acquired present status 1990.

Academic Year: August to June

Admission Requirements: Secondary school diploma

Fees: (Norwegian Kroner): 1,020 per annum

Main Language(s) of Instruction: Norwegian, English

International Co-operation: With universities in Sweden, Denmark, France, Russia, China.

Degrees and Diplomas: *Bachelor*: Civil Engineering; Computer Technology; Electrical Engineering; Electronics Engineering; Space Technology; Mechanical Engineering; Economics and Business Administration; Science Education; *Bachelor*: Nursing, 3 yrs; *Master*: Civil Engineering; Computer Technology; Electrical Engineering; Space Technology Engineering; Design; Production Engineering. Also 1 yr study programme in Computer Technology building on the title of "Bachelor" (3 years' study), 1 yr study programme in Economics and Management building on "Bachelor", 1 yr study programme in drug prevention building on Bachelor in Nursing, 1 yr study programme qualifying for studies in Engineering.

Student Services: Academic counselling, Canteen, Cultural centre, Handicapped facilities, Health services, Social counselling, Sports facilities

Libraries: Main Library

Academic Staff *2010-2011*	**TOTAL**
FULL-TIME	**170**
STAFF WITH DOCTORATE	
FULL-TIME	c. **20**

Student Numbers *2010-2011*	
All (Foreign Included)	**1,700**
FOREIGN ONLY	**130**

Last Updated: 22/09/11

NESNA UNIVERSITY COLLEGE

Høgskolen i Nesna (HINE)
8700 Nesna
Tel: +47 75-05-78-00
Fax: +47 75-05-79-00
EMail: postmottak@hinesna.no
Website: http://www.hinesna.no

Rector: Sven Erik Forfang
Tel: +47 75-05-78-01 EMail: sefo@hinesna.no

Colleges

Education (Education)

History: Founded 1918. Acquired present status 1994. Basically a teacher training college, now expanded into other fields such as nursing, informatics, earth sciences, musicology, and others.

Main Language(s) of Instruction: Norwegian

Degrees and Diplomas: *Bachelor*, *Master*

NORD-TRØNDELAG UNIVERSITY COLLEGE

Høgskolen i Nord-Trøndelag (HINT)
Postboks 2501, 7729 Steinkjer
Tel: +47 74-11-20-00
Fax: +47 74-11-20-01
EMail: postmottak@hint.no; hint@hint.no
Website: http://www.hint.no

Rector: Steinar Nebb EMail: steinar.nebb@hint.no

International Relations: Ole C. Tidemann, International Coordinator Tel: +47 74-11-22-73 EMail: ole.c.tidemann@hint.no

Faculties

Agriculture and Information Technology (Agriculture; Animal Husbandry; Information Technology; Multimedia); **Economics, Organization and Leadership** (Accountancy; Administration; Economics; Leadership; Management; Public Administration); **Education of Driving Instructors** (Teacher Training); **Health Sciences** (Health Sciences; Nursing; Pharmacy); **Teacher Education** (Music Education; Physical Education; Preschool Education; Primary Education; Secondary Education)

History: Founded 1839. Acquired present status and title 1994.

Academic Year: August to June

Admission Requirements: Secondary school certificate (Videregående skole)

Fees: None

Main Language(s) of Instruction: Norwegian

Degrees and Diplomas: *Bachelor (BA)*: 3 yrs; *Master (MA)*: a further 2 yrs

Student Services: Academic counselling, Canteen, Cultural centre, Foreign student adviser, Handicapped facilities, Social counselling

Student Residential Facilities: For 520 students

Libraries: 3 Libraries

Last Updated: 27/10/11

NORWEGIAN ACADEMY OF MUSIC

Norges musikkhøgskole (NMH)
Postboks 5190, Majorstua, 0302 Oslo
Tel: +47 23-36-70-00
Fax: +47 23-36-70-01
EMail: mh@nmh.no
Website: http://www.nmh.no

Rector: Eirik Birkeland
Tel: +47 23-36-70-11 EMail: eirik.birkeland@nmh.no

Director: Ingeborg Harsten
Tel: +47 23-36-70-31 EMail: ingeborg.harsten@nmh.no

International Relations: Knut Myhre, International Coordinator
Tel: +47 23-36-70-22 EMail: knut.myrhe@nmh.no

Programmes

Music (Jazz and Popular Music; Music; Music Education; Music Theory and Composition; Musical Instruments; Religious Music)

History: Founded 1973. A State Institution governed by an elected Board.

Academic Year: September to June (September-December; January-June)

Admission Requirements: Secondary school certificate (examen artium) and entrance examination

Fees: None

Main Language(s) of Instruction: Norwegian

International Co-operation: Participates in Erasmus; Nordplus; ABAM

Degrees and Diplomas: *Bachelor*; *Master*; *Ph.D. (PhD)*: 4 yrs

Student Services: Academic counselling, Canteen, Foreign student adviser, Handicapped facilities

Student Residential Facilities: None

Special Facilities: Recording Studio

Libraries: Music Literature, Music Sheets, Music Scores, Sound, Video, etc

Last Updated: 27/10/11

NORWEGIAN POLICE UNIVERSITY COLLEGE

Politihøgskolen
Slemdalsveien 5, Postboks 5027, Majorstua, 0301 Oslo
Tel: +47 23-19-99-00
Fax: +47 23-19-99-01
EMail: postmottak@phs.no; postoslophs@phs.no
Website: http://www.phs.no

Rector: Håkon Skulstad

Programmes

Police Studies (Police Studies)

Further Information: Also campus in Bodø Stavern and Kongsvinger.

History: Founded 1992. Acquired present status 2004.

Main Language(s) of Instruction: Norwegian

Degrees and Diplomas: *Bachelor*; *Master*

Student Numbers *2010-2011*: Total: c. 340

Last Updated: 19/09/11

IAU NORWEGIAN SCHOOL OF ECONOMICS

Norges Handelshøyskole (NHH)
Helleveien 30, 5045 Bergen
Tel: +47 55-95-92-16
Fax: +47 55-95-10-00
EMail: nhh.postmottak@nhh.no
Website: http://www.nhh.no

Rector: Jan I. Haaland (2005-)
Tel: +47 55-95-92-17 EMail: jan.haaland@nhh.no

International Relations: John Andersen, Director International Relations Tel: +47 55-95-92-20 EMail: john.andersen@nhh.no

Centres

Administrative Research (Leadership; Management); **Applied Research** (Business Administration; Economics)

Departments

Accounting, Auditing and Law (Accountancy; Law); **Economics** (Economics); **Finance and Management Sciences** (Finance; Management); **Professional and Intercultural Communication** (Communication Studies; Modern Languages); **Strategy and Management** (Management)

History: Founded 1936 following legislation passed in 1917. A State Institution of University rank.

Governing Bodies: Executive Board comprising 11 members; Department Boards. The students have elected representatives in all governing bodies

Academic Year: August to June (August-December; January-June)

Admission Requirements: Upper secondary school certificate

Fees: None

Main Language(s) of Instruction: Norwegian at undergraduate level, Norwegian and English at graduate and Ph.D levels

International Co-operation: With 140 Universities (Business Schools). Also participates in the Global Network Programme in International Management (PIM) and The Global Alliance in Management Education (CEMS).

Accrediting Agencies: EQUIS

Degrees and Diplomas: *Bachelor*: Economics, Business Administration, 3 yrs; *Master*: Economics; Business Administration, a further 2 yrs; *Ph.D.*: Economics; Business Administration (Ph.D.), 3 yrs, by dissertation

Student Services: Academic counselling, Canteen, Cultural centre, Employment services, Foreign student adviser, Handicapped facilities, Social counselling, Sports facilities

Student Residential Facilities: Some residential facilities for students. International students are guaranteed housing

Libraries: Main Library, 250,000 vols

Publications: NHH-Bulletin *(quarterly)*; Research and Publications (in English) *(annually)*

Student Numbers *2012-2013*: Total 3,100

Last Updated: 11/03/13

NORWEGIAN SCHOOL OF SPORT SCIENCES

Norges idrettshøgskole (NIH)

PO Box 4014, Ullevaal Stadion, 0806 Oslo
Tel: +47 23-26-20-00
Fax: +47 22-23-42-20
EMail: postmottak@nih.no
Website: http://www.nih.no

Rector: Sigmund Loland (2005-)
Tel: +47 23-26-20-08, Fax: +47 23-26-20-13
EMail: sigmund.loland@nih.no

Director-General: Baard Wist
Tel: +47 23-26-20-06, Fax: +47 23-26-20-14
EMail: baard.wist@nih.no

International Relations: Kristin Dybvad, Senior Executive Officer
Tel: +47 23-26-20-16 EMail: kristin.dybvad@nih.no

Departments

Coaching and Psychology (Psychology; Sports); **Cultural and Social Studies** (Sociology; Sports; Sports Management); **Physical Education** (Physical Education); **Physical Performance** (Biological and Life Sciences; Sports); **Sports Medicine** (Sports; Sports Medicine)

History: Founded 1968. A State Institution financially supported by the Ministry of Education and Research.

Governing Bodies: Styre (Board)

Academic Year: August to June (August-December; January-June)

Admission Requirements: Secondary school certificate (examen artium) and physical fitness examination

Fees: None; Fees for part-time students

Main Language(s) of Instruction: Norwegian

International Co-operation: Participates in Erasmus and Nordplus programmes.

Degrees and Diplomas: *Bachelor*: Sports Sciences; *Master*: Sports Sciences; *Ph.D.*

Student Services: Academic counselling, Canteen, Foreign student adviser, Handicapped facilities, Health services, Sports facilities

Libraries: c. 70,000 vols

Last Updated: 27/10/11

NORWEGIAN SCHOOL OF VETERINARY SCIENCE

Norges veterinærhøgskole (NVH)

Postboks 8146 Dep., 0033 Oslo
Tel: +47 22-96-45-00
Fax: +47 22-59-73-09
EMail: post@nvh.no
Website: http://www.veths.no

Rector: Yngvild Wasteson
Tel: +47 22-96-45-01 EMail: Yngvild.Wasteson@veths.no

Director: Knut Børve
Tel: +47 22-96-45-02 EMail: knut.borve@veths.no

International Relations: Melanie Etchell
Tel: +47 22-59-71-20 EMail: melanie.etchell@veths.no

Departments

Animal Companion Clinical Science (Radiology; Veterinary Science); **Animal Production Clinical Science** (Animal Husbandry; Veterinary Science; Zoology); **Basic Sciences and Aquatic Medicine** (Anatomy; Biochemistry; Genetics; Marine Biology; Medicine; Nutrition; Pathology; Physiology); **Food Safety and Infection Biology** (Biology; Food Science)

Divisions

Farm Research (Farm Management)

Units

Animal Laboratory

History: Founded 1935, an autonomous State institution responsible to the Ministry of Education and Research. Financed by the State, Agricultural Research Council, other research councils, and industry.

Governing Bodies: Styre (Board)

Academic Year: August to June (August-December; January-June)

Admission Requirements: Secondary school certificate (examen artium)

Fees: None

Main Language(s) of Instruction: Norwegian, English (for Master)

Degrees and Diplomas: *Candidata/Candidatus*: Veterinary Medicine, 5 1/2 yrs; *Master*: Food Safety; Aquatic Medicine, 2 yrs; *Doctor Philosophiae*: 4-5 yrs by thesis showing independent research; *Ph.D.*: Natural Sciences (Dr.scient.); Veterinary Medicine, a further 3-4 yrs. Also Veterinary Nursing Education, 2 yrs

Special Facilities: Veterinary Museum

Libraries: College Library, c. 77,000 vols

Last Updated: 27/10/11

IAU NORWEGIAN UNIVERSITY OF LIFE SCIENCES

Universitetet for miljø og biovitenskap (UMB)

Postboks 8985 (Merkes: 3533/5000), 7439 Trondheim
Tel: +47 64-96-50-00
Fax: +47 64-96-50-01
EMail: postmottak@umb.no
Website: http://www.umb.no

Rector: Hans Fredrik Hoen
Tel: +47 64-96-50-03 EMail: rektor@umb.no

Centres

Animal Production Experimental Station *(SHE)* (Animal Husbandry); **Plant Research in Controlled Climates** *(SKP)* (Plant and Crop Protection)

Departments

Chemistry, Biotechnology and Food Science (Biotechnology; Chemistry; Food Science; Microbiology); **Ecology and Natural Resource Management** (Agricultural Management; Biology; Forestry); **Economics and Resource Management** (Economics; Natural Resources; Social Sciences); **International Environment and Development Studies,** (Development Studies; Environmental Studies); **Landscape Architecture and Spatial Planning** (Landscape Architecture); **Mathematical Sciences and Technology** (Mathematics; Technology); **Plant and Environmental Sciences** (Agriculture; Botany; Chemistry; Ecology; Natural Resources; Soil Science)

History: Founded 1859 as the only Norwegian agricultural postgraduate college. Renamed Agricultural University of Norway. Acquired present status and title 2005. Under the jurisdiction of the Ministry of Education and Research since 1997.

Governing Bodies: Executive Board, comprising 11 members. The students are represented in the Board

Academic Year: August to August (August-December; January-May; May-August)

Admission Requirements: Secondary school certificate or equivalent

Fees: Tuition, none

Main Language(s) of Instruction: Norwegian; English

Degrees and Diplomas: *Bachelor*: 3 yrs; *Master*: 2 yrs; *Ph.D.*: Agriculture (Dr.Scient), 3 yrs

Student Services: Academic counselling, Canteen, Employment services, Foreign student adviser, Foreign Studies Centre, Nursery care, Social counselling, Sports facilities

Student Residential Facilities: Yes

Special Facilities: Agricultural Museum of Norway; The Dairy Museum

Libraries: Main Library, c. 365,000 vols

Last Updated: 27/10/11

NORWEGIAN UNIVERSITY OF SCIENCE AND TECHNOLOGY

Norges teknisk-naturvitenskaplige universitet (NTNU)

7491 Trondheim
Tel: +47 73-59-50-00
Fax: +47 73-59-53-10
EMail: postmottak@adm.ntnu.no
Website: http://www.ntnu.no

Rector: Torbjørn Digernes
Tel: +47 73-59-80-11, Fax: +47 73-59-80-90
EMail: torbjorn.digernes@ntnu.no; gry.fiksdal@ntnu.no

International Relations: Hilde Skeie, Head, International Office
Tel: +47 73-59-02-50, Fax: +47 73-59-52-10
EMail: international@ntnu.no; hilde.skeie@ntnu.no

Faculties

Architecture and Fine Arts (Architectural and Environmental Design; Architecture; Building Technologies; Development Studies; Fine Arts; Real Estate; Regional Planning; Town Planning); **Engineering Science and Technology** (Building Technologies; Construction Engineering; Ecology; Environmental Engineering; Geological Engineering; Geophysics; Heating and Refrigeration; Hydraulic Engineering; Industrial Engineering; Marine Engineering; Materials Engineering; Mining Engineering; Petroleum and Gas Engineering; Production Engineering; Railway Engineering; Road Engineering; Safety Engineering; Technology; Thermal Engineering; Transport Engineering); **Humanities** (Applied Linguistics; Archaeology; Art Criticism; Art History; Arts and Humanities; Comparative Literature; Cultural Studies; Dance; English; European Studies; Film; Germanic Languages; Heritage Preservation; History; Linguistics; Literature; Media Studies; Medieval Studies; Music; Musicology; Nordic Studies; Philosophy; Religious Studies; Romance Languages; Technology; Theatre); **Information Technology, Mathematics and Electrical Engineering** (Automation and Control Engineering; Electrical Engineering; Energy Engineering; Environmental Engineering; Information Sciences; Mathematics; Mathematics and Computer Science; Statistics; Telecommunications Engineering); **Medicine** (Anaesthesiology; Behavioural Sciences; Biomedical Engineering; Cardiology; Child Care and Development; Community Health; Gastroenterology; Gynaecology and Obstetrics; Laboratory Techniques; Medical Technology; Medicine; Molecular Biology; Neurosciences; Paediatrics; Physiology; Pneumology; Psychiatry and Mental Health; Rheumatology; Sports); **Natural Sciences and Technology** (Biotechnology; Botany; Chemical Engineering; Chemistry; Materials Engineering; Nanotechnology; Natural Resources; Physical Chemistry; Physics; Zoology); **Social Sciences and Technology Management** (Adult Education; African Studies; Anthropology; Child Care and Development; Clinical Psychology; Demography and Population; Development Studies; Economics; Education; Engineering Management; Geography; Health Sciences; Management; Mass Communication; Media Studies; Political Sciences; Psychology; Social Sciences; Social Work; Sociology; Teacher Training)

Further Information: Also close working relations with St. Olav's University Hospital.

History: Founded 1968, replacing the University of Trondheim which included the Norwegian Institute of Technology, the College of Arts and Science, and the Natural History and Archaeology Museum. Acquired present title 1996.

Governing Bodies: Board

Academic Year: August to June (August-December; January-June)

Admission Requirements: Secondary school certificate (examen artium) or equivalent

Fees: None

Main Language(s) of Instruction: Norwegian

Degrees and Diplomas: *Bachelor*: Science; Social Sciences; Humanities; Music; Fine Art; *Candidata/Candidatus*: Medicine; Clinical Psychology; *Master*: Humanities; Science; Social Sciences; Health Science; Social Work; Fine Arts; Technology; Architecture; Science (Biotechnology); Technology; Architecture; Social Sciences (Economy); *Doctor Philosophiae*: Humanities, Social Sciences, Science, Medicine; Technology; Architecture; *Ph.D.*: Humanities; Social Sciences; Science; Medicine; Clinical Psychology; Technology; Architecture. Also Diploma in Teacher Training, 1 yr.

Student Services: Academic counselling, Canteen, Cultural centre, Employment services, Foreign student adviser, Handicapped facilities, Health services, Language programs, Nursery care, Social counselling, Sports facilities

Student Residential Facilities: Students hostels and flats

Special Facilities: Natural History and Archeology Museum; Centre for Medieval Studies; Trondhjem Biologiske Stasjon (Marine Station); Ringve Botanical Garden; Svinvik Arboretum; Kongsvoll Alpine Botanical Garden

Libraries: University Library; University Library of Trondheim

Publications: Gemini *(biennially)*; Spor *(biennially)*; Universitetsavisa

Press or Publishing House: Tapir Forlag. NTNU Information Division

Last Updated: 27/09/11

OSLO AND AKERSHUS UNIVERSITY COLLEGE OF APPLIED SCIENCES

Høgskolen i Oslo og Akershus (HIOA/OAUC)

Postboks 4, St. Olavs plass, 0130 Oslo
Tel: +47 22-45-20-00
Fax: +47 22-45-30-65
EMail: postmottak@hio.no
Website: http://www.hioa.no/

Rector: Kari Toverud Jensen (2011-)
Tel: +47(22) 45-30-21, Fax: +47(22) 45-30-05
EMail: KariToverud.Jensen@hio.no

International Relations: Dagrun Kvammen, Director, International Office
Tel: +47(22) 45-20-72, Fax: +47(22) 45-28-25
EMail: dagrun.kvammen@hio.no

Faculties

Education and International Studies (Education; International Studies; Preschool Education; Primary Education; Secondary Education; Teacher Training; Translation and Interpretation; Vocational Education); **Health Sciences** (Behavioural Sciences; Biomedicine; Dental Technology; Health Administration; Health Sciences; Laboratory Techniques; Medical Technology; Nursing; Nutrition; Occupational Therapy; Orthodontics; Pharmacy; Physical Therapy; Radiology); **Social Sciences** (Archiving; Business Administration; Information Sciences; Journalism; Library Science; Media Studies; Public Relations; Social Policy; Social Work); **Technology, Art and Design** (Civil Engineering; Computer Science; Design; Energy Engineering; Fine Arts; Industrial Design; Theatre)

Further Information: Also Campus in Kjeller.

History: Founded 1994. Acquired present title 2011 following merger between Høgskolen i Oslo (Oslo University College) and Høgskolen i Akershus (Akershus University College).

Governing Bodies: OAUC Board

Academic Year: August to June (August-December; January-June)

Admission Requirements: Formal qualification for entry to higher education

Main Language(s) of Instruction: Norwegian, English

International Co-operation: Participates in Nordplus, Erasmus, Erasmus Mundus, Quota, EU Framework Programme, NOMA, NUCOOP, Leonardo da Vinci, Interreg IV, EU Health Programme, Culture 2000, CIP (Competitiveness and Innovation Framework Programme), eContent-plus project (DG Information Society and Media), Eureka programme – Celtic.

Accrediting Agencies: Norwegian Agency for Quality Assurance in Education (NOKUT)

Degrees and Diplomas: *Bachelor*: Administration and Management; Applied Computer Technology; Information Management ;Child Welfare; Library and Information Science; Bioengineering; Drama and Theatre Communications; Occupational Therapy; Teacher in Arts and Crafts; Biotechnology and Chemical Engineering; Civil Engineering; Computer Engineering; Electronics Engineering and Information Technology; Energy and Environmental Engineering in Buildings; Mechanical Engineering; Dentistry; Sign Language and Interpreting; Engineering Education; Development Studies; Welfare; Nursing; Finance and Administration; Journalism; Cost Economics, Nutrition and Management; Art and Design; Learning

Psychology; Media and Communications; Orthopaedic Engineering; Product; Radiography; Auditing; Community Nutrition; Social Work; Nursing; Teacher Training for Bilingual Teachers; Pharmaceuticals; Photo Journalism; Physiotherapy; Physiotherapy; Pre-school Teacher; Home Economics and Hospitality Management; Sport, Recreation and Health Science; Information Technology; Vocational Teacher (Building and Construction, Design and Craftsmanship, Electrical Engineering, Health and Social Care, Media and Communication, Restaurant and Food Processing, Service and Transport, Technical and Industrial Production).; *Master*: ICT-supported Learning; International Education and Development; International Social Welfare and Health Policy; Journalism; Clinical Nursing Science; Learning in Complex Systems; Network and System Administration; Product Design; Kindergarten Education; Library and Information Science; Biomedicine; Energy and Environment in Buildings; Family Treatment; Multicultural and International Education; Design, Arts and Crafts; Elementary Education; Health Science and Empowerment; Mental Health; Rehabilitation and Therapy; Community Nutrition; Social work; Corporate Governance; Vocational Education; *Ph.D.*: Behavioral Analysis; Professional studies; Social work and Social Policy. Also 4 yr programme in Elementary Teacher Teacher; Courses and Graduate Programmes in File and document management; Library and Information Science; Design and Communication in Digital Media; Drama and Theatre Communication; Ekspresstudium in sign language; Preparatory Course for Engineering; Physical education and sports; Cultural Leadership; Art and Design; Textile Design; Organization and Management; Policy and management; Teacher Training; Sign Language; Development Studies; Economics and Management.

Student Services: Academic counselling, Canteen, Foreign student adviser, Foreign Studies Centre, Handicapped facilities, Language programs, Nursery care, Social counselling, Sports facilities

Libraries: c. 200,000 vols; Six Learning Centres

Press or Publishing House: In House Publishing

Academic Staff *2010-2011*: Total: c. 1,600

Student Numbers *2011-2012*: Total: c. 16,000

Last Updated: 21/09/11

OSLO NATIONAL ACADEMY OF THE ARTS

Kunsthøgskolen i Oslo (KHIO)
Postboks 6853, St Olavs Plass, 0130 Oslo
Tel: +47 22-99-55-00
Fax: +47 22-99-55-02
EMail: khio@khio.no
Website: http://www.khio.no

Rector: Cecilie Broch Knudsen
Tel: +47 22-99-55-11 EMail: ceciliebroch.knudsen@khio.no

Secretary-General: Erling W. Wist
Tel: +47 22-99-55-04 EMail: erling.wist@khio.no

International Relations: Anne-Cathrine Andersen, Coordinator
Tel: +47 22-99-55-05 EMail: anne.andersen@khio.no

Faculties

Design (Design); **Fine Arts** (Fine Arts; Painting and Drawing; Performing Arts; Sculpture); **Performing Arts** (Dance; Opera; Performing Arts; Theatre); **Visual Arts** (Visual Arts)

History: Founded 1818 as National College of Art and Design. Acquired present name and status 1996, after merger with five formerly independent colleges. It is now a University College.

Governing Bodies: Board of the ONCA (11 members).

Academic Year: August to Mid-June

Admission Requirements: Secondary school certificate and entrance examination

Fees: (Norwegian Kroner): 280 per semester

Main Language(s) of Instruction: Norwegian

International Co-operation: With universities in Belgium, France, Ireland, Italy, Netherlands, Sweden, Spain, United Kingdom, Germany, Austria. Participates in Erasmus and Nordplus programmes.

Accrediting Agencies: Nasjonalt organ for kvalitet i utdanningen (NOKUT)

Degrees and Diplomas: *Bachelor (BA)*: 3 yrs; *Master*

Student Services: Academic counselling, Canteen, Foreign student adviser, Nursery care

Special Facilities: Art Galleries. Studios. Auditorium with stage (for opera, theatre and ballet). Stages.

Libraries: Main Library; library for Performing Arts; library for Art and Design; library for Fine Arts

Press or Publishing House: Akademisk Publisering

Last Updated: 27/10/11

ØSTFOLD UNIVERSITY COLLEGE

Høgskolen i Østfold (HIØ)
Os Alle 9 N-1757, 1757 Halden
Tel: +47 69-21-50-00
Fax: +47 69-21-50-02
EMail: postmottak@hiof.no
Website: http://www.hiof.no

Rector: Elin Nesje Vestli (2006-)
Tel: +47 69-21-50-06 EMail: elin.n.vestli@hiof.no

Høgskoledirektør: Carl-Morten Gjeldnes

International Relations: Ellen Hoy-Petersen, Senior Executive Officer Tel: +47 69-21-50-13 EMail: ellen.hoy-petersen@hiof.no

Academies

Theatre *(Norwegian Academy)* (Acting; Display and Stage Design)

Faculties

Business, Social Sciences and Foreign Languages (Accountancy; Business Administration; Economics; English; French; German; International Business; Management; Political Sciences); **Computer Science** (Computer Engineering; Computer Networks; Computer Science; Software Engineering); **Education** (Education; Higher Education Teacher Training; Preschool Education; Teacher Training); **Engineering** (Chemical Engineering; Civil Engineering; Engineering; Mechanical Engineering; Telecommunications Engineering); **Health and Social Work Studies** (Health Sciences; Social Work); **Health Studies** (Health Education; Laboratory Techniques; Medical Technology; Nursing)

History: Founded 1994.

Academic Year: August to June (August-December; January-June)

Admission Requirements: Secondary school certificate or recognized equivalent

Fees: None

Main Language(s) of Instruction: Norwegian

International Co-operation: With universities in United Kingdom, Germany, France, Italy, Belgium, Ireland, Finland, Sweden, Denmark, Austria, Netherlands, USA.

Accrediting Agencies: National Academic Information Centre (NAIC)

Degrees and Diplomas: *Bachelor*: 3 yrs; *Master*: a further 2 yrs

Student Services: Academic counselling, Canteen, Language programs, Social counselling, Sports facilities

Student Residential Facilities: Yes

Libraries: Faculty Libraries

Last Updated: 14/02/08

SAAMI UNIVERSITY COLLEGE

Sámi allaskuvla/Sámi University College (SA/SUC)
Hánnoluohkká 45, 9520 Guovdageaidnu
Tel: +47 78-44-84-00
Fax: +47 78-44-84-02
EMail: postmottak@samiskhs.no
Website: http://www.samiskhs.no

Rector: Jelena Porsanger EMail: jelenap@samiskhs.no

Director: Maaren Palismaa
Tel: +47 78-44-84-99 EMail: maaren.palismaa@samiskhs.no

International Relations: Lena Susanne Gaup
Tel: +47 78-48-77-21 EMail: lena-sunsanne.gaup@samiskhs.no

Departments

Education (Education); **Journalism** (Journalism); **Reindeer Husbandry and Natural Science** (Animal Husbandry; Natural Sciences); **Sámi Language and Literature** (Literature; Scandinavian

Languages); **Sámi Traditional and Applied Arts** (Fine Arts); **Teachers Education** (Teacher Trainers Education)

History: Founded 1989. Acquired present status 1994.

Main Language(s) of Instruction: North-Sámi

Degrees and Diplomas: *Bachelor*: Reindeer Husbandry; Sámi language and Sámi Literature; Duodji, Sámi Traditional and Applied Arts; Sámi Pre-School Teachers Education; Sámi JournalismSámi Teachers Education; *Master*: Duodji, Sámi Traditional and Applied Arts; Sámi language and Sámi Literature

Last Updated: 20/09/11

SOGN OG FJORDANE UNIVERSITY COLLEGE

Høgskolen i Sogn og Fjordane (HSS)

Postboks 133, 6851 Sogndal
Tel: +47 57-67-60-00
Fax: +47 57-67-61-00
EMail: post@hisf.no
Website: http://www.hisf.no

Rector: Åse Løkeland (2007-)
Tel: +47(57) 67-61-11 EMail: ase.lokeland@hisf.no

Director: Hans Jørgen Binningsbø
Tel: +47(57) 67-61-10 EMail: hans.binningsbo@hisf.no

International Relations: Kari Thorsen
Tel: +47(57) 67-61-41 EMail: kari.thorsen@hisf.no

Centres

The Sandane Study Centre (Special Education)

Faculties

Engineering and Science (Automation and Control Engineering; Ecology; Engineering; Geology; Instrument Making; Landscape Architecture); **Health Studies** (Community Health; Nursing; Psychiatry and Mental Health); **Social Sciences** (English; Social Policy; Social Sciences; Social Work; Teacher Training)

Further Information: 3 sites: Sogndal, Førde and Sandane

History: Founded 1994.

Academic Year: August to June

Admission Requirements: Secondary school certificate (International Baccalaureate) or equivalent. Proficiency in English and Norwegian

Fees: None

Main Language(s) of Instruction: Norwegian

International Co-operation: With universities in Europe, USA, Australia. Also participates in Nordplus, Erasmus, and Leonardo programmes.

Degrees and Diplomas: *Bachelor*, *Master*

Student Services: Academic counselling, Canteen, Foreign student adviser, Handicapped facilities, Nursery care, Social counselling, Sports facilities

Libraries: Yes

Last Updated: 27/10/11

SØR-TRØNDELAG UNIVERSITY COLLEGE

Høgskolen i Sør-Trøndelag (HIST)

N-7004 Trondheim
Tel: +47 73-55-90-00
Fax: +47 73-93-90-51
EMail: postmottak@hist.no
Website: http://www.hist.no

Rector: Trond Michael Andersen
Tel: +47 73-55-90-64, Fax: +47 95-26-91-64
EMail: trond.m.andersen@hist.no

Director: Ann Elisabeth Wedø
Tel: +47 73-55-90-61 EMail: a.e.wedo@hist.no

International Relations: Marit Sandtrø
Tel: +47 73-55-90-70 EMail: marit.sandtro@hist.no

Faculties

Business Administration (Business Administration); **Health Education and Social Work** (Child Care and Development; Health Sciences; Occupational Therapy; Physical Therapy; Social Work; Speech Therapy and Audiology); **Informatics and E-Learning** (Distance Education; Information Technology); **Nursing** (Nursing); **Teacher and Interpreter Education** (Teacher Training; Translation and Interpretation); **Technology** (Biomedicine; Chemical Engineering; Civil Engineering; Electrical Engineering; Food Technology; Materials Engineering; Mechanical Engineering; Technology)

Schools

Business *(Trondheim)* (Business Administration; Economics; Health Administration) *Dean*: Ove Gustafsson

History: Founded 1994 by merging eight colleges in Trondheim.

Governing Bodies: Board

Academic Year: August to June

Admission Requirements: Generell Studiekompetanse

Main Language(s) of Instruction: Norwegian

International Co-operation: With universities in Sweden, Denmark, the Netherlands, Ireland, United Kingdom, USA, and Russia.

Degrees and Diplomas: *Bachelor*: 3 yrs; *Master*: 2 yrs

Student Services: Academic counselling, Canteen, Foreign student adviser, Handicapped facilities, Health services, Social counselling, Sports facilities

Libraries: Yes

Last Updated: 27/10/11

STORD/HAUGESUND UNIVERSITY COLLEGE

Høgskolen Stord / Haugesund (HSH/SHUC)

Postboks 5000, 5409 Stord
Tel: +47 53-49-13-00
Fax: +47 53-49-14-01
EMail: postmottak@hsh.no
Website: http://www.hsh.no

Rector: Liv Reidun Grimstvedt
Tel: +47 53-49-14-06, Fax: +47 53-49-14-01
EMail: liv.grimstvedt@hsh.no

Faculties

Engineering (Engineering; Mechanical Engineering); **Health and social sciences** (Health Sciences; Social Sciences); **Teacher Education** (Teacher Training)

Programmes

Economics (Economics); **Nautical Operations** (Nautical Science); **Nurse Training** (Nursing); **Safety Engineering** (Safety Engineering)

History: Founded 1994.

Main Language(s) of Instruction: Norwegian

Degrees and Diplomas: *Bachelor*: 3 yrs; *Master*: a further 2 yrs

Last Updated: 27/10/11

TELEMARK UNIVERSITY COLLEGE

Høgskolen i Telemark (HIT)

Postboks 203, 3901 Porsgrunn
Tel: +47 35-02-62-00
Fax: +47 35-57-50-02
EMail: postmottak@hit.no
Website: http://www.hit.no

Rector: Kristian Bogen
Tel: +47 35-57-50-06 EMail: kristian.bogen@hit.no

Director: John W. Viflot
Tel: +47 35-57-50-05 EMail: john.viflot@hit.no

International Relations: Pål Augestad
Tel: +45 35-57-50-23 EMail: pal.augestad@hit.no

Faculties

Art, Design and Traditional Art (Art Education; Design; Folklore; Visual Arts); **Business, Administration and Computer Studies** (Accountancy; Business Administration; Computer Science; Management; Marketing; Real Estate; Tourism); **Culture and Humanities** (Arts and Humanities; Cultural Studies; History; Literature; Scandinavian Languages; Writing); **Environmental Studies** (Ecology; Environmental Management; Natural Resources); **Health and Social Studies** (Health Sciences; Nursing; Social Studies; Social Work); **Sport, Physical Education and Outdoor Life Studies** (Physical Education; Sports); **Technology / Engineering**

(Automation and Control Engineering; Civil Engineering; Computer Graphics; Mechanical Engineering; Soil Science; Surveying and Mapping; Technology; Water Science)

History: Founded 1994.

Main Language(s) of Instruction: Norwegian and English

International Co-operation: Participates in Erasmus; Nordplus

Degrees and Diplomas: *Bachelor*, *Master*, *Ph.D.*

Student Services: Academic counselling, Canteen, Foreign student adviser, Handicapped facilities, Social counselling

Libraries: Yes

Last Updated: 27/10/11

THE OSLO SCHOOL OF ARCHITECTURE AND DESIGN

Arkitektur- og designhøgskolen i Oslo (AHO)

PO Box 6768, St. Olavs plass, 0130 Oslo
Tel: +47 22-99-70-00
Fax: +47 22-11-71-90
EMail: postmottak@aho.no
Website: http://www.aho.no

Rector: Karl Otto Ellefsen
Tel: +47 22-99-70-01
EMail: rektor@aho.no; karl.o.ellefsen@aho.no

International Relations: Kjersti Bergheim, Senior Academic Officer, Student and Academic Affairs
Tel: +47 22-99-70-24, Fax: +47 22-99-71-89
EMail: kjersti.bergheim@adm.aho.no

Institutes

Architecture (Architecture); **Design** (Design; Industrial Design); **Form, Theory and History** (Architecture; Design; History; Museum Studies); **Urbanism and Landscape** (Landscape Architecture; Town Planning; Urban Studies)

History: Founded 1945 as Statens Arkitektskole, acquired present title 1969. A State Institution governed by a Board appointed by the Ministry of Education and Research.

Academic Year: August to June (August-December; January-June)

Admission Requirements: Secondary school certificate (Vitnemål fra videregående skole) and entrance examination

Fees: None

Main Language(s) of Instruction: Norwegian

International Co-operation: Participates in Ilaud, Nordplus, Cirrus/ Cumulus, EAAE and Nofua programmes.

Degrees and Diplomas: *Master*: Architecture, 5 1/2 yrs; *Master*: Industrial Design, 5 yrs; *Ph.D.*

Student Services: Academic counselling, Canteen, Foreign student adviser, Handicapped facilities, Health services, Nursery care, Social counselling, Sports facilities

Student Residential Facilities: Yes

Special Facilities: Gallery AHO

Libraries: c. 44,000 vols

Last Updated: 25/10/11

UNIVERSITY OF AGDER

Universitetet i Agder (UIA)

Post Box 422, 4604 Kristiansand
Tel: +47 38-14-10-00
Fax: +47 38-14-10-01
EMail: postmottak@uia.no
Website: http://www.uia.no

Rector: Torunn Lauvdal (2011-2015)
Tel: +47 38-14-11-02 EMail: torunn.lauvdal@uia.no

International Relations: Svein A. Pedersen, Director, International Relations Tel: +47 38-14-11-59 EMail: Svein.A.Pedersen@uia.no

Faculties

Economics and Social Sciences (Accountancy; Business Administration; Development Studies; Economics; Information Sciences; Law; Management; Political Sciences; Public Administration; Social Sciences; Social Work); **Engineering, Mathematics and Science** (Analytical Chemistry; Biology; Chemistry; Civil Engineering; Computer Engineering; Computer Science; Electrical and Electronic Engineering; Electronic Engineering; Energy Engineering; Engineering; Industrial Management; Information Management; Information Technology; Mathematics; Mathematics Education; Mechanical Engineering; Natural Sciences; Telecommunications Engineering); **Fine Arts** (Art Management; Fine Arts; Handicrafts; Music; Theatre; Visual Arts); **Health and Sports** (Educational Psychology; Health Sciences; Nursing; Nutrition; Physical Education; Public Health; Sports); **Humanities and Education** (Arts and Humanities; Education; Educational Sciences; English; French; German; History; Mass Communication; Modern Languages; Nordic Studies; Philosophy; Religion; Scandinavian Languages; Special Education; Theology)

Units

Teacher Education *(Inter-disciplinary)* (Preschool Education; Primary Education; Secondary Education; Teacher Training)

History: Founded as Høgskolen i Agder Agder (University College) 1994. Acquired present status and title September 2007.

Main Language(s) of Instruction: Norwegian; English

Degrees and Diplomas: *Bachelor*, *Master*, *Ph.D.*

Libraries: c. 300,000 vols; c. 18,500 periodical subscriptions.

Student Numbers *2010-2011*	**TOTAL**
All (Foreign Included)	c. **2,500**
FOREIGN ONLY	**270**

Last Updated: 21/09/11

UNIVERSITY OF BERGEN

Universitetet i Bergen (UIB)

Postboks 7800, Muséplass 1, N 5020 Bergen
Tel: +47 55-58-00-00
Fax: +47 55-58-96-43
EMail: post@uib.no
Website: http://www.uib.no

Rector: Sigmund Grønmo (2005-)
Tel: +47 55-58-20-02, Fax: +47 55-58-96-43
EMail: rektor@rektor.uib.no

University Director: Kari Tove Elvbakken
Tel: +47 55-58-00-00, Fax: +47 55-58-96-43
EMail: Karitove.Elvbakken@udir.uib.no

International Relations: Astri Andresen, Vice Rector for International Relations (2009)
Tel: +47 55-58-20-51, Fax: +47 55-58-96-43
EMail: astri.andresen@rektor.uib.no

Centres

Geobiology (Natural Sciences; Technology); **International Health** (Health Sciences); **Medieval Studies** (Medieval Studies); **Middle East and Islamic Studies** (Islamic Studies; Middle Eastern Studies); **Sciences and Humanities** (Arts and Humanities; Natural Sciences); **Women's and Gender Studies** (Gender Studies; Women's Studies)

Faculties

Humanities (Arts and Humanities); **Law** (Law); **Mathematics and Natural Sciences** (Mathematics; Natural Sciences); **Medicine and Dentistry** (Dentistry; Medicine); **Psychology** (Psychology); **Social Sciences** (Social Sciences)

Research Centres

Climate *(Bjerknes)* (Meteorology); **Petroleum** *(Integrated)* (Petroleum and Gas Engineering)

Further Information: Approx. 300 courses taught in English for exchange students, including courses in Scandinavia Area Studies (10 courses at the Faculty of Humanities and the Faculty of Social Sciences). Approx. 30 Master's programmes taught in English (2 yrs). Residents of developing countries and Eastern Europe are eligible for scholarship programmes of the Norwegian Ministry of Education (through the Quota Scheme). Norwegian language courses taught during the semester. For further information, foreign students should contact: Eli Ertresvaag Zachariadis Telephone: +47(55) 58-49-53; E-mail: eli.zachariadis@adm.uib.no

History: Founded as Bergen Museum 1825, became University 1948. A State institution enjoying considerable autonomy in both academic and financial matters. Financed by a grant voted by Parliament.

Governing Bodies: University Board

Academic Year: August to June (August-December; January-June)

Admission Requirements: Secondary school certificate (examen artium) or recognized equivalent

Fees: None

Main Language(s) of Instruction: Norwegian (English in selected programmes, in particular M.Phil. degrees)

International Co-operation: Participates in COIMBRA group, COMPOSTELA group, and Utrecht network programmes, World-wide Universities Network, The Inter-University Centre of Dubrovnik, Nordic Centre in China, Nordic Centre in India, The Southern African-Nordic Centre, University of the Arctic, European University Association, International Association of Universities

Degrees and Diplomas: *Bachelor*: Arts and Social Sciences; Dental Hygiene; Science, 3 yrs; *Bachelor*: Music; Natural Sciences Education, 4 yrs; *Candidata/Candidatus*: Medicine (cand.Med.); Psychology (cand.psychol.), 6 yrs; *Master*: Arts and Social Sciences, a further 2 yrs; *Master*: Arts and Social Sciences Education; Dentistry; Integrated one-tier programme; Law; Natural Sciences Education; Pharmacy, 5 yrs; *Master*: Experience-based, 1-1 1/2 yrs; *Master*: Health Sciences, 1-2 yrs; *Master*: Natural Sciences, 2 yrs

Student Services: Canteen, Cultural centre, Foreign student adviser, Handicapped facilities, Health services, Language programs, Nursery care, Social counselling, Sports facilities

Student Residential Facilities: For c. 3,000 students

Special Facilities: Bergen Museum; Bryggen Museum of Medieval Archaeology; Museum of Theatre and Drama. Botanical Garden. Norwegian Arboretum

Libraries: Bergen University Library, c. 1.4m. vols

Academic Staff *2010-2011*	MEN	WOMEN	**TOTAL**
FULL-TIME	c. 1,670	1,680	**3,350**
Student Numbers *2012-2013*			
All (Foreign Included)	–	–	c. **14,500**

Last Updated: 25/02/13

UNIVERSITY OF NORDLAND

Universitetet i Nordland (HIBO)

8049 Bodø
Tel: +47 75-51-72-00
Fax: +47 75-51-74-57
EMail: postmottak@hibo.no
Website: http://www.hibo.no

Rector: Pål Pedersen
Tel: +47 41 57 56 25 EMail: paal.pedersen@hibo.no

University College Director: Stig Fossum
EMail: stig.fossum@hibo.no

International Relations: Tine Viveka Westerberg
Tel: +47 75-51-78-03 EMail: international@hibo.no

Departments

Fisheries and Natural Sciences (Aquaculture; Economics; Fishery; Marine Science and Oceanography; Marketing; Natural Sciences); **Nursing and Health Sciences** (Anaesthesiology; Gerontology; Health Sciences; Nursing; Occupational Health; Oncology; Psychiatry and Mental Health; Social Welfare; Welfare and Protective Services); **Professional Studies** (Cultural Studies; Dance; Education; Pedagogy; Preschool Education; Primary Education; Secondary Education; Sports; Teacher Training); **Social Sciences** (Administration; History; Political Sciences; Social Sciences; Social Work; Sociology)

Graduate Schools

Business (Accountancy; Business Administration; Business and Commerce; Environmental Management; Information Technology; International Business; Management; Marketing; Transport Management)

History: Founded 1994 as Høgskolen i Bodø. Acquired present title and status 2010.

Main Language(s) of Instruction: English and Norwegian

Degrees and Diplomas: *Bachelor*: Business; Sports Administration; Information Technology; Economy; Auditing; Child Protection; History; Social Work; Sociology; Political Science; Circumpolar Studies; Fisheries; Aquaculture; Export Marketing; Fisheries Economy; Economy and Export; Honours: Quality Management and Manufacturing of Marine Raw Materials; Nursing; Honours: Aging and Welfare Services for Old People; Occupational Health and Safety; Practice Mentoring within Health and Social Welfare Studies; Mental Health; Anaesthetics; Child Nursing; Intensive Care; Operating Theatre Nursing; Cancer Nursing; *Master*: Arts: Social Science; Sociology; Social Work (M.A.); Ocean Farming; Practical Knowledge; Science: Business; *Ph.D.*: Business Administration

Special Facilities: 5 laboratories with 170 computers; Auditorium; Study Halls; Radio; Television Facilities; Research vessel 'Oscar Sund'

Libraries: Library, 75,000 vols; 600 periodicals

Last Updated: 03/01/11

UNIVERSITY OF OSLO

Universitetet i Oslo (UIO)

Postboks 1072, Blindern, 0316 Oslo
Tel: +47 22-85-50-50
Fax: +47 22-85-43-74
EMail: informasjon@uio.no; postmottak@admin.uio.no
Website: http://www.uio.no

Rector: Ole Petter Ottersen (2009-2013)
Tel: +47 22-85-63-03, Fax: +47 22-85-44-42 EMail: rektor@uio.no

University Director: Gunn-Elin Aa. Bjørneboe
Tel: +47 22-85-63-01, Fax: +47 22-85-44-42
EMail: g.e.bjorneboe@admin.uio.no

International Relations: Svein Hullstein, Special Adviser
Tel: +47 22-85-84-64, Fax: +47 22-85-44-42
EMail: svein.hullstein@admin.uio.no; h.m.ullero@admin.uio.no

Centres

Ethics (Ethics); **Functional Materials and Nanotechnology** *(FUNMAT)* (Materials Engineering; Nanotechnology); **Ibsen Studies**; **Technology, Innovation and Culture Studies** (Cultural Studies; Technology); **Viking and Medieval Studies** (Medieval Studies; Nordic Studies); **Women's Studies and Gender Research** (Gender Studies; Women's Studies)

Faculties

Dentistry (Dentistry); **Education** (Education; Educational Research; Special Education; Teacher Training); **Humanities** (Archaeology; Art History; Arts and Humanities; Classical Languages; Communication Studies; Comparative Literature; Cultural Studies; Eastern European Studies; Germanic Studies; Heritage Preservation; History; Linguistics; Media Studies; Museum Studies; Music; Musicology; Oriental Studies; Philosophy; Romance Languages; Theatre); **Law** (Criminology; Human Rights; International Law; Law; Maritime Law; Private Law; Public Law) *Dean*: John T. Johnsen; **Mathematics and Natural Sciences** (Astrophysics; Biochemistry; Biology; Chemistry; Computer Science; Ecology; Geography; Geology; Geophysics; Mathematics; Molecular Biology; Nanotechnology; Natural Sciences; Pharmacy; Physics); **Medicine** (Biotechnology; Community Health; Health Administration; Health Sciences; Medicine; Nursing); **Social Sciences** (Anthropology; Economics; European Studies; Geography (Human); Political Sciences; Psychology; Social Sciences; Sociology); **Theology** (Theology) *Dean*: Helge S. Kvanvig

Institutes

Human Rights *(Norwegian Institute)* (Human Rights) *Director*: Nils Butenschøn

History: Founded 1811 as Kongelige Frederiks Universitet, named after the King of Denmark. Acquired present title 1939.

Governing Bodies: Universitetsstyret (University Board)

Academic Year: August to June (August-December; January-June)

Admission Requirements: Secondary school certificate or recognized equivalent

Fees: None

Main Language(s) of Instruction: Norwegian and English

International Co-operation: Participates in Erasmus; Erasmus Mundus; Nordplus

Degrees and Diplomas: *Bachelor*: 3 yrs; *Master*: 2 yrs; *Ph.D.*: 3 yrs

Student Services: Academic counselling, Canteen, Cultural centre, Employment services, Foreign student adviser, Foreign Studies Centre, Handicapped facilities, Health services, Language programs, Nursery care, Social counselling, Sports facilities

Student Residential Facilities: Yes

Special Facilities: Museums: Historical Museum; The Viking Ship Museum; The Classical Antiquities Collection; Ethnographic collection; Coin Cabinet; Collection of national antiquities; The Runic Archives. Botanical Garden.

Libraries: Universitetsbiblioteket

Publications: Apollon *(quarterly)*

Last Updated: 28/10/11

UNIVERSITY OF STAVANGER

Universitetet i Stavanger (UIS)

N-4036 Stavanger
Tel: +47 51-83-10-00
Fax: +47 51-83-10-50
EMail: post@uis.no
Website: http://www.uis.no

Rector: Marit Boyesen EMail: marit.boyesen@uis.no

University Director: John Branem Møst
Tel: +47(51) 83-30-01 EMail: john.b.most@uis.no

Faculties

Arts and Education (Behavioural Sciences; Cultural Studies; Dance; Education; Modern Languages; Music; Preschool Education); **Science and Technology** (Computer Engineering; Electrical Engineering; Industrial and Production Economics; Materials Engineering; Mathematics; Mechanical Engineering; Natural Sciences; Petroleum and Gas Engineering; Structural Architecture); **Social Sciences** (Business Administration; Cultural Studies; Health Sciences; Hotel Management; Journalism; Management; Mass Communication; Multimedia; Nursing; Social Sciences; Social Work; Tourism)

History: Founded 1994 as Stavanger University College. Acquired present status 2005.

Main Language(s) of Instruction: Norwegian and English

Degrees and Diplomas: *Bachelor*, *Master*, *Ph.D.*

Libraries: University library

Last Updated: 28/10/11

UNIVERSITY OF TROMSØ

Universitetet i Tromsø (UIT)

Breivika, 9037 Tromsø
Tel: +47 77-64-40-00
Fax: +47 77-64-49-00
EMail: postmottak@uit.no
Website: http://www.uit.no

Rector: Jarle Aarbakke (2002-)
Tel: +47 77-64-49-88, Fax: +47 77-64-47-60
EMail: rektor@adm.uit.no; jarle.aarbakke@adm.uit.no

Director: Lasse Lønnum
Tel: +47 77-64-49-90, Fax: +47 77-64-47-60
EMail: lasse.lonnum@adm.uit.no

International Relations: Astrid Revhaug, International Advisor
Tel: +47 77-64-49-72 EMail: astrid.revhaug@adm.uit.no

Faculties

Biosciences, Fisheries and Economics (Aquaculture; Economics; Marine Biology; Marketing; Social Sciences); **Fine Arts** (Dance; Fine Arts; Music; Theatre; Writing); **Health Sciences** (Biomedicine; Community Health; Dentistry; Health Sciences; Pharmacy; Public Health); **Humanities, Social Sciences and Education** (Anthropology; Archaeology; Archiving; Art History; Classical Languages; Comparative Literature; Education; English; Finnish; French; German; Greek; History; Latin; Library Science; Linguistics; Nordic Studies; Political Sciences; Religious Studies; Russian; Sociology); **Law** (Law); **Science and Technology** (Biology; Chemistry; Engineering; Geology; Mathematics and Computer Science; Physics; Statistics)

History: Founded 1968, officially opened by King Olav V 1972. A State institution enjoying considerable autonomy in both academic and financial matters. Financed primarily by the government. Merged with Tromso University College 2009.

Governing Bodies: University Board

Academic Year: August to June (August-December; January-June)

Admission Requirements: Secondary school certificate (examen artium) or recognized equivalent

Fees: None

Main Language(s) of Instruction: Norwegian

International Co-operation: Participates in Nordplus, Socrates, and Barents Region programmes.

Accrediting Agencies: National Agency for Accreditation (NOKU)

Degrees and Diplomas: *Bachelor*: Aquaculture; Biology; Physics; Chemistry; Geology; Computer Science; Mathematics; Statistics; Economics; History; Religious Studies; Archaeology; Philosophy; Sociology; Social Anthropology; Political Science; Planning and Cultural Studies; Psychology; Education Research; Art History; Classical Studies; Documentation Studies; Literature; Languages; Fisheries; Business Administration; Past and Present Multicultural Norway; Russian Studies; Health Administration; Language and Economics; Business Economics and Logistics (Interdisciplinary Programmes), 3 yrs; *Master*: Fish Health; Fisheries Biology; Aquaculture; Economics; Business Economics and Marketing; Business Administration; Coastal Planning and Management; International Fisheries Management; Physics; Geology; Computer Science; Chemistry; Mathematics; Statistics; Medical Biology; Health Science; Public Health; Archaeology; History; Religious Studies; Philosophy; Sociology; Political Science; Educational Research; Special Needs Education; Social Anthropology; Planning and Cultural Studies; Management and Organisation; Science; Nordic Medieval Studies; Peace and Conflict Transformation; Visual Cultural Studies; Indigenous Studies; Documentation Studies; Art History; Literature; Language, 2 yrs; *Master*: Land Use and Agriculture in Arctic Areas; Teacher Training in Natural Science and Mathematics (for Secondary Schools), in Science and Mathematics (for Comprehensive Schools); Teacher Training in Languages and Social Sciences; Fish Health (Integrated Programmes), 5 yrs; *Master*: Public Health; Action Learning; Adult Education, 18 months; *Ph.D.*: Arts and Humanities (Dr.art.); Law (Dr.juris); Medicine (Dr.med.); Psychology (Dr.psychol.); Science (Dr.scient.); Social Sciences. Also Technological Programmes in Industrial Mathematics, Computer Science, Molecular Biotechnology, Electrical Engineering, Space Geophysics; Professional Degree Studies in Medicine, Psychology (6 yrs), Odonthology, Pharmacy, Law (5 yrs); One-year Studies in Library Studies, Foundation Course in Medicine; Postgraduate Certificate in Education (1 yr)

Student Services: Academic counselling, Canteen, Cultural centre, Foreign student adviser, Handicapped facilities, Health services, Language programs, Nursery care, Social counselling, Sports facilities

Special Facilities: Museology Museum. Botanical Garden. Planetarium

Libraries: 989,210 vols

Last Updated: 28/10/11

VESTFOLD UNIVERSITY COLLEGE

Høgskolen i Vestfold (HVE)

P.O. Box N-2243, 3103 Tønsberg
Tel: +47 33-03-10-00
Fax: +47 33-03-11-00
EMail: postmottak@hive.no
Website: http://www.hive.no

Rector: Petter Aasen (2007-)
Tel: +47 33-03-10-10 EMail: Petter.Aasen@hive.no

Director: Olav Refsdal
Tel: +47 33-03-10-23 EMail: olav.refsdal@hive.no

International Relations: Jan Håkon Olsson
Tel: +47 33-03-10-98 EMail: jan.h.olsson@hive.no

Faculties

Business and Social Sciences (Business Administration; Management; Social Sciences; Sociology); **Health Sciences** (Nursing)

Dean: Inger Johanne Kraver; **Humanities and Education** (Arts and Humanities; Education; History; Modern Languages; Pedagogy; Preschool Education; Sociology; Teacher Training); **Technology and Maritime Studies** (Marine Engineering; Marine Science and Oceanography; Nanotechnology; Nautical Science; Technology)

History: Founded 1994.

Governing Bodies: College Board

Academic Year: August to June

Admission Requirements: 3 years' upper secondary school in Norway. Minimum requirements in English and Norwegian. TOEFL minimum score of 500 points; IELTS minimum score of 5.0. Minimum score of 450 points in Bergenstesten

Fees: None

Main Language(s) of Instruction: Norwegian

International Co-operation: Bilateral agreements. Also participates in Erasmus and Nordplus

Accrediting Agencies: The Norwegian Agency for Quality Assurance in Education (NOKUT)

Degrees and Diplomas: *Bachelor*: 3 yrs; *Master*; *Ph.D.*

Student Services: Academic counselling, Canteen, Cultural centre, Foreign student adviser, Handicapped facilities, Language programs, Social counselling, Sports facilities

Libraries: Yes

Last Updated: 27/10/11

VOLDA UNIVERSITY COLLEGE

Høgskolen i Volda (HVO)

Postboks 500 / P.O Box 500, 6101 Volda

Tel: +47 70-07-50-00

Fax: +47 70-07-50-51

EMail: postmottak@hivolda.no

Website: http://www.hivolda.no

Rector: Per Halse Tel: +47 70-07-50-20

Director: Jacob Kjøde Jr
Tel: +47 70-07-50-10 EMail: jacob.kjode@hivolda.no

International Relations: Cecilie Wilhelmsen
Tel: +47 70-07-51-20 EMail: cecilie.wilhelmsen@hivolda.no

Faculties

Arts and Physical Education (Design; Fine Arts; Media Studies; Music; Physical Education; Theatre); **Humanities and Education** (Arts and Humanities; Communication Studies; Cultural Studies; Education; Literature; Media Studies; Modern Languages); **Media and Journalism** (Journalism; Media Studies); **Social Sciences and History** (Administration; History; Social Sciences; Social Work)

History: Founded 1994.

Governing Bodies: Administrative Board (11 members), Faculty Board

Academic Year: August to June (August-December; January-June)

Admission Requirements: Secondary school leaving certicate

Fees: (Norwegian Kroner): 550 per semester

Main Language(s) of Instruction: Norwegian. Several courses in English

International Co-operation: With universities in the Nordic countries, Austria, China, Hungary, India, Ireland, Lithuania, Malawi, Namibia, Spain, Turkey, United Kingdom and USA.

Degrees and Diplomas: *Bachelor*: Pre-school Teacher Education; Social Work; Child Care; Journalism; Public Information; Animation; Planning and Governance; Media Studies; Information and Communication Technology and Design; Theology, 3 yrs; *Master*: Planning and Governance; New Norwegian Written Culture; Special Needs, 2 further 2 yrs. Also Postgraduate Diplomas in Film and Television Documentaries; Certificate of Education

Student Services: Academic counselling, Canteen, Foreign student adviser, Handicapped facilities, Language programs, Nursery care, Social counselling, Sports facilities

Student Residential Facilities: Yes

Libraries: c. 95,000 vols

Last Updated: 27/10/11

PRIVATE INSTITUTIONS

BERGEN NLA UNIVERSITY COLLEGE

NLA Høgskolen i Bergen

PO Box 74, Sandviken, 5812 Bergen

Tel: +47 55-54-07-00

Fax: +47 55-54-07-01

Website: http://www.nla.no

Rector: Bjarne Kvam

International Relations: Siri Elisabeth Haug EMail: seh@nla.no

Programmes

Education (Christian Religious Studies; Cultural Studies; Curriculum; Education; Educational Administration; Educational Psychology; Ethics; History of Religion; International and Comparative Education; Preschool Education; Religious Education; Religious Studies; Social Sciences; Special Education; Sports; Teacher Training; Theology)

History: Founded 1966 as Norwegian Teacher Academy. Acquired present title 2010.

Degrees and Diplomas: *Bachelor*, *Master*

Last Updated: 08/11/11

BERGEN SCHOOL OF ARCHITECTURE

Bergen Arkitet Skole

Sandviksboder 59-61a, 5035 Bergen

Tel: +47(55) 36 38 80

EMail: adm@bergenarkitektskole.no

Website: http://www.bergenarkitektskole.no/

Rector: Marianne Skjulhaug (2007-)

Programmes

Architecture (Architecture; Landscape Architecture)

History: Founded 1986.

Main Language(s) of Instruction: Norwegian

Degrees and Diplomas: *Master*

Last Updated: 28/10/11

BI NORWEGIAN BUSINESS SCHOOL

Handelshøyskolen BI

Nydalsveien 37, 0484 Oslo

Tel: +47 46-41-00-00

Fax: +47 21-04-80-00

EMail: info@bi.no

Website: http://www.bi.no

Head: Tom Colbjørnsen

Provost: Dag Morten Dalen

Programmes

Business Administration (Accountancy; Business Administration; Economics; English; Finance; Industrial and Organizational Psychology; International Business; Leadership; Management; Marketing; Mathematics; Public Relations; Real Estate; Retailing and Wholesaling; Statistics; Tourism); **Graduate Studies** (Accountancy; Business Administration; Economics; Finance; Industrial and Organizational Psychology; International Business; Management; Marketing; Political Sciences); **Shipping Management** (Marine Transport; Transport Management)

Further Information: Six study locations in Norway: Oslo (main campus with all international programmes), Bergen, Trondheim, Stavanger, Kristiansand, and Drammen. Also eight Research Departments

History: Founded 1943 as Institute for Business Economics "Bedriftsøkonomisk Institut" (BI). Acquired present status 2008.

Degrees and Diplomas: *Bachelor*, *Master*, *Ph.D.*

Last Updated: 08/11/11

DIAKONHJEMMET UNIVERSITY COLLEGE

Diakonhjemmet Høgskole
Postboks 184, Vinderen, 0319 Oslo
Tel: +47 22-45-19-45
Fax: +47 22-45-19-50
EMail: dhs@diakonhjemmet.no
Website: http://www.diakonhjemmet.no

Rector: Ingunn Moser
Tel: +47 22-45-19-00 EMail: moser@diakonhjemmet.no

Schools
Nursing (Nursing); **Social Work** (Social Work); **Theology and Diaconal Ministry** (Theology)

History: Founded 1980.

Main Language(s) of Instruction: Norwegian

International Co-operation: With universities in Germany, United Kingdom, Sweden, Portugal, Italy, Austria, Spain, Belgium, Nordic Countries and Malawi; Participates in the Erasmus Programme

Degrees and Diplomas: *Bachelor*; *Master (M.A.)*

Student Services: Academic counselling, Canteen, Foreign student adviser, Handicapped facilities, Health services, Nursery care, Social counselling, Sports facilities

Student Residential Facilities: Yes

Libraries: Yes

Last Updated: 25/10/11

LOVISENBERG DIACONAL UNIVERSITY COLLEGE

Lovisenberg Diakonale Høgskole (LDH)
Lovisenberggt. 15b, 0456 Oslo
Tel: +47 22-35-82-00
Fax: +47 22-37-49-34
EMail: admin@ldh.no
Website: http://www.ldh.no

Rector (Acting): Margrete Hestetun
EMail: margrete.hestetun@ldh.no

Director: Vidar Haukeland EMail: vidar.haukeland@lovisenberg.no

Programmes
Nursing (Child Care and Development; Gerontology; Nursing; Occupational Therapy; Physical Therapy; Radiology; Social Work)

History: Founded 1994.

Degrees and Diplomas: *Bachelor*; *Master*

Last Updated: 08/11/11

QUEEN MAUD UNIVERSITY COLLEGE OF EARLY CHILDHOOD EDUCATION

Dronning Mauds Minne Høgskole for Førskolelærerutdanning
Thoning Owesensgt. 18, 7044 Trondheim
Tel: +47 73-80-52-00
Fax: +47 73-80-52-52
EMail: post@dmmh.no
Website: http://www.dmmh.no

Rector: Elin Alvestrand EMail: ea@dmmh.no

Director, Administration: Geir Inge Lien EMail: gil@dmmh.no

Programmes
Education (Art Education; Child Care and Development; Cultural Studies; Education; Environmental Studies; Music Education; Physical Education; Preschool Education; Science Education; Special Education; Technology Education; Theatre; Vocational Education)

History: Founded 1947. Acquired present status 2008.

Degrees and Diplomas: *Bachelor*; *Master*

Last Updated: 08/11/11

THE NORWEGIAN SCHOOL OF IT

Norges Informasjonsteknologiske Høgskole (NITH)
Schweigaardsgate 14, 0185 Oslo
Tel: +47 22-05-99-99
Fax: +47 22-05-99-60
EMail: oslo@nith.no
Website: http://www.nith.no

Rector: Bjorn Jarle Hansen EMail: bjh@nith.no

Administrator: Stale Andersen EMail: staander@nith.no

Programmes
Information Technology (Computer Graphics; Computer Networks; Computer Science; Data Processing; E-Business/Commerce; English; Information Management; Management Systems; Mathematics; Norwegian; Physics; Software Engineering; Technology)

Degrees and Diplomas: *Bachelor*; *Master*

Last Updated: 08/11/11

Oman

STRUCTURE OF HIGHER EDUCATION SYSTEM

Description:

Higher education is provided by public and private universities, several specialized institutes, technical and vocational colleges and colleges of education. The public university is an autonomous institution. Its governing bodies are the university council and the academic council. All private education institutions and colleges of education are under the supervision of the Ministry of Higher Education.

Stages of studies:

University level first stage: *Undergraduate level*
The national qualification framework of the Sultanate of Oman comprises four undergraduate levels (degrees in academic scales) and offers the following qualifications: certificate (1 year); diploma (2 years); advanced diploma (3 years); Bachelor's degree (4 years); graduate diploma (one year after the Bachelor's degree at level 4).

University level second stage: *Postgraduate level*
The national qualification framework of the Sultanate of Oman comprises two postgraduate levels (degree in academic scales) and offers the following qualifications: Postgraduate Diploma (1 year at level 5); Master's degree (1 to 2 years after the Bachelor's degree); Doctorate (2 to 4 years after the Master's degree).

ADMISSION TO HIGHER EDUCATION

Admission to university-level studies:

Name of secondary school credential required: General Certificate/ General Education Diploma

Minimum score/requirement: 65% but 80% is normally required to enter undergraduate study, whilst 90-95% may be required to enter the Faculty of Medicine

For entry to: Universities

RECOGNITION OF STUDIES

Quality assurance system:

The Accreditation Council is responsible for the accreditation, evaluation and quality assurance of all higher education institutions in the Sultanate of Oman.

Bodies dealing with recognition:

Oman Accreditation Council

Acting Chairman: Hamed Al-Dhahab
Chief Executive Officer: Salim Razvi
P.O.Box 1255
Al Khuwair 133
Tel: +968 2412-1226
Fax: +968 2412-1231
EMail: enquiries@oaaa.gov.om
WWW: http://www.oac.gov.om/
Deals with credential recognition for entry to institution: Yes

NATIONAL BODIES

Ministry of Higher Education

Minister: Rawya Bint Saoud al-Bossaeidi
PO Box 82
Ruwi 112
Tel: +968 24795400
Fax: +968 24701929
EMail: dgpd@mohe.gov.om
WWW: http://www.mohe.gov.om

Role of national body: Supervises all higher education institutions and is responsible for overseas students, for formulating higher education policies and administering the Law on Grants and Scholarships.

Data for academic year: 2007-2008

Source: IAU from Oman Permanent Delegation to UNESCO, 2007. Bodies, 2012.

INSTITUTIONS

PUBLIC INSTITUTIONS

SULTAN QABOOS UNIVERSITY (SQU)

Al Khoudh, PO Box 50, 123 Muscat
Tel: +968 2414-1111
Fax: +968 2441-3391
EMail: vcoffice@squ.edu.om
Website: http://www.squ.edu.om

Vice-Chancellor: Ali Al-Bemani
Tel: +968 2414-1167, Fax: +968 2441-3254

Vice-Chancellor for Administrative and Financial Affairs: Hamed Suleiman Al-Salmi
Tel: +968 2414-1167, Fax: +968 2441-3179

International Relations: Salahaddin Al-Saadi, Deputy Director, International Relations
Tel: +968 2414-1978, Fax: +968 2414-13075
EMail: ir@squ.edu.om

Centres

Community Services and Continuing Education (Continuing Education; Social and Community Services) *Director*: Rashid Al-Kiyumi; **Educational Technology** (Educational Technology) *Director*: Houmoud Al-Moqbali; **Human Resource and Staff Development** *Director*: Khamis Al-Rasbi; **Information Systems** (Computer Science); **Language** (Linguistics; Modern Languages)

Colleges

Agriculture and Marine Sciences (Agricultural Engineering; Agriculture; Animal Husbandry; Crop Production; Economics; Fishery; Food Science; Marine Science and Oceanography; Natural Resources; Nutrition; Soil Management; Veterinary Science; Water Management; Water Science); **Arts and Social Sciences** (Arabic; Archaeology; Arts and Humanities; Communication Studies; English; Geography; History; Information Sciences; Journalism; Library Science; Social and Community Services; Social Sciences; Sociology; Theatre; Tourism); **Commerce and Economics** (Accountancy; Business Computing; Economics; Finance; Management; Marketing; Statistics; Systems Analysis); **Education** (Art Education; Curriculum; Education; Educational Administration; Educational Psychology; Educational Technology; Islamic Studies; Pedagogy; Physical Education; Preschool Education; Psychology); **Engineering** (Architecture; Chemical Engineering; Civil Engineering; Computer Engineering; Electrical Engineering; Engineering; Industrial Engineering; Mechanical Engineering; Mining Engineering; Petroleum and Gas Engineering); **Law** (Criminal Law; Law; Public Law); **Medicine and Health Sciences** (Anaesthesiology; Anatomy; Behavioural Sciences; Biochemistry; Child Care and Development; Community Health; Epidemiology; Gynaecology and Obstetrics; Haematology; Health Sciences; Immunology; Medicine; Microbiology; Ophthalmology; Oral Pathology; Paediatrics; Pathology; Pharmacology; Physiology; Radiology; Statistics; Surgery); **Nursing** (Community Health; Nursing; Psychiatry and Mental Health); **Science** (Applied Chemistry; Biology; Biotechnology; Chemistry; Computer Science; Earth Sciences; Geophysics; Laboratory Techniques; Mathematics; Medical Technology; Natural Sciences; Physics; Statistics)

Research Centres

Communication; **Earthquake Monitoring** (Seismology); **Environmental Studies and Research** (Environmental Studies); **Oil and Gas**; **Omani**; **Remote Sensing and Geographical Information System** (Geography; Information Technology; Surveying and Mapping); **Water Science** (Water Science)

Further Information: Also University Hospital

History: Founded 1980 with construction starting 1983. First students admitted 1986. An autonomous institution.

Governing Bodies: University Council; Academic Council

Academic Year: September to June (September-January; February-June)

Admission Requirements: Secondary school certificate (Shahada Amma) or equivalent

Fees: For postgraduate studies

Main Language(s) of Instruction: Arabic, English

International Co-operation: With universities in the United Kingdom, United States, France, Italy, Germany, Japan, Netherlands, Iran, China, Korea, UAE, Pakistan, Australia, Thailand

Degrees and Diplomas: *Diploma*: Educational Supervision; Learning Difficulties; Medical Librarianship; School Administration, 1 yr; *Bachelor's Degree*: Agriculture (Bagr), 4 yrs including foundation yr; *Bachelor's Degree*: Arts (BA); Education (BEd); Health Sciences (BSc); Law (BSc); Science (Commerce and Economics) (BSc), 4 yrs; *Bachelor's Degree*: Engineering (BEng); Nursing (BSc); Science (BSc), 5 yrs; *Master's Degree*: Agriculture (MSc); Arts (MA); Education (MEd); Engineering (MSc); Medicine (MSc); Science (MSc), a further 2 yrs; *Master's Degree*: Business Administration; Law, 2 yrs; *Master's Degree*: Health Sciences (MSc), 3 yrs following Health Sciences Bachelor's degree; *Doctorate*

Student Services: Academic counselling, Canteen, Cultural centre, Employment services, Handicapped facilities, Health services, Language programs, Nursery care, Sports facilities

Student Residential Facilities: Yes

Libraries: Central Library. Medical Library. Mosque Library. Commerce Library. Arts Library

Publications: Journal for Scientific Research - Agricultural Science *(biannually)*; Journal for Scientific Research - Medical Science *(biannually)*; Journal for Scientific Research - Science and

Technology *(biannually)*; Journal of Scientific Research - Engineering *(annually)*

Press or Publishing House: University Printing Press

Last Updated: 30/11/11

PRIVATE INSTITUTIONS

AL ZAHRA COLLEGE FOR WOMEN

PO Box 1197, Muscat
Tel: +968 24607678
EMail: info@zahracol.edu.om
Website: http://www.zahracol.edu.om

Programmes

Accountancy (Accountancy); **Business Administration** (Business Administration); **Computer Science** (Computer Science); **English Language and Literature** (English; Literature); **Finance and Banking** (Banking; Finance); **Graphic Design** (Graphic Design)

History: Founded 1999.

Degrees and Diplomas: *Diploma*; *Bachelor's Degree*

Libraries: Yes

Last Updated: 29/11/11

DHOFAR UNIVERSITY

P.O. Box 2509, 211 Salalah
EMail: du@du.edu.om
Website: http://www.du.edu.om

Vice-Chancellor: Hassan Said Mahad Kashoob

Colleges

Arts and Applied Sciences (Arabic; Chemistry; Computer Science; Education; English; Mathematics; Physics; Social Work; Translation and Interpretation); **Commerce and Business Administration** (Accountancy; Finance; Management; Marketing); **Engineering** (Chemical Engineering; Computer Engineering; Electrical Engineering; Graphic Design; Interior Design; Mechanical Engineering)

History: Founded 2004.

Main Language(s) of Instruction: Arabic

Degrees and Diplomas: *Diploma*; *Bachelor's Degree*; *Master's Degree*

Student Residential Facilities: Yes

Libraries: Yes

Last Updated: 29/11/11

MAJAN COLLEGE

PO Box 710, 112 Ruwi, Muscat
Tel: +968 2475-1573
Fax: +968 2475-1570
EMail: mcucom@omantel.net.om
Website: http://www.majancollege.edu.om

Dean (Acting): Maha Kobei

Faculties

Business Administration (Accountancy; Business Administration; E-Business/Commerce; Finance; Human Resources; Marketing; Tourism); **English Language** (English); **Information Technology** (Computer Networks; Computer Science; Information Technology)

History: Founded 1995.

Degrees and Diplomas: *Bachelor's Degree*; *Master's Degree*

Last Updated: 30/11/11

OMAN MEDICAL COLLEGE

PO Box 620, 130 Azaiba, Muscat
Tel: +968 2450-4608
Fax: +968 2450-4820
EMail: admissions@omc.edu.om
Website: http://www.omc.edu.om

Dean: Saleh Mohamed Al Khusaiby

Departments

Natural Sciences (Natural Sciences)

Programmes

Medicine (Anatomy; Gynaecology and Obstetrics; Medicine; Neurosciences; Pathology; Physiology; Psychiatry and Mental Health; Surgery); **Pharmacy** (Pharmacology; Pharmacy)

Further Information: Also branch in Sohar

History: Founded 2001.

Degrees and Diplomas: *Diploma*; *Bachelor's Degree*. Doctor of Medicine, 7 yrs

Last Updated: 23/10/09

SOHAR UNIVERSITY

PO Box 44, 311 Sohar
Tel: +968 2672-0101
Fax: +968 2672-0102
EMail: soharuni@omantel.net.om
Website: http://www.soharuni.edu.om

Vice-Chancellor: Abood Hamad Al-Sawafi

Faculties

Business (Accountancy; Business Administration; Commercial Law; Management; Marketing); **Computing and Information Technology** (Computer Engineering; Computer Networks; Computer Science; Multimedia; Software Engineering); **Engineering** (Chemical Engineering; Civil Engineering; Computer Engineering; Electrical and Electronic Engineering; Mechanical Engineering); **Humanities and Social Sciences** (Arabic; Arts and Humanities; Biology; Education; English; Journalism; Media Studies; Physical Education; Social Sciences; Translation and Interpretation)

History: Founded 2001.

Degrees and Diplomas: *Diploma*: 2 yrs; *Advanced Diploma*; *Bachelor's Degree*: 4 yrs; *Master's Degree*

Libraries: Yes

Last Updated: 30/11/11

UNIVERSITY OF NIZWA

P.O. Box 33, 616 Birkat Al Mouz
Website: http://www.unizwa.edu.om

Chancellor: Ahmad bin Khalfan Al Rawahi

Colleges

Arts and Sciences (Arabic; Biotechnology; Chemistry; Computer Science; English; French; German; Mathematics; Physics; Statistics; Translation and Interpretation); **Economics, Administration and Information Systems** (Accountancy; Business Administration; Finance; International Business; Management; Marketing); **Engineering and Architecture** (Architecture; Chemical Engineering; Civil Engineering; Computer Engineering; Electrical Engineering; Environmental Engineering; Interior Design); **Nursing and Pharmacy** (Nursing; Pharmacy)

History: Founded 2004.

Main Language(s) of Instruction: Arabic

Degrees and Diplomas: *Diploma*; *Bachelor's Degree*; *Master's Degree*

Libraries: University Library

Last Updated: 30/11/11

WALJAT COLLEGES OF APPLIED SCIENCES

PO Box 197, Rusayl, 124 Muscat
Tel: +968 2444-6660 +968 2444-9194
Fax: +968 2444-9196 +968 2444-9197
EMail: waljatcm@omantel.net.om; registrar@waljatcolleges.edu.om
Website: http://www.waljatcolleges.edu.om

Dean: A.M. Agrawal EMail: dean@waljat.net

Director, Administration and Finance: Nasser Al Ghilani
EMail: admndept@waljat.net

Departments

Biotechnology; **Computer Science and Engineering** (Computer Engineering; Computer Science); **Electrical Engineering** (Electrical Engineering); **Electronic Engineering**; **English Language** (English); **Management** (Management); **Mathematics**; **Mechanical Engineering** (Mechanical Engineering); **Physics** (Physics)

Degrees and Diplomas: *Bachelor's Degree*; *Master's Degree*

Last Updated: 03/10/08

Pakistan

STRUCTURE OF HIGHER EDUCATION SYSTEM

Description:

Since 2002, the Higher Education Commission (HEC) has been empowered to carry out evaluation, improvement and promotion of higher education, research and development, to formulate policies, guiding principles and priorities for higher education institutions and to prescribe conditions under which institutions, including those that are not part of the State educational system, may be opened and operated.
The mandate of HEC encompasses all degree granting universities and institutions, both in public and private sectors and supports the attainment of quality education by facilitating and co-ordinating self-assessment of academic programmes and their external review by national and international experts. HEC also supervises the planning, development and accreditation of public and private sector higher education institutions.
Its goal is to facilitate the reform process.

Stages of studies:

University level first stage: *Bachelor's degree*
Bachelor's Pass degrees are normally obtained after a two-year course and Honours degrees after a four-year course in Arts, Science, Commerce, Engineering, and Computer Science and a five-year course in Veterinary Medicine, Pharmacy, Medicine and Architecture.

University level second stage: *Master's degree, B.Ed., LLB*
A Master's degree (16 years of education) requires two years of study after the Bachelor's degree (pass). For Master's (honours) degree it takes 1 and a half to 2 years for 4-year Bachelor's degrees in Agriculture, Engineering, Pharmacy, Medical studies, etc. These degrees are equated to M.Phil degrees. B.ed. requires one-year study beyond a Bachelor's degree (pass). The LLB is a three-year post Bachelor's degree (pass) qualification. Postgraduate diplomas are offered in various fields of studies by many universities and generally require one-year study.

University level third stage: *M.Phil., Ph.D.*
The Master of Philosophy (M.Phil.) takes two years after the Master's Degree. It is a research-based programme that also requires a thesis. The Ph.D. (Doctorate of Philosophy) is a research degree which requires, on average, three years' study/research after the M.Phil. degree and 4 to 5 years study/research after the Master's Degree.

University level fourth stage: *Doctor's degree*
The degrees of Doctor of Literature (D.Litt.), Doctor of Science (D.Sc.) and Doctor of Law (LLD) are awarded after five to seven years of study.
Distance higher education:
Distance higher education is offered by the Allama Iqbal Open University and the Virtual University of Pakistan. The first provides a wide range of courses at different levels in Humanities, Teacher Education, Technical Education, Business Management, Commerce, Social Sciences, Arabic, Pakistan Studies, Islamic Studies, and Home Economics and Women's Studies. It uses multi-media techniques, such as correspondence packages, radio and television broadcasts, tutorial instruction... The second is specifically established to cater for the needs of students at tertiary level of education in the field of computer science and provides on-line knowledge-based instruction.

ADMISSION TO HIGHER EDUCATION

Admission to university-level studies:

Name of secondary school credential required: Higher Secondary School Certificate (Intermediate Certificate)
Minimum score/requirement: 45%
For entry to: Bachelors' degree (Pass/Hons)
Alternatives to credentials: Shahadatul Sanvia Khasa

Entrance exam requirements: A National Test is required for entry to Engineering, Medicine and Architecture. Some universities also conduct their own admission tests.

Foreign students admission:

Definition of foreign student: A student who does not hold Pakistani nationality falls in the category of foreign student.

Quotas: 5% of total seats are reserved for foreign students.

Entrance exam requirements: Foreign students should submit details concerning previous studies and qualifications within 45 days from the last date fixed for receiving applications. Applications must be sponsored by candidates' governments and forwarded through embassies in Islamabad or through Pakistan embassies abroad.

Entry regulations: After being admitted, foreign students are required to send an admission letter to the Embassy of Pakistan in their respective countries. A visa will be issued and the university concerned will provide hostel facilities. For other expenditures, studentsl must present their financial guarantee certificate.

Health requirements: Admitted foreign students have to produce a medical certificate issued by a government medical officer of their respective countries.

Language requirements: Good knowledge of English is essential for all regular students.

RECOGNITION OF STUDIES

Quality assurance system:

The Higher Education Commission validates/recognizes and accredits educational qualifications and higher education institutions in the country.

Special provisions for recognition:

Recognition for university level studies: IBCC

For access to advanced studies and research: Higher Education Commission (HEC)

For exercising a profession: Pakistan Engineering Council (PEC); Pakistan Medical and Dental Council (PMDC)

NATIONAL BODIES

Ministry of Education and Training

Minister: Sheikh Waqas Akram
Room No.101 1st Floor, C block Pak Secretariat
Islamabad 44000
Tel: +92(51) 9213933
Fax: +92(51) 9203742
WWW: http://moptt.gov.pk/

Higher Education Commission - HEC

Chairman: Javaid R. Laghari
Executive Director: Syed Sohail H. Naqvi
Sector H-9
Islamabad
Tel: +92(51) 904 0000
EMail: info@hec.gov.pk
WWW: http://www.hec.gov.pk
Role of national body: Governing body for the promotion and improvement of higher education in Pakistan.

Data for academic year: 2006-2007
Source: IAU from Higher Education Commission, Islamabad, 2006. Bodies, 2012.

INSTITUTIONS

PUBLIC INSTITUTIONS

ABDUL WALI KHAN UNIVERSITY

Mardan, Khyber-Pakhtookhwa
Tel: +92(93) 7929-094
Fax: +92(93) 7923-0571
EMail: webmaster@awkum.edu.pk
Website: http://www.awkum.edu.pk/

Vice-Chancellor: Ihsan Ali

Registrar: Sher Ali Khan Tel: +92(93) 7923-0618

Departments

Botany (Botany); **Chemistry** (Chemistry); **Computer Science** (Computer Science); **Education** (Education); **English** (English); **Islamic studies** (Islamic Studies); **Law** (Law); **Management Sciences** (Management); **Mathematics** (Mathematics); **Physics** (Physics); **Political Sciences** (Political Sciences); **Zoology** (Zoology)

Accrediting Agencies: Higher Education Commission

Degrees and Diplomas: *Bachelor's Degree (Honours)*; *Master's Degree*; *Doctor's Degree*

Last Updated: 24/08/10

AIR UNIVERSITY

E-9, PAF Complex, Islamabad 44000
Tel: +92(51) 9262557-58
Fax: +92(51) 9200158
EMail: information@mail.au.edu.pk
Website: http://www.au.edu.pk

Vice-Chancellor: Ijaz Ahmad Malik EMail: amjad@mail.au.edu.pk

Registrar: Zafar Ahmed
Tel: +92(51) 9262557-58 Ext 203, Fax: +92(51) 9260158
EMail: registrar@mail.au.edu.pk

Faculties

Administrative Sciences (Business Administration; Finance; Human Resources; Marketing); **Basic and Applied Sciences** (Computer Engineering; Computer Science; Mathematics; Physics); **Engineering** (Electronic Engineering; Engineering; Mechanical Engineering; Software Engineering; Systems Analysis; Telecommunications Engineering); **Social Sciences and Humanities** (Arts and Humanities; English)

Institutes

Avionics and Aeronautics (Aeronautical and Aerospace Engineering; Mechanical Engineering)

History: Created 2002.

Degrees and Diplomas: *Bachelor's Degree*; *Bachelor's Degree (Honours)*; *Master's Degree*; *Master of Philosophy*; *Doctor's Degree*

Last Updated: 23/05/12

ALLAMA IQBAL OPEN UNIVERSITY (AIOU)

Sector H-8, Islamabad 44000
Tel: +92(51) 925-0101
EMail: vcaiou@isb.paknet.com.pk
Website: http://www.aiou.edu.pk

Vice-Chancellor: Mahmood H. Butt (2005-)
EMail: vc@aiou.edu.pk

Registrar: Ilyas Ahmed
Tel: +92(51) 925-0025, Fax: +92(51) 925-0026
EMail: reg@aiou.edu.pk

International Relations: Ilyas Ahmed
Tel: +92(51) 925-0025 EMail: reg@aiou.edu.pk

Centres

Research and Evaluation (Educational Research; Educational Testing and Evaluation) *Director*: Masooda Chaudhry

Faculties

Arabic and Islamic Studies (Arabic; Cultural Studies; History; History of Religion; Holy Writings; Islamic Law; Islamic Studies; Islamic Theology; Literature; Religion; Religious Education; Religious Studies) *Dean*: Muhammad Baqir Khan Khakwani; **Education** (Adult Education; Continuing Education; Curriculum; Distance Education; Education; Educational Administration; Educational Sciences; Leadership; Literacy Education; Primary Education; Science Education; Secondary Education; Special Education; Teacher Trainers Education) *Dean*: Zafar Iqbal; **Sciences** (Agriculture; Biology; Chemistry; Community Health; Computer Science; Electronic Engineering; Engineering; Environmental Studies; Forestry; Health Sciences; Mathematics; Natural Sciences; Ophthalmology; Optometry; Physics; Statistics; Telecommunications Engineering) *Dean*: Muhammad Kaleem Tahir; **Social Sciences and Humanities** (Applied Linguistics; Arts and Humanities; Banking; Business Administration; Business and Commerce; Demography and Population; Design; Economics; English; Finance; Fine Arts; Geography; History; Human Resources; Information Sciences; Information Technology; Journalism; Law; Library Science; Management; Marketing; Mass Communication; Modern Languages; Radio and Television Broadcasting; Regional Studies; Social Sciences; Social Studies; Social Work; Sociology; Urdu; Women's Studies) *Dean*: Inam-ul-Haq Javed

Institutes

Educational Technology (Educational Technology; Engineering; Fine Arts; Graphic Design; Media Studies; Radio and Television Broadcasting; Video) *Director*: Mujahid Nizami; **Mass Education** (Education; Hotel Management; Media Studies; Primary Education; Secondary Education) *Director*: Lubna Saif

History: Founded 1974 by Act of Parliament to provide equality of educational opportunities for the largest population (workers, housewives, and others who wish to upgrade their education or acquire knowledge for professional advancement or love of learning). Acquired present title 1977.

Governing Bodies: Executive Council; Academic Council; Selection Board; Finance Committee; Academic Planning and Development Committee; Committee for Research Technology; Board of Advanced Studies and Research; Faculty Board and Committee of Courses

Academic Year: June to April (June-October; December-April)

Admission Requirements: Intermediate or higher secondary certificate

Fees: (PK Rupees): 690-22,000 per semester

Main Language(s) of Instruction: Urdu, English

International Co-operation: With universities in Bangladesh, India, Sri Lanka, United Kingdom and Thailand.

Accrediting Agencies: Higher Education Commission (HEC)

Degrees and Diplomas: *Bachelor's Degree (BA)*: 2 yrs with majors in 5 disciplines; *Bachelor's Degree*: Computer Science (BSCS); Engineering; Telecommunications (BE), 4 yrs; *Bachelor's Degree*: Vision Sciences (BSc), 2 yrs; *Master's Degree*: Agriculture (MSc Honors), a further 3 yrs following Bachelor's Degree; *Master's Degree*: Business Administration; Information Technology; Marketing Management; Banking and Finance; Human Resources Management (MBA); Teaching English as a Foreign language (TEFL); History; Urdu; Islamic Studies; Arabic (MA), a further 2 -3 yrs following Bachelor's Degree; *Master's Degree*: Commonwealth Executive Business Administration (MPA); Pakistan Studies; Economics; Mass Communication; Food and Nutrition; Physics; Computer Science; Mathematics; Chemistry; Environmental Design; Forestry (MSc), a further 2 yrs following Bachelor's Degree; *Master's Degree*: Education (MA/Med), a further 1-2 yrs following Bachelor's Degree; *Master's Degree*: Library and Information Science (MLIS), a further 2 yrs; *Master of Philosophy*: Islamic Studies; Iqbal Studies; Urdu; Teacher Education; Educational Administration; Distance Education; Special Education; Physics; Mass Communication; Economics; Chemistry; Food and Nutrition; Pakistani Languages and Literarture, a further 2 yrs following MPhil or 4 yrs following Master's Degree; *Doctor's Degree*: Islamic Studies; Iqbal Studies; Urdu; Teacher's Training Education; Educational

Administration; Distance Education; Special Education; Arabic; Mathematics; Statistics; Economics (PhD), a further 2-5 yrs following Master of Philosophy. Also postgraduate diplomas in Women Studies; Mass Communication; Dietetics; Nutrition; English as a Foreign Language; Computer Science; Educational Administration; Public Administration; CYP-Youth in Develpoment Work; Environmental Design

Student Services: Academic counselling, Canteen, Health services, Language programs, Sports facilities

Student Residential Facilities: Yes

Special Facilities: Inter-disciplinary laboratory/workshop; Computer labs; Free Internet

Libraries: c. 135,000 vols; Arabic collection 7,000; Audio/Visual 3,000 periodicals

Publications: Pakistan Journal of Education *(biannually)*; Pakistan Journal of Social Sciences *(biannually)*

Last Updated: 01/12/08

BAHAUDDIN ZAKARIYA UNIVERSITY (BZU)

Bosan Road, Multan, Punjab 60800
Tel: +92(61) 921-00-71
Fax: +92(61) 921-00-98
EMail: info@bzu.edu.pk
Website: http://www.bzu.edu.pk

Vice-Chancellor: Muhammad Zafarullah
Tel: +92(61) 9210069 EMail: vc@bzu.edu.pk

Registrar: Muhammad Asharaf Ch.
Tel: +92(61) 9210097 EMail: registrar@bzu.edu.pk

Faculties

Arts and Social Sciences (Arts and Humanities; Asian Studies; Economics; Education; History; International Relations; International Studies; Mass Communication; Political Sciences; Social Sciences); **Engineering**; **Islamic Studies and Languages** (Arabic; English; Islamic Studies; Urdu); **Law, Commerce and Business Administration** (Business Administration; Business and Commerce; Law); **Pharmacy** (Pharmacy); **Science and Agriculture** (Agriculture; Botany; Chemistry; Computer Science; Engineering; Materials Engineering; Mathematics; Natural Sciences; Physics; Statistics; Zoology); **Veterinary Sciences**

History: Founded 1975 as University of Multan, acquired present title 1979. An autonomous body, financed by the central government through the University Grants Commission.

Governing Bodies: Syndicate; Senate

Academic Year: September to June

Admission Requirements: Intermediate or higher secondary certificate

Fees: (PK Rupees): c. 3,000-20,000

Main Language(s) of Instruction: English, Urdu

Degrees and Diplomas: *Bachelor's Degree*: 4 yrs; *Master's Degree*: a further 1-2 yrs; *Doctor's Degree*: Agriculture; Arabic; Botany; Zoology; Business Administration; Sociology; Applied Psychology; Chemistry; Business Finance; Economics; Education; Linguistics; History; Islamiat; Mathematics; Pakistan Studies; Pharmacy; Physics; Political Science (PhD); Statistics; Urdu

Student Residential Facilities: Yes

Special Facilities: Botanical Garden. Agriculture Farm

Libraries: Central Library, total, c. 100,000 vols

Publications: Research journals (Humanities, Science)

BAHRIA UNIVERSITY (BU)

Shangrila Road, Sector E-8, Islamabad 44000
Tel: +92(51) 9260002
Fax: +92(51) 9260885
EMail: info@bahria.edu.pk
Website: http://www.bahria.edu.pk

Rector: Shahid Iqbal (2012-)
Tel: +92(51) 9260821 EMail: rector@bahria.edu.pk

Registrar: Mumtaz Raza EMail: registrar@bahria.edu.pk

International Relations: Awais Mehmood, International Relations Officer
Tel: +92(51) 9263422 EMail: internationaloffice@bahria.edu.pk

Centres

National Centre for Maritime Policy Research *(Karachi)* (Marine Science and Oceanography; Maritime Law)

Colleges

Medicine and Dentistry *(Karachi)* (Dentistry; Medicine)

Departments

Computer and Software Engineering (Computer Engineering; Computer Science; Software Engineering); **Earth and Environmental Sciences** (Earth Sciences; Environmental Studies); **Electrical Engineering** (Electrical Engineering); **Graduate Studies and Applied Sciences** (Natural Sciences); **Humanities and Social Sciences** (Arts and Humanities; Social Sciences); **Law** (Law); **Management Sciences** (Management)

Institutes

Professional Psychology *(Karachi)* (Psychology)

Further Information: Campuses in Karachi, Islamabad. The following affiliated units: Frontier Medical and Dental College,Abbottabad; Shifa College of Medicine, Shifa College of Nursing, Islamabad Medical and Dental College, Yusra Medical and Dental College, Islamabad; Institute of Teachers' Education, Rawalpindi

History: Created 2002.

Degrees and Diplomas: *Bachelor's Degree*: Anthropology; International Relations; Development Studies; Media Studies; Geology; Geophysics; Environmental Sciences; Finance; Marketing; HRM; Law; Medicine; Software Engineering; Computer Engineering; Electrical Engineering; Telecommunications Engineering; Computer Science; Nursing; Dental Surgery; Psychology, 4-5 yrs; *Master's Degree*: Telecom and Networking; Software Engineering; Geology; Geophysics; Business Administration; Management Sciences; Psychology, 1 1/2 - 3 yrs; *Master of Philosophy*: Psychology; Management Sciences; *Doctor's Degree*: Clinical Psychology; Educational Psychology; Organizational Psychology; Networking; Management Sciences. Also Postgraduate Diploma in Primary Teaching

Student Services: Sports facilities

Student Residential Facilities: Private student hostel

Academic Staff *2011-2012*	MEN	WOMEN	TOTAL
FULL-TIME	463	363	**826**
PART-TIME	381	153	**534**
STAFF WITH DOCTORATE			
FULL-TIME	24	17	**41**
PART-TIME	39	5	**44**
Student Numbers *2011-2012*			
All (Foreign Included)	6,836	3,445	**10,281**
FOREIGN ONLY	8	2	**10**

Last Updated: 14/02/12

BALOCHISTAN UNIVERSITY OF ENGINEERING AND TECHNOLOGY (BUET)

Khuzdar, Balochistan 413197
Tel: +92(0848) 412-524
Fax: +92(0848) 413-364
EMail: info@buetk.edu.pk
Website: http://buetk.edu.pk/

Vice-Chancellor: Mukhtar Ahmad Khan
Tel: +92(0848) 412-834 EMail: vc@buetk.edu.pk

Registrar: Sher Ahmed Qambrani EMail: registrar@buetk.edu.pk

International Relations: Muhammad Yousaf Bangulzai, Deputy Registrar Tel: +92(0848) 550-299 EMail: mybangulzai@yahoo.com

Departments

Basic Sciences *Chairman*: Shakoor Qaisrani; **Civil Engineering** (Civil Engineering) *Chairman*: Ali Akbar; **Computer Systems Engineering & Sciences** (Computer Engineering; Computer Science; Information Technology) *Chairman*: Sohrab Khan Bizanjo; **Electrical Engineering** (Electrical Engineering) *Chairman*: Sikandar Ali Abbasi; **Mechanical Engineering** (Mechanical Engineering) *Chairman*: Fazli Rehman

History: Founded 1987 as a College. Acquired present status 1994.

Governing Bodies: Syndicate

Academic Year: March to December

Admission Requirements: Intermediate (pre-Engineering) with a score of 50% and D.A.E. with a score of 60%

Main Language(s) of Instruction: English

Accrediting Agencies: Pakistan Engineering Council

Degrees and Diplomas: *Bachelor's Degree*: Civil Engineering; Electrical Engineering; Mechanical Engineering; Computer Engineering; Computer Science, 4 yrs. Also Diploma in Information Technology

Student Services: Academic counselling, Canteen, Health services, Social counselling, Sports facilities

Student Residential Facilities: Yes

Libraries: Yes

Last Updated: 18/11/09

BALOCHISTAN UNIVERSITY OF INFORMATION TECHNOLOGY AND MANAGEMENT SCIENCES (BUITMS)

Jinnah Town, Quetta, Balochistan
Tel: +92(81) 2880493-9202463
Fax: +92(81) 9201064
EMail: info@buitms.edu.pk
Website: http://www.buitms.edu.pk

Vice-Chancellor: M.A.K. Malghani Tel: +92(81) 9202463

Registrar: Mohammad Azam Baloch Tel: +92(81) 9202483

Faculties

Computer and Emerging Sciences (Computer Engineering; Computer Science; Continuing Education; Electronic Engineering; Information Technology; Mathematics); **Management Sciences** (Accountancy; Arts and Humanities; Development Studies; Finance; Management; Marketing; Social Sciences)

History: Founded 2002.

Governing Bodies: Senate

Degrees and Diplomas: *Bachelor's Degree*; *Master's Degree*; *Doctor's Degree*: Mathematics. Also Postgraduate Diploma

BOLAN UNIVERSITY OF MEDICAL AND HEALTH SCIENCES

Quetta
Website: http://www.bmc.edu.pk/

Principal: Shahnaz Naseer Baloch EMail: principal@bmc.edu.pk

Departments

Basic Sciences (Anatomy; Biochemistry; Community Health; Forensic Medicine and Dentistry; Pathology; Pharmacology; Physiology); **Clinical Main Line Sciences** (Gynaecology and Obstetrics; Medicine; Ophthalmology; Paediatrics; Surgery); **Compulsory Clinical Sub Specialities** (Anaesthesiology; Dentistry; Dermatology; Orthopaedics; Psychiatry and Mental Health; Radiology); **Optional Clinical Sub Specialities** (Cardiology; Endocrinology; Gastroenterology; Nephrology; Neurology; Paediatrics; Plastic Surgery; Surgery; Urology)

Degrees and Diplomas: *Master's Degree*

Last Updated: 23/08/10

COMSATS INSTITUTE OF INFORMATION TECHNOLOGY (CIIT)

Plot No 30, Sector H8/1, Islamabad 44000
Tel: +92(51) 925-8481-3
Fax: +92(51) 444-2805
Website: http://www.ciit.edu.pk

Rector: Syed M. Junaid Zaidi EMail: rector@comsats.edu.pk

Registrar: Arshad Salim Malik EMail: registrar@comsats.edu.pk

Faculties

Architecture and Design *Dean*: S. M. Junaid Zaidi; **Business Administration** *Dean*: Talat Afza; **Engineering** (Chemical Engineering; Electrical Engineering; Engineering; Mechanical Engineering) *Dean*: Shahid Ahmad Khan; **Information Science and Technology** *Dean*: Muhammad Rafiq Asim; **Science** *Dean*: Raheel Qamar

History: Founded 1998 by the Commission on Science and Technology for Sustainable Development in the South (COMSATS). Acquired present status 2000.

Governing Bodies: Board of Governors

Academic Year: September to July (September-January; March-July)

Admission Requirements: Intermediate or higher secondary certificate with minimum 50% marks from an accredited institution

Fees: (PK Rupees): Tuition, 36,500-40,500 per semester; 41,500 (Engineering). (US Dollars): 1,500 per semester for overseas students, 100 graduation fee

Main Language(s) of Instruction: English

International Co-operation: With universities in Germany and Italy

Accrediting Agencies: Higher Education Council (HEC); Pakistan Engineering Council (PEC); Pakistan Council of Architects and Town Planners (PCAT-P)

Degrees and Diplomas: *Bachelor's Degree*: Science; Architecture; Business Administration (BS; B Arch); *Master's Degree*: Science; Business Administration; Development Studies (MS; MBA); *Doctor's Degree (PhD)*

Student Services: Academic counselling, Canteen, Cultural centre, Employment services, Health services, Language programs, Sports facilities

Student Residential Facilities: Yes (for male and female students)

Libraries: c. 69,560 vols

Last Updated: 01/12/08

DOW UNIVERSITY OF HEALTH SCIENCES

Baba-E-Urdu Road, P.O.BOX 942943, Karachi, Sindh 74200
Tel: +92(21) 9215754-7
EMail: info@duhs.edu.pk
Website: http://www.duhs.edu.pk/index.asp

Vice-Chancellor: Masood Ahmeed Khan EMail: vc@duhs.edu.pk

Colleges

Dow International Medical College (Medicine); **Dow Medical College**; **Pharmacy** (Pharmacy); **Sindh Medical College** (Medicine)

Institutes

Health Management; **Nursing**; **Ojha Institute**; **Oral Health Sciences** *(Dr. Ishrat-ul-Ebad Khan Institute)* (Health Sciences); **Physical Medicine and Rehabilitation**

History: Founded 2004.

Degrees and Diplomas: *Bachelor's Degree*; *Master's Degree*; *Doctor's Degree*: Medicine

IAU FATIMA JINNAH WOMEN UNIVERSITY (FJWU)

The Mall, Rawalpindi, Punjab 46000
Tel: +92(51) 9271167
Fax: +92(51) 9271168
EMail: fjwuvc@comsats.net.pk
Website: http://www.fjwu.edu.pk

Vice-Chancellor: Samina Amin Qadir (2011-)

Registrar: Maryam Rab
Tel: +92(51) 9271170, Fax: +92(51) 9271170
EMail: fjwudreg@comsats.net.pk

International Relations: Fareena Mahmood, Deputy Director, Quality Enhancement Cell
Tel: +92(51) 9272733, Fax: +92(51) 9272733
EMail: ddir_qec@fjwu.edu.pk

Centres

Research and Resource (WRRC) *(Women) Head*: Samina Amin Qadir

Faculties

Arts and Social Sciences (Arts and Humanities; Fine Arts; Social Sciences) *Programme Coordinator*: Rukhsana Hasan; **Education**

Dean: Saeeda Asadullah Khan; **Islamic and Oriental Learning** (Arabic; Islamic Law; Islamic Studies; Oriental Studies) *Dean*: Saeeda Asadullah Khan; **Law, Commerce and Management Sciences** (Agricultural Economics; Economics; Finance; International Business; International Economics) *Dean*: Naheed Zia Khan; **Science and Technology** *Dean*: Naheed Zia Khan

History: Founded 1998.

Governing Bodies: Syndicate

Academic Year: September to June (September-January; February-June)

Admission Requirements: A-Levels and Intermediate

Fees: (PK Rupees): Bachelor's degree programmes, 10,875; Master's degree programmes, 6,025

Main Language(s) of Instruction: English

International Co-operation: With universities in the USA; United Kingdom; Sweden; Canada

Degrees and Diplomas: *Bachelor's Degree*: Software Engineering; Computer Arts; Economics; Education; English; Environmental Sciences; Fine Arts, 4 yrs; *Master's Degree*: Behavioural Sciences; Business Administration; Communication Sciences; Public Administration; Computer Sciences; Defence and Diplomatic Studies (M.BEH.SC; MBA; MCMM.SC; M.DDS), a further 2 1/2 yrs; *Doctor's Degree*: Behavioural Sciences; Economics; Education; English; Environmental Sciences; Gender Studies, 3 yrs

Student Services: Academic counselling, Canteen, Cultural centre, Foreign student adviser, Health services, Language programs, Nursery care, Sports facilities

Student Residential Facilities: 9 hostels

Special Facilities: Printing and Photocopying; Computer Lab

Libraries:c. 25,000 vols; 500 journals; Digital Library; Subscription to Pakistan Education Research Network (PERN), Virtual Software for Library

Publications: Journal of Gender and Social Studies *(quarterly)*

Last Updated: 14/11/08

FEDERAL URDU UNIVERSITY OF ARTS, SCIENCE AND TECHNOLOGY

House No D1-59, Block 7, Gulshane-Iqbal, Karachi, Sindh
Tel: +92(21) 497-3296
Fax: +92(21) 482-4852
EMail: info.gc@fuuast.edu.pk
Website: http://www.fuuast.edu.pk/english/

Vice-Chancellor: Syed Iqbal Mohsin
Tel: +92(21) 924-3716 EMail: vicechancellor@fuuast.edu.pk

Departments

Biochemistry; **Botany** (Botany); **Business Administration** (Business Administration); **Chemistry** (Chemistry); **Computer Science** (Computer Science); **Environmental Sciences** (Environmental Studies); **Geography** (Geography); **Geology**; **Mathematical Sciences** (Mathematics); **Microbiology**; **Pakistan Studies**; **Pharmaceutical Sciences**; **Physics** (Physics); **Statistics** (Statistics); **Zoology**

Further Information: Also Abdul Haq Campus, Islamabad Campus

History: Founded by a presidential ordinance on Nov. 13, 2002. Upgrading two existing colleges, Federal Urdu Science College and Federal Urdu College at Karachi.

Degrees and Diplomas: *Bachelor's Degree*; *Bachelor's Degree (Honours)*; *Master's Degree*; *Doctor's Degree*

FRONTIER WOMEN UNIVERSITY (FWU)

Asamia Road, Peshawar
Tel: +92(91) 9212-422
EMail: Info@fwu.edu.pk
Website: http://www.fwu.edu.pk

Vice-Chancellor: Syeda Farhana Jahangir

Faculties

Arts (Arts and Humanities); **Numerical and Physical Sciences** (Computer Science; Mathematics; Statistics); **Pure Sciences** (Biology; Computer Science; Microbiology); **Social Sciences** (Social Sciences); **Theology** (Theology)

History: Founded 2004.

Degrees and Diplomas: *Bachelor's Degree*; *Master's Degree*; *Doctor's Degree*

Last Updated: 23/08/10

GOMAL UNIVERSITY (GU)

Dera Ismail Khan, Peshawar, North West Frontier Province
Tel: +92(966) 750-239 +92(966) 750-266
Fax: +92(961) 750-255
Website: http://www.gu.edu.pk

Vice-Chancellor: Muhammad Farid Khan (2007-)
Tel: +92(966) 750-279, Fax: +92(966) 750-255
EMail: vc@gu.edu.pk

Registrar: Muhammad Jan Khan Fax: +92(966) 750-172

International Relations: Faridullah Khan, Director Academics
Tel: +92(966) 750-079 EMail: vc@gu-edu-pk

Faculties

Agriculture (Agriculture) *Dean*: Muhammad Qasim Khan; **Art and Humanities** (Arts and Humanities) *Dean*: Ashia Bibi; **Pharmacy** (Pharmacy) *Dean*: Gul Majeed Khan; **Sciences** (Mathematics; Natural Sciences) *Dean*: Muhammad Ayub

History: Founded 1974.

Governing Bodies: Syndicate; Senate

Academic Year: September to June (September-January; February-June)

Admission Requirements: Intermediate or higher secondary certificate

Main Language(s) of Instruction: English

Degrees and Diplomas: *Diploma (DPEd)*; *Bachelor's Degree (DVM, Pharmacy-D, LLB, BBA(H), BSc Agri, BCs, Bed)*; *Bachelor's Degree (BCom(H), DPA(H), BS Telecom: BSBio Tech, BPEd,)*; *Master's Degree (MA, Msc, Med)*

Student Services: Canteen, Foreign Studies Centre, Health services, Sports facilities

Student Residential Facilities: Yes

Libraries: Total, 40,500 vols

Publications: Gomal University Research *(biennially)*

Last Updated: 18/08/08

WENSAM COLLEGE

Dera Ismail Khan, North West Frontier Province

Principal: Said Rauf Khan (1992-)
Tel: +92(966)-731919, Fax: +92(966)-719782

History: Founded 1979.

GOVERNMENT COLLEGE UNIVERSITY, FAISALABAD

Faisalabad
Tel: +92(41) 920-0670
Fax: +92(41) 920-0671
EMail: gcuf@gcuf.edu.pk; info@gcuf.edu.pk
Website: http://www.gcuf.edu.pk

Vice-Chancellor: Asif Iqbal Khan EMail: asif.iqbal@hotmail.com

Registrar: Muhammad Aslam Chaudhary

Faculties

Arts and Social Sciences (Applied Linguistics; Asian Studies; Economics; Education; English; Fine Arts; Geography; Mass Communication; Psychology; Sociology); **Business and Administration** (Banking; Business Administration; Business and Commerce; Finance; Industrial Management; Public Administration); **Islamic and Oriental Learning** (Arabic; Islamic Studies; Urdu); **Law**; **Science and Technology** (Biology; Botany; Computer Science; Environmental Studies; Home Economics; Industrial Chemistry; Mathematics; Pharmacy; Physics; Statistics; Telecommunications Engineering; Zoology)

History: Founded 1897. Acquired university status 2002.

Degrees and Diplomas: *Bachelor's Degree*; *Master's Degree*; *Master of Philosophy*

GOVERNMENT COLLEGE UNIVERSITY, LAHORE (GCU)

Lower Mall, Katchehri Road, Lahore, Punjab 54600
Tel: +92(42) 9213340
Fax: +92(42) 9213341
Website: http://www.gcu.edu.pk

Vice-Chancellor: Khalid Aftab (1993-) Fax: +92(42) 9213337
EMail: vicechancellor@gcu.edu.pk

Registrar: Zahir Ahmed Siddiqi Fax: +92(42) 9213341
EMail: registrar@gcu.edu.pk

Centres
Advanced Studies in Physics (Physics) *Director*: Ijaz Mutaba Ghauri

Faculties
Arts (Arts and Humanities; Economics; English; History; Persian; Philosophy; Political Sciences; Urdu) *Dean*: Sohail Ahmed Khan; **Management Studies** *Chairperson*: Faisal Khokhar; **Science** (Botany; Chemistry; Computer Science; Mathematics; Physics; Psychology; Statistics; Zoology) *Dean*: Muhammad Akram Kashmiri

Schools
Mathematical Sciences *Director-General*: Alla Ditta Raza Chaudry

History: Founded 1864. Acquired present status 2002.

Governing Bodies: Syndicate

Admission Requirements: Intermediate and Secondary Education Certificate or equivalent

Main Language(s) of Instruction: English

International Co-operation: With universities in UK; Malaysia; Iran; Morocco; Italy

Degrees and Diplomas: *Bachelor's Degree*: 2 yrs; *Master's Degree*; *Master of Philosophy*; *Doctor's Degree*: Botany, Biotechnology, Chemistry, Clinical Psychology, Economics, English, Environmental Sciences, History, Mathematics, Persian, Physics, Political Science, Psychology, Statistics, Urdu, Zoology. Also Postgraduate Diploma

Student Services: Academic counselling, Canteen, Cultural centre, Employment services, Foreign student adviser, Handicapped facilities, Health services, Language programs, Social counselling, Sports facilities

Student Residential Facilities: Yes

Special Facilities: Zoology Museum

Libraries: Yes

HAZARA UNIVERSITY (HU)

Dhodial, Mansehra
Tel: +92(997) 414004
Fax: +92(997) 414152
EMail: hazara_university@yahoo.com
Website: http://www.hu.edu.pk

Vice-Chancellor: Ihsan Ali
Tel: +92(997) 530732, Fax: +92(997) 530046
EMail: vicechancellor@hu.edu.pk

Registrar: Sher Ali Khan Tel: +92(997) 531551

Departments
Education (English); **Education** (Education); **Management Sciences** (Management); **Mathematics and Computer Science** (Mathematics and Computer Science); **Mathematics and Computer Sciences** (Mathematics); **Natural Sciences** (Natural Sciences); **Natural Sciences** (Natural Sciences); **Natural Sciences**

History: Founded 2001. Acquired present status 2003.

Governing Bodies: Senate; Syndicate; Academic Council; Board of Faculties; Board of Studies; Board of Advanced Studies; Selection Board; Finance Committee; Planning and Development Committee

Academic Year: August to June (August-January; February-June)

Admission Requirements: Intermediate or higher secondary school certificate (with a minimum of 45% marks)

Fees: (PK Rupees): 7,000 per semester

Main Language(s) of Instruction: English

Accrediting Agencies: Government of Pakistan, Higher Education Commission

Degrees and Diplomas: *Bachelor's Degree (Honours)*: Biochemistry (BSC); Business Administration (BBA); Computer Science (BCS); Education (BA); English (BA); Microbiology (BSc), 4 yrs; *Master's Degree*: Business Administration (MBA); Chemistry (MSc); Computer Science (MCS), a further 2 yrs; *Master's Degree*: Business and Commerce (M.COM), 1 further yr; *Master's Degree*: English (MA), 2 yrs; *Doctor's Degree*: Botany; Chemistry; Biochemistry; Microbiology. Also Postgraduate Diploma (PGD-IT) evening

Student Services: Academic counselling, Canteen, Employment services, Foreign student adviser, Foreign Studies Centre, Health services, Language programs, Sports facilities

Student Residential Facilities: Yes

Libraries: Departmental and Central Library; Internet

Press or Publishing House: Government Printing Press

INSTITUTE OF BUSINESS ADMINISTRATION (IBA)

University Road, Karachi, Sindh 75270
Fax: +92(21) 926-1510
EMail: info@iba.edu.pk
Website: http://www.iba.edu.pk

Director: Ishrat Husain (2008-)
Tel: +92(21) 926-1501, Fax: +92(21) 926-1508
EMail: director@iba.edu.pk; ihusain@iba.edu.pk

Associate Dean, Faculty of Business Administration: Muhammad Nishat
Tel: +92(21) 926-1528, Fax: +92(21) 926-1508
EMail: mnishat@iba.edu.pk

Centres
Access to Finance; **Computer Studies**; **Entrepreneurship Development**; **Executive Education**

Departments
Accounting and Law; **Economics and Finance**; **Management** (Management); **Marketing** (Marketing); **Social Sciences**

Further Information: Also City Campus

History: Created 1955 as a USAID financed project. Acquired current status 1994.

Governing Bodies: Board of Governors.

Academic Year: September to August

Admission Requirements: Undergraduate, Higher Secondary Certificate with minimum 60% up to intermediate level, or 3 'A' levels, minimum one 'B' and two 'Cs'; Postgraduate, at least a Bachelor's degree from a reognized institution.

Fees: (PK Rupees): Full-time, 36,300-83,300; postgraduate, 13,600 - 13,900

Main Language(s) of Instruction: English

Accrediting Agencies: HEC, Pakistan

Degrees and Diplomas: *Bachelor's Degree*: Business Administration (BBA); Business Administration - Management Information Systems (BBA-MIS), 4 yrs full-time (Day study); *Bachelor's Degree*: Computer Science; Software Engineering; Information Technology (BS), 4 yrs full-time; *Master's Degree*: Business Administration (MBA), up to 5 yrs part-time study (Evening study); *Master's Degree*: Business Administration (MBA); Business Administration - Management Information Systems (MBA-MIS), 2 yrs full-time (Day study); *Master's Degree*: Business Administration - Management Information Systems (MBA-MIS), 3-6 yrs part-time (Evening study); *Master's Degree*: Computer Science; Software Engineering; Information Technology (MS); Finance (MS), 2 yrs full-time; *Master's Degree*: Economics (MS), 1 1/2 to 2 yrs full-time; *Doctor's Degree*: Computer Science and Engineering; Information and Communication Technology; Operations Research; Artificial Intelligence; Cryptography; Numerical Analysis; Numerical Computing, 5 yrs

Student Services: Academic counselling, Canteen, Employment services, Sports facilities

Student Residential Facilities: Male hostel.

Libraries: 30,953 vols.

Publications: Business Review *(biannually)*

Last Updated: 01/12/09

INSTITUTE OF MANAGEMENT SCIENCES (PESHAWAR) (IMSCIENCES)

1-A, Sector E / 5, Phase – VII, Hayatabad, Peshawar, North West Frontier Province
EMail: info@imsciences.edu.pk
Website: http://www.imsciences.edu.pk/

Director: Nasser Ali Khan

Programmes

Business Administration

History: Founded 2002.

Degrees and Diplomas: *Bachelor's Degree*; *Master's Degree*

INSTITUTE OF SPACE TECHNOLOGY (IST)

P.O. Box 2750, Islamabad 44000
Tel: +92(51) 9273316-20
Fax: +92(51) 9273310
EMail: info@ist.edu.pk
Website: http://www.ist.edu.pk/

Vice Chancellor: Imran Rahman (2004-)
Tel: +92(51) 9273301 EMail: vcist@ist.edu.pk

Director Academics: Ayaz Aziz
Tel: +92(51) 9273302 EMail: director@ist.edu.pk

International Relations: Najam Naqvi
Tel: +92(51) 9075454
EMail: najm_naqvi@yahoo.com, najam.naqvi@ist.edu.pk

Programmes

Aerospace Engineering *Head of Department*: Sarwar Naqvi; **Communication Systems Engineering** (Computer Science; Electrical and Electronic Engineering; Information Technology; Telecommunications Engineering) *Head*: Qamar ul-Islam

History: Founded 2002.

Governing Bodies: Principal officers; Senate

Admission Requirements: Higher Secondary School Certificate (HSSC); A-Level or Equivalent and entry test.

Fees: (PK Rupees): Undergraduate Programmes :40,000 per semester; Graduate Programmes: 50,000per semester (local students)

Main Language(s) of Instruction: English

International Co-operation: With universities in United Kingdom and China

Accrediting Agencies: Higher Education Commission of Pakistan (HEC); Pakistan Engineering Council (PEC)

Degrees and Diplomas: *Bachelor's Degree*: Aerospace Engineering (BS-AE); Communication Systems Engineering (BS-CSE), 4 yrs; *Master's Degree*: Aerospace Engineering (MS-AE); Communication Systems Engineering (MS-CSE), 2 yrs

Student Services: Academic counselling, Canteen, Cultural centre, Employment services, Foreign student adviser, Foreign Studies Centre, Health services, Language programs, Social counselling, Sports facilities

Student Residential Facilities: Hostels

Special Facilities: Aero modelling club; Student clubs and societies; Internet facilities

Libraries: c. 5,000 technical books, more than 50 magazines of international reputation, e-books, 600 cdroms; 120 audiovisual cassettes, 50 DVD, access to different archives and libraries

Press or Publishing House: Private Printing

Academic Staff *2008*	MEN	WOMEN	TOTAL
FULL-TIME	187	27	**214**
STAFF WITH DOCTORATE			
FULL-TIME	8	1	**9**

Last Updated: 26/11/08

INTERNATIONAL ISLAMIC UNIVERSITY (IIU)

PO Box 1243, Islamabad 44000
Tel: +92(51) 9261761
Fax: +92(51) 2250821
EMail: dir-pr@iiu.edu.pk
Website: http://www.iiu.edu.pk

Rector: Manzoor Ahmad
Tel: +92(51) 2254707, Fax: +92(51) 2254879
EMail: rector@iiu.edu.pk

Registrar: Gulzar Ahmed Khwaja
Tel: +92(51) 9258044, Fax: +92(51) 9258044
EMail: dir-acad@iiu.edu.pk

Academies

Dawah; **Shari'ah** (Islamic Law)

Faculties

Arabic (Arabic); **Linguistics and Languages** (Linguistics; Modern Languages); **Management Sciences** (Management); **Shari'ah and Law** (Islamic Law; Law); **Usuluddin (Islamic Studies)** (Islamic Studies)

Institutes

Islamic Economics (Economics); **Islamic Research** (Islamic Studies); **Languages** (Modern Languages)

Schools

Economics (Economics)

History: Founded 1980 as Islamic University, acquired present title 1985.

Governing Bodies: Board of Trustees; Board of Governors

Academic Year: September to June

Admission Requirements: Intermediate or higher secondary certificate

Main Language(s) of Instruction: Arabic, English

Degrees and Diplomas: *Bachelor's Degree*: 4 yrs; *Master's Degree*: a further 1-3 yrs; *Doctor's Degree (PhD)*: 3-5 yrs

KARAKURAM INTERNATIONAL UNIVERSITY (KIU)

University Road, Northern Areas, Gilgit
Tel: +92(5811) 504-40
Fax: +92(5811) 582-45
EMail: vc@kiu.edu.pk
Website: http://www.kiu.edu.pk/

Vice-Chancellor: Aziz Ali Najam (2004-)

Registrar: Ghulam Hussain
Tel: +92 (5811) 565-88 EMail: m.hussain@kiu.edu.pk

Departments

Biological Science (Biotechnology; Genetics; Microbiology; Molecular Biology) *Dr.* Rachel Louise Alexandra Jack; **Business Management and Economics** *Head*: Saranjam Muhmmad Baig; **Educational Development** *Head*: Abdul Hameed Lone; **Food Agriculture and Chemical Technology** (Analytical Chemistry; Chemistry; Food Technology; Inorganic Chemistry; Physical Chemistry) *Head*: Jahangir Khan Khalil; **International Relations and Political Science** (International Law; International Relations) *Head*: Zahid Mehmood; **Mathematics and Information Technology** (Applied Mathematics; Computer Networks; Computer Science; Data Processing; Mathematics) *Head*: Aftab Khan; **Modern Languages** (Linguistics; Literature) *Head*: Matthew Stott

History: Founded 2002.

Governing Bodies: The Syndicate, Academic Council, Finance and Planning Committee, Advanced Studies and Research Board, Discipline Committee, Affiliation Committee

Academic Year: February - December

Admission Requirements: Higher Secondary School Certificate

Fees: (PK Rupees): 15,000 per semester

Main Language(s) of Instruction: English

Accrediting Agencies: Higher Education Commission (HEC)

Degrees and Diplomas: *Bachelor's Degree*: Science and Arts (BA/BSc), 4 yrs; *Master's Degree*: Science and Arts (MA/MSc), 2 yrs

Student Services: Academic counselling, Canteen, Cultural centre, Health services, Language programs, Social counselling, Sports facilities

Student Residential Facilities: Yes

Libraries: Yes

KHYBER MEDICAL UNIVERSITY (KMU)

PDA Building Block IV, Phase-5, Hayatabad, Peshawar NWFP
Tel: +92(91) 921-7695
Fax: +92(91) 921-7704
EMail: info@kmu.edu.pk
Website: http://www.kmu.edu.pk

Vice Chancellor: Mohammad Hafizullah EMail: vc@kmu.edu.pk

Registrar: Jalil-Ur-Rahman

Faculties

Biomedical Engineering (Biomedical Engineering); **Dentistry** (Dentistry); **Health Care and Hospital Management** (Health Administration); **Medicine and Allied Sciences** (Medicine); **Nursing** (Nursing); **Paramedical Sciences** (Paramedical Sciences); **Postgraduate Studies and Research**; **Public Health and Preventive Science** (Public Health; Social and Preventive Medicine); **Surgical and Allied Sciences** (Surgery)

Degrees and Diplomas: *Bachelor's Degree*: Dental Surgery, Medicine, Surgery (BDS; MBBS)

Last Updated: 06/01/10

KING EDWARD MEDICAL UNIVERSITY (KEMU)

Nelagumbad, Anarkali, Lahore, Punjab 54000
Tel: +92(42) 735-4005
Fax: +92(42) 723-3796
EMail: kemcol@brain.net.pk
Website: http://www.kemc.edu/

Vice-Chancellor: Mumtaz Hasan (2006-)

Centres

Nuclear Medicine (CENUM) (Medical Technology) *Director*: Syed Waqar Haider

Departments

Anaesthesiology I *Head*: Abdul Qayyum; **Anaesthesiology II** *Head*: Syed Millat Hussain; **Anatomy** *Head*: Attaya Khalid; **Biochemistry** *Head*: Kamran Aziz; **Cardiac Surgery** (Cardiology; Surgery) *Head*: Mansoor Hussain; **Cardiology** (Cardiology) *Head*: Bilal Zakariah Khan; **Chest Medicine** (Pneumology) *Head*: Shamshad Rasul Awan; **Clinical Oncology (Radiotherapy)** (Oncology) *Head*: D. Shaharyar; **Community Medicine** (Community Health) *Head*: Maaz Ahmad; **Dermatology I** *Head*: Syed Atif Hasnain Kazmi; **Dermatology II** *Head*: Sabrina Suhail Pal; **ENT I** *Head*: Azhar Hameed; **ENT II** (Otorhinolaryngology) *Head*: Mansoor Baseer Pal; **Forensic Medicine** (Forensic Medicine and Dentistry) *Head*: Saeed Ahmed Malik; **Neurology** *Head*: Muhammad Nasrullah; **Neurosurgery** (Neurology; Surgery) *Head*: Anjum Habib Vora; **Obstetrics and Gynaecology I** *(Lady Willingdon Hospital, Lahore)* (Gynaecology and Obstetrics) *Head*: Yasmin Raashid; **Obstetrics and Gynaecology II** *(Lady Willingdon Hospital, Lahore) Head*: Ahmed Wasim Yusuf; **Obstetrics and Gynaecology III** *(Lady Willingdon Hospital, Lahore)* (Gynaecology and Obstetrics) *Head*: Tabinda Rana; **Obstetrics and Gynaecology IV** *(Lady Aitchison Hospital, Lahore)* (Gynaecology and Obstetrics) *Head*: Nasim Niaz; **Ophthalmology I** (Ophthalmology) *Head*: Muhammad Saleem Akhtar; **Ophthalmology II** (Ophthalmology) *Head*: Mumtaz Hussain; **Ophthalmology III** *Head*: Asad Aslam Khan; **Oral and Maxillofacial Surgery** (Dentistry; Oral Pathology; Surgery) *Head*: Riaz Ahmad Warriach; **Orthopaedics I** *Head*: Iqbal Ahmed Bhutta; **Orthopaedics II** (Orthopaedics) *Head*: Syed Muhammad Awais; **Paediatric Medicine I** *Head*: Ghazanfar Ali Sheikh; **Paediatric Medicine II** *Head*: Muhammad Ashraf Sultan; **Paediatric Surgery** (Paediatrics; Surgery) *Head*: Mehmood Shaukat; **Pathology** (Pathology) *Head*: Samina Naeem; **Pharmacology** (Pharmacology) *Head*: A. Shabbir Ahmad; **Physiology** *Head*: Muhammad Akram; **Plastic Surgery** *Head*: Farid Ahmad Khan; **Psychiatry and Behavioural Sciences** (Behavioural Sciences; Psychiatry and Mental Health) *Head*: Muhammad Riaz Bhatti; **Radiology** (Radiology) *Head*: Muhammad Nawaz Anjum; **Social and Prentive Paediatrics** *Head*: Rifat Nisar Ashraf; **Thoracic Surgery** *Head*: Aamir Mahmud Ijaz; **Urology** (Urology) *Head*: Muhammad Nawaz Chughati

Institutes

Punjab Institute of Preventive Ophthalmology (PIPO) *Director*: Asad Aslam Khan

Research Centres

Pakistan Medical Research Centre (PMRC) *Director*: Iffat Shabbir

Schools

Nursing *Principal*: Nusrat Sultana; **Orthopaedic Technology** *Manager*: Sultan Mehmood; **Paramedics** (Medical Auxiliaries; Paramedical Sciences) *Superintendent*: Fayyaz Ahmed Ranjha; **Physiotherapy** *(Mayo Hospital)* (Physical Therapy) *Principal*: Saleha Saleem Bukhari

Further Information: Mayo Hospital, Lady Willingdon Hospital, Lady Aitchison Hospital

History: Established 1860 as Medical School. Previously part of University of the Punjab under Faculty of Medicine and Dentistry (known as King Edward Medical College). Acquired current status and title 2005.

Governing Bodies: Board of Management

Academic Year: October to December; January to March; April to June.

Admission Requirements: Pakistani FSc (Secondary School Certificate) in pre-medical with an unadjusted score of 715/1,100; entrance exam

Fees: (PK Rupees): 10,474.00 per annum

Main Language(s) of Instruction: English

Degrees and Diplomas: *Bachelor's Degree (BSc)*; *Master's Degree (MSc)*; *Master of Philosophy (Mphil)*; *Doctor's Degree (PhD)*. Also: MBBS; BDS; FCPS; MD; MS; MDS

Student Residential Facilities: Separate male and female hostels

Special Facilities: Various hospitals and teaching clinics

Libraries: Yes

KOHAT UNIVERSITY OF SCIENCE AND TECHNOLOGY (KUST)

Jarma, Bannu Road, Kohat, North West Frontier Province 26000
Tel: +92(922) 554-505 +92(922) 554-575
Fax: +92(922) 554-556
EMail: kust@psh.paknet.com.pk
Website: http://www.kust.edu.pk

Vice-Chancellor: Zabta Khan Shinwari Tel: +92(922) 554-565

Director: Muhammad Saleem Gandapur
Tel: +92(0922) 554-557 EMail: msjgandapur@yahoo.com

International Relations: Muhammad Ramazan

Departments

Computer Science (Computer Science; Information Technology) *Vice-Chancellor*: Shair Ali Shinwari

History: Founded 2001.

Governing Bodies: Government of NWFP Pakistan

Fees: (PK Rupees): 12,000 per semester

Main Language(s) of Instruction: English

Degrees and Diplomas: *Bachelor's Degree (Honours)*; *Master's Degree*

Student Services: Academic counselling, Canteen, Employment services, Language programs, Sports facilities

Libraries: Main Library, Internet

Press or Publishing House: Imperial Press Kohat

LAHORE COLLEGE FOR WOMEN UNIVERSITY (LCWU)

Jail Road, Lahore, Punjab 54600
Tel: +92(42) 920-1950
Fax: +92(42) 920-3077
EMail: info@lcwu.edu.pk
Website: http://www.lcwu.edu.pk

Vice-Chancellor: Bushra Mateen
Tel: +92(42) 920-3072 EMail: vc@lcwu.edu.pk

Registrar: Shaista Vine EMail: registrar@lcwu.edu.pk

Faculties

Arts and Social Sciences *Dean*: Riffat Saqlain; **Islamic and Oriental Learning** (Arabic; Islamic Studies; Native Language; Oriental Studies; Persian; Urdu) *Dean*: Shagufta Zakria; **Management Sciences and Information Technology** (Business Education; Computer Science; Electronic Engineering; Information Technology; Management) *Dean*: Farhat Saleemi; **Natural Sciences** (Botany; Chemistry; Environmental Studies; Geography; Natural Sciences; Physics; Zoology) *Dean*: Kausar J. Cheema

History: Founded 1922 as Lahore College for Women. Acquired present status 2002.

Governing Bodies: Syndicate

Academic Year: September to July

Admission Requirements: Matriculation Certificate

Main Language(s) of Instruction: English, Urdu

Degrees and Diplomas: *Bachelor's Degree*: 4-5 yrs; *Master's Degree*: 2 yrs

Student Services: Academic counselling, Canteen, Cultural centre, Health services, Language programs, Nursery care, Social counselling, Sports facilities

Student Residential Facilities: Yes

Libraries: Yes

LASBELAA UNIVERSITY OF AGRICULTURE, WATER AND MARINE SCIENCES

District Lasbela, Uthal, Balochistan 90150
Tel: +92(853) 610-846 +92(853) 610-246
Website: http://www.luawms.pk

Vice-Chancellor: Abdul Hameed Bajoi (2007-)
Tel: +92(853) 610-847, Fax: +92(853) 610-903
EMail: bajoi03@yahoo.com

Registrar: Ghulam Hussain Jaffar
Tel: +92(853) 610-846, Fax: +92(853) 610-294
EMail: luawms@gmail.com

Departments

Economics (Agricultural Economics; Econometrics; Economics; Finance; Human Resources; International Business; Public Administration) *Head*: Gulawar Khan; **English** *Head*: Ashfaque Sawar

Faculties

Crop and Plant Sciences (Agronomy; Entomology; Horticulture; Plant Pathology; Soil Science) *Dean*: Muhammad Faheem Malik; **Marine Sciences** (Marine Biology; Marine Science and Oceanography) *Dean*: Shahid Amjad; **Veterinary and Animal Sciences** *Dean*: Muhammad Israel Rind; **Water Sciences** (Energy Engineering; Environmental Management; Irrigation; Water Management) *Head*: Muhammad Ejaz

History: Created 2005.

Governing Bodies: University Senate

Academic Year: November - March; April - July;

Admission Requirements: HSC (Higher School Certificate), with a score of at least 45%; age limit of 21

Fees: (PK Rupees): 3,750 for students from Balochistan; 5,000 for students from other provinces.

Main Language(s) of Instruction: English

International Co-operation: With universities in Pakistan and United Kingdom (Glasgow University)

Accrediting Agencies: Veterinary Accrediation Council & Agriculture Council

Degrees and Diplomas: *Bachelor's Degree*: Agronomy; Horticulture; Entomology; Plant Pathology; Soil Science (BS Agriculture); Human Resource Development; International Trade; Public Finance; Agricultural Economics; Microeconomics/Macroeconomics; Applied Econometrics (BS Economics); Linguistics; Literature (BS English); Marine Geology & Geophysics; Fisheries Biology & Shrimp Aquaculture; Coastal Zone Management (BS Marine Sciences), 4 yrs; *Bachelor's Degree*: Livestock & Poultry Production; Animal Nutrition & Production; Biosciences; Pre-clinical Sciences; Clinical Sciences (Doctor of Veterinary Medicine), 5 yrs; *Master of Philosophy*: Modern Languages; Literature; Linguistic; English, 2 yrs

Student Services: Canteen, Health services, Social counselling, Sports facilities

Student Residential Facilities: 300 places in separate male/female accommodation

Special Facilities: Computer laboratories

Libraries: Yes

Last Updated: 10/10/08

LIAQUAT UNIVERSITY OF MEDICAL AND HEALTH SCIENCES (LUMHS)

Jamshoro, Sindh
Tel: +92(22) 2772230-3878440
Fax: +92(22) 2772827
EMail: registrar@lumhs.edu.pk
Website: http://www.lumhs.edu.pk

Vice-Chancellor: Noushad Ahmed Shaikh
Tel: +92(22) 2771303, Fax: +92(22) 2772389
EMail: vcsect@lumhs.edu.pk

Registrar: Syed Ghulam Kadir Shah
Tel: +92(22) 2772230, Fax: +92(22) 2772827

Faculties

Basic Medical and Health Sciences (Health Sciences; Medicine) *Dean*: Shaheen Shah; **Community and Public Health Sciences** *(Jamshoro and Hyderabad)* (Community Health; Health Sciences; Public Health) *Dean*: Rafique Ahmed Soomro; **Dentistry** *(Jamshoro and Hyderabad)* (Dentistry) *Dean*: Rafique Ahmed Memon; **Medicine and Allied Sciences** *(Jamshoro and Hyderabad)* (Health Sciences; Medicine) *Dean*: Muhammad Anwar Memon; **Surgery and Allied Sciences** *(Jamshoro and Hyderabad)* (Health Sciences; Surgery) *Dean*: Abdul Sattar Memon

History: Founded 1881 as Medical School, 1951 as Medical College, acquired present status 2001.

Governing Bodies: Syndicate and Senate

Academic Year: March to December

Admission Requirements: Inter Science (Class XII) Biology group or equivalent qualification

Fees: (PK Rupees): Undergraduate, 15,000 per annum; Postgraduate Degree, 20,000 per annum; Postgraduate Diploma, 12,000 per annum

Main Language(s) of Instruction: English

International Co-operation: With universities in the United Kingdom and USA

Accrediting Agencies: Higher Education Commission; Pakistan Medical and Dental Council

Degrees and Diplomas: *Diploma*: Child Health; Cardiology; Dermatology; Nuclear Medicine; Psychiatric Medicine; Medical Radiotherapy; Gynaecology & Obstetrics; Otorhinolaryngology; Ophtalmology; Medical Radio Diagnosis; Clinical Pathology; Anaesthesiology; Family Medicine; General Dental Surgery; Medical Jurisprudence, 2 yrs; *Bachelor's Degree*: Dental Surgery (BDS); Nursing (BSc), 4 yrs; *Bachelor's Degree*: Medicine, Surgery, Health Sciences (MBBS), 5 yrs; *Master's Degree*: Cardiology; General Medicine; Paediatrics; Psychiatry; General Surgery; Orthopaedics; Gynaecology & Obstetrics; Ophtalmology; Urology; Otorhinolaryngology; Public Health; Forensic Medicine; Neurosurgery; Plastic Surgery (MS), 4 yrs; *Master's Degree*: Orthodontics; Prosthetics; Oral Surgery (M.Sc.), a further 2 yrs; *Master of Philosophy*: Pathology; Anatomy; Physiology; Pharmacology; Biochemistry (M.Phil), a further 3 yrs; *Doctor's Degree*: Anatomy; Biochemistry; Pharmacology; Physiology; Anatomy; Biochemistry; Pharmacology (PhD)

Student Services: Academic counselling, Canteen, Foreign student adviser, Foreign Studies Centre, Health services, Language programs, Social counselling, Sports facilities

Student Residential Facilities: 4 girls and 7 boys hostels

Special Facilities: Museum; Training and IT facilities (Mega lab, Dental Computer Lab)

Libraries: Central Library, Computer and Internet services; Digital Resource Library for Postgraduate students; Reading Hall
Publications: JLUMHS, A Scientific Journal *(quarterly)*
Last Updated: 05/12/08

MEHRAN UNIVERSITY OF ENGINEERING AND TECHNOLOGY JAMSHORO (MUET)

Jamshoro, Sindh 76062
Tel: +92(22) 2772250-73
Fax: +92(22) 2771382
EMail: registrar@muet.edu.pk
Website: http://www.muet.edu.pk

Vice-Chancellor: Abdul Qadeer Khan Rajput (1993-)
Tel: +92(221) 771-197 EMail: vc@muet.edu.pk

Registrar: Mohammad Aslam Uqaili
International Relations: Mushtaque Ahmed Baloch
EMail: pro@muet.edu.pk

Centres
English Language *Director*: M. H. Bodlo

Faculties
Architecture (Architecture; Town Planning) *Dean*: Dost A. Khowaja; **Engineering** (Chemical Engineering; Civil Engineering; Computer Engineering; Electrical and Electronic Engineering; Industrial Engineering; Mechanical Engineering; Metallurgical Engineering; Mining Engineering; Petroleum and Gas Engineering; Textile Technology) *Dean*: Riaz A. Sohag; **Technology** (Technology) *Dean*: Muhammad Ibrahim Panhwar

Institutes
Environmental Engineering and Management (Environmental Engineering; Environmental Management) *Director*: Abdul Rasheed Memon; **Irrigation and Drainage Engineering** (Irrigation) *Director*: Bakhshal Khan Lashari

Further Information: Also affiliated colleges and institutes:Government College of Technology; The Hyderabad Institute of Arts, Science and Technology

History: Founded 1963 as Sind University Engineering College, acquired present status and title 1977.

Academic Year: October to August

Fees: (PK Rupees): c. 14,000-40,000 per annum

Main Language(s) of Instruction: English

Degrees and Diplomas: *Bachelor's Degree*: 4-5 yrs; *Master's Degree*: a further 1 1/2 yrs; *Master of Philosophy (PhD)*: a further 2 yrs; *Doctor's Degree*: Engineering (PhD), 2 yrs

Libraries: Central Library, 100,000 vols, 30 periodical subscriptions
Last Updated: 28/11/08

MIRPUR UNIVERSITY OF SCIENCE AND TECHNOLOGY (MUST)

Mirpur, Azad Jammu and Kashmir
Website: http://www.must.edu.pk

Vice-Chancellor: Habib-ur-Rehman Tel: +92(5827) 961034

Registrar: Muhammad Shabir Mirza

Faculties
Arts (Economics; Education; English; Fine Arts; Islamic Studies); **Engineering And Technology** (Civil Engineering; Computer Engineering; Electrical Engineering; Mechanical Engineering; Software Engineering); **Home Economics** (Home Economics); **Sciences**

History: Founded 1980 as Ali Ahmed Shah University College of Engineering & Technology. Acquired present name and title 2008.

Accrediting Agencies: Higher Education Commission

Degrees and Diplomas: *Bachelor's Degree*; *Master's Degree*; *Master of Philosophy*; *Doctor's Degree*

Student Services: Academic counselling, Canteen, Health services, Social counselling, Sports facilities
Last Updated: 24/08/10

NATIONAL COLLEGE OF ARTS (NCA)

4-Shahra-e-Quaid-e-Azam, Lahore, Punjab 54600
Tel: +92(42) 9210599-601
Fax: +92(42) 9210500
EMail: info@nca.edu.pk
Website: http://www.nca.edu.pk/

Principal: Sajida Haider Vandal

Registrar: Murtaza Jafri

Departments
Architecture (Architecture); **Design**; **Fine Arts** (Fine Arts; Painting and Drawing; Printing and Printmaking; Sculpture); **Musicology**

Degrees and Diplomas: *Bachelor's Degree*; *Master's Degree*; *Doctor's Degree*: Communication and Cultural Studies

NATIONAL UNIVERSITY OF MODERN LANGUAGES (NUML)

Sector H-9, Islamabad 44000
Tel: +92(51) 925-7636
Fax: +92(51) 925-7679
EMail: info@numl.edu.pk
Website: http://www.numl.edu.pk

Rector: Aziz Ahmad Khan (2004-)

Director Administration: Muhammad Yasin
Tel: +92(51) 925-7637, Fax: +92(51) 925-7294

International Relations: Kamran Jahangir, Registrar
Tel: +92(51) 925-7674 EMail: kamranjahangir@hotmail.com

Faculties
Advanced Integrated Studies and Research (Arabic; Arts and Humanities; Asian Studies; Business Administration; Cultural Studies; Education; English; Finance; French; German; Hindi; Human Resources; Islamic Studies; Management; Marketing; Persian; Russian; Social Sciences; Urdu) *Dean*: Shazra Munawar; **European Languages** (English; French; German; Italian; Russian; Spanish; Turkish) *Dean*: Rubina Kamran; **Information Technology and Management Sciences** (Business Administration; Computer Education; Computer Science; Information Sciences; Information Technology; Management; Software Engineering; Telecommunications Engineering) *Dean*: Rasheed Ahmad Khan; **Near Eastern Languages and Culture** *Dean*: Syed Ali Anwar; **Social Sciences** (Asian Studies; Economics; Education; Government; History; International Relations; Islamic Studies; Mass Communication) *Dean*: Muhammad Azam Khan

Further Information: Regional Campuses in Faisalabad, Hyderabad, Karachi; Lahore; Multan; Peshawar; Quetta
History: Founded 1970 as National Institute of Modern Languages, acquired present status 2000.

Governing Bodies: Board of Governors

Academic Year: January to December (January-June; July-December)

Admission Requirements: Intermediate or higher secondary certificate, entry test and interview for Language Proficiency and undergraduate courses; Bachelor's Degree, test and interview for Post Graduate Courses; Master in 1st division and GRE test for Masters and PhD.

Fees: (PK Rupees): 10,000-38,000 per semester

Main Language(s) of Instruction: English

International Co-operation: With universities in France, China, Kazakhstan, Netherlands, Ukraine, United Kingdom, USA,

Accrediting Agencies: Higher Education Commission

Degrees and Diplomas: *Bachelor's Degree*: Languages; Information Technology; Management Sciences; Humanities and Social Sciences, Modern Languages, Computer Sciences, Business Administration, Education, Computer Engineering, Telecom Engineering, Software Engineering, Economics, 4 yrs; *Master's Degree*: Languages; Translation Studies; Social Sciences; Information Technology and Management Sciences; Business Administration; Computer Sciences; Information Technology; Education, 2 yrs; *Master of Philosophy*: Arabic; English; Education; French; German; Islamic Studies; Linguistics; Persian; Urdu; Sociology; Human Resource Development; Management; Finance; Marketing; Business Administration, 2-3 yrs; *Doctor's Degree*: Arabic; English;

Education; French; German; Islamic Studies; Linguistics; Persian; Urdu; Human Resource Development; Management (PhD), 3-5 yrs

Student Services: Academic counselling, Canteen, Cultural centre, Employment services, Foreign student adviser, Foreign Studies Centre, Handicapped facilities, Health services, Language programs, Social counselling, Sports facilities

Student Residential Facilities: 4 Male and 1 Female Hostels

Special Facilities: Movie studio. Confucius Centre, Language Labs; Computer Labs; FM Radio Station

Libraries: Main Library with over 150.000 books; UN Reference Library:15.000 books/journals; Confucius Institute Library : 10,000 books, Departmental libraries

Publications: Daryaft, Research Articles in Urdu *(biannually)*; Journal of Educational Research, Research Articles in Education *(biannually)*; Journal of Management & Technology, Research Articles in Engineering, Management Sciences; Social Sciences; Information Technology *(biannually)*; Research Magazine, Research Articles in English *(biannually)*; Takhleeqi Adab, Articles in Urdu *(biannually)*

Last Updated: 09/10/08

NATIONAL UNIVERSITY OF SCIENCES AND TECHNOLOGY (NUST)

Sector H-12 Campus, Islamabad 297
Tel: +92(51) 111-11-6878
EMail: info@nust.edu.pk
Website: http://www.nust.edu.pk

Rector: Muhammad Asghar (2007-)
Tel: +92(51) 9085-1001, Fax: +92(51) 9085-1007
EMail: rector@nust.edu.pk

Pro-Rector, Planning and Resources: Muhammad Mushtaq
Tel: +92(51) 908-51021, Fax: +92(51) 831-7363
EMail: pro-rector@nust.edu.pk

Pro-Rector, Academics and Research: Asif Raza
EMail: prorectoranr@nust.edu.pk

International Relations: Muhammad Ismail, Director, Quality Assurance
Tel: +92(51) 9085-1431, Fax: +92(51) 9085-1432
EMail: dqa@nust.edu.pk

Centres

Advanced Mathematics and Physics *(CAMP-Rawalpindi)* (Mathematics; Physics); **Modelling and Simulation** *(RCMC-Islamabad)* (Chemical Engineering; Materials Engineering); **Professional Development** *(PDC-Islamabad)* (Staff Development); **Technology Incubation** *(TIC-Rawalpindi)* (Technology); **Virology and Immunology** *(NCVI-Rawalpindi)* (Immunology; Virology)

Colleges

Aeronautical Engineering *(CAE -Risalpur)* (Aeronautical and Aerospace Engineering); **Civil Engineering** *(MCE-Risalpur)* (Civil Engineering); **Electrical and Mechanical Engineering** *(CE&ME-Rawalpindi)* (Electrical Engineering; Mechanical Engineering); **Marine Engineering** *(PNEC-Karachi)* (Marine Engineering); **Medical Sciences** *(AMC-Rawalpindi)* (Medicine); **Telecommunications Engineering** *(MCS-Rawalpindi)* (Telecommunications Engineering)

Schools

Business *(NBS-Islamabad)* (Business Education); **Chemical and Materials Engineering** *(SCME-Islamabad)* (Chemical Engineering; Energy Engineering; Materials Engineering); **Civil and Environmental Engineering** *(SCEE-Islamabad)* (Civil Engineering; Construction Engineering; Environmental Engineering; Surveying and Mapping; Water Management); **Electrical Engineering and Computer Engineering** *(SEECS-Islamabad)* (Computer Engineering; Electrical Engineering); **Mechanical and Manufacturing Engineering** *(SMME-Islamabad)* (Mechanical Engineering)

History: Founded 1991 by the Ministry of Science and Technology.

Governing Bodies: Board of Governors, Executive Committee, Academic Council, Faculty Board of Studies,

Academic Year: September to August

Admission Requirements: Undergraduate: Minimum 60% aggregate marks each in Matric and in FSC (excluding NCC marks) equivalent exams. No deviation in this regard is allowed. Postgraduate: sixteen years of schooling or 4 years (130 credit hours) calculated afterFA/FSC/A Level mandatory for admission in MS/M Phil programme leading to PhD and MBA. The previous (terminal) degree or academic transcript on the basis of which applicant is eligible to apply for MS Engineering/IT/ M Phil leading to PhD must be PEC/HEC/PM&DC (as applicable) recognized with a minimum CGPA of 2.50 of 4.00 (3.50 of 5.00) or 1st Division (60% marks).

Fees: (PK Rupees): Undergraduate: Engineering/IT/Medical/ Management Rs 8,500Postgraduate: Engineering/IT/Medical/ Management Rs 7,000

Main Language(s) of Instruction: English

International Co-operation: With 42 universities in United Kingdom, USA, Germany, Australia, Thailand, Singapore, China, Japan, Ukraine, Korea, Denmark, France, South Africa, Netherlands, Malaysia, Switzerland, Pakistan.

Accrediting Agencies: Higher Education Commission (HEC), Pakistan Engineering Council (PEC), Pakistan Medical and Dental Council (PMD&C), National Computing Education and Accreditation Council (NCEAC)

Degrees and Diplomas: *Bachelor's Degree*: Dental Surgery (BDS); Economics (BS); Engineering (BE); Information Technology (BIT); Virology and Immunology, 4 yrs; *Bachelor's Degree*: Medical Sciences (MBBS), 5 yrs; *Bachelor's Degree (Honours)*: Business Administration (BBA(Hons)), 4 yrs; *Master's Degree*: Engineering (MS), a further 1 1/2 yrs; *Master's Degree*: Information Technology (MIT), 11/2 yrs; *Master's Degree*: Management Sciences (MBA), 2 yrs; *Master of Philosophy*: Anatomy; Physiology; Biochemistry; Pharmacology; Chemical Pathology; Mathematics and Physics; *Doctor's Degree*: Medical Sciences; Management Sciences; Information Technology; Mathematics; Transport Engineering; Geotechnical Engineering; Structural Engineering; Telecommunications Engineering; Computer Software Engineering; Computer Engineering; Information Security; Electrical Engineering; Mechanical Engineering; Environmental Engineering (PhD)

Student Services: Academic counselling, Canteen, Cultural centre, Employment services, Foreign student adviser, Health services, Social counselling, Sports facilities

Student Residential Facilities: Yes

Special Facilities: Museums

Libraries: Total, 340,274 vols; E-book: 50,000; Journals/Magazines: 21,867; E-Journals: 23,000; Library: 178

Publications: Corps of Engineers Journal - Journal of Corps of Engineering; NUST Journal of Engineering Sciences (NJES); NUST Newsletter; Qasid; Research Chronicle; Signals Technology Window; Technocrat

Student Numbers *2011-2012*: Total 9,479

Last Updated: 03/12/09

NED UNIVERSITY OF ENGINEERING AND TECHNOLOGY (NEDUET)

University Road, Karachi, Sindh 75270
Tel: +92(21) 926-1261
Fax: +92(21) 926-1255
EMail: vc@neduet.edu.pk
Website: http://www.neduet.edu.pk

Vice-Chancellor: Abul Kalam Tel: +92(21) 926-1253

Registrar: Javed Aziz Khan
Tel: +92(21) 926-1257 EMail: registrar@neduet.edu.pk

Faculties

Biomedical Engineering (Bioengineering; Biomedical Engineering) *Division Head*: Muzzaffar Mahmood; **Chemical and Materials Engineering** (Chemical Engineering; Materials Engineering; Metallurgical Engineering; Polymer and Plastics Technology) *Head*: Muhammad Tufail; **Civil Engineering and Architecture** (Architecture; Civil Engineering; Engineering; Environmental Engineering; Petroleum and Gas Engineering; Urban Studies) *Dean*: Sahibzada Farooq Ahmed Rafeeqi; **Electrical and Computer Engineering** *Dean*: Talat Altaf; **Information, Science and Humanities** (Arts and Humanities; Computer Science; Information Technology; Management; Mathematics; Natural Sciences) *Dean*: Mahmood Khan Pathan; **Mechanical and Manufacturing Engineering** (Automotive Engineering; Industrial Engineering; Marine Engineering;

Mechanical Engineering; Textile Technology) *Dean*: Nazimuddin Qureshi

Further Information: Also 4 affiliated colleges: Pak-Swiss Training Centre (PCSIR); Institute of Industrial Electronics Engineering (IIEE), Karachi; PAF Institute of Aviation Technology, Karachi; Government College of Technology, Karachi

History: Founded 1922 as Engineering College, acquired present status and title 1977.

Governing Bodies: Syndicate; Senate

Admission Requirements: Higher secondary certificate (Pre-Engineering)

Fees: (PK Rupees): c. 13,900; foreign students, c. 162,000

Main Language(s) of Instruction: English

Accrediting Agencies: Pakistan Engineering Council; Pakistan Council of Architecture and Town Planners

Degrees and Diplomas: *Bachelor's Degree (BE/BCIT)*: 4 yrs; *Bachelor's Degree*: Architecture; Bioengineering; Medical Engineering, 5 yrs; *Master's Degree (MEngg/MCIT/MURP)*: 1 1/2-2 1/2 yrs; *Doctor's Degree (PhD)*: 3 yrs. Postgraduate Diploma in Land Surveying

Student Services: Academic counselling, Canteen, Employment services, Foreign student adviser, Health services, Social counselling, Sports facilities

Student Residential Facilities: For students from other regions and foreign students only

Libraries: Central Library, 135,000 vols, 22,000 periodicals. Digital Library

Publications: NED University Journal of Research *(biennially)*

Last Updated: 28/11/08

NORTH WEST FRONTIER PROVINCE AGRICULTURAL UNIVERSITY (NWFPAU)

PO Pakistan Forest Institute, Peshawar, North West Frontier Province
Tel: +92(91) 921-6572
Fax: +92(91) 921-6520
EMail: registraraup@yahoo.com
Website: http://www.aup.edu.pk/

Vice-Chancellor: Said Khan Khalil Tel: +92(91) 921-6518

Registrar: Dilawar Khan Tel: +92(91) 921-6521

International Relations: Muhammad Afzal Tel: +92(91) 921-6532

Faculties

Animal Husbandry and Veterinary Science (Animal Husbandry; Veterinary Science) *Dean*: Muhammad Taj; **Crop Production Sciences** (Crop Production) *Dean*: Fazal Hayat Taj; **Crop Protection Sciences** (Plant and Crop Protection) *Dean*: Sher Hassan; **Nutritional Sciences** (Dietetics; Nutrition) *Dean*: Iqtidar Ahmad Khalil; **Rural Social Sciences** (Rural Studies; Social Sciences) *Dean*: Zahid Hussain

Institutes

Biotechnology and Genetic Engineering (Biotechnology; Genetics) *Director*: Zahoor Ahmad Swati; **Business and Management Sciences/Computer Science** (Business and Commerce; Computer Science; Information Technology; Management) *Director*: Farzand Ali Jan

Further Information: Also 12 constituent Research Institutes and 20 affiliated Institutes

History: Founded 1981.

Governing Bodies: Academic Council; Syndicate

Academic Year: January to December

Admission Requirements: Higher secondary certificate

Fees: (PK Rupees): 9,000-73,000

Main Language(s) of Instruction: English

Degrees and Diplomas: *Bachelor's Degree*: 4 yrs; *Master's Degree*: a further 4 terms; *Doctor's Degree (PhD)*: a further 4 yrs

Student Services: Academic counselling, Canteen, Employment services, Foreign student adviser, Foreign Studies Centre, Health services, Social counselling, Sports facilities

Libraries: Central Library, c. 90,000 vols; Institute of Development Studies, c. 20,000 vols

NORTH WEST FRONTIER PROVINCE UNIVERSITY OF ENGINEERING AND TECHNOLOGY (NWFPUET)

PO Box 814, Peshawar, North West Frontier Province
Tel: +92(91) 921-6796
Fax: +92(91) 921-8097
EMail: uetp@paknet.1.ptc.pk
Website: http://web.nwfpuet.edu.pk/index.php

Vice-Chancellor: Syed Imtiaz Hussain Gillani
Tel: +92(91) 921-6493

Registrar: Imtiaz Ahmad Khan
Tel: +92(91) 921-6496 EMail: registrar@nwfpuet.edu.pk

International Relations: Muhammad Sarwar Khan, Adviser Finance and Planning
Tel: +92(91) 921-6497, Fax: +92(91) 921-6663
EMail: df@nwfpuet.edu.pk

Departments

Agricultural Engineering (Agricultural Engineering) *Chairman*: Zahid Mahmood; **Architecture and Regional Planning** *(Abbottabad Campus)* (Architecture; Regional Planning) *Chairman*: Shabir Ullah Qureshi; **Basic Sciences and Islamic Studies** (Islamic Studies; Natural Sciences) *Chairman*: Saeed-ur-Rehman; **Chemical Engineering** (Chemical Engineering) *Chairman*: Hisham Taha Abdullah El-Dessouky; **Civil Engineering** (Civil Engineering) *Chairman*: Noor-Ul-Amin; **Civil Engineering** (Civil Engineering) *Chairman*: Akhtar Naeem; **Computer Science and Information Technology** *(Non Engineering Programme))* (Computer Science; Information Technology) *Chairman*: Inayat Ullah Khan Babar; **Computer Software Engineering** *(Mardan Campus)* (Software Engineering) *Chairman*: Inayatullah Khan Babar; **Computer Systems Engineering** (Computer Engineering; Information Technology) *Chairman*: Khwaja Muhammad Yahya; **Electrical and Electronic Engineering** (Electrical Engineering; Power Engineering; Telecommunications Engineering) *Chairman*: Azzam-ul-Asar; **Electrical Engineering** *(Bannu Campus)* (Electrical Engineering) *Chairman*: Syed Waqar Shah; **Electronic Engineering** *(Abbottabad Campus)* (Electronic Engineering) *Chairman*: Riaz Ul Husnain; **Industrial Engineering** (Industrial Engineering) *Chairman*: Iftikhar Hussain; **Mechanical Engineering** (Mechanical Engineering; Metallurgical Engineering) *Chairman*: Saeed Jeved Tajik; **Mechatronics Engineering** (Electronic Engineering; Mechanical Engineering) *Chairman*: Riaz Akber Shah; **Mining Engineering** (Mining Engineering) *Chairman*: Khan Gul Jadoon; **Telecommunications** *(Madran Campus)* (Telecommunications Engineering) *Chairman*: Shagufta Naz

Institutes

Urban Infrastructure Planning (Town Planning; Urban Studies) *Head*: Akhtar Naeem

Further Information: Also 3 affiliated colleges: 2 for Bachelor and Master of Sciences in Engineering; and 1 for Bachelor of Technology

History: Founded 1952 as College of Engineering in University of Peshawar. Acquired present status 1980.

Governing Bodies: Boards of Study; Academic Council; Syndicate; Finance and Planning Committee; Board of Advanced Studies and Research; Selection Board

Academic Year: September to June

Admission Requirements: Higher secondary certificate, Advanced ('A') levels (Cambridge/Oxford)

Fees: (PK Rupees): Bachelor Level: 62,000 (foreign students, US$ 7,000); Master Level: 50,000 (foreign students, US$ 1,140; PhD, 42,000

Main Language(s) of Instruction: English

International Co-operation: With universities in United Kingdom; United States; Thailand; Italy; Turkey; Malaysia; South Korea

Accrediting Agencies: Pakistan Engineering Council; Pakistan Council of Architects and Town Planner

Degrees and Diplomas: *Bachelor's Degree*: Engineering, 4 yrs; *Master's Degree*: Engineering, a further 2 yrs; *Doctor's Degree*: 3 yrs after MSc.Engg

Student Services: Academic counselling, Canteen, Employment services, Foreign student adviser, Health services, Sports facilities

Student Residential Facilities: Yes

Libraries: Central Library. Also reference libraries for each department. Digital library

Publications: Journal of Engineering and Applied Sciences *(biannually)*

Last Updated: 01/12/08

PAKISTAN INSTITUTE OF DEVELOPMENT ECONOMICS

Quaid-i-Azam University Campus, PO Box 1091, Islamabad 44000
Tel: +92(51) 920-1140
Fax: +92(51) 921-0886
EMail: pide@apollo.net.pk
Website: http://www.pide.org.pk/

Vice-Chancellor: Rashid Amjad
Tel: +92(51) 921-7,879; +92(51) 260-1146
EMail: vc@pide.org.pk; rashidamjad@pide.org.pk

Registrar: Abdul Qayyum
EMail: registrar@pide.org.pk; qayyum@gmail.com

Departments

Business Studies (Business Administration; Business and Commerce) *Head*: Fazal Husain; **Econometrics and Statistics** (Econometrics; Statistics) *Head*: Abdul Qayyum; **Economics** (Economics) *Head*: Ejaz Ghani; **Population Sciences** (Anthropology; Demography and Population) *Head*: Durr-e-Nayab

History: Created in 1957 in Karachi. Obtained status of an autonomous research organization. Acquired current status 2006.

Governing Bodies: Senate; Syndicate

Admission Requirements: Undergraduate degree; TEOFL qualification.

Fees: (PK Rupees): Home students, 20,000 - 45,000 per semester, (US Dollars), Overseas students, 600 - 1,500 per semester

Degrees and Diplomas: *Master's Degree*: Business Administration (MBA); Economics; Econometrics and Statistics; Population Sciences, 2 yrs; *Master of Philosophy*: Economics, 2 yrs; *Doctor's Degree*: Economics, 4 yrs

Libraries:c. 32,500 vols.

Last Updated: 22/10/08

PAKISTAN INSTITUTE OF ENGINEERING AND APPLIED SCIENCES (PIEAS)

P.O. Nilore, Islamabad 44000
Tel: +92(51) 9290273-4
Fax: +92(51) 9223727
EMail: registrar@pieas.edu.pk
Website: http://www.pieas.edu.pk

Rector: Muhammad Aslam

Faculties

Applied Sciences (Computer Science; Information Sciences; Medicine; Physics); **Engineering**

Degrees and Diplomas: *Bachelor's Degree*; *Master's Degree*; *Doctor's Degree*: Chemical and Process Engineering; Computer Sciences and Informatics; Mechanical Engineering; Nuclear Engineering; Physics; Systems Engineering

PEOPLES UNIVERSITY OF MEDICAL AND HEALTH SCIENCES FOR WOMEN, NAWABSHAH (SHAHEED BENAZIRABAD) (PUMHSW)

Nawabshah, Shaheed Benazirabad, Sindh
Tel: +92(244) 937 0428 +92(244) 937 0259
Fax: +92(244) 937 0263
EMail: vc@pumhs.edu.pk
Website: http://www.pumhs.edu.pk

Vice-Chancellor: Azam Hussain Yousifani

Faculties

Basic and Allied Sciences (Anatomy; Biochemistry; Forensic Medicine and Dentistry; Pathology; Pharmacology; Physiology); **Community and Allied Sciences** (Community Health; Public Health); **Medicine and Allied Sciences** (Cardiology; Dermatology; Diabetology; Medicine; Neurology; Paediatrics; Pneumology; Psychiatry and Mental Health; Venereology); **Surgery and Allied Sciences** (Anaesthesiology; Gynaecology and Obstetrics; Neurology; Operations Research; Orthopaedics; Otorhinolaryngology; Paediatrics; Radiology; Surgery; Urology)

History: Created 1974 as part of Liaquat University of Medical and Health Sciences. Acquired current title and status 2010.

Degrees and Diplomas: *Bachelor's Degree (Honours)*; *Master's Degree*

Last Updated: 13/04/12

QUAID-E-AWAM UNIVERSITY OF ENGINEERING, SCIENCES AND TECHNOLOGY, NAWABSHAH (QUEST)

Sakrand road, Nawabshah, Sindh 67480
Tel: +92(241) 937-0366
Fax: +92(241) 937-0367
EMail: information@quest.edu.pk
Website: http://quest.edu.pk

Vice-Chancellor: Wahid Bux Soomro
Tel: +92(241) 937-0366 EMail: vc@quest.edu.pk

Registrar: Syed Ghulam Qadir Shah
Tel: +92(241) 937-0373 EMail: registrar@quest.edu.pk

Faculties

Engineering (Civil Engineering; Computer Engineering; Electrical Engineering; Information Technology; Mechanical Engineering) *Dean*: Ali Bux Soomro; **Science** *Dean*: Ali Bux Soomro; **Technology** *Dean*: Sadaruddin Shaikh

History: Founded 1974. Acquired present title 1996.

Governing Bodies: Syndicate; Senate

Academic Year: January to December

Admission Requirements: Higher secondary school certificate

Fees: (PK Rupees): 13,475-20,975 per annum

Main Language(s) of Instruction: English

Accrediting Agencies: Pakistan Engineering Council

Degrees and Diplomas: *Bachelor's Degree*: 3-4 yrs; *Bachelor's Degree*: Industrial Technology; *Bachelor's Degree (Honours)*: Technology; *Bachelor's Degree (Pass)*: Technology; *Master of Philosophy*; *Doctor's Degree*

Student Services: Academic counselling, Canteen, Employment services, Foreign student adviser, Health services, Language programs, Social counselling, Sports facilities

Student Residential Facilities: Yes

Special Facilities: Auditorium

Libraries: Central Library c. 40,000 vols

Publications: Quaid-E-Awam University Research Journal of Engineering, Science and Technology, Publication of Research papers *(biannually)*

Last Updated: 27/03/09

QUAID-I-AZAM UNIVERSITY, ISLAMABAD (QAU)

PO Box 1090, Islamabad 45320
Tel: +92(51) 90643063-2002
Fax: +92(51) 921-9888
Website: http://www.qau.edu.pk

Vice-Chancellor: U.A.G. Isani EMail: vc@qau.edu.pk

Registrar: Hussain Manzoor Sheikh EMail: registrar@qau.edu.pk

International Relations: Rashid Khalid Tel: +92(51) 921-9899

Faculties

Medicine (Medicine) *Dean*: Fazle Hadi; **Natural Sciences** (Biology; Chemistry; Computer Science; Earth Sciences; Electronic

Engineering; Mathematics; Natural Sciences; Physics; Statistics) *Dean*: Ali Khawaja Azam; **Social Sciences** (Administration; Anthropology; Asian Studies; Economics; History; International Relations; Psychology; Social Sciences) *Dean*: Mohammad Waseem

Further Information: Also 1affiliated college and 6 other institutions at national level

History: Founded 1965 as University of Islamabad, acquired present status 1967 and present title 1976. A postgraduate institution.

Governing Bodies: Syndicate and Academic Council

Academic Year: January to December (January-June; July-December)

Admission Requirements: University degree

Fees: (PK Rupees): 10,765 to 14,000 per annum; international students, 61,000-80,800

Main Language(s) of Instruction: English

Degrees and Diplomas: *Master's Degree*: 2 yrs; *Master of Philosophy*: 2 yrs; *Doctor's Degree (PhD)*: 2 yrs. Also Postgraduate Diploma and Certificate in Computer Science

Student Services: Academic counselling, Canteen, Sports facilities

Student Residential Facilities: Yes

Libraries: 156,000 vols; special collections, c. 25,000

Publications: Journal of Natural Sciences *(biannually)*; Journal of Social Sciences *(biannually)*

SARDAR BAHADUR KHAN WOMEN'S UNIVERSITY

Brewery Road, Quetta, Balochistan
Tel: +92(81) 920-2098 +92(81) 920-1377 +92(81) 920-2106
Fax: +92(81) 285-1680
EMail: info@sbkwu.edu.pk
Website: http://www.sbkwu.edu.pk

Vice-Chancellor: Shahida Jaffrey (2004-)
EMail: vc_secretariat@sbkwu.edu.pk

Registrar: Jamila Qazi EMail: registrar@sbkwu.edu.pk

Departments

Botany; **Chemistry** (Chemistry); **Computer Science** (Computer Science); **Economics** (Economics); **Education** (Education); **English Literature** (English; Literature); **Fine Arts** (Fine Arts); **Mathematics** (Mathematics); **Pakistan Studies**; **Social Work** (Social Work); **Sociology** (Sociology); **Urdu** (Urdu); **Zoology** (Zoology)

History: Founded 2004 as Balochistan's first women's university.

Admission Requirements: Entrance exam

Fees: (PK Rupees): 2,250 per semester

Degrees and Diplomas: *Bachelor's Degree*: Chemistry; Mathematics; Zoology; Environmental Science; Genetics; Computer Science; Economics (BSc); English; Sociology; Fine Arts (BA), 4 yrs; *Master's Degree*: Botany; Chemistry; Mathematics; Zoology; Economics (MSc); Education; English; Pakistan Studies; Sociology; Social Work; Urdu (MA), a further 2 yrs

Student Services: Academic counselling, Canteen, Cultural centre, Nursery care, Sports facilities

Student Residential Facilities: Yes with priority for students from outside Quetta.

Special Facilities: Day care centre

Libraries: Yes - with specialised sections for Physical and Biological Sciences, Law, and Education

Last Updated: 21/11/08

SHAH ABDUL LATIF UNIVERSITY (SALU)

Khairpur, Sindh
Tel: +92(792) 9280051-4
Fax: +92(792) 9280060
EMail: info@salu.edu.pk
Website: http://www.salu.edu.pk/

Vice-Chancellor: Abdul Rahim Malik EMail: vc@salu.edu.pk

Faculties

Arts (Arts and Humanities; Business and Commerce; Economics; English; Indic Languages; International Relations; Urdu); **Commerce and Business Administration** (Business Administration); **Law** (Law); **Science** (Archaeology; Botany; Chemistry; Computer Science; Mathematics; Microbiology; Natural Sciences; Physics; Statistics)

History: Founded 1987. Originally Campus of the University of Sindh.

Academic Year: February to December (February-June; September-December)

Admission Requirements: Higher secondary certificate (HSC) or equivalent, pre-entry written test

Main Language(s) of Instruction: English

Degrees and Diplomas: *Bachelor's Degree (Honours)*: Arts (BA Hons); Commerce (BCom Hons); Science (BSc Hons), 3 yrs; *Master's Degree*: a further yr

Student Residential Facilities: Yes

Libraries: Central Library, c. 27,500 vols

Publications: Ashkar (in English) *(annually)*; Bhittai Journal (in Sindhi) *(annually)*; Sachal Sarmast (in English) *(annually)*; The Commerce and Economic Review (in English) *(annually)*

SINDH AGRICULTURAL UNIVERSITY (SAU)

Tandojam, Sindh 70060
Tel: +92(22) 2765869
Fax: +92(22) 2765300
EMail: info@sau.edu.pk
Website: http://www.sau.edu.pk/

Vice-Chancellor: A.Q. Mughal
Registrar: Hafizullah Memon
Tel: +92(22) 2765387, Fax: +92(22) 2765387
EMail: riasat2k_sau@yahoo.com

Centres

Information Technology (Information Technology) *Director*: Fateh Mohammad Soomro

Faculties

Agricultural Engineering (Agricultural Engineering) *Dean*: Hussain Bux Bhutto; **Agricultural Social Sciences** (Agriculture; Social Sciences) *Dean*: Khalid Hussain Mahar; **Animal Husbandry and Veterinary Sciences** (Animal Husbandry; Veterinary Science) *Dean*: Gul Mohammad Baloch; **Crop Production** (Crop Production) *Dean*: Shamasdduin Tunio; **Crop Protection** (Plant and Crop Protection) *Dean*: Shafi Muhammad Nizamani; **Institute of Food Science and Technology** *Director*: Saghir Ahmed Sheikh

Further Information: Also 2 experimental farms

History: Founded 1939 as King George V Institute of Agriculture at Sakrand. Moved to Tandojam 1954 and became University 1977. A State institution enjoying considerable autonomy in both financial and academic matters. Financed through the University Grants Commission.

Governing Bodies: Senate

Academic Year: October to July (October-February; March-July)

Admission Requirements: Intermediate or higher secondary certificate (Science group)

Main Language(s) of Instruction: English

Degrees and Diplomas: *Bachelor's Degree*: Agricultural Engineering (BE); Agriculture; Agricultural Engineering and Veterinary Science; Information Technology (BS); Social Sciences, 4 yrs; *Master's Degree*: Agriculture and Veterinary Science; Agriculture Engineering (ME); Social Sciences, a further 2 yrs; *Doctor's Degree*: Agriculture Engineering, Veterinary Science (DVM)

Student Services: Academic counselling, Canteen, Cultural centre, Employment services, Health services, Nursery care, Social counselling, Sports facilities

Special Facilities: Botanical Garden; Horticulture Garden

Libraries: Central Library, c. 165,000 items

Publications: Agricultural Engineering and Veterinary Sciences *(biannually)*; Pakistan Journal of Agriculture; Sindh Agriculture University News *(quarterly)*

Last Updated: 20/11/08

SUKKUR INSTITUTE OF BUSINESS ADMINISTRATION (SIBA)

Airport Road, Sukkur, Sindh 65200
Tel: +92(71) 563-0272 +92(71) 563-3490
Fax: +92(71) 563-2465
EMail: info@iba-suk.edu.pk
Website: http://www.iba-suk.edu.pk/

Director: Nisar Ahmed Siddiqui
Tel: +92(71) 563-3491 EMail: director@iba-suk.edu.pk

Registrar: Mohammad Aslam Pathan
Tel: +92(71) 563-0272, Ext.109 EMail: registrar@iba-suk.edu.pk

International Relations: Madad Ali Shah
Tel: +92(71) 563-0272, Ext.119 EMail: madad@iba-suk.edu.pk

Faculties

Business Administration (Accountancy; Banking; Business Administration; Economics; Finance; Human Resources; Management; Marketing; Statistics) *Head*: Syed Mir Mohammad Shah; **Information Technology** (Computer Networks; Computer Science; Data Processing; E-Business/Commerce; Information Sciences; Information Technology; Management Systems; Software Engineering; Telecommunications Engineering) *Head*: Zahid Hussain Khand

History: Created in 1994. Affiliated to IBA Karachi

Governing Bodies: Senate; Syndicate; Academic Council

Academic Year: September to December; January to May

Admission Requirements: Secondary School certificate with minimum 50% marks for undergraduate programmes; Bachelor-level degree for postgraduate programmes.

Fees: (PK Rupees): Bachelor Programmes: 34,800 1st semester and 26,800 subsequent semesters; Master Programmes: 38,800 1st semester and 30,800 subsequent semesters

Main Language(s) of Instruction: English

Accrediting Agencies: Higher Education Commission (HEC)

Degrees and Diplomas: *Bachelor's Degree*: Business Administration; Management; Marketing; Finance; Human Resource; Computer Science; Telecommunication Engineering (BBA; BSCS; BSTS), 4 yrs (8 semesters); *Master's Degree*: Marketing; Finance; Human Resource; Business Administration; Information System; Banking and Finance (MBA), a further 2 yrs (4 semesters)

Student Services: Academic counselling, Canteen, Employment services, Foreign student adviser, Foreign Studies Centre, Handicapped facilities, Health services, Language programs, Nursery care, Social counselling, Sports facilities

Student Residential Facilities: 4 boys hostels for 200 students; 3 girls hostel for 150

Special Facilities: Auditorium; Video Conference; Wi-Fi

Libraries: 15,000 vols, 1,000 CDs; Access to 10,000 online journals; E-brary: http://site.ebrary.com/lib/ibasukkur

Last Updated: 28/11/08

THE ISLAMIA UNIVERSITY OF BAHAWALPUR (IU)

Bahawalpur, Punjab
Tel: +92(621) 925-5518
Fax: +92(621) 925-5519
EMail: vc@iub.edu.pk
Website: http://www.iub.edu.pk/

Vice-Chancellor: Belal A. Khan (2005-)

Registrar: Mahboob A. Shah
Tel: +92(621) 925-0235, Fax: +92(621) 925-0235

International Relations: Saqib Aziz Tel: +92(621) 925-0236

Faculties

Arts (Arts and Humanities; Economics; English; Indic Languages; Information Sciences; Library Science; Mass Communication; Political Sciences; Urdu) *Head*: Najeebuddin Jamal; **Education** *Dean*: Aslam Adeeb; **Islamic Learning** (Arabic; History; Islamic Studies; Law; Persian) *Dean*: A.R. Rehmat; **Science** (Chemistry; Computer Science; Geography; Mathematics; Natural Sciences; Pharmacy; Physics; Statistics) *Dean*: Muhammad Moazzam

Institutes

Desert Studies *(Cholistan)* (Arid Land Studies) *Director*: R.M. Iqbal

Further Information: Also 86 affiliated colleges

History: Founded 1975. The University promotes studies and research in Islamic disciplines, social and natural sciences, and humanities.

Governing Bodies: Senate; Syndicate; Academic Council

Academic Year: September to August

Admission Requirements: Intermediate or higher secondary certificate

Fees: (PK Rupees): c. 5,000

Main Language(s) of Instruction: English, Urdu

Accrediting Agencies: Higher Education Commission

Degrees and Diplomas: *Bachelor's Degree*: Arts; Science; Commerce, 2 yrs; *Master's Degree*: a further 2 yrs; *Doctor's Degree (PhD)*: a further 3-6 yrs. Also Doctor of Pharmacy, 5 yrs

Student Services: Academic counselling, Canteen, Foreign student adviser, Health services, Sports facilities

Student Residential Facilities: Yes

Libraries: 125,000 vols, 162 periodical subscriptions

Publications: Journal of Pure and Applied Sciences *(biannually)*; Majulla Uloom-e-Islamia *(biannually)*

UNIVERSITY OF AGRICULTURE, FAISALABAD (UAF)

Faisalabad, Punjab 38040
Tel: +92(41) 920-0161
Fax: +92(41) 6920-0764
EMail: academics@uaf.edu.pk
Website: http://www.uaf.edu.pk

Vice-Chancellor: Iqrar Ahmad Khan
Tel: +92(41) 920-0200, Fax: +92(41) 920-0764
EMail: uaf@fsd.paknet.com.pk

Registrar: Muhammad Hussain
Tel: +92(41) 920-0161, Ext.2000, Fax: +92(41) 920-0764
EMail: registrar@uaf.edu.pk

Divisions

Education and Extension (Education) *Director*: Sher Muhammad

Faculties

Agricultural Economics (Agricultural Economics; Management; Marketing; Rural Studies; Sociology) *Dean*: Zakir Hussain; **Agricultural Engineering and Technology** (Agricultural Engineering; Technology) *Dean*: Muhammad Shafi Sabir; **Agriculture** (Agriculture; Entomology; Soil Science) *Dean*: Muhammed Ashfaq; **Animal Husbandry** (Animal Husbandry) *Dean*: Ihsan Ul-Haq; **Sciences** (Mathematics; Natural Sciences; Statistics) *Dean*: Muhammad Ashraf; **Veterinary Science** (Veterinary Science) *Dean*: Muhammad Siddique

Institutes

Animal Sciences and Food Technology (Food Technology; Zoology) *Director*: Muhammad Sarwar; **Food Science and Technology** *Director*: Faqir Muhammed Anjum; **Horticultural Sciences** (Horticulture) *Director*: Muhammed Aslam Pervez; **Soil and Environmental Sciences** (Environmental Engineering; Soil Science) *Director*: Maqsood Ahmad

History: Founded 1909 as Punjab Agricultural College and Research Institute, acquired present status and title 1961.

Governing Bodies: Syndicate: Senate

Academic Year: Two semesters of 19 weeks, starting September

Admission Requirements: Intermediate Science Certificate, following secondary school education

Fees: (PK Rupees): 275-440 per semester; International students, 45,000-50,000 per annum

Main Language(s) of Instruction: English

International Co-operation: With institutions in USA; China; Germany; United Kingom; France; Korea; Egypt

Degrees and Diplomas: *Bachelor's Degree*: Agriculture; Agricultural Engineering; Veterinary Science, 4 yrs; *Master's Degree*: Agriculture; Agricultural Engineering; Veterinary Science; Social

Science; Basic Science, a further 2 yrs; *Doctor's Degree*: Agriculture; Agricultural Engineering; Veterinary; Social Science; Basic Science (PhD), a further 3-4 yrs

Student Services: Academic counselling, Canteen, Employment services, Foreign Studies Centre, Handicapped facilities, Health services, Language programs, Social counselling, Sports facilities

Student Residential Facilities: Yes

Libraries: c. 181,750 vols

Publications: Pakistan Journal of Agricultural Sciences *(quarterly)*; Pakistan Veterinary Journal *(quarterly)*

Press or Publishing House: University Press

UNIVERSITY OF ARID AGRICULTURE (UAAR)

Shamsabad, Murree Road, Rawalpindi, Punjab 46300
Tel: +92(51) 9290151-2
Fax: +92(51) 9290160
EMail: uaar@yahoo.com
Website: http://www.uaar.edu.pk

Vice-Chancellor: Khalid Mehmood Khan

Registrar: Aslam Farooq Butt

Divisions

Continuing Education, Home Economics and Women Development (Continuing Education; Home Economics; Women's Studies)

Faculties

Agriculture (Agronomy; Animal Husbandry; Crop Production; Entomology; Farm Management; Food Science; Genetics; Horticulture; Plant Pathology; Soil Science) *Dean*: Mushtaq Shaudhry; **Science** (Agricultural Economics; Biology; Botany; Economics; Natural Sciences; Sociology; Statistics; Zoology) *Dean*: Afsar Mian

Institutes

Education and Research (Educational Research) *Director*: Muhammad Iqbal; **Information Technology** *(Barani)* (Information Technology) *Director*: Jamil Sawar; **Management Sciences** (Management) *Director*: M.A. Zaheer

History: Founded 1979 as the Barani (Rain-fed) Agricultural College, Rawalpindi affiliated with the University of Agriculture, Faisalabad. Acquired present status and title 1994.

Governing Bodies: University Syndicate

Academic Year: October to July (Optional Summer session)

Admission Requirements: Higher secondary school certificate

Fees: (PK Rupees): 400-46,000 per annum

Main Language(s) of Instruction: English

Accrediting Agencies: Higher Education Commission

Degrees and Diplomas: *Bachelor's Degree (Honours)*: Business Administration (BBA(Hons)), 3 yrs; *Bachelor's Degree (Honours)*: Science in Agriculture (BSc(Hons)), 4 yrs; *Master's Degree*: Business Administration (MBA), 18 months-2 yrs; *Master's Degree*: Science; Agriculture; Education (MSc), a further 2 yrs; *Master of Philosophy*: Education; *Doctor's Degree*: Agriculture; Biological Sciences; Agro-Economics; Forestry

Student Services: Academic counselling, Canteen, Cultural centre, Employment services, Foreign student adviser, Foreign Studies Centre, Handicapped facilities, Health services, Language programs, Nursery care, Social counselling, Sports facilities

Student Residential Facilities: Yes

Libraries: University Library, 10,500 vols; 1,500 serial titles

Publications: Pakistan Journal of Arid Agriculture *(biannually)*

UNIVERSITY OF AZAD JAMMU AND KASHMIR (AJKU)

Muzaffarabad, Azad Jammu El Kashmir
Tel: +92(5881) 433-28
Fax: +92(5881) 447-17
Website: http://www.ajku.edu.pk/

Vice-Chancellor: Manzoor H. Khan
Tel: +92(51) 9259151, Fax: +92(51) 9259152
EMail: vice.chancellor@ajku.edu.pk

Registrar: Arshad Iqbal Tel: +92(58) 81043228

Centres

Computer Science (Computer Science)

Colleges

Administration *(Kotli)* (Administration; Business Administration; Business and Commerce) *Dean*: Ghalulam Ghous; **Agriculture** *(Rawalakot)* (Agriculture) *Dean*: M. B. Choudhry; **Engineering and Technology** *(Mirpur)* (Electrical Engineering; Electronic Engineering; Engineering; Telecommunications Engineering) *Dean*: M. Nusrullah; **Home Economics** *(Mirpur)* (Home Economics) *Dean*: Saeeda J. A. Shah; **Textile Design** *(Muzaffarabad)* (Textile Design) *Dean*: Saleema Atta

Faculties

Arts *(University College, Muzaffarabad)* (Arts and Humanities; Economics; English; Linguistics; Literature) *Dean*: Ch. Khairat; **Science** *(University College, Muzaffarabad)* (Botany; Chemistry; Computer Science; Mathematics; Natural Sciences; Physics; Zoology) *Dean*: Abdul R. Khan

Institutes

Development Studies (Development Studies); **Geology** (Geology); **Islamic Studies** (Arabic; Economics; Islamic Studies); **Kashmir Studies** (History; Regional Studies)

History: Founded 1980. Constituent units are the main campus (Muzaffarabad) for postgraduate teaching in Natural and Social Sciences; and University Colleges of Engineering (Mirpur); Agriculture (Rawalakot); and Administrative Sciences (Kotli).

Academic Year: September to December (September-May; March-December)

Admission Requirements: Intermediate or higher secondary certificate

Main Language(s) of Instruction: Urdu, English

Degrees and Diplomas: *Bachelor's Degree*: Engineering (BSc); Textile Design (BA), 4 yrs; *Bachelor's Degree*: Law (LLB), a further 2 yrs; *Bachelor's Degree (Honours)*: Agriculture, 4 yrs; *Master's Degree*: Arts (MA); Science (MSc), a further 2 yrs

Student Residential Facilities: For c. 540 students

Libraries: Main Library, 7,000 vols

UNIVERSITY OF BALOCHISTAN (UOB)

Sariab Road, Quetta, Balochistan
Tel: +92(81) 9211288
Fax: +92(81) 9211277
EMail: netadmin@uob.edu.pk; syedarif1999@yahoo.com
Website: http://www.uob.edu.pk/

Vice-Chancellor: Abdul Nabi
Tel: +92(81) 9211288, Fax: +92(81) 9211277
EMail: vc@uob.edu.pk

Director Quality Enhancement Cell: Syed Arif Agha
Tel: +92(82) 9211457 EMail: syedarif1999@yahoo.com

Registrar: Muhammad Iqbal Kasi EMail: registrar@uob.edu.pk

International Relations: Mazar Shai, Principal Staff Officer
Tel: +92(81) 9211268 EMail: mazoo78@hotmail.com

Centres

Mineralogy

Colleges

Law

Faculties

Basic Sciences (Chemistry; Mathematics; Natural Sciences; Physics); **Earth and Enviromental Studies** (Environmental Studies; Geography; Geology; Natural Resources); **Education & Arts and Humanities** (Arts and Humanities; Development Studies; Education; Fine Arts; Gender Studies; History; Islamic Studies; Media Studies; Philosophy; Psychology); **Life Sciences** (Botany; Microbiology; Pharmacy; Zoology); **Litterature and Language** (English; Literature; Native Language Education; Persian; Urdu); **Management Sciences, Business and Information Technology** (Business and Commerce; Computer Science; Economics; Information

Sciences; Information Technology; Library Science; Management); **Social Sciences** (International Relations; Law; Political Sciences; Social Sciences; Social Work)

Institutes

Biochemistry (Biochemistry)

History: Founded 1970.

Academic Year: March to December

Admission Requirements: Intermediate or higher secondary certificate

Main Language(s) of Instruction: English, Urdu

International Co-operation: With universities in Thailand; Iran; Poland

Accrediting Agencies: Quality Assurance Agency; Higher Education Commission

Degrees and Diplomas: *Bachelor's Degree*: 4 yrs; *Master's Degree*: 2 yrs; *Master of Philosophy*: 2 yrs; *Doctor's Degree (PhD)*: 2-3 yrs

Libraries: 3,500 periodical subscriptions. Access to electronic networks: International Journals, E-books

Academic Staff *2009-210*	MEN	WOMEN	TOTAL
FULL-TIME	1,364	245	**1,609**
PART-TIME	117	20	**137**
STAFF WITH DOCTORATE			
FULL-TIME	46	14	**60**
Student Numbers *2009-2010*			
All (Foreign Included)	9,169	1,617	**10,786**
FOREIGN ONLY	17	2	**19**

Last Updated: 29/03/11

UNIVERSITY OF EDUCATION (UE)

College Road, Township, Lahore,
Punjab 54770
Tel: +92(42) 521-6525
Fax: +92(42) 521-6524
EMail: registrar@ue.edu.pk
Website: http://www.ue.edu.pk

Vice-Chancellor: Munawar Sultana Mirza
Tel: +92(42) 521-6521 EMail: vc@ue.edu.pk

Registrar (Acting): Muhammad Saeed Akhtar
Tel: +92(42) 543-5071

International Relations: Muhammad Saeed Akhtar, Registrar (Acting) Tel: +92(42) 543-5072, Fax: +92(42) 543-3634

Divisions

Islamic and Oriental Learning (Islamic Studies; Oriental Studies) *Director*: Khalid Amjad; **Management and Administration** (Administration; Management) *Director*: Zarina Khattak

Faculties

Arts and Social Sciences (Arts and Humanities; Social Sciences) *Dean*: Muzaffar Abbas; **Education** (Education; Teacher Training) *Dean*: Basharat Ali; **Science and Technology** (Natural Sciences; Technology) *Dean*: F. M. Nazar

Institutes

Teacher Education *(Provincial (PITE))* (Distance Education; Teacher Trainers Education) *Director*: Naz Rizvi

Further Information: Also Campuses in Attock; Bank Road (Lahore); Dera Ghazi Khan; Garden Town (Lahore); Faisalabad; Jauharabad, Lower Mall (Lahore); Multan; Okara; Township (Lahore); Vehari

History: Founded 2002.

Governing Bodies: Syndicate

Fees: (PK Rupees): 12,225-52,750

Main Language(s) of Instruction: English

Accrediting Agencies: Higher Education Commission

Degrees and Diplomas: *Bachelor's Degree (Honours)*: Mathematics, Chemistry, Zoology (BS(Hons), BBA(Hons)), 4 1/2 yrs; *Bachelor's Degree (Pass)*: Elementary, Secondary, Special Education (Bed; BA Bed, BSc Bed, BFA Bed), 1 1/2-2 1/2 yrs; *Master's Degree*: Education, Special Education, Physics, Chemistry, Mathematics; Education Leadership and Management (Med), 1 1/2 - 2 1/2 yrs; *Master of Philosophy*: Urdu, English, 2 1/2 yrs; *Doctor's Degree*: Education, Urdu (PhD), 4 1/2 yrs

Student Services: Academic counselling, Canteen, Health services

Student Residential Facilities: Yes

Special Facilities: Computer

Libraries: Yes

Last Updated: 20/11/08

UNIVERSITY OF ENGINEERING AND TECHNOLOGY, LAHORE (UETL)

Grand Trunk Road, Lahore, Punjab 54890
Tel: +92(42) 6822012
Fax: +92(42) 6822566
EMail: webmaster@uet.edu.pk
Website: http://www.uet.edu.pk

Departments

Architecture (Architecture and Planning) *Chairman*: Ikram Ali Shah Gilani; **Chemical Engineering** (Chemical Engineering; Polymer and Plastics Technology) *Chairman*: A.K. Salariya; **Chemistry** (Chemistry) *Chairman*: M. Amjad; **Civil Engineering** (Civil Engineering) *Chairman*: Faiz Ahmad Chishti; **Computer Science** (Computer Science) *Chairman*: Aftab Ahmad Malik; **Electrical Engineering** (Electrical Engineering) *Chairman*: Noor Muhammad Sheikh; **Environmental Engineering and Research** (Environmental Engineering) *Chairman*: Javed Anwar Aziz; **Humanities** (Arts and Humanities) *Chairman*: Syed Masood Haider Zaidi; **Islamic Studies** (Islamic Studies) *Chairman*: M. Yahya Chaudhry; **Mathematics** (Mathematics) *Chairman*: Nawazish Ali Shah; **Mechanical Engineering** (Industrial Engineering; Mechanical Engineering; Production Engineering) *Chairman*: Iqbal Hussain; **Metallurgical and Materials Engineering** (Materials Engineering; Metallurgical Engineering) *Chairman*: Faizul Hassan; **Mining and Geological Engineering** (Geological Engineering; Mining Engineering) *Chairman*: Rana M. Tayyub; **Petroleum Engineering** (Petroleum and Gas Engineering) *Chairman*: Ahmad Saeed Khan; **Physics** (Physics) *Chairman*: M. Khaleeq-ur-Rehman; **Town and Regional Planning** (Regional Planning; Town Planning; Transport Engineering) *Chairman*: S. Shabihul Hassan Zaidi

Faculties

Architecture and Planning (Architecture and Planning) *Dean*: Mahmood Hussain; **Chemical, Mineral and Metallurgical Engineering** (Chemical Engineering; Metallurgical Engineering; Mining Engineering) *Dean*: Ali Ahmad Khokhar; **Civil Engineering** (Civil Engineering) *Dean*: Javed Anwar Aziz; **Electrical Engineering** (Electrical and Electronic Engineering) *Dean*: K.E. Durrani; **Mechanical Engineering** (Industrial Engineering; Mechanical Engineering; Production Engineering) *Dean*: Iqbal Hussain; **Natural Sciences, Humanities, and Islamic Studies** (Arts and Humanities; Islamic Studies; Natural Sciences) *Dean*: M. Nasir Chaudhry

Further Information: Also 1 constituent and 9 affiliated colleges

History: Founded 1923 as Maclegon Technical College, acquired present name and status 1961.

Governing Bodies: Senate; Syndicate; Academic Council

Academic Year: January to December

Admission Requirements: Higher secondary school certificate or equivalent

Fees: (PK Rupees): Tuition, 500-5,000 per month

Main Language(s) of Instruction: English

Accrediting Agencies: Pakistan Engineering Council

Degrees and Diplomas: *Bachelor's Degree*: Architecture (BArch), 5 yrs; *Bachelor's Degree*: Engineering (BSc/BScEng), 4 yrs; *Master's Degree*: Engineering (MSc/MScEng), a further 2 yrs; *Master of Philosophy (MPhil)*; *Doctor's Degree (PhD)*: 4 yrs

Student Residential Facilities: Yes

Special Facilities: Museum. Observatory

Libraries: National Library of Engineering Sciences

UNIVERSITY OF ENGINEERING AND TECHNOLOGY, TAXILA (UET)

Taxila, Punjab 47050
Tel: +92(596) 9314216-23
Fax: +92(596) 9047420
Website: http://www.uettaxila.edu.pk

Vice-Chancellor: Habibullah Jamal
Tel: +92(51) 9047401 EMail: dr_hjamal@uettaxila.edu.pk

Registrar: Aziz-ur-Rehman Tel: +92(51) 9047405

Faculties

Basic Sciences and Humanities (Arts and Humanities; Mathematics; Natural Sciences); **Civil and Environmental Engineering** (Civil Engineering; Environmental Engineering); **Computer Engineering** (Computer Engineering); **Electronics and Electrical Engineering** (Electrical Engineering; Electronic Engineering); **Industrial Engineering** (Industrial Engineering); **Mechanical and Aeronautical Engineering** (Aeronautical and Aerospace Engineering; Mechanical Engineering)

History: Founded 1975 as Constituent College of University of Engineering and Technology, Lahore, acquired present status and title 1993.

Governing Bodies: Academic Council; Syndicate

Academic Year: September to May

Admission Requirements: Intermediate pre-Engineering Science Certificate, following secondary school certificate

Main Language(s) of Instruction: English

Degrees and Diplomas: *Bachelor's Degree*: Engineering, 4 yrs; *Master's Degree*: a further 1-2 yrs; *Doctor's Degree*: Engineering

Student Residential Facilities: For c. 1,100 students

Libraries: c. 23,000 vols

UNIVERSITY OF GUJRAT

Fowra Chock, Gujrat
Tel: +92(53) 9260271-3
Fax: +92(53) 9260270
EMail: info@uog.edu.pk
Website: http://www.uog.edu.pk/

Vice-Chancellor: Mohammad Nizamuddin
Tel: +92(53) 9260272-3 Ext: 801

Deputy Registrar: Tanzeela Qamar
Tel: +92(53) 9260272-3 Ext: 801 EMail: tanzilagill@hotmail.com

Faculties

Arts, Crafts and Product Design; **Basic Sciences** (Mathematics and Computer Science; Natural Sciences); **Behavioral and Social Sciences** (Behavioural Sciences; Social Sciences); **Business Administration** (Business Administration); **Information Technology**

Degrees and Diplomas: *Bachelor's Degree*; *Master's Degree*: Arts, Crafts and Design; Business Administration; Business Information Technology; Computer Sciences and Information Technology; Mathematics; Statistics; Sociology; Psychology; English

UNIVERSITY OF HEALTH SCIENCES

Khayaban-e-Jamia Punjab, Lahore, Punjab 54600
Tel: +92(42) 923-1304-9
Fax: +92(42) 923-0870
EMail: vc@uhs.edu.pk
Website: http://www.uhs.edu.pk

Vice-Chancellor: Malik Hussain Mubbashar (2003-)
Tel: +92(42) 923-0396, Fax: +92(42) 923-0131
EMail: vcuhspk@gmail.com; malikh@isb.paknet.com.pk

Departments

Allied Health Sciences (Health Sciences); **Anatomy**; **Biochemistry** (Biochemistry); **Biomedical Engineering**; **Environmental Health**; **Family Medicine** (Medicine); **Human Genetics and Biotechnology** (Biotechnology; Genetics); **Immunology**; **Microbiology** (Microbiology); **Nursing** (Nursing); **Pathology** (Pathology); **Pharmacology**; **Physiology**

Further Information: Also 20 Medical & Dental Colleges, 7 Institutes of post graduate education, 18 Allied Health Sciences and 5 post graduate Nursing Colleges, located in different cities of the province of Punjab.

History: History of affiliated colleges dates back to 1930s. University regulates and coordinates all the activities of Medical Education throughout the province of Punjab.

Governing Bodies: Board of Governors, Academic Council, Syndicate and Board of Studies

Academic Year: January to December

Fees: (PK Rupees): public colleges, 15,000 per annum; private colleges, 375,000

Main Language(s) of Instruction: English

International Co-operation: With universities in the USA, China, Germany, France, United Kingdom

Accrediting Agencies: Pakistan Medical and Dental Council, World Health Organization (WHO), United States Medical Licensing Authority, General Medical Council UK, Medical Council Ireland

Degrees and Diplomas: *Bachelor's Degree*: Dentistry (BDS); Nursing; Allied Health Sciences (BSc), 4 yrs; *Bachelor's Degree*: Medicine; Surgery (MBBS), 5 yrs; *Bachelor's Degree*: Paramedical Sciences; Electro-Medical Engineering; Laboratory Technology; Physiotherapy (B.Sc.); *Bachelor's Degree (Honours)*: Medical Imaging Technology (B.Sc.(Hons)); *Master's Degree*: Nursing; Medical Technology; Biomedical Engineering (MSc); *Master's Degree*: Surgery; Dental Surgery; Public Health; Hospital Management; Maternal and Child Health, a further 2 yrs; *Master of Philosophy*: Anatomy; Physiology; Cell Biology; Histopathology and Morbid Anatomy; Immunology; Microbiology; Human Genetics, Biotechnology; Pharmacology; Biochemistry (Mphil), 2-4 yrs; *Doctor's Degree*: Medicine (PhD), 2-6 yrs. Also MBBS; BDS and Postgraduate Diplomas

Student Services: Academic counselling, Canteen, Foreign student adviser, Foreign Studies Centre, Health services, Social counselling, Sports facilities

Student Residential Facilities: Yes

Libraries: Yes
Last Updated: 28/11/08

UNIVERSITY OF KARACHI (KU)

University Road, Karachi, Sindh 75270
Tel: +92(21) 926-1336 +92(21) 926-1337
Fax: +92(21) 926-13340
EMail: vcku@cyber.net.pk
Website: http://www.uok.edu.pk/

Vice-Chancellor: Muhammad Qaiser EMail: vc@ku.edu.pk

Registrar: Muhammad Raees Alvi
Tel: +92(21) 926-1326, Fax: +92(21) 926-1343

Faculties

Arts (Arabic; Economics; Education; English; History; Indic Languages; Information Sciences; International Relations; Islamic Studies; Library Science; Mass Communication; Persian; Philosophy; Political Sciences; Psychology; Public Administration; Social Work; Sociology; Special Education; Urdu) *Dean*: Muhammad Shamsuddin; **Business Administration and Commerce** (Business Administration; Business and Commerce) *Head*: Muhammad Shamsuddin; **Education** (Education) *Dean*: Muhammad Shamsuddin; **Islamic Studies** (Islamic Studies) *Dean*: Jalauddin Ahmed Noori; **Law** (Law) *Dean*: Mamoon Hussain; **Medicine** (Medicine) *Dean*: Saadiya Aziz Karim; **Pharmacy** (Chemistry; Pharmacology; Pharmacy) *Dean*: Najma Sultana; **Science** (Applied Chemistry; Applied Physics; Biochemistry; Botany; Chemistry; Computer Science; Food Science; Food Technology; Genetics; Geography; Geology; Mathematics; Microbiology; Physics; Physiology; Statistics; Zoology) *Dean*: Shaikh Ajaz Rasool

Further Information: Also 8 Affiliated Institutes/Centres

History: Founded 1950.

Governing Bodies: Senate; Syndicate

Academic Year: January to December

Admission Requirements: Intermediate or higher secondary certificate

Fees: (PK Rupees): Morning courses, 1,000-14,000 per semester; evening courses, 6,000-20,000 per semester

Main Language(s) of Instruction: English; Urdu

Accrediting Agencies: Higher Education Commission

Degrees and Diplomas: *Bachelor's Degree*: Business & Commerce (B.Com), 2 yrs; *Bachelor's Degree*: Food Science & Technology; Computer Science; Applied Chemistry; Software Engineering (BS; BCT; BSSE), 4 yrs; *Bachelor's Degree*: Law; Business Administration; Public Administration (BL; BBA; BPA), 3 yrs; *Bachelor's Degree*: Medicine; Pharmacy (MBBS; Pharm-D), 5 yrs; *Bachelor's Degree (Honours)*: Architecture (BSc (Hons.)), 5 yrs; *Bachelor's Degree (Honours)*: Arts; Science (BA (Hons); BSc (Hons)), 3 yrs; *Bachelor's Degree (Honours)*: Industrial Design; Graphic Design; Textile Design; Ceramic Art; Fine Arts; Islamic Art; Art History (BA (Hons.)), 4 yrs; *Master's Degree*: Business Administration; Computer Science; Public Administration (MBA; MCS; MPA/ MAS), a further 2 yrs; *Master's Degree*: Natural Sciences; Mathematics & Computer Science; Business & Commerce; Law (MSc; MA; M.Com; LL.M), 1 further yr; *Master of Philosophy (M.Phil)*: a further 2 yrs; *Doctor's Degree (PhD)*: 3 yrs following MA, MSc

Student Services: Academic counselling, Canteen, Cultural centre, Employment services, Foreign student adviser, Health services, Language programs, Social counselling, Sports facilities

Student Residential Facilities: Boys Hostel; Girl Hostel

Special Facilities: Museum; Art Gallery; Observatory; Movie studio

Libraries: Dr. Mahmoud Husain Library, c. 300,000 vols; 42 foreign journals

Publications: Journal of Botany *(biannually)*; Journal of Pharmaceutical Science *(biannually)*; Journal of Pharmacology *(biannually)*; Journal of Science *(biannually)*; Karachi University Journal of Islamic Studies *(biannually)*; Karachi University Journal of Mass Communication *(annually)*; Karachi University Journal of Social Sciences *(annually)*; The Islamic Culture *(quarterly)*

Press or Publishing House: Karachi University Press

UNIVERSITY OF MALAKAND (UOM)

Chakdara, Dir, Malakand, North West Frontier Province
Tel: +92(945) 763442
Fax: +92(945) 763491
EMail: ajabk66@yahoo.com
Website: http://www.uom.edu.pk/

Programmes

Biotechnology (Biotechnology); **B-Pharmacy** (Pharmacy); **Computer Science** (Computer Science); **English** (English); **Forestry** (Forestry); **Management Studies** (Business Administration); **Mathematics** (Mathematics); **Sociology** (Sociology)

History: Founded 2001.

Degrees and Diplomas: *Bachelor's Degree*; *Master's Degree*; *Master of Philosophy*; *Doctor's Degree*: Botany; Management; Mathematics; Organic Chemistry

UNIVERSITY OF PESHAWAR (PUP)

Peshawar, North West Frontier Province
Tel: +92(91) 9216469
Fax: +92(91) 9216470
EMail: administration@upesh.edu.pk
Website: http://www.upesh.edu.pk

Vice-Chancellor: Haroon Rashid
Tel: +92(91) 9216469 EMail: vice_chancellor@upesh.edu.pk

Registrar: Sher Bahadur
Tel: +92(91) 9216471 EMail: registrar@upesh.edu.pk

International Relations: Rubina Khilji
Tel: +92(91) 9216285 EMail: rubina_khilji@hotmail.com

Centres

Area Studies (Regional Studies) *Director*: Azmat Hayat Khan; **Geology** (Geology) *Director*: Mohd. Asif Khan; **Pakistan Studies** (Southeast Asian Studies) *Director*: Peruaiz-A Toru; **Physical Chemistry** (Physical Chemistry) *Director*: Mustafa Syed

Colleges

Commerce *(Quaid-E-.Azam)* (Business and Commerce) *Principal (Acting)*: Ghulam Taqi; **Home Economics** (Home Economics) *Principal*: Simin Masud; **Women** *(Jinnah)* (Women's Studies) *Principal*: Sajida Noor

Faculties

Arts (Anthropology; Archaeology; Economics; English; European Languages; Fine Arts; History; Information Sciences; International Relations; Journalism; Library Science; Management; Philosophy; Political Sciences; Psychology; Social Work; Sociology) *Dean*: Ghulam Taqi Bangash; **Education** (Education) *Dean*: Zulfiqar-H. Gillani; **Islamic Studies and Arabic** (Arabic; Islamic Studies) *Dean*: Saeed Ullah Gazi; **Law** (Law) *Dean*: Ahmed Ali Khan; **Oriental Languages** (Oriental Languages; Persian; Urdu) *Dean*: Ghulam Nasir; **Science** (Botany; Chemistry; Computer Science; Electronic Engineering; Environmental Studies; Geography; Geology; Mathematics; Natural Sciences; Pharmacy; Physics; Statistics) *Dean*: Nasiruddin Nasir

Institutes

Management Studies (Management)

Further Information: Also 43 Affiliated Colleges and 14 constituent Research Institutes/Stations

History: Founded 1950.

Governing Bodies: Syndicate; Senate

Admission Requirements: Higher secondary certificate, at least second class (Pre-medical or Pre-engineering)

Fees: According to programme

Main Language(s) of Instruction: English

International Co-operation: With universities in Germany, United Kingdom

Degrees and Diplomas: *Bachelor's Degree (Honours) (B.A., B.Sc (Hon))*: 4 yrs; *Master's Degree (M.A., M.Sc)*: a further 2 yrs; *Master of Philosophy (M.Phil)*; *Doctor's Degree (Ph.D)*. The Master's Degree is also awarded with honours

Student Services: Canteen, Health services, Language programs, Sports facilities

Student Residential Facilities: Yes

Special Facilities: Museum

Libraries: c. 80,000 vols

Publications: Al-Suna Sharquia (Peshawar University Journal) *(annually)*; Arts and Letters; Central Asia *(annually)*; Geological Bulletin *(annually)*; Journal of Education and Research *(annually)*; Journal of Humanities and Social Sciences *(annually)*; Journal of Law and Society *(annually)*; Journal of Science and Technology *(annually)*; Pakistan Journal of Geography *(annually)*; Pashto *(annually)*; Research Journal *(annually)*; Scientific Khyber

UNIVERSITY OF SARGODHA

Sargodha, Punjab
Tel: +92(451) 9230170
Fax: +92(451) 3222121
EMail: vc@uos.edu.pk
Website: http://www.uos.edu.pk/

Vice-Chancellor: Mohammad Akram Chaudary
EMail: akramch50@hotmail.com

Registrar: M.B. Awan
Tel: +92(451) 9230802, Fax: +92(451) 9230837
EMail: registrar@uos.edu.pk

Faculties

Agriculture (Agriculture; Food Science; Nutrition); **Arts and Social Sciences and Law** (Communication Studies; Education; English; Fine Arts; History; Law; Library Science; Physical Education; Political Sciences; Psychology; Social Work; Sociology); **Islamic and Oriental Languages** (Islamic Studies; Oriental Languages); **Management and Business Administration** (Business Administration; Business and Commerce; Economics); **Medical and Health Science** (Dietetics; Medicine; Physical Therapy); **Pharmacy** (Pharmacy); **Science** (Biological and Life Sciences; Chemistry; Computer Science; Earth Sciences; Mathematics; Physics; Statistics)

History: Founded 2002.

Degrees and Diplomas: *Diploma*; *Bachelor's Degree*; *Master's Degree*; *Master of Philosophy*; *Doctor's Degree*

Last Updated: 01/12/08

UNIVERSITY OF SCIENCE AND TECHNOLOGY

Miran Shah Road, Bannu
Tel: +92(928) 621-123 +92(928) 620-829
Website: http://www.ustb.edu.pk/documents/23.html

Vice-Chancellor: Asmatullah Khan Tel: +91(928) 624-088
Registrar: Sifath Ullah Khan Tel: +91(928) 620-827

Departments

Chemistry (Chemistry) *Chair*: Saeed Ahmed; **Physics** (Physics) *Coordinator*: Aman Ullah Khan

Institutes

Biotechnology and Botany (Biotechnology; Botany) *Coordinator*: D Subhan; **Education and Research** *Coordinator*: Saeed Khan; **Information Technology** (Computer Science; Software Engineering) *Coordinator*: Aurangzeb Khan; **Management Sciences** *Coordinator*: Aman Ullah Awan

Governing Bodies: Chancellor's Committee

Admission Requirements: HSC or equivalent for undergraduate; Bachelor's degree or equivalent for postgraduate

Degrees and Diplomas: *Bachelor's Degree*: Banking and Finance; Software Engineering; Computer Sciences (BSc); Business Administration and Information Technology (BBA (IT)), 4 yrs; *Bachelor's Degree*: Education (Bed), 1 yr; *Bachelor's Degree (Honours)*: Business Administration (BBA); Chemistry; Physics; Botany; Biotechnology (BSc), 4 yrs; *Master's Degree*: Business Administration (MBA); Chemistry; Physics; Botany; Computer Sciences (MSc); Education (Med), a further 2 yrs; *Master of Philosophy*: Education (Mphil), a further 2 yrs

UNIVERSITY OF SINDH (SU)

Allama I.I. Kazi Campus, Jamshoro, Sindh 76080
Tel: +92(221) 771-681
Fax: +92(221) 771-372
EMail: info@usindh.edu.pk
Website: http://www.usindh.edu.pk

Vice-Chancellor: Mazharul Haq Siddiqui (2001-)
Tel: +92(221) 771-363, Fax: +92(221) 771-246
EMail: vc@usindh.edu.pk

Registrar: Saeed Ahmed Soomro
Tel: +92(221) 771-284, Fax: +92(221) 772-002
EMail: registrar@usindh.edu.pk

International Relations: M. Rais Ahmed, Consultant on Higher Education
Tel: +92(221) 772-657 +92(221) 771-681 Ext. 681,
Fax: +92(221) 772-002 EMail: consultantonh_ed@yahoo.com

Centres

Analytical Chemistry *(Excellence)* (Analytical Chemistry; Chemistry; Industrial Chemistry) *Director*: Iqbal A. Bhangar; **Environmental Sciences** (Ecology; Environmental Studies; Sanitary Engineering) *Director*: Mushtaque Ahmed Baloch; **Far East and South East Asian Studies** (East Asian Studies; Southeast Asian Studies) *Director*: Lutfullah Mangi; **Health and Physical Education** (Health Sciences; Physical Education; Physical Therapy; Sports Management; Sports Medicine) *Director*: Yasmeen Iqbal Qureshi; **Pakistan Studies** (Cultural Studies; Economics; Geography; Industrial and Production Economics; Middle Eastern Studies; Political Sciences) *Director*: Rafia Ahmed Shaikh; **Pure and Applied Geology** (Geology) *Director*: Parveen Akhtar Usmani; **Sindh Development Studies** (Development Studies; Economics; Regional Studies; Rural Studies) *Director*: Abida Tahrani

Faculties

Arts *(Master)* (Arabic; Arts and Humanities; English; Fine Arts; Oriental Languages; Persian; Philosophy; Urdu) *Dean*: Muhammad Qasim Bughio; **Commerce and Business Administration** *(Also MBA Executive Evening programme at Elsa Kazi Campus, Hyderabad)* (Business Administration; Business and Commerce) *Dean*: Anwar Ali Shah G. Syed; **Education** *(Elsa Kazi Campus, Hyderabad)* (Adult Education; Distance Education; Education; Educational Sciences; Higher Education; Primary Education; Secondary Education) *Dean*: Iqbal Ahmed Panhwar; **Islamic Studies** *(Elsa Kazi Campus, Hyderabad)* (Comparative Religion; History of Religion; Islamic Studies; Religion; Religious Practice; Religious Studies; Sociology) *Dean*: Sanaullah Bhutto; **Law** *(Restricted to Bachelor degree at Colleges in Hyderabad, Dadu and Nawabshah)* (Law) *Dean*: Ahmed Ali Shaikh; **Natural Sciences** (Biological and Life Sciences; Chemistry; Computer Science; Earth Sciences; Information Technology; Mathematics; Natural Sciences; Physics) *Dean*: Muhammad Yar Khuhawar; **Social Sciences** (Communication Studies; Criminology; Economics; International Studies; Political Sciences; Psychology; Social Sciences; Sociology; Sports; Welfare and Protective Services) *Dean*: Rafia Ahmed Shaikh

Institutes

Arts and Design (Design; Fine Arts) *Director*: Muhammad Ali Bhatti; **Biochemistry** (Biochemistry) *Director*: Allah Nawaz Memon; **Biotechnology and Genetic Engineering** (Biotechnology; Genetics) *Director*: Muhammad Umar Dahot; **Information Technology** (Information Technology) *Director*: Abdul Wahab Ansari; **Mathematics and Computer Science** (Mathematics and Computer Science) *Director*: Noor Ahmed Shaikh; **Physics** (Physics) *Director*: Muhammad Maroof Khushk

Further Information: Also 74 affiliated colleges, (58 general degree colleges and 5 law colleges offering Bachelor courses in Humanities, Science, Commerce (2 yrs) and in Law (3 yrs), 18 private affiliated colleges offering courses in Computer Science, Business Administration (3 yrs))

History: Founded 1947 in Karachi. Relocated in Hyderabad and acquired present status and title 1951.

Governing Bodies: Senate, Syndicate, Academic Council

Academic Year: January to December

Admission Requirements: Intermediate or higher secondary certificate and pre-entry test for all programmes

Fees: (PK Rupees): 600-1,200 per semester

Main Language(s) of Instruction: English

International Co-operation: With universities in United Kingdom, USA, China, Japan, Bangladesh, Malaysia

Accrediting Agencies: Higher Education Commission

Degrees and Diplomas: *Bachelor's Degree*: Information Technology; Computer Science; Mathematics; Statistics; Biotechnology; Biochemistry; Botany; Entomology; Genetics; Microbiology; Physiology; Zoology; Chemistry; Earth Sciences (BS), 4 yrs; *Bachelor's Degree (Honours)*: Arts and Humanities; Commerce; Education; Sciences (BSc, BA, BEd, Bcom), 3 yrs; *Bachelor's Degree (Pass)*: Arts and Humanities; Commerce; Education; Science (BSc, BA, BEd, Bcom), 2 yrs; *Bachelor's Degree (Pass)*: Education (Bed); Health and Physical Education (BHPEd); *Master's Degree*: Arts and Humanities; Islamic Studies; Social Sciences (MA); Business Administration (MBA); Commerce (MCom); Public Administration (MPA), a further 1-2 yrs; *Master's Degree*: Education (MEd), a further 1-2 yrs after Bed; *Master's Degree*: Health and Physical Education (MHPE), a further 1 yr after BHPE; *Master of Philosophy*: Arts and Humanities; Natural Sciences; Social Sciences (Mphil), a further 2 yrs; *Master of Philosophy*: Science (MS), a further 1-2 yrs; *Doctor's Degree*: Arts and Humanities; Natural Sciences; Social Sciences (PhD), at least 3 yrs following Master's. Post-graduate Diploma in Library, Information Science and Archives, Special Education and Public Administration. Master's Degree in Rural Development Studies under distance education (off campus) programme. Post Graduate Diploma in various branches of Medical and Health Computer Sciences, Information Technology

Student Services: Academic counselling, Canteen, Cultural centre, Foreign Studies Centre, Health services, Social counselling, Sports facilities

Student Residential Facilities: For 2,600 students

Special Facilities: Anthropological Research Museum. Mohtarma Benazir Bhutto Gallery. Photography Gallery. Musical Gallery. Departmental Geology and Zoology Museum. Herbarium in Botany. Greenhouse

Libraries: c. 255,800 vols

Publications: 'ARIAL' Journal of the English Department *(annually)*; 'KEENJHAR' Journal of Sindhi Department *(annually)*; 'PEACE' Research Journal of the Faculty of Islamic Studies *(annually)*; Sindh University Journal of Education *(annually)*; Sindh University Research Journal (Arts Series) *(annually)*; Sindh University Research Journal (Science Series) *(biannually)*; Sindh University Research Journal of Social Sciences *(annually)*; 'TAHQIQUE' Research Journal of Urdu Department *(annually)*

Press or Publishing House: Sindh University Press

UNIVERSITY OF SWAT

Mingora, Khyber Pakhtunkhwa 19300
Tel: +92(946) 924-0006
Fax: +92(946) 726-166
EMail: info@uswat.edu.pk
Website: http://uswat.edu.pk/

Vice-Chancellor: Muhammad Jahanzeb Khan
EMail: vc@uswat.edu.pk

Registrar: Mehboob ur Rahman Rahman
Tel: +92(946) 924-0066, Fax: +92(946) 726-165
EMail: registrar@uswat.edu.pk

Departments

Computer and Software Technology (Computer Science; Software Engineering); **Environmental Science** (Environmental Management; Environmental Studies); **Journalism and Mass Communication** (Journalism; Mass Communication); **Law and Shari'a** (Islamic Law; Law); **Mathematics and Statistics** (Mathematics; Statistics); **Psychology** (Psychology); **Zoology** (Zoology)

Institutes

Biotechnology and Microbiology (Biotechnology; Microbiology); **Cultural Heritage, Tourism and Hospitality Management** (Cultural Studies; Heritage Preservation; Hotel Management; Tourism); **Economics, Social and Development Studies** (Development Studies; Economics); **Plant Sciences** (Botany; Plant and Crop Protection)

Schools

Education and Staff Training (Education; Teacher Training); **Management and Commerce** (Business Administration; Business and Commerce)

History: Created 2010,

Governing Bodies: Senate; Syndicate

Academic Year: spring (Sep to Jan); autumn (Mar to July)

Admission Requirements: Undergraduate, minimum 45% in HSSC (12 years of education)

Fees: (PKR): 9,300, undergraduate; 13,900, postgraduate,

Main Language(s) of Instruction: English

Accrediting Agencies: Higher Education Commission (HEC)

Degrees and Diplomas: *Bachelor's Degree*: Software Engineering; Biotechnology; Microbiology; Economics; Development Studies; Education; Environmental Sciences; Law and Shari'a; Statistics; Botany; Zoology; Psychology; *Bachelor's Degree (Honours)*: Business Administration; *Master's Degree*: Computer Science; Business Administration; Botany; Environmental Sciences; Microbiology; Psychology; Zoology; Journalism and Mass Communication; Law; *Master of Philosophy*: Botany; *Doctor's Degree*: Botany

Student Services: Canteen, Sports facilities

Publications: Pakistan Journal of Applied Social Sciences *(annually)*

Academic Staff *2012-2013*	MEN	WOMEN	**TOTAL**
FULL-TIME	163	19	**182**
PART-TIME	21	6	**27**
STAFF WITH DOCTORATE			
FULL-TIME	6	–	**6**
Student Numbers *2012-2013*			
All (Foreign Included)	1,248	163	**1,411**

Evening students, 465.
Last Updated: 31/01/13

UNIVERSITY OF THE PUNJAB, LAHORE (PU)

P.O. Box No. 54590, Lahore, Punjab 54590
Tel: +92(55) 9200985
Fax: +92(55) 9201223
EMail: registrar@pu.edu.pk
Website: http://www.pu.edu.pk

Vice-Chancellor: Arshad Mahmood
Tel: +92(42) 9231099, Fax: +92(42) 9231101
EMail: vc@pu.edu.pk

Registrar: Muhammad Naeem Khan
Tel: +92(42) 9231102, Fax: +92(42) 9231103

International Relations: Rashid Khan Barak Zai
Tel: +92(42) 923-1127

Colleges

Commerce *(Hailey)* (Business and Commerce) *Principal*: Nazir Ahmad; **Information Technology** *(PUCIT)* (Computer Science; Information Technology) *Director*: Asad Maqbool; **Law** (Law) *Principal*: D.M. Malik; **Oriental Studies** (Arabic; Asian Studies; French; Indic Languages; Middle Eastern Studies; Oriental Languages; Persian; Urdu) *Principal*: Akram M. Chaudhary

Faculties

Arts (Administration; Business Administration; Design; Economics; English; Fine Arts; French; History; Library Science; Mass Communication; Philosophy; Political Sciences; Social Work; Sociology) *Dean*: A.R. Butt; **Commerce** (Business and Commerce) *Dean*: M.A. Akram; **Education** (Education) *Dean*: Zafar M. Iqbal; **Engineering and Technology** (Chemical Engineering; Engineering; Materials Engineering; Metallurgical Engineering; Petroleum and Gas Engineering; Technology) *Dean*: Arif M. Butt; **Islamic and Oriental Studies** (Arabic; French; Indic Languages; Islamic Studies; Persian; Urdu) *Dean*: Akram M. Chaudhary; **Pharmacy** (Pharmacy); **Science** (Applied Mathematics; Astronomy and Space Science; Biochemistry; Biotechnology; Botany; Environmental Studies; Geography; Geology; Home Economics; Information Technology; Mathematics; Natural Sciences; Physics; Psychology; Statistics; Zoology) *Dean*: Waheed M. Akhtar

Institutes

Business Administration (Business Administration) *Director*: Ehsan M. Malik; **Chemical Engineering and Technology** (Chemical Engineering; Engineering; Materials Engineering; Metallurgical Engineering; Petroleum and Gas Engineering; Technology) *Director*: Shafqat Nawaz; **Chemistry** (Chemistry) *Director*: Jamil A. Chaudhary; **Education and Research** (Education; Educational Research) *Director*: Munawar S. Mirza; **Geology** (Geology) *Director*: Shafiq Ahmad; **Statistics** (Statistics) *Director*: A.S. Akhtar

Further Information: Also 13 research centres, and 373 affiliated colleges

History: Founded 1882, the University is the oldest in Pakistan. Acquired present status 2002. Former Faculty of Medicine and Dentistry (Kind Edward Medical College) granted full university status 2005. See 'King Edward Medical University'.

Governing Bodies: Senate

Academic Year: September to August

Admission Requirements: Intermediate Certificate or recognized equivalent

Main Language(s) of Instruction: English, Urdu

International Co-operation: 36 International Research Collaboration programmes

Accrediting Agencies: Higher Education Commission

Degrees and Diplomas: *Diploma*: Education; Library Science; Law; Linguistics, 1 yr; *Bachelor's Degree*: Applied Geology (BScAppGeo); Fine Arts (BFA); Science Education (BScEd), 3 yrs; *Bachelor's Degree*: Arts (BA); Commerce (BCom); Law (LLB); Physiotherapy; Science (BSc); Space Science (BScSpSc), 2 yrs; *Bachelor's Degree*: Dental Surgery (BDS); Engineering (BScEng); Home Economics (BSc(HEco)); Medicine and Surgery (MBBS); Pharmacy (Ppharm), 4 yrs; *Master's Degree*: Arts; Commerce (Mcom); Dental Surgery (MDS); Education (MEd); Home Economics (MSc(HEco)); Law (LLM); Pharmacy (MPharm), a further 1-2 yrs; *Master's Degree*: Engineering; Science Education (MSed), 2 yrs; *Master of Philosophy*: a further 1-2 yrs; *Master of Philosophy*: Surgery (MS), a further 1-2 yrs; *Doctor's Degree*: Botany; Zoology; Biology; Economics; Management; Business Administration; Education; Medicine; Pharmacy (MD); Philosophy; History; Political Sciences; Communication Studies; English; Arabic; South Asian Studies; Pakistan Studies; Islamic Studies (PhD). Also 1- to 2- year Postgraduate Diplomas

Student Services: Academic counselling, Canteen, Cultural centre, Employment services, Foreign student adviser, Foreign Studies Centre, Health services, Language programs, Nursery care, Social counselling, Sports facilities

Student Residential Facilities: Yes

Special Facilities: Observatory

Libraries: Punjab University Library, 1,120,495 vols; 42 Department Libraries, c. 8.9m. Vols

Press or Publishing House: Punjab University Press

UNIVERSITY OF VETERINARY AND ANIMAL SCIENCES

Out Fall Road, Lahore, Punjab 54000
Tel: +92(42) 920-0476
Fax: +92(42) 921-1461
EMail: uvas@yahoo.com
Website: http://www.uvas.edu.pk

Vice-Chancellor: Talat Naseer Pasha Tel: +92(42) 921-1476

Registrar: Attique Ahmad

International Relations: Nasim Ahmad
EMail: drnasim@yahoo.com

Divisions

Advanced Studies *Director*: Makhdoom Abdul Jabbar; **Research** *Director*: Nasim Ahmad

Faculties

Animal Production and Technology *(FAPT) Dean*: Muhammad Abdullah; **Bio-Sciences** *(FBS)* (Anatomy; Biochemistry; Histology; Pharmacology; Physiology; Social Sciences; Toxicology) *Dean*: Muhammad Ashraf; **Fisheries and Wildlife** *(FFWM)* (Aquaculture; Ecology; Fishery; Wildlife) *Dean*: Naureen Aziz Qureshi; **Life Sciences Business Management** (Animal Husbandry; Business Administration; Computer Science; Information Technology; Statistics) *Dean*: Talat Naseer Pasha; **Livestock Business Management** *(FLBM)* (Business Administration; Computer Science; Economics; Statistics) *Dean*: Talat Naseer Pasha; **Veterinary Sciences** (Animal Husbandry; Epidemiology; Medicine; Microbiology; Parasitology; Pathology; Public Health; Surgery; Veterinary Science) *Dean*: Nasim Ahmad

Institutes

Continuing Education and Extension *Director*: Zafar Iqbal Choudry

History: Founded 1882 as Veterinary School and Veterinary College 1921. Acquired present status 2002.

Governing Bodies: Academic Council; Syndicate

Admission Requirements: Higher Secondary School Certificate (in English)

Fees: (PK Rupees): 17,650-25,080 per semester

Main Language(s) of Instruction: English

International Co-operation: With institutions in Switzerland, Korea, United Kingdom, France, USA, Indonesia

Accrediting Agencies: Pakistan Veterinary Medical Council

Degrees and Diplomas: *Master's Degree*: 2 yrs; *Doctor's Degree (PhD)*: 3 yrs. Doctor of Veterinary Medicine 5 yrs

Student Services: Academic counselling, Canteen, Cultural centre, Employment services, Foreign student adviser, Foreign Studies Centre, Handicapped facilities, Health services, Language programs, Nursery care, Social counselling, Sports facilities

Libraries: 28,892 vols; 10 subscriptions to periodicals

Publications: Pakistan Journal of Veterinary and Animal Science

Last Updated: 09/10/08

VIRTUAL UNIVERSITY OF PAKISTAN

M.A. Jinnah Campus, Defence Road Off Raiwind Road, Lahore, Punjab
Tel: +92(42) 111-880
Fax: +92(42) 920-0604
EMail: info@vu.edu.pk
Website: http://www.vu.edu.pk/

Faculties

Arts (Accountancy; Business and Commerce; Finance; Mass Communication; Psychology); **Computer Science and Information Technology** (Computer Science; Information Technology); **Management** (Business Administration; Management; Public Administration)

History: Founded 2002.

Degrees and Diplomas: *Diploma*; *Bachelor's Degree*; *Master's Degree*

PRIVATE INSTITUTIONS

ABASYN UNIVERSITY

Ring Road (Charsadda Link), Peshawar, North West Frontier Province 25000
Tel: +92(91) 225-0820 +92(91) 258-2835
Fax: +92(91) 258-2834
EMail: abasyn.university@gmail.com
Website: http://www.abasyn.edu.pk/

Chancellor: Imran Ummah Mohammad
Tel: +92(321) 902-6228 EMail: mimranuk04@gmail.com

Vice-Chancellor: Fida Mohammad
EMail: vicechancellor@abasyn.edu.pk

International Relations: Muhammad Haneef Muhammad, Public Relations Officer
Tel: +92(333) 915-7310 EMail: hanifkhasksar@gmail.com

Departments

Management Sciences

History: Created 2007.

Academic Year: January to December

Fees: (PK Rupees): per course, 18,000 to 350,000

Main Language(s) of Instruction: English

Accrediting Agencies: HEC, Pakistan

Degrees and Diplomas: *Bachelor's Degree*: Computer Science; Physics, 4 yrs; *Bachelor's Degree (Honours)*: Business Administration, 4 yrs; *Master's Degree*: Business Administration; Management; Development Studies; Commerce; Health Policy & Management; Computer Science; Education; Educational Planning & Management, 2 yrs; *Master's Degree*: Education, 1 yr; *Master of Philosophy*: Education, 2 yrs. Some Bachelor's degrees offered in two years as top-up courses.

Student Services: Academic counselling, Canteen, Cultural centre, Employment services, Foreign student adviser, Health services, Social counselling, Sports facilities

Student Residential Facilities: Yes

Libraries: c. 10,000 vols.

Publications: Abasyn University Journal of Social Science *(annually)*

Last Updated: 25/04/08

AGA KHAN UNIVERSITY (AKU)

Stadium Road, Karachi, Sindh 74800
Tel: +92(21) 493-0051
Fax: +92(21) 493-4294 +92(21) 493-2095
EMail: aku@aku.edu
Website: http://www.aku.edu

President: Firoz Rasul EMail: president@aku.edu

Provost and Chief Academic Officer (Acting): William Doe
EMail: provost@aku.edu

Colleges

Medicine (Medicine) *Dean*: Mohammad Khurshid

Institutes

Educational Development (Educational Sciences; Teacher Trainers Education; Teacher Training) *Director*: Muhammad Memon; **Study of Muslim Civilizations** *(London)* (Islamic Studies) *Director*: Abdou Filali-Ansary

Schools

Nursing *Dean*: Yasmin Amarsi

Further Information: Also University Teaching Hospital and branches in Pakistan, Kenya, Tanzania (Aga Khan University - Tanzania Institute of Higher Education), Uganda, United Kingdom, Afghanistan, Syria, United Arab Emirates.

History: Founded 1983.

Governing Bodies: Board of Trustees

Academic Year: October to August

Admission Requirements: Higher Secondary Certificate, or equivalent

Main Language(s) of Instruction: English

Degrees and Diplomas: *Diploma*: Nursing (RN), 3 yrs; *Bachelor's Degree*: Medicine (MB/BS), 5 yrs; *Bachelor's Degree*: Nursing (BScN), 4 yrs; *Bachelor's Degree*: Nursing (BScN (PostRN)), 2 yrs; *Master's Degree*: Education (MEd); Epidemiology and Biostatics (MSc); Medicine (Mmed); Muslim Cultures (MA), a further 2 yrs; *Master's Degree*: Health Policy and Management (MSc), a furher 2 yrs; *Master's Degree*: Nursing (MScN), 2 yrs; *Doctor's Degree*: Education (PhD); Health Sciences (PhD), a further 4 yrs. Also Advanced Diploma (1 yr of study) in Primary Education, English Language Teaching, School Management, Specialist Teachers, Education Leadership & Management

Student Services: Academic counselling, Canteen, Employment services, Foreign student adviser, Health services, Social counselling, Sports facilities

Student Residential Facilities: Yes

Special Facilities: Learning Resource Centre. Teaching and learning through multimedia technology. For computer assisted learning, a number of software packages including ADAMS, ILIAD, QMR and ECG are available

Libraries: Jivraj Health Sciences Library, c. 26,000 vols. The Kurji Periodical Library subscribes to c. 500 journals.

Publications: AKHUWAT

Last Updated: 10/10/08

AL-HAMD ISLAMIC UNIVERSITY

Quetta Zargoon Road Near Nadra office, Sariab, Quetta, Balochistan 87300
Tel: +92 (81) 2451-342
Fax: +92 (81) 2451-439
EMail: president@aiu.edu.pk
Website: http://www.aiu.edu.pk

President: Shakeel Ahmed Roshan

Departments

Business Administration (Business Administration); **Social Sciences** (Social Sciences)

Degrees and Diplomas: *Bachelor's Degree*; *Master's Degree*; *Doctor's Degree*

Last Updated: 23/08/10

ALKHAIR UNIVERSITY, AJK (AU)

Camp Office, 88-W, Fazal-Ul-Haq Road, Blue Area, Islamabad
Tel: +92(51) 287-9907
Fax: +92(51) 287-9906
EMail: headoffice_alkhair@yahoo.com.edu
Website: http://www.alkhair.edu.pk

Vice-Chancellor: Khan Ahmed Goraya (2004-)
Tel: +92(51) 287-9908

Registrar: Muhammad Sharif Sabir Tel: +92(51) 227-1366

Campuses

Business Administration *(Peshawar)* (Business Administration) *Chairman*: G. Mustafa

Colleges

Business Administration *(Lahore)* (Business Administration) *Dean*: M. Salim Alvi; **Business Administration** *(Islamabad)* (Business Administration); **Business Administration** *(Karachi)* (Business Administration; Computer Science; Management); **Business Administration** *(Sargodha)* (Business Administration) *Principal*: Muhammad Javaid; **Computer and Management Sciences** *(Islamabad)* (Computer Science; Management) *Principal*: Muhammad Afzal; **Engineering** *(Abbottabad)* (Engineering) *Principal*: Zafar M. Khilji; **Engineering and Technology** *(Rawalpindi)* (Engineering; Technology); **Engineering and Technology** *(Mirpur)* (Engineering; Technology) *Dean*: Mahabat Khan; **Management Sciences** *(Faisalabad)* (Management) *Principal*: Muhammad A. Mian

Faculties

Education (Education) *Dean*: M. Tahir Qadri; **Engineering** (Engineering) *Dean*: M. Salim Alvi; **Management Sciences** (Management) *Dean*: Muhammad Afzal

Further Information: North-West Frontier Province Branch, Peshawar

History: Founded 1994. Has 44 Affiliated colleges through out Pakistan

Governing Bodies: Board of Governors

Academic Year: February to January (February to June; September to January)

Main Language(s) of Instruction: English

Accrediting Agencies: Higher Education Commission of Pakistan

Degrees and Diplomas: *Bachelor's Degree*: Business Administration; Commerce; Education; Technology; Law (BBA, BIT, BGS, BED), 2-3 yrs; *Bachelor's Degree (Honours)*: Technology (BTech), 4 yrs; *Master's Degree*: Management Sciences, Computer Sciences, Information Technology (MBA, MIT (IT), MBA(EX), MCS,), 2 yrs

Libraries: c. 5,000 vols

Last Updated: 05/12/08

BAQAI MEDICAL UNIVERSITY (BMU)

PO Box 2407, 51 Deh Tor, Gadap Road, near Toll Plaza, Super Highway, Karachi, Sindh 74600
Tel: +92(21) 441-0293-8
Fax: +92(21) 441-0317; +92(21) 661-7968
EMail: bmckarachi@yahoo.com
Website: http://www.baqai.edu.pk

Vice-Chancellor: Syed Azhar Ahmed (1996-)
Tel: +92(21) 441-0311, Fax: +92(21) 441-0439
EMail: syed_azhar2000@hotmail.com

Registrar: Khursheed Ali Khan (2006-)
Tel: +92(21) 441-0331, Fax: +92(21) 441-0439
EMail: israrkhan_js@yahoo.com

International Relations: Masood Ahmed
Tel: +92(21) 441-0293, Fax: +92(21) 441-0439

Centres

Medical Education *Dean*: Syed Mohib Mehmoodrab

Departments

Anatomy (Anatomy) *Chairperson*: Kishwar Sultana; **Biochemistry** (Biochemistry) *Chairman*: Muhammad Sarwar; **Forensic Medicine and Toxicology** (Forensic Medicine and Dentistry; Toxicology) *Chairman*: Tariq Mirza; **Neurosurgery** (Surgery) *Assistant Professor*: Jamshed Butt; **Paediatrics** (Paediatrics) *Chairperson*: Saddiqua Ibrahim; **Pakistan Studies and Islamiat** (Islamic Studies) *Director*: Uzma Khan; **Pharmacology & Therapeutics** (Pharmacy; Philosophy) *Chairman*: Muhammad Shamim Syed; **Physiology** (Physiology) *Chairman*: Sikandar Ali Sheikh; **Radiology** (Radiology); **Surgery** (Surgery) *Chairman*: Fareed Uddin Baqai

Faculties

Basic Medical Sciences (Anatomy; Biochemistry; Community Health; Forensic Medicine and Dentistry; Pathology; Pharmacology; Physiology; Toxicology) *Dean*: Sikandar Ali Shaikh; **Health Management** (Health Administration; Health Sciences; Information Technology; Management) *Dean*: Muhammad Aslam; **Medicine and Dentistry**; **Nursing** *Dean*: Muhammad Aslam; **Pharmaceutical Sciences** (Pharmacy; Philosophy) *Chief Executive Officer*: Fazal Hussain Syed

Institutes

Haematology *(Baqai Institute of Hematology (BIH))* (Haematology); **Health Sciences** *(Baqai Institute of Health Sciences (BIHS))* (Health Administration; Health Sciences) *Dean*: Muhammad Aslam; **Information Technology** (Information Technology) *Head*: Farrukh Zaman Hai; **Management Sciences** *(Baqai Institute of Management Sciences (BIMS))* (Management) *Director*: Ghulam Asghar; **Medical Technology** *(Baqai Institute of Medical Technology (BIMT))* (Medical Technology) *Director*: Nazar Hussain; **Pathology and Molecular Medicine** (Pathology) *Executive Director*: Azhar Ahmed Syed; **Physiotherapy and Rehabilitation Medicine** *(Baqai Institute of Physical Therapy and Rehabilitation Medicine)* (Rehabilitation and Therapy) *Director*: A. A. Kamal; **Reproduction and**

Developmental Sciences *(Baqai Institute of Reproduction & Developmental Sciences (BIRDS))* (Embryology and Reproduction Biology) *Director*: Zahida Baqai

History: Founded 1988 as Baqai Medical College. Acquired present status and title 1996.

Governing Bodies: Board of Governors, Academic Council

Academic Year: January to December

Admission Requirements: Secondary school certificate or intermediate certificate with A Level/Grade 12, with minimum 60% marks for undergraduate admissions. For postgraduate admissions the regulations and guidelines of Higher Education Commission, Pakistan Medical and Dental Council ans Pakistan Pharmacy are followed

Fees: Depending on programmes (undergraduate/postgraduate)

Main Language(s) of Instruction: English

Accrediting Agencies: Higher Education Commission (HEC); Pakistan Medical and Dental Council (PMDC); Pakistan Pharmacy Council; Pakistan Nursing Council

Degrees and Diplomas: *Bachelor's Degree*: Business Administration (BBA); Medical Technology (BS(Med.Tech)), 2 yrs; *Bachelor's Degree*: Dentistry; Physical Therapy and Rehabilitation Medicine (BDS; BS Physiotherapy); Software Engineering; Telecommunication Engineering; Bio Informatics (BS), 4 yrs; *Bachelor's Degree*: Medicine and Surgery; Veterinary ; Pharmacy (MBBS; DVM; Pharm D), 5 yrs; *Master's Degree*: Hematology; Medical Technology; Public Health; Business and Health Administration (MSc; MBA; EMBA), 2 yrs; *Master's Degree*: Medicine and Allied; Surgery and Allied (MD; MS), 4 yrs; *Doctor's Degree*: Medicine; Pharmacy (PhD), 2 -7 yrs. Also Postgraduate Diploma in Diabetology; Endocrinology and Hematology

Student Services: Academic counselling, Canteen, Health services, Sports facilities

Student Residential Facilities: Separate residences for 150 female students and 50 male students

Special Facilities: Internet; Museum; Learning Resources Centre

Libraries: Yes. Online journals

Publications: Baqa-e-Sehat (Urdu Magazine) *(quarterly)*; The Journal of Baqai Medical University, Scientific Research Journal *(biannually)*

Press or Publishing House: BMU Press

Last Updated: 28/11/08

BEACONHOUSE NATIONAL UNIVERSITY

3-C, Zafar Ali Road, Lahore, Punjab
Tel: +92(42) 5718260-3
Fax: +92(42) 5760254
EMail: info@bnu.edu.pk
Website: http://www.bnu.edu.pk/index.htm

Vice Chancellor: Sartaj Aziz

Registrar: Farzana Shahid

Schools

School of Architecture and Design; **School of Computer and Information Technology**; **School of Education**; **School of Liberal Arts**; **School of Media and Mass Communication**; **School of Social Sciences**; **School of Visual Arts**

Degrees and Diplomas: *Bachelor's Degree*; *Bachelor's Degree (Honours)*; *Master's Degree*: English Literature; English; Women Studies; Mass Communication; Education; Educational Leadership and Management; Applied Psychology

CECOS UNIVERSITY OF INFORMATION TECHNOLOGY AND EMERGING SCIENCES

F-5, Phase-6, Peshawar, North West Frontier Province
Tel: +92(91) 272-662 +92(91) 279-662
Fax: +92(91) 276-663
Website: http://www.cecos.com/

President: Muhammad Tanveer Javed

Colleges

Business Education *(CECOS Frontier)* (Business Education)

Faculties

Engineering (Architecture; Civil Engineering; Electrical Engineering; Mechanical Engineering)

Institutes

Data *(CECOS)* (Computer Science); **Management and Information Sciences** (Computer Science; Information Technology; Management)

History: Founded 2001.

Degrees and Diplomas: *Diploma*; *Bachelor's Degree*; *Master's Degree*

CITY UNIVERSITY OF SCIENCE AND INFORMATION TECHNOLOGY (CUSIT)

G.T. Road, Nishtarabad, Peshawar, North West Frontier Province 25000
Tel: +92(91) 256-7923-26
Fax: +92(91) 256-7927
EMail: info@cityuniversity.edu.pk
Website: http://www.cityuniversity.edu.pk

Vice-Chancellor: Muhammad Asrar
EMail: vc@cityuniversity.edu.pk

President: M. Sabur Sethi EMail: president@cityuniversity.edu.pk

International Relations: Amjad Ali
EMail: registrar@cityuniversity.edu.pk

Faculties

Arts *Dean*: Shaheen Quli Khan; **Computer Science and Information Technology** *Dean*: Sardar Mohammad; **Education** *Dean*: Mehmooda Rahman; **Management** *Dean*: Inamullah Khan

History: Founded 2001.

Academic Year: January to December (January-June; August-December)

Admission Requirements: A level or equivalent with at least 45% marks for Bachelors. BA/BSC with at least 45% marks for Masters.

Fees: (PK Rupees): Bachelor's programmes, 24,000 per semester; Master's programmes, 24,500 per semester

Main Language(s) of Instruction: English

Accrediting Agencies: Higher Education Commission, British Accreditation Council

Degrees and Diplomas: *Bachelor's Degree*: 4 yrs; *Master's Degree*: a further 2 yrs; *Master of Philosophy*: Education; *Doctor's Degree*: Education

Student Services: Academic counselling, Canteen, Employment services, Health services, Sports facilities

DADABHOY INSTITUTE OF HIGHER EDUCATION (DIHE)

SNPA-17/B, Block 3, K.C.H.S. Union Ltd. Behind Hill Park General Hospital, Shaheed-e-Millat Road, Karachi, Sindh
EMail: info@dadabhoy.edu.pk
Website: http://www.dadabhoy.edu.pk

Chancellor: Abdullah Dadabhoy

Faculties

Computer and Mathematical Science (Mathematics and Computer Science); **Education** (Education); **Law** (Law); **Management, Media and Social Sciences** (Management; Media Studies; Social Sciences)

Degrees and Diplomas: *Bachelor's Degree*; *Master's Degree*; *Master of Philosophy*

FORMAN CHRISTIAN COLLEGE

Ferozepur Road, Lahore, Punjab 54600
Tel: +92(42) 923 1581 +92(42) 923 1588
Fax: +92(42) 923 0703
EMail: info@fccollege.edu.pk
Website: http://www.fccollege.edu.pk/

Rector: Peter H. Armacost

Departments

Biological Science; **Business and Management** (Business Administration; Business and Commerce; Management); **Chemistry** (Chemistry); **Computer Science and Information Technology** (Computer Science; Information Technology); **Economics**; **Education**; **English**; **Geography**; **Health and Physical Education** (Health Education; Physical Education); **History and Pakistan Studies** (History); **Mass Communication**; **Mathematics**; **Physics**; **Political Science** (Political Sciences); **Psychology** (Psychology); **Religious Studies**; **Sociology** (Sociology); **Statistics** (Statistics); **Urdu** (Urdu)

History: Created in 1864 as Lahore Mission College. Became Forman Christian College 1894. Acquired current status 2004.

Governing Bodies: Academic Council; Board of Governors

Academic Year: October to February; February to May

Admission Requirements: Secondary school certificate or equivalent, undergraduate programmes; Bachelor's degree, postgradute programmes.

Fees: (PK Rupees): Undergraduate, c. 43,500-120,000 per annum; Master's courses, 46,000-49,000; MBA, 190,000

International Co-operation: With University of Kentucky, USA

Degrees and Diplomas: *Bachelor's Degree*: Biological Science; Business and Management; Chemistry; Computer Science & Information Technology; Economics; Education; English; Geography; History & Pakistan Studies; Mass Communication; Mathematics; Physics; Political Science; Psychology; Religious Studies; Statistics; Urdu, 4 yrs; *Master's Degree*: Botany; Mathematics; Political Science (MSc); Business Administration (MBA); English; Urdu (MA), 2 yrs

Student Services: Canteen, Cultural centre, Employment services, Health services, Sports facilities

Student Residential Facilities: Six hostels for c. 600 students.

Special Facilities: Centre for Learning and Teaching.

Libraries: Ewing Memorial Library, c. 100,000 vols.

FOUNDATION UNIVERSITY

198, St. No. 50, F-10/4, Islamabad 44000
Tel: +92(51) 229-6971
Fax: +92(51) 210-0282
EMail: registrar@fui.edu.pk
Website: http://www.fui.edu.pk

Rector: Asrar-ul-Haq Sheikh (2006-)
Tel: +92(51) 210-0280 EMail: rector@fui.edu.pk

Administrator: Qamar uz-Zaman Tel: +92(51) 210-0281

International Relations: Tanwir ul-Islam

Colleges

Liberal Arts and Science

Faculties

Education *(New Lalazar, Rawalpindi)* (Education; Educational Sciences; International Relations; Linguistics; Literature; Special Education) *Head*: Muhammad Akram Khan; **Engineering and Information Technology** (Computer Science; Engineering; Information Technology; Software Engineering; Telecommunications Engineering); **Management Sciences** *Head*: Muhammad Iqbal Saif; **Medical Sciences** (Anatomy; Behavioural Sciences; Biochemistry; Forensic Medicine and Dentistry; Gynaecology and Obstetrics; Medicine; Otorhinolaryngology; Paediatrics; Pathology; Pharmacology; Physiology; Surgery) *Head*: Ashraf Ali Mallhi

History: Founded 2002.

Governing Bodies: Board of Governors; Executive Committee; Academic Council

Academic Year: January to December

Admission Requirements: BA/BSc degree for Postgraduates, and FA/FSc for Bachelor and MBBS degrees

Fees: (PK Rupees): Residents, 50,000-275,000 per annum

Main Language(s) of Instruction: English

Accrediting Agencies: Higher Education Commission; College of Physicians and Surgeons of Pakistan; Pakistan Engineering Council

Degrees and Diplomas: *Bachelor's Degree*: 4 yrs; *Master's Degree (MA)*: a further 2 yrs; *Master of Philosophy (Mphil)*: a further 2 yrs; *Doctor's Degree*: a further 3-5 yrs

Student Services: Academic counselling, Canteen, Health services, Social counselling, Sports facilities

Student Residential Facilities: Yes

Special Facilities: Laboratories.

Libraries: Yes.

Publications: Fauji Foundation Health Journal, Medical Journal *(biannually)*

GANDHARA UNIVERSITY

57 Gulmohar Lane, University Town, Peshawar, North West Frontier Province
Tel: +92(91) 844-429
Fax: +92(91) 844-428
EMail: gandhara@brain.net.pk
Website: http://www.gandhara.edu.pk

Vice-Chancellor: R.A.K. Tahirkheli Tel: +92(91) 844-432

Faculties

Computer Studies (Computer Science; Information Technology); **Dental Sciences**; **Engineering and Technology** (Engineering; Technology); **Medicine and Allied Sciences** (Medicine; Nursing); **Pharmaceutical Sciences** (Pharmacology; Pharmacy)

History: Founded 2002.

GHULAM ISHAQ KHAN INSTITUTE OF ENGINEERING SCIENCES AND TECHNOLOGY (GIKIEST)

Topi, Distt. Swabi, North West Frontier Province 23460
Tel: +92(938) 271858
Fax: +92(938) 271865
Website: http://www.giki.edu.pk

Rector: Abdullah Sadiq
Tel: +92(938) 271897, Fax: +92(938) 271862
EMail: rector@giki.edu.pk

Faculties

Computer Science and Engineering (Artificial Intelligence; Computer Engineering; Computer Science; Multimedia; Software Engineering); **Electronic Engineering** (Electronic Engineering); **Engineering Sciences** (Engineering); **Humanities and Management Science** (Arts and Humanities; Management); **Mechanical Engineering** (Mechanical Engineering); **Metallurgy and Materials** (Materials Engineering; Metallurgical Engineering)

Degrees and Diplomas: *Bachelor's Degree*; *Master's Degree*; *Doctor's Degree*: Computer Science; Electronic Engineering; Metallurgy and Materials Engineering

GIFT UNIVERSITY

Near GIFT University Chowk, Gurjanwala 52250
Tel: +98(55) 389-9289
Fax: +92(55) 389-0266
Website: http://www.gift.edu.pk

President: Muhammad Anwar Dar
Tel: +92(55) 389-2988, Fax: +92(55) 389-2986
EMail: president@gift.edu.pk

Rector: Khawja Zahid Parwaiz
Tel: +92(55) 389-2981-2, Fax: +92(55) 389-2980
EMail: rector@gift.edu.pk

Registrar: Rizwan Rashid
Tel: +92(55) 389-2984 EMail: registrar@gift.edu.pk

Schools

Accountancy and Finance (Accountancy; Finance); **Art, Design and Architecture** (Architecture; Design; Fine Arts); **Arts and Social Sciences** (Social Sciences); **Business and Commerce** (Business Administration; Business and Commerce); **Computer Science** (Computer Science); **Management** (Management)

History: Founded 2002.

Governing Bodies: Board of governors

Main Language(s) of Instruction: English

Degrees and Diplomas: *Bachelor's Degree (Honours)*: Accounting and Finance (BSc); Business Administration (BSc); Computer Science (BSc); Textile and Fashion Design (BOD), 4 yrs; *Master's Degree (MBA)*: 2 yrs; *Master's Degree*: Accounting and Finance (MSc); English (Language and Literature) (MA), 2 yrs

Special Facilities: 5 computer labs

Libraries:c. 10,000 vols

GREENWICH UNIVERSITY (GU)

Greenwich House, DK-10, 38th Street, Darakshan, Phase-VI, DHA, Karachi, Sindh 75500
Tel: +92(21) 3584-7663
Fax: +92(21) 3585-1910
EMail: gu@greenwichuniversity.edu.pk
Website: http://www.greenwichuniversity.edu.pk

Vice-Chancellor: Seema Mughal (1998-)
EMail: vc@greenwichuniversity.edu.pk

Director of Administration: Saeed Mughal Tel: +92(21) 584-0398

International Relations: Rab Nawaz
EMail: rub@greenwichuniversity.edu.pk

Faculties

Management Sciences and Information Studies (Business Administration; Computer Science); **Social Sciences and Humanities** (Arts and Humanities; Mass Communication; Media Studies)

History: Founded 1987, acquired present status 1998. Chartered by Government of Sindh Pakistan 1998.

Governing Bodies: Board of Governors

Academic Year: August to June (August-October; November-March; March-June)

Admission Requirements: Intermediate (H.S.C)/O/A Levels

Fees: (PK Rupees): 40,000-50,000 per semester

Main Language(s) of Instruction: English

Accrediting Agencies: Higher Education Commission

Degrees and Diplomas: *Bachelor's Degree (BS)*: 3-4 yrs; *Master's Degree*: 1-2 yrs; *Master of Philosophy*; *Doctor's Degree*

Student Services: Academic counselling, Canteen, Employment services, Foreign student adviser, Handicapped facilities, Health services, Social counselling, Sports facilities

Libraries: c. 20,000 vols; 50 periodical subscriptions.

Academic Staff *2010-2011*	**TOTAL**
FULL-TIME	63
PART-TIME	47
STAFF WITH DOCTORATE	
FULL-TIME	24
Student Numbers *2010-2011*	
All (Foreign Included)	948

HAJVERY UNIVERSITY (HU)

43-52 Industrial Area, Gulberg III, Lahore, Punjab
Tel: +92(42) 111-777-007
Fax: +92(42) 575-5564
EMail: info@hajveryuniversity.com
Website: http://www.hajveryuniversity.com

Board of Governors: Atif Mushtaq
Tel: +92(42) 576-0136-7 EMail: chairman@hajveryuniversity.com

Director: Usman M. Ghauri EMail: admin@hajveryuniversity.com

Academic Advisor: Abbass Nazar

Colleges
Women's

Faculties

Business Administration (Banking; Business Administration; Business Computing; E-Business/Commerce; Finance; Human Resources; Management; Marketing); **Commerce and Banking** (Banking; Business and Commerce); **Engineering** (Electrical and Electronic Engineering; Engineering; Telecommunications Engineering; Textile Technology); **Fine Arts and Fashion Design**; **Humanities and Social Sciences** (Arts and Humanities; Economics; Finance; French; Mass Communication; Mathematics; Psychology; Social Sciences; Statistics); **Information Technology and Computer Science** (Computer Science; Information Technology); **Language and Literature**

Institutes

Fashion Technology *(FIT)* (Fashion Design)

Schools

Pharmacy (Pharmacy)

Further Information: Also Euro Campus in Lahore and branch in Multan

History: Founded 1992 as Hajvery College. Acquired present status 2002.

Governing Bodies: Board of Governors

Admission Requirements: 12 years' intermediate schooling or A Levels or American High School

Main Language(s) of Instruction: English

Accrediting Agencies: Higher Education Commission of Pakistan; Accreditation Committee Punjab Provincial Government

Degrees and Diplomas: *Bachelor's Degree*; *Bachelor's Degree (Honours)*; *Master's Degree*; *Master of Philosophy*; *Doctor's Degree*: Pharmacy (Pharm D)

Student Services: Academic counselling, Canteen, Employment services, Health services, Language programs, Social counselling, Sports facilities

Student Residential Facilities: Yes

Libraries: Yes

HAMDARD UNIVERSITY (HU)

Sharae Madinat al-Hikmah, Muhammad Bin Qasim Avenue, Karachi, Sindh 74600
Tel: +92(21) 644-0035-42
Fax: +92(21) 644-0045
EMail: huvc@hamdard.edu.pk
Website: http://www.hamdard.edu.pk

Vice-Chancellor: Nasim A. Khan (2008-)
Tel: +92(21) 644-0017 +92(21) 644-0030, Fax: +92(21) 644-0066

Registrar: Ameer Haider Ali
Tel: +92(21) 644-0019, Fax: +92(21) 644-0016
EMail: registrar@hamdard.edu.pk

International Relations: M. Azmat Ataka
EMail: ataka@hamdard.edu.pk

Colleges

Eastern Medicine *Dean*: Hakim Abdul Hannan; **Medicine and Dentistry** (Dentistry; Health Sciences; Medicine) *Dean*: M. Sarwar

Institutes

Education and Social Sciences (Education; Social Sciences) *Director*: Muhammad Ali Siddiqui; **Information Technology** *Director*: Nazeer Ahmed; **Management Sciences** (Management) *Dean*: Matin A. Khan

Schools

Law (Law) *Dean*: Nasir Arlam Zahid

Further Information: Campuses in Islamabad

History: Founded 1991. A private chartered University.

Governing Bodies: Board of Governors

Academic Year: August to June (August-December; January-June)

Admission Requirements: Intermediate certificate/A level or equivalent

Main Language(s) of Instruction: English

Accrediting Agencies: HEC, PEC, PMDC, NCT,CISCO - Canada/USA

Degrees and Diplomas: *Bachelor's Degree*: Management; Computer Science; Education (BBA, BCS, BEd), 2-3 yrs; *Bachelor's Degree*: Medicine; Dentistry; Information Technology; Eastern Medicine; Engineering and Technology (MBBS, BDS, BE(IT); BEMS), 4-5 yrs; *Master's Degree*: Management; Information Technology; Computer Science; Education (MBA; MS-IT; MEd; MCS), a further 2 yrs; *Doctor's Degree*: Education and Social

Sciences; Management; Medicine; Engineering; Pharmacy; Eastern Medicine (PhD), a further 3 yrs

Student Services: Academic counselling, Canteen, Employment services, Health services, Social counselling, Sports facilities

Student Residential Facilities: Yes

Libraries: 494,763 vols

Last Updated: 07/04/08

IMPERIAL COLLEGE OF BUSINESS STUDIES (ICBS)

49 Zafar Ali Road, Lahore, Punjab 54660
Tel: +92(42) 5710480-1
Fax: +92(42) 5711651
EMail: registrar@imperial.edu.pk
Website: http://www.imperial.edu.pk

Rector: Azmat Abbas Syed EMail: president@imperial.edu.pk

Programmes

Business Administration (Business Administration; Information Technology); **Information Technology and Computer Science** (Computer Science; Information Technology)

History: Founded 1991.

Degrees and Diplomas: *Bachelor's Degree (BSc; BBA)*; *Master's Degree (MBA; MSc; MBIT)*

Last Updated: 21/11/08

INDUS UNIVERSITY

ST-2D, Block-17, Gulshan-e-Iqbal, Karachi, Sindh
Tel: +92(21) 3497-7457 +92(21) 3480-1430
Fax: +92(21) 3498-5320
EMail: indus@indus.edu.pk
Website: http://www.indus.edu.pk/

Vice-Chancellor: Khalid Amin (2010-)

International Relations: Wahid Farooqui, Director
EMail: director@indus.edu.pk

Faculties

Business Administration and Commerce (Business Administration; Business and Commerce); **Engineering** (Bioengineering; Civil Engineering; Electrical Engineering; Electronic Engineering; Engineering; Petroleum and Gas Engineering); **Fashion and Textile Design** (Fashion Design; Interior Design; Textile Design); **Information Science and Technology** (Information Sciences; Information Technology); **Social Sciences** (Social Sciences)

History: Created 2006 as Indus Institute of Higher Education. Acquired current title 2012.

Degrees and Diplomas: *Bachelor's Degree*: Textile Management and Marketing; Textile Design; Fashion Design, 3 yrs; *Bachelor's Degree (Honours)*: Computer Systems Engineering; Telecommunications Engineering; Electronics and Information Systems; Electronic Engineering; Business Administration; Computer Science; Textile, 4 yrs; *Master's Degree*: Human Resources, Marketing, Finance, Management & IT, a further 2 yrs. Also: Postgraduate Diploma (2 semesters) in Wet Processing

Last Updated: 31/07/12

INDUS VALLEY SCHOOL OF ART AND ARCHITECTURE (IVS)

Street 33, Block-2, Sheme-5, Clifton, Karachi, Sindh 75600
Tel: +92(21) 5861039-40
Fax: +92(21) 5861048
EMail: info@indusvalley.edu.pk
Website: http://www.indusvalley.edu.pk

Chairman: Manzoor Ahmed

Faculties

Architecture (Architecture); **Design** (Design); **Fine Arts** (Fine Arts)

History: Founded 1989. An ordinance issued by the Governor of Sindh authorized officially Degree granting 1993, and was subsequently ratified in 1994 as an Act of the Provincial Assembly of Sindh.

Governing Bodies: Board of Governors; Executive Committee

Academic Year: January to December (January-May; July-December).

Admission Requirements: Intermediate (High School) 55% marks 'B' grade or 'A' Level 2 subjects pass other than English

Fees: Registration: Rs. 30,000 (including Rs. 10,000 refundable security deposit); per semester (2 per year): Rs. 30,000

Main Language(s) of Instruction: English

Degrees and Diplomas: *Bachelor's Degree*: Architecture, 5 yrs; *Bachelor's Degree*: Design; Fine Arts, 4 yrs. Also postgraduate diploma

Student Services: Academic counselling, Canteen, Cultural centre, Employment services, Handicapped facilities, Health services, Social counselling, Sports facilities

Libraries: 4,000 vols

INSTITUTE OF BUSINESS AND TECHNOLOGY BITZTEK

Main Ibrahim Hydri Road, Korangi Creek, Karachi, Sindh 75190
Tel: +92(21) 3509-1871
Fax: +92(21) 3509-2384
EMail: info@biztek.edu.pk
Website: http://www.biztek.edu.pk

Rector: Muhammad Ali Siddiqui (2011-)
EMail: drmuhammadali@biztekian.com

International Relations: Syed Kashif Rafi, Registrar
Tel: +92(21) 3512-0462 EMail: skashifrafi@biztekian.com

Programmes

Business Administration (Accountancy; Banking; Economics; Finance; Human Resources; International Business; Management; Marketing); **Computer Science** (Computer Networks; Computer Science; Multimedia); **Information Technology** (Computer Networks; Information Technology; Multimedia)

History: Created 2001. Acquired status 2004.

Degrees and Diplomas: *Bachelor's Degree*; *Master's Degree*

Libraries: 9,200 vols

Student Numbers *2011-2012*: Total 2,525

Last Updated: 29/09/11

INSTITUTE OF BUSINESS MANAGEMENT (IOBM)

Korangi Creek, Karachi, Sindh 75190
Tel: +92(21) 3509-1915
Fax: +92(21) 3509-0968
EMail: admissions@cbm.edu.pk; sskarim@iobm.edu.pk
Website: http://www.iobm.edu.pk/

President: Shahjehan S. Karim
Tel: +92(21) 3509-1915 EMail: sskarim@iobm.edu.pk

Executive Director, Administration, Admissions and Finance: Sabina Mohsin EMail: sabina@iobm.edu.pk

International Relations: Khalid Amin, Head, International Relations EMail: Khalid.amin@iobm.edu.pk

Colleges

Business Management (Accountancy; Banking; Economics; Finance; Management); **Computer Science and Information Systems** (Computer Science; Industrial Engineering; Industrial Management; Information Sciences; Statistics); **Economics and Social Development** (Development Studies; Economics)

History: Founded 1995. Acquired present status 1998.

Accrediting Agencies: Higher Education Commission

Degrees and Diplomas: *Bachelor's Degree (Pass)*: 4 yrs; *Master's Degree*: 2 yrs following Bachelor's Degree; *Master of Philosophy*

Libraries: c. 10,000 vols; 43 periodical subscriptions

Publications: Pakistan Business Review *(quarterly)*

Student Numbers *2012-2013*: Total: c. 4,000

Last Updated: 14/03/13

INSTITUTE OF MANAGEMENT SCIENCES (LAHORE) (IMS)

23-E-III, Gulberg III, Lahore, Punjab 54600
Tel: +92(42) 111 19 19 38
Fax: +92(42) 575 86 65
EMail: info@pakaims.edu.pk
Website: http://www.pakaims.edu.pk

Rector: Khalid Ranjha

Faculties

Business Management (Business Administration; Commercial Law; Finance; Marketing) *Dean*: Afzal Beg; **Computer Science** (Computer Science; Information Technology) *Dean*: Shujaat Ali Shah

History: Founded 1986. Acquired present status 2002.

Governing Bodies: Board of Governors

Academic Year: Sept - Dec; Jan - April; May - August

Admission Requirements: Undergraduate: 'A' levels or equivalent, aptitute test and interview; postgraduate: Bachelor's degree or equivalent

Fees: (PK Rupees): Undergraduate, 19,800 per semester; postgraduate, 22,000 - 29,500

Degrees and Diplomas: *Bachelor's Degree*: Business Administration; Computer Science (BBA, BCS), 4 yrs; *Master's Degree*: Business Administration; Computer Science (MBA, MCS), a further 2 yrs

IQRA UNIVERSITY, KARACHI (IU)

Shaheed-e-Millat Road (Ext.), Defence View, Karachi, Sindh 75500
Tel: +92(21) 111-264-264
Fax: +92(21) 5894806
EMail: info@iqra.edu.pk
Website: http://www.iqra.edu.pk

President: U.A.G Issani (2006-)
Tel: +92(21) 111-264-264 (114), Fax: +92(21) 538-5739
EMail: vc@iqra.edu.pk

Registrar: Syed Akif Hasan
Tel: +92(21) 111-264-264 (153), Fax: +92(21) 589-4806
EMail: registrar@iqra.edu.pk

International Relations: Shafaq Habib
Tel: +92(21) 111-264-264 (135) EMail: shafaqhabib@iqra.edu.pk

Faculties

Education (Education) *Dean*: Ismail Saad; **Engineering and Technology** (Electronic Engineering; Engineering; Technology; Telecommunications Engineering) *Dean*: Kamran Raja; **Fashion Design** (Fashion Design; Textile Design) *Dean*: Shama Saeed; **Management** (Management) *Dean*: Akif Hasan

Further Information: Also campuses in Peshawar, Quetta and Lahore

History: Founded 1998. Acquired present status 2000.

Governing Bodies: Board of Governors; Academic Council; Board of Studies; Board of Faculties; Board of Advanced Studies and Research (BASR), Selection Board; Finance and Planning Committee

Academic Year: January to December (January-May; June-July; August-December)

Admission Requirements: High School Certificate / A-Levels (minimum 3 courses passed)

Fees: (PK Rupees): Bachelors : 10,800-52,800 per semester; Masters: 9,600-43,350; PhD: 40,000

Main Language(s) of Instruction: English

International Co-operation: With universities in USA and United Kingdom

Accrediting Agencies: Government of Sindh; Higher Education Commission (HEC); Pakistan Engineering Council (PEC)

Degrees and Diplomas: *Bachelor's Degree*: Business Administration; Computer Science; Information Technology; Fashion & Textile Design; Engineering; Education; Social Science; Development Studies; Media (BBA Honors), 4 yrs; *Master's Degree*: Business Administration; Computer Sciences; Education; Development Studies; International Relations (MS; MBA; Med; MSDS; Mphil; MS(IR& DS)), 2 yrs; *Doctor's Degree*: Business Administration; Computer Science; Education (PhD), 3 yrs. Also Diploma in Fashion Design

Student Services: Academic counselling, Canteen, Employment services, Foreign student adviser, Handicapped facilities, Health services, Social counselling, Sports facilities

Student Residential Facilities: No

Special Facilities: Auditoriums; Sound Editing Studio

Libraries: 4 Central Libraries.c. 30,000 vols; Online journals

Publications: South Asian Journal of Management Sciences, Peer Reviewed Journal *(bimonthly)*

Press or Publishing House: Iqra University Press

Last Updated: 27/11/08

IQRA UNIVERSITY, QUETTA

8-B/2 Zarghoon Road, Quetta, Balochistan
Tel: +92(81) 841-583-99
Fax: +92-81) 840-105
EMail: info@iqraqta.edu.pk
Website: http://www.iqraqta.edu.pk

Director: Sher Akber Khan

Registrar: Mansoor-ul-Huda Abbasi EMail: abbasi@iqraqta.edu.pk

Faculties

Computer Science (Computer Science); **Management Science** (Management)

Admission Requirements: Higher Secondary School Certificate (HSC) or equivalent

Main Language(s) of Instruction: English

Degrees and Diplomas: *Bachelor's Degree (BCS, BBA)*; *Master's Degree (MCS; MBA; EMBA)*

ISRA UNIVERSITY (IU)

PO Box 313, Hala Road, Hyderabad, Sindh
Tel: +92(022) 2030181-4
Fax: +92(022) 2030180
EMail: info@isra.edu.pk
Website: http://www.isra.edu.pk

Vice-Chancellor: Asadullah Kazi (1997-)

Registrar: Muhammad Nawaz Qureshi

Faculties

Computer Science (Artificial Intelligence; Computer Networks; Computer Science; Data Processing; Software Engineering) *Chairperson*: Asadullah Shah Syed; **Management Sciences** (Banking; Finance; Management; Marketing) *Chairperson*: Amanat Ali Jalbani; **Medicine and Allied Medical Sciences** (Medicine; Ophthalmology; Surgery) *Dean*: Ghulamqadir Kazi

History: Founded 1996, the university is owned, managed and administrated by Isra Foundation. Acquired present status 1997.

Governing Bodies: Board of Governors

Admission Requirements: F.Sc, British Advanced Level Certificate or equivalent for Bachelor degree programmes, Bachelors degree for Masters programmes, Pre-Admission Test followed by Interview on merit basis

Fees: (PK Rupees): 20,000-80,000 per semester

Main Language(s) of Instruction: English

Accrediting Agencies: Higher Education Commission, Ministry of Education, Government

Degrees and Diplomas: *Bachelor's Degree*: Information Technology (BIT); Management Sciences (Specialization in IT) (BBA IT); Medicine & Surgery (MBBS); *Bachelor's Degree (Honours)*: Computer Science (BCS); Management Sciences (BBA); *Master's Degree*: Business Administration (MBA); Computer Science (MCS); Information Technology Management (MITM); *Doctor's Degree*: Computer Science; Information Technology; Management; Basic Medical Sciences

Student Services: Academic counselling, Canteen, Employment services, Health services, Language programs, Sports facilities

Libraries: Main Library; Audiovisual Library, Anatomy Museum Library

JINNAH UNIVERSITY FOR WOMEN (JUW)

5-C Nazimabad, Karachi, Sindh 74600
Tel: +92(21) 6620857-59
Fax: +92(21) 6620614
EMail: info@juw.edu.pk
Website: http://www.juw.edu.pk

Vice-Chancellor: Riaz Ahmed Hashmi (1999-)

Registrar: Qazi Nawab Manzar

Faculties

Arts (Arts and Humanities; Business Administration; Economics; Education; English; Islamic Studies; Mass Communication; Political Sciences; Urdu) *Dean*: Jamila Khanum; **Commerce and Business Administration**; **Pharmacy**; **Science** (Biochemistry; Botany; Chemistry; Computer Science; Mathematics; Microbiology; Natural Sciences; Pharmacy; Physics; Zoology) *Dean*: Rukhsana Talat

History: Founded 1998.

Governing Bodies: Board of Governors

Admission Requirements: Higher School Leaving Certificate

Fees: (PK Rupees): Humanities: 2,800-3,400 per semester; Science: 3,200-4,900 per semester; Business Administration: 15,000 per semester; Computer Science: 18,000 per semester; Pharmacy: 13,000 per semester

Main Language(s) of Instruction: English and Urdu

Degrees and Diplomas: *Bachelor's Degree*: Commerce; Pharmacy; Computer Science and Information Technology, 2-5 yrs; *Bachelor's Degree*: Education, 1 yr; *Bachelor's Degree (Honours)*: Economics; Education; English; Islamic Studies; Mass Communication; Political science; Urdu; Biochemistry; Botany; Chemistry; Microbiology; Zoology (B.A (Honours); B.Sc (Honours)), 3 yrs; *Master's Degree*: Business Administration (MBA); Computer Science (MCS); Economics; Education; English; Islamic Studies; Mass Communication Political Science; Urdu; Biochemistry; Botany; Chemistry Microbiology; Zoology (M.A.; M.Sc), 2 yrs; *Master's Degree*: Information Technology (MIT). Also Postgraduate Diploma in Computer Science

Student Services: Canteen, Handicapped facilities, Language programs, Sports facilities

Student Residential Facilities: None

Special Facilities: Botanical and Zoology Museums

Libraries: Yes

Publications: Aayan *(annually)*; Dareecha *(annually)*

KARACHI INSTITUTE OF ECONOMICS AND TECHNOLOGY (KIET)

PAF Base, Korangi Creek, Karachi, Sindh 75190
Tel: +92(21) 5091114-7
Fax: +92(21) 5091118
EMail: info@pafkiet.edu.pk
Website: http://www.pafkiet.edu.pk

Chancellor: Mohammad Izhar-ul-Hasan

Director, Administration: Ubaid M. Abbasi

Colleges

Computing and Information Technology (Computer Networks; Computer Science; Telecommunications Engineering) *Dean*: Irfan Hyder; **Management Sciences** (Business Administration; Management) *Dean*: Manzoor Khalidi

Departments

Engineering *Dean*: Irfan Hyder

Further Information: City Campus

History: Established 1997. Obtained status 2000.

Governing Bodies: Board of Governors

Admission Requirements: 'A' levels (or equivalent) with a score of at least 50% for undergraduate programmes plus aptitude test; Bachelor's degree or equivalent for postgraduate programmes.

Fees: (PK Rupees): 2,165 - 2,675 per credit hour

Degrees and Diplomas: *Bachelor's Degree*: Computer Science; Telecommunications and Networks; Business Administration; Computer Arts; Electronics; Telecommunications; Computer Systems; Engineering (Industrial Electronics); Engineering (Avionics), 4 yrs; *Master's Degree*: Telecommunications Engineering; Business Administration; Management Science; Computer Science; Telecommunications & Networking;, a further 2 yrs; *Master of Philosophy*: Business Management, 1 yr; *Doctor's Degree*: Computer Science

KHADIM ALI SHAH BUKHARI INSTITUTE OF TECHNOLOGY (KASBIT)

84-B, S.M.C. H.S., Karachi, Sindh 74400
Tel: +92(21) 431-4970-3
Fax: +92(21) 452-5525
EMail: info@kasbit.edu.pk
Website: http://www.kasbit.edu.pk

Director: Muhammad Saleem EMail: msaleem@kasbit.edu.pk

Rector: Wali Khan Durrani EMail: wali@kasbit.edu.pk

International Relations: S. Waqar-ul-Hassan EMail: waqar@kasbit.edu.pk

Faculties

Computer Science (Computer Science) *Dean*: Kamran Ali Khan; **Engineering** (Applied Chemistry; Applied Mathematics; Electrical Engineering; Electronic Engineering; Information Sciences) *Dean*: Jamshed ur Rehman Khan; **Management** (Accountancy; Business Administration; Business Computing; Economics; Finance; Human Resources; Management; Marketing; Statistics; Taxation) *Dean*: Muhammad Mahmud

History: Founded 1999. Acquired present status 2001.

Governing Bodies: Board of Governors; Academic Council; Selection Board; Board of Faculties; Board of Studies

Academic Year: February to January (February-June; September-January)

Admission Requirements: HSC A level

Fees: (PK Rupees): 34,500-44,500 per semester

Main Language(s) of Instruction: English

Accrediting Agencies: Government of Pakistan

Degrees and Diplomas: *Bachelor's Degree*: Business Administration; Computer Science; Engineering, 4 yrs; *Master's Degree*: Computer Science; Business Administration, 2 yrs

Student Services: Academic counselling, Canteen, Employment services, Foreign student adviser, Health services, Social counselling, Sports facilities

Student Residential Facilities: None

Libraries: c. 4,000.18 periodicals

KINNAIRD COLLEGE FOR WOMEN (KCW)

93, Jail Road, Lahore, Punjab 54800
Tel: +92(42) 756-9532
Fax: +92(42) 758-7018
EMail: kcw@wol.net.pk
Website: http://www.kinnaird.edu.pk/

Principal: Mira Phailbus Tel: +92(42) 756-9533

Faculties

Arts and Humanities (Economics; English; Environmental Studies; Fine Arts; French; Geography; International Relations; Journalism; Mathematics; Political Sciences; Psychology; Statistics; Urdu); **General Studies**; **Science** (Botany; Business Computing; Chemistry; Physics; Zoology)

History: Created in 1913 with Intermediate classes. Bachelor's degree classes began 1917. Obtained current title and status 2002.

Governing Bodies: Board of Governors

Academic Year: September to January; January to May.

Admission Requirements: Satisfactory 'A' level grades or FSc (Pakistani High School Certificate).

Fees: (PK Rupees): 22,000 per annum.

Degrees and Diplomas: *Bachelor's Degree (Honours) (BA; BSc)*: 4 yrs; *Master's Degree*: Environmental Science; English; Applied Language Studies; Media Studies

LAHORE SCHOOL OF ECONOMICS

Intersection Main Boulevard, Phase VI DHA and Burki Road, Burki, Lahore, Punjab 53200
Tel: +92(42) 6560936
Fax: +92(42) 6560905
EMail: admin@lahoreschool.edu.pk
Website: http://www.lahoreschoolofeconomics.edu.pk/

Rector: Shahid Amjad Chaudhry Tel: +92(42) 656-0938

Registrar: Viqar Ahmed Tel: +92(42) 656-0938

Administrative Officer: Mohsin Ijaz Malik
Tel: +92(42) 656-1041, Fax: +92(42) 656-0905

International Relations: Saman Zahra Khan, Deputy Registrar
Tel: +92(42) 656-1232

Faculties

Business Administration (Business Administration) *Dean*: Sohail Zafar; **Economics** (Economics) *Dean*: Azam Amjad Chaudry

History: Founded 1993. Acquired present status 1997.

Governing Bodies: Board of Governors. Chairman of the Board of Governors

Academic Year: September to August

Admission Requirements: Undergraduate: High School Diploma or equivalent, entrance examination and Inteview. Bachelors degree with a CGPA of above 3, for Graduate Programmes

Fees: (PK Rupees): Bachelor's programmes (4 yrs): 705,000; Master's programmes (2 yrs): 476,000; EMBA programme (2 yrs): 288,000

Main Language(s) of Instruction: English

International Co-operation: With Bachesehir University (Turkey)

Accrediting Agencies: Higher Education Commission

Degrees and Diplomas: *Bachelor's Degree (Honours)*: Economics; Business Administration (BSc(Hons); BBA(Hons)), 4 yrs; *Master's Degree*: Economics; Business Administration (MSc; MBA), 2 yrs; *Master of Philosophy*: Economics; Business Administration (MS/ Mphil), 4 yrs; *Doctor's Degree*: Economics; Business Administration (PhD), 4 yrs

Student Services: Academic counselling, Canteen, Cultural centre, Employment services, Foreign student adviser, Foreign Studies Centre, Handicapped facilities, Health services, Language programs, Social counselling, Sports facilities

Student Residential Facilities: Women Hostel capacity of 64 of visiting Faculty Cottage 4

Special Facilities: Media Centre for video production and computer editing. Collaboration with Lahore Chitrkar (Studio& Gallery) for Music and Art lessons

Libraries: Main Campus (Burki Road); City Campus (Gulberg). Electronic journals including J-Stor.

Publications: Lahore Journal of Economics *(biannually)*; Lahore Journal of Policy Studies *(annually)*; Lahore School Case Study Journal *(biannually)*

Press or Publishing House: Lahore School of Economics Press
Last Updated: 21/11/08

LAHORE UNIVERSITY OF MANAGEMENT SCIENCES (LUMS)

Opposite Sector U, DHA, Lahore, Punjab 54792
Tel: +92(42) 5722670-9
Fax: +92(42) 5722591
EMail: zahoor@lums.edu.pk
Website: http://www.lums.edu.pk

Vice-Chancellor: Syed Zahoor Hassan
Tel: +92(42) 572-2141, Fax: +92(42) 572-2592

Assistant Manager: Mubarika Aijazuddin
Tel: +92(42) 5722670 (ext: 2,269) EMail: mubarika@lums.edu.pk

International Relations: Nuzhat Kamran, Head, Marketing and External Relations Office
Tel: +92(42) 5722670 (ext: 4,208) EMail: nuzhatk@lums.edu.pk

Centres

Executive Development *(Rausing)* (Economics; Finance; Management; Marketing) *Associate Dean*: Bashir Ahmed Khan; **Management and Economic Research** (Economics; Management) *Director*: Naim Sipra; **Small and Medium Entreprises** (Small Business) *Director*: Jamshed Hassan Khan

Schools

Arts and Science (Arts and Humanities; Computer Science) *Dean*: Arif Zaman; **Business Administration** *Dean*: Ehsan-Ul Haque

History: Founded 1985.

Governing Bodies: Board of Governors; Board of Trustees; National Management Foundation

Academic Year: August/September to June

Admission Requirements: Intermediate or secondary certificate and test, SAT I & II. (For MBA, University degree at Bachelor level; work experience)

Fees: (PK Rupees): Admission Fee 20,000; Bachelor and Master 9,800 per quarter; MBA 257,200 the first year

Main Language(s) of Instruction: English

International Co-operation: With universities in Canada

Degrees and Diplomas: *Bachelor's Degree (Honours)*: Economics, Mathematics, Computer Engineering, Finance and Accountancy, Computer Science, Social Sciences (BSc Hons), 4 yrs; *Master's Degree*: Business Administration (EMBA), 2 yrs; *Master's Degree*: Business Administration (MBA), a further 2 yrs; *Master's Degree*: Computer Science (MS), 1-5 yrs; *Master's Degree*: Economics (MSc), 1-2 yrs; *Doctor's Degree*: Computer Science and Computer Engineering; Mathematics (PhD)

Student Services: Academic counselling, Canteen, Employment services, Foreign student adviser, Handicapped facilities, Health services, Social counselling, Sports facilities

Student Residential Facilities: Yes

Libraries: 45,000 Books, CDS and Videos, Virtual Library and 260 Journals from the year 1,800 onwards

Press or Publishing House: Case and Publication Unit

MINHAJ UNIVERSITY

Near Hamdard Chowk, Township, Lahore, Punjab
Tel: +92(42) 514 5621-6
Fax: +92(42) 511 6779
EMail: info@mul.edu.pk
Website: http://www.mul.edu.pk/home/home.php

Vice-Chancellor: Muhammad Nazir Roomani

Faculties

Basic Science and Mathematics (Biology; Chemistry; Mathematics; Physics; Statistics) *Dean*: Ali Muhammad; **Commerce and Management Sciences** (Banking; Business and Commerce; Finance; Management; Marketing) *Dean*: Naseer Akhtar; **Computer Science and Information Technology** (Computer Networks; Computer Science; Information Technology; Software Engineering) *Dean*: Muhammad Nazir Romani; **Islamic Studies** *Dean*: Muhammad Tahir-UL-Qardi; **Languages** *Dean*: Zahoor Ahmed Azhar; **Social Sciences and Humanities** (Economics; History; Political Sciences) *Dean*: Muhammad Zahid Khan Lodhi

Further Information: Also: Minhaj College for Women (Lahore); Gulburg Campus (Gulburg); College of Shariah and Islamic Studies (Lahore)

History: Created 2003. Obtained status 2005.

Governing Bodies: Board of Governors

Academic Year: Oct - Mar; April - July

Fees: (PK Rupees): undergraduate, 50,000 - 198,000; postgraduate, 50,000 - 145,000 per programme

Degrees and Diplomas: *Diploma*: English Language; *Bachelor's Degree (Honours)*: Islamic Studies; Political Science; Mathematics; Chemistry; Computer Science; Information Technology; Commerce; Business Administration; Physics; Statistics; Economics (BA; BS; BSc; BBA; Bcom), 4 yrs; *Bachelor's Degree (Pass)*: Mathematics; Chemistry; Physics; Computer Science; Commerce; Business Administration; (BA; BBA; BSc), 2 yrs; *Master's Degree*: English Literature; English Language Teaching; Arabic; Urdu; Islamic Studies (MA; Mphil); Mathematics; Chemistry; Economics; Computer Science; Commerce and IT; Business Administration; Banking & Finance; Marketing; Industrial Management; IT; Political Science; History and Pak Studies (MA; MBA; MSc), a further 2 yrs; *Doctor's*

Degree: English; Islamic Studies/Shariah (PhD), a further 3-5 yrs. Also: Postgraduate Diploma in English Language Teaching;

Student Residential Facilities: Two male hostels and one female hostel

MOHAMMAD ALI JINNAH UNIVERSITY (MAJU)

Jinnah Avenue, Blue Area, Islamabad 75400
Tel: +92(51) 2822446 - Ext 0
Fax: +92(51) 2822743
EMail: info@jinnah.edu.pk
Website: http://www.jinnah.edu.pk

President: Abdul Wahab (2002-) EMail: awahab@jinnah.edu.pk

Registrar: G.A. Naqi Syed

Departments

Business Administration *Chairman*: Mumtaz Khan; **Electrical Engineering and Computer Science** *Chairman*: Sibghatullah Siddiqi; **Executive Education** (Business Administration; Information Technology) *Chairman*: Saud Masud; **General Education**

History: Founded 1998, acquired present status 2000. Follows the modern American system of education. It has two campuses: one in Karachi and one in Islamabad.

Governing Bodies: Board of Governors, Chancellor, President

Academic Year: September to May

Admission Requirements: Bachelor's Degree. Minimum score 19 on ACT, 500 on TOEFL, or clear Jinnah's admission test

Fees: (PK Rupees): Admission fee 15,000; 32,250 per trimester

Main Language(s) of Instruction: English

Accrediting Agencies: Higher Education Commission

Degrees and Diplomas: *Bachelor's Degree*: Computer Science (BS); Information Technology (BBA), 3 yrs; *Master's Degree*: Computer Science (MS), 1 yr; *Master's Degree*: Finance, Marketing, Banking, Management (MBA), 2 yrs; *Master's Degree*: Information Technology (EMBA), 1-2 yrs; *Doctor's Degree*: Computer Sciences; Electronic Engineering; Management Sciences

Student Services: Academic counselling, Canteen, Employment services, Social counselling, Sports facilities

Student Residential Facilities: None

Special Facilities: Hardware interface laboratory, Research laboratory, Computer laboratory

Libraries: 2,525 vols, 12 periodicals. Also equipped with Internet.

MOHI-UD-DIN ISLAMIC UNIVERSITY

Nerian Sharif, AJK
Tel: +92(51) 4859658-60
Website: http://www.miu.edu.pk

Vice-Chancellor: Muhammad Khurshid

Registrar: S. Akhtar Hussain

Faculties

Arabic and Islamic Studies (Arabic; Islamic Law; Islamic Studies); **Commerce, Chartered Accountancy, Banking, Business Administration, Hospital Management, Hotel Management** (Accountancy; Banking; Business Administration; Computer Science; Health Administration; Hotel Management); **Education, Technical and Vocational** (Education; Vocational Education); **Engineering and Textile** (Engineering; Textile Design; Textile Technology); **Health and Medical Sciences** (Health Sciences; Medicine); **Languages, Social Sciences and Humanities** (Economics; English; History; Social Work; Urdu); **Law** (Law); **Natural Sciences** (Botany; Chemistry; Physics)

History: Founded 2000.

Degrees and Diplomas: *Bachelor's Degree*; *Master's Degree*; *Master of Philosophy*

NATIONAL COLLEGE OF BUSINESS ADMINISTRATION AND ECONOMICS

40-E /1, Gulberg III, Lahore, Punjab
Tel: +92(42) 5752716
EMail: info@ncbae.edu.pk
Website: http://www.ncbae.edu.pk/

Rector: Munir Ahmad EMail: drmunir@ncbae.edu.pk

Registrar: B.A. Chishty EMail: bachishty@ncbae.edu.pk

Centres

Executive Development Center; Population Research Center

Schools

Arts and Media Studies (Arts and Humanities; Media Studies); **Computer Science and Information Technology** (Computer Science; Information Technology); **Economics and Commerce** (Business and Commerce; Economics); **Environmental Science** (Environmental Studies); **Management Studies** (Management); **Mathematical Sciences** (Mathematics)

Degrees and Diplomas: *Bachelor's Degree*; *Master's Degree*; *Doctor's Degree*: Computer Science; Environmetrics; Environmental Management Science; Management; Population Studies; Statistics; Mathematics; Demography

NATIONAL TEXTILE UNIVERSITY (NTU)

Mannawala, Sheikhupura Road, Faisalabad, Punjab
Tel: +92(41) 9230081-82
Fax: +92(41) 9230098
EMail: info@ntu.edu.pk
Website: http://www.ntu.edu.pk

Vice-Chancellor: Anjum M. Saleem
Tel: +92(41) 9230099 EMail: vc@ntu.edu.pk

Administrative Officer: Muhammad Latif Chaudhry
EMail: latif@ntu.edu.pk

Departments

Applied Sciences; **Fabric Manufacturing** (Textile Technology); **Garment Manufacturing** (Clothing and Sewing); **Textile Chemistry** (Chemistry; Textile Technology); **Yarn Manufacturing** (Textile Technology)

History: Founded 1954 as Institute of Textile Technology. Acquired present status 2002.

Degrees and Diplomas: *Bachelor's Degree*: Textile Engineering; Polymer Science; Textile and Apparel Design; Business Administration, 4 yrs

NATIONAL UNIVERSITY OF COMPUTER AND EMERGING SCIENCES (NU/NUCES)

FAST House, Rohtas Road, G-9/4, Islamabad 44000
Tel: +92(51) 285-5072
Fax: +92(51) 285-5070; +92(51) 285-5075
EMail: info@nu.edu.pk
Website: http://www.nu.edu.pk

Rector: Amir Muhammed (2000-) EMail: amir@nu.edu.pk

Registrar: Mohammad Latif Virk
Tel: +92(51) 226-4629
EMail: latif.virk@nu.edu.pk; virk99@hotmail.com

International Relations: Mohammad Latif Virk, Registrar
Tel: +92(51) 226-4629

Campuses

Islamabad (Computer Engineering; Computer Science; Management; Telecommunications Engineering) *Director*: Aftab Ahmed Maroof; **Karachi** (Computer Engineering; Computer Science; Management; Telecommunications Engineering) *Director*: Zubair Ahmed Shaikh; **Lahore** (Computer Engineering; Computer Science; Management; Mathematics; Telecommunications Engineering) *Director*: S.M. Husnine; **Peshawar** (Computer Engineering; Computer Science; Management; Telecommunications Engineering) *Director*: Farooq Ahmad

History: Founded 1980. Sponsored by the Foundation for Advancement of Science and Technology (FAST). Acquired present status 2000.

Governing Bodies: Board of Trustees; Board of Governors

Academic Year: August/September to June

Admission Requirements: Intermediate/higher secondary certificate/ A level and entry test

Fees: (PK Rupees): 118,000

Main Language(s) of Instruction: English

Accrediting Agencies: Higher Education Commission; Pakistan Engineering Council

Degrees and Diplomas: *Bachelor's Degree*: Computer Science; Telecom Engineering; Computer Engineering; Business Administration (BS), 4 yrs; *Master's Degree*: Computer Science; Software Project Management; Telecom Engineering; Mathematics; Business Administration (MS), a further 1 1/2-2 yrs; *Doctor's Degree*: Computer Science; Mathematics (Ph.D.), 3-5 yrs

Student Services: Academic counselling, Canteen, Employment services, Language programs, Social counselling, Sports facilities

NEWPORTS INSTITUTE OF COMMUNICATIONS AND ECONOMICS (NICE)

159/0, Block-3, Kashmir Road, PECHS, Karachi, Sindh
Tel: +92(21) 4547417
Fax: +92(21) 4541089
EMail: info@newports.edu.pk
Website: http://www.newports.edu.pk

Chairman: Sadiq Jamal EMail: sadiq@newports.edu.pk

Registrar: Salman Jamal EMail: salman@newports.edu.pk

Faculties

Business and Administration (Business Administration); **Computer Science**

History: Founded 2002.

Degrees and Diplomas: *Bachelor's Degree*; *Master's Degree*

NORTHERN UNIVERSITY (NU)

3-The Mall, Nowshera Cantt, Nowshera, North West Frontier Province
Tel: +92(923) 613485-86
EMail: admin@biit.edu.pk
Website: http://www.northern.edu.pk

Rector: Mohammad Khan

Faculties

Administrative Sciences; **Arts and Social Sciences**; **Engineering and Information Technology**; **Science** (Mathematics; Statistics)

Further Information: Also branch in Islamabad.

History: Founded 2002.

Degrees and Diplomas: *Bachelor's Degree*; *Bachelor's Degree (Honours)*; *Master's Degree*

PRESTON INSTITUTE OF MANAGEMENT SCIENCES AND TECHNOLOGY

177/2, IEP Building, Sharah-e-Faisal, Karachi, Sindh
Tel: +92(21) 2789888-90
Fax: +92(21) 2789891
EMail: info@pimsat-khi.edu.pk
Website: http://pimsat-khi.edu.pk/

Rector: M.A. Jan

Deputy Registrar: Khawar Nehal

Programmes

Management (Management); **Technology** (Technology)

Degrees and Diplomas: *Bachelor's Degree*; *Master's Degree*: Business Administration

PRESTON UNIVERSITY KOHAT AND KARACHI

KDA Scheme II, Kohat, North West Frontier Province
Tel: +92(922) 515-081
Fax: +92(922) 515-084
Website: http://www.preston.edu.pk

Chancellor: Abdul Basit Tel: +92(922) 515-084

Faculties

Business Administration (Business Administration; E-Business/Commerce); **Doctoral Programmes** (Business Administration; Computer Science; Development Studies; Economics; International Relations; Philosophy; Technology); **Engineering** (Electrical and Electronic Engineering; Telecommunications Engineering; Textile Technology); **Information Technology** (Information Technology); **Natural Sciences** (Mathematics; Natural Sciences; Statistics); **Social Sciences** (Economics; International Relations; Psychology; Social Sciences); **Technology** (Electronic Engineering; Technology; Telecommunications Engineering)

Further Information: Also Islamabad, Peshawar, Lahore Canal, Lahore OPSTeC, Multan, Faisalabad, Gujranwala, Quetta, Karachi (IT, Business, B&F, BIS-1, BIS-2), Hyderabad and Dubai Campuses

History: Founded 1984. Acquired present status 2002. Also Campus in Karachi (founded 2004).

Accrediting Agencies: Higher Education Commission

Degrees and Diplomas: *Bachelor's Degree*: Business Administration, Information Technology, E-Commerce, Textile, Technology; *Master's Degree*: Business Administration, E-Commerce, Textile, Technology; *Master of Philosophy*

QURTUBA UNIVERSITY OF SCIENCE AND INFORMATION TECHNOLOGY (QUSIT)

Sheikh Yousuf Road, Desa Ismail Khan, Peshawar, North West Frontier Province
Tel: +92(966) 714-007 +92(966) 715-206
Fax: +92(966) 714-008
EMail: info@qurtuba.edu.pk
Website: http://www.qurtuba.edu.pk

Vice-Chancellor: Hameed Ullah Khan Alizai (2004-)
Tel: +92(966) 714-007, Fax: +92(966) 714-008

President: Abdul Aziz Khan Niazi (2001-)
Tel: +92(91) 581-2117, Fax: +92(91) 582-5837

International Relations: Qadar Bakhsh Baloch, Coordinator, Academic Programmes
Tel: +92(91) 5825-707, Fax: +92(91) 5825-837
EMail: qbuzdar@hotmail.com; qbuzdar@yahoo.com

Faculties

Basic Sciences (Mathematics; Natural Sciences) *Chairman*: Hamidullah Khan Alizai; **Information Technology and Computer Science** (Computer Science; Information Technology) *Chairman (Acting)*: Ehsanullah Marwat; **Linguistics** (Linguistics) *Chairman*: Khatir Ghaznavi; **Management Sciences** (Management) *Chairman*: Muhammad Khan Niazi; **Social Sciences and Humanities** (Arts and Humanities; Social Sciences) *Dean*: Muhammad Saleem

Further Information: Also a campus in Peshawar

History: Founded 2001.

Governing Bodies: Board of Governors; Academic Council

Admission Requirements: Intermediate or higher secondary certificate

Fees: (PK Rupees): c. 9,000-30,000 per semester

Main Language(s) of Instruction: English

Accrediting Agencies: Higher Education Commission of Pakistan

Degrees and Diplomas: *Diploma*: 1 sem; *Bachelor's Degree*: 1-4 yrs; *Master's Degree*: 1-3 yrs; *Master of Philosophy (M.Phil)*: 2 yrs; *Doctor's Degree (PhD)*: 3 yrs

Student Services: Academic counselling, Canteen, Employment services, Foreign student adviser, Health services, Social counselling, Sports facilities

Student Residential Facilities: Yes

Libraries: Yes

Publications: The Dialogue, Research Journal of Social Sciences and Humanities *(quarterly)*

RIPHAH INTERNATIONAL UNIVERSITY (RIU)

48th Street, G-6/1-1, Islamabad
Tel: +92(51) 2877-391 +92(51) 2877-392 +92(51) 2877-393
Fax: +92(51) 2828-189
EMail: Contact@riphah.edu.pk
Website: http://www.riphah.edu.pk

Vice-Chancellor: Anis Ahmad Tel: +92(51) 2877-390

International Relations: Muhammad Hafeez, Registrar and International Relations Officer EMail: mhafeez@riphah.edu.pk

Faculties
Computer Science (Computer Science; Information Technology; Software Engineering) *Dean*: Muhammad Sharif Bhatti; **Engineering and Applied Sciences** *Dean*: Muhammad Sharif Bhatti; **Health and Medical Sciences** (Health Sciences; Medicine; Surgery) *Dean*: Najam Khan; **Management Sciences** *Dean*: Muhammad Zaheer Akhtar; **Media Sciences** (Media Studies); **Pharmaceutical Sciences** (Pharmacology; Pharmacy) *Dean*: Inam ul Haq; **Social Sciences and Humanities** (Arts and Humanities; Social Sciences)

History: Founded 2002.

Governing Bodies: Board of Governors

Academic Year: September to August

Admission Requirements: Secondary school certificate

Main Language(s) of Instruction: English

International Co-operation: With universities in Malaysia, China, Jordan, Bahrain, United Kingdom

Accrediting Agencies: Higher Education Commission; Pakistan Medical and Dental Council; Pakistan Engineering Council; Pharmacy Council of Pakistan

Degrees and Diplomas: *Bachelor's Degree*: Medicine; Surgery; Pharmacy (MBBS), 5 yrs; *Bachelor's Degree*: Software Engineering; Computer Science; Information Technology; Computer Engineering; Telecommunication Engineering; Biomedical Engineering; Electronics Engineering; Dental Surgery (BS; BDS; BBA), 4 yrs; *Master's Degree*: Software Engineering; Business Administration; Pain Medicine (MS), a further 2 yrs; *Doctor's Degree*: Medicine; Surgery; Gynaecology and Obstetrics, Paediatrics, Anasthaesia, a further 5 yrs

Student Services: Academic counselling, Canteen, Cultural centre, Foreign Studies Centre, Health services, Language programs, Social counselling, Sports facilities

Student Residential Facilities: Separate hostels for boys & girls

Special Facilities: Yes

Libraries: Yes

SARHAD UNIVERSITY OF SCIENCE AND INFORMATION TECHNOLOGY

36-B, Chinar Road, University Town, Peshawar, North West Frontier Province
Tel: +92(91) 584-6508-9
Fax: +92(91) 584-1460
EMail: info@suit.edu.pk
Website: http://www.suit.edu.pk/mai

Vice-Chancellor: Salim ur Rehman EMail: vc@suit.edu.pk

Registrar: Muhammad Nasir EMail: registrar@suit.edu.pk

Faculties
Arts, Social Sciences and Education (Arts and Humanities; Education; Social Sciences; Urdu); **Computer Science/IT** (Computer Science; Information Technology; Telecommunications Engineering); **Engineering** (Electrical Engineering; Electronic Engineering; Engineering; Mechanical Engineering); **Life Sciences**; **Management** (Management)

History: Founded 2001.

Degrees and Diplomas: *Bachelor's Degree (BBA)*; *Bachelor's Degree*: Computer Science, Information Technology (BS-CS; BS-IT; BS-Telecommunication); Engineering; Management; Education (Btech; BBA; Bed); *Master's Degree*: Business Administration; Management (MBA; MPH); Urdu; Education (MA; Med); *Master of Philosophy*: Arts and Humanities, Education (Mphil); *Doctor's Degree*: Urdu; Education (PhD)

Last Updated: 21/11/08

SHAHEED ZULFIKAR ALI BHUTTO INSTITUTE OF SCIENCE AND TECHNOLOGY (SZABIST)

90, Clifton, Karachi, Sindh 75600
Tel: +92(21) 1119-22478
Fax: +92(21) 583-0446
EMail: info@szabist.edu.pk
Website: http://www.szabist.edu.pk

President: Saqib Rizavi EMail: saqib.rizavi@szabist.edu.pk

Registrar: Azeem Muhammad EMail: azeem@szabist.edu.pk

International Relations: Jaya S. Loungani, Manager, External Relations and Financial Assistance EMail: jaya@szabist.edu.pk

Faculties
Computer Science (Computer Science; E-Business/Commerce; Software Engineering) *Coordinator*: Mohammad Nadeem; **Management Sciences** (Finance; Human Resources; Information Management; Information Technology; Management; Marketing) *Coordinator*: Zia Ul Haq Memon; **Social Sciences** (Social Sciences) *Coordinator*: Amanat Ali Jalbani

History: Founded 1995. In the process of development.

Governing Bodies: Board of Trustees

Academic Year: August to July, (August-December; January-May; June-July) for Undergraduate and Postgraduate programmes

Admission Requirements: Intermediate or Higher Secondary Certificate, A level or equivalent. (For MBA and MS, First Degree or equivalent)

Fees: (PK Rupees): Undergraduate, 47,250 per semester; Graduate, 42,240-54,900

Main Language(s) of Instruction: English

International Co-operation: With universities in USA and Korea

Accrediting Agencies: Provincial Assembly; Government of Sindh; Higher Education Commission (HEC); Government of Pakistan

Degrees and Diplomas: *Bachelor's Degree*: Law (LLB), 3 yrs; *Bachelor's Degree*: Management; Marketing; Finance; Information Technology (BBA); Software Engineering; Computer Systems; Technology Management (BS), 4 yrs; *Master's Degree*: Database Management Systems; Networking (MS); International Relations; Sociology; Political Science; Economics (MS); Management; Marketing; Finance; Information Technology (MS), 1 further yr; *Master's Degree*: Management; Marketing; Finance; Information Technology (MBA); Software Engineering; Computer Systems; Technology Management (MCS), a further 2 yrs; *Doctor's Degree*: Database Management Systems; Networking (PhD), 2-3 yrs; *Doctor's Degree*: International Relations; Sociology; Political Science; Economics (PhD), a further 2-3 yrs; *Doctor's Degree*: Management; Marketing; Finance; Information Technology (PhD), a further 3 yrs

Student Services: Academic counselling, Canteen, Employment services, Foreign student adviser, Language programs, Social counselling

Student Residential Facilities: None

Special Facilities: Multimedia Room; Auditorium

Libraries: 5,571 vols

Publications: Journal of Independent Studies and Research (JISR) *(biannually)*; Phoenix *(biannually)*

Student Numbers *2011-2012*: Total 3,496
Last Updated: 07/04/08

SIR SYED UNIVERSITY OF ENGINEERING AND TECHNOLOGY (SSUET)

University Road, Karachi, Sindh 75300
Tel: +92(21) 498-8000
Fax: +92(21) 498-2393
EMail: info@ssuet.edu.pk
Website: http://www.ssuet.edu.pk

Vice-Chancellor: Saiyid Nazir Ahmad (1997-)
Tel: +92(21) 498-8777
EMail: nazir@ssuet.edu.pk; vc@ssuet.edu.pk

Registrar: Shah Mehmood Syed
Tel: +92(21) 498-6585 EMail: registrar@ssuet.edu.pk

International Relations: Khan Zaman Mubarak
EMail: mubarak_zaman@yahoo.com

Departments
Applied Mathematics (Applied Mathematics) *Director*: Syed Jawaid Hassan Rizvl; **Biomedical Engineering** (Biomedical Engineering) *Director*: M.A. Haleem; **Civil Engineering** (Civil Engineering) *Director*: Makhdumi Maqbool Saeed; **Computer Engineering** (Computer Engineering) *Director*: Tasadduq Ali Imran;

Electronic Engineering (Electronic Engineering) *Dean*: Siddiqui Najeeb; **Science** (Natural Sciences) *Dean*: Jawaid Hassan Rizvi Syed

Research Centres

International *Director*: Farooqui Amir

Further Information: 39 Research Laboratories

History: Founded 1993.

Academic Year: January to December (January-June; July-December)

Admission Requirements: Intermediate or Higher Secondary Certificate (Pre-Engineering Group)

Main Language(s) of Instruction: English

Degrees and Diplomas: *Bachelor's Degree*: Biomedical Engineering; Civil Engineering; Computer Engineeering; Electronic Engineering, 4 yrs; *Master's Degree*: Computer Engineering; Electronic Engineering, 2 yrs; *Doctor's Degree (PhD)*: 3-5 yrs

Student Services: Academic counselling, Canteen, Employment services, Foreign student adviser, Health services, Sports facilities

Last Updated: 07/04/08

SUPERIOR UNIVERSITY

31 Tipu Block, New Garden Town, Lahore, Punjab
Tel: +92(42) 5858031-3
Fax: +92(42) 5858033
EMail: info@superior.edu.pk
Website: http://www.superior.edu.pk

Rector: Abdul Rehman

Colleges

Business and Management; **Computer Science and Information Technology** (Computer Science; Telecommunications Services); **Economics and Commerce**; **Intermediate**; **Law**

Degrees and Diplomas: *Bachelor's Degree*: Business Administration (BBA), 3 yrs; *Bachelor's Degree*: Commerce (B.Com); Law (BA), 2 yrs; *Bachelor's Degree (Honours)*: Aviation Management (BS); Business Administration (BBA); Computer Science (BSc); Telecommunication (BSc), 4 yrs; *Master's Degree*: Business Administration (MBA (Professional)); Computer Science (MS); Economics (MSc); Mass Communication (MS); Telecommunication (MSc), 2 yrs; *Master's Degree*: Business Administration (MBA (Executive)); Commerce (M.Com), $2\frac{1}{2}$ yrs; *Master's Degree*: Law (LL.M), $1\frac{1}{2}$ yrs; *Master of Philosophy*: Business Administration (MS; M.Phil), 1 yr

TEXTILE INSTITUTE OF PAKISTAN

10/F, Block-6 PECHS, Karachi, Sindh 75400
Tel: +92(21) 4549734
Fax: +92(21) 4533525
EMail: info@tip.edu.pk
Website: http://www.tip.edu.pk

Chancellor: Arif Hasan

Programmes

Textile Design Technology (Textile Design); **Textile Management and Marketing** (Management; Marketing); **Textile Science** (Textile Technology); **Textile Technology** (Textile Technology)

History: Founded 1994. Obtained status 2001

Governing Bodies: Board of Governors; Academic Council

Fees: (PK Rupees): 60,000 per semester

Degrees and Diplomas: *Bachelor's Degree (Honours)*: Textile Science; Textile Design Technology; Textile Management & Marketing; Apparel Manufacturing & Merchandising (BSc, BBA), 4 yrs

Student Residential Facilities: Yes

Special Facilities: Science laboratories; Textile testing laboratories; CAD/CAM laboratories

Libraries: c. 6,500 vols

THE UNIVERSITY OF FAISALABAD (TUF)

4 km-Sargodha Road, Faisalabad, Punjab 38850
Tel: +92(41) 8868326-30
Fax: +92(41) 8868220
EMail: info@tuf.edu.pk
Website: http://tuf.edu.pk

Pro-Rector: Abdul Majeed (2003-)

Director, Administration and Registrar: Izhar Ul Ahsan

Faculties

Engineering Technology and Computer Science *Dean*: Syed Ather Hashmi; **Islamic and Oriental Learning** (Arabic; Islamic Studies; Oriental Studies) *Dean*: Zahoor Azhar; **Management Sciences and Business Administration** (Business Administration; Management) *Dean*: Tariq Kaleem; **Medical Sciences** (Biochemistry; Medicine; Physiology; Surgery) *Dean*: Muhammad Ali; **Social Sciences and Humanities** (Arabic; Economics; English; Social Sciences) *Dean*: Akram Khan Khan

Institutes

Fashion Design (Fashion Design; Interior Design; Textile Design)

History: Founded 2002.

Governing Bodies: Board of Governors

Academic Year: September to August (September-January; February-June; July-August)

Admission Requirements: 50 % marks in 'A' level or intermediate certificate

Fees: (PK Rupees): 14,250-195,000

Main Language(s) of Instruction: English

Degrees and Diplomas: *Bachelor's Degree*; *Bachelor's Degree (Honours)*; *Master's Degree*

Student Services: Academic counselling, Canteen, Cultural centre, Employment services, Foreign student adviser, Foreign Studies Centre, Health services, Social counselling, Sports facilities

Student Residential Facilities: Yes

Special Facilities: Museum, Auditorium

Libraries: Yes

THE UNIVERSITY OF LAHORE (UOL)

1 Km Raiwind Road, Lahore, Punjab 54600
Tel: +92(42) 5411901-17
Fax: +92(42) 5413036
EMail: info@uol.edu.pk
Website: http://www.uol.edu.pk

Rector: M. H. Qazi
Tel: +92(42) 541-2082 EMail: mhqazi@ulhr.edu.pk

Colleges

Medicine and Dentistry (Anaesthesiology; Anatomy; Biochemistry; Cardiology; Community Health; Dentistry; Dermatology; Forensic Medicine and Dentistry; Gynaecology and Obstetrics; Medicine; Ophthalmology; Orthopaedics; Paediatrics; Pathology; Pharmacology; Physical Therapy; Psychiatry and Mental Health; Radiology; Surgery; Urology)

Departments

Computer Science and Information Technology (Computer Science; Information Technology); **Management Science**; **Mathematics and Statistics**; **Pharmacy** (Pharmacy)

History: Founded 1999. Acquired present status 2002.

Degrees and Diplomas: *Bachelor's Degree*; *Master's Degree*. Also Postgraduate Diploma

UNIVERSITY OF CENTRAL PUNJAB (UCP)

31, Main Gulberg, Lahore, Punjab 54000
Tel: +92(42) 5755314-7
Fax: +92(42) 5710881
EMail: info@ucp.edu.pk
Website: http://www.ucp.edu.pk

Pro-Rector: Fehmida Fehmida
Tel: +92(42) 5755314-17, Fax: +92(42) 5710881
EMail: prorector@ucp.edu.pk

Executive Director Planning & Coordination/Registrar: Ejaz Ahmad Qureshi
Tel: +92(42) 5755314-17, Fax: +92(42) 5710881
EMail: exec.dir.pc@ucp.edu.pk

Faculties
Commerce (Business and Commerce); **Information Technology** (Computer Science; Information Technology); **Law** (Law); **Management Studies** (Business Administration; Management)

History: Founded 2002.

Degrees and Diplomas: *Bachelor's Degree*; *Master's Degree*; *Doctor's Degree*: Information Technology

UNIVERSITY OF EAST (UOE)
640/B, Unit No: 2, Latifabad, Hyderabad, Sindh
Tel: +92(22) 3868612
Fax: +92(22) 3863990
EMail: Info@universityofeast.com
Website: http://www.uoe.edu.pk/

Rector: Abdul Qadeer

Registrar: Mirza Hammad Baig
EMail: registrar@universityofeast.com

Departments
Business Administration; **English** (English); **Information Technology** (Information Technology); **Law** (Law); **Media Science**

Degrees and Diplomas: *Bachelor's Degree*; *Master's Degree*: Business Administration; English

UNIVERSITY OF MANAGEMENT AND TECHNOLOGY (IMT)
C-II, Johar Town, Lahore, Punjab
Tel: +92(42) 5212801-10
Fax: +92(42) 5184789
EMail: admissions@umt.edu.pk
Website: http://www.umt.edu.pk/

Rector: Hasan Sohaib Murad

Schools
Business and Economics; **Education and Arts** (Education; English; Islamic Studies); **Science and Technology** (Computer Engineering; Computer Science; Mathematics; Natural Sciences; Telecommunications Engineering; Textile Technology)

Further Information: Also branch in Islamabad

Degrees and Diplomas: *Bachelor's Degree*; *Master's Degree*; *Master of Philosophy*; *Doctor's Degree*: Computer Science; Education; Electrical Engineering; Management; Textile Chemistry; Applied Linguistics

UNIVERSITY OF SOUTH ASIA (USA)
47 Tufail Road, Lahore, Punjab 54810
Tel: +92(42) 667-2942-5
Fax: +92(42) 665-0983
EMail: solutions@usa.edu.pk
Website: http://www.usa.edu.pk

Vice Chancellor: Mohammed Salim Akhter (2006-)
Fax: +92(42) 667-3810 EMail: msakhter@yahoo.com

Registrar: Anwar ul Haq Anwar EMail: m.anwarul.haq@usa.edu.pk

International Relations: Nadeem Farooki Farooki, Director, Admissions and Academics

Faculties
Art and Fashion Design *Associated Dean*: Khalid Ejaz Ahmad Khan; **Commerce** (Accountancy; Economics; Finance) *Head*: Muhammad Nadeem; **Computer Science** *Head*: Adnan Nabeel Qureshi; **Engineering** (Electrical and Electronic Engineering) *Head*: Muhammad Rauf Butt; **Law** *Dean*: Mohammad Naeem; **Management** *Dean*: Ejaz Sandhu

Governing Bodies: Board of Governors

Admission Requirements: Intermediate (FA / FSc) or equivalent (A-levels) for Bachelor's programme; Bachelor's degree required for Master's programme

Fees: (PK Rupees): 15,000 for admission; 36,000 per semester for tuition

Main Language(s) of Instruction: English

Accrediting Agencies: Higher Education Commission (HEC)

Degrees and Diplomas: *Bachelor's Degree*: Architecture, Fashion Design (Barch); Business Administration (BBA); Computer Science (BSCS), 4 yrs; *Bachelor's Degree*: Commerce (Bcom), 2 yrs; *Bachelor's Degree*: Law (LLB), 3 yrs; *Master's Degree*: Business Administration (MBA); Fashion Design (MFD); Fine Arts (MFA), a further 2 yrs; *Master's Degree*: Computer Science (MSCS), a further 2 yrs / 1 yr after BSCS; *Master's Degree*: Law (LLM), a further year

Student Services: Academic counselling, Canteen, Employment services, Foreign student adviser, Language programs, Social counselling, Sports facilities

Student Residential Facilities: Separate accommodation for male and female students

Libraries: yes

UNIVERSITY OF WAH
Wah, Punjab 47040
Website: http://www.uw.edu.pk/

Head: Khalid Parvez Lone

Faculties
Basic Sciences (Biology; Chemistry; Mathematics; Physics; Statistics); **Computer Science** (Computer Science); **Engineering**; **Management**; **Social Sciences and Humanities**

History: Founded 2005.

Governing Bodies: Board of Governors

Fees: (PK Rupees): 22,575 - 38,175 depending on programmes

Degrees and Diplomas: *Bachelor's Degree (Honours)*; *Master's Degree*; *Doctor's Degree (PhD)*

Student Services: Sports facilities

Last Updated: 06/01/10

IAU ZIAUDDIN UNIVERSITY (ZU)
4/B, Shahra-e-Ghalib, Block-6, Clifton, Karachi, Sindh 75600
Tel: +92(21) 3586-2937
Fax: +92(21) 3586-2940
EMail: info@zu.edu.pk
Website: http://www.zu.edu.pk/

Vice-Chancellor: Pirzada Qasim Raza Siddiqui (2012-)
Tel: +92(21) 3530-5451, Fax: +92(21) 3583-3674
EMail: vc@zu.edu.pk

Registrar: Mohammad Yousaf (2008-2013)
Tel: 021 3582 3519, Fax: 021 3582 2940

International Relations: Kamran Hameed, Dean, Ziauddin Medical College (2008-2013)
Tel: +92(21) 3582-3519, Fax: +92(21) 3582-940
EMail: deanzmc@zu.edu.pk

Colleges
Dentistry (Dentistry); **Media Sciences** (Media Studies); **Medicine** (Anaesthesiology; Cardiology; Dermatology; Gastroenterology; Gynaecology and Obstetrics; Haematology; Laboratory Techniques; Medicine; Neurology; Oncology; Ophthalmology; Orthopaedics; Otorhinolaryngology; Paediatrics; Psychiatry and Mental Health; Radiology; Surgery); **Nursing and Midwifery** (Midwifery; Nursing); **Pharmacy** (Pathology; Pharmacology; Pharmacy); **Physical Therapy** (Physical Therapy; Speech Therapy and Audiology)

Faculties
Arts; **Business Administration** (Business Administration); **Engineering** (Biomedical Engineering; Biomedicine); **Fine Arts** (Fine Arts); **Law** (Law)

History: Founded 1995 as Ziauddin Medical University. Acquired current title 2005.

Academic Year: November to October

Admission Requirements: A-Level or higher secondary school certificate (pre-medical), minimum 60% marks in Pre-Medical Group

Fees: (PK Rupees): 24,000-475,000 per annum for local residents. (US Dollar): 6,000-12,000 for overseas applicants, depending on programmes

Main Language(s) of Instruction: English

Accrediting Agencies: Higher Education Commission; Pakistan Medical and Dental Council; Pharmacy Council of Pakistan; Pakistan Nursing Council; Pakistan Engineering Council; College of Physicians and Surgeon of Pakistan for Fellowship training

Degrees and Diplomas: *Bachelor's Degree*: Media Studies; Biomedical Engineering; Medical Technology (BSc); Medicine; Surgery (MBBS); Nursing; Physical Therapy; Speech Language Therapy; Dental Surgery; *Master's Degree*: Medical Technology (MS); Surgery (Master of Surgery); *Master of Philosophy*: Basic Health Sciences and Periondotology (MPhil); *Doctor's Degree*: Basic Health Sciences and Periondotology (PhD); Medicine (MD). Also Postgraduate Diploma in: Medical Librarianship and Medical Record Science. Diploma in Pharmacy (4yrs)

Student Services: Academic counselling, Canteen, Employment services, Foreign student adviser, Foreign Studies Centre, Handicapped facilities, Health services, Language programs, Social counselling, Sports facilities

Student Residential Facilities: None

Special Facilities: Anatomy Museum; Pathology and Research lab

Libraries: c. 8,000 vols; 25 jounals; Selected books and periodicals avalaible online

Student Numbers *2011-2012*: Total 1,720

Last Updated: 18/02/10

Palestine

STRUCTURE OF HIGHER EDUCATION SYSTEM

Description:

Higher education is mainly provided by universities and community colleges. All universities have their own administrative organization with a President, a Vice-President, and a Board of Trustees. Colleges are headed by a Dean and Administrative Councils. The Ministry of Higher Education is the national organization which supervises and coordinates the activities of the higher education institutions within the framework of national policies.

Stages of studies:

University level first stage: *Bachelor's degree*
The Bachelor's degree is generally conferred after four years' study by universities and some university colleges. Engineering and Agricultural studies last for five years.

University level second stage: *Master's degree, Postgraduate diploma*
Master's degrees are conferred in certain subjects two years beyond the Bachelor's degree. Postgraduate diplomas are conferred in certain subjects after one or two years' study beyond the Bachelor's degree without research training.

University level third stage: *Doctorate (PhD)*
Doctorates are awarded in certain subjects after three years of study beyond the Master's degree.

Distance higher education:
Distance education is offered at Al-Quds Open University which comprises 20 regional centres. The University offers undergraduate Degrees and Continuing Education and Training courses.

ADMISSION TO HIGHER EDUCATION

Admission to university-level studies:

Name of secondary school credential required: Tawjihi

Minimum score/requirement: 65%

For entry to: Access to universities and university colleges

Alternatives to credentials: Palestinian Tawjihi; Foreign secondary school certificate equivalent to the Tawjihi

Entrance exam requirements: University entrance exam in Mathematics, and English or Arabic in some universities.

Foreign students admission:

Definition of foreign student: Any student who is not of Palestinian origin.

Entrance exam requirements: Secondary school Certificate level. If students continue their studies, universities take their grades into consideration.

Health requirements: Health certificate.

Language requirements: Students should have a good knowledge of English and/or Arabic.

RECOGNITION OF STUDIES

Quality assurance system:

All programmes officially registered and accredited by the Ministry of Education and Higher Education.

NATIONAL BODIES

Ministry of Education and Higher Education

P.O. Box 576
Al-Masioun
Ramallah
Tel: +972(2) 298 3200
Fax: +972(2) 298 3222
EMail: irp@mohe.gov.ps
WWW: http://www.mohe.gov.ps

Role of national body: Supervising and coordinating all activities related to education in Palestine.

Accreditation and Quality Assurance Commission - AQAC

Head of AQAC: Mirvat Bulbul
PO Box 1932
Ramallah
Tel: +970(2) 298 0140
Fax: +970(2) 295 4518
EMail: aqac.head@mohe.gov.ps
WWW: http://www.aqac.mohe.gov.ps

Role of national body: Licenses and accredits higher education institutions and academic programmes and carries out institutional and academic programme evaluation.

Data for academic year: 2006-2007

Source: IAU from Ministry of Education and Higher Education, Higher Education Sector, Palestine, 2006. Bodies, 2012.

INSTITUTIONS

PUBLIC INSTITUTIONS

AL-AQSA UNIVERSITY

Gaza, Gaza Strip
Tel: +972(8) 282-6809 +972(8) 282-6819
Fax: +972(8) 286-5309
EMail: alaqsa@alaqsa.edu.ps
Website: http://www.alaqsa.edu.ps

President: Ali Zidan Abu Zuhri (2002-)
Tel: +972(8) 283-943, Fax: +972(8) 282-7996
EMail: president@alaqsa.edu.ps

Vice-president for Academic Affairs: Ayman Mahmoud Subh
Tel: +972(8) 284-5478, Fax: +972(8) 284-5478

Faculties

Administration (Accountancy; Banking; Business Administration; Finance); **Arts** (Arabic; English; French; Geography; History; Islamic Studies; Library Science; Sociology); **Education** (Education; Pedagogy; Psychology); **Fine Arts** (Ceramic Art; Graphic Design; Photography; Textile Design; Weaving); **Media** (Journalism; Media Studies; Multimedia; Radio and Television Broadcasting); **Science** (Biology; Chemistry; Computer Science; Mathematics; Physics; Technology)

History: Founded 1991. Acquired present status and title 2001.

Governing Bodies: Ministry of Education and Higher Education

Academic Year: September to June. Also summer session (June to August)

Admission Requirements: Secondary school certificate

Fees: (Jordanian Dinars): 10 per credit hour per semester

Main Language(s) of Instruction: Arabic

Accrediting Agencies: Ministry of Education and Higher Education

Degrees and Diplomas: *Bachelor's Degree*: Science (BSc), 4 yrs

Student Services: Academic counselling, Canteen, Health services, Social counselling, Sports facilities

Libraries: Two libraries

Publications: Journal of Applied Sciences *(biennially)*; Journal of Human Sciences, Arts, human sciences, education, information *(biennially)*

Press or Publishing House: Al-Aqsa University Press

Last Updated: 27/07/11

AL-AZHAR UNIVERSITY - GAZA

Jame'at Al-Azhar Bi Ghazza (AUG)
PO Box 1277, Gaza, Gaza Strip
Tel: +970(8) 282-4010
Fax: +970(8) 282-3180
EMail: alazhar@alazhar.edu.ps
Website: http://www.alazhar.edu.ps

President: Jawad A. Wadi (2006-) EMail: jwadi@hotmail.com

Vice-President for Planning and Quality Assurance: Mahmoud K. Okasha EMail: m.okasha@palnet.com

International Relations: Mahmoud K. Okasha, Vice-President for Planning and Quality Assurance EMail: m.okasha@palnet.com

Faculties

Agriculture and Environment (Agriculture; Animal Husbandry; Environmental Management; Food Science; Plant and Crop Protection); **Applied Medical Sciences** (Laboratory Techniques; Physical Therapy; Radiology); **Arts and Human Sciences** (Arabic; English; French; Geography; History; Literature; Middle Eastern Studies; Sociology); **Dentistry** (Dentistry); **Economics and Administrative Sciences** (Accountancy; Business Administration; Economics; Political Sciences; Statistics); **Education** (Foreign

Languages Education; Mathematics Education; Native Language Education; Primary Education; Science Education; Teacher Trainers Education); **Engineering and Information Technology** (Engineering; Information Technology; Software Engineering); **Law** (Law; Private Law; Public Law); **Medicine** (Anatomy; Gynaecology and Obstetrics; Immunology; Paediatrics; Pathology; Pharmacology; Physiology; Social and Preventive Medicine); **Pharmacy** (Pharmacy); **Science** (Biology; Chemistry; Geography; Geology; Industrial Chemistry; Mathematics; Physics); **Sharia** (Islamic Law)

History: Founded 1991. Acquired status 1992.

Governing Bodies: University Council; Board of Trustees; Academic Council

Academic Year: September to August (Sept to Jan; Feb to June; June to Aug)

Admission Requirements: Secondary school certificate, with an average of at least 65%

Fees: (US Dollars): 30 per credit hour

Main Language(s) of Instruction: Arabic, English

International Co-operation: With universities in Egypt; United Kingdom; France; Germany; Turkey; Belgium; USA

Accrediting Agencies: Ministry of Education and Higher Education

Degrees and Diplomas: *Bachelor's Degree*: Administration; Accounting; Economics; Applied Statistics; Political Sciences (B.Sc); Agriculture and Environment (B.Agric); Education; Law (B.Ed; B.Law); Physical Therapy; Laboratory Medicine; Physics; Computing; Microbiology; Chemistry; Mathematics; Geology; Geography (B.Sc); Sociology; English; French; History; Geography; English Literature; Middle Eastern Studies; Arabic Literature (B.A), 4 yrs; *Bachelor's Degree*: Dentistry; Pharmacy; Computer System Engineering (B.Dent; B.Pharm; B.Eng), 5 yrs; *Bachelor's Degree*: Medicine (MB), 6 yrs; *Master's Degree*: Administration; Accounting; Economics; Applied Statistics; Political Sciences (M.Sc); Agriculture and Environment (M.Agric); Engineering; Law (M.Eng; M.Law); Physical Therapy; Laboratory Medicine; Physics; Computing; Microbiology; Chemistry; Mathematics; Geology; Georgraphy (M.Sc); Sociology; English; French; History; Geography; English Literature; Middle Eastern Studies; Arabic Literature (M.A), 2 yrs; *Master's Degree*: Education (M.Edu), 3 yrs. also: Diploma of Education, 1 yr.

Student Services: Academic counselling, Canteen, Cultural centre, Handicapped facilities, Health services, Language programs, Nursery care, Social counselling, Sports facilities

Special Facilities: Art gallery

Libraries: 69,000 vols; 150 journal subscriptions; access to electronic networks.

Publications: Journal of Al-Azhar University-Gaza (Humanities), Scientific research journal *(quarterly)*; Journal of Al-Azhar University-Gaza (Natural Sciences), Scientific research journal *(quarterly)*

Last Updated: 27/07/11

AL-QUDS OPEN UNIVERSITY (QOU)

PO Box 51800, Sheikh Jarrah, Musa Feidi Street, East Jerusalem, West Bank

Tel: +972(2) 581-6239 +972(2) 581-7237 +972(2) 581-6283

Fax: +972(2) 581-6734

EMail: pub_relations@qou.edu

Website: http://www.qou.edu

President: Younes Amro (2001-)
Tel: +972(2) 296-4571, Fax: +972(2) 296-4570
EMail: yamro@qou.edu

Vice-President for Administrative Affairs: Samir Al-Najdi
Tel: +972(2) 581-6239, Fax: +972(2) 581-6734
EMail: administrative@qou.edu

International Relations: Lucy Hishmeh, Head, Public Relations Department
Tel: +972(2) 240-3160, Fax: +972(2) 240-6077
EMail: lhishmeh@qou.edu

Centres

Continuing Education and Communication Service (Communication Studies; Continuing Education); **Information and Communication Technology** (Information Technology; Telecommunications Engineering); **Media Production** (Media Studies)

Departments

Research and Postgraduate Studies (Distance Education; Information Sciences; Public Administration; Social Work)

Faculties

Administration and Economic Sciences (Accountancy; Administration; Economics; Finance; Marketing); **Agriculture** (Agriculture; Animal Husbandry; Horticulture; Plant and Crop Protection); **Education** (Arabic; History; Islamic Studies; Mathematics; Natural Sciences); **Social and Family Development** (Child Care and Development; Family Studies; Social Work); **Technology and Applied Sciences** (Computer Science; Information Technology)

Further Information: Also branches outside Palestine: two in Saudi Arabia (Riyadh Studt Center and Jeddah Study Centre) and one in the United Arab Emirates.

History: Founded 1985. Acquired present status 1991. At present there are 22 educational areas and Study Centres in the major cities of Palestine, .

Governing Bodies: Board of Trustees; the University Council

Academic Year: October to July (October-January; March-July); also Summer semester,(July-August; August to September)

Admission Requirements: Secondary school Certificate (Tawjihi)

Fees: (Jordanian Dinars): 13 per credit hour

Main Language(s) of Instruction: Arabic

Accrediting Agencies: Ministry of Higher Education, Association of Arab Universities

Degrees and Diplomas: *Diploma*: Education, 2 yrs; *Bachelor's Degree*: Education; Management and Economics Science; Agriculture; Social and Family Development; Technology and Applied Sciences, 4-12 yrs

Student Services: Academic counselling, Canteen, Employment services, Handicapped facilities, Language programs, Social counselling

Student Residential Facilities: None

Special Facilities: Studio for Multimedia instruction material; Video-Conference

Libraries: Central library in Ramallah and one small library in every Educational Areas and Studies Centres

Publications: QOU's Refereed Research Journal *(biannually)*; Resalat Jamiat Al-Quds Al Maftooha *(quarterly)*

Last Updated: 21/06/11

AL-QUDS UNIVERSITY

PO Box 51000, Abdel Hamaid Shoman Street, Beit Hanina, East Jerusalem

Tel: +972(2) 2627-4979

Fax: +972(2) 2627-7166

EMail: alqudsu@planet.edu

Website: http://www.alquds.edu

President: Sari Anwar Nusseibeh (1995-)
Tel: +972(2) 583-8652, Fax: +972(2) 583-8653
EMail: president@admin.alquds.edu

International Relations: Samira Barghouthi, International Academic Cooperation (2009-)
Tel: +972(2) 791-293, Fax: +972(2) 791-293
EMail: sbarghouthi@planet.edu

Centres

Advancement of Peace and Democracy *(Issam Sartawi)* (Peace and Disarmament); **Islamic Research** (Islamic Studies); **Jerusalem Studies** (Linguistics; Modern Languages); **Political Prisoners Affairs** *(Abu-Jihad)* (Civil Law); **Women and Gender Studies** *(INSAN)* (Gender Studies; Women's Studies)

Colleges

Graduate Studies

Faculties

Arts (Arabic; Archaeology; Arts and Humanities; Development Studies; English; Fine Arts; Geography; History; Media Studies; Music; Philosophy; Physical Education; Political Sciences; Social

Work; Urban Studies); **Business and Economics** (Accountancy; Administration; Banking; Business Administration; Economics; Finance; Marketing); **Da'wa and Religious Studies** (Islamic Law; Islamic Theology; Religious Studies); **Dentistry** (Dentistry; Orthodontics; Periodontics); **Education** (Curriculum; Primary Education; Psychology); **Engineering** (Computer Engineering; Electronic Engineering; Engineering; Materials Engineering); **Health Professions** (Health Education; Laboratory Techniques; Midwifery; Nursing; Physical Therapy); **Law** (Law); **Medicine** (Medicine); **Pharmacy** (Pharmacy); **Public Health** (Public Health); **Quran and Islamic Studies** (Islamic Studies; Koran); **Science and Technology** (Biology; Chemistry; Computer Science; Earth Sciences; Environmental Studies; Food Technology; Information Technology; Mathematics; Natural Sciences; Technology)

Institutes
Applied Research (Regional Studies); **Archaeology** (Archaeology); **Economics and Business Studies** (Business and Commerce; Economics); **Modern Media** (Media Studies); **Regional Studies** (American Studies; Asian Studies; Middle Eastern Studies); **Sustainable Development**

Research Centres
Health (Health Education)

History: Founded 1984.

Governing Bodies: Board of Trustees, comprising 7 public and academic personalities; Executive Committee; Academic Council

Academic Year: October to June (October-January; February-June); Also summer course from Augsut to September

Admission Requirements: Secondary school Certificate (Tawjeihi) or recognized foreign equivalent and entrance examination

Main Language(s) of Instruction: Arabic, English

Degrees and Diplomas: *Bachelor's Degree*: Administration and Economic Sciences; Arts (BA); Da'wa and Principles of Religion; Health Professions; Law; Public Health; Quran and Islamic Studies; Science and Technology (BSc), 4 yrs; *Bachelor's Degree*: Computer Engineering; Dentistry; Electronic Engineering (BElEng); Pharmacy, 5 yrs; *Bachelor's Degree*: Medicine, 5 yrs + 2 yrs; *Bachelor's Degree*: Science and Culture; *Master's Degree*: Accountancy; Applied and Industrial Technology; Applied Mathematics; Arabic Language and Literature; Area Studies (Israeli/Middle Eastern Studies); Business Administration; Chemistry; Community Mental Health; Economics; Educational Administration; Educational Counselling; Islamic Archaeology (MA); Maternal-Child Health Nursing; Media Studies; Modern Islamic Studies; Nursing Management; Organic Chemistry and Molecular Biology; Physics; Public and Civil Law; Public Health; Speech and Language Disorders; Teaching Methods. Also posgraduate Diplomas

Special Facilities: Palestinian Heritage Museum

Libraries: c. 81,000 vols

Publications: Science Journal *(annually)*

Last Updated: 21/06/11

AN-NAJAH NATIONAL UNIVERSITY (ANU)

PO Box 7, Omar Ibn Al-Khattab Street 00972, Nablus, West Bank
Tel: +972(9) 234-5115 +972(9) 239-4988
Fax: +972(9) 234-5982
EMail: info@najah.edu
Website: http://www.najah.edu

President: Rami Hamdallah (1998-)
EMail: president@najah.edu; rami@najah.edu

Vice-President for Academic Affairs: Maher Al-Natsheh
EMail: natsheh@najah.edu

International Relations: Kherieh Rasass, Director, Office of International and Strategic Affairs
Tel: +972(9) 239-4960, Ext. 4486 EMail: international@najah.edu

Centres
Energy Research (Natural Resources); **Biological, Chemical and Drug Analysis** (Biology; Chemistry; Toxicology); **Community Service** (Social and Community Services); **Computer Science** (Computer Science); **Construction and Transportation Research** (Construction Engineering; Transport and Communications); **Continuing Education** (Continuing Education); **Earth Sciences and Seismic Engineering** (Earth Sciences; Seismology); **Human Rights and Democracy** *(UNESCO Chair)* (Human Rights); **Measurement and Evaluation**; **Opinion Polls and Survey Studies** (Social Studies); **Poison Control and Drug Information** (Toxicology); **Urban and Regional Planning** (Regional Planning; Urban Studies); **Water and Environmental Studies** (Environmental Studies; Water Science)

Colleges
Community *(An-Najah)* (Accountancy; Banking; Business Administration; Finance; Marketing; Medical Auxiliaries; Pharmacy); **Technology** *(Hisham Hijawi)* (Computer Engineering; Electrical Engineering; Electronic Engineering; Graphic Design; Heating and Refrigeration; Industrial Engineering; Mechanical Engineering; Technology)

Faculties
Agriculture (Agricultural Economics; Animal Husbandry; Crop Production; Food Technology; Nutrition; Plant and Crop Protection); **Arts** (Arabic; Archaeology; Arts and Humanities; English; French; Geography; History; Literature; Social Work; Sociology; Tourism); **Economics and Administration** (Accountancy; Banking; Business Administration; Economics; Finance; Marketing; Political Sciences); **Educational Sciences and Psychology** (Educational Administration; Educational and Student Counselling; Educational Sciences; Educational Technology; Pedagogy; Primary Education; Psychology); **Engineering** (Architecture; Building Technologies; Chemical Engineering; Civil Engineering; Computer Engineering; Construction Engineering; Electrical Engineering; Engineering; Industrial Engineering; Mechanical Engineering; Telecommunications Engineering); **Fine Arts** (Ceramic Art; Design; Fine Arts; Graphic Design; Music; Painting and Drawing; Sculpture); **Graduate Studies** (Animal Husbandry; Applied Linguistics; Arabic; Arts and Humanities; Business Administration; Construction Engineering; Curriculum; Educational Administration; Energy Engineering; Engineering; Environmental Studies; Geography; Health Sciences; History; Islamic Law; Law; Management; Medicine; Natural Sciences; Nursing; Pedagogy; Pharmacy; Physical Education; Plant and Crop Protection; Political Sciences; Private Law; Psychiatry and Mental Health; Public Health; Public Law; Road Engineering; Taxation; Town Planning; Water Science); **Human Medicine and Health Sciences** (Biomedicine; Laboratory Techniques; Medical Auxiliaries; Medicine; Midwifery; Nursing; Optometry; Pharmacy); **Information Technology** (Business Computing; Computer Science; Information Management; Information Sciences; Information Technology); **Islamic Law (Shari'a)** (Banking; Islamic Law; Religious Studies); **Law** (Private Law; Public Law); **Science** (Applied Chemistry; Biology; Chemistry; Electronic Engineering; Mathematics; Physics; Statistics); **Veterinary Medicine** (Veterinary Science)

Institutes
Water and Environmental Studies (Environmental Engineering; Environmental Studies; Water Management)

Laboratories
Central Medical (Medicine)

Programmes
Study of Involuntary Migration (Demography and Population)

History: Founded 1918 as An-Najah Nabulsi School, acquired present status and title 1977.

Governing Bodies: Board of Trustees

Academic Year: August to May (August-December; January-May)

Admission Requirements: Undergraduate admissions occur through Tertiary Matriculation Examination (UTME) or Direct Entry (DE). UTME Candidates must hold one of the following qualifications: General Certificate of Eduction (GCE) ordinary level, Senior Secondary Certificate Examination (SSCE), National Business and Technical Examination Board Certificate (NABTEB), National Examination Council Certificate (NECO), Teachers Grade II Certificate; passed with at least five credits, which must include English Language and Mathematics, passed at one or two sittings. DE candidates should possess one of the following qualifications which must also be acceptable to the University: Higher National Diploma (HND), National Certificate in Education (NCE), Ordinary National Diploma (OND; obtained from any recognized institution in at least credit level.

Fees: (Jordanian Dinars): varies according to subject.

Main Language(s) of Instruction: Arabic and English

International Co-operation: Participates in Tempus and Erasmus

Degrees and Diplomas: *Diploma*: 2 yrs; *Bachelor's Degree*: 4 yrs; *Master's Degree*: a further 2 yrs; *Doctorate (PhD)*: 5 yrs

Student Services: Academic counselling, Canteen, Cultural centre, Foreign student adviser, Health services, Language programs, Nursery care, Social counselling, Sports facilities

Student Residential Facilities: For Faculty members

Special Facilities: Medical Lab Centre; Health Clinics; Computer Centre; Computer Laboratory for Disabled Students; Poison and Drug Control Centre

Libraries: 400,000 vols

Publications: An-Najah Journal of Research (Humanities); An-Najah Journal of Research (Medicine); An-Najah Journal of Research (Natural Sciences)

Academic Staff *2011-2012*	MEN	WOMEN	TOTAL
FULL-TIME	1,211	405	**1,616**
PART-TIME	299	97	**396**
STAFF WITH DOCTORATE			
FULL-TIME	316	29	**345**
PART-TIME	92	11	**103**
Student Numbers *2011-2012*			
All (Foreign Included)	–	–	**21,237**

Last Updated: 19/02/13

BETHLEHEM UNIVERSITY

PO Box 11407, Jerusalem 92248
Tel: +972(2) 274-1241
Fax: +972(2) 274-4440
EMail: webmaster@bethlehem.edu
Website: http://www.bethlehem.edu

Vice-Chancellor: Peter Bray (2009-)
Tel: +972(2) 274-1241, Fax: +972(2) 274-4440
EMail: pbray@bethlehem.edu

International Relations: Irene Hazou, Assistant Vice-President for Accademic Affairs EMail: ihazou@bethlehem.edu

Centres

Biotechnology Education and Training *(UNESCO)* (Biotechnology); **Palestinian Heritage** *(Turathuna)* (Heritage Preservation); **Teaching Excellence** (Teacher Training)

Faculties

Arts (Arabic; Arts and Humanities; English; Religious Studies; Social Sciences); **Business Administration** (Accountancy; Business Administration); **Education** (Education; Pedagogy; Preschool Education; Primary Education); **Nursing** (Midwifery; Nursing; Occupational Therapy; Physical Therapy); **Science** (Biology; Chemistry; Computer Science)

Institutes

Community Partnership; **Hotel Management** (Hotel Management; Tourism); **Leadership** *(Cardinal Martini)* (Leadership)

Research Laboratories

Heridiary (Genetics)

Research Units

Water and Soil Environment *Head*: Alfred Abed Rabbo

History: Founded 1973 by the American De La Salle Brothers and tracing its origins to a College they opened in 1893. A private Institution recognized by the Ministry of Higher Education and sponsored by the Holy See.

Governing Bodies: Board of Trustees

Academic Year: August to June (August-December; January-June)

Admission Requirements: Secondary school Certificate or recognized equivalent, and entrance examination

Fees: (Jordanian Dinars): 700 per semester

Main Language(s) of Instruction: Arabic, English

International Co-operation: Wth universities in Germany, Ireland, Italy, Mexico, Norway, Philippines, Sweden, USA, Spain, France

Accrediting Agencies: Ministry of Higher Education

Degrees and Diplomas: *Diploma*: Neonatal; Travel Agency Management, 2 yrs; *Associate Degree*: Hotel Management, 2 yrs; *Bachelor's Degree*: Arts; Business Administration; Education; Hotel Management; Nursing; Science, 4 yrs; *Postgraduate Diploma*: Education, a further 2 yrs; *Postgraduate Diploma*: Neonatal, 2 yrs; *Master's Degree*: Biotechnology, 2 yrs; *Master's Degree*: International Cooperation and Development, a further 2 yrs

Student Services: Academic counselling, Canteen, Cultural centre, Handicapped facilities, Health services, Social counselling, Sports facilities

Student Residential Facilities: Yes

Libraries: Central Library, c. 190,000 vols

Publications: Journal *(annually)*

Last Updated: 19/04/11

BIRZEIT UNIVERSITY

Jami'at Birzeit (BZU)
PO Box 14, Birzeit, West Bank
Tel: +972(2) 298-2000
Fax: +972(2) 281-0656
EMail: webinfo@birzeit.edu
Website: http://www.birzeit.edu

President: Khalil S. Hindi
Tel: +972(2) 298-2008 EMail: president@birzeit.edu

Vice-President for Administrative and Financial Affairs: Sami El-Sayrafi
Tel: +972(2) 298-2001, Fax: +972(2) 298-2078
EMail: vpadmin@birzeit.edu

Vice-President for Academic Affairs: Adnan Yahya
Tel: +972(2) 298-2239 EMail: vp.academic@birzeit.edu

International Relations: Lubna Abdel-Hadi, Deputy Director, Public Relations Office EMail: labdhadi@birzeit.edu; pr@birzeit.edu

Centres

Continuing Education *(Ramallah)* (Continuing Education); **Development Studies** (Development Studies); **Information Technology Centre of Excellence** *(Najjad Zeenii (NZITCE))* (Information Technology); **Media Development** (Media Studies)

Faculties

Arts (Anthropology; Arabic; Archaeology; Cultural Studies; Education; English; French; Geography; History; Literature; Media Studies; Philosophy; Physical Education; Psychology; Sociology; Translation and Interpretation); **Commerce and Economics** (Accountancy; Business Administration; Business and Commerce; Economics; Finance; Management); **Education** (Education); **Engineering** (Civil Engineering; Electrical Engineering; Mechanical Engineering; Structural Architecture); **Graduate Studies** (Applied Chemistry; Arabic; Business Administration; Community Health; Development Studies; Education; Environmental Engineering; Environmental Studies; Gender Studies; Geography; Health Sciences; History; Human Rights; Hydraulic Engineering; International Studies; Islamic Studies; Islamic Theology; Laboratory Techniques; Law; Mathematics and Computer Science; Public Health; Sociology; Statistics; Town Planning; Water Science); **Information Technology** (Computer Science; Information Technology; Systems Analysis); **Law and Public Administration** (Law; Political Sciences; Public Administration); **Nursing and Allied Health Professions** (Dietetics; Nursing; Nutrition); **Science** (Biology; Chemistry; Mathematics; Physics)

Institutes

Community and Public Health (Community Health; Public Health); **Environmental and Water Studies** (Environmental Studies; Water Science); **International Studies** *(Ibrahim Abu Lughod)* (International Studies); **Law** (Law); **Women's Studies** (Women's Studies)

Laboratories

Testing Laboratory (Environmental Studies; Occupational Health) *Director*: Aqel Abu Qare

Units

Palestine and Arab Studies *(International Students Programme)* (Arabic; Social Sciences)

History: Founded 1924 as school, acquired present status and title 1972. A public/non-governmental Institution financed by student fees and contributions.

Governing Bodies: Board of Trustees

Academic Year: September to July (September-January; February to July). Summer session, July to August.

Admission Requirements: General certificate of secondary education (Tawjihi) or foreign equivalent

Fees: (Jordanian Dinars): Bachelor's degrees, 20-30 per credit hour; Master's degrees, 67-90

Main Language(s) of Instruction: Arabic, English

International Co-operation: Participates in Tempus; cooperation agreements with a number of Universities worldwide

Degrees and Diplomas: *Bachelor's Degree*: Arts; Economics and Commerce; Science; Law and Public Administration, 4 yrs; *Bachelor's Degree*: Engineering, 5 yrs; *Bachelor's Degree*: Information Technology, 4-5 yrs; *Postgraduate Diploma*: Education, 1-2 yrs; *Master's Degree*: Applied Statistics; Arabic Islamic Studies; Business Administration; Community and Public Health; Contemporary Arab Studies; Democracy and Human Rights; Economics; Education; Gender, Law and Development; Geography; International Relations; Law; Medical Laboratory Technology; Scientific Computing; Sociology; Water and Environmental Engineering; Water and Environmental Science; Urban Planning and Landscape Architecture, 1-2 yrs

Student Services: Academic counselling, Canteen, Foreign student adviser, Foreign Studies Centre, Health services, Social counselling, Sports facilities

Student Residential Facilities: For women students

Special Facilities: Diana Tamari Sabbagh Gallery; Virtual Gallery

Libraries: Yusuf Alghanim Library, 152,800 vols. (94,800 in English; 58,000 in Arabic). Archaeology, 6,000; Women's Studies, 8,854; Law 17,506; Development Studies and Community Health 27,394; E-books 13,140; E-journals 12,856 titles

Academic Staff *2010-2011*	MEN	WOMEN	TOTAL
FULL-TIME	263	96	**359**
PART-TIME	78	38	**116**
STAFF WITH DOCTORATE			
FULL-TIME	179	33	**212**
PART-TIME	32	12	**44**
Student Numbers *2010-2011*			
All (Foreign Included)	3,665	5,587	**9,252**

Last Updated: 18/05/11

COLLEGE OF ISLAMIC CALL - GAZA

Gaza, Gaza Strip
Tel: +972(8) 253-9180
Fax: +972(8) 253-9180

Director: Shukri Al Taweel

Programmes

Islamic Studies (Islamic Studies; Islamic Theology)

History: Founded 2000.

Degrees and Diplomas: *Bachelor's Degree*

Last Updated: 27/02/12

COLLEGE OF ISLAMIC CALL - QALQILIAH

Qalqiliah, West Bank
Tel: +972(9) 294-2266
Fax: +972(9) 294-0266

Director: Rasheed Mansour

Programmes

Islamic Religious Studies (Islamic Studies; Islamic Theology; Koran)

History: Founded 1992.

Degrees and Diplomas: *Bachelor's Degree*

Last Updated: 27/02/12

EDUCATION SCIENCE FACULTY - RAMALLAH MEN'S TRAINING CENTRE (RMTC)

Alma'ahed Street, Ramallah, West Bank 160
Tel: +972(2) 295-6423
Fax: +972(2) 295-4966
EMail: m.omran@unrmtc.org

Dean: Mohammad Omram Tel: +972(2) 298-4967

Vice-Dean: Samir Abdel-Wahad

Departments

Commercial Professions; **Teaching Professions**

History: Founded 1960. Formaerly known as College of Educational Sciences for Men (UNRWA).

Degrees and Diplomas: *Bachelor's Degree*

Last Updated: 27/02/12

EDUCATION SCIENCE FACULTY - RAMALLAH WOMEN'S TRAINING CENTRE (ESF/RWTC)

Tireh Street, Ramallah, West Bank 214
Tel: +972(2) 295-6533
Fax: +972(2) 295-6534
EMail: t.jarbawi@unrwa.org
Website: http://www.unrwa.org

Dean: Tafeeda Al-Jarbawee

Vice-Dean for Academic affairs: Muneer Rafeedi
EMail: mrafidioo@yahoo.com

Departments

Arabic Language; **Education and Psychology**; **Mathematics**; **Science**

History: Founded 1962. Formerly known as College of Educational Sciences for Women (UNRWA). Acquired present title 1993.

Degrees and Diplomas: *Bachelor's Degree*

Last Updated: 27/02/12

HEBRON UNIVERSITY

Al-Khalil University

PO Box 40, Hebron, West Bank
Tel: +972(2) 222-0995
Fax: +972(2) 222-9303
EMail: info@hebron.edu
Website: http://www.hebron.edu

President: Awni A. Khatib
Tel: +972(2) 222-0995 Ext.153 EMail: AwniK@Hebron.edu

Vice-President for Academic Affairs: Radwan Barakat
Tel: +972(2) 222-0995 Ext.200

Departments

Continuing Education *Director*: Hanis Al-Said

Faculties

Agriculture (Agricultural Economics; Agriculture; Animal Husbandry; Food Technology; Irrigation; Management; Nutrition; Plant and Crop Protection; Soil Science); **Arts** (Arabic; Arts and Humanities; English; Foreign Languages Education; Geography; History; Literature; Mass Communication; Political Sciences); **Education and Psychology** (Education; Psychology); **Graduate Studies and Scientific Research** (Agriculture; Arabic; History; Islamic Law; Linguistics; Literature; Management; Plant and Crop Protection); **Islamic Studies and Shari'a** (Education; Islamic Law; Islamic Studies) *Dean*: Hussein Al-Tartori; **Nursing** (Nursing); **Pharmacy** (Pharmacy); **Science and Technology** (Biology; Chemistry; Computer Science; Education; Mathematics; Natural Sciences) *Dean*: Mahmoud Edheidel

Schools

Finance and Management (Accountancy; Business Administration; Finance; Marketing; Public Administration)

Further Information: Also Liaison Offices in Jerusalem and Amman.

History: Founded 1971 as Theological College, acquired present status and title 1980. A public institution.

Governing Bodies: Board of Trustees; University Council

Academic Year: September to June (September-January; February-June)

Admission Requirements: Secondary school certificate

Fees: (US Dollars): 450 per semester

Main Language(s) of Instruction: Arabic, English

International Co-operation: With universities in United Kingdom

Accrediting Agencies: Ministry of Education and Higher Education

Degrees and Diplomas: *Bachelor's Degree*: Agriculture; Islamic Law; Science; Nursing; Education; Science and Technology; Finance and Management, 4 yrs; *Master's Degree*: Arabic; Nursing; Islamic Law; Natural Agricultural Resources and Sustainable Management (MA), 1 yr. Also Higher Diploma in Management, 1 yr

Student Services: Academic counselling, Canteen, Employment services, Health services, Nursery care, Social counselling, Sports facilities

Libraries: Central Library, c. 40,000 vols

Publications: Hebron University Research Journal *(annually)*

Press or Publishing House: Hebron University Publishing Office

Last Updated: 21/06/11

IBN SINA NURSING AND MIDWIFERY COLLEGE

Ramallah, West Bank
Tel: +972(2) 900-399
Fax: +972(2) 981-137
EMail: ibnsina00@yahoo.com

Director: Zahira Habash

Faculties

Nursing (Nursing)

Accrediting Agencies: Ministry of Health

Degrees and Diplomas: *Bachelor's Degree*

ISLAMIC UNIVERSITY OF GAZA

Al Jami'ah Al Eslamiyah

PO Box 108, Jamal Abed El_Naser Street, Gaza, Gaza Strip
Tel: +972(8) 286-0700
Fax: +972(8) 286-0800
EMail: public@iugaza.edu.ps; webmasters@mail.iugaza.edu
Website: http://www.iugaza.edu.ps

President: Kamalain Sha'at (2004-)
Tel: +972(8) 282-3310, Fax: +972(8) 286-3552
EMail: pres@iugaza.edu.ps

Vice-President for Administrative Affairs: Salem Helles

International Relations: Nazmi Al-Masri, Assistant to Vice-President, External Relations
Tel: +972(7) 282-5106, Fax: +972(7) 282-5106
EMail: nmasri@mail.iugaza.edu

Centres

Aural History (Folklore; History; Social Studies); **Continuing Education and Community Service** (Development Studies; Social and Community Services); **Environmental and Rural Studies** (Ecology; Environmental Studies; Marine Science and Oceanography; Natural Resources; Rural Studies; Waste Management); **Holy Koran** (Islamic Studies; Koran); **IT Affairs** (Computer Networks; Computer Science; Information Technology) *Director*: Hatem Hammad

Faculties

Arts (Arabic; Archaeology; Arts and Humanities; English; Geography; History; Information Sciences; Journalism; Public Relations; Social and Community Services) *Dean*: Mahmoud Alamoudy; **Commerce** (Accountancy; Business Administration; Business and Commerce; Economics; Political Sciences) *Dean*: Rushdy Wady; **Education** (Arabic; Computer Education; Education; Educational and Student Counselling; Educational Technology; English; Foreign Languages Education; Islamic Studies; Mathematics; Mathematics Education; Primary Education; Science Education; Social Studies) *Dean*: Mahmoud Abu Daff; **Engineering** (Civil Engineering; Computer Engineering; Electrical Engineering; Engineering; Environmental Engineering; Industrial Engineering; Structural Architecture) *Dean*: Adnan Enshasi; **Fundamentals of Religion** *Dean*: Naseem Yaseen; **Information Technology** (Computer Science; Information Technology; Software Engineering) *Dean*: Ala'a Alhalees; **Medicine** (Medicine; Surgery) *Dean*: Mufeed Almukhalalati; **Nursing** (Health Sciences; Nursing) *Dean*: Ashraf Aljedy; **Science** (Biochemistry; Biology; Biotechnology; Chemistry; Computer Science; Earth Sciences; Environmental Studies; Mathematics; Mathematics and Computer Science; Medical Technology; Natural Sciences; Optometry; Physics; Statistics) *Dean*: Naser Farhat; **Shari'a** (Islamic Law; Islamic Theology; Koran; Religious Education) *Dean*: Maher Alholi

Laboratories

Food Analysis (Food Science; Food Technology) *Director*: Ahmed Thabet; **Medical Technology** (Medical Technology) *Director*: Ahmad Selmi; **Nursing Skills** (Nursing) *Supervisor*: Ahmed Abu Rahma; **Psychology** (Psychology) *Supervisor*: Samir Quta; **Soil and Materials Testing** (Building Technologies; Materials Engineering; Soil Science) *Director*: Ahmed Al Kurd; **Support Technology** *Director*: Hazem Shehada

Units

Architecture Conservation and Urban Rehabilitation *Director*: Husam Dawood; **Business Research and Studies** (Business Education) *Director*: Ramadan Alhendy; **Energy Research and Development** *Director*: Mohamed Auda; **Projects and Research** (Engineering) *Director*: Mohamed El-Hanjoury

History: Founded 1978 as direct continuation of Palestine Religious Institute (Al-Azhar) in Gaza.

Governing Bodies: Council of Founders, Board of Trustees, University Council

Academic Year: October to June (September-January; February-June). Also Summer Semester (July-August)

Admission Requirements: General Secondary Education Certificate (Tawjihi) or equivalent for Bachelor's degree; Bachelor's degree or Master's degree for Master's degree.

Fees: (US Dollars): 20-35 per credit hour

Main Language(s) of Instruction: Arabic, English

International Co-operation: With universities in Egypt, Jordan, UK, Italy, USA

Accrediting Agencies: Palestinian Ministry of Higher Education.

Degrees and Diplomas: *Bachelor's Degree*: Arts; Commerce; Education; Fundamentals of Religion (Usul Addeen); Information Technology; Nursing; Science; Sharia, 4 yrs; *Bachelor's Degree*: Engineering, 5 yrs; *Postgraduate Diploma*: Educational Habilitation; General Education; Islamic Studies; Mental Health; Psychological Guidance; School Administration, 1 further yr; *Master's Degree*: Accounting and Finance; Business Administration; Engineering; Civil Engineering; Design and Rehabilitation of Structure; Architectural Engineering; Computer Engineering; Foundations of Jurisprudence; Comparative Jurisprudence; Islamic Jurisdiction; Hadith Sciences; Aqidah & Contemporary Schools; Interpretation and Quran Sciences; Literature; Rhetoric and Criticism; Modern History; Islamic History; Mathematics; Physics; Chemistry; Biological Sciences; Psychology; Curricula and Methodology; Fundamentals of Education; Rehabilitation Sciences, a further 2 yrs. Also undergraduate Diplomas at the Community College for Professional and Applied Sciences in Programming and System Analysis, Library Science and Information Management, Office Administration and Executive Secretary, Accounting, Multimedia Technology, Design and Administration of Web sites, Supervision of Building and Civil Engineering Projects, Kindergarten Teacher Training, Geographical Information Systems, Computer Maintenance, Architecture, Engineering, Creative Drawing, Nursing, Disability Rehabilitation Sciences and Islamic Studies

Student Services: Academic counselling, Canteen, Employment services, Handicapped facilities, Health services, Social counselling, Sports facilities

Special Facilities: Computer Facilities

Libraries: 69,435 vols in Arabic; 37,921 vols in English; 839 periodical titles in Arabic; 584 titles in English; 18 Manuscripts (Arabic); theses

Publications: University Research Journal *(other/irregular)*

Press or Publishing House: Islamic University Press

Student Numbers *2010-2011*: Total 19,972
Last Updated: 29/03/13

PALESTINE POLYTECHNIC UNIVERSITY (PPU)

P.O. Box 198, Ein Sara Street, Hebron, West Bank
Tel: +970(2) 222-8912
Fax: +970(2) 221-7248
EMail: info@ppu.edu
Website: http://www.ppu.edu

President: Ibrahim Al-Masri (2008-)
Tel: +970(2) 222-8912 Ext.24
EMail: presidentoffice@ppu.edu; imasri@ppu.edu

International Relations: Ruba Sunokrot, Public Relations Officer
Tel: +970(2) 222-8912 Ext.17 EMail: rubast@ppu.edu

Colleges

Administrative Science and Informatics (Business Administration; Computer Science; E-Business/Commerce; Information Technology; Marketing); **Applied Professions** (Administration; Computer Science; Engineering); **Applied Sciences** (Applied Physics; Computer Science; Electronic Engineering; Mathematics; Modern Languages); **Engineering and Technology** (Architecture; Automotive Engineering; Civil Engineering; Computer Engineering; Electrical Engineering; Mechanical Engineering)

Departments

Continuing Education (Continuing Education)

Research Units

Biotechnology (Biotechnology)

History: Founded 1978.

Degrees and Diplomas: *Diploma*: 2 yrs; *Bachelor's Degree*: Engineering, 5 yrs; *Bachelor's Degree*: Science, 4 yrs; *Master's Degree*: 2 yrs

Libraries: 26,000 vols; 110 periodical subscriptions

Last Updated: 21/06/11

PALESTINE TECHNICAL COLLEGE - AL-AROUB (PTC-AL-AR)

Bethlehem Street, P.O. Box 14, Hebron, West Bank
Tel: +972(2) 252-2346
Fax: +972(2) 252-2347
EMail: bqumsieh@ptca.edu.ps
Website: http://www.ptca.edu.ps

Dean: Basem Qumsieh

History: Founded 1958.

Degrees and Diplomas: *Bachelor's Degree*

PALESTINE TECHNICAL COLLEGE - DEIR EL BALAH (PTC-DEIR-E)

PO Box 6037, Deir El Balah, Gaza
Tel: +972(8) 253-1171
Fax: +972(8) 253-8101
EMail: ayman_ptc@hotmail.com
Website: http://www.ptcdb.edu.ps/mainsite

Dean: Hamid Mahdi

Programmes

Fashion Design (Fashion Design); **Hotel Management** (Hotel Management); **Information Technology** (Information Technology); **Photography** (Film; Photography)

History: Founded 1992.

Main Language(s) of Instruction: Arabic

Degrees and Diplomas: *Bachelor's Degree*

PALESTINE TECHNICAL COLLEGE - RAMALLAH (PTC - RAMALL)

Alma'ahed Street, Ramallah, West Bank
Tel: +972(2) 298-4298
Fax: +972(2) 295-6526
EMail: ptc_college1952@yahoo.com
Website: http://www.ptcr.edu.ps

Dean: Najwa Arafat

History: Founded 1952.

Degrees and Diplomas: *Bachelor's Degree*

Last Updated: 24/02/12

PALESTINE TECHNICAL UNIVERSITY - KADOORIE

P.O. Box 7, Yafa Street, Tulkarem, West Bank
Tel: +970(92) 688-199 +970(92) 677-923
Fax: +970(92) 677-922
EMail: info@ptuk.edu.ps
Website: http://www.ptuk.edu.ps/

Acting President: Saed Mallak (2012-)
Tel: +970(92) 680-173 EMail: s.mallak@ptuk.edu.ps

International Relations: Omar Jouda, International Relations Officer Tel: +970(92) 688-188 EMail: o.jouda@ptuk.edu.ps

Colleges

Economics, Management and Business (Administration; Banking; Business Computing; Finance); **Engineering and Technology** (Computer Engineering; Electrical Engineering; Industrial Engineering; Mechanical Engineering; Telecommunications Engineering); **Science and Education** (Applied Mathematics; Physical Education; Physics; Technology Education)

History: Founded 1930 as Palestine Technical College - Tulkam-Khadoury. Acquired present status 2007.

Governing Bodies: University Council

Academic Year: September to June

Admission Requirements: Tawjihi (Secondary School Leaving Certificate)

Fees: (JOD): 24 per credit hour, BSc; 20 per credit hour, BA

Main Language(s) of Instruction: Arabic, English

Degrees and Diplomas: *Diploma*; *Bachelor's Degree*: Electrical Engineering; Industrial Automation; Computer Systems Engineering; Communications Engineering and Technology Programme (CET); Mechatronics Engineering., 5 yrs; *Bachelor's Degree*: Physical Education; Technological Education; Applied Mathematics; Physics; Computerized Banking and Financial Sciences; Industrial Administration; Accounting Information System, 4 yrs

Student Services: Academic counselling, Canteen, Cultural centre, Employment services, Handicapped facilities, Health services, Language programs, Social counselling, Sports facilities

Special Facilities: Access to the following electronic networks: Eerald; E-brary; Sprigers; IEEE; EBISCO

Libraries: c. 30,000 vols; 4,692 periodical subscriptions.

Academic Staff *2011*	MEN	WOMEN	**TOTAL**
FULL-TIME	151	69	**220**
PART-TIME	49	10	**59**
STAFF WITH DOCTORATE			
FULL-TIME	35	3	**38**
PART-TIME	–	2	**2**
Student Numbers *2013*			
All (Foreign Included)	–	–	c. **4,950**

Last Updated: 12/02/13

WAJDI UNIVERSITY COLLEGE OF TECHNOLOGY (WUCT)

Mount of Olives, JerusalemJerusalem
Tel: +972(2) 6286357
Fax: +972(2) 6261096
EMail: info@wuct.edu.ps
Website: http://www.wit.edu.ps

Director: Nadeerah Abu Gharbieh

Programmes

Business Informatics (Business Computing); **Computer and Information Technology** (Business Computing; Computer Networks; Computer Science; Information Technology)

History: Founded 2004.

Accrediting Agencies: Ministry of Higher Education (MoHE)
Degrees and Diplomas: *Bachelor's Degree*
Last Updated: 24/02/12

PRIVATE INSTITUTIONS

PALESTINE AHLIYA UNIVERSITY COLLEGE (PAUC)

PO Box 1041, West Bank, Bethlehem
Tel: +970(2) 275-1566
Fax: +970(2) 274-9652
EMail: college@paluniv.edu.ps
Website: http://www.paluniv.edu.ps

President: Ghassan Abu Hijleh (2011-)
EMail: abuhijleh@paluniv.edu.ps

Presidential Assistant for Administration and Finance: Imad Al-Zeer EMail: imad@paluniv.edu.ps

International Relations: Samer Ghabboun, Director of Public and International Affairs EMail: samer@paluniv.edu.ps

Departments
Allied Health Sciences (Physical Therapy; Radiology); **Arts and Science** (Arabic; English; Social Sciences); **Banking Administration and Finance** (Accountancy; Banking; Business Administration); **Information Technology** (Information Technology); **Islamic Studies** (Islamic Studies); **Law** (Law)

History: Created 2007. First graduation in 2010/2011.

Governing Bodies: Administration Board

Academic Year: Sept to Jan; Feb to June

Admission Requirements: Secondary School Certificate.

Fees: (Jordanian Dinars): 670 to 880 per semester.

Main Language(s) of Instruction: Arabic, with some courses taught in English

Accrediting Agencies: Minister of Higher Education, Palestine

Degrees and Diplomas: *Bachelor's Degree*: 4 yrs

Student Services: Academic counselling, Canteen, Cultural centre, Employment services, Foreign student adviser, Foreign Studies Centre, Handicapped facilities, Health services, Language programs, Nursery care, Social counselling, Sports facilities

Student Residential Facilities: None

Special Facilities: Special Education Centre; Human Rights and Democracy Centre

Libraries: 16,000 vols plus electronic and printed journals.

Academic Staff *2011-2012*	MEN	WOMEN	**TOTAL**
FULL-TIME	29	5	**34**
PART-TIME	30	10	**40**
STAFF WITH DOCTORATE			
FULL-TIME	17	2	**19**
PART-TIME	10	–	**10**
Student Numbers *2011-2012*			
All (Foreign Included)	743	447	**1,190**

Distance students, 1,204. **Evening students**, 14.
Last Updated: 16/01/12

PALESTINE COLLEGE OF NURSING - KHAN YOUNIS

Khan Younis, Gaza Strip
Tel: +972(8) 205-0240
Fax: +972(8) 205-0230
EMail: pcngaza@hotmail.com

Dean: Adnan Al Sibakhi

Programmes
Nursing (Nursing)

History: Founded 1997.

Degrees and Diplomas: *Bachelor's Degree*

THE ARAB AMERICAN UNIVERSITY - JENIN (AAUJ)

PO Box 240, Jenin, West Bank
Tel: +972(4) 251-0801 +972(4) 251-0802
Fax: +972(4) 251-0801 +972(4) 251-0810
EMail: admin@aauj.edu
Website: http://www.aauj.edu

President: Adli Saleh (2000-)
Tel: +972(4) 252-0107 EMail: asaleh@aauj.edu

Vice President for Planning and Development: Zaki Saleh
Tel: +972(4) 251-0801 Ext.:153 EMail: zsaleh@aauj.edu

International Relations: Mohammad Sabaneh, Director, International and Public Relations Department EMail: pr@aauj.edu

Centres
Computer (Computer Science) *Director*: Mohammad Hannon; **Continuing Education and Community Service** *(CECSC)* (Banking; Finance) *Director*: Haj-Hamad Zakarya; **Dental** (Dentistry) *Director*: Baraa Sabha; **English Language** *(ELC)* (English) *Director*: Suhad Aboushi; **Information Technologies** *(Hasseeb Sabbagh - HSITCE)* (Information Technology) *Director*: Sami Awad

Faculties
Administrative and Financial Sciences *Dean*: Sulaiman Abbadi; **Allied Medical Sciences** *Dean*: Thaer Abd Elghani; **Arts and Science** *Dean*: Saed Malak; **Dentistry** *Dean*: Mahmoud Abu-Mowais; **Engineering and Information Technology** (Computer Science; Information Technology; Multimedia; Telecommunications Engineering) *Dean*: Osamah Salameh; **Law** *Dean*: Ghassan Eleyyan

History: Founded 1996 as the first private university in Palestine. Started programs 2000.

Governing Bodies: Palestinian Ministry of Education and Higher Education. Board of Directors; Board of Trustees; University Council; Deans Council

Academic Year: September to May (September-December; January-May)

Admission Requirements: High School Diploma or its equivalent

Fees: (Euros): Arts and Science Faculty, 35-45; Allied Medical Sciences Faculty, 39-52; Dentistry Faculty, 150; Administrative and Financial Sciences Faculty, 30-40; Engineering and Information Technology Faculty, 45-60; Law Faculty, 30-40

Main Language(s) of Instruction: English

International Co-operation: With universities in Germany and Belgium; participates in the Erasmus Mundus, DAAD Foundation and Tempus Programmes

Accrediting Agencies: Palestinian Ministry of Education and Higher Education

Degrees and Diplomas: *Diploma*: Finance and Banking Sciences, 1 yr; *Diploma*: Programming and Database Analysis; *Bachelor's Degree*: Business Administration; Accountancy; Marketing; Banking and Finance; Operations Management/Management Information System; Operations Management/Hospital and Health Care Management (B.Sc); Computer Science; Computer Information Technology; Multi-media Technology; Telecommunications Engineering (B.Sc); Law (concentration on international law public/Private) (B.Sc); Mathematics and Statistics; Biology and Biotechnology; English Language; Physics; Chemistry; Arabic Language and Media (B.Sc.); Medical Laboratory Sciences; Health Sciences-Occupational Therapy; Health Sciences-Physiotherapy Therapy; Enviromental and Community Healh; Nursing; Medical Imaging (B.Sc), 4 yrs; *Bachelor's Degree*: Dentistry, 5 yrs

Student Services: Academic counselling, Canteen, Employment services, Handicapped facilities, Health services, Language programs, Nursery care, Social counselling, Sports facilities

Student Residential Facilities: Two female dormitories; One academic staff building

Libraries: c. 65,000 vols; 250 periodicals; ISDIS System, Internal Services/Oracle System: Directory of Open Access Journals, Bio One Databse, Cambridge Journals, IOP Institute of Physics
Last Updated: 05/01/09

UNIVERSAL STUDIES ACADEMY

P.O. Box: 5353, Omar Mukhtar Street, Harazine Bld., Gaza
Tel: +972(8) 2828428
EMail: President@usacademy.info
Website: http://www.usacademy.info/english.htm

Colleges

Information Studies (Journalism; Mass Communication; Media Studies; Public Relations); **Administration and Economics** (Banking; Business Administration; Economics; Finance; Hotel Management; Human Resources; International Relations; Management; Marketing; Political Sciences; Public Administration; Tourism); **Arts and Letters** (Arabic; Education; English; Geography; History; Library Science; Linguistics; Sociology); **Education** (Education; Educational Administration; Islamic Studies; Pedagogy); **Law** (International Law; Law; Private Law; Public Law); **Science and Technology** (Botany; Chemistry; Environmental Studies; Geophysics; Information Technology; Medicine; Physics; Public Health)

History: Founded 2001. Acquired present status 2006.

Accrediting Agencies: Council for Higher Education Quality (CHEQ), Palestine.Society of Scientific Research and Studies, Palestine.Palestinian Chamber of Commerce.

Degrees and Diplomas: *Bachelor's Degree*; *Master's Degree*; *Doctorate*

Last Updated: 24/02/12

UNIVERSITY COLLEGE OF APPLIED SCIENCES (UCAS)

P.O. Box 1415, Khan Younis, Gaza Strip
Tel: +970(8) 286-8999
Fax: +970(8) 284-7404
EMail: IR@ucas.edu.ps
Website: http://www.ucas.edu.ps

Rector: Rifat Rustom (2011-)
Tel: +970(8) 286-8999
EMail: rector@ucas.edu.ps; rustom@ucas.edu.ps

Vice-Rector for Administrative Affairs: Wesam Sakallah
Tel: +970(8) 286-8999, Fax: +970(8) 286-4888
EMail: wsakallah@ucas.edu.ps

International Relations: Mohammed H. Al-Afifi, International Relations Officer EMail: ir@ucas.edu.ps

Departments

Business (Accountancy; Administration; Business and Commerce; Sales Techniques; Secretarial Studies); **Educational Sciences** (Physical Education; Preschool Education; Primary Education; Technology Education); **Engineering Sciences** (Architecture; Automation and Control Engineering; Building Technologies; Civil Engineering; Crafts and Trades; Interior Design; Surveying and Mapping); **Health Sciences** (Medical Auxiliaries; Midwifery; Nursing); **Humanities** (Advertising and Publicity; Islamic Studies; Public Relations; Secretarial Studies; Social Work); **Information Technology** (Information Technology; Multimedia; Surveying and Mapping); **Rehabilitation Sciences** (Physical Therapy; Speech Therapy and Audiology)

History: Created 1998 as Community College of Applied Sciences and Technology. Acquired current title 2007.

Governing Bodies: University Council

Academic Year: Sep - Jan; Feb - May; June - Aug

Admission Requirements: General Certificate of Secondary Education or equivalent.

Fees: (Jordanian Dinar): 25 per credit hour.

Main Language(s) of Instruction: Arabic

International Co-operation: with institutions in France, USA, Italy, Turkey. Also Erasmus, Tempus and FP7.

Degrees and Diplomas: *Bachelor's Degree*: Administrative Sciences; Educational Sciences; Engineering Sciences; Information Technology, 4-5 yrs

Student Services: Academic counselling, Canteen, Employment services, Handicapped facilities, Health services, Language programs, Nursery care, Social counselling, Sports facilities

Libraries: 74,505 vols; 1,347 periodical subscriptions; access to 48 electronic networks.

Academic Staff *2011-2012*	MEN	WOMEN	**TOTAL**
FULL-TIME	96	34	**130**
PART-TIME	178	88	**266**
STAFF WITH DOCTORATE			
FULL-TIME	8	2	**10**
PART-TIME	2		**2**
Student Numbers *2011-2012*			
All (Foreign Included)	4,494	4,091	**8,585**
FOREIGN ONLY	4	2	**6**

Part-time students, 971. **Distance students**, 188. **Evening students**, 0.

Last Updated: 19/02/13

Panama

STRUCTURE OF HIGHER EDUCATION SYSTEM

Description:

Higher education is mainly provided by universities, higher schools and institutes. There are both public and private universities. Higher education is directed by the Ministry of Education but controlled by the University of Panama by law. The Consejo de Rectores de Panama coordinates several universities.

Stages of studies:

University level first stage: *Licenciatura*

The Licenciatura is generally conferred after studies lasting between four and five years. Professional titles are conferred in several fields, generally after five years (three in Nursing and six in Medicine).

University level second stage: *Maestria*

The Maestría is conferred after one to two years' further study beyond the Licenciatura. Students must submit a thesis or other requirement.

University level third stage: *Doctorado*

Distance higher education:

Distance education is offered by the Universidad Interamericana de Educación a Distancia (UNIEDPA) and the Universidad Abierta y a Distancia de Panamá (UNADP).

ADMISSION TO HIGHER EDUCATION

Admission to university-level studies:

Name of secondary school credential required: Bachiller

Alternatives to credentials: Certificado de Maestro de Nivel Superior

Entrance exam requirements: Entrance examination for some state universities.

Foreign students admission:

Entrance exam requirements: Foreign students must hold a Secondary School Leaving Certificate or its equivalent.

Entry regulations: Foreign students must ask for information from Panamean consulates abroad.

Language requirements: Students must have a good knowledge of Spanish.

NATIONAL BODIES

Ministerio de Educación (Ministry of Education)

Minister: Lucinda Molinar
Villa Cárdenas, Ancón
Apartado postal 0816-04049
Panama
Tel: +507 511 4400
EMail: meduca@meduca.gob.pa
WWW: http://www.meduca.gob.pa/

Consejo de Rectores de Panamá (Council of Rectors of Panama)

President: Bruno Garisto Petrovich
Albrook, Ancón, Edificio N° 868
Panama
Tel: +507 315 1601
WWW: http://www.consejo.ac.pa/

Asociación de Universidades Privadas de Panamá - AUPPA (Association of Private Universities of Panama)

President: Rosario Coya Navarro
Vía España, Calle Elvira Méndez, Edificio. Interseco Piso N°3
Panama
Tel: +507 265 0641
Fax: +507 265 0638
EMail: auppa@auppa.org.pa
WWW: http://www.auppa.org.pa/

Data for academic year: 2006-2007
Source: IAU from Ministry of Education, Panama, 2006. Bodies 2012.

INSTITUTIONS

PUBLIC INSTITUTIONS

AUTONOMOUS UNIVERSITY OF CHIRIQUÍ

Universidad Autónoma de Chiriquí (UNACHI)
El Cabrero, David, Provincia de Chiriquí
Tel: +507 775-1114
Fax: +507 774-4050
EMail: sitioweb@unachi.ac.pa
Website: http://www.unachi.ac.pa/

Rector: Héctor Requena Núñez
Tel: +507 775-7243, Fax: +507 774-2679

Secretario General: Daniel Carrillo Tel: +507 774-4050

International Relations: Juana Ramos, Vicerrectora
Tel: +507 774-5992, Fax: +507 774-5992
EMail: jramos@mail.chiriqui.com

Faculties
Business Administration; **Economics**; **Educational Sciences**; **Humanities**; **Natural Sciences**; **Public Administration**; **Social Communication**

Programmes
Law and Political Science; **Medicine** (Medicine); **Nursing**

Further Information: Also Branches in Boquete, Oriente, Barú.

History: Founded 1994, acquired present status and title 1995.

Admission Requirements: Secondary school certificate and entrance examination

Main Language(s) of Instruction: Spanish

International Co-operation: Participates in Intercampus programme (Spain); Fondo Mixto (Mexico); ANUIES; CSUCA; IFARHU (Canada)

Degrees and Diplomas: *Técnico Superior (TEC)*; *Licenciatura (LIC)*; *Maestría (MSc)*; *Doctorado*: Educational Sciences (DR). Posgrado de Especialización

Student Services: Canteen, Employment services, Health services, Language programs, Nursery care, Social counselling, Sports facilities

Special Facilities: Auditorium. Laboratories. Clinic of Psychological Orientation

Libraries: Central Library

Publications: Bitacora, Social, cultural and scientific topics *(quarterly)*; Econometrín, Economic topics; El Observator, Faculty social communication *(quarterly)*; Supra, Spanish magazine

INTERNATIONAL MARITIME UNIVERSITY OF PANAMA

Universidad Marítima Internacional de Panamá
La Boca, Edificio 911, Panamá
Tel: 507-314-3701
EMail: info@umip.ac.pa
Website: http://www.umip.ac.pa/spanish/index.php

Rector: Victor Luna

Centres
Language *(Maritime)* (English)

Faculties
Marine Sciences (Marine Biology; Marine Science and Oceanography); **Maritime Transport** (Marine Engineering; Marine Transport); **Nautical Sciences** (Nautical Science; Naval Architecture)

History: Founded 2005.

Main Language(s) of Instruction: Spanish

Degrees and Diplomas: *Licenciatura*; *Maestría*. Also posgrados

Last Updated: 26/10/09

SPECIALIZED UNIVERSITY OF THE AMERICAS

Universidad Especializada de Las Américas (UDELAS)
Apartado Postal 0843-01041, Albrook Edificios 806 y 808, Balboa
Tel: +507 501-1000
EMail: rectoria@udelas.ac.pa
Website: http://www.udelas.ac.pa

Rectora: Berta Torrijos de Arosemena
Tel: +507 315-0102, Fax: +507 315-1068
EMail: btarect@psi.net.pa

Vicerrector: Juan Bosco Bernal EMail: vicerectoria@udelas.ac.pa

Secretario General: Eric Garcia

Faculties
Health and Integral Rehabilitation (Education of the Handicapped; Gerontology; Occupational Therapy; Orthopaedics; Rehabilitation and Therapy; Special Education; Speech Therapy and Audiology); **Social and Special Education**

History: Founded 1997.

Main Language(s) of Instruction: Spanish

Degrees and Diplomas: *Licenciatura*; *Maestría*; *Doctorado*

Last Updated: 26/10/09

TECHNOLOGICAL UNIVERSITY OF PANAMÁ

Universidad Tecnológica de Panamá
Apartado 6-2894, El Dorado, Panamá
Tel: +507 360-3000 +507 360-3120
Fax: +507 264-9149
EMail: utp@utp.ac.pa
Website: http://www.utp.ac.pa

Rector: Marcela Paredes de Vásquez (2003-)
Tel: +507 236-9723, Fax: +507 360-3181

Vicerrectora Administrativa: Myriam González Boutet
Tel: +507 236-0654, Fax: +507 236-2512
EMail: benigo.vargas@utp.ac.pa

International Relations: Gregorio Urriola, Director de Relaciones Internationales
Tel: +507 236-1802, Fax: +507 236-6510
EMail: gregorio.urriola@utp.ac.pa

Centres

Computer (Computer Networks; Computer Science; Data Processing; Information Management); **Experimental Engineering** *(Experimental Engineering Research Centre)* (Engineering); **Hydraulic and Hydrotechnical Research** (Hydraulic Engineering); **Production and Agroindustry Research** (Agricultural Engineering; Production Engineering); **Project Centre** (Engineering); **Virtual UTP** (Computer Engineering)

Faculties

Civil Engineering (Civil Engineering); **Computer Systems Engineering** (Computer Engineering); **Electrical Engineering** (Electrical Engineering); **Industrial Engineering** (Industrial Engineering); **Mechanical Engineering** (Mechanical Engineering); **Science and Technology** (Mathematics and Computer Science; Natural Sciences; Technology)

Further Information: Regional Centres in different provinces: Cocle, Chiriqui, Bocas del Toro, Azuero, Panama Oeste Colón and Veraguas

History: Founded 1941 as Department of Engineering of the University of Panamá, became Polytechnic Institute 1975, and acquired present status and title 1981.

Governing Bodies: General Council; Academic Council; Administrative Council and Research; Master and Extension Council

Academic Year: March to December

Admission Requirements: Secondary school certificate (bachillerato) obtained in a five year or more study plan

Fees: (US Dollars): 30 plus 7.5 per laboratory per semester for an engineer degree; for postgraduate, 30 plus 75 per credit

Main Language(s) of Instruction: Spanish

International Co-operation: Programa de Cooperacion Interuniversitaria con Ibero America(PCI)

Accrediting Agencies: Global Marine Survey Inc., Representatives of ICONTEC

Degrees and Diplomas: *Técnico Superior (TEC)*: 3 yrs; *Licenciatura (LIC)*: 5 yrs; *Maestría*: a further 2 yrs; *Doctorado*: 1 yr; *Doctorado (DR)*

Student Services: Canteen, Employment services, Language programs, Nursery care, Sports facilities

Libraries: General Library and Specialized libraries in each Faculty and Regional Center

Publications: Memoria Institucional *(annually)*
Last Updated: 27/03/09

UNIVERSITY OF PANAMÁ

Universidad de Panamá
Ciudad Universitaria, Dr. Octavio Méndez Pereira,
El Cangrejo-Estafeta Universitaria, Panamá 3
Tel: +507 223-0654
Fax: +507 523-5011
EMail: rectoria@ancon.up.ac.pa
Website: http://www.up.ac.pa

Rector: Gustavo García de Paredes (2006-)
Tel: +507 523-5000, Fax: +507 269-2820

General Secretary: Miguel Angel Candanedo
Tel: +507 523-5027, Fax: +507 264-4127
EMail: sgral@hotmail.com

International Relations: Vielka de Escobar, Director, International Cooperation Tel: +507 264-3055 EMail: diciat@ancon.up.ac.pa

Faculties

Agricultural Sciences (Agriculture; Education; Welfare and Protective Services); **Architecture** (Architecture; Architecture and Planning; Fine Arts); **Business Administration and Accountancy** (Accountancy; Business Administration; Service Trades); **Computer Science, Electronics and Communication**; **Dentistry** (Dentistry); **Economics** (Business Administration; Economics; Social Sciences); **Educational Sciences** (Educational Sciences); **Fine Arts** (Fine Arts; Performing Arts); **Humanities** (Arts and Humanities; Information Sciences; Social Sciences); **Law and Political Science** (Law; Political Sciences); **Medicine** (Medicine); **Natural and Exact Sciences and Technology** (Education; Engineering; Mathematics and Computer Science; Natural Sciences); **Nursing** (Nursing); **Pharmacy** (Pharmacy); **Psychology** (Psychology); **Public Administration** (Public Administration; Social Sciences; Welfare and Protective Services); **Social Communication** (Business Administration; Communication Studies; Information Sciences); **Veterinary Science** (Veterinary Science)

Institutes

Analysis; **Criminology** (Criminology); **Environmental Sciences and Biodiversity** *(ICAB)* (Environmental Studies); **Ethnic Traditions and Cultures**; **Food and Nutrition** (Food Science; Nutrition); **Geosciences** (Earth Sciences; Geology); **Human Genome**; **National Studies**; **Panama Canal and International Studies** (International Studies); **Physical Education** (Physical Education); **Women's Studies**

History: Founded 1935. Autonomy granted by decree 1946. The institution falls under the jurisdiction of the Ministry of Education. Reorganized 1981.

Governing Bodies: Consejo General Universitario; Consejo Académico; Consejo Administrativo

Academic Year: April to January (April-September; September-January)

Admission Requirements: Secondary school certificate (bachillerato) or recognized equivalent

Fees: (Balboa): 24.50 per semester

Main Language(s) of Instruction: Spanish

Degrees and Diplomas: *Maestro a Nivel Superior*: Secondary Education, 1 1/2 yr; *Técnico Superior*: 1-3 yrs; *Licenciatura*: Accountancy; Agricultural Engineering; Agriculture and Cattle Raising Development; Anthropology; Applied Arts; Architecture; Archiving; Biology; Business Administration; Chemistry; Commerce; Computer Science and Engineering; Customs; Public Administration; Dance; Economics; Education; Educational and Professional Counselling; Electronic and Communication Engineering; Engineering; English; Finance and Banking; Food Science and Technology; French; Geography; Geography and History; Graphic Design; History; Home Economics Education; Interior Design; International Relations; Journalism; Law and Political Science; Library Science; Mathematics; Music; Musical Instruments and Singing; Nursing; Nutrition and Dietetics; Philosophy and History; Physical Education; Physics; Phytotechnical Agronomy Engineering; Plastic Arts; Police Public Administration; Psychology; Public Administration; Public Relations; Publicity; Radio and Television Broadcasting; Secretarial and Office Management; Social Work; Sociology; Spanish; Statistics; Theatre; Visual Arts; Zootechnical Engineering, 4 yrs; *Licenciatura*: Pharmacy, 4 1/2 yrs; *Maestría*: a further 2 yrs; *Doctorado*: Dentistry, 5 yrs; *Doctorado*: Medicine; Veterinary Medicine, 6 yrs. Also Specialization, 9-12 months

Student Services: Academic counselling, Health services, Social counselling

Special Facilities: Art Gallery. Theatre. Museums. TV Studio. Radio Studio

Libraries: Central Library, c. 300,000 vols

Publications: Acción y Reflexión Educativa *(quarterly)*; Memoria, revista *(annually)*; Temas, revista *(bimonthly)*

Press or Publishing House: Imprenta Universitaria

AZUERO REGIONAL CENTRE

CENTRO REGIONAL UNIVERSITARIO DE AZUERO

Chitrá, Provincia de Herrera
Tel: +507 296-4712
Fax: +507 296-5910

Director: Milcíades Pinzón

Faculties
Animal Husbandry (Animal Husbandry); **Architecture** (Architecture); **Business Administration and Accountancy** (Accountancy; Business Administration); **Economics** (Economics); **Education** (Education); **Humanities** (Arts and Humanities); **Law** (Law); **Natural Sciences** (Natural Sciences); **Nursing** (Nursing); **Public Administration** (Public Administration); **Social Communication** (Communication Studies)

Degrees and Diplomas: *Técnico Superior*, *Licenciatura*

CHIRIQUI REGIONAL CENTRE

CENTRO REGIONAL UNIVERSITARIO DE CHIRIQUÍ

David, Provincia de Chiriquí
Tel: +507 275-3485
Fax: +507 274-2679

Director: Roque Lagrotta

COCLÉ REGIONAL CENTRE

CENTRO REGIONAL UNIVERSITARIO DE COCLÉ

Penonomé, Provincia de Coclé
Tel: +507 297-8868
Fax: +507 297-9642

Director: Fulgencio Álvarez

Faculties
Animal Husbandry (Animal Husbandry); **Business Administration and Accountancy**; **Education**; **Humanities**; **Law and Political Science** (Law; Political Sciences); **Natural and Exact Sciences** (Natural Sciences); **Public Administration** (Architecture; Public Administration); **Social Communication** (Communication Studies)

Degrees and Diplomas: *Técnico Superior*: 3 yrs; *Licenciatura*: 4-6 yrs

COLÓN REGIONAL CENTRE

CENTRO REGIONAL UNIVERSITARIO DE COLÓN

Ciudad Arco Iris, Provincia de Colón
Tel: +507 245-2567
Fax: +507 241-5857

Director: Dorindo Cortés

Faculties
Business Administration and Accountancy (Accountancy; Business Administration); **Economics** (Economics); **Education** (Education); **Humanities** (Arts and Humanities); **Natural and Exact Sciences** (Natural Sciences); **Public Administration** (Public Administration)

LOS SANTOS REGIONAL CENTRE

CENTRO REGIONAL UNIVERSITARIO DE LOS SANTOS

Las Tablas, Provincia de Los Santos
Tel: +507 294-6813
Fax: +507 294-8080

Director: Argelidis Cedeño

SAN MIGUELITO REGIONAL CENTRE

CENTRO REGIONAL UNIVERSITARIO DE SAN MIGUELITO

Distrito de San Miguelito, Provincia de Panamá
Tel: +507 267-8960
Fax: +507 267-8185

Director: Israel Pérez

VERAGUAS REGIONAL CENTRE

CENTRO REGIONAL UNIVERSITARIO DE VERAGUAS

Distrito de Santiago, Provincia de Veraguas
Tel: +507 298-4587
Fax: +507 298-4056

Director: Nemecio Donoso

Degrees and Diplomas: *Licenciatura*

WEST PANAMA REGIONAL CENTRE

CENTRO REGIONAL UNIVERSITARIO DE PANAMÁ OESTE

Distrito La Chorrera, Provincia de Panamá
Tel: +507 253-5058
Fax: +507 253-2114

Director: Germán Beitia

Faculties
Business Management and Accountancy (Accountancy; Business Administration); **Education** (Education); **Humanities** (Arts and Humanities); **Natural Sciences and Technology** (Natural Sciences; Technology); **Public Administration** (Public Administration); **Social Communication** (Communication Studies)

PRIVATE INSTITUTIONS

AMERICAN UNIVERSITY

Universidad Americana

Area Bancaria, Calle Ricardo Arias y Ave 3ra Sur, Panamá
Tel: +507 213-1967 +507 213-1214
Fax: +507 213-0976
EMail: info@uam.ac.pa
Website: http://www.uam.ac.pa

Rectora: Veronica de Barrios

Faculties
Business Studies (Accountancy; Banking; Business Administration; Finance; Marketing); **Communication**; **Computer Science** (Computer Graphics; Computer Science); **Education** (English; Teacher Training); **Law** (Law; Political Sciences)

History: Founded 1997.

Degrees and Diplomas: *Técnico Superior*, *Licenciatura*; *Maestría*
Last Updated: 26/10/09

CHRISTIAN UNIVERSITY OF PANAMA

Universidad Cristiana de Panama (UCP)

Calle Omega, Vista Alegre, Arraiján
Tel: +507 251-5532 251-6413
Fax: +507 251-5236
Website: http://www.ucp.ac.pa

Rector: Prudencia Raquel de Delgado
Vicerectora Administrativa: Norma Estela González de De León
Secretaria General: Nannett Rodríguez

Programmes
Advertising and Publicity (Advertising and Publicity); **Business, Finance and Banking** (Banking; Business and Commerce; Finance); **English**; **Graphic Design**; **Human Resources** (Human Resources); **Law and Political Science** (Law; Political Sciences); **Marketing**; **Systems Analysis** (Systems Analysis); **Tourism** (Hotel and Restaurant; Hotel Management; Tourism)

Degrees and Diplomas: *Licenciatura*; *Maestría*

COLUMBUS UNIVERSITY

Universidad Columbus

Edificio Columbus Calle 50 y Celso Carbonell, , Bella Vista, Panamá
Tel: +507 263-3888
Fax: +507 263-3896
EMail: columbus@columbus.edu
Website: http://www.columbus.edu

Rector: Carlos A. Arellano Lennox

Vicerrector Académico: Carlos A. Bonilla G.

International Relations: Librada Fernández

Faculties

Economics and Commerce (Advertising and Publicity; Banking; Business Administration; Business and Commerce; Finance; Hotel Management; Insurance; Marketing; Sales Techniques; Tourism); **Education and Linguistics** (Education; Educational Administration; Linguistics; Modern Languages; Teacher Training); **Environmental and Agro-industrial Sciences**; **Law and Political Science** (Civil Law; Constitutional Law; Criminal Law; Human Rights; Political Sciences); **Marine Sciences**; **Medicine and Health Sciences** (Dietetics; Health Sciences; Hygiene; Medicine; Nutrition; Physical Therapy; Surgery); **Social and Information Sciences**; **Technology**

History: Founded 1994.

Main Language(s) of Instruction: Spanish

DELPHI UNIVERSITY

Universidad Delphi

Bocas del Toro, Panamá

Rector: Maria de Tousenkm

Programmes

Investigative Medicine

FLORIDA STATE UNIVERSITY - PANAMA (FSU PANAMA)

P.O. Box 6-4794 El Dorado, Panama 6A, Calle Ernesto J. Castillero 1033, La Boca Balboa - Ancon, Panamá

Tel: +507 314-0367

Fax: +507 314-0366

EMail: fsupanama@mailer.fsu.edu; admissions_fsupanama@fsu.edu

Website: http://panama.fsu.edu

Rector: Carlos Langoni

Programmes

Computer Science; **Environmental Studies**; **Information Studies**; **International Affairs** (International Business); **Latin American and Carribean Studies**; **Liberal Studies**; **Social Science** *(Interdisciplinary)* (Social Sciences)

Fees: (US Dollars): 154 per credit hour; Application Fee (first semester only), 30.

Degrees and Diplomas: *Licenciatura*; *Maestría*; *Doctorado*

Libraries: c. 50,000 vols; 280 databases; c. 100,000 e-books; 19,000 e-journals.

INTERAMERICAN DISTANCE EDUCATION UNIVERSITY OF PANAMA

Universidad Interamericana de Educación a Distancia de Panamá (UNIEDPA)

Calle 30 e y Avenida Mexico, Panamá

Tel: +507 227-2902 +507 227-2898

Fax: +507 227-5565

EMail: uniedpa@cwp.net.pa

Website: http://www.uniedpa.com

Rector: Laurentiño Gudiño

Programmes

Administration and Accountancy (Accountancy; Administration); **Educational Sciences** (Educational Sciences); **Law and Political Science** (Law; Political Sciences); **Secretarial Studies** (Secretarial Studies)

Further Information: Also campuses in Colón, Penonome, Veraguas, Herera, Chiriqui, Darién, Chorrera, Ocú y Tonosi.

History: Founded 1986.

Degrees and Diplomas: *Maestro a Nivel Superior*, *Técnico Superior*, *Licenciatura*; *Maestría*; *Doctorado*

Last Updated: 26/10/09

INTERAMERICAN UNIVERSITY OF PANAMÁ

Universidad Interamericana de Panamá

Apartado 9865, Zona 9, Panamá

Tel: +507 263-7787

Fax: +507 264-2544

EMail: info@uinteramericana.edu

Website: http://www.uinteramericana.edu

Rector: Antonio Fletcher

Faculties

Administration and Social Sciences; **Engineering and Architecture** (Architecture; Civil Engineering; Electronic Engineering; Industrial Engineering; Information Sciences; Interior Design; Mechanical Engineering)

Schools

Hotel Management (Hotel Management)

History: Founded 1992.

Academic Year: January to December

Admission Requirements: Secondary school certificate or equivalent

Fees: (US Dollars): 120-350 per subject/course

Main Language(s) of Instruction: Spanish

Accrediting Agencies: University of Panamá

Degrees and Diplomas: *Licenciatura*: 3 1/2 yrs; *Maestria*: a further 1 1/2 yrs

Student Services: Academic counselling, Employment services, Foreign student adviser, Language programs, Social counselling

Libraries: Yes

Last Updated: 26/10/09

INTERNATIONAL UNIVERSITY

Universidad Internacional

55 Street, El Cangrejo, (next to the Egyptian Embassy), Panamá

Tel: +507 269-1515

EMail: info@internationaluniversity.edu

Website: http://www.internationaluniversity.edu

Rector: Pablo Tuñón Vejas

Programmes

Accounting and Audit (Accountancy; Banking); **Business Administration** (Administration; Business Administration; Business Computing; Marketing); **Education** (Education; Educational Administration); **Health** (Health Administration; Health Sciences); **Law and Political Sciences**; **Tourism and Hotel Management** (Hotel Management; Tourism)

Further Information: Also campus in La Chorrera.

History: Created 2000. Acquired current status 2003.

Degrees and Diplomas: *Licenciatura*: Administration; Accounting and Audit; Law and Political Sciences; Education; Tourism and Hotel Management; *Maestría*: Business Administration; Education; Law; Health; *Doctorado*: Education. Also: Post-Grado in: Education; Business Administration

Last Updated: 25/09/09

INTERNATIONAL UNIVERSITY OF BUSINESS AND EDUCATION

Universidad Internacional de Comercio y Educación (UICE)

Via Argentina entrando por la calle del trapìchito, Panamá

Tel: +507 227-6644 +507 227-4192

Fax: +507 227-1642

Website: http://www.uniced.ac.pa

Rectora: Mirla Arjona F.

Programmes

Business and Commerce (Accountancy; Business and Commerce); **Education** (Education); **Law and Political Science**

Degrees and Diplomas: *Licenciatura*

Last Updated: 26/10/09

ISAE UNIVERSITY

Universidad ISAE

Transistmica y Avenida Ramón Arias, Edifico Maheli, frente al McDonald local #4, Panamá
Tel: +507 278-1432 +507 278-1433
Fax: +507 278-1434
EMail: mailto:isaeuniv@cwpanama.net
Website: http://www.isaeuniversidad.com/Pages/Default.aspx

Rector: Xiomara de Arrocha

Programmes

Business Administration (Accountancy; Business Administration; Marketing); **Law and Political Science**

LATIN AMERICAN UNIVERSITY OF INTERNATIONAL BUSINESS

Universidad Latinoamericana de Comercio Exterior (ULACEX)

El Cangrejo, Calle F, al lado del Teatro la Cúpula, Panamá
Tel: +507 223-7941
Fax: +507 213-1792
EMail: ulacex@cwpanama.net
Website: http://www.ulacex.com

Rector: Bruno Garisto

Programmes

Accountancy (Accountancy); **Banking and Finance** (Administration; Banking; Finance); **Business Administration** (Business Administration; Marketing); **Engineering** (Engineering); **International Business** (International Business); **Law and Political Science**; **Psychology** (Psychology); **Tourism and Hotel Management**

Main Language(s) of Instruction: Spanish

Degrees and Diplomas: *Licenciatura*; *Maestría*. Also posgrados
Last Updated: 27/10/09

LATIN AMERICAN UNIVERSITY OF SCIENCES AND TECHNOLOGY

Universidad Latinoamericana de Ciencias y Tecnologia (ULACIT)

Via España, Calle 74E, Antigua Entrada al Club de Golf, Panamá
Tel: +507 224-5377
Fax: +507 222-3607 +507 224-0318
EMail: info@ulacit.ac.pa
Website: http://www.ulacit.ac.pa

Rector: Noemi Castillo

Faculties

Administration (Accountancy; Banking; Business Administration; Finance; International Business); **Design, Communication and Marketing** (Advertising and Publicity; Graphic Design; Interior Design; Marketing; Sales Techniques); **Engineering** (Computer Engineering; Computer Networks; Electronic Engineering; Industrial Engineering; Mechanical Engineering; Software Engineering; Transport Engineering); **Health Sciences** (Dentistry; Health Sciences; Medicine; Nutrition; Surgery); **Hotel Management and Tourism** (Hotel Management; Tourism); **Law and Political Science** (Criminology; Law; Political Sciences)

History: Founded 1991. Acquired present status 2004.

Main Language(s) of Instruction: Spanish

Degrees and Diplomas: *Licenciatura*; *Maestría*
Last Updated: 26/10/09

LATIN UNIVERSITY OF PANAMÁ

Universidad Latina de Panamá

Apartado 87-0887, Vía Ricardo J. Alfaro, Calle Aragón, Urbanización Castilla, Panamá 7
Tel: +507 230-8600
Fax: +507 230-8600 +507 230-8605
EMail: web@ns.ulat.ac.pa
Website: http://www.ulat.ac.pa

Rectora: Sonia de Smith
Tel: +507 230-8610, Fax: +507 230-8604
EMail: zsmith@ns.ulat.ac.pa

Directora: Claudia Marín
Tel: +507 230-8652, Fax: +507 230-8603
EMail: clmarin@ns.ulat.ac.pa

International Relations: Eneida López
Tel: +507 230-8659, Fax: +507 230-8604
EMail: elopez@ns.ulat.ac.pa

Centres

Postgraduate Studies

Faculties

Administration and Economics (Administration; Economics); **Communication** (Communication Studies); **Educational Sciences** (Educational Sciences); **Law and Political Science** (Law; Political Sciences); **Medicine and Health Sciences** (Health Sciences; Medicine); **Technology** (Technology)

Institutes

Language *(Latina)*

History: Founded 1989. Acquired present status 1991.

Governing Bodies: Board of Directors

Admission Requirements: High school diploma

Fees: (Balboa): 1,500 per annum

Main Language(s) of Instruction: Spanish

International Co-operation: Fulbright, AECI

Degrees and Diplomas: *Licenciatura*: Business, Technology, Education, Communication, 3-4 yrs; *Maestría*: Business, Education, Marketing (MBA, MED), 1 yr and 4 months; *Doctorado*: Education, Business, 2 yrs

Student Services: Foreign student adviser, Handicapped facilities, Language programs, Sports facilities

Student Residential Facilities: None

AZUERO REGIONAL CENTRE

CENTRO REGIONAL DE AZUERO

Calle Ing. Roberto Reyna Chitré, Azuero, Provincia de Herrera
Tel: +507 996-1155
Fax: +507 996-1170
Website: http://www.ulat.ac.pa/centros_regionales

Faculties

Administration and Economics; **Education**; **Law and Political Science**; **Medical and Health Sciences**; **Technology**

DAVID REGIONAL CENTRE

CENTRO REGIONAL DE DAVID

Calle 5ta, David, Provincia de Chiriqui
Tel: +507 774-8821
Fax: +507 774-8821
Website: http://www.ulat.ac.pa/centros_regionales

Departments

English; **Postgraduate and Master's Studies**

Faculties

Administration and Economics; **Education**; **Law and Political Science**; **Technology**

SANTIAGO REGIONAL CENTRE

CENTRO REGIONAL DE SANTIAGO

Calle 2da Final vía la Colorada, Santiago, Provincia de Veraguas
Tel: +507 998-5412
Fax: +507 998-5812
Website: http://www.ulat.ac.pa/centros_regionales/

Faculties
Administration and Economics; **Education**; **Law and Political Science**; **Natural Sciences**; **Technology**

METROPOLITAN UNIVERSITY OF SCIENCE AND TECHNOLOGY

Universidad Metropolitana de Ciencia y Tecnología (UMECIT)
Calle L A Edificio 49 B, Oeste; Via Venetto, Frente a la Embajada de Egipto. Corregimiento Bella Vista, Rianjo
Tel: +507 264-9908 +507 264-8154
Fax: +507 263-2471
Website: http://www.umecit.edu.pa

Rector: José Alberto Nieto Rojas

Faculties
Economics and Administration (Accountancy; Administration; Advertising and Publicity; Banking; Business Administration; Finance; Human Resources; International Business; International Relations; Marketing; Tourism); **Health Sciences**; **Humanities and Educational Sciences** (Curriculum; Education; English; Pedagogy; Physical Education; Preschool Education; Psychology; Social Work); **Law and Forensic Sciences** (Criminology; Forensic Medicine and Dentistry; Law; Political Sciences); **Nautical Sciences** (Marine Transport; Nautical Science); **Technology, Construction and Environment** (Computer Networks; Construction Engineering; Electrical Engineering; Environmental Engineering; Graphic Design; Industrial Design; Radio and Television Broadcasting; Systems Analysis; Telecommunications Engineering)

Degrees and Diplomas: *Técnico Superior*, *Licenciatura*; *Maestría*; *Doctorado*
Last Updated: 27/10/09

NOVA SOUTHEASTERN UNIVERSITY

Universidad Nova Southeastern
Albrook -Eduf- 869, PO Box 3318, Balboa Panamá, Panamá
Tel: +507 232-7062
Fax: +507 232-7064
EMail: rroman@nova.edu

OPEN AND DISTANCE UNIVERSITY OF PANAMÁ

Universidad Abierta y a Distancia de Panamá (UNADP)
Avenida Perú, Edificio Brumas No 39-12 Zona 7, Panamá
Tel: +507 227-7242
Fax: +507 227-7243
EMail: generalunadp@cwpanama.net
Website: http://www.unadp.ac.pa

Rector: Rosa E. Sánchez

Programmes
Accountancy (Accountancy); **Adult Education**; **Banking and Finance** (Banking; Finance); **Business Administration** (Business Administration); **Educational Administration**; **Human Resource Management** (Human Resources); **International Commerce**

History: Founded 1994.
Main Language(s) of Instruction: Spanish
Degrees and Diplomas: *Técnico Superior*, *Licenciatura*; *Maestría*
Last Updated: 23/10/09

OTEIMA TECHNOLOGICAL UNIVERSITY

Universidad Tecnológica OTEIMA
Edificio Plaza Oteima, Calle D. Norte entre Ave. 1era y 2da Este, David, Provincia de Chiriquí
EMail: oteima@oteima.ac.pa
Website: http://www.oteima.ac.pa/nueva

Rectora: Nixa Gnaegi de Ríos EMail: rectoria@oteima.ac.pa

Programmes
Business Administration (Business Administration; Hotel Management; International Business); **Computer Science** (Computer Networks; Computer Science); **English** (English); **Law and Political Science** (Law; Political Sciences)

History: Founded 1987. Acquired present status 2005.
Main Language(s) of Instruction: Spanish
Degrees and Diplomas: *Licenciatura*; *Maestría*
Last Updated: 26/10/09

PANAMERICAN UNIVERSITY

Universidad Panamericana
Vía España y Calle Elvira Méndez, Edificio Interseco, Piso 7, Panamá
Tel: +507 265-0706 +507 265-0641
Fax: +507 265-0638
EMail: upam@cableonda.net
Website: http://www.upam.ac.pa

Rector: Rosario Coya Navarro EMail: rosariocoya@upam.ac.pa

Programmes
Banking (Banking); **Business Administration**; **Law and Political Science** (Law; Political Sciences); **Management Engineering**; **Tourism** (Tourism)

Main Language(s) of Instruction: Spanish
Degrees and Diplomas: *Técnico Superior*, *Licenciatura*; *Maestría*. Also offers "Post-grado" degree, 1yr following Licenciatura.
Last Updated: 27/10/09

SAN MARTÍN UNIVERSITY OF PANAMÁ

Universidad San Martín de Panamá
"Ciudad del Saber", Forte Clayton, Edificio 811, Panamá
Tel: +507 317-1076
Fax: +507 317-1075
EMail: tceville@sanmartin.edu.co
Website: http://www.sanmartin.edu.co

Rector: Julio Delgado

Faculties
Biological Sciences (Biotechnology)

Degrees and Diplomas: *Licenciatura*
Last Updated: 26/10/09

SANTA MARÍA LA ANTIGUA CATHOLIC UNIVERSITY, PANAMÁ

Universidad Católica Santa María La Antigua (USMA)
Apartado 0819-08550, Panamá
Tel: +507 230-8200 +507 230-8300
Fax: +507 230-3593
EMail: info@usma.edu.pa
Website: http://www.usma.ac.pa

Rector: Pablo Varela Server
Tel: +507 230-8201 EMail: ppvarela@usma.ac.pa

Secretaria General: Ingrid M. Chang Valdés
Tel: +507 230-8210 EMail: pichang@usma.ac.pa

International Relations: Justiniano Montenegro
Tel: +507 230-8378, Fax: +507 230-4467
EMail: pjmonten@usma.ac.pa

Faculties
Administration (Accountancy; Administration; Business Administration; Finance; International Business; Marketing; Tourism); **Humanities and Religious Sciences** (Arts and Humanities; Ethics; Preschool Education; Religion; Teacher Training); **Law and Political Science** (Law; Political Sciences); **Social Sciences**; **Technology and Natural Sciences** (Architecture; Civil Engineering; Computer Engineering; Electronic Engineering; Graphic Design; Industrial Engineering; Interior Design; Telecommunications Engineering)

History: Founded 1965 with the Archbishop of Panamá as Grand Chancellor of the University. Reorganized 1973.
Governing Bodies: Board of Directors
Academic Year: January to December (January-April; May-August; September-December)
Admission Requirements: Secondary school certificate and admission course
Fees: (US Dollars): 600-900 per semester

Main Language(s) of Instruction: Spanish

Degrees and Diplomas: *Técnico Superior*: 2 yrs; *Licenciatura*: 4-5 yrs; *Maestría*: a further 2 yrs; *Doctorado*: 4 yrs

Student Services: Academic counselling, Employment services, Foreign student adviser, Handicapped facilities, Health services, Language programs, Social counselling, Sports facilities

Libraries: c. 65,000 vols

Publications: Revista "Iustitia et Pulchritudo"; Revista 'La Antigua'

Press or Publishing House: Editorial Santa María La Antigua

Academic Staff *2007-2008*	MEN	WOMEN	TOTAL
FULL-TIME	25	18	**43**
PART-TIME	–	–	**380**
STAFF WITH DOCTORATE			
FULL-TIME	6	6	**12**
PART-TIME	–	–	**70**
Student Numbers *2007-2008*			
All (Foreign Included)	–	–	**4,500**

Last Updated: 23/10/09

SPECIALIZED UNIVERSITY OF AUTHORIZED PUBLIC ACCOUNTANCY

Universidad Especializada del Contador Público Autorizado (UNESCPA)

Urbanzación Los Angeles, Calle 60, Oeste Na J-18, Panamá
Tel: +507 236-6571
Fax: +507 236-7194
EMail: unescpa@pa.inter.net
Website: http://www.colegiocpapanama.org/unescpa.shtml

President: Américo Quintero

Secretario General: Eduardo Casal

Programmes
Auditing (Accountancy); **Taxation**
History: Founded 2004.
Degrees and Diplomas: Offers "Post-grados" degree, 1 yr.

UNIVERSITY OF ARTS GANEXA

Universidad del Arte GANEXA

Apartado 844, Zona 1, Panamá
Tel: +507 223-9140 +507 264-3961
Fax: +507 264-6949
EMail: info@ganexa.edu.pa
Website: http://www.ganexa.edu.pa

Rector: Ricauter Martínez

Schools
Architecture; **Fashion Design**; **Gastronomy**; **Graphic Design** (Graphic Design); **Photography** (Photography); **Plastic Arts** (Painting and Drawing; Sculpture)

Degrees and Diplomas: *Licenciatura*; *Maestría*
Last Updated: 23/10/09

UNIVERSITY OF CARTAGO

Universidad de Cartago

Plaza Oteima, David, Provincia de Chiriquí
Tel: +507 774-4472 +507 774-9963
Fax: +507 777-4104
EMail: informacion@ucapanama.org
Website: http://www.ucapanama.org

Rector: Carlos Fajardo EMail: cfajardo@ucapanama.org

Faculties
Administrative Sciences (Accountancy; Banking; Business Administration; Finance; Human Resources; Insurance); **Humanities, Ecology and Tourism** (Arts and Humanities; Ecology; Tourism); **Law and Political Sciences** (Law; Political Sciences); **Science and Technology** (Computer Science; Technology)

Degrees and Diplomas: *Licenciatura*; *Maestría*: School Management; Educational Technology; University Teaching; Finance; Marketing; Corporative Management; Tourism; Human Resources Management; *Doctorado*: Business Administration, Administration
Last Updated: 23/10/09

UNIVERSITY OF LOUISVILLE - PANAMA

Universidad de Louisville

cl. 45 Bella Vista, Panamá
Tel: +507 264-0777
Fax: +507 264-7962
EMail: info@louisville.com.pa
Website: http://www.louisville.com.pa

Rector: Oscar León

Programmes
Business Administration; **Engineering** (Business and Commerce; Engineering); **English** (English); **Human Resources** (Human Resources); **International Relations** (International Relations); **Psychology and Counseling**; **Science** (Industrial Engineering)
History: Founded 1997.
Degrees and Diplomas: *Licenciatura*; *Maestría*
Last Updated: 26/10/09

UNIVERSITY OF PEACE

Universidad de la Paz

Apartado 1507, Balboa Ancón, Panamá
Tel: +507 232-7650
Fax: +507 232-7647

Rectora: Lucrecia Herrera Cozzarelli (1994-)
Tel: +507 232-7650 EMail: lucrehc@ayayai.com

Administrative Officer: Otto Zapata Gordon
Tel: +507 232-8583, Fax: +507 232-7647

International Relations: Natividad Pérez Martinez, Vicerrectora
Tel: +507 232-7647, Fax: +507 232-7647

Faculties
Accountancy; **Administration**; **Agriculture**; **Education**; **Exact Sciences**; **Finance**; **Fine Arts**; **Humanities**; **Law and Political Science**; **Marketing**; **Professional Studies**; **Social Communication**; **Technology**
History: Founded 1994.
Main Language(s) of Instruction: Spanish
Student Services: Academic counselling, Employment services

UNIVERSITY OF SANTANDER - PANAMÁ

Universidad de Santander - Panamá (UDES - PANAMA)

Paitilla, en La Escuela Las Esclavas, Panamá

Rector: Rafael Serrano

UNIVERSITY OF THE ISTHMUS

Universidad del Istmo (UDI)

Avenida Justo Arosemena entre Calle 40 y 41, Bella Vista (antiguo Colegio María Inmaculada), Panamá
Tel: +507 277-8822 +507 277-8823
Fax: +507 227-8831
EMail: informacion@udi.edu
Website: http://www.udi.edu

Rector: Pablo Michelsen Niño

Vicerrector Administrativo: Oswaldo Moreno

Faculties
Business Studies (Accountancy; Business Administration; Finance; International Business); **Communication Sciences** (Journalism; Media Studies); **Engineering and Information Technology** (Computer Engineering; Industrial Engineering; Information Technology; Safety Engineering; Systems Analysis; Telecommunications Engineering); **Law and Political Science** (Law; Political Sciences); **Marine Sciences** (Marine Science and Oceanography; Transport Management); **Marketing and Advertisment**; **Technical Careers** (English; Teacher Trainers Education); **Tourism** (Hotel Management; Tourism)

Further Information: Also branches in David, Chorrera, Colón, Santiago, Los Pueblos
History: Founded 1963.
Degrees and Diplomas: *Técnico Superior*, *Licenciatura*; *Maestría*; *Doctorado*
Last Updated: 26/10/09

Papua New Guinea

STRUCTURE OF HIGHER EDUCATION SYSTEM

Description:

Higher education is mainly provided by universities and specialized institutions. The Office for Higher Education is responsible for coordinating higher education. Its objectives include fostering a rational development of higher education in the light of the country's needs in terms of resources and delivering higher education efficiently and cost-effectively and maintaining quality.

Stages of studies:

University level first stage: *Certificate, Diploma, Bachelor's degree*

Certificates and diplomas are awarded after studies lasting between two and three years. The Bachelor's degree is conferred after four years' study with an additional year for Honours. Students who hold the Secondary School Leaving Certificate follow a one-year preliminary course at the university before studying for the Bachelor's degree. Some degree courses start as two-year Diploma courses followed by a further two years for a degree. Degree courses in Law and Medicine last for five years. There are also five-year Diploma courses at the higher technician level.

University level second stage: *Master's degree*

The Master's degree is conferred after studies lasting between one and three years beyond the Bachelor's degree. Candidates must submit a thesis. Candidates for the Master's degree in Education must have obtained an appropriate Bachelor's degree, completed one year's graduate work and have two years' experience in teaching or other educational work. Initial preliminary studies and the qualifying examination may be waived for candidates with Honours Degrees.

University level third stage: *Doctor's degree*

The Doctor of Philosophy is conferred after a minimum of three years' study on candidates who hold a Master's degree or a Bachelor's degree after an additional minimum preliminary training period. Candidates must submit a thesis.

Distance higher education:

Correspondence courses are run by the Institute of Distance and Continuing Education of the University of Papua New Guinea.

ADMISSION TO HIGHER EDUCATION

Admission to university-level studies:

Name of secondary school credential required: Higher School Certificate

Other admission requirements: Most students also follow a one-year foundation course.

Foreign students admission:

Entrance exam requirements: Foreign students must have credit passes at form IV level in English, Mathematics and Sciences; University of Papua New Guinea and Papua New Guinea University of Technology and Goroka Teachers College accept students with good grades from Grade 12.

Entry regulations: Students must have a visa.

Language requirements: Students must have a good command of English for all courses. An orientation programme is organized at the University of Papua New Guinea.

NATIONAL BODIES

Ministry for Higher Education, Research, Science and Technology

Minister: David Arore
PO Box 5117
2nd Floor Mutual Rumana Building
Boroko
Tel: +675 327 7528
Fax: +675 327 7480

Office for Higher Education

Director General: David Kavanamur
2nd Floor Mutual Rumana, Waigani Drive
Boroko
Tel: +675 301 2052
Fax: +675 325 8386
WWW: http://www.ohe.gov.pg
Role of national body: OHE is advising the Minister for Higher Education, Research, Science and Technology on all matters concerning higher education.

Data for academic year: 2002-2003
Source: IAU from IBE website, 2003. Bodies, 2012.

INSTITUTIONS

DIVINE WORD UNIVERSITY (DWU)

PO Box 483, Madang, Madang Province
Tel: +675(422) 2937
Fax: +675(422) 2812
EMail: info@dwu.ac.pg
Website: http://www.dwu.ac.pg

President: Jan Czuba (1995-)
Tel: +675(422) 1135, Fax: +675(422) 2853
EMail: jczuba@dwu.ac.pg

Vice-President: Cecilia Nembou
EMail: cnembou@dwu.ac.pg; cnembou@gmail.com

Vice-President, Academic: Andrew Simpson
EMail: asimpson@dwu.ac.pg

International Relations: Michael McManus
EMail: mmcmanus@dwu.ac.pg

Faculties

Arts (Communication Arts; Regional Studies; Religious Studies; Social Studies) *Dean*: Linda Crowl; **Business and Management** (Business Administration; Information Management; Mathematics and Computer Science; Tourism) *Dean*: Romulo Lindio; **Education** *Dean*: Catherine Nongkas; **Flexible Learning** (Business Administration; Curriculum; Educational Administration; Educational and Student Counselling; Higher Education; Higher Education Teacher Training; Human Resources; Justice Administration; Management; Peace and Disarmament; Public Administration; Social Studies; Special Education; Teacher Training) *Director*: Philip Smith; **Health Sciences** *Professor*: Francis Hombhanje; **Theology** (Catholic Theology)

History: Founded 1980, acquired present status 1996.

Governing Bodies: University Council

Academic Year: January to November (January-June; July-November)

Admission Requirements: Completion of high school education Grade 12

Fees: (Kina): 10,200-17,000 per annum

Main Language(s) of Instruction: English

International Co-operation: With universities in Australia; Philippines, Japan, Poland, Germany

Accrediting Agencies: Commission of Higher Education

Degrees and Diplomas: *Certificate/Diploma*: 1-2 yrs; *Bachelor's Degree*: 4 yrs; *Master's Degree*: 5-6 yrs; *Doctor's Degree*: 4 yrs full-time, 6 yrs part-time

Student Services: Academic counselling, Canteen, Foreign student adviser, Foreign Studies Centre, Health services, Language programs, Social counselling, Sports facilities

Student Residential Facilities: Yes

Libraries: Central Library

Press or Publishing House: Divine Word University Press

Academic Staff *2010*	MEN	WOMEN	**TOTAL**
FULL-TIME	62	46	**108**
PART-TIME	14	11	**25**
STAFF WITH DOCTORATE			
FULL-TIME	32	26	**58**
PART-TIME	26	9	**35**
Student Numbers *2010*			
All (Foreign Included)	883	1,013	**1,896**
FOREIGN ONLY	35	24	**59**

Part-time students, 170. **Distance students**, 1,200.

Last Updated: 18/03/10

PACIFIC ADVENTIST UNIVERSITY (PAU)

Private Mail Bag, Boroko, National Capital District 111
Tel: +675(328) 0200 +675(328) 0200
Fax: +675(328) 1257
EMail: information@pau.ac.pg; admin@pau.ac.pg
Website: http://www.pau.ac.pg

Vice-Chancellor: Branamir Schubert (2007-)
EMail: b.schubert@pau.ac.pg

International Relations: Glynn Galo, Deputy-Vice-Chancellor (2008-)
Tel: 675 328 0200, Fax: 675 328 1257 EMail: glynn.galo@pau.ac.pg

Schools

Arts and Humanities *Dean*: Jillian Thiele; **Business and Management** *Dean*: Luka Titimanu; **Education** (Education; Primary Education; Secondary Education) *Dean*: Carol Tasker; **Health Sciences** *Dean*: Rosaline Lapau-Baker; **Science and Technology** (Biology; Chemistry; Mathematics; Natural Sciences; Physics; Technology); **Theology** (Bible; Religion; Theology)

History: Founded 1983 as Pacific Adventist College. Acquired present status 1996. Became Pacific Adventist University 1997.

Governing Bodies: Pacific Adventist University Council

Academic Year: February to December (February-June; August-December)

Admission Requirements: Higher School Certificate

Fees: (Kina): c. 10,000 per annum

Main Language(s) of Instruction: English

Accrediting Agencies: Adventist Accrediting Association

Degrees and Diplomas: *Bachelor's Degree*: Accountancy and Management; Accountancy and Computing; Business (BBus), 4 1/2 yrs; *Bachelor's Degree*: Theology; Education; Accountancy; Nursing; Management; Office Administration; Science (BA, BEd, BBus, BSc), 4 yrs; *Master's Degree*: Theology, 4 yrs part-time or 3 semesters full-time. Also Diploma in Nursing 3 yrs

Student Services: Academic counselling, Canteen, Employment services, Health services, Social counselling, Sports facilities

Student Residential Facilities: Yes

Special Facilities: Bird sanctuary

Libraries: 102,951 vols; 466 subscriptions to periodicals

Press or Publishing House: Pacific Adventist University Press

Last Updated: 18/07/08

PAPUA NEW GUINEA UNIVERSITY OF TECHNOLOGY

Private Mail Bag, Lae, Morobe Province 411
Tel: +675(473) 4999
Fax: +675(475) 7667
Website: http://www.unitech.ac.pg

Vice-Chancellor: Misty Baloiloi (2001-)
EMail: vice-chancellor@unitech.ac.pg

Registrar: Alan Sako EMail: asako@admin.unitech.ac.pg

Departments

Agriculture (Agriculture); **Applied Physics** (Applied Physics; Forestry); **Applied Sciences** (Natural Sciences); **Architecture and Building Science** (Architecture; Building Technologies); **Business Studies** (Business and Commerce); **Civil Engineering** (Civil Engineering); **Electrical and Communication Engineering** (Electrical Engineering; Telecommunications Engineering); **Forestry** (Forestry); **Language and Communication** (Communication Studies; Modern Languages); **Mathematics and Computer Science** (Mathematics; Statistics); **Mechanical Engineering** (Energy Engineering; Industrial Design; Mechanical Engineering; Mechanics; Production Engineering); **Mining Engineering** (Mining Engineering); **Surveying and Land Studies** (Rural Studies; Surveying and Mapping)

History: Founded 1965 as Papua New Guinea Institute of Higher Technical Education. Acquired present status and title 1973.

Academic Year: February to November (February-June; July-November)

Admission Requirements: Completion of high school education, Grade 12 level or equivalent

Main Language(s) of Instruction: English

Degrees and Diplomas: *Bachelor's Degree*: 4-5 yrs; *Master's Degree*: a further 1-2 yrs; *Doctor's Degree (PhD)*: a further 3-5 yrs

Student Services: Academic counselling, Canteen, Health services, Social counselling, Sports facilities

Student Residential Facilities: Yes

Libraries: c. 100,000 vols

FORESTRY COLLEGE

PO Box 92, Bulolo, Morobe Province
Tel: +675(474) 5226
Fax: +675(474) 5311

Principal: Tommy Nahuet

Programmes

Forestry

TIMBER INDUSTRY TRAINING COLLEGE

PO Box 92, Lae, Morobe Province
Tel: +675(472) 1083
Fax: +675(472) 3586
EMail: tftc@global.net.pg
Website: http://www.unitech.ac.pg

Programmes

Forestry

UNIVERSITY OF GOROKA (UOG)

PO Box 1078, Goroka, Eastern Highlands Province 441
Tel: +675(731) 1700
Fax: +675(732) 2620
EMail: vcsecretary@uog.ac.pg
Website: http://www.uog.ac.pg

Vice-Chancellor: Gairo Onagi
Tel: +675(731) 1701, Fax: +675(732) 1914

Pro-Vice-Chancellor (Acting): Jerry Semos
Tel: +675(731) 1731, Fax: +675(732) 1914
EMail: semosj@uog.ac.pg

International Relations: Veronica Thomas
Tel: +675(731) 1822 EMail: thomasv@uog.ac.pg

Faculties

Education (Curriculum; Education; Educational Sciences); **Humanities** (Arts and Humanities; Business and Commerce; Literature; Modern Languages; Performing Arts; Religious Education; Social Sciences); **Science** (Agriculture; Computer Science; Design; Home Economics; Mathematics; Natural Sciences; Physical Education; Technology)

History: Founded 1968, acquired present status and title 1997.

Governing Bodies: University Council

Academic Year: February to December

Admission Requirements: Completion of high school education, Grade 12 level ('B' level grades)

Fees: (Kina): c. 11,000-13,000 per annum

Main Language(s) of Instruction: English

International Co-operation: With universities in Australia

Accrediting Agencies: Office of Higher Education

Degrees and Diplomas: *Bachelor's Degree*: Education (with Honours), 1 yr; *Bachelor's Degree*: Education; Science; Humanities, 4 yrs; *Master's Degree*: Education, 2 yrs full-time; 4 yrs part-time. Also Diploma in Education, 1 yr

Student Services: Academic counselling, Canteen, Cultural centre, Foreign student adviser, Health services, Social counselling, Sports facilities

Student Residential Facilities: Yes

Libraries: Central Library, 100,000 vols, 400 periodicals

Publications: PNG Journal of Education *(annually)*; PNG Journal of Teacher Education *(quarterly)*

Press or Publishing House: University Press

Last Updated: 23/02/10

UNIVERSITY OF PAPUA NEW GUINEA

PO Box 320, University Post Office, Port Moresby, National Capital District
Tel: +675(326) 0900
Fax: +675(326) 7187
EMail: webmaster@upng.ac.pg
Website: http://www.upng.ac.pg

Vice-Chancellor: Ross Hynes (2006-) EMail: vcoffice@upng.ac.pg

Registrar: Vincent Malaibe Tel: +675(326) 7143

Centres

Biodiversity and Natural Products Research *(CBNPR)*; **Disaster Reduction**; **Distance Education Research** *Director*: Paraka Pena;

Human Rights; **Public Health**; **Research and Postgraduate Studies** *Dean*: Simon Saulei; **Teaching, Learning and In-House Training** *Director*: Boe Lahui-Ako

Institutes

Arts and Communication *(Melanesian)*

Research Centres

Melanesian and Pacific Studies; **Motupore Island** *Director*: Mark Baine

Schools

Business Administration (Banking; Business Administration; Business and Commerce; Economics; Finance; Management; Political Sciences; Psychology; Tourism) *Dean*: Albert Mellam; **Humanities and Social Sciences** (Administration; Anthropology; Arts and Humanities; Business and Commerce; Communication Studies; Demography and Population; Development Studies; Economics; English; Fine Arts; Gender Studies; Geography; History; Information Sciences; Journalism; Linguistics; Literature; Modern Languages; Performing Arts; Philosophy; Political Sciences; Psychology; Public Relations; Social Work; Sociology; Visual Arts) *Dean*: Kenneth Sumbuk; **Law** (Law) *Dean (Acting)*: S. Kaipu; **Natural and Physical Sciences** (Biology; Chemistry; Computer Science; Environmental Studies; Geology; Mathematics; Natural Sciences; Physics; Statistics) *Dean (Acting)*: L. Hill

History: Founded 1966.

Governing Bodies: University Council

Academic Year: February to November (February-June; July-November)

Admission Requirements: Successful completion of preliminary year's studies, Grade 12 level of high school, or by Australian Matriculation, or recognized equivalent

Main Language(s) of Instruction: English

Degrees and Diplomas: *Bachelor's Degree*: 4-5 yrs; *Master's Degree*: a further 1-3 yrs; *Doctor's Degree (PhD)*: a further 3-4 yrs

Student Residential Facilities: For c. 1,680 students

Libraries: Michael Jomare Library, c. 450,000 vols, 2,000 current periodicals

Press or Publishing House: Unipress

ENGA UNIVERSITY CENTRE

PO Box 379, Wabag, Enga Province
Tel: +675(547) 1048

MADANG OPEN CAMPUS

PO Box 2036, Madang, Madang Province
Tel: +675(852) 3003
Fax: +675(852) 2528

TAURAMA CAMPUS

PO Box 5623, Boroko,
National Capital District 111
Tel: +675(311) 2626 + 675(311) 2504
Fax: +675(325) 6809

Schools

Medicine and Health Sciences (Community Health; Dentistry; Health Sciences; Laboratory Techniques; Medical Auxiliaries; Medicine; Nursing; Pharmacy; Radiology) *Dean*: Isi Kevau

UNIVERSITY OF VUDAL (UOV)

Private Mail Bag, Rabaul,
East New Britain Province 611
Tel: +675(983) 9144
Fax: +675(983) 9166
EMail: ntali@daltron.com.pg

Vice-Chancellor: Philip Siaguru
Tel: +675(983) 9277, Fax: +675(983) 9277

Deputy-Director, Division of Administration: Aria Hailaeavila

Departments

Agriculture (Agriculture; Tropical Agriculture) *Head*: Terence Price

Further Information: Oro Campus

History: Founded 1965 as Vudal Agricultural College, became University College of Papua New Guinea University 1991, and acquired present status and title 1997.

Governing Bodies: University Council

Academic Year: February to November

Admission Requirements: Completion of high school education, Grade 12

Fees: (Kina): 150-7,500 per annum

Main Language(s) of Instruction: English

Accrediting Agencies: Office of Higher Education

Degrees and Diplomas: *Certificate/Diploma*: Agriculture, 3 yrs; *Bachelor's Degree*: Agriculture, 4 yrs; *Master's Degree*: Management Studies, 2 yrs part-time. Bachelor of Fisheries Science, Bachelor of Business Information Systems, and Master of Management Studies, in process of development

Student Services: Academic counselling, Canteen, Employment services, Health services, Social counselling, Sports facilities

Student Residential Facilities: Yes

Special Facilities: University Farm

Libraries: Central Library

Paraguay

STRUCTURE OF HIGHER EDUCATION SYSTEM

Description:

Higher education is provided by universities and institutes, both public and private, and other professional tertiary level institutions. The Ministry of Education and Culture is in charge of the implementation of the law on education. All public and private universities are created by law.

Stages of studies:

University level first stage: *Título de Grado: Licenciado, Professional Title*

The Licenciatura or professional title is usually conferred after four to six years' study (Medicine, Engineering, Law).

University level second stage: *Título de Postgrado: Especialista, Magister, Doctor*

These titles are awarded by Universities and Institutos Superiores after completion of the Licenciatura. The Curso de especialización aims at professional habilitation, the Maestría at deeper knowledge of the field studied, the Doctorado at training researchers.

ADMISSION TO HIGHER EDUCATION

Admission to university-level studies:

Name of secondary school credential required: Bachillerato

Entrance exam requirements: Examen de ingreso to enter most universities.

NATIONAL BODIES

Ministerio de Educación y Cultura - MEC (Ministry of Education and Culture)

Minister: Horacio Galeano Perrone
Director-General, Universities: Norys Cubilla
15 de Agosto e/ General Díaz y E. V. Haedo
Asunción
Tel: +595 450 014/15
WWW: http://www.mec.gov.py

Agencia Nacional de Evaluación y Acreditación de la Educación Superior - ANEAES (Higher Education Evaluation and Accreditation Agency)

President: Héctor Rojas Sanabria
Jejuí N° 530 c/ 14 de Mayo
Asunción
Tel: +595(21) 445 362
EMail: info@aneaes.gov.py
WWW: http://www.aneaes.gov.py/

Role of national body: Agency responsible for the promotion of higher education quality through the creation and implementation of mechanisms for the evaluation and accreditation of undergraduate and graduate programmes.

Consejo Nacional de Educación y Cultura (National Council for Education and Culture)

President: Horacio Galeano Perrone
Sgto. Martinez 240 e/ Dr. Telmo Aquino
Asunción
Tel: +595(21) 660-763
EMail: secretaria@conec.gov.py
WWW: http://www.conec.gov.py/

Data for academic year: 2010-2011
Source: IAU from the Ministry, ANEAES and IBE websites, 2010. Bodies updated 2012.

INSTITUTIONS

AMERICAN UNIVERSITY

Universidad Americana
Avenida Brasilia 1100, Asunción
Tel: +595(21) 295-710
Fax: +595(21) 295-710
EMail: universidad@uamericana.edu.py
Website: http://www.uamericana.edu.py

President of the Council: Andrés Benkö (1996-)
Tel: +595(21) 291-965, Ext.102
EMail: abenko@uamericana.edu.py

Academic Vice-Dean: Cecilio Jara
EMail: cjara@uamericana.edu.py

Administrative and Financial Vice-Director: Francisco Montecinos EMail: fmontecinos@uamericana.edu.py

Faculties
Communication, Arts and Technology (Advertising and Publicity; Architecture; Communication Studies; Computer Engineering; Fashion Design; Industrial Engineering; Interior Design; Marketing; Public Relations); **Economics and Administration** (Accountancy; Administration; Business and Commerce; Farm Management; Finance; Hotel Management; Human Resources; Labour and Industrial Relations; Management; Marketing; Public Administration; Public Relations; Sports Management; Tourism); **Health Sciences**; **Law, Political and Social Sciences** (International Relations; Law; Political Sciences)

History: Founded 1991 as Institute (INCADE), acquired present status and title 1993.

Governing Bodies: Board of Directors

Academic Year: March to December (March-July; August-December)

Admission Requirements: Secondary school certificate or equivalent

Fees: (Guaranis): 495,000 per month

Main Language(s) of Instruction: Spanish

International Co-operation: With universities in USA; Europe and Latin America

Accrediting Agencies: AAACSB

Degrees and Diplomas: *Licenciatura*: Accountancy; International Trade, 4 yrs; *Licenciatura*: Architecture; Commercial Engineering; Information Systems; Law; Marketing; Psychology, 5 yrs; *Maestría*: Business Administration; *Doctorado*: Economy and Administration; Law; Education (PhD)

Student Services: Academic counselling, Canteen, Cultural centre, Employment services, Handicapped facilities, Health services, Language programs, Nursery care, Sports facilities

Student Residential Facilities: Yes

Libraries: c. 10,000 vols

Publications: American News, Institutional Magazine *(monthly)*

Last Updated: 18/12/09

AUTONOMOUS UNIVERSITY OF ASUNCIÓN

Universidad Autónoma de Asunción (UAA)
Jejuí n° 667 e/O'Leary y 15 de Agosto, Asunción
Tel: +595(21) 495-873
Fax: +595(21) 495-873
EMail: info@uaa.edu.py
Website: http://www.uaa.edu.py

Rector: Julio Miguel Martin Puertas (2001-)
Tel: +595(21) 498 873, Ext. 132 EMail: jmartin@uaa.edu.py

Vicerrectora: Kitty Gaona Franco EMail: kgaona@uaa.edu.py

International Relations: Liz Alcazar (2002)
Tel: +595(21) 495 873, Ext. 199 EMail: ealcaraz@uaa.edu.py

Faculties
Business Administration and Economics (Accountancy; Business Administration; Economics; Engineering Management; Finance; International Business; Marketing); **Health Sciences**; **Humanities Sciences and Communication**; **Law, Political and Social Sciences** (International Relations; Law; Notary Studies); **Science and Technology** (Computer Engineering; Software Engineering; Systems Analysis)

History: Founded 1978 as Escuela Superior de Administración de Empresas, acquired present status 2002.

Governing Bodies: Consejo Superior Universitario

Academic Year: March to March (March-July; August-December; January-March)

Admission Requirements: Secondary school certificate (bachiller) or equivalent, and entrance examination

Fees: (US Dollars): 500 per semester

Main Language(s) of Instruction: Spanish

International Co-operation: With Universities in Argentina; Bolivia; Brazil; Canada; Chile; Colombia; Costa Rica; Mexico; Cuba; Ecuador; France; Australia; Portugal; Spain and USA.

Degrees and Diplomas: *Licenciatura*: Business Administration; International Business; Accountancy; Economics; Marketing; Engineering of Business; Finance; Computer Engineering; Systems Engineering; Systems Analysis; Law; Notary Studies; International Relations; Educational Sciences; Audiovisual Communication; Publicity; Public Relations; Journalism, 4-5 yrs; *Maestría*: Business Administration; Accounting and Audit; Educational Sciences; Law; Natural Resources Management; Computer Science; Tourism; Psycho-pedagogy, 2 yrs; *Doctorado*: Business Administration; Educational Sciences; Law; Natural Resources Management, 2-3 yrs

Student Services: Academic counselling, Canteen, Employment services, Social counselling, Sports facilities

Last Updated: 18/12/09

COLUMBIA UNIVERSITY OF PARAGUAY

Universidad Columbia del Paraguay
Av. España 1239 c/ Padre Cardozo, Asunción
Tel: +595(21) 206-526
Fax: +595(21) 206-527
EMail: susana.leon@columbia.edu.py
Website: http://www.columbia.edu.py/

Rector: Roberto Elías Canese
Tel: +595(21) 222-662, Fax: +595(21) 206-526
EMail: roberto.elias@columbia.edu.py

Secretaria General: María Elena Urbieta Tel: +595(21) 490-811

International Relations: Teresa Riveros
Tel: +595(21) 206-527 EMail: teresa.rivero@columbia.edu.py

Programmes
Accountancy and Administration; **Architecture and Design** (Architecture; Design); **Business Administration** (Business Administration); **Commerce** (Business and Commerce); **Computer Engineering**; **Graphic Design** (Graphic Design); **Hotel and Tourism**; **International Business** (International Business); **Law**; **Marketing** (Marketing); **Psychology** (Psychology); **Social Engineering**

Further Information: Also other site: 25 de mayo 658 y Antequera; Mexico y Mariscal Estigarribia y Ciudad de Pedro Juan Caballero

History: Founded 1942 as Dactilography Academy. Acquired present title and status 1991.

Academic Year: March to December

Admission Requirements: High School Certificate

Main Language(s) of Instruction: Spanish

International Co-operation: With universities in Argentina; Canada; Spain

Accrediting Agencies: Agencia Nacional de Evaluación y Acreditación de la Educación Superior (ANEAES)

Degrees and Diplomas: *Técnico Superior*; *Licenciatura*: 4-5 yrs; *Maestría*; *Doctorado*. Also Law and Architect Degrees (5 yrs)

Student Services: Academic counselling, Employment services, Sports facilities

Libraries: Yes

Last Updated: 18/12/09

COMUNERA UNIVERSITY

Universidad Comunera (UCOM)

San José 630 y Artigas, Asunción

Tel: +595(21) 223-892 +595(21) 222-036

EMail: educom@ucom.edu.py

Website: http://www.ucom.edu.py/

Rectora: Alex Prieto de Martínez

Faculties

Agricultural Administration; **Business Administration** (Business Administration); **Computer Science** (Computer Science); **Law**; **Public Administration** (Public Administration); **Public Relations**; **Social Economics** (Banking; Finance; Insurance); **Tourism and Environment** (Environmental Studies; Tourism)

History: Founded 1992.

Main Language(s) of Instruction: Spanish

Degrees and Diplomas: *Licenciatura*; *Maestría*. Also Ingeniero

Last Updated: 18/12/09

DR. RAÚL PEÑA INSTITUTE OF EDUCATION

Instituto Superior de Educación Dr. Raúl Peña

Avenida Eusebio Ayala Km. 4.5, Asunción

Tel: +595(21) 503-012

Fax: +595(21) 503-015

EMail: ise-mec@sce.cnc.una.py

Website: http://www.ise.edu.py

Director General: Juan María Carrón Rivarola

Programmes

Education (Education)

History: Founded 1968.

Main Language(s) of Instruction: Spanish

Degrees and Diplomas: *Licenciatura*: 4 yrs; *Especializacion*: 1 yr; *Maestría*: 2 yrs

Last Updated: 18/12/09

EVANGELICAL UNIVERSITY OF PARAGUAY

Universidad Evangélica del Paraguay (UEP)

Casilla de Correo 27070, Chaco Boreal N° 511, Asunción, Central C.P. 1808

Tel: +595(21) 609-141

Fax: +595(21) 607-931

EMail: unievangelica@rieder.net.py

Website: http://www.uep.edu.py/

Rector: Dionisio Órtiz Mutti

Secretario General: Esteban G. Missena

International Relations: Melita Wall

Faculties

Accountancy, Administration and Economics *Dean*: Guillermo Nagy; **Educational Sciences and Humanities** (Arts and Humanities; Educational Sciences; Preschool Education; Primary Education; Social Work) *Dean*: Alfred Neufel; **Health Sciences** (Nursing) *Dean*: Benedicto Ortellado; **Modern Languages** (English; Modern Languages; Spanish) *Dean*: Alexis Aquino; **Music** (Music) *Dean*: Werner Franz; **Psychology and Human Development** (Educational Psychology) *Dean*: Ermelinda Cuenca; **Theology** (Religion; Theology) *Dean*: Alfred Neufel

History: Founded 1994.

Governing Bodies: Consejo superior

Academic Year: March to December

Admission Requirements: Secondary school certificate

Fees: (Guaranis): 3.3m. per annum

Main Language(s) of Instruction: Spanish

International Co-operation: With universities in Canada,USA, Germany, Spain

Accrediting Agencies: National Council of Universities

Degrees and Diplomas: *Licenciatura*: Accountancy; Business Administration; Educational Psychology; English; Spanish; Music; Nursing; Social Work; Guarani; Bilingual Education; Theology, 4 yrs; *Licenciatura*: Kindergarden and Preschool Education; Elementary and High School, 5 yrs. Also Health Technician in Nursing, 3 yrs and Emergency Services, 2 yrs

Student Services: Academic counselling, Canteen, Cultural centre, Language programs, Sports facilities

Student Residential Facilities: Yes

Libraries: Yes

IBEROAMERICAN UNIVERSITY

Universidad Iberoamericana

15 de Agosto esq. Ygatimí (frente a la Plaza Italia), Asunción

Tel: +595(44) 7207 +595(44) 4822

Fax: +595(44) 7207 +595(44) 4822

EMail: samparo@quanta.com.py; iberoamericano@quanta.com.py

Website: http://www.unibe.edu.py/

Rectora: Nidia Sanabria de Romero

Vicerrector: Sanie Romero de Velásquez

Programmes

Accountancy; **Art Education**; **Computer Engineering** (Computer Engineering; Systems Analysis); **Educational Sciences**; **Journalism**; **Languagues and Literature** (Literature; Modern Languages); **Mathematics**; **Nursing** (Nursing); **Nutrition** (Nutrition); **Psychology** (Psychology); **Social Sciences**

Degrees and Diplomas: *Licenciatura*; *Especializacion*; *Maestría*

Last Updated: 18/12/09

INTERCONTINENTAL UNIVERSITY OF TECHNOLOGY

Universidad Tecnológica Intercontinental (UTIC)

Fulgencio R. Moreno 189 y Yegros, Asunción

Tel: +595(49) 7047 +595(49)1148

EMail: informes@utic.edu.py

Website: http://www.utic.edu.py/

Rector: Hugo Ferreira González

Faculties

Arts and Humanities (Arts and Humanities); **Business Administration**; **Computer Engineering** (Computer Engineering); **Health Sciences**; **Law and Social Sciences** (Law; Social Sciences)

Degrees and Diplomas: *Licenciatura*; *Maestría*; *Doctorado*

Last Updated: 21/12/09

METROPOLITAN UNIVERSITY OF ASUNCIÓN

Universidad Metropolitana de Asunción

Avenida Mcal. López N° 1104 esquina Mayor Bullo, Asunción

Tel: +595(22) 9399 +595(22) 2029

EMail: uma@uma.edu.py

Website: http://www.uma.edu.py

Rectora: María Liz García de Arnold

Faculties

Business Administration and Economics (Accountancy; Advertising and Publicity; Business Administration; Economics; International Business; Management; Marketing); **Computer Science**; **Education and Art** (Arts and Humanities; Education; Fine Arts);

Humanities and Educational Sciences; **Law, Political and Social Sciences** (Law; Political Sciences; Social Sciences)

History: Founded 2003.

Main Language(s) of Instruction: Spanish

Degrees and Diplomas: *Licenciatura*; *Especializacion*; *Maestría*; *Doctorado*

Last Updated: 18/12/09

NATIONAL UNIVERSITY OF ASUNCIÓN

Universidad Nacional de Asunción (UNA)
Ciudad Universitaria San Lorenzo, Asunción 2064
Tel: +595(21) 211-419
Fax: +595(21) 213-734
EMail: rector@una.py
Website: http://www.una.py

Rector: Pedro Gerardo González González Tel: +595(21) 585-546

Secretario General: Julio Renán Paniagua
Tel: +595(21) 585-540 EMail: sgeneral@rec.una.py

Colleges

Paraguay-Brazil (Regional Studies)

Faculties

Agricultural Sciences (Agriculture; Ecology; Forestry); **Architecture** (Architecture); **Chemistry** (Biochemistry; Chemical Engineering; Food Technology; Pharmacy); **Dentistry** (Dentistry); **Economics** (Accountancy; Administration; Economics); **Engineering** (Civil Engineering; Electrical Engineering; Electronic Engineering; Geography; Industrial Engineering; Materials Engineering; Mechanical Engineering); **Exact and Natural Sciences** (Biological and Life Sciences; Chemistry; Geology; Mathematics; Natural Sciences; Physics; Production Engineering; Statistics); **Law** (Civil Law; Commercial Law; Criminal Law; Human Rights; International Law; Labour Law; Law; Private Law; Public Law; Sociology); **Medicine** (Gynaecology and Obstetrics; Medicine; Nursing; Physical Therapy; Social Work; Surgery); **Philosophy** (Arts and Humanities; Communication Studies; Education; History; Philosophy; Psychology); **Polytechnic** (Computer Science; Electrical Engineering; Electronic Engineering; Hotel Management; Information Technology; Library Science; Meteorology; Systems Analysis); **Veterinary Science** (Anatomy; Animal Husbandry; Epidemiology; Genetics; Histology; Microbiology; Parasitology; Pathology; Physiology; Veterinary Science)

Institutes

Art (Art Education; Visual Arts); **Modern Languages** (English; French; German; Modern Languages; Native Language)

Research Institutes

Health Sciences (Endocrinology; Immunology; Pathology; Public Health; Tropical Medicine)

History: Founded1890. Granted autonomous status 1929. Financed by the State.

Governing Bodies: Consejo Superior Universitario

Academic Year: March to December (March-June; August-December)

Admission Requirements: Secondary school certificate (bachillerato) or equivalent, and entrance examination

Main Language(s) of Instruction: Spanish

Degrees and Diplomas: *Técnico Superior*: 3 yrs; *Licenciatura*: Accountancy; Administration; Agricultural Engineering; Economics; Human Ecology Engineering; Library Science; Pharmacy; Social Work, 5 yrs; *Licenciatura*: Analytical Chemistry; Art Critic; Arts; Food Technology; Geography; Graphic Design; History; Languages; Letters; Nursing; Philosophy, 3-4 yrs; *Licenciatura*: Architecture; Engineering; Geographical Engineering; Psychology, 6 yrs; *Licenciatura*: Forestry, 5 yrs and thesis; *Maestría*; *Doctorado*: Accountancy; Administration; Dentistry; Economics; Education Sciences; History; Law; Letters; Medicine and Surgery; Social Sciences; Veterinary Science, 5-6 yrs

Special Facilities: Natural History Museum. Herbarium of Botanical Sciences

Libraries: University Library, c. 30,000 vols

Press or Publishing House: EDUNA

Last Updated: 18/12/09

NATIONAL UNIVERSITY OF ITAPÚA

Universidad Nacional de Itapúa (UNI)
Tarumá N° 255 c/Ruta 1 Km 25 (B° Káaguy Rory), Encarnación, Itapúa
Tel: +595(71) 206-990 +595(71) 206-991
Fax: +595(71) 206-990 +595(71) 206-991
EMail: unirec@itacom.com.py
Website: http://www.uni.edu.py/

Rector: Hildegardo González

Faculties

Agronomy and Forestry; **Economics and Administration** (Administration; Economics); **Engineering** (Engineering); **Humanities, Social Sciences and Guarani Studies**; **Law** (Law); **Medicine** (Medicine); **Science and Technology** (Business Computing; Electronic Engineering; Food Technology)

Degrees and Diplomas: *Licenciatura*; *Especializacion*; *Maestría*; *Doctorado*

Last Updated: 18/12/09

NATIONAL UNIVERSITY OF PILAR

Universidad Nacional de Pilar (UNP)
Mello 208 e Iturbe, Pilar
Tel: +595(86) 30059 +595(86) 32148
EMail: rectorado@unp.edu.py
Website: http://www.unp.edu.py/

Rector: Víctor Ríos Ojeda

Faculties

Accountancy, Administration and Economics (Accountancy; Administration; Economics); **Agriculture and Cattle Breeding**; **Applied Sciences**; **Humanities and Educational Sciences** (Arts and Humanities; Educational Sciences); **Law and Political Science**

Degrees and Diplomas: *Licenciatura*; *Maestría*; *Doctorado*

NATIONAL UNIVERSITY OF THE EAST

Universidad Nacional del Este (UNE)
Campus Km 8 Acaray, Calle Universidad Nacional del Este y Rca. del Paraguay - Barrio San Juan, Ciudad del Este, Alto Paraná
Tel: +595(61) 63804
Fax: +595(61) 68664
EMail: rectorado@une.edu.py
Website: http://www.une.edu.py

Rector: Victor Alfredo Britez EMail: victor_britez@une.edu.py

Secretario General: Julio Cesar Meaurio
EMail: jcemeaurio@hotmail.com

Director Académico: Rosa Medina Pavon
EMail: rosa_medina@une.edu.py

International Relations: Rolando Segovia Páez
EMail: rolando_segovia@une.edu.py

Faculties

Agricultural Engineering; **Economics** (Accountancy; Administration; Economics); **Health Sciences** (Health Sciences; Medicine; Surgery) *Dean*: Humberto Raul Fanego; **Law and Social Sciences** (Law; Political Sciences; Social Sciences); **Philosophy** (Communication Studies; Educational Sciences; History; Literature; Mathematics; Philosophy; Psychology); **Polytechnic** (Electrical Engineering; Systems Analysis; Tourism)

History: Founded 1993.

Academic Year: February to December

Admission Requirements: High School Certificate

Main Language(s) of Instruction: Spanish; Guarani

International Co-operation: With universities in Latin America and Europe

Degrees and Diplomas: *Técnico Superior*: Electrical Engineering, 3 yrs; *Técnico Superior*: Tourism; Computer Engineering, 2 yrs; *Licenciatura*: History; Philosophy; Communication Sciences; Mathematics; Psychology; Computer Engineering; *Licenciatura*: Nursing, 5 yrs; *Maestría*: 5 yrs; *Doctorado*: Surgery

Last Updated: 18/12/09

OUR LADY OF THE ASSUMPTION CATHOLIC UNIVERSITY

Universidad Católica 'Nuestra Señora de la Asunción' (UC)

Independencia Nacional y Comuneros, Casilla 1718, Asunción
Tel: +595(21) 441-044
Fax: +595(21) 445-245
EMail: uca@mmail.com.py
Website: http://www.uc.edu.py

Rector: Antonio Tellechea Solís (1997-)
Tel: +595(21) 442-192, Fax: +595(21) 442-192
EMail: uca3@mmail.com.py
Vicerrector Administrativo: Enrique Cáceres Rojas
Tel: +595(21) 490-401, Fax: +595(21) 490-401
EMail: uca5@mmail.com.py
International Relations: Minerva Izquierdo Centurión
Tel: +595(21) 492-284 EMail: uca6@mmail.com.py

Conservatories
Music (Music)

Departments
Admissions Courses *Director*: Elizabeth Tonina; **Theology and Pastoral Action** (Pastoral Studies; Theology)

Faculties
Business, Administration and Accountancy (Accountancy; Administration; Business and Commerce) *Dean*: Darío Turrini; **Law and Diplomatic Studies** (International Relations; Law) *Dean*: Ernesto Velásquez; **Philosophy and Human Sciences** (Arts and Humanities; Education; Philosophy; Political Sciences) *Dean*: Carmen Quintana; **Science and Technology** (Architecture; Mathematics and Computer Science; Natural Sciences; Technology) *Dean*: Carlos Sánchez

Higher Institutes
Theology (Theology) *Director*: Michel Gibaud

History: Founded 1960 by the Conferencia Episcopal del Paraguay. Recognized by the State on the same basis as the National University. The Archbishop of Asunción is Grand Chancellor of the University.

Governing Bodies: Consejo Superior Universitario; Consejo Ejecutivo; Consejo Administrativo Plenario

Academic Year: March to December (March-July; August-December)

Admission Requirements: Secondary school certificate (bachillerato) or equivalent, and completion of preparatory course (curso probatorio de ingreso)

Main Language(s) of Instruction: Spanish

International Co-operation: With Universities in Spain, Brazil, France, Canada, USA

Degrees and Diplomas: *Licenciatura*: Accountancy; Business Administration; Diplomatic Studies; Education; History; Letters; Mathematics; Midwifery; Nursing; Pastoral Studies; Philosophy; Political Science; Psychology; Sociology, 5-6 yrs; *Licenciatura*: Architecture (Arquitecto); Engineering (Ingeniero); Law (Abogado); Medicine and Surgery (Médico Cirujano), 6 yrs; *Licenciatura*: Chemistry; Pharmacy (Químico Farmacéutico); Economics (Economista); Nursing (Enfermero), 4 yrs; *Maestría*: Business and Administration, a further 2 yrs; *Doctorado*: Law, a further 2 yrs

Special Facilities: University Radio 'Radio Cáritas' - Universidad Católica

Libraries: Central Library, c. 45,000 vols

Publications: Anuario; Anuario, Facultad de Ciencias Jurídicas y Diplomáticas; Anuario, Facultad de Filosofía y Ciencias Humanas; Estudios Antropológicos, Revista del Centro de Estudios Antropológicos; Revista Jurídica; Universitas

Press or Publishing House: Centro de Publicaciones de la Universidad Católica (CEPUC)

ALTO PARANÁ REGIONAL BRANCH
SEDE REGIONAL ALTO PARANÁ
Paraná Country Club, Ciudad del Este
Tel: +595(61) 572-466

Prorrector: Emilio Zaragoza

Faculties
Accountancy (Accountancy) *Dean*: Genaro García; **Health Sciences** (Health Sciences) *Dean*: Petrona Cardozo; **Law** (Law) *Dean*: Porfirio Zacarías León; **Science and Technology** (Mathematics and Computer Science; Natural Sciences; Technology) *Dean*: Manuel Chamorro

CONCEPCIÓN REGIONAL BRANCH
SEDE REGIONAL CONCEPCIÓN
Iturbe 783, Concepción
Tel: +595(31) 2329

Prorrector: Nery Sanabria

Faculties
Accountancy (Accountancy) *Dean*: María Victoria Coelho; **Educational Sciences** (Education; Educational Sciences) *Dean*: Teresa López

GUAIRÁ REGIONAL BRANCH
SEDE REGIONAL GUAIRÁ
Ruta a Ñumi, Villarrica
Tel: +595(541) 3118-2670

Prorrector: Modesto Escobar

Faculties
Business, Administration and Accountancy (Accountancy; Administration; Business and Commerce) *Dean*: Stella Decoud; **Chemistry and Pharmacy** (Chemistry; Pharmacy) *Dean*: Nilsa Battaglia; **Educational Sciences** (Education; Educational Sciences) *Dean*: Herminio Leiva; **Law** (Law) *Dean*: Esther Lisboa; **Medicine** (Medicine) *Dean*: Francisco Duarte

ITAPÚA REGIONAL BRANCH
SEDE REGIONAL ITAPÚA
Antequera y Tomás Romero Pereira, Encarnación
Tel: +595(71) 203-627
Fax: +595(71) 203-165
EMail: rrpp@uci.edu.py
Website: http://www.uci.edu.py

Prorrector: Jesús René Haurón

Faculties
Economics (Economics) *Dean*: Francisco Maciel; **Educational Sciences** (Education; Educational Sciences) *Dean*: Isabel Madrazzo; **Law** (Law) *Dean*: Martial Cantero; **Sciences and Technology** (Mathematics and Computer Science; Natural Sciences; Technology) *Dean*: Mario Zaputovich

PIERRE FAUCHARD AUTONOMOUS UNIVERSITY OF PARAGUAY

Universidad Autónoma del Paraguay Pierre Fauchard

General Díaz 1053, Colón 568, Asunción
Tel: +595(21) 441-924
Fax: +595(21) 447-579
Website: http://www.uap.edu.py

Rector: Arnaldo Lataza M. Fax: +595(21) 493-296
EMail: rectorado@uap.edu.py

Director Administrativo: Hugo Giménez

International Relations: Fernando Carmona

Faculties
Accountancy and Business Administration (Accountancy; Business Administration); **Behavioural Sciences**; **Dentistry** *(Pierre Fauchard)*; **Optical Technology** (Optical Technology); **Speech Therapy** (Speech Therapy and Audiology)

Programmes
Nutrition (Nutrition)

History: Founded 1992.

Main Language(s) of Instruction: Spanish

Degrees and Diplomas: *Licenciatura*; *Especializacion*; *Doctorado*
Last Updated: 18/12/09

POLYTECHNIC AND ARTS UNIVERSITY OF PARAGUAY

Universidad Politécnica y Artística del Paraguay

Av. Mariscal López casi Mayor Bullo, Asunción
Tel: +595(21) 448-162
Fax: +595 (21) 212-079
EMail: webmaster@upap.edu.py
Website: http://www.upap.edu.py/

Rector: Manuel Viedma Romero

Faculties
Arts and Technology; **Business Studies** (Accountancy; Business Administration; Business and Commerce; Economics; Hotel Management; Marketing; Tourism); **Dentistry and Health Sciences**; **Law** (Law); **Social Sciences, Humanities and Law**; **Sports**

Further Information: Traditional and Open Learning Institution

Degrees and Diplomas: *Licenciatura*; *Maestria*; *Doctorado*. Also professional title
Last Updated: 21/12/09

PRIVATE UNIVERSITY OF THE EAST

Universidad Privada del Este (UPE)

Av. Neembucú y Caazapá, Area 5, Ciudad Pte. Franco, Alto Paraná
Tel: +595(61) 550-055
Fax: +595(61) 550-055
EMail: upe@cde.uninet.com.py
Website: http://www.upe.edu.py

Rector: Juan Bautista González (1997-)

Secretario General: Nicolás Flores González
Tel: +595(61) 552-304

International Relations: Nathalia Soria Tel: +595(61) 552-305

Faculties
Administration and Accountancy (Accountancy; Business Administration); **Architecture** (Architecture); **Computer Engineering** (Computer Engineering; Software Engineering); **Dentistry** (Dentistry); **Educational Sciences** (Distance Education; Educational Administration; Educational Sciences; Primary Education; Science Education; Secondary Education); **Environmental Studies**; **Health Sciences** (Medicine; Nursing; Podiatry; Surgery); **Law, Political and Social Sciences** (Law; Political Sciences; Social Sciences)

History: Founded 1992.

Governing Bodies: Consejo Superior Universitario; Consejo de Facultad

Academic Year: March to December (March-July; August-December)

Admission Requirements: Seconday school certificate (bachillerato) or equivalent

Main Language(s) of Instruction: Spanish

Degrees and Diplomas: *Licenciatura*: 4-6 yrs

Student Services: Academic counselling, Canteen, Language programs, Sports facilities

Libraries: c. 2,600 vols
Last Updated: 21/12/09

UNIVERSITY OF THE INTEGRATION OF THE AMERICAS

Universidad de la Integración de las Américas (UNIDA)

Av. Venezuela 1353 c, Tte. Insaurralde, Asunción
Tel: +595(21) 211-667
EMail: info@unida.edu.py; internacional@unida.edu.py
Website: http://www.unida.edu.py/

Head: Mario Paz (1974-)
Tel: +595(21) 211-667 EMail: mpaz@unida.edu.py

Administrative Officer: Alvaro Barcel EMail: barcel@unida.edu.py

International Relations: Ursula López
EMail: ulopez@unida.edu.py

Faculties
Computer Science (Computer Science; Information Sciences; Information Technology); **Health Sciences** (Medicine; Nursing; Nutrition; Physical Therapy); **Management** (Accountancy; Administration; Management; Marketing)

Schools
Postgraduate Studies (Education; Higher Education; Management; Public Health)

History: Founded 2003.

Governing Bodies: Director-General, Rector and Academic Director

Admission Requirements: Certificado de Estudios recognized by Ministry

Main Language(s) of Instruction: Spanish

International Co-operation: With universities in Brazil

Degrees and Diplomas: *Licenciatura*; *Especializacion*; *Maestría*; *Doctorado*. Also Diplomado

Student Services: Canteen, Employment services, Health services, Language programs, Nursery care

Student Residential Facilities: No

Special Facilities: Laboratories (Anatomy, Chemistry, Nutrition, Physiotherapy)

Libraries: University Library

Publications: Luis de Gaspari, Laws research *(annually)*; Paradigma, Research magazine of Health *(annually)*
Last Updated: 03/07/12

UNIVERSITY OF THE NORTH

Universidad del Norte (UNINORTE)

Avenida España 676 c/Boquerón, Asunción
Tel: +595(21) 229-450
Fax: +595(21) 228-217
EMail: info@uninorte.edu.py
Website: http://www.uninorte.edu.py

President: Juan Manuel Marcos (1993-)
Tel: +595(21) 229-450, Fax: +595(21) 610-651
EMail: rectorado@uninorte.edu.py

Executive Vice-President: Max Fraenkel
Tel: +595(21) 229-450, Fax: +595(21) 228-217
EMail: rectorado@uninorte.edu.py

International Relations: María José Peña, Director Continuing Education
Tel: +595(21) 203-576, Fax: +595(21) 204-235
EMail: econtinua@uninorte.edu.py

Faculties
Business Studies; **Chemistry**; **Education and Humanities**; **Engineering**; **Graduate Studies** *Dean*: Juan Manuel Marcos; **Health Sciences**; **Law and Political Science**; **Medicine** (Gynaecology and Obstetrics; Medicine; Nursing; Nutrition); **Medicine** *Dean*: Juan Carlos Chaparro

Further Information: Also 17 Community Colleges outside Asunción

History: Founded 1991.

Governing Bodies: Council

Academic Year: March to December

Admission Requirements: Secondary school certificate

Main Language(s) of Instruction: Spanish

International Co-operation: With universities in Brazil; Argentina; Chile; Bolivia; Korea; Puerto Rico; Australia; Spain; France; Uruguay

Degrees and Diplomas: *Licenciatura*: Biochemistry; Chemistry; Pharmacy; Industrial Chemistry; Agricultural Business; Accountancy; Marketing; Business and Commerce; Education; Arts and Humanities; Journalism; Advertizing and Publicity; Civil Engineering; Electrical Engineering; Telecommunications Engineering; Industrial Engineering; Electromechanical Engineering; Graphic Design; System Analysis; Computer Science; Medicine; Gynaecology and Obstetrics; Nursing; Nutrition; Physical Education; Sports Management; Psychology; Physiotherapy; Dentistry; Political Science; Notary Studies; International Relations; International Business, 4 yrs; *Maestría*: Journalism; Education; Literature; Law;

Health; Environment; Nutrition; Accounting, 2 yrs; *Doctorado*: Dentistry; Medicine; Law, 1 yr

Student Services: Academic counselling, Canteen, Cultural centre, Employment services, Foreign student adviser, Foreign Studies Centre, Handicapped facilities, Health services, Language programs, Nursery care, Social counselling, Sports facilities

Special Facilities: Art Galleries. Ancient Books Museum. Technical Laboratories. Movie Studio. Voice Recording Studio. Auditoruim. Academic Research Centre

Libraries: Yes

Publications: Journal of Law Studies *(biennially)*

Press or Publishing House: Universidad del Norte Press

Last Updated: 18/12/09

UNIVERSITY OF THE PACIFIC

Universidad del Pacífico

México 775 c/Fulgencio R. Moreno, Asunción

Tel: +595(21) 450-287 +595(21) 444-728

Fax: +595(21) 444-728

EMail: info@up.edu.py

Website: http://www.upacifico.edu.py/

Rector: Luis H. Berganza Perasso

Faculties

Agriculture and Cattle Breeding (Agriculture; Cattle Breeding); **Arts and Communication**; **Business Administration** (Accountancy; Business Administration; Marketing); **Health Sciences**; **Law and Social Sciences**

Degrees and Diplomas: *Licenciatura*. Also Ingeniero

Last Updated: 18/12/09

UNIVERSITY OF THE SOUTHERN CONE OF THE AMERICAS

Universidad del Cono Sur de las Américas (UCSA)

Av. España 372 c/Brasil, Asunción

Tel: +595(21) 213-978

EMail: ucsa@ucsa.edu.py

Website: http://www.ucsa.edu.py/

Rector: Luis Lima EMail: luislima@ucsa.edu.py

Secretaria General: Carolina Scholz
EMail: sgeneral@ucsa.edu.py

Areas

Business Studies (Accountancy; Business Administration; Finance; International Business; Marketing); **Engineering** (Computer Engineering; Electrical Engineering; Industrial Engineering; Mathematics); **Humanities**

History: Founded 1996.

Governing Bodies: Rector; Vicerrectores; Directores; Coordinadores

Admission Requirements: High School Certificate

Main Language(s) of Instruction: Spanish

Degrees and Diplomas: *Licenciatura*. Also Ingeniero

Student Services: Academic counselling, Canteen, Employment services, Foreign student adviser, Nursery care, Social counselling, Sports facilities

Publications: TODO USCA, Magazine *(biennially)*

Last Updated: 18/12/09

Peru

STRUCTURE OF HIGHER EDUCATION SYSTEM

Description:

Higher education is provided by universities, both public and private, schools, higher institutes and postgraduate centres. Universities are autonomous. Each has a University Assembly made up of the Rector, the Vice-Rectors, the Deans of the faculties, the Director of the graduate school and representatives from teaching and student groups. The Assembly is the ultimate authority. It elects the Rector and the Vice-Rectors. State universities are publicly funded. They are coordinated by the Asemblea Nacional de Rectores which defines the objectives of university activities, ensures their coordination and oversees their economic development.

Stages of studies:

University level first stage: *Pregrado*
Studies for the Bachiller last for ten academic semesters.
According to Article 23 of the Law on Universities, the professional qualifications of Licenciado require not less than ten academic semesters or approval of the years/credits including those of general knowledge that preceded them. It also requires having passed the corresponding Bachillerato, and when applicable, some professional practice. To obtain the title of Licenciado, the submission of a thesis or a professional exams is required.

University level second stage: *Postgrado*
The second stage leads to the titles of Maestro and Doctor. The minimum duration of studies is four semesters in each case. Candidates must defend original research work.

Distance higher education:
Teacher training is available through distance education.

ADMISSION TO HIGHER EDUCATION

Admission to university-level studies:

Name of secondary school credential required: Certificado de Educación Secundaria

Foreign students admission:

Entry regulations: Foreign students must hold a Secondary School Leaving Certificate. They may obtain scholarships and financial assistance and may be employed on campus. Foreign nationals from countries with which Peru has concluded agreements can obtain a convalidación of their studies, degrees and diplomas; when Peru has not signed such agreements they obtain the revalidación.
Language requirements: Students must have a satisfactory command of Spanish.

NATIONAL BODIES

Ministerio de Educación (Ministry of Education)

Minister: Emma Patricia Salas O'Brien
Calle Comercio s/n
San Borja
Lima
Tel: +51(1) 215 5800
WWW: http://www.minedu.gob.pe/

Dirección General de Educación Superior y Técnico profesional – Ministerio de Educación

Director General: Pilar Saavedra Paredes
Calle Comercio s/n, San Borja
Lima
Tel: +51(1) 615 5800

Role of national body: The Directorate for Higher Education and Technical Training is responsible for developing and implementing the higher education policy.

Asamblea Nacional de Rectores - ANR (Rectors' National Assembly)

President: Orlando Velásquez Benites
Calle Aldabas No. 337, Urb. Las Gardenias-Surco
Lima
Tel: +51(1) 275 4608
Fax: +51(1) 275 5017
WWW: http://www.anr.edu.pe

Role of national body: Public organization of public and private universities' rectors whose aim is to study, coordinate and direct the academic sector of the country.

Data for academic year: 2010-2011
Source: IAU from Ministerio de Educación, 2010. Bodies updated 2012.

INSTITUTIONS

PUBLIC INSTITUTIONS

DANIEL ALCIDES CARRIÓN NATIONAL UNIVERSITY

Universidad Nacional Daniel Alcides Carrión (UNDAC)
Edificio Estatal 4, San Juan Pampa, Cerro de Pasco
Tel: +51(63) 722197-722220
Fax: +51(63) 721813
EMail: informatica@undac.edu.pe
Website: http://www.undac.edu.pe

Rector: Santos Salvador Blanco Muñoz
EMail: sblancom1@yahoo.es

Vicerrector Académico: Luis Enrique Almeyda Vásquez
EMail: viceacad@undac.edu.pe

Vicerrector Administrativo: Flaviano Armando Zenteno Ruiz
EMail: viceadm@undac.edu.pe

Faculties
Accountancy, Economics and Administration (Accountancy; Administration; Economics); **Agricultural Sciences** (Agriculture; Agronomy; Animal Husbandry; Food Science); **Dentistry** (Dentistry); **Education, Communication and Law** (Communication Studies; Education; Law; Political Sciences; Primary Education; Secondary Education); **Engineering** (Computer Engineering; Engineering; Environmental Engineering; Geology; Metallurgical Engineering; Mining Engineering); **Health Sciences** (Gynaecology and Obstetrics; Health Sciences; Midwifery; Nursing)

Schools
Postgraduate Studies (Business Administration; Community Health; Ecology; Educational Administration; Environmental Studies; Leadership; Public Health) *Director*: Félix Rivera Serrano

History: Founded 1965.

Main Language(s) of Instruction: Spanish

Degrees and Diplomas: *Bachiller*, *Titulo Profesional de Licenciado*; *Maestría*; *Doctorado*: Education
Last Updated: 11/10/10

ENRIQUE GUZMÁN Y VALLE NATIONAL UNIVERSITY OF EDUCATION

Universidad Nacional de Educación Enrique Guzmán y Valle
La Cantuta - Lurigancho - Chosica, Lima, Lima
Tel: +51(1) 3600626
Fax: +51(1) 3600634
EMail: rectorado@une.edu.pe
Website: http://www.une.edu.pe/

Rector: Juan Tutuy Aspauza EMail: jtutuy@une.edu.pe

Vicerrector Académico: Luis Alberto Rodriguez de los Rios
EMail: lrodriguez@une.edu.pe

Faculties
Administration and Tourism (Administration; Tourism); **Pedagogy and Physical Education** (Education; Pedagogy; Physical Education); **Science** (Biology; Chemistry; Computer Science; Mathematics; Physics); **Social Sciences and Humanities** (Art History; Communication Studies; Modern Languages; Social Sciences); **Stockbreeding and Nutrition** (Cattle Breeding; Food Science; Food Technology; Nutrition); **Technology** (Construction Engineering; Electrical Engineering; Electronic Engineering; Industrial Engineering; Telecommunications Engineering; Textile Technology)

Schools
Postgraduate Studies

History: Founded 1905 as Escuela Normal, became college 1960 and then national university. A State institution.

Academic Year: April to December (April-July; August-December)

Admission Requirements: Secondary school certificate and entrance examination

Fees: None

Main Language(s) of Instruction: Spanish

Degrees and Diplomas: *Bachiller*, *Título Profesional de Licenciado*: Teaching qualification, primary, secondary, and technical levels; *Maestría*; *Doctorado*: Educational Psychology; Educational Sciences. Also Especialidades

Libraries: College Library
Last Updated: 11/10/10

FEDERICO VILLARREAL NATIONAL UNIVERSITY

Universidad Nacional Federico Villarreal (UNFV)
Jr. Carlos Gonzáles 285, Maranga, San Miguel, Lima
Tel: +51(14) 2193600
EMail: rector@unfv.edu.pe
Website: http://www.unfv.edu.pe

Rector: Juan Néstor Escudero Román
Tel: +51(14) 219-3661, Fax: +51(14) 219-3661

Vicerrector Académico: Hernán Humberto Álvarez Sotomayor

Secretaria General: Patricia Velasco Valderas
Tel: +51(14) 451-4653, Fax: +51(14) 451-4653
EMail: drpattyvel@hotmail.com

Faculties

Administration (Administration; Business Administration; International Business; Marketing; Private Administration; Tourism); **Architecture and Town Planning** (Architecture; Town Planning); **Civil Engineering** (Civil Engineering); **Dentistry** (Dentistry); **Economics** (Economics); **Education** (Education; Physical Education; Primary Education; Secondary Education; Special Education); **Electronic Engineering and Computer Science** (Computer Science; Electronic Engineering; Telecommunications Engineering); **Finance and Accountancy** (Accountancy; Finance); **Geographic and Environmental Engineering and Ecotourism** (Ecology; Environmental Engineering; Geography; Tourism); **Humanities** (Anthropology; Archaeology; Arts and Humanities; History; Linguistics; Literature; Philosophy); **Industrial and Systems Engineering** (Agricultural Engineering; Computer Engineering; Industrial Engineering; Transport Engineering); **Law and Political Science** (Law; Political Sciences); **Medical Technology** (Laboratory Techniques; Medical Technology; Optometry; Physical Therapy; Rehabilitation and Therapy; Speech Therapy and Audiology); **Medicine** *('Hipólito Unanue')* (Gynaecology and Obstetrics; Medicine; Nursing; Nutrition; Surgery); **Natural Sciences and Mathematics** (Biology; Chemistry; Mathematics; Natural Sciences; Physics; Statistics); **Oceanography, Fishery, and Food Sciences** (Fishery; Food Science; Marine Science and Oceanography); **Psychology** (Psychology); **Social Sciences** (Communication Studies; Social Sciences; Social Work; Sociology)

Schools

Postgraduate Studies

Further Information: Also 10 Research Centres

History: Founded 1963. An autonomous institution financed by the State.

Governing Bodies: Asamblea Universitaria

Academic Year: April to December

Admission Requirements: Secondary school certificate and entrance examination

Fees: None

Main Language(s) of Instruction: Spanish

Degrees and Diplomas: *Bachiller*: 5 yrs; *Maestría*: 2 yrs following Bachiller; *Doctorado*: 2 yrs. Also diplomados

Student Services: Academic counselling, Cultural centre, Health services, Language programs, Nursery care, Social counselling, Sports facilities

Special Facilities: Museum

Libraries: Total, c. 54,000 vols

Publications: Journal of the Faculty of Law and Political Science; Research Publications

Last Updated: 12/10/10

HERMILIO VALDIZÁN NATIONAL UNIVERSITY

Universidad Nacional Hermilio Valdizán (UNHEVAL)

Avenida Universitaria No 601, Cayhuayna, Huánuco, Huánuco

Tel: +51(62) 512341

Fax: +51(62) 513360

EMail: rectorado_unheval@hotmail.com

Website: http://www.unheval.edu.pe

Rector: Víctor Pedro Cuadros Ojeda Tel: +51(62) 519594

Vicerrector Administrativo: Erasmo Fernández Síxto Tel: +51(62) 513363

Vicerrector Académico: Pedro G. Villavícencio Guardía Tel: +51(62) 513144

Faculties

Accountancy and Finance (Accountancy; Finance); **Administration and Tourism** (Administration; Hotel Management; Tourism); **Agronomy** (Agricultural Engineering; Agronomy; Industrial Engineering); **Civil Engineering and Architecture** (Architecture; Civil Engineering; Engineering); **Economics** (Economics); **Education** (Education; Primary Education; Secondary Education); **Human Medicine and Psychology** (Dentistry; Medicine; Psychology); **Industrial and Systems Engineering** (Industrial Engineering; Systems Analysis); **Law and Political Science** (Law; Political Sciences); **Nursing** (Nursing); **Obstetrics** (Gynaecology and Obstetrics); **Social Sciences** (Communication Studies; Social Sciences; Sociology); **Veterinary Science and Zoology** (Veterinary Science; Zoology)

History: Founded 1964.

Admission Requirements: Secondary school certificate and entrance examination

Main Language(s) of Instruction: Spanish

Degrees and Diplomas: *Bachiller*: 5 yrs; *Maestría*: a further 2 yrs; *Doctorado*

Student Services: Academic counselling, Canteen, Health services, Language programs, Nursery care, Social counselling, Sports facilities

Libraries: Central Library

Publications: Valdizana, Research and Programmes Information *(biannually)*

Last Updated: 12/10/10

JAIME BAUSATE Y MEZA UNIVERSITY

Universidad Jaime Bausate y Meza

Jr. Río de Janeiro N° 560, Jesús María, (Esquina con Jr. Costa Rica), Lima

EMail: bausate@bausate.edu.pe

Website: http://www.bausate.edu.pe

Presidente: Roberto Marcos Mejía Alarcón

Programmes

Journalism (Journalism)

History: Founded 1958 as Escuela de Periodismo Jaime Bausate y Meza. Acquired present status and title 2008.

Main Language(s) of Instruction: Spanish

Degrees and Diplomas: *Bachiller*, *Título Profesional de Licenciado*. Also Diplomados

Last Updated: 21/10/10

JORGE BASADRE GROHMANN NATIONAL UNIVERSITY

Universidad Nacional Jorge Basadre Grohmann

Alto De Lima N°1594, Apdo. 316, Tacna, Tacna

Tel: +51(52) 714090

Fax: +51(54) 721385

EMail: viad@unjbg.edu.pe

Website: http://www.unjbg.edu.pe

Presidente: Luis Alberto Iberico Rojas EMail: redo@unjbg.edu.pe

Vice-Presidente Académico: Domingo Jesús Cabel Moscoso EMail: viac@unjbg.edu.pe

Vice-Presidente Administrativo: Juan Vitaliano Rodríguez Pantigoso

Faculties

Accountancy and Finance (Accountancy; Finance); **Administration** (Administration); **Agriculture** (Agricultural Economics; Agriculture; Agronomy; Animal Husbandry; Veterinary Science); **Architecture and Town Planning** (Architecture; Town Planning); **Education** (Education; Educational Administration; Environmental Studies; Literature; Mathematics and Computer Science; Modern Languages; Social Sciences; Technology; Translation and Interpretation); **Engineering** (Civil Engineering; Engineering; Geological Engineering); **Fishery** (Fishery); **Food Industries** (Food Technology); **Letters and Law** (Arts and Humanities; Communication Studies; Law; Political Sciences); **Medical Science** (Biochemistry; Dentistry; Medicine; Pharmacy); **Metallurgical Engineering** (Metallurgical Engineering); **Mining Engineering** (Mining Engineering); **Nursing** (Nursing); **Obstetrics** (Gynaecology and Obstetrics; Midwifery); **Science** (Applied Physics; Biology; Chemical Engineering; Mathematics and Computer Science; Microbiology; Natural Sciences; Physics)

Schools

Postgraduate (Accountancy; Agriculture; Business Administration; Computer Science; Development Studies; Educational Technology; Food Technology)

History: Founded 1971 as Universidad Nacional de Tacna. Acquired present title 1983.

Governing Bodies: Asamblea Universitaria; Consejo Universitario

Academic Year: April to December

Admission Requirements: Secondary school certificate and entrance examination

Fees: None

Main Language(s) of Instruction: Spanish

Degrees and Diplomas: *Bachiller*; *Título Profesional de Licenciado*: Accountancy (Contador público); Engineering (Ingeniero); *Maestría*; *Doctorado*: Educational Sciences

Libraries: Central Library; Ciudad Universitaria Library

Last Updated: 12/10/10

JOSÉ FAUSTINO SÁNCHEZ CARRIÓN NATIONAL UNIVERSITY

Universidad Nacional José Faustino Sánchez Carrión (UNJFSC)

Ciudad Universitaria, Av. Mercedes Indacochea S/N, Huacho, Lima
Tel: +51(1) 2323359
Fax: +51(1) 2324298
EMail: vrac@unjfsc.edu.pe
Website: http://www.unjfsc.edu.pe

Rector: Alberto Coayla Vilca (2009-)
EMail: rectorado@unjfsc.edu.pe

Vicerrector Académico: Elsa Oscuvilca Tapia

Vicerrector Administrativo: Aurora Rios Colan
EMail: vadministrativo@unjfsc.edu.pe

Faculties

Accountancy, Economics and Finance (Accountancy; Economics; Finance); **Administration, Tourism and International Business** (Administration; Hotel Management; International Business; Tourism); **Agrarian Science and Food Industry** (Agronomy; Food Technology; Zoology); **Bromatology and Nutrition** (Food Science; Nutrition); **Chemical, Metallurgical and Environmental Engineering** (Chemical Engineering; Environmental Engineering; Metallurgical Engineering); **Education** (Education; Educational Technology; Physical Education; Preschool Education; Primary Education; Secondary Education; Sports); **Engineering** (Computer Engineering; Industrial Engineering; Systems Analysis); **Fishing Engineering** (Fishery); **Human Medicine** (Medicine); **Law and Political Science** (Law; Political Sciences); **Science and Engineering** (Applied Mathematics; Civil Engineering; Computer Science; Electronic Engineering; Engineering; Physics; Statistics); **Social Sciences** (Communication Studies; Social Work; Sociology)

History: Founded 1968. A State Institution.

Governing Bodies: Reorganization Commission

Academic Year: April to December

Admission Requirements: Secondary school certificate and entrance examination

Main Language(s) of Instruction: Spanish

Degrees and Diplomas: *Bachiller*: 5 yrs; *Maestría*; *Doctorado*. Also diplomados

Student Services: Academic counselling, Health services, Language programs, Nursery care, Social counselling, Sports facilities

Libraries: Central and Specific Libraries

Last Updated: 12/10/10

JOSÉ MARÍA ARGUEDA NATIONAL UNIVERSITY

Universidad Nacional José María Arguedas

Jr. Tupac Amaru N° 123, Andahuaylas
Tel: +51(83) 421992
EMail: info@unajma.edu.pe
Website: http://unajma.edu.pe

Presidente: Augusto Padilla Yépez

Faculties

Agro-industrial Engineering (Agricultural Engineering; Industrial Engineering); **Business Administration** (Business Administration); **Systems Engineering** (Systems Analysis)

History: Founded 2004.

Main Language(s) of Instruction: Spanish

Degrees and Diplomas: *Bachiller*; *Título Profesional de Licenciado*

Last Updated: 12/10/10

LA MOLINA NATIONAL UNIVERSITY OF AGRICULTURE

Universidad Nacional Agraria La Molina (UNALM)

Avenida La Molina s/n, La Molina, Lima, Lima
Tel: +51(1) 349-5877
EMail: rectorado@lamolina.edu.pe
Website: http://www.lamolina.edu.pe

Rector: Jesús Abel Mejia Marcacuzco (2009-2014)
EMail: jabel@lamolina.edu.pe

Vicerrector Academico: Jorge Luis Aliaga Gutiérrez
EMail: vguevara@lamolina.edu.pe

Faculties

Agricultural Engineering (Agricultural Engineering); **Agronomy** (Agriculture; Agronomy; Entomology; Horticulture; Plant Pathology; Soil Science); **Animal Husbandry** (Animal Husbandry; Nutrition); **Economics and Planning** (Arts and Humanities; Business Administration; Economics; Rural Planning; Statistics); **Fishery** (Fishery); **Food Technology** (Food Technology); **Forestry** (Forestry); **Science** (Biology; Chemistry; Environmental Engineering; Mathematics; Meteorology; Natural Sciences; Physics)

Institutes

Biotechnology (Biotechnology); **Small Sustainable Production**

Further Information: Also 4 Institutes (Biodiversity, Biotechnology, Agroindustrial Development, Total Quality Laboratories), 3 Institutes for Regional Development (Coast, Highlands, Amazonia, all covering more than 6000 hectares), and 15 research programmes and centres. Fundación para el Desarrollo Agrario deals with projects' management

History: Founded 1902 at Santa Beatriz as National School of Agriculture (ENA), moved to La Molina 1933. Postgraduate school established 1958. Became University 1960. An autonomous institution financed by the State and by its own resources.

Governing Bodies: Asamblea Universitaria; Consejo Universitario

Academic Year: April to December (April-July; August-December)

Admission Requirements: Secondary school certificate, and entrance examination

Main Language(s) of Instruction: Spanish

Degrees and Diplomas: *Bachiller*: by thesis following Bachillerato; *Maestría (MSc)*: a further 2 yrs and thesis; *Doctorado*: a further 2 yrs and thesis. Also Diplomado

Student Services: Academic counselling, Canteen, Cultural centre, Foreign student adviser, Health services, Language programs, Nursery care, Social counselling, Sports facilities

Special Facilities: Anthropology Museum. Botanical Garden. Meteorological Observatory; University Farm

Libraries: National Agricultural Library, c. 50,000 vols; faculty libraries

Publications: Anales Científicos, Órgano Científico Oficial de la Universidad

Press or Publishing House: Ediagria

Last Updated: 11/10/10

MICAELA BASTIDAS NATIONAL UNIVERSITY OF APURIMAC

Universidad Nacional Micaela Bastidas de Apurimac

Avenida Arenas 121, Abancay
Tel: +51(83) 322577
Website: http://www.unamba.edu.pe

Rector: Leoncio Teófilo Carnero Carnero

Vicerrectora Académica: Lucy Marisol Guanuchi Orellana

Schools

Agro-industrial Engineering (Agricultural Engineering; Industrial Engineering); **Business Administration** (Business Administration); **Computer and Systems Engineering** (Computer Engineering; Systems Analysis); **Mathematics and Computer Science** (Mathematics and Computer Science); **Mining Engineering** (Mining Engineering); **Physical Education and Dance** (Dance;

Physical Education); **Veterinary Science and Zoology** (Veterinary Science; Zoology)

History: Founded 2000.

Main Language(s) of Instruction: Spanish

Degrees and Diplomas: *Bachiller*
Last Updated: 12/10/10

NATIONAL AMAZON UNIVERSITY OF MADRE DE DIOS

Universidad Nacional Amazonica de Madre de Dios
Ciudad Universitaria Av. Jorge Chávez s/n, Puerto Maldonado, Madre de Dios
Tel: +51(82) 572652
Website: http://www.unamad.edu.pe

Presidente: Augusto Bacco Montes Gutiérrez
Tel: +51(82) 573186 EMail: presidencia@unamad.edu.pe

Vicepresidente Administrativo: Lorenzo Melquiades Alvites Velezmoro
Tel: +51(82) 573880 EMail: vpadministrativo@unamad.edu.pe

Vicepresidente Académico: Bertha Lucia Ikeda Araujo
Tel: +51(82) 573789 EMail: vpacademica@unamad.edu.pe

Faculties

Education (Mathematics and Computer Science); **Engineering** (Agricultural Engineering; Environmental Engineering; Forestry; Industrial Engineering)

History: In the process of being organized and institutionalized.

Degrees and Diplomas: *Bachiller*; *Título Profesional de Licenciado*

Special Facilities: Museum

Libraries: Yes.
Last Updated: 30/05/08

NATIONAL INTERCULTURAL UNIVERSITY OF THE CENTRAL AMAZON

Universidad Nacional Intercultural de la Amazonia Central
Carretera a San José Km. 1/2, Yarinacochas, Pucallpa, Ucayali
Tel: +51(61) 596438
EMail: informes@unia.edu.pe
Website: http://www.unia.edu.pe

Presidente: Luis Freddy Vilcatoma Salas
EMail: presidente@unia.edu.pe

Vice Presidente Administrativo: María Yrene Cortez Mondragón
EMail: vice_administrativo@unia.edu.pe

Vice Presidente Académico: Isidro Rimarachin Cabrera
EMail: vice_academico@unia.edu.pe

Divisions

Education (Bilingual and Bicultural Education; Primary Education); **Engineering** (Agricultural Engineering; Forestry; Industrial Engineering)

History: Founded 2000.

Main Language(s) of Instruction: Spanish

Degrees and Diplomas: *Bachiller*; *Título Profesional de Licenciado*
Last Updated: 12/10/10

NATIONAL TECHNOLOGICAL UNIVERSITY OF THE SOUTHERN CONE OF LIMA

Universidad Nacional Tecnológica del Cono Sur de Lima
Av. Revolución s/n, Sector 3, Grupo 10, Mz. "M" Lt. 17 - Villa El Salvador, Lima, Lima
EMail: informes@untecs.edu.pe
Website: http://www.untecs.edu.pe

Presidente: Francisco Mario Piscoya Hermoza

Programmes

Business Administration (Business Administration); **Electronic and Telecommunications Engineering** (Electronic Engineering; Telecommunications Engineering); **Environmental Engineering** (Environmental Engineering); **Mechanical and Electrical Engineering** (Electrical Engineering; Mechanical Engineering); **Systems Engineering** (Systems Analysis)

History: Founded 2001.

Main Language(s) of Instruction: Spanish

Degrees and Diplomas: *Bachiller*
Last Updated: 13/10/10

NATIONAL UNIVERSITY OF AGRICULTURE OF LA SELVA

Universidad Nacional Agraria de la Selva (UNAS)
Avenida Universitaria s/n Km. 1.5, Tingo María, Huánuco
Tel: +51(62) 562342 +51(62) 562190
Fax: +51(62) 561156
EMail: unas@unas.edu.pe
Website: http://www.unas.edu.pe

Rector: Milthon Muñoz Berrocal
Tel: +51(62) 562702 EMail: mmunoz@unas.edu.pe

Vicerrector Académico: Wilfredo Zavala Solorzano
Tel: +51(62) 561781, Fax: +51(62) 561156
EMail: vacad@unas.edu.pe

Faculties

Agronomy (Agriculture; Agronomy); **Animal Husbandry** (Animal Husbandry); **Computer Science and Systems** (Computer Engineering; Computer Science); **Economics and Administration** (Accountancy; Administration; Economics); **Food Technology** (Food Technology); **Renewable Natural Resources** (Natural Resources)

History: Founded in 1964.

Governing Bodies: Asemblea Univarsitaria. Consejo Universitario y consejos de Facultad

Admission Requirements: Secondary school certificate and entrance examination

Fees: (Nuevos Soles): Matricula, 750 per semerster

Main Language(s) of Instruction: Spanish

International Co-operation: With universities in Europe and Brazil

Accrediting Agencies: Asamblea Nacional de Rectores

Degrees and Diplomas: *Título Profesional de Licenciado*: Agronomy; Animal Husbandry; Food Technology, Natural Resources; Ecology, 5 yrs; *Título Profesional de Licenciado*: Economics; Accountancy; Administration; Computer Engineering; *Maestría*: Economics; Agriculture; Animal Husbandry, 2 yrs

Student Services: Academic counselling, Cultural centre, Employment services, Health services, Language programs, Nursery care, Social counselling, Sports facilities

Student Residential Facilities: Yes

Special Facilities: Museum; Zoological Garden; Experimental Station

Libraries: Central library; 6 Faculty libraries

Publications: Tropicultura, Scientific journal *(annually)*

Press or Publishing House: Fondo Editorial de la Universidad Nacional Agraria de la Selva
Last Updated: 07/10/10

NATIONAL UNIVERSITY OF CAJAMARCA

Universidad Nacional de Cajamarca
Av Atahualpa N° 1050, Cajamarca
Tel: +51(76) 363263
Fax: +51(76) 362796
EMail: rector@unc.edu.pe
Website: http://www.unc.edu.pe

Rector: Carlos Segundo Tirado Soto Fax: +51(76) 822796
EMail: catirso@unc.edu.pe

Vicerrector Académico: Oscar R. Silva Rodríguez

Faculties

Agriculture (Agricultural Business; Agriculture; Environmental Engineering; Food Technology; Forestry); **Economics, Accountancy, and Administration** (Accountancy; Administration; Economics); **Education** (Education); **Engineering** (Civil Engineering; Engineering; Engineering Management; Geological Engineering;

Hydraulic Engineering); **Health Sciences** (Gynaecology and Obstetrics; Health Sciences; Midwifery; Nursing); **Human Medicine**; **Law and Political Science** (Law; Political Sciences); **Social Sciences** (Hotel Management; Social Sciences; Sociology; Tourism); **Veterinary Science** (Veterinary Science); **Zoology** (Zoology); **Zoology** *Dean*: José Antonio Mantilla Guerra

Further Information: Also branches in Jaén, Celendin, and Chota

History: Founded 1962. A State institution.

Governing Bodies: Asamblea Universitaria; Consejo Universitario

Academic Year: March to December

Admission Requirements: Secondary school certificate

Main Language(s) of Instruction: Spanish

Degrees and Diplomas: *Bachiller*; *Título Profesional de Licenciado*; *Maestría*; *Doctorado*

Student Services: Health services

Special Facilities: Natural History Museum. Archaeological Museum. Herbarium

Libraries: Central Library, c. 40,000 vols

Press or Publishing House: Editorial Universitaria de la Universidad Nacional de Cajamarca

Last Updated: 11/10/10

NATIONAL UNIVERSITY OF CALLAO

Universidad Nacional del Callao (UNAC)

Av Juan Pablo II 306, Bellavista, Callao, Lima

Tel: +51(1) 4296608

Fax: +51(1) 4296607

EMail: rector@unac.edu.pe

Website: http://www.unac.edu.pe

Rector: Manuel Alberto Mori Paredes (2010-2015)

Centres

Technological and Experimental Research

Faculties

Accountancy (Accountancy); **Administration** (Administration; Business Administration); **Chemical Engineering** (Chemical Engineering); **Economics** (Economics); **Electrical and Electronic Engineering** (Computer Engineering; Electrical Engineering; Electronic Engineering; Engineering; Industrial Engineering; Mechanical Engineering; Systems Analysis); **Environmental Engineering and Natural Resources** (Environmental Engineering; Natural Resources); **Fishing and Food Engineering** (Fishery; Food Technology); **Health Sciences** (Health Sciences; Nursing); **Mechanical Engineering and Energy** (Energy Engineering; Mechanical Engineering); **Natural Sciences and Mathematics** (Mathematics; Natural Sciences)

Schools

Postgraduate

Further Information: Also English and French as Foreign Language courses.

History: Founded 1966 as Universidad Nacional Técnica del Callao. Acquired present status and title 1983.

Governing Bodies: Consejo Universitario

Academic Year: April to December (April-July; August-December)

Admission Requirements: Secondary school certificate and entrance examination in Spanish

Fees: (US Dollars): c. 400 per annum

Main Language(s) of Instruction: Spanish

International Co-operation: Study Abroad Programme with Alliance française, France

Degrees and Diplomas: *Bachiller*: 5 yrs; *Título Profesional de Licenciado*: 5 yrs; *Maestría*: Economics; Health Sciences; Engineering; Accountancy; Administration, 2 yrs. Also Diplomado

Student Services: Academic counselling, Canteen, Cultural centre, Employment services, Health services, Language programs, Social counselling, Sports facilities

Student Residential Facilities: For 10,000 students

Libraries: Central Library, 15,000 vols. Specialized libraries in each academic division, 5,000 vols

Publications: Research Papers Catalogue *(annually)*

Last Updated: 11/10/10

NATIONAL UNIVERSITY OF CENTRAL PERU

Universidad Nacional del Centro del Perú (UNCP)

Av. Mariscal Castilla N° 3909 - 4089 El Tambo, Huancayo, Junín

Tel: +51(64) 481062

EMail: viceadministrativo@uncp.edu.pe

Website: http://www.uncp.edu.pe

Rector: Carlos Antonio Adauto Justo EMail: rector@uncp.edu.pe

Vicerrector Administrativo: Edgar López Quilca
Tel: +51(64) 481072

Faculties

Accountancy (Accountancy); **Agronomy** (Agronomy); **Architecture** (Architecture; Town Planning); **Biology and Chemistry** (Biology; Chemistry); **Business Administration** (Business Administration); **Chemical Engineering** (Chemical Engineering); **Communication**; **Economics**; **Electrical and Electronic Engineering** (Electrical Engineering; Electronic Engineering); **Food Industries** (Food Technology); **Forestry and Environmental Sciences** (Environmental Studies; Forestry); **Human Medicine**; **Mathematics and Physics** (Mathematics; Physics); **Mechanical Engineering** (Mechanical Engineering); **Metallurgical and Materials Engineering** (Materials Engineering; Metallurgical Engineering); **Mining Engineering** (Mining Engineering); **Nursing** (Nursing); **Pedagogy and Humanities** (Art Education; Arts and Humanities; Education; Geography; History; Linguistics; Literature; Mathematics; Natural Sciences; Pedagogy; Philosophy; Physical Education; Primary Education; Psychology); **Social Work** (Social Work); **Sociology** (Sociology); **Zoology**

Schools

Postgraduate (Business Administration; Education; Environmental Management; Rural Planning) *Director*: Juan Lino Quispe; **Professional Studies** *(Junín)* (Automation and Control Engineering; Food Science) *Director*: Dilfredo Mallma Capcha; **Professional Studies** *(Tarma)* (Automation and Control Engineering; Business Administration; Food Science; Hotel Management; Technology; Tourism) *Director*: Rubén Cortez Galindo; **Professional Studies** *(Satipo)* (Agronomy; Animal Husbandry; Food Science; Forestry) *Director*: Edgar Acosta López

History: Founded 1959, acquired present status 1961. A State institution.

Governing Bodies: Consejo Universitario, Asamblea Universitaria

Academic Year: April to December (April-July; July-December)

Admission Requirements: Secondary school certificate and entrance examination

Main Language(s) of Instruction: Spanish

Degrees and Diplomas: *Bachiller*; *Bachiller*: Anthropology; Business Administration; Journalism; Nursing; Social Work; Sociology; *Título Profesional de Licenciado*: Accountancy (Contador público); Architecture (Arquitecto); Economics (Economista); Engineering (Ingeniero), 5 yrs; *Título Profesional de Licenciado*: Teacher; *Maestría*: Rural Development; Business Administration; Higher Education; Environment Management; Production Systems; Biotechnology; *Doctorado*. Also specialization degrees.

Student Services: Academic counselling, Canteen, Health services, Language programs, Social counselling

Special Facilities: Museums of Ethnology, History an Regional Archaeology.

Libraries: c. 4,000 vols

Publications: Revista de Ciencias Agrarias

Last Updated: 11/10/10

NATIONAL UNIVERSITY OF ENGINEERING

Universidad Nacional de Ingeniería (UNI)

Avenida Túpac Amaru No 210, Distrito del Rímac, Lima, Lima

Tel: +51(1) 4819830-4811070

EMail: rrpp@uni.edu.pe

Website: http://www.uni.edu.pe

Rector: Aurelio Marcelo Padilla Ríos
Tel: +51(1) 4811035 EMail: rector22@uni.edu.pe

Secretario General: L. Luis Acuña Pinaud Tel: +51(1) 4817914

Faculties
Architecture, Town Planning and Arts (Architecture; Fine Arts; Regional Planning; Town Planning); **Chemical Engineering and Textiles** (Chemical Engineering; Materials Engineering; Textile Technology); **Civil Engineering** (Civil Engineering); **Economic Engineering and Social Sciences** (Economics; Engineering; Social Sciences; Statistics); **Electrical and Electronic Engineering** (Electrical and Electronic Engineering); **Environmental Engineering** (Environmental Engineering; Health Administration; Hygiene); **Geological, Mining, and Metallurgical Engineering** (Geological Engineering; Metallurgical Engineering; Mining Engineering); **Industrial and Systems Engineering** (Computer Engineering; Industrial Engineering; Systems Analysis); **Mechanical Engineering** (Electrical Engineering; Electronic Engineering; Mechanical Engineering; Naval Architecture); **Petroleum and Petro-chemical Engineering** (Petroleum and Gas Engineering); **Science** (Chemistry; Mathematics; Natural Sciences; Physics)

History: Founded 1955.

Governing Bodies: University Assembly; University Council

Academic Year: April to December (April-July; August-December)

Admission Requirements: Secondary school certificate and entrance examination

Fees: None

Main Language(s) of Instruction: Spanish

International Co-operation: Participates in the Programa de Cooperación Interuniversitaria América Latina-España and the Alfa Programme

Accrediting Agencies: Secretaría Ejecutiva de Cooperación Técnica Internacional

Degrees and Diplomas: *Bachiller*: Architecture; Physics; Mathematics; Chemistry; Physics Engineering; Sanitary Engineering; Hygiene and Industrial Safety; Civil Engineering; Economics Engineering; Statistics Engineering; Electrical Engineering; Electronical Engineering (Bach.); Geological Engineering; Metallurgical Engineering; Mining Engineering; Industrial Engineering; Systems Engineering; Mechanical Engineering; Naval Engineering; Mecatronics Engineering; Petroleum Engineering; Petrochemical Engineering; Chemical Engineering (Bach.); Textile Engineering; Telecommunications Engineering (Bach.), 5 yrs; *Bachiller*: Science; Physics; Mathematics; Chemistry (Lic.), 5 yrs by thesis; *Título Profesional de Licenciado*: Architecture (Arq) (Arquitecto), by thesis following Bachiller; *Maestría*: Architecture and Town Planning; Regional Planning; Urban Renovation; Applied Mathematics; Chemistry; Physics; Medical and Instrumental Physics; Aeronautics; Water management; Environmental Management; Hydraulics; Systems Engineering (Mag.); Environmental Engineering; Telematics; Automation; Power Engineering; Telecommunications; Signal Processing; Materials Science; Machine Design; Energy Engineering; Aeronautics; Chemical Engineering; Process Engineering; Systems Engineering (Mag.); Geotechnical Engineering; Transport Engineering; Business Management; Building technology; Building Management; Management and Development; Foreign Trade; Mining Engineering; Geological Engineering; Metallurgical Engineering; Mining Engineering (Mag.); Industrial Engineering (Mag.), a further 2 yrs; *Doctorado*: Physics; Mathematics; Mechanical Engineering, 2 yrs. Also Segunda especialización 1 yr

Student Services: Academic counselling, Cultural centre, Employment services, Health services, Language programs, Nursery care, Social counselling, Sports facilities

Student Residential Facilities: Yes

Special Facilities: Mineralogy Museum; Paleontology Museum; Art Gallery

Libraries: Central Library, 37,090 vols; faculty libraries, 101,784 vols

Last Updated: 11/10/10

NATIONAL UNIVERSITY OF HUANCAVELICA

Universidad Nacional de Huancavelica (UNH)
Ciudad Universitaria de Paturpampa, Huancavelica, Huancavelica
Fax: +51(67) 451380
EMail: rectorado@unh.edu.pe
Website: http://www.unh.edu.pe

Rectora: Yda Flor Camposano Córdova (2007-)
EMail: ycamposano@unh.edu.pe

Vicerrectora Académico: Ruggerths Neil De La Cruz Marcos
Tel: +51(67) 451121 EMail: rdelacruz@unh.edu.pe

Faculties
Agriculture (Agricultural Management; Agriculture; Agronomy); **Business Administration** (Accountancy; Business Administration); **Education** (Education; Primary Education; Secondary Education); **Electronic and Systems Engineering** (Electronic Engineering; Systems Analysis); **Engineering** (Civil Engineering); **Health Sciences** (Gynaecology and Obstetrics); **Law and Political Science** (Law; Political Sciences); **Mining and Civil Engineering** (Civil Engineering; Mining Engineering); **Nursing** (Nursing)

History: Founded 1992.

Governing Bodies: Asamblea Universitaria; Consejo Universitario; Rectorado; Vicerretorado Administrativo; Vicerrectorado Académico; Consejo de Facultad; Decanatura

Admission Requirements: High School Certificate and entrance examination

Fees: (US Dollars): c. 30,00

Main Language(s) of Instruction: Spanish

International Co-operation: With universities in Spain, Cuba, Mexico, Colombia and Brazil

Degrees and Diplomas: *Bachiller*: Nursery; Obstetrics; Civil Engineering; Systems Engineering; Electronic Engineering; Zootechnics; Metallurgical Engineering; Agricultural Engineering; Agronomy; Education; Administration; Accountancy; Law, 5 yrs; *Maestría*: Business Administration; Accountancy; Public Administration; Education; Higher Education; Educational Administration; Bilingual and Bicultural Education; Law; Public Health; Health Administration, 2 yrs; *Maestría*: Engineering; Environmental Management; Engineering Management; Animal Husbandry

Student Services: Academic counselling, Canteen, Cultural centre, Foreign student adviser, Health services, Language programs, Nursery care, Social counselling, Sports facilities

Student Residential Facilities: None

Special Facilities: Videoconference room

Libraries: Central Library

Publications: Revista Institucional "Wamanrazu", Scientific and Cultural Magazine *(biennially)*

Press or Publishing House: Centro de Impresiones de la UNH

Last Updated: 11/10/10

NATIONAL UNIVERSITY OF JULIACA

Universidad Nacional de Juliaca
Av. Nueva Zelandia 631, Juliaca, Puno
EMail: informes@unaj.edu.pe
Website: http://www.unaj.edu.pe

Programmes
Agro-industrial Engineering (Food Technology); **Business Studies** (International Business; Marketing); **Dentistry** (Dentistry); **Environmental Engineering** (Environmental Engineering)

History: Founded 2007.

Main Language(s) of Instruction: Spanish

Degrees and Diplomas: *Bachiller*

Last Updated: 27/10/10

NATIONAL UNIVERSITY OF MOQUEGUA

Universidad Nacional de Moquegua
Calle Antigua de Samegua, Moquegua, Moquegua
EMail: correo@unam.edu.pe
Website: http://www.unam.edu.pe

Presidente: Eli Joaquín Espinoza Atencia

Programmes
Agro-industrial Engineering (Agricultural Engineering; Industrial Engineering); **Environmental Engineering** (Environmental Engineering); **Fishing Engineering** (Fishery); **Mining Engineering** (Mining Engineering); **Public Administration and Social Development** (Development Studies; Public Administration); **Systems**

and Computer Engineering (Computer Engineering; Systems Analysis)

History: Founded 2005.

Main Language(s) of Instruction: Spanish

Degrees and Diplomas: *Bachiller*; *Título Profesional de Licenciado*

Last Updated: 11/10/10

NATIONAL UNIVERSITY OF PIURA

Universidad Nacional de Piura (UNP)

Campus Universitario, Urb. Miraflores s/n, Castilla, Apartado Postal 295, Piura, Piura

Tel: +51(73) 343181

Fax: +51(73) 343184

EMail: viceadmin@unp.edu.pe

Website: http://www.unp.edu.pe

Rector: José Raúl Rodriguez Lichtenheldt

EMail: rectorado@unp.edu.pe

Vicerrector Académico: Eddy William Gives Mujica

EMail: viceacad@unp.edu.pe

Vicerrector Administrativo: Oscar Armando Vásquez Ramos

Faculties

Accountancy and Finance (Accountancy; Finance); **Administration** (Administration; Business Administration; Public Administration); **Agronomy** (Agricultural Engineering; Agriculture; Agronomy; Hygiene; Soil Science); **Architecture and Town Planning** (Architecture; Town Planning); **Civil Engineering** (Civil Engineering); **Economics** (Economics); **Fishery Engineering** (Aquaculture; Fishery); **Human Medicine** (Anatomy; Community Health; Health Sciences; Medicine; Pathology); **Industrial Engineering** (Computer Engineering; Industrial Engineering); **Mining Engineering** (Chemical Engineering; Geological Engineering; Mining Engineering; Petroleum and Gas Engineering); **Political Science and Law** (Law; Political Sciences); **Science** (Biology; Electronic Engineering; Mathematics; Natural Sciences; Physics; Telecommunications Engineering); **Social Sciences and Education** (Education; Social Sciences); **Zoology** (Zoology)

Schools

Postgraduate Studies

History: Founded 1961 as a technical institution, reorganized 1969 as national university.

Governing Bodies: Asamblea Universitaria; Consejo Universitario

Academic Year: April to December (April-July; August-December)

Admission Requirements: Secondary school certificate

Fees: None

Main Language(s) of Instruction: Spanish

Degrees and Diplomas: *Bachiller*; *Título Profesional de Licenciado*: 5 yrs; *Maestría*; *Doctorado*

Libraries: Central Library, 23,000 vols

Publications: Revistas

Last Updated: 11/10/10

NATIONAL UNIVERSITY OF SAN AGUSTÍN

Universidad Nacional de San Agustín (UNSA)

Casilla postal 23, Santa Catalina 117, Arequipa

Tel: +51(54) 237808-224839

EMail: vmedina@unsa.edu.pe

Website: http://www.unsa.edu.pe

Rector: Valdemar Medina Hoyos (2009-)

Tel: +51(54) 237808 EMail: rectorado@unsa.edu.pe

Vice Rectora Administrativa: Elisa Castañeda Huamán

Tel: +51(54) 229830 EMail: vrad@ac.unsa.edu.pe

Centres

Languages

Faculties

Accountancy, Admnistration and ActuarialSciences (Accountancy; Actuarial Science; Administration); **Architecture and Town Planning** (Architecture; Town Planning); **Biology and Cattle Breeding** (Agriculture; Biology; Cattle Breeding; Nutrition); **Civil Engineering** (Civil Engineering); **Economics** (Economics); **Education** (Education); **Geology, Geophysics and Mining** (Geology; Geophysics; Mining Engineering); **History and Social Sciences** (Anthropology; History; Hotel Management; Social Sciences; Social Work; Sociology; Tourism); **Law** (Law; Private Law; Public Law); **Medicine** (Anatomy; Gynaecology and Obstetrics; Medicine; Microbiology; Neurology; Paediatrics; Pathology; Physiology; Psychiatry and Mental Health; Surgery); **Natural and Exact Sciences** (Chemistry; Mathematics; Natural Sciences; Physics); **Nursing** (Nursing); **Philosophy and Humanities** (Arts and Humanities; Linguistics; Literature; Philosophy); **Process Engineering** (Chemical Engineering; Chemistry; Engineering Management; Food Science; Materials Engineering; Metallurgical Engineering); **Production and Services Engineering** (Electrical and Electronic Engineering; Industrial Engineering; Mechanical Engineering; Production Engineering; Systems Analysis); **Psychology, Industrial Relations, and Communication Sciences** (Communication Studies; Labour and Industrial Relations; Psychology)

Institutes

Computer Science; **Geophysics** *(Characato)* (Geophysics)

History: Founded 1714 as Universidad Real y Pontificia "Intra Claustra". Became Universidad Nacional del Gran Padre San Agustín 1828. Reorganized 1969.

Governing Bodies: Asamblea Universitaria; Consejo Ejecutivo

Academic Year: September to August (September-January; March-August)

Admission Requirements: Secondary school certificate and entrance examination

Fees: None

Main Language(s) of Instruction: Spanish

Degrees and Diplomas: *Bachiller*: Anthropology; Chemistry; Education; History; Industrial Relations; Literature and Languages; Mathematics; Nutrition; Philosophy; Physics; Sociology, 5 yrs; *Título Profesional de Licenciado*: Accountancy (Contador público); Agricultural Engineering (Ingeniero agropecuario); Architecture (Arquitecto); Biology (Biólogo); Chemical Engineering (Ingeniero químico); Civil Engineering (Ingeniero civil); Geological Engineering (Ingeniero Geólogo); Geophysic Engineering (Ingeniero Geofísico); Metallurgical Engineering (Ingeniero metalurgista); Nursing (Enfermera); Social Services (Asistente social), 5 yrs; *Título Profesional de Licenciado*: Law (Abogado); Psychology (Psicólogo), 6 yrs; *Título Profesional de Licenciado*: Medicine and Surgery (Médico-Cirujano), 7 1/2 yrs; *Maestría*; *Doctorado*

Special Facilities: Archaeology and History Museums

Libraries: Central Library, c. 41,000 vols; Medicine, c. 14,500; programme libraries

Last Updated: 11/10/10

IAU NATIONAL UNIVERSITY OF SAN MARCOS

Universidad Nacional Mayor de San Marcos (UNMSM)

Av. Germán Amézaga s/n, Ciudad Universitaria, Lima, 1 Lima

Tel: +51(1) 619-7000

EMail: rectorado@unmsm.edu.pe

Website: http://www.unmsm.edu.pe

Rector: Pedro Atilio Cotillo Zegara (2011-)

EMail: rectunmsm@unmsm.edu.pe

International Relations: Maria Lau Luyo, Head of Cooperation and Interinstitutional Affairs Office

EMail: ccoperacion.unmsm@gmail.com

Faculties

Accountancy (Accountancy); **Administration** (Administration; International Business; Tourism); **Arts and Humanities** (Art Education; Arts and Humanities; Communication Studies; Information Sciences; Library Science; Linguistics; Literature; Philosophy); **Biological Sciences** (Biological and Life Sciences; Biotechnology; Genetics; Microbiology; Parasitology); **Chemistry and Chemical Engineering** (Agricultural Engineering; Chemical Engineering; Chemistry; Industrial Engineering); **Dentistry** (Dentistry); **Economics** (Economics); **Education** (Education; Physical Education; Primary Education; Secondary Education); **Electronic and Electrical Engineering** (Electrical Engineering; Electronic Engineering; Telecommunications Engineering); **Geology, Mining, Metallurgy and Geography** (Geography; Geology; Metallurgical Engineering; Mining Engineering); **Industrial Engineering** (Industrial

Engineering); **Law and Political Science** (Law; Political Sciences); **Mathematics** (Computer Science; Mathematics; Operations Research; Statistics); **Medicine** (Anatomy; Gynaecology and Obstetrics; Laboratory Techniques; Medical Technology; Medicine; Nursing; Nutrition; Occupational Therapy; Physical Therapy; Radiology; Rehabilitation and Therapy); **Pharmacy and Biochemistry** (Biochemistry; Food Science; Pharmacy; Toxicology); **Physics** (Physics); **Psychology** (Psychology); **Social Sciences** (Anthropology; Archaeology; Geography; History; Social Sciences; Social Work; Sociology); **Systems and Computer Engineering** (Computer Engineering; Systems Analysis); **Veterinary Science** (Veterinary Science)

Institutes

Raúl Porras; **Tropical Medicine**

Research Centres

Rural Andine History (Anthropology; Archaeology; Fine Arts; History)

Further Information: Also Research Centres and Institutes

History: Founded 1551 by Royal Decree and reorganized by Papal Bull 1571. Closed at the time of the establishment of the Republic, reinaugurated 1861. Became an autonomous Institution 1874, reorganized 1946 and 1969. Receives financial assistance from the State.

Governing Bodies: University Assembly; University Council; Deans Council

Academic Year: April to December (April-July; September-December)

Admission Requirements: Secondary school certificate and entrance examination

Main Language(s) of Instruction: Spanish

Degrees and Diplomas: *Bachiller*: Administration; Anthropology; Archaeology; Art; Hispanic Literature; Languages; Mathematics; Philosophy; Physics; Social Work; Sociology; Statistics; *Título Profesional de Licenciado*: Accountancy (Contador público); Biomathematics (Biólogo matemático); Chemical Engineering (Ingeniero químico); Chemistry (Químico); Dentistry (Cirujano Dentista); Economics (Economista); Electronics (Ingeniero electrónico); Fluid Mechanics (Ingeniero mecánico de Fluidos); Geography (Geógrafo); Geology (Ingeniero geólogo); Industrial Engineering (Ingeniero industrial); Journalism (Periodista); Law (Abogado); Medicine and Surgery (Médico-Cirujano); Midwifery (Obstétriz); Pharmacy (Químico farmacéutico); Psychology (Psicólogo); Teaching qualification, secondary level; Veterinary Medicine (Médico veterinario); *Maestría*; *Doctorado*

Special Facilities: Museums: Archaeology and Ethnology; Natural History; Art and History

Libraries: Biblioteca Central "Pedro Zulen"; specialized libraries

Publications: Anales de Medicina; Anales del Programa de Farmacia y Bioquímica; Archivos del Instituto de Biología Andina; Boletín Bibliográfico de la Biblioteca Central; Boletín del Instituto de Investigaciones Económicas; Boletín del Programa de Medicina; Ciencias Comerciales; Derecho de Trabajo; Derecho y Ciencias Políticas; Farmacia; Investigaciones Pecuarias; Letras; Medicina Veterinaria; Neuro-Psiquiatría-Sphinx; Nueva Crónica (History); Odontología; Peruana de Medicina Tropical; Revistas de: Educación; Sanidad Avícola

Student Numbers *2011-2012*: Total 35,000

Last Updated: 13/09/11

NATIONAL UNIVERSITY OF SAN MARTÍN

Universidad Nacional de San Martín

Jr. Maynas N° 177, Tarapoto, San Martín
Tel: +51(42) 524253
EMail: informes@unsm.edu.pe
Website: http://www.unsm.edu.pe

Rector: Alfredo Quinteros Garcia EMail: rectorunsm@hotmail.com

Vicerrector Académico: Julio Ríos Ramirez

Vicerrector Administrativo: Jorge Sanchez Ríos

Faculties

Agro-Industrial Engineering (Agricultural Engineering; Industrial Engineering); **Agronomy** (Agriculture; Agronomy); **Civil Engineering** (Civil Engineering); **Ecology** (Ecology); **Economics** (Economics); **Education and Humanities** (Education; Modern Languages); **Health Sciences** (Gynaecology and Obstetrics; Health Sciences; Nursing); **Systems Engineering** (Systems Analysis)

History: Founded 1979.

Main Language(s) of Instruction: Spanish

Degrees and Diplomas: *Bachiller*; *Título Profesional de Licenciado*

Last Updated: 11/10/10

NATIONAL UNIVERSITY OF SANTA

Universidad Nacional del Santa (UNS)

Av. Pacífico N°508 Urb. Buenos Aires Apdo.10, Nuevo Chimbote, Ancash
Tel: +51(43) 310445
Fax: +51(43) 311650
EMail: secgral@uns.edu.pe
Website: http://www.uns.edu.pe

Rector: Pedro Eliseo Moncada Becerra
Tel: +51(43) 311556 EMail: pmoncada@uns.edu.pe

Vicerrector Académico: Victor Augusto Castro Zavaleta
EMail: vracad@uns.edu.pe

Vicerrector Administrativo: Damián Manayay Sanchez
EMail: vradmin@uns.edu.pe

Centres

Educational Research; **Teacher Training**

Faculties

Education and Humanities (Communication Studies; Cultural Studies; Mathematics; Modern Languages; Philosophy; Physics; Preschool Education; Primary Education; Psychology; Secondary Education); **Engineering** (Agricultural Engineering; Civil Engineering; Computer Engineering; Energy Engineering; Engineering; Industrial Engineering); **Science** (Aquaculture; Biology; Natural Sciences; Nursing)

History: Founded 1984. Acquired present status 1998.

Governing Bodies: Asamblea Universitaria; Consejo Universitario; Consejos de Facultades

Admission Requirements: Secondary School Certificate

Main Language(s) of Instruction: Spanish

Accrediting Agencies: Asamblea Nacional de Rectores

Degrees and Diplomas: *Bachiller*: Education; *Título Profesional de Licenciado*: Civil Engineering; Agricultural Engineering; Energy Engineering; Computer Engineering, 5 yrs

Student Services: Academic counselling, Cultural centre, Health services, Language programs, Nursery care, Social counselling, Sports facilities

Last Updated: 12/10/10

NATIONAL UNIVERSITY OF THE ALTIPLANO

Universidad Nacional del Altiplano

Ciudad Universitaria, Av. Floral 1153, Puno
Tel: +51(54) 356081
Fax: +51(54) 368590
EMail: unapnet@unap.edu.pe
Website: http://www.unap.edu.pe/portal/wiraqocha/ukhu-pacha

Rector: Lucio Avila Rojas
Tel: +51(54) 352206 EMail: lucioavila24@yahoo.com

Vicerrector Administrativo: Edgardo Pineda Quispe
Tel: +51(54) 366186, Fax: +51(54) 352992

Vicerrector Académico: Germán Yabar Pilco
Tel: +51(54) 368099, Fax: +51(54) 366142

Faculties

Accountancy and Administration (Accountancy; Administration); **Agricultural Engineering** (Agricultural Engineering; Electrical Engineering; Mechanical Engineering; Physics); **Agriculture** (Agricultural Engineering; Agriculture); **Biology** (Biology); **Chemical Engineering** (Chemical Engineering); **Civil Engineering, Architecture and Town Planning** (Architecture; Civil Engineering; Mathematics; Physics; Town Planning; Urban Studies); **Economics** (Economics); **Education** (Education; Physical Education; Preschool Education; Primary Education; Secondary Education); **Geological**

and Metallurgical Engineering (Geological Engineering; Metallurgical Engineering); **Health Sciences** (Dentistry; Health Sciences; Medicine; Nutrition); **Human Medicine** (Medicine); **Law and Political Science** (Law; Political Sciences); **Metallurgical and Geological Engineering** (Geological Engineering; Metallurgical Engineering); **Mining Engineering** (Mining Engineering); **Nursing** (Nursing); **Social Sciences** (Anthropology; Communication Studies; Social Sciences; Sociology; Tourism); **Social Work** (Social Work); **Statistics and Computer Science** (Electronic Engineering; Statistics; Systems Analysis); **Veterinary Medicine and Animal Husbandry** (Animal Husbandry; Veterinary Science)

History: Founded 1856. Closed for almost 100 years. Reopened 1961. A national autonomous University financed by the State.

Governing Bodies: Asamblea Universitaria with two-thirds academic staff and one-third student membership; Consejo Universitario

Academic Year: April to December (April-July; August-December)

Admission Requirements: Secondary school certificate and entrance examination

Fees: None

Main Language(s) of Instruction: Spanish

International Co-operation: With universities in Bolivia, Argentina, Chile (CRISCOS)

Degrees and Diplomas: *Bachiller*: Accountancy and Administration; Agricultural Engineering, 5 yrs; *Bachiller*: Administration; Agronomy, Agro-industry, Topography; Anthropology; Biology; Chemistry; Civil Engineering, Architecture, Physics, Mathematics; Economics; Education; Geological and Metallurgical Engineering; Human Medicine, Nutrition, Odontology; Law; Mining Engineering; Nursing; Nutrition; Social Work; Sociology; Sociology, Tourism, Anthropology, Communication; Statistics; Tourism; Veterinary Medicine and Animal Husbandry; *Título Profesional de Licenciado*: Accountancy (Contador Público); Agricultural Engineering (Ingeniero agroindustrial); Agricultural Engineering (Ingeniero agrónomo); Architecture; Biology (Biólogo); Chemical Engineering (Ingeniero químico); Civil Engineering; Dentistry (Odontólogo); Economics (Ingeniero economista); Electrical Engineering; Electronic Engineering; Geology Engineering; Law (Abogado); Mechanical Engineering; Medicine (Médico); Metallurgical Engineering; Mining Engineering (Ingeniero de Minas); Nursing (Enfermera); Social Work (Trabajador social); Statistics; Surgery (Médico Cirujano); Surveying (Ingeniero Topográfico y Agrimensor); Systems Engineering; Veterinary Medicine and Animal Husbandry (Médico Veterinario y Zootecnista); *Maestría*; *Doctorado*

Student Services: Academic counselling, Canteen, Cultural centre, Foreign Studies Centre, Health services, Language programs, Nursery care, Social counselling, Sports facilities

Libraries: Central Library, c. 25,000 vols; libraries of the faculties, c. 4,200

Publications: Boletín Universitario de Investigación *(monthly)*

Last Updated: 11/10/10

NATIONAL UNIVERSITY OF THE PERUVIAN AMAZON

Universidad Nacional de la Amazonía Peruana

P.O. Box 496, Sargento Lores No 385, Iquitos, Loreto
Tel: +51(65) 234140
Fax: +51(65) 233657
EMail: infounap@unapiquitos.edu.pe
Website: http://www.unapiquitos.edu.pe

Rector: Antonio Pasquel Ruiz
Tel: +51(65) 266303 EMail: rectorado@unapiquitos.edu.pe

Faculties

Agronomy (Agronomy; Animal Husbandry); **Biology** (Aquaculture; Biology; Ecology; Microbiology; Parasitology); **Chemical Engineering** (Chemical Engineering); **Computer Science and Systems Engineering** (Computer Science; Systems Analysis); **Dentistry** (Dentistry); **Economics and Trade** (Accountancy; Administration; Economics; International Business; Tourism); **Education and Humanities** (Education; Preschool Education; Primary Education; Secondary Education; Teacher Training); **Food Industry** (Food Science; Food Technology); **Forestry** (Forestry); **Law and Political Science** (Law; Political Sciences); **Medicine** (Medicine; Surgery); **Nursing** (Nursing); **Pharmacy and Biochemistry** (Biochemistry; Pharmacy); **Zoology** (Zoology)

History: Founded 1961. Reorganized 1969.

Governing Bodies: Asamblea Universitaria; Consejo Universitario

Academic Year: April to December (April-July; August-December)

Admission Requirements: Secondary school certificate and entrance examination

Main Language(s) of Instruction: Spanish

Degrees and Diplomas: *Bachiller*: Administration; Education; *Título Profesional de Licenciado*: Agronomy (Ingeniero agrónomo); Animal Husbandry (Ingeniero Zootecnista); Chemical Engineering (Ingeniero químico); Food Technology (Ingeniero Industria alimentaria); Forestry Engineering (Ingeniero forestal); *Maestría*: 2 yrs. Also Diplomas

Student Services: Academic counselling, Foreign student adviser, Health services, Social counselling, Sports facilities

Libraries: Yes

Publications: Informe anual de los trabajos de investigación *(annually)*

Last Updated: 11/10/10

NATIONAL UNIVERSITY OF TRUJILLO

Universidad Nacional de Trujillo (UNT)

Av. Juan Pablo II S/N; Ciudad Universitaria, Trujillo, La Libertad
Tel: +51(44) 205448
Fax: +51(44) 256629
EMail: rectorado@unitru.edu.pe
Website: http://www.unitru.edu.pe

Rector: Orlando Velásquez Benites

Secretario General: Pedro Luis Lavalle Dios
Tel: +51(44) 232961, Fax: +51(44) 256629
EMail: secgral@unitru.edu.pe

Faculties

Agriculture and Stockbreeding (Agriculture; Cattle Breeding); **Biology** (Biochemistry; Biology; Fishery; Microbiology; Parasitology; Physiology); **Chemical Engineering** (Chemical Engineering; Chemistry); **Economics** (Economics); **Education and Communication** (Communication Studies; Education); **Engineering** (Engineering); **Law and Political Science** (Law; Political Sciences); **Medicine** (Medicine); **Nursing** (Nursing); **Pharmacy and Biochemistry** (Biochemistry; Pharmacy); **Physics and Mathematics** (Mathematics; Physics); **Social Sciences** (Social Sciences)

Further Information: Also Stomatology Clinic

History: Founded 1824 by decree of Simón Bolívar, opened 1831. The university was closed between 1878 and 1894. Reorganized 1969.

Academic Year: April to December (April-July; August-December)

Admission Requirements: Secondary school certificate and entrance examination

Fees: None

Main Language(s) of Instruction: Spanish

Degrees and Diplomas: *Bachiller*: Agriculture Engineering; Agronomy; Animal Husbandry; Archaeology; Anthropology; Biology; Business Administration; Chemical Engineering; Communication Sciences; Computer Engineering; Computer Sciences; Economics; Education; Communication Studies; Environmental Engineering; History; Industrial Engineering; Mechanical Engineering; Metallurgical Engineering; Materials Engineering; Electronical Engineering; Mining Engineering; Mathematics; Physics; Physics and Mathematics; Social Sciences; Social Work; Statistics; Tourism, 5 yrs; *Bachiller*: Law; *Bachiller*: Political Science, 6 yrs; *Título Profesional de Licenciado*: Accountancy (Contador público); Agricultural Engineering; Agronomy; Animal Husbandry (Ingeniero); Biology; Microbiology; Fishery (Biólogo); Computer Engineering, Industrial Engineering; Mechanical Engineering; Metallurgical Engineering; Materials Engineering; Mining Engineering; Electronic Engineering; Chemical Engineering; Environmental Engineering; Economics (Economista); Education; Preschool Education; Primary School Education; Secondary School Education; Mathematics Education; English; French; German; Litterature; Physics; Chemistry; Biology; Medicine and Surgery (Médico-Cirujano); Nursing; Philosophy; Psychology; Social Sciences; Statistics, 5 yrs; *Título Profesional de*

Licenciado: Dentistry and Stomatology; Law and Political Science (Abogado); Pharmaceutical Chemistry (Químico Farmacéutico); Pharmacy and Biochemistry, 6 yrs; *Título Profesional de Licenciado*: Medicine, 7 yrs; *Maestría*; *Doctorado*

Student Services: Employment services, Handicapped facilities, Language programs, Nursery care, Social counselling, Sports facilities

Student Residential Facilities: none

Special Facilities: Archeological Museum; Zoological Museum; Astronomic Hall Observatory

Libraries: Central Library, c. 18,000 vols; Education and Social Sciences, c. 11,000 vols; Engineering, c. 9,000 vols; Physics and Mathematics, c. 5,600 vols; Languages, c. 5,200 vols; Biology, c. 10,000 vols; Pharmacy, c. 5,800 vols; Medicine, c. 6,200 vols; Economics, c. 11,000 vols; Law and Political Science, c. 10,000; Nursing, c. 1,600 vols; Archaeology, c. 3,400 vols; Peruvian-Mexican Library, c. 2,100 vols

Publications: Revistas Universitarias, Revista de Ciencia y Tecnología; Sciendo, Ciencia para el Desarrollo; Revista Médica *(annually)*

Last Updated: 11/10/10

NATIONAL UNIVERSITY OF TUMBES

Universidad Nacional de Tumbes
Centro Cívico 3er Piso, Tumbes, Tumbes
Tel: +51(72) 523952
Fax: +51(72) 523081
EMail: rectorado@untumbes.edu.pe

Rector: Napoleón Puño Lecarnaqué
Tel: +51(72) 523081 EMail: rector@untumbes.edu.pe

Vicerrector Administrativo: Gino Antonio Moretti Otoya
Tel: +51(72) 523441, Ext. 120
EMail: vicerrector_adm@untumbes.edu.pe

Faculties

Agronomy (Agriculture; Agronomy); **Economics** (Accountancy; Administration; Business Administration; Economics); **Fishery** (Aquaculture); **Health Sciences** (Gynaecology and Obstetrics; Medicine; Nursing); **Law and Social Science**

History: Founded 1984.

Governing Bodies: Asamblea Universitaria; Consejo Universitario; Consejos de Facultad

Admission Requirements: Secondary school certificate

Main Language(s) of Instruction: Spanish

Degrees and Diplomas: *Bachiller*, *Título Profesional de Licenciado*; *Maestría*

Student Services: Academic counselling, Cultural centre, Health services, Language programs, Nursery care, Social counselling, Sports facilities

Libraries: Central and specialized libraries

Last Updated: 04/01/10

NATIONAL UNIVERSITY OF UCAYALI

Universidad Nacional de Ucayali
Apartado postal 90, Carretera Federico Basadre km 6, Pucallpa, Ucayali
Tel: +51(64) 573-779
Fax: +51(64) 592-236
EMail: rectorado@unu.edu.pe
Website: http://www.unu.edu.pe/

Rector: Edgar Juan Díaz Zuñiga EMail: ediazz@unu.edu.pe

Faculties

Agronomy (Agriculture; Agronomy); **Economics, Administration and Accountancy** (Accountancy; Administration; Economics); **Education and Social Sciences** (Education; Social Sciences); **Forestry and Environmental Studies** (Environmental Studies; Forestry); **Health Sciences** (Health Sciences; Nursing); **Law and Political Science**; **Systems and Civil Engineering** (Civil Engineering; Systems Analysis)

History: Founded 1979.

Academic Year: April to December

Admission Requirements: Secondary school certificate

Fees: None

Main Language(s) of Instruction: Spanish

Degrees and Diplomas: *Título Profesional de Licenciado*; *Maestría*

Libraries: c. 7,380 vols

Last Updated: 11/10/10

PEDRO RUÍZ GALLO NATIONAL UNIVERSITY

Universidad Nacional Pedro Ruíz Gallo
Avenida Juan XXIII 339, Chiclayo, Lambayeque
Tel: +51(74) 282081
Fax: +51(74) 282069
EMail: jmontenegrov@unprg.edu.pe
Website: http://www.unprg.edu.pe

Rector: Francis Villena Rodríguez
Tel: +51(74) 590393, Fax: +51(74) 283638
EMail: fvillena@unprg.edu.pe

Vicerrector Académico: José Faustino Montenegro Vasquez

Vicerrector Administrativo: Manuel Tafur Moran
EMail: mtafur@unprg.edu.pe

Faculties

Agricultural Engineering; **Agronomy** (Agronomy; Plant and Crop Protection; Soil Science); **Biology** (Biology; Microbiology); **Chemical Engineering and Food Industries** (Chemical Engineering; Food Technology); **Civil Engineering, Systems Engineering and Architecture** (Architecture; Civil Engineering; Engineering; Systems Analysis); **Economics, Administration and Accountancy** (Accountancy; Administration; Economics); **History, Social Sciences and Education** (Communication Studies; Education; Sociology); **Human Medicine** (Medicine); **Law and Political Science** (Law; Political Sciences); **Mechanical and Electrical Engineering**; **Nursing** (Nursing); **Physics and Mathematics**; **Veterinary Science** (Veterinary Science); **Zoology** (Zoology)

History: Founded 1960 as high school, acquired present title and status 1970, incorporating the former Universidad Nacional Agraria del Norte and the Universidad Nacional de Lambayeque. Reorganized 1972.

Academic Year: July to January (July-November; February-June; September-January)

Admission Requirements: Secondary school certificate and entrance examination

Fees: None

Main Language(s) of Instruction: Spanish

Degrees and Diplomas: *Bachiller*: Biology; *Título Profesional de Licenciado*: Accountancy (Contador Público); Agricultural Engineering (Ingeniero agrícola); Agricultural Engineering (Ingeniero agrónomo); Animal Husbandry (Ingeniero Zootecnista); Biology (Biólogo); Civil Engineering (Ingeniero civil); Law (Abogado); Nursing (Enfermera); Sociology (Sociólogo); Veterinary Medicine (Médico Veterinario), 5 yrs; *Maestría*; *Doctorado*: Educational Sciences; Health Sciences; Higher Education; Law

Libraries: c. 16,000 vols

Last Updated: 13/10/10

SAN ANTONIO ABAD DEL CUSCO NATIONAL UNIVERSITY

Universidad Nacional de San Antonio Abad del Cusco (UNSAAC)
Apartado Postal N° 921, Avenida de la Cultura No 733, Cusco
Tel: +51(84) 232398
Fax: +51(84) 222271
EMail: rectorado@unsaac.edu.pe
Website: http://www.unsaac.edu.pe

Rector: Víctor Raúl Aguilar Callo

Vicer Rector Administrativo: René Concha Lezama

Vice Rector Académico: Lauro Enciso Rodas
EMail: vrac@unsaac.edu.pe

Faculties

Accountancy and Finance (Accountancy; Finance); **Administration and Tourism** (Administration; Tourism); **Agrarian and**

Tropical Sciences *(Quillabamba)* (Agronomy; Tropical Agriculture); **Agro-ecological Engineering and Rural Development** *(Vilcabamba - Grau)* (Agriculture; Ecology; Rural Planning); **Agro-Industrial Engineering** *(Sicuani)* (Agricultural Engineering; Industrial Engineering); **Agronomy and Zoology** (Agronomy; Animal Husbandry; Zoology); **Architecture and Plastic Arts** (Architecture; Painting and Drawing; Sculpture); **Biological Sciences** (Biological and Life Sciences); **Chemical and Metallurgical Engineering** (Chemical Engineering; Metallurgical Engineering); **Chemistry, Physics and Mathematics** (Chemistry; Mathematics; Physical Therapy); **Civil Engineering** (Civil Engineering); **Economics** (Economics); **Education** *(Canas, Espinar)* (Education); **Electrical, Mechanical and Mining Engineering** (Electrical Engineering; Mechanical Engineering; Mining Engineering); **Forestry and Environmental Studies** *(Pto Maldonado)* (Environmental Studies; Forestry); **Geological Engineering and Geography** (Geography; Geological Engineering); **Human Medicine** (Medicine); **Law and Political Science** (Law; Political Sciences); **Nursing** (Nursing); **Social Communication and Languages** (Communication Studies; Modern Languages); **Social Sciences** (Anthropology; Archaeology; History; Social Sciences)

Schools

Postgraduate Studies (Administration; Civil Engineering; Economics; Education; Law; Rural Planning)

History: Founded 1692. Acquired present status 1983.

Governing Bodies: Asamblea Universitaria

Main Language(s) of Instruction: Spanish

Degrees and Diplomas: *Título Profesional de Licenciado*; *Maestría*; *Doctorado*

Last Updated: 11/10/10

SAN CRISTÓBAL OF HUAMANGA NATIONAL UNIVERSITY

Universidad Nacional San Cristóbal de Huamanga

Portal Independencia N°57, Ayacucho
Tel: +51(66) 312230
Fax: +51(66) 812510
EMail: rector@unsch.edu.pe
Website: http://www.unsch.edu.pe

Rector: Víctor Humberto Alegría Valeriano

Vicerrector Administrativo: José A. Cancio Alvárez

Vicerrector Académico: Marcial Molina Ritcher

Faculties

Agriculture (Agriculture; Rural Planning; Veterinary Science); **Biology** (Biochemistry; Biology; Pharmacy); **Chemical and Metallurgical Engineering** (Chemical Engineering; Engineering; Metallurgical Engineering); **Economics, Administration and Accountancy** (Accountancy; Business Administration; Economics); **Education** (Education; Physical Education; Primary Education; Secondary Education); **Law and Political Science** (Law; Political Sciences); **Mining, Geological and Civil Engineering** (Civil Engineering; Computer Engineering; Geological Engineering; Mathematics; Mining Engineering; Physics); **Nursing** (Nursing); **Obstetrics** (Gynaecology and Obstetrics); **Social Sciences** (Anthropology; Archaeology; Communication Studies; History; Social and Community Services; Social Sciences)

History: Founded 1677. Closed in 1886 and reopened 1957. Reorganized 1969 and faculties replaced by academic programmes. Financed by the government and under the jurisdiction of the Ministry of Education.

Governing Bodies: Consejo Universitario; Consejos de Programas; Consejo de Administración Económica; Consejo de Instituto

Academic Year: April to December (April-July; August-December)

Admission Requirements: Secondary school certificate and entrance examination

Main Language(s) of Instruction: Spanish

Degrees and Diplomas: *Bachiller*: Anthropology; Biology; Chemistry; Education; Social Service; *Título Profesional de Licenciado*: Agriculture; Law; Midwifery; Mining; Teaching qualifications, primary level; Teaching qualifications, secondary level; *Maestría*; *Doctorado*: Anthropology; Biology; Education; Midwifery; Social Service

Student Residential Facilities: Yes

Special Facilities: Natural History Museum; Archaeology and Petrology Museum

Libraries: c. 12,000 vols

Publications: Universidad y Wamaní

Last Updated: 13/10/10

SAN LUIS GONZAGA NATIONAL UNIVERSITY OF ICA

Universidad Nacional San Luis Gonzaga de Ica

Prolongación Ayabaca C.9 Urb. San José, Ica
Tel: +51(56) 226039-233971
Fax: +51(56) 235991
EMail: unica@correo.dnet.com.pe
Website: http://www.unica.edu.pe/

Rector: Alejandro Encinas Fernández (2012-)
EMail: rector_unica@hotmail.com

Vicerrector Administrativo: Francisco Chaparro Zapana

Vicerrector Académico: Rulman Franco Linares

Faculties

Agronomy (Agriculture; Agronomy); **Business Administration** (Administration; Business Administration); **Chemical Engineering** (Chemical Engineering); **Civil Engineering** (Civil Engineering); **Communication, Tourism and Archaeology** (Archaeology; Communication Studies; Tourism); **Dentistry** (Dentistry); **Economics and Accountancy** (Accountancy; Economics); **Fisheries and Food** (Fishery; Food Science); **Humanities and Education** (Arts and Humanities; Education); **Law and Political Science** (Law; Political Sciences); **Mechanical, Electrical and Electronic Engineering** (Electrical Engineering; Electronic Engineering; Mechanical Engineering); **Medicine** (Medicine); **Mining and Metallurgy Engineering** (Metallurgical Engineering; Mining Engineering); **Nursing** (Nursing); **Pharmacy and Biochemistry** (Biochemistry; Pharmacy); **Science** (Biology; Mathematics and Computer Science; Natural Sciences; Physics); **Veterinary Medicine and Animal Husbandry** (Animal Husbandry; Veterinary Science)

History: Founded 1955, became university 1961. An autonomous institution.

Academic Year: April to December (April-July; August-December)

Main Language(s) of Instruction: Spanish

Degrees and Diplomas: *Bachiller*; *Maestría*; *Doctorado*

Last Updated: 10/09/12

SANTIAGO ANTÚNEZ DE MAYOLO NATIONAL UNIVERSITY

Universidad Nacional Santiago Antúnez de Mayolo (UNASAM)

Avenida Centenario N°200, Huaraz, Ancash
Tel: +51(43) 721452
Fax: +51(43) 721393
EMail: sec_gral@unasam.edu.pe
Website: http://www.unasam.edu.pe

Rector: Dante Sánchez Rodríguez (2012-)

Vicerrector Administrativo: César Augusto Narro Cachay

Vicerrector Académico: Roosevelt Villalobos Díaz

Faculties

Administration and Tourism (Administration; Tourism); **Agriculture** (Agricultural Engineering); **Civil Engineering** (Civil Engineering); **Economics and Accountancy** (Accountancy; Administration; Economics); **Education and Communication** (Communication Studies; Education); **Environmental Studies** (Environmental Engineering; Environmental Studies); **Food Industries** (Food Science); **Law and Political Science** (Law; Political Sciences); **Medicine** (Medicine); **Mining** (Geology; Metallurgical Engineering; Mining Engineering)

Schools

Postgraduate Studies *Director*: Fernando Castillo Picón

History: Founded 1977.

Governing Bodies: Asamblea Universitaria; Consejo

Main Language(s) of Instruction: Spanish
Degrees and Diplomas: *Bachiller*, *Maestría*
Last Updated: 13/10/10

TORIBIO RODRIGUEZ DE MENDOZA NATIONAL UNIVERSITY OF THE AMAZONAS

Universidad Nacional Toribio Rodriguez de Mendoza de Amazonas

Ciudad Universitaria: El Franco - Barrio de Higos Urco., Chachapoyas, Amazonas
Tel: +51(41) 477955
EMail: informes@unatamazonas.edu.pe
Website: http://www.unatamazonas.edu.pe/

Rector: Vicente Marino Castañeda Chávez
EMail: vcastaneda@unatamazonas.edu.pe

Vicerrector Académico: Miguel Ángel Barrena Gurbillón
EMail: mbarrena@unatamazonas.edu.pe

Vicerrectora Administrativa: Flor Teresa García Huamán
EMail: fgarcia@unatamazonas.edu.pe

Faculties

Agro-industrial Engineering (Agricultural Engineering; Industrial Engineering); **Nursing** (Nursing); **Primary Education** (Primary Education; Teacher Training); **Tourism and Administration** (Administration; Tourism)

Institutes

Archaeology and Anthropology *(Kuelap)* (Anthropology; Archaeology)

Research Institutes

Sustainable Development (Development Studies)

History: Founded 2000.

Main Language(s) of Instruction: Spanish

Degrees and Diplomas: *Bachiller*
Last Updated: 13/10/10

PRIVATE INSTITUTIONS

ADA A. BYRON PRIVATE UNIVERSITY

Universidad Privada Ada A. Byron

Av. Abelardo Alva Maúrtua N° 499, Chincha, Ica
Tel: +51(56) 262-439
Website: http://upab.edu.pe

Presidente: Fortunato Basílides Sánchez Ramirez

Programmes

Administration and Finance (Administration; Finance); **Food Industry** (Food Technology); **Nursing** (Nursing); **Psychology** (Psychology); **Systems Engineering** (Systems Analysis)

History: Founded 2005.

Main Language(s) of Instruction: Spanish

Degrees and Diplomas: *Bachiller*, *Título Profesional de Licenciado*
Last Updated: 21/10/10

ALAS PERUANAS UNIVERSITY

Universidad Alas Peruanas

Av. San Felipe N°1109 - Jesús María, Lima, Lima
Tel: +51(1) 2660195
Fax: +51(1) 4709838
EMail: c_hinojosa@uap.edu.pe
Website: http://www.uap.edu.pe

Rector: Fidel Ramírez Prado EMail: f_ramirez@uap.edu.pe

Faculties

Agricultural Science (Veterinary Science); **Business Sciences** (Accountancy; Administration; Economics; Finance; Hotel and Restaurant; Hotel Management; International Business; Management; Tourism); **Communication Sciences** (Communication Studies); **Education and Humanities** (Education; English); **Engineering and Architecture** (Aeronautical and Aerospace Engineering; Architecture; Civil Engineering; Electrical Engineering; Engineering; Environmental Engineering; Geological Engineering; Marine Engineering; Mechanical Engineering; Natural Resources; Naval Architecture; Telecommunications Engineering); **Health Sciences** (Biochemistry; Gerontology; Gynaecology and Obstetrics; Medical Technology; Nursing; Nutrition; Pharmacy; Psychology; Sports; Sports Medicine; Stomatology); **Law and Political Science** (Law; Political Sciences)

Further Information: Branches in Piura, Arequipa, Ayacucho , Cajamarca, Chiclayo, Huancayo, Ica, Juliaca, Moyobamba, Pucallpa, Trujillo and Tumbes

History: Founded 1996.

Main Language(s) of Instruction: Spanish

Degrees and Diplomas: *Bachiller*, *Maestría*; *Doctorado*
Last Updated: 21/09/10

ANDEAN UNIVERSITY OF CUSCO

Universidad Andina del Cusco

Urb. Ingeniería Larapa Grande A-5 San Jerónimo, Cusco
Tel: +51(84) 273390
Fax: +51(84) 271438
EMail: webmaster@uandina.edu.pe
Website: http://www.uandina.edu.pe

Rector: Gloria Charca Puente de la Vega (2001-)
Tel: +51(84) 273885

Faculties

Administration, Economics and Accountancy (Accountancy; Administration; Economics); **Engineering** (Chemistry; Civil Engineering; Engineering; Industrial Engineering; Mathematics; Physics; Systems Analysis); **Health Sciences** (Midwifery; Nursing; Paediatrics; Psychology; Stomatology); **Law and Political Science** (Law; Political Sciences); **Social Sciences and Education** (Education; Tourism)

History: Founded 1979.

Main Language(s) of Instruction: Spanish

Degrees and Diplomas: *Bachiller*, *Título Profesional de Licenciado*
Last Updated: 21/09/10

ANTENOR ORREGO PRIVATE UNIVERSITY

Universidad Privada Antenor Orrego (UPAO)

Av. América Del Sur N°3145, Urb. Monserrate, Trujillo, La Libertad
Tel: +51(44) 604444
Fax: +51(44) 282900
Website: http://www.upao.edu.pe

Rector: Vìctor Raúl Lozano Ibáñez
Tel: +51(44) 604469 EMail: rector@upao.edu.pe

Vicerrector académico: Guillermo Guerra Cruz
Tel: +51(44) 604477

Faculties

Agriculture (Agricultural Engineering; Food Science; Veterinary Science); **Architecture, Town Planning and Arts** (Architecture); **Communication Sciences** (Communication Studies); **Economics** (Accountancy; Administration; Economics; Finance); **Education and Humanities** (Arts and Humanities; Primary Education); **Engineering** (Civil Engineering; Computer Engineering; Computer Networks; Electronic Engineering; Software Engineering; Telecommunications Engineering); **Health Sciences** (Gynaecology and Obstetrics; Nursing); **Law and Political Science** (Law; Political Sciences); **Medicine** (Medicine; Psychology; Stomatology)

History: Founded 1988.

Governing Bodies: University Assembly; University Council

Admission Requirements: Secondary school certificate

Fees: (Nuevo Soles): 180 per semester for all courses. Monthly: 1,000 for Medicine; 650 for Stomatology; 400 for Psychology and Veterinary Medicine; 200 for Education and 330 for other courses

Main Language(s) of Instruction: Spanish

International Co-operation: With universities in the USA; Denmark; Spain; Germany; Brazil; Argentina

Degrees and Diplomas: *Bachiller*: Administration, Economics, Accountancy; *Bachiller*: Agronomy (Bach. Ing.) (Ingeniero Agrónomo); Architecture (Bach.) (Arquitecto); Civil Engineering;

Electronical Engineering (Bach. Ing. Civil) (Ingeniero Civil); Communication Sciences (Contador Público); Computer and Systems Engineering (Bach.) (Ingeniero de Computación y Sistemas); Economics (Economista); Education; Food Technology (Bach. Ing.) (Ingeniero); Nursing (Bach. Lic.) (Licenciada en Enfermeria); Obstetrics (Bach. Obst.) (Obstetriz/ Obstetra), 5 yrs; *Bachiller*: Law (Bach. Abog.) (Abogado), 6 yrs; *Bachiller*: Medicine (Bach. Med.) (Médico Cirujano), 7 yrs; *Maestría*: Agronomy; Architecture; Business Administration; Communication Sciences; Education; Law; Medicine; Obstetrics; Systems Engineering, 2 yrs; *Maestría*: Environmental Management; *Doctorado*: Education, 2 yrs; *Doctorado*: Law; Constitutional Law; Private Law; Public Law; History of Law. Also Diplomado in Law; Administration (4 months)

Student Services: Canteen, Employment services, Health services, Language programs, Nursery care, Sports facilities

Special Facilities: Museum; Movie Studio

Libraries: A central library and 10 small libraries according to each speciality

Publications: Amauta, Scientific Magazine *(annually)*; Arnaldoa, Scientific Magazine *(biannually)*; Arq'am, Scientific Magazine *(biannually)*; Campus, Scientific Magazine *(biennially)*; Esculapio, Scientific Magazine *(biennially)*; Hampi Runa, Scientific Magazine *(biennially)*; Negocios, Informative Bulletin *(monthly)*; Pueblo Continente (Official Magazine), Scientific Magazine *(biennially)*; Scientia et Humanitas, Informative Bulletin *(monthly)*

Last Updated: 21/10/10

ANTONIO GUILLERMO URRELO PRIVATE UNIVERSITY

Universidad Privada Antonio Guillermo Urrelo (UPAGU)

Jr. José Sabogal 913 / Jr. Primavera 140, Cajamarca, Cajamarca

Tel: +51(76) 366991

Fax: +51(76) 366991

EMail: Vicerrectorado@upagu.edu.pe

Website: http://www.upagu.edu.pe

Rector: Wilman Ruiz Vigo (2006-) EMail: rectorado@upagu.edu.pe

Vicerrector académico: Homero Bazán Zurta

Tel: +51(76) 342554 EMail: vicerrectorado@upagu.edu.pe

Gerente General: Carmen Rosa Díaz Camacho

Tel: +51(76) 365819-123

Faculties

Administration (Accountancy; Business Administration; Finance; International Business); **Engineering** (Computer Engineering; Systems Analysis); **Health Sciences** (Biochemistry; Pharmacy); **Law and Political Science** (Law; Political Sciences); **Nursing** (Nursing); **Psychology** (Psychology); **Tourism, Hotel Management and Gastronomy** (Cooking and Catering; Hotel Management; Tourism)

History: Founded 1999.

Academic Year: April to December

Admission Requirements: Secondary school certificate and admission test

Fees: (Nuevos Soles): 1,350 per semester

Main Language(s) of Instruction: Spanish

Degrees and Diplomas: *Bachiller*: 5 yrs; *Título Profesional de Licenciado*

Student Services: Academic counselling, Employment services, Foreign Studies Centre, Handicapped facilities, Health services, Language programs, Social counselling, Sports facilities

Libraries: Central library, c. 6,000 publications

Last Updated: 21/10/10

ANTONIO RUIZ DE MONTOYA UNIVERSITY

Universidad Antonio Ruiz de Montoya

Av. Paso de los Andes 970, Pueblo Libre, Lima, 21 Lima

Tel: +51(1) 423-5697

Fax: +51(1) 423-1126

EMail: informes@uarm.edu.pe

Website: http://www.uarm.edu.pe

Presidente: Vicente Santuc Laborde EMail: vsantuc@uarm.edu.pe

Programmes

Education (Education); **Humanities** (Arts and Humanities); **Journalism** (Journalism); **Philosophy** (Philosophy); **Political Science** (Political Sciences); **Tourism** (Tourism)

History: Founded 2003.

Main Language(s) of Instruction: Spanish

Degrees and Diplomas: *Bachiller*. Also especialización

Last Updated: 21/09/10

ARCHBISHOP LOAYZA PRIVATE UNIVERSITY

Universidad Privada Arzobispo Loayza

Av. Arequipa N° 979 Santa Beatriz, Lima

Tel: +51(1) 330-9090

EMail: informes@ual.edu.pe

Website: http://www.ual.edu.pe

Presidente: Alberto Silva del Águila

Vice Presidente Académico: Augusto Aquilino Díaz Sánchez

Faculties

Computer Engineering (Computer Engineering; Systems Analysis); **Nursing** (Nursing); **Obstetrics** (Gynaecology and Obstetrics)

History: Founded 2009.

Degrees and Diplomas: *Título Profesional de Licenciado*

Last Updated: 11/10/10

AUTONOMOUS UNIVERSITY OF PERU

Universidad Autónoma del Perú

Panamerica Sur km 16.3, Lima

EMail: informes@autonoma.edu.pe

Website: http://www.autonoma.pe/2010

Presidente: Cesar Acuña Peralta

Programmes

Accountancy (Accountancy); **Administration** (Administration); **Law** (Law); **Psychology** (Psychology); **Systems Engineering** (Systems Analysis)

History: Founded 2007.

Main Language(s) of Instruction: Spanish

Degrees and Diplomas: *Bachiller*

Last Updated: 25/10/10

CATHOLIC UNIVERSITY OF TRUJILLO

Universidad Católica de Trujillo

Aguamarina S/N Mz.K Lt.13, Urbanización Los Cedros, Trujillo, La Libertad

Tel: +51(44) 204421

Fax: +51(44) 204159

EMail: presidencia@uct.edu.pe; admision@uct.edu.pe

Website: http://www.uct.edu.pe

Presidente: Letelier Mass Villanueva

EMail: presidencia@uct.edu.pe

Faculties

Administration and Finance (Accountancy; Administration; Finance; Hotel Management; Tourism); **Engineering** (Industrial Engineering); **Humanities** (Communication Studies; Law; Preschool Education; Primary Education; Psychology); **Theology** (Theology)

History: Founded 2000.

Main Language(s) of Instruction: Spanish

Degrees and Diplomas: *Bachiller*, *Título Profesional de Licenciado*

Last Updated: 22/09/10

CAYETANO HEREDIA PERUVIAN UNIVERSITY

Universidad Peruana Cayetano Heredia (UPCH)

Avenida Honorio Delgado N°932, Urb. Ingeniería, San Martín de Porres, 31 Lima

Tel: +51(1) 319-0000 +51(1) 482-1130

Fax: +51(1) 482-3435

EMail: rector@upch.edu.pe

Website: http://www.upch.edu.pe

Rectora: Fabiola León Velarde Tel: +51(1) 482-4045

Centres

Ecology *(CCEA)*; **Environmental Studies** (Environmental Studies)

Faculties

Education (Education); **Medicine** *(Alberto Hurtado)* (Medical Technology; Medicine); **Nursing** (Nursing); **Psychology** *(Leopoldo Chiappo Galli)* (Psychology); **Public Health and Administration** *(Carlos Vidal Layseca)* (Administration; Public Health); **Science and Philosophy** *(Alberto Cazorla Talleri)* (Arts and Humanities; Biochemistry; Biology; Chemistry; Environmental Studies; Mathematics and Computer Science; Microbiology; Molecular Biology; Mountain Studies; Natural Sciences; Philosophy; Physics; Physiology); **Stomatology** (Stomatology); **Veterinary Science and Zoology** (Veterinary Science; Zoology)

Schools

Postgraduate *(Victor Alzamora Castro)*

History: Founded 1961 by the faculty members of the National University of San Marcos Medical School. An autonomous private institution.

Governing Bodies: Asamblea Universitaria; Consejo Universitario

Academic Year: April to December (April-July; August-December)

Admission Requirements: Secondary school certificate and entrance examination

Fees: (Nuevos Soles): c. 2,600 per month

Main Language(s) of Instruction: Spanish

International Co-operation: With universities in Spain, France, USA and Latin American countries. Also participates in different programmes with :Programa de Movilidad Estudiantil-Uniòn de Universidades de América Latina (PAME-UDUAL), Centro Interuniversitario de Desarrollo (CINDA), Organisatión Universitaria Interamericana (OUI), Consorcio de Universidades (Péru)

Accrediting Agencies: Instituto Internacional para el Aseguramiento de la Calidad-Centro Interuniversitario de Desarrollo (IAC-CINDA); Consejo Nacional de Acreditación de la República de Colombia (CAN-Colombia)

Degrees and Diplomas: *Bachiller*: Administration; Biology; Chemistry; Computer Engineering; Dentistry and Stomatology; Medical Technology; Nursing; Pharmacy and Biochemistry; Psychology; Sports; Physical Education; Veterinary Science, 5 yrs; *Bachiller*: Education, 2 yrs (Programa de Complenentacíon; requiere estudios superiores previos y convalidación); *Bachiller*: Medicine, 7 yrs; *Título Profesional de Licenciado*: Computer Engineering; Dentistry and Stomatology; Heath Administration; Laboratory Technics; Radiology; Rehabilitation and Physical Therapy; Speech Therapy and Audiology; Occupational Therapy; Mathematics; Medical Technology; Medicine; Nursing; Pharmacy and Biochemistry (Químico Farmacéutico); Sports and Physical Education; Veterinary Science, 5 yrs; *Título Profesional de Licenciado*: Education, 1 further year after Bachillerato; *Título Profesional de Licenciado*: Statistics, 6 yrs; *Título Profesional de Licenciado*: Surgery (Médico-Cirujano), 7 yrs (simultáneos con los estudios del Bachillerato); *Maestría*: Clinical Psychology; Educational Psychology; Toxicology; Computer Engineering; Demography and Population Studies; Dentistry and Stomatology; Education; Higher Education; Literacy Education; Natural Science Education; Environmental and Developpment Studies; Environmental Sciences; Gender Studies; Governement and Social and Community Services; Health Sciences; Health Administration; Medicine; Epidemiology; Gerontology; Biochemistry and Molecular Biology; Physiology; Immunology; Microbiology; Tropical Medicine; Nursing; Psychiatry and Mental Health; Public Health; Social Welfare; Statistical; Veterinary Science, 2 yrs following Bachiller; *Doctorado*: Biochemistry and Molecular Biology; Medicine; Physiology; Public Health, 2 yrs following Maéstria; *Doctorado*: Stomatology, 2 yrs after Maestría

Student Services: Academic counselling, Canteen, Cultural centre, Health services, Language programs, Social counselling, Sports facilities

Student Residential Facilities: Yes

Special Facilities: Videoconference

Libraries: Central Library: 16,137 vols.; Theses 7,242; Monographs 1,128; Peruvian Literature 18,900 vols; CD-ROM 589; Videos 1,761; Journal database 251,663; E-book database 29,608. Psychology Library: 650 vols and 316 thesis; Nursing Library: 840 vols; Tropical Medicine Library 1,500 vols

Publications: Acta Herediana, Cultural Magazine *(biennially)*; Hontanar, Scientific Magazine of the Faculty of Sciences and Philosophy *(biennially)*; Revista Estomatológica Herediana, Scientific Magazine of the Faculty of Stomatology *(biennially)*; Revista Médica Herediana, Scientific Magazine of the Faculty of Medicine *(quarterly)*; Revista Psicológica Herediana, Scientific Magazine of the Faculty of Psychology *(biennially)*

Last Updated: 15/10/10

CÉSAR VALLEJO PRIVATE UNIVERSITY

Universidad Privada César Vallejo

Avenida Larco cdra. 17, Trujillo, La Libertad
Tel: +51(44) 485020
Fax: +51(44) 485019
EMail: trujillo@ucv.edu.pe
Website: http://www.ucv.edu.pe

Rector: César Acuña Peralta EMail: infor@ucv.edu.pe

Faculties

Architecture (Architecture); **Business Studies** (Administration); **Communication** (Communication Studies; Journalism); **Education and Languages** (Modern Languages; Primary Education; Translation and Interpretation); **Engineering** (Agricultural Engineering; Civil Engineering; Industrial Engineering; Mechanical Engineering; Systems Analysis); **Humanities** (Psychology); **Law** (Law); **Medicine** (Gynaecology and Obstetrics; Medicine; Nursing; Nutrition)

Further Information: Also branches in Lima,Tarapoto, Chiclayo, Piura and Chimbote

History: Founded 1991.

Academic Year: April to December

Admission Requirements: Secondary school certificate

Main Language(s) of Instruction: Spanish

International Co-operation: With universities in Spain; China; Mexico; Chile; USA; Colombia; Brazil

Degrees and Diplomas: *Bachiller*: 5 yrs; *Título Profesional de Licenciado*: 5 yrs; *Maestría*: 2 yrs; *Doctorado*: Economics and Social Studies

Student Services: Academic counselling, Cultural centre, Handicapped facilities, Language programs, Nursery care, Social counselling, Sports facilities

Last Updated: 21/10/10

CONTINENTAL UNIVERSITY OF SCIENCE AND ENGINEERING

Universidad Continental de Ciencias e Ingeniería (UCCI)

Calle Real 125, Huancayo, Junín
Tel: +51(64) 212738
Fax: +51(64) 221929
Website: http://www.continental.edu.pe/

Rector: Esaú Caro Meza

Areas

Administration and Marketing (Accountancy; Administration; Economics; Marketing); **Computing and Information Technology** (Computer Science; Information Technology); **Engineering and Architecture** (Agricultural Engineering; Architecture; Civil Engineering; Electrical Engineering; Environmental Engineering; Industrial Engineering; Mining Engineering)

Programmes

Education (Education); **Law** (Law)

Further Information: Also branch in Lima

History: Founded 1998.

Main Language(s) of Instruction: Spanish

Degrees and Diplomas: *Bachiller*, *Título Profesional de Licenciado*; *Maestría*. Also Diplomados

Last Updated: 22/09/10

ESAN UNIVERSITY

Universidad ESAN

Alonso de Molina 1652, Monterrico, Surco, Lima, Lima
Tel: +51(1) 317-7200
Fax: +51(1) 345-1328
Website: http://www.esan.edu.pe

Rector: Jorge Talavera Traverso
Tel: +51(1) 345-1331, Fax: +51(1) 345-1325

Vicerrector: Jaime Serida Nishimura

Graduate Schools

Business Administration (Business Administration)

History: Founded 1963 as Escuela de Administración de Negocios para Graduados. Acquired present status and title 2003.

Governing Bodies: General Assembly, University Council

Main Language(s) of Instruction: Spanish, English

International Co-operation: With universities in USA, Spain, France and Germany

Accrediting Agencies: AMBAs, Member of AACSB, EFMD

Degrees and Diplomas: *Maestría (MSc)*. ESAN offers a Ph. D. in Management Sciences, in Business Administration and Management in partnership with ESADE

Special Facilities: Art Gallery

Libraries: c. 50,000 vols of books, printed documents and other bibliographic material; 15,000 periodicals (printed and digital), c. 70,000 articles in Spanish and Portuguese published in over 200 Iberoamerican periodicals. Specialised bibiographic data bases in business and economics: online, on CD-ROM. An online catalogue is avalaible via Internet and Intranet :http://cendoc.esan.edu.pe

Last Updated: 07/10/10

FACULTY OF PONTIFICAL AND CIVIL THEOLOGY OF LIMA

Facultad de Teología Pontificia y Civil de Lima

Jr Carlos Bondy 700, Pueblo Libre, Lima, Lima
Tel: +51(1) 4610013
Fax: +51(1) 4610245
Website: http://www.ftpcl.edu.pe

Rector: Pedro Rufino Hidalgo Díaz

Higher Institutes

Ecclesiastic Studies (Canon Law; Christian Religious Studies; Holy Writings; Logic; New Testament; Pastoral Studies; Philosophy; Religious Studies; Theology)

Programmes

Education (Catholic Theology; Christian Religious Studies; Curriculum; Education; Educational Administration; Educational Psychology; Ethics; History of Religion; Holy Writings; Human Rights; Mathematics; Pedagogy; Philosophy; Teacher Training); **Philosophy** (Philosophy); **Theology** (Canon Law; Hebrew; Holy Writings; Pastoral Studies; Theology)

History: Founded 1551. Acquired present status 1994.

Main Language(s) of Instruction: Spanish

Degrees and Diplomas: *Bachiller*, *Título Profesional de Licenciado*; *Maestría*

Libraries: 16,000 vols

Last Updated: 21/09/10

FRANKLIN ROOSEVELT PRIVATE UNIVERSITY OF HUANCAYO

Universidad Privada de Huancayo Franklin Roosevelt

Av. Giráldez N° 542, Huancayo
Tel: +51(64) 219-604
Website: http://www.ufr.edu.pe

Presidente: Víctor Raúl Orhuela Paredes

Programmes

Nursing (Nursing); **Obstetrics** (Gynaecology and Obstetrics); **Pharmacy and Biochemistry** (Biochemistry; Pharmacy)

History: Founded 2009.

Main Language(s) of Instruction: Spanish

Degrees and Diplomas: *Título Profesional de Licenciado*

Last Updated: 25/10/10

INCA GARCILASO DE LA VEGA UNIVERSITY

Universidad Inca Garcilaso de la Vega

Av. Bolival N°165 - Pueblo Libre, Lima, Lima
Tel: +51(1) 4632626
Fax: +51(1) 4635260
EMail: secretariageneral@uigv.edu.pe
Website: http://www.uigv.edu.pe

Rector: Luis Cervantes Liñan (2004-)
EMail: rectorado@uigv.edu.pe

Vicerrector: Jorge Lazo Manrique
Tel: +51(1) 4714142 EMail: vrac@uigv.edu.pe

Faculties

Accountancy (Accountancy; Business Administration; Economics); **Administration and Economics** (Administration; Economics); **Communication Studies and Tourism** (Communication Studies; Hotel Management; Tourism); **Education** (Education); **Foreign Trade and International Marketing** (International Business; Marketing); **Industrial Engineering** (Industrial Engineering); **Law and Political Science** (Law; Political Sciences); **Nursing** (Nursing); **Pharmacy and Biochemistry** (Biochemistry; Pharmacy); **Psychology and Social Sciences** (Psychology; Social Sciences; Social Work; Sociology); **Stomatology** (Stomatology); **Systems Engineering, Computer Science and Telecommunications** (Computer Engineering; Engineering; Systems Analysis; Telecommunications Engineering)

Schools

Postgraduate

History: Founded 1964. Reorganized 1969.

Governing Bodies: Asamblea Universitaria; Consejo Universitario

Main Language(s) of Instruction: Spanish

Degrees and Diplomas: *Bachiller*, *Maestría*; *Doctorado*: Accountancy; Administration; Economics; Education; Environmental Management; Law; Mass Communication; Psychology; Public Health; Sociology

Last Updated: 07/10/10

JOSÉ CARLOS MARIATEGUI UNIVERSITY

Universidad José Carlos Mariategui

Calle Ayacucho 393, Moquegua, Moquegua
Tel: +51(54) 461110
EMail: educa@ujcm.edu.pe
Website: http://www.ujcm.edu.pe

Rector: Ayar Chaparro Guerra EMail: achaparro@ujcm.edu.pe

Vicerrector: Edgar Bedoya Justo EMail: ebedoya@ujcm.edu.pe

Secretario General: Oscar Paredes Vargas
EMail: oparedes@ujcm.edu.pe

Faculties

Engineering (Agricultural Engineering; Civil Engineering; Engineering; Environmental Engineering; Industrial Engineering; Mechanical Engineering); **Health Sciences** (Dentistry; Gynaecology and Obstetrics; Nursing); **Law, Business Studies and Education** (Accountancy; Business and Commerce; Education; Law; Primary Education; Secondary Education)

History: Founded 1989 as Universidad de Moquegua. Acquired present status and title 2002.

Main Language(s) of Instruction: Spanish

Degrees and Diplomas: *Título Profesional de Licenciado*; *Maestría*; *Doctorado*

Last Updated: 07/10/10

JUAN MEJÍA BACA PRIVATE UNIVERSITY

Universidad Privada Juan Mejía Baca

Av. Quiñonez N° 640, Urb. San Martín, Chiclayo
Tel: +51(74) 22-5763
Website: http://www.umb.edu.pe

Presidente: Pedro Gaspar Casanova Chirinos

Programmes
Commercial Engineering (Banking; Finance; International Business); **Computer Engineering** (Computer Engineering); **Education** (Education); **Hotel Management and Ecotourism** (Hotel Management; Tourism); **Psychology** (Psychology)

History: Founded 2008.

Main Language(s) of Instruction: Spanish

Degrees and Diplomas: *Bachiller*; *Título Profesional de Licenciado*
Last Updated: 11/10/10

LE CORDON BLEU UNIVERSITY

Universidad Le Cordon Bleu
Av. Vasco Nuñez de Balboa 530 - Miraflores, Lima
Tel: +51(1) 617-8310
EMail: informes@ulcb.edu.pe
Website: http://www.ulcb.edu.pe

Rector: Sixtilio Dalmau Castañón

Programmes
Food Industry Engineering (Food Technology); **Gastronomy and Culinary Arts** (Cooking and Catering); **Nutrition, Health and Food Techniques** (Food Technology; Health Administration; Nutrition); **Tourism and Hotel Management** (Hotel Management; Management; Tourism)

History: Founded 2009.

Main Language(s) of Instruction: Spanish

Degrees and Diplomas: *Bachiller*
Last Updated: 22/10/10

LOS ANGELES CATHOLIC UNIVERSITY OF CHIMBOTE

Universidad Católica Los Angeles de Chimbote
Av. Bolognesi N° 835, Chimbote, Ancash
Tel: +51(43) 343-444
EMail: rectorado@uladech.edu.pe
Website: http://www.uladech.edu.pe

Rector: Julio Domínguez Granda
EMail: jdominguez@uladech.edu.pe

Faculties
Accountancy, Finance and Administration (Accountancy; Administration; Finance; Tourism); **Education and Humanities** (Computer Education; Education; Humanities and Social Science Education; Preschool Education; Primary Education; Science Education); **Engineering** (Civil Engineering; Engineering; Systems Analysis); **Health Sciences** (Biochemistry; Dentistry; Gynaecology and Obstetrics; Nursing; Pharmacology; Psychology); **Law and Political Science** (Law; Political Sciences)

History: Founded 1985.

Academic Year: February to December

Admission Requirements: Secondary school certificate

Main Language(s) of Instruction: Spanish

Degrees and Diplomas: *Bachiller*; *Título Profesional de Licenciado*; *Maestría*
Last Updated: 22/09/10

MARCELINO CHAMPAGNAT UNIVERSITY

Universidad Marcelino Champagnat
Av. Mariscal Castilla N°1270, Santiago de Surco, Lima, 33 Lima
Tel: +51(1) 4490449
EMail: informes@umch.edu.pe
Website: http://www.umch.edu.pe/

Rector: Antonio Castagnetti Morini (1995-)
EMail: rector@umch.edu.pe

Vicerrector: Pablo González Franco
EMail: vicerector@umch.edu.pe

Faculties
Education (Education; Educational Psychology; Natural Sciences; Religious Studies; Teacher Training)

History: Founded 1990.

Governing Bodies: Asamblea Universitaria. Consejo Universitario.

Academic Year: March to December (March-July; August-December)

Admission Requirements: Secondary school certificate

Fees: (US Dollars): 1,100 per annum. 550 per term. Distance Education, 320

Main Language(s) of Instruction: Spanish

International Co-operation: With Universidad Complutense de Madrid and Universidad Pontifica de Salamanca (Spain)

Accrediting Agencies: Asamblea Nacional de Rectores

Degrees and Diplomas: *Bachiller*: Education, 5 yrs; *Maestría*: Education, a further 2 yrs; *Doctorado*: a further 2 yrs following Maestría. Also Diplomados and Especialistas

Student Services: Academic counselling, Employment services, Language programs

Student Residential Facilities: For 300 students of Distance Education

Libraries: Biblioteca de la Universidad, c. 42,300 vols
Last Updated: 07/10/10

NÉSTOR CÁCERES VELÁSQUEZ ANDEAN UNIVERSITY

Universidad Andina Néstor Cáceres Velásquez (UANCV)
Edificio El Campin Of. 301 Apdo. 231, Juliaca, Puno
Tel: +51(51) 322213
Fax: +51(51) 321142
EMail: uancv@uancv.edu.pe
Website: http://www.uancv.edu.pe

Rector: Juan Luque Mamani EMail: rectorado@uancv.edu.pe

Faculties
Administration and Accountancy (Accountancy; Business Administration; Hotel Management; Management; Marketing; Tourism); **Engineering and Pure Sciences** (Architecture; Civil Engineering; Electrical Engineering; Environmental Engineering; Industrial Engineering; Mechanical Engineering; Systems Analysis; Town Planning); **Health Sciences** (Biochemistry; Gynaecology and Obstetrics; Health Sciences; Medicine; Midwifery; Nursing; Pharmacy); **Law and Political Science** (Law; Political Sciences); **Science Education** (Education; Science Education); **Systems Engineering** (Engineering; Systems Analysis)

Institutes
Computer Science (Computer Science); **Languages** (Modern Languages)

History: Founded 1981.

Governing Bodies: University Assembly. University Council

Admission Requirements: Secondary School Leaving Certificate

Main Language(s) of Instruction: Spanish and English

Degrees and Diplomas: *Bachiller*; *Título Profesional de Licenciado*; *Maestría*; *Doctorado*

Student Services: Language programs, Sports facilities

Libraries: Yes
Last Updated: 21/09/10

NORBERT WIENER PRIVATE UNIVERSITY

Universidad Privada Norbert Wiener
Avenida Arequipa 440, Lima, Lima
Tel: +51(14) 4339119-4459898
EMail: info@uwiener.edu.pe
Website: http://www.uwiener.edu.pe

Rector: César Lip Licham EMail: c78@wienergroup.com

Vicerrector: Juan Pedro Matzumura Kasano
EMail: j67@wienergroup.com

Secretaria General: Dorina Rivera Gallegos
EMail: d83@wienergroup.com

Faculties
Administration and International Business (Accountancy; Administration; Hotel Management; International Business; Tourism); **Engineering** (Industrial Engineering; Systems Analysis);

Health Sciences (Dentistry; Gynaecology and Obstetrics; Medical Technology; Nursing); **Law and Political Science** (Law; Political Sciences); **Pharmacy and Biochemistry** (Biochemistry; Pharmacy)

History: Founded 1996. Acquired present status 2004.

Main Language(s) of Instruction: Spanish

Degrees and Diplomas: *Bachiller*, *Título Profesional de Licenciado*; *Maestría*; *Doctorado*

Libraries: Yes

Last Updated: 21/10/10

ORVAL PERUVIAN ART UNIVERSITY

Universidad Peruana de Arte Orval

Primavera 207, Chacarilla, San Borja, Lima

Tel: +51(1) 719-2319

EMail: imagen@uorval.edu.pe

Website: http://www.uorval.edu.pe

Presidente: Ernesto Neptali Ríos Montenegro

Programmes

Archeo-architecture and Tourism Management (Archaeology; Architecture; Management; Tourism); **Graphic Arts and Advertising** (Advertising and Publicity; Graphic Arts); **Interior Design** (Interior Design)

History: Founded 2010.

Main Language(s) of Instruction: Spanish

Degrees and Diplomas: *Bachiller*

Last Updated: 22/10/10

PERUVIAN SCIENTIFIC UNIVERSITY

Universidad Cientifica del Perú (UCP)

Av. Abelardo Quiñones KM 2.5 San Juan Bautista, Iquitos, Loreto

Tel: +51(65) 261-092

EMail: jruiz@ucp.edu.pe

Website: http://www.ucp.edu.pe

Rector: Juan Remigio Saldaña Rojas (2010-)
EMail: jsaldana@ucp.edu.pe

International Relations: Julio Ruiz Murrieta, Director, International Relations

Faculties

Architecture and Urban Planning (Architecture; Town Planning); **Business Administration** (Accountancy; Business Administration; Finance); **Education and Humanities** (Arts and Humanities; Education); **Health Sciences** (Health Sciences); **Law and Political Science** (Law; Political Sciences); **Science and Engineering** (Engineering; Natural Sciences)

Graduate Schools

Law (Law); **Telematics** (Information Technology; Surveying and Mapping; Telecommunications Services)

History: Founded 1990 as Universidad Particular de Iquitos (Private University of Iquitos). Acquired current title 2009.

Governing Bodies: University Council; Faculty Council

Academic Year: August to April (August-December; January-April)

Admission Requirements: High school Certificate

Fees: (US Dollars): 1,000 per annum

Main Language(s) of Instruction: Spanish

Degrees and Diplomas: *Bachiller*: Law; Ecology; Tourism; Communication; Education; Architecture and Urban Development; Computer Sciences; Civil Engineering; Business Administration; Accounting and Finance; Dentistry; Medical Technology; Obstetrics; Psychology, 5 yrs; *Maestría*: Law; Telematics, a further 2 yrs

Student Services: Academic counselling, Cultural centre, Health services, Language programs, Social counselling, Sports facilities

Libraries: 17,000 vols; 6 periodical subscriptions; virtual library with 35,000 titles of books

Last Updated: 17/03/11

PERUVIAN UNION UNIVERSITY

Universidad Peruana Unión

Carretera Central Km 19, Ñaña, Lima, Lima

Tel: +51(1) 3590060

Fax: +51(1) 3590063

EMail: wilbg@upeu.edu.pe

Website: http://www.upeu.edu.pe

Rector: Leonor Bustinza Cabala de Carbo

Vicerrector: Juan Choque Fernández

Gerente General: César Palacios Pinedo

Faculties

Business Studies (Accountancy; Administration; Business Computing); **Education and Humanities** (Arts and Humanities; Communication Studies; Education; Psychology); **Engineering and Architecture** (Architecture; Engineering); **Health Sciences** (Health Sciences; Nursing); **Theology** (Philosophy; Public Health; Religion; Theology)

Institutes

Languages (Modern Languages); **Theological Research** (Education; Religion; Theology) *Director*: Enrique Treiyer

Further Information: Also branches in Ayacucho and Pucalipa

History: Founded 1919. Acquired present status 1983.

Governing Bodies: Consejo Universitario; Asamblea Universitaria

Academic Year: March to December (March-July; August-December)

Admission Requirements: Secondary school certificate and entrance examination

Fees: (Nuevos Soles): 5,474 per semester

Main Language(s) of Instruction: Spanish

Accrediting Agencies: Asamblea Nacional de Rectores; Adventist Accrediting Association

Degrees and Diplomas: *Bachiller*: 5 yrs; *Maestría*: a further 2 yrs; *Doctorado*

Student Services: Academic counselling, Nursery care, Sports facilities

Student Residential Facilities: For c. 400 students

Libraries: 'Daniel Hammerly Dupuy' Library, c. 35,000 vols

Publications: Theologika, Theological Research *(biannually)*

Press or Publishing House: Imprenta Editorial Unión

Last Updated: 05/01/10

PERUVIAN UNIVERSITY OF APPLIED SCIENCES

Universidad Peruana de Ciencias Aplicadas (UPC)

Prolongación Primavera 2390, Monterrico, 33 Lima

Tel: +51(1) 3133333

Fax: +51(1) 3133344

EMail: lbustame@upc.edu.pe

Website: http://www.upc.edu.pe

Rector: Luis Bustamante Beláunde (1995-)

International Relations: Josefina Camet, Directora de la Oficina Internacional EMail: fcamet@upc.edu.pe

Faculties

Architecture (Architecture); **Business Studies** (Accountancy; Administration; Business and Commerce; Finance; Human Resources; Marketing); **Communication Sciences** (Advertising and Publicity; Communication Studies; Journalism); **Contemporary Arts** (Music); **Economics** (Economics; Finance; International Business); **Engineering** (Civil Engineering; Electrical Engineering; Engineering; Industrial Engineering; Software Engineering; Systems Analysis; Telecommunications Engineering); **Health Sciences** (Dentistry; Dietetics; Medicine; Nutrition; Physical Therapy); **Hotel Management and Tourism** (Hotel Management; Tourism); **Human Sciences** (Psychology; Translation and Interpretation); **Law** (Law)

History: Founded 1994. Acquired present status 1999.

Admission Requirements: Secondary school certificate and entrance examination

Main Language(s) of Instruction: Spanish

International Co-operation: With universities in USA; UK; Sweden; Chile; Mexico; Spain

Degrees and Diplomas: *Bachiller*: 5 yrs; *Maestría*: Business Administration (MBA); Law; Operation Management; Business Law; Industrial Relations; Construction Management;, 1.5 yrs; *Doctorado*: Business Administration

Student Services: Academic counselling, Canteen, Employment services, Foreign student adviser, Health services, Language programs, Sports facilities

Student Residential Facilities: None

Libraries: c. 42,000 vols; 87,343 digital vols (53,454 books, 33,889 periodicals).

Publications: Revista de Economía y Derecho *(quarterly)*

Press or Publishing House: UPC University Press

Last Updated: 15/10/10

PERUVIAN UNIVERSITY OF GLOBAL INTEGRATION

Universidad Peruana de Integración Global

Av. Circunvalación N° 653 - San Ignacio de Monterrico, Santiago de Surco, Lima, Lima

Tel: +51(1) 2750500

EMail: admision@upig.edu.pe

Website: http://www.upig.edu.pe

Presidente: Luis Bernardo Guzmán Cabrera

Programmes

Civil Engineering (Civil Engineering); **Law and Political Science** (Law; Political Sciences); **Marketing and International Business** (International Business; Marketing); **Nursing** (Nursing); **Systems Engineering and Computer Science** (Computer Science; Systems Analysis)

History: Founded 2007.

Main Language(s) of Instruction: Spanish

Degrees and Diplomas: *Bachiller*, *Título Profesional de Licenciado*

Last Updated: 15/10/10

PERUVIAN UNIVERSITY OF SCIENCE AND COMPUTER SCIENCE

Universidad Peruana de Ciencias e Informática

Jr.Talara 748 752 Jesús Maria, Lima, Lima

Tel: +51(1) 4241832

EMail: informes@upci.edu.pe

Website: http://www.upci.edu.pe/index.php

Presidente: Héctor Vilca Palacios EMail: presidencia@upci.edu.pe

Gerente General: Juan Salazar Luza

Programmes

Accountancy, Audit and Finance (Accountancy; Finance); **Administration and International Business** (Administration; International Business); **Law** (Law); **Systems Engineering** (Systems Analysis); **Telecommunications Engineering** (Telecommunications Engineering); **Tourism, Hotel Management and Gastronomy** (Cooking and Catering; Hotel Management; Tourism)

History: Founded 2002.

Main Language(s) of Instruction: Spanish

Degrees and Diplomas: *Bachiller*

Last Updated: 15/10/10

PERUVIAN UNIVERSITY OF THE AMERICAS

Universidad Peruana de las Americas

Av. Garcilaso De la Vega N°1880, Lima, Lima

Tel: +51(1) 3327461

EMail: informes@ulasamericas.edu.pe

Website: http://campus.ulasamericas.edu.pe/upea/index.php

Rector: Luis Efraín Hurtado

Vicerrectora Académica: Maria Elena Arana

Faculties

Business Studies (Accountancy; Administration; Business Administration; International Business; Marketing); **Communication** (Communication Studies); **Law** (Law); **Systems Engineering and Computer Science** (Computer Engineering; Computer Science; Systems Analysis)

History: Founded 2002.

Main Language(s) of Instruction: Spanish

Degrees and Diplomas: *Bachiller*, *Título Profesional de Licenciado*

Last Updated: 15/10/10

PERUVIAN UNIVERSITY OF THE CENTRE

Universidad Peruana del Centro

Jr. Moquegua N° 474, Huancayo

Tel: +51(64) 202-005

Website: http://www.upecen.edu.pe

Presidente: Telésforo León Colonia

Programmes

Business Administration (Business Administration); **Civil Engineering** (Civil Engineering); **Law and Political Science** (Law; Political Sciences); **Nursing** (Nursing); **Obstetrics** (Gynaecology and Obstetrics)

History: Founded 2009.

Main Language(s) of Instruction: Spanish

Degrees and Diplomas: *Bachiller*

Last Updated: 21/10/10

PERUVIAN UNIVERSITY OF THE EAST

Universidad Peruana del Oriente

Av Abelardo Quiñonez N° 2725, Iquitos

EMail: uperuanadeloriente@hotmail.com

Website: http://uperuanadeloriente.blogspot.com/2007/07/upo.html

Presidente: José Torres Vásquez

Programmes

Law and Political Science (Law; Political Sciences); **Nursing** (Nursing); **Stomatology** (Stomatology); **Systems Engineering** (Systems Analysis); **Tourism, Hotel Management and Gastronomy** (Cooking and Catering; Hotel Management; Tourism)

History: Founded 2006.

Main Language(s) of Instruction: Spanish

Degrees and Diplomas: *Bachiller*

Last Updated: 22/10/10

PONTIFICAL CATHOLIC UNIVERSITY OF PERU

Pontificia Universidad Católica del Perú (PUCP)

Avenida Universitaria 1801, Distrito San Miguel, Lima, 32 Lima

Tel: +51(1) 626-2000

Fax: +51(1) 626-2000 Ext. 2847

EMail: secgen@pucp.edu.pe

Website: http://www.pucp.edu.pe

Rector: Marcial Rubio Correa (2009-)

Tel: +51(1) 626-2000, ext 2002 EMail: mrubio@pucp.edu.pe

Centres

Advanced Manufacturing Technologies (Production Engineering; Technology); **Applied Geographical Research** (Geography); **Architecture and Urban Studies Research**; **Centrum Business Centre of PUCP**; **Conflict Analysis and Resolution** (Peace and Disarmament); **Continuing Education**; **Cultural**; **Education and Research** (Education); **Foreign Languages** (Modern Languages); **Innovation and Development**; **Music and Dance** (Dance; Music); **Oriental Studies** (Asian Studies; Middle Eastern Studies; Oriental Languages); **Pastoral University Counselling** (Religion); **Philosophical Studies** (Philosophy); **Pre-University** (Education); **Research and Juridical Counselling**; **Social, Economic, Political and Anthropological Research** (Anthropology; Economics; Political Sciences; Social Sciences); **Study, Research and Dissemination of Latin American Music** (Latin American Studies; Music); **University Teaching** (Higher Education)

Faculties

Administration and Accountancy (Accountancy; Business Administration); **Architecture and Town Planning** (Architecture;

Town Planning); **Communication Arts** (Advertising and Publicity; Cinema and Television; Communication Studies; Journalism; Performing Arts; Visual Arts); **Education** (Education; Preschool Education; Primary Education); **Fine Arts** (Engraving; Fine Arts; Graphic Design; Industrial Design; Painting and Drawing; Sculpture); **Humanities** (Archaeology; Arts and Humanities; Environmental Studies; Geography (Human); History; Information Sciences; Linguistics; Literature; Philosophy; Psychology); **Law** (Law); **Management** (Leadership; Management); **Science and Engineering** (Chemistry; Civil Engineering; Computer Engineering; Electronic Engineering; Engineering; Industrial Engineering; Mathematics; Mathematics and Computer Science; Mechanical Engineering; Mining Engineering; Natural Sciences; Physics; Telecommunications Engineering); **Social Sciences** (Anthropology; Economics; Political Sciences; Social Sciences; Sociology)

Institutes

Computing (Computer Science); **Corrosion and Protection** (Environmental Studies); **Environmental Studies** (Ecology; Environmental Studies); **Ethno-musicology** (Musicology); **Human Rights and Democracy** (Human Rights); **International Studies** (International Studies); **Languages** (Literature; Modern Languages); **Quality** (Business Administration; Environmental Management); **Radio-astronomy** (Astronomy and Space Science)

Research Institutes

Riva-Agüero (Arts and Humanities)

Schools

Theatre (Theatre)

Units

General Arts Studies (Arts and Humanities); **General Science Studies** (Engineering; Mathematics and Computer Science; Natural Sciences); **Graduate School**

History: Founded 1917 as a Catholic university. Classified by law 1949 in the category of national universities and entitled to award degrees and titles under the same condition. Honorary title of Pontifical University conferred by the Vatican 1942. Reorganized 1969 and faculties replaced by major academic programmes. An Episcopal Council, presided over by the Archbishop of Lima, Grand Chancellor of the University, has since been established by decree of the Sacred Congregation of Seminaries and Universities.

Governing Bodies: University Assembly; University Council

Academic Year: March to December (March-July; August-December)

Admission Requirements: Secondary school certificate or foreign equivalent, and entrance examination

Main Language(s) of Instruction: Spanish

International Co-operation: Participates in the Centro Interuniversitario de Desarrollo (CINDA); Alban Programme (European Union), Alfa Programme;Co-operation programme between European and Latin American higher education institutions (Colombus); Union of Universities of Latin America and the Caribbean (UDUAL); Inter-american Organization for Higher Education (IOHE)

Degrees and Diplomas: *Bachiller*: Administration; Accountancy; Arts and Humanities; Archaeology; Geography; Philosophy; Linguistics; Literature; History; Education; Information Sciences; Mathematics and Computer Science; Fine Arts; Graphic Design; Industrial Design; Art Education; Sculpture; Painting and Drawing; Performing Arts; Journalism; Publicity; Communication Arts; Communication Studies; Social Sciences; Psychology; Social Work; Sociology; Anthropology; Economics, 5 yrs; *Bachiller*: Law, 6 yrs; *Título Profesional de Licenciado*: Arts and Humanities; Archaeology; Business Administration; Accountancy; Communication Studies; Journalism; Education; Primary Education; Secondary Education; Natural Sciences Education; Art Education; Philosophy; Social Sciences; Physics; Chemistry; History; Geography; Modern Languages; Literature; English; Mathematics; Theology; Development Studies; Engineering; Civil Engineering; Telecommunications Engineering; Mining Engineering; Electronic Engineering; Industrial Engineering; Computer Engineering; Mechanical Engineering; Fine Arts; Graphic Design; Sculpture; Painting and Drawing; Information Sciences; Philosophy; Geography; History; Linguistics; Literature; Spanish; Natural Sciences; Physics; Chemistry; Mathematics and Computer Science; Performing Arts; Audiovisual Communications; Advertizing; Social Sciences; Anthroplogy; Economics; Sociology; Law; Psychology; Educational Psychology; Social Psychology, 5 yrs; *Maestría*: Andean Studies; Anthropology; Archaeology; History; Linguistics; Arts and Humanities; Philosophy; History; Linguistics; Hispano-American Literature; Communication Studies; Computer Science; Economics; Industrial Relations; Regulation of Public Services; Education; Educational Administration; Physics Education; Chemistry Education; Mathematics Education; Curriculum; Education and Human Communication Disorders; Educational Policies; Engineering; Biomedical Engineering; Civil Engineering; Automatization and Control Engineering; Mechanical Engineering; Industrial Engineering; Welding Engineering; Materials Engineering; Law; Civil Law; Constitutional Law; Business Law; International Business Law; Jurisdictional Policy; Intellectual Property and Competition; Procedural Law; Criminal Law; Tributary Law; Management; Direction of Construction and Real Estate Compagnies; Mathematics; Natural Sciences; Applied Physics; Physics; Social Management; Social Sciences; Anthropology; Political Science; Forensic Anthropology and Bioarchaeology; Social Sciences; Psychology; Sociology; Social Sciences; Theoretical Psychoanalytic Studies; Psychology with specialization in Clinical Evaluation, 2 yrs; *Maestría*: Business Administration, 1-2 yrs; *Doctorado*: Andean Studies (Anthropology; Archaeology; History; Linguistics; Business Administration, 4 yrs; *Doctorado*: Arts and Humanities; Law; Mathematics; Social Sciences; Antropology, 2 yrs

Student Services: Academic counselling, Canteen, Cultural centre, Employment services, Foreign student adviser, Foreign Studies Centre, Health services, Language programs, Nursery care, Social counselling, Sports facilities

Special Facilities: 62 laboratories; 13 libraries. Art Gallery; Theatre; Cinema; 'Josefina Ramos de Cox' Museum; 'Georg Petersen' Geological Museum

Libraries: Central Library, c. 543,200 vols

Publications: Agenda Internacional, Research in International Law *(biannually)*; Antropológica *(annually)*; Areté, Revista de Filosophía *(biannually)*; Boletín de Arqueología PUCP *(annually)*; Boletín del Instituto Riva-Agüero-BIRA, Research on Humanities *(annually)*; Coyuntura *(bimonthly)*; Derecho PUCP *(annually)*; Economía PUCP *(annually)*; Educación PUCP *(biannually)*; Electro Electrónica *(biannually)*; Espacio y Desarrollo, Research on Applied Geography *(annually)*; Estudios de Filosofía *(biannually)*; Histórica, Research on History *(biannually)*; Lexis, Linguistic and Literature publication *(biannually)*; Magister en Derecho Civil *(annually)*; Pensamiento Constitucional, Constitutional Law and Political Science Research *(annually)*; Pro-Mathemática *(biannually)*; Revista de Psicología PUCP *(biannually)*; Revista de Química *(biannually)*; Synergias Péru, Research on French Linguistics *(annually)*

Last Updated: 21/09/10

PRIVATE UNIVERSITY OF ICA

Universidad Privada de Ica

Avenida Túpac Arnaru n° 336, Ica

EMail: informes@upav.net

Website: http://www.oocities.com/upav/index.htm

Presidente: Nicanor Ninahuamán Mucha

Faculties

Agro-industrial Engineering (Agricultural Engineering; Industrial Engineering); **Education** (Education); **Obstetrics** (Gynaecology and Obstetrics)

History: Founded 1997 as Universidad Privada Abraham Valdelomar. Acquired present title 2009.

Main Language(s) of Instruction: Spanish

Degrees and Diplomas: *Bachiller*

Last Updated: 21/10/10

PRIVATE UNIVERSITY OF PUCALLPA

Universidad Privada de Pucallpa

Jr. Coronel Portillo Nro. 298, Jr. Huáscar Nro. 679, Pucallpa, Ucayali

Tel: +51(61) 575035

Fax: +51(61) 570670

EMail: informes@upp.edu.pe

Website: http://www.uppucallpa.org

Presidente: Jorge Flores Buitrón EMail: presidente@upp.edu.pe

Programmes

Accountancy and Finance (Accountancy; Finance); **Business Administration** (Business Administration); **Law and Political Science** (Law; Political Sciences); **Systems Engineering** (Systems Analysis)

History: Founded 2005.

Main Language(s) of Instruction: Spanish

Degrees and Diplomas: *Bachiller*
Last Updated: 21/10/10

PRIVATE UNIVERSITY OF TACNA

Universidad Privada de Tacna (UPT)
Avenida Bolognesi N° 1177, Apdo. 126, Tacna, Tacna
Tel: +51(52) 426881
Fax: +51(52) 426881
EMail: odesar@upt.edu.pe
Website: http://www.upt.edu.pe

Rectora: Elva Inés Acevedo Velásquez
EMail: rectorado@upt.edu.pe

Vicerrector Administrativo: Arcadio Atencio Vargas
Tel: +51(52) 427212 +51(52) 415851
EMail: vadministrativo@upt.edu.pe

Faculties

Architecture and Town Planning (Architecture; Town Planning); **Business Administration** (Accountancy; Business Administration; Business and Commerce; Finance; Hotel Management; International Business; Production Engineering; Tourism); **Education, Communication and Humanities** (Arts and Humanities; Communication Studies; Education; Primary Education; Secondary Education); **Engineering** *(Capanique, Pocollay)* (Agricultural Engineering; Civil Engineering; Electronic Engineering; Engineering; Industrial Engineering; Systems Analysis); **Health Sciences** *(Capanique, Pocollay)* (Dentistry; Medical Technology; Medicine); **Law and Political Science** *(Capanique, Pocollay)* (Law; Political Sciences)

Schools

Postgraduate Studies (Administration; Business Administration; Computer Science; Educational Administration; Law; Nursing; Physical Therapy)

History: Founded 1985, acquired present status 1993.

Admission Requirements: Secondary school certificate or foreign equivalent

Main Language(s) of Instruction: Spanish

Degrees and Diplomas: *Bachiller*: 5-6 yrs; *Maestría*: a further 2 yrs; *Doctorado*

Student Services: Academic counselling, Canteen, Foreign student adviser, Health services, Language programs, Nursery care, Social counselling, Sports facilities
Last Updated: 21/10/10

PRIVATE UNIVERSITY OF THE NORTH

Universidad Privada del Norte
Avenida del Ejército No. 920, Urb. El Molino, Trujillo, La Libertad
Fax: +51(44) 220062
EMail: informes@upnorte.edu.pe
Website: http://www.upn.edu.pe/

Rector: Daniel Rodríguez Risco EMail: drr@upnorte.edu.pe

Vicerrector: Alfredo Muñoz Gonzales

Faculties

Accountancy (Accountancy); **Administration** (Administration); **Architecture** (Architecture; Interior Design); **Communication Studies** (Communication Studies); **Industrial Engineering** (Industrial Engineering); **Law** (Law); **Systems Engineering** (Systems Analysis)

History: Founded 1993.

Main Language(s) of Instruction: Spanish

Degrees and Diplomas: *Bachiller*, *Maestría*
Last Updated: 05/01/10

PRIVATE UNIVERSITY OF TRUJILLO

Universidad Privada de Trujillo
Av. Industrial Carretera a Laredo Km. 4, Trujillo
Tel: +51(44) 211-557
Fax: +51(44) 608-725
EMail: informes@uptrujillo.edu.pe
Website: http://www.uptrujillo.edu.pe/v3/

Presidente: José Gregorio Silva Lara

Programmes

Accountancy (Accountancy); **Civil Engineering** (Civil Engineering); **Law**; **Marketing** (Marketing); **Systems Engineering and Computer Science** (Computer Science; Systems Analysis)

History: Founded 2006.

Main Language(s) of Instruction: Spanish

Degrees and Diplomas: *Título Profesional de Licenciado*
Last Updated: 15/10/10

RICARDO PALMA UNIVERSITY

Universidad Ricardo Palma (URP)
Av. Benávides N°5440, Las Gardenias - Surco, Lima, Lima
Tel: +51(1) 2750450
Fax: +51(1) 2750468
EMail: sec_gral@urp.edu.pe
Website: http://www.urp.edu.pe

Rector: Iván Rodríguez Chávez (1996-)
Tel: +51(1) 2753644 EMail: rector@urp.edu.pe

Vicerrector Administrativo: Ronal Figueroa Ávila
EMail: vice.administrativo@urp.edu.pe

Centres

Research (Architecture; Biology; Economics; Engineering; Medicine; Modern Languages; Psychology; Town Planning) *Director*: Victor La Torre Aguilar

Faculties

Architecture and Town Planning (Architectural and Environmental Design; Architecture; Interior Design; Surveying and Mapping; Town Planning); **Biology** (Biology; Cell Biology; Histology; Immunology; Veterinary Science); **Economics** (Accountancy; Administration; Economics); **Engineering** (Civil Engineering; Electronic Engineering; Engineering; Industrial Engineering; Information Technology; Mechanical Engineering); **Law and Political Science** (Law; Political Sciences); **Medicine** (Genetics; Gynaecology and Obstetrics; Medicine; Parasitology); **Modern Languages** (Communication Studies; Cultural Studies; Modern Languages; Spanish; Translation and Interpretation); **Psychology** (Developmental Psychology; Neurosciences; Pathology; Psychology; Psychometrics)

Institutes

Classical and Oriental Studies (Classical Languages; Oriental Studies); **Ethnobiology** (Biology; Ethnology); **Museology and Artistic Research** (Museum Studies); **Natural Resources** (Natural Resources); **Philosophy** (Philosophy); **Ricardo Palma**; **Science and Technology** (Science Education; Technology); **Sports and Leisure** (Leisure Studies; Sports)

Schools

Postgraduate Studies (Higher Education; Industrial and Organizational Psychology; Industrial Engineering)

History: Founded 1969. A private autonomous institution.

Governing Bodies: Asamblea Universitaria; Consejo Universitario

Academic Year: April to March (April-July; August-December; January-March)

Admission Requirements: Secondary school certificate

Main Language(s) of Instruction: Spanish

Degrees and Diplomas: *Bachiller*: Accountancy; Administration; Architecture; Biology; Civil Engineering; Computer Science; Economics; Industrial Engineering; Mechanical Engineering, Electronic Engineering; Psychology; Translation and Interpretation; Veterinary Science, 5 yrs; *Bachiller*: Medicine, 7 yrs; *Título Profesional de Licenciado*: Accountancy (Contador público); Administration; Economics (Economista); Engineering (Ingeniero); Medicine and Surgery (Médico-Cirujano); Translation and Interpretation; Veterinary Science; *Maestría*: Administration; Architecture; Education;

Ecology; Psychology; Tourism and Hotel Management; Political Science; *Doctorado*: Political Sciences and International Relations

Student Services: Canteen, Cultural centre, Health services, Language programs, Nursery care, Social counselling, Sports facilities

Special Facilities: Natural History Museum. Visual Arts Gallery

Libraries: Humanities Library, c. 6,600 vols; Technology, 6,100; Economics, 5,400; Sciences, 5,320

Publications: Caminos *(biannually)*; Nexus *(biannually)*; Perfiles de Ingeniería *(annually)*; Revista Arquitextos *(biannually)*; Revista Aula Palma; Revista de Investigación BIOTEMPO *(annually)*; Revista de la Facultad de Ciencias Económicas *(annually)*; Revista de la Facultad de Lenguas Modernas *(biannually)*; Revista de la Facultad de Psicología *(annually)*; Revista Pirámides; Revista Tradición *(biannually)*; Revista URPI

Press or Publishing House: Fondo Editorial de la Universidad Ricardo Palma

Last Updated: 21/10/10

SAINT IGNATIUS OF LOYOLA UNIVERSITY

Universidad San Ignacio de Loyola
Avenida La Fontana 550, La Molina, Lima, Lima
Tel: +51(1) 3171000
Fax: +51(1) 3171025
EMail: admision@usil.edu.pe
Website: http://www.usil.edu.pe/

Rector: Edward Roekaert Embrechts

Vicerrector Académico: Henry Barclay Rey De Castro

Faculties

Administration (Administration; Business Administration; Economics; Environmental Management; Finance; International Business; International Relations; Law; Marketing); **Education** (Education); **Engineering and Architecture** (Agricultural Engineering; Architecture; Civil Engineering; Computer Engineering; Industrial Engineering; Systems Analysis; Town Planning); **Hotel Management, Tourism and Gastronomy** (Cooking and Catering; Hotel Management; Tourism); **Humanities** (Art Education; Communication Disorders; Design; Psychology)

Schools

Postgraduate Studies

History: Founded 1996.

Main Language(s) of Instruction: Spanish

Degrees and Diplomas: *Título Profesional de Licenciado*; *Maestría*

Last Updated: 21/10/10

SAINT JOHN THE BAPTIST PRIVATE UNIVERSITY

Universidad Privada San Juan Bautista (UPSJB)
Avenida José Antonio Lavalle s/n, Hacienda Villa, Chorrillos
Tel: +51(254) 7601
EMail: rchavez@upsjb.edu.pe
Website: http://www.upsjb.edu.pe

Rector: Víctor Mayhuasca Cabrera
EMail: vmayhuasca@upsjb.edu.pe

Vicerrector académico: Abilio Anaya Pajuelo
EMail: aanaya@upsjb.edu.pe

Faculties

Communication and Administration (Accountancy; Administration; Communication Studies; Hotel Management; Tourism); **Engineering** (Computer Engineering; Systems Analysis); **Health Sciences** (Medicine; Nursing; Stomatology; Veterinary Science; Zoology); **Law** (Administrative Law; Civil Law; Commercial Law; Constitutional Law; International Law; Labour Law; Law)

History: Founded 1997.

Main Language(s) of Instruction: Spanish

Degrees and Diplomas: *Bachiller*. Business Administration; Computer Science; *Bachiller*. Information Sciences; Nursing; Stomatology; Veterinary Medicine, 5 years; *Bachiller*. Law, 6 years; *Bachiller*. Surgery, 7 years; *Título Profesional de Licenciado*; *Maestría*; *Doctorado*

Last Updated: 21/10/10

SAN CARLOS PRIVATE UNIVERSITY

Universidad Privada San Carlos
Jiron Conde de Lemos N° 128, Puno
Website: http://www.upsc.edu.pe

Presidente: Fernando Cáceda Diaz

Programmes

Accountancy (Accountancy; Finance); **Engineering** (Computer Engineering; Environmental Engineering); **Law** (Law); **Nursing** (Nursing)

History: Founded 2006.

Main Language(s) of Instruction: Spanish

Degrees and Diplomas: *Bachiller*

Last Updated: 21/10/10

SAN PABLO CATHOLIC UNIVERSITY

Universidad Católica San Pablo
Avenida Salaverry 301, Vallecito, Arequipa
Tel: +51(54) 605600
Fax: +51(54) 281517
EMail: info@ucsp.edu.pe; institucional@ucsp.edu.pe
Website: http://www.usp.edu.pe

Rector: Alonso Quintanilla Pérez-Wicht
Tel: +51(54) 605600 Anexo 230 EMail: a.quintanilla@ucsp.edu.pe

Faculties

Business Administration (Accountancy; Business Administration); **Engineering** (Computer Engineering; Industrial Engineering; Telecommunications Engineering); **Humanities** (Education; Psychology); **Law** (Law)

History: Founded 1997. Acquired present status 2001.

Governing Bodies: Consejo Superior; Consejo Universitario

Admission Requirements: Secundaria completa

Main Language(s) of Instruction: Spanish

International Co-operation: With universities in USA; Spain

Degrees and Diplomas: *Bachiller*, *Título Profesional de Licenciado*. Also diplomados

Libraries: Yes

Last Updated: 22/09/10

SAN PEDRO PRIVATE UNIVERSITY

Universidad Privada San Pedro
Urb. Los Pinos s/n, Chimbote, Ancash
Tel: +51(43) 323505
Fax: +51(43) 341079
EMail: upsp@lanet.com.pe
Website: http://infoupsp.tripod.com

Rector: Jorge Arturo Benites Robles
Tel: +51(43) 341078, Fax: +51(43) 328034
EMail: rectorsp@upsp.edu.pe

Vicerrector Administrativo: Javier Azparrent Taipe

Vicerrector Académico: Arnulfo Becerra Alfaro

Faculties

Accountancy and Administration (Accountancy; Administration); **Education and Humanities** (Clinical Psychology; Primary Education; Secondary Education); **Engineering** (Civil Engineering; Computer Engineering; Systems Analysis); **Health Sciences** (Gynaecology and Obstetrics; Medical Technology; Nursing); **Human Medicine** (Medicine); **Law and Political Science** (Law; Political Sciences)

History: Founded 1988.

Admission Requirements: Secondary school certificate

Main Language(s) of Instruction: Spanish

Degrees and Diplomas: *Bachiller*, *Maestría*

Last Updated: 21/10/10

SANTA MARÍA CATHOLIC UNIVERSITY

Universidad Católica de Santa María

Urb. San José s/n, Umacollo, Arequipa
Tel: +51(54) 382-038
Fax: +51(54) 251-213
EMail: ucsm@ucsm.edu.pe
Website: http://www.ucsm.edu.pe

Rector: Abel Andrés Tapia Fernandez
Tel: +51(54) 251-112, Fax: +51(54) 252-542

Centres
Investigation

Faculties
Accountancy and Finance (Accountancy; Business Administration; Finance); **Architecture and Civil Engineering** (Architecture; Civil Engineering; Environmental Engineering); **Biological and Chemical Science and Engineering** (Agricultural Engineering; Agronomy; Bioengineering; Biology; Chemical Engineering; Chemistry; Food Technology; Veterinary Science); **Economics and Business Administration** (Business Administration; Economics); **Human Medicine** (Medicine); **Law and Political Science** (Law; Political Sciences); **Nursing** (Nursing); **Obstetrics and Paediatrics** (Gynaecology and Obstetrics; Paediatrics); **Odontology** (Dentistry); **Pharmacy, Biochemistry and Biotechnology** (Biochemistry; Biotechnology; Pharmacy); **Physics and Formal Sciences** (Civil Engineering; Computer Engineering; Electrical Engineering; Industrial Engineering; Mechanical Engineering; Physics); **Social Sciences and Humanities** (Advertising and Publicity; Archaeology; Communication Studies; Education; Hotel Management; Psychology; Public Administration; Social Work; Theology; Tourism)

Institutes
Computer Science (Computer Science); **Languages** (Modern Languages)

History: Founded 1961. Reorganized 1969.

Academic Year: March to December (March-July; August-December)

Admission Requirements: Secondary school certificate and entrance examination

Main Language(s) of Instruction: Spanish

International Co-operation: With universities in Latin America; Europe; China

Degrees and Diplomas: *Bachiller*; *Maestría*; *Doctorado*. Also Professional Titles

Student Services: Academic counselling, Cultural centre, Employment services, Foreign student adviser, Health services, Language programs, Sports facilities

Special Facilities: 4 Museums; 4 Art galleries

Libraries: University Library.

Last Updated: 22/09/10

SANTO TORIBIO DE MOGROVEJO CATHOLIC UNIVERSITY

Universidad Católica Santo Toribio de Mogrovejo

Avenida Panamericana Norte N°855, Chiclayo, Lambayeque
Tel: +51(74) 222-703
Fax: +51(74) 222-703
EMail: informacion@usat.edu.pe
Website: http://www.usat.edu.pe

Rector: Hugo Calienes Bedoya

Faculties
Business Administration (Accountancy; Administration; Business Administration; Economics; Hotel Management; Tourism); **Engineering** (Architecture; Civil Engineering; Computer Engineering; Electrical Engineering; Environmental Engineering; Industrial Engineering; Mechanical Engineering; Systems Analysis); **Humanities** (Arts and Humanities; Communication Studies; Education); **Law** (Law); **Medicine** (Dentistry; Health Sciences; Medicine; Nursing; Psychology)

History: Founded 1998. Acquired present status 2005.

Main Language(s) of Instruction: Spanish

Degrees and Diplomas: *Bachiller*; *Título Profesional de Licenciado*; *Maestría*; *Doctorado*. Also Especialización

Libraries: Yes.

Last Updated: 22/09/10

SCIENTIFIC UNIVERSITY OF THE SOUTH

Universidad Científica del Sur

Panamerica Sur Km 19, Lima, Lima
Tel: +51(1) 6106400
EMail: informes@ucsur.edu.pe
Website: http://www.ucsur.edu.pe

Rector: Agustín Iza Stoll
Tel: +51(1) 2546403, Fax: +51(1) 4465335

Areas
Agronomy and Environment (Agronomy; Environmental Engineering; Environmental Management; Environmental Studies; Forestry; Hotel and Restaurant; Marine Biology; Tourism; Veterinary Science; Zoology); **Arts and Humanities** (Architecture; Law; Literature; Theatre; Town Planning); **Engineering and Business** (Administration; Advertising and Publicity; Business and Commerce; Economics; Engineering; Marketing); **Health Studies** (Dietetics; Health Sciences; Medicine; Nutrition; Psychology; Stomatology)

History: Founded 1998.

Main Language(s) of Instruction: Spanish

Degrees and Diplomas: *Bachiller*; *Título Profesional de Licenciado*. Also Diplomados

Libraries: Yes

Last Updated: 24/12/09

SEDES SAPIENTIAE CATHOLIC UNIVERSITY

Universidad Católica Sedes Sapentiae (UCSS)

Esquina Constelaciones y Sol de Oro, Los Olivos, Lima, 39 Lima
Tel: +51(1) 5330008 +51(1) 5330079
Fax: +51(1) 5330008 Ext.220
EMail: universidad@ucss.edu.pe
Website: http://www.ucss.edu.pe

Rector: Joaquín Martínez Valls EMail: jmartinez@ucss.edu.pe

Faculties
Agricultural Engineering (Agricultural Engineering); **Economics and Commerce** (Accountancy; Administration; Economics); **Economics and Commerce** *(Sede Huacho)* (Accountancy; Administration; Finance; International Business); **Education and Humanities** (Archiving; Documentation Techniques; Foreign Languages Education; Library Science; Preschool Education; Primary Education; Religious Education; Secondary Education; Special Education); **Engineering** (Computer Engineering; Industrial Engineering); **Health Sciences** (Dietetics; Health Sciences; Nursing; Nutrition; Physical Therapy; Psychology)

History: Founded 1998. Acquired present status 2006.

Governing Bodies: Rector; Administración general; Vicepresidencia Académica

Admission Requirements: Secondary school certificate and entrance examination

Fees: (Nuevos Soles): 304-396 monthly

Main Language(s) of Instruction: Spanish; English

International Co-operation: With universities in Spain; Italy; Peru

Accrediting Agencies: Asamblea Nacional de Rectores

Degrees and Diplomas: *Bachiller*. 5 yrs; *Título Profesional de Licenciado*; *Maestría*. Also Diplomados

Student Services: Academic counselling, Canteen, Employment services, Health services, Language programs, Social counselling

Student Residential Facilities: None

Special Facilities: Auditorium; Movie Studio; 4 Computer Labs

Libraries: Yes

Publications: Cuadernos Literarios *(biennially)*; Riesgo de Educar *(biennially)*; Studium Veritatis *(annually)*

Press or Publishing House: Fondo Editorial Universidad Católica Sedes Sapientiae

Last Updated: 22/09/10

SEÑOR DE SIPÁN UNIVERSITY

Universidad Señor de Sipán (USS)
Carretera a Pimentel Km 5, Chiclayo, Lambayeque
Tel: +51(74) 203723
Fax: +51(74) 203861
EMail: hacuna@uss.edu.pe
Website: http://www.uss.edu.pe

Rector: Humberto Llempén Coronel (2000-)
Tel: +51(74) 203723, Ext.6002 EMail: hllempen@uss.edu.pe

Gerente: Humberto Acuña Peralta Tel: +51(74) 203723, Ext.6002

Faculties

Business Studies (Accountancy; Administration; Business and Commerce; International Business; Tourism); **Engineering, Architecture and Town Planning** (Agricultural Engineering; Architecture; Civil Engineering; Electrical Engineering; Industrial Engineering; Mechanical Engineering; Systems Analysis; Town Planning); **Health Sciences** (Health Sciences; Nursing; Stomatology); **Humanities** (Art Education; Communication Studies; Graphic Design; Psychology); **Law** (Law)

History: Founded 1999.

Main Language(s) of Instruction: Spanish

Degrees and Diplomas: *Bachiller*: 5 yrs; *Título Profesional de Licenciado*: Accountancy; Administration; Communication; Psychology; Tourism and Business Administration; Civil Engineering; Industrial Engineering; Mechanical Engineering; Electrical Engineering; Computer Engineering; Law, 5 yrs

Student Services: Academic counselling, Canteen, Cultural centre, Foreign Studies Centre, Health services, Language programs, Nursery care, Social counselling, Sports facilities

Libraries: Electronic Library

Last Updated: 21/10/10

SERGIO BERNALES PRIVATE UNIVERSITY

Universidad Privada Sergio Bernales S.A.C.
Esq. Calle Santa Rosa e Hipólito Unanue Urb. Los Libertadores, Cañete, Lima
Tel: +51(1) 5811438
EMail: informes@upsb.edu.pe
Website: http://www.upsb.edu.pe/

Rector: Vicente M. Castañeda Chávez

Vicerrector Académico: Norvil. E. Cieza Montenegro

Programmes

Law and Political Science (Law; Political Sciences); **Obstetrics**; **Systems and Computer Engineering**

History: Founded 2002.

Main Language(s) of Instruction: Spanish

Degrees and Diplomas: *Bachiller*; *Título Profesional de Licenciado*

Last Updated: 05/01/10

SIMÓN BOLIVAR PERUVIAN UNIVERSITY

Universidad Peruana Simón Bolivar
Av. Juan Pablo Fernandini N° 1255, Pueblo Libre, Lima, Lima
Website: http://www.usb.edu.pe

Presidente: Carroll Dale Salinas

Programmes

Accountancy and Auditing (Accountancy); **Administration, Hotel Management and Ecotourism** (Administration; Ecology; Hotel Management; Tourism); **Commercial Engineering** (Business and Commerce); **Communication and Advertising** (Advertising and Publicity; Journalism); **Systems Engineering and Computer Safety** (Software Engineering; Systems Analysis)

History: Founded 2006.

Main Language(s) of Instruction: Spanish

Degrees and Diplomas: *Bachiller*; *Título Profesional de Licenciado*

Last Updated: 21/10/10

TECHNOLOGICAL UNIVERSITY OF PERU

Universidad Tecnológica del Perú
Esquina Av. 28 de Julio y Avenida Petit Thouars 116, Lima, Lima
Tel: +51(1) 3329393
EMail: informes@utp.edu.pe
Website: http://www.utp.edu.pe

Rector: Enrique Bedoya Sánchez

Faculties

Accountancy and Administration (Accountancy; Business Administration; Finance; Hotel Management; International Business; Marketing; Tourism); **Engineering** (Aeronautical and Aerospace Engineering; Automation and Control Engineering; Automotive Engineering; Computer Engineering; Electrical Engineering; Graphic Design; Industrial Engineering; Mechanical Engineering; Naval Architecture; Safety Engineering; Software Engineering; Systems Analysis; Telecommunications Engineering; Textile Technology); **Humanities** (Communication Studies; International Relations; Law; Political Sciences)

History: Founded 1997.

Main Language(s) of Instruction: Spanish

Degrees and Diplomas: *Bachiller*

Libraries: Yes

Last Updated: 25/10/10

TECHNOLOGICAL UNIVERSITY OF THE ANDES

Universidad Tecnológica de Los Andes
Avenida Perú 700, Abancay, Apurimac
Tel: +51(84) 321-559
Fax: +51(84) 321-181
EMail: secgeneral@utea.edu.pe
Website: http://www.utea.edu.pe

Rector: David Terrazas Estacio EMail: rectorado@utea.edu.pe

Vicerrector Académico: Toribio Tapia Molina
EMail: vacademico@utea.edu.pe

Faculties

Accountancy and Finance (Accountancy; Finance); **Agronomy** (Agriculture; Agronomy); **Education and Humanities** (Arts and Humanities; Education); **Engineering**; **Law and Political Science** (Law; Political Sciences); **Stomatology** (Stomatology); **Tourism and Gastronomy** (Cooking and Catering; Tourism)

History: Founded 1984 as Universidad de Apurimac, acquired present status and title 1994.

Academic Year: April to December (April-July; September-December)

Admission Requirements: Secondary school certificate

Main Language(s) of Instruction: Spanish

Degrees and Diplomas: *Bachiller*, *Título Profesional de Licenciado*

Last Updated: 21/10/10

TELESUP PRIVATE UNIVERSITY

Universidad Privada Telesup
Av. 28 de Julio 1233, Lima
Tel: +51(1) 244-6445
EMail: informes@telesup.edu.pe
Website: http://www.utelesup.com

Presidente: Rafael Castañeda Castañeda

Vicerrector Académico: Elías Castillo Rosa Pérez

Programmes

Accountancy and Finance (Accountancy; Finance); **Agro-industrial Engineering** (Agricultural Engineering; Industrial Engineering); **Business Administration** (Business Administration); **Law and Political Science** (Law; Political Sciences); **Systems Engineering** (Systems Analysis)

History: Founded 2004.

Main Language(s) of Instruction: Spanish

Degrees and Diplomas: *Bachiller*. Also Diplomado

Libraries: Yes

Last Updated: 15/10/10

THE ANDES PERUVIAN UNIVERSITY

Universidad Peruana Los Andes
Av. Giráldez N°230, Huancayo, Junín
Tel: +51(64) 223838
Fax: +51(64) 223848
EMail: admision@mail.upla.edu.pe
Website: http://www.upla.edu.pe

Rector: Dimas Hugo Fernández Barrantes

Vicerrector Académico: José Castillo Custodio

Vicerrector Administrativo: Vidal Fernández Sullca

Centres

Languages (Modern Languages)

Faculties

Administration and Accountancy (Accountancy; Business Administration); **Education and Human Sciences** (Primary Education; Secondary Education); **Engineering** (Architecture; Civil Engineering; Computer Engineering; Industrial Engineering); **Health Sciences** (Biochemistry; Dentistry; Gynaecology and Obstetrics; Health Sciences; Medical Technology; Medicine; Nursing; Nutrition; Optometry; Pharmacy; Psychology; Veterinary Science; Zoology)

History: Founded 1983 as Universidad Privada Los Andes, acquired present status and title 1996.

Academic Year: April to December (April-July; September-December)

Admission Requirements: Secondary school certificate and entrance examination

Main Language(s) of Instruction: Spanish

Degrees and Diplomas: *Bachiller*: 5-6 yrs; *Título Profesional de Licenciado*; *Maestría*

Last Updated: 21/10/10

UNIVERSITY FOR THE DEVELOPMENT OF THE ANDEAN REGION

Universidad para el Desarrollo Andino
Av. Ricardo Fernández 103, Pueblo Nuevo - Lircay - Angaraes, Huancavelica, Huancavelica
Fax: +51(67) 458193
EMail: universidad@udea.edu.pe
Website: http://www.udea.edu.pe/

Presidente: Luz María Alvarez Calderón

Vicerrector Académico: Adrico Via Ortega

Faculties

Engineering (Computer Engineering; Engineering); **Humanities and Social Sciences** (Arts and Humanities; Primary Education; Secondary Education; Social Sciences)

History: Founded 2002.

Main Language(s) of Instruction: Quechua and Spanish

Degrees and Diplomas: *Título Profesional de Licenciado*: Agronomy; Computer Engineering; Education

Last Updated: 13/10/10

UNIVERSITY OF CHICLAYO

Universidad de Chiclayo (UDCH)
Av. Salaverry 235, Chiclayo, Chiclayo
Tel: +51(74) 222-610
Fax: +51(74) 222-610
EMail: información@udch.edu.pe
Website: http://www.udch.edu.pe

Rector: Augusto Virgilio Tello Amenero
EMail: rectorado@udch.edu.pe

Faculties

Architecture and Civil Engineering (Architecture; Civil Engineering; Town Planning); **Business Administration** (Accountancy; Administration; Economics; Marketing); **Communication** (Communication Studies; Journalism; Public Relations); **Computer Science** (Computer Science); **Education** (Education; Primary Education; Secondary Education; Special Education); **Health Sciences** (Gynaecology and Obstetrics; Health Sciences; Medical Technology; Nursing; Nutrition); **Law** (Law); **Medicine** (Medicine); **Psychology** (Psychology)

History: Founded 1985, acquired present status 1991.

Governing Bodies: University Assembly, comprising 51 members; University Council, comprising 17 members

Academic Year: March to December (March-July; August-December)

Admission Requirements: Secondary school certificate

Main Language(s) of Instruction: Spanish

Degrees and Diplomas: *Bachiller*: 5 yrs; *Maestría*; *Doctorado*

Student Services: Canteen, Employment services, Language programs, Social counselling, Sports facilities

Libraries: Central Library, c. 20,000 vols. Specialized libraries for each school

Last Updated: 22/09/10

UNIVERSITY OF HUÁNUCO

Universidad de Huánuco
Jr. Hermilio Valdizán 871, Huánuco, Huánuco
Tel: +51(64) 511-113
Fax: +51(64) 513-154
EMail: info@udh.edu.pe
Website: http://www.udh.edu.pe

Rector: José Antonio Beraún Barrantes

Faculties

Business Administration (Accountancy; Business Administration; Cooking and Catering; Finance; Hotel and Restaurant; Hotel Management; International Business; Marketing; Tourism); **Education** (Foreign Languages Education; Preschool Education; Primary Education); **Engineering** (Architecture; Civil Engineering; Computer Engineering; Environmental Engineering); **Health Sciences** (Dentistry; Gynaecology and Obstetrics; Health Sciences; Nursing; Psychology); **Law and Political Science** (Law; Political Sciences)

Further Information: Also branches in Tingo María, Cerro de Pasco, Lima and Pucalpa

History: Founded 1989. Previously Universidad 'Víctor Andrés Belaúnde'.

Academic Year: April to December (April-July; September-December)

Admission Requirements: Secondary school certificate

Main Language(s) of Instruction: Spanish

Degrees and Diplomas: *Bachiller*, *Título Profesional de Licenciado*; *Maestría*; *Doctorado*

Last Updated: 22/09/10

UNIVERSITY OF LAMBAYEQUE

Universidad de Lambayeque
Calle Tacna 065, Chiclayo
Tel: +51(74) 208-836
Website: http://www.udl.edu.pe

Presidente: Juan Pablo Moreno Muro

Programmes

Accountancy (Accountancy); **Commercial Engineering** (Business and Commerce); **Environmental Engineering** (Environmental Engineering); **Systems Engineering** (Systems Analysis); **Tourism Administration** (Administration; Tourism)

History: Founded 2010.

Main Language(s) of Instruction: Spanish

Degrees and Diplomas: *Título Profesional de Licenciado*

Last Updated: 11/10/10

UNIVERSITY OF LIMA

Universidad de Lima
Avenida Javier Prado Este cuadra 46, Monterrico, Lima, 33 Lima
Tel: +51(1) 437-6767
Fax: +51(1) 435-6552
EMail: dusar@correo.ulima.edu.pe
Website: http://www.ulima.edu.pe

Rector: Ilse Wisotzki (1994-)
Tel: +51(1) 435-1689 EMail: iwisotzki@correo.ulima.edu.pe

Schools

Business (Accountancy; Administration; Economics; Finance); **Engineering** (Architecture; Industrial Engineering; Systems Analysis); **Humanities** (Communication Studies; Law; Psychology); **Postgraduate Studies** (Banking; Business Administration; Commercial Law; Communication Studies; Educational Administration; Finance; Industrial Engineering; Systems Analysis)

History: Founded 1962 as a private autonomous institution.

Governing Bodies: University Assembly; Directive Council; School Council

Academic Year: March to December (March-July; August-December)

Admission Requirements: Secondary school certificate and entrance examination

Main Language(s) of Instruction: Spanish

International Co-operation: With universities in Germany; Australia; Brazil; Canada; Chile; South Korea; Spain; USA; Netherlands; Italy; France; Also coopeerates with member countries of the CINDA : Argentina; Chile; Colombia; Mexico; Panama; Dominican Republic; Venezuela

Degrees and Diplomas: *Bachiller*, *Título Profesional de Licenciado*; *Maestría*

Student Services: Academic counselling, Cultural centre, Employment services, Foreign student adviser, Foreign Studies Centre, Handicapped facilities, Health services, Social counselling, Sports facilities

Special Facilities: Capital Markets Lab; Movie and TV studio; Computer Assisted Flexible Manufacturing Lab; Auditoriums

Libraries: CentralLibrary, c. 97,000 vols

Publications: Contratexto, Articles written by members of the College of Communications *(annually)*; Ingeniería Industrial, Articles written by members of the College of Industrial Engineering *(annually)*; Interfaces, Digital Journal published by the College of Systems Engineering *(annually)*; Lienzo, Articles on art and culture *(annually)*; Lus et Praxis, Articles written by members of the College of Law *(annually)*; Persona, Articles written by members of the College of Psychology *(annually)*; Un vicio absurdo, Collection of poems published by the Department of University Welfare *(annually)*

Press or Publishing House: Fondo de Editorial de la Universidad de Lima

Last Updated: 22/09/10

UNIVERSITY OF PIURA

Universidad de Piura
Avenida Ramón Múgica 131, Urb. San Eduardo, Piura, 353 Piura
Tel: +51(73) 284500
Fax: +51(73) 284510
EMail: info@udep.edu.pe
Website: http://www.udep.edu.pe

Rector: Antonio Abruña Puyol (2003-)
EMail: aabruna@udep.edu.pe

Departments

Biomedical Sciences (Biomedicine)

Faculties

Communication Sciences (Communication Studies; Journalism; Marketing); **Economics and Business Administration** (Accountancy; Business Administration; Economics); **Educational Sciences** (Education; Educational Sciences; Teacher Training); **Engineering** (Civil Engineering; Computer Engineering; Electrical Engineering; Engineering; Industrial Engineering; Mechanical Engineering); **Humanities** (Arts and Humanities; Cultural Studies; Heritage Preservation; History; Philosophy); **Law** (Law)

Institutes

Family Sciences (Family Studies); **Hydraulics** (Hydraulic Engineering)

Schools

Leadership *(Lima)* (Business Administration; Leadership); **Technology** (Technology)

Further Information: Also branch in Lima

History: Founded 1968. A corporate Institution of the Prelature of Opus Dei.

Governing Bodies: Consejo Superior

Academic Year: March to December (March-July; August-December)

Admission Requirements: Secondary school certificate and entrance examination

Fees: (US Dollars): 1,000-3,825 per term (c. 25 credits per term)

Main Language(s) of Instruction: Spanish

International Co-operation: With universities in Spain; México; Argentina; Chile; Ecuador

Degrees and Diplomas: *Bachiller*, *Título Profesional de Licenciado*; *Maestría*

Student Services: Academic counselling, Canteen, Cultural centre, Employment services, Foreign student adviser, Health services, Language programs, Nursery care, Sports facilities

Student Residential Facilities: Yes

Special Facilities: Radar; Physics and Chemistry Labs

Libraries: Central Library, c. 100.836 vols

Publications: Colección Algarrobo *(annually)*; Colección de Ciencias Sociales *(annually)*; Colección de Derecho *(annually)*; Colección de Temas Empresariales *(annually)*; Colección Persona y Comunicación *(annually)*; Colección Temas de Humanidades *(annually)*

Press or Publishing House: University of Piura Press

Distance students, 436.
Last Updated: 22/09/10

UNIVERSITY OF SAN MARTÍN DE PORRES

Universidad de San Martín de Porres (USMP)
Avenida las Calandrias s/n, Santa Anita, Lima, Lima
Tel: +51(1) 3620064
Fax: +51(1) 3630557
EMail: admision@usmp.edu.pe
Website: http://www.usmp.edu.pe

Rector: Raúl Eduardo Bao García

Faculties

Accountancy, Economics and Finance (Accountancy; Economics; Finance); **Administration and Human Resources** (Administration; Human Resources; International Business; Marketing); **Communication Sciences, Tourism and Psychology** (Advertising and Publicity; Communication Studies; Journalism; Psychology; Tourism); **Dentistry** (Dentistry); **Engineering and Architecture**; **Human Medicine** (Medicine; Surgery); **Law** (Law; Political Sciences); **Nursing and Obstetrics** (Gynaecology and Obstetrics; Nursing)

Institutes

Arts (Music); **Quality of Education**

Schools

Postgraduate Studies

History: Founded 1962. Reorganized 1969.

Governing Bodies: Asamblea Universitaria; Consejo Universitario

Academic Year: March to December

Admission Requirements: Secondary school certificate

Fees: According to socio-economic evaluation. Average semester tuition fee: (US Dollars): 1,000

Main Language(s) of Instruction: Spanish

Degrees and Diplomas: *Bachiller*, *Título Profesional de Licenciado*; *Maestría*: 2 yrs; *Doctorado*: Accountancy and Finance; Education; Law; Medicine; Psychology; Public Administration; Tourism; *Doctorado*: Public Relations, 2 yrs

Student Services: Academic counselling, Canteen, Cultural centre, Employment services, Foreign student adviser, Handicapped facilities, Health services, Language programs, Sports facilities

Special Facilities: Maternity Hospital; Wine Institute; TV Studio; Radio laboratory

Libraries: Yes
Publications: Veritas *(monthly)*
Last Updated: 07/10/10

UNIVERSITY OF SCIENCE AND ARTS OF LATIN AMERICA

Universidad de Ciencias y Artes de América Latina
Avenida Primavera n° 970, Urb. Chacarilla, Surco, Lima
EMail: informes@ucal.edu.pe
Website: http://www.ucal.edu.pe

Presidente: Antonio Palomino

Programmes

Communication Studies (Communication Studies); **Graphic Design** (Advertising and Publicity; Graphic Design); **Interior Design** (Interior Design)

History: Founded 2010.

Main Language(s) of Instruction: Spanish

Degrees and Diplomas: *Bachiller*
Last Updated: 22/10/10

UNIVERSITY OF SCIENCE AND HUMANITIES

Universidad de Ciencias y Humanidades
Av. Universitaria 5175, Los Olivos
Website: http://www.uch.edu.pe/portal/index.php

Presidente: César Augusto Ángeles Caballero

Programmes

Accountancy (Accountancy; Finance); **Electronic Engineering** (Electronic Engineering; Telecommunications Engineering); **Nursing** (Nursing); **Primary Education** (Primary Education); **Systems Engineering** (Systems Analysis)

History: Founded 2006.

Main Language(s) of Instruction: Spanish
Degrees and Diplomas: *Bachiller*
Last Updated: 22/10/10

UNIVERSITY OF THE PACIFIC

Universidad del Pacífico
Apartado 4683, Avenida Salaverry 2020, Jesús María, Lima, 11 Lima
Tel: +51(1) 219-0100
Fax: +51(1) 219-0128
EMail: ori@up.edu.pe
Website: http://www.up.edu.pe

Rector: Felipe Portocarrero Fax: +51(1) 219-0140
Vicerrectora: María Matilde Schwalb Helguero

Centres

Business Management Consulting (Management) *Director*: Pedro Franco Concha; **Languages** (English; Modern Languages) *Director*: María de la Lama Eggerstedt; **Research** (Arts and Humanities; Business Administration; Economics; Mathematics; Political Sciences; Social Sciences) *Director*: Eduardo Morón Pastor

Departments

Humanities (Arts and Humanities; Cultural Studies; History; Literature; Modern Languages; Philosophy); **Social and Political Science** (Political Sciences; Social Sciences)

Faculties

Business Administration and Accountancy (Accountancy; Administration; Business Administration); **Business Engineering** (Business Administration; Information Technology); **Economics** (Economics); **Law** (Law)

Schools

Graduate *Director*: Alejandro Flores Castro

History: Founded 1962. A private institution.

Governing Bodies: University Assembly; Steering Committee

Academic Year: March to December (March-July; August-December)

Admission Requirements: Secondary school certificate and entrance examination

Main Language(s) of Instruction: Spanish

International Co-operation: With universities and institutions in Austria, Belgium, Bolivia, Costa Rica, Ecuador, El Salvador, Slovenia, Netherlands, Germany, Spain, Italy, Finland, France, Guatemala, Island, Nicaragua, Switzerland, Sweden, USA, Canada, Mexico, Colombia, Brazil, Chile, Panama, Paraguay, United Kingdom, Denmark, Czech Republic, Poland, Hungary, Norway, Singapore, Argentina, Uruguay, Venezuela. Also participates in the UNESCO Colombus Programme, CINDA and AUSJAL. Work with ISA and CIEE.

Degrees and Diplomas: *Bachiller*: Accountancy; Business Administration, Economics; Business and Commerce, 5 yrs; *Bachiller*: Law, 6 yrs; *Título Profesional de Licenciado*; *Maestría*: Business Administration; Economics; Finance; Human Resources; Marketing, a further 2 yrs. Also Diplomado

Student Services: Academic counselling, Employment services, Foreign student adviser, Social counselling, Sports facilities

Special Facilities: PC laboratories. Exposition Rooms.

Libraries: General Library, 57,957 vols; Newspaper and magazine Library, 1,197 titles

Press or Publishing House: Editorial de la Universidad del Pacífico
Last Updated: 07/10/10

WOMEN'S UNIVERSITY OF THE SACRED HEART

Universidad Femenina del Sagrado Corazón (UNIFE)
Avenida Los Frutales 954, Urb. Camacho-La Molina, Lima, 12 Lima
Tel: +51(1) 4364641
Fax: +51(1) 4350853
EMail: tsegura@unife.edu.pe
Website: http://www.unife.edu.pe

Rectora: Elga García Aste (1995-) EMail: egarcia@unife.edu.pe

Vicerrectora Académica: Victoria Garcia Garcia
EMail: vgarcia@unife.edu.pe

Vicerrector Administrativo: Jorge Silva Merino
EMail: vicad@unife.edu.pe

Faculties

Architecture (Architecture); **Education** (Education; Preschool Education; Primary Education; Special Education); **Engineering, Nutrition and Administration** (Administration; Computer Engineering; Engineering; Nutrition); **Law** (Law); **Psychology and Humanities** (Humanities and Social Science Education; Psychology); **Translation, Interpretation and Communication** (Communication Studies; Translation and Interpretation)

Schools

Postgraduate Studies *Director*: Rosa María Reusche Lari

History: Founded 1962, opened 1963 by the Sisters of the Sacred Heart. An autonomous institution.

Governing Bodies: University Assembly, University Council

Academic Year: January to December (Januay-March; April-July; August-December)

Admission Requirements: Secondary school certificate and entrance examination

Main Language(s) of Instruction: Spanish

Degrees and Diplomas: *Bachiller*, *Título Profesional de Licenciado*; *Maestría*: 2 yrs; *Doctorado*: a further 2 yrs

Student Services: Academic counselling, Cultural centre, Foreign student adviser, Health services, Language programs, Nursery care, Social counselling, Sports facilities

Special Facilities: Art Gallery

Libraries: c. 60,000 vols

Publications: Revista de Arquitectura *(annually)*; Revista de Educación *(annually)*; Revista de Ing. Sistemas *(annually)*; Revista de la Universidad *(annually)*; Revista de Psicología *(annually)*; Revista 'Puente' *(annually)*
Last Updated: 07/10/10

Philippines

STRUCTURE OF HIGHER EDUCATION SYSTEM

Description:

Higher education is provided by higher education institutions (HEI) composed of public and private universities and colleges. The state universities and colleges (SUCs) on which charters have been conferred are autonomous. In terms of enrolment, a huge majority of students are enrolled in private HEIs. The Commission on Higher Education (CHED) created in 1994 oversees both private and public tertiary schools; the Technical Education and Skills Development Authority (TESDA) is responsible for postsecondary technical and vocational education, while the Department of Education is in charge of basic education (elementary and high school).

Stages of studies:

University level first stage: *Bachelor's degree*

A Bachelor's degree is generally conferred after four years' study. The minimum number of credits required for four-year Bachelor's degrees ranges from 120 to 190. In some fields, such as Business, Teacher Education, Engineering and Agriculture, one semester's work experience is required. In Pharmacy, some HEIs choose to offer the five-year programme with permission from CHED. An internship is required prior to the board examination in Community Pharmacy, Hospital Pharmacy and Industrial Pharmacy. Medical Technology and Radiology Technology are four-year courses with a one-year internship at the 4th year level in an accredited training centre/hospital. Physical Therapy/Occupational Therapy is a five-year course with a clinical internship at the fifth-year level in an accredited training centre/hospital. Nutrition and Dietetics is a four-year course with supervised field experience in the second semester of the fourth-year level in Hospital, Food Service and Public Health. In Engineering, Architecture and Music the Bachelor's degree is conferred after five years' study and in Dentistry and Veterinary Medicine after six years. Medicine and other Health-related programmes require one year's internship or clerkship in an accredited training centre/hospital. In Dentistry, there is a two-year preparatory course and a four-year course. The Veterinary Medicine course comprises two clerkship, three internship units and 14 field experience units. The Bachelor of Science in Nursing is obtained after four years' study at a college or university. Related learning experiences start during the second semester of the 1st year level.

University level second stage: *Post Baccalaureate (Certificate/Diploma); Master's degree*

Certificates and Diplomas are conferred on completion of one or two years of study beyond the Bachelor's degree. They are not equivalent to a Master's degree.

To be admitted to the Master's degree, students must have a general average of at least 85 or B or 2 in the undergraduate course. The Master's degree normally requires a further two years' study (in Architecture five). In Law, students must already have obtained a four-year Bachelor's degree in another subject and secured a Certificate of Eligibility for Law from the institution in which they wish to enroll. The degree often takes eight years to obtain. In Medicine, students must first obtain a Bachelor's degree in another relevant subject before beginning a four-year course in Medicine.

University level third stage: *PhD*

To be admitted to a Doctorate programme, students must have an average of at least 1.75 in the Master's degree. The PhD requires a further two to three years' study (minimum) following upon the Master's degree and a dissertation. In Medicine, after having followed a three-year course, students follow a one-year clinical clerkship, a one-year internship and three to five years' residency for specialization.

ADMISSION TO HIGHER EDUCATION

Admission to university-level studies:

Name of secondary school credential required: High School Diploma

Entrance exam requirements: Students must sit for an Entrance Examination.

Other admission requirements: Certificate of good moral character.

Foreign students admission:

Entrance exam requirements: Students must have graduated from a recognized secondary or high school and should apply directly to the higher education institution where they wish to enrol.

Entry regulations: Foreign students must be in possession of a visa and a financial guarantee. They must present a copy of the Alien Certificate of Registration. In Medicine and Dentistry, they must present a Certificate of Eligibility.

Health requirements: Health certificate.

Language requirements: Students should be proficient in English or Filipino. Special language and other preparatory courses are organized by some universities either before or during regular studies.

RECOGNITION OF STUDIES

Quality assurance system:

The accreditation system is currently under revision. At the moment, it consists in four phases as follows:
Level I (applicant) - refers to programmes which have at least undergone a preliminary survey visit and are certified by the FAAP for private and AACUP for public HEIs;
Level II (accredited status) - refers to programmes which have at least been granted initial accredited status by any of the member agencies of the FAAP and AACUP, whose status is certified by the latter;
Level III (accredited status) - refers to programmes which have been re-accredited and which have met the additional criteria or guidelines set by FAAP and AACUP, whose status is certified by the latter.
Level IV - institutions which have distinguished themselves in a broad area of academic disciplines and enjoy prestige and authority comparable to that of international universities.
The CHED issues a "Special Order" for students who graduated from private HEIs, which are not identified as having a Deregulated and Autonomous Status. A "Special Order" is the authority granted to a private HEI to graduate students, from a specific course on a certain date, provided they have satisfied the requirements. It is required for the graduation of students from the formal tertiary levels in private schools.
The Expanded Tertiary Education Equivalency and Accreditation Programme (ETEEAP) is a certification mechanism for non-school based learning that is integrated into the country's educational system. This programme is a comprehensive education assessment scheme at the tertiary level which recognizes, accredits and gives equivalency of the knowledge, skills, attitudes and values gained by individuals from relevant work experiences, high-level non-formal training and informal experiences parallel to those obtained through the formal system, through modalities.
Foreign students' credentials are assessed by the HEI where they wish to study.

NATIONAL BODIES

Department of Education - DepEd

Secretary: Armin Altamirano Luistro
DepEd Complex, Meralco Avenue
Pasig City
Tel: +63(2) 632 1361-71
WWW: http://www.deped.gov.ph
Role of national body: Responsible for education at elementary and secondary levels. Determines curricula.

Commission on Higher Education - CHED

Chairman: Patricia B. Licuanan
Higher Education Development Center (HEDC) Bldg., C.P. Garcia Avenue, U.P. Diliman
Quezon City
EMail: info@ched.gov.ph
WWW: http://www.ched.gov.ph
Role of national body: Promotes quality education; takes steps to ensure that education is accessible to all; ensures academic freedom; sets minimum standards for programmes; monitors and evaluates the performance of programmes and institutions of higher learning.

Technical Education and Skills Development Authority - TESDA

Director-General: Joel J. Villanueva

TESDA Complex, East Service Road South Super Highway, Taguig

Manila

Tel: +63(2) 877 7777

EMail: contactcenter@tesda.gov.ph;tesdacontactcenter@gmai

WWW: http://www.tesda.gov.ph

Role of national body: Responsible for post-secondary, middle level manpower training and development.

Accrediting Agency of Chartered Colleges and Universities in the Philippines - AACCUP

President and Chairman: Serafin L. Ngohayon

Executive Director: Manuel T. Corpus

Unit 812 Future Point Plaza I

112 Panay Avenue, South Triangle

Quezon City

Tel: +63(2) 415 9016

Fax: +63(2) 415 8995

EMail: mail@aaccupqa.org.ph

WWW: http://www.aaccupqa.org.ph/

Role of national body: Non-Stock, non-profit, non-governmental organization that aims to upgrade the quality of education through voluntary accreditation for public HEIs.

Philippine Accrediting Association of Schools, Colleges and Universities - PAASCU

President: Fr. Joel E. Tabora, SJ

Unit 107

The Tower at Emerald Square

J.P. Rizal Corner P. Tuazon Streets

Quezon City 1109

Tel: +63(2) 911 2845

Fax: +63(2) 911 0807

EMail: info@paascu.org.ph;cpijano@paascu.org.ph

WWW: http://www.paascu.org.ph/

Coordinating Council of Private Educational Associations - COCOPEA

#89-C 9th Avenue

Cubao

Quezon City

Tel: +63(2) 913 2932

Fax: +63(2) 911 5888

Role of national body: Maintains links with the private higher education institutions and the Commission on Higher Education to attain excellence in higher education.

Catholic Educational Association of the Philippines - CEAP

President: Gregorio L. Bañaga

No 7 Road 16 Bgy. Bagong Pag-Asa

Quezon City 1105

Tel: +63(2) 926 5153

Fax: +63(2) 926 5150

EMail: info@ceap.org.ph

WWW: http://www.ceap.org.ph/

Fund Assistance to Private Education - FAPE

7th Floor, Concorde Condominium

Salcedo Corner Benavides Streets

Legaspi Village

Makati City

Tel: +63(2) 892 1466

Fax: +63(2) 818 0013

EMail: info@peac-fape.org.ph
WWW: http://www.fape.org.ph/

Data for academic year: 2006-2007
Source: IAU from Commission on Higher Education (CHED), 2006. Bodies, 2012.

INSTITUTIONS

PUBLIC INSTITUTIONS

ABRA STATE INSTITUTE OF SCIENCE AND TECHNOLOGY

Lagangilang, Lagangilang, Abra
Tel: +63(74) 752-8414
Fax: +63(74) 904-1973

President: Roberto P. Tubaña

Programmes
Agricultural Business (Agricultural Business); **Agricultural Education** (Agricultural Education); **Agricultural Engineering** (Agricultural Engineering); **Agriculture**; **Biology** (Biology); **Education** *(Bangued, Abra)* (Education; English; Filipino; Foreign Languages Education; Home Economics Education; Mathematics Education; Native Language Education; Primary Education; Science Education; Secondary Education); **Forestry** (Forestry; Wood Technology); **Home Economics** (Home Economics); **Industrial Engineering** *(Bangued, Abra)*; **Mathematics** (Mathematics); **Natural Sciences** (Natural Sciences); **Primary Education** (Primary Education)

Further Information: Also Satellite Campus in Bangued, Abra

History: Founded 1908. Acquired present status and title 1983.

Degrees and Diplomas: *Certificate/Diploma*; *Bachelor's Degree*; *Master's Degree*
Last Updated: 21/07/10

ADIONG MEMORIAL POLYTECHNIC STATE COLLEGE

Ditsaan, Ramain, Marawi City, Lanao del Sur 9713

Officer In-Charge: Bashier D. Salic

Programmes
Agriculture (Agricultural Engineering; Agriculture; Crop Production; Forestry); **Computer Science** (History); **Education** (Education; History; Primary Education; Secondary Education)

History: Founded 1999.

Degrees and Diplomas: *Certificate/Diploma*: Agricultural Technology, Forest Ranger; *Associate Degree*: Computer Science; *Bachelor's Degree*: Agriculture, Secondary Education, Forestry; *Master's Degree*: Education
Last Updated: 22/07/10

AGUSAN DEL SUR STATE COLLEGE OF AGRICULTURE AND TECHNOLOGY

San Teodoro, Bunawan, Agusan del Sur 8506

President: Doroteo E. Jaquias

Programmes
Agriculture (Agricultural Business; Agricultural Engineering; Agriculture; Animal Husbandry; Forestry; Horticulture); **Education** (Education; Primary Education; Secondary Education); **Information Technology** (Information Technology)

History: Founded 1908.

Degrees and Diplomas: *Bachelor's Degree*: 4-6 yrs
Last Updated: 23/07/10

AKLAN STATE UNIVERSITY (ASU)

Barangay Bacan, Kalibo, Aklan 5601
Tel: +63(36) 267-5801
Fax: +63(36) 267-5801
Website: http://www.asu.edu.ph

President: Benny A. Palma EMail: bpalma_5@yahoo.com.ph

Vice-President, Administration: Ma. Merline I. Marcelino

Campuses
ASU Ibajay (Agriculture; Computer Science; Crop Production; English; Filipino; Hotel and Restaurant; Hotel Management; Mathematics; Primary Education; Secondary Education; Secretarial Studies; Tourism; Zoology) *Dean*: Theodore R. Rowan; **ASU Kalibo** (Automotive Engineering; Civil Engineering; Cosmetology; Education; Educational Administration; Electrical Engineering; Food Technology; Heating and Refrigeration; Home Economics; Industrial Arts Education; Industrial Engineering; Machine Building; Painting and Drawing; Textile Technology) *Dean*: Loneto R. Berlandino; **ASU Makato** (Education; Educational Administration; English; Filipino; Home Economics Education; Mathematics; Secondary Education; Technology Education) *Head, TEC*: Eleonor T. Mationg; **ASU New Washington** (Education; Fishery; Food Technology; Hotel and Restaurant; Hotel Management; Marine Biology; Physical Education; Primary Education; Secondary Education; Taxation) *Dean*: Elenita B. Andrade

Centres
Teacher Education (Education; English; Home Economics; Mathematics; Secondary Education; Teacher Training; Technology; Technology Education)

Colleges
Agriculture, Forestry and Environmental Sciences (Agricultural Economics; Agricultural Engineering; Agriculture; Crop Production; Environmental Management; Environmental Studies; Food Science; Forestry; Home Economics; Nutrition; Soil Science; Zoology); **Fisheries and Marine Sciences** (Coastal Studies; English; Filipino; Fishery; Food Science; Food Technology; Health Sciences; Hotel and Restaurant; Hotel Management; Marine Biology; Marine Science and Oceanography; Mathematics; Music; Natural Resources; Physical Education; Taxation; Tourism); **Hospitality and Rural Resources Management** (Agriculture; Computer Science; Crop Production; English; Filipino; Hotel and Restaurant; Hotel Management; Mathematics; Natural Resources; Rural Studies; Tourism; Zoology); **Industrial Technology** (Architecture; Automotive Engineering; Civil Engineering; Cosmetology; Electronic Engineering; Food Technology; Home Economics; Hotel and Restaurant; Hotel Management; Industrial Arts Education; Industrial Engineering; Information Technology; Technology; Textile Technology); **Teacher Education** (Biological and Life Sciences; Education; English; Mathematics; Physics; Primary Education; Social Studies; Teacher Training)

Schools
Arts and Sciences (Applied Mathematics; Biology; English; Health Education; Health Sciences; Mathematics; Nursing); **Management Sciences** (Accountancy; Business Administration; Economics; Finance; Human Resources; Information Management; Management; Marketing; Public Administration); **Veterinary Medicine** (Veterinary Science)

History: Founded 1918. Acquired present status 2001.

Degrees and Diplomas: *Certificate/Diploma*; *Associate Degree*; *Bachelor's Degree*; *Post Baccalaureate Certificate/Diploma*; *Master's Degree*; *PhD*
Last Updated: 28/03/11

ALTAVAS COLLEGE

Altavas, Aklan 5616
Tel: +63(36) 269-1287
Fax: +63(36) 269-1059
EMail: altavas_college@yahoo.com

President: Denny D. Refol

Programmes

Business Administration (Business Administration); **Education** (Education; English; Mathematics Education; Primary Education; Secondary Education); **Hotel and Restaurant Management** (Hotel and Restaurant; Hotel Management)

History: Founded 2003.

Degrees and Diplomas: *Bachelor's Degree*
Last Updated: 26/07/10

APAYO STATE COLLEGE

Malama, Conner, Apayao 3807
Tel: +63(918) 080-5897

President: Zacarias Baluscang Jr.

Programmes

Agriculture *(Also Luna Campus)* (Agriculture; Animal Husbandry; Crop Production; Forestry; Zoology); **Architecture** *(Luna Campus)* (Architecture); **Business Administration** (Business Administration; Management; Management Systems; Public Administration; Secretarial Studies); **Computer Science** (Computer Science); **Education** *(Also Luna Campus)* (Education; Educational Administration; Foreign Languages Education; Home Economics Education; Mathematics Education; Primary Education; Secondary Education); **Engineering and Technology** *(Also Luna Campus)* (Automotive Engineering; Civil Engineering; Electronic Engineering; Food Technology; Industrial Engineering; Information Technology; Interior Design; Textile Technology)

History: Founded 1971.

Degrees and Diplomas: *Certificate/Diploma*: 2 yrs; *Associate Degree*: 2 yrs; *Bachelor's Degree*: 4 yrs
Last Updated: 27/07/10

AURORA STATE COLLEGE OF TECHNOLOGY

Sitio Dicaloyungan Brgy, Zabali, Baler, Aurora 3200
Tel: +63(42) 209-4354
Fax: +63(42) 209-4354
EMail: ascot@mindgate.net
Website: http://ascot.edu.ph/

President: Eusebio V. Angara

Departments

Agriculture and Aquatic Science (Agriculture; Aquaculture; Crop Production; Fishery); **Engineering** (Civil Engineering; Electrical Engineering; Engineering; Mechanical Engineering); **Forestry and Environmental Sciences** (Environmental Management; Environmental Studies; Forestry); **General Education** (Biology; Education; Educational Administration; English; Hotel and Restaurant; Hotel Management; Mathematics Education; Physical Education; Primary Education; Science Education; Secondary Education; Tourism); **Graduate Studies**; **Industrial Technology** (Automotive Engineering; Building Technologies; Civil Engineering; Electrical Engineering; Food Technology; Industrial Engineering; Technology); **Information Technology** (Information Technology)

Programmes

Management (Educational Administration; Management; Public Administration)

Further Information: Also campus in Bazal.

History: Founded 1994.

Degrees and Diplomas: *Certificate/Diploma*; *Bachelor's Degree*; *Master's Degree*
Last Updated: 28/07/10

BACOLOD CITY COLLEGE

Barangay Taculing, Bacolod City, Negros Occidental 6100
Tel: +63(34) 708-6200
Fax: +63(34) 708-6200

Administrator: Reynaldo P. Parreñas

Programmes

Business Administration (Business Administration; Business Computing; Management; Secretarial Studies); **Education** (Education; English; Mathematics Education); **Industrial Technology** (Civil Engineering; Industrial Engineering); **Information Systems** (Information Management; Information Technology)

History: Founded 1997.

Degrees and Diplomas: *Bachelor's Degree*: 4 yrs
Last Updated: 29/07/10

BAGANGA COLLEGE

Poblacion, Baganga, Davao Oriental 8204
Tel: +63(82) 440-3433

Dean: Vilma Labad

Programmes

Education (Education; English; Mathematics Education; Primary Education; Secondary Education)

History: Founded 2005.

Degrees and Diplomas: *Bachelor's Degree*; *Master's Degree*
Last Updated: 29/07/10

BAGO CITY COLLEGE

Barangay Balingasad, Bago City, Negros Occidental 6101
Tel: +63(34) 461-1363
Fax: +63(34) 461-0199
EMail: bagocc_regofc@yahoo.com

Administrator: Ramona C. Lamo

Programmes

Agriculture (Animal Husbandry; Horticulture); **Computer Science** (Computer Science); **Criminology** (Criminology); **Engineering and Technology** (Agricultural Engineering; Automotive Engineering; Building Technologies; Electrical and Electronic Engineering); **English** (English); **Hotel and Restaurant Services** (Cooking and Catering; Hotel and Restaurant; Hotel Management); **Mathematics** (Mathematics); **Primary Education** (Primary Education); **Secondary Education** (Secondary Education)

History: Founded 1980.

Degrees and Diplomas: *Certificate/Diploma*; *Associate Degree*; *Bachelor's Degree*
Last Updated: 29/07/10

BALABAGAN TRADE SCHOOL

Narra Street, Balabagan, Lanao Del Sur 9302
EMail: BTS/lanao@yahoo.com

Administrator: Sarbaya Bonsalagan

Programmes

Education (Education; Primary Education; Secondary Education); **Industrial Arts** (Industrial Arts Education)

History: Founded 1967.

Degrees and Diplomas: *Bachelor's Degree*
Last Updated: 07/04/11

BALUD MUNICIPAL COLLEGE

Abelita, Sr., Balud, Masbate 5412

Dean: Fausto Ibañez

Programmes

Education (Education; English; Native Language; Native Language Education; Primary Education; Secondary Education)

History: Founded 2006.

Degrees and Diplomas: *Bachelor's Degree*
Last Updated: 29/07/10

BASILAN STATE COLLEGE

Sumagdang, Isabela City, Basilan 7300
Tel: +63(62) 200-7523

President: Idris Hakim

Programmes

Arts and Sciences (Agricultural Engineering; Computer Science; Criminology; Dietetics; English; Filipino; Islamic Studies; Mathematics; Native Language; Nursing; Nutrition); **Business Administration** (Business Administration; Business Computing; Management; Public Administration); **Education** (Agricultural Education; Education; Educational Administration; Educational Sciences; Primary Education; Secondary Education); **Government and Political Sciences** (Government; Political Sciences); **Law** (Law)

History: Founded 1984.

Degrees and Diplomas: *Bachelor's Degree*; *Master's Degree*; *PhD*
Last Updated: 29/07/10

BATAAN PENINSULA STATE UNIVERSITY

Capitol Compound, Balanga City, Bataan 2100
Tel: +63(47) 237-2350
Fax: +63(47) 237-2350
Website: http://www.bpsu.edu.ph

President: Delfin O. Magpantay
EMail: domagpantay@bpsu.edu.ph

Vice-President for Administration and Finance: Gregorio J. Rodis EMail: gjrodis@bpsu.edu.ph

Vice-President for Academic Affairs: Mercedes G. Sanchez
EMail: mgsanchez@bpsu.edu.ph

Campuses

Abucay (Agricultural Business; Agricultural Engineering; Agricultural Equipment; Agriculture; Agronomy; Secondary Education; Technology Education; Zoology); **Dinalupihan** (Biology; Civil Engineering; Electrical Engineering; Hotel and Restaurant; Hotel Management; Mathematics; Nursing; Physics; Primary Education; Secondary Education; Social Studies); **Orani** (Cosmetology; Electronic Engineering; Food Technology; Home Economics; Home Economics Education; Hotel and Restaurant; Hotel Management; Industrial Arts Education; Industrial Engineering; Nursing; Primary Education)

Colleges

Arts and Sciences (Hotel and Restaurant; Hotel Management; Nursing); **Business and Accountancy** *(Balanga Campus)* (Accountancy; Business Administration; Human Resources; Management; Management Systems; Marketing); **Education** *(Balanga Campus)* (Art Education; Biological and Life Sciences; English; Filipino; Health Education; Mathematics Education; Music Education; Native Language; Native Language Education; Physical Education; Physics; Secondary Education; Social Studies); **Engineering and Architecture** (Architecture; Civil Engineering; Electronic Engineering; Mechanical Engineering; Structural Architecture; Telecommunications Engineering); **Industrial Technology** (Automotive Engineering; Electrical and Electronic Engineering; Food Technology; Heating and Refrigeration; Mechanical Equipment and Maintenance; Metal Techniques; Production Engineering); **Nursing and Midwifery** *(Balanga Campus)* (Midwifery; Nursing); **Social and Behavioural Sciences** (Behavioural Sciences; Social Sciences); **Technical - Vocational Training**

Institutes

Advanced Studies (Business Administration; Education; Educational Administration; Educational and Student Counselling; Engineering Management; Filipino; Foreign Languages Education; Home Economics Education; Mathematics Education; Native Language; Native Language Education; Nursing; Physical Education; Public Administration; Science Education; Social Studies; Sports; Technology Education)

Further Information: Campuses in Abucay, Balanga, Dinalupihan and Orani

History: Founded 1953. Acquired present status and title 2007 following merger of Bataan Polytechnic State College and Bataan State College.

Degrees and Diplomas: *Certificate/Diploma*: 1-3 yrs; *Associate Degree*: 2 yrs; *Bachelor's Degree*: 4 yrs; *Bachelor's Degree*: Engineering, 5 yrs; *Master's Degree*: a further 2 yrs; *PhD*: a further 2 yrs
Last Updated: 30/07/10

BATANES STATE COLLEGE

San Antonio, Basco, Batanes 3900

President: Aleth M. Mamauag

Programmes

Undergraduate and Professional (Agriculture; Hotel and Restaurant; Hotel Management; Industrial Engineering; Information Technology; Primary Education; Secondary Education; Software Engineering; Tourism)

History: Founded 1967. Acquired present status 1995. Formerly known as Batanes Polytechnic College.

Degrees and Diplomas: *Certificate/Diploma*; *Bachelor's Degree*: 4 yrs
Last Updated: 30/07/10

BATANGAS STATE UNIVERSITY

Rizal Avenue, Batangas City, Batangas 4200
Tel: +63(43) 723-0339
Fax: +63(43) 723-5373
Website: http://www.batstate-u.edu.ph/

President: Nora Lumbera-Magnaye
EMail: noramagnaye@yahoo.com

Vice-President for Academic Affairs: Leonila V. Antonio

Vice-President for Administration and Finance: Luzviminda C. Catapang-Rosales

Campuses

Alangilan (Advertising and Publicity; Architecture; Automation and Control Engineering; Chemical Engineering; Civil Engineering; Computer Engineering; Electrical and Electronic Engineering; Engineering; Environmental Engineering; Fine Arts; Food Technology; Hotel and Restaurant; Hotel Management; Industrial Engineering; Information Management; Information Technology; Interior Design; Marine Transport; Mechanical Engineering; Metal Techniques; Petroleum and Gas Engineering; Sanitary Engineering; Telecommunications Engineering; Tourism); **Apolinario R. Apacible School of Fisheries - Nasugbu** *(ARASOF Campus)* (Accountancy; Agricultural Engineering; Agriculture; Biological and Life Sciences; Business Administration; Business and Commerce; Computer Engineering; Computer Science; Criminology; Economics; Education; Electrical and Electronic Engineering; English; Finance; Fishery; Food Technology; Hotel and Restaurant; Hotel Management Human Resources; Industrial Engineering; Information Technology; Management; Marine Transport; Marketing; Mass Communication; Mathematics Education; Nursing; Primary Education; Psychology; Secondary Education; Teacher Training; Tourism); **Balayan** (Accountancy; Architecture; Business Administration; Business and Commerce; Computer Science; Education; Electrical and Electronic Engineering; Engineering; Fine Arts; Hotel and Restaurant; Hotel Management; Industrial Arts Education; Industrial Engineering; Teacher Training; Tourism); **Jose P. Laurel Polytechnic College - Malvar** *(JPLPC Malvar Campus)* (Accountancy; Art Education; Automation and Control Engineering; Biological and Life Sciences; Business Administration; Business and Commerce; Civil Engineering; Computer Engineering; Computer Science; Criminology; Economics; Education; Electronic Engineering; Engineering; English; Finance; Food Technology; Health Education; Hotel and Restaurant; Hotel Management; Human Resources; Industrial Engineering; Management; Marketing; Mathematics Education; Mechanical Engineering; Metal Techniques; Music Education; Physical Education; Primary Education; Production Engineering; Psychology; Secondary Education; Teacher Training; Tourism); **Lemery** (Accountancy; Architecture; Business Administration; Business and Commerce; Computer Engineering; Computer Science; Education; Electrical and Electronic Engineering; Engineering; Finance; Fine Arts; Industrial Arts Education; Industrial Engineering; Management; Marketing; Teacher Training; Tourism); **Lipa City** (Accountancy; Business Administration; Business and Commerce; Communication Studies; Computer Engineering; Computer Science; Engineering; Human Resources; Industrial Engineering; Management; Marketing; Psychology); **Lobo** (Agricultural Engineering; Agriculture;

Education; Educational Administration; Forestry; Secondary Education; Tropical Agriculture); **Rosario** (Accountancy; Architecture; Automotive Engineering; Business Administration; Business and Commerce; Computer Engineering; Computer Science; Economics; Education; Electrical and Electronic Engineering; Engineering; Fine Arts; Industrial Engineering; Primary Education; Secondary Education; Teacher Training; Tourism); **San Juan** (Business Administration; Computer Engineering; Education; Electrical and Electronic Engineering; English; Industrial Engineering; Marketing; Mathematics; Mathematics Education; Primary Education; Science Education; Secondary Education); **Taysan** (Computer Engineering; Education; Electrical Engineering; Electronic Engineering; Food Technology; Home Economics; Industrial Arts Education; Primary Education; Public Administration; Secondary Education)

Colleges

Accountancy, Business, Economics and International Hospitality Management (Accountancy; Business Administration; Business and Commerce; Economics; Finance; Hotel and Restaurant; Hotel Management; Human Resources; Management; Marketing; Tourism); **Arts and Science** (Biology; Chemistry; Cinema and Television; Communication Studies; Criminology; English; Journalism; Mathematics; Psychology; Public Administration; Radio and Television Broadcasting; Taxation); **Engineering, Architecture, Fine Arts and Computer Science** (Architecture; Automation and Control Engineering; Chemical Engineering; Civil Engineering; Computer Engineering; Computer Science; Electrical and Electronic Engineering; Environmental Engineering; Fine Arts; Food Technology; Industrial Engineering; Information Technology; Interior Design; Mechanical Engineering; Petroleum and Gas Engineering; Sanitary Engineering; Structural Architecture; Telecommunications Engineering; Visual Arts); **Industrial Technology** (Automation and Control Engineering; Automotive Engineering; Civil Engineering; Computer Engineering; Electrical Engineering; Electronic Engineering; Food Technology; Metal Techniques; Production Engineering); **Law** (Law); **Nursing** (Dietetics; Nursing); **Teacher Education** (Art Education; Child Care and Development; Computer Education; Education; English; Filipino; Health Education; Home Economics Education; Industrial Arts Education; Mathematics Education; Music Education; Native Language; Native Language Education; Physical Education; Preschool Education; Primary Education; Science Education; Secondary Education; Social Sciences; Technology)

Schools

Graduate Studies (Business Administration; Chemistry; Computer Engineering; Computer Science; Education; Educational Administration; Electronic Engineering; Engineering; English; Foreign Languages Education; Information Technology; Literature; Mathematics Education; Mechanical Engineering; Philosophy; Public Administration; Technology; Telecommunications Engineering)

History: Founded 1903. Acquired present status 2001.

Degrees and Diplomas: *Certificate/Diploma*; *Associate Degree*; *Bachelor's Degree*; *Master's Degree*; *PhD*

Last Updated: 30/07/10

BENGUET STATE UNIVERSITY

Km. 5, La Trinidad, La Trinidad, Benguet 2601
Tel: +63(74) 442-2127
Fax: +63(74) 442-2281
EMail: admin@bsu.edu.ph
Website: http://www.bsu.edu.ph

President: Rogelio D. Colting EMail: op@bsu.edu.ph

Vice-President for Academic Affairs: Tessie M. Merestela

Vice-President: Alfredo C. Tipayno

Colleges

Agriculture (Agricultural Business; Agricultural Economics; Agriculture; Agronomy; Entomology; Forestry; Horticulture; Plant Pathology; Rural Planning; Rural Studies; Soil Science; Zoology); **Arts and Sciences** (Biology; Environmental Studies; Information Technology; Mathematics; Native Language; Native Language Education; Physics; Science Education; Statistics); **Engineering and Applied Technology** (Agricultural Engineering; Engineering; Technology); **Forestry** (Forestry); **Home Economics and Technology** (Dietetics; Home Economics; Nutrition; Technology); **Nursing** (Nursing); **Teacher Education** (Art Education; Biological and Life Sciences; Education; English; Ethics; Filipino; Health Education; Mathematics; Mathematics Education; Music Education; Native Language; Native Language Education; Physical Education; Physics; Preschool Education; Primary Education; Secondary Education; Social Studies); **Veterinary Medicine**

Institutes

Physical Education and Sports (Physical Education; Sports)

Schools

Graduate Studies (Agricultural Education; Agriculture; Agronomy; Biology; Botany; Education; Educational Administration; Educational and Student Counselling; Entomology; Foreign Languages Education; Forestry; Horticulture; Native Language; Native Language Education; Natural Resources; Physics; Primary Education; Public Administration; Rural Studies; Science Education; Soil Science; Technology Education; Water Management; Zoology)

Further Information: Also Open University. Branches in Buguias and Bokod

History: Founded 1916, acquired present status and title 1985.

Governing Bodies: Board of Regents

Academic Year: June to March (June-October; November-March)

Admission Requirements: Graduation from high school and entrance examination

Fees: (Pesos): c. 25 per unit; graduate, c. 110-200 per unit

Main Language(s) of Instruction: Filipino, English

Degrees and Diplomas: *Certificate/Diploma*; *Associate Degree*; *Bachelor's Degree*; *Post Baccalaureate Certificate/Diploma*; *Master's Degree*; *PhD*

Student Residential Facilities: Yes

Special Facilities: Regional Information Technology Centre. Museums. Tissue Culture Laboratory.

Libraries: Main Library and College Libraries, c. 40,000 vols

Publications: Academic Chronicle *(quarterly)*; BSU Research Journal; Rangtay *(quarterly)*; Research and Extension Newsletter *(quarterly)*

Last Updated: 02/08/10

BICOL UNIVERSITY

Rizal Street, Legazpi City, Albay 4500
Tel: +63(52) 821-7939
Fax: +63(52) 821-7939
EMail: bumps@isp.bicol-u.edu.ph
Website: http://www.bicol-u.edu.ph

President: Fay Lea Patria M. Lauraya

Vice-President for Academic Affairs: Helen M. Llenaresas

Vice-President for Administration: Eduardo M. Loria

Colleges

Agriculture and Forestry (Agricultural Business; Agricultural Engineering; Agricultural Management; Agronomy; Coastal Studies; Crop Production; Forestry; Natural Resources; Zoology); **Arts and Letters** (Cinema and Television; Communication Arts; Communication Studies; English; Journalism; Media Studies; Radio and Television Broadcasting; Speech Studies; Theatre); **Business, Economics and Management** (Accountancy; Business Administration; Economics; Government; Management; Physical Education; Political Sciences; Public Administration; Social Work; Sociology); **Education** (Art Education; Biological and Life Sciences; Biology; Chemistry; Education; Educational Administration; Educational and Student Counselling; Educational Technology; English; Ethics; Filipino; Health Education; History; Home Economics; Home Economics Education; Library Science; Mathematics Education; Music Education; Native Language; Native Language Education; Physical Education; Physics; Primary Education; Science Education; Secondary Education; Social Studies; Social Work; Speech Studies; Technology Education; Theatre); **Engineering** (Automotive Engineering; Computer Engineering; Computer Science; Electrical and Electronic Engineering; Engineering; Food Technology; Information Technology; Mechanical Engineering; Telecommunications Engineering); **Fisheries** (Aquaculture; Coastal Studies; Fishery; Food Technology; Natural Resources); **Industrial Technology** (Automotive Engineering; Chemical Engineering; Civil Engineering; Electrical and Electronic Engineering; Food Science; Food

Technology; Industrial Engineering; Information Technology; Mechanical Engineering; Metal Techniques; Mining Engineering; Thermal Engineering); **Nursing** (Nursing); **Science** (Biology; Chemistry; Computer Science)

Programmes

Architecture (Architecture); **Peace and Security Administration** (Peace and Disarmament)

Further Information: Also Daraga, Polangui and Tabaco campuses

History: Founded 1969 incorporating Bicol Teachers' College; Roxas Memorial Agricultural School; Bicol Regional School of Arts and Trades; and Bicol School of Fisheries. A State Institution.

Governing Bodies: Board of Regents

Academic Year: June to March (June-October; November-March)

Admission Requirements: Graduation from high school and entrance examination

Main Language(s) of Instruction: Filipino, English

Degrees and Diplomas: *Certificate/Diploma*; *Associate Degree*; *Bachelor's Degree*; *Master's Degree*; *PhD (EdD)*

Student Residential Facilities: Yes

Special Facilities: Natural History Museum

Libraries: Central Library c. 70,000 vols

Publications: Bicol Universitarian; BU Bulletin and Outreach Publication; Coverall; Gearcast (Engineering); Publications of the Colleges; Rand D Journal

Press or Publishing House: Extension Service Centre

Last Updated: 02/08/10

BUKIDNON STATE UNIVERSITY (BSC)

Fortich Street, Malaybalay City, Bukidnon 8700
Tel: +63(88) 841-2237
Fax: +63(88) 841-2237
Website: http://www.bsc.edu.ph

President: Victor M. Barroso
Tel: +63(88) 841-2196, Fax: +63(88) 813-2717
EMail: presoffice@bsc.edu.ph

Vice-President for Administration, Planning and Development: Oscar B. Cabañelez

Vice-President for Academic Affairs: Cornelia T. Partosa

Colleges

Arts and Science (Economics; English; Mathematics; Physics; Social Sciences; Sociology; Technology); **Business Administration and Information Technology** (Accountancy; Banking; Business Administration; Computer Engineering; Electronic Engineering; Finance; Information Technology; Software Engineering); **Community Education and Industrial Technology** (Automotive Engineering; Communication Studies; Cooking and Catering; Cosmetology; Development Studies; Electrical and Electronic Engineering; Electronic Engineering; Food Technology; Government; Hotel and Restaurant; Hotel Management; Public Administration; Social and Community Services; Technology; Textile Technology; Wood Technology); **Law** (Law); **Nursing** (Nursing); **Teacher Education** (Biological and Life Sciences; English; Filipino; Home Economics Education; Mathematics; Mathematics Education; Native Language; Native Language Education; Physics; Preschool Education; Primary Education; Science Education; Secondary Education; Social Studies; Technology; Technology Education)

Schools

Graduate Studies (Biological and Life Sciences; Education; Educational Administration; Educational and Student Counselling; Educational Technology; English; Mathematics Education; Public Administration; Science Education; Sociology)

History: Founded 1924. Formerly known as Bukidnon State College. Acquired present status and title 2007.

Admission Requirements: Admission examination and psychological test

Fees: (Pesos): c. 6,000

Main Language(s) of Instruction: Filipino, English

International Co-operation: With universities in USA; Australia; United Kingdom; Singapore; Japan

Accrediting Agencies: CHED's IQuAME; Accrediting Agency of Chartered Colleges and Universities in the Philippines (AACCUP)

Degrees and Diplomas: *Bachelor's Degree*; *Master's Degree*; *PhD*

Student Services: Academic counselling, Canteen, Cultural centre, Health services, Language programs, Nursery care, Sports facilities

Last Updated: 03/08/10

BULACAN AGRICULTURAL STATE COLLEGE

Pinaod, San Ildefonso, Bulacan 3010
Tel: +63(44) 901-1427
Fax: +63(47) 901-1427
EMail: administration@buasc.winsys.net
Website: http://www.basc.org.ph/

President: Josie A. Valdez

Programmes

Agriculture (Agricultural Business; Agricultural Economics; Agricultural Education; Agricultural Engineering; Animal Husbandry; Crop Production; Food Technology; Forestry; Home Economics; Technology; Zoology); **Business Administration** (Business Administration); **Education** (Biology; Chemistry; Education; Educational Administration; English; Mathematics Education; Primary Education; Science Education; Secondary Education); **Hospitality Management** (Hotel and Restaurant; Hotel Management; Tourism); **Information Technology** (Information Technology)

Further Information: Also Doña Remedios Trinidad Campus (Doña Remedios Trinidad, Bulacan)

History: Founded 1953. Formerly known as Bulacan National Agricultural State College.

Degrees and Diplomas: *Certificate/Diploma*; *Associate Degree*; *Bachelor's Degree*; *Master's Degree*

Last Updated: 03/08/10

BULACAN STATE UNIVERSITY

McArthur Hi-Way, City of Malolos, Bulacan 3000
Tel: +63(44) 791-0153 +63(44) 791-0852 +63(44) 791-2165
Fax: +63(97) 791-0153
EMail: bsu-ice@bulsu.edu.ph
Website: http://www.bulsu.edu.ph

President: Mariano C. de Jesus

Colleges

Architecture and Fine Arts (Advertising and Publicity; Architecture; Fine Arts; Landscape Architecture; Painting and Drawing; Visual Arts); **Arts and Letters** (Communication Arts; Fine Arts; Journalism; Mass Communication; Performing Arts; Radio and Television Broadcasting; Visual Arts); **Education** (Automotive Engineering; Biology; Chemistry; Computer Education; Electrical Engineering; Electronic Engineering; English; Filipino; Food Technology; Heating and Refrigeration; Information Sciences; Library Science; Mathematics Education; Music Education; Native Language Education; Physics; Preschool Education; Primary Education; Science Education; Secondary Education; Social Sciences; Special Education; Teacher Training; Technology Education; Textile Technology); **Engineering** (Aeronautical and Aerospace Engineering; Civil Engineering; Computer Engineering; Electrical Engineering; Electronic Engineering; Industrial Engineering; Mechanical Engineering; Production Engineering; Telecommunications Engineering); **Home Economics** (Home Economics; Hotel and Restaurant; Hotel Management; Tourism); **Industrial Technology** (Automation and Control Engineering; Automotive Engineering; Electronic Engineering; Food Technology; Heating and Refrigeration; Technology; Textile Technology); **Information and Communications Technology** (Computer Engineering; Information Technology); **Nursing** (Nursing); **Physical Education, Recreation and Sports** (Parks and Recreation; Physical Education; Sports); **Science** (Biology; Computer Science; Mathematics; Statistics); **Social Sciences and Philosophy** (Accountancy; Business Administration; Criminology; Law; Management; Psychology)

Schools

Graduate Studies (Biology; Business Administration; Chemistry; Civil Engineering; Computer Engineering; Curriculum; Education; Educational Administration; Educational and Student Counselling; Electronic Engineering; Filipino; Foreign Languages Education; Home Economics Education; Information Technology; Law;

Mathematics Education; Mechanical Engineering; Native Language; Native Language Education; Physics; Preschool Education; Primary Education; Public Administration; Science Education; Social Studies; Technology Education; Telecommunications Engineering)

Further Information: Campuses: Bustos (Bustos, Bulacan), Meneses (Matungao, Bulacan) and San José del Monte (Bulacan)

History: Founded 1904 as Bulacan Trade School. Renamed Bulacan College of Arts and Trades 1965-1993. Acquired present status and title 1993.

Governing Bodies: Board of Regents

Academic Year: June to March (June-October; November-March)

Admission Requirements: Graduation from high school and entrance examination

Main Language(s) of Instruction: English

Degrees and Diplomas: *Certificate/Diploma*; *Bachelor's Degree*; *Master's Degree*; *PhD*

Last Updated: 04/08/10

CAGAYAN STATE UNIVERSITY (CSU)

Carig, Tuguegarao City, Cagayan 3500
Tel: +63(78) 846-7455
Fax: +63(78) 844-4119
EMail: inquiry@csu.edu.ph
Website: http://www.csu.edu.ph

President: Roger P. Perez

Vice-President for Administration and Business: Perfecto V. Vivit

Campuses

Aparri *(Aparri, Cagayan)* (Accountancy; Automotive Engineering; Biology; Business Administration; Criminology; Educational Administration; Electrical Engineering; Electronic Engineering; English; Filipino; Fishery; Food Technology; Health Education; Home Economics; Hotel and Restaurant; Hotel Management; Human Resources; Industrial Engineering; Industrial Management; Information Technology; Management; Marine Biology; Mathematics Education; Music Education; Native Language; Native Language Education; Physical Education; Police Studies; Primary Education; Public Administration; Science Education; Secondary Education; Social Sciences; Technology; Tourism) *Campus Executive Officer*: Simeon Rabanal, Jr.; **Gonzaga** *(Gonzaga, Cagayan)* (Agriculture; Business Administration; Criminology; Crop Production; Economics; Educational Administration; English; Filipino; Forestry; Hotel and Restaurant; Hotel Management; Information Technology; Management; Native Language Education; Primary Education; Public Administration; Secondary Education; Social Sciences; Zoology) *Campus Executive Officer*: Jana S. Quirino; **Lallo** *(Lal-Lo, Cagayan)* (Agricultural Engineering; Agriculture; Biology; Business Administration; Crop Production; English; Health Education; Hotel and Restaurant; Hotel Management; Information Technology; Mathematics Education; Music Education; Physical Education; Political Sciences; Primary Education; Science Education; Secondary Education; Social Sciences; Technology; Tourism; Zoology) *Campus Executive Officer*: Ferdinand C. Oli; **Lasam** *(Lasam, Cagayan)* (Business Administration; Electronic Engineering; English; Hotel and Restaurant; Hotel Management; Industrial Engineering; Information Technology; Primary Education; Public Administration; Science Education) *Campus Executive Officer*: Bernardino Allag; **Piat** *(Piat, Cagayan)* (Agriculture; Crop Production; English; Home Economics Education; Horticulture; Information Technology; Mathematics Education; Primary Education; Secondary Education; Social Sciences; Social Studies; Technology Education; Zoology) *Campus Executive Officer*: Vicente S. Binasoy, Jr.; **Sanchez Mira** *(Sanchez Mira, Cagayan)* (Accountancy; Agriculture; Business Administration; Computer Science; Criminology; Crop Production; Educational Administration; English; Hotel and Restaurant; Hotel Management; Industrial Engineering; Information Technology; Mass Communication; Mathematics; Mathematics Education; Police Studies; Primary Education; Public Administration; Science Education; Secondary Education; Tourism; Zoology) *Campus Executive Officer*: Aurelio C. Caldez

Colleges

Agriculture (Agriculture); **Arts and Sciences** (Biology; Chemistry; Economics; English; Environmental Management; Environmental Studies; Information Technology; Law; Management; Mass Communication; Mathematics; Political Sciences; Psychology); **Business, Entrepreneurship and Accountancy** (Accountancy; Business Administration; Finance; Management; Marketing); **Education** (Automotive Engineering; Biological and Life Sciences; Education; Electrical Engineering; Electronic Engineering; English; Filipino; Food Technology; Mathematics Education; Native Language; Native Language Education; Physics; Primary Education; Secondary Education; Social Sciences; Technology Education; Textile Design; Textile Technology); **Engineering** (Agricultural Engineering; Chemical Engineering; Civil Engineering; Computer Engineering; Electrical Engineering; Electronic Engineering; Engineering; Telecommunications Engineering); **Fisheries and Marine Science** (Fishery; Marine Biology; Marine Science and Oceanography); **Hospitality Industry Management** (Hotel and Restaurant; Hotel Management; Tourism); **Information Technology** (Computer Science; Information Technology); **Law** (Law); **Medical Technology** (Laboratory Techniques; Medical Technology); **Medicine** (Medicine; Public Health); **Public Administration** (Public Administration); **Technology** (Automotive Engineering; Electrical Engineering; Electronic Engineering; Food Technology; Heating and Refrigeration; Mechanical Engineering; Technology; Textile Technology); **Veterinary Medicine** (Animal Husbandry; Aquaculture; Environmental Management; Epidemiology; Food Science; Food Technology; Nutrition; Parasitology; Veterinary Science; Wildlife; Zoology)

Schools

Graduate Studies (Agriculture; Biology; Business Administration; Chemistry; Criminal Law; Criminology; Crop Production; Education; Educational Administration; Educational and Student Counselling; Educational Psychology; English; Filipino; Foreign Languages Education; Government; Human Resources; Humanities and Social Science Education; Information Technology; Law; Management; Mathematics; Medicine; Native Language; Native Language Education; Physical Education; Physics; Psychology; Public Administration; Public Health; Public Law; Rural Studies; Social Sciences; Surgery; Technology Education; Zoology)

History: Founded 1907.

Degrees and Diplomas: *Certificate/Diploma*; *Bachelor's Degree*; *Post Baccalaureate Certificate/Diploma*; *PhD*

Student Services: Academic counselling, Canteen, Cultural centre, Health services, Sports facilities

Special Facilities: Museum.

Libraries: Computer, library automation

Last Updated: 04/08/10

CAMARINES SUR POLYTECHNIC COLLEGE

San Isidro, Nabua, Camarines Sur 4434
Tel: +63(54) 631-1321
Fax: +63(54) 631-1321
EMail: presilarde@yahoo.com
Website: http://www.cspc.edu.ph

President: Monsito G. Ilarde

Vice-President for Administration: Ferdinand B. Valencia

Programmes

Graduate (Business Administration; Education; Engineering; Midwifery; Nursing; Technology); **Undergraduate and Professional** (Architecture; Automotive Engineering; Business Administration; Civil Engineering; Computer Engineering; Construction Engineering; Crafts and Trades; Education; Electrical Engineering; Electronic Engineering; Engineering; Food Science; Food Technology; Heating and Refrigeration; Home Economics Education; Hotel and Restaurant; Hotel Management; Information Technology; Management; Mathematics Education; Mechanical Engineering; Medical Technology; Midwifery; Nursing; Physics; Primary Education; Secondary Education; Secretarial Studies; Structural Architecture; Teacher Training; Technology; Technology Education; Telecommunications Engineering; Textile Technology; Tourism)

Further Information: Also Bicol College of Arts and Trades-Naga City Campus (Naga City, Camarines Sur)

History: Founded 1985.

Degrees and Diplomas: *Certificate/Diploma*; *Bachelor's Degree*; *Master's Degree*

Last Updated: 05/08/10

CAMIGUIN POLYTECHNIC STATE COLLEGE

Balbagon, Mambajao, Camiguin 9100
Tel: +63(88) 387-0044
Fax: +63(88) 387-0044

President: Venus Irving A. Lammawin

Programmes

Agriculture (Agricultural Education; Agricultural Engineering; Agriculture; Animal Husbandry; Crop Production; Plant and Crop Protection); **Business Administration** (Business Administration; Ecology; Management; Public Administration; Tourism); **Education** (Biology; Chemistry; Education; Science Education; Secondary Education; Teacher Training); **Engineering and Technology** (Agricultural Engineering; Automotive Engineering; Construction Engineering; Electrical Engineering; Electronic Engineering; Engineering; Technology; Telecommunications Engineering; Textile Technology); **Nursing** (Nursing); **Science** (Computer Science; Marine Biology)

History: Founded 1995. Formerly known as Camiguin School of Arts & Trades.

Degrees and Diplomas: *Bachelor's Degree*; *Master's Degree*

Last Updated: 06/08/10

CAPIZ STATE UNIVERSITY

Fuentes Drive, Roxas City, Capiz 5800
Tel: +63(36) 621-4220
Fax: +63(36) 621-4578
EMail: capizstateuniversity@yahoo.com

President: Rochellir D. Dadivas

Campuses

Dayao *(Dayao, Capiz)* (Business Computing; Criminology; Education; Fishery; Primary Education; Secretarial Studies; Software Engineering); **Dumarao** *(Dumarao, Capiz)* (Agricultural Engineering; Computer Science; Criminology; Education; Home Economics Education; Primary Education; Social Studies; Veterinary Science; Zoology); **Pilar** *(Pilar, Capiz)* (Education; Food Technology; Hotel and Restaurant; Hotel Management; Management; Primary Education; Social and Community Services; Social Work); **Población** *(Capiz)* (Agronomy; Computer Science; Economics; Educational Administration; English; Filipino; Food Technology; Home Economics; Management; Mathematics; Native Language; Political Sciences; Public Administration; Science Education; Social Sciences; Sociology; Zoology); **Población Mambusao** *(Roxas City)* (Accountancy; Agricultural Business; Agricultural Engineering; Agriculture; Art Education; Biology; Business Administration; Business and Commerce; Crop Production; Curriculum; English; Environmental Management; Environmental Studies; Filipino; Finance; Foreign Languages Education; Forestry; Health Education; Home Economics; Home Economics Education; Horticulture; Management; Marketing; Mathematics Education; Music Education; Native Language; Native Language Education; Physical Education; Plant and Crop Protection; Preschool Education; Primary Education; Science Education; Secondary Education; Social Studies; Soil Science; Technology Education; Zoology); **Pontevedra** *(Pontevedra, Capiz)* (Agricultural Economics; Agricultural Engineering; Agriculture; Agronomy; Animal Husbandry; Aquaculture; Business Administration; Business and Commerce; Coastal Studies; Computer Science; Crop Production; Economics; Education; Educational Administration; English; Filipino; Fishery; Food Science; Food Technology; Foreign Languages Education; Health Education; Home Economics; Home Economics Education; Hotel and Restaurant; Hotel Management; Marketing; Mathematics; Mathematics Education; Music Education; Native Language; Native Language Education; Physical Education; Primary Education; Science Education; Social Studies; Teacher Training; Technology Education; Tourism; Zoology); **Sapian** *(Sapian, Capiz)* (English; Food Science; Hotel and Restaurant; Hotel Management; Household Management; Management; Primary Education); **Sigma** *(Sigma, Capiz)* (Automotive Engineering; Electronic Engineering; Food Science; Food Technology; Home Economics; Hotel and Restaurant; Hotel Management; Textile Technology); **Tapaz** *(Tapaz, Capiz)* (Agriculture; Automotive Engineering; Business Computing; Crop Production; Curriculum; Electrical Engineering; Landscape Architecture; Mathematics Education; Primary Education; Secretarial Studies; Zoology)

Programmes

Architecture (Architecture); **Business Administration** (Business Administration; Management; Public Administration); **Education** (Art Education; Biological and Life Sciences; Education; Educational Administration; Health Education; Home Economics Education; Music Education; Physical Education; Physics; Technology Education); **Engineering and Industrial Technology** (Automotive Engineering; Civil Engineering; Cosmetology; Electrical Engineering; Electronic Engineering; Engineering; Food Science; Food Technology; Furniture Design; Heating and Refrigeration; Home Economics; Home Economics Education; Mechanical Engineering; Technology; Textile Technology)

History: Founded 1969.

Degrees and Diplomas: *Bachelor's Degree*; *Master's Degree*; *PhD*

Last Updated: 06/08/10

CARAGA STATE UNIVERSITY

Ampayon, Butuan City, Agusan del Norte 8600
Tel: +63(85) 342-3047
Fax: +63(85) 342-1079
EMail: op_ewi@normisist.edu.ph
Website: http://www.carsu.edu.ph

President: Joanna B. Cuenca

Vice-President for Academic Affairs: Luisito I. Tabada
EMail: litabada@normisist.edu.ph

Campuses

Cabadbaran (Automotive Engineering; Civil Engineering; Electrical Engineering; Engineering; Food Science; Food Technology; Heating and Refrigeration; Hotel and Restaurant; Hotel Management; Industrial Arts Education; Information Technology; Structural Architecture; Technology Education; Textile Technology; Tourism)

Colleges

Agricultural Sciences and Natural Resources (Agricultural Business; Agricultural Engineering; Agricultural Management; Agriculture; Forestry; Horticulture; Natural Resources; Zoology); **Arts and Sciences** (Applied Mathematics; Biology; Entomology; Environmental Studies; Mathematics; Mathematics and Computer Science; Statistics); **Engineering and Information Technology** (Agricultural Engineering; Computer Engineering; Computer Networks; Computer Science; Engineering; Geological Engineering; Information Technology; Materials Engineering; Software Engineering); **Graduate Studies** (Anatomy; Biology; Chemistry; Crop Production; Ecology; Education; Educational Administration; Educational and Student Counselling; English; Environmental Management; Foreign Languages Education; Genetics; Health Education; Information Technology; Literacy Education; Mathematics; Mathematics Education; Physics; Physiology; Science Education); **Science Education** (Biology; Mathematics Education; Primary Education; Science Education; Secondary Education)

History: Founded 1946. Formerly known as Northern Mindanao State Institute of Science and Technology (NORMISIST). Acquired present status 2009 following incorporation of Northern Mindanao College of Science and Technology (NMCAST).

Degrees and Diplomas: *Certificate/Diploma*; *Bachelor's Degree*; *Master's Degree*; *PhD*

Last Updated: 22/12/10

CARLOS HILADO MEMORIAL STATE COLLEGE

Mabini Street, Talisay, Negros Occidental 6115
Tel: +63(34) 708-6451
Fax: +63(34) 433-4611
EMail: chmsc_talisay@chmsc.edu.ph
Website: http://www.chmsc.edu.ph/

President (Acting): Benny Palma

Vice-President for Academic Affairs: Orlando Z. Beñales

Vice-President for Administration: Salvador B. Zaragosa, Jr.

Campuses

Alijis *(Alijis Road, Bacolod City, Negros Occidental)* (Automotive Engineering; Computer Engineering; Education; Electrical Engineering; Electronic Engineering; Food Technology; Mechanical

Engineering; Teacher Training; Textile Technology); **Bacolod** *(Bacolod City, Negros Occidental)* (Accountancy; Business Administration; Finance; Management; Management Systems; Public Administration); **Binalbagan** *(College of Fisheries-Binalbagan, Negros Occidental)* (Aquaculture; Biology; Business Administration; Coastal Studies; Criminology; Fishery; Food Science; Food Technology; Home Economics; Information Technology; Natural Resources; Physics; Primary Education; Science Education; Technology)

Colleges

Education (Art Education; Education; English; Foreign Languages Education; Health Education; Home Economics Education; Mathematics Education; Music Education; Physical Education; Physics; Preschool Education; Primary Education; Secondary Education; Special Education; Technology Education); **Industrial Technology** (Automotive Engineering; Civil Engineering; Electrical and Electronic Engineering; Food Technology; Heating and Refrigeration; Hotel and Restaurant; Hotel Management; Industrial Engineering; Information Technology; Technology; Textile Technology)

Schools

Arts and Science (Arts and Humanities; English; Social Sciences)

History: Founded 1954 as the Negros Occidental School of Arts and Trade. Acquired present title 1994.

Degrees and Diplomas: *Associate Degree*; *Bachelor's Degree*; *Master's Degree*; *PhD*
Last Updated: 06/08/10

CATAINGAN MUNICIPAL COLLEGE

Poblacion, Cataingan, Masbate 5405

Head: Wilton T. Kho

Programmes

Education (Education; English; Mathematics Education; Primary Education; Secondary Education); **Literature** (English; Literature)

History: Founded 1986.

Degrees and Diplomas: *Bachelor's Degree*
Last Updated: 10/08/10

CATANDUANES STATE COLLEGE

Calatagan, Virac, Catanduanes 4800
Tel: +63(52) 811-1485
Fax: +63(52) 811-1295
EMail: csc@catnet.edu.ph;
catanduanes_state_colleges@yahoo.com
Website: http://www.csc.edu.ph

President: Asuncion V. Asetre

Campuses

Panganiban (Agricultural Education; Agriculture; Building Technologies; Crop Production; Curriculum; Education; English; Food Science; Food Technology; Industrial Arts Education; Mathematics Education; Primary Education; Science Education; Zoology)

Programmes

Agriculture (Agricultural Education; Agriculture; Crop Production; Fishery; Zoology); **Arts and Sciences** (Accountancy; Biology; Civil Engineering; Dietetics; Economics; English; Forestry; Home Economics; Information Management; Information Technology; Marketing; Mathematics; Nursing; Nutrition; Political Sciences); **Business Administration** (Agricultural Business; Business Administration; Management; Public Administration); **Education** (Agricultural Education; Art Education; Biological and Life Sciences; Biology; Business Education; Chemistry; Education; Educational Administration; Educational and Student Counselling; English; Ethics; Filipino; Health Education; Home Economics Education; Industrial Arts Education; Library Science; Literacy Education; Mathematics Education; Music Education; Native Language; Native Language Education; Physical Education; Physics; Primary Education; Science Education; Secondary Education; Social Studies; Teacher Trainers Education); **Industrial Education and Technology** (Automotive Engineering; Civil Engineering; Electrical Engineering; Electronic Engineering; Food Technology; Heating and Refrigeration; Industrial Arts Education; Mechanical Engineering; Textile Technology)

History: Founded 1971.

Degrees and Diplomas: *Certificate/Diploma*; *Associate Degree*; *Bachelor's Degree*; *Master's Degree*; *PhD*
Last Updated: 10/08/10

CAVITE STATE UNIVERSITY

Bancod, Indang, Cavite 4122
Tel: +63(46) 415-0013
Fax: +63(46) 415-0012
EMail: cvsu_rc@cavite.net
Website: http://www.cvsu.edu.ph/

President: Divinia C. Chavez

Campuses

Bacoor (Business Administration; Computer Science; English; Hotel and Restaurant; Hotel Management; Mathematics Education; Secondary Education) *Dean*: Henry O. Garcia; **Carmona** (Biology; Business Administration; Computer Engineering; Computer Science; Health Education; Hotel and Restaurant; Hotel Management; Industrial Engineering; Information Technology; Secondary Education) *Dean*: Cristina F. Olo; **Cavite City** (Business Administration; Computer Engineering; Computer Science; Education; English; Filipino; Hotel and Restaurant; Hotel Management; Information Technology; Marketing; Mathematics Education; Native Language; Native Language Education; Primary Education; Secondary Education) *Dean*: Cristeta Montano; **Imus** (Business Administration; Business Computing; Computer Science; Hotel and Restaurant; Hotel Management; Information Technology; Management; Secretarial Studies) *Dean*: Gilchor P. Cubilo; **Naic** *(Formerly Cavite College of Fisheries)* (Biological and Life Sciences; Business Administration; Computer Engineering; Computer Science; Economics; English; Fishery; Food Technology; Health Education; Hotel and Restaurant; Hotel Management; Information Technology; Marketing; Mathematics Education; Primary Education; Secondary Education) *Dean*: Lorenzo L. Lapitan, Jr.; **Rosario** *(Formerly Cavite College of Arts and Trades)* (Computer Engineering; Education; Electrical Engineering; Hotel and Restaurant; Hotel Management; Industrial Arts Education; Industrial Engineering; Management; Secondary Education; Technology) *Dean*: Lorna L. Penales; **Silang** (Business Administration; Business Computing; Computer Science; Education; Hotel and Restaurant; Hotel Management; Information Technology; Landscape Architecture; Secondary Education; Secretarial Studies; Tourism) *Dean*: Julio G. Alava; **Tanza** (Business Administration; Computer Engineering; Computer Science; Hotel and Restaurant; Hotel Management) *Dean*: Reynaldo B. Samonte; **Trece Martires City** (Business Administration; Business Computing; Hotel and Restaurant; Hotel Management; Industrial Engineering; Information Technology; Secretarial Studies) *Dean*: Corazon Y. Mercado

Colleges

Agriculture, Forestry, Environment and Natural Resources (Agricultural Business; Agriculture; Environmental Management; Environmental Studies; Food Technology; Forestry; Natural Resources) *Dean*: Adolfo C. Manuel, Jr.; **Arts and Sciences** (Applied Mathematics; Biology; English; Mass Communication; Political Sciences; Psychology) *Dean*: Evelyn O. Singson; **Economics, Management and Development Studies** (Accountancy; Business Administration; Development Studies; Economics; International Studies; Management) *Dean*: Roderick M. Rupido; **Education** (Education; Hotel and Restaurant; Hotel Management; Preschool Education; Primary Education; Secondary Education; Tourism) *Dean*: Agnes P. Nuestro; **Engineering and Information Technology** (Agricultural Engineering; Architecture; Automotive Engineering; Business Administration; Business Computing; Civil Engineering; Computer Engineering; Computer Science; Earth Sciences; Electrical and Electronic Engineering; Engineering; Industrial Engineering; Information Management; Information Technology; Regional Planning; Secretarial Studies; Structural Architecture; Telecommunications Engineering; Town Planning) *Dean*: Renato B. Cubilla; **Nursing** (Health Education; Medical Technology; Midwifery; Nursing) *Dean*: Lenila A. de Vera; **Sports, Physical Education and Recreation** (Criminology; Parks and Recreation; Physical Education; Sports) *Dean*: Romeo C. Reyes Jr.; **Veterinary Medicine and Biomedical Sciences** (Animal Husbandry; Veterinary Science) *Dean*: Eugene Principe

Schools

Graduate Studies *(Graduate School And Open Learning College)* (Adult Education; Agricultural Economics; Agricultural Engineering; Agriculture; Biology; Business Administration; Chemistry; Civil Engineering; Computer Engineering; Computer Science; Construction Engineering; Crop Production; Curriculum; Design; Education; Educational Administration; Educational and Student Counselling; Electrical and Electronic Engineering; Engineering; Food Science; Human Resources; Information Technology; Management; Mathematics; Mathematics Education; Nursing; Physical Education; Plant and Crop Protection; Primary Education; Public Administration; Regional Planning; Secondary Education; Soil Management; Structural Architecture; Telecommunications Engineering; Town Planning; Water Management; Water Science; Zoology) *Dean*: Lilibeth P. Novicio

Further Information: Also General Trias Campus, Cavit

History: Founded 1906. Acquired present status 1998. Formerly known as Don Severino Agricultural College.

Degrees and Diplomas: *Certificate/Diploma*; *Associate Degree*; *Bachelor's Degree*; *Master's Degree*; *PhD*

Last Updated: 10/08/10

CEBU NORMAL UNIVERSITY (CNU)

Osmeña Boulevard, Cebu City, Cebu 6000
Tel: +63(32) 253-9611
Fax: +63(32) 254-1130
EMail: cnu@cvis.net.ph
Website: http://www.cnu.edu.ph

President: Marcelo Lopez
Tel: +63(32) 253-6211 EMail: cnupres@cvis.net.ph

Colleges

Arts and Sciences (Arts and Humanities; Biological and Life Sciences; Biology; Chemistry; Communication Studies; English; Filipino; Health Sciences; Hotel and Restaurant; Hotel Management; Mathematics; Native Language; Nursing; Physics; Political Sciences; Secondary Education; Social Studies; Tourism); **Teacher Education** (Art Education; Biological and Life Sciences; English; Filipino; Foreign Languages Education; Home Economics Education; Mathematics Education; Music Education; Native Language Education; Physical Education; Physics; Preschool Education; Primary Education; Science Education; Social Studies; Special Education; Technology Education)

Graduate Schools

Graduate Studies (Child Care and Development; Community Health; Education; Educational Administration; Educational and Student Counselling; Educational Psychology; Educational Research; English; Filipino; Foreign Languages Education; Health Administration; Health Education; Home Economics; Home Economics Education; Library Science; Literature; Mathematics Education; Music Education; Native Language Education; Nursing; Physical Education; Preschool Education; Psychiatry and Mental Health; Public Administration; Science Education; Social Studies; Special Education)

Further Information: Nursing practicum provided by the Don Vincente Sotto Medical Memorial Hospital. Also Centre for National Language (Pilipino) in Central Visayas

History: Founded 1915 as Cebu Normal School, became Cebu State College 1976, acquired present status and title 1998.

Governing Bodies: Board of Regents

Academic Year: June to March (June-October; November-March), Summer session, April-May (Graduate Studies only)

Admission Requirements: Graduation from high school, and entrance examination in English

Fees: (Pesos): Tuition, c. 30-50 per unit; graduate, c. 200-250 per unit

Main Language(s) of Instruction: Filipino, English, Spanish. Also Cebuano in Liberal Arts.

International Co-operation: With universities in USA, Spain, Singapore, Canada, Japan, Australia and UK

Accrediting Agencies: Accrediting Agency of Chartered Colleges and Universities in the Philippines (AACCUP)

Degrees and Diplomas: *Bachelor's Degree*; *Master's Degree*; *PhD*

Student Services: Academic counselling, Canteen, Health services, Language programs, Social counselling, Sports facilities

Student Residential Facilities: Yes

Special Facilities: Museum of Visayan Culture (education and culture of Cebuanos from Hindu-Malay to American Eras). Laboratories for Biology, Chemistry and Physics. Speech Laboratory. Audio-Visual,Teacher Excellence and Computer Centres

Libraries: University Libraries

Publications: CNU Graduate School Journal, Research by academics *(biennially)*; Nexus (Connection), Journal of academic papers and research, creative writing *(quarterly)*; Usisa (Investigation), Journal of research for the university *(biennially)*

Last Updated: 11/08/10

CEBU STATE COLLEGE OF SCIENCE AND TECHNOLOGY (CSCST)

R. Palma St., M.J. Cuenco Avenue, Cebu City, Cebu 6000
Tel: +63(32) 256-2164
Fax: +63(32) 416-6706
EMail: information@cscst.ph
Website: http://www.cscst.edu.ph

President: Bonifacio S. Villanueva

Campuses

Argao *(Argao, Cebu)* (Agricultural Engineering; Agriculture; Agronomy; Animal Husbandry; Computer Engineering; Education; Educational Administration; Electronic Engineering; Forestry; Hotel and Restaurant; Hotel Management; Industrial Design; Primary Education; Public Administration; Secondary Education; Technology Education; Textile Technology; Tourism; Zoology) *College Superintendent*: Pedrito C. Pontillas; **Carmen** *(College of Fisheries Technology-Carmen, Cebu)* (Aquaculture; Computer Engineering; Education; Fishery; Home Economics Education; Hotel and Restaurant; Hotel Management; Industrial Engineering; Marine Engineering; Mathematics Education; Primary Education; Science Education; Technology Education; Tourism) *College Superintendent*: Venerando D. Cuñado; **Daanbantayan** *(Daanbantayan, Cebu)* (Aquaculture; Curriculum; Education; Electronic Engineering; Fishery; Harvest Technology; Home Economics; Home Economics Education; Hotel and Restaurant; Hotel Management; Industrial Engineering; Primary Education; Secondary Education; Technology; Technology Education) *College Superintendent*: Severino R. Romano; **Danao City** *(Danao City, Cebu)* (Automotive Engineering; Civil Engineering; Computer Engineering; Education; Electrical Engineering; Electronic Engineering; Heating and Refrigeration; Home Economics Education; Hotel and Restaurant; Hotel Management; Industrial Engineering; Mechanical Engineering; Metal Techniques; Primary Education; Secondary Education; Technology Education; Textile Technology; Tourism) *College Superintendent*: Florencio L. Ramos; **Main** (Automotive Engineering; Education; Educational Administration; Electrical and Electronic Engineering; Home Economics Education; Hotel and Restaurant; Hotel Management; Industrial Engineering; Mathematics; Mechanical Engineering; Nursing; Primary Education; Public Administration; Secondary Education; Special Education; Technology; Technology Education) *President*: Bonifacio S. Villanueva; **Mandaue City** *(Mandaue City, Cebu)* (Automotive Engineering; Civil Engineering; Cosmetology; Electrical Engineering; Electronic Engineering; Engineering; Food Technology; Metal Techniques; Technology; Textile Technology; Wood Technology) *College Superintendent*: Ponciano C. Bontia; **Moalboal** *(Moalboal, Cebu)* (Aquaculture; Education; Educational Administration; Fishery; Harvest Technology; Home Economics Education; Hotel and Restaurant; Hotel Management; Industrial Engineering; Primary Education; Secondary Education) *College Superintendent*: Romeo Pableo; **San Francisco** *(San Francisco, Cebu)* (Aquaculture; Computer Engineering; Curriculum; Education; Electronic Engineering; Fishery; Harvest Technology; Home Economics Education; Hotel and Restaurant; Hotel Management; Industrial Engineering; Primary Education; Tourism) *College Superintendent*: Panfilo E. Ciriaco; **Sudlon/Barili** *(College of Agriculture-Sudlon/Barili, Barili, Cebu)* (Agricultural Economics; Agricultural Engineering; Agriculture; Agronomy; Education;

Forestry; Home Economics Education; Horticulture; Hotel and Restaurant; Hotel Management; Primary Education; Secondary Education; Technology Education; Tourism; Zoology) *College Superintendent*: Hospicio S. Saniel; **Tuburan** *(Tuburan, Cebu)* (Automotive Engineering; Civil Engineering; Cosmetology; Curriculum; Education; Electrical Engineering; Electronic Engineering; Food Technology; Home Economics Education; Hotel and Restaurant; Hotel Management; Industrial Engineering; Metal Techniques; Primary Education; Secondary Education; Technology Education; Textile Technology; Wood Technology) *College Superintendent*: Wilma M. Reyes

Programmes

Graduate Studies (Automotive Engineering; Education; Educational Administration; Electrical and Electronic Engineering; Public Administration; Technology; Technology Education)

History: Founded 1911. Formerly known as Cebu School of Arts and Trades. Acquired present status and title 1982.

Degrees and Diplomas: *Certificate/Diploma*; *Bachelor's Degree*; *Master's Degree*; *PhD*
Last Updated: 11/08/10

CENTRAL BICOL STATE UNIVERSITY OF AGRICULTURE (CBSUA)

San Jose, Pili, Camarines Sur 4418
Tel: +63(54) 3577-3341
Fax: +63(54) 3577-7206
Website: http://www.cssac.edu.ph

President: Marito T. Bernales

Vice-President for Administration andFinance: Ramon C. Arimado

Vice-President for Academic Affairs: Eden C. Paz

Campuses

Calabanga (Arts and Humanities; Automotive Engineering; Curriculum; Education; Electrical and Electronic Engineering; Engineering; English; Filipino; Food Technology; Heating and Refrigeration; Hotel and Restaurant; Hotel Management; Mathematics; Mathematics Education; Native Language; Native Language Education; Preschool Education; Primary Education; Secondary Education; Technology; Textile Technology); **Sipocot** (Automotive Engineering; Biological and Life Sciences; Criminology; Curriculum; Education; Electrical and Electronic Engineering; English; Filipino; Food Science; Food Technology; Home Economics Education; Information Technology; Mathematics; Mathematics Education; Mechanical Engineering; Native Language; Native Language Education; Physics; Primary Education; Secondary Education; Software Engineering; Teacher Training; Technology Education; Textile Technology)

Institutes

Agricultural Sciences and Environmental Management (Agricultural Engineering; Agricultural Equipment; Agriculture; Agronomy; Botany; Entomology; Environmental Management; Environmental Studies; Forestry; Horticulture; Landscape Architecture; Plant Pathology; Soil Science; Waste Management; Water Management; Water Science; Zoology); **Arts and Sciences** (Applied Chemistry; Applied Mathematics; Applied Physics; Arts and Humanities; Computer Science; Engineering; Modern Languages; Physical Education; Social Sciences); **Development Education** (Agriculture; Biological and Life Sciences; Curriculum; English; Filipino; Foreign Languages Education; Home Economics; Mathematics; Mathematics Education; Native Language; Native Language Education; Physics; Preschool Education; Primary Education; Secondary Education); **Economics and Management** (Agricultural Business; Agricultural Economics; Agricultural Engineering; Management; Tourism); **Engineering and Technology** (Agricultural Engineering; Engineering; Food Science; Food Technology; Technology); **Veterinary Medicine** (Veterinary Science)

Programmes

Graduate (Agronomy; Botany; Education; Educational Research; Environmental Management; Horticulture; Natural Resources; Plant and Crop Protection)

Further Information: Also Pasacao Extension Campus (PEC)

History: Founded 1918. Formerly known as Camarines Sur State Agricultural College.

Degrees and Diplomas: *Bachelor's Degree*; *Master's Degree*; *PhD*
Last Updated: 06/08/10

CENTRAL LUZON STATE UNIVERSITY (CLSU)

Maharlika Highway, Science City of Múñoz,
Nueva Ecija 3120
Tel: +63(44) 456-0107
Fax: +63(44) 456-0107
EMail: administrator@clsu-ph.net
Website: http://www.clsu.edu.ph

President: Rodolfo C. Undan (1999-)
Tel: +63(44) 456-0688, Fax: +63(44) 456-5202
EMail: rcundan@mozcom.com

Vice-President for Administration: Raul D. Divina

Vice-President for Academic Affairs: Danilo G. Tan

Colleges

Agriculture (Agricultural Business; Agricultural Economics; Animal Husbandry; Crop Production; Dairy; Pest Management; Plant and Crop Protection; Soil Science; Zoology); **Arts and Science** (Arts and Humanities; Behavioural Sciences; Biological and Life Sciences; Biology; Chemistry; English; Filipino; Mathematics; Modern Languages; Native Language; Physics; Psychology; Social Sciences; Statistics); **Business Administration and Accountancy** (Accountancy; Business Administration; Economics; Human Resources; Management; Marketing); **Education** (Curriculum; Education; Primary Education; Secondary Education; Teacher Training); **Engineering** (Agricultural Engineering; Agricultural Equipment; Civil Engineering; Information Technology); **Fisheries** (Aquaculture; Biotechnology; Fishery; Molecular Biology); **Home Sciences and Industry** (Food Technology; Home Economics; Home Economics Education; Textile Design); **Veterinary Science and Medicine** (Veterinary Science)

Institutes

Graduate Studies (Agricultural Business; Agricultural Economics; Agricultural Education; Agricultural Engineering; Agronomy; Animal Husbandry; Aquaculture; Biology; Botany; Chemistry; Communication Studies; Crop Production; Development Studies; Education; Educational Administration; Educational and Student Counselling; Educational Research; Entomology; Environmental Management; Fishery; Home Economics Education; Horticulture; Literature; Microbiology; Modern Languages; Plant and Crop Protection; Plant Pathology; Rural Planning; Rural Studies; Soil Management; Soil Science; Teacher Training; Veterinary Science; Water Management; Zoology)

Further Information: Also 3 laboratory schools

History: Founded 1907 as Central Luzon Agricultural School, reorganized as Central Luzon Agricultural College 1950, and acquired present status and title 1964.

Governing Bodies: Board of Regents

Academic Year: June to March (June-October; November-March)

Admission Requirements: Graduation from high school and entrance examination

Fees: (Pesos): c. 100 per unit, per annum; graduate c. 300

Main Language(s) of Instruction: English

International Co-operation: With universities in Thailand; China; Japan; Nepal; Uganda

Accrediting Agencies: Accrediting Agency of Chartered Colleges and Universities in the Philippines (AACCUP)

Degrees and Diplomas: *Bachelor's Degree*; *Master's Degree*; *PhD*

Student Services: Academic counselling, Canteen, Cultural centre, Employment services, Foreign Studies Centre, Health services, Social counselling, Sports facilities

Student Residential Facilities: For c. 2,500 students

Special Facilities: University Museum. Biological Garden

Libraries: c. 45,000 vols

Publications: Scientific Journal *(biannually)*

Press or Publishing House: CLSU Publishing House
Last Updated: 12/08/10

CENTRAL MINDANAO UNIVERSITY (CMU)

University Town, Musuan, Bukidnon 8710
Tel: +63(88) 356-1910
Fax: +63(88) 356-1912
EMail: info@cmu.edu.ph
Website: http://www.cmu.edu.ph

President: Rodrigo L. Malunhao

Colleges

Agriculture (Agricultural Business; Agricultural Economics; Agricultural Education; Agriculture; Agronomy; Communication Studies; Entomology; Horticulture; Plant Pathology; Soil Science; Zoology); **Arts and Science** (Arts and Humanities; Biology; Chemistry; English; History; Library Science; Mathematics; Political Sciences; Psychology; Sociology); **Commerce and Accountancy** (Accountancy; Business Administration; Business and Commerce; Management); **Education** (Biology; Education; English; Filipino; Foreign Languages Education; Mathematics Education; Native Language; Native Language Education; Physical Education; Science Education); **Engineering** (Agricultural Engineering; Civil Engineering; Electrical Engineering; Information Technology; Mechanical Engineering); **Forestry** (Environmental Engineering; Forestry); **Home Economics** (Dietetics; Food Science; Food Technology; Home Economics; Home Economics Education; Hotel and Restaurant; Hotel Management; Nutrition); **Nursing** (Nursing); **Veterinary Science** (Veterinary Science)

Schools

Graduate (Agricultural Business; Agricultural Economics; Agricultural Education; Agriculture; Agronomy; Anthropology; Arts and Humanities; Biology; Chemistry; Education; Educational Administration; English; Entomology; Filipino; Food Science; Foreign Languages Education; Forestry; Home Economics; Home Economics Education; Horticulture; Mathematics Education; Native Language Education; Natural Sciences; Physics; Plant Pathology; Primary Education; Science Education; Soil Science; Zoology)

History: Founded 1910, became Mindanao Agricultural College 1952 and acquired present status 1965.

Governing Bodies: Board of Regents

Academic Year: June to March (June-October; November-March)

Admission Requirements: Graduation from high school and entrance examination

Fees: (Pesos): c. 10 per unit, per semester

Main Language(s) of Instruction: Filipino, English

Accrediting Agencies: Accrediting Agency of Chartered Colleges and Universities in the Philippines (AACCUP)

Degrees and Diplomas: *Certificate/Diploma*; *Bachelor's Degree*; *Post Baccalaureate Certificate/Diploma*; *Master's Degree*; *PhD*

Student Services: Academic counselling, Canteen, Health services, Sports facilities

Student Residential Facilities: Yes

Special Facilities: Anthropological Museum; Herbariums; Biological and Medicinal Garden; Arboretum; Radio Station

Libraries: Central Library, c. 17,400 vols

Publications: Journal of Science and Agriculture *(biannually)*

Press or Publishing House: CMU Printing Press

Last Updated: 12/08/10

CENTRAL VISAYAS STATE COLLEGE OF AGRICULTURE, FORESTRY AND TECHNOLOGY

Zamora, Bilar, Bohol 6317
Tel: +63(38) 535-9022
Fax: +63(38) 535-9055

President: Elpidio T. Magante

Campuses

Calape *(Calape Polytechnic College)* (Education; English; Fishery; Industrial Engineering; Mathematics Education; Primary Education; Secondary Education; Technology) *College Director*: Inocencio L. Cosare; **Candijay** (Aquaculture; Biological and Life Sciences; Biology; Coastal Studies; Computer Science; Curriculum; Education; English; Filipino; Fishery; Foreign Languages Education; Home Economics; Hotel and Restaurant; Hotel Management; Marine Biology; Mathematics Education; Native Language Education; Natural Resources; Physics; Primary Education; Science Education; Secondary Education; Technology Education; Tourism) *College Director*: Arnulfo C. Olandria; **Clarin** (Coastal Studies; Curriculum; Education; Home Economics Education; Hotel and Restaurant; Hotel Management; Mathematics Education; Natural Resources; Primary Education; Technology Education) *College Director*: Dioscoro A. Avergonzado; **Main Campus** (Agricultural Education; Agricultural Engineering; Agricultural Management; Agriculture; Automotive Engineering; Civil Engineering; Computer Science; Crop Production; Curriculum; Development Studies; Education; Environmental Studies; Food Technology; Forestry; Home Economics; Hotel and Restaurant; Mathematics Education; Primary Education; Rural Planning; Rural Studies; Secondary Education; Social and Community Services; Technology; Tourism; Zoology); **Tagbilaran** (Aquaculture; Architecture; Automotive Engineering; Civil Engineering; Computer Engineering; Computer Science; Cosmetology; Curriculum; Education; Electrical Engineering; Electronic Engineering; English; Environmental Management; Filipino; Fishery; Food Technology; Foreign Languages Education; Heating and Refrigeration; Hotel and Restaurant; Hotel Management; Management; Marine Biology; Marine Science and Oceanography; Mathematics; Mathematics Education; Mechanical Engineering; Metal Techniques; Native Language Education; Natural Resources; Primary Education; Public Administration; Secondary Education; Technology Education; Textile Technology; Tourism; Wood Technology) *College Director*: Fernando L. Restificar

History: Founded in 1912. Formerly Bilar Rural High School (1912-1960). Acquired present status 1998.

Degrees and Diplomas: *Certificate/Diploma*; *Bachelor's Degree*; *Master's Degree*

Last Updated: 06/09/10

CITY COLLEGE OF CALAMBA

Barreto Street, Calamba City, Laguna 4027
Tel: +63(49) 545-0055
Fax: +63(49) 545-0160
EMail: city_college_of_calamba@yahoo.com.ph

President: Alin Aldea

Programmes

Accountancy (Accountancy); **Computer Science** (Computer Science); **Education** (Education; English; Mathematics Education; Primary Education; Science Education); **Information Technology** (Information Technology)

History: Founded 2006.

Degrees and Diplomas: *Bachelor's Degree*

Last Updated: 07/09/10

CITY COLLEGE OF LUCENA

Maharlika H-Way, Lucena City, Quezon 4301
Tel: +63(42) 373-1483
Fax: +63(42) 710-8890

Chairman (Acting): Azucena Romulo

Programmes

Undergraduate and Professional (Information Management; Management; Public Administration)

History: Founded 2002.

Degrees and Diplomas: *Bachelor's Degree*

Last Updated: 17/03/11

CITY OF MALABON UNIVERSITY

Maya-Maya Cor. Pampano Street, Dagat-Dagatan, Malabon City, Third District, Metro Manila 1404
Tel: +63(2) 287-8948
Fax: +63(2) 287-8948

President: Ramon M. Maronillo

Programmes

Arts and Science (Information Technology; Journalism; Political Sciences); **Business Administration** (Accountancy; Business Administration; Business and Commerce; Business Computing;

Management; Public Administration); **Education** (Education; Educational Administration; English; Mathematics Education; Preschool Education; Primary Education; Secondary Education; Social Studies); **Engineering** (Engineering; Mechanical Engineering)

History: Founded 1994. Acquired present status and title 2003.

Degrees and Diplomas: *Associate Degree*; *Bachelor's Degree*; *Master's Degree*: Business Administration; Educational Management; Public Administration; Education; *PhD*: Education; Public Administration

Last Updated: 07/09/10

COLLEGE OF BATANGAS CITY

Kolehiyo ng Lungsod ng Batangas

Batangas City, Batangas 4200

Programmes

Commerce (Business Administration; Business and Commerce; Management); **Education** (Curriculum; Education; Primary Education)

Degrees and Diplomas: *Bachelor's Degree*

Last Updated: 27/10/10

COTABATO CITY STATE POLYTECHNIC COLLEGE

Sinsuat Avenue, Maguindanao, Cotabato City, Cotabato 9600

Tel: +63(64) 421-2982

EMail: balucasf@yahoo.com

President: Dingan C. Ali

Programmes

Agriculture (Agricultural Engineering; Agriculture; Agronomy; Crop Production; Fishery; Forestry; Zoology); **Arts and Sciences** (Computer Science; Industrial and Organizational Psychology; Islamic Studies; Mathematics; Psychology; Social and Community Services; Social Work); **Business Administration** (Business and Commerce; Management; Public Administration); **Education** (Art Education; Education; English; Foreign Languages Education; Health Education; Mathematics Education; Music Education; Physical Education; Secondary Education; Teacher Training; Technology Education); **Engineering and Technology** (Civil Engineering; Electrical Engineering; Engineering; Information Technology; Technology; Technology Education)

History: Founded 1983.

Degrees and Diplomas: *Bachelor's Degree*; *Master's Degree*; *PhD*

Last Updated: 10/09/10

COTABATO FOUNDATION COLLEGE OF SCIENCE AND TECHNOLOGY

Doroluman, Arakan, North Cotabato 9417

Tel: +63(64) 288-1343

Fax: +63(64) 288-1343

President: Makalutang B. Luna

Programmes

Agriculture (Agricultural Business; Agricultural Education; Agriculture; Agronomy; Forestry; Horticulture; Zoology); **Computer Science** (Computer Science); **Education** (Art Education; Biology; Education; Educational Administration; Health Education; Mathematics Education; Music Education; Physical Education; Primary Education; Secondary Education; Technology Education); **Home Economics** (Home Economics); **Information Technology** (Information Technology); **Social Work and Communication Development** (Communication Studies; Social Work)

History: Founded 1967. Formerly known as Children's Educational Foundation Village (1967-1983).

Degrees and Diplomas: *Bachelor's Degree*; *Master's Degree*; *PhD*

Last Updated: 10/09/10

DAVAO DEL NORTE STATE COLLEGE

New Visayas, Panabo City, Davao del Norte 8105

Tel: +63(84) 628-4301

Fax: +63(84) 628-4301

President: Edgardo M. Santos

Programmes

Education (Biology; Education; Educational Administration; Higher Education; Home Economics Education; Mathematics Education; Physics; Science Education; Secondary Education; Technology Education); **Science** (Aquaculture; Fishery; Food Technology; Information Technology; Marine Biology; Marine Engineering; Marine Science and Oceanography)

History: Founded 1969. Formerly known as Davao del Norte School of Fisheries (1988-1995).

Degrees and Diplomas: *Bachelor's Degree*; *Master's Degree*; *PhD*

Last Updated: 22/09/10

DAVAO ORIENTAL STATE COLLEGE OF SCIENCE AND TECHNOLOGY

Guang-Guang, Mati, Davao Oriental 8200

Tel: +63(82) 388-3195

Fax: +63(87) 388-3195

EMail: doscst@yahoo.com

President: Grace G. Lopez

Programmes

Education (Biological and Life Sciences; Education; English; Foreign Languages Education; Mathematics Education; Physics; Primary Education; Science Education; Secondary Education); **Engineering** (Agricultural Engineering; Automotive Engineering; Data Processing; Industrial Engineering; Industrial Management); **Science** (Agricultural Business; Biology; Civil Engineering; Communication Studies; Development Studies; Environmental Studies; Information Technology; Mathematics; Nursing)

Further Information: Also Cateel Extension and San Isidro campuses

History: Founded 1989.

Degrees and Diplomas: *Bachelor's Degree*; *Master's Degree*

Last Updated: 22/09/10

DEVELOPMENT ACADEMY OF THE PHILIPPINES (DAP)

PO Box 12788, DAP Building, San Miguel Avenue, Ortigas Center, Pasig City, Second District, Metro Manila 1605

Tel: +63(2) 631-0921

Fax: +63(2) 361-2123

EMail: academy@dap.edu.ph

Website: http://www.dap.edu.ph

President: Antonio D. Kalaw, Jr

Centres

Governance (Government); **Knowledge Management**; **Quality and Competitiveness** (Safety Engineering); **Sustainable Human Development** (Development Studies; Human Resources)

Graduate Schools

Public and Development Management (Development Studies; Public Administration)

Further Information: Also regional offices in Mindanao and Visayas.

History: Founded 1973.

Degrees and Diplomas: *Bachelor's Degree*; *Master's Degree*

Last Updated: 27/09/10

DON HONORIO VENTURA TECHNOLOGICAL STATE UNIVERSITY

Poblacion, Bacolor, Pampanga 2001

Tel: +63(45) 900-0691

Fax: +63(45) 910-0046

Website: http://www.dhvtsu.edu.ph

President: Enrique G. Baking

Vice-President for Administration, Finance and Auxiliary Services: Rohel S. Serrano

Campuses
Mexico - Pampanga (Architecture; Art Education; Civil Engineering; Economics; Electrical Engineering; Electronic Engineering; English; Filipino; Fine Arts; Foreign Languages Education; Health Education; Industrial Engineering; Information Technology; Management; Marketing; Mathematics Education; Mechanical Engineering; Music Education; Native Language Education; Physical Education; Primary Education; Secondary Education; Technology Education; Telecommunications Engineering)

Colleges
Business Administration (Business Administration; Economics; Management; Marketing); **Engineering and Architecture** (Architecture; Civil Engineering; Electrical Engineering; Electronic Engineering; Fine Arts; Industrial Engineering; Information Technology; Mechanical Engineering; Structural Architecture; Telecommunications Engineering); **Industrial Technology** (Automotive Engineering; Civil Engineering; Computer Education; Cosmetology; Electrical Engineering; Fashion Design; Food Science; Heating and Refrigeration; Industrial Engineering; Information Technology; Mechanical Engineering; Metal Techniques); **Teacher Education** (Art Education; Curriculum; Education; English; Filipino; Foreign Languages Education; Health Education; Mathematics Education; Music Education; Native Language Education; Physical Education; Primary Education; Science Education; Secondary Education; Technology Education)

Institutes
Arts and Sciences (Arts and Humanities; Economics; Management; Marketing)

Schools
Graduate Studies (Education; Educational Administration; Industrial Management; Public Administration)

History: Founded 1861 as Escuela de Artes y Oficios de Bacolor. Formerly known as Don Honorio Ventura College of Arts and Trades. Acquired present status and title 2009.

Degrees and Diplomas: *Certificate/Diploma*; *Bachelor's Degree*; *Master's Degree*; *PhD*

Last Updated: 28/09/10

DON MARIANO MARCOS MEMORIAL STATE UNIVERSITY

Sapilang, North La Union-Main Campus, Bacnotan, La Union 2515
Tel: +63(72) 242-5641 +63(72) 888-5677
Fax: +63(72) 242-5641
EMail: ergapasin@eudoramail.com

President: Ernesto R. Gapasin EMail: ergapasin@dmmmsu.edu.ph

Programmes
Agriculture (Agricultural Business; Agricultural Education; Agricultural Engineering; Agricultural Management; Agriculture; Agronomy; Animal Husbandry; Crop Production; Environmental Studies; Forestry; Rural Planning; Rural Studies; Soil Science; Zoology); **Education** (Curriculum; Home Economics Education; Primary Education; Secondary Education; Technology Education); **Information Management and Technology** (Information Management; Information Technology); **Veterinary Medicine** (Veterinary Science)

History: Founded 1960, reorganized 1972. Acquired present status 1981. A State Institution.

Governing Bodies: Board of Regents

Academic Year: June to May (June-October; November-March; April-May)

Admission Requirements: Graduation from high school and entrance examination

Main Language(s) of Instruction: Filipino, English

Degrees and Diplomas: *Bachelor's Degree*; *Post Baccalaureate Certificate/Diploma*; *Master's Degree*; *PhD*

Student Services: Academic counselling, Canteen, Cultural centre, Employment services, Foreign Studies Centre, Health services, Social counselling, Sports facilities

Libraries: c. 22,000 vols

Last Updated: 28/03/11

MID LA UNION CAMPUS

Catbangen, City of San Fernando, La Union 2500
Tel: +63(72) 242-3608 +63(72) 888-2266
Fax: +63(72) 242-5906
EMail: mluc@dmmmsu.edu.ph
Website: http://www.dmmmsu.edu.ph

Chancellor: Rogelio C. Tanagon

Programmes
Arts and Science (Arts and Humanities; Business Administration; Electrical Engineering; Electronic Engineering; Food Technology; Hotel and Restaurant; Hotel Management; Industrial Engineering; Information Technology; Management; Mechanical Engineering; Technology; Textile Technology); **Education** (Education; Primary Education); **Graduate Studies** (Administration; Development Studies; Management Systems; Mathematics Education; Science Education; Teacher Training; Technology Education); **Law** (Law)

History: Founded 1981.

Degrees and Diplomas: *Certificate/Diploma*; *Bachelor's Degree*; *Master's Degree*; *PhD*

OPEN UNIVERSITY

Catbangen, City of San Fernando, La Union 2500
Tel: +63(72) 242-3608 +63(72) 888-2266
Fax: +63(72) 242-3608
EMail: mluc@dmmmsu.edu.ph; dous_dlc@yahoo.com
Website: http://www.dmmmsu.edu.ph

Director: Concepcion L Bederio

Programmes
Graduate Studies (Administration; Child Care and Development; Development Studies; Government; Law; Police Studies; Preschool Education; Public Administration; Science Education; Teacher Training); **Undergraduate and Professional** (Agriculture; Education; Horticulture; Management)

Further Information: Traditional and Open Learning Institution

History: Founded 1981.

Degrees and Diplomas: *Bachelor's Degree*; *Post Baccalaureate Certificate/Diploma*; *Master's Degree*; *PhD*

SOUTH LA UNION CAMPUS

Dona Toribia Aspiras Road, Agoo, La Union 2504
Tel: +63(72) 521-0020
Fax: +63(72) 710-7959
Website: http://www.dmmmsu.edu.ph

Chancellor: Inocencio D. Mangaoang, Jr.

Programmes
Education (Art Education; Biological and Life Sciences; Chemistry; Curriculum; English; Filipino; Foreign Languages Education; Health Education; Home Economics; Mathematics Education; Music Education; Native Language Education; Physical Education; Physics; Preschool Education; Primary Education; Science Education; Secondary Education; Social Studies; Special Education); **Science** *(Bachelor of Science programme)* (Agricultural Engineering; Agriculture; Biology; Computer Science; Education; Fishery; Mathematics; Nursing; Psychology)

History: Founded 1977. Acquired present status 1980.

Degrees and Diplomas: *Certificate/Diploma*; *Bachelor's Degree*

DR. EMILIO B. ESPINOSA, SR. MEMORIAL STATE COLLEGE OF AGRICULTURE AND TECHNOLOGY

Cabitan, Mandaon, Masbate 5411
Tel: +63(912) 886-3629
Fax: +63(912) 834-6378
EMail: debesmscat@yahoo.com

President: Magno S. Conag, Jr.

Programmes
Agriculture (Agricultural Education; Agricultural Engineering; Agriculture; Animal Husbandry; Crop Production; Forestry; Zoology); **Computer Science** (Computer Science); **Education** (Biological and Life Sciences; Education; English; Filipino; Foreign Languages Education; Home Economics Education; Mathematics Education; Native Language Education; Preschool Education; Primary Education; Secondary Education; Technology Education); **Graduate** (Agricultural Education; Agriculture; Animal Husbandry; Crop Production; Education; Educational Administration; Home Economics Education; Zoology); **Industrial Technology** (Automotive Engineering; Civil Engineering; Electrical Engineering; Food Technology; Home Economics; Technology); **Veterinary Medicine** (Veterinary Science)

History: Founded 1952. Formerly known as Dr. Emilio B. Espinosa, Sr. Memorial Agricultural College (DEBESMAC).

Degrees and Diplomas: *Associate Degree*; *Bachelor's Degree*; *Post Baccalaureate Certificate/Diploma*; *Master's Degree*

Last Updated: 28/09/10

DR. FILEMON C. AGUILAR MEMORIAL COLLEGE

Golden Gate Subd. Talon III, City of Las Piñas, Fourth District, Metro Manila 1740
Tel: +63(2) 805-8425
Fax: +63(2) 805-8522

President: Conrado C. Aguilar

Programmes
Undergraduate and Professional (Accountancy; Banking; Business Administration; Finance; Management; Marketing)

History: Founded 1998.

Degrees and Diplomas: *Bachelor's Degree*

Last Updated: 28/09/10

EASTERN SAMAR STATE UNIVERSITY

Baranguay Maypangdan, Borongan, Eastern Samar 6800
Tel: +63(55) 261-2500
Fax: +63(55) 261-2725
Website: http://www.essu.edu.ph

President: Reynaldo A. Lombrio

Campuses
Can-Avid *(Can-Avid, Eastern Samar)* (Agricultural Education; Agricultural Engineering; Agriculture; Education; Forestry; Home Economics Education; Mathematics Education; Primary Education; Science Education; Secondary Education; Social Sciences; Technology Education); **Guiuan** *(Guiuan, Eastern Samar)* (Automotive Engineering; Civil Engineering; Cosmetology; Electrical Engineering; Electronic Engineering; Filipino; Food Technology; Home Economics Education; Hotel and Restaurant; Hotel Management; Industrial Engineering; Mathematics Education; Native Language Education; Primary Education; Secondary Education; Social Sciences; Social Studies; Technology Education; Textile Technology; Tourism); **Maydolong** *(Maydolong, Eastern Samar)* (Art Education; Education; Health Education; Industrial Engineering; Music Education; Physical Education; Preschool Education; Primary Education; Secondary Education; Technology Education); **Salcedo** *(Salcedo, Eastern Samar)* (Agricultural Business; Agricultural Engineering; Agriculture; Computer Science; Education; Management; Primary Education; Secondary Education)

Programmes
Agriculture (Agriculture; Animal Husbandry; Crop Production; Fishery; Zoology); **Business Administration** (Business and Commerce; Economics; Management); **Computer Science** (Computer Science); **Education** (Biology; Education; Educational Administration; English; Filipino; Foreign Languages Education; Home Economics Education; Library Science; Mathematics Education; Modern Languages; Native Language Education; Primary Education; Science Education; Secondary Education; Social Sciences; Technology Education); **Engineering** (Civil Engineering; Computer Engineering; Electrical Engineering; Engineering); **Environmental Management** (Environmental Management); **Information Technology** (Information Technology); **Mass Communication** (Mass Communication); **Nursing** (Nursing); **Tourism, Hotel and Restaurant Management** (Hotel and Restaurant; Hotel Management; Tourism)

History: Founded 1960.

Degrees and Diplomas: *Bachelor's Degree*; *Master's Degree*; *PhD*

Last Updated: 29/09/10

EASTERN VISAYAS STATE UNIVERSITY (ESVU)

Salazar Street, Tacloban City, Leyte 6500
Tel: +63(53) 321-2185
Fax: +63(53) 321-2186
EMail: helpdesk@evsu.edu.ph
Website: http://www.evsu.edu.ph

President: Catalino B. Beltran

Director, Administrative Services Division: Doris Ann S. Espina

Campuses
Burauen *(Buaruen, Leyte)* (Agricultural Engineering; Business Administration; English; Foreign Languages Education; Home Economics Education; Mathematics Education; Science Education; Secondary Education); **Carigara** *(Carigara College of Fisheries, Leyte)* (Education; Fishery; Information Technology); **Dulag** *(Dulag, Leyte)* (Agricultural Engineering; Civil Engineering; Information Technology; Secondary Education); **Ormoc** *(Ormoc City, Leyte)* (Civil Engineering; Cooking and Catering; Electrical Engineering; Hotel and Restaurant; Hotel Management; Industrial Engineering; Information Technology; Mechanical Engineering; Secondary Education; Teacher Training; Thermal Engineering); **Tanauan** *(Tanauan, Leyte)* (Civil Engineering; Fishery; Industrial Engineering; Information Technology)

Colleges
Architecture (Architecture; Interior Design); **Arts and Sciences** (Chemistry; Economics; Environmental Studies; Statistics); **Business and Entrepreneurship** (Accountancy; Business Administration; Management; Marketing); **Education** (Education; Home Economics Education; Primary Education; Secondary Education; Technology Education); **Engineering** (Chemical Engineering; Civil Engineering; Electrical Engineering; Electronic Engineering; Engineering; Industrial Engineering; Information Technology; Mechanical Engineering; Telecommunications Engineering); **Technology** (Cooking and Catering; Hotel and Restaurant; Industrial Engineering; Marine Engineering; Mechanical Engineering)

Schools
Graduate Studies (Business Administration; Curriculum; Education; Educational Administration; Management; Public Administration)

History: Founded 1907. Acquired present status and title 2004.

Governing Bodies: Board of Regents

Admission Requirements: High School Diploma

Main Language(s) of Instruction: Filipino, English

Degrees and Diplomas: *Bachelor's Degree*; *Bachelor's Degree*; *Master's Degree*; *PhD*

Student Services: Academic counselling, Canteen, Cultural centre, Health services, Language programs, Social counselling, Sports facilities

Last Updated: 29/09/10

EULOGIO AMAN RODRIGUEZ INSTITUTE OF SCIENCE AND TECHNOLOGY

Nagtahan Street, Sampaloc, Manila, First District, Metro Manila 1008
Tel: +63(2) 715-1319
Fax: +63(2) 715-1307
EMail: sap_headoffice@earist.edu.ph
Website: http://www.earist.edu.ph

President: Eduardo S. Caillo EMail: op@earist.edu.ph

Colleges
Architecture and Fine Arts (Advertising and Publicity; Architecture; Fine Arts; Interior Design; Painting and Drawing; Structural Architecture); **Arts and Sciences** (Applied Physics; Computer Science; Industrial and Organizational Psychology; Mathematics); **Business and Public Administration** (Accountancy; Business Administration; Business Education; Human Resources; Marketing;

Public Administration; Secretarial Studies); **Education** (Education; Educational Administration; Educational and Student Counselling; Mathematics Education; Science Education; Special Education; Technology Education); **Engineering** (Chemical Engineering; Civil Engineering; Computer Engineering; Electrical Engineering; Electronic Engineering; Engineering; Mechanical Engineering; Telecommunications Engineering); **Hotel and Restaurant Management** (Hotel and Restaurant; Hotel Management); **Industrial Technology** (Automotive Engineering; Electrical Engineering; Electronic Engineering; Food Technology; Heating and Refrigeration)

Further Information: Also campus in Cavite City, Cavite

History: Founded 1946, acquired present status and title 1978.

Degrees and Diplomas: *Associate Degree*; *Bachelor's Degree*; *Master's Degree*; *PhD*
Last Updated: 30/09/10

FORTUNATO F. HALILI NATIONAL AGRICULTURAL SCHOOL

Guyong, Santa Maria, Bulacan 3022
Tel: +63(44) 641-1847

Programmes

Agricultural Technology (Agricultural Engineering; Technology)

History: Founded 1959. Formerly know as Philippine National Agricultural School.

Degrees and Diplomas: *Certificate/Diploma*; *Bachelor's Degree*
Last Updated: 01/10/10

GOV. ALFONSO D. TAN COLLEGE

Maloro, Tangub City, Misamis Occidental 7214

President: Jennifer Wee Tan

Programmes

Arts (Arts and Humanities; Economics; English; Mass Communication; Political Sciences); **Business Administration** (Accountancy; Business Administration; Business Computing; Human Resources; Management; Marketing); **Computer Science** (Computer Science); **Criminology** (Criminology); **Education** (Education; English; Filipino; Foreign Languages Education; Mathematics Education; Native Language Education; Primary Education; Secondary Education)

History: Founded 1984. Formerly known as Gov. Alfonso D. Tan Memorial College.

Degrees and Diplomas: *Bachelor's Degree*
Last Updated: 04/10/10

GOVERNOR GENEROSO COLLEGE OF ARTS, SCIENCE AND TECHNOLOGY

Poblacion, Gov. Generoso, Davao Oriental

President: Rosita J. Bustamante

Programmes

Arts and Science (English; Mathematics); **Education** (Education; Educational Administration; English; Foreign Languages Education; Mathematics Education; Primary Education; Secondary Education); **Public Administration** (Public Administration)

Degrees and Diplomas: *Bachelor's Degree*; *Master's Degree*: Education (Educational Management); Public Administration
Last Updated: 04/10/10

GUIMARAS STATE COLLEGE

Mclain, Buenavista, Guimaras 5044
Tel: +63(33) 580-8244

President: Sofronio Dignomo

Campuses

Mosqueda *(Guimaras)* (Education; Food Technology; Home Economics Education; Mathematics Education; Primary Education; Textile Technology)

Programmes

Graduate (Education; Educational Administration; English; Foreign Languages Education; Public Administration; Social Sciences); **Undergraduate and Professional** (Business and Commerce; Business Computing; Cosmetology; Criminology; Education; English; Filipino; Food Technology; Foreign Languages Education; Home Economics Education; Hotel and Restaurant; Hotel Management; Industrial Arts Education; Information Technology; Mathematics Education; Native Language Education; Primary Education; Secondary Education; Secretarial Studies; Social Sciences; Technology; Technology Education)

Further Information: Also Branch in Jordan

History: Founded 1968.

Degrees and Diplomas: *Certificate/Diploma*; *Bachelor's Degree*; *Master's Degree*: Education (English/Social Sciences; Educational Management); Public Administration; *PhD*: Education (Educational Management)
Last Updated: 04/10/10

HADJI BUTO SCHOOL OF ARTS AND TRADES

Scott Road, Jolo, Sulu 7400

Officer In-Charge: Amilbangsa Ladja

Programmes

Arts and Trades (Industrial Engineering; Secondary Education; Secretarial Studies; Technology; Technology Education)

History: Founded 1928. Formerly National School of Arts (1928-1963).

Degrees and Diplomas: *Associate Degree*; *Bachelor's Degree*
Last Updated: 04/10/10

IFUGAO STATE UNIVERSITY (IFSU)

Nayon, Lamut, Ifugao 3605
Tel: +63(918) 387-2952
Fax: +63(74) 382-2108
EMail: iscaf@hotmail.com
Website: http://www.ifsu.edu.ph/

President: Serafin L. Ngohayon EMail: ngohayon@yahoo.com

Campuses

Lagawe *(Lagawe, Ifugao)* (Art Education; Civil Engineering; Computer Education; Education; Finance; Food Technology; Health Education; Home Economics Education; Hotel and Restaurant; Hotel Management; Human Resources; Industrial Arts Education; Industrial Engineering; Management; Marketing; Mathematics Education; Music Education; Physical Education; Primary Education; Public Administration; Science Education; Secondary Education; Technology Education); **Potia** *(Potia, Alfonso Lista, Ifugao)* (Agricultural Education; Agriculture; Animal Husbandry; Computer Science; Criminology; Crop Production; Curriculum; Education; Educational Administration; English; Filipino; Food Technology; Foreign Languages Education; Forestry; Health Education; Home Economics Education; Hotel and Restaurant; Hotel Management; Household Management; Mathematics Education; Midwifery; Music Education; Native Language Education; Natural Sciences; Physical Education; Primary Education; Secondary Education; Social Studies; Technology Education; Zoology); **Tinoc** *(Tinoc, Ifugao)* (Curriculum; Education; Industrial Engineering; Primary Education)

Institutes

Agriculture and Forestry (Agricultural Engineering; Agriculture; Animal Husbandry; Crop Production; Forest Products; Forestry; Harvest Technology; Rural Studies; Zoology); **Arts and Sciences** (Criminology; Political Sciences); **Computer Science** (Computer Science); **Education** (Curriculum; Education; Educational Administration; English; Filipino; Foreign Languages Education; Home Economics Education; Native Language Education; Physical Education; Science Education; Social Studies); **Graduate Studies** (Agricultural Education; Education; Educational Administration; English; Filipino; Foreign Languages Education; Forestry; Management; Mathematics Education; Native Language Education; Nursing; Public Administration; Science Education); **Health** (Health Sciences)

History: Started in 1920 as a Farm settlement school. Renamed Ifugao Agricultural and Technical College 1973. Became Ifugao

State College of Agriculture and Forestry in 1982. Acquired current title and status 2010.

Degrees and Diplomas: *Certificate/Diploma*; *Associate Degree*; *Bachelor's Degree*; *Master's Degree*; *PhD*
Last Updated: 10/01/12

ILOCOS SUR POLYTECHNIC STATE COLLEGE (ISPSC)

National Highway, Sta. Maria, Ilocos Sur 2705
Tel: +63(77) 732-5549; +63(77) 732-5512; +63(77) 325-5549
Fax: +63(77) 732-5512
EMail: ispsc_2705@yahoo.com
Website: http://www.ispsc.edu.ph/

President: Alejandro V. Directo (1999-)

Vice-President for Administration and Resource Generation: Corazon A. Gines

Vice-President for Academic Affairs: Wilma M. Ponce

Colleges

Agriculture *(Santa Maria Campus, Ilocos Sur)* (Agricultural Education; Agricultural Engineering; Agricultural Equipment; Agricultural Management; Agriculture; Agronomy; Crop Production; Forestry; Harvest Technology; Home Economics; Home Economics Education; Horticulture; Hotel and Restaurant; Hotel Management; Information Technology; Primary Education; Rural Planning; Secondary Education; Technology; Zoology); **Agro-Industrial Technology** *(Cervantes Campus, Ilocos Sur)* (Agricultural Engineering; Home Economics; Home Economics Education; Hotel and Restaurant; Hotel Management; Information Technology; Primary Education; Secondary Education; Teacher Training; Technology; Technology Education); **Commercial and Social Services** *(Candon Campus, Candon City)* (Computer Engineering; Education; Fishery; Home Economics Education; Hotel and Restaurant; Hotel Management; Information Technology; Science Education; Secondary Education; Tourism); **Engineering and Technology** *(Santiago Campus, Ilocos Sur)* (Automotive Engineering; Cosmetology; Electrical and Electronic Engineering; Home Economics; Home Economics Education; Industrial Engineering; Primary Education; Social Studies; Teacher Training; Technology; Technology Education); **Fisheries and Marine Science** *(Narvacan Campus, Ilocos Sur)* (Aquaculture; Fishery; Harvest Technology; Home Economics Education; Information Technology; Marine Science and Oceanography; Secondary Education; Technology Education); **Teacher Education** *(Tagudin Campus, Ilocos Sur)* (Agricultural Education; Business Administration; Education; English; Foreign Languages Education; Health Education; Information Management; Management; Mathematics; Mathematics Education; Music Education; Physical Education; Physics; Primary Education; Psychology; Science Education; Secondary Education; Social Sciences; Technology Education)

Schools

Graduate Studies *(Santa Maria/Tagudin/Cervantes Campuses)* (Agricultural Education; Agriculture; Agronomy; Education; Horticulture; Rural Planning; Zoology)

Further Information: Campuses: Santiago, Tagudin, Candon City, Cervantes, Narvacan (Ilocos Sur)

History: Founded 1963.

Governing Bodies: Board of Trustees

Admission Requirements: High School Diploma

Fees: (Pesos): 50.00 - 130.00 per unit

Main Language(s) of Instruction: Filipino, English

Accrediting Agencies: Institutional Monitoring and Evaluation for Quality Assurance (IQUAME); Accrediting Agency of Chartered Colleges and Universities in the Philippines (AACCUP)

Degrees and Diplomas: *Certificate/Diploma*; *Bachelor's Degree*; *Master's Degree*
Last Updated: 07/10/10

ILOILO STATE COLLEGE OF FISHERIES

Bargangay Tiwi, Barotac Nuevo, Iloilo 5007
Tel: +63(33) 361-2413
Fax: +63(33) 361-2439
EMail: IscofSUCpresident@yahoo.com
Website: http://www.iscof.ilo.onevirtual.com

President: Ma. Rosario Panes

Campuses

Barotac Nuevo (Art Education; Biological and Life Sciences; Education; Electrical Engineering; Electronic Engineering; English; Food Technology; Foreign Languages Education; Hotel and Restaurant; Hotel Management; Industrial Engineering; Information Sciences; Information Technology; Music Education; Physical Education; Primary Education; Science Education; Secondary Education; Secretarial Studies; Teacher Training); **Dingle** (Agricultural Engineering; Agriculture; Animal Husbandry; Crop Production; Environmental Management; Filipino; Food Technology; Forestry; Health Education; Information Technology; Mathematics Education; Native Language Education; Primary Education; Science Education; Secondary Education; Teacher Training; Tourism; Zoology); **Dumangas** (Biological and Life Sciences; Computer Engineering; Electrical and Electronic Engineering; Electronic Engineering; English; Filipino; Food Technology; Foreign Languages Education; Heating and Refrigeration; Hotel and Restaurant; Hotel Management; Mathematics Education; Metal Techniques; Native Language Education; Primary Education; Science Education; Secondary Education; Textile Technology); **San Enrique** (Agriculture; Animal Husbandry; Automotive Engineering; Computer Engineering; Crop Production; Educational and Student Counselling; Electrical Engineering; Electronic Engineering; English; Filipino; Foreign Languages Education; Hotel and Restaurant; Hotel Management; Industrial Arts Education; Information Technology; Native Language Education; Primary Education; Secondary Education; Secretarial Studies; Teacher Training; Zoology)

Schools

Graduate (Fishery; Government; Marine Transport; Rural Planning; Rural Studies)

History: Founded 1957.

Degrees and Diplomas: *Certificate/Diploma*; *Bachelor's Degree*; *Master's Degree*; *PhD*
Last Updated: 07/10/10

INITAO COLLEGE

National Highway Bagares Street, Initao, Misamis Oriental 9022

College Administrator: Rodenio N. Obsioma

Programmes

Business Administration (Business Administration; Public Administration); **Education** (Education; Mathematics Education; Primary Education; Secondary Education); **Hotel and Restaurant Management** (Hotel and Restaurant; Hotel Management)

History: Founded 2003.

Degrees and Diplomas: *Bachelor's Degree*
Last Updated: 20/10/10

ISABELA STATE UNIVERSITY

San Fabian, Echague, Isabela 3309
Tel: +63(78) 672-2013
Fax: +63(78) 672-2029
EMail: isue@isu.edu.ph
Website: http://www.isu.edu.ph

President: Romeo R. Quilang

Campuses

Angadanan *(Formerly Isabela State University - Angadanan Agro-Industrial College)* (Automotive Engineering; Computer Engineering; Criminology; Education; Electrical Engineering; Electronic Engineering; English; Filipino; Food Technology; Foreign Languages Education; Hotel and Restaurant; Hotel Management; Industrial Engineering; Mathematics Education; Native Language Education; Physics; Primary Education; Secondary Education; Technology Education) *Executive Director*: Felipe Ammungauan; **Cabagan** *(Formerly Cagayan Valley Institute of Technology, 1,963-1979)* (Agricultural Business; Agricultural Education; Agricultural Engineering; Agricultural Equipment; Agriculture; Art Education; Biology; Botany; Communication Studies; Criminology; Crop Production; Ecology; Education; Educational Administration; English; Environmental Management; Environmental Studies; Filipino; Food Technology; Foreign Languages Education; Forest Biology; Forest Management; Forest Products; Forestry; Health Education; Home Economics Education; Hotel and Restaurant; Hotel Management;

Information Technology; Journalism; Mathematics Education; Microbiology; Music Education; Native Language Education; Natural Resources; Physical Education; Primary Education; Radio and Television Broadcasting; Science Education; Secondary Education; Social Sciences; Social Studies; Sociology; Special Education; Technology Education; Waste Management; Zoology) *Executive Director*: Edwin C. Macaballug; **Cauayan** *(Formerly Isabela State University - Cauayan Polytechnic College)* (Agricultural Engineering; Art Education; Automotive Engineering; Business Administration; Commercial Law; Computer Engineering; Criminology; Education; Electronic Engineering; English; Foreign Languages Education; History; Hotel and Restaurant; Hotel Management; Industrial Engineering; Information Technology; Law; Management; Mathematics Education; Music Education; Physical Education; Political Sciences; Primary Education; Science Education; Secondary Education) *Executive Director*: Rimalu B. Serrano; **Echague (Main)** *(Formerly Isabela state College of Agriculture, 1,972-1978)* (Accountancy; Agricultural Business; Agricultural Economics; Agricultural Engineering; Agriculture; Animal Husbandry; Art Education; Biology; Business Administration; Chemical Engineering; Chemistry; Civil Engineering; Criminology; Crop Production; Education; Educational Administration; English; Filipino; Food Technology; Foreign Languages Education; Forestry; Harvest Technology; Health Education; Home Economics Education; Hotel and Restaurant; Hotel Management; Human Resources; Information Management; Information Technology; Library Science; Management; Marketing; Mass Communication; Mathematics; Mathematics Education; Music Education; Native Language Education; Nursing; Physical Education; Political Sciences; Primary Education; Psychology; Public Administration; Rural Planning; Rural Studies; Science Education; Secondary Education; Social and Community Services; Social Sciences; Soil Management; Soil Science; Technology Education; Tourism; Veterinary Science; Zoology) *President*: Romeo R. Quilang; **Ilagan** *(Formerly Isabela School of Arts & Trades)* (Automotive Engineering; Building Technologies; Business Computing; Civil Engineering; Computer Engineering; Construction Engineering; Cosmetology; Electrical Engineering; Electronic Engineering; Food Technology; Furniture Design; Home Economics; Home Economics Education; Industrial Arts Education; Information Technology; Mathematics; Mechanical Engineering; Midwifery; Nursing; Technology Education; Textile Technology) *Executive Director*: Aurea A. de la Cruz; **Jones** *(Formerly Jones Rural School (College Department))* (Agriculture; Criminology; English; Foreign Languages Education; Information Technology; Primary Education; Secondary Education; Zoology) *Executive Director*: Joel L. Reyes; **Roxas** *(Formerly Roxas Memorial Agricultural & Industrial School)* (Agricultural Business; Agricultural Education; Agricultural Management; Agriculture; Crop Production; Filipino; Fishery; Information Technology; Mathematics Education; Native Language Education; Secondary Education; Zoology) *Executive Director*: Wilfredo G. Lim; **San Mariano** *(Formerly Isabela State University - Delfin Albano Memorial Institute of Agriculture & Technology)* (Agricultural Engineering; Agricultural Equipment; Computer Engineering; Crop Production; Education; English; Food Technology; Foreign Languages Education; Forestry; Home Economics Education; Hotel and Restaurant; Hotel Management; Mathematics Education; Science Education; Secondary Education; Technology Education; Zoology) *Executive Director (Acting)*: Clarinda C. Galiza; **San Mateo** *(Formerly San Mateo Vocational and Industrial High School, 1,971-1977)* (Agriculture; Education; Electrical Engineering; Electronic Engineering; Food Technology; Industrial Arts Education; Information Technology; Mathematics Education; Political Sciences; Secondary Education; Technology Education; Textile Technology) *Administrator*: Leon M. Gonzales

History: Founded 1926, reorganized 1963 and 1978. A State Institution.

Degrees and Diplomas: *Certificate/Diploma*; *Associate Degree*; *Bachelor's Degree*; *Post Baccalaureate Certificate/Diploma*; *Master's Degree*; *PhD*
Last Updated: 21/10/10

JOSEFINA H. CERILLES STATE COLLEGE

Mati, San Miguel, Zamboanga del Sur 7029
Tel: +63(62) 353-1644
Fax: +63(62) 353-1644
EMail: karlsaniel@yahoo.com

President: Carlicita A. Saniel

Colleges

Arts and Trades *(Canuto M.S. Enerio College of Arts and Trades)* (Automotive Engineering; Electrical Engineering; Electronic Engineering; Home Economics; Home Economics Education; Hotel and Restaurant; Hotel Management; Industrial Arts Education; Industrial Engineering; Mathematics; Technology; Technology Education)

Programmes

Agricultural Technology (Agricultural Engineering); **Agriculture** (Agriculture); **Allied Health Sciences** (Health Sciences); **Arts and Humanities** (Arts and Humanities); **Computer Technology** (Computer Engineering); **Education** (Education; Primary Education; Secondary Education); **Fishery** (Aquaculture; Fishery); **Forestry** (Forestry); **Hotel and Restaurant Management** (Hotel and Restaurant; Hotel Management); **Industrial Education** (Industrial Arts Education); **Industrial Technology** (Industrial Engineering); **Laws** (Law); **Nursing** (Nursing)

Further Information: Also Bayog, Dimataling, Josefina, Kumalarang, Lapuyan, Mahayag, Margosatubig, Midsalip, Pagadian, Ramon Magsaysay, San Pablo, Tabina, Tambulig, Tigbao, Tukuran and Vincenzo Sagun campuses (Zamboanga del Sur Province)

History: Founded 1995. Formerly Western Mindanao State University - ESU, and Josefina H. Cerilles Polytechnic College.

Degrees and Diplomas: *Associate Degree*; *Bachelor's Degree*
Last Updated: 27/10/10

JOSÉ RIZAL MEMORIAL STATE COLLEGE

Gov. Guading Adasa Street, Sta. Cruz, Dapitan City, Zamboanga del Norte 7120
Tel: +63(65) 213-6361
Fax: +63(65) 213-6444
EMail: jrmscmain@yahoo.com

President: Edgar S. Balbuena

Campuses

Dipolog (Computer Education; Criminology; Education; Electrical Engineering; Electronic Engineering; Engineering; English; Ethics; Filipino; Foreign Languages Education; Health Education; Home Economics Education; Hotel and Restaurant; Hotel Management; Industrial Arts Education; Mass Communication; Mathematics Education; Music Education; Native Language Education; Physical Education; Primary Education; Science Education; Social Sciences; Telecommunications Engineering; Tourism) *Campus Administrator*: Emma T. Tapales; **Katipunan** *(Katipunan National Agricultural School)* (Agricultural Business; Agricultural Engineering; Agriculture; Animal Husbandry; Art Education; Biological and Life Sciences; Computer Science; Crop Production; English; Foreign Languages Education; Forestry; Home Economics Education; Hotel and Restaurant; Hotel Management; Mathematics Education; Music Education; Physical Education; Physics; Primary Education; Secondary Education; Social Studies; Soil Science; Zoology) *Campus Administrator*: Aida O. Lanioso; **Siocon** (Accountancy; Agriculture; Animal Husbandry; Automotive Engineering; Business and Commerce; Civil Engineering; Computer Science; Criminology; Crop Production; Education; Electrical Engineering; Electronic Engineering; English; Filipino; Fishery; Food Technology; Foreign Languages Education; Forestry; Hotel and Restaurant; Hotel Management; Industrial Engineering; Mathematics Education; Midwifery; Native Language Education; Nursing; Primary Education; Science Education; Social Studies; Structural Architecture; Textile Technology; Zoology) *Campus Administrator*: Ideltruda D. Ybarsabal; **Zamboanga del Norte** (Accountancy; Agriculture; Automotive Engineering; Biology; Business Administration; Civil Engineering; Computer Education; Computer Engineering; Computer Science; Criminology; Education; Educational Administration; Electrical Engineering; Electronic Engineering; English; Filipino; Food Technology; Foreign Languages Education; Health Education; Hotel and Restaurant; Hotel Management; Human Resources; Industrial Engineering; Information Technology; Management; Marine Biology; Marine Engineering; Marine Transport; Mass Communication; Mathematics; Mathematics Education; Midwifery; Music Education; Native Language Education; Nursing; Physical Education; Political Sciences; Psychology; Public Administration; Science Education; Social Sciences; Social Studies; Structural Architecture; Technology Education; Telecommunications Engineering; Textile Technology; Tourism; Vocational Education) *President*: Edgar S. Balbuena

Programmes

Undergraduate (Computer Science; Education; Engineering; Engineering Management; Management; Marine Biology; Political Sciences; Technology)

History: Founded 1947. Formerly Dapitan Junior High School (1947-1948); Dapitan High School (1949-1959); and Rizal Memorial National Vocational School.

Degrees and Diplomas: *Associate Degree*; *Bachelor's Degree*; *Master's Degree*; *PhD*

Last Updated: 27/10/10

KALINGA-APAYAO STATE COLLEGE

Purok 6, Bulanao, Tabuk, Kalinga 3800
Tel: +63(74) 872-2045
Fax: +63(74) 872-2045
EMail: kasc@yahoo.com

President: Eduardo Bagtang

Campuses

Dagupan (Arts and Humanities; Biology; Business Administration; Business and Commerce; Chemistry; Development Studies; Education; English; History; Management; Political Sciences; Psychology; Public Administration)

Programmes

Graduate (Business Administration; Development Studies; Education; English; Filipino; Foreign Languages Education; Mathematics Education; Native Language Education; Public Administration; Rural Planning; Social and Community Services; Social Studies; Teacher Training); **Undergraduate and Professional** (Agricultural Engineering; Agriculture; Biology; Civil Engineering; Communication Studies; English; Filipino; Foreign Languages Education; Forestry; Health Education; History; Literature; Mathematics; Mathematics Education; Native Language Education; Primary Education; Science Education; Secondary Education; Social Studies)

History: Founded 1974.

Degrees and Diplomas: *Certificate/Diploma*; *Bachelor's Degree*; *Master's Degree*: Education (Development Education; English; Filipino; Mathematics; Social Studies); Business Administration; Public Administration; Rural Development; *PhD*: Education (Community Development; Development Education)

Last Updated: 27/10/10

KAPALONG COLLEGE OF AGRICULTURAL SCIENCES AND TECHNOLOGY

Poblacion Kapalong, Sto. Tomas, Davao del Norte
Tel: +63(84) 371-0334

Administrator: Emiliana M. Alegre

Programmes

Accountancy (Accountancy); **Agriculture** (Agriculture); **Arts and Humanities** (Arts and Humanities); **Education** (Education; Primary Education; Secondary Education)

History: Founded 2005.

Degrees and Diplomas: *Bachelor's Degree*

Last Updated: 27/10/10

LA CARLOTA CITY COLLEGE

Gurea Street, La Carlota City, Negros Occidental 6130
EMail: lcctcollege@yahoo.com

President: Lydia V. Peñafiel

Programmes

Graduate (Business Administration; Education; Educational Administration; English; Foreign Languages Education; Mathematics Education; Primary Education; Public Administration); **Undergraduate and Professional** (Accountancy; Agriculture; Agronomy; Automotive Engineering; Business Administration; Business and Commerce; Child Care and Development; Criminal Law; Criminology; Economic History; Education; English; Finance; Foreign Languages Education; Management; Mathematics Education; Midwifery; Police Studies; Preschool Education; Primary Education; Secondary Education)

History: Founded 1966.

Degrees and Diplomas: *Certificate/Diploma*; *Associate Degree*; *Bachelor's Degree*; *Master's Degree*: Business Administration; Public Administration; Education (Primary Education; English; Mathematics; Educational Management)

Last Updated: 27/10/10

LAGUNA STATE POLYTECHNIC UNIVERSITY

L. De Leon Street, Siniloan, Laguna 4019
Tel: +63(49) 813-0452
Fax: +63(49) 813-0273
Website: http://www.lspu.edu.ph/

President: Ricardo A. Wagan

Vice-President for Administration: Nerrida P. Baja

Vice-President for Academic Affairs: Olivia P. Magpily

International Relations: Ricardo F. Wagan III, Vice-President for External Affairs

Colleges

Agricultural Science and Technology *(Siniloan Campus)* (Agricultural Business; Agricultural Education; Agricultural Engineering; Agricultural Management; Agriculture; Animal Husbandry; Crop Production; Environmental Studies; Forestry; Home Economics; Technology; Zoology); **Arts and Sciences** *(Siniloan Campus)* (Business Computing; Computer Engineering; Computer Science; Economics; Information Technology; Psychology; Secretarial Studies); **Education** *(Siniloan Campus)* (Education; English; Filipino; Foreign Languages Education; Home Economics Education; Mathematics Education; Native Language Education; Physical Education; Primary Education; Secondary Education; Social Studies; Technology Education); **Hospitality Management and Tourism** *(Siniloan Campus)* (Home Economics; Hotel and Restaurant; Hotel Management; Management; Technology; Tourism)

Programmes

Engineering *(Sta Cruz Campus)* (Civil Engineering; Electrical Engineering; Electronic Engineering; Engineering; Mechanical Engineering; Telecommunications Engineering); **Engineering** *(San Pablo Campus)* (Electronic Engineering; Telecommunications Engineering); **Graduate Studies and Applied Research** *(Siniloan Campus)* (Agriculture; Animal Husbandry; Crop Production; Education; Educational Administration; Educational and Student Counselling; English; Filipino; Foreign Languages Education; Home Economics; Home Economics Education; Mathematics; Mathematics Education; Native Language Education; Physical Education; Science Education; Social Sciences; Speech Studies; Teacher Training; Technology; Technology Education; Zoology); **Industrial Technology** *(San Pablo Campus)* (Automotive Engineering; Civil Engineering; Cosmetology; Electrical Engineering; Electronic Engineering; Food Technology; Heating and Refrigeration; Information Technology; Mechanical Engineering; Structural Architecture; Textile Technology); **Science and Technology** *(Sta Cruz Campus)* (Biology; Chemistry; Hotel and Restaurant; Hotel Management; Information Technology; Management; Marketing; Mathematics; Physics; Production Engineering; Radio and Television Broadcasting); **Teacher Education** *(Sta Cruz Campus)* (Automotive Engineering; Chemistry; Electrical Engineering; Electronic Engineering; English; Filipino; Heating and Refrigeration; History; Home Economics Education; Industrial Arts Education; Mathematics; Mathematics Education; Physics; Secondary Education; Teacher Training); **Teacher Education** *(San Pablo Campus)* (Automotive Engineering; Biology; Chemistry; Civil Engineering; Cosmetology; Education; Electronic Engineering; English; Filipino; Food Technology; Foreign Languages Education; Heating and Refrigeration; History; Home Economics Education; Industrial Arts Education; Mathematics Education; Native Language Education; Physics; Preschool Education; Primary Education; Psychology; Science Education; Secondary Education; Social Studies; Structural Architecture; Teacher Training; Technology Education; Textile Technology; Wood Technology); **Technology Education** *(Sta Cruz Campus)* (Automotive Engineering; Electrical Engineering; Electronic Engineering; Food Technology; Heating and Refrigeration; Industrial Engineering; Textile Technology); **Undergraduate Studies** *(Los Baños Campus)* (Computer Education; Dietetics; English; Filipino; Fishery; Food Technology; Foreign Languages Education; History; Hotel and Restaurant; Hotel Management; Information Technology; Journalism; Mathematics Education; Native Language Education; Nutrition; Preschool Education; Primary Education; Science Education; Secondary Education; Technology Education; Tourism)

Further Information: Campuses: Siniloan (formerly Baybay National College of Agriculture & Technology and Laguna State Polytechnic College); San Pablo City (formerly San Pablo City National School of Arts & Trades); Sta Cruz (formerly Laguna College of Arts & Trades); Los Baños (formerly Los Baños College of Fisheries)

History: Founded 1952 as Baybay Provincial High School. Renamed Baybay National Agricultural and Vocational School 1957, Baybay National College of Agriculture and Technology 1971. Converted into a state college, known as the Laguna State Polytechnic College 1983. Acquired present university status and title 2007.

Degrees and Diplomas: *Certificate/Diploma*; *Associate Degree*; *Bachelor's Degree*; *Master's Degree*; *PhD*
Last Updated: 29/10/10

LAGUNA UNIVERSITY

Brgy. Bubukal, Sta. Cruz, Laguna 4009
Tel: +63(49) 808-4360
Fax: +63(49) 808-1126

President: Teresita S. Lazaro

Programmes
Accountancy (Accountancy); **Communication Arts** (Communication Arts); **Computer Science** (Computer Science); **Education** (Biology; Education; English; Foreign Languages Education; Mathematics; Mathematics Education; Physics; Primary Education; Secondary Education); **Entrepreneurship** (Management); **Information and Communication Technology** (Communication Studies; Information Technology); **Mechanical Engineering** (Mechanical Engineering)

History: Founded 2006.

Degrees and Diplomas: *Bachelor's Degree*
Last Updated: 29/10/10

LANAO AGRICULTURAL COLLEGE

Poblacion, Lumbatan, Lanao del Sur 9307

Superintendent: Arimao S. Asum

Programmes
Agriculture (Agricultural Education; Agricultural Engineering; Agriculture; Crop Production)

Degrees and Diplomas: *Bachelor's Degree*
Last Updated: 29/10/10

LAPAK AGRICULTURAL COLLEGE

East Kuntad, Siasi, Sulu 7412

Administrator: Abdulmunap E. Abbarani

Programmes
Graduate Studies (Education; Educational Administration); **Undergraduate and Professional Studies** (Agricultural Education; Agriculture; Crop Production; Education; English; Filipino; Foreign Languages Education; Mathematics Education; Native Language Education; Primary Education)

History: Founded 1916. Formerly Lapak Agricultural School (1974-1996).

Degrees and Diplomas: *Bachelor's Degree*; *Master's Degree*
Last Updated: 29/10/10

LEYTE NORMAL UNIVERSITY (LNU)

P. Paterno Street, Tacloban City, Leyte 6500
Tel: +63(53) 321-2176
Fax: +63(53) 325-6122
EMail: webmaster@lnu.edu.ph
Website: http://lnu.edu.ph

President: Evelyn C. Cruzada
Vice-President for Administration: Marietta B. Arinto

Colleges
Arts and Science (Arts and Humanities; Biology; Communication Studies; Information Sciences; Information Technology; Library Science; Mathematics and Computer Science; Social Work); **Arts and Science - Graduate Studies** (Biology; English; Foreign Languages Education; Mathematics Education; Native Language Education; Physical Education; Social Sciences); **Education** (Art Education; Biological and Life Sciences; Curriculum; Education; English; Ethics; Filipino; Foreign Languages Education; Health Education; Mathematics Education; Music Education; Native Language Education; Physical Education; Physics; Preschool Education; Primary Education; Secondary Education; Social Sciences; Special Education; Technology Education); **Education - Graduate Studies** (Education; Educational Administration; Filipino; Foreign Languages Education; Literacy Education; Mathematics Education; Native Language Education; Natural Sciences; Social Sciences); **Management and Entrepreneurship - Graduate Studies** (Human Resources; Management)

Programmes
Management and Entrepreneurship (Home Economics; Hotel and Restaurant; Hotel Management; Tourism)

History: Founded 1921 as Provincial Normal School. Converted into Leyte State College 1976. Acquired present status and title 1995.

Governing Bodies: Board of Regents

Academic Year: June to May (June-October; November-March; April-May)

Admission Requirements: Graduation from high school and entrance examination

Main Language(s) of Instruction: Filipino, English

International Co-operation: With universities in Korea, China, Singapore, Australia and Spain

Accrediting Agencies: Commission on Higher Education (CHED); Accrediting Agency of Chartered Colleges and Universities in the Philippines (AACCUP)

Degrees and Diplomas: *Bachelor's Degree*; *Master's Degree*: Education (Physical Education; Elementary Mathematics; Social Sciences; Natural Sciences; Reading; Filipino; Modern Languages); English; Management; Social Work; Educational Management; Secondary and Tertiary; College Teaching; Mathematics Education; Special Education; Biology; Information Technology; *PhD*: Management; Hotel and Restaurant Management; Language Teaching; Social Sciences Research

Student Services: Academic counselling, Canteen, Cultural centre, Employment services, Health services, Social counselling, Sports facilities

Student Residential Facilities: For c. 6,000 students

Special Facilities: Botanical Garden; Theatre; Museum; Audio-visual Studio

Libraries: Learning Resource Centre (Automated)

Publications: LNU Research Journal and LNU Forum *(biannually)*

Press or Publishing House: None
Last Updated: 29/10/10

LIBACAO COLLEGE OF SCIENCE AND TECHNOLOGY

Malanga, Libacao, Aklan 5602
Tel: +63(36) 273-2224
Fax: +63(36)-273-2028

Administrator: Renato Z. Gepty

Programmes
Hotel and Restaurant Technology (Cooking and Catering; Hotel and Restaurant); **Industrial Education** (Automotive Engineering; Electrical Engineering; Food Technology; Home Economics; Home Economics Education; Technology Education; Textile Technology)

History: Founded 2003.

Degrees and Diplomas: *Bachelor's Degree*
Last Updated: 29/10/10

LIMAY POLYTECHNIC COLLEGE

Limay, Bataan 2103
Tel: +63(47) 244-6939
Fax: +63(47) 244-7872

President: Annie S. Gomez

Programmes
Accountancy (Accountancy); **Business Administration** (Business Administration; Finance; Leadership; Management); **Elementary Education** (English; Foreign Languages Education; Health Education; Mathematics; Primary Education; Science Education); **Information Technology** (Information Technology); **Secondary Education** (English; Foreign Languages Education; Mathematics; Science Education; Secondary Education)

History: Founded 1999.

Degrees and Diplomas: *Certificate/Diploma*; *Associate Degree*; *Bachelor's Degree*
Last Updated: 29/10/10

LIPA CITY PUBLIC COLLEGE

B. Morada Avenue, Lipa City, Batangas 4217
Tel: +63(43) 757-0243
Fax: +63(43) 756-7303
EMail: lcpc2001mbn@yahoo.com

Administrator: Romulo H. Valencia

Programmes
Computer Science (Computer Science); **Education** (Art Education; Biological and Life Sciences; Education; English; Ethics; Filipino; Foreign Languages Education; Health Education; Music Education; Native Language Education; Physical Education; Preschool Education; Primary Education; Secondary Education; Social Studies; Special Education)
History: Founded 1994.

Degrees and Diplomas: *Certificate/Diploma*; *Associate Degree*; *Bachelor's Degree*
Last Updated: 02/11/10

MARIANO MARCOS STATE UNIVERSITY

Barangay 16, City of Batac, Ilocos Norte 2906
Tel: +63(77) 792-3191 +63(77) 792-3878
Fax: +63(77) 792-3191
EMail: mmsu_op@mmsu.edu.ph
Website: http://www.mmsu.edu.ph

President: Miriam E. Pascua Tel: +63(77) 792-3878

Vice-President, Academic Affairs: Epifania O. Agustin

Vice-President, Administration and Corporate Affairs: Ramon A. Leano

Centres
Teaching Excellence *(Laoag Campus)* (Education; Teacher Training)

Colleges
Agriculture and Forestry - Dingras Campus (Agricultural Engineering; Animal Husbandry; Crop Production; Fishery; Forestry; Horticulture); **Agriculture, Food and Sustainable Development** *(CAFSD)* (Agricultural Engineering; Agriculture; Agronomy; Animal Husbandry; Development Studies; Environmental Management; Environmental Studies; Food Technology; Forestry; Home Economics; Technology); **Arts and Sciences** *(CAS)* (Biological and Life Sciences; Biology; Chemistry; Communication Studies; Computer Science; English; Environmental Studies; Filipino; Literature; Mathematics; Modern Languages; Native Language; Physical Education; Social Sciences); **Business, Economics and Accountancy** *(CBEA)* (Accountancy; Business Administration; Economics; Human Resources; Management; Marketing; Tourism); **Engineering** *(COE)* (Ceramics and Glass Technology; Chemical Engineering; Civil Engineering; Computer Engineering; Electrical Engineering; Electronic Engineering; Engineering; Mechanical Engineering; Telecommunications Engineering); **Fisheries - Currimao Campus** (Aquaculture; Fishery; Marine Biology); **Health Sciences** (Curriculum; Health Sciences; Nursing; Pharmacy; Physical Therapy; Special Education); **Industrial Technology - Paoay Campus (Satellite Campus)** (Automotive Engineering; Ceramics and Glass Technology; Civil Engineering; Computer Engineering; Electrical Engineering; Electronic Engineering; Food Technology; Industrial Engineering; Technology; Textile Technology); **Law** (Law); **Teacher Education - Laoag Campus** (Art Education; Biology; Chemistry; Curriculum; Education; Educational Administration; Educational and Student Counselling; English; Filipino; Foreign Languages Education; Health Education; Home Economics Education; Industrial Arts Education; Information Management; Library Science; Literature; Mathematics Education; Music Education; Native Language Education; Physical Education; Physics; Preschool Education; Primary Education; Science Education; Secondary Education; Social Studies; Special Education; Teacher Training; Technology Education); **Technology - Laoag City** (Architecture; Automotive Engineering; Electrical Engineering; Electronic Engineering; Fashion Design; Food Technology; Heating and Refrigeration; Home Economics; Industrial Arts Education; Industrial Design; Industrial Engineering; Technology; Telecommunications Engineering; Textile Technology)

Schools
Graduate Studies - Laoag Campus (Agriculture; Animal Husbandry; Biology; Chemistry; Child Care and Development; Crop Production; Education; Educational Administration; Educational and Student Counselling; English; Filipino; Foreign Languages Education; Forestry; Health Education; Home Economics Education; Information Management; Library Science; Linguistics; Mathematics Education; Music Education; Native Language Education; Nursing; Physical Education; Physics; Preschool Education; Public Administration; Rural Planning; Rural Studies; Science Education; Social Studies; Special Education; Teacher Training; Technology Education; Zoology)

Further Information: Also Research and Development Directorate; Extension Services/Technology Promotion and Utilization Directorate; Commission on Higher Education (CHED) Zonal Research Centre; Ilocos Agriculture and Resources Research and Development Consortium; Ilocos Norte Science Community; Regional Center on Poverty

History: Founded 1978, incorporating the Mariano Marcos Memorial College of Science and Technology; Northern Luzon State College, Laoag City; Ilocos Norte College of Arts and Trades; and Ilocos Norte Agricultural College. A State Institution.

Governing Bodies: Board of Regents; University Council

Academic Year: June to March (June-October; November-March)

Admission Requirements: Graduation from high school and entrance examination

Main Language(s) of Instruction: Filipino, English

Degrees and Diplomas: *Certificate/Diploma*; *Bachelor's Degree*: Agricultural Engineering; Agriculture, 4-5 yrs; *Bachelor's Degree*: Agriculural Technology; Biology; Business Administration; Computer Science; Cooperative Management; Development Communication; Economics; Elementary Education; English Studies; Environmental Science; Forestry; Home Technology; Industrial Education; Industrial Technology; Marine Biology, Fisheries; Mathematics; Nursing; Pharmacy; Secondary Education; Sociology, 4 yrs; *Bachelor's Degree*: Ceramics Engineering; Chemical Engineering; Civil Engineering; Computer Engineering; Electrical Engineering, Electronics and Communication Engineering; Mechanical Engineering; Physical Therapy, 5 yrs; *Master's Degree*: Arts (Public Administration; Nursing - Major in Maternal and Child Health and Medical Surgical Nursing); Public Administration; Rural Development; Nursing (Major in Maternal and Child Health and Medical Surgical Nursing); Agriculture (Major in Animal Science and Crop Science); Science (Rural Development; Agriculture - Major in Animal Science and Crop Science; Agroforestry); *Master's Degree*: Arts in Education (English/Linguistics; Teacher Education; MSEPK/PEHM; Technology and Home Economics; Biology; Chemistry; Science Education; Mathematics; Physics); Arts in Education (Filipino; Educational Management; Social Studies; Guidance and Counselling; Livelihood Education; Library and Information Management; Special Education)); Education (English/Linguistics; Teacher Education; MSEPK/PEHM; Technology and Home Economics); Education (Filipino; Educational Management; Social Studies; Guidance and Counselling; Early Childhood Education; Library Information Management; Special Education), a further 2 yrs; *PhD*: Crop Production Management; Linguistics; Rural Development (PhD); Education, 2-3 yrs following Master's. Also Graduate Diploma (Major in Science Education; Mathematics Education; English Education)

Student Services: Academic counselling, Canteen, Cultural centre, Employment services, Health services, Social counselling, Sports facilities

Student Residential Facilities: Yes

Special Facilities: Iloko Museum. University Art Gallery
Libraries: Central Library, c. 60,000 vols
Last Updated: 29/11/10

MARIKINA POLYTECHNIC COLLEGE

Shoe Avenue, Sta. Elena, City of Marikina, Second District, Metro Manila 1800
Tel: +63(2) 682-0596
Fax: +63(2) 682-0591

President: Henry L. Lanada

Programmes

Education (Education; Educational Administration); **Industrial Technology** (Automotive Engineering; Civil Engineering; Electrical Engineering; Electronic Engineering; Fashion Design; Food Technology; Heating and Refrigeration; Mechanical Engineering; Metal Techniques; Technology; Textile Design; Textile Technology); **Teaching** (Biology; Chemistry; Civil Engineering; Education; Electrical Engineering; Mathematics; Mechanical Engineering; Physics; Science Education; Teacher Training; Textile Technology); **Technician/Technical Teacher Education** (Applied Chemistry; Applied Mathematics; Applied Physics; Automation and Control Engineering; Automotive Engineering; Chemistry; Civil Engineering; Education; Electrical Engineering; Electronic Engineering; Fashion Design; Food Technology; Heating and Refrigeration; Mechanical Engineering; Metal Techniques; Physics; Secondary Education; Technology Education; Textile Technology)

History: Founded 1947. Acquired present status and title 2004. Formerly known as Marikina Institute of Science and Technology. Acquired current status 2004.

Degrees and Diplomas: *Bachelor's Degree*; *Master's Degree*: Arts in Teaching (Biology; Drafting, Electrical, Garments, Mechanical, Civil and Instructional Technology; Chemistry; Elementary Mathematics and Science; Physics; Applied Arts and Crafts; Mathematics; Science; Practical Arts); Education (Educational Management); Technical Education (Mechanical, Civil, Electrical, Electronic and Automotive Technology; Refrigeration and Air Conditioning; Welding and Fabrication; Chemistry; Physics; Technical English)
Last Updated: 29/11/10

MARINDUQUE STATE COLLEGE (MSC)

Tanza, Boac, Marinduque 4900
Tel: +63(42) 332-2028
Fax: +63(42) 332-2028
EMail: msc_president@yahoo.com
Website: http://www.mscollege.net

President: Romulo H. Malvar

Campuses

Gasan (Fishery) *Director*: Euloguio R. Medina, Jr.; **Sta. Cruz** (Child Care and Development; Communication Arts; Curriculum; Education; Home Economics Education; Hotel Management; Information Management; Political Sciences; Preschool Education; Primary Education; Tourism); **Torrijos** (Agricultural Engineering)

Programmes

Arts (Communication Arts; English); **Education** (Art Education; Biological and Life Sciences; Biology; Curriculum; Education; Educational Administration; Health Education; Home Economics Education; Mathematics Education; Music Education; Physical Education; Physics; Secondary Education; Social Studies; Technology Education); **Public Administration** (Public Administration); **Science** (Automotive Engineering; Civil Engineering; Electrical Engineering; Food Technology; Heating and Refrigeration; Hotel Management; Industrial Engineering; Information Management; Information Technology; Management; Mechanical Engineering; Metal Techniques; Midwifery; Nursing; Textile Technology; Tourism)

Further Information: Branches in Gasan, Santa Cruz, Torrijos

History: Founded 1983. Formerly Marinduque School of Arts and Trades (1953-1982 and Marinduque Institute of Science and Technology (1983-1991).

Degrees and Diplomas: *Certificate/Diploma*; *Associate Degree*; *Bachelor's Degree*; *Master's Degree*: Education (Educational Management); Public Administration (Organizational Studies)
Last Updated: 01/12/10

MAUBAN UNIVERSITY COLLEGE

Pambayang Kolehiyo ng Mauban

African Daisy II, Sitio, Mauban, Quezon 4330
Tel: +63(42) 784-1252
Fax: +63(42) 784-1252
EMail: pkm_maubanin@yahoo.com

Dean: Rexito P. Bantayan

Programmes

Education (Education; English; Filipino; Foreign Languages Education; Mathematics Education; Native Language Education; Primary Education; Secondary Education)

History: Founded 2005.

Degrees and Diplomas: *Bachelor's Degree*
Last Updated: 20/01/11

MINDANAO STATE UNIVERSITY (MSU)

MSU Main Campus, Marawi City, Lanao del Sur 9700
Tel: +63(63) 352-1002
Fax: +63(63) 352-1002
Website: http://www.msumain.edu.ph/

President: Macapado A. Muslim EMail: op@msumain.edu.ph

Centres

Islamic, Arabic and Asian Studies *(King Faisal Center)* (Arabic; Asian Studies; Islamic Law; Islamic Studies)

Colleges

Agriculture (Agricultural Business; Agricultural Education; Agricultural Engineering; Agricultural Equipment; Agricultural Management; Agriculture; Agronomy; Animal Husbandry; Crop Production; Farm Management; Food Science; Horticulture; Management; Zoology); **Business Administration and Accountancy** (Accountancy; Business Administration; Economics; Management; Marketing); **Education** (Chemistry; Curriculum; Education; Educational Administration; Educational and Student Counselling; English; Filipino; Foreign Languages Education; Home Economics Education; Literacy Education; Mathematics Education; Native Language Education; Physics; Preschool Education; Teacher Training; Technology Education); **Engineering** (Automotive Engineering; Building Technologies; Chemical Engineering; Civil Engineering; Electrical Engineering; Electronic Engineering; Engineering; Mechanical Engineering; Telecommunications Engineering); **Fisheries** (Aquaculture; Fishery); **Forestry and Environmental Studies** (Environmental Studies; Forestry); **Health Sciences** (Health Education; Health Sciences; Midwifery; Nursing); **Hotel and Restaurant Management** (Hotel and Restaurant; Hotel Management; Tourism); **Information Technology** (Computer Science; Information Technology); **Law** (Islamic Law; Law); **Medicine** (Medicine); **Natural Sciences and Mathematics** (Biology; Chemistry; Mathematics; Mathematics and Computer Science; Natural Sciences; Physics; Statistics; Zoology); **Public Affairs** (Development Studies; Government; Public Administration; Social and Community Services; Social Work); **Social Sciences and Humanities** (Anthropology; Arts and Humanities; Communication Studies; Development Studies; English; Filipino; History; Information Sciences; Journalism; Library Science; Modern Languages; Peace and Disarmament; Philosophy; Political Sciences; Psychology; Social Psychology; Social Sciences; Sociology; Speech Studies; Theatre); **Sports, Physical Education and Recreation** (Environmental Studies; Parks and Recreation; Physical Education; Sports)

Institutes

Science Education (Biology; Chemistry; Mathematics; Physics; Science Education)

Schools

Graduate (Agriculture; Asian Studies; Biology; Chemistry; Development Studies; Education; Educational Administration; Educational and Student Counselling; English; Filipino; Foreign Languages Education; Government; History; Islamic Law; Islamic Studies; Literacy Education; Mathematics; Modern Languages; Native Language Education; Nursing; Peace and Disarmament; Physical Education; Physics; Public Administration; Science Education; Social and Community Services; Social Psychology; Statistics; Zoology)

History: Founded 1961, first students admitted June 1966. A State Institution.

Governing Bodies: Board of Regents; University Council

Academic Year: June to March (June-October; November-March)

Admission Requirements: Graduation from high school and entrance examination

Main Language(s) of Instruction: English

Degrees and Diplomas: *Certificate/Diploma*; *Bachelor's Degree*; *Master's Degree*: Arts in: Public Administration; Animal Science; Education (Reading; Educational Management; Guidance and Counselling; School Administration) English; Filipino; History; Islamic Law; Psychology; Science in: Educational Mathematics; Farming System; Mathematics; Physical Education; Teaching (Elementary & High School Mathematics; Elementary Science; Physical Science; General Science); *PhD*: Philippine Studies; Educational Management; Education

Student Services: Academic counselling, Canteen, Cultural centre, Foreign Studies Centre, Health services, Social counselling, Sports facilities

Student Residential Facilities: Yes

Special Facilities: Aga Khan Museum; Natural Sciences Museum

Libraries: c. 110,000 vols

Publications: Arts and Science Journal; Development Administration Journal; Fisheries and Aquaculture Journal; Mindanao Journal

Press or Publishing House: University Publishing House

Last Updated: 02/05/11

GENERAL SANTOS CAMPUS
(MSU GENERAL SANTOS)

Fatima Campus, Fatima, General Santos City, South Cotabato 9500
Tel: +63(83) 380-7164
Fax: +63(83) 380-7167

Chancellor: Macapado A. Muslim

Programmes

Graduate (Education; Educational Administration; Public Administration); **Undergraduate and Professional**

History: Founded 1973.

Degrees and Diplomas: *Associate Degree*; *Bachelor's Degree*; *Master's Degree*: Education (Reading; General Education); Public Administration (Public Fiscal Administration; Public Personnel Administration; Organization and Management; Local Government Administration)

ILIGAN INSTITUTE OF TECHNOLOGY
(MSU-IIT)

Andres Bonifacio Drive, Iligan City, Lanao del Norte 9200
Tel: +63(63) 221-4050 +63(63) 221-4055
Fax: +63(63) 221-4056
EMail: msuiit@sulat.edu.ph
Website: http://www.msuiit.edu.ph

Chancellor: Marcelo P. Salazar (2000-)
EMail: oc-mps@sulat.msuiit.edu.ph

International Relations: Leo.L. Dagaerag
EMail: pemo-leo@sulat.msuiit.edu.ph

Colleges

Arts and Social Sciences (Arts and Humanities; English; Filipino; History; Political Sciences; Psychology; Social Sciences; Sociology); **Business Administration and Accountancy** (Accountancy; Agricultural Economics; Banking; Business Administration; Economics; Finance; Information Technology; International Economics; Management; Marketing; Taxation); **Education** (Biology; Chemistry; Education; Home Economics Education; Industrial Arts Education; Physical Education; Physics; Science Education; Technology Education); **Engineering** (Ceramics and Glass Technology; Chemical Engineering; Civil Engineering; Computer Engineering; Computer Science; Electrical and Electronic Engineering; Engineering; Materials Engineering; Mechanical Engineering; Metallurgical Engineering; Telecommunications Engineering); **Science and Mathematics** (Biology; Botany; Chemistry; Health Sciences; Marine Biology; Mathematics; Natural Sciences; Physics; Statistics; Zoology)

Schools

Computer Studies (Computer Science; Electronic Engineering; Information Technology); **Engineering Technology** (Automation and Control Engineering; Automotive Engineering; Chemical Engineering; Civil Engineering; Electrical and Electronic Engineering; Engineering; Heating and Refrigeration; Mechanical Engineering; Metallurgical Engineering); **Graduate** (Accountancy; Biology; Business Administration; Chemistry; Civil Engineering; Computer Science; Development Studies; Education; Engineering; English; Environmental Studies; Filipino; History; Information Management; Information Sciences; Information Technology; Library Science; Marine Biology; Mathematics; Mathematics Education; Mechanical Engineering; Physical Education; Physics; Science Education; Sociology; Statistics); **Research**

History: Founded 1946 as High School, became Technical School 1958 and acquired present title 1968. Attached to Mindanao State University. Financially supported by the Government.

Governing Bodies: Board of Regents

Academic Year: June to May (June-October; November-March; April-May)

Admission Requirements: Graduation from high school and entrance examinatiuon

Main Language(s) of Instruction: English

Accrediting Agencies: Accrediting Agency of Chartered Colleges and Universities in the Philippines (AACCUP)

Degrees and Diplomas: *Bachelor's Degree*; *Master's Degree*: Business Management in: Finance; Human Resources; Institutional Management; Marketing; Production Management); Chemistry; English Language Studies; History; Information & Library Systems; Information Management & Technology; Science Education in: Biology, Chemistry, General Science, Mathematics, Physics; Science in: Biology, Chemistry, Civil Engineering, Computer Applications, Computer Science, Environmental Science, Information Management; Science in: Information Technology, Marine Biology, Mathematics, Mechanical Engineering, Physical Education, Physics, Statistics; Sociology; Sustainable Development Studies; Applied Statistics; Arts in: English, Filipino, Sociology; Biology; Computer Applications; Computer Science; Engineering; Mathematics; Physics; *PhD*: Sustainable Development Studies; Engineering; Mathematics; Chemistry; Mathematics; Physics; Science Education

Student Residential Facilities: For 9,000 students

Special Facilities: Natural Science Museum. Marine Biology Experimental Station, Camiguin Island

LANAO DEL NORTE AGRICULTURAL COLLEGE
(MSU LNAC)

Barangay Ramain, Sultan Naga Dimaporo, Lanao del Norte 9223
EMail: msulnac_snd@yahoo.com

Superintendent: Zenaida C. Ali

Programmes

Undergraduate and Professional (Agricultural Engineering; Agriculture; Agronomy; Animal Husbandry; Crop Production; Education; English; Foreign Languages Education; Forestry; Information Technology; Mathematics Education; Primary Education; Secondary Education; Zoology)

History: Founded 1916.

Degrees and Diplomas: *Bachelor's Degree*

LANAO NATIONAL COLLEGE OF ARTS AND
TRADES (MSU LNCAT)

Saduc, Marawi City, Lanao del Sur 9700
Tel: +63(63) 520-681
Website: http://www.msumain.edu.ph

Superintendent: Bangki Mimbantas

Programmes

Undergraduate and Professional (Education; Industrial Arts Education; Primary Education; Secondary Education)

History: Founded 1974.

Degrees and Diplomas: *Associate Degree*; *Bachelor's Degree*

MAGUINDANAO CAMPUS (MSU MAGUINDANAO)

Dalican, Datu Odin Sinsuat, Shariff Kabunsuan 9601
Tel: +63(64)486-0039
Fax: +63(64)486-0039
Website: http://www.msumain.edu.ph

Chancellor: Nazarollah R. Macalandong

Programmes

Graduate (Curriculum; Education; English; English Studies; Public Administration); **Undergraduate** (Agricultural Business; Agricultural Education; Agricultural Engineering; Agricultural Management; Agronomy; Animal Husbandry; Computer Science; Development Studies; Education; English; Fishery; Food Science; Foreign Languages Education; Forestry; Government; Mathematics Education; Public Administration; Secondary Education; Social and Community Services; Zoology)

History: Founded 1973 as Dinaig Agricultural and Technical College, acquiring current title 1982.

Degrees and Diplomas: *Certificate/Diploma*; *Bachelor's Degree*; *Master's Degree*: Education; English Language Studies; Public Administration

MAIGO SCHOOL OF ARTS AND TRADES (MSU MSAT)

Poblacion, Maigo, Lanao del Norte 9206
EMail: israellabastilla@yahoo.com
Website: http://www.msumain.edu.ph

Superintendent: Magadapa A. Ringia

Programmes

Undergraduate and Professional (Automotive Engineering; Building Technologies; Computer Engineering; Computer Science; Construction Engineering; Cooking and Catering; Cosmetology; Education; Electrical Engineering; Electronic Engineering; Food Science; Food Technology; Furniture Design; Heating and Refrigeration; Home Economics Education; Hotel and Restaurant; Hotel Management; Industrial Arts Education; Industrial Engineering; Mathematics; Metal Techniques; Primary Education; Technology Education; Textile Technology)

History: Founded 1948.

Degrees and Diplomas: *Certificate/Diploma*; *Bachelor's Degree*

MINDANAO STATE UNIVERSITY-BUUG COLLEGE

Barangay Datu Panas, Buug, Zamboanga del Sur 7009
Tel: +63(920) 320-9397
Fax: +63(920) 320-9397
EMail: msubc_od@yahoo.com
Website: http://www.msubuug.blogspot.com/

Director: Mohammad Ali T. Mariga

Campuses

Alicia Extension *(Zamboanga Sibugay)* (Fishery); **Ipil Extension** (Nursing); **Tabina Extension** (Agriculture; Computer Science; Fishery; Hotel and Restaurant; Hotel Management)

Colleges

Agriculture (Agricultural Engineering; Agriculture; Agronomy); **Education** (Biology; Education; English; Filipino; Foreign Languages Education; Mathematics Education; Native Language Education; Primary Education; Secondary Education); **Forestry** (Forestry); **Social Sciences** (English; Filipino; Hotel and Restaurant; Hotel Management; Information Technology; Nursing; Social Sciences)

Schools

Graduate (Development Studies; Educational Administration; Peace and Disarmament)

History: Founded 1971.

Degrees and Diplomas: *Bachelor's Degree*; *Master's Degree*: Arts in: Education (School Administration); Peace and Development Education

MINDANAO STATE UNIVERSITY-NAAWAN (MSU NAAWAN)

Purok 6, Poblacion, Naawan, Misamis Oriental 9023
Tel: +63(8822) 720-552
Fax: +63(8822) 720-552
EMail: msu_naawan@yahoo.com
Website: http://www.msunaawan.edu.ph/

Chancellor: Jusie C. Roxas

Programmes

Graduate (Aquaculture; Biology; Development Studies; Education; Environmental Management; Environmental Studies; Marine Biology; Mathematics Education; Public Administration; Science Education); **Undergraduate** (Accountancy; Agriculture; Agronomy; Aquaculture; Biology; Business Administration; Chemistry; Education; Environmental Studies; Fishery; Forestry; Hotel and Restaurant; Hotel Management; Information Technology; Management; Marine Biology; Marketing; Mathematics Education; Primary Education; Science Education; Secondary Education; Zoology)

History: Founded as a marine research laboratory in 1973. Merged with the MSU academic branch, School of Marine Fisheries and Technology, acquiring its current status and title in 1988.

Degrees and Diplomas: *Bachelor's Degree*; *Master's Degree*: Public Administration; Science in: Aquaculture, Education (Mathematics; General Science; Biology), Environmental Science, Marine Biology; *PhD*: Marine Biology; Sustainable Development

SULU DEVELOPMENT TECHNICAL COLLEGE (MSU SULU)

Jolo, Sulu
Website: http://www.msumain.edu.ph

Chancellor: Asjada Kiram

Programmes

Graduate (Government; Public Administration); **Undergraduate** (Agriculture; Biology; Business Administration; Development Studies; Education; English; Fishery; Government; Islamic Studies; Mathematics; Political Sciences; Primary Education; Public Administration; Secondary Education; Social and Community Services; Sociology)

Degrees and Diplomas: *Bachelor's Degree*; *Master's Degree*: Government Management; Public Administration

TAWI-TAWI COLLEGE OF TECHNOLOGY AND OCEANOGRAPHY (MSU TAWI-TAWI)

Tubig Sallang, Tubig Sallang, Sanga-Sanga, Bongao, Tawi-Tawi 7500
EMail: eddiemalih@yahoo.com

Chancellor: Hji. Muh'd Zahran Eddie M. Alih

Programmes

Graduate (Educational Administration; English; Foreign Languages Education; Government; Mathematics Education; Public Administration); **Undergraduate** (Aquaculture; Arabic; Computer Science; Curriculum; Education; English; Filipino; Fishery; Foreign Languages Education; History; Islamic Law; Islamic Studies; Marine Biology; Mathematics; Mathematics Education; Native Language Education; Physical Education; Political Sciences; Preschool Education; Primary Education; Secondary Education; Statistics)

History: Founded 2004.

Degrees and Diplomas: *Bachelor's Degree*; *Master's Degree*: English Language Teaching; Educational Administration and Supervision; Educational Organization and Management; English &

Mathematics Teaching; Public Administration (Public Personnel Administration; Fiscal Administration; Local Government Administration)

MINDANAO UNIVERSITY OF SCIENCE AND TECHNOLOGY

Claro M. Recto Avenue, Lapasan, Cagayan de Oro City, Misamis Oriental 9000
Tel: +63(88) 856-3811
Fax: +63(88) 856-4696
EMail: info@mpsc.edu.ph; mpsc@mpsc.edu.ph
Website: http://www.mpsc.edu.ph

President: Ricardo E. Rotoras EMail: re_rotoras@mpsc.edu.ph

Campuses

Jasaan (Automotive Engineering; Education; Electrical Engineering; Home Economics Education; Industrial Engineering; Information Technology; Mechanical Engineering; Secondary Education; Technology Education); **Oroquieta City** (Curriculum; Education; Information Technology; Primary Education); **Panaon** (Education; Information Technology; Marine Biology; Natural Resources; Physics; Primary Education)

Programmes

Graduate (Agricultural Engineering; Applied Mathematics; Chemistry; Education; Educational Administration; Engineering; English; Environmental Engineering; Environmental Studies; Foreign Languages Education; Industrial Arts Education; Industrial Engineering; Information Technology; Mathematics; Mathematics Education; Physics; Public Administration; Science Education; Special Education; Teacher Training; Technology Education); **Undergraduate and Professional** (Applied Mathematics; Applied Physics; Architecture; Automotive Engineering; Chemistry; Civil Engineering; Computer Engineering; Education; Electrical Engineering; Electronic Engineering; Environmental Engineering; Environmental Management; Environmental Studies; Food Science; Food Technology; Home Economics Education; Industrial Arts Education; Information Technology; Mathematics Education; Mechanical Engineering; Physics; Primary Education; Public Administration; Secondary Education; Special Education; Structural Architecture; Teacher Training; Technology Education; Telecommunications Engineering)

History: Founded 1927. Formerly known as Mindanao Polytechnic State College.

Degrees and Diplomas: *Certificate/Diploma*; *Bachelor's Degree*; *Master's Degree*: Agro-Industrial Technology Management; Applied Mathematics; Environmental Science and Technology; Mathematics Education; Physical Sciences Education; Technology Communications Management; Science Education; English as a Second Language; Special Education Teaching; Educational Planning and Management; Industrial Technology; Public Administration; Technician Teacher Education; Industrial Education; Engineering; Information Technology; *PhD*: Public Administration; Technology Education; Mathematics; Mathematics Education; Applied Mathematics; Science Education; Chemistry; Educational Planning and Management
Last Updated: 06/12/10

MINDORO STATE COLLEGE OF AGRICULTURE AND TECHNOLOGY

Alcate, Victoria, Oriental Mindoro 5205
Tel: +63(43) 286-7371
Fax: +63(43) 286-2368
EMail: minscat_main@yahoo.com

President: Jesse T. Zamora

Campuses

Bongabong *(Formerly Bongabong College of Fisheries)* (Aquaculture; Biological and Life Sciences; Criminology; Education; English; Fishery; Foreign Languages Education; Hotel and Restaurant; Hotel Management; Information Technology; Mathematics Education; Primary Education; Tourism); **Calapan City** *(Formerly Polytechnic College of Calapan)* (Automotive Engineering; Criminology; Electrical Engineering; Electronic Engineering; English; Filipino; Food Science; Food Technology; Foreign Languages Education; Home Economics Education; Hotel and Restaurant; Hotel Management; Industrial Arts Education; Mathematics Education; Native Language Education; Physics; Science Education; Secondary Education; Teacher Training; Technology Education; Textile Technology)

Programmes

Graduate (Agriculture; Biology; Crop Production; Education; Educational Administration; Mathematics Education; Science Education); **Undergraduate** (Agricultural Business; Agricultural Engineering; Agriculture; Biology; Crop Production; Education; English; Filipino; Foreign Languages Education; Forestry; Information Technology; Management; Mathematics Education; Native Language Education; Primary Education; Science Education; Secondary Education; Zoology)

History: Founded 1951. Formerly known as Mindoro College of Agriculture and Technology.

Degrees and Diplomas: *Bachelor's Degree*; *Master's Degree*: Education (Educational Management; Biology; General Science; Mathematics); Agriculture (Crop Science)
Last Updated: 06/12/10

MISAMIS ORIENTAL STATE COLLEGE OF AGRICULTURE AND TECHNOLOGY (MOSCAT)

Magsaysay Street, Claveria, Misamis Oriental 9004
Tel: +63(912) 358-1116
Fax: +63(912) 358-1465
EMail: info@moscat.edu.ph
Website: http://www.moscat.edu.ph

President: Elpidio R. Bautista

Programmes

Graduate (Agricultural Business; Agricultural Engineering; Agriculture; Animal Husbandry; Crop Production; Harvest Technology; Teacher Training); **Undergraduate and Professional** (Agricultural Education; Agricultural Engineering; Agricultural Management; Agriculture; Animal Husbandry; Biological and Life Sciences; Biology; Communication Studies; Computer Education; Computer Engineering; Crop Production; English; Environmental Engineering; Environmental Management; Farm Management; Filipino; Food Technology; Foreign Languages Education; Forestry; Harvest Technology; Horticulture; Hotel and Restaurant; Hotel Management; Information Technology; Native Language Education; Primary Education; Science Education; Secondary Education; Social Work; Tourism; Zoology)

History: Founded 1963.

Degrees and Diplomas: *Certificate/Diploma*; *Bachelor's Degree*; *Master's Degree*: Agricultural Science and Technology (Crop Production; Animal Production; Postharvest Processing; Agribusiness Management); Teaching Sciences
Last Updated: 07/12/10

MOUNTAIN PROVINCE STATE POLYTECHNIC COLLEGE

Poblacion, Bontoc, Mt. Province 2616
Tel: +63(74) 602-1014
Fax: +63(74) 602-1014
EMail: joycetimidan@yahoo.com

President: Nieves Dacyon

Campuses

Mt. Data (Agricultural Business; Agricultural Engineering; Animal Husbandry; Biology; Harvest Technology; Industrial Engineering; Mathematics; Plant and Crop Protection); **Tadian** (Agricultural Business; Agricultural Engineering; Civil Engineering; Education; Educational Administration; Environmental Management; Environmental Studies; Forestry; Harvest Technology; Home Economics Education; Hotel and Restaurant; Hotel Management; Industrial Arts Education; Industrial Engineering; Mathematics Education; Primary Education; Science Education; Secondary Education; Social Studies; Technology Education)

Programmes

Graduate (Business Administration; Curriculum; Education; Educational Administration; English; Foreign Languages Education; Public Administration; Rural Planning; Science Education); **Undergraduate and Professional** (Accountancy; Administration; Arts and Humanities; Business Administration; Business and Commerce;

Computer Engineering; Criminology; English; Foreign Languages Education; History; Hotel and Restaurant; Hotel Management; Mathematics Education; Nursing; Primary Education; Science Education; Secondary Education; Secretarial Studies; Social Studies; Tourism)

History: Founded 1969.

Degrees and Diplomas: *Certificate/Diploma*; *Bachelor's Degree*; *Master's Degree*: Business Administration; Public Administration; Science Education; English Teaching; General Education; *PhD*: Educational Management; Rural Development
Last Updated: 07/12/10

NAVAL INSTITUTE OF TECHNOLOGY

P.I. Garcia Street, Naval, Biliran 6543
Tel: +63(53) 500-9045
Fax: +63(53) 500-9045
EMail: esgvpaa@yahoo.com

President: Editha S. Genson

Campuses

Biliran (Agricultural Business; Agricultural Engineering; Agriculture; Agrobiology; Animal Husbandry; Education; Fishery; Forestry; Home Economics Education; Mathematics Education; Natural Sciences; Science Education; Secondary Education; Technology Education) *Administrator*: Nicasio R. Elatico

Programmes

Graduate Studies (Communication Arts; Economics; Education; Educational Administration; English; Filipino; Foreign Languages Education; Human Resources; Industrial Arts Education; Management; Mathematics Education; Native Language Education; Primary Education; Public Administration; Science Education; Teacher Training); **Undergraduate and Professional** (Biology; Business Administration; Civil Engineering; Computer Engineering; Computer Science; Criminology; Electrical Engineering; Hotel and Restaurant; Hotel Management; Industrial Arts Education; Information Management; Information Technology; Law; Marine Engineering; Marine Transport; Mechanical Engineering; Nursing; Primary Education; Secondary Education; Tourism)

History: Founded 1945.

Degrees and Diplomas: *Certificate/Diploma*; *Associate Degree*; *Bachelor's Degree*; *Master's Degree*; *PhD*
Last Updated: 16/12/10

NAVOTAS POLYTECHNIC COLLEGE

Bangus Street, North Bay Boulevard South, City of Navotas, Third District, Metro Manila 1485
Tel: +63(2) 283-2361
Fax: +63(2) 281-8861

President: Fransisca S. Roque

Programmes

Arts and Science (Filipino; History; Mathematics); **Business Administration** (Accountancy; Business Administration; Business Computing; Management); **Computer Studies** (Computer Engineering; Computer Networks; Computer Science); **Education** (Curriculum; Education; English; Filipino; Foreign Languages Education; History; Mathematics Education; Native Language Education; Preschool Education; Primary Education; Secondary Education)

History: Founded 1994.

Degrees and Diplomas: *Associate Degree*; *Bachelor's Degree*
Last Updated: 16/12/10

NEGROS ORIENTAL STATE UNIVERSITY

Main Campus, Kagawasan Avenue, Dumaguete City, Negros Oriental 6200
Tel: +63(35) 225-4751
Fax: +63(35) 225-0777
EMail: sojor@cvpc.edu.ph
Website: http://www.norsu.edu.ph

President: Henry A. Sojor

Vice-President, Administration, Development and Special Concerns: Maria Elsa Ilona A. Bulado

Vice-President, Academic Affairs: Victoria P. Dinopol

International Relations: Peter T. Dayot, Vice-President, Planning, Research, Extension and International Linkages

Campuses

Bais1 (Accountancy; Agricultural Engineering; Agriculture; Air Transport; Architecture; Biology; Business Administration; Business and Commerce; Chemistry; Civil Engineering; Computer Engineering; Computer Science; Criminology; Electrical Engineering; Electronic Engineering; Fishery; Forestry; Geological Engineering; Geology; Hotel and Restaurant; Hotel Management; Industrial Arts Education; Industrial Engineering; Information Technology; Law; Management Systems; Marine Engineering; Marine Transport; Mass Communication; Mathematics; Mechanical Engineering; Nursing; Pharmacy; Primary Education; Psychology; Secondary Education; Social Sciences; Software Engineering; Technology; Technology Education; Telecommunications Engineering; Thermal Engineering; Tourism) *Campus Administrator*: Bernardina E. Dueñas; **Bayawan** (Accountancy; Agricultural Engineering; Agriculture; Air Transport; Architecture; Biology; Chemistry; Civil Engineering; Computer Engineering; Computer Science; Criminology; Electrical Engineering; Electronic Engineering; Forestry; Geological Engineering; Hotel and Restaurant; Hotel Management; Industrial Arts Education; Industrial Engineering; Information Technology; Law; Management Systems; Marine Engineering; Marine Transport; Mass Communication; Mathematics; Mechanical Engineering; Midwifery; Nursing; Pharmacy; Primary Education; Psychology; Secondary Education; Social Sciences; Technology; Technology Education; Telecommunications Engineering; Thermal Engineering; Tourism) *College Administrator*: Bernadette O. Tan; **Genaro Goñi Memorial College** (Accountancy; Business Administration; Business and Commerce; Computer Education; Filipino; Foreign Languages Education; Health Education; Home Economics Education; Law; Management; Mathematics; Mathematics Education; Music Education; Native Language Education; Physical Education; Primary Education; Science Education; Social Sciences) *Campus Administrator*: Bernardina E. Dueñas; **Guihulngan** (Accountancy; Agricultural Engineering; Agriculture; Air Transport; Architecture; Biology; Business Administration; Business and Commerce; Chemistry; Civil Engineering; Computer Engineering; Computer Science; Criminology; Electrical Engineering; Electronic Engineering; Fishery; Forestry; Geological Engineering; Geology; Hotel and Restaurant; Hotel Management; Industrial Arts Education; Industrial Engineering; Information Technology; Management Systems; Marine Engineering; Marine Transport; Mass Communication; Mathematics; Mechanical Engineering; Nursing; Pharmacy; Primary Education; Psychology; Secondary Education; Social Sciences; Technology; Technology Education; Telecommunications Engineering; Thermal Engineering; Tourism) *Campus Director*: Jose S. Baquilta; **Mabinay Institute of Technology** (Engineering); **Main II** (Building Technologies); **Siaton Community College** (Accountancy; Agricultural Engineering; Agriculture; Air Transport; Architecture; Biology; Business Administration; Business and Commerce; Chemistry; Civil Engineering; Computer Engineering; Computer Science; Criminology; Electrical Engineering; Electronic Engineering; Fishery; Forestry; Geological Engineering; Geology; Industrial Arts Education; Industrial Engineering; Information Technology; Management Systems; Marine Engineering; Marine Transport; Mass Communication; Mathematics; Mechanical Engineering; Nursing; Pharmacy; Primary Education; Psychology; Secondary Education; Social Sciences; Technology; Technology Education; Telecommunications Engineering; Thermal Engineering; Tourism) *College Administrator*: Juanita B. Somido-Solis

Colleges

Agriculture and Forestry (Agricultural Engineering; Agriculture; Fishery; Forestry; Rubber Technology); **Arts and Sciences** (Biology; Chemistry; Computer Science; Criminology; English; Geology; Information Technology; Management Systems; Mass Communication; Mathematics; Social Sciences; Tourism); **Education** (Education; Industrial Arts Education; Primary Education; Secondary Education); **Engineering and Architecture** (Architecture; Civil Engineering; Computer Engineering; Electrical Engineering; Electronic Engineering; Engineering; Geological Engineering; Mechanical Engineering; Mining Engineering; Telecommunications Engineering; Thermal Engineering); **Industrial Technology** (Automotive Engineering; Civil Engineering; Computer Engineering; Electrical and Electronic Engineering; Food Technology; Industrial Design; Industrial Engineering; Mechanical Engineering; Textile

Technology); **Maritime Education** (Marine Engineering; Marine Transport); **Tourism and Hospitality Management** (Business Computing; Dentistry; Hotel and Restaurant; Hotel Management; Midwifery; Nursing; Technology; Technology Education; Tourism)

Schools

Graduate Studies (Agriculture; Agronomy; Animal Husbandry; Automotive Engineering; Biology; Civil Engineering; Curriculum; Education; Educational Administration; Electrical Engineering; Electronic Engineering; English; Filipino; Fishery; Foreign Languages Education; Government; Health Sciences; History; Human Resources; Industrial Design; Information Technology; Library Science; Management; Marine Science and Oceanography; Mathematics; Mechanical Engineering; Native Language Education; Physical Education; Psychology; Public Administration; Science Education; Sociology; Technology; Technology Education; Zoology)

Further Information: Also Manibay, Bayawan City, Bais City, Siaton, Guihulgan, and Pamplona campuses

History: Founded 1927 as Negros Oriental Provincial School. Renamed Negros Oriental Trade School 1927, East Visayan School of Arts and Trade 1956and Central Visayas Polytechnic College 1983. Acquired present status and title 2004.

Degrees and Diplomas: *Bachelor's Degree*; *Master's Degree*: Arts in: Business Administration; Educational Management; English; Filipino; History; Maritime Education; Mathematics Teaching; Physical Education; Psychology; Science Teaching; Sociology; Special Education; Vocational Education; Public Health; Public Management; Technological Education; Science in: Agriculture (Agricultural Extension); Biology; Fisheries; Information Technology; Library Science; Mathematics; *PhD*: Educational Management; Public Management; Applied Linguistics
Last Updated: 17/12/10

NEGROS STATE COLLEGE OF AGRICULTURE

City of Kabankalan, Negros Occidental 6109
Fax: +63(34) 471-3425
President: Freddie C. Maningo

Campuses

Candoni; **Cauayan** (Agricultural Business; Agriculture; Crop Production; Primary Education; Secondary Education; Zoology); **Hinoba-an**; **Ilog** (Agricultural Engineering; Agriculture; Aquaculture; Crop Production; Fishery) *President*: Freddie C. Maningo; **Moises Padilla**; **San Carlos**; **Sipalay** (Agricultural Engineering; Agriculture; Animal Husbandry; Crop Production; Curriculum; Education; Health Education; Home Economics Education; Primary Education; Science Education) *Campus Director*: Agnes L. Paraba

Programmes

Graduate (Agricultural Education; Agriculture; Animal Husbandry; Crop Production; Education; Educational Administration; English; Filipino; Foreign Languages Education; Horticulture; Human Resources; Mathematics Education; Native Language Education; Physical Education; Preschool Education; Public Administration; Rural Planning; Rural Studies; Science Education; Social Sciences; Zoology); **Undergraduate and Professional** (Agricultural Business; Agricultural Education; Agricultural Engineering; Animal Husbandry; Crop Production; Education; Electrical Engineering; English; Food Technology; Forestry; Hotel and Restaurant; Hotel Management; Information Technology; Mechanical Engineering; Primary Education; Secondary Education; Social Sciences; Statistics; Zoology)

History: Founded 1946.

Degrees and Diplomas: *Certificate/Diploma*; *Bachelor's Degree*; *Master's Degree*: Public Administration (Human Resources Management); Education (Mathematics; Physical Education; Science; Social Sciences; Filipino; English; Early Childhood Education; Educational Management (Vocational Productivity); *PhD*: Educational Management
Last Updated: 17/12/10

NEW LUCENA POLYTECHNIC COLLEGE

Don Epifanio Sonza Sr. Avenue, New Lucena, Iloilo 5005
Tel: +63(33) 526-2015
Fax: +63(33) 526-2015
Administrator: Buen S. Mondejar

Programmes

Hotel and Restaurant Services Technology (Hotel and Restaurant); **Information Technology** (Information Technology); **Midwifery** (Midwifery)

History: Founded 1971.

Degrees and Diplomas: *Certificate/Diploma*; *Bachelor's Degree*
Last Updated: 21/12/10

NORTHERN ILOILO POLYTECHNIC STATE COLLEGE

V. Cudilla Sr. Avenue, Estancia, Iloilo 5017
Tel: +63(33) 397-0314
Fax: +63(33) 397-0315
EMail: nipsc_main@yahoo.com

President: Joel P. Limson

Campuses

Ajuy (Business Administration; Computer Engineering; Criminology; Education; English; Foreign Languages Education; Hotel and Restaurant; Hotel Management; Management; Mathematics Education; Physical Therapy; Secondary Education; Small Business; Software Engineering); **Barotac Nuevo** (Agriculture; Education; Technology); **Barotac Viejo** (Agricultural Engineering; Agriculture; Crop Production; Education; English; Foreign Languages Education; Home Economics Education; Mathematics Education; Primary Education; Secondary Education; Technology Education; Zoology); **Batad** (Agriculture; Crop Production; Education; Electronic Engineering; English; Food Technology; Foreign Languages Education; Home Economics; Home Economics Education; Industrial Arts Education; Information Technology; Secondary Education; Technology Education; Zoology); **Concepcion** (Aquaculture; Computer Engineering; Cooking and Catering; Education; Electrical Engineering; Filipino; Fishery; Food Technology; Home Economics Education; Hotel and Restaurant; Hotel Management; Marine Science and Oceanography; Mathematics Education; Native Language Education; Secondary Education; Technology Education); **Lemery** (Education; Electronic Engineering; Filipino; Food Technology; Foreign Languages Education; Industrial Arts Education; Information Management; Information Technology; Primary Education; Secondary Education); **Sara** (Civil Engineering; Criminology; Electrical Engineering; Food Technology; Hotel and Restaurant; Hotel Management; Textile Technology; Tourism); **Victorino Salcedo** *(Victorino Salcedo Polytechnic College)* (Hotel and Restaurant; Secretarial Studies; Technology)

Programmes

Graduate *(Estancia Campus)* (Education; Educational Administration; English; Foreign Languages Education; Mathematics Education; Public Administration; Science Education); **Undergraduate and Professional** *(Estancia Campus)* (Aquaculture; Automotive Engineering; Biology; Business Administration; Civil Engineering; Computer Engineering; Computer Science; Education; Electrical Engineering; Engineering; English; Fishery; Food Technology; Foreign Languages Education; Industrial Engineering; Management; Marine Engineering; Marine Science and Oceanography; Mathematics Education; Midwifery; Primary Education; Public Administration; Secondary Education; Teacher Training)
History: Founded 1956.

Degrees and Diplomas: *Certificate/Diploma*; *Bachelor's Degree*; *Master's Degree*: Public Administration; Education (Educational Management); Professional Studies Education (Educational Management); Teaching (English; Mathematics; Science); *PhD*: Education (Development Management)
Last Updated: 21/12/10

NORTHERN NEGROS STATE COLLEGE OF SCIENCE AND TECHNOLOGY

Old Sagay, Sagay City, Negros Occidental 6122
Tel: +63(34) 722-4120 +63(34) 722-4169
Fax: +63(34) 722-4120

President: Rogelio T. Artajo

Programmes

Graduate (Educational Administration; Nursing; Public Administration); **Undergraduate and Professional** (Agricultural Engineering; Aquaculture; Biology; Chemistry; Coastal Studies; Criminal Law;

Crop Production; Education; Fishery; Hotel and Restaurant; Hotel Management; Information Technology; Marine Biology; Marine Transport; Mathematics; Natural Resources; Nursing; Science Education; Secondary Education; Zoology)

History: Founded 1971. Acquired present status 1983.

Degrees and Diplomas: *Bachelor's Degree*; *Master's Degree*: Nursing (Nursing Leadership); Public Administration; Education (Educational Management); *PhD*: Educational Management

Last Updated: 22/12/10

NORTHWESTERN MINDANAO STATE COLLEGE OF SCIENCE AND TECHNOLOGY

Tangub City, Misamis Occidenal 7214
Tel: +63(88) 354-1183
Fax: +63(88) 354-1183

President: Philip T. Tan

Programmes

Agriculture (Agriculture; Animal Husbandry; Crop Production; Zoology); **Education** (Biology; Curriculum; Education; Health Education; Home Economics Education; Mathematics Education; Primary Education; Science Education; Secondary Education; Technology Education); **Hospitality Management** (Hotel and Restaurant; Hotel Management); **Industrial Technology** (Automotive Engineering; Civil Engineering; Computer Engineering; Electrical Engineering; Electronic Engineering; Food Technology; Heating and Refrigeration); **Information Technology** (Information Management; Information Technology; Management Systems)

History: Founded 1971. Formerly known as Tangub Agro-Industrial Technology.

Degrees and Diplomas: *Bachelor's Degree*

Last Updated: 22/12/10

NUEVA EJICA UNIVERSITY OF SCIENCE AND TECHNOLOGY

Pamantasan ng Agham at Teknolohiya sa Nueva Ecija (NEUST)

General Tinio Street, Cabanatuan City, Nueva Ecija 3100
Tel: +63 (44) 464-3674 +63(44) 463-0226
Fax: +63 (44) 463-0226
EMail: neustmain@yahoo.com
Website: http://www.neust.edu.ph

President: Hilario C. Ortiz EMail: president@neust.edu.ph

Campuses

Aliaga (Education; Information Technology; Management); **Atate** (Education; Information Technology; Management); **Fort Magsaysay** (Education; Management); **Gapan City** (Education; Information Technology; Management); **Peñaflorida** (Education; Information Technology; Management); **San Isidro** (Education; Industrial Arts Education; Information Technology; Management); **Sebani Estate Agricultural College** (Agriculture; Education; Food Technology; Industrial Arts Education); **Sumacab** (Architecture; Education; Management)

Programmes

Graduate Studies (Business Administration; Civil Engineering; Computer Education; Computer Networks; Curriculum; Data Processing; Education; Educational Administration; Electrical Engineering; Engineering; Engineering Management; Industrial Arts Education; Information Technology; Mathematics Education; Mechanical Engineering; Physics; Public Administration; Science Education; Software Engineering; Teacher Training; Technology Education); **Undergraduate Studies** (Agricultural Engineering; Agriculture; Agronomy; Architecture; Art Education; Banking; Building Technologies; Business Administration; Chemistry; Civil Engineering; Computer Graphics; Criminology; Crop Production; Economics; Education; Electrical Engineering; English; Environmental Studies; Finance; Food Technology; Foreign Languages Education; Forestry; Health Education; Home Economics Education; Hotel and Restaurant; Hotel Management; Industrial Arts Education; Information Technology; Interior Design; Management; Marketing; Mathematics Education; Mechanical Engineering; Music Education; Nursing; Physical Education; Physics; Primary Education; Science Education; Secondary Education; Systems Analysis; Technology Education; Zoology)

Further Information: Also campuses in Aliaga, Atate, Fort Magsaysay, San Isidro and Sumacab.

History: Founded 1929, as the Nueva Ecija Trade School. Became state college 1964. Acquired present status- of state university-1998.

Governing Bodies: Board of Regents

Admission Requirements: High school diploma, entrance examination

Main Language(s) of Instruction: Filipino; English

International Co-operation: With universities in Japan, Singapore, Australia, China, Hong Kong and Macau

Accrediting Agencies: Accrediting Agency of Chartered Colleges and Universities in the Philippines (AACCUP)

Degrees and Diplomas: *Certificate/Diploma*; *Associate Degree*; *Bachelor's Degree*; *Master's Degree*: Business Administration; Public Administration; Education Management; Engineering Management; Engineering Education; Arts in Teaching; Arts in Industrial Education; *PhD*: Industrial Technological Education; Mathematics Education; Management; Management; Business Administration; Public Administration; Educational Administration; Engineering Management; Science Education

Student Services: Academic counselling, Canteen, Cultural centre, Employment services, Health services, Language programs, Social counselling, Sports facilities

Student Residential Facilities: Dormitories; Guest House

Special Facilities: University Museum

Publications: NEUST Research Journal, Publication of research studies/projects conducted by faculty and staff *(biennially)*

Press or Publishing House: The NEUST Printing Press

Last Updated: 07/01/11

NUEVA VIZCAYA STATE UNIVERSITY-BAYOMBONG CAMPUS (NVSU)

Main Campus, Bayombong, Nueva Vizcaya 3700
Tel: +63(78) 321-2280
Fax: +63(78) 321-2112
EMail: bayombong@nvsu.edu.ph
Website: http://www.nvsu.edu.ph

President: Marilou S. Gilo-Abon (2005-)
EMail: president@nvsu.edu.ph

VIce-President for Administration: Elmer T. Castañeto
EMail: vpad@nvsu.edu.ph

Colleges

Agriculture (Agricultural Business; Agricultural Education; Agricultural Engineering; Agrobiology; Agronomy; Aquaculture; Crop Production; Fishery; Horticulture; Soil Science; Veterinary Science; Water Management; Zoology); **Arts and Sciences** (Arts and Humanities; Computer Science; Information Technology; Mathematics; Modern Languages; Natural Sciences; Social Sciences); **Engineering** (Agricultural Engineering; Civil Engineering; Construction Engineering; Crop Production; Farm Management; Hydraulic Engineering; Soil Management; Structural Architecture; Transport Engineering; Water Management); **Forestry** (Agronomy; Environmental Studies; Forestry); **Human Ecology** (Clothing and Sewing; Cooking and Catering; Home Economics Education; Hotel and Restaurant; Hotel Management; Nutrition; Textile Technology; Tourism); **Teacher Education** (Art Education; Automotive Engineering; Biology; Foreign Languages Education; Furniture Design; Health Education; Industrial Arts Education; Music Education; Native Language Education; Physical Education; Primary Education; Science Education; Secondary Education; Social Studies; Technology Education)

Graduate Schools

Graduate School (Agricultural Business; Agricultural Education; Agricultural Engineering; Agricultural Management; Animal Husbandry; Art Education; Chemistry; Crop Production; Education; Educational Administration; Environmental Studies; Forest Management; Forestry; Health Education; Home Economics; Industrial Engineering; Literacy Education; Mathematics Education; Music Education; Natural Resources; Physical Education; Primary

Education; Rural Planning; Science Education; Soil Management; Teacher Training; Technology; Water Management; Zoology)

History: Nueva Vizcaya State University was created in 2004 out of a merger between Nueva Vizcaya State Institute of Technology (created 1916) and Nueva Vizcaya State Polytechnic College (created 1946).

Governing Bodies: Academic Council; Administrative Council

Admission Requirements: (Undergraduate): High School Diploma and entrance exam; (Postgraduate): Bachelor's degree or equivalent with a GPA of at least 2.00 for Master's programme; Master's degree or equivalent with a GPA of at least 1.75 for Doctorate programmes

Fees: (Pesos): Undergraduate, 150.00 per unit; Postgraduate, 235.00-435.00

Main Language(s) of Instruction: Filipino, English

Degrees and Diplomas: *Certificate/Diploma*; *Associate Degree*; *Bachelor's Degree (BA, BSc)*; *Master's Degree (MA, MSc)*; *PhD*

Last Updated: 04/01/11

NUEVA VIZCAYA STATE UNIVERSITY-BAMBANG CAMPUS

Heroes Boulevard, Bambang, Nueva Vizcaya 3702
Tel: +63(78) 321-3037
Fax: +63(78) 321-3037
EMail: bambang@nvsu.edu.ph
Website: http://www.nvsu.edu.ph

Campus Administrator: Leodevico M. Fronda

Colleges

Arts and Sciences (Arts and Humanities; Biology; English; Modern Languages; Natural Sciences; Public Administration); **Engineering** (Computer Engineering; Electrical Engineering; Electronic Engineering; Industrial Engineering; Mechanical Engineering; Telecommunications Engineering); **Industrial Technology** (Automotive Engineering; Civil Engineering; Computer Science; Cosmetology; Electrical and Electronic Engineering; Food Technology; Heating and Refrigeration; Hotel Management; Industrial Engineering; Information Management; Information Technology; Mechanical Engineering; Metal Techniques; Textile Technology; Tourism); **Teacher Education** (Art Education; Biology; Chemistry; English; Filipino; Foreign Languages Education; Health Education; History; Home Economics Education; Industrial Arts Education; Mathematics Education; Music Education; Native Language Education; Physical Education; Preschool Education; Primary Education; Science Education; Secondary Education; Social Studies; Technology Education)

Graduate Schools

Graduate School (Business Administration; Educational Administration; Educational Technology; Engineering Management; English; Filipino; Foreign Languages Education; Government; Home Economics Education; Mathematics Education; Native Language Education; Pedagogy; Public Administration; Science Education; Technology Education)

History: Founded 1946. Formerly known as Nueva Vizcaya State Polytechnic College.

Degrees and Diplomas: *Certificate/Diploma*; *Bachelor's Degree*; *Master's Degree*; *PhD*

OCCIDENTAL MINDORO NATIONAL COLLEGE

San Jose, Occidental Mindoro 5100
Tel: +63(42) 491-1460
Fax: +63(42) 491-1460

President: Arnold N. Venturina

Programmes

Business Administration (Accountancy; Business Administration; Business and Commerce; Management); **Education** (Education; English; Filipino; Foreign Languages Education; Mathematics Education; Native Language Education; Primary Education; Secondary Education); **Graduate Studies** (Education; Public Administration; Teacher Training); **Information Technology** (Information Technology)

History: Founded 1966. Formerly known as San Jose National High School. Acquired present status 1983.

Degrees and Diplomas: *Certificate/Diploma*; *Associate Degree*; *Bachelor's Degree*; *Master's Degree*: Development Education; Public Administration; Teaching

Last Updated: 28/03/11

OCCIDENTAL MINDORO NATIONAL COLLEGE-LABANGAN CAMPUS

San José, Occidental Mindoro 5100

Campus Director: Theresita G. Macaraig

Programmes

Criminology (Criminology); **Hotel and Restaurant Management** (Hotel and Restaurant; Hotel Management); **Industrial Education** (Automotive Engineering; Electrical and Electronic Engineering; Industrial Arts Education)

History: Founded 2002.

Degrees and Diplomas: *Bachelor's Degree*

OCCIDENTAL MINDORO NATIONAL COLLEGE-MAMBURAO

Mamburao, Occidental Mindoro 5106

Campus Director: Judith G. Gamit

OCCIDENTAL MINDORO NATIONAL COLLEGE-MURTHA CAMPUS

San Jose, Occidental Mindoro 5100

Campus Director: Liberato D. Calanza, Jr.

Programmes

Agricultural Education (Agricultural Education; Crop Production; Food Technology); **Agricultural Technology** (Agricultural Engineering; Animal Husbandry; Crop Production); **Agriculture** (Agriculture; Crop Production; Forestry)

History: Founded 2002.

Degrees and Diplomas: *Bachelor's Degree*

ORMOC CITY SCHOOL OF ARTS AND TRADES

Brgy. Don Felipe, Ormoc City, Leyte 6541
Tel: +63(53) 255-7497

Programmes

Undergraduate and Professional

History: Founded 2000.

Degrees and Diplomas: *Bachelor's Degree*

Last Updated: 04/01/11

PALAWAN STATE UNIVERSITY (PSU)

Tiniguiban Heights, Puerto Princesa City, Palawan 5300
Tel: +63(48) 433-2379
Fax: +63(48) 433-5303
EMail: Psuam@hotmail.com
Website: http://www.psu.itgo.com

President: Teresita L. Salva

Campuses

Araceli (Asian Studies; Education; Electrical Engineering; English; Foreign Languages Education; Management; Primary Education; Social Studies); **Balabac** (Education; Management; Primary Education); **Bataraza** (Business Administration; Civil Engineering; Education; Electrical Engineering; Filipino; Management; Marketing; Mechanical Engineering; Native Language Education; Primary Education); **Brooke's Point** (Art Education; Business Administration; Civil Engineering; Education; Electrical Engineering; English; Filipino; Foreign Languages Education; Health Education; Hotel and Restaurant; Hotel Management; Management; Marketing; Mathematics Education; Mechanical Engineering; Music Education; Native

Language Education; Physical Education; Political Sciences; Primary Education; Science Education; Secondary Education); **Coron** (Education; English; Health Education; Hotel and Restaurant; Hotel Management; Management; Music Education; Physical Education; Primary Education; Secondary Education; Social Studies; Tourism); **Cuyo** (Art Education; Asian Studies; Education; Electrical Engineering; English; Filipino; Foreign Languages Education; Management; Mathematics Education; Music Education; Physical Education; Primary Education; Secondary Education); **Dumaran** (Asian Studies; Education; Electrical Engineering; Management; Mechanical Engineering; Primary Education); **Narra** (Art Education; Civil Engineering; Education; Electrical Engineering; Health Education; Hotel and Restaurant; Hotel Management; Management; Music Education; Physical Education; Political Sciences; Primary Education; Science Education; Secondary Education; Tourism); **New Ibajay, El Nido** (Education; Hotel and Restaurant; Hotel Management; Management; Primary Education; Secondary Education; Tourism); **Palawan College of Arts and Trades-Cuyo** (Automotive Engineering; Building Technologies; Civil Engineering; Cosmetology; Curriculum; Education; Electrical Engineering; Electronic Engineering; English; Filipino; Food Technology; Foreign Languages Education; Furniture Design; Heating and Refrigeration; Home Economics; Hotel and Restaurant; Hotel Management; Industrial Arts Education; Marine Engineering; Mathematics Education; Mechanical Engineering; Metal Techniques; Native Language Education; Nutrition; Secondary Education; Social Studies; Structural Architecture; Technology; Telecommunications Engineering; Textile Technology; Tourism); **Pasadena, El Nido**; **Quezon** (Art Education; Business Administration; Education; Electrical Engineering; English; Filipino; Foreign Languages Education; Health Education; Hotel and Restaurant; Hotel Management; Management; Marketing; Mathematics Education; Music Education; Native Language Education; Physical Education; Primary Education; Secondary Education; Tourism); **Rizal** (Art Education; Biology; Education; English; Environmental Studies; Foreign Languages Education; Management; Marine Biology; Music Education; Physical Education; Political Sciences; Primary Education); **Roxas** (Art Education; Business Administration; Civil Engineering; Education; Filipino; Hotel and Restaurant; Hotel Management; Management; Music Education; Native Language Education; Physical Education; Political Sciences; Primary Education; Social Studies; Tourism); **Sofronio Española** (Education; Management; Primary Education); **Taytay** (Business Administration; Education; Electrical Engineering; Filipino; Home Economics Education; Hotel and Restaurant; Hotel Management; Management; Marketing; Mathematics Education; Native Language Education; Primary Education; Secondary Education; Tourism)

Colleges

Arts and Humanities (Arts and Humanities; English; History; Journalism; Mass Communication; Philosophy; Political Sciences; Psychology; Radio and Television Broadcasting; Tourism); **Business Administration** (Accountancy; Agricultural Business; Banking; Business Administration; Finance; Hotel and Restaurant; Hotel Management; Management; Marketing); **Education** (Art Education; Education; Educational and Student Counselling; English; Ethics; Filipino; Foreign Languages Education; Health Education; History; Home Economics Education; Library Science; Mathematics Education; Music Education; Native Language Education; Physical Education; Preschool Education; Primary Education; Science Education; Secondary Education; Social Studies; Social Work; Technology Education); **Engineering, Architecture and Technology** (Architecture; Civil Engineering; Electrical Engineering; Mechanical Engineering; Petroleum and Gas Engineering; Structural Architecture; Technology); **Science** (Biology; Computer Science; Environmental Management; Environmental Studies; Marine Biology; Mathematics; Midwifery; Nursing)

History: Founded 1972. Acquired present status 1984. Formerly known as Palawan Teachers College (1972-1984) and Palawan State College (1984-1994).

Degrees and Diplomas: *Certificate/Diploma*; *Associate Degree*; *Bachelor's Degree*; *Master's Degree*: Literature; Management (Environmental Management); Public Administration; Teaching (Language Studies; Mathematics; Physics; Biology; Chemistry); Environmental Management; Public Administration; Education (Mathematics; Social Sciences; Physical Education; Guidance and Counselling; Filipino; English; Educational Administration; School Leardership and Instruction); *PhD*: Education (Educational Management)

Last Updated: 05/01/11

PALOMPON INSTITUTE OF TECHNOLOGY

Evangelista Street, Palompon, Leyte 6538
Tel: +63(53) 338-2082
Fax: +63(53) 338-2501
EMail: pitmep@yahoo.com

President: Delia T. Combista

Campuses

Tabango *(Formerly Marcelino R. Veloso National Polytechnic College-PIT Tabango Campus)* (Automotive Engineering; Education; Electrical Engineering; Fishery; Food Technology; Home Economics Education; Hotel and Restaurant; Hotel Management; Industrial Engineering; Information Technology; Primary Education; Science Education; Technology Education; Tourism)

Programmes

Graduate (Curriculum; Development Studies; Educational Administration; Educational and Student Counselling; English; Filipino; Foreign Languages Education; Home Economics Education; Industrial Arts Education; Management; Marine Engineering; Mathematics Education; Native Language Education; Nautical Science; Physical Education; Rural Planning; Science Education; Social and Community Services; Teacher Training; Technology); **Undergraduate and Professional** (Automotive Engineering; Communication Arts; Cosmetology; Curriculum; Education; Electrical Engineering; English; Filipino; Food Technology; Foreign Languages Education; Handicrafts; Heating and Refrigeration; Home Economics Education; Industrial Arts Education; Information Technology; Marine Engineering; Marine Transport; Mathematics Education; Mechanical Engineering; Native Language Education; Natural Sciences; Primary Education; Secondary Education; Technology; Technology Education; Telecommunications Engineering; Textile Technology)

History: Founded 1964.

Degrees and Diplomas: *Associate Degree*; *Bachelor's Degree*; *Master's Degree*: Teaching (Physical Education; Filipino; English; Mathematics; Marine Engineering/Nautical Studies; Science); Management; Technology Education (Industrial Education; Home Economics; General Programme); Community Development; Development Education (Mathematics; Language; English); Educational Management; Elementary Education; Guidance and Counselling; *PhD*: Management; Technology Management; Community Development; Industrial Education; Development Education Management; Educational Management

Last Updated: 06/01/11

PAMPANGA AGRICULTURAL COLLEGE (PAC)

Magalang, Pampanga 2011
Tel: +63(45) 866-0800
Fax: +63(45) 866-0800
EMail: pac@comclark.com
Website: http://www.instanet.com.ph/pac/

President: Honorio M. Soriano, Jr.

Programmes

Graduate (Agricultural Business; Agricultural Management; Agriculture; Biology; Business Administration; Crop Production; Education; Educational Administration; English; Foreign Languages Education; Horticulture; Management; Mathematics Education; Physical Education; Science Education; Zoology); **Undergraduate and Professional** (Agricultural Business; Agricultural Economics; Agricultural Engineering; Agriculture; Agronomy; Biology; Communication Studies; Crop Production; Development Studies; English; Forestry; Health Education; Home Economics; Home Economics Education; Horticulture; Information Technology; Mathematics; Music Education; Physical Education; Primary Education; Science Education; Secondary Education; Technology Education; Veterinary Science; Zoology)

History: Founded 1918. Formerly known as La Granja Modelo. Acquired present status 1974.

Degrees and Diplomas: *Certificate/Diploma*; *Associate Degree*; *Bachelor's Degree*; *Post Baccalaureate Certificate/Diploma*:

Veterinary Medicine; *Master's Degree*: Agriculture (Crop Science; Horticulture; Animal Science); Education (Mathematics; Educational Management; General Science; English; Physical Education; Biology); Business Management; Professional Studies (Science Education; Business Management; Educational Management); *PhD*: Education (Educational Management); Agricultural Business Management; Agricultural Sciences (Animal Science; Crop Science); Management
Last Updated: 20/01/11

PANGASINAN STATE UNIVERSITY

Alvear Street, Lingayen, Pangasinan 2401
Tel: +63(75) 542-6464/67
Fax: +63(75) 542-4261
EMail: webmaster@psu.edu.ph
Website: http://www.psu.edu.ph

President: Victoriano C. Estira Tel: +63(75) 542-4057

Vice-President, Administration and Planning: Lydia C. Buduhan

Campuses

Asingan (Automotive Engineering; Communication Studies; Computer Engineering; Curriculum; Dietetics; Education; Electrical Engineering; Electronic Engineering; English; Food Technology; Foreign Languages Education; Health Education; Home Economics Education; Information Technology; Mathematics Education; Mechanical Engineering; Nutrition; Physics; Primary Education; Science Education; Secondary Education; Technology Education; Textile Technology); **Bayambang** (Art Education; Biological and Life Sciences; Business Administration; Chemistry; Child Care and Development; Communication Studies; Curriculum; Education; English; Filipino; Foreign Languages Education; Home Economics Education; Information Technology; Management; Mathematics Education; Music Education; Native Language Education; Nursing; Physical Education; Physics; Preschool Education; Primary Education; Public Administration; Science Education; Secondary Education; Social Studies; Technology Education; Telecommunications Engineering); **Binmaley** (Criminology; Education; Environmental Studies; Fishery; Hotel and Restaurant; Hotel Management; Marine Biology; Marine Transport; Tourism; Transport Management); **Infanta** (Agricultural Education; Agricultural Engineering; Agricultural Equipment; Agriculture; Crop Production; Farm Management; Forestry; Zoology); **Lingayen** (Automotive Engineering; Business Administration; Ceramics and Glass Technology; Civil Engineering; Communication Studies; Computer Engineering; Computer Science; Cosmetology; Dietetics; Economics; Education; Electrical Engineering; Electronic Engineering; English; Food Technology; Foreign Languages Education; Hotel and Restaurant; Hotel Management; Industrial Engineering; Information Technology; Mathematics; Nutrition; Physics; Public Administration; Science Education; Social Studies; Social Work; Statistics; Technology Education; Textile Technology; Tourism); **Open University** (Agriculture; Aquaculture; Development Studies; Education; Educational Administration; Management; Public Administration); **San Carlos City** (Agricultural Education; Agricultural Engineering; Agriculture; Communication Studies; Crop Production; Education; Information Technology; Primary Education; Secondary Education; Technology Education; Zoology); **Sta. Maria** (Agricultural Business; Agricultural Education; Agricultural Engineering; Agricultural Equipment; Agricultural Management; Agriculture; Crop Production; Secondary Education; Zoology); **Urdaneta City** (Agriculture; Architecture; Civil Engineering; Communication Arts; Communication Studies; Computer Education; Computer Engineering; Crop Production; Curriculum; Education; Educational Administration; Educational and Student Counselling; Electrical Engineering; English; Filipino; Foreign Languages Education; Home Economics Education; Information Technology; Management; Management Systems; Mathematics; Mathematics Education; Mechanical Engineering; Native Language Education; Science Education; Social Studies; Special Education; Statistics; Technology Education; Zoology)

Schools

Graduate (Agriculture; Aquaculture; Communication Arts; Computer Education; Crop Production; Development Studies; Education; Educational Administration; Educational and Student Counselling; English; Filipino; Foreign Languages Education; Home Economics Education; Management Systems; Mathematics Education; Native Language Education; Public Administration; Science Education; Social Sciences; Special Education; Technology Education; Zoology)

History: Founded 1922 as Normal School, became College 1969 and University 1978, incorporating 7 previously existing Institutions. A State Institution receiving financial support from the Government.

Governing Bodies: Board of Regents

Academic Year: June to April (June-October; October-April)

Admission Requirements: Graduation from high school and entrance examination

Main Language(s) of Instruction: Filipino, English

Accrediting Agencies: Accrediting Agency of Chartered Colleges and Universities in the Philippines (AACCUP)

Degrees and Diplomas: *Bachelor's Degree*; *Master's Degree*: Development Management (Educational Management); Public Management; Management Engineering); Agriculture (Animal Science; Crop Science); Education (Educational Management; Instructional Leadership; Communication Arts English/Filipino; Computer Education; Guidance and Counselling; Mathematics; Science; Social Studies; Special Education; Technology; Home Economics); *PhD*: Education (Educational Management; Guidance and Counselling; Instruction and Curriculum; Mathematics)

Student Residential Facilities: Yes

Libraries: c. 30,000 vols

Publications: Academic Review *(biannually)*; Journal of Education Research *(biannually)*

Last Updated: 21/01/11

PARTIDO STATE UNIVERSITY (PARSU)

San Juan Bautista Street, Goa, Camarines Sur 4422
Tel: +63(54) 453-0235
Fax: +63(54) 453-1083
EMail: psu_goa@asia.com

President: Nita V. Morallo

Campuses

Caramoan (Automotive Engineering; Electrical Engineering; Food Technology; Heating and Refrigeration; Hotel and Restaurant; Hotel Management; Information Technology; Technology Education; Tourism); **Goa - San Jose** *(Formerly San Jose Polytechnic Institute)* (Automotive Engineering; Civil Engineering; Criminology; Curriculum; Education; Food Technology; Heating and Refrigeration; Hotel and Restaurant; Hotel Management; Information Technology; Management Systems; Secretarial Studies; Technology; Tourism); **Lagonoy - Caramon** *(Formerly Lagonoy Fishery School)* (Dietetics; Nutrition); **Main** (Accountancy; Automotive Engineering; Banking; Biological and Life Sciences; Biology; Business Administration; Business Computing; Chemistry; Civil Engineering; Communication Studies; Computer Education; Computer Science; Curriculum; Education; Electrical Engineering; English; Environmental Engineering; Filipino; Finance; Foreign Languages Education; Geology; Health Education; Heating and Refrigeration; Information Technology; Management; Mathematics; Mathematics Education; Native Language Education; Physics; Political Sciences; Preschool Education; Primary Education; Sanitary Engineering; Science Education; Secondary Education; Secretarial Studies; Special Education; Textile Technology); **Sagñay** (Agriculture; Aquaculture; Automotive Engineering; Education; Fishery; Harvest Technology; Secondary Education); **Salogon** (Agricultural Management); **Tinambac** (Automotive Engineering; Business Computing; Computer Education; Environmental Studies; Food Technology; Hotel and Restaurant; Hotel Management; Management Systems; Secretarial Studies; Technology)

Programmes

Graduate Studies *(Main Campus)* (Education; Educational Administration; English; Foreign Languages Education; Mathematics Education; Science Education)

History: Founded 1941, acquired present status and title 2001.

Governing Bodies: Board of Regents

Admission Requirements: Graduation from high school and entrance examination

Fees: (Pesos): 47-100 per unit

Main Language(s) of Instruction: Filipino, English

Accrediting Agencies: Accrediting Agency of Chartered Colleges and Universities in the Philippines (AACCUP)

Degrees and Diplomas: *Certificate/Diploma*; *Associate Degree*; *Bachelor's Degree*; *Master's Degree*: Education (English; Mathematics; Science); Public Affairs (Local Governance and Development); Arts in Education (Instructional Management); *PhD*: English Language Education; Mathematics Education

Student Services: Academic counselling, Canteen, Cultural centre, Health services, Language programs, Sports facilities

Student Residential Facilities: For 90 students plus six new housing units for staff and faculty

Special Facilities: Information Technology Centre, Speech Laboratory, Audio Visual Room, Sanitary Engineering Laboratory, Biology Laboratory, Tissue Culture Laboratory, Microbiology Laboratory

Libraries: 13,947 vols

Publications: PSU R&D Journal, Research Journal *(annually)*

Last Updated: 21/01/11

PASSI CITY COLLEGE

Passi City, Iloilo 5037
Tel: +63(33) 311-6087
Fax: +63(33) 311-5087

Programmes

Business Administration (Accountancy; Business Administration; Business and Commerce; Finance; Management); **Criminal Justice** (Criminal Law; Criminology); **Education** (Education; English; Foreign Languages Education; Mathematics Education; Primary Education; Secondary Education); **Hotel and Restaurant Management** (Hotel and Restaurant); **Information Technology** (Information Technology)

Degrees and Diplomas: *Bachelor's Degree*

Last Updated: 21/01/11

PATEROS TECHNOLOGICAL COLLEGE

College Street, Sto. Rosario Kanluran, Pateros, Fourth District, Metro Manila
Tel: +63(2) 640-5375

Administrator: Rosalinda S. Zambrano

Programmes

Computer Science (Business Computing; Computer Engineering; Computer Science; Secretarial Studies)

Degrees and Diplomas: *Bachelor's Degree*

Last Updated: 21/01/11

PHILIPPINE MERCHANT MARINE ACADEMY

New PMMA Complex Site, San Narciso, Zambales 2205
Tel: +63(47) 913-4396
EMail: secretariat@pmmaai.org

President: Fidel Diñoso

Programmes

Marine and Maritime Studies (Marine Engineering; Marine Transport)

Further Information: Also annex in Pulilan.

History: Founded 1998.

Degrees and Diplomas: *Bachelor's Degree*; *Master's Degree*: Maritime Education and Training; Ship Management; Shipping Business Management

Last Updated: 24/01/11

PHILIPPINE NORMAL UNIVERSITY

Pamantasang Normal ng Pilipinas (PNU)

Taft Avenue, Corner Ayala Boulevard, Manila, Metro Manila 1000
Tel: +63(2) 302-6763
Fax: +63(2) 527-0375
Website: http://www.pnu.edu.ph

President: Ester B. Ogena (2011-2014) Tel: +63(2) 527-0375

Vice-President for Academics: Adelaida C. Gines

Vice-President for Administration,Finance and Development: Rebecca C. Nueva España

International Relations: René Romero
Tel: +63(2) 527-0367, Fax: +63(2) 527-0367
EMail: rcromero@email.com

Campuses

Agusan (Educational Administration; English; Filipino; Foreign Languages Education; Home Economics Education; Humanities and Social Science Education; Mathematics; Mathematics Education; Native Language Education; Physical Education; Primary Education; Science Education; Secondary Education; Teacher Training); **Cadiz** (Art Education; Curriculum; Education; Educational Administration; English; Filipino; Foreign Languages Education; Home Economics Education; Literature; Mathematics Education; Music Education; Native Language Education; Physical Education; Primary Education; Science Education; Social Sciences; Teacher Training); **Lopez** (Education; English; Mathematics Education; Physical Education; Primary Education; Secondary Education)

Programmes

Education *(Undergraduate programme)* (Art Education; Bilingual and Bicultural Education; Biology; Chemistry; Education; English; Ethics; Filipino; Foreign Languages Education; History; Home Economics Education; Information Sciences; Journalism; Library Science; Linguistics; Literature; Mathematics Education; Music Education; Native Language Education; Physical Education; Physics; Preschool Education; Primary Education; Science Education; Secondary Education; Social Sciences; Speech Studies; Technology Education; Theatre; Writing); **Graduate** (Bilingual and Bicultural Education; Biology; Chemistry; Child Care and Development; Curriculum; Educational Administration; Educational and Student Counselling; Educational Psychology; Educational Technology; Educational Testing and Evaluation; English; Ethics; Filipino; Foreign Languages Education; Health Education; History; Home Economics Education; Information Sciences; Library Science; Linguistics; Literature; Mathematics Education; Music Education; Physical Education; Primary Education; Science Education; Secondary Education; Social Sciences; Special Education; Teacher Training; Theatre); **Library and Information Sciences** *(Undergraduate programme)* (Information Sciences; Library Science); **Psychology** *(Undergraduate programme)* (Educational and Student Counselling; Educational Psychology; Psychology); **Science** *(Undergraduate programme)* (Biology; Chemistry; Dietetics; Home Economics; Information Technology; Mathematics; Nutrition; Physics; Technology); **Undergraduate Certificate and Specialization** (Art Education; Chemistry; Educational and Student Counselling; English; Ethics; Filipino; Foreign Languages Education; Health Education; Home Economics Education; Information Sciences; Library Science; Literacy Education; Mathematics Education; Music Education; Native Language Education; Physical Education; Physics; Preschool Education; Primary Education; Science Education; Special Education; Speech Studies; Teacher Training; Theatre; Women's Studies; Writing)

History: Founded as Normal School 1901, became College 1949 and University 1991.

Governing Bodies: Board of Regents

Academic Year: June to March (June-November; November-March)

Admission Requirements: Graduation from high school and entrance examination

Fees: (Pesos): 450 per unit

Main Language(s) of Instruction: Filipino, English

Degrees and Diplomas: *Certificate/Diploma*; *Bachelor's Degree*; *Master's Degree*: Education; Non Formal Education; Science Education; Teaching; *PhD*: Education (Educational Administration; Educational Management; Bilingual Education; Curriculum and Instriction; Filipino; Guidance and Counselling; Mathematics; Reading Education; Science Education); Lingusitics (Applied Linguistics; Filipino Linguistics and Literature) Literature

Student Services: Academic counselling, Language programs, Sports facilities

Student Residential Facilities: Yes

Special Facilities: Museum of Health Sciences

Libraries: c. 138,870 vols

Publications: Siyasik Research Journal
Press or Publishing House: PNU Press
Last Updated: 20/01/11

PHILIPPINE STATE COLLEGE OF AERONAUTICS (PHILSCA)

Manlunas Street, Villamor Air Base, Pasay City, Fourth District, Metro Manila 1309
Tel: +63(2) 513-0847
Fax: +63(2) 853-5127

Officer-In-Charge: Carmelita P. Yadao-Sison

Campuses

Fernando Air Base (Air Transport; Computer Science; Electronic Engineering; English; Maintenance Technology); **Mactan Air Base** (Aeronautical and Aerospace Engineering; Computer Science; Electronic Engineering; Food Technology; Heating and Refrigeration; Maintenance Technology; Metal Techniques; Textile Technology; Wood Technology); **Pampanga Extension** (Aeronautical and Aerospace Engineering; Computer Science; Electronic Engineering; English; Information Management; Maintenance Technology; Mathematics; Transport Management)

Programmes

Graduate (Aeronautical and Aerospace Engineering; Air Transport; Mathematics; Public Administration; Transport Management); **Undergraduate and Professional** (Aeronautical and Aerospace Engineering; Air Transport; Computer Engineering; Computer Science; Education; Electronic Engineering; English; Maintenance Technology; Mathematics; Public Administration; Transport Management)

History: Founded 1969.

Degrees and Diplomas: *Associate Degree*; *Bachelor's Degree*; *Master's Degree*: Public Administration (Government and Airport Administration); Mathematics Education; Aeronautical Management; *PhD*: Aeronautical Education

Last Updated: 24/01/11

POLYTECHNIC UNIVERSITY OF THE PHILIPPINES (PUP)

2/F South Wing, Academic Building, Anonas Street, Sta. Mesa, Manila, First District, Metro Manila 01008
Tel: +63(2) 716-2644
Fax: +63(2) 716-1143
EMail: inquire@pup.edu.ph
Website: http://www.pup.edu.ph

President: Dante G. Guevarra

Vice-President for Administration: Augustus F. Cezar

International Relations: Juan C. Birion, Vice-President for Student Services and External Affairs

Campuses

Commonwealth (Business Administration; Business Education; Human Resources; Information Technology; Management; Marketing); **Lepanto**; **Lopez** (Accountancy; Administration; Agricultural Business; Agricultural Management; Business Administration; Business Education; Civil Engineering; Electrical Engineering; Hotel and Restaurant; Hotel Management); **Main (Rizal)** (Education; English; Mathematics); **Main (San Pedro)** (Education; English; Foreign Languages Education; Information Technology; Management; Mathematics Education); **Maragondon** (Accountancy; Business Administration; Education; Electrical Engineering; Electronic Engineering; Mechanical Engineering; Telecommunications Engineering); **Mariveles** (Accountancy; Business Administration; Business Education; Education; Electronic Engineering; Human Resources; Industrial Engineering; Information Technology; Management; Nursing; Primary Education; Secondary Education; Teacher Training; Telecommunications Engineering); **Mulanay** (Administration; Agricultural Business; Agricultural Management; Business Education; Management; Primary Education); **Open University** (Computer Science; Construction Engineering; Educational Administration; Information Sciences; Library Science; Management; Mass Communication; Public Administration; Radio and Television Broadcasting); **Pulilan** (Business Administration; Computer Science; Educational Administration; Management; Secondary Education); **Ragay** (Accountancy; Administration; Business Administration; Computer Science; English; Foreign Languages Education; Government; Information Technology; Marketing; Mathematics Education; Primary Education; Public Administration; Secondary Education); **San Juan** (Accountancy; Computer Science; Hotel and Restaurant; Hotel Management; Information Technology; Management; Secondary Education); **Sta. Maria, Bulacan** (Accountancy; Civil Engineering; Education; English; Foreign Languages Education; Hotel and Restaurant; Hotel Management; Information Technology; Management; Mathematics Education); **Sta. Rosa** (Accountancy; Clinical Psychology; Computer Science; Education; Electronic Engineering; English; Foreign Languages Education; Health Education; Industrial Engineering; Information Technology; Management; Marketing; Mathematics Education; Nursing; Secondary Education; Telecommunications Engineering); **Sto. Tomas** (Accountancy; Business Education; Computer Science; Electrical Engineering; Electronic Engineering; Government; Hotel and Restaurant; Hotel Management; Industrial and Organizational Psychology; Industrial Engineering; Information Technology; Management; Public Administration; Secondary Education; Telecommunications Engineering); **Taguig** (Accountancy; Administration; Applied Mathematics; Business Administration; Electronic Engineering; English; Foreign Languages Education; Human Resources; Information Technology; Management; Marketing; Mathematics; Mathematics Education; Mechanical Engineering; Secondary Education; Telecommunications Engineering); **Unisan** (Agricultural Business; Agricultural Management; Business Education; Management; Primary Education)

Colleges

Accountancy (Accountancy); **Architecture and Fine Arts** (Architecture; Fine Arts; Interior Design); **Arts** (Arts and Humanities; History; Information Sciences; Library Science; Philosophy; Psychology; Sociology); **Business** (Advertising and Publicity; Business Administration; Business and Commerce; Hotel and Restaurant; Management; Marketing; Public Relations; Tourism); **Communication** (Journalism; Mass Communication; Radio and Television Broadcasting); **Computer Management and Information Technology** (Business Computing; Computer Science; Information Technology); **Cooperatives** (Accountancy; Banking; Finance; Management; Small Business; Social and Community Services); **Economics, Finance and Politics** (Banking; Economic and Finance Policy; Economics; Finance; Government; Political Sciences; Public Administration); **Engineering** (Civil Engineering; Computer Engineering; Electrical Engineering; Electronic Engineering; Engineering; Geological Engineering; Industrial Engineering; Mechanical Engineering; Railway Engineering; Telecommunications Engineering); **Languages and Linguistics** (English; Filipino; Linguistics; Modern Languages); **Law** (Law); **Nutrition and Food Science** (Dietetics; Food Science; Nutrition); **Office Administration and Business Teacher Education** (Administration; Business Education); **Physical Education and Sports** (Physical Education; Sports); **Science** (Chemistry; Dietetics; Food Technology; Mathematics; Natural Sciences; Nutrition; Physics; Statistics); **Tourism and Hotel and Restaurant Management** (Hotel and Restaurant; Hotel Management; Tourism)

Schools

Graduate Sudies (Business Administration; Communication Studies; Economics; Educational Administration; Engineering; Filipino; Foreign Languages Education; Geological Engineering; Industrial Engineering; Information Sciences; Information Technology; Library Science; Management; Mass Communication; Mathematics Education; Native Language Education; Philosophy; Physical Education; Psychology; Public Administration; Science Education; Seismology; Sports; Statistics)

History: Founded 1904 as the Manila Business School under the Manila City School system organized by the American Colonial Government in the Philippines. Acquired present title 1978.

Governing Bodies: Board of Regents

Admission Requirements: Graduation from high school and entrance examination

Main Language(s) of Instruction: English

Degrees and Diplomas: *Certificate/Diploma*; *Associate Degree*; *Bachelor's Degree*; *Master's Degree*: Applied Statistics; Business Administration; Business Education; Communication; Construction Management; Educational Management; Industrial Engineering Management; Library and Information Sciences; Mass

Communication; Physical Education and Sports; Public Administration; Science and Mathematics Education; Arts in: Economics; Filipino; Language Teaching; Philosophy; Psychology; Science in: Earthquake Engineering; Information Technology; *PhD*: Business Administration; Educational Management; Public Administration

Libraries: Central Library, c. 120,000 vols

Publications: Annual Report *(annually)*; Graduate Forum; Monograph; Panday; PUP Studies; Statistical Bulletin

Press or Publishing House: PUP Printing Press

Last Updated: 25/01/11

QUIRINO POLYTECHNIC COLLEGE

Capitol Hills, Cabarroguis, Quirino 3400
Tel: +63(917) 340-3859
Fax: +63(78) 692-5044
EMail: qpc@indigo.net.ph

Administrator: Edilberto S. Acio

Programmes

Arts and Humanities (Arts and Humanities; English); **Civil Engineering** (Civil Engineering); **Commerce** (Business and Commerce; Management); **Computer Science** (Computer Science); **Criminology** (Criminology); **Elementary Education** (Education; Mathematics Education; Primary Education); **Hotel and Restaurant Management** (Hotel and Restaurant; Hotel Management)

History: Founded 1983, acquiring current status in 1988.

Degrees and Diplomas: *Certificate/Diploma*; *Bachelor's Degree*

Last Updated: 26/01/11

QUIRINO STATE COLLEGE

Andres Bonifacio, Diffun, Quirino 3401
Tel: +63(78) 694-7056
Fax: +63(78) 694-7056
EMail: qsc_edu_ph@yahoo.com

President: Raynaldo P. Villamayor

Programmes

Agriculture (Agricultural Engineering; Agricultural Equipment; Agriculture; Animal Husbandry; Crop Production; Forestry; Zoology); **Criminology** (Criminology); **Education** (Education; Educational Administration; English; Filipino; Foreign Languages Education; Health Education; Home Economics; Home Economics Education; Mathematics Education; Native Language Education; Primary Education; Science Education; Secondary Education; Technology Education); **Graduate** (Crop Production; Educational Administration; Management; Public Administration); **Home Technology** (Cooking and Catering; Food Technology; Home Economics; Home Economics Education; Household Management; Nutrition; Technology; Technology Education); **Hotel and Restaurant Management** (Hotel and Restaurant; Hotel Management; Tourism); **Information Technology** (Information Technology); **Nutrition and Dietetics** (Dietetics; Nutrition)

History: Formerly known as Quirino National Agriculture School.

Degrees and Diplomas: *Certificate/Diploma*; *Associate Degree*; *Bachelor's Degree (BA; BSc)*; *Master's Degree*: Education (Educational Management; Supervision and Administration); Public Management; Crop Science (MA; MSc)

Last Updated: 26/01/11

RAMON MAGSAYSAY TECHNOLOGICAL UNIVERSITY - RAMON MAGSAYSAY POLYTECHNIC COLLEGE (RMTU)

Palanginan, Iba, Zambales 2201
Tel: +63(47) 811-1683
Fax: +63(47) 811-1683
EMail: fe_2218@yahoo.com

President: Feliciano S. Rosete EMail: rmtupresident@yahoo.com

Vice-President for Administration and Finance: Jose Docuyanan

International Relations: Felipa M. Rico, Director, Public Information, International Exchange and Cooperation

Campuses

Botolan *(Agro-Forestry Research and Wildlife Breeding Center)* (Agricultural Business; Agricultural Education; Agricultural Engineering; Agricultural Equipment; Agriculture; Forestry; Geological Engineering; Industrial Engineering; Rural Planning; Rural Studies; Secondary Education); **Candelaria** *(Research Center for Fisheries Technology and Marine Biology)* (Computer Science; Fishery; Hotel and Restaurant; Hotel Management; Marine Biology; Nursing); **Castillejos** (Accountancy; Business Administration; Computer Science; Education; Primary Education; Public Administration; Secondary Education; Social Sciences); **Masinloc** *(Center for Business and Entrepreneurial Education)* (Accountancy; Banking; Business Administration; Computer Science; Economics; Education; Finance; Hotel and Restaurant; Hotel Management; Political Sciences); **San Marcelino** *(Center of Agricultural Research; formerly Western Luzon Agricultural College (WLAC))* (Agricultural Engineering; Animal Husbandry; Applied Mathematics; Education; Food Technology; Home Economics; Hotel and Restaurant; Hotel Management; Primary Education; Secondary Education; Social Sciences; Sociology; Veterinary Science; Zoology); **Sta. Cruz** (Computer Science; Education; Primary Education; Secondary Education)

Colleges

Accountancy and Business Administration (Accountancy; Business Administration); **Arts and Sciences** (Biology; Economics; English; Management; Psychology); **Communication and Information Technology** (Computer Engineering; Computer Science; Information Technology); **Education** (Education; Industrial Arts Education; Primary Education; Secondary Education); **Engineering and Architecture** (Architecture; Civil Engineering; Electrical Engineering; Engineering; Mechanical Engineering; Naval Architecture); **Industrial Technology** (Industrial Engineering; Marine Transport); **Law** (Law); **Mondriaan Aura** (Business Administration; Computer Science; Education; Health Education; Nursing; Public Administration); **Nursing** (Nursing); **Physical Education** (Physical Education); **Public Administration** (Public Administration); **Tourism, Home, Hotel and Restaurant Management** (Food Technology; Home Economics; Hotel and Restaurant; Hotel Management; Technology; Tourism)

Schools

Graduate (Business Administration; Education; Public Administration; Teacher Training)

History: Founded 1912. Acquired present status 1998.

Governing Bodies: Board of Regents

Admission Requirements: Form 138; Medical Certificate; Entrance Examination

Fees: (Pesos): 4,000-6,500 per semester

Main Language(s) of Instruction: English

International Co-operation: With universities in South Korea

Accrediting Agencies: Accrediting Agency of Chartered Colleges and Universities in the Philippines (AACCUP); State University and Colleges Levelling

Degrees and Diplomas: *Certificate/Diploma*; *Associate Degree*; *Bachelor's Degree*; *Master's Degree*: Agriculture; Business Administration; Education; Forestry; Public Administration; *PhD*: Agriculture; Education

Student Services: Academic counselling, Canteen, Cultural centre, Employment services, Health services, Social counselling, Sports facilities

Student Residential Facilities: Yes

Special Facilities: Research and Extension Training; Audio-visual Room; Museum

Libraries: yes

Press or Publishing House: Ramon Magsaysay Technological University-Iba Campus

Last Updated: 26/01/11

REGIONAL MADRASAH GRADUATE ACADEMY

SPDA Dorm Bldg., Buluan, Maguindanao

President: Benjamin P. Dumato

Programmes

Agriculture (Agriculture); **Computer Science** (Computer Science); **Computer Technology** (Computer Engineering); **Education**

(Islamic Studies; Primary Education; Secondary Education); **Islamic Studies** (Islamic Studies)

Degrees and Diplomas: *Bachelor's Degree*
Last Updated: 26/01/11

RIZAL TECHNOLOGICAL UNIVERSITY

Boni Avenue, City of Mandaluyong, Third District, Metro Manila 1550
Tel: +63(2) 534-8267
Fax: +63(2) 534-9710
EMail: op@rtu.edu.ph
Website: http://www.rtu.edu.ph/

President: Jesus Rodrigo F. Torres (2010-)

Colleges

Arts and Sciences (Biology; Biotechnology; Political Sciences; Psychology; Statistics); **Business and Entrepreneurial Technology** (Accountancy; Business Administration; Business Computing; Management; Marketing; Secretarial Studies); **Education** (Computer Education; Education; English; Foreign Languages Education; Humanities and Social Science Education; Mathematics Education; Native Language Education; Physics; Science Education; Secondary Education; Social Studies); **Engineering and Industrial Technology** (Architecture; Automation and Control Engineering; Civil Engineering; Computer Engineering; Electrical Engineering; Electronic Engineering; Engineering; Industrial Engineering; Information Technology; Instrument Making; Mechanical Engineering; Structural Architecture; Technology; Telecommunications Engineering); **Nursing** (Nursing)

Institutes

Physical Education (Parks and Recreation; Physical Education; Sports)

Schools

Graduate (Astronomy and Space Science; Automation and Control Engineering; Business Administration; Computer Engineering; Educational Administration; Educational Technology; Engineering; English; Foreign Languages Education; Industrial Engineering; Information Technology; Instrument Making; Literature; Mathematics Education; Public Administration; Science Education; Technology Education)

History: Founded 1969 as College of Rizal. Renamed Rizal Technological Colleges (RTC) 1975. Acquired present university status and title 1997.

Degrees and Diplomas: *Certificate/Diploma*; *Bachelor's Degree*; *Master's Degree*: Astronomy; Educational Management; English Major in Language Instruction; English Major in Literature; Industrial Psychology; Instructional Technology; Mathematics Education; Public Administration; Teaching Major in Educational Management; Engineering Major in Instrumentation and Control Engineering; Business Administration; Engineering Education; Engineering Education (Major in Computer Engineering and Industrial Engineering); *PhD*: Business Administration; Public Administration; Technology Education
Last Updated: 27/01/11

ROMBLON STATE UNIVERSITY (RSU)

Bgy. Liwanag, Odiongan, Romblon 5505
Tel: +63(42) 567-5270 +63(42) 567-5273
Fax: +63(42) 567-5341
Website: http://www.rsu.edu.ph/

President: Jeter S. Sespeñe

Campuses

Romblon College of Fisheries and Forestry-Calatrava *(Formerly Romblon College of Fisheries and Forestry, Calatrava)* (Education; English; Fishery; Foreign Languages Education; Home Economics Education; Information Technology; Primary Education; Science Education; Secondary Education; Technology Education); **Romblon College of Fisheries and Forestry-Ferriol** (Fishery; Forestry); **Romblon College of Fisheries and Forestry-San Agustin** (Education; Educational Administration; Fishery; Hotel and Restaurant; Hotel Management; Information Technology; Mathematics Education; Primary Education; Secondary Education; Software Engineering); **Romblon College of Fisheries and Forestry-San Andres** (Education; Fishery; Primary Education; Science Education); **Romblon College of Fisheries and Forestry-Sibuyan, Cajidiocan** (Agricultural Engineering; Education; Information Technology; Primary Education; Secondary Education); **Romblon College of Fisheries and Forestry-Sta. Fe** (Education; English; Filipino; Foreign Languages Education; Mathematics Education; Native Language Education; Primary Education; Secondary Education); **Romblon College of Fisheries and Forestry-Sta. Maria** (Education; Fishery; Primary Education); **Romblon College of Fisheries and Forestry-Tanagan**; **Sawang** (Education; Primary Education; Secondary Education); **Sibuyan Polytechnic College-San Fernando** *(Formerly Romblon State College - San Fernando Campus)* (Automotive Engineering; Civil Engineering; Cosmetology; Curriculum; Education; Educational Administration; Electrical Engineering; English; Filipino; Food Technology; Foreign Languages Education; Health Education; Home Economics Education; Hotel and Restaurant; Hotel Management; Industrial Arts Education; Industrial Engineering; Mathematics Education; Native Language Education; Primary Education; Science Education; Structural Architecture; Technology Education; Textile Technology)

Programmes

Graduate (Agriculture; Business Administration; Education; Educational Administration; English; Foreign Languages Education; Public Administration; Science Education; Teacher Training); **Undergraduate and Professional** (Accountancy; Agricultural Engineering; Banking; Biology; Business Administration; Civil Engineering; Education; Electrical Engineering; English; Filipino; Finance; Foreign Languages Education; Health Education; Home Economics Education; Hotel and Restaurant; Hotel Management; Information Technology; Management; Mathematics; Mathematics Education; Mechanical Engineering; Native Language Education; Physical Education; Political Sciences; Primary Education; Science Education; Secondary Education; Technology Education)

History: Founded 1948. Formerly Romblon State College. Acquired present title and status 2009.

Degrees and Diplomas: *Bachelor's Degree*; *Master's Degree*: Business Administration; Public Administration; Agriculture; Education (Science; Educational Administration; Educational Management; English)
Last Updated: 27/01/11

SAMAR STATE COLLEGE OF AGRICULTURE AND FORESTRY

Maharlika Highway, San Jorge, Western Samar 6707

President: Aida L. Tobes

Programmes

Undergraduate and Professional (Agricultural Business; Agricultural Education; Agricultural Engineering; Agriculture; Animal Husbandry; Crop Production; Environmental Studies; Food Science; Food Technology; Forestry; Information Technology; Nutrition; Rural Planning; Secondary Education; Zoology)

History: Founded 1954.

Degrees and Diplomas: *Certificate/Diploma*; *Associate Degree*; *Bachelor's Degree*
Last Updated: 17/02/11

SAMAR STATE UNIVERSITY (SSU)

Arteche Boulevard, Guindapunan, Catbalogan, Western Samar 6700
Tel: +63(55) 251-2139, +63(55) 251-2016
Fax: +63(55) 543-8394
Website: http://www.ssu.edu.ph/

President: Simon P. Babalcon Jr (2003-)
EMail: op_simon@ssu.edu.ph

Vice-President, Administrative Affairs: Jose S. Labro
Tel: +63(55) 251-6806 EMail: jose@ssu.edu.ph

International Relations: Felissa E. Gomba, Vice-President, Research and Development EMail: felissa@ssu.edu.ph

Campuses

Basey (Education; Electronic Engineering; Food Technology; Primary Education; Technology; Textile Technology); **Mercedes** (Agricultural Education; Aquaculture; Education; Fishery; Marine

Engineering); **Paranas** (Automotive Engineering; Chemistry; Education; Electrical Engineering; Engineering; Food Technology; Home Economics Education; Mathematics Education; Physical Education; Physics; Primary Education; Secondary Education; Technology; Technology Education; Textile Technology)

Programmes

Applied Statistics (Statistics); **Engineering** (Civil Engineering; Computer Engineering; Electrical Engineering; Electronic Engineering; Engineering; Telecommunications Engineering); **Graduate** (Automotive Engineering; Chemistry; Civil Engineering; Construction Engineering; Education; Educational Administration; Educational and Student Counselling; Electrical Engineering; Electronic Engineering; Engineering; Filipino; Fishery; Home Economics; Mathematics Education; Modern Languages; Native Language Education; Physical Education; Physics; Primary Education; Public Administration; Science Education; Technology; Water Management; Water Science); **Industrial Technology** (Automotive Engineering; Electrical Engineering; Electronic Engineering; Food Technology; Heating and Refrigeration; Metal Techniques; Structural Architecture; Technology); **Information Studies** (Information Management; Information Technology); **Nursing** (Nursing); **Primary Education** (Art Education; Education; English; Foreign Languages Education; Health Education; Mathematics Education; Music Education; Physical Education; Primary Education; Science Education; Social Studies); **Psychology** (Psychology); **Secondary Education** (Chemistry; Health Education; Home Economics Education; Mathematics Education; Physical Education; Physics; Secondary Education; Technology Education); **Technician Education** (Automotive Engineering; Civil Engineering; Cosmetology; Electrical Engineering; Electronic Engineering; Food Technology; Home Economics Education; Industrial Arts Education; Mechanical Engineering; Technology; Technology Education; Textile Technology); **Technology** (Automotive Engineering; Civil Engineering; Computer Science; Cosmetology; Electrical Engineering; Electronic Engineering; Food Technology; Information Technology; Technology; Textile Technology)

History: Founded 2005.

Governing Bodies: Board of Regents

Academic Year: June to March

Admission Requirements: High School Diploma; Entrance exam

Fees: (Pesos): 100 per unit

Main Language(s) of Instruction: English

International Co-operation: With universities in Korea and Japan

Accrediting Agencies: Accrediting Agency of Chartered Colleges and Universities in the Philippines (AACCUP)

Degrees and Diplomas: *Bachelor's Degree*; *Master's Degree*: Education and Teaching (Educational Management; Primary Education; Chemistry; Language; Fishery Education; Mathematics; Vocational Technology; Physics); Engineering (Construction Engineering and Management; Water Resource Engineering and Management); Public Management; Arts in: Filipino; Guidance and Counselling; English; Home Economics; Physical Education; Technician Education (Drafting Technology; Civil Technology; Automotive Technology; Electrical Technology; Electronic Technology); *PhD*: Educational Management; Technology Management

Student Services: Academic counselling, Canteen, Employment services, Handicapped facilities, Health services, Social counselling, Sports facilities

Special Facilities: film studio

Publications: SSU and R&D Updates, Newsletter of SSU research and development activities *(quarterly)*; The Tradesman, News magazine for the tertiary sector *(biennially)*

Last Updated: 17/02/11

SAN PABLO CITY COLLEGE

Dalubhasaan Ng Lungsod Ng San Pablo

Brgy. San Jose, San Pablo City, Laguna 4000
Tel: +63(49) 800-4948
Fax: +63(49) 800-3285

College Administrator (Acting): Edelio B. Panaligan

Programmes

Arts and Science (Economics; Hotel and Restaurant; Hotel Management; Information Technology; Political Sciences; Psychology); **Business Administration** (Banking; Business Administration; Finance; Human Resources; Management; Marketing); **Education** (Biological and Life Sciences; Curriculum; Education; English; Foreign Languages Education; Health Education; Mathematics Education; Preschool Education; Primary Education; Science Education; Secondary Education; Social Studies; Special Education)

History: Founded 1997.

Degrees and Diplomas: *Bachelor's Degree*

Last Updated: 21/09/10

SIQUIJOR STATE COLLEGE

North Poblacion, Larena, Siquijor 6225
Tel: +63(35) 377-2041
Fax: +63(35) 377-2041
EMail: webmaster@siquijorstatecollege.every1.net

President: Baldomero Martinez, Jr.

Programmes

Arts (English); **Business Administration** (Business Administration); **Education** (Education; English; Foreign Languages Education; Mathematics; Physics; Primary Education; Secondary Education; Social Studies); **Graduate** (Educational Administration; Industrial Arts Education; Public Administration); **Science** (Automotive Engineering; Civil Engineering; Communication Studies; Criminology; Development Studies; Electrical Engineering; Electronic Engineering; Food Technology; Hotel and Restaurant; Hotel Management; Industrial Engineering; Information Technology; Marine Engineering; Marine Transport; Mathematics; Mechanical Engineering; Political Sciences; Structural Architecture; Technology; Textile Technology; Tourism)

History: Founded in 1920, acquiring current status and title in 1983.

Degrees and Diplomas: *Associate Degree*; *Bachelor's Degree*; *Master's Degree*: Educational Management; Industrial Education; Public Management

Last Updated: 21/02/11

SORSOGON STATE COLLEGE

Magsaysay, City of Sorsogon, Sorsogon 4700
Tel: +63(56) 211-1869
Fax: +63(56) 211-1845
EMail: Sorsogonstatecollege@yahoo.com
Website: http://www.sorsogonstatecollege.edu.ph/

President: Antonio E. Fuentes

Campuses

Bulan - Institute of Management and Information Technology (Automotive Engineering; Cinema and Television; Computer Science; Educational Administration; Electronic Engineering; Government; Information Management; Information Technology; Management; Public Administration; Technology Education); **Castilla - School of Agriculture and Agriculture-Based Technology** *(Mayon)* (Agricultural Education; Agricultural Engineering; Agricultural Equipment; Agriculture; Veterinary Science); **Magallanes - School of Fisheries and Fisheries-Based Technology** (Aquaculture; Education; Fishery; Harvest Technology; Marine Biology; Marine Engineering; Natural Resources)

Programmes

Graduate (Administration; Crafts and Trades; Education; Educational Administration; English; Filipino; Foreign Languages Education; Home Economics Education; Management; Mathematics; Native Language Education; Public Administration; Technology Education); **Undergraduate and Professional** (Architecture; Art Education; Arts and Humanities; Automotive Engineering; Biological and Life Sciences; Biology; Chemistry; Civil Engineering; Curriculum; Electrical Engineering; Electronic Engineering; Engineering; English; Filipino; Food Technology; Health Education; Home Economics Education; Mathematics Education; Mechanical Engineering; Music Education; Native Language Education; Physical Education; Primary Education; Science Education; Secondary Education; Structural Architecture; Technology; Textile Technology)

History: Founded 1908.

Degrees and Diplomas: *Associate Degree*; *Bachelor's Degree*; *Master's Degree*: Arts in Education (English; Mathematics; Filipino);

Arts in Teaching (Livelihood Technology Education; Technology and Home Economics Education); Management (Administration and Supervision; Public Administration; Educational Management)
Last Updated: 21/02/11

SOUTHERN LEYTE STATE UNIVERSITY (SLSU)

Barangay San Roque, Sogod, Southern Leyte 6606
Tel: +63(53) 382-3294 +63(53) 382-2003
Fax: +63(53) 382-2003
EMail: admin@slsuonline.edu.ph
Website: http://www.slsuonline.edu.ph

President: Gloria M. Reyes

Vice-President: Jude A. Duarte

Campuses

Bontoc (Agricultural Engineering; Aquaculture; Fishery; Information Technology; Marine Biology; Secondary Education) *College Administrator*: Rosario L. Paulo; **Hinunangan** (Agricultural Business; Agricultural Engineering; Biology; English; Foreign Languages Education; Mathematics Education; Physics; Secondary Education) *Campus Administrator*: Valerio B. Cabalo; **San Juan** (Automotive Engineering; Crafts and Trades; Electrical Engineering; Electronic Engineering; English; Filipino; Foreign Languages Education; Home Economics Education; Industrial Engineering; Information Technology; Management Systems; Mathematics Education; Native Language Education; Science Education; Secondary Education; Secretarial Studies; Technology Education) *College Administrator*: Joel T. Guasa; **Tomas Oppus** (Art Education; Biological and Life Sciences; Biology; Chemistry; Communication Arts; Communication Studies; Curriculum; Economics; Education; Educational Administration; Educational and Student Counselling; English; Filipino; Foreign Languages Education; Health Education; History; Human Resources; Management; Marketing; Mathematics; Mathematics Education; Music Education; Native Language Education; Physical Education; Physics; Preschool Education; Primary Education; Public Administration; Science Education; Secondary Education; Social Sciences; Social Studies; Special Education) *Campus Administrator*: Prose Ivy G. Yepes

Programmes

Civil Engineering (Civil Engineering); **Criminal Justice** (Criminal Law; Criminology); **Electrical Engineering** (Electrical Engineering); **Food Technology** (Food Technology); **Graduate** *(Main Campus and Tomas Oppus Campus)* (Education; English; Filipino; Foreign Languages Education; Management; Mathematics Education; Native Language Education; Natural Sciences; Teacher Training; Technology Education); **Hotel, Restaurant and Tourism Management** (Hotel and Restaurant; Hotel Management; Tourism); **Industrial Education** (Curriculum; Home Economics Education; Technology Education); **Industrial Technology** (Automotive Engineering; Electrical Engineering; Electronic Engineering; Food Technology; Heating and Refrigeration; Textile Technology); **Information Technology** (Information Technology); **Mechanical Engineering** (Mechanical Engineering)

History: Founded in 1963 as the Sogod National Trade School, acquiring current status and title in 1981.

Degrees and Diplomas: *Associate Degree*; *Bachelor's Degree*; *Master's Degree*: Public Administration; Arts in Education (Language Teaching; Guidance & Counselling; Mathematics; Science Education; Social Sciences; Filipino; Educational Management); Teaching (Filipino; Mathematics; English; Natural Sciences); Management; Technology Education
Last Updated: 21/02/11

SOUTHERN LUZON STATE UNIVERSITY

Brgy. Kulapi, Lucban, Quezon 4328
Tel: +63(42) 416-4168 +63(42) 540-4816
Fax: +63(42) 416-4168 +63(42) 911-1252
EMail: slsuniv@yahoo.com
Website: http://www.slsu.edu.ph/

President: Cecilia N. Gascon

Campuses

Alabat (Aquaculture; Electrical and Electronic Engineering; English; Fishery; Foreign Languages Education; Secondary Education) *Campus Director*: Jimson F. Oliveros; **Infanta** (Agricultural Engineering; Agriculture; Art Education; Education; Electrical Engineering; Electronic Engineering; Engineering; Home Economics Education; Mathematics Education; Music Education; Physical Education; Secondary Education; Technology Education) *Campus Director*: Eleuterio R. De Vela; **Judge Guillermo Eleazar Polytechnic College -Tagkawayan** *(Formerly J. Guillermo Eleazar Polytechnic College)* (Aquaculture; Business Administration; Computer Engineering; Curriculum; Education; English; Finance; Fishery; Food Technology; Foreign Languages Education; Human Resources; Management; Marketing; Mathematics Education; Physics; Public Administration) *Campus Director*: Cesar I. Nazareno; **Lucena** *(Formerly Lucena Dual Training and Livelihood Center)* (Computer Engineering; Industrial Engineering) *Campus Director*: Carmen M. Barron; **Polilio** *(Formerly SLPC-Polillo Junior Community College)* (Curriculum; Education; Primary Education; Public Administration) *Campus Director*: Virgilio B. Buelva; **Sampaloc** *(Formerly Sampaloc Junior Community College)* (Agricultural Engineering) *Campus Director*: Enrico S. Sajul; **Tiaong** (Agricultural Engineering; Computer Engineering; Curriculum; Education; Engineering; Industrial Engineering; Primary Education) *Campus Director*: Wenceslao Durante

Colleges

Agriculture (Agricultural Engineering; Agriculture; Environmental Management; Environmental Studies; Forestry); **Allied Medicine** (Midwifery; Nursing); **Arts and Sciences** (Biology; Communication Studies; History; Mathematics; Psychology; Public Administration); **Business Administration** (Accountancy; Business Administration; Finance; Human Resources; Management; Marketing); **Engineering** (Civil Engineering; Computer Engineering; Electrical Engineering; Electronic Engineering; Engineering; Industrial Engineering; Mechanical Engineering; Telecommunications Engineering); **Industrial Technology** (Automotive Engineering; Civil Engineering; Computer Engineering; Electrical and Electronic Engineering; Food Technology; Hotel and Restaurant; Hotel Management; Industrial Design; Mechanical Engineering); **Teacher Education** (Art Education; Curriculum; Education; English; Filipino; Foreign Languages Education; Mathematics Education; Music Education; Native Language Education; Physical Education; Physics; Preschool Education; Primary Education; Secondary Education; Social Studies; Teacher Training)

Schools

Graduate (Business Administration; Education; Educational Administration; Forestry; Linguistics; Management; Mathematics Education; Nursing; Primary Education; Public Administration; Science Education)

Further Information: Also Branches in Lucena, Alabat, Infanta, Tagkawayan (Judge Guillermo Eleazar Polytechnic College), Polilio, Sampaloc

History: Founded 1964. Formerly known as Southern Luzon Polytechnic College. Acquired present status and title 2005.

Degrees and Diplomas: *Certificate/Diploma*; *Associate Degree*; *Bachelor's Degree*; *Master's Degree*: Education (Primary Education; Educational Administration and Supervision); Nursing; Arts in: Mathematics Education; Science Education; Applied Lingusitics; Management; Business Administration; Forestry; *PhD*: Development Education; Science Education
Last Updated: 21/02/11

SOUTHERN PHILIPPINE AGRICULTURAL BUSINESS, MARINE AND AQUATIC SCHOOL OF TECHNOLOGY

Poblacion, Malita, Davao del Sur 8012
Tel: +63(973) 221-7627
Fax: +63(973) 221-7627
EMail: spamast_campus@digos.mozcom.com

President: Alexander M. Campaner

Programmes

Digos (Agricultural Business; Agricultural Education; Agricultural Engineering; Agricultural Management; Crop Production; Fishery; Forestry; Home Economics Education; Information Technology; Mathematics Education; Science Education; Secondary Education); **Graduate** (Agricultural Business; Agricultural Management; Business Administration; Education; Educational Administration; Mathematics Education); **Undergraduate and Professional**

Studies (Agricultural Business; Agricultural Engineering; Agricultural Management; Crop Production; Fishery; Forestry; Home Economics Education; Information Technology; Mathematics Education; Science Education; Secondary Education)

History: Founded 1982.

Degrees and Diplomas: *Bachelor's Degree*; *Master's Degree*: Education (Educational Management; Mathematics Teaching); Agri-Business Management; Business Administration
Last Updated: 22/02/11

SULTAN KUDARAT POLYTECHNIC STATE COLLEGE

E. J.C. Montilla, Tacurong City, Sultan Kudarat 9800
Tel: +63(64) 200-4264
Fax: +63(64) 200-4261

President: Teresita Cambel

Campuses

Isulan (Automotive Engineering; Civil Engineering; Computer Engineering; Electrical Engineering; Electronic Engineering; Food Technology; Industrial Engineering; Information Management; Information Technology; Structural Architecture; Telecommunications Engineering) *Campus Dean*: Edwin C. Alido; **Kalamansig** (Agricultural Education; Aquaculture; Computer Engineering; Education; Fishery; Information Technology) *Campus Dean*: Rex F. Dapitan; **Lutayan** (Agricultural Engineering; Agricultural Management; Agriculture; Development Studies; Primary Education) *Campus Dean*: Jesusa D. Oruoste

Programmes

Agriculture (Agricultural Engineering; Agriculture; Aquaculture; Fishery); **Education** (Agricultural Education; Education; English; Filipino; Fishery; Foreign Languages Education; History; Native Language Education; Physical Education; Social Sciences); **Graduate** (Agricultural Engineering; Agriculture; Crop Production; Educational Administration; English; Filipino; Foreign Languages Education; History; Mathematics Education; Native Language Education; Physical Education; Public Administration; Science Education; Zoology); **Hotel and Restaurant Management** (Hotel and Restaurant; Hotel Management); **Industrial Technology** (Automotive Engineering; Civil Engineering; Electrical Engineering; Food Technology; Industrial Engineering; Information Sciences; Structural Architecture); **Science** *(Bachelor of Science programmes)* (Biology; Chemistry; Civil Engineering; Computer Engineering; Hotel and Restaurant; Hotel Management; Information Sciences; Mathematics; Primary Education; Secondary Education); **Social Sciences** (Economics; Educational and Student Counselling); **Teaching** (Education; Primary Education; Secondary Education; Teacher Training)

History: Founded 1966. Formerly known as Tacurong Municipal High School (1990-1991).

Degrees and Diplomas: *Bachelor's Degree*; *Master's Degree*: Science Teaching (Mathematics; English; History; Science; Physical Education; Filipino); Management (Educational Management; Public Management); Arts in Agricultural Science and Technology (Animal and Crop Science); *PhD*: Agricultural Science; Institutional Development and Management
Last Updated: 28/02/11

SULU STATE COLLEGE

Capitol Site, Jolo, Sulu 7400
Tel: +63 (68) 341-8911
Fax: +63 (68) 341-8911

President: Hamsali S. Jawali

Programmes

Graduate Studies (Agriculture; Business Administration; Education; Educational Administration; Filipino; Human Resources; Mathematics Education; Modern Languages; Native Language Education; Public Administration; Social Sciences); **Undergraduate and Professional Studies** (Agricultural Engineering; Agriculture; Business Administration; Computer Engineering; Computer Science; Crop Production; Education; Educational Administration; English; Filipino; Foreign Languages Education; History; Home Economics Education; Information Technology; Management; Mathematics Education; Native Language Education; Nursing; Primary Education; Secondary Education; Social Sciences; Zoology)

History: Foinded 1924. Formerly known as Dayang Dayang Hadji Piandao Memorial High School.

Degrees and Diplomas: *Bachelor's Degree*; *Master's Degree*: Education (Mathematics Education; Filipino; Language Teaching; Educational Administration); Social Sciences; Business Administration; Public Administration (Personnel Administration); Agriculture; *PhD*: Education; Public Administration
Last Updated: 28/02/11

SURALLAH NATIONAL AGRICULTURAL SCHOOL

Dajay, Surallah, South Cotabato 9512
Tel: +63(83) 238-3050
Fax: +63(83) 238-3050
EMail: sunas-tesda@yahoo.com

Superintendent: Isidro H. Cambel Sr.

Programmes

Agriculture (Agricultural Engineering; Agriculture; Aquaculture; Food Technology; Horticulture)

History: Founded 1975.

Degrees and Diplomas: *Certificate/Diploma*; *Bachelor's Degree*
Last Updated: 28/02/11

SURIGAO DEL SUR POLYTECHNIC STATE COLLEGE (SSPSC)

National Highway, Tandag, Surigao del Sur 8300
Tel: +63 (86) 211-3509
Fax: +63 (86) 211-3509

President: Remegita C. Olvida EMail: remegita_olvida@yahoo.com

Chief Administrative Officer: Wivina A. Tering
EMail: wivina_tering@yahoo.com

International Relations: Aldy B. Novo
EMail: aldybnovo@yahoo.com

Campuses

Cagwait (Automotive Engineering; Civil Engineering; Computer Engineering; Electrical Engineering; Food Technology; Industrial Engineering; Technology; Textile Technology) *Campus Director*: Julio A. Lamigo; **Cantilan** (Automotive Engineering; Biological and Life Sciences; Business Administration; Civil Engineering; Computer Education; Computer Engineering; Computer Science; Electrical and Electronic Engineering; Filipino; Finance; Home Economics Education; Hotel and Restaurant; Hotel Management; Industrial Arts Education; Management; Mathematics Education; Mechanical Engineering; Metal Techniques; Native Language Education; Physics; Science Education; Secondary Education; Social Studies; Structural Architecture; Technology Education; Textile Technology) *Campus Director*: Cirila O. De Los Arcos; **Lianga** (Aquaculture; Biology; Business Administration; Computer Science; Cooking and Catering; Fishery; Home Economics Education; Hotel and Restaurant; Hotel Management; Management; Marine Biology; Marine Engineering; Primary Education; Technology Education) *Campus Director*: Elenita S. Santamaria; **San Miguel** (Administration; Agricultural Education; Agricultural Engineering) *Campus Chancellor*: Romeo A. Patan; **Tagbina** (Agricultural Business; Agricultural Education; Agricultural Engineering; Agriculture; Business Administration; Computer Science; Primary Education; Secondary Education; Technology) *Campus Chancellor*: Ariston C. Ronquillo

Programmes

Arts *(Bachelor of Arts programme)* (Economics; English; Mathematics; Political Sciences; Public Administration); **Business Administration** (Banking; Business Administration; Finance; Hotel and Restaurant; Hotel Management); **Chemical Engineering** (Chemical Engineering); **Computer Science** (Computer Science); **Education** (Biological and Life Sciences; Education; English; Filipino; Foreign Languages Education; Mathematics Education; Native Language Education; Primary Education; Science Education; Secondary Education); **Graduate Studies** (Education; Educational Administration; English; Filipino; Foreign Languages Education; Home Economics Education; Mathematics Education; Public Administration; Science Education; Social Studies; Technology

Education); **Marine Biology** (Marine Biology); **Public Administration** (Public Administration)

History: Founded 1993.

Governing Bodies: Board of Trustees

Admission Requirements: Prescribed by the Academic Council and approved by the President

Fees: (Pesos): 90 per unit

Main Language(s) of Instruction: Filipino, English

Accrediting Agencies: Accrediting Agency of Chartered Colleges and Universities in the Philippines (AACCUP)

Degrees and Diplomas: *Associate Degree*: 2 yrs; *Bachelor's Degree*; *Master's Degree*: Education (Educational Management); Teaching (Technology and Home Economics; English; Mathematics; Filipino; Science; Social Studies); Public Administration; *PhD*: Education (Educational Management)

Student Services: Academic counselling, Canteen, Employment services, Health services, Social counselling

Student Residential Facilities: Yes

Libraries: Yes

Last Updated: 28/02/11

SURIGAO STATE COLLEGE OF TECHNOLOGY (SSCT)

Narciso Street, Surigao City, Surigao del Norte 8400
Tel: +63(86) 826-6346
Fax: +63(86) 826-6346
EMail: ssctsurigao@gmail.com
Website: http://ssct.edu.ph/

President: Gloria C. Gemparo (2010-)

Campuses

Del Carmen (Industrial Arts Education; Industrial Engineering; Information Technology; Secondary Education); **Malimono** (Aquaculture; Fishery; Marine Biology; Primary Education; Secondary Education)

Colleges

Industrial Technology (Automotive Engineering; Electrical Engineering; Electronic Engineering; Heating and Refrigeration; Industrial Engineering; Mechanical Engineering; Metal Techniques)

Divisions

Engineering (Civil Engineering; Computer Engineering; Electrical Engineering; Electronic Engineering; Engineering; Telecommunications Engineering); **Information Technology** (Computer Science; Information Technology; Technology); **Teacher Education** (Biological and Life Sciences; English; Filipino; Food Technology; Foreign Languages Education; Hotel and Restaurant; Hotel Management; Mathematics Education; Native Language Education; Physics; Primary Education; Secondary Education; Technology Education)

Programmes

Graduate Studies (Automotive Engineering; Civil Engineering; Education; Electrical and Electronic Engineering; English; Filipino; Food Technology; Foreign Languages Education; Industrial Engineering; Information Technology; Mathematics Education; Mechanical Engineering; Native Language Education; Science Education; Structural Architecture); **Hotel and Restaurant Management** (Hotel and Restaurant; Hotel Management)

History: Founded 1969 as Surigao del Norte School of Arts and Trade.

Degrees and Diplomas: *Certificate/Diploma*; *Bachelor's Degree*; *Master's Degree*: Arts in Education (Mathematics); Industrial Education

Last Updated: 28/02/11

TALISAY CITY COLLEGE

Cor. V.H. Garces & Rizal Streets, Talisay City, Cebu 6045

Director: Tomas L. Ramos

Programmes

Education (Education; Filipino; Mathematics Education; Native Language Education; Physical Education; Primary Education; Secondary Education); **Hotel and Restaurant Services Technology** (Hotel and Restaurant); **Industrial Technology** (Industrial Engineering); **Nursing** (Nursing)

History: Founded 2004.

Degrees and Diplomas: *Associate Degree*; *Bachelor's Degree*
Last Updated: 01/03/11

TARLAC COLLEGE OF AGRICULTURE

Malacampa, Camiling, Tarlac 2306
Tel: +63(45) 934-0216
Fax: +63(45) 934-0216
EMail: tca@mozcom.com

President: Philip B. Ibarra

Programmes

Agriculture (Agricultural Engineering; Agriculture; Forestry; Zoology); **Business Administration** (Business Administration; Economics; Management); **Education** (Education; Primary Education; Secondary Education); **Food Technology** (Food Technology); **Geodetic Engineering** (Earth Sciences; Geological Engineering); **Graduate Studies** (Agricultural Engineering; Agriculture; Education; Forestry; Teacher Training); **Home Technology** (Home Economics; Technology); **Information Technology** (Information Technology); **Nursing** (Nursing); **Psychology** (Psychology); **Veterinary Medicine** (Veterinary Science)

History: Founded 1945. Formerly Tarlac College of Technology - College of Agriculture (1965 -1974).

Degrees and Diplomas: *Certificate/Diploma*; *Associate Degree*; *Bachelor's Degree*; *Post Baccalaureate Certificate/Diploma*: Veterinary Medicine; *Master's Degree*: Arts in: Education; Teaching; Science in: Agricultural Engineering; Agriculture; Forestry; *PhD*
Last Updated: 01/03/11

TARLAC STATE UNIVERSITY

Romulo Boulevard, San Vicente, City of Tarlac, Tarlac 2300
Tel: +63(45) 982-1624 +63(45) 982-2605
Fax: +63(45) 982-0110
EMail: tsu@mozcom.com.ph
Website: http://www.tsu.edu.ph/Homepage.aspx

President: Priscilla C. Viuya

Vice-President for Administration: Dalisay V. Rigor

Campuses

Lucinda (Art Education; Curriculum; Education; English; Filipino; Foreign Languages Education; Health Education; Home Economics Education; Industrial Arts Education; Mathematics Education; Music Education; Native Language Education; Nursing; Physical Education; Physics; Preschool Education; Primary Education; Secondary Education; Social Studies; Technology Education); **San Isidro** (Advertising and Publicity; Architecture; Automotive Engineering; Electrical Engineering; Electronic Engineering; Fine Arts; Food Technology; Industrial Engineering; Information Technology; Nutrition)

Colleges

Arts and Social Sciences (Communication Arts; English; Psychology); **Business and Accountancy** (Accountancy; Business Administration; Economics; Finance; Hotel and Restaurant; Hotel Management; Management; Marketing); **Computer Studies** (Computer Science; Information Technology); **Engineering** (Civil Engineering; Electrical Engineering; Electronic Engineering; Engineering; Industrial Engineering; Mechanical Engineering; Telecommunications Engineering); **Human Kinetics** (Physical Therapy); **Law** (Criminal Law; Criminology; Law); **Public Administration** (Public Administration); **Science** (Chemistry)

Programmes

Graduate Studies (Business Administration; Education; Educational Administration)

History: Founded 1906 as Trade School, acquired present status and title 1989.

Governing Bodies: Board of Regents

Academic Year: June to March (June-October; November-March)

Admission Requirements: Graduation from high school and entrance examination

Degrees and Diplomas: *Bachelor's Degree*; *Post Baccalaureate Certificate/Diploma*: Information Technology; *Master's Degree*: Business Administration; Education (Administration and Supervision; Technology and Livelihood Education; Mathematics; Guidance and Counselling; Educational Management); Public Administration (Health Management); Civil Engineering; Electrical Engineering; Information Technology; *PhD*: Education (Industrial Education Management; Educational Management); Business Administration; Public Administration
Last Updated: 01/03/11

TAWI-TAWI REGIONAL AGRICULTURAL COLLEGE

Nalil, Bongao, Tawi-Tawi 7500
Tel: +63(918) 416-0659

Officer In-Charge: Moh. Asady M. Hussin

Programmes

Agriculture (Agricultural Business; Agricultural Education; Agriculture; Crop Production; Zoology); **Computer Science** (Computer Science); **Forestry** (Forestry); **Graduate Studies** (Agricultural Education; Agricultural Management; Agriculture; Crop Production; Education; Educational Administration; Zoology)

History: Founded 1957. Formerly known as Tawi-Tawi National Agricultural College (1957-1974).

Degrees and Diplomas: *Bachelor's Degree*; *Master's Degree*: Education (Administration and Supervision); Agricultural Education (Animal Science; Crop Science); Agricultural Management; Agriculture (Animal Science; Crop Science)
Last Updated: 01/03/11

TECHNOLOGICAL UNIVERSITY OF THE PHILIPPINES (TUP)

Ayala Boulevard, Ermita, Manila, First District, Metro Manila 1001
Tel: +63(2) 521-4063
Fax: +63(2) 523-2293
Website: http://www.tup.edu.ph

President: Godofredo E. C. Gallega

Vice-President for Administration and Finance: Cresenciano Laza

International Relations: Viola Delos T. Reyes, Vice-President for Academic Affairs

Campuses

Cavite (Automotive Engineering; Civil Engineering; Computer Education; Computer Engineering; Electrical Engineering; Electronic Engineering; Industrial Arts Education; Mechanical Engineering; Power Engineering; Production Engineering; Structural Architecture); **Taguig** (Automation and Control Engineering; Automotive Engineering; Chemical Engineering; Civil Engineering; Computer Engineering; Electrical Engineering; Electronic Engineering; Engineering; Heating and Refrigeration; Instrument Making; Mechanical Engineering; Structural Architecture; Teacher Training; Technology; Technology Education; Telecommunications Engineering); **Visayas** (Automotive Engineering; Chemical Engineering; Computer Engineering; Electrical Engineering; Electronic Engineering; Engineering; Heating and Refrigeration; Mechanical Engineering; Technology; Telecommunications Engineering)

Colleges

Architecture and Fine Arts (Architecture; Fine Arts; Graphic Design); **Engineering** (Civil Engineering; Electrical Engineering; Electronic Engineering; Mechanical Engineering; Telecommunications Engineering); **Industrial Education** (Industrial Arts Education; Technology Education); **Industrial Technology** (Automation and Control Engineering; Automotive Engineering; Civil Engineering; Computer Engineering; Electronic Engineering; Food Technology; Graphic Arts; Heating and Refrigeration; Hotel and Restaurant; Hotel Management; Mechanical Engineering; Metal Techniques; Nutrition; Power Engineering; Printing and Printmaking; Production Engineering; Railway Engineering; Telecommunications Engineering; Textile Technology); **Liberal Arts** (Arts and Humanities; Dietetics; Fine Arts; Industrial Management; Management; Nutrition); **Science** (Applied Chemistry; Applied Mathematics; Applied Physics; Environmental Studies; Information Management; Information Technology; Laboratory Techniques)

Programmes

Graduate Studies (Architecture; Civil Engineering; Education; Electrical Engineering; Engineering; Graphic Arts; Graphic Design; Industrial Arts Education; Information Technology; Management; Mechanical Engineering; Teacher Training; Technology; Technology Education)

History: Founded 1901 as School, became College of Arts and Trades 1959. Reorganized as University 1978 including the Manila Technician Institute, Taguig, Bocolod Technician Institute, Talisay, and Iligan Institute of Technology, and 10 Regional Manpower Training Centres. Financed partly by the State and partly from tuition fees.

Governing Bodies: Board of Regents

Academic Year: June to March (June-October; November-March). Also Summer Session (April-May)

Admission Requirements: Graduation from high school and entrance examination

Fees: (Pesos) 3,460 per semester

Main Language(s) of Instruction: English

Accrediting Agencies: Accrediting Agency of Chartered Colleges and Universities in the Philippines (AACCUP)

Degrees and Diplomas: *Certificate/Diploma*; *Associate Degree*; *Bachelor's Degree*; *Master's Degree*: Graphics Technology; Management; Engineering (Civil; Electrical; Mechanical); Information Technology; Technology; Technology Education; Industrial Education (Administration and Supervision; Curriculum and Instruction; Educational Technology; Guidance and Counselling); Management; Teaching (Chemistry; General Science; Mathematics; Non-Formal Education; Physics; Technology and Home Economics); Architecture (Construction Technology Management); *PhD*: Management Science; Technology Management; Technology; Education (Career Guidance; Industrial Education Management)

Student Services: Academic counselling, Canteen, Cultural centre, Employment services, Foreign Studies Centre, Health services, Social counselling, Sports facilities

Special Facilities: TUP Museum, Gallery

Libraries: Central Library, c. 25,000 vols

Publications: Phil. Journal of Industrial Education and Technology, Research publication of the university. *(biannually)*

Press or Publishing House: University Press
Last Updated: 01/03/11

TIBURCIO TANCINCO MEMORIAL INSTITUTE OF SCIENCE AND TECHNOLOGY

Rueda Street, Calbayog City, Western Samar 6710
Tel: +63(55) 209-3657
Fax: +63(55) 209-3657
EMail: ttmist@ttmist.edu.ph; ttmist1982@yahoo.com
Website: http://www.ttmist.edu.ph

President: Socorro O. Bohol

Programmes

Graduate (Business Administration; Education; Educational and Student Counselling; Engineering Management; Industrial Arts Education; Library Science; Management; Public Administration; Science Education); **Undergraduate and Professional** (Agricultural Engineering; Agriculture; Agronomy; Automotive Engineering; Biological and Life Sciences; Business Administration; Civil Engineering; Communication Studies; Computer Engineering; Computer Science; Criminology; Curriculum; Development Studies; Education; Educational and Student Counselling; Electrical Engineering; Electronic Engineering; English; Environmental Management; Food Technology; Foreign Languages Education; Health Education; Home Economics Education; Horticulture; Hotel and Restaurant; Hotel Management; Industrial Engineering; Information Management; Information Sciences; Information Technology; Management Systems; Mathematics Education; Mechanical Engineering; Primary Education; Science Education; Secondary Education; Secretarial Studies; Social and Community Services; Structural Architecture; Telecommunications Engineering; Textile Technology; Tourism; Urban Studies)

History: Founded 1959.

Degrees and Diplomas: *Certificate/Diploma*; *Associate Degree*; *Bachelor's Degree*; *Master's Degree*: Education (Administration and Supervision; Curriculum and Development); Engineering Management; Library Administration; Public Management; Science in Guidance and Counselling; Industrial Education (Technology and Home Economics); Science Teaching (Mathematics; General Science); Information Technology; Business Administration; *PhD*: Education (Educational Management); Management

Last Updated: 02/03/11

TRINIDAD MUNICIPAL COLLEGE

Población, Trinidad, Bohol 6324
Tel: +63(38) 516-1023
Fax: +63(38) 516-1023

President: Leo Armando B. Boncales

Programmes

English (English); **Information Technology** (Information Technology); **Political Sciences** (Political Sciences); **Secretarial Administration** (Management Systems; Secretarial Studies)

History: Founded 1985.

Degrees and Diplomas: *Associate Degree*; *Bachelor's Degree*

Last Updated: 02/03/11

UNIVERSITY OF ANTIQUE (UA)

Mayor Santiago A. Lotilla Street, Sibalom, Antique 5713
Tel: +63(36) 543 - 8124 +63(36) 543-8161
Fax: +63(36) 543-8161
EMail: ua@antiquespride.edu.ph
Website: http://www.antiquespride.edu.ph

President: Victor E. Navarra EMail: psca@psca.edu.ph

Vice-President for Academics: Elena M. Calumbiran

Chief Administrative Officer: Ronilo C. Soriano
EMail: ronisoriano@yahoo.com

Campuses

Hamtic (Agricultural Education; Agricultural Engineering; Agricultural Equipment; Animal Husbandry; Computer Science; Crop Production; Dairy; English; Food Technology; Foreign Languages Education; Forestry; Harvest Technology; Home Economics Education; Mathematics Education; Secondary Education; Technology Education; Zoology)

Colleges

Arts and Sciences (Arts and Humanities; Criminology; English; Political Sciences; Psychology; Urban Studies); **Business Education** (Accountancy; Business Administration; Management Systems; Marketing; Secretarial Studies; Small Business); **Computer Studies** (Computer Engineering; Computer Science; Information Technology); **Education** (Education; Education of the Gifted; Education of the Handicapped; Engineering; English; Filipino; Foreign Languages Education; Health Education; Home Economics Education; Industrial Arts Education; Mathematics Education; Native Language Education; Primary Education; Science Education; Secondary Education; Social Studies; Special Education; Teacher Training; Technology Education); **Engineering and Architecture** (Architecture; Civil Engineering; Electronic Engineering; Engineering; Structural Architecture; Telecommunications Engineering); **Maritime Education** (Cooking and Catering; Marine Engineering); **Technology** (Automotive Engineering; Cosmetology; Electronic Engineering; Food Technology; Heating and Refrigeration; Hotel and Restaurant; Hotel Management; Industrial Engineering; Mechanical Engineering; Technology; Textile Technology)

Schools

Graduate (Curriculum; Education; Educational Administration; English; Foreign Languages Education; Human Resources; Mathematics Education; Philosophy; Public Administration; Science Education)

History: Founded 1954. Formerly known as Antique School of Arts and Trades and Polytechnic State College of Antique. Acquired present university status and title 2009.

Degrees and Diplomas: *Bachelor's Degree*; *Master's Degree*: Teaching (English; Mathematics); Education (Curriculum and Instruction; Vocational Technology; Educational Management); Public Administration (Human Resources); *PhD*: Public Administration

Last Updated: 25/01/11

UNIVERSITY OF CABUYAO

Pamantasan ng Cabuyao

Katapatan Village, Brgy. Banay-Banay, Cabuyao, Laguna 4025
Tel: +63(49) 832-3036
Fax: +63(49) 531-4554

President: Roberto Atmosfera

Programmes

Undergraduate and Professional (Accountancy; Banking; Business Administration; Business Computing; Computer Engineering; Computer Science; Electronic Engineering; English; Finance; Heating and Refrigeration; Industrial Engineering; Information Management; Information Technology; Management; Marketing; Mass Communication; Mathematics; Mechanical Engineering; Midwifery; Nursing; Preschool Education; Primary Education; Psychology; Public Relations; Secondary Education; Telecommunications Engineering)

History: Founded 2003.

Degrees and Diplomas: *Certificate/Diploma*; *Associate Degree*; *Bachelor's Degree*

Last Updated: 07/01/11

UNIVERSITY OF CALOOCAN CITY

General San Miguel Street, Sangandan Road, Caloocan City, Third District, Metro Manila 1400
Tel: +63(2) 324-6855 +63(2) 324-6581
Fax: +63(2) 324-6855

President: Enrico "Recom" Echiverri

Colleges

Arts and Sciences (Criminology; Educational and Student Counselling; English; Foreign Languages Education; Industrial and Organizational Psychology; Journalism; Law; Mathematics Education; Political Sciences; Psychology; Public Administration; Radio and Television Broadcasting; Special Education; Tourism); **Business and Accountancy** (Accountancy; Business Administration; Finance; Human Resources; Management; Marketing); **Computer Studies** (Business Computing; Computer Science; Information Technology; Management Systems; Secretarial Studies); **Education** (Biology; Education; Home Economics Education; Industrial Arts Education; Physics; Primary Education; Secondary Education; Technology Education); **Graduate Studies** (Education; Educational Administration; Public Administration; Science Education)

History: Founded 1971 as Caloocan City Polytechnic College. Acquired present status and title 2004.

Degrees and Diplomas: *Bachelor's Degree*; *Master's Degree*: Public Administration; Education (Educational Management; Science Educatio); *PhD*: Public Administration

Last Updated: 04/03/11

UNIVERSITY OF EASTERN PANGASINAN

Binalonan, Pangasinan 2436

Chairman of the Board: Mayor Ramon N. Guico Jr

Programmes

Undergraduate and Professional (Business Administration; Criminology; Finance; Hotel and Restaurant; Hotel Management; Industrial Arts Education; Information Technology; Management; Marketing; Nursing; Tourism)

Degrees and Diplomas: *Bachelor's Degree*

Last Updated: 04/03/11

UNIVERSITY OF EASTERN PHILIPPINES (UEP)

University Town, Catarman, Northern Samar 6400
Tel: +63(55) 251-8008
Fax: +63(55) 251-8405
EMail: uephil@lycos.com
Website: http://www.uep.edu.ph/

President: Mar P. de Asis

Campuses
Catubig (Agricultural Engineering; Business Computing; Computer Engineering; Computer Networks; Computer Science; Food Technology; Secretarial Studies); **Laoang** (Automotive Engineering; Biology; Civil Engineering; Computer Education; Cosmetology; Criminology; Education; Electrical Engineering; Electronic Engineering; English; Fishery; Food Technology; Foreign Languages Education; Health Education; Home Economics Education; Mathematics Education; Mechanical Engineering; Music Education; Physical Education; Primary Education; Science Education; Secondary Education; Technology Education; Textile Technology; Wood Technology)

Colleges
Agriculture *(Pedro Rebadulla Memorial Agricultural College)* (Agricultural Business; Agricultural Education; Agricultural Engineering; Agriculture; Aquaculture; Fishery; Forestry); **Arts and Communication** (Arts and Humanities; Communication Studies; Development Studies; Information Technology; Journalism; Literature; Modern Languages; Political Sciences; Public Administration; Radio and Television Broadcasting; Sociology; Urban Studies); **Business Administration** (Accountancy; Business Administration; Economics; Management; Marketing; Secretarial Studies); **Education** (Education; Home Economics Education; Industrial Arts Education; Institutional Administration; Primary Education; Secondary Education; Technology Education); **Engineering** (Agricultural Engineering; Automotive Engineering; Civil Engineering; Computer Engineering; Electrical Engineering; Engineering; Industrial Engineering; Information Technology; Mechanical Engineering; Natural Resources; Structural Architecture; Technology; Technology Education; Water Science); **Law** (Law); **Nursing** (Nursing); **Science** (Biology; Chemistry; Environmental Studies; Home Economics; Hotel and Restaurant; Hotel Management; Marine Biology; Mathematics; Natural Sciences; Physics; Zoology); **Veterinary Science** *(Graduate)* (Veterinary Science)

Schools
Graduate (Agriculture; Biology; Business Administration; Chemistry; Civil Engineering; Development Studies; Economics; Education; Educational Administration; Educational and Student Counselling; English; Environmental Studies; Filipino; Foreign Languages Education; Management; Mathematics Education; Modern Languages; Native Language Education; Nursing; Physical Education; Physics; Primary Education; Public Administration; Science Education; Social Studies; Water Management; Water Science; Zoology)

History: Founded 1918 as Catarman Farm School supported by municipal and provincial funds of the Province of Samar. Became Catarman Agricultural School 1951, supported by national and provincial funds and then Catarman National Agricultural High School supported entirely by the national Government. Became Samar Institute of Technology 1957 and University 1964.

Governing Bodies: Board of Regents

Academic Year: June to March (June-October; October-March). Also Summer Session (April to May)

Admission Requirements: Graduation from high school or foreign equivalent, and entrance examination

Main Language(s) of Instruction: Filipino, English

Accrediting Agencies: Accrediting Agency of Chartered Colleges and Universities in the Philippines (AACCUP)

Degrees and Diplomas: *Certificate/Diploma*; *Bachelor's Degree*; *Post Baccalaureate Certificate/Diploma*: Veterinary Medicine; *Master's Degree*: Business Administration; Education (Physical Education; Guidance and Counselling; Administration and Supervision); Language and Literature (English); Language Teaching (Filipino; English); Nursing; Community Development; Economics; Environmental Studies; Physics; Teaching Chemistry; Teaching (Elementary Education; Mathematics; Social Studies); Public Administration; Public Management; Agricultural Extension; Animal Science; Biological Science; Civil Engineering (Water Resources); *PhD*: Arts in Language and Literature; Business Administration; Educational Management; Public Administration

Student Services: Academic counselling, Canteen, Cultural centre, Health services, Nursery care, Social counselling, Sports facilities

Student Residential Facilities: For c. 8,000 students

Special Facilities: UEP Biodiversity.

Libraries: Central Library, c. 30,000 vols

Publications: Pacific Journal *(annually)*

Last Updated: 04/03/11

UNIVERSITY OF MAKATI

J. P. Rizal Extension, West Rembo, City of Makati, Fourth District, Metro Manila 1215
Tel: +63(2) 882-0535
Fax: +63(2) 882-0675
Website: http://www.universityofmakati.net

President: Tomas B. Lopez

Vice-President for Administration and Finance: Raymundo P. Arcega

Programmes
Graduate Studies (Business Administration; Child Care and Development; Education; Education of the Handicapped; Educational Administration; Educational and Student Counselling; Educational Technology; Finance; Health Administration; Human Resources; Management; Nursing; Public Administration; Public Health; Special Education); **Undergraduate and Professional** (Accountancy; Aeronautical and Aerospace Engineering; Biological and Life Sciences; Biology; Business Administration; Child Care and Development; Civil Engineering; Communication Studies; Computer Networks; Computer Science; Education; Electrical Engineering; Electronic Engineering; English; Filipino; Finance; Foreign Languages Education; Government; Human Resources; Industrial Engineering; Management; Management Systems; Marketing; Mathematics Education; Media Studies; Native Language Education; Nursing; Political Sciences; Preschool Education; Psychology; Radio and Television Broadcasting; Secretarial Studies; Social Studies; Special Education; Teacher Training; Telecommunications Engineering; Tourism)

History: Founded 1972 as Makati Poytechnic Community College, renamed Makati College 1987, merged 1990 with Fort Andres Bonifacio College and acquired present status 1991.

Governing Bodies: Board of Regents

Admission Requirements: Graduation from high school and entrance examination

Fees: (Pesos): Makati city residents, 1,000, non-residents, 3,000. Graduate School: residents, 2,000, non-residents, 4,000

Main Language(s) of Instruction: Filipino, English

Degrees and Diplomas: *Bachelor's Degree*; *Master's Degree*: Arts in: Nursing (Public Health Administration; Maternal and Child Nursing; Nursing Service Administration); Special Education (Mental Retardation and Autism); Education (Instructional Design and Media; Administration and Supervision; Guidance and Counselling); Business Administration (Human Resources Management; Property Management; Entrepreneurship and Microfinance); *PhD*: Education (Educational Management; Innovative Education Management)

Student Services: Academic counselling, Canteen, Cultural centre, Employment services, Health services, Social counselling, Sports facilities

Student Residential Facilities: Yes

Libraries: Main Library

Last Updated: 04/03/11

UNIVERSITY OF MANILA
Universidad de Manila (UDM)

PNB Bldg., Escolta, Santa Cruz, City of Manila, First District, Metro Manila 1000
Tel: +63(2) 309-0582 +63(2) 302-6558
Fax: +63(2) 309-0954

President: Justice Rodolfo G. Palattao

Programmes
Undergraduate and Professional (Accountancy; Automotive Engineering; Business Administration; Computer Engineering; Computer Science; Criminology; Economics; Electrical Engineering; Electronic Engineering; Finance; Food Technology; Heating and Refrigeration; Hotel and Restaurant; Industrial Engineering; Management; Marketing; Mass Communication; Mathematics; Nursing; Physical Education; Physical Therapy; Political Sciences; Psychology; Public Administration; Secondary Education; Social

Work; Technology; Telecommunications Engineering; Textile Technology)

History: Founded 1995 as City College of Manila. Acquired present title 2006.

Degrees and Diplomas: *Bachelor's Degree*

Last Updated: 03/03/11

UNIVERSITY OF MARIKINA CITY

Pamantasan ng Lungsod ng Marikina

Brazil Street, Greenhights Subd., Phase I, Concepcion Uno, Marikina City, Second District, Metro Manila

Tel: +63(2) 998-5254

Fax: +63(2) 998-5254

President: Dalisay G. Brawner

Programmes

Undergraduate and Professional (Business Administration; Criminology; Education; English; Filipino; Foreign Languages Education; Hotel and Restaurant; Hotel Management; Management; Marketing; Mass Communication; Mathematics Education; Native Language Education; Nursing)

History: Founded 2003.

Degrees and Diplomas: *Associate Degree*; *Bachelor's Degree*; *Master's Degree*: Business Administration; Educational Management

Last Updated: 07/01/11

UNIVERSITY OF MONTALBAN

Pamantasan ng Montalban

Montalban, Rizal 1860

EMail: pamantasan_ng_montalban@yahoo.com

President: Pedro C. Cuerpo

Programmes

Education (Biology; Curriculum; Education; Physics; Preschool Education; Primary Education; Technology Education); **Science** (Business and Commerce; Civil Engineering; Computer Engineering; Human Resources; Information Technology; Management)

History: Founded 2004.

Degrees and Diplomas: *Bachelor's Degree*

Last Updated: 20/01/11

UNIVERSITY OF MUNTINLUPA CITY

Pamantasan ng Lungsod ng Muntinlupa

NBP Reservation, City of Muntinlupa, Fourth District, Metro Manila 1770

Tel: +63(2) 560-1488

Fax: +63(2) 560-1492

Website: http://www.plmun.edu.ph

President: Fe Nazareno Martinez

Programmes

Graduate (Business Administration; Educational Administration; Educational and Student Counselling); **Undergraduate and Professional** (Accountancy; Art Education; Business Administration; Business and Commerce; Child Care and Development; Computer Science; Criminal Law; Criminology; Education; English; Filipino; Finance; Foreign Languages Education; Health Education; Human Resources; Management; Marketing; Mass Communication; Mathematics Education; Music Education; Native Language Education; Physical Education; Political Sciences; Primary Education; Psychology; Science Education; Secondary Education; Social Sciences; Special Education)

History: Founded 1991. Formerly known as Muntinlupa Polytechnic College (1991-2003).

Degrees and Diplomas: *Certificate/Diploma*; *Associate Degree*; *Bachelor's Degree*; *Master's Degree*: Arts in Guidance and Counselling; Educational Management; Business Administration

Last Updated: 07/01/11

UNIVERSITY OF NORTHERN PHILIPPINES

Quirino Boulevard, Vigan City, Ilocos Sur 2700

Tel: +63(77) 722-2810 +63(77) 722-2812

Fax: +63(77) 722-2810

EMail: unp@vigan.amanet.net

Website: http://www.unp.edu.ph/

President: Lauro B. Tacbas

Campuses

Candon (Art Education; Business Administration; Computer Science; Curriculum; Education; English; Filipino; Foreign Languages Education; Health Education; Home Economics Education; Management; Mathematics Education; Music Education; Native Language Education; Nursing; Physical Education; Political Sciences; Primary Education; Secondary Education; Social Sciences) *Campus Dean*: Lumen Almachar

Colleges

Architecture (Architecture); **Arts and Science** (Biology; Computer Science; English; Environmental Studies; History; Information Sciences; Library Science; Marine Biology; Mass Communication; Mathematics; Physics; Political Sciences; Psychology; Social Sciences; Statistics; Tourism); **Business Administration and Accountancy** (Accountancy; Banking; Business Administration; Finance; Hotel and Restaurant; Hotel Management; Management); **Communication and Information Technology** (Communication Studies; Information Technology); **Criminology** (Criminal Law; Criminology); **Engineering** (Civil Engineering; Computer Science; Engineering; Geological Engineering; Sanitary Engineering); **Fine Arts** (Advertising and Publicity; Fine Arts; Interior Design; Painting and Drawing); **Health Sciences** (Community Health; Health Sciences; Medicine; Midwifery; Nursing); **Law** (Law); **Social Work** (Social Work); **Teacher Education** (Art Education; Curriculum; Education; Educational and Student Counselling; English; Ethics; Filipino; Foreign Languages Education; Health Education; Home Economics Education; Library Science; Mathematics Education; Music Education; Native Language Education; Natural Sciences; Physical Education; Physics; Preschool Education; Primary Education; Science Education; Secondary Education; Social Sciences; Social Studies; Teacher Training); **Technology** (Automotive Engineering; Electrical Engineering; Electronic Engineering; Heating and Refrigeration; Industrial Engineering; Technology)

Programmes

Environmental Science (Environmental Management; Environmental Studies); **Graduate Studies** (Art Education; Business Administration; Chemistry; Education; Educational Administration; Educational and Student Counselling; English; Filipino; Foreign Languages Education; Government; Health Education; Home Economics Education; Mathematics Education; Native Language Education; Nursing; Physical Education; Physics; Police Studies; Public Administration; Science Education; Statistics); **Industrial Education** (Automotive Engineering; Electrical Engineering; Electronic Engineering; Home Economics; Industrial Arts Education)

History: Founded 1902 as Trade School, became Northern Luzon School of Arts and Trades 1951, acquired present status and title 1965.

Governing Bodies: Board of Regents

Academic Year: June to March (June-October; November-March)

Admission Requirements: Graduation from high school or recognized foreign equivalent, and entrance examination

Main Language(s) of Instruction: Filipino, English, Ilocano

Degrees and Diplomas: *Certificate/Diploma*; *Associate Degree*; *Bachelor's Degree*; *Master's Degree*: Arts in Teaching (English; Filipino; Home Economics; Health Education; Physical Education; Practical Arts; Nursing); Science in Teaching (Physics; Chemistry); Arts in: Business Administration; Education (Mathematics Education; Guidance; Educational Management; Science Education); Mathematics Education; Nursing; Social Work; Public Administration (Local Government; Governmental Administration; Police Administration); Statistics; *PhD*: Education (Educational Management and Supervision); Business Administration; Public Administration

Student Residential Facilities: Yes

Special Facilities: Ilocano Museum

Libraries: Central Library, c. 9,000 vols; Graduate School, c. 1,000

Publications: New Vision *(biannually)*; Tandem *(quarterly)*

Last Updated: 07/03/11

UNIVERSITY OF PASAY CITY

Pamantasan ng Lungsod ng Pasay

Pasadeña Street, Pasay City, Fourth District, Metro Manila 1300

Tel: +63(2) 551-0525

President: Yolanda F. Cruz

Programmes

Graduate (Education); **Undergraduate and Professional** (Accountancy; Business Administration; Business and Commerce; Computer Science; Education; English; Filipino; Foreign Languages Education; History; Hotel and Restaurant; Hotel Management; Law; Management; Marketing; Mass Communication; Mathematics Education; Midwifery; Native Language Education; Nursing; Political Sciences; Primary Education; Secondary Education; Secretarial Studies; Software Engineering)

History: Founded 1994.

Degrees and Diplomas: *Associate Degree*; *Bachelor's Degree*; *Master's Degree*: Education

Last Updated: 19/01/11

UNIVERSITY OF PASIG CITY

Pamantasan ng Lungsod ng Pasig (PLP)

Alcalde Jose Street, Kapasigan, City of Pasig, Second District, Metro Manila 1600

Tel: +63(2) 628-1014

Fax: +63(2) 628-1015

EMail: admin@plp.edu.ph

Website: http://www.plp.edu.ph

President: Rosalinda V. Tirona

Colleges

Business Administration (Accountancy; Business Administration; Management); **Computer Science** (Computer Science; Mathematics); **Education** (Education; Foreign Languages Education; Native Language Education; Preschool Education; Primary Education; Science Education; Secondary Education); **Engineering** (Electronic Engineering; Engineering; Telecommunications Engineering); **Hospitality Management** (Cooking and Catering; Hotel and Restaurant; Hotel Management; Tourism); **Information Technology** (Information Technology); **Nursing**

History: Founded 2000.

Degrees and Diplomas: *Associate Degree*; *Bachelor's Degree*

Last Updated: 19/01/11

UNIVERSITY OF RIZAL SYSTEM - TANAY (MAIN CAMPUS) (URS)

University Main Campus, Sampaloc, Tanay, Rizal 1980

Tel: +63(2) 674-2545

Fax: +63(2) 674-2543

EMail: olive_deleon@yahoo.com

Website: http://www.urs.edu.ph

President: Olivia F. De Leon

Tel: +63(2) 653-1735, Fax: +63(2) 674-1735

Vice-President for Administration and Finance: Demetria A. San Juan Tel: +63 691-6081, Fax: +63 653-1082

Programmes

Agriculture (Agricultural Engineering; Agricultural Equipment; Agriculture; Agronomy; Animal Husbandry; Forestry; Harvest Technology; Zoology); **Arts and Science** (Biology; English; Mathematics; Political Sciences; Psychology; Public Administration; Tourism); **Business Administration** (Banking; Business Administration; Finance; Management; Management Systems; Marketing; Secretarial Studies); **Education** (Computer Science; Curriculum; English; Filipino; Foreign Languages Education; Home Economics Education; Mathematics Education; Native Language Education; Primary Education; Secondary Education; Technology Education); **Environmental Sciences** (Environmental Studies); **Home Technology** (Home Economics; Technology)

History: Founded 2001 through merger of the Rizal Polytechnic College, Rizal State College and the Rizal Technological University extension campus.

Governing Bodies: Board of Regents

Admission Requirements: Secondary school certificate and entrance examination

Main Language(s) of Instruction: Filipino, English

Accrediting Agencies: Accrediting Agency of Chartered Colleges and Universities in the Philippines (AACCUP)

Degrees and Diplomas: *Bachelor's Degree*; *Master's Degree*: Agriculture (Crop Science; Animal Science; Agricultural Management); *PhD*: Agriculture (Agronomy)

Student Services: Academic counselling, Cultural centre, Employment services, Handicapped facilities, Health services, Language programs, Sports facilities

Student Residential Facilities: Dormitory

Special Facilities: Museum; Auditorium; Gymnasium; Language Learning Centre; Audio-Visual Education Centre; Medical and Dental Clinic; Research and Production Centre; Agronomy Building

Libraries: Yes. Also E-Library.

Last Updated: 08/03/11

UNIVERSITY OF RIZAL SYSTEM - ANGONO

Angono, Rizal 1930

Tel: +63(2) 451-0102

Fax: +63(2) 651-0346

Chancellor: Gloria P. Sarabia

Programmes

Arts and Science (Biology; English; Journalism; Mass Communication; Mathematics; Political Sciences; Psychology; Public Administration; Tourism); **Elementary Education** (Curriculum; Educational and Student Counselling; English; Filipino; Foreign Languages Education; Health Education; Home Economics Education; Native Language Education; Preschool Education; Primary Education; Science Education; Technology Education); **Fine Arts** (Advertising and Publicity; Fine Arts); **Hotel and Restaurant Management** (Hotel and Restaurant; Hotel Management); **Music** (Music; Music Education); **Secondary Education** (Art Education; Computer Education; Curriculum; English; Filipino; Foreign Languages Education; Health Education; History; Mathematics Education; Music Education; Native Language Education; Physical Education; Science Education; Secondary Education; Social Studies)

Degrees and Diplomas: *Certificate/Diploma*; *Bachelor's Degree*

UNIVERSITY OF RIZAL SYSTEM - ANTIPOLO

Marigman Street, Barangay San Roque, Antipolo City, Rizal 1970

Tel: +63(2) 696-3496

Fax: +63(2) 697-1362

President: Olivia F. de Leon

Programmes

Arts and Science (Biology; English; Political Sciences; Psychology; Tourism); **Business Administration** (Banking; Business Administration; Finance; Management; Management Systems; Marketing; Secretarial Studies); **Education** (Biological and Life Sciences; English; Foreign Languages Education; Mathematics Education; Physical Education; Primary Education; Science Education; Secondary Education); **Graduate** (Business Administration; Education; Educational Administration; Educational and Student Counselling; Mathematics Education; Physical Education; Public Administration; Science Education; Teacher Training); **Hotel and Restaurant Management** (Hotel and Restaurant; Hotel Management)

Degrees and Diplomas: *Certificate/Diploma*; *Bachelor's Degree*; *Master's Degree*: Education (Educational Management; Guidance and Counselling); Business Administration; Public Administration; Teaching (Physical Education; Mathematics; Science)

UNIVERSITY OF RIZAL SYSTEM - BINANGONAN

Manila East Road, Calumpang, Binangonan, Rizal 1940

Tel: +63(2) 652-1018

Fax: +63(2) 652-1018

Chancellor: Gloria P. Sarabia

Programmes

Business Administration and Accountancy (Accountancy; Banking; Business Administration; Economics; Finance; Information Management; Information Technology; Marketing); **Graduate** (Business Administration; Management; Public Administration); **Information Management** (Information Management); **Office Administration** (Management Systems; Secretarial Studies)

Degrees and Diplomas: *Certificate/Diploma*; *Bachelor's Degree*; *Master's Degree*: Business Administration; Management; Public Administration; *PhD*: Public Administration

UNIVERSITY OF RIZAL SYSTEM - CAINTA

Cainta, Rizal 1900
Tel: +63(2) 248-0860
Fax: +63(2) 653-3020

Chancellor: Reneecilia B. Paz de Leon

Programmes

Elementary Education (Curriculum; English; Foreign Languages Education; Mathematics Education; Primary Education; Science Education); **Secondary Education** (English; Foreign Languages Education; Home Economics Education; Mathematics Education; Physics; Secondary Education; Technology Education); **Technology** (Automotive Engineering; Electrical Engineering; Electronic Engineering; Hotel and Restaurant; Hotel Management; Technology)

History: Founded 1999.

Degrees and Diplomas: *Certificate/Diploma*; *Bachelor's Degree*

UNIVERSITY OF RIZAL SYSTEM - CARDONA

Dalig, Cardona, Rizal 1950
Tel: +63(2) 653-1159

Campus Director: Alex C. Pili

Programmes

Fishery (Fishery)

History: Founded 2000.

Degrees and Diplomas: *Bachelor's Degree*

UNIVERSITY OF RIZAL SYSTEM - MORONG

Sumulong Street, Morong, Rizal 1960
Tel: +63(2) 653-1735
Fax: +63(2) 653-1082

President: Olivia F. de Leon

Programmes

Engineering and Technology (Automotive Engineering; Civil Engineering; Computer Engineering; Electrical Engineering; Electronic Engineering; Hotel and Restaurant; Hotel Management; Mechanical Engineering; Production Engineering; Telecommunications Engineering); **Graduate** (Education; Educational Administration; Educational and Student Counselling; English; Filipino; Foreign Languages Education; Home Economics Education; Management; Mathematics Education; Native Language Education; Physical Education; Science Education; Social Studies; Teacher Training; Technology Education); **Industrial Education** (Automotive Engineering; Electrical Engineering; Electronic Engineering; Industrial Arts Education; Technology; Technology Education); **Information Management** (Information Management); **Primary Education** (Art Education; Curriculum; Education; English; Foreign Languages Education; Health Education; Library Science; Mathematics Education; Music Education; Physical Education; Preschool Education; Primary Education; Science Education; Special Education); **Science** (Biology; Computer Science; Educational and Student Counselling; Mathematics; Mechanical Engineering; Psychology); **Secondary Education** (Biological and Life Sciences; Chemistry; English; Foreign Languages Education; Home Economics Education; Mathematics Education; Physics; Secondary Education; Technology Education); **Technician Teacher Education** (Automotive Engineering; Civil Engineering; Electrical and Electronic Engineering; Mechanical Engineering; Production Engineering; Technology Education)

History: Founded 1944.

Degrees and Diplomas: *Certificate/Diploma*; *Bachelor's Degree*; *Master's Degree*: Management; Education (Guidance and Counselling; Educational Management); Teaching (Social Studies; Science and Technology; Physical Education; Mathematics; English; Technology and Home Economics; Filipino); *PhD*: Education (Educational Management)

UNIVERSITY OF RIZAL SYSTEM - PILILIA

Pililia, Rizal 1910
Tel: +63(2) 674-3558

Chancellor: Gloria P. Sarabia

Programmes

Graduate (Business Administration; Education; Educational Administration; English; Filipino; Foreign Languages Education; Home Economics Education; Mathematics Education; Native Language Education; Physical Education; Public Administration; Social Studies; Teacher Training); **Undergraduate and Professional** (Accountancy; Banking; Biological and Life Sciences; Business Administration; Civil Engineering; Computer Education; Curriculum; Education; English; Finance; Foreign Languages Education; Geological Engineering; History; Hotel and Restaurant; Hotel Management; Management; Management Systems; Marketing; Mathematics Education; Physical Education; Political Sciences; Primary Education; Psychology; Public Administration; Science Education; Secondary Education; Secretarial Studies; Social Studies)

Degrees and Diplomas: *Certificate/Diploma*; *Associate Degree*; *Bachelor's Degree*; *Master's Degree*: Business Administration; Public Administration; Education (Educational Management; Physical Education; Home Economics); Teaching (English; Mathematics; Social Studies; Filipino); *PhD*: Public Administration; Educational Management

UNIVERSITY OF RIZAL SYSTEM - RODRIGUEZ

Amityville, San Jose, Rodriguez, Rizal 1860
Tel: +63(2) 997-9765
Fax: +63(2) 997-9765

Campus Director: Allen U. Bautista

Programmes

Graduate (Business Administration; Education; Educational Administration; Educational and Student Counselling; English; Filipino; Foreign Languages Education; Mathematics Education; Native Language Education; Public Administration; Science Education; Teacher Training); **Undergraduate and Professional** (Agricultural Engineering; Art Education; Banking; Biological and Life Sciences; Business Administration; Curriculum; Development Studies; Education; English; Filipino; Finance; Foreign Languages Education; History; Home Economics Education; Management; Management Systems; Marketing; Mathematics; Mathematics Education; Music Education; Native Language Education; Physical Education; Political Sciences; Primary Education; Psychology; Science Education; Secondary Education; Secretarial Studies; Social and Community Services; Social Work; Tourism)

Degrees and Diplomas: *Certificate/Diploma*; *Associate Degree*; *Bachelor's Degree*; *Master's Degree*: Business Administration; Public Administration; Arts in Education (Guidance and Counselling; Educational Management); Arts in Teaching (Filipino; Science Education; English; Mathematics)

UNIVERSITY OF RIZAL SYSTEM - TAYTAY

Highway 2000, Taytay, Rizal 1920
Tel: +63(2) 401-7928
EMail: urs_taytaycampus@yahoo.com

Campus Director: Concepcion C. Ofamen

Programmes

Undergraduate and Professional (Business Administration; Civil Engineering; Education; English; Foreign Languages Education;

Home Economics Education; Management; Nursing; Secondary Education; Technology Education; Textile Technology)

Degrees and Diplomas: *Bachelor's Degree*

UNIVERSITY OF SOUTHEASTERN PHILIPPINES (USEP)

Bo. Obrero, Davao City, Davao del Sur 8000
Tel: +63(82) 221-7737
Fax: +63(82) 221-7738
Website: http://www.usep.edu.ph

President: Perfecto A. Alibin

Vice-President for Administration: Rodulfo Sumugat

International Relations: Adelaide Pagkalunagan
EMail: pio@usep.edu.ph

Campuses

Bislig (Art Education; Automotive Engineering; Civil Engineering; Education; Electrical Engineering; Electronic Engineering; English; Foreign Languages Education; Forestry; Mechanical Engineering; Music Education; Physical Education; Secondary Education); **Mabini** (Agricultural Economics; Agricultural Education; Agricultural Engineering; Agriculture; Agronomy; Communication Arts; Crop Production; Education; Educational Administration; English; Environmental Engineering; Foreign Languages Education; Forest Products; Forestry; Health Education; Home Economics Education; Horticulture; Information Technology; Literacy Education; Mathematics Education; Natural Resources; Plant and Crop Protection; Science Education; Soil Science; Technology Education); **Mintal** (Agricultural Business; Agricultural Economics; Agricultural Engineering; Anthropology; Biology; Business Administration; Development Studies; Education; Educational Administration; English; Farm Management; Filipino; Foreign Languages Education; Mathematics Education; Native Language Education; Primary Education; Public Administration; Science Education); **Tagum - College of Agriculture** (Agricultural Economics; Agricultural Engineering; Agriculture; Agronomy; Animal Husbandry; Communication Arts; Crop Production; Education; Educational Administration; Educational Research; English; Environmental Engineering; Foreign Languages Education; Forest Products; Forestry; Harvest Technology; Health Education; Home Economics; Horticulture; Information Technology; Literacy Education; Mathematics Education; Natural Resources; Plant and Crop Protection; Primary Education; Science Education; Secondary Education; Soil Science; Technology Education; Water Management; Water Science; Zoology)

Colleges

Arts and Science (Applied Linguistics; Applied Mathematics; Arts and Humanities; Biology; Linguistics; Literature; Mathematics; Modern Languages; Natural Sciences; Statistics); **Education** (Art Education; Biological and Life Sciences; Biology; Communication Studies; Education; Educational Administration; Educational and Student Counselling; Educational Sciences; English; Filipino; Foreign Languages Education; Health Education; Home Economics Education; Music Education; Native Language Education; Physical Education; Physics; Primary Education; Science Education; Secondary Education; Special Education; Teacher Training); **Engineering** (Civil Engineering; Electrical and Electronic Engineering; Engineering; Geological Engineering; Mechanical Engineering; Metallurgical Engineering; Mining Engineering; Telecommunications Engineering); **Governance, Business and Economics** (Agricultural Business; Agricultural Economics; Business Administration; Development Studies; Economics; Environmental Management; Environmental Studies; Government; Management; Public Administration; Taxation); **Technology** (Computer Engineering; Industrial Engineering; Technology; Technology Education)

Institutes

Computing (Computer Science; Information Sciences; Information Technology)

History: Founded 1978.

Governing Bodies: Board of Regents

Academic Year: June to March (June-October; November-March)

Admission Requirements: Graduation from high school and entrance examination

Fees: (Pesos): Undergraduate, 100 per unit; Graduate, 300 per unit

Main Language(s) of Instruction: English

International Co-operation: With universities in South Korea, Australia, USA

Accrediting Agencies: Accrediting Agency of Chartered Colleges and Universities in the Philippines (AACCUP)

Degrees and Diplomas: *Certificate/Diploma*: Arts, Technology, 2-3 yrs; *Bachelor's Degree*: Agri-Business; Agri-Economics; Agricultural Economics; Computer Technology; Industrial Technology; Technology Education; Agricultural Education; Extension Education; Agricultural Technology; Biology; Computer Science; Information Technology; Economics; Agriculture; Community Development; English; Forestry; Industrial Education; Industrial Technology; Mathematics; Public Administration; Elementary Education; Secondary Education; Statistics, 4 yrs; *Bachelor's Degree*: Agricultural Engineering; Civil Engineering; Electrical Engineering; Mechanical Engineering; Electronics and Communications Engineering, 5 yrs; *Master's Degree*: Business Administration; Education; Engineering; Information Technology; Econometrics; Economics; Environmental and Resource Management; Development Communication; Local and Regional Governance; Public Administration; Development Administration; Industrial Technology; Vocational Technology; Forestry; Professional Studies in Development Education; Extension Education; Agriculture; Agricultural Engineering; Teaching Mathematics; Applied Mathematics; Biology; Language Teaching; Instructional Leadership, a further 2-3 yrs; *PhD*: Education (Educational Planning and Management); Philosophy (Horticulture), 2-5 yrs following Master. Also Graduate Diploma in Econometrics and Economics: 2 yrs

Student Services: Academic counselling, Employment services, Health services, Language programs, Social counselling

Special Facilities: Speech Laboratory

Libraries: Total, c. 12,000 vols

Publications: Southeastern Philippines Journal of Research and Development *(biannually)*

Last Updated: 11/03/11

UNIVERSITY OF SOUTHERN MINDANAO (USM)

USM Avenue, Kabacan, Cotabato 9407
Tel: +63(64) 248-2138
Fax: +63(64) 248-2138
Website: http://www.usm.edu.ph

President: Jesus Antonio Derije

Campuses

Kidapawan City (Automotive Engineering; Civil Engineering; Electrical and Electronic Engineering; Food Technology; Heating and Refrigeration; Industrial Arts Education; Industrial Engineering; Mechanical Engineering; Metal Techniques; Technology; Technology Education)

Colleges

Agriculture (Agriculture; Agronomy; Animal Husbandry; Entomology; Farm Management; Genetics; Horticulture; Plant and Crop Protection; Plant Pathology; Soil Science); **Arts and Science** (Applied Chemistry; Arts and Humanities; Behavioural Sciences; Biology; Chemistry; Communication Studies; English; Information Sciences; Journalism; Library Science; Modern Languages; Natural Sciences; Psychology); **Business, Development Economics and Management** (Accountancy; Agricultural Business; Agricultural Economics; Business Administration; Development Studies; Human Resources; Management; Marketing); **Education** (Art Education; Biological and Life Sciences; Education; English; Filipino; Foreign Languages Education; Home Economics Education; Mathematics Education; Music Education; Native Language Education; Physical Education; Physics; Primary Education; Secondary Education; Social Studies; Technology Education); **Education** *(Buluan Extension)* (Education; Primary Education; Secondary Education); **Engineering and Computing** (Agricultural Engineering; Civil Engineering; Computer Engineering; Computer Science; Electronic Engineering; Engineering; Information Management; Information Technology; Technology Education); **Graduate** (Agricultural Economics; Agricultural Education; Agricultural Engineering; Agriculture; Agronomy; Aquaculture; Biology; Communication Studies; Crop Production; Education; Educational Administration; English; Filipino; Foreign Languages Education; Home Economics Education; Horticulture; Industrial Arts Education; Information

Management; Islamic Studies; Mathematics Education; Native Language Education; Plant and Crop Protection; Public Administration; Rural Planning; Rural Studies; Soil Science; Zoology); **Human Ecology and Food Sciences** (Dietetics; Food Technology; Hotel and Restaurant; Hotel Management; Nutrition; Tourism); **Industry and Technology** *(Department of Industrial Technology)* (Automotive Engineering; Electrical Engineering; Heating and Refrigeration; Industrial Engineering; Mechanical Equipment and Maintenance; Mechanics; Metal Techniques; Structural Architecture); **Nursing** (Midwifery; Nursing); **Veterinary Medicine** (Veterinary Science)

Institutes

Middle East and Asian Studies (Asian Studies; International Relations; Islamic Studies; Middle Eastern Studies)

Further Information: Also Centre of Excellence in Agriculture Education and Nodal Centre in Biology.

History: Founded 1954 as Mindanao Institute of Technology, acquired present status and title 1978.

Governing Bodies: Board of Regents

Academic Year: June to March

Admission Requirements: Graduation from high school and entrance examination (USMICET)

Fees: (Pesos): 40 per unit

Main Language(s) of Instruction: Filipino, English

Accrediting Agencies: Accrediting Agency of Chartered Colleges and Universities of the Philippines (AACCUP)

Degrees and Diplomas: *Bachelor's Degree*; *Master's Degree*; *PhD*: Education (Educational Management); Agricultural Sciences (Agricultural Education; Seed Technology; Extension Education; Soil Science; Crop Protection; Crop Production and Management; Animal Science); Extension Education; Rural Development

Student Services: Academic counselling, Cultural centre, Employment services, Health services, Social counselling, Sports facilities

Libraries: c. 500,000 vols; internet facilities

Publications: RDEP Monitor *(quarterly)*; USM Abstract Bibliography *(annually)*; USM CA Research Journal *(biannually)*; USM R & D Journal *(biannually)*

Press or Publishing House: USM Multi-media Center and GP Printing Press, Davao City

Last Updated: 11/03/11

UNIVERSITY OF TAGUIG CITY

Pamantasan ng Lungsod ng Taguig

Sunshine Mall, FTI, Taguig City, Fourth District, Metro Manila
Tel: +63(2) 628-1999
Fax: +63(2) 642-3588

Vice-President, Academic and Student Affairs: Anna Maria Theresa N. Umali

Programmes

Business Administration (Agricultural Business; Business Administration; Management; Marketing); **Computer Science** (Computer Science); **Criminology** (Criminology); **Hotel and Restaurant Management** (Hotel and Restaurant; Hotel Management); **Industrial Technology** (Automotive Engineering; Electrical Engineering; Electronic Engineering; Food Technology; Heating and Refrigeration; Industrial Engineering; Metal Techniques; Textile Technology); **Tourism** (Tourism)

History: Founded 2006.

Degrees and Diplomas: *Bachelor's Degree*

Last Updated: 19/01/11

UNIVERSITY OF THE CITY OF MANILA

Pamantasan ng Lungsod ng Maynila (PLM)

Gen. Luna Corner Muralla Streets, Intramuros, City of Manila, First District, Metro Manila 1002
Tel: +63(2) 527-7941
Fax: +63(2) 527-3552
EMail: info@plm.edu.ph
Website: http://www.plm.edu.ph

President: Adel A. Tamano
Tel: +63(2) 527-3551, Fax: +63(2) 528-4594
EMail: president@plm.edu.ph

Vice-President for Administration: Danilo A. Baluyot

International Relations: Tio Jacob
Tel: +63(2) 528-4584, Fax: +63(2) 528-4594
EMail: oiil@plm.edu.ph

Colleges

Accountancy and Economics (Accountancy; Economics); **Architecture and Urban Planning** (Architecture; Town Planning); **Engineering and Technology** (Chemical Engineering; Civil Engineering; Communication Studies; Computer Science; Electrical and Electronic Engineering; Engineering; Industrial Engineering; Mechanical Engineering; Production Engineering; Technology; Telecommunications Engineering); **Human Development** (Clinical Psychology; Industrial and Organizational Psychology; Psychology; Social Work; Teacher Training); **Law** (Law); **Liberal Arts** (Arts and Humanities; English; Filipino; Social Sciences); **Management and Entrepreneurship** (Banking; Business Administration; Finance; Management; Marketing; Public Administration); **Mass Communication** (Mass Communication); **Medicine** (Community Health; Health Sciences; Medicine); **Nursing** (Midwifery; Nursing); **Physical Education, Recreation and Sports** (Parks and Recreation; Physical Education; Sports); **Physical Therapy** (Physical Therapy); **Science** (Biology; Biotechnology; Chemistry; Mathematics; Physics); **Tourism, Hotel and Travel Industry Management** (Hotel and Restaurant; Hotel Management; Tourism)

Graduate Schools

Arts, Sciences and Education (Arts and Humanities; Education; Mass Communication; Mathematics; Natural Sciences; Nursing; Psychology); **Engineering** (Computer Engineering; Electronic Engineering; Engineering; Engineering Management); **Health Sciences** (Health Sciences; Nursing); **Law** (Law); **Management** (Business Administration; Government; Management)

History: Founded 1967. Responsible to the authorities of the City of Manila.

Governing Bodies: Board of Regents; University Council

Academic Year: June to March (June-October; November-March)

Admission Requirements: Graduation from high school and entrance examination

Main Language(s) of Instruction: Filipino, English

Accrediting Agencies: Association of Local Colleges and Universities - Commission on Accreditation

Degrees and Diplomas: *Bachelor's Degree*; *Post Baccalaureate Certificate/Diploma*; *Master's Degree*: Business Administration; Government Management; Communication; Communication Management; Education (Biological Science; Social Studies; Educational Administration; Physical Science); Engineering Management; Science in Mathematics Education; Family Science; Nursing; Psychology (Clinical; Industrial); School Principalship; Engineering (System Management; Construction Management; Structural Engineering; Manufacturing; Computer Engineering); *PhD*: Business Administration; Education; Public Management

Student Services: Academic counselling, Canteen, Cultural centre, Employment services, Health services, Language programs, Nursery care, Social counselling, Sports facilities

Libraries: c. 50,000 vols

Last Updated: 07/01/11

UNIVERSITY OF THE PHILIPPINES SYSTEM (U.P. DILIMAN)

Diliman, Quezon City, Second District, Metro Manila 1101
Tel: +63(2) 981-8500 +63(2) 436-7537
Fax: +63(2) 926-1572 +63(2) 928-3014
EMail: upsio@up.edu.ph
Website: http://www.up.edu.ph/

President: Alfredo E. Pascual (2011-) EMail: op@up.edu.ph

Vice-President for Administration, UP System: Maragtas Sofronio V. Amante

Vice-President for Academic Affairs: Gisela P. Concepcion

Centres

Asian Studies (Asian Studies; East Asian Studies; South Asian Studies; Southeast Asian Studies); **Statistics** (Statistics); **Technology Management** (Engineering Management; Technology); **Third World Studies Programme**

Colleges

Architecture (Architecture; Building Technologies; Landscape Architecture); **Arts and Letters** (American Studies; Art Criticism; Art History; Arts and Humanities; Asian Studies; Communication Studies; Comparative Literature; English Studies; European Languages; Filipino; French; French Studies; German; Germanic Studies; Italian; Literature; Modern Languages; Spanish; Speech Studies; Theatre; Writing); **Business Administration** (Accountancy; Business Administration; Finance; Management); **Education** (Anthropology; Art Education; Biology; Chemistry; Communication Arts; Curriculum; Education; Educational Administration; Educational and Student Counselling; Educational Psychology; Educational Testing and Evaluation; English; Filipino; Foreign Languages Education; Health Administration; Health Education; Literacy Education; Mathematics Education; Modern Languages; Native Language Education; Philosophy of Education; Physics; Preschool Education; Primary Education; Science Education; Secondary Education; Social Studies; Special Education); **Engineering** (Chemical Engineering; Civil Engineering; Computer Engineering; Computer Science; Electrical and Electronic Engineering; Electrical Engineering; Electronic Engineering; Energy Engineering; Engineering; Environmental Engineering; Industrial Engineering; Materials Engineering; Mechanical Engineering; Metallurgical Engineering; Mining Engineering; Surveying and Mapping; Telecommunications Engineering; Thermal Engineering; Water Science); **Fine Arts** (Art Education; Art History; Communication Arts; Fine Arts; Industrial Design; Painting and Drawing; Sculpture; Visual Arts); **Home Economics** (Child Care and Development; Clothing and Sewing; Community Health; Family Studies; Food Science; Food Technology; Home Economics; Hotel and Restaurant; Hotel Management; Interior Design; Nutrition; Textile Technology); **Human Kinetics** (Physical Education; Sports); **Law** (Law); **Mass Communication** (Communication Studies; Film; Journalism; Mass Communication; Radio and Television Broadcasting; Visual Arts); **Music** (Conducting; Music; Music Education; Music Theory and Composition; Musical Instruments; Musicology; Performing Arts); **Public Administration and Governance** *(National College)* (Government; Public Administration; Regional Planning); **Science** (Applied Mathematics; Applied Physics; Biology; Biotechnology; Cell Biology; Chemistry; Computer Science; Ecology; Environmental Studies; Genetics; Geology; Marine Biology; Marine Science and Oceanography; Materials Engineering; Mathematics; Meteorology; Microbiology; Molecular Biology; Natural Sciences; Operations Research; Physics; Physiology); **Social Sciences and Philosophy** (Anthropology; Demography and Population; Geography; Geography (Human); History; International Studies; Linguistics; Philosophy; Political Sciences; Psychology; Social Sciences; Sociology); **Social Work and Community Development** (Social Work; Urban Studies; Women's Studies)

Institutes

Islamic Studies (Islamic Studies); **Library and Information Sciences** (Information Sciences; Library Science); **Tourism** *(Asian Institute of Tourism)* (Tourism)

Programmes

Archaeological Studies (Archaeology)

Research Centres

Applied Geodesy and Photogrammetry *(Training Centre)* (Civil Engineering; Earth Sciences); **Building Research Service** (Building Technologies); **Hydraulics** *(National Centre)*; **Leadership, Citizenship and Democracy** (Leadership); **Local and Regional Governance** (Government); **Policy and Executive Development** (Administration); **Science and Mathematics Education Development** (Mathematics Education; Science Education)

Research Institutes

Biology (Biology); **Chemistry** (Chemistry); **Geological Sciences** *(National)* (Geology); **Government and Law Reform** (Government; Law); **Human Rights** (Human Rights); **Judicial Administration**; **Legal Studies** (International Law); **Marine Science** (Marine Science and Oceanography); **Molecular Biology and Biotechnology** *(NIMBB-UPD)* (Biotechnology; Molecular Biology); **Natural Sciences** (Natural Sciences); **Physics** *(National)* (Physics); **Population** (Demography and Population); **Small Scale Industries** (Small Business); **Transportation Studies** *(National)* (Engineering; Management; Transport Management)

Schools

Economics (Economics); **Labour and Industrial Relations** (Human Resources; Labour and Industrial Relations); **Urban and Regional Planning** (Regional Planning; Town Planning; Transport Management)

Further Information: Also Extension Programmes in Pampanga and Olongapo City. Diliman (Olongapo City) and Diliman (Pampanga) campuses

History: Founded 1908. An autonomous unit of the University System. Acquired current status 1982

Governing Bodies: Board of Regents

Academic Year: June to May (June-October; November-March; April-May)

Fees: (Pesos): c. 300 per unit

Main Language(s) of Instruction: Filipino, English

International Co-operation: Participates in the Programme of Southeast Asian Area Studies with Academica Senica; La Trobe University; University of Montreal; Kansai University; Northern Territory University

Degrees and Diplomas: *Certificate/Diploma*; *Bachelor's Degree*; *Master's Degree*; *PhD*

Student Services: Academic counselling, Canteen, Cultural centre, Employment services, Foreign student adviser, Foreign Studies Centre, Health services, Language programs, Social counselling, Sports facilities

Special Facilities: Vargas Museum. UP Film Center. Radio Station. Marine Biological Station. Science and Technology Park

Libraries: Central Library, c. 1,100,000 vols; c. 40,000 serial titles; c. 26,000 microforms

Publications: Alipato, Journal of Basic Education *(biannually)*; Asian Studies *(biannually)*; Carillon *(monthly)*; Diliman Review *(monthly)*; Economics Observer *(bimonthly)*; Education Quarterly *(quarterly)*; Home Economics Journal *(biannually)*; Human Rights Agenda *(monthly)*; Index to Philippine Periodicals *(biannually)*; Journal of Communication Studies *(annually)*; Journal of Industrial Relations *(biannually)*; Journal of Industrial Relations *(biannually)*; Law and Development *(annually)*; Law Monitor *(monthly)*; Natural and Applied Sciences Bulletin *(quarterly)*; Philippine Engineering Journal *(quarterly)*; Philippine Journal of Labour and Industrial Relations *(biannually)*; Philippine Journal of Public Administration *(quarterly)*; Philippine Journal of Veterinary Medicine *(biannually)*; Philippine Law Journal *(quarterly)*; Philippine Planning Journal *(biannually)*; Philippine Social Sciences and Humanities Review *(quarterly)*; Review of Business and Economics *(quarterly)*; Science Diliman *(biannually)*; The Acta Medica Philippina Journal *(quarterly)*; The National Administrative Register *(biannually)*; The Philippine Review of Business and Economics *(biannually)*; The Pterocarpus Journal *(biannually)*

Last Updated: 17/03/11

UNIVERSITY OF THE PHILIPPINES - DILIMAN

Diliman, Quezon City, Second District, Metro Manila 1101
Tel: +63(2) 981-8500
Fax: +63(2) 920-5302
Website: http://www.upd.edu.ph/

Chancellor: Caesar Saloma EMail: oc.upd@up.edu.ph

Centres

Statistics

Colleges

Architecture (Architecture; Building Technologies; Landscape Architecture); **Arts and Letters** (Art History; Asian Studies; Comparative Literature; English; English Studies; European Languages; Filipino; French; German; Italian; Performing Arts; Russian; Spanish; Speech Studies; Theatre; Writing); **Business Administration** (Accountancy; Business Administration); **Education** (Art Education; Biology; Chemistry; Education; Educational

Administration; Educational Technology; English; Filipino; Foreign Languages Education; Health Education; Humanities and Social Science Education; Mathematics Education; Native Language Education; Physics; Preschool Education; Primary Education; Science Education; Secondary Education; Social Studies; Special Education); **Engineering** (Chemical Engineering; Civil Engineering; Computer Engineering; Computer Science; Electrical and Electronic Engineering; Engineering; Geological Engineering; Industrial Engineering; Mechanical Engineering; Metallurgical Engineering; Mining Engineering; Operations Research; Telecommunications Engineering); **Fine Arts** (Art Education; Art History; Communication Arts; Fine Arts; Industrial Design; Painting and Drawing; Sculpture; Visual Arts); **Home Economics** (Child Care and Development; Clothing and Sewing; Family Studies; Food Technology; Home Economics; Hotel and Restaurant; Hotel Management; Interior Design; Nutrition; Textile Design); **Human Kinetics** (Physical Education; Sports); **Law** (Administrative Law; Constitutional Law; Criminal Law; Government; Human Rights; Insurance; International Law; Justice Administration; Labour Law; Law; Private Law; Public Law; Taxation); **Mass Communication** (Communication Studies; Film; Journalism; Mass Communication; Radio and Television Broadcasting); **Music** (Conducting; Dance; Music; Music Education; Music Theory and Composition; Musical Instruments; Performing Arts; Singing; Theatre); **Public Administration and Governance** *(National)* (Government; Public Administration); **Science** (Applied Physics; Biology; Biotechnology; Chemistry; Environmental Studies; Geology; Marine Science and Oceanography; Mathematics; Mathematics and Computer Science; Meteorology; Molecular Biology; Natural Sciences; Physics); **Social Sciences and Philosophy** (Anthropology; Geography; Geography (Human); History; Linguistics; Philosophy; Political Sciences; Psychology; Social Sciences; Sociology); **Social Work and Community Development** (Development Studies; Social and Community Services; Social Work)

Institutes

Islamic Studies (Islamic Studies); **Library and Information Studies** (Information Sciences; Library Science); **Tourism** *(Asian)* (Tourism)

Programmes

Graduate Studies (Accountancy; Actuarial Science; Administration; Anthropology; Applied Mathematics; Architectural and Environmental Design; Architecture; Art Criticism; Art Education; Art History; Asian Studies; Bioengineering; Biology; Biotechnology; Business Administration; Cell Biology; Chemical Engineering; Chemistry; Child Care and Development; Civil Engineering; Communication Studies; Comparative Literature; Computer Science; Conducting; Cultural Studies; Curriculum; Dance; Demography and Population; Development Studies; Ecology; Economics; Education; Educational Administration; Educational and Student Counselling; Educational Psychology; Educational Research; Educational Technology; Educational Testing and Evaluation; Electrical Engineering; Electronic Engineering; Energy Engineering; Engineering; English; English Studies; Environmental Engineering; Environmental Studies; Family Studies; Filipino; Fine Arts; Food Science; Foreign Languages Education; French; Genetics; Geography; Geography (Human); Geology; Government; Health Education; History; Home Economics; Human Resources; Industrial Engineering; Information Sciences; International Studies; Islamic Studies; Journalism; Labour and Industrial Relations; Landscape Architecture; Library Science; Linguistics; Literacy Education; Management; Marine Biology; Marine Science and Oceanography; Materials Engineering; Mathematics; Mathematics Education; Mechanical Engineering; Metallurgical Engineering; Meteorology; Microbiology; Modern Languages; Molecular Biology; Music; Music Education; Music Theory and Composition; Musical Instruments; Musicology; Native Language Education; Nutrition; Operations Research; Performing Arts; Philosophy; Philosophy of Education; Physical Education; Physics; Physiology; Political Sciences; Prehistory; Preschool Education; Psychology; Public Administration; Radio and Television Broadcasting; Real Estate; Regional Planning; Singing; Social Studies; Social Work; Sociology; Spanish; Special Education; Speech Studies; Statistics; Surveying and Mapping; Taxation; Theatre; Thermal Engineering; Town Planning; Translation and Interpretation; Transport and Communications; Water Science; Women's Studies; Writing)

Schools

Economics (Economics); **Labour and Industrial Relations** (Human Resources; Labour and Industrial Relations); **Urban and Regional Planning** (Regional Planning; Town Planning)

Further Information: Extensions Programmes in Pampanga and Olongapo City.

History: Founded 1908.

Degrees and Diplomas: *Certificate/Diploma*; *Associate Degree*; *Bachelor's Degree*; *Master's Degree*; *PhD*

UNIVERSITY OF THE PHILIPPINES - MANILA

Padre Faura Corner, Maria Orosa Street,
Ermita, City of Manila, First District,
Metro Manila 1000
Tel: +63(2) 741-1950
Fax: +63(2) 741-6603
EMail: oc@mail.upm.edu.ph
Website: http://www.upm.edu.ph/

Chancellor: Ramon L. Arcadio

Vice-Chancellor for Academic Affairs: Josefina G. Tayag

Centres

Health Professions Teacher Training *(National)* (Health Education; Health Sciences); **National Telehealth** *(NTC)* (Ophthalmology); **Newborn Screening Reference** *(NSRC)*

Colleges

Allied Medical Professions (Occupational Therapy; Physical Therapy; Speech Therapy and Audiology); **Arts and Science** (Arts and Humanities; Biology; Communication Arts; Mathematics; Natural Sciences; Physical Education; Social Sciences); **Dentistry** (Dentistry); **Medicine** (Medicine); **Nursing** (Nursing); **Pharmacy** (Pharmacy); **Public Health** (Public Health)

Departments

Clinical Epidemiology *(DCE)* (Epidemiology); **Health Sciences** *(National Graduate Office)*

Institutes

Health *(NIH)* (Health Sciences)

Programmes

Graduate Studies (Applied Chemistry; Biochemistry; Child Care and Development; Community Health; Dentistry; Environmental Studies; Epidemiology; Ethics; Gynaecology and Obstetrics; Health Administration; Health Education; Health Sciences; Management; Medicine; Microbiology; Nursing; Nutrition; Occupational Health; Oncology; Orthodontics; Orthopaedics; Parasitology; Pharmacology; Pharmacy; Physiology; Public Administration; Public Health; Rehabilitation and Therapy; Speech Therapy and Audiology; Surgery)

Schools

Health Sciences (Health Sciences)

Further Information: Also Philippine General Hospital. Extension programmes in Palo Leyte

History: Founded 1908. Reorganized into the University of the Philippines System 1972.

Academic Year: June to May (June-October; November-March; April-May)

Admission Requirements: Graduation from accredited high school or equivalent (PEPT) and entrance examination (UPCAT)

Main Language(s) of Instruction: Filipino, English

Degrees and Diplomas: *Certificate/Diploma*; *Bachelor's Degree*: 4-5 yrs; *Post Baccalaureate Certificate/Diploma*: a further 1-2 yrs; *Master's Degree*: a further 1-2 yrs; *PhD*: a further 1-2 yrs

Student Services: Academic counselling, Cultural centre, Employment services, Foreign Studies Centre, Handicapped facilities, Health services, Nursery care, Social counselling, Sports facilities

Libraries: c. 161,000 vols

Publications: ACTA Medica Philippina; Ang Pahinungód ng Unibersidad ng Pilipinas Manila *(monthly)*; Bagumbayan; Department of Surgery Newsletter *(weekly)*; Library Guide *(annually)*; Philippine Development Forum; Post Graduate Pediatrics *(biannually)*; Surgical Bulletin; University Library New Acquisition List *(quarterly)*; UP College of Dentistry Newsletter; UP College of Medicine Newsletter; UPCN Journal; UPCN Research Bulletin

UNIVERSITY OF THE PHILIPPINES BAGUIO (UPB)

Governor Park Road, Baguio City, Benguet 2600
Tel: +63(74) 442-3888
Fax: +63(74) 442-3888
EMail: our@upb.edu.ph
Website: http://www.upb.edu.ph

Chancellor: Priscilla Supnet-Macansantos
EMail: psmacansantos@lycos.com

Vice-Chancellor for Administration: Bienvenido C. Marzan

Centres
Cordillera Studies

Colleges
Arts and Communication (Communication Studies; Fine Arts; Journalism; Literature; Mass Communication; Modern Languages; Visual Arts); **Science** (Biology; Mathematics; Mathematics and Computer Science; Natural Sciences; Physics); **Social Sciences** (Anthropology; Development Studies; Economics; History; Management; Philosophy; Political Sciences; Psychology; Social Sciences)

Institutes
Management (Economics; Management)

Programmes
Human Kinetics (Physical Education; Sports)

History: Founded 1961. Became an autonomous college 1999. Acquired present status 2002.

Governing Bodies: Executive Committee (Execom); Academic Personnel Fellowship Committee (APFC); Administrative Personnel Committee (AdPC); University Council (UC)

Academic Year: June to May

Admission Requirements: Graduation from accredited high school or equivalent and entrance examination (UPCAT)

Fees: (Pesos): 200-600 per unit

Main Language(s) of Instruction: Filipino, English

International Co-operation: East Meets West Centre. Also participates in the FAAP, PACUCOA, PAASCU programmes, and in the Southeast Asian Universities.

Degrees and Diplomas: *Certificate/Diploma*; *Bachelor's Degree*; *Master's Degree*

Student Services: Academic counselling, Canteen, Cultural centre, Employment services, Handicapped facilities, Health services, Language programs, Social counselling, Sports facilities

Student Residential Facilities: UPB Ladies Residence Hall; UPB Walk-up Housing (for faculty and staff plus one unit for guests)

Special Facilities: Museum; Art Gallery

Libraries: On-line Public Access Catalogues; CD-Rom and Database access; Microfilms and Microfiches

UNIVERSITY OF THE PHILIPPINES CEBU COLLEGE

Gorordo Avenue, Lahug, Cebu City, Cebu 6000
Tel: +63(32) 231-3086
Fax: +63(32) 232-8104
EMail: irc@letech.net.ph
Website: http://www.cebu.upv.edu.ph/

Dean: Jesus V. Juario

Programmes
Graduate (Biology; Chemistry; English; Environmental Studies; Filipino; Foreign Languages Education; Management; Mathematics; Physics; Regional Planning; Social Studies; Town Planning); **Undergraduate** (Applied Mathematics; Biology; Business Administration; Computer Science; Fine Arts; Industrial Design; Management; Mass Communication; Mathematics; Painting and Drawing; Political Sciences; Psychology)

History: Founded 1908. An autonomous unit of the University of the Philippines System.

Academic Year: June to March (June-October; November-March)

Admission Requirements: Graduation from high school recognized by the Department of Education and entrance examination

Main Language(s) of Instruction: Filipino, English

Degrees and Diplomas: *Bachelor's Degree*; *Master's Degree*

Student Services: Academic counselling, Canteen, Employment services, Health services, Social counselling, Sports facilities

Special Facilities: University Theatre

Press or Publishing House: University of the Philippines Press

UNIVERSITY OF THE PHILIPPINES LOS BAÑOS

College, Los Baños, Laguna 4031
Tel: +63(49) 536-2894
Fax: +63(49) 536-3673
EMail: rlv@mudspring.uplb.edu.ph
Website: http://www.uplb.edu.ph

Chancellor: Luis Rey I. Velasco

Vice-Chancellor for Administration: Roberto F. Rañola, Jr.

Centres
National Crop (Crop Production)

Colleges
Agriculture (Agriculture; Applied Chemistry; Biotechnology; Entomology; Food Technology; Horticulture); **Arts and Sciences** (Arts and Humanities; Biological and Life Sciences; Chemistry; Computer Science; Environmental Studies; Mathematics; Natural Sciences; Physical Therapy; Physics; Social Sciences); **Economics and Management** (Economics; Management); **Engineering and Agro-Industrial Technology** (Agricultural Equipment; Chemical Engineering; Civil Engineering; Electrical Engineering; Meteorology; Production Engineering; Soil Science; Water Science); **Forestry** (Forestry); **Human Ecology** (Development Studies; Environmental Studies; Family Studies; Nutrition; Social Studies); **Veterinary Science** (Veterinary Science)

Institutes
Biotechnology (Biotechnology); **Chemistry** (Chemistry); **Forest Conservation** (Forest Management); **Plant Breeding** (Botany)

Research Centres
Management (Management)

Research Institutes
Agrarian Studies (Agriculture); **Animal Husbandry** (Animal Husbandry); **Biological Sciences** (Biological and Life Sciences); **Computer Science** (Computer Science); **Dairy** (Dairy); **Development Communication** (Development Studies); **Environmental Science and Management** (Environmental Management); **Food Science and Technology** (Food Technology); **Human Nutrition and Food** (Food Science; Nutrition); **Mathematical Sciences and Physics** (Mathematics; Physics)

History: Founded 1909, acquired present status and title 1972. An autonomous unit of the University of the Philippines System.

Academic Year: June to March (June-October; November-March). Also Summer Session (April-May)

Admission Requirements: Graduation from high school and entrance examination

Main Language(s) of Instruction: English

Degrees and Diplomas: *Certificate/Diploma*; *Bachelor's Degree*; *Post Baccalaureate Certificate/Diploma*; *Master's Degree*; *PhD*

Student Services: Academic counselling, Cultural centre, Employment services, Health services, Nursery care, Sports facilities

Special Facilities: Natural History Museum. Makiling Botanic Gardens. Science and Technology Park

Libraries: c. 260,000 vols

UNIVERSITY OF THE PHILIPPINES MINDANAO (UPMIN)

Bago Oshiro, Mintal, Davao City, Davao del Sur 8000
Tel: +63(82) 293-0310
Fax: +63(82) 293-0310
EMail: upmin@upmin.edu.ph
Website: http://www.upmin.edu.ph

President: Alfredo E. Pascual

Vice-President for Administration: Maragtas Sofronio V. Amante

Colleges

Humanities and Social Sciences (Anthropology; Architecture; Arts and Humanities; Communication Arts; Economics; English; Social Sciences); **Science and Mathematics** (Applied Mathematics; Biology; Computer Science; Food Technology)

Schools

Management (Agricultural Business; Economics; Management; Rural Planning; Town Planning)

History: Founded 1995

Admission Requirements: High school diploma and UPCAT (admission tests)

Fees: (Pesos): 4,234-10,751 per annum

Main Language(s) of Instruction: Filipino, English

Degrees and Diplomas: *Bachelor's Degree*; *Master's Degree*: Management; Urban and Regional Planning

Student Services: Academic counselling, Canteen, Cultural centre, Social counselling, Sports facilities

Student Residential Facilities: Yes

Publications: BANWA *(annually)*

UNIVERSITY OF THE PHILIPPINES OPEN UNIVERSITY (UPOU)

Los Baños, Laguna 4031
Tel: +63(49) 536-6001to 6006
Fax: +63(49) 536-6015
EMail: info@upou.edu.ph
Website: http://www.upou.edu.ph/

Chancellor: Grace J. Alfonso EMail: upouoc@upou.edu.ph

Faculties

Education (Literacy Education; Mathematics; Mathematics Education; Modern Languages; Science Education; Social Studies); **Information and Communication Studies** (Computer Science; Information Sciences; Information Technology; Mass Communication; Multimedia; Systems Analysis); **Management and Development Studies** (Computer Science; Development Studies; Environmental Studies; Health Administration; Health Sciences; Natural Resources; Nursing; Public Administration; Public Health; Social Work)

Programmes

Graduate (Biology; Chemistry; Communication Studies; Development Studies; Distance Education; Education; Environmental Management; Foreign Languages Education; Health Administration; Information Management; Information Technology; Literacy Education; Management; Mathematics; Native Language Education; Natural Resources; Nursing; Physics; Public Administration; Public Health; Social Studies; Social Work)

Further Information: Open Higher Education Institution

History: Founded 1995 as the 5th constituent of the University of the Philippines system.

Governing Bodies: The University of the Philippines system's Board of Regents

Academic Year: June to March (June-October; November-March). Also Summer session, April to May.

Admission Requirements: Secondary School Certificate. Admission Test.

Fees: (Peso): Tuition, 300-450 per unit according to diploma

Main Language(s) of Instruction: Filipino, English

Degrees and Diplomas: *Certificate/Diploma*; *Associate Degree*; *Bachelor's Degree*; *Master's Degree*: Education (Language and Literacy; Social Studies); Information Systems; Social Work; Development Communication; Distance Education; Public Health; Hospital Administration; Nursing; Public Management; Environment and Natural Resources Management; *PhD*: Communication; Education (Biology; Chemistry; Physics; Mathematics)

Student Services: Academic counselling, Foreign student adviser, Social counselling

Special Facilities: Computer laobratory. Theatre.

Libraries: On-line Library, c. 1,673 Books, 100 VHS tapes, 90 CD-Roms

Publications: UPOU Research Monograph, Research by Faculty and Staff

Press or Publishing House: UPOU Printing and Production Unit

UNIVERSITY OF THE PHILIPPINES VISAYAS (UPV)

Main Administration Building, UPV Miagao Campus, Miagao, Iloilo 5023
Tel: +63(33) 338-1535
Fax: +63(33) 338-1534
EMail: webmaster@upv.edu.ph; disp.ovcpd@upv.edu.ph; efrain.servento@up.edu.ph
Website: http://www.upv.edu.ph/

Chancellor: Glenn D. Aguilar

Colleges

Arts and Science (Applied Mathematics; Biology; Chemistry; Communication Studies; Computer Science; Development Studies; Economics; History; Literature; Mathematics; Media Studies; Physics; Political Sciences; Psychology; Public Health; Sociology; Statistics); **Fisheries and Ocean Sciences** (Aquaculture; Fishery; Marine Science and Oceanography); **Management** (Accountancy; Business Administration; Management; Marketing)

Research Centres

Central Visayas Studies *(Cebu City Campus)*; **Institute of Molecular Biology and Biotechnology** (Biology; Biotechnology); **Leyte-Samar Heritage** *(Tacloban City Campus)* (Regional Studies); **West Visayan Studies** *(Iloilo City Campus)* (Regional Studies)

Schools

Graduate (Aquaculture; Biological and Life Sciences; Biology; Business Administration; Chemistry; Educational and Student Counselling; English; Filipino; Fishery; Foreign Languages Education; Literacy Education; Management; Marine Biology; Marine Science and Oceanography; Mathematics Education; Microbiology; Native Language Education; Physics; Regional Planning; Social Sciences; Town Planning); **Technology** (Chemical Engineering; Food Technology; Technology)

Further Information: Also Colleges in Cebu and in Tacloban

History: Founded 1947. Acquired present status 1979. An autonomous unit of the University of the Philippines System. It has 4 campuses.

Governing Bodies: Board of Regents

Academic Year: June to March (June-October and November-March); Summer session (April-May)

Admission Requirements: Must qualify in the University of the Philippines College Admission Test(UPCAT); must have graduated from an accredited high school

Fees: (Pesos): Undergraduate, 200 per unit; Graduate, 600 per unit; Laboratory, 100-1,000

Main Language(s) of Instruction: English

Degrees and Diplomas: *Certificate/Diploma*; *Bachelor's Degree*; *Master's Degree*: Aquaculture; Marine Affairs; Fisheries (Aquaculture; Fisheries Biology; Fish Processing Technology); Ocean Studies; Education (Biology; Chemistry; English as Second Language; Filipino; Guidance; Mathematics; Physics; Reading; Social Sciences); Biological Sciences (Developmental Biology; Environmental Biology; Marine Biology; Microbiology); Management (Business Management); Urban and Regional Planning; *PhD*: Fisheries (Aquaculture)

Student Services: Academic counselling, Canteen, Employment services, Foreign student adviser, Health services, Language programs, Nursery care, Social counselling, Sports facilities

Student Residential Facilities: Yes

Special Facilities: Art Museum and Gallery; Natural Science Museum. Science and Technology Park. Botanical Garden; Iloilo City Campus Little Theater; UPV Cebu College Little Gallery

Libraries: 109,681 vols

Publications: DANYAG: the UPV Journal of Humanities and Social Sciences *(biannually)*; Research Training Centres and Facilities; UPV Journal of Natural Sciences *(biannually)*

Press or Publishing House: UP Press

UNIVERSITY OF THE PHILIPPINES VISAYAS TACLOBAN COLLEGE

Magsaysay Blvd, Tacloban City, Leyte 6500
EMail: uptaclrc@mozcom.com

Programmes

Graduate (Business Administration; Management; Public Administration; Taxation); **Undergraduate** (Accountancy; Biology; Business Administration; Communication Arts; Computer Science; Economics; Management; Political Sciences; Psychology; Social Sciences)

History: Founded 1973.

Degrees and Diplomas: *Bachelor's Degree*; *Master's Degree*

UNIVERSITY OF VALENZUELA CITY

Pamantasan ng Lungsod ng Valenzuela

Poblacion II Malinta, City of Valenzuela, Third District, Metro Manila
Tel: +63(2) 277-6495
Fax: +63(2) 277-6100

President: Nedeña C. Torralba

Programmes

Graduate (Education; Educational Administration; Public Administration); **Undergraduate and Professional** (Biological and Life Sciences; Business Administration; Education; Electrical Engineering; English; Filipino; Finance; Foreign Languages Education; Human Resources; Management; Marketing; Mathematics Education; Native Language Education; Primary Education; Secondary Education)

History: Founded 2002.

Degrees and Diplomas: *Bachelor's Degree*; *Master's Degree*: Education (Educational Administration); Public Administration

Last Updated: 19/01/11

UPI AGRICULTURAL COLLEGE - PROVINCIAL TECHNOLOGICAL INSTITUTE OF TECHNOLOGY

Upi, Shariff Kabunsuan 9602
EMail: uasptia1919@yahoo.com.ph

School Administrator II: Sukarno B. Datukan

Programmes

Undergraduate and Professional (Agricultural Business; Agricultural Education; Agricultural Engineering; Agriculture; Forestry; Home Economics; Technology)

History: Founded 1919.

Degrees and Diplomas: *Associate Degree*; *Bachelor's Degree*

Last Updated: 17/03/11

URDANETA CITY UNIVERSITY

San Vincente West, City of Urdaneta, Pangasinan 2428
Tel: +63(75) 568-7612 +63(75) 568-5062
Fax: +63(75) 568-7612
EMail: ccu@gdigitelone.com

President: Elizabeth A. Montero

Programmes

Graduate (Business Administration; Education; Educational Administration; Nursing; Preschool Education; Public Administration; Public Health; Special Education); **Undergraduate** (Accountancy; Banking; Business and Commerce; Civil Engineering; Criminology; Education; Electrical Engineering; English; Filipino; Finance; Foreign Languages Education; Health Education; Hotel and Restaurant; Hotel Management; Information Sciences; Information Technology; Library Science; Management; Management Systems; Mass Communication; Mathematics Education; Midwifery; Music Education; Native Language Education; Nursing; Pharmacy; Physical Education; Political Sciences; Preschool Education; Primary Education; Psychology; Science Education; Secondary Education; Secretarial Studies; Social Studies; Social Work; Special Education; Tourism)

History: Founded 1966. Formerly known as City College of Urdaneta.

Degrees and Diplomas: *Associate Degree*; *Bachelor's Degree*; *Master's Degree*: Nursing; Public Administration; Public Health; Education (Special Education; Early Childhood Education; Educational Management); Business Administration; *PhD*: Education

Last Updated: 17/03/11

VALENZUELA CITY POLYTECHNIC COLLEGE

VMTC Cmpd., Kamagong Street, Fortune Village 6, Parada, City of Valenzuela, Third District, Metro Manila
Tel: +63(2) 445-0470
Fax: +63(2) 293-0775

Officer-In-Charge: Nedena C. Torralba

Programmes

Undergraduate and Professional (Automotive Engineering; Civil Engineering; Computer Engineering; Education; Electrical Engineering; Electronic Engineering; Heating and Refrigeration; Industrial Arts Education; Mechanical Engineering; Teacher Training; Technology Education; Textile Technology)

History: Founded 1996.

Degrees and Diplomas: *Bachelor's Degree*

Last Updated: 17/03/11

VISAYAS STATE UNIVERSITY (VSU)

Brgy. Visca, Baybay, Leyte 6521
Tel: +63(53) 335-2600
Fax: +63(53) 335-2601
EMail: opvisca@mozcom.com
Website: http://www.vsu.edu.ph

President: Jose L. Bacusmo

Campuses

Alang-Alang (Agricultural Education; Agricultural Engineering; Agriculture; Education; Environmental Management; Mathematics Education; Primary Education; Secondary Education); **Isabel** (Agricultural Business; Art Education; Computer Engineering; Education; Home Economics; Industrial Engineering; Information Technology; Mathematics Education; Mechanical Engineering; Music Education; Physical Education; Primary Education; Secondary Education; Technology Education); **Open University** (Biotechnology; Civil Engineering; Economics; Home Economics; Hotel and Restaurant; Hotel Management; Nursing; Tourism); **Tolosa** (Education; Fishery; Primary Education; Secondary Education); **Villaba** (Agricultural Engineering; Agriculture; Crop Production; Education; English; Foreign Languages Education; Home Economics Education; Mathematics Education; Primary Education; Science Education; Secondary Education; Technology Education; Zoology)

Colleges

Agriculture (Agriculture; Agronomy; Communication Studies; Food Science; Food Technology; Horticulture; Pest Management; Soil Science; Zoology); **Arts and Science** (Applied Chemistry; Arts and Humanities; Behavioural Sciences; Biological and Life Sciences; Chemistry; Mathematics; Physics; Statistics); **Education** (Agricultural Management; Art Education; Biology; Chemistry; Education; Health Education; Mathematics Education; Music Education; Physical Education; Primary Education; Rural Planning; Science Education; Secondary Education); **Engineering and Agri-Industries** (Agricultural Engineering; Civil Engineering; Computer Science; Engineering; Geological Engineering; Mechanical Engineering); **Forestry and Natural Resources** (Environmental Management; Forest Products; Forestry; Natural Resources; Wildlife); **Management and Economics** (Accountancy; Agricultural Business; Agricultural Economics; Agricultural Management; Business

Administration; Farm Management; Food Science; Home Economics; Hotel and Restaurant; Hotel Management; Management; Tourism; Zoology); **Nursing** (Nursing); **Veterinary Medicine** (Veterinary Science)

Institutes

Human Kinetics (Dance; Parks and Recreation; Physical Education; Sports)

Schools

Graduate (Agricultural Business; Agricultural Economics; Agricultural Education; Agricultural Engineering; Agricultural Management; Agronomy; Animal Husbandry; Biology; Business Administration; Chemistry; Communication Studies; Development Studies; Education; English; Entomology; Food Science; Food Technology; Foreign Languages Education; Home Economics; Horticulture; Management; Mathematics Education; Modern Languages; Physical Education; Physics; Plant and Crop Protection; Plant Pathology; Rural Planning; Rural Studies; Social Sciences; Soil Science; Tropical Agriculture; Zoology)

History: Founded 1924 as Baybay Agricultural School. Renamed Baybay Agricultural High School 1934 and converted into Baybay National Agricultural School and into Visayas Agricultural College 1960, and reconverted into Visayas State College of Agriculture 1974. Renamed Leyte State University (LSU) 2001. Acquired present title 2007.

Governing Bodies: Board of Regents

Admission Requirements: Application form for admission; original copy of form 138; 6 photos; copy of birth certificate authentified by NSO

International Co-operation: Participates in various programmes (Apan, ADB, Answer, Aciar, Cirad, Ciat, Cip, CFTU, Ciifad, GTZ, Euronatur, Fao-UN, Icraf, Jica, Jsps, Searca, Usaid, Upward, Winrock

Degrees and Diplomas: *Certificate/Diploma*; *Bachelor's Degree*; *Post Baccalaureate Certificate/Diploma*; *Master's Degree*: Agricultural Development; Education; Management; Science; *PhD*: Entomology; Agricultural Education; Animal Science; Horticulture; Plant Pathology

Student Services: Academic counselling, Canteen, Cultural centre, Employment services, Health services, Sports facilities

Student Residential Facilities: Yes.

Special Facilities: Museum. Radio station.

Publications: Annals of Tropical Research *(biennially)*; Science and Humanities Journal, Referred graduate journal *(annually)*

Last Updated: 18/03/11

WEST VISAYAS STATE UNIVERSITY

Luna Street, La Paz, Iloilo City, Iloilo 5000
Tel: +63(33) 320-0870
Fax: +63(33) 320-0879
EMail: wvsu@mail.com
Website: http://www.wvsu.edu.ph/

President: Pablo E. Subong, Jr.

Vice-President for Academic Affairs: Editha Y. Sillorequez
EMail: rccabag2000@yahoo.com

Vice-President for Administration and Finance: Ramon G. Zarceno

Campuses

Calinog (Agriculture; Crop Production; Curriculum; Education; Educational Administration; English; Food Technology; Foreign Languages Education; Hotel and Restaurant; Hotel Management; Industrial Engineering; Management; Mathematics Education; Primary Education; Public Administration; Science Education; Secondary Education; Zoology) *Campus Administrator*: Rosario Clarabel C. Contreras; **Janiuay** (Automotive Engineering; Computer Education; Curriculum; Education; Electrical Engineering; Electronic Engineering; English; Food Technology; Foreign Languages Education; Home Economics Education; Hotel and Restaurant; Industrial Arts Education; Information Technology; Mathematics Education; Primary Education; Secondary Education; Social Sciences; Technology Education; Textile Technology) *Campus Administrator*: Raymund G. Gemora; **Lambunao East Branch** (Applied Chemistry; Automotive Engineering; Criminology; Curriculum; Education; Educational Administration; Electrical and Electronic Engineering; English; Food Technology; Foreign Languages Education; Forensic Medicine and Dentistry; Hotel and Restaurant; Hotel Management; Industrial Arts Education; Industrial Engineering; Literacy Education; Mathematics Education; Primary Education; Secondary Education; Technology Education) *Campus Administrator*: Dominador C. Lisao; **Pototan** (Automotive Engineering; Computer Education; Curriculum; Education; Electrical Engineering; English; Food Technology; Foreign Languages Education; Home Economics Education; Hotel and Restaurant; Industrial Engineering; Information Management; Information Technology; Mathematics Education; Secondary Education; Technology Education) *Campus Administrator*: Rodeline M. Pasuelo

Centres

Regional (Science Education)

Colleges

Agriculture and Forestry (Agriculture; Forestry); **Arts and Science** (Anatomy; Arts and Humanities; Biological and Life Sciences; Biology; Biotechnology; Cell Biology; Ecology; Environmental Studies; Genetics; Histology; Immunology; Microbiology; Molecular Biology; Parasitology; Physiology; Social Sciences; Virology); **Business and Management** (Business and Commerce; Hotel and Restaurant; Hotel Management; Management; Small Business; Tourism); **Education** (Biology; Chemistry; Education; Educational and Student Counselling; English; Filipino; Foreign Languages Education; Health Education; Library Science; Literacy Education; Mathematics Education; Native Language Education; Physics; Preschool Education; Primary Education; Science Education; Secondary Education; Social Sciences; Social Studies; Special Education); **Mass Communication** (Development Studies; Journalism; Mass Communication; Radio and Television Broadcasting); **Medicine** (Medicine); **Nursing** (Nursing); **Physical and Music Education** (Music; Music Education; Physical Education)

Institutes

Information and Communications Technology (Information Technology)

Further Information: Also Non-Formal Education. Extension Programmes. Teaching Hospital

History: Founded 1924 as Iloilo Normal School, became West Visayas State College 1962, acquired present status and title 1987.

Governing Bodies: Board of Regents

Academic Year: June to May (June-October; November-March; April-May)

Admission Requirements: Graduation from high school and entrance examination; Nursing, Aptitude Test; Medicine, National Medical Admission Test (NMAT)

Main Language(s) of Instruction: Filipino, English

Accrediting Agencies: Accrediting Agency of Chartered Colleges and Universities of the Philippines (AACCUP)

Degrees and Diplomas: *Certificate/Diploma*; *Bachelor's Degree*; *Post Baccalaureate Certificate/Diploma*: Medicine; *Master's Degree*; *PhD*

Student Services: Academic counselling, Cultural centre, Health services, Social counselling, Sports facilities

Student Residential Facilities: Dormitory, WVSU -Hometel

Special Facilities: Media Centre. Wildlife Conservation Facility for Indigenous Species

Libraries: Central Library, 16,430 vols; Medical Library, 1,633 vols

Publications: College of Education Research Journal *(annually)*; Research Journal *(annually)*; West Visayas State University (WVSU) Graduate Journal *(quarterly)*

Last Updated: 31/03/11

WESTERN MINDANAO STATE UNIVERSITY (WMSU)

Normal Road, Baliwasan, Zamboanga City, Zamboanga del Sur 7000
Tel: +63(62) 991-2837 +63(62) 991-1040 +63(62) 991-1771
Fax: +63(62) 991-3065
EMail: op-misto@wmsu.edu.ph
Website: http://www.wmsu.edu.ph

President: Grace J. Rebollos

Vice-President for Planning, Administration and Finance: Loyda A. Bangahan

International Relations: Armando A. Arquiza, University and Board Secretary EMail: dsa-arquiza@yahoo.com

Campuses

Zamboanga Del Norte Agricultural College-Tampilisan (Agricultural Business; Agricultural Education; Agricultural Engineering; Business and Commerce; Computer Science; Criminology; Crop Production; Curriculum; Education; English; Filipino; Foreign Languages Education; Forestry; Home Economics; Hotel and Restaurant; Hotel Management; Information Technology; Mathematics Education; Plant Pathology; Police Studies; Political Sciences; Primary Education; Secondary Education; Social Studies; Soil Science; Technology; Zoology); **Zamboanga Del Sur Agricultural College** (Agricultural Education; Computer Science; Criminology; Crop Production; Curriculum; Education; Educational Administration; English; Food Technology; Foreign Languages Education; Information Technology; Mathematics Education; Police Studies; Primary Education; Secondary Education)

Centres

Research (Economics; Education; Health Sciences; Natural Sciences; Social Sciences; Technology)

Colleges

Agriculture *(San Ramon)* (Agricultural Business; Agricultural Engineering; Agriculture; Crop Production; Zoology); **Architecture** (Architectural and Environmental Design; Architecture; Architecture and Planning; Construction Engineering); **Asian and Islamic Studies** (Arabic; Asian Studies; Islamic Studies); **Criminal Justice Education** (Criminal Law; Criminology; Police Studies); **Education** (Art Education; Biology; Chemistry; Education; Educational Administration; Educational and Student Counselling; English; Ethics; Filipino; Foreign Languages Education; Health Education; Mathematics Education; Music Education; Native Language Education; Physical Education; Physics; Preschool Education; Science Education; Social Studies; Special Education); **Engineering and Technology** (Architecture; Civil Engineering; Ecology; Electrical Engineering; Engineering; Environmental Engineering; Environmental Management; Geological Engineering; Industrial Engineering; Industrial Management; Information Technology; Mechanical Engineering; Safety Engineering; Sanitary Engineering; Structural Architecture; Water Management; Water Science); **Forestry and Environmental Studies** (Environmental Studies; Forestry); **Home Economics and Nutrition** (Dietetics; Food Technology; Health Education; Home Economics; Home Economics Education; Nutrition); **Law** (Law); **Liberal Arts** (Accountancy; Arts and Humanities; Economics; Education; English; Filipino; Foreign Languages Education; History; Journalism; Mass Communication; Native Language Education; Philosophy; Political Sciences; Psychology; Radio and Television Broadcasting; Social Studies); **Nursing** (Community Health; Health Education; Nursing); **Public Administration and Development Studies** (Administration; Development Studies; Government; Human Resources; Management; Public Administration); **Science and Mathematics** (Biology; Chemistry; Education; Mathematics; Mathematics Education; Natural Sciences; Physics; Science Education; Statistics); **Social Work and Community Development** (Social and Community Services; Social Work; Town Planning)

Departments

Extension Services (Automotive Engineering; Clothing and Sewing; Electronic Engineering; Graphic Arts; Secretarial Studies; Textile Design); **Physical Education, Recreation and Sports** (Parks and Recreation; Physical Education; Sports; Sports Management)

Schools

Graduate (Biology; Chemistry; Child Care and Development; Civil Engineering; Dance; Education; Educational Administration; Educational and Student Counselling; Electrical Engineering; Engineering; English; Environmental Engineering; Environmental Management; Filipino; Foreign Languages Education; Government; Health Education; Home Economics Education; Human Resources; Information Technology; Management; Mathematics Education; Mechanical Engineering; Native Language Education; Nursing; Parks and Recreation; Physical Education; Physics; Political Sciences; Psychiatry and Mental Health; Psychology; Public Administration; Science Education; Social Studies; Social Work; Special Education; Sports; Taxation; Water Management)

History: Founded 1918 as Secondary School. Became Teacher Training School 1955 and College 1961. Acquired present status and title 1978. An autonomous State Institution financed by the Government.

Governing Bodies: Board of Regents

Academic Year: June to March (June-October; November-March)

Admission Requirements: Graduation from high school and entrance examination

Main Language(s) of Instruction: Filipino, English, Spanish, Arabic

Degrees and Diplomas: *Associate Degree*; *Bachelor's Degree*; *Master's Degree*; *PhD*

Student Residential Facilities: Yes

Special Facilities: Ethnological Museum

Libraries: Central Library, c. 21,000 vols.; specialized Libraries, Law, c. 1,550; Agriculture, c. 2,000; Graduate School, c. 2,200; Science, Mathematics and Forestry Library, c. 3,500

Publications: Research Journal

Last Updated: 31/03/11

WESTERN PHILIPPINES UNIVERSITY

San Juan, Aborlan, Palawan 5302
Tel: +63(48) 433-4480 +63(48) 433-4367
Fax: +63(48) 433-4367
EMail: wpuwebsite@yahoo.com
Website: http://www.wpu.edu.ph/main/

President: Concepto B. Magay

Campuses

Busuanga (Agricultural Engineering; Hotel and Restaurant; Hotel Management; Sociology; Tourism); **Culion** (Agricultural Engineering; Electrical Engineering; Fishery; Sociology); **El Nido** (Agricultural Business; Criminology; Hotel and Restaurant; Hotel Management; Tourism); **Puerto Princesa** (Agricultural Business; Agronomy; Aquaculture; Business Administration; Civil Engineering; Criminology; Education; Educational Administration; Electrical Engineering; Horticulture; Management; Marine Biology; Marine Engineering; Marine Transport; Mechanical Engineering; Primary Education; Public Administration; Rural Planning; Secondary Education; Social Work; Sociology); **Quezon** (Agricultural Business; Criminology; Development Studies; Education; Forestry; Primary Education; Rural Planning; Secondary Education; Sociology); **Rio Tuba** (Agricultural Business; Mechanical Engineering)

Programmes

Graduate (Agronomy; Development Studies; Educational Administration; Horticulture; Public Administration; Rural Planning); **Undergraduate and Professional** (Agricultural Business; Agricultural Engineering; Agriculture; Automotive Engineering; Business Administration; Civil Engineering; Criminology; Development Studies; Electrical Engineering; Environmental Management; Forestry; Home Economics; Hotel and Restaurant; Hotel Management; Management; Mechanical Engineering; Primary Education; Public Administration; Rural Planning; Secondary Education; Social Work; Sociology; Tourism)

Further Information: Campuses: Busuanga, Culion, El Nido, Puerto Princesa, Quezon and Rio Tuba

History: Founded 2004. Formerly known as State Polytechnic College of Palawan-Main.

Degrees and Diplomas: *Certificate/Diploma*; *Bachelor's Degree*; *Master's Degree*; *PhD*

Last Updated: 06/04/11

WESTERN VISAYAS COLLEGE OF SCIENCE AND TECHNOLOGY

Burgos St., La Paz, Iloilo City, Iloilo 5000
Tel: +63(33) 335-0584
Fax: +63(33) 329-4274
EMail: wvcst@stealth.iloilo.net
Website: http://www.wvcst.edu.ph

President: Luis M. Sorolla, Jr.

Vice-President, Administration and Finance: Edwin T. Fos

Campuses

Barotac Nuevo (Automotive Engineering; Computer Engineering; Education; Electrical Engineering; Electronic Engineering; Hotel and Restaurant; Industrial Engineering); **Dumangas** (Automotive Engineering; Electrical Engineering; Electronic Engineering; Hotel and Restaurant; Industrial Engineering; Information Technology); **Leon** (Agricultural Education; Agricultural Engineering; Agriculture; Crop Production; Forestry; Information Technology; Zoology); **Miagao** (Automotive Engineering; Biological and Life Sciences; Building Technologies; Civil Engineering; Cooking and Catering; Cosmetology; Curriculum; Education; Educational Administration; Electrical Engineering; Electronic Engineering; English; Environmental Studies; Filipino; Food Technology; Foreign Languages Education; Heating and Refrigeration; Home Economics Education; Hotel and Restaurant; Industrial Arts Education; Industrial Engineering; Information Technology; Marine Engineering; Mathematics Education; Metal Techniques; Native Language Education; Primary Education; Science Education; Secondary Education; Social Studies; Technology Education; Textile Technology)

Colleges

Arts and Sciences (Computer Science; Information Technology; Mathematics; Urban Studies); **Education** (Architecture; Biology; Civil Engineering; Education; Heating and Refrigeration; Home Economics Education; Industrial Arts Education; Mathematics Education; Mechanical Engineering; Physics; Primary Education; Science Education; Secondary Education; Teacher Training; Technology Education; Textile Technology); **Engineering and Architecture** (Architecture; Automotive Engineering; Electrical Engineering; Electronic Engineering; Marine Engineering; Mechanical Engineering); **Industrial Technology** (Automotive Engineering; Civil Engineering; Cooking and Catering; Cosmetology; Electrical and Electronic Engineering; Heating and Refrigeration; Hotel and Restaurant; Industrial Engineering; Metal Techniques; Textile Technology)

Schools

Graduate Studies (Computer Science; Education; Educational Administration; Electronic Engineering; Home Economics; Industrial Arts Education; Industrial Engineering; Mathematics; Mechanical Engineering; Technology)

History: Founded 1905. Acquired present status 1983.

Degrees and Diplomas: *Certificate/Diploma*; *Bachelor's Degree*; *Master's Degree*; *PhD*

Last Updated: 07/04/11

ZAMBOANGA CITY STATE POLYTECHNIC COLLEGE

R.T. Lim Boulevard, Baliwasan, Zamboanga City, Zamboanga del Sur 7000
Tel: +63(62) 991-4012 +62(62) 991-3815
Fax: +63(62) 993-0023
EMail: zcspc@yahoo.com

President: Nora Ponce

Programmes

Graduate (Curriculum; Educational and Student Counselling; Home Economics Education; Industrial Arts Education; Mathematics Education; Vocational Counselling; Vocational Education); **Undergraduate and Professional** (Automotive Engineering; Civil Engineering; Computer Engineering; Electrical Engineering; Electronic Engineering; Food Technology; Heating and Refrigeration; Home Economics Education; Industrial Arts Education; Marine Engineering; Technology; Technology Education; Textile Technology)

History: Founded in 1905, acquiring present title and status in 2001.

Degrees and Diplomas: *Bachelor's Degree*; *Master's Degree*: Arts in Teaching Vocational Education (Curriculum and Instruction; Vocational Guidance and Counselling; Vocational Administration and Supervision; Home Economics; Mathematics; Industrial Arts)

Last Updated: 31/03/11

ZAMBOANGA STATE COLLEGE OF MARINE SCIENCE AND TECHNOLOGY

Fort Pilar, Zamboanga City, Zamboanga del Sur 7000
Tel: +63(62) 991-0643
Fax: +63(62) 991-0777
EMail: ZSCMST@zambo.ph.net
Website: http://www.zscmst.edu.ph

President: Milavel D. Nazario
Tel: +63(62) 992-3092, Fax: +63(62) 991-0777
EMail: mnazario@zscmst.edu.ph

Vice-President for Academic Affairs: Gloria D. Cabato

Vice-President for Administration, Finance and Corporate Affairs: Rico R. Mabalod

Programmes

Graduate (Aquaculture; Education; Fishery; Home Economics; Management; Marine Engineering; Marine Science and Oceanography; Marine Transport; Public Administration); **Undergraduate and Professional** (Aquaculture; Biological and Life Sciences; English; Fishery; Food Technology; Foreign Languages Education; Hotel and Restaurant; Hotel Management; Marine Biology; Marine Engineering; Marine Transport; Physics; Secondary Education; Tourism)

History: Founded in 1956, acquiring present title and status in 1986.

Degrees and Diplomas: *Certificate/Diploma*; *Bachelor's Degree*; *Master's Degree*: Education (Alternative Learning System); Home Economics; Fisheries Management; Maritime Management; Public Management; Teaching English/Marine Engineering/Marine Transportation; Fisheries; Marine Biodiversity; Marine Management

Last Updated: 31/03/11

PRIVATE INSTITUTIONS

ABADA COLLEGE

Marfrancisco, Pinamalayan, Oriental Mindoro 5208
Tel: +63(43) 443-1356 +63(43) 284-41-50
Fax: +63(43) 443-1356

President: Miguel D. Ansaldo Jr.

Programmes

Undergraduate and Professional (Business Administration; Computer Science; Criminology; Education; History; Law)

History: Founded 1950.

Degrees and Diplomas: *Certificate/Diploma*; *Associate Degree*; *Bachelor's Degree*

Last Updated: 28/03/11

ABE INTERNATIONAL COLLEGE OF BUSINESS AND ECONOMICS

2578 Legarda Avenue, Sampaloc, Manila, Metro Manila 1010
Tel: +63(2) 736-2893 +63(2) 736-2894
Fax: +63(2) 736-3978
Website: http://www.abecollege.com

President: Amable C. Aguiluz IX

Director: Rowena M. Panuncio EMail: rmpanuncio@amaes.edu.ph

Campuses

Bulacan *(Malolos, Bulacan) Director*: Anselmo Leano, Jr.; **Caloocan** *(Caloocan City) Director*: Rossana A. Buzeta; **Cebu** *(Lahug, Cebu) Director*: Luis D. Canora; **Cubao** *(Cubao, Quezon City) Director*: Marites R. Gamboa; **Fairview** *(Quezon City) Director*: Glenda Esguerra; **Iloilo** *(Sampaguita, Iloilo City) Director*: Peter John Gener; **Las Piñas** *(Las Piñas City) Director*: Jesusa B. Alberto; **Leyte** *(Tacloban City, Leyte) Director*: Jocelyn Tan; **Makati** *(Makati City) Director*: Susana Arcan; **Negros Occidental** *(Bacolod City, Negros Occidental) Director*: Joretta Abraham; **Nueva Ecija** *(Cabanatuan City, Nueva Ecija) Director*: Tita C. Agsunod; **Pangasinan** *(Urdaneta City, Pangasinan) Director*: Osmundo B. Corpuz; **Rizal** *(Cainta, Rizal) Director*: Mary Ann Q. Manuel; **Taft** *(Ermita, Manila) Director*: Rizza Abayari

Programmes
Accountancy (Accountancy); **Business Administration** (Business Administration; E-Business/Commerce; Management; Marketing); **Computer Science** (Computer Science); **Hotel and Restaurant** (Hotel and Restaurant; Hotel Management); **Information Management and Technology** (Information Management; Information Technology); **Tourism** (Tourism)
History: Founded 1999.
Degrees and Diplomas: *Bachelor's Degree*
Last Updated: 20/07/10

ABRA VALLEY COLLEGES

Taft Street, Bangued, Abra
Tel: +63(74) 752-7747
EMail: registrar@avc.educ.ph

President: Francis A. Borgoña

Programmes
Undergraduate and Professional (Arts and Humanities; Business Administration; Business and Commerce; Civil Engineering; Criminology; Education; English; Filipino; Finance; Foreign Languages Education; History; Hotel and Restaurant; Humanities and Social Science Education; Information Technology; Law; Management; Mass Communication; Mathematics; Mathematics Education; Native Language Education; Natural Sciences; Nursing; Political Sciences; Primary Education; Secondary Education; Secretarial Studies; Social Studies; Social Work)
History: Founded 1948.
Degrees and Diplomas: *Certificate/Diploma*: 2 yrs; *Bachelor's Degree*: 4 yrs; *Bachelor's Degree*: Computer Engineering, 5 yrs
Last Updated: 28/03/11

ABRAHAM DUMLAO COLLEGES OF THE PHILIPPINES

12, Salvia St., Dominic Subd., Zabarte, Novaliches, Quezon City, Second District, Metro Manila 1124
Tel: +63(2) 936-0957
Fax: +63(2) 936-0957
EMail: dumlaocollege@yahoo.com

President: Abraham C. Dumlao

Programmes
Engineering (Electronic Engineering; Engineering; Heating and Refrigeration; Mechanical Engineering); **Food Technology** (Food Technology); **Hotel and Restaurant Management** (Hotel and Restaurant; Hotel Management); **Tourism** (Tourism)
History: Founded 1979, acquired current status in 1999. Formerly Dumlao Technical Institute (1985-1996).
Degrees and Diplomas: *Certificate/Diploma*: 1 yr; *Bachelor's Degree*
Last Updated: 22/07/10

ABUBAKAR COMPUTER LEARNING CENTER FOUNDATION

Brgy. Simandagit, Bongao, Tawi-Tawi 7500
EMail: aclcfi_edu@yahoo.com
President: Ponchita S. Abubakar

Programmes
Arts and Humanities (Arts and Humanities; Political Sciences); **Business Administration** (Accountancy; Business Administration; Management); **Computer Science and Information** (Computer Graphics; Computer Science; Information Technology; Mass Communication); **Criminology** (Criminology); **Education** (Education; English; Foreign Languages Education; Primary Education; Secondary Education); **Nursing** (Nursing)
History: Founded 1996.
Degrees and Diplomas: *Bachelor's Degree*; *Master's Degree*: Arts; *PhD*: Education
Last Updated: 22/07/10

ACCESS COMPUTER AND TECHNICAL COLLEGE

2nd Flr & 3rd Flr Access Main Bldg, CM Recto Avenue corner Quezon Blvd, Quiapo, Manila, Metro Manila 1004
Tel: +63(2) 733-9474
Fax: +63(2) 734-8517
EMail: accessrec@pldtdsl.net
Website: http://accesscomputercollege.com

President: Romeo T. Zarate

Programmes
Business Administration (Business Administration); **Computer Engineering** (Computer Engineering); **Computer Science** (Computer Science); **Hotel and Restaurant Management** (Hotel and Restaurant; Hotel Management); **Information Technology** (Information Technology); **Tourism Management** (Tourism)
Further Information: Also campus in Quezon City
History: Founded 1981.
Degrees and Diplomas: *Certificate/Diploma*: 2 yrs; *Bachelor's Degree*: 4 yrs; *Bachelor's Degree*: Computer Engineering, 5 yrs
Last Updated: 28/03/11

ACES TAGUM COLLEGE

Purok Pag-ibig, Makilam, Tagum City, Davao del Norte 8100
Tel: +63(84) 217-2623
Fax: +63(84) 217-2623
EMail: atcregoffice@gmail.com
President: Francisco P. De la Peña, Jr.

Programmes
Business Administration (Accountancy; Business Administration; Business and Commerce; Management); **Education** (Education; English; Filipino; Mathematics Education; Primary Education; Secondary Education); **Hotel and Restaurant Management** (Hotel and Restaurant; Hotel Management); **Information Technology** (Information Technology)
History: Founded 2000.
Degrees and Diplomas: *Bachelor's Degree*: 4 yrs
Last Updated: 22/07/10

ACLC COLLEGE OF BUTUAN CITY

999 J.C. Aquino Avenue, Butuan City, Agusan del Norte 8600
Tel: +63(85) 341-5719
Fax: +63(85) 815-3248
EMail: aclcbtn@yahoo.com

Director: Alan L. Atega

Programmes
Business Administration (Business Administration; Finance; Management; Marketing); **Computer Science** (Computer Science); **Information Management and Technology** (Information Management; Information Technology)
Further Information: Also ACLC College - Ormoc; ACLC College of Bukidnon; ACLC College of Meycauayan and ACLC-Tagbilaran.
History: Founded in 1997 as ACLC College. Acquired present title 2005.
Degrees and Diplomas: *Bachelor's Degree*: 4 yrs
Last Updated: 28/03/11

ACMCL COLLEGE

Poblacion 1, Victoria, Oriental Mindoro 5205
Tel: +63(43) 285-5381
Fax: +63(43) 450-0072
EMail: acmontessoricollege@yahoo.com
President: Tito Tony H. Dolor

Programmes
Computer Science (Computer Engineering; Computer Science; Software Engineering); **Education** (Education; English; Mathematics Education; Primary Education; Secondary Education); **Electronics and Communications Technology** (Electronic Engineering; Telecommunications Engineering); **Food and Beverage Services** (Food Science; Food Technology); **Hotel and Restaurant**

Management (Hotel and Restaurant; Hotel Management); **Tour Guiding Services** (Tourism)

History: Founded 1993.

Degrees and Diplomas: *Bachelor's Degree*

Last Updated: 22/07/10

ACSI BUSINESS AND COMPUTER SCHOOL

J.M. Basa St., Iloilo City, Iloilo 5000
Tel: +63(33) 509-9160
EMail: acsi@easycom.net

Director: Nima Forro Sanchez

Programmes

Computer Science (Computer Science); **Information Systems** (Information Technology)

History: Founded 1984.

Degrees and Diplomas: *Associate Degree*; *Bachelor's Degree*

Last Updated: 22/07/10

ACTS COMPUTER COLLEGE

P. Guevarra Ave. cor. A. Bonifacio St., Sta. Cruz, Laguna 4009
Tel: +63(49) 808-1484
Fax: +63(49) 808-1863

President: Elma Macalinao

Programmes

Undergraduate and Professional (Business Administration; Computer Engineering; Information Sciences; Information Technology; Secretarial Studies)

History: Founded 1987. Acquired present 1994.

Degrees and Diplomas: *Associate Degree*: 2 yrs; *Bachelor's Degree*: 4 yrs

Last Updated: 22/07/10

ADAMSON UNIVERSITY

Universidad ng Adamson

900 San Marcelino Street, Ermita, City of Manila, First District, Metro Manila 1000
Tel: +63(2) 524-2011 +63(2) 521-0690
Fax: +63(2) 524-6590 +63(2) 522-5526
EMail: aducommunity@adamson.edu.ph; registrar@adamson.edu.ph
Website: http://www.adamson.edu.ph

President: Gregorio L. Bañaga Jr, C.M. (2003-)
Tel: +63(2) 525-7013, Fax: +63(2) 525-7013
EMail: glbanaga@gmail.com

Vice-President, Academic Affairs: Francisco Nicolas P. Magnaye, Jr., C.M.
Tel: +63(2) 522-2211, Fax: +63(2) 522-2211
EMail: heescurel@adamson.edu.ph

International Relations: Venusmar Quevedo
EMail: vcquevedo@adamson.edu.ph

Colleges

Architecture (Architecture) *Dean*: Peter A. Villanueva; **Business Administration** (Business Administration; Business and Commerce) *Dean*: Carl Mark B. Miniano; **Engineering** (Ceramic Art; Chemical Engineering; Civil Engineering; Computer Engineering; Electrical Engineering; Electronic Engineering; Engineering; Environmental Engineering; Geology; Industrial Engineering; Mechanical Engineering; Mining Engineering) *Dean*: Jesus Manalastas; **Law** (Law) *Dean*: Antonio Abad; **Liberal Arts and Education** (Arts and Humanities; Computer Education; Economics; Education; Educational Technology; English; Mass Communication; Philosophy; Physical Education; Political Sciences; Religious Education; Social Studies) *Dean*: Servillano T. Marquez; **Nursing** (Nursing) *Dean*: Naressia Ballena; **Pharmacy** (Pharmacy) *Dean*: Ryan Pekson; **Science** (Biology; Chemistry; Computer Science; Mathematics; Natural Sciences; Psychology) *Dean*: Ma. Gladiola Santos

Schools

Graduate Studies (Business Administration; Chemistry; Education; Educational Administration; Educational Technology; Engineering; Information Technology; Management; Management Systems; Pastoral Studies; Pharmacy; Theology) *Dean*: Jose Genaro R. Yap-Aizon

History: Founded 1932 as Adamson School of Industrial Chemistry by Dr. George Lucas Adamson, acquired University status 1941. A private Institution operating under the supervision of the Department of Education, Culture and Sports.

Governing Bodies: Board of Trustees, comprising 10 members; Executive Committee; Academic Council; Administrative Council; Student Council; Economic Coouncil

Academic Year: June to March (June-October; November-March)

Admission Requirements: Graduation from high school or foreign qualifications accredited by the Bureau of Private Schools, and entrance examination

Main Language(s) of Instruction: Filipino, English

International Co-operation: With institutions in Bangladesh, Indonesia, Thailand, USA

Accrediting Agencies: Philippine Accrediting Association of Schools, Colleges and Universities (PAASCU); Philippine Association of Colleges and Universities, Commission on Accreditation (PACUCOA); Educational Associations Federation of Accrediting Agencies of the Philippines (FAAP); Commission on Higher Education (CHED)

Degrees and Diplomas: *Certificate/Diploma*; *Bachelor's Degree*; *Master's Degree*: Education (Supervision and Administration; Computer-Aided Instruction); Business Administration; Chemistry; Management Engineering; Information Technology; Engineering; Pharmacy; Theology (Pastoral Ministry; Dogmatic Studies; Vincentian Studies); *PhD*: Education (Education Administration); Management

Student Services: Academic counselling, Canteen, Cultural centre, Employment services, Foreign student adviser, Health services, Language programs, Social counselling, Sports facilities

Special Facilities: Theatre; Art Gallery; Radio Station

Libraries: c. 81,000 vols

Press or Publishing House: Adamson Printing Press

Last Updated: 03/03/11

ADIONG MEMORIAL COLLEGE FOUNDATION

Carumba Street, Wao, Lanao del Sur 9716

President: Mamintal A. Adiong Jr.

Programmes

Agriculture (Agriculture; Agronomy); **Business Administration** (Accountancy; Business Administration); **Computer Technology** (Computer Engineering); **Education** (Education; Primary Education; Secondary Education); **Political Sciences** (Political Sciences)

History: Founded 2002.

Degrees and Diplomas: *Associate Degree*; *Bachelor's Degree*

Last Updated: 22/07/10

ADVANCED INSTITUTE OF TECHNOLOGY

Sangi, New Road, Pajo, Lapu-Lapu City, Cebu 6015
Tel: +63(32) 340-5534
Fax: +63(32) 340-5534
EMail: ait_96@yahoo.com

President: Fernanda E. Ybañez

Programmes

Aircraft Maintenance (Air Transport); **Computer Science and Technology** (Computer Engineering; Computer Science); **Education** (Education; Mathematics Education; Preschool Education; Primary Education; Secondary Education); **Hotel and Restaurant Management** (Hotel and Restaurant; Hotel Management)

History: Founded 1994.

Degrees and Diplomas: *Associate Degree*; *Bachelor's Degree*

Last Updated: 22/07/10

ADVENTIST COLLEGE OF TECHNOLOGY

Acmonan, Tupi, South Cotabato 9505
EMail: act_inbox@yahoo.com

Director: Ismael R. Asunsion

Programmes

Education (Mathematics Education; Primary Education; Religious Education; Secondary Education)

History: Founded 1994.

Degrees and Diplomas: *Certificate/Diploma*; *Bachelor's Degree*

Last Updated: 22/07/10

ADVENTIST INTERNATIONAL INSTITUTE OF ADVANCED STUDIES (AIIAS)

PO Box 038, Silang, Cavite 4118
Tel: +63(46) 414-4300
Fax: +63(46) 414-4301
EMail: oberholster@aiias.edu
Website: http://www.aiias.edu

President: Stephen Guptill (2007-)
Tel: +63(46) 414-43-06
EMail: sguptill@aiias.edu; president@aiias.edu

Registrar: Maria T. Cairus EMail: registrar@aiias.edu

Vice-President, Finance: Max Langi

International Relations: Frederick Oberholster, Vice-President, Academic
Tel: +63(46) 414-4311, Fax: +63(46) 414-4381 +63(46) 414-4309

Graduate Departments

Business *(Graduate School)* (Business Administration) *Chair*: Eustacio Penniecook; **Education** *(Graduate School)* (Education) *Chair*: Prema Gaikwad; **Health Sciences** *(Graduate School)* (Public Health) *Chair*: Gina Segovia-Siapco

Schools

Theology *(Seminary)* (Bible; Missionary Studies; Theology) *Dean*: Gerald Klingbeil

History: Founded 1957 as Philippine Union College. Acquired present status 1987.

Accrediting Agencies: Commission on Higher Education (CHED); Philippine Accrediting Association of Schools, Colleges and Universities (PAASCU); Association for Theological Education in Southeast Asia

Degrees and Diplomas: *Post Baccalaureate Certificate/Diploma*: Business Administration; Public Health (Advanced Certificate in Public Health); *Master's Degree*: Public Health (MPH); Religion; Education (MA); Theology; Ministry; Divinity (MTh; MMin; MDiv); *PhD*: Ministry (DMin); Religion; Business; Christian Education (PhD). Also: Education Specialist (EdS) degree, 18 months after Master's

Libraries: 48,278 vols; 122 periodical subscriptions

Last Updated: 22/07/10

ADVENTIST TECHNOLOGICAL INSTITUTE

Dicoloc, Jimenez, Misamis Occidental 7204
Tel: +63(88)272-2826
Fax: +63(88)272-2826
EMail: aurora_1217@yahoo.com.ph

President: Albert D. Quiza

Programmes

Business Administration (Business Administration; Finance; Human Resources; Management)

History: Founded 2004.

Degrees and Diplomas: *Bachelor's Degree*

Last Updated: 23/07/10

ADVENTIST UNIVERSITY OF THE PHILIPPINES (AUP)

PO Box 1834, Putting Kahoy, Silang, Cavite 4118
Tel: +63(49) 541-1211
Fax: +63(49) 521-1228
EMail: info@aup.edu.ph
Website: http://www.aup.edu.ph/

President: Gladden Flores EMail: president@aup.edu-.ph

Colleges

Arts, Sciences and Technology (Advertising and Publicity; Agricultural Engineering; Agriculture; Automotive Engineering; Biology; Chemistry; Computer Engineering; Computer Science; Crop Production; Dentistry; Design; Electronic Engineering; English; Fine Arts; History; Industrial and Organizational Psychology; Mathematics; Music; Musical Instruments; Painting and Drawing; Psychology; Theology; Zoology); **Business** (Accountancy; Business Administration; Business and Commerce; Hotel and Restaurant; Information Management; Marketing; Secretarial Studies); **Education** (Administration; Biology; Child Care and Development; Educational Administration; Educational and Student Counselling; English; Filipino; Health Education; Health Sciences; History; Home Economics; Information Sciences; Leadership; Library Science; Mathematics; Mathematics Education; Music; Music Education; Physical Education; Primary Education; Psychology; Religious Education; Science Education; Secondary Education; Social Studies; Technology); **Health** (Dietetics; Health Education; Medical Technology; Nutrition; Public Health); **Nursing** (Health Education; Nursing); **Theology** (History of Religion; Philosophy; Theology)

History: Founded 1917, acquired present status and title 1996.

Governing Bodies: Board of Trustees

Admission Requirements: Graduation from high school

Main Language(s) of Instruction: English

Accrediting Agencies: Association of Christian Schools and Colleges; Adventist Accrediting Association

Degrees and Diplomas: *Certificate/Diploma*: 2 yrs; *Associate Degree*: 2 yrs; *Bachelor's Degree*: 4 yrs; *Master's Degree*: a further 2 yrs; *PhD*: a further 2 yrs

Student Services: Academic counselling, Canteen, Foreign student adviser, Health services, Nursery care, Social counselling, Sports facilities

Publications: Graduate Research Journal *(annually)*; University Research Journal *(annually)*

Press or Publishing House: AUP Printing Press

Last Updated: 23/07/10

AEMILIANUM INSTITUTE

Rizal Street, Piot, City of Sorsogon, Sorsogon 4700
Tel: +63(56) 211-1297
Fax: +63(56) 211-2330
EMail: aemilianum@yahoo.com; paolutto@yahoo.com

President: Richard Germanetto

Programmes

Undergraduate and Professional (Automotive Engineering; Business Administration; Communication Studies; Computer Engineering; Computer Networks; Computer Science; Construction Engineering; Education; Electronic Engineering; Engineering; English; Information Technology; Law; Mechanical Engineering; Metal Techniques; Political Sciences; Preschool Education; Primary Education; Secondary Education; Secretarial Studies; Telecommunications Engineering)

History: Founded 1985.

Degrees and Diplomas: *Certificate/Diploma*: 1-3 yrs; *Bachelor's Degree*: 4 yrs; *Bachelor's Degree*: Engineering, 5 yrs; *Master's Degree*: a further 2 yrs

Last Updated: 23/07/10

AERONAUTICAL ACADEMY OF THE PHILIPPINES

Baras, Camarines Sur
Tel: +63(54) 472-9866 +63(54) 811-8880
Fax: +63(54) 472-9866

President: Raul P. Hebrio

Programmes

Aeronautical Engineering (Aeronautical and Aerospace Engineering); **Aircraft Maintenance Technology** (Air Transport); **Avionics Technology** (Aeronautical and Aerospace Engineering)

History: Founded 1998.

Degrees and Diplomas: *Bachelor's Degree*: 4 yrs; *Bachelor's Degree*: Engineering, 5 yrs

Last Updated: 23/07/10

AGO FOUNDATION COLLEGE

Concepcion Grande, Naga City, Camarines Sur 4400
Tel: +63(54) 811-6520
Fax: +63(54) 811-1355

President: Angelita F. Ago

Programmes

Business Administration (Business Administration; Secretarial Studies); **Hotel and Restaurant Management** (Hotel and Restaurant; Hotel Management); **Medical Technology** (Medical Technology); **Nursing** (Nursing); **Radiologic Technology** (Radiology)

History: Founded 1985.

Degrees and Diplomas: *Certificate/Diploma*: 2 yrs; *Bachelor's Degree*: 3-4 yrs

Last Updated: 23/07/10

AGO MEDICAL AND EDUCATIONAL CENTER - BICOL CHRISTIAN COLLEGE OF MEDICINE

Rizal St., Legazpi City, Albay 4500
Tel: +63(52) 481-1155
Fax: +63(52) 245-5058
EMail: amecbccm@malcity.com

President: Angelita F. Ago

Programmes

Graduate (Health Education; Public Health); **Undergraduate and Professional** (Dentistry; Health Sciences; Hotel and Restaurant; Hotel Management; Mass Communication; Medical Technology; Medicine; Nursing; Physical Therapy; Psychology; Radiology)

History: Founded 1975. Acquired present status 1979.

Degrees and Diplomas: *Certificate/Diploma*: 1 1/2 yr; *Bachelor's Degree*: 3 1/2-4 yrs; *Post Baccalaureate Certificate/Diploma*: 5 yrs; *Master's Degree*: a further 1 1/2 yrs

Last Updated: 23/07/10

AGONCILLO COLLEGE

Agoncillo, Batangas 4211
Tel: +63(43) 210-2228
Fax: +63(43) 210-3320
EMail: Agoncillocollege_inc@yahoo.com

President: Anna Queen Gloria M. Camad

Programmes

Computer Studies (Computer Engineering; Computer Science); **Criminology** (Criminology); **Customs Administration** (Taxation); **Education** (Education; Preschool Education; Primary Education; Secondary Education)

History: Founded 2006.

Degrees and Diplomas: *Bachelor's Degree*

Last Updated: 23/07/10

AGOO COMPUTER COLLEGE PHILS.

Cases Boulevard, Agoo, La Union 2504
Tel: +63(72) 710-0087
Fax: +63(72) 521-0165

EMail: agoocomputercollege@yahoo.com; philippines@justice.com

President: Alex A. Valdez

Programmes

Computer Studies (Computer Engineering; Computer Science; Software Engineering); **Secretarial Administration** (Computer Science; Secretarial Studies)

History: Founded 1987. Acquired present status 1996.

Degrees and Diplomas: *Bachelor's Degree*

Last Updated: 23/07/10

AGRO-INDUSTRIAL FOUNDATION COLLEGE OF THE PHILIPPINES - DAVAO

Bolton Riverside, Ecoland, Matina, Davao City, Davao del Sur 8000
Tel: +63(82)303-0377
Fax: +63(82) 301-0041
EMail: agrocollege@yahoo.com

President: Sofia R. Basalo

Programmes

Education (Education; Preschool Education; Primary Education; Secondary Education); **Electrical Engineering** (Electrical Engineering); **Hotel and Restaurant Management** (Hotel and Restaurant; Hotel Management); **Marine Studies** (Marine Engineering; Marine Transport)

History: Founded 1978.

Degrees and Diplomas: *Bachelor's Degree*: 4 yrs

Last Updated: 23/07/10

AGRO-INDUSTRIAL FOUNDATION COLLEGE OF THE PHILIPPINES - STA. MARIA

Avila Street, Sta. Maria, Davao del Sur 8011
Tel: +63(82) 276-0210

President: Sofia R. Basalo

Programmes

Education (Education; English; Mathematics Education; Primary Education; Secondary Education)

History: Founded 1974.

Degrees and Diplomas: *Bachelor's Degree*: 4 yrs

Last Updated: 23/07/10

AGUSAN BUSINESS AND ARTS FOUNDATION

Capitol Drive, Butuan City, Agusan del Norte 8600
Tel: +63(85) 342-8185
EMail: abafi@email.com

Administrator: Mercedes G. Pag-ong

Programmes

Business Administration (Accountancy; Business Administration; Management; Secretarial Studies); **Education** (Education; Primary Education; Science Education; Secondary Education)

History: Founded 1983. Acquired present status 1988.

Degrees and Diplomas: *Bachelor's Degree*: 4 yrs

Last Updated: 23/07/10

AGUSAN COLLEGES

Del Pilar Street, Butuan City, Agusan del Norte 8600
Tel: +63 (85) 341-1523
Fax: +63 (85) 342-8004
EMail: sargon@mozcom.com

President: Thucydides Chanjueco-Sadiasa

Programmes

Arts and Humanities (Arts and Humanities); **Business Administration** (Accountancy; Business Administration; Business and Commerce; Finance; Human Resources; Management; Marketing; Secretarial Studies); **Computer Studies** (Business Computing; Computer Science); **Education** (Education; Primary Education; Secondary Education)

History: Founded 1951.

Degrees and Diplomas: *Bachelor's Degree*; *Master's Degree*

Last Updated: 23/07/10

AGUSAN DEL SUR COLLEGE

Narra Avenue, Bayugan, Agusan del Sur 8502
Tel: +63(85) 343-6958
Fax: +63(85) 231-2150
EMail: adsco_pres@yahoo.com

President: Inocencio P. Angeles, Sr.

Programmes

Arts and Humanities (Arts and Humanities; English; Political Sciences); **Business Administration** (Accountancy; Business Administration; Business and Commerce; Computer Science; English; Finance; Marketing; Secretarial Studies); **Education** (English; Primary Education; Secondary Education); **Nursing** (Nursing)

History: Founded 1966 as Southern Agusan Institute (1966-1994). Acquired present status and title 1994.

Degrees and Diplomas: *Associate Degree*; *Bachelor's Degree*: 4 yrs
Last Updated: 23/07/10

AGUSAN INSTITUTE OF TECHNOLOGY

North Montilla Blvd., Butuan City, Agusan del Norte 8600
Tel: +63 (85) 342-9996 +63 (85) 342-5430
Fax: +63 (85) 342-5430
EMail: ait@yahoo.com

President: Shirley T. Lim EMail: ait_stlim@hotmail.com

Programmes

Business Administration (Accountancy; Business Administration; Business and Commerce; Management; Public Administration); **Criminology** (Criminology); **Elementary Education** (English; Filipino; History; Home Economics; Home Economics Education; Mathematics Education; Primary Education; Science Education); **Engineering** (Automotive Engineering; Electronic Engineering; Mechanical Engineering); **Hotel and Restaurant Management** (Hotel and Restaurant; Hotel Management); **Marine Studies** (Marine Transport); **Marine Transportation**; **Secondary Education** (English; Filipino; History; Home Economics; Home Economics Education; Mathematics Education; Physical Education; Science Education; Secondary Education)

History: Founded 1985.

Degrees and Diplomas: *Associate Degree*; *Bachelor's Degree*: 4 yrs; *Master's Degree*
Last Updated: 23/07/10

AIR LINK INTERNATIONAL AVIATION COLLEGE

Domestic Airport Rd., Pasay City, Fourth District, Metro Manila 1301
Tel: +63(2) 834-1060 +63(2) 851-8485
Fax: +63(2) 854-8682

President: Geronimo A. Amurao

Programmes

Business Administration (Business Administration); **Computer Science** (Computer Science); **Engineering and Technology** (Aeronautical and Aerospace Engineering; Air Transport); **Tourism** (Tourism)

History: Founded 1984. Formerly known as Air Link International Aviation School.

Degrees and Diplomas: *Certificate/Diploma*; *Bachelor's Degree*: 4 yrs; *Bachelor's Degree*: Aerosapace Engineering, 5 yrs
Last Updated: 28/03/11

AKLAN CATHOLIC COLLEGE

Archbishop Reyes Street, Kalibo, Aklan 5600
Tel: +63(36) 268-4152
Fax: +63(36) 268-4010
EMail: info@acc.edu.ph
Website: http://www.acc.edu.ph/

President: Jose Gualberto I. Villasis

Registrar: Cecilia S. Calizo

Vice-President, Administration: Reynold G. Corcino

Colleges

Business Education (Accountancy; Banking; Business Administration; Business Computing; Finance; Human Resources; Management; Marketing); **Criminology** (Criminology); **Hospitality Management** (Cooking and Catering; Hotel and Restaurant; Hotel Management; Tourism); **Information and Computer Studies** (Computer Engineering; Computer Science; Information Technology); **Law** (Law); **Nursing** (Nursing); **Teacher Education and Liberal Arts** (Biology; Education; Educational Administration; Educational and Student Counselling; Educational Psychology; English; Filipino; Health Education; Mathematics Education; Political Sciences; Primary Education; Science Education; Secondary Education; Teacher Training)

Schools

Graduate Studies (Education; Educational Administration; Educational and Student Counselling; Educational Psychology)

History: Founded 1945.

Degrees and Diplomas: *Certificate/Diploma*; *Associate Degree*: 2 yrs; *Bachelor's Degree*: 4 yrs; *Master's Degree*: a further 2 yrs
Last Updated: 23/07/10

AKLAN POLYTECHNIC INSTITUTE

Quezon Avenue, Kalibo, Aklan 5600
Tel: +63(36) 262-3202 +63(36) 262-5751
Fax: +63(36) 262-3203
EMail: api-mtc@kalibo-cable.tv

President: Rodillo L. Policarpio

Programmes

Undergraduate and Professional (Business Administration; Business Computing; Computer Engineering; Computer Science; Engineering; Marine Engineering; Marine Transport; Nursing; Taxation)

History: Founded 1986.

Degrees and Diplomas: *Certificate/Diploma*; *Associate Degree*: 2 yrs; *Bachelor's Degree*: 4 yrs; *Bachelor's Degree*: Engineering, 5 yrs
Last Updated: 23/07/10

ALBAY INSTITUTE OF TECHNOLOGY

Sta. Cruz, Ligao City, Albay 4504
Tel: +63(52) 837-7403
EMail: aitligao@yahoo.com; frdelossantos@yahoo.com

President: Reynaldo B. Belleza

Programmes

Business Administration (Business Administration; Business Computing; Management; Secretarial Studies); **Computer Technology** (Computer Engineering)

History: Founded 1993.

Degrees and Diplomas: *Associate Degree*: 2 yrs; *Bachelor's Degree*: 4 yrs
Last Updated: 23/07/10

ALDERSGATE COLLEGE

Bonfal Street, Solano, Nueva Vizcaya 3709
Tel: +63(78) 326-5085 +63(78) 326-5645
Fax: +63(78) 326-5085
EMail: aldersgate@hotmail.com
Website: http://www.aldersgate-college.com

President: Junifen F. Gauuan EMail: junifenf.gauuan@yahoo.com

Colleges

Arts, Science and Education *(Also Graduate School of Education)* (Astronomy and Space Science; Automation and Control Engineering; Biology; Education; Educational Administration; Educational Technology; Electrical and Electronic Engineering; English; Health Sciences; Media Studies; Microbiology; Modern Languages; Multimedia; Preschool Education; Primary Education; Religious Education; Robotics; Secondary Education; Social Sciences; Special Education); **Engineering and Technology** (Civil Engineering; Computer Engineering; Computer Science; Electrical Engineering; Engineering; Information Technology; Technology)

Schools

Business and Accountancy *(Also Graduate School of Management)* (Accountancy; Business Administration; Business and Commerce; Finance; Human Resources; International Business; Management; Marketing; Public Administration); **Criminology** (Criminology); **Hospitality Management** (Cooking and Catering; Hotel and Restaurant; Hotel Management; Tourism); **Informatics** (Computer Science; Information Technology; Media Studies);

Medical Sciences *(Also Graduate School of Nursing)* (Midwifery; Nursing)

History: Founded 1965.

Degrees and Diplomas: *Associate Degree*: 2 yrs; *Bachelor's Degree*: 4-5 yrs; *Master's Degree*: a further 2-3 yrs

Last Updated: 23/07/10

ALEJANDRO COLLEGES

Gen. Luis Street, Novaliches, Quezon City, Second District, Metro Manila
Tel: +63(2) 937-2639 +63(2) 937-2640
Fax: +63(2) 977-5555
EMail: alejandrocolleges@yahoo.com

President: Constancia C. Sarmiento

Programmes

Undergraduate and Professional (Architectural and Environmental Design; Architecture; Business Administration; Civil Engineering; Computer Science; Education; Electrical Engineering; Electronic Engineering; Engineering; Hotel and Restaurant; Hotel Management; Industrial Engineering; Marine Transport; Primary Education; Secondary Education; Secretarial Studies)

History: Founded 1986. Formerly known as Alejandro Institute of Technology.

Degrees and Diplomas: *Certificate/Diploma*: 1-2 yrs; *Associate Degree*: 2 yrs; *Bachelor's Degree*: 4 yrs; *Bachelor's Degree*: Computer Engineering; Civil Engineering; Electrical Engineering; Electronics and Telecommunications Engineering, 5 yrs

Last Updated: 26/07/10

ALEMARZ SCHOOL OF SCIENCE AND TECHNOLOGY

Purok 3A Upland, Valencia City, Bukidnon 8709
Tel: +63(88) 828-3303
Fax: +63(88) 828-3303
EMail: alemarzs@yahoo.com

Director: Orlando C. Cabahug

Programmes

Undergraduate and Professional (Business Administration; Education; Primary Education)

History: Founded 1972.

Degrees and Diplomas: *Certificate/Diploma*: 1 yr; *Associate Degree*: 2 yrs; *Bachelor's Degree*

Last Updated: 26/07/10

ALEXIAN COLLEGE OF PARANG

Atis St., Parang, Shariff Kabunsuan 9604

President: Subaida Akil-Lineses

Programmes

Education (Education; Primary Education; Secondary Education)

History: Founded 2004.

Degrees and Diplomas: *Bachelor's Degree*

Last Updated: 28/03/11

ALFELOR SR. MEMORIAL COLLEGE

Poblacion Zone 2, Del Gallego, Camarines Sur 4411
Tel: +63(42) 304-8549
Fax: +63(42) 304-8549
EMail: asmc1985@yahoo.com

President: Eduardo B. Tibi

Programmes

Business Administration (Business and Commerce; Management); **Criminology** (Criminology); **Education** (Education; English; Filipino; Mathematics Education; Preschool Education; Primary Education; Science Education; Secondary Education); **Political Sciences** (Political Sciences)

History: Founded 1985.

Degrees and Diplomas: *Bachelor's Degree*: 4 yrs

Last Updated: 26/07/10

ALITAGTAG COLLEGE

Poblacion West, Alitagtag, Batangas 4205
Tel: +63(43) 211-4985
Fax: +63(43) 772-0552
EMail: alitagtagcollege@hotmail.com

President: Catherine R. Banta

Programmes

Education (Education; English; Mathematics Education; Preschool Education; Primary Education; Secondary Education); **Engineering and Technology** (Computer Engineering; Computer Science; Industrial Engineering; Technology)

History: Founded 1948. Acquired present status 1999.

Degrees and Diplomas: *Certificate/Diploma*: 2 yrs; *Bachelor's Degree*: 4 yrs

Last Updated: 26/07/10

ALL NATIONS COLLEGE

VV Soliven, Mayamot, Antipolo City, Rizal 1870
Tel: +63(2) 647-2899
Fax: +63(2) 250-1386
EMail: all_nations_college@yahoo.com

President: Teodora Sarmiento

Programmes

Education (Art Education; Education; English; Health Education; Music Education; Physical Education; Preschool Education; Primary Education; Secondary Education); **Theology** (Bible; Theology)

History: Founded 2005.

Degrees and Diplomas: *Bachelor's Degree*

Last Updated: 26/07/10

AMA COMPUTER UNIVERSITY (AMACU)

Maximina Street, Villa Arca Subd., Proj. 8, Quezon City, Second District, Metro Manila 1106
Tel: +63(2) 330-0378
Fax: +63(2) 330-0358
EMail: info@amaes.edu.ph
Website: http://www.ama-university.com/

President: Amable C. Aguiluz IX

Colleges

Arts and Science (Arts and Humanities; Economics; English; Mass Communication; Political Sciences; Psychology); **Business Administration and Accountancy** (Accountancy; Business Administration; Finance; Health Administration; Information Management; Management; Marketing); **Computer Studies** (Computer Networks; Computer Science; Information Management; Information Technology; Multimedia; Robotics; Software Engineering; Systems Analysis); **Education** (Computer Education; Computer Science; Education; English; Mathematics; Primary Education; Secondary Education; Special Education); **Engineering** (Automation and Control Engineering; Computer Engineering; Computer Networks; Electrical Engineering; Electronic Engineering; Industrial Engineering; Production Engineering; Robotics; Telecommunications Engineering)

Courses

Call Centre *(Short Course)*; **Maritime Studies** (Marine Engineering; Marine Transport)

Schools

Graduate Studies (Business Administration; Computer Education; Computer Science); **Medicine and Allied Health care** *(AMA School of Medicine, Makati City and East Rizal)* (Health Sciences; Nursing)

Further Information: 40 AMA colleges all over the Philippines: National Capital Region: Manila Campus; Caloocan Campus; Fairview Campus; Las Piñas Campus; Makati Campus; Parañaque Campus; Pasig Campus; Quezon City Campus. Region I: Laoag Campus; La Union Campus. Region II: Tuguegarao Campus; Baguio Campus; Santiago Campus. Region III: Malolos Campus; Pampanga Campus; Angeles Campus; Cabanuatan Campus; Tarlac Campus; Olongapo Campus. Region IV: East Rizal Campus; Biñan Campus; Calamba Campus; Cavite Campus; Batangas

Campus; Lipa Campus; Lucena Campus; AMA Sta. Cruz Campus. Region V: Legazpi Campus; Naga Campus. Region VI: Bacolod Campus; Iloilo Campus; Dumaguete Campus. Region VII: Cebu Campus. Region VIII: Tacloban Campus. Region IX: Zamboanga Campus. Region X: Cagayan de Oro Campus. Region XI: General Santos Campus; Davao Campus. Also AMA Computer Learning Center College (General Santos City (Dadiangas), South Cotabato and Tacloban City, Leyte)

History: Founded 1987 as AMA Computer College. Acquired present status and title 2001.

Degrees and Diplomas: *Bachelor's Degree*: 4-5 yrs; *Master's Degree*; *PhD*

Last Updated: 26/07/10

AMANDO COPE COLLEGE

Baranghawon, Tabaco City, Albay 4511
Tel: +63(52) 487-4455
Fax: +63(52) 830-1334

President: Antonio C. Cope

Programmes

Education (Education; Mathematics Education; Primary Education; Secondary Education); **Nursing** (Nursing)

History: Founded 2004.

Degrees and Diplomas: *Bachelor's Degree*: 4 yrs

Last Updated: 26/07/10

AMORE COLLEGE

Colegio de Amore
Trece Martires City, Cavite

Vice-President: Raul Bolante

Programmes

Computer Science (Computer Science); **Criminology** (Criminology); **Hotel and Restaurant Management** (Hotel and Restaurant; Hotel Management)

Degrees and Diplomas: *Bachelor's Degree*

Last Updated: 08/09/10

ANDRES BONIFACIO COLLEGE

College Park, Miputak, Dipolog City, Zamboanga del Norte 7100
Tel: +63 212-2937
Fax: +63 212-9178
EMail: andres_bonifacio_college@yahoo.com
Website: http://www.abcollege.edu.ph/

President: Sancho S. Amatong

Programmes

Business Administration (Accountancy; Business Administration; Business and Commerce; Finance; Human Resources; Management; Public Administration); **Criminology** (Criminology); **Education** (Art Education; Education; Educational Administration; English; Filipino; Health Education; Home Economics; Home Economics Education; Literature; Mathematics Education; Music Education; Physical Education; Primary Education; Science Education; Social Studies; Technology Education); **Engineering** (Agricultural Engineering; Civil Engineering; Computer Engineering; Computer Science; Electrical Engineering; Electronic Engineering; Engineering; Mechanical Engineering; Telecommunications Engineering); **Mass Communication** (Mass Communication); **Political Sciences** (Political Sciences)

History: Founded 1940, acquired present status and title 1946.

Degrees and Diplomas: *Bachelor's Degree*: 4-5 yrs; *Master's Degree*

Last Updated: 26/07/10

ANDRES SORIANO COLLEGE

Andres Soriano Avenue, Bislig City, Surigao del Sur 8311
Tel: +63(86) 853-2306
Fax: +63(86) 828-2065
EMail: asc1185@panabo.philcom.com.ph

President: Inocencio C. Sayawan

Programmes

Arts and Humanities (Arts and Humanities; English; History; Social Studies); **Commerce** (Accountancy; Banking; Business and Commerce; Finance; Management); **Computer Science and Technology** (Computer Science); **Education** (English; Mathematics; Primary Education; Secondary Education; Social Studies)

History: Founded in 1951 as Andrers Soriano Junior College. Acquired present status in 1981.

Degrees and Diplomas: *Bachelor's Degree*; *Master's Degree*

Last Updated: 26/07/10

ANDRES SORIANO MEMORIAL COLLEGE

Bo. Don Andres Soriano, Toledo City, Cebu 6038
Tel: +63(32) 235-2026
Fax: +63(32) 235-2170

Director: Nonita P. Legaspi

Programmes

Education (Education; English; Mathematics Education; Preschool Education; Primary Education; Secondary Education); **Engineering and Technology** (Automotive Engineering; Business Computing; Computer Engineering; Technology)

History: Founded 1965.

Degrees and Diplomas: *Bachelor's Degree*

Last Updated: 26/07/10

ANGELES SYSTEMS PLUS COMPUTER COLLEGE

Sta Isabel Building, Balibago, Angeles City, Pampanga 2009
Tel: +63(45) 322-6966
Fax: +63(45) 322-6966
EMail: spccbal@mail.ang.sequel.net

President: Lourdes R. Bustamante

Programmes

Business Administration (Accountancy; Business Administration; Hotel and Restaurant; Hotel Management; Tourism); **Education** (Art Education; Education; English; Mathematics Education; Music Education; Physical Education; Primary Education; Secondary Education); **Engineering and Technology** (Computer Engineering; Computer Science; Electronic Engineering; Information Technology; Telecommunications Engineering); **Nursing** (Nursing)

History: Founded 1985, acquiring present status in 2204.

Degrees and Diplomas: *Certificate/Diploma*: 6 months - 2 yrs; *Associate Degree*: 2 yrs; *Bachelor's Degree*: 4 yrs; *Bachelor's Degree*: Engineering, 5 yrs; *Master's Degree*: a further 2 yrs

Last Updated: 26/07/10

ANGELES UNIVERSITY FOUNDATION

MacArthur Highway, Angeles City, Pampanga 2009
Tel: +63(45) 888-2663
Fax: +63(45) 845-1491
EMail: auf@auf.edu.ph
Website: http://www.auf.edu.ph

President: Ricardo P. Pama

Vice-President for Administration: Sylvia M. Soriano

International Relations: Lourdes (LOU) T. Nepomuceno, Director, Office of International Affairs EMail: ltnepomuceno@auf.edu.ph

Colleges

Allied Medical Professions (Medical Technology; Medicine; Nursing; Occupational Therapy; Pharmacy; Physical Therapy; Public Health); **Arts and Sciences** (Biology; Communication Studies; Psychology); **Business and Accountancy** (Accountancy; Business Administration; Hotel and Restaurant; Hotel Management; Human Resources; Management; Marketing; Tourism); **Computer Studies** (Computer Science; Information Technology); **Criminal Justice Education** (Criminal Law; Criminology); **Education** (Biological and Life Sciences; Education; English; Ethics; Filipino; Health Education; Mathematics Education; Music Education; Physical Education; Preschool Education; Primary Education; Science Education; Secondary Education; Social Studies; Special Education); **Engineering** (Aeronautical and Aerospace Engineering; Civil Engineering;

Computer Engineering; Electrical Engineering; Electronic Engineering; Engineering; Engineering Management); **Nursing** (Nursing)

Schools

Graduate Studies (Business Administration; Civil Engineering; Computer Engineering; Education; Educational Administration; Educational and Student Counselling; Engineering; English; Filipino; Information Technology; Management; Mathematics; Mathematics Education; Nursing; Physical Education; Public Administration; Public Health; Science Education); **Law** (Law); **Medicine** (Medicine)

History: Founded 1962 as Angeles Institute of Technology, became University 1971 and University Foundation 1975. Formally inaugurated as Catholic University 1978. Granted autonomous status by CHED 2003. A private Institution financed by students' fees and donations.

Governing Bodies: Board of Trustees

Academic Year: June to March (June-October; November-March)

Admission Requirements: Graduation from high school and passing the Angeles University Foundation admission test (AUFCAT)

Main Language(s) of Instruction: English

Accrediting Agencies: Philippine Accreditation Association of Schools, Colleges and Universities

Degrees and Diplomas: *Bachelor's Degree*: 4-5 yrs; *Post Baccalaureate Certificate/Diploma*: Medicine (MD), 4 yrs; *Master's Degree*: Business Administration; Mathematics; Public Administration, a further 2 yrs; *PhD*: Educational Management; Public Administration (PhD), a further 3 yrs

Student Services: Academic counselling, Canteen, Cultural centre, Employment services, Foreign student adviser, Foreign Studies Centre, Health services, Language programs, Social counselling, Sports facilities

Student Residential Facilities: Yes

Libraries: Central Library, c. 40,000 vols

Publications: AUF Journal *(biannually)*; Researcher's Digest *(quarterly)*

Press or Publishing House: Angeles Publishing House

Last Updated: 26/07/10

ANGELICUM COLLEGE

112, M.J. Cuenco Street, Quezon City, Second District, Metro Manila 1114
Tel: +63(2) 712-1745
Fax: +63(2) 412-5860
EMail: academicaffairs@angelicum.edu.ph
Website: http://www.angelicum.edu.ph

Rector: Ferdinand L. Bautista, O.P.
EMail: rector@angelicum.edu.ph

Programmes

Business Administration (Business Administration; Human Resources; Management); **Communication Arts** (Cinema and Television; Communication Arts); **Computer Science** (Computer Science); **Education** (Education; Mathematics Education; Preschool Education; Primary Education; Science Education; Secondary Education); **Information Management and Technology** (Information Management; Information Technology)

History: Founded 1972. Acquired present status 1995. Previously known as Angelicum School.

Degrees and Diplomas: *Associate Degree*; *Bachelor's Degree*: 4 yrs

Last Updated: 27/07/10

ANNUNCIATION COLLEGE OF BACON SORSOGON UNIT

479 Magsaysay Avenue, City of Sorsogon, Sorsogon 4700
Tel: +63(56) 211-1659
Fax: +63(56) 211-1659
EMail: acbsui_sorcity@yahoo.com

President: Divinagracia Dino-Barcelo

Programmes

Graduate (Education; Educational Administration; Educational and Student Counselling; English; Public Administration); **Undergraduate and Professional** (Accountancy; Agricultural Engineering; Arts and Humanities; Business Administration; Business and Commerce; Business Computing; Civil Engineering; Computer Science; Economics; Education; Engineering; English; Filipino; Health Education; Management; Mathematics; Mathematics and Computer Science; Mathematics Education; Natural Sciences; Political Sciences; Primary Education; Public Administration; Science Education; Secondary Education; Social Studies)

History: Founded 1961, acquired present status and title 1967.

Degrees and Diplomas: *Certificate/Diploma*: 2 yrs; *Bachelor's Degree*: 4 yrs; *Bachelor's Degree*: Engineering, 5 yrs; *Master's Degree*: a further 3 yrs; *PhD*: 4 yrs

Last Updated: 27/07/10

ANTONIO R. PACHECO COLLEGE

#36 San Gregorio Ext., Kimpo Subd., Maguindanao, Cotabato City, Cotabato 9600
Tel: +63(64) 421-7173
EMail: pacheco@mozcom.com

President: Maria T. Pacheco

Programmes

Business Administration (Business Administration; Business and Commerce; Management); **Education** (Education; English; Filipino; History; Mathematics Education; Preschool Education; Primary Education; Secondary Education); **Information Technology** (Computer Science; Information Technology)

History: Founded 1996.

Degrees and Diplomas: *Bachelor's Degree*: 4 yrs

Last Updated: 27/07/10

AQUINAS UNIVERSITY OF LEGAZPI

Peñaranda Street, Rawis, Legazpi City, Albay 4500
Tel: +63(52) 482-0543
Fax: +63(52) 482-0540
EMail: registrar@aq.edu.ph
Website: http://www.aq.edu.ph/

Rector and President: Ramonclaro G. Mendez, O.P.
EMail: rector@aq.edu.ph

Registrar: Leticia R. Roque

Colleges

Arts, Sciences and Education (Art Education; Communication Studies; Education; English; Health Education; Information Sciences; Library Science; Music Education; Philosophy; Physical Education; Political Sciences; Primary Education; Psychology; Science Education; Secondary Education); **Business Management and Accountancy** (Accountancy; Business Administration; Economics; Finance; Hotel and Restaurant; Hotel Management; Human Resources; Management; Marketing; Tourism); **Law** (Law); **Nursing and Health Sciences** (Health Sciences; Midwifery; Nursing)

Institutes

Polytechnic (Advertising and Publicity; Architecture; Civil Engineering; Computer Engineering; Computer Science; Electronic Engineering; Engineering; Fine Arts; Industrial Engineering; Telecommunications Engineering)

History: Founded 1948 as Junior College, administration transferred to the Dominican Fathers 1965, acquired University status 1969. A private institution.

Governing Bodies: Board of Trustees

Academic Year: June to March (June-October; November-March)

Admission Requirements: Graduation from high school or foreign equivalent, and entrance examination

Main Language(s) of Instruction: Filipino, English

Degrees and Diplomas: *Certificate/Diploma*: Accountancy Aide (AA); Junior Secretarial Course (JSC), 2 yrs; *Associate Degree*: 2 yrs; *Bachelor's Degree*: Accountancy (BSA); Arts (AB); Business

Administration (BSBA); Computer Science (BSCoS); Elementary Education (BSEd); Nursing (BSN); Secondary Education (BSEd); Secretarial Administration (BSSA), 4 yrs; *Bachelor's Degree*: Architecture (BSArch); Civil Engineering (BSCE), 5 yrs; *Bachelor's Degree*: Law (LlB), 4 yrs following first degree; *Master's Degree*: Arts in Education (MAEd); Arts in Nursing (MAN); Arts in Teaching Science Education (MAT); Business Administration (MBA); Public Administration (MPA); Science in Management Engineering (MSME), a further 3 yrs; *PhD*: Business Administration (DBA); Education, a further 3 yrs

Student Services: Academic counselling, Canteen, Cultural centre, Employment services, Health services, Social counselling, Sports facilities

Student Residential Facilities: Yes

Libraries: Central Library, c. 62,000 vols

Publications: Aquinas Bulletin *(quarterly)*; Page Journal *(quarterly)*

Last Updated: 27/07/10

ARELLANO UNIVERSITY (AU)

2600 Legarda Street, Sampaloc, Manila, First District, Metro Manila 1008
Tel: +63(2) 734-7371
Fax: +63(2) 736-9450
EMail: info@arellano.edu.ph
Website: http://www.arellano.edu.ph

Chairman: Francisco V. Cayco (1995-) Fax: +63(2) 735-3684

Colleges

Arts and Science (Dance; Economics; English; Filipino; History; Performing Arts; Political Sciences; Psychology; Special Education; Translation and Interpretation); **Hospitality and Tourism Management** (Cooking and Catering; Food Science; Food Technology; Hotel and Restaurant; Hotel Management; Tourism)

Graduate Schools

Business (Business Administration; Finance; Management; Marketing); **Education** (Child Care and Development; Education; Educational Administration; Educational and Student Counselling; Educational Psychology; English; Filipino; Home Economics Education; Mathematics Education; Preschool Education; Psychology; Special Education); **Nursing** (Community Health; Nursing; Occupational Health; Psychiatry and Mental Health)

Institutes

Accountancy (Accountancy); **Allied Medical Services** (Laboratory Techniques; Medical Technology; Physical Therapy)

Schools

Business and Commerce (Business Administration; Business and Commerce; Finance; Management; Marketing; Physical Education; Sports); **Computer Science** (Computer Science; Information Technology; Multimedia; Software Engineering); **Education** (Art Education; Biology; Cultural Studies; Education; English; Filipino; Health Education; History; Home Economics; Library Science; Mathematics; Music Education; Natural Sciences; Physical Education; Physics; Preschool Education; Primary Education; Secondary Education; Social Studies); **Law** (Law); **Nursing** (Nursing)

Further Information: Also branches in Malabon, Pasay and Pasig.

History: Founded 1938 as Arellano Law College, acquired present status and title 1947.

Governing Bodies: Board of Trustees

Academic Year: June to March (June-October; October-March)

Admission Requirements: Graduation from high school or recognized equivalent, and entrance examination

Main Language(s) of Instruction: Filipino, English

Degrees and Diplomas: *Certificate/Diploma*; *Bachelor's Degree*; *Master's Degree*; *PhD*

Student Services: Academic counselling, Canteen, Cultural centre, Employment services, Foreign Studies Centre, Health services, Social counselling, Sports facilities

Libraries: c. 35,000 vols

Publications: Philippine Education Quarterly *(quarterly)*

Last Updated: 27/07/10

ARRIESGADO COLLEGE FOUNDATION

201 Bonifacio Street, Tagum City, Davao del Norte 8100
Tel: +63(84) 217-3691
Fax: +63(84) 218-5885
EMail: arriesgadocollege@yahoo.com.ph

President: Vicente C. Arriesgado, Sr.

Programmes

Education (Education; Primary Education); **Nursing** (Nursing)

History: Founded in 1989, acquiring present status in 1995.

Degrees and Diplomas: *Bachelor's Degree*

Last Updated: 27/07/10

ASBURY COLLEGE

Luna St., Anda, Pangasinan 2405
Tel: +63(75) 557-5052
Fax: +63(75) 557-5052
EMail: asburycollege@sbcglobal.net
Website: http://www.asburycollege-anda.org

Director: Harrison M. Caasi

Programmes

Arts and Humanities (English; History; Religious Education; Sociology); **Education** (Education; English; Filipino; Mathematics; Preschool Education; Primary Education; Secondary Education); **Theology**

History: Founded 1947.

Degrees and Diplomas: *Bachelor's Degree*

Last Updated: 27/07/10

ASIA COLLEGE OF ADVANCED STUDIES IN ARTS, SCIENCES AND TECHNOLOGY

Bgy. Sta. Clara, Bobon, Northern Samar 6401

President: Ernesto B. Aban

Programmes

Business Administration (Business Administration; Management); **Education** (Education; English; Mathematics Education; Primary Education; Secondary Education); **Political Sciences** (Political Sciences)

History: Founded 2000.

Degrees and Diplomas: *Certificate/Diploma*; *Bachelor's Degree*

Last Updated: 27/07/10

ASIA PACIFIC COLLEGE

3 Humabon Place, Magallanes Village, Makati City, Metro Manila 1232
Tel: +63(2) 852-9232
Fax: +63(2) 852-2648
EMail: phil77@ibm.net
Website: http://www.apc.edu.ph

President: Paulino Y. Tan

Graduate Schools

Information Management (Information Management; Information Technology)

Schools

Business Administration and Accountancy (Accountancy; Advertising and Publicity; Business Administration; Finance; Human Resources; Management; Marketing; Tourism); **Computer Science and Information Technology** (Computer Engineering; Computer Networks; Computer Science; Information Technology; Software Engineering; Systems Analysis); **Engineering** (Computer Engineering; Electronic Engineering; Engineering); **Multimedia Arts** (Aesthetics; Computer Graphics; Computer Science; Design; Graphic Arts; Multimedia; Painting and Drawing; Photography; Video; Visual Arts)

History: Founded 1991. Formerly known as Asia Pacific Computer Technology Center and Asia Pacific Computer College.

Degrees and Diplomas: *Certificate/Diploma*; *Bachelor's Degree*: 4 yrs; *Master's Degree*: Information Management, a further 2 yrs. Also Executive Program, 2yrs

Student Residential Facilities: Residence Hall for 88 Students
Special Facilities: Computer Laboratories; Auditorium
Last Updated: 27/07/10

ASIA PACIFIC COLLEGE OF ADVANCED STUDIES

A.H. Banzon Street, Ibayo, Balanga City, Bataan 2100
Tel: +63(47) 237-6713 +63(47) 791-1769
Fax: +63(47) 791-3548
EMail: fea@moscom.com

President: Flocerfida E. Ayangco

Programmes

Communication (Communication Studies); **Education** (Biological and Life Sciences; Education; English; Preschool Education; Primary Education; Secondary Education); **Hotel and Restaurant Management** (Hotel and Restaurant; Hotel Management); **Nursing** (Nursing); **Tourism** (Tourism)

History: Founded 1999 as Asia Pacific Academy. Acquired present status 2001.

Degrees and Diplomas: *Bachelor's Degree*
Last Updated: 27/07/10

ASIA SCHOOL OF ARTS AND SCIENCES - THE COLLEGE OF INFORMATION TECHNOLOGY

433, Jorjog Building, Tandang Sora Avenue, Barangay Culiat, Quezon City, Second District, Metro Manila 1126
Tel: +63(2) 455-1926
Fax: +63(2) 455-1924
EMail: asas_cit@indanet.com

President: Cecilia A. Platilla

Programmes

Business Administration (Business Administration; Finance; Human Resources; Management; Marketing); **Computer Science** (Computer Science); **Education** (Education; English; Filipino; Mathematics Education; Primary Education; Secondary Education)

History: Founded 1996 as FASS Institute of Technology -Tandang Sora Inc. Acquired present title 1998.

Degrees and Diplomas: *Certificate/Diploma*: 2 yrs; *Bachelor's Degree*: 4 - 5 yrs
Last Updated: 27/07/10

ASIAN COLLEGE FOUNDATION

Km 3, J.C. Aquino Avenue, Butuan City, Agusan del Norte 8600
Tel: +63(85) 342-3356
Fax: +63(85) 342-3356
EMail: asian_acf@yahoo.com.ph

President: Wenifredo D. Osigan

Programmes

Health Science Education (Health Education; Health Sciences); **Nursing** (Nursing); **Optometry** (Optometry); **Radiologic Technology** (Radiology)

History: Founded 1991.

Degrees and Diplomas: *Certificate/Diploma*; *Associate Degree*; *Bachelor's Degree*: 4 yrs
Last Updated: 27/07/10

ASIAN COLLEGE OF SCIENCE AND TECHNOLOGY (ACSAT)

1013 Aurora Blvd., Cubao, Quezon City, Second District, Metro Manila 1109
Tel: +63(2) 912-3236 +63(2) 434-8868 +63(2) 433-0267
Fax: +63(2) 912-3238
EMail: acsatcenter@acsat.edu.ph
Website: http://www.acsat.edu.ph/

President: Gloria D. Sia Sia

Campuses

Alabang *(Alabang, City of Muntinlupa, Fourth District)* (Business Administration; Business Computing; Computer Engineering; Computer Science; Electronic Engineering; Hotel and Restaurant; Hotel Management; Management; Nursing); **Baliuag** *(Baliuag, Bulacan)* (Business Administration; Computer Engineering; Computer Science; Human Resources; Information Technology; Management; Marketing) *Director*: Orlando C. Verniz; **Bayawan** *(Bayawan, Negros Oriental) Director*: Raoul Francisco D. Sia; **Cabanatuan** *(Cabanatuan City, Nueva Ecija)* (Business Administration; Computer Science; Electronic Engineering) *Director*: Constacio A. Sia; **Cagayan De Oro** *(Cagayan De Oro City, Misamis Oriental)* (Business Administration; Business Computing; Computer Education; Computer Engineering; Computer Science; Electronic Engineering; Human Resources; Information Technology; Management; Marketing) *Director*: Vergie L. Baclaya; **Caloocan** *(Kalookan City, Third District)* (Business Administration; Business Computing; Computer Engineering; Computer Science; Electronic Engineering; Hotel and Restaurant; Hotel Management; Management; Marketing; Nursing); **Dumaguete** *(Dumaguete City, Negros Oriental)* (Accountancy; Business Administration; Computer Engineering; Computer Science; Electronic Engineering; Hotel and Restaurant; Hotel Management; Human Resources; Information Technology; Management; Marketing; Tourism) *Director*: Ma. Renee Sol D. Calumpang

Colleges

Business and Management (Business Administration; Business Computing; Management); **Engineering** (Computer Engineering; Computer Networks; Electronic Engineering; Engineering); **Hotel and Restaurant Management** (Hotel and Restaurant; Hotel Management); **Information and Communications Technology** (Computer Engineering; Computer Science; Electronic Engineering; Information Technology); **Nursing** (Nursing)

History: Founded 1972 as Asian Institute of Electronics. Acquired present status and title 1994.

Degrees and Diplomas: *Certificate/Diploma*; *Associate Degree*; *Bachelor's Degree*: 4 yrs; *Bachelor's Degree*: Computer Engineering, 5 yrs
Last Updated: 27/07/10

ASIAN COLLEGE OF TECHNOLOGY - TALISAY

Colon St., Brgy. Kalubihan, Talisay City, Cebu 6045
Tel: +63(32) 412-3428
Fax: +63(32) 253-1628
EMail: asian_college@yahoo.com

President: Rodrigo A. Abellanosa

Programmes

Business Administration (Business Administration); **Computer Accounting and Management** (Business Computing; Management); **Computer Engineering** (Computer Engineering); **Computer Science** (Computer Science); **Education** (Computer Education; Education; Preschool Education; Primary Education; Secondary Education); **Hotel and Restaurant Management** (Hotel and Restaurant; Hotel Management); **Information Management and Technology** (Information Management; Information Technology); **Nursing** (Nursing); **Physical Therapy** (Physical Therapy)

History: Founded 1992.

Degrees and Diplomas: *Bachelor's Degree*: 4-5 yrs
Last Updated: 27/07/10

ASIAN DEVELOPMENT FOUNDATION COLLEGE

P. Burgos St., Tacloban City, Leyte 6500
Tel: +63(53) 325-8698
Fax: +63(53) 325-7654
EMail: adfc_tac_leyte@yahoo.com

Chief Executive Officer: Edward Y. Chua

Programmes

Business Administration (Accountancy; Business Administration; Business and Commerce; Management); **Criminology** (Criminology); **Education** (Education; Primary Education; Secondary Education); **Engineering** (Civil Engineering; Computer Engineering; Computer Science); **Hotel and Restaurant** (Business Computing; Hotel and Restaurant; Hotel Management); **Information Sciences** (Information Sciences; Information Technology; Journalism; Mass Communication; Radio and Television Broadcasting); **Law** (Law);

Nursing and Midwifery (Midwifery; Nursing); **Philippine Studies** (Cultural Studies; South Asian Studies)

History: Founded 1984.

Degrees and Diplomas: *Certificate/Diploma*: 2 yrs; *Associate Degree*: 2 yrs; *Bachelor's Degree*: 4-5 yrs; *Master's Degree*: a further 2 yrs

Last Updated: 27/07/10

ASIAN INSTITUTE FOR DISTANCE EDUCATION

Unit 302, Greenbelt Mansion, 106 Perea St., Legaspi Village, Makati City, Fourth District, Metro Manila 1229

Tel: +63(2) 810-0968 +63(2) 819-3286

Fax: +63(2) 813-0565

President: Antonio O. Cojuangco

Programmes

Business Administration (Business Administration; Management); **Economics** (Economics); **English** (English); **Political Sciences** (Political Sciences)

History: Founded 1984.

Degrees and Diplomas: *Bachelor's Degree*: 4 yrs

Last Updated: 27/07/10

ASIAN INSTITUTE OF COMPUTER STUDIES

3/F A. Francisco, Ten Commandments Bldg., Rizal Avenue Ext., Grace Park, Caloocan City, Third District, Metro Manila

Tel: +63(2) 363-0497

Fax: +63(2) 935-1651

EMail: admission@aics.edu.ph

Website: http://www.aics.edu.ph

President: Manuel T. Asis

Programmes

Computer Science (Computer Engineering; Computer Networks; Computer Science; Information Management; Secretarial Studies)

Further Information: Branches: Fairview (Quezon City); España (Sampaloc, Manila); Caloocan (Caloocan City); Bicutan (Paranaque City); Taytay (Rizal); Bacoor (Cavite); Dau (Mabalacat, Pampanga); San Fernando (Pampanga); Marilao (Bulacan); Tarlac (Tarlac City); Urdaneta (Pangasinan); Marikina (Marikina City); Guadalupe (Makati); Commonwealth (Quezon City); Cubao (Quezon City); Dasmariñas (Cavite); Baliuag (Bulacan); Tanay (Rizal); Cogeo (Antipolo City); Sta. Rosa (Laguna); San Pedro (San Pedro City, Laguna); Calamba (Laguna); Gma (Cavite); Montalban (Rizal); Balagtas (Bulacan)

History: Founded 1996.

Degrees and Diplomas: *Associate Degree*: 2 yrs; *Bachelor's Degree*: 4 yrs

Last Updated: 28/07/10

ASIAN INSTITUTE OF E-COMMERCE

Poblacion East, Calasiao, Pangasinan 2418

Tel: +63(75) 517-6560

Fax: +63(75) 517-6460

EMail: aie_college@yahoo.com

President: Aveleo Q. Fuentes

Programmes

Computer Studies (Computer Education; Computer Engineering; Computer Science); **E-Commerce** (Accountancy; Business Administration; E-Business/Commerce; Finance; Management; Marketing); **Health Care Services** (Health Sciences); **Hotel and Restaurant Management** (Hotel and Restaurant; Hotel Management); **Information Management and Technology** (Information Management; Information Technology)

History: Founded 2005.

Degrees and Diplomas: *Bachelor's Degree*

Last Updated: 28/07/10

ASIAN INSTITUTE OF JOURNALISM AND COMMUNICATION

Unit 902 Annapolis Wilshire Plaza, Annapolis St., Greenhills, San Juan, Second District, Metro Manila 1008

Tel: +63(2) 724-4564 +63(2) 725-4227 +63(2) 725-4228

Fax: +63(2) 725-4228

EMail: info@aijc.com.ph; gs@aijc.com.ph

Website: http://www.aijc.com.ph

President: Rogelio V. Cuyno

Vice-President, Administration and Finance: Imelda E. Samson

Programmes

Communication Management (Communication Studies); **Journalism** (Journalism)

History: Founded 1980. Formerly known as Asian Institute of Journalism. Acquired present title 1994.

Degrees and Diplomas: *Master's Degree*: 2 yrs

Last Updated: 28/07/10

ASIAN INSTITUTE OF MANAGEMENT

123 Paseo de Roxas, Makati City, Fourth District, Metro Manila 1260

Tel: +63(2) 892-4011

Fax: +63(2) 893-7631

EMail: aimnet@aim.edu

Website: http://www.aim.edu

Head: Francis G. Estrada

Tel: +63(2) 892-4011 Ext. 167, Fax: +63(2) 893-3338

EMail: president@aim.edu

Centres

Development Management (Development Studies; Management); **Entrepreneurship** *(Asia)* (Business Administration; Management); **Executive Education and Lifelong Learning** *(EXCELL)* (Banking; Finance; Fine Arts; Health Administration; Management; Marketing)

Graduate Schools

Business Administration *(Washington SyCip)* (Business Administration)

Research Centres

Banking and Finance *(Gov. Jose B. Fernandez, Jr.)* (Banking; Finance); **Corporate Responsibility** *(Ramon V. del Rosario)* (Business Administration); **Hills Governance** *(AIM-HGC)*; **Policy** *(AIM)*

History: Founded 1968.

Degrees and Diplomas: *Master's Degree*: Business Administration; Entrepreneurship; Management; Development Management. Also Executive MBA, 18 months

Last Updated: 28/07/10

ASIAN INSTITUTE OF MARITIME STUDIES

AIMS CMET Bldg., A. Arnaiz Ave., cor. F.B. Harrison St., Pasay City, Fourth District, Metro Manila

Tel: +63(2) 834-5782 +63(2) 831-5747

Fax: +63(2) 831-8499

EMail: webmaster@aims.ph

Website: http://www.aims.ph

President: Arlene Abuid-Paderanga

Tel: +63 833-4035 EMail: aoap@aims.ph

Vice President for Administration: Elisa Abuid-Cayab

Centres

Advanced Studies and Training (Marine Transport); **Languages, Arts and Social Sciences** (Arts and Humanities; Modern Languages; Social Sciences)

Colleges

Business Education and Training (Business Administration); **Maritime Education and Training** (Marine Engineering; Marine Transport)

History: Founded 1993.

Degrees and Diplomas: *Bachelor's Degree*: 4 yrs; *Master's Degree*
Special Facilities: Media Centre; Computer and Internet Laboratory; Audio-Visual Room
Libraries: Yes
Last Updated: 28/07/10

ASIAN INSTITUTE OF TECHNOLOGY AND EDUCATION

Quezon, Bukidnon

President: Virginia Balmes

Programmes

Information Technology (Information Technology); **Secondary Education** (English; Mathematics Education; Secondary Education)

History: Founded 2005.

Degrees and Diplomas: *Bachelor's Degree*
Last Updated: 28/07/10

ASIAN SOCIAL INSTITUTE

1518 Leon Guinto Street, Malate, Manila, First District, Metro Manila 1004
Tel: +63(2) 523-8265 +63(2) 523-8266
Fax: +63(2) 526-6155
EMail: info@asinet-online.org
Website: http://www.asinet-online.org

President: Mina M. Ramirez Tel: +63(2) 523-3483

Programmes

Applied Cosmic Anthropology *(Doctoral programme)* (Anthropology); **Bachelor** (Social Work); **Master** (Economics; Education; Educational Administration; Pastoral Studies; Social and Community Services; Social Work; Sociology)

History: Founded 1962.

Degrees and Diplomas: *Bachelor's Degree*: 1 1/2 yr; *Master's Degree*: a further 3 yrs; *PhD*: a further 3 yrs
Last Updated: 28/07/10

ASSUMPTION COLLEGE

San Lorenzo Drive, San Lorenzo Village, Makati City, Fourth District, Metro Manila 1223
Tel: +63(2) 847-0757
Fax: +63(2) 817-4289
EMail: ac-info@assumption.edu.ph
Website: http://www.assumption.edu.ph/

President: Mary Gertrude M. Borres
Tel: +63(2) 894-3603 EMail: gertrude@assumption.edu.ph

Schools

Arts and Science (Advertising and Publicity; Communication Studies; Education; Fine Arts; Interior Design; Media Studies; Natural Sciences; Psychology); **Business** (Accountancy; Business Administration; Information Management; International Business; International Economics; Management; Marketing); **Graduate Studies** (Education; Psychology)

History: Founded 1940.

Degrees and Diplomas: *Certificate/Diploma*; *Bachelor's Degree*; *Master's Degree*
Last Updated: 28/07/10

ASSUMPTION COLLEGE OF DAVAO

Cabaguio Avenue, Davao City, Davao del Sur 8000
Tel: +63(82) 221-5698
Fax: +63(82) 226-3201
EMail: assumption@skyinet.net

President: Marietta B. Banayo

Programmes

Arts and Humanities (English; Sociology); **Education** (Biological and Life Sciences; Communication Arts; Education; Health Education; Mathematics Education; Primary Education; Science Education; Secondary Education); **Hotel and Restaurant Management** (Hotel and Restaurant; Hotel Management); **Information Technology** (Information Technology)

History: Founded 1958.

Degrees and Diplomas: *Bachelor's Degree*: 4 yrs
Last Updated: 28/07/10

ASSUMPTION COLLEGE OF NABUNTURAN

Poblacion Nabunturan, Compostela Valley, Davao del Norte 8106
Tel: +63(84) 376-0626
EMail: acn_excelsior@yahoo.com.ph

President: Clarita L. Villaflor

Programmes

Arts and Humanities (Arts and Humanities; English); **Business Administration** (Accountancy; Business Administration; Business and Commerce; Business Computing; Finance; Management); **Education** (Art Education; Biological and Life Sciences; Education; Educational Administration; Educational and Student Counselling; English; Ethics; Filipino; Home Economics Education; Mathematics Education; Music Education; Preschool Education; Primary Education; Secondary Education); **Mathematics; Biology** (Biology; Mathematics)

History: Founded 1955 as Assumption Academy of Compostela, acquired present status and title 1960.
Degrees and Diplomas: *Bachelor's Degree*; *Master's Degree*
Last Updated: 28/07/10

ATENEO DE DAVAO UNIVERSITY

E. Jacinto Street, Davao City, Davao del Sur 8000
Tel: +63(82) 221-2411
Fax: +63(82) 226-4416
EMail: psspdvo@addu.edu.ph
Website: http://www.addu.edu.ph

President: Antonio S. Samson EMail: pres@addu.edu.ph

Registrar: Rene Alexis P. Villarente

Colleges

Law (Law); **Nursing** (Nursing)

Schools

Arts and Sciences (Architecture; Biological and Life Sciences; Biology; Chemical Engineering; Chemistry; Civil Engineering; Clinical Psychology; Computer Engineering; Computer Science; Development Studies; Economics; Education; Educational Administration; Educational and Student Counselling; Electrical Engineering; Electronic Engineering; Engineering; English; Filipino; Foreign Languages Education; History; Industrial Engineering; Information Technology; International Studies; Literature; Mass Communication; Mathematics; Mathematics Education; Mechanical Engineering; Philosophy; Physical Education; Physics; Political Sciences; Preschool Education; Primary Education; Psychology; Social Sciences; Social Work; Sociology; Structural Architecture; Telecommunications Engineering; Theology); **Business and Governance** (Accountancy; Business Administration; Finance; Government; Human Resources; Management; Marketing; Public Administration)

History: Founded 1948 as a College, acquired present status and title 1977. A private institution under the supervision of the Society of Jesus and recognized by the Department of Education, Culture and Sports.

Governing Bodies: Board of Trustees

Academic Year: June to March (June-October; November-March)

Admission Requirements: Graduation from high school and entrance examination

Main Language(s) of Instruction: Filipino, English

Degrees and Diplomas: *Bachelor's Degree*; *Post Baccalaureate Certificate/Diploma*; *Master's Degree*; *PhD*

Student Residential Facilities: Yes

Libraries: c. 70,000 vols
Publications: Tambara
Last Updated: 28/07/10

ATENEO DE MANILA UNIVERSITY - QUEZON CITY

Loyola Heights Campus, Katipunan Avenue, Loyola Heights, PO Box 1168, Quezon City Central Post Office, Quezon City, Second District; Metro Manila 1108
Tel: +63(2) 426-6001
EMail: oip@admu.edu.ph
Website: http://www.admu.edu.ph

President: Bienvenido F. Nebres, S.J. (1993-)
Tel: +63(2) 426-6078, Fax: +63(2) 426-6079
EMail: president@admu.edu.ph

Vice-President for Administration and Planning: Edna P. Franco
Academic Vice-President: Antonette Palma-Angeles
Tel: +63(2) 426-6038 EMail: avp@admu.edu.ph

International Relations: Glenn de Leon
Tel: +63(2) 426-5907, Fax: +63(2) 426-5907
EMail: gdeleon@ateneo.edu.ph

Schools

Humanities (Art Criticism; Art History; Arts and Humanities; Catholic Theology; Christian Religious Studies; English; Filipino; Fine Arts; French; German; Indonesian; Italian; Modern Languages; Philosophy; Portuguese; Spanish; Theatre; Theology; Visual Arts; Writing); **Management** *(John Gokongwei School)* (Accountancy; Commercial Law; English; Finance; Information Technology; Law; Management; Marketing; Taxation); **Science and Engineering** (Biology; Chemistry; Computer Engineering; Computer Science; Electronic Engineering; Environmental Engineering; Environmental Management; Environmental Studies; Health Sciences; Information Technology; Mathematics; Physics; Telecommunications Engineering); **Social Sciences** (Anthropology; Asian Studies; Chinese; Communication Studies; Development Studies; East Asian Studies; European Studies; History; Japanese; Psychology; Social Sciences; Sociology)

History: Founded 1859. Became College 1865, and a private institution 1901. Granted University status 1959.

Academic Year: June to March (June-October; November-March); summer classes, April to May

Admission Requirements: Graduation from high school and entrance examination

Main Language(s) of Instruction: Filipino, English

International Co-operation: With Asia-Europe Foundation (ASEF), Association of Christian Universities and Colleges in Asia (ACUCA), Association of Southeast and East Asian Catholic Colleges and Universities (ASEACCU), Association of Universities of Asia and the Pacific (AUAP), University Mobility in Asia and the Pacific (UMAP), Consortium for Iberoamerican Studies, European Studies Consortium, Forum for East Asia-Latin American Coopertion (FEALAC), International Federation of Catholic Universities (IFCU).

Accrediting Agencies: Commission on Higher Education (CHED); Philippine Accreditation Association of Schools, Colleges and Universities (PAASCU)

Degrees and Diplomas: *Certificate/Diploma*; *Bachelor's Degree (BA)*: 4 yrs; *Bachelor's Degree (BSc)*: 4-5 yrs; *Master's Degree (MSc; MA; MHA; MBA)*: a further 2 yrs; *PhD*

Student Services: Academic counselling, Canteen, Cultural centre, Employment services, Foreign student adviser, Foreign Studies Centre, Health services, Language programs, Social counselling, Sports facilities

Student Residential Facilities: For c. 370 students

Special Facilities: Ateneo Art Gallery. Manila Observatory

Libraries: Loyola Heights Campus: Rizal Library, Institute of Philippine Culture Library, Centre for Social Policy Library. Rockwell Campus: Ateneo Professional Schools (APS) Library

Publications: Budhi; Law School Journal; Loyola Schools Review; Philippine Studies Journal

Press or Publishing House: Ateneo de Manila University Press
Last Updated: 28/07/10

ATENEO DE NAGA UNIVERSITY (ADNU)

Ateneo Avenue, Naga City, Camarines Sur 4400
Tel: +63(54) 473-8447
Fax: +63(54) 473-9253
Website: http://www.adnu.edu.ph

President: Joel E. Tabora (1999-) EMail: tabora@adnu.edu.ph

Vice-President for Academic Affairs: Rebecca Torres
Tel: +63(54) 473-0821

International Relations: Nilo Benjamin

Colleges

Arts and Sciences (Arts and Humanities; Communication Studies; Economics; Journalism; Library Science; Literature; Mathematics; Mathematics and Computer Science; Modern Languages; Natural Sciences; Nursing; Philosophy; Political Sciences; Psychology; Radio and Television Broadcasting; Social Sciences; Tourism); **Commerce** (Accountancy; Banking; Business Administration; Business and Commerce; Business Computing; Finance; Health Administration; Management; Marketing; Public Administration); **Computer Studies and Engineering** (Civil Engineering; Computer Engineering; Computer Science; Engineering; Environmental Management; Information Management; Information Sciences; Information Technology; Mathematics); **Education** (Biology; Chemistry; Computer Education; Curriculum; Education; Educational and Student Counselling; Educational Psychology; Educational Technology; English; Environmental Studies; Filipino; Health Education; Information Sciences; Library Science; Mathematics Education; Music Education; Parks and Recreation; Physical Education; Physics; Preschool Education; Primary Education; Science Education; Secondary Education; Social Studies; Special Education; Sports)

History: Founded 1940. Acquired present status 1999.

Governing Bodies: Board of Trustees; Council of Administrators

Admission Requirements: Graduation from high school

Main Language(s) of Instruction: English

Accrediting Agencies: Philippine Accrediting Association of Schools, Colleges and Universities (PAASCU)

Degrees and Diplomas: *Bachelor's Degree*; *Master's Degree*; *PhD*

Student Services: Academic counselling, Canteen, Handicapped facilities, Health services, Social counselling, Sports facilities

Special Facilities: Recording studio

Libraries: Electronic Resource Centre (Internet)
Last Updated: 28/07/10

ATENEO DE ZAMBOANGA UNIVERSITY (ADZU)

La Purisima Street, Zamboanga City, Zamboanga del Sur
Tel: +63(62) 991-0871
Fax: +63(62) 991-0870
EMail: president@adzu.edu.ph
Website: http://www.adzu.edu.ph

President: Antonio F. Moreno
Tel: +63(62) 991-1151, Fax: +63(62) 991-08790
EMail: president@central.adzu.edu.ph

Assistant for Finance and Administration: Raymund E. Belleza, SJ

Colleges

Nursing (Nursing); **Science and Information Technology** (Biology; Computer Engineering; Computer Networks; Computer Science; Electronic Engineering; Mathematics; Telecommunications Engineering)

Schools

Education (Art Education; Biology; Business Education; Chemistry; Child Care and Development; Computer Education; Education; Educational Administration; English; Filipino; Health Education; History; Mathematics Education; Music Education; Physical Education; Physics; Preschool Education; Primary Education; Science Education; Secondary Education); **Graduate Studies**; **Liberal Arts** (Arts and Humanities; Development Studies; Economics; English; Filipino; Industrial and Organizational Psychology; Information Sciences; Library Science; Mass Communication; Philosophy; Psychology; Social Studies); **Management and Accountancy** (Accountancy; Business Administration; Business and Commerce; Commercial Law; Finance; Information Management; Management;

Public Administration); **Medicine** *(Zamboanga Medical School Foundation, founded 1991)* (Health Education; Medicine; Public Health)

History: Founded 1912. Acquired present status and title 2001.

Governing Bodies: Board of Trustees

Academic Year: June to May (June-March; April-May)

Admission Requirements: High school Diploma, entrance examination

Main Language(s) of Instruction: English

Accrediting Agencies: Philippine Accrediting Association of Schools, Colleges and Universities (PAASCU)

Degrees and Diplomas: *Associate Degree*; *Bachelor's Degree*; *Master's Degree*; *PhD*

Student Services: Academic counselling, Canteen, Cultural centre, Health services, Language programs, Social counselling, Sports facilities

Special Facilities: Audiovisual Centre; Internet Access Area; Computer Laboratories; Science Laboratories

Libraries: c. 67,550 vols plus a number of periodical subscriptions

Publications: Ateneo de Zamboanga Journal *(biennially)*; Journal of Multi-Disciplinary Studies, Publication of Graduate Students Research *(biennially)*; Peace and Culture Studies, Publication of Graduate Students Research *(biennially)*; The Graduate School Review, Publication of Graduate Students Research *(annually)*

Press or Publishing House: ADZU Press

Last Updated: 28/07/10

ATENEO GRADUATE SCHOOL OF BUSINESS

20 APS Bldg., Rockwell Drive, Rockwell Center, City of Makati, Fourth District, Metro Manila 1200
Tel: +63(2) 899-7691
Fax: +63(2) 898-5006

President: Bienvenido F. Nebres, S.J.

Programmes

Business (Business Administration; Health Administration; Information Management; Information Technology; Management; Public Administration)

History: Founded 1963.

Degrees and Diplomas: *Master's Degree*

Last Updated: 28/07/10

AURORA PIONEER MEMORIAL COLLEGE

Aurora, Zamboanga del Sur 7020
Tel: +63(62) 331-2334

President: Danilo P. Ceniza

Programmes

Commerce (Business Administration; Business and Commerce); **Computer Science** (Computer Science); **Education** (Education; English; Mathematics Education; Primary Education; Secondary Education)

History: Founded 1950.

Degrees and Diplomas: *Bachelor's Degree*: 4 yrs

Last Updated: 28/07/10

BAGUIO CENTRAL UNIVERSITY

18 Bonifacio Street, Baguio City, Benguet 2600
Tel: +63(74) 442-4949
Fax: +63(74) 444-9247
EMail: B_C_U_@hotmail.com

President: Margarita J. Fernández (1980-)
Tel: +63(74) 442-4949, Fax: +63(74) 442-3109
EMail: bcu@hotmail.com

Vice-President for Administration: Elizabeth F. Bulaqueña
Tel: +63(74) 442-4949, Fax: +63(74) 443-3949
EMail: bcu@hotmail.com

International Relations: Wilhelmina F Drummond, Vice President for Academic Affairs
Tel: +63(74) 442-4949, Fax: +63(74) 9247
EMail: bcu@hotmail.com

Programmes

Arts and Humanities (Arts and Humanities; English; History; Library Science; Political Sciences); **Business Administration** (Accountancy; Banking; Business Administration; Business and Commerce; Business Computing; Finance; Management; Marketing; Public Administration); **Criminal Law** (Criminal Law; Criminology); **Education** (Art Education; Biology; Education; Educational Administration; Educational and Student Counselling; English; Filipino; Health Education; History; Home Economics Education; Library Science; Mathematics; Mathematics Education; Music Education; Native Language; Native Language Education; Physical Education; Preschool Education; Primary Education; Science Education; Secondary Education; Social Studies; Technology Education); **Engineering** (Civil Engineering; Computer Engineering; Computer Science; Engineering; Geophysics); **Health Sciences** (Health Sciences; Medicine; Midwifery; Nursing; Physical Therapy); **Tourism, Hotel and Restaurant Management** (Hotel and Restaurant; Hotel Management; Tourism)

Further Information: Clinics

History: Founded 1945 as Centro Academy offering Vocational Education, acquired present status and title 1977.

Governing Bodies: Board of Trustees; Office of Administration

Academic Year: June to May (June-October; November-March); summer session, April to May

Admission Requirements: Baccalaureate Level - Graduate from High School, College Admission Test(CAT); Certificate of good moral character and other requirements; international students see Registrar; Graduate Lever- holder of Baccalaureate degree for Master Degree

Main Language(s) of Instruction: English

International Co-operation: With Presbyterian Seminary and Colleges (Seoul Korea); Veterans Administration (USA)

Accrediting Agencies: Philippine Association of Colleges and Universities (PACUCOA); Commission on Accreditation; Coordinating Council of Private Education Association; Fund for the Assistance for Private Education(FAPE)

Degrees and Diplomas: *Certificate/Diploma*; *Associate Degree*; *Bachelor's Degree*; *Master's Degree*; *PhD*

Student Services: Academic counselling, Canteen, Employment services, Foreign student adviser, Health services, Language programs, Nursery care, Social counselling, Sports facilities

Special Facilities: Kiva Museum. Guidance and Testing Centre; Speech Clinic; Research Center

Libraries: 8 libraries of the faculties

Publications: College of Business Management *(annually)*; Flame *(quarterly)*

Press or Publishing House: Baguio Midland Publishing House

Last Updated: 29/07/10

BAGUIO COLLEGE OF TECHNOLOGY

37 Harrison Rd, Baguio City, Benguet 2600
Tel: +63(74) 424-0859
Fax: +63(74) 442-3743
EMail: info@beticollege.edu.ph; beticollege_baguio@yahoo.com.ph
Website: http://www.beticollege.edu.ph

Director: Wilfredo F. Abad, Sr.

Registrar: Ligaya R. Abad

Programmes

Computer Engineering (Computer Engineering); **Industrial Education** (Computer Engineering; Electrical and Electronic Engineering); **Industrial Engineering** (Industrial Engineering); **Industrial Technology** (Electrical and Electronic Engineering; Industrial Engineering); **Information Technology** (Information Technology)

History: Founded 1972. Formerly known as Beti College of Technology.

Degrees and Diplomas: *Bachelor's Degree*: 4-5 yrs

Last Updated: 29/07/10

BAI MALGEN MAMA COLLEGE

Capiton, Datu Odin Sinsuat, Shariff Kabunsuan 9601
EMail: bmmci.dosmag@yahoo.com

President: Bai Myrna B. Mama

Programmes
Computer Science (Computer Science); **Criminology** (Criminology); **Education** (Education; Preschool Education; Primary Education; Secondary Education)

History: Founded 2006.

Degrees and Diplomas: *Bachelor's Degree*
Last Updated: 29/07/10

BALAYAN COLLEGES

Balayan, Batangas 4213
Tel: +63(43) 221-4273 +63(43) 921-2160
Fax: +63(43) 221-4273

President: Gil G. Martinez

Programmes
Accountancy (Accountancy); **Computer Technology** (Computer Engineering); **Education** (Education; English; Filipino; Mathematics Education; Native Language Education; Preschool Education; Primary Education; Secondary Education); **Hotel and Restaurant Management** (Hotel and Restaurant; Hotel Management)

History: Founded 1926. Acquired present status 1964.

Degrees and Diplomas: *Certificate/Diploma*: 2 yrs; *Bachelor's Degree*: 4 yrs
Last Updated: 29/07/10

BALITE INSTITUTE OF TECHNOLOGY

Siquijor, Central Visayas 6225
Tel: +63(35) 480-3314
Fax: +63(35) 411-4856
EMail: epson@bit.mozcom.com

President: Alma Bella Balite-Diputado

Programmes
Administration (Accountancy; Business Administration; Business and Commerce; Management; Public Administration); **Education** (Education; Educational Administration; Primary Education; Secondary Education); **English** (English)

Further Information: Also campus in Butuan City (Agusan Del Norte), founded 2001

History: Founded 1993.

Degrees and Diplomas: *Associate Degree*; *Bachelor's Degree*; *Master's Degree*
Last Updated: 29/07/10

BALIUAG MARITIME FOUNDATION

Km. 54 Cagayan Calley Road, San Rafael, Bulacan 3008
Tel: +63(44) 766-1263
Fax: +63(44) 766-0316
EMail: bma@bul.info.com

President: Mauro M. Bautro

Programmes
Marine Engineering (Marine Engineering); **Marine Transport** (Marine Transport)

History: Founded 1994.

Degrees and Diplomas: *Bachelor's Degree*: 4 yrs
Last Updated: 29/07/10

BALIUAG UNIVERSITY

Gil Carlos Street, Baliuag, Bulacan 3006
Tel: +63(44) 766-2045 +63(44) 766-3344
Fax: +63(44) 766-3345
Website: http://www.baliuagu.edu.ph/

President: Alicia S. Bustos
EMail: asbustos@baliuaguniversity.edu.ph
Vice President for Academic Affairs: Flordeliza A. Castro
Vice-President for Administration: Patricia B. Lagunda
EMail: pblagunda@baliuaguniversity.edu.ph

Colleges
Arts and Sciences (Communication Studies; Economics; English; History; Information Sciences; Library Science; Mathematics; Political Sciences; Psychology; Social Work); **Business Administration and Accountancy** (Accountancy; Banking; Business Administration; Business Computing; Economics; Finance; Human Resources; Marketing); **Education** (Biological and Life Sciences; Education; Educational and Student Counselling; English; Filipino; Library Science; Mathematics; Mathematics Education; Native Language; Native Language Education; Preschool Education; Primary Education; Secondary Education; Social Studies; Teacher Trainers Education); **Environmental Design and Engineering** (Civil Engineering; Computer Engineering; Computer Science; Electrical Engineering; Electronic Engineering; Environmental Studies; Information Management; Information Technology; Mechanical Engineering; Telecommunications Engineering); **Nursing** (Health Education; Nursing)

Schools
Hospitality Management and Tourism (Hotel and Restaurant; Hotel Management; Tourism)

History: Founded 1925, acquired present status and title 2001.

Governing Bodies: Board of Trustees

Academic Year: June to March

Admission Requirements: High school diploma, entrance examination and Placement Test

Fees: (Pesos): c. 27,000 per semester

Main Language(s) of Instruction: English

International Co-operation: With universities in Korea

Accrediting Agencies: Philippine Association of Colleges and Universities - Commission on Accreditation (PACU-COA)

Degrees and Diplomas: *Associate Degree*; *Bachelor's Degree*; *Master's Degree*; *PhD*

Student Services: Academic counselling, Canteen, Cultural centre, Health services, Language programs, Nursery care, Social counselling, Sports facilities

Special Facilities: Internet Laboratory; Call Centre Laboratory; Speech Laboratory; Information Technology and Computer Centre; Language Centre

Libraries: Yes

Publications: Graduate School Journal *(annually)*; HARVEST - Research Journal *(annually)*

Press or Publishing House: Baliuag University Press
Last Updated: 29/07/10

BANTAYAN SOUTHERN INSTITUTE

M.L. Quezon St., Bantigue, Bantayan, Cebu 6052
Tel: +63(32) 352-5263

President: Alicia P. Cabatingan

Programmes
Commerce (Business Administration; Business and Commerce; Management); **Computer Science and Technology** (Computer Engineering; Computer Science); **Education** (Education; Primary Education; Secondary Education)

History: Founded 1947 as Southern College. Acquired present title 1960.

Degrees and Diplomas: *Bachelor's Degree*
Last Updated: 29/07/10

BATAAN HEROES MEMORIAL COLLEGE

Roman Highway, Balanga City, Bataan 2100
Tel: +63(47) 237-2383
Fax: +63(47) 237-1938
EMail: bhmc@mozcom.com

President: Laurena S. Rosales

Programmes
Civil Engineering (Civil Engineering); **Computer Engineering** (Computer Engineering); **Computer Science** (Computer Science);

Criminology (Criminology); **Electrical Engineering** (Electrical Engineering); **Electronics and Communications Engineering** (Electronic Engineering; Telecommunications Engineering); **Mechanical Engineering** (Mechanical Engineering); **Secondary Education** (Mathematics Education; Secondary Education)

History: Founded 1979.

Degrees and Diplomas: *Certificate/Diploma*: 2 yrs; *Bachelor's Degree*: 4 yrs; *Bachelor's Degree*: Engineering, 5 yrs

Last Updated: 29/07/10

BATANGAS COLLEGE OF ARTS AND SCIENCES

Banaybanay Concepcion, Lipa City, Batangas 4217
Tel: +63(43) 756-1232
EMail: bssan2005@yahoo.com

President: Jose de Castro

Programmes

Communication Studies (Communication Studies); **Education** (Education; Preschool Education; Primary Education; Secondary Education); **Information Technology** (Information Technology)

History: Founded 2000. Formerly known as Batangas Science College.

Degrees and Diplomas: *Bachelor's Degree*

Last Updated: 30/07/10

BATANGAS EASTERN COLLEGE

01 Javier Street, San Juan, Batangas 4226
Tel: +63(43) 575-3616
Fax: +63(43) 575-3616

President: Katherine Johanna B. de Villa

Programmes

Business Administration (Accountancy; Banking; Business Administration; Finance; Human Resources; Management); **Education** (Art Education; Computer Education; Education; English; Filipino; Mathematics Education; Music Education; Native Language; Native Language Education; Physical Education; Preschool Education; Primary Education; Secondary Education); **Health Care Services** (Nursing)

History: Founded 1940. Acquired present status 2001.

Degrees and Diplomas: *Certificate/Diploma*: 1-2 yrs; *Bachelor's Degree*: 4 yrs

Last Updated: 30/07/10

BATO INSTITUTE OF SCIENCE AND TECHNOLOGY

Brgy. Dolho, Bato, Leyte 6525
Tel: +63(53) 336-2589
Fax: +63(53) 336-2589
EMail: bitsreg@yahoo.com.ph

President: Josephine K. Germano

Programmes

Business Administration (Business Administration; Business and Commerce); **Education** (Education; Primary Education; Secondary Education); **Hotel and Restaurant Management** (Hotel and Restaurant; Hotel Management); **Nursing** (Nursing)

History: Founded 1995.

Degrees and Diplomas: *Certificate/Diploma*: 1-2 yrs; *Bachelor's Degree*: 4 yrs

Last Updated: 30/07/10

BATUAN COLLEGES

Poblacion Sur, Batuan, Bohol 6318
Tel: +63(38) 533-9016
Fax: +63(38) 533-9016
EMail: bcilink@bohol-on-line.com; batuancolleges@yahoo.com

President: Consolacion Vinluan

Programmes

Business Administration (Business Administration; Hotel and Restaurant; Hotel Management; Tourism); **Information Technology** (Information Technology); **Teacher Training** (Education; English; Mathematics Education; Primary Education; Science Education; Secondary Education)

History: Founded 1994.

Degrees and Diplomas: *Bachelor's Degree*: 4 yrs

Last Updated: 30/07/10

BAYAWAN COLLEGE

Bollos Street, Ubos, Bayawan, Negros Oriental 6221

Dean: Elena D. Abella

Programmes

Arts and Science (Automotive Engineering; Filipino; History; Mathematics; Metal Techniques; Native Language; Software Engineering); **Business Administration** (Business Administration; Public Administration); **Education** (Education; Educational Administration; English; History; Mathematics Education; Primary Education; Secondary Education)

History: Founded 1986.

Degrees and Diplomas: *Bachelor's Degree*; *Master's Degree*

Last Updated: 30/07/10

BENEDICTO COLLEGE

A.S. Fortuna Street, Mandaue City, Cebu 6014
Tel: +63(32) 345-5790
Fax: +63(32) 345-6873
EMail: info@benedictocollege.com.ph

President: Samuel L. Chioson

Programmes

Business Administration (Accountancy; Business Administration; Finance; Management); **Computer and Technology Studies** (Computer Engineering; Computer Science; Information Technology); **Education** (Education; Preschool Education; Primary Education); **Hospitality Management** (Hotel and Restaurant; Hotel Management; Tourism); **Mass Communication** (Mass Communication); **Nursing** (Midwifery; Nursing)

History: Founded 2000. Formerly Benedicto Computer College.

Degrees and Diplomas: *Associate Degree*: 2 yrs; *Bachelor's Degree*: 4 yrs

Last Updated: 30/07/10

BENGUET CENTRAL COLLEGE

JF-05 Pico Rd., La Trinidad, Benguet 2601
Tel: +63(75) 422-7084
EMail: benguetbcc@yahoo.com

President: Claro Q. Esoen

Programmes

Undergraduate and Professional (Accountancy; Administration; Automotive Engineering; Business Administration; Business and Commerce; Computer Science; Education; Electrical Engineering; Electronic Engineering; English; Filipino; Finance; Health Education; History; Industrial Arts Education; Mathematics Education; Mechanical Engineering; Native Language Education; Political Sciences; Primary Education; Public Administration; Secondary Education; Secretarial Studies)

History: Founded 1984 as Benguet School of Technology. Acquired present title 1996.

Degrees and Diplomas: *Bachelor's Degree*: 4 yrs

Last Updated: 28/03/11

BERNARDO COLLEGE

Pulang Lupa, Las Piñas City, Fourth District, Metro Manila 1742
Tel: +63(2) 873-3330
Fax: +63(2) 872-1129
EMail: eeg@impactnet.com

President: Jesusan Bernardo-Guinto

Programmes

Arts and Humanities (Arts and Humanities; English); **Business Administration** (Business Administration; Economics; Management; Marketing; Secretarial Studies); **Computer Science** (Computer Science); **Computer Technology** (Computer Science;

Technology); **Education** (Education; English; Filipino; Foreign Languages Education; Native Language Education; Secondary Education); **Hotel and Restaurant** (Hotel and Restaurant; Hotel Management)

History: Founded 1984 as Bernardo Foundation Institute.

Degrees and Diplomas: *Certificate/Diploma*: 2 yrs; *Associate Degree*; *Bachelor's Degree*
Last Updated: 02/08/10

BICOL COLLEGE

Cor. J.P. Rizal & R.F. Tabuena Sts., Daraga, Albay 4501
Tel: +63(52) 483-0904 +63(52) 824-2093
Fax: +63(52) 483-0904
EMail: bc@cats.edu.ph; bicolcollege@yahoo.com

President: Pedro Marcellana

Programmes
Arts (Arts and Humanities; Economics; English; Library Science; Political Sciences); **Business Administration** (Banking; Business Administration; Business and Commerce; Finance; Management); **Computer Science** (Computer Science); **Criminology** (Criminology); **Education** (Biological and Life Sciences; Biology; Education; English; Filipino; Health Education; Mathematics Education; Native Language; Native Language Education; Physics; Primary Education; Science Education; Secondary Education); **Graduate Studies** (Criminology; Education; Management); **Hospitality Management** (Hotel and Restaurant; Hotel Management; Tourism); **Law** (Law); **Nursing** (Nursing)

History: Founded 1941, acquired present status and title 1964.

Degrees and Diplomas: *Certificate/Diploma*: 2 yrs; *Bachelor's Degree*: 4 yrs; *Master's Degree*: a further 2 yrs; *PhD*: 3 yrs
Last Updated: 02/08/10

BICOL COLLEGE OF AGRICULTURE

Camagong, Camarines Sur 5152
Tel: +63(54) 454 2640

President: Eduardo Pilapil

Programmes
Agriculture (Agricultural Engineering; Agriculture; Horticulture; Zoology)

History: Founded 1998.

Degrees and Diplomas: *Bachelor's Degree*
Last Updated: 02/08/10

BICOL MERCHANT MARINE COLLEGE

Piot, City of Sorsogon, Sorsogon 4700
Tel: +63(56) 211-1257
Fax: +63(56) 211-2430
EMail: bmmci02@hotmail.com

President: Leon V. Pangilinan

Programmes
Customs Administration (Taxation); **Hospitality Management** (Hotel and Restaurant; Hotel Management; Tourism); **Marine Engineering** (Marine Engineering); **Marine Transport** (Marine Transport)

History: Founded 1993, acquired present status and title 1994.

Degrees and Diplomas: *Certificate/Diploma*: 1-2 yrs; *Bachelor's Degree*: 4 yrs
Last Updated: 28/03/11

BINALBAGAN CATHOLIC COLLEGE

Carmen Street, Binalbagan, Negros Occidental 6107
Tel: +63(34) 388-8383
Fax: +63(34) 388-8927

Administrative Team Member: Victoria E. Embate

Programmes
Agriculture (Agriculture; Food Technology); **Business Administration** (Accountancy; Business Administration; Economics; Finance; Human Resources; Management; Management Systems; Secretarial Studies); **Education** (Biological and Life Sciences; Education; English; Filipino; Foreign Languages Education; Health Education; Mathematics Education; Native Language; Native Language Education; Primary Education; Science Education; Secondary Education; Social Studies)

History: Founded 1957.

Degrees and Diplomas: *Certificate/Diploma*; *Bachelor's Degree*: 4 yrs
Last Updated: 02/08/10

BINANGONAN CATHOLIC COLLEGE

Libid, Binangonan, Rizal 1940
Tel: +63(2) 652-0098
Fax: +63(2) 652-0098
EMail: BinangonanCatholicCollege@yahoo.com; bcc1947@yahoo.com

President: Paquito Gallego

Programmes
Business Administration (Business Administration; Business Computing; Secretarial Studies); **Information Technology** (Computer Engineering; Information Technology)

History: Founded 1947.

Degrees and Diplomas: *Associate Degree*: 2 yrs; *Bachelor's Degree*
Last Updated: 02/08/10

BLANCIA CARREON COLLEGE FOUNDATION

Barangay Sudlon, Molave, Zamboanga del Sur 7023
Tel: +63(62) 225-1406
EMail: info@bccfi.com

Administrator: Nida Grace P. Arcayos

Programmes
Commerce (Business and Commerce; Management); **Computer Science** (Computer Science); **Education** (Education; Primary Education; Secondary Education); **Information Technology** (Information Technology); **Nursing** (Nursing)

History: Founded 1992.

Degrees and Diplomas: *Certificate/Diploma*: 1 yr; *Bachelor's Degree*
Last Updated: 02/08/10

BLESSED MOTHER COLLEGE

Iponan, Cagayan de Oro City, Misamis Oriental 9000
Tel: +63(88) 728-205 +63(88) 2273-5593
Fax: +63(88) 728-205 +63(88) 2273-7272

President: Elma G. Dueñas

Programmes
Education (Education; Primary Education; Secondary Education); **Nursing** (Nursing)

History: Founded 1994.

Degrees and Diplomas: *Bachelor's Degree*
Last Updated: 02/08/10

BLESSED TRINITY COLLEGE

Poblacion, Talibon, Bohol 6325
Tel: +63(38) 515-0030

Director: Corazon L. Caberte

Programmes
Business Administration (Accountancy; Business Administration; Business and Commerce; Human Resources); **Education** (Education; English; Filipino; Mathematics Education; Native Language; Primary Education; Secondary Education)

History: Founded 1947. Formerly known as Blessed Child Academy.

Degrees and Diplomas: *Associate Degree*; *Bachelor's Degree*: 4 yrs
Last Updated: 02/08/10

BOHOL INSTITUTE OF TECHNOLOGY - CARMEN

Carmen, Bohol 6319
Tel: +63(35) 411-2861
Fax: +63(35) 411-4856
EMail: epson@bit.mozcom.com

President: Alma Bella Balite-Diputado

Programmes

Undergraduate and Professional Studies (Agricultural Engineering; Automotive Engineering; Computer Engineering; English; Primary Education; Secretarial Studies)

History: Founded in 1998.

Degrees and Diplomas: *Associate Degree*: 2 yrs; *Bachelor's Degree*: 4 yrs
Last Updated: 03/08/10

BOHOL INSTITUTE OF TECHNOLOGY - JAGNA

Población, Jagna, Bohol 6308
Tel: +63(38) 238-2489
Fax: +63(35) 411-4856
EMail: epson@bit.mozcom.com

President: Alma Bella Balite-Diputado

Programmes

Undergraduate and Professional (Arts and Humanities; Business and Commerce; Computer Engineering; Education; Primary Education; Public Administration; Secondary Education)

History: Founded 1996.

Degrees and Diplomas: *Bachelor's Degree*
Last Updated: 03/08/10

BOHOL INSTITUTE OF TECHNOLOGY - TALIBON

San José, Talibon, Bohol 6325
Tel: +63(35) 411-2861
Fax: +63(35)411-4856
EMail: epson@bit.mozcom.com

President: Alma Bella Balite-Diputado

Programmes

Graduate (Arts and Humanities; Public Administration); **Undergraduate and Professional** (Accountancy; Arts and Humanities; Computer Engineering; Education; Primary Education; Public Administration; Secondary Education; Secretarial Studies)

History: Founded 1992.

Degrees and Diplomas: *Bachelor's Degree*; *Master's Degree*
Last Updated: 03/08/10

BOHOL INSTITUTE OF TECHNOLOGY INTERNATIONAL COLLEGE - TAGBILARAN

100 Gallares Street, Tagbilaran City, Bohol 6300
Tel: +63(35) 411-4856
Fax: +63(35) 411-2656
EMail: epson@bit.mozcom.com

President: Alma Bella Balite-Diputado

Programmes

Business Administration (Accountancy; Business Administration; Business and Commerce; Hotel and Restaurant; Hotel Management; Information Management; Management; Public Administration; Taxation); **Education** (Educational Administration; Primary Education; Secondary Education); **Engineering and Computer Science** (Civil Engineering; Computer Engineering; Computer Science; Electrical Engineering; Electronic Engineering; Engineering; Information Technology; Laboratory Techniques; Marine Engineering; Marine Transport; Mechanical Engineering; Radiology; Telecommunications Engineering); **Health Sciences** (Midwifery; Nursing; Physical Therapy); **Social Sciences** (Criminology; Mass Communication; Social Sciences)

Further Information: Branches in Bohol-Carmen, Bohol-Jagna, Bohol-Talibon

History: Founded 1981.

Degrees and Diplomas: *Bachelor's Degree*; *Master's Degree*; *PhD*
Last Updated: 03/08/10

BOHOL NORTHEASTERN COLLEGE

Isaac Garces St., Ubay, Bohol 6315
Tel: +63(38) 518-0279

President: Amalia R. Tirol

Programmes

Business Administration (Business Administration; Business and Commerce; Finance); **Education** (Education; English; Preschool Education; Primary Education; Secondary Education); **Engineering and Technology** (Automotive Engineering; Computer Engineering; Computer Science; Electrical and Electronic Engineering); **Hotel and Restaurant Management** (Hotel and Restaurant; Hotel Management); **Information Technology** (Information Technology); **Political Sciences** (Political Sciences)

History: Founded in 1996.

Degrees and Diplomas: *Bachelor's Degree*: 4 yrs
Last Updated: 03/08/10

BOHOL NORTHERN STAR COLLEGE INC.

Poblacion, Ubay, Bohol 6315
Tel: +63(38) 518-0279
Fax: +63(38) 518-0279

President: Amalia R. Tirol

Programmes

Business Administration (Accountancy; Business Administration; Finance; Management; Marketing); **Education** (Education; English; Mathematics Education; Preschool Education; Primary Education; Secondary Education); **Engineering and Technology** (Automotive Engineering; Electrical and Electronic Engineering; Information Technology); **Political Sciences** (Political Sciences); **Psychology** (Psychology)

History: Founded 1996.

Degrees and Diplomas: *Bachelor's Degree*
Last Updated: 03/08/10

BOHOL NORTHWESTERN COLLEGE

Población, Catigbian, Bohol 6343
EMail: rising-star-ph@yahoo.com

President: Doris Dinorog Obeña

Programmes

Computer Science and Technology (Computer Engineering; Computer Science); **Teacher Training** (Filipino; Mathematics Education; Native Language; Native Language Education; Primary Education; Secondary Education)

History: Founded 1997.

Degrees and Diplomas: *Associate Degree*; *Bachelor's Degree*
Last Updated: 03/08/10

BOHOL WISDOM SCHOOL

CPG North Avenue, Tagbilaran City, Bohol 6300
Tel: +63(38) 411-5150
Fax: +63(38) 411-2467

Administrator: Maria Socorro M. Navarrete

Programmes

Education (Education; English; Mathematics Education; Preschool Education; Primary Education; Science Education; Secondary Education)

History: Founded 2004.

Degrees and Diplomas: *Bachelor's Degree*
Last Updated: 03/08/10

BRENT HOSPITAL AND COLLEGES INC.

R.T. Lim Boulevard, Zamboanga City, Zamboanga del Sur 7000
Tel: +63(62) 992-4447
Fax: +63(62) 991-5358
EMail: bhci@zambo.l-nExt.net

Chief Operations Officer: Virgilio Anaud

Programmes

Undergraduate and Professional Studies (Health Education; Medical Technology; Midwifery; Nursing; Physical Therapy; Science Education)

History: Founded 1983. Formerly known as Brent Colleges of Allied Medicine.

Degrees and Diplomas: *Bachelor's Degree*: 4-5 yrs
Last Updated: 03/08/10

BRENTWOOD COLLEGE OF ASIA INTERNATIONAL SCHOOL

Blumentrit Street, Naga City, Camarines Sur 4400

Head: Carmelo D. Carcido

Programmes

Business Administration (Accountancy; Business Administration; Communication Studies; Management; Marketing); **Computer Science** (Computer Science); **Education** (Education; Primary Education; Secondary Education); **Information Technology** (Information Technology)

History: Founded 2002 as Brentwood College of Asia.

Degrees and Diplomas: *Bachelor's Degree*
Last Updated: 03/08/10

BROKENSHIRE COLLEGE

Madapo Hills, Davao City, Davao del Sur 8000
Tel: +63(82) 221-4457
Fax: +63(82) 222-4085
EMail: registrar@brokenshire.edu.ph
Website: http://www.brokenshire.edu.ph

President: Leopoldo R. Naïve

Programmes

Business Administration (Accountancy; Business Administration; Finance; Human Resources; Management; Marketing); **Computer Science**; **Education** (Biological and Life Sciences; Education; Educational and Student Counselling; English; Mathematics Education; Physical Education; Preschool Education; Primary Education; Secondary Education; Sports); **Hotel and Restaurant Management** (Hotel and Restaurant; Hotel Management; Tourism); **Information Technology** (Information Technology); **Nursing** (Midwifery; Nursing); **Political Sciences** (Political Sciences); **Psychology** (Psychology); **Theology** (Theology)

Further Information: Also Socsksargen Campus, General Santos City (Dadiangas), South Cotabato (founded 2004)

History: Founded 1954, acquired present status and title 1978.

Degrees and Diplomas: *Bachelor's Degree*
Last Updated: 03/08/10

BROOKFIELD COLLEGE

Dasmariñas, Cavite
Tel: +63(46) 973-0442
Fax: +63(46) 973-0442

President: Albert C. Paulin

Programmes

Hotel and Restaurant Management (Hotel and Restaurant; Hotel Management)

Degrees and Diplomas: *Bachelor's Degree*
Last Updated: 03/08/10

BSBT COLLEGE

434 Magsaysay Avenue, Baguio City, Benguet 2600
Tel: +63(74) 442-2986
Fax: +63(74) 446-0521
EMail: bsbt@mozcom.com; bsbtcollege@yahoo.com

President: Galo D. Wegan

Programmes

Business Administration (Business Administration; Business Computing; Finance; Human Resources; Management)

History: Founded 1972.

Degrees and Diplomas: *Bachelor's Degree*
Last Updated: 03/08/10

BUAD AGRICULTURAL SCHOOL

Marantao, Marawi City, Lanao del Sur

President: Datu Blo Umpar Adiong

Programmes

Agriculture (Agriculture; Agronomy)

History: Founded 2006.

Degrees and Diplomas: *Bachelor's Degree*
Last Updated: 03/08/10

BUBONG MARZOK MEMORIAL FOUNDATION COLLEGE

Officer's Line, Bubong A Marawi, Marawi City, Lanao del Sur 9700
Tel: +63(62) 352-0220

President: Minoma 'Hadji Malik' Bubong

Programmes

Commerce (Business and Commerce; Management); **Computer Science** (Computer Science); **Education** (Education; English; Filipino; Native Language; Native Language Education; Preschool Education; Primary Education; Secondary Education); **Nursing** (Midwifery; Nursing)

History: Founded 2000.

Degrees and Diplomas: *Associate Degree*; *Bachelor's Degree*
Last Updated: 03/08/10

BUCAS GRANDE FOUNDATION COLLEGE

Timcang St., Brgy., Taruc, Soccoro, Surigao del Norte 8416
Tel: +63(918) 594-3466
EMail: bgfc.registrar@yahoo.com

President: Warlito L. Noguera

Programmes

Computer Science (Computer Science); **Education** (Education; English; Mathematics Education; Primary Education; Secondary Education); **Entrepreneurship** (Management); **Information Technology** (Information Technology)

History: Founded in 2003, formerly known as Vice West Caraga Colleges.

Degrees and Diplomas: *Bachelor's Degree*
Last Updated: 03/08/10

BUTUAN CITY COLLEGES

Montilla Boulevard, Butuan City, Agusan del Norte 8600
Tel: +63(85) 341-5561
Fax: +63(85) 225-7875
EMail: bcc1950@yahoo.com

President: Remedios M. Famador EMail: rmfamador@yahoo.com

Programmes

Arts and Humanities (Arts and Humanities; History; Political Sciences); **Business Administration** (Banking; Business and Commerce; Finance; Human Resources; Management; Marketing; Secretarial Studies); **Criminology** (Criminology); **Hospitality Management** (Hotel and Restaurant; Hotel Management; Tourism); **Primary Education** (English; Filipino; Mathematics Education; Native Language Education; Primary Education; Social Studies);

Secondary Education (English; Filipino; Mathematics Education; Secondary Education; Social Studies)
History: Founded 1950. Formerly known as Agusan Institute (1950-1966).
Degrees and Diplomas: *Bachelor's Degree*: 4 yrs
Last Updated: 04/08/10

BUTUAN DOCTORS' COLLEGES

J.C. Aquino Avenue, Butuan City, Agusan del Norte 8600
Tel: +63(85) 342-8572 +63(85) 225-3616
Fax: +63(85) 225-3616
EMail: college@butuandoctors.com; bdc@skyinet.net

Executive Administrative Officer: Therese M. Estacio

Programmes

Arts and Humanities (Arts and Humanities); **Science** (Biology; Medical Technology; Midwifery; Nursing; Physical Therapy; Radiology)
History: Founded 1971 as Bututan Doctor's Hospital School of Nursing, acquiring present title and status in 1978.
Degrees and Diplomas: *Associate Degree*; *Bachelor's Degree*
Last Updated: 04/08/10

BVS COLLEGE

Km. 5, La Trinidad, Benguet 2601
Tel: +63(74) 309-3719
Fax: +63(74) 309-3719
EMail: bvx.colleges@yahoo.com

Chancellor: Narciso A. Somyden

Programmes

Business Administration (Business Administration; Finance; Management; Management Systems; Marketing); **Tourism** (Tourism)
History: Founded 1999. Formerly known as BVS School of Technology.
Degrees and Diplomas: *Certificate/Diploma*: 1-2 yrs
Last Updated: 04/08/10

CABALUM WESTERN COLLEGE

Dr. Fermin Caram, Sr. Ave., Iloilo City, Iloilo 5000
Tel: +63(33) 337-3636
Fax: +63(33) 337-8226
EMail: cwc@fastmail.net; cwc@cabalum.fapenet.org

President: Johnny C. Cabalum

Programmes

Business Administration (Banking; Business Administration; Business Computing; Computer Education; Computer Engineering; Computer Science; Data Processing; Finance; Management; Marketing; Secretarial Studies); **Computer Engineering and Science** (Computer Engineering; Computer Science)
History: Founded 1945. Acquired present status 1984.
Degrees and Diplomas: *Associate Degree*; *Bachelor's Degree*
Last Updated: 04/08/10

CABARRUS CATHOLIC COLLEGE

San Jose, Sipalay, City of Sipalay, Negros Occidental 6113
Director: Teodora B. Jalea, OSS

Programmes

Education (Business Computing; Education; English; Mathematics Education; Primary Education; Secondary Education); **English** (English)
History: Founded 1963.
Degrees and Diplomas: *Bachelor's Degree*: 4 yrs
Last Updated: 04/08/10

CAGAYAN COLLEGES TUGUEGARAO

Don Matias P. Perez Bldg., College Avenue, Tuguegarao City, Cagayan 3500
Tel: +63(78) 844-0416 +63(78) 844-0417
Fax: +63(78) 844-3694
EMail: admin@ctc-cct.edu.ph
Website: http://www.ctc-cct.edu.ph/

President: Victor V. Perez EMail: cos@ctc-cct.edu.ph
Registrar: Adarito V. Corsino
Vice-President for Administration: Estela B. Perez

Colleges

Arts and Sciences (Biology; Economics; English; Environmental Studies; Fishery; Government; History; Marine Biology; Mass Communication; Mathematics; Political Sciences; Radio and Television Broadcasting; Social Work; Sociology); **Business Education** (Accountancy; Banking; Business Administration; Business Education; Finance; Human Resources; Management; Marketing; Public Administration; Secretarial Studies); **Criminology** (Criminology; Police Studies); **Education** (Education; Educational Administration; English; Filipino; Health Education; Humanities and Social Science Education; Mathematics Education; Music Education; Native Language; Native Language Education; Physical Education; Preschool Education; Primary Education; Science Education; Secondary Education; Social Sciences; Social Studies); **Engineering and Technology** (Automotive Engineering; Chemical Engineering; Civil Engineering; Computer Engineering; Computer Science; Electrical and Electronic Engineering; Engineering; Engineering Management; Geophysics; Home Economics; Information Technology; Marine Engineering; Marine Transport; Mechanical Engineering; Technology; Telecommunications Engineering); **Health** (Health Sciences; Midwifery; Nursing); **Hospitality Industry Management** (Hotel and Restaurant; Hotel Management; Tourism); **Law** (Commercial Law; Law); **Maritime Education**
History: Founded 1948.
Degrees and Diplomas: *Certificate/Diploma*; *Associate Degree*; *Bachelor's Degree*; *Master's Degree*; *PhD*
Last Updated: 04/08/10

CAGAYAN DE ORO COLLEGE

Max Suniel Street, Carmen, Cagayan de Oro City, Misamis Oriental 9000
Tel: +63(88) 858-5869
Fax: +63(88) 858-3880
EMail: mmbeley@yahoo.com.ph
Website: http://www.coc.phinma.edu.ph

President: Meliton B. Salazar, Jr.

Colleges

Arts and Science (Economics; English; History; Mass Communication; Mathematics; Radio and Television Broadcasting; Sociology); **Commerce and Accountancy** (Accountancy; Banking; Business Administration; Business and Commerce; Finance; Government; Management; Marketing); **Criminology** (Criminology; Police Studies); **Education** (Education; Educational Administration; English; Filipino; Mathematics Education; Native Language; Native Language Education; Physics; Primary Education; Science Education; Secondary Education; Social Studies); **Engineering and Architecture** (Architecture; Chemical Engineering; Civil Engineering; Computer Engineering; Computer Science; Electrical and Electronic Engineering; Engineering; Engineering Management; Geophysics; Information Technology; Mechanical Engineering; Telecommunications Engineering); **Hotel and Restaurant Management** (Hotel and Restaurant; Hotel Management); **Nursing** (Nursing)
History: Founded 1948. Formerly known as Parents Teacher College.
Degrees and Diplomas: *Bachelor's Degree*; *Master's Degree*; *PhD*
Last Updated: 04/08/10

CAGAYAN VALLEY COLLEGES OF QUIRINO

Magandingay, Cabarroguis, Quirino 3400
President: Perla Mitra-Aldaba

Programmes
Arts and Humanities (Economics; English; Political Sciences); **Criminology** (Criminology); **Elementary Education** (Education; Primary Education); **Public Safety Administration** (Public Administration; Welfare and Protective Services); **Secondary Education** (Education; Secondary Education); **Secretarial Studies** (Secretarial Studies)

History: Founded 1974.

Degrees and Diplomas: *Certificate/Diploma*: 2 yrs; *Bachelor's Degree*: 4 yrs
Last Updated: 05/08/10

CAGAYAN VALLEY COMPUTER AND INFORMATION TECHNOLOGY COLLEGE

28 Carreon St., Centro East, City of Santiago, Isabela 3311
Tel: +63(78) 682-1842 +63(78) 682-7976
Fax: +63(78) 682-1842 +63(78) 682-7976
EMail: cvcitci@yahoo.com
Website: http://www.cvcitc.edu.ph/

President: Redentor B. Taguinod

Programmes
Arts (Arts and Humanities; Economics; English; Political Sciences); **Business Administration** (Accountancy; Business Administration; Business Computing; Finance; Management; Marketing; Secretarial Studies); **Information Technology** (Information Technology)

History: Founded 1997.

Degrees and Diplomas: *Bachelor's Degree*
Last Updated: 05/08/10

CAINTA CATHOLIC COLLEGE

A. Bonifacio Avenue, Cainta, Rizal 1900
Tel: +63(2) 655-0841
EMail: info@caintacatholic.every1.net

President: Arnel Lagarejos

Programmes
Undergraduate and Professional (Business Administration; Computer Science; Education; Primary Education; Religious Education; Secondary Education)

History: Founded 1960.

Degrees and Diplomas: *Associate Degree*; *Bachelor's Degree*
Last Updated: 05/08/10

CALAMBA DOCTORS' COLLEGE

Parian, Calamba City, Laguna 4027
Tel: +63(49) 545-9921
Fax: +63(49) 545-9922

President: Juan Lagunzad

Programmes
Nursing (Midwifery; Nursing); **Secondary Education** (Education; English; Mathematics Education; Science Education; Secondary Education)

History: Founded 2002. Formerly known as CDH Allied Medical Colleges.

Degrees and Diplomas: *Bachelor's Degree*
Last Updated: 05/08/10

CALAUAG CENTRAL COLLEGE

Rizal Street, Calauag, Quezon 4318
Tel: +63(42) 301-7260
Fax: +63(42) 301-8408
EMail: calauagcentral@yahoo.com

Executive Vice-President: Leticia F. Aguilar

Programmes
Business Administration (Business Administration; Management); **Education** (Education; Filipino; Native Language; Native Language Education; Preschool Education; Primary Education; Secondary Education); **Literature** (Literature)

History: Founded 1931. Formerly Calauag Institute.

Degrees and Diplomas: *Bachelor's Degree*
Last Updated: 05/08/10

CALAYAN EDUCATIONAL FOUNDATION

Red V, Lucena City, Quezon 4301
Tel: +63(42) 710-2514
Fax: +63(42) 710-4563
EMail: cefi@mozcom.com

President: Ronaldo Antonio D.V. Calayan

Programmes
Arts and Humanities (Arts and Humanities); **Education** (Education; Preschool Education; Primary Education; Secondary Education); **Health Sciences** (Medical Technology; Midwifery; Nursing; Physical Therapy; Radiology); **Hotel and Restaurant Management** (Hotel and Restaurant; Hotel Management); **Tourism** (Tourism)

History: Founded 1973.

Degrees and Diplomas: *Bachelor's Degree*
Last Updated: 05/08/10

CALBIGA WESTERN SAMAR COLLEGE

Polangi, Calbiga, Western Samar 6715

President: Juan C. Teoco Jr.

Programmes
Business Administration (Business Administration); **Education** (Education; Primary Education; Secondary Education)

History: Founded 2006.

Degrees and Diplomas: *Bachelor's Degree*
Last Updated: 05/08/10

CALI PARAMEDICAL COLLEGE FOUNDATION

Gaus Bldg. Quezon Avenue, Marawi City, Lanao del Sur 9700
Tel: +63(916) 927-8463

President: Camal A. Cali

Programmes
Computer Science (Computer Science); **Hotel and Restaurant Management** (Hotel and Restaurant; Hotel Management); **Midwidery** (Midwifery); **Teacher Training** (Health Education; Primary Education; Secondary Education)

History: Founded 2002 as Cali Sa Marawi Memorial School Foundation. Acquired present status and title 2003.

Degrees and Diplomas: *Associate Degree*; *Bachelor's Degree*: 4 yrs
Last Updated: 05/08/10

CALUMPIT COLLEGE

Colegio de Calumpit

Mc Arthur Hi-way, Calumpit, Bulacan 3003

President: Oscar A. del Rosario

Programmes
Education (Education; English; Preschool Education; Primary Education; Secondary Education); **Entrepreneurship** (Management)

Degrees and Diplomas: *Bachelor's Degree*
Last Updated: 08/09/10

CAMARINES NORTE COLLEGE

Maharlika Highway, Labo, Camarines Norte 4604
Tel: +63(54)447-6130
Fax: +63(54)447-6130

President: Teresa V. Soriano

Programmes
Commerce (Business and Commerce; Management; Secretarial Studies); **Education** (Education; English; Filipino; Mathematics Education; Native Language Education; Primary Education; Secondary Education); **English** (English); **Filipino** (Filipino; Native Language); **Political Sciences** (Political Sciences)

History: Founded 1946.

Degrees and Diplomas: *Certificate/Diploma*: 2 yrs; *Bachelor's Degree*: 4 yrs
Last Updated: 05/08/10

CAMARINES NORTE SCHOOL OF LAW, ARTS AND SCIENCES

Itomang, Talisay, Camarines Norte 6402
Tel: +63(54) 445-1256
Fax: +63(54) 445-1256

President: Andres Rommel C. De Jesus

Programmes

Business Administration (Business Administration; Justice Administration); **Criminology** (Criminology); **Law** (Law); **Political Sciences** (Political Sciences)

History: Founded 2000. Formerly Camarines Norte School of Law.

Degrees and Diplomas: *Bachelor's Degree*
Last Updated: 05/08/10

CAMARINES NORTE STATE COLLEGE

Froilan Pimentel Avenue, Daet, Camarines Norte 4600
Tel: +63(54) 721-4496
Fax: +63(54) 721-4545

President: Wenifredo T. Oñate

Campuses

Entienza *(Sta. Elena, Camarines Norte)* (Agriculture; Education; Management; Secondary Education) *Dean*: Manolo A. Carbonell; **Labo** *(Labo, Camarines Norte)* (Agricultural Business; Agricultural Economics; Agricultural Education; Agricultural Engineering; Crop Production; Environmental Management; Zoology) *Dean*: Reynaldo U. Sale; **Mercedes** *(San Roque, Camarines Norte)* (Fishery; Food Science; Food Technology; Marine Biology; Marine Transport) *Dean*: Sylvia B. Salvan; **Panganiban** *(Jose Panganiban, Camarines Norte)* (Automotive Engineering; Civil Engineering; Computer Engineering; Electrical Engineering; Electronic Engineering; Engineering; Food Technology; Information Technology; Mechanical Engineering; Technology; Textile Technology) *Dean*: Jackson B. De Chavez

Programmes

Arts and Humanities (Arts and Humanities; English; Filipino; History; Native Language; Sociology); **Business Administration** (Accountancy; Business Administration; Economics; Educational Administration; Finance; Human Resources; Management; Marketing; Public Administration); **Education** (Art Education; Biological and Life Sciences; Chemistry; Education; English; Filipino; Health Education; Home Economics Education; Mathematics Education; Music Education; Native Language Education; Physical Education; Preschool Education; Primary Education; Science Education; Secondary Education; Social Studies; Technology Education); **Science** (Biology; Chemistry; Mathematics; Physics); **Undergraduate and Professional** (Agricultural Education; Agricultural Engineering; Agriculture; Biology; Chemistry; Civil Engineering; Economics; Education; Electrical Engineering; English; Environmental Management; Fishery; History; Industrial Arts Education; Industrial Engineering; Management; Marine Transport; Marketing; Mechanical Engineering; Primary Education; Public Administration; Secondary Education; Sociology)

Further Information: Also Campus in Mercedes, Labo and Panganiban.

History: Founded 1992.

Degrees and Diplomas: *Certificate/Diploma*; *Bachelor's Degree*; *Master's Degree*
Last Updated: 05/08/10

CAMILING COLLEGES

Gomez Street, Camiling, Tarlac 2306
Tel: +63(45) 934-0575

President: Rodolfo G. Romulo

Programmes

Elementary Education (Primary Education); **Secondary Education** (English; Secondary Education)

History: Founded 1946.

Degrees and Diplomas: *Associate Degree*; *Bachelor's Degree*
Last Updated: 06/08/10

CANOSSA COLLEGE

Brgy. VI-D, Lakeside Park Subdivision, San Pablo City, Laguna 4000
Tel: +63(49) 562-3891
Fax: +63(49) 562-3890
EMail: sr-ling@qnet1.net

Director: Ludivina Z. Sangel

Programmes

Commerce and Economics (Accountancy; Banking; Business and Commerce; Economics; Finance; Management); **Computer Science** (Computer Science); **Education** (Education; Preschool Education; Primary Education; Religious Education; Secondary Education); **Hotel and Restaurant Management** (Hotel and Restaurant; Hotel Management); **Nursing** (Nursing); **Psychology** (Psychology)

History: Founded 1955, acquired present status and title 1963.

Degrees and Diplomas: *Bachelor's Degree*
Last Updated: 06/08/10

CAP COLLEGE FOUNDATION

149 Legaspi St., Legaspi Village, City of Makati, Fourth District, Metro Manila 1229
Tel: +63(2) 812-6923
Fax: +63(2) 818-0560
EMail: capcol@mnl.sequel.net
Website: http://www.cap.com.ph

President: Quintin S. Doromal

Programmes

Arts, Humanities, Science and Social Sciences (Arts and Humanities; Criminology; Economics; English; History; Information Technology; Journalism; Mathematics; Pastoral Studies; Political Sciences; Psychology; Radio and Television Broadcasting; Sociology); **Business Administration** (Accountancy; Banking; Business Administration; Economics; Finance; Management; Marketing; Public Administration)

Further Information: Traditional and Open Learning Institution

History: Founded 1988 as Correspondence Accreditation Program for College Foundation. Acquired present title 1995.

Degrees and Diplomas: *Certificate/Diploma*; *Associate Degree*; *Bachelor's Degree*; *Master's Degree*
Last Updated: 06/08/10

CAPALONGA COLLEGE

Alayao, Capalonga, Camarines Norte 4607

President: Estrella A. Retiro

Programmes

Agriculture (Agriculture; Crop Production; Zoology); **Education** (Education; English; Mathematics Education; Primary Education; Secondary Education)

History: Founded 2002.

Degrees and Diplomas: *Bachelor's Degree*
Last Updated: 06/08/10

CAPITOL MEDICAL CENTRE COLLEGES

No. 4 Sto. Domingo Avenue, Quezon City, Second District, Metro Manila 1103
Tel: +63(2) 742-5531
Fax: +63(2) 374-2568
EMail: info@capitolmedical.org
Website: http://www.capitolmedical.org/CMCcolleges

President: Thelma Navarette Clemente

Programmes

Nursing (Nursing)

History: Founded 2004.

Degrees and Diplomas: *Bachelor's Degree*
Last Updated: 06/08/10

CAPITOL UNIVERSITY

President Osmeña St./Corrales Ave. Extension, Cagayan de Oro City, Misamis Oriental 9000
Tel: +63(8822) 723-349
Fax: +63(8822) 856-1272
EMail: cu@cu-cdo.edu.ph
Website: http://www.cu.edu.ph/

President: Casimiro B. Juarez Jr. (1988-) Tel: +63 (8822) 726-136

Vice-President for Academic Affairs: Luvismin S. Aves

Executive Vice-President: Fe R. Juarez
Tel: +63 (8822) 729-864, Fax: +63 (8822) 856-1272
EMail: fejuarez@cu-cdo.edu.ph

International Relations: Marites A. Khanser, Vice-President, Research and Extension
Tel: +63 (8822) 726-136, Fax: +63 (8822) 856-1272
EMail: ntmadale@yahoo.com

Colleges

Arts and Sciences (Arts and Humanities; English; Filipino; Native Language); **Business Administration** (Accountancy; Business Administration; Business and Commerce; Finance; Management; Marketing; Public Administration; Taxation); **Computer Studies** (Computer Science); **Criminology** (Criminology); **Education** (Education; Educational Administration; Educational and Student Counselling; English; Filipino; Humanities and Social Science Education; Literacy Education; Native Language Education; Primary Education; Science Education; Secondary Education); **Engineering** (Civil Engineering; Electronic Engineering; Engineering; Marine Engineering; Marine Transport; Mechanical Engineering; Nautical Science; Telecommunications Engineering); **Health Sciences** (Midwifery; Nursing)

History: Founded 1971 as Cagayan Capitol College. Acquired university status 2003.

Governing Bodies: Board of Directors

Admission Requirements: Entrance examination

Main Language(s) of Instruction: English

International Co-operation: With Northen Illinois University (USA); Soka University and Soka Gakkai International (Japan). Also participates in the CISCO Networking Academy Programme

Accrediting Agencies: Philippine Association of Colleges and Universities Commission on Accreditation (PACUVOA)

Degrees and Diplomas: *Associate Degree*: Computer Technology (ACT), 2 yrs; *Bachelor's Degree*: Civil Engineering (BSCE); Electronics and Communication Engineering (BSECE); Mechanical Engineering (BSME), 5 yrs; *Bachelor's Degree*: Commerce (Management, Banking and Finance, Management Accounting) (BSC); Computer Science (BSc); Criminology (BSCrim); Elementary Education (English, Filipino, Mathematics) (BEED); English (AB); Marine Transport (BSc); Nursing (BSN); Secondary Education (English, Filipino, Mathematics) (BSEd), 4 yrs; *Bachelor's Degree*: Marine Engineering (BSMarE), 3 yrs; *Master's Degree*: Business Management (MBM); Public Service Management (MPSM), a further 2 yrs; *Master's Degree*: Education (Educational Administration, English, Reading, Social Sciences Education) (MA); Guidance and Counselling, Filipino (MA), 3 yrs; *PhD*: Educational Management (PhD); Management (DM), a further 3 yrs. Also: Graduate in Midwifery (GM) after 2 yrs

Student Services: Academic counselling, Canteen, Cultural centre, Employment services, Foreign student adviser, Health services, Sports facilities

Special Facilities: Museum of Three Cultures; Hospital Facilities; Research and Extension Office; Gift shop and book centre; Ecumenical Prayer Room

Libraries: Lending library; Reference and Special Collections

Publications: Kayamag Interdisciplinary Forum on Science, Society and Letters, Features Ethnographs and Research Articles on Social Sciences, Humanities as well as Poetry, Literary Essays and Book Reviews. *(annually)*; Lamdag, Graduate School Journal. *(biennially)*; Mentor's Journal, Articles on Pedagogy *(annually)*; MINDAyawan Journal of Culture and Society, Official Journal of the University, a Multidisciplinary Forum of Scholarly Articles *(biannually)*; Salabutan (The Power of Understanding), Research journal of the university's Guidance and Counselling Centre *(annually)*; Ventures Articles, Articles of special significance for Business Education *(biennially)*

Press or Publishing House: Capitol University Press
Last Updated: 06/08/10

CARAGA INSTITUTE OF TECHNOLOGY

National Highway, Songkoy, Kitcharao, Agusan del Norte 8609
Tel: +63(917) 7031-261

President: Napoleon G. Sandiasa

Programmes

Computer Secretarial Studies (Business Computing; Secretarial Studies); **Education** (Education; English; Foreign Languages Education; Primary Education)

History: Founded 1996.

Degrees and Diplomas: *Bachelor's Degree*
Last Updated: 06/08/10

CARTHEL SCIENCE EDUCATIONAL FOUNDATION (CSEF)

San Manuel, Tarlac 2309
Tel: +63(915) 712-4606
EMail: carthel9002@yahoo.com

President: Carlito V. Arenas (1987-)
Tel: +63(917) 522-2254 EMail: carl_md2000@yahoo.com

Executive Vice-President: Thelma Arenas
Tel: +63(917) 508-2647

International Relations: Sharon Mae Carolino

Programmes

Computer Science (Computer Science); **Elementary Education** (Primary Education) *Dean*: Annabelle Lacbayan; **Hotel and Restaurant Management** (Hotel and Restaurant; Hotel Management); **Nursing** (Nursing); **Physical Therapy** (Physical Therapy); **Radiologic Technology** (Radiology; Technology); **Secondary Education** (English; Secondary Education)

History: Founded 1949 as Ofra College Foundation. Acquired present title and status 1987.

Admission Requirements: Graduation from high school

Fees: (Pesos): c. 5,000-19,600

Main Language(s) of Instruction: English

Degrees and Diplomas: *Associate Degree*: Computer Science; Hotel and Restaurant Management, 2 yrs; *Associate Degree*: Radiology Technology, 3 yrs; *Bachelor's Degree*: Elementary Education; Nursing; Radiologic Technology; Secondary Education, 4 yrs; *Bachelor's Degree*: Physical Therapy, 5 yrs

Student Services: Academic counselling, Canteen, Cultural centre, Employment services, Foreign student adviser, Foreign Studies Centre, Handicapped facilities, Health services, Language programs, Nursery care, Social counselling, Sports facilities

Student Residential Facilities: Yes

Libraries: Yes
Last Updated: 10/08/10

CASA DEL NIÑO COLLEGE

San Pedro, Laguna 4023

President: Rosario G. Acierto

Programmes

Computer Science (Computer Science); **Education** (Education; English; Mathematics Education; Preschool Education; Primary Education; Science Education; Secondary Education); **Information Technology** (Information Technology)

History: Founded 2002. Formerly known as Casa del Niño Schools System.

Degrees and Diplomas: *Bachelor's Degree*: 4 yrs; *Bachelor's Degree*: Engineering, 5 yrs
Last Updated: 28/03/11

CATANDUANES COLLEGES

Salvacion, Virac, Catanduanes 4800
Tel: +63(52) 811-1280
Fax: +63(52) 811-1280
EMail: catcoll@digitelone.com; Catanduanes.Colleges@yahoo.com

President: Ephraim Antonio A. Gianan Tel: +63(52) 811-0337

Programmes

Graduate (Education; Educational Administration; Management); **Undergraduate and Professional** (Accountancy; Arts and Humanities; Business Administration; Business and Commerce; Computer Education; Computer Engineering; Computer Science; Economics; Education; English; Management; Political Sciences; Primary Education; Secondary Education; Social Sciences)

History: Founded 1937. Acquired present status 1965.

Degrees and Diplomas: *Certificate/Diploma*; *Associate Degree*; *Bachelor's Degree*; *Master's Degree*
Last Updated: 10/08/10

CATANDUANES INSTITUTE OF TECHNOLOGY FOUNDATION

San Juan, Virac, Catanduanes 4800
EMail: CITFI@yahoo.com

President: Gaudioso L. Ocol

Programmes

Engineering (Automotive Engineering; Computer Engineering; Electronic Engineering; Engineering; Telecommunications Engineering)

History: Founded 1994.

Degrees and Diplomas: *Certificate/Diploma*; *Bachelor's Degree*
Last Updated: 10/08/10

CAVITE WEST POINT COLLEGE

Ciudad Silangan, Ternate, Cavite 4111
Tel: +63(46) 412-0153
Fax: +63(46) 412-0165
EMail: cavitewestpointcollege@yahoo.com

President: Evangelino Z. Nigoza

Programmes

Business Administration (Business Administration; Public Administration); **Education** (Education; Primary Education; Secondary Education); **Hotel and Restaurant Management** (Hotel and Restaurant; Hotel Management)

History: Founded 2000.

Degrees and Diplomas: *Certificate/Diploma*; *Bachelor's Degree*
Last Updated: 10/08/10

CBD COLLEGE

F. Jaca St., Inayawan, Cebu City, Cebu 6000
Tel: +63(32) 272-7810
Fax: +63(32) 272-2139
EMail: cbdil@lycos.com

Director: Clarita B. Dacua

Programmes

Business Administration (Business Administration); **Computer Engineering** (Computer Engineering); **Education** (Education; Primary Education; Secondary Education)

History: Founded 1998.

Degrees and Diplomas: *Associate Degree*; *Bachelor's Degree*
Last Updated: 10/08/10

CEBU AERONAUTICAL TECHNICAL SCHOOL

Salinas Drive, Lahug, Cebu City, Cebu 6000
Tel: +63(32) 233-0090
Fax: +63(32) 233-0097

President: Galdino G. Varona

Programmes

Air Transport and Aeronautics (Aeronautical and Aerospace Engineering; Air Transport; Management)

History: Founded 1953, acquired present status and title 1978.

Degrees and Diplomas: *Associate Degree*; *Bachelor's Degree*
Last Updated: 10/08/10

CEBU DOCTORS' UNIVERSITY (CDU)

North Reclamation Area, Mandaue City, Cebu 6014
Tel: +63(32) 253-8001
Fax: +63(32) 412-4907
EMail: records@cdc-cdh.edu
Website: http://www.cebudoctorsuniversity.edu

President: Potenciano V. Larrazabal, Jr.

Colleges

Allied Medical Sciences (Laboratory Techniques; Medical Technology; Radiology); **Arts and Sciences** (Biology; Computer Engineering; Computer Science; Psychology); **Dentistry** (Dental Technology; Dentistry; Orthodontics; Periodontics); **Nursing** (Nursing); **Optometry** (Optometry); **Pharmacy** (Pharmacy); **Rehabilitative Sciences** (Occupational Therapy; Physical Therapy; Rehabilitation and Therapy)

Schools

Graduate Studies (Development Studies; Educational Administration; Health Administration; Health Education; Nursing)

Further Information: Has eight colleges, including Cebu Doctor's University College of Medicine

History: Founded 1972 as Cebu Doctors' College, became the first institute dedicated to teaching Health Sciences and Medicine that was authorised to operate by the Ministry of Education. Acquired present title 2003.

Degrees and Diplomas: *Associate Degree*; *Bachelor's Degree*; *Master's Degree*; *PhD*
Last Updated: 10/08/10

CEBU DOCTOR'S UNIVERSITY COLLEGE OF MEDICINE (CDU-CM)

1 Dr. P. V. Larrazabal Jr. Avenue, North Reclamation Area, Mandaue City, Cebu 6014
Tel: +63(32) 253-4919
Fax: +63(32) 253-4919
EMail: record@cdc.edu.ph
Website: http://www.cebudoctorsuniversity.edu/colleges/medicine/

President: Potenciano V. Larrazabal, Jr.

Programmes

Medicine (Medicine)

History: Founded 1977 by the Cebu Doctor's University. Formerly known as formerly Cebu Doctors' College of Medicine (1973-2003).

Degrees and Diplomas: Doctor of Medicine
Last Updated: 10/08/10

CEBU EASTERN COLLEGE

40 Leon Kilat Street, Cebu City, Cebu 6000
Tel: +63(32) 254-2761
Fax: +63(32) 256-2526
EMail: cec_direct@pacific.net.ph; cec_college_registrar@yahoo.com.ph

Administrator: Kho Siok We

Programmes

Education (Education; Preschool Education; Primary Education; Secondary Education)

History: Founded 1915 as Cebu Chinese High School. Acquired present status 1974.

Degrees and Diplomas: *Bachelor's Degree*
Last Updated: 10/08/10

CEBU INSTITUTE OF MEDICINE (CIM)

79 F. Ramos St., Cebu City, Cebu 6000
Tel: +63(32) 253-7412/3124
Fax: +63(32) 256-5756
EMail: admin@cim.edu.ph
Website: http://www.cim.edu.ph

President: Josefina L. Poblete

Programmes

Medicine (Biology; Biomedicine; Community Health; Gynaecology and Obstetrics; Medicine; Ophthalmology; Otorhinolaryngology; Paediatrics; Surgery)

History: Founded 1957, acquiring present status and title in 1967.

Admission Requirements: Undergraduate Degree and successfully passed the National Medical Admission Test (NMAT) .

Degrees and Diplomas: *Bachelor's Degree*: Biology
Last Updated: 10/08/10

CEBU INSTITUTE OF TECHNOLOGY (CIT)

N. Bacalso Avenue, Cebu City, Cebu 6000
Tel: +63(32) 261-7741
Fax: +63(32) 261-7743
EMail: registrar@cit.edu
Website: http://www.cit.edu

President: Gregorio L. Escario EMail: president@cit.edu

Colleges

Arts and Sciences (Applied Linguistics; Biology; English; Graphic Arts; Mass Communication; Mathematics; Psychology); **Commerce** (Accountancy; Banking; Business Administration; Hotel and Restaurant; Human Resources; Management; Management Systems; Marketing; Public Administration; Tourism); **Computer Studies**; **Education** (English; Filipino; Foreign Languages Education; Mathematics Education; Native Language Education; Preschool Education; Primary Education; Science Education; Special Education); **Engineering and Architecture**; **Nurisng** (Nursing)

History: Founded 1946. Acquired present status and title 1957.

Admission Requirements: Secondary School Certificate; National Secondary Assessment Test (NSAT); Entrance examination

Degrees and Diplomas: *Associate Degree*; *Bachelor's Degree*; *Master's Degree*: Computer Science
Last Updated: 05/08/09

CEBU INTERNATIONAL DISTANCE EDUCATION COLLEGE

Wilson St., Cebu City, Cebu 6000
EMail: cidecedu@yahoo.com
Website: http://www.cidec.schoolpad.ph

President: Pureza V. Veloso

Registrar: Blanca A. Alejandro

Vice-President, Academic Affairs: Nenita V. Lapingcao

Programmes

Arts (English; Political Sciences; Psychology); **Business Administration** (Business Administration; Human Resources; Management; Marketing); **Education** (Education; Primary Education; Secondary Education; Special Education); **Information Technology** (Information Technology)

History: Founded 2005. Formerly known as Cebu Distance Learning Institute.

Degrees and Diplomas: *Bachelor's Degree*
Last Updated: 11/08/10

CEBU MARY IMMACULATE COLLEGE

Borbajo Street, Talamban, Cebu City, Cebu 6000
EMail: info@cmic.edu.ph

President: Marc Achilles M. Phua

Programmes

Arts and Humanities (Arts and Humanities; English); **Business Administration** (Business Administration); **Education** (Education; English; Mathematics Education; Physics; Preschool Education; Primary Education; Secondary Education; Special Education); **Information Technology** (Information Technology)

History: Founded 2005.

Degrees and Diplomas: *Bachelor's Degree*
Last Updated: 11/08/10

CEBU ROOSEVELT MEMORIAL COLLEGE

San Vicente Street, Bogo, Cebu 6010
Tel: +63(32) 251-2313
Fax: +63(32) 251-2494

President: Victor Eliot V. Lepiten, Jr.

Programmes

Arts and Sciences (Computer Science; Cooking and Catering; Criminology; Educational Administration; Hotel and Restaurant; Hotel Management; Information Management; Information Technology; Mass Communication; Mathematics; Political Sciences; Psychology; Tourism); **Business Administration** (Accountancy; Business Administration; Business and Commerce; Management; Marketing); **Education** (Education; English; Filipino; Foreign Languages Education; Home Economics Education; Native Language Education; Preschool Education; Primary Education; Secondary Education; Social Studies; Technology Education)

History: Founded 1947.

Degrees and Diplomas: *Bachelor's Degree*; *Master's Degree*
Last Updated: 11/08/10

CEBU SACRED HEART COLLEGE

Lawaan, Talisay City, Cebu 6045
Tel: +63(32) 272-4347 +63(32) 272-4438

Head: Dee San T. Magdadaro

Programmes

Hotel and Restaurant Management (Hotel and Restaurant; Hotel Management); **Nursing** (Nursing); **Tourism Management** (Tourism)

History: Founded 1995, acquiring current status in 2003.

Degrees and Diplomas: *Bachelor's Degree*
Last Updated: 11/08/10

CEGUERA TECHNOLOGICAL COLLEGE

Highway 1, Francia, District IV, Iriga City, Camarines Sur 4431
Tel: +63(54) 299-2224
Fax: +63(54) 299-2224
EMail: ctc_irg@yahoo.com; cistjdc@mozcom.com

President: Fe Dilanco-Ceguera

Programmes

Arts and Sciences (Automotive Engineering; Civil Engineering; Computer Science; Criminology; Electrical Engineering; Electronic Engineering; English; Heating and Refrigeration; Industrial Arts Education; Information Management; Information Technology; Mathematics; Mechanical Engineering; Technology); **Business Administration** (Business Administration; Human Resources; Marketing); **Education** (Computer Education; English; Mathematics Education; Secondary Education)

History: Founded 1984. Formerly known as Ceguera Institute of Science and Technology.

Degrees and Diplomas: *Certificate/Diploma*; *Bachelor's Degree*
Last Updated: 12/08/10

CENTRAL BASAK ISLAMIC REGIONAL COLLEGE

Rumayas, Lumba-Bayabao, Lanao del Sur 9705

President: Gloria Galo-Darimbang

Programmes

Arts (Political Sciences); **Commerce** (Business and Commerce; Management); **Education** (Education; Filipino; Native Language;

Native Language Education; Primary Education; Secondary Education)

History: Founded 1997.

Degrees and Diplomas: *Bachelor's Degree*
Last Updated: 12/08/10

CENTRAL COLLEGE OF PANGASINAN

Ilang District, San Carlos City, Pangasinan 2420
Tel: +63(75) 532-2194
Fax: +63(75) 532-2194
EMail: central_pang@yahoo.com; mcc@mozcom.com

President: Roberto G. Ferrer

Programmes

Business Administration (Business Administration); **Business Data Processing** (Business Administration; Business Computing; Data Processing); **Computer Education** (Computer Education); **Computer Science** (Computer Science); **Office Administration** (Business Administration)

History: Founded 1992. Formerly Marian Computer College (1997-2003)

Degrees and Diplomas: *Associate Degree*; *Bachelor's Degree*
Last Updated: 12/08/10

CENTRAL COLLEGES OF THE NORTH

Luna St., Ugac Highway, Tuguegarao City, Cagayan 3500
Tel: +63(78) 501-0597

President: Raldy C. Palattao

Programmes

Criminology (Criminology); **Information Technology** (Information Technology)

History: Founded 1998.

Degrees and Diplomas: *Bachelor's Degree*
Last Updated: 12/08/10

CENTRAL COLLEGES OF THE PHILIPPINES

52, Aurora Boulevard, Quezon City, Second District, Metro Manila 1100
Tel: +63(2) 715-5170
Fax: +63(2) 715-0848
EMail: bobcat@ccp.edu.ph
Website: http://www.ccp.edu.ph

President: Crispino T. Reyes

Colleges

Accountancy (Accountancy); **Architecture** (Architecture); **Arts and Sciences** (Arts and Humanities; Economics; English; Natural Sciences; Psychology; Social Sciences); **Business Administration** (Banking; Business Administration; Business Computing; Economics; Finance; Management; Marketing); **Computer Science** (Computer Science; Information Management; Information Technology); **Education** (Education; English; Filipino; Foreign Languages Education; History; Mathematics; Native Language Education); **Engineering** (Civil Engineering; Computer Engineering; Electrical Engineering; Electronic Engineering; Engineering; Industrial Engineering; Mechanical Engineering; Telecommunications Engineering); **Nursing** (Nursing); **Office Administration** (Business Administration; Secretarial Studies); **Optometry** (Optometry)

Schools

Graduate Studies (Business Administration; Information Technology; Public Administration; Teacher Training)

History: Founded 1954. Formerly Polytechnic Colleges of the Philippines (1954-1969).

Degrees and Diplomas: *Associate Degree*; *Bachelor's Degree*; *Master's Degree*
Last Updated: 12/08/10

CENTRAL LUZON COLLEGE OF TECHNOLOGY - OLONGAPO

1 CBMU Upper Kalaklan, East Bajac-Bajac, Olongapo City, Zambales 2200
Tel: +63(47) 224-8042
Fax: +63(47) 223-5855
EMail: clct@svisp.com

President: Renato P. Legaspi

Programmes

Accountancy (Accountancy); **Business Administration** (Business Administration; Management); **Criminology** (Criminology); **Customs Administration** (Administration; Taxation); **Information Technology** (Information Technology); **Marine Engineering** (Marine Engineering); **Marine Transportation** (Marine Transport); **Nursing** (Midwifery; Nursing)

History: Founded 1970.

Degrees and Diplomas: *Certificate/Diploma*; *Bachelor's Degree*
Last Updated: 12/08/10

CENTRAL LUZON DOCTORS' HOSPITAL EDUCATIONAL INSTITUTION

Hospital Drive, San Vicente, City of Tarlac, Tarlac 2300
Tel: +63(45) 982-0264
Fax: +63(45) 982-4430
EMail: cldh@mozcom.com

President: Rocardo Hipolito

Programmes

Medical Technology (Medical Technology); **Nursing** (Nursing); **Pharmacy** (Pharmacy); **Physical Therapy** (Physical Therapy); **Radiologic Technology** (Radiology); **Respiratory Therapy** (Respiratory Therapy)

History: Founded 1966.

Degrees and Diplomas: *Certificate/Diploma*; *Associate Degree*; *Bachelor's Degree*; *Master's Degree*
Last Updated: 12/08/10

CENTRAL MINDANAO COLLEGES

Osmeña Drive, City of Kidapawan, North Cotabato 9400
Tel: +63(84) 288-1708
Fax: +63(84) 288-5299

President: Cesar Sabulao

Programmes

Arts and Sciences (Criminology; Economics; English; Filipino; History; Mathematics; Native Language; Political Sciences); **Business Administration** (Banking; Business Administration; Business and Commerce; Finance; Marketing); **Civil Engineering** (Civil Engineering); **Education** (Art Education; Education; English; Filipino; Foreign Languages Education; History; Mathematics Education; Music Education; Native Language; Native Language Education; Physical Education; Primary Education; Science Education; Secondary Education); **Graduate Studies** (Business Administration; Education; Educational Administration)

History: Founded 1946, acquired present status and title 1947.

Degrees and Diplomas: *Bachelor's Degree*; *Master's Degree*
Last Updated: 12/08/10

CENTRAL MINDANAO COMPUTER SCHOOL

2nd-F Villasor Bldg., Burgos Street, M'lang, North Cotabato 9402
Tel: +63(64) 452-0216
EMail: cmcs_mlang@yahoo.com

President: Jonathan F. Abasquez

Programmes

Information Management and Technology (Computer Science; Information Management; Information Technology)

History: Founded 1999.

Degrees and Diplomas: *Bachelor's Degree*
Last Updated: 12/08/10

CENTRAL NEGROS COLLEGE

S. Carmona Street, San Carlos City, Negros Occidental 6127
Tel: +63(34) 312-5439
Fax: +63(34) 312-5439
EMail: cnc@mozcom.com

Director: Mario S. Ledesma Tel: +63(34) 312-5522

Programmes

Arts and Humanities (Arts and Humanities; English; History); **Business Administration** (Banking; Business Administration; Business and Commerce; Finance; Marketing); **Education** (Education; English; Filipino; Foreign Languages Education; Home Economics Education; Mathematics Education; Native Language Education; Primary Education; Secondary Education; Social Studies; Technology Education)

History: Founded 1929. Formerly known as Central Negros Institute (1950-1974). Acquired present status and title 1974.

Degrees and Diplomas: *Certificate/Diploma*; *Bachelor's Degree*
Last Updated: 12/08/10

CENTRAL PHILIPPINE ADVENTIST COLLEGE

Alegria, Murcia, Negros Occidental 6129
Tel: +63(34) 710-0307
Fax: +63(34) 710-0585
EMail: cpac@mozcom.com

President: Alfredo T. Amada EMail: president@cpac.edu.ph

Programmes

Agriculture (Agricultural Engineering; Agriculture; Crop Production); **Biology** (Biology); **Business Administration** (Accountancy; Business Administration; Business Computing; Management; Secretarial Studies); **Civil Engineering** (Civil Engineering); **Education** (Biology; Education; English; Health Education; Mathematics Education; Primary Education; Secondary Education); **Information Management** (Information Management; Information Technology); **Mathematics** (Mathematics); **Nursing** (Nursing); **Theology** (Theology)

History: Founded 1982.

Degrees and Diplomas: *Associate Degree*; *Bachelor's Degree*
Last Updated: 12/08/10

CENTRAL PHILIPPINE UNIVERSITY (CPU)

Lopez Jaena Street, Jaro, Iloilo City, Iloilo 5000
Tel: +63(33) 329-1971
Fax: +63(33) 329-5861
EMail: admin@cpu.edu.ph
Website: http://www.cpu.edu.ph

President: Teodoro C. Robles Tel: +63(33) 320-3824

Colleges

Agriculture (Agricultural Business; Agricultural Economics; Agricultural Education; Agricultural Engineering; Agriculture; Animal Husbandry; Crop Production; Horticulture; Zoology); **Arts and Science** (Arts and Humanities; Biological and Life Sciences; Chemistry; English; Mass Communication; Mathematics; Medical Technology; Modern Languages; Natural Sciences; Nutrition; Physics; Political Sciences; Social Sciences; Social Work); **Business and Accountancy** (Accountancy; Business Administration; Economics; Management); **Computer Studies** (Computer Science; Information Management; Information Technology; Software Engineering); **Education** (Biological and Life Sciences; Dietetics; Education; English; Filipino; Foreign Languages Education; Health Education; Home Economics; Information Sciences; Library Science; Music Education; Native Language Education; Nutrition; Physical Education; Preschool Education; Primary Education; Secondary Education; Social Studies; Special Education); **Engineering** (Chemical Engineering; Civil Engineering; Communication Studies; Electrical and Electronic Engineering; Engineering; Mechanical Engineering); **Law** (Law); **Medicine** (Medicine); **Nursing** (Nursing); **Theology** (Ethics; Religion; Theology)

Programmes

Hotel and Restaurant Management (Hotel and Restaurant; Hotel Management)

Schools

Graduate Studies (Agricultural Economics; Agronomy; Business Administration; Computer Science; Education; Educational and Student Counselling; Engineering; English; Information Sciences; Library Science; Management; Nursing; Public Administration; Social Work; Sociology; Theology)

History: Founded 1905 as Jaro Industrial School by American Baptist Foreign Mission Society. Became High School 1915, Junior College 1922, Senior College 1938. Acquired University status 1953 and placed under Filipino control 1969. The University is a private institution, financed by tuition fees and grants, operating under the supervision of the Commission of Higher Education and the Department of Education, Culture and Sports.

Governing Bodies: Board of Trustees

Academic Year: June to May (June-October; November-March; April-May)

Admission Requirements: Graduation from high school and entrance examination

Fees: (Pesos): c. 5,000-15,000 per semester

Main Language(s) of Instruction: Filipino, English

Accrediting Agencies: Philippine Accrediting Association of Schools, Colleges and Universities; Association of Christian Schools; Association of Theological Education in South East Asia

Degrees and Diplomas: *Certificate/Diploma*; *Associate Degree*; *Bachelor's Degree*; *Master's Degree*; *PhD*

Student Services: Academic counselling, Canteen, Cultural centre, Employment services, Health services, Social counselling, Sports facilities

Student Residential Facilities: Yes

Special Facilities: Museum. Art gallery. Observatory. Movie studio. Radio station

Libraries: Henry Luce III Library, c. 180,000 vols. Special Collections (American Studies Resource Center, Food and Agriculture Organization, World War II Documents, Meyer-Asian Collection, Elizabeth Knox Sacred Music Collection). Repository of c. 40,000 United Nations Documents

Publications: The South East Asia Journal, Publication of University research *(biennially)*
Last Updated: 06/09/10

CENTRAL SULU COLLEGE

Poblacion, Siasi, Sulu 7412

President: Orlando V. Kong

Programmes

Commerce (Business Administration; Business and Commerce); **Education** (Education; Primary Education; Secondary Education; Teacher Training)

History: Founded 1951as Siasi Academy. Acquired present title 1967.

Degrees and Diplomas: *Associate Degree*; *Bachelor's Degree*; *Master's Degree*
Last Updated: 06/09/10

CENTRE FOR INTERNATIONAL EDUCATION GLOBAL COLLEGES, INC.

168, Pres. Magsaysay Street, Villa Aurora, Mabolo, Cebu City, Cebu 6000
Tel: +63(32) 232-4333
Fax: +63(32) 233-2566
EMail: info@cie.edu
Website: http://www.cie.edu

President: Nelia Cruz Sarcol

Programmes

Business Administration (Business Administration); **Information Technology** (Information Technology)

History: Founded 1998. Formerly known as Global Foundation for International Education.

Degrees and Diplomas: *Bachelor's Degree*
Last Updated: 28/03/11

CENTRO ESCOLAR UNIVERSITY (CEU)

Mendiola Street, San Miguel, Manila, Metro Manila 1005
Tel: +63(2) 735-6861 +63(2) 735-8851
Fax: +63(2) 735-5991
EMail: celao@ceu.edu.ph
Website: http://www.ceu.edu.ph

President: María Cristina D. Padolina (2006-)
Tel: +63(2) 735-5991 EMail: mcdpadolina@ceu.edu.ph

Executive Vice-PresidentInformation Officer: Ricardo F. de Leon
EMail: rfdeleon@ceu.edu.ph

Vice-President and Registrar: Lucia D. Gonzales
EMail: ldgonzales@ceu.edu.ph

Colleges

Business and Technology (Accountancy; Business Administration; Finance; Information Technology; Management; Marketing; Technology) *Dean*: Nilo V. Francisco; **Education, Liberal Arts and Science** *(Malolos)* (Arts and Humanities; Education; Journalism; Mass Communication; Natural Sciences; Psychology; Radio and Television Broadcasting; Science Education) *Dean*: Elizabeth C. Roces; **Medical Technology** (Medical Technology) *Dean*: Charito M. Bermido; **Nursing** (Nursing) *Dean*: Merlina V. Locquiao; **Optometry** (Optometry) *Dean*: Jessica F. Torre

Schools

Accountancy and Management (Accountancy; Business Administration; Finance; Management; Marketing) *Dean*: Flordeliza L. Anastacio; **Dentistry** (Dentistry) *Dean*: Maria Jona D. Godoy; **Education, Liberal Arts, Music and Social Work** (Arts and Humanities; Biological and Life Sciences; Curriculum; Education; English; Information Sciences; Journalism; Library Science; Mass Communication; Mathematical Physics; Music; Music Education; Musical Instruments; Performing Arts; Physics; Political Sciences; Preschool Education; Primary Education; Secondary Education; Social Work; Special Education) *Dean*: Teresita G. Carey; **Graduate** (Biology; Business Administration; Cosmetology; Curriculum; Dentistry; Dietetics; Educational Administration; Educational and Student Counselling; Higher Education; Hotel and Restaurant; Hotel Management; Information Technology; Library Science; Management; Mathematics; Mathematics Education; Music Education; Nursing; Nutrition; Orthodontics; Periodontics; Pharmacy; Psychology; Public Administration; Science Education; Social Work; Southeast Asian Studies; Special Education; Teacher Training; Tourism) *Assistant Dean*: Juliana M. Laraya; **Nutrition and Hospitality Management** (Dietetics; Hotel and Restaurant; Hotel Management; Nutrition; Tourism) *Dean*: Cecilia C. Uncad; **Pharmacy** (Pharmacy) *Dean*: Olivia M. Limuaco; **Science and Technology** (Biology; Computer Engineering; Computer Science; Cosmetology; Information Technology; Psychology) *Dean*: Betty M. Lontoc

Further Information: Campuses in Malolos City and Makati City.

History: Founded 1907 as a private Institution, recognized by the State. Acquired present status 1932.

Governing Bodies: Board of Directors; Administrative Council

Academic Year: June to March (June-October; November-March)

Admission Requirements: Graduation from high school or recognized foreign equivalent, entrance examination, interview.

Fees: (Pesos): 24,000-37,000

Main Language(s) of Instruction: Filipino, English

International Co-operation: With universities in China, Thailand, Australia, Japan, Korea, Taiwan.

Accrediting Agencies: Philippine Association of Colleges and Universities Commission on Accreditation (PACUCOA), Philippine Accrediting Association of Schools, Colleges and Universities (PAASCU)

Degrees and Diplomas: *Certificate/Diploma*; *Associate Degree*; *Bachelor's Degree*; *Master's Degree*; *PhD*. Also Proficiency as Dental Technician; Ophthalmic Technician and Post-Doctorate in Total Quality Management in Higher Education.

Student Services: Academic counselling, Canteen, Employment services, Foreign student adviser, Foreign Studies Centre, Health services, Language programs, Sports facilities

Special Facilities: Centro Escolar University Archives and Museum

Libraries: University Library

Publications: Cienca y Virtud, Creative Writings Magazine; Graduate and Faculty Studies, Research Abstracts Journal *(biannually)*

Press or Publishing House: CEU Press

Last Updated: 07/09/10

CHIANG KAI SHEK COLLEGE

1477 Narra Street, Tondo, Manila, First District, Metro Manila 1012
Tel: +63(2) 252-6161
Fax: +63(2) 252-6161
EMail: info@cksc.edu.ph
Website: http://www.cksc.edu.ph

President: Bee Ching U. Ong Kian Koc Tel: +63(2) 252-6125

Colleges

Undergraduate and Professional (Accountancy; Artificial Intelligence; Business Administration; Chinese; Computer Networks; Computer Science; Education; Foreign Languages Education; Graphic Arts; Hotel and Restaurant; Hotel Management; Information Management; Information Sciences; Information Technology; Management; Marketing; Mathematics; Mathematics Education; Multimedia; Nursing)

Schools

Graduate Studies (Business Administration; Education; Educational Administration; English; Foreign Languages Education; Mathematics Education; Science Education)

History: Founded 1939, acquired present status and title 1965.

Degrees and Diplomas: *Certificate/Diploma*; *Bachelor's Degree*; *Master's Degree*

Last Updated: 07/09/10

CHILD JESUS COLLEGE

Phase IV, Bagong Silang, Caloocan City, Third District, Metro Manila 1428
Tel: +63(2) 446-9963
EMail: childjesuscollegecaloocan@yahoo.com

Director: Crispina B. Bragado

Programmes

Business Administration (Business Administration; Economics; Finance; Management; Marketing); **Computer and Information Technology** (Computer Engineering; Information Technology); **Computer Science** (Computer Science); **Education** (Education; English; Foreign Languages Education; Mathematics Education; Primary Education; Science Education; Secondary Education); **Hotel and Restaurant Management** (Hotel and Restaurant; Hotel Management); **Nursing** (Nursing)

History: Founded 1990. Acquired present status 1997.

Degrees and Diplomas: *Bachelor's Degree*: 4 yrs

Last Updated: 07/09/10

CHILDREN OF MARY IMMACULATE COLLEGE

22 Maisan Road, Malinta, Valenzuela City, Third District, Metro Manila 1441
Tel: +63(2) 293-3149
Fax: +63(2) 291-8821

President: Eleanor De Leon Llenado Tel: +63(2) 291-8821

Programmes

Undergraduate and Professional (Business Administration; Business and Commerce; Education; English; Management; Primary Education; Secondary Education)

History: Founded 1978 as Children of Mary Immaculate School.

Degrees and Diplomas: *Associate Degree*: 2 yrs; *Bachelor's Degree*: 4 yrs

Last Updated: 07/09/10

CHINESE GENERAL HOSPITAL COLLEGE OF NURSING AND LIBERAL ARTS

286 Blumentritt Street, Sta. Cruz, Manila, First District, Metro Manila 1003
Tel: +63(2) 711-0075
Fax: +63(2) 741-5166
EMail: cghcnregistrar@yahoo.com.ph

President: James Dy

Programmes

Health Sciences (Health Sciences); **Nursing** (Nursing)

History: Founded 1921 as Chinese General Hospital School of Nursing. Acquired present status and title 1980.

Degrees and Diplomas: *Associate Degree*: Health Science Education; *Bachelor's Degree*: Nursing

Last Updated: 07/09/10

CHRIST THE KING COLLEGE - CALBAYOG CITY

499 Magsaysay Boulevard, Calbayog City, Western Samar 6710
Tel: +63(55) 209-3626
Fax: +63(55) 533-9526
EMail: info@ckc.edu.ph
Website: http://www.ckc.edu.ph

President: Prisco A. Cajes, OFM Tel: +63(55) 209-2400

Programmes

Graduate (Computer Science; Education; Educational Administration; English; Filipino; Foreign Languages Education; Mathematics Education; Native Language Education; Science Education); **Undergraduate** (Accountancy; Banking; Biology; Business Administration; Business and Commerce; Computer Education; Computer Science; Economics; Education; Educational Administration; English; Filipino; Finance; Foreign Languages Education; History; Hotel and Restaurant; Hotel Management; Human Resources; Information Management; Information Technology; Law; Management; Marketing; Mathematics Education; Native Language Education; Nursing; Political Sciences; Preschool Education; Primary Education; Psychology; Science Education; Secondary Education; Social Studies; Social Work)

History: Founded 1905, acquired present status and title 1951.

Degrees and Diplomas: *Associate Degree*; *Bachelor's Degree*; *Master's Degree*

Last Updated: 07/09/10

CHRIST THE KING COLLEGE - GINGOOG CITY

National Highway, Gingoog City, Misamis Oriental 9014
Tel: +63(88) 861-4229
Fax: +63(88) 861-0149
Website: http://ckc.philcom.ph

President: Ma. Aida L. Mariano, RVM

Programmes

Undergraduate and Professional Studies (Arts and Humanities; Biology; Business Administration; Education; Law; Mathematics and Computer Science; Midwifery; Social Sciences; Social Work)

History: Founded 1947, acquired present status and title 1950.

Degrees and Diplomas: *Bachelor's Degree*

Last Updated: 07/09/10

CHRIST THE KING COLLEGE - MARANDING

Lala, Maranding, Lanao del Norte 9211
Tel: +63(63) 388-7373
Fax: +63(63) 388-7373

President: Elenito de los Reyes Galido, D.D

Programmes

Business Administration (Business Administration; Finance; Management); **Criminology** (Criminology); **Education** (Education; English; Foreign Languages Education; Health Education; Mathematics Education; Primary Education; Science Education; Secondary Education)

History: Founded 1999.

Degrees and Diplomas: *Bachelor's Degree*

Last Updated: 07/09/10

CHRISTIAN COLLEGE OF TANAUAN

J.V. Pagaspas Street, Tanauan City, Batangas 4232
Tel: +63(43) 778 -5468
Fax: +63(43) 778 -5469

President: Vinson B. Pineda

Programmes

Business Administration (Accountancy; Business Administration; Business and Commerce; Human Resources; Management); **Computer Science** (Computer Science); **Criminology** (Criminology); **Customs Administration** (Taxation); **Education** (Education; Primary Education); **Hotel and Restaurant Management** (Hotel and Restaurant; Hotel Management); **Industrial Engineering** (Industrial Engineering); **Information Technology** (Information Technology); **Nursing** (Nursing)

History: Founded 2003.

Degrees and Diplomas: *Bachelor's Degree*

Last Updated: 07/09/10

CHRISTIAN COLLEGES OF SOUTHEAST ASIA

Tulip Drive, Matina, Davao City, Davao del Sur 8000
Tel: +63(82) 298-4526
Fax: +63(82) 296-9455

President: Michael Ang

Programmes

Business Administration (Accountancy; Banking; Business Administration; Finance; Management; Marketing); **Computer Science** (Computer Science); **Education** (Biological and Life Sciences; Education; English; Filipino; Foreign Languages Education; Health Education; Mathematics Education; Music Education; Native Language Education; Physical Education; Preschool Education; Social Studies; Special Education); **Mathematics** (Mathematics)

History: Founded 2004.

Degrees and Diplomas: *Bachelor's Degree*

Last Updated: 07/09/10

CICOSAT COLLEGES

Lingsat, City of San Fernando, La Union 2500
Tel: +63(72) 242-2698
Fax: +63(72) 700-0103
EMail: cicosat_colleges@yahoo.com; cicosat@launion.com

President: Jose B. Abella

Programmes

Aeronautical Engineering (Aeronautical and Aerospace Engineering); **Automotive Engineering** (Automotive Engineering); **Commerce** (Banking; Business and Commerce; Finance); **Criminology** (Criminology); **Electrical Engineering** (Electrical Engineering); **Electronics and Communications Engineering** (Communication Studies; Electronic Engineering; Engineering; Telecommunications Engineering); **Elementary Education** (Education; Primary Education); **Industrial Education** (Automotive Engineering; Education; Electrical and Electronic Engineering; Industrial Arts Education); **Industrial Technology** (Industrial Engineering; Technology); **Management** (Management); **Mechanical Engineering** (Mechanical Engineering); **Nursing** (Nursing); **Pharmacy** (Pharmacy); **Secondary Education** (Education; Mathematics Education; Secondary Education)

History: Founded 1991. Formerly known as Central Ilocandia College of Science and Technology.

Degrees and Diplomas: *Certificate/Diploma*; *Bachelor's Degree*; *Master's Degree*

Last Updated: 12/08/10

CIT COLLEGES

Burgos Street, Paniqui, Tarlac 2307
Tel: +63(45)931-0512
Fax: +63(45)931-0512

President: Domingo C. Palarca

Programmes

Arts and Science (Business Administration; English; Filipino; Industrial Arts Education; Management; Modern Languages; Native Language); **Education** (Art Education; Education; English; Filipino; Foreign Languages Education; Health Education; History; Mathematics Education; Music Education; Native Language Education; Physical Education; Primary Education; Science Education; Secondary Education; Social Studies)

History: Founded 1948. Formerly Central Institute of Technology (1948-1999).
Degrees and Diplomas: *Bachelor's Degree*
Last Updated: 07/09/10

CLARENDON COLLEGE

Odiong, Roxas, Oriental Mindoro 5212
Tel: +63(45) 289-2638 +63(43) 289-2538

President: Juanito A. Bagay, Jr.

Programmes

Business Administration (Business Administration; Management); **Education** (English; Foreign Languages Education; Mathematics Education; Primary Education; Secondary Education)
History: Founded 1996. Acquired present status 2002.
Degrees and Diplomas: *Bachelor's Degree*
Last Updated: 07/09/10

CLARET COLLEGE OF ISABELA

Sta. Cruz, Isabela City, Basilan 7300
Tel: +63(62) 200-3865
Fax: +63(62) 200-3865
EMail: claret_college_of_isabela@yahoo.com

President: Felimon P. Libot, CMF

Programmes

Arts and Science (Arts and Humanities; Computer Science; Information Management; Information Technology); **Business Administration** (Accountancy; Business Administration; Finance; Secretarial Studies); **Education** (Education; Primary Education; Secondary Education)
History: Founded 1949, acquired present status and title 1967.
Degrees and Diplomas: *Bachelor's Degree*
Last Updated: 07/09/10

CLCC INSTITUTE OF COMPUTER ARTS AND TECHNOLOGY

J.P. Rizal Street, Lalud, Calapan City, Oriental Mindoro 5200
Tel: +63(43) 286-7289
EMail: rtm_ph@yahoo.com

School Administrator: Erlina D. Caringal

Programmes

Business Administration (Business Administration; Business Computing; Computer Education; Management); **Computer Science** (Computer Science)
History: Founded 1991. Acquired present status 1995.
Degrees and Diplomas: *Certificate/Diploma*; *Bachelor's Degree*
Last Updated: 07/09/10

COLLEGE FOR RESEARCH AND TECHNOLOGY - CABANATUAN CITY

Beedle Street, Padre Burgos, Cabanatuan City, Nueva Ecija 3100
Tel: +63(44) 463-2735
Fax: +63(44) 463-2735
EMail: crtcab@mozcom.com

President: Reynato C. Arimbuyutan

Programmes

Computer Studies (Business Computing; Computer Engineering); **Information Technology** (Information Technology)
History: Founded 1990.
Degrees and Diplomas: *Certificate/Diploma*; *Associate Degree*; *Bachelor's Degree*
Last Updated: 09/09/10

COLLEGE OF MARY IMMACULATE

J.P. Rizal Street, Pandi, Bulacan 3014
Tel: +63(44) 661-1527
Fax: +63(44) 661-1055
EMail: cmi_pandi@yahoo.com

President: Cecille Santos Andres

Programmes

Accountancy (Accountancy); **Business Administration** (Business Administration); **Computer Technology** (Computer Engineering); **Elementary Education** (Primary Education); **Hotel and Restaurant Management** (Hotel and Restaurant; Hotel Management); **Secondary Education** (Secondary Education)
History: Founded 2001.
Degrees and Diplomas: *Associate Degree*; *Bachelor's Degree*
Last Updated: 09/09/10

COLLEGE OF SAINT GABRIEL THE ARCHANGEL

Colegio de San Gabriel Arcangel
Blk 13 lot 26 Brgy Fatima 1 Area E, City of San Jose del Monte, Bulacan 3023
Tel: +63(917) 469-9352 +63(44) 691-6630

President: Gabriel G. Uriarte

Programmes

Arts and Science (Arts and Humanities; Computer Engineering; Criminology; Hotel and Restaurant; Hotel Management; Information Technology; Psychology; Tourism); **Business Administration** (Business Administration; Management); **Education** (Educational and Student Counselling; English; Filipino; Foreign Languages Education; Mathematics Education; Native Language Education; Primary Education; Secondary Education)
History: Founded 1993. Acquired present status 2005.
Degrees and Diplomas: *Associate Degree*; *Bachelor's Degree*
Last Updated: 08/09/10

COLLEGE OF SAN ANTONIO OF PADUA

Colegio de San Antonio de Padua
Ramon Durano Foundation Compound, Danao City, Cebu 6004
Tel: +63(32) 200-5388
Fax: +63(32) 200-5388

President: Ramon H. Durano VI

Programmes

Nursing (Nursing)
History: Founded 2004.
Degrees and Diplomas: *Associate Degree*; *Bachelor's Degree*
Last Updated: 08/09/10

COLLEGE OF ST. CATHERINE

362 Quirino Hi-way, Baesa, Quezon, Quezon City, Second District, Metro Manila 1116
Tel: +63(2) 330-4883

President: Arlene S.C. Maningding

Programmes

Information Technology (Information Technology); **Secondary Education** (Art Education; Education; English; Foreign Languages Education; Health Education; Mathematics Education; Music Education; Physical Education; Secondary Education; Social Studies)
History: Founded 1993.
Degrees and Diplomas: *Bachelor's Degree*
Last Updated: 09/09/10

COLLEGE OF ST. JOHN - ROXAS

Teodorica Avenue, Brgy. Banica, Roxas City, Capiz 5800
Tel: +63(36) 621-2377
Fax: +63(36) 621-5688
EMail: emacen@yahoo.com

Chancellor: Emma A. Encarnacion

Programmes
Accountancy (Accountancy); **Business Administration** (Business Administration); **Nursing** (Nursing); **Psychology** (Psychology)

History: Founded 1998.

Degrees and Diplomas: *Bachelor's Degree*
Last Updated: 09/09/10

COLLEGE OF ST. LAWRENCE

Balagtas, Bulacan 3016
Tel: +63(44) 693-3471
Fax: +63(44) 693-3452

President: Jerry B. Coloma

Programmes
Business Administration (Accountancy; Banking; Finance; Management); **Computer Science** (Computer Science); **Criminology**; **Education** (Education; Mathematics Education; Science Education; Secondary Education)

History: Founded 1997.

Degrees and Diplomas: *Bachelor's Degree*
Last Updated: 09/09/10

COLLEGE OF TECHNOLOGICAL SCIENCES - CEBU

Natalio Bacalso Avenue, Cebu City, Cebu 6000
Tel: +63(32) 256-1303
Fax: +63(32) 254-2434
EMail: ctscebu@cts.edu.ph
Website: http://www.cts.edu.ph

President: Jose Mari T. Bigornia

Programmes
Automotive Technology (Automotive Engineering); **Electronic and Communications Engineering** (Electronic Engineering; Telecommunications Engineering); **Engineering** (Civil Engineering; Computer Engineering); **Industrial Technology** (Industrial Engineering); **Information Technology** (Information Technology); **Nursing** (Nursing)

History: Founded 1950. Formerly known as Cebu Technological School.

Degrees and Diplomas: *Associate Degree*; *Bachelor's Degree*
Last Updated: 09/09/10

COLLEGE OF THE HOLY FAMILY

Colegio de la Sagrada Familia
Tangos, Baliuag, Bulacan 3006

President: Alfredo M. Santos

Programmes
Education (Education; English; Foreign Languages Education; Preschool Education; Primary Education); **Entrepreneurship** (Management); **Hospitality Management** (Hotel and Restaurant; Hotel Management; Tourism); **Information Technology** (Information Technology)

Degrees and Diplomas: *Bachelor's Degree*
Last Updated: 08/09/10

COLLEGE OF THE HOLY SPIRIT OF MANILA

163 E. Mendiola Street, San Miguel, Manila, Metro Manila 1005
Tel: +63(2) 735-5980 +63(2) 735-5981
Fax: +63(2) 735-5981
EMail: info@holyspirit.edu.ph
Website: http://www.chsmanila.edu.ph

President: Ancille B. Elveña EMail: president@holyspirit.edu.ph

Programmes
Arts *(Bachelor of Arts programme)* (Communication Arts; Human Resources; International Studies; Psychology; Tourism); **Fine Arts** *(Bachelor of Fine Arts programme)* (Advertising and Publicity); **Science** *(Bachelor of Science programme)* (Accountancy; Biology; Business Administration; Business and Commerce; Computer Science; Hotel and Restaurant; Hotel Management; Interior Design; Management; Marketing; Mathematics; Medical Technology; Nursing; Psychology; Tourism); **Secondary Education** (Education; English; Ethics; Foreign Languages Education; Religious Education; Secondary Education)

History: Founded 1913.

Degrees and Diplomas: *Certificate/Diploma*; *Bachelor's Degree*
Last Updated: 09/09/10

COLLEGE OF THE HOLY SPIRIT OF TARLAC

F. Tañedo Street, City of Tarlac, Tarlac 2300
Tel: +63(45) 982-1230
Fax: +63(45) 982-1230
EMail: chstarlac@digitelone.com

Director: Teresita Eugenio

Programmes
Arts and Humanities (Arts and Humanities; English; Psychology); **Business Administration** (Accountancy; Banking; Business Administration; Economics; Finance; Management; Marketing); **Education** (Biological and Life Sciences; Education; English; Ethics; Filipino; Foreign Languages Education; Health Education; Mathematics Education; Native Language Education; Preschool Education; Primary Education; Science Education; Secondary Education); **Nursing** (Nursing)

History: Founded 1939, acquired present status and title 1968.

Degrees and Diplomas: *Associate Degree*; *Bachelor's Degree*
Last Updated: 09/09/10

COLLEGE OF THE IMMACULATE CONCEPTION

Del Pilar Street, Cabanatuan City, Nueva Ecija 3100
Tel: +63(44) 463-0048
Fax: +63(44) 463-7481
EMail: cab.cic@mozcom.com; cicØØ1ph@digitelone.com

President: Michael Feliciano I. Veneracion

Programmes
Arts *(Bachelor of Arts programme)* (Mass Communication; Political Sciences); **Business Administration** (Accountancy; Banking; Business Administration; Economics; Finance; Human Resources; Management; Marketing); **Computer Science** (Computer Science); **Education** (Art Education; Biological and Life Sciences; Child Care and Development; Education; Educational Administration; Educational and Student Counselling; Educational Psychology; English; Ethics; Filipino; Foreign Languages Education; Health Education; Home Economics Education; Mathematics Education; Music Education; Native Language Education; Physical Education; Physics; Preschool Education; Psychology; Science Education; Social Studies; Sociology; Special Education; Technology Education); **Hotel and Restaurant Management** (Hotel and Restaurant; Hotel Management); **Information Technology** (Information Technology); **Nursing** (Nursing); **Social Work** (Social Work)

History: Founded 1926.

Degrees and Diplomas: *Associate Degree*; *Bachelor's Degree*; *Master's Degree*; *PhD*
Last Updated: 09/09/10

COLLEGES OF THE REPUBLIC

Maharlika Highway, San Jose City, Nueva Ecija 3121
Tel: +63(44) 511-1609
Fax: +63(44) 511-2278
EMail: republic@mozcom.com

President: Anacleto K. Agaton

Programmes
Commerce (Accountancy; Banking; Business Administration; Business and Commerce; Computer Science; Finance; Management; Marketing); **Education** (Art Education; Education; Educational Administration; Educational and Student Counselling; Educational Psychology; English; Filipino; Foreign Languages Education; Health Education; History; Mathematics Education; Music Education; Native Language Education; Physical Education; Physics; Science Education; Social Studies); **Political Sciences** (Political Sciences); **Psychology** (Psychology)

History: Founded 1948.

Degrees and Diplomas: *Associate Degree*; *Bachelor's Degree*; *Master's Degree*
Last Updated: 09/09/10

COLLEGIUM SOCIETATIS ANGELI PACIS

Washington Street, Cansojong, Talisay City, Cebu 6045
Tel: +63(38) 272-7775
Fax: +63(38) 272-3810

President/Director: Cristobal E. Garcia

Programmes

Philosophy (Philosophy); **Theology** (Theology)

History: Founded 1997.

Degrees and Diplomas: *Bachelor's Degree*; *Master's Degree*
Last Updated: 09/09/10

COLUMBAN COLLEGE - OLONGAPO CITY

N°1 Mt. Apo Street, New Asinan, Olongapo City, Zambales 2200
Tel: +63(47) 222-3329
Fax: +63(47) 222-7782 +63(47) 222-5181
EMail: inquiry@columban.edu.ph
Website: http://www.columban.edu.ph

President: Crisostomo A. Cacho

Vice-President for Academic Affairs: Marymerlin Ladiza Espolong

Vice-President for Finance and Administration: Amelia Cecilia Santos Reyes

Centres

Industrial Technology (Electronic Engineering; Industrial Engineering)

Colleges

Architecture (Architecture); **Arts and Sciences** (Communication Studies; Information Sciences; Library Science; Political Sciences; Social Work); **Business Administration** (Accountancy; Business Administration; Finance; Hotel and Restaurant; Hotel Management; Human Resources; Management; Marketing; Tourism); **Computer Studies** (Computer Science; Information Technology); **Education** (Art Education; Biological and Life Sciences; Education; English; Ethics; Filipino; Foreign Languages Education; Mathematics Education; Music Education; Native Language Education; Physical Education; Primary Education; Religious Education; Secondary Education; Social Studies); **Engineering** (Civil Engineering; Computer Engineering; Electrical Engineering; Electronic Engineering; Engineering; Industrial Engineering); **Nursing** (Nursing)

Schools

Graduate Studies (Business Administration; Educational Administration; English; Ethics; Foreign Languages Education; Public Administration; Religious Education; Science Education); **Midwifery** (Midwifery)

History: Founded 1952 as Naval Reservation Junior College. Acquired present status and title 1962.

Governing Bodies: Board of Trustees

Academic Year: June to March

Admission Requirements: Secondary School Certificate and College Entrance Test

Fees: (Pesos): c. 1.500 per semester

Main Language(s) of Instruction: Filipino, English

Accrediting Agencies: Philippine Accrediting Association of Schools, Colleges and Universities (PAASCU)

Degrees and Diplomas: *Certificate/Diploma*; *Associate Degree*; *Bachelor's Degree*; *Master's Degree*; *PhD*

Student Services: Academic counselling, Canteen, Cultural centre, Employment services, Health services, Language programs, Nursery care, Social counselling, Sports facilities

Publications: Columban College The Journal *(biannually)*
Last Updated: 09/09/10

COLUMBAN COLLEGE - STA. CRUZ, ZAMBALES

Naulo, Santa Cruz, Zambales 2213
Tel: +63(47) 222-3329
Fax: +63(47) 222-7782

President: Crisostomo Cacho

Programmes

Business Administration (Business Administration; Finance; Human Resources; Management); **Education** (Education; English; Foreign Languages Education; Mathematics Education; Physical Education; Primary Education; Science Education; Secondary Education); **Information Systems** (Information Technology)

History: Founded 1995.

Degrees and Diplomas: *Associate Degree*; *Bachelor's Degree*: 4 yrs
Last Updated: 09/09/10

COLUMBUS COLLEGE

Lucena City, Quezon 4301
Tel: +63(42) 710-6377
Fax: +63(42) 660-6083

President: Numerita M. Buen

Programmes

Undergraduate and Professional (Automotive Engineering; Business Administration; Business Education; Computer Engineering; Computer Science; Education; Electronic Engineering; Hotel and Restaurant; Hotel Management; Information Technology; Marine Engineering; Secondary Education; Secretarial Studies)

History: Founded 1993.

Degrees and Diplomas: *Certificate/Diploma*; *Associate Degree*; *Bachelor's Degree*
Last Updated: 09/09/10

COMPUTER ARTS AND TECHNOLOGICAL COLLEGE

Balintawak Street, Legazpi City, Albay 4500
Tel: +63(52) 280-1645 +63(52) 214-4324
Fax: +63(52) 480-1924
EMail: admin@cats.edu.ph
Website: http://www.cats.edu.ph

President: Reynaldo A. Belleza

Programmes

Undergraduate and Professional (Accountancy; Administration; Business Administration; Communication Studies; Computer Education; Computer Engineering; Computer Science; Criminology; E-Business/Commerce; Electrical Engineering; Information Technology; Radio and Television Broadcasting; Telecommunications Engineering)

History: Founded 1988 as Computer Arts and Technology School. Acquired present status and title 1999.

Degrees and Diplomas: *Certificate/Diploma*; *Associate Degree*; *Bachelor's Degree*
Last Updated: 09/09/10

COMPUTER COLLEGE OF THE VISAYAS

Mabini Street, Iloilo City, Iloilo 5000
Tel: +63(33) 337-3052 +63(33) 337-4278
Fax: +63(33) 335-0848
EMail: ccv-iloilo@hotmail.com

President: Nestor C. Salajog

Programmes

Computer Science (Computer Science); **Computer Technology** (Computer Engineering)

History: Founded 1983 as Visayan Computer Data Processing Inc. Acquired present status and title 1986.

Degrees and Diplomas: *Associate Degree*; *Bachelor's Degree*
Last Updated: 09/09/10

COMPUTER COMMUNICATION DEVELOPMENT INSTITUTE - SORSOGON (CCDI)

Rizal Street, City of Sorsogon, Sorsogon
Tel: +63(56) 421-5575
EMail: ecbalasta@yahoo.com
Website: http://www.ccdi-sorsogon.net

President: Felix R. Alfelor, Jr.

Administrator: Edgar C. Balasta

Programmes

Computer Science (Computer Science); **Information Management** (Information Management); **Information Technology** (Information Technology)

Further Information: CCDI campuses: Iriga City; Naga City; Goa; Legaspi City; Pili, Camarines Sur; Tabaco City

History: Founded 1997.

Degrees and Diplomas: *Certificate/Diploma*: 1-2 yrs; *Associate Degree*: 2 yrs; *Bachelor's Degree*: 4 yrs
Last Updated: 09/09/10

COMPUTER TECHNOLOGIES INSTITUTE OF ZAMBOANGA CITY

Baliwasan Chico, Zamboanga City, Zamboanga del Sur 7000
Tel: +63(62) 991-2365 +63(62) 991-4367
Fax: +63(62) 991-2365
EMail: ctiz_zc@yahoo.com; comtech_institute@yahoo.com

President: Cleofe Carmelita C. Cajucom

Programmes

Undergraduate and Professional Studies (Computer Engineering; Hotel and Restaurant; Hotel Management; Information Management; Software Engineering; Systems Analysis)

Further Information: Also campus in Isabela City, Basilan.

History: Founded 1991 as Comtech Software Center. Acquired present status and title 1996.

Degrees and Diplomas: *Bachelor's Degree*
Last Updated: 09/09/10

COMTEQ COMPUTER AND BUSINESS COLLEGE

Bldg-8722 Tabing Ilog Road, Subcom Area, SBMA, Olongapo City, Zambales 2200
Tel: +63(47) 252-3335
Fax: +63(47) 252-3335
EMail: comteq@subictel.Com
Website: http://www.comteq.edu.ph/

President: Conrado B. Joaquin

Programmes

Business Administration (Business Administration; Human Resources; Information Management); **Computer Science** (Computer Science); **Information Technology**

History: Founded 1997as Comteq Center for Information Technology, and changed to Comteq Computer and Business School 1998. Acquired present status and title 1999.

Degrees and Diplomas: *Certificate/Diploma*; *Associate Degree*; *Bachelor's Degree*
Last Updated: 10/09/10

CONCEPCION HOLY CROSS COLLEGE

San Nicolas, Concepcion, Tarlac 2316
Tel: +63(45) 923-0406

President: Raquel T. Sta Ines

Programmes

Business Administration (Business Administration; Business and Commerce; Management); **Computer Science and Technology** (Computer Engineering; Computer Science); **Education** (English; Foreign Languages Education; Mathematics Education; Primary Education; Secondary Education; Social Sciences)

History: Founded 1996.

Degrees and Diplomas: *Associate Degree*; *Bachelor's Degree*
Last Updated: 10/09/10

CONCORD TECHNICAL INSTITUTE

Cabreros St. Basak, San Nicolas, Cebu City, Cebu 6000
Tel: +63(32) 254-6147
Fax: +63(32) 255-1571

Director: Vicenta B. Ty

Programmes

Marine Studies (Marine Engineering; Marine Transport)

History: Founded 1956.

Degrees and Diplomas: *Bachelor's Degree*
Last Updated: 10/09/10

CONCORDIA COLLEGE

1739, Pedro Gil Street, Paco, Manila, Metro Manila 1007
Tel: +63(2) 564-2001 +63(2) 564-2002
Fax: +63(2) 563-4352
EMail: concordia@dcphilippines.org
Website: http://concordia.dcphilippines.org/

President: Ma. Corazon Manalo, D.C.

Programmes

Business Administration (Accountancy; Business Administration; Business and Commerce; Management); **Education** (Computer Education; Education; English; Foreign Languages Education; Music Education; Primary Education); **Graduate** (Health Administration; Nursing; Psychiatry and Mental Health); **Medical Technology** (Medical Technology); **Music** (Music; Musical Instruments); **Nursing** (Nursing); **Social Work** (Social Work)

History: Founded 1868 as Colegio Dela Immaculada Concepcion Dela Concordia. Acquired present status and title 1993.

Degrees and Diplomas: *Certificate/Diploma*; *Associate Degree*; *Bachelor's Degree*; *Master's Degree*
Last Updated: 10/09/10

CONGRESS COLLEGE

San Nicolas Sur, Agoo, La Union 2504
Tel: +63(72) 710-1373

President: Higinio T. Panay

Programmes

Business Administration (Business and Commerce; Management; Secretarial Studies); **Education** (Art Education; Education; Educational Administration; Music Education; Physical Education; Primary Education; Secondary Education)

History: Founded 1946.

Degrees and Diplomas: *Bachelor's Degree*; *Master's Degree*
Last Updated: 10/09/10

CONSOLATRIX COLLEGE OF TOLEDO CITY

Magsaysay Street, Toledo City, Cebu 6038
Tel: +63(32) 322-5844
EMail: consolatrix_college@yahoo.com

Director: Ma. Editha Lina Escalanina

Programmes

Computer Science (Computer Science); **Education** (English; Foreign Languages Education; Mathematics Education; Primary Education; Science Education; Secondary Education); **Hotel and Restaurant Management** (Hotel and Restaurant; Hotel Management); **Information Technology** (Information Technology)

History: Founded in 1961.

Degrees and Diplomas: *Bachelor's Degree*
Last Updated: 10/09/10

COR JESU COLLEGE

Sacred Heart Avenue, Digos City, Davao del Sur 8002
Tel: +63(82) 553-2433
Fax: +63(82) 553-2333
EMail: cjcregistrar@cjc.edu.ph

President: Rolando A. Fabiana

Divisions

Arts and Sciences (Criminology; Economics; English; History; Information Sciences; Library Science; Psychology; Social Studies); **Business Administration** (Accountancy; Business Administration; Finance; Hotel and Restaurant; Hotel Management; Human Resources; Management); **Computer Studies** (Computer Science; Information Technology); **Education** (Art Education; Education; Educational and Student Counselling; English; Filipino; Foreign Languages Education; Health Education; Library Science; Mathematics Education; Music Education; Native Language Education; Physical Education; Primary Education; Science Education; Secondary Education; Social Studies); **Engineering and Technology** (Automotive Engineering; Civil Engineering; Computer Engineering; Electronic Engineering; Mechanical Engineering; Metal Techniques; Telecommunications Engineering); **Health and Sciences** (Health Sciences; Midwifery; Nursing)

Schools

Graduate Studies (Business Administration; Education; Educational Administration; Educational and Student Counselling; Library Science; Mathematics Education; Public Administration); **Law** (Law)

History: Founded 1959, acquired present status and title 1961.

Degrees and Diplomas: *Bachelor's Degree*; *Master's Degree*
Last Updated: 10/09/10

CORDILLERA A+ COMPUTER TECHNOLOGY COLLEGE

Quezon Street, Dagupan, Tabuk, Kalinga 3800
EMail: angieyumul@yahoo.com

Programmes

Undergraduate and Professional (Business Administration; Business Computing; Computer Science; Criminal Law; Electronic Engineering; Hotel and Restaurant; Hotel Management; Information Technology; Secretarial Studies; Telecommunications Engineering)

History: Founded 1997.

Degrees and Diplomas: *Bachelor's Degree*: 4 yrs; *Bachelor's Degree*: Electronic Engineering; Telecommunications Engineering, 5 yrs
Last Updated: 10/09/10

CORDILLERA CAREER DEVELOPMENT COLLEGE

Buyagan, La Trinidad, Benguet 2601
Tel: +63(74) 432-2737
Fax: +63(74) 422-2221
EMail: ccdc@ccdc.org.ph
Website: http://www.ccdc.edu.ph/

President: James M. Malaya Tel: +63(74) 432-2221

Programmes

Business Administration (Accountancy; Business Administration; Business and Commerce; Public Administration); **Criminology** (Criminology); **Education** (Art Education; Education; English; Foreign Languages Education; History; Mathematics Education; Music Education; Physical Education; Preschool Education; Primary Education; Secondary Education; Social Studies); **Hotel and Restaurant Management** (Hotel and Restaurant; Hotel Management); **Laws** (Law); **Nursing** (Nursing); **Social Work** (Social Work)

History: Founded 1993.

Degrees and Diplomas: *Certificate/Diploma*; *Bachelor's Degree*; *Master's Degree*
Last Updated: 10/09/10

CORJESU COMPUTER COLLEGE

898-A Pili Drive cor. Mangga Road, Butuan City, Agusan del Norte 8600
Tel: +63(85) 815-0439
Fax: +63(85) 225-7162
EMail: corjesu_2006@yahoo.com

President: Mamerto P. Prochina

Programmes

Business Administration (Business Administration); **Elementary Education** (Primary Education)

History: Founded 1994.

Degrees and Diplomas: *Bachelor's Degree*
Last Updated: 10/09/10

COTABATO MEDICAL FOUNDATION COLLEGE

CMFCI Complex, Quezon Avenue, Poblacion 8, Midsayap, North Cotabato 9410
Tel: +63(64) 229-8207
Fax: +63(64) 229-8426

President: Arturo C. Sobong

Programmes

Health Care Services (Health Education); **Nursing and Midwifery** (Midwifery; Nursing)

History: Founded 1993.

Degrees and Diplomas: *Associate Degree*: 2 yrs; *Bachelor's Degree*
Last Updated: 10/09/10

CRIMINAL JUSTICE COLLEGE

81 Jusmin Street, Lodora Village, Muntinlupa City, Fourth District, Metro Manila 1773
Tel: +63(2) 861-8253 +63(2) 862-5392
Fax: +63(2) 861-8253 +63(2) 862-5392

President: Alejandro P. Foronda

Programmes

Criminology (Criminal Law; Criminology)

History: Founded 1998.

Degrees and Diplomas: *Bachelor's Degree*
Last Updated: 10/09/10

CRISTAL E-COLLEGE

50-A Cristal Towers, Ma. Clara Street, Tagbilaran City, Bohol 6300
Tel: +63(38) 411-2509
Fax: +63(38) 235-5980
EMail: cec@mozcom.com

President: Will Tyron Tirol

Programmes

Arts *(Bachelor of Arts programme, Panglao Campus)* (Communication Studies; Mass Communication); **Computer Science** (Computer Science); **Education** *(Panglao Campus)* (Education; English; Foreign Languages Education; Mathematics Education; Primary Education; Secondary Education; Social Studies); **Information Technology** (Information Technology); **Science** *(Bachelor of Science programme, Panglao Campus)* (Business Administration; Civil Engineering; Criminology; Electrical Engineering; Electronic Engineering; Hotel and Restaurant; Hotel Management; Marine Engineering; Marine Transport; Mechanical Engineering; Telecommunications Engineering; Tourism)

History: Founded 2002. Acquired present status and title 2003.

Degrees and Diplomas: *Bachelor's Degree*
Last Updated: 10/09/10

CS COLLEGES OF TABUK

Provincial Road, Tabuk, Kalinga 3800

Programmes

Education and Performing Arts (Education; Performing Arts; Secondary Education)

History: Founded 2001. Formerly known as C.S. School of Music and the Performing Arts.
Degrees and Diplomas: *Bachelor's Degree*
Last Updated: 10/09/10

CVE COLLEGES

T.R. Alvarez Brgy. del Carmen, Pagbilao, Quezon 4302
Tel: +63(42) 731-3180
Fax: +63(42) 731-3181
EMail: cvecolleges@yahoo.com

President: Evelina E. Villena

Programmes

Business Administration (Business Administration; Finance); **Education** (Education; Primary Education; Secondary Education; Technology Education)
History: Founded 2002.
Degrees and Diplomas: *Bachelor's Degree*
Last Updated: 21/09/10

DAGUPAN COLLEGE

Colegio de Dagupan
Arellano Street, Dagupan City, Pangasinan 2400
Tel: +63(75) 522-2405 +63(75) 522•0682
Fax: +63(75) 522-3629
EMail: webmaster@computronix.edu.ph; webmaster@computronix.edu.ph
Website: http://www.colegiodedagupan.net

Managing Director: Voltaire P. Arzadon Tel: +63(75) 522-0632

Colleges

Arts, Sciences and Education (Arts and Humanities; Education; Mass Communication; Natural Sciences; Political Sciences; Primary Education; Psychology; Secondary Education); **Business and Accountancy** (Accountancy; Banking; Business Administration; Business and Commerce; Finance; Hotel and Restaurant; Hotel Management; Management; Marketing; Tourism); **Engineering and Technology** (Civil Engineering; Computer Engineering; Electrical Engineering; Electronic Engineering; Engineering; Technology; Telecommunications Engineering); **Information and Computing Studies** (Computer Engineering; Computer Science; Information Technology); **Nursing** (Health Education; Health Sciences; Nursing)
History: Founded 1984. Formerly known as Computronix College.
Degrees and Diplomas: *Certificate/Diploma*; *Associate Degree*; *Bachelor's Degree*
Last Updated: 08/09/10

DAGUPAN COLLEGES FOUNDATION

Perez Boulevard, Dagupan City, Pangasinan 2400
Tel: +63(75) 515-5792 +63(75) 515-5793
Fax: +63(75) 515-5793 +63(75) 515-5792

President: Nicanor J. Valdez

Programmes

Dental Technology (Dental Technology); **Education** (Computer Science; Education; English; Foreign Languages Education; Mathematics Education; Primary Education; Secondary Education); **Midwifery** (Midwifery); **Radiologic Technology** (Medical Technology; Radiology)
History: Founded 1992 as Dagupan City Colleges of Science and Technology. Acquired present title 1996.
Degrees and Diplomas: *Associate Degree*; *Bachelor's Degree*
Last Updated: 21/09/10

DANIEL B. PEÑA MEMORIAL COLLEGE FOUNDATION

Ziga Avenue, Tabaco City, Albay 4511
Tel: +63(52) 487-5671
Fax: +63(52) 830-3003
EMail: admin@dbpmcf.edu.ph
Website: http://www.dbpmcf.edu.ph

President: Salvador V. Rios, Jr.

Registrar: Miguel Molato

Programmes

Graduate (Business Administration; Education; Management; Public Administration); **Undergraduate and Professional** (Accountancy; Arts and Humanities; Banking; Business and Commerce; Computer Engineering; Computer Science; Criminology; Curriculum; Education; English; Foreign Languages Education; Management; Mathematics Education; Preschool Education; Primary Education; Secondary Education; Secretarial Studies; Social Studies; Software Engineering)
History: Founded 1949, acquired present status and title 1962.
Degrees and Diplomas: *Certificate/Diploma*; *Associate Degree*; *Bachelor's Degree*; *Master's Degree*; *PhD*
Last Updated: 21/09/10

DANSALAN POLYTECHNIC COLLEGE

5th Floor, Al-Shiek Building, Quezon Avenue, Marawi City, Lanao del Sur 9700
Tel: +63(63) 352-0738
Fax: +63(92) 723-0161
EMail: dpc_ched04@yahoo.com

President: Zaanoding D. Esmail

Programmes

Undergraduate and Professional Studies (Accountancy; Computer Engineering; Computer Science; Criminology; Education; Information Technology; Primary Education; Secondary Education)
History: Founded 1999.
Degrees and Diplomas: *Certificate/Diploma*; *Bachelor's Degree*
Last Updated: 21/09/10

DATA CENTER COLLEGE OF THE PHILIPPINES - BAGUIO CITY

A. Bonifacio St., Baguio City, Benguet 2600
Tel: +63(74) 444-3539 +63(74) 442-4160
Fax: +63(74) 444-3539
EMail: DCCP@moscom.com

President: Wilfredo M. Bactad

Programmes

Computer Engineering (Computer Engineering); **Computer Science** (Computer Science); **Information Technology** (Information Technology); **Office Administration** (Business Administration; Secretarial Studies)
History: Founded 1980 as Data Center Philippines, Inc.
Degrees and Diplomas: *Bachelor's Degree*
Last Updated: 21/09/10

DATA CENTER COLLEGE OF THE PHILIPPINES - BANGUED, ABRA

Ubbog, Lipcan, Bangued, Abra 2800
Tel: +63(74) 444-3539 +63(74) 752-8585
Fax: +63(74) 752-5162
EMail: dcpiabra@eudoramail.com

President: Artemio A. Feraren

Programmes

Business Administration (Business Administration); **Computer Science** (Computer Science); **Criminology** (Criminology); **Hotel and Restaurant Management** (Hotel and Restaurant; Hotel Management); **Information Technology** (Information Technology)
History: Founded 1995 as Data Center Philippines of Bangued, Inc. Acquired present title 2001.
Degrees and Diplomas: *Bachelor's Degree*
Last Updated: 21/09/10

DATA CENTER COLLEGE OF THE PHILIPPINES - LAOAG CITY

A.G.Tupaz, Cor Fariñas Street, Brgy. 8, San Vicente, Laoag City, Ilocos Norte 2900
Tel: +63(77) 772-0371 +63(77) 770-3975
Fax: +63(77) 772-3652
EMail: dccplaoag@yahoo.com

President: Joseph D. Sicco

Programmes

Arts and Humanities (Arts and Humanities; English); **Business Administration** (Banking; Business and Commerce; Economics; Finance; Management; Marketing; Secretarial Studies); **Computer Engineering** (Computer Engineering); **Computer Science** (Computer Science); **Criminology** (Criminology); **Education** (Education; Mathematics Education; Primary Education; Secondary Education); **Information Management** (Information Management); **Information Technology** (Information Technology); **Mathematics** (Mathematics)

History: Founded 1985.

Degrees and Diplomas: *Certificate/Diploma*; *Bachelor's Degree*
Last Updated: 21/09/10

DATA CENTER COLLEGE OF THE PHILIPPINES - VIGAN CITY

3rd. Floor, Landmark Building, Jose Singson Street, Vigan City, Ilocos Sur 2700
Tel: +63(77) 722-1953
Fax: +63(77) 444-3539
EMail: dcpi_vg@mozcom.com

President: Wilfredo M. Bactad

Programmes

Computer Science (Computer Science); **Information Management** (Information Management); **Information Technology** (Information Technology)

History: Founded 1998.

Degrees and Diplomas: *Certificate/Diploma*; *Bachelor's Degree*
Last Updated: 21/09/10

DATU IBRAHIM PAGLAS MEMORIAL COLLEGE

Poblacion, Datu Paglas, Maguindanao 9617
EMail: dipmc_paglas@yahoo.com

President: Mohammed Youssef Paglas

Programmes

Agriculture (Agriculture; Agronomy); **Business Administration** (Business Administration; Management); **Computer Science** (Computer Science); **Criminology** (Criminology); **Education** (Education; English; Filipino; Foreign Languages Education; Mathematics Education; Native Language Education; Primary Education; Secondary Education)

History: Founded 2002.

Degrees and Diplomas: *Associate Degree*; *Bachelor's Degree*
Last Updated: 22/09/10

DATU MALA - MUSLIM MINDANAO ISLAMIC COLLEGE

Quezon Avenue, Marawi City, Lanao del Sur 9700

President: Gamal P. Mala

Programmes

Undergraduate and Professional (Business and Commerce; English; Foreign Languages Education; History; Management; Preschool Education; Primary Education; Secondary Education)

History: Founded 1997.

Degrees and Diplomas: *Bachelor's Degree*
Last Updated: 22/09/10

DAV COLLEGE

Magallanes Street, Roxas City, Capiz 5800
EMail: sticc@roxas-online.net.ph

President: Alberto A. Villaruz, Jr.

Programmes

Computer Science (Computer Science)

History: Founded 1996 as STI College - Roxas. Acquired present status and title 1998.

Degrees and Diplomas: *Bachelor's Degree*
Last Updated: 22/09/10

DAVAO CENTRAL COLLEGE

Juan de La Cruz Street, Toril, Davao City, Davao del Sur 8000
Tel: +63(82) 291-1882
Fax: +63(82) 291-2480
EMail: deliaadvincula@hotmail.com

Director: Delia C. Advincula

Programmes

Arts (History; Political Sciences); **Business Administration** (Business Administration; Finance; Management); **Education** (Biological and Life Sciences; Education; English; Foreign Languages Education; Mathematics Education; Primary Education; Secondary Education; Social Studies)

History: Founded in 1948, acquiring its present status in 1993.

Degrees and Diplomas: *Bachelor's Degree*
Last Updated: 22/09/10

DAVAO DEL NORTE AGRICULTURAL COLLEGE FOUNDATION

Poblacion, New Corrella, Davao Del Norte

President-Emiritus: Senforiano I. Alterado, Sr.

Programmes

Agriculture (Agricultural Engineering; Agriculture; Crop Production; Zoology)

History: Founded 2006.

Degrees and Diplomas: *Bachelor's Degree*
Last Updated: 22/09/10

DAVAO DOCTOR'S COLLEGE

General Malvar Street, Davao City, Davao del Sur 8000
Tel: +63(82) 227-5972
Fax: +63(82) 221-1074
EMail: admin@davaodoctors.edu.ph; ddc@davaodoctors.edu.ph
Website: http://www.davaodoctors.edu.ph

President: Rizalina M. Pañgan

Director for Administration and Business Affairs: Lino Fabio Cesar A. Suñer Jr.

Centres

Continuing Education

Colleges

Allied Health Sciences (Health Education; Medical Technology; Occupational Therapy; Optometry; Physical Therapy; Radiology); **Arts, Sciences, Business, and Education** (Biology; Communication Arts; Computer Science; English; Ethics; Filipino; Foreign Languages Education; Hotel and Restaurant; Hotel Management; Mathematics Education; Native Language Education; Primary Education; Psychology; Secondary Education; Tourism); **Nursing** (Nursing)

History: Founded 1974 as Davao Doctors Hospital School of Nursing. Acquired present status and title 1980.

Degrees and Diplomas: *Bachelor's Degree*
Last Updated: 22/09/10

DAVAO MEDICAL SCHOOL FOUNDATION COLLEGE

Circumferential Road, Bajada, Davao City, Davao del Sur 8000
Tel: +63(82) 226-2344
Fax: +63(82) 224-3510
EMail: dmsf@dmsf.edu.ph
Website: http://www.dmsf.edu.ph

President: Jonathan A. Alegre

Registrar: Mila Maruya EMail: registrar@dmsf.edu.ph

Colleges

Dentistry (Anaesthesiology; Anatomy; Botany; Dental Hygiene; Dental Technology; Dentistry; Genetics; Microbiology; Nutrition; Oral Pathology; Organic Chemistry; Orthodontics; Pathology); **Medicine** (Anatomy; Biochemistry; Community Health; Dermatology; Embryology and Reproduction Biology; Epidemiology; Forensic Medicine and Dentistry; Gynaecology and Obstetrics; Histology; Medicine; Microbiology; Neurology; Paediatrics; Parasitology; Pathology; Pharmacology; Physiology; Psychiatry and Mental Health; Surgery); **Nursing** (Nursing)

History: Founded 1976, acquired present status and title 1980.

Degrees and Diplomas: *Bachelor's Degree*; *Master's Degree*

Last Updated: 22/09/10

DAVAO WINCHESTER COLLEGES

Población, Sto. Tomas, Davao del Norte 8112
Tel: +63(84) 374-0718
Fax: +63(84) 829-2344

President: Felizardo E. Gentapanan

Programmes

Computer Science (Computer Science); **Criminology** (Criminology); **Education** (Education; Primary Education; Secondary Education); **Hotel and Restaurant Management** (Cooking and Catering; Food Technology; Hotel and Restaurant; Hotel Management)

Degrees and Diplomas: *Bachelor's Degree*

Last Updated: 22/09/10

DEAF EVANGELISTIC ALLIANCE FOUNDATION

Brgy. Paowin, Cavinti, Laguna 4013
Tel: +63(02) 823-8072 +63(02) 823-8079
EMail: Deafincoryell@yahoo.com

Director: Salvador Q. Cuare

Programmes

Primary Education (Primary Education)

History: Founded 1972.

Degrees and Diplomas: *Bachelor's Degree*

Last Updated: 27/09/10

DEE HWA LIONG COLLEGE FOUNDATION

Sapang Masaic, Brgy. Duquit, Mabalacat, Pampanga 2010
Tel: +63(45) 323-5631 +63(45) 323-5632
Fax: +63(45) 323-5631
EMail: dhlcf@datelnet.net

President: Antonio Dee

Programmes

Business Administration (Business Administration; Finance; Human Resources; Management; Marketing); **Education** (Education; English; Foreign Languages Education; Mathematics Education; Primary Education; Science Education; Secondary Education); **Nursing** (Midwifery; Nursing); **Physical Therapy** (Physical Therapy)

History: Founded 2000.

Degrees and Diplomas: *Bachelor's Degree*: 4 yrs

Last Updated: 27/09/10

DE LA SALLE - ARANETA UNIVERSITY (DLS-AU)

Victoneta Avenue, Malabon, Third District, Metro Manila 1400
Tel: +63(2) 330-9128 +63(2) 361-9053
Fax: +63(2) 361-9054
EMail: webmaster@araneta.dlsu.edu.ph
Website: http://www.araneta.dlsu.edu.ph

President: Ricardo P. Loguda Tel: +63(2) 524-4611

Executive Vice-President: Oscar Bautista Tel: +63(2) 361-9054

Colleges

Arts, Science, Education and Technology (Art Education; Arts and Humanities; Computer Engineering; Computer Science; Education; English; Filipino; Food Technology; Foreign Languages Education; Forestry; Health Education; Home Economics; Home Economics Education; Mathematics Education; Mechanical Engineering; Music Education; Native Language Education; Natural Sciences; Physical Education; Preschool Education; Psychology; Science Education; Secondary Education; Technology; Technology Education); **Business and Accountancy** (Accountancy; Banking; Business Administration; Business and Commerce; Finance; Hotel and Restaurant; Hotel Management; Management); **Veterinary Medicine and Agricultural Sciences** (Agriculture; Agronomy; Animal Husbandry; Crop Production; Forestry; Veterinary Science)

Schools

Graduate (Administration; Agricultural Engineering; Agriculture; Agrobiology; Animal Husbandry; Biology; Business Administration; Crop Production; Education; Educational Administration; Educational and Student Counselling; Educational Psychology; Filipino; Forestry; Management; Mathematics Education; Native Language Education; Physical Education; Public Administration; Zoology)

History: Founded 1946 as Araneta Institute of Agriculture, acquired University status 1958 (Gregorio Araneta University Foundation Manila). Acquired present status and title 2002.

Governing Bodies: Board of Trustees

Academic Year: June to March (June-October; October-March)

Admission Requirements: Graduation from high school or recognized foreign equivalent and entrance examination

Fees: (Pesos): c. 150-500 per unit

Main Language(s) of Instruction: Filipino, English

Accrediting Agencies: Philippine Association of Colleges and Universities - Commission on Accreditation

Degrees and Diplomas: *Associate Degree*; *Bachelor's Degree*; *Master's Degree*; *PhD*

Student Services: Academic counselling, Canteen, Employment services, Foreign Studies Centre, Health services, Nursery care, Social counselling, Sports facilities

Student Residential Facilities: Yes

Libraries: c. 34,000 vols

Publications: Research Journal *(quarterly)*

Last Updated: 23/09/10

DE LA SALLE COLLEGE OF SAINT BENILDE

2544 Taft Avenue, Malate, Manila, First District, Metro Manila 1004
Tel: +63(2) 524-0657
Fax: +63(2) 523-8896
EMail: registrar@dls-csb.edu.ph; evp@dls-csb.edu.ph
Website: http://www.dls-csb.edu.ph

President and Chief Executive Officer: Victor A. Franco

Schools

Deaf Education and Applied Studies (Business Administration; Education of the Handicapped; Multimedia; Special Education); **Design and Arts** (Architecture; Dance; Fashion Design; Industrial Design; Interior Design; Management; Multimedia; Music; Performing Arts; Photography; Theatre); **Hotel, Restaurant and Institution Management** (Cooking and Catering; Hotel and Restaurant; Hotel Management; Tourism); **Management and Information Technology** (Business Administration; Business Computing; Human Resources; Information Technology; Management; Marketing; Systems Analysis); **Multidisciplinary Studies** (International Relations; International Studies)

History: Founded 1988.

Governing Bodies: Board of Trustees, Academic Council, Operations Council

Academic Year: June to April

Admission Requirements: High School diploma

Main Language(s) of Instruction: Filipino, English

International Co-operation: With universities in Japan, USA, New Zealand

Accrediting Agencies: Philippine Accrediting Association of Schools, Colleges and Universities (PAASCU)

Degrees and Diplomas: *Certificate/Diploma*; *Bachelor's Degree*

Student Services: Academic counselling, Canteen, Employment services, Foreign student adviser, Handicapped facilities, Health services, Language programs, Social counselling, Sports facilities

Student Residential Facilities: Yes

Special Facilities: Theatre

Libraries: Yes

Publications: Learning Edge *(annually)*

Press or Publishing House: De La Salle University Press

Last Updated: 22/09/10

DE LA SALLE FOUNDATION COLLEGE OF TACLOBAN

Colegio de la Salle Fondation de Tacloban

Magsaysay Boulevard, Tacloban City, Leyte 6500

Tel: +63(53) 523-0400

Fax: +63(53) 325-5757

EMail: colegiodelasallefdti@yahoo.com

President: Ireen M. Nodado-Reyna

Programmes

Hotel and Restaurant (Cooking and Catering; Hotel and Restaurant; Hotel Management); **Tourism** (Tourism)

History: Founded 2002.

Degrees and Diplomas: *Bachelor's Degree*

Last Updated: 08/09/10

DE LA SALLE HEALTH SCIENCES INSTITUTE

Bagongbayan, Dasmariñas, Cavite 4115

Tel: +63(46) 416-0226

Fax: +63(46) 416-0465

EMail: registrar@hsc.dlsu.edu.ph; vpegg@hsc.dlsu.edu.ph

Website: http://www.hsc.dlsu.edu.ph

President: Augustine L. Boquer (2006-)

Vice-Chancellor for Academics: Ramona Luisa Pablo-Santos

Colleges

Medical Radiation Technology (Medical Technology; Radiology); **Medicine** (Anatomy; Biochemistry; Community Health; Forensic Medicine and Dentistry; Gynaecology and Obstetrics; Health Sciences; Medicine; Microbiology; Ophthalmology; Orthopaedics; Otorhinolaryngology; Paediatrics; Parasitology; Pathology; Pharmacology; Physiology; Psychiatry and Mental Health; Radiology; Surgery); **Nursing and Midwifery** (Midwifery; Nursing); **Physical Therapy** (Health Sciences; Physical Therapy; Rehabilitation and Therapy)

History: Founded 1979, acquired present status 1987.

Governing Bodies: Presidents Council, Executive Council

Academic Year: June to May

Admission Requirements: Graduation from high school and entrance examination

Main Language(s) of Instruction: English

Accrediting Agencies: Philippine Accrediting Association of Schools, Colleges and Universities (PAASCU)

Degrees and Diplomas: *Bachelor's Degree*; *Post Baccalaureate Certificate/Diploma*; *Master's Degree*

Student Services: Academic counselling, Foreign student adviser, Health services, Social counselling

Publications: Medical Journal of De La Salle University *(biennially)*

Last Updated: 22/09/10

DE LA SALLE - LIPA (DLSL)

1962 J.P. Laurel National Highway, Lipa City, Batangas 4217

Tel: +63(43) 756-5555

Fax: +63(43) 756-3117

EMail: webmaster@alvernia.edu.ph

Website: http://www.lasalipa.edu.ph/

President: Manuel Fajarillo (2003-)
Tel: +63(43) 756-3118 EMail: bro.manuel.pajarillo@lasapila.edu.ph

Vice-President: Juan Lozano EMail: juan.lozano@lasalipa.edu.ph

Colleges

Arts and Sciences (Biology; Communication Studies; Mathematics; Primary Education; Psychology; Secondary Education); **Business Administration** (Accountancy; Business Administration; Business and Commerce; Finance; Management; Management Systems; Marketing); **Information Technology and Engineering** (Computer Engineering; Computer Science; Electrical Engineering; Electronic Engineering; Industrial Engineering; Information Technology; Telecommunications Engineering); **International Hospitality and Tourism Management** (Cooking and Catering; Hotel and Restaurant; Hotel Management; Tourism); **Law** (Law); **Nursing** (Nursing)

History: Founded 1962.

Governing Bodies: Board of Trustees

Academic Year: June to March (June-October; November-March); Also Summer session (April-May)

Admission Requirements: Secondary school certificate; Sealed recommendation form filled out and duly signed by any of the following: Principal, Class Adviser or Guidance Counselor

Fees: (US Dollars): foreign students, 200

Main Language(s) of Instruction: English

International Co-operation: With universities in USA

Accrediting Agencies: Philippine Accrediting Association of Schools, Colleges & Universities (PAASCU)

Degrees and Diplomas: *Certificate/Diploma*; *Bachelor's Degree*

Student Services: Academic counselling, Canteen, Employment services, Handicapped facilities, Health services, Nursery care, Social counselling, Sports facilities

Student Residential Facilities: None

Special Facilities: Hotel and Restaurant Laboratory for HRM students

Libraries: Yes

Last Updated: 22/09/10

DE LA SALLE UNIVERSITY (DLSU)

2401 Taft Avenue, Malate, Manila, Metro Manila 1004

Tel: +63(2) 523-4333

Fax: +63(2) 523-4152

EMail: fscbrrd@dlsu.edu.ph

Website: http://www.dlsu.edu.ph

President: Armin Luistro
Tel: +63(2) 526-4281, Fax: +63(2) 526-1403
EMail: luistroa@dlsu.edu.ph

Executive Vice-President: Carmelita Quebengco
Tel: +63(2) 523-4148 EMail: quebengcoc@dlsu.edu.ph

International Relations: Benison Cu Fax: +63(2) 523-3911
EMail: cub@dlsu.edu.ph

Colleges

Business and Economics (Accountancy; Business Administration; Business and Commerce; Commercial Law; Economics; Finance; Management; Marketing); **Computer Studies** (Computer Engineering; Computer Science; Information Technology; Software Engineering); **Education** (Curriculum; Education; Educational Administration; Educational and Student Counselling; Educational Research; English; Foreign Languages Education; Linguistics; Physical Education; Science Education; Sports Management); **Engineering** (Chemical Engineering; Civil Engineering; Electronic

Engineering; Engineering; Industrial Engineering; Management; Mechanical Engineering; Production Engineering; Telecommunications Engineering); **Liberal Arts** (Arts and Humanities; Asian Studies; Behavioural Sciences; Communication Arts; Communication Studies; Development Studies; Economics; English; Filipino; History; International Studies; Literature; Philosophy; Political Sciences; Psychology; Religious Studies; Translation and Interpretation; Writing); **Science** (Biology; Chemistry; Environmental Studies; Mathematics; Natural Sciences; Physics)

History: Founded 1911. Formally granted University status 1975. A private Institution conducted by the Brothers of the Christian Schools. Degrees recognized by the Government.

Governing Bodies: Board of Trustees

Academic Year: June to April (June-August; September-December; January-April)

Admission Requirements: Graduation from high school and entrance examination

Fees: (Pesos): c. 1,560-1,950 per unit

Main Language(s) of Instruction: English

Accrediting Agencies: Philippine Accrediting Association of Schools, Colleges and Universities (PAASCU); Philippine Commission on Higher Education

Degrees and Diplomas: *Bachelor's Degree*; *Master's Degree*; *PhD*

Student Services: Academic counselling, Canteen, Cultural centre, Employment services, Foreign Studies Centre, Handicapped facilities, Health services, Language programs, Social counselling, Sports facilities

Student Residential Facilities: Yes

Special Facilities: European documentation Centre; Art Gallery; Science and Technology Research Centre

Libraries: Central Library, c. 215,000 vols

Publications: Asia-Pacific Social Science Review; Business and Economics Review *(biannually)*; Computer Studies *(quarterly)*; Journal of the College of Engineering *(biannually)*; Malate Literary Journal *(quarterly)*; The Manila Journal of Science *(3 per annum)*

Press or Publishing House: De La Salle University Press, Inc

Last Updated: 23/09/10

DE LA SALLE UNIVERSITY - CANLUBANG

Leandro V. Locsin Campus, Laguna Boulevard LTI Spine Road, Biñan, Laguna 4024
Tel: +63(2) 6700-1111
Fax: +63(2) 6700-1111
EMail: dlsucanlubang@dlsu.edu.ph; inquiries@canlubang.dlsu.edu.ph
Website: http://www.canlubang.dlsu.edu.ph/

President: Joaquin S. Martinez

Director for Academic Services/Registrar: Karen R. Hebron

Schools

Arts and Sciences (Mathematics; Modern Languages; Religious Studies; Social Sciences); **Engineering** (Computer Engineering; Electronic Engineering; Engineering; Industrial Engineering; Telecommunications Engineering); **Information and Communication Studies** (Communication Arts; Communication Studies); **Information Technology and Computing** (Computer Science; Information Technology); **Management and Technopreneurship** (Business Administration; Management)

History: Founded 2003.

Degrees and Diplomas: *Bachelor's Degree*

Last Updated: 23/09/10

DE LA SALLE UNIVERSITY - DASMARIÑAS (DLSU-D)

Bagong Bayan, Dasmariñas, Cavite 4114
Tel: +63(46) 416-4531 +63(46) 416-4533
Fax: +63(46) 416-0338
EMail: postmaster@linux1.dasma.dlsu.edu.ph; webmaster@dasma.dlsu.edu.ph
Website: http://www.dasma.dlsu.edu.ph

President: Augustine Boquer EMail: op@dlsud.edu.ph

Vice-Chancellor for Finance and Administrative Services: Epifania D. Anfone EMail: edanfone@dlsud.edu.ph

Vice-Chancellor for Academics and Research: Olivia M. Legaspi Tel: +63(46) 416-4435 EMail: omlegaspi@dlsud.edu.ph

Colleges

Business Administration (Accountancy; Administration; Advertising and Publicity; Agricultural Business; Business Administration; Economics; Human Resources; Management; Marketing) *Dean*: Willington Okechukwu Onuh; **Criminal Justice Education** (Criminal Law; Criminology; Police Studies) *Head*: Alrien F. Dausan; **Education** (Educational Administration; Educational and Student Counselling; Educational Psychology; English; Ethics; Foreign Languages Education; Primary Education; Religious Education; Secondary Education; Social Sciences) *Dean*: Manuel G. Camarse; **Engineering and Technology** (Civil Engineering; Electrical Engineering; Electronic Engineering; Environmental Engineering; Industrial Engineering; Information Technology; Mechanical Engineering; Safety Engineering; Technology; Telecommunications Engineering) *Head*: Jose Rizaldy A. De Armas; **International Hospitality Management** (Hotel and Restaurant; Hotel Management; Tourism) *Head*: Jefferson S. Buenviaje; **Liberal Arts** (Communication Arts; Communication Studies; Development Studies; Filipino; Journalism; Native Language; Philosophy; Political Sciences; Psychology; Radio and Television Broadcasting) *Dean*: Emmanuel F. Calairo; **Science** (Applied Mathematics; Architecture; Biology; Computer Science; Environmental Engineering; Environmental Studies; Mathematics; Physics) *Dean*: Carmelita C. Cervillon

History: Founded 1977 as Emilio Aguinaldo College. A private Institute under the supervision of the Brothers of the Christian Schools. Acquired present status and title 1987.

Governing Bodies: Board of Trustees

Academic Year: June to May

Admission Requirements: Graduation from High School and entrance examination

Fees: (Pesos): c. 15,000 per semester

Main Language(s) of Instruction: English

International Co-operation: With universities in China, Indonesia, Taiwan

Accrediting Agencies: Philippines Accrediting Association of Schools, Colleges and Universities

Degrees and Diplomas: *Certificate/Diploma*; *Associate Degree*; *Bachelor's Degree*; *Master's Degree*; *PhD*

Student Services: Academic counselling, Canteen, Cultural centre, Employment services, Foreign student adviser, Handicapped facilities, Health services, Language programs, Sports facilities

Student Residential Facilities: Yes

Special Facilities: Museum

Libraries: University Library

Publications: Faculty Publications, Professional journal; Sinag, Kamalayan *(biannually)*

Last Updated: 23/09/10

DE LA VIDA COLLEGE

Notre Dame Avenue, Cotabato City, Cotabato 9600
Tel: +63(64) 421-6973
EMail: delavida@microweb.com.ph

President: Eladio V. Abueva

Programmes

Arts (English; History); **Business Administration** (Business Administration; Finance; Government; Management; Marketing; Public Administration); **Criminology** (Criminal Law; Criminology); **Education** (Education; Educational Administration; English; Filipino; Foreign Languages Education; History; Mathematics; Native Language Education; Primary Education; Secondary Education; Social Studies)

History: Founded 1991. Formerly known as De La Vida Institute (1991-1994).

Degrees and Diplomas: *Bachelor's Degree*; *Master's Degree*

Last Updated: 23/09/10

DE LOS SANTOS COLLEGE - STI COLLEGE

201 E., Rodriguez Sr. Boulevard, Quezon City, Second District, Metro Manila 1101
Tel: +63(2) 413-4968 +63(2) 723-0041
Fax: +63(2) 721-7871
EMail: delocoll@hotmail.com

President: Efren V. De Los Santos

Programmes

Undergraduate and Professional (Health Education; Hotel and Restaurant; Hotel Management; Midwifery; Nursing; Physical Therapy)

History: Founded 1975 as De Los Santos School of Nursing. Formerly known as De Los Santos College; and De Los Santos College - STI College of Health Professions, Inc. (2002-2005).

Degrees and Diplomas: *Associate Degree*; *Bachelor's Degree*
Last Updated: 23/09/10

DE LOS SANTOS COLLEGE - STI COLLEGE OF QUEZON AVENUE

1050 CDC Bldg. Quezon Avenue, Quezon City, Second District, Metro Manila
Tel: +63(2) 373-3360
Fax: +63(2) 373-3350
EMail: jantipuesto21@yahoo.com.ph

Chief Executive Officer: Cheryl Jean M. Perez

Programmes

Business Administration (Business Administration); **Computer and Electronic Technology** (Computer Engineering; Electronic Engineering); **Computer Science** (Computer Science); **Information Technology** (Information Technology); **Nursing** (Nursing)

History: Founded 2000. Formerly known as STI Sta. Mesa.

Degrees and Diplomas: *Bachelor's Degree*
Last Updated: 23/09/10

DEL SUR GOOD SHEPHERD COLLEGE

Wao, Lanao del Sur

President: Cecilia D. Sanes

Programmes

Administration (Business Administration; Business and Commerce; Business Computing; Public Administration; Secretarial Studies); **Arts and Humanities** (Arts and Humanities); **Education** (Educational Administration; Primary Education; Secondary Education; Teacher Training)

Degrees and Diplomas: *Bachelor's Degree*; *Master's Degree*
Last Updated: 27/09/10

DE OCAMPO MEMORIAL COLLEGE

3222 Ramon Magsaysay Boulevard, Santa Mesa, Manila, First District, Metro Manila
Tel: +63(2) 715-1891
Fax: +63(2) 715-0967

President: Vicente Antonio A. de Ocampo

Programmes

Dental Medicine (Dentistry); **Hotel and Restaurant Management** (Hotel and Restaurant; Hotel Management; Tourism); **Liberal Arts** (Economics; English; History); **Medical Technology** (Medical Technology); **Nursing** (Midwifery; Nursing); **Nutrition** (Nutrition); **Office Administration** (Business Administration; Business Computing; Computer Science); **Optometry** (Optometry)

History: Founded 1962.

Degrees and Diplomas: *Certificate/Diploma*; *Associate Degree*; *Bachelor's Degree*
Last Updated: 27/09/10

DE PAUL COLLEGE

E. Lopez Street, Iloilo City, Iloilo 5000
Tel: +63(33) 329-7036 +63(33) 320-4133
Fax: +63(33) 320-7389
EMail: registrar@depulcm.edu.ph

Rector (Acting): Danilo M. Failadona

Programmes

Undergraduate and Professional (Biological and Life Sciences; Business Administration; Computer Education; Computer Science; Data Processing; English; Filipino; Foreign Languages Education; Health Education; Information Management; Information Technology; Management; Marketing; Mathematics; Mathematics Education; Native Language Education; Natural Sciences; Political Sciences; Primary Education; Psychology; Science Education; Secondary Education)

History: Founded 1948.

Degrees and Diplomas: *Associate Degree*; *Bachelor's Degree*
Last Updated: 27/09/10

DEVELOPMENT FOR ADVANCED TECHNOLOGY ACHIEVEMENT (DATA) COLLEGE

Del Pilar, Capitol Boulevard, City of San Fernando, Pampanga 2000
Tel: +63(45) 961-5653
Fax: +63(45) 860-6649
EMail: info@datacollege.edu.ph; data@manila.com.ph

President: Maria Lourdes M. Sulit

Programmes

Business Administration (Accountancy; Business Administration; Data Processing); **Computer Science and Engineering** (Computer Engineering; Computer Science); **Hotel and Restaurant Management** (Hotel and Restaurant; Hotel Management)

History: Founded 1986.

Degrees and Diplomas: *Certificate/Diploma*; *Associate Degree*; *Bachelor's Degree*
Last Updated: 27/09/10

DE VERA INSTITUTE OF TECHNOLOGY

Sagpon, Legazpi City, Albay 4500
Tel: +63(52) 820-1945
Fax: +63(52) 820-1945
EMail: devera_office@yahoo.com

Executive Vice-President: Delfin G. De Vera II

Programmes

Engineering and Technology (Computer Engineering; Electrical Engineering; Electronic Engineering; Industrial Engineering; Technology; Telecommunications Engineering)

History: Founded 1967 as Albay School of Electronics. Acquired present status and title 2001.

Degrees and Diplomas: *Certificate/Diploma*; *Bachelor's Degree*
Last Updated: 27/09/10

DIAZ COLLEGE

Lawton Street, Tanjay, Negros Oriental 6204
Tel: +63(85) 2725 +63(85) 527-0152

President: Roberto A. Diaz

Programmes

Business Administration (Accountancy; Banking; Finance; Management); **Computer Science and Technology** (Computer Engineering; Computer Science); **Education** (Education; Educational Administration; Educational and Student Counselling; English; Filipino; Foreign Languages Education; History; Mathematics Education; Native Language Education; Primary Education; Secondary Education)

History: Founded 1947. Formerly known as East Negros Institute (1947-1998).

Degrees and Diplomas: *Bachelor's Degree*; *Master's Degree*
Last Updated: 27/09/10

DIPOLOG CITY INSTITUTE OF TECHNOLOGY

National Highway, Minaog, Dipolog City, Zamboanga del Norte 7100
Tel: +63(65) 212-2979
Fax: +63(65) 212-2979

President: Florentino Diana

Programmes

Undergraduate and Professional Studies (Computer Science; Hotel and Restaurant; Hotel Management; Marine Engineering; Marine Transport; Midwifery; Primary Education; Taxation)

History: Founded 1987.

Degrees and Diplomas: *Certificate/Diploma*; *Bachelor's Degree*

Last Updated: 27/09/10

DIPOLOG MEDICAL CENTER COLLEGE FOUNDATION

Mibang, Sta. Filomena, Dipolog City, Zamboanga del Norte 7100
Tel: +63(62) 212-3827
EMail: info@dmc.edu.ph

President: Alberto P. Concha

Vice-President for Academic Affairs and Research: Albert T. Concha, Jr.

Programmes

Undergraduate Studies (Accountancy; Computer Science; Criminology; Hotel and Restaurant; Hotel Management; Information Technology; Laboratory Techniques; Management; Marketing; Mass Communication; Medical Technology; Nursing; Physical Therapy; Political Sciences; Radiology)

Schools

Graduate Studies (Educational Administration; Management; Public Administration)

History: Founded 1976. Formerly known as Dipolog Medical Center School of Midwifery/Dipolog Medical Center College of Health Sciences.

Degrees and Diplomas: *Bachelor's Degree*; *Master's Degree*

Last Updated: 27/09/10

DIVINA PASTORA COLLEGE

Malgapo Street, San Vincente, City of Gapan, Nueva Ecija 3105
Tel: +63(44) 486-0569
Fax: +63(44) 486-0569
EMail: Divina.pastora.college@mail.com

President: Maria D. Paule

Programmes

Education (Education; English; Filipino; Foreign Languages Education; Mathematics Education; Native Language Education; Primary Education; Secondary Education; Social Studies); **Liberal Arts** (Economics; English; Mathematics)

History: Founded 1958.

Degrees and Diplomas: *Certificate/Diploma*; *Associate Degree*; *Bachelor's Degree*

Last Updated: 27/09/10

DIVINE MERCY COLLEGE FOUNDATION

129 University Avenue, Caloocan City, Third District, Metro Manila 1400
Tel: +63(2) 361-1922
Fax: +63(2) 361-0762

President: Benedicta B. Martinez

Programmes

Business Administration (Business Administration; Economics; Finance; Management; Marketing); **Computer Science** (Computer Science); **Education** (Education; English; Foreign Languages Education; Mathematics Education; Primary Education; Science Education; Secondary Education); **Hotel and Restaurant Management** (Hotel and Restaurant; Hotel Management); **Information Technology** (Information Technology); **Nursing** (Nursing)

History: Founded 1997.

Degrees and Diplomas: *Associate Degree*; *Bachelor's Degree*

Last Updated: 27/09/10

DIVINE MERCY COMPUTER COLLEGE

Tanchan Building, Colon Street, Cebu City, Cebu 6000
Tel: +63(32) 412-1075
Fax: +63(32) 255-1034
EMail: divina_bono@yahoo.com

President: None E. Bono, Jr.

Programmes

Computer Studies (Computer Engineering; Computer Science; Information Management; Information Technology)

History: Founded 1995.

Degrees and Diplomas: *Bachelor's Degree*

Last Updated: 27/09/10

DIVINE WORD COLLEGE OF BANGUED

Rizal Street Zone 6, Bangued,
Abra 2800
Tel: +63(74) 752-8373
Fax: +63(74) 752-8003
EMail: dwcb@sflu.com

President: Cirilo O. Ortega

Programmes

Graduate Studies (Business Administration; Education; Ethics; Filipino; Management; Mathematics Education; Native Language Education; Public Administration; Religious Education; Science Education); **Undergraduate Studies** (Accountancy; Biology; Business Administration; Communication Studies; Computer Science; Development Studies; Education; English; Filipino; Finance; Foreign Languages Education; History; Industrial Engineering; Information Technology; Management; Mathematics; Mathematics Education; Native Language Education; Natural Sciences; Nursing; Political Sciences; Preschool Education; Primary Education; Science Education; Secondary Education; Social Studies)

History: Founded 1920 as Colegio del Sagrado Corazon. Acquired present status and title 1948.

Degrees and Diplomas: *Certificate/Diploma*; *Associate Degree*; *Bachelor's Degree*; *Master's Degree*

Last Updated: 27/09/10

DIVINE WORD COLLEGE OF CALAPAN

Infantado St., Sta. Marcia Village, Calapan City, Oriental Mindoro 5200
Tel: +63(43) 288-4567 +63(43) 288-4303
Fax: +63(43) 288-5085
EMail: divine@dwcc.edu.ph
Website: http://www.dwcc.edu.ph

President: Anthony Ibarra B. Fabella
EMail: ibarra_svd@yahoo.com

Programmes

Accountancy (Accountancy); **Banking and Finance** (Banking; Finance); **Business Administration** (Business Administration; Management); **Civil Engineering** (Civil Engineering); **Computer Engineering** (Computer Engineering); **Economics** (Economics); **Education** (Art Education; Biological and Life Sciences; Biology; Chemistry; Educational and Student Counselling; English; Ethics; Filipino; Foreign Languages Education; Health Education; Mathematics Education; Music Education; Native Language Education; Physical Education; Physics; Preschool Education; Primary Education; Religious Education; Science Education; Secondary Education; Social Studies; Special Education); **Electronics and Communications Engineering** (Electronic Engineering; Telecommunications Engineering); **English** (English); **History** (History); **Information Technology** (Information Technology); **Journalism** (Journalism); **Management** (Management); **Marketing** (Marketing); **Mass Communication** (Mass Communication); **Political Sciences**; **Psychology and Human Resources** (Human Resources; Psychology); **Public Administration** (Education; Public Administration); **Science** (Computer Science; Mathematics; Natural Sciences); **Social Sciences** (Social Sciences); **Social Studies** (Social Studies); **Tourism, Hotel and Restaurant Management** (Hotel and Restaurant; Hotel Management; Tourism)

History: Founded 1946.

Governing Bodies: SVD Schools Board of Trustees; Commission on Higher Education

Main Language(s) of Instruction: English

Accrediting Agencies: Philippine Accrediting Association of Schools, Colleges and Universities (PAASCU)

Degrees and Diplomas: *Associate Degree*; *Bachelor's Degree*; *Master's Degree*: Business Administration; Public Administration; Education (Mathematics; English; Social Sciences; Filipino; Science); *PhD*: Management

Student Services: Academic counselling, Canteen, Health services, Social counselling, Sports facilities

Student Residential Facilities: Ladies dormitory

Last Updated: 27/09/10

DIVINE WORD COLLEGE OF LAOAG

General Segundo Avenue, Brgy. 12, Laoag City, Ilocos Norte 2900
Tel: +63(77) 772-1228 +63(77) 771-5126
Fax: +63(77) 772-1625 +63(77) 772-0736
EMail: dwcl@dwcl.edu.ph; divine@dwclaoag.com

President: Rodel Arellano, SVD

Programmes

Arts and Science (Architecture; Civil Engineering; Computer Science; English; Information Management; Information Technology; Management; Mass Communication; Nursing; Political Sciences); **Business Administration** (Accountancy; Banking; Business Administration; Finance; Hotel and Restaurant; Hotel Management; Management); **Education** (Education; English; Ethics; Filipino; Foreign Languages Education; Health Education; History; Mathematics Education; Music Education; Native Language Education; Physical Education; Primary Education; Science Education; Secondary Education); **Engineering** (Civil Engineering; Computer Engineering; Electrical Engineering; Electronic Engineering; Engineering; Telecommunications Engineering); **Graduate Studies** (Business Administration; Development Studies; Ethics; Management; Preschool Education; Special Education)

History: Founded 1946. Formerly known as Saint William College (1946-1964).

Degrees and Diplomas: *Certificate/Diploma*; *Associate Degree*; *Bachelor's Degree*; *Master's Degree*; *PhD*

Last Updated: 27/09/10

DIVINE WORD COLLEGE OF LEGAZPI

Rizal Street, Legazpi City, Albay 4500
Tel: +63(52) 480-1239
Fax: +63(52) 480-2148
EMail: dwclinfo@gmail.com
Website: http://www.dwc-legazpi.edu/

President: Crispin A. Cordero, SVD

Vice-President for Administration and Finance: Alejandro F. Gobenciong, SVD

Vice-President for Academic Affairs: Ricardo Francisco C. Miranda, SVD

Colleges

Arts and Sciences (Accountancy; Biology; Computer Science; Economics; English; Finance; Hotel and Restaurant; Hotel Management; Human Resources; Information Technology; Marketing; Mathematics; Political Sciences; Psychology; Social Sciences; Tourism); **Business Education** (Accountancy; Banking; Business Administration; Business and Commerce; Business Education; Environmental Management; Finance; Human Resources; Management; Marketing; Public Administration); **Computer Studies**; **Education** (Art Education; Education; English; Filipino; Foreign Languages Education; Health Education; History; Mathematics Education; Music Education; Native Language Education; Physical Education; Primary Education; Religious Education; Secondary Education; Social Studies; Special Education); **Engineering** (Civil Engineering; Electrical Engineering; Engineering); **Nursing** (Nursing)

History: Founded 1961, acquired present status and title 1965.

Degrees and Diplomas: *Certificate/Diploma*: 2 yrs; *Bachelor's Degree*: 4 yrs; *Bachelor's Degree*: Engineering, 5 yrs; *Master's Degree*: a further 2 yrs

Last Updated: 27/09/10

DIVINE WORD COLLEGE OF SAN JOSE

General Lukban Street, San Jose, Occidental Mindoro 5100
Tel: +63(43) 491-4505 +63(43) 491-4504
Fax: +63(43) 491-1523
EMail: dwcsjpresoffice@yahoo.com

President: Ernesto F. Vitor, SVD
Tel: +63(43) 491-4503, Fax: +63(43) 491-4503

Programmes

Business Administration (Accountancy; Business Administration; Finance; Management); **Computer Science** (Computer Science); **Education** (Education; Educational Administration; English; Filipino; Foreign Languages Education; Mathematics Education; Native Language Education; Primary Education; Science Education; Secondary Education); **Graduate Studies** (Business Administration; Education; Educational Administration; Science Education); **Hotel and Restaurant Management** (Hotel and Restaurant; Hotel Management); **Nursing** (Nursing); **Tourism** (Tourism)

History: Founded 1960.

Degrees and Diplomas: *Certificate/Diploma*; *Associate Degree*; *Bachelor's Degree*; *Master's Degree*

Last Updated: 27/09/10

DIVINE WORD COLLEGE OF URDANETA

J.P. Rosal Street, Bayaoas, Pangasinan 2428
Tel: +63(75) 568-2588 +63(75) 568-2796
Fax: +63(75) 568-2588
EMail: dwcurd@yahoo.com

President: Limneo O. Dangupon, S.V.D.

Programmes

Arts (Economics; English; History; Mathematics; Psychology); **Commerce** (Accountancy; Banking; Business Administration; Business and Commerce; Economics; Finance; Management; Marketing); **Computer Science** (Computer Science); **Education** (Computer Education; Data Processing; Education; English; Filipino; Foreign Languages Education; Home Economics Education; Mathematics Education; Native Language Education; Primary Education; Science Education; Technology Education)

History: Founded 1966.

Degrees and Diplomas: *Bachelor's Degree*

Last Updated: 27/09/10

DIVINE WORD COLLEGE OF VIGAN

Burgos Street, Vigan City, Ilocos Sur 2700
Tel: +63(75) 722-2033 +63(75) 722-1783
Fax: +63(75) 722-1821
EMail: diwocovi@mozcom.com

President: Dominador O. Ramos, SVD
EMail: president_dwcv@yahoo.com

Programmes

Arts (Economics; English; Filipino; History; Library Science; Mathematics; Natural Sciences; Political Sciences; Psychology; Social Sciences); **Business Administration** (Accountancy; Banking; Business Administration; Finance; Human Resources; Management; Marketing); **Computer Science** (Computer Science); **Education** (Educational and Student Counselling; English; Ethics; Filipino; Foreign Languages Education; Health Education; Mathematics Education; Music Education; Native Language Education; Physical Education; Preschool Education; Primary Education; Religious Education; Science Education; Secondary Education; Social Sciences; Special Education); **Hotel and Restaurant Management** (Cooking and Catering; Hotel and Restaurant; Hotel Management); **Information Technology** (Information Technology)

History: Founded 1945. Acquired present status and title 1994.

Degrees and Diplomas: *Bachelor's Degree*: 4 yrs; *Master's Degree*: Business Administration

Last Updated: 28/03/11

DMMA COLLEGE OF SOUTHERN PHILIPPINES

Tigatto Road, Buhangin, Davao City, Davao del Sur 8000
Tel: +63(82) 241-1356
Fax: +63(82) 241-1351
EMail: dmma@dctech.com.ph

President: Lorenzo Edwin F. Eusebio

Programmes
Undergraduate and Professional Studies (Banking; Business and Commerce; Computer Science; English; Filipino; Finance; Foreign Languages Education; Hotel and Restaurant; Hotel Management; Information Technology; Management; Marine Engineering; Marine Transport; Native Language Education; Nursing; Primary Education; Secondary Education; Taxation; Tourism)

History: Founded 1993 as Davao Merchant Marine Academy. Acquired present status and title 2000.

Degrees and Diplomas: *Bachelor's Degree*
Last Updated: 28/09/10

DMMC INSTITUTE OF HEALTH SCIENCES

143 Narra Street, Mt. View Subd., Tanauan City, Batangas 4232
Tel: +63(43) 778-1810 +63(43) 778-6893
Fax: +63(43) 778-4322 +63(43) 778-6352
EMail: dmmc@pacific.net.ph
Website: http://www.dmmcinc.com/dmmcihs.edu.ph.html

President: Edwin M. Mercado

Programmes
Health Sciences (Business Administration; Chemistry; Child Care and Development; Education; English; Foreign Languages Education; Mathematics Education; Medical Technology; Nursing; Occupational Therapy; Physical Therapy; Physics; Preschool Education; Primary Education; Psychology; Radiology; Secondary Education; Special Education)

History: Founded 2002. Acquired present status and title 2003.

Degrees and Diplomas: *Bachelor's Degree*
Last Updated: 28/09/10

DOMINICAN COLLEGE

179 Blumentritt Street, City of San Juan, Second District, Metro Manila 1500
Tel: +63(2) 725-0953 +63(2) 724-5406
Fax: +63(2) 744-7021 +63(2) 724-5406
EMail: dominican@dcan.edu.ph
Website: http://www.dcan.edu.ph

Director: Ma. Rosalinda F. Calong, O.P.

Programmes
Undergraduate and Professional (Business and Commerce; Computer Science; Hotel and Restaurant; Hotel Management; Management; Mass Communication; Nursing; Physical Therapy; Psychology; Tourism)

History: Founded 1924 as Academia de Santa Catalina. Formerly known as Colegio de Jesus-Maria (1947-1965).

Degrees and Diplomas: *Bachelor's Degree*
Last Updated: 28/09/10

DOMINICAN COLLEGE OF ILOILO

Aldeguer Street, Iloilo City, Iloilo 5000
Tel: +63(33) 336-1433
Fax: +63(33) 336-1431
EMail: dcil@mail.com

President: Mary Laurencia S. Camayodo, O.P.

Programmes
Undergraduate and Professional (Business Administration; Computer Science; Education; English; Finance; Management; Primary Education; Religious Education; Secondary Education)

History: Founded 1998.

Degrees and Diplomas: *Certificate/Diploma*; *Bachelor's Degree*
Last Updated: 28/09/10

DOMINICAN COLLEGE OF SANTA ROSA LAGUNA

San Lorenzo South, Balibago, Sta. Rosa City, Laguna 4026
Tel: +63(49) 247-4076
Fax: +63(49) 247-0686
EMail: dcsr@pacific.net.ph

Director: Rosalinda F. Calong, O.P.

Programmes
Undergraduate and Professional (Accountancy; Business and Commerce; Computer Science; English; Foreign Languages Education; Hotel and Restaurant; Hotel Management; Information Management; Information Technology; Management; Marketing; Mathematics Education; Nursing; Secondary Education)

History: Founded 1994.

Degrees and Diplomas: *Bachelor's Degree*
Last Updated: 28/09/10

DOMINICAN COLLEGE OF TARLAC

Tarlac City, Tarlac 2315
Tel: +63(45) 615-0015
Fax: +63(45) 925-0519
EMail: dom.ct@mozcom.com

Director: Caridad S. Bayani OP

Programmes
Arts and Humanities (Arts and Humanities; Literature; Political Sciences); **Elementary Education** (English; Foreign Languages Education; Mathematics Education; Primary Education); **Hotel and Restaurant Management** (Hotel and Restaurant; Hotel Management); **Nursing** (Nursing); **Secondary Education** (English; Foreign Languages Education; Mathematics Education; Secondary Education)

History: Founded as San Nicolas Academy 1947.

Degrees and Diplomas: *Associate Degree*; *Bachelor's Degree*
Last Updated: 28/09/10

DON BOSCO CENTER OF STUDIES

Michael Rua Street, Better Living Subdivision, City of Parañaque, Fourth District, Metro Manila
Tel: +63(2) 823-3290
Fax: +63(2) 822-3613
Website: http://www.dbcs.ph/index.php

President: Vitaliano S. Dimaranan

Programmes
Theology (Religious Studies; Theology)

History: Founded 1984.

Degrees and Diplomas: *Master's Degree*
Last Updated: 28/09/10

DON BOSCO COLLEGE - CANLUBANG

Jose Yulo Sr. Boulevard, Canlubang, Laguna 4028
Tel: +63(49) 549-3404 +63(49) 549-2307
Fax: +63(49) 549-2343
EMail: db_col@laguna.net

Rector: Luisito M. Castaneda, SDB

Programmes
Arts (Arts and Humanities; Philosophy); **Industrial and Technical Education** (Automotive Engineering; Electronic Engineering; Information Technology; Mechanical Engineering); **Secondary Education** (Computer Education; English; Foreign Languages Education; Mathematics Education; Physics; Religious Education; Secondary Education)

History: Founded 1963.

Degrees and Diplomas: *Certificate/Diploma*; *Bachelor's Degree*
Last Updated: 28/09/10

DON BOSCO TECHNICAL COLLEGE

736, General Kalentong Street, City of Mandaluyong, Third District, Metro Manila 1550
Tel: +63(2) 531-8081
Fax: +63(2) 531-6644
EMail: dbtc@donbosco.net
Website: http://www.dbtc.edu.ph

Rector: Martin M. Macasaet, SDB

Programmes

Undergraduate and Professional (Architecture; Computer Engineering; Computer Science; Electrical Engineering; Electronic Engineering; Heating and Refrigeration; Information Technology; Management; Mechanical Engineering; Structural Architecture; Telecommunications Engineering)

History: Founded 1953.

Degrees and Diplomas: *Associate Degree*; *Bachelor's Degree*
Last Updated: 28/09/10

DON BOSCO TECHNOLOGY CENTER

Pleasant Homes Subdivision, Punta Princesa, Cebu City, Cebu 6000
Tel: +63(32) 273-1127
Fax: +63(32) 273-2302
EMail: lansdb@yahoo.com
Website: http://www.dbtc-cebu.edu.ph

Rector: Honesto "Noiret" Geronimo, SDB
EMail: rector@dbtc-cebu.edu.ph

Colleges

Computer Studies (Computer Science; Information Management; Information Technology); **Engineering** (Electronic Engineering; Engineering; Industrial Engineering; Materials Engineering; Mechanical Engineering; Telecommunications Engineering); **Religious Education and Pastoral Communication** (Pastoral Studies; Religious Education); **Technical Education** (Industrial Engineering; Mechanical Engineering)

History: Founded 1954.

Degrees and Diplomas: *Bachelor's Degree*
Last Updated: 28/09/10

DON CARLOS POLYTECHNIC COLLEGE

Purok 2, Norte, Don Carlos, Bukidnon 8712

President: Ma. Victoria O. Pizzaro

Programmes

Community Development (Development Studies; Social and Community Services); **Economics** (Economics); **Engineering** (Automotive Engineering); **Hotel and Restaurant Management** (Hotel and Restaurant; Hotel Management); **Public Administration** (Public Administration)

History: Founded 2006. Formerly known as Bukidnon State College Extension.

Degrees and Diplomas: *Bachelor's Degree*
Last Updated: 28/09/10

DON JOSE ECLEO MEMORIAL FOUNDATION COLLEGE OF SCIENCE AND TECHNOLOGY

Justiniana Edera, San Jose, Dinagat Islands 8427
Tel: +63(86) 826-5320

Director: Violeta B. Omega

Programmes

Arts and Sciences (Arts and Humanities; English; Filipino; Mathematics); **Commerce** (Banking; Business and Commerce; Finance; Management); **Education** (English; Filipino; Foreign Languages Education; Mathematics Education; Native Language Education; Primary Education; Secondary Education); **Electrical and Electronic Engineering** (Electrical and Electronic Engineering); **Information Technology** (Business Computing; Computer Engineering; Information Technology; Software Engineering)

History: Founded 1981.

Degrees and Diplomas: *Bachelor's Degree*
Last Updated: 28/09/10

DOÑA JACINTA L. ESTEVES MEMORIAL COLLEGE

Población, Baganga, Davao Oriental

President: Vicente L. Esteves, Jr.

Programmes

Education (Education; Educational and Student Counselling; Primary Education; Secondary Education)

History: Founded 2004.

Degrees and Diplomas: *Bachelor's Degree*
Last Updated: 28/09/10

DOÑA REMEDOS TRINIDAD MEDICAL FOUNDATION

Calanipawan Road, Sagkahan, Tacloban City, Leyte 6500
Tel: +63(53) 321-2345
Fax: +63(53) 327-5004
EMail: rtr1980@yahoo.com

President: Ferdinand Martin G. Romualdez

Programmes

Health Sciences (Biology; Medical Technology; Medicine; Nursing; Physical Engineering)

History: Founded 1980.

Degrees and Diplomas: *Bachelor's Degree*; *Post Baccalaureate Certificate/Diploma*; *Master's Degree*
Last Updated: 28/09/10

DR. AURELIO MENDOZA MEMORIAL COLLEGE

Dr. Aurelio Mendoza Street, Ipil, Zamboanga Sibugay 7001
Tel: +63(62) 333-5537
Fax: +63(62) 333-5537

President: Bayani P. Mendoza

Programmes

Arts and Science (Computer Engineering; Computer Science; Criminology; English; History); **Commerce** (Accountancy; Business Administration; Computer Science; Management; Secretarial Studies); **Education** (Education; English; Foreign Languages Education; History; Home Economics Education; Primary Education; Secondary Education)

History: Founded 1968.

Degrees and Diplomas: *Certificate/Diploma*; *Bachelor's Degree*
Last Updated: 28/09/10

DR. CARLOS S. LANTING COLLEGE - QUEZON CITY

16, Tandang Sora Avenue, Sangandaan Novaliches, Quezon City, Second District, Metro Manila 1116
Tel: +63(2) 938-7782 +63(2) 938-7789
Fax: +63(2) 939-7229
EMail: dclc_casaul@yahoo.com.ph

President: Ruby L. Casaul

Programmes

Graduate (Education; Educational Administration; Nursing); **Undergraduate and Professional** (Arts and Humanities; Banking; Business Administration; Computer Engineering; Computer Science; Cosmetology; Dentistry; Education; Educational Administration; Electrical Engineering; Electronic Engineering; English; Fashion Design; Filipino; Finance; Food Technology; Health Sciences; Hotel and Restaurant; Hotel Management; Information Technology; Management; Marine Engineering; Marine Transport; Marketing; Medical Technology; Midwifery; Nursing; Physical Therapy; Political Sciences; Psychology; Radiology; Secondary Education; Secretarial Studies; Taxation; Tourism)

Further Information: Also campus in City of Tabaco, Albay

History: Founded 1984.

Degrees and Diplomas: *Associate Degree*; *Bachelor's Degree*; *Master's Degree*
Last Updated: 28/09/10

DR. DOMINGO B. TAMONDONG MEMORIAL SCHOOL

Brgy. Ala, Esperanza, Sultan Kudarat 9806
EMail: ddbtmsi@yahoo.com

President: Elizabeth Bayuga

Programmes

Health Sciences (Medical Technology; Midwifery; Nursing; Radiology)

History: Founded 1989.

Degrees and Diplomas: *Associate Degree*; *Bachelor's Degree*
Last Updated: 28/09/10

DR. FRANCISCO L. CALINGASAN MEMORIAL COLLEGES FOUNDATION

Camp Avejar, Nasugbu, Batangas 4231
Tel: +63(43) 931-1312
Fax: +63(43) 931-1312

President: Maribelle Calingasan

Programmes

Education (Biological and Life Sciences; Communication Arts; Education; English; Filipino; Foreign Languages Education; Health Education; Home Economics Education; Mathematics Education; Native Language Education; Primary Education; Science Education; Secondary Education; Social Studies; Technology Education); **Graduate Studies** (Education; Educational Administration; Mathematics Education; Science Education); **Science** *(Bachelor of Science programme)* (Accountancy; Business and Commerce; Computer Science; Finance; Management; Marketing; Medical Technology; Nursing; Physical Therapy; Radiology)

History: Founded 1976. Formerly known as I.B. Calingasan Memorial Institution.

Degrees and Diplomas: *Certificate/Diploma*; *Associate Degree*; *Bachelor's Degree*; *Master's Degree*
Last Updated: 28/09/10

DR. GLORIA D. LACSON FOUNDATION COLLEGES

National Highway, Castellano, San Leonardo, Nueva Ecija 3102
Tel: +63(44) 486-2919
Fax: +63(44) 486-2432
EMail: dg_lacson_fci@hotmail.com

President: Crescencia V.C. Shamsoddin

Programmes

Business Administration (Accountancy; Business Administration; Economics; Finance; Human Resources; Management; Marketing); **Computer Science** (Computer Science); **Criminology** (Criminology); **Education** (Education; Educational Administration; Educational and Student Counselling; English; Filipino; Foreign Languages Education; Mathematics Education; Native Language Education; Primary Education; Secondary Education); **Nursing** (Community Health; Nursing); **Physical Therapy** (Physical Therapy); **Psychology** (Psychology); **Radiologic Technology** (Medical Technology; Radiology)

Further Information: Also campus in Cabanatuan City (Nueva Ecija)

History: Founded 1993.

Degrees and Diplomas: *Certificate/Diploma*; *Associate Degree*; *Bachelor's Degree*; *Master's Degree*
Last Updated: 29/09/10

DR. PEDRO P. OCAMPO COLLEGES

De Mazenod Avenue Extension, Cotabato City, Cotabato 9600
Tel: +63(64) 421-6548 +63(64) 421-5697
Fax: +63(64) 421-6549
EMail: dprocampocollegesinc@yahoo.com

President: Pedro S. Ocampo, Jr.

Programmes

Criminology (Criminology); **Education** (Education; Health Education; Primary Education; Secondary Education); **Medical Technology** (Medical Technology; Radiology); **Nursing** (Midwifery; Nursing)

History: Founded 1987 as Dr. P. Ocampo Institute of Technology. Acquired present status and title in 1991.

Degrees and Diplomas: *Bachelor's Degree*
Last Updated: 29/09/10

DR. SOLOMON V. MOLINA COLLEGE

Oroquieta City, Misamis Occidental 7207

Director: Solomon U. Molina

Programmes

Business Administration (Business Administration; Human Resources; Management; Marketing; Public Administration); **Education** (Preschool Education; Primary Education)

History: Founded 1992. Formerly known as Solomon Molina School and Development Center.

Degrees and Diplomas: *Bachelor's Degree*
Last Updated: 21/02/11

DR. SUN YAT SEN MEMORIAL SCHOOL AND MARITIME INSTITUTE

C. Gotladera Street, Zone 2, Bulan, Sorsogon 4706
Tel: +63(56) 411-1149 +63(56) 411-1731
Fax: +63(56) 411-1149 +63(56) 411-1731

President: Samuel Z. Lee

Programmes

Business Administration (Business Administration; Finance; Management; Tourism); **Primary Education** (Preschool Education; Primary Education)

History: Founded 1950. Formerly known as Dr. Sun Yat Sen Memorial School.

Degrees and Diplomas: *Certificate/Diploma*; *Bachelor's Degree*
Last Updated: 29/09/10

DR. V. ORESTES ROMUALDEZ EDUCATIONAL FOUNDATION

Real Street, Tacloban City, Leyte 6500
Tel: +63(53) 321-2345 +63(53) 325-7074
Fax: +63(53) 325-8353

President: Ferdinand Martin G. Romualdez

Programmes

Law (Law)

History: Founded 1995. Formerly known as Dr. Vicente Orestes Romualdez Educational Foundation.

Degrees and Diplomas: *Bachelor's Degree*
Last Updated: 29/09/10

DR. YANGA'S FRANCISCO BALAGTAS COLLEGES

McArthur Highway, Wakas, Bocaue, Bulacan 3018
Tel: +63(44) 692-5291
Fax: +63(44) 692-5291
EMail: msyanga@blcn.net.ph; msyanga@blcn.pworld.net.ph

President: Marciano D. Yanga

Programmes

Accountancy (Accountancy); **Agriculture** (Agriculture; Animal Husbandry); **Commerce** (Banking; Business and Commerce; Finance; Management; Marketing); **Computer Science** (Computer Science); **Economics and Political Sciences** (Arts and Humanities; Economics; Political Sciences); **Education** (Biology; English; Filipino; Foreign Languages Education; Mathematics Education; Native Language Education; Primary Education; Secondary Education); **Hotel and Restaurant Management** (Hotel and Restaurant; Hotel Management); **Marine Engineering and Transportation** (Marine Engineering; Marine Transport); **Nursing**

(Nursing); **Tourism** (Tourism); **Veterinary Medicine** (Veterinary Science)

History: Founded 1950. Formerly known as Dr. Yanga's Francisco Balagtas Colleges (1987-2001).

Degrees and Diplomas: *Certificate/Diploma*; *Associate Degree*; *Bachelor's Degree*; *Post Baccalaureate Certificate/Diploma*
Last Updated: 29/09/10

EAST CENTRAL COLLEGES

B. Mendoza Street, City of San Fernando, Pampanga 2000
Tel: +63(45) 963-1536
Fax: +63(45) 961-2175 +63(45) 963-1536
EMail: eccbase@sfp.irnet.ph; eccbase@comclark.com

President: Joseh C. Tolentino

Programmes

Accountancy (Accountancy); **Arts and Humanities** (Arts and Humanities; Economics; English; Psychology); **Business Administration** (Accountancy; Business Administration; Management; Public Administration); **Civil Engineering** (Civil Engineering); **Computer Science** (Computer Science); **Education** (English; Filipino; Foreign Languages Education; History; Library Science; Mathematics Education; Native Language Education; Physical Education; Science Education); **Information Technology** (Information Technology); **Laws** (Law)

History: Founded 1945.

Degrees and Diplomas: *Associate Degree*; *Bachelor's Degree*; *Master's Degree*
Last Updated: 29/09/10

EAST COAST COLLEGE

Población, Cateel, Davao Oriental 8205

President: Lerma M. Valenzuela

Programmes

Education (Education; Educational and Student Counselling; Primary Education)
History: Founded 1999. Acquired present status and title 2004.

Degrees and Diplomas: *Bachelor's Degree*
Last Updated: 29/09/10

EAST PACIFIC COMPUTER COLLEGE

Brgy. Baybay, Catarman, Northern Samar 6400
Tel: +63(55) 251-8336
Fax: +63(55) 251-8333
EMail: epcc@yahoo.com.ph

President: Raul C. Gacusan

Programmes

Computer Studies (Computer Engineering; Computer Science); **Customs Administration** (Taxation); **Information Management and Technology** (Information Management; Information Technology)

History: Founded 1995.

Degrees and Diplomas: *Bachelor's Degree*
Last Updated: 29/09/10

EAST PANGASINAN COLLEGES OF SCIENCE AND TECHNOLGY

3 Bonifacio Street, Tayug, Pangasinan 2445

President: Romeo T. Padilla

Programmes

Business Administration (Accountancy; Business Administration; Management); **Commerce** (Banking; Business and Commerce; Finance); **Computer Science** (Computer Science); **Criminology** (Criminology); **Education** (Education; English; Filipino; Foreign Languages Education; Mathematics Education; Native Language Education; Primary Education; Secondary Education); **Electrical and Electronic Technology** (Electrical and Electronic Engineeering); **Hotel and Restaurant Management** (Hotel and Restaurant; Hotel Management); **Information Technology** (Information Technology)

History: Founded 2004.

Degrees and Diplomas: *Bachelor's Degree*
Last Updated: 29/09/10

EASTER COLLEGE

Easter School Road, Guisad, Baguio City, Benguet 2600
Tel: +63(74) 442-6242 +63(74) 424-6764
Fax: +63(74) 442-3164
EMail: iceman@eastercollege.ph
Website: http://www.eastercollege.ph

President: Brigitt S. Santiago (2010-)

Colleges

Business Administration (Business Administration; Development Studies; Environmental Studies; Management; Marketing); **Education** (Development Studies; Education; English; Foreign Languages Education; Health Education; History; Library Science; Mathematics Education; Music Education; Physical Education; Primary Education; Secondary Education); **Hotel and Restaurant Management** (Cooking and Catering; Hotel and Restaurant; Hotel Management); **Nursing** (Nursing)

History: Founded 1906 as Easter School. Acquired present status and title 1995.

Degrees and Diplomas: *Bachelor's Degree*
Last Updated: 29/09/10

EASTERN KUTAWATO COLLEGE

Poblacion, Buluan, Maguindanao
EMail: nando_501@yahoo.com

President: Hisham S. Nando

Programmes

Undergraduate and Professional (Agriculture; Computer Science; Primary Education)

History: Founded 2003.

Degrees and Diplomas: *Bachelor's Degree*
Last Updated: 29/09/10

EASTERN LAGUNA COLLEGES

J. Rizal Street, Paete, Laguna 4016
Tel: +63(49) 557-0183
Fax: +63(49) 557-0183

President: Marina Dalagan

Programmes

Asian History and Culture (Asian Studies; History); **Commerce** (Business Administration; Business and Commerce; Management); **Education** (Education; English; Foreign Languages Education; Primary Education; Secondary Education; Social Studies); **Hotel and Restaurant Management** (Hotel and Restaurant; Hotel Management)

History: Founded 1947, acquired present status and title 1971.

Degrees and Diplomas: *Certificate/Diploma*; *Associate Degree*; *Bachelor's Degree*; *Master's Degree*
Last Updated: 29/09/10

EASTERN LUZON COLLEGES

Magsaysay Hills, Bambang, Nueva Vizcaya 3702
Tel: +63(78) 803-2185
Fax: +63(78) 803-2185
Website: http://www.elc.edu.ph

President: Carlos M. Alacdis

Campuses

Benguet *(La Trinidad, Benguet)* (Accountancy; Administration; Business and Commerce; Computer Science; Criminology; Education; English; Foreign Languages Education; Mathematics Education; Primary Education; Secondary Education)

Programmes

Accountancy (Accountancy); **Commerce** (Business and Commerce; Finance; Management); **Computer Science** (Computer Science); **Criminology** (Criminology); **Education** (Education;

English; Filipino; Foreign Languages Education; Mathematics Education; Native Language Education; Physics; Primary Education; Secondary Education; Social Sciences); **Hotel and Restaurant Management** (Hotel and Restaurant; Hotel Management); **Information Systems and Technology** (Information Technology); **Office Administration** (Administration; Business Computing; Computer Science; Secretarial Studies); **Public Administration** (Public Administration)

History: Founded 2004.

Degrees and Diplomas: *Certificate/Diploma*; *Bachelor's Degree*
Last Updated: 29/09/10

EASTERN MINDANAO COLLEGE OF TECHNOLOGY (EMCOTECH)

Pagadian City, Zamboanga del Sur 7016
Tel: +63(62)214-4171

President: Avelino J. Lozada

Programmes

Computer Science (Computer Science); **Information Technology** (Information Technology)

History: Founded 2006. Formerly known as Pagadian Technological Center.

Degrees and Diplomas: *Certificate/Diploma*; *Bachelor's Degree*
Last Updated: 29/09/10

EASTERN MINDORO COLLEGE

Bagong Bayan II, Bongabong, Oriental Mindoro 5211
Tel: +63(43) 488-0169
EMail: emc_1945@yahoo.com

President: Honorio F. Pastor

Programmes

Arts and Humanities (History); **Commerce** (Banking; Business and Commerce; Finance; Management); **Education** (Biology; Computer Education; Education; English; Filipino; Foreign Languages Education; History; Mathematics Education; Native Language Education; Physics; Preschool Education; Primary Education; Secondary Education)

History: Founded 1945, acquired present status and title 1967.

Degrees and Diplomas: *Associate Degree*; *Bachelor's Degree*
Last Updated: 29/09/10

EASTERN MINDORO INSTITUTE OF TECHNOLOGY AND SCIENCES (EMITS)

Del Pilar Street, Pinamalayan, Oriental Mindoro 5208
Tel: +63(43) 284-3974
Fax: +63(43) 284-3974
EMail: eqc_gumaca@yahoo.com

President: Sheridan Edmundo Alexander S. Semilla

Programmes

Commerce (Business and Commerce; Management); **Computer Science** (Computer Science); **Economics** (Economics); **Education** (Education; English; Foreign Languages Education; Mathematics Education; Primary Education; Science Education; Secondary Education); **Hotel and Restaurant Management** (Hotel and Restaurant; Hotel Management)

History: Founded 1985.

Degrees and Diplomas: *Certificate/Diploma*; *Associate Degree*; *Bachelor's Degree*
Last Updated: 29/09/10

EASTERN QUEZON COLLEGE

R. Marco Street, Brgy. Peñafrancia, Gumaca, Quezon 4307
Tel: +63(42) 317-5639
EMail: eqc_gumaca@yahoo.com
President: Antonio T. Villar

Programmes

Arts (English; History); **Commerce** (Banking; Business and Commerce; Finance; Management; Marketing); **Education** (Education; English; Foreign Languages Education; Primary Education; Secondary Education; Social Studies)

History: Founded 1947.

Degrees and Diplomas: *Certificate/Diploma*; *Associate Degree*; *Bachelor's Degree*
Last Updated: 29/09/10

EASTERN VISAYAS CENTRAL COLLEGES

Dalakit, Catarman, Northern Samar 6400
EMail: evcc07@yahoo.com.ph

President: Jacob Chino F. Meimban

Programmes

Undergraduate and Professional (Criminology; English; Foreign Languages Education; Information Management; Law; Nursing; Political Sciences; Primary Education)

History: Founded 2000.

Degrees and Diplomas: *Bachelor's Degree*
Last Updated: 29/09/10

EBENEZER INTERNATIONAL COLLEGES

Barangay Biclatan, General Trias, Cavite 4107
Tel: +63(46) 509-0500
Fax: +63(46) 509-0500
EMail: mduranaeic@yahoo.com

President: Hernando R. Gomez

Programmes

Business Administration (Accountancy; Business Administration; Business Computing; Economics; Finance; Human Resources; Management; Marketing)

History: Founded 2004.

Degrees and Diplomas: *Bachelor's Degree*
Last Updated: 29/09/10

ECUMENICAL CHRISTIAN COLLEGE

Zamora Street, City of Tarlac, Tarlac 2300
Fax: +63(45) 982-6125
EMail: ecumcollege@yahoo.com

President: Alfredo M. Conte

Programmes

Education (Biological and Life Sciences; Child Care and Development; Ethics; Physics; Preschool Education; Primary Education; Secondary Education; Special Education); **Nursing** (Nursing)

History: Founded 1963.

Degrees and Diplomas: *Bachelor's Degree*
Last Updated: 29/09/10

EDENTON MISSION COLLEGE

Sison, Maitum, Sarangani 9515

President: Abenir C. Garanzo

Programmes

Undergraduate and Professional (Curriculum; Education; Literature; Primary Education; Secondary Education)

History: Founded 1947.

Degrees and Diplomas: *Bachelor's Degree*
Last Updated: 29/09/10

EDNOR COLLEGES

Romulo Highway, San Vicente, Bamban, Tarlac 2317
Tel: +63(45) 982-3577
Fax: +63(45) 982-3577
EMail: ednor@mozcom.com

President: Eduardo D. Santos

Programmes

Business Administration (Business Administration; Management); **Computer Science** (Computer Science); **Education**

(Education; English; Foreign Languages Education; Primary Education; Secondary Education)

History: Founded 1986 as Ednor Academy.

Degrees and Diplomas: *Certificate/Diploma*; *Associate Degree*; *Bachelor's Degree*

Last Updated: 29/09/10

EDUCATIONAL SYSTEMS TECHNOLOGICAL INSTITUTE

Murallon, Boac, Marinduque 4900
Tel: +63(42) 332-2068
Fax: +63(42) 332-2068
EMail: esti.admin.boac@hotmail.com

President: Cita J. Larga

Programmes

Computer Science (Computer Science); **Criminology** (Criminology); **Education** (Computer Education; Secondary Education); **Information Management** (Information Management); **Marine Transport** (Marine Transport)

History: Founded 1990.

Degrees and Diplomas: *Bachelor's Degree*

Last Updated: 29/09/10

EMILIO AGUINALDO COLLEGE

1113-1117 San Marcelino Street, Paco, Manila, First District, Metro Manila 1000
Tel: +63(2) 521-2710 +63(2) 523-3117
Fax: +63(2) 523-3100
EMail: info@eac.edu.ph
Website: http://www.eac.edu.ph

President: Jose Paulo E. Campos

Head, Finance and Administration: Fernando U. Campaña

International Relations: Cecilia P. Reyes, International Officer

Schools

Business Administration (Accountancy; Business Administration; Finance; Management; Marketing; Taxation); **Criminology** (Criminology); **Dentistry** (Dentistry); **Education** (Education; Educational Technology; Educational Testing and Evaluation; English; Foreign Languages Education; Health Education; Music Education; Physical Education; Primary Education; Secondary Education; Social Studies); **Engineering and Technology** (Computer Engineering; Computer Science; Electrical Engineering; Electronic Engineering; Engineering; Industrial Engineering; Software Engineering; Technology; Telecommunications Engineering); **Hotel and Restaurant Management** (Cooking and Catering; Hotel and Restaurant; Hotel Management; Tourism); **Liberal Arts** (Arts and Humanities; Communication Studies; Mass Communication; Modern Languages; Psychology; Social Sciences); **Medical Technology** (Health Education; Laboratory Techniques; Medical Technology); **Medicine** (Anatomy; Biochemistry; Dentistry; Dietetics; Forensic Medicine and Dentistry; Gynaecology and Obstetrics; Health Sciences; Medical Technology; Medicine; Midwifery; Nursing; Nutrition; Occupational Therapy; Ophthalmology; Otorhinolaryngology; Paediatrics; Parasitology; Pathology; Pharmacology; Pharmacy; Physical Therapy; Physiology; Psychiatry and Mental Health; Radiology; Rehabilitation and Therapy; Respiratory Therapy; Social and Preventive Medicine; Surgery); **Nursing and Midwifery** (Midwifery; Nursing); **Nutrition and Dietetics** (Dietetics; Nutrition); **Pharmacy** (Pharmacy); **Physical, Occupational and Respiratory Therapy** (Occupational Health; Occupational Therapy; Physical Therapy; Respiratory Therapy); **Radiologic Technology** (Laboratory Techniques; Radiology); **Science** (Biology; Biotechnology; Botany; Cell Biology; Chemistry; Mathematics; Molecular Biology; Natural Sciences; Physics; Statistics; Zoology)

History: Founded 1973.

Degrees and Diplomas: *Certificate/Diploma*; *Bachelor's Degree*; *Master's Degree*

Last Updated: 30/09/10

EMMANUEL COLLEGE

Atis Street, General Santos City, South Cotabato 9500
Tel: +63(83) 552-3202
Fax: +63(83) 552-3202
EMail: emco_gsc@yahoo.com

President: Rose Rio Cerezo

Programmes

Arts and Humanities (English; History)

History: Founded 1962.

Degrees and Diplomas: *Bachelor's Degree*

Last Updated: 30/09/10

ENDERUN COLLEGE

2/F Wynsum Corporate Plaza, 22 F. Ortigas Jr. Road, City of Pasig, Second District, Metro Manila
Tel: +63(2) 638-5555
Fax: +63(2) 636-1614
EMail: admissions@enderun.com.ph

President: Javier B. Infante

Programmes

International Hospitality Management (Cooking and Catering; Hotel and Restaurant; Hotel Management; Tourism)

History: Founded 2005.

Degrees and Diplomas: *Bachelor's Degree*

Last Updated: 30/09/10

ENTREPRENEURS SCHOOL OF ASIA

27 Calle Industria Bagumbayan, Libis, Quezon City, Second District, Metro Manila
Tel: +63(2) 638-1188
Fax: +63(2) 638-2680

Chairman, Board of Trustees: Vivienne K. Tan

Programmes

Entrepreneurship (Business Administration; Management)

History: Founded 2000 as Thames International School-Greenhills Inc. Acquired present title 2007.

Degrees and Diplomas: *Bachelor's Degree*

Last Updated: 30/09/10

ERHARD SYSTEMS TECHNOLOGICAL INSTITUTE

M.L. Quezon Street, Odiongan, Romblon 4900
Tel: +63(42) 567-5561
Fax: +63(42) 567-5561
EMail: erhard_sti@yahoo.com

President: Idella G. Formilleza

Programmes

Computer Science (Computer Science); **Criminology** (Criminology)

History: Founded 1990.

Degrees and Diplomas: *Bachelor's Degree*

Last Updated: 30/09/10

ESTELA COLLEGE

No. 2, Fdr Road, Sto. Tomas, Davao del Norte 8112
Tel: +63(84) 829-2389
Fax: +63(84) 374-0201

President: Socorro L. Estela

Programmes

Business Administration (Business Administration); **Computer Science** (Computer Science); **Information Technology** (Information Technology)

History: Founded 2001.

Degrees and Diplomas: *Bachelor's Degree*

Last Updated: 30/09/10

EULOGIO R. DIZON COLLEGE OF NUEVA ECIJA

Saranay District, Guimba, Nueva Ecija 3115
Tel: +63(44) 611-0413
Fax: +63(44) 611-3207
EMail: erd_college@yahoo.com

President: Jose R. Dizon

Programmes

Arts and Science (Arts and Humanities; English; Mathematics; Political Sciences); **Commerce** (Business and Commerce; Business Computing; Computer Science; Management; Public Administration); **Computer Science** (Computer Science); **Criminology** (Criminology); **Education** (Education; Educational Administration; English; Filipino; Foreign Languages Education; Mathematics Education; Native Language Education; Primary Education; Secondary Education)

History: Founded 1927 as Corregidor College. Acquired present status and title 1996.

Degrees and Diplomas: *Bachelor's Degree*; *Master's Degree*
Last Updated: 30/09/10

EVANGELICAL THEOLOGICAL COLLEGE OF THE PHILIPPINES

R. Duterte Street, Banawa, Cebu City, Cebu 6000
Tel: +63(32) 254-0070
Fax: +63(32) 254-0070
EMail: admin@etcp.net

President: Reuben V. Quijano

Programmes

Theology (Christian Religious Studies; Religious Education; Theology)

History: Founded 1986 as Evangelical Theological School.

Degrees and Diplomas: *Bachelor's Degree*
Last Updated: 30/09/10

EVELAND CHRISTIAN COLLEGE

Bonifacio Street, San Mateo, Isabela 3318
Tel: +63(78) 664-2434

President: Melanio A. Castillo EMail: melaniocastillo@yahoo.com

Programmes

Computer Secretarial (Business Computing; Secretarial Studies); **Theology** (Theology)

History: Founded 1947.

Degrees and Diplomas: *Bachelor's Degree*
Last Updated: 30/09/10

FAR EASTERN POLYTECHNIC COLLEGE

Sta Lucia, DBB1, Dasmariñas, Cavite 4114
Tel: +63(46) 506-0297
Fax: +63(46) 506-0297
EMail: fepc_educ@yahoo.com

President: Ben I. Gomez

Programmes

Business Administration (Business Administration; Management; Marketing); **Computer Science** (Computer Science); **Hotel and Restaurant Management** (Hotel and Restaurant; Hotel Management); **Technical Teacher Education** (Technology Education)

History: Founded 2005.

Degrees and Diplomas: *Bachelor's Degree*
Last Updated: 30/09/10

FAR EASTERN UNIVERSITY (FEU)

Nicanor Reyes Street, Sampaloc, Manila, Metro Manila 1015
Tel: +63(2) 735-5621
Fax: +63(2) 735-0232
EMail: admissions@feu.edu.ph
Website: http://www.feu.edu.ph

President: Lydia Balatbat-Echauz
Tel: +63(2) 735-5621, Fax: +63(2) 735-0232

Colleges

Engineering and Computer Studies *(FEU-East Asia College)* (Civil Engineering; Computer Engineering; Computer Networks; Computer Science; Electrical Engineering; Electronic Engineering; Engineering; Industrial Engineering; Information Technology)

Institutes

Accountancy, Business and Finance (Accountancy; Business Administration; Economics; Finance; Hotel and Restaurant; Hotel Management; Human Resources; Law; Management; Marketing; Secretarial Studies; Tourism); **Architecture and Fine Arts** (Advertising and Publicity; Architecture; Fine Arts; Painting and Drawing); **Arts and Science** (Applied Mathematics; Arts and Humanities; Biology; English; Filipino; Information Technology; International Studies; Literature; Mass Communication; Medical Technology; Natural Sciences; Political Sciences; Psychology); **Education** (Art Education; Curriculum; Education; Educational Administration; Foreign Languages Education; Mathematics Education; Native Language Education; Physical Education; Primary Education; Science Education; Secondary Education; Special Education; Sports); **Graduate Studies** (Arts and Humanities; Business Administration; Curriculum; Education; Educational Administration; English; Mass Communication; Nursing; Physical Education; Psychology; Special Education; Teacher Training); **Law** (Commercial Law; Law); **Nursing** (Health Sciences; Nursing)

Further Information: Campuses: Diliman, Makati and Silang

History: Founded 1928 as Institute of Accountancy and Business Administration, consolidated with Far Eastern College and incorporated under present title 1933. East Asia College of Information Technology (EACIT). FEU took over East Asia College of Information Technology (EACIT) and merged it with its own College of Engineering to form FEU - East Asia College (FEU - EAC) 2002.

Governing Bodies: Board of Trustees

Academic Year: June to March (June-October; November-March)

Admission Requirements: Graduation from high school and entrance examination

Fees: (Pesos): Registration and tuition, 18,870 per semester

Main Language(s) of Instruction: English

Accrediting Agencies: Philippine Association of Colleges and Universities Commission on Accreditation (PACUCUOA); Philippine Accrediting Association of Schools, Colleges and Universities (PAASCU)

Degrees and Diplomas: *Associate Degree*; *Bachelor's Degree*; *Master's Degree*: Business Administration; Mass communication; Political Science; History; Library Science; Letters; Mathematics; Physical Education; Filipino; Educational Administration; Nursing; Psychology; Government Administration; Library Science; *PhD*: Education; Educational Administration

Student Services: Academic counselling, Canteen, Cultural centre, Employment services, Foreign student adviser, Handicapped facilities, Health services, Language programs, Social counselling, Sports facilities

Special Facilities: Auditorium; University Conference Centre

Libraries: Audi-visual Centre, E-Library

Publications: Ambon, Literary publication featuring the winning entries of the yearly literary contest in Filipino for undergraduates, together with literary works of invited guest writers *(annually)*; Arts and Sciences Review, Interdisciplinary journal in English and Filipino published by the Institute of Arts and Sciences *(biannually)*; Far Eastern University Journal, Publication featuring scholarly works on education and related topics *(biannually)*; Global Insights, Journal published by the Institute of Accountancy, Business and Finance *(quarterly)*; Research Digest, Publication of the Institute of Graduate Studies featuring scholarly works of the Institute's faculty and students and guest researchers *(annually)*; Transition, Literary publication featuring the winning entries of the yearly literary contest in English for undergraduates, together with literary works of invited guest writers *(annually)*

Last Updated: 30/09/10

FATHER SATURNINO URIOS UNIVERSITY (FSUU)

San Francisco Street cor. J.C. Aquino Avenue, Butuan City, Agusan del Norte 8600
Tel: +63(85) 342-1830
Fax: +63(85) 815-3418
EMail: info@urios.edu.ph; registrar@urios.edu.ph
Website: http://www.urios.edu.ph

President: John Christian U. Young

Vice-President for Academic Affairs: Randy Jasper C. Odchigue

Academies
Law Enforcement (Criminal Law; Criminology)

Programmes
Accountancy (Accountancy); **Arts and Science** (Applied Mathematics; Biology; Economics; Educational and Student Counselling; Political Sciences); **Business Administration** (Accountancy; Business Administration; Business and Commerce; Computer Science; Finance; Hotel and Restaurant; Hotel Management; Human Resources; Management; Management Systems; Marketing); **Computer Studies** (Computer Science; Information Technology); **Engineering** (Civil Engineering; Industrial Engineering); **Law** (Law); **Nursing** (Nursing); **Teacher Education** (Computer Education; English; Filipino; Foreign Languages Education; Health Education; History; Mathematics Education; Music Education; Native Language Education; Physical Education; Primary Education; Science Education; Secondary Education; Social Studies; Special Education)

History: Founded 1900. Acquired present status 1949.

Degrees and Diplomas: *Associate Degree*; *Bachelor's Degree*; *Master's Degree*; *PhD*
Last Updated: 01/10/10

FATIMA COLLEGE OF CAMIGUIN

Lumad, Mambajao, Camiguin 9100
Tel: +63(88) 387-0953
Fax: +63(88) 387-1038

Director: Raphael B. Amante

Programmes
Undergraduate and Professional Studies (Accountancy; Banking; Business Administration; Business and Commerce; Educational and Student Counselling; English; Filipino; Finance; Foreign Languages Education; Mathematics; Mathematics Education; Native Language Education; Primary Education; Secondary Education)

History: Founded 1922. Formerly known as Camiguin Institute and Fatima Junior College of Camiguin.

Degrees and Diplomas: *Bachelor's Degree*
Last Updated: 01/10/10

FEATI UNIVERSITY

Helios Street, Santa Cruz, Manila, First District, Metro Manila 1003
Tel: +63(2) 733-8321 +63(2) 733-8322
Fax: +63(2) 733-7043
EMail: info@featiu.edu.ph
Website: http://www.featiu.edu.ph

President: Adolfo Jesus R. Gopez EMail: president@featiu.edu.ph

Executive Vice-President: Gabriel P. Intengan

International Relations: Leopoldo V. Abis, Vice-President for Academic Affairs

Colleges
Architecture (Architecture); **Arts, Sciences and Education** (Applied Mathematics; Arts and Humanities; Computer Engineering; Electronic Engineering; English; Filipino; Foreign Languages Education; Mass Communication; Native Language Education; Secondary Education; Vocational Education); **Business** (Banking; Business Administration; Finance; Management; Marketing; Tourism); **Engineering** (Aeronautical and Aerospace Engineering; Chemical Engineering; Civil Engineering; Computer Engineering; Computer Science; Electrical Engineering; Electronic Engineering; Engineering; Geological Engineering; Industrial Engineering; Information Technology; Maintenance Technology; Mechanical Engineering; Telecommunications Engineering); **Maritime Education** (Marine Engineering; Marine Transport; Taxation)

Schools
Fine Arts (Design; Fine Arts); **Graduate** (Management)

History: Founded 1946 as the Far Eastern School of Aeronautics, became Feati Institute of Technology 1947, acquired University status 1959.

Governing Bodies: Board of Trustees

Academic Year: June to March (June-October; October-March)

Admission Requirements: Graduation from high school and entrance examination

Fees: (Pesos): c. 15,700 per semester

Main Language(s) of Instruction: English

Degrees and Diplomas: *Certificate/Diploma*; *Associate Degree*; *Bachelor's Degree*; *Master's Degree*

Libraries: c. 25,000 vols
Last Updated: 01/10/10

FELIPE R. VERALLO MEMORIAL FOUNDATION- BOGO

Clotilde Hills, Dakit, Bogo, Cebu 6010
Tel: +63(32) 351-4216
EMail: frvmfi@hotmail.com
Website: http://www.frvmfi.4t.com

President: Clomen M.V. Jamoral

Senior Vice-President: Ma. Corazon Jamoral-Maglasang

Colleges
Commerce and Computer Science (Accountancy; Business and Commerce; Computer Science); **Education** (Education; Home Economics Education; Primary Education; Secondary Education; Technology Education)

Courses
Para-Medical Studies (Midwifery; Nursing; Physical Therapy)

History: Founded 1989.

Degrees and Diplomas: *Bachelor's Degree*; *Master's Degree*: Educational Administration and Supervision
Last Updated: 01/10/10

FELIX O. ALFELOR SR. FOUNDATION COLLEGE

San Juan Avenue, Sipocot, Carmarines Sur 4408
Tel: +63(54) 450-7102

President: Emmanuel R. Alfelor

Programmes
Undergraduate and Professional (Business Administration; Business and Commerce; English; Filipino; Foreign Languages Education; Mathematics Education; Native Language Education; Political Sciences; Primary Education; Secondary Education)

History: Founded 1986.

Degrees and Diplomas: *Certificate/Diploma*; *Bachelor's Degree*
Last Updated: 01/10/10

FELLOWSHIP BAPTIST COLLEGE

Rizal Street, Barangay 9, City of Kabankalan, Negros Occidental 6111
Tel: +63(34) 471-2167 +63(34) 471-2156
Fax: +63(34) 471-2167

President: Anecito D. Villaluz, Jr.

Programmes
Undergraduate and Professional (Accountancy; Biological and Life Sciences; Business Administration; Civil Engineering; Computer Engineering; Computer Science; Cooking and Catering; Education; Electronic Engineering; English; Finance; Foreign Languages Education; History; Management; Medical Technology; Nursing; Primary Education; Psychology; Science Education; Secondary Education; Telecommunications Engineering; Theology; Tourism)

History: Founded 1954.

Degrees and Diplomas: *Certificate/Diploma*; *Associate Degree*; *Bachelor's Degree*: 4 yrs

Last Updated: 01/10/10

FERNANDEZ COLLEGE OF ARTS AND TECHNOLOGY

Gil Carlos Street, Baliuag, Bulacan 3006
Tel: +63(44) 673-1876 +63(44) 766-1194
Fax: +63(44) 673-1712
EMail: fcatmain@yahoo.com

President: Marcelo V. Fernandez

Programmes

Arts and Science *(BA & BSc programmes)* (Accountancy; Business Administration; Communication Studies; Computer Engineering; Computer Science; Criminology; Finance; Hotel and Restaurant; Hotel Management; Marine Transport; Midwifery; Nursing; Physical Education; Political Sciences); **Education** (Biological and Life Sciences; Education; Primary Education; Secondary Education)

History: Founded 1997.

Degrees and Diplomas: *Certificate/Diploma*; *Bachelor's Degree*

Last Updated: 01/10/10

FEU-DR. NICANOR REYES MEDICAL FOUNDATION

Regalado Avenue cor. Dahlia Street, West Fairview, Quezon City, Second District, Metro Manila 1122
Tel: +63(2) 427-0213 +63(2) 938-4884
Fax: +63(2) 427-5624
EMail: info@feu-nrmf.ph
Website: http://www.feu-nrmf.ph

Chairman: Josephine C. Reyes

Programmes

Medical Technology (Medical Technology); **Medicine** (Biochemistry; Child Care and Development; Community Health; Dermatology; Gynaecology and Obstetrics; Laboratory Techniques; Medicine; Microbiology; Neurology; Nutrition; Ophthalmology; Otorhinolaryngology; Paediatrics; Parasitology; Pathology; Pharmacology; Physiology; Rehabilitation and Therapy; Surgery); **Nursing** (Nursing); **Physical Therapy** (Physical Therapy)

History: Founded 1971. Formerly known as Far Eastern University - Institute of Medicine (1952-1971).

Degrees and Diplomas: *Bachelor's Degree*; *Post Baccalaureate Certificate/Diploma*: Medicine

Last Updated: 01/10/10

FEU-EAST ASIA COLLEGE

Nicanor Reyes Sr. Street, Sampaloc, City of Manila, First District, Metro Manila 1008
Tel: +63(2) 736-0015 +63(2) 736-0017
Fax: +63(2) 736-0025
EMail: info@feu-eastasia.edu.ph
Website: http://www.feu-eastasia.edu.ph/

President: Lydia B. Echauz

Senior Director for Academic Affairs: May Rose C. Imperial

Executive Director: Benson T. Tan

Departments

Civil Engineering (Civil Engineering); **Computer Engineering** (Computer Engineering; Computer Networks; Software Engineering); **Computer Science** (Computer Science; Software Engineering); **Computer Technology** (Computer Engineering; Information Technology); **Electrical Engineering** (Electrical Engineering); **Electronic Engineering** (Electronic Engineering); **Industrial Engineering** (Industrial Engineering); **Information Technology** (Computer Graphics; Computer Networks; Information Technology)

History: Founded 1992. Formerly known as FEU-East Asia College of Information Technology (1998-2003).

Degrees and Diplomas: *Associate Degree*; *Bachelor's Degree*

Last Updated: 01/10/10

FEU-FERN COLLEGE

Sampaguita Avenue, Mapayapa Village, Quezon City, Second District, Metro Manila 1101
Tel: +63(2) 931-6064
Fax: +63(2) 931-1453
EMail: info@feufern.edu.ph
Website: http://www.feufern.edu.ph

President: Lydia B. Echauz

Vice-President: Paulino Y. Tan

Programmes

Undergraduate and Professional (Accountancy; Business Administration; Computer Science; Finance; Information Management; Information Sciences; Information Technology; Law; Management; Marketing)

History: Founded 1994.

Degrees and Diplomas: *Bachelor's Degree*

Last Updated: 01/10/10

FILAMER CHRISTIAN COLLEGE

Roxas Avenue, Roxas City, Capiz 5800
Tel: +63(36) 621-0807
Fax: +63(36) 621-3075
EMail: filamer_christian@yahoo.com.ph
Website: http://www.filamer.edu.ph

President: Expedito A. Señeres Tel: +63(36) 212-317

Vice-President for Academic Affairs: George O. Cortel

Programmes

Arts and Science (Accountancy; Biology; Business Administration; Business and Commerce; Communication Studies; Computer Science; Criminology; Development Studies; Economics; Electronic Engineering; English; Hotel and Restaurant; Hotel Management; Information Technology; Management; Mathematics; Nursing; Political Sciences; Theology); **Education** (Education; English; Ethics; Filipino; Foreign Languages Education; Literacy Education; Mathematics Education; Native Language Education; Preschool Education; Primary Education; Science Education; Secondary Education); **Graduate Studies** (Education; English; Foreign Languages Education; Mathematics Education; Science Education; Social Sciences)

History: Founded 1904.

Degrees and Diplomas: *Certificate/Diploma*; *Associate Degree*; *Bachelor's Degree*; *Master's Degree*: Education (General Science; Mathematics; Physical Education; Social Sciences; English)

Last Updated: 01/10/10

FIRST ASIA INSTITUTE OF TECHNOLOGY AND HUMANITIES

2 Pres. Laurel Highway, Tanauan City, Batangas 4232
Tel: +63(43) 778-0656
Fax: +63(43) 405-2326
EMail: inquries@firstasia.edu.ph
Website: http://www.firstasia.edu.ph

President: Saturnino G. Belen, Jr.

Schools

Humanities (Arts and Humanities; Communication Studies; Education; Fine Arts; Mathematics; Natural Sciences; Nursing; Primary Education; Psychology; Secondary Education); **Management** (Accountancy; Business Administration; Hotel and Restaurant; Hotel Management; Management; Tourism); **Technology** (Civil Security; Computer Engineering; Computer Science; Criminology; Electronic Engineering; Engineering; Industrial Engineering; Information Technology)

History: Founded 2001.

Degrees and Diplomas: *Bachelor's Degree*

Last Updated: 01/10/10

FL VARGAS COLLEGE - ABULUG

Calog Sur, Abulug, Cagayan 3517

Dean: Mildred T. Daranay

Programmes

Business Administration (Accountancy; Banking; Business Administration; Business and Commerce; Finance); **Criminology** (Criminology); **Education** (Education; English; Foreign Languages Education; Health Education; Mathematics Education; Primary Education; Science Education); **Engineering** (Electrical Engineering; Electronic Engineering; Engineering; Telecommunications Engineering); **Hotel and Restaurant Management** (Hotel and Restaurant; Hotel Management); **Information Technology** (Information Technology); **Nursing** (Nursing)

History: Founded 2001.

Degrees and Diplomas: *Bachelor's Degree*
Last Updated: 01/10/10

FL VARGAS COLLEGE - TUGUEGARO

Corner Blumentritt and Gonzaga Streets, Abulug, Cagayan 3500
Tel: +63(78) 846-3947
Fax: +63(78) 846-3947
EMail: FLV_MainCampus@Eudoramil.com

Executive Vice-President: Dante B. Pasicolon

Programmes

Business Administration (Accountancy; Banking; Business Administration; Business and Commerce; Finance; Management; Taxation); **Computer Science** (Computer Science); **Criminology** (Criminology); **Education** (Chemistry; Education; English; Foreign Languages Education; Mathematics Education; Primary Education; Secondary Education); **Engineering** (Civil Engineering; Computer Engineering; Electrical Engineering; Engineering; Mechanical Engineering); **Hotel and Restaurant Management** (Hotel and Restaurant; Hotel Management)

History: Founded 1995.

Degrees and Diplomas: *Certificate/Diploma*; *Bachelor's Degree*
Last Updated: 01/10/10

FLIGHT DYNAMIC SCHOOL OF AERONAUTICS

Gen. Aviation Road Corner Basak-Iba, Lapu-Lapu City, Cebu 6015
Tel: +63(32) 340-0325
Fax: +63(32) 340-0325
EMail: flightdynamics_jdc@yahoo.com

President: Juanito de la Cruz

Programmes

Aeronautic and Airline Studies (Aeronautical and Aerospace Engineering; Air Transport; Maintenance Technology)

History: Founded 1995.

Degrees and Diplomas: *Bachelor's Degree*
Last Updated: 01/10/10

FLIGHT SCHOOL INTERNATIONAL

124 Domestic Road, Pasay City, Fourth District, Metro Manila 1300
Tel: +63(2) 851-7161
Fax: +63(2) 851-0012

President: Crisolita S. Rebusi Navarro

Programmes

Aircraft Maintenance Engineering and Technology (Aeronautical and Aerospace Engineering; Maintenance Technology)

History: Founded 2004.

Degrees and Diplomas: *Associate Degree*; *Bachelor's Degree*
Last Updated: 01/10/10

FORD ACADEMY OF THE ARTS

Ladislawa Village, Buhangin, Davao City, Davao del Sur 8000
Tel: +63(82) 227-1096
Fax: +63(82) 224-1835

President: Aida R. Ford

Programmes

Fine Arts (Fine Arts; Painting and Drawing)

History: Founded 1980 as Learning Center of the Arts. Acquired present title 1992.

Degrees and Diplomas: *Bachelor's Degree*
Last Updated: 01/10/10

FOUNDATION UNIVERSITY (FU)

Dr. Miciano Road, Dumaguete City, Negros Oriental 6200
Tel: +63(35) 422-9167
Fax: +63(35) 225-0617
EMail: op@foundationu.com
Website: http://www.foundationu.com

President: Mira D. Sinco
Tel: +63(35) 422-9167, Fax: +63(35) 225-0617
EMail: mdsinco@yahoo.com

Vice-President for Academic Affairs (Acting): Eva C. Melon
EMail: eva.melon@foundationu.com

Colleges

Agriculture (Agricultural Business; Agriculture; Agronomy; Animal Husbandry; Harvest Technology); **Arts and Science** (Arts and Humanities; Biology; Economics; English; Mathematics; Natural Sciences; Physics; Political Sciences); **Business and Administration** (Accountancy; Business and Commerce; Computer Science; Economics; Finance; Information Management; Information Technology; Management; Marketing; Public Administration); **Education** *(Elementary and Secondary Levels)* (Education; Primary Education; Secondary Education); **Law** (Law)

Schools

Computer Studies (Computer Science; Information Technology); **Graduate** (Business Administration; Education; Public Administration); **Hospitality Management** (Hotel and Restaurant; Hotel Management; Tourism); **Industrial Engineering** (Industrial Engineering)

Units

Extension Services *(Bacong; Valencia)*; **Research**

History: Founded 1949 as College, a private and independent institution. Acquired present status 1969.

Governing Bodies: Board of Trustees

Academic Year: June to March (June-October; November-March)

Admission Requirements: Graduation from high school and entrance examination

Main Language(s) of Instruction: Filipino, English

Accrediting Agencies: Philippine Accrediting Association of Schools, Colleges and Universities; Philippine Association of Colleges and Universities Commission on Accreditation

Degrees and Diplomas: *Bachelor's Degree*: Agriculture; Arts; Biology; Commerce; Elementary Education; Secondary Education, 4 yrs; *Bachelor's Degree*: Industrial Engineering, 5 yrs; *Bachelor's Degree*: Law, 4 yrs following first degree; *Master's Degree*: Education; Agricultural Education; Science in Business Administration, a further 2-3 yrs; *PhD*: Education (EdD); Public Administration (DPA)

Student Services: Academic counselling, Canteen, Cultural centre, Employment services, Health services, Social counselling, Sports facilities

Student Residential Facilities: None

Special Facilities: Museum

Libraries: c. 55,110 vols

Publications: Graduate Research Journal *(biennially)*; Law Forum; R & D Journal *(annually)*

Last Updated: 01/10/10

FRANCISCAN COLLEGE OF THE IMMACULATE CONCEPTION

A. Bonifacio Street, Baybay, Leyte 6521
Tel: +63(53) 335-2282
Fax: +63(53) 335-3382

President: M. Adrianne Siano, OSF

Programmes

Graduate (Education; Educational Administration; Educational and Student Counselling; Educational Technology; English; Filipino; Foreign Languages Education; Native Language Education; Science Education); **Undergraduate and Professional** (Banking;

Biology; Business Administration; Business and Commerce; Computer Science; Economics; Education; English; Filipino; Finance; Foreign Languages Education; Hotel and Restaurant; Hotel Management; Human Resources; Information Technology; Management; Mathematics Education; Native Language Education; Primary Education; Secondary Education)

History: Founded 1947.

Degrees and Diplomas: *Certificate/Diploma*; *Associate Degree*; *Bachelor's Degree*; *Master's Degree*
Last Updated: 01/10/10

FRANCISCO HOMES LEARNING ACADEMY

San Jose del Monte, Bulacan 3023
President: Leonardo D. Simon

Programmes
Education (Education; English; Filipino; Foreign Languages Education; Mathematics Education; Native Language Education; Physics; Primary Education; Secondary Education); **Hotel and Restaurant Management** (Hotel and Restaurant; Hotel Management); **Nursing** (Nursing)

History: Founded 2004.

Degrees and Diplomas: *Bachelor's Degree*
Last Updated: 01/10/10

FULLBRIGHT COLLEGE

Km 5, National Highway Corner Mangga Street, Brg. San Jose, Puerto Princesa City, Palawan 5300
Tel: +63(48) 434-3095
Fax: +63(48) 434-3097
EMail: fulbritpalawan@hotmail.com

President: Eustacio Q. Edualino

Programmes
Business Administration (Banking; Business Administration; Finance; Management; Marketing); **Computer Science** (Computer Science); **Criminology** (Criminology); **Education** (Art Education; Education; English; Filipino; Foreign Languages Education; Mathematics Education; Music Education; Native Language Education; Physical Education; Social Studies); **Engineering** (Computer Engineering; Electronic Engineering; Engineering; Telecommunications Engineering); **Information Technology** (Information Technology)

History: Founded 1998.

Degrees and Diplomas: *Bachelor's Degree*
Last Updated: 01/10/10

FUNDAMENTAL BAPTIST COLLEGE FOR ASIANS

5085, Buno-Matatalaib, City of Tarlac, Tarlac 2300
Tel: +63(45) 982-7250 +63(45) 982-7251
Fax: +63(45) 985-7250
EMail: fbca@mozcom.com

President: Emmanuel T. Quizon

Programmes
Elementary Education (Education; English; Foreign Languages Education; Primary Education); **Theology** (Theology)

History: Founded 1983.

Degrees and Diplomas: *Bachelor's Degree*
Last Updated: 01/10/10

GANI L. ABPI COLLEGES

Buayan, Datu Piang, Maguindanao 9607
Tel: +63(91) 694-11738
EMail: glaci-cmi@yahoo.com

Director/President: Ysmael Nasser Abpi

Programmes
Economics (Economics); **Education** (Education; English; Foreign Languages Education; History; Primary Education; Secondary Education)

History: Founded 1960.

Degrees and Diplomas: *Bachelor's Degree*
Last Updated: 01/10/10

GARCIA COLLEGE OF TECHNOLOGY

Osmeña Avenue, Capitol Site, Kalibo, Aklan 5600
Tel: +63(36) 262-4751
Fax: +63(36) 262-3280
EMail: gctkalibo@yahoo.com

President: Edwin R. Garcia Tel: +63(36) 868-5131

Programmes
Business Administration (Accountancy; Business Administration; Business and Commerce; Business Computing; Finance; Human Resources; Management; Marketing); **Computer Science** (Computer Science); **Engineering** (Civil Engineering; Electrical Engineering; Engineering; Geological Engineering); **Hotel and Restaurant Management** (Hotel and Restaurant; Hotel Management; Mechanical Engineering); **Information Technology** (Information Technology)

History: Founded 1968.

Degrees and Diplomas: *Associate Degree*; *Bachelor's Degree*
Last Updated: 01/10/10

GENERAL DE JESUS COLLEGE

Vallarta Street, San Isidro, Nueva Ecija 3106
Tel: +63(44) 486-0149 +63(44) 486-3813
Fax: +63(44) 486-0149
EMail: gjc@ne-link.net

President: Noemi Villanueva

Programmes
Commerce (Banking; Business Administration; Business and Commerce; Business Computing; Computer Science; Finance; Management); **Education** (English; Filipino; Foreign Languages Education; Mathematics Education; Native Language Education; Primary Education; Science Education; Secondary Education; Social Studies)

History: Founded 1946 as General de Jesus Academy. Acquired present title 1997.

Degrees and Diplomas: *Associate Degree*; *Bachelor's Degree*
Last Updated: 04/10/10

GENERAL SANTOS DOCTORS' MEDICAL SCHOOL FOUNDATION

Vensu Building, National Highway, General Santos City, South Cotabato 9500
Tel: +63(83) 302-3507
Fax: +63(83) 552-9793
EMail: gsdmsfi@yahoo.com

President: Gerano B. Valencia

Programmes
Nursing (Midwifery; Nursing); **Psychology** (Psychology); **Radiologic Technology** (Medical Technology; Radiology)

History: Founded 2002.

Degrees and Diplomas: *Bachelor's Degree*
Last Updated: 04/10/10

GENSANTOS FOUNDATION

1245 Nuestra Señora de la Paz Street, General Santos City, South Cotabato 9500
Tel: +63(83) 554-6286
Fax: +63(83) 552-3008
EMail: cadcanad@gsc.weblinq.com

President: Dominador S. Dizon

Programmes
Undergraduate and Professional (Accountancy; Banking; Business and Commerce; Education; Human Resources; Management; Marketing; Mathematics Education; Physics; Secondary Education)

History: Founded 1994.

Degrees and Diplomas: *Bachelor's Degree*
Last Updated: 04/10/10

GINGOOG CHRISTIAN COLLEGE

National Highway, Gingoog City, Misamis Oriental 9014
Tel: +63(8) 842-7376
Fax: +63(8) 842-7914

Director: Rodolfo Z. Alegado

Programmes

Education (Education; Physics; Primary Education; Secondary Education)

History: Founded 1946 as Gingoog Institute. Acquired present status and title 1998.

Degrees and Diplomas: *Bachelor's Degree*
Last Updated: 04/10/10

GLOBAL CITY INNOVATIVE COLLEGE

3F Bonifacio Technology Center, 31st Street, Bonifacio SEZ, Fort Bonifacio, Taguig City, Fourth District, Metro Manila 1634
Tel: +63(2) 818-0945
Fax: +63(2) 818-0946
Website: http://www.gcic.edu.ph

President: Michael S. Tan

Colleges

Business Administration (Business Administration; Finance; International Business; Management); **Education** (Education; Primary Education; Secondary Education); **Information Technology** (Information Technology); **International Hospitality Management** (Cooking and Catering; Hotel and Restaurant; Hotel Management; Tourism); **Nursing and International Health Studies** (Health Sciences; Nursing)

Further Information: Also Subic Campus, Olongapo City, Zambales

History: Founded 2002.

Degrees and Diplomas: *Bachelor's Degree*
Last Updated: 04/10/10

GOLDEN GATE COLLEGES

P. Prieto Street, Batangas City, Batangas 4200
Tel: +63(43) 723-2663
Fax: +63(43) 723-2077

President: Wilfredo Jacinto

Programmes

Graduate (Business Administration; Education; Educational Administration; Nursing; Public Administration); **Undergraduate and Professional** (Business Administration; Chemical Engineering; Education; English; Finance; Foreign Languages Education; Health Education; Management; Mathematics Education; Mechanical Engineering; Midwifery; Nursing; Primary Education; Secondary Education)

History: Founded 1946.

Degrees and Diplomas: *Associate Degree*; *Bachelor's Degree*; *Master's Degree*
Last Updated: 04/10/10

GOLDEN HERITAGE POLYTECHNIC COLLEGE

Vamenta Boulevard, Cagayan de Oro City, Misamis Oriental 9000
Tel: +63(8822) 727-781 +63(8822) 858-220
Fax: +63(8822) 727-781

President: Tito P. Dichosa

Programmes

Business Administration (Business Administration; Business Computing; Management); **Education** (Education; English; Foreign Languages Education)

History: Founded 1987.

Degrees and Diplomas: *Bachelor's Degree*
Last Updated: 04/10/10

GOLDENSTATE COLLEGE

P. Acharon Boulevard, General Santos City, South Cotabato 9500
Tel: +63(83) 552-5544
Fax: +63(83) 552-5544

President: Josie Yap-Tirador

Programmes

Business Administration (Business Administration; Computer Science; Secretarial Studies); **Hotel and Restaurant Management** (Hotel and Restaurant; Hotel Management); **Nursing and Midwifery** (Midwifery; Nursing); **Tourism** (Tourism)

History: Founded 1992. Formerly Goldenstate Institute, Inc. (1992-2001).

Degrees and Diplomas: *Bachelor's Degree*: Tourism; Hotel and Restaurant Management; Business Administration
Last Updated: 04/10/10

GOLDEN SUCCESS COLLEGE

1297 Corner Singson Street, Cebu City, Cebu 6000
Tel: +63(32) 255-6691
Fax: +63(32) 255-6691
EMail: goldensuccess_academy@yahoo.com

President: Rolando C. Sangalang

Programmes

Education (Education; English; Foreign Languages Education; Mathematics Education; Preschool Education; Primary Education; Science Education; Secondary Education; Special Education); **Hotel and Restaurant Management** (Hotel and Restaurant; Hotel Management)

Degrees and Diplomas: *Bachelor's Degree*
Last Updated: 04/10/10

GOLDEN WEST COLLEGES

Don Jose Drive, City of Alaminos, Pangasinan 2404
Tel: +63(75) 552-7382
Fax: +63(75) 552-7382
EMail: golden_west_colleges@yahoo.com

President: Nicanor J. Valdez

Programmes

Business Administration (Accountancy; Business and Commerce; Management); **Computer Science** (Computer Science); **Criminology** (Criminology); **Education** (Primary Education; Secondary Education); **Nursing** (Nursing); **Technology and Engineering** (Automotive Engineering; Civil Engineering; Electrical and Electronic Engineering; Information Technology)

History: Founded 1994.

Degrees and Diplomas: *Associate Degree*; *Bachelor's Degree*
Last Updated: 04/10/10

GOOD SAMARITAN COLLEGES

Burgos Avenue, Cabanatuan City, Nueva Ecija 3100
Tel: +63(44) 463-1582 +63(44) 463-1585
Fax: +63(44) 463-0891
EMail: goodsam@mozcom.com

President: Peregrin T. De Guzman, Jr.

Programmes

Graduate Studies (Child Care and Development; Education; Educational Administration; Nursing; Science Education); **Undergraduate and Professional Studies** (Education; Medical Technology; Midwifery; Nursing; Physical Therapy; Physics; Primary Education; Radiology; Respiratory Therapy; Secondary Education)

History: Founded 1973. Formerly known as The Good Samaritan School of Nursing and Midwifery.

Degrees and Diplomas: *Associate Degree*; *Bachelor's Degree*; *Master's Degree*
Last Updated: 04/10/10

GORDON COLLEGE

East Tapinac, Olongapo City, Zambales 2200
Tel: +63(47) 224-2088
Fax: +63(47) 224-2089
EMail: occ_admin@subicnet.com

President: Katherine H. Gordon

Programmes
Accountancy (Accountancy); **Business Administration** (Business Administration; Management); **Computer Science and Technology** (Computer Engineering; Computer Science); **Hotel and Restaurant Management** (Hotel and Restaurant; Hotel Management); **Information Management** (Information Management); **Information Technology** (Information Technology); **Nursing** (Midwifery; Nursing)

History: Founded 1999. Formerly known as Olongapo City Colleges (1999-2003).

Degrees and Diplomas: *Associate Degree*; *Bachelor's Degree*
Last Updated: 04/10/10

GOV. ANGEL MEDINA FOUNDATION COLLEGE

Panes, Passi City, Iloilo 5037
Tel: +63(33) 367-1189

President: Marianita Acuna

Programmes
Computer Science (Computer Science); **Criminology** (Criminology); **Elementary Education** (Primary Education)

History: Founded 2004.

Degrees and Diplomas: *Bachelor's Degree*: 4 yrs
Last Updated: 04/10/10

GOVERNOR ANDRES PASCUAL COLLEGE

1045 M. Naval Street, City of Navotas, Third District, Metro Manila
Tel: +63(2) 282-9036
Fax: +63(2) 282-9035
EMail: gapc@compass.com.ph

President: Olivia S. Pascual

Programmes
Graduate Studies (Education; Educational Administration); **Undergraduate and Professional Studies** (Accountancy; Business Administration; Computer Engineering; Computer Science; Cooking and Catering; Education; Filipino; Hotel and Restaurant; Hotel Management; Management; Mathematics Education; Native Language Education; Primary Education; Science Education; Secondary Education; Social Studies)

History: Founded 1995. Formerly known as Governor Andres Pascual College in Business and Arts and Computer Science.

Degrees and Diplomas: *Associate Degree*; *Bachelor's Degree*; *Master's Degree*: Education (Administration and Supervision); *PhD*: Education (Educational Management)
Last Updated: 04/10/10

GRACE CHRISTIAN COLLEGE

Grace Village, Sto. Domingo Street, Quezon City, Second District, Metro Manila
Tel: +63(2) 366-2000
Fax: +63(2) 364-1971

President: James L. Tan

Programmes
Business Administration (Accountancy; Business Administration; Business Computing; Human Resources; Management); **Education** (Education; English; Foreign Languages Education; Mathematics Education; Secondary Education); **Engineering and Technology** (Electronic Engineering; Information Technology; Telecommunications Engineering)

History: Founded 1950.

Degrees and Diplomas: *Bachelor's Degree*
Last Updated: 04/10/10

GRACE MISSION COLLEGE

Catiningan, Socorro, Oriental Mindoro 5207
Tel: +63(43) 284-5000

President: Romeo C. Santiago

Programmes
Midwifery (Midwifery); **Secondary Education** (English; Foreign Languages Education; Mathematics Education)

History: Founded 1976, acquired present status and title 1983.

Degrees and Diplomas: *Certificate/Diploma*; *Bachelor's Degree*
Last Updated: 04/10/10

GREAT PLEBIAN COLLEGE

Don P. Reinoso, City of Alaminos, Pangasinan 2404
Tel: +63(75) 552-7250
Fax: +63(75) 552-7250
EMail: gpcalaminos@yahoo.com

Director: Lourdes B. Garcia

Programmes
Arts (Arts and Humanities; English; History); **Business Administration** (Accountancy; Business Administration; Business and Commerce; Management); **Education** (Education; English; Filipino; Foreign Languages Education; History; Native Language Education; Primary Education; Science Education; Secondary Education)

History: Founded 1948. Formerly Northern Luzon School of Arts and Trade (1951-1960).

Degrees and Diplomas: *Bachelor's Degree*
Last Updated: 04/10/10

GREEN VALLEY COLLEGE FOUNDATION

Km. 2., General Santos Drive, Koronadal City, South Cotabato 9506
Tel: +63(83) 228-4034
Fax: +63(83) 228-2949
EMail: gvgate@mozcom.com; greenvalley_101795@yahoo.com

President: Romeo S. Sustiguer Sr.

Programmes
Business Administration (Accountancy; Banking; Business Computing; Computer Education; Finance; Management; Secretarial Studies); **Hotel and Restaurant Management** (Hotel and Restaurant; Hotel Management); **Information Technology** (Information Technology)

History: Founded 1995.

Degrees and Diplomas: *Bachelor's Degree*
Last Updated: 04/10/10

GREENVILLE COLLEGE

112 Belfast-San Salvador Streets Greenpark Village, Pasig City, Second District, Metro Manila 1600
Tel: +63(2) 681-3554 +63(2) 682-5063
Fax: +63(2) 646-3277

President: Erlinda Cuison

Programmes
Graduate (Business Administration; Education; Educational Administration; Public Administration); **Undergraduate and Professional** (English; Filipino; Foreign Languages Education; Native Language Education; Primary Education; Psychology; Public Administration; Secondary Education)

History: Founded 1987 as Development Education Center, Inc. Acquired present title 1998.

Degrees and Diplomas: *Associate Degree*; *Bachelor's Degree*; *Master's Degree*: Education (Educational Management); Public Administration; Business Administration; *PhD*: Education (Educational Management)
Last Updated: 04/10/10

GUAGUA NATIONAL COLLEGES (GNC)

Sta. Filomena, Guagua, Pampanga 2003
Tel: +63(45) 900-0841 +63(45) 900-0341
Fax: +63(45) 910-0841 +63(45) 900-0341
EMail: gnc.ph.edu@yahoo.com; gnc_edu_ph@yahoo.com
Website: http://www.gnc.edu.ph/

President: Ricardo Puno

Colleges
Accountancy (Accountancy); **Arts** (English); **Business Administration** (Accountancy; Banking; Business Administration; Computer Engineering; Computer Science; Finance; Hotel and Restaurant; Hotel Management; Management); **Education** (Education; English; Filipino; Foreign Languages Education; Mathematics Education; Native Language Education; Physical Education; Science Education; Social Sciences); **Engineering** (Civil Engineering; Engineering); **Nursing** (Nursing)

Graduate Schools
Graduate Studies (Business Administration; Education; Educational Administration; Public Administration)

History: Founded 1918.

Governing Bodies: Board of Trustees; Board of Administrators

Admission Requirements: Secondary school certificate and entrance examination

Fees: (Pesos): 16,000 per semester

Main Language(s) of Instruction: English

Accrediting Agencies: Philippine Association of Colleges and Universities Commission on Accreditation

Degrees and Diplomas: *Associate Degree*; *Bachelor's Degree*; *Master's Degree*: Education (Educational Management); Business Administration; Public Administration; *PhD*: Education (Educational Management)

Student Services: Academic counselling, Canteen, Employment services, Health services, Language programs, Social counselling, Sports facilities

Libraries: Yes

Last Updated: 04/10/10

GUZMAN COLLEGE OF SCIENCE AND TECHNOLOGY

509, Zacarias P. De Guzman St. Quiapo, Manila, First District, Metro Manila 1001
Tel: +63(2) 733-9456 +63(2) 733-9458
Fax: +63(2) 733-9464

President: Renato S. Relampagos

Programmes
Undergraduate and Professional (Business Administration; Industrial Arts Education; Secretarial Studies)

History: Founded 1947.Formerly known as Guzman Institute of Electronics.

Degrees and Diplomas: *Bachelor's Degree*

Last Updated: 04/10/10

HARRIS MEMORIAL COLLEGE

G.K. Bunyi, Taytay, Rizal 1920
Tel: +63 658-2798
Fax: +63 658-2797
EMail: harrismemorial@l-manila.com.ph

President: Cristina N. Mañabat

Programmes
Undergraduate and Professional (English; Foreign Languages Education; History; Preschool Education; Primary Education; Religious Education; Religious Music; Secondary Education; Social Studies)

History: Founded 1903. Formerly known as Harris Memorial School.

Degrees and Diplomas: *Bachelor's Degree*

Last Updated: 04/10/10

HARVARDIAN COLLEGES

Lourdes Street, City of San Fernando, Pampanga 2000
Tel: +63(45) 963-6832
Fax: +63(45) 963-6832

President: Manuel D. Tagle

Programmes
Graduate Studies (Education; Educational Administration; Educational and Student Counselling); **Undergraduate and Professional Studies** (Banking; Business Administration; Business and Commerce; Education; English; Filipino; Finance; Foreign Languages Education; History; Law; Management; Mathematics Education; Native Language Education; Political Sciences; Primary Education; Secondary Education)

History: Founded 1955.

Degrees and Diplomas: *Bachelor's Degree*; *Master's Degree*: Education (Guidance and Counselling; Administration and Supervision)

Last Updated: 04/10/10

HEADSTART COLLEGE OF COTABATO

Tamontaka MB, Maguindanao, Cotabato City, Cotabato 9600
Tel: +63(64) 390-3592
Fax: +63(64) 421-6571

President: Joy Bulosan

Programmes
Criminology (Criminology); **Education** (Education; Mathematics Education; Primary Education; Secondary Education)

History: Founded 1994.

Degrees and Diplomas: *Bachelor's Degree*

Last Updated: 04/10/10

HERCOR COLLEGE

Altavas, Roxas City, Capiz 5800
Tel: +63(36) 621-6897

President: José A. Hernández

Programmes
Undergraduate and Professional (Business Administration; Computer Science; Criminology; Hotel and Restaurant; Hotel Management; Tourism)

History: Founded 2004.

Degrees and Diplomas: *Certificate/Diploma*; *Bachelor's Degree*

Last Updated: 04/10/10

HGB COLLEGE

Centro 1, Tumauini, Isabela 3325
Tel: +63(78) 632-4026
Fax: +63(78) 632-4026
EMail: hgbc_reg2005@yahoo.com.ph

President: Romeo Z. Tarun

Programmes
Business Administration (Business Administration; Cooking and Catering; Finance; Hotel and Restaurant; Hotel Management; Household Management; Human Resources; Management; Secretarial Studies); **Criminology** (Criminology); **Education** (Education; English; Foreign Languages Education; Mathematics Education; Primary Education; Secondary Education); **Software Engineering**

History: Founded 2005.

Degrees and Diplomas: *Bachelor's Degree*

Last Updated: 04/10/10

HILAND INSTITUTE COLLEGES

Sitio Kabutoyen, Brgy, Blensong, Nuro, Upi, Shariff Kabunsuan 9602
Tel: +63(64) 390-2735
EMail: hici@yahoo.com

Administrator: Romulo H.N. Millan

Programmes

Undergraduate and Professional (Business Administration; Criminology)

History: Founded 2006.

Degrees and Diplomas: *Bachelor's Degree*: Criminology, Business Administration

Last Updated: 04/10/10

HILLSDALE COLLEGE

City of San Jose del Monte, Bulacan 3023

Programmes

Education (Education; English; Foreign Languages Education; Mathematics Education; Preschool Education; Primary Education; Secondary Education)

Degrees and Diplomas: *Bachelor's Degree*

Last Updated: 04/10/10

HMIJ - PHILIPPINE ISLAMIC COLLEGE

BCC Compound, Baliwasan Grande, Zamboanga City, Zamboanga del Sur 7000
Tel: +63(62) 993-1793
Fax: +63(62) 993-1783

President: Mejal B. Jammang

Programmes

Undergraduate and Professional Studies (Business and Commerce; Computer Science; Criminology; Education; English; Foreign Languages Education; Health Education; Management; Primary Education; Science Education; Secondary Education)

History: Founded 1999.

Degrees and Diplomas: *Bachelor's Degree*

Last Updated: 04/10/10

HOLY ANGEL UNIVERSITY (HAU)

Santo Rosario Street, Angeles City, Pampanga 2009
Tel: +63(45) 888-8691
Fax: +63(45) 888-1754 +63(45) 888-2514
EMail: registrar@hau.edu.ph
Website: http://www.hau.edu.ph

President: Bernadette M. Nepomuceno (1995-)
Tel: +63(45) 322-3862, Fax: +63(45) 888-2514

Colleges

Arts, Sciences and Education (Advertising and Publicity; Biological and Life Sciences; Communication Studies; Education; English; Filipino; Foreign Languages Education; Health Education; Information Sciences; Journalism; Library Science; Mathematics Education; Native Language Education; Physical Education; Physics; Preschool Education; Primary Education; Psychology; Public Relations; Radio and Television Broadcasting; Secondary Education; Social Studies; Special Education; Sports); **Business and Accountancy** (Accountancy; Banking; Business Administration; Commercial Law; Human Resources; Marketing); **Criminal Justice Education and Forensics** (Criminal Law; Criminology; Forensic Medicine and Dentistry); **Engineering and Architecture** (Aeronautical and Aerospace Engineering; Architecture; Civil Engineering; Computer Engineering; Electrical Engineering; Electronic Engineering; Industrial Engineering; Mechanical Engineering; Structural Architecture; Telecommunications Engineering); **Hospitality Management** (Cooking and Catering; Hotel and Restaurant; Hotel Management; Tourism); **Information and Communications Technology** (Computer Networks; Computer Science; Information Technology; Multimedia); **Nursing** (Nursing)

Schools

Graduate Studies (Accountancy; Business Administration; Educational Administration; Educational and Student Counselling; Electrical Engineering; Electronic Engineering; Engineering; Engineering Management; English; English Studies; Filipino; Foreign Languages Education; Government; Industrial Engineering; Information Technology; Library Science; Literature; Management; Mathematics Education; Native Language Education; Nursing; Public Administration; Science Education; Special Education; Telecommunications Engineering)

History: Founded 1933 as Academy, became College 1962 and acquired University status 1981. A private Institution under the supervision of the Department of Education.

Governing Bodies: Board of Trustees

Academic Year: June to April (June-October; November-April)

Admission Requirements: Graduation from high school and entrance examination

Main Language(s) of Instruction: Filipino, English

Accrediting Agencies: Philippine Accrediting Association of Schools, Colleges and Universities (PAASCU)

Degrees and Diplomas: *Associate Degree*; *Bachelor's Degree*; *Master's Degree*; *PhD*

Student Services: Academic counselling, Canteen, Employment services, Foreign student adviser, Health services, Language programs, Social counselling, Sports facilities

Special Facilities: Don Juan D. Nepomuceno Center for Kapampangan Studies

Libraries: Central Library, c. 24,790 vols

Publications: Holy Angel University Graduate Journal *(biannually)*; Indung Ibatan, Kapampangan Language Magazine of the Centre for Kapampangan Studies; Sing-sing, Publication of the Don Juan D. Nepomuceno Center for Kapampangan Studies of Holy Angel University *(quarterly)*

Last Updated: 04/10/10

HOLY CHILD COLLEGE OF INFORMATION TECHNOLOGY

Allah Valley Drive, Surallah, South Cotabato 9512
Tel: +63(83) 238-3036
Fax: +63(83) 238-3036
EMail: hecitine@yahoo.com

President: Henry A. Agan

Programmes

Information Technology (Information Technology)

History: Founded 2008.

Degrees and Diplomas: *Bachelor's Degree*

Last Updated: 05/10/10

HOLY CHILD COLLEGES OF BUTUAN CITY

2nd St., Guingona Sudb., Butuan City, Agusan del Norte 8600
Tel: +63(85) 342-3875
Fax: +63(85) 342-3875
EMail: holychildcollegesofbutuan@yahoo.com

President: Rudolfo Pimentel Esteves

Programmes

Business Administration (Business Administration; Business and Commerce; Economics; Management); **Criminolgy**; **Education** (Biological and Life Sciences; Child Care and Development; Educational and Student Counselling; English; Foreign Languages Education; Mathematics Education; Preschool Education; Primary Education; Secondary Education; Special Education); **Nursing** (Nursing); **Tourism** (Hotel and Restaurant; Hotel Management; Tourism)

History: Founded 2000.

Degrees and Diplomas: *Bachelor's Degree*

Last Updated: 05/10/10

HOLY CHILD JESUS COLLEGE

Padre Burgos Street, Gumaca, Quezon 4307
Tel: +63(42) 317-4753
Fax: +63(42) 317-4753
EMail: hcjc_2001@yahoo.com

President: Buenaventura M. Famadico, DD

Programmes

Undergraduate and Professional (Biological and Life Sciences; English; Foreign Languages Education; Health Education; Management; Marketing; Primary Education; Science Education; Secondary Education)

History: Founded 2001.

Degrees and Diplomas: *Bachelor's Degree*
Last Updated: 05/10/10

HOLY CHILD SCHOOL OF DAVAO

E. Jacinto Street, Davao City, Davao del Sur 8000
Tel: +63(82) 222-9404
Fax: +63(82) 221-1815
EMail: info@holychilddavao.edu.ph
Website: http://www.holychilddavao.edu.ph/

Director: Victoria D. Leuterio

Departments

Commerce (Business and Commerce; Finance; Management; Marketing); **Computer Science** (Computer Science); **Education** (Education; English; Foreign Languages Education; Preschool Education; Primary Education; Secondary Education; Special Education); **Information Technology** (Information Technology); **Nursing** (Nursing)

History: Founded 1981.

Degrees and Diplomas: *Bachelor's Degree*
Last Updated: 05/10/10

HOLY CONCEPTION COLLEGE

Colegio de la Purisima Concepcion
CPC Main Bldg., Arzobispo Street, Roxas City, Capiz 5800
Tel: +63(36) 210-286
EMail: cpc_scss@capznet.mozcom.com

Rector: Vicente F. Hilata

Programmes

Graduate (Business Administration; Education; Educational Administration; Educational and Student Counselling; English; Filipino; Foreign Languages Education; Native Language Education; Public Administration); **Undergraduate and Professional** (Accountancy; Art Education; Business Administration; Civil Engineering; Computer Engineering; Computer Science; Criminology; Education; Electrical Engineering; English; Ethics; Filipino; Finance; Foreign Languages Education; Home Economics Education; Hotel and Restaurant; Hotel Management; Law; Management; Marine Engineering; Marketing; Mass Communication; Mathematics Education; Music Education; Native Language Education; Philosophy; Physical Education; Political Sciences; Primary Education; Public Administration; Religious Education; Science Education; Secondary Education)

History: Founded 1948.

Degrees and Diplomas: *Certificate/Diploma*; *Bachelor's Degree*; *Master's Degree*; *PhD*
Last Updated: 08/09/10

HOLY CROSS ACADEMY OF SASA

Km.9, Sasa, Davao City, Davao del Sur 8000
Tel: +63(82) 234-0857
Fax: +63(82) 234-3385

Director: Ma. Nena B. Heramil, TDM

Programmes

Business Administration (Business Administration; Finance; Management; Marketing); **Hotel and Restaurant Management** (Hotel and Restaurant; Hotel Management); **Tourism** (Tourism)

History: Founded 2005.
Last Updated: 05/10/10

HOLY CROSS COLLEGE - NUEVA ECIJA

Poblacion Brgy Rizal, Santa Rosa, Nueva Ecija 3101
Tel: +63(44) 311-2017
Fax: +63(44) 311-3039

President: David P. Sta. Ines, Jr.

Programmes

Commerce (Banking; Business and Commerce; Finance; Management); **Computer Science** (Computer Science); **Elementary Education** (Education; Primary Education)

History: Founded 1946. Formerly known as Holy Cross Academy (1946-1986).

Degrees and Diplomas: *Bachelor's Degree*
Last Updated: 05/10/10

HOLY CROSS COLLEGE - PAMPANGA

Sta. Lucia, Santa Ana, Pampanga 2022
Tel: +63(45) 631-0309
Fax: +63(45) 631-0036
EMail: hccpamp@mozcom.com; hccinfocom@speed.info.com.ph

President: Paterno H. Dizon

Programmes

Arts and Humanities; **Commerce** (Accountancy; Business and Commerce; Management); **Elementary Education**; **Mathematics and Computer Science** (Computer Science; Mathematics); **Secondary Education** (English; Filipino; Mathematics; Physical Education; Secondary Education)

History: Founded 1945. Formerly Holy Cross Academy (1945-1984).

Degrees and Diplomas: *Bachelor's Degree*
Last Updated: 05/10/10

HOLY CROSS COLLEGE OF CALINAN

Davao-Bukidnon Hi-way, Calinan, Davao City, Davao del Sur 8000
Tel: +63(82) 295-0145 +63(82) 295-0797
Fax: +63(82) 295-0145
EMail: hcc.calinan@eudoramail.com

Director: Donatila Cruz

Programmes

Arts (Arts and Humanities; History; Literature; Social Studies); **Business Administration** (Accountancy; Business Administration; Business and Commerce; Finance; Management; Marketing); **Education** (Biological and Life Sciences; Communication Arts; Education; English; Filipino; Foreign Languages Education; Health Education; History; Mathematics Education; Native Language Education; Primary Education; Science Education; Secondary Education; Social Studies); **Science** (Biology; Mathematics)

History: Founded 1948. Formerly known as Holy Cross of Calinan High School (1948-1966).

Degrees and Diplomas: *Bachelor's Degree*
Last Updated: 05/10/10

HOLY CROSS COLLEGE OF CARIGARA

Rebolledo Street, Ponong, Carigara, Leyte 6529
Tel: +63(53) 331-2099
Fax: +63(53) 331-2601
EMail: holycrosscollege_carigara@yahoo.com

Head: M. Anthony Kuizon

Programmes

Business Administration (Banking; Business Administration; Business Computing; Finance; Management); **Computer Science and Technology** (Computer Engineering; Computer Science); **Education** (Education; English; Filipino; Foreign Languages Education; Health Education; Library Science; Mathematics Education; Music Education; Native Language Education; Physical Education; Primary Education; Secondary Education)

History: Founded 1945.

Degrees and Diplomas: *Bachelor's Degree*
Last Updated: 05/10/10

HOLY CROSS OF BANSALAN COLLEGE

Dahlia Street, Bansalan, Davao del Sur 8005
Tel: +63(82) 553-9246
Fax: +63(82) 553-9246
EMail: hcbansalan@gmail.com

Director/Dean: Ma. Fe D. Gerodias, RVM

Programmes

Commerce (Accountancy; Business and Commerce; Management); **Education** (Education; English; Foreign Languages Education; Primary Education; Science Education; Secondary Education)

History: Founded 1959, acquired present status and title 1984.

Degrees and Diplomas: *Bachelor's Degree*

Last Updated: 05/10/10

HOLY CROSS OF DAVAO COLLEGE

Sta. Ana Avenue, Davao City, Davao del Sur 8000
Tel: +63(82) 221-9071
Fax: +63(82) 221-9079
EMail: hcdc@hcdc.edu.ph
Website: http://www.hcdc.edu.ph

President: Irish A. Melleza Tel: +63(82) 221-8071

Campuses

Babak *(Island Garden, City of Samal)* (Business Administration; Business and Commerce; Education; English; Foreign Languages Education; Mathematics Education; Primary Education; Secondary Education)

Colleges

Arts and Sciences (Economics; English; Filipino; History; Information Sciences; Library Science; Mass Communication; Mathematics; Natural Sciences; Physical Education; Political Sciences; Psychology; Social Work); **Business** (Accountancy; Business Administration; Economics; Finance; Hotel and Restaurant; Hotel Management; Human Resources; Marketing; Taxation); **Criminology** (Criminology); **Education** (Biological and Life Sciences; Education; English; Filipino; Foreign Languages Education; Health Education; Mathematics Education; Music Education; Native Language Education; Physical Education; Physics; Preschool Education; Primary Education; Religious Education; Secondary Education; Social Studies; Special Education); **Engineering and Technology** (Engineering; Technology); **Maritime** (Marine Transport)

Schools

Graduate Studies (Economics; Education; Educational Administration; Management; Pastoral Studies; Philosophy; Religious Education; Theology)

History: Founded 1951.

Degrees and Diplomas: *Bachelor's Degree*; *Master's Degree*; *PhD*

Last Updated: 05/10/10

HOLY FAMILY CENTRE OF STUDIES FOUNDATION

Rangas, Juban, Sorsogon 4703

Dean: Lemuel W. Galias

Programmes

Philosophy (Philosophy); **Religious Studies** (Religious Studies)

History: Founded 1995.

Degrees and Diplomas: *Bachelor's Degree*

Last Updated: 05/10/10

HOLY INFANT COLLEGE

Benigno Aquino Street, Utap, Tacloban City, Leyte 6500
Tel: +63(53) 321-2960
Fax: +63(53) 325-6212
EMail: hic_registrar@yahoo.com

President: M. Carmela Cabactulan

Programmes

Arts (Communication Studies; English; Filipino; Political Sciences; Psychology); **Business Administration** (Banking; Business Administration; Business Computing; Computer Science; Finance; Human Resources; Management); **Education** (Art Education; Biological and Life Sciences; Computer Education; Education; Educational Administration; Educational and Student Counselling; English; Ethics; Filipino; Foreign Languages Education; Health Education; Information Sciences; Library Science; Mathematics Education; Music Education; Native Language Education; Physical Education; Physics; Preschool Education; Science Education; Secondary Education; Social Studies; Special Education); **Graduate** (Education; Educational Administration; Educational and Student Counselling; English; Ethics; Filipino; Foreign Languages Education; Music Education; Native Language Education; Pedagogy; Science Education; Teacher Training); **Nursing** (Midwifery; Nursing); **Radiologic Technology** (Medical Technology; Radiology)

History: Founded 1924.

Degrees and Diplomas: *Certificate/Diploma*; *Associate Degree*; *Bachelor's Degree*; *Master's Degree*: Education (Reading; General Science; Educational Management; English Language; Music Education; Values Education; Guidance and Counselling; Filipino)

Last Updated: 05/10/10

HOLY INFANT JESUS COLLEGE

Mayumi Street, Sta. Rita, Olongapo City, Zambales 2200
Tel: +63(47) 222-4907
Fax: +63(47) 222-4907
EMail: hijc@hvisions.com

President: Antonio M. Crispin

Programmes

Arts and Humanities (Arts and Humanities; Political Sciences); **Commerce** (Banking; Business and Commerce; Finance; Hotel and Restaurant; Hotel Management; Management); **Computer Studies** (Computer Science; Software Engineering); **Criminology** (Criminology); **Education** (Education; Primary Education; Secondary Education)

History: Founded 1999.

Degrees and Diplomas: *Bachelor's Degree*

Last Updated: 05/10/10

HOLY NAME UNIVERSITY (HNU)

Lesage and Gallares Streets, Tagbilaran City, Bohol 6300
Tel: +63(38) 411-3764 +63(38) 411-3432
Fax: +63(38) 411-3387
EMail: webteam@hnu.edu.ph
Website: http://www.hnu.edu.ph

President: Ernesto M. Lagura, SVD
Tel: +63(38) 411-3387 EMail: pres@hnu.edu.ph

Vice President for Academic Affairs: Teodoro P. Gapuz, SVD
Tel: +63(38) 411-2766, Fax: +63(38) 411-2766
EMail: research@hnu.edu.ph

Vice-President for Administration: Andres B. Guban, SVD

Colleges

Arts and Sciences (Biology; Criminology; Information Sciences; Library Science; Mass Communication; Mathematics; Philosophy; Political Sciences; Psychology); **Business and Accountancy** (Accountancy; Business Administration; Business Computing; Economics; Finance; Hotel and Restaurant; Hotel Management; Human Resources; Management; Marketing; Tourism); **Computer Science** (Computer Engineering; Computer Science; Information Technology); **Education** (Art Education; Biological and Life Sciences; Curriculum; Education; English; Filipino; Foreign Languages Education; Health Education; History; Mathematics Education; Music Education; Native Language Education; Physical Education; Preschool Education; Primary Education; Secondary Education; Social Studies; Special Education; Technology); **Engineering** (Civil Engineering; Computer Engineering; Electronic Engineering; Engineering; Telecommunications Engineering); **Law** (Civil Law; Criminal Law; Labour Law; Law; Maritime Law); **Nursing** (Nursing)

Schools

Graduate Studies (Business Administration; Education; Educational Administration; Educational and Student Counselling; English; Filipino; Foreign Languages Education; Library Science; Mathematics Education; Native Language Education; Nursing; Philosophy; Primary Education; Public Administration; Science Education; Secondary Education)

History: Founded 1947. Known as Holy Name College (1947-1963). Became Divine Word College and acquired present status 1964. Acquired present title 2001.

Governing Bodies: Board of Trustees

Academic Year: June to March

Admission Requirements: High school certificate; Certificate of good moral character

Fees: (Pesos): undergraduate, c. 9,200; Graduate and Law, c. 8,500

Main Language(s) of Instruction: English

International Co-operation: With Seisen University (Japan)

Accrediting Agencies: Philippine Accrediting Agency of Schools, Colleges and Universities (PAASCU)

Degrees and Diplomas: *Associate Degree*; *Bachelor's Degree*; *Master's Degree*: Education (Native Language Education; Primary Education; Secondary Education; Science Education; Nursing Education; Mathematics Education; Educational Guidance and Counselling; English); Public Administration; Business Administration; Library Science; Philosophy; Nursing; *PhD*: Education; Educational Management

Student Services: Academic counselling, Canteen, Employment services, Handicapped facilities, Health services, Language programs, Sports facilities

Student Residential Facilities: None

Special Facilities: Photo Museum; Multimedia Centre

Publications: Ang Kinaadman, Faculty Journal *(biennially)*

Last Updated: 05/10/10

HOLY ROSARY COLLEGE FOUNDATION

1427 Fr. Hofstee Street, Tala, Caloocan City, Third District, Metro Manila 1427
Tel: +63(2) 962-8118
Fax: +63(2) 962-8418

Director: Rosita M. Yaya

Campuses

Calaba *(Calaba, San Isidro, Nueva Ecija)* (Preschool Education; Primary Education; Special Education)

Programmes

Secondary Education (English; Foreign Languages Education; Mathematics Education; Secondary Education)

History: Founded 1951. Formerly known as Holy Rosary College.

Degrees and Diplomas: *Bachelor's Degree*

Last Updated: 05/10/10

HOLY SPIRIT FOUNDATION OF LEYTE (HSFLI)

65-A Real Street, Tacloban City, Leyte 6500
Tel: +63(53) 523-5676

President: Corazon C. Kierulf

Programmes

Business Administration (Business Administration); **Criminology** (Criminology)

History: Founded 2000.

Degrees and Diplomas: *Bachelor's Degree*

Last Updated: 05/10/10

HOLY TRINITY COLLEGE OF GENERAL SANTOS CITY

Fiscal Daproza Avenue, General Santos City, South Cotabato 9500
Tel: +63(83) 552-3905 +63(83) 552-5578
Fax: +63(83) 552-3905
EMail: holytrinitycollege@htcgsc.edu.ph
Website: http://main.htcgsc.edu.ph/

President: Rey T. Albano EMail: president@htcgsc.edu.ph

Vice-President for Administration: Josemar T. Albano

Registrar: Jennifer O. Oñas EMail: collegeregistrar@htcgsc.edu.ph

Colleges

Business Management Education (Accountancy; Banking; Business Administration; Economics; Finance; Human Resources; Management; Marketing); **Criminal Justice Education** (Criminal Law; Criminology); **Humanities and Social Sciences** (English; Filipino; Political Sciences; Social and Community Services); **Information Technology Education** (Computer Science; Information Technology); **Teacher Education** (Biological and Life Sciences; Education; Educational and Student Counselling; English; Ethics; Filipino; Foreign Languages Education; Mathematics Education; Native Language Education; Primary Education)

Programmes

Graduate Studies (Educational Administration; Educational and Student Counselling; English; Foreign Languages Education; Mathematics Education)

History: Founded 1989.

Degrees and Diplomas: *Bachelor's Degree*; *Master's Degree*: Education

Last Updated: 06/10/10

HOLY TRINITY COLLEGE OF PUERTO PRINCESA

Quezon Street, Puerto Princesa City, Palawan 5300
Tel: +63(48) 433-2061
Fax: +63(48) 433-2161
EMail: admin@htc.edu.ph
Website: http://www.htc.edu.ph

President: Estrella Tangan, OP (2000-)
EMail: tangan@mozcom.com

Colleges

Business and Accountancy (Accountancy; Business Administration; Business and Commerce; Finance; Management; Marketing); **Education, Arts and Sciences** (Biological and Life Sciences; Biology; Economics; Education; English; Filipino; Foreign Languages Education; History; Mathematics Education; Native Language Education; Political Sciences; Primary Education; Religious Education; Secondary Education; Social Studies); **Engineering** (Civil Engineering; Computer Engineering; Computer Science; Engineering; Geological Engineering); **Information and Communication Technology** (Computer Science; Information Technology); **Nursing and Health Sciences** (Health Sciences; Nursing; Physical Therapy); **Public Safety** (Criminology); **Tourism and Hospitality Management** (Hotel and Restaurant; Hotel Management; Tourism)

Programmes

Graduate Studies (Business Administration; Chemical Engineering; Civil Engineering; Computer Engineering; Education; Educational Administration; Educational and Student Counselling; Electronic Engineering; Engineering Management; English; Filipino; Foreign Languages Education; Mathematics Education; Mechanical Engineering; Native Language Education; Public Administration; Science Education; Telecommunications Engineering)

History: Founded 1940.

Governing Bodies: Board of Trustees; Educational Council

Admission Requirements: Graduation from high school

Fees: (Pesos): c. 400 per unit

Main Language(s) of Instruction: English

Accrediting Agencies: Philippine Accrediting Association of Schools, Colleges and Universities (PAASCU); Dominican Sisters of St. Catherine of Siena

Degrees and Diplomas: *Associate Degree*; *Bachelor's Degree*; *Master's Degree*; *PhD*

Student Services: Academic counselling, Canteen, Health services, Sports facilities

Last Updated: 06/10/10

HOLY VIRGIN OF SALVATION FOUNDATION COLLEGE

Burayan, San Jose, Tacloban City, Leyte 6500
Tel: +63(53) 323-2440
Fax: +63(53) 323-2440
EMail: chitmerin@yahoo.com

President: Cesar M. Merin

Programmes

Economics (Economics); **Education** (Education; Mathematics Education; Primary Education; Secondary Education); **Political Sciences** (Political Sciences)

History: Founded 1995.

Degrees and Diplomas: *Certificate/Diploma*; *Bachelor's Degree*
Last Updated: 06/10/10

HOMEFRONT INSTITUTE

Tenorio, Datu Odin Sinsuat, Shariff Kabunsuan

President: Dominga E. Navidad

Programmes

Computer Science (Computer Science); **Secondary Education** (Secondary Education)

History: Founded 2006.

Degrees and Diplomas: *Bachelor's Degree*
Last Updated: 06/10/10

IATEC COMPUTER COLLEGE

Nautical Highway, Bgy. Sta. Rita, Pinamalayan, Oriental Mindoro 5208
Tel: +63(43) 284-3964
Fax: +63(43) 284-3363
EMail: info@iatecnet.com; maxgui20@yahoo.com

President: Efren J. Mason

Programmes

Business Administration (Business Administration); **Computer Engineering** (Computer Engineering); **Computer Science** (Computer Science); **Electronic and Communications Engineering** (Electronic Engineering; Telecommunications Engineering); **Hotel and Restaurant Management** (Hotel and Restaurant; Hotel Management)

History: Founded 2002.

Degrees and Diplomas: *Bachelor's Degree*
Last Updated: 06/10/10

ICCT COLLEGES

V.V. Soliven Ave., II Bgy. San Isidro, Cainta, Rizal 1900
Tel: +63(02) 249-1050
Fax: +63(02) 678-5538
Website: http://www.icct.edu.ph

President: Consuelo L. Co

Colleges

Arts and Sciences (Communication Studies; English; Mass Communication; Mathematics; Psychology); **Business** (Business Administration; Business and Commerce; Commercial Law; Economics; Information Management); **Computer Studies** (Computer Science; Information Technology; Software Engineering); **Criminology** (Criminology; Protective Services); **Education** (Chemistry; Education; English; Filipino; Foreign Languages Education; Information Technology; Mathematics Education; Native Language Education; Physical Education; Physics; Science Education); **Engineering** (Computer Engineering; Electronic Engineering; Engineering); **Hospitality Management** (Cooking and Catering; Hotel and Restaurant; Hotel Management; Tourism); **Nursing** (Nursing)

Further Information: Campuses: San Mateo; Cogeo; Sumulong; Taytay; Angono; Binangonan

History: Founded 1992, acquired present status 2001. Formerly known as Institute of Creative Computer Technology Colleges.

Degrees and Diplomas: *Certificate/Diploma*; *Associate Degree*; *Bachelor's Degree*
Last Updated: 06/10/10

ICTI - POLYTECHNIC COLLEGE

Sabayle Street, Iligan City, Lanao del Norte 9200
Tel: +63(63) 221-2020
Fax: +63(63) 221-2020
EMail: ictipc@yahoo.com.ph

President: Jennifer P. Densing

Programmes

Business and Commerce (Hotel and Restaurant; Hotel Management; Secretarial Studies)

History: Founded 1966. Formerly known as Iligan City Technical Institute.

Degrees and Diplomas: *Bachelor's Degree*
Last Updated: 06/10/10

IETI COLLEGE OF SCIENCE AND TECHNOLOGY

161 Purok 2 Magsaysay Avenue, Brgy. Magsaysay, San Pedro, Laguna 4028
Tel: +63(49) 868-1505
Fax: +63(49) 869-7775
EMail: ieti_sanpedro@yahoo.com.ph
Website: http://www.ieti.edu.ph

President: Cesar S. Ochoa

Campuses

Alabang *(Alabang, City of Muntinlupa, Fourth District, Metro Manila)* (Business Administration; Computer Engineering; Computer Science; Education; Information Technology; Mathematics Education; Secondary Education; Telecommunications Engineering); **Marikina** *(City of Marikina, Second District, Metro Manila)* (Computer Engineering; Electronic Engineering; Hotel and Restaurant; Hotel Management; Information Technology; Mechanical Engineering; Telecommunications Engineering)

Programmes

Business Administration (Business Administration; Management; Taxation); **Education** (Computer Education; Education; English; Foreign Languages Education; Mathematics Education; Primary Education; Science Education; Secondary Education; Social Studies); **Engineering and Technology** (Computer Engineering; Industrial Engineering; Information Technology); **Hotel and Restaurant Management** (Hotel and Restaurant; Hotel Management); **Psychology** (Psychology)

History: Founded 1998.

Degrees and Diplomas: *Associate Degree*; *Bachelor's Degree*
Last Updated: 07/10/10

IGNATIAN COLLEGE

Gonzalo Javier Street, Cotabato City, Cotabato 9600
Tel: +63(64) 421-4488
Fax: +63(64) 421-2334

President: Aniceto S. Bitayo

Programmes

Education (Education; Primary Education)

History: Founded 1992.

Degrees and Diplomas: *Bachelor's Degree*
Last Updated: 07/10/10

ILIGAN CAPITOL COLLEGE

Roxas Street Avenue, Mahayahay, Iligan City, Lanao del Norte 9200
Tel: +63(63) 221-2247
Fax: +63(63) 221-5217
EMail: iligan_capitol_college@yahoo.com
Website: http://www.icc.edu.ph

President: Laureana S. Rosales

Colleges

Arts and Sciences (English; Political Sciences); **Business Administration** (Accountancy; Banking; Business Administration; Finance; Human Resources; Management; Marketing; Public Administration); **Computer Studies** (Computer Engineering; Computer Science); **Criminology** (Criminology); **Education** (Education; English; Filipino; Foreign Languages Education; Home Economics Education; Mathematics Education; Native Language Education; Primary Education; Secondary Education)

History: Founded 1964.

Degrees and Diplomas: *Bachelor's Degree*
Last Updated: 07/10/10

ILIGAN MEDICAL CENTER COLLEGE

San Miguel Village, Pala-o, Iligan City, Lanao del Norte 9200
Tel: +63(63) 221-4661
Fax: +63(63) 221-6581
EMail: imccnet@imcc.edu.ph
Website: http://www.imcc.edu.ph/

President: Royce S. Torres

Programmes

Arts and Sciences (Biology; Computer Science; Criminology; Information Management; Information Technology; Mass Communication; Social Work); **Business Administration** (Accountancy; Business Administration; Economics; Finance; Hotel and Restaurant; Hotel Management; Human Resources; Management; Marketing; Public Administration; Tourism); **Education** (Educational Administration; English; Filipino; Foreign Languages Education; Health Education; Mathematics Education; Native Language Education; Science Education; Secondary Education; Special Education); **Health Sciences** (Health Sciences; Medical Technology; Midwifery; Nursing; Physical Therapy; Radiology)

History: Founded 1975.

Degrees and Diplomas: *Bachelor's Degree*; *Master's Degree*: Human Resources Management; Educational Management
Last Updated: 07/10/10

ILOILO DOCTORS' COLLEGE

West Avenue, Iloilo City, Iloilo 5000
Tel: +63(33) 337-9122
Fax: +63(33) 337-9122
EMail: roqueza@i-iloilo.com.ph; community@idc.edu.ph
Website: http://www.idc.edu.ph/

President: Alejandro A. Rivera, Jr.

Colleges

Arts and Sciences (Biological and Life Sciences; Social Work); **Commerce** (Banking; Business and Commerce; Finance; Management; Secretarial Studies); **Criminology** (Criminology); **Information Technology** (Computer Engineering; Computer Science; Information Management; Information Technology); **Medicine** *(Iloilo Doctors' College of Medicine is affiliated to Iloilo Doctors' College)* (Medicine); **Nursing** (Nursing); **Paramedicine** (Medical Technology; Paramedical Sciences; Radiology)

Schools

Dentistry (Dentistry); **Midwifery** (Midwifery); **Physical Therapy** (Physical Therapy)

Further Information: Iloilo Doctors' College of Medicine affiliated to Iloilo Doctors' College

History: Founded 1972.

Degrees and Diplomas: *Certificate/Diploma*; *Associate Degree*; *Bachelor's Degree*; *Post Baccalaureate Certificate/Diploma*
Last Updated: 07/10/10

IMMACULADA CONCEPCION COLLEGE

Miramonte Avenue, Soldier's Hills III Subd., Tala, Caloocan City, Third District, Metro Manila 1427
Tel: +63(2) 937-5428 +63(2) 721-4777
Fax: +63(2) 721-2982

President: Mercedes Molina

Programmes

Business Administration (Banking; Business Administration; Business Computing; Finance; Management; Marketing); **Computer Science** (Computer Science); **Education** (Education; English; Foreign Languages Education; Mathematics Education; Primary Education; Secondary Education)

History: Founded 1984.

Degrees and Diplomas: *Associate Degree*; *Bachelor's Degree*
Last Updated: 07/10/10

IMMACULADA CONCEPCION (SOLDIER'S HILLS) COLLEGES

Soldiers Hills IV, Molino, Bacoor, Cavite 4102
Tel: +63(46) 572-0867
Fax: +63(02) 7212982
EMail: icc_cavite@yahoo.com; iccshiv@cavite.inExt.net

President: Mercedes Molina

Programmes

Undergraduate and Professional (Business Administration; Computer Engineering; Computer Science; Secretarial Studies)

History: Founded 1992.

Degrees and Diplomas: *Associate Degree*; *Bachelor's Degree*
Last Updated: 07/10/10

IMMACULATE CONCEPTION ARCHDIOCESAN SCHOOL

Fr. Barua Street, Tetuan, Zamboanga City, Zamboanga del Sur 7000
Tel: +63(62) 991-2490
Fax: +63(62) 991-2774
EMail: icastetuanschool@yahoo.com

Director: David Alonzo

Programmes

Undergraduate and Professional (Accountancy; Business Administration; Business and Commerce; Finance; Hotel and Restaurant; Hotel Management; Management; Marketing; Mass Communication; Philosophy)

History: Founded 1980.

Degrees and Diplomas: *Bachelor's Degree*
Last Updated: 07/10/10

IMMACULATE CONCEPTION COLLEGE - ALBAY

Rizal Street, Daraga, Albay 4501
Tel: +63(52) 824-1074
Fax: +63(52) 824-1789
EMail: icc_albay@yahoo.com

President: Belen Baylon Francisco

Programmes

Undergraduate and Professional (Environmental Management; Environmental Studies; Hotel and Restaurant; Hotel Management; Midwifery; Nursing)

History: Founded 1963. Formerly Baylon Memorial Colleges (Daraga, Albay).

Degrees and Diplomas: *Certificate/Diploma*; *Bachelor's Degree*
Last Updated: 07/10/10

IMMACULATE CONCEPTION COLLEGE - BALAYAN

Plaza Mabini, Balayan, Batangas 4213
Tel: +63(43) 211-4363
Fax: +63(43) 211-4363

Director: Modesta San Jose, AR

Programmes

Business Administration (Accountancy; Business Administration; Business and Commerce; Finance; Management; Secretarial Studies); **Computer Studies** (Computer Engineering; Computer Science); **Education** (Education; English; Filipino; Foreign Languages Education; History; Home Economics Education; Mathematics Education; Native Language Education; Primary Education; Secondary Education); **English** (English); **Hotel and Restaurant Management** (Hotel and Restaurant; Hotel Management); **Information Management** (Information Management)

History: Founded 1935, acquired present status and title 1955.

Degrees and Diplomas: *Certificate/Diploma*; *Associate Degree*; *Bachelor's Degree*
Last Updated: 20/10/10

IMMACULATE HEART OF MARY COLLEGE - PARAÑAQUE

Dominic Savio Street, Better Living Subd, City of Parañaque, Fourth District, Metro Manila 1711
Tel: +63(2) 823-4109
Fax: +63(2) 823-5628
EMail: immaculate_college@yahoo.com

Director: Lydia D. Canon, SFSCF

Programmes

Undergraduate and Professional (Accountancy; Business Administration; Education; English; Foreign Languages Education; Information Technology; Management; Marketing; Preschool Education; Primary Education; Psychology; Secondary Education)

History: Founded 1979. Formerly Immaculate Heart of Mary School.

Degrees and Diplomas: *Bachelor's Degree*
Last Updated: 20/10/10

IMUS INSTITUTE

Nueno Avenue, Imus, Cavite 4103
Tel: +63(46) 471-2997
Fax: +63(46) 471-2555
EMail: info@imusinstitute.edu.ph

President: Encarnacion N. Ranalio

Programmes

Undergraduate and Professional (Accountancy; Business and Commerce; Business Computing; Child Care and Development; English; Filipino; Finance; Foreign Languages Education; Hotel and Restaurant; Hotel Management; Human Resources; Information Technology; Management; Marketing; Native Language Education; Primary Education; Special Education; Tourism)

History: Founded 1952.

Degrees and Diplomas: *Associate Degree*; *Bachelor's Degree*
Last Updated: 20/10/10

INDIANA SCHOOL OF AERONAUTICS

Magellan Business Park, Kagudoy Road, Basak, Lapu-Lapu City, Cebu 6015
Tel: +63(32) 340-0771
Fax: +63(32) 341-0098
EMail: Indiana@col.net.ph

President: Jovenal B. Toring

Programmes

Undergraduate and Professional Studies (Aeronautical and Aerospace Engineering; Air Transport; Computer Science; Hotel and Restaurant; Hotel Management; Maintenance Technology; Management; Primary Education; Secondary Education; Taxation; Tourism; Transport Engineering; Transport Management)

History: Founded 1993.

Degrees and Diplomas: *Bachelor's Degree*: 4-5 yrs
Last Updated: 20/10/10

INFORMATICS COLLEGE CALOOCAN

380 Rizal Avenue Ext. Cor. 11th Avenue, Grace Park, Caloocan City, Third District, Metro Manila 1400
Tel: +63(2) 365-2361
Fax: +63(2) 363-7010
Website: http://www.informatics.edu.ph

President: Ramon Mitra

Programmes

Undergraduate and Professional (Business Computing; Computer Science; Information Technology; Software Engineering)

History: Founded 1999. Formerly known as Informatics Kalookan Computer Institute.

Degrees and Diplomas: *Certificate/Diploma*; *Bachelor's Degree*
Last Updated: 20/10/10

INFORMATICS COLLEGE EASTWOOD

Orchard Road, Bagumbayan Libis, Quezon City, Second District, Metro Manila
Tel: +63(2) 667-30-92
Fax: +63(2) 667-30-92
Website: http://www.informatics.edu.ph

President: Leonardo A. Riingen

Programmes

Business Administration (Business Administration; Finance; Marketing); **Computer Science** (Computer Science); **Information Management** (Information Management); **Information Technology** (Information Technology)

History: Founded 1993. Formerly Informatics College Ortigas.

Degrees and Diplomas: *Bachelor's Degree*
Last Updated: 20/10/10

INFORMATICS COLLEGE MANILA

1882 Tandem Bldg., C.M. Recto Ave., Manila, Metro Manila
Tel: +63(2) 313-0081 +63(2) 313-0084
Fax: +63(2) 313-0080
EMail: ihe@informatics.com.ph
Website: http://www.informatics.edu.ph

President: Leonardo A. Ringler
EMail: president@informatics.com.ph

Programmes

ICT (Computer Graphics; Computer Networks; Computer Science; Data Processing)

History: Founded 1995.

Degrees and Diplomas: *Bachelor's Degree*: 4 yrs
Last Updated: 28/03/11

INFORMATICS COLLEGE NORTHGATE

Indo-China Drive, Northgate Cyberzone, Filinvest Corporate City, Alabang, City of Muntinlupa, Fourth District, Metro Manila
Tel: +63(2) 772-2472
Fax: +63(2) 772-2476
Website: http://www.informatics.edu.ph

President: Leonardo A. Riingen

Programmes

Business Administration (Business Administration; Finance; Marketing); **Computer Studies** (Computer Networks; Computer Science; Multimedia; Software Engineering); **Information Management and Technology** (Information Management; Information Technology)

History: Founded 1995. Formerly known as Informatics International College (2001-2003).

Degrees and Diplomas: *Bachelor's Degree*
Last Updated: 20/10/10

INFORMATICS COLLEGE QUEZON CITY

29 North Avenue, North EDSA, Quezon City, Second District, Metro Manila 1015
Tel: +63(2) 925-5640
Fax: +63(2) 925-5202
EMail: iic_quezoncity@informatics.com.ph
Website: http://www.informatics.edu.ph

President: Daniel A. Ongchoco

Programmes

Undergraduate and Professional (Business Administration; Computer Engineering; Computer Networks; Computer Science; Information Management; Information Technology; Marketing; Multimedia; Software Engineering)

History: Founded 1995.

Degrees and Diplomas: *Associate Degree*; *Bachelor's Degree*: 4 yrs
Last Updated: 28/03/11

INFORMATICS COMPUTER INSTITUTE - UPTOWN CEBU

General Maxilom Avenue, Cebu City, Cebu 6000
EMail: ucicii@yahoo.com
Website: http://www.informaticsgroup.com

Vice-President, Administration: Maria Teresa T. Celis

Programmes

Computer Science (Computer Science)
History: Founded 2001.
Degrees and Diplomas: *Bachelor's Degree*
Last Updated: 20/10/10

INFORMATICS INTERNATIONAL COLLEGE - RIZAL

The Brick Road, Sta Lucia East Grand Mall, Cainta, Rizal 1900
Tel: +(63) 645-5270
EMail: iic-cainta@informatics.com.ph
Website: http://www.informatics.com.ph

President: Daniel Ongchoco

Programmes

Undergraduate and Professional (Business Administration; Computer Science; Information Technology; Marketing)
Degrees and Diplomas: *Bachelor's Degree*
Last Updated: 11/03/11

INFORMATION AND COMMUNICATIONS TECHNOLOGY ACADEMY

3rd Floor, Phil First Bldg, 6764 Ayala Avenue, City of Makati, Fourth District, Metro Manila 1226
Tel: +63(2) 891-3865
Fax: +63(2) 891-3727
EMail: inquire@iacademy.ph

Chief Operating Officer: Reuel Virtucio

Programmes

Undergraduate and Professional (Business Administration; Computer Science; Information Technology)
History: Founded 2003.
Degrees and Diplomas: *Bachelor's Degree*
Last Updated: 20/10/10

INNOVATIVE COLLEGE OF SCIENCE AND TECHNOLOGY

Malitbog, Bongabong, Oriental Mindoro 5211
Tel: +63(43) 283-5521
Fax: +63(43) 283-5561
EMail: icst_2004@yahoo.com.ph

President: Anthony L. Yap

Programmes

Civil Engineering (Civil Engineering); **Commerce** (Accountancy; Business and Commerce); **Criminology** (Criminology); **Education** (Child Care and Development; Education; English; Filipino; Mathematics Education; Native Language Education; Preschool Education; Primary Education; Secondary Education); **Hospitality Management** (Hotel and Restaurant; Hotel Management; Tourism); **Information Technology** (Information Technology)
History: Founded 2004.
Degrees and Diplomas: *Bachelor's Degree*
Last Updated: 20/10/10

INSTITUTE OF BUSINESS, SCIENCE AND MEDICAL ARTS

Francisco Street, Pinamalayan, Oriental Mindoro 5208
Tel: +63(43) 284-3056
Fax: +63(43) 284-3056
EMail: ibsma_2003@yahoo.com

President: Dennis B. Mambil

Programmes

Undergraduate and Professional (Information Technology; Midwifery)
History: Founded 2003.
Degrees and Diplomas: *Bachelor's Degree*
Last Updated: 20/10/10

INSTITUTE OF COMMUNITY AND FAMILY HEALTH, INC.

4th flr. Medical Arts Bldg, 11 Banawe cor. Cardiz St.Barangay Doña Josefa, Quezon City, Second District, Metro Manila 1113
Tel: +63(2) 712-0815
Fax: +63(2) 712-0815
EMail: icfh_inc@yahoo.com
Website: http://www.geocities.com/icfhi_ph

Executive Director and Dean: Remigio D. Mercado

Programmes

Public Health (Community Health; Public Health)
History: Founded 1993.
Degrees and Diplomas: *Master's Degree*: Public Health
Last Updated: 20/10/10

INTERCITY COLLEGE OF SCIENCE & TECHNOLOGY

Araullo Ext. Street, Davao City, Davao del Sur 8000
Tel: +63(82) 222-9766 +63(82) 222-9769
Fax: +63(82) 222-9767
EMail: intercity_edu@gmail.com

Administrator: Ma. Riza F. Dayrit

Programmes

Undergraduate and Professional (Computer Science; Information Management; Information Technology; Management; Nursing)
History: Founded 2005. Formerly known as Davao Informatics Computer Institute.
Degrees and Diplomas: *Certificate/Diploma*; *Bachelor's Degree*
Last Updated: 20/10/10

INTERFACE COMPUTER COLLEGE

1881 Henry Yang Complex, C.M. Recto Avenue, Sampaloc, Manila, First District, Metro Manila 1001
Tel: +63(2) 736-3912
Fax: +63(2) 736-4150
EMail: info@interface.edu.ph
Website: http://www.interface.edu.ph

President: Jaime B. Espadilla

Campuses

Caloocan (Business Administration; Business Computing; Computer Education; Computer Science; Information Management; Information Technology); **Cebu** (Computer Science; Hotel and Restaurant; Hotel Management; Information Management; Information Technology); **Iloilo** (Business Administration; Business and Commerce; Computer Engineering; Computer Science; Information Management; Information Technology; Software Engineering); **Manila** (Business Administration; Business Computing; Computer Engineering; Computer Science; Information Management; Information Technology)
Further Information: Traditional and Open Learning Institution. Also campuses in Cabanatuan and Davao
History: Founded 1982. Acquired present status and title 1994.
Degrees and Diplomas: *Certificate/Diploma*; *Associate Degree*; *Bachelor's Degree*
Last Updated: 20/10/10

INTER-GLOBAL MARITIME COLLEGE

Brgy. Bocohan, Lucena City, Quezon 4301
Tel: +63(42) 660-3632
Fax: +63(42) 660-5074
EMail: igcfi@yahoo.com

President: Carmencita L. Medina

Programmes

Undergraduate and Professional (Hotel and Restaurant; Hotel Management; Marine Transport; Taxation)

History: Founded 1996.

Degrees and Diplomas: *Associate Degree*; *Bachelor's Degree*
Last Updated: 20/10/10

INTERNATIONAL ACADEMY OF MANAGEMENT AND ECONOMICS (IAME)

1061, Metropolitan Avenue, San Antonio Village, Makati City, Metro Manila 1203
Tel: +63 896-2358 +63 896-2318
Fax: +63 896-2351
EMail: chairman@iame.edu.ph
Website: http://www.iame.edu.ph

Chairman and Chief Executive Officer: Emmanuel T. Santos (1985-)

Vice-President: Primavera S. Donohue
EMail: psdonohue@sbcglobal.net

Graduate Schools

Graduate Studies (Management)

Institutes

Strategic and International Studies (International Studies)

Schools

Management and Economics (Economics; Finance; Human Resources; Management; Marketing)

History: Founded 1978 as International University Foundation. Acquired present status and title 1985.

Governing Bodies: Board of Trustees; International Advisory Council

Admission Requirements: High school diploma

Fees: (US Dollars): Bachelor's Degree, 5,488; Master's Degree, 1,660; Ph.D., 2,800

Main Language(s) of Instruction: English

International Co-operation: With universities in USA, United Kingdom, Switzerland, Australia

Degrees and Diplomas: *Certificate/Diploma*; *Bachelor's Degree*; *Master's Degree*: Business Administration; Management, Thesis and Non-Thesis; *PhD*: Management

Student Services: Academic counselling, Canteen, Employment services, Foreign student adviser, Foreign Studies Centre, Handicapped facilities, Health services, Language programs, Social counselling, Sports facilities

Student Residential Facilities: Hostel; Condominium units

Special Facilities: TV Studio; Theatre

Publications: IAME Journal of Management, Law & Economics, Research works *(annually)*; Manila Observer, Magazine *(other/irregular)*

Press or Publishing House: IAME Design Studio; The Printing Press
Last Updated: 20/10/10

INTERNATIONAL BAPTIST COLLEGE

474 Arayat Street, Brgy. Malamig, City of Mandaluyong, Third District, Metro Manila 1550
Tel: +63(2) 533-6378 +63(2) 533-0090
Fax: +63(2) 531-4227
EMail: ibc@ibc.org.ph
Website: http://www.ibc.org.ph

President: Gavino S. Tica

Programmes

Arts *(Bachelor of Arts programme)* (Economics; English; Psychology; Religious Education; Theology); **Education** (Education; English; Filipino; Foreign Languages Education; History; Mathematics Education; Native Language Education; Preschool Education); **Information Technology** (Information Technology)

History: Founded 1972.

Degrees and Diplomas: *Bachelor's Degree*
Last Updated: 20/10/10

INTERNATIONAL CHRISTIAN COLLEGES

Upper Tadiangan, Tuba, Benguet 2603
Tel: +63(74) 445-6479
Fax: +63(74) 445-6480
EMail: bbcc594@hanmail.net

President: Rosalia D. Guadaña

Programmes

Education (Education; English; Foreign Languages Education; Mathematics Education; Preschool Education; Primary Education; Secondary Education); **Social Work** (Social Work)

Degrees and Diplomas: *Bachelor's Degree*
Last Updated: 20/10/10

INTERNATIONAL COLLEGE OF EXCELLENCE

Poblacion, Urdaneta City, Pangasinan 2428
EMail: ice2007_urdanetapangasinan@yahoo.com

President: Danilo B. Lim

Programmes

Business Administration (Business Administration; Economics; Finance; Human Resources; Management; Marketing); **Education** (Education; English; Filipino; Foreign Languages Education; Health Education; Mathematics Education; Music Education; Native Language Education; Physical Education; Primary Education; Secondary Education; Technology Education)

Degrees and Diplomas: *Bachelor's Degree*
Last Updated: 20/10/10

INTERNATIONAL COLLEGES OF ASIA

Tambac, Pangasinan 2400
Tel: +63(75) 515-3250
Fax: +63(75) 522-8173
EMail: ica@angasinan.net

President: Andres Justino F. Abalos

Programmes

Education (English; Filipino; Foreign Languages Education; Mathematics Education; Native Language Education; Primary Education; Secondary Education); **Engineering** (Electrical Engineering; Mechanical Engineering); **Marine Transport** (Marine Transport)

History: Founded 1976. Formerly known as International Maritime and Technical Institute Foundation (1992-2001).

Degrees and Diplomas: *Bachelor's Degree*: 4 yrs; *Bachelor's Degree*: Engineering, 5 yrs
Last Updated: 20/10/10

INTERNATIONAL PEACE LEADERSHIP COLLEGE

Maya-maya Drive Corner Santana Drive, Victoria Valley Subd., Antipolo City, Rizal 1870
Tel: +63(2) 658-4875
Fax: +63(2) 658-0067

President: Celso C. Talaba

Programmes

Business Administration (Business Administration; Human Resources; Management; Marketing); **Journalism** (Journalism); **Philosophy** (Philosophy); **Political Sciences** (Political Sciences); **Secondary Education** (English; Ethics; Foreign Languages Education; Secondary Education)

History: Founded 2004. Formerly UTS-Asia.

Degrees and Diplomas: *Bachelor's Degree*
Last Updated: 21/10/10

INTERNATIONAL SCHOOL OF ASIA AND THE PACIFIC

Alimannao Hills, Peñablanca, Cagayan 3502
Tel: +63(78) 844-1010
Fax: +63(78) 844-1010
EMail: mcnp_isap@yahoo.com

President: Ronald P. Guzman

Programmes
Business Administration (Business Administration); **Criminology** (Criminology); **Customs Administration** (Taxation); **Hotel and Restaurant Management** (Hotel and Restaurant; Hotel Management); **Information Technology** (Information Technology); **Public Administration** (Public Administration); **Secondary Education** (Secondary Education); **Social Work** (Social Work)

History: Founded 1998.

Degrees and Diplomas: *Bachelor's Degree*
Last Updated: 21/10/10

INTERWORLD COLLEGE OF TECHNOLOGY FOUNDATION - TARLAC

Ninoy Aquino Avenue, Tibag, City of Tarlac, Tarlac 2300
Tel: +63(45) 982-6551 +63(45) 982-7138
Fax: +63(45) 982-6252 +63(45) 982-1928
EMail: interworldcolleges_tarlac@yahoo.com

President: Edwin Sagun

Programmes
Accountancy (Accountancy); **Business Administration** (Business Administration); **Computer Science** (Computer Science); **Criminology** (Criminology); **Elementary Education** (Primary Education); **Hotel and Restaurant Management** (Hotel and Restaurant; Hotel Management); **Liberal Arts** (Arts and Humanities); **Secondary Education** (Secondary Education)

History: Founded 1998.

Degrees and Diplomas: *Certificate/Diploma*; *Bachelor's Degree*
Last Updated: 21/10/10

INTERWORLD COLLEGES FOUNDATION INCORPORATED - PANIQUI

Burgos Street, Paniqui, Tarlac 2307
Tel: +63(45) 931-1031
Fax: +63(45) 931-0652 +63(45) 931-1077
EMail: icf-p@comclark.com

President: Eleanor C. Coliamco EMail: eleanorc@mozcom.com

Programmes
Business Administration (Accountancy; Business Administration; Finance; Management); **Computer Science** (Computer Science); **Education** (English; Filipino; Foreign Languages Education; Health Education; History; Mathematics Education; Native Language Education; Primary Education; Secondary Education)

History: Founded 1991.

Degrees and Diplomas: *Certificate/Diploma*; *Associate Degree*; *Bachelor's Degree*
Last Updated: 21/10/10

IRENE B. ANTONIO TECHNOLOGICAL COLLEGE

Brgy Salawagan, Quezon, Bukidnon 8715
Tel: +63(88)828-1337
Fax: +63(88)828-1337

President: Irene B. Antonio EMail: irenebantonio@yahoo.com

Programmes
Criminology (Criminology); **Entrepreneurship** (Management); **Primary Education** (Primary Education); **Public Administration** (Public Administration)

History: Founded 2005.

Degrees and Diplomas: *Bachelor's Degree*
Last Updated: 21/10/10

ISABELA COLLEGE OF ARTS AND TECHNOLOGY

Tagaran, City of Cauayan, Isabela 3305
Tel: +63(78) 652-1038
Fax: +63(78) 652-1038

President: Andy Domingo

Programmes
Computer Science (Computer Science); **Criminology** (Criminology); **Hotel and Restaurant Management** (Hotel and Restaurant; Hotel Management); **Information Technology** (Information Technology); **Marine Engineering** (Marine Engineering); **Marine Transportation** (Marine Transport); **Mechanical Engineering** (Mechanical Engineering)

History: Founded 1996. Formerly Isabela Maritime Institute of Technology.

Degrees and Diplomas: *Certificate/Diploma*; *Bachelor's Degree*
Last Updated: 21/10/10

ISABELA COLLEGES

Don Jose Africano, City of Cauayan, Isabela 3305
Tel: +63(918) 200-8969
Fax: +63(78) 652-2312

President: Arturo R. Toledo

Programmes
Arts and Humanities (Arts and Humanities); **Business Administration** (Accountancy; Business Administration; Public Administration); **Computer Studies** (Computer Engineering; Computer Science); **Criminology** (Criminology); **Education** (Business Education; Education; Primary Education; Secondary Education); **Information Technology** (Information Technology); **Philosophy** (Philosophy)

History: Founded 1948.

Degrees and Diplomas: *Associate Degree*; *Bachelor's Degree*; *Master's Degree*: Education; Business Administration; Public Administration; *PhD*: Education; Philosophy
Last Updated: 21/10/10

ISHRM SCHOOL SYSTEM

Bacoor, Cavite 4102
Tel: +63(46) 870-1451
Fax: +63(46) 870-1451

President: Alexander T. Gramaje

Programmes
Business Administration (Business Administration); **Hotel and Restaurant** (Hotel and Restaurant; Hotel Management)

History: Founded 2004.

Degrees and Diplomas: *Bachelor's Degree*
Last Updated: 26/10/10

JAMIATU MARAWI AL-ISLAMIA FOUNDATION

Upper Marinaut, Marawi City, Lanao del Sur 9700
Tel: +63(63) 352-0237

President: Rashid D. Sampaco

Programmes
Undergraduate and Professional Studies (Accountancy; Arts and Humanities; Business and Commerce; English; Filipino; Foreign Languages Education; History; Native Language Education; Nursing; Political Sciences; Primary Education; Secondary Education)

History: Founded 1994.

Degrees and Diplomas: *Bachelor's Degree*: Arts; Education; Commerce; Nursing
Last Updated: 26/10/10

JAMIATU MUSLIM MINDANAO

Darrusalam, Matampay, Marawi City, Lanao del Sur 9700

President: Alim Zainal Abedin Salih

Programmes
Graduate (Education; Public Administration); **Undergraduate and Professional** (Business and Commerce; English; Filipino; Foreign Languages Education; Management; Mathematics Education; Native Language Education; Primary Education; Secondary Education; Social Studies)
History: Founded 1987.
Degrees and Diplomas: *Bachelor's Degree*; *Master's Degree*: Education, Public Administration
Last Updated: 26/10/10

JAMIATUL PHILIPPINE AL-ISLAMIA

Amai-Manabilang Street, Raya Madaya, Marawi City, Lanao del Sur 9700
Tel: +63(63) 520-136
EMail: jpi50@yahoo.com

President: Abdulgafuur Madki Alonto

Programmes
Graduate Studies (Education; Public Administration); **Undergraduate and Professional Studies** (Accountancy; Business and Commerce; Computer Science; Criminology; Educational Sciences; English; Filipino; Foreign Languages Education; Islamic Law; Management; Mathematics Education; Native Language Education; Political Sciences; Primary Education; Public Administration; Secondary Education; Social Work)
History: Founded 1950. Formerly Kamilol Islam Colleges (1956-1963).
Degrees and Diplomas: *Bachelor's Degree*; *Master's Degree*: Education; Public Administration
Last Updated: 26/10/10

JESUS IS LORD COLLEGES FOUNDATION

101, Bunlo, Bocaue, Bulacan 3018
Tel: +63(44) 692-1894
Fax: +63(44) 692-1867
EMail: jilcf@hotmail.com

President: Eduardo C. Villanueva

Programmes
Arts and Humanities (Arts and Humanities; Psychology); **Commerce and Business Administration** (Banking; Business Administration; Business and Commerce; Finance; Management); **Elementary Education** (Primary Education; Science Education); **Secondary Education** (English; Filipino; Foreign Languages Education; Mathematics Education; Native Language Education; Science Education; Secondary Education; Social Studies)
History: Founded 1983. Formerly Jesus Is Lord Christian School (1983-1997).
Degrees and Diplomas: *Bachelor's Degree*
Last Updated: 26/10/10

JESUS REIGNS CHRISTIAN COLLEGE FOUNDATION, INC.

811 Julio Nakpil Street, Malate, City of Manila, First District, Metro Manila
Tel: +63(2) 307-0883
Fax: +63(2) 400-3820
EMail: jesusreignscc@yahoo.com

President: Ligaya B. Javier

Programmes
Undergraduate and Professional (Business Administration; Education; English; Foreign Languages Education; Information Technology; Management; Preschool Education; Primary Education; Psychology; Secondary Education)
History: Founded 2005.
Degrees and Diplomas: *Bachelor's Degree*
Last Updated: 26/10/10

J & K INTERNATIONAL COLLEGE

Angeles City, Pampanga
Tel: +63(45) 893-4048
Fax: +63(45) 893-4048

President: Florencia Marfil

Programmes
Education (Education; English; Foreign Languages Education; Physical Education; Secondary Education); **Hotel and Restaurant Management** (Hotel and Restaurant; Hotel Management)
Degrees and Diplomas: *Bachelor's Degree*
Last Updated: 26/10/10

J.P. SIOSON GENERAL HOSPITAL AND COLLEGES

75 Bukidnon Street, Bagong Bantay, Quezon City, Second District, Metro Manila 1105
Tel: +63(2) 927-3683 +63(2) 455-4281
Fax: +63(2) 927-3683

President: Juanito P. Sioson

Programmes
Nursing and Midwifery (Midwifery; Nursing)
History: Founded 1991. Formerly J. P. Sioson Colleges, Inc. (1993-1996).
Degrees and Diplomas: *Associate Degree*; *Bachelor's Degree*
Last Updated: 26/10/10

JOHN B. LACSON COLLEGES FOUNDATION - AREVALO

Sto. Niño Sur, Arevalo, Iloilo City, Iloilo 5000
Tel: +63(33) 336-1080
Fax: +63(33) 336-1080
EMail: admin@jblcf-arevalo.com
Website: http://www.arevalo.jblfmu.edu.ph/

Administrator: Ralph L. Pador

Programmes
Graduate (Management; Marine Transport; Public Administration; Transport Management)
History: Founded 1948. Formerly Iloilo Maritime Academy (1948-1984).
Degrees and Diplomas: *Master's Degree*; *PhD*
Last Updated: 27/10/10

JOHN B. LACSON COLLEGES FOUNDATION - BACOLOD

Pauline Village, Bacolod City, Negros Occidental 6100
Tel: +63(34) 434-2278
Fax: +63(34) 434-2279
EMail: info@jblcf-bacolod.edu.ph
Website: http://www.jblcf-bacolod.edu.ph

Programmes
Undergraduate and Professional (Hotel and Restaurant; Hotel Management; Marine Engineering; Marine Transport; Taxation; Tourism)
History: Founded 1976.
Degrees and Diplomas: *Certificate/Diploma*; *Bachelor's Degree*
Last Updated: 27/10/10

JOHN B. LACSON FOUNDATION MARITIME UNIVERSITY - MOLO

M.H. Del Pilar Street, Iloilo City, Iloilo 5000
Tel: +63(35) 336-5451
Fax: +63(35) 336-5449
EMail: info@jblcf.fapenet.org

Administrator: Lorna Gellada

Programmes
Undergraduate and Professional (Business Administration; Information Technology; Marine Engineering; Marine Transport; Taxation; Transport Management)
History: Founded 1948.
Degrees and Diplomas: *Bachelor's Degree*
Last Updated: 27/10/10

JOHN BOSCO COLLEGE

La Salle Drive, Bislig City, Surigao del Sur 8311
Tel: +63(86) 853-3415
Fax: +63(86) 853-3415
EMail: jbosco_c@panabo.philcom.com.ph

Director: Ophelia S. Fugoso

Programmes
Arts and Humanities (English; Filipino); **Business Administration** (Business Administration; Business and Commerce; Finance; Management); **Computer Science** (Computer Science); **Education** (English; Foreign Languages Education; Mathematics Education; Native Language Education; Primary Education; Science Education; Secondary Education); **Information Technology** (Information Technology)
History: Founded 1963.
Degrees and Diplomas: *Bachelor's Degree*
Last Updated: 27/10/10

JOHN PAUL COLLEGE

MG Andaya Compound, Odiong, Roxas, Oriental Mindoro 5212
Tel: +63(43) 299-2240
EMail: jpc_roxas@yahoo.com

President: Manuel "Manny" G. Andaya

Programmes
Business Administration (Business Administration; Management); **Civil Engineering** (Civil Engineering); **Computer Science** (Computer Science); **Criminology** (Criminology); **Education** (Education; English; Foreign Languages Education; Mathematics Education; Primary Education; Secondary Education); **Political Sciences** (Political Sciences)
History: Founded 1998.
Degrees and Diplomas: *Associate Degree*; *Bachelor's Degree*
Last Updated: 27/10/10

JOHN PAUL II COLLEGE OF DAVAO

Ecoland, Matina, Davao City, Davao del Sur 8000
Tel: +63(82) 297-8755
Fax: +63(82) 299-3375
EMail: junlim07@yahoo.com

President: Ernesto C. Evangelista

Programmes
Business Administration (Accountancy; Business Administration; Economics; Finance; Human Resources; Management; Marketing); **Computer Science** (Computer Science); **Education** (Art Education; Health Education; Music Education; Physical Education; Primary Education; Secondary Education; Special Education); **Engineering** (Computer Engineering; Electrical Engineering; Electronic Engineering; Geological Engineering; Telecommunications Engineering); **Information Technology** (Information Technology); **Nursing** (Nursing)
History: Founded 2000.Formerly Philippine College of Innovative Education.
Degrees and Diplomas: *Bachelor's Degree*
Last Updated: 27/10/10

JOHN WESLEY COLLEGE

57 College Avenue, Tuguegarao City, Cagayan 3500
Tel: +63(78) 846-4084
EMail: jwc_tug@yahoo.com

President: Rodel M. Acdal

Programmes
Theology (Religious Music; Theology)
History: Founded 1989.
Degrees and Diplomas: *Bachelor's Degree*
Last Updated: 27/10/10

JOJI ILAGAN CAREER CENTER FOUNDATION

Gov.Chavez Street, Davao City, Davao del Sur 8000
Tel: +63(82) 227-5602
Fax: +63(82) 221-0315
EMail: jib@jibcareercenter.com
Website: http://www.jojiilagancareercenter.com/

President: Jose Edgar J. Ilagan

Programmes
Hotel and Restaurant Management (Hotel and Restaurant; Hotel Management; Tourism)
History: Founded 1982.
Degrees and Diplomas: *Bachelor's Degree*
Last Updated: 27/10/10

JOSE C. FELICIANO COLLEGE

Dau Expressway, Dau, Mabalacat, Pampanga 2010
Tel: +63(45) 331-2531 +63(45) 331-2531
Fax: +63(45) 331-2530
EMail: jcfc@mozcom.com

President: Angelina F. Paras

Programmes
Hotel and Restaurant Management (Hotel and Restaurant; Hotel Management); **Marine Transportation** (Marine Transport); **Nursing and Midwifery** (Midwifery; Nursing); **Secondary Education** (English; Foreign Languages Education; Secondary Education); **Tourism** (Management; Tourism)
History: Founded 1994. Formerly Jose C. Feliciano School of Science and Technology (1994-1995).
Degrees and Diplomas: *Bachelor's Degree*; *Post Baccalaureate Certificate/Diploma*
Last Updated: 27/10/10

JOSÉ MARIA COLLEGE

JC Comp., Phil-Japan Highway, Buhangin, Davao City, Davao del Sur 8000
Tel: +63(82) 234-7272
Fax: +63(82) 234-7272
Website: http://www.jmc.edu.ph

President: Apollo C. Quiboloy
Executive Vice-President: Ingrid C. Canada

Programmes
Arts and Science *(Bachelor in Arts and Science programmes)* (Civil Engineering; Computer Science; English; Information Technology; Mass Communication; Psychology; Theology); **Business Administration** (Accountancy; Business Administration; Finance; Management); **Education** (Education; English; Foreign Languages Education; Mathematics Education; Primary Education; Secondary Education)
History: Founded 2003.
Degrees and Diplomas: *Bachelor's Degree*
Last Updated: 27/10/10

JOSÉ NAVARRO POLYTECHNIC COLLEGE

200 Naghalin, Kananga, Leyte 6531
Tel: +63(53) 553-0087
Fax: +63(53) 553-0087

President: Erlinda N. Verendia

Programmes
Undergraduate and Professional (Agricultural Business; Banking; Business and Commerce; Computer Education; Finance; Hotel and Restaurant; Hotel Management; Information Technology; Management; Primary Education)
History: Founded 1990 as José Navarro Technical Centre. Acquired present title 2001.
Degrees and Diplomas: *Bachelor's Degree*
Last Updated: 27/10/10

JOSE RIZAL UNIVERSITY

80 Shaw Boulevard, Mandaluyong City, Third District, Metro Manila 1550
Tel: +63(2) 531-8031
Fax: +63(2) 531-6087
EMail: jru@jru.edu
Website: http://www.jru.edu

President: Vicente K. Fabella EMail: president@jru.edu

Colleges

Undergraduate and Professional (Accountancy; Business and Commerce; Computer Engineering; Computer Science; Economics; Education; English; Finance; Foreign Languages Education; History; Hotel and Restaurant; Hotel Management; Information Technology; Management; Marketing; Mathematics Education; Nursing; Primary Education; Secondary Education; Secretarial Studies)

Schools

Graduate Studies (Business Administration; Education; Government; Public Administration); **Law** (Law)

History: Founded 1919. Formerly Jose Rizal Colege (1922-2000). Acquired present status 2009.

Degrees and Diplomas: *Certificate/Diploma*; *Bachelor's Degree*; *Master's Degree*: Business Administration; Public Administration; Education; *PhD*: Business Administration; Public Administration
Last Updated: 27/10/10

KABANKALAN CATHOLIC COLLEGE

Guanzon Street, City of Kabankalan, Negros Occidental 6111
Tel: +63(34) 471-2479
Fax: +63(34) 471-2462

President: Patricio A. Buzon

Programmes

Undergraduate and Professional (Anthropology; Business and Commerce; Computer Science; Education; English; Filipino; Foreign Languages Education; Home Economics Education; Information Technology; Mathematics Education; Native Language Education; Philosophy; Primary Education; Religious Education; Secondary Education; Social Studies; Sociology; Technology Education)

History: Founded 1963.

Degrees and Diplomas: *Certificate/Diploma*; *Associate Degree*; *Bachelor's Degree*
Last Updated: 27/10/10

KALAYAAN COLLEGE

84 A. Bonifacio Avenue, Riverbanks Center, Barangka, City of Marikina, Second District, Metro Manila 1803
Tel: +63(2) 998-1724
Fax: +63(2) 934-4865
EMail: info@kalayaan.edu.ph
Website: http://www.kalayaan.edu.ph

President: José V. Abueva

Campuses

Bataan (Accountancy; Business Administration; Computer Engineering; Computer Science; Education; English; Finance; Foreign Languages Education; Management; Preschool Education; Primary Education; Public Administration; Secondary Education)

Divisions

Education (Child Care and Development; Education; Preschool Education; Primary Education; Secondary Education); **Humanities and Communication** (Fine Arts; Graphic Design; Journalism; Literature; Painting and Drawing); **Science and Technology** (Computer Engineering; Computer Science); **Social Sciences** (Accountancy; Business Administration; Hotel and Restaurant; Hotel Management; Psychology; Public Administration; Social Sciences)

History: Founded 2001.

Degrees and Diplomas: *Certificate/Diploma*; *Associate Degree*; *Bachelor's Degree*
Last Updated: 27/10/10

KALINGA COLLEGES OF SCIENCE AND TECHNOLOGY

Provincial Road, Purok 5, Bulanao, Tabuk, Kalinga 3800
EMail: kcst_2000@yahoo.com

President: Estella P. Dulin

Programmes

Computer Engineering (Computer Engineering); **Computer Science** (Computer Science); **Criminology** (Criminology); **Geodetic Engineering** (Geological Engineering); **Information Technology** (Information Technology); **Political Sciences** (Political Sciences)

History: Founded 2001.

Degrees and Diplomas: *Associate Degree*; *Bachelor's Degree*
Last Updated: 27/10/10

KALOS M.A. COLLEGE

28 Lower P. Burgos, Baguio City, Benguet 2600
Tel: +63(74) 442-1890

President: Brandino P. Bestre

Programmes

Education (Education; Information Technology; Primary Education; Secondary Education); **Theology** (Theology)

History: Founded 1998.

Degrees and Diplomas: *Bachelor's Degree*
Last Updated: 27/10/10

KESTER GRANT COLLEGE PHILIPPINES

1608 Quezon Avenue, Quezon City, Second District, Metro Manila 1106
Tel: +63(2) 928-9125
Fax: +63(2) 928-91-19

President: George U. Lim

Programmes

Business Administration (Business Administration; Management; Marketing); **Education** (Education; English; Foreign Languages Education; Mathematics Education; Primary Education; Science Education; Secondary Education); **Nursing** (Nursing)

History: Founded 2003.

Degrees and Diplomas: *Bachelor's Degree*
Last Updated: 27/10/10

KIDAPAWAN COLLEGE

Colegio de Kidapawan

Quezon Boulevard, Kidapawan City, North Cotabato 9400
Tel: +63(64) 288-1340
Fax: +63(64) 288-1340
EMail: cdkregistrar@yahoo.com.ph

President: Janice R. Mearns Martinez

Programmes

Undergraduate and Professional Studies (Business Administration; Computer Engineering; Computer Science; Criminology; Education; Electrical and Electronic Engineering; Hotel and Restaurant; Hotel Management; Information Technology; Midwifery; Nursing; Primary Education)

History: Founded 1986, aquiring present title and status in 2006.

Degrees and Diplomas: *Bachelor's Degree*
Last Updated: 08/09/10

KINGFISHER SCHOOL OF BUSINESS AND FINANCE

1131 McArthur Hi-way, Lucao, Pangasinan 2400
Tel: +63 (75) 515-4697
Fax: +63 (75) 515-4697
EMail: info@kingfisher.edu.ph; kingfisher@usatv1.net
Website: http://www.kingfisher.edu.ph

President: Augustues P. Lambino

Programmes
Accountancy (Accountancy); **Entrepreunership** (Management); **Finance** (Finance); **Management** (Accountancy; Finance; Information Management; Information Technology; Management); **Marketing** (Marketing)

History: Founded 2004.

Degrees and Diplomas: *Bachelor's Degree*
Last Updated: 27/10/10

KING'S COLLEGE OF ISULAN

Kalawag Extension, Isulan, Sultan Kudarat 9805
Tel: +63(64) 201-3386
Fax: +63(64) 201-3386
EMail: kci@peei.org; jaelbar@ndtc.fapenet.org

Director/College Dean: Elena G. Barker

Programmes
Undergraduate and Professional Studies (Business and Commerce; Data Processing; English; Filipino; Foreign Languages Education; Mathematics Education; Native Language Education; Primary Education; Secondary Education; Social Studies)

History: Founded 1958. Formerly Kalawag Institute (1958-1965).

Degrees and Diplomas: *Bachelor's Degree*
Last Updated: 27/10/10

KING'S COLLEGE OF MARBEL

Brgy. Morales, Koronadal City, South Cotabato 9506
Tel: +63(83) 228-5063

Head: Sonnie P. Laraño

Programmes
Undergraduate and Professional Studies (Agricultural Engineering; English; Filipino; Foreign Languages Education; Mathematics Education; Native Language Education; Preschool Education; Secondary Education)

History: Founded 1959.

Degrees and Diplomas: *Bachelor's Degree*
Last Updated: 27/10/10

KUTAWATO DARRUSALAM COLLEGE

Purok Zailon, NB Bagua, Campo Muslim, Cotabato City, Cotabato 9600
Tel: +63(64) 421-5914
Fax: +63(64) 421-5914
EMail: kutdar@yahoo.com

President: Abdullah Rastan K. Manan

Programmes
Education (Education; Primary Education; Social Studies)

History: Founded 1979. Formerly Mahad Kutawato College, Inc. (1979- 2002).

Degrees and Diplomas: *Bachelor's Degree*
Last Updated: 27/10/10

KUTAWATO INSTITUTE OF TECHNOLOGY FOUNDATION

Poblacion 8, Kakar Extension, Cotabato City, Cotabato 9600
Tel: +63(64) 390-2318

Administrator: Muslim K. Pananguilan

Programmes
Computer Science (Computer Science); **Education** (Primary Education; Secondary Education)

History: Founded 1992.

Degrees and Diplomas: *Certificate/Diploma*; *Bachelor's Degree*
Last Updated: 27/10/10

LAAK INSTITUTE FOUNDATION

Poblacion, Laak, Compostela Valley 8115
Tel: +63(84)217-3766
Fax: +63(84)217-3766

President: John E. Natavio

Programmes
Business Administration (Business Administration; Management; Marketing); **Education** (Biological and Life Sciences; Education; English; Foreign Languages Education; Mathematics Education; Primary Education; Secondary Education)

History: Founded 2006.

Degrees and Diplomas: *Bachelor's Degree*
Last Updated: 28/10/10

LA CONCEPCION COLLEGE

Francisco Avenue, City of San Jose del Monte, Bulacan 3023
Tel: +63(44) 691-7349 +63(44) 691-6347
EMail: laconcepcioncollege@yahoo.com

President: Francisco C. Magpantay

Programmes
Criminology (Criminology); **Education** (Education; Filipino; History; Mathematics Education; Native Language Education; Primary Education; Secondary Education; Social Studies)

History: Founded 1998.

Degrees and Diplomas: *Bachelor's Degree*
Last Updated: 27/10/10

LA CONSOLACION COLLEGE - BACOLOD

Galo-Gatuslao Streets, Bacolod City, Negros Occidental 6100
Tel: +63(34) 433-9664
Fax: +63(34) 433-0634
EMail: lcc-main@lcc-b.lasaltech.com
Website: http://www.lcc.lasaltech.com

President: Maria Myrna S.T. Concepcion, OSA

Programmes
Graduate (Accountancy; Business Administration; Education; Educational Administration; Educational Technology; English; Filipino; Foreign Languages Education; Human Resources; Literature; Mathematics Education; Native Language Education; Physical Education; Religious Studies; Science Education; Teacher Training); **Undergraduate and Professional** (Accountancy; Advertising and Publicity; Architecture; Architecture and Planning; Arts and Humanities; Business Administration; Business and Commerce; Communication Arts; Computer Science; Educational Administration; Ethics; Fine Arts; Hotel Management; Industrial Design; Interior Design; Mathematics Education; Painting and Drawing; Physical Education; Primary Education; Religious Education; Science Education; Secondary Education; Secretarial Studies; Teacher Training; Tourism)

History: Founded 1912.

Degrees and Diplomas: *Certificate/Diploma*; *Bachelor's Degree*; *Master's Degree*: Business Administration (Accountancy Management, Human Resources Management); Education (English/Literature, Filipino, Religious Studies, Science, Physical Education, Educational Technology, Mathematics, Educational Management)
Last Updated: 28/10/10

LA CONSOLACION COLLEGE - BAIS

Aglipay Street, Bais City, Negros Oriental 6206
EMail: lccbaiscity@yahoo.com

Director: Teresita Azañes, OSA

Programmes
Business Administration (Business Administration); **Education** (Curriculum; Education; English; Ethics; Filipino; Foreign Languages Education; Native Language Education; Primary Education; Secondary Education; Social Sciences); **Hotel and Restaurant Management** (Hotel and Restaurant; Hotel Management); **Information Technology** (Information Technology)

History: Founded 1947.

Degrees and Diplomas: *Bachelor's Degree*
Last Updated: 28/10/10

LA CONSOLACION COLLEGE - BIÑAN

Sto. Tomas, Biñan, Laguna 4024
Tel: +63(49) 512-7120
Fax: +63(49) 512-7120
EMail: lccbndirectress@lccbn.mozcom.com

Director: Ana Isabel V. Marcelo, OSA

Programmes

Undergraduate and Professional (Accountancy; Banking; Business and Commerce; Computer Education; Computer Science; Cooking and Catering; Educational and Student Counselling; English; Ethics; Filipino; Finance; Foreign Languages Education; History; Home Economics Education; Hotel and Restaurant; Hotel Management; Human Resources; Management; Marketing; Mathematics Education; Native Language Education; Natural Sciences; Psychology; Technology Education; Tourism)

History: Founded 1985.

Degrees and Diplomas: *Associate Degree*; *Bachelor's Degree*
Last Updated: 28/10/10

LA CONSOLACION COLLEGE - CALOOCAN

496 A. Mabini Street, Caloocan City, Third District, Metro Manila 1400
Tel: +63(2) 287-9703
Fax: +63(2) 287-0429
Website: http://www.lcc-c.edu.ph

President: Puri Alma Peña, OSA

Programmes

Undergraduate and Professional (Business Administration; Business Computing; Computer Education; Computer Science; Education; Ethics; Filipino; Hotel and Restaurant; Hotel Management; Information Management; Information Technology; Management; Marketing; Mathematics Education; Native Language Education; Nursing; Primary Education; Secondary Education; Tourism)

History: Founded 1940.

Degrees and Diplomas: *Bachelor's Degree*
Last Updated: 28/10/10

LA CONSOLACION COLLEGE - DAET

Froilan Pimentel Avenue, Daet, Camarines Norte 4600
Tel: +63(54) 571-2237 +63(54) 721-2181
Fax: +63(54) 721-1102
EMail: lcc-college-daet@yahoo.com

President: Cecilia C. Ibana, O.S.A.

Programmes

Graduate (Education; Educational Administration; Filipino; Native Language Education); **Undergraduate and Professional** (Accountancy; Business and Commerce; Computer Science; Education; Primary Education; Secondary Education; Tourism)

History: Founded 1948.

Degrees and Diplomas: *Certificate/Diploma*; *Associate Degree*; *Bachelor's Degree*; *Master's Degree*
Last Updated: 28/10/10

LA CONSOLACION COLLEGE - DEPARO

St. Peter Street, Villa Maria Subdivision, Caloocan City, Third District, Metro Manila 1420
Tel: +63(2) 935-81-82 +63(2) 930-8155
Fax: +63(2) 935-81-82

President: Gavina F. Barrera, OSA
EMail: srgbarreraosa@yahoo.com

Programmes

Business Administration (Business Administration); **Computer Science** (Computer Science); **Hotel and Restaurant Management** (Hotel and Restaurant; Hotel Management); **Tourism** (Tourism)

History: Founded 1995.

Degrees and Diplomas: *Bachelor's Degree*
Last Updated: 28/10/10

LA CONSOLACION COLLEGE - IRIGA CITY

San Francisco, Iriga City, Camarines Sur 4431
Tel: +63(54) 299-2340
Fax: +63(54) 655-0950
EMail: lcci-2004@yahoo.com
Website: http://www.lcci.edu.ph/lcci/default.asp

President: Adelina H. Segismundo, OSA

Programmes

Undergraduate and Professional (Computer Education; Computer Engineering; Computer Science; Cooking and Catering; Education; English; Foreign Languages Education; Hotel and Restaurant; Hotel Management; Mathematics Education; Primary Education; Science Education; Secondary Education; Tourism)

History: Founded 1949. Formerly La Consolacion Academy.

Degrees and Diplomas: *Bachelor's Degree*
Last Updated: 28/10/10

LA CONSOLACION COLLEGE - LA CARLOTA CITY

La Paz Street, La Carlota City, Negros Occidental 6130
Tel: +63(34) 460-2567
Fax: +63(34) 460-2215
EMail: laconsolacion_lacarlota@yahoo.com.ph

Director: Maria Corazon L. De Jesus, OSA

Programmes

Business Administration (Accountancy; Business Administration; Business and Commerce; Data Processing; Finance; Management); **Education** (Education; Filipino; Native Language Education; Primary Education; Secondary Education); **English** (English); **Hotel and Restaurant Management** (Hotel and Restaurant; Hotel Management); **Information Management and Technology** (Information Management; Information Technology)

History: Founded 1941.

Degrees and Diplomas: *Bachelor's Degree*
Last Updated: 28/10/10

LA CONSOLACION COLLEGE - LILOAN

Poblacion, Liloan, Cebu 6002
Tel: +63 564-2866
Fax: +63 564-2866
EMail: anajuan_lcc@yahoo.com

Director: Ma. Corazon Del Carmen, OSA

Programmes

Education (Education; English; Filipino; Foreign Languages Education; Mathematics Education; Native Language Education; Primary Education; Science Education; Secondary Education; Social Studies); **Information Technology** (Information Technology)

History: Founded 1965.

Degrees and Diplomas: *Bachelor's Degree*
Last Updated: 28/10/10

LA CONSOLACION COLLEGE - MANILA

8 Mendiola Street, San Miguel, Manila, First District, Metro Manila 1005
Tel: +63(2) 736-0235 +63(2) 313-0513
Fax: +63(2) 736-7602
EMail: lccm@lccm.edu.ph; admissionsoffice@lccm.edu.ph
Website: http://www.lccm.edu.ph

President: Ma. Imelda A. Mora, OSA

Institutes

International Culinary Arts (Cooking and Catering)

Schools

Arts and Science (Mass Communication; Psychology; Secondary Education); **Business** (Accountancy; Advertising and Publicity; Banking; Business Administration; Finance; Human Resources; International Business; Management; Marketing); **Graduate Studies** (Hotel and Restaurant; Hotel Management; Management; Technology; Tourism); **Hotel and Restaurant and Tourism Management** (Hotel and Restaurant; Hotel Management; Tourism);

Information Technology and Computer Studies (Computer Science; Information Management; Information Sciences; Information Technology); **Music** (Conducting; Jazz and Popular Music; Music; Music Theory and Composition; Musical Instruments; Religious Music; Singing); **Nursing** (Nursing)

History: Founded 1956.

Degrees and Diplomas: *Associate Degree*; *Bachelor's Degree*; *Master's Degree*: Technology and Entrepreneurship; Hotel and Tourism Management
Last Updated: 28/10/10

LA CONSOLACION COLLEGE - PASIG

641 Mercedes Avenue, San Miguel, City of Pasig, Second District, Metro Manila
Tel: +63(2) 641-8599
Fax: +63(2) 641-8599
EMail: info@lcc-p.edu.ph
Website: http://www.lcc-p.edu.ph

President: Editha S. Zerna, OSA EMail: sredith@lcc-p.edu.ph

Programmes

Undergraduate and Professional (Business Administration; Business and Commerce; Computer Science; Education; English; Foreign Languages Education; Hotel and Restaurant; Hotel Management; Human Resources; Management; Marketing; Nursing; Primary Education; Secondary Education)

History: Founded 1993.

Degrees and Diplomas: *Bachelor's Degree*
Last Updated: 28/10/10

LA CONSOLACION COLLEGE TANAUAN

Tanuan, Batangas 4232
Tel: +63(43) 778-1020
Fax: +63(43) 778-8850
EMail: OLFA_community@yahoo.com

President: Emilia Lacuarta, OSA

Programmes

Business Administration (Accountancy; Banking; Business Administration; Business Computing; Finance; Human Resources; Management; Marketing); **Education** (Biology; Child Care and Development; Education; English; Filipino; Foreign Languages Education; Mathematics Education; Native Language Education; Preschool Education; Primary Education); **Hospitality Management** (Hotel and Restaurant; Hotel Management; Tourism)

History: Founded 1948. Formerly Our Lady of Fatima Academy / College of Our Lady of Fatima.

Degrees and Diplomas: *Bachelor's Degree*
Last Updated: 28/10/10

LACSON COLLEGE

1852-C Taft Avenue, Pasay City, Fourth District, Metro Manila 1800
Tel: +63(2) 831-7423
Fax: +63(2) 831-7423

President: Rosalia G. Kapauan

Programmes

Undergraduate and Professional (Arts and Humanities; Business and Commerce; Criminology)

History: Founded 1938.

Degrees and Diplomas: *Bachelor's Degree*
Last Updated: 28/10/10

LADY OF LOURDES HOSPITAL AND COLLEGES OF CAYBIGA

15 Gen. Luis Street, Caybiga, Caloocan City, Third District, Metro Manila 1400
Tel: +63(2) 983-5581
Fax: +63(2) 984-1409

President: Erlinda B. Mauricio

Programmes

Business Administration (Management; Marketing); **Nursing** (Midwifery; Nursing); **Secondary Education** (Education; English; Foreign Languages Education; Secondary Education)

History: Founded 2004.

Degrees and Diplomas: *Bachelor's Degree*
Last Updated: 28/10/10

LADY OF PEÑAFRANCIA COLLEGE

Bagasbas Road, Daet, Camarines Norte 4600
Tel: +63(54) 721-5466
EMail: ladylpc83@yahoo.com

President: Nenita T. Sto. Domingo

Programmes

Hotel and Restaurant Management (Hotel and Restaurant; Hotel Management); **Secondary Education** (Biology; Computer Education; Secondary Education)

History: Founded 1983.

Degrees and Diplomas: *Certificate/Diploma*; *Bachelor's Degree*
Last Updated: 28/10/10

LA FORTUNA COLLEGE

1121 Del Pilar Street, Cabanatuan City, Nueva Ecija 3100
Tel: +63(44) 463-8465
Fax: +63(44) 463-8464
EMail: vino.job@yahoo.com

President: Carmelita G. Espinoza

Programmes

Business Administration (Business Administration); **Computer Engineering** (Computer Engineering); **Computer Science** (Computer Science); **Education** (Education; Primary Education); **Hotel and Restaurant Management** (Hotel and Restaurant; Hotel Management); **Mass Communication** (Mass Communication)

History: Founded 1995.

Degrees and Diplomas: *Associate Degree*; *Bachelor's Degree*
Last Updated: 28/10/10

LAGUNA COLLEGE

Paseo de Escudero, San Pablo City, Laguna 4000
Tel: +63(49) 562-8077 +63(49) 562-8078
Fax: +63(49) 562-8077
EMail: lcpride@skyinet.net

President: Gertrude S. Evangelista-Thomas

Programmes

Arts (Arts and Humanities; Economics; English); **Civil Engineering** (Civil Engineering); **Commerce** (Accountancy; Business and Commerce; Management; Marketing); **Computer Science** (Computer Science); **Education** (Education; English; Filipino; Foreign Languages Education; Health Education; Mathematics Education; Native Language Education; Primary Education; Public Administration; Science Education; Secondary Education); **Graduate Studies** (Business Administration; Education; Educational Administration; Management; Public Administration); **Industrial Engineering** (Industrial Engineering); **Nursing** (Nursing)

History: Founded 1923.

Degrees and Diplomas: *Certificate/Diploma*; *Associate Degree*; *Bachelor's Degree*; *Master's Degree*: Education (Administration and Supervision); Business Management; Public Administration
Last Updated: 28/10/10

LAGUNA COLLEGE OF BUSINESS AND ARTS

Burgos Street, Calamba City, Laguna 4027
Tel: +63(49) 545-4769 +63(49) 545-4766
Fax: +63(49) 545-3309
EMail: LCBARegistrar@yahoo.com

President: Cristina A. Ymson

Programmes

Graduate (Business Administration; Education; Educational Administration; Educational and Student Counselling; English;

Filipino; Foreign Languages Education; Management; Native Language Education; Psychology; Public Administration; Social Studies; Teacher Training); **Undergraduate and Professional** (Accountancy; Business Administration; Computer Education; Computer Engineering; Computer Science; Economics; Education; English; Filipino; Foreign Languages Education; Management; Marketing; Mathematics Education; Native Language Education; Political Sciences; Primary Education; Psychology; Secondary Education; Secretarial Studies; Social Studies)

History: Founded 1930 as Laguna Institute.

Degrees and Diplomas: *Certificate/Diploma*; *Bachelor's Degree*; *Master's Degree*
Last Updated: 28/10/10

LAGUNA NORTHWESTERN COLLEGE

194 Mabini Street, San Antonio, San Pedro, Laguna 4023
Tel: +63(49) 846-0738
Fax: +63(49) 846-0738
EMail: lnc_registrar@yahoo.com

President: Rolando A. Entilla

Centres
Corinthian (Business and Commerce; Education; Management; Primary Education; Secondary Education)

Programmes
Graduate (Business Administration; Education; Public Administration); **Undergraduate and Professional** (Accountancy; Business and Commerce; Computer Engineering; Computer Science; Education; Hotel and Restaurant; Hotel Management; Human Resources; Literature; Management; Nursing; Occupational Therapy; Philosophy; Physical Therapy; Primary Education; Psychology; Secondary Education)

History: Founded 1978.

Degrees and Diplomas: *Certificate/Diploma*; *Associate Degree*; *Bachelor's Degree*; *Master's Degree*: Business Administration; Public Administration; Education, a further 2 yrs
Last Updated: 28/10/10

LAGUNA SANTIAGO EDUCATIONAL FOUNDATION

F. Sario Street, Sta. Cruz, Laguna 4009
Tel: +63(49) 808-1431
Fax: +63(49) 810-1435
EMail: lagunasantiago@yahoo.com

President: Enrico Ariel T. Ting

Programmes
Undergraduate and Professional (Accountancy; Business Administration; Computer Science; Management)

History: Founded 1947.

Degrees and Diplomas: *Certificate/Diploma*; *Associate Degree*; *Bachelor's Degree*
Last Updated: 28/10/10

LAGUNA SCIENCE AND TECHNOLOGY COLLEGE

12 Sto. Niño, San Pedro, Laguna 4023
Tel: +63(2) 868-1347
Fax: +63(2) 868-1347
EMail: lti@stream.net.ph; lti@digitelone.com

President: Danilo A. Pelindario

Programmes
Undergraduate and Professional (Computer Science; Software Engineering; Technology; Technology Education)

History: Founded 1984. Formerly known as Laguna Technological Institute.

Degrees and Diplomas: *Certificate/Diploma*; *Bachelor's Degree*
Last Updated: 28/10/10

LAKE LANAO COLLEGE

Cabili Street, Marawi City, Lanao del Sur 9700

President: Taharoden Ampaso Wahab

Programmes
Arts (Islamic Law; Islamic Studies; Political Sciences); **Education** (Education; English; Foreign Languages Education; History; Primary Education; Secondary Education)

History: Founded 2003.

Degrees and Diplomas: *Bachelor's Degree*
Last Updated: 29/10/10

LANAO COLLEGE OF CRIMINOLOGY

Buadiamaloy, Masiu, Lanao del Sur

President: Nairah M. Macalawi

Programmes
Criminology (Criminology)

Degrees and Diplomas: *Bachelor's Degree*
Last Updated: 29/10/10

LANAO EDUCATIONAL INSTITUTE

Camp Jose Abad Santos, Malabang, Lanao del Sur 9300

President: Hadja Aisah D.R. Mikunug

Programmes
Arts and Science (Banking; Business and Commerce; English; Filipino; Finance; History; Mathematics; Political Sciences); **Education** (Education; Educational Administration; English; Filipino; Foreign Languages Education; History; Mathematics Education; Native Language Education; Primary Education; Secondary Education; Teacher Training); **Graduate Studies** (Education; Educational Administration; Teacher Training)

History: Founded 1986.

Degrees and Diplomas: *Bachelor's Degree*; *Master's Degree*: Education (Administration and Supervision)
Last Updated: 29/10/10

LANAO ISLAMIC PARAMEDICAL COLLEGE FOUNDATION

Sohaya Bldg. 2, Pumping Street, Marawi City, Lanao del Sur 9700
Tel: +63(63) 352-0329
EMail: lipci_188@yahoo.com

President: Sohaya M. Sampal

Programmes
Computer Science (Computer Science); **Education** (Education; Health Education; Primary Education; Secondary Education); **Nursing** (Nursing)

History: Founded 2005.

Degrees and Diplomas: *Bachelor's Degree*
Last Updated: 29/10/10

LANAO SCHOOL OF SCIENCE AND TECHNOLOGY

Maranding, Lanao del Norte 9211
Tel: +63(63) 388-7199
Fax: +63(63) 388-7199
EMail: rizalyntabanao@yahoo.com

President: Rizalyn M. Tabanao

Programmes
Commerce (Business and Commerce); **Computer Science** (Computer Science); **Education** (Education; English; Foreign Languages Education; Health Education; Mathematics Education; Primary Education; Secondary Education); **Nursing** (Nursing)

History: Founded 1998.

Degrees and Diplomas: *Associate Degree*; *Bachelor's Degree*
Last Updated: 29/10/10

LARMEN DE GUIA MEMORIAL COLLEGE

U.N. Avenue, Alang-alang, Mandaue City, Cebu 6014
Tel: +63(32) 344-8593
EMail: rois_lgmc@yahoo.com

President: Jose Mari L. De Guia

Programmes

Undergraduate and Professional Studies (Computer Engineering; English; Foreign Languages Education; Mathematics Education; Nursing; Physics; Primary Education; Science Education; Secondary Education; Special Education)

History: Founded 2003.

Degrees and Diplomas: *Bachelor's Degree*
Last Updated: 29/10/10

LA SALLE COLLEGE - ANTIPOLO

Bo. San Luis, Antipolo City, Rizal 1870
Tel: +63(2) 644-0506
Fax: +63(2) 644-2224

President: Crisanto M. Moreno, FSC

Programmes

Commerce (Accountancy; Banking; Business and Commerce; Economics; Finance; Management; Marketing); **Communication Studies** (Communication Studies); **Education** (Education; English; Foreign Languages Education; Primary Education; Secondary Education); **Hospitality Management** (Tourism); **Psychology** (Psychology)

History: Founded 1985. Formerly La Salle School Antipolo.

Degrees and Diplomas: *Bachelor's Degree*
Last Updated: 28/10/10

LA SALLE COLLEGE - VICTORIAS

Paz Avenue, Canetown Subdivision, Vicmico, City of Victorias, Negros Occidental 6119
Tel: +63(34) 198-5132
EMail: lasalle_victorias@yahoo.com

President: Gus Boquer

Programmes

Undergraduate and Professional (Accountancy; Business Administration; Business and Commerce; Computer Science; Data Processing; Finance)

History: Founded 1980. Formerly University of St. La Salle-Vicmico (1988-1992).

Degrees and Diplomas: *Associate Degree*; *Bachelor's Degree*
Last Updated: 28/10/10

LA SALLE UNIVERSITY

Valconcha Street, Ozamis City, Misamis Occidental
Tel: +63(88) 521-1010
Fax: +63(88) 521-1010
EMail: jerguiza@yahoo.com; icclasalle@ozamiz.com
Website: http://www.lsu.edu.ph

President: Narciso S. Erguiza Jr. FSC

Colleges

Accountancy (Accountancy; Taxation); **Arts and Science** (Communication Studies; Criminology; Economics; English; History; Information Sciences; Journalism; Library Science; Mathematics; Natural Sciences; Political Sciences; Psychology; Social Work); **Business and Economics** (Agricultural Business; Business Administration; Business Computing; Finance; Human Resources; Management; Marketing); **Computer Studies** (Computer Science; Information Technology); **Education** (Art Education; Biology; Chemistry; Computer Engineering; Education; English; Ethics; Filipino; Foreign Languages Education; Health Education; Mathematics Education; Music Education; Native Language Education; Physical Education; Physics; Preschool Education; Primary Education; Secondary Education; Social Studies; Special Education; Technology Education); **Engineering** (Civil Engineering; Computer Engineering; Electrical Engineering; Electronic Engineering; Engineering; Geological Engineering; Structural Architecture); **Nursing** (Midwifery; Nursing)

Programmes

Graduate Studies (Biology; Business Administration; Chemistry; Education; Educational Administration; Educational and Student Counselling; English; Filipino; Foreign Languages Education; Home Economics Education; Literature; Mathematics Education; Native Language Education; Nursing; Physical Education; Physics; Public Administration; Religious Education; Science Education; Social Studies)

Schools

Tourism and Hospitality Management (Hotel and Restaurant; Hotel Management; Tourism)

History: Founded 1929. Formerly Immaculate Conception College-La Salle; Immaculate Conception College; Immaculate Conception School. Acquired present status and title 2006.

Degrees and Diplomas: *Bachelor's Degree*; *Master's Degree*; *PhD*
Last Updated: 20/10/10

LA UNION COLLEGE OF NURSING (LUCN)

181 Purok 3 Biday, City of San Fernando, La Union 2500
Tel: +63(72) 888-5016
Fax: +63(72) 888-5199
EMail: lucn@sflu.com

President: Zenaida C. Finn

Programmes

Nursing (Nursing)

History: Founded 2003.

Degrees and Diplomas: *Bachelor's Degree*
Last Updated: 28/10/10

LA UNION COLLEGE OF SCIENCE AND TECHNOLOGY

Pezcadores Street, Bauang, La Union 2501
Tel: +63(72) 705-3922
Fax: +63(72) 705-3629
EMail: lucst_blu_06@yahoo.com.ph

President: Arturo C. Quinto

Programmes

Education (Education; English; Ethics; Filipino; Foreign Languages Education; Native Language Education; Secondary Education); **Hotel and Restaurant Management** (Hotel and Restaurant; Hotel Management); **Information Technology** (Information Technology)

History: Founded 2002.

Degrees and Diplomas: *Bachelor's Degree*
Last Updated: 28/10/10

LAS NAVAS COLLEGE

Colegio de Las Navas

Poblacion, H. Jolejole District, Las Navas, Northern Samar 6420

College Administrator: Gregorio M. Orsolino

Programmes

Business Administration (Business Administration); **Computer Science** (Computer Science); **Criminology** (Criminology); **Education** (Education; English; Foreign Languages Education; Primary Education; Secondary Education; Special Education)

History: Founded 2005.

Degrees and Diplomas: *Bachelor's Degree*
Last Updated: 08/09/10

LAS PIÑAS COLLEGE

Dr. Faustino L. Uy Avenue, Pilar Village, Almaza, City of Las Piñas, Fourth District, Metro Manila 1750
Tel: +63(2) 801-0245 +63(2) 800-3086
Fax: +63(2) 800-3086 +63(2) 805-60-06

President: Luz Co-Uy

Programmes

Graduate (Business Administration); **Undergraduate and Professional** (Banking; Business Administration; Economics; English; Filipino; Finance; History; Hotel and Restaurant; Hotel

Management; Industrial Engineering; Management; Marketing; Mechanical Engineering; Nursing; Political Sciences; Psychology)

History: Founded 1975.

Degrees and Diplomas: *Certificate/Diploma*; *Associate Degree*; *Bachelor's Degree*; *Master's Degree*: Business Administration

Last Updated: 29/10/10

L.D. WOOSLEY BETHANY COLLEGES

1714 Dian Street, Palanan, City of Makati, Fourth District, Metro Manila 1235

Tel: +63(2) 833-4576

Fax: +63(2) 831-4132

EMail: bethanymakati@yahoo.com

President: Gerardo G. Nalde

Programmes

Education (Education; English; Foreign Languages Education; Preschool Education; Primary Education; Secondary Education); **Theology** (Missionary Studies; Theology)

History: Founded 1999.

Degrees and Diplomas: *Certificate/Diploma*; *Bachelor's Degree*

Last Updated: 27/10/10

LEGACY COLLEGE OF COMPOSTELA

Población, Compostela, Compostela Valley 8115

Tel: +63(84) 822-0492

EMail: legacycomp@yahoo.com

President: Jovita R. Ancog

Programmes

Business Administration (Accountancy; Business Administration; Finance; Management); **Education** (English; Foreign Languages Education; Primary Education; Secondary Education)

History: Founded 1996. Formerly known as Philippine Institute of Medical Sciences and Technology.

Degrees and Diplomas: *Bachelor's Degree*

Last Updated: 29/10/10

LEMERY COLLEGES

055 WCC Bldg. Ilustre Avenue, Lemery, Batangas 4209

Tel: +63(43) 411-1887

Fax: +63(43) 411-1887

EMail: lemecoll@mozcom.com

President: Oscarito M. Hernandez

Programmes

Undergraduate and Professional (Business Administration; Business Computing; Computer Science; Education; Hotel and Restaurant; Hotel Management; Primary Education; Secondary Education)

History: Founded 1994.

Degrees and Diplomas: *Certificate/Diploma*; *Bachelor's Degree*

Last Updated: 29/10/10

LEON GUINTO MEMORIAL COLLEGE

Mabini Street, Atimonan, Quezon 4331

Tel: +63(42) 316-5471

Fax: +63(42) 511-1356

President: Nestor M. Parafina

Programmes

Business Administration (Accountancy; Business Administration; Management; Marketing); **Economics** (Economics); **Education** (Education; English; Filipino; Foreign Languages Education; Health Education; Mathematics Education; Music Education; Native Language Education; Physical Education; Primary Education; Secondary Education; Special Education)

History: Founded 1971.

Degrees and Diplomas: *Bachelor's Degree*

Last Updated: 29/10/10

LEYTE COLLEGES

Sta. Cruz Street, Tacloban City, Leyte 6500

Tel: +63(53) 321-1501

Fax: +62(53) 325-2433

President: Violeta Astilla-Aparis

Programmes

Business Administration (Banking; Business Administration; Business and Commerce; Finance; Management); **Criminology** (Criminology); **Education** (English; Filipino; Foreign Languages Education; Mathematics Education; Native Language Education; Primary Education; Secondary Education; Social Sciences); **Law** (Law); **Political Sciences** (Political Sciences)

History: Founded 1946 as Leyte Institute, acquiring present title 1949.

Degrees and Diplomas: *Bachelor's Degree*

Last Updated: 29/10/10

LEYTE POLYTECHNIC COLLEGE

Private Road, Sto. Niño Ext., Tacloban City, Leyte 6500

Tel: +63(53) 321-2384

EMail: leyteploytechnic@yahoo.com

Programmes

Customs Administration (Taxation)

History: Founded 1996.

Degrees and Diplomas: *Bachelor's Degree*

Last Updated: 29/10/10

LEYTE SCHOOL OF PROFESSIONALS

Real St. cor. Calanipawan Road, Sagkahan, Tacloban City, Leyte 6500

Tel: +63(53) 325-3930

Fax: +63(53) 325-3482

EMail: lst@evis.net.ph

Website: http://www.lsp.evis.net.ph/

President: Francisco S. Tantuico, Jr.

Programmes

Accountancy (Accountancy); **Business Administration** (Business Administration); **Public Administration** (Public Administration)

History: Founded in 2002.

Degrees and Diplomas: *Bachelor's Degree*

Last Updated: 29/10/10

L.F. GONZALES COLLEGE OF SCIENCE AND TECHNOLOGY

Maharlika Hi-Way 3102, San Leonardo, Nueva Ecija 3102

Tel: +63(44) 604-1314

President: Leonardo F. Gonzales

Programmes

Nursing (Nursing)

Degrees and Diplomas: *Bachelor's Degree*

Last Updated: 27/10/10

LICEO DE CAGAYAN UNIVERSITY (LDECU)

Rodolfo N. Pelaez Boulevard, Carmen, Cagayan de Oro City, Misamis Oriental 9000

Tel: +63(8822) 722-244

Fax: +63(8822) 727-044

Website: http://www.liceo.edu.ph

President: Mariano M. Lerin

Tel: +63(88) 858-4093, Fax: +63(88) 858-3123

Vice-President for Administration: Alain Marc P. Golez

International Relations: Teresita T. Tumapon, Vice-President for Academic Affairs

Colleges

Arts and Sciences (Biology; Chemistry; Economics; English; English Studies; Filipino; Hotel and Restaurant; Hotel Management; Human Resources; International Studies; Literature; Mass

Communication; Mathematics; Modern Languages; Natural Sciences; Physics; Political Sciences; Psychology; Social Sciences; Sociology; Tourism); **Business and Accountancy** (Accountancy; Business Administration; Business and Commerce; Data Processing; Finance; Hotel and Restaurant; Hotel Management; Information Technology; Tourism); **Education** (Education; English; Filipino; Foreign Languages Education; Health Education; Mathematics Education; Music Education; Native Language Education; Physical Education; Primary Education; Secondary Education; Social Studies); **Engineering** (Civil Engineering; Computer Engineering; Electrical Engineering; Electronic Engineering; Engineering; Industrial Engineering; Telecommunications Engineering); **Information Technology** (Computer Networks; Computer Science; Information Technology); **Law** (Law); **Law Enforcement and Public Safety** (Civil Security; Criminal Law; Criminology); **Medical Laboratory Science** (Laboratory Techniques; Medical Technology); **Nursing** (Nursing); **Pharmacy** (Pharmacy); **Physical Therapy** (Physical Therapy); **Radiologic Technology** (Medical Technology; Radiology)

Schools

Graduate Studies (Business Administration; Education; English; Environmental Management; Foreign Languages Education; Government; Health Education; Human Resources; Information Management; Information Technology; Management; Management Systems; Nursing; Public Administration)

History: Founded 1955. Formerly known as Liceo de Cagayan.

Governing Bodies: Board of Directors

Admission Requirements: Entrance examination

Main Language(s) of Instruction: English

Accrediting Agencies: Philippine Association of Colleges and Universities Commission on Accreditation

Degrees and Diplomas: *Bachelor's Degree*; *Master's Degree*: Management; Nursing; Education; *PhD*: Management

Student Services: Academic counselling, Canteen, Cultural centre, Employment services, Handicapped facilities, Health services, Language programs, Nursery care, Social counselling, Sports facilities

Special Facilities: Museum. Botanical garden.

Libraries: Central Library, c. 36,500 vols

Last Updated: 29/10/10

LICEO DE DAVAO

Briz District, Tagum City, Davao del Norte 8100
Tel: +63(84) 217-3554
EMail: liceo_de_davao@yahoo.com

President: Antero C. De los Reyes, Jr.

Programmes

Undergraduate and Professional Studies (Business and Commerce; Education; English; Foreign Languages Education; Mathematics Education; Nursing; Primary Education; Secondary Education)

History: Founded 1980.

Degrees and Diplomas: *Bachelor's Degree*

Last Updated: 29/10/10

LICEO DE MASBATE

Quezon Street, Masbate, Masbate 5400
Tel: +63(52) 333-2276
Fax: +63(52) 333-2276

President: Claro V. Caluya, III, V.G.

Programmes

Business Administration (Accountancy; Banking; Business Administration; Business and Commerce; Finance; Management); **Education** (Education; English; Filipino; Foreign Languages Education; Mathematics Education; Native Language Education; Primary Education; Science Education; Secondary Education); **English** (English); **Hospitality Management** (Hotel and Restaurant; Hotel Management)

History: Founded 1948.

Degrees and Diplomas: *Certificate/Diploma*; *Associate Degree*; *Bachelor's Degree*

Last Updated: 29/10/10

LICEO DE SAN JACINTO FOUNDATION

Almonte Street, San Jacinto, Masbate 5417

President: Isidro C. Merillo

Programmes

Undergraduate and Professional (Computer Science; Education; English; Foreign Languages Education; Mathematics Education; Political Sciences; Primary Education; Secondary Education)

History: Founded 2003. Formerly Liceo de San Jacinto, Inc.

Degrees and Diplomas: *Bachelor's Degree*

Last Updated: 29/10/10

LIPA CITY COLLEGES

G-A Solis Street, Lipa City, Batangas 4217
Tel: +63(43) 756-1943 +63(43) 756-3768
Fax: +63(43) 757-3768
EMail: lcc@lipacitycolleges.net
Website: http://www.lipacitycolleges.net/

President: Carlos R. Mojares

Programmes

Graduate (Education; Educational Administration); **Undergraduate and Professional** (Accountancy; Banking; Business Administration; Business and Commerce; Computer Science; Criminology; Education; English; Filipino; Finance; Foreign Languages Education; Health Education; Hotel and Restaurant; Hotel Management; Human Resources; Mathematics Education; Native Language Education; Nursing; Primary Education; Science Education; Secondary Education; Tourism)

History: Founded 1947 as Lipa Business Institute.

Degrees and Diplomas: *Certificate/Diploma*; *Associate Degree*; *Bachelor's Degree*; *Master's Degree*: Educational Management

Last Updated: 02/11/10

LORMA COLLEGES

Carlatan, City of San Fernando, La Union 2500
Tel: +63(72) 888-4341 +63(72) 242-3624
Fax: +63(72) 242-3628
EMail: joema@lorma.edu.ph
Website: http://www.lorma.edu.ph

Director: Jose P. Mainggang

Courses

Engineering (Computer Engineering; Engineering); **Information and Communications Technology** (Computer Science; Information Technology); **Liberal Arts** (Applied Chemistry; Biology; Chemistry; Computer Education; English; Family Studies; Foreign Languages Education; Human Resources; Mathematics Education; Physical Chemistry; Physics; Psychology; Secondary Education; Theology); **Management and Accountancy** (Accountancy; Business Administration; Finance; Health Administration; Hotel and Restaurant; Hotel Management; Human Resources; Management; Marketing); **Paramedical** (Laboratory Techniques; Medical Technology; Nursing; Physical Therapy; Respiratory Therapy)

Schools

Graduate Studies (Child Care and Development; Community Health; Information Technology; Nursing)

History: Founded 1970.

Degrees and Diplomas: *Certificate/Diploma*; *Bachelor's Degree*; *Master's Degree*: Nursing; Information Technology

Last Updated: 02/11/10

LOS BAÑOS COLLEGE

Colegio de Los Baños

Lopez Avenue, Los Baños, Laguna 4030
Tel: +63(49) 536-1977
Fax: +63(49) 536-1982
EMail: cdlba@gateway.edu.ph; chinkysanagustin@yahoo.com

President: Marina L. San Agustin

Programmes
Graduate (Educational Administration; Management; Public Administration); **Undergraduate and Professional** (Accountancy; Arts and Humanities; Business Administration; Computer Science; Economics; Education; Primary Education; Secondary Education)

History: Founded 1984.

Degrees and Diplomas: *Bachelor's Degree*; *Master's Degree*
Last Updated: 08/09/10

LOURDES COLLEGE

7 General Capistrano Street, Cagayan de Oro City, Misamis Oriental 9000
Tel: +63(8822) 723-464
Fax: +63(88) 857-1487
EMail: lc@lccdo.edu.ph
Website: http://www.lccdo.edu.ph/index3.htm

President: Ma. Adelaida C. Huiso

Programmes
Arts and Sciences (Dietetics; English; Filipino; History; Home Economics; Information Sciences; Library Science; Mass Communication; Music; Nutrition; Psychology); **Business and Accountancy** (Accountancy; Business Administration; Business and Commerce; Human Resources); **Hotel and Restaurant Management** (Hotel and Restaurant; Hotel Management); **Nursing** (Nursing); **Social Work** (Social Work); **Teacher Education** (Curriculum; English; Filipino; Foreign Languages Education; Health Education; History; Mathematics Education; Music Education; Native Language Education; Physical Education; Preschool Education; Primary Education; Religious Education; Science Education; Secondary Education)

History: Founded 1928. Formerly San Agustin Parochial School and Lourdes Junior College.

Degrees and Diplomas: *Associate Degree*; *Bachelor's Degree*; *Master's Degree*: Education (Physical Education; Elementary Education; English Communication Arts; Childhood Education; Educational Management); Home Economics; Human Resources Development
Last Updated: 02/11/10

LOURDES COLLEGE OF BULACAN

Veteransville, Angat, Bulacan 3012
Tel: +63(44) 671-0324
Fax: +63(44) 671-0324

Director: Wilfredo R. Reyes

Programmes
Business Administration (Business Administration; Business Computing; Management; Secretarial Studies); **Elementary Education** (Primary Education)

History: Founded 1974.

Degrees and Diplomas: *Associate Degree*; *Bachelor's Degree*
Last Updated: 02/11/10

LOWER ISAROG FOUNDATION EXPONENT

Barangay Gingaroy, Tigaon, Camarines Sur 4420
Tel: +63(54) 452-3043

President: Gregorio B. Chavez

Programmes
Computer Science and Technology (Computer Engineering; Computer Science)

History: Founded 1995.

Degrees and Diplomas: *Associate Degree*; *Bachelor's Degree*
Last Updated: 02/11/10

LOYOLA COLLEGE OF CULION

Upper Libis Street, Culion, Palawan 5315

Director: Rogel Anecito L. Abais, S.J.

Programmes
Arts and Humanities (Literature)

History: Founded 1985.

Degrees and Diplomas: *Bachelor's Degree*
Last Updated: 02/11/10

LUCAN POLYTECHNIC COLLEGE

San Francisco District, Pagadian City, Zamboanga Del Sur 7016
Tel: +63(62) 215-3307
Fax: +63(62) 215-3307

President: Lucas V. Leonardo

Programmes
Business Administration (Business Administration); **Computer Science** (Computer Science); **Education** (Education; Primary Education); **Information Technology** (Information Technology)

History: Founded 2000.

Degrees and Diplomas: *Bachelor's Degree*
Last Updated: 02/11/10

LUIS H. DILANCO SR. FOUNDATION COLLEGE

Bahay, Libmanan, Camarines Sur 4407
Tel: +63(54) 511-9155
Fax: +63(54) 299-2224
EMail: lhdsfcollege@yahoo.com

President: Fe Dilanco-Ceguera

Programmes
Computer Science (Computer Science); **Information Management** (Information Management; Information Technology)

History: Founded 2004.

Degrees and Diplomas: *Bachelor's Degree*
Last Updated: 02/11/10

LUNA COLLEGES

Lopez-Jaena Street, Tayug, Pangasinan 2445
Tel: +63(75) 572-2915

President: Linda Mamenta-Ramos

Programmes
Arts (English; History); **Education** (Education; English; Filipino; Foreign Languages Education; History; Native Language Education; Primary Education); **Graduate Studies** (Educational Administration; Psychology)

History: Founded 1935.

Degrees and Diplomas: *Certificate/Diploma*; *Associate Degree*; *Bachelor's Degree*; *Master's Degree*: Educational Management; Psychology
Last Updated: 02/11/10

LUNA GOCO COLLEGES

Lalud, Calapan City, Oriental Mindoro 5200
Tel: +63(43) 286-7208
Fax: +63(43) 286-7208
EMail: lgcolleges@yahoo.com

President: Emelita C. Luna-Goco

Programmes
Criminology (Criminology); **Nursing** (Midwifery; Nursing); **Primary Education**; **Radiologic Technology** (Medical Technology; Radiology); **Social Work** (Social Work)

Further Information: Also Luna Goco Colleges-Pinamalayan, Oriental Mindoro

History: Founded 1987.

Degrees and Diplomas: *Certificate/Diploma*; *Associate Degree*; *Bachelor's Degree*
Last Updated: 02/11/10

LUZON COLLEGE OF SCIENCE AND TECHNOLOGY (URDANETA)

Mc Arthur Hi-way, Nancayasan, City of Urdaneta, Pangasinan 2428
Tel: +63(75) 624-2389
Fax: +63(75) 568-3474
EMail: aida1050@hotmail.com

President: Nelia A. De Leon

Programmes

Commerce (Banking; Business and Commerce; Finance; Management); **Computer Science** (Computer Science; Management); **Elementary Education** (Primary Education); **Hotel and Restaurant Management** (Hotel and Restaurant; Hotel Management); **Secondary Education** (English; Filipino; Foreign Languages Education; Mathematics Education; Native Language Education; Physical Education; Secondary Education; Social Studies)

History: Founded 1999 as Luzon Institute and Technology. Also previously known as Luzon Colleges of Science and Technology.

Degrees and Diplomas: *Certificate/Diploma*: 1-2 yrs; *Bachelor's Degree*
Last Updated: 03/11/10

LYCEUM NORTHWESTERN - FLORENCIA T. DUQUE COLLEGE

Nancayasan, City of Urdaneta, Pangasinan 2428
Tel: +63(75) 568-7342
Fax: +63(75) 522-1907

President: Gonzalo T. Duque

Programmes

Commerce (Accountancy; Banking; Business and Commerce; Finance; Management); **Computer Engineering** (Computer Engineering); **Computer Science** (Computer Science); **Criminology** (Criminology); **Education** (Education; English; Foreign Languages Education; Mathematics Education; Primary Education; Secondary Education); **Nursing** (Nursing); **Political Sciences** (Political Sciences); **Tourism** (Tourism)

History: Founded 2000.

Degrees and Diplomas: *Bachelor's Degree*
Last Updated: 03/11/10

LYCEUM NORTHWESTERN UNIVERSITY

Tapuac District, Dagupan City, Pangasinan 2400
Tel: +63(75) 515-8684 +63(75) 515-8682
Fax: +63(75) 522-1907
EMail: info@lyceum.edu.ph
Website: http://www.lyceum.edu.ph

President: Gonzalo T. Duque

Programmes

Architecture (Architecture); **Arts** (Arts and Humanities; English; Mass Communication; Political Sciences); **Biology** (Biology); **Business Administration** (Accountancy; Banking; Business Administration; Business and Commerce; Finance; Management); **Computer Science** (Computer Science); **Criminology** (Criminology); **Education** (Education; English; Filipino; Foreign Languages Education; Mathematics Education; Native Language Education; Physics; Primary Education; Secondary Education); **Engineering** (Civil Engineering; Computer Engineering; Electrical Engineering; Electronic Engineering; Engineering; Mechanical Engineering; Telecommunications Engineering); **Information Technology** (Information Technology); **Laws** (Law); **Marine Transport and Engineering** (Marine Engineering; Marine Transport); **Medical Technology** (Medical Technology); **Medicine** (Dentistry; Health Sciences; Medicine; Optometry); **Nursing** (Nursing); **Pharmacy** (Pharmacy); **Physical Therapy** (Physical Therapy); **Psychology** (Psychology); **Radiologic Technology** (Medical Technology; Radiology); **Tourism** (Hotel and Restaurant; Hotel Management; Tourism)

Schools

Graduate Studies (Business Administration; Education; Nursing; Public Administration; Public Health)

History: Founded 1969 as the Dagupan City School of Nursing. Renamed Lyceum-Northwestern 1974. Acquired present status and title 2003.

Degrees and Diplomas: *Certificate/Diploma*; *Associate Degree*; *Bachelor's Degree*; *Post Baccalaureate Certificate/Diploma*; *Master's Degree*: Business Administration; Public Health; Education; Nursing; *PhD*: Business Administration; Education
Last Updated: 03/11/10

LYCEUM OF ALABANG

88 GNT Business Center, National Road, Putatan, City of Muntinlupa, Fourth District, Metro Manila
Tel: +63(2) 861-5199
Fax: +63(2) 861-5100

President: Danilo V. Ayap

Programmes

Undergraduate and Professional (Business Administration; Computer Engineering; Computer Science; Hotel and Restaurant; Hotel Management; Information Technology)

History: Founded 2003. Formerly known as National College of Science and Technology (2003-2005).

Degrees and Diplomas: *Associate Degree*; *Bachelor's Degree*
Last Updated: 29/10/10

LYCEUM OF APARRI

Macanaya District, Aparri, Cagayan 3515
Tel: +63(78) 888-2075
Fax: +63(78) 888-2736
EMail: admin@lyceumofaparri.com
Website: http://www.lyceumofaparri.com/

Executive Vice-President: Joel M. Reyes

Programmes

Business Administration (Accountancy; Business Administration; Management; Public Administration); **Computer Science** (Computer Science); **Criminology** (Criminology); **Education** (Education; Educational Administration; Primary Education; Secondary Education); **Engineering** (Civil Engineering; Computer Engineering; Engineering; Geological Engineering); **Hotel and Restaurant Management** (Hotel and Restaurant; Hotel Management); **Information Technology** (Information Technology); **Library and Information Sciences** (Information Sciences; Library Science); **Nursing** (Nursing)

History: Founded 1967.

Degrees and Diplomas: *Certificate/Diploma*; *Associate Degree*; *Bachelor's Degree*; *Master's Degree*: Business Administration; Education; *PhD*: Education (Educational Management)
Last Updated: 03/11/10

LYCEUM OF ILIGAN FOUNDATION

Corpus Christi Village, Iligan City, Lanao del Norte 9200
Tel: +63(63) 221-1818
Fax: +63(63) 221-1817
EMail: info@lif.edu.ph

President: Rosalinda Rosales-Deleste

Programmes

Undergraduate and Professional Studies (Architecture; Business and Commerce; Computer Engineering; Computer Science; Electrical Engineering; Electronic Engineering; English; Filipino; Foreign Languages Education; Marine Transport; Mathematics Education; Midwifery; Native Language Education; Nursing; Primary Education; Taxation; Telecommunications Engineering)

History: Founded 1997.

Degrees and Diplomas: *Certificate/Diploma*; *Bachelor's Degree*
Last Updated: 03/11/10

LYCEUM OF NORTHERN LUZON

Mc Arthur Hi-way, San Vicente Central, Pangasinan 2428
Tel: +63(75) 568-7966
Fax: +63(75) 568-7963

President: Mariano M. Gandia

Programmes
Business Administration (Accountancy; Banking; Business Administration; Business and Commerce; Finance; Management); **Computer Studies** (Computer Engineering; Computer Science); **Criminology** (Criminology); **Education** (English; Filipino; Foreign Languages Education; Health Education; Mathematics Education; Native Language Education; Physical Education; Primary Education; Secondary Education); **Engineering** (Electronic Engineering; Telecommunications Engineering); **Hotel and Restaurant Management** (Hotel and Restaurant; Hotel Management); **Information Technology** (Information Technology); **Nursing and Midwifery** (Midwifery; Nursing)

History: Founded 1994.

Degrees and Diplomas: *Certificate/Diploma*; *Associate Degree*; *Bachelor's Degree*
Last Updated: 03/11/10

LYCEUM OF SUBIC BAY

Lot 73, Central Business District, Subic Bay Freeport Zone, Olongapo City, Zambales 2200
Tel: +63(47) 252-5940
Fax: +63(47) 252-3157
Website: http://www.lyceumsubicbay.com.ph

President: Alfonso F. Borda

Programmes
Business Administration (Accountancy; Business Administration; Finance; Human Resources; Management; Taxation); **Computer Science** (Computer Science); **Engineering** (Electronic Engineering; Engineering; Telecommunications Engineering); **Hotel and Restaurant Management** (Hotel and Restaurant; Hotel Management); **Information Technology** (Information Technology); **Nursing** (Nursing)
History: Founded 2003 as National College of Science and Technology. Acquired present title 2005.
Degrees and Diplomas: *Associate Degree*; *Bachelor's Degree*
Last Updated: 03/11/10

LYCEUM OF THE PHILIPPINES UNIVERSITY

Cor. Muralla and Real Streets, Intramuros, Manila, First District, Metro Manila 1002
Tel: +63(2) 527-8251 +63(2) 527-8255
Fax: +63(2) 527-1758
EMail: lpumktg@gmail.com; admissionsinfo@lyceumphil.edu.ph
Website: http://www.manila.lpu.edu.ph/

President: Roberto P. Laurel

Executive Director for Administration/Director, Human Resources: Pompeyo Adamos

Centres
Professional and Continuing Education (Arts and Humanities; Business Administration; Chinese; Computer Science; Cooking and Catering; Dance; Engineering; English; Filipino; French; German; Hotel and Restaurant; Information Management; Journalism; Modern Languages; Spanish; Sports; Textile Design; Theatre)

Colleges
Arts and Sciences (Advertising and Publicity; Arts and Humanities; English; Environmental Studies; Filipino; Journalism; Law; Literature; Mass Communication; Media Studies; Multimedia; Political Sciences; Psychology; Public Relations; Radio and Television Broadcasting; Town Planning; Urban Studies); **Business Administration** (Accountancy; Business Administration; Finance; Management; Marketing; Taxation); **Computer Studies** (Computer Science; Information Sciences; Information Technology); **Engineering** (Computer Engineering; Electrical Engineering; Electronic Engineering; Engineering; Industrial Engineering; Telecommunications Engineering); **International Relations** (Cultural Studies; Economics; French; International Relations; Japanese; Political Sciences; Spanish); **International Relations** (International Business; International Relations); **International Tourism and Hospitality Management** (Cooking and Catering; Hotel and Restaurant; Hotel Management; Tourism); **Nursing** (Nursing)

Schools
Graduate Studies *(Claro M. Recto Academy of Advanced Studies)* (Business Administration; Economics; Education; Educational Administration; Educational and Student Counselling; International Relations; Political Sciences; Public Administration; Taxation; Tourism)

History: Founded 1952. Formerly known as Lyceum of the Philippines. Acquired present title 2005.

Degrees and Diplomas: *Certificate/Diploma*; *Associate Degree*; *Bachelor's Degree*; *Master's Degree*: Business Administration; Public Administration; Education (Educational Management; Educational Guidance and Counselling); Fiscal Management; International Relations; Economics; Political Science; *PhD*: Fiscal Management; Public Policy and Management
Last Updated: 03/11/10

LYCEUM OF THE PHILIPPINES UNIVERSITY - BATANGAS

Capitol Site, Batangas City, Batangas 4200
Tel: +63(43) 723-2038
Fax: +63(43) 723-3549
EMail: info@lyceumbatangas.edu.ph
Website: http://www.lyceumbatangas.edu.ph/

President: Peter P. Laurel

Colleges
Allied Health Professions (Laboratory Techniques; Medical Technology; Physical Therapy; Radiology); **Business Administration** (Accountancy; Banking; Business Administration; Economics; Finance; Human Resources; Management; Marketing; Taxation); **Computer Studies** (Computer Science; Information Technology); **Criminology** (Criminal Law; Criminology); **Dentistry** (Dentistry); **Education, Arts and Sciences** (Advertising and Publicity; Education; Journalism; Marketing; Mass Communication; Primary Education; Psychology; Radio and Television Broadcasting; Secondary Education); **Engineering** (Computer Engineering; Electronic Engineering; Energy Engineering; Engineering; Engineering Management; Industrial Engineering; Mechanical Engineering; Power Engineering; Production Engineering; Robotics; Telecommunications Engineering); **International Tourism and Hospitality Management** (Cooking and Catering; Hotel and Restaurant; Hotel Management; Tourism); **Marine Engineering and Transport** *(Lyceum International Maritime Academy)* (Marine Engineering; Marine Transport); **Nursing** (Nursing)

Schools
Graduate Studies (Business Administration; Public Administration)

History: Founded 1966. Formerly known as Lyceum of the Philippines - Batangas.

Degrees and Diplomas: *Certificate/Diploma*; *Associate Degree*; *Bachelor's Degree*; *Master's Degree*
Last Updated: 03/11/10

LYCEUM OF THE PHILIPPINES UNIVERSITY - CAVITE

Governor's Drive, General Trias, Cavite 4107
Tel: +63(46) 484-8095
Fax: +63(46) 484-8095
EMail: lpucavite@yahoo.com

President: Peter P. Laurel

Programmes
4-Year Studies (Accountancy; Business Administration; Communication Studies; Computer Science; Cooking and Catering; Education; English; Foreign Languages Education; Hotel and Restaurant; Hotel Management; Human Resources; Information Technology; International Relations; Law; Management; Marketing; Multimedia; Primary Education; Secondary Education; Tourism); **5-Year Studies** (Accountancy; Civil Engineering; Computer Engineering; Electrical Engineering; Electronic Engineering; Industrial Engineering; Mechanical Engineering); **Graduate Studies** (Business Administration; Education; Educational Administration; Educational and Student Counselling; Management; Public Administration; Tourism)
History: Founded 2008.

Degrees and Diplomas: *Bachelor's Degree*; *Master's Degree*
Last Updated: 03/11/10

LYCEUM OF THE PHILIPPINES UNIVERSITY - LAGUNA

Km. 54, Makiling Highway, Calamba City, Laguna 4027
Tel: +63(49) 545-0972
Fax: +63(49) 545-0974
EMail: litph@yahoo.com
Website: http://www.lpl.edu.ph/home.php

Vice-President: Peter P. Laurel

Colleges

Arts and Sciences (Advertising and Publicity; Communication Studies; Film; Marketing; Photography; Public Relations; Radio and Television Broadcasting; Theatre); **Business and Accountancy** (Accountancy; Business Administration; Government; Management; Marketing; Public Administration; Taxation); **Computer Studies** (Computer Science; Information Technology); **Engineering** (Automation and Control Engineering; Computer Engineering; Computer Networks; Electrical Engineering; Electronic Engineering; Energy Engineering; Engineering; Industrial and Organizational Psychology; Industrial Engineering; Information Technology; Microelectronics; Power Engineering; Software Engineering; Telecommunications Engineering); **International Tourism and Hospitality Management** (Cooking and Catering; Hotel and Restaurant; Hotel Management; Tourism)

Further Information: Also St Cabrini College of Allied Medicine

History: Founded 2001. Formerly known as Lyceum Institute of Technology.

Degrees and Diplomas: *Associate Degree*; *Bachelor's Degree*
Last Updated: 03/11/10

LYCEUM OF THE PHILIPPINES UNIVERSITY - ST. CABRINI COLLEGE OF ALLIED MEDICINE

Maharlika H-Way, Sto. Tomas, Batangas 4234
Tel: +63(43) 778-6218
Fax: +63(43) 778-6218

President: Feliciano Torres

Programmes

Nursing (Nursing)

History: Founded 2002.

Degrees and Diplomas: *Bachelor's Degree*
Last Updated: 03/11/10

LYCEUM OF TUAO

Centro 02, Tuao, Cagayan 3528
Tel: +63(78) 826-2157

President: Federico B. Fabian

Programmes

Business Administration (Business Administration; Business and Commerce; Human Resources; Management); **Criminology** (Criminology); **Education** (Education; English; Foreign Languages Education; Primary Education)

History: Founded 1996.

Degrees and Diplomas: *Bachelor's Degree*
Last Updated: 03/11/10

MABA COMPUTER ORIENTED HIGH SCHOOL & COLLEGE LABORATORY AND TUTORIAL CENTER FOUNDATION

Lakandula Drive, Legazpi City, Albay 4500
Tel: +63(52) 480-3035
Fax: +63(52) 480-8575

President: Myrna B. Andes

Programmes

Computer Science (Computer Science)

History: Founded 1990. Formerly known as Maba Computer College.

Degrees and Diplomas: *Certificate/Diploma*; *Associate Degree*; *Bachelor's Degree*
Last Updated: 03/11/10

MABINI COLLEGE OF BATANGAS

J. Ponopio Street, Poblacion, Mabini, Batangas 4202
Tel: +63(43) 487-0117
Fax: +63(43) 487-0117
EMail: info@mabinicollege.com
Website: http://www.mabinicollege.com/

President: Aida Solis Domecillo

Programmes

Undergraduate and Professional Studies (Banking; Business Administration; Business and Commerce; Computer Science; Curriculum; Education; English; Finance; Foreign Languages Education; Political Sciences; Preschool Education; Primary Education; Secondary Education)

History: Founded 1948 as Mabini High School. Renamed Mataas na Paaralang Mabini (1974-2002).

Degrees and Diplomas: *Bachelor's Degree*
Last Updated: 04/11/10

MABINI COLLEGES

Governor Panotes Avenue, Daet, Camarines Norte 4600
Tel: +63(54) 721-1281
Fax: +63(54) 721-5743
EMail: mabinicollege@hotmail.com

Executive Committee Chairman: Luz I. Garcia

Programmes

Business Administration (Accountancy; Banking; Business Administration; Finance; Management; Secretarial Studies); **Computer Science** (Computer Science); **Education** (Art Education; Education; English; Filipino; Foreign Languages Education; Health Education; History; Mathematics Education; Native Language Education; Physical Education; Preschool Education; Primary Education; Secondary Education; Social Studies; Special Education); **Graduate** (Education; Educational Administration; Special Education); **Home Economics** (Home Economics); **Nursing** (Midwifery; Nursing); **Social Work** (Social Work)

History: Founded 1924 as Camarines Sur Institute. Acquired present status and title 1954.

Degrees and Diplomas: *Certificate/Diploma*; *Associate Degree*; *Bachelor's Degree*; *Master's Degree*: Education (Leadership Education; Educatoinal Administration and Supervision; Special Education)
Last Updated: 04/11/10

MACRO COMPUTER COLLEGE

Govantes Dike, Bantay, Ilocos Sur 2727
Tel: +63(77) 722-2097
Fax: +63(77) 722-2097
EMail: admin@macro.edu.ph

President: Cirilo A. Para

Programmes

Business Administration (Business Administration; E-Business/Commerce); **Education** (Education; Secondary Education; Technology Education); **Information Systems** (Information Management; Information Technology); **Information Technology** (Information Technology)

History: Founded 1989.

Degrees and Diplomas: *Certificate/Diploma*; *Bachelor's Degree*
Last Updated: 04/11/10

MAGSAYSAY MEMORIAL COLLEGE OF ZAMBALES

Libertad, San Narciso, Zambales 2205
Tel: +63(47) 913-4603

President: Daniel Presto

Programmes
Commerce (Banking; Business and Commerce; Finance; Management); **Computer Science** (Computer Science); **Education** (Education; English; Filipino; Foreign Languages Education; Home Economics Education; Mathematics Education; Native Language Education; Primary Education; Science Education; Secondary Education; Technology Education); **English** (English); **Hotel and Restaurant Management** (Hotel and Restaurant; Hotel Management)

History: Founded 1947.

Degrees and Diplomas: *Certificate/Diploma*; *Associate Degree*; *Bachelor's Degree*
Last Updated: 04/11/10

MAHARDIKA INSTITUTE OF TECHNOLOGY

Ilmoh Street, Bongao, Tawi-Tawi 7500
Tel: +63(68) 268-1259
Fax: +63(68) 268-1259
EMail: mitechnology2005@yahoo.com

Director: Sambas I. Hassan

Programmes
Undergraduate and Professional Studies (Business Administration; Criminology; Electrical Engineering; English; Foreign Languages Education; Management; Nursing; Police Studies; Primary Education; Secondary Education)

History: Founded 1998. Formerly known as Mahardika Institute of Computer Technology.

Degrees and Diplomas: *Bachelor's Degree*
Last Updated: 04/11/10

MAILA ROSARIO COLLEGES

Diversion Road, San Gabriel, Tuguegarao City, Cagayan 3500
Tel: +63(78) 846-3236
Fax: +63(78) 846-3236
EMail: mrc_2006@yahoo.com

Executive Vice-President: Manuel S. Tan, Jr.

Programmes
Criminology (Criminology)

History: Founded 2006.

Degrees and Diplomas: *Bachelor's Degree*
Last Updated: 04/11/10

MAKATI MEDICAL CENTER COLLEGE OF NURSING

Makati Medical Center, 2 Amorsolo Street, City of Makati, Fourth District, Metro Manila 1200
Tel: +63(2) 815-9910 +63(2) 893-3284
Fax: +63(2) 893-3284
Website: http://www.mmccn.edu.ph

President: Richard N. Ferrer

Programmes
Undergraduate and Professional (Health Education; Health Sciences; Nursing; Psychology)

History: Founded 1975. Formerly known as Remedios Trinidad Romualdez Memorial School. Acquired present title 2010.

Degrees and Diplomas: *Associate Degree*; *Bachelor's Degree*
Last Updated: 26/01/11

MALASIQUI AGNO VALLEY COLLEGE

Bonifacio Street, Malasiqui, Pangasinan 2421
Tel: +63(75) 536-5372 +63(75) 536-5111
Fax: +63(75) 536-6738

President: Osmundo B. Lambino

Programmes
Education (English; Filipino; Foreign Languages Education; History; Mathematics Education; Native Language Education; Primary Education; Secondary Education)

History: Founded 1936.

Degrees and Diplomas: *Bachelor's Degree*
Last Updated: 04/11/10

MALAYAN COLLEGES

Pulo Diezmo Road, Cabuyao, Laguna 4025
Tel: +63(49) 832-4000
EMail: info@mcl.edu.ph

President: Reynaldo B. Vea

Programmes
Accountancy (Accountancy); **Chemical Engineering** (Chemical Engineering); **Civil Engineering** (Civil Engineering); **Computer Engineering** (Computer Engineering); **Computer Science** (Computer Science); **Electrical Engineering** (Electrical Engineering); **Electronic and Communication Engineering** (Electronic Engineering; Telecommunications Engineering); **Entrepreneurship** (Management); **Hotel and Restaurant Management** (Hotel and Restaurant; Hotel Management); **Industrial Engineering** (Industrial Engineering); **Information Technology** (Information Technology); **Marine Transport and Engineering** (Marine Engineering; Marine Transport); **Mechanical Engineering** (Mechanical Engineering)

History: Founded 2006. Formerly Malayan Colleges Laguna.

Degrees and Diplomas: *Bachelor's Degree*
Last Updated: 04/11/10

MALLIG PLAINS COLLEGE

Casili, Mallig, Isabela 3323
Tel: +63(78) 642-8867
Fax: +63(78) 642-8958
EMail: mpc_edu_ph@yahoo.com; mpc_edu_ph@hotmail.com

President: Leocadio E. Ignacio

Programmes
Graduate (Business Administration; Education); **Undergraduate and Professional** (Accountancy; Automotive Engineering; Computer Engineering; Computer Science; Criminology; Electrical Engineering; Electronic Engineering; English; Filipino; Food Technology; Foreign Languages Education; History; Hotel and Restaurant; Hotel Management; Industrial Engineering; Mathematics Education; Native Language Education; Political Sciences; Primary Education; Psychology; Science Education; Secondary Education)

History: Founded 1951. Formerly known as Western Isabela Polytechnic College.

Degrees and Diplomas: *Certificate/Diploma*; *Bachelor's Degree*; *Master's Degree*: Business Administration; Education
Last Updated: 04/11/10

MANILA ADVENTIST MEDICAL CENTER AND SCHOOL OF MEDICAL ARTS

1975 Donada Street, Pasay City, Fourth District, Metro Manila 1300
Tel: +63(2) 525-9191
Fax: +63(2) 524-3256
EMail: mamc@mamc-sma.org
Website: http://www.mamc-sma.org

President: Bibly L. Macaya

Schools
Medical Arts (Health Sciences; Midwifery; Nursing; Physical Therapy; Radiology)

History: Founded 1993. Formerly known as Manila Sanitarium and Hospital School of Medical Arts and Manila Adventist Medical Center and School of Medical Arts. Acquired present title 2007.

Degrees and Diplomas: *Associate Degree*; *Bachelor's Degree*
Last Updated: 04/11/10

MANILA BUSINESS COLLEGE

1671-1689 Alvarez St. cor. M. Hizon Street, Santa Cruz, City of Manila, First District, Metro Manila 1003
Tel: +63(2) 314-6861
Fax: +63(2) 314-6884
EMail: admin@mbc.edu.ph
Website: http://www.mbc.edu.ph

Executive Vice-President: Frederick Stephen L. Ding, Jr.

Colleges
Arts and Sciences (Economics; English; Hotel and Restaurant; Hotel Management; Information Technology; Mass Communication; Tourism); **Business Management** (Accountancy; Banking; Business Administration; Business Computing; E-Business/Commerce; Economics; Finance; Human Resources; International Business; Management; Marketing; Transport Management); **Public Administration** (Public Administration)

Programmes
Graduate Studies (Business Administration; Education; Educational Administration; Information Technology; Management; Public Administration)

History: Founded 1979. Formerly known as Metro Data Computer College (1993-2002).

Degrees and Diplomas: *Certificate/Diploma*; *Bachelor's Degree*
Last Updated: 04/11/10

MANILA CENTRAL UNIVERSITY (MCU)

Epifanio de los Santos Avenue, Caloocan City, Third District, Metro Manila 1400
Tel: +63(2) 364-1071
Fax: +63(2) 364-1070
EMail: admin@mcu.edu.ph; registrar@mcu.edu.ph
Website: http://www.mcu.edu.ph

President: Aristotle T. Mabbaran

Colleges
Arts and Sciences (Arts and Humanities; Biology; Natural Sciences; Psychology); **Business Administration** (Accountancy; Business Administration; Management; Marketing); **Computer Studies** (Computer Science; Information Management; Information Technology); **Dentistry** (Dental Hygiene; Dental Technology; Dentistry; Periodontics); **Medical Technology** (Medical Technology); **Medicine** (Anatomy; Biochemistry; Community Health; Gynaecology and Obstetrics; Medicine; Neurology; Ophthalmology; Otorhinolaryngology; Paediatrics; Parasitology; Pathology; Pharmacology; Physiology; Psychiatry and Mental Health; Surgery); **Nursing** (Midwifery; Nursing); **Optometry** (Optical Technology; Optometry); **Pharmacy** (Inorganic Chemistry; Microbiology; Parasitology; Pharmacology; Pharmacy; Public Health; Toxicology); **Physical Therapy** (Physical Therapy)

Schools
Graduate Studies (Business Administration; Education; Educational Administration; Nursing; Philosophy; Secondary Education)

Further Information: Also Teaching Hospital (MCU-FDT Medical Foundation Hospital)

History: Founded 1904 as School of Pharmacy, became Manila College of Pharmacy and Dentistry 1929. Renamed Manila Central College 1946. Acquired present status and title 1948.

Governing Bodies: Board of Trustees

Academic Year: June to March (June-November; November-March)

Admission Requirements: Graduation from high school and entrance examination

Main Language(s) of Instruction: Filipino, English

Accrediting Agencies: Philippine Association of Colleges and Universities Commission on Accreditation

Degrees and Diplomas: *Certificate/Diploma*: Dental Technician; Dental Hygiene; Midwifery; Optical Laboratory Technician; *Bachelor's Degree*; *Post Baccalaureate Certificate/Diploma*: Dental Medicine (DMD); Medicine (MD); Optometry (OD); *Master's Degree*: Business Administration; College Teaching; Education; Nursing; Optometry; Orthodontics; *PhD*: Education; Philosophy; Educational Administration. Also Postgraduate Certificate in Orthodontics/ Dentistry 2 yrs

Student Services: Academic counselling, Canteen, Cultural centre, Employment services, Foreign student adviser, Foreign Studies Centre, Handicapped facilities, Health services, Social counselling, Sports facilities

Libraries: Central Library, c. 21,000 specialized libraries, total, c. 8,000 vols

Publications: MCU Research Journal *(quarterly)*; Philippine Scientific Journal *(biannually)*
Last Updated: 04/11/10

MANILA DOCTORS COLLEGE

Pres. Diosdado Macapagal Boulevard, Metropolitan Park, Pasay City, Fourth District; Metro Manila 1000
Tel: +63(2) 832-0712
Fax: +63(2) 832-0711
EMail: mdcol@compass.com.ph

President: Teresita O. Turla

Programmes
Nursing (Nursing); **Psychology** (Psychology); **Pulmonary Therapy** (Respiratory Therapy); **Zoology** (Zoology)

History: Founded 1975. Campus moved from Manila City to Pasay City 2004.

Degrees and Diplomas: *Certificate/Diploma*; *Bachelor's Degree*
Last Updated: 04/11/10

MANILA LAW COLLEGE

641 Sales Street, Santa Cruz, City of Manila, First District, Metro Manila
Tel: +63(2) 314-8513
Fax: +63(2) 735-8624
Website: http://www.pccr.edu.ph/mlc/mlc_home.htm

President: Gregory Alan F. Bautista

Programmes
Law (Law)

History: Founded 1899. Formerly Manila Law College Foundation.

Degrees and Diplomas: *Bachelor's Degree*
Last Updated: 04/11/10

MANILA MONTESSORI COLLEGE - BIÑAN

Biñan, Laguna 4024
Tel: +63(2) 411-7221
Fax: +63(2) 372-6910

President: Teresita C. Dy

Programmes
Hotel and Restaurant Management (Hotel and Restaurant; Hotel Management)

Degrees and Diplomas: *Certificate/Diploma*; *Bachelor's Degree*
Last Updated: 04/11/10

MANSFIELD TECHNOLOGICAL COLLEGE

A. Soriano H-way, Naic, Cavite 4110
Tel: +63(46) 412-1190
Fax: +63(46) 412-1190
EMail: mtci@yahoo.com

President: Midel A. Gonzales

Programmes
Undergraduate and Professional (Accountancy; Business Administration; Computer Science; Hotel and Restaurant; Hotel Management; Management; Marketing)

History: Founded 2000.

Degrees and Diplomas: *Bachelor's Degree*
Last Updated: 04/11/10

MANTO MEMORIAL FOUNDATION COLLEGE

A. Bonifacio and S. Duterte Streets, Danao City, Cebu 6004
Tel: +63(32) 200-3208

Board Chairperson: Pacita M. Veloso

Programmes
Commerce (Business and Commerce; Management); **Computer Technology** (Computer Engineering); **Education** (Education; Preschool Education; Primary Education; Secondary Education); **Graduate Studies** (Education; Educational Administration); **Nursing and Midwifery** (Midwifery; Nursing)

History: Founded 1979. Formerly Gregoria R. Manto Memorial Technical School (1979-1984).

Degrees and Diplomas: *Bachelor's Degree*; *Master's Degree*: Education (Educational Management and Supervision)
Last Updated: 04/11/10

MANUEL L. QUEZON UNIVERSITY

916 R. Hidalgo Street, Quiapo, Manila, Metro Manila 1001
Tel: +63(4) 742-4204 +63(4) 734-0121
Fax: +63(4) 733-79-76 +63(4) 733-9974
EMail: mlq@mlqu.edu.ph
Website: http://www.mlqu.edu.ph

President: Eduardo D. De Los Angeles EMail: pres@mlqu.edu.ph

Executive Officer/Vice President for Administration: Ma. Victoria O. Chan EMail: mvoc@info.com.ph

Schools

Accountancy and Business Arts (Accountancy; Business Administration; Business and Commerce; Finance; Management; Marketing; Secretarial Studies); **Architecture** (Architecture); **Criminal Justice** (Criminal Law; Criminology; Police Studies); **Education, Arts and Sciences** (Education; International Relations; Journalism; Political Sciences; Primary Education; Psychology; Secondary Education); **Engineering** (Chemical Engineering; Civil Engineering; Computer Engineering; Electrical Engineering; Electronic Engineering; Engineering; Industrial Engineering; Mechanical Engineering; Telecommunications Engineering); **Graduate Studies** (Arts and Humanities; Business Administration; Business and Commerce; Education; Educational Administration; Educational and Student Counselling; English; Filipino; History; Industrial Management; Law; Library Science; Mathematics; Mathematics and Computer Science; Mathematics Education; Philosophy; Political Sciences; Psychology; Public Administration; Science Education; Special Education; Taxation; Teacher Training); **Information Technology** (Computer Science; Information Management; Information Technology); **Law** (Fiscal Law; Law)

History: Founded 1947 as School of Law. Faculty of Arts and Science opened 1948, Faculty of Education, Elementary School, and High School added 1949. Graduate School and Faculty of Commerce established 1952, Faculty of Engineering and Architecture 1954. Granted University status 1958. Operating under the supervision of the Ministry of Education, Culture and Sports.

Governing Bodies: Board of Regents

Academic Year: June to March (June-October; November-March)

Admission Requirements: Graduation from high school or recognized foreign equivalent, and entrance examination

Main Language(s) of Instruction: English

Degrees and Diplomas: *Bachelor's Degree*; *Master's Degree*: Business Administration; Computer Management; General Management; Industrial Management; Information Systems; Marketing Management; Commerce (Taxation); Library Science; Mathematics; Education (Mathematics Education; Science Education); English; History; Guidance; Filipino; Political Science; Psychology; Special Education; Educational Management and Planning; Teaching English as a Second Language; Law; Taxation; Public Administration; *PhD*: Business Management; English; Filipino; Psychology; Education (Educational Management and Planning; Educational Guidance and Counseling); Public Administration

Student Residential Facilities: For c. 12,000 students

Libraries: Central Library, c. 11,250 vols; Faculty Libraries c. 13,640 vols

Publications: Acquitas; Graduate School Review; Law Quarterly; Quezonian

Last Updated: 04/11/10

MANUEL S. ENVERGA UNIVERSITY FOUNDATION - CANDELARIA

Brgy. Malabanan Norte, Candelaria, Quezon 4323
Tel: +63(42) 585-8320
Fax: +63(42) 585-4274
EMail: eucandelaria_registrar@yahoo.com

President: Naila Leveriza

Programmes

Undergraduate and Professional (Accountancy; Arts and Humanities; Business Administration; Computer Engineering; Electronic Engineering; Hotel Management; Midwifery; Police Studies; Primary Education; Secondary Education; Secretarial Studies)

History: Founded 1992.

Degrees and Diplomas: *Certificate/Diploma*; *Associate Degree*; *Bachelor's Degree*
Last Updated: 04/11/10

MANUEL S. ENVERGA UNIVERSITY FOUNDATION - CATANAUAN

Don Manuel Abella Drive, Brgy. 09 Poblacion, Catanauan, Quezon 4311
Tel: +63(42) 315-8203
Fax: +63(42) 315-8203

President: Naila Leveriza

Programmes

Business Administration (Business Administration; Human Resources; Management); **Education** (Curriculum; Education; English; Filipino; Foreign Languages Education; Mathematics Education; Native Language Education; Primary Education; Secondary Education); **Public Administration** (Public Administration)

History: Founded 1948.

Degrees and Diplomas: *Certificate/Diploma*; *Bachelor's Degree*
Last Updated: 04/11/10

MANUEL S. ENVERGA UNIVERSITY FOUNDATION - LUCENA

University Site, Lucena City, Quezon 4301
Tel: +63(42) 710-2541
Fax: +63(42) 373-6065
Website: http://www.mseuf.edu.ph

President: Naila E. Leveriza

Programmes

Accountancy (Accountancy); **Arts and Sciences** (Advertising and Publicity; Communication Studies; Comparative Literature; Computer Science; Criminology; Economics; English; Filipino; Fine Arts; History; Information Management; Information Technology; Journalism; Literature; Marine Engineering; Marine Transport; Mathematics; Natural Sciences; Philosophy; Political Sciences; Psychology; Public Administration; Radio and Television Broadcasting; Sociology); **Biology** (Biology); **Business Administration** (Banking; Business Administration; Business Computing; Finance; Human Resources; Industrial Management; Management; Marketing); **Elementary Education** (English; Foreign Languages Education; Health Education; Mathematics Education; Preschool Education; Primary Education; Science Education; Social Studies); **Environmental Science** (Environmental Management; Environmental Studies); **Hotel and Restaurant Management** (Hotel and Restaurant; Hotel Management); **Laws** (Law); **Library and Information Sciences** (Information Sciences; Library Science); **Management** (Management; Public Administration); **Nursing** (Nursing); **Office Administration** (Business Administration; Secretarial Studies); **Secondary Education** (Biology; Education; English; Ethics; Filipino; Foreign Languages Education; Health Education; History; Home Economics Education; Library Science; Mathematics Education; Music Education; Native Language Education; Physical Education; Science Education; Secondary Education); **Tourism** (Tourism)

History: Founded 1947 as College, acquired present status 1968.

Governing Bodies: Board of Trustees

Academic Year: June to March (June-October; October-March)

Admission Requirements: Graduation from high school and entrance examination

Main Language(s) of Instruction: Filipino, English

Degrees and Diplomas: *Certificate/Diploma*; *Associate Degree*; *Bachelor's Degree*; *Master's Degree*: Business Administration; Information Technology; Management (Engineering Management; Human Resources Management; Human Resources Management); Physical Education, Public Administration; Teaching; Education (School Administration; Mathematics; Guidance; Filipino; English); Criminology; *PhD*: Education (Educational Management); Management

Libraries: c. 45,000 vols

Publications: The Luzonian *(quarterly)*
Last Updated: 04/11/10

MANUEL S. ENVERGA UNIVERSITY FOUNDATION - SAN ANTONIO

Quizon Street, Poblacion, San Antonio, Quezon 4324
Tel: +63(42) 545-4113
Fax: +63(42) 545-4113

President: Naila Leveriza

Programmes
Business Administration (Business Administration; Human Resources; Management); **Education** (Education; Mathematics Education; Primary Education; Secondary Education)

History: Founded 2005.

Degrees and Diplomas: *Bachelor's Degree*
Last Updated: 04/11/10

MANUEL V. GALLEGO FOUNDATION COLLEGES

Zulueta St., Cabanatuan City, Nueva Ecija 3100
Tel: +63(44) 463-0863
Fax: +63(44) 463-7738
EMail: mvgallego@digitelone.com

President: Joseph L. Gallego

Programmes
Accountancy (Accountancy); **Commerce** (Business and Commerce; Management); **Computer Science** (Computer Science); **Criminology** (Criminology); **Education** (Education); **Nursing** (Nursing)

History: Founded 1952 as Central Luzon School of Nursing. Formerly Central Luzon Educational Center (1963 - 1974). Acquired present title 1998.

Degrees and Diplomas: *Associate Degree*; *Bachelor's Degree*; *Master's Degree*: Education (Primary Education; Secondary Education; Educational Management; Guidance and Counselling; Filipino; English; Mathematics); Nursing (Administration of Nursing Schools and Services; Community Health Nursing)
Last Updated: 04/11/10

MAPANDI MEMORIAL COLLEGE

048 Buanda Boulevard Saduc, Marawi City, Lanao del Sur 9700
Tel: +63(63) 352-0357
Fax: +63(63) 520-357
EMail: mapandicenter@lycos.com
Website: http://mapandicenter.tripod.com/

President: Mohammad Gonaranao U. Mapandi Jr.

Programmes
Computer Science (Computer Science); **Education** (Preschool Education; Primary Education; Secondary Education); **Health Sciences** (Health Education; Medical Technology; Midwifery; Nursing); **Management Accounting** (Accountancy; Management)

Further Information: Part of the Mapandi Memorial Medical and Education Centre

History: Founded 1978. Formerly Mapandi Memorial Hospital School of Midwifery (1978-1987).

Degrees and Diplomas: *Associate Degree*; *Bachelor's Degree*
Last Updated: 04/11/10

MAPUA INSTITUTE OF TECHNOLOGY

658 Muralla Street Intramuros, Manila, First District, Metro Manila 1002
Tel: +63(2) 247-5000
Fax: +63(2) 527-3680
EMail: info@mapua.edu.ph
Website: http://www.mapua.edu.ph

President and Chief Executive Officer: Reynaldo V. Bea
Tel: +63(2) 527-7190, Fax: +63(2) 527-5161
EMail: jbjuson@mapua.edu.ph

Executive Vice-President for Academic Affairs: Bonifacio T. Doma Jr

Campuses
Makati (Accountancy; Business Administration; Computer Science; Hotel and Restaurant; Hotel Management; Information Management; Information Technology; Management; Nursing)

Departments
Earth Sciences and Engineering *(EMSE)* (Earth Sciences; Materials Engineering; Metallurgical Engineering; Mining Engineering); **Multimedia Arts and Sciences** (Cinema and Television; Media Studies; Multimedia)

Schools
Architecture, Industrial Design and the Built Environment *(AR-ID-BE)* (Architecture; Construction Engineering; Industrial Design; Interior Design); **Basic Studies** (Mathematics; Physical Education; Physics; Sports); **Business and Management** *(R.T. Yuchengco School)* (Accountancy; Business Administration; Hotel and Restaurant; Hotel Management; Management); **Chemical Engineering and Chemistry** *(CHE-Chm)* (Biochemistry; Biotechnology; Cell Biology; Chemical Engineering; Chemistry; Microbiology; Molecular Biology); **Civil Engineering, Environmental and Sanitary Engineering** *(CE-EnSE)* (Civil Engineering; Construction Engineering; Environmental Engineering; Sanitary Engineering); **Electrical, Electronic and Computer Engineering** *(EE-ECE-CoE)* (Computer Engineering; Electrical Engineering; Electronic Engineering; Telecommunications Engineering); **Graduate Studies** *(GS)* (Architecture; Chemical Engineering; Chemistry; Civil Engineering; Computer Engineering; Computer Science; Construction Engineering; Electrical Engineering; Engineering; Engineering Management; Environmental Engineering; Geological Engineering; Industrial Engineering; Materials Engineering; Mechanical Engineering; Power Engineering; Structural Architecture; Water Science); **Health Sciences** *(San Lorenzo Ruiz School)* (Anatomy; Health Education; Health Sciences; Microbiology; Nursing; Nutrition; Parasitology; Pathology; Physiology); **Industrial Engineering and Engineering Management** (Engineering Management; Industrial Engineering); **Information Technology** *(IT)* (Computer Science; Information Technology); **Languages, Humanities and Social Sciences** (Arts and Humanities; Human Resources; Modern Languages; Psychology; Social Sciences); **Mechanical Engineering** *(ME)* (Mechanical Engineering)

History: Founded 1925.

Degrees and Diplomas: *Certificate/Diploma*; *Bachelor's Degree*: 4 yrs; *Bachelor's Degree*: Geology-Geological Engineering; Biotechnology; Chemistry; Chemical Engineering, 5 yrs; *Bachelor's Degree*: Information Management; Information Technology; Computer Science, 3 yrs; *Master's Degree*: Chemistry; Civil Engineering; Environmental Engineering; Materials Science and Engineering; Geotechnical Engineering; Computer Science; Construction Engineering; Architecture Education; Structural Engineering; Geoinformatics, a further 2 yrs; *Master's Degree*: Engineering Management; Electrical Engineering; Electronics and Communications Engineering; *PhD*: Chemistry; Environmental Engineering
Last Updated: 29/11/10

MARAWI CAPITOL COLLEGE FOUNDATION

Quezon Avenue, Marawi City, Lanao del Sur 9700
Tel: +63(63) 352-0347

President: Pendatum C. Macarambon

Programmes
Undergraduate and Professional Studies (Business and Commerce; Computer Science; Education; Primary Education; Secondary Education)

History: Founded 1991.

Degrees and Diplomas: *Associate Degree*; *Bachelor's Degree*
Last Updated: 29/11/10

MARAWI ISLAMIC COLLEGE

Panggao Saduc, Marawi City, Lanao del Sur

Officer In-Charge: Sultan Mangompia M. Abdul

Programmes
Education (Education; Primary Education; Secondary Education)

History: Founded 2003.

Degrees and Diplomas: *Bachelor's Degree*
Last Updated: 29/11/10

MARBEL SCHOOL OF SCIENCE AND TECHNOLOGY

Prk. Uper Valley, Brgy. Sto. Niño, Koronadal City, South Cotabato 9506
Tel: +63(83) 228-3147
Fax: +63(83) 228-3147

President: Godofredo N. Guya

Programmes
Undergraduate and Professional Studies (Computer Science; Criminology)

History: Founded 1992. Formerly known as Moverstate (1992 - 1994).

Degrees and Diplomas: *Bachelor's Degree*
Last Updated: 29/11/10

MARCELINO FULE MEMORIAL COLLEGE

Del Pilar Street, Alaminos, Laguna 4001
Tel: +63(49) 567-1450
Fax: +63(49) 567-1450
EMail: giunelric@yahoo.co.uk

President: Cesar G. Fule

Programmes
Undergraduate and Professional (Business and Commerce; English; Finance; Foreign Languages Education; Mathematics Education; Primary Education; Secondary Education)

History: Founded 1946.

Degrees and Diplomas: *Associate Degree*; *Bachelor's Degree*
Last Updated: 29/11/10

MARIAM SCHOOL OF NURSING

Flores Street corner Rizal Avenue, Lamitan City, Basilan 7302
EMail: msn05_nsg@yahoo.com.ph

President: Carmelita C. Cajucom

Programmes
Nursing (Nursing)

History: Founded 2005.

Degrees and Diplomas: *Bachelor's Degree*
Last Updated: 29/11/10

MARIAN COLLEGE

Climaco Street, Ipil, Zamboanga Sibugay 7001
Tel: +63(62) 991-4367
Fax: +63(62) 991-2365
EMail: chedsalud@yahoo.com

Director: Mercedes Salud, SFIC

Programmes
Commerce (Business and Commerce; Management); **Computer Science** (Computer Science; Software Engineering); **Education** (Curriculum; Education; English; Filipino; Foreign Languages Education; Mathematics Education; Native Language Education; Primary Education; Secondary Education); **Science, Arts and Humanities** (English; History; Mathematics)

Further Information: Also Marian College of Baliuag.

History: Founded 1958.

Degrees and Diplomas: *Bachelor's Degree*
Last Updated: 29/11/10

MARINA CHING COLLEGE

359 National Highway, San Pedro, Laguna 4023
Tel: +63(2) 868-9523
Fax: +63(2) 868-9523
EMail: marina_college@yahoo.com

President: Arthur Ching

Programmes
Business Administration (Business Administration; Finance; Management; Marketing)

History: Founded 2007.

Degrees and Diplomas: *Bachelor's Degree*
Last Updated: 29/11/10

MARINDUQUE MIDWEST COLLEGE

Dili, Gasan, Marinduque 4905
Tel: +63(42) 342-1014
Fax: +63(42) 342-1014
EMail: mmc@dreamvsat.ph

President: Milton V. Mendoza

Programmes
Business Administration (Accountancy; Business Administration; Management); **Computer Science** (Computer Science); **Computer Technology** (Computer Engineering); **Economics** (Economics); **Education** (Education; Primary Education; Secondary Education); **English** (English)

History: Founded 1945. formerly known as Marinduque Midwest School. Acquired present title 1957.

Degrees and Diplomas: *Certificate/Diploma*; *Associate Degree*; *Bachelor's Degree*
Last Updated: 29/11/10

MARINERS' POLYTECHNIC COLLEGES - PANGANIBAN

Panganiban Drive, Naga City, Camarines Sur 4400
Tel: +63(5421) 473-1434
Fax: +63(5421) 472-6721
EMail: marinerssytem@yahoo.com; mpc75@mozcom.com

President: Marilissa J. Ampuan

Programmes
Undergraduate and Professional (Business Administration; Hotel and Restaurant; Hotel Management; Mass Communication; Radio and Television Broadcasting; Taxation; Tourism)

History: Founded 1974.

Degrees and Diplomas: *Certificate/Diploma*: 2 yrs; *Bachelor's Degree*: 4 yrs
Last Updated: 01/12/10

MARINERS' POLYTECHNIC COLLEGES FOUNDATION - BARAS

Baras, Canaman, Camarines Sur 4402
Tel: +63(54) 473-9726
Fax: +63(54) 811-7300
EMail: baras75@yahoo.com

President: Dante LA. Jimenez

Programmes
Undergraduate and Professional (Marine Engineering; Marine Transport; Nautical Science; Taxation)

History: Founded 1975.

Degrees and Diplomas: *Certificate/Diploma*; *Bachelor's Degree*: 4 yrs; *Bachelor's Degree*: Engineering, 5 yrs
Last Updated: 01/12/10

MARINERS' POLYTECHNIC COLLEGES FOUNDATION - LEGAZPI

Purok 2, Brgy. 42, Legazpi City, Albay 4500
Tel: +63(52) 482-0997
Fax: +63(52) 482-0166
EMail: mariners@globalink.net.ph
Website: http://www.mariners.edu.ph

President: Dante LA. Jimenez

Programmes
Undergraduate and Professional (Hotel and Restaurant; Hotel Management; Marine Engineering; Marine Transport; Mechanical Engineering; Taxation; Tourism)

History: Founded 1985.

Degrees and Diplomas: *Certificate/Diploma*; *Bachelor's Degree*: 4 yrs; *Bachelor's Degree*: Engineering, 5 yrs
Last Updated: 01/12/10

MARITIME ACADEMY OF ASIA AND THE PACIFIC

Brgy. Alas-Asin, Mariveles, Bataan 2105
Tel: +63(917) 533-8263 +63(917) 535-4832 +63(2) 527-2110
Fax: +63(47) 244-5809 +63(47) 532-7990
EMail: info@maap.edu.ph
Website: http://maap.edu.ph

President: Eduardo M.R. Santos

Programmes

Marine Engineering (Marine Engineering); **Marine Transportation** (Marine Transport)

History: Founded 2000.

Degrees and Diplomas: *Bachelor's Degree*
Last Updated: 01/12/10

MARTINEZ MEMORIAL COLLEGE

198 A. Mabini Street, Caloocan City, Third District, Metro Manilia 1400
Tel: +63(2) 288-8861 +63(2) 288-8863
Fax: +63(2) 288-4279

President: Ferdinand A. Martinez

Programmes

Graduate (Educational Administration); **Undergraduate and Professional** (Business Administration; Health Education; Health Sciences; Medical Technology; Nursing; Physical Therapy; Psychology; Radiology)

History: Founded 1962. Formerly known as Martinez Memorial Colleges.

Degrees and Diplomas: *Associate Degree*; *Bachelor's Degree*; *Master's Degree*: Educational Management
Last Updated: 01/12/10

MARY CHILES COLLEGE

667 F.T. Dalupan Sr. Street (formerly Gastambide), Sampaloc, Manila, First District, Metro Manila 1008
Tel: +63(2) 735-5341
Fax: +63(2) 735-5437
EMail: marychilescollege@yahoo.com

Administrator: Vanessan Florendo-Santos Tel: +63 722-5043

Programmes

Undergraduate and Professional (Health Education; Midwifery; Nursing; Respiratory Therapy)

History: Founded 1913. Formerly Mary Chiles General Hospital - School of Nursing and Midwifery (1964-1979).

Degrees and Diplomas: *Certificate/Diploma*: Respiratory Therapy, 2 yrs; *Bachelor's Degree*: Nursing. Also programme in Midwifery
Last Updated: 01/12/10

MARY JOHNSTON COLLEGE

1221 Juan Nolasco Street, Tondo I / II, Manila, First District, Metro Manila 1013
Tel: +63(2) 245-0765 +63(2) 241-1729
Fax: +63(2) 245-0765 +63(2) 245-0763
EMail: mjcoll@i-nExt.net

President: Myrna Puno Velasquez

Programmes

Undergraduate and Professional (Midwifery; Physical Therapy; Respiratory Therapy)

History: Founded 1994.

Degrees and Diplomas: *Bachelor's Degree*: Physical Therapy, 5 yrs; *Bachelor's Degree*: Respiratory Therapy, 4 yrs. Also Midwifery Course, 2 yrs
Last Updated: 01/12/10

MARY THE QUEEN COLLEGE OF SCIENCE AND TECHNOLOGY

Road 44 Commonwealth Avenue, Quezon City, Second District, Metro Manila
Tel: +63(2) 434-4460
Fax: +63(2) 434-7192

President: Elias S. Cipriano

Programmes

Nursing (Nursing)

Degrees and Diplomas: *Bachelor's Degree*
Last Updated: 01/12/10

MARY THE QUEEN COLLEGE - PAMPANGA

Gapan-Olongapo Road, Guagua, Pampanga 2003
Fax: +63(45) 961-7079

President: Michael Lapid

Programmes

Accountancy (Accountancy); **Business Administration** (Accountancy; Business Administration; Finance; Management; Marketing); **Computer Technology** (Computer Engineering); **Information Systems** (Information Management; Information Technology); **Secondary Education** (Education; Mathematics Education; Secondary Education)

History: Founded 2002.

Degrees and Diplomas: *Bachelor's Degree*
Last Updated: 01/12/10

MARYHILL COLLEGE

PO Box 13, Ciudad Maharlika Subd., Iyam, Lucena City, Quezon 4301
Tel: +63(42) 373-6177
Fax: +63 42) 373-0165
EMail: maryhill@usa.net

President: Emilio Z. Marquez, D.D.

Programmes

Undergraduate and Professional (Accountancy; Advertising and Publicity; Biological and Life Sciences; Business Administration; Economics; Education; English; Environmental Studies; Ethics; Foreign Languages Education; Marketing; Nursing; Philosophy; Secondary Education; Social Studies)

History: Founded 1996.

Degrees and Diplomas: *Certificate/Diploma*; *Associate Degree*; *Bachelor's Degree*
Last Updated: 01/12/10

MASBATE COLLEGE

Rosero Street, Masbate, Masbate 5400
Tel: +63(56) 333-2103
Fax: +63(56) 333-5717
EMail: masbate_colleges@yahoo.com

President: Manuel G. Bunan

Programmes

Arts and Science *(Bachelor's degree programmes)* (Accountancy; Banking; Business and Commerce; Computer Engineering; Computer Science; Criminology; Electronic Engineering; English; Finance; History; Management; Mathematics; Medical Technology; Nursing; Political Sciences; Radiology; Telecommunications Engineering); **Education** (Education; English; Filipino; Foreign Languages Education; History; Home Economics Education; Mathematics Education; Native Language Education; Political Sciences; Primary Education); **Graduate** (Education; Educational Administration); **Laws** (Law)

History: Founded 1964.

Degrees and Diplomas: *Certificate/Diploma*; *Associate Degree*; *Bachelor's Degree*; *Master's Degree*: Educational Management; *PhD*: Educational Management
Last Updated: 07/04/11

MASIRICAMPO-ABANTAS MEMORIAL COLLEGE

Buadi Sacayo Basak, Marawi City, Lanao del Sur

President: H. Moomina Tawano Abantas

Programmes

Education (Education; Primary Education; Secondary Education)

History: Founded 2002.

Degrees and Diplomas: *Bachelor's Degree*

Last Updated: 01/12/10

MASTERS TECHNOLOGICAL INSTITUTE OF MINDANAO

0013 M. Badelles Sr. Street Cor. Zamora Street, Poblacion, Iligan City, Lanao del Norte 9200

Tel: +63(63) 221-6472

Chairman, Board of Trustees: Edwin O. Deiparine

Programmes

Undergraduate and Professional Studies (Accountancy; Computer Engineering; Computer Science; Electrical and Electronic Equipment and Maintenance; Maintenance Technology; Mechanics; Technology)

History: Founded in 1996.

Degrees and Diplomas: *Certificate/Diploma*; *Bachelor's Degree*

Last Updated: 01/12/10

MATER DEI COLLEGE - BOHOL

Cabulijan, Tubigon, Bohol 6329

Tel: +63(38) 237-2394

Fax: +63(38) 508-8166

President: Lourdes H. Torrefranca

Programmes

Arts (Economics; English); **Business Administration** (Accountancy; Business Administration; Computer Science; Economics; Finance; Hotel and Restaurant; Hotel Management; Management; Marketing; Tourism); **Criminology** (Criminology; Police Studies); **Education** (Economics; Educational Administration; Educational Sciences; Ethics; Filipino; Foreign Languages Education; History; Mathematics Education; Preschool Education; Primary Education; Secondary Education; Social Studies); **Graduate Studies** (Business Administration; Educational Administration; English; Ethics; Foreign Languages Education; Mathematics Education; Public Administration); **Information Systems and Technology** (Information Management; Information Technology); **Mathematics** (Mathematics); **Nursing** (Nursing)

History: Founded 1984.

Degrees and Diplomas: *Associate Degree*; *Bachelor's Degree*; *Master's Degree*: Educational Management; Public Service Management; English Language Teaching; Business Management; Values Education; Mathematics Teaching

Last Updated: 01/12/10

MATER DEI COLLEGE - SILAY CITY

St. Francis Natures Park Subdivision, Silay City, Negros Occidental 6116

Tel: +63(34) 495-2711

Fax: +63(34) 495-2711

EMail: materdeicollege_mmhc@yahoo.com.ph

President: Matthew Frederick Ma. Fernandez, MMHC

Programmes

Secondary Education (Education; English; Foreign Languages Education; Philosophy; Secondary Education)

History: Founded 1999.

Degrees and Diplomas: *Bachelor's Degree*

Last Updated: 01/12/10

MATER DIVINAE GRATIAE COLLEGE

Camp Picardo, Dolores, Eastern Samar 6817

Tel: +63 830-0314

Head/Principal: Ma. Gracia T. Osida, SFSC

Programmes

Undergraduate and Professional Studies (Computer Education; Education; English; Foreign Languages Education; Primary Education)

History: Founded in 1995

Degrees and Diplomas: *Associate Degree*; *Bachelor's Degree*

Last Updated: 01/12/10

MATER REDEMPTORIS COLLEGE OF SAN JOSE CITY

San Jose City, Nueva Ecija 3121

Rector: Francid Ma. Tiquiq

Programmes

Arts and Science (Communication Studies; Curriculum; Education; English; Foreign Languages Education; Philosophy; Primary Education; Secondary Education; Theology)

Degrees and Diplomas: *Associate Degree*; *Bachelor's Degree*

Last Updated: 01/12/10

MATI DOCTORS COLLEGE

National Highway, Fronting Provincial Hospital, Mati, Davao Oriental 8200

EMail: matidoctorscollege@yahoo.com

President: Noreen Jane P. Teodoro

Programmes

Health Sciences (Health Education; Health Sciences; Midwifery; Nursing)

History: Founded 1999.

Degrees and Diplomas: *Associate Degree*; *Bachelor's Degree*

Last Updated: 01/12/10

MATI POLYTECHNIC COLLEGE

Mapantad, Sainz Street, Mati, Davao Oriental 8200

Tel: +63(87) 388-3526

Fax: +63(87) 388-4347

EMail: mpc_edu@yahoo.com

President: Aresio M. Agbong

Programmes

Undergraduate and Professional Studies (Banking; Business and Commerce; Criminology; Curriculum; Finance; Marketing; Primary Education; Social Studies)

History: Founded 1991. Formerly known as Mati Polytechnic Institute (1992-2000).

Degrees and Diplomas: *Bachelor's Degree*

Last Updated: 02/12/10

MATS COLLEGE OF TECHNOLOGY

R. Castillo Street, Agdao, Davao City, Davao del Sur 8000

Tel: +63(82) 226-4560

Fax: +63(82) 225-3576

President: Eduardo I. Alterado

Programmes

Aircraft Technology (Air Transport; Technology); **Airline Management and Accountancy** (Accountancy; Air Transport); **Business Administration** (Accountancy; Business Administration; Business and Commerce; Management; Taxation); **Criminology** (Criminology); **Dentistry** (Dentistry); **Education** (Education; English; Foreign Languages Education; Primary Education; Secondary Education); **Engineering** (Aeronautical and Aerospace Engineering; Electrical Engineering; Electronic Engineering; Industrial Engineering; Marine Engineering; Marine Transport; Mechanical Engineering; Telecommunications Engineering); **Optometry** (Optometry); **Tourism, Hotel and Restaurant Management** (Hotel and Restaurant; Hotel Management)

History: Founded 1970 as Mindanao Aeronautical Technical School. Acquired present title 1977.

Degrees and Diplomas: *Bachelor's Degree*

Last Updated: 02/12/10

MAXINO COLLEGE

Bagacay, Magnao Road, Dumaguete City, Negros Oriental 6200
Tel: +63(35) 225-1612 +63(35) 422-6703
Fax: +63(35) 422-6703
EMail: maxinocollege@yahoo.com.ph

President: Gerardo C. Maxino

Programmes

Business Administration (Business Administration; Human Resources; Management); **Computer Engineering** (Computer Engineering); **Information Technology** (Information Technology); **Physics** (Physics); **Political Sciences** (Political Sciences)

History: Founded 2006.

Degrees and Diplomas: *Bachelor's Degree*
Last Updated: 02/12/10

MCN COLLEGE

39 Rizal Street, Tuguegarao City, Cagayan 3500
Tel: +63(78) 846-1820
EMail: MCN_College@yahoo.com

President: Nora C. Navarro

Programmes

Accountancy (Accountancy); **Business Management and Entrepreneurship** (Business Administration; Management); **Computer Engineering** (Computer Engineering); **Computer Science** (Computer Science; Software Engineering); **Information Technology** (Information Technology)

History: Founded 1989.

Degrees and Diplomas: *Certificate/Diploma*; *Bachelor's Degree*: 4 yrs; *Bachelor's Degree*: Computer Engineering, 5 yrs
Last Updated: 02/12/10

MEDICAL COLLEGES OF NORTHERN PHILIPPINES

Alimannao Hills, Peñablanca, Cagayan 3502
Tel: +63(78) 844-1010
Fax: +63(78) 844-1010
EMail: mcnp_isap@yahoo.com

President: Ronald P. Guzman

Programmes

Dental Technology (Dental Technology); **Nursing** (Midwifery; Nursing); **Physical Therapy** (Physical Therapy); **Radiologic Technology** (Medical Technology; Radiology)

History: Founded 1994.

Degrees and Diplomas: *Certificate/Diploma*; *Associate Degree*; *Bachelor's Degree*: 4 yrs; *Bachelor's Degree*: Physical Therapy, 5 yrs
Last Updated: 02/12/10

MEDINA COLLEGE

Jose Abad Santos Street, Carmen Annex, Ozamis City, Misamis Occidental 7200
Tel: +63(65) 521-0036 +63(65) 521-1466
Fax: +63(65) 521-1466
EMail: medina_regoff_oza@hotmail.com

President: Rico M. Medima, Jr.

Campuses

Ipil (Arts and Humanities; Computer Science; Criminology; Nursing; Primary Education); **Pagadian** (Arts and Humanities; English; Foreign Languages Education; Hotel and Restaurant; Hotel Management; Medical Technology; Midwifery; Nursing; Primary Education; Radiology; Tourism)

Programmes

Arts (English; History; Political Sciences); **Dental Medicine** (Dentistry); **Education** (Education; English; Foreign Languages Education; Health Education; Health Sciences; Primary Education; Secondary Education); **Graduate** (Business Administration; Education; Educational and Student Counselling; Government; Nursing; Primary Education; Public Administration; Public Health); **Science** (Agriculture; Banking; Biology; Business Administration; Business and Commerce; Civil Engineering; Computer Engineering; Computer Science; Electrical Engineering; Finance; Food Science; Food Technology; Home Economics; Mechanical Engineering; Medical Technology; Midwifery; Nursing; Nutrition; Occupational Therapy; Pharmacy; Physical Therapy; Public Administration; Radiology; Secretarial Studies; Tourism)

History: Founded in 1963.

Degrees and Diplomas: *Bachelor's Degree*; *Master's Degree*: Business Administration; Elementary Education; Guidance and Counseling; Nursing; Public Administration (Non-Thesis and with thesis); Arts in Education; Nursing; Public Health; *PhD*: Education
Last Updated: 02/12/10

MEDINA FOUNDATION COLLEGE

Jasmine Street, Poblacion, Sapang Dalaga, Misamis Occidental 7212
Tel: +63(65) 586-0088

Administrator: Eduardo De Los Santos

Programmes

Business Administration (Business Administration; Management; Secretarial Studies); **Economics** (Economics); **Education** (English; Foreign Languages Education; Health Education; Music Education; Physical Education; Primary Education; Secondary Education)

Degrees and Diplomas: *Bachelor's Degree*
Last Updated: 02/12/10

MEGABYTE COLLEGE OF SCIENCE AND TECHNOLOGY - GUAGUA

Calle McKinley Sto. Cristo, Guagua, Pampanga 2003
Tel: +63(45) 900-2412
Fax: +63(45) 900-2412
EMail: mcst@mozcom.com

Director: Crisencio B. Buenarte

Programmes

Computer Technology (Computer Engineering); **Information Technology** (Information Technology)

Further Information: Also Florida Campus in Floridablanca, Pampanga

History: Founded 1985.

Degrees and Diplomas: *Certificate/Diploma*; *Associate Degree*; *Bachelor's Degree*
Last Updated: 02/12/10

MEIN COLLEGE

San Jose Gusu, Zamboanga City, Zamboanga del Sur 7000
Tel: +63(62) 992-3319
Fax: +63(62) 991-1954
EMail: mcengracia@yahoo.com

President: Loureli C. Siy

Programmes

Commerce (Business and Commerce; Business Computing; Human Resources; Management); **Computer Engineering** (Computer Engineering); **Computer Science** (Computer Science; Software Engineering); **Electronics and Computer Engineering** (Computer Engineering; Electronic Engineering); **Secondary Education** (Education; English; Foreign Languages Education; Secondary Education)

History: Founded in 1985.

Degrees and Diplomas: *Associate Degree*; *Bachelor's Degree*
Last Updated: 02/12/10

METRO BUSINESS COLLEGE - PASAY

2052 Taft Avenue Cor. Buendia Avenue, Pasay City, Fourth District, Metro Manila 1300
Tel: +63(2) 888-0432
Fax: +63(2) 887-7236

President: Ileana N. Ibay

Programmes
Undergraduate and Professional (Business Administration; Computer Science)

Further Information: Also Metro Business College-Quezon City

History: Founded 1985. Formerly known as Metro Data Computer College (1993-2002).

Degrees and Diplomas: *Associate Degree*; *Bachelor's Degree*
Last Updated: 02/12/10

METRO-DAGUPAN COLLEGES

Serafica Street, Mangaldan, Pangasinan 2432
Tel: +63(75) 513-3954 +63(75) 522-5492
Fax: +63(75) 522-6367
EMail: mdc@pangasinan.com

President: Mae T. De Los Reyes

Programmes
Arts (Mass Communication); **Business Administration** (Accountancy; Business Administration; Management; Marketing); **Civil Engineering** (Civil Engineering); **Computer Science** (Computer Engineering; Computer Science; Industrial Engineering; Information Technology); **Criminology** (Criminology; Police Studies); **Education** (Curriculum; Education; English; Ethics; Filipino; Foreign Languages Education; Health Education; Home Economics Education; Mathematics Education; Music Education; Native Language Education; Physical Education; Primary Education; Science Education; Secondary Education; Social Studies; Technology Education); **Graduate** (Business Administration; Child Care and Development; Educational Administration; English; Ethics; Filipino; Government; Health Education; International Business; Management; Mathematics Education; Music Education; Physical Education; Police Studies; Preschool Education; Primary Education; Public Administration; Science Education; Small Business; Social and Community Services; Social Studies; Social Work; Special Education; Technology Education); **Tourism** (Hotel and Restaurant; Hotel Management; Tourism)

History: Founded 1996.

Degrees and Diplomas: *Associate Degree*; *Bachelor's Degree*; *Master's Degree*: Business Administration (Business Management; Small and Medium-Scale Enterprise Management; International Business Management); Public Administration
Last Updated: 02/12/10

METRO DUMAGUETE COLLEGE

3rd Floor Noreco II Bldg., Real Street, Dumaguete City, Negros Oriental 6200
Tel: +63(35) 225-9170
Fax: +63(35) 422-9728

President: Delma P. Manila

Programmes
Business Administration (Business Administration); **Communication** (Communication Studies); **Computer Science** (Computer Science); **Information Technology** (Information Technology); **Tourism Management** (Tourism)

History: Founded 2007.

Degrees and Diplomas: *Bachelor's Degree*
Last Updated: 02/12/10

METRO MANILA COLLEGE

No.1 72nd Avenue Munich Olympic Bo. Kaligayahan, Novaliches, Quezon City, Second District, Metro Manila 1123
Tel: +63(2) 939-1162 +63(2) 936-3082
Fax: +63(2) 419-1482
EMail: Memaco@yahoo.com

President: Erlinda M. Da'lag

Programmes
Graduate (Business Administration; Criminology; Education; Educational Administration; Educational and Student Counselling; English; Foreign Languages Education; Mathematics Education); **Undergraduate and Professional** (Accountancy; Art Education; Banking; Business Administration; Business and Commerce; Criminology; Education; Educational Administration; Educational Sciences; English; Finance; Foreign Languages Education; Human Resources; Management; Marketing; Mathematics Education; Music Education; Native Language Education; Physical Education; Police Studies; Primary Education; Real Estate; Secondary Education; Secretarial Studies; Social Studies)

History: Founded 1947 as Novaliches Academy. Acquired present title 1977.

Degrees and Diplomas: *Bachelor's Degree*: 4 yrs; *Master's Degree*: Business Administration; Criminology; English and Mathematics Education; Educational Administration and Supervision; Educational Guidance and Counselling, a further 2 yrs; *PhD*: Development Education, a further 3 yrs
Last Updated: 02/12/10

METRO SUBIC COLLEGES

East Tapinac, Sta. Rita, Olongapo City, Zambales 2200
Tel: +63(47) 223-7875
Fax: +63(47) 223-7875

Dean: Teresita O. Oliver

Programmes
Nursing (Midwifery; Nursing); **Radiologic Technology** (Medical Technology; Radiology)

History: Founded 1993.

Degrees and Diplomas: *Certificate/Diploma*; *Associate Degree*; *Bachelor's Degree*
Last Updated: 02/12/10

METROPOLITAN HOSPITAL COLLEGE OF NURSING

1357 Masangkay Street, Santa Cruz, City of Manila, First District, Metro Manila
Tel: +63(2) 255-0401
Fax: +63(2) 254-7356

President: Joel T. Go

Programmes
Nursing (Nursing)
History: Founded 1976.

Degrees and Diplomas: *Bachelor's Degree*
Last Updated: 02/12/10

METROPOLITAN SCHOOL OF SCIENCE AND TECHNOLOGY

Maharlika Road, City of Santiago, Isabela 3311
Tel: +63(78) 682-7381
Fax: +63(78) 682-7381
EMail: mcst@yahoo.com

Director: Marivic Valdez-Eclipse

Programmes
Criminology (Criminology)

History: Founded 1993.

Degrees and Diplomas: *Bachelor's Degree*
Last Updated: 02/12/10

METROPOLYTECHNIC COLLEGE

Block 1 Lot 1 Phase 1 Package 2, Bagong Silang, Caloocan City, Third District, Metro Manila 1428
Tel: +63(2) 962-9823
Fax: +63(2) 962-9823
EMail: metro_polytechnic1998@yahoo.com.ph

President: Benjamin U. Gagni, Jr.

Programmes
Education (Education; English; Foreign Languages Education; Mathematics Education; Primary Education; Secondary Education)

History: Founded 1998.

Degrees and Diplomas: *Certificate/Diploma*; *Bachelor's Degree*
Last Updated: 02/12/10

MEYCAUAYAN COLLEGE

Mc Arthur Highway, Calvario, City of Meycauayan, Bulacan 3020
Tel: +63(44) 840-6190 +63(44) 840-0899
Fax: +63(44) 935-3539
EMail: mcian@bulacan.ph

President: Vicente A. Hermoso, Jr.

Programmes
Business Administration (Accountancy; Business Administration; Finance; Management; Marketing); **Computer Science** (Computer Science); **Education** (Biology; Chemistry; Child Care and Development; Education; English; Filipino; Foreign Languages Education; Mathematics Education; Native Language Education; Preschool Education; Primary Education; Social Studies); **Graduate** (Educational Administration; English; Filipino; Foreign Languages Education; Mathematics Education; Native Language Education; Physical Education; Psychology); **Psychology** (Psychology)

History: Founded 1925.

Degrees and Diplomas: *Bachelor's Degree*; *Master's Degree*: Arts in: Psychology; Educational Administration and Supervision; Management; English; Filipino; Mathematics; Physical Education
Last Updated: 02/12/10

MICRO ASIA COLLEGE OF SCIENCE AND TECHNOLOGY

Paulien Zone 1, Iba, Zambales 2201
Tel: +63(47) 811-1365 +63(47) 811-2463
Fax: +63(47) 811-1365
EMail: mahlyvj@digetelone.com; macsatatiba@yahoo.com

President: Ricardo Z. Torio

Programmes
Business Administration (Accountancy; Banking; Business Administration; Finance; Management); **Computer Science and Engineering** (Computer Engineering; Computer Science); **Information Management** (Information Management)

History: Founded 1994 as IBA Institute of Technology.

Degrees and Diplomas: *Certificate/Diploma*; *Bachelor's Degree*
Last Updated: 02/12/10

MICROCITY COMPUTER COLLEGES FOUNDATION

Narra Street, San Jose, Balanga City, Bataan 2100
Tel: +63(47) 237-3242
Fax: +63(47) 237-3242
EMail: microcity1992@digitelone.com

President: Carmen Morales

Programmes
Computer Science and Engineering (Computer Engineering; Computer Science); **Electronics and Communication Engineering** (Electronic Engineering; Telecommunications Engineering); **Information Management** (Information Management)

History: Founded 1992. Formerly known as Microcity Computer Colleges. Acquired present title 2002.

Degrees and Diplomas: *Certificate/Diploma*; *Associate Degree*; *Bachelor's Degree*
Last Updated: 02/12/10

MICROSYSTEM INTERNATIONAL INSTITUTE OF TECHNOLOGY

3rd Floor Cebu Appliance Bldg., Highway Sangi, Tabunok, Talisay City, Cebu 6045
Tel: +63(32) 272-9277 +63(32) 491-7461
Fax: +63(32) 272-9277
EMail: miit_educ2002@ymail.com

Administrator: Alfredo S. Moreno Jr.

Programmes
Business Administration (Business Administration; Finance); **Computer Science** (Computer Science); **Information Systems and Technology** (Information Management; Information Technology)

Degrees and Diplomas: *Bachelor's Degree*
Last Updated: 02/12/10

MIDWAY MARITIME FOUNDATION

10 Bitas, Maharlika Highway, Cabanatuan City, Nueva Ecija 3100
Tel: +63(44) 463-7020 +63(44) 463-7021
Fax: +63(44) 463-5093
EMail: midway_1993@digitelone.com

President: Sabino M. Manglicmot

Programmes
Customs Administration (Administration; Taxation); **Marine Engineering** (Marine Engineering); **Marine Transportation** (Marine Transport)

History: Founded 1988.

Degrees and Diplomas: *Certificate/Diploma*; *Bachelor's Degree*
Last Updated: 02/12/10

MINA DE ORO INSTITUTE OF SCIENCE AND TECHNOLOGY

Poblacion 4, Victoria, Oriental Mindoro 5205

Programmes
Commerce (Business and Commerce; Management); **Midwifery** (Midwifery); **Nursing** (Nursing)

Further Information: Also campus in Roxas, Oriental Mindoro

Degrees and Diplomas: *Certificate/Diploma*; *Bachelor's Degree*
Last Updated: 03/12/10

MINDANAO ARTS AND TECHNOLOGICAL INSTITUTE

Brgy. 09, Malaybalay City, Bukidnon 8700
Tel: +63(88) 813-4770
Fax: +63(88) 813-4770
EMail: mati@mozcom.com

Director: Tito P. Dichosa

Programmes
Undergraduate and Professional Studies (Business Administration; Criminology; Hotel and Restaurant; Hotel Management; Information Technology; Midwifery)

History: Founded 1988.

Degrees and Diplomas: *Certificate/Diploma*; *Bachelor's Degree*
Last Updated: 03/12/10

MINDANAO AUTONOMOUS COLLEGE FOUNDATION

D. Flores Street, Lamitan City, Basilan 7302
EMail: macfi_lamitan@yahoo.com

Chief Executive Officer: Rima H.Hassan Al-Hadja

Programmes
Graduate (Education; Educational Administration; Educational and Student Counselling; English; Filipino; Foreign Languages Education; Mathematics Education; Native Language Education; Science Education; Social Studies); **Undergraduate and Professional Studies** (Computer Engineering; Computer Science; Criminology; English; Filipino; Foreign Languages Education; Health Education; Islamic Studies; Mathematics Education; Native Language Education; Nursing; Political Sciences; Primary Education; Science Education; Secondary Education)

History: Founded 2003.

Degrees and Diplomas: *Bachelor's Degree*; *Master's Degree*: Education (Filipino; Social Studies; Science; Guidance; English; Mathematics; Educational Administration); Public Administration (Organization and Management)
Last Updated: 03/12/10

MINDANAO CAPITOL COLLEGE

Don. Roman Vilo Street, Cotabato City, Cotabato 9600

President: Bai Habiba A. Wahab

Programmes

Commerce (Banking; Business and Commerce; Finance; Management); **Education** (Economics; Education; English; Filipino; Foreign Languages Education; History; Mathematics Education; Native Language Education; Primary Education; Secondary Education); **History** (History); **Political Sciences** (Political Sciences)

History: Founded 1992.

Degrees and Diplomas: *Bachelor's Degree*
Last Updated: 03/12/10

MINDANAO INTERNATIONAL UNIVERSITY

Mindanao Kokosai Daigaku

Mamay Road, Lanang, Davao City, Davao del Sur 8000
Tel: +63(82) 223-0013
Fax: +63(82) 235-1863
EMail: docnlvitto@yahoo.com

President: Escovilla Nieto Latorre Vitto

Programmes

Community Development (Urban Studies); **Education** (Biological and Life Sciences; Curriculum; Education; Mathematics Education; Preschool Education; Primary Education; Science Education; Secondary Education; Special Education); **International Studies** (International Studies); **Social Services** (Child Care and Development; Gerontology; Social and Community Services)

History: Founded 2001.

Degrees and Diplomas: *Bachelor's Degree*
Last Updated: 03/12/10

MINDANAO ISLAMIC COMPUTER COLLEGE

Quezon Avenue, Marawi City, Lanao del Sur 9700

President: Cairoden I. Alonto

Programmes

Computer Science (Computer Science); **Education** (Education; Primary Education; Secondary Education)

History: Founded 1992.

Degrees and Diplomas: *Associate Degree*; *Bachelor's Degree*
Last Updated: 03/12/10

MINDANAO MEDICAL FOUNDATION COLLEGE

R. Castillo Street, Agdao, Davao City, Davao del Sur 8000
Tel: +63(82) 221-6225
Fax: +63(82) 226-4560

President: Amie Theresa Alterado Bautista

Programmes

Health Sciences (Medical Technology; Nursing; Pharmacy; Physical Therapy)

History: Founded 1979.

Degrees and Diplomas: *Bachelor's Degree*
Last Updated: 03/12/10

MINDANAO POLYTECHNIC COLLEGE

Crossing Makar, General Santos City, South Cotabato 9500
Tel: +63(83) 552-2671
Fax: +63(83) 552-7898
EMail: mpcweb@mpc-ph.com

President: J. Apolinario L. Lozada, Jr., DBE

Programmes

Undergraduate and Professional Studies (Accountancy; Business Administration; Business and Commerce; Hotel and Restaurant; Hotel Management; Information Technology; Management; Marine Engineering; Marine Transport; Mechanical Engineering; Taxation; Tourism)

History: Founded 1980 as Mindanao Polytechnic School. Acquired current title 1985.

Degrees and Diplomas: *Bachelor's Degree*
Last Updated: 03/12/10

MINDANAO SANITARIUM AND HOSPITAL COLLEGE OF MEDICAL ARTS FOUNDATION

Pinesville, Iligan City, Lanao del Norte 9200
Tel: +63(63) 221-9219
Fax: +63(63) 223-2114
EMail: mshcnet@yahoo.com

President: Edgar Claude A. Nadal

Programmes

Computer Science (Computer Science); **Health Sciences** (Health Education; Medical Technology; Midwifery; Nursing; Physical Therapy; Radiology); **Information Technology** (Information Technology)

History: Founded 1994.

Degrees and Diplomas: *Associate Degree*; *Bachelor's Degree*
Last Updated: 03/12/10

MIRIAM COLLEGE

Katipunan Rd., Loyola Heights, Quezon City, Second District, Metro Manila 1101
Tel: +63(2) 580-5400 +63(2) 927-2421 +63(2) 927-2431
Fax: +63(2) 423-0169
EMail: coll-admission@mc.edu.ph
Website: http://www.mc.edu.ph

President: Patricia B. Licuanan EMail: president@mc.edu.ph

Programmes

Graduate (Child Care and Development; Education; Environmental Studies; Family Studies; Human Resources; International Studies; Psychology); **Undergraduate and Professional** (Accountancy; Business Administration; Child Care and Development; Communication Arts; Computer Engineering; E-Business/Commerce; Environmental Management; Environmental Studies; International Studies; Management; Marketing; Psychology; Social Work)

History: Founded 1923. Formerly known as Maryknoll College (1929-1989).

Degrees and Diplomas: *Certificate/Diploma*; *Associate Degree*; *Bachelor's Degree*; *Master's Degree*: Arts in: International Studies; Migration; Science in Environmental Studies; Management; Education (Childhood Education; Special Education; Measurement and Evaluation; Values Education and Development; Instructional Management); Arts in: Family Psychology; Guidance and Counselling; Human Resources; *PhD*: Environmental Studies; Child and Family Psychology; Environmental Education
Last Updated: 06/12/10

MISAMIS INSTITUTE OF TECHNOLOGY

Bañadero, Highway, Ozamis City, Misamis Occidental 7200
Tel: +63(88) 521-2189
Fax: +63(88) 521-2189
EMail: mit.mtc@ozamiz.com

President: Allan A. Maglasang

Programmes

Accountancy (Accountancy); **Computer Science** (Computer Science); **Customs Administration** (Taxation); **Engineering** (Civil Engineering; Electrical Engineering; Electronic Engineering; Engineering; Marine Engineering; Marine Transport; Mechanical Engineering; Telecommunications Engineering); **Mass Communication** (Journalism; Mass Communication; Radio and Television Broadcasting)

History: Founded 1965. Formerly known as Misamis Technical School and Misamis Technical Institute.

Degrees and Diplomas: *Associate Degree*; *Bachelor's Degree*
Last Updated: 07/12/10

MISAMIS ORIENTAL INSTITUTE OF SCIENCE AND TECHNOLOGY

Balingasag, Misamis Oriental 9005
Tel: +63(88) 333-2306
Fax: +63(88) 333-2535
EMail: moist_rv@yahoo.com

President: Romulo P. Valmores

Programmes

Business Administration (Business Administration; Management; Marketing); **Criminology** (Criminology); **Education** (Education; English; Foreign Languages Education; Primary Education; Secondary Education); **Hotel and Restaurant Management** (Hotel and Restaurant; Hotel Management)

History: Founded 2002.

Degrees and Diplomas: *Bachelor's Degree*
Last Updated: 07/12/10

MISAMIS UNIVERSITY

Hilarion T. Feliciano Street, Ozamis City, Misamis Occidental 7200
Tel: +63(88) 521-0367
Fax: +63(65) 521-2917
EMail: mu@mu.edu.ph
Website: http://www.mu.edu.ph

President: Karen Belina F. De Leon

Executive Vice-President and Vice-President for Academic Affairs: Sonia S. Feliciano

International Relations: Gloria M. Feliciano, Vice-President for External Affairs

Colleges

Agriculture and Forestry (Agricultural Education; Agricultural Engineering; Agriculture; Forestry); **Allied Health Sciences** (Occupational Therapy; Physical Therapy); **Arts and Science** (Arts and Humanities; Biology; Economics; English; History; Journalism; Mathematics; Natural Sciences; Political Sciences; Psychology; Social and Community Services; Social Work; Zoology); **Business and Management** (Business Administration; Business and Commerce; Economics; Human Resources; Management; Marketing); **Computer Studies** (Computer Science; Information Technology); **Criminology** (Criminal Law; Criminology); **Dentistry** (Dentistry); **Education** (Biological and Life Sciences; Education; English; Filipino; Foreign Languages Education; Mathematics Education; Native Language Education; Preschool Education; Primary Education; Secondary Education; Social Studies); **Engineering and Technology** (Civil Engineering; Computer Engineering; Electrical Engineering; Engineering; Mechanical Engineering; Technology); **Law** (Law); **Maritime Education** (Marine Engineering; Marine Transport); **Medical Technology** (Medical Technology); **Nursing** (Nursing)

Schools

Graduate Studies (Business Administration; Educational Administration; Educational and Student Counselling; Educational Sciences; English; Filipino; Foreign Languages Education; Government; Mathematics Education; Midwifery; Native Language Education; Nursing; Public Administration); **Midwifery** (Midwifery)

Further Information: Also Oroquieta City Campus, Misamis Occidental. Teaching Hospital.

History: Founded 1929 as School. Became Institute 1931 and College 1955. Acquired present status and title 1977. A private Institution.

Governing Bodies: Board of Trustees

Academic Year: June to March (June-October; November-March)

Admission Requirements: Graduation from high school and entrance examination

Main Language(s) of Instruction: Filipino, English

Degrees and Diplomas: *Certificate/Diploma*; *Bachelor's Degree*; *Post Baccalaureate Certificate/Diploma*; *Master's Degree*: Arts in Education (Educational Management, Guidance and Counseling; Mathematics Education, Filipino and English Language Teaching); Arts in Nursing (Community Health Nursing; Maternal and Child Nursing; Nursing Education Administration); Nursing (Community Health Nursing; Maternal and Child Nursing; Nursing Education Administration); Public Administration; Business Administration; *PhD*: Education (Educational Management)

Student Residential Facilities: Forc. 110 students

Libraries: Central Library, c. 28,000 vols; Oroquieta Unit, c. 14,000 vols

Publications: Misamis Collegian *(biannually)*
Last Updated: 07/12/10

MLG COLLEGE OF LEARNING

Brgy. Atabay, Hilangos, Leyte 6524
Tel: +63(53) 336-2932
Fax: +63(53) 336-2932

Director: Giovanni G. Olo

Programmes

Undergraduate and Professional Studies (Computer Education; Computer Science; Education; Information Technology; Management; Primary Education; Secondary Education)

History: Founded 1999.

Degrees and Diplomas: *Bachelor's Degree*
Last Updated: 07/12/10

MONDRIAAN AURA COLLEGE

22-14th Street, East Tapinac, SBFZ, Olongapo City, Zambales 2200
Tel: +63(47) 252-3808
Fax: +63(47) 252-3801
EMail: aura@svisp.com

President: Edgar G. Geniza

Programmes

Arts and Humanities (Arts and Humanities; Mass Communication); **Business Administration** (Business Administration; Human Resources; Management; Public Administration); **Computer Science** (Computer Science); **Education** (Educational Administration; English; Filipino; Foreign Languages Education; Health Education; Mathematics Education; Native Language Education; Primary Education; Science Education; Secondary Education; Social Studies; Teacher Training); **Engineering** (Computer Engineering; Electronic Engineering; Industrial Engineering; Telecommunications Engineering)

History: Founded 1993.

Degrees and Diplomas: *Associate Degree*; *Bachelor's Degree*; *Master's Degree*: Arts (Teaching; Educational Administration); Management (Public Administration; Business Administration; Human Resource Management)
Last Updated: 07/12/10

MONTASHIR ISLAMIC COLLEGES

Dayawan, Masiu, Lanao del Sur 9706

President: Hadji Amer Macadupang

Programmes

Education (Education; Primary Education; Secondary Education)

Degrees and Diplomas: *Bachelor's Degree*
Last Updated: 07/12/10

MONTESSORI PROFESSIONAL COLLEGE - IMUS

Imus, Cavite 4103
Tel: +63(2) 697-6650
Fax: +63(2) 697-6650

President: Danilo Dy

Programmes

Business Administration (Business Administration; Management); **Computer Science** (Computer Science); **Hotel and Restaurant Management** (Hotel and Restaurant; Hotel Management)

History: Founded 1998.

Degrees and Diplomas: *Bachelor's Degree*
Last Updated: 07/12/10

MONTICELLO INTERNATIONAL COLLEGE

Camp 7, Kennon Rd., Maryheights, Camp 7, Kennon Road, Baguio City, Benguet 2600
Tel: +63(74) 447-4031
Fax: +63(74) 447-4030
EMail: mmcmlijauco@gmail.com
Website: http://www.haksanila.net

President: Ruben A. Corpuz

Programmes

Undergraduate and Professional (Education; English; Foreign Languages Education; Primary Education; Secondary Education)

History: Founded 2002 as Haksan International Language Academy. Acquired present title 2003.

Degrees and Diplomas: *Bachelor's Degree*
Last Updated: 07/12/10

MOUNT CARMEL COLLEGE

Carmelite Street, City of Escalante, Negros Occidental 6124
Tel: +63(34) 454-0211
Fax: +63(34) 454-0213
EMail: mcc@yahoo.com.ph

President: Perfecto Ll. Adeva, Jr., O.Carm.

Campuses

Baler (Arts and Humanities; Business Administration; Business and Commerce; Computer Engineering; Criminology; Economics; Education; English; Ethics; Filipino; Foreign Languages Education; History; Management; Marketing; Native Language Education; Philosophy; Primary Education; Religious Education; Science Education; Secondary Education; Social Studies; Sociology); **Bocaue, Bulacan** (Education; Hotel and Restaurant; Hotel Management; Medical Technology; Midwifery; Nursing; Physical Therapy; Radiology; Secondary Education); **Casiguran** (Education; Religious Education; Secondary Education); **San Francisco** (Accountancy; Business Administration; Education; English; Finance; Foreign Languages Education; Management; Primary Education; Secondary Education)

Programmes

Arts (English; Sociology); **Business Administration** (Accountancy; Business Administration; Computer Science; Finance; Management); **Computer Science** (Computer Science); **Education** (Curriculum; Education; English; Filipino; Foreign Languages Education; Health Education; Mathematics Education; Native Language Education; Primary Education; Science Education; Secondary Education)

History: Founded 1961.

Degrees and Diplomas: *Certificate/Diploma*; *Associate Degree*; *Bachelor's Degree*
Last Updated: 07/12/10

MOUNT MORIAH COLLEGE

Mabini, Poro, Cebu 6049
Tel: +63(32) 272-4347
Fax: +63(32) 272-0003

President: Aguido A. Magadaro

Programmes

Undergraduate and Professional Studies (Business and Commerce; Computer Engineering; Computer Networks; Criminology; English; Foreign Languages Education; Information Technology; Management; Police Studies; Primary Education; Secondary Education)

History: Founded 1994.

Degrees and Diplomas: *Bachelor's Degree*
Last Updated: 07/12/10

MOUNTAIN VIEW COLLEGE

College Heights, Mt. Nebo, Bukidnon 8709
Tel: +63(88) 222-5519
Fax: +63(88) 222-5516
EMail: mvcollege@eudoramail.com
Website: http://www.mvcollege.org

President: Daniel D. Dial

Programmes

Undergraduate and Professional Studies (Accountancy; Agriculture; Animal Husbandry; Art Education; Biology; Business Administration; Computer Education; Crop Production; Education; English; Ethics; Finance; Foreign Languages Education; Health Education; Home Economics Education; Human Resources; Management; Mathematics Education; Music Education; Nursing; Physical Education; Primary Education; Religion; Religious Education; Secondary Education; Technology Education; Theology; Zoology)

History: Founded in 1953.

Degrees and Diplomas: *Bachelor's Degree*
Last Updated: 07/12/10

MYSTICAL ROSE COLLEGE OF SCIENCE AND TECHNOLOGY

Pogon lomboy, Mangatarem, Pangasinan 2413
Tel: +63(75) 546-0513
EMail: mysticalrosecollege@yahoo.com

President: Vigilio V. Valmonte

Programmes

Elementary Education (Primary Education; Special Education); **Secondary Education** (Secondary Education)

History: Founded 1996. Formerly known as Mystical Rose Montessori.

Degrees and Diplomas: *Bachelor's Degree*
Last Updated: 07/12/10

NAGA COLLEGE FOUNDATION

Peñafrancia Avenue, Naga City, Camarines Sur 4400
Tel: +63(54) 473-8486
Fax: +63(54) 472-4011
EMail: info@ncf.edu.ph

President: Carlo P. Villanueva

Programmes

Graduate (Business Administration; Criminal Law; Criminology; Education; Educational Administration; English; Filipino; Foreign Languages Education; Home Economics Education; Human Resources; Mathematics Education; Native Language Education; Physical Education; Public Administration; Science Education); **Undergraduate and Professional** (Art Education; Banking; Biological and Life Sciences; Business and Commerce; Civil Engineering; Computer Science; Criminology; Economics; Education; Engineering; English; Filipino; Finance; Foreign Languages Education; Health Education; History; Home Economics Education; Management; Marketing; Mathematics Education; Music Education; Native Language Education; Nursing; Physical Education; Primary Education; Science Education; Secondary Education; Social Studies; Speech Studies; Technology Education; Theatre)

History: Founded 1947. Formerly known as Naga College, Inc.

Degrees and Diplomas: *Certificate/Diploma*; *Associate Degree*; *Bachelor's Degree*; *Master's Degree*: Business Administration; Public Administration; Criminology; Education (Administration and Supervision; Educational Management; English; Filipino; Home Economics; Mathematics Education; Physical Education; Science Education); *PhD*: Human Resources Management
Last Updated: 07/12/10

NAGA VIEW ADVENTIST COLLEGE

Panicuason, Naga City, Camarines Sur 4400
Tel: +63(54) 473-5811
Fax: +63(54) 473-5811
EMail: nesdayson_nvac_pres@yahoo.com.ph

President: Nestor D. Dayson

Programmes

Education (Art Education; Education; English; Filipino; Foreign Languages Education; Health Education; Mathematics Education; Music Education; Native Language Education; Physical Education; Primary Education; Secondary Education); **Theology** (Theology)

History: Founded 1965. Formerly known as Philippine Union College-Naga View Campus.

Degrees and Diplomas: *Certificate/Diploma*; *Bachelor's Degree*
Last Updated: 07/12/10

NAMEI POLYTECHNIC INSTITUTE

123 A. Mabini Street, City of Mandaluyong, Third District, Metro Manila 1550
Tel: +63(2) 531-7328
Fax: +63(2) 531-8561
EMail: namei@pacific.net.ph

President: Ma. Celedonia P. Patag

Programmes

Undergraduate and Professional (Marine Engineering; Marine Transport; Naval Architecture)

History: Founded 1947 as Naval Architecture and Marine Engineering Institute. Acquired present title 1997.

Degrees and Diplomas: *Bachelor's Degree*
Last Updated: 07/12/10

NATIONAL CHRISTIAN LIFE COLLEGE (NCLC)

7 1st Street, Sto. Niño, City of Marikina, Second District, Metro Manila 1800
Tel: +63(2) 941-7401
Fax: +63(2) 941-4048
EMail: nclc.org@yahoo.com

Director: Leticia S. Ferriol

Programmes

Undergraduate and Professional (Computer Graphics; Education; Information Technology; Primary Education; Software Engineering)

History: Founded 2002.

Degrees and Diplomas: *Bachelor's Degree*
Last Updated: 07/12/10

NATIONAL COLLEGE OF BUSINESS AND ARTS

Brgy. San Juan, Taytay, Rizal 1920
Tel: +63(2) 658-6992
Fax: +63(2) 660-6253
EMail: webmaster@ncba.edu.ph
Website: http://www.ncba.edu.ph

President: Jose R. Torres

Campuses

Cubao (Accountancy; Banking; Biological and Life Sciences; Business Administration; Computer Education; Education; English; Finance; Foreign Languages Education; Health Education; Hotel and Restaurant; Hotel Management; Human Resources; Information Technology; Management; Marketing; Mathematics Education; Political Sciences; Primary Education; Public Administration; Science Education; Secondary Education); **Fairview** (Accountancy; Banking; Biological and Life Sciences; Business Administration; Computer Education; Education; English; Finance; Foreign Languages Education; Health Education; Hotel and Restaurant; Hotel Management; Human Resources; Information Technology; Management; Marketing; Mathematics Education; Political Sciences; Primary Education; Science Education; Secondary Education)

Programmes

Graduate *(Cubao and Fairview campuses)* (Business Administration; Finance; Human Resources; Public Administration); **Undergraduate and Professional** (Accountancy; Banking; Business Administration; Computer Education; Education; English; Finance; Foreign Languages Education; Hotel and Restaurant; Hotel Management; Human Resources; Management; Marketing; Mathematics Education; Nursing; Political Sciences; Primary Education; Science Education; Secondary Education)

History: Founded 1968.

Degrees and Diplomas: *Certificate/Diploma*; *Bachelor's Degree*; *Master's Degree*: Business Administration; Financial Management; Human Resources Management; Public Administration
Last Updated: 07/12/10

NATIONAL COLLEGE OF SCIENCE AND TECHNOLOGY

Amafel Bldg., Aguinaldo Highway, Dasmariñas, Cavite 4114
Tel: +63(46) 416-4779
EMail: Registrar@ncst.ph.com
Website: http://www.ncst.edu.ph/

President: Emerson B. Atanacio

Campuses

La Union *(Founded 1964)* (Accountancy; Automotive Engineering; Business Administration; Computer Engineering; Computer Science; Criminology; Education; Electrical Engineering; Electronic Engineering; Hotel and Restaurant; Hotel Management; Industrial Engineering; Information Technology; Mass Communication; Mechanical Engineering; Primary Education; Secondary Education; Telecommunications Engineering) *President*: Blanchita B. Ignacio

Programmes

Accountancy (Accountancy); **Architecture** (Architecture); **Comminication Studies** (Advertising and Publicity; Communication Studies; Film; Journalism; Mass Communication; Media Studies; Photography; Public Relations; Radio and Television Broadcasting; Theatre); **Criminology** (Criminology); **Customs Administration** (Taxation); **Education** (Education; English; Foreign Languages Education; Mathematics Education; Physics; Science Education; Secondary Education); **Engineering** (Computer Engineering; Electronic Engineering; Industrial Engineering; Information Technology; Telecommunications Engineering); **Hotel and Restaurant Management** (Hotel and Restaurant; Hotel Management); **Office Management** (Business Administration; Management; Marketing)

History: Founded 1998.

Degrees and Diplomas: *Associate Degree*: 2 yrs; *Bachelor's Degree*: 4 yrs; *Bachelor's Degree*: Engineering, 5 yrs
Last Updated: 16/12/10

NATIONAL POLYTECHNIC COLLEGE OF SCIENCE AND TECHNOLOGY

892 Alfina Bldg., Gulod, Novaliches, Quezon City, Second District, Metro Manila 1117
Tel: +63(2) 936-0622
Fax: +63(2) 418-7080

President: Eugenio P. Palaruan

Programmes

Computer Studies (Computer Networks; Computer Science); **Education** (Education; English; Filipino; Foreign Languages Education; Native Language Education; Primary Education; Secondary Education)

History: Founded 2006.

Degrees and Diplomas: *Bachelor's Degree*
Last Updated: 16/12/10

NATIONAL UNIVERSITY (NU)

551 Mariano F. Jhocson Street, Sampaloc, Manila, First District, Metro Manila 1008
Tel: +63(2) 749-8221
Fax: +63(2) 749-8210
EMail: teddyo@nu.edu.ph
Website: http://www.national-u.edu.ph

President and CEO: Teodoro Jhocson Ocampo
Tel: +63(2) 749-8210

Registrar: Arline P. Royo
Tel: +63(2) 749-8209, Fax: +63(2) 749-8209

International Relations: Carla P. Falconit, Vice-President for External Affairs and University Relations
Tel: +63(2) 749-8205, Fax: +63(2) 749-8205

Campuses

CEDCE *(Baguio City)* (Hotel and Restaurant; Hotel Management; Information Technology; Management; Nursing; Political Sciences)

Colleges

Architecture (Architecture; Architecture and Planning; Real Estate) *Dean*: Ma. Lourdes C. Gaite; **Commerce** (Banking; Business Administration; Business and Commerce; Finance; Management)

Dean: Rolando T. Averilla; **Computer Studies** (Computer Networks; Computer Science; Information Technology; Software Engineering) *Dean*: Rolando R. Lansigan; **Dentistry** (Dentistry) *Dean*: Joseph D. Lim; **Education** (Education; English; Filipino; History; Mathematics; Natural Sciences; Social Studies) *Dean*: Estrellita V. Gruenberg; **Engineering** (Chemical Engineering; Civil Engineering; Computer Engineering; Computer Science; Electrical Engineering; Electronic Engineering; Engineering; Geophysics; Industrial Engineering; Marine Science and Oceanography; Mechanical Engineering; Sanitary Engineering; Telecommunications Engineering) *Dean*: Dolores S.D. Cleofas; **Hotel and Restaurant Management** (Hotel and Restaurant; Hotel Management); **Liberal Arts** (Mathematics; Physical Education; Physics; Social Sciences) *Dean*: Jessica B. Constantino; **Nursing** (Nursing) *Dean*: Jumar T. Ubalde; **Pharmacy** (Pharmacy) *Dean*: Priscilla D. Miranda

Schools

Graduate Studies (Education; Educational Administration; Environmental Engineering; Public Administration; Sanitary Engineering; Special Education) *Dean*: Estrellita V. Gruenberg

History: Founded 1900 as Colegio Pilipino, became Colegio Mercantil 1905. English replaced Spanish as medium of instruction 1913. Became National Academy 1916, present title adopted 1921. A private Institution.

Governing Bodies: Board of Trustees; University Council

Academic Year: June to March (June-October; November-March)

Admission Requirements: Graduation from high school or equivalent and aptitude test, or foreign equivalent recognized by the Government Department of Education

Main Language(s) of Instruction: English

Degrees and Diplomas: *Certificate/Diploma*; *Associate Degree*; *Bachelor's Degree*; *Post Baccalaureate Certificate/Diploma*; *Master's Degree*: Public Administration; Special Education; Environmental Sanitary Engineering; Educational Management; *PhD*: Educational Management

Student Services: Academic counselling, Canteen, Cultural centre, Employment services, Foreign Studies Centre, Health services, Social counselling, Sports facilities

Libraries: c. 120,000 vols

Last Updated: 16/12/10

NAZARENUS COLLEGE FOUNDATION

MacArthur Highway, Saluysoy, City of Meycauayan, Bulacan 3020
Tel: +63(44) 840-7837
Fax: +63(44) 711-5429
EMail: nazarenuscollege@yahoo.com

President: Juan C.M. Tordesillas

Programmes

Education (Education; Health Education; Primary Education; Secondary Education); **Nursing** (Midwifery; Nursing); **Radiologic Technology** (Medical Technology; Radiology)

History: Founded 1989.

Degrees and Diplomas: *Certificate/Diploma*; *Bachelor's Degree*

Last Updated: 16/12/10

NEGROS COLLEGE

Ricardo Garcia Street, Ayungon, Negros Oriental 6210
Tel: +63(916) 769-1045
EMail: negroscollege@hotmail.com

President: Mauvito Y. Grapa

Programmes

Undergraduate and Professional Studies (Business Administration; Business Computing; Computer Education; Computer Engineering; Curriculum; Education; Primary Education)

History: Founded 1999.

Degrees and Diplomas: *Associate Degree*; *Bachelor's Degree*

Last Updated: 16/12/10

NEGROS MARITIME COLLEGE FOUNDATION

Airport Area, National Highway, Sibulan, Negros Oriental 6201
Tel: +63(35) 225-5215
Fax: +63(35) 225-5215

Chair/President: Edith A. Vera

Programmes

Undergraduate and Professional Studies (Marine Engineering; Marine Transport; Taxation)

History: Founded 1994.

Degrees and Diplomas: *Bachelor's Degree*

Last Updated: 16/12/10

NETWORK COMPUTER AND BUSINESS COLLEGES

No. 32 18th Street, SBFZ, East Bajac-Bajac, Olongapo City, Zambales 2200
Tel: +63(47) 222-3912
EMail: ncbc_pcf@yahoo.com

President: Alexander C. Nozuelo

Programmes

Business Administration (Business Administration; Business Computing; Human Resources; Information Management; Information Technology); **Computer Science** (Computer Science); **Information Technology** (Information Technology)

History: Founded 1993.

Degrees and Diplomas: *Certificate/Diploma*; *Associate Degree*; *Bachelor's Degree*

Last Updated: 17/12/10

NEW ENGLAND COLLEGE

40 Quezon Avenue, Quezon City, Second District, Metro Manila
Tel: +63(2) 711-3406 +63(2) 711-9379
Fax: +63(2) 711-0857
EMail: info@nec.edu.ph
Website: http://www.nec.edu.ph

President: Norma Ong Ching

Vice-President for Academic Affairs: Eduardo R. Alicias, Jr.

International Relations: Henry Wong, Vice-President for International Linkages

Programmes

Business Administration (Accountancy; Business Administration; Finance; Human Resources; Management; Marketing); **Education** (Education; English; Foreign Languages Education; Primary Education; Secondary Education; Special Education); **Information Technology** (Computer Graphics; Computer Networks; Computer Science; Information Technology; Multimedia; Software Engineering); **Nursing** (Community Health; Health Administration; Health Sciences; Nursing; Nutrition)

History: Founded 2004.

Degrees and Diplomas: *Bachelor's Degree*

Last Updated: 21/12/10

NEW ERA UNIVERSITY

Pamantasan ng New Era (NEU)

No. 9 Central Avenue, New Era, Quezon City, Second District, Metro Manila 1107
Tel: +63(2) 921-4221
Fax: +63(2) 981-4240
EMail: registrar@neu.edu.ph
Website: http://www.neu.edu.ph

President: Corazon C. Osorio
Tel: +63(2) 981-3803, Fax: +63(2) 981-4240

Vice-President: Alberto R. Domingo Jr

Colleges

Arts and Sciences (Biology; Educational and Student Counselling; Journalism; Mass Communication; Political Sciences; Psychology); **Business Education and Administration** (Accountancy; Banking; Business Administration; Business Education; Commercial Law; Finance; Human Resources; Management); **Education**

(Curriculum; Education; English; Filipino; Foreign Languages Education; Mathematics Education; Native Language Education; Preschool Education; Social Studies; Special Education; Technology Education); **Engineering and Technology** (Civil Engineering; Computer Science; Electrical Engineering; Electronic Engineering; Engineering; Industrial Engineering; Mechanical Engineering; Telecommunications Engineering); **Evangelical Ministry** (Pastoral Studies); **Law** (Constitutional Law; Criminal Law; Law); **Nursing** (Nursing)

Schools

Graduate Studies (Business Administration; Education; Educational Administration; Educational Psychology; Filipino; Mathematics Education; Native Language Education; Social Sciences; Special Education)

Further Information: Batangas Branch in Lipa City, Gensan Branch in General Santos City and Central Luzon Branch in San Fernando City

History: Founded 1975 as New Era Educational Institute (NEEI). Renamed New Era College (1981-1995). Acquired present status and title 2010.

Governing Bodies: Board of Trustees

Academic Year: June to May (June-October; October-March; April-May)

Admission Requirements: Graduation from high school and entrance examination

Fees: (Pesos): 9,500 per semester

Main Language(s) of Instruction: Filipino, English

International Co-operation: With the World Bank and with the Asian Institute of Management

Accrediting Agencies: Philippine Association of Colleges & Universities Commission on Accreditation (PACUCOA)

Degrees and Diplomas: *Bachelor's Degree*; *Master's Degree*: Education (Educational Management; Educational Psychology; Filipino; Language Education; Mathematics; Social Sciences; Special Education); Business Administration; *PhD*: Education (Educational Management)

Student Services: Academic counselling, Canteen, Cultural centre, Employment services, Foreign student adviser, Foreign Studies Centre, Health services, Social counselling, Sports facilities

Student Residential Facilities: Yes. Dormitories; condominium units for some employees

Special Facilities: Biological Garden

Libraries: Central Library, 13,000 vols; School Libraries and Reading Centres, c. 40,000

Publications: CAS Journal, A compilation of faculty research and articles *(biennially)*; Graduate Journal; Knowledge, A compilation of institutional research of New Era Faculty; Mind and Ways *(biannually)*; SGS Bulletin

Press or Publishing House: LCD Publishing/ Iglesia Ni Cristo Publication Office

Last Updated: 21/12/10

NEW NORTHERN MINDANAO COLLEGES (NORMI)

Atega Street, Cabadbaran, Agusan del Norte 8605
Tel: +63(85) 343-1231
Fax: +63(85) 343-1231
EMail: nmc_cabadbaran@yahoo.com

President: Ricardo D. Gonzales

Programmes

Arts and Humanities (Arts and Humanities; English; Filipino; Political Sciences); **Business and Commerce** (Accountancy; Business and Commerce; Management); **Education** (Education; English; Filipino; Foreign Languages Education; Native Language Education; Primary Education; Secondary Education)

History: Founded 1946.

Admission Requirements: Graduation from high school

Main Language(s) of Instruction: English

Degrees and Diplomas: *Bachelor's Degree*; *Master's Degree*: Education (English). Also two-year course in Hotel and Restaurant Management and Information Technology

Student Services: Academic counselling, Canteen, Health services

Student Residential Facilities: Yes

Special Facilities: Audio-visual rooms

Libraries: Yes

Publications: The Norminian *(biennially)*

Last Updated: 21/12/10

NJ VALDEZ COLLEGES FOUNDATION

Bacag, Villasis, Pangasinan 2427
Tel: +63(75) 564-5054
Fax: +63(75) 564-5054

President: Nicanor Valdez

Programmes

Accountancy (Accountancy); **Commerce** (Business and Commerce; Management); **Education** (Education; Primary Education; Secondary Education); **Industrial Education** (Automotive Engineering; Electrical Engineering; Electronic Engineering); **Information Technology** (Information Technology)

History: Founded 1990. Formerly known as Urdaneta College of Technology.

Degrees and Diplomas: *Associate Degree*; *Bachelor's Degree*

Last Updated: 21/12/10

NORTH CENTRAL MINDANAO COLLEGE

Prk. Lemon Tree, Maranding, Lala, Lanao del Norte 9211
Tel: +63(63) 496-0109 +63(63) 388-7213
EMail: northcentralmindanaocolleges@yahoo.com.ph

President: Myrna Y. Undag

Programmes

Undergraduate and Professional Studies (Accountancy; Biology; Business Administration; Computer Science; Criminology; Curriculum; Education; English; Filipino; Foreign Languages Education; Health Education; Hotel and Restaurant; Hotel Management; Management; Marketing; Mathematics Education; Midwifery; Native Language Education; Nursing; Primary Education; Science Education; Secondary Education; Social Work; Tourism)

History: Founded 1989.

Degrees and Diplomas: *Associate Degree*; *Bachelor's Degree*

Last Updated: 21/12/10

NORTH DAVAO COLLEGE - PANABO

Quirino Street, Bgy. Gredo, Panabo City, Davao del Norte 8105
Tel: +63(84) 628-5264
Fax: +63(84) 628-5264
EMail: absndc85@mozcom.com

President: Anita B. Somoso

Programmes

Arts (English); **Education** (Education; English; Foreign Languages Education; Mathematics Education; Primary Education; Secondary Education)

History: Founded 1985.

Degrees and Diplomas: *Bachelor's Degree*

Last Updated: 21/12/10

NORTH DAVAO COLLEGE - TAGUM FOUNDATION

Apokon Road, Tagum City, Davao del Norte 8100
Tel: +63(84) 217-3766
Fax: +63(84) 400-3138

President: Anita B. Somoso

Programmes

Business Administration (Business Administration; Finance; Management); **Education** (Biological and Life Sciences; Curriculum; Education; English; Foreign Languages Education;

Mathematics Education; Primary Education; Secondary Education); **Nursing** (Nursing)

History: Founded 1989.

Degrees and Diplomas: *Bachelor's Degree*
Last Updated: 21/12/10

NORTH NEGROS COLLEGE

Villena - Juan Luna Streets, Cadiz City, Negros Occidental 6121
Tel: +63(34) 493-0396
EMail: nncolleg@lasaltech.com
Website: http://www.northnegroscollege.com

President: Agustin Jesmar C. Desuyo

Programmes

Undergraduate and Professional (Business Administration; Computer Science; Management)

History: Founded 1979.

Degrees and Diplomas: *Bachelor's Degree*
Last Updated: 21/12/10

NORTHEASTERN CEBU COLLEGES

F. Ralota Street cor. Pio del Pilar Street, Danao City, Cebu 6004
Tel: +63(32) 200-3349
EMail: ncc_inc@ncitsolutions.com

President: Agnes A. Magpale

Programmes

Business Administration (Business Administration); **Education** (Education; English; Filipino; Foreign Languages Education; Mathematics Education; Native Language Education; Primary Education; Secondary Education); **Information Technology** (Information Technology); **Tourism, Hotel and Restaurant Management** (Hotel and Restaurant; Hotel Management; Tourism)

History: Founded 2000.

Degrees and Diplomas: *Bachelor's Degree*
Last Updated: 21/12/10

NORTHEASTERN COLLEGE

National Highway, Villasis, Santiago City, Isabela 3311
Tel: +63(78) 682-8454
Fax: +63(78) 682-8454
Website: http://www.northeasterncollege.edu.ph/

President: Tomas C. Bautista

Colleges

Commerce and Accountancy (Accountancy; Banking; Business and Commerce; Finance; Management; Marketing); **Criminology** (Criminology); **Education** (Education; Primary Education; Secondary Education); **Engineering** (Engineering); **Hotel and Restaurant Management** (Hotel and Restaurant; Hotel Management); **Information Technology** (Information Technology); **Law** (Law); **Liberal Arts** (Arts and Humanities; Economics; English; Mass Communication; Mathematics; Political Sciences); **Nursing** (Nursing)

Courses

Computer Secretarial (Business Computing; Secretarial Studies); **Geodetic Engineering** (Geological Engineering)

Schools

Graduate Studies (Business Administration; Education; Educational Administration; Public Administration); **Midwifery** (Midwifery)

History: Founded 1941.

Degrees and Diplomas: *Bachelor's Degree*; *Master's Degree*: Education; Business Administration; Public Administration; *PhD*: Education (Educational Management)
Last Updated: 21/12/10

NORTHEASTERN MINDANAO COLLEGES

Rizal Cor. Amat Streets, Surigao City, Surigao del Norte 8400
Tel: +63(86) 231-9356
Fax: +63(86) 826-1764
EMail: nemco_registrar@yahoo.com; campus@balanghai.com
Website: http://www.nemco.edu.ph/

President: Josefa J. Paloma

Programmes

Arts and Humanities (Arts and Humanities; English); **Business Administration and Commerce** (Accountancy; Banking; Business and Commerce; Economics; Finance; Human Resources; Management; Marketing; Public Administration); **Computer Science** (Computer Science); **Criminology** (Criminology); **Education** (English; Filipino; Foreign Languages Education; Mathematics Education; Native Language Education; Primary Education; Secondary Education; Social Studies); **Information Technology** (Computer Science; Information Management; Information Technology)

History: Founded 1947.

Degrees and Diplomas: *Bachelor's Degree*
Last Updated: 21/12/10

NORTHERN CAGAYAN COLLEGES FOUNDATION

Centro East, Ballesteros, Cagayan 3516
Tel: +63(62) 862-3031
Fax: +63(78) 862-3089

President: Estella P. Fernandez

Programmes

Education (Education; Educational Administration; English; Foreign Languages Education; Primary Education)

History: Founded 1931. Formerly known as Northern Cagayan Academy.

Degrees and Diplomas: *Bachelor's Degree*: 4 yrs; *Master's Degree*: 2 yrs
Last Updated: 21/12/10

NORTHERN CEBU COLLEGE

San Vicente Street, Bogo, Cebu 6010
Tel: +63(32) 251-2643
Fax: +63(32) 251-2643

President: Frankie V. Fernan

Programmes

Secondary Education (Education; English; Filipino; Foreign Languages Education; Native Language Education; Secondary Education; Social Studies)

History: Founded 1932 as Cebu Northern Institute. Acquired present title 1950.

Degrees and Diplomas: *Bachelor's Degree*
Last Updated: 21/12/10

NORTHERN CHRISTIAN COLLEGE

Mabini Street, Laoag City, Ilocos Norte 2900
Tel: +63(77) 772-0687 +63(77) 772-0052
Fax: +63(77) 772-1864
EMail: cia@iln.csi.com.ph
Website: http://www.ncc.edu.ph/

President: Caesar I. Agnir

Programmes

Arts *(Bachelor of Arts programme)* (English; Environmental Studies; History; Political Sciences; Theology); **Business Administration and Commerce** (Accountancy; Banking; Business Administration; Business Computing; Finance; Human Resources; Management; Marketing); **Education** (Curriculum; Education; Educational and Student Counselling; English; Ethics; Filipino; Foreign Languages Education; Health Education; History; Home Economics Education; Mathematics Education; Music Education; Native Language Education; Physical Education; Preschool Education; Primary Education; Science Education; Secondary Education; Special Education; Technology Education); **Graduate Studies** (Education; Educational Administration; Educational and Student Counselling); **Nursing** (Nursing); **Religious Education** (Religious Education); **Social Work** (Social Work); **Tourism, Hotel and Restaurant Technology** (Hotel and Restaurant; Tourism)

History: Founded 1946.

Degrees and Diplomas: *Certificate/Diploma*; *Associate Degree*; *Bachelor's Degree*; *Master's Degree*: Public Administration; Education (Administration and Management; Guidance and Counselling; Instructional Management); *PhD*: Education (Educational Management)
Last Updated: 21/12/10

NORTHERN COTABATO COLLEGES FOUNDATION

Mapanao Extension, Kabacan, Cotabato 9407
Tel: +63(64) 248-2107

President: Aida B. Abrenilla

Programmes

Business and Commerce (Accountancy; Business and Commerce; Management); **Computer Science** (Computer Science); **Criminology** (Criminology; Police Studies)

History: Founded 1993. Formerly Cotabato Technological Institute (1990-1993).

Degrees and Diplomas: *Bachelor's Degree*
Last Updated: 21/12/10

NORTHERN ILOCANDIA COLLEGE OF SCIENCE AND TECHNOLOGY

Oaig Daya, City of Candon, Ilocos Sur 2710
Tel: +63(77)742-5413

President: Jocelyn Abella-Galang

Programmes

Criminology (Criminology); **Hotel and Restaurant Management** (Hotel and Restaurant; Hotel Management); **Industrial Education** (Education; Industrial Design; Technology)

History: Founded 2004.

Degrees and Diplomas: *Bachelor's Degree*
Last Updated: 21/12/10

NORTHERN LEYTE COLLEGE

Zamora Street, Palompon, Leyte 6538
Tel: +63(53) 338-2306
Fax: +63(53) 338-2306
EMail: northernleytecollege@yahoo.com

Director: Apolonio A. Abordo

Programmes

Undergraduate and Professional Studies (Business and Commerce; Computer Science; Management; Primary Education)

History: Founded 1945.

Degrees and Diplomas: *Bachelor's Degree*
Last Updated: 21/12/10

NORTHERN LUZON ADVENTIST COLLEGE

Artacho, Sison, Pangasinan 2434
Tel: +63(75) 567-7096
Fax: +63(75) 567-2627
EMail: info@nlac.educ.ph
Website: http://www.nlac.edu.ph

President: Nestor C. Rilloma
EMail: castilloarnulfo@eudoramail.com

Programmes

Arts *(Bachelor of Arts programme)* (English; Filipino; History; Mass Communication; Mathematics; Natural Sciences; Political Sciences; Theology); **Business Administration** (Accountancy; Business Administration; Business and Commerce; Management; Marketing; Secretarial Studies); **Education** (English; Filipino; Foreign Languages Education; History; Mathematics Education; Native Language Education; Primary Education; Science Education; Secondary Education); **Graduate** (Education); **Information and Computer Science** (Computer Science; Information Sciences; Information Technology); **Nursing** (Nursing); **Psychology** (Psychology)

History: Founded 1923.

Degrees and Diplomas: *Associate Degree*; *Bachelor's Degree*; *Master's Degree*: Education
Last Updated: 22/12/10

NORTHERN PHILIPPINES COLLEGE FOR MARITIME SCIENCE AND TECHNOLOGY

National Highway, Lingsat, San Fernando City, La Union 2500
Tel: +63(72) 888-3167 +63(72) 242-5676
Fax: +63(77) 242-5676
EMail: npcmst_sfc@yahoo.com.ph

President: Arturo C. Quinto EMail: arturo@net.com.ph

Programmes

Computer Science (Computer Science); **Criminology** (Criminology); **Electrical Engineering** (Electrical Engineering); **Marine Engineering** (Marine Engineering); **Marine Transportation** (Marine Transport); **Mechanical Engineering** (Mechanical Engineering)

History: Founded 1979. Formerly Technological Studies, Inc. (1990-2001).

Degrees and Diplomas: *Bachelor's Degree*
Last Updated: 22/12/10

NORTHERN QUEZON COOPERATIVE COLLEGE

Brgy. Omon, Infanta, Quezon 4336
Tel: +63(42) 535-2871
Fax: +63(42) 563-7327
EMail: fbl@psdn.org.ph

President: Francis B. Lucas

Programmes

Graduate (Education; Educational Administration); **Undergraduate and Professional** (Business Administration; Business and Commerce; Education; English; Filipino; Finance; Foreign Languages Education; Human Resources; Management; Marketing; Mathematics Education; Native Language Education; Primary Education; Secondary Education; Social Studies)

History: Founded 1968. Formerly known as Infanta Commuinty College.

Degrees and Diplomas: *Certificate/Diploma*; *Bachelor's Degree*; *Master's Degree*: Education (Educational Management)
Last Updated: 22/12/10

NORTHERN SAMAR COLLEGES

Cor. Annunciation and Roxas Streets, Catarman, Northern Samar 6400
Tel: +63(55) 500-9538
Fax: +63(55) 500-9538
EMail: northernsamarcolleges@yahoo.com

President: Leah Moore-Mangada

Programmes

Business Administration (Business Administration; Management); **Education** (Computer Education; Education; Primary Education; Secondary Education); **Information Technology** (Information Technology)

Degrees and Diplomas: *Bachelor's Degree*
Last Updated: 22/12/10

NORTHERN ZAMBALES COLLEGE

Masinloc, Zambales 2211
Tel: +63(47) 821-1026
Fax: +63(47) 821-1257

President: Emma E. Edano

Programmes

Commerce (Accountancy; Business and Commerce; Management); **Criminology** (Criminology); **Education** (Curriculum; Primary Education)

History: Founded 1995. Formerly known as Virgen De los Remedios College (1995-2000).

Degrees and Diplomas: *Bachelor's Degree*
Last Updated: 22/12/10

NORTH VALLEY COLLEGE FOUNDATION

Lanao, Cotabato, City of Kidapawan, North Cotabato 9400
Tel: +63(64) 288-5628
Fax: +63(64) 288-5628

President: Samuel Jeff S. Babol

Programmes

Health Sciences (Medical Technology; Nursing; Radiology)

History: Founded 1994. Formerly Dr. S.J. Babol Foundation College (until 1993).

Degrees and Diplomas: *Bachelor's Degree*
Last Updated: 21/12/10

NORTHWESTERN AGUSAN COLLEGES

Bay View Hill, Nasipit, Agusan del Norte 8602
Tel: +63(85) 343-2122
Fax: +63(85) 283-3759

President: Maria Erlinda N. Magtibay

Programmes

Arts and Humanities (Arts and Humanities; History); **Business Administration** (Business Administration; Management); **Education** (English; Foreign Languages Education; Primary Education; Secondary Education; Special Education)
History: Founded 1967 as Nasipit Institute, acquired present title1997.
Degrees and Diplomas: *Bachelor's Degree*
Last Updated: 22/12/10

NORTHWESTERN MINDANAO CHRISTIAN COLLEGES

Upper Centro, Tudela, Misamis Occidental 7202
Tel: +63(92) 206-7165
EMail: jysnmcc@yahoo.com

Director: Glenda S. Hapitan

Programmes

Arts (Economics; English; Political Sciences); **Office Administration** (Business Administration; Computer Education; Management); **Science** (Mathematics)
History: Founded 1946, acquiring current title and status in 1987.
Degrees and Diplomas: *Associate Degree*; *Bachelor's Degree*
Last Updated: 22/12/10

NORTHWESTERN UNIVERSITY

Airport Avenue, Laoag City, Ilocos Norte 2900
Tel: +63(77) 670-8510 +63(77) 670-86-07
Fax: +63(77) 771-3814
EMail: info@nwu.edu.ph
Website: http://www.nwu.edu.ph

President: Ben A. Nicolas (1988-)
EMail: nwupresident@yahoo.com

Vice-President for Administration: Ferdinand S. Nicolas

Registrar: Grace G. Sales

Colleges

Allied Health Sciences (Medical Technology; Midwifery; Nursing; Physical Therapy); **Arts and Sciences** (Communication Arts; Computer Science; Economics; English Studies; Environmental Management; Environmental Studies; Literature; Mass Communication; Mathematics; Modern Languages; Political Sciences; Psychology); **Business Education** (Accountancy; Banking; Business Administration; Business and Commerce; Finance; Hotel and Restaurant; Hotel Management; Management; Tourism); **Criminal Justice Education** (Criminal Law; Criminology); **Engineering, Architecture and Technology** (Architecture; Civil Engineering; Electrical Engineering; Electronic Engineering; Mechanical Engineering; Structural Architecture; Telecommunications Engineering); **Law** (Law); **Maritime Education** (Marine Engineering; Marine Transport); **Teacher Education** (Child Care and Development; Education; English; Filipino; Foreign Languages Education; Health Education; Library Science; Mathematics Education; Music Education; Native Language Education; Physical Education; Preschool Education; Science Education; Secondary Education; Teacher Training)

Schools

Graduate Studies *(Vedasto J. Samonte)* (Business Education; Comparative Literature; Education; Educational Administration; Educational and Student Counselling; English; Filipino; Foreign Languages Education; Management; Mathematics Education; Native Language Education; Nursing; Preschool Education; Public Administration)

History: Founded 1932 as Northwestern Academy. Acquired University status 1992.
Governing Bodies: Board of Directors
Academic Year: June to March (June-October; October-March)
Admission Requirements: Graduation from high school and NWU Placement Examination
Fees: (Pesos): c. 12,000 per semester
Main Language(s) of Instruction: Filipino, English
International Co-operation: With universities in Korea, Canada
Accrediting Agencies: International Organization for Standardization, Philippine Association of Colleges and Universities
Degrees and Diplomas: *Associate Degree*; *Bachelor's Degree*; *Master's Degree*: Business Administration; Arts in: Education; Nursing; Public Administration; Science in: Management Engineering; *PhD*: Education (Educational Management; Development Education). Also Professional Degree in Law, 4 yrs
Student Services: Academic counselling, Canteen, Cultural centre, Employment services, Health services, Language programs, Sports facilities
Student Residential Facilities: Yes
Last Updated: 22/12/10

NORTHWESTERN VISAYAN COLLEGES

19 Martyrs Street Cor Pastrana Street, Kalibo, Aklan 5600
Tel: +63(36) 262-3439
Fax: +63(36) 262-3439
EMail: nvcalumni@yahoo.com
Website: http://www.nvc.edu.ph/

President: Allen S. Quimpo

Programmes

Graduate (Education; Educational Administration; Public Administration); **Undergraduate and Professional** (Accountancy; Aeronautical and Aerospace Engineering; Air Transport; Art Education; Banking; Business Administration; Business and Commerce; Computer Science; Education; English; Filipino; Finance; Foreign Languages Education; History; Home Economics Education; Hotel and Restaurant; Hotel Management; Mass Communication; Mathematics Education; Music Education; Native Language Education; Physical Education; Primary Education; Secondary Education; Technology Education)
History: Founded 1948.
Degrees and Diplomas: *Associate Degree*; *Bachelor's Degree*; *Master's Degree*: Public Administration; Arts in: Education (Educational Management)
Last Updated: 22/12/10

NOTRE DAME OF DADIANGAS UNIVERSITY

Marist Avenue, General Santos City, South Cotabato 9500
Tel: +63(83) 552-4444
Fax: +63(83) 552-3385
Website: http://www.nddu.edu.ph/

President: John Y. Tan

Colleges

Arts and Sciences (Arts and Humanities; Biology; Economics; English; Mass Communication; Political Sciences; Psychology); **Business Administration** (Accountancy; Business Administration; Economics; Finance; Hotel and Restaurant; Hotel Management;

Management; Marketing; Tourism); **Education** (Art Education; Biological and Life Sciences; Curriculum; Education; English; Foreign Languages Education; Health Education; Information Sciences; Library Science; Mathematics Education; Music Education; Physical Education; Preschool Education; Primary Education; Religious Education; Secondary Education); **Engineering and Technology** (Architecture; Civil Engineering; Computer Engineering; Computer Science; Electrical Engineering; Electronic Engineering; Engineering; Industrial Engineering; Information Technology; Structural Architecture; Technology; Telecommunications Engineering); **Nursing** (Nursing)

Schools

Graduate Studies (Biology; Business Administration; Civil Engineering; Education; Educational Administration; Educational and Student Counselling; Engineering; Foreign Languages Education; Human Resources; Management; Mathematics Education; Modern Languages; Native Language Education; Nursing; Preschool Education; Public Administration; Religious Education; Science Education)

History: Founded 1953. Formerly known as Notre Dame of Dadiangas College (1953-2006).

Degrees and Diplomas: *Bachelor's Degree*; *Master's Degree*: Business Administration; Business Education; Engineering (Civil Engineering); Public Administration; Science in Mathematics and Biology; Arts in Nursing; Education (Guidance and Counselling; Biology; Religious Education; Early Childhood Education; Science Education; Teaching English as Second Language; Mathematics; Administration and Supervision; Filipino; Educational Management); *PhD*: Management (Human Resources Management); Language Education; Science Education (Biology); Education

Last Updated: 22/12/10

NOTRE DAME OF JOLO COLLEGE

Jolo, Sulu 7400

President: Emmanual A. Sison

Programmes

Graduate Studies (Business Administration; Education; Educational Administration; Government; Nursing; Public Administration); **Undergraduate and Professional Studies** (Accountancy; Biological and Life Sciences; Business and Commerce; Criminology; Education; English; Filipino; Foreign Languages Education; Information Technology; Management; Mathematics Education; Native Language Education; Nursing; Primary Education; Science Education; Secondary Education; Social Studies; Social Work)

History: Founded 1954.

Degrees and Diplomas: *Bachelor's Degree*; *Master's Degree*: Business Administration; Public Administration; Education (Educational Management); Nursing; *PhD*: Education (Educational Management)

Last Updated: 22/12/10

NOTRE DAME OF KIDAPAWAN COLLEGE

Datu Ingkal Street, Kidapawan City,
North Cotabato 9400
Tel: +63(64) 288-1673
Fax: +63(64) 288-5235
EMail: btedf@ndkc.edu.ph

President: Teodulo A. Fernandez

Programmes

Undergraduate and Professional Studies (Accountancy; Business Administration; Business and Commerce; Civil Engineering; Computer Science; Curriculum; Economics; Education; Electronic Engineering; English; Ethics; Foreign Languages Education; Information Management; Information Technology; Mass Communication; Nursing; Political Sciences; Primary Education; Secondary Education; Telecommunications Engineering)

History: Founded 1958.

Degrees and Diplomas: *Bachelor's Degree*

Last Updated: 22/12/10

NOTRE DAME OF MARBEL UNIVERSITY

Alunan Avenue, Koronadal City, South Cotabato 9506
Tel: +63(83) 228-2218
Fax: +63(83) 228-2819
EMail: president@ndmu.edu.ph
Website: http://www.ndmu.edu.ph

President: Wilfredo E. Lubrico

Registrar: Ruel Biboso

Colleges

Business (Accountancy; Business Administration; Business and Commerce; Public Administration; Secretarial Studies); **Education** (Education; Educational Administration; Educational and Student Counselling; Foreign Languages Education; Primary Education); **Liberal Arts** (Arts and Humanities; Economics; English; Filipino; History; Library Science; Philosophy); **Nursing** (Nursing); **Science and Technology** (Agricultural Engineering; Agriculture; Applied Mathematics; Biology; Chemical Engineering; Chemistry; Civil Engineering; Computer Engineering; Computer Science; Electrical Engineering; Electronic Engineering; Entomology; Food Technology; Geological Engineering; Industrial Engineering; Mathematics; Medical Technology; Natural Sciences; Physics; Technology; Telecommunications Engineering)

Schools

Graduate (Biology; Business Administration; Chemistry; Crop Production; Education; Educational Administration; Educational and Student Counselling; English; Filipino; Foreign Languages Education; Information Technology; Library Science; Mathematics; Mathematics Education; Native Language Education; Physical Education; Physics; Public Administration; Religious Education; Rural Planning)

History: Founded 1946 as secondary school and expanded in 1955 into college. Acquired present status and title 1992.

Governing Bodies: Board of Trustees

Academic Year: June to May (June-October; November-March; April-May)

Admission Requirements: Graduation from high school and entrance examination

Main Language(s) of Instruction: English

Degrees and Diplomas: *Associate Degree*; *Bachelor's Degree*; *Master's Degree*: Arts in Education (Mathematics; Biology; Chemistry; Educational Management; Guidance and Counselling; Physical Education; Physics; Religious Education; Teaching English as a Second Language; Library Science; Filipino); Arts in: Library Science; Nursing; Science in: Biology; Chemistry; Crop Science; Information Technology; Mathematics; Physics; Rural Extension and Development; Biology; Business Administration; Chemistry; English; Information Technology; Mathematics; Nursing; Physics; Public Administration; *PhD*: Educational Management; Science Education (Chemistry; Physics)

Student Services: Academic counselling, Canteen, Cultural centre, Employment services, Health services, Social counselling, Sports facilities

Libraries: Central Library, c. 75,000 vols; 3,000 e-journal subscriptions

Publications: Research Journal *(annually)*

Last Updated: 22/12/10

NOTRE DAME OF MIDSAYAP COLLEGE

Quezo Avenue, Midsayap, North Cotabato 9410
Tel: +63(64) 229-8455
Fax: +63(64) 229-8024
EMail: info@ndmc.edu.ph
Website: http://www.ndmc.edu.ph/

President: Romeo S. Saniel EMail: ndmcpresident@yahoo.com

Programmes

Undergraduate and Professional Studies (Accountancy; Banking; Biological and Life Sciences; Business Administration; Business and Commerce; Computer Science; Economics; Education; English; Filipino; Finance; Foreign Languages Education; History; Information Management; Information Technology; Management; Marketing; Mathematics; Mathematics Education; Native Language

Education; Natural Sciences; Nursing; Physical Education; Primary Education; Science Education; Secondary Education)

History: Founded 1941.

Degrees and Diplomas: *Bachelor's Degree*

Last Updated: 22/12/10

NOTRE DAME OF SALAMAN COLLEGE

Provincial Highway, Lebak, Sultan Kudarat 9807
Tel: +63(64) 205-3041
Fax: +63(64) 205-3041
EMail: notredameofsalamancollege@yahoo.com

President: Antonio P. Pueyo

Programmes

Arts (English; Filipino; Mathematics; Natural Sciences); **Business Administration** (Business Administration; Management); **Criminology** (Criminology); **Education** (English; Filipino; Foreign Languages Education; Mathematics Education; Native Language Education; Primary Education; Science Education; Secondary Education)

History: Founded 1965.

Degrees and Diplomas: *Bachelor's Degree*

Last Updated: 22/12/10

NOTRE DAME OF TACURONG COLLEGE

Lapu-Lapu Street, Tacurong City, Sultan Kudarat 9800
Tel: +63(64) 200-3364
Fax: +63(64) 200-3631
EMail: ndtc_excel@yahoo.com

President: Jose Colin M. Bagaforo

Programmes

Arts (Economics; English; History; Political Sciences); **Business Administration** (Accountancy; Banking; Business Administration; Business and Commerce; Economics; Finance; Human Resources; Management; Marketing); **Computer Studies** (Computer Education; Computer Engineering; Computer Science); **Criminology** (Criminology); **Education** (Education; English; Ethics; Filipino; Foreign Languages Education; Health Education; History; Mathematics Education; Music Education; Native Language Education; Physical Education; Primary Education; Secondary Education); **Graduate Studies** (Education; Educational Administration; Educational and Student Counselling; English; Filipino; Foreign Languages Education; Mathematics Education; Native Language Education); **Hotel and Restaurant Management** (Hotel and Restaurant; Hotel Management); **Nursing** (Nursing); **Social Work** (Social Work)

History: Founded 1950. Formerly known as Notre Dame of Tacurong, Inc. (1968-1978).

Degrees and Diplomas: *Bachelor's Degree*: 4 yrs; *Master's Degree*: Education (Educational Administration; Educational Guidance and Counselling; English; Filipino; Mathematics), a further 2 yrs

Last Updated: 22/12/10

NOTRE DAME RVM COLLEGE OF COTABATO

74 Sinsuat Avenue, Cotabato City, Cotabato 9600
Tel: +63(64) 421-6238
Fax: +63(64) 421-2845

President: Jocelyn G. Gerarde

Programmes

Business Administration (Accountancy; Business Administration; Finance; Management; Marketing); **Education** (Curriculum; Education; English; Foreign Languages Education; Mathematics Education; Primary Education; Secondary Education); **Hotel and Restaurant Management** (Hotel and Restaurant; Hotel Management); **Information Technology** (Information Technology)

History: Founded 1904. Formerly known as Notre Dame of Cotabato for Girls.

Degrees and Diplomas: *Bachelor's Degree*

Last Updated: 23/12/10

NOTRE DAME-SIENA COLLEGE OF POLOMOLOK

Pitimini Street, Polomolok, South Cotabato 9504
Tel: +63(83) 500-8401
Fax: +63(83) 500-8414
EMail: ndscp2004@gmail.com

President: Anna Marie G. Gatmaytan

Programmes

Computer Science (Computer Science); **Education** (Curriculum; Education; English; Foreign Languages Education; Primary Education; Secondary Education); **English** (English); **Entrepreneurship** (Management)

History: Founded 1966.

Degrees and Diplomas: *Bachelor's Degree*

Last Updated: 23/12/10

NOTRE DAME UNIVERSITY (NDU)

Notre Dame Avenue, Cotabato City, Cotabato 9600
Tel: +63(64) 421-2698 +63(64) 421-4312
Fax: +63(64) 421-4312
EMail: registrar@nducotabato.org
Website: http://www.nducotabato.org/

President: Eduardo G. Tanudtanud, OMI

Centres

Peace Education (Peace and Disarmament); **Policy, Advocacy and Strategic Studies** (Communication Studies; Law)

Colleges

Arts and Sciences (Biology; Economics; Mass Communication; Philosophy; Psychology; Public Administration; Sociology); **Business and Accountancy** (Accountancy; Business Administration; Business and Commerce; Finance; Management; Public Administration; Secretarial Studies); **Education** (Education; English; Filipino; Food Technology; Foreign Languages Education; History; Home Economics Education; Library Science; Mathematics Education; Native Language Education; Physical Education; Primary Education; Science Education; Secondary Education); **Engineering and Computer Studies** (Civil Engineering; Computer Engineering; Computer Science; Electrical Engineering; Electronic Engineering; Engineering; Mechanical Engineering; Telecommunications Engineering); **Health sciences** (Nursing); **Law** (Administrative Law; Civil Law; Commercial Law; Constitutional Law; Criminal Law; International Law; Law; Public Law)

Departments

Infrastructure and Maintenance (Maintenance Technology)

Schools

Graduate (Business Administration; Education; Educational Administration; Educational and Student Counselling; Educational Psychology; English; Filipino; History; Library Science; Mathematics Education; Native Language Education; Peace and Disarmament; Physical Education; Public Administration; Religious Education)

History: Founded 1948 as Notre Dame College, acquired University status 1969. A private Institution under the supervision of the Oblates of Mary Immaculate.

Governing Bodies: Board of Trustees

Academic Year: June to March (June-October; November-March)

Admission Requirements: Graduation from high school and entrance examination

Main Language(s) of Instruction: Filipino, English, Spanish

Degrees and Diplomas: *Certificate/Diploma*; *Associate Degree*; *Bachelor's Degree*; *Master's Degree*: Arts (English; Humanities; Peace and Development); Business Administration; Business Education; Public Administration; Education (Educational Administration; Counselling and Psychology; Guidance and Counselling; Religious Education; Science Education; Teaching Strategies; Physical Education; Mathematics Education; History; Filipino); *PhD*: Education (Educational Management; Peace and Development); Peace and Development Education

Student Services: Academic counselling, Canteen, Cultural centre, Employment services, Health services, Social counselling

Special Facilities: Cultural Artifacts Museum; NDU N'Musa Museum

Libraries: Central Library c. 83,000 vols; Jr. Oblate Seminary, c. 6,600; Peace Education: Socio-Economic Research Library, c. 745; Elementary Training Department, c. 8,000

Publications: Balinghad *(quarterly)*; Notre Dame Journal *(biannually)*; Occasional Papers

Press or Publishing House: Notre Dame Press

Last Updated: 23/12/10

NOVA COMPUTER COLLEGE

3rd Floor Gonzales Bldg., 1197 Edsa, Quezon City, Second District, Metro Manila 1105
Tel: +63(2) 374-2104
Fax: +63(2) 371-5945
EMail: admin@ncc.edu.ph
Website: http://www.ncc.edu.ph/

President: Jesus U. Hao

Programmes

Undergraduate and Professional (Computer Engineering; Computer Science; Information Management; Information Technology; Secretarial Studies)

History: Founded 1992.

Degrees and Diplomas: *Associate Degree*; *Bachelor's Degree*

Last Updated: 23/12/10

NOVAGEN COLLEGE OF QUEZON CITY

797 Quirino Highway, Gulod, Novaliches, Quezon City, Second District, Metro Manila
Tel: +63(2) 938-1449
Fax: +63(2) 937-9672

President: Nena Eng Tan

Programmes

Nursing (Nursing)

History: Founded 2005.

Degrees and Diplomas: *Bachelor's Degree*

Last Updated: 23/12/10

NUEVA ECIJA COLLEGES

Cagayan Valley Road, Cabanatuan City, Nueva Ecija 3100
Tel: +63(44) 463-2191
Fax: +63(44) 463-1323
EMail: nec_parmed@yahoo.com

President: Rocio S. Baltao

Programmes

Computer Science (Computer Science); **Hotel and Restaurant Management** (Hotel and Restaurant; Hotel Management); **Medical Technology** (Medical Technology); **Nursing** (Nursing); **Occupational Therapy** (Occupational Therapy); **Pharmacy** (Pharmacy); **Physical Therapy** (Physical Therapy); **Tourism** (Tourism)

History: Founded 1970. Formerly known as Nueva Ecija Doctors School of Nursing (1970-1979).

Degrees and Diplomas: *Certificate/Diploma*; *Associate Degree*; *Bachelor's Degree*; *Master's Degree*: Nursing

Last Updated: 23/12/10

NYK-TDG MARITIME ACADEMY

Canlubang, Laguna 4037
Tel: +63(49) 549-0923
Fax: +63(49) 549-0923
EMail: ntma@ntma.edu.ph

President: Wilson P. Travina

Programmes

Maritime Studies (Marine Engineering; Marine Transport)

Last Updated: 04/01/11

OBLATES OF ST. JOSEPH COLLEGE OF PHILOSOPHY

Bo. Marawoy, Lipa City, Batangas 4217
Tel: +63(43) 756-2550
EMail: osjcp@yahoo.com

President: Ranulfo B. Alkonga, OSJ

Programmes

Philosophy (Philosophy)

History: Founded 1998.

Degrees and Diplomas: *Bachelor's Degree*

Last Updated: 04/01/11

O.B. MONTESSORI CENTER

No. 3 Eisenhower Street, Greenhills, City of San Juan, Second District, Metro Manila
Tel: +63(2) 722-9720 +63(2) 229-727
Fax: +63(2) 721-2673
EMail: registrar@obmontessori.edu.ph
Website: http://www.obmontessori.edu.ph

President: Preciosa S. Soliven

Programmes

Education (Education; Philosophy of Education; Preschool Education); **Food Management** (Cooking and Catering; Food Science; Food Technology)

Further Information: Branches: Las Piñas, Sta Anna, Angeles, Fairview

History: Founded 1966.

Degrees and Diplomas: *Certificate/Diploma*; *Bachelor's Degree*. Also Proficiency Course in Montessori Pre-SchoolEducation.

Last Updated: 04/01/11

OLIVAREZ COLLEGE

Dr. Arcadio Santos Avenue, Sucat, City of Parañaque, Fourth District, Metro Manila 1700
Tel: +63(2) 825-4517
Fax: +63(2) 825-8712
EMail: info@olivarezcollege.edu.ph
Website: http://www.olivarezcollege.edu.ph

President: Pablo R. Olivarez

Programmes

Undergraduate and Professional (Arts and Humanities; Business Administration; Business and Commerce; Computer Science; Education; English; Filipino; Foreign Languages Education; Health Sciences; Hotel and Restaurant; Hotel Management; Management; Marketing; Mass Communication; Medical Technology; Midwifery; Native Language Education; Nursing; Physical Education; Physical Therapy; Political Sciences; Preschool Education; Primary Education; Psychology; Radiology; Science Education; Secondary Education; Tourism)

Schools

Graduate Studies (Business Administration; Education; Educational Administration; Educational and Student Counselling; Management; Nursing)

History: Founded 1976.

Degrees and Diplomas: *Certificate/Diploma*; *Associate Degree*; *Bachelor's Degree*; *Master's Degree*: Business Management; Education (Guidance and Counselling; Educational Management); Nursing, a further 2 yrs

Last Updated: 04/01/11

OLIVAREZ COLLEGE TAGAYTAY

E. Aguinaldo Highway, Tagaytay City, Cavite 4120
Tel: +63(46) 860-2301
Fax: +63(46) 860-2301
EMail: oct@itrac.com

Vice-President for Academics and Services: Eric L. Olivarez

Programmes

Undergraduate and Professional (Business Administration; Business and Commerce; Cooking and Catering; Education; Hotel and Restaurant; Hotel Management; Management; Nursing; Primary Education)

History: Founded 2003.

Degrees and Diplomas: *Certificate/Diploma*; *Bachelor's Degree*

OSIAS COLLEGES

F. Tañedo Street, San Nicolas, City of Tarlac, Tarlac 2300
Tel: +63(45) 982-0245
EMail: osias@mozcom.com

Director: Paz L. Concepcion

Programmes

Graduate Studies (Business Administration; Education; Educational Administration; Educational and Student Counselling); **Undergraduate and Professional Studies** (Administration; Business and Commerce; Education; Filipino; History; Literature; Management; Mathematics Education; Primary Education; Secondary Education)

History: Founded 1949.

Degrees and Diplomas: *Certificate/Diploma*; *Associate Degree*; *Bachelor's Degree*; *Master's Degree*: Arts (Educational Administration and Supervision; Guidance and Counselling); Business Administration
Last Updated: 04/01/11

OSIAS EDUCATIONAL FOUNDATION

Balaoan, La Union 2517
Tel: +63(72) 794-2160
Fax: +63(72) 794-2161
EMail: osiasbalaoan@yahoo.com

President: Danilo Concepcion

Programmes

Arts and Humanities (Arts and Humanities; English; History); **Business Administration** (Banking; Business Administration; Business and Commerce; Finance; Human Resources; Management); **Education** (English; Foreign Languages Education; History; Primary Education; Secondary Education; Social Studies); **Graduate** (Education; Educational Administration; Primary Education; Secondary Education)

History: Founded 1947.

Degrees and Diplomas: *Certificate/Diploma*; *Bachelor's Degree*
Last Updated: 04/01/11

OSMEÑA COLLEGE

Osmeña, Masbate, Masbate 5400
Tel: +63(56) 333-2899
Fax: +63(56) 333-4444

President: Wilfredo M. Peliño

Programmes

Arts and Sciences (Economics; English; History; Mass Communication; Mathematics; Political Sciences); **Business Administration** (Accountancy; Banking; Business Administration; Finance; Human Resources; Management; Marketing); **Computer Science** (Computer Science); **Criminology** (Criminology); **Education** (Education; English; Filipino; History; Home Economics Education; Mathematics Education; Native Language Education; Primary Education; Secondary Education; Social Studies; Technology Education); **Graduate** (Business Administration; Education; English; Filipino; History; Mathematics Education; Public Administration); **Hospitality Management/Hotel and Restaurant Management** (Hotel and Restaurant; Hotel Management; Tourism)

History: Founded 1948.

Degrees and Diplomas: *Certificate/Diploma*; *Bachelor's Degree*; *Master's Degree*: Education; Teaching (History; Mathematics; Filipino; English); Business Administration; Public Administration (Administration and Supervision); *PhD*: Education (Educational Management)
Last Updated: 04/01/11

OUR LADY OF ASSUMPTION COLLEGE SYSTEM

San Pedro, Laguna 4023
Tel: +63(2) 529-6707
Fax: +63(2) 808-2902

President: Ethelwyn Acierto

Campuses

Cabuyao (Business Administration; Taxation; Tourism)

Programmes

Undergraduate and Professional (Business Administration; Computer Science; Education; Hotel and Restaurant; Hotel Management; Information Technology; Management; Marketing; Political Sciences; Primary Education; Secondary Education; Taxation; Tourism)

History: Founded 1989.

Degrees and Diplomas: *Associate Degree*; *Bachelor's Degree*
Last Updated: 04/01/11

OUR LADY OF FATIMA UNIVERSITY

120 McArthur Highway, City of Valenzuela, Third District, Metro Manila 1440
Tel: +63(2) 293-2703 +63(2) 293-2706
Fax: +63(2) 293-2704
EMail: info@fatima.edu.ph; admissions@fatima.edu.ph
Website: http://www.fatima.edu.ph

President: Juliet O. Santos

Campuses

Antipolo City; Quezon City (Biology; Computer Science; Hotel and Restaurant; Hotel Management; Nursing; Physical Therapy; Psychology; Tourism)

Colleges

Arts and Sciences (Biology; English; Filipino; Health Sciences; Mathematics; Natural Sciences; Philosophy; Physical Education; Physics; Psychology; Social Sciences; Zoology); **Business Administration** (Business Administration; Management; Marketing); **Computer Science** (Computer Engineering; Computer Science; Information Technology); **Criminology** (Criminology); **Dentistry** (Dentistry); **Education** (Education; English; Foreign Languages Education; Preschool Education; Primary Education; Secondary Education); **Hospitality and Institutional Management** (Cooking and Catering; Dietetics; Hotel and Restaurant; Hotel Management; Nutrition; Tourism); **Maritime Education** (Marine Engineering; Marine Transport); **Medical Technology** (Medical Technology); **Medicine** (Medicine); **Nursing** (Midwifery; Nursing); **Pharmacy** (Pharmacy); **Physical Therapy** (Physical Therapy)

Schools

Graduate Studies (Anatomy; Business Administration; Education; Educational Administration; Nursing; Physical Therapy; Physiology; Public Administration; Public Health; Teacher Training; Tourism)

History: Founded 1973 as Our Lady of Fatima College (Valenzuela).

Degrees and Diplomas: *Associate Degree*; *Bachelor's Degree*; *Master's Degree*: Arts in Business Administration; College Teaching; Education; Nursing; Public Administration
Last Updated: 04/01/11

OUR LADY OF GUADALUPE COLLEGES

Sierra Madre Street cor. I Esteban Street, City of Mandaluyong, Third District, Metro Manila 1200
Tel: +63(2) 535-5886
Fax: +63(2) 535-5885
EMail: olgc@pldtdsl.net
Website: http://www.olgc.edu.ph

President: Conrado S. Dayrit

Programmes

Nursing (Nursing)

History: Founded 2003.

Degrees and Diplomas: *Bachelor's Degree*
Last Updated: 04/01/11

OUR LADY OF LA SALETTE SCHOOL

Escuela de Nuestra Señora de la Salette

Tapuac Dist., Dagupan City, Pangasinan 2400
Tel: +63(75) 522-3279
Fax: +63(75) 522-3279
EMail: enlas@mozcom.com

President: Lina Galvan-Tan

Programmes
Education (Education; Primary Education); **Nursing and Midwifery** (Midwifery; Nursing); **Secretarial Administration** (Business Administration; Secretarial Studies)
History: Founded 1989.
Degrees and Diplomas: *Bachelor's Degree*; *Post Baccalaureate Certificate/Diploma*
Last Updated: 30/09/10

OUR LADY OF LOURDES COLLEGE

5031 Gen. T. de Leon Street, City of Valenzuela, Third District, Metro Manila 1442
Tel: +63(2) 293-9372
Fax: +63(2) 293-5009

President: Emelita Demetillo-Liwanag

Programmes
Undergraduate and Professional (Arts and Humanities; Business Administration; Computer Science; Criminology; Education; English; Foreign Languages Education; Hotel and Restaurant; Hotel Management; Information Technology; Management; Mathematics Education; Primary Education; Secondary Education)
History: Founded 1986. Formerly known as Our Lady of Lourdes Learning Center (1986-1994).
Degrees and Diplomas: *Associate Degree*; *Bachelor's Degree*
Last Updated: 04/01/11

OUR LADY OF LOURDES COLLEGE FOUNDATION

Vinzons Avenue, Daet, Camarines Norte 4600
Tel: +63(54) 721-1368
Fax: +63(54) 721-2610

President: Abundio P. Palencia

Programmes
Undergraduate and Professional (Business Administration; Business and Commerce; Computer Science; Criminology; Economics; Education; Marine Engineering; Marine Transport; Medical Technology; Midwifery; Nursing; Physical Therapy; Primary Education; Psychology; Radiology; Secondary Education; Secretarial Studies)
History: Founded 1977. Formerly known as Our Lady of Lourdes School of Midwifery.
Degrees and Diplomas: *Certificate/Diploma*; *Associate Degree*; *Bachelor's Degree*
Last Updated: 04/01/11

OUR LADY OF LOURDES TECHNOLOGICAL COLLEGE

105 General Luis Street, Novaliches, Quezon City, Second District, Metro Manila 1123
Tel: +63(2) 419-6019
Fax: +63(2) 419-2967

President: Ismael J. Alamares I

Programmes
Undergraduate and Professional (Accountancy; Business and Commerce; Computer Science; Criminology; Education; English; Foreign Languages Education; Hotel and Restaurant; Hotel Management; Information Technology; Management; Primary Education; Secondary Education)
History: Founded 1997. Formerly known as Our Lady of Lourdes Technological Institute (1997-2005).
Degrees and Diplomas: *Certificate/Diploma*; *Associate Degree*; *Bachelor's Degree*
Last Updated: 05/01/11

OUR LADY OF MANAOAG COLLEGE

Poblacion, Manaoag, Pangasinan 2430
Tel: +63(75) 529-0121
Fax: +63(75) 529-0121
EMail: olmc_mail@yahoo.com.ph

President: Patricio A. Apa, OP

Programmes
Undergraduate and Professional (Business Administration; Business and Commerce; Computer Science; Education; English; Filipino; Foreign Languages Education; Information Technology; Mathematics Education; Native Language Education; Primary Education; Secondary Education)
History: Founded 1949 as Holy Rosary Academy. Acquired present status and title 2001.
Degrees and Diplomas: *Bachelor's Degree*
Last Updated: 05/01/11

OUR LADY OF MERCY COLLEGE

National Highway, Bgy. Locsoon, Borongan, Eastern Samar 6800
Tel: +63(55) 560-0073
Fax: +63(55) 560-0073

President: Diosdado A. Obligar, Jr.

Programmes
Undergraduate and Professional Studies (Criminology; Education; Law; Midwifery; Nursing; Primary Education)
Further Information: Also Bacolod Campus (Bacolod City, Negros Occidental)
History: Founded 1995.
Degrees and Diplomas: *Bachelor's Degree*
Last Updated: 05/01/11

OUR LADY OF MT. CARMEL INSTITUTE OF MEDICAL STUDIES

Brgy. Saguin, City of San Fernando, Pampanga 2000
Tel: +63(72) 860-1265
Fax: +63(72) 860-5977

President: Monette E. Briones

Programmes
Business Administration (Business Administration); **Hotel and Restaurant Management** (Hotel and Restaurant; Hotel Management); **Nursing** (Nursing); **Tourism Management** (Tourism)
Last Updated: 05/01/11

OUR LADY OF PERPETUAL SUCCOR COLLEGE

General Ordoñez Street, City of Marikina, Second District, Metro Manila 1807
Fax: +63(2) 942-0114 +63(2) 942-0672
EMail: olopsc@yahoo.com; olopss@edsamail.com.ph
Website: http://www.geocities.com/olopsc

Rector: Carmen C. Salvador

Programmes
Undergraduate and Professional (Business Administration; Computer Engineering; Computer Science; Curriculum; Education; English; Foreign Languages Education; Hotel and Restaurant; Hotel Management; Human Resources; Information Technology; Management; Management Systems; Marketing; Mathematics Education; Preschool Education; Primary Education; Secondary Education)
History: Founded 1978 as Our Lady of Perpetual Succor School. Acquired present status and title 1994.
Degrees and Diplomas: *Certificate/Diploma*; *Associate Degree*; *Bachelor's Degree*
Last Updated: 05/01/11

OUR LADY OF SALVATION COLLEGE

808 San Lorenzo Poblacion, Tiwi, Albay 4513
Tel: +63(52) 488-5185
Fax: +63(52) 488-5185
EMail: olsc_2006@yahoo.com

President: Vicente Tomas C. Vera VII

Programmes

Education (Education; Mathematics Education; Primary Education; Science Education; Secondary Education)

History: Founded 2000. Formerly known as Nazareth Learning Center.

Degrees and Diplomas: *Bachelor's Degree*
Last Updated: 05/01/11

OUR LADY OF THE PILLAR COLLEGE-CAUAYAN (OLPC-C)

New Site, San Fermin, City of Cauayan, Isabela 3305
Tel: +63(78) 652-0685 +63(78) 652-2605
Fax: +63(78) 652-0685
EMail: registrar@olpcc.edu.ph
Website: http://www.olpcc.edu.ph/

President: Mariano D. Gatan Tel: +63(78) 652-0685

Executive Vice-President: Exuperio V. Flores
EMail: evp@pldtdel.net

Programmes

Accountancy (Accountancy); **Arts and Humanities** (Arts and Humanities; Economics; English; Philosophy; Political Sciences; Sociology); **Business Administration** (Business Administration; Computer Education; Finance; Hotel and Restaurant; Hotel Management; Management; Marketing); **Computer Engineering** (Computer Engineering); **Criminology** (Criminology); **Electrical Engineering** (Electrical and Electronic Equipment and Maintenance); **Electronics and Communications Engineering** (Electronic Engineering; Telecommunications Engineering); **Elementary Education** (English; Filipino; Foreign Languages Education; Health Education; Mathematics Education; Native Language Education; Preschool Education; Primary Education; Religious Education; Science Education); **Graduate Studies** (Administration; Education; Educational Administration; English; Filipino; Foreign Languages Education; Management; Mathematics Education; Native Language Education; Preschool Education; Religious Education; Science Education); **Information Technology** (Information Technology); **Nursing** (Nursing); **Office Administration**; **Public Administration** (Public Administration); **Secondary Education** (Biological and Life Sciences; Business Education; Ethics; Filipino; Foreign Languages Education; Mathematics Education; Native Language Education; Physics; Religious Education; Science Education; Secondary Education; Technology Education)

History: Founded 1956, acquiring current status and title 1969.

Admission Requirements: High School Diploma

Fees: (Pesos): c. 30,000

Main Language(s) of Instruction: Filipino, English

Accrediting Agencies: Philippine Association of Colleges and Universities, Commission on Accreditation (PACUCOA); Philippine Accrediting Association of Schools, Colleges and Universities (PAASCU)

Degrees and Diplomas: *Bachelor's Degree*; *Master's Degree*: Education (Science Education; Preschool Education; Filipino; Mathematics; English; Educational Management; Religious Education); Business Administration; Public Administration; *PhD*: Administration and Supervision

Student Services: Academic counselling, Canteen, Employment services, Health services, Sports facilities

Special Facilities: Audio-visual room, speech lab
Last Updated: 05/01/11

OUR LORD'S GRACE MONTESSORI SCHOOL AND COLLEGES

Commonwealth Avenue, Diliman, Quezon City, Second District, Metro Manila 1104
Tel: +63(2) 455-3228
Fax: +63(2) 931-8950
EMail: olgm@nsclub.net

School Administrator: Rasia Honeylet H. Ortañez

Programmes

Undergraduate and Professional (Economics; Mass Communication; Psychology)

History: Founded 1984 as Our Lady of Grace Montessori School. Acquired current title 1996.

Degrees and Diplomas: *Bachelor's Degree*
Last Updated: 05/01/11

OVILLA TECHNICAL COLLEGE

38 Danao Street, Masbate, Masbate 5400
Tel: +63(56) 333-6090

President: Julius D. Ovilla

Programmes

Undergraduate and Professional (Education; Industrial Arts Education; Political Sciences; Primary Education)

History: Founded 1962 as Ovilla Fashion School. Acquired present status and title 1964.

Degrees and Diplomas: *Bachelor's Degree*
Last Updated: 05/01/11

OXFORDIAN COLLEGES

Dasmariñas, Cavite 4114
Tel: +63(46) 686-0259

President: Rey Balibago

Programmes

Business Administration (Accountancy; Business Administration); **Education** (Education; Filipino; Mathematics Education; Native Language Education; Primary Education; Secondary Education); **Hotel and Restaurant Management** (Hotel and Restaurant; Hotel Management)

History: Created 2006.

Degrees and Diplomas: *Bachelor's Degree*
Last Updated: 05/01/11

PACASUM COLLEGE

Perez Street, Marawi City, Lanao del Sur 9700
Tel: +63(63) 352-0403

President: Johairah P. Pangarungan Tel: +63 520-691

Programmes

Business Administration (Business Administration; Management); **Education** (Education; English; Filipino; Foreign Languages Education; History; Mathematics Education; Native Language Education; Primary Education; Secondary Education); **English** (English); **Political Sciences** (Political Sciences)

History: Founded 1966.

Degrees and Diplomas: *Bachelor's Degree*
Last Updated: 05/01/11

PACE GRADUATE SCHOOL OF CHRISTIAN EDUCATION

22 3rd Avenue, Cubao, Quezon City, Second District, Metro Manila 1109
Tel: +63(2) 722-0943
Fax: +63(2) 722-0943

President: Romulo G. Pizaña

Programmes

Christian Education (Christian Religious Studies; Curriculum; Educational Administration; Educational and Student Counselling; Preschool Education; Primary Education; Religious Education)

History: Founded 1991.

Degrees and Diplomas: *Certificate/Diploma*; *Master's Degree*: Christian Education (Educational Management; Guidance and Counselling; Curriculum and Instruction; Early Childhood Education)
Last Updated: 05/01/11

PADOVA COLLEGE

McArthur Highway, Dau, Mabalacat, Pampanga 2010
Tel: +63(45) 331-4856
Fax: +63(45) 331-7292
EMail: smmc@comclark.com

President: Antonio S. Yap

Programmes

Arts and Humanities (Arts and Humanities; Communication Arts); **Business Administration** (Business Administration; Management)

History: Founded 1966. Formerly known as Padova Polytechnic College.

Degrees and Diplomas: *Bachelor's Degree*
Last Updated: 05/01/11

PAGADIAN CAPITOL COLLEGE

Rizal Avenue, Pagadian City, Zamboanga del Sur 7016
Tel: +63(62) 214-4364
Fax: +63(62) 214-4364
EMail: registrarpcc@yahoo.com.ph

President: Ricardo F. Santiago

Programmes

Arts and Humanities (Arts and Humanities); **Commerce** (Accountancy; Business and Commerce; Management); **Computer Science** (Computer Science); **Criminology** (Criminology); **Education** (Education; Filipino; Primary Education; Secondary Education); **Electrical Engineering** (Electrical Engineering); **Information Technology** (Information Technology); **Laws** (Law)

History: Founded 1993. Formerly known as Pagadian College of Criminology and Sciences.

Degrees and Diplomas: *Associate Degree*; *Bachelor's Degree*
Last Updated: 05/01/11

PALARIS COLLEGE

01 Perez Boulevard, San Carlos City, Pangasinan 2420
Tel: +63(75) 532-3847
Fax: +63(75) 634-1039
EMail: palariscollege@yahoo.com; alaris@pang.pworld.net.ph

President: Alice Ilalo S. Baun

Programmes

Business Administration (Banking; Business Administration; Finance); **Education** (Education; English; Foreign Languages Education; Primary Education; Secondary Education); **English** (English; Modern Languages); **Graduate** (Education; Educational Administration); **Hotel and Restaurant Management** (Hotel and Restaurant; Hotel Management)

History: Founded 1946 as Palaris Junior College. Acquired present title 1971.

Degrees and Diplomas: *Certificate/Diploma*; *Bachelor's Degree*; *Master's Degree*: Education (Administration and Supervision)
Last Updated: 05/01/11

PALAWAN POLYTECHNIC COLLEGE

Manalo Extension, Puerto Princesa City, Palawan 5300
Tel: +63(48) 434-2393
Fax: +63(48) 434-2393
EMail: ppci_mats@yahoo.com

President/Registrar: Aileen A. Alterado

Programmes

Business Administration (Business Administration; Management); **Computer Science** (Computer Science); **Customs Administration** (Taxation); **Engineering** (Civil Engineering; Engineering; Marine Engineering; Marine Transport; Mechanical Engineering); **Nursing** (Nursing); **Tourism** (Tourism)

History: Founded 1979 as MATS College of Technology. Acquired present status and title 1986.

Degrees and Diplomas: *Certificate/Diploma*; *Bachelor's Degree*
Last Updated: 05/01/11

PALAWAN TECHNOLOGICAL COLLEGE

245 Malvar Street, Puerto Princesa City, Palawan 5300
Tel: +63(48) 434-4518
Fax: +63(48) 434-2775
EMail: ptci_ppc@yahoo.com

President: Celestino C. Mauleon

Programmes

Hotel and Restaurant Management (Hotel and Restaurant; Hotel Management); **Information Technology** (Cooking and Catering; Information Technology)

History: Founded 1995.

Degrees and Diplomas: *Certificate/Diploma*; *Bachelor's Degree*
Last Updated: 06/01/11

PAMPANGA COLLEGES

Plobacion, Macabebe, Pampanga 2018
Tel: +63(45) 921-1416
Fax: +63(45) 921-1242
EMail: pampangacolleges@digitelone.com

President: Fidel L. Isip Jr.

Programmes

Commerce (Banking; Business and Commerce; Finance); **Education** (English; Foreign Languages Education; Primary Education; Secondary Education)

History: Founded 1938, acquiring present status in 1950.

Degrees and Diplomas: *Bachelor's Degree*
Last Updated: 20/01/11

PANAY TECHNOLOGICAL COLLEGE

M. Laserna Street, Kalibo, Aklan 5600
Tel: +63(36) 268-5152
Fax: +63(36) 268-5239
EMail: ptci@yahoo.com

President/Director: Bernardino C. Arguelles

Programmes

Undergraduate and Professional (Business and Commerce; Business Computing; Computer Engineering; Computer Science; Hotel and Restaurant; Hotel Management; Tourism)

History: Founded 1982.

Degrees and Diplomas: *Certificate/Diploma*; *Associate Degree*; *Bachelor's Degree*
Last Updated: 20/01/11

PANGASINAN MEMORIAL COLLEGE

95 Artacho Street, Lingayen, Pangasinan 2401
Tel: +63(75) 542-2818
Fax: +63(75) 662-0840

President: Rajewen B. Pulido

Programmes

Education (Education; English; Filipino; Foreign Languages Education; Mathematics Education; Native Language Education; Primary Education; Science Education; Secondary Education)

History: Founded 1949.

Degrees and Diplomas: *Certificate/Diploma*; *Bachelor's Degree*
Last Updated: 20/01/11

PANGASINAN MERCHANT MARINE ACADEMY

Perez Boulevard, Dagupan City, Pangasinan 2400
Tel: +63(75) 515-7870 +63(75) 515-3331
Fax: +63(75) 515-7870
EMail: Pamma_acad@digitelone.com

President: Michelle B. De la Cruz

Programmes

Criminology (Criminology; Police Studies); **Education** (Education; Primary Education; Science Education; Secondary Education); **Hotel and Restaurant Management** (Hotel and Restaurant; Hotel

Management); **Marine Engineering** (Marine Engineering); **Marine Transportation** (Marine Transport); **Tourism** (Tourism)

History: Founded 1976. Formerly known as Pangasinan Marine Academy (1978 -1983).

Degrees and Diplomas: *Associate Degree*; *Bachelor's Degree*
Last Updated: 20/01/11

PANPACIFIC UNIVERSITY NORTH PHILIPPINES (PUNP)

McArthur Highway, San Vicente, Urdaneta City, Pangasinan 2428
Tel: +63(75) 568-2672
Fax: +63(75) 568-7662
EMail: info@punp.edu.ph
Website: http://www.punp.edu.ph

President: Romeo T. Padilla

Senior Vice-President: Corazon Padilla

Colleges

Arts and Science (Arts and Humanities; Biology; English; Mathematics); **Business and Accountancy** (Accountancy; Business Administration; Business and Commerce; Finance; Hotel and Restaurant; Hotel Management; Management; Marketing; Tourism); **Computer Studies** (Computer Science; Information Technology); **Criminology** (Criminal Law; Criminology); **Engineering** (Civil Engineering; Computer Engineering; Electrical Engineering; Electronic Engineering; Engineering; Telecommunications Engineering); **Law**; **Maritime Education** (Marine Transport); **Nursing** (Nursing); **Teacher Education** (Biology; Education; English; Filipino; Foreign Languages Education; Health Education; Mathematics Education; Music Education; Native Language Education; Physical Education; Primary Education; Secondary Education; Social Sciences)

Departments

Pharmacy (Pharmacy)

Schools

Graduate (Biology; Business Administration; Criminal Law; Criminology; Education; Educational Administration; English; Foreign Languages Education; Health Education; Mathematics Education; Music Education; Physical Education; Public Administration; Special Education)

Further Information: Also Tayug Campus

History: Founded 1993 as Pangasinan Colleges of Science and Technology.

Accrediting Agencies: Philippine Association of Colleges and Universities, Commission on Accreditation (PACUCOA)

Degrees and Diplomas: *Associate Degree*; *Bachelor's Degree*; *Master's Degree*: Business Administration; Public Administration; Education (Educational Management); Criminology; *PhD*: Educational Management

Student Services: Academic counselling, Canteen, Foreign student adviser, Health services, Language programs, Sports facilities
Last Updated: 20/01/11

PARADIGM COLLEGE OF SCIENCE AND TECHNOLOGY

Roxas, Oriental Mindoro 5212
Tel: +63(43) 289-2827
Fax: +63(43) 289-2827
EMail: lynxletter1@yahoo.com

President: Hernan C. Erorita

Programmes

Business Administration (Business Administration; Finance; Management); **Hotel and Restaurant Management** (Hotel and Restaurant; Hotel Management); **Secondary Education** (Industrial Arts Education; Secondary Education)

Degrees and Diplomas: *Bachelor's Degree*
Last Updated: 21/01/11

PARANG FOUNDATION COLLEGE

Making, Parang, Shariff Kabunsuan 9604
President: Gabasan P. Ali , Al-Hadj

Programmes

Arts (Arts and Humanities); **Criminology** (Criminology); **Education** (Education; Primary Education; Secondary Education)

History: Founded 1989.

Degrees and Diplomas: *Bachelor's Degree*
Last Updated: 21/01/11

PARTIDO COLLEGE

Tambuco Street, Goa, Camarines Sur 4422
Tel: +63(54) 453-0278
Fax: +63(54) 453-0278
EMail: partidocollege@yahoo.com

President: Emma G. Alfelor

Programmes

Graduate (Business Administration; Educational Administration; Educational and Student Counselling; Filipino; Management; Native Language Education; Public Administration); **Undergraduate and Professional** (Accountancy; Banking; Business and Commerce; Criminology; Education; English; Filipino; Finance; Foreign Languages Education; History; Management; Mathematics Education; Native Language Education; Political Sciences; Primary Education; Secondary Education)

History: Founded 1979. Formerly known as Camarines Sur Institute.

Degrees and Diplomas: *Certificate/Diploma*; *Bachelor's Degree*; *Master's Degree*: Business Administration; Management; Public Administration; Education (Filipino; Administration and Supervision; Mathematics; Guidance and Counselling); *PhD*: Education (Educational Management)
Last Updated: 21/01/11

PASIG CATHOLIC COLLEGE

Justice Ramon Jabson Street, Malinao, Pasig City, Second District, Metro Manila 1600
Tel: +63(2) 642-7451 +63(2) 641-1791 +63(2) 628-2577
Fax: +63(2) 641-3134
EMail: info@pasigcatholic.edu.ph
Website: http://www.pasigcatholic.edu.ph/

President: Gerardo O. Santos

Graduate Schools

Education (Education; Educational Administration)

Programmes

Undergraduate and Professional (Accountancy; Biology; Business Administration; Chemistry; Computer Education; Computer Engineering; English; Filipino; Foreign Languages Education; Information Technology; Literacy Education; Management; Management Systems; Marketing; Mathematics; Mathematics Education; Native Language Education; Preschool Education; Psychology; Social Studies)

History: Founded 1913.

Degrees and Diplomas: *Associate Degree*; *Bachelor's Degree*; *Master's Degree*: Arts in Educational Management
Last Updated: 21/01/11

PASS COLLEGE

Quezon Avenue, City of Alaminos, Pangasinan 2404
Tel: +63(75) 654-0001 +63(75) 551-3364
Fax: +63(75) 654-0001
EMail: pass_col@mozcom.com

President: Ruben D. Morante

Programmes

Accountancy (Accountancy); **Business Administration** (Business Administration; Business and Commerce); **Computer Science** (Computer Science); **Education** (Education; Primary Education)

History: Founded 1997 as Philippine Accountancy and Science School. Acquired present title 2001.

Degrees and Diplomas: *Certificate/Diploma*; *Associate Degree*; *Bachelor's Degree*
Last Updated: 21/01/11

PATRIA SABLE CORPUS COLLEGE

8 Guzman Street, Calao West, City of Santiago, Isabela 3311
Tel: +63(78) 682-7046
Fax: +63(78) 682-7754
EMail: pscorpuscollege@yahoo.com

President: Laures S.C. Moreno

Programmes

Accountancy (Accountancy); **Arts and Humanities** (Arts and Humanities; English; Mass Communication); **Commerce** (Banking; Business and Commerce; Business Computing; Finance; Management; Marketing); **Computer Engineering** (Computer Engineering); **Computer Science** (Computer Science); **Criminology** (Criminology); **Education** (Child Care and Development; Preschool Education; Primary Education; Secondary Education); **Electrical Engineering** (Electrical Engineering); **Electronics and Communication Engineering** (Electronic Engineering; Telecommunications Engineering); **Hotel and Restaurant Management** (Hotel and Restaurant; Hotel Management); **Industrial Education** (Automotive Engineering; Electrical Engineering; Electronic Engineering; Industrial Arts Education); **Industrial Technology** (Automotive Engineering; Electrical Engineering; Electronic Engineering; Industrial Engineering; Technology)

History: Founded 1947 as Sable Fashion School. Formerly Sable Vocational Academy (1983-1992).

Degrees and Diplomas: *Certificate/Diploma*; *Associate Degree*; *Bachelor's Degree*

Last Updated: 21/01/11

PATTS COLLEGE OF AERONAUTICS

Lombos Avenue, Sucat Road, San Isidro, City of Parañaque, Fourth District, Metro Manila 1700
Tel: +63(2) 825-8823
Fax: +63(2) 825-8824
EMail: admin@patts.edu.ph
Website: http://www.patts.edu.ph

President: Maria Felisa S. Valdez

Programmes

Undergraduate and Professional (Aeronautical and Aerospace Engineering; Air Transport; Business Administration; Hotel and Restaurant; Hotel Management; Maintenance Technology; Marketing; Tourism; Transport Management)

History: Founded 1969.

Degrees and Diplomas: *Bachelor's Degree*: 4-5 yrs

Last Updated: 21/01/11

PERPETUAL HELP COLLEGE OF MANILA

V. Concepcion Street, Sampaloc, Manila, First District, Metro Manila 1008
Tel: +63(2) 731-8199 +63(2) 731-1550
Fax: +63(2) 731-1550
Website: http://www.perpetual.edu.ph

President: Antonio L. Tamayo

Programmes

Undergraduate and Professional (Accountancy; Business Administration; Computer Science; Hotel and Restaurant; Hotel Management; Information Technology; Management; Mass Communication; Nursing; Occupational Therapy; Physical Therapy; Respiratory Therapy; Secretarial Studies; Zoology)

History: Founded 1968. Formerly known as Perpetual Help Hospital School of Nursing, Paramedical & Special Courses Inc. (1968-1976).

Degrees and Diplomas: *Associate Degree*; *Bachelor's Degree*: 4-5 yrs

Last Updated: 21/01/11

PERPETUAL HELP COLLEGE OF PANGASINAN

Montemayor Street, Malasiqui, Pangasinan 2421
Tel: +63(75) 536-4955 +63(75) 536-4503
Fax: +63(75) 536-4955
EMail: perpetualpangasinan@yahoo.com
Website: http://www.uphsl.edu.ph/pangasinan/index.htm

President: Antonio L. Tamayo

Programmes

Arts (English); **Business Administration** (Accountancy; Business Administration; Human Resources; Management); **Education** (English; Foreign Languages Education; Mathematics Education; Primary Education; Science Education; Secondary Education; Social Studies); **Hotel and Restaurant Management** (Hotel and Restaurant; Hotel Management); **Nursing** (Nursing)

History: Founded 1976.

Degrees and Diplomas: *Associate Degree*; *Bachelor's Degree*

Last Updated: 21/01/11

PERPETUAL HELP PARAMEDICAL COLLEGE

Happy Homes Subdivision, Tagas, City of Tabaco, Albay 4511
Tel: +63(52) 435-0943
EMail: phpcollege@yahoo.com

Registrar/Administrator: Elizabeth B. Binalingbing

Programmes

Health Sciences (Midwifery; Nursing)

History: Founded 1993.

Degrees and Diplomas: *Certificate/Diploma*; *Bachelor's Degree*

Last Updated: 21/01/11

PHILIPPINE ADVENT COLLEGE

Ramon Magsaysay, Sindangan, Zamboanga del Norte 7112
EMail: pmcernal@gmail.com

President: Pio M. Cernal

Programmes

Undergraduate and Professional Studies (Accountancy; Arts and Humanities; Business Administration; Business and Commerce; Computer Science; Information Technology; Law; Management; Midwifery; Nursing; Political Sciences; Primary Education; Secondary Education)

History: Founded 1975 as Hillside View College, acquiring present title 1985.

Degrees and Diplomas: *Bachelor's Degree*

Last Updated: 21/01/11

PHILIPPINE CAMBRIDGE SCHOOL OF LAW, ARTS, SCIENCES, BUSINESS ECONOMICS AND TECHNOLOGY

Burol Main, Dasmariñas, Cavite 4114
Tel: +63(46) 850-2071
Fax: +63(46) 973-2855

Chancellor: Bong Caluntad

Programmes

Undergraduate and Professional (Accountancy; Advertising and Publicity; Banking; Business Administration; Computer Education; Computer Engineering; Education; Electronic Engineering; English; Filipino; Finance; Foreign Languages Education; Hotel and Restaurant; Hotel Management; Information Technology; Law; Management; Marketing; Mathematics Education; Native Language Education; Primary Education; Secondary Education; Secretarial Studies; Social Studies; Software Engineering; Tourism)

History: Founded 2001.

Degrees and Diplomas: *Bachelor's Degree*

Last Updated: 21/01/11

PHILIPPINE CENTRAL COLLEGE OF ARTS, SCIENCE AND TECHNOLOGY

Natividad, Naguilian, La Union 2511
Tel: +63(72) 609-1040
Fax: +63(72) 609-1428
EMail: lvlandingin@pccast.edu.ph

President: Ludivina V. Landingin

Programmes

Computer Science (Computer Science); **Education** (Education; English; Foreign Languages Education; Primary Education;

Secondary Education); **Information Technology** (Information Technology); **Office Management** (Administration; Management)

History: Founded 2000. Formerly known as Naguilian Institute of Science and Technology.

Degrees and Diplomas: *Certificate/Diploma*; *Bachelor's Degree*
Last Updated: 21/01/11

PHILIPPINE CHRISTIAN UNIVERSITY

PO Box 907, 1648 Taft Avenue, corner Pedro Gil Street, Ermita, Manila, First District, Metro Manila 1004
Tel: +63(2) 526-2261 +63(2) 524-6671
Fax: +63(2) 526-5110
EMail: regis@pcu.edu.ph
Website: http://www.pcu.edu.ph

Chairman, Management Committee: Felix D. Carao, Jr. (2009-)
Tel: +63(2) 523-2372

President: Oscar S. Suarez

Vice-President, Academic Affairs: Greg Melchor C. de Lara
Tel: +63(2) 525-5435, Fax: +63(2) 525-5435
EMail: gmcdelara@yahoo.com

International Relations: Origen P. Pascua, University Registrar
Tel: +63(2) 523-2162, Fax: +63(2) 525-5435
EMail: genepascua@yahoo.com

Centres

Institutional Reseach and Planning Development *(CIRPD)*; **Instructional Media** *(IMC)* (Educational Technology); **Resource Learning** *(RLC)*

Colleges

Arts, Sciences and Social Work *(Manila)* (Development Studies; English; History; Mass Communication; Mathematics; Psychology; Social Work); **Arts, Sciences and Teacher Education** *(Dasmarinas)* (Education; Health Education; Nursing; Primary Education; Secondary Education); **Business Administration and Accounting** *(Manila)* (Accountancy; Administration; Business Administration; Management; Secretarial Studies; Tourism); **Business and Technology** *(Dasmarinas)* (Business Administration; Computer Science; Hotel and Restaurant; Hotel Management; Information Technology; Tourism); **Computer Studies** *(Manila)* (Computer Engineering; Computer Science; Information Sciences; Information Technology); **Education and Allied Programmes** *(Manila)* (Education; Educational Administration; Preschool Education; Primary Education; Secondary Education); **Law** *(Manila)* (Law); **Nursing and Allied Health** *(Manila)* (Dietetics; Health Education; Hotel and Restaurant; Hotel Management; Nursing; Nutrition)

Graduate Schools

Religion and Philosophy *(Manila)* (Religious Studies; Theology)

Programmes

Seminary *(Manila)* (Pastoral Studies; Religious Education; Theology)

Further Information: Also PCU Dasmarinas, Cavitas Campus.

History: Founded 1946 as College, acquired present status and title 1976. A private institution supported by the United Methodist Church and United Church of Christ in the Philippines.

Governing Bodies: The Management Committee

Academic Year: June to March (June-October; November-March)

Admission Requirements: Graduation from high school and entrance examination

Fees: (Pesos): c. 470 per unit; graduate, c. 1,370

Main Language(s) of Instruction: Filipino, English

International Co-operation: With universities in Korea, Indonesia, Pakistan

Accrediting Agencies: Association of Christian Schools, Colleges and Universities Accrediting Agency

Degrees and Diplomas: *Bachelor's Degree*; *Master's Degree*: Business Administration; Information Technology; Management; Nursing; Psychology; Theology Studies; Education (Educational Administration; Filipino; Psychology/Guidance and Counselling; Mathematics/Science Teaching; Early Childhood; English); *PhD*: Education; Missiology; Philosophy in: Business Administration; Development Administration; Religious Studies

Student Services: Academic counselling, Canteen, Cultural centre, Employment services, Foreign student adviser, Foreign Studies Centre, Health services, Language programs, Nursery care, Social counselling, Sports facilities

Student Residential Facilities: None

Special Facilities: Instructional Media Centre

Libraries: 51,902 vols (Manila campus); 21,917 (Dasmarinas campus)

Publications: Academic Review, Journal *(biannually)*; Journal of Education Research, Publication of the Graduate School *(biannually)*

Academic Staff *2008-2009*: Total 533

Student Numbers *2008-2009*: Total 14,015
Last Updated: 21/01/11

PHILIPPINE COLLEGE FOUNDATION

Hagkol, Valencia City, Bukidnon 8709
Tel: +63(88) 222-2657
Fax: +63(88) 222-2657
EMail: adelapagonzaga@yahoo.com
Website: http://philippinecollegefoundation.net

Director: Amable S. Pagonzaga

Programmes

Business Administration (Business Administration); **Criminology** (Criminology); **Elementary Education** (Education; English; Foreign Languages Education; Primary Education); **Hotel and Restaurant Management** (Hotel and Restaurant; Hotel Management); **Office Administration** (Administration)

History: Founded 1988.

Degrees and Diplomas: *Bachelor's Degree*
Last Updated: 24/01/11

PHILIPPINE COLLEGE OF AERONAUTICS, SCIENCE AND TECHNOLOGY

EL 98 . Jaro, Iloilo City, Iloilo 5000
Tel: +63(33) 509-3403

President: Lyn A. Rosales

Programmes

Airline Management (Air Transport); **Hotel, Restaurant and Tourism Management** (Hotel and Restaurant; Hotel Management; Tourism)

Degrees and Diplomas: *Bachelor's Degree*
Last Updated: 24/01/11

PHILIPPINE COLLEGE OF CRIMINOLOGY

650 Sales Street, Sta. Cruz, City of Manila, First District, Metro Manila 1003
Tel: +63(2) 314-8513
Fax: +63(2) 734-7856
EMail: pccr@pccr.edu.ph
Website: http://www.pccr.edu.ph/

President: Gregory Alan F. Bautista
Tel: +63(2) 733-1607, Fax: +63(2) 733-1608

Departments

Chemistry (Chemistry); **Criminology** (Criminology); **Law** (Law); **Law Enforcement** (Police Studies); **Mathematics** (Mathematics); **Modern Languages** (Modern Languages)

History: Founded 1954.

Degrees and Diplomas: *Bachelor's Degree*: Criminology; *Master's Degree*: Criminology; *PhD*: Criminology
Last Updated: 24/01/11

PHILIPPINE COLLEGE OF HEALTH SCIENCES

1813 C.M. Recto Avenue, Quiapo, City of Manila, First District, Metro Manila 1015
Tel: +63(2) 733-9480 +63(2) 734-0340
Fax: +63(2) 734-0339

President: George C. Cordero

Programmes
Graduate (Education; Educational Administration; English; Foreign Languages Education; Health Administration; Management; Mathematics Education; Nursing; Public Administration); **Undergraduate and Professional** (English; Medical Technology; Midwifery; Nursing; Occupational Therapy; Physical Therapy; Political Sciences; Psychology; Radiology)
History: Founded 1993.
Degrees and Diplomas: *Associate Degree*; *Bachelor's Degree*; *Master's Degree*: Nursing (Nursing Administration and Management); Public Administration; Education (English; Educational Management; Mathematics); *PhD*: Management; Educational Management
Last Updated: 24/01/11

PHILIPPINE COLLEGE OF NORTHWESTERN LUZON

Agoo, La Union 2504
Tel: +63(72) 522-1038

President: Alfredo A. Durante

Programmes
Business Administration (Accountancy; Business Administration; Finance; Human Resources; Management)
Degrees and Diplomas: *Bachelor's Degree*
Last Updated: 24/01/11

PHILIPPINE COLLEGE OF SCIENCE AND TECHNOLOGY

Nalsian, Calasiao, Pangasinan 2418
Tel: +63(75) 522-8032
Fax: +63(75) 523-0894
EMail: philcst@hotmail.com
Website: http://www.philcst.edu.ph/.edu.ph/

President: Lourdes S. Fernandez

Colleges
Accountancy and Business Administration (Accountancy; Business Administration); **Computer Studies** (Computer Science; Information Technology); **Criminology** (Criminology); **Education and Mass Communication** (Curriculum; Education; Journalism; Mass Communication; Mathematics Education; Primary Education; Science Education; Secondary Education); **Engineering and Architecture** (Architecture; Civil Engineering; Computer Engineering; Electrical Engineering; Electronic Engineering; Engineering; Industrial Engineering; Mechanical Engineering; Structural Architecture; Telecommunications Engineering); **Hotel and Restaurant Management** (Hotel and Restaurant; Hotel Management; Tourism); **Maritime Studies** (Marine Engineering; Marine Transport); **Nursing and Midwifery** (Midwifery; Nursing); **Technical Studies** (Technology)
History: Founded 1994.
Degrees and Diplomas: *Bachelor's Degree*
Last Updated: 24/01/11

PHILIPPINE COLLEGE OF TECHNOLOGY

Davao Medical School Drive, J.P. Laurel Avenue, Davao City, Davao del Sur 8000
Tel: +63(82) 222-4808
Fax: +63(82) 221-0381
EMail: pctdavao@philwebinc.com

President: Ma. Rossini L. Balili

Programmes
Business Administration (Accountancy; Business Administration; Finance; Human Resources; Management); **Computer Science** (Computer Science); **Education** (Curriculum; Education; English; Foreign Languages Education; Mathematics Education; Primary Education; Secondary Education); **Environmental Science** (Environmental Studies); **Hotel and Restaurant Management** (Hotel and Restaurant; Hotel Management); **Tourism Management** (Hotel Management; Tourism); **Travel Management** (Tourism)
History: Founded 1993. Formerly known as Philippine School of Technology (1993-2000).
Degrees and Diplomas: *Bachelor's Degree*
Last Updated: 24/01/11

PHILIPPINE COMPUTER COLLEGE

Dionesio Micayabas Street, Purok 4 South Poblacion, Maramag, Bukidnon 8714
Tel: +63(88) 356-1633 +63(88) 226-4072
Fax: +63(88) 356-1633
EMail: pccbukidnon@hotmail.com

President: Fe A. Torres

Programmes
Undergraduate and Professional (Business Administration; Computer Engineering; Computer Science; Information Technology; Management; Marketing)
History: Founded 1997.
Degrees and Diplomas: *Certificate/Diploma*; *Bachelor's Degree*
Last Updated: 24/01/11

PHILIPPINE CULTURAL COLLEGE

1253 Jose Abad Santos Avenue, Tondo, City of Manila, First District, Metro Manila 1012
Tel: +63(2) 252 - 0501
Fax: +63(2) 254 - 0814
EMail: info@pchsonline.org
Website: http://www.pchsonline.org

President: Lily C. Go

Programmes
Business Administration (Accountancy; Business Administration; Human Resources; Management; Marketing); **Education** (Chinese; Education; Foreign Languages Education; Preschool Education; Primary Education; Secondary Education); **Hotel and Restaurant Management** (Hotel and Restaurant; Hotel Management); **Information Technology** (Information Technology); **Tourism Management** (Tourism)
Further Information: Also special English classes for foreign students
History: Founded 1923 as Philippine Chinese High School. Acquired present status and title 2008.
Degrees and Diplomas: *Bachelor's Degree*
Last Updated: 24/01/11

PHILIPPINE DOMINICAN CENTER OF INSTITUTIONAL STUDIES

Sto. Domingo Convent, 537 Quezon Avenue, Quezon City, Second District, Metro Manila 1114
Tel: +63(2) 743-7764
Fax: +63(2) 743-7760

Director: Stephen R. Redillas, O.P.

Programmes
Philosophy (Philosophy; Religious Studies)
History: Founded 1968.
Degrees and Diplomas: *Bachelor's Degree*; *Master's Degree*
Last Updated: 24/01/11

PHILIPPINE LAW ENFORCEMENT COLLEGE

Patria Building Corner Gomez and Rizal Streets, Tuguegarao City, Cagayan 3500
Tel: +63(78) 844-4910
Fax: +63(78) 844-4910
EMail: Philippine_Law_Enforcement_College@yahoo.com

President: Emmanuel M. Aldaba

Programmes
Arts (Economics; English; Political Sciences); **Criminology** (Criminology); **Customs Administration** (Taxation); **Public Safety Administration** (Civil Security; Public Administration)
History: Founded 1997.
Degrees and Diplomas: *Bachelor's Degree*
Last Updated: 24/01/11

PHILIPPINE LAW SCHOOL

1852 Taft Avenue, Pasay City, Fourth District, Metro Manila 1300
Tel: +63(2) 521-4988

President: Niczon Yao

Programmes
Law (Law)

History: Founded 1915.

Degrees and Diplomas: *Bachelor's Degree*
Last Updated: 24/01/11

PHILIPPINE MERCHANT MARINE SCHOOL - MANILA (PMMS)

1571 Lope de Vega St., corner Rizal Avenue, Santa Cruz, City of Manila, First District, Metro Manila 1003
Tel: +63(2) 742-3372
Fax: +63(2) 742-3375
Website: http://pmms-online.com

President: Juan O. Nolasco III

Programmes
Marine Transport (Marine Transport)

History: Founded 1950.

Degrees and Diplomas: *Bachelor's Degree*
Last Updated: 24/01/11

PHILIPPINE MISSIONARY INSTITUTE

Biga, Silang, Cavite 4118
Tel: +63(46) 414-0494
Fax: +63(46) 414-0561
EMail: hbelandres@hotmail.com

President: Hector T. Belandres

Programmes
Theology (Christian Religious Studies; Cultural Studies; Pastoral Studies; Religious Education; Religious Music; Theology)

History: Founded 1969.

Degrees and Diplomas: *Bachelor's Degree*
Last Updated: 24/01/11

PHILIPPINE MUSLIM TEACHERS' COLLEGE

Bo. Green, Bangon, Marawi City, Lanao del Sur 9700

President (Acting): A. M. Sharief

Programmes
Education (Education; Primary Education; Secondary Education)

History: Founded 2000.

Degrees and Diplomas: *Bachelor's Degree*
Last Updated: 24/01/11

PHILIPPINE REHABILITATION INSTITUTE FOUNDATION

56 Banawe Street, Quezon City, Second District, Metro Manila 1114
Tel: +63(2) 743-7592
Fax: +63(2) 712-9821
EMail: info@prifnet.com; admission@prifnet.com
Website: http://www.prifnet.com

President: Ricardo N. Lim

Programmes
Health Sciences (Health Administration; Health Sciences; Medical Technology; Nursing; Occupational Therapy; Physical Therapy; Radiology)

Further Information: Also branch in San Matias, Guagua, Pampanga

History: Founded 1995.

Degrees and Diplomas: *Bachelor's Degree*
Last Updated: 24/01/11

PHILIPPINE SCHOOL OF BUSINESS ADMINISTRATION - MANILA

826 R. Papa Street, Sampaloc, City of Manila, First District, Metro Manila 1008
Tel: +63(2) 741-4608 +63(2) 735-1355
Fax: +63(2) 735-1384
EMail: psbamla@pacific.net.ph
Website: http://www.psba.edu

President: Jose F. Peralta

Registrar: B. Erlinda

Campuses
Quezon City (Accountancy; Banking; Business Administration; Computer Science; Finance; Human Resources; Management; Management Systems; Marketing) *President*: Benjamin P. Paulino

Programmes
Graduate *(Manila and Quezon City)* (Business Administration); **Undergraduate and Professional** (Accountancy; Banking; Business Administration; Finance; Management; Management Systems; Marketing)

History: Founded 1963. Acquired present status and title 1966.

Degrees and Diplomas: *Bachelor's Degree*; *Master's Degree*: Business Administration; *PhD*: Business Administration
Last Updated: 24/01/11

PHILIPPINE STATESMAN COLLEGE

Burgos Avenue, Cabanatuan City, Nueva Ecija 3100
Tel: +63(44) 463-6695

President: Manuel A. Estrella

Programmes
Psychology (Psychology)

History: Founded 1947.

Degrees and Diplomas: *Master's Degree*: Psychology
Last Updated: 24/01/11

PHILIPPINE TECHNOLOGICAL & MARINE SCIENCES - ZAMBOANGA DEL SUR

Purok Tugas Ballesteros Street, Rizal Avenue, Balangasan District, Pagadian City, Zamboanga del Sur 7016
Tel: +63(62) 353-1633
Fax: +63(62) 353-1633
EMail: ptmspagadian@yahoo.com

President: Marietta Tahadlangit Cañete

Campuses
Zamboanga Sibugay (Accountancy; Business and Commerce; Business Computing; Computer Science; Electronic Engineering; Hotel and Restaurant; Hotel Management; Information Technology; Management; Marine Transport; Mass Communication; Mechanical Engineering; Radio and Television Broadcasting; Telecommunications Engineering; Tourism)

Programmes
Undergraduate and Professional (Accountancy; Business and Commerce; Business Computing; Computer Engineering; Computer Science; Electronic Engineering; Hotel and Restaurant; Hotel Management; Information Technology; Management; Marine Transport; Mass Communication; Mechanical Engineering; Radio and Television Broadcasting; Telecommunications Engineering; Tourism)

History: Founded 1999. Formerly known as Pagadian Technological and Marine Sciences (1999-2003).

Degrees and Diplomas: *Bachelor's Degree*
Last Updated: 24/01/11

PHILIPPINE WESTERN UNION COLLEGE

07 Carlos P. Garcia Street, City of Alaminos, Pangasinan 2404
Tel: +63(75) 551-2092

President: Emilio O. Palisoc Jr.

Programmes

Business Administration (Business Administration); **Business Management** (Business Administration; Management)

History: Founded 2004.

Degrees and Diplomas: *Bachelor's Degree*
Last Updated: 24/01/11

PHILIPPINE WOMEN'S UNIVERSITY (PWU)

1743 Taft Avenue, Manila, First District, Metro Manila 1004
Tel: +63(2) 526-8421
Fax: +63(2) 522-4002
EMail: pwu@pwu.edu.ph
Website: http://www.pwu.edu.ph/

President: José Francisco Benitez (2010-)
Tel: +63(2) 526-8421 Ext 109/114
EMail: fbb@pwu.edu.ph; kikobenitez@gmail.com

Vice-President for Academics, Research and Publications: Kristina Benitez
Tel: +63(2) 339-2582 EMail: kasbenitez@gmail.com

Vice President, Administration: Ma. Louisa Mirasol
Tel: +63(2) 526-8288, Fax: +63(2) 526-6935
EMail: mirasol_marlu@yahoo.com

International Relations: Alfredo Reyes, Vice-President for External Affairs
Tel: +63(2) 526-8421 Ext 171, Fax: +63(2) 526-7595
EMail: freddie.reyes@gmail.com

Faculties

Business Education and Information Technology (Business Administration; Business Education; Computer Science; Information Management; Information Technology; Management); **Food Technology and Hospitality Management** (Food Science; Food Technology; Hotel and Restaurant; Hotel Management; Tourism); **Health and Wellness** (Dietetics; Medical Technology; Nursing; Nutrition; Pharmacy); **Humanities and Social Sciences** (Advertising and Publicity; Clinical Psychology; Communication Arts; Education; Environmental Studies; Gender Studies; Industrial and Organizational Psychology; International Relations; Media Studies; Performing Arts; Psychology; Public Relations; Social Work); **Visual and Performing Arts** (Design; Fine Arts; Industrial Design; Interior Design; Music)

Further Information: Traditional and Open Learning Institution and has two campuses located at Quezon City and Davao.

History: Founded 1919. Acquired present status and title 1932.

Governing Bodies: University Council

Academic Year: June to May

Admission Requirements: High School Certificate (or equivalent)

Fees: (PHP): 31,000 per semester

Main Language(s) of Instruction: English, Filipino

International Co-operation: with institutions in South Korea, Thailand, Qatar, Vietnam, USA, Japan, Indonesia

Accrediting Agencies: Philippine Association of Colleges and Universities Commission on Accreditation (PACUCOA); Philippine Accrediting Association of Schools, Colleges and Universities (PAASCU); and Commission on Higher Education – Regional Quality Assessment Team

Degrees and Diplomas: *Bachelor's Degree*; *Master's Degree*; *PhD*

Student Services: Academic counselling, Canteen, Cultural centre, Employment services, Foreign student adviser, Foreign Studies Centre, Health services, Language programs, Social counselling, Sports facilities

Special Facilities: Museum; Art gallery

Libraries: c. 80,000 vols; 142 periodical subscriptions

Academic Staff *2012-2013*	MEN	WOMEN	TOTAL
FULL-TIME	69	88	**157**
PART-TIME	29	99	**128**
STAFF WITH DOCTORATE			
FULL-TIME	2	3	**5**
PART-TIME	18	25	**43**
Student Numbers *2012-2013*			
All (Foreign Included)	3,584	8,782	**12,366**
FOREIGN ONLY	167	287	**454**

Distance students, 1,448.
Last Updated: 11/03/13

PHILIPPINE WOMEN'S UNIVERSITY - QUEZON CITY

Epifanio De Los Santos Avenue, Quezon City, Second District, Metro Manila 1104
Tel: +63(2) 920-6309
Fax: +63(2) 920-6313
EMail: pwumanila@pwu.edu.ph
Website: http://www.pwuquezoncity.com/

Officer-in-Charge: Hipolito P. Palcon

Programmes

Graduate (Business Administration; Education; Public Administration; Special Education); **Undergraduate and Professional** (Accountancy; Business Administration; Communication Arts; Computer Education; Computer Science; Education; Hotel and Restaurant; Hotel Management; International Studies; Management; Nursing; Peace and Disarmament; Preschool Education; Psychology)

History: Founded 1956.

Degrees and Diplomas: *Bachelor's Degree*; *Master's Degree*

PHILIPPINES WOMEN'S COLLEGE OF DAVAO

Davao City, Davao del Sur 8000
Tel: +63(82) 296-0403
Fax: +63(82) 299-2838
EMail: info@thepwcofdavao.com
Website: http://www.pwu.edu.ph/pwcdavao/main.html

President: Rosa Santos Munda

Dean and Executive Officer: Ma. Gracia C. Conde

Programmes

Business Administration (Banking; Business Administration; Finance; Management; Marketing); **Education** (Curriculum; Educational and Student Counselling; Ethics; Mathematics Education; Primary Education; Secondary Education); **Entrepreneurship** (Management); **Fine Arts** (Advertising and Publicity; Fashion Design; Industrial Design; Interior Design; Painting and Drawing); **Fine Arts** (Design; Fine Arts); **Food Technology** (Food Technology); **Hotel and Restaurant Management** (Cooking and Catering; Hotel and Restaurant; Hotel Management); **Tourism** (Tourism)

History: Founded 1953.

Degrees and Diplomas: *Associate Degree*; *Bachelor's Degree*

PHILSIN COLLEGE FOUNDATION, INC.

3153 R. Magsaysay Blvd., Sta. Mesa, City of Manila, First District, Metro Manila 1016
Tel: +63(2) 715-0010 +63(2) 715-0018
Fax: +63(2) 715-0018

President: James T. Pahati

Programmes

Marine Transport (Marine Transport)

Further Information: Also branch in Rizal

History: Founded 1995 as Philsin Marine Technology College Foundation.

Degrees and Diplomas: *Bachelor's Degree*
Last Updated: 25/01/11

PILAR COLLEGE

Justice Roseller T. Lim Blvd., Zamboanga City, Zamboanga del Sur 7000
Tel: +63(62) 991-4682
EMail: pilarczc@jetlink.com.ph; pilarcol@zambo.I-nExt.net
Website: http://www.geocities.com/pilar_collegezam

Director: Ma. Bernadette G. Suico, RVM

Programmes

Undergraduate and Professional Studies (Accountancy; Business Administration; Business and Commerce; Computer Education; Computer Science; Education; English; Filipino; Finance; Foreign Languages Education; Health Education; Hotel and Restaurant; Hotel Management; Information Management; Information Sciences; Information Technology; Library Science; Management; Mathematics Education; Native Language Education; Nursing; Primary Education; Science Education; Secondary Education; Tourism)

History: Founded 1894. Formerly known as Pilar Institution (1984-1997).

Degrees and Diplomas: *Bachelor's Degree*
Last Updated: 25/01/11

PILGRIM CHRISTIAN COLLEGE

Akut-Tiano Streets, Cagayan de Oro City, Misamis Oriental 9000
Tel: +63(88) 856-4232
Fax: +63(88) 856-4232

President: Pio Baconga

Programmes

Undergraduate and Professional Studies (Accountancy; Business Administration; Curriculum; Education; English; Finance; Foreign Languages Education; Health Education; Human Resources; Management; Marketing; Mass Communication; Music; Physical Education; Preschool Education; Special Education)

History: Founded 1948.

Degrees and Diplomas: *Bachelor's Degree*
Last Updated: 25/01/11

PILI CAPITAL COLLEGE

San Isidro, Pili, Camarines Sur 4418
Tel: +63(54) 477-7003
Fax: +63(54) 477-7155

President: Gabriel C. Cayetano

Programmes

Criminology (Criminology); **Education** (Education; English; Foreign Languages Education; Mathematics Education; Primary Education; Secondary Education)

History: Founded 1988. Formerly Pili Capital Educational Center.

Degrees and Diplomas: *Bachelor's Degree*
Last Updated: 25/01/11

PIMSAT COLLEGES

Mc Arthur Hi-way, Bolosan, Pangasinan 2400
Tel: +63(75) 523-6667 +63(75) 522-6667 +63(75) 515-5754
Fax: +63(75) 522-1808
EMail: pimsatcolleges@yahoo.com

President: Rebene C. Carrera

Programmes

Business Administration (Accountancy; Business Administration); **Computer Science** (Computer Science); **Criminology** (Criminology); **Education** (Mathematics Education; Primary Education; Secondary Education); **Engineering** (Civil Engineering; Computer Engineering; Electrical Engineering; Electronic Engineering; Engineering; Marine Engineering; Mechanical Engineering; Telecommunications Engineering); **Hotel and Restaurant Management** (Hotel and Restaurant; Hotel Management); **Information Technology** (Information Technology); **Marine Transport** (Marine Transport); **Nursing** (Nursing)

History: Founded 1983. Formerly known as Philippine Institute for Maritime Studies and Technology College (1983-1995).

Degrees and Diplomas: *Certificate/Diploma*; *Associate Degree*; *Bachelor's Degree*
Last Updated: 25/01/11

PINES CITY COLLEGES

Magsaysay Avenue, Baguio City, Benguet 2600
Tel: +63(74) 445-9064
Fax: +63(74) 445-2208

Programmes

Undergraduate and Professional (Biology; Chemistry; Dental Technology; Dentistry; Education; Educational and Student Counselling; English; Ethics; Foreign Languages Education; History; Home Economics; Home Economics Education; Hotel and Restaurant; Mathematics; Mathematics Education; Medical Technology; Midwifery; Nursing; Occupational Therapy; Optometry; Pharmacy; Physical Therapy; Respiratory Therapy; Science Education; Secondary Education; Secretarial Studies; Social Studies; Technology; Technology Education; Tourism)

History: Founded 1969.

Degrees and Diplomas: *Associate Degree*; *Bachelor's Degree*; *Post Baccalaureate Certificate/Diploma*: Dental Medicine, 4 yrs; *Post Baccalaureate Certificate/Diploma*: Optometry, 6 yrs
Last Updated: 25/01/11

PLT COLLEGE

Zulueta Street, Bayombong, Nueva Vizcaya 3700
Tel: +63(78) 805-3682
Fax: +63(78) 805-3682
EMail: pltc@pltcollege.edu.ph

President: Purisimo L. Tiam

Programmes

Commerce (Business and Commerce; Economics); **Computer Management** (Computer Science; Management); **Criminology** (Criminology); **Education** (Education; Primary Education; Secondary Education); **Hotel and Restaurant Management** (Hotel and Restaurant; Hotel Management); **Information and Computer Science** (Computer Science; Information Sciences); **Nursing** (Nursing); **Office Administration** (Administration; Business Administration); **Radiologic Technology** (Medical Technology; Radiology)

History: Founded 1989. Formerly known as Programming Language Technique College.

Degrees and Diplomas: *Associate Degree*; *Bachelor's Degree*
Last Updated: 25/01/11

PMI COLLEGES - BOHOL

Carlos P. Garcia Avenue, Tagbilaran City, Bohol 6300
Tel: +63(38) 411-2601 +63(38) 411-2158
Fax: +63(38) 411-2601
EMail: pmib-edu@mozcom.com

Director: Misoro A. Salamera

Programmes

Customs Administration (Taxation); **Marine Engineering** (Marine Engineering); **Marine Transport** (Marine Transport)

History: Founded in 1973.

Degrees and Diplomas: *Bachelor's Degree*
Last Updated: 25/01/11

PMI COLLEGES - MANILA

419 William Burke Street, Sta. Cruz, City of Manila, First District, Metro Manila 1003
Tel: +63(2) 242-0265 +63(2) 242-0266
Fax: +63(2) 243-4853

President: Rizabel Cloma-Santos

Programmes

Customs Administration (Taxation); **Marine Transport** (Marine Transport)

History: Founded 1948. Formerly known as Philippine Maritime Institute - Manila.

Degrees and Diplomas: *Associate Degree*; *Bachelor's Degree*; *Master's Degree*: Customs Administration
Last Updated: 24/01/11

PMI COLLEGES - QUEZON CITY

73 Roosevelt Avenue, San Francisco del Monte, Quezon City, Second District, Metro Manila 1105
Tel: +63(2) 347-4769
Fax: +63(2) 347-4770

President: Rizabel Cloma-Santos

Programmes

Undergraduate and Professional (Marine Engineering; Marine Transport; Taxation)

History: Founded 1948. Formerly known as Philippine Maritime Institute - Quezon City.

Degrees and Diplomas: *Associate Degree*; *Bachelor's Degree*
Last Updated: 24/01/11

PMMS COLLEGES

San Antonio Valley Road, Talon 1, City of Las Piñas, Fourth District, Metro Manila 1747
Tel: +63(2) 805-0243 +63(2) 805-0239
Fax: +63(2) 805-0243

President: Alberto C. Compas

Centres

PMMS Caregiver Training

Courses

Marine Transportation (Marine Transport); **Technical Education and Skills Development Authority** *(Technical Education and Skills Development Authority - TESDA)* (Maintenance Technology; Marine Engineering; Marine Transport; Metal Techniques; Technology)

Programmes

Customs Administration (Taxation); **Hotel and Restaurant Management** (Hotel and Restaurant; Hotel Management); **Marine Engineering** (Marine Engineering)

History: Founded 1950. Formerly known as Philippine Merchant Marine School.

Degrees and Diplomas: *Certificate/Diploma*; *Associate Degree*; *Bachelor's Degree*
Last Updated: 25/01/11

PNTC COLLEGES (PNTC COLLEGES)

Zone III, Lt. Cantimbuhan, Poblacion, Dasmariñas, Cavite 4115
Tel: +63(46) 416-5111
Fax: +63(46) 416-2584
EMail: philnautical@pntc.com.ph
Website: http://www.pntc.com.ph

President: Hernani N. Fabia

Programmes

Business Administration (Business Administration); **Customs Administration** (Taxation); **Marine Engineering** (Marine Engineering); **Marine Transportation** (Marine Transport)

Further Information: Locations: Dasmarinas, Cavite; Intramuros, Manila; Tanza, Cavite

History: Founded 1994 as Philippine Nautical Training Institute, Inc. (PNTI). Formerly known as Philippine Nautical and Technological College.

Degrees and Diplomas: *Bachelor's Degree*
Last Updated: 24/01/11

POLYTECHNIC COLLEGE OF DAVAO DEL SUR

MacArthur Highway, City of Digos, Davao del Sur 8002
Tel: +63(82) 553-3441
EMail: pcds101@mail.com

President: Nestor Ledesma

Programmes

Undergraduate and Professional Studies (Computer Science; Criminology; Medical Technology; Midwifery; Nursing; Radiology)

History: Founded 1986.

Degrees and Diplomas: *Associate Degree*; *Bachelor's Degree*
Last Updated: 25/01/11

POLYTECHNIC COLLEGE OF LA UNION

San Joaquin Sur, Agoo, La Union 2504
Tel: +63(72) 710-0242
Fax: +63(72) 521-0592
EMail: pcluph@yahoo.com

President: Rodolfo T. Panay

Programmes

Graduate (Educational Administration; English; Mathematics; Public Administration); **Undergraduate and Professional** (Banking; Business and Commerce; Computer Engineering; Criminology; Educational Administration; English; Filipino; Finance; Foreign Languages Education; Information Technology; Law; Management; Marine Transport; Mathematics; Mathematics Education; Native Language Education; Nursing; Primary Education; Public Administration; Secondary Education)

History: Founded 1992. Formerly known as PAMETS Colleges.

Degrees and Diplomas: *Associate Degree*; *Bachelor's Degree*; *Master's Degree*
Last Updated: 25/01/11

POLYTECHNIC INSTITUTE OF TABACO

100 Panal, City of Tabaco, Albay 4511
Tel: +63(52) 487-5928
EMail: jlg_pita888@yahoo.com

President: Jaime L. Guardino

Programmes

Undergraduate and Professional (Arts and Humanities; Business Administration; Computer Engineering; Computer Science; Electrical Engineering; Electronic Engineering; Information Technology; Primary Education; Telecommunications Engineering)

History: Founded 1985.

Degrees and Diplomas: *Certificate/Diploma*; *Associate Degree*; *Bachelor's Degree*
Last Updated: 25/01/11

POWER SCHOOL OF TECHNOLOGY

Tanza, Cavite 4108
Tel: +63(46) 885-1149

President: Jesus Villongco

Programmes

Undergraduate and Professional (Business Administration; Computer Science; Management; Marketing)

History: Founded 2002.

Degrees and Diplomas: *Bachelor's Degree*
Last Updated: 25/01/11

PRINCE OF PEACE COLLEGE

Balete, Poblacion, Puerto Galera, Oriental Mindoro 5203
Tel: +63(43) 287-3012

President: Maria Concepcion R. Atienza

Programmes

Undegraduate and Professional (Education; Primary Education)

History: Founded 1994 as Prince of Peace Montessori School.

Degrees and Diplomas: *Certificate/Diploma*; *Bachelor's Degree*
Last Updated: 25/01/11

PROFESSIONAL MONTESSORI COLLEGE

M.L. Quezon Extn., Antipolo City, Rizal 1870
Tel: +63(2) 697-6650
Fax: +63(2) 697-6650

President: Danilo D. Dy

Programmes
Undergraduate and Professional (Business Administration; Computer Science; Hotel and Restaurant; Hotel Management; Secretarial Studies)
History: Founded 1998.
Degrees and Diplomas: *Bachelor's Degree*
Last Updated: 25/01/11

PROGRAMMING LANGUAGE TECHNIQUE COLLEGE

San Francisco, Guinobatan, Albay 4503
Tel: +63(52) 484-6250
Fax: +63(52) 484-6250
EMail: pltcollege@yahoo.com

President: Nenita R. Osia

Programmes
Undergraduate and Professional (Administration; Business Administration; Computer Education; Hotel and Restaurant; Hotel Management; Secondary Education)
History: Founded 1995.
Degrees and Diplomas: *Certificate/Diploma*; *Bachelor's Degree*
Last Updated: 25/01/11

QUEZON CENTER FOR RESEARCH AND STUDIES

8th Flr., Garcia Carporate Tower, Corner Rizal & Granja Streets, Lucena City, Quezon 4301
Tel: +63(42) 373-3852
Fax: +63(42) 660-5630
EMail: qcrsim@gmail.com

President: Leandro P. Garcia

Programmes
Business Administration (Business Administration; Business Computing; Finance; Management; Marketing)
Degrees and Diplomas: *Bachelor's Degree*
Last Updated: 26/01/11

QUEZON CITY POLYTECHNIC UNIVERSITY

673 Quirino Highway, San Bartolome, Quezon City, Second District, Metro Manila 1116
Tel: +63(2) 936-0526

President: Ofelia M. Carague

Programmes
Entrepreneurial Management (Business Administration; Management); **Industrial Engineering** (Industrial Engineering); **Information Communications Technology** (Information Technology); **Information Technology** (Information Technology)
History: Founded 1989.
Degrees and Diplomas: *Bachelor's Degree*
Last Updated: 26/01/11

QUEZON COLLEGES OF SOUTHERN PHILIPPINES

Alunan Highway, Tacurong City, Sultan Kudarat 9800
Tel: +63(64) 200-5766
EMail: qcsp_educ_ph@yahoo.com.ph

Director: Eduardo V. Quezon

Programmes
Graduate (Educational Administration); **Undergraduate and Professional Studies** (Banking; Business and Commerce; Economics; Education; English; Filipino; Finance; Foreign Languages Education; Management; Mathematics; Mathematics Education; Native Language Education; Primary Education; Secondary Education)
History: Founded 1958. Formerly known as Lyceum of Southern Philippines (1975-1978).
Degrees and Diplomas: *Bachelor's Degree*; *Master's Degree*: Educational Management
Last Updated: 26/01/11

QUEZON COLLEGES OF THE NORTH

Cortez Street, Centro East, Ballesteros, Cagayan 3516

President: Leoncia A. Alonzo

Programmes
Business Administration (Business Administration; Business and Commerce; Management; Marketing)
Degrees and Diplomas: *Certificate/Diploma*; *Bachelor's Degree*
Last Updated: 26/01/11

QUEZON INSTITUTE OF TECHNOLOGY

Poblacion, Quezon, Bukidnon 8715
Tel: +63(88) 355-1190
EMail: jp_zonealert@yahoo.com

President: Restituto S. Gumanid

Programmes
Arts (Economics; Political Sciences); **Business Administration** (Business Administration; Management); **Education** (Filipino; Mathematics Education; Native Language Education; Primary Education; Secondary Education)
History: Founded 1986.
Degrees and Diplomas: *Bachelor's Degree*
Last Updated: 26/01/11

QUEZON MEMORIAL INSTITUTE OF SIQUIJOR

Canal, Siquijor, Central Visayas 6225
Tel: +63(35) 344-2037

President: Richard C. Quezon

Programmes
Undergraduate and Professional (Art Education; Curriculum; Education; Health Education; History; Music Education; Physical Education; Preschool Education)
History: Founded 1947.
Degrees and Diplomas: *Certificate/Diploma*; *Bachelor's Degree*
Last Updated: 26/01/11

QUEZONIAN EDUCATIONAL COLLEGE

633 R. Soler Street, Atimonan, Quezon 4331
Tel: +63(42) 361-4129
EMail: qzunian@mozcom.com

President: Ma. Aurora A. Tamayo

Programmes
Undergraduate and Professional (Business Administration; Computer Science; Economics; Education; English; Filipino; Finance; Foreign Languages Education; Human Resources; Management; Mathematics Education; Native Language Education; Primary Education; Secondary Education)
History: Founded 1985.
Degrees and Diplomas: *Certificate/Diploma*; *Associate Degree*; *Bachelor's Degree*
Last Updated: 26/01/11

RAMON MAGSAYSAY MEMORIAL COLLEGES

Pioneer Avenue, General Santos City, South Cotabato 9500
Tel: +63(83) 552-3348 +63(83) 552-4189
Fax: +63(83) 552-3264
EMail: rmmc@rmmc.edu.ph
Website: http://www.rmmc.edu.ph/

President: Kristoffer Franz Mari R. Millado
EMail: kfmillado@rmmc.edu.ph

Registrar: Rodriga Gallogo EMail: registrar@rmmc.edu.ph

Programmes
Accountancy (Accountancy); **Business Education** (Business Administration; Economics; Finance; Management; Marketing); **Criminology** (Criminology); **Customs Administration** (Taxation); **Education** (Education; English; Filipino; Foreign Languages Education; Mathematics Education; Native Language Education; Primary Education; Science Education; Secondary Education);

Engineering (Civil Engineering; Engineering); **Information Technology** (Computer Engineering; Computer Science; Information Technology); **Liberal Arts** (Economics; English; Filipino; Mass Communication; Psychology); **Office Administration** (Administration; Management; Secretarial Studies); **Social Work** (Social Work)

Schools

Graduate (Education; Educational Administration; Educational and Student Counselling; English; Foreign Languages Education)

History: Founded 1960. Formerly known as Magsaysay Memorial Colleges.

Degrees and Diplomas: *Bachelor's Degree*; *Master's Degree*: Arts (Educational Management and Administration; English; Guidance and Counselling)

Last Updated: 26/01/11

READ DATA ACCESS COMPUTER COLLEGE

027 Juan dela Cruz Street, City of Kidapawan, North Cotabato 9400
Tel: +63(64) 278-3044
EMail: rdacc_registrar@yahoo.com

President: Simelisa M. Eñola

Programmes

Computer Science (Computer Science); **Information Systems** (Information Technology); **Information Technology** (Information Technology)

History: Founded 1992. Formerly known as Computer Learning Center (1997-2000).

Degrees and Diplomas: *Bachelor's Degree*

Last Updated: 26/01/11

REGENCY POLYTECHNIC COLLEGE

Lower Balmores - Peredes Street, Brgy GPS, Koronadal City, South Cotabato 9506
Tel: +63(83) 228-4059
Fax: +63(83) 228-4059

President: Roberto F. Escaro III

Programmes

Criminology (Criminology); **Marine Transportation and Engineering** (Marine Engineering; Marine Transport)

History: Founded 1986 as Cotabato City Technical School. Renamed Cotobato City Central College (1993-2004).

Degrees and Diplomas: *Bachelor's Degree*

Last Updated: 26/01/11

REGINA MONDI COLLEGE

Hi-Way 1, San Nicolas, Iriga City, Camarines Sur 4431
Tel: +63(54) 456-2525 +63(54) 299-1498
Fax: +63(54) 299-1498
EMail: regina_mondi@yahoo.com

President: Eufemia C. Ceguera

Programmes

Accountancy (Accountancy); **Business Administration** (Banking; Business Administration; Business Computing; Finance; Management)

History: Founded 2004.

Degrees and Diplomas: *Bachelor's Degree*

Last Updated: 26/01/11

REGIS MARIE COLLEGE

Dr. A. Santos Avenue, Sucat, City of Parañaque, Fourth District, Metro Manila 1700
Tel: +63(2) 826-9267

President: Jose Ricardo Custodio Masias
EMail: jcmasias@hotmail.com

Programmes

Undergraduate and Professional (Business Computing; Computer Science; Education; English; Filipino; Foreign Languages Education; Mathematics Education; Native Language Education; Primary Education; Science Education; Secondary Education; Secretarial Studies)

History: Founded 1993.

Degrees and Diplomas: *Associate Degree*; *Bachelor's Degree*

Last Updated: 26/01/11

REPUBLIC CENTRAL COLLEGES

Plaridel Street, Angeles City, Pampanga 2009
Tel: +63(45) 322-5863 +63(45) 322-5656
Fax: +63(45) 322-6670

President: Victoria L. Angeles

Programmes

Accountancy (Accountancy); **Arts** (Economics; English); **Civil Engineering** (Civil Engineering); **Commerce** (Accountancy; Business and Commerce; Computer Science; Management); **Computer Science** (Computer Science); **Education** (Biology; English; Filipino; Foreign Languages Education; Mathematics Education; Native Language Education; Primary Education; Secondary Education); **Graduate** (Business Administration; Education; Management; Public Administration); **Hotel and Restaurant Management** (Hotel and Restaurant; Hotel Management); **Nursing** (Nursing)

History: Founded 1946. Formerly known as Republic Academy.

Degrees and Diplomas: *Associate Degree*; *Bachelor's Degree*; *Master's Degree*: Business Management; Public Management; Arts in Education

Last Updated: 26/01/11

REPUBLIC COLLEGES OF GUINOBATAN

G. Alban Street, Guinobatan, Albay 4503
Tel: +63(52) 484-6580
Fax: +63(52) 484-6401
EMail: rc_gbtn_inc@yahoo.com

President: Emmanuel Flores

Programmes

Graduate (Agricultural Education; Education; Educational Administration; Filipino; Home Economics Education; Native Language Education; Public Administration); **Undergraduate and Professional** (Biology; Business Administration; Computer Science; Education; English; Filipino; Foreign Languages Education; Home Economics Education; Management; Mathematics Education; Native Language Education; Primary Education; Secondary Education; Technology Education)

History: Founded 1947.

Degrees and Diplomas: *Certificate/Diploma*; *Bachelor's Degree*; *Master's Degree*: Education (Agriculture; Administration and Supervision; Filipino; Home Economics); Public Administration

Last Updated: 26/01/11

REPUBLICAN COLLEGE

42-18th Avenue, Quezon City, Second District, Metro Manila 1109
Tel: +63(2) 912-1286
Fax: +63(2) 912-5579

President: Horosi S. Aguiling

Programmes

Graduate (Business Administration; Criminology; Education); **Undergraduate and Professional** (Business and Commerce; Business Computing; Criminology; Education; English; Filipino; Foreign Languages Education; Management; Native Language Education; Political Sciences; Secondary Education; Secretarial Studies)

History: Founded 1949.

Degrees and Diplomas: *Bachelor's Degree*; *Master's Degree*: Business Administration; Education; Criminology

Last Updated: 26/01/11

R.G. DE CASTRO COLLEGES

Gerona Street, Bulan, Sorsogon 4706
Tel: +63(56) 411-1583
Fax: +63(56) 411-1583
EMail: rgccbulan@yahoo.com

President: Gary R. de Castro

Programmes

Undergraduate and Professional (Business and Commerce; Education; English; Information Technology; Management; Marketing; Primary Education; Secondary Education)
History: Founded 1950.
Degrees and Diplomas: *Bachelor's Degree*
Last Updated: 26/01/11

RICHMOND MONTESSORI COLLEGE

Dipolog City, Zamboanga Del Norte 7100
Tel: +63(65) 212-7688
EMail: rmc_dipolog@yahoo.com
President: Francisco Geronilla

Programmes

Undergraduate and Professional (Curriculum; Education; Preschool Education; Primary Education)
History: Founded 1983.
Degrees and Diplomas: *Bachelor's Degree*
Last Updated: 27/01/11

RIVERSIDE COLLEGE

Dr. Pablo O. Torre Sr. Street, Bacolod City, Negros Occidental 6100
Tel: +63(34) 432-7624
Fax: +63(34) 709-7460
EMail: info@riverside.edu.ph

President: Jean T. Rivera

Programmes

Graduate (Nursing); **Undergraduate and Professional** (Medical Technology; Midwifery; Nursing; Physical Therapy; Psychology; Radiology; Special Education)
History: Founded 1959.
Degrees and Diplomas: *Certificate/Diploma*; *Associate Degree*; *Bachelor's Degree*; *Master's Degree*: Nursing
Last Updated: 27/01/11

RIZAL COLLEGE OF LAGUNA

National Highway Parian, Calamba City, Laguna 4027
Tel: +63(49) 545-1180
EMail: rcl@laguna.net
President: Roldan M. Noynay

Programmes

Undergraduate and Professional (Business Administration; English; Filipino; Foreign Languages Education; History; Industrial Arts Education; Management; Management Systems; Marketing; Native Language Education; Secondary Education; Secretarial Studies)
History: Founded 1974. Formerly Rizal Technical Institute.
Degrees and Diplomas: *Certificate/Diploma*; *Bachelor's Degree*
Last Updated: 27/01/11

RIZAL COLLEGE OF TAAL

G. Marella Street, Taal, Batangas 4208
Tel: +63(43) 421-1160
Fax: +63(43) 421-1160
EMail: rizalcollegeoftaal@yahoo.com

President: Fe Cabrera

Programmes

Graduate (Education; Educational Administration); **Undergraduate and Professional** (Accountancy; Banking; Business Administration; Business and Commerce; Computer Science; Criminology; Education; English; Filipino; Finance; Foreign Languages Education; Health Education; History; Home Economics Education; Management; Mathematics Education; Music Education; Native Language Education; Physical Education; Primary Education; Science Education; Technology Education)
History: Founded 1923.
Degrees and Diplomas: *Certificate/Diploma*; *Bachelor's Degree*; *Master's Degree*: Education (Educational Administration)
Last Updated: 27/01/11

RIZAL MARINE AND TECHNO-COMPUTER COLLEGE

Brgy. Ilog, Infanta, Quezon 4336
Tel: +63(2) 535-3284
Fax: +63(2) 535-3284
Director: Fermina Q. Villaluna

Programmes

Undergraduate and Professional (Education; English; Foreign Languages Education; Home Economics Education; Hotel and Restaurant; Hotel Management; Information Technology; Mathematics Education; Primary Education; Secondary Education; Technology Education)
History: Founded 2002.
Degrees and Diplomas: *Certificate/Diploma*; *Bachelor's Degree*
Last Updated: 27/01/11

RIZAL MEMORIAL COLLEGES

A. Pichon Sr. Street, Davao City, Davao del Sur 8000
Tel: +63(82) 225-3940
Fax: +63(82) 222-4355
Website: http://www.rmcdavao.com

President: Evelyn Abellera Magno

Programmes

Accountancy (Accountancy); **Agriculture** (Agriculture); **Arts** (Communication Arts; Economics; English; Political Sciences); **Civil Engineering** (Civil Engineering); **Commerce** (Accountancy; Banking; Business Administration; Business and Commerce; Finance; Management; Marketing); **Criminology** (Criminology); **Education** (Art Education; Education; Educational and Student Counselling; English; Ethics; Filipino; Foreign Languages Education; Health Education; History; Home Economics Education; Literacy Education; Mathematics Education; Music Education; Native Language Education; Preschool Education; Primary Education; Science Education; Secondary Education; Social Studies; Technology Education); **Electrical Engineering** (Electrical Engineering); **Graduate** (Business Administration; Economics; Educational Administration; Educational and Student Counselling; English; Filipino; Foreign Languages Education; Home Economics Education; Management; Native Language Education); **Mathematics** (Mathematics); **Mechanical Engineering** (Mechanical Engineering); **Office Administration** (Administration; Business Computing; Secretarial Studies); **Psychology** (Psychology)
History: Founded 1948.
Degrees and Diplomas: *Bachelor's Degree*; *Master's Degree*; *Master's Degree*: Arts in: Teaching English; Educational Management; Teaching Home Economics; Filipino; Guidance and Counselling; Economics; *PhD*: Business Management
Last Updated: 27/01/11

RIZAL MEMORIAL INSTITUTE OF DAPITAN CITY

Gov. Carnicero Street, Dapitan City, Zamboanga Del Norte 7101
Tel: +63(62) 213-6620

President: Jose R. Manguiran Tel: +63(62) 415-2691

Programmes

Undergraduate and Professional (Arts and Humanities; Business Administration; Business and Commerce; Education; English; Foreign Languages Education; Human Resources; Management; Marketing; Primary Education; Secondary Education)
History: Founded 1946. Formerly known as Rizal Memorial Institute.
Degrees and Diplomas: *Bachelor's Degree*

Last Updated: 27/01/11

ROGATIONIST COLLEGE

Km. 52 Aguinaldo High-way, Lalaan II, Silang, Cavite 4118
Tel: +63(46) 414-0448 +63(46) 414-1015
Fax: +63(46) 414-2039
EMail: infodesk@rog.edu.ph
Website: http://www.rog.edu.ph

Rector: Eduardo L. Fernandez

Director, Finance and Administration: Herman Abcede

Programmes
Undergraduate and Professional (Accountancy; Automotive Engineering; Business Administration; Computer Engineering; Computer Science; Cooking and Catering; Education; Electrical Engineering; Electronic Engineering; English; Foreign Languages Education; Graphic Arts; Hotel and Restaurant; Hotel Management; Industrial Engineering; Information Technology; Management; Management Systems; Marketing; Mathematics Education; Mechanical Engineering; Primary Education; Printing and Printmaking; Religious Education; Secondary Education; Secretarial Studies; Telecommunications Engineering; Tourism)

Further Information: Also campuses in Parañaque and Davao

History: Founded 1987.

Degrees and Diplomas: *Certificate/Diploma*; *Associate Degree*; *Bachelor's Degree*
Last Updated: 27/01/11

ROMAN C. VILLALON MEMORIAL COLLEGES FOUNDATION

Sayre Highway, East Kibawe, Kibawe, Bukidnon 8720
Tel: +63(88) 357-1256
Fax: +63(88) 357-1426

President: Concepcion S. Villalon

Programmes
Education (Education; Primary Education)

History: Founded 2000.

Degrees and Diplomas: *Bachelor's Degree*
Last Updated: 27/01/11

ROMBLON COLLEGE

M. Formilleza, Odiongan, Romblon 5505
Tel: +63(42) 508-3008
Fax: +63(42) 508-3008

President: Nellie G. De Castro

Programmes
Undergraduate and Professional (Computer Science; Education; English; Foreign Languages Education; History; Primary Education; Secondary Education)

History: Founded 1948.

Degrees and Diplomas: *Bachelor's Degree*
Last Updated: 27/01/11

ROOSEVELT COLLEGE - CAINTA

Sumulong Highway, Cainta, Rizal 1900
Tel: +63(2) 681-6202
Fax: +63(2) 681-6222
EMail: ruzveltcal@info.com.ph
Website: http://www.rooseveltcollege.edu.ph

President: Romeo P. De la Paz

Programmes
Undergraduate and Professional (Business and Commerce; Civil Engineering; Computer Engineering; Computer Science; Education; Electrical Engineering; Nursing; Primary Education; Radio and Television Broadcasting; Secondary Education)

History: Founded 1933.

Degrees and Diplomas: *Bachelor's Degree*
Last Updated: 27/01/11

ROOSEVELT COLLEGE - MARIKINA

J.P Rizal Street, Lamuan, City of Marikina, Second District, Metro Manila 1800
Tel: +63(2) 941-5683 +63(2) 942-09-49
Fax: +63(2) 941-5683

President: Romeo P. De la Paz

Programmes
Commerce (Accountancy; Business and Commerce; Finance; Management); **Computer Science** (Computer Science); **Information Management** (Information Management); **Information Technology** (Information Technology); **Office Administration** (Management Systems; Secretarial Studies)

History: Founded 1933.

Degrees and Diplomas: *Bachelor's Degree*
Last Updated: 27/01/11

ROXAS COLLEGE

Bagumbayan, Roxas, Oriental Mindoro 5212
Tel: +63(43) 289-2487

President: Arnulfo C. Sison

Programmes
Undergraduate and Professional (Banking; Business and Commerce; Education; English; Filipino; Finance; Foreign Languages Education; History; Mathematics Education; Native Language Education; Primary Education; Secondary Education)

History: Founded 1946.

Degrees and Diplomas: *Bachelor's Degree*
Last Updated: 27/01/11

ROYAL CHRISTIAN COLLEGE

Highway Wireless, Mandaue City, Cebu 6014
Tel: +63(32) 345-4194
Fax: +63(32) 345-4195

President: Antero Roy N. Book

Programmes
Airline Management (Air Transport; Transport Management); **Commerce** (Accountancy; Business Administration; Business and Commerce; Management; Marketing); **Tourism and Travel Management** (Air Transport; Tourism; Transport Management)

History: Founded in 1980. Formerly known as Technological Institute of Cebu City.

Degrees and Diplomas: *Bachelor's Degree*
Last Updated: 27/01/11

SACRED HEART COLLEGE OF CALAMBA

Southwestern Poblacion, Calamba, Misamis Occidental 7210
Tel: +63(88) 271-3372
Fax: +63(88) 271-3372
EMail: shcc_inc@yahoo.com

Director: Alfredo M. Malalis

Programmes
Undergraduate and Professional Studies (Business Administration; Criminology; Education; English; Foreign Languages Education; Political Sciences; Primary Education; Secondary Education)

History: Founded 1979. Formerly known as Sacred Heart High School and Sacred Heart School.

Degrees and Diplomas: *Associate Degree*; *Bachelor's Degree*
Last Updated: 27/01/11

SACRED HEART COLLEGE OF LUCENA

1 Merchan St., Lucena City, Quezon 4301
Tel: +63(42) 710-2505 +63(42) 710-3888
Fax: +63(42) 373-4240
EMail: shc@shc.edu.ph
Website: http://www.shc.edu.ph

President: Fe G. Gedalanga, DC

Programmes

Graduate (Biological and Life Sciences; Biology; Education; Educational Administration; English; Filipino; Foreign Languages Education; Mathematics Education; Native Language Education; Nursing; Physics; Primary Education; Religious Education; Secondary Education; Social Sciences); **Undergraduate and Professional** (Accountancy; Art Education; Biological and Life Sciences; Business Administration; Child Care and Development; Communication Studies; Computer Education; Computer Science; Economics; Education; English; Filipino; Finance; Foreign Languages Education; Health Education; Home Economics Education; Human Resources; Literature; Management; Management Systems; Mathematics; Mathematics Education; Music Education; Native Language Education; Nursing; Physical Education; Physics; Preschool Education; Primary Education; Psychology; Religious Education; Secondary Education; Secretarial Studies; Social Studies; Social Work; Special Education; Technology Education)

History: Founded 1884. Formerly known as Jesus Sacred Heart College.

Degrees and Diplomas: *Associate Degree*; *Bachelor's Degree*; *Master's Degree*: Education (Social Sciences; Religious Education; Physical Science; Biological Science; Filipino; Mathematics; Educational Management; English); Teaching (College Teaching; Mathematics; Social Sciences; Reading Education; Filipino); Nursing

Last Updated: 27/01/11

SACRED HEART COLLEGE OF TACLOBAN CITY

T. Claudio Street, Tacloban City, Leyte 6500
Tel: +63(53) 321-2424
Fax: +63(53) 325-3467
EMail: shstacloban@yahoo.com

President: Angelica Shen

Programmes

Arts (English); **Business Administration** (Business Administration); **Education** (Education; Secondary Education)

History: Founded 1958.

Degrees and Diplomas: *Bachelor's Degree*

Last Updated: 27/01/11

SACRED HEART OF JESUS COLLEGE

Colegio del Sagrado Corazon de Jesus
General Hughes Street, Iloilo City, Iloilo 5000
Tel: +63(33) 337-4654
Fax: +63(33) 336-9408

President: Ma. Lourdes S. Verzosa

Programmes

Undergraduate and Professional (Accountancy; Business Administration; Education; Hotel and Restaurant; Hotel Management; Primary Education; Social Work)

History: Founded 1917.

Degrees and Diplomas: *Associate Degree*; *Bachelor's Degree*

Last Updated: 08/09/10

SAFFRULLAH M. DIPATUAN FOUNDATION ACADEMY

Menor Street Extension, Pangarungan Village, Marawi City, Lanao del Sur 9700
EMail: smd_fa@yahoo.com

President: Saffrullah M. Dipatuan

Programmes

Computer Science (Computer Science); **Nursing** (Health Education; Midwifery; Nursing); **Secondary Education** (Secondary Education)

History: Founded 2004.

Degrees and Diplomas: *Bachelor's Degree*

Last Updated: 27/01/11

SAINT ANNE COLLEGE OF LUCENA

Brgy. Gulang-Gulang, Lucena City, Quezon 4301
Tel: +63(42) 710-5624 +63(42) 373-6150
Fax: +63(42) 373-6150

President: Potenciano A. Andaman

Programmes

Undergraduate and Professional (Accountancy; Business Administration; Criminology; Curriculum; Education; English; Foreign Languages Education; Home Economics Education; Hotel and Restaurant; Hotel Management; Management; Midwifery; Nursing; Physical Therapy; Physics; Primary Education; Psychology; Secondary Education; Technology Education; Tourism)

History: Founded 1986. Formerly known as St. Anne School of Medical Sciences.

Degrees and Diplomas: *Certificate/Diploma*; *Bachelor's Degree*

Last Updated: 27/01/11

SAINT ANTHONY COLLEGE OF TECHNOLOGY

Dau, Mabalacat, Pampanga 2010
Tel: +63(45) 331-7292
Fax: +63(45) 331-7292
EMail: sact@comclark.com

President: Antonio S. Yap

Programmes

Aeronautical Engineering (Aeronautical and Aerospace Engineering); **Arts and Humanities** (History); **Computer Science** (Computer Science); **Elementary Education** (Communication Arts; English; Foreign Languages Education; Primary Education); **Graduate** (Education; Educational Administration; Teacher Training); **Secondary Education** (Biochemistry; English; Filipino; Foreign Languages Education; History; Mathematics Education; Native Language Education; Science Education; Secondary Education)

History: Founded 1945.

Degrees and Diplomas: *Bachelor's Degree*; *Master's Degree*: Education (Educational Management); Teaching

Last Updated: 27/01/11

SAINT ANTHONY MARY CLARET COLLEGE

48 Cenacle Drive, Sanville Subdivision, Culiat, Tandang Sora, Quezon City, Second District, Metro Manila 1107
Tel: +63(2) 932-0343 +63(2) 920-1442
Fax: +63(2) 920-5420

President: Victor F. Sadaya

Programmes

Missiology (Bible; Missionary Studies); **Philosophy** (Philosophy); **Theology** (Bible; Theology)

History: Founded 1995. Formerly known as Claret Formation Center.

Degrees and Diplomas: *Bachelor's Degree*; *Master's Degree*: Missiology; Biblical Studies; Theology

Last Updated: 27/01/11

SAINT ANTHONY'S COLLEGE

Sta. Cruz, Sta. Ana, Cagayan 3514

President: Irene C. Anapi

Programmes

Undergraduate and Professional (Business Administration; Education; English; Foreign Languages Education; Mathematics; Mathematics Education; Primary Education; Secondary Education)

History: Founded 1953. Formerly St. Anthony's Academy (1953-1973).

Degrees and Diplomas: *Certificate/Diploma*; *Associate Degree*; *Bachelor's Degree*

Last Updated: 28/01/11

SAINT ANTHONY'S COLLEGE - ANTIQUE

San Miguel, San Jose, Antique 5700
Tel: +63(36) 540-9236
Fax: +63(36) 540-9971
EMail: postmaster@sac.edu.ph

President: Jose S. Bantolo

Programmes

Undergraduate and Professional (Accountancy; Art Education; Business and Commerce; Civil Engineering; Computer Engineering; Computer Science; Criminology; Curriculum; Education; English; Foreign Languages Education; Hotel and Restaurant; Hotel Management; Management; Mathematics Education; Music Education; Philosophy; Physical Education; Political Sciences; Preschool Education; Primary Education; Science Education; Secondary Education; Social Studies; Special Education; Tourism)

History: Founded 1958.

Degrees and Diplomas: *Certificate/Diploma*; *Bachelor's Degree*
Last Updated: 28/01/11

SAINT AUGUSTINE COLLEGES FOUNDATION

Burgos Street, Paniqui, Tarlac
Tel: +63(45) 931-0107 +63(931) 931-1590
Fax: +63(45) 931-1590
EMail: cec_clhs@mozcom.com

President: Cesar E. Cuchapin

Programmes

Business Administration (Business Administration; Management); **Computer Technology** (Computer Engineering); **Elementary Education** (Primary Education); **Secondary Education** (English; Filipino; Foreign Languages Education; Mathematics Education; Native Language Education; Secondary Education)

History: Founded 1999.

Degrees and Diplomas: *Associate Degree*; *Bachelor's Degree*
Last Updated: 28/01/11

SAINT BERNADETTE COLLEGE OF ALABANG

Km. 23.6 East Service Road, Uding's Compound I, Alabang, City of Muntinlupa, Fourth District, Metro Manila 1770
Tel: +63(2) 842-2139 +63(2) 850-57-09
Fax: +63(2) 842-2139

President: Felicitas C. Rabonza

Programmes

Undergraduate and Professional (Administration; Business Administration; Business and Commerce; Business Computing; Computer Engineering; Education; English; Foreign Languages Education; Hotel and Restaurant; Hotel Management; Information Technology; Management; Marketing; Primary Education; Secondary Education; Teacher Training)

History: Founded 1983. Formerly Saint Bernadette School of Alabang.

Degrees and Diplomas: *Certificate/Diploma*; *Associate Degree*; *Bachelor's Degree*
Last Updated: 28/01/11

SAINT BERNADETTE COLLEGE OF HEALTH AND SCIENCE

3rd Floor, R&J Bldg., Quirino Highway, Novaliches, Quezon City, Second District, Metro Manila
Tel: +63(2) 930-4358
Fax: +63(2) 938-2309

President: Ceferino A. Baltazar, Jr.

Programmes

Business Administration (Business Administration; Human Resources; Management; Marketing); **Health Science Education** (Health Education; Health Sciences); **Nursing** (Midwifery; Nursing)

History: Founded 2002.

Degrees and Diplomas: *Bachelor's Degree*
Last Updated: 28/01/11

SAINT BRIDGET'S COLLEGE

M.H. del Pilar Street, Brgy 1, Batangas City, Batangas 4200
Tel: +63(43) 723-3616
Fax: +63(43) 723-3616
EMail: college@saintbridgetbatangas.edu.ph

President: Mary Lydia Ebora

Programmes

Undergraduate and Professional (Biological and Life Sciences; Business Administration; Communication Arts; Curriculum; Education; English; Filipino; Finance; Foreign Languages Education; Health Education; Human Resources; Information Technology; Management; Management Systems; Marketing; Mathematics Education; Native Language Education; Physics; Preschool Education; Primary Education; Science Education; Secondary Education; Social Studies; Social Work; Special Education)

History: Founded 1913.

Degrees and Diplomas: *Certificate/Diploma*; *Bachelor's Degree*
Last Updated: 28/01/11

SAINT CATHERINE'S COLLEGE

Poblacion I, Carcar, Cebu 6019
Tel: +63(32) 487-9708
Fax: +63(32) 487-9708

President: Ma. Rosalinda Calong

Programmes

Accountancy (Accountancy); **Arts** (English); **Business Administration** (Business Administration); **Computer Engineering** (Computer Engineering); **Computer Science** (Computer Science); **Education** (Education; English; Foreign Languages Education; Mathematics Education; Primary Education; Science Education; Secondary Education); **Graduate** (Educational Administration; Educational and Student Counselling; Management; Mathematics Education; Public Administration; Science Education)

History: Founded 1993.

Degrees and Diplomas: *Associate Degree*; *Bachelor's Degree*; *Master's Degree*: Management; Public Management; Arts in Student Personnel Services; Education in Educational Management; Science in Mathematics and Science Teaching
Last Updated: 28/01/11

SAINT COLUMBAN COLLEGE

Corner Alano and Sagun Streets, San Francisco District, Pagadian City, Zamboanga del Sur 7016
Tel: +63(62) 215-1799 +63(62) 215-1800
Fax: +63(62) 214-1290
EMail: ghingone@yahoo.com

President: Emmanuel T. Cabajal

Programmes

Arts *(Bachelor of Arts programme)* (Economics; English; History; Mathematics; Philosophy; Political Sciences; Psychology); **Business Administration** (Accountancy; Banking; Business Administration; Computer Science; Finance; Human Resources; Management); **Education** (Biology; Curriculum; Education; English; Ethics; Filipino; Foreign Languages Education; History; Home Economics Education; Library Science; Mathematics Education; Native Language Education; Primary Education; Religious Education; Science Education; Secondary Education); **Graduate** (Business Administration; Education; Educational Administration; Educational and Student Counselling; English; Filipino; Foreign Languages Education; Native Language Education; Public Administration; Teacher Training); **Science** *(Bachelor of Science programme)* (Accountancy; Computer Science; Hotel and Restaurant; Hotel Management; Information Technology; Management Systems; Secretarial Studies)

History: Founded 1957.

Degrees and Diplomas: *Associate Degree*; *Bachelor's Degree*; *Master's Degree*: Educational Management (English; Filipino); Guidance and Counselling; Business Administration; Public Administration; Teaching (Filipino; English); Arts in Education (English)
Last Updated: 28/01/11

SAINT COLUMBAN'S COLLEGE

Poblacion, Lingayen, Pangasinan 2401
Tel: +63(75) 542-4864
Fax: +63(75) 542-4864
EMail: st_columbanscg@yahoo.com

Director: Nicasio A. Villamil, Jr.

Programmes

Accountancy (Accountancy); **Business Administration** (Accountancy; Banking; Business Administration; Finance; Human Resources; Management; Marketing); **Education** (Education; English; Filipino; Foreign Languages Education; Mathematics Education; Native Language Education; Religious Education; Secondary Education)

History: Founded 1947.

Degrees and Diplomas: *Certificate/Diploma*; *Associate Degree*; *Bachelor's Degree*
Last Updated: 28/01/11

SAINT DOMINIC COLLEGE OF BATANES

Lizardo Street, Basco, Batanes 3900
EMail: sdcbi@yahoo.com

President: Brigido R. Casas

Programmes

Business Administration (Business Administration); **Commerce** (Business and Commerce); **Education** (Primary Education; Secondary Education); **Graduate** (Education; Educational Administration; Science Education)

History: Founded 1968.

Degrees and Diplomas: *Certificate/Diploma*; *Bachelor's Degree*; *Master's Degree*: Education (Educational Management; Science Education)
Last Updated: 28/01/11

SAINT ESTANISLAO KOSTKA COLLEGE

Sagario Street, Manukan, Zamboanga del Norte 7110

Director: Edgardo A. Calumba

Programmes

Commerce (Accountancy; Business and Commerce; Management); **Criminology** (Criminology); **Education** (Business Administration; Computer Education; Education; English; Foreign Languages Education; Mathematics Education; Primary Education; Science Education; Secondary Education); **Mathematics** (Mathematics)

History: Founded 1955.

Degrees and Diplomas: *Bachelor's Degree*
Last Updated: 31/01/11

SAINT FERDINAND COLLEGE

Centro, Cabagan, Isabela 3328
Tel: +63(78) 636-3376
Fax: +63(78) 636-3376

President: Cesar B. Malenab

Programmes

Undergraduate and Professional (Criminology; Education; English; Foreign Languages Education; Mathematics Education; Police Studies; Primary Education; Secondary Education)

History: Founded 1999.

Degrees and Diplomas: *Certificate/Diploma*; *Bachelor's Degree*
Last Updated: 31/01/11

SAINT FRANCIS COLLEGE

Pascual B. Gutay Street, Sabang II, Allen, Northern Samar 6405
Tel: +63(55) 300-2169

Director: Edgardo A. Alutaya

Programmes

Undergraduate and Professional Studies (Education; English; Primary Education)

History: Founded 1948. Formerly known as Saint Francis Educational Institute.

Degrees and Diplomas: *Bachelor's Degree*
Last Updated: 31/01/11

SAINT FRANCIS COLLEGE - GUIHULNGAN

Bataria, Guihulngan, Negros Oriental 6214
Tel: +63(35) 368-4213
Fax: +63(35) 368-4213
EMail: jcalvin@epic.net; fcao_jcb@epic.net

Director: Salvador Tumaca, Jr.

Programmes

Undergraduate and Professional Studies (Banking; Business Administration; Computer Science; Curriculum; Economics; Education; English; Finance; Foreign Languages Education; Human Resources; Information Technology; Literature; Management; Marketing; Primary Education; Secondary Education)

History: Founded 1962.

Degrees and Diplomas: *Bachelor's Degree*
Last Updated: 31/01/11

SAINT FRANCIS DIVINE COLLEGE

Salvia St., St. Dominic No.12, Subd. Novaliches, Quezon City, Second District, Metro Manila 1124
Tel: +63(2) 939-9304

Director: Milagros B. Palacio

Programmes

Undergraduate and Professional (Computer Science; Education; English; Filipino; Foreign Languages Education; Management; Mathematics Education; Midwifery; Native Language Education; Primary Education; Secondary Education)

History: Founded 1978 as St. Francis Guidance School. Changed name to St. Francis Divine Institute. Acquired present title 1999.

Degrees and Diplomas: *Associate Degree*; *Bachelor's Degree*
Last Updated: 31/01/11

SAINT FRANCIS INSTITUTE OF COMPUTER STUDIES

National Highway, San Pedro, Laguna 4023
Tel: +63(2) 868-9639
Fax: +63(2) 868-3197
EMail: lamante@yahoo.com

President: Luisito V. Amante

Programmes

Business Administration (Business Administration; Finance; Management; Marketing); **Information Technology** (Information Technology); **Office Management** (Management Systems; Secretarial Studies)

History: Founded 1998.

Degrees and Diplomas: *Bachelor's Degree*
Last Updated: 31/01/11

SAINT FRANCIS OF ASSISI COLLEGE (SFAC)

045 Admiral Road, Admiral Village, Talon Tres, City of Las Piñas, Fourth District, Metro Manila
Tel: +63(2) 800-4507 +63(2) 805-8014
Fax: +63(2) 805-8014
EMail: info@stfrancis.edu.ph
Website: http://www.stfrancis.edu.ph

President: Evangeline O. Orosco

Colleges

Business Administration (Business Administration; Management; Management Systems; Marketing; Secretarial Studies); **Computer Studies** (Computer Engineering; Computer Science); **Education and Liberal Arts** (Biology; Education; English; Filipino; Foreign Languages Education; Health Education; Mathematics Education; Native Language Education; Physics; Preschool Education; Primary Education; Psychology; Science Education; Secondary Education; Special Education); **Engineering** (Electrical Engineering; Electronic

Engineering; Engineering; Telecommunications Engineering); **Hotel and Restaurant Management** (Hotel and Restaurant; Hotel Management; Tourism); **Nursing** (Nursing)

Programmes

Graduate (Business Administration; Education; Educational Administration; Educational and Student Counselling; Management)

Further Information: Campuses: Bacoor (Cavite); Taguig; Alabang (Muntinlupa); Saint Anthony School (Las Piñas & Los Baños); Pamplona (Las Piñas); Biñan (Laguna); Dasmariñas

History: Founded 1981.

Degrees and Diplomas: *Associate Degree*; *Bachelor's Degree*; *Master's Degree*: Education; Business Management

Last Updated: 31/01/11

SAINT FRANCIS XAVIER COLLEGE

Brgy. 5, San Francisco, Agusan del Sur 8501
Tel: +63(85) 343-9322
Fax: +63(85) 839-2284
EMail: sfxc@cdo.philcom.com.ph

Director: Herberto O. Villarazo

Programmes

Accountancy (Accountancy); **Arts and Humanities** (Arts and Humanities; English); **Business Administration** (Accountancy; Administration; Business Administration; Business and Commerce; Computer Science; Finance; Management; Marketing); **Criminology** (Criminology); **Education** (English; Foreign Languages Education; Primary Education; Secondary Education); **Office Administration** (Computer Education; Management Systems; Secretarial Studies)

History: Founded 1991 as Saint Francis Institute of Technology.

Degrees and Diplomas: *Associate Degree*; *Bachelor's Degree*

Last Updated: 31/01/11

SAINT GABRIEL COLLEGE

Kalibo, Aklan 5600
Tel: +63(36) 268-9055
Fax: +63(36) 268-9317
EMail: stgabrielcollege@yahoo.com

President: Ramon Gabriel S. Legaspi, Jr.

Programmes

Undergraduate and Professional (Health Education; Midwifery; Nursing)

History: Founded 1970.

Degrees and Diplomas: *Certificate/Diploma*; *Associate Degree*; *Bachelor's Degree*

Last Updated: 31/01/11

SAINT JAMES COLLEGE OF PADRE BURGOS

Teodorico Esclamado, Sr. Street, Padre Burgos, Southern Leyte 6602
Tel: +63(53) 573-0183
EMail: sjcpbsl@yahoo.com

Programmes

Arts - English Language (Arts and Humanities; English); **Commerce** (Banking; Business and Commerce; Finance)

History: Founded 1946.

Degrees and Diplomas: *Bachelor's Degree*

Last Updated: 31/01/11

SAINT JOHN COLLEGE OF BUUG FOUNDATION

National Highway, Buug, Zamboanga del Sur 7009
Tel: +63(62) 344-8133
Fax: +63(62) 344-8133

President: Juan C. Vergara

Programmes

Undergraduate and Professional Studies (Banking; Business Administration; Criminology; Curriculum; Education; Finance; Health Education; Management; Nursing; Primary Education; Social Sciences)

History: Founded 1992. Formerly known as Saint John General Hospital School of Midwifery.

Degrees and Diplomas: *Bachelor's Degree*

Last Updated: 31/01/11

SAINT JOHN COLLEGES

Chipeco Avenue, Calamba City, Laguna 4027
Tel: +63(49) 545-1948
Fax: +63(49) 545-3521
EMail: phil_sja_sjc@yahoo.com

President: Alberto Rivera

Programmes

Arts (Economics; History; Political Sciences); **Business Administration** (Accountancy; Banking; Business Administration; Business Computing; Finance); **Computer Science** (Computer Science); **Education** (Curriculum; Education; English; Filipino; Foreign Languages Education; Mathematics Education; Native Language Education; Primary Education; Secondary Education; Social Studies)

History: Founded 1951.

Degrees and Diplomas: *Bachelor's Degree*

Last Updated: 31/01/11

SAINT JOSEPH COLLEGE - CAVITE CITY

Plaridel Street, San Roque, Cavite City, Cavite 4100
Tel: +63(46) 431-1937
Fax: +63(46) 431-1937
EMail: stjosephcollegecavite@yahoo.com.ph

Director: Ma. Flora Silverio

Programmes

Graduate (Education; Educational Administration; Educational and Student Counselling; Nursing); **Undergraduate and Professional** (Education; Hotel and Restaurant; Midwifery; Nursing; Primary Education; Secondary Education; Secretarial Studies)

History: Founded 1945.

Degrees and Diplomas: *Certificate/Diploma*; *Associate Degree*; *Bachelor's Degree*; *Master's Degree*

Last Updated: 31/01/11

SAINT JOSEPH COLLEGE - MAASIN CITY

Tomas Oppus Street, Tunga-Tunga, Maasin City, Southern Leyte 6600
Tel: +63(53) 381-2126
Fax: +63(53) 570-8662

President: Precioso D. Cantillas

Programmes

Graduate (Business Administration; Education; Educational Administration; Educational and Student Counselling; Health Administration; Nursing); **Undergraduate and Professional** (Accountancy; Business Administration; Business and Commerce; Civil Engineering; Computer Education; Computer Science; Criminology; Economics; Education; English; Filipino; Finance; Foreign Languages Education; Hotel and Restaurant; Hotel Management; Law; Management; Management Systems; Mathematics Education; Native Language Education; Primary Education; Science Education; Secondary Education)

History: Founded 1928.

Degrees and Diplomas: *Associate Degree*; *Bachelor's Degree*; *Master's Degree*: Business Administration; Education (Guidance and Counselling; Educational Management); Nursing (Nursing Administration; Administration and Supervision)

Last Updated: 31/01/11

SAINT JOSEPH COLLEGE OF BULACAN

San Jose Patag, Saint Maria, Bulacan 3022
Tel: +63(44) 641-4872
Fax: +63(44) 641-4872
EMail: stjosephcollege@digitelone.com

President: Felisa P. Nepomuceno

Programmes
Business Administration (Business Administration); **Computer Science** (Computer Science); **Elementary Education** (Primary Education); **Psychology** (Psychology); **Secondary Education** (Secondary Education)
History: Founded 1996. Formerly St. Joseph Academy (1996-1999).
Degrees and Diplomas: *Associate Degree*; *Bachelor's Degree*
Last Updated: 31/01/11

SAINT JOSEPH COLLEGE OF CANLAON

Samaka Village, Canlaon City, Negros Oriental 6223

Director: Adela M. Pabon

Programmes
Undergraduate and Professional Studies (Business and Commerce; English; Foreign Languages Education; History; Management; Mathematics Education; Primary Education; Secondary Education)
History: Founded 1957.
Degrees and Diplomas: *Bachelor's Degree*
Last Updated: 31/01/11

SAINT JOSEPH INSTITUTE OF TECHNOLOGY (SJIT)

Montilla Blvd. corner Rosales Street, Butuan City, Agusan del Norte 8600
Tel: +63(85) 342-5694 +63(85) 225-5039
Fax: +63(85) 815-4248
EMail: info@sjit.edu.ph
Website: http://www.sjit.edu.ph

President: Leticia C. Salas

Academies
Maritime (Marine Engineering; Marine Transport)

Colleges
Business Administration (Business Administration; Business and Commerce; Hotel Management; Management; Marketing; Tourism); **Criminology** (Criminology); **Education and Liberal Arts** (Educational and Student Counselling; English; Mass Communication; Mathematics Education; Primary Education; Psychology; Secondary Education); **Engineering and Architecture** (Architecture; Civil Engineering; Computer Engineering; Electrical and Electronic Engineering; Mechanical Engineering); **Information Technology** (Computer Science; Information Management; Information Technology); **Nursing** (Nursing)
History: Founded 1971. Acquired present status 1974.
Degrees and Diplomas: *Bachelor's Degree*; *Master's Degree*: Management (Public Service Management; Business Management); Education; Teaching; *PhD*: Management
Last Updated: 31/01/11

SAINT JOSEPH'S COLLEGE OF BAGGAO

San Jose, Baggao, Cagayan 3506
Tel: +63(917) 379-5466

President: Ma. Adela M. Pabon

Programmes
Undergraduate and Professional (Business Administration; Curriculum; Economics; Education; English; Foreign Languages Education; Human Resources; Management; Mathematics Education; Primary Education; Secondary Education)
History: Founded 1950. Formerly Saint Joseph College (1950-1994).
Degrees and Diplomas: *Certificate/Diploma*; *Bachelor's Degree*
Last Updated: 31/01/11

SAINT JUDE THADDEUS INSTITUTE OF TECHNOLOGY

Borromeo Street, Surigao City, Surigao Del Norte 8400
Tel: +63(86) 826 0139
Fax: +63(86) 826-0139

President: George M. Salabao EMail: george@ns.sjit.edu.ph

Programmes
Broadcasting (Radio and Television Broadcasting); **Computer Science** (Computer Science); **Criminology** (Criminology); **Customs Administration** (Taxation); **Education** (English; Primary Education; Secondary Education); **Electronics and Communications** (Electronic Engineering; Telecommunications Engineering); **Public Administration and Commerce** (Business and Commerce; Public Administration; Secretarial Studies)
History: Founded in 1977 as the St. Jude Technical Institute, receiving its current status in 1980.
Degrees and Diplomas: *Bachelor's Degree*
Last Updated: 01/02/11

SAINT LOUIS ANNE COLLEGES

Old National Highway, Brgy. Nueva, San Pedro, Laguna 4023
Tel: +63(49) 808-4064
Fax: +63(2) 868-8706
EMail: slac.educ@yahoo.com

President: Louis Anne Marcos-Perez

Programmes
Undergraduate and Professional (Accountancy; Art Education; Biology; Business Administration; Computer Engineering; Computer Science; Education; English; Foreign Languages Education; Hotel and Restaurant; Hotel Management; Management; Mathematics Education; Medical Technology; Music Education; Physical Education; Physical Therapy; Physics; Primary Education; Respiratory Therapy; Secondary Education)
History: Founded 1986.
Degrees and Diplomas: *Certificate/Diploma*; *Associate Degree*; *Bachelor's Degree*
Last Updated: 01/02/11

SAINT LOUIS COLLEGE - CITY OF SAN FERNANDO

National Highway, Lingsat, La Union 2500
Tel: +63(72) 242-5535 +63(72) 242-5536
Fax: +63(72) 888-3955
EMail: slc_lu@hotmail.com

President: Norma Maria P. Rutab

Programmes
Graduate (Business Administration; Education; Educational Administration; Finance; Library Science; Management; Marketing; Mathematics Education; Public Administration; Science Education); **Undergraduate and Professional** (Accountancy; Architecture; Banking; Biological and Life Sciences; Business Administration; Business and Commerce; Business Computing; Civil Engineering; Economics; English; Ethics; Filipino; Finance; Foreign Languages Education; Geological Engineering; Health Education; Hotel and Restaurant; Hotel Management; Human Resources; Industrial Engineering; Information Sciences; Information Technology; Law; Library Science; Management; Marketing; Mathematics; Mathematics Education; Music Education; Native Language Education; Natural Sciences; Physical Education; Political Sciences; Psychology; Public Administration; Religious Education; Science Education; Secondary Education; Secretarial Studies; Structural Architecture; Tourism; Water Management; Water Science)
History: Founded 1948.
Degrees and Diplomas: *Associate Degree*; *Bachelor's Degree*; *Master's Degree*: Business Administration (Marketing; Finance); Public Administration; Education (Mathematics; Educational Management; Library Science; Science Education); *PhD*: Education (Educational Management); Management
Last Updated: 01/02/11

SAINT LOUIS COLLEGE OF BULANAO

Tabuk, Kalinga 3800
Tel: +63(74) 872-2385

President: Prudencio P. Andaya Jr.

Programmes
Graduate (Education; Educational Administration; English; Filipino; Foreign Languages Education; Native Language Education; Public Administration); **Undergraduate and Professional** (Biology; Education; English; Filipino; Foreign Languages Education; History; Mathematics Education; Native Language Education; Political Sciences; Primary Education; Secondary Education)

History: Founded 1967.

Degrees and Diplomas: *Bachelor's Degree*; *Master's Degree*: Public Administration; Education (English; Filipino; Administration and Supervision)

Last Updated: 01/02/11

SAINT LOUIS UNIVERSITY (SLU)

A. Bonifacio Street, Baguio City, Benguet 2600
Tel: +63(74) 442-3043
Fax: +63(74) 442-2842
EMail: sluregis@slu.edu.ph
Website: http://www.slu.edu.ph

President: Jessie M. Hechanova (2005-)
Tel: +63(74) 444-8908 EMail: jesse@slu.edu.ph

Vice-President for Administration: Arnulfo Soriano
Tel: +63(74) 443-2001 EMail: vpadm@slu.edu.ph

International Relations: Carmen Sia, Registrar

Centres
Child and Youth Health (Child Care and Development) *Director*: Geraldo Costa; **Regional Science Teaching** (Science Education) *Director*: Oscar Bautista; **SLU Network** (Management Systems) *Director*: Winston Chugsayan

Colleges
Accountancy and Commerce (Accountancy; Business Administration; Business and Commerce; Finance; Hotel Management; Management; Marketing; Public Administration; Tourism) *Dean*: Reynaldo Bautista; **Education** (Education; Educational Administration; Information Technology; Library Science; Mathematics Education; Physical Education; Preschool Education; Primary Education; Religious Education; Science Education; Secondary Education; Sports) *Dean*: Roque Bernardez; **Engineering and Architecture** (Architecture; Chemical Engineering; Civil Engineering; Electrical Engineering; Electronic Engineering; Engineering; Engineering Management; Environmental Engineering; Geological Engineering; Industrial Engineering; Mechanical Engineering; Mining Engineering; Town Planning) *Dean*: Bonifacio De la Pena; **Information and Computing Sciences** (Computer Science; Information Management; Information Sciences; Information Technology; Library Science; Mathematics; Statistics) *Dean*: Cecilia Mercado; **Law** (Law) *Dean*: Ceasar Oracion; **Medicine** (Medicine) *Dean*: Elizabeth Dacanay; **Natural Sciences** (Biology; Medical Technology; Natural Sciences; Pharmacy; Radiology) *Dean*: Gaudelia Reyes; **Nursing** (Nursing)

Departments
Management Information Systems (Information Technology; Management Systems) *Director*: Angelito Peralta

Institutes
Foreign Languages and International Studies (International Studies; Modern Languages) *Director*: Edmundo Ceniza; **Philosophy and Religion** (Philosophy; Religion) *Director*: Pacita Vizcarra; **Small-Scale Industries** (Small Business) *Director*: Edmund Benavidez

Further Information: Also Hospital of the Sacred Heart and University Medical and Dental Clinic

History: Founded 1911 as Saint Louis School. Began offering College courses 1952 and acquired University status 1963. Granted autonomy status 2001.

Governing Bodies: Board of Trustees

Academic Year: June to May (June-October; November-March; April-May)

Admission Requirements: Graduation from high school or recognized foreign equivalent, and entrance examination

Fees: (Pesos): 14,000 - 57,000 per semester; post-graduate 10,200

Main Language(s) of Instruction: English

International Co-operation: With universities in Belgium, China, France, Indonesia, Vietnam, Sweden and USA.

Accrediting Agencies: Philippine Accrediting Association of Schools, Colleges and Universities (PAASCU)

Degrees and Diplomas: *Associate Degree*: Health Science Education; Accountancy Technology; *Bachelor's Degree*: Accountancy; Civil Engineering; Chemical Engineering; Electrical Engineering; Electronics and Communication Engineering; Geodetic Engineering; Industrial Engineering; Mechanical Engineering; Architecture; Commerce; Elementary Education; Secondary Education; Psychology; Social Work; Computer Science; Information Technology; Mathematics; Statistics; Biology; Medical Technology; Pharmacy; Radiologic Technology; Nursing; Law (LLB); Mass Communication; Economics; English; Political Science; Philosophy (PhB); *Master's Degree*: Accountancy; Business Administration; Public Management; Special Education; Educational Management; Education; Library and Information Technology; Engineering; Civil Engineering; Environmental Engineering; Management Engineering; Mountain Engineering; Environmental and Habitat Planning; Philosophy; Religious Studies; Guidance and Counseling; Biological Sciences; Biology; Environmental Sciences; Pharmacy; Nursing; Medicine (MD); *PhD*: Management; Educational Management; Language Education. Also Special Programme for Graduate Nurses, 2 yrs

Student Services: Academic counselling, Canteen, Cultural centre, Employment services, Foreign student adviser, Foreign Studies Centre, Health services, Language programs, Social counselling, Sports facilities

Student Residential Facilities: Dormitory accommodation for c. 640 Women and c. 260 Men

Special Facilities: Museums: Arts and Culture; Natural Sciences Archives

Libraries: Total: c. 134,040 vols

Publications: Research Journal *(biennially)*

Press or Publishing House: Saint Louis University Printing Press

Last Updated: 01/02/11

SAINT LOUISE DE MARILLAC COLLEGE - BOGO

Sor D. Rubio Street, Bogo, Cebu 6010
Tel: +63(32) 251-2036 +63(32) 251-2037
Fax: +63(32) 251-2036
EMail: demarillac@yahoo.com

Director: Minda P. Penaredondo

Programmes
Undergraduate and Professional Studies (Accountancy; Business Administration; Computer Education; Computer Science; Curriculum; Education; English; Foreign Languages Education; Hotel and Restaurant; Hotel Management; Information Technology; Management; Primary Education; Secondary Education; Tourism)

History: Founded 1936.

Degrees and Diplomas: *Bachelor's Degree*

Last Updated: 01/02/11

SAINT LOUISE DE MARILLAC COLLEGE OF SORSOGON

Burgos Street, Talisay, City of Sorsogon, Sorsogon 4700
Tel: +63(56) 211-1186
Fax: +63(56) 421-5556
EMail: marillac_sor@yahoo.com

President: Lourdes L. Albis

Programmes
Graduate (Education; Educational Administration; Educational and Student Counselling; Educational Technology; Ethics; Religious Education); **Undergraduate and Professional** (Accountancy; Biochemistry; Biology; Business Administration; Communication Studies; Economics; Education; Educational and Student Counselling; English; Filipino; Finance; Foreign Languages Education; Health Education; History; Human Resources; Management; Marketing; Mathematics; Mathematics Education; Native Language Education; Physics; Primary Education; Science Education; Secondary Education; Social Studies)

History: Founded 1937. Formerly Colegio de la Milagrosa.

Degrees and Diplomas: *Certificate/Diploma*; *Associate Degree*; *Bachelor's Degree*; *Master's Degree*: Education (Religious Education; Non Formal Education; Instructional Methods; Values Education; Educational Management; Guidance and Counselling)

Last Updated: 01/02/11

SAINT MARY'S COLLEGE

Poblacion Sur, Sta. Maria, Ilocos Sur 2705
Tel: +63(77) 732-5629
Fax: +63(77) 732-5629
EMail: smcian_2005@yahoo.com

President: Godofredo S. Reyes

Programmes

Arts and Humanities (Arts and Humanities; English); **Education** (Education; English; Foreign Languages Education; Primary Education; Secondary Education)

History: Founded 1948.

Degrees and Diplomas: *Bachelor's Degree*; *Master's Degree*: Education (Educational Management in Administration and Supervision)

Last Updated: 01/02/11

SAINT MARY'S COLLEGE OF BALIUAG

Racelis, Baliuag, Bulacan 3006
Tel: +63(44) 766-2265
Fax: +63(44) 766-2265
EMail: smcb03@yahoo.com

Director: Marissa Rebosura

Programmes

Business Administration (Accountancy; Business Administration; Finance; Human Resources; Management); **Education** (Computer Education; Education; English; Foreign Languages Education; Mathematics Education; Primary Education; Science Education; Secondary Education); **Hotel and Restaurant Management** (Hotel and Restaurant; Hotel Management); **Information Technology** (Information Technology); **Nursing** (Nursing)

History: Founded 1912. Formerly known as formerly St. Mary's Academy (1959-2002).

Degrees and Diplomas: *Bachelor's Degree*

Last Updated: 01/02/11

SAINT MARY'S COLLEGE OF CATBALOGAN

Del Rosario Street, Catbalogan, Western Samar 6700
Tel: +63(55) 251-2074
Fax: +63(55) 251-2074
EMail: saintmaryscatbalogan@yahoo.com
Website: http://www.rvmonline.net/smccatbalogan/

President: Ma. Lorina A. Jumawan

Colleges

Arts and Sciences (English; Mass Communication); **Business and Technology** (Accountancy; Business Administration; Business and Commerce; Computer Science; Hotel and Restaurant; Hotel Management); **Education** (Education; Primary Education; Secondary Education)

History: Founded 1946

Degrees and Diplomas: *Bachelor's Degree*

Last Updated: 01/02/11

SAINT MARY'S COLLEGE OF MARINDUQUE

Isok, Boac, Marinduque 4900
Tel: +63(42) 332-1870
Fax: +63(42) 332-1870
EMail: smc_marinduque@yahoo.com

Director: Ma. Magdalena L. Leocadio

Programmes

Undergraduate and Professional (Accountancy; Business Administration; Business and Commerce; Business Computing; Education; English; Finance; Foreign Languages Education; Human Resources; Management; Management Systems; Primary Education; Secondary Education; Secretarial Studies)

History: Founded 1920.

Degrees and Diplomas: *Certificate/Diploma*; *Associate Degree*; *Bachelor's Degree*

Last Updated: 01/02/11

SAINT MARY'S COLLEGE OF MEYCAUAYAN

McArthur Hi-Way, City of Meycauayan, Bulacan 3020
Tel: +63(44) 840-9781
Fax: +63(44) 840-2947
EMail: misnet@globe.com.ph
Website: http://www.smcm.edu.ph

Director: Maria Clarita R. Balleque

Programmes

Accountancy, Business Administration and Commerce (Accountancy; Business and Commerce; Business Computing; Computer Science; Finance; Human Resources; Management; Marketing); **Computer Science** (Computer Science); **Education** (Curriculum; Education; English; Filipino; Foreign Languages Education; Mathematics Education; Native Language Education; Preschool Education; Primary Education; Religious Education; Science Education; Secondary Education); **Information Systems and Technology** (Information Management; Information Technology); **Nursing** (Nursing); **Tourism, Hospitality, Hotel and Restaurant Management** (Hotel and Restaurant; Hotel Management; Tourism)

History: Founded 1916. Formerly known as St. Marys's Academy.

Degrees and Diplomas: *Bachelor's Degree*

Last Updated: 01/02/11

SAINT MARY'S COLLEGE OF SAN JUAN

11 J. de Mesa Street, Little Baguio, San Juan, Second District, Metro Manila
Tel: +63(2) 721-8938
Fax: +63(2) 721-8939
Website: http://www.stmarycollege.net

President: Elizabeth C. Ong EMail: president@stmarycollege.net

Programmes

Nursing (Nursing)

History: Founded 1995.

Degrees and Diplomas: *Bachelor's Degree*

Last Updated: 01/02/11

SAINT MARY'S COLLEGE OF TAGUM

National Highway, Tagum City, Davao del Norte 8100
Tel: +63(84) 217-3687
Fax: +63(84) 400-3130
EMail: webmaster@smct.edu.ph

President: Ma. Preciosa Russiana

Programmes

Accountancy (Accountancy); **Arts** (Economics; English; Psychology); **Business Administration** (Accountancy; Business Administration; Economics; Finance; Human Resources; Management); **Civil Engineering** (Civil Engineering); **Commerce** (Accountancy; Administration; Banking; Economics; Finance; Management); **Computer Science** (Computer Science); **Criminology** (Criminology); **Education** (Education; Educational and Student Counselling; English; Filipino; Foreign Languages Education; Health Education; Library Science; Mathematics Education; Music Education; Native Language Education; Physical Education; Primary Education; Science Education; Secondary Education); **Hospitality Management** (Hotel and Restaurant; Hotel Management); **Nursing** (Nursing)

History: Founded in 1948, acquiring its present status in 1969. Formerly known as Holy Cross College (1960-1967).

Degrees and Diplomas: *Bachelor's Degree*; *Master's Degree*: Education (Teaching Science; Physical Education; Administration and Supervision; Mathematics; Guidance and Counselling; English; Filipino; Primary Education)

Last Updated: 03/02/11

SAINT MARY'S UNIVERSITY (SMU)

Bayombong, Nueva Vizcaya 3700
Tel: +63(78) 321-2221
Fax: +63(78) 321-2117
EMail: smunet@smu.edu.ph; smunet@hotmail.com
Website: http://www.smu.edu.ph/

President: Renillo H. Sta. Ana

Vice-President for Administration: John Octavios S. Palina

Colleges

Computer Science and Information Technology (Computer Science; Information Technology); **Law** (Law)

Schools

Accountancy (Accountancy); **Arts and Sciences** (Biology; Chemistry; Education; Educational and Student Counselling; English; Foreign Languages Education; History; Journalism; Mathematics; Mathematics Education; Natural Sciences; Philosophy; Physics; Psychology; Religious Education; Science Education; Social Sciences; Teacher Training; Theology); **Business** (Business Administration; Business and Commerce; Finance; Hotel and Restaurant; Hotel Management; Human Resources; Management; Tourism); **Education** (Art Education; Biology; Child Care and Development; Education; Educational Administration; Ethics; Filipino; Health Education; Information Sciences; Library Science; Literacy Education; Mathematics Education; Music Education; Native Language Education; Pedagogy; Physical Education; Physics; Preschool Education; Primary Education; Religious Education; Secondary Education; Social Studies); **Engineering and Architecture** (Architecture; Civil Engineering; Computer Engineering; Electrical Engineering; Electronic Engineering; Engineering; Geological Engineering; Management; Structural Architecture); **Health Sciences** (Health Sciences; Midwifery; Nursing); **Public Administration and Governance** (Criminology; Government; Law; Political Sciences; Public Administration)

History: Founded 1928 as a Graduate School, started as a College 1947. Acquired present status and title 1994.

Governing Bodies: Board of Trustees

Academic Year: June to May (June-October; November-March; April-May)

Admission Requirements: Graduation from high school or equivalent

Fees: (Pesos): c. 5,000 per semester

Main Language(s) of Instruction: Filipino, English

Accrediting Agencies: Philippine Accrediting Association of Schools, Colleges and Universities (PAASCU)

Degrees and Diplomas: *Certificate/Diploma*: Geodetic Surveying Aide (AGE), 3 yrs; *Certificate/Diploma*: Office Administration (AOA), 2 yrs; *Bachelor's Degree*: Accountancy (BSA); Arts (AB); Commerce (BSC); Criminology (BSCrim); Electrical Engineering (BSEE); Elementary Education (BEEd); Hotel and Restaurant Management (BSHRM); Information Technology (BSIT); Management Accountancy (BSMA); Natural Sciences / Mathematics (BS); Public Administration (BSPA); Tourism (BS), 4 yrs; *Bachelor's Degree*: Civil Engineering (BSCE); Computer Engineering (BSComp E); Electronics and Communications (BSECE); Geodesic Engineering (BSGE); Mechatronics (BSMecha), 5 yrs; *Bachelor's Degree*: Law (LIB); Nursing (BSN); Secondary Education (BSEd), 4-5 yrs; *Master's Degree*: Accountancy (MSA); Arts in Education (MAEd); Arts in English (MAEngl); Arts in Teaching (MAT); Business Administration (MBA); Business Administration (MSBA); Engineering (MSME); Engineering (ME); Nursing (MSN); Public Administration (IMPA); Public Administration (MPA-Non -Thesis); Public Administration (MPA); *PhD*: Commerce (PhD-Comm); Education (EdD)

Student Services: Academic counselling, Canteen, Cultural centre, Employment services, Foreign student adviser, Health services, Language programs, Nursery care, Social counselling, Sports facilities

Student Residential Facilities: Ladies dormitory.

Special Facilities: Educational Media Centre. Gymnasium-Auditorium. Cultural Affairs Office. Research Centre. Human Resources Development Centre. SMUNet Office. Internet Library.

Libraries: Rev. John van Bauwel Building. Jubilee Library Building; CL Building.

Publications: Journal of Northern Luzon *(annually)*

Press or Publishing House: SMU Printing Press

Last Updated: 03/02/11

SAINT MICHAEL COLLEGE-HINDANG CAMPUS

Bonifacio Street, Hindang, Leyte 6523
EMail: Saintmichaelcollege@yahoo.com

President: Manolito M. Ybañez

Programmes

Commerce (Business Administration; Business and Commerce; Human Resources; Management); **Education** (Education; Primary Education; Secondary Education); **Information and Communications Technology** (Communication Studies; Information Technology; Software Engineering)

History: Founded 1948.

Degrees and Diplomas: *Bachelor's Degree*

Last Updated: 03/02/11

SAINT MICHAEL COLLEGE OF CARAGA (SMCC)

C. Atupan Street, Nasipit, Agusan del Norte 8602
Tel: +63(85) 343-3251 +63(85) 283-3113
Fax: +63(85) 343-3607
EMail: sitemaster@smccnasipit.edu.ph
Website: http://www.smccnasipit.edu.ph

President: Bienvenido Jose A. Betaizer

Departments

Business Administration and Commerce (Business Administration; Business and Commerce; Finance); **Computer Science** (Computer Science); **Education** (Education; English; Foreign Languages Education; Primary Education; Secondary Education); **Hotel and Restaurant Management** (Hotel and Restaurant; Hotel Management); **Information Technology** (Information Technology); **Technical Programs** (Accountancy; Computer Science; Hotel and Restaurant; Technology; Tourism)

History: Founded 1948. Formerly known as Saint Michael Institute.

Degrees and Diplomas: *Bachelor's Degree*

Last Updated: 03/02/11

SAINT MICHAEL'S COLLEGE

San Roque, Guagua, Pampanga 2003
Tel: +63(45) 900-0719
Fax: +63(45) 900-0719 +63(45) 900-0219

President: Antonio A Ramos

Programmes

Accountancy (Accountancy); **Arts and Humanities** (Arts and Humanities; Political Sciences); **Commerce** (Banking; Business and Commerce; Finance); **Computer Technology** (Computer Engineering); **Education** (Education; English; Filipino; Foreign Languages Education; Mathematics Education; Native Language Education; Primary Education; Secondary Education; Social Studies)

History: Founded 1941.

Degrees and Diplomas: *Certificate/Diploma*; *Associate Degree*; *Bachelor's Degree*

Last Updated: 03/02/11

SAINT MICHAEL'S COLLEGE CANTILAN

Rizal Street, Cantilan, Surigao Del Sur 8317
EMail: smc_cantilan@yahoo.com

Directress: Vivina M. Init

Programmes

Arts and Humanities (Arts and Humanities; Economics; English; History); **Commerce** (Banking; Business Administration; Business and Commerce; Finance; Management); **Computer Science** (Computer Science); **Education** (Education; English; Filipino; Foreign Languages Education; Mathematics Education; Native Language Education; Primary Education; Secondary Education; Social Studies)

History: Founded 1915.

Degrees and Diplomas: *Bachelor's Degree*

Last Updated: 03/02/11

SAINT MICHAEL'S COLLEGE OF ILIGAN

74 Quezon Avenue, Iligan City, Lanao del Norte 9200
Tel: +63(63) 221-3812
Fax: +63(63) 221-8109
EMail: smc_rvm04@yahoo.com

President: Ma. Yolanda C. Reyes

Programmes

Arts and Sciences (Accountancy; Banking; Business Administration; Business and Commerce; Computer Engineering; Computer Science; Criminology; English; Finance; Hotel and Restaurant; Hotel Management; Human Resources; Information Technology; Management; Marketing; Nursing; Philosophy; Psychology); **Education** (Computer Education; Curriculum; Education; English; Foreign Languages Education; Mathematics Education; Primary Education; Secondary Education); **Graduate** (Education; Educational and Student Counselling; English; Filipino; Foreign Languages Education; Native Language Education)

History: Founded 1915. Formerly known as Escuela de San Miguel and St. Michael's Academy.

Degrees and Diplomas: *Bachelor's Degree*; *Master's Degree*: Education (Filipino; English Language Teaching; Educational Management; Guidance and Counselling)

Last Updated: 25/02/11

SAINT MICHAEL'S COLLEGE OF LAGUNA

Platero, Biñan, Laguna 4024
Tel: +63(49) 511-9359 +63(2) 699-2417
Fax: +63(49) 511-9359 +63(2) 699-2417
EMail: mec@smcl.edu.ph
Website: http://www.smcl.edu.ph/

President: Lourdes Almeda-Sese

Director for Academics and Research: Maria Regina M.C. Manabat

International Relations: Flordeliza C. Reyes, Executive Vice-President for External Relations

Programmes

Graduate (Business Administration; Education; Educational Administration); **Undergraduate and Professional** (Accountancy; Business Administration; Business and Commerce; Computer Engineering; Computer Science; Education; English; Filipino; Foreign Languages Education; Health Education; Hotel and Restaurant; Hotel Management; Human Resources; Management; Marketing; Mathematics Education; Native Language Education; Nursing; Primary Education; Secondary Education)

History: Founded 1975.

Degrees and Diplomas: *Certificate/Diploma*; *Associate Degree*; *Bachelor's Degree*; *Master's Degree*: Education (Educational Management); Business Administration

Last Updated: 03/02/11

SAINT PATRICK COLLEGE

Ma. Fe Subd., Arellano Avenue, Orani, Bataan 2112
Tel: +63(47) 431-1453
Fax: +63(47) 431-1453
EMail: bei@mozcom.com

President: José Henry V. Bello

Programmes

Undergraduate and Professional (Banking; Business Administration; Business and Commerce; English; Finance; Management)

History: Founded 1977. Formerly Bataan Central Colleges (2000-2002).

Degrees and Diplomas: *Certificate/Diploma*; *Associate Degree*; *Bachelor's Degree*

Last Updated: 03/02/11

SAINT PAUL COLLEGE FOUNDATION

279 Bulacao, Pardo, Cebu City, Cebu 6000
Tel: +63(32) 272-2985
Fax: +63(32) 272-8475
EMail: spcfi@yahoo.com

President: Lourdes Libres Rosaroso

Programmes

Undergraduate and Professional Studies (Computer Engineering; Computer Science; Education; English; Foreign Languages Education; Information Technology; Mathematics Education; Nursing; Primary Education; Science Education; Secondary Education)

History: Founded 1984.

Degrees and Diplomas: *Associate Degree*; *Bachelor's Degree*

Last Updated: 03/02/11

SAINT PAUL COLLEGE OF ILOCOS SUR

Rizal, Bantay, Ilocos Sur 2727
Tel: +63(77) 722-4782 +63(77) 632-0791
Fax: +63(77) 632-0791 +63(77) 674-2457

President: Marie Celine Santos

Programmes

Accountancy (Accountancy); **Arts** (English; Filipino; Mathematics; Religious Education); **Business Administration** (Accountancy; Business Administration; Finance; Human Resources; Management; Marketing); **Computer Science** (Computer Science); **Education** (Education; English; Filipino; Foreign Languages Education; Home Economics Education; Mathematics Education; Native Language Education; Primary Education); **Hotel and Restaurant Management** (Hotel and Restaurant; Hotel Management); **Information Technology** (Information Technology); **Nursing** (Nursing); **Tourism** (Tourism)

History: Founded 1905. Formerly known as Rosary College of Vigan, Inc. (1961-1968).

Degrees and Diplomas: *Associate Degree*; *Bachelor's Degree*

Last Updated: 03/02/11

SAINT PAUL COLLEGE OF SAN MIGUEL

Salangan, San Miguel, Bulacan 3011
Tel: +63(44) 764-0349
Fax: +63(44) 764-0656

President: Victoria L. Lavente

Programmes

Accountancy (Accountancy); **Business Administration** (Business Administration; Management); **Computer Science** (Computer Science); **Elementary Education** (Education; English; Foreign Languages Education; Primary Education); **Secondary Education** (Education; English; Ethics; Secondary Education)

History: Founded 1938 as San Miguel Catholic Institute. Acquired present title 1956.

Degrees and Diplomas: *Associate Degree*; *Bachelor's Degree*

Last Updated: 03/02/11

SAINT PAUL COLLEGE OF TECHNOLOGY

3/F Cedasco Bldg., Paniqui, Tarlac 2307
Tel: +63(45) 931-1033
Fax: +63(45) 934-0484 +63(45) 931-1003
EMail: mario_b_gana@yahoo.com

President: Nintha Lucilla Baldado

Programmes

Computer Science (Computer Science); **Elementary Education** (Education; Mathematics Education; Primary Education; Social Sciences)

History: Founded 1999. Formerly St. Paul Technical School, Inc. (1989-1994).

Degrees and Diplomas: *Bachelor's Degree*

Last Updated: 03/02/11

SAINT PAUL'S BUSINESS SCHOOL

Campetic, Palo, Leyte 6501
Tel: +63(53) 323-7558
Fax: +63(53) 323-7558
EMail: aga_josie@yahoo.com
Website: http://www.spbspalo.edu.ph/

President: Absalon G. Apostol

Programmes

Undergraduate and Professional (Accountancy; Banking; Business and Commerce; Economics; Finance; Management; Management Systems; Marketing)

History: Founded 1994.

Degrees and Diplomas: *Bachelor's Degree*
Last Updated: 04/02/11

SAINT PEDRO POVEDA COLLEGE

EDSA, Corner Poveda Street, Quezon City, Second District, Metro Manila 1100
Tel: +63(2) 631-8756 +63(2) 631-8756
Fax: +63(2) 635-2696
EMail: registrar@poveda.edu.ph
Website: http://www.poveda.edu.ph/

President: Emma T. Melgarejo

Programmes

Business Administration (Business Administration; Human Resources; Management); **Education** (Curriculum; Education; English; Foreign Languages Education; Mathematics Education; Preschool Education; Primary Education; Secondary Education)

History: Founded 1960 as Institucion Teresiana School.

Degrees and Diplomas: *Bachelor's Degree*
Last Updated: 04/02/11

SAINT PETER COLLEGE SEMINARY

Km 6, Butuan City, Agusan del Norte 8600
Tel: +63(85) 341-6601
Fax: +63(85) 3423757
EMail: rslasco@hotmail.com

Rector: Ruel S. Lasco

Programmes

Arts and Humanities (Arts and Humanities; English; Religious Education)

History: Founded 1959.

Degrees and Diplomas: *Bachelor's Degree*
Last Updated: 04/02/11

SAINT PETER'S COLLEGE

15 de Septiembre Street, Balingasag, Misamis Oriental 9005
Tel: +63(88) 333-2072
Fax: +63(88) 333-2072

President: Gerardo D. Paguio

Programmes

Arts and Humanities, Business and Education (Arts and Humanities; Business Administration; Education)

History: Founded 1950.

Degrees and Diplomas: *Bachelor's Degree*
Last Updated: 04/02/11

SAINT PETER'S COLLEGE OF ORMOC

Fr. Ismael Cataag Street, Ormoc City, Leyte 6541
Tel: +63(53) 255-4391
Fax: +63(53) 255-3406
EMail: spcpres@spc-ormoc.edu.ph
Website: http://www.spc-ormoc.edu.ph

President: Susan Abellana

Programmes

Accountancy (Accountancy); **Business Administration and Commerce** (Accountancy; Banking; Business Administration; Finance; Human Resources; Management); **Computer Science** (Computer Science); **Education** (Computer Education; Education; English; Filipino; Foreign Languages Education; Native Language Education; Primary Education; Science Education; Secondary Education; Special Education); **Hotel and Restaurant Management** (Hotel and Restaurant; Hotel Management); **Liberal Arts** (English; Literature; Political Sciences)

History: Founded 1914, acquiring current status and title in 1966.

Degrees and Diplomas: *Associate Degree*; *Bachelor's Degree*
Last Updated: 04/02/11

SAINT PETER'S COLLEGE OF TORIL

Mcarthur Highway, Toril, Davao City, Davao del Sur 8000
Tel: +63(82) 291-2007
Fax: +63(82) 291-0257
EMail: SPCT@Davao.Fapenet.com

Director: Samuelita P. Enriquez

Programmes

Undergraduate and Professional Studies (Accountancy; Business Administration; Curriculum; Education; English; Filipino; Finance; Foreign Languages Education; Health Education; Management; Marketing; Mathematics Education; Native Language Education; Primary Education; Science Education)

History: Founded 1948.

Degrees and Diplomas: *Bachelor's Degree*
Last Updated: 04/02/11

SAINT PETER'S COLLEGE-ILIGAN CITY

Sabayle Street, Iligan City, Lanao del Norte 9200
Tel: +63(63) 221-6246 +63(63) 221-6247
Fax: +63(63) 221-3223
EMail: ray-alfar@yahoo.com

President: Sotero A. Punongbayan

Programmes

Business Administration (Administration; Business Administration; Economics; Finance; Human Resources; Management; Marketing); **Civil Engineering** (Civil Engineering); **Commerce** (Business and Commerce); **Computer Engineering** (Computer Engineering); **Computer Science** (Computer Science); **Education** (Curriculum; Education; English; Filipino; Foreign Languages Education; History; Mathematics Education; Native Language Education; Primary Education; Secondary Education; Social Studies); **Electrical Engineering** (Electrical Engineering); **Electronics and Communication Engineering** (Electronic Engineering; Telecommunications Engineering); **Information Technology** (Information Technology); **Liberal Arts** (Economics; English; Filipino; History; Political Sciences); **Mechanical Engineering** (Mechanical Engineering)

History: Founded 1952.

Degrees and Diplomas: *Bachelor's Degree*
Last Updated: 04/02/11

SAINT RITA COLLEGE - MANILA

Plaza del Carmen, Quiapo, City of Manila, First District, Metro Manila
Tel: +63(2) 736-4360
Fax: +63(2) 736-3988

Director: Ma. Ninfa Inzon

Programmes

Undergraduate and Professional (Education; English; Foreign Languages Education; Hotel and Restaurant; Hotel Management; Primary Education; Secondary Education)

History: Founded 1907. Acquired present status 1945.

Degrees and Diplomas: *Associate Degree*; *Bachelor's Degree*
Last Updated: 04/02/11

SAINT RITA COLLEGE - PARAÑAQUE

Dr. A. Santos Avenue, Sucat, City of Parañaque, Fourth District, Metro Manila 1700
Tel: +63(2) 826-5241
Fax: +63(2) 826-4523

Director: Ma. Goretti Cui

Programmes
Undergraduate and Professional (Business and Commerce; Education; Educational and Student Counselling; English; Foreign Languages Education; Management; Mathematics Education; Primary Education)
History: Founded 1964.
Degrees and Diplomas: *Associate Degree*; *Bachelor's Degree*
Last Updated: 04/02/11

SAINT RITA'S COLLEGE OF BALINGASAG

Tres Martires, Balingasag, Misamis Oriental 9005

Director: Ma. Adelaida C. Huiso

Programmes
Undergraduate and Professional (Accountancy; Arts and Humanities; Banking; Biological and Life Sciences; Biology; Business Administration; Business and Commerce; Curriculum; Education; English; Filipino; Finance; Foreign Languages Education; Health Education; History; Human Resources; Management; Marketing; Mathematics; Mathematics Education; Native Language Education; Natural Sciences; Primary Education; Science Education; Secondary Education)
History: Founded 1901. Formerly known as St. Rita's Parochial School; St. Rita's School; St. Rita's High School and St. Rita's College.
Degrees and Diplomas: *Bachelor's Degree*
Last Updated: 07/02/11

SAINT ROSE COLLEGE EDUCATIONAL FOUNDATION

McArthur Highway, Barangay Samput, Paniqui, Tarlac 2307
Tel: +63(45) 931-1162
Fax: +63(45) 931-0703
EMail: srcefi_paniqui@hotmail.com

Director: Joaquin A. Siongco

Programmes
Accountancy (Accountancy); **Business Administration** (Business Administration; Management); **Computer Science** (Computer Science); **Elementary Education** (Preschool Education; Primary Education); **Secondary Education** (Educational and Student Counselling; Mathematics Education; Secondary Education)
History: Founded 2002.
Degrees and Diplomas: *Bachelor's Degree*
Last Updated: 07/02/11

SAINT SCHOLASTICA'S COLLEGE OF HEALTH SCIENCES

Sta. Cruz Street, Tacloban City, Leyte 6500
Tel: +63(53) 325-2187
Fax: +63(53) 325-4089

President: Rosario Obibiana

Programmes
Undergraduate and Professional (Biology; Laboratory Techniques; Medical Technology; Nursing; Pharmacy)
History: Founded 2000.
Degrees and Diplomas: *Bachelor's Degree*
Last Updated: 07/02/11

SAINT THERESA COLLEGE (STC)

Rizal Street Corner Magsaysay Street, Tandag, Surigao del Sur 8300
Tel: +63(86) 211-3046
Fax: +63(86) 211-3046
Website: http://sttheresacollege.edu.ph

President: Carlos P. Bautista (2002-) Tel: +63(86) 211-3913

Programmes
Arts and Humanities (Arts and Humanities; Biology; Economics; English; Political Sciences; Psychology); **Commerce and Business Administration** (Accountancy; Banking; Business Administration; Business and Commerce; Computer Education; Finance; Management; Marketing; Operations Research; Public Administration; Secretarial Studies); **Elementary Education** (English; Filipino; Foreign Languages Education; Mathematics Education; Native Language Education; Primary Education; Religious Education; Science Education); **Graduate Studies** (Business Administration; Educational Administration; Educational and Student Counselling); **Mathematics** (Mathematics); **Secondary Education** (Biological and Life Sciences; English; Filipino; Foreign Languages Education; Mathematics Education; Native Language Education; Religious Education; Science Education; Secondary Education; Social Studies); **Secretarial Administration** (Administration; Computer Education; Management; Secretarial Studies)
History: Founded as Cartilla Class in 1916 by Missionaries of The Sacred Heart of Jesus
Governing Bodies: Board of Trustees, Administrative Council, Academic Council
Admission Requirements: High School Diploma
Fees: (Peso): 153.50 per unit per semester
Main Language(s) of Instruction: English
Degrees and Diplomas: *Associate Degree*; *Bachelor's Degree*: Arts, Teacher Education, Business Management and Education (BA, BSc); *Master's Degree*: Business Administration; Educational Administration; Guidance and Counselling
Last Updated: 07/02/11

SAINT THERESA'S COLLEGE OF CEBU

Ramon Aboitiz Street, Cebu City, Cebu 6000
Tel: +63(37) 253-6337
Fax: +63(32) 253-6335
EMail: stccomus@yahoo.com

Director: Merced Sanchez

Programmes
Accountancy (Accountancy); **Arts** (English; Mass Communication; Music Education; Psychology); **Commerce** (Business Administration; Business and Commerce; Management; Marketing); **Education** (Education; Educational and Student Counselling; English; Filipino; Foreign Languages Education; Mathematics Education; Music Education; Native Language Education; Primary Education; Religious Education; Science Education; Secondary Education; Social Studies); **Social Work** (Social Work)
History: Founded 1933.
Degrees and Diplomas: *Bachelor's Degree*
Last Updated: 07/02/11

SAINT THERESE COLLEGE

Soriano Street, San Carlos City, Pangasinan 2420
Tel: +63(75) 955-5539

President: Armand F. Magleo

Programmes
Criminology (Criminology)
History: Founded 1993.
Degrees and Diplomas: *Bachelor's Degree*
Last Updated: 07/02/11

SAINT THOMAS AQUINAS COLLEGE

Bagares Street, Sogod, Southern Leyte 6606
Tel: +63(53) 382-2146
Fax: +63(53) 382-2637
EMail: stac_ssl@yahoo.com

Director: Merwin L. Kangleon

Programmes
Business Administration (Business Administration; Human Resources; Management); **Education** (Education; Primary Education; Secondary Education)
History: Founded 1946.
Degrees and Diplomas: *Bachelor's Degree*
Last Updated: 07/02/11

SAINT TONIS COLLEGE

Purok 4, Bulanao, Tabuk, Kalinga 3800

Programmes
Nursing (Nursing)
Degrees and Diplomas: *Bachelor's Degree*
Last Updated: 07/02/11

SAINT VINCENT DE PAUL COLLEGE

Andres Soriano Avenue, Mangagoy, Bislig City, Surigao del Sur 8311
Tel: +63(86) 628-2004
Fax: +63(86) 853-1635
EMail: svpcnet@eudoramail.com

President: Erwin Rommel C. Torres

Programmes
Arts (Economics; English); **Business Administration** (Business Administration; Finance; Management; Marketing); **Commerce** (Business Administration; Business and Commerce); **Education** (Education; English; Foreign Languages Education; Primary Education; Secondary Education)
History: Founded 1983.
Degrees and Diplomas: *Associate Degree*; *Bachelor's Degree*
Last Updated: 07/02/11

SAINT VINCENT'S COLLEGE

Padre Ramon Street, Estaka, Dipolog City, Zamboanga del Norte 7100
Tel: +63(62) 212-2691

President: Jose R. Maguiran

Programmes
Accountancy (Accountancy); **Arts** (Communication Arts; English; Filipino; Philosophy; Political Sciences); **Business Administration** (Business Administration); **Commerce** (Accountancy; Banking; Business and Commerce; Finance; Management); **Computer Engineering** (Computer Engineering); **Computer Science** (Computer Science); **Education** (Art Education; Curriculum; Economics; Education; Educational and Student Counselling; English; Filipino; Foreign Languages Education; Health Education; Mathematics Education; Music Education; Native Language Education; Physical Education; Primary Education; Religious Education; Science Education; Secondary Education); **Electronics and Communication Engineering** (Electronic Engineering; Telecommunications Engineering); **Graduate** (Business Administration; Education; Educational Administration; Public Administration); **Hotel and Restaurant Management** (Hotel and Restaurant; Hotel Management); **Mathematics** (Mathematics); **Secretarial Administration** (Administration; Computer Education; Management; Management Systems; Secretarial Studies); **Tourism Management** (Tourism)
History: Founded 1917.
Degrees and Diplomas: *Bachelor's Degree*; *Master's Degree*: Business Administration; Public Management; Education; *PhD*: Educational Management
Last Updated: 07/02/11

SAINTS JOHN AND PAUL COLLEGES

Halang, Calamba City, Laguna 4030
Tel: +63(49) 834-4013 +63(49) 834-6732
Fax: +63(49) 545-6858
EMail: sjpc_211994.educ@yahoo.com.ph

President: Razul Z. Requesto

Programmes
Undergraduate and Professional (Chemistry; Curriculum; Education; Hotel and Restaurant; Hotel Management; Mathematics Education; Midwifery; Nursing; Occupational Therapy; Physical Therapy; Primary Education; Psychology; Respiratory Therapy; Secondary Education)
History: Founded 1994.
Degrees and Diplomas: *Certificate/Diploma*; *Bachelor's Degree*
Last Updated: 07/02/11

SALAZAR COLLEGES OF SCIENCE AND INSTITUTE OF TECHNOLOGY

211 N. Bacalso Avenue, Cebu City, Cebu 6000
Tel: +63(32) 261-0234
Fax: +63(32) 261-0235
EMail: dmsalazar@yahoo.com

President: Doroteo M. Salazar

Programmes
Undergraduate and Professional Studies (Business and Commerce; Civil Engineering; Computer Engineering; Criminology; Education; Electrical Engineering; Hotel and Restaurant; Hotel Management; Management; Marine Engineering; Mathematics Education; Mechanical Engineering; Police Studies; Primary Education; Secondary Education; Software Engineering)
History: Founded 1983. Formerly SALCON Institute of Technology (1983-1986).
Degrees and Diplomas: *Bachelor's Degree*
Last Updated: 17/02/11

SAL FOUNDATION COLLEGE

Marhaban, Salimbao, Sultan Kudarat, Shariff Kabunsuan 9605

President: Subaida Akil-Lineses

Programmes
Criminology (Criminology); **Education** (Education; Secondary Education)
History: Founded 2002.
Degrees and Diplomas: *Bachelor's Degree*
Last Updated: 17/02/11

SAMAR COLLEGE

Mabini Avenue, Catbalogan, Western Samar 6700
Tel: +63(53) 251-3021
Fax: +63(53) 251-3021

Chairman: Fidelindo G. Fernandez

Programmes
Arts (English; Social Sciences); **Business Administration** (Business Administration); **Commerce** (Accountancy; Business and Commerce; Finance; Management; Marketing); **Criminology** (Criminology); **Graduate** (Communication Studies; Education; Educational Administration; Filipino; Foreign Languages Education; Literacy Education; Native Language Education; Primary Education); **information Studies** (Information Management; Information Technology); **Law** (Law); **Primary Education** (Art Education; Curriculum; English; Filipino; Foreign Languages Education; Health Education; Home Economics Education; Mathematics Education; Music; Native Language Education; Physical Education; Preschool Education; Primary Education; Science Education; Social Studies; Special Education); **Secondary Education** (Art Education; Biological and Life Sciences; English; Filipino; Foreign Languages Education; Health Education; Mathematics Education; Music Education; Native Language Education; Physical Education; Physics; Science Education; Secondary Education; Social Studies)
History: Founded 1949.
Degrees and Diplomas: *Bachelor's Degree*; *Master's Degree*: Arts in Education (Educational Management; Reading; Filipino; Elementary Education; Language Teaching; Communication Language Learning
Last Updated: 17/02/11

SAMSON COLLEGE OF SCIENCE AND TECHNOLOGY - QUEZON CITY

587 EDSA, Cubao, Quezon City, Second District, Metro Manila 1111
Tel: +63(2) 414-6429 +63(2) 721-4129
Fax: +63(2) 723-1648
EMail: admin@samson.edu.ph
Website: http://www.samson.edu.ph

President: Gerald S. Aycardo

Programmes
Undergraduate and Professional (Computer Science; Electronic Engineering; Information Management; Information Technology; Mechanics; Secretarial Studies)

History: Founded 1948. Formerly known as Samson Institute of Technology (1987-1998).

Degrees and Diplomas: *Certificate/Diploma*; *Associate Degree*; *Bachelor's Degree*
Last Updated: 17/02/11

SAN AGUSTIN COLLEGE - BACOLOD

Colegio San Agustin - Bacolod
Benigno S. Aquino Drive, Bacolod City, Negros Occidental 6100
Tel: +63(34) 433-1248
Fax: +63(34) 433-9187
EMail: csabacolod@yahoo.com

President: Mamerto A. Alfeche, O.S.A.

Programmes
Arts *(Bachelor of Arts programme)* (English; Mathematics; Natural Sciences; Psychology); **Education** (Art Education; Biology; English; Ethics; Filipino; Foreign Languages Education; Health Education; Mathematics Education; Music Education; Native Language Education; Physical Education; Physics; Preschool Education; Primary Education; Science Education; Secondary Education; Social Studies); **Science** *(Bachelor of Science programme)* (Accountancy; Banking; Biology; Business Administration; Business and Commerce; Chemical Engineering; Chemistry; Computer Engineering; Computer Science; Economics; Electronic Engineering; Finance; Human Resources; Information Technology; Management; Marketing; Mathematics; Mechanical Engineering; Medical Technology; Nursing; Psychology; Telecommunications Engineering; Tourism)

History: Founded 1962.

Degrees and Diplomas: *Certificate/Diploma*; *Associate Degree*; *Bachelor's Degree*
Last Updated: 09/09/10

SAN AGUSTIN COLLEGE - BIÑAN

Colegio San Agustin - Biñan
San Francisco Juana Complex I, Biñan, Laguna 4024
Tel: +63(2) 478-0167
Fax: +63(2) 478-0180
EMail: csa_southwoods07@yahoo.com.ph
Website: http://www.csabinan.edu.ph

President: Richard L. Pido

Programmes
Business Administration (Business Administration; Economics; Management; Marketing; Real Estate); **Communication** (Communication Studies); **Computer Science** (Computer Science); **Foreign Service**; **Hotel and Restaurant Management** (Hotel and Restaurant; Hotel Management); **Information Technology** (Information Technology); **Psychology** (Psychology); **Tourism** (Tourism)

History: Founded 1985. Acquired present status 1998.

Degrees and Diplomas: *Bachelor's Degree*
Last Updated: 09/09/10

SAN AGUSTIN INSTITUTE OF TECHNOLOGY

Mabini Street, Poblacion, Valencia City, Bukidnon 8709
Tel: +63(88) 222-3711 +63(88) 828-1499
Fax: +63(88) 828-1499

Director: Felisa P. Batusin

Programmes
Undergraduate and Professional Studies (Business Administration; Business and Commerce; Economics; Filipino; Finance; Human Resources; Industrial Arts Education; Literacy Education; Management; Marketing; Mathematics Education; Midwifery; Native Language Education; Primary Education; Secondary Education)

History: Founded 1960. Formerly known as San Agustin Technical Institute.

Degrees and Diplomas: *Bachelor's Degree*
Last Updated: 17/02/11

SAN ANTONIO DE PADUA COLLEGE

Sta. Clara Sur, Pila, Laguna 4010
Tel: +63(49) 559-0501 +63(49) 559-0079
Fax: +63(49) 559-0452
EMail: sapc@mozcom.com

Executive Vice-President: Elisa T. Martinez

Programmes
Undergraduate and Professional (Business and Commerce; Hotel and Restaurant; Hotel Management; Management; Psychology)

History: Founded 1979.

Degrees and Diplomas: *Certificate/Diploma*; *Associate Degree*; *Bachelor's Degree*
Last Updated: 17/02/11

SAN BEDA COLLEGE

638 Mendiola Street, San Miguel, City of Manila, First District, Metro Manila 1005
Tel: +63(2) 735-6011 +63(2) 735-6015
Fax: +63(2) 735-5994
EMail: pro@sanbeda.edu.ph
Website: http://www.sanbeda.edu.ph

Rector: Mateo Ma. J. De Jesus (2007-)
Tel: +63(2) 741-7786 EMail: rector@sanbeda.edu.ph

Colleges
Arts and Science (Accountancy; Arts and Humanities; Economics; Finance; Human Resources; Information Technology; Management; Natural Sciences; Philosophy; Psychology; Public Administration; Telecommunications Engineering); **Law** (Law); **Medicine** (Medicine); **Nursing** (Nursing)

Graduate Colleges
Law (Law)

Graduate Schools
Business; **Liturgy** (History of Religion; Philosophy; Religion)

History: Founded 1901. Formerly known as Colegio De San Beda (1901-1917).

Degrees and Diplomas: *Bachelor's Degree*; *Master's Degree*: Business Administration; Business Administration in Organization Development; Entrepreneurial Management; Liturgy; Laws; Criminal Justice Administration; *PhD*: Business Administration; Liturgy
Last Updated: 17/02/11

SAN BEDA COLLEGE - ALABANG

Don Manolo Blvd., Alabang Hills Village, Alabang, City of Muntinlupa, Fourth District, Metro Manila 1702
Tel: +63(2) 842-3508 +63(2) 809-3179
Fax: +63(2) 842-3511
EMail: sbca@sanbeda-alabang.edu.ph
Website: http://www.sanbeda-alabang.edu.ph

President: Dom Clemen H. Roque

Programmes
Laws (Law)

History: Founded 1972. Formerly known as St. Benedict College (1994-2004).

Degrees and Diplomas: *Bachelor's Degree*
Last Updated: 17/02/11

SAN CARLOS COLLEGE

Mabini Street, San Carlos City, Pangasinan 2420
Tel: +63(75) 955-5190 +63(75) 634-1094
Fax: +63(75) 955-5190
EMail: scc@sancarloscollege.edu.ph
Website: http://www.sancarloscollege.edu.ph

President: Arturo B. de Veyra

Registrar: Veronica M. Buna Cruz
EMail: registrar@sancarloscollege.edu.ph

Administrative/Planning Officer: Richard A. de Veyra

Colleges

Accountancy (Accountancy); **Business Administration** (Business Administration; Human Resources; Management); **Education** (Art Education; Biological and Life Sciences; Curriculum; Education; English; Filipino; Foreign Languages Education; Mathematics Education; Music Education; Native Language Education; Physical Education; Preschool Education; Primary Education; Secondary Education; Social Studies; Special Education); **Graduate Studies** (Education; Educational Administration); **Information and Computer Studies** (Computer Science; Information Technology; Software Engineering); **Liberal Arts** (Arts and Humanities; English; Mathematics; Political Sciences)

History: Founded 1946.

Degrees and Diplomas: *Associate Degree*; *Bachelor's Degree*; *Master's Degree*: Education (Educational Administration)
Last Updated: 17/02/11

SAN FRANCISCO COLLEGES

Brgy. 3, San Francisco, Agusan del Sur 8501
Tel: +63 (85) 839-2200
Fax: +63 (85) 839-2200
EMail: sfc_registrar@yahoo.com

President: Jose Mari D. Amador

Programmes

Business Administration (Accountancy; Business Administration; Management); **Elementary Education** (Education; Filipino; Native Language Education; Primary Education); **Political Sciences** (Political Sciences)

History: Founded 1977.

Degrees and Diplomas: *Bachelor's Degree*
Last Updated: 17/02/11

SAN FRANCISCO JAVIER COLLEGE

National Highway, Narra, Palawan 5303

Director: Marilyn N. Cula

Programmes

Undergraduate and Professional (Accountancy; Banking; Business Administration; Education; English; Finance; Foreign Languages Education; History; Home Economics Education; Mathematics Education; Primary Education; Secondary Education)
History: Founded 1957.
Degrees and Diplomas: *Associate Degree*; *Bachelor's Degree*
Last Updated: 17/02/11

SAN FRANCISCO JAVIER COLLEGE
Colegio de San Francisco Javier

East Poblacion, Rizal, Zamboanga del Norte 7104
Tel: +63(65) 906-0059
EMail: cdsfj_rizal@yahoo.com

Director: Ranulfo M. Suarez

Programmes

Undergraduate and Professional Studies (Business Administration; Business and Commerce; Computer Science; Economics; Hotel and Restaurant; Hotel Management; Human Resources; Management; Primary Education; Secondary Education; Social Work)

History: Founded in 1950, acquiring its present status and title in 1999.

Degrees and Diplomas: *Bachelor's Degree*
Last Updated: 08/09/10

SAN ILDEFONSO COLLEGE

M.H. Del Pilar Street, Tanay, Rizal 1980
Tel: +63(2) 654-3278
Fax: +63(2) 654-1399
EMail: registration_admission2005@yahoo.com

President: Pedro C. Canonero

Programmes

Undergraduate and Professional (Business Administration; Business and Commerce; Curriculum; Education; Finance; Hotel and Restaurant; Hotel Management; Management; Preschool Education; Primary Education; Secondary Education)

History: Founded 1918.

Degrees and Diplomas: *Associate Degree*; *Bachelor's Degree*
Last Updated: 17/02/11

SAN ISIDRO COLLEGE

Impalambong, Malaybalay City, Bukidnon 8700
Tel: +63(88) 221-2440
Fax: +63(88) 221-2368
EMail: Sicmly@moscom.com

President: Virgelio H. Delfin

Programmes

Undergraduate and Professional (Accountancy; Administration; Business Administration; Business and Commerce; Economics; Education; English; Filipino; Finance; Foreign Languages Education; Human Resources; Management; Marketing; Native Language Education; Nursing; Philosophy; Primary Education; Religious Education; Secondary Education; Theology)

History: Founded 1949. Formerly known as San Isidro High School.

Degrees and Diplomas: *Bachelor's Degree*
Last Updated: 18/02/11

SAN JOSÉ CHRISTIAN COLLEGES

Sto. Niño 1st., San Jose City, Nueva Ecija 3121
Tel: +63(44) 511-4858
Fax: +63(44) 947-3114

President: Narciso V. Salvador

Programmes

Commerce (Banking; Business and Commerce; Finance); **Education** (Education; English; Foreign Languages Education; History; Mathematics Education; Primary Education; Secondary Education); **Graduate Studies** (Education; Educational Administration; Educational and Student Counselling; Public Administration)

History: Founded 1947. Formerly San Jose Colleges (1947-2001).

Degrees and Diplomas: *Bachelor's Degree*; *Master's Degree*: Education (Educational Management; Guidance and Counselling)
Last Updated: 18/02/11

SAN JOSE COLLEGE - JARO
Colegio de San Jose - Jaro

E. Lopez Street, Jaro, Iloilo City, Iloilo 5000
Tel: +63(33) 329-1595
Fax: +63(33) 320-4605
EMail: lariosa_ph@yahoo.com

President: Maria Lourdes S. Verzosa

Programmes

Business Administration (Accountancy; Business Administration; Business and Commerce; Finance; Management); **Education** (Computer Education; Education; English; Filipino; Foreign Languages Education; Home Economics Education; Mathematics Education; Native Language Education; Primary Education; Secondary Education; Technology Education)

History: Founded 1872, acquired present status and title 1946.

Degrees and Diplomas: *Certificate/Diploma*; *Bachelor's Degree*
Last Updated: 08/09/10

SAN JOSE COLLEGE OF ALAMINOS

Colegio San Jose de Alaminos

Quezon Avenue, City of Alaminos, Pangasinan 2404
Tel: +63(75) 551-2979
Fax: +63(75) 552-7062
EMail: csja@cbcpworld.com

President: Jesus A. Cabrera

Programmes

Arts and Humanities (Arts and Humanities; Mass Communication; Philosophy); **Business Administration** (Banking; Business Administration; Business and Commerce; Finance; Management; Marketing); **Education** (Education; English; Foreign Languages Education; History; Mathematics Education; Primary Education; Religious Education; Science Education; Secondary Education)

History: Founded 2001.

Degrees and Diplomas: *Bachelor's Degree*
Last Updated: 09/09/10

SAN JUAN DE DIOS EDUCATIONAL FOUNDATION

2772-2774 Roxas Boulevard, Pasay City, Fourth District, Metro Manila 1300
Tel: +63(2) 831-9817 +63(2) 551-2756
Fax: +63(2) 551-9214
EMail: dadoy@dcphilippines.org
Website: http://www.sanjuandedios.org

President: Josefina R. Quiachon

Programmes

Undergraduate and Professional (Hotel and Restaurant; Hotel Management; Laboratory Techniques; Medical Technology; Nursing; Physical Therapy)

History: Founded 1913. Formerly known as San Juan de Dios Hospital School of Nursing (1913-1965).

Degrees and Diplomas: *Bachelor's Degree*
Last Updated: 18/02/11

SAN JUAN DE LETRAN COLLEGE - ABUCAY, BATAAN

Colegio de San Juan de Letran - Abucay, Bataan

Dominican Avenue, Abucay, Bataan 2114
Website: http://bataan.letran.edu/

President: Tamerlane R. Lana

Courses

Accountancy (Accountancy); **Business Administration** (Business Administration; Finance; Human Resources; Management; Marketing); **Communication Arts** (Communication Arts); **Electrical Engineering** (Electrical Engineering); **Electronic Engineering**; **Hospitality Management** (Hotel and Restaurant; Hotel Management; Tourism); **Industrial Engineering** (Industrial Engineering); **Information Technology** (Computer Engineering; Computer Networks; Information Technology; Software Engineering); **Secondary Education** (Biology; English; Foreign Languages Education; Mathematics Education; Physics; Secondary Education)

Degrees and Diplomas: *Bachelor's Degree*
Last Updated: 08/09/10

SAN JUAN DE LETRAN COLLEGE - CALAMBA, LAGUNA

Colegio de San Juan de Letran - Calamba, Laguna

Barrio Bucal, Calamba City, Laguna 4027
Tel: +63(49) 545-5453
Fax: +63(49) 545-1829
Website: http://www.letran-calamba.edu.ph

Rector and President: Honorato C. Castigador, OP.

Vice-President for Administration and Planning Division: Nelson C. Taclobos, O.P.

Graduate Schools

Professional Studies (Business Administration; Educational Administration; Engineering Management; Government; Human Resources; Information Technology; Management)

Schools

Arts and Sciences (Advertising and Publicity; Communication Studies; Education; English; Foreign Languages Education; Human Resources; Marketing; Mathematics Education; Preschool Education; Primary Education; Psychology; Public Relations; Radio and Television Broadcasting; Secondary Education; Teacher Training); **Business, Management, and Accountancy** (Accountancy; Business and Commerce; Economics; Hotel and Restaurant; Hotel Management; Human Resources; Management; Marketing; Tourism); **Computer Studies and Information Technology** (Computer Engineering; Computer Networks; Computer Science; Information Technology; Software Engineering); **Engineering** (Computer Engineering; Electrical Engineering; Electronic Engineering; Engineering; Industrial Engineering; Mechanical Engineering; Telecommunications Engineering); **Nursing** (Nursing)

History: Founded 1979.

Degrees and Diplomas: *Bachelor's Degree*; *Master's Degree*; *PhD*
Last Updated: 08/09/10

SAN JUAN DE LETRAN COLLEGE - MANILA

Colegio de San Juan de Letran - Manila

151, Muralla Street, Intramuros, Manila, First District, Metro Manila
Tel: +63(2) 527-7693
Fax: +63(2) 527-1783
Website: http://www.letran.edu

Rector: Tamerlane Lana EMail: rectors@letran.edu

Vice-President, Academic Affairs: Juan Ponce, O.P.

Colleges

Business Administration and Accountancy (Accountancy; Business Administration; Economics; Finance; Hotel and Restaurant; Hotel Management; Human Resources; Management; Marketing; Tourism); **Education** (Education; English; Foreign Languages Education; Physical Education; Science Education; Secondary Education); **Liberal Arts and Sciences** (Advertising and Publicity; Communication Arts; Computer Engineering; Information Technology; Journalism; Multimedia; Political Sciences; Psychology; Public Relations; Radio and Television Broadcasting; Software Engineering)

Schools

Graduate Studies (Business Administration)

History: Founded 1620, acquired present status and title 1930.

Degrees and Diplomas: *Associate Degree*; *Bachelor's Degree*; *Master's Degree*; *PhD*
Last Updated: 08/09/10

SAN JUAN SAMAR COLLEGE

Colegio de San Juan Samar

Feeder Road, Libertad, Lavezares, Northern Samar 6404
Tel: +63(917) 423-9292

President: Eufemia A. Jatap

Programmes

Business Administration (Business Administration; Management); **Computer Science** (Computer Science; Software Engineering); **Criminology** (Criminology); **Education** (Education; English; Filipino; Foreign Languages Education; Mathematics Education; Native Language Education; Science Education; Secondary Education); **Information Technology** (Information Technology)

History: Founded 2002.

Degrees and Diplomas: *Bachelor's Degree*
Last Updated: 08/09/10

SAN LORENZO COLLEGE

Colegio de San Lorenzo

Congressional Avenue, Project 6, Quezon City, Second District, Metro Manila 1106

Tel: +63(2) 454-6644

Fax: +63(2) 926-0413

Website: http://www.cdsl.edu.ph

President: Mary Claire Therese F. Balgan

Programmes

Arts (Communication Arts; Psychology); **Business Administration** (Business Administration; Information Management; Information Technology; Management; Marketing); **Education** (Computer Education; Education; Preschool Education; Primary Education; Secondary Education); **Science** (Accountancy; Computer Engineering; Computer Science; Electronic Engineering; Hotel and Restaurant; Hotel Management; Industrial Engineering; Nursing; Telecommunications Engineering)

History: Founded 1987.

Degrees and Diplomas: *Bachelor's Degree*: Electronics and Telecommunication Engineering; Computer Engineering; Industrial Engineering, 5 yrs; *Bachelor's Degree*: Hotel and Restaurant Management; Computer Science; Business Administration; Marketing; Psychology; Accountancy; Communication Arts; Education; Preschool Education; Management; Computer Education; Computer Based Information System, 4 yrs

Last Updated: 08/09/10

SAN LORENZO DEMA ALA ACADEMY

Academia de San Lorenzo Dema Ala

San Jose del Monte, Bulacan 3023

President: Edana G. Dema-Ala

Programmes

Business Administration (Business Administration; Economics; Finance; Human Resources; Marketing); **Criminology** (Criminology); **Education** (Education; English; Mathematics Education; Primary Education; Secondary Education)

Degrees and Diplomas: *Bachelor's Degree*

Last Updated: 22/07/10

SAN LORENZO RUIZ CENTER OF STUDIES AND SCHOOL

St. Dominic Subv., Dolores, City of San Fernando, Pampanga 2000

Tel: +63(45) 961-1092

Fax: +63(45) 961-1091

EMail: slrcss@yahoo.com

President: Lourdes M. Javier

Programmes

Elementary Education (English; Foreign Languages Education; Mathematics Education; Preschool Education; Primary Education; Science Education); **Secondary Education** (English; Mathematics Education; Science Education; Secondary Education)

History: Founded 1998. Formerly San Lorenzo Ruiz Child Study Center and Special Studies (1991-1994).

Degrees and Diplomas: *Bachelor's Degree*

Last Updated: 18/02/11

SAN LORENZO RUIZ COLLEGE OF MANILA, NORTHERN SAMAR

Colegio de San Lorenzo Ruiz de Manila, Northern Samar

J. P. Rizal Street, Catarman, Northern Samar 6400

Tel: +63(55) 500-9260

Fax: +63(55) 500-9260

EMail: cslrm@yahoogroups.com

President: Rolando R. Carpio

Programmes

Commerce (Banking; Business and Commerce; Finance); **Computer Science** (Computer Science); **Criminology** (Criminology); **Elementary Education** (Primary Education); **Hotel and Restaurant Management** (Hotel and Restaurant; Hotel Management; Tourism); **Information and Computer Technology** (Computer Engineering; Information Technology); **Medical Technology** (Medical Technology); **Nursing and Midwifery** (Midwifery); **Political Sciences** (Political Sciences)

History: Founded 1990.

Degrees and Diplomas: *Certificate/Diploma*; *Associate Degree*; *Bachelor's Degree*

Last Updated: 08/09/10

SAN LORENZO RUIZ COLLEGE OF ORMOC

Bgy. San Pablo, Ormoc City, Leyte 6541

Tel: +63(53) 255-5643

Fax: +63(53) 255-8564

EMail: slrc_ormoc@yahoo.com

President: Potenciano V. Larrazabal,Jr.

Programmes

Medical Laboratory Science (Laboratory Techniques; Medical Technology); **Nursing** (Nursing)

History: Founded 2004.

Degrees and Diplomas: *Bachelor's Degree*

Last Updated: 18/02/11

SAN PABLO COLLEGES

Hermanos Belen St., San Pablo City, Laguna 4000

Tel: +63(49) 562-4041

Fax: +63(49) 562-0957

EMail: spcccs2008@yahoo.com

Website: http://www.sanpablocolleges.edu.ph/

President: Quintin C. Eala

Vice-President for Academic Affairs: Lucy G. Del Rio

Vice-President for Administrative Affairs: Rufino L. Tanio

Colleges

Accountancy (Accountancy); **Arts and Sciences** (Economics; English; Mass Communication; Mathematics; Political Sciences; Psychology); **Business Administration** (Business Administration; Finance; Hotel and Restaurant; Hotel Management; Human Resources; Management; Marketing; Public Administration); **Computer Studies** (Business Computing; Computer Engineering; Computer Science); **Education** (Art Education; Education; English; Filipino; Foreign Languages Education; Health Education; Home Economics Education; Mathematics Education; Music Education; Native Language Education; Physical Education; Physics; Secondary Education; Social Studies; Technology Education); **Law** (Law); **Nursing** (Midwifery; Nursing); **Physical Therapy** (Physical Therapy)

History: Founded 1947.

Degrees and Diplomas: *Certificate/Diploma*; *Associate Degree*; *Bachelor's Degree*; *Master's Degree*: Business Administration; Education (Guidance and Counselling; Filipino; English; Administration and Supervision); Nursing; *PhD*: Education (Educational Management)

Last Updated: 18/02/11

SAN PASCUAL BAYLON COLLEGE

Colegio de San Pascual Baylon

Pag-Asa, Obando, Bulacan 3021

Tel: +63(2) 292-4534

Fax: +63(2) 299-1617

President: Danilo G. de los Reyes

Programmes

Accountancy; **Business Administration** (Business Administration); **Computer Science** (Computer Science); **Elementary Education** (Primary Education); **Secondary Education** (English; Filipino; Foreign Languages Education; Mathematics Education; Native Language Education; Science Education; Secondary Education)

History: Founded 1913.

Degrees and Diplomas: *Certificate/Diploma*: 2 yrs; *Bachelor's Degree*

Last Updated: 08/09/10

SAN PEDRO COLLEGE

Colegio de San Pedro

Phase IA, Pacita Complex I, San Pedro, Laguna 4023
Tel: +63(49) 847-5535
EMail: cdsp@ambitec.com.ph

President: Maximo Abesamis

Programmes

Computer Science (Computer Science); **Information Systems and Technology** (Information Technology); **Office Administration** (Business Administration; Business Computing; Computer Engineering)

History: Founded 1995.

Degrees and Diplomas: *Associate Degree*; *Bachelor's Degree*
Last Updated: 08/09/10

SAN PEDRO COLLEGE

12 C. Guzman Street, Davao City, Davao del Sur 8000
Tel: +63(82) 221-0634
Fax: +63(82) 226-4461
EMail: srpat@spcnet.edu.ph
Website: http://www.spcdavao.edu.ph

President: Nanita M. Handugan

Vice-President for Academic Affairs: Desiderio N. Noveno, Jr.

Vice-President for Administration and Planning: Sergio V. Opeña

Programmes

Arts (English; Human Resources; Psychology); **Business Administration** (Business Administration; Finance; Human Resources; Management; Marketing); **Commerce** (Accountancy; Business and Commerce; Management; Marketing); **Computer Science** (Computer Science); **Graduate** (Educational and Student Counselling; Health Administration; Industrial and Organizational Psychology; Nursing; Social and Community Services); **Guidance and Counselling** (Educational and Student Counselling); **Information Technology** (Information Technology); **Medical Laboratory Science** (Laboratory Techniques; Medical Technology); **Nursing** (Nursing); **Pharmacy** (Pharmacy); **Physical Therapy** (Physical Therapy); **Psychology** (Psychology); **Respiratory Therapy** (Respiratory Therapy); **Science** (Biology); **Secondary Education** (Biological and Life Sciences; Biology; Chemistry; English; Foreign Languages Education; Physics; Science Education; Secondary Education)

History: Founded 1956, acquiring present status 1977.

Degrees and Diplomas: *Bachelor's Degree*; *Master's Degree*: Nursing (Nursing Education); Arts in: Guidance and Counselling; Hospital Administration; Industrial Counselling; Nursing; *PhD*: Philosophy in: Community Counselling; School Counselling; Industrial Counselling
Last Updated: 18/02/11

SAN PEDRO COLLEGE OF BUSINESS ADMINISTRATION

National Highway, San Pedro, Laguna 4023
Tel: +63(2) 808-2258
Fax: +63(2) 808-2258
Website: http://www.spcba.edu.ph

Chief Administrator: Jowell Jo N. Ching

Programmes

Graduate (Business Administration; Government); **Undergraduate and Professional** (Accountancy; Administration; Banking; Business Administration; Computer Engineering; Computer Science; Economics; Education; English; Finance; Foreign Languages Education; Health Education; Hotel and Restaurant; Hotel Management; Human Resources; Industrial Engineering; Information Technology; Management; Marketing; Mathematics Education; Political Sciences; Primary Education; Psychology; Science Education; Secondary Education; Secretarial Studies; Tourism)

History: Founded 1988.

Degrees and Diplomas: *Certificate/Diploma*; *Associate Degree*; *Bachelor's Degree*; *Master's Degree*: Business Administration; Government Management
Last Updated: 18/02/11

SAN SEBASTIAN COLLEGE - RECOLETOS

C.M. Recto Avenue, Sampaloc, City of Manila, First District, Metro Manila 1000
Tel: +63(2) 734-8931 +63(2) 734-8939
Fax: +63(2) 734-8918
EMail: hrd@sscrmnl.edu.ph
Website: http://www.sscrmnl.edu.ph/

President: Dionisio Cachero Tel: +63(2) 734-8917

Vice-President for Admistration: Dionisio Selma

Colleges

Accountancy, Business and Computer Studies (Accountancy; Business Administration; Computer Science; Law; Management; Marketing; Mathematics); **Arts and Science** (Arts and Humanities; Mass Communication; Modern Languages; Natural Sciences; Physical Education; Political Sciences; Psychology); **International Hospitality Management** (Hotel and Restaurant; Hotel Management; Tourism)

Institutes

Graduate Studies (Accountancy; Business Administration; Economics; Finance; Marketing; Theology); **Law** (Administrative Law; Civil Law; Commercial Law; Constitutional Law; Criminal Law; Ethics; Fiscal Law; Forensic Medicine and Dentistry; Insurance; International Law; Labour Law; Law; Public Law; Taxation); **Religious Education and Philosophy** (Philosophy; Religious Education)

Further Information: Also San Sebastian College - Recoletos - Canlubang

History: Founded 1946.

Degrees and Diplomas: *Bachelor's Degree*; *Master's Degree*: Business Administration; Theology
Last Updated: 18/02/11

SAN SEBASTIAN COLLEGE - RECOLETOS DE CAVITE

Manila Blvd., Sta. Cruz, Cavite City, Cavite 4100
Tel: +63(46) 431-0861
Fax: +63(46) 431-1461
EMail: admin@sscr.edu
Website: http://www.sscr.edu/

President: Emil Jaruda

Colleges

Accountancy, Business Administration and Hospitality Management (Accountancy; Business Administration; Finance; Hotel and Restaurant; Hotel Management; Marketing; Tourism); **Arts and Sciences** (Economics; English; Industrial and Production Economics; Mass Communication; Psychology; Public Relations); **Criminal Justice Education** (Criminal Law; Criminology); **Engineering, Computer Studies and Technology** (Computer Engineering; Computer Science; Electronic Engineering; Engineering; Industrial Engineering; Information Management; Information Technology; Technology; Telecommunications Engineering); **Nursing** (Nursing)

Graduate Schools

Business (Business Administration)

History: Founded 1966. Formerly known as San Sebastian College - Recoletos.

Degrees and Diplomas: *Certificate/Diploma*; *Bachelor's Degree*; *Master's Degree*: Business Administration
Last Updated: 18/02/11

SAN SEBASTIAN COLLEGE - SABLAYAN

Colegio de San Sebastian - Sablayan

Dangeros, Sablayan, Occidental Mindoro 5104

President: Wilfredo M. Del Parto, SVD

Programmes

Undergraduate and Professional (Accountancy; Business and Commerce; Education; Management; Mathematics Education; Nursing; Primary Education)

History: Founded 1976, acquired present status and title 1988.

Degrees and Diplomas: *Certificate/Diploma*; *Bachelor's Degree*
Last Updated: 08/09/10

SANTA CATALINA DE ALEJANDRIA COLLEGE

Colegio de Santa Catalina de Alejandria

Bishop Epifanio B. Surban Street, Dumaguete City, Negros Oriental 6200
Tel: +63(35) 225-4831
Fax: +63(35) 225-7435
EMail: cosca1@globelines.com.ph

President: John F. Du

Programmes

Commerce (Accountancy; Business Administration; Computer Science; Hotel and Restaurant; Hotel Management; Information Management; Management; Taxation); **Criminology** (Criminology); **Education** (Education; Physical Education; Secondary Education; Teacher Training)

History: Founded 1959, acquired present status and title 1969.

Degrees and Diplomas: *Bachelor's Degree*; *Master's Degree*
Last Updated: 08/09/10

SANTA CLARA DE MONTEFALCO

City of Meycauayan, Bulacan 3020
Tel: +63(44) 695-3647
Fax: +63(44) 695-3656

President: Carolina Yumul

Programmes

Nursing (Nursing)

Degrees and Diplomas: *Bachelor's Degree*
Last Updated: 18/02/11

SANTA CRUZ INSTITUTE

Bonifacio St. Brgy. Banahaw, Sta. Cruz, Marinduque 4902
Tel: +63(42) 321-1037
Fax: +63(42) 321-1037
EMail: santacruzinstitute_marinduque@yahoo.com

President: Raquel Retardo Pedro

Programmes

Undergraduate and Professional (Business and Commerce; Computer Science; English; Filipino; Foreign Languages Education; Information Management; Management; Mathematics Education; Native Language Education; Secondary Education; Social Sciences)

Degrees and Diplomas: *Certificate/Diploma*; *Bachelor's Degree*
Last Updated: 18/02/11

SANTA CRUZ MISSION SCHOOL

Lem-Ehek, Poblacion, Lake Sebu, South Cotabato 9512
Tel: +63(83) 228-2313
Fax: +63(83) 228-2313
EMail: scmsilakesebu@yahoo.com

President: Maria L. Gandam

Programmes

Community Development (Town Planning; Urban Studies)

History: Founded 1984.

Degrees and Diplomas: *Bachelor's Degree*
Last Updated: 18/02/11

SANTA ISABEL COLLEGE

210 Taft Avenue, City of Manila, First District, Metro Manila 1000
Tel: +63(2) 525-9416
Fax: +63(2) 524-7340
EMail: santaisabel@dcphilippines.org
Website: http://santaisabel.dcphilippines.org/

President: Josefina R. Quiachon

Programmes

Business Administration and Accountancy (Accountancy; Business Administration; Finance; Hotel and Restaurant; Hotel Management; Human Resources; Management; Marketing; Public Relations); **Computer Science** (Computer Science; Information Technology); **Liberal Arts and Education** (Arts and Humanities; Education; Educational and Student Counselling; Primary Education; Secondary Education; Teacher Training); **Music** (Music; Music Education; Music Theory and Composition; Musical Instruments; Singing)

History: Founded 1632.

Degrees and Diplomas: *Certificate/Diploma*; *Associate Degree*; *Bachelor's Degree*; *Master's Degree*: Arts in Education; Music (Composition; Voice; Piano; Music Education)
Last Updated: 18/02/11

SANTA MONICA - MANILA COLLEGE

Colegio de Santa Monica - Manila

98 Marcos Alvarez Avenue, Las Piñas City, Fourth District, Metro Manila

President: Jose Luis G. Tribiño

Programmes

Business Administration (Business Administration); **Nursing** (Nursing)

History: Founded 2003.

Degrees and Diplomas: *Bachelor's Degree*
Last Updated: 08/09/10

SANTA MONICA INSTITUTE OF TECHNOLOGY

Cabili Avenue, Iligan City, Lanao del Norte 9200
Tel: +63(63) 221-2678
Fax: +63(63) 221-2678
EMail: smit@mozcom.com

President: Felicisimo M. Ungui, Jr.

Programmes

Education (Education; English; Filipino; Foreign Languages Education; Mathematics Education; Native Language Education; Primary Education; Secondary Education); **Industrial Education** (Automotive Engineering; Electrical Engineering; Electronic Engineering; Heating and Refrigeration; Home Economics Education; Industrial Arts Education; Technology Education)

History: Founded 1985.

Degrees and Diplomas: *Certificate/Diploma*; *Bachelor's Degree*
Last Updated: 18/02/11

SANTA MONICA OF POLANGUI COLLEGE

Colegio de Santa Monica of Polangui

Centro, Polangui, Albay 4506
Tel: +63(52) 486-2245

President: Merly R. Ortiz

Programmes

Undergraduate and Professional (Banking; Business Administration; Business and Commerce; Economics; English; Finance; Management; Marketing; Political Sciences)

History: Founded 1997.

Degrees and Diplomas: *Certificate/Diploma*; *Bachelor's Degree*
Last Updated: 08/09/10

SANTA RITA COLLEGE

Colegio de Santa Rita

Atienza Avenue, San Carlos City, Negros Occidental 6127
Tel: +63(34) 312-6212
Fax: +63(34) 312-6824
EMail: csr@greendot.com.ph

Director: Ma. Benecia A. Olaño

Programmes

Graduate (Education; Educational Administration; Educational and Student Counselling; Filipino; Native Language Education); **Undergraduate and Professional** (Accountancy; Business Administration; Computer Science; Education; Educational and Student Counselling; English; Filipino; Finance; Foreign Languages Education; Home Economics Education; Information Technology;

Management; Mathematics Education; Midwifery; Native Language Education; Nursing; Philosophy; Primary Education; Secondary Education)

History: Founded 1933, acquired present status and title 1946.

Degrees and Diplomas: *Certificate/Diploma*; *Bachelor's Degree*; *Master's Degree*

Last Updated: 08/09/10

SANTIAGO CITY COLLEGES

National Highway, City of Santiago, Isabela 3311
Tel: +63(78) 682-6366
EMail: santiagocitycolleges@yahoo.com

President: Eligio A. Montero III

Programmes

Criminology (Criminology)

Degrees and Diplomas: *Bachelor's Degree*

Last Updated: 18/02/11

SANTO NIÑO DE CABUYAO COLLEGE

Colegio de Santo Niño de Cabuyao

Sto. Niño Street, Poblacion, Cabuyao, Laguna 4025
Tel: +63(49) 531-4771
Fax: +63(49) 531-4771
EMail: csnc@laguna.net

Director: Jasmin H. Acuña

Programmes

Undergraduate and Professional (Business Administration; Business and Commerce; Education; Management; Primary Education; Secondary Education)

History: Founded 1990.

Degrees and Diplomas: *Bachelor's Degree*

Last Updated: 08/09/10

SANTO NINO DE JASAAN COLLEGE

Colegio de Santo Nino de Jasaan

San Francisco Street, Upper Jasa-An, Misamis Oriental 9003
Tel: +63(8822)760-429
Fax: +63(8822)760-429

Director: Tarcisio G. Absin

Programmes

Undergraduate and Professional Studies (Business Administration; Criminology; Economics; Education; English; Foreign Languages Education; Mathematics Education; Midwifery; Primary Education; Secondary Education)

History: Founded 1972.

Degrees and Diplomas: *Bachelor's Degree*

Last Updated: 08/09/10

SEA AND SKY COLLEGE

Greenhills Subdivision, Pagdaraoan, La Union 2500
Tel: +63(72) 242-5224 +63(72) 700-2702
Fax: +63(72) 242-3869
EMail: Lucia_saint@yahoo.com

President: Daniel Bolong, Jr.

Programmes

Airline Secretarial Administration (Air Transport; Secretarial Studies; Transport Management); **Broadcasting** (Radio and Television Broadcasting); **Business Administration** (Business Administration; Finance; Management; Marketing); **Communication Arts** (Communication Arts); **Foreign Service** (International Relations; Tourism); **Hotel and Restaurant Management** (Hotel and Restaurant; Hotel Management); **Journalism** (Journalism)

History: Founded 1994. Formerly known as Sea and Sky School (1994-1996).

Degrees and Diplomas: *Certificate/Diploma*; *Bachelor's Degree*

Last Updated: 18/02/11

SENATOR NINOY AQUINO COLLEGE FOUNDATION

Cataluña Street, Sen. Ninoy Aquino, Sultan Kudarat 9811

President: Hadja Sittie Aisha Helen P. Acoon

Campuses

Marawi (Business Administration; Business and Commerce; Computer Science; Education; Mathematics Education; Primary Education; Secondary Education)

Programmes

Undergraduate and Professional Studies (Agricultural Engineering; Animal Husbandry; Business and Commerce; Computer Science; Management; Primary Education)

History: Founded 1994.

Degrees and Diplomas: *Associate Degree*; *Bachelor's Degree*

Last Updated: 18/02/11

SERAPION C. BASALO MEMORIAL FOUNDATION COLLEGE

Poblacion, Kiblawan, Davao del Sur 8008

President: Sofia R. Basalo

Programmes

Undergraduate and Professional Studies (Agricultural Engineering; Agriculture; Crop Production; English; Foreign Languages Education; History; Secondary Education)

History: Founded 1964.

Degrees and Diplomas: *Bachelor's Degree*

Last Updated: 18/02/11

SHARIFF KABUNSUAN COLLEGE

Bagua I, Lugay Lugay, Cotabato City, Mindanao 9600
Tel: +63(64) 421-8865
Fax: +63(64) 421-8865
EMail: skci_cot@yahoo.com

President: Bai Cabaybay D. Abubakar

Campuses

Parang (Annex) (Education; Educational Administration; Teacher Training)

Programmes

Arts (Economics; English; Political Sciences; Psychology); **Business Administration** (Banking; Business Administration; Finance; Management); **Education** (Education; English; Filipino; Foreign Languages Education; History; Mathematics Education; Native Language Education; Primary Education; Secondary Education)

History: Founded 1986.

Degrees and Diplomas: *Bachelor's Degree*; *Master's Degree*: Education (Educational Administration and Supervision; Teaching)

Last Updated: 18/02/11

SHEPHERDS COLLEGE

Saluysoy, City of Meycauayan, Bulacan 3020
Tel: +63(44) 840-7025 +63(44) 228-3406
Fax: +63(44) 840-7025

President: Rustica L. Carlos

Programmes

Computer Studies (Business Computing; Computer Engineering; Computer Science); **Education** (Education; English; Foreign Languages Education; Mathematics Education; Primary Education)

History: Founded 1938. Formerly known as Meycauayan Legaspi College (1993-1999).

Degrees and Diplomas: *Certificate/Diploma*; *Associate Degree*; *Bachelor's Degree*

Last Updated: 18/02/11

SIARGAO ISLAND INSTITUTE OF TECHNOLOGY

Sto. Niño Street, Dapa, Surigao del Norte 8417
Tel: +63(86) 231-7762
Fax: +63(86) 826-4259
EMail: siit_94@yahoo.com
Website: http://www.siit.edu.ph/

President: Rolando A. Cuartero

Programmes

Criminology (Criminology); **Elementary Education** (English; Foreign Languages Education; Mathematics Education; Primary Education); **Office Administration** (Administration; Management Systems; Secretarial Studies); **Secondary Education** (English; Foreign Languages Education; Mathematics Education; Secondary Education)

History: Founded 1996.

Degrees and Diplomas: *Bachelor's Degree*
Last Updated: 18/02/11

SIBUGAY TECHNICAL INSTITUTE

Lower Taway, Ipil, Zamboanga Sibugay 7001
Tel: +63(62) 333-2469
Fax: +63(62) 333-2469
EMail: sibugaytech@yahoo.com

President: Eufemio D. Javier, Jr.

Programmes

Business Administration (Business Administration); **Computer Science** (Computer Science); **Information Technology** (Information Technology)

History: Founded 2003.

Degrees and Diplomas: *Bachelor's Degree*
Last Updated: 18/02/11

SIENA COLLEGE

Del Monte Avenue, Quezon City, Second District, Metro Manila 1105
Tel: +63(2) 712-3668 +63(2) 414-1157
Fax: +63(2) 712-3672
EMail: admin@siena.edu.ph
Website: http://www.siena.edu.ph

President: Estrella T. Tangan

Programmes

Graduate (Pastoral Studies; Religious Education); **Undergraduate and Professional** (Accountancy; Banking; Business Administration; Computer Science; Finance; Hotel and Restaurant; Hotel Management; Management; Mass Communication; Religious Education; Secondary Education; Tourism)

History: Founded 1959. Formerly Sienna College.

Degrees and Diplomas: *Associate Degree*; *Bachelor's Degree*; *Master's Degree*: Arts in: Pastoral Ministry; Religious Education
Last Updated: 18/02/11

SIENA COLLEGE OF TAYTAY

E. Rodriguez Avenue, Taytay, Rizal 1920
Tel: +63(2) 658-8765
Fax: +63(2) 660-4761
EMail: sct@skuyinet.net

President: Mesalina E. Cloma, OP

Programmes

Undergraduate and professional (Computer Engineering; Computer Science; Curriculum; Education; Educational and Student Counselling; Electronic Engineering; English; Foreign Languages Education; Hotel and Restaurant; Hotel Management; Industrial Engineering; Management; Mathematics Education; Nursing; Primary Education; Religious Education; Science Education; Secondary Education; Special Education; Telecommunications Engineering; Tourism)

History: Founded 1982. Formerly known as Siena College.

Degrees and Diplomas: *Bachelor's Degree*
Last Updated: 18/02/11

SIENNA COLLEGE OF SAN JOSE

City of San Jose del Monte, Bulacan 3023
Tel: +63(44) 691-0936
Fax: +63(44) 691-0935
EMail: opsiena@bulacan.ph

President: Caroline Capili

Programmes

Business Administration (Business Administration; Leadership; Management); **Computer Science** (Computer Science); **Elementary Education** (Primary Education); **Hotel and Restaurant Management** (Hotel and Restaurant; Hotel Management); **Secondary Education** (English; Foreign Languages Education; Mathematics Education; Religious Education; Secondary Education)

History: Founded 1998. Formerly Siena School of San Jose (1989-1997).

Degrees and Diplomas: *Bachelor's Degree*
Last Updated: 18/02/11

SIERRA COLLEGE

9 Baliton Street, Bonfal West, Bayombong, Nueva Vizcaya 3700
Tel: +63(78) 321-4355 +63(78) 321-4449
Fax: +63(78) 321-4449
EMail: sierracoll@yahoo.com

President: Randy V. Mason

Programmes

Information Technology (Information Technology)

History: Founded 1999. Formerly known as Sierra Computer Learning Center, Inc.

Degrees and Diplomas: *Bachelor's Degree*
Last Updated: 18/02/11

SILAY INSTITUTE

Silay City, Negros Occidental 6116
Tel: +63(34) 495-1833
Fax: +63(34) 495-6390
EMail: info@silayinstitute.edu.ph; silayinstitute@yahoo.com
Website: http://silayinstitute.edu.ph

President: Rosario J. de Guzman

Programmes

Business and Commerce (Accountancy; Business Administration; Business and Commerce; Data Processing; Information Management; Management; Secretarial Studies); **Computer Science** (Computer Science); **Elementary Education** (Curriculum; Primary Education)

History: Founded 1925.

Degrees and Diplomas: *Certificate/Diploma*; *Bachelor's Degree*
Last Updated: 18/02/11

SILLIMAN UNIVERSITY (SU)

Hibbard Avenue, Dumaguete City, Negros Oriental 6200
Tel: +63(35) 422-6002 +63(35) 422-2295
Fax: +63(35) 225-4768
EMail: oip@su.edu.ph
Website: http://www.su.edu.ph

President: Ben S. Malayang III EMail: pres@su.edu.ph

Vice-President for Finance and Administration: Cleonico Y. Fontelo

Registrar: Annabelle Pa-a EMail: ora@su.edu.ph

Centres

Law and Development *(Salonga Center)* (Development Studies; Law); **Research and Environmental Management** *(Angelo King Center)* (Environmental Management; Environmental Studies)

Colleges
Agriculture (Agricultural Business; Agriculture; Agronomy; Zoology); **Arts and Sciences** (American Studies; Anthropology; Arts and Humanities; Asian Studies; Biology; Chemistry; Coastal Studies; English; Environmental Management; Environmental Studies; Filipino; History; Industrial and Organizational Psychology; Literature; Marine Biology; Mathematics; Mathematics Education; Modern Languages; Natural Resources; Natural Sciences; Philosophy; Physics; Political Sciences; Psychology; Public Health; Religion; Science Education; Social Psychology; Social Work; Sociology; Southeast Asian Studies; Speech Studies; Theatre; Writing); **Business Administration** (Accountancy; Business Administration; Business and Commerce; Business Computing; Economics; Management; Management Systems; Public Administration; Secretarial Studies); **Computer Studies** (Computer Science; Information Technology); **Education** (Art Criticism; Biological and Life Sciences; Chemistry; Curriculum; Dietetics; Education; Educational Administration; Educational and Student Counselling; English; Filipino; Foreign Languages Education; Health Education; Home Economics Education; Library Science; Music Education; Native Language Education; Nutrition; Physical Education; Physics; Preschool Education; Primary Education; Secondary Education; Social Studies; Special Education; Technology Education); **Engineering and Design** (Civil Engineering; Computer Engineering; Electrical Engineering; Engineering; Mechanical Engineering); **Law** (Law); **Mass Communication** (Mass Communication); **Nursing** (Medical Technology; Physical Therapy; Psychiatry and Mental Health; Public Health); **Performing Arts** (Acting; Conducting; Fine Arts; Music; Music Education; Music Theory and Composition; Musical Instruments; Musicology; Singing; Speech Studies; Theatre)

Institutes
Environmental and Marine Sciences *(Silliman University Marine Laboratory)* (Coastal Studies; Environmental Management; Natural Resources)

History: Founded 1901 as Silliman Institute, following donation by Dr. Horace B. Silliman to the Presbyterian Board of Foreign Missions (USA). Became University 1938. A private Institution supported by fees, donations, and grants. Since 1957 support from the United States has been channelled through the United Board for Christian Higher Education in Asia, New York.

Governing Bodies: Board of Trustees

Academic Year: June to March (June-October; November-March)

Admission Requirements: Graduation from high school and entrance examination

Main Language(s) of Instruction: English

Degrees and Diplomas: *Associate Degree*; *Bachelor's Degree*; *Master's Degree*; *PhD*

Student Residential Facilities: Yes

Special Facilities: Anthropology Museum; Biology Museum

Libraries: Total, c. 180,000 vols

Publications: Sands and Coral *(annually)*; Silliman Journal *(quarterly)*

Press or Publishing House: University Press
Last Updated: 18/02/11

SKILL POWER INSTITUTE

2/F Lores Country Plaza, MLQuezon Ext., Brgy San Roque, Antipolo City, Rizal 1870
Tel: +63(2) 696-4715
Fax: +63(2) 696-5579
EMail: spi_antipolo@yahoo.com; spi_headoffice@yahoo.com

President: Eladio A. Guevarra

Programmes
Business Administration (Business Administration; Finance; Human Resources; Management; Marketing); **Computer Science** (Computer Science); **Education** (Biological and Life Sciences; Education; Physics; Preschool Education; Primary Education; Secondary Education; Special Education); **Hospitality Management** (Hotel and Restaurant; Hotel Management; Tourism)

History: Founded 2005.

Degrees and Diplomas: *Bachelor's Degree*
Last Updated: 21/02/11

SOFTNET COLLEGE OF SCIENCE AND TECHNOLOGY

Ibayo Street, Balanga City, Bataan 2100
Tel: +63(47) 237-0077 +63(47) 791-1141
Fax: +63(47) 791-2791
EMail: softnet.colleget@yahoo.com

President: Gregorio M. Sison Jr.

Programmes
Computer Engineering (Computer Engineering); **Computer Science** (Computer Science); **Hotel and Restaurant Management** (Hotel and Restaurant; Hotel Management); **Nursing** (Nursing)

History: Founded 1999.

Degrees and Diplomas: *Certificate/Diploma*; *Associate Degree*; *Bachelor's Degree*
Last Updated: 21/02/11

SOLIS INSTITUTE OF TECHNOLOGY

Loilo Street, Managanaga, Bulan, Sorsogon 4706
Tel: +63(56) 411-1478 +63(56) 411-1001
Fax: +63(56) 411-1478
EMail: sit_97@yahoo.com

President: Flocerfida G. Solis

Programmes
Undergraduate and Professional (Business Administration; Criminology; Education; English; Filipino; Foreign Languages Education; Native Language Education; Primary Education; Secondary Education)

History: Founded 1997. Formerly known as Data Masters Incorporated Computer School.

Degrees and Diplomas: *Certificate/Diploma*; *Bachelor's Degree*
Last Updated: 21/02/11

SORSOGON COLLEGE OF CRIMINOLOGY

3928 Rizat Street, Piot, City of Sorsogon, Sorsogon 4700
Tel: +63(56) 211-2302
Fax: +63(56) 421-5417
EMail: sorcriminology@yahoo.com

President: Jose Manuel P. Marcial

Programmes
Criminology (Criminology)

History: Founded 1998.

Degrees and Diplomas: *Bachelor's Degree*
Last Updated: 21/02/11

SOUTHDALE INTERNATIONAL SCHOOL OF SCIENCE, ARTS AND TECHOLOGY (SISSAT)

Emilio Aguinaldo Highway, Palico IV, Imus, Cavite 4103
Tel: +63(46) 472-0511
Fax: +63(46) 472-0511
EMail: joepeter_ibtc2004@yahoo.com

President: Joe Peter A. Simeon

Programmes
Business Administration (Business Administration; Economics; Finance; Human Resources; Management; Marketing); **Computer Science** (Computer Science); **Information Technology** (Information Technology); **Secondary Education** (English; Foreign Languages Education; Secondary Education)

History: Founded 2002 Formerly known as Imus Business and Technological College.

Degrees and Diplomas: *Bachelor's Degree*
Last Updated: 21/02/11

SOUTHEAST ASIA INTERDISCIPLINARY DEVELOPMENT INSTITUTE (SAIDI - SCHOOL OF OD)

Taktak Drive, Antipolo City, Rizal 1870
Tel: +63(2) 658-9302
Fax: +63(2) 658-9302
EMail: inquiry@saidi.edu.ph
Website: http://www.saidi.edu.ph

President: Eligio Ma. P. Santos EMail: emaps@agila.com.ph

Programmes
Graduate Studies (Business Administration; Educational Technology; Finance; Management)

History: Founded 1965. Acquired present status 1975.

Degrees and Diplomas: *Master's Degree*: Instruction Development and Technology; Organization Development (Enterprise Leadership; Microfinance Management); *PhD*: Organization
Last Updated: 21/02/11

SOUTHEAST ASIAN COLLEGE

290 Espana Corner N. Ramirez Street, Quezon City, Second District, Metro Manila 1100
Tel: +63(2) 781-6362 +63(2) 712-3640
Fax: +63(2) 712-3209
EMail: information@saci.edu.ph; saci@yahoo.com
Website: http://www.saci.edu.ph

President: Delfin A. Tan Tel: +63(2) 711-3532

Programmes
Business Administration (Business Administration; Secretarial Studies); **Education** (Education; English; Foreign Languages Education; Home Economics Education; Mathematics Education; Primary Education; Secondary Education; Technology Education); **Health Sciences** (Medical Technology; Midwifery; Nursing; Radiology); **Hotel and Restaurant Management** (Hotel and Restaurant; Hotel Management); **Psychology** (Psychology); **Tourism** (Tourism)

History: Founded 1975 as United Doctors' Medical Center College. Acquired present title 1977.

Degrees and Diplomas: *Associate Degree*; *Bachelor's Degree*
Last Updated: 21/02/11

SOUTH EAST ASIAN INSTITUTE OF TECHNOLOGY

National Highway, Tupi, South Cotabato
Tel: +63(83) 822-0010
Fax: +63(83) 822-0010
EMail: seritine@yahoo.com

President: Milagros S. Tamayo

Programmes
Information Technology (Information Technology)

History: Founded 2008.

Degrees and Diplomas: *Bachelor's Degree*
Last Updated: 21/02/11

SOUTH MANSFIELD COLLEGE

Roman Cruz Avenue, Soldier Hills, City of Muntinlupa, Fourth District, Metro Manila
Tel: +63(2) 862-1976

President: Marl V. Ferenal

Programmes
Business Administration (Business Administration; Management; Marketing); **Science** (Hotel and Restaurant; Hotel Management; Information Management; Information Technology; Management)

Degrees and Diplomas: *Associate Degree*; *Bachelor's Degree*
Last Updated: 21/02/11

SOUTH UPI COLLEGE

Timanan, South Upi, Maguindanao 9603

President: Amil B. Kamid

Programmes
Agriculture (Agriculture); **Secondary Education** (Secondary Education)

History: Founded 2004.
Last Updated: 21/02/11

SOUTHEASTERN COLLEGE

College Road, Taft Avenue, Pasay City, Fourth District, Metro Manila 1300
Tel: +63(2) 831-8484 +63(2) 551-5693
Fax: +63(2) 831-7532
EMail: info@southeastern.com.ph
Website: http://www.southeastern.com.ph

Director: Conrad Miguel Mañalac

Programmes
Accountancy (Accountancy); **Arts** (English; Filipino; History; Psychology); **Business Administration** (Business Administration; Computer Networks; Computer Science; Finance; Management; Marketing; Secretarial Studies; Software Engineering); **Education** (Education; English; Filipino; Foreign Languages Education; History; Mathematics Education; Primary Education; Secondary Education); **Office Administration** (Management Systems; Secretarial Studies)

History: Founded 1946.

Degrees and Diplomas: *Certificate/Diploma*; *Bachelor's Degree*
Last Updated: 21/02/11

SOUTHEASTERN COLLEGE OF PADADA

National Highway, Padada, Davao del Sur 8007

Director: Peter Paul Sarabia

Programmes
Undergraduate and Professional Studies (Arts and Humanities; English; Filipino; Foreign Languages Education; Native Language Education; Secondary Education; Social Studies)

History: Founded 1951.

Degrees and Diplomas: *Bachelor's Degree*
Last Updated: 21/02/11

SOUTHERN BAPTIST COLLEGE

Barangay Bialong, Mlang, North Cotabato 9402
Tel: +63(64) 268-4020
Fax: +63(64) 268-4020

President: Pedro S. Gape

Programmes
Accountancy (Accountancy); **Arts** (Arts and Humanities; English; Public Administration; Social Sciences); **Commerce** (Accountancy; Banking; Business Administration; Business and Commerce; Finance; Management; Management Systems; Secretarial Studies); **Computer Science** (Computer Science); **Education** (Biology; Education; English; Filipino; Foreign Languages Education; Mathematics Education; Native Language Education; Primary Education; Science Education; Secondary Education; Social Studies); **Graduate** (Education); **Theology and Arts** (Theology)

History: Founded 1952.

Degrees and Diplomas: *Bachelor's Degree*; *Master's Degree*: Education
Last Updated: 21/02/11

SOUTHERN BICOL COLLEGES

Mabini Street, Masbate, Masbate 5400
Tel: +63(56) 333-2794
Fax: +63(56) 333-2794

President: Maria Luisa M. Bakunawa

Programmes
Undergraduate and Professional (Biology; Civil Engineering; Law; Mechanical Engineering; Midwifery; Nursing; Philosophy; Primary Education; Psychology; Secondary Education; Sociology)

History: Founded 1993.

Degrees and Diplomas: *Certificate/Diploma*; *Bachelor's Degree*
Last Updated: 21/02/11

SOUTHERN BUKIDNON FOUNDATION ACADEMY

Don Carlos Norte, Don Carlos, Bukidnon 8712
Tel: +63(88) 226-2424
EMail: sbfa_doncar@yahoo.com

Director: Elpidio D. Aranggo, Jr.

Programmes

Undergraduate and Professional (Business Education; English)

History: Founded 1985.

Degrees and Diplomas: *Certificate/Diploma*; *Bachelor's Degree*
Last Updated: 21/02/11

SOUTHERN CAPITAL COLLEGES

Atty. P. Conol Sr. Street, Cor. Barrientos Street, Pob. 2, Oroquieta City, Misamis Occidental 7207
Tel: +63(88) 531-1170
Fax: +63(88) 531-1170

President: Bayani P. Mendoza

Programmes

Accountancy (Accountancy); **Arts** (English); **Business Administration** (Business Administration; Economics); **Commerce** (Accountancy; Business Administration; Business and Commerce); **Criminology** (Criminology); **Education** (Education; English; Foreign Languages Education; History; Home Economics Education; Mathematics Education; Primary Education; Secondary Education; Social Studies; Technology Education)

History: Founded 1946.

Degrees and Diplomas: *Certificate/Diploma*; *Bachelor's Degree*
Last Updated: 21/02/11

SOUTHERN CHRISTIAN COLLEGE

Quezon Avenue, Midsayap, North Cotabato 9410
Tel: +63(64) 229-8323
Fax: +63(64) 229-8753
EMail: enssc@yahoo.com

President: Erlinda N. Senturias

Programmes

Graduate (Business Administration; Curriculum; Educational Administration; Management; Public Administration); **Undergraduate and Professional Studies** (Agricultural Business; Agricultural Engineering; Biology; Business Administration; Curriculum; Development Studies; English; Filipino; Foreign Languages Education; Health Education; History; Home Economics Education; Hotel and Restaurant; Hotel Management; Information Sciences; Information Technology; Library Science; Management; Management Systems; Mathematics; Mathematics Education; Midwifery; Music Education; Native Language Education; Physical Education; Primary Education; Science Education; Secondary Education; Secretarial Studies; Theology; Urban Studies)

History: Founded 1949.

Degrees and Diplomas: *Bachelor's Degree*; *Master's Degree*: Education (Curriculum and Instruction); Management (Business/ Public Administration)
Last Updated: 21/02/11

SOUTHERN CITY COLLEGES

Pilar Street, Zamboanga City, Zamboanga del Sur 7000
Tel: +63(62) 991-1847
Fax: +63(62) 992-0819
EMail: scc_1946@hotmail.com

President: Edwin M. Caliolio

Programmes

Accountancy (Accountancy); **Business Administration** (Business Administration; Economics; Finance; Human Resources; Management; Marketing); **Civil Engineering** (Civil Engineering); **Commerce** (Accountancy; Banking; Business Administration; Business and Commerce; Finance; Management; Marketing); **Computer Science** (Computer Science); **Criminology** (Criminology); **Customs Administration** (Taxation); **Education** (Curriculum; Education; English; Filipino; Foreign Languages Education; Mathematics Education; Native Language Education; Primary Education; Secondary Education); **Information** (Information Technology); **Information Management** (Information Management); **Liberal Arts** (English; Filipino); **Office Administration** (Business Computing; Computer Education; Secretarial Studies)

History: Founded 1946.

Degrees and Diplomas: *Bachelor's Degree*
Last Updated: 21/02/11

SOUTHERN DE ORO PHILIPPINES COLLEGE

Julio Pacana, Cagayan de Oro City, Misamis Oriental 9000
Tel: +63(88) 856-2609 +63(88) 856-2610
Fax: +63(88) 856-2610
EMail: southphilcollege@yahoo.com
Website: http://www.southphilcollege.com

President: Alfredo A. Delgado

Programmes

Arts and Humanities (Arts and Humanities; Economics; English); **Business and Commerce** (Banking; Business Administration; Business and Commerce; Business Computing; Criminology; Finance; Hotel and Restaurant; Management; Management Systems; Marketing; Secretarial Studies); **Education** (Education; Educational Administration; English; Filipino; Foreign Languages Education; Mathematics Education; Native Language Education; Secondary Education); **Graduate** (Educational Administration; Secondary Education); **Hotel and Restaurant Management** (Hotel and Restaurant; Hotel Management); **Science** (Criminology; Marine Transport; Primary Education)

History: Founded 1982. Formerly known as Southern Philippines Academy.

Degrees and Diplomas: *Associate Degree*; *Bachelor's Degree*; *Master's Degree*: Arts in: Educational Management; Secondary Education
Last Updated: 21/02/11

SOUTHERN LUZON COLLEGE

Congressional East Avenue, Dasmariñas, Cavite 4114
Tel: +63(46) 416-4166
Fax: +63(46) 416-4168

Chairperson, Management Committee: Marilou V. Pagaduan

Programmes

Undergraduate and Professional (Accountancy; Business Administration; Computer Science; Hotel and Restaurant; Hotel Management; Industrial Arts Education; Marine Transport; Taxation)

History: Founded 1994. Formerly known as Southern Luzon College of Business, Maritime Science and Technology.

Degrees and Diplomas: *Certificate/Diploma*; *Associate Degree*; *Bachelor's Degree*
Last Updated: 21/02/11

SOUTHERN LUZON INSTITUTE

San Buenaventura, Bulan, Sorsogon 4706
Tel: +63(58) 411-1612
EMail: slikrams@hotmail.com

President: Remedios A. Villamor

Programmes

Undergraduate and Professional (Business and Commerce; Education; English; Foreign Languages Education; Management; Primary Education; Secondary Education)

History: Founded 1924. Formerly known as K. R. Asuncion Memorial School.

Degrees and Diplomas: *Bachelor's Degree*
Last Updated: 21/02/11

SOUTHERN LUZON TECHNOLOGICAL COLLEGE FOUNDATION

Astillero Bldg., Oro Site, Legazpi City, Albay 4500
Tel: +63(52) 480-8939 +63(52) 820-1474
Fax: +63(52) 480-8939
EMail: sltfi@yahoo.com

President: Rosemarie Quinto-Rey

Programmes

Computer Engineering (Computer Engineering); **Computer Science** (Computer Science); **Information Systems** (Information Technology); **Secondary Education** (Education; English; Foreign Languages Education; Mathematics Education; Secondary Education)

History: Founded 1990.

Degrees and Diplomas: *Certificate/Diploma*; *Bachelor's Degree*
Last Updated: 21/02/11

SOUTHERN MASBATE ROOSEVELT COLLEGE

Katipunan, Placer, Masbate 5408
Director/Registrar: Melba A. Calipay

Programmes

Undergraduate and Professional (English; Foreign Languages Education; Primary Education; Secondary Education)

History: Founded 1949.Formerly known as Southern Masbate Roosevelt Junior College.

Degrees and Diplomas: *Bachelor's Degree*
Last Updated: 22/02/11

SOUTHERN MINDANAO COLLEGE - AGRO TECH

Sumadat, Dumalinao, Zamboanga del Sur 7015
President: Romeo C. Hofileña

Programmes

Agricultural Technology (Agricultural Engineering)

History: Founded 1969.

Degrees and Diplomas: *Bachelor's Degree*
Last Updated: 22/02/11

SOUTHERN MINDANAO COLLEGES

Jamisola Street, Sta. Lucia District, Pagadian City, Zamboanga del Sur 7016
Tel: +63(62) 214-4804 +63(62) 215-2257
Fax: +63(62) 215-2589
EMail: gavenia_2003@yahoo.com
President: Romeo C. Hofileña Tel: +63(62) 215-1624

Programmes

Arts (English; History; Political Sciences; Psychology; Public Administration; Sociology); **Business Administration** (Business Administration); **Civil Engineering** (Civil Engineering); **Commerce** (Accountancy; Banking; Business and Commerce; Finance; Management); **Computer Engineering** (Computer Engineering); **Computer Science** (Computer Science); **Criminology** (Criminology); **Electrical Engineering** (Electrical Engineering); **Electronics and Communication Engineering** (Electronic Engineering; Telecommunications Engineering); **Geodetic Engineering** (Earth Sciences; Geological Engineering); **Graduate** (Business Administration; Education; Educational Administration; Educational and Student Counselling; Educational Psychology; Public Administration); **Hotel and Restaurant Management** (Hotel and Restaurant; Hotel Management); **Industrial Education** (Industrial Arts Education); **Information Management** (Information Management); **Information Technology** (Information Technology); **Office Administration** (Computer Education; Management Systems; Secretarial Studies); **Primary Education** (Education; English; Filipino; Foreign Languages Education; Health Education; Home Economics Education; Mathematics Education; Native Language Education; Primary Education; Science Education); **Secondary Education** (Art Education; Biological and Life Sciences; English; Ethics; Filipino; Foreign Languages Education; Health Education; Home Economics Education; Mathematics Education; Music Education; Native Language Education; Physical Education; Physics; Science Education; Secondary Education; Social Studies; Technology Education); **Social Work** (Social Work)

History: Founded 1940.

Degrees and Diplomas: *Bachelor's Degree*; *Master's Degree*: Business Administration; Public Administration; Arts in Education (Guidance and Counselling; Educational Management; Psychology); *PhD*: Educational Management
Last Updated: 22/02/11

SOUTHERN MINDANAO INSTITUTE OF TECHNOLOGY

National Highway, Tacurong City, Sultan Kudarat 9800
Tel: +63(64) 200-3549
Fax: +63(64) 200-3549

President: Federico S. Señeres, Sr.

Programmes

Undergraduate and Professional Studies (Business and Commerce; Criminology; Education; Electronic Engineering; English; Foreign Languages Education; Hotel and Restaurant; Hotel Management; Industrial Arts Education; Information Technology; Management Systems; Mass Communication; Primary Education; Secondary Education; Secretarial Studies)

History: Founded 1985.

Degrees and Diplomas: *Certificate/Diploma*; *Bachelor's Degree*
Last Updated: 22/02/11

SOUTHERN NEGROS COLLEGE

Crossing Da-an, Binalbagan, Negros Occidental 6107
Tel: +63(34) 388-8244 +63(34) 432-5515

President and Director: David V. Lopez

Programmes

Commerce (Business and Commerce)

History: Founded 1947.

Degrees and Diplomas: *Bachelor's Degree*
Last Updated: 22/02/11

SOUTHERN PENINSULA COLLEGE

Corner Padre Zamora-Tamblots Streets, Labason, Zamboanga del Norte 7117
Tel: +63(65) 377-2144
Fax: +63(65) 377-2144
EMail: spenc_04@yahoo.com.ph

President: Romeo E. Delgado

Programmes

Commerce (Business and Commerce; Management); **Education** (Education; English; Foreign Languages Education; Mathematics Education; Primary Education; Secondary Education)

History: Founded 2004.

Degrees and Diplomas: *Certificate/Diploma*; *Bachelor's Degree*
Last Updated: 22/02/11

SOUTHERN PHILIPPINE ADVENTIST COLLEGE

Camanchiles, Matanao, Davao del Sur 8002
Tel: +63(82) 511-8075
Fax: +63(82) 511-8074
EMail: venus_escobidal@yahoo.com.ph

President: Chliejvferwyn C. Catolico

Programmes

Arts (Theology); **Business and Office Administration** (Accountancy; Business Administration; Management; Management Systems; Secretarial Studies); **Computer Science** (Computer Science); **Education** (Education; English; Foreign Languages Education; Mathematics Education; Primary Education; Secondary Education)

History: Founded 1950.

Degrees and Diplomas: *Bachelor's Degree*
Last Updated: 22/02/11

SOUTHERN PHILIPPINE COLLEGE

Corner Padre Zamora - Tamblots Streets, Labason, Zamboanga del Norte 7117

Chairman: Neo E. Orendain

Programmes

Undergraduate and Professional Studies (Business and Commerce; Curriculum; Data Processing; Education; English; Foreign Languages Education; Management; Primary Education; Secondary Education; Software Engineering)

History: Founded 1946.

Degrees and Diplomas: *Bachelor's Degree*

Last Updated: 22/02/11

SOUTHERN PHILIPPINES COLLEGE OF SCIENCES AND HEALTH EDUCATION

Lidasan-Ayunan Bldg., Poblacion 1, Parang, Shariff Kabunsuan 9604

Tel: +63(64) 425-0066

Fax: +63(64) 421-1969

College Administrator: Ma. Carmen Echavez

Programmes

Business Administration (Business Administration; Management); **Criminology** (Criminology); **Nursing** (Midwifery; Nursing); **Primary Education** (English; Filipino; Foreign Languages Education; History; Mathematics Education; Primary Education; Science Education); **Secondary Education** (English; Filipino; Foreign Languages Education; History; Mathematics Education; Native Language Education; Science Education; Secondary Education)

History: Founded 2005.

Degrees and Diplomas: *Bachelor's Degree*

Last Updated: 22/02/11

SOUTHERN PHILIPPINES INSTITUTE OF SCIENCE AND TECHNOLOGY

Anabu II-A, Imus, Cavite 4103

Tel: +63(46) 875-3458

Fax: +63(46) 471-0712

President: Erlinda Manzanero

Programmes

Undergraduate and Professional (Accountancy; Business Administration; Computer Engineering; Computer Science; Electronic Engineering; English; Finance; Foreign Languages Education; Hotel and Restaurant; Hotel Management; Information Technology; Management; Management Systems; Marketing; Mathematics Education; Preschool Education; Primary Education; Psychology; Science Education; Secondary Education; Social Studies; Telecommunications Engineering; Tourism)

History: Founded 1999.

Degrees and Diplomas: *Certificate/Diploma*; *Bachelor's Degree*

Last Updated: 22/02/11

SOUTHERN PHILIPPINES METHODIST COLLEGE

Spottswood Methodist Center, City of Kidapawan, North Cotabato 9400

Tel: +63(64) 278-4297

EMail: spmckidapawan@yahoo.com

President (Acting): Lina D. Villanueva

Programmes

Education (Education; Preschool Education; Primary Education); **Theology** (Theology)

History: Founded 1994.

Degrees and Diplomas: *Bachelor's Degree*

Last Updated: 22/02/11

SOUTHERN TECHNOLOGICAL INSTITUTE OF THE PHILIPPINES

Andres Soriano Avenue, Brgy. Mangagoy, Bislig City, Surigao del Sur 8311

Tel: +63(86) 853-5005

EMail: stip@eudoramail.com

President/Chairperson: Josephina Toyco Franco

Programmes

Criminology (Criminology); **Education** (Education; English; Foreign Languages Education)

History: Founded 1976 as Saint Josph Technical School, acquiring present title and status in 1986.

Degrees and Diplomas: *Bachelor's Degree*

Last Updated: 22/02/11

SOUTH ILOCANDIA COLLEGE OF ARTS AND TECHNOLOGY

San Eugenio, Aringay, La Union 2503

Tel: +63(72) 521-3207 +63(72) 714-0213

Fax: +63(72) 521-0101

EMail: sicatcollege_aringay@yahoo.com

Chief Executive Officer: Petronilo B. Floragues

Programmes

Accountancy (Accountancy); **Computer Science** (Computer Science); **Criminology** (Criminology); **Secondary Education** (English; Filipino; Foreign Languages Education; Native Language Education; Secondary Education)

History: Founded 2000.

Degrees and Diplomas: *Certificate/Diploma*; *Bachelor's Degree*

Last Updated: 21/02/11

SOUTHLAND COLLEGE

Don Emilio Village, Kabankalan City, Negros Occidental

President: Anecito Villaluz, Jr.

Programmes

Undergraduate and Professional (Accountancy; Business Administration; Midwifery; Nursing)

History: Founded 2009.

Degrees and Diplomas: *Bachelor's Degree*

Last Updated: 22/02/11

SOUTHVILLE INTERNATIONAL SCHOOL AND COLLEGES (SISC)

2181 Tropical Avenue corner Luxembourg Street, BF Homes International, City of Las Piñas, Fourth District, Metro Manila 1700

Tel: +63(2) 825-2358 +63(2) 820-8702

Fax: +63(2) 829-3960

EMail: pr@southville.edu.ph

Website: http://www.sville.edu.ph

Programmes

Undergraduate and Professional (Business Administration; Communication Arts; Computer Science; Education; Fashion Design; Finance; Health Education; Human Resources; Information Technology; Management; Marketing; Mass Communication; Mathematics Education; Media Studies; Nursing; Primary Education; Psychology; Secondary Education; Special Education; Tourism)

History: Founded 2002. Formerly Southville International School.

Degrees and Diplomas: *Bachelor's Degree*

Last Updated: 22/02/11

SOUTHWAY COLLEGE OF TECHNOLOGY

National Highway, Brgy.3, San Francisco, Agusan del Sur 8501

Tel: +63(85) 839-4476

EMail: socotech95@yahoo.com

President/Director: Melecerio S. Flores

Programmes

Accounting Technology (Accountancy); **Criminology** (Criminology); **Health Services** (Health Education; Midwifery; Nursing);

Hotel and Restaurant Management (Hotel and Restaurant; Hotel Management); **Information Technology** (Information Technology); **Public and Business Adminstration** (Business Administration; Government; Management; Public Administration)

History: Founded 1995.

Degrees and Diplomas: *Associate Degree*; *Bachelor's Degree*

Last Updated: 22/02/11

SOUTHWESTERN INSTITUTE OF BUSINESS AND TECHNOLOGY

Nautical Highway, Panggulayan, Pinamalayan, Oriental Mindoro 5208

Tel: +63(43) 284-4318

Fax: +63(43) 284-4317

President: Gregorio R. Lamanilao

Programmes

Graduate (Business Administration; Educational Administration; Mathematics Education; Public Administration); **Undergraduate and Professional** (Business Administration; Hotel and Restaurant; Hotel Management; Information Technology; Primary Education; Taxation)

History: Founded 2006.

Degrees and Diplomas: *Bachelor's Degree*; *Master's Degree*: Business Administration; Educational Management; Mathematics Education; Public Administration

Last Updated: 22/02/11

SOUTHWESTERN MINDANAO ISLAMIC INSTITUTE

Serantes Street, Jolo, Sulu 7000

EMail: smii@smii-edu.org

President: Mohammad Yusop S. Ismi

Programmes

Undergraduate and Professional Studies (Business and Commerce; Civil Engineering; Law; Pharmacy)

History: Founded 1997.

Degrees and Diplomas: *Bachelor's Degree*

Last Updated: 22/02/11

SOUTHWESTERN PHILIPPINES FOUNDATION COLLEGE

Jupiter Street, Imelda, Zamboanga Sibugay 7007

Tel: +63(62) 211-6554

EMail: spfc_lmelda@yahoo.com

President: Samad L. Balabagan

Programmes

Business Administration (Accountancy; Business Administration; Business and Commerce; Management; Public Administration); **Computer Science** (Computer Science); **Primary Education** (Education; English; Filipino; Foreign Languages Education; Mathematics Education; Native Language Education; Primary Education); **Secondary Education** (English; Filipino; Foreign Languages Education; Mathematics Education; Native Language Education; Secondary Education)

History: Founded 2003.

Degrees and Diplomas: *Bachelor's Degree*

Last Updated: 23/02/11

SOUTHWESTERN UNIVERSITY

Villa Aznar-Urgello Street, Cebu City, Cebu 6000

Tel: +63(32) 415-5681 +63(32) 415-5689

Fax: +63(32) 253-7501

EMail: registrar@swu.edu.ph

Website: http://www.swu.edu.ph

President: Elsa A. Suralta (2010-) EMail: president@swu.edu.ph

Colleges

Arts and Sciences (Biology; English; Hotel and Restaurant; Hotel Management; Information Management; Journalism; Mass Communication; Political Sciences; Psychology; Social Work; Tourism); **Computer Studies** (Computer Engineering; Computer Science); **Criminology** (Criminology); **Dental Medicine** (Dentistry); **Education** (Education; Health Education; Physical Education; Primary Education; Secondary Education); **Engineering** (Civil Engineering; Engineering; Mechanical Engineering); **Law** (Law); **Maritime Studies** (Marine Transport); **Medical Technology** (Medical Technology); **Medicine** *(Matias H. Aznar Memorial College of Medicine)* (Anatomy; Biochemistry; Community Health; Gynaecology and Obstetrics; Medicine; Microbiology; Paediatrics; Pathology; Pharmacology; Physiology; Social and Preventive Medicine); **Nursing** (Nursing); **Optometry** (Optometry); **Pharmacy** (Pharmacy); **Physical Therapy** (Physical Therapy); **Veterinary Medicine** (Veterinary Science)

Graduate Schools

Health Sciences, Management and Pedagogy (Business Administration; Communication Studies; Community Health; Cultural Studies; Education; Educational Administration; Educational and Student Counselling; English; Filipino; Foreign Languages Education; Health Administration; Health Sciences; Hotel and Restaurant; Hotel Management; Human Resources; Information Technology; Management; Mathematics Education; Music Education; Native Language Education; Nursing; Pedagogy; Physical Education; Physical Therapy; Preschool Education; Psychiatry and Mental Health; Public Administration; Public Health; Real Estate; Science Education; Social Studies; Special Education; Surgery; Teacher Training; Tourism)

Schools

Business (Accountancy; Banking; Business Administration; Business and Commerce; Finance; Management; Marketing)

History: Founded 1946 as Southwestern Colleges, became University 1959.

Governing Bodies: Board of Directors

Academic Year: June to March (June-October; November-March)

Admission Requirements: Graduation from high school and entrance examination

Main Language(s) of Instruction: English, Tagalog, Cebuano

Degrees and Diplomas: *Bachelor's Degree*; *Post Baccalaureate Certificate/Diploma*: Dental Medicine; Medicine; Optometry; Veterinary Medicine (DDM), 4-6 yrs following first degree; *Master's Degree*: Arts in Nursing (Medical-Surgical Nursing; Psychiatric Nursing; Nursing Service Administration; Community Health Nursing; Maternal and Chiled Health Nursing; Nursing Education); Arts in Teaching (English Language & Literature; Science; Human Kinetics; Information & Comunications Technology; Mathematics; Social Studies; Physical Therapy; Music Education; Special Education; Filipino); Business Administration (Human Resource and Organizational Management; Hospital Administration; Real Estate and Property Management; Hotel and Restaurant Management; Tourism and Recreation Management); Public Health; Business Administration (for executives); Public Administration; Education (Educational Leadership & Management; Early Childhood Education; Guidance and Counselling; Cultural Education); *PhD*: Public Administration; Education (Educational Leadership & Management; Physical Education; Special Education); Education (Filipino Language Teaching; English Language Teaching)

Student Services: Academic counselling, Canteen, Cultural centre, Employment services, Health services, Nursery care, Social counselling, Sports facilities

Student Residential Facilities: Yes

Special Facilities: Cultural Museum. Biological Garden. Aznar Coliseum. Amphitheatre

Libraries: Central Library, c. 50,000 vols; Medicine, c. 11,000; Graduate Library, c. 5,000 vols; Engineering, c. 4,000 vols

Publications: Southwestern Research Journal *(biannually)*; The Beacon *(annually)*; The Quill

Press or Publishing House: Southwestern University Press

Last Updated: 23/02/11

SPA COLLEGE

Datu Ugalingan Piang Street, Datu Piang, Maguindanao

President: Solaiman M. Sandigan

Programmes
Arts and Sciences (Economics; English; Filipino; History; Political Sciences); **Commerce** (Banking; Business Administration; Business and Commerce; Finance; Management); **Criminology** (Criminology); **Graduate Studies** (Education; Educational Administration; Management; Public Administration); **Primary Education** (English; Filipino; Foreign Languages Education; Mathematics Education; Native Language Education; Primary Education; Science Education; Social Studies); **Secondary Education** (English; Filipino; Foreign Languages Education; Mathematics Education; Native Language Education; Science Education; Secondary Education; Social Studies)
History: Founded 2003.
Degrees and Diplomas: *Bachelor's Degree*; *Master's Degree*: Public Administration (Management and Organization); Education (School Administration and Supervision)
Last Updated: 23/02/11

SPEED COMPUTER COLLEGE

Cogon Street, City of Sorsogon, Sorsogon 4700
Tel: +63(56) 211-1057

President: Perry Auxillos

Programmes
Undergraduate and Professional (Information Technology; Midwifery)
History: Founded 1991.
Degrees and Diplomas: *Certificate/Diploma*; *Bachelor's Degree*
Last Updated: 23/02/11

ST. ALPHONSUS SCHOOL OF THEOLOGY

Brgy. Isabang, Lucena City, Quezon 4301
Tel: +63(42) 710-3127
Fax: +63(42) 660-3846
EMail: alfonsino72@yahoo.com.ph

Dean: Nelson L. Valle

Programmes
Arts (Religious Studies; Theology)
History: Founded 1972.
Degrees and Diplomas: *Master's Degree*: Theology; Religious Studies
Last Updated: 27/01/11

ST. ANNE COLLEGE OF ILOILO

Cor. M.H. del Pilar and Lopez Jaena Streets, Iloilo City, Iloilo 5000
Tel: +63(33) 337-9480
Fax: +63(33) 336-20-86
EMail: stannecol@eudoramail.com

President: Alma E. Natividad

Programmes
Undergraduate and Professional (Accountancy; Business Administration; Business and Commerce; Hotel and Restaurant; Hotel Management; Management)
History: Founded 1986.
Degrees and Diplomas: *Associate Degree*; *Bachelor's Degree*
Last Updated: 27/01/11

ST. ANTHONY COLLEGE OF CALAPAN CITY

Gov. Infantado Street, Calapan City, Oriental Mindoro 5200
Tel: +63(43) 288-8552
Fax: +63(43) 288-4255
EMail: jirsacst@globelines.com.ph

Chief Operating Officer: Jamesy I. Reyes

Programmes
Business Administration (Business Administration; Management; Marketing); **Computer Engineering** (Computer Engineering); **Hotel and Restaurant Management** (Hotel and Restaurant; Hotel Management); **Information Technology** (Information Technology); **Nursing** (Nursing); **Secondary Education** (Biology; Chemistry; English; Foreign Languages Education; Mathematics Education; Secondary Education); **Tourism Management** (Tourism)
History: Founded 2004.
Degrees and Diplomas: *Bachelor's Degree*
Last Updated: 25/02/11

STA. CATALINA COLLEGE

2260 Legarda Street, Sampaloc, City of Manila, First District, Metro Manila 1008
Tel: +63(2) 734-6861
Fax: +63(2) 734-6817

President: Ana C. Celestial

Programmes
Business Administration (Banking; Business Administration; Finance; Management; Management Systems; Marketing); **Economics** (Economics); **Hotel and Restaurant Management** (Hotel and Restaurant; Hotel Management); **Primary Education** (Primary Education; Religious Education)
History: Founded 1706. Formerly known as Colegio De Sta. Catalina (1706-1953).
Degrees and Diplomas: *Associate Degree*; *Bachelor's Degree*
Last Updated: 18/02/11

STA. CECILIA COLLEGE

108 Gen. T. de Leon Street, City of Valenzuela, Third District, Metro Manila 1442
Tel: +63(2) 293-6015 +63(2) 293-6017
Fax: +63(2) 293-6016

President: Emerson B. Atanacio

Programmes
Business Administration (Business Administration; Management; Management Systems; Marketing); **Computer Technology** (Computer Engineering); **Hotel and Restaurant Management** (Hotel and Restaurant; Hotel Management); **Information Technology** (Information Technology)
History: Founded 2003.
Degrees and Diplomas: *Bachelor's Degree*
Last Updated: 25/02/11

STA. CLARA COLLEGE

Aguinaldo Street, Tigaon, Camarines Sur 4420
Tel: +63(54) 452-3006
Fax: +63(54) 452-3006

President: Gina M. Galang

Programmes
Business Administration (Business Administration; Human Resources; Management; Marketing); **Education** (Biological and Life Sciences; Education; English; Foreign Languages Education; Mathematics Education; Physics; Primary Education; Secondary Education)
History: Founded 1951. Formerly known as Sta. Clara Academy.
Degrees and Diplomas: *Bachelor's Degree*
Last Updated: 25/02/11

STA. ELENA (CAMARINES NORTE) COLLEGE

M. Roxas Street, Sta. Elena, Camarines Norte 4611
Tel: +63(54) 201-3155
Fax: +63(54) 201-3688
EMail: secnc@yahoo.com

President: Noli D. Bayani

Programmes
Undergraduate and Professional (Accountancy; English; Foreign Languages Education; Primary Education; Secondary Education)
History: Founded 1995.
Degrees and Diplomas: *Certificate/Diploma*; *Bachelor's Degree*: 4 yrs
Last Updated: 25/02/11

STA. ISABEL UNIVERSITY

Universidad de Sta. Isabel

Elias Angeles Street, Naga City, Camarines Sur 4400
Tel: +63(54) 473-8417 +63(54) 473-9954
Fax: +63(54) 472-2871
EMail: usi-naga@eudoramail.com
Website: http://www.usi.edu.ph/

President: Ma. Asuncion G. Evidente

Registrar: Marlene C. Pacis

Vice-President for Administrative Services & Finance: Remedios T. Tidor

Colleges

Arts, Sciences and Teacher Education (Art Education; Biological and Life Sciences; Biology; Development Studies; Ecology; Economics; Education; English; Environmental Studies; Filipino; Foreign Languages Education; Management; Mass Communication; Mathematics; Mathematics Education; Music Education; Musical Instruments; Native Language Education; Physical Education; Physics; Political Sciences; Preschool Education; Primary Education; Psychology; Religious Education; Secondary Education; Singing; Social Studies; Special Education; Urban Studies); **Business Education** (Accountancy; Business and Commerce; Cooking and Catering; Hotel and Restaurant; Hotel Management; Management; Tourism); **Health Education** (Dietetics; Health Sciences; Nursing; Nutrition; Physical Therapy)

Further Information: Also USI Panganiban Campus, Naga City

History: Founded 1868 as Colegio de Santa Isabel and acquired University status 2002.

Degrees and Diplomas: *Certificate/Diploma*; *Bachelor's Degree*; *Post Baccalaureate Certificate/Diploma*: Medicine; *Master's Degree*: Management; Education (Religious Education; Mathematics; Filipino; English; Administration and Supervision; Music Education; Guidance and Counselling); Nursing (Medical-Surgical Nursing; Community Health Nursing; Nursing Administration; Maternal-Child Nursing); Social Work; Disaster Management; *PhD*: Human Development
Last Updated: 03/03/11

STA. LOURDES OF LEYTE FOUNDATION COLLEGE

Colegio de Sta. Lourdes of Leyte Foundation

Brgy. I Quezon, Tabontabon, Leyte 6504
Tel: +63(53) 323-9392
Fax: +63(53) 323-9392
EMail: csllfi@yahoo.com

President: Rustico B. Balderian

Programmes

Commerce (Business and Commerce); **Nursing** (Nursing)

History: Founded 2003.

Degrees and Diplomas: *Bachelor's Degree*
Last Updated: 08/09/10

STA. ROSA COLLEGE OF BUSINESS AND COMPUTER - CONTINENTAL UNIVERSITY CENTRE

Market Area, Sta. Rosa City, Laguna 4026
Tel: +63(49) 534-4166
Fax: +63(49) 534-4166
EMail: presking@continental.edu.ph

Programmes

Undergraduate and Professional (Business Administration; Computer Science)

History: Founded 1996. Formerly Sta Rosa College of Business and Computer (1996-2001).

Degrees and Diplomas: *Associate Degree*; *Bachelor's Degree*
Last Updated: 18/02/11

STA. TERESA COLLEGE

Kapitan Ponso Street, Bauan, Batangas 4201
Tel: +63(43) 727-1174
Fax: +63(43) 727-3718
EMail: stc_bauan@yahoo.com

President: Carlo Magno C. Ilagan

Programmes

Business Administration (Administration; Business Administration; Finance; Human Resources; Management); **Computer Science** (Computer Science); **Education** (Biological and Life Sciences; Curriculum; Education; English; Filipino; Foreign Languages Education; Health Education; Mathematics Education; Native Language Education; Physics; Preschool Education; Primary Education; Religious Education; Science Education; Secondary Education; Social Studies); **Information System and Technology** (Information Technology)

History: Founded 1940.

Degrees and Diplomas: *Associate Degree*; *Bachelor's Degree*
Last Updated: 18/02/11

STA. VERONICA COLLEGE

National Highway, Baroro, Bacnotan, La Union 2515
Tel: +63(72) 720-0174 +63(72) 242-5479
Fax: +63(72) 720-2604

President: Veronica P. Conanan

Programmes

Criminology (Criminology)

History: Founded 1998.

Degrees and Diplomas: *Certificate/Diploma*; *Bachelor's Degree*
Last Updated: 18/02/11

ST. ANTHONY COLLEGE OF ROXAS CITY

San Roque Extension, Roxas City, Capiz 5800
Tel: +63(36) 621-4185
Fax: +63(36) 621-2129

President: Paz T. Marfori

Programmes

Midwifery (Midwifery); **Nursing** (Nursing)

History: Founded 1956. Formerly St. Anthony School of Nursing and Midwifery (1956-1980).

Degrees and Diplomas: *Associate Degree*; *Bachelor's Degree*
Last Updated: 28/01/11

ST. BENEDICT COLLEGE OF COTABATO

Bishop Mongue Avenue, Cotabato City, Cotabato 9600
Tel: +63(64) 421-1969
Fax: +63(64) 421-1969

Chairman, Board of Trustees: Victoria R. Franco

Programmes

Undergraduate and Professional Studies (Accountancy; Banking; Business Administration; Business and Commerce; Criminology; Economics; Education; English; Finance; Foreign Languages Education; Human Resources; Management; Marketing; Mathematics Education; Nursing; Primary Education; Science Education; Secondary Education)

History: Founded 1993.

Degrees and Diplomas: *Bachelor's Degree*
Last Updated: 28/01/11

ST. BERNADETTE OF LOURDES COLLEGE

47 Dahlia Avenue cor. Fairlane Avenue, West Fairview, Quezon City, Second District, Metro Manila 1118
Tel: +63(2) 930-7494 +63(2) 938-2504
Fax: +63(2) 930-7494

President: Conrado M. Yap

Programmes

Nursing (Nursing)

History: Founded 2003.

Degrees and Diplomas: *Bachelor's Degree*
Last Updated: 28/01/11

ST. CAMILLUS COLLEGE OF MANAOAG

Barangay Licsi, Manaoag, Pangasinan 2430
Tel: +63(75) 519-5200
Fax: +63(75) 519-2463
Website: http://www.stcamillus.edu.ph/

President: Isabel R. Mendoza

Programmes
Midwifery (Midwifery); **Primary Education** (Primary Education); **Secondary Education** (Secondary Education)

History: Founded 2006.

Degrees and Diplomas: *Certificate/Diploma*; *Bachelor's Degree*
Last Updated: 25/02/11

ST. CLARE COLLEGE OF CALOOCAN

Old Zabarte Road, Camarin, Caloocan City, Third District, Metro Manila 1422
Tel: +63(2) 951-5224 +63(2) 962-2317
Fax: +63(2) 961-0191 +63(2) 962-1643

President: Clarita G. Adalem

Programmes
Undergraduate and Professional (Business Administration; Computer Science; Education; English; Foreign Languages Education; Management; Mathematics Education; Political Sciences; Primary Education; Secondary Education)
History: Founded 1997.

Degrees and Diplomas: *Bachelor's Degree*
Last Updated: 28/01/11

ST. CONSTANTINE INSTITUTE OF SCIENCE AND TECHNOLOGY

518 National Road, Darangan, Binangonan, Rizal 1940
Tel: +63(2) 652-1514
Fax: +63(2) 652-1514
EMail: scistech_01@yahoo.com

President: Teresa D. Vanguardia

Programmes
Business Administration (Accountancy; Business Administration; Economics; Finance; Human Resources; Management; Marketing); **Computer Science** (Computer Science); **Hotel and Restaurant Management** (Hotel and Restaurant; Hotel Management); **Office Management** (Management Systems; Secretarial Studies)

History: Founded 2005.

Degrees and Diplomas: *Bachelor's Degree*
Last Updated: 25/02/11

ST. DOMINIC COLLEGE OF ARTS AND SCIENCES OF CAVITE

Aguinaldo HighWay, Talaba IV, Bacoor, Cavite 4102
Tel: +63(46) 970-4145
Fax: +63(46) 970-4140

Administrator: Marita A. Rillo

Programmes
Undergraduate and Professional (Banking; Business Administration; Education; English; Finance; Foreign Languages Education; Hotel and Restaurant; Hotel Management; Human Resources; Information Technology; Management; Marketing; Mathematics; Nursing; Primary Education; Psychology; Science Education; Secondary Education; Special Education)

History: Founded 2003.

Degrees and Diplomas: *Bachelor's Degree*
Last Updated: 28/01/11

ST. DOMINIC SAVIO COLLEGE

Blk 1 Lot 6 Mountain Heights Subdivision Quirino Highway, Caloocan City, Third District, Metro Manila
Tel: +63(2) 961-5497 +63(2) 961-7755
Fax: +63(2) 961-5499
EMail: inquiry@sdsc.edu.ph
Website: http://www.sdsc.edu.ph

President: Nestor B. De La Cruz

Colleges
Accountancy, Business and Related Courses (Accountancy; Business Administration; Hotel and Restaurant; Hotel Management; Management; Management Systems; Marketing; Secretarial Studies); **Education and Liberal Arts** (Criminology; Education; Mass Communication; Primary Education; Psychology; Secondary Education); **Engineering, Computer Related and Technical Courses** (Computer Engineering; Computer Science; Electronic Engineering; Engineering; Technology; Telecommunications Engineering); **Health Related Courses** (Midwifery; Nursing)

Schools
Graduate Studies (Business Administration; Education; Educational Administration; Public Administration)

History: Founded 1993 as St. Dominic Savio School. Acquired present title 1996.

Degrees and Diplomas: *Bachelor's Degree*; *Master's Degree*: Business Administration; Education (Educational Management); Public Administration
Last Updated: 28/01/11

STELLA MARIS COLLEGE - OROQUIETA CITY

Independence Street, Oroquieta City, Misamis Occidental 7207
Tel: +63(88) 531-180
Fax: +63(88) 531-1675
EMail: smc_oroquieta@greendot.com.ph

Director: Isabelita P. Suarez

Programmes
Undergraduate and Professional (Accountancy; Business and Commerce; Primary Education; Religious Education; Secondary Education)

History: Founded 1964.

Degrees and Diplomas: *Bachelor's Degree*
Last Updated: 25/02/11

STELLA MARIS COLLEGE - QUEZON CITY

891 Cambridge Street, Cubao, Quezon City, Second District, Metro Manila 1109
Tel: +63(2) 912-4085
Fax: +63(2) 912-4210

Director: Adelaida Florendo

Programmes
Accountancy (Accountancy); **Arts** (English); **Business Administration** (Accountancy; Business Administration; Business and Commerce; Economics; Finance; Human Resources; Management; Marketing); **Elementary Education** (Education; English; Foreign Languages Education; Home Economics Education; Mathematics Education; Primary Education); **Religious Education** (Religious Education)

History: Founded 1955.
Last Updated: 25/02/11

ST. FERDINAND COLLEGE - ILAGAN

Sta. Ana, Ilagan, Isabela 3300
Tel: +63(78) 622-3137
Fax: +63(78) 622-3137
EMail: sfc@sfc.edu.ph; saintferdinandcollege@yahoo.com
Website: http://www.sfc.edu.ph

President: Salome S. Carino

Vice-President for Administration: Elena Ariola
EMail: elen_ariola@yahoo.com

International Relations: Elena Ariola
EMail: elen_ariola@yahoo.com

Colleges

Accountancy (Accountancy); **Business Education and Office Administration** (Administration; Business and Commerce; Business Education; Public Administration; Secretarial Studies); **Criminology** (Criminology); **Education, Arts and Science** (Arts and Humanities; Economics; Education; English; Filipino; Mathematics; Political Sciences; Primary Education; Science Education; Secondary Education); **Health and Sciences** (Health Sciences; Midwifery; Nursing; Psychology); **Information and Technology**; **Law** (Law)

Schools

Graduate (Business Administration; Education; Educational Administration; English; Foreign Languages Education; Mathematics Education; Public Administration)

History: Founded 1951

Governing Bodies: Board of Trustees

Admission Requirements: Secondary School Certificate

Fees: (Pesos): 344.00

Main Language(s) of Instruction: Filipino, English

Accrediting Agencies: Philippine Accrediting Association of Schools, Colleges and Universities (PAASCU)

Degrees and Diplomas: *Associate Degree*; *Bachelor's Degree*; *Master's Degree*: Business Administration; Public Administration; Education (Management; Mathematics; English); *PhD*: Education Management

Student Services: Academic counselling, Canteen, Cultural centre, Employment services, Health services, Nursery care, Social counselling, Sports facilities

Student Residential Facilities: 1 Ladies Dormitory

Libraries: Yes

Last Updated: 31/01/11

STI COLLEGE

6/F STI Academic Center, University Parkway Drive, Bonifacio Global City, Taguig, Metro Manila 1229
Tel: +63(2) 887-8447
Fax: +63(2) 891-3725
Website: http://www.sti.edu/

President: Augusto C. Lagman

Campuses

Alabang (Business Administration; Computer Engineering; Computer Science; Electronic Engineering; Hotel and Restaurant; Hotel Management; Information Technology; Management; Management Systems; Secretarial Studies; Tourism); **Angeles City** (Computer Engineering; Computer Science; Electronic Engineering; Information Technology; Management Systems; Secretarial Studies); **Bacolod** (Computer Engineering; Computer Science; Electronic Engineering; Information Technology); **Bacoor** (Business Administration; Business Computing; Computer Engineering; Computer Networks; Computer Science; Information Technology; Management; Robotics; Secretarial Studies; Software Engineering); **Balagtas** (Business Administration; Computer Engineering; Computer Science; Curriculum; Education; Hotel and Restaurant; Hotel Management; Information Technology; Management; Primary Education; Secondary Education); **Balanga** (Computer Engineering; Computer Science; E-Business/Commerce; Electronic Engineering; Information Technology; Media Studies; Multimedia); **Balayan** (Business Administration; Computer Education; Computer Engineering; Computer Graphics; Computer Networks; Computer Science; Electronic Engineering; Graphic Design; Hotel and Restaurant; Hotel Management; Information Technology; Management; Multimedia; Secondary Education; Tourism); **Baliuag** (Business Administration; Computer Science; Hotel and Restaurant; Hotel Management; Information Technology; Management; Multimedia); **Batangas** (Business Administration; Computer Education; Computer Engineering; Computer Science; Electronic Engineering; Information Technology; Management; Management Systems; Mathematics Education; Secondary Education; Secretarial Studies); **Cabanatuan City** (Computer Engineering; Computer Science; Electronic Engineering; Information Technology); **Cainta** (Business Administration; Computer Engineering; Computer Networks; Computer Science; E-Business/Commerce; Electronic Engineering; Hotel and Restaurant; Information Technology; Management Systems; Multimedia; Secondary Education; Secretarial Studies; Software Engineering; Tourism); **Caloocan** (Business Administration; Computer Engineering; Computer Science; Education; Electronic Engineering; Hotel and Restaurant; Hotel Management; Information Technology; Management; Management Systems; Mathematics Education; Multimedia; Secretarial Studies); **Cebu City** (Business Administration; Computer Engineering; Computer Science; E-Business/Commerce; Electronic Engineering; Information Management; Information Technology; Management; Management Systems; Nursing; Secretarial Studies); **City of San Fernando** (Computer Engineering; Computer Science; Information Technology; Management Systems; Secretarial Studies); **City of Tarlac** (Computer Engineering; Computer Science; Electronic Engineering; Information Technology); **College of Mindanao** (Computer Engineering; English; Information Technology; Nursing); **Cotabato** (Computer Engineering; Computer Science; Hotel and Restaurant; Information Technology; Tourism); **Cubao** (Computer Engineering; Computer Science; Cooking and Catering; E-Business/Commerce; Hotel and Restaurant; Information Technology; Management Systems; Nursing; Secretarial Studies); **Dagupan City** (Computer Engineering; Computer Science; Electronic Engineering; Information Technology); **Dasmariñas** (Computer Engineering; Computer Science; Electronic Engineering; Hotel and Restaurant; Hotel Management; Information Technology; Tourism); **E-College Baguio** (Business Administration; Computer Engineering; Computer Science; E-Business/Commerce; Hotel and Restaurant; Information Technology; Management; Mathematics Education; Multimedia; Nursing; Secondary Education; Tourism); **E-College Southwoods** (Business Administration; Computer Engineering; Computer Science; Hotel and Restaurant; Hotel Management; Information Management; Information Technology; Management; Management Systems; Nursing; Secondary Education; Secretarial Studies); **EDSA Crossing** (Computer Engineering; Computer Science; Information Technology; Management Systems; Secretarial Studies); **General Santos** (Computer Engineering; Computer Science; Electronic Engineering; Hotel and Restaurant; Hotel Management; Information Technology; Tourism); **Global City** (Business Administration; Computer Engineering; Computer Science; Electronic Engineering; Information Technology; Management; Nursing); **Iloilo** (Business Administration; Computer Science; Information Technology); **Kalibo** (Business Administration; Computer Engineering; Computer Science; Electronic Engineering; Hotel and Restaurant; Information Technology; Management; Tourism); **Las Piñas** (Business Administration; Business Computing; Computer Engineering; Computer Science; Electronic Engineering; Information Technology; Management Systems; Mathematics Education; Multimedia; Nursing; Secondary Education; Secretarial Studies); **Legazpi** (Business Administration; Computer Engineering; Computer Science; Electronic Engineering; Information Technology; Management; Telecommunications Engineering); **Lipa** (Business Administration; Computer Engineering; Computer Science; E-Business/Commerce; Electronic Engineering; Information Technology; Management); **Lucena** (Business Administration; Business Computing; Computer Engineering; Computer Networks; Computer Science; Electronic Engineering; Information Technology; Management; Management Systems; Nursing; Secretarial Studies); **Luzon - Calamba Branch** *(STI College of Luzon-Calamba Branch)* (Computer Engineering; Computer Science; Nursing); **Luzon-San Pablo Branch** (Computer Engineering; Computer Science; Electronic Engineering; Information Technology; Nursing); **Makati** (Accountancy; Business Administration; Computer Engineering; Computer Science; Electronic Engineering; Hotel and Restaurant; Information Technology; Nursing; Tourism); **Malolos** (Computer Science); **Marikina** (Computer Engineering; Computer Science; Hotel and Restaurant; Information Technology; Tourism); **Metro Manila (STI-Fairview)** (Business Administration; Computer Engineering; Computer Science; Electronic Engineering; Hotel and Restaurant; Hotel Management; Information Technology; Management; Nursing; Tourism); **Meycauayan** (Computer Engineering; Computer Science; Electronic Engineering; Information Technology; Management Systems; Secretarial Studies; Telecommunications Engineering); **Mindanao** (Computer Engineering; Computer Science; E-Business/Commerce; Electronic Engineering; Information Technology; Nursing; Software Engineering); **Munoz EDSA** (Computer Engineering; Computer Networks; Computer Science; E-Business/Commerce; Electronic Engineering; Information Technology; Multimedia);

Novaliches (Business Administration; Business Computing; Computer Engineering; Computer Networks; Computer Science; Electronic Engineering; Hotel and Restaurant; Information Technology; Management; Mathematics Education; Secondary Education; Tourism); **Olongapo City** (Computer Engineering; Computer Science); **Ormoc** (Computer Engineering; Computer Science; Cooking and Catering; Electronic Engineering; Hotel and Restaurant; Information Technology); **Parañaque** (Business Administration; Computer Engineering; Computer Science; Electronic Engineering; Hotel and Restaurant; Management; Management Systems; Secretarial Studies; Tourism); **Recto** (Business Administration; Computer Engineering; Computer Science; Information Management; Information Technology; Management; Nursing; Secondary Education); **Rosario** (Computer Engineering; Computer Science; Cooking and Catering; Electronic Engineering; Hotel and Restaurant; Information Technology; Nursing; Tourism); **San Fernando City, La Union** (Computer Engineering; Computer Science; Electronic Engineering; Hotel and Restaurant; Hotel Management; Tourism); **Santiago City** (Business Administration; Computer Science; Information Technology; Management Systems; Secretarial Studies); **Sta. Cruz** (Business Administration; Computer Engineering; Computer Science; Hotel and Restaurant; Hotel Management; Information Technology; Management; Management Systems; Nursing; Secretarial Studies); **Sta. Maria** (Business Administration; Computer Science; Information Management; Management Systems; Nursing); **Sta. Rosa** (Business Administration; Computer Education; Computer Engineering; Computer Science; Hotel and Restaurant; Hotel Management; Information Technology; Management; Secondary Education); **Surigao** (Computer Engineering; Computer Science; Electronic Engineering; Hotel and Restaurant; Hotel Management; Information Technology; Tourism); **Tacloban** (Computer Engineering; Electronic Engineering; Information Technology; Management Systems; Secretarial Studies); **Taft** (Computer Science; Hotel and Restaurant; Information Technology; Tourism); **Tagbilaran** (Computer Engineering; Computer Science; Electronic Engineering; Hotel and Restaurant; Hotel Management; Information Technology); **Tanauan** (Computer Science; E-Business/Commerce; Electronic Engineering; Hotel and Restaurant; Information Technology; Tourism); **Tanay** (Business Administration; Hotel and Restaurant; Information Technology; Tourism); **Tuguegarao** (Computer Engineering; E-Business/Commerce; Electronic Engineering; Information Technology); **Zamboanga** (Business Administration; Business Computing; Computer Education; Computer Engineering; Computer Science; Electronic Engineering; Information Management; Information Technology; Management; Midwifery; Nursing; Secondary Education)

Programmes

Business and Management (Business Administration; Business and Commerce; Management; Management Systems; Secretarial Studies); **Engineering** (Computer Engineering; Computer Networks; Electronic Engineering; Telecommunications Engineering); **Healthcare** (Behavioural Sciences; Health Education; Health Sciences; Natural Sciences; Nursing); **Hospitality and Tourism Management** (Cooking and Catering; Hotel and Restaurant; Hotel Management; Tourism; Transport Management); **ICT (Information and Communications Technology)** (Computer Science; Information Management; Information Technology; Multimedia)

History: Founded in 1983, focusing on computer education . In 2001, STI expanded its programme to Include non-ICT programmes.

Degrees and Diplomas: *Certificate/Diploma*; *Associate Degree*; *Bachelor's Degree*; *Master's Degree*: Information Technology
Last Updated: 28/02/11

ST. JAMES COLLEGE OF PARAÑAQUE

8408 Dr. A. Santos Avenue, Sucat Road, City of Parañaque, Fourth District, Metro Manila 170
Tel: +63(2) 820-7110 +63(2) 825-8755
Fax: +63(2) 820-7112

President: James Kenley M. Torres

Programmes

Undergraduate and Professional (Business Administration; Education; English; Foreign Languages Education; Hotel and Restaurant; Hotel Management; Management; Mathematics; Primary Education; Psychology; Secondary Education; Tourism)

History: Founded 1987.

Degrees and Diplomas: *Bachelor's Degree*
Last Updated: 31/01/11

ST. JAMES COLLEGE OF QUEZON CITY

736 Tandang Sora Avenue cor. Mindanao Avenue, Quezon City, Second District, Metro Manila 1116
Tel: +63(2) 926-3930 +63(2) 928-9259
Fax: +63(2) 926-5049

President: James Kenley M. Torres

Programmes

Undergraduate and Professional (Education; English; Foreign Languages Education; Hotel and Restaurant; Hotel Management; Mathematics Education; Nursing; Primary Education; Psychology; Secondary Education)

History: Founded 1976. Renamed Saint James School of Quezon City (1978-1995).

Degrees and Diplomas: *Associate Degree*; *Bachelor's Degree*
Last Updated: 31/01/11

ST. JOHN BERCHMANS SCHOOL OF MANILA FOUNDATION

815 R. Papa Street, Sampaloc, City of Manila, First District, Metro Manila
Tel: +63(2) 735-4670 +63(2) 735-4695
Fax: +63(2) 735-4670
EMail: saintjohnberchmans@gmail.com
Website: http://www.stjohnberchmans.co.nr

President: Lily Lim

Programmes

Undergraduate and Professional (Business Administration; Business Computing; Computer Science; Information Management; Information Technology; Management; Management Systems)

History: Founded 1991. Formerly known as A-Advance Academy.

Degrees and Diplomas: *Associate Degree*; *Bachelor's Degree*
Last Updated: 31/01/11

ST. JOHN BOSCO COLLEGE OF NORTHERN LUZON

Lingsat, City of San Fernando, La Union 2500
Tel: +63(72) 700-0164
Fax: +63(72) 700-0164

Chairman, Board of Trustees: Renato M. Abat

Programmes

Civil Engineering (Civil Engineering); **Computer Science** (Computer Science); **Criminology** (Criminology); **Hotel and Restaurant Management** (Hotel and Restaurant; Hotel Management)

Degrees and Diplomas: *Bachelor's Degree*
Last Updated: 25/02/11

ST. JOHN OF BEVERLY SCHOOL

749 Quirino Highway, San Bartolome, Novaliches, Quezon City, Second District, Metro Manila 1116
Tel: +63(2) 936-1603 +63(2) 417-9068
Fax: +63(2) 936-1603

President: Erlinda P. Mercado

Programmes

Undergraduate and Professional (Business Administration; Education; English; Foreign Languages Education; Management; Primary Education; Secondary Education)

History: Founded 1995.

Degrees and Diplomas: *Bachelor's Degree*
Last Updated: 25/02/11

ST. JOHN TECHNOLOGICAL COLLEGE OF THE PHILIPPINES

29 Jewel Street, Forest Hills Subd., Gulod, Novaliches, Quezon City, Second District, Metro Manila 1117
Tel: +63(2) 936-0622 +63(2) 937-9956
Fax: +63(2) 937-9956

President: Elpidio J. Cardenas

Programmes

Undergraduate and Professional (Business Administration; Computer Engineering; Computer Science; Electrical Engineering; Electronic Engineering; Management Systems; Mechanical Engineering; Secretarial Studies; Telecommunications Engineering)

History: Founded 1989.

Degrees and Diplomas: *Associate Degree*; *Bachelor's Degree*

Last Updated: 25/02/11

ST. JOHN THE EVANGELIST SCHOOL OF THEOLOGY

Brgy. Salvation, Leyte, Leyte 6501
Tel: +63(53) 323-3115
Fax: +63(53) 323-9299
EMail: hrvillamil@yahoo.com

Rector: Hector R. Villamil

Programmes

Theology (Bible; Pastoral Studies; Theology)

History: Founded 1988.

Degrees and Diplomas: *Master's Degree*: Pastoral Ministry; Biblical Theology; Systematic Theology

Last Updated: 31/01/11

ST. JOSEPH'S COLLEGE OF QUEZON CITY

295 E. Rodriguez Avenue, Quezon City, Second District, Metro Manila 1102
Tel: +63(2) 723-0221 +63(2) 723-0223
Fax: +63(2) 725-5197
EMail: info@sjcqc.edu.ph
Website: http://www.sjcqc.edu.ph

President: Esperanza L. Vistro Tel: +63(2) 725-5197

Colleges

Arts and Sciences (Arts and Humanities; Business Administration; Business and Commerce; Business Computing; Education; English; Finance; Foreign Languages Education; Human Resources; Information Technology; Literature; Management; Management Systems; Marketing; Mass Communication; Mathematics Education; Primary Education; Psychology; Religious Education; Secondary Education; Secretarial Studies; Social Work; Special Education)

Institutes

Nursing (Nursing)

Schools

Graduate Studies (Education; Educational Administration; Educational and Student Counselling; Educational Testing and Evaluation; Foreign Languages Education; Gerontology; Mathematics Education; Native Language Education; Special Education)

History: Founded 1932 as St. Joseph's Academy of Manila. Acquired present status 1949 and title 1957.

Degrees and Diplomas: *Associate Degree*; *Bachelor's Degree*; *Master's Degree*: Education (Special Education; Early Childhood Education; Pre-Elementary Education; Educational Management; Guidance and Counselling; Applied Gerontology; Language Teaching; Christian Formation Education); Education (Teaching English as a Foreign Language; Instructional Supervision)

Last Updated: 31/01/11

ST. JUDE COLLEGE

Dimasalang cor Don Quijote Streets, Sampaloc, City of Manila, First District, Metro Manila 1008
Tel: +63(2) 314-5833 +63(2) 731-4244
Fax: +63(2) 740-4149
EMail: stjude@stjude.edu.ph
Website: http://www.stjude.edu.ph

President: Evangeline Atienza Del Rosario

Colleges

St. Jude Cavite *(Dasmariñas, Cavite)* (Business Administration; Computer Science; Education; Hotel and Restaurant; Hotel Management; Medical Technology; Nursing; Primary Education; Psychology; Radiology; Secondary Education; Tourism)

Schools

Business Administration And Information Technology (Business Administration; Computer Science; Economics; Finance; Human Resources; Information Technology; Management; Marketing); **Graduate Studies** (Education; Educational Administration; Health Administration; Health Education; Nursing); **International Hospitality Management** (Cooking and Catering; Hotel and Restaurant; Hotel Management; Tourism); **Liberal Arts and Education** (Education; English; Filipino; Foreign Languages Education; Health Education; Mathematics Education; Native Language Education; Primary Education; Psychology; Science Education; Secondary Education); **Nursing** (Midwifery; Nursing); **Pharmacy** (Pharmacology; Pharmacy); **Radiologic Technology** (Medical Technology; Radiology); **Rehabilitation Sciences** (Occupational Therapy; Physical Therapy; Respiratory Therapy)

History: Founded 1968.

Degrees and Diplomas: *Associate Degree*; *Bachelor's Degree*; *Master's Degree*: Hospital Administration; Education (Educational Administration); Nursing; Nursing Education

Last Updated: 01/02/11

ST. LOUIS COLLEGE - VALENZUELA

005 Maysan Road, City of Valenzuela, Third District, Metro Manila 1443
Tel: +63(2) 277-9753 +63(2)292-0481
Fax: +63(2) 292-3137
Website: http://www.slcv.edu.ph/college.html

President: Raymond O. Luciano

Departments

Commerce (Accountancy; Banking; Business Administration; Finance; Management); **Computer Science** (Computer Engineering; Computer Science); **Hotel and Restaurant Management** (Cooking and Catering; Hotel and Restaurant; Hotel Management); **Office Management** (Management Systems; Secretarial Studies)

History: Founded 1978.

Degrees and Diplomas: *Associate Degree*; *Bachelor's Degree*

Last Updated: 01/02/11

ST. LUKE'S COLLEGE OF MEDICINE - WILLIAM H. QUASHA MEMORIAL

Cathedral Heights, Sta. Ignaciana Street, New Manila, Quezon City, Second District, Metro Manila 1102
Tel: +63(2) 723-0101 +63(2) 727-7610
Fax: +63(2) 727-7609
EMail: info@stlukesmedcollege.edu.ph
Website: http://stlukesmedcollege.edu.ph

President: Brigido L. Carandang, Jr. Tel: +63(2) 724-4331

Departments

Anatomy and Histology (Anatomy; Histology); **Anesthesiology** (Anaesthesiology); **Behavioral Science and Psychiatry** (Behavioural Sciences; Psychiatry and Mental Health); **Biochemistry** (Biochemistry); **Clinical Research** (Medicine); **Clinical Evaluation** (Medicine); **Clinical Integration**; **Dermatology** (Dermatology); **Emergency Medicine** (Medicine); **Foundations of Medicine** (Medicine); **Legal Medicine** (Forensic Medicine and Dentistry); **Medicine** (Medicine); **Molecular Biology and Basic Science Research** (Biological and Life Sciences; Molecular Biology; Natural Sciences); **Neurosciences** (Neurosciences); **Nuclear Medicine**

(Medicine); **Obstetrics and Gynecology** (Gynaecology and Obstetrics); **Ophthalmology** (Ophthalmology); **Orthopedics** (Orthopaedics); **Otorhinolaryngology** (Otorhinolaryngology); **Paediatrics** (Paediatrics); **Pathology** (Pathology); **Pharmacology** (Pharmacology); **Physiology** (Physiology); **Preventive and Community Medicine** (Community Health; Social and Preventive Medicine); **Radiation Oncology** (Oncology); **Radiology** (Radiology); **Rehabilitation Medicine** (Rehabilitation and Therapy); **Surgery** (Surgery); **Urology** (Urology)

History: Founded 1994.

Degrees and Diplomas: *Post Baccalaureate Certificate/Diploma*: Medicine, 5 yrs

Last Updated: 01/02/11

ST. LUKE'S INSTITUTE

Rizal Street, Kabacan, Cotabato 9407
Tel: +63(64) 248-2130 +63(64) 248-2130
Fax: +63(64) 248-2130
EMail: sli_kabacan@yahoo.com.ph

President: Edmundo J. Apuhin

Programmes

Undergraduate and Professional Studies (Business Administration; Business and Commerce; Computer Engineering; Computer Science; English; Foreign Languages Education; Hotel and Restaurant; Hotel Management; Management; Mathematics Education; Secondary Education)

History: Founded 1991. Formerly known as St. Luke's School of Midwifery and Paramedical Institute.

Degrees and Diplomas: *Bachelor's Degree*

Last Updated: 01/02/11

ST. MARY'S ANGEL COLLEGE OF PAMPANGA

San Pedro, Santa Ana, Pampanga 2022
Tel: +63(45) 875-2368
Fax: +63(45) 875-2368

President: Susan C. Ramos

Programmes

Business Administration (Business Administration; Human Resources; Marketing); **Civil Engineering** (Civil Engineering); **Communication Studies** (Communication Studies); **Hotel and Restaurant Management** (Hotel and Restaurant; Hotel Management); **Information Technology** (Information Technology); **Primary Education** (Primary Education); **Secondary Education** (English; Foreign Languages Education; Mathematics Education; Science Education; Secondary Education); **Tourism Management** (Tourism)

Degrees and Diplomas: *Bachelor's Degree*

Last Updated: 25/02/11

ST. MARY'S COLLEGE

37 Mother Ignacia Avenue, Paligsahan, Quezon City, Second District, Metro Manila
Tel: +63(2) 373-6846 +63(2) 373-6849
Fax: +63(2) 374-3073
EMail: info@smcqc.edu.ph
Website: http://www.smcqc.edu.ph

President: Ma. Anicia B. Co

Programmes

Undergraduate and Professional (Art Education; Biological and Life Sciences; Communication Studies; Curriculum; Education; English; Foreign Languages Education; Mathematics Education; Music Education; Nursing; Preschool Education; Primary Education; Secondary Education; Teacher Training)

History: Founded 1725 as Colegio del Beaterio. Renamed St. Mary's College 1912.

Degrees and Diplomas: *Certificate/Diploma*; *Bachelor's Degree*

Last Updated: 01/02/11

ST. MARY'S COLLEGE BAGANGA

Poblacion, Baganga, Davao Oriental 8204

Director: Ma. Jocelyn G. Gerarde

Programmes

Business Administration (Business Administration; Human Resources); **Education** (Education; English; Foreign Languages Education; Physics; Primary Education; Secondary Education)

Degrees and Diplomas: *Bachelor's Degree*

Last Updated: 25/02/11

ST. MARY'S COLLEGE OF BORONGAN

E. Cinco Street, Baybay, Borongan, Eastern Samar 6800
Tel: +63(55) 261-2038
Fax: +63(55) 261-2038

Director: Ma. Myrna B. Querol

Programmes

Arts (Philosophy); **Commerce** (Accountancy; Business Administration; Business and Commerce; Economics; Human Resources; Management; Marketing); **Computer Science** (Computer Science); **Education** (Computer Education; Education; English; Filipino; Foreign Languages Education; History; Home Economics Education; Mathematics Education; Native Language Education; Physical Education; Preschool Education; Primary Education; Secondary Education); **Hotel and Restaurant Management** (Hotel and Restaurant; Hotel Management)

History: Founded 1946. Later changed title of St. Joseph College - Eastern Samar to present one.

Degrees and Diplomas: *Bachelor's Degree*

Last Updated: 01/02/11

ST. MARY'S COLLEGE OF LABASON

Imelda Street, Labason, Zamboanga del Norte 7117
Tel: +63(65) 377-2157
Fax: +63(65) 377-2169
EMail: smclabason@yahoo.com

Director: Ma. Virginia C. Amadlao

Programmes

Computer Technology (Computer Engineering); **Education** (Education; English; Foreign Languages Education; Primary Education; Secondary Education); **Information Technology** (Information Technology)

History: Founded 1947. Formerly Ferrer College (1997-2000) and Saint Mary's Academy.

Degrees and Diplomas: *Certificate/Diploma*; *Bachelor's Degree*

Last Updated: 03/02/11

ST. MATTHEW COLLEGE

Miguel Cristi Street, San Mateo, Rizal 1850
Tel: +63 997-5947
EMail: matthean@gmail.com

President: Grace Ramos

Programmes

Undergraduate and Professional

History: Founded 1982.

Degrees and Diplomas: *Bachelor's Degree*

Last Updated: 03/02/11

ST. PAUL COLLEGE FOUNDATION - F. RAMOS

F. Ramos Corner Junquera Street, Cebu City, Cebu 6000
Tel: +63(32) 255-7414

President: Lourdes Libres Rosaroso

Programmes

Midwifery (Midwifery); **Nursing** (Nursing)

History: Founded 2002. Formerly know as Cebu St. Paul College Foundation - F. Ramos.

Degrees and Diplomas: *Associate Degree*; *Bachelor's Degree*

Last Updated: 25/02/11

ST. PAUL COLLEGE FOUNDATION - MANDAUE

Highway, Maguikay, Mandaue City, Cebu 6000
Tel: +63(32) 272-2985 +63(32) 346-5764
Fax: +63(32) 272-8475

President: Lourdes Libres Rosaroso

Programmes

Computer Engineering (Computer Engineering); **Computer Science** (Computer Science); **Information Technology** (Information Technology)

History: Founded 2000. Formerly know as Cebu St. Paul College Foundation - Mandaue.

Degrees and Diplomas: *Associate Degree*; *Bachelor's Degree*
Last Updated: 25/02/11

ST. PAUL UNIVERSITY DUMAGUETE

L. Rovira Road, Bantayan, Dumaguete City, Negros Oriental 6200
Tel: +63(35) 225-1506
Fax: +63(35) 225-7217

President: Ma. Nilda C. Masirag

Programmes

Graduate (Business Administration; Curriculum; Education; Educational Administration; Educational and Student Counselling; English; Foreign Languages Education; Hotel and Restaurant; Hotel Management; Nursing; Preschool Education; Primary Education; Public Administration; Religious Education); **Undergraduate and Professional** (Accountancy; Administration; Art Education; Arts and Humanities; Biological and Life Sciences; Business Administration; Computer Science; Curriculum; Education; English; Filipino; Foreign Languages Education; Health Education; History; Hotel and Restaurant; Hotel Management; Human Resources; Information Technology; International Business; Management; Management Systems; Marketing; Mass Communication; Mathematics; Mathematics Education; Music Education; Native Language Education; Natural Sciences; Nursing; Physical Education; Preschool Education; Primary Education; Psychology; Religious Education; Science Education; Secondary Education; Special Education; Tourism)

History: Founded 1904. Formerly known as Saint Paul College of Dumaguete.

Degrees and Diplomas: *Bachelor's Degree*; *Master's Degree*: Business Administration; Public Administration; English; Hotel and Restaurant Management; Nursing; Religious Education; Education (English Language Teaching; Guidance and Counselling; Curriculum and Instruction; Early Childhood Education; Educational Management; Elementary Education); *PhD*: Business Administration; Public Administration; Education
Last Updated: 03/02/11

ST. PAUL UNIVERSITY OF ILOILO

General Luna Street, Iloilo City, Iloilo 5000
Tel: +63(33) 338-1097 +63(33) 336-3648
Fax: +63(33) 336-3648 +63(33) 336-5619
EMail: spuiloilo@yahoo.com.edu.ph
Website: http://www.spuiloilo.edu.ph

Head: Carolina Agravante

Programmes

Graduate (Nursing); **Undergraduate and Professional** (Accountancy; Biology; Business Administration; Computer Science; English; Finance; Hotel and Restaurant; Hotel Management; Information Technology; Management; Marketing; Mass Communication; Nursing; Physical Therapy; Psychology; Secondary Education; Theatre; Tourism)

History: Founded 1946. Formerly known as Saint Paul College of Iloilo.

Degrees and Diplomas: *Certificate/Diploma*; *Associate Degree*; *Bachelor's Degree*; *Master's Degree*: Nursing
Last Updated: 03/02/11

ST. PAUL UNIVERSITY PHILIPPINES (SPUP)

Mabini Street, Tuguegarao City, Cagayan 3500
Tel: +63(78) 844-1863
Fax: +63(78) 846-4305
EMail: Sr_Remy@yahoo.com
Website: http://www.spup.edu.ph/

President: Remy Angela Junio EMail: sr-remy@eudoramail.com;
Vice-President for Academic Affairs: Nicole de Marie Dabalus

Programmes

Graduate (Business Administration; Civil Engineering; Computer Engineering; Education; Educational Administration; Educational and Student Counselling; Electronic Engineering; Engineering; English; Environmental Engineering; Ethics; Filipino; Foreign Languages Education; Home Economics; Information Sciences; Information Technology; Library Science; Literature; Management; Mathematics Education; Modern Languages; Native Language Education; Nursing; Physical Education; Psychology; Public Administration; Religious Education; Sanitary Engineering; Science Education; Social Psychology; Social Studies; Social Work; Teacher Training; Telecommunications Engineering)

Schools

Accountancy and Business (Accountancy; Business Administration; Business and Commerce; Finance; Hotel and Restaurant; Hotel Management; Management; Marketing; Tourism); **Arts and Sciences** (Biology; Literature; Modern Languages; Psychology; Public Administration; Social Work); **Education** (Art Education; Education; English; Foreign Languages Education; Home Economics Education; Information Sciences; Library Science; Mathematics Education; Music Education; Physical Education; Primary Education; Religious Education; Science Education; Secondary Education; Social Studies); **Health Sciences** (Health Sciences; Medical Technology; Nursing; Nutrition; Pharmacy; Physical Therapy; Radiology); **Information Technology and Engineering** (Computer Engineering; Electronic Engineering; Information Technology; Sanitary Engineering; Telecommunications Engineering)

History: Founded 1907 as Colegio de San Pablo. Renamed St. Paul College of Tuguegarao 1949. Granted university status 1982.

Governing Bodies: Board of Trustees

Academic Year: June to March (June-October; November-March). Also summer session, April-May

Admission Requirements: Graduation from high school and entrance examination for Undergraduate courses; Original transcript of Records of Undergraduate course or Masteral course for Master's or Doctarate degree respectively

Fees: (Pesos):For Undergraduate courses, 280.00-290.00 per unit; for Master's, 483.00 per unit; for Doctarate, 668.00 per unit

Main Language(s) of Instruction: English

International Co-operation: With Universities in Canada, Honduras, San Antonio and Philippines

Accrediting Agencies: Philippine Accrediting Association of Schools, Colleges and Universities (PAASCU)

Degrees and Diplomas: *Certificate/Diploma*; *Bachelor's Degree*: 4-5 yrs; *Master's Degree*: Arts in: Home Economics; Religious Education; Nursing; Arts in: Language and Literature; Psychology; Public Administration; Education (Administration and Supervision; Mathematics; Science; Guidance; Filipino; English; Physical Education; Religious Education/Values Education); Business Administration; Science in: Social Work; Teaching (English; Mathematics; Biology; Filipino; Home Economics; Social Studies; Physical Education); Nursing (Adult Nursing; Women's Health; Nursing Administration; Primary Health Care; Library and Information Science; Engineering (Civil Engineering; Computer Engineering; Electronics and Communication Engineering; Sanitary and Environmental Engineering); Information Technology, a further 2-3 yrs; *PhD*: Business Management; Psychology (Major in Social Psychology); Public Administration; Education (Major in Educational Management); Mathematics Education; Information Technology; Nursing Science, a further 2 yrs

Student Services: Academic counselling, Canteen, Cultural centre, Employment services, Health services, Nursery care, Social counselling, Sports facilities

Student Residential Facilities: For 60 Women students

Special Facilities: Botanical garden

Libraries: 49,200 vols

Publications: Pauleen *(biannually)*; Paulinette *(biannually)*; Search (Faculty Journal) *(annually)*; TECH TALK *(quarterly)*; The Paulinian *(quarterly)*; Y Gamu Na Pattaraddayan *(3 per annum)*

Last Updated: 03/02/11

ST. PAUL UNIVERSITY SURIGAO

Corner San Nicolas and Rizal Streets, Surigao City, Surigao Del Norte 8400
Tel: +63(86) 826-1725
Fax: +63(86) 826-1724
EMail: spus@spusurigao.edu.ph
Website: http://www.spusurigao.edu.ph/

President: Merceditas Ang, SPC EMail: president@snc.fapenet.org

Programmes

Accountancy (Accountancy); **Accountancy Technology** (Accountancy); **Arts** (English; Mass Communication; Philosophy; Political Sciences; Sociology); **Business Administration** (Banking; Business Administration; Finance; Human Resources; Management); **Civil Engineering** (Civil Engineering); **Computer Engineering** (Computer Engineering); **Computer Science** (Computer Science); **Criminology** (Criminology); **Education** (Biology; Business Computing; Business Education; Education; English; Filipino; Foreign Languages Education; Health Education; Home Economics Education; Library Science; Mathematics Education; Native Language Education; Physical Education; Primary Education; Science Education; Secondary Education; Social Studies); **Electronics and Communication Engineering** (Electronic Engineering; Telecommunications Engineering); **Graduate Studies** (Business Administration; Educational Administration; English; Filipino; Home Economics; Mathematics Education; Public Administration; Science Education); **Hotel and Restaurant Management** (Hotel and Restaurant; Hotel Management); **Information Management** (Information Management); **Information Technology** (Information Technology); **Nursing** (Nursing); **Office Administration** (Administration; Management Systems; Secretarial Studies); **Psychology** (Psychology); **Tourism Management** (Tourism)

History: Founded 1906, acquiring current status in 1947.

Degrees and Diplomas: *Certificate/Diploma*; *Associate Degree*; *Bachelor's Degree*; *Master's Degree*: Business Administration; Public Administration; Arts in: Mathematics Teaching; Educational Management; English; Science Teaching; Filipino; Home Economics; *PhD*: Educational Management

Last Updated: 03/02/11

ST. PAUL UNIVERSITY-MANILA (ST. PAUL UNIVERITY SYSTEM)

680 Pedro Gil Street, Malate, Manila, Metro Manila 1004
Tel: +63(2) 526-6620 +63(2) 524-5687
Fax: +63(2) 526-0410
Website: http://www.spumanila.edu.ph

President: Wynna Marie A. Medina
EMail: wmedina@spumanila.edu.ph

Vice President, Administrative Services: Milagros Amos
EMail: srmilaspc@spumanila.edu.ph

Programmes

Arts and Sciences (Advertising and Publicity; Biochemistry; Clinical Psychology; Communication Studies; Educational and Student Counselling; English; Journalism; Mass Communication; Mathematics; Philosophy; Psychology); **Business and Management** (Accountancy; Business Administration; Business and Commerce; Computer Science; Cooking and Catering; Hotel and Restaurant; Hotel Management; Human Resources; Information Technology; Management; Marketing; Tourism; Transport Management); **Education** (Art Education; Biological and Life Sciences; Curriculum; Education; English; Foreign Languages Education; Health Education; Mathematics Education; Music Education; Physical Education; Physics; Preschool Education; Primary Education; Secondary Education; Special Education); **Graduate** (Business Administration; Conducting; Curriculum; Education; Educational Administration; Educational and Student Counselling; Health Administration; Hotel and Restaurant; Hotel Management; Music; Music Education; Music Theory and Composition; Musical Instruments; Musicology; Nursing; Performing Arts; Special Education); **Music and the Performing Arts** (Music; Music Education; Musical Instruments; Performing Arts; Singing); **Nursing and Allied Health Services** (Health Sciences; Nursing; Psychology)

History: Founded 1912 as St. Paul Institution. Become Saint Paul College of Manila in 1940, and accredited in 1957. Acquired current name and became part of the St Paul University System in 2004.

Degrees and Diplomas: *Certificate/Diploma*; *Bachelor's Degree*; *Master's Degree*: Business Administration (Organizational Development; Hotel and Restaurant Management); Music (Choral Conducting; Music Education; Musicology; Performance; Piano Pedagogy; Theory Pedagogy); Nursing (Academic Management; Clinical Management); Education (Educational Leadership and Management; Guidance Counseling; Curriculum and Instruction); Special Education (Developmental Disabilities); *PhD*: Nursing Education (Leadership and Management); Education (Educational Leadership and Management)

Last Updated: 25/02/11

ST. PAUL UNIVERSITY-QUEZON CITY (ST. PAUL QC)

Gilmore Avenue Aurora Boulevard, Quezon City, Second District, Metro Manila
Tel: +63(2) 726-7986 +63(2) 726-7988
Fax: +63(2) 723-0552
Website: http://www.spuqc.edu.ph

President: Nintha Lucilla Baldado

Programmes

Arts *(Bachelor of Arts programme)* (Journalism; Mass Communication; Media Studies; Psychology; Radio and Television Broadcasting; Religious Education; Religious Studies; Theatre); **Education** (Biology; Education; Educational Technology; English; Foreign Languages Education; Mathematics Education; Preschool Education; Religious Education; Science Education; Secondary Education; Special Education); **Graduate Studies** (Biology; Business Administration; Communication Studies; Hotel and Restaurant; Hotel Management; Management; Operations Research; Psychology; Religious Education; Tourism; Transport Management); **Science** *(Bachelor of Science programme)* (Accountancy; Biology; Business Administration; Business and Commerce; Clinical Psychology; Educational and Student Counselling; Hotel and Restaurant; Hotel Management; Industrial and Organizational Psychology; Information Management; Information Technology; International Business; Management; Nursing; Psychology; Tourism)

History: Founded 1946. Formerly known as Saint Paul College of Quezon City.

Degrees and Diplomas: *Certificate/Diploma*; *Bachelor's Degree*; *Master's Degree*: Arts in: Communication; Psychology; Religious Education; Teaching Biology; Business Administration (Operations Research and Logistics; Management; Hospitality and Tourism)

Last Updated: 04/02/11

ST. PETER BAPTIST COLLEGE FOUNDATION

Poblacion, Lupi, Camarines Sur 4409

President: Medardo B. Castroverde

Programmes

Education (English; Foreign Languages Education; Mathematics Education; Primary Education; Secondary Education)

History: Founded 1965.

Degrees and Diplomas: *Bachelor's Degree*

Last Updated: 04/02/11

STO. NIÑO COLLEGE OF ORMOC

Sto. Niño Avenue, Ormoc City, Leyte 6541
Tel: +63(53) 255-3153 +63(53) 5614338
Fax: +63(53) 255-3153
EMail: snc-ormocCity@yahoo.com

Chief Executive Officer and Chairman of the Board: Nepomuceno P. Aparis I

Programmes
Arts (English; Political Sciences); **Business Administration** (Administration; Business Administration; Management Systems); **Criminology** (Criminology); **Education** (Education; English; Foreign Languages Education; Mathematics Education; Primary Education; Science Education; Secondary Education); **Tourism Management** (Tourism)

History: Founded 1986.

Degrees and Diplomas: *Bachelor's Degree*
Last Updated: 28/02/11

STO. ROSARIO SAPANG PALAY COLLEGE

Area I Sapang Palay, City of San Jose del Monte, Bulacan 3023
Tel: +63(917) 384-7094

Rector: Virgilio Wilfredo M. Cruz

Programmes
Accountancy (Accountancy); **Arts and Humanities** (Arts and Humanities; Psychology); **Business Administration** (Accountancy; Business Administration; Management); **Computer Science** (Computer Science); **Elementary Education** (Primary Education); **Office Administration** (Administration; Computer Networks); **Secondary Education** (English; Foreign Languages Education; Mathematics Education; Secondary Education)

History: Founded 1966. Formerly known as Assumption Sapang Palay College (1982-1995).

Degrees and Diplomas: *Associate Degree*; *Bachelor's Degree*
Last Updated: 28/02/11

STO. TOMAS COLLEGE

Bonifacio Street, Danao City, Cebu 6004
Tel: +63(32) 200-3037
Fax: +63(32) 200-3037
EMail: stsdanao@yahoo.com.ph; negritasabc@yahoo.com.ph

Director: Alma C. Melicor

Programmes
Education (Education; English; Science Education; Secondary Education); **Information Technology** (Information Technology)

History: Founded 2006.

Degrees and Diplomas: *Bachelor's Degree*
Last Updated: 28/02/11

ST. RITA HOSPITAL COLLEGE OF NURSING AND SCHOOL OF MIDWIFERY

2407 T. Earnshaw Street, Gagalangin, Tondo, City of Manila, First District, Metro Manila
Tel: +63(2) 251-4729
Fax: +63(2) 251-4729

President: Federico S. Marquez

Programmes
Nursing and Midwifery (Midwifery; Nursing)

History: Founded 1958. Formerly known as Scout Ramon V. Albano Memorial College (1978-1991).

Degrees and Diplomas: *Bachelor's Degree*
Last Updated: 07/02/11

ST. SCHOLASTICA'S COLLEGE

PO Box 3153, 2560 Leon Guinto Street, Malate, City of Manila, First District, Metro Manila 1004
Tel: +63(2) 567-7686
Fax: +63(2) 521-2593
EMail: sscinfo@ssc.edu.ph
Website: http://www.ssc.edu.ph

President: Angelica Leviste EMail: president@ssc.edu.ph

Schools
Accountancy (Accountancy); **Arts and Sciences** (Arts and Humanities; Education; Fine Arts; History; Information Technology; Interior Design; Literature; Mass Communication; Mathematics; Modern Languages; Natural Sciences; Nutrition; Philosophy; Physical Education; Political Sciences; Psychology; Sociology; Special Education; Theology; Visual Arts; Women's Studies); **Commerce** (Business Administration; Business and Commerce; Economics; Finance; Information Management; International Business; International Economics; International Relations; Management; Marketing); **Music** (Music; Music Education; Music Theory and Composition; Musical Instruments; Singing)

History: Founded 1906.

Accrediting Agencies: Philippine Accrediting Association of Schools, Colleges and Universities (PAASCU)

Degrees and Diplomas: *Certificate/Diploma*; *Bachelor's Degree*; *Master's Degree*: Arts in: Education (Primary Education; Special Education; Preschool Management and Education); Humanities (Women's Studies); Business (Business Management); Music (Musical Instruments; Music Education); Science (Franchise Management; Guidance and Counselling; Clinical Psychology; Accountancy; Management Psychology and Counselling; nternational Hospitality Management; Family Psychology and Counselling)
Last Updated: 07/02/11

ST. THERESE - MTC COLLEGES - LA FIESTA

M.H. Del Pilar St., Molo, Iloilo City, Iloilo 5000
Tel: +63(33) 336-1408
Fax: +63(33) 337-9508

Programmes
Computer Science (Computer Science); **Hotel and Restaurant Management** (Hotel and Restaurant; Hotel Management); **Nursing** (Nursing)

Degrees and Diplomas: *Certificate/Diploma*; *Associate Degree*; *Bachelor's Degree*
Last Updated: 07/02/11

ST. THERESE - MTC COLLEGES - MAGDALO

Magdalo Street, La Paz, Iloilo City, Iloilo 5000
Tel: +63(33) 320-8275
Fax: +63(33) 320-8434
EMail: stclib@iloilo.fapenet.org

President: Arturo A. Sebastian

Programmes
Criminology (Criminology); **Marine Engineering** (Marine Engineering); **Marine Transport** (Marine Transport)

History: Founded 1986.

Degrees and Diplomas: *Bachelor's Degree*
Last Updated: 07/02/11

ST. THERESE - MTC COLLEGES - TIGBAUAN

Brgy. Tan Pael, Tigbauan, Iloilo 5021
Tel: +63(33) 511-8679
Fax: +63(33) 511-8679

President: Arturo A. Sebastian

Programmes
Marine Engineering and Transport (Marine Engineering; Marine Transport)

History: Founded 1983.

Degrees and Diplomas: *Certificate/Diploma*; *Bachelor's Degree*
Last Updated: 07/02/11

SULTAN KUDARAT EDUCATIONAL INSTITUTION

25 National Highway, Tacurong City, Sultan Kudarat 9800
Tel: +63(64) 384-1503
Fax: +63(64) 384-1503
EMail: skei_edu@yahoo.com

President: Soledad Tamondong-Eugenio

Programmes
Business Administration (Business Administration); **Hotel and Restaurant Management** (Hotel and Restaurant; Hotel Management); **Nursing** (Midwifery)

History: Founded 1978. Formerly known as Tamondong-Eugenio Gen. Hospital - School of Midwifery (1978-1983).

Degrees and Diplomas: *Certificate/Diploma*; *Bachelor's Degree*
Last Updated: 28/02/11

SULTAN KUDARAT ISLAMIC ACADEMY FOUNDATION COLLEGE (SKIA)

Bulalo, Sultan Kudarat (Nuring), Shariff Kabunsuan 9605
Tel: +63(64) 421-4386
Fax: +63(64) 421-4386
EMail: skia_online@yahoo.com
Website: http://skiaonline.cyow.com/

President/Founder: Michael O. Mastura

Programmes

Undergraduate and Professional (Criminology; Curriculum; Education; English; Filipino; Foreign Languages Education; History; Information Technology; Islamic Studies; Management Systems; Mathematics Education; Native Language Education; Political Sciences; Primary Education; Science Education; Secondary Education; Secretarial Studies)

History: Founded 1991.

Degrees and Diplomas: *Certificate/Diploma*; *Associate Degree*; *Bachelor's Degree*
Last Updated: 28/02/11

SUNRISE CHRISTIAN COLLEGE FOUNDATION OF THE PHILIPPINES

Purok 2-B, Butuan City, Agusan del Norte 8600
Tel: +63(85) 226-5024
Fax: +63(85) 226-5024
EMail: rolina@butuan.philcom.com.ph
Website: http://sunrisechristiancollege.wordpress.com

President: Roman G. Cariaga

Programmes

Arts and Humanities (Religious Education); **Education** (Business Administration; Computer Science; Criminology; English; Foreign Languages Education; Hotel and Restaurant; Hotel Management; Primary Education; Secondary Education)

History: Founded 1994.

Degrees and Diplomas: *Bachelor's Degree*
Last Updated: 28/02/11

SUPERIOR INSTITUTE OF SCIENCE AND TECHNOLOGY OF SANTIAGO CITY

Maharlika Highway, Plaridel, City of Santiago, Isabela 3311
Tel: +63(78) 682-4068
Fax: +63(78) 682-4068
EMail: sistch@digitelone.com

Administrator: Irene B. Mendoza

Programmes

Information Technology (Information Technology); **Office Administration** (Administration; Management Systems; Secretarial Studies)

History: Founded 1998. Formerly known as Golden Lion Computer Training & Services.

Degrees and Diplomas: *Certificate/Diploma*; *Associate Degree*; *Bachelor's Degree*
Last Updated: 28/02/11

SURIGAO EDUCATION CENTER

Km 2, Surigao City, Surigao del Norte 8400
Tel: +63(86) 826-2007
Fax: +63(86) 826-2007
EMail: secreg_surigao@yahoo.com
Website: http://www.sec.edu.ph

President: Bienvenido Alex K. Bautista

Colleges

Allied Medical Sciences (Medical Technology; Midwifery; Nursing); **Business Education** (Accountancy; Business Administration; Economics; Finance; Hotel and Restaurant; Hotel Management; Human Resources; Management; Marketing); **Engineering and Architecture** (Architecture; Civil Engineering; Computer Engineering; Electrical and Electronic Engineering; Electronic Engineering; Engineering; Mechanical Engineering; Structural Architecture; Telecommunications Engineering); **Information Technology** (Computer Science; Information Technology); **Maritime Studies** (Marine Engineering; Marine Transport); **Teacher Training** (Mathematics Education; Primary Education; Science Education; Secondary Education; Teacher Trainers Education)

History: Founded in 1978 as Surigao Medical Center School of Midwifery, acquiring current title in 1989.

Degrees and Diplomas: *Associate Degree*; *Bachelor's Degree*
Last Updated: 28/02/11

SURIGAO SUR COLLEGES

Purok 6, Poblacion, Barobo, Surigao del Sur 8309
President: Carlos G. Gambe, Sr.

Programmes

Elementary Education (Filipino; Native Language Education; Primary Education); **Secondary Education** (Filipino; Native Language Education; Secondary Education)

History: Founded 1993.

Degrees and Diplomas: *Bachelor's Degree*
Last Updated: 28/02/11

SYNTACS COMPUTER COLLEGE - ORMOC

Lilia Avenue, Cogon, Ormoc City, Leyte 6541
Tel: +63(53)255-5632 +63(53) 561-1509
EMail: info@syntacs.edu.ph
Website: http://www.syntacs.edu.ph

Programmes

Computer Studies (Computer Engineering; Computer Science)

History: Founded 1999.

Degrees and Diplomas: *Bachelor's Degree*: 4 yrs
Last Updated: 28/02/11

SYSTEMS PLUS COMPUTER COLLEGE - CALOOCAN

141-143 Cor. 6th & 7th Streets, Caloocan City, Third District, Metro Manila 1400
Tel: +63(2) 367-7502 +63(2) 330-29-52
Fax: +63(2) 365-4743

President: Lourdes R. Bustamante

Programmes

Undergraduate and Professional (Business Administration; Computer Engineering; Computer Science; Information Management; Information Technology; Management; Technology)

History: Founded 1997.

Degrees and Diplomas: *Certificate/Diploma*; *Associate Degree*; *Bachelor's Degree*
Last Updated: 28/02/11

SYSTEMS PLUS COMPUTER COLLEGE - QUEZON CITY

1707 E. Rodriguez Sr. Avenue, Quezon City, Second District, Metro Manila 1109
Tel: +63(2) 412-2419
Fax: +63(2) 448-6960

President: Lourdes R. Bustamante

Programmes

Business Administration (Business Administration; Management; Management Systems; Secretarial Studies); **Computer Engineering** (Computer Engineering); **Computer Science** (Computer Science); **Information Management and Technology** (Information Management; Information Technology)

History: Founded 1989.

Degrees and Diplomas: *Bachelor's Degree*
Last Updated: 01/03/11

TABACO COLLEGE

5 Tomas Cabiles Avenue, Tabaco City, Albay 4511
Tel: +63(52) 487-5443
Fax: +63(52) 487-5443
EMail: tabcol82@yahoo.com
Website: http://www.tabacocollege.net/

President: Marie D. Biglaen

Programmes

Arts *(Bachelor of Arts programme)* (Economics; English; History; Mass Communication; Political Sciences); **Business Administration** (Banking; Business Administration; Computer Science; Economics; Finance; Information Technology; Management; Marketing); **Computer Science** (Computer Science); **Criminology** (Criminology); **Education** (Education; English; Filipino; Foreign Languages Education; History; Mathematics Education; Native Language Education; Primary Education; Secondary Education; Social Studies); **Hospitality Management** (Hotel and Restaurant; Hotel Management; Tourism); **Law** (Law); **Nursing** (Midwifery; Nursing)

Schools

Graduate Studies (Business Administration; Educational Administration; English; Filipino; Foreign Languages Education; Management; Native Language Education; Police Studies; Public Administration)

History: Founded 1982.

Degrees and Diplomas: *Certificate/Diploma*; *Associate Degree*; *Bachelor's Degree*; *Master's Degree*: Management (Business Management; Public Administration; Public Management); Arts in Teaching (Filipino; English); *PhD*: Management (Public Management; Educational Management; Business Management)

Last Updated: 01/03/11

TAGUM DOCTORS COLLEGE

Mahogany Street, Rabe Subd., Tagum City, Davao Del Norte 8100
Tel: +63(84) 400-5071
Fax: +63(84) 370-7441

President: Jonathan A. Alegre

Programmes

Nursing (Nursing)

History: Founded 2008.

Degrees and Diplomas: *Bachelor's Degree*

Last Updated: 01/03/11

TANAUAN INSTITUTE

4232 J.V. Pagaspas Street, Tanauan City, Batangas 4232
Tel: +63(43) 778-1742
Fax: +63(43) 778-1742
EMail: ti@cybat.sequel.net

President: Maria Theresa Collantes

Programmes

Graduate (Education; Educational Administration; English; Filipino; Foreign Languages Education; Native Language Education); **Undergraduate and Professional** (Accountancy; Banking; Business and Commerce; Computer Science; Criminology; Economics; Education; English; Filipino; Finance; Foreign Languages Education; Management; Mathematics Education; Midwifery; Native Language Education; Preschool Education; Primary Education; Secondary Education)

History: Founded 1924.

Degrees and Diplomas: *Associate Degree*; *Bachelor's Degree*; *Master's Degree*: Arts in Education (Educational Administration and Supervision; English; Filipino)

Last Updated: 01/03/11

TANCHULING COLLEGE

Imperial Court Subdivision Phase II, Legazpi City, Albay 4500
Tel: +63(52) 480-6106
Fax: +63(52) 480-6104
EMail: registrar1@tanchuling.edu.ph
Website: http://www.tanchuling.edu.ph/

President: Vicente N.Y. Tanchuling

Programmes

Undergraduate and Professional (Business Administration; Finance; Hotel and Restaurant; Hotel Management; Information Technology; Midwifery; Nursing; Physical Therapy)

History: Founded 1976. Formerly known as Tanchuling School of Midwifery.

Degrees and Diplomas: *Certificate/Diploma*; *Associate Degree*; *Bachelor's Degree*

Last Updated: 01/03/11

TAÑON COLLEGE

Ylagan, San Carlos City, Negros Occidental 6127
Tel: +63(34) 312-6239
Fax: +63(34) 729-9254
EMail: tañon@mozcom.com

President: Belenda A. Menchaca

Programmes

Business Administration (Accountancy; Business Administration; Finance; Management); **Computer science** (Computer Science); **Education** (Curriculum; English; Foreign Languages Education; Physical Education; Primary Education; Secondary Education); **Hotel and Restaurant Management** (Hotel and Restaurant; Hotel Management); **Political Science** (Political Sciences)

History: Founded 1952.

Degrees and Diplomas: *Certificate/Diploma*; *Bachelor's Degree*

Last Updated: 01/03/11

TASASHYASS COLLEGE

9 Zabarte Road, Ma. Luisa Subd., Brgy. 177 Camarin, Caloocan City, Third District, Metro Manila
Tel: +63(2) 961-5879 +63(2) 961-1574
Fax: +63(2) 961-3267

President: Moca Dilabakun

Programmes

Business Administration (Business Administration; Finance; Human Resources; Management; Marketing); **Health Care** (Nursing); **Hotel and Restaurant Management** (Cooking and Catering; Hotel and Restaurant; Hotel Management); **Information Technology** (Computer Science; Information Technology; Software Engineering); **Secondary Education** (Biological and Life Sciences; English; Foreign Languages Education; Mathematics Education; Secondary Education)

History: Founded 2008.

Degrees and Diplomas: *Bachelor's Degree*

Last Updated: 01/03/11

TAYABAS WESTERN ACADEMY

De Gala Street, Candelaria, Quezon 4323
Tel: +63(42) 585-7877
Fax: +63(42) 585-7400

President: Rizalina M. Sagullo

Programmes

Undergraduate and Professional (Accountancy; Business Administration; Business and Commerce; Management Systems; Primary Education; Secondary Education)

History: Founded 1928.

Degrees and Diplomas: *Certificate/Diploma*; *Bachelor's Degree*

Last Updated: 01/03/11

TECARRO COLLEGE FOUNDATION, INC.

Sandawa Road, New Matina, Davao City, Davao del Sur 8000
Tel: +63(82) 297-2511
Fax: +63(82) 297-2511
EMail: ednatec@yahoo.com

President: Edna S. Tecarro

Programmes

Undergraduate and Professional Studies (Midwifery; Nursing)

History: Founded 1989.
Degrees and Diplomas: *Bachelor's Degree*
Last Updated: 01/03/11

TECH PACIFIC COLLEGE

91 14th Avenue Murphy Cubao, Quezon City, Second District, Metro Manila 1109
Tel: +63(2) 438-1607
Fax: +63(2) 438-1604

President: Sheila O. Versoza

Programmes

Undergraduate and Professional (Business Computing; Computer Engineering; Computer Science; Electronic Engineering; Information Technology; Secretarial Studies)

History: Founded 1997 as Global School of Technology. Acquired present title 2005.

Degrees and Diplomas: *Bachelor's Degree*
Last Updated: 01/03/11

TECHNOLOGICAL INSTITUTE OF THE PHILIPPINES - MANILA (TIP P. CASAL)

363 P. Casal Street, Quiapo, City of Manila, First District, Metro Manila 1001
Tel: +63(2) 736-4208 +63(2) 733-9117
Fax: +63(2) 734-3614
EMail: tesyq@mnl.net
Website: http://www.tip.edu.ph

President: Elizabeth Q. Lahoz

Campuses

Quezon City (Accountancy; Architecture; Business and Commerce; Chemical Engineering; Civil Engineering; Computer Engineering; Computer Science; Education; Electrical Engineering; Electronic Engineering; English; Finance; Foreign Languages Education; Industrial Engineering; Information Management; Information Technology; Management; Marine Engineering; Marketing; Mathematics Education; Mechanical Engineering; Physics; Sanitary Engineering; Telecommunications Engineering; Transport Management)

Colleges

Business Education (Accountancy; Business Administration; Finance; Human Resources; Management; Marketing; Transport Management); **Education** (Education; English; Foreign Languages Education; Mathematics Education; Physics; Science Education; Secondary Education); **Engineering and Architecture** (Architecture; Chemical Engineering; Civil Engineering; Computer Engineering; Electrical Engineering; Electronic Engineering; Engineering; Environmental Engineering; Industrial Engineering; Mechanical Engineering; Sanitary Engineering; Telecommunications Engineering); **Information Technology Education** *(Bachelor and Master programmes)* (Computer Science; Information Management; Information Technology); **Maritime Education** (Marine Engineering; Marine Transport)

History: Founded 1962.

Degrees and Diplomas: *Certificate/Diploma*; *Associate Degree*; *Bachelor's Degree*; *Master's Degree*: Information Technology
Last Updated: 01/03/11

TEODORO M. LUANSING COLLEGE OF ROSARIO

Rosario, Batangas 4225
Tel: +63(43) 321-0626
Fax: +63(43) 321-0626
EMail: tmlcr_04@yahoo.com
Website: http://www.tmlcr.741.com

President: Toeodoro Karr M. Luansing

Programmes

Business Administration (Banking; Business Administration; Finance; Management); **Computer Studies** (Computer Science); **Criminology** (Criminology); **Education** (Education; English; Foreign Languages Education; Mathematics; Primary Education; Secondary Education)

History: Founded 2004.

Degrees and Diplomas: *Bachelor's Degree*
Last Updated: 01/03/11

THE ADELPHI COLLEGE

New Street East, Lingayen, Pangasinan 2401
Tel: +63(75) 542-4543
Fax: +63(75) 542-4543
EMail: rvnald@yahoo.com

President: Gladys Maricar Lopez De Guzman

Programmes

Arts and Humanities (Arts and Humanities); **Commerce** (Banking; Business and Commerce; Finance); **Education** (Education; Mathematics Education; Primary Education; Secondary Education); **Graduate Studies** (Education; Educational Administration; Educational and Student Counselling)

History: Founded 1945.

Degrees and Diplomas: *Associate Degree*; *Bachelor's Degree*; *Master's Degree*: Education (Guidance and Counselling; Educational Management)
Last Updated: 01/03/11

THE COLLEGE OF MAASIN

R. Kangleon Street, Tunga-tunga, Maasin City, Southern Leyte 6600
Tel: +63(53) 381-2014
Fax: +63(53) 570-9575
EMail: collegeofmaasin1925@yahoo.com

President: Miguel T. Udtohan

Programmes

Arts (Economics; English; Political Sciences); **Business Administration** (Business Administration; Business and Commerce; Economics; Human Resources; Management); **Computer Science** (Computer Science); **Education** (Biological and Life Sciences; Curriculum; Education; English; Foreign Languages Education; Mathematics Education; Preschool Education; Primary Education; Secondary Education; Special Education); **Graduate** (Public Administration); **Information Technology** (Information Technology); **Laws** (Law); **Nursing** (Nursing)

History: Founded 1924.

Degrees and Diplomas: *Associate Degree*; *Bachelor's Degree*; *Master's Degree*: Public Administration
Last Updated: 01/03/11

THE DOCTOR'S CLINIC AND HOSPITAL SCHOOL FOUNDATION

Gen. Santos Drive, Koronadal City, South Cotabato 9506
Tel: +63(83) 228-2019
Fax: +63(83) 228-4015

President: Arturo P. Pingoy

Programmes

Health Sciences (Health Education; Health Sciences; Medical Technology; Midwifery; Nursing; Radiology)

History: Founded 1971 as The Doctor's Clinic and Hospital, School of Midwifery. Renamed The Doctors' Clinic & Hospital, College of Nursing & Midwifery (1991-1994).

Degrees and Diplomas: *Associate Degree*; *Bachelor's Degree*
Last Updated: 01/03/11

THE FAMILY CLINIC

1452 A. H. Lacson Avenue, Sampaloc, City of Manila, First District, Metro Manila 1008
Tel: +63(2) 731-2901
Fax: +63(2) 731-2536

President: Emma C. Garcia

Programmes
Nursing (Nursing); **Physical Therapy** (Physical Therapy); **Psychology** (Psychology); **Radiologic Technology** (Medical Technology; Radiology)

History: Founded 1953. Formerly known as Family Colleges.

Degrees and Diplomas: *Bachelor's Degree*
Last Updated: 01/03/11

THE FISHER'S VALLEY COLLEGE

5 Manuel L. Quezon Street, Hagunoy, Taguig City, Fourth District, Metro Manila 1636
Tel: +63(2) 837-4259 +63(2) 839-1903
Fax: +63(2) 837-4261

President: Ronald R. Yap

Programmes
Undergraduate and Professional (Accountancy; Business Administration; Computer Science; Education; English; Foreign Languages Education; Hotel and Restaurant; Hotel Management; Information Technology; Management; Mathematics Education; Primary Education; Secondary Education)

History: Founded 1986 as The Fisher Valley School. Formerly known as The Fisher Valley Academy (1993-1995).

Degrees and Diplomas: *Associate Degree*; *Bachelor's Degree*
Last Updated: 01/03/11

THE LEWIS COLLEGE

479 Magsaysay Avenue, City of Sorsogon, Sorsogon 4700
Tel: +63(56) 211-3446
Fax: +63(56) 211-3845
EMail: tlcphil2000@yahoo.com

President: Loida Nicolas-Lewis

Programmes
Undergraduate and Professional (Accountancy; Business Administration; Computer Engineering; Education; English; Foreign Languages Education; Information Technology; Management; Marketing; Mathematics Education; Primary Education; Secondary Education)

History: Founded 2000.

Degrees and Diplomas: *Bachelor's Degree*
Last Updated: 02/03/11

THE MANILA TIMES SCHOOL OF JOURNALISM

371 A Bonifacio Drive, Port Area, City of Manila, First District, Metro Manila
Tel: +63(2) 301-9625 +63(2) 404-2543
Fax: +63(2) 301-9625

President: Dante Francis M. Ang II

Programmes
Journalism (Journalism)

History: Founded 2003.

Degrees and Diplomas: *Bachelor's Degree*
Last Updated: 02/03/11

THE NATIONAL TEACHERS COLLEGE

629 Nepomuceno Street, Quiapo, Manila, Metro Manila 101
Tel: +63(2) 734-5601 +63(2) 734-5602 63(2) 734-5605
Fax: +63(2) 734-1885
EMail: webmaster@ntc.edu.ph
Website: http://www.ntc.edu.ph

President: Priscilla Y. Arguelles

Administrative Assistant to the Vice-President and Registrar: Evangeline Q. Mallillin

Programmes
Graduate (Education; Educational Administration; Educational and Student Counselling; English; Filipino; Foreign Languages Education; Home Economics Education; Humanities and Social Science Education; Information Sciences; Library Science; Mathematics Education; Native Language Education; Preschool Education; Primary Education; Science Education; Secondary Education; Technology Education); **Undergraduate and Professional** (Administration; Art Education; Arts and Humanities; Biological and Life Sciences; Computer Education; Economics; Education; Educational Administration; Educational and Student Counselling; English; Ethics; Filipino; Foreign Languages Education; Health Education; Home Economics Education; Hotel and Restaurant; Humanities and Social Science Education; Information Sciences; Library Science; Management Systems; Mathematics; Mathematics Education; Music Education; Native Language Education; Physical Education; Preschool Education; Primary Education; Psychology; Science Education; Secondary Education; Secretarial Studies; Social Sciences; Social Studies; Special Education; Technology Education)

History: Founded 1928.

Degrees and Diplomas: *Bachelor's Degree*; *Master's Degree*: Education (Home Economics; Science Education; Guidance and Counselling; Social Science Education; Secondary Mathematics; Elementary Mathematics); Education (Technology and Home Management; Secondary Education; English; Filipino; Administration and Supervision; Library and Information Science; Educational Management; Mathematics; Library Science); *PhD*: Educational Management; Educational Leadership (Ed.D). Also Non-degree programmes in Medical Office Assistantship, Computerised Office Management; Food Service Management (2 yrs). Short-term Courses.
Last Updated: 02/03/11

THE NEW EL SALVADOR COLLEGE

El Salvador, Northern Mindanao 9017

Chairman: John Mark T. Magallanes

Programmes
Education (Education; Primary Education; Secondary Education)

Degrees and Diplomas: *Bachelor's Degree*
Last Updated: 02/03/11

THE UNIVERSITY OF MANILA (UM, UNIVMAN)

546 Dr. M.V. De los Santos Street, Sampaloc, City of Manila, First District, Metro Manila 1008
Tel: +63(2) 735-5098 +63(2) 735-5256
Fax: +63(2) 735-5089
EMail: admin@um.edu.ph
Website: http://www.um.edu.ph/

President: Emily D. de Leon

Programmes
Arts (Arts and Humanities; Cultural Studies; Economics; English; History; Japanese; Modern Languages; Political Sciences; Public Administration); **Business Administration** (Banking; Business Administration; Economics; Finance; Management; Marketing); **Education** (Computer Education; Computer Science; Education; Educational and Student Counselling; English; Filipino; Foreign Languages Education; History; Library Science; Mathematics Education; Native Language Education; Physics; Primary Education; Science Education; Secondary Education; Social Studies); **Foreign Service** (International Relations); **Graduate Studies** (Education; Educational Administration; Educational and Student Counselling; Law; Political Sciences; Public Administration); **Hotel and Restaurant Management** (Hotel and Restaurant; Hotel Management); **Industrial Engineering** (Industrial Engineering)

History: Founded 1913 as Instituto de Manila, a private High School. Became University 1921. A private institution under the supervision of the Commission on Higher Education.

Governing Bodies: Board of Trustees; Administrative Council

Academic Year: June to March (June-October; November-March)

Admission Requirements: Graduation from accredited high school or equivalent, and entrance examination

Fees: (Pesos) c. 12,000

Main Language(s) of Instruction: English

International Co-operation: With universities in Japan, Korea, Taiwan

Accrediting Agencies: Philippines Association of Universities and Colleges

Degrees and Diplomas: *Associate Degree*; *Bachelor's Degree*; *Master's Degree*: Business Administration; Public Administration; Arts in: Education (Administration and Supervision; Guidance and Counselling); Political Sciences; *PhD*: Education; Public Administration

Student Services: Academic counselling, Canteen, Cultural centre, Employment services, Foreign student adviser, Foreign Studies Centre, Health services, Language programs, Social counselling, Sports facilities

Student Residential Facilities: For Women students only

Special Facilities: Dr. M.V. de los Santos Memorial Museum

Libraries: Central Library, c. 20,980 vols; High School and Elementary Library, c. 5,990; Bayani Virata Faylona Law Library, c. 2,080; Business and Education, c. 5,600

Publications: Business Logbook; Journal of East Asiatic Studies; Law Gazette

Last Updated: 02/03/11

TOMAS CLAUDIO MEMORIAL COLLEGE

T. Claudio Street, Morong, Rizal 1960
Tel: +63(2) 691-5592
Fax: +63(2) 691-5595
EMail: registrar@tcmc.edu.ph
Website: http://www.tcmc.edu.ph/

President: Felino SM. Angeles, Jr.

Programmes

Arts and Sciences (Criminology; Economics; English; History; Midwifery; Nursing; Police Studies; Public Administration); **Business Administration** (Accountancy; Business Administration; Business Computing; Economics; Finance; Hotel and Restaurant; Hotel Management; Human Resources; Management; Marketing; Secretarial Studies); **Education** (Art Education; Biology; Education; English; Ethics; Filipino; Foreign Languages Education; History; Mathematics Education; Music Education; Native Language Education; Physical Education; Physics; Primary Education; Secondary Education; Social Studies); **Graduate** (Business Administration; Education; Educational Administration; Educational and Student Counselling; Public Administration)

History: Founded 1950.

Degrees and Diplomas: *Associate Degree*; *Bachelor's Degree*; *Master's Degree*: Business Administration; Public Administration; Arts in Education (Guidance and Counselling; Educational Management; Administration and Supervision)

Last Updated: 02/03/11

TOMAS DEL ROSARIO COLLEGE

San Jose, Balanga City, Bataan 2100
Tel: +63(47) 237-3115 +63(47) 791-6082
Fax: +63(47) 791-6152
EMail: aaa@btn.csi.com.ph

President: Antonio Ortiguera

Programmes

Accountancy (Accountancy); **Business Administration** (Banking; Business Administration; Finance; Management; Marketing); **Computer Science** (Computer Science); **Education** (Education; English; Filipino; Foreign Languages Education; Native Language Education; Primary Education; Secondary Education); **Nursing** (Nursing); **Nursing** (Nursing); **Secondary Education** (English; Filipino; Secondary Education)

History: Founded 1950.

Degrees and Diplomas: *Certificate/Diploma*; *Bachelor's Degree*; *Master's Degree*: Arts in Education (Educational Management)

Last Updated: 02/03/11

TRACE COLLEGE

El Danda Street, Batong Malake, Los Baños, Laguna 4030
Tel: +63(49) 536-3944
Fax: +63(49) 536-4193

President: Erwin F. Genuino

Programmes

Undergraduate and Professional (Business Administration; Computer Education; Computer Engineering; Computer Science; Hotel and Restaurant; Hotel Management; Information Technology; Management; Management Systems; Marketing; Nursing; Secondary Education; Secretarial Studies)

Further Information: Also City of Makati Campus

History: Founded 1993. Formerly known as Trace Computer and Business College.

Degrees and Diplomas: *Certificate/Diploma*; *Associate Degree*; *Bachelor's Degree*

Last Updated: 02/03/11

TRADE-TECH INTERNATIONAL SCIENCE INSTITUTE

Hi-way Estancia, Mandaue City, Cebu 6014
Tel: +63(32) 346-4433
Fax: +63(32) 346-4436
EMail: ttsi@skyinet.net

President: Jose O. Cuevas

Programmes

Science (Computer Engineering; Computer Science; Information Management; Information Technology; Management Systems)

History: Founded 2005.

Degrees and Diplomas: *Bachelor's Degree*

Last Updated: 02/03/11

TRINITAS SCHOOL

3A Jupiter St., Phase II Sto. Niño, City of Meycauayan, Bulacan 3020
Tel: +63(44) 695-1484
Fax: +63(44) 695-1484
EMail: trinitas_school@digitalone.com

President: Maria Trinitas F. Canias

Programmes

Business Administration (Business Administration; Management; Marketing); **Education** (Biology; Education; English; Filipino; Foreign Languages Education; History; Mathematics Education; Native Language Education; Primary Education; Secondary Education); **Information Technology** (Information Technology); **Nursing** (Nursing); **Psychology** (Psychology)

History: Founded 1992.

Degrees and Diplomas: *Bachelor's Degree*

Last Updated: 02/03/11

TRINITY UNIVERSITY OF ASIA (TUA)

Cathedral Heights, 275 E. Rodriguez Street, Quezon City, Second District, Metro Manila 1100
Tel: +63(2) 415-0634 +63(2) 723-9057
Fax: +63 (2) 725-5924
EMail: webmaster@tua.edu.ph
Website: http://www.tua.edu.ph/

President: Josefina S. Sumaya

Vice-President for Academic Affairs: Epitacio S. Palispis

Vice President, Administration and Finance: Leonora N. Yngente

Colleges

Arts and Science (Biology; Computer Science; English; Justice Administration; Mass Communication; Psychology; Religious Music); **Business Administration** (Accountancy; Business Administration; Finance; Human Resources; Management; Marketing; Public Administration); **Computing and Information Sciences** (Computer Engineering; Computer Networks; Computer Science; Information Technology); **Education** (Curriculum; English; Filipino; Foreign Languages Education; Health Education; Mathematics Education; Music Education; Native Language Education; Physical Education; Preschool Education; Primary Education; Secondary Education; Special Education); **Hospitality and Tourism Management** (Hotel and Restaurant; Hotel Management; Tourism);

Medical Technology (Medical Technology); **Nursing** *(St. Luke's)* (Nursing)

Schools

Graduate Studies (Business Administration; Education; Health Administration; Management; Nursing; Public Administration)

History: Founded 1963. Previously known as Trinity College of Quezon City. Acquired current status and title 2006.

Governing Bodies: Board of Trustees

Academic Year: June to March (June-October; November-March)

Admission Requirements: Entrance exam; Secondary school certificate.

Fees: (Peso): 20,000-25,000 per semester

Main Language(s) of Instruction: English

International Co-operation: With institutions in Czech Republic, Ecuador, France, India, Israel, Jamaica, Mexico, Russia, Thailand, UK, USA

Accrediting Agencies: Commission on Higher Education of the Philippines

Degrees and Diplomas: *Associate Degree*; *Bachelor's Degree*; *Master's Degree*: Business Administration; Management; Public Administration; Education; Nursing; *PhD*: Education; Public Administration. Also Certificate in Professional Education

Student Services: Academic counselling, Canteen, Handicapped facilities, Sports facilities

Special Facilities: Centre for Community and Extension Services

Libraries: Yes

Last Updated: 02/03/11

UM BANSALAN COLLEGE

R. Delos Cientos Street, Poblacion Dos, Bansalan, Davao del Sur 8005
Tel: +63(82) 510-0110
Fax: +63(82) 510-0110

Director: Salvador C. Tagalog Jr.

Programmes

Undergraduate and Professional Studies (Accountancy; Art Education; Banking; Biological and Life Sciences; Business Administration; Business and Commerce; Criminology; English; Finance; Foreign Languages Education; Health Education; History; Human Resources; Management; Marketing; Nursing; Physical Education; Secondary Education)

History: Founded 1962.

Degrees and Diplomas: *Bachelor's Degree*

Last Updated: 02/03/11

UM COTABATO COLLEGE

Bishop Mongeau Avenue, Cotabato City, Cotabato 9600
Tel: +63(64) 421-5726 +63(64) 421-7220
Fax: +63(64) 421-7220
EMail: umcot@mozcom.com

Director: Elias G. Cuevas

Programmes

Undergraduate and Professional Studies (Accountancy; Business and Commerce; Criminology; Management)

History: Founded 1958. Formerly known as UM Radio School (1959-1986).

Degrees and Diplomas: *Bachelor's Degree*

Last Updated: 02/03/11

UM DIGOS COLLEGE

Roxas Extension, City of Digos, Davao del Sur 8002
Tel: +63(82) 553-2914
Fax: +63(82) 553-2914

Director: Warlita C. Canque

Programmes

Undergraduate and Professional Studies (Business and Commerce; Curriculum; Education; English; Filipino; Foreign Languages Education; History; Mathematics Education; Music Education; Native Language Education; Political Sciences; Primary Education; Secondary Education)

History: Founded 1949.

Degrees and Diplomas: *Bachelor's Degree*

Last Updated: 02/03/11

UM GUIANGA COLLEGE

Tugbok, Davao City, Davao del Sur 8000
Tel: +63(82) 293-0264
Fax: +63(82) 293-0264
EMail: um_guianga@yahoo.com

President: Matias L. Mercado, Jr.

Programmes

Undergraduate and Professional (Business and Commerce; Communication Arts; Education; English; Foreign Languages Education; Management; Primary Education; Secondary Education)

History: Founded in 1965. Formerly known as UM Guianga Junior College (1970 - 1997).

Degrees and Diplomas: *Bachelor's Degree*

Last Updated: 02/03/11

UM PANABO COLLEGE

Pedro N. Arguelles Street, Brgy. San Francisco, Panabo City, Davao del Norte 8105
Tel: +63(84) 628-5427
EMail: um@mozom.com

Director: Evelyn P. Saludes

Programmes

Undergraduate and Professional Studies (Accountancy; Business Administration; Business and Commerce; Curriculum; English; Filipino; Foreign Languages Education; Management; Mathematics Education; Native Language Education; Primary Education; Secondary Education)

History: Founded 1948.

Degrees and Diplomas: *Bachelor's Degree*

Last Updated: 02/03/11

UM PEÑAPLATA COLLEGE

Obenza, Samal District, Island Garden City of Samal, Davao del Norte 8119

Director: Alberto M. Condes

Programmes

Undergraduate and Professional Studies (Business and Commerce; Education; English; Foreign Languages Education; Information Technology; Mathematics Education; Primary Education; Secondary Education)

History: Founded 1950. Formerly known as University of Mindanao Peñaplata Junior College (1966-1999).

Degrees and Diplomas: *Bachelor's Degree*

Last Updated: 02/03/11

UM TAGUM COLLEGE

Mabini Street, Tagum City, Davao del Norte 8100
Tel: +63(84) 217-3225
Fax: +63(84) 400-3355
EMail: tagum@umindanao.edu.ph
Website: http://www.tagum.umindanao.edu.ph/

Director: Fely D. Rabaca

Programmes

Graduate Studies (Business Administration; Education; Educational Administration; Educational and Student Counselling; English; Filipino; Foreign Languages Education; Human Resources; Management; Mathematics Education; Native Language Education; Public Administration; Science Education); **Undergraduate and Professional Studies** (Accountancy; Art Education; Biological and Life Sciences; Business and Commerce; Computer Engineering; Curriculum; Economics; Education; Educational and Student Counselling; Electrical Engineering; English; Filipino; Finance; Foreign Languages Education; History; Hotel and Restaurant; Hotel

Management; Human Resources; Library Science; Management; Marketing; Mathematics; Mathematics Education; Music Education; Native Language Education; Nursing; Philosophy; Physical Education; Primary Education; Public Administration; Secondary Education)

History: Founded 1950.

Degrees and Diplomas: *Bachelor's Degree*; *Master's Degree*: Arts in Education (Administration and Supervision; Teaching English; Teaching Filipino; Teaching Science; Teaching Mathematics; Educational Guidance and Counselling; Educational Management); Business Administration; Management (Human Resource Management); Public Administration

Last Updated: 02/03/11

UNCIANO COLLEGES (ANTIPOLO)

Circumferential Road, Antipolo City, Rizal 1780
Tel: +63(2) 697-0174
Fax: +63(2) 650-7096

President: Natividad V. Unciano

Programmes

Undergraduate and Professional (Hotel and Restaurant; Hotel Management; Medical Technology; Midwifery; Nursing; Physical Therapy; Radiology; Tourism)

History: Founded 1975.

Degrees and Diplomas: *Bachelor's Degree*: 4 yrs; *Bachelor's Degree*: Physical Therapy, 5 yrs

Last Updated: 02/03/11

UNCIANO COLLEGES AND GENERAL HOSPITAL

V.Mapa-Guadalcanal Street, Santa Mesa, City of Manila, First District, Metro Manila 1070
Tel: +63(2) 716-7292
Fax: +63(2) 716-7291

President: Natividad V. Unciano

Programmes

Health Sciences and Psychology (Dental Technology; Dentistry; Health Sciences; Medical Technology; Midwifery; Nursing; Physical Therapy; Psychology; Radiology)

History: Founded 1976. Formerly known as Unciano Paramedical College (1980-1990).

Degrees and Diplomas: *Associate Degree*; *Bachelor's Degree*: 4-5 yrs; *Post Baccalaureate Certificate/Diploma*: Dental Medicine. Also Graduate in Midwifery and Dental Technology, 2yrs; Health Care Giver programme, 6 months

Last Updated: 02/03/11

UNIDA CHRISTIAN COLLEGE

Anabu I-F, Imus, Cavite 4103
Tel: +63(46) 472-3755
Fax: +63(46) 472-2591
EMail: lsrtriple5@yahoo.com

Administrator: Gloria Silla Tonggian

Programmes

Undergraduate and Professional (Accountancy; Business Administration; Computer Engineering; Computer Science; Curriculum; English; Foreign Languages Education; Primary Education; Secondary Education)

History: Founded 2002. Formerly known as Unida Evangelical College.

Degrees and Diplomas: *Associate Degree*; *Bachelor's Degree*

Last Updated: 02/03/11

UNION CHRISTIAN COLLEGE

Barangay 2, Widdoes Street, City of San Fernando, La Union 2500
Tel: +63(72) 888-2865 +63(72) 888-3340 +63(72) 700-0282
Fax: +63(72) 888-3340
EMail: uccpres@sflu.com

President: Felimon Lagon

Programmes

Accoutancy; **Arts** (English; History; Political Sciences); **Commerce/Business Administration** (Banking; Business Administration; Business and Commerce; Economics; Finance; Management); **Computer Science** (Computer Engineering; Computer Science); **Education** (Biological and Life Sciences; Child Care and Development; Curriculum; English; Filipino; Foreign Languages Education; Health Education; History; Library Science; Mathematics Education; Music Education; Native Language Education; Physical Education; Preschool Education; Primary Education; Science Education; Social Sciences); **Graduate Studies** (Education; Nursing; Teacher Training); **Nursing** (Nursing); **Office Administration** (Administration; Computer Education; Management; Management Systems; Secretarial Studies)

History: Founded 1910.

Degrees and Diplomas: *Certificate/Diploma*; *Associate Degree*; *Bachelor's Degree*; *Master's Degree*: Education (Teacher Education); Nursing

Last Updated: 02/03/11

UNION COLLEGE

A. Mabini Street, Sta. Cruz, Laguna 4009
Tel: +63(49) 808-1083
Fax: +63(49) 808-3893
EMail: ucl@union.mozcom.com

President: David S. Sobrepeña

Programmes

Accountancy and Commerce (Accountancy; Business and Commerce; Economics; Management; Marketing); **Arts** (Economics; English; Political Sciences; Psychology; Public Administration); **Computer Science** (Computer Science); **Education** (Education; English; Filipino; Foreign Languages Education; Mathematics Education; Native Language Education; Primary Education; Secondary Education); **Graduate** (Education; Educational Administration; Educational and Student Counselling; Educational Psychology; Public Administration); **Hotel and Restaurant Management** (Hotel and Restaurant; Hotel Management); **Information Technology** (Information Technology); **Science** (Computer Education; Computer Engineering; Computer Science; Hotel and Restaurant; Hotel Management; Information Management; Information Technology; Secretarial Studies)

History: Founded 1946.

Degrees and Diplomas: *Certificate/Diploma*; *Bachelor's Degree*; *Master's Degree*: Education (Psychology; Guidance and Counselling; Administration and Supervision); Public Administration (Organisation and Management)

Last Updated: 02/03/11

UNITED SCHOOL OF SCIENCE AND TECHNOLOGY COLLEGES

TRITC Bldg, City of Tarlac, Tarlac 2300
Tel: +63(45) 982-3304 +63(45) 982-7710
Fax: +63(45) 982-7722
EMail: usstnfc@mozcom.com

President: Guillermina J. Tabamo

Programmes

Business Administration (Business Administration; Management); **Computer Science** (Computer Science); **Criminology** (Criminology); **Hotel and Restaurant Management** (Hotel and Restaurant; Hotel Management); **Mass Communication** (Mass Communication); **Nursing** (Nursing); **Secondary Education** (Secondary Education; Social Studies)

History: Founded 1994. Formerly known as United School of Science and Technology

Degrees and Diplomas: *Certificate/Diploma*; *Bachelor's Degree*

Last Updated: 03/03/11

UNIVERSAL COLLEGE OF NURSING

8273 Dr. A. Santos Avenue, San Dionisio, Sucat, City of Parañaque, Fourth District, Metro Manila 1700
Tel: +63(2) 820-4276
Fax: +63(2) 829-8615

President: Domingo T. Tay

Programmes

Hotel and Restaurant Management (Hotel and Restaurant; Hotel Management); **Information Management** (Information Management); **Nursing** (Nursing); **Tourism Management** (Tourism)

History: Founded 2005.

Degrees and Diplomas: *Bachelor's Degree*
Last Updated: 03/03/11

UNIVERSITY OF ARAULLO

Pamantasan ng Araullo

Maharlika Highway, Bitas, Cabanatuan City, Nueva Ecija 3100
Tel: +63(44) 463-0952
Fax: +63(44) 463-0952
EMail: inquiries@aupen.edu.ph
Website: http://www.au.phinma.edu.ph

President: Rolan C. Esteban

Programmes

Graduate (Arts and Humanities; Business Administration); **Undergraduate and Professional** (Accountancy; Architecture; Business and Commerce; Civil Engineering; Computer Science; Criminology; Education; Geological Engineering; Industrial Engineering; Law; Nursing; Primary Education; Secondary Education)

History: Founded 1950 as Law School, became College 1953 and acquired University status 1983.

Governing Bodies: Board of Trustees

Academic Year: June to March (June-October; November-March)

Admission Requirements: Graduation from high school and entrance examination

Main Language(s) of Instruction: Filipino, English

Degrees and Diplomas: *Bachelor's Degree*; *Master's Degree*: Arts; Science in Business Administration; *PhD*

Student Services: Academic counselling, Canteen, Cultural centre, Foreign Studies Centre, Health services, Nursery care, Social counselling, Sports facilities

Libraries: Central Library, c. 50,000 vols; Law, c. 2,500; Graduate School, c. 4,500

Publications: Araullian *(quarterly)*; Sandigan *(quarterly)*; The Horizon *(annually)*

Press or Publishing House: Gonzales Printing House
Last Updated: 07/01/11

UNIVERSITY OF ASIA AND THE PACIFIC (UA&P)

Pearl Drive, Ortigas Complex, Pasig City, Second District, Metro Manila 1600
Tel: +63(2) 637-0912
Fax: +63(2) 631-2174
EMail: email@uap.edu.ph; registrar@uap.edu.ph
Website: http://uap.edu.ph/

President: Jose Maria Arsenio G. Mariano
EMail: josemaria.mariano@uap.asia

Vice-President for Administrative Affairs: Rolando Sison
EMail: rsison@uap.edu.ph

Vice-President for Academic Affairs (Acting): Arwin Vibar
EMail: arwin.vibar@uap.asia

Programmes

Graduate (Arts and Humanities; Child Care and Development; Civics; Communication Arts; Communication Studies; Development Studies; Economics; Education; Ethics; Food Science; Industrial and Production Economics; Information Technology; International Relations; Management; Nursing; Preschool Education); **Undergraduate and Professional** (Arts and Humanities; Child Care and Development; Communication Arts; Communication Studies; Development Studies; Economics; Industrial and Production Economics; Information Technology; Management; Preschool Education)

History: Founded 1967 as Center for Research and Communication, a project of the Southeast Asia Science Foundation, Inc. Acquired present status and title 1995.

Academic Year: June to March (June-October; November-March)

Admission Requirements: Graduation from high school or foreign equivalent and entrance examination

Fees: (Pesos): 58,000 per semester

Main Language(s) of Instruction: English

International Co-operation: With universities in France, Germany, Spain, Netherlands, Hong Kong, Korea, Australia, USA, Mexico

Degrees and Diplomas: *Bachelor's Degree*; *Master's Degree*: Applied Business Economics (Food Systems Management); Communication (Integrated Marketing Communications); Economics Education; Education (Values Education; Liberal Education; Child Development Education; Development Education); Nursing; Political Economy (International Relations and Development); Humanities; Industrial Economics; Information Technology; Management; *PhD*: Development Management (with Specialization in Economics)

Student Services: Academic counselling, Canteen, Employment services, Health services, Social counselling, Sports facilities

Libraries: Central Library, 42,950 vols

Publications: Agribusiness Monitor *(monthly)*; Industry Monitor, Industry updates and analyses for sound business planning *(monthly)*; Recent Economic Indicators, Comprehensive macroeconomic advice from experts *(monthly)*
Last Updated: 03/03/11

UNIVERSITY OF BAGUIO

77 General Luna Road, Baguio City, Benguet 2600
Tel: +63(74) 442-3540 +63(74) 442-4915
Fax: +63(74) 442-3071
EMail: ub@ubaguio.edu
Website: http://www.ubaguio.edu

President: Herminio C. Bautista (1992-)
Tel: +63(74) 442-2867, Fax: +63(74) 442-3071
EMail: herminiob@yahoo.com

Vice-President for Administration: Rebecca C. Cajilog
EMail: beccajilog@yahoo.com

Schools

Business Administration and Accountancy (Accountancy; Business Administration; Business and Commerce; Business Education; Finance; Management; Secretarial Studies); **Dentistry** (Dental Technology; Dentistry); **Engineering and Architecture** (Architecture; Civil Engineering; Computer Engineering; Computer Science; Electronic Engineering; Environmental Engineering; Industrial Engineering; Sanitary Engineering; Structural Architecture; Telecommunications Engineering); **Graduate Studies** (Business Administration; Business Education; Criminology; Dentistry; Education; English; Filipino; Philosophy; Public Administration; Secondary Education); **Human Sciences** (English; Mass Communication; Political Sciences; Psychology; Public Administration; Radio and Television Broadcasting); **Information Technology** (Computer Engineering; Computer Science; Information Technology); **International Hospitality and Tourism Management** (Hotel and Restaurant; Hotel Management; Tourism); **Law** (Law); **Law Enforcement and Administration** (Criminal Law; Criminology); **Natural Sciences** (Biology; Laboratory Techniques; Physical Therapy); **Nursing** (Dietetics; Midwifery; Nursing; Nutrition); **Teacher Education** (Development Studies; Education; Educational Administration; Primary Education; Secondary Education; Special Education; Teacher Training)

History: Founded 1948 as Technical Institute, acquired University status 1969.

Governing Bodies: Board of Trustees

Academic Year: June to March (June-October; October-March). Also summer session, April to May

Admission Requirements: Graduation from high school and entrance examination

Main Language(s) of Instruction: Filipino, English, Spanish

Degrees and Diplomas: *Associate Degree*; *Bachelor's Degree*: 4-5 yrs; *Post Baccalaureate Certificate/Diploma*: Dental Medicine (DDM); *Master's Degree*: Business Administration (MBA); Business Education; College Teaching (MACT); Criminology; Dental Science; Education (MAEd); English (MAEnglish); Filipino; Public

Administration; Science Education (MASE); Secondary Teaching, a further 2 yrs; *PhD*: Education; Philosophy

Student Residential Facilities: Yes

Special Facilities: Anthropology Museum

Libraries: c. 80,000 vols

Publications: Journal *(biannually)*; Research Journal *(biannually)*

Press or Publishing House: AJ Press

Last Updated: 03/03/11

UNIVERSITY OF BATANGAS

Hilltop, Batangas City, Batangas 4200
Tel: +63(43) 723-1446 +63(43) 980-0041
Fax: +63(43) 723-0695
EMail: info@ub.edu.ph; admin@ub.edu.ph
Website: http://www.ub.edu.ph

President: Hernando B. Perez

Colleges

Allied Medical Sciences (Occupational Therapy; Physical Therapy; Respiratory Therapy); **Arts and Sciences** (Communication Studies; Law; Management; Mathematics; Political Sciences; Psychology); **Business and Accountancy** (Accountancy; Banking; Business and Commerce; Finance; Information Management; Information Technology; Management; Management Systems; Marketing); **Education** (Child Care and Development; Computer Education; Education; English; Filipino; Foreign Languages Education; Health Education; Home Economics Education; Information Sciences; Library Science; Mathematics Education; Music Education; Native Language Education; Physical Education; Preschool Education; Primary Education; Science Education; Secondary Education; Social Studies; Teacher Training; Technology Education); **Engineering** (Civil Engineering; Computer Engineering; Electrical Engineering; Electronic Engineering; Environmental Engineering; Industrial Engineering; Mechanical Engineering; Sanitary Engineering; Telecommunications Engineering); **Graduate Studies** (Administration; Business Administration; Education; Educational Administration; English; Filipino; Foreign Languages Education; Human Resources; Management; Mathematics; Native Language Education; Public Administration); **Law** (Law); **Nursing and Midwifery** (Midwifery; Nursing; Public Health); **Tourism and Hospitality Management** (Cooking and Catering; Hotel and Restaurant; Hotel Management; Tourism)

History: Founded 1946, acquired present status 1996. Formerly known as Western Philippine Colleges.

Admission Requirements: Graduation from high school

Degrees and Diplomas: *Certificate/Diploma*; *Associate Degree*; *Bachelor's Degree*; *Master's Degree*: Business Management (Business Administration; Human Resources Management); Public Administration; Education (English; Filipino; Social Studies; Educational Management); Science (Mathematics); *PhD*: Business Management; Public Administration; Education (Educational Management; English; Filipino)

Student Services: Academic counselling, Canteen, Health services, Sports facilities

Publications: U of B Forum, Official Publication of the University; UB Graduate School Journal; UB Law Journal

Last Updated: 03/03/11

UNIVERSITY OF BOHOL (UB)

Maria Clara Street, Tagbilaran City, Bohol 6300
Tel: +63(38) 411-2081 +63(38) 411-3101
Fax: +63(38) 411-3101 +63(38) 411-3106
EMail: info@universityofbohol.com
Website: http://www.universityofbohol.com

President: David Tirol

Registrar: Dalia Melda T. Magno Tel: +63(38) 411-2081

Vice-President for Administration: Nuevas T. Montes

Programmes

Doctorate Courses (Business Administration; Educational Administration; Human Resources; Management); **Master Courses** (Community Health; Educational Administration; Educational and Student Counselling; English; Filipino; Health Administration; History; Mathematics Education; Native Language Education; Nursing; Psychology; Social Sciences); **Undergraduate Courses** (Accountancy; Air Transport; Architecture; Arts and Humanities; Banking; Business and Commerce; Civil Engineering; Computer Engineering; Computer Science; Criminology; Dietetics; Earth Sciences; Economics; Education; Electrical Engineering; Electronic Engineering; English; Filipino; Finance; Fine Arts; Foreign Languages Education; Geological Engineering; History; Home Economics Education; Hotel and Restaurant; Hotel Management; Human Resources; Industrial Engineering; Law; Library Science; Management; Marketing; Mathematics; Mathematics Education; Mechanical Engineering; Midwifery; Native Language Education; Nursing; Nutrition; Pharmacy; Physical Education; Physical Therapy; Political Sciences; Primary Education; Psychology; Science Education; Secondary Education; Social Studies; Taxation; Technology Education; Telecommunications Engineering; Tourism; Transport Management)

Further Information: Also Family Care and Rehabilitation Centres

History: Founded 1946 as College, acquired present status and title 1970.

Governing Bodies: Board of Trustees

Academic Year: June to March (June-October; November-March)

Admission Requirements: Graduation from high school and entrance examination

Main Language(s) of Instruction: Filipino, English, Spanish

Degrees and Diplomas: *Certificate/Diploma*; *Associate Degree*; *Bachelor's Degree*: 4-5 yrs; *Master's Degree*: Nursing (Community Health Nursing; Medical-Surgical Nursing; Nursing Service Administration); Educational Management; English; Guidance and Counselling; History; Psychology; Teaching Social Sciences/Filipino/Mathematics/Physical Education; Public Administration; Business Administration, a further 2-3 yrs; *PhD*: Educational Management; Business Management; Human Resources Management, a further 3-4 yrs

Student Services: Academic counselling, Canteen, Cultural centre, Employment services, Health services, Social counselling, Sports facilities

Special Facilities: Research Centre. Museum

Libraries:c. 19,500 vols

Publications: The Academe; The Beginner; The Forum; The Penmasters; Varsitarian

Last Updated: 03/03/11

UNIVERSITY OF CEBU (UC)

Osmeña Sr. Boulevard, Corner Sanciangko Street, Cebu City, Cebu 6000
Tel: +63(32) 254-1501 +63(32) 255-7777
Fax: +63(32) 253-0729
EMail: info@uc.edu.ph; ycg@uc.edu.ph
Website: http://www.uc.edu.ph

President: Augusto W. Go

Chancellor: Yvette Candice G. Gotianuy Tel: +63(32) 255-0655

Vice-Chancellor for Administrative Affairs: Nendell Hanz L. Abella EMail: hla@uc.edu.ph

Campuses

Banilad (Accountancy; Business Administration; Business and Commerce; Computer Engineering; Computer Science; Criminology; Education; Electronic Engineering; Hotel and Restaurant; Hotel Management; Information Management; Information Technology; Law; Midwifery; Nursing; Primary Education; Secondary Education; Telecommunications Engineering; Tourism); **Lapulapu and Mandaue** (Accountancy; Art Education; Biological and Life Sciences; Business Administration; Business Computing; Computer Education; Computer Engineering; Computer Science; Cooking and Catering; Criminology; Education; Electrical Engineering; Electronic Engineering; English; Filipino; Finance; Foreign Languages Education; Health Education; Hotel and Restaurant; Hotel Management; Human Resources; Industrial Engineering; Information Technology; Management; Management Systems; Marine Engineering; Marine Transport; Marketing; Mathematics Education; Music Education; Native Language Education; Nursing; Physical Education; Physics; Primary Education; Science Education; Secondary Education; Secretarial Studies; Social Studies; Taxation; Telecommunications Engineering)

Programmes

Graduate Studies *(Main Campus)* (Art Education; Business Administration; Computer Education; Computer Science; Criminal Law; Criminology; Education; Educational Administration; Educational Technology; English; Filipino; Foreign Languages Education; Marine Science and Oceanography; Mathematics Education; Native Language Education; Nautical Science; Nursing; Science Education); **Undergraduate Studies** (Accountancy; Art Education; Banking; Business Administration; Business and Commerce; Business Computing; Civil Engineering; Computer Engineering; Computer Science; Criminology; Curriculum; Economics; Education; Electrical Engineering; English; Ethics; Filipino; Finance; Foreign Languages Education; Health Education; Home Economics Education; Hotel and Restaurant; Hotel Management; Industrial and Organizational Psychology; Industrial Engineering; Information Sciences; Information Technology; Marine Engineering; Marine Transport; Mathematics Education; Mechanical Engineering; Music Education; Native Language Education; Naval Architecture; Physical Education; Political Sciences; Primary Education; Science Education; Secondary Education; Secretarial Studies; Social Studies; Special Education; Taxation; Technology Education)

Further Information: Also Mambaling Campus

History: Founded 1964 as College of Commerce, became Cebu Central College 1983, and acquired present status and title 1992.

Governing Bodies: Board of Trustees

Academic Year: June to March (June-October; November-March)

Admission Requirements: Graduation from high school

Fees: (Pesos): c. 7,000-10,000 per semester

Main Language(s) of Instruction: English

Accrediting Agencies: Philippine Association of Colleges and Universities Commission on Accreditation (PACU-COA)

Degrees and Diplomas: *Bachelor's Degree*; *Master's Degree*: Business Administration; Science in Teaching (Computer Science; Marine and Nautical; English; Educational Technology; Mathematics; Integrated Arts in Education; Filipino); Criminology; Nursing; Business Administration; Criminal Justice; Elementary School Management); *PhD*: Education

Student Services: Academic counselling, Canteen, Cultural centre, Employment services, Foreign Studies Centre, Health services, Social counselling, Sports facilities

Libraries: Main Library, c. 54,000 vols.; Graduate School, c. 5,000 vols; South Campus, c. 12,000 vols; METC, c. 7,500 vols; High School Library, c. 7,200 vols

Publications: College Publication (Lakandiwa) *(other/irregular)*

Last Updated: 04/03/11

UNIVERSITY OF ILOILO

Rizal Street, Iloilo City, Iloilo 5000
Tel: +63(33) 338-1071
Fax: +63(33) 337-3743
EMail: uiadm@ui.edu.ph
Website: http://www.ui.edu.ph

President: Alberto Lopez
Tel: +63(33) 338-1081 EMail: presoffice@ui.edu.ph

Executive Vice-President: Rosario Alberto
Tel: +63(33) 338-1081 EMail: rosepalberto@yahoo.com

Colleges

Arts and Sciences (Arts and Humanities; Mass Communication; Political Sciences; Psychology); **Criminal Justice** (Civil Security; Criminology; Police Studies); **Education** (Curriculum; Education; English; Ethics; Filipino; Foreign Languages Education; Home Economics; Mathematics Education; Native Language Education; Primary Education; Secondary Education; Special Education; Technology Education); **Information Technology and Engineering** (Civil Engineering; Computer Science; Engineering; Information Technology; Marine Engineering; Mechanical Engineering); **Law** (Law); **Management and Accountancy** (Accountancy; Business Administration; Business and Commerce; Finance; Hotel and Restaurant; Hotel Management; Information Management; Management; Marketing; Secretarial Studies); **Nursing** (Health Education; Nursing)

Programmes

Graduate (Business Administration; Education; Educational Administration; English; Filipino; Foreign Languages Education; Mathematics Education; Public Administration; Science Education)

History: Founded 1947, acquired University status 1968. Became part of the Philippine Investment Management (PHINMA), Inc. 2009.

Governing Bodies: Board of Directors

Academic Year: June to May

Admission Requirements: High School Diploma and College Entrance Test

Fees: (Pesos): 15,000 per semester

Main Language(s) of Instruction: English

Accrediting Agencies: Philippine Accrediting Association of Schools, Colleges and Universities (PAASCU)

Degrees and Diplomas: *Certificate/Diploma*; *Associate Degree*; *Bachelor's Degree*; *Master's Degree*: Business Administration; Public Administration; Education (Filipino; Mathematics; Science; Teaching English as Second Language; Administration and Supervision); *PhD*: Educational Management

Student Services: Canteen, Health services, Language programs, Sports facilities

Press or Publishing House: Makinaugalingon Press

Last Updated: 04/03/11

UNIVERSITY OF LA SALETTE (ULS)

Arranz Street, Dubinan East, City of Cauayan, Isabela 3311
Tel: +63(78) 682-4771
Fax: +63(78) 682-5170
EMail: webmaster@lasalette.edu.ph
Website: http://www.lasalette.edu.ph

President: Romeo B. Gonzales (1979-)
EMail: frromy@lasalette.net

Vice-President for Administration: Franklin G. Picio
Tel: +63(78) 682-5167

International Relations: Maria Purificacion Obra
Tel: +63(78) 682-8362 EMail: mariaapro@yahoo.com

Colleges

Agriculture and Fisheries Technology (Agricultural Business; Agriculture; Fishery; Food Science; Forestry; Rural Planning; Town Planning); **Allied Medical Programmes** (Laboratory Techniques; Medical Technology; Optometry; Pharmacy; Physical Therapy; Radiology); **Arts and Sciences** (Architecture; Arts and Humanities; Biology; Chemistry; Economics; English; Environmental Studies; Home Economics; Library Science; Mass Communication; Mathematics; Philosophy; Physics; Political Sciences; Psychology; Public Administration; Rural Planning; Social Work; Town Planning); **Commerce** (Accountancy; Business Administration; Business Computing; Computer Science; Finance; Hotel and Restaurant; Hotel Management; Management; Management Systems; Marketing; Secretarial Studies; Taxation; Tourism); **Community Health and Midwifery** (Community Health; Midwifery; Public Health); **Criminology** (Criminology; Police Studies); **Education** (Art Education; Civics; Computer Education; Educational and Student Counselling; English; Environmental Studies; Ethics; Filipino; Foreign Languages Education; Health Education; History; Home Economics; Home Economics Education; Library Science; Literacy Education; Mathematics Education; Music Education; Native Language Education; Physical Education; Preschool Education; Primary Education; Religious Education; Science Education; Social Sciences; Social Studies; Technology Education; Tourism); **Engineering** (Civil Engineering; Computer Engineering; Electronic Engineering; Environmental Engineering; Geological Engineering; Marine Engineering; Sanitary Engineering; Telecommunications Engineering); **Information Technology** (Information Management; Information Technology); **Laws** (Law); **Nursing** (Nursing)

Schools

Graduate (Business Administration; Computer Science; Criminology; Education; Engineering; Engineering Management; Environmental Studies; Health Administration; Information Technology; Nursing; Public Administration; Public Health; Science Education; Social Work)

History: Founded 1951 as La Sallette of Santiago, acquired present status and title 1998. A private Institution under the supervision of the Missionaries of our Lady of La Salette.

Governing Bodies: Board of Incorporators; Board of Trustees

Academic Year: June to March (June-October; November-March). Summer Session April to May

Admission Requirements: Graduation from high school and entrance examination

Fees: (Pesos): 10,000-12,000 per semester

Main Language(s) of Instruction: English

Accrediting Agencies: Philippine Accrediting Association of Schools, Colleges and Universities (PAASCU)

Degrees and Diplomas: *Certificate/Diploma*; *Associate Degree*; *Bachelor's Degree*: 4-5 yrs; *Post Baccalaureate Certificate/Diploma*: Dentistry; Medicine; Optometry; *Master's Degree*: Arts in: Nursing; Religious Education; Education (Social Sciences; Physical Education; Educational Management; Filipino; English; Mathematics; Science; Home Economics; Guidance; Preschool Education); Science in: Accountancy; Computer Science; Criminology; Education; Engineering Education; Engineering Management; Environmental Sciences; Information Technology; Library Science; Nursing; Public Health; Science Education; Social Work; *Master's Degree*: Business Management; Hospital Administration; Information Technology; Public Administration, 2 yrs; *PhD*: Business Management; Public Administration; Philosophy in: Educational Management; English; Filipino; Mathematics; Social Sciences; Science, 3 yrs

Student Services: Academic counselling, Canteen, Cultural centre, Foreign student adviser, Foreign Studies Centre, Health services, Language programs, Social counselling, Sports facilities

Student Residential Facilities: Yes

Special Facilities: Museum. Filipiniana Collections. Internet Laboratory

Libraries: Special Libraries

Publications: Research Journal and Graduate School Journal, Official Publication of Research Center and Graduate School *(annually)*

Last Updated: 04/03/11

UNIVERSITY OF LUZON (UL)

Perez Boulevard, Dagupan City, Pangasinan 2400
Tel: +63(75) 522-8295 +63(75) 515-7707 +63(75) 522-1623
Fax: +63(75) 515-5767
EMail: webmaster@ul.edu.ph; registrar@ul.edu.ph
Website: http://www.ul.edu.ph

President: Macarthur M. Samson Tel: +63(75) 1623

Vice-President for Administrative Affairs: Liberato Reyna EMail: webmaster@ul.edu.ph

International Relations: Aurora Reyna
Tel: +63(75) 515-7707 EMail: assr_7145@yahoo.com

Programmes

Architecture (Architecture); **Arts** (Economics; English; Filipino; Mass Communication; Political Sciences; Psychology; Social Work); **Business and Commerce** (Accountancy; Banking; Business Computing; Finance; Hotel and Restaurant; Hotel Management; Management; Management Systems; Marketing; Public Administration; Secretarial Studies); **Criminology** (Criminology); **Education** (Education; English; Filipino; Foreign Languages Education; Library Science; Mathematics Education; Native Language Education; Primary Education; Science Education; Secondary Education); **Engineering** (Chemical Engineering; Civil Engineering; Computer Engineering; Computer Science; Electrical Engineering; Electronic Engineering; Engineering; Industrial Engineering; Mechanical Engineering; Telecommunications Engineering); **Graduate Studies** (Business Administration; Criminology; Curriculum; Development Studies; Education; Educational Administration; Educational and Student Counselling; English; Filipino; Foreign Languages Education; Government; Health Administration; Library Science; Management; Native Language Education; Nursing; Physical Education; Primary Education; Public Administration; Secondary Education; Sports; Urban Studies); **Information Management and Technology** (Information Management; Information Technology); **Journalism** (Journalism); **Medical Technology** (Medical Technology); **Nursing** (Nursing); **Pharmacy** (Pharmacy); **Tourism** (Tourism)

History: Founded 1948 as Luzon College of Commerce and Business Administration. Renamed Luzon Colleges 1952. Acquired present status and title 2003.

Governing Bodies: Board of Trustees

Fees: (Pesos): Tuition fees: 325 per unit

Main Language(s) of Instruction: English

Accrediting Agencies: Philippine Association of Colleges and Universities Commission on Accreditation (PACUCOA)

Degrees and Diplomas: *Associate Degree*; *Bachelor's Degree*; *Master's Degree*: Arts in Education (College Teaching; Guidance and Counselling; Filipino; Library Science; Physical Education and Sports Science; Management of Elementary/Secondary Schools; English; Elementary Education); Business Administration; Public Administration (Police Administration; Community Development; Local Government; Development Planning and Management); Nursing (Nursing Administration); Criminology; *PhD*: Business Management; Arts (Educational Management; Business Management; Curriculum and Instruction); Public Administration

Student Services: Academic counselling, Canteen, Cultural centre, Employment services, Foreign student adviser, Foreign Studies Centre, Handicapped facilities, Health services, Language programs, Nursery care, Social counselling, Sports facilities

Libraries: Yes

Publications: Research Vistas *(annually)*

Last Updated: 04/03/11

UNIVERSITY OF MINDANAO

Bolton Street, Davao City, Davao del Sur 8000
Tel: +63(82) 226-3526
Fax: +63(82) 226-3527
EMail: um@mozcom.com
Website: http://www.umindanao.edu.ph

President: Guillermo P. Torres

Vice-President, Administration and General Services: Antonio M. Pilpil EMail: pdg@mail.dvo.info.com.ph

Colleges

Accountancy (Accountancy); **Architecture** (Architecture; Fine Arts; Painting and Drawing); **Arts and Science** (Agriculture; Arts and Humanities; Chemistry; Computer Science; English; Environmental Studies; Forestry; Information Sciences; Information Technology; Library Science; Mass Communication; Mathematics; Physics; Political Sciences; Psychology; Social Work); **Business Administration** (Accountancy; Banking; Business Administration; Business Computing; Economics; Finance; Hotel and Restaurant; Hotel Management; Human Resources; Management; Management Systems; Marketing; Secretarial Studies); **Criminology** (Criminology); **Education** (Art Education; Biological and Life Sciences; Curriculum; Education; Educational and Student Counselling; English; Filipino; Foreign Languages Education; Mathematics Education; Music Education; Native Language Education; Physical Education; Preschool Education; Primary Education; Secondary Education; Social Studies; Special Education); **Engineering** (Chemical Engineering; Civil Engineering; Computer Engineering; Electrical Engineering; Electronic Engineering; Engineering; Mechanical Engineering); **Law** (Law); **Nursing** (Nursing)

Schools

Graduate (Business Administration; Chemical Engineering; Civil Engineering; Criminology; Economics; Education; Educational and Student Counselling; Electrical Engineering; Electronic Engineering; Engineering; English; Environmental Engineering; Environmental Management; Filipino; Foreign Languages Education; Home Economics Education; Human Resources; Information Sciences; Library Science; Management; Mathematics Education; Mechanical Engineering; Native Language Education; Physical Education; Public Administration; Science Education; Social Work; Technology Education; Telecommunications Engineering)

Further Information: Also Medical Dental Clinic. Branches: Bansalan, Digos, Guianga, Ilang-Tibungco, Panabo, Peñaplata, Tagum and Toril

History: Founded as a private non-sectarian College 1946. Became University 1963. An independent private institution under the supervision of the Ministry of Education, Culture and Sports.

Governing Bodies: Board of Trustees

Academic Year: June to March (June-October; November-March)

Admission Requirements: Graduation from high school or recognized foreign equivalent, and entrance examination

Main Language(s) of Instruction: Filipino, English

Degrees and Diplomas: *Bachelor's Degree*; *Post Baccalaureate Certificate/Diploma*: Education; *Master's Degree*: Arts in Education (Teaching Science; Library Science; Administration and Supervision; Guidance and Counselling; Home Economics; Teaching Values Education; Teaching English/Filipino; Physical Education; Mathematics; Educational Management); Business Administration; Environmental Planning; Public Administration; Social Work (Direct Social Work Practice; Social Administration); Arts in College Teaching (Law Enforcement Administration); Engineering (Chemical Engineering; Mechanical Engineering; Electrical Engineering; Environmental Engineering; Electronics and Communications Engineering; Civil Engineering); Science in Criminology (Criminalistics); *PhD*: Business Administration; Education (Educational Management); Public Administration; Management; Criminal Justice (Criminology)

Student Services: Academic counselling, Canteen, Employment services, Health services, Language programs, Social counselling, Sports facilities

Special Facilities: Mini-Theatre

Libraries: Central Library, c. 73,300 vols

Publications: The Mindanao Collegian *(quarterly)*

Last Updated: 07/03/11

UNIVERSITY OF NEGROS OCCIDENTAL - RECOLETOS (UNO-RECOLETOS)

Lizares Avenue, Bacolod City, Negros Occidental 6100
Tel: +63(34) 433-2449 +63(34) 433-1848
Fax: +63(34) 433-1709
Website: http://www.uno-r.edu.ph/

President: Demetrio S. Peñascoza, OAR

Colleges

Agriculture (Agricultural Business; Agriculture; Crop Production; Zoology); **Arts and Science** (Arts and Humanities; Mass Communication; Natural Sciences; Philosophy; Political Sciences; Psychology; Social Work); **Business and Accountancy** (Accountancy; Banking; Business Administration; Business and Commerce; Computer Engineering; Economics; Finance; Management; Management Systems; Marketing; Secretarial Studies); **Criminology** (Criminology); **Education** (Art Education; Biological and Life Sciences; Curriculum; Education; English; Filipino; Foreign Languages Education; Health Education; Home Economics Education; Industrial Arts Education; Mathematics Education; Music Education; Native Language Education; Physical Education; Preschool Education; Primary Education; Science Education; Secondary Education; Social Studies; Special Education); **Engineering** (Chemical Engineering; Civil Engineering; Computer Science; Electrical Engineering; Electronic Engineering; Engineering; Mechanical Engineering; Telecommunications Engineering); **Hospitality Management** (Hotel and Restaurant; Hotel Management; Tourism); **Information Management and Technology** (Information Management; Information Technology); **Law** (Law); **Nursing** (Medical Technology; Nursing)

Schools

Graduate (Business Administration; Development Studies; Education; Educational Administration; Educational and Student Counselling; English; Filipino; Foreign Languages Education; Management; Mathematics Education; Native Language Education; Physical Education; Physics; Political Sciences; Social Sciences; Special Education)

History: Founded 1941 as Institute, became University 1957. Administered since 1962 by the Recollect Fathers of St. Augustine. Under the supervision of the Ministry of Education, Culture, and Sports.

Academic Year: June to March (June-October; November-March)

Admission Requirements: Graduation from high school and entrance examination

Main Language(s) of Instruction: English

Accrediting Agencies: Philippine Accrediting Association of Schools, Colleges and Universities (PAASCU)

Degrees and Diplomas: *Certificate/Diploma*; *Bachelor's Degree*; *Master's Degree*: Business Administration; Public Administration; Science in Computer Science; Education (Special Education; School Administration and Supervision; Political Sciences; Teaching Physics/Filipino/Physical Education/Mathematics/English; Guidance and Counselling; Social Science); *PhD*: Education (Educational Management); Philosophy in Business Management; Development Management; Educational Management

Student Services: Academic counselling, Canteen, Cultural centre, Employment services, Health services, Sports facilities

Libraries: Central Library, c. 80,000 vols

Publications: Journal *(quarterly)*

Last Updated: 07/03/11

UNIVERSITY OF NORTHEASTERN PHILIPPINES (UNEP)

San Roque, Iriga City, Camarines Sur 4431
Tel: +63(54) 299-2698
Fax: +63(54) 456-0293
EMail: info@unep.edu.ph
Website: http://www.unep.edu.ph

President: Remelisa G. Alfelor-Moraleda (2001-)

Colleges

Arts and Science, Social Work and General Education (Arts and Humanities; Botany; Chemistry; Communication Studies; Economics; English; History; Mass Communication; Political Sciences; Psychology; Social Studies; Social Work; Zoology); **Business Education** (Accountancy; Agricultural Business; Banking; Business Administration; Business and Commerce; Business Computing; Economics; Finance; Human Resources; Management; Management Systems; Marketing; Public Administration; Secretarial Studies; Taxation); **Criminology** (Criminology); **Education** (Education; Educational Administration; Educational and Student Counselling; English; Ethics; Filipino; Foreign Languages Education; Health Education; History; Home Economics Education; Literacy Education; Mathematics Education; Music Education; Native Language Education; Natural Sciences; Physical Education; Primary Education; Science Education; Secondary Education; Social Studies; Technology Education); **Engineering, Architecture and Technology** (Architecture; Civil Engineering; Electrical and Electronic Engineering; Engineering; Geological Engineering; Industrial Engineering; Mechanical Engineering; Structural Architecture; Surveying and Mapping; Telecommunications Engineering); **International Hospitality Management** (Hotel and Restaurant; Hotel Management; Tourism); **Law** (Law); **Maritime Education** (Marine Engineering; Marine Transport); **Nursing** (Midwifery; Nursing)

Schools

Graduate (Agricultural Education; Business Administration; Education; Educational Administration; Educational and Student Counselling; English; Filipino; Foreign Languages Education; Human Resources; Management; Native Language Education; Primary Education; Public Administration)

History: Founded 1948. Acquired present status 1974.

Governing Bodies: Board of Trustees

Academic Year: June to March

Admission Requirements: Graduation from high school and entrance examination

Main Language(s) of Instruction: Filipino, English

Accrediting Agencies: Federation of Accrediting Agencies of the Philippines

Degrees and Diplomas: *Certificate/Diploma*; *Associate Degree*; *Bachelor's Degree*; *Master's Degree*: Business Administration; Public Administration; Education (Elementary Education; Administration and Supervision; Guidance and Counselling; Englis; Filipino); *PhD*: Education (Educational Administration and Supervision); Human Resources; Public Management; Business Management

Student Services: Academic counselling, Canteen, Cultural centre, Employment services, Handicapped facilities, Health services, Language programs, Nursery care, Social counselling, Sports facilities

Student Residential Facilities: Alumni Hall, hostel accomodations

Special Facilities: Theatre; Campus FM Radio; TV Studio and Station

Libraries: c. 25,000 vols

Last Updated: 07/03/11

UNIVERSITY OF NUEVA CACERES

Jaima Hernandez Avenue, Naga City, Camarines Sur 4400
Tel: +63(54) 811-6100
Fax: +63(54) 811-1015
EMail: dhs@unc.edu.ph
Website: http://www.unc.edu.ph

President: Dolores H. Sison

Executive Vice-President: Lourdes S. Anonas

Registrar: Nelia E. San Jose

Colleges

Arts and Science (Arts and Humanities; Biology; Botany; Chemistry; Economics; English; Environmental Studies; Literature; Mathematics; Natural Sciences; Political Sciences; Psychology; Zoology); **Business and Accountancy** (Accountancy; Business Administration; Business and Commerce; Economics; Finance; Hotel and Restaurant; Hotel Management; Human Resources; Management Systems; Marketing; Public Administration; Secretarial Studies); **Computer Studies** (Computer Engineering; Computer Science; Information Management; Information Technology); **Education** (Biological and Life Sciences; Biology; Computer Education; Curriculum; Education; Educational and Student Counselling; English; Filipino; Foreign Languages Education; Health Education; History; Home Economics Education; Information Sciences; Library Science; Mathematics Education; Music Education; Native Language Education; Physical Education; Physics; Preschool Education; Primary Education; Secondary Education; Social Studies; Special Education); **Engineering and Architecture** (Architecture; Civil Engineering; Computer Engineering; Computer Science; Electrical Engineering; Electronic Engineering; Engineering; Industrial Engineering; Mechanical Engineering; Sanitary Engineering; Telecommunications Engineering); **Law** (Law); **Nursing** (Nursing)

Departments

Higher Education (Higher Education); **Primary Education** (Primary Education)

Schools

Graduate (Business Administration; Education; Educational Administration; Educational and Student Counselling; English; Filipino; Management; Mathematics Education; Public Administration; Special Education)

History: Founded 1948 as the Nueva Caceres Colleges. Became University 1954. Supervised by the Ministry of Education, Culture and Sports.

Governing Bodies: Board of Trustees

Academic Year: June to March (June-October; November-March)

Admission Requirements: Graduation from high school and entrance examination

Main Language(s) of Instruction: Filipino, English

Degrees and Diplomas: *Certificate/Diploma*; *Associate Degree*; *Bachelor's Degree*; *Master's Degree*: Arts in Education (Administration Supervision; Guidance and Counselling; Educational Management; Special Education); Arts in English; Filipino; Library Science; Teaching Mathematics; Business Administration; Management; Public Administration; Environmental Sciences (Chemistry; General Science Education; Ecology); *PhD*: Education (Educational Management; Filipino Language and Literature); Philosophy in Management (Behavioural Management)

Student Residential Facilities: Yes

Special Facilities: University Museum

Libraries: Central Library, c. 15,000 vols; Division libraries, c. 13,000

Publications: Bikol Culture; Education Journal; Journal of Graduate Studies and Research; University of Nueva Caceres Bulletin *(monthly)*

Last Updated: 07/03/11

UNIVERSITY OF PANGASINAN

Arellano Street, Dagupan City, Pangasinan 2400
Tel: +63(75) 522-5635 +63(75) 522-3459
Fax: +63(75) 522-2496
EMail: msorio@upang.edu.ph
Website: http://up.phinma.edu.ph

President: Catalino P. Rivera
Tel: +63(75) 671-6330, Fax: +63(75) 671-6333

Colleges

Education (Education; English; Filipino; Foreign Languages Education; Mathematics Education; Midwifery; Native Language Education; Primary Education; Science Education; Secondary Education); **Law** (Law); **Liberal Arts** (Economics; English; History; Mass Communication; Political Sciences; Psychology)

Schools

Graduate (Business Administration; Education; Educational Administration; Filipino; Higher Education; Management; Management Systems; Secondary Education)

Units

Business (Accountancy; Banking; Business Administration; Business and Commerce; Economics; Finance; Hotel and Restaurant; Hotel Management; Human Resources; Management; Marketing; Tourism); **Engineering** (Architecture; Building Technologies; Civil Engineering; Computer Engineering; Electrical Engineering; Electronic Engineering; Engineering; Information Technology; Structural Architecture; Telecommunications Engineering); **Nursing and Health** (Health Sciences; Medical Technology; Midwifery; Nursing; Physical Therapy)

Further Information: Also Pangasinan Medical Centre

History: Founded 1925, acquired University status 1968. Under the supervision of the Commission on Higher Education.

Governing Bodies: Board of Trustees

Academic Year: June to March (June-October; November-March)

Admission Requirements: Graduation from high school and entrance examination/ interview

Main Language(s) of Instruction: Filipino, English

Accrediting Agencies: Philippine Association of Colleges Universities Commission on Accreditation (PACUCOA)

Degrees and Diplomas: *Certificate/Diploma*; *Associate Degree*; *Bachelor's Degree*; *Master's Degree*: Arts in Education; Business Administration; Science in Management Engineering; *PhD*: Education (Higher Education)

Student Services: Academic counselling, Canteen, Cultural centre, Employment services, Foreign Studies Centre, Health services, Social counselling, Sports facilities

Special Facilities: Audio-Visual Centre; Gymnasium

Libraries: Yes

Publications: Researcher *(biennially)*

Press or Publishing House: SLA Publishing House

Last Updated: 07/03/11

UNIVERSITY OF PERPETUAL HELP RIZAL

Alabang-Zapote Avenue, Pamplona 3, City of Las Piñas, Fourth District, Metro Manila 1740
Tel: +63(2) 871-0639 +63(2) 800-0638
Fax: +63(2) 875-0194
EMail: uphsd@perpetualdalta.edu.ph
Website: http://perpetualdalta.edu.ph

President: Antonio L. Tamayo

Campuses

Calamba (Accountancy; Biology; Business Administration; Business and Commerce; Civil Engineering; Computer Engineering; Computer Science; Criminology; Electrical Engineering; Electronic Engineering; Finance; Hotel and Restaurant; Hotel Management; Human Resources; Industrial Engineering; Information Technology; Journalism; Management; Marketing; Mass Communication; Mechanical Engineering; Medical Technology; Nursing; Pharmacy; Political Sciences; Primary Education; Psychology; Radio and Television Broadcasting; Secondary Education; Telecommunications Engineering; Tourism); **GMA** (Accountancy; Business and

Commerce; Communication Studies; Computer Science; Education; English; Filipino; Foreign Languages Education; Health Education; Home Economics Education; Hotel and Restaurant; Hotel Management; Information Technology; Management; Mathematics Education; Music Education; Native Language Education; Nursing; Physical Education; Physical Therapy; Primary Education; Psychology; Secondary Education; Social Sciences; Tourism); **Isabela** (Accountancy; Business Administration; Business and Commerce; Computer Engineering; Education; Hotel and Restaurant; Hotel Management; Information Technology; Management; Mass Communication; Midwifery; Nursing; Political Sciences; Primary Education; Psychology; Secondary Education; Tourism); **Laguna** (Accountancy; Biology; Business Administration; Business and Commerce; Child Care and Development; Civil Engineering; Computer Engineering; Computer Science; Criminology; Curriculum; Dietetics; Education; Educational Administration; Educational and Student Counselling; Educational Psychology; Electrical Engineering; Electronic Engineering; English; Filipino; Foreign Languages Education; Health Education; Health Sciences; History; Home Economics Education; Hotel and Restaurant; Hotel Management; Industrial Engineering; Information Management; Information Technology; Journalism; Law; Library Science; Management; Management Systems; Marine Engineering; Marine Transport; Mass Communication; Mathematics Education; Mechanical Engineering; Microbiology; Music Education; Native Language Education; Nursing; Nutrition; Physical Education; Political Sciences; Preschool Education; Primary Education; Psychology; Radio and Television Broadcasting; Science Education; Secretarial Studies; Social Sciences; Social Studies; Special Education; Technology Education; Telecommunications Engineering); **Molino** (Accountancy; Biology; Business Administration; Business Computing; Computer Engineering; Computer Science; Curriculum; Education; Electrical Engineering; Electronic Engineering; English; Filipino; Foreign Languages Education; Health Education; History; Home Economics Education; Hotel and Restaurant; Hotel Management; Human Resources; Industrial Engineering; Information Technology; Journalism; Management; Marketing; Mass Communication; Native Language Education; Nursing; Preschool Education; Primary Education; Psychology; Radio and Television Broadcasting; Secondary Education; Secretarial Studies; Technology Education; Telecommunications Engineering; Tourism)

Centres

Flight Cabin Crew *(WINGS Career Center for Flight Cabin Crew)* (Air Transport)

Colleges

Animation (Multimedia; Video); **Arts and Sciences** (Biology; Cinema and Television; Journalism; Mass Communication; Photography; Political Sciences; Psychology; Public Relations; Radio and Television Broadcasting); **Aviation** (Aeronautical and Aerospace Engineering; Air Transport); **Aviation Maintenance** (Aeronautical and Aerospace Engineering; Air Transport); **Computer Studies** (Computer Engineering; Computer Science; Information Technology; Software Engineering); **Criminology** (Criminology; Police Studies); **Dentistry** (Dental Hygiene; Dental Technology; Dentistry); **Education** (Art Education; Curriculum; Education; English; Foreign Languages Education; Health Education; Mathematics Education; Music Education; Physical Education; Preschool Education; Primary Education; Secondary Education; Social Studies; Special Education); **Engineering** (Civil Engineering; Computer Engineering; Electrical Engineering; Electronic Engineering; Engineering; Industrial Engineering; Mechanical Engineering; Telecommunications Engineering); **International Hospitality Management** (Cooking and Catering; Hotel and Restaurant; Hotel Management; Tourism); **Law** (Law); **Maritime Education** (Marine Engineering; Marine Transport; Mechanical Engineering; Naval Architecture); **Medical Technology** (Laboratory Techniques; Medical Technology); **Nursing and Midwifery** (Dietetics; Midwifery; Nursing; Nutrition); **Pharmacy** (Pharmacy); **Physical and Occupational Therapy** (Occupational Therapy; Physical Therapy); **Radiologic Technology** (Medical Technology; Radiology); **Respiratory Therapy** (Respiratory Therapy)

Schools

Business Administration and Accountancy (Accountancy; Banking; Business Administration; Finance; Human Resources; Management; Marketing); **Medicine** *(Jonelta Foundation School of Medicine. Campuses: Biñan Laguna Campus; Cavite; Manila; Pangasinan and Isabela)* (Dentistry; Medical Technology; Medicine; Midwifery; Nursing; Occupational Therapy; Pharmacy; Physical Therapy; Radiology; Respiratory Therapy)

History: Founded 1975. Formerly known as Perpetual Help College of Rizal (1975-1997). Acquired present status and title 1997.

Degrees and Diplomas: *Associate Degree*; *Bachelor's Degree*; *Master's Degree*: Business Administration; Education (Special Education; Science; Computer Education Management; English; Health Sciences; Nursing Education Management; Psychology; Social Sciences; Guidance and Counselling; Educational Management; Mathematics; Teaching Health Education); Teaching (English; Health; Biology; Livelihood); *PhD*: Business Administration; Philosophy in Education (Educational Management, Administration and Supervision)

Last Updated: 07/03/11

UNIVERSITY OF REGINA CARMELI

Barasoain and Catmon, City of Malolos,
Bulacan 3000
Tel: +63(44) 791-0271 +63(44) 791-1142
Fax: +63(44) 791-1349
EMail: registrar@urc.edu.ph
Website: http://www.urc.edu.ph

President: Niceta M. Vargas, O.S.A. (1984-)
Tel: +63(97) 791-1142, Fax: +63(97) 791-1142
EMail: nmvargas@urc.edu.ph

Vice-President for Academic Affairs: Belen De Jesus
EMail: bbdejesus@urc.edu.ph

Colleges

Allied Medical Science (Midwifery; Nursing); **Business Administration** (Accountancy; Business Administration; Business and Commerce; Economics; Finance; Human Resources; Jewelry Art; Management); **Computer Science and Engineering** (Computer Engineering; Computer Science; Industrial Engineering); **Education** (Education; English; Ethics; Filipino; Foreign Languages Education; Mathematics Education; Native Language Education; Preschool Education; Primary Education; Science Education; Secondary Education); **Hospitality Management** (Hotel and Restaurant; Hotel Management; Tourism); **Liberal Arts** (Biology; Chemistry; Communication Studies; English; Information Sciences; Library Science; Mathematics; Physics; Political Sciences; Psychology; Zoology)

Programmes

Graduate Studies (Anthropology; Behavioural Sciences; Business Administration; Development Studies; Education; Educational Administration; Educational Technology; English; Filipino; Foreign Languages Education; Hotel and Restaurant; Hotel Management; Information Technology; Library Science; Literature; Management; Mathematics Education; Modern Languages; Native Language Education; Nursing; Performing Arts; Preschool Education; Psychology; Public Administration; Religious Studies; Social Studies; Sociology; Taxation; Theatre)

History: Founded 1937 as Regina Carmeli College (formerly Colegio de Nuestra Señora del Carmen). Acquired present status and title 1997.

Main Language(s) of Instruction: English, Tagalog

Degrees and Diplomas: *Certificate/Diploma*; *Associate Degree*; *Bachelor's Degree*; *Master's Degree*: Arts in Nursing; Science in: Information Technology; Library Science; Behavioural Sciences (Psychology; Sociology; Anthropology); Business Administration (Hotel and Restaurant Management; Cooperative Education and Management); Education (English; Filipino; Mathematics; Drama and Arts; Early Childhood Education; Social Studies; Educational Management; Computer Aided Instruction; Religious Studies); Public Administration (Research and Development; Fiscal Administration); *PhD*: Business Administration; Public Administration; Education (Educational Management); Language and Literature; Philosophy (Educational Leadership and Management)

Student Services: Academic counselling, Canteen, Cultural centre, Employment services, Foreign student adviser, Health services, Language programs, Nursery care, Social counselling, Sports facilities

Last Updated: 08/03/11

UNIVERSITY OF SAINT ANTHONY (USANT)

Ortega Street, Iriga City, Camarines Sur 4431
Tel: +63(54) 299-2401
Fax: +63(54) 299-2403
EMail: usant@mozcom.com

President: Santiago D. Ortega, Jr. (1984-)

Colleges

Arts and Science (Arts and Humanities; Biology; Communication Studies; Computer Science; Economics; English; History; Mathematics; Political Sciences; Psychology); **Commerce and Business Administration** (Accountancy; Banking; Business Administration; Business and Commerce; Economics; Finance; Hotel and Restaurant; Hotel Management; Management; Management Systems; Marketing; Secretarial Studies); **Criminology** (Civil Security; Criminology); **Education** (Education; English; Filipino; Foreign Languages Education; Health Education; History; Home Economics Education; Industrial Arts Education; Library Science; Mathematics Education; Native Language Education; Physical Education; Primary Education; Science Education; Secondary Education); **Engineering and Architecture** (Architecture; Civil Engineering; Engineering); **Maritime Studies** (Marine Engineering; Marine Transport); **Nursing** (Midwifery; Nursing); **Physical Therapy** (Physical Therapy)

Graduate Schools

Graduate Studies (Business Administration; Criminology; Education; Educational Administration; Educational and Student Counselling; English; Filipino; Foreign Languages Education; History; Home Economics Education; Mathematics Education; Native Language Education; Nursing; Physical Education; Preschool Education; Primary Education; Science Education; Secondary Education; Special Education)

History: Founded 1947 as Academy, became College 1963. Acquired present status and title 1973. Under the supervision of the Commission on Higher Education.

Governing Bodies: Board of Trustees

Academic Year: June to March (June-October; November-March)

Admission Requirements: Graduation from high school and entrance examination

Fees: (Pesos): c. 15,000 per semester

Main Language(s) of Instruction: English

Accrediting Agencies: Philippine Association of Colleges & Universities Commission on Accreditation (PACUCOA)

Degrees and Diplomas: *Certificate/Diploma*; *Associate Degree*; *Bachelor's Degree*; *Master's Degree*: Arts in Education (Elementary and Secondary Science Teaching; English; Guidance and Counselling; History; Filipino; Mathematics; Physical Education); Arts in Education (Special Education for the Hearing Impaired; Administration and Supervision; Non-Formal Education; Home Economics; Preschool Education); Business Administration; Criminology (Law Enforcement Administration and Correction); Nursing (Psychiatric Nursing; Medical Surgical Nursing; Maternal Child Nursing); *PhD*: Education (Resource Management; Filipino; Educational Management)

Student Services: Academic counselling

Student Residential Facilities: Yes

Special Facilities: Audio-visual Centre

Libraries: c. 26,500 vols

Publications: Research Journal /Graduate Forum *(annually)*

Last Updated: 08/03/11

UNIVERSITY OF SAINT LA SALLE

La Salle Avenue, Bacolod City, Negros Occidental 6100
Tel: +63(34) 434-6100 +63(34) 432-3027
Fax: +63(34) 434-1063
EMail: reg@usls.edu
Website: http://www.usls.edu

President: Augustine Boquer (1998-) EMail: president@usls.edu

Vice-President for Academic Affairs: Elsie Coscolluela
Tel: +63(34) 433-0078, Fax: +63(34) 433-0415
EMail: vpaa@usis.edu

International Relations: Marie Therese Jochico
Fax: +63(34) 435-2594 EMail: tvjdera@usls.edu

Colleges

Arts and Science (Arts and Humanities; Biology; Communication Studies; Computer Science; Economics; Information Technology; Marketing; Mass Communication; Political Sciences; Psychology); **Business and Accountancy** (Accountancy; Agricultural Business; Business and Commerce; Economics; Human Resources; Management; Marketing; Tourism); **Education** (Art Education; Education; English; Foreign Languages Education; Health Education; Mathematics Education; Music Education; Physical Education; Physics; Primary Education; Secondary Education; Social Studies; Special Education; Teacher Training); **Engineering** (Chemical Engineering; Computer Engineering; Electronic Engineering; Engineering; Environmental Engineering; Materials Engineering; Telecommunications Engineering); **Law** (Law); **Medicine** (Medicine); **Nursing** (Nursing)

Schools

Graduate (Business Administration; Chemistry; Development Studies; Education; Educational Administration; Educational and Student Counselling; Electronic Engineering; Engineering; English; Environmental Engineering; Family Studies; Foreign Languages Education; Information Management; Information Technology; Linguistics; Literacy Education; Literature; Management; Mathematics Education; Modern Languages; Natural Sciences; Nursing; Preschool Education; Public Administration; Religious Studies; Special Education; Teacher Training; Telecommunications Engineering)

Further Information: Also AffiliateCollege in Roxas City and Research Centre (URC)

History: Founded as College 1952 by the La Salle Brothers of the Christian Schools. Acquired present status 1988.

Governing Bodies: Board of Trustees

Academic Year: June to March (June-October; November-March)

Admission Requirements: Graduation from high school or foreign equivalent and entrance examination

Fees: (Pesos): 35,000-40,000 per annum

Main Language(s) of Instruction: Filipino, English

International Co-operation: With universities in Belgium; Korea; Japan; Canada; Mexico; USA; Australia

Degrees and Diplomas: *Bachelor's Degree*; *Master's Degree*: Arts (Conflict and Reconciliation Studies); Arts in Teaching (Reading; Language and Literature); Science in Guidance and Counselling; Business Administration; Educational Management; Engineering (Electronics and Communications Engineering); Environmental Engineering; Information Management; Nursing; Public Management; Education (Early Childhood Education; English Language; Special Education; Guidance and Counselling; Chemistry; Natural Sciences; Marriage and Family; Mathematics); *PhD*: Education (Educational Management); Philosophy (Nursing; Religious Studies; Educational Management; Development Studies; Applied Linguistics; Business Management; Mathematics Education)

Student Services: Academic counselling, Canteen, Health services, Social counselling, Sports facilities

Special Facilities: Museo Negrense de la Salle; American Studies Resource Centre

Libraries: College Library, 70,385 vols; Graduate School Library, 5,466; Law library, 3,100

Publications: Handurao *(biennially)*; Management Review

Last Updated: 09/03/11

UNIVERSITY OF SAN AGUSTÍN (USA)

General Luna Street, Iloilo City, Iloilo 5000
Tel: +63(33) 337-4841 +63(33) 337-4855
Fax: +63(33) 337-4403
EMail: info@usa.edu.ph
Website: http://www.usa.edu.ph

President: Manuel M. Vergara, OSA (2004-)
Tel: +63(33) 337-4841 EMail: president@usa.edu.ph

Registrar: Gemma Halili
Tel: +63(33) 337-4841 EMail: registrar@usa.edu.ph

Colleges

Arts and Science (Arts and Humanities; Biology; Chemistry; Communication Arts; Computer Science; Criminology; Economics; English; Information Technology; International Relations; Mass Communication; Natural Sciences; Philosophy; Political Sciences; Psychology; Public Administration; Tourism); **Commerce and Accountancy** (Accountancy; Business Administration; Business and Commerce; Human Resources; Management; Marketing); **Education** (Art Education; Curriculum; Dietetics; English; Ethics; Filipino; Foreign Languages Education; Health Education; Home Economics Education; Hotel and Restaurant; Hotel Management; Mathematics Education; Music Education; Native Language Education; Nutrition; Physical Education; Preschool Education; Religious Education; Science Education; Social Studies; Special Education; Teacher Training; Technology Education); **Engineering and Architecture** (Architecture; Chemical Engineering; Civil Engineering; Computer Engineering; Electronic Engineering; Engineering; Fine Arts; Interior Design; Mechanical Engineering; Painting and Drawing; Telecommunications Engineering); **Law** (Law); **Nursing** (Nursing); **Pharmacy and Medical Technology** (Alternative Medicine; Health Sciences; Medical Technology; Pharmacy; Toxicology)

Conservatories

Music (Music; Music Education; Singing)

Schools

Graduate Studies (Administration; Business Administration; Chemistry; Economics; Education; Educational Administration; Educational and Student Counselling; Educational Psychology; English; Filipino; Government; Human Resources; Literature; Mathematics; Natural Sciences; Physics; Psychology; Public Administration; Religious Education; Social Sciences; Taxation)

History: Founded 1904 by the Augustinian Fathers, became University 1953. Granted autonomous status by the Commission on Higher Education of the Philippines 2004.

Governing Bodies: Board of Trustees

Academic Year: June to March (June-October; October-March)

Admission Requirements: Graduation from high school or foreign equivalent and entrance examination

Main Language(s) of Instruction: Filipino, English

Accrediting Agencies: Philippine Accrediting Association of Schools, Colleges and Universities (PAASCU)

Degrees and Diplomas: *Certificate/Diploma*; *Associate Degree*; *Bachelor's Degree*; *Master's Degree*: Arts in Education (Social Sciences; Preschool Education; Educational Management; Psychology and Guidance; Religious Education; Catechetics; Chemistry; Physics; Mathematics; English; Filipino; Natural Sciences; Special Education); Arts in Guidance and Counselling; Literature; Nursing; Pastoral Theology; Philosophy; Psychology; Religious Studies; Arts in Teaching; Business Administration; Nursing; Management in Human Resources Management; Public Administration; Economics; Medical Technology; *PhD*: Business Management; Philosophy in: Education (Psychology and Guidance); Psychology

Student Services: Academic counselling, Canteen, Employment services, Health services, Social counselling, Sports facilities

Special Facilities: Museum, Archives, Conference Halls and Auditorium

Libraries: 127,521 vols; 1,211 periodical subscriptions

Publications: Augustinian *(annually)*; Augustinian Legacy *(annually)*; Augustinian Research Journal *(annually)*; SANAG *(annually)*; Scientific Augustinian *(annually)*

Press or Publishing House: University Press; USA Publishing House; Libro Agustino

Last Updated: 09/03/11

UNIVERSITY OF SAN CARLOS (USC)

P. del Rosario Street, Cebu City, Cebu 6000
Tel: +63(32) 253-1000
Fax: +63(32) 255-4341
EMail: information@usc.edu.ph
Website: http://www.usc.edu.ph

President: Dionisio Marcelo Miranda, SVD

Vice-President for Academic Affairs: Felino Javines, Jr.

Vice-President for Administration: Ernesto Lagura

Colleges

Architecture and Fine Arts (Advertising and Publicity; Architecture; Fine Arts; Interior Design; Landscape Architecture; Painting and Drawing); **Arts and Sciences** (Anthropology; Applied Physics; Arts and Humanities; Biology; Chemistry; Computer Engineering; Computer Networks; Computer Science; Data Processing; Economics; Environmental Studies; History; Information Sciences; Information Technology; Library Science; Linguistics; Literature; Marine Biology; Mathematics; Multimedia; Philosophy; Political Sciences; Psychology; Sociology); **Commerce** (Accountancy; Business Administration; Business and Commerce; Economics; Environmental Management; Finance; French; German; Hotel and Restaurant; Hotel Management; Human Resources; Management; Marketing; Secretarial Studies; Tourism; Transport Management); **Education** (Art Education; Biology; Chemistry; Civics; Communication Arts; Cooking and Catering; Dietetics; Education; Ethics; Mathematics Education; Music Education; Nutrition; Physical Education; Physics; Preschool Education; Primary Education; Religious Education; Science Education; Secondary Education; Special Education; Textile Design); **Engineering** (Chemical Engineering; Civil Engineering; Computer Engineering; Computer Networks; Electrical and Electronic Engineering; Engineering; Industrial Engineering; Mechanical Engineering; Software Engineering; Telecommunications Engineering); **Law** (Law); **Nursing** (Health Sciences; Nursing); **Pharmacy** (Health Sciences; Pharmacy)

Schools

Graduate (Accountancy; Anthropology; Architecture; Biology; Botany; Business Administration; Chemical Engineering; Chemistry; Child Care and Development; Civil Engineering; Community Health; Computer Engineering; Computer Networks; Curriculum; Economics; Education; Educational Administration; Educational and Student Counselling; Educational Testing and Evaluation; Electrical Engineering; Electronic Engineering; Energy Engineering; Engineering; Engineering Management; English; Environmental Engineering; Environmental Studies; Foreign Languages Education; Geological Engineering; History; Industrial and Organizational Psychology; Industrial Engineering; Information Sciences; Information Technology; Landscape Architecture; Library Science; Linguistics; Literature; Management; Marine Biology; Mathematics; Mathematics Education; Mechanical Engineering; Microelectronics; Nursing; Pharmacy; Philosophy; Philosophy of Education; Physical Education; Physics; Political Sciences; Psychology; Religious Education; Science Education; Social Psychology; Sociology; Software Engineering; Special Education; Structural Architecture; Taxation; Telecommunications Engineering; Thermal Engineering; Urban Studies; Water Management; Water Science; Zoology)

Further Information: Also Research Centres and Laboratory

History: Founded 1595 as Parish School by Jesuit Fathers. Closed between 1768 and 1783 following the expulsion of the Jesuits from the Philippines. Reopened 1783 and renamed Seminario-Colegio de San Carlos. Administered by Dominican Fathers until 1862; by Vincentian Fathers, 1867 and subsequently by the Society of the Divine Word (SVD). Became an Institution of Higher Learning for the laity 1924. Suspended 1941, reopened 1945. Acquired University status 1948. Under the authority of the Society of the Divine Word, recognized by the Commission on Higher Education.

Governing Bodies: Board of Trustees

Academic Year: June to March (June-October; November-March). Summer session April-May

Admission Requirements: Graduation from high school and entrance examination

Main Language(s) of Instruction: English

Accrediting Agencies: Philippine Accrediting Association of Schools, Colleges and Universities

Degrees and Diplomas: *Certificate/Diploma*; *Associate Degree*; *Bachelor's Degree*; *Master's Degree*; *PhD*: Education; Philosophy in Anthropology; Business Administration; Management; Philosophy; Science Education (Physics; Biology; Chemistry); Philosophy in Education (Research and Evaluation; Educational Administration; Curriculum and Instruction)

Student Services: Academic counselling, Canteen, Cultural centre, Health services, Sports facilities

Student Residential Facilities: Yes

Special Facilities: Museums: Anthropological and Ethnological; Science (Biology and Geology)

Libraries: c. 250,000 vols

Publications: Philippine Quarterly of Culture and Society *(quarterly)*; Philippine Scientist *(annually)*; Semper Fidelis *(annually)*

Last Updated: 09/03/11

UNIVERSITY OF SAN JOSE - RECOLETOS (USJ-R)

Magallanes Street, Cebu City, Cebu 6000
Tel: +63(32) 253-7900
Fax: +63(32) 254-1720
EMail: pres@usjr.edu.ph; usj-r@fapenet.org
Website: http://www.usjr.edu.ph

President: Enrico Peter A. Silab OAR
EMail: president@usjr.edu.ph

Vice-President, Administration: Raul M. Buhay

Colleges

Arts and Sciences (Arts and Humanities; Biology; English; Information Sciences; Library Science; Mass Communication; Philosophy; Political Sciences; Psychology); **Commerce** (Accountancy; Banking; Business Administration; Business and Commerce; Economics; Finance; Hotel and Restaurant; Hotel Management; Human Resources; Management; Marketing; Tourism); **Education** (Art Education; Biochemistry; Biology; Computer Education; Education; Educational and Student Counselling; English; Ethics; Filipino; Foreign Languages Education; Health Education; Home Economics Education; Library Science; Mathematics Education; Music Education; Native Language Education; Physical Education; Preschool Education; Religious Education; Science Education; Secondary Education; Social Sciences; Social Studies; Special Education); **Engineering** (Civil Engineering; Electrical Engineering; Electronic Engineering; Engineering; Environmental Engineering; Industrial Engineering; Mechanical Engineering; Sanitary Engineering; Telecommunications Engineering); **Information, Computer, Communications Technology** (Computer Engineering; Computer Science; Information Management; Information Technology; Journalism; Management Systems; Mass Communication; Media Studies; Secretarial Studies); **Law** (Law); **Nursing** (Health Education; Nursing)

Schools

Graduate (Art Education; Biology; Business Administration; Business and Commerce; Chemistry; Communication Studies; Development Studies; Education; Educational Administration; Educational and Student Counselling; English; Ethics; Filipino; Foreign Languages Education; Human Resources; Industrial and Organizational Psychology; Information Technology; Journalism; Literature; Management; Mathematics Education; Media Studies; Native Language Education; Physical Education; Preschool Education; Primary Education; Psychology; Radio and Television Broadcasting; Science Education; Secondary Education; Social Psychology; Special Education; Sports)

History: Founded 1947 as College by the Recollect Fathers; Graduate School established 1960. Acquired University status 1984. Became a grantee of the International Development Research Centre (Ottawa, Canada) for research on Primary Health Care 1989-1991.

Governing Bodies: Academic Council, School Board

Academic Year: June to March (June-October; November-March)

Admission Requirements: Graduation from high school and entrance examination

Main Language(s) of Instruction: Filipino, English

Accrediting Agencies: Association of Southeast and East Asian Catholic Colleges and Universities; Philippine Accrediting Association of Schools, Colleges and Universities

Degrees and Diplomas: *Certificate/Diploma*; *Associate Degree*; *Bachelor's Degree*; *Master's Degree*; *PhD*: Business Administration; Management (Educational Management; Human Resources Management); Philosophy in English; Education (Instructional System and Resource Management)

Student Services: Academic counselling, Canteen, Cultural centre, Employment services, Health services, Language programs, Sports facilities

Special Facilities: Mass Communication Studio; Centre for Performing Arts

Libraries: c. 80,300 vols

Publications: Forward *(3 per annum)*; Journal of Research, Faculty research journal *(annually)*

Last Updated: 09/03/11

UNIVERSITY OF SANTO TOMAS

Pamantasan ng Santo Tomas (UST)
España Street, Sampaloc, City of Manila, First District, Metro Manila 1015
Tel: +63(2) 786-1611 +63(2) 406-1611
Fax: +63(2) 732-7486
Website: http://www.ust.edu.ph/

Rector: Rolando V. De La Rosa, O.P. (1998-)
Tel: +63(2) 731-3123 EMail: rector@mnl.ust.edu.ph

Secretary General: Florentino A. Bolo, Jr., O.P.

Assistant to the Rector for Administration: Pilar I. Romero

International Relations: Mafel C. Ysrael, Executive Assistant to the Vice-Rector for Academic Affairs
Tel: +63(2) 749-9730, Fax: +63(2) 749-9730
EMail: mcysrael@mnl.ust.edu.ph

Centres

Applied Ethics *(CAE)* (Ethics); **Conservation of Cultural Property and Environment in the Tropics** *(CCCPET)* (Cultural Studies; Environmental Management; Environmental Studies); **Creative Writing and Studies** *(CCWS)* (Writing); **Education and Research Development** *(CERD)* (Development Studies; Education); **Social Research** *(SRC)* (Social Studies)

Colleges

Accountancy *(UST-AMV)* (Accountancy; Management); **Architecture** (Architecture); **Commerce and Business Administration** (Business Administration; Business and Commerce; Management); **Education** (Dietetics; Education; Food Technology; Information Sciences; Library Science; Nutrition; Preschool Education; Primary Education; Secondary Education; Special Education; Teacher Training); **Fine Arts and Design** (Advertising and Publicity; Design; Fine Arts; Industrial Design; Interior Design; Painting and Drawing); **Nursing** (Nursing); **Rehabilitation Sciences** (Occupational Therapy; Physical Therapy; Speech Therapy and Audiology; Sports); **Science** (Actuarial Science; Applied Physics; Biology; Chemistry; Mathematics; Microbiology; Psychology); **Tourism and Hospitality Management** (Hotel and Restaurant; Hotel Management; Tourism)

Conservatories

Music (Conducting; Music; Music Education; Music Theory and Composition; Musical Instruments; Singing)

Faculties

Arts and Letters (Arts and Humanities; Asian Studies; Behavioural Sciences; Communication Arts; Communication Studies; Economics; Journalism; Justice Administration; Literature; Media Studies; Philosophy; Political Sciences; Social Sciences; Sociology); **Civil Law** (Administrative Law; Civil Law; Commercial Law; Constitutional Law; Criminal Law; Insurance; International Law; Labour Law; Political Sciences; Private Law; Public Law); **Ecclesiastical Studies** (Canon Law; Pastoral Studies; Philosophy; Theology); **Engineering** (Chemical Engineering; Civil Engineering; Computer Science; Electrical Engineering; Electronic Engineering; Engineering; Industrial Engineering; Information Technology; Mechanical Engineering; Telecommunications Engineering); **Medicine and Surgery** (Anaesthesiology; Anatomy; Biochemistry; Community Health; Dermatology; Epidemiology; Forensic Medicine and Dentistry; Gynaecology and Obstetrics; Histology; Medicine; Microbiology; Neurology; Neurosciences; Nutrition; Ophthalmology; Otorhinolaryngology; Paediatrics; Parasitology; Pathology; Pharmacology; Physiology; Psychiatry and Mental Health; Radiology; Rehabilitation and Therapy; Social and Preventive Medicine; Surgery); **Pharmacy** (Biochemistry; Botany; Medical Technology; Pharmacy)

Institutes

Physical Education and Athletics (Physical Education; Sports); **Technological Courses** (Electronic Engineering; Management; Technology)

Research Centres

Ecclesiastical Sciences *(John Paul II - JPIIRCES)* (Religious Studies); **Health Sciences** *(RCHS)* (Health Sciences); **Movement Science** *(CRMS)* (Natural Sciences); **Natural Sciences** *(RCNS)* (Natural Sciences)

Schools

Graduate (Accountancy; Advertising and Publicity; Applied Physics; Architecture; Arts and Humanities; Banking; Biological and Life Sciences; Biology; Business Administration; Business and Commerce; Canon Law; Chemistry; Civil Law; Clinical Psychology; Communication Studies; Cultural Studies; Curriculum; Development Studies; Economics; Education; Educational Administration; Educational and Student Counselling; Engineering; English; Ethics; Finance; Fine Arts; Food Science; Health Administration; Health Education; Heritage Preservation; History; Human Resources; Industrial and Organizational Psychology; Law; Library Science; Literature; Management; Management Systems; Marketing; Mathematics Education; Medical Technology; Microbiology; Music; Natural Sciences; Nursing; Oriental Studies; Pastoral Studies; Pharmacy; Philosophy; Physical Therapy; Political Sciences; Psychology; Public Administration; Religious Studies; Science Education; Social Sciences; Theology; Writing)

History: Founded 1611 as College of Our Lady of the Rosary by the Most Rev. Fr. Miguel de Benavides, O.P., Archbishop of Manila and the Dominican Fathers. Became College of Santo Tomas 1616. Royal confirmation granted 1785 by the Spanish Government. In 1902 Pope Leo XIII decreed and granted the title of Pontifical University. Pope Pius XII granted the title of Catholic University of the Philippines in 1947. A private Institution under the supervision of the Department of Education, Culture and Sports (for elementary and high school levels) and Commission on Higher Education (for college level).

Governing Bodies: Board of Trustees; Council of Regents; Economic Council; Academic Senate

Academic Year: June to March (June-October; November-March)

Admission Requirements: Graduation from high school or equivalent approved by the Government Bureau of Private Schools and entrance examination

Fees: (Pesos): College, 27,000-36,000 per semester; Medicine, 73,000-75,000; Law, 26,000-38,000 per semester; Graduate School, 1,189.90/ unit for Master; 1,385.40/unit for Doctorate

Main Language(s) of Instruction: Filipino, English

Accrediting Agencies: PACUCOA

Degrees and Diplomas: *Certificate/Diploma*; *Bachelor's Degree*: Architecture; Arts; Computer Science; Education; Engineering; Fine Arts; Information Management; Information Technology; Law; Music; Nursing; Pharmacy; Science; *Post Baccalaureate Certificate/ Diploma*: Medicine; *Master's Degree*: Arts; Science (MA; MS); *PhD*: Biology. Chemistry; Commerce; Education (Guidance and Counselling; Curriculum and Instruction; Educational Management); Development Studies; English; History; Law; Literature; Philosophy; Political Sciences; Psychology; Public Administration; Economics; Human Resoource Management; Theology

Student Services: Academic counselling, Canteen, Cultural centre, Employment services, Foreign student adviser, Foreign Studies Centre, Handicapped facilities, Health services, Language programs, Nursery care, Social counselling, Sports facilities

Student Residential Facilities: Yes

Special Facilities: Museum of Arts and Sciences; Research Complex; Auditoria

Libraries: 177,412 vols; 32 e-journals; 338 e-books; 604 serial subscriptions; 1,516 gifts and exchange

Publications: Academia *(quarterly)*; Acta Manilana *(annually)*; Boletin Eclesiastico *(bimonthly)*; Chemical Bulletin; College of Science Journal *(biennially)*; Journal of Graduate Research *(biennially)*; Journals of Medicine, Nursing, Law, Education, Commerce; Medical Forum; Pax Roman Bulletin; Philippiniana Sacra *(quarterly)*; Purple Gazette *(biennially)*; Research Report *(biennially)*; The Flame *(monthly)*; The Varsitarian *(monthly)*; Thomasian Engineer; Unitas *(quarterly)*; Veritas; Vision

Press or Publishing House: UST Publishing House

Student Numbers *2008-2009*: Total 40,447

Last Updated: 20/01/11

UNIVERSITY OF SOUTHERN PHILIPPINES FOUNDATION

Salinas Drive, Lahug, Cebu City, Cebu 6000
Tel: +63(32) 232-5939
Fax: +63(32) 231-0178
Website: http://uspf.edu.ph

President: Alicia P. Cabatingan

Vice-President, Administration: Oscar P. Jereza, Jr.

Centres

Computer Studies (Computer Education; Computer Science; Information Technology)

Colleges

Accountancy (Accountancy); **Arts and Science** (Arts and Humanities; Behavioural Sciences; Computer Science; English; Ethics; Filipino; Hotel and Restaurant; Mathematics; Music; Natural Sciences; Philosophy; Political Sciences; Social Welfare; Social Work); **Education** (Education; Primary Education; Secondary Education; Special Education); **Engineering and Architecture** (Architecture; Civil Engineering; Electrical Engineering; Electronic Engineering; Engineering; Geological Engineering; Mechanical Engineering; Structural Architecture; Telecommunications Engineering; Waste Management); **Law** (Administrative Law; Civil Law; Constitutional Law; Criminal Law; Human Rights); **Nursing** (Nursing); **Pharmacy** (Pharmacy)

Schools

Business and Management (Accountancy; Business Administration; Business and Commerce; Hotel and Restaurant; Management); **Graduate** (Curriculum; Education; Environmental Management; Law; Preschool Education; Primary Education; Social Work)

Further Information: Don Felix Montinola Memorial Centre

History: Founded 1927 as Southern Institute, became Southern College 1933, acquired University status 1949.

Governing Bodies: Board of Trustees

Academic Year: June to March (June-October; October-March)

Admission Requirements: Secondary school certificate or recognized equivalent and entrance examination

Main Language(s) of Instruction: Filipino, English

Degrees and Diplomas: *Associate Degree*; *Bachelor's Degree*; *Master's Degree*: Public Administration. Education; Law; Environmental Management; Social Work; *PhD*: Education

Special Facilities: Philipiniana Museum

Libraries: Central Library, c. 26,000 vols; Graduate School, c. 1,100; Engineering, c. 3,000; Commerce, c. 3,000

Publications: Indepth; The Southern Scholar

Last Updated: 14/03/11

UNIVERSITY OF ST. LOUIS - TUGUEGARAO

Mabini Street, Tuguegarao City, Cagayan 3500
Tel: +63(78) 844-1873 +63(78) 844-1872 +63(78) 844-1872
Fax: +63(78) 844-0889
EMail: president@uslt.edu.ph
Website: http://www.uslt.edu.ph/

President: Rosalinda P. Valdepeñas
EMail: rosalindavaldepenas@uslt.edu.ph

Vice-President for Administration: Emmanuel James Pattaguan
EMail: jamespattaguan@uslt.edu.ph

Colleges

Health and Allied Sciences (Nursing); **Tourism and Technical-Vocational Education** (Electrical and Electronic Engineering; Environmental Management; Hotel and Restaurant; Hotel Management; Management Systems; Nursing; Secretarial Studies; Tourism)

Schools

Business Administration and Accountancy (Accountancy; Business Administration; Finance; Human Resources; Management; Public Administration); **Education, Arts and Sciences** (Art Education; Arts and Humanities; Biological and Life Sciences; Education; English; Ethics; Filipino; Foreign Languages Education;

Health Education; Mass Communication; Mathematics Education; Music Education; Native Language Education; Philosophy; Physical Education; Physics; Political Sciences; Primary Education; Psychology; Public Administration; Secondary Education; Social Studies); **Engineering, Architecture and Fine Arts** (Architecture; Civil Engineering; Computer Engineering; Electrical Engineering; Electronic Engineering; Engineering; Fine Arts; Geological Engineering; Industrial Engineering; Interior Design; Mining Engineering); **Graduate** (Business Administration; Civil Engineering; Education; Education of the Socially Disadvantaged; Electrical Engineering; Engineering; English; Foreign Languages Education; Geological Engineering; Information Technology; Management; Mathematics Education; Public Administration); **Information and Computing Sciences** (Computer Engineering; Computer Science; Information Sciences; Information Technology; Library Science)

History: Founded 1965. Formerly known as Saint Louis College.

Degrees and Diplomas: *Certificate/Diploma*; *Associate Degree*; *Bachelor's Degree*; *Master's Degree*: Education (Mathematics; English); Business Administration; Engineering (Geodetic Engineering; Civil Engineering; Electrical Engineering); Information Technology; Public Administration; Teaching (English); *PhD*: Business Management; Public Administration; Education

Last Updated: 14/03/11

UNIVERSITY OF THE ASSUMPTION

Unisite Subd., Del Pilar, City of San Fernando, La Union 2000
Tel: +63(45) 961-1482 +63(45) 961-3617
Fax: +63(73) 961-5675 +63(45) 961-6059
Website: http://www.ua.edu.ph

President: Roberto C. Mallari

Vice-President for Administration: Manuel C. Sta. Maria

Colleges

International Hospitality and Tourism Management (Hotel and Restaurant; Hotel Management; Tourism); **Nursing** (Nursing); **Professional Teacher Education** (Art Education; Biology; Chemistry; Education; English; Ethics; Filipino; Foreign Languages Education; Health Education; Mathematics Education; Music Education; Native Language Education; Physical Education; Preschool Education; Primary Education; Religious Education; Secondary Education; Teacher Training)

Institutes

Theology and Religious Studies (Religious Studies; Theology)

Schools

Arts and Sciences (Communication Studies; Linguistics; Modern Languages; Psychology; Social Sciences); **Business** (Accountancy; Business Administration; Management Systems); **Graduate** (Business Administration; Civil Engineering; Education; Educational Administration; Educational and Student Counselling; Electrical Engineering; Engineering; English; Foreign Languages Education; Geological Engineering; Information Technology; Mathematics Education; Public Administration; Theology); **Technological Studies** (Architecture; Computer Science; Engineering; Interior Design; Technology)

History: Founded 1963 as College, became University 1980.

Governing Bodies: Board of Trustees

Academic Year: June to March (June-October; November-March)

Admission Requirements: Graduation from high school and entrance examination

Main Language(s) of Instruction: Filipino, English, Spanish

Degrees and Diplomas: *Bachelor's Degree*; *Master's Degree*: Business Administration; Public Administration; Theological Studies; Education (Early Childhood; Teaching Filipino; Physical Education; Mathematics; English; Educational Management; Guidance and Counselling); *PhD*: Education (Educational Management)

Special Facilities: Archdiocesan Museum

Libraries: c. 27,000 vols

Publications: Regina *(quarterly)*; Research Journal *(biannually)*; Veritas *(quarterly)*

Last Updated: 17/03/11

UNIVERSITY OF THE CORDILLERAS

Governor Pack Road, Baguio City, Benguet 2600
Tel: +63(74) 442-3316 +63(074) 442-2564
Fax: +63(74) 442-6268
EMail: inbox-uc@uc-bcf.edu.ph
Website: http://www.uc-bcf.edu.ph

Programmes

Graduate (Business Administration; Civil Engineering; Computer Science; Education; Engineering; Foreign Languages Education; Management; Native Language Education; Public Administration; Teacher Training); **Undergraduate and Professional** (Accountancy; Architecture; Biology; Business Administration; Civil Engineering; Computer Engineering; Computer Science; Criminology; Education; Electronic Engineering; English; Finance; Hotel and Restaurant; Hotel Management; Information Management; Information Technology; Law; Management; Management Systems; Mass Communication; Nursing; Political Sciences; Primary Education; Psychology; Public Administration; Secondary Education; Secretarial Studies; Telecommunications Engineering; Tourism)

History: Founded 1946. Acquired present status and title 2004.

Degrees and Diplomas: *Bachelor's Degree*; *Master's Degree*: Education; Teaching; Business Administration; Computer Science; Developmental Management; Information Technology; Public Administration; Mountain Engineering; Civil Engineering; *PhD*: Language Education; Management

Last Updated: 17/03/11

UNIVERSITY OF THE EAST - CALOOCAN

105 Samson Road, Caloocan City, Third District, Metro Manila 1400
Tel: +63(2) 367-4572
Fax: +63(2) 364-2659
EMail: uec@ue.edu.ph
Website: http://www.ue.edu.ph/caloocan

Chancellor: Fedeserio C. Camarao

Colleges

Arts and Science (Advertising and Publicity; Arts and Humanities; Communication Arts; Cooking and Catering; Hotel and Restaurant; Hotel Management; Journalism; Media Studies; Natural Sciences; Public Relations; Radio and Television Broadcasting; Tourism); **Business Administration** (Accountancy; Banking; Business Administration; Business Computing; Economics; Finance; Management; Marketing); **Engineering** (Civil Engineering; Computer Engineering; Electrical and Electronic Engineering; Engineering; Industrial Engineering; Information Technology; Mechanical Engineering; Telecommunications Engineering); **Fine Arts** (Advertising and Publicity; Fine Arts; Industrial Design; Interior Design; Painting and Drawing)

Further Information: Also Site in Quezon

History: Founded 1954.

Governing Bodies: Board of Trustees

Academic Year: June to March

Admission Requirements: Graduation from high school and entrance examination

Main Language(s) of Instruction: Filipino, English

Accrediting Agencies: Philippine Association of Colleges and Universities Commission on Accreditation

Degrees and Diplomas: *Bachelor's Degree*

Student Services: Academic counselling, Canteen, Health services, Social counselling, Sports facilities

Last Updated: 17/03/11

IAU UNIVERSITY OF THE EAST - MANILA

2219 Claro M. Recto Avenue, Sampaloc, City of Manila, First District, Metro Manila 1008
Tel: +63(2) 735-5471 +63(2) 735-6973
Fax: +63(2) 735-6972
Website: http://www.ue.edu.ph

President: Ester Albano-Garcia (2007-)
Tel: +63(2) 735-6973, Fax: +63(2) 338-1400
EMail: president@ue.edu.ph

Registrar: Romeo Q. Armada
Tel: +63(2) 735-5604 EMail: rqarmada@ue.edu.ph

International Relations: Edilberto B. Sulat, Jr.
Tel: +63(2) 735-8545 EMail: uro@ue.edu.ph

Colleges

Arts and Science (Arts and Humanities; Biology; Chinese; Communication Studies; Economics; English; Filipino; History; Hotel and Restaurant; Hotel Management; International Studies; Journalism; Justice Administration; Library Science; Mass Communication; Mathematics; Natural Sciences; Physics; Political Sciences; Psychology; Radio and Television Broadcasting; Sociology; Spanish; Statistics); **Business Administration** (Accountancy; Banking; Business Administration; Economics; Finance; Management; Marketing); **Computer Studies and Systems** (Computer Science; Information Management; Information Technology); **Dentistry** (Dentistry; Health Education); **Education** (Biology; Chemistry; Dietetics; Education; Educational Administration; Educational and Student Counselling; Foreign Languages Education; History; Home Economics; Mathematics Education; Native Language Education; Nutrition; Physical Education; Preschool Education; Primary Education; Science Education; Secondary Education; Social Studies; Special Education); **Engineering** (Civil Engineering; Computer Engineering; Electrical Engineering; Electronic Engineering; Industrial Engineering; Mechanical Engineering; Telecommunications Engineering); **Fine Arts** (Advertising and Publicity; Fine Arts; Industrial Design; Interior Design; Painting and Drawing); **Law** (Law)

Schools

Graduate (Administration; Arts and Humanities; Biology; Business Administration; Construction Engineering; Education; Educational Administration; Educational and Student Counselling; Engineering; English; Environmental Studies; Filipino; Finance; History; Human Resources; Information Sciences; Leadership; Library Science; Management; Marketing; Mathematics; Mathematics and Computer Science; Natural Sciences; Physical Education; Political Sciences; Public Administration; Social Sciences; Teacher Training)

History: Founded 1946 as Philippine College of Commerce and Business Administration. Acquired present status and title 1950.

Governing Bodies: Board of Trustees

Academic Year: June to March (June-October; November-March). Also Summer Session, April-May

Admission Requirements: Graduation from high school or recognized foreign equivalent, and entrance examination

Fees: (Pesos): Educational/College Undergraduate: 1,040 per unit, except Dentistry: 30,000-40,000 per semester; graduate Studies (MBA Executive): 1,500 per unit

Main Language(s) of Instruction: Filipino, English

Accrediting Agencies: Philippine Association of Colleges and Universities-Commission on Accreditation (PACUCOA); Philippine Accrediting Association of Schools, Colleges and Universities (PAASCU)

Degrees and Diplomas: *Bachelor's Degree*; *Bachelor's Degree*; *Master's Degree*: Business Administration; Construction Management; Dentistry; Education; Teaching; Public Administration; Library and Information Science; Environmental Science; Information Management; *PhD*: Education (Educational Administration and Leadership); Business Administration

Student Services: Academic counselling, Canteen, Cultural centre, Employment services, Foreign student adviser, Foreign Studies Centre, Health services, Social counselling, Sports facilities

Special Facilities: University Theatre

Libraries: 204,872 vols (includes vols at Caloocan)

Publications: Research Bulletin *(annually)*; UE Annual Report *(annually)*; UE Graduates School Research Journal, UE Journal *(annually)*; UE Today *(monthly)*

Academic Staff *2008-2009*	MEN	WOMEN	**TOTAL**
FULL-TIME	354	354	**708**
PART-TIME	19	6	**25**
Student Numbers *2008-2009*			
All (Foreign Included)	21,224	17,418	**38,642**
FOREIGN ONLY	721	479	**1,200**

Last Updated: 17/03/11

UNIVERSITY OF THE EAST - RAMON MAGSAYSAY MEMORIAL MEDICAL CENTER

62 Aurora Boulevard, Quezon City, Second District, Metro Manila 1113
Tel: +63(2) 715-0861 +63(2) 713-3315
Fax: +63(2) 715-1070
Website: http://www.uerm.edu.ph

President: Romeo A. Divinagracia

Colleges

Medicine (Anatomy; Biochemistry; Community Health; Epidemiology; Gastroenterology; Gynaecology and Obstetrics; Medicine; Microbiology; Neurosciences; Ophthalmology; Otorhinolaryngology; Paediatrics; Parasitology; Pathology; Pharmacology; Physiology; Psychiatry and Mental Health; Surgery); **Nursing** (Nursing); **Physical Therapy** (Physical Therapy)

Schools

Graduate (Child Care and Development; Community Health; Diabetology; Health Administration; Health Education; Nursing; Occupational Health; Psychiatry and Mental Health; Public Health; Traditional Eastern Medicine; Tropical Medicine)

History: Founded 1957.

Degrees and Diplomas: *Bachelor's Degree*; *Master's Degree*: Nursing (Nursing Service; Nursing Education Administration; Mental Health and Psychiatric Nursing; Matelnal Child Nursing; Adult Health Nursing); Asian Health Practices; Internal Medicine (Diabetology); Public Health (Epidemiology; Health Facility Management); Tropical Medicine; Health Science Education

Last Updated: 17/03/11

UNIVERSITY OF THE IMMACULATE CONCEPTION

Father Selga Street, Davao City, Davao del Sur 8000
Tel: +63(82) 221-8090 +63(82) 221-8181
Fax: +63(82) 226-2676
Website: http://www.uic.edu.ph

President: María Assumpta M. David (1999-)
Tel: +63(82) 226-2676

Vice-President, Administration and Finance: Maria Mauricia Villarmil

Programmes

Arts, Music and Education (Art Education; Arts and Humanities; Communication Arts; Curriculum; Education; Educational and Student Counselling; English; Filipino; Foreign Languages Education; Health Education; History; Home Economics Education; Literature; Mathematics Education; Music; Music Education; Musical Instruments; Native Language Education; Natural Sciences; Physical Education; Preschool Education; Primary Education; Psychology; Science Education; Singing; Social Sciences; Social Studies; Special Education); **Business** (Accountancy; Business Administration; Business and Commerce; Management; Marketing); **Health Sciences** (Chemistry; Dietetics; Health Sciences; Medical Technology; Nursing; Nutrition; Pharmacy); **Science and Technology** (Civil Engineering; Computer Engineering; Computer Science; Electronic Engineering; Engineering; Information Management; Information Technology; Telecommunications Engineering)

Schools

Graduate Studies (Business Administration; Chemistry; Education; Educational Administration; Educational and Student Counselling; Engineering; English; Foreign Languages Education; Information Management; Information Technology; Mathematics Education; Pharmacy; Physical Education; Physics; Primary Education; Religious Education; Social Sciences); **Postgraduate** (Business Administration; Education; Educational Administration; Linguistics; Management)

Further Information: Traditional and Open Learning Institution

History: Founded 1905, acquired present status 1992.

Governing Bodies: Board of Trustees

Admission Requirements: Report card; Entrance examination and interview; Certificate of Good Moral Character

Main Language(s) of Instruction: English

Accrediting Agencies: Philippine Accrediting Association for Schools, Colleges and Universities

Degrees and Diplomas: *Bachelor's Degree*; *Master's Degree*: Business Administration; Religious Education; Educational Management; Teaching College Physics; Teaching College Chemistry; Elementary Education; Education (Mathematics; Social Sciences; Guidance and Counselling); Engineering Education; Physical Education; Pharmacy; Information Technology; Information Management; *PhD*: Educational Leadership; Linguistics; Business Management

Student Services: Academic counselling, Canteen, Cultural centre, Employment services, Health services, Nursery care, Social counselling, Sports facilities

Student Residential Facilities: Yes

Special Facilities: Clinical Laboratory, Science Resource Centre, Information Technology Research Centre, Computer Laboratory

Libraries: Yes. Educational Research Centre (ERIC); Thomas Jefferson Information Centre (On-line); Microfiche Reader/ Printer

Publications: Research Journal *(biennially)*

Last Updated: 17/03/11

UNIVERSITY OF THE VISAYAS (UV)

D. Jakosalem Corner Colon Street, Cebu City, Cebu 6000
Tel: +63(32) 254-9902
Fax: +63(32) 121-1391
EMail: registrar@uv.edu.ph
Website: http://www.uv.edu.ph/

President: Eduardo R. Gullas (1964-)
Tel: +63(32) 254-5759, Fax: +63(32) 253-2752

Campuses

Dalaguete (Technology); **Gullas College Danao City Branch** (Accountancy; Art Education; Business Administration; Criminology; Economics; Education; English; Filipino; Finance; Foreign Languages Education; Health Education; Hotel and Restaurant; Hotel Management; Human Resources; Information Technology; Management; Marketing; Mathematics Education; Music Education; Native Language Education; Physical Education; Primary Education; Secondary Education); **Gullas College Toledo Branch** (Business Administration; Computer Engineering; Computer Science; Education; Primary Education; Secondary Education); **Mandaue** (Computer Engineering; English; Foreign Languages Education; Literature; Secondary Education); **UV-Gullas College Minglanilla** (Civil Security; Environmental Management); **UV-Gullas College of Medicine** (Medicine)

Colleges

Arts and Science (Arts and Humanities; Biology; Economics; English; Hotel and Restaurant; Journalism; Literature; Natural Sciences; Political Sciences; Psychology; Public Administration; Tourism); **Commerce and Business Administration** (Accountancy; Banking; Business Administration; Business and Commerce; Finance; Management; Marketing; Secretarial Studies; Taxation; Tourism); **Computer Studies** (Computer Engineering; Computer Science); **Criminology** (Criminal Law; Criminology; Police Studies); **Education and Teacher Training** (Economics; English; Filipino; Foreign Languages Education; Home Economics Education; Mathematics Education; Native Language Education; Physical Education; Primary Education; Science Education; Secondary Education; Social Studies; Special Education); **Engineering and Architecture** (Architecture; Civil Engineering; Electrical Engineering; Electronic Engineering; Engineering; Industrial Engineering; Information Technology; Marine Engineering; Marine Transport; Mechanical Engineering; Telecommunications Engineering); **Law** (Civil Law; Constitutional Law; International Law; Labour Law; Law; Political Sciences); **Medicine** (Medicine); **Nursing** (Midwifery; Nursing); **Pharmacy** (Biochemistry; Microbiology; Pharmacology; Pharmacy; Zoology)

Schools

Graduate Studies (Business Administration; Child Care and Development; Community Health; Economics; Education; Educational Administration; Educational and Student Counselling; English; Filipino; Foreign Languages Education; Health Education; Home Economics Education; Human Resources; Literacy Education; Management; Management Systems; Marine Science and Oceanography; Marketing; Mathematics Education; Native Language; Nursing; Physical Education; Preschool Education; Public Administration; Science Education; Social Studies; Special Education; Technology Education)

History: Founded 1919 as Institute, became University 1948. A private Institution, financed by tuition fees.

Governing Bodies: Board of Trustees

Academic Year: June to March (June-October; November-March)

Admission Requirements: Graduation from high school or recognized foreign equivalent

Fees: (Pesos): 7,000 per semester

Main Language(s) of Instruction: English

Accrediting Agencies: Philippine Association of Colleges and Universities - Commission on Accreditation (PACU-COA)

Degrees and Diplomas: *Certificate/Diploma*; *Associate Degree*; *Bachelor's Degree*; *Master's Degree*: Public Administration; Education; Nursing; Teaching; Business Administration; Public Administration; Management Engineering; *PhD*: Management (Human Resources Management); Education (School Administration); Public Administration

Student Services: Academic counselling, Canteen, Cultural centre, Employment services, Foreign student adviser, Handicapped facilities, Health services, Language programs, Social counselling, Sports facilities

Student Residential Facilities: Yes

Libraries: Main College Library, c. 65,000 vols; Graduate School, c. 18,500; Medicine, c. 14,000; Law, c. 8,000

Publications: Humanitas Folio *(quarterly)*; Research Journal *(biannually)*; UV Journal *(annually)*; Visayanian *(biannually)*

Last Updated: 17/03/11

VALENCIA COLLEGES

Hagkol, Valencia City, Bukidnon 8709
Tel: +63(88) 828-4023 +63(88) 828-1338
Fax: +63(88) 828-4023
EMail: valencia_colleges@yahoo.com

Director: Pablito L. Intong

Programmes

Graduate (Education; Government; Public Administration); **Undergraduate** (Arts and Humanities; Business Administration; Criminology; Economics; Primary Education; Secondary Education; Social Studies; Sociology)

History: Founded 1989.

Degrees and Diplomas: *Bachelor's Degree*; *Master's Degree*: Government Administration; Arts in Teaching

Last Updated: 17/03/11

VELEZ COLLEGE

79 F. Ramos Street, Cebu City, Cebu 6000
Tel: +63(32) 253-6887 +63(32) 253-7388
Fax: +63(32) 253-7996
EMail: velez@mozcom.com

President: Teodoro V. Diez Tel: +63(32) 253-7388

Programmes

Undergraduate and Professional (Biology; Medical Technology; Nursing; Occupational Therapy; Physical Therapy)

History: Founded 1996.

Degrees and Diplomas: *Bachelor's Degree*

Last Updated: 18/03/11

VERITAS COLLEGE OF IROSIN

San Julian, Irosin, Sorsogon 4707
Tel: +63(56) 557- 3249
Fax: +63(56) 557- 3249

Director: Elias F. Escanilla

Programmes

Undergraduate and Professional (Agricultural Engineering; Business Administration; Business and Commerce; Computer Science; Criminology; Curriculum; Economics; Education; English; Filipino;

Finance; Foreign Languages Education; Health Education; Information Technology; Management; Mathematics Education; Music Education; Native Language Education; Physical Education; Political Sciences; Primary Education; Science Education; Secondary Education)

History: Founded 1985.

Degrees and Diplomas: *Certificate/Diploma*; *Bachelor's Degree*
Last Updated: 18/03/11

VILLAFLORES COLLEGE

Legaspi Street, Tanjay, Negros Oriental 6204
Tel: +63(35) 415-9015

President: Nora V. Pilas

Programmes

Graduate (Education; Educational Administration; Educational and Student Counselling); **Undergraduate and Professional** (Accountancy; Banking; Business Administration; Business and Commerce; Education; English; Filipino; Finance; Foreign Languages Education; Human Resources; Management; Mathematics Education; Native Language Education; Political Sciences; Primary Education; Secondary Education)

History: Founded 1952.

Degrees and Diplomas: *Certificate/Diploma*; *Bachelor's Degree*; *Master's Degree*: Education (Administration and Supervision; Guidance and Counselling)
Last Updated: 18/03/11

VILLAGERS MONTESSORI COLLEGE

Dalsol Street, GSIS Village, Project 8, Quezon City, Second District, Metro Manila 1106
Tel: +63(2) 926-2431
Fax: +63(2) 929-0857

President: Armando M. Lascano

Programmes

Undergraduate and Professional (Business Administration; Economics; Education; English; Finance; Foreign Languages Education; Management; Marketing; Mathematics Education; Preschool Education; Primary Education; Secondary Education; Special Education)

History: Founded 1983. Formerly known as Villagers Montessori School (1984-2003).

Degrees and Diplomas: *Bachelor's Degree*
Last Updated: 18/03/11

VIRGEN DE LOS REMEDIOS COLLEGE - OLONGAPO CITY

No. 10 Fontaine Street, East Bajac-Bajac, Olongapo City, Zambales 2200
Tel: +63(47) 222-3045
Fax: +63(47) 222-7649

President: Remedios M. Dela Peña

Programmes

Graduate (Business Administration; Education; Management; Philosophy; Public Administration); **Undergraduate and Professional** (Accountancy; Arts and Humanities; Business Administration; Computer Engineering; Computer Science; Criminology; Education; Primary Education; Secondary Education)

History: Founded 1983.

Degrees and Diplomas: *Bachelor's Degree*; *Master's Degree*: Business Management; Public Management; Arts in Education; *PhD*: Education; Philosophy
Last Updated: 18/03/11

VIRGEN MILAGROSA UNIVERSITY FOUNDATION AND VMU INSTITUTE OF MEDICAL FOUNDATION (VMUF)

Martin P. Posadas Avenue, San Carlos City, Pangasinan 2420
Tel: +63(75) 531-2222 +63(75) 532-2380
Fax: +63(75) 955-5707 +63(75) 634-2692
EMail: vmuf@mozcom.com
Website: http://www.vmuf.edu.ph

President: Maria Lilia Posadas Juan
Tel: +63(75) 955-5054, Fax: +63(75) 6 34-2692

Vice-President Finance: Avelino GeagaFax: +63(75) 634-2692

International Relations: Angelo Juan
Tel: +63(75) 634-2693, Fax: +63(75) 6 34-2692

Programmes

Graduate (Biology; Business Administration; Education; Educational Research; Engineering Management; Medicine; Nursing; Philosophy; Public Administration; Public Health; Science Education; Teacher Training; Veterinary Science); **Undergraduate and Professional** (Accountancy; Banking; Biology; Business Administration; Civil Engineering; Computer Science; Economics; Education; Electrical Engineering; Electronic Engineering; English; Finance; Hotel and Restaurant; Hotel Management; Information Sciences; Law; Library Science; Management; Management Systems; Marketing; Mechanical Engineering; Medical Technology; Midwifery; Nursing; Pharmacy; Physical Education; Physical Therapy; Political Sciences; Primary Education; Psychology; Radiology; Secondary Education; Secretarial Studies; Sports; Telecommunications Engineering; Veterinary Science)

Further Information: Also Teaching Hospital and VMU Medical Foundation Institute

History: Founded 1958, acquired present status and title 1994.

Governing Bodies: Board of Trustees

Academic Year: June to May (June-October; October March; April-May)

Admission Requirements: Graduation from high school and entrance examination; Bachelor of Science degree for Medicine and Law

Main Language(s) of Instruction: Filipino, English

Accrediting Agencies: Commission on Higher Education (CHED); Technical Skills and Development Authority (TESDA)

Degrees and Diplomas: *Associate Degree*; *Bachelor's Degree*; *Post Baccalaureate Certificate/Diploma*; *Master's Degree*: Nursing; Business Administration; Public Administration; Public Health; Biology; Engineering Management; Teaching; *PhD*: Dental Medicine; Medicine; Veterinary Medicine

Student Services: Academic counselling, Canteen, Employment services, Foreign student adviser, Health services, Social counselling, Sports facilities

Student Residential Facilities: Yes

Libraries: Main Library

Publications: Virginian *(quarterly)*; VMUF Research Journal *(biannually)*

Press or Publishing House: VMUF Printing Press
Last Updated: 18/03/11

VISAYAN MARITIME ACADEMY

East Carol Street, Sum-ag, Bacolod City, Negros Occidental 6100
Tel: +63(34) 444-1090 +63(34) 444-1093
Fax: +63(34) 444-1090
Website: http://www.vma.edu.ph/

President: Elisabeth Orola Salabas

Programmes

Undergraduate and Professional (Business and Commerce; Computer Science; Cooking and Catering; Hotel and Restaurant; Hotel Management; Information Management; Information Technology; Marine Engineering; Marine Transport; Tourism)

History: Founded 1987. Formerly known as Visayan Maritime Academy. Acquired present title 2006.

Degrees and Diplomas: *Bachelor's Degree*
Last Updated: 18/03/11

WESLEYAN COLLEGE OF MANILA

1706 Leveriza Street, Pasay City, Manila, Fourth District, Metro Manila 1300
Tel: +63(2) 303-4031 +63(2) 524-3497
Fax: +63(2) 303-4031
EMail: iso@wcm.edu.ph
Website: http://www.wcm.edu.ph

President: Florita V. Miranda

Programmes

Undergraduate and Professional (Accountancy; Business Administration; Communication Studies; Computer Engineering; Criminology; Education; English; Foreign Languages Education; Information Technology; Management; Preschool Education; Primary Education; Psychology; Secondary Education; Special Education)

History: Founded 2000.

Degrees and Diplomas: *Associate Degree*; *Bachelor's Degree*
Last Updated: 18/03/11

WESLEYAN UNIVERSITY - PHILIPPINES

Mabini Extension, Cabanatuan City, Nueva Ecija 3100
Tel: +63(44) 463-2162
Fax: +63(44) 463-0596
EMail: admin@wesleyan.edu.ph
Website: http://www.wesleyan.edu.ph

President: Manuel G. Palomo

Campuses

Aurora (Banking; Business Administration; Business and Commerce; Computer Science; Criminology; Curriculum; Economics; Education; Educational and Student Counselling; Finance; Management; Marketing; Political Sciences; Preschool Education; Primary Education)

Colleges

Allied Medical and Health Courses (Medical Technology; Midwifery; Radiology); **Arts and Sciences** (Arts and Humanities; Economics; English; Mass Communication; Mathematics; Political Sciences; Psychology; Social Work); **Business and Accountancy** (Accountancy; Business Administration; Business and Commerce; Finance; Marketing); **Computer Studies** (Computer Science; Information Technology; Software Engineering); **Criminal Justice** (Criminology); **Education** (Art Education; Curriculum; Education; English; Ethics; Filipino; Foreign Languages Education; History; Mathematics Education; Music Education; Native Language Education; Physical Education; Preschool Education; Primary Education; Science Education; Secondary Education); **Hotel, Restaurant and Institutional Management** (Hotel and Restaurant; Hotel Management; Management); **Nursing** (Nursing); **Technology** (Computer Engineering; Electronic Engineering; Technology; Telecommunications Engineering)

Schools

Graduate Studies (Business Administration; Education; Educational Administration; Nursing)

History: Founded 1946 as Philippine Wesleyan College. Acquired present status and title 1978.

Governing Bodies: Board of Trustees

Main Language(s) of Instruction: English

Degrees and Diplomas: *Bachelor's Degree*; *Master's Degree*: Education (Filipino; English Language Teaching; Educational Management; Mathematics); Nursing; *PhD*: Education (Educational Management)

Student Services: Academic counselling, Canteen, Cultural centre, Employment services, Health services, Language programs, Nursery care, Social counselling, Sports facilities
Last Updated: 18/03/11

WEST AGUSAN COLLEGES

Purok #4, Zillovia, Talacognon, Agusan del Sur 8510
Tel: +63(918) 595-0677
Fax: +63(918) 595-0677

President: Roberto T. Justo

Programmes

Accountancy (Accountancy)
History: Founded 1991
Degrees and Diplomas: *Associate Degree*; *Bachelor's Degree*
Last Updated: 18/03/11

WEST BAY COLLEGE

Ilaya Street, Alabang, City of Muntinlupa, Fourth District, Metro Manila 1770
Tel: +63(2) 850-2966 +63(2) 842-4298
Fax: +63(2) 850-3027
EMail: Info_wbc@westbaycollege.edu.ph
Website: http://www.westbaycollege.edu.ph

President: Benito P. Chiongbian

Colleges

Arts and Science (Mass Communication; Psychology); **Business** (Accountancy; Business Administration; Management; Marketing; Taxation); **Engineering** (Computer Engineering; Computer Science; Electrical Engineering; Electronic Engineering; Engineering; Marine Engineering; Mechanical Engineering; Telecommunications Engineering); **Hotel and Restaurant Management** (Hotel and Restaurant; Hotel Management); **Maritime Studies** (Marine Engineering; Marine Transport); **Nursing** (Nursing)

History: Founded 1996.

Degrees and Diplomas: *Bachelor's Degree*
Last Updated: 18/03/11

WEST COAST COLLEGE

Rizal Street, Pioduran, Albay 4516

President: Salvador Gnilo

Programmes

Undergraduate and Professional (Business and Commerce; Business Education; English; Foreign Languages Education; Primary Education; Secondary Education)

History: Founded 2000.

Degrees and Diplomas: *Bachelor's Degree*
Last Updated: 18/03/11

WEST NEGROS COLLEGE

Burgos Street, Bacolod City, Negros Occidental 6100
Tel: +63(34) 434-4561 +63(34) 434-4569
Fax: +63(34) 433-4818
EMail: registrar@wnu.edu.ph
Website: http://www.wnu.edu.ph/index.asp

President: Suzette Lilian A. Agustin
Tel: +63(34) 435-3829 EMail: presidents-office@wnu.edu.ph

Colleges

Arts and Science (English; Mathematics; Psychology; Public Administration); **Business and Management** (Accountancy; Business Administration; Economics; Hotel and Restaurant; Hotel Management; Human Resources; Management; Management Systems; Marketing; Secretarial Studies; Tourism); **Criminal Justice Education** (Civil Security; Criminology); **Education** (Art Education; Cultural Studies; Education; Educational Administration; Educational and Student Counselling; Educational Psychology; English; Filipino; Foreign Languages Education; Mathematics Education; Music Education; Native Language Education; Physical Education; Preschool Education; Primary Education; Secondary Education; Special Education; Teacher Training); **Engineering** (Chemical Engineering; Civil Engineering; Electrical Engineering; Electronic Engineering; Mechanical Engineering; Telecommunications Engineering); **Information and Communication Technology** (Computer Science; Information Technology); **Maritime Studies** (Marine Engineering; Marine Transport); **Nursing and Allied Health Sciences** (Health Education; Midwifery; Nursing)

Schools

Graduate (Education; Educational Administration; Educational and Student Counselling; Educational Psychology; Filipino; Native Language Education; Nursing; Physical Education; Public Administration)

History: Founded 1948.

Degrees and Diplomas: *Certificate/Diploma*; *Associate Degree*; *Bachelor's Degree*; *Master's Degree*: Education (Guidance and Psychology; Administration and Supervision; Physical Education; Filipino); Nursing; Public Administration; *PhD*: Public Administration; Philosophy in Educational Management
Last Updated: 18/03/11

WESTERN COLLEGES

Capt. C. Nazareno Street, Naic, Cavite 4110
Tel: +63(46) 522-4294
EMail: Westerncollegesnaiccavite@yahoo.com

Director: Precilla T. Baylosis

Programmes

Graduate (Education; Educational Administration); **Undergraduate and Professional** (Accountancy; Business Administration; Business and Commerce; Economics; English; Filipino; Finance; Foreign Languages Education; Hotel and Restaurant; Hotel Management; Management; Marketing; Mathematics Education; Native Language Education; Primary Education; Secondary Education; Social Studies)

History: Founded 1945. Acquired present status 1946.

Degrees and Diplomas: *Certificate/Diploma*; *Bachelor's Degree*; *Master's Degree*: Education (Administration and Supervision)
Last Updated: 31/03/11

WESTERN INSTITUTE OF TECHNOLOGY

Luna Street, La Paz, Iloilo City, Iloilo 5000
Tel: +63(33) 320-0902 +63(33) 320-9767
Fax: +63(33) 320-1484
EMail: wit@edu.ph
Website: http://www.wit.edu.ph

President: Richard S. Salas Tel: +63(33) 320-0259

Registrar: Lorna T. Balcena

Colleges

Arts and Sciences (Biology; Computer Education; Hotel and Restaurant; Hotel Management; Mathematics); **Business Administration** (Accountancy; Business Administration; Finance; Management; Management Systems; Secretarial Studies); **Engineering** (Civil Engineering; Computer Engineering; Electrical Engineering; Engineering; Information Technology; Marine Engineering; Mechanical Engineering)

Schools

Graduate (Business Administration; Chemical Engineering; Computer Education; Electrical Engineering; Engineering; Management; Mechanical Engineering)

History: Founded 1957. Acquired present status 1964.

Degrees and Diplomas: *Certificate/Diploma*; *Bachelor's Degree*; *Master's Degree*: Business Management; Engineering
Last Updated: 31/03/11

WESTERN LEYTE COLLEGE OF ORMOC CITY

A. Bonifacio Street, Ormoc City, Leyte 6541
Tel: +63(53) 255-8549
Fax: +63(53) 561-5308

President: Manuel T. Fiel

Programmes

Accountancy (Accountancy); **Arts and Humanities** (Arts and Humanities; Economics; English; Filipino; Political Sciences; Psychology); **Business Administration and Commerce** (Accountancy; Banking; Business Administration; Business Computing; Human Resources; Management; Marketing; Secretarial Studies); **Education** (Art Education; Cultural Studies; Economics; Education; English; Filipino; Foreign Languages Education; Health Education; Mathematics Education; Music Education; Native Language Education; Physical Education; Primary Education; Science Education; Secondary Education); **Graduate** (Education; Educational Administration); **ICT** (Computer Science; Information Technology); **Law** (Law); **Nursing** (Nursing)

History: Founded 1945.

Degrees and Diplomas: *Bachelor's Degree*; *Master's Degree*: Education (Educational Administration and Supervision)
Last Updated: 31/03/11

WESTERN MINDANAO COOPERATIVE COLLEGE

Doña Vicenta Bldg., Gov. Lim Avenue, Zamboanga City, Zamboanga del Sur 7000
Tel: +63(62) 992-6550

Chairman: Diolito C. Sonido

Programmes

Arts (Journalism; Management; Small Business; Social Sciences); **Education** (Curriculum; Education; English; Primary Education; Secondary Education)

History: Founded 2002.

Degrees and Diplomas: *Bachelor's Degree*
Last Updated: 31/03/11

WESTMEAD INTERNATIONAL SCHOOL

Gulod West, Batangas City, Batangas 4200
Tel: +63(43) 300-2235
Fax: +63(43) 722-1868
EMail: westmeadinternational@yahoo.com.ph

Chairperson/President: Iluminada L. de Chavez

Programmes

Undergraduate and Professional (Accountancy; Business Administration; Computer Science; Cooking and Catering; Education; Hotel Management; Information Technology; Mechanical Engineering; Primary Education; Secondary Education; Software Engineering; Taxation; Tourism)

History: Founded 2007.

Degrees and Diplomas: *Bachelor's Degree*
Last Updated: 07/04/11

WISDOM INTERNATIONAL SCHOOL FOR HIGHER EDUCATION STUDIES

PMTC Bldg., 037 Bo. Green, Bangon, Marawi City, Lanao del Sur
Website: http://wisdom.edu.ph

President: Mamarinta P. Mababaya

Programmes

Business Administration (Business Administration); **Islamic Studies** (Islamic Studies)

History: Founded 2005.

Degrees and Diplomas: *Bachelor's Degree*
Last Updated: 07/04/11

WORLD CITI COLLEGES (WCC)

960 Aurora Blvd. Cor. T. Morato Ave., Quezon City, Second District, Metro Manila 1100
Tel: +63(2) 913-8380 +63(2) 913-6367
Fax: +63(2) 913-8383
EMail: info@worldciti.edu.ph
Website: http://www.worldciti.edu.ph

President: Arlyn Grace V. Guico

Campuses

Antipolo (Accountancy; Air Transport; Business Administration; Criminology; Education; Hotel and Restaurant; Hotel Management; Information Technology; Midwifery; Nursing; Technology; Tourism); **Caloocan** (Business Administration; Criminology; Education; Hotel and Restaurant; Hotel Management; Information Technology; Midwifery; Nursing; Tourism)

Colleges

Arts and Sciences (Biology; Business Administration; Chemistry; Modern Languages; Natural Sciences; Philosophy; Psychology; Social Sciences); **Business Administration** (Business Administration); **Information Technology** (Information Technology); **Medical Radiologic Technology** (Medical Technology; Radiology); **Medical Technology** (Laboratory Techniques; Medical

Technology); **Nursing and Midwifery** (Midwifery; Nursing); **Pharmacy** (Pharmacy); **Rehabilitation Sciences** (Physical Therapy; Rehabilitation and Therapy; Respiratory Therapy)

Departments
Medical Transcription

Schools
International Hospitality Management (Cooking and Catering; Hotel and Restaurant; Hotel Management; Tourism)

Further Information: Also campuses in Caloocan City (formerly Holy Trinity School) and WCC in Antipolo City (formerly Westminster College)

History: Founded 1971. Formerly known as formerly Quezon City Medical Center and Colleges.

Degrees and Diplomas: *Certificate/Diploma*; *Associate Degree*; *Bachelor's Degree*; *Master's Degree*

Last Updated: 07/04/11

WORLDTECH RESOURCES FOUNDATION - IRIGA CITY

Alfelor Street, Iriga City, Camarines Sur 4431
Tel: +63(54) 456-0259 +63(54) 655-1620
EMail: wri-iriga@digitelone.com

President/Chief Executive Officer: Daniel A. de Leon

Programmes
Computer Science (Computer Science)

History: Founded 1992-1993.

Degrees and Diplomas: *Associate Degree*; *Bachelor's Degree*

Last Updated: 07/04/11

WORLDTECH RESOURCES FOUNDATION - NAGA CITY

National Highway, Concepcion Grande, Naga City, Camarines Sur 4400
Tel: +63(54) 472-8733 +63(54) 472-8729
Fax: +63(54) 472-8733
EMail: wri_naga@yahoo.com

President/Chief Executive Officer: Daniel A. de Leon

Programmes
Undergraduate and Professional (Business Administration; Computer Engineering; Computer Science; Management; Marketing)

History: Founded 1989.

Degrees and Diplomas: *Associate Degree*; *Bachelor's Degree*

Last Updated: 07/04/11

XAVIER UNIVERSITY (XU)

Corrales Avenue, Cagayan de Oro City, Misamis Oriental 9000
Tel: +63(8822) 726-335 +63(8822) 723-116
Fax: +63(8822) 727-163
Website: http://www.xu.edu.ph

President: José Ramon T. Villarin

Registrar: Aurora M. Gapuz
Tel: +63(8822) 723-116, Ext. 2011 EMail: apaa@xu.edu.ph

Colleges
Agriculture (Agricultural Engineering; Agriculture; Animal Husbandry; Crop Production; Food Technology); **Arts and Sciences** (Arts and Humanities; Biology; Chemistry; Economics; English; Filipino; History; International Studies; Literature; Marine Biology; Mathematics; Natural Sciences; Philosophy; Psychology; Sociology); **Business and Management** (Accountancy; Agricultural Business; Business Administration; Business and Commerce; Information Management; Management); **Education** (Education; Primary Education; Secondary Education); **Engineering** (Chemical Engineering; Civil Engineering; Computer Science; Electrical Engineering; Electronic Engineering; Engineering; Industrial Engineering; Mechanical Engineering; Technology; Telecommunications Engineering); **Nursing** (Nursing)

Schools
Graduate (Anthropology; Biology; Business Administration; Economics; Education; Educational Administration; Educational and Student Counselling; Engineering; English; History; Information Technology; Mathematics Education; Nursing; Psychology; Public Administration; Sociology); **Law** (Law); **Medicine** (Medicine)

History: Founded 1933 as Ateneo de Cagayan by Jesuit missionary Fr. James T.G. Hayes, S.J. Acquired present title 1958. A private Institution recognized by the Department of Education, Culture and Sports, and the Commission on Higher Education. The University works in consortium with 'Ateneo de Davao' and 'Ateneo de Zamboanga' Universities.

Governing Bodies: Board of Trustees

Academic Year: June to March (June-October; November-March)

Admission Requirements: Graduation from high school or equivalent and entrance examination

Fees: (Pesos): c. 15,000-25,000 per semester

Main Language(s) of Instruction: English

Accrediting Agencies: Philipine Accrediting Association for Schools, Colleges, and Universities

Degrees and Diplomas: *Certificate/Diploma*: Mechanical Engineering (BSME), 5 yrs; *Bachelor's Degree*: Accountancy (BSAc); Agribusiness (BSAB); Agriculture (BSA); Biology (BSBio); Business Management (BSBM); Chemistry (BSChem); Computer Science (BSCS); Development Communication (BSDC); Elementary Education (BSEEd); English Literature; Food Technology (BSFT); Information Management (BSIM); International Studies; Marine Biology (BSN); Mathematics (BSMath); Psychology (BSPsy); Secondary Education (BSE); Sociology (AB), 4 yrs; *Bachelor's Degree*: Agricultural Engineering (BSAE); Chemical Engineering (BSChE); Civil Engineering (BSCE); Electrical Engineering (BSEE); Electronics and Communication Engineering (BSCE); Industrial Engineering (BSIE), 5 yrs; *Bachelor's Degree*: Law (LLB), 4 yrs following first degree; *Post Baccalaureate Certificate/Diploma*: Medicine (MD), 4 yrs following first degree; *Master's Degree (MA)*: a further 2 yrs; *Master's Degree*: Business Administration (MBA); Public Administration (MPA), a further 2 yrs; *PhD*: Education; Public Administration (DPA); Sociology; Anthropology, a further 3-5 yrs

Student Services: Academic counselling, Canteen, Cultural centre, Health services, Social counselling, Sports facilities

Special Facilities: Folk-Life Museum

Libraries: Undergraduate library, c. 75,000 vols; Graduate library, c. 6,000 vols; Law library, c. 4,000 vols; Medical library, c. 7,500 vols

Publications: Kinaadman Journal *(annually)*

Last Updated: 31/03/11

XIJEN COLLEGE OF MT. PROVINCE

Upper Caluttit, Bontoc, Mt. Province 2616
Tel: +63(74) 606-8132
Fax: +63(74) 606-8132

President: Joel T. Fagsao

Programmes
Entrepreneurship (Management); **Information Technology** (Information Technology); **Secondary Education** (Filipino; Native Language Education; Secondary Education)

History: Founded 1992.

Degrees and Diplomas: *Bachelor's Degree*

Last Updated: 31/03/11

YAMAN LAHI FOUNDATION - EMILIO AGUINALDO COLLEGE

Congressional Avenue - East, Dasmariñas, Cavite 4114
Tel: +63(46) 416-4341
Fax: +63(46) 416-0260

President: Jose Paolo E. Campos

Programmes
Undergraduate and Professional (Accountancy; Banking; Biology; Business Administration; Civil Engineering; Communication Studies; Computer Engineering; Computer Science; Criminology; Education; Electrical Engineering; Electronic Engineering; English; Filipino; Finance; Foreign Languages Education; History; Hotel and

Restaurant; Hotel Management; Management; Marketing; Mathematics Education; Mechanical Engineering; Native Language Education; Nursing; Primary Education; Psychology; Science Education; Secondary Education; Taxation; Telecommunications Engineering)

History: Founded 1996. Formerly known as Emilio Aguinaldo College.

Degrees and Diplomas: *Certificate/Diploma*: 2-3 yrs; *Bachelor's Degree*: 4 yrs; *Bachelor's Degree*: Electrical Engineering, 5 yrs
Last Updated: 31/03/11

ZAMBOANGA DEL SUR MARITIME INSTITUTE OF TECHNOLOGY

Pagadian City, Zamboanga del Sur 7016
Tel: +63(62) 214-1336 +63(62) 215-2232
Fax: +63(62) 214-3613
EMail: zsmit_balangasan@yahoo.com

President: Manuel A. Maglasang

Programmes

Undergraduate and Professional Studies (Accountancy; Business and Commerce; Computer Engineering; Computer Science; Criminology; Hotel and Restaurant; Hotel Management; Management; Marine Engineering; Marine Transport; Mass Communication; Mechanical Engineering; Radio and Television Broadcasting)

History: Founded 1994.

Degrees and Diplomas: *Bachelor's Degree*: 4-5 yrs
Last Updated: 31/03/11

ZAMBOANGA UNIVERSITY

Universidad de Zamboanga

A. Eustaquio Quadrangle, Zamboanga City, Zamboanga del Sur 7000
Tel: +63(62) 991-3929 +63(62) 991-5677
Fax: +63(62) 991-9371 +63(62) 992-7677
EMail: comm_centre@uz.edu.ph
Website: http://www.uz.edu.ph/

President: Arturo F. Eustaquio III

Vice-President Academic Affairs: Bashiruddin A. Ajihil

Vice-President for Administration: Ronald S. Eustaquio

Campuses

Ipil (Accountancy; Business Administration; Computer Engineering; Computer Science; Criminology; Political Sciences; Primary Education; Secondary Education)

Colleges

Business Management (Accountancy; Agricultural Engineering; Business Administration; Business and Commerce; Economics; Finance; Human Resources; Management; Management Systems; Marketing; Secretarial Studies; Taxation); **Engineering and Information Technology** (Civil Engineering; Computer Engineering; Computer Science; Electronic Engineering; Engineering; Information Technology; Telecommunications Engineering)

Institutes

Technical Education (Agricultural Engineering; Computer Engineering; Computer Science; Dental Technology; Electrical Engineering; Electronic Engineering; Health Administration; Hotel and Restaurant; Hotel Management; Nursing)

Schools

Allied Medicine (Medical Technology; Nursing; Pharmacy; Radiology; Respiratory Therapy); **Criminal Justice** (Civil Security; Criminology; Police Studies); **Education, Arts and Science** (Art Education; Biology; Chemistry; Civics; Curriculum; Economics; Education; English; Ethics; Filipino; Foreign Languages Education; History; Home Economics Education; Information Sciences; Islamic Studies; Library Science; Mathematics; Mathematics Education; Music Education; Native Language Education; Natural Sciences; Physical Education; Physics; Political Sciences; Preschool Education; Primary Education; Public Administration; Secondary Education; Social Studies; Social Work; Technology Education); **Graduate** (Business Administration; Business Education; Criminology; Curriculum; Education; Educational Administration; English; Filipino; Foreign Languages Education; Information Management; Library Science; Mathematics Education; Native Language Education; Preschool Education; Public Administration; Science Education)

History: Founded 1948 as Zamboanga Arturo Eustaquio Colleges.

Degrees and Diplomas: *Bachelor's Degree*; *Master's Degree*: Business Administration; Public Administration; Arts in Education (School Administration and Supervision; English; Mathematics; Filipino; Science Education; Early Childhood Education); Science in Criminology; Library Science (Library and Management Information Service); *PhD*: Education (Educational Management; Curriculum and Supervision; English; Filipino; Science Education; Mathematics; Business Education)
Last Updated: 03/03/11

ZAMORA MEMORIAL COLLEGE

Sto. Nino Street, Bacacay, Albay 4509
Tel: +63(52) 558-3274
EMail: venice_bellen@yahoo.com.ph

President: Aida B. Vergara

Programmes

Undergraduate and Professional (Art Education; Education; English; Filipino; Foreign Languages Education; Health Education; Home Economics Education; Music Education; Native Language Education; Physical Education; Primary Education; Secondary Education; Social Studies; Technology Education)

History: Founded 1948. Formerly known as Zamora Memorial Institute.

Degrees and Diplomas: *Bachelor's Degree*
Last Updated: 31/03/11

Poland

STRUCTURE OF HIGHER EDUCATION SYSTEM

Description:

Higher education is currently provided for by the Law on Higher Education of 27 July 2005. The higher education system comprises both public and nonpublic institutions. Before 1990, there were only state higher education institutions (with the exception of the Catholic University of Lublin). The Higher Education Act, introduced in 1990, enabled the creation of nonstate higher education institutions. When the Schools of Higher Professional Education Act came into force in 1997, courses of higher professional education were created. Thus, at present, there are both university-type and non university-type (professional education) institutions in Poland. Graduates of first cycle courses are awarded the professional title of licencjat or inżynier (or equivalent) after 34 years' study. Graduates of a second cycle course are awarded the professional title of magister or equivalent after 1.5 to 2 years of studies. There are also magisterlevel studies which run as longcycle programmes (jednolite studia magisterskie) of 4,5-6 years' duration. Most higher education institutions come under the supervision of the Ministry of Science and Higher Education. Some, however, come under the control of other competent Ministries: Ministry of Health (medical higher education institutions) and Ministry of Culture and National Heritage (for academies of music, fine arts, theatre, and cinematography). There are also schools that are supervised by the Ministry of National Defence (military schools), the Ministry of Internal Affairs and Administration (Main School of Fire Service, Higher School of Police) and the Ministry of Infrastructure (merchant navy academies).
The credential giving access to higher education is the maturity certificate. Admission to higher education is based on the results of the maturity examination. Higher education institutions may also organize entrance examinations, and check the knowledge and abilities which were not tested in the maturity examination.

Stages of studies:

University level first stage: *First cycle (licencjat, inzynier)*

First cycle programmes are provided by both university-type higher education institutions and institutions of higher professional education. Graduates are awarded the professional title of licencjat (after 3 years of study) or inżynier (after 3.5-4 years of study) following a thesis or a diploma project. As from 2009, graduates obtain a diploma of completion of the first cycle programme (dyplom ukończenia studiów pierwszego stopnia). They may proceed to study for a second cycle degree (magister or equivalent).
The professional title of licencjat has been awarded as from 1992. Additionally, as from 2005, the title of licencjat położnictwa has been granted to graduates of higher professional studies in midwifery and the title of licencjat pielęgniarstwa to graduates in nursing.
The graduates of first cycle programmes in architecture are awarded the title of inżynier architect and in landscape architecture, the magister inżynier krajobrazu.
Military and police schools award their graduates the title of oficer dyplomowany, and the Main School of Fire Service grants them the title of inżynier pożarnictwa.

University level second stage: *Second cycle (magister)*

Studies at this stage can be of two types: a second cycle of 1.52-year duration or a longcycle course of 5-6 years. Both programmes are provided at university and non-university higher education institutions to holders of the professional titles of licencjat or inżynier or equivalent. The graduates are awarded the title of magister or one of its equivalents after submitting and defending a thesis or a diploma project (if envisaged in the curricula). As from 2009, the graduates of secondcycle programmes obtain the diploma of completion of second cycle studies (dyplom ukończenia studiów drugiego stopnia) and the graduates of longcycle programmes obtain the diploma of completion of long-cycle magister studies (dyplom ukończenia jednolitych studiów magisterskich). The holders of the title of magister or its equivalent may continue their education at the postgraduate level.

University level third stage: *Third cycle (doktorat)*

The academic degree of doktor can be obtained by graduates of third cycle (post-graduate) studies, which usually last for 3 to 4 years, or by persons who combine their professional work with academic research and the writing of a dissertation. All candidates must hold the professional title of magister or its equivalent. To be awarded the degree of doktor, the candidate must submit and successfully defend a doctoral dissertation that is assessed positively by two supervisors, and pass doctorate examinations. The degree of doktor can be conferred either by higher education institutions or by the research institutes entitled to award it. Since March 2003, the name of the qualification awarded as an equivalent to the degree of doktor in artistic disciplines is doktor sztuki.

University level fourth stage: *Higher doctorate (habilitacja)*
The academic degree of doktor habilitowany is awarded to candidates who already hold the degree of doktor. It can be obtained either by academic staff of higher education institutions and research units, or by persons who combine their research work with other professional activities. To be awarded the academic degree of doktor habilitowany, the candidate must have made remarkable scientific or artistic achievements, submit a dissertation which contributes to the development of a given scientific discipline, receive a favorable assessment of his/her dissertation from three supervisors, pass an examination, and deliver a favorably assessed lecture.
Since March 2003, the name of the qualification awarded in artistic disciplines as an equivalent to the degree of doktor habilitowany is doktor habilitowany sztuki.
The holders of the doktor habilitowany degree are eligible for the academic post of professor at higher education institutions and can be awarded the academic title of professor conferred by the President of the Republic of Poland.

ADMISSION TO HIGHER EDUCATION

Admission to university-level studies:

Name of secondary school credential required: Świadectwo dojrzałości

Minimum score/requirement: 30% in the grading system introduced in 2005 (grade 2 before)

For entry to: all higher education institutions.

Entrance exam requirements: There is an entrance examination for some courses (according to the institution). Some institutions also have qualifying tests or qualifying interviews for access to some of their courses. Specific ability requirements are demanded for artistic studies, physical education and architecture, as well as for military and police schools.

Numerus clausus/restrictions: Higher education institutions are autonomous in this matter. The number of students is decided by the senate of each institution.

Other admission requirements: Prize-winners of national competitions (olimpiada) in various secondary-school subjects are exempt from entrance examinations.

Foreign students admission:

Entry regulations: Students must be in possession of a valid passport and a student visa or other document entitling them to stay in Poland. Polish diplomatic missions abroad offer information on studies in Poland (application forms) and assistance in applying.

Health requirements: Candidates seeking to be admitted to higher studies should submit a health certificate enabling them to study in the selected discipline.

RECOGNITION OF STUDIES

Quality assurance system:

The State Accreditation Committee (Państwowa Komisja Akredytacyjna) is responsible for quality assurance, and the supervision of the foundation of new higher education institutions and branch campuses of the existing ones. Study programmes of higher education institutions must fulfil the requirements of the Central Council of Higher Education. The Minister of Science and Higher Education decides on the basis of the State Accreditation Committee's statement.
According to the Law of Higher Education (2005), a foreign higher education institution may establish an institution with a seat in Poland upon the consent of the Minister responsible for higher education.

Bodies dealing with recognition:

Ministerstwo Nauki i Szkolnictwa Wyższego (Ministry of Science and Higher Education)

Ul. Wspólna 1/3
Warszawa 00-529
Tel: +48(22) 529 2718
Fax: +48(22) 628 0922
EMail: sekretariat.bm@nauka.gov.pl
WWW: http://www.nauka.gov.pl

Departament Nadzoru i Organizacji Szkolnictwa Wyższego (Department of Higher Education Organisation and Supervision)

ul. Wspólna 1/3
Warszawa 00-529
Tel: +48(22) 628 6776
Fax: +48(22) 529 3534
EMail: sekretariat.dns@mnisw.gov.pl

ENIC/NARIC Polska (ENIC/NARIC Poland)

Head: Hanna Reczulska
ul. Wspólna 1/3
Warszawa 00-529
Tel: +48(22) 628 6776
Fax: +48(22) 628 3534
EMail: enic-naric@nauka.gov.pl

Polska Komisja Akredytacyjna - PKA (Polish Accreditation Committee)

ul. Żurawia 32/34
Warszawa 00-515
Tel: +48(22) 622 0718
Fax: +48(22) 621 1584
EMail: pka@pka.edu.pl
WWW: http://www.pka.edu.pl/

Special provisions for recognition:

Recognition for university level studies: All applicants must submit a secondary-school leaving certificate recognised as equivalent to the Polish maturity certificate, either on the basis of a bilateral/multilateral agreement on mutual recognition of school credentials, or if such an agreement does not exist, the certificate must be recognised by an appropriate local educational authority (kuratorium oświaty).

For access to advanced studies and research: All applicants must submit complete official academic documents together with their application form to the higher education institution or research institute. In case there is no bilateral agreement between Poland and the country in which the credentials were obtained, their studies must first be recognised as equivalent to a given type of studies in Poland. For access to second cycle studies, the applicants can be exempted from the recognition procedure. For access to doctoral studies, only the holders of credentials from EU/EEA can be exempted from the recognition procedure, provided that their credentials give them the right to access similar studies in their home countries.

For exercising a profession: In the case of graduates from countries with which Poland has signed bilateral agreements on mutual recognition of education, the applicants must present relevant documents to the appropriate Ministry, and in some cases (e.g. medical professions) fulfill the requirements of the professional body conferring the right to exercise the given profession. In the case of regulated professions, the qualifications of EU/EEA citizens are recognized under the EU directives. The graduates from other countries must have their credentials recognized at a higher education institution first, and then fulfill the requirements of professional bodies.

NATIONAL BODIES

Ministerstwo Nauki i Szkolnictwa Wyższego (Ministry of Science and Higher Education)

Minister: Barbara Kudrycka
Ul. Wspólna 1/3
Warszawa 00-529
Tel: +48(22) 529 2718
Fax: +48(22) 628 0922
EMail: sekretariat.bm@nauka.gov.pl
WWW: http://www.nauka.gov.pl

Role of national body: Elaborating educational policies at the national level, coordinating other governing bodies, controlling higher education institutions supervised by this Ministry.

Departament Nadzoru i Organizacji Szkolnictwa Wyższego (Department of Higher Education Organisation and Supervision)

Director: Ewa Sieczek
ul. Wspólna 1/3
Warszawa 00-529
Tel: +48(22) 628 6776
Fax: +48(22) 529 3534
EMail: sekretariat.dns@mnisw.gov.pl

Rada Główna Szkolnictwa Wyższego (Central Council of Higher Education)

President: Józef Lubacz
ul. Wspólna 1/3
Warszawa 00-529
Tel: +48 22 5292661
Fax: +48 22 5292768
EMail: radaglowna@mnisw.gov.pl
WWW: http://www.rgnisw.nauka.gov.pl/

Role of national body: Cooperates with the Minister of Science and Higher Education and the other national bodies in the implementation of tasks concerning higher education; in particular, defines the requirements for organizing new fields of study an the conferring of professional titles, as well as minimum curriculum requirements for each field of study.

Centralna Komisja do Spraw Stopni Naukowych i Tytułów (Central Commission for Academic Degrees and Titles)

President: Tadeusz Kaczorek
Secretary: Osman Achmatowicz
pl. Defilad 1 (PKiN)
Warszawa 00-901
Tel: +48(22) 826 8238
Fax: +48(22) 620 3324
EMail: kancelaria@ck.gov.pl
WWW: http://www.ck.gov.pl

Role of national body: Supervises the conferring of the academic degrees of Doktor and Doktor habilitowany; entitles the faculties of the higher education institutions and research units to award these academic degrees.

Polska Komisja Akredytacyjna - PKA (Polish Accreditation Committee)

Director: Barbara Wojciechowska
ul. Żurawia 32/34
Warszawa 00-515
Tel: +48(22) 622 0718
Fax: +48(22) 621 1584
EMail: pka@pka.edu.pl
WWW: http://www.pka.edu.pl/

Role of national body: Quality assurance, advisory and controlling tasks in establishing new higher education institutions and award of licences to organize new fields of study in the existing ones.

Konferencja Rektorów Akademickich Szkół Polskich - KRASP (Conference of Rectors of Academic Schools in Poland)

President: Wieslaw Banys
Secretary General: Andrzej Kraśniewski
Warsaw University of Technology, Nowowiejska 15/19
Warsaw 00-665
Tel: +48(22) 234 7537
Fax: +48(22) 234 5885
EMail: biuro@krasp.org.pl
WWW: http://www.krasp.org.pl

Role of national body: A voluntary association of rectors representing Polish institutions of higher education which have the right to award the doctor's degree (or equivalent) in at least one scientific discipline. It safeguards traditional academic values, including the constitutional principle of higher education institutions autonomy which guarantees the right of these institutions to present their positions on all issues of interest to the academic community.

Konferencja Rektorów Zawodowych Szkół Polskich - KRZASP (Conference of Rectors of Higher Professional Schools in Poland)

President: Waldemar Tłokiński
ul. Wały Piastowskie 1
Gdańsk 80-855
Tel: +48 (58) 307 4400
EMail: krzasp@krzasp.pl
WWW: http://www.krzasp.pl/

Role of national body: A voluntary association of rectors representing Polish institutions of higher professional education.

Data for academic year: 2011-2012

Source: IAU from the Department of Higher Education Organisation and Supervision, Ministry of Science and Higher Education, 2011. Bodies 2012.

INSTITUTIONS

PUBLIC INSTITUTIONS

ACADEMY OF FINE ARTS, GDAŃSK

Akademia Sztuk Pięknych w Gdańsku (ASP)
ul. Targ Węglowy 6, 80-836 Gdańsk, pomorskie
Tel: +48(58) 301-28-01
Fax: +48(58) 301-22-00
EMail: office@asp.gda.pl
Website: http://www.asp.gda.pl

Rektor: Ludmiła Ostrogórska (2008-)
Tel: +48(58) 301-44-40 EMail: rektorat@asp.gda.pl

Kanclerz: Jolanta Ewartowska
Tel: +48(58) 301-29-59 EMail: jolanta.ewartowska@asp.gda.pl;

International Relations: Magdalena Wiacek, Student Exchange Co-ordinator EMail: magda@asp.gda.pl

Faculties
Architecture and Interior Design (Architecture; Furniture Design; Industrial Design; Interior Design); **Graphic Design** (Graphic Arts; Graphic Design; Media Studies); **Painting** (Anatomy; Fine Arts; Painting and Drawing; Visual Arts); **Sculpture** (Ceramic Art; Painting and Drawing; Photography; Sculpture)

Institutes
Art *(Interfaculty)* (Arts and Humanities; Painting and Drawing; Sculpture)

Programmes
Doctoral Studies (Architecture; Design; Environmental Studies; Graphic Arts; Painting and Drawing; Sculpture)

History: Founded 1945 as State School of Arts, acquired present status and title 1996.

Governing Bodies: Senate

Academic Year: October to June

Admission Requirements: Secondary school certificate (Matura) and entrance examination

Fees: (US Dollars): Foreign students, 3,500 - 5,000 per annum

Main Language(s) of Instruction: Polish

International Co-operation: With universities in Switzerland, Netherlands, Germany

Accrediting Agencies: Ministry of Science and Higher Education

Degrees and Diplomas: *Licencjat*; *Magister*; *Doktor*

Student Services: Academic counselling, Canteen, Cultural centre, Foreign student adviser, Foreign Studies Centre, Language programs, Sports facilities

Student Residential Facilities: Yes

Special Facilities: Art Gallery

Libraries: 13,374 vols
Last Updated: 07/09/11

ACADEMY OF FINE ARTS, KATOWICE

Akademia Sztuk Pięknych w Katowicach (ASP)

ul. Raciborska 37, 40-074 Katowice, śląskie
Tel: +48(32) 251-69-89
Fax: +48(32) 251-89-67
EMail: rektorat@aspkat.edu.pl
Website: http://www.aspkat.edu.pl

Rector: Marian Oślisło (2005-)
Tel: 48(32) 205-50-23 EMail: oslislo@aspkat.edu.pl

Kanclerz: Iwona Herszlikowicz
Tel: +48(32) 251-69-89 EMail: iwonah@aspkat.edu.pl

International Relations: Jacek Rykała, Vice-Rector
Tel: 48(32) 205-50-23 EMail: rykala@aspkat.edu.pl

Departments
Foreign Languages and Physical Education (English; French; German; Modern Languages; Physical Education)

Faculties
Art (Fine Arts; Graphic Arts; Painting and Drawing; Visual Arts); **Design** (Design; Fine Arts; Graphic Design; Industrial Design; Visual Arts)

Institutes
Art Theory and History (Art History; Fine Arts)

History: Founded 1947 as Branch of State College of Fine Arts in Wrocław. Incorporated as Branch of the Academy of Fine Arts 'Jan Matejko', Cracow 1952. Acquired present status 2001.

Governing Bodies: Rector, Senate

Academic Year: October to June (October-February; February-June)

Admission Requirements: Secondary school certificate; three-stage exam (two-stage for foreign students)

Fees: (New Zloty): Evening studies (BA and MA complementary studies) 3,200 per semester. (Euros): Foreign students 2,000; Evening studies (BA and MA complementary studies) 2,000 per year

Main Language(s) of Instruction: Polish

International Co-operation: Participates in Socrates/Erasmus programme; CEEPUS programme; Agreements with universities in Spain, Portugal, Slovakia, United Kingdom, Greece, Germany, Belgium, Italy, France, Czech Republic, Romania, Finland, Austria, Croatia.

Accrediting Agencies: Ministry of Science and Higher Education

Degrees and Diplomas: *Licencjat*; *Magister*

Student Services: Foreign student adviser, Handicapped facilities, Language programs

Libraries: Computerized data base

Publications: Folia Academiae *(annually)*; Wiadomości ASP *(annually)*

Last Updated: 07/09/11

ACADEMY OF FINE ARTS, POZNAŃ

Uniwersytet Artystyczny w Poznaniu (UAP)

al. Marcinkowskiego 29, 60-967 Poznań, wielkopolskie
Tel: +48(61) 855-25-21
Fax: +48(61) 852-80-91
EMail: office@uap.edu.pl
Website: http://uap.edu.pl/

Rektor: Marcin Berdyszak (2008-)
Tel: +48(61) 863-16-21, Fax: +48(61) 852-80-91

Kanclerz: Wieslaw Szokalewicz
Tel: +48(61) 852-35-41 EMail: Szokalewicz@asp.poznan.pl

International Relations: Marek Boruczkowski, Pełnomocnik Rektora ds. Wspólpracy z Zagranica
Tel: +48(61) 855-25-21 Ext. 360, Fax: +48(61) 852-80-91
EMail: marek.boruczkowski@uap.edu.pl

Courses
Pedagogy (Pedagogy)

Departments
Foreign Languages (English; French; German; Modern Languages)

Faculties
Architecture and Design (Architecture; Art History; Design; Display and Stage Design; Furniture Design; Interior Design; Philosophy; Town Planning); **Art Education** (Art Criticism; Art Education; Pedagogy); **Graphic Design** (Communication Arts; Graphic Arts; Graphic Design; Visual Arts); **Multimedia Communication** (Communication Arts; Film; Multimedia; Photography; Visual Arts); **Painting** (Painting and Drawing); **Sculpture and Spatial Practice** (Sculpture)

History: Founded 1919. Acquired status of Academy of Fine Arts and named Akademia Sztuk Pięknych w Poznaniu (Academy of Fine Arts, Poznań) 1996. Acquired present title 2010.

Governing Bodies: Senate

Academic Year: October to June

Admission Requirements: Secondary school certificate (Matura), and entrance examination

Fees: (US Dollars): 5,000 per annum for foreign and postgraduate students

Main Language(s) of Instruction: Polish; English

International Co-operation: With universities in France, Spain, USA, United Kingdom, Germany, Slovak Republic, The Netherlands, Czech Republic. Also participates in Erasmus and CEEPUS programmes.

Accrediting Agencies: Ministry of Science and Higher Education

Degrees and Diplomas: *Licencjat*; *Świadectwo ukończenia studiów podyplomowych*; *Magister*

Student Services: Academic counselling, Foreign student adviser, Social counselling

Student Residential Facilities: Yes

Special Facilities: Art Galleries

Publications: Zeszyty Artystyczne *(quarterly)*; Zeszyty Naukowe *(biennially)*

Student Numbers *2010-2011*: Total 1,480

Part-time students, 757.

Last Updated: 07/09/11

ACADEMY OF FINE ARTS, WARSAW

Akademia Sztuk Pięknych w Warszawie (ASP)

ul. Krakowskie Przedmieście 5, 00-068 Warszawa, mazowieckie
Tel: +48(22) 320-02-00
Fax: +48(22) 320-02-14
EMail: rektorat@asp.waw.pl
Website: http://www.asp.waw.pl

Rektor: Ksawery Piwocki (2002-) Tel: +48(22) 826-19-72

Kanclerz: Jacek Mogilski
Tel: +48(22) 320-02-30 EMail: dyrekcja@asp.waw.pl

International Relations: Wiktor Jędrzejec, Prorektor

Departments
History and Art Theory *(Interfaculty)* (Art History; Fine Arts; Philosophy)

Faculties
Conservation and Restoration of Works of Art (Architectural Restoration; Chemistry; Information Technology; Laboratory Techniques; Painting and Drawing; Restoration of Works of Art; Sculpture); **Design** (Art History; Communication Arts; Design; Painting and Drawing; Sculpture; Visual Arts); **Graphic Arts** (Communication Arts; Graphic Arts; Multimedia; Painting and Drawing; Visual Arts); **Interior Design** (Architecture; Art History; Communication Arts; Computer Graphics; Construction Engineering; Design; Furniture Design; Interior Design; Landscape Architecture; Painting and Drawing; Visual Arts); **Media Art and Stage Design** (Communication Arts; Display and Stage Design; Fine Arts; Graphic Design; Multimedia; Painting and Drawing; Photography; Visual Arts); **Painting** (Painting and Drawing; Weaving); **Sculpture** (Ceramic Art; Handicrafts; Painting and Drawing; Photography; Sculpture; Visual Arts)

Institutes
Conservation and Restoration of Works of Art *(Intercollegiate)* (Restoration of Works of Art)

Schools
Foreign Language (English; French; German; Modern Languages; Russian)

Units
Education (Pedagogy)

History: Founded 1904 as School, acquired present status and title 1932.

Governing Bodies: Senate

Academic Year: October to May (October-January; February-May)

Admission Requirements: Secondary school certificate (matura), art works, entrance examination

Fees: (New Złoty): tuition fee for local students, 5,000-9,000 per annum; For foreign students (Euros), 5,000-10,000 per annum.

Main Language(s) of Instruction: Polish, English, German

International Co-operation: Socrates/Erasmus EU Programmes

Accrediting Agencies: Ministry of Science and Higher Education, Minstry of Culture and National Heritage

Degrees and Diplomas: *Licencjat*; *Magister*, *Doktor*

Student Services: Foreign Studies Centre, Health services, Social counselling, Sports facilities

Student Residential Facilities: Yes

Special Facilities: Museum ASP Warszawa. Art Gallery

Libraries: Central Library, 25,750 vols; 350 exhibition catalogs; 5,630 journals.

Publications: Zeszyty Naukowe Akademii Sztuk Pięknych

Press or Publishing House: Komisja Wydawnicza

Last Updated: 08/09/11

ACADEMY OF MUSIC, CRACOW

Akademia Muzyczna w Krakowie (AM)

ul. Św. Tomasza 43, 31-027 Kraków, małopolskie

Tel: +48(12) 422-04-55

Fax: +48(12) 422-23-43

EMail: zbrektor@cyfronet.pl

Website: http://www.amuz.krakow.pl

Rektor: Stanisław Krawczyński (2005-) Tel: +48(12) 422-32-50

Dyrektor Administracyjny: Krzysztof Rymarczyk
Tel: +48(12) 423-20-78, Fax: +48(12) 422-44-55
EMail: krzysztof.rymarczyk@amuz.krakow.pl

International Relations: Agata Kubik, Head, International Cooperation Centre
Tel: +48(12) 422-04-55 Ext. 147 +48(12) 426-29-70,
Fax: +48(12) 426-29-70
EMail: international@amuz.krakow.pl; agata.kubik@amuz.krakow.pl

Courses
Teacher Training *(Interfaculty)* (Teacher Training)

Divisions
Comprehensive Piano Studies *(Interfaculty)* (Music; Musical Instruments); **Foreign Languages** *(Interfaculty)* (English; French; German; Italian; Modern Languages); **Humanities and Physical Education** *(Interfaculty)* (Arts and Humanities; Education; History; Philosophical Schools; Philosophy; Physical Education; Psychology)

Faculties
Composition, Interpretation and Musical Education (Conducting; Music; Music Education; Music Theory and Composition; Religious Music; Singing); **Instrumental Studies** (Jazz and Popular Music; Music; Musical Instruments); **Vocal and Acting Studies** (Acting; Music; Singing)

Programmes
Postgraduate Studies (Art Criticism; Art Therapy; Music; Music Theory and Composition; Musical Instruments)

History: Founded 1888. Acquired present status 1946, became Academy of Music 1979. Under the jurisdiction of the Ministry of Culture and Art.

Governing Bodies: Senate

Academic Year: October to June (October-February; February-June)

Admission Requirements: Secondary school graduate, musical secondary school graduate, matriculation leaving examination

Fees: (New Złoty): 350-5,000 per semester; Postgraduate programmes, 1,600-2,500 per semester; Doctorate, 2,500 per semester.

Main Language(s) of Instruction: Polish

International Co-operation: 26 ERASMUS Partners in Italy; Germany; Austria; United Kingdom; Portugal; Czech Republic; Lithuania; Turkey; Sweden; France

Accrediting Agencies: Ministry of Science and Higher Education

Degrees and Diplomas: *Licencjat*; *Świadectwo ukończenia studiów podyplomowych*; *Magister*, *Doktor*

Student Residential Facilities: For c. 135 students

Special Facilities: Electro-Acoustic Music Studio, Multimedia Studio

Libraries: Central Library, c. 43,000 vols; Record Library, c. 7,000 vols

Publications: 'Introductio Musicae'; 'Muzyka i Liryka', Music and Lyrics series; ''Vivo' and 'Modi' *(annually)*

Press or Publishing House: University Press

Last Updated: 06/09/11

ACADEMY OF PHYSICAL EDUCATION, WROCŁAW

Akademia Wychowania Fizycznego we Wrocławiu (AWF)

al. Ignacego Jana Paderewskiego 35, 51-612 Wrocław, dolnośląskie

Tel: +48(71) 347-32-00

Fax: +48(71) 348-25-27

EMail: rektor@awf.wroc.pl

Website: http://www.awf.wroc.pl

Rektor: Juliusz Migasiewicz (2002-)
Tel: +48(71) 347-31-01, Fax: +48(71) 347-31-81

International Relations: Tadeusz Skolimowski, Vice-Rector
Tel: +48(71) 347-31-13, Fax: +48(71) 347-31-79

Faculties
Physical Education (Anatomy; Biochemistry; Biological and Life Sciences; Biophysics; Education; Health Education; History; Nutrition; Parks and Recreation; Physical Education; Physiology; Psychology; Sports; Sports Management; Sports Medicine; Tourism); **Physiotherapy** (Biology; Ecology; Medicine; Neurology; Orthopaedics; Paediatrics; Philosophy; Physical Therapy; Physiology; Sociology; Surgery)

History: Founded 1946 as Physical Education Centre, reorganized 1950 as Physical Education College, reorganized 1972 as Academy of Physical Education, and acquired present status and title 1990.

Governing Bodies: Senate

Academic Year: September to June (September-January; February-June)

Admission Requirements: Secondary school certificate (Świadectwo maturalne), entrance exam

Fees: (New Złoty): Extramural studies, 1,000 per semester

Main Language(s) of Instruction: Polish

International Co-operation: Erasmus programme (Germany, Belgium), CEEPUS programme (Czech Republic, Slovakia, Croatia, Bulgaria)

Accrediting Agencies: Ministry of Science and Higher Education

Degrees and Diplomas: *Licencjat*; *Świadectwo ukończenia studiów podyplomowych*; *Magister*, *Doktor*

Student Services: Canteen, Cultural centre, Foreign student adviser, Handicapped facilities, Health services, Sports facilities

Student Residential Facilities: For 500 students

Special Facilities: Olympic Stadium

Libraries: Central Library

Publications: Fizjoterapia (Physiotherapy) *(quarterly)*; Human Movement (Człowiek I Ruch) *(biennially)*; Studia i Monografie AWF we Wrocławiu *(biennially)*; Życie Akademickie *(monthly)*

Press or Publishing House: Wydawnictwo AWF

Last Updated: 09/09/11

ADAM MICKIEWICZ UNIVERSITY, POZNAŃ

Uniwersytet im. Adama Mickiewicza w Poznaniu (UAM)

H. Wieniawskiego 1, 61-712 Poznań, Wielkopolskie

Tel: +48(61) 829-40-00

Fax: +48(61) 829-41-11

EMail: rectorof@amu.edu.pl

Website: http://www.amu.edu.pl

Rektor: Bronisław Marciniak (2008-)
Tel: +48(61) 829-43-08, Fax: +48(61) 829-44-44
EMail: marcinia@amu.edu.pl

Chancellor: Stanisław Wachowiak
Tel: +48(61) 829-43-37, Fax: +48(61) 829-40-00
EMail: kanclerz@amu.edu.pl

International Relations: Jacek Witkoś, Vice-Rector for Research and International Relations
Tel: +48(61) 829-43-67, Fax: +48(61) 829-44-44
EMail: wjacek@amu.edu.pl

Centres

Advanced Technology (Technology) *Director*: Bogdan Marciniec; **Foreign Language Teaching** (Modern Languages) *Head*: Mateusz Kaszyński; **Innovation and Technology Transfer** (Technology) *Head*: Jacek Wajda; **IT Infrastructure and Project Management** (Information Technology; Management) *Director*: Przemysław Stolarski; **Physical Training and Sports** (Physical Education; Sports) *Head*: Piotr Szafarkiewicz; **Teaching and Multimedia - University Film Studio** (Film; Multimedia) *Head*: Stefan Habryło

Faculties

Biology (Anthropology; Biology; Biotechnology; Computer Science; Laboratory Techniques; Molecular Biology) *Dean*: Bogdan Jackowiak; **Chemistry** (Analytical Chemistry; Biochemistry; Chemical Engineering; Chemistry; Crystallography; Inorganic Chemistry; Materials Engineering; Organic Chemistry; Physics; Science Education; Water Science) *Dean*: Andrzej Molski; **Educational Studies** (Adult Education; Art Education; Child Care and Development; Education; Educational Psychology; Educational Sciences; Educational Technology; Environmental Studies; Pedagogy; Psychotherapy; Sociology; Special Education) *Dean*: Zbyszko Melosik; **Geographical and Geological Sciences** (Development Studies; Ecology; Environmental Management; Environmental Studies; Geography; Geology; Parks and Recreation; Surveying and Mapping; Tourism) *Dean*: Marek Marciniak; **History** (Anthropology; Art History; Cultural Studies; East Asian Studies; Ethnology; History; Musicology; Prehistory) *Dean*: Hanna Kóčka-Krenz; **Law and Administration** (Administration; Administrative Law; Civil Law; Commercial Law; Constitutional Law; Criminal Law; Economics; European Union Law; Fiscal Law; Forensic Medicine and Dentistry; History of Law; International Law; Labour Law; Law; Political Sciences; Public Law) *Dean*: Tomasz Sokołowski; **Mathematics and Computer Science** (Linguistics; Logic; Mathematics; Mathematics and Computer Science; Mathematics Education; Statistics) *Dean*: Marek Nawrocki; **Modern Languages and Literature** (Applied Linguistics; Asian Religious Studies; Communication Studies; German; Linguistics; Literature; Modern History; Oriental Studies; Philology; Romance Languages; Russian; Scandinavian Languages) *Dean*: Teresa Tomaszkiewicz; **Pedagogy and Fine Arts** *(KALISZ)* (Art Education; Art Therapy; Cognitive Sciences; English; Environmental Studies; Fine Arts; Heritage Preservation; Information Sciences; Music Education; Painting and Drawing; Pedagogy; Philology; Religious Music; Teacher Training) *Dean*: Marian Walczak; **Physics** (Astronomy and Space Science; Physics; Sound Engineering (Acoustics)) *Dean*: Ryszard Naskręcki; **Polish and Classical Philology** (Philology; Polish; Slavic Languages) *Dean*: Józef Tomasz Pokrzywiak; **Political Science and Journalism** (Economics; German; Government; History; International Relations; Journalism; Law; Marketing; Political Sciences; Psychology; Social Sciences) *Dean*: Tadeusz Wallas; **Social Sciences** (Cultural Studies; Philosophy; Psychology; Social Sciences; Sociology) *Dean*: Zbigniew Drozdowicz; **Theology** (Bible; Canon Law; Christian Religious Studies; History of Religion; Holy Writings; New Testament; Pastoral Studies; Philosophy; Religion; Religious Education; Social Sciences; Theology) *Dean*: Jan Szpet

Laboratories

14C AMS *Director*: Tomasz Goslar

Research Centres

"Multicultural Discourse" Humanities Study (Arts and Humanities; Cultural Studies) *Director*: Halina Chałacińska; **Central Asian Study** (Asian Studies) *Director*: Marek Gawęcki; **Edyta Stein Study** (History) *Director*: Anna Grzegorczyk; **Ethics** (Ethics) *Director*: Paweł Bortkiewicz; **European Integration** (European Studies) *Director*: Stefan Jurga; **Gender Studies** *(Interdisciplinary)* (Gender Studies) *Director*: Ewa Kraskowska; **Humanities/Art/ Technology** *(Interdisciplinary)* (Arts and Humanities; Fine Arts; Technology) *Director*: Dobrochna Ratajczak; **Institute of Wielkopolska** (Geography (Human); Social Sciences) *Director*: Witold Molik; **Integrated Monitoring of Natural Environment** (Environmental Studies); **International Education** *(AMU-Programme for International Exchange)* (Education) *Director*: Rafał Witkowski; **Metropolitan Study** (Regional Studies; Urban Studies) *Director*: Tomasz Kaczmarek; **Migration Study** (Demography and Population) *Director*: Michał Buchowski; **Open Studies** *Director*: Jacek Sójka; **Public Policy Studies** (Government) *Director*: Marek Kwiek; **Regional Culture Observatory** (Cultural Studies) *Director*: Jacek Sójka; **Speech Processing and Language** *(Interdisciplinary)* (Linguistics; Speech Studies) *Director*: Katarzyna Dziubalska-Kołaczyk; **Study of the Quality of Life** (Safety Engineering) *Director*: Ryszard Cichocki; **Ultrafast Laser Spectroscopy Study** (Laser Engineering) *Director*: Jerzy Karolczak; **University Coordination and Programme Teacher Training** (Teacher Training) *Director*: Ewa Muszyńska; **University Park of Earth History** (History) *Director*: Jerzy Fedorowski; **University Study Centre - Musical Theatre** (Music; Theatre) *Director*: Elżbieta Nowicka

Schools

Polish Language for Foreign Students (Polish) *Director*: Agnieszka Mielczarek; **Translation, Interpreting and Languages** (Modern Languages; Translation and Interpretation) *Director*: Witold Skowroński

Further Information: Also Collegium Polonicum in Słubice - joint unit run by Adam Mickiewicz University and European University of Viadrina (Frankfurt/Oder, Germany); Collegium Europaeum in Gniezno - developes research on the ideas of unified Europe in a historical context, with particular emphasis on Polish-German relationships and provides studies in European Education and Social Communication.

History: Founded 1919.

Governing Bodies: Senate; Faculty Council

Academic Year: October to June (October-January; February-June)

Admission Requirements: Secondary School Leaving Certificate (Matura) or recognized foreign equivalent and entrance examination

Fees: (US Dollars): 2,000-3,000 per annum.

Main Language(s) of Instruction: Polish

International Co-operation: LLP Erasmus; Erasmus-Mundus; CEEPUS; DAAD; Leonardo da Vinci; GFPS; Fulbright; MSPC; SERP-Chem; EMCC; E.MA

Accrediting Agencies: Ministry of Science and Higher Education;, Polish Accreditation Committee; University Accreditation Commission

Degrees and Diplomas: *Licencjat (lic.)*: 3 yrs; *Magister (mgr)*: a further 2 yrs; *Doktor (dr)*: a further 4 yrs; *Doktor habilitowany*: Teaching Qualification, university level (D. Litt), by thesis after doctorate. The D. Litt. (Doctor of Letters) can be obtained either at the university level or at the level of The Central Committee for Academic Degrees and Scientific Titles. Submission of a monograph or a set of publications is required.

Student Services: Canteen, Health services, Sports facilities

Student Residential Facilities: Yes

Special Facilities: Conference Centers (Ciążeń, Gułtowy, Obrzycko); Botanical Garden; Foreign Studies Centres (Alliance

Francaise, British Council Library, Austrian Centre for Culture, Confucius Institutes); Weather and Climate Monitoring Stations;

Libraries: University Library, c. 2,7 m. vols; Faculty and institute libraries, c. 2,3 m. vols; Archives

Publications: Acta Arithmetica, Scientific Paper; Annales Missiologiceae Posnanienses, Scientific Paper; Anthropological Review, Scientific Paper; Artium Questiones, Scientific Paper; Baltic Pontic Studies, Scientific Paper; Biodiversity: Research and Conversation, Scientific Paper; Current Topics in Biophysics, Scientific Paper; Folia Malacologica, Scientific Paper; Folia Praehistorica Posnaniensia, Scientific Paper; Folia Scandinavica Posnaniensia, Scientific Paper; Functiones et Approximatio, Scientific Paper; Geologos, Scientific Paper; Glottodidactica, Scientific Paper; Lingua ac Communitas, Scientific Paper; Neodidagmata, Scientific Paper; Poznań Studies in Contemporary Linguistics, Scientific Paper; Poznan Studies in the Philosophy of Sciences and the Humanities, Scientific Paper; Przegląd Politologiczny, Scientific Paper; Questiones Geographicae, Scientific Paper; Random Structures and Algorithms, Scientific Paper; Roczniki Socjologii Rodziny, Scientific Paper; Ruch Prawniczy, Ekonomiczny i Socjologiczny, Scientific Paper; Silva Iaponicarum, Scientific Paper; Studia Anglica Posnaniensia, Scientific Paper; Symbolae Philologorum Posnaniensium Graecae et Latinae, Scientific Paper; Werkwinkel. Journal of Low Countries and South African Studies, Scientific Paper

Press or Publishing House: Adam Mickiewicz University Press

Last Updated: 29/08/11

AGH UNIVERSITY OF SCIENCE AND TECHNOLOGY, CRACOW

Akademia Górniczo-Hutnicza im. Stanisława Staszica w Krakowie (AGH-UST)

Al. A. Mickiewicza 30, 30-059 Kraków, małopolskie
Tel: +48(12) 617-36-84
Fax: +48(12) 617-32-63
EMail: rekrutacja@agh.edu.pl
Website: http://www.agh.edu.pl

Rektor: Antoni Tajduś (2005-)
Tel: +48(12) 617-20-02, Fax: +48(12) 633-46-72
EMail: rektorat@agh.edu.pl; tajdus@agh.edu.pl

Kanclerz: Henryk Ziolo
Tel: +48(12) 617-20-08 EMail: ziolo@regent.uci.agh.edu.pl

International Relations: Marta Foryś, Head, International Relations
Tel: +48(12) 617-47-83, Fax: +48(12) 617-32-57
EMail: dwz@agh.edu.pl

Centres

Academic Business Incubator (Business Administration; Management); **Computer** (Computer Education); **Cyfronet Academic Computer** (Computer Science); **E-learning** (Distance Education); **Electron Microscopy for Materials Science** *(International)* (Materials Engineering); **Energy Problems** (Energy Engineering); **Foreign Languages** (English; Foreign Languages Education; French; German; Modern Languages; Russian); **Materials and Nanotechnology** *(Academic)* (Materials Engineering; Nanotechnology); **Museum of the History of Technology** (Archiving; Art History; Heritage Preservation; Museum Studies); **Technology Transfer** (Technology)

Chairs

Science, Technology and Engineering Education *(UNESCO)* (Engineering; Science Education; Technology Education)

Departments

Sport and Physical Education (Physical Education; Sports)

Faculties

Applied Mathematics (Applied Mathematics; Mathematics); **Drilling, Oil and Gas** (Geological Engineering; Geology; Mining Engineering; Petroleum and Gas Engineering); **Electrical Engineering, Automatics, Computer Science and Electronics** (Automation and Control Engineering; Computer Science; Electrical Engineering; Electronic Engineering; Measurement and Precision Engineering; Robotics; Sound Engineering (Acoustics); Telecommunications Engineering); **Energy and Fuels** (Chemistry; Energy Engineering; Environmental Engineering; Nuclear Engineering; Power Engineering; Thermal Engineering); **Foundry Engineering** (Chemistry; Engineering Management; Metal Techniques; Metallurgical Engineering; Polymer and Plastics Technology; Technology); **Geology, Geophysics and Environmental Protection** (Computer Science; Environmental Engineering; Environmental Studies; Geochemistry; Geology; Geophysics; Mineralogy; Mining Engineering; Natural Resources; Surveying and Mapping; Tourism); **Humanitites** (Anthropology; Communication Studies; Contemporary History; Cultural Studies; Economics; Philosophy; Political Sciences; Sociology); **Management** (Industrial Management; Management); **Materials Science and Ceramics** (Analytical Chemistry; Biochemistry; Biology; Building Technologies; Ceramics and Glass Technology; Chemistry; Inorganic Chemistry; Materials Engineering; Neurosciences); **Mechanical Engineering and Robotics** (Engineering Management; Environmental Studies; Machine Building; Mechanical Engineering; Power Engineering; Production Engineering; Robotics; Sound Engineering (Acoustics); Transport Engineering); **Metals Engineering and Industrial Computer Science** (Computer Education; Computer Science; Environmental Engineering; Materials Engineering; Metallurgical Engineering; Polymer and Plastics Technology; Technology Education; Thermal Engineering); **Mining and Geoengineering** (Civil Engineering; Economics; Environmental Engineering; Geology; Industrial Management; Materials Engineering; Mining Engineering; Production Engineering); **Mining Surveying and Environmental Engineering** (Construction Engineering; Environmental Engineering; Environmental Studies; Mining Engineering; Surveying and Mapping); **Non-Ferrous Metals** (Chemistry; Materials Engineering; Metal Techniques; Metallurgical Engineering; Polymer and Plastics Technology); **Physics and Applied Computer Science** (Applied Physics; Biophysics; Computer Science; Medical Technology; Nuclear Physics; Physics; Solid State Physics)

Schools

Engineering in Biomedicine *(Multidisciplinary)* (Biomedical Engineering); **Environmental Protection and Engineering** *(Walerego Goetla)* (Energy Engineering; Environmental Engineering; Environmental Studies; Waste Management)

History: Founded 1919 as Akademia Górnicza (Academy of Mining). Renamed as Akademia Górniczo-Hutnicza 1949. Acquired present title 1969.

Governing Bodies: Senate

Academic Year: October to June (October-January; February-June)

Admission Requirements: Secondary school (or secondary technical school) certificate (Świadectwo Dojrzałości) and entrance examination

Fees: (Euros): 2,000-13,000 per annum (depends on Faculty and study level)

Main Language(s) of Instruction: Polish; English

International Co-operation: Participates in the Ceepus, Tempus, Socrates, Leonardo (France, Germany), 5 FP, 6 FP of the EU, eContent, Eureka, Cost, NATO

Accrediting Agencies: State Accreditation Committee at the Ministry of Science and Higher Education

Degrees and Diplomas: *Licencjat*: Sociology; Cultural Studies; Management; Marketing; *Magister*: Automatics Control and Robotics; Civil Engineering; Ceramics; Education in Technology and Informatics; Electronics and Telecommunications; Electrical Engineering; Power Engineering; Medical Physics; Technical Physics; Geodesy, Surveying and Cartography; Environmental Protection; Chemical Technology; Management; Management and Production Engineering; Geophysics; Mining and Geology; Informatics; Applied Computer Science; Biomedical Engineering; Materials Engineering; Oil and Gas Engineering; Environmental Engineering; Mathematics; Mechatronics; Engineering and Construction of Machines; Metallurgy; *Doktor*: Machinery Construction and Exploitation; Geophysics; Geology; Geodesy, Surveying and Cartography; Environmental Engineering; Management science; Chemical Technology; Chemistry; Metallurgy; Power Engineering; Physics; Mathematics (Ph.D.); Mining and Geology Engineering; Environmental Engineering; Metallurgy; Materials Engineering; Automatics Control and Robotics; Electronics; Telecommunications; Electrical Engineering; Informatics; Biocybernetics and Biomedical Engineering; Mechanics; *Doktor habilitowany*: Geophysics; Geology;

Geodesy, Surveying and Cartography; Environmental Engineering; Chemical Technology; Chemistry; Metallurgy; Power Engineering; Physics; Mining and Geology Engineering; Environmental Engineering; Metallurgy; Materials Engineering; Automatics Control and Robotics; Electronics; Telecommunications; Electrical Engineering; Informatics; Mechanics; Machinery Construction and Exploitation. Switched to the Bologna System of education in 2007. Bachelor's degree in: Automatics Control and Robotics; Civil Engineering; Ceramics; Education in Technology and Informatics; Electronics and Telecommunications; Electrical Engineering; Power Engineering; Medical Physics; Technical Physics; Geodesy, Surveying and Cartography; Geophysics; Mining and Geology; Informatics; Applied Computer Science; Informatics and Econometrics; Acoustic Engineering; Biomedical Engineering; Materials Engineering; Mechanical and Materials Engineering; Oil and Gas Engineering; Environmental Engineering; Mathematics; Mechatronics; Engineering and Construction of Machines; Metallurgy; Environmental Protection; Tourism and Recreation; Chemical Technology; Virtotechnology; Management; Management and Production Engineering. Master's degree in: Automatics Control and Robotics; Civil Engineering; Ceramics; Education in Technology and Informatics; Electronics and Telecommunications; Electrical Engineering; Power Engineering; Medical Physics; Technical Physics; Geodesy, Surveying and Cartography; Geophysics; Mining and Geology; Informatics; Applied Computer Science; Biomedical Engineering; Materials Engineering; Oil and Gas Engineering; Environmental Engineering; Mathematics; Mechatronics; Engineering and Construction of Machines; Metallurgy; Environmental Protection; Chemical Technology; Management; Management and Production Engineering. Ph.D. in: Mining and Geology Engineering; Environmental Engineering; Metallurgy; Materials Engineering; Automatics Control and Robotics; Electronics; Telecommunications; Electrical Engineering; Informatics; Biocybernetics and Biomedical Engineering; Mechanics; Machinery Construction and Exploitation; Geophysics; Geology; Geodesy, Surveying and Cartography; Environmental Engineering; Management science; Chemical Technology; Chemistry; Metallurgy; Power Engineering; Physics; Mathematics.

Student Services: Canteen, Cultural centre, Employment services, Handicapped facilities, Health services, Language programs, Nursery care, Sports facilities

Student Residential Facilities: For c. 5,500 students

Special Facilities: Museum of Geology. Centre for History of Science and Technology. Museum and Archives of the University of Mining and Metallurgy. RAK Cracow Students Radio

Libraries: Central Library, 1,314,867 vols; 31 specialized libraries of the Institutes, 388,346,000 vols

Publications: Automatyka *(biennially)*; Computer Science *(annually)*; Elektrotechnika *(biennially)*; Geodezja *(biennially)*; Geologia *(quarterly)*; Górnictwo *(quarterly)*; Inżynieria Środowiskowa *(biennially)*; Mechanika *(quarterly)*; Metallurgy and Foundry Engineering *(biennially)*; Opuscula Mathematica *(annually)*; Telekomunikacja Cyfrowa *(annually)*

Academic Staff *2010-2011*	**TOTAL**
FULL-TIME	**4,042**
STAFF WITH DOCTORATE FULL-TIME	**300**
Student Numbers *2010-2011*	
All (Foreign Included)	**36,562**
FOREIGN ONLY	**101**

Part-time students, 8,193.

Last Updated: 01/09/11

BIALYSTOK UNIVERSITY OF TECHNOLOGY

Politechnika Białostocka (PB)

ul. Wiejska 45a, 15-351 Białystok, podlaskie
Tel: +48(85) 746-90-00
Fax: +48(85) 742-90-15
EMail: rektorat@pb.bialystok.pl
Website: http://www.pb.bialystok.pl

Rektor: Tadeusz Citko
Tel: +48(85) 746-90-10 EMail: rektor@pb.edu.pl

Kanclerz: Mirosław Milewski
Tel: +48(85) 746-97-61, Fax: +48(85) 746-97-63
EMail: mirekm@pb.edu.pl; kancelaria@pb.edu.pl

International Relations: Lech Dzienis, Vice-Rector, Promotion and Cooperation
Tel: +48(85) 746-90-10, Fax: +48(85) 746-90-15
EMail: prorektor.wspolpraca@pb.edu.pl

Centres

Foreign Language (English; German; Modern Languages; Russian); **Physical Education and Sport** (Physical Education; Sports)

Faculties

Architecture (Architectural and Environmental Design; Architecture; Architecture and Planning; Graphic Arts; Interior Design; Town Planning; Visual Arts); **Civil and Environmental Engineering** (Bridge Engineering; Building Technologies; Civil Engineering; Construction Engineering; Ecology; Economics; Environmental Engineering; Environmental Studies; Geological Engineering; Heating and Refrigeration; Landscape Architecture; Road Engineering; Soil Conservation; Structural Architecture; Water Science); **Computer Science** (Business Computing; Computer Engineering; Computer Networks; Computer Science; Information Technology; Mathematics; Software Engineering); **Electrical Engineering** (Automation and Control Engineering; Electrical Engineering; Electronic Engineering; Industrial Engineering; Power Engineering; Telecommunications Engineering); **Environmental Management** *(BTU Branch - Hajnówka)* (Environmental Management; Forestry); **Management** (Accountancy; Business Administration; Business Computing; Economics; Finance; Industrial Management; Management; Marketing; Parks and Recreation; Social Sciences; Tourism; Transport Management); **Mechanical Engineering** (Agricultural Engineering; Agriculture; Automation and Control Engineering; Biomedical Engineering; Computer Education; Food Technology; Forestry; Heating and Refrigeration; Information Sciences; Information Technology; Machine Building; Mechanical Engineering; Medical Technology; Production Engineering; Rehabilitation and Therapy; Robotics; Technology Education; Thermal Engineering)

History: Founded 1949 as college, acquired present status and title 1974

Governing Bodies: Senate

Academic Year: October to June (October-February; February-June)

Admission Requirements: Secondary school certificate (matura) and entrance examination

Fees: (New Złoty): 1,600 per semester; Foreign students, 3,000 euros per annum

Main Language(s) of Instruction: Polish; English

International Co-operation: With universities in Portugal, Italy, United Kingdom, Germany, Denmark. Also participates in the Socrates/Erasmus, Jean Monnet, Leonardo and 5TH FP programmes

Accrediting Agencies: Ministry of Science and Higher Education

Degrees and Diplomas: *Inżynier*, *Licencjat*, *Świadectwo ukończenia studiów podyplomowych*; *Magister*, *Doktor*

Student Services: Academic counselling, Canteen, Cultural centre, Employment services, Health services, Nursery care, Social counselling, Sports facilities

Student Residential Facilities: 4 students hostels

Special Facilities: Art Gallery "Politechnika"

Libraries: Central Library, 346,000 vols

Publications: Architektura *(other/irregular)*; Budowa i Eksplotacja Maszyn *(other/irregular)*; Budownictwo *(other/irregular)*; Ekonomia i Zarzadzanie *(other/irregular)*; Elektryka *(other/irregular)*; Inzynieria Środowiska *(other/irregular)*; Matematyka, Fizyka, Chemia *(other/irregular)*; Mechanika *(other/irregular)*

Press or Publishing House: Politechnika Bialostocka, Dial Wydawnictw i Poligrafii

Academic Staff *2010-2011*: Total 700

Student Numbers *2010-2011*: Total 13,500

Last Updated: 21/09/11

CARDINAL STEFAN WYSZYNSKI UNIVERSITY, WARSAW

Uniwersytet Kardynała Stefana Wyszyńskiego w Warszawie (UKSW)

ul. Dewajtis 5, 01-815 Warszawa, mazowieckie
Tel: +48(22) 561-89-48
Fax: +48(22) 561-88-51
EMail: info@uksw.edu.pl
Website: http://www.uksw.edu.pl

Rector: Henryk Skorowski (2010-)

Administrative Director: Marek Lepa
Tel: +48(22) 561-89-33, Fax: +48(22) 561-89-02
EMail: da@uksw.edu.pl

International Relations: Tadeusz Klimski, Vice-Rector
Tel: +48(22) 561-89-52, Fax: +48(22) 561-88-08
EMail: bwm@uksw.edu.pl

Faculties

Biology and Natural Sciences (Biological and Life Sciences; Biology; Environmental Engineering) *Dean*: Kinga Suwinska; **Canon Law** (Canon Law) *Dean*: Józef Wrocenski; **Christian Philosophy** (Environmental Studies; Philosophy; Psychology) *Dean*: Jan Krokos; **Family Studies** (Family Studies) *Dean*: Mieczyslaw Ozorowski; **History and Social Sciences** (Ancient Civilizations; Archaeology; Art History; European Studies; History; Musicology; Political Sciences; Religious Music; Social Work; Sociology) *Dean*: Jaroslaw Koral; **Humanities** (Cultural Studies; Pedagogy; Philology; Polish) *Dean*: Jadwiga Kuczynska-Kwapisz; **Law and Administration** (Administration; International Relations; Law) *Dean*: Marek Michalski; **Mathematics and Natural Sciences. College of Science** (Chemistry; Computer Science; Econometrics; Mathematics; Physics) *Dean*: Michal Krynicki; **Theology** (Family Studies; Journalism; Media Studies; Missionary Studies; Theology; Tourism) *Dean*: Stanisław Dziekonski

Institutes

Antiques (Ancient Civilizations) *Director*: Dorota Folga-Januszewska; **Archaeology** (Archaeology) *Director*: Zbigniew Kobylinski; **Art History** (Art History) *Director*: Zbigniew Bania; **Cultural Knowledge** (Cultural Studies) *Director*: Witold Kawecki; **Ecology and Bioethics** (Environmental Studies) *Director*: Zbigniew Lepko; **Historical Sciences** *Director*: Józef Naumowicz; **International Law, European Union and International Relations** (European Union Law; International Law; International Relations) *Director*: Cezary Mik; **Media Education and Journalism** (Journalism; Theology) *Director*: Andrzej Adamski; **Pedagogy** *(St. Jan Bosco)* (Pedagogy) *Director*: Jan Chrobak; **Philosophy** (Philosophy) *Director*: Ryszard Mon; **Polish Philology** (Cultural Studies; Philology; Polish) *Director*: Wojciech Kudyba; **Political Science** (Political Sciences) *Director*: Aniela Dylus; **Psychology** (Psychology) *Director*: Henryk Gasiul; **Sociology** (Sociology) *Director*: Władysław Majkowski; **Theology** (Theology) *Director*: Stanislaw Dziekonski; **Theology** *(Radom)* (Theology) *Director*: Zbigniew Skrok; **Theology of the Apostolate** *(Oltarzew)* (Religion; Theology) *Director*: Marian Kowalczyk

Further Information: Branch in Radom

History: Founded 1954 as Academy of Catholic Theology. Acquired present status and title 1999.

Governing Bodies: Senate

Academic Year: October to June (October-February; February-June)

Admission Requirements: Graduation from high school (Matura)

Fees: None for daytime studies. Extramural studies fees depend on faculty

Main Language(s) of Instruction: Polish

International Co-operation: With universities in China, Czech Republic, Egypt, France, Germany, Italy, Lithuania, Slovakia, Ukraine, Russia. Also participates in the Erasmus programme

Accrediting Agencies: Ministry of Science and Higher Education

Degrees and Diplomas: *Licencjat*: International Relations; Biology; Environmental Engineering; Journalism and Social Communication; Family Studies (lic.); Philosophy; Environmental Studies; History; Art History; Sociology; European Studies; Archaeology; Philology; Polish Philology; Cultural Studies; Political Science; Mathematics; Physics; Sciences; Computer Science; Econometrics; Administration (lic.), 3 yrs; *Magister*: Pedagogy; International Relations (mgr.), 2 yrs; *Magister*: Theology; Canon Law; Psychology; Pedagogy (mgr), 5 yrs; *Doktor*: History; Theology; Canon Law; Political Science; Philosophy; Psychology; Sociology (dr), 4 yrs; *Doktor habilitowany*: Theology; Canon Law; Political Science; Philosophy (dr hab.)

Student Services: Academic counselling, Canteen, Employment services, Handicapped facilities, Health services, Nursery care, Social counselling, Sports facilities

Libraries: 345,790 vols

Publications: Collectanea Theologica *(quarterly)*; Jus Matrimoniale *(annually)*; Kroniki UKSW *(quarterly)*; Maqom *(biennially)*; Prawo Kanoniczne *(quarterly)*; Saeculum Christianum *(biennially)*; Studia nad Rodziną *(biennially)*; Studia Philosophiae Christianae *(biennially)*; Studia Psychologica *(annually)*; Studia Theologica Varsaviensia *(biennially)*; Zeszyty Prawnicze *(annually)*

Press or Publishing House: Publishing House of UKSW

Last Updated: 25/08/11

CHRISTIAN THEOLOGICAL ACADEMY IN WARSAW

Chrześcijańska Akademia Teologiczna w Warszawie (CHAT)

ul. Miodowa 21 c, 00-246 Warszawa, mazowieckie
Tel: +48(22) 831-95-97
Fax: +48(22) 635-95-44
EMail: chat@chat.edu.pl
Website: http://nowa.chat.edu.pl

Rektor: Jeremiasz Jan Anchimiuk (2008-) Tel: +48(22) 831-95-97

Kanclerz: Jerzy Machaj Tel: +48(22) 635-68-55

Departments

Ecumenism *(Intersection)* (Religion); **Foreign Languages** *(Intersection)* (English; German; Modern Languages; Russian; Slavic Languages); **Philosophy, Ethics and Sociology** *(Intersection)* (Ethics; Philosophy; Sociology); **Physical Education and Sport** *(Intersection)* (Physical Education; Sports); **Religious and Canon** *(Intersection)* (Religion); **Sciences of Religions** *(Intersection)* (Religion)

Institutes

Education *(Ecumenical)* (Education; Religious Education; Social Work)

Sections

Evangelical Theology (Greek (Classical); Hebrew; Holy Writings; New Testament; Religious Practice; Theology); **Old Catholic Theology** (Bible; Catholic Theology; History of Religion; Religious Practice); **Orthodox Theology** (History of Religion; Holy Writings; New Testament; Orthodox Theology; Religious Studies)

History: Founded 1954 through separtation of the Evangelical Theological Faculty from the Warsaw University.

Accrediting Agencies: National Accreditation Commission

Degrees and Diplomas: *Licencjat*; *Świadectwo ukończenia studiów podyplomowych*; *Magister*; *Doktor*

Last Updated: 09/09/11

CRACOW UNIVERSITY OF ECONOMICS

Uniwersytet Ekonomiczny w Krakowie (AE)

ul. Rakowicka 27, 31-510 Kraków, małopolskie
Tel: +48(12) 293-52-00
Fax: +48(12) 293-50-10
EMail: janek@ae.krakow.pl
Website: http://www.ae.krakow.pl

Rektor: Roman Niestrój (2008-)
Tel: +48(12) 293-54-21, Fax: +48(21) 293-50-02
EMail: rektor@ae.krakow.pl

Kanclerz: Mirosław Chechelski
Tel: +48(12) 293-54-22, Fax: +48(21) 293-50-06
EMail: miroslaw.chechelski@uek.krakow.pl

International Relations: Agnieszka Nawrocka, Head of International Cooperation
Tel: +48(12) 293-51-03
EMail: Agnieszka.Nawrocka@uek.krakow.pl

Departments

Foreign Languages (English; French; German; Italian; Modern Languages; Russian; Spanish); **Physical Education and Sports** (Physical Education; Sports)

Faculties

Commodity Science (Applied Chemistry; Chemistry; Ecology; Economics; Food Technology; Management; Measurement and Precision Engineering; Microbiology; Natural Sciences; Packaging Technology; Production Engineering; Safety Engineering; Technology); **Economics and International Relations** (Comparative Law; Economic and Finance Policy; Economics; European Studies; Human Resources; International Business; International Economics; International Law; International Relations; Management; Philosophy; Political Sciences; Public Administration; Public Law; Real Estate; Small Business; Sociology); **Finance** (Accountancy; Ecology; Economics; Finance; Home Economics; Household Management; Industrial Management; Insurance; Law; Mathematics); **Management** (Accountancy; Behavioural Sciences; Computer Science; Econometrics; Economics; Labour and Industrial Relations; Management; Marketing; Operations Research; Statistics; Tourism)

Schools

Business (Business Administration; International Business); **Public Administration** (Public Administration)

Further Information: Also International Business Study (3 years, intermediate university level qualification, in English); Poland Economy in Transition (1 year, course for foreign students, in English); Interfaculty Pedagogic Course (2 years, in Polish)

History: Founded 1925 as College of Commerce, granted academic status 1938. Closed 1939, reopened 1950 as Cracow Higher School of Economics. 1974 - Academy of Economics and acquired present status and title 2007.

Governing Bodies: Senate

Academic Year: October to June (October-January; February-June)

Admission Requirements: Secondary school certificate (matura) and entrance examination

Fees: (New Złoty): c. 1,600-2,600 per semester; Studies in English 3,600.

Main Language(s) of Instruction: Polish. English for special programmes

International Co-operation: With universities in Albania, Australia, Austria, Belgium, Bulgaria, Croatia, Montenegro, Czech Republic, Denmark, Estonia, Finland, France, Greece, Spain, Netherlands, Iceland, Japan, Canada, Korea, Lithuania, Latvia, Mexico, Moldova, Germany, Norway, Peru, Portugal, Russia, Romania, Serbia, Slovakia, Slovenia, USA, Switzerland, Sweden, Taiwan, Turkey, Ukraine, Venezuela, Hungary, Great Britain, Italy. Participates in the Erasmus, ATLANTIS, CEEPUS and TEMPUS programmes.

Accrediting Agencies: Ministry of Science and Higher Education

Degrees and Diplomas: *Inżynier*, *Licencjat*, *Świadectwo ukończenia studiów podyplomowych*; *Magister*, *Doktor*. Also dual degrees with foreign partner university in Germany, Sweden, France and USA; Master in Business Administration (MBA) and in Public Administration (MPA), a further 2 yrs following first degree

Student Services: Canteen, Cultural centre, Employment services, Foreign student adviser, Foreign Studies Centre, Handicapped facilities, Health services, Language programs, Nursery care, Social counselling, Sports facilities

Student Residential Facilities: Yes

Special Facilities: Computer Centre; Museum

Libraries: Central Library (Economics), c. 425,000 vols; 80,000 periodicals, World Economic CD-ROM database

Press or Publishing House: Wydawnictwo Akademii Ekonomicznej w Krakowie (Academic Publishing House)
Last Updated: 28/09/11

CZESTOCHOWA UNIVERSITY OF TECHNOLOGY

Politechnika Częstochowska (PCZ)
ul. J.H. Dąbrowskiego 69, 42-200 Częstochowa, śląskie
Tel: +48(34) 325-52-11
Fax: +48(34) 361-23-85
EMail: rektor@adm.pcz.czest.pl
Website: http://www.pcz.pl

Rektor: Maria Nowicka-Skowron (2008-)

Kanclerz: Katarzyna Pikuła
Tel: +48(34) 325-17-76, Fax: +48(34) 325-17-76
EMail: kanclerz@adm.pcz.czest.pl

International Relations: Sebastian Goldsztajn, International Cooperation Officer
Tel: +48(34) 325-04-31, Fax: +48(34) 325-40-66
EMail: sgoldsztajn@adm.pcz.czest.pl

Centres

Foreign Languages (English; French; German; Modern Languages; Russian); **Physical Education and Sports** (Physical Education; Sports); **Vocational Studies and Teacher Training** (Communication Studies; Education; Psychology; Teacher Training)

Faculties

Civil Engineering (Architecture; Architecture and Planning; Building Technologies; Civil Engineering; Construction Engineering; Energy Engineering; Metal Techniques; Real Estate; Road Engineering; Structural Architecture; Town Planning); **Electrical Engineering** (Automation and Control Engineering; Computer Engineering; Computer Networks; Computer Science; Electrical Engineering; Electronic Engineering; Multimedia; Power Engineering; Robotics; Telecommunications Engineering); **Environmental Protection and Engineering** (Biotechnology; Energy Engineering; Engineering; Environmental Engineering; Environmental Management; Heating and Refrigeration; Power Engineering; Waste Management; Water Management; Water Science); **Management** (Accountancy; Business Administration; Computer Science; Econometrics; English; Finance; German; Management; Marketing; Production Engineering; Safety Engineering; Taxation; Transport Management); **Materials Processing Technology and Applied Physics** (Applied Physics; Biomedical Engineering; Ceramics and Glass Technology; Engineering Management; Environmental Engineering; Information Technology; Materials Engineering; Metal Techniques; Metallurgical Engineering; Physics; Production Engineering; Safety Engineering); **Mechanical Engineering and Computer Science** (Biomedical Engineering; Energy Engineering; Engineering Management; Information Technology; Mathematics; Mathematics and Computer Science; Mechanical Engineering; Mechanics; Production Engineering)

Further Information: Also Distance Education Unit.

History: Founded 1949 as engineering school, became Technical University 1955.

Governing Bodies: Senate

Academic Year: October to June (October-February; February-June)

Admission Requirements: Secondary school certificate (matura) and entrance examination

Main Language(s) of Instruction: Polish; English

International Co-operation: Participates in the Tempus, Socrates-Erasmus, Leornado da Vinci, Eureka, Cost and Copernicus programmes.

Accrediting Agencies: Ministry of Science and Higher Education

Degrees and Diplomas: *Inżynier*, *Licencjat*, *Świadectwo ukończenia studiów podyplomowych*; *Magister*, *Doktor*

Student Residential Facilities: Yes

Special Facilities: Museum of Artistic Casts

Libraries: Central Library, c. 400,000 vols

Publications: Seria Monografie, Series Monographies *(other/irregular)*; Turbulence *(annually)*

Press or Publishing House: University Publishing House
Last Updated: 22/09/11

EUGENIUSZ GEPPERT ACAEMY OF ART AND DESIGN IN WROCLAW

Akademia Sztuk Pięknych im. 'Eugeniusza Gepperta' we Wrocławiu (ASP)
ul. Plac Polski 3/4, 50-156 Wrocław, dolnośląskie
Tel: +48(71) 343-80-31
Fax: +48(71) 343-15-58
EMail: info@asp.wroc.pl
Website: http://www.asp.wroc.pl

Rector: Jacek Szewczyk
Tel: +48(71) 343-15-58, Fax: +48(71) 343-15-58

Kanclerz: Wojciech Orzechowski
Tel: +48(71) 343-36-68 EMail: kanclerz@asp.wroc.pl

International Relations: Beata Ludwiczak, International Relations Officer
Tel: +48(71) 343-80-31 Ext. 232, Fax: +48(71) 343-80-31 Ext. 232
EMail: blu@asp.wroc.pl

Faculties

Ceramic and Glass (Ceramic Art; Design; Economics; Glass Art; Marketing; Painting and Drawing; Restoration of Works of Art; Sculpture) *Dean*: Jerzy Chodurski; **Graphic Arts and Media Arts** (Computer Graphics; Graphic Arts; Graphic Design; Multimedia; Painting and Drawing; Photography; Printing and Printmaking; Visual Arts); **Interior Architecture and Industrial Design** (Civil Engineering; Computer Graphics; Design; Furniture Design; Industrial Design; Interior Design); **Painting and Sculpture** (Art Education; Ceramic Art; Computer Graphics; Multimedia; Painting and Drawing; Sculpture)

Institutes

Foreign Languages (English; French; German; Modern Languages); **History of Art and Philosophy** (Art History; Philosophy)

Units

Postgraduate studies *(Interfaculty)* (Art History; Ceramic Art; Computer Graphics; Cultural Studies; Fine Arts; Glass Art; Interior Design; Painting and Drawing)

History: Founded 1791 as School of Fine Arts, acquired present status and title 1946.

Governing Bodies: Senate

Academic Year: October to June

Admission Requirements: Secondary School Certificate (Matura) and entrance examinations

Fees: (US Dollars): Foreign students, 5,000 per annum

Main Language(s) of Instruction: Polish

International Co-operation: With universities in Italy, United Kingdom, Sweden, Finland, France, Germany, Slovakia, Romania, Czech Republic, Ukraine. Also participate in Socrates/Erasmus programme

Accrediting Agencies: Ministry of Culture

Degrees and Diplomas: *Licencjat*; *Świadectwo ukończenia studiów podyplomowych*; *Magister*

Student Services: Academic counselling, Canteen, Employment services, Foreign student adviser, Foreign Studies Centre, Handicapped facilities, Language programs, Social counselling

Student Residential Facilities: Dormitory

Special Facilities: Museum; Art Gallery

Libraries: c. 14,000 vols; 1,000 magazine vols and 3,700 catalogues from Polish and foreign exhibitions.

Publications: Format *(quarterly)*

Last Updated: 07/09/11

GDANSK UNIVERSITY OF TECHNOLOGY

Politechnika Gdańska (PG)

ul. Narutowicza 11/12, 80-233 Gdańsk, pomorskie
Tel: +48(58) 347-29-99
Fax: +48(58) 341-58-21
EMail: rekrutacja@pg.gda.pl
Website: http://www.pg.gda.pl

Rektor: Henryk Krawczyk (2008-)
Tel: +48(58) 347-12-69, Fax: +48(58) 347-27-47
EMail: rektor@pg.gda.pl

Kanclerz: Marek Tłok
Tel: +48(58) 347-12-15, Fax: +48(58) 341-78-45
EMail: dyrad@pg.gda.pl

International Relations: Andrzej Zieliński, Vice-Rector for International Cooperation and European Programmes
Tel: +48(58) 347-22-80, Fax: +48(58) 347-12-90
EMail: prorew@pg.gda.pl

Centres

Academic Sports (Sports); **Language** (English; French; German; Italian; Japanese; Modern Languages; Russian; Spanish; Swedish); **Mathematics and Distance Education** (Distance Education; Mathematics Education)

Faculties

Applied Physics and Mathematics (Applied Physics; Mathematics; Nuclear Physics; Physics; Solid State Physics); **Architecture** (Architectural and Environmental Design; Architectural Restoration; Architecture; Regional Planning; Town Planning; Visual Arts); **Chemistry** (Analytical Chemistry; Biochemistry; Biotechnology; Chemical Engineering; Chemistry; Engineering Management; Environmental Engineering; Environmental Studies; Food Technology; Inorganic Chemistry; Materials Engineering; Microbiology; Organic Chemistry; Pharmacology; Physical Chemistry; Polymer and Plastics Technology); **Civil and Environmental Engineering** (Bridge Engineering; Building Technologies; Civil Engineering; Environmental Engineering; Geological Engineering; Hydraulic Engineering; Marine Engineering; Materials Engineering; Mechanics; Railway Engineering; Road Engineering; Structural Architecture; Surveying and Mapping; Transport Engineering; Waste Management; Water Management); **Electrical and Control Engineering** (Automation and Control Engineering; Computer Engineering; Electrical and Electronic Engineering; Electronic Engineering; Power Engineering; Robotics); **Electronics, Telecommunications and Informatics** (Automation and Control Engineering; Biomedical Engineering; Computer Engineering; Computer Networks; Computer Science; Electronic Engineering; Information Technology; Robotics; Telecommunications Engineering); **Management and Economics** (Economics; Management; Small Business); **Mechanical Engineering** (Electronic Engineering; Engineering Management; Materials Engineering; Mechanical Engineering; Medical Technology; Production Engineering; Safety Engineering); **Ocean Engineering and Ship Technology** (Automation and Control Engineering; Marine Engineering; Marine Transport; Materials Engineering; Mechanics; Power Engineering; Safety Engineering)

History: Founded 1904 as Königliche Technische Hochschule zu Danzig, Germany. Following First World War belonged to the Free City of Gdańsk. In 1945 became Polish state academic institution called Politechnika Gdanska.

Governing Bodies: Senate, Rector

Academic Year: October to June (October-February; February-June)

Admission Requirements: Secondary school diploma (Matura)

Fees: (Euros): Tuition fee, Foreign students, 2,000-5,000 per annum

Main Language(s) of Instruction: Polish, English

International Co-operation: Participates in the Erasmus programmes.

Accrediting Agencies: Ministry of Science and Higher Education; National Accreditation Commission

Degrees and Diplomas: *Inżynier*; *Licencjat*; *Świadectwo ukończenia studiów podyplomowych*; *Magister*; *Doktor*. Also non-degree short cycle programmes; MBA

Student Services: Canteen, Foreign student adviser, Health services, Sports facilities

Libraries: Central Library, c. 1,2m. Vols

Publications: Pismo PG *(monthly)*; Zeszyty Naukowe Politechniki Gdańskiej, Scientific Papers

Academic Staff *2010-2011*: Total: c. 2,500

Student Numbers *2010-2011*: Total: c. 26,000

Last Updated: 22/09/11

GDYNIA MARITIME UNIVERSITY

Akademia Morska w Gdyni (AM)

ul. Morska 81-87, 81-225 Gdynia, pomorskie
Tel: +48(58) 620-75-12
Fax: +48(58) 620-67-01
EMail: pror1@am.gdynia.pl
Website: http://www.am.gdynia.pl

Rektor: Romuald Cwilewicz (2008-)
Tel: +48(58) 620-75-12, Fax: +48(58) 690-13-51
EMail: rektor@am.gdynia.pl

Kanclerz: Sławomir Polański EMail: kanclerz@am.gdynia.pl

International Relations: Isabella Dudek-Muczyńska, International Programmes Officer
Tel: +48(58) 690-14-63, Fax: +48(58) 690-12-88
EMail: izabela@am.gdynia.pl

Departments

Foreign Languages (English; German; Modern Languages); **Physical Education and Sports** (Physical Education; Sports)

Faculties

Electrical Engineering (Automation and Control Engineering; Electrical Engineering; Electronic Engineering; Marine Engineering; Power Engineering; Telecommunications Engineering); **Entrepreneurship and Quality Science** (Chemistry; Economics; Hotel Management; Information Sciences; Management; Safety Engineering; Service Trades; Tourism; Transport Management); **Marine Engineering** (Engineering; Machine Building; Maintenance Technology; Marine Engineering; Mechanical Engineering; Physics; Safety Engineering); **Navigation** (Marine Science and Oceanography; Marine Transport; Mathematics; Meteorology; Nautical Science; Transport and Communications)

History: Founded 1920 as Maritime School, reorganized 1959, and acquired present status and title 1968.

Governing Bodies: Senate

Academic Year: October to May (October-January; January-May)

Admission Requirements: Secondary school certificate (Matura) and entrance examination

Main Language(s) of Instruction: Polish

International Co-operation: Participates in the Socrates/ Erasmus and 5th Framework (5FP) programmes

Accrediting Agencies: Ministry of Science and Higher Education

Degrees and Diplomas: *Inżynier*; *Licencjat*; *Świadectwo ukończenia studiów podyplomowych*; *Magister*

Student Services: Academic counselling, Canteen, Social counselling

Student Residential Facilities: Four student hostels

Special Facilities: Museum

Libraries: 100,000 vols

Publications: Akademicki Kurier Morski, University's life and maritime matters *(quarterly)*; Zeszyty Naukowe/Joint Proceedings, Science and research works *(other/irregular)*

Last Updated: 02/09/11

GENERAL TADEUSZ KOŚCIUSZKO MILITARY ACADEMY OF LAND FORCES IN WROCŁAW

Wyższa Szkoła Oficerska Wojsk Lądowychim. generała Tadeusza Kościuszki (WSO)

ul. Czajkowskiego 109, 51-150 Wrocław, dolnośląskie
Tel: +48(71) 765-81-34
Website: http://www.wso.wroc.pl/

Rektor-Komendant: Mariusz Wiatr
Tel: +48(71) 765-82-22, Fax: +48(71) 765-82-25
EMail: komendant@wso.wroc.pl

Kanclerz: Zbigniew Gawlik Tel: +48(71) 765-84-28

Departments

Computer Science *(Interfaculty)* (Computer Science); **Foreign Languages** *(Interfaculty)* (English; Modern Languages); **Physical Education** *(Interfaculty)* (Physical Education; Sports)

Faculties

Management (Accountancy; Computer Engineering; Computer Science; Econometrics; Economics; Finance; Management; Mathematics; Natural Sciences; Operations Research; Statistics); **Security** (Anthropology; Arts and Humanities; Civil Engineering; Demography and Population; Education; Ethnology; History; Industrial Engineering; Journalism; Machine Building; Philosophy; Political Sciences; Protective Services; Safety Engineering; Social Studies; Sociology)

Institutes

Command (Military Science; Safety Engineering; Transport Management)

History: Founded 2001. Acquired present title 2003.

Governing Bodies: Senate

Main Language(s) of Instruction: Polish

Accrediting Agencies: Ministry of Science and Higher Education and Ministry of Defence

Degrees and Diplomas: *Inżynier*, *Licencjat*, *Świadectwo ukończenia studiów podyplomowych*; *Magister*

Last Updated: 26/10/11

GRAŻYNA AND KIEJSTUT BACEWICZ ACADEMY OF MUSIC, ŁÓDŹ

Akademia Muzyczna im. Grażyny i Kiejstuta Bacewiczów w Łodzi (AM)

ul. Gdańska 32, 90-716 Łódź, łódzkie
Tel: +48(42) 662-16-00
Fax: +48(42) 633-79-36
EMail: kancelaria@amuz.lodz.pl
Website: http://www.amuz.lodz.pl

Rektor: Antoni Wierzbiński
Tel: +48(42) 662-16-01, Fax: +48(42) 662-16-60
EMail: rektorat@amuz.lodz.pl

Kanclerz: Agnieszka Grochulska Tel: +48(42) 662-16-65

International Relations: Sławomir Kaczorowski, Vice-Rector
Tel: +48(42) 662-16-15 EMail: international@amuz.lodz.pl

Faculties

Composition, Theory of Music, Eurhythmics and Art Education (Art Education; Music; Music Education; Music Theory and Composition; Performing Arts); **Instrumental Studies** (Music; Musical Instruments); **Piano, Harpsichord and Organ** (Music; Music Education; Performing Arts); **Vocal and Acting Performance** (Acting; Music; Singing)

Programmes

Music Therapy and Rehabilitation (Art Therapy; Rehabilitation and Therapy)

History: Founded 1945 as State Music Conservatory, became State Higher School of Music 1946. Acquired present status 1982 and title 1999, named after Grażyna and Kiejstut Bacewicz.

Governing Bodies: Senate

Academic Year: October to June (October-January; February-June)

Admission Requirements: Secondary school certificate, diploma of completion of secondary music school, and entrance examinations

Fees: (Euros): Foreign students: c. 5,000 per annum; (New Złoty): Polish students: c. 3,400-4,600

Main Language(s) of Instruction: Polish

International Co-operation: Participates in the Socrates/Erasmus programme

Accrediting Agencies: Ministry of Culture

Degrees and Diplomas: *Licencjat*; *Świadectwo ukończenia studiów podyplomowych*; *Magister*, *Doktor*

Student Services: Canteen, Sports facilities

Student Residential Facilities: For c. 100 students

Special Facilities: Recording Studio

Libraries: Central Music Library, 9,063 vols; 6,100 records and CDs

Publications: Zeszyty Naukowe

Press or Publishing House: Komisja Wydawnicza Akademii Muzycznej w Łodzi

Last Updated: 06/09/11

HE PRESIDENT STANISŁAW WOJCIECHOWSKI HIGHER VOCATIONAL STATE SCHOOL IN KALISZ

Państwowa Wyższa Szkoła Zawodowa im. Prezydenta Stanisława Wojciechowskiego w Kaliszu (PWSZ)
ul. Nowy Świat 4, 62-800 Kalisz, wielkopolskie
Tel: +48(62) 757-36-74
Fax: +48(62) 767-95-06
EMail: kancelaria@pwsz.kalisz.pl
Website: http://www.pwsz.kalisz.pl

Rektor: Jan Chajda (2008-)
Tel: +48(62) 767-95-00, Fax: +48(62) 767-95-10
EMail: rektorat@pwsz.kalisz.pl

Kanclerz: Kazimierz Matusiak
Tel: +48(62) 767-95-50, Fax: +48(62) 767-95-06

International Relations: Tatiana Manasterska, Vice-Rector
Tel: +48(62) 767-95-03 EMail: t.manasterska@izb.pwsz.kalisz.pl

Departments
Foreign Languages (English; German; Modern Languages; Russian; Spanish)

Faculties
Management (Accountancy; Business Administration; Economics; Finance; Government; International Business; Management; Marketing; Mathematics; Media Studies; Public Administration; Real Estate; Social Sciences; Statistics; Transport Management); **Medicine** (Biochemistry; Cosmetology; Gynaecology and Obstetrics; Health Sciences; Medicine; Midwifery; Nursing; Pharmacology; Radiology); **Rehabilitation and Sports** (Physical Education; Physical Therapy; Rehabilitation and Therapy; Sports); **Technology** (Architecture; Automation and Control Engineering; Computer Science; Construction Engineering; Electrical Engineering; Environmental Engineering; Heating and Refrigeration; Machine Building; Mechanical Engineering; Technology)

Programmes
Postgraduate studies (Agricultural Business; Environmental Engineering; Higher Education; Law; Management; Mathematics Education; Physical Therapy; Safety Engineering)

Further Information: Also postgraduate studies

History: Founded 1999.

Governing Bodies: Senate

Fees: (New Zloty): 1,700-2,000 per semester.

Main Language(s) of Instruction: Polish

International Co-operation: With universities in Germany, Italy, Turkey, Slovakia, Bulgaria, Portugal, Hungary, Latvia, Ukraine, Belarus, Russia, USA. Participates in the LLP-Erasmus programme.

Accrediting Agencies: Ministry of Science and Higher Education

Degrees and Diplomas: *Inżynier*; *Licencjat*; *Świadectwo ukończenia studiów podyplomowych*; *Magister*

Student Services: Sports facilities

Student Residential Facilities: Hostel (343 beds)

Special Facilities: 65 laboratories and specialized

Libraries: c. 110,000 vols; 325 periodical subscriptions; 1,950 e-books, electronic journals and other digital documents; 75 electronic databases.

Academic Staff *2010-2011*: Total 366

Student Numbers *2010-2011*: Total 4,036

Last Updated: 21/09/11

HIGHER SCHOOL OF THE AIR FORCE, DĘBLIN

Wyższa Szkoła Oficerska Sił Powietrznych (WSOSP)
ul. Dywizjonu 303 nr 12, 08-521 Dęblin, lubelskie
Tel: +48(81) 883-71-00
Fax: +48(81) 883-71-03
EMail: rzecznik@wsosp.deblin.pl
Website: http://www.wsosp.deblin.pl

Rektor-Komendant: Jan Rajchel
Tel: +48(81) 551-71-00, Fax: +48(81) 551-71-03
EMail: sekretariatrektora@wsosp.deblin.pl

Kanclerz: Waldemar Bieniek
Tel: +48(81) 551-74-51, Fax: +48(81) 551-74-52
EMail: kanclerz_wsosp@wsosp.deblin.pl

Departments
Aviation and Aerospace *(Military)* (Aeronautical and Aerospace Engineering; Air Transport); **Aviation and Aerospace** *(Civilian)* (Aeronautical and Aerospace Engineering; Air Transport); **National Security and Logistics** (Military Science; Protective Services; Transport Management); **Postgraduate Studies** (Air Transport; Safety Engineering; Transport Management)

Degrees and Diplomas: *Inżynier*, *Świadectwo ukończenia studiów podyplomowych*; *Magister*

Last Updated: 23/10/11

HIGHER VOCATIONAL SCHOOL IN SUWALKI

Państwowa Wyższa Szkoła Zawodowa w Suwałkach (PWSZ)
ul. Teofila Noniewicza 10, 16-400 Suwałki, podlaskie
Tel: +48(87) 562-84-29
Fax: +48(87) 562-84-30
EMail: sekretariat@pwsz.suwalki.pl
Website: http://www.pwsz.suwalki.pl/

Rektor: Jerzy Sikorski (2010-)
Tel: +48(87) 562-84-32, Fax: +48(87) 562-84-55
EMail: sekretariat.rektor@pwsz.suwalki.pl

Kanclerz: Zdzisław Siemaszko
Tel: +48(87) 562-84-56, Fax: +48(87) 562-84-55
EMail: sekretariat.kanclerz@pwsz.suwalki.pl

Institutes
Building (Architecture; Building Technologies; Construction Engineering; Road Engineering; Town Planning); **Health Protection** (Health Sciences; Medicine; Nursing); **Humanities and Economics** (Accountancy; Arts and Humanities; Economics; English; Finance; Philology; Russian; Tourism); **Technology and Life Sciences** (Agricultural Business; Agriculture; Biological and Life Sciences; Environmental Management; Food Technology; Management; Production Engineering; Technology; Tourism; Transport and Communications)

Programmes
Postgraduate Studies (Accountancy; Computer Engineering; Education; Energy Engineering; Management)

History: Founded 2005.

Governing Bodies: Senate

Degrees and Diplomas: *Inżynier*, *Licencjat*; *Licencjat*: Nursing; *Świadectwo ukończenia studiów podyplomowych*

Last Updated: 04/09/11

HIGHER VOCATIONAL STATE SCHOOL IN WŁOCŁAWEK

Państwowa Wyższa Szkoła Zawodowa we Włocławku (PWSZ)
ul. 3 Maja 17, 87-800 Włocławek, kujawsko-pomorskie
Tel: +48(54) 231-60-80
Fax: +48(54) 231-43-52
EMail: rekrutacja@pwsz.wloclawek.pl
Website: http://www.psww.pl/

Rector: Tadeusz Dubicki (2011-)
Tel: +48(54) 231-60-88, Fax: +48(54) 231-60-88
EMail: rektorat@pwsz.wloclawek.pl

Kanclerz: Teresa M. Bieniek EMail: kancelaria@pwsz.wloclawek.pl

Departments
Foreign Languages (English; German; Modern Languages; Russian; Spanish); **Physical Education and Sports** (Physical Education; Sports)

Institutes
Humanities (Arts and Humanities; Education; English; German; Philology; Polish; Russian); **Social Sciences and Informatics** (Administration; Computer Science; International Relations; Management; Social Sciences)

Programmes

Postgraduate Studies (Business Administration; Ethics; Finance; Law; Occupational Health; Pedagogy; Preschool Education; Psychology; Public Administration; Safety Engineering; Speech Therapy and Audiology)

History: Founded 2001.

Governing Bodies: Senate

Degrees and Diplomas: *Licencjat*; *Świadectwo ukończenia studiów podyplomowych*

Last Updated: 05/09/11

I.J. PADEREWSKI ACADEMY OF MUSIC, POZNAŃ

Akademia Muzyczna im. Ignacego Jana Paderewskiego w Poznaniu (AMUZ)

ul. Święty Marcin 87, 61-808 Poznań, wielkopolskie

Tel: +48(61) 856-89-00

Fax: +48(61) 853-66-76

EMail: amuz@amuz.edu.pl

Website: http://www.amuz.edu.pl

Rektor: Bogumił Nowicki

Tel: +48(61) 856-89-10 EMail: msworek@amuz.edu.pl

Kanclerz: Elizabeth Mikołajczyk

Tel: +48(61) 856-89-26 EMail: emikolajczyk@amuz.edu.pl

International Relations: Barbara Baszuk, LLP Erasmus Institutional Coordinator

Tel: +48(61) 856-89-53 EMail: bbaszuk@amuz.edu.pl

Colleges

Chamber Music *(Interfaculty)* (Music)

Departments

Foreign Languages *(Interfaculty)* (English; German; Modern Languages); **Historical Instruments** (Musical Instruments); **Pedagogy** *(Interfaculty)* (Music Education; Pedagogy); **Physical Education and Sports** *(Interfaculty)* (Physical Education; Sports); **Social and Humanities Sciences** *(Interfaculty)* (Aesthetics; Art History; Arts and Humanities; Cultural Studies; Ethics; History; Media Studies; Modern Languages; Philosophy; Social Sciences)

Faculties

Choral Conducting, Music Education and Church Music (Art Education; Art Therapy; Conducting; Musical Instruments; Religious Music; Singing); **Composition, Conducting, Theory of Music and Eurhythmics** (Conducting; Music; Music Theory and Composition); **Instruments** (Jazz and Popular Music; Music; Musical Instruments); **String Instruments, Harp, Guitar and Violin - Making** (Instrument Making; Musical Instruments); **Vocal Studies** (Music; Singing)

Programmes

Postgraduate Studies (Art Therapy; Music)

Further Information: Branch in Szczecin

History: Founded 1920, acquired present status and title 1981.

Governing Bodies: Senate

Admission Requirements: Secondary school certificate (matura) and entrance examinations

Main Language(s) of Instruction: Polish

Accrediting Agencies: Ministry of Science and Higher Education

Degrees and Diplomas: *Licencjat*; *Świadectwo ukończenia studiów podyplomowych*: Arts and Music Therapy; *Magister*

Last Updated: 06/09/11

JAGIELLONIAN UNIVERSITY, CRACOW

Uniwersytet Jagielloński w Krakowie (UJ)

ul. Gołębia 24, 31-007 Kraków, małopolskie

Tel: +48(12) 422-10-33

Fax: +48(12) 422-32-29

EMail: rektor@adm.uj.edu.pl

Website: http://www.uj.edu.pl

Rektor: Karol Musioł (2008-)

Tel: +48(12) 422-66-89, Fax: +48(12) 422-63-06

Chancellor (Director of Administration: Tadeusz Skarbek

Tel: +48(12) 422-95-40, Fax: +48(12) 421-95-05

EMail: skarbek@adm.uj.edu.pl

International Relations: Szczepan Biliński, Vice-Rector

Tel: +48(12) 431-06-53, Fax: +48(12) 422-66-65

EMail: prorektor.nauka@uj.edu.pl

Centres

Central and Eastern Studies (Central European Studies; Eastern European Studies; International Relations); **European Studies** (European Studies); **Innovations Technology Transfer and University Development** *(CITTRU)* (Technology); **Jagiellonian Language** (Baltic Languages; Chinese; English; Foreign Languages Education; French; German; Italian; Latin; Russian; Spanish; Teacher Trainers Education); **Teachers' Training** (Education; Pedagogy)

Faculties

Biochemistry, Biophysics and Biotechnology (Biochemistry; Biophysics; Biotechnology; Botany; Cell Biology; Immunology; Microbiology; Virology); **Biology and Earth Sciences** (Biology; Botany; Earth Sciences; Geography; Geology; Molecular Biology; Zoology); **Chemistry** (Analytical Chemistry; Applied Chemistry; Chemistry; Inorganic Chemistry; Organic Chemistry; Physical Chemistry); **Health Care** *(Collegium Medicum)* (Health Sciences; Nursing; Public Health); **History** (Archaeology; Art History; Ethnology; History; Music Theory and Composition; Musicology); **International and Political Studies** (International Studies; Political Sciences); **Law and Administration** (Administration; Canon Law; European Union Law; International Law; Law; Police Studies; Political Sciences; Private Law); **Management and Social Communication** (Cinema and Television; Communication Studies; Film; Information Sciences; Journalism; Library Science; Public Relations); **Mathematics and Computer Science** (Computer Science; Mathematics); **Medicine** *(Collegium Medicum)* (Dentistry; Medicine); **Pharmacy** *(Collegium Medicum)* (Analytical Chemistry; Biochemistry; Cell Biology; Food Science; Histology; Inorganic Chemistry; Medical Technology; Organic Chemistry; Pharmacology; Pharmacy; Toxicology); **Philology** (Classical Languages; English; German; Hungarian; Italian; Linguistics; Oriental Languages; Philology; Romance Languages; Russian; Slavic Languages; Spanish; Swedish; Theatre); **Philosophy** (Education; Philosophy; Psychology; Religious Studies; Sociology); **Physics, Astronomy and Applied Computer Science** (Astronomy and Space Science; Computer Science; Physics); **Polish Studies** (Arts and Humanities; Cultural Studies; Philology; Polish)

Laboratories

Physico-Chemical Analyses and Structural Research *(Regional, Inter-University)* (Analytical Chemistry; Atomic and Molecular Physics; Optics; Physical Chemistry; Radiology)

Research Centres

Jewish Culture and History *(Interdisciplinary)* (Cultural Studies; Hebrew; Jewish Studies)

Schools

Medicine for Foreigners *(Teaching in English)* (Medicine); **Polish Language and Culture** *(Summer School)* (Cultural Studies; Polish)

Units

Medical Centre for Post-Graduate Education Collegium Medicum (Medicine); **Physical Education** *(Interfaculty, Physical Education and Sports Studium)* (Physical Education; Sports)

History: Founded 1364 by Casimir the Great on the model of the universities of Padua and Bologna. Reorganized 1400 by Ladislaus Jagiello on the pattern of the Sorbonne. Copernicus studied at the university in the 15th century. Reorganized in the 19th century in keeping with the ideas of rationalism. University closed and nearly two hundred professors were deported during the German occupation 1939. Operated as an underground university with 800 students after 1942. Extensive reconstruction began after 1945. Acquired present status and title 1964.

Governing Bodies: Senate

Academic Year: October to June (October-February; February-June)

Admission Requirements: Secondary school certificate (Matura) and entrance examination

Fees: (Euro): Foreign students: registration, 200; tuition: undergraduate, postgraduate, c. 4,000-8,000 per annum; Medical College: 11,000-12,000 per annum.

Main Language(s) of Instruction: Polish

International Co-operation: Participates in the Socrates/Erasmus programme

Accrediting Agencies: Ministry of Science and Higher Education

Degrees and Diplomas: *Licencjat*: All except Law, Medicine, Pharmacy, Biophysics, Psychology (lic.), 3 yrs; *Magister (mgr)*: a further 2 yrs; *Doktor*: Legal Science; Humanities; Mathematical Sciences; Computer Science; Physical Sciences; Life Sciences; Earth Sciences; Chemical Science; Pharmaceutical Science; Medical Science (PhD), at least a further 3 yrs by thesis; *Doktor habilitowany*: Legal Science; Humanities; Mathematical Sciences; Computer Science; Physical Sciences; Life Sciences; Earth Sciences; Chemical Science; Pharmaceutical Science; Medical Science (Dr.hab.), by further research

Student Services: Academic counselling, Canteen, Employment services, Foreign student adviser, Foreign Studies Centre, Handicapped facilities, Health services, Language programs, Sports facilities

Student Residential Facilities: For 5,000 students (6 dormitories)

Special Facilities: University Museum (Collegium Maius); Museum of Geology; Museum of Natural History; Museum of Anthropology. Botanical Garden. University Computer and Network Centre

Libraries: Central Library, c. 2,900,000 vols; institute libraries, c. 21. LIBRARY FACILITIES: Central Library, c. 2,900,000 vols; institute libraries, c. 1,310,000.

Publications: Biuletyn Biblioteki Jagiellońskiej, The Jagiellonian Library Bulletin *(annually)*; Rocznik Astronomiczny (The Astronomical) *(annually)*; Zeszyty Naukowe Uniwersytetu Jagiellońskiego, The Jagiellonian University Scientific Papers, in 26 series *(annually)*

Press or Publishing House: Drukarnia Uniwersytetu Jagiellońskiego (Jagellonian University Press)

Academic Staff *2010-2011*	MEN	WOMEN	**TOTAL**
FULL-TIME	3,093	4,159	**7,252**
PART-TIME	255	402	**657**
STAFF WITH DOCTORATE			
FULL-TIME	1,720	1,378	**3,098**
PART-TIME	87	95	**182**
Student Numbers *2010-2011*			
All (Foreign Included)	19,924	30,640	**50,564**
FOREIGN ONLY	538	746	**1,284**

Last Updated: 26/08/11

JAN AMOS KOMIENSKI STATE SCHOOL OF HIGHER VOCATIONAL EDUCATION IN LESZNO

Państwowa Wyższa Szkoła Zawodowa im. J.A. Komeńskiego w Lesznie (PWSZ)

ul. Mickiewicza 5, 64-100 Leszno, wielkopolskie
Tel: +48(65) 529-60-60
Fax: +48(65) 529-60-98
EMail: asystent@pwsz.edu.pl
Website: http://www.pwsz.edu.pl

Rector: Czeslaw Krolikowski
Tel: +48(65) 529-60-61, Fax: +48(65) 529-60-82
EMail: rektor@pwsz.edu.pl

Administrative Director: Zbigniew Mocek
Tel: +48(65) 529-60-64, Fax: +48(65) 529-60-74
EMail: kanclerz@pwsz.edu.pl

International Relations: Magdalena Cebula

Departments

Foreign Languages (English; Modern Languages)

Institutes

Agriculture (Agriculture); **Computer Science** (Computer Science); **Economics and Management** (Economics; Management); **Educational Sciences** (Education; Teacher Training); **Electrical Engineering** (Electrical Engineering); **Mechanical Engineering** (Mechanical Engineering); **Music** (Music); **Physical Education** (Physical Education; Sports); **Tourism** (Tourism)

History: Founded 1999.

Governing Bodies: Senate

Main Language(s) of Instruction: Polish

Accrediting Agencies: Ministry of Science and Higher Education

Degrees and Diplomas: *Inżynier*; *Licencjat*; *Świadectwo ukończenia studiów podyplomowych*

Last Updated: 03/09/11

JAN DLUGOSZ UNIVERSITY IN CZĘSTOCHOWA

Akademia im. Jana Długosza w Częstochowie (AJD)

ul. Waszyngtona 4/8, 42-200 Częstochowa, śląskie
Tel: +48(34) 378-41-00 +48(34) 378-41-18
Fax: +48(34) 378-42-22
EMail: rektor@ajd.czest.pl
Website: http://www.ajd.czest.pl

Rektor: Zygmunt Bąk (2008-)

Dyrektor Administracyjny: Mariola Ptaszek
Tel: +48(34) 378-41-82 EMail: kanclerz@ajd.czest.pl

International Relations: Miroslaw Skowronski, Head, International Relations Office
Tel: +48(34) 378-43-64, Fax: +48(34) 378-43-68
EMail: dwz@ajd.czest.pl

Departments

Foreign Languages (English; French; German; Modern Languages; Russian); **Physical Education and Sports** (Physical Education; Sports)

Faculties

Art Education (Art Education; Conducting; Fine Arts; Graphic Arts; Jazz and Popular Music; Multimedia; Music; Music Education; Music Theory and Composition; Musical Instruments; Painting and Drawing; Physics; Sculpture; Visual Arts); **Education** (Education; Educational Sciences; Parks and Recreation; Pedagogy; Physical Education; Preschool Education; Primary Education; Rehabilitation and Therapy; Social Work; Sports; Tourism; Vocational Counselling; Welfare and Protective Services); **Mathematics and Natural Sciences** (Analytical Chemistry; Biology; Biophysics; Biotechnology; Botany; Chemistry; Computer Graphics; Computer Science; Ecology; Environmental Engineering; Environmental Studies; Information Technology; Inorganic Chemistry; Materials Engineering; Mathematics; Mathematics and Computer Science; Medical Technology; Microbiology; Multimedia; Natural Sciences; Organic Chemistry; Physical Chemistry; Physics; Safety Engineering; Software Engineering; Solid State Physics; Sound Engineering (Acoustics); Tourism; Zoology); **Philology and History** (Ancient Civilizations; Archiving; English; English Studies; European Studies; German; Germanic Studies; History; International Studies; Journalism; Medieval Studies; Native Language Education; Philology; Polish; Tourism); **Social Sciences** (Administration; Administrative Law; Business Administration; Comparative Law; Economics; History; International Law; Management; Marketing; Philosophy; Private Law; Psychology; Public Law; Social Sciences; Sociology)

History: Founded as Teacher Training College in 1971. Until 2004 Wyższa Szkoła Pedagogiczna. Acquired present status and title in 2004.

Governing Bodies: Senate

Academic Year: October to June (October-January; February-June)

Admission Requirements: Secondary school certificate of education (matura) or equivalent and entrance examinations

Fees: (New Złoty): 1,600-2,000 per semester

Main Language(s) of Instruction: Polish

International Co-operation: With universities in Algeria, Belarus, Czech Republic, France, Germany, Ukraine, Russian Federation. Also participates in the Socrates/Erasmus Programme (Germany, France, Belgium, Denmark)

Accrediting Agencies: Ministry of Science and Higher Education

Degrees and Diplomas: *Inżynier*; *Licencjat*; *Świadectwo ukończenia studiów podyplomowych*; *Magister*; *Doktor*. Also Vocational and Higher Professional Degrees.

Student Services: Canteen, Foreign student adviser

Student Residential Facilities: For 842 students

Special Facilities: Astronomical Observatory

Libraries: Central Library, c. 257,000 vols

Publications: Art Education, Music Education *(annually)*; Historical Notebook *(annually)*; Neophilological Studies *(annually)*; Polish Philology *(annually)*; Polish-Ukrainian Annually *(annually)*; Scientific Papers (Mathematics, Physics, Chemistry) *(annually)*; Sociology *(annually)*

Press or Publishing House: WSP Publishing House

Academic Staff *2010-2011*: Total: c. 500

Student Numbers *2010-2011*: Total: c. 9,000

Last Updated: 01/09/11

JAN MATEJKO ACADEMY OF FINE ARTS IN KRAKOW

Akademia Sztuk Pięknych im. Jana Matejki w Krakowie (ASP)

pl. Jana Matejki 13, 31-157 Kraków, małopolskie
Tel: +48(12) 299-20-00
Fax: +48(12) 422-65-66
EMail: rektor@asp.krakow.pl
Website: http://www.asp.krakow.pl

Rektor: Adam Wsiołkowski (2008-)
Tel: +48(12) 422-24-50, Fax: +48(12) 422-65-66

Kanclerz: Adam Oleszko Tel: +48(12) 422-05-72

International Relations: Anna Tomczykiewicz, Senior International Officer
Tel: +48(12) 299-20-33, Fax: +48(12) 299-20-33
EMail: erasmus@asp.krakow.pl; atomczykiewicz@asp.krakow.pl

Centres

Foreign Languages *(Interfaculty)* (English; French; German; Modern Languages)

Departments

Theory and History of Art *(Interfaculty)* (Art History; Fine Arts)

Faculties

Conservation and Restoration of Works of Art (Laboratory Techniques; Restoration of Works of Art); **Graphic Arts** (Film; Graphic Arts; Painting and Drawing; Photography); **Industrial Design** (Communication Arts; Design; Industrial Design; Visual Arts); **Interior Design** (Design; Furniture Design; Interior Design; Painting and Drawing; Sculpture); **Painting** (Art Education; Display and Stage Design; Painting and Drawing; Textile Design); **Sculpture** (Architecture; Computer Graphics; Design; Multimedia; Painting and Drawing; Sculpture)

Programmes

Doctoral studies (Design; Fine Arts; Restoration of Works of Art; Visual Arts)

Sections

Physical Education *(Interfaculty)* (Physical Education; Sports)

History: Founded 1818 as School of Drawing and Painting branch of Department of Literature of Jagiellonian University, Cracow. Reorganized, and acquired present status and title 1950.

Governing Bodies: Senate; Faculty Councils

Academic Year: October to June (October-February; February-June)

Admission Requirements: Secondary school certificate (świadectwo dojrzałości) and portfolio

Fees: (Euro): Euro-residents, 3,350-11,240 per annum (except for Postgraduate and Doctorate programmes, 3,000 per annum); Euro-residents, 5,800-8,000 per annum.

Main Language(s) of Instruction: Polish

International Co-operation: Participates in Erasmus and CEEPUS programmes. Agreements with universities in U.S.A., Germany, Switzerland, Mexico.

Accrediting Agencies: Ministry of Science and Higher Education, Ministry of Culture

Degrees and Diplomas: *Licencjat*; *Świadectwo ukończenia studiów podyplomowych*; *Magister*, *Doktor*

Student Services: Canteen, Cultural centre, Foreign student adviser, Health services, Sports facilities

Student Residential Facilities: Student Residence for 234 students

Special Facilities: Art Gallery; Museum; Archives; Fasion Design Laboratory

Libraries: Central Library, c. 150,000 vols

Publications: Wiadomości Asp *(monthly)*

Last Updated: 07/09/11

JĘDRZEJ ŚNIADECKI ACADEMY OF PHYSICAL EDUCATION AND SPORT IN GDAŃSK

Akademia Wychowania Fizycznego i Sportu im. Jędrzeja Śniadeckiego w Gdańsku (AWFIS)

ul. Kazimierza Górskiego 1, 80-336 Gdańsk, pomorskie
Tel: +48(58) 552-17-69
Fax: +48(58) 552-07-51
EMail: rektor@awf.gda.pl
Website: http://www.awf.gda.pl

Rektor: Waldemar Moska (2010-)

Dyrektor Administracyjny: Olgierd Bojke
Tel: +48(58) 554-71-23, Fax: +48(58) 552-17-92
EMail: biuroda@awf.gda.pl

Vice-Rector for Student Affairs and Sport: Kazimierz Kochanowicz
Tel: +48(58) 554-74-67, Fax: +48(58) 554-72-59
EMail: kochk@awf.gda.pl; prorektorzy@awf.gda.pl

Vice-Rector for Education and Development: Andrzej Suchanowski
Tel: +48(58) 554-74-67, Fax: +48(58) 554-72-59
EMail: asuchan@awf.gda.pl; prorektorzy@awf.gda.pl

International Relations: Anna Szczęsna-Kaczmarek, Vice-Rector for Science and International Cooperation
Tel: +48(58) 554-72-97, Fax: +48(58) 554-73-87
EMail: annaszk@awf.gda.pl

Centres

Foreign Languages (Modern Languages) *Head*: Krzysztof Pniewski

Faculties

Physical Education (Anatomy; Anthropology; Biochemistry; Biology; Dance; Ecology; Health Sciences; Information Technology; Music; Pedagogy; Philosophy; Physical Education; Physical Therapy; Physiology; Psychology; Rehabilitation and Therapy; Social Sciences; Sociology; Sports; Sports Medicine; Statistics) *Dean*: Andrzej Szwarc; **Tourism and Recreation** (Economics; Hotel and Restaurant; Hotel Management; Leisure Studies; Marketing; Parks and Recreation; Physical Education; Psychology; Sports; Tourism) *Dean*: Stanisław Sawczyn

History: Founded 1969 as Technical School of Physical Education. Acquired Academy status and renamed Jędrzej Śniadecki Academy of Physical Education in Gdańsk acquired present status and title 1981. Acquired present status and title 2002.

Main Language(s) of Instruction: Polish

Accrediting Agencies: Ministry of Science and Higher Education

Degrees and Diplomas: *Licencjat*; *Magister*; *Doktor*

Last Updated: 26/08/11

JÓZEF PIŁSUDSKI ACADEMY OF PHYSICAL EDUCATION, WARSAW

Akademia Wychowania Fizycznego Józefa Piłsudskiego w Warszawie (AWF)

ul. Marymoncka 34, 00-968 Warszawa, mazowieckie
Tel: +48(22) 834-04-31
Fax: +48(22) 865-10-80
EMail: rektor@awf.edu.pl
Website: http://www.awf.edu.pl

Rektor: Alicja Przyłuska-Fiszer Tel: +48(22) 865-10-80

Kanclerz: Tomasz Iwańczuk
Tel: +48(22) 834-05-14, Fax: +48(22) 834-76-65
EMail: kanclerz@awf.edu.pl

International Relations: Zbigniew Trzaskoma, Vice-Rector for Science and International Co-operation
EMail: prorektor.nauka@awf.edu.pl

Faculties

Physical Education (Anatomy; Anthropology; Arts and Humanities; Biological and Life Sciences; Biology; Physical Education; Physiology; Psychology; Social Sciences; Sports; Sports Medicine); **Rehabilitation** (Biology; Physical Therapy; Rehabilitation and Therapy); **Tourism and Recreation** (Economics; English; French; German; Italian; Management; Modern Languages; Parks and Recreation; Russian; Spanish; Tourism)

History: Founded 1929 as Central Institute of Physical Education (CIWF), acquired present status and title 1938.

Governing Bodies: Senate

Academic Year: October to September

Admission Requirements: Secondary school certificate (Matura) and entrance examinations

Main Language(s) of Instruction: Polish

Accrediting Agencies: Ministry of Science and Higher Education

Degrees and Diplomas: *Licencjat*; *Świadectwo ukończenia studiów podyplomowych*; *Magister*, *Doktor*

Student Services: Canteen, Cultural centre, Employment services, Health services, Sports facilities

Student Residential Facilities: For c. 1,040 students

Libraries: Central Library, 110,000 vols

Publications: Kultura Fizyczna, (Physical Culture) *(bimonthly)*; Postępy Rehabilitacji, (Rehabilitation Development) *(quarterly)*; Scientific Yearbook, (in English and Polish) *(annually)*; Wychowanie Fizyczne i Sport, (Physical Education and Sports) *(quarterly)*

Press or Publishing House: Division of Scientific Publishing

Last Updated: 09/09/11

KAROL SZYMANOWSKI ACADEMY OF MUSIC, KATOWICE

Akademia Muzyczna im. Karola Szymanowskiego w Katowicach (AM)

ul Zacisze 3, 40-025 Katowice, śląskie
Tel: +48(32) 255-40-17
Fax: +48(32) 256-44-85
EMail: kancelaria@am.katowice.pl
Website: http://www.am.katowice.pl

Rektor: Tomasz Miczka (2008-)
Tel: +48(32) 779-21-11, Fax: +48(32) 779-21-24
EMail: biurorektora@am.katowice.pl

Kanclerz: Katarzyna Pleśniak
Tel: +48(32) 779-21-11 EMail: kanclerz@am.katowice.pl

International Relations: Joanna Mentel-Imielska, International Relations Officer - Socrates Erasmus Coordinator
Tel: +48(32) 779-22-22, Fax: +48(32) 779-22-22
EMail: J.Mentel@am.katowice.pl

Departments

Pedagogy *(Interfaculty)* (Music Education; Pedagogy); **Physical Education and Sport** (Physical Education; Sports); **Piano Accompaniment** *(Interfaculty)* (Music; Musical Instruments)

Faculties

Composition, Interpretation, Education and Jazz (Conducting; Jazz and Popular Music; Music; Music Education; Music Theory and Composition; Singing); **Vocal and Instrumental Performance** (Acting; Music; Musical Instruments; Singing)

History: Founded 1929 as State Conservatory of Music, renamed 1934 as Silesian Conservatory of Music. Reorganized 1945 as State Music College, named after Karol Szymanowski. Acquired present status and title 1979.

Governing Bodies: Senate

Academic Year: October to June (October-January; February-June)

Admission Requirements: Secondary school certificate (Matura) and entrance examination

Fees: (US Dollars): Foreign Students, 5,000 per annum. EU students free

Main Language(s) of Instruction: Polish

International Co-operation: With universities in EU countries. Also participates in the Socrates/Erasmus, USA-Louiseville, K4

Accrediting Agencies: Ministry of Science and Higher Education; Ministry of Culture

Degrees and Diplomas: *Licencjat*; *Magister*

Student Services: Academic counselling, Canteen, Cultural centre, Health services, Social counselling, Sports facilities

Student Residential Facilities: Students' dorm "Parnas"

Special Facilities: Computerised Recording Studio; Theatre Hall; Silesian Organ Museum

Libraries: Main Library: 31,071 volumes of books; 4,850 periodicals, 50,000 sets of music notes

Publications: Main Library Papers, Silesian Music Culture Archives *(biennially)*; Publication of Music Academy *(other/irregular)*

Last Updated: 06/09/11

KASIMIR PUŁASKI TECHNICAL UNIVERSITY OF RADOM

Politechnika Radomska im. Kazimierza Pułaskiego (PR)

ul. J. Malczewskiego 29, 26-600 Radom, mazowieckie
Tel: +48(48) 361-70-00
Fax: +48(48) 361-70-21
EMail: dwa@pr.radom.pl
Website: http://www.pr.radom.pl

Rektor: Mirosław Luft
Tel: +48 (48) 361-70-10, Fax: +48 (48) 361-70-12
EMail: rektor@pr.radom.pl

Kanclerz: Mariusz Początek
Tel: +48(48) 361-72-00, Fax: +48(48) 361-72-03
EMail: m.poczatek@pr.radom.pl

International Relations: Blajer Wojciech, Vice Rector, Human Resources Development and International Cooperation
EMail: rektorn@pr.radom.pl

Centres

Distance Education (Electrical Engineering; Mechanical Engineering; Transport Engineering)

Departments

Foreign Languages *(Interfaculty)* (English; French; German; Polish; Russian); **Physical Education and Sports** *(Interfaculty)* (Physical Education)

Faculties

Art (Architecture; Design; Fine Arts; Graphic Arts; Graphic Design; Interior Design; Painting and Drawing; Performing Arts; Photography; Sculpture; Video; Visual Arts); **Economics** (Accountancy; Administration; Applied Mathematics; Banking; Business Administration; Business Computing; Development Studies; Econometrics; Economic and Finance Policy; Economics; Finance; Insurance; International Business; International Relations; Management; Marketing; Mathematics and Computer Science; Operations Research; Philosophy; Safety Engineering; Sociology; Statistics); **Materials Science, Technology and Design** (Chemical Engineering; Chemistry; Cosmetology; Design; Environmental Engineering; Materials Engineering; Production Engineering; Textile Design); **Mechanical Engineering** (Automotive Engineering; Computer Engineering; Electronic Engineering; Energy Engineering; Engineering Management; Heating and Refrigeration; Machine Building; Materials Engineering; Mechanical Engineering; Mechanics; Physics; Production Engineering; Thermal Engineering); **Teacher Training** (Computer Science; Data Processing; Health Education; Mathematics; Mathematics and Computer Science; Pedagogy; Physical Education; Teacher Training; Technology Education); **Transport and Electrical Engineering** (Automation and Control Engineering; Electrical Engineering; Electronic Engineering; Energy Engineering; Marketing; Measurement and Precision Engineering; Transport Engineering; Transport Management)

Institutes

Health Sciences (Health Sciences; Nursing; Physical Therapy); **Philology and Pedagogy** (Communication Studies; English;

German; Journalism; Literature; Modern Languages; Pedagogy; Philology; Polish; Tourism; Translation and Interpretation)

History: Founded 1950 as Evening Engineering School, reorganized 1978, and acquired present status and title 1996.

Governing Bodies: Senate

Academic Year: October to June (October-January; February-June)

Admission Requirements: Secondary school certificate (Matura)

Fees: (New Złoty): c. 4,000 per semester

Main Language(s) of Instruction: Polish

International Co-operation: Participates in the Tempus and Socrates/Erasmus programmes

Accrediting Agencies: Ministry of Science and Higher Education

Degrees and Diplomas: *Inżynier*; *Licencjat*; *Świadectwo ukończenia studiów podyplomowych*; *Magister*, *Doktor*

Student Services: Academic counselling, Canteen, Cultural centre, Foreign student adviser, Handicapped facilities, Health services, Social counselling, Sports facilities

Student Residential Facilities: For c. 1,200 students

Special Facilities: Radio Station. Art Gallery. Sport Centre

Libraries: Central Library and Libraries of Faculties

Press or Publishing House: Publishing Office

Last Updated: 22/09/11

KAZIMIERZ WIELKI UNIVERSITY IN BYDGOSZCZ

Uniwersytet Kazimierza Wielkiego w Bydgoszczy (AB IM. KW)

ul. J. K. Chodkiewicza 30, 85-064 Bydgoszcz, kujawsko-pomorskie
Tel: +48(52) 341-91-00
Fax: +48(52) 341-91-60
EMail: rekrutacja@ukw.edu.pl
Website: http://www.ukw.edu.pl

Rektor: Józef Kubik (2006-)
Tel: +48(52) 341-35-33, Fax: +48(52) 341-35-33
EMail: rektor@ukw.edu.pl

Kanclerza: Wanda Kmieć
Tel: +48(52) 341-34-64, Fax: +48(52) 360-82-06
EMail: kanclerz@ukw.edu.pl

International Relations: Janusz Ostoja-Zagorski, Vice-Rector for Science and International Relations
Tel: +48(52) 341-91-08, Fax: +48(52) 341-47-73
EMail: dnauki@ukw.edu.pl

Faculties

Administration and Social Sciences (Administration; Administrative Law; Anthropology; Civil Law; Computer Science; Criminal Law; Criminology; Economics; Environmental Studies; Ethics; Finance; Information Sciences; Law; Library Science; Logic; Management; Philosophy; Police Studies; Public Administration; Social Sciences; Sociology); **Humanities** (Ancient Civilizations; Applied Linguistics; Arabic; Archaeology; Arts and Humanities; Communication Studies; Contemporary History; Cultural Studies; Demography and Population; English; German; Grammar; History; International Relations; Journalism; Library Science; Literature; Mass Communication; Media Studies; Medieval Studies; Modern History; Modern Languages; Philology; Polish; Political Sciences; Russian; Sociology); **Mathematics, Physics and Technology** (Biology; Biomedical Engineering; Chemistry; Computer Science; Electrical and Electronic Equipment and Maintenance; Engineering; Geography; Information Technology; Mathematics; Mathematics Education; Mechanics; Natural Sciences; Physics; Technology; Wood Technology); **Natural Sciences** (Biochemistry; Biology; Biotechnology; Botany; Cell Biology; Ecology; Economic History; Environmental Studies; Genetics; Geography; Geography (Human); Microbiology; Natural Sciences; Physical Education; Physiology; Sports; Tourism; Toxicology; Water Management; Water Science; Zoology); **Pedagogy and Psychology** (Art Education; Conducting; Development Studies; Education; Educational Sciences; Environmental Studies; Health Education; Music Education; Music Theory and Composition; Musical Instruments; Neurological Therapy; Pedagogy; Philosophy of Education; Preschool Education; Psychology; Rehabilitation and Therapy; Singing; Social Psychology; Sociology; Special Education)

Units

Foreign Languages *(Interfaculty)* (English; Foreign Languages Education; French; German; Italian; Latin; Russian); **Pedagogy** *(Interfaculty)* (Pedagogy); **Physical Education and Sports** *(Interfaculty)* (Physical Education; Sports); **Study Internship** *(Interfaculty)* (Police Studies)

History: Founded 1969 as Teacher Training College (Wyższa Szkoła Pedagogiczna w Bydgoszczy), Academia Bydgoska im. Kazimierza Wielkiego until 2007.

Governing Bodies: Rector, Senate

Academic Year: October to June (October-January; February-June)

Admission Requirements: Secondary school certificate (świadectwo dojrzałości) and entrance examination

Fees: Full-time students, none; Foreign students, yes (except students with special grants, e.g. Socrates/Erasmus, government grants)

Main Language(s) of Instruction: Polish

International Co-operation: With universities in Finland, Germany, Russian Federation; Participates in the Erasmus programme.

Accrediting Agencies: Ministry of Science and Higher Education

Degrees and Diplomas: *Inżynier*; *Licencjat*; *Świadectwo ukończenia studiów podyplomowych*; *Magister*, *Doktor*

Student Services: Academic counselling, Canteen, Cultural centre, Employment services, Health services, Nursery care, Social counselling, Sports facilities

Libraries: Central Library, 365,000 vols, 32,000 special collection units. Libraries of the faculties and departments

Press or Publishing House: Wydawnictwo Akademii Bydgoskiej im. Kazimierza Wielkiego

Academic Staff *2010-2011*: Total 700

STAFF WITH DOCTORATE: Total 150

Student Numbers *2010-2011*: Total: c. 15,000

Last Updated: 28/09/11

KIELCE UNIVERSITY OF TECHNOLOGY

Politechnika Świętokrzyska (PŚK)

al. 1000 Państwa Polskiego 7, 25-314 Kielce, świętokrzyskie
Tel: +48(41) 344-16-84
Fax: +48(41) 344-29-97
EMail: promocja@tu.kielce.pl
Website: http://www.tu.kielce.pl

Rektor: Stanisław Adamczak (2008-)
Tel: +48(41) 342-41-00, Fax: +48(41) 344-29-97
EMail: rektor@tu.kielce.pl

Kanclerz: Andrzej Sęk
Tel: +48(41) 342-41-50, Fax: +48(41) 344-38-74
EMail: kanclerz@tu.kielce.pl

International Relations: Zbigniew Rusin, Vice-Rector for International Cooperation
Tel: +48(41) 342-47-73, Fax: +48(41) 344-23-06
EMail: zbigniew.rusin@tu.kielce.pl

Centres

Continuing Education (Automotive Engineering; Computer Engineering; Computer Graphics; Computer Networks; Data Processing; English; French; German; Italian; Laser Engineering; Materials Engineering; Multimedia; Protective Services; Software Engineering)

Faculties

Civil and Environmental Engineering (Architectural Restoration; Architecture and Planning; Bridge Engineering; Civil Engineering; Computer Science; Construction Engineering; Environmental Engineering; Geological Engineering; Heating and Refrigeration; Hydraulic Engineering; Materials Engineering; Road Engineering; Sanitary Engineering; Structural Architecture; Surveying and Mapping; Telecommunications Engineering; Transport Engineering; Waste Management; Water Management); **Electrical Engineering,**

Automatics and Computer Science (Automation and Control Engineering; Computer Engineering; Computer Graphics; Computer Networks; Computer Science; Data Processing; Electrical Engineering; Electronic Engineering; Energy Engineering; Measurement and Precision Engineering; Physics; Power Engineering; Robotics; Software Engineering; Telecommunications Engineering); **Management and Computer Modelling** (Business Administration; Computer Education; Computer Engineering; Computer Graphics; Computer Science; Data Processing; Economics; Engineering Management; Finance; Industrial Management; Information Technology; Management; Materials Engineering; Mathematics; Mathematics and Computer Science; Production Engineering; Rubber Technology); **Mechatronics and Machine Building** (Automation and Control Engineering; Automotive Engineering; Heating and Refrigeration; Hydraulic Engineering; Information Technology; Laser Engineering; Machine Building; Materials Engineering; Mathematics and Computer Science; Mechanical Engineering; Mechanics; Metal Techniques; Metallurgical Engineering; Road Transport; Robotics; Safety Engineering; Transport Engineering; Transport Management)

History: Founded 1965 as School of Engineering. Acquired present status and title 1974.

Governing Bodies: Senate

Academic Year: October to June (October-February; February-June)

Admission Requirements: Secondary school certificate (Matura) and entrance examination

Fees: (New Złoty): 1,300 - 1,550 per term

Main Language(s) of Instruction: Polish

International Co-operation: With universities in Austria, Belarus, Belgium, Bulgaria, Croatia, Czech Republic, France, Germany, Hungary, Ireland, Latvia, Lithuania, Portugal, Romania, Russian Federation, Slovakia, Slovenia, Spain, Sweden, Ukraine, UK, USA

Accrediting Agencies: Ministry of Science and Higher Education

Degrees and Diplomas: *Inżynier*, *Licencjat*, *Świadectwo ukończenia studiów podyplomowych*; *Magister*, *Doktor*

Student Services: Academic counselling, Canteen, Cultural centre, Employment services, Handicapped facilities, Health services, Language programs, Nursery care, Social counselling, Sports facilities

Student Residential Facilities: Yes

Special Facilities: Sports centre, student club, catering facilities

Libraries: Central Library, 147,587 vols

Publications: Zeszyty Naukowe *(other/irregular)*

Press or Publishing House: Publishing House

Last Updated: 23/09/11

KOSZALIN UNIVERSITY OF TECHNOLOGY

Politechnika Koszalińska (PK)

ul. Śniadeckich 2, 75-453 Koszalin, zachodniopomorskie
Tel: +48(94) 347-86-20
Fax: +48(94) 347-86-19
EMail: jmr@tu.koszalin.pl
Website: http://www.tu.koszalin.pl

Rektor: Tomasz Krzyżyński (2005-)
Tel: +48(94) 347-86-20, Fax: +48(94) 347-86-19

Kanclerz: Artur Wezgraj
Tel: +48(94) 347-86-10, Fax: +48(94) 342-59-63
EMail: artur.wezgraj@tu.koszalin.pl

International Relations: Ewa Glijerska-Balasz
Tel: +48(94) 347-86-65, Fax: +48(94) 346-03-74
EMail: egbalasz@tu.koszalin.pl

Faculties

Civil and Environmental Engineering (Civil Engineering; Construction Engineering; Energy Engineering; Environmental Engineering; Environmental Management; Environmental Studies; Heating and Refrigeration; Road Engineering; Soil Conservation; Surveying and Mapping; Toxicology; Waste Management; Water Management); **Economics and Management** (Accountancy; Banking; Business Administration; Ecology; Economics; Finance; Insurance; Management; Marketing; Public Administration; Real Estate; Regional Studies; Rural Studies; Tourism; Urban Studies); **Electronics and Computer Science** (Automation and Control Engineering; Business Computing; Computer Engineering; Computer Networks; Computer Science; Data Processing; Educational Psychology; Electronic Engineering; Information Management; Information Technology; Medical Technology; Optical Technology; Pedagogy; Preschool Education; Primary Education; Software Engineering; Telecommunications Engineering); **Industrial Design** (Industrial Design; Interior Design; Visual Arts); **Mechanical Engineering** (Agricultural Business; Agricultural Engineering; Agriculture; Biotechnology; Building Technologies; Computer Engineering; Engineering; Food Technology; Forestry; Heating and Refrigeration; Industrial Management; Information Management; Information Technology; Machine Building; Management; Mechanical Engineering; Mechanics; Nutrition; Plant and Crop Protection; Production Engineering; Road Transport; Safety Engineering; Thermal Engineering; Transport and Communications; Transport Management); **Mechatronics, Nanotechnology and Vacuum Technique** (Automation and Control Engineering; Biomedical Engineering; Electronic Engineering; Film; Graphic Design; Materials Engineering; Measurement and Precision Engineering; Mechanical Engineering; Medical Technology; Nanotechnology; Rehabilitation and Therapy; Software Engineering; Visual Arts); **Modern Languages** (Communication Studies; English; German; Journalism; Media Studies; Modern Languages; Public Relations); **Social Policy and International Relations** (Central European Studies; Eastern European Studies; European Studies; International Relations; Public Administration)

History: Founded 1968 as Koszalin Higher School of Engineering, acquired present status and title 1996.

Governing Bodies: Senate

Academic Year: October to June (October-February; February-June)

Admission Requirements: Secondary school certificate (Matura)

Fees: (New Złoty): 1,700-2,900 per semester (part-time degree programmes)

Main Language(s) of Instruction: Polish

International Co-operation: Lifelong Learning Programme - Erasmus; Tempus Programme; Ceepus Programme; Baltic Sea Region Programme; 6/7 Framework Programmes; Jean Monnet Programme.

Accrediting Agencies: Ministry of Science and Higher Education

Degrees and Diplomas: *Inżynier*, *Licencjat*, *Magister*, *Doktor (Ph.D.)*

Student Services: Academic counselling, Canteen, Cultural centre, Employment services, Foreign student adviser, Health services, Language programs, Nursery care, Social counselling, Sports facilities

Student Residential Facilities: Student hostels

Special Facilities: Science and Technology Park with academic incubator; Laboratory of Vacuum Technology; 6/7 Framework Programme Subregional Contact Point; Centre of Foreign Languages; Computer Centre; Sport Centre; The University of the Third Age

Libraries: Main and Departmental libraries, 136,639 vols; Special collections, 55,545 vols; 16,977 periodicals

Publications: Koszalińskie Studia i Materiały *(biennially)*; Na Temat *(biennially)*; Zeszyty Naukowe, Civil and Environmental Engineering; Economics and Management; Mechanical Engineering; Electronics and Computer Engineering *(annually)*

Press or Publishing House: Publishing Service

Student Numbers *2010-2011*: Total: c. 18,500

Last Updated: 26/08/11

LUBLIN UNIVERSITY OF TECHNOLOGY

Politechnika Lubelska (PL)

ul. Nadbystrzycka 38 D, 20-618 Lublin, lubelskie
Tel: +48(81) 538-46-57
Fax: +48(81) 532-26-12
EMail: politechnika@pollub.pl
Website: http://www.pollub.pl

Rektor: Marek Opielak (2008-)
Tel: +48(81) 538-41-00, Fax: +48(81) 538-46-57
EMail: rektor@pollub.pl

Kanclerz: Mieczysław Hasiak
Tel: +48(81) 538-41-03, Fax: +48(81) 532-46-95
EMail: kanclerz@pollub.pl; m.hasiak@pollub.pl

International Relations: Beata Kijak-Mitura, International Relations Officer
Tel: +48(81) 538-41-10, Fax: +48(81) 532-46-78
EMail: b.kijak@pollub.pl

Departments

Foreign Languages (English; French; German; Modern Languages); **Physical Education and Sports** (Physical Education; Sports)

Faculties

Civil Engineering and Architecture (Architectural Restoration; Architecture; Bridge Engineering; Building Technologies; Civil Engineering; Geological Engineering; Mechanics; Road Engineering; Town Planning); **Electrical Engineering and Computer Science** (Automation and Control Engineering; Computer Engineering; Computer Science; Electrical Engineering; Electronic Engineering; Energy Engineering; Mathematics); **Environmental Engineering** (Environmental Engineering; Environmental Studies; Thermal Engineering; Waste Management; Water Management); **Fundamentals of Technology** (Applied Mathematics; Applied Physics; Teacher Training; Technology; Technology Education); **Management** (Accountancy; Business Administration; Business Computing; Computer Networks; E-Business/Commerce; Economics; Finance; Information Management; Information Technology; Management; Marketing; Safety Engineering); **Mechanical Engineering** (Automation and Control Engineering; Automotive Engineering; Computer Graphics; Engineering Management; Food Technology; Information Technology; Machine Building; Materials Engineering; Mechanical Engineering; Mechanics; Polymer and Plastics Technology; Production Engineering; Thermal Physics; Transport Engineering)

History: Founded 1953 as Evening Engineering School. Acquired present status and title 1977.

Governing Bodies: Academic Senate

Academic Year: October to June (October-February; February-June)

Admission Requirements: Secondary school certificate (Matura) and qualifying interview or entrance examination

Fees: (New Złoty): Extramural courses, 1,100-1,900 per semester. Foreign students, US$ 3,000-5,000 per annum

Main Language(s) of Instruction: Polish

International Co-operation: With 50 bilateral international cooperative agreements. Also participates in the CEEPUS, 6 Framework Programme, LdV II, Polonium 2000 and Socrates-Erasmus programmes

Accrediting Agencies: Ministry of Science and Higher Education

Degrees and Diplomas: *Inżynier (inż.)*: 4 1/2 yrs; *Licencjat*; *Świadectwo ukończenia studiów podyplomowych*; *Magister*; *Doktor*. Also MBA

Student Services: Academic counselling, Canteen, Cultural centre, Employment services, Foreign Studies Centre, Health services, Nursery care, Social counselling, Sports facilities

Student Residential Facilities: For c. 1,400 students

Special Facilities: Computer Centre; Centre for Innovation and Advanced Technology; Technology Transfer Centre;Business Incubator

Libraries: Central Library c. 150,000 vols; 300 Polish and 40 foreign periodical subscriptions.

Publications: Informatyka Stosowana, Applied Computer Science *(annually)*; Zeszyty Naukowe *(annually)*

Press or Publishing House: Wydawnictwa Politechniki Lubelskiej

Academic Staff *2010-2011*	**TOTAL**
FULL-TIME	c. **550**
Student Numbers *2010-2011*	
All (Foreign Included)	c. **11,000**

Part-time students, 3,600.
Last Updated: 22/09/11

MARIE CURIE-SKŁODOWSKA UNIVERSITY

Uniwersytet Marii Curie-Skłodowskiej w Lublinie (UMCS)

Pl. M. Curie-Skłodowskiej 5, 20-031 Lublin, lubelskie
Tel: +48(81) 537-51-00
Fax: +48(81) 533-36-69 +48(81) 537-51-02
EMail: promocja@umcs.lublin.pl
Website: http://www.umcs.lublin.pl

Rector: Andrzej Dabrowski (2008-)
Tel: +48(81) 537-51-09 +48(81) 537-51-07
EMail: andrzej.dabrowski@umcs.lublin.pl

Kanclerz: Mirosław Urbanek
Tel: +48(81) 537-53-13, Fax: +48(81) 537-51-13
EMail: kanclerz@umcs.lublin.pl; Miroslaw.Urbanek@umcs.lublin.pl

International Relations: Ryszard Straszyński, Director
Tel: +48(81) 537-52-18, Fax: +48(81) 537-54-10
EMail: rstraszy@ramzes.umcs.lublin.pl

Centres

Eastern Europe *(UMCS)* (Eastern European Studies); **Polish Language and Culture for Foreigners** (Classical Languages; Cultural Studies; English; German; Polish; Romance Languages; Russian)

Colleges

Fine Arts *(Kazimierz Dolny)* (Art Therapy; Communication Arts; Design; Film; Fine Arts; Graphic Arts; Graphic Design; Multimedia; Painting and Drawing; Photography; Publishing and Book Trade)

Faculties

Art (Art Education; Art History; Art Therapy; Ceramic Art; Communication Arts; Conducting; Fine Arts; Graphic Arts; Graphic Design; Jazz and Popular Music; Music; Music Education; Music Theory and Composition; Musical Instruments; Painting and Drawing; Religious Music; Sculpture; Singing; Visual Arts); **Biology and Earth Sciences** (Biochemistry; Biology; Biotechnology; Earth Sciences; Environmental Management; Environmental Studies; Geography; Laboratory Techniques; Microbiology; Natural Resources; Parks and Recreation; Science Education; Tourism); **Chemistry** (Chemical Engineering; Chemistry; Environmental Studies; Inorganic Chemistry; Laboratory Techniques; Optical Technology; Organic Chemistry; Physical Chemistry); **Economics** (Accountancy; Economics; Finance; Information Technology; Management; Marketing); **Humanities** (Archaeology; Arts and Humanities; Cultural Studies; English; German; History; Information Sciences; Library Science; Linguistics; Philology; Polish; Romance Languages; Slavic Languages; Speech Therapy and Audiology); **Law and Administration** (Administration; Administrative Law; Civil Law; Commercial Law; Constitutional Law; Criminal Law; Criminology; Economics; European Union Law; Finance; Fiscal Law; Forensic Medicine and Dentistry; History of Law; Labour Law; Law; Management; Occupational Health; Public Administration; Public Law; Safety Engineering); **Mathematics, Physics and Computer Science** (Applied Physics; Computer Science; Mathematics; Physics); **Pedagogy and Psychology** (Adult Education; Clinical Psychology; Developmental Psychology; Education; Educational Psychology; Family Studies; Health Education; Neurological Therapy; Pedagogy; Preschool Education; Primary Education; Psychology; Rehabilitation and Therapy; Social Psychology; Special Education; Teacher Training; Vocational Counselling); **Philosophy and Sociology** (Aesthetics; Anthropology; Communication Studies; Cultural Studies; Economics; Education; Ethics; European Studies; Family Studies; Laboratory Techniques; Logic; Philosophy; Religious Studies; Rural Studies; Sociology); **Political Science** (Communication Studies; Ethnology; Government; Human Rights; International Relations; Journalism; Philosophy; Political Sciences; Sociology)

Further Information: Also Branch University in Rzeszów. Colleges in Bilgoraj, Biała Podlaska and Radom. Distance Education Center.

History: Founded 1944 as a State University. Faculties of Medicine and Pharmacy detached in 1950 to form separate College of Medicine. Faculties of Veterinary Medicine and Agriculture detached 1955 to form separate College of Agriculture.

Governing Bodies: Senate

Academic Year: October to June (October-February; February-June). Also Summer Semester (July-August)

Admission Requirements: Secondary school certificate (matura) and entrance examination

Fees: (New Złoty): Part-time students, 2,650-6,000 per semester; Foreign students, US$ 3,000-5,000.

Main Language(s) of Instruction: Polish; English

International Co-operation: Participates in the Erasmus programme.

Accrediting Agencies: Ministry of Science and Higher Education

Degrees and Diplomas: *Licencjat*; *Świadectwo ukończenia studiów podyplomowych*; *Magister*, *Doktor*

Student Residential Facilities: For c. 3,240 students

Special Facilities: Zoology Museum; Biology Museum. Botanical Garden. Astrological Observatory. Audiovisual Studio

Libraries: Central Library, c. 1,481,000 vols; Department Libraries, total, c. 1 m. vols

Publications: Annales Universitatis Maria Curie-Skłodowska *(annually)*

Press or Publishing House: Wydawnictwo UMCS

Academic Staff *2010-2011*	**TOTAL**
FULL-TIME	**49**
Student Numbers *2010-2011*	
All (Foreign Included)	**26,872**
FOREIGN ONLY	**16**

Part-time students, 7,786.

Last Updated: 28/09/11

MARITIME UNIVERSITY OF SZCZECIN

Akademia Morska w Szczecinie (AMS)

ul. Wały Chrobrego 1-2, 70-500 Szczecin, zachodniopomorskie
Tel: +48(91) 480-94-00
Fax: +48(91) 480-95-75
EMail: rektor@am.szczecin.pl
Website: http://www.am.szczecin.pl

Rektor: Stanisław Gucma (2008-)
Tel: +48(91) 480-93-02, Fax: +48(91) 480-95-85

Chancellor: Andrzej Durajczyk
Tel: +48(91) 480-93-36 EMail: kanclerz@am.szczecin.pl

International Relations: Wojciech Czyżewski
Tel: +48(91) 480-94-80 EMail: w.czyzewski@am.szczecin.pl

Faculties

Engineering and Economics of Transport (Production Engineering; Transport and Communications; Transport Management) *Dean*: Zofia Jóźwiak; **Marine Engineering** (Electronic Engineering; Marine Engineering; Mechanical Engineering) *Dean*: Cezary Behrendt; **Navigation** (Computer Science; Marine Transport; Nautical Science; Surveying and Mapping; Transport and Communications) *Dean*: Jerzy Hajduk

Further Information: Also Marine Officers' Training Center; Marine Rescue Training Centre; LNG European Training Center; Marine Training Centre in Świnoujście; Maritime English Center (MEC).

History: Founded 1947 incorporating the State School of Sea Fisheries and the State Maritime School. Until 2004 Wyższa Szkoła Morska. Acquired present status and title 2004.

Governing Bodies: Senate

Academic Year: September to June (September-January; February-June)

Admission Requirements: Secondary school certificate (Matura), and entrance examination (age limit 23 yrs)

Fees: (US Dollars): Foreign students, 4,400 per annum

Main Language(s) of Instruction: Polish

International Co-operation: Baltic Sea Region 2007-2,013; Erasmus; Leonardo da Vinci; South Baltic Programme; CIP IEE.

Accrediting Agencies: Ministry of Science and Higher Education; National Accreditation Board in Poland

Degrees and Diplomas: *Inżynier*: Navigation; Transport; Geodesy and Cartography; Computer Science; Mechanical Engineering; Mechatronics; Transport; Management and Production; Engineering; Logistics; *Magister*: Navigation; Mechanical Engineering; Transport; Management and Production Engineering

Student Services: Canteen, Cultural centre, Employment services, Foreign student adviser, Health services, Sports facilities

Student Residential Facilities: For 965 students

Special Facilities: Laboratory of electronic navigational aids; ECDIS simulator; Planetarium; GMDSS simulator; Electronics laboratory; Communications laboratory; Computer laboratories; Laboratory of hydrographical survey and aids to navigation; Ship stability laboratory; Loading simulator; Four up-to-date simulators of LNG European Training Center: integrated bridge simulator of Q-Flex vessels (LNG tankers); Dynamic positioning system simulator; Ship loading simulator; LNG tanker crew members and managerial staff of all gas transport operations.

Libraries: Central Library, 124 thousand vols; 7,950 Polish and foreign magazine vols and c. 24,400 special items; Collection of IMO documents, supported by the IMO VEGA database.

Publications: Akademickie Aktualności Morskie *(bimonthly)*; Studia, Serial; Zeszyty Naukowe Akademii Morskiej *(quarterly)*

Press or Publishing House: Dział Wydawnictw WSM

Last Updated: 26/08/11

MEDICAL UNIVERSITY OF BIALYSTOK

Uniwersytet Medyczny w Białymstoku (AM)

ul. J. Kilińskiego 1, 15-089 Białystok, podlaskie
Tel: +48(85) 748-54-00 +48(85) 879-54-00
Fax: +48(85) 748-54-08
EMail: kancelaria@umb.edu.pl
Website: http://www.amb.edu.pl

Rektor: Jacek Nikliński (2008-)
Tel: +48(85) 748-54-03 EMail: rektor@amb.edu.pl

Kanclerz: Konrad Raczkowski
Tel: +48(85) 748-54-15, Fax: +48(85) 748-54-16

International Relations: Małgorzata Laudanska, Head, Department of Science, International Relations
Tel: +48(85) 748-54-12, Fax: +48(85) 748-54-90
EMail: dzialnau@umwb.edu.pl; malgorzata.laudanska@umb.edu.pl

Faculties

Health Science (Anaesthesiology; Dietetics; Epidemiology; Food Technology; Gerontology; Gynaecology and Obstetrics; Hygiene; Medicine; Midwifery; Neurology; Nursing; Nutrition; Paediatrics; Pathology; Pharmacology; Public Health; Radiology; Rehabilitation and Therapy; Speech Therapy and Audiology; Statistics); **Medicine** (Anatomy; Biochemistry; Biology; Biophysics; Dental Technology; Dentistry; Embryology and Reproduction Biology; Forensic Medicine and Dentistry; Genetics; Health Education; Histology; Immunology; Medical Technology; Medicine; Microbiology; Molecular Biology; Orthodontics; Paediatrics; Pathology; Pharmacology; Physiology; Radiology; Social and Preventive Medicine; Surgery); **Pharmacy** (Analytical Chemistry; Biochemistry; Biology; Chemistry; Cosmetology; Haematology; Health Sciences; Histology; Immunology; Inorganic Chemistry; Laboratory Techniques; Medical Technology; Microbiology; Organic Chemistry; Paediatrics; Pharmacology; Pharmacy; Physical Chemistry; Physiology; Toxicology)

Further Information: Also University Hospital and University Children's Hospital in Bialystok.

History: Founded 1950.

Governing Bodies: Senate; Faculty Council

Academic Year: October to June (October-February; February-June)

Admission Requirements: Graduation from high school (matura) and entrance examination

Fees: (US Dollars): Foreign students, c. 5,000 per annum

Main Language(s) of Instruction: Polish, English

International Co-operation: With universities in Germany, Sweden, Lithuania, Belarus. Participates in the Erasmus programme.

Accrediting Agencies: Ministry of Health

Degrees and Diplomas: *Licencjat*; *Lekarz*; *Lekarz*: Dentistry; *Magister*, *Doktor*

Student Services: Academic counselling, Canteen, Cultural centre, Employment services, Foreign student adviser, Foreign Studies Centre, Handicapped facilities, Health services, Language programs, Nursery care, Social counselling, Sports facilities

Student Residential Facilities: For c. 850 students

Special Facilities: Pharmacy Museum.

Libraries: Central Library, 134,300 vols

Publications: Bibliografia Publikacji Naukowych Pracowników AMB *(annually)*; Roczniki Akademii Medycznej w Białymstoku *(annually)*; Spis Wykładów i Spis Pracowników Uczelni *(annually)*

Academic Staff *2010-2011*: Total: c. 750
Student Numbers *2010-2011*: Total: c. 4,000
Last Updated: 29/09/11

MEDICAL UNIVERSITY OF GDAŃSK

Gdański Uniwersytet Medyczny (GUMED)
ul. Marii Skłodowskiej-Curie 3a, 80-210 Gdańsk, pomorskie
Tel: +48(58) 349-22-22
Fax: +48(58) 301-61-15
EMail: webadmin@amg.gda.pl
Website: http://www.amg.gda.pl

Rektor: Janusz Moryś
Tel: +48(58) 349-10-00, Fax: +48(58) 520-40-38
EMail: rektor@gumed.edu.pl

Kanclerz: Marek Langowski
Tel: +48(58) 349-10-10 +48(58) 34910-30,
Fax: +48(58) 344-73-36 EMail: kanclerz@gumed.edu.pl

International Relations: Ewa Kiszka, Head, International Relations Office
Tel: +48(58) 349-11-61, Fax: +48(58) 349-11-62
EMail: ekiszka@gumed.edu.pl

Departments

Foreign Languages *(Interfaculty)* (English; French; German; Latin; Modern Languages; Polish; Spanish); **Physical Education and Sport** *(Interfaculty)* (Physical Education; Sports)

Faculties

Biotechnology *(Intercollegiate UG-MUG)* (Biochemistry; Biotechnology; Cell Biology; Molecular Biology; Virology); **Health Sciences** (Biochemistry; Cardiology; Gerontology; Health Sciences; Medical Technology; Nursing; Nutrition; Oncology; Physiology; Rehabilitation and Therapy; Social and Preventive Medicine; Toxicology; Treatment Techniques); **Medicine** (Anaesthesiology; Anatomy; Biochemistry; Biology; Biophysics; Cardiology; Dental Technology; Dentistry; Diabetology; Endocrinology; Epidemiology; Ethics; Forensic Medicine and Dentistry; Genetics; Gerontology; Gynaecology and Obstetrics; Haematology; Hepatology; Histology; Hygiene; Immunology; Medicine; Microbiology; Nephrology; Neurology; Oncology; Ophthalmology; Orthodontics; Orthopaedics; Otorhinolaryngology; Pathology; Periodontics; Pharmacology; Physics; Physiology; Pneumology; Psychiatry and Mental Health; Statistics; Surgery; Treatment Techniques; Urology); **Pharmacy** (Analytical Chemistry; Biochemistry; Biology; Botany; Chemistry; Computer Science; Inorganic Chemistry; Laboratory Techniques; Mathematics; Microbiology; Organic Chemistry; Pathology; Pharmacy; Physical Chemistry; Physiology; Statistics; Toxicology)

Institutes

Maritime and Tropical Medicine *(Interfaculty)* (Endocrinology; Medicine; Microbiology; Parasitology; Tropical Medicine)

Further Information: Also 2 clinical hospitals: the Academic Clinical Center – the MUG Hospital and the Academic Maritime and Tropical Medicine Center.

History: Founded 1945 as Akademię Lekarską. Changed name to Akademia Medyczna w Gdańsku (Academy of Medicine, Gdańsk) 1950. Acquired present status 1956. Acquired present title 2009. One of the largest medical universities on the southern coast of the Baltic Sea.

Governing Bodies: Senate; Faculty Boards

Academic Year: October to June (October-February; February-June)

Admission Requirements: Secondary school certificate (matura) or equivalent

Fees: (Euros) None for Polish students; Foreign students, tuition, 6,000 per annum; students of Polish origin living abroad, tuition, 5,000 per annum

Main Language(s) of Instruction: Polish

International Co-operation: With universities in Germany, Finland, Italy, UK, the Netherlands, Sweden, France, Spain. Also participates in the Socrates/Erasmus, Tempus, Inco-Copernicus programmes

Accrediting Agencies: Ministry of Science and Higher Education, Ministry of Health

Degrees and Diplomas: *Licencjat*; *Lekarz*; *Świadectwo ukończenia studiów podyplomowych*; *Magister*; *Doktor*

Student Services: Cultural centre, Foreign student adviser, Language programs, Social counselling, Sports facilities

Student Residential Facilities: 4 dormitories (1138 beds).

Special Facilities: Botanical Garden. Laboratory of Scientific Photography. Tri-City Academic Experimental Animal Centre

Libraries: Central Library, total, 366,000 vols; 103,000 printed magazines vols; c. 106,000 special collection units; 26 databases; Over 5,000 online magazines.

Publications: Annales Academiae Medicae Gedanensis *(annually)*; Bibliography of AMG Publications *(annually)*; Report of Current Research activities, Annual Report *(annually)*

Academic Staff *2010-2011*	**TOTAL**
FULL-TIME	**1,000**
STAFF WITH DOCTORATE	
FULL-TIME	**c. 573**
Student Numbers *2010-2011*	
All (Foreign Included)	**6,505**
FOREIGN ONLY	**39**

Part-time students, 1,276.
Last Updated: 02/09/11

MEDICAL UNIVERSITY OF ŁÓDŹ

Uniwersytet Medyczny w Łodzi (UM)
al. Kościuszki 4, 90-419 Łódź, łódzkie
Tel: +48(42) 272-59-66
Fax: +48(42) 272-58-06 +48(42) 272-58-07
EMail: rektor@umed.lodz.pl
Website: http://www.umed.lodz.pl

Rektor: Paweł Górski (2008-)
Tel: +48(42) 272-58-02, Fax: +48(42) 272-58-06
EMail: rektor@rkt.umed.lodz.pl

Kanclerz: Jacek Grabowski
Tel: +48(42) 272-58-18, Fax: +48(42) 272-58-20
EMail: kanclerz@umed.lodz.pl

International Relations: Justyna Strumiłło, International Relations Officer
Tel: +48(42) 272-59-60 EMail: justyna.strumillo@umed.lodz.pl

Centres

foreign Language Teaching (English; French; German; Modern Languages; Russian)

Faculties

Biomedical Sciences and Postgraduate Training (Biomedicine; Biotechnology; Cardiology; Medical Technology; Medicine; Nursing; Radiology); **Health Sciences, with the Division of Nursing and Midwifery** (Anatomy; Arts and Humanities; Biology; Biophysics; Chemistry; Economics; Epidemiology; Ethics; Gerontology; Health Sciences; Immunology; Medicine; Microbiology; Midwifery; Nursing; Organic Chemistry; Paediatrics; Pathology; Pedagogy; Pharmacology; Philosophy; Physiology; Public Health; Social Sciences; Sociology; Statistics; Surgery); **Medicine with the Division of Dentistry** (Anatomy; Arts and Humanities; Biology; Biophysics; Chemistry; Dental Technology; Dentistry; Dermatology; Endocrinology; English; Ethics; Immunology; Latin; Medicine; Microbiology; Modern Languages; Neurology; Organic Chemistry; Orthodontics; Paediatrics; Pathology; Periodontics; Pharmacology; Philosophy; Physical Education; Physiology; Psychology; Radiology; Social Sciences; Sociology; Surgery; Venereology); **Military Medicine, with the Division of Studies in English and the Division of Physiotherapy** (Anatomy; Arts and Humanities; Biology; Biophysics; Chemistry; Dermatology; Endocrinology; English; Ethics; Immunology; Latin; Medicine; Microbiology; Modern Languages; Neurology; Organic Chemistry; Paediatrics; Pathology;

Pharmacology; Philosophy; Physical Education; Physical Therapy; Physiology; Psychology; Social Sciences; Sociology; Surgery; Venereology); **Pharmacy** (Biochemistry; Biology; Biotechnology; Chemistry; Cosmetology; Food Science; Laboratory Techniques; Organic Chemistry; Pharmacology; Pharmacy; Toxicology)

Further Information: Also 5 Teaching Hospitals (600 beds); 34 hospital wards and departments with c. 12,00 beds localized in non-University municipal hospitals.

History: Founded 1945 as part of the University of Łódź. 1950 - Medical Academy of Łódź. 2002 - acquired present status through merger of Medical Academy of Łódź (founded 1950) and Military Medical Academy of Łódź (founded 1958).

Governing Bodies: Senate

Academic Year: October to June

Admission Requirements: Secondary school certificate (Matura) or equivalent, and entrance examination

Fees: (US Dollar): Foreign students, 5,500-7,500 per annum

Main Language(s) of Instruction: Polish; English

International Co-operation: With universities in Italy, the Netherlands, UK and Switzerland; Agreements for practices in hospitals in Italy, Germany, France, Slovakia, the U.K; Participates in the Erasmus/Socrates and 5th Framework programmes

Accrediting Agencies: Ministry of Science and Higher Education, National Accreditation Commission

Degrees and Diplomas: *Licencjat*; *Lekarz*; *Lekarz*: Dentistry; *Świadectwo ukończenia studiów podyplomowych*; *Magister*; *Doktor*

Student Services: Canteen, Cultural centre, Foreign student adviser, Foreign Studies Centre, Handicapped facilities, Health services, Language programs, Social counselling, Sports facilities

Student Residential Facilities: For 964 students

Special Facilities: Anatomy Museum; History of Medicine and Pharmacy Museum

Libraries: Main Library, 293,567 vols

Publications: Annales Academiae Lodzensis *(quarterly)*; Index Seminum *(annually)*

Press or Publishing House: Division of Publications of the Medical University of Łódź

Academic Staff *2010-2011*	**TOTAL**
FULL-TIME	**1,600**
STAFF WITH DOCTORATE	
FULL-TIME	c. **900**
Student Numbers *2010-2011*	
All (Foreign Included)	c. **8,500**
FOREIGN ONLY	**400**

Last Updated: 29/09/11

MEDICAL UNIVERSITY OF SILESIA IN KATOWICE

Śląski Uniwersytet Medyczny w Katowicach (ŚLAM)

ul. Warszawska 14, 40-006 Katowice, śląskie
Tel: +48(32) 208-36-00
Fax: +48(32) 208-36-34
EMail: rektor@sum.edu.pl
Website: http://www.sum.edu.pl

Rector: Ewa Małecka-Tendera (2005-)
Tel: +48(32)208-35-55, Fax: +48(32)208-35-61

Chancellor: Bernadeta Kuraszewska
Tel: +48(32) 251-50-46 +48(32) 208-35-48,
Fax: +48(32) 208-35-77 EMail: kanclerz@sum.edu.pl

International Relations: Blazej Śmigas, International Relations Officer
Tel: +48(32) 208-36-40, Fax: +48(32) 208-36-05
EMail: rekwz@slam.katowice.pl

Faculties

Health Care *(Katowice)* (Gynaecology and Obstetrics; Nursing; Physical Therapy); **Medicine** *(Katowice)* (English; Medicine); **Medicine and Dentistry** *(Zabrze)* (Dentistry; Medicine); **Pharmacy and Medical Analysis** *(Sosnowiec)* (Biotechnology; Cosmetology; Laboratory Techniques; Pharmacy); **Public Health** *(Bytom)* (Dietetics; Environmental Studies; Epidemiology; Health Sciences; Occupational Health; Public Health; Statistics)

History: Founded 1948, Slaska Akademia Medyczna until 2007.

Governing Bodies: Senate

Academic Year: October to September

Admission Requirements: Secondary school certificate (matura), and entrace examination

Fees: (Euros): Undergraduate programmes, 3,300-6,830 per annum; Graduate programmes, 26,000-36,000 per annum.

Main Language(s) of Instruction: Polish; English

International Co-operation: With 20 medical universities in Czech Republic, Denmark, Estonia, France, Holland, Germany, Slovakia, Hungary, Italy, Romania, Turkey. Participates in the Socrates/ Erasmus programme.

Accrediting Agencies: State Accreditation Commision

Degrees and Diplomas: *Licencjat*; *Lekarz*; *Lekarz*: Dentistry; *Świadectwo ukończenia studiów podyplomowych*; *Magister*; *Doktor*

Student Services: Academic counselling, Canteen, Cultural centre, Employment services, Foreign student adviser, Foreign Studies Centre, Health services, Language programs, Nursery care, Social counselling, Sports facilities

Student Residential Facilities: Yes

Special Facilities: Animal Laboratory, Computer Laboratory, Language Laboratory

Libraries: Central Library, c. 149,000 vols; over 29,000 specialised magazines.

Publications: Annales Academiae Silesiensis; Annales Societatis Doctrinae Studentium *(quarterly)*; Biuletyn Informacyjny *(bimonthly)*; Wiadomości Lekarskie *(monthly)*

Press or Publishing House: Publishing House

Academic Staff *2010-2011*: Total 1,449
STAFF WITH DOCTORATE: Total 34
Student Numbers *2010-2011*: Total 6,402
Last Updated: 28/09/11

MEDICAL UNIVERSITY OF WARSAW

Warszawski Universytet Medyczny (AM)

ul. Żwirki i Wigury 61, 02-091 Warszawa, mazowieckie
Tel: +48(22) 572-09-13
Fax: +48(22) 572-01-54
EMail: sekretariat.rektora@am.edu.pl
Website: http://www.am.edu.pl

Rektor: Marek Krawczyk
Tel: +48(22) 572-01-01 +48(22) 572-01-51,
Fax: +48(22) 572-01-61 EMail: rektor@wum.edu.pl

Kanclerz: Małgorzata Kozłowska
Tel: +48(22) 572-03-01, Fax: +48(22) 572-03-61
EMail: malgorzata.kozlowska@wum.edu.pl

International Relations: Slawomir Majewski, Vice Rector for Science and International Relations
Tel: +48(22) 572-01-06, Fax: +48(22) 572-01-66
EMail: slawomir.majewski@wum.edu.pl

Centres

Postgraduate Studies (Clinical Psychology; Gender Studies; Health Administration; Human Resources; Insurance; Management; Psychology)

Faculties

Health Sciences (Anaesthesiology; Biochemistry; Biology; Dietetics; Gerontology; Gynaecology and Obstetrics; Health Sciences; Immunology; Laboratory Techniques; Medicine; Nephrology; Neurology; Nursing; Nutrition; Oncology; Physiology; Public Health; Surgery); **Medicine I with Division of Dentistry** (Anaesthesiology; Anatomy; Biochemistry; Biology; Cardiology; Chemistry; Dental Technology; Dentistry; Dermatology; Embryology and Reproduction Biology; Endocrinology; Forensic Medicine and Dentistry; Gastroenterology; Genetics; Gynaecology and Obstetrics; Haematology; Health Sciences; Histology; Hygiene; Immunology; Medical Technology; Medicine; Microbiology; Nephrology; Neurological Therapy; Neurology; Oncology; Ophthalmology; Orthodontics; Orthopaedics;

Otorhinolaryngology; Paediatrics; Parasitology; Pathology; Pharmacology; Physiology; Pneumology; Public Health; Radiology; Rehabilitation and Therapy; Social and Preventive Medicine; Speech Therapy and Audiology; Surgery; Tropical Medicine); **Medicine II with Division of Physical Therapy** (Biochemistry; Cardiology; Dermatology; English; Epidemiology; Ethics; Gynaecology and Obstetrics; Health Sciences; Medical Technology; Medicine; Neurological Therapy; Neurology; Oncology; Ophthalmology; Orthopaedics; Paediatrics; Pathology; Physical Therapy; Polish; Psychiatry and Mental Health; Psychology; Radiology; Rehabilitation and Therapy; Social and Preventive Medicine; Surgery; Venereology); **Pharmacy** (Analytical Chemistry; Biochemistry; Biology; Chemistry; Environmental Studies; Inorganic Chemistry; Laboratory Techniques; Microbiology; Molecular Biology; Organic Chemistry; Pathology; Pharmacology; Pharmacy; Physiology; Toxicology)

Further Information: 5 affiliated teaching hospitals: Public Central Teaching Hospital, he Infant Jesus Teaching Hospital – Emergency and Trauma Centre, Public Ophthalmic Teaching Hospital, Duchess Anna Mazowiecka Public Teaching Hospital and Public Paediatric Teaching Hospital.

History: Founded 1789, reorganized as Academy of Medicine 1809, and acquired present status and title 1950. Change of the name in 2008 - 'Warsaw University of Medicine'.

Governing Bodies: Rektorat

Academic Year: October to June (October-January; February-June)

Admission Requirements: Secondary School certificate (Matura) and entrance examinations. Foreign students: Knowledge of Polish, no entrance examinations

Fees: (New Złoty): 4,000 - 15,000 per annum

Main Language(s) of Instruction: Polish, English

International Co-operation: With universities in Germany, Austria, Spain, Italy, Finland, Belgium, France, Slovenia, Czech Republic, Bulgaria. Also participates in Erasmus and CEEPUS programmes

Accrediting Agencies: Komisja Akredytacyjna Uczelni Medycznych

Degrees and Diplomas: *Licencjat*; *Lekarz*; *Lekarz*: Dentistry; *Świadectwo ukończenia studiów podyplomowych*; *Magister*, *Doktor*

Student Services: Academic counselling, Canteen, Cultural centre, Foreign student adviser, Health services, Language programs, Social counselling, Sports facilities

Student Residential Facilities: For 726 students

Libraries: Main Library and department libraries, total, 296,988 vols, 108 486 periodicals

Publications: Medycyna, Dydaktyka, Wychowanie *(quarterly)*; Z Życia Akademii Medycznej w Warszawie *(monthly)*

Academic Staff *2010-2011*: Total 1,414

STAFF WITH DOCTORATE: Total 140

Student Numbers *2010-2011*: Total: c. 9,000

Last Updated: 03/10/11

MILITARY UNIVERSITY OF TECHNOLOGY IN WARSAW

Wojskowa Akademia Techniczna im Jarosława Dąbrowskiego (WAT)

ul. Gen. Sylwestra Kaliskiego 2, 00-908 Warszawa, mazowieckie
Tel: +48(22) 683-79-38 +48(22) 683-79-56
Fax: +48(22) 683-79-38 +48(22) 683-91-59
EMail: rekrutacja@wat.edu.pl
Website: http://www.wat.edu.pl

Rektor: Zygmund Mierczyk (2008-)
Tel: +48(22) 683-90-01, Fax: +48(22) 683-76-60
EMail: zmierczyk@wat.edu.pl

Kanclerz: Jan Klejszmit
Tel: +48(22) 683-90-61, Fax: +48(22) 683-79-77
EMail: jan.klejszmit@wat.edu.pl

International Relations: Marek Malawski
Tel: +48(22) 683-79-20, Fax: +48(22) 666-77-45
EMail: mmalawski@wat.waw.pl

Departments

Foreign Languages (English; French; German; Modern Languages; Russian); **Physical Education** (Physical Education; Sports)

Faculties

Chemistry and New Technologies *(CCT)* (Chemistry; Materials Engineering; Physics; Solid State Physics; Technology); **Civil Engineering and Geodesy** *(WIG)* (Building Technologies; Civil Engineering; Construction Engineering; Geological Engineering; Information Technology; Telecommunications Engineering); **Cybernetics** *(WCY)* (Applied Mathematics; Arts and Humanities; Automation and Control Engineering; Computer Engineering; Computer Networks; Computer Science; Economics; Engineering Management; Information Management; Information Technology; Mathematics; Operations Research; Protective Services; Software Engineering); **Electronics** *(WEL)* (Electrical and Electronic Equipment and Maintenance; Electrical Engineering; Electronic Engineering; Measurement and Precision Engineering; Microwaves; Technology; Telecommunications Engineering); **Mechanical Engineering** *(WME)* (Computer Science; Mechanical Engineering; Mechanics; Transport Management); **Mechatronics** *(WMT)* (Aeronautical and Aerospace Engineering; Air Transport; Industrial Design; Military Science; Safety Engineering; Technology)

Institutes

Optoelectronics (Electronic Engineering; Engineering; Laser Engineering; Optical Technology)

Further Information: Also Branch in Bemowo

History: Founded 1951.

Governing Bodies: Senate

Academic Year: 1 October - 30 June

Admission Requirements: Secondary school certificate (matura) and competitive entrance examinations

Fees: For part-time students

Main Language(s) of Instruction: Polish

International Co-operation: With universities in UK, France, Germany, Slovakia, Czech Republic, Russia, Ukraine, China, Japan, South Korea., USA. Participates in Erasmus LLP programme.

Accrediting Agencies: Ministry of Science and Higher Education

Degrees and Diplomas: *Inżynier*, *Licencjat*; *Świadectwo ukończenia studiów podyplomowych*; *Magister*, *Doktor*

Student Services: Academic counselling, Canteen, Cultural centre, Employment services, Foreign student adviser, Health services, Language programs, Nursery care, Social counselling, Sports facilities

Student Residential Facilities: Dormitory

Special Facilities: Sport Center, Health Center, Students Club

Libraries: Yes

Publications: Journal of Technical Physics *(quarterly)*

Last Updated: 04/10/11

NATIONAL DEFENCE UNIVERSITY IN WARSAW

Akademia Obrony Narodowej (AON)

al. gen Chruściela 103 blok 25, 00-910 Warszawa, mazowieckie
Tel: +48(22) 681-34-01
EMail: rzecznik@aon.edu.pl
Website: http://www.aon.edu.pl

Rektor-Komendant: Romuald Ratajczak

Departments

Postgraduate Studies (Military Science; Protective Services)

Faculties

Administration (Administration; Public Administration); **European studies** (European Studies); **History** (History); **Internal Security** (Protective Services); **International Relations** (International Relations); **Logistics** (Transport and Communications; Transport Management); **Management** (Air Transport; Management); **National Security** (Protective Services)

History: Founded 1765.

Main Language(s) of Instruction: Polish

International Co-operation: Participates in the Erasmus programme

Degrees and Diplomas: *Licencjat*; *Świadectwo ukończenia studiów podyplomowych*; *Magister*, *Doktor*

Student Services: Canteen, Sports facilities

Student Residential Facilities: Residential halls (c. 1,000 places)

Special Facilities: Internet reading room; TV studio.

Libraries: c. 800,000 vols

Last Updated: 27/10/11

NICOLAUS COPERNICUS UNIVERSITY, TORUŃ

Uniwersytet Mikołaja Kopernika w Toruniu (UMK)

ul. Gagarina 11, 87-100 Toruń, kujawsko-pomorskie
Tel: +48(56) 611-40-10
Fax: +48(56) 654-29-44
EMail: kontakt@umk.pl
Website: http://www.umk.pl

Rektor: Andrzej Radzimiński (2005-)
Tel: +48(56) 654-29-51 +48(56) 611-42-42,
Fax: +48(56) 654-29-44 EMail: rektor@umk.pl

Kanclerz: Paweł Modrzyński
Tel: +48(56) 611-42-32, Fax: +48(56) 611-47-97
EMail: kanclerz@umk.pl

International Relations: Elizabeth M. Wisniewska, Head, Department of International Relations
Tel: +48(56) 611-42-85 +48(56) 611-42-29,
Fax: +48(56) 611-22-45 EMail: eladwz@umk.pl; iro@umk.pl

Centres

Archaeology of Middle Ages (Archaeology; Medieval Studies); **European Studies** *(Jean Monnet)* (European Studies); **Foreign Languages** (English; French; German; Latin; Modern Languages; Russian); **Nonlinear Studies** *(J. Schauder)* (Mathematics); **Polish Language and Culture for Foreigners** (Cultural Studies; Polish)

Faculties

Biology and Earth Sciences (Animal Husbandry; Biology; Biotechnology; Earth Sciences; Ecology; Environmental Studies; Farm Management; Geography; Laboratory Techniques; Leisure Studies; Molecular Biology; Plant and Crop Protection; Tourism); **Chemistry** (Chemistry; Materials Engineering); **Economic Sciences and Management** (Accountancy; Business and Commerce; Econometrics; Economics; European Studies; Finance; Human Resources; Management; Marketing; Real Estate; Regional Studies; Statistics; Transport Management); **Education Sciences** (Education; Educational Administration; Pedagogy; Psychology; Special Education; Welfare and Protective Services); **Fine Arts** (Art Education; Fine Arts; Graphic Arts; Graphic Design; Heritage Preservation; Painting and Drawing; Sculpture); **Health Sciences** *(Collegium Medicum w Bydgoszczy)* (Dietetics; Gynaecology and Obstetrics; Health Sciences; Midwifery; Nursing; Public Health); **History** (Anthropology; Archaeology; Archiving; Art History; Cultural Studies; Ethnology; History; Information Sciences; Library Science); **Humanities** (Arts and Humanities; Logic; Philosophy; Sociology); **Law and Administration** (Administration; Banking; Commercial Law; European Studies; European Union Law; Finance; Government; Insurance; Italian; Labour Law; Law; Management; Philology; Public Administration; Taxation); **Mathematics and Computer Science** (Computer Science; Data Processing; Information Sciences; Information Technology; Mathematics; Mathematics and Computer Science; Mathematics Education; Statistics); **Medicine** *(Collegium Medicum w Bydgoszczy)* (Biotechnology; Cosmetology; Medicine; Physical Therapy); **Pharmacy** *(Collegium Medicum w Bydgoszczy)* (Pharmacy); **Philology** (Applied Linguistics; Arabic; Central European Studies; Classical Languages; Cultural Studies; English; European Languages; French; German; Greek (Classical); Italian; Japanese; Linguistics; Literature; Mediterranean Studies; Modern Languages; Philology; Romance Languages; Russian; Speech Therapy and Audiology); **Physics, Astronomy and Informatics** (Applied Physics; Astronomy and Space Science; Astrophysics; Atomic and Molecular Physics; Automation and Control Engineering; Biophysics; Computer Science; Electronic Engineering; Engineering; Materials Engineering; Optics; Physics; Robotics; Science Education); **Political Sciences and International Studies** (International Relations; International Studies; Journalism; Mass Communication; Political Sciences; Protective Services); **Theology** (Catholic Theology; Family Studies; Pastoral Studies; Social Work; Theology)

History: Founded 1945. Incorporated Ludwik Rydygier Medical Academy in Bydgoszcz in 2004.

Governing Bodies: Senate

Academic Year: October to June (October-February; February-June)

Admission Requirements: Secondary school certificate (Matura) and entrance examination

Fees: (US Dollars): Foreign students, 2,700-7,000 per annum

Main Language(s) of Instruction: Polish

International Co-operation: Socrates/Erasmus, Leonardo da Vinci, 7FP, 6FP programmes

Accrediting Agencies: Ministry of Science and Higher Education

Degrees and Diplomas: *Licencjat*; *Świadectwo ukończenia studiów podyplomowych*; *Magister*, *Doktor*. Also Executive MBA

Student Services: Academic counselling, Canteen, Cultural centre, Employment services, Handicapped facilities, Health services, Sports facilities

Student Residential Facilities: For 3,350 students

Special Facilities: Natural History Museum; Astronomical Observatory; Computer Centre; University Online TV

Libraries: Central Library, c. 2.2m. vols; British Library, 8,000 ; Alliance francaise Library, 5,800, and University Archives

Publications: Eastern European Countryside; Logic and Logical Philosophy; Open Systems and Information Dynamics in Physical and Life Sciences; Reports on Mathematical Physics; Theoria et Historia Scientiarum; Topological Methods in Nonlinear Analysis

Press or Publishing House: Wydawnictwo UMK

Academic Staff *2010-2011*	**TOTAL**
FULL-TIME	**2,222**
STAFF WITH DOCTORATE	
FULL-TIME	**1,144**
Student Numbers *2010-2011*	
All (Foreign Included)	c. **31,000**
FOREIGN ONLY	**250**

Part-time students, 12,000.

Last Updated: 29/09/11

OPOLE UNIVERSITY

Uniwersytet Opolski (UO)

pl. Kopernika 11a, 45-040 Opole, opolskie
Tel: +48(77) 452-70-00 +48(77) 541-60-70
Fax: +48(77) 541-60-00
EMail: sekretariat@uni.opole.pl
Website: http://www.uni.opole.pl

Rektor: Krystyna Czaja (2008-)
Tel: +48(77) 541-59-03, Fax: +48(77) 541-59-00
EMail: rektorat@uni.opole.pl; krystyna.czaja@uni.opole.pl

Dyrektor Administracyjny: Andrzej Kimla
Tel: +48(77) 541-60-70, Fax: +48(77) 541-60-00
EMail: andrzej.kimla@uni.opole.pl;

International Relations: Piotr Paweł Wieczorek, Vice-Rector for Science and International Relations
Tel: +48(77) 541-59-04, Fax: +48(77) 541-59-00
EMail: rektorat@uni.opole.pl; piotr.wieczorek@uni.opole.pl

Faculties

Chemistry (Analytical Chemistry; Biochemistry; Chemistry; Inorganic Chemistry; Organic Chemistry; Physical Chemistry; Polymer and Plastics Technology); **Economics** (Accountancy; Econometrics; Economic and Finance Policy; Economics; Finance; Geography; Information Sciences; Management; Marketing; Real Estate; Safety Engineering; Social Policy; Transport Management); **History and Pedagogy** (Archaeology; Art Education; Central European Studies; Communication Arts; Contemporary History; Eastern European Studies; Educational Sciences; Fine Arts; Graphic Design; History; Medieval Studies; Mediterranean Studies; Modern History; Pedagogy; Philosophy; Political Sciences; Preschool Education; Psychology; Sociology); **Law and Administration** (Administration; Commercial Law; Criminology; Economics; Environmental

Studies; European Union Law; Finance; Human Resources; Information Management; Justice Administration; Law; Management; Protective Services; Psychology; Public Administration; Safety Engineering; Sociology); **Mathematics, Physics and Informatics** (Applied Physics; Astronomy and Space Science; Astrophysics; Computer Science; Electronic Engineering; Laboratory Techniques; Mathematics; Nuclear Physics; Physics; Science Education); **Natural and Technical** (Biology; Biotechnology; Computer Science; Educational Technology; Environmental Engineering; Environmental Management; Environmental Studies; Geology; Industrial Design; Information Technology; Molecular Biology; Production Engineering; Soil Conservation; Soil Science; Waste Management; Water Management); **Philology** (Cultural Studies; English; Film; Folklore; French; French Studies; German; Linguistics; Literature; Media Studies; Philology; Polish; Romance Languages; Russian; Slavic Languages; Theatre); **Theology** (Bible; Canon Law; Ethics; Family Studies; History of Religion; Holy Writings; Music Education; Pastoral Studies; Philosophy; Religious Art; Religious Music; Religious Practice; Theology)

Further Information: Also Study Abroad programme

History: Founded 1950 as higher pedagogical school, incorporating the Teacher Training College and Theological-Pastoral Institute. Acquired present status and title 1994.

Governing Bodies: Senate

Academic Year: October to September

Admission Requirements: Secondary school certificate (Matura) and entrance examination

Fees: (New Złoty): Recurrent Education students, 1,800-4,600 per annum

Main Language(s) of Instruction: Polish

International Co-operation: Also participates in the Tempus, Socrates and CEEPUS, Leonardo Da Vinci programmes.

Accrediting Agencies: Ministry of Science and Higher Education

Degrees and Diplomas: *Inżynier*, *Licencjat*; *Świadectwo ukończenia studiów podyplomowych*; *Magister*, *Doktor*

Student Services: Cultural centre, Social counselling, Sports facilities

Student Residential Facilities: For c. 1,680 students

Special Facilities: Observatory

Libraries: Central Library, 430,000 vols

Publications: Economic and Environmental Studies, Research Journals *(annually)*; Liturgia Sacra *(biennially)*; Scriptura Sacra, Biblical Studies *(annually)*; Stylisties *(annually)*; Theological-historical Studies of the Opole Silesia *(annually)*; Zeszyty Naukowe Uniwersytetu Opolskiego, Research Journals *(other/irregular)*

Press or Publishing House: Dział Wydawniczy (University Publisher)

Last Updated: 29/09/11

OPOLE UNIVERSITY OF TECHNOLOGY

Politechnika Opolska (PO)

ul. Stanisława Mikołajczyka 5, 45-271 Opole, opolskie
Tel: +48(77) 400-60-00
Fax: +48(77) 400-60-50
EMail: biurorektora@po.opole.pl
Website: http://www.po.opole.pl

Rector: Jerzy Skubis (2002-)
Tel: +48(77) 400-61-27, Fax: +48(77) 400-05-71
EMail: j.skubis@po.opole.pl

Kanclerz: Barbara Hetmańska
Tel: +48(77) 400-61-90 EMail: b.hetmanska@po.opole.pl

International Relations: Joanna Boguniewicz-Zabłocka, Head, Department of International Cooperation
Tel: +48(77) 400-61-53, Fax: +48(77) 400-63-49
EMail: j.boguniewicz@po.opole.pl

Centres

Foreign Languages (English; French; German; Italian; Modern Languages; Russian; Spanish)

Faculties

Civil Engineering (Architecture; Bridge Engineering; Building Technologies; Civil Engineering; Construction Engineering; Geological Engineering; Materials Engineering; Mechanics; Physics; Road Engineering; Town Planning); **Economy and Management** (Accountancy; Administration; Business Administration; Business Computing; Economics; European Studies; Finance; Human Resources; Management; Marketing); **Electrical Engineering, Automatic Control and Informatics** (Automation and Control Engineering; Computer Science; Electronic Engineering; Information Sciences; Measurement and Precision Engineering; Mechanical Engineering; Power Engineering; Robotics); **Mechanical Engineering** (Agricultural Engineering; Automation and Control Engineering; Chemical Engineering; Engineering Management; Environmental Engineering; Food Technology; Forestry; Industrial Engineering; Machine Building; Materials Engineering; Mechanical Engineering; Mechanics; Nutrition; Power Engineering; Production Engineering; Road Engineering; Thermal Engineering); **Physical Education and Physiotherapy** (Hotel Management; Parks and Recreation; Physical Education; Physical Therapy; Rehabilitation and Therapy; Tourism); **Production Engineering and Logistics** (Engineering Management; Information Technology; Management; Production Engineering; Safety Engineering; Transport Engineering)

History: Founded 1966 as Higher School of Engineering, acquired present status and title 1996.

Governing Bodies: Senate

Academic Year: October to September (October-January; February-June)

Admission Requirements: Secondary school certificate (Matura) or equivalent

Fees: (Euros): 2,500 per annum

Main Language(s) of Instruction: Polish, German, English

International Co-operation: Participates in the CEEPUS, Leonardo da Vinci, Tempus, Socrates/Erasmus and Seventh Framework (7FP) programmes

Accrediting Agencies: Ministry of Science and Higher Education

Degrees and Diplomas: *Inżynier*, *Licencjat*; *Świadectwo ukończenia studiów podyplomowych*; *Magister*, *Doktor*

Student Services: Academic counselling, Canteen, Cultural centre, Employment services, Foreign student adviser, Handicapped facilities, Health services, Language programs, Social counselling, Sports facilities

Student Residential Facilities: 4 hostels for 1,500 students

Special Facilities: Computer Centre. Multimedia Centre

Libraries: Total, c. 420,000 vols

Publications: Skrypty *(annually)*; Studies and Monographs *(annually)*; Zeszyty Naukowe, Scientific Papers *(annually)*

Press or Publishing House: Oficina Wydawnicza

Academic Staff *2010-2011*: Total 957
STAFF WITH DOCTORATE: Total 304
Student Numbers *2010-2011*: Total: c. 12,000
Last Updated: 22/09/11

PEDAGOGICAL UNIVERSITY OF CRACOW

Uniwersytet Pedagogiczny im. Komisji Edukacji Narodowej w Krakowie (UP)

ul. Podchorążych 2, 30-084 Kraków, małopolskie
Tel: +48(12) 662-60-14
Fax: +48(12) 637-22-43
EMail: info@up.krakow.pl
Website: http://www.ap.krakow.pl

Rektor: Michał Śliwa
Tel: +48(12) 662-60-03 EMail: rektor@up.krakow.pl

Kanclerz: Jan Kałużny
Tel: +48(12) 662-60-08, Fax: +48(12) 635-88-85
EMail: Kanclerz@ap.krakow.pl

International Relations: Tadeusz Budrewicz, Vice-Rector for Science and International Cooperation Tel: +48(12) 662-60-43

Departments

Foreign Languages (English; French; German; Latin; Modern Languages; Philology; Polish; Russian; Spanish); **Physical Education and Sports** (Physical Education; Sports)

Faculties
Art (Art Education; Fine Arts; Graphic Design; Painting and Drawing; Sculpture; Visual Arts); **Geography and Biology** (Biology; Earth Sciences; Geography); **Humanities** (Arts and Humanities; History; Journalism; Philosophy; Political Sciences; Sociology); **Mathematics, Physics and Technology** (Computer Science; Mathematics; Physics; Technology); **Pedagogy** (Child Care and Development; Civics; Education; Educational Sciences; Educational Technology; Media Studies; Pedagogy; Psychology; Special Education); **Philology** (Arts and Humanities; Information Sciences; Library Science; Linguistics; Literature; Modern Languages; Philology; Polish)

Further Information: Also branch in Bielsko Biała, Tarnów, Nowy Sącz

History: Founded in 1946 as State Higher School of Education. Bears the name of the Commission of the National Education created in Poland in 1773 as the first ministry of national education in Europe. MA awarded 1954, renamed 1973. Became Akademia Pedagogiczna im. Komisji Edukacji Narodowej w Krakowie (Pedagogical Academy of Cracow of the National Education Commission) 1999. Acquired present title 2008.

Governing Bodies: Senate

Academic Year: October-September

Admission Requirements: Secondary school certificate and entrance examination

Fees: (New Zoty): 1,600-5,100 per annum; Postgraduate programmes, 1,100-2,000 per semester (except for Personalized education, 764-1,275 for the whole programme).

Main Language(s) of Instruction: Polish

International Co-operation: With universities in France, Germany, Spain, Portugal, Sweden, Greece, Finland, Lithuania. Also participates in Socrates, Jean-Monnet

Accrediting Agencies: Ministry of Science and Higher Education

Degrees and Diplomas: *Inżynier*; *Licencjat*; *Świadectwo ukończenia studiów podyplomowych*; *Magister*; *Doktor*; *Doktor habilitowany*

Student Services: Canteen, Cultural centre, Employment services, Foreign student adviser, Handicapped facilities, Health services, Nursery care, Sports facilities

Student Residential Facilities: Student hostels for c. 2 458 students

Special Facilities: Astronomical Observatory; Conference Centre

Libraries: c. 645,000 vols

Publications: Konspekt *(quarterly)*

Academic Staff *2010-2011*: Total 800

STAFF WITH DOCTORATE: Total 190

Student Numbers *2010-2011*: Total: c. 19,000

Last Updated: 06/09/11

POLICE ACADEMY IN SZCZYTNO

Wyższa Szkoła Policji w Szczytnie (WSPOL)

ul. Marszałka Józefa Piłsudskiego 111,
12-100 Szczytno, warmińsko-mazurskie
Tel: +48(89) 621-59-00
Fax: +48(89) 624-26-10
EMail: wspol@wspol.edu.pl
Website: http://www.wspol.edu.pl

Komendant-Rektor: Arkadiusz Letkiewicz (2008-)
Tel: +48(89) 621-51-00 EMail: rektor@wspol.edu.pl

Kanclerz: Jan Michał Chojnowski
Tel: +48(89) 621-51-13 EMail: kanclerz@wspol.edu.pl

Departments
Postgraduate Studies (Administration; Criminal Law; Forensic Medicine and Dentistry; Protective Services; Public Administration; Safety Engineering)

Programmes
Administration (Administration); **Internal Security** (Protective Services)

History: Founded 1972, acquired present status and title 1990.

Governing Bodies: Senate

Main Language(s) of Instruction: Polish

International Co-operation: Participates in the Erasmus programme.

Accrediting Agencies: Ministry of Science and Higher Education

Degrees and Diplomas: *Licencjat*; *Świadectwo ukończenia studiów podyplomowych*; *Magister*

Student Services: Canteen, Cultural centre, Health services, Language programs, Nursery care, Sports facilities

Student Residential Facilities: Hotel accommodation (for 1,020 people in student hostels - three-person rooms; and for 180 people in hotels - twin rooms).

Special Facilities: Movie Studio

Libraries: Central Library, 200,000 vols

Publications: Policyjny Biuletyn Szkoleniowy *(quarterly)*; Przegląd Policyjny *(quarterly)*

Last Updated: 24/10/11

POLISH NAVAL ACADEMY IN GDYNIA

Akademia Marynarki Wojennej im. Bohaterow Westerplatte w Gdynia (AMW)

ul. Jana Śmidowicza 69, 81-103 Gdynia, pomorskie
Tel: +48(58) 626-27-53
Fax: +48(58) 626-29-96
EMail: int.cont@amw.gdynia.pl
Website: http://www.amw.gdynia.pl

Rektor: Czesław Dyrcz
Tel: +48(58) 626-25-14, Fax: +48(58) 626-29-63
EMail: rektor@amw.gdynia.pl

Kanclerz: Boguslaw Bąk
Tel: +48(58) 626-26-13, Fax: +48(58) 626-26-13
EMail: kanclerz@amw.gdynia.pl

International Relations: Adam Duczmal, Head, International Relations
Tel: +48(58) 626-25-20, Fax: +48(58) 626-25-20
EMail: aduczmal@amw.gdynia.pl

Faculties
Command and Faculty Maritime Operation (Military Science; Safety Engineering); **Humanities and Social Sciences** (Child Care and Development; Education; Educational Technology; History; Human Resources; International Relations; Management; Marketing; Military Science; Pedagogy; Social Sciences; Social Work); **Mechanical and Electrical Engineering** (Automation and Control Engineering; Electrical Engineering; Machine Building; Marine Engineering; Mathematics; Mechanical Engineering; Power Engineering); **Navigation and Naval Weapons** (Marine Engineering; Marine Science and Oceanography; Military Science; Nautical Science; Sound Engineering (Acoustics); Surveying and Mapping)

History: Founded 1922 as Oficerska Szkoła Marynarki Wojennej w Toruniu. Acquired present title 1987.

Governing Bodies: Rectorate

Academic Year: October to September

Admission Requirements: High School Certificate (Matura) and entrance examination

Fees: (New Złoty): c. 1,500 (for extramural and evening courses only)

Main Language(s) of Instruction: Polish, English

Accrediting Agencies: Ministry of Science and Higher Education; Ministry of National Defence; Ministry of Transport and Construction; The State Accreditation Committee; Technical Universities Accreditation Committee

Degrees and Diplomas: *Inżynier*, *Licencjat*, *Świadectwo ukończenia studiów podyplomowych*; *Magister*

Student Services: Academic counselling, Canteen, Cultural centre, Employment services, Foreign student adviser, Health services, Language programs, Nursery care, Social counselling, Sports facilities

Student Residential Facilities: 3 dormitories

Special Facilities: Observatory. Movie studio

Libraries: c. 179,000 vols; 130 Polish and 56 International periodical subscriptions; 21 online magazines.

Last Updated: 02/09/11

POMERANIAN ACADEMY IN SŁUPSK

Akademia Pomorska w Słupsku (PAP)

ul. Arciszewskiego 22a, 76-200 Słupsk, pomorskie
Tel: +48(59) 840-53-28
Fax: +48(59) 840-54-75
EMail: rektor@apsl.edu.pl
Website: http://www.apsl.edu.pl

Rector: Roman Drozd (2008-)
Tel: +48(59) 840-59-30, Fax: +48(59) 840-59-35

Kanclerz: Ewa Sobolewska
Tel: +48(59) 840-53-27 EMail: kanclerz@apsl.edu.pl

International Relations: Mirosław Roll-Maksyśko, International Relations Officer
Tel: +48(59) 840-59-46 EMail: biurokarier@apsl.edu.pl

Centres

Clean Energy *(Academic)* (Energy Engineering); **Sports and Rehabilitation** (Physical Education; Rehabilitation and Therapy; Sports; Tourism)

Faculties

Education and Philosophy (Computer Education; Education; Foreign Languages Education; Music; Music Education; Pedagogy; Philosophy; Preschool Education; Psychology; Rehabilitation and Therapy; Social Work); **Mathematics and Natural Sciences** (Anatomy; Biological and Life Sciences; Data Processing; Environmental Engineering; Environmental Studies; Geography; Health Sciences; Laboratory Techniques; Mathematics; Medical Technology; Medicine; Nanotechnology; Natural Sciences; Nursing; Parks and Recreation; Physics; Physiology; Public Health; Regional Studies; Statistics; Tourism); **Philology and History** (Ancient Civilizations; Archiving; Cultural Studies; East Asian Studies; English; Foreign Languages Education; German; Government; History; International Relations; Journalism; Linguistics; Literature; Medieval Studies; Modern History; Modern Languages; Philology; Police Studies; Polish; Political Sciences; Protective Services; Regional Studies; Russian; Safety Engineering; Sociology)

Schools

Computer Science (Computer Science)

History: Founded 1969 as teacher training college; acquired present status 1974 and title 2000.2006 - change of name (previous name Pomorska Akademia Pedagogiczna w Słupsku)

Governing Bodies: Senate

Academic Year: October to June (October-January; February-June)

Admission Requirements: Secondary school certificate (matura)

Fees: yes, for distance students

Main Language(s) of Instruction: Polish

International Co-operation: Participates in Leonardo da Vinci, Socrates-Comenius programmes

Accrediting Agencies: Ministry of Science and Higher Education, National Commission of Accreditation

Degrees and Diplomas: *Licencjat*; *Świadectwo ukończenia studiów podyplomowych*; *Magister*

Student Services: Academic counselling, Canteen, Cultural centre, Employment services, Health services, Nursery care, Social counselling, Sports facilities

Libraries:c. 272,330 vols

Publications: Słupsk History Studies *(annually)*; Słupsk Humanities Works *(annually)*; Słupsk Mathematics and Natural Sciences Works *(annually)*

Press or Publishing House: School Publishers

Last Updated: 07/09/11

POMERANIAN MEDICAL UNIVERSITY

Pomorski Uniwersytet Medyczny (PUM)

ul. Rybacka 1, 70-204 Szczecin, zachodniopomorskie
Tel: +48(91) 480-08-01
Fax: +48(91) 480-07-05
EMail: rektor@sci.pam.szczecin.pl
Website: http://www.ams.edu.pl

Rektor: Przemysław Nowacki (2005-)
Tel: +48(91) 480-08-01

Kanclerz: Jerzy Łuczak
Tel: +48(91) 480-07-01 EMail: kanclerz@sci.pam.szczecin.pl

International Relations: Hanna Białek, Registrar
Tel: +48(91) 480-08-10 EMail: ep@sci.pam.szczecin.pl

Centres

International Hereditary Cancer - IHCC *(Interdepartmental)* (Oncology)

Faculties

Medicine (Biochemistry; Cardiology; Chemistry; Embryology and Reproduction Biology; Endocrinology; Epidemiology; Ethics; Forensic Medicine and Dentistry; Gynaecology and Obstetrics; Haematology; Histology; Hygiene; Immunology; Laboratory Techniques; Medical Technology; Medicine; Neurology; Oncology; Ophthalmology; Orthopaedics; Paediatrics; Parasitology; Pathology; Pharmacology; Physics; Physiology; Psychiatry and Mental Health; Psychology; Radiology; Rheumatology; Sociology; Surgery; Urology); **Medicine and Dentistry** (Anatomy; Dental Technology; Dentistry; Dermatology; Medicine; Oncology; Ophthalmology; Orthodontics; Otorhinolaryngology; Paediatrics; Periodontics; Radiology; Stomatology; Surgery; Venereology); **Nursing** (Health Sciences; Nursing; Rehabilitation and Therapy)

Laboratories

Family Physician Education *(Interdepartmental)* (Community Health; Medical Technology)

Units

Calamity Medicine *(Interdepartmental)* (Dentistry; Medicine); **Doctoral Studies** *(Interdepartmental)* (Medicine); **Foreign Languages Learning** *(Interdepartmental)* (English; French; German; Latin; Modern Languages; Polish; Russian); **Physical Education and Sports** *(Interdepartmental)* (Physical Education; Sports); **Postgraduate Education Study** *(Interdepartmental)* (Community Health; Medicine; Public Health)

Further Information: Also 2 Clinical Hospitals (1,370 beds).

History: Founded 1948 as Pomorska Akademia Medyczna w Szczecinie (Pomeranian Academy of Medicine, Szczecin). Acquired present title 2010.

Governing Bodies: Senate

Academic Year: October to June (October-January; February-June)

Admission Requirements: Secondary school certificate (matura) and entrance examinations

Fees: (US Dollars):Tuition, Polish students, c. 6,000 per annum; Program in English, c. 9,000.

Main Language(s) of Instruction: Polish; English

International Co-operation: With universities in Germany. Also participates in Socrates/Erasmus Program

Accrediting Agencies: Ministry of Science and Higher Education

Degrees and Diplomas: *Licencjat*; *Lekarz*; *Świadectwo ukończenia studiów podyplomowych*; *Magister*; *Doktor*

Student Services: Health services

Libraries: Main Library, c. 260,000 vols

Publications: University Annals

Press or Publishing House: PAM Publishing Division

Academic Staff *2010-2011*: Total 620

Last Updated: 26/09/11

PONTIFICAL FACULTY OF THEOLOGY IN WARSAW

Papieski Wydział Teologiczny w Warszawie (PWTW)
ul. Rakowiecka 61, 02-532 Warszawa, mazowieckie
Tel: +48(22) 542-87-17
Fax: +48(22) 849-02-72
EMail: sekretariat@bobolanum.edu.pl
Website: http://www.bobolanum.edu.pl

Rektor: Zbigniew Kubacki EMail: z.kubacki@jezuici.pl

Prorektor: Krzysztof Pawlina
EMail: sekretariat-pwtw@pwtw.mkw.pl

Sections

St. Andrew Bobola *(Collegium Bobolanum)* (Christian Religious Studies; Ethics; Greek (Classical); Hebrew; Latin; Pastoral Studies; Political Sciences; Religious Studies; Teacher Training; Theology); **St. John the Baptist** (Anthropology; Bible; Canon Law; Christian Religious Studies; Ethics; History of Religion; New Testament; Pastoral Studies; Philosophy; Religious Education; Religious Music; Theology)

Further Information: An open and traditional education institution.

History: Founded 1988.

Main Language(s) of Instruction: Polish

Degrees and Diplomas: *Licencjat*; *Świadectwo ukończenia studiów podyplomowych*; *Doktor*

Libraries: Library Bobolanum, 310,000 vols and 110,000 periodical subscritpions;

Last Updated: 26/10/11

POPE JOHN PAUL II STATE SCHOOL OF HIGHER EDUCATION IN BIAŁA PODLASKA

Państwowa Szkoła Wyższa im. Papieża Jana Pawła II w Białej Podlaskiej (PSWBP)
ul. Sidorska 95/97, 21-500 Biała Podlaska, lubelskie
Tel: +48(83) 344-99-00
Fax: +48(83) 344-99-50
EMail: psw@pswbp.pl
Website: http://www.pswbp.pl/

Rector: Mieczysław Adamowicz (2009-) EMail: rektor@pswbp.pl

Kanclerz: Leszek Petruczenko EMail: kanclerz@pswbp.pl

International Relations: Małgorzata Mikołajczuk, Manager
EMail: nauczanie@pwsz.bialapodlaska.pl

Institutes

Agriculture (Agriculture; Economics; Mass Communication; Sociology); **Computer Science** (Computer Engineering; Computer Graphics; Computer Networks; Computer Science; Information Management; Information Technology); **Construction Engineering** (Construction Engineering; Ecology); **Management** (International and Comparative Education; Management; Taxation); **Neophilology** (English; German; Philology; Russian); **Nursing** (Nursing); **Pedagogy** (Child Care and Development; Educational and Student Counselling; Pedagogy; Preschool Education; Rehabilitation and Therapy; Social and Preventive Medicine; Social Work); **Public Health** (Cosmetology; Health Administration; Public Health; Rehabilitation and Therapy; Sports); **Rescue Medicine** (Medicine); **Sociology** (Economics; Mass Communication; Sociology); **Tourism and Recreation** (Hotel Management; Management; Marketing; Parks and Recreation; Tourism)

Programmes

Postgraduate Studies (Agricultural Management; Computer Graphics; Computer Networks; Computer Science; Distance Education; Education; Educational Administration; Health Sciences; Human Resources; Information Technology; Multimedia; Pedagogy; Rehabilitation and Therapy; Speech Therapy and Audiology)

History: Founded 2000. Formerly known as Państwowa Wyższa Szkoła Zawodowa w Białej Podlaskiej (State School of Higher Vocational Education, Biała Podlaska).

Governing Bodies: Senate

Admission Requirements: Secondary school certificate (matura) and entrance examinations

Main Language(s) of Instruction: Polish

Accrediting Agencies: Ministry of Science and Higher Education

Degrees and Diplomas: *Inżynier*; *Licencjat*; *Świadectwo ukończenia studiów podyplomowych*; *Magister*

Academic Staff *2010-2011*: Total 38

Student Numbers *2010-2011*: Total: c. 3,500

Last Updated: 20/09/11

POZNAŃ UNIVERSITY OF ECONOMICS

Uniwersytet Ekonomiczny w Poznaniu (UE)
al. Niepodległości 10, 61-875 Poznań, wielkopolskie
Tel: +48(61) 856-90-00
Fax: +48(61) 866-89-24
EMail: promocja@ue.poznan.pl
Website: http://www.ue.poznan.pl/

Rektor: Marian Gorynia (2008-)
Tel: (+48) 61-856-91-50 EMail: rektor@ue.poznan.pl

Kanclerz: Krzysztof Czajkowski
Tel: +48(61) 856-95-00, Fax: +48(61) 854-39-88
EMail: kanclerz@ue.poznan.pl

International Relations: Elżbieta Szwejk, Head, Department for Research and International Cooperation
Tel: +48(61) 856-93-80, Fax: +48(61) 854-39-87
EMail: swz@ae.poznan.pl

Departments

Sport and Physical Education (Physical Education; Sports)

Faculties

Commodity Science (Biochemistry; Chemistry; Ecology; Environmental Studies; Food Science; Food Technology; Maintenance Technology; Management; Marketing; Microbiology); **Economics** (Banking; Demography and Population; Economic and Finance Policy; Economics; Education; Finance; Human Resources; Insurance; Journalism; Labour and Industrial Relations; Marketing; Philosophy; Public Relations; Social Policy; Sociology; Statistics); **Informatics and Electronic Economy** (Applied Mathematics; Business Computing; Computer Science; E-Business/Commerce; Econometrics; Economics; Information Sciences; Information Technology; Operations Research; Statistics); **International Business and Economics** (Economics; European Studies; Finance; International Business; International Economics; Marketing; Tourism; Transport Management); **Management** (Accountancy; Business and Commerce; Commercial Law; Computer Science; Cultural Studies; Economics; Environmental Studies; Finance; Information Technology; International Studies; Management; Marketing; Mathematics; Real Estate; Service Trades; Statistics; Transport and Communications; Transport Economics; Transport Management)

Programmes

Foreign Languages *(SPNJO)* (English; French; German; Modern Languages; Russian; Spanish)

Further Information: Also Branch in Wielkopolska; Also Distance Learning Center.

History: Founded 1926 as commercial college, reorganized as higher school of commerce 1950. Became Akademia Ekonomiczna w Poznaniu (Academy of Economics, Poznań) 1974. Introduced the three-tier Bologna system of education 2006. Acquired present status and title 2008.

Governing Bodies: Senate

Academic Year: October to June

Admission Requirements: Secondary school certificate (Matura) and entrance examination

Fees: (Euros): Tuition fees for foreign students,(Euro) 2,000 per annum; For Polish students (New Złoty): 6,000 per annum.

Main Language(s) of Instruction: Polish; English

International Co-operation: With universities in Austria, Belgium, Belarus, Bulgaria, China, Croatia, Czech Republic, Denmark, Estonia, Finland, France, Greece, Spain, the Netherlands, Ireland, Iceland, Canada, Lithuania, Latvia, Macau, Germany, Norway , Portugal, Russia, Romania, Slovakia, Slovenia, USA, Sweden, Taiwan, Thailand, Turkey, Ukraine, Hungary, UK, Italy, . Also participates in Socrates/Erasmus, V and VI Framework programmes

Accrediting Agencies: Ministry of Science and Higher Education

Degrees and Diplomas: *Inżynier*; *Licencjat*; *Świadectwo ukończenia studiów podyplomowych*; *Magister*; *Doktor*. Also MBA in cooperation with Georgia State University in Atlanta, the European Academy of Economics in Berlin (Germany), the University of Rennes (France) and the Nottingham Trent University (UK).

Student Services: Academic counselling, Canteen, Cultural centre, Foreign student adviser, Health services, Language programs, Social counselling, Sports facilities

Student Residential Facilities: For 800 students

Special Facilities: Computer Centre

Libraries: Main Library 390,000 vols

Publications: The Poznań University of Economics Bulletin *(quarterly)*; The Poznań University of Economics Review *(biennially)*

Academic Staff *2010-2011*: Total 500
STAFF WITH DOCTORATE: Total 140
Last Updated: 28/09/11

POZNAŃ UNIVERSITY OF LIFE SCIENCES

Uniwersytet Przyrodniczy w Poznaniu (AR)

ul. Wojska Polskiego 28, 60-637 Poznań, wielkopolskie
Tel: +48(61) 848-72-00
Fax: +48(61) 848-71-45
EMail: rzecznik@up.poznan.pl
Website: http://puls.edu.pl/

Rektor: Grzegorz Skrzypczak
Tel: +48(61) 848-70-01, Fax: +48(61) 848-71-45
EMail: rektorat@up.poznan.pl

Kanclerz: Marek Klimecki
Tel: +48(61) 848-70-19 EMail: klimecki@up.poznan.pl

International Relations: Jan Pikul, Vice-Rector for Science and International Relations
Tel: +48(61) 848-70-04 EMail: dznn@up.poznan.pl

Faculties

Agriculture and Bioengineering (Agricultural Engineering; Agriculture; Agronomy; Biochemistry; Bioengineering; Biotechnology; Botany; Chemistry; Environmental Engineering; Genetics; Mathematics; Microbiology; Soil Conservation; Soil Science; Statistics); **Animal Breeding and Biology** (Animal Husbandry; Biology; Chemistry; Ecology; Geography; History; Mathematics; Modern Languages; Parks and Recreation; Social Studies; Tourism; Veterinary Science); **Economics and Social Sciences** (Accountancy; Agricultural Business; Agricultural Economics; Economics; Education; Finance; Forest Economics; Law; Management; Marketing; Social Sciences); **Food Science and Nutrition** (Animal Husbandry; Biochemistry; Biotechnology; Dairy; Dietetics; Engineering; Food Science; Food Technology; Meat and Poultry; Microbiology; Nutrition; Physics; Safety Engineering; Toxicology); **Forestry** (Environmental Management; Forest Economics; Forestry); **Horticulture and Landscape Architecture** (Botany; Crop Production; Entomology; Environmental Studies; Forestry; Horticulture; Landscape Architecture; Physiology; Plant and Crop Protection; Plant Pathology); **Land Reclamation and Environmental Engineering** (Ecology; Environmental Engineering; Geological Engineering; Hydraulic Engineering; Mechanical Engineering; Mechanics; Meteorology; Soil Science; Surveying and Mapping); **Wood Technology** (Chemical Engineering; Chemistry; Environmental Engineering; Machine Building; Maintenance Technology; Mechanical Engineering; Thermal Engineering; Wood Technology)

Units

Foreign Languages (English; French; German; Modern Languages; Russian); **Household Management** (Aesthetics; Education; Health Sciences; Home Economics; Household Management; Nutrition; Social Work); **Physical Education** (Physical Education; Sports)

History: Founded 1870 as Agricultural School, became Faculty of Agriculture and Forestry within Poznań University 1919, detached as Higher School of Agriculture 1951. Became Agricultural University 1972 and August Cieszkowski Agricultural University as of 1996. Acquired title 2008.

Governing Bodies: Senate

Academic Year: October to September (October-February; February-September)

Admission Requirements: High School certificate and entrance examination

Main Language(s) of Instruction: Polish, English

Accrediting Agencies: Ministry of Science and Higher Education

Degrees and Diplomas: *Inżynier*; *Licencjat*; *Świadectwo ukończenia studiów podyplomowych*; *Magister*; *Doktor*

Student Services: Academic counselling, Canteen, Cultural centre, Foreign student adviser, Handicapped facilities, Health services, Social counselling, Sports facilities

Student Residential Facilities: For 2,687 students

Special Facilities: History of the University Museum. 12 Experimental Farms. Research Wildlife Station (wolf)

Libraries: University Library, 674,746 vols

Publications: Publikacje Informacyjne Akademii Rolniczej w Poznaniu *(other/irregular)*; Roczniki Akademii Rolniczej w Poznaniu *(annually)*

Press or Publishing House: Agricultural University Press

Student Numbers *2010-2011*: Total: c. 13,000
Last Updated: 29/09/11

POZNAN UNIVERSITY OF MEDICAL SCIENCES

Uniwersytet Medyczny im. Karola Marcinkowskiego w Poznaniu (AM IM K.M.)

ul. Fredry 10, 61-701 Poznań, wielkopolskie
Tel: +48(61) 854-60-00
Fax: +48(61) 852-04-55
EMail: info@ump.edu.pl
Website: http://www.amp.edu.pl

Rektor: Jacek Wysocki
Tel: +48(61) 854-62-28, Fax: +48(61) 852-04-55
EMail: rektor@ump.edu.pl

Kanclerz: Bogdan Poniedziałek
Tel: +48(61) 852-62-59, Fax: +48(61) 852-62-59
EMail: bponiedzialek@ump.edu.pl; sekr_dyr@ump.edu.pl

International Relations: Bożena Raducha, Manager, International Relations Tel: +48(61) 854-60-36 EMail: braducha@amp.edu.pl

Centres

Medical Simulation *(Inter-faculty)* (Medicine); **Teaching in English** *(Inter-faculty)* (Dentistry; English; Health Sciences; Medicine; Natural Sciences; Pharmacy; Physical Therapy)

Departments

Foreign Languages *(Inter-faculty)* (English; German; Modern Languages); **Occupational Medicine Clinic** *(Inter-faculty)* (Medicine; Occupational Health); **Physical Education and Sports** *(Inter-faculty)* (Physical Education; Sports)

Faculties

Health Sciences (Biological and Life Sciences; Cell Biology; Clinical Psychology; Community Health; Health Administration; Health Sciences; Medicine; Midwifery; Natural Sciences; Neurology; Nursing; Occupational Health; Physical Therapy; Psychology; Public Health; Social and Preventive Medicine; Social Sciences); **Medicine I** (Anaesthesiology; Biological and Life Sciences; Biology; Endocrinology; Epidemiology; Gastroenterology; Genetics; Gynaecology and Obstetrics; Haematology; Health Sciences; Medicine; Microbiology; Neurology; Oncology; Ophthalmology; Orthopaedics; Otorhinolaryngology; Paediatrics; Parasitology; Pathology; Physiology; Radiology; Rheumatology; Surgery); **Medicine II** *(Medical Education in English, Postgraduate)* (Anatomy; Biological and Life Sciences; Biophysics; Biotechnology; Cardiology; Chemistry; Dental Hygiene; Dental Technology; Dentistry; Dermatology; Dietetics; Gastroenterology; Haematology; Health Education; Health Sciences; Histology; Immunology; Laboratory Techniques; Medicine; Microbiology; Nephrology; Optometry; Oral Pathology; Orthodontics; Orthopaedics; Paediatrics; Periodontics; Physiology; Psychiatry and Mental Health; Rheumatology; Surgery; Tropical Medicine; Urology); **Pharmacy** (Analytical Chemistry; Applied Chemistry; Biochemistry; Biological and Life Sciences; Biotechnology; Botany; Chemistry; Cosmetology; Economics; Health Sciences; Inorganic Chemistry; Laboratory Techniques; Medical Technology; Medicine; Molecular Biology; Natural Resources;

Natural Sciences; Organic Chemistry; Pharmacology; Pharmacy; Physical Chemistry; Plant Pathology; Toxicology)

History: Founded 1919, acquired present status and title 1950. Akademia Medyczna im. Karola Marcinkowskiego w Poznaniu until 2007.

Governing Bodies: Senate, elected every 3 years

Academic Year: October to June (October-January; February-June)

Admission Requirements: Secondary school certificate (Matura) and entrance examinations

Main Language(s) of Instruction: Polish, English

International Co-operation: With universities in Belarus, Denmark, Finland, France, Germany, Japan, the Netherlands, Papua New Guinea, Sweden, Ukraine, USA, Italy, Spain, Netherlands. Also participates in the Socrates/Erasmus, Leonardo programmes

Accrediting Agencies: Ministry of Health; Ministry of Science and Higher Education

Degrees and Diplomas: *Lekarz*; *Lekarz*: Dentistry; *Magister*; *Doktor*

Student Services: Academic counselling, Canteen, Cultural centre, Employment services, Foreign student adviser, Foreign Studies Centre, Health services, Social counselling, Sports facilities

Special Facilities: Museum of Medicine

Libraries: Central Medical Library, c. 332,437 vols

Publications: Bibliografia prac Akademii Medycznej im. Karola Marcinkowskiego w Poznaniu; Biuletyn Informacyjny AM; Fakty AM; Nowiny Lekarskie; Pielęgniarstwo Polskie; Polski Przegląd Nauk o Zdrowiu

Press or Publishing House: Wydawnictwo Naukowe Akademii Medycznej im. Karola Marcinkowskiego w Poznaniu

Academic Staff *2010-2011*	**TOTAL**
FULL-TIME	**1,300**
STAFF WITH DOCTORATE FULL-TIME	c. **130**
Student Numbers *2010-2011*	
All (Foreign Included)	**8,137**
FOREIGN ONLY	**1,011**

Distance students, 2,500.

Last Updated: 29/09/11

POZNAN UNIVERSITY OF TECHNOLOGY

Politechnika Poznańska (PP)

pl. Marii Skłodowskiej-Curie 5, 60-965 Poznań, wielkopolskie
Tel: +48(61) 665-37-35
Fax: +48(61) 665-35-30
EMail: sekretariat.rektora@put.poznan.pl
Website: http://www.put.poznan.pl

Rektor: Adam Hamrol
Tel: +48(61) 665-35-37, Fax: +48(61) 665-37-70
EMail: rector@put.poznan.pl

Klanclerz: Janusz Napierala
Tel: +48(61) 665-35-24, Fax: +48(61) 665-35-30
EMail: Kanclerz@put.poznan.pl

International Relations: Aleksandra Rakowsak, Prorektor, International Relations
Tel: +48(61) 665-36-92, Fax: +48(61) 665-36-99
EMail: prorector.education@put.poznan.pl

Centres

Computer Network Management (Computer Science); **Innovation and Technology Transfer** *(Comprehensive community based - PUT - CIRITT)* (Technology)

Departments

Foreign Languages *(Interfaculty unit)* (English; French; German; Modern Languages; Russian); **Physical Education and Sport** *(Interfaculty unit)* (Physical Education; Sports)

Faculties

Architecture (Architecture; Painting and Drawing; Sculpture; Town Planning; Visual Arts); **Chemical Technology** (Chemical Engineering; Chemistry; Engineering Management; Environmental Engineering); **Civil and Environmental Engineering** (Architecture; Civil Engineering; Environmental Engineering); **Computer Science** (Automation and Control Engineering; Biological and Life Sciences; Computer Engineering; Computer Science; Robotics); **Electrical Engineering** (Automation and Control Engineering; Computer Engineering; Electrical Engineering; Electronic Engineering; Energy Engineering; Information Technology; Mathematics; Power Engineering; Robotics); **Electronics and Telecommunications** (Computer Networks; Electronic Engineering; Mass Communication; Microelectronics; Multimedia; Telecommunications Engineering); **Management** (Economics; Industrial Management; Management; Marketing; Safety Engineering; Transport Management); **Mechanical Engineering and Management** (Biomedical Engineering; Electronic Engineering; Engineering Management; Materials Engineering; Mechanical Engineering; Mechanics; Production Engineering); **Technical Physics** (Applied Physics; Nuclear Physics); **Working Machines and Transportation** (Machine Building; Materials Engineering; Mechanical Engineering; Thermal Engineering; Transport and Communications; Transport Engineering)

History: Founded 1919 as college, closed 1939, reopened 1945 and acquired full University status 1955

Governing Bodies: Senate

Academic Year: October to June (October-February; February-June)

Admission Requirements: Secondary school certificate (Matura) and entrance examination

Fees: (New Złoty): 1,200-3,500 per semester. For foreign students (Euro): for first cycle programmes, 1,500 per annum; second cycle programmes, 2,000 per annum; third cycle programmes, 3,000 per annum. Postgraduate programmes, 2,000 per annum.

Main Language(s) of Instruction: Polish

International Co-operation: Socrates-Erasmus, Tempus, Phare, Nato, CEEPUS, Jean Monet, Leonardo da Vinci programmes

Accrediting Agencies: Ministry of Science and Higher Education

Degrees and Diplomas: *Inżynier*; *Licencjat*; *Świadectwo ukończenia studiów podyplomowych*; *Magister*; *Doktor*

Student Services: Canteen, Cultural centre, Employment services, Foreign student adviser, Handicapped facilities, Language programs, Sports facilities

Student Residential Facilities: 6 student houses (2,000 beds).

Special Facilities: Student Broadcasing Station

Libraries: Main Library, 800,033 vols

Publications: Zeszyty Naukowe, Scientific Papers

Press or Publishing House: Wydawnictwo Uczelniane Politechniki Poznańskiej

Academic Staff *2008-2009*	MEN	WOMEN	**TOTAL**
FULL-TIME	884	323	**1,207**
STAFF WITH DOCTORATE FULL-TIME	712	204	**916**
Student Numbers *2007-2008*			
All (Foreign Included)	–	–	**17,848**
FOREIGN ONLY	–	–	**135**

Evening students, 5,983.

Last Updated: 22/09/11

PUBLIC HIGHER MEDICAL PROFESSIONAL SCHOOL IN OPOLE

Państwowa Medyczna Wyższa Szkoła Zawodowa w Opolu (WMWSZ)

ul. Katowicka 68, 45-060 Opole, opolskie
Tel: +48(77) 441-08-82
Fax: +48(77) 442-35-25
EMail: rektorat@wsm.opole.pl
Website: http://www.wsm.opole.pl

Rector: Andrzej Steciwko Tel: +48(77) 442-35-25

Kanclerz: Zdzislaw Sworowski
EMail: sekretariatkanclerza@wsm.opole.pl

Programmes

Cosmetology (Cosmetology); **Nursing** (Nursing); **Obstetrics** (Gynaecology and Obstetrics); **Physiotherapy** (Physical Therapy); **Public Health** (Public Health)

History: Founded 2003.

Degrees and Diplomas: *Licencjat*; *Licencjat*: Nursing; *Świadectwo ukończenia studiów podyplomowych*

Last Updated: 03/09/11

PUBLIC HIGH VOCATIONAL SCHOOL NAMED BY PROF. STANISLAW TARNOWSKI IN TARNOBRZEG

Państwowa Wyższa Szkoła Zawodowa im. prof. Stanisława Tarnowskiego w Tarnobrzegu (PWSZ)

Ul. Sienkiewicza 50, 39-400 Tarnobrzeg, 39-400 Tarnobrzeg, podkarpackie
Tel: +48(15) 822-90-15 +48(15) 823-65-16
Fax: +48(15) 823-57-88
EMail: uczelnia@pwsz.tarnobrzeg.pl
Website: http://www.pwsz.tarnobrzeg.pl

Rector: Kazimierz Jaremczuk (2002-)
Tel: +48(15) 823-64-94 EMail: aga_pwsz@op.pl

Chancellor: Jacek Maślanka
Tel: +48(15) 822-90-15 +48(15) 822-90-23 Ext.223
EMail: pwsz_t@poczta.onet.pl

International Relations: Stanisław Domaradzki, Prorector
Tel: +48(15) 822-90-15 +48(15) 822-90-23 Ext. 229
EMail: prore_pwsz@interia.pl

Institutes

Business and Management (Accountancy; Administration; Business Administration; Finance; Human Resources; Management; Parks and Recreation; Tourism); **Pedagogy** (Child Care and Development; Health Education; Pedagogy; Rehabilitation and Therapy; Special Education); **Sociology** (Communication Studies; Development Studies; European Studies; European Union Law; Family Studies; Insurance; Labour and Industrial Relations; Media Studies; Protective Services; Regional Studies; Social Policy; Social Problems; Sociology)

History: Founded 2001.

Degrees and Diplomas: *Licencjat*; *Świadectwo ukończenia studiów podyplomowych*

Last Updated: 04/09/11

RZESZÓW UNIVERSITY OF TECHNOLOGY

Politechnika Rzeszowska im. Ignacego Łukaszewicza (PRZ)

ul. Wincentego Pola 2, 35-959 Rzeszów, podkarpackie
Tel: +48(17) 865-11-00
Fax: +48(17) 854-12-60
EMail: rektor@prz.edu.pl
Website: http://www.prz.edu.pl

Rektor: Andrzej Sobkowiak (2005-) Tel: +48(17) 854-12-60

Kanclerz: Janusz Bury
Tel: +48(17) 854-23-40 EMail: ra@prz.adu.pl

International Relations: Feliks Stachowicz, Vice-Rector
Tel: +48(17) 854-11-27, Fax: +48(17) 854-11-27
EMail: ro@prz.edu.pl

Departments

Foreign Languages (Modern Languages) *Head*: Małgorzata Kołodziej; **Physical Education and Sports** (Physical Education) *Head*: Jacek Lutak

Faculties

Chemistry (Biotechnology; Chemical Engineering; Chemistry; Materials Engineering) *Dean*: Ireneusz Opaliński; **Civil and Environmental Engineering** (Civil Engineering; Environmental Engineering) *Dean*: Leonard Ziemiański; **Electrical and Computer Engineering** (Computer Engineering; Computer Science; Electrical Engineering; Telecommunications Engineering) *Dean*: Kazimierz Buczek; **Management** (Economics; European Studies; Food Science; Management; Transport Management) *Dean*: Grzegorz Ostasz; **Mathematics and Applied Physics** (Applied Physics; Engineering; Mathematics) *Dean*: Dov Wajnryb; **Mechanical Engineering and Aeronautics** (Aeronautical and Aerospace Engineering; Electronic Engineering; Mechanical Engineering; Mechanics; Production Engineering; Transport Engineering) *Dean*: Krzysztof Kubiak

History: Founded 1951 as a branch of the Technical University of Cracow, became independent as college 1963. Acquired present status and title 1974.

Governing Bodies: Senate

Academic Year: October to June (October-February; February-June)

Admission Requirements: Secondary school certificate (Matura)

Fees: (US Dollars): Foreign students, 2,000-3,500 per annum

Main Language(s) of Instruction: Polish

International Co-operation: With universities in Germany, France, Portugal, Belgium, Great Britain, Spain, Austria, Denmark, Greece, Turkey, Iceland, Norway, Finland, Bulgaria, Slovakia, Japan, USA, Ukraine, Russia, Czech Republic, Hungary, Romania, Croatia

Accrediting Agencies: Ministry of Science and Higher Education

Degrees and Diplomas: *Licencjat (lic.)*: 3 yrs; *Magister*; *Doktor (Dr)*: a further 2-3 yrs by thesis

Student Services: Canteen, Cultural centre, Health services, Social counselling, Sports facilities

Student Residential Facilities: Yes

Special Facilities: Computer Centre; Aviation Training Centre; University Gliding Centre in Bezmiechowa

Libraries: Central Library, 157,000 vols; 158,000 technical standards, catalogues, certificates; 35,000 magazines 8,600 on-line periodicals.

Publications: Electrical Engineering, Computer Science, Chemistry, Economy and Humanities *(other/irregular)*; Journal of Mathematics and Applications *(annually)*; Mechanics, Civil and Environmental Engineering, Management and Marketing *(quarterly)*

Press or Publishing House: Oficyna Wydawnicza (Publishing House of Rzeszów UT)

Last Updated: 25/08/11

SIEDLCE UNIVERSITY OF NATURAL SCIENCES AND HUMANITIES

Uniwersytet Przyrodniczo-Humanistyczny w Siedlcach (UPH)

ul. Konarskiego 2, 08-110 Siedlce, mazowieckie
Tel: +48(25) 644-20-48
Fax: +48(25) 644-20-45
EMail: rektor@uph.edu.pl
Website: http://www.uph.edu.pl

Rektor: Antoni Jówko
Tel: +48(25) 643-19-20, Fax: +48(25) 644-20-45

Dyrektor Administracyjny: Andrzej Tarasiuk
Tel: +48(25) 643-19-15 EMail: dyrektor@uph.edu.pl

International Relations: Ewa Bańkowska, Head, Department of Science and International Cooperation
Tel: +48(25) 643-19-43 EMail: bankowskae@uph.edu.pl

Centres

Education and Rehabilitation of the Disabled (Rehabilitation and Therapy) *Director*: Beata Harań; **Foreign Languages** (Modern Languages) *Director*: Ewa Wyrzykowska; **Horsemanship** (Sports) *Director*: Wiesław Augustyniak; **Physical Education and Sports** (Physical Education; Sports) *Director*: Dariusz Izdebski

Faculties

Agriculture (Agricultural Economics; Agricultural Education; Agriculture; Animal Husbandry; Bioengineering; Biology; Farm Management) *Dean*: Piotr Gulinski; **Humanities** (Education; History; Modern Languages; Pedagogy; Polish; Political Sciences; Primary Education; Social Sciences; Teacher Training) *Dean*: Jerzy Kunikowski; **Management** (Management) *Dean*: Jaroslaw Kardas; **Sciences** (Chemistry; Computer Science; Education; Mathematics; Physics) *Dean*: Iwona Szamrej-Forys

History: Founded 1969 as College of Teacher Training, reorganized 1974 as University of Agriculture and Teacher Education. Became Akademia Podlaska w Siedlcach (Podlasie Academy, Siedlce) 1999. Acquired present status and title 2010.

Governing Bodies: Senate

Academic Year: October to June (October-January; February-June)

Admission Requirements: Secondary school certificate (matura) or foreign equivalent; foreign students - examination in the Polish language

Main Language(s) of Instruction: Polish; English

International Co-operation: With universities in Belarus, Russian Federation,Georgia, Lithuania, Ukraine, Germany, Italy, France, Spain

Accrediting Agencies: Polish State Accreditation Committee

Degrees and Diplomas: *Inżynier*: Agriculture; Animal Husbandry; Computer Science; Bioengineering in Food Production; *Licencjat*: Modern Languages; Administration; Management; Logistic; Political Science; National Security; Biology; Dietetics, Polish Studies; History; Pedagogy; International Relations; Chemistry; Physics; Mathematics; Tourism and Recreation; *Magister*: Agriculture; Animal Husbandry; Computer Science; Polish Studies; History; Pedagogy; National Security; Political Science; Management; Marketing; Administration; Chemistry; Biology; Computer Science; Mathematics; *Doktor*: Agronomy; Biology; Chemistry; History; Animal Husbandry; *Doktor habilitowany*: Agronomy; Animal Husbandry

Student Services: Cultural centre, Handicapped facilities, Health services, Sports facilities

Student Residential Facilities: For 958 students

Special Facilities: Art Gallery

Libraries: Main Library 330,000 vols

Publications: Agriculture *(quarterly)*; Akta Scienciarum Polonarum, Biology *(biennially)*; Manager; Podlaskie Zeszyty Pedagogiczne *(biennially)*; Studia Informatika *(biennially)*

Last Updated: 29/08/11

SILESIAN UNIVERSITY OF TECHNOLOGY

Politechnika Śląska (SUT)

ul. Akademicka 2A, 44-100 Gliwice, śląskie

Tel: +48(32) 237-10-00 +48(32) 237-19-87

Fax: +48(32) 237-23-62

EMail: RD1@polsl.pl

Website: http://www.polsl.pl

Rektor: Andrzej Karbownik (2008-)
Tel: +48(32) 237-12-55 EMail: R-BR@polsl.pl

Kanclerz: Krzysztof Pałucha
Tel: +48(33) 237-22-55 EMail: RA@polsl.pl

International Relations: Jerzy Rutkowski, Vice-Rector for International Cooperation
Tel: +48(32) 237-12-22, Fax: +48(32) 237-80-85
EMail: RW-S@polsl.pl

Colleges

Foreign Languages (English; French; Italian; Modern Languages; Philology)

Faculties

Architecture (Architecture; Architecture and Planning; Building Technologies; Design; Fine Arts; Interior Design; Town Planning); **Automatic Control, Electronics and Computer Science** (Automation and Control Engineering; Computer Science; Data Processing; Electronic Engineering; Robotics; Software Engineering; Telecommunications Engineering); **Biomedical Engineering** (Biomedical Engineering; Computer Science; Health Sciences; Medical Technology); **Chemistry** (Analytical Chemistry; Biotechnology; Chemical Engineering; Chemistry; Engineering Management; Industrial Chemistry; Inorganic Chemistry; Organic Chemistry; Petroleum and Gas Engineering; Physical Chemistry; Polymer and Plastics Technology); **Civil Engineering** (Bridge Engineering; Building Technologies; Civil Engineering; Geological Engineering; Mechanics; Road Engineering; Structural Architecture); **Electrical Engineering** (Automation and Control Engineering; Computer Science; Electrical and Electronic Engineering; Electrical and Electronic Equipment and Maintenance; Electrical Engineering; Electronic Engineering; Industrial Engineering; Measurement and Precision Engineering; Mechanical Engineering; Power Engineering; Robotics); **Energy and Environmental Engineering** (Biotechnology; Energy Engineering; Environmental Engineering; Environmental Studies; Heating and Refrigeration; Machine Building; Power Engineering; Safety Engineering; Thermal Engineering; Waste Management; Water Management); **Materials Science and Metallurgy** (Computer Education; Electronic Engineering; Energy Engineering; Materials Engineering; Mechanical Engineering; Medical Technology; Metallurgical Engineering; Production Engineering; Technology; Technology Education); **Mathematics and Physics** (Applied Physics; Computer Science; Electronic Engineering; Mathematics; Physics; Telecommunications Engineering); **Mechanical Engineering** (Automation and Control Engineering; Computer Education; Computer Science; Engineering Management; Machine Building; Materials Engineering; Mechanical Engineering; Mechanics; Metal Techniques; Nanotechnology; Production Engineering; Robotics; Technology); **Mining and Geology** (Electrical Engineering; Geological Engineering; Geology; Mechanical Engineering; Mineralogy; Mining Engineering; Safety Engineering; Waste Management); **Organization and Management** (Administration; Computer Science; Econometrics; Economics; Engineering Management; Environmental Management; Finance; Law; Management; Marketing; Production Engineering; Safety Engineering; Social Sciences; Sociology; Transport Management); **Transport** (Automotive Engineering; Computer Science; Railway Engineering; Road Engineering; Transport and Communications; Transport Management)

History: Founded 1945

Governing Bodies: Senate

Academic Year: October to September (October-February; February-September)

Admission Requirements: Secondary school certificate (Matura) and entrance examination

Fees: (Euro): For foreign students enrolment fee, 200; Tuition fee, 3,000-6,000 per annum.

Main Language(s) of Instruction: Polish, English

International Co-operation: Erasmus Programme (Austria, Belgium, Czech Republic, Germany, Greece, Portugal, Spain, Italy, Ireland, Netherlands, Sweden, United Kingdom, France, Denmark, Finland), Other cooperation programmes: USA, Ukraine, Ukraine, Egypt, Russian Federation, canada, Vietnam.

Accrediting Agencies: Ministry of Science and Higher Education

Degrees and Diplomas: *Inżynier*; *Licencjat*; *Świadectwo ukończenia studiów podyplomowych*; *Magister (mgr.inż.)*: 5 -5 1/2 yrs; *Doktor*

Student Services: Academic counselling, Canteen, Cultural centre, Employment services, Health services, Language programs, Sports facilities

Student Residential Facilities: Hostels

Special Facilities: Geological Museum

Libraries: Central Library, 570,990 vols; faculty libraries, 219,609

Publications: Zeszyty naukowe Politechniki Sląskiej, Scientific journal

Press or Publishing House: The Printing House

Academic Staff *2010-2011*: Total 1,700

STAFF WITH DOCTORATE: Total 300

Student Numbers *2010-2011*: Total: c. 30,000

Last Updated: 23/09/11

STANISŁAW STASZIC STATE SCHOOL OF HIGHER VOCATIONAL EDUCATION IN PIŁA

Państwowa Wyższa Szkoła Zawodowa im. Stanisława Staszica w Pile (PWSZ)

ul. Podchorążych 10, 64-920 Piła, wielkopolskie

Tel: +48(67) 352-26-00

Fax: +48(67) 352-26-09

EMail: info@pwsz.pila.pl

Website: http://www.pwsz.pila.pl

Rector: Stanislaus Staszic
Tel: +48(67) 352-26-01 EMail: rektor@pwsz.pila.pl

Kanclerz: Sylvester M. Sieradzki
Tel: +48(67) 352-26-03 EMail: kanclerz@pwsz.pila.pl

International Relations: Lukasz Marczak, Senior Officer for International Relations and Science and Institutional Erasmus Coordinator

Tel: +48(673) 522-680, Fax: +48(673) 522-609
EMail: lukasz.marczak@pwsz.pila.pl

Departments

Foreign Languages (English; German; Latin; Modern Languages; Russian); **Physical Education and Sport** (Physical Education; Sports)

Institutes

Economics (Accountancy; Business Administration; Business Computing; Economics; Hotel and Restaurant; Management; Real Estate; Small Business; Tourism); **Health Protection** (Health Sciences; Medicine; Nursing; Physical Therapy); **Humanities** (Applied Linguistics; Arts and Humanities; English; Government; History; Philology; Political Sciences; Social Work); **Polytechnic** (Automation and Control Engineering; Automotive Engineering; Building Technologies; Construction Engineering; Electrical Engineering; Electronic Engineering; Energy Engineering; Industrial Engineering; Mechanical Engineering; Road Transport; Transport Engineering; Transport Management)

History: Founded 2000.

Governing Bodies: Senate

Fees: (New Złoty): 1,700-2,500 per semester

Main Language(s) of Instruction: Polish

Accrediting Agencies: Ministry of Science and Higher Education; State Accreditation Committee; National Council for Accreditation of Medical Education

Degrees and Diplomas: *Inżynier*; *Licencjat*; *Licencjat*: Nursing; *Świadectwo ukończenia studiów podyplomowych*

Student Services: Sports facilities

Student Residential Facilities: Dormitory

Special Facilities: Computer Networking Centre

Libraries: Yes

Last Updated: 03/09/11

STATE HIGHER VOCATIONAL SCHOOL IN GORZÓW WIELKOPOLSKI

Państwowa Wyższa Szkoła Zawodowa w Gorzowie Wielkopolskim (PWSZ)

ul. Teatralna 25, 66-400 Gorzów Wielkopolski, lubuskie
Tel: +48(95) 721-60-23
Fax: +48(95) 721-60-22
EMail: kancelaria@pwsz.pl
Website: http://www.pwsz.pl

Rector: Elżbieta Skorupska-Raczyńska (2011-)
EMail: rektor@pwsz.pl

Kanclerz: Roman Gawroniak
Tel: +48(95) 721-60-11, Fax: +48(95) 721-60-10
EMail: kanclerz@pwsz.pl

International Relations: Aleksandra Kubacka, Coordinator of International Cooperation
Tel: +48(95) 721-60-70, Fax: +48(95) 721-60-05
EMail: koordynator@pwsz.pl

Institutes

Administration and National Security (Administration; Economics; Finance; Government; Protective Services; Public Administration); **Humanities** (Arts and Humanities; Child Care and Development; English; German; Pedagogy; Philology; Polish; Preschool Education; Social Work); **Management** (Accountancy; Business Administration; Business Computing; Engineering; Engineering Management; Finance; Human Resources; Information Technology; Leisure Studies; Management; Real Estate; Small Business; Tourism; Transport Management); **Technology** (Computer Engineering; Computer Graphics; Computer Networks; Computer Science; Data Processing; Multimedia; Operations Research)

History: Founded 1998.

Governing Bodies: Senate

Fees: (New Złoty): 1,600-2,200 per semester.

Main Language(s) of Instruction: Polish

Accrediting Agencies: Ministry of Science and Higher Education

Degrees and Diplomas: *Inżynier*; *Licencjat*; *Świadectwo ukończenia studiów podyplomowych*; *Magister*: Polish Studies

Libraries: c. 70,000 vols

Academic Staff *2010-2011*: Total 300
STAFF WITH DOCTORATE: Total 60

Student Numbers *2010-2011*: Total: c. 5,000

Last Updated: 21/09/11

STATE HIGHER VOCATIONAL SCHOOL IN KROSNO

Państwowa Wyższa Szkoła Zawodowa w Krośnie (PWSZ)

ul. Rynek 1, 38-400 Krosno, podkarpackie
Tel: +48(13) 437-55-00
Fax: +48(13) 437-55-11
EMail: pwsz@pwsz.krosno.pl
Website: http://www.pwsz.krosno.pl

Rector: Janusz Gruchała

Kanclerz: Franciszek Tereszkiewicz

International Relations: Bartłomiej Michalski, International Cooperation Officer
Tel: +48(13) 437-55-15, Fax: +48(13) 437-55-11
EMail: iro@pwsz.krosno.pl; b.michalski@pwsz.krosno.pl

Academies

Linux IT (Computer Science); **Microsoft IT** (Information Technology); **Young** *(Krosno)* (Advertising and Publicity; Agriculture; Arts and Humanities; Computer Science; Construction Engineering; English; Environmental Engineering; German; Mechanical Engineering; Nursing; Parks and Recreation; Pedagogy; Philology; Physical Education; Polish; Russian; Tourism)

Institutes

Economic and Social Policy (Agriculture; Development Studies; Economic and Finance Policy; Nursing; Rural Studies; Social Policy); **Humanities** (Arts and Humanities; Education; English; German; Philology; Polish; Russian; Translation and Interpretation); **Physical Education** (Parks and Recreation; Physical Education; Sports; Tourism); **Technology** (Architecture; Computer Engineering; Energy Engineering; Environmental Engineering; Mechanical Engineering; Technology)

Schools

Foreign Languages *(Academia)* (English; French; German; Italian; Modern Languages; Polish; Russian; Spanish)

Units

Foreign Languages (English; Modern Languages); **Mathematics, Sciences and Natural Sciences** (Mathematics; Natural Sciences); **Pedagogy Studies and Humanities** (Arts and Humanities; History; Pedagogy; Philosophy; Psychology; Sociology); **Physical Education and Sport** (Physical Education; Sports)

History: Founded 1999.

Governing Bodies: Senate

Academic Year: October to June (October-February; February-June)

Main Language(s) of Instruction: Polish; English

Accrediting Agencies: Ministry of Science and Higher Education

Degrees and Diplomas: *Inżynier*; *Licencjat*; *Świadectwo ukończenia studiów podyplomowych*

Last Updated: 21/09/11

STATE HIGHER VOCATIONAL SCHOOL IN NOWY SĄCZ

Państwowa Wyższa Szkoła Zawodowa w Nowym Sączu (PWSZ)

ul. Staszica 1, 33-300 Nowy Sącz, małopolskie
Tel: +48(18) 443-45-45 +48(18) 547-56-02
Fax: +48(18) 443-46-08
EMail: sog@pwsz-ns.edu.pl
Website: http://www.pwsz-ns.edu.pl

Rektor: Zbigniew Ślipek (2008-) EMail: balanda@if.uj.edu.pl

Kanclerz: Zbigniew Zieliński
Tel: +48(18) 443-45-45, Fax: +48(18) 443-45-45
EMail: zzielinski@pwsz-ns.edu.pl

International Relations: Zdzisława Zacłona, Pro-Rector for Science, Development and Cooperation EMail: briw@pwsz-ns.edu.pl

Institutes
Economics (Accountancy; Administration; Economics; Finance; International Business; Tourism); **Foreign Languages** (English; German; Modern Languages; Philology; Russian; Translation and Interpretation); **Health Sciences** (Health Sciences; Medicine; Nursing); **Pedagogy** (Art Education; Child Care and Development; Computer Education; Cultural Studies; Foreign Languages Education; Mathematics; Mathematics and Computer Science; Natural Resources; Pedagogy; Preschool Education; Visual Arts); **Physical Education** (Physical Education); **Technology** (Computer Science; Electronic Engineering; Energy Engineering; Food Technology; Mechanical Engineering; Production Engineering; Technology)

Programmes
Distance Education (Administration; Art Education; Child Care and Development; Computer Science; Economics; Electronic Engineering; Energy Engineering; Finance; Food Technology; Management; Mechanical Engineering; Medicine; Nursing; Pedagogy; Physical Education; Rehabilitation and Therapy; Sports; Tourism)

Further Information: Also postgraduate studies

History: Founded 1998.

Governing Bodies: Senate

Main Language(s) of Instruction: Polish

Accrediting Agencies: Ministry of Science and Higher Education

Degrees and Diplomas: *Inżynier*, *Licencjat*; *Świadectwo ukończenia studiów podyplomowych*
Last Updated: 03/09/11

STATE HIGHER VOCATIONAL SCHOOL IN RACIBÓRZ

Państwowa Wyższa Szkoła Zawodowa w Raciborzu (PWSZ)

ul. Słowackiego 55, 47-400 Racibórz, śląskie
Tel: +48(32) 415-50-20
Fax: +48(32) 415-50-20 Ext. 129
EMail: pwszwraciborzu@pro.onet.pl; rektorat@pwsz.raciborz.edu.pl
Website: http://www.pwsz-raciborz.prv.pl

Rector: Michał Szepelawy
Tel: +48(32) 415-50-02
EMail: barbara.zobek@pwsz.raciborz.edu.pl

Kanclerz: Cezary M. Raczek
EMail: kancelaria@pwsz.raciborz.edu.pl

Departments
Foreign Languages (Modern Languages)

Institutes
Art (Art Therapy; Fine Arts; Graphic Design; Interior Design; Painting and Drawing; Photography; Visual Arts); **Educational Sciences** (Educational Psychology; Educational Sciences; English; Foreign Languages Education; German; Media Studies; Pedagogy; Primary Education); **Engineering and Mathematics** (Automation and Control Engineering; Computer Science; Economics; Educational Psychology; Engineering; English; Finance; German; Mathematics; Mathematics Education; Robotics); **Modern Languages** (Czech; English; English Studies; Foreign Languages Education; German; Modern Languages; Philology; Russian; Slavic Languages); **Physical Education** (Physical Education; Sports); **Social Studies** (Communication Studies; Finance; Government; Human Resources; Leadership; Management; Media Studies; Public Administration; Social Studies)

Degrees and Diplomas: *Inżynier*, *Licencjat*, *Świadectwo ukończenia studiów podyplomowych*
Last Updated: 04/09/11

STATE HIGHER VOCATIONAL SCHOOL IN SANDOMIERZ

Państwowa Wyższa Szkoła Zawodowa w Sandomierzu (PWSZ)

ul. Schinzla 13a, 27-600 Sandomierz, świętokrzyskie
Tel: +48(15) 644-60-06
Fax: +48(15) 644-60-06
EMail: rektorat@pwsz.sandomierz.pl
Website: http://www.pwsz.sandomierz.pl/

Rektor: Antoni Gawron

Administrative Officer: Józef Burkowski
EMail: kanclerz@pwsz.sandomierz.pl

Programmes
Cosmetology (Cosmetology); **Gardening** (Horticulture); **Mechatronics** (Electronic Engineering; Mechanical Engineering); **Philology** (English; German; Philology); **Postgraduate Studies** (Child Care and Development; Ethics; Information Sciences; Library Science; Pedagogy; Preschool Education; Speech Therapy and Audiology)

History: Founded 2007.

Degrees and Diplomas: *Inżynier*, *Licencjat*, *Świadectwo ukończenia studiów podyplomowych*
Last Updated: 04/09/11

STATE HIGHER VOCATIONAL SCHOOL OF PODHALE IN NOWY TARG

Podhalańska Państwowa Wyższa Szkoła Zawodowa w Nowym Targu (PPWSZ)

ul. Kokoszków 71, 34-400 Nowy Targ, małopolskie
Tel: +48(18) 266-70-24
Fax: +48(18) 261-07-08
EMail: rektorat@ppwsz.edu.pl
Website: http://www.ppwsz.edu.pl

Rector: Stanisław Hodorowicz (2001-) Tel: +48(18)26-10-711

Kanclerz: Andrzej Sasuła

International Relations: Anna Śmiałkowska
EMail: asmialkowska@ppwsz.nowotarski.pl

Institutes
Architecture and Town Planning (Architecture; Town Planning); **Emergency Medicine** (Medicine); **Environmental Protection** (Environmental Studies); **Humanities** (Arts and Humanities; Philology; Polish); **Nursing** (Nursing); **Physiotherapy** (Physical Therapy); **Tourism and Recreation** (Parks and Recreation; Tourism)

History: Founded 2001.

Degrees and Diplomas: *Inżynier*, *Licencjat*; *Licencjat*: Nursing; *Świadectwo ukończenia studiów podyplomowych*
Last Updated: 03/09/11

STATE HIGHER VOCATIONAL SCHOOL, SULECHÓW

Państwowa Wyższa Szkoła Zawodowa w Sulechowie (PWSZ)

ul. Armii Krajowej 51, 66-100 Sulechów, lubuskie
Tel: +48(68) 352-83-14
Fax: +48(68) 352-83-08
EMail: rektorat@pwsz.sulechow.pl
Website: http://www.pwsz.sulechow.pl

Rector: Wiesław Miczulski (2008-)
Tel: +48(68) 352-83-03 EMail: w.miczulski@pwsz.sulechow.pl

Chancellor: Janusz Mstowski
Tel: +48(68) 352-84-18, Fax: +48(68) 352-84-18
EMail: j.mstowski@pwsz.sulechow.pl

International Relations: Roman Bajor
Tel: +48(68) 352-83-14 EMail: roman.bajor@pwsz.sulechow.pl

Centres
Equestrian (Sports)

Departments
Foreign Languages (English; French; German; Italian; Modern Languages; Russian); **Physical Education** (Physical Education; Sports)

Institutes
Law and Administration (Administration; Law); **Managing and Agricultural Engineering** (Agricultural Engineering; Management); **Polytechnic** (Energy Engineering; Information Technology); **Tourism and Recreation** (Parks and Recreation; Tourism)

Programmes
Postgraduate Studies (Energy Engineering; Parks and Recreation; Public Administration; Real Estate; Tourism)

History: Founded 1998 as Wyższa Szkoła Administracji Publicznej. Acquired present title 2001.

Fees: (New Złoty): 1,650-1,800 per semester

Accrediting Agencies: Ministry of Science and Higher Education

Degrees and Diplomas: *Inżynier*, *Licencjat*; *Świadectwo ukończenia studiów podyplomowych*

Last Updated: 04/09/11

STATE HIGHER VOCATIONAL SCHOOL, TARNÓW

Państwowa Wyższa Szkoła Zawodowa w Tarnowie (PWSZ)
ul. Mickiewicza 8, 33-100 Tarnów, małopolskie
Tel: +48(14) 631-66-20
Fax: +48(14) 631-66-00
EMail: pwsz@pwsztar.edu.pl
Website: http://www.pwsztar.edu.pl

Rektor: Stanisław Komornicki (1998-)
Tel: +48(14) 631-65-00 EMail: rektorat@pwsztar.edu.pl

International Relations: Marek Frankowicz
Tel: +48(14) 602-75-37-02 EMail: frankowi@chemia.uj.edu.pl

Institutes
Administration and Economics (Administration; Economics; Management); **Health Sciences** (Health Sciences; Nursing; Physical Education; Physical Therapy); **Humanities** (Arts and Humanities; English; French; German; Modern Languages; Philology; Polish; Romance Languages); **Mathematics and Natural Sciences** (Chemistry; Environmental Studies; Mathematics and Computer Science; Natural Sciences); **Polytechnics** (Computer Science; Electrical Engineering; Electronic Engineering; Engineering; Materials Engineering; Telecommunications Engineering)

Programmes
Postgraduate Studies *(KLEKSS Project)* (Energy Engineering)

History: Founded 1998.

Governing Bodies: Senate

Main Language(s) of Instruction: Polish

International Co-operation: With universities in Austria, Belgium, Germany, France, Finland, Great Britain, Greece, Italy, Ireland and Turkey

Accrediting Agencies: Ministry of Science and Higher Education

Degrees and Diplomas: *Inżynier*, *Licencjat*; *Świadectwo ukończenia studiów podyplomowych*

Student Numbers *2009-2010*: Total: c. 6,000

Last Updated: 04/09/11

STRZEMIŃSKI ACADEMY OF ART ŁÓDŹ

Akademia Sztuk Pięknych im. Władysława Strzemińskiego w Łodzi (ASP ŁÓDŹ)
ul. Wojska Polskiego 121, 91-726 Łódź, łódzkie
Tel: +48(42) 254-75-98
Fax: +48(42) 254-75-60
EMail: kancelaria@asp.lodz.pl
Website: http://www.asp.lodz.pl

Rektor: Grzegorz Chojnacki
Tel: +48(42) 254-74-05 EMail: rektor@asp.lodz.pl

Kanclerz: Aleksandra Sowińska Banaszkiewicz
Tel: +48(42) 254-74-08 EMail: kanclerz@asp.lodz.pl

International Relations: Lena Szymborska, International Relations Officer
Tel: +48(42) 254-75-34, Fax: +48(42) 254-75-34
EMail: lena.szymborska@asp.lodz.pl; ioffice@asp.lodz.pl

Faculties
Graphic Desing and Painting (Graphic Design; Multimedia; Painting and Drawing; Photography; Printing and Printmaking; Sculpture); **Industrial Design and Interior Design** (Communication Arts; Industrial Design; Interior Design); **Textile and Fashion** (Fashion Design; Fine Arts; Jewelry Art; Painting and Drawing; Textile Design); **Visual Arts** (Art History; Film; Graphic Design; Multimedia; Painting and Drawing; Photography; Sculpture; Visual Arts)

Programmes
Postgraduate studies (Aesthetics; Art Education; Communication Arts; Design; Fashion Design; Graphic Design; Interior Design; Marketing; Painting and Drawing; Photography; Printing and Printmaking; Visual Arts)

History: Founded 1945 as State Art School of Łódź, acquired present status and title 1987.

Governing Bodies: Senate

Academic Year: October to June

Admission Requirements: Secondary school certificate (matura) and entrance examinations

Main Language(s) of Instruction: Polish

International Co-operation: With universities in Germany, Italy, Ukraine, Sweden, Slovakia

Accrediting Agencies: Ministry of Science and Higher Education

Degrees and Diplomas: *Licencjat*; *Świadectwo ukończenia studiów podyplomowych*; *Magister*. Also Joint Master Programmes

Student Services: Academic counselling, Canteen, Foreign student adviser, Health services, Language programs, Sports facilities

Special Facilities: Art Gallery

Libraries: Central Library

Publications: Zeszyty ASP

Last Updated: 07/09/11

SZCZECIN UNIVERSITY

Uniwersytet Szczeciński (US)
Al. Papieża Jana Pawła II 22a, 70-453 Szczecin, zachodniopomorskie
Tel: +48(91) 444-10-00
Fax: +48(91) 444-11-74
EMail: rzecznik@univ.szczecin.pl
Website: http://www.univ.szczecin.pl

Rector: Waldemar Tarczynski
Tel: +48(91) 444-11-72 EMail: rektor@univ.szczecin.pl

Dyrektor Administracyjny: Eugeniusz Kisiel
Tel: +48(91) 444-11-05, Fax: +48(91) 444-11-04
EMail: sekretariat.kanclerza@univ.szczecin.pl

International Relations: Andrzej Witkowski, Vice Rector for Science and International Cooperation
Tel: +48(91) 444-11-99, Fax: +48(91) 444-11-99
EMail: pronauk@univ.szczecin.pl

Faculties
Administration in Jarocin *(Jarocin - Distance Education)* (Administration; Civil Security; Government); **Earth Sciences** (Coastal Studies; Earth Sciences; Geography; Geography (Human); Geology; Leisure Studies; Marine Science and Oceanography; Meteorology; Regional Studies; Surveying and Mapping; Tourism; Urban Studies; Water Management); **Economics** *(Wałcz - Distance Education)* (Economics; English; German; International Studies; Polish); **Economics and Management Services** (Accountancy; Banking; E-Business/Commerce; Economic and Finance Policy; Economics; European Studies; Finance; Human Resources; Insurance; Management; Marine Science and Oceanography; Parks and Recreation; Social Policy; Tourism; Transport and Communications; Transport Management); **Humanities** (Anthropology; Arts and Humanities; Bible; Canon Law; Eastern European Studies;

Education; English; Ethnology; European Studies; French; German; Germanic Studies; History; History of Religion; International Relations; Music Education; Pastoral Studies; Peace and Disarmament; Pedagogy; Polish; Political Sciences; Primary Education; Psychology; Slavic Languages; Sociology; Special Education; Teacher Training); **Law and Administration** (Administration; Administrative Law; Business Administration; Civil Law; Commercial Law; Constitutional Law; Criminal Law; Economics; Environmental Studies; European Union Law; Fiscal Law; Government; History of Law; Information Management; International Law; Labour Law; Law; Public Administration; Public Law; Social Policy); **Management and Economics** (Banking; Computer Science; Econometrics; Economics; Finance; Management; Marketing); **Mathematics and Physics** (Astronomy and Space Science; Astrophysics; Computer Science; Educational Technology; Environmental Management; Information Technology; Mathematics; Medical Technology; Multimedia; Nanotechnology; Nuclear Physics; Optics; Physics; Polymer and Plastics Technology; Solid State Physics; Technology; Telecommunications Engineering); **Natural Sciences** (Anatomy; Anthropology; Biochemistry; Biology; Biotechnology; Botany; Cell Biology; Chemistry; Ecology; Environmental Studies; Genetics; Immunology; Microbiology; Physiology; Water Management; Zoology); **Philology** (Cultural Studies; Foreign Languages Education; German; Journalism; Mass Communication; Philology; Polish; Romance Languages; Slavic Languages; Translation and Interpretation); **Physical Education and Health Promotion** (Health Sciences; Parks and Recreation; Physical Education; Public Health; Sports; Tourism); **Socio-Economics** *(Gorzow Wielkopolski - Distance Education)* (Economics; English; German; International Studies; Polish; Social Sciences); **Theology** (Family Studies; Theology)

History: Founded 1973 as Higher School of Pedagogy and the Faculty of Economics of Transport of Szczecin Technical University and the Academy of Commerce (founded 1946). Acquired present name and status 1985.

Governing Bodies: Universities Council; Senate

Academic Year: October to July (October-January; February-July)

Admission Requirements: Secondary school certificate (matura) and entrance examination

Fees: (Euros): 3,000 per year plus 200 for first year. Students from EU countries are free of charge.

Main Language(s) of Instruction: Polish, German, English

International Co-operation: With universities in Germany, Italy, Sweden, France, Finland, Belgium, Spain, United Kingdom, Greece. Also participates in Erasmus Programme

Accrediting Agencies: Ministry of Science and Higher Education

Degrees and Diplomas: *Licencjat*; *Świadectwo ukończenia studiów podyplomowych*; *Magister*, *Doktor*

Student Services: Academic counselling, Cultural centre, Foreign student adviser, Handicapped facilities, Health services, Language programs, Social counselling, Sports facilities

Student Residential Facilities: Halls of residence with c. 1,800 places

Special Facilities: Geological Museum

Libraries: Central Library, c. 1.2 m.

Publications: Nowa Krytyka, Philosophical studies *(quarterly)*; Przeglad Universytecki *(quarterly)*; Przeglad Zachodniopomorski, Interdisciplinary periodical *(quarterly)*; Studia i Rozprawy, Dissertations and monographic works; Zeszyty Naukowe

Press or Publishing House: Wydawnictwa Naukowe

Last Updated: 30/09/11

TADEUSZ KOŚCIUSKO CRACOW UNIVERSITY OF TECHNOLOGY

Politechnika Krakowska im. Tadeusza Kościuszki (PK)

ul. Warszawska 24, 31-155 Kraków, małopolskie
Tel: +48(12) 628-20-00
Fax: +48(12) 628-20-71
EMail: kancelaria@pk.edu.pl
Website: http://www.pk.edu.pl

Rektor: Kazimierz Furtak
Tel: +48(12) 628-22-01, Fax: +48(12) 628-22-62
EMail: rektor@pk.edu.pl

Kanclerz: Lucjan Tabaka
Tel: +48(12) 628-22-05, Fax: +48(12) 628-30-03
EMail: kanclerz@pk.edu.pl

International Relations: Jolanta Rak, Head, International Relations Office
Tel: +48(12) 628-26-42, Fax: +48(12) 628-26-42
EMail: jolar@pk.edu.pl

Centres

Academic Business Incubator (Business Administration); **Foreign Languages** (English; German; Russian; Spanish); **International Education** *(Interfaculty)* (Cultural Studies; English; Polish); **New Technology and Medical Technology** *(Intercollegiate)* (Biomedical Engineering; Medical Technology; Technology); **Pedagogy and Psychology** (Educational Psychology; Pedagogy); **Sports and Recreation** (Parks and Recreation; Physical Education; Sports); **Technology Transfer** (Business Administration; Management; Technology)

Faculties

Architecture (Architecture; Landscape Architecture; Town Planning); **Chemical Engineering and Technology** (Biotechnology; Chemical Engineering; Chemistry; Nanotechnology; Petroleum and Gas Engineering); **Civil Engineering** (Architecture; Civil Engineering; Construction Engineering; Transport Engineering); **Electrical and Computer Engineering** (Computer Engineering; Electrical Engineering; Energy Engineering; Information Technology); **Environmental Engineering** (Architecture; Environmental Engineering; Environmental Studies); **Mechanical Engineering** (Automation and Control Engineering; Biomedical Engineering; Energy Engineering; Engineering Management; Information Technology; Materials Engineering; Mechanical Engineering; Mechanics; Production Engineering; Robotics; Safety Engineering; Transport Engineering); **Physics, Mathematics and Computer Science** (Information Technology; Mathematics; Mathematics and Computer Science; Nanotechnology; Physics)

History: Founded 1945, acquired present status 1954

Governing Bodies: Senate

Academic Year: October to June (October-February; February-June)

Admission Requirements: Secondary school certificate (Matura) and entrance examination

Fees: (New Złoty): External students, c. 2,000-12,000

Main Language(s) of Instruction: Polish

International Co-operation: Participates in the Socrates/Erasmus, Ceepus, Leonardo da Vinci

Accrediting Agencies: Ministry of Science and Higher Education

Degrees and Diplomas: *Inżynier*, *Świadectwo ukończenia studiów podyplomowych*; *Magister*, *Doktor*

Student Services: Academic counselling, Canteen, Cultural centre, Employment services, Foreign student adviser, Foreign Studies Centre, Handicapped facilities, Health services, Language programs, Social counselling, Sports facilities

Student Residential Facilities: Yes

Special Facilities: Conference and Exhibition Centre, Museum

Libraries: Central Library, c. 750,000 vols; 81,650 periodicals

Publications: Czasopismo Techniczne, Technical Bulletin; Nasza Politechnika *(bimonthly)*; Zeszyty Naukowe, Scientific Papers

Press or Publishing House: Redakcja Wydawnictw Politechniki Krakowskiej

Academic Staff *2010-2011*	**TOTAL**
FULL-TIME	**1,181**
Student Numbers *2010-2011*	
All (Foreign Included)	**16,374**

Part-time students, 4,349.

Last Updated: 22/09/11

TECHNICAL UNIVERSITY OF ŁÓDŹ

Politechnika Łódzka (PL)

ul. Żeromskiego 116, 90-924 Łódź, łódzkie
Tel: +48(42) 631-20-80
Fax: +48(42) 631-85-22
EMail: intrel@p.lodz.pl
Website: http://www.p.lodz.pl

Rektor: Stanisław Bielecki (2008-)
Tel: +48(42) 631-20-02 EMail: office.rector@adm.p.lodz.pl

Executive Dyrektor: Stanisław Starzak
Tel: +48(42) 631-20-12, Fax: +48(42) 636-56-15
EMail: stanislaw.starzak@p.lodz.pl

International Relations: Ireneusz Zbicinski, Vice-Rector
Tel: +48(42) 631-20-80, Fax: +48(42) 636-53-79

Colleges

Commodity Science (Economics; Food Science; Safety Engineering) *Director*: Izabella Krucińska; **Logistics** (Transport Management) *Dierctor*: Grzegorz Bąk; **Spatial Economy** (Economics) *Director*: Dariusz Gawin

Faculties

Biotechnology and Food Science (Biotechnology; Environmental Studies; Food Technology; Nutrition) *Dean*: Maria Koziołkiewicz; **Chemistry** (Chemical Engineering; Chemistry; Environmental Studies; Materials Engineering; Nanotechnology; Organic Chemistry; Polymer and Plastics Technology) *Dean*: Piotr Paneth; **Civil Engineering, Architecture and Environmental Engineering** (Architecture; Civil Engineering; Environmental Engineering; Interior Design; Town Planning) *Dean*: Dariusz Gawin; **Electrical, Electronic, Computer and Control Engineering** (Automation and Control Engineering; Computer Science; Electrical and Electronic Engineering; Electrical Engineering; Electronic Engineering; Power Engineering; Robotics; Safety Engineering; Telecommunications Engineering; Transport Engineering) *Dean*: Sławomir Wiak; **Engineering** *(International)* (Biomedical Engineering; Biotechnology; Business and Commerce; Computer Science; Engineering; Information Technology; Management; Mechanical Engineering; Structural Architecture; Technology; Telecommunications Engineering) *Dean*: Tomasz Saryusz-Wolski; **Material Technologies and Textiles Design** (Computer Education; Design; Materials Engineering; Polymer and Plastics Technology; Safety Engineering; Technology Education; Textile Design; Textile Technology) *Dean*: Ryszard Korycki; **Mechanical Engineering** (Automation and Control Engineering; Electronic Engineering; Management; Materials Engineering; Mechanical Engineering; Power Engineering; Production Engineering; Robotics; Transport Engineering) *Dean*: Bogdan Kruszyński; **Organization and Management** (European Studies; Management; Production Engineering; Safety Engineering) *Dean*: Ryszard Grądzki; **Process and Environmental Engineering** (Chemical Engineering; Engineering Management; Environmental Engineering; Safety Engineering) *Dean*: Stanisław Ledakowicz; **Technical Physics, Computer Science and Applied Mathematics** (Applied Mathematics; Computer Science; Information Technology; Mathematics; Physics) *Dean*: Grzegorz Bąk

Institutes

Papermaking and Printing (Paper Technology; Printing and Printmaking) *Director*: Barbara Surma-Ślusarska

History: Founded 1945.

Governing Bodies: Senate

Academic Year: October to June (October-February; February-June)

Admission Requirements: Secondary school certificate (Matura) and entrance examination

Fees: (Euro): Foreign students 2,000-4,000 per annum

Main Language(s) of Instruction: Polish; English; French

International Co-operation: with over 400 universities, research centres, institutes and companies in 40 countries around the world

Accrediting Agencies: Ministry of Science and Higher Education; State Accreditation Commission; Technical Universities Accreditation Commission

Degrees and Diplomas: *Inżynier*: Engineering; Science (Inż.), 3 1/2-4 yrs; *Świadectwo ukończenia studiów podyplomowych*; *Magister*: Engineering; Science (Mgr.inż.); *Doktor*: Architecture and Urban Planning, Automatic Control and Robotics, Biotechnology, Civil Engineering, Computer Science, Chemical Engineering, Chemical Technology Electronics, Electrical Engineering, Environmental Engineering; Materials Engineering, Mechanical Engineering, Textile Engineering, Theoretical Mechanics; *Doktor*: Management Studies; Chemistry; Physics; Mathematics (Dr inż.), by thesis, a further 3-4 yrs; *Doktor habilitowany*: Automation, Control Engineering and Robotics; Biotechnology; Chemical Engineering; Chemical Technology; Civil Engineering; Electronics; Electrical Engineering; Environmental Engineering; Materials Eng.; Mechanical Eng; Theoretical Mechanics; Textile Eng. (Dr.hab), by thesis, following Doctor; *Doktor habilitowany*: Chemistry

Student Services: Academic counselling, Canteen, Cultural centre, Employment services, Foreign student adviser, Foreign Studies Centre, Handicapped facilities, Health services, Language programs, Nursery care, Social counselling, Sports facilities

Student Residential Facilities: For 3,000 students

Special Facilities: Computer Centre;Museum; Art Galleries; Students' Radio "Żak".

Libraries: Central Library, c. 500,000 vols; specialized libraries (Chemical, Electrical, Mechanical, Civil Engineering,Food Chemistry), 240,000 vols

Publications: Journal of Applied Analysis; Scientific Papers published by the various faculties *(biannually)*; Zeszyty Historyczne *(biennially)*; Życie Uczelni *(quarterly)*

Press or Publishing House: Redakcja Wydawnictw Naukowych Politechniki Łódzkiej

Academic Staff *2010-2011*	MEN	WOMEN	TOTAL
FULL-TIME	928	473	**1,401**
PART-TIME	57	29	**86**
STAFF WITH DOCTORATE			
FULL-TIME	843	374	**1,217**
PART-TIME	27	10	**37**
Student Numbers *2010-2011*			
All (Foreign Included)	12,472	7,407	**19,879**

Evening students, 5,017.

Last Updated: 25/08/11

THE ALEKSANDER ZELWEROWICZ STATE THEATRE ACADEMY

Akademia Teatralna im. Aleksandra Zelwerowicza w Warszawie (AT)

ul. Miodowa 22/24, 00-246 Warszawa, mazowieckie
Tel: +48(22) 831-02-16
Fax: +48(22) 831-91-01
EMail: rektorat@at.edu.pl
Website: http://www.at.edu.pl

Rektor: Andrzej Strzelecki (2008-)
Tel: +48(22) 831-95-45 +48(22) 831-69-25,
Fax: +48(22) 831-91-01

Chancellor: Beata Kowal
Tel: +48(22) 831-12-16 Ext. 112 EMail: International@at.edu.pl

International Relations: Cezary Morawski, Rector's Representative for International Relations EMail: cezary.morawski@at.edu.pl

Departments

Acting (Acting; Anthropology; Art History; Dance; English; Film; Literature; Modern Languages; Music; Philosophy; Singing; Sports; Theatre); **Directing** (Acting; Art History; Theatre); **Puppet - Theatre Arts** (Acting; Performing Arts; Theatre); **Theatre Studies** (Anthropology; Art Criticism; Art History; Art Management; Film; Literature; Philosophy; Radio and Television Broadcasting; Theatre)

History: Founded 1932, acquired present status and title 1996.

Governing Bodies: Senate; Theatre Council

Academic Year: October to June

Admission Requirements: Secondary school certificate (matura) and entrance examination

Main Language(s) of Instruction: Polish

Accrediting Agencies: Państwowa Komisja Akredytacyjna

Degrees and Diplomas: *Świadectwo dojrzałości*; *Licencjat*; *Magister*

Student Services: Canteen, Health services

Student Residential Facilities: Yes

Special Facilities: Theatre

Libraries: Main Library. Department library in Białystok

Last Updated: 08/09/11

THE ANGELUS SILESIUS STATE SCHOOL OF HIGHER VOCATIONAL EDUCATION IN WAŁBRZYCH

Państwowa Wyższa Szkoła Zawodowa im. Angelusa Silesiusa w Wałbrzychu (PWSZ)

ul. Zamkowa 4, 58-300 Wałbrzych, dolnośląskie
Tel: +48(74) 641-92-00 +48(74) 641-92-01
Fax: +48(74) 641-92-02
EMail: pwsz@pwsz.com.pl
Website: http://www.pwsz.com.pl/

Rector: Elżbieta LoncLonc

Kanclerz: Jan Zwierko EMail: kancelaria@pwsz.com.pl

International Relations: Justyna Jaskólska, Institutional Erasmus Coordinator
Tel: +48(74) 641-92-08, Fax: +48(74) 641-92-08
EMail: erasmus@pwsz.com.pl

Institutes

Humanities (Arts and Humanities; English; German; Pedagogy; Philology; Polish; Spanish); **Natural and Technical Sciences** (Landscape Architecture; Natural Sciences; Transport Management); **Social and Legal Sciences** (Administration; Journalism; Law; Marketing; Occupational Health; Public Administration; Social Sciences); **Tourism and Recreation** (Cosmetology; Economics; Leisure Studies; Parks and Recreation; Tourism)

Programmes

Postgraduate Studies (Forensic Medicine and Dentistry; Horticulture; Parks and Recreation; Safety Engineering; Speech Therapy and Audiology; Tourism; Welfare and Protective Services)

History: Founded 1999.

Governing Bodies: Senate

Admission Requirements: Secondary school certificate (matura) and entrance examinations

Main Language(s) of Instruction: Polish

International Co-operation: With universities in Belgium, Czech Republic, France, Lithuania, Greece, Spain, Malta, Portugal, Romania, Turkey, Belarus and Russia.

Accrediting Agencies: Ministry of Science and Higher Education

Degrees and Diplomas: *Inżynier*, *Licencjat*; *Świadectwo ukończenia studiów podyplomowych*

Last Updated: 05/09/11

THE BRONISŁAW MARKIEWICZ STATE SCHOOL OF HIGHER VOCATIONAL EDUCATION IN JAROSŁAW

Państwowa Wyższa Szkoła Techniczno-Ekonomiczna im. ks. Bronisława Markiewicza w Jarosławiu (PWSZ JAROSŁAW)

ul. Kasprowicza 1, 37-500 Jarosław, podkarpackie
Tel: +48(16) 621-02-04
Fax: +48(16) 621-08-44
EMail: pwsz@pwszjar.edu.pl
Website: http://www.pwszjar.edu.pl

Rector: Zbigniew Makieła (2008-)

Dyrektor Administracyjny: Zofia Kukla
Tel: +48(16) 624-26-00, Fax: +48(16) 621-02-04

International Relations: Roman Fedan
Tel: +48(16) 621-08-44, Fax: +48(16) 621-08-44

Institutes

Health Sciences (Health Education; Health Sciences; Nursing); **Humanities** (Arts and Humanities; English; German; Health Education; Nursing; Pedagogy; Philology; Primary Education; Rehabilitation and Therapy); **International Relations** (Cultural Studies; European Union Law; Hotel Management; International Relations; Leisure Studies; Public Administration; Tourism); **Technical Engineering** (Bridge Engineering; Civil Engineering; Computer Engineering; Computer Graphics; Computer Networks; Computer Science; Construction Engineering; Geological Engineering; Multimedia; Road Engineering; Software Engineering; Surveying and Mapping); **Tourism and Hotel Management** (Finance; Hotel and Restaurant; Hotel Management; Management; Real Estate; Safety Engineering; Tourism)

History: Founded 1998. Acquired present title 2010. Formerly known as Państwowa Wyższa Szkoła Zawodowa 'im. Ksw Jarosławiu (State Higher Vocational School, Jarosław).

Governing Bodies: Senate

Fees: (New Złoty): 1,150 per semester

Main Language(s) of Instruction: Polish

International Co-operation: Paricipates in the Ersamus.

Accrediting Agencies: Ministry of Science and Higher Education

Degrees and Diplomas: *Inżynier*, *Licencjat*; *Świadectwo ukończenia studiów podyplomowych*

Student Numbers *2010-2011*: Total: c. 5,000

Last Updated: 20/09/11

THE EAST EUROPEAN STATE HIGHER SCHOOL IN PRZEMYŚL

Państwowa Wyższa Szkoła Wschodnioeuropejska w Przemyślu (PWSZ)

ul. Tymona Terleckiego 6, 37-700 Przemyśl, podkarpacie
Tel: +48(16) 678-37-90
Fax: +48(16) 678-94-69
EMail: rektorat@pwsw.pl
Website: http://www.pwsw.pl

Rector: Jan Draus (2003-)

Kanclerz: Wacław Szkoła

Programmes

Applied Linguistics (Applied Linguistics); **English Studies** (English Studies); **Environmental Engineering** (Environmental Engineering); **History** (History); **Interior design** (Interior Design); **International Relations** (Central European Studies; European Studies; International Relations; Protective Services); **Materials Engineering** (Materials Engineering); **Mechatronics** (Electronic Engineering; Mechanical Engineering); **Polish Studies** (Journalism; Native Language Education; Polish); **Political Science** (Political Sciences; Protective Services; Public Administration); **Postgraduate Studies** (Adult Education; Commercial Law; European Studies; Human Resources; Information Management; Management; Police Studies; Tourism); **Sociology** (Communication Studies; Economics; Media Studies; Social Work; Sociology); **Ukrainian Philology** (Philology; Slavic Languages)

History: Founded 2001.

Fees: Free of charge

Degrees and Diplomas: *Inżynier*, *Licencjat*; *Świadectwo ukończenia studiów podyplomowych*

Last Updated: 03/09/11

THE FELIKS NOWOWIEJSKI ACADEMY OF MUSIC IN BYDGOSZCZ

Akademia Muzyczna im. Feliksa Nowowiejskiego w Bydgoszczy (AM)

ul. J. Słowackiego 7, 85-008 Bydgoszcz, kujawsko-pomorskie
Tel: +48(52) 321-05-82 +48(52) 321-06-87
Fax: +48(52) 321-23-50
EMail: sekr@amuz.bydgoszcz.pl
Website: http://www.amuz.bydgoszcz.pl

Rektor: Maria Murawska (2005-)
Tel: +48(52) 321-11-42, Fax: +48(52) 321-05-82 Ext. 27
EMail: rektor@amuz.bydgoszcz.pl

Kanclerz: Marek Czerski
Tel: +48(52) 321-11-42 EMail: kanclerz@amuz.bydgoszcz.pl

Departments

Piano Chamber Music *(Interfaculty)* (Music; Musical Instruments)

Faculties

Choir Conducting and Music Education (Conducting; Jazz and Popular Music; Music Education; Musicology; Opera; Religious Music); **Composition and Theory of Music** (Music Theory and Composition; Sound Engineering (Acoustics)); **Instrumental Music**

(Musical Instruments); **Vocal and Drama Studies** (Acting; Music; Singing)

Programmes

Contemporary Music *(Interfaculty)* (Music); **Early Music** *(Interfaculty)* (Music); **Foreign Languages** *(Interfaculty)* (English; French; German; Italian; Modern Languages); **Jazz and Popular Music** *(Interfaculty)* (Jazz and Popular Music); **Music Pedagogy** *(Interfaculty)* (Music Education)

Units

Recording Studio and Library *(Interfaculty)*

History: Founded 1974 as branch of State Academy of Music in Łódź, became an independent institution 1979 as State Academy of Music, Bydgoszcz and acquired present title 1981, named after Feliks Nowowiejski.

Governing Bodies: Senate

Admission Requirements: Secondary school certificate (Świadectwo dojrzałości)

Fees: (New Złoty): Extramural studies, c. 1,500 per semester

Main Language(s) of Instruction: Polish

International Co-operation: With universities in Poland, Slovakia, Serbia, Bulgaria, Japan, Germany, Italy, France, Austria, Ukraine and Latvia. Participates in the European Culture Project FABREC (Fabrique Culturelle Européenne).

Accrediting Agencies: Ministry of Culture and National Heritage

Degrees and Diplomas: *Licencjat*; *Świadectwo ukończenia studiów podyplomowych*; *Magister*, *Doktor*

Student Services: Academic counselling, Employment services, Language programs, Social counselling, Sports facilities

Special Facilities: Concert hall (170 seats);

Libraries: c. 63,000 vols

Publications: Zeszyt Naukowy, Scientific Newsletter

Press or Publishing House: Publishing House

Last Updated: 05/09/11

THE FRYDERYK CHOPIN UNIVERSITY OF MUSIC, WARSAW

Uniwersytet Muzyczny Fryderyka Chopina (UMFC)

ul. Okólnik 2, 00-368 Warszawa, mazowieckie
Tel: +48(22) 827-72-41
Fax: +48(22) 827-83-09
EMail: info@chopin.edu.pl
Website: http://www.chopin.edu.pl

Rektor: Stanisław Moryto (2005-)
Tel: +48(22) 827-83-03, Fax: +48(22) 827-83-09
EMail: rektor@chopin.edu.pl

Kanclerz: Marek Bykowski
Tel: +48(22) 827-83-09 +48(22) 827-72-41 Ext. 242,
Fax: +48(22) 827-83-09 EMail: dyrektoradm@chopin.edu.pl

International Relations: Natalia Sukiennik, Head, International Relations and Promotion Office
Tel: +48(22) 827-83-10, Fax: +48(22) 827-83-10
EMail: promocja@chopin.edu.pl

Departments

Choir Conducting, Music Education, Church Music, Rhythmics and Dance (Conducting; Dance; Music; Music Education; Musical Instruments; Pedagogy; Religious Music); **Composition, Conducting and Theory of Music** (Aesthetics; Art History; Arts and Humanities; Conducting; Music; Music Theory and Composition; Philosophy); **Instrumental and Educational Studies in Białystok** (Music; Music Education; Musical Instruments; Psychology); **Instrumental Studies** (Music; Musical Instruments); **Piano, Harpsichord and Organ** (Music; Musical Instruments); **Sound Engineering** (Music; Sound Engineering (Acoustics)); **Vocal Studies** (Music; Singing; Speech Therapy and Audiology)

Further Information: Also Branch in Białystok

History: Founded 1810, acquired present status and named Akademia Muzyczna im. Fryderyka Chopina w Warszawie (The Frederic Chopin Academy of Music, Warsaw) 1979. Acquired present title 2008.

Admission Requirements: Secondary school certificate and entrance examination

Fees: (US Dollar): Foreign students, c. 6,000 per annum

International Co-operation: Participates in the Erasmus programme

Accrediting Agencies: Ministry of Science and Higher Education

Degrees and Diplomas: *Licencjat*; *Świadectwo ukończenia studiów podyplomowych*; *Magister*, *Doktor*

Special Facilities: Concert Hall

Libraries: c. 100,000 vols and c. 20,000 audio items; Sound library

Last Updated: 05/09/11

THE JAN GRODEK HIGHER VOCATIONAL STATE SCHOOL IN SANOK

Państwowa Wyższa Szkoła Zawodowa im. Jana Grodka w Sanoku (PWSZ)

ul. Mickiewicza 21, 38-500 Sanok, podkarpackie
Tel: +48(13) 465-59-50
Fax: +48(13) 465-59-59
EMail: rektorat@pwsz-sanok.edu.pl
Website: http://www.pwsz-sanok.edu.pl/

Rector: Halina Mieczkowska
Tel: +48(13) 465-59-52, Fax: +48(13) 465-59-59

Kanclerz: Lesław Siedlecki
Tel: +48(13) 465-59-62 EMail: kanclerz@pwsz-sanok.edu.pl

Institutes

Agriculture (Agricultural Business; Agricultural Economics; Agriculture; Landscape Architecture; Production Engineering; Transport Engineering); **Humanities and Art** (Arts and Humanities; Czech; Education; Media Studies; Music; Pedagogy; Philology; Polish; Preschool Education; Regional Studies; Russian; Slavic Languages; Social Work; Tourism); **Medicine** (Medicine; Nursing); **Technology** (Computer Science; Materials Engineering; Mechanical Engineering; Mechanics)

Programmes

Postgraduate Studies (Advertising and Publicity; Agriculture; European Studies; Family Studies; Health Education; Health Sciences; Mechanical Engineering; Nursing; Safety Engineering; Social Work)

History: Founded 2001.

Fees: (New Złoty): 1,400-2,000 per semester

Degrees and Diplomas: *Inżynier*, *Licencjat*; *Licencjat*: Nursing; *Świadectwo ukończenia studiów podyplomowych*

Special Facilities: Computer labs; Audio-visual rooms; Laboratory of physical education; Laboratories (Agriculture; Nursing; Fine Arts; Engineering)

Last Updated: 04/09/11

THE JAN KOCHANOWSKI UNIVERSITY OF HUMANITIES AND SCIENCE IN KIELCE

Uniwersytet Humanistyczno-Przyrodniczy Jana Kochanowskiego w Kielce (AŚ)

ul. S. Żeromskiego 5, 25-369 Kielce, świętokrzyskie
Tel: +48(41) 344-20-11
Fax: +48(41) 344-88-05
EMail: rector@pu.kielce.pl
Website: http://www.pu.kielce.pl

Rektor: Regina Renz (2000-)
Tel: +48(41) 344-23-14 EMail: Rektor@ujk.edu.pl

Kanclerz: Janina Pierścińska
Tel: +48(41) 349-72-13 EMail: Kanclerz@ujk.edu.pl

International Relations: Joanna Wilk, Head, Department of Science and International Relations
Tel: +48(41) 349-72-30 EMail: Dzial.Nauki@ujk.edu.pl

Campuses

Piotrków (Administration; Economic History; Education; History; International Relations; Management; Philology; Polish; Protective Services; Social Sciences; Sociology)

Faculties

Health Sciences (Gynaecology and Obstetrics; Health Sciences; Medicine; Midwifery; Nursing; Physical Therapy; Public Health); **Humanities** (Arts and Humanities; English; German; History; Information Sciences; Journalism; Library Science; Literature; Mass Communication; Philology; Polish; Russian); **Management and Administration** (Administration; Business Administration; Economics; European Studies; Management; Political Sciences; Transport Management); **Mathematics and Natural Sciences** (Applied Physics; Biology; Biotechnology; Chemistry; Computer Science; Econometrics; Environmental Management; Environmental Studies; Geography; Mathematics; Natural Sciences; Physics); **Pedagogy and Art** (Art Education; Design; Education; Fine Arts; Music Education; Pedagogy; Psychology; Social Work)

Units

Foreign Languages *(Interfaculty)* (Danish; Dutch; English; French; German; Italian; Modern Languages; Portuguese; Russian; Spanish); **Physical Education and Sports** *(Interfaculty)* (Physical Education; Sports)

Further Information: Branch in Piotrkow Trybulnaski

History: Founded 1969 as Higher School of Pedagogy. Reorganized as Pedagogical University 1973, named after Jan Kochanowski 1979, and acquired present status and title 2000.

Governing Bodies: Senate

Academic Year: October to June (October-January; February-June)

Admission Requirements: Secondary school certificate (Matura) and entrance examination

Fees: (US Dollars): Foreign students, c. 1,500 per annum

Main Language(s) of Instruction: Polish

International Co-operation: Participates in LLP-Erasmus programme.

Accrediting Agencies: Ministry of Science and Higher Education

Degrees and Diplomas: *Inżynier*; *Licencjat*; *Świadectwo ukończenia studiów podyplomowych*; *Magister*; *Doktor*

Student Services: Canteen, Cultural centre, Health services, Sports facilities

Libraries: Central Library, c. 452,460 vols; 17,000 periodical subscriptions

Publications: Głos Akademicki *(monthly)*; Zeszyty Naukowe

Academic Staff *2010-2011*	**TOTAL**
FULL-TIME	**996**
Student Numbers *2009-2010*	
All (Foreign Included)	**19,831**
FOREIGN ONLY	**9**

Part-time students, 7,472.

Last Updated: 28/09/11

THE JERZY KUKUCZKA ACADEMY OF PHYSICAL EDUCATION

Akademia Wychowania Fizycznego im. Jerzego Kukuczki w Katowicach (AWF)

ul. Mikołowska 72A, 40-065 Katowice, śląskie
Tel: +48(32) 207-51-00
Fax: +48(32) 207-52-00
EMail: rektorat@awf.katowice.pl
Website: http://www.awf.katowice.pl

Rektor: Zbigniew Waśkiewicz
Tel: +48(32) 207-51-52, Fax: +48(32) 207-52-00

Kanclerz: Maciej Górski
Tel: +48(32) 207-51-16, Fax: +48(32) 251-68-68
EMail: secretariat@awf.katowice.pl

International Relations: Piotr Rodak, International Affairs Officer
Tel: +48(32) 207-52-34, Fax: +48(32) 207-52-00
EMail: p.rodak@awf.katowice.pl

Departments

Foreign Languages *(Interdepartmental)* (English; Modern Languages)

Faculties

Physical Education (Anatomy; Anthropology; Biochemistry; Dance; Hygiene; Law; Medicine; Pedagogy; Philosophy; Physical Education; Physical Therapy; Physiology; Sociology; Sports; Sports Medicine; Statistics); **Physiotherapy** (Cardiology; Neurological Therapy; Neurology; Orthopaedics; Physical Therapy; Pneumology; Rehabilitation and Therapy; Safety Engineering; Sports); **Sports and Tourism Management** (Ecology; Environmental Studies; Sports; Sports Management; Tourism; Yoga)

Programmes

Postgraduate studies (Health Education; Physical Education; Physical Therapy; Protective Services; Rehabilitation and Therapy; Sports; Sports Management; Tourism)

History: Founded 1970 as Higher School, acquired present status and title 1979.

Governing Bodies: Senate

Academic Year: October to June

Admission Requirements: Secondary school certificate (Matura) and entrance examinations

Fees: (US Dollars): Foreign students, c. 4,000 per annum

Main Language(s) of Instruction: Polish

Accrediting Agencies: Ministry of Science and Higher Education

Degrees and Diplomas: *Licencjat*; *Świadectwo ukończenia studiów podyplomowych*; *Magister*; *Doktor*

Student Services: Sports facilities

Student Residential Facilities: For c. 250 students

Libraries: Central Library, c. 40,000 vols

Publications: Roczniki Naukowe Akademii Wychowania Fizycznego w Katowicach, Silesian Scientific Annual of AWF *(annually)*; Zeszyty Naukowe Akademii Wychowania Fizycznego w Katowicach, AWF Scientific Letters *(biennially)*

Last Updated: 08/09/11

THE KARKONOSZE STATE HIGHER SCHOOL IN JELENIA GÓRA

Karkonoska Państwowa Szkoła Wyższa w Jeleniej Górze (KK PWSZ)

ul. Lwówecka 18, 58-503 Jelenia Góra, dolnośląskie
Tel: +48(75) 645-33-00
Fax: +48(75) 645-33-10
EMail: rektorat@kpswjg.pl
Website: http://www.kk.jgora.pl

Rektor: Henryk Gradkowski (2008-)
Tel: +48(75) 645-33-11 EMail: tomasz.winnicki@kk.jgora.pl

Chancellor: Grażyna Malczuk
Tel: +48(75) 642-05-26 EMail: kkpwsz@go2.pl

International Relations: Andrzej Mochola, Rector's Plenipotentiary for International Relations
Tel: +48(75) 642-05-13 EMail: kkpwsz@go2.pl

Faculties

Humanities (Arts and Humanities; Communication Studies; History; Journalism; Pedagogy; Philology; Polish); **Natural Sciences** (Natural Sciences; Nursing; Physical Education; Physical Therapy); **Technology** (Computer Education; Electronic Engineering; Production Engineering; Safety Engineering; Technology; Technology Education; Telecommunications Engineering)

Programmes

Postgraduate Studies (Child Care and Development; Computer Engineering; Computer Networks; Computer Science; Education; Health Sciences; Information Technology; Preschool Education; Rehabilitation and Therapy; Safety Engineering; Sports; Sports Management)

History: Founded 1998, a higher State vocational education institution. Formerly know as Kolegium Karkonoskie - Państwowa Wyższa Szkoła Zawodowa w Jeleniej Górze (Karkonosze College - State Higher Vocational School, Jelenia Góra).

Governing Bodies: Senate

Main Language(s) of Instruction: Polish

Accrediting Agencies: Ministry of Science and Higher Education

Degrees and Diplomas: *Inżynier*; *Licencjat*; *Świadectwo ukończenia studiów podyplomowych*
Last Updated: 19/09/11

THE KAROL LIPIŃSKI ACADEMY OF MUSIC, WROCŁAW

Akademia Muzyczna im. Karola Lipińskiego we Wrocławiu (AMUZ)

pl. Jana Pawła II nr 2, 50-043 Wrocław, dolnośląskie
Tel: +48(71) 355-55-43
Fax: +48(71) 355-28-49
EMail: info@amuz.wroc.pl
Website: http://www.amuz.wroc.pl

Rektor: Krystian Kiełb (2008-)
Tel: +48(71) 355-90-56, Fax: +48(71) 355-91-05
EMail: rektor@amuz.wroc.pl

Kanclerz: Danuta Koprowska
Tel: +48(71) 355-28-49, Fax: +48(71) 355-28-49
EMail: danuta.koprowska@amuz.wroc.pl

International Relations: Maria Brzuchowska, International Relations Coordinator
Tel: +48(71) 355-55-43 Ext. 115, Fax: +48(71) 355-28-49
EMail: maria.brzuchowska@amuz.wroc.pl

Faculties

Composition, Conducting, Music Theory and Music Therapy (Art Therapy; Conducting; Music; Music Theory and Composition); **Music Education** (Music; Music Education; Religious Music; Singing); **Musical Instruments** (Jazz and Popular Music; Music; Musical Instruments); **Vocal Studies** (Music; Singing)

Units

Foreign Languages *(Interfaculty)* (English; German; Italian; Modern Languages)

Further Information: Also postgraduate studies

History: Founded 1948 as School of Music, acquired present status and title 1981.

Governing Bodies: Senate

Academic Year: October to June

Admission Requirements: Secondary school of music certificate (Dyplom)

Fees: (Euros): 2,000 per annum

Main Language(s) of Instruction: Polish

International Co-operation: Socrates/Erasmus programme

Accrediting Agencies: Ministry of Culture

Degrees and Diplomas: *Licencjat*; *Świadectwo ukończenia studiów podyplomowych*; *Magister*; *Doktor*

Student Services: Academic counselling, Canteen, Cultural centre, Foreign student adviser, Foreign Studies Centre, Handicapped facilities, Health services, Language programs, Sports facilities

Student Residential Facilities: For 150 students

Special Facilities: Audiovisual Studio. Computer Music Studio

Libraries: Central Library, c. 10,000 vols

Publications: Zeszyty Naukowe, Academic publication

Last Updated: 06/09/11

THE LUDWIK SOLSKI STATE DRAMA SCHOOL IN KRAKÓW

Państwowa Wyższa Szkoła Teatralna im. Ludwika Solskiego w Krakowie (PWST)

ul. Straszewskiego 21/22, 31-109 Kraków, małopolskie
Tel: +48(12) 422-18-55 +48(12) 422-57-01
Fax: +48(12) 422-02-09
EMail: sekretariat@pwst.krakow.pl
Website: http://www.pwst.krakow.pl/

Rektor: Ewa Kutrys (2008-)
Tel: +48(12) 422-81-96 EMail: rektor@pwst.krakow.pl

Dyrektor Administracyjny: Franciszek Gałuszka
Tel: +48(12) 430-15-91 EMail: secretariat@pwst.krakow.pl

International Relations: Ewa Domagała
EMail: ewad@pwst.krakow.pl

Faculties

Acting *(Wrocław)* (Acting; Theatre); **Acting** (Acting; Performing Arts; Singing; Theatre); **Dance Theatre** *(Bytom)* (Acting; Dance; Performing Arts; Theatre); **Drama Directing** (Management; Performing Arts; Theatre); **Puppetry** *(Wrocław)* (Theatre); **Theatre Directing for Children and Youth** *(Postgraduate - Wrocław)* (Performing Arts; Theatre)

History: Founded 1946, the first State theatre academy created after World War II by the Ministry of Culture and Art, incorporating three Drama Workshops. Acquired present status and title 1991, named after Ludwik Solski.

Governing Bodies: Senate; Faculty Council

Academic Year: October to June (October-January; February-June)

Admission Requirements: Secondary school certificate (świadectwo maturalne)

Fees: (US Dollars): Foreign students, c. 8,000 per annum; none for Polish students

Main Language(s) of Instruction: Polish

International Co-operation: With universities in Czech Republic, Slovakia, Spain, Latvia, Estonia, Russia, Ukraine, France, Italy and Germany; Participates in the Socrates/Erasmus programme

Accrediting Agencies: Ministry of Science and Higher Education

Degrees and Diplomas: *Świadectwo ukończenia studiów podyplomowych*; *Magister*

Student Services: Canteen, Cultural centre, Employment services, Foreign student adviser, Foreign Studies Centre, Health services, Language programs, Nursery care, Sports facilities

Student Residential Facilities: Yes

Special Facilities: Art Gallery. Sound Studio

Libraries: Central Library, c. 30,000 vols

Publications: Zeszyty Teatralne PWST, Theatrical Publication

Last Updated: 20/09/11

THE MAIN SCHOOL OF FIRE SERVICE IN WARSAW

Szkoła Główna Służby Pożarniczej w Warszawie (SGSP)

ul. J. Słowackiego 52/54, 01-629 Warszawa, mazowieckie
Tel: +48(22) 561-77-00
Fax: +48(22) 833-07-24
EMail: sgsp@sgsp.edu.pl
Website: http://www.sgsp.edu.pl

Rektor: Ryszard Dąbrowa (2009-) EMail: rektor@sgsp.edu.pl

Prorektor: Elżbieta Kępka-Wnęk Tel: +48(22) 833-39-80

International Relations: Thomas Zwęglińsk, Head, International Cooperation Department
Tel: +48(22) 561-77-46 EMail: tzweglinski@sgsp.edu.pl

Faculties

Civil Safety Engineering (Construction Engineering; Environmental Engineering; Fire Science; Information Management; Management; Mass Communication; Peace and Disarmament; Safety Engineering; Social Sciences); **Fire Safety Engineering** (Building Technologies; Chemistry; Communication Studies; Construction Engineering; Electrical Engineering; Engineering Management; Fire Science; Information Management; Information Technology; Mass Communication; Mathematics; Mechanics; Medicine; Physics; Protective Services; Safety Engineering)

Units

Foreign Languages *(Inter-faculty)* (English; German; Modern Languages; Russian); **Physical Education** *(Inter-faculty)* (Physical Education)

History: Founded 1971 as Wyższa Oficerska Szkoła Pożarnicza, acquired present status and title 1982.

Governing Bodies: Senate

Academic Year: October - June

Admission Requirements: Secondary school certificate (Matura) and entrance examinations

Fees: (New Złoty): Extra-mural students, 2,100 per semester; postgraduate students, 3,000-4,200 per annum (day students, none)

Main Language(s) of Instruction: Polish

Accrediting Agencies: Ministry of Science and Higher Education; Ministry of Interior and Administration

Degrees and Diplomas: *Inżynier*; *Świadectwo ukończenia studiów podyplomowych*; *Magister*

Student Services: Academic counselling, Canteen, Cultural centre, Employment services, Health services, Social counselling, Sports facilities

Libraries: SGSP Main Library

Publications: Zeszyty Naukowe Szkoły Głównej Służby Pożarniczej *(other/irregular)*

Last Updated: 27/09/11

THE MARIA GRZEGORZEWSKA ACADEMY OF SPECIAL EDUCATION

Akademia Pedagogiki Specjalnej im. Marii Grzegorzewskiej w Warszawie (APS)

ul. Szczęśliwicka 40, 02-353 Warszawa, mazowieckie
Tel: +48(22) 589-36-00
Fax: +48(22) 658-11-18
EMail: aps@aps.edu.pl
Website: http://www.aps.edu.pl

Rektor: Jan Łaszczyk (2008-)
Tel: +48(22) 822-71-34 +48(22) 589-36-00
EMail: laszczyk@aps.edu.pl

Kanclerz: Maciej Olejniczak
Tel: +48(22) 589-36-23 +48(22) 589-36-00 Ext. 3224
EMail: molejniczak@aps.edu.pl

International Relations: Anna Firkowska-Mankiewicz, Deputy Rector Tel: +48(22) 824-36-94 EMail: naukapro@aps.edu.pl

Colleges

Foreign Languages (English; French; German; Modern Languages; Russian)

Faculties

Applied Social Sciences (Clinical Psychology; Psychology; Social Policy; Social Psychology; Social Sciences; Social Work; Sociology; Welfare and Protective Services); **Pedagogical Sciences** (Art Education; Art Therapy; Education; Educational Administration; Educational Psychology; Information Technology; Occupational Therapy; Pedagogy; Preschool Education; Psychology; Rehabilitation and Therapy; Special Education; Speech Therapy and Audiology)

History: Founded 1922 as State Institute of Special Education, reorganized as College for Special Education 'Maria Grzegorzewska' 1976, and acquired present status and title 2000.

Governing Bodies: Senate

Academic Year: October to June

Admission Requirements: Secondary school certificate (Świadectwo dojrzałości)

Fees: (New Złoty): Extramural studies, 2,450 per year. Postgraduate studies: 1,200-2,500 per term

Main Language(s) of Instruction: Polish; Some Postgraduate programmes in English

Accrediting Agencies: Ministry of Science and Higher Education, The State Accreditation Committee

Degrees and Diplomas: *Licencjat*; *Świadectwo ukończenia studiów podyplomowych*; *Magister*, *Doktor*

Student Services: Academic counselling, Canteen, Cultural centre, Employment services, Handicapped facilities, Health services, Social counselling, Sports facilities

Student Residential Facilities: For 478 students

Special Facilities: Maria Grzegorzewska Museum. Maria Grzegorzewska Foundation

Libraries: Main Library, 120,642 vols

Publications: APSolut *(bimonthly)*; Szkoła Specjalna (Special School) *(bimonthly)*

Press or Publishing House: ASE Publishing House

Academic Staff *2008-2009*	MEN	WOMEN	**TOTAL**
FULL-TIME	–	–	**289**
Student Numbers *2008-2009*			
All (Foreign Included)	1,400	5,600	c. **7,000**
FOREIGN ONLY	–	–	**10**

Last Updated: 06/09/11

THE POLISH NATIONAL FILM, TELEVISION AND THEATER SCHOOL IN ŁÓDŹ

Państwowa Wyższa Szkoła Filmowa, Telewizyjna i Teatralna im. Leona Schillera w Łodzi (PWSFTVIT)

ul. Targowa 61/63, 90-323 Łódź, łódzkie
Tel: +48(42) 634-58-00
Fax: +48(42) 674-81-39
EMail: rektorat@filmschool.lodz.pl
Website: http://www.filmschool.lodz.pl

Rektor: Robert Gliński (2008-)
Tel: +48(42) 634-58-14, Fax: +48(42) 674-81-39
EMail: wozniak@filmschool.lodz.pl

Kanclerz: Igor Duniewski
EMail: administracja@filmschool.lodz.pl; iduniewski@filmschool.lodz.pl

International Relations: Andrzej Bednarek, Vice President of International Affairs
Tel: +48(42) 634-58-20, Fax: +48(42) 634-59-28
EMail: swzfilm@filmschool.lodz.pl

Departments

Acting (Acting; Art History; Cultural Studies; Music; Physical Education; Sports); **Animation Directing and Special Effects** (Aesthetics; Art History; Cinema and Television; Display and Stage Design; Film; Literature; Music; Philosophy; Software Engineering; Technology; Theatre; Visual Arts); **Cinematography** (Cinema and Television; Music; Photography; Technology; Visual Arts); **Editing** (Film; Technology); **Film and Television Directing** (Cinema and Television; Film); **Film and Television Production Management** (Film; Management; Mass Communication; Radio and Television Broadcasting); **Photography** (Photography); **Screenwriting** (Cinema and Television; Writing)

Programmes

Postgraduate Studies (Film; Management; Mass Communication; Radio and Television Broadcasting)

History: Founded 1948.

Academic Year: October to June (October-January; February-June)

Admission Requirements: Secondary school certificate (Matura) and entrance examinations

Fees: (New Złoty): Undergraduate programmes, 2,000-10,000 per annum; Graduate programmes, 6,000-13,000 per annum.

Main Language(s) of Instruction: Polish

International Co-operation: With institutions in UK; Germany; France; Russian Federation

Accrediting Agencies: Ministry of Science and Higher Education

Degrees and Diplomas: *Licencjat*; *Świadectwo ukończenia studiów podyplomowych*; *Magister*

Student Services: Academic counselling, Canteen, Foreign student adviser, Health services, Language programs, Sports facilities

Student Residential Facilities: Student hostel

Special Facilities: Movie Studio. TV Studio. Theatre

Libraries: Main Library, c. 50,000 vols; c. 450 periodical subscriptions.

Last Updated: 20/09/11

THE SCHOOL OF HIGHER VOCATIONAL EDUCATION IN NYSA

Państwowa Wyższa Szkoła Zawodowa w Nysie (PWSZ)

ul. Armii Krajowej 7, 48-300 Nysa, opolskie
Tel: +48(77) 448-47-00
Fax: +48(77) 435-29-89
EMail: sekretariat@pwsz.nysa.pl
Website: http://www.pwsz.nysa.pl

Rector: Zofia Wilimowska (2008-)
Tel: +48(77) 448-47-03 EMail: rektor@pwsz.nysa.pl

Chancellor: Zbigniew Szlempo Tel: +48(77) 409-22-70

International Relations: Monika Witt, Prorector
Tel: +48(77) 409-08-60 EMail: mwitt@pwsz.nysa.pl

Institutes

Architecture (Architecture); **Cosmetology** (Cosmetology); **Finance** (Accountancy; Finance); **Foreign Languages** (Modern Languages); **Fundamental Sciences** (Natural Sciences); **History** (History); **Informatics** (Computer Networks; Computer Science); **Internal Security** (Economic History; Information Sciences; Protective Services); **Jazz** (Jazz and Popular Music); **Management** (Management; Production Engineering); **Modern Languages** (English; German; Modern Languages; Philology); **Nursing** (Nursing); **Nutrition** (Nutrition); **Physical Education** (Physical Education; Sports); **Public Health** (Public Health)

History: Founded 2001.

Degrees and Diplomas: *Inżynier*; *Licencjat*; *Świadectwo ukończenia studiów podyplomowych*

Libraries: 31,316 vols; 154 magazines; special collections, 1,073 items.
Last Updated: 03/09/11

THE STANISŁAW MONIUSZKO ACADEMY OF MUSIC

Akademia Muzyczna im. S. Moniuszki w Gdańsku (AMUZ)
ul. Łąkowa 1/2, 80-743 Gdańsk, pomorskie
Tel: +48(58) 300-92-01
Fax: +48(58) 300-92-10
EMail: muzyczna@amuz.gda.pl
Website: http://www.amuz.gda.pl

Rektor: Bogdan Kułakowski EMail: rektor@amuz.gda.pl

Dyrektor Administracyjny: Piotr Żerko
Tel: +48(58) 300-92-01, Fax: +48(58) 300-92-10
EMail: kanclerz@amuz.gda.pl

International Relations: Elizabeth Rosińska, Erasmus Coordinator
Tel: +48(58) 300-92-13 EMail: e.rosinska@amuz.gda.pl

Departments

Foreign Languages (English; French; German; Italian; Latin; Modern Languages; Russian; Swedish); **Pedagogy** (Music Education; Pedagogy); **Physical Education** (Physical Education)

Faculties

Choral Conducting, Music Education and Rhythmics (Conducting; Jazz and Popular Music; Multimedia; Music; Music Education; Music Theory and Composition; Religious Music; Singing); **Conducting, Composition and Theory of Music** (Conducting; Music; Music Theory and Composition); **Musical Instruments** (Music; Music Education; Musical Instruments); **Vocal and Acting** (Acting; Music; Singing)

Programmes

Postgraduate Studies (Conducting; Music Theory and Composition; Musical Instruments)

History: Founded 1947, acquired present status 1962.

Fees: (New Złoty): Undergraduate programmes, 500-2,900 per semester; Postgraduate courses, c. 1,800 per semester. Foreign students, (Euro) c. 2,800 per annum.

Main Language(s) of Instruction: Polish

International Co-operation: Participates in the Erasmus programme: agreements with universities in Austria, Belgium, Bulgaria, Denmark, Estonia, Finland, France, Germany, Iceland, Italy, Latvia, Lithuania, Netherlands, Portugal, Sweden, Turkey, United Kingdom.

Accrediting Agencies: Ministry of Science and Higher Education

Degrees and Diplomas: *Licencjat*; *Świadectwo ukończenia studiów podyplomowych*; *Magister*

Libraries: c. 90,000 vols; Audio library: 15,000 audio recordings;

Publications: Prace specjalne-Zeszyty Naukowe *(other/irregular)*

Press or Publishing House: Wydawnictwo Akademii Muzycznej w Gdańsku

Student Numbers *2010-2011*: Total: c. 700
Last Updated: 06/09/11

THE STATE HIGHER SCHOOL OF VOCATIONAL EDUCATION IN ZAMOŚĆ

Państwowa Wyższa Szkoła Zawodowa im. Szymona Szymonowica w Zamościu (PWSZ)
ul. Akademicka 8, 22-400 Zamość, lubelskie
Tel: +48(84) 638-34-44 +48(84) 638-35-55
Fax: +48(84) 638-35-00
EMail: rektorat@pwszzamosc.pl
Website: http://www.pwszzamosc.pl

Rektor: Waldemar Martyn

Kanclerz: Jerzy Korniluk

Centres

Entrepreneurship (Business Administration; Management)

Departments

Foreign Languages (English; French; German; Modern Languages; Russian); **Physical Education** (Physical Education; Sports)

Institutes

Humanities (Arts and Humanities; English; Foreign Languages Education; Hotel Management; Native Language Education; Parks and Recreation; Philology; Polish; Political Sciences; Public Relations; Regional Studies; Russian; Tourism; Translation and Interpretation); **Mathematics and Technology Innovation** (Computer Engineering; Mathematics; Technology); **Natural Sciences and Technology** (Biology; Construction Engineering; Energy Engineering; Environmental Studies; Health Sciences; Materials Engineering; Natural Sciences; Safety Engineering; Technology)

History: Founded 2005. Acquired present title 2009.

Governing Bodies: Senate

Main Language(s) of Instruction: Polish

Degrees and Diplomas: *Inżynier*; *Licencjat*; *Świadectwo ukończenia studiów podyplomowych*

Student Residential Facilities: Yes

Libraries: c. 8,000 vols

Press or Publishing House: FACT Simonidis
Last Updated: 05/09/11

THE STATE HIGHER VOCATIONAL SCHOOL IN KOSZALIN

Państwowa Wyższa Szkoła Zawodowa w Koszalinie (PWSZ)
ul. Leśna 1, 75-582 Koszalin, zachodniopomorskie
Tel: +48(94) 342-67-66
Fax: +48(94) 341-65-86
EMail: pwsz-koszalin@wp.pl
Website: http://www.pwsz-koszalin.pl/

Rektor: Waldemar Żarski

Kanclerz: Beata Koronkiewicz

Institutes

Human Sciences (Arts and Humanities; Education; Nursing; Philology; Polish); **Modern Languages** (English; French; German; Modern Languages; Philology; Physical Education; Tourism)

Programmes

Postgraduate Studies (Child Care and Development; Communication Studies; Education; Media Studies; Physical Education; Psychology; Rehabilitation and Therapy)

History: Founded 2009.

Fees: (New Złoty): Postgraduate programmes, 1,000-1,500 per semester

Degrees and Diplomas: *Licencjat*; *Licencjat*: Nursing; *Świadectwo ukończenia studiów podyplomowych*

Libraries: c. 20,000 vols
Last Updated: 05/09/11

THE STATE HIGHER VOCATIONAL SCHOOL IN SKIERNIEWICE

Państwowa Wyższa Szkoła Zawodowa w Skierniewicach (PWSZ)

ul. Batorego 64C, 96-100 Skierniewice, łódzkie
Tel: +48(46) 834-40-00
Fax: +48(46) 834-40-07
EMail: dziekanat@pwsz.skierniewice.pl
Website: http://www.pwsz.skierniewice.pl

Rektor: Tadeusz Janusz
Tel: +48(46) 834-40-01 EMail: rektorat@pwsz.skierniewice.pl

Kanclerz: Jacek Śmiłowski
Tel: +48(46) 834-40-04 EMail: kanclerz@pwsz.skierniewice.pl

Faculties

Economics and Business Administration (Accountancy; Business Administration; Computer Science; Econometrics; Economics; European Studies; Finance; Information Technology; Management; Real Estate; Small Business; Taxation); **Natural Sciences and Engineering** (Computer Engineering; Computer Graphics; Cosmetology; Data Processing; Engineering; Food Technology; Health Sciences; Horticulture; Multimedia; Natural Sciences; Nutrition); **Sociology and Philology** (Communication Studies; Human Resources; Media Studies; Philology; Polish; Social Work; Sociology)

Programmes

Postgraduate Studies (Agricultural Economics; Agriculture; Horticulture; Landscape Architecture; Rural Planning)

History: Founded 2005.

Degrees and Diplomas: *Inżynier*, *Licencjat*, *Świadectwo ukończenia studiów podyplomowych*
Last Updated: 04/09/11

THE STATE SCHOOL OF HIGHER EDUCATION IN CHEŁM

Państwowa Wyższa Szkoła Zawodowa w Chełmie (PWSZ)

ul. Pocztowa 54, 22-100 Chełm, lubelskie
Tel: +48(82) 565-88-95
Fax: +48(82) 565-88-94
EMail: rektorat@pwsz.chelm.pl
Website: http://www.pwsz.chelm.pl/

Rector: Józef Zając

Kanclerz: Marian Różański
Tel: +48(82) 565-54-11 EMail: kanclerz@pwsz.chelm.pl

International Relations: Arkadiusz Tofil, Vice Rector for Development and International Relations Tel: +48(82) 562-06-07

Centres

Postgraduate studies (Agricultural Economics; Agriculture; Air Transport; Biology; Child Care and Development; Civics; Computer Graphics; Computer Science; Cultural Studies; Design; Educational Administration; Higher Education; History; Information Technology; Labour and Industrial Relations; Mathematics; Mathematics Education; Peace and Disarmament; Philology; Physics; Polish; Preschool Education; Protective Services)

Departments

Foreign Languages *(Interfaculty Unit)* (English; Modern Languages); **Physical Education** *(Interfaculty Unit)* (Physical Education; Sports)

Institutes

Agricultural Sciences (Agriculture); **Humanities** (Arts and Humanities; History; Philology; Polish); **Mathematics and Information Technology** (Computer Science; Information Technology; Mathematics; Pedagogy); **Neophilology** (English; German; International Relations; Modern Languages; Philology); **Technical Sciences** (Building Technologies; Electrical Engineering; Mechanical Engineering; Mechanics)

Degrees and Diplomas: *Inżynier*, *Licencjat*, *Świadectwo ukończenia studiów podyplomowych*
Last Updated: 20/09/11

THE STATE SCHOOL OF HIGHER EDUCATION IN OŚWIĘCIM

Państwowa Wyższa Szkoła Zawodowa im. rotmistrza Witolda Pileckiego w Oświęcimiu (PWSZ)

ul. Kolbego 8, 32-600 Oświęcim
Tel: +48(33) 843-06-91 +48(33) 843-06-87
Fax: +48(33) 843-05-30
EMail: sekretariat@pwsz-oswiecim.edu.pl
Website: http://www.pwsz-oswiecim.edu.pl/

Rektor: Lucjan Suchanek Tel: +48(33) 843-07-14

Kanclerz: Adam Bilski
Tel: +48(33) 843-06-87, Fax: +48(33) 843-06-91
EMail: kanclerz@pwsz-oswiecim.edu.pl

Institutes

Management (Business Administration; Cultural Studies; Educational Administration; Management; Public Administration; Social Sciences; Tourism); **Nursing** (Biomedicine; Nursing); **Pedagogy** (Pedagogy); **Philology** (English; German; Linguistics; Philology; Russian; Translation and Interpretation); **Political Sciences** (Communication Studies; Germanic Studies; Human Rights; International Relations; Jewish Studies; Media Studies; Political Sciences)

Programmes

Postgraduate Studies (Computer Graphics; Management)

History: Founded 2005.

Fees: (New Złoty): Postgraduate programme, 2,950 per annum.

Main Language(s) of Instruction: Polish

International Co-operation: Participates in the Erasmus programme

Degrees and Diplomas: *Licencjat*, *Świadectwo ukończenia studiów podyplomowych*
Last Updated: 05/09/11

THE STATE SCHOOL OF HIGHER PROFESSIONAL EDUCATION IN ELBLĄG

Państwowa Wyższa Szkoła Zawodowa w Elblągu (PWSZ)

ul. Wojska Polskiego 1, 82-300 Elbląg, warmińsko-mazurskie
Tel: +48(55) 239-88-50
Fax: +48(55) 239-88-52
EMail: pwsz@pwsz.elblag.pl
Website: http://www.pwsz.elblag.pl

Rektor: Zbigniew Walczyk
Tel: +48(55) 239-88-55, Fax: +48(55) 239-88-92
EMail: rektor@pwsz.elblag.pl

Kanclerz: Bohdan Niemirycz Tel: +48(55) 239-88-50

International Relations: Iwona Dwojacka, International Officer, Erasmus Coordinator
Tel: +48(55) 239-88-09 EMail: br@pwsz.elblag.pl

Institutes

Applied Informatics (Computer Education; Computer Engineering; Computer Graphics; Computer Networks; Data Processing; Multimedia; Software Engineering); **Economics** (Administration; Business Administration; Economics; Educational Administration; Finance; Management); **Pedagogy and Languages** (Computer Education; Educational and Student Counselling; English; German; Modern Languages; Pedagogy; Philology; Polish; Translation and Interpretation); **Technology** (Automation and Control Engineering; Construction Engineering; Electrical Engineering; Environmental Engineering; Machine Building; Mechanical Engineering)

History: Founded 1998.

Main Language(s) of Instruction: Polish

International Co-operation: With universities in Russia, Sweden, Lithuania, Norway, Czech Republic, Greece, Spain, Germany, Romania, Slovakia, Hungary. Participates in the Erasmus Programme.

Accrediting Agencies: Ministry of Science and Higher Education

Degrees and Diplomas: *Inżynier*, *Licencjat*, *Świadectwo ukończenia studiów podyplomowych*

Student Services: Sports facilities

Special Facilities: Lecture hall with audio-visual equipment for 160 students; 19 computer laboratories; 2 languages laboratories; 11 specialistics laboratories.
Libraries: c. 62,000 vols.

Academic Staff *2010-2011*: TOTAL 204
STAFF WITH DOCTORATE 75
Student Numbers *2010-2011*: Total: c. 3,500
Last Updated: 21/09/11

THE STATE SCHOOL OF HIGHER PROFESSIONAL EDUCATION IN KONIN

Państwowa Wyższa Szkoła Zawodowa w Koninie (PWSZ)
ul. Przyjaźni 1, 62-510 Konin, wielkopolskie
Tel: +48(63) 249-72-02
Fax: +48(63) 249-72-01
EMail: rektorat@konin.edu.pl
Website: http://www.pwsz.konin.edu.pl

Rector: Wojciech Poznaniak (2008-)
Kanclerz: Zdzisław Dębowski
Tel: +48(63) 249-72-15, Fax: +48(63) 249-72-11
EMail: kanclerz@konin.edu.pl
International Relations: Renata Pietrzak
Tel: +48(63) 249-72-05 EMail: renatap@konin.edu.pl

Departments
Foreign Languages *(SPNJO - Interfaculty)* (English; Modern Languages); **Physical Education and Sports** *(SWFiS - Interfaculty)* (Physical Education; Sports)

Faculties
Civil Engineering and Municipal Installations *(Turku)* (Architecture; Civil Engineering; Environmental Engineering); **Physical Education and Health** *(Interdepartmental Unit)* (Parks and Recreation; Physical Education; Physical Therapy; Sports; Tourism); **Socio-Engineering** (Accountancy; Art Education; Automation and Control Engineering; Business Administration; Economics; Education; Engineering; English; European Studies; Finance; Foreign Languages Education; Geography; German; Government; Information Management; Information Sciences; Information Technology; Journalism; Machine Building; Management; Marketing; Materials Engineering; Media Studies; Modern Languages; Music Education; Philology; Polish; Political Sciences; Preschool Education; Production Engineering; Public Administration; Real Estate; Rehabilitation and Therapy; Social Work; Transport Engineering; Transport Management)

History: Founded 1998.
Governing Bodies: Senate
Admission Requirements: Secondary school certificate (matura) and entrance examinations
Main Language(s) of Instruction: Polish
Accrediting Agencies: Ministry of Science and Higher Education
Degrees and Diplomas: *Inżynier*; *Licencjat*; *Świadectwo ukończenia studiów podyplomowych*

Student Numbers *2010-2011*: Total: c. 4,000
Last Updated: 21/09/11

THE STATE SCHOOL OF HIGHER PROFESSIONAL EDUCATION IN PŁOCK

Państwowa Wyższa Szkoła Zawodowa w Płocku (PWSZ)
Plac Dąbrowskiego 2, 09-402 Płock, mazowieckie
Tel: +48(24) 366-54-20
Fax: +48(24) 366-54-20 Ext. 218
EMail: pwsz@pwszplock.pl
Website: http://www.pwszplock.pl/

Rector: Jacek Grzywacz (2008-)
Administrative Manager: Monika Nowakowska
International Relations: Agnieszka Dłużniewska

Departments
Foreign Languages (English; German; Modern Languages; Russian); **Physical Education and Sport** (Physical Education; Sports)

Institutes
Economics (Accountancy; Agricultural Business; Agricultural Economics; Economics; European Studies; Finance; International Business; Marketing; Public Administration; Tourism); **Education** (Art Education; Education; English; German; Music Education; Pedagogy; Preschool Education; Primary Education); **Health Sciences** (Health Sciences); **Mathematics and Computer Science** (Banking; Computer Graphics; Computer Networks; Data Processing; Insurance; Mathematics; Mathematics and Computer Science; Software Engineering); **Modern Languages** (English; German; Information Technology; Literature; Modern Languages; Philology; Russian; Social Studies)

Programmes
Computer Science (Computer Science)

History: Founded 1999.
Governing Bodies: Senate
Admission Requirements: Secondary school certificate (matura) and entrance examinations
Main Language(s) of Instruction: Polish
Accrediting Agencies: Ministry of Science and Higher Education
Degrees and Diplomas: *Licencjat*; *Świadectwo ukończenia studiów podyplomowych*
Last Updated: 03/09/11

THE STATE SCHOOL OF HIGHER VOCATIONAL EDUCATION IN CIECHANÓW

Państwowa Wyższa Szkoła Zawodowa w Ciechanowie (PWSZ)
ul. Narutowicza 9, 06-400 Ciechanów, mazowieckie
Tel: +48(23) 672-20-50
Fax: +48(23) 672-20-50
EMail: rektorat@pwszciechanow.edu.pl; kanclerz@pwszciechanow.edu.pl
Website: http://www.pwszciechanow.edu.pl

Rector: Andrzej Kolasa
Tel: +48(23) 672-20-50 EMail: rektorat@pwszciechanow.edu.pl
Kanclerz: Piotr Wójcik
Tel: +48(23) 673-75-78 EMail: kanclerz@pwszciechanow.edu.pl

Departments
Computer Science (Computer Engineering; Computer Science; Information Technology; Software Engineering)

Institutes
Economics (Administration; Banking; Business Administration; Econometrics; Economics; Finance; Law; Marketing; Mathematics; Statistics); **Engineering** (Engineering; Production Engineering); **Health Protection** (Health Sciences; Nursing; Public Health; Rehabilitation and Therapy); **History and Philology** (Electronic Engineering; History; Journalism; Mass Communication; Philology; Polish; Telecommunications Engineering); **Social and Cultural Studies** (Cultural Studies; Ethics; Literature; Philosophy; Social Sciences; Theatre)

Degrees and Diplomas: *Inżynier*; *Licencjat*; *Świadectwo ukończenia studiów podyplomowych.* Also Certificate.

Student Numbers *2010-2011*: Total: c. 1,800
Last Updated: 21/09/11

THE WITELON UNIVERSITY OF APPLIED SCIENCES IN LEGNICA

Państwowa Wyższa Szkoła Zawodowa im. Witelona w Legnicy (PWSZ)
ul. Parliamentary 5a, 59-220 Legnica, dolnośląskie
Tel: +48(76) 723-21-50 +48(76) 723-21-51
Fax: +48(76) 723-29-05
EMail: powsz@powsz.legnica.edu.pl
Website: http://www.pwsz.legnica.edu.pl

Rektor: Ryszard K. Pisarski (2008-)
Tel: +48(76) 723-20-82 EMail: niedzielaa@pwsz.legnica.edu.pl

Kanclerz: Robert M. Burba
Tel: +48(76) 723-20-81 EMail: burbar@pwsz.legnica.edu.pl

International Relations: Malgorzata Witkowska, Vice-Rector for Science and International Relations
Tel: +48(76) 723-23-47, Fax: +48(76) 723-29-05
EMail: witkowskam@pwsz.legnica.edu.pl

Faculties

Administration (Administration; Business Administration; Civil Security; Environmental Management; Environmental Studies; Management; Public Administration); **Education, Tourism and Recreation** (Adult Education; Education; English; Hotel and Restaurant; Parks and Recreation; Preschool Education; Primary Education; Rehabilitation and Therapy; Social Work; Tourism); **Humanities** (Arts and Humanities; English; German; Literature; Philology; Russian); **Management and Informatics** (Accountancy; Automation and Control Engineering; Computer Graphics; Computer Networks; Computer Science; Economics; Energy Engineering; Finance; Human Resources; Information Management; Information Technology; Management; Marketing; Multimedia; Production Engineering; Real Estate; Safety Engineering; Small Business; Transport Management); **Medicine** (Health Education; Law; Medicine; Nursing); **Political Science** (Communication Studies; European Studies; Political Sciences; Public Administration; Public Relations)

History: Founded 1998. Acquired present title 2003.

Governing Bodies: Senate; Assembly

Main Language(s) of Instruction: Polish

Accrediting Agencies: Ministry of Science and Higher Education

Degrees and Diplomas: *Inżynier*; *Świadectwo ukończenia studiów podyplomowych*; *Magister*

Last Updated: 03/09/11

UNIVERSITY OF AGRICULTURE IN KRAKOW

Uniwersytet Rolniczy w Krakowie im. Hugona Kołłątaja w Krakowie (AR)

al. A. Mickiewicza 21, 31-120 Kraków, małopolskie
Tel: +48(12) 662-42-83
Fax: +48(12) 633-62-45
EMail: rector@ar.krakow.pl
Website: http://www.ar.krakow.pl

Rektor: Janusz Żmija (2002-)
Tel: +48(12) 633-13-36, Fax: +48(12) 632-62-45

Kanclerz: Krzysztof Ziółkowski
Tel: +48(12) 662-42-80, Fax: +48(12) 662-42-98
EMail: k.ziolkowski@ur.krakow.pl

International Relations: Krystyna Koziec, Vice Rector for Research and International Relations
Tel: +48(12) 662-42-59, Fax: +48(12) 663-62-45
EMail: recsci@ar.krakow.pl

Centres

Continuing Education (Agricultural Business; Agricultural Management; Agriculture; Environmental Management; European Union Law; Food Technology; Forestry; Information Technology; Management; Marketing; Nutrition; Rural Planning; Safety Engineering)

Departments

Foreign Languages *(Interfaculty)* (English; French; German; Modern Languages; Russian); **Physical Education** *(Interfaculty)* (Physical Education; Sports)

Faculties

Agriculture and Economics (Agricultural Business; Agricultural Economics; Agriculture; Biology; Chemistry; Crop Production; Ecology; Economic and Finance Policy; Economics; English; Environmental Studies; European Union Law; Management; Marketing; Mathematics; Microbiology; Physics; Physiology; Plant and Crop Protection; Social Sciences; Sociology; Soil Conservation; Soil Science; Statistics; Tourism); **Animal Sciences** (Agricultural Economics; Anatomy; Animal Husbandry; Biology; Ecology; Embryology and Reproduction Biology; Endocrinology; Environmental Management; Fishery; Genetics; Hygiene; Meat and Poultry; Nutrition; Physiology; Zoology); **Environmental Engineering and Land Surveying** (Agriculture; Applied Mathematics; Building Technologies; Ecology; Environmental Engineering; Geological Engineering; Hydraulic Engineering; Meteorology; Regional Planning; Rural Planning; Surveying and Mapping; Waste Management; Water Management); **Food Technology** (Animal Husbandry; Biotechnology; Engineering; Food Technology; Home Economics; Machine Building; Microbiology; Nutrition; Safety Engineering; Vegetable Production); **Forestry** (Agricultural Engineering; Botany; Ecology; Entomology; Environmental Management; Forest Biology; Forest Management; Forestry; Genetics; Pathology; Soil Science; Transport Management; Wildlife); **Horticulture** (Agricultural Economics; Apiculture; Biochemistry; Bioengineering; Botany; Ecology; Environmental Management; Genetics; Horticulture; Marketing; Physiology; Plant and Crop Protection; Soil Management; Vegetable Production); **Production and Power Engineering** (Agricultural Engineering; Automation and Control Engineering; Computer Science; Ecology; Engineering Management; Food Technology; Forestry; Information Technology; Mechanical Engineering; Physics; Power Engineering; Production Engineering; Transport Management)

Programmes

Biotechnology *(Interfaculty)* (Biotechnology); **Landscape Architecture** *(Interfaculty)* (Landscape Architecture)

Units

Experimental Forestry *(Interfaculty)* (Forestry)

Further Information: Also Courses in English for foreign students in Agroecology ofered by the Faculty of Agriculture and Economics

History: Founded 1890 as Agronomy Department of Jagiellonian University, Cracow. Became faculty 1923 and independent institution 1953 as Higher College of Agriculture. Acquired present status and title 1972. Known as Academia Rolinicza until 2008.

Governing Bodies: Senate; Faculty Council

Academic Year: October to June (October-February; February-June)

Admission Requirements: Secondary school certificate (matura)

Fees: (New Złoty): Undergraduate, 1,500-1,700 per annum; postgraduate, 1,800-2,000 per semester. Foreign students, EUR 2,000 per annum

Main Language(s) of Instruction: Polish

International Co-operation: With universities in Czech Republic, Slovak Republic, Austria, Belgium, Belarus, Switzerland, Germany, USA, Ukraine, Russia, Taiwan, Finland, Greece, Netherland, Norway, France

Accrediting Agencies: Ministry of Science and Higher Education

Degrees and Diplomas: *Inżynier*; *Licencjat*; *Świadectwo ukończenia studiów podyplomowych*; *Magister*; *Doktor*

Student Services: Canteen, Cultural centre, Handicapped facilities, Health services, Sports facilities

Student Residential Facilities: For 1,548 students

Special Facilities: Experimental Forestry Station in Krynica

Libraries: Central Library, 625 256 vols

Publications: Acta Scientarum Polonoru, Krakow ed. series: Formatio Circumiectus; Zeszyty Naukowe Akademii Rolniczej, Scientific papers in Polish and English

Press or Publishing House: Dział Wydawnictw Akademii Rolniczej

Student Numbers *2010-2011*: Total: c. 13,000
Last Updated: 30/09/11

UNIVERSITY OF BIAŁYSTOK

Uniwersytet w Białymstoku (UWB)

ul. M. Skłodowskiej-Curie 14, 15-097 Białystok, podlaskie
Tel: +48(85) 745-70-00
Fax: +48(85) 745-70-73
EMail: uniwersytet@uwb.edu.pl
Website: http://www.uwb.edu.pl

Rektor: Jerzy Nikitorowicz
Tel: +48(85) 745-70-01 EMail: rektorat@uwb.edu.pl

Kanclerz: Tomasz Zalewski
Tel: +48(85) 745-71-15, Fax: +48(85) 745-70-73
EMail: kanclerz@uwb.edu.pl

International Relations: Beata Godlewska-Żyłkiewicz, Vice-Rector for Science and International Relations
Tel: +48(85) 745-70-65, Fax: +48(85) 745-70-73
EMail: prekt-n@uwb.edu.pl; ac-dwz@uwb.edu.pl

Faculties

Administration *(Siedlce)* (Administration; European Union Law; Finance; Management; Political Sciences; Private Law; Public Law); **Biology and Chemistry** (Biology; Chemistry; Environmental Studies); **Economics and Informatics** *(Vilnius, Lithuania)* (Computer Science; Economics); **Economics and Management** (Accountancy; Computer Science; Econometrics; Economics; Environmental Studies; Finance; Government; International Economics; International Relations; Management; Statistics); **History and Sociology** (Archiving; Central European Studies; Civics; Eastern European Studies; Heritage Preservation; History; International Relations; Sociology); **Law** (Administration; Commercial Law; Criminal Law; Development Studies; European Studies; European Union Law; Finance; Fiscal Law; Government; Health Administration; Law; Public Administration; Public Law); **Mathematics and Informatics** (Computer Education; Computer Science; Econometrics; Mathematics; Mathematics and Computer Science; Technology Education); **Pedagogy and Psychology** (Art History; Art Therapy; Child Care and Development; Cultural Studies; Education; Educational Administration; Educational and Student Counselling; Educational Psychology; Family Studies; Health Education; Pedagogy; Preschool Education; Primary Education; Protective Services; Psychology; Rehabilitation and Therapy; Safety Engineering; Social Work); **Philology** (Cultural Studies; English; French; Information Sciences; Journalism; Library Science; Philology; Polish; Public Relations; Russian; Slavic Languages; Speech Therapy and Audiology); **Physics** (Computer Science; Physics)

History: Founded 1968 as branch of Warsaw University, acquired present status and title 1997.

Governing Bodies: Senate

Academic Year: October to June (October-January; February-June)

Admission Requirements: Secondary school certificate (matura)

Main Language(s) of Instruction: Polish

International Co-operation: Participates in the Tempus, Socrates, Ceepus, and Lingua programmes

Accrediting Agencies: Ministry of Science and Higher Education

Degrees and Diplomas: *Licencjat*; *Świadectwo ukończenia studiów podyplomowych*; *Magister*, *Doktor*

Student Services: Canteen, Cultural centre, Handicapped facilities, Health services, Sports facilities

Student Residential Facilities: 3 Student's Houses

Libraries: Central library, 400,000 vols; specialized libraries, total, 320,000 vols

Publications: Nasz Uniwersytet - Our University *(quarterly)*

Academic Staff *2010-2011*: Total: c. 900

Student Numbers *2010-2011*: Total: c. 18,000

Last Updated: 03/10/11

UNIVERSITY OF BIELSKO-BIALA

Akademia Techniczno-Humanistyczna w Bielsku-Białej (ATH)

ul. Willowa 2, 43-309 Bielsko-Biała, śląskie
Tel: +48(33) 827-93-50
Fax: +48(33) 827-93-55
EMail: rektorat@ath.bielsko.pl
Website: http://www.ath.bielsko.pl

Rector: Ryszard TrombskiBarcik (2008-)
Tel: +48(33) 827-92-01, Fax: +48(33) 827-93-55
EMail: mtrombski@ath.bielsko.pl

Kanclerz: Leszek Zaporowski
Tel: +48(33) 827-93-20, Fax: +48(33) 827-93-00
EMail: lzaporowski@ath.bielsko.pl

International Relations: Hanna Lamers, Head, International Cooperation Department
Tel: +48(33) 827-92-39, Fax: +48(33) 827-93-56
EMail: hlamers@ath.bielsko.pl; international@ath.bielsko.pl

Centres

Computer Science (Computer Science)

Departments

Foreign Languages (English; French; German; Italian; Latin; Modern Languages); **Physical Education and Sports** (Physical Education; Sports); **Science** (Natural Sciences)

Faculties

Health Sciences (Health Sciences; Nursing); **Humanities and Social Sciences** (Anthropology; Arts and Humanities; Central European Studies; Czech; English; Pedagogy; Polish; Psychology; Russian; Slavic Languages; Social Sciences; Spanish); **Management and Computer Science** (Computer Science; Economics; European Union Law; Information Technology; International Relations; Management; Marketing; Sociology; Transport Management); **Materials and Environment Sciences** (Biology; Chemistry; Ecology; Engineering; Environmental Engineering; Environmental Studies; Hydraulic Engineering; Materials Engineering; Physics; Polymer and Plastics Technology; Textile Technology); **Mechanical Engineering and Computer Science** (Automation and Control Engineering; Automotive Engineering; Computer Science; Electrical Engineering; Engineering; Measurement and Precision Engineering; Mechanical Engineering; Mechanics; Production Engineering)

History: Founded 2001. An independent governmental academic institution. Previously, since 1969, a branch of the Technical University of Lodz (Politechnika Lódzka).

Academic Year: October to June (October - January; February - June)

Admission Requirements: Secondary school certificate "Matura", entrance examination for some faculties

Main Language(s) of Instruction: Polish

International Co-operation: Socrates, Ceepus, 6th Framework Program, Thematic networks, Open Distant Learning, Leonardo

Accrediting Agencies: Polish Accreditation Commission

Degrees and Diplomas: *Inżynier*, *Licencjat*; *Świadectwo ukończenia studiów podyplomowych*; *Magister*, *Doktor*

Student Services: Academic counselling, Foreign student adviser, Health services, Sports facilities

Special Facilities: Art Gallery

Libraries:c. 129,000 vols. Electronic access

Academic Staff *2010-2011*: Total 400

STAFF WITH DOCTORATE: Total 200

Student Numbers *2010-2011*: Total: c. 8,000

Last Updated: 08/09/11

UNIVERSITY OF ECONOMICS IN KATOWICE

Uniwersytet Ekonomiczny w Katowicach (UE)

ul. 1 Maja 50, 40-287 Katowice, śląskie
Tel: +48(32) 257-70-00
Fax: +48(32) 257-71-89
EMail: kancelaria@ue.katowice.pl; biuro.promocji@ue.katowice.pl
Website: http://www.ue.katowice.pl/

Rektor: Jan Pyka (2008-) Fax: +48(32) 257-71-13
EMail: rektor.sekretariat@ue.katowice.pl

Director of Administration: Włodzimierz Mitoraj
EMail: kancelaria@ue.katowice.pl

International Relations: Barbara Centkowska, Director, International Cooperation
Tel: +48(32) 257-71-22, Fax: +48(32) 257-71-25
EMail: barbara.centkowska@ue.katowice.pl

Academies

Economics for the Young (Business Administration; Economics; Finance; Management; Marketing)

Centres

Studies Conducted in Foreign Languages (Accountancy; Business Administration; English; Finance; Insurance; International Business; Management)

Faculties

Computer Science and Communication (Business Computing; Communication Studies; Computer Engineering; Computer Science; Data Processing; E-Business/Commerce; Information Management; Journalism; Management; Mass Communication; Media Studies; Multimedia; Public Relations; Software Engineering); **Economics** (Business Administration; Communication Studies; E-Business/Commerce; Economics; Environmental Studies; Human Resources; International Business; International Economics; Management; Public Administration; Public Relations; Real Estate; Regional Planning; Safety Engineering; Service Trades; Town Planning; Transport Economics; Transport Engineering; Transport Management); **Finance and Insurance** (Accountancy; Engineering; Finance; Health Administration; Insurance; Real Estate); **Management** (Computer Science; Econometrics; Economics; Finance; Human Resources; International Business; Management; Marketing; Statistics; Tourism; Transport Management)

Schools

Economics of Foreign Languages *(Silesian)* (Economics; English; French; German; Italian; Modern Languages; Russian); **International Business** *(Silesian)* (Accountancy; Business Administration; Civil Law; Commercial Law; E-Business/Commerce; Economics; English; Finance; French; Human Resources; Insurance; International Business; Management; Marketing; Operations Research; Real Estate; Statistics; Transport Management); **Stock Exchange** (Finance)

Units

Children's University of Economics *(EUD)* (Economics)

Further Information: Also Branch in Bielsko-Biała and Rybnik.

History: Founded 1936 as a private college (College of Social and Economic Sciences). Reorganized 1950 as Higher School of Economics, named after Karol Adamiecki 1972, and acquired present status and named Akademia Ekonomiczna im. Karola Adamieckiego w Katowicach (Karol Adamiecki University of Economics in Katowice) 1974. Acquired present title 2010.

Governing Bodies: Rector and Senate

Academic Year: October to June (October-February, February-June)

Admission Requirements: Secondary school certificate (matura), and entrance examination

Fees: (New Złoty): 2,100-2,400 per semester.

Main Language(s) of Instruction: Polish; English

International Co-operation: With universities in Austria, Belgium, Bulgaria, Czech Republic, Finland, France, Germany, Greece, Hungary, Ireland, Island, Italy, Latvia, Lithuania, Netherlands, Norway, Portugal, Romania, Spain, Slovakia, Slovenia,UK. Also participates in the Leonardo da Vinci, Ceepus, Tempus, Socrates/ Erasmus

Accrediting Agencies: State Accrediting Committee

Degrees and Diplomas: *Inżynier*; *Licencjat*; *Świadectwo ukończenia studiów podyplomowych*; *Magister*; *Doktor*

Student Services: Academic counselling, Canteen, Employment services, Foreign student adviser, Foreign Studies Centre, Handicapped facilities, Health services, Language programs, Sports facilities

Student Residential Facilities: For c. 690 students

Libraries: Central Library, c. 301,000 vols; specialized libraries, c. 34,700 vols

Publications: Journal of Economics and Management *(other/irregular)*; Studia Ekonomiczne *(3 per annum)*

Press or Publishing House: Wydawnictwo Uczelniane

Student Numbers *2010-2011*: Total: c. 2,100

Last Updated: 28/09/11

UNIVERSITY OF GDAŃSK

Uniwersytet Gdański (UG)

ul. Bażyńskiego 1a, 80-952 Gdańsk, pomorskie

Tel: +48(58) 552-91-00

Fax: +48(58) 552-03-11

EMail: rekug@univ.gda.pl

Website: http://www.ug.gda.pl

Rektor: Bernard Lammek (2008-)
Tel: +48(58) 523-24-07, Fax: +48(58) 523-57-00
EMail: rekug@ug.edu.pl

Kanclerz: Jerzy Gwizdała
Tel: +48(58) 523-20-08 EMail: kanclerz@ug.edu.pl

International Relations: Teresa Chocholska, Manager, International Relations Office
Tel: +48(32) 523-23-04 +48(32) 523-24-60,
Fax: +48(32) 523-24-37
EMail: rektc@ug.edu.pl; zagranica@ug.edu.pl

Centres

German Culture and Language *(Herder)* (German; Germanic Studies)

Departments

Foreign Languages (Arabic; Chinese; Economics; English; French; German; Information Technology; Italian; Japanese; Law; Modern Languages; Polish; Russian; Spanish; Swedish); **Physical Education and Sports** (Physical Education; Sports)

Faculties

Biology (Biology; Natural Sciences); **Biotechnology** *(Intercollegiate - UG and MUG)* (Biotechnology); **Chemistry** (Agriculture; Chemistry; Environmental Studies); **Economics** (Economics; Finance; International Business; International Economics; International Relations); **History** (Archaeology; Art History; Ethnology; History; Religious Studies; Tourism); **Law and Administration** (Administration; Law); **Management** (Accountancy; Computer Science; Econometrics; Finance; Management); **Mathematics, Physics and Informatics** (Computer Science; Mathematics; Medical Technology; Physics); **Oceanography and Geography** (Economics; Environmental Studies; Geography; Geology; Marine Science and Oceanography); **Philology** (Applied Linguistics; Cultural Studies; English; German; Philology; Polish; Romance Languages; Russian; Scandinavian Languages; Slavic Languages; Speech Therapy and Audiology; Theatre); **Social Sciences** (Journalism; Mass Communication; Pedagogy; Philosophy; Political Sciences; Psychology; Social Sciences; Social Welfare; Sociology; Special Education)

History: Founded 1970.

Governing Bodies: Senate

Academic Year: October to June (October-February; February-June)

Admission Requirements: Secondary school certificate (Matura) and entrance examination

Fees: (New Złoty): 2,850-5,400 per annum.

Main Language(s) of Instruction: Polish

International Co-operation: Participates in the the LLP-Erasmus Programme.

Accrediting Agencies: Ministry of Science and Higher Education

Degrees and Diplomas: *Inżynier*; *Licencjat*; *Świadectwo ukończenia studiów podyplomowych*; *Magister*; *Doktor*

Student Services: Language programs

Student Residential Facilities: 10 student hostels (2,117 beds).

Libraries: Central Library, c. 1,5m. Vols; 38,850 Electronic periodical subscriptions.

Publications: Publications of the Faculties

Press or Publishing House: Gdańsk University Press

Academic Staff *2010-2011*: Total: c. 1,720

Student Numbers *2010-2011*: Total: c. 33,000

Last Updated: 28/09/11

UNIVERSITY OF LIFE SCIENCES IN LUBLIN

Uniwersytet Przyrodniczy w Lublinie (AR)
ul. Akademicka 13, 20-950 Lublin, lubelskie
Tel: +48(81) 445-66-77
Fax: +48(81) 533-35-49
EMail: poczta@up.lublin.pl; biuro.rektora@up.lublin.pl; sekretariat.uczelni@up.lublin.pl
Website: http://www.ar.lublin.pl

Rektor: Marian Wesołowski (2008-)
Tel: +48(81) 533-35-49, Fax: +48(81) 445-66-77
EMail: biuro@ursus.ar.lublin.pl

Kanclerz: Henryk Bichta
Tel: +48(81) 445-66-22, Fax: +48(81) 533-37-52
EMail: dyradm@ursus.ar.lublin.pl

International Relations: Grazyna Gregorczyk, Head, Department of Science and International Relations
Tel: +48(81) 445-69-68, Fax: +48(81) 445-68-58
EMail: grazyna.gregorczyk@up.lublin.pl

Centres

Continuing Education (Agricultural Business; Agriculture; Animal Husbandry; Energy Engineering; Environmental Management; Food Technology; Health Sciences; Marketing; Safety Engineering; Tourism)

Deaneries

Physical Education and Sports *(Interfaculty)* (Physical Education; Sports)

Departments

Foreign Languages *(Interfaculty)* (English; Modern Languages)

Faculties

Agricultural Business (Agricultural Business; Agronomy; Biotechnology; Chemistry; Ecology; Economics; Environmental Engineering; Environmental Studies; Farm Management; Forestry; Genetics; Landscape Architecture; Leisure Studies; Meteorology; Parks and Recreation; Plant and Crop Protection; Soil Science; Tourism); **Agriculture** *(Zamosc)* (Agricultural Business; Agriculture; Animal Husbandry; Biochemistry; Biology; Child Care and Development; Environmental Management; Environmental Studies; Plant and Crop Protection; Plant Pathology); **Biology and Animal Breeding** (Animal Husbandry; Biochemistry; Biology; Ecology; Environmental Management; Hygiene; Nutrition; Science Education; Toxicology; Wildlife; Zoology); **Food Science and Biotechnology** (Biotechnology; Food Science; Food Technology; Nutrition); **Horticulture and Landscape Architecture** (Agricultural Economics; Botany; Ecology; Economics; Genetics; Horticulture; Landscape Architecture; Physiology; Plant and Crop Protection; Plant Pathology; Soil Science); **Production Engineering** (Agricultural Engineering; Agricultural Equipment; Applied Mathematics; Applied Physics; Automation and Control Engineering; Biophysics; Computer Science; Energy Engineering; Food Technology; Forestry; Heating and Refrigeration; Horticulture; Industrial Engineering; Information Sciences; Maintenance Technology; Mathematics; Physics; Production Engineering; Safety Engineering; Statistics; Technology; Thermal Engineering); **Veterinary Medicine** (Anatomy; Animal Husbandry; Biochemistry; Biotechnology; Dermatology; Embryology and Reproduction Biology; Environmental Management; Food Science; Histology; Microbiology; Parasitology; Pathology; Pharmacology; Physiology; Radiology; Surgery; Toxicology; Veterinary Science)

Further Information: Also Experimental Farms in Bezek, Sosnowica, Parczew and Felin

History: Founded 1955 as Higher Agricultural School, acquired present status and title 1972. Akademia Rolicza until 2008.

Governing Bodies: Senate

Academic Year: October to June

Admission Requirements: Secondary school certificate (matura) and entrance examinations

Fees: (New Złoty) Extramural 1,000 - 1,500; Evening 2,200 -3,000

Main Language(s) of Instruction: Polish

International Co-operation: Tempus, Socrates/Erasmus (Belgium, France)

Accrediting Agencies: Ministry of Science and Higher Education

Degrees and Diplomas: *Inżynier*; *Licencjat*; *Świadectwo ukończenia studiów podyplomowych*; *Magister*; *Doktor*

Student Services: Academic counselling, Canteen, Cultural centre, Foreign student adviser, Foreign Studies Centre, Health services, Language programs, Nursery care, Sports facilities

Student Residential Facilities: 6 hostels for 2,181 students

Special Facilities: Experimental Farms, Modern Conference Centre

Libraries: Central Library

Publications: Aktualności *(quarterly)*; Excerpta Veterinaria *(annually)*

Press or Publishing House: The Agricultural University Publishing House

Last Updated: 29/09/11

UNIVERSITY OF ŁÓDŹ

Uniwersytet Łódzki (UL)
ul. G. Narutowicza 65, 90-131 Łódź, łódzkie
Tel: +48(42) 635-40-00
Fax: +48(42) 665-57-71
EMail: rektoratul@uni.lodz.pl
Website: http://www.uni.lodz.pl

Rektor: Włodzimierz Nykiel
Tel: +48(42) 635-40-02, Fax: +48(42) 665-57-71

Kanclerz: Rafał Majda
Tel: +48(42) 635-40-10, Fax: +48(42) 678-60-23
EMail: kanclerzul@uni.lodz.pl

International Relations: Zofia Wysokińska, Prorektor
Tel: +48(42) 635-40-08 EMail: bwz@uni.lodz.pl

Centres

English Language (English); **European Studies** (European Studies); **Foreign Languages** (Modern Languages); **French** (French); **New Media and Distance Learning** (Distance Education); **Physical Education and Sports** (Physical Education; Sports); **Translation and Interpretation Studies**

Faculties

Biology and Environmental Protection (Biology; Biotechnology; Environmental Studies; Microbiology) *Dean*: Elżbieta Żądzińska; **Chemistry** (Chemistry) *Dean*: Bogusław Kryczka; **Economics and Sociology** (Accountancy; Computer Science; Econometrics; Economics; European Studies; Finance; International Economics; Social Work; Sociology; Transport Management) *Dean*: Jan Gajda; **Educational Sciences** (Educational Psychology; Educational Sciences; Pedagogy; Psychology) *Dean*: Grzegorz Michalski; **Geographical Sciences** (Economics; Geography; Tourism) *Dean*: Tadeusz Marszał; **International and Political Studies** (Cultural Studies; International Economics; International Studies; Political Sciences) *Dean*: Tomasz Domański; **Law and Administration** (Administration; Law; Social Policy) *Dean*: Agnieszka Liszewska; **Management** (Accountancy; Computer Science; Finance; Management; Transport Management) *Dean*: Ewa Walińska; **Mathematics and Computer Science** (Computer Science; Mathematics) *Dean*: Ryszard Pawlak; **Philology** (Communication Studies; Cultural Studies; Information Sciences; Journalism; Library Science; Philology; Polish) *Dean*: Piotr Stalmaszczyk; **Philosophy and History** (Archaeology; Art History; Ethnology; History; Philosophy) *Dean*: Zbigniew Anusik; **Physics and Applied Informatics** (Computer Science; Physics) *Dean*: Anna Urbaniak-Kucharczyk; **Tomaszów Maz.** *(Branch Office)* (Administration; Computer Science; Economics; Management; Tourism)

Schools

Polish for Foreign Students (Polish) *Director*: Grażyna Zarzycka

History: Founded 1945.

Governing Bodies: Senate

Academic Year: October to June (October-February; February-June)

Admission Requirements: Secondary school certificate (matura). Qualification is based on score comparison.

Fees: (New Złoty): Extramural and evening studies, 2,600-4,800 per annum; Law and Administration, 4,800-5,500 per annum.

Main Language(s) of Instruction: Polish; English

International Co-operation: With universities in France, USA and Germany. Participates in exchange and research programmes such as Campus Europae, Norwegian Financial Mechanism, Compostela Group of Universities, Erasmus Mundus - GEMMA, Erasmus IP, Comenius, Leonardo da Vinci.

Accrediting Agencies: Ministry of Science and Higher Education

Degrees and Diplomas: *Licencjat (Lic.)*: 3-3 1/2 yrs; *Magister (Mgr.)*: 2 yrs; *Magister*: Law, 5 yrs; *Doktor (Ph.D.)*: 4 yrs; *Doktor habilitowany (Dr. hab.)*: Following Doktor. Also MBA

Student Services: Canteen, Cultural centre, Handicapped facilities, Health services, Sports facilities

Special Facilities: School of Polish for Foreigners; Museum of Geology; Museum of Natural History; Accelerator of Technology; Innovation Center; Lead Slowing-down spectrometer (LSDS); Archaeological and biological external research stations; Computer Centre linked up to Earn, Internet, Decnet; Unit of New Media and Distance Learning; American Corner; Alliance Franēaise; Publishing House; Conference Centres

Libraries: University Library, c. 3 mln. vols. Libraries of the faculties

Publications: Acta Universitatis Lodziensis, Research bulletin, 20 fields of Science *(1-2 per annum)*; Kronika Uniwersytetu Łódzkiego *(bimonthly)*

Press or Publishing House: Wydawnictwo Uniwersytetu Łódzkiego

Academic Staff *2010-2011*	MEN	WOMEN	TOTAL
FULL-TIME	–	–	**2,238**
PART-TIME	–	–	**122**
Student Numbers *2010-2011*			
All (Foreign Included)	14,299	28,646	**42,945**
FOREIGN ONLY	121	172	**293**

Part-time students, 15,243.

Last Updated: 25/08/11

UNIVERSITY OF MEDICINE OF LUBLIN

Uniwersytet Medyczny w Lublinie (AM LUBLIN)

al. Racławickie 1, 20-059 Lublin, lubelskie
Tel: +48(81) 528-84-00
Fax: +48(81) 532-89-03
EMail: biuro.rektora@am.lublin.pl
Website: http://www.am.lublin.pl

Rektor: Andrzej Książek
Tel: +48(81) 532-46-33, Fax: +48(81) 532-46-33

Senior Administrative Officer: Andrzej Niedzielski
Tel: +48(81) 532-15-02

International Relations: Maria Grudzińska, International Relations Officer
Tel: +48(81) 532-29-39, Fax: +48(81) 532-10-75
EMail: margrudz@eskulap.am.lublin.pl

Faculties

Medicine and Dentistry (Anaesthesiology; Anatomy; Biology; Cell Biology; Chemistry; Dental Technology; Dentistry; Dermatology; Embryology and Reproduction Biology; English; Gastroenterology; Genetics; German; Gynaecology and Obstetrics; Haematology; Health Sciences; Histology; Immunology; Italian; Latin; Medicine; Modern Languages; Oncology; Ophthalmology; Oral Pathology; Orthopaedics; Paediatrics; Parasitology; Periodontics; Physiology; Psychiatry and Mental Health; Radiology; Russian; Spanish; Surgery; Venereology; Virology); **Medicine and English-speaking Division** (Anaesthesiology; Biochemistry; Biophysics; Cardiology; Economics; Endocrinology; English; Epidemiology; Forensic Medicine and Dentistry; Gastroenterology; Genetics; Gynaecology and Obstetrics; Haematology; Immunology; Medical Technology; Medicine; Microbiology; Molecular Biology; Nephrology; Neurology; Oncology; Orthopaedics; Otorhinolaryngology; Paediatrics; Pathology; Pharmacology; Physiology; Pneumology; Public Health; Radiology; Rehabilitation and Therapy; Rheumatology; Speech Therapy and Audiology; Surgery; Urology); **Nursing and Health Sciences** (Anaesthesiology; Arts and Humanities; Clinical Psychology; Cosmetology; Dietetics; Endocrinology; Environmental Studies; Epidemiology; Ethics; Gynaecology and Obstetrics; Health Sciences; Laboratory Techniques; Mathematics; Medicine; Neurology; Nursing; Paediatrics; Pharmacology; Philosophy; Physical Therapy; Plastic Surgery; Psychiatry and Mental Health; Public Health; Rehabilitation and Therapy; Speech Therapy and Audiology; Sports; Statistics); **Pharmacy** (Analytical Chemistry; Biochemistry; Biology; Biotechnology; Botany; Chemistry; Computer Science; Food Science; Genetics; Haematology; Inorganic Chemistry; Laboratory Techniques; Microbiology; Nutrition; Organic Chemistry; Pharmacology; Pharmacy; Physical Chemistry; Toxicology)

Further Information: Also 2 independent University Hospitals, 1 Children hospital and 1 Clinical Dental Center. Courses for foreign students from USA

History: Founded 1944 as Faculty of Maria Skłodowska University in Lublin, acquired present status 1950.

Governing Bodies: Senate

Academic Year: October to June (October-January; February-June)

Admission Requirements: Secondary school certificate (matura) and entrance examination

Fees: (New Złoty): Poish students, 2,100-12,000 per semester; Foreign students (Euro), 7,500 per annum.

Main Language(s) of Instruction: Polish, English

International Co-operation: With universities in Belgium, France, Ireland, Norway, Portugal, Spain. Also participates in Erasmus and Leonardo da Vinci programmes

Accrediting Agencies: Ministry of Science and Higher Education

Degrees and Diplomas: *Inżynier*; *Licencjat*; *Lekarz*; *Lekarz*: Dentistry; *Świadectwo ukończenia studiów podyplomowych*; *Magister*; *Doktor*

Student Services: Academic counselling, Canteen, Cultural centre, Foreign student adviser, Foreign Studies Centre, Health services, Nursery care, Social counselling, Sports facilities

Student Residential Facilities: Students House (1,250 beds).

Special Facilities: Pharmacy Museum

Libraries: Central Library, 130,535 vols; 10,592 serial publications (foreign, foreign, 433 Polish, 10,000 digital); Special collection, 48,905 vols.

Publications: Alma Mater *(quarterly)*

Academic Staff *2010-2011*: Total 100

STAFF WITH DOCTORATE: Total 660

Student Numbers *2010-2011*: Total: c. 5,000

Last Updated: 29/09/11

UNIVERSITY OF RZESZÓW

Uniwersytet Rzeszowski (UR)

ul. Rejtana 16c, 35-959 Rzeszów, podkarpackie
Tel: +48(17) 872-10-10 +48(17) 872-12-65
Fax: +48(17) 872-12-65
EMail: info@univ.rzeszow.pl
Website: http://www.univ.rzeszow.pl

Rektor: Stanisław Uliasz (2008-) EMail: rektorur@univ.rzeszow.pl

Kanclerz: Jarosław Szlęzak
Tel: +48(17) 872-10-08, Fax: +48(17) 852-21-02
EMail: kanclerz@univ.rzeszow.pl

International Relations: Lucyna Kustra, Head, Department of International Relations
Tel: +48(17) 872-10-71, Fax: +48(17) 872-10-71
EMail: dzwz@univ.rzeszow.pl

Academies

Carpathian Studies *(European - Interfaculty)* (Central European Studies; Eastern European Studies)

Campuses

Branch Campus of the Faculty of Biotechnology *(Kolbuszowa)* (Animal Husbandry; Biotechnology; Chemistry; Computer Science; Ecology; Genetics; Microbiology; Physiology; Toxicology)

Centres

Culture and Education Studies *(Interfaculty)* (Dance; Music; Singing); **Polish Culture and Language for Poles from Abroad and Foreigners** *(POLONUS - Interfaculty)* (Cultural Studies; Polish)

Colleges

Physical Education and Sports *(Interfaculty)* (Physical Education; Sports); **Practical Foreign Languages Teaching** *(Interfaculty)* (English; French; German; Latin; Modern Languages; Russian)

Faculties

Art (Art Education; Fine Arts; Graphic Arts; Graphic Design; Painting and Drawing; Sculpture); **Biology and Agriculture** (Agricultural Engineering; Agriculture; Agrobiology; Animal Husbandry; Anthropology; Biology; Botany; Business and Commerce; Chemistry; Crop Production; Ecology; Economics; Environmental Management; Environmental Studies; Food Science; Food Technology; Physical Chemistry; Physiology; Production Engineering; Soil Science; Tourism; Zoology); **Economics** (Agricultural Business; Agricultural Economics; Econometrics; Economic and Finance Policy; Economics; Finance; Information Technology; International Economics; International Relations; Marketing; Statistics); **Law and Administration** (Administration; Civil Law; Commercial Law; Comparative Law; Constitutional Law; Criminal Law; European Union Law; History; International Law; Labour Law; Law; Philosophy; Public Law; Sociology); **Mathematics and Natural Sciences** (Applied Mathematics; Artificial Intelligence; Computer Education; Computer Engineering; Computer Networks; Computer Science; Data Processing; Mathematics; Mathematics Education; Medical Technology; Natural Sciences; Physics; Science Education; Technology; Technology Education); **Medicine** (Epidemiology; Health Sciences; Medicine; Neurological Therapy; Neurology; Nursing; Oncology; Orthopaedics; Paediatrics; Physical Therapy; Physiology; Public Health; Radiology; Rehabilitation and Therapy; Surgery); **Pedagogy - Art** (Adult Education; Conducting; Dance; Educational Technology; Music; Music Education; Musical Instruments; Pedagogy; Preschool Education; Primary Education; Rehabilitation and Therapy; Singing; Social Psychology; Vocational Education); **Philology** (Applied Linguistics; Cultural Studies; English; English Studies; German; Grammar; Linguistics; Literature; Philology; Polish; Russian); **Physical Education** (Physical Education; Physical Therapy; Rehabilitation and Therapy; Sports); **Sociology and History** (Ancient Civilizations; Anthropology; Archaeology; Contemporary History; Cultural Studies; Eastern European Studies; European Studies; Government; History; International Relations; International Studies; Marketing; Medieval Studies; Military Science; Modern History; Political Sciences; Public Administration; Rural Studies; Social Policy; Sociology; Urban Studies)

Institutes

Philosophy (Logic; Philosophy)

History: Established 2001 through the merger of Pedagogical University of Rzeszów, Maria Curie Skłodowska University of Lublin, Rzeszów branch and Rzeszów Economies Faculty of the Agricultural University of Cracow.

Governing Bodies: Senate

Academic Year: October to June (October-February; February-June)

Admission Requirements: Secondary school certificate (matura)

Fees: (New Złoty): 3,000 per annum

Main Language(s) of Instruction: Polish

International Co-operation: With universities in Italy, France, Russian Federation, Ukraine, USA. Also participates in Socrates/Erasmus, and CEEPUS programmes.

Accrediting Agencies: Ministry of Science and Higher Education

Degrees and Diplomas: *Inżynier*, *Licencjat*; *Świadectwo ukończenia studiów podyplomowych*; *Magister*, *Doktor*, *Doktor habilitowany*

Student Services: Academic counselling, Canteen, Cultural centre, Employment services, Foreign student adviser, Foreign Studies Centre, Handicapped facilities, Health services, Language programs, Nursery care, Social counselling, Sports facilities

Student Residential Facilities: For 2,906 students

Special Facilities: Pigon's Museum; Astronomical Observatory; Archive

Libraries: Central Library, 1,040,000 vols

Publications: University press *(monthly)*; Zeszyty Naukowe UR *(3 per annum)*

Academic Staff *2010-2011*: Total: c. 2,000

Student Numbers *2010-2011*: Total: c. 25,000

Last Updated: 30/09/11

UNIVERSITY OF SILESIA

Uniwersytet Śląski w Katowicach (US)

ul. Bankowa 12, 40-007 Katowice, śląskie

Tel: +48(32) 359-19-56 +48(32) 359-22-22

Fax: +48(32) 359-20-52

EMail: info@us.edu.pl; admission@us.edu.pl

Website: http://www.us.edu.pl

Rektor: Wiesław Banyś (2008-)
Tel: +48(32) 359-13-00, Fax: +48(32) 359-20-55
EMail: rektor@us.edu.pl; wieslaw.banys@us.edu.pl

Kanclerz: Ewa Magiera
Tel: +48(32) 359-18-91, Fax: +48(32) 359-19-45
EMail: kanclerz@us.edu.pl; ewa.magiera@us.edu.pl

International Relations: Adam Kurzeja
Tel: +48(32) 359-13-67 EMail: adku@adm.us.edu.pl

Centres

Polish Committee for Cooperation with Alliance Francaise at the University of Silesia (French)

Faculties

Art (Art Education; Conducting; Fine Arts; Graphic Arts; Graphic Design; Music; Music Education; Musical Instruments; Painting and Drawing; Sculpture); **Biology and Environmental Protection** (Anatomy; Biochemistry; Biology; Biophysics; Botany; Cell Biology; Ecology; Embryology and Reproduction Biology; Environmental Studies; Genetics; Histology; Microbiology; Physiology; Science Education; Toxicology; Zoology); **Computer Science and Materials Science** (Chemistry; Computer Graphics; Computer Science; Information Sciences; Materials Engineering; Polymer and Plastics Technology); **Earth Sciences** (Earth Sciences; Geochemistry; Geography; Geology; Geophysics; Meteorology; Mineralogy; Paleontology; Petroleum and Gas Engineering; Regional Studies; Surveying and Mapping; Tourism); **Ethnology and Science Education** (Anthropology; Arts and Humanities; Civics; Cultural Studies; Education; Educational Sciences; Ethnology; Geography; Humanities and Social Science Education; Preschool Education; Science Education; Special Education); **Law and Administration** (Administration; Administrative Law; Agriculture; Canon Law; Civil Law; Commercial Law; Constitutional Law; Criminal Law; Criminology; Economics; Environmental Studies; European Union Law; Fiscal Law; Government; History of Law; International Law; Labour Law; Law; Mining Engineering; Private Law; Public Law; Rural Planning; Social Policy); **Mathematics, Physics and Chemistry** (Analytical Chemistry; Astronomy and Space Science; Astrophysics; Biophysics; Chemistry; Environmental Studies; Inorganic Chemistry; Mathematics; Mathematics and Computer Science; Mathematics Education; Nuclear Physics; Organic Chemistry; Physical Chemistry; Physics; Polymer and Plastics Technology; Science Education; Solid State Physics); **Pedagogy and Psychology** (Art Therapy; Child Care and Development; Clinical Psychology; Education; Educational Sciences; Forensic Medicine and Dentistry; Health Education; Music Education; Pedagogy; Preschool Education; Psychology; Rehabilitation and Therapy; Social Psychology; Special Education); **Philology** (American Studies; Applied Linguistics; Canadian Studies; Chemistry; Classical Languages; Communication Studies; Comparative Literature; Cultural Studies; English; English Studies; Film; French; French Studies; Gender Studies; German; Greek (Classical); History; Information Sciences; Italian; Latin; Library Science; Linguistics; Literature; Marketing; Media Studies; Modern Languages; Philology; Polish; Romance Languages; Russian; Slavic Languages; Spanish; Speech Studies; Theatre; Translation and Interpretation); **Radio and Television** *(Krzysztof Kieslowski)* (Cinema and Television; Display and Stage Design; Film; Media Studies; Radio and Television Broadcasting); **Social Sciences** (Ancient Civilizations; Anthropology; Art History; Central European Studies; Contemporary History; Eastern European Studies; Ethics; History; International Relations; Journalism; Logic; Mass Communication; Medieval Studies; Modern History; Philosophy; Political Sciences; Social Policy; Social Sciences; Social Work; Sociology); **Theology** (Bible; Canon Law; Christian Religious Studies; Family Studies; History of Religion; Holy Writings;

Missionary Studies; New Testament; Pastoral Studies; Philosophy; Religious Art; Religious Practice; Theology)

Programmes

Intensive English Language Arts (English)

Schools

International Business *(Silesian)* (Accountancy; Business Administration; Finance; International Business)

Further Information: Branches in: Sosnowiec, Chorzów, Jastrzębie, Rybnik and Cieszyn

History: Founded 1968 incorporating former branch of Jagiellonian University in Cracow and Higher School of Pedagogy, Katowice.

Governing Bodies: Senate

Academic Year: October to June (October-January; February-June)

Admission Requirements: Secondary school certificate (Matura) or foreign equivalent, and a knowledge of Polish

Fees: (Euros): Registration, 200, tuition, 3,000-4,000 per annum; postgraduate, 5,000

Main Language(s) of Instruction: Polish, English

International Co-operation: Participates in the Socrates/Erasmus, Tempus, Leonardo da Vinci, Copernicus, and Lingua programmes

Accrediting Agencies: Ministry of Science and Higher Education

Degrees and Diplomas: *Inżynier*; *Licencjat*; *Świadectwo ukończenia studiów podyplomowych*; *Magister*; *Doktor*; *Doktor habilitowany*

Student Services: Academic counselling, Canteen, Cultural centre, Employment services, Foreign student adviser, Health services, Language programs, Social counselling, Sports facilities

Student Residential Facilities: For 3,400 students

Special Facilities: Museum of the Earth. Meteorological Observatory; Centre of Human and Natural Environment. Faculty Zoo. Experimental Field.

Libraries: Central Library and libraries of the faculties and departments, total, c. 1m. vols

Publications: Zeszty Naukowe Wydziałów, Scientific Papers

Press or Publishing House: University Press

Academic Staff *2010-2011*	**TOTAL**
FULL-TIME	**1,995**
STAFF WITH DOCTORATE FULL-TIME	**1,085**
Student Numbers *2010-2011*	
All (Foreign Included)	**32,268**

Part-time students, 12,651.

Last Updated: 30/09/11

UNIVERSITY OF TECHNOLOGY AND LIFE SCIENCES IN BYDGOSZCZ

Uniwersytet Technologiczno-Przyrodniczy im. J.J. Śniadeckich w Bydgoszczy (ATR)

ul. Ks. Kordeckiego 20, 85-225 Bydgoszcz, kujawsko-pomorskie

Tel: +48(52) 373-02-80

Fax: +48(52) 374-93-27

EMail: rdd@utp.edu.pl

Website: http://www.utp.edu.pl

Rektor: Antoni Bukaluk (2008-)
Tel: +48(52) 374-94-44, Fax: +48(52) 374-93-02
EMail: rektor@utp.edu.pl

Kanclerz: Krystyna Nowak
Tel: +48(52) 373-02-80, Fax: +48(52) 374-94-55
EMail: dyrektor@utp.edu.pl

International Relations: Małgorzata Gawinecka, International Cooperation Officer
Tel: +48(52) 374-94-32, Fax: +48(52) 374-93-99
EMail: gawi@utp.edu.pl

Faculties

Agriculture and Biotechnology (Agricultural Business; Agriculture; Biochemistry; Biotechnology; Botany; Chemistry; Ecology; Economics; Entomology; Food Technology; Genetics; Meteorology; Microbiology; Pathology; Plant and Crop Protection; Soil Conservation; Soil Science; Vegetable Production); **Animal Breeding and Biology** (Animal Husbandry; Biochemistry; Biology; Biotechnology; Ecology; Embryology and Reproduction Biology; Environmental Studies; Genetics; Hygiene; Meat and Poultry; Microbiology; Nutrition; Physiology; Tourism; Zoology); **Chemical Technology and Engineering** (Bioengineering; Chemical Engineering; Chemistry; Environmental Studies; Food Technology; Inorganic Chemistry; Organic Chemistry; Physical Chemistry; Polymer and Plastics Technology; Technology); **Civil and Environmental Engineering** (Administration; Architecture; Architecture and Planning; Building Technologies; Civil Engineering; Construction Engineering; Economics; Environmental Engineering; Environmental Management; Geological Engineering; Heating and Refrigeration; Mechanics; Painting and Drawing; Road Engineering; Sculpture; Town Planning); **Management** (Arts and Humanities; Economics; Engineering Management; Finance; Information Management; Law; Management; Social Sciences); **Mathematics and Physics** (Applied Chemistry; Mathematics; Physics); **Mechanical Engineering** (Agricultural Engineering; Automation and Control Engineering; Automotive Engineering; Electronic Engineering; Food Technology; Machine Building; Maintenance Technology; Materials Engineering; Mechanical Engineering; Mechanics; Polymer and Plastics Technology; Production Engineering; Thermal Engineering); **Telecommunications and Electrical Engineering** (Automation and Control Engineering; Computer Engineering; Electrical Engineering; Electronic Engineering; Power Engineering; Telecommunications Engineering)

History: Founded 1951 as Evening Engineering School, reorganized as Engineering College, incorporating the branch of Poznań Agricultural College. Akademia Techniczno-Rolnicza im. J.J.Sniadeckich w Bydgoszczy until 2007

Governing Bodies: Senate

Academic Year: September to June

Admission Requirements: Secondary school certificate (Matura)

Fees: (US Dollars): Foreign students, 3,000 per annum

Main Language(s) of Instruction: Polish; English

International Co-operation: With universities in Belarus, Ukraine, Germany; Slovakia; Czech Republic, Russia, Sweden, France, Lithuania, the Netherlands, Spain. Participates in the Socrates, Erasmus, Tempus, Visby, Leonardo da Vinci; 6th Framework and Ceepus programmes.

Accrediting Agencies: Ministry of Science and Higher Education

Degrees and Diplomas: *Inżynier*; *Licencjat*; *Świadectwo ukończenia studiów podyplomowych*; *Magister*; *Doktor*

Student Services: Academic counselling, Canteen, Cultural centre, Employment services, Foreign student adviser, Handicapped facilities, Health services, Language programs, Nursery care, Social counselling, Sports facilities

Student Residential Facilities: For 1,991 students

Libraries: Central Library, 273,000 vols

Publications: Biuletyn Informacyjny ATR *(quarterly)*

Academic Staff *2010-2011*: Total 680
STAFF WITH DOCTORATE: Total 140
Student Numbers *2010-2011*: Total: c. 10,000

Last Updated: 30/09/11

UNIVERSITY OF WARMIA AND MAZURY IN OLSZTYN

Uniwersytet Warmińsko-Mazurski w Olsztynie (UWM)

ul. Michała Oczapowskiego 2, 10-719 Olsztyn-Kortowo, warmińsko-mazurskie

Tel: +48(89) 523-49-13

Fax: +48(89) 523-44-56

EMail: ewa.burska@uwm.edu.pl

Website: http://www.uwm.edu.pl

Rector: Józef Górniewicz (2008-)
Tel: +48(89) 523-33-30, Fax: +48(89) 523-44-56
EMail: rektor@uwm.edu.pl

Kanclerz: Wojciech Cymerman
Tel: +48(89) 523-33-44 EMail: kanclerz@uwm.edu.pl

International Relations: Tomasz Dusza, Head, International Relations Office
Tel: +48(89) 523-35-21, Fax: +48(89) 524-04-94
EMail: tomasz.dusza@uwm.edu.pl

Faculties

Animal Bioengineering (Animal Husbandry; Bioengineering); **Biology** (Biology; Biotechnology; Environmental Studies); **Economics** (Accountancy; Banking; Business Administration; Business and Commerce; European Studies; Finance; Human Resources; Insurance; Management; Marketing; Public Administration; Real Estate; Social Policy); **Environmental Management and Agriculture** (Agricultural Business; Agricultural Engineering; Agricultural Management; Environmental Management; Environmental Studies; Horticulture; Landscape Architecture; Soil Science); **Environmental Sciences and Fisheries** (Aquaculture; Biotechnology; Environmental Engineering; Environmental Studies; Fishery; Food Technology; Natural Resources; Safety Engineering; Water Management); **Fine Arts** (Art Therapy; Fine Arts; Music); **Food Science** (Biotechnology; Cooking and Catering; Dairy; Food Science; Food Technology; Hotel and Restaurant; Meat and Poultry; Nutrition; Production Engineering; Tourism); **Geodesy and Land Management** (Environmental Studies; Geological Engineering; Information Sciences; Mathematics; Real Estate; Regional Planning; Rural Planning; Statistics; Surveying and Mapping; Town Planning); **Humanities** (Arts and Humanities; Central European Studies; German; History; International Relations; Journalism; Literature; Modern Languages; Polish; Russian; Slavic Languages); **Law and Administration** (Administration; Law); **Mathematics and Computer Science** (Applied Mathematics; Astronomy and Space Science; Computer Science; Information Technology; Mathematics; Mathematics Education; Nuclear Physics; Physics; Statistics); **Medicine** (Medicine; Neurology; Nursing; Surgery); **Social Sciences** (Education; Government; International Economics; International Relations; Marketing; Pedagogy; Political Sciences; Preschool Education; Rehabilitation and Therapy; Social Sciences; Social Work; Sociology; Special Education; Teacher Training); **Technical Sciences** (Agricultural Engineering; Architecture and Planning; Automation and Control Engineering; Building Technologies; Civil Engineering; Electronic Engineering; Energy Engineering; Engineering; Environmental Engineering; Food Technology; Forestry; Materials Engineering; Mechanical Engineering; Production Engineering); **Theology** (Bible; Canon Law; Christian Religious Studies; History of Religion; Pedagogy; Philosophy; Religion; Religious Studies); **Veterinary Medicine** (Molecular Biology; Pathology; Physiology; Public Health; Veterinary Science)

History: Founded 1999 from the merger of Olsztyn University of Agriculture and Technology 'Michał Oczapowski', Higher School of Pedagogy, and Warmian Theological Institute.

Governing Bodies: Senate

Academic Year: October to September (October-January; February-September)

Admission Requirements: Secondary school certificate (matura) and entrance examinations

Main Language(s) of Instruction: Polish

International Co-operation: Participates in the Socrates/Erasmus, Erasmus/Mundus and Leonardo da Vinci programmes

Accrediting Agencies: Ministry of Science and Higher Education

Degrees and Diplomas: *Inżynier*, *Licencjat*; *Lekarz*: Veterinary Science; *Świadectwo ukończenia studiów podyplomowych*; *Magister*, *Doktor*, *Doktor habilitowany*

Student Services: Academic counselling, Canteen, Cultural centre, Employment services, Foreign Studies Centre, Handicapped facilities, Health services, Nursery care, Social counselling, Sports facilities

Special Facilities: Observatory. Biological Garden. Movie Studio

Libraries: Central Library, c. 1m. vols

Publications: Acta Neophilologica *(annually)*; Acta Polono-Ruthenica *(annually)*; Acta Scientiarum Polonorum : Administration Locorum; Economic Sciences *(annually)*; Forum Oświatowe *(biennially)*; Forum Teologiczne *(annually)*; Humanistyka i Przyrodoznawstwo *(annually)*; Polish Journal of Natural Sciences *(annually)*; Rolnicze ABC *(quarterly)*; Technical Sciences *(biennially)*; Wiadomości Uniwersyteckie UWM *(monthly)*

Academic Staff *2010-2011*: Total 2,000

STAFF WITH DOCTORATE: Total 214

Student Numbers *2010-2011*: Total: c. 31,000

Last Updated: 03/10/11

UNIVERSITY OF WARSAW

Uniwersytet Warszawski (UW)

ul. Krakowskie Przedmieście 26/28, 00-927 Warszawa, mazowieckie
Tel: +48(22) 552-00-00
Fax: +48(22) 552-40-29
EMail: rektor@adm.uw.edu.pl
Website: http://www.uw.edu.pl

Rektor: Katarzyna Chałasińska-Macukow
Tel: +48(22) 552-03-55 +48(22) 552-03-42,
Fax: +48(22) 552-40-00 EMail: kmacukow@adm.uw.edu.pl

Kanclerz: Jerzy Pieszczurykow
Tel: +48(22) 552-04-56, Fax: +48(22) 552-08-00
EMail: jerzyp@adm.uw.edu.pl

International Relations: Włodzimierz Lengauer, Vice-Rector for Research and International Cooperation
Tel: +48(22) 552-03-50, Fax: +48(22) 552-40-21
EMail: wlengauer@adm.uw.edu.pl

Centres

Behaviour Genetics *(interdisciplinary)* (Genetics); **British Studies** (English Studies); **Environmental Studies** (Environmental Studies); **European** *(Warsaw)* (European Studies); **Foreign Language Teacher Training and European Education** (English; Foreign Languages Education; French; German); **Foreign Languages** (Modern Languages); **Forensic Sciences** (Forensic Medicine and Dentistry); **French Culture Studies and La Francophonie** (French; French Studies); **Humanities** *(Interfaculty, individual studies)* (Arts and Humanities); **Local Government and Local Development** (Development Studies; Government); **Mathematical and Computational Modelling - ICM** *(Interdisciplinary)* (Computer Science; Mathematics; Mathematics and Computer Science); **Mediterranean Archaeology** *(Kazimierz Michałowski)* (Archaeology; Mediterranean Studies); **New Technologies** *(CeNT)* (Information Technology); **Open Multimedia Education** (Educational Technology; Multimedia); **Political Analysis** (Political Sciences); **Preclinical Research and Technology** *(CEPT)* (Technology); **Technology Transfer** *(UOTT)* (Technology)

Chairs

Erasmus of Rotterdam (Arts and Humanities; Social Sciences); **Sustainable Development** *(UNESCO)* (Development Studies)

Departments

Physical Education and Sports (Physical Education; Sports)

Faculties

Applied Linguistics (Applied Linguistics; Central European Studies; Cultural Studies; Eastern European Studies; Foreign Languages Education; Linguistics; Russian; Slavic Languages); **Applied Social Sciences and Rehabilitation** (Higher Education; Rehabilitation and Therapy; Social Sciences; Social Studies); **Biology** (Biochemistry; Biology; Biotechnology; Botany; Environmental Management; Genetics; Microbiology; Zoology); **Chemistry** (Chemistry); **Economics** (Banking; Econometrics; Economics; Finance; International Relations; Statistics); **Education** (Education; Pedagogy; Primary Education); **Geography and Regional Studies** (Computer Education; Geography; Information Sciences; Regional Studies; Surveying and Mapping); **Geology** (Environmental Studies; Geological Engineering; Geology; Mineralogy; Natural Resources; Petroleum and Gas Engineering; Water Science); **History** (Anthropology; Archaeology; Art History; Ethnology; History; Information Sciences; Library Science; Musicology; Publishing and Book Trade); **Journalism and Political Science** (European Studies; International Relations; Journalism; Political Sciences; Social Policy); **Law and Administration** (Administration; Civil Law; Criminal Law; History of Law; International Law; Law); **Management** (Economics; Industrial and Organizational Psychology; Management; Management Systems; Marketing; Sociology); **Mathematics, Informatics and Mechanics** (Applied Mathematics; Computer Science; Mathematics; Mechanics); **Modern Languages** (English; French; German; Hungarian; Italian; Linguistics; Modern

Languages; Romance Languages; Spanish); **Oriental Studies** (African Languages; African Studies; Ancient Civilizations; Arabic; Asian Religious Studies; Asian Studies; Chinese; Cultural Studies; Eastern European Studies; Hebrew; Islamic Studies; Japanese; Korean; Oriental Languages; Oriental Studies; Persian; Turkish); **Philosophy and Sociology** (Philosophy; Sociology); **Physics** (Astronomy and Space Science; Geophysics; Mathematical Physics; Physics); **Polish Language** (Baltic Languages; Classical Languages; Cultural Studies; East Asian Studies; Foreign Languages Education; Linguistics; Literature; Philology; Polish; Slavic Languages); **Psychology** (Clinical Psychology; Cognitive Sciences; Neurology; Psychiatry and Mental Health; Psychology; Psychotherapy; Social Psychology)

Institutes

Interdisciplinary Studies *(Artes Liberales)* (Arts and Humanities); **Social Studies** *(Interfaculty - Robert Zajonc)* (Social Studies); **The Americas and Europe** (American Studies; European Studies; Latin American Studies)

Laboratories

Heavy Ions *(Environmental)* (Nuclear Physics)

Programmes

Environmental Studies *(Interdisciplinary)* (Environmental Studies); **Mathematics and Natural Sciences** *(Individual Interfaculty - College MISMap)* (Mathematics; Natural Sciences)

Research Centres

Antiques South-East Europe (Ancient Civilizations; Archaeology); **Migration** *(Warsaw University)* (Demography and Population)

Units

Polish Committee of Alliance Franêaise (French Studies); **The Open University of Warsaw University** *(UOUW)* (Arabic; Architecture; Art History; Arts and Humanities; Business Administration; Cultural Studies; Economics; English; Environmental Studies; Fine Arts; French; German; Greek (Classical); Health Sciences; History; Italian; Japanese; Latin American Studies; Law; Literature; Mathematics; Medieval Studies; Multimedia; Philosophy; Physics; Polish; Psychology; Russian; Slavic Languages; Spanish; Technology)

Further Information: Also Courses of Polish Language and Culture for foreign students

History: Founded 1808 as school of law, became University 1816. Reorganized 1945. Since new Act on Higher Education 1990, University authorities are elected, and faculties are given freedom to decide on research and instruction. Branch in Białystok, founded 1968, became separate University 1997.

Governing Bodies: Senate

Academic Year: October to May (October-February; February-May)

Admission Requirements: Secondary school certificate (matura) and entrance examination

Main Language(s) of Instruction: Polish

International Co-operation: Participates in the Socrates/Erasmus and Leonardo da Vinci programmes

Accrediting Agencies: Ministry of Science and Higher Education

Degrees and Diplomas: *Licencjat*; *Świadectwo ukończenia studiów podyplomowych*; *Magister*, *Doktor*, *Doktor habilitowany*

Student Services: Canteen, Cultural centre, Employment services, Foreign Studies Centre, Handicapped facilities, Health services, Sports facilities

Student Residential Facilities: For c. 3,570 students

Special Facilities: University Museum. Museum of Geology. Astronomical Observatory. Botanical Garden

Libraries: Central Library, c. 2,360,000 vols; libraries of the faculties/centres, c. 2,370.000

Publications: American Bulletin; Anglica; Cahiers de Varsovie; Japonica; Kwartalnik Neofilologiczny; Prace Filologiczne; Publications of the Faculties; Studia Iuridica

Press or Publishing House: University Press

Academic Staff *2010-2011*: Total: c. 3,100

Student Numbers *2010-2011*: Total: c. 56,000

Last Updated: 03/10/11

UNIVERSITY OF WROCŁAW

Uniwersytet Wrocławski (UWR)

pl. Uniwersytecki 1, 50-137 Wrocław, dolnośląskie

Tel: +48(71) 375-22-15

Fax: +48(71) 344-34-21

EMail: rektorat@uni.wroc.pl

Website: http://www.uni.wroc.pl

Rektor: Marek Bojarski (2008-)
Tel: +48(71) 343-68-47 EMail: rektor@uni.wroc.pl

Kanclerz: Ryszard Żukowski
Tel: +48(71) 343-55-35 +48(71) 375-23-03,
Fax: +48(71) 341-04-82 EMail: dyrektor@adm.uni.wroc.pl

International Relations: Adam Jezierski, Vice-Rector for Research and International Relations
Tel: +48(71) 375-22-70, Fax: +48(71) 343-68-48
EMail: prorscie@uni.wroc.pl

Faculties

Biological Sciences (Anthropology; Biological and Life Sciences; Biology; Biotechnology; Botany; Environmental Studies; Genetics; Geography; Geology; Microbiology; Natural Sciences; Zoology); **Biotechnology** (Biochemistry; Biotechnology; Microbiology); **Chemistry** (Chemistry); **Earth Sciences and Environmental Management** (Development Studies; Earth Sciences; Environmental Management; Geography); **Historical and Pedagogical Sciences** (Archaeology; Art History; Educational Sciences; Ethnology; History; Musicology; Pedagogy; Primary Education; Psychology); **Law, Administration and Economy** (Administration; Civil Law; Constitutional Law; Criminal Law; Criminology; Economics; European Union Law; International Law; Law); **Mathematics and Computer Science** (Computer Science; Mathematics; Mathematics and Computer Science); **Philology** (Classical Languages; Dutch; English; German; Information Sciences; Journalism; Library Science; Mass Communication; Mediterranean Studies; Modern Languages; Oriental Languages; Oriental Studies; Philology; Polish; Romance Languages; Slavic Languages); **Physics and Astronomy** (Astronomy and Space Science; Physics); **Social Sciences** (European Studies; German; International Studies; Logic; Philosophy; Political Sciences; Psychology; Social Sciences; Sociology)

Institutes

Individual Studies in the College of Humanities *(Interfaculty)* (Administration; Ancient Civilizations; Anthropology; Archaeology; Art History; Classical Languages; Cultural Studies; Dutch; Economics; Education; English; Ethnology; German; History; Information Sciences; International Studies; Journalism; Law; Library Science; Logic; Mass Communication; Musicology; Pedagogy; Philology; Philosophy; Polish; Political Sciences; Psychology; Romance Languages; Slavic Languages; Social Sciences; Sociology)

Units

Interdisciplinary Study of Environmental Protection (Biochemistry; Biology; Chemistry; Ecology; Economics; Energy Engineering; Environmental Studies; Geology; Health Sciences; Law; Mathematics; Meteorology; Microbiology; Physics; Soil Science; Technology; Toxicology)

Further Information: interdisciplinary studies in English (www.interstudies.uni.wroc.pl)

History: Founded 1505 as Generale Litterarum Gymnasium by decree of Ladislas Jagellon, King of Bohemia and Hungary. Jesuit College founded 1702 by Emperor Leopold I. Became a University 1811 after union with the University of Frankfurt-am-Oder. Closed as a German University and opened in 1945 as Polish University with academic staff from different Polish schools.

Governing Bodies: Senate

Academic Year: October to June (October-February; February-June)

Admission Requirements: Secondary school certificate (Matura) and entrance examination

Fees: (US Dollars): c. 3,000-4,000 per annum

Main Language(s) of Instruction: Polish

International Co-operation: Participates in the Tempus, Ceepus, Socrates, Leonardo da Vinci and Jean Monnet programmes, VI Framework Program

Accrediting Agencies: Ministry of Science and Higher Education

Degrees and Diplomas: *Inżynier*; *Licencjat*; *Świadectwo ukończenia studiów podyplomowych*; *Magister*; *Doktor*

Student Services: Language programs

Special Facilities: Museum of Natural History; Geological Museum; Museum of Minerals. Botanical Garden. Centre de l'Alliance Francaise. Astronomical Observatory; Meteorological Observatory

Libraries: University Library and the libraries of specialized institutes and departments, c. 3,8m. vols.

Publications: Acta Universitatis Wratislaviensis; Classica Wratislaviensia; Monografie i Raporty Centrum Studiow Niemieckich i Europeajskich im. Willy Brandta; Prace; Raporty; Studia

Press or Publishing House: University Press

Academic Staff *2010-2011*: Total: c. 1,900

Student Numbers *2010-2011*: Total: c. 37,000

Last Updated: 03/10/11

UNIVERSITY OF ZIELONA GÓRA

Uniwersytet Zielonogórski (UZ)

ul. Licealna 9, 65-417 Zielona Góra, lubuskie
Tel: +48(68) 328-20-00
Fax: +48(68) 327-07-35
EMail: rektorat@uz.zgora.pl
Website: http://www.uz.zgora.pl

Rektor: Czesław Osekowski
Tel: +48(68) 328-22-02 EMail: Rektor@uz.zgora.pl

Kanclerz: Franciszek Orlik
Tel: +48(68) 328-24-50, Fax: +48(68) 328-27-21
EMail: Dyrektor@adm.uz.zgora.pl

International Relations: Tadeusz Kuczynski, Vice-Rector for Science and International Relations
Tel: +48(68) 328-32-90, Fax: +48(68) 328-32-98
EMail: ProrektorDN@uz.zgora.pl

Faculties

Arts (Architecture; Art Education; Arts and Humanities; Fine Arts; Graphic Arts; Interior Design; Jazz and Popular Music; Music; Music Education; Painting and Drawing; Visual Arts); **Biological Sciences** (Biological and Life Sciences; Biology; Biotechnology; Botany; Environmental Studies; Molecular Biology); **Civil and Environmental Engineering** (Architecture and Planning; Biological and Life Sciences; Building Technologies; Civil Engineering; Construction Engineering; Environmental Engineering; Laboratory Techniques; Sanitary Engineering; Soil Science; Structural Architecture; Town Planning); **Education, Sociology and Health Sciences** (Education; Health Sciences; Information Technology; Media Studies; Nursing; Pedagogy; Physical Education; Preschool Education; Psychology; Public Health; Rehabilitation and Therapy; Social Work; Sociology); **Electrical Engineering, Computer Science and Telecommunications** (Automation and Control Engineering; Computer Engineering; Computer Science; Electrical Engineering; Electronic Engineering; Industrial Engineering; Measurement and Precision Engineering; Robotics; Telecommunications Engineering; Telecommunications Services); **Humanities** (Arts and Humanities; Cultural Studies; English; German; Histology; Information Sciences; Library Science; Literature; Mass Communication; Media Studies; Modern Languages; Philology; Polish; Political Sciences; Romance Languages; Russian); **Management** (Automation and Control Engineering; Business Computing; Communication Arts; Economics; Finance; Human Resources; Management; Marketing; Protective Services; Psychology; Public Administration; Safety Engineering; Social Policy); **Mathematics, Computer Science and Econometrics** (Computer Science; Econometrics; Mathematics; Mathematics and Computer Science; Statistics); **Mechanical Engineering** (Biomedical Engineering; Computer Education; Computer Science; Information Technology; Maintenance Technology; Mechanical Engineering; Mechanics; Occupational Health; Production Engineering; Safety Engineering; Technology Education); **Physics and Astronomy** (Applied Physics; Astronomy and Space Science; Computer Science; Physics)

History: Founded 1965 as engineering school. Acquired present status 1996 and merged with the Pedagogical University 'Tadeusz Kotarbiński', Zielona Góra 2001.

Governing Bodies: Rector and Vice-Rectors

Academic Year: October to June (October-February; February-June)

Admission Requirements: Secondary school certificate (Matura) or foreign equivalent, and entrance examination

Fees: (New Zloty): part-time, evening and postgraduate studies: 1,300-1,800 per semester

Main Language(s) of Instruction: Polish

International Co-operation: With universities in Germany, UK, France, Spain, Portugal, the Netherlands, Finland, Ukraine, Belarus, Czech Republic, Slovakia, China, Russia

Accrediting Agencies: State Accreditation Committee

Degrees and Diplomas: *Inżynier*; *Licencjat*; *Świadectwo ukończenia studiów podyplomowych*; *Magister*; *Doktor*; *Doktor habilitowany*

Student Services: Academic counselling, Canteen, Employment services, Foreign student adviser, Handicapped facilities, Health services, Language programs, Social counselling, Sports facilities

Student Residential Facilities: For c. 2,400 students, partially adapted to the needs of the disabled

Special Facilities: Art galleries, sports hall, tennis field, concert and assembly hall, student clubs, horse-riding centre, astronomical observatory

Libraries: Central Library, 800,000 vols

Publications: Applied Mathematics and Computer Science *(quarterly)*; Applied Mechanics and Engineering *(quarterly)*; Discussiones Mathematicea, Series *(annually)*; Management *(biennially)*

Academic Staff *2010-2011*	**TOTAL**
FULL-TIME	**934**
Student Numbers *2010-2011*	
All (Foreign Included)	**16,290**

Part-time students, 5,884.

Last Updated: 03/10/11

UNIVERSITY SCHOOL OF PHYSICAL EDUCATION IN KRAKOW

Akademia Wychowania Fizycznego im. Bronisława Czecha w Krakowie (AWF)

Al. Jana Pawła II 78, 31-571 Kraków, małopolskie
Tel: +48(12) 683-10-00 +48(12) 683-12-27
Fax: +48(12) 683-11-21
EMail: rektor@awf.krakow.pl
Website: http://www.awf.krakow.pl

Rektor: Andrzej Klimek (2008-)
Tel: +48(12) 683-12-27 +48(12) 683-11-21

Kanclerz: Franciszek Romaniak
Tel: +48(12) 683-15-16, Fax: +48(12) 648-12-10
EMail: kanclerz@awf.krakow.pl

International Relations: Dorota Madejska
Tel: +48(12) 683-15-80 EMail: rekolacz@skok.awf.krakow.pl

Departments

Foreign Languages (English; German; Modern Languages; Romance Languages; Russian; Spanish)

Faculties

Motor Rehabilitation (Anatomy; Biochemistry; Gerontology; Health Education; Hygiene; Neurology; Orthopaedics; Physical Therapy; Physiology; Psychiatry and Mental Health; Rehabilitation and Therapy; Rheumatology; Social Sciences; Sports); **Physical Education and Sport** (Anthropology; Arts and Humanities; Biochemistry; Biology; Dance; History; Nutrition; Pedagogy; Philosophy; Physical Education; Physiology; Psychology; Rehabilitation and Therapy; Sports; Sports Medicine); **Tourism and Leisure** (Art History; Cultural Studies; Ecology; Economics; Geography; History; Hotel Management; Information Technology; Law; Leisure Studies; Management; Natural Sciences; Philosophy; Rehabilitation and Therapy; Sociology; Statistics; Tourism)

History: Founded 1893 as department of the Jagiellonian University, became independant institution and acquired present status and title 1951.

Governing Bodies: Senate; Rector

Academic Year: October-June

Admission Requirements: Secondary school certificate (matura) and entrance examinations

Fees: (New Zoty): 1,800-3,000 per semester for local students; (Euro): 4,000 per annum for foreign students (2,500 for part-time studies).

Main Language(s) of Instruction: Polish

International Co-operation: With universities in Portugal, France, The Netherlands

Accrediting Agencies: Ministry of Science and Higher Education

Degrees and Diplomas: *Licencjat*; *Świadectwo ukończenia studiów podyplomowych*; *Magister*; *Doktor*

Student Services: Canteen, Cultural centre, Employment services, Handicapped facilities, Health services, Sports facilities

Student Residential Facilities: 3 dormitories (c. 900 beds); Teachers quarters

Special Facilities: Scientific Information Centre

Libraries: Central Library

Publications: Antropomotoryka *(biennially)*; Folia Turistica *(biennially)*; Studia Humanistyczne *(biennially)*

Student Numbers *2009-2010*: Total: c. 5,000

Last Updated: 08/09/11

UNIVERSITY SCHOOL OF PHYSICAL EDUCATION IN POZNAN

Akademia Wychowania Fizycznego im. Eugeniusza Piaseckiego w Poznaniu (AWF)

ul. Królowej Jadwigi 27/39, 61-871 Poznań, wielkopolskie
Tel: +48(61) 835-50-00
Fax: +48(61) 835-50-98
EMail: office@awf.poznan.pl
Website: http://www.awf.poznan.pl

Rektor: Jerzy Smorawiński (2008-)
Tel: +48(61) 852-51-85, Fax: +48(61) 835-51-03
EMail: rektor@awf.poznan.pl

p.o. Kanclerz: Stanisław Wiesław Kuhnert
Tel: +48(61) 835-50-30, Fax: +48(61) 833-00-87
EMail: sekretariat@awf.poznan.pl

International Relations: Małgorzata Nawrocka, International Relations Officer
Tel: +48(61) 835-50-66, Fax: +48(61) 833-00-39
EMail: nawrocka@awf.poznan.pl

Departments

Foreign Languages *(Interdepartment)* (English; German; Modern Languages; Russian)

Faculties

Physical Education *(Gorzow Wielkopolski)* (Anthropology; Arts and Humanities; Biochemistry; Biology; Computer Science; English; History; Modern Languages; Natural Sciences; Parks and Recreation; Philosophy; Physical Education; Physiology; Psychology; Sociology; Sports; Sports Medicine; Statistics; Tourism); **Physical Education, Sport and Rehabilitation** (Anatomy; Anthropology; Biochemistry; Biology; Education; Environmental Studies; Ethnology; Health Education; History; Hygiene; Neurology; Philosophy; Physical Education; Physical Therapy; Physiology; Psychology; Rehabilitation and Therapy; Respiratory Therapy; Rheumatology; Sociology; Sports; Sports Medicine); **Tourism and Recreation** (Computer Science; Ecology; Economics; Environmental Studies; Food Science; Geography; Nutrition; Parks and Recreation; Statistics; Tourism)

Further Information: Branch in Gorzów Wielkopolski

History: Founded 1919 as faculty of University of Poznań, reorganized as higher school of physical education 1950, and acquired present status and title 1973.

Governing Bodies: Senate

Academic Year: September to May (September-January; January-May)

Admission Requirements: Secondary school certificate (Matura) and entrance examination

Fees: (US Dollars): Foreign students, 5,000 per annum

Main Language(s) of Instruction: Polish

International Co-operation: Participates in Socrates/Erasmus (Germany, Greece, Spain, France, Finland, Denmark, Netherlands, Portugal, Sweden) and CEEPUS (Slovenia, Slovak Republic, Czech Republic, Bulgaria) programmes

Accrediting Agencies: Ministry of Science and Higher Education

Degrees and Diplomas: *Licencjat*; *Świadectwo ukończenia studiów podyplomowych*; *Magister*; *Doktor*

Student Services: Academic counselling, Employment services, Health services, Social counselling, Sports facilities

Student Residential Facilities: For 800 students

Libraries: Main Library, 146,145 vols

Publications: Biuletyn Informacyjny AWF *(quarterly)*; Monografie, Podręczniki, Skrypty AWF w Poznaniu, Series; Roczniki Naukowe, Scientific Annuals *(annually)*; Studies in Physical Culture and Tourism *(annually)*

Press or Publishing House: The AWF's Publishers

Last Updated: 09/09/11

WARSAW SCHOOL OF ECONOMICS

Szkoła Główna Handlowa w Warszawie (SGH)

al. Niepodległości 162, 02-554 Warszawa, mazowieckie
Tel: +48(22) 564-60-00 +48(22) 564-64-64
Fax: +48(22) 849-53-12
EMail: informacja@sgh.waw.pl
Website: http://www.sgh.waw.pl

Rector: Adam Budnikowski (2008-)
Tel: +48(22) 564-62-01, Fax: +48(22) 849-51-95
EMail: adam.budnikowski@sgh.waw.pl

Kanclerz: Witold Włodarczyk EMail: joachim.osinski@sgh.waw.pl

International Relations: Elzbieta Kawecka-Wyrzykowska, Vice-Rector for International Relations
EMail: Elzbieta.Kawecka@sgh.waw.pl

Centres

Economic Studies Development (Development Studies; Economics); **Foreign Languages** (English; French; German; Italian; Modern Languages; Polish; Romance Languages; Russian; Spanish); **Physical Education and Sport** (Physical Education; Sports)

Colleges

Business Administration (Accountancy; Administration; Administrative Law; Agricultural Business; Business Administration; Business and Commerce; Economic and Finance Policy; Finance; Geography (Human); Human Resources; Management; Management Systems; Marketing; Real Estate; Small Business; Transport Management); **Economic Analysis** (Business Computing; Demography and Population; Econometrics; Economic and Finance Policy; Economics; International Studies; Mathematics; Mathematics and Computer Science; Statistics); **Management and Finance** (Accountancy; Banking; Business Administration; Commercial Law; Consumer Studies; Economic and Finance Policy; Economics; Finance; Government; Insurance; Management; Marketing; Safety Engineering; Transport and Communications); **Socio-Economics** (Economic and Finance Policy; Economics; European Union Law; Government; History; History of Societies; Insurance; International Relations; International Studies; Labour and Industrial Relations; Management; Natural Resources; Philosophy; Political Sciences; Public Administration; Social Policy; Social Sciences; Social Studies; Sociology); **World Economy** (Banking; Business and Commerce; Ecology; Economic and Finance Policy; Economics; European Studies; Finance; Insurance; International Business; International Economics; International Law; International Relations; Management; Marketing; Tourism)

Departments

Accounting Teaching (Accountancy); **Education** (Economics; Education); **Logistics** (Transport Management); **Science**

History: Founded 1906, as a private school, reorganized 1933 as Central School of Commerce, acquired present status 1949 as

Central School of Planning and Statistics, and acquired present title 1991.

Governing Bodies: Senate

Academic Year: October to June (October-February; February-June)

Admission Requirements: Secondary school certificate (Matura)

Fees: None for full-time Polish students

Main Language(s) of Instruction: Polish; English

International Co-operation: With universities in the EU, USA, Canada, Japan, Korea, Singapore, China and India, New Zealand, Russia, Eastern Europe and Australia.

Accrediting Agencies: Ministry of Science and Higher Education

Degrees and Diplomas: *Licencjat*: with universities SGH Asian countries, including Japan, Korea, Singapore, China and India as well as with the countries of South and Central America and New Zealand, Russia and Eastern Europe. Since 2010, the exchange will be implemented in Australian; *Świadectwo ukończenia studiów podyplomowych*; *Magister*; *Doktor*. Also post-graduate studies in foreign languages: two English-language programmes, MBA - American and Canadian, and Polish-French programme "Management of the European economy" in collaboration with Groupe HEC; American MBA programme (Warsaw Executive MBA - Wemba) in collaboration with the University of Minnesota; and Canadian programme (Canadian Executive MBA - CEMB) with the University of Quebec at Montreal.

Student Services: Academic counselling, Canteen, Cultural centre, Employment services, Foreign student adviser, Foreign Studies Centre, Health services, Language programs, Social counselling, Sports facilities

Student Residential Facilities: For 1,160 students

Special Facilities: Student's Movie Studio 'Underground'. Computer Laboratories

Libraries: Central Library, over 1m. Vols; 221 periodical subscriptions

Publications: Bulletin of Institute of the Social Economy *(quarterly)*; Condition of Agriculture, Research Institute of Economic Development *(quarterly)*; Condition of Home Markets, Research Institute of Economic Development *(quarterly)*; Economic Papers in foreign languages *(annually)*; Economic Papers, Institute of International Studies *(annually)*; Economic Policy *(biennially)*; Outlook for Building Industry, Research Institute of Economic Development *(quarterly)*; Outlook for Industry, Research Institute of Economic Development *(monthly)*; Outlook for Trade, Research Institute of Economic Development *(monthly)*; Poland International Economic Report, Institute of World Economy *(annually)*; Publications of IFGN, Institute of National Economy; Studies and Materials, Collegium of Management and Finance; Studies and Materials, Economic Studies Development Centre; Studies and Materials, Institute of International Studies *(annually)*

Press or Publishing House: Oficyna Wydawnicza Szkoły Głównej Handlowej

Academic Staff *2010-2011*: Total: c. 900

Student Numbers *2010-2011*: Total: c. 16,000

Last Updated: 27/09/11

WARSAW UNIVERSITY OF LIFE SCIENCES

Szkoła Główna Gospodarstwa Wiejskiego w Warszawie (SGGW-WULS)

ul. Nowoursynowska 166, 02-787 Warszawa, mazowieckie
Tel: +48(22) 593-10-00
Fax: +48(22) 593-10-87 +48(22) 593-10-89
EMail: info@sggw.waw.pl
Website: http://www.sggw.pl/

Rektor: Alojzy Szymański (2008-)
Tel: +48(22) 593-10-10, Fax: +48(22) 593-10-06
EMail: rektor@sggw.pl

Chancellor: Władysław Skarżyński
Tel: +48(22) 593-10-01, Fax: +48(22) 593-10-03
EMail: kanclerz@sggw.pl

International Relations: Mieczyslaw Rygalski, Head of International Relations Office
Tel: +48(22) 593-10-40, Fax: +48(22) 593-10-42
EMail: mieczyslaw.rygalski@sggw.pl

Faculties

Agriculture and Biology (Agriculture; Agrobiology; Agronomy; Biochemistry; Biology; Botany; Crop Production; Natural Sciences; Plant and Crop Protection; Soil Science; Statistics); **Animal Sciences** (Animal Husbandry; Cattle Breeding; Environmental Studies; Fishery; Food Science; Genetics; Nutrition; Physiology; Tourism); **Applied Informatics and Mathematics** (Applied Mathematics; Computer Science; Econometrics; Information Technology; Mathematics; Statistics); **Civil and Environmental Engineering** (Applied Mathematics; Civil Engineering; Construction Engineering; Engineering; Environmental Engineering; Environmental Studies; Geological Engineering; Geophysics; Hydraulic Engineering); **Economics** (Accountancy; Agricultural Economics; Econometrics; Economic and Finance Policy; Economics; Finance; Management; Transport Management); **Food Science** (Agrobiology; Biotechnology; Brewing; Chemistry; Crop Production; Dairy; Food Science; Food Technology; Industrial Management; Inorganic Chemistry; Meat and Poultry; Microbiology; Organic Chemistry; Physical Chemistry; Safety Engineering); **Forestry** (Botany; Ecology; Forest Biology; Forest Economics; Forest Management; Forest Products; Forestry; Soil Management; Tourism); **Horticulture and Landscape Architecture** (Biotechnology; Botany; Entomology; Environmental Management; Genetics; Horticulture; Landscape Architecture; Plant Pathology; Vegetable Production); **Human Nutrition and Consumer Science** (Consumer Studies; Cooking and Catering; Dietetics; Food Science; Food Technology; Home Economics; Human Resources; Marketing; Nutrition; Physiology; Safety Engineering); **Humanities** (Arts and Humanities; Communication Studies; Education; International Relations; Pedagogy; Philosophy; Psychology; Sociology); **Production Engineering** (Agricultural Engineering; Agricultural Equipment; Business Administration; Energy Engineering; Engineering; Engineering Management; Forestry; Industrial Management; Information Technology; Management; Production Engineering); **Veterinary Medicine** (Anatomy; Biochemistry; Embryology and Reproduction Biology; Epidemiology; Histology; Hygiene; Microbiology; Parasitology; Pathology; Pharmacology; Physiology; Public Health; Surgery; Toxicology; Veterinary Science); **Wood Technology** (Applied Physics; Biophysics; Building Technologies; Forest Products; Industrial Management; Physics; Wood Technology)

Units

Biotechnology *(Interfaculty)* (Biotechnology); **Commodity Science** *(Interdisciplinary)* (Home Economics); **Environmental Protection** *(Interfaculty)* (Biology; Ecology; Energy Engineering; Environmental Engineering; Environmental Management; Environmental Studies; Forestry; Health Sciences; Meteorology; Microbiology; Surveying and Mapping; Tourism; Wildlife); **Foreign Language Education** (English; French; German; Modern Languages; Russian); **Inter-regional Planning and Management** *(Interfaculty)* (Management; Public Administration; Regional Planning); **Physical Education and Sports** (Physical Education; Sports); **Tourism and Recreation** (Hotel and Restaurant; Leisure Studies; Parks and Recreation; Tourism)

History: Founded 1816 as Institute of Agronomy in Marymont, reorganized and relocated several times during Car's government, became Polish Royal School of Agriculture 1918 and acquired present status and title 1919 after Poland gained independence.

Governing Bodies: Senate

Academic Year: October to June (October-January; February-June)

Admission Requirements: Secondary school certificate (Matura) or foreign equivalent, no examination

Fees: (US Dollars): 1,800-4,000 per semester.

Main Language(s) of Instruction: Polish; English

International Co-operation: With universities in Denmark, Netherlands, Germany,Canada, UK, Hungary, France, Slovak Republic, Ukraine, Japan, USA, Egypt, Lithuania, Russian Federation, Belarus. Also participates in the Socrates/Erasmus, Tempus, Erasmus Mundus programmes

Accrediting Agencies: Ministry of Science and Higher Education

Degrees and Diplomas: *Inżynier*; *Licencjat*; *Lekarz*; *Świadectwo ukończenia studiów podyplomowych*; *Magister*; *Doktor*. Also MBA

Student Services: Academic counselling, Canteen, Cultural centre, Employment services, Handicapped facilities, Health services, Language programs, Nursery care, Sports facilities

Student Residential Facilities: 12 students houses (c. 4,000 beds).

Special Facilities: Historical Museum of SGGW, Experimental Field Station for Plant Genetics, Breeding and Biotechnology; Horse Clinic; Experimental Field of Vaccinium Plants; Experimental Agricultural Stations; Experimental Forestry Station, Animal Husbandry Station

Libraries: Main Library, 450,000 vols; 3 Faculty Libraries

Publications: Acta Scientarum Polonarum Architectura *(biennially)*; Acta Scientarum Polonarum Oeconomia *(biannually)*; Agricola, University periodical *(quarterly)*; Annals of Warsaw University of Life Sciences, Scientific publications, 7 thematic series *(biannually)*; Information Booklets *(bimonthly)*; Scientific publications, Handbooks, scripts, monographs *(other/irregular)*; Scientific Review, Engineering and Environmental Protection *(quarterly)*

Press or Publishing House: Warsaw University of Life Sciences Press

Academic Staff *2010-2011*	MEN	WOMEN	**TOTAL**
FULL-TIME	660	560	**1,220**
PART-TIME	–	–	**10**
STAFF WITH DOCTORATE			
FULL-TIME	390	420	**810**
PART-TIME	–	–	c. **10**
Student Numbers *2011-2012*			
All (Foreign Included)	–	–	c. **27,145**

Last Updated: 27/09/11

WARSAW UNIVERSITY OF TECHNOLOGY

Politechnika Warszawska (PW)

pl. Politechniki 1, 00-661 Warszawa, mazowieckie
Tel: +48(22) 234-72-11 +48(22) 629-74-84
Fax: +48(22) 621-68-92
EMail: pw@pw.edu.pl
Website: http://www.pw.edu.pl

Rektor: Włodzimierz Kurnik
Tel: +48(22) 234-72-20 EMail: jmr@rekt.pw.edu.pl

Kanclerz: Krzysztof Dziedzic
Tel: +48(22) 628-61-29, Fax: +48(22) 628-84-68
EMail: ka@ca.pw.edu.pl

International Relations: Marek Polak, Director, Centre for International Cooperation
Tel: +48(22) 660-71-85, Fax: +48(22) 660-57-77
EMail: mpolak@cwm.pw.edu.pl

Centres

Computer (Computer Science); **Foreign Languages** *(Interfaculty)* (English; French; German; Italian; Modern Languages; Polish; Russian; Spanish); **Physical Education and Sports** (Physical Education; Sports)

Colleges

Economics and Social Sciences *(Płock)* (Economics; Industrial and Production Economics; Social Sciences)

Faculties

Administration and Social Science (Administration; Economics; History; Law; Philosophy; Safety Engineering; Social Sciences; Sociology); **Architecture** (Architectural and Environmental Design; Architectural Restoration; Architecture; Heritage Preservation; Rural Planning; Structural Architecture; Town Planning); **Automotive and Construction Machinery Engineering** (Automotive Engineering; Machine Building; Mechanical Engineering; Mechanical Equipment and Maintenance; Power Engineering; Railway Engineering); **Chemical and Process Engineering** (Biotechnology; Chemical Engineering; Engineering Management; Environmental Engineering; Mechanical Engineering; Thermal Physics); **Chemistry** (Analytical Chemistry; Biotechnology; Chemistry; Inorganic Chemistry; Organic Chemistry; Physical Chemistry; Polymer and Plastics Technology; Solid State Physics; Technology); **Civil Engineering** (Civil Engineering; Construction Engineering; Mechanical Engineering); **Civil Engineering, Mechanics and Petrochemistry** *(Płock)* (Agricultural Equipment; Building Technologies; Chemistry; Civil Engineering; Environmental Engineering; Machine Building; Mechanical Engineering; Mechanics; Petroleum and Gas Engineering); **Electrical Engineering** (Automation and Control Engineering; Electrical and Electronic Engineering; Electrical and Electronic Equipment and Maintenance; Industrial Engineering; Measurement and Precision Engineering; Power Engineering); **Electronics and Information Technology** (Automation and Control Engineering; Computer Engineering; Computer Networks; Computer Science; Electronic Engineering; Information Technology; Measurement and Precision Engineering; Microelectronics; Microwaves; Optometry; Software Engineering; Telecommunications Engineering); **Environmental Engineering** (Biotechnology; Environmental Engineering; Heating and Refrigeration; Hydraulic Engineering; Petroleum and Gas Engineering; Waste Management; Water Management); **Geodesy and Cartography** (Earth Sciences; Geophysics; Printing and Printmaking; Surveying and Mapping); **Management** (Business Administration; Business Computing; Economics; Finance; Information Sciences; Management; Production Engineering; Safety Engineering; Transport Management); **Materials Science and Engineering** (Ceramics and Glass Technology; Materials Engineering; Metal Techniques; Polymer and Plastics Technology); **Mathematics and Information Sciences** (Computer Science; Information Sciences; Mathematics); **Mechatronics** (Automation and Control Engineering; Biomedical Engineering; Electronic Engineering; Measurement and Precision Engineering; Mechanical Engineering; Mechanical Equipment and Maintenance; Mechanics; Microelectronics; Optical Technology; Optics; Optometry; Robotics); **Physics** (Nuclear Physics; Optics; Physics; Solid State Physics); **Power and Aeronautical Engineering** (Aeronautical and Aerospace Engineering; Automation and Control Engineering; Environmental Engineering; Heating and Refrigeration; Mechanical Engineering; Mechanics; Nuclear Engineering; Power Engineering; Robotics); **Production Engineering** (Automation and Control Engineering; Building Technologies; Engineering Drawing and Design; Machine Building; Management Systems; Materials Engineering; Mechanical Engineering; Mechanics; Metal Techniques; Production Engineering; Robotics); **Transport** (Air Transport; Automotive Engineering; Railway Transport; Road Transport; Transport and Communications; Transport Engineering; Transport Management) *Dean*: Andrzej Chudzikiewicz

Schools

Business *(Interfaculty)* (Business Administration; Economics; Finance; International Business; Management; Marketing)

Further Information: Also Branch in Płock

History: Founded 1826 as Preparatory School for the Institute of Technology. Closed in 1830 and reopened 1898. Acquired present title and status 1915.

Governing Bodies: Senate

Academic Year: October to June (October-February; February-June)

Admission Requirements: Secondary school certificate (Matura), or foreign equivalent and entrance examination

Fees: Foreign students, (US Dollars): 3,000-5,000

Main Language(s) of Instruction: Polish; English

International Co-operation: With 63 universities all around the world. Participates in the Socrates/Erasmus, Leonardo da Vinci, Eureka, Grungwig, Minerwa, 6th Framework programmes

Accrediting Agencies: Ministry of Science and Higher Education

Degrees and Diplomas: *Inżynier*, *Licencjat*, *Magister*, *Doktor*

Student Services: Canteen, Cultural centre, Employment services, Foreign student adviser, Foreign Studies Centre, Health services, Language programs, Sports facilities

Student Residential Facilities: For 5,400 students

Special Facilities: Museum

Libraries: c. 1,2m vols

Publications: Demonstratio Matematica *(quarterly)*; Machine Dynamics Problems *(quarterly)*; Miesięcznik Politechniki Warszawskiej *(monthly)*; Reports on Geodesy *(quarterly)*

Press or Publishing House: Warsaw University of Technology Publications

Academic Staff *2010-2011*	TOTAL
FULL-TIME	2,453
STAFF WITH DOCTORATE	
FULL-TIME	1,519
Student Numbers *2010-2011*	
All (Foreign Included)	36,156
FOREIGN ONLY	612

Last Updated: 26/09/11

WEST POMERANIAN UNIVERSITY OF TECHNOLOGY, SZCZECIN

Zachodniopomorski Uniwersytet Technologiczny w Szczecinie (ZUT)

al. Piastów, 70-310 Szczecin, zachodniopomorskie
Tel: +48(91) 449-41-11
Fax: +48(91) 449-40-14
EMail: zut@zut.edu.pl
Website: http://zut.edu.pl/

Rector: Włodzimierz Kiernożycki
Tel: +48(91) 434-67-51 +48(91) 449-40-15,
Fax: +48(91) 449-40-14 EMail: rektor@zut.edu.pl

Kanclerz: Jarosław Potaczek
Tel: +48(91) 449-41-20, Fax: +48(91) 434-73-26
EMail: kanclerz@zut.edu.pl

International Relations: Stanisław Heropolitański, University Spokesman
Tel: +48(91) 449-48-30, Fax: +48(91) 449-48-30
EMail: rzecznik@zut.edu.pl

Faculties

Biotechnology and Animal Breeding (Animal Husbandry; Biology; Biotechnology; Crop Production; Ecology; Environmental Studies; Tourism); **Chemical Technology and Engineering** (Biotechnology; Chemical Engineering; Environmental Engineering; Environmental Studies; Information Technology; Inorganic Chemistry; Nanotechnology; Organic Chemistry; Polymer and Plastics Technology; Technology); **Civil Engineering and Architecture** (Architecture; Architecture and Planning; Civil Engineering; Construction Engineering; Design; Energy Engineering; Environmental Engineering; Real Estate; Road Engineering; Town Planning); **Computer Science and Information Technology** (Computer Engineering; Computer Graphics; Computer Science; Information Technology; Management; Multimedia; Production Engineering; Software Engineering; Telecommunications Engineering); **Economics** (Accountancy; Business Administration; Business Computing; Economics; Finance; Government; Health Administration; Human Resources; International Business; International Relations; Management; Real Estate; Safety Engineering; Tourism; Transport Management); **Electrical Engineering** (Automation and Control Engineering; Computer Graphics; Electrical Engineering; Electronic Engineering; Information Technology; Multimedia; Physical Engineering; Robotics; Telecommunications Engineering); **Environment Management and Agriculture** (Agricultural Economics; Agricultural Engineering; Agricultural Management; Agriculture; Agronomy; Environmental Studies; Farm Management; Forestry; Horticulture; Landscape Architecture); **Food Sciences and Fisheries** (Bioengineering; Fishery; Food Science; Food Technology; Marine Biology; Marine Science and Oceanography; Microbiology; Nutrition; Tourism); **Marine Engineeeing and Transport** (Energy Engineering; Engineering; Heating and Refrigeration; Marine Engineering; Marine Transport; Mechanics; Naval Architecture; Power Engineering; Safety Engineering; Thermal Engineering; Transport Economics; Transport Engineering; Transport Management); **Mechanical Engineering and Mechatronics** (Automation and Control Engineering; Automotive Engineering; Electronic Engineering; Machine Building; Maintenance Technology; Materials Engineering; Mechanical Engineering; Mechanics; Metal Techniques; Physics; Polymer and Plastics Technology; Production Engineering; Solid State Physics; Thermal Engineering)

History: Founded 1946 as School of Engineering, merged with School of Economics, and acquired present status and title 1955. Acquried present title 2009 after merger with Akademia Rolnicza w Szczecinie (Academy of Agriculture, Szczecin).

Governing Bodies: Senate

Academic Year: October to June (October-February; February-June)

Admission Requirements: Secondary school certificate (Matura) and entrance examinations

Fees: (Euros): Foreign students, 2,000-, 3,000 per annum

Main Language(s) of Instruction: Polish

International Co-operation: Participates in the Socrates/Erasmus, Leonardo, FP5, FP6, Culture, Polonium programmes

Accrediting Agencies: Ministry of Science and Higher Education; National Accreditation Commission

Degrees and Diplomas: *Inżynier*; *Licencjat*; *Świadectwo ukończenia studiów podyplomowych*; *Magister*; *Doktor*. Also Certificates

Student Services: Academic counselling, Canteen, Cultural centre, Employment services, Foreign student adviser, Foreign Studies Centre, Handicapped facilities, Health services, Language programs, Nursery care, Social counselling, Sports facilities

Student Residential Facilities: Yes

Special Facilities: Astronomical Observatory

Libraries: Central Library, 404,714 vols

Publications: Monographic Series *(other/irregular)*; Zeszyty Naukowe "Ekoplast" *(biennially)*

Academic Staff *2009-2010*: Total: c. 1,100

Student Numbers *2009-2010*: Total: c. 13,000

Last Updated: 07/09/11

WROCLAW MEDICAL UNIVERSITY

Akademia Medyczna im. Piastów Śląskich we Wrocławiu (AM)

Wybrzeże L. Pasteura 1, 50-367 Wrocław, dolnośląskie
Tel: +48(71) 784-10-01
Fax: +48(71) 784-01-09
EMail: rektor@am.wroc.pl
Website: http://www.am.wroc.pl

Rektor: Marek Ziętek

Kanclerz: Artur Parafiński
Tel: +48(71) 784-10-02, Fax: +48(71) 784-00-07
EMail: dyrektor@adm.am.wroc.pl

International Relations: Peter Mittelstaedt
Tel: +48(71) 784-11-44, Fax: +48(71) 784-00-33
EMail: mitel@zagr.am.wroc.pl

Departments

Foreign Languages *(Interdepartmental Unit)* (English; French; German; Latin; Modern Languages; Polish; Russian); **Physical Education** *(Interdepartmental Unit)* (Physical Education)

Divisions

Studies in English (Anaesthesiology; Anatomy; Biochemistry; Biology; Biophysics; Chemistry; Dentistry; Embryology and Reproduction Biology; Endocrinology; English; Gastroenterology; Genetics; Histology; Hygiene; Immunology; Medicine; Microbiology; Nutrition; Oncology; Paediatrics; Pathology; Pharmacology; Physiology; Surgery)

Faculties

Dentistry (Anatomy; Dental Technology; Dentistry; Orthodontics; Orthopaedics; Otorhinolaryngology; Periodontics; Surgery); **Health Sciences** (Cardiology; Dietetics; Gerontology; Gynaecology and Obstetrics; Health Administration; Health Sciences; Nursing; Paediatrics; Physical Therapy; Pneumology; Public Health; Rehabilitation and Therapy); **Medicine** (Anaesthesiology; Anatomy; Arts and Humanities; Biochemistry; Biology; Biophysics; Cardiology; Chemistry; Embryology and Reproduction Biology; Endocrinology; Forensic Medicine and Dentistry; Gastroenterology; Genetics; Germanic Studies; Gynaecology and Obstetrics; Health Education; Histology; Hygiene; Immunology; Medicine; Microbiology; Nutrition; Occupational Health; Oncology; Paediatrics; Parasitology; Pathology; Pedagogy; Pharmacology; Physiology; Rheumatology; Surgery); **Pharmacy** (Analytical Chemistry; Biochemistry; Biology; Biomedicine; Botany; Chemistry; Food Science; Inorganic Chemistry; Laboratory Techniques; Medicine; Nutrition; Organic Chemistry; Pharmacology; Pharmacy; Physical Chemistry; Toxicology); **Postgraduate Medical Training** (Cardiology; Dermatology; Diabetology; Dietetics; Endocrinology; Gastroenterology; Gynaecology and Obstetrics; Haematology; Hepatology; Medicine; Nephrology;

Neurology; Oncology; Ophthalmology; Orthopaedics; Otorhinolaryngology; Paediatrics; Pneumology; Psychiatry and Mental Health; Radiology; Rehabilitation and Therapy; Social and Preventive Medicine; Sports Medicine; Surgery; Urology; Venereology)

Further Information: Also Wroclaw Medical University Fundation; Private Health Centre - University Dental Polyclinic; 2 University Hospitals.

History: Founded 1945 as high school, became Academy of Medicine 1950, and acquired present status and title 1994.

Governing Bodies: Senate and Rector

Academic Year: October to June (October-January; February-June)

Admission Requirements: Secondary school certificate (Matura) and entrance examination

Fees: (Euros): 2,500-7,000 per annum

Main Language(s) of Instruction: Polish; English

International Co-operation: With universities in Germany; Italy; France; Spain; Finland; Sweden; Portugal; Netherlands; Czech Republic; Slovak Republic; Lithuania; Russian Federation; Belarus; Hungary. Also participates in the Socrates/Erasmus, Leonardo da Vinci, COST, Wellcome Trust, TRIGR, 5th and 6th Framework programmes

Accrediting Agencies: Ministry of Science and Higher Education, State Accreditation Commission

Degrees and Diplomas: *Licencjat*; *Lekarz*; *Lekarz*: Dentistry; *Świadectwo ukończenia studiów podyplomowych*; *Magister*; *Doktor*

Student Services: Academic counselling, Canteen, Cultural centre, Employment services, Foreign student adviser, Foreign Studies Centre, Health services, Language programs, Nursery care, Social counselling, Sports facilities

Special Facilities: Forensic Medicine Museum. Medical Plants Garden

Libraries: Main Library

Publications: Dental and Medical Problems *(other/irregular)*; Mycology in Medicine *(quarterly)*; Postępy Medycyny Klinicznej i Doświadczalnej (Advances in Clinical and Experimental Medicine) *(quarterly)*

Press or Publishing House: Publishing House, Wrocław

Academic Staff *2010-2011*: Total 1,072

STAFF WITH DOCTORATE: Total 676

Last Updated: 02/09/11

WROCŁAW UNIVERSITY OF ECONOMICS

Uniwersytet Ekonomiczny we Wrocławiu (WUE)

Komandorska 118/120, 53-345 Wrocław, dolnośląskie
Tel: +48(71) 368-01-00
Fax: +48(71) 367-27-78
EMail: kontakt@ue.wroc.pl
Website: http://ue.wroc.pl

Rector: Bogusław Fiedor (2005-)
Tel: +48(71) 368-01-41, Fax: +48(71) 368-09-21
EMail: rektor@ue.wroc.pl

Dyrektor Administracyjny: Edward Bratek
Tel: +48(71) 368-01-44, Fax: +48(71) 368-09-21
EMail: kanclerz@ue.wroc.pl

International Relations: Jaroslaw Witkowski, Vice-Rector for International Cooperation
Tel: +48(71) 368-01-60, Fax: +48(71) 367-09-21
EMail: jwit@ae.jgora.pl

Faculties

Economic Sciences (Accountancy; Economics; Finance; International Business; International Economics; International Relations; Management) *Dean*: Andrzej Graczyk; **Engineering and Economics** (Management; Production Engineering) *Dean*: Władysław Czupryk; **Management, Computer Science and Finance** (Accountancy; Business Computing; Computer Science; Econometrics; Finance; Management) *Dean*: Jozef Dziechciarz; **Regional Economics and Tourism** (Economics; Management; Tourism) *Dean*: Marek Walesiak

Further Information: Also Branches in Świdnica, Wałbrzych, Głogów, and Brzeg

History: Founded 1947 as Higher Commercial School. Acquired present title 2008. Formerly known as Akademia Ekonomiczna im. Oskara Langego we Wrocławiu until 2008.

Governing Bodies: Senate

Academic Year: October to June (October-January; February-June)

Admission Requirements: Secondary school certificate (świadectwo maturalne) and entrance examination

Fees: (Euro): 2,500 per annum for non-European students.

Main Language(s) of Instruction: Polish; English

International Co-operation: With universities in European countries, Japan, USA, Canada, Russia, Ukraine.

Accrediting Agencies: Ministry of Science and Higher Education

Degrees and Diplomas: *Licencjat*: Economics; Management; *Magister*: Economics; Management; *Doktor*: Economics; Management. Also Bachelor's degree; Master's degree; MBA and executive MBA

Student Services: Academic counselling, Canteen, Cultural centre, Employment services, Foreign student adviser, Foreign Studies Centre, Handicapped facilities, Health services, Language programs, Social counselling, Sports facilities

Student Residential Facilities: For c. 17,000 students

Libraries: Central Library, c. 400,000 vols

Publications: Argumenta Oeconomica, ISI Master Journal List; Prace Naukowe Uniwersytetu Ekonomicznego we Wroclawiu

Press or Publishing House: Wydawnictwo Akademii Ekonomicznej we Wrocławiu

Academic Staff *2010-2011*: Total 1,379

Student Numbers *2010-2011*: Total: c. 17,000

Last Updated: 29/08/11

WROCŁAW UNIVERSITY OF ENVIRONMENTAL AND LIFE SCIENCES

Uniwersytet Przyrodniczy we Wrocławiu (AR)

ul. C.K. Norwida 25/27, 50-375 Wrocław, dolnośląskie
Tel: +48(71) 320-50-20
Fax: +48(71) 320-54-04 +48(71) 328-35-76
EMail: dos@up.wroc.pl; info.rekrutacja@up.wroc.pl
Website: http://www.ar.wroc.pl

Rektor: Roman Kołacz (2008-)
Tel: +48(71) 320-51-01, Fax: +48(71) 320-54-04
EMail: rektor@up.wroc.pl

Kanclerz: Marian Rybarczyk
Tel: +48(71) 320-51-09 +48(71) 320-51-51-30,
Fax: +48(71) 328-35-76 EMail: kanclerz@up.wroc.pl

International Relations: Alina Wieliczko, Vice-Rector for International Relations
Tel: +48(71) 320-10-25, Fax: +48(71) 328-48-49
EMail: AGM@up.wroc.pl

Departments

Foreign Languages *(Interfaculty)* (English; French; German; Modern Languages; Russian); **Inter-Pedagogical** *(Interfaculty)* (Teacher Training); **Physical Education and Sport** *(Interfaculty)* (Physical Education; Sports)

Faculties

Biology and Animal Science (Animal Husbandry; Biology; Computer Science; Fishery; Genetics; Hygiene; Meat and Poultry; Nutrition); **Environmental Engineering and Geodesy** (Architecture and Planning; Building Technologies; Civil Engineering; Economics; Environmental Engineering; Environmental Management; Geological Engineering; Landscape Architecture; Mathematics; Measurement and Precision Engineering; Parks and Recreation; Real Estate; Safety Engineering; Surveying and Mapping); **Food Science** (Biotechnology; Chemistry; Cooking and Catering; Crop Production; European Union Law; Food Science; Food Technology; Fruit Production; Health Sciences; Hotel Management; Microbiology; Nutrition; Safety Engineering; Social and Preventive Medicine); **Life Sciences and Technology** (Agricultural Engineering; Agriculture; Agronomy; Biological and Life Sciences; Biophysics; Botany; Ecology; Economics; Engineering Management; Environmental Management;

Environmental Studies; Forestry; Genetics; Horticulture; Nutrition; Physics; Plant and Crop Protection; Production Engineering; Social Sciences; Soil Science); **Veterinary Medicine** (Biochemistry; Embryology and Reproduction Biology; Food Science; Hygiene; Immunology; Parasitology; Pathology; Pharmacology; Physiology; Surgery; Toxicology; Veterinary Science; Zoology)

History: Founded 1951 as Higher School of Agriculture, renamed the Agricultural University of Wrocław 1972, acquired present status and title 2006.

Governing Bodies: Senate

Academic Year: October to June (October-February; February-June)

Admission Requirements: Secondary school certificate (Matura)

Fees: (US Dollars): Part-time students 1,000; Foreign students from non-EU member states 1,200 per semester, 4,000-5,000 per annum

Main Language(s) of Instruction: Polish

International Co-operation: Participates in the LLP-Erasmus, CEEPUS, 7th PR EU, and TEMPUS programmes.

Accrediting Agencies: Ministry of Science and Higher Education

Degrees and Diplomas: *Inżynier*, *Licencjat*; *Świadectwo ukończenia studiów podyplomowych*; *Magister*, *Doktor*, *Doktor habilitowany*

Student Services: Academic counselling, Canteen, Cultural centre, Foreign Studies Centre, Health services, Social counselling, Sports facilities

Student Residential Facilities: For 1,800 students

Special Facilities: Weather Station

Libraries: Central Library, 212,000 vols; faculty libraries

Publications: Zeszyty Naukowe, Scientific Journals (in Polish, abstracts and headings in English) *(annually)*

Press or Publishing House: Wydawnictwo Akademii Rolniczej we Wrocławiu

Academic Staff *2010-2011*: Total 710

STAFF WITH DOCTORATE: Total 170

Student Numbers *2010-2011*: Total: c. 10,400

Last Updated: 30/09/11

WROCŁAW UNIVERSITY OF TECHNOLOGY

Politechnika Wrocławska (PWR)

Wybrzeże Wyspiańskiego 27, 50-370 Wrocław, dolnośląskie
Tel: +48(71) 320-26-00
Fax: +48(71) 322-36-64
EMail: Kancelaria.Rektora@pwr.wroc.pl
Website: http://www.pwr.wroc.pl

Rektor: Tadeusz Więckowski (2008-)
Tel: +48(71) 320-22-17 EMail: jmr@pwr.wroc.pl

Dyrektor Administracyjny: Alicja Samołyk
Tel: +48(71) 320-22-77, Fax: +48(71) 322-36-64
EMail: sekrpwr@ac.pwr.wroc.pl

International Relations: Izabela Hutchins, Head of International Office
Tel: +48(71) 320-41-14, Fax: +48(71) 320-35-70
EMail: izabela.hutchins@pwr.wroc.pl

Departments

Fundamental Studies (Computer Science; Mathematics; Physics)

Faculties

Architecture (Architecture; Town Planning); **Chemistry** (Biotechnology; Chemical Engineering; Chemistry; Materials Engineering); **Civil Engineering** (Civil Engineering); **Computer Science and Management** (Computer Engineering; Computer Science; Management); **Electrical Engineering** (Automation and Control Engineering; Electrical Engineering; Electronic Engineering; Mechanical Engineering; Robotics); **Electronics** (Automation and Control Engineering; Computer Science; Electronic Engineering; Robotics; Telecommunications Engineering); **Environmental Engineering** (Environmental Engineering; Environmental Studies); **Fundamental Problems of Technology** (Applied Physics; Biomedical Engineering; Computer Science; Mathematics; Physics); **Geoengineering, Mining and Geology** (Geological Engineering; Geology; Mining Engineering; Surveying and Mapping); **Mechanical and Power Engineering** (Machine Building; Mechanical Engineering; Power Engineering); **Mechanical Engineering** (Automation and Control Engineering; Biomedical Engineering; Electronic Engineering; Engineering Management; Machine Building; Mechanical Engineering; Production Engineering; Robotics; Transport Engineering); **Microsystem Electronics and Photonics** (Electronic Engineering; Mechanical Engineering; Physics; Telecommunications Engineering)

History: Founded 1945 as a State institution with four faculties. Reorganized 1968 with some 29 institutes replacing a large number of individual chairs. Under the jurisdiction of the Ministry of National Education. At present times it includes 12 faculties, 30 institutes and 5 Chairs.

Governing Bodies: Senate

Academic Year: October to June (October-January; February-June)

Admission Requirements: Secondary school certificate (Matura)

Fees: Tuition fees for Programmes in English, Bachelor, 3,000 per annum; Master, 4,000 per annum; PhD, 4,000 per annum. For Programmes in Polish, Bachelor 2,500 per annum; Master, 3,000 per annum; PhD, 4,000 per annum.

Main Language(s) of Instruction: Polish; English

International Co-operation: Agreements with over 250 partner universities all over the world. Participates in LLP-Erasmus, Erasmus-Mundus, the 7th Framework, and Leonardo da Vinci programmes.

Accrediting Agencies: Ministry of Science and Higher Education

Degrees and Diplomas: *Inżynier*, *Magister*, *Doktor*

Student Services: Academic counselling, Canteen, Cultural centre, Employment services, Foreign student adviser, Foreign Studies Centre, Handicapped facilities, Health services, Social counselling, Sports facilities

Student Residential Facilities: Yes

Special Facilities: Scientific Information Centre

Libraries: 900,000 vols

Publications: Environment Protection Engineering; Optica Applicata; Studia Geotechnica et Mechanica; Systems Science; Zeszyty Naukowe Politechniki Wrocławskiej, Scientific Papers

Press or Publishing House: Wrocław University of Technology Press

Academic Staff *2009-2010*: Total: c. 2,000

Student Numbers *2009-2010*: Total 32,929

Last Updated: 26/09/11

BRANCH AT BIELAWA

FILIA W BIELAWIE

ul. Żeromskiego 41-41a, 58-260 Bielawa
Tel: +48(74) 833-96-03 +48(74) 832-87-28
Fax: +48(74) 833-46-71
EMail: zod.bielawa@pwr.wroc.pl
Website: http://www.bielawa.pwr.wroc.pl

Dean: Maciej Chorowski

Departments

Mechanical and Power Engineering (Energy Engineering; Mechanical Engineering; Nuclear Engineering; Power Engineering; Thermal Engineering)

Degrees and Diplomas: *Inżynier*

BRANCH AT JELENIA GÓRA

FILIA W JELENIEJ GÓRZE

pl. Piastowski 27, 58-560 Jelenia Góra, dolnośląskie
Tel: +48(75) 755-10-48
Fax: +48(75) 755-15-99
EMail: sekretariat@pwr.jgora.pl; dziekanat@pwr.jgora.pl
Website: http://www.pwr.jgora.pl

Dyrektor: Maciej Pawłowski Tel: +48(71) 320-22-76

Faculties

Civil Engineering (Bridge Engineering; Civil Engineering; Construction Engineering; Road Engineering); **Computer Science and Management** (Computer Science; Management); **Electronics**

(Automation and Control Engineering; Computer Engineering; Computer Networks; Electronic Engineering; Telecommunications Engineering); **Environmental Engineering** (Environmental Engineering; Heating and Refrigeration; Soil Management; Waste Management; Water Management); **Fundamental Problems of Technology** (Biomedical Engineering; Data Processing; Medical Technology); **Mechanical Engineering** (Mechanical Engineering)

History: Founded 1976 as Branch of Wrocław University of Technology.

Degrees and Diplomas: *Inżynier*

STAFF WITH DOCTORATE: Total 47

Student Numbers *2010-2011*: Total: c. 600

BRANCH AT LEGNICA

FILIA W LEGNICY

ul. S. Batorego 8, 59-220 Legnica, dolnośląskie
Tel: +48(76) 850-29-66
Fax: +48(76) 850-29-81
EMail: zod.legnica@pwr.wroc.pl
Website: http://www.pwr.legnica.pl

Dyrektor: Jerzy Bartoszewski
Tel: +48(76) 850-29-66 EMail: Jerzy.Bartoszewski@pwr.wroc.pl

Faculties
Civil Engineering (Civil Engineering); **Electrical Engineering** (Electrical Engineering); **Geoengineering, Mining and Geology** (Geological Engineering; Geology; Mining Engineering); **Mechanical Engineering** (Mechanical Engineering)

History: Founded 1969 as Branch of Wrocław University of Technology.

Degrees and Diplomas: *Inżynier*

BRANCH AT WAŁBRZYCH

FILIA W WAŁBRZYCHU

ul. Armii Krajowej 78, 58-302 Wałbrzych, dolnośląskie
Tel: +48(74) 847-56-58
Fax: +48(74) 780-24
EMail: zod.walbrzych@pwr.wroc.pl
Website: http://www.walbrzych.pwr.wroc.pl

Dyrektor: Andrzej Figiel
Tel: +48(74) 847-65-94 EMail: andrzej.figiel@pwr.wroc.pl

Faculties
Civil Engineering (Bridge Engineering; Civil Engineering; Road Engineering); **Environmental Engineering** (Environmental Engineering; Heating and Refrigeration); **Mechanical Engineering** (Engineering Management; Mechanical Engineering; Production Engineering)

History: Founded 1968 as Branch of Wrocław University of Technology.

Degrees and Diplomas: *Inżynier*

Student Residential Facilities: Student house (c. 100 beds).

Academic Staff *2010-2011*: Total: c. 30

Student Numbers *2010-2011*: Total: c. 800

PRIVATE INSTITUTIONS

ACADEMY OF BUSINESS ADMINISTRATION AND HEALTH SCIENCES IN LODZ

Wyższa Szkoła Biznesu i Nauk o Zdrowiu (WSBINOZ)

ul. Piotrkowska 278, 90-361 Łódź, łódzkie
Tel: +48(42) 683-44-18
Fax: +48(42) 683-44-22
EMail: uczelnia@medyk.edu.pl
Website: http://www.medyk.edu.pl/

Rektor: Marian Szpakowski

Kanclerz: Michal Orski

Departments
Postgraduate Studies (Art Education; Child Care and Development; Dietetics; Education; Educational Administration; Health Sciences; Information Sciences; Information Technology; Library Science; Mathematics Education; Pedagogy; Physical Education; Physical Therapy; Physics; Podiatry; Preschool Education; Rehabilitation and Therapy; Safety Engineering; Science Education; Speech Therapy and Audiology; Sports; Technology Education; Transport Management)

Faculties
Administration (Administration; Economics; European Union Law; Finance; Government); **Cosmetology** (Cosmetology; Nutrition; Podiatry; Sports; Technology); **Dietetics** (Dietetics; Psychology); **Pedagogy** (Child Care and Development; Education; Pedagogy; Preschool Education; Protective Services)

History: Founded 2006.

Governing Bodies: Senate

Main Language(s) of Instruction: Polish

Accrediting Agencies: State Accreditation Commission

Degrees and Diplomas: *Licencjat*; *Świadectwo ukończenia studiów podyplomowych*

Last Updated: 19/10/11

ACADEMY OF BUSINESS IN DĄBROWA GÓRNICZA

Wyższa Szkoła Biznesu w Dąbrowie Górniczej (WSB)

ul. Cieplaka 1c, 41-300 Dąbrowa Górnicza, śląskie
Tel: +48(32) 295-93-16
Fax: +48(32) 295-93-44
EMail: international@wsb.edu.pl
Website: http://www.wsb.edu.pl

Rector: Zdzisława Dacko-Pikiewicz (2008-)
EMail: zdacko@wsb.edu.pl

International Relations: Agata Czerwienska
Tel: +48(32) 295-93-16 EMail: aczerwienska@wsb.edu.pl

Centres
English (English); **Physical Education and Sports** (Physical Education; Sports)

Faculties
Administration (Administration); **Economics** (Econometrics); **English Philology** (English; Philology); **Information Technology** (Computer Science); **International Relations** (International Relations); **Logistics** (Transport Management); **Management** (Management); **Pedagogy** (Pedagogy); **Production Management** (Industrial Management); **Sociology** (Sociology)

History: Founded 1995.

Accrediting Agencies: Ministry of Science and Higher Education

Degrees and Diplomas: *Inżynier*: Information technology (inż.); *Licencjat*: Management; Law; Finance (lic.); *Magister*: Management; Law; Finance (mgr)

Last Updated: 29/08/11

ACADEMY OF COMPUTER SCIENCE AND MANAGEMENT IN BIELSKO-BIALA

Wyższa Szkoła Informatyki i Zarządzania w Bielsku-Białej (WSIZ)

ul. Legionów 81, 43-300 Bielsko-Biała, śląskie
Tel: +48(33) 822-90-70
Fax: +48(33) 822-90-71
EMail: wsiz@wsi.edu.pl; wsiz@wsi.net.pl
Website: http://www.wsi.edu.pl

Rektor: Elzbieta Marecka (2008-)

Kanclerz: Franciszek Marecki

International Relations: Józef Ober Tel: +48(33) 818-44-62

Chairs

Computer Science and Information Technology (Computer Science; Information Technology); **Database and Artificial Intelligence** (Artificial Intelligence; Data Processing); **Design of Information Systems** (Computer Engineering; Information Technology; Transport Management); **Information Management Systems** (Business Computing; Computer Graphics; Information Management); **Internet and Multimedia Systems** (Information Technology; Multimedia); **Telecommunication Systems and Information Security** (Information Management; Telecommunications Engineering)

Departments

Postgraduate Studies (Computer Graphics; Data Processing; Information Management; Information Technology; Multimedia; Telecommunications Engineering; Transport Management)

History: Founded 1996.

Governing Bodies: Senate

Main Language(s) of Instruction: Polish

Accrediting Agencies: Ministry of Science and Higher Education

Degrees and Diplomas: *Inżynier*; *Świadectwo ukończenia studiów podyplomowych*

Last Updated: 23/10/11

ACADEMY OF COMPUTER SCIENCE AND MANAGEMENT IN PRZEMYSL

Wyższa Szkoła Informatyki i Zarządzania w Przemyślu (WSIIZ)

ul. Słowackiego 85, 37-700 Przemyśl, podkarpackie
Tel: +48(16) 676-05-91
EMail: info@wsiiz.edu.pl
Website: http://www.wsiiz.edu.pl

Rektor: Henryk Fedewicz

Departments

Postgraduate Studies (Business Computing; Data Processing; Dietetics; Information Technology; Physical Therapy; Rehabilitation and Therapy; Software Engineering)

Faculties

Computer Science (Computer Engineering; Computer Graphics; Computer Science; Industrial Engineering; Information Technology; Multimedia; Robotics; Software Engineering); **Cosmetology** (Alternative Medicine; Cosmetology; Nutrition; Pharmacy; Plastic Surgery; Sports)

History: Founded 2002.

Main Language(s) of Instruction: Polish

Degrees and Diplomas: *Inżynier*; *Licencjat*; *Świadectwo ukończenia studiów podyplomowych*

Last Updated: 23/10/11

ACADEMY OF EUROPEAN INTEGRATION IN SZCZECIN

Wyższa Szkoła Integracji Europejskiej w Szczecinie (WSIE)

ul. Adama Mickiewicza 47, 70-385 Szczecin, zachodniopomorskie
Tel: +48(91) 423-14-10
Fax: +48(91) 423-83-33
EMail: dziekanat@wsie.pl
Website: http://www.wsie.pl

Rektor: Edward Wiktor Radecki

Kanclerz: Renata Bugaj

Faculties

International Relations (Cultural Studies; European Studies; International Business; International Economics; International Relations; Protective Services); **Management** (Accountancy; Banking; Business Administration; Health Administration; Health Sciences; Home Economics; Industrial and Organizational Psychology; Information Management; Insurance; Management; Welfare and Protective Services)

History: Founded 1999.

Governing Bodies: Senate

Admission Requirements: Secondary school certificate (matura)

Main Language(s) of Instruction: Polish

Accrediting Agencies: Ministry of Science and Higher Education

Degrees and Diplomas: *Licencjat*; *Świadectwo ukończenia studiów podyplomowych*; *Magister*

Last Updated: 23/10/11

ACADEMY OF FINANCE, WARSAW

Akademia Finansów (WSUIB)

ul. Modlińska 51, 03-199 Warszawa, mazowieckie
Tel: +48(22) 811-60-01 +48(22) 811-60-02
Fax: +48(22) 811-70-04
EMail: af@af.edu.pl; dziekanat@af.edu.pl
Website: http://www.af.edu.pl/

Rektor: Miroslaw Zdanowski (1991-)

Prorektor ds. Organizacyjnych: Tadeusz Terlikowski
Tel: +48(22) 614-37-77

International Relations: Agnieszka Beer
Tel: +48(22) 614-44-30 EMail: abeer@af.edu.pl

Departments

Finance and Accounting (Accountancy; Banking; Economics; European Studies; Finance; Insurance); **International Relations** (American Studies; Finance; International Business; International Relations; Journalism; Service Trades)

Institutes

Finance (Finance); **Risk Management** (Banking; Economics; Finance; Insurance; International Economics; International Relations; Mathematics); **Social Affairs and International Relations** (American Studies; Economics; European Studies; Germanic Studies; History; International Relations; Journalism; Mass Communication; Political Sciences; Social Policy)

History: Founded 1991, acquired present status 1992 . Change of the name in 2005 – Akademia Finansów (previous named Wyższa Szkoła Ubezpieczeń i Bankowości w Warszawie)

Governing Bodies: Senate

Academic Year: October to June

Admission Requirements: Secondary school certificate (matura) and entrance examinations

Fees: (New Złoty): 240-800

Main Language(s) of Instruction: Polish, German, French, Russian, Spanish

International Co-operation: Participates in the Socrates, Erasmus, Tempus, Leonardo da Vinci programmes

Accrediting Agencies: Ministry of Science and Higher Education

Degrees and Diplomas: *Inżynier*, *Licencjat*; *Świadectwo ukończenia studiów podyplomowych*; *Magister*, *Doktor*. Also Certified Accountant diploma; University of the Third Age Programmes.

Student Services: Academic counselling, Canteen, Foreign student adviser, Language programs, Sports facilities

Libraries: Central Library; 195 periodical subscriptions

Publications: Journal of Financial Services *(biannually)*; Studia Finansowe; Zarządzanie Ryzykiem; Zeszyty Naukowe

Press or Publishing House: Univeristy Publishing house

Student Numbers *2010-2011*: Total: c. 3,000

Last Updated: 31/08/11

ACADEMY OF HEALTH EDUCATION IN ŁÓDŹ

Wyższa Szkoła Edukacji Zdrowotnej I Nauk Społecznych (WSEZINS)

ul. Kamińskiego 2, 90-229 Łódź, łódzkie
Tel: +48(42) 678-78-25
Fax: +48(42) 678-78-24
EMail: info@wsez.pl
Website: http://www.wsez.pl

Rector: Zygfryd Juczyński

Kanclerz: Zbigniew Domzal

International Relations: Anna Gulej, International Relations Officer EMail: anna.gulej@wsez.pl

Departments

Education (Civics; Continuing Education; Education; Educational Psychology; Health Education; Media Studies; Rehabilitation and Therapy; Social and Preventive Medicine; Speech Therapy and Audiology; Tourism); **Humanities and Cultural Studies** (Arts and Humanities; Cultural Studies); **Social Sciences** (Development Studies; Social Sciences; Social Work); **Special Education** (Special Education)

History: Founded 2002 as Wyższa Szkoła Edukacji Zdrowotnej w Łodzi (Higher School of Health Education, Łódź). Acquired present title 2010.

International Co-operation: Participates in the Leonardo/Erasmus programmes

Degrees and Diplomas: *Licencjat*; *Świadectwo ukończenia studiów podyplomowych*; *Magister*

Last Updated: 04/10/11

ACADEMY OF HOTEL MANAGEMENT AND CATERING INDUSTRY

Wyższa Szkoła Hotelarstwa i Gastronomii w Poznaniu (WSHIG)

ul. Nieszawska 19, 61-022 Poznań, wielkopolskie

Tel: +48(61) 871-15-50

Fax: +48(61) 871-15-33

EMail: wshig@wshig.poznan.pl

Website: http://www.wshig.pl/

Rector: Roman David Tauber (1992-) EMail: rektor@wshig.poznan.pl

Director, Administration and Human Resources: Irena Czyżewska Tel: +48(61) 871-15-47 EMail: irena@wshig.poznan.pl

International Relations: Anna Górniak, International Programmes Coordinator
Tel: +48(61) 871-15-57, Fax: +48(61) 871-15-33
EMail: agorniak@wshig.poznan.pl

Centres

Postgraduate Studies (Dietetics; Hotel and Restaurant; Hotel Management; Management; Nutrition; Sports)

Departments

Foreign Languages (English; French; German; Italian; Modern Languages; Russian; Spanish); **Hospitality and Catering** (Cooking and Catering; Food Science; Food Technology; Hotel and Restaurant; Hotel Management; Nutrition); **Management and Marketing** (Economics; Hotel and Restaurant; Management; Marketing; Parks and Recreation; Tourism); **Tourism and Recreation** (Hotel Management; International Business; Parks and Recreation; Tourism)

Programmes

Recreation Movement (Hotel Management; Physical Education; Rehabilitation and Therapy; Sports)

History: Founded 1992 as higher school, acquired present status and title 2000.

Governing Bodies: Senate

Admission Requirements: Secondary school certificate (matura)

Fees: (New Złoty): 5,400-6,000 per annum.

Main Language(s) of Instruction: Polish

Accrediting Agencies: Ministry of Science and Higher Education

Degrees and Diplomas: *Licencjat*; *Świadectwo ukończenia studiów podyplomowych*; *Magister*. Also certificates.

Student Services: Canteen, Sports facilities

Special Facilities: 10 seminar rooms and classrooms; 18 lecture halls; 4 computer rooms and the assembly hall; Internet reading room

Last Updated: 06/10/11

ACADEMY OF HUMANITIES AND ECONOMICS IN PABIANICE

Wyższa Szkoła Humanistyczno-Ekonomiczna w Pabianicach

ul. Św. Jana 33, 95-200 Pabianice, łódzkie

Tel: 48(42) 212-16-88

Fax: 48(42) 212-16-89

EMail: sekretariat@wshe.pabianice.pl

Website: http://www.wshe.pabianice.pl

Rector: Marian Lelonek

Prorektor: Gabriela Idzikowska

Departments

Postgraduate Studies (Child Care and Development; Preschool Education)

Faculties

Economics (Accountancy; Economics; Finance; Town Planning; Transport Management); **Pedagogy** (English; Pedagogy; Preschool Education; Social Work); **Sociology** (Regional Studies; Social Work; Sociology)

History: Founded 2001.

Fees: (New Złoty): Part-time mode, 30 per month; Postgraduate studies, 700 per semester.

Main Language(s) of Instruction: Polish

Accrediting Agencies: National Accreditation Commission

Degrees and Diplomas: *Licencjat (Lic.)*; *Świadectwo ukończenia studiów podyplomowych*

Last Updated: 21/10/11

ACADEMY OF INTERNATIONAL RELATIONS AND AMERICAN STUDIES

Wyższa Szkoła Stosunków Międzynarodowych i Amerykanistyki w Warszawie (WSSMIA)

Aleje Jerozolimskie 44, 01-310 Warszawa, mazowieckie

Tel: +48(22) 665-81-38 +48(22) 255-39-52

Fax: +48(22) 255-39-53

EMail: sekretariat@wssmia.edu.pl

Website: http://www.wssmia.edu.pl

Rektor: Paweł Bromski EMail: rektoratwssmia@wssmia.edu.pl

Prorektor: Marek Grzelewski EMail: admin@wssmia.edu.pl

Departments

Political Sciences (Administration; American Studies; Cultural Studies; Economic and Finance Policy; European Studies; Government; Health Administration; History; Human Resources; International Relations; Journalism; Management; Mass Communication; Political Sciences; Protective Services; Public Administration; Public Relations; Radio and Television Broadcasting; Social Studies; Sociology); **Postgraduate studies** (Cultural Studies; Government; International Relations; International Studies; Political Sciences)

History: Founded 1997.

Governing Bodies: Senate

Admission Requirements: Secondary school certificate (Matura)

Fees: (New Zoty): Undergaduate tuition fee, 2,540-3,405 per semester; Master and Postgraduate, 2,640-2,905 per semester.

Main Language(s) of Instruction: Polish

Accrediting Agencies: Ministry of Science and Higher Education

Degrees and Diplomas: *Licencjat*; *Świadectwo ukończenia studiów podyplomowych*; *Magister*

STAFF WITH DOCTORATE: Total 32

Last Updated: 08/10/11

ACADEMY OF LAW AND DIPLOMACY IN GDYNIA

Szkoła Wyższa Prawa i Dyplomacji (SWPD)

ul. Śląska 35/37, 81-310 Gdynia, pomorskie

Tel: +48(58) 661-83-91

Fax: +48(58) 661-83-93

EMail: rektorat@wsms.edu.pl

Website: http://http://swpd.edu.pl/

Rector: Wojciech Lamentowicz (1999-)
Tel: +48(58) 661-86-01 EMail: prawo@wsms.edu.pl

Administrative Director: Kamila Adrianek
Tel: +48(58) 621-65-19, Fax: +48(58) 621-65-22
EMail: rekrutacja@wsms.edu.pl

International Relations: Adam Kosidło
Tel: +48(58) 661-83-92 EMail: dziekanat@wsms.edu.pl

Departments

Computer Science (Computer Science); **Foreign Languages** (Arabic; Chinese; English; French; German; Japanese; Modern Languages; Spanish; Swedish); **Postgraduate Studies** (Accountancy; Business Administration; E-Business/Commerce; Finance; Government; Health Administration; International Business; International Economics; Labour Law; Law; Public Administration; Public Law; Welfare and Protective Services)

Faculties

Finance and Accounting (Accountancy; Banking; Finance; Insurance); **International Relations** (Automotive Engineering; Business Administration; Insurance; International Business; International Relations; Marketing; Political Sciences); **Law** (Civil Law; Comparative Law; Constitutional Law; Criminal Law; European Union Law; International Law; Law; Public Law)

Programmes

China Studies *(interdisciplinary)* (Asian Studies; Chinese); **Energy Policy** (Economics; Energy Engineering; International Relations); **Japan Studies** (Asian Studies; Japanese); **Sports** (International Business; Sports; Sports Management)

History: Founded 1996. Formerly know as Wyższa Szkoła Międzynarodowych Stosunków Gospodarczych i Politycznych w Gdyni (Higher School of International Economic and Political Relations, Gdynia).

Governing Bodies: Rector

Academic Year: October-June

Admission Requirements: Secondary school certificate (Matura)

Fees: (New Złoty): c. 2,000-4,000 per semester

Main Language(s) of Instruction: Polish, English

International Co-operation: With universities in Sweden, France, Turkey. Participate in the Erasmus/Socrates programmes.

Accrediting Agencies: Ministry of Science and Higher Education; National Accreditation Commission

Degrees and Diplomas: *Licencjat*; *Magister*; *Doktor*. Also MBA

Student Services: Academic counselling, Employment services, Foreign student adviser, Handicapped facilities, Language programs, Social counselling, Sports facilities

Publications: Studia Europejskie *(quarterly)*

Last Updated: 07/10/11

ACADEMY OF MANAGEMENT AND ADMINISTRATION IN OPOLE

Wyższa Szkoła Zarządzania i Administracji w Opolu

ul. Niedziałkowskiego 18, 45-085 Opole, opolskie
Tel: +48(77) 402-19-00
Fax: +48(77) 456-64-94
EMail: info@poczta.wszia.opole.pl
Website: http://www.wszia.opole.pl/

Rector: Marian Duczmal (2002-)
Tel: +48(77) 402-19-03 EMail: rektorat@wszia.opole.pl

Dyrektor Administracyjny: Józef Kaczmarek
Tel: +48(77) 402-16-03 EMail: kanclerz@poczta.wszia.opole.pl

International Relations: Witold Potwora

Campuses

Kluczbork (Administration; Management); **Tarnów** (Accountancy; Economic and Finance Policy; Economics; Educational Administration; Finance; Foreign Languages Education; Gerontology; Health Sciences; International Economics; Preschool Education; Psychology; Public Administration; Regional Studies; Rehabilitation and Therapy; Safety Engineering; Social Work; Teacher Training; Urban Studies)

Colleges

Management and Administration *(Kedzierzyn-Kozle)* (Accountancy; Administration; Business Administration; Finance; Health Administration; Human Resources; Information Management; Information Technology; Management; Sports Management; Transport Management)

Faculties

Economics (Accountancy; Banking; Business Administration; Computer Science; Economic and Finance Policy; Economics; German; Health Administration; Human Resources; Information Management; Information Technology; International Economics; Management; Marketing; Operations Research; Philology; Public Relations; Sports Management; Transport Management); **Education** (Child Care and Development; Education; Educational Administration; English; Foreign Languages Education; German; Gerontology; Pedagogy; Preschool Education; Psychology; Rehabilitation and Therapy; Social and Preventive Medicine; Social Work); **Postgraduate Studies** (Accountancy; Administration; Child Care and Development; Civics; Ethics; Health Administration; Human Resources; Marketing; Mass Communication; Occupational Health; Pedagogy; Preschool Education; Public Administration; Rehabilitation and Therapy; Social Work; Sports Management; Teacher Training; Transport Management; Welfare and Protective Services); **Sociology and Administration** (Administration; Ethics; European Union Law; Gender Studies; Government; Justice Administration; Law; Marketing; Political Sciences; Protective Services; Public Administration; Regional Studies; Social Work; Sociology)

History: Founded 1996.

Admission Requirements: Secondary school certificate (Matura)

Main Language(s) of Instruction: Polish

Accrediting Agencies: Ministry of Science and Higher Education

Degrees and Diplomas: *Licencjat*; *Świadectwo ukończenia studiów podyplomowych*; *Magister*

Special Facilities: Auditorium hall; 2 lecture halls; Audio-visual rooms; Computer labs.

Libraries: Main library, c. 25,000 vols; Branch campus library, c. 12,000 vols.

Last Updated: 10/10/11

ACADEMY OF SPORT EDUCATION IN WARSAW

Wyższa Szkoła Edukacja w Sporcie (EWS WARSZAWA)

ul. Powązkowska 59 (Forty Bema), 01-728 Warszawa, mazowieckie
Tel: +48(22) 392-96-31
Fax: +48(22) 435-68-83
EMail: bos.wsews@interia.pl
Website: http://www.ews.edu.pl/

Rector: Wojciech Ryszkowski Tel: +48(22) 532-13-31

Kanclerz: Marek Rybiński
Tel: +48(22) 392-96-36 EMail: marekrybinski@wp.pl

Departments

Postgraduate Studies (Sports)

Faculties

Physical Education (Dance; Physical Education; Sports; Sports Management); **Tourism and Recreation** (Leisure Studies; Sports; Tourism)

Further Information: Also centers in Wrocław and Wisła.

History: Founded 2002.

Main Language(s) of Instruction: Polish

Accrediting Agencies: State Accreditation Commission

Degrees and Diplomas: *Licencjat*; *Świadectwo ukończenia studiów podyplomowych*

Last Updated: 19/10/11

ACADEMY OF TOURISM AND HOTEL MANAGEMENT IN WARSAW

Wyższa Szkoła Organizacji Turystyki i Hotelarstwa w Warszawie (WSOTIH)

ul. 17 Stycznia 32, 02-148 Warszawa, mazowieckie
Tel: +48(22) 576-47-36
Fax: +48(22) 576-47-37
EMail: dziekanat@wsotih.edu.pl
Website: http://www.wsotih.edu.pl

Rektor: Piotr Zientarski
Tel: +48(22) 576-46-16 EMail: rektorat@wsotih.edu.pl

Kanclerz: Joanna Grzegorzewska
Tel: +48(22) 576-40-35 EMail: kanclerz@wsotih.edu.pl

Centres

Language (English; French; Modern Languages; Russian); **Polish Language** *(For Foreigners)* (Polish)

Departments

Postgraduate Studies (Health Administration; Management; Marketing; Sports; Teacher Training; Tourism)

Faculties

European Studies (European Studies; International Relations); **Management** (Business Administration; Human Resources; Management; Marketing; Protective Services; Public Relations); **Tourism** (Alternative Medicine; Health Sciences; Hotel and Restaurant; International Business; Leisure Studies; Parks and Recreation; Tourism)

History: Founded 2002.

Main Language(s) of Instruction: Polish

Degrees and Diplomas: *Licencjat*; *Świadectwo ukończenia studiów podyplomowych*

Last Updated: 23/10/11

ALCIDE DE GASPERI UNIVERSITY OF EUROREGIONAL ECONOMY IN JÓZEFÓW

Wyższa Szkoła GosWyższa Szkoła Gospodarki Euroregionalnej im. Alcide De Gasperi w Józefowie (WSGE)

ul. Sienkiewicza 2, 05-410 Józefów, mazowieckie
Tel: +48(22) 789-19-03
Fax: +48(22) 789-19-03
EMail: sekretariat@wsge.edu.pl
Website: http://www.wsge.edu.pl

Rektor: Wincenty Bednarek
Tel: +48(22) 789-19-03 Ext.18, Fax: +48(22) 780-10-07
EMail: rektorat@wsge.edu.pl

Kanclerz: Jan Jakimowicz
Tel: +48(22) 789-19-03 Ext.15, Fax: +48(22) 780-10-07
EMail: rektorat@wsge.edu.pl

International Relations: Iwona Niedziółka, International Relations Officer Tel: +48(22) 789-19-03 Ext.17 EMail: iwona@wsge.edu.pl

Courses

Foreign language (English; Modern Languages)

Departments

Postgraduate Studies (Administration; Educational Administration; European Union Law; Health Education; Human Resources; Mass Communication; Pedagogy; Preschool Education; Protective Services; Public Law; Rehabilitation and Therapy; Safety Engineering; Teacher Training)

Faculties

Administration (Administration; Business Administration; European Studies; Finance; Police Studies; Protective Services; Public Administration); **Education** (Education; Leisure Studies; Pedagogy; Preschool Education; Rehabilitation and Therapy; Teacher Training; Tourism); **Environmental Protection** (Environmental Engineering; Environmental Studies; Landscape Architecture; Public Health); **Internal Security** (Civil Law; Police Studies; Protective Services; Safety Engineering); **Management** (Hotel and Restaurant; Human Resources; Leisure Studies; Management; Tourism)

Fees: (Euro): Tuition fees, 3,500-3,800 per annum

Main Language(s) of Instruction: Polish; English

International Co-operation: With universities in Lithuania, Spain, Hungary, Italy, Ukraine. Participates in LLP Erasmus and Leonardo da Vinci programmes.

Degrees and Diplomas: *Inżynier*; *Licencjat*; *Świadectwo ukończenia studiów podyplomowych*; *Magister*

Libraries: c. 11,000 vols

Last Updated: 06/10/11

ALEKSANDER GIEYSZTOR ACADEMY OF HUMANITIES, PUŁTUSK

Akademia Humanistyczna im. Aleksandra Gieysztora (WSH)

ul. Daszyńskiego 17, 06-100 Pułtusk, mazowieckie
Tel: +48(23) 692-98-13
Fax: +48(23) 692-50-82
EMail: rektorat@ah.edu.pl
Website: http://ah.edu.pl/

Rektor: Adam Koseski (2002-) Tel: +48(23) 692-98-14

Dyrektor Administracyjny: Adam Koseski Tel: +48(23) 692-53-38

International Relations: Anna Iwanowska
Tel: +48(23) 692-18-75, Fax: +48(23) 692-84-92
EMail: aiwanowska@wsh.edu.pl

Centres

Foreign Languages Teaching *(CNJO)* (English; Foreign Languages Education; French; German; Italian; Russian; Spanish)

Faculties

Administrative Studies (Accountancy; Administration; European Union Law; Finance; Law; Public Administration; Taxation; Tourism; Welfare and Protective Services); **Education** (Child Care and Development; Education; English; Family Studies; Foreign Languages Education; German; Health Sciences; Labour and Industrial Relations; Nursing; Police Studies; Preschool Education; Primary Education; Protective Services; Russian; Special Education); **History** (African Languages; Archaeology; Archiving; Central European Studies; Eastern European Studies; History; Information Sciences; Library Science; Museum Studies; Teacher Training); **Polish Language and Literature** (Cultural Studies; Journalism; Literature; Mass Communication; Polish; Public Relations; Speech Therapy and Audiology; Teacher Training); **Political Science** (Advertising and Publicity; Ecology; European Studies; International Relations; International Studies; Journalism; Marketing; Political Sciences; Public Administration; Welfare and Protective Services); **Sociology** (Communication Studies; Human Resources; Marketing; Social Work; Sociology); **Tourism, Hotel Management and Environmental Promotion** (Agriculture; Environmental Studies; Hotel Management; Physical Education; Sports; Tourism)

History: Founded 1994, acquired present status 2001. Known as Wyższa Szkoła Humanistyczna im. Aleksandra Gieystora w Pułtusku until 2006.

Governing Bodies: Senate

Admission Requirements: Secondary school certificate (matura)

Main Language(s) of Instruction: Polish

Accrediting Agencies: Ministry of Science and Higher Education

Degrees and Diplomas: *Licencjat*; *Świadectwo ukończenia studiów podyplomowych*; *Magister*: Philology; History; Political science; Pedagogy; *Doktor*: History; Political science; Pedagogy (dr)

Student Residential Facilities: Hostel (105 beds)

Libraries: c. 135,000 vols; periodical 134 Polish and 20 international subscriptions.

Student Numbers *2010-2011*: Total: c. 4,000

Last Updated: 01/09/11

ALMAMER HIGHER SCHOOL OF ECONOMICS, WARSAW

ALMAMER Wyższa Szkoła Ekonomiczna w Warszawie (ALMAMER WSE)

ul. Wolska 45, 01-201 Warszawa, mazowieckie
Tel: +48(22) 321-85-85
Fax: +48(22) 321-85-84
EMail: almamer@almamer.pl
Website: http://www.almamer.pl

Rector: Janusz Merski (2002-)
Tel: +48(22) 321-85-85 EMail: rektor@almamer.pl

Kanclerz: Małgorzata Merska
Tel: +48(22) 636-74-00, Fax: +48(22) 826-38-46
EMail: kanclerz@almamer.pl

International Relations: Irena Skuba, International Relations Officer
Tel: +48(22) 321-85-39, Fax: +48(22) 321-85-04
EMail: irena.skuba@almamer.pl

Centres

Postgraduate and Specialised Courses (Accountancy; Business Administration; Communication Studies; Health Administration; Hotel Management; Human Resources; Journalism; Management; Pedagogy; Public Administration; Real Estate; Safety Engineering; Tourism; Transport Management)

Departments

Foreign Languages (English; German; Modern Languages; Russian); **Physical Education and Sports** (Physical Education; Sports)

Faculties

Administration (Administration; Government; Public Administration); **Cosmetology** (Cosmetology); **Economics** (Accountancy; Banking; Business Administration; Economics; European Studies; Finance; International Business; Management; Small Business; Transport Management); **Physiotherapy** (Physical Therapy); **Political Science** (International Relations; Journalism; Marketing; Media Studies; Political Sciences; Public Administration); **Tourism and Recreation** (Cooking and Catering; Hotel and Restaurant; Hotel Management; Parks and Recreation; Tourism)

Institutes

Vietnamese Studies (Asian Studies; Vietnamese)

History: Founded as College in 1994, acquired present status and title 1998.

Governing Bodies: Senate

Academic Year: October to June

Admission Requirements: Secondary school certificate (A-level Exams) and qualifying interview

Fees: (New Złoty): Registration, c. 600; evening study 1,700 - 2,350 per semester, full time study 2,850 per semester; postgraduate study c. 200 registration, 3,000 tuition per year

Main Language(s) of Instruction: Polish

International Co-operation: With universities in UK, Germany, Australia, Czech Republic, Slovakia. Also participates in Leonardo da Vinci Programme

Accrediting Agencies: Ministry of Science and Higher Education

Degrees and Diplomas: *Licencjat*; *Świadectwo ukończenia studiów podyplomowych*; *Magister*

Student Services: Academic counselling, Canteen, Cultural centre, Health services, Language programs, Social counselling, Sports facilities

Libraries: c. 60,000 vols

Publications: Zeszyty Naukowe *(quarterly)*
Last Updated: 09/09/11

ANDRZEJ FRYCZ MODRZEWSKI KRAKOW UNIVERSITY

Krakowska Akademia im. Andrzeja Frycza Modrzewskiego (KSW)

ul. Kanoniczna 9, 31-126 Kraków, małopolskie
Tel: +48(12) 433-99-00
Fax: +48(12) 429-28-00
EMail: rektorat@afm.edu.pl
Website: http://www.ka.edu.pl/

President: Jerzy Malec
Tel: +48(12) 252-46-50, Fax: +48(12) 252-46-75

Prorektor: Klemens Budzowski
Tel: +48(12) 252-46-50, Fax: +48(12) 252-46-51

International Relations: Jerzy Marcinkowski, International Relations Officer
Tel: +48(12) 252-46-96 EMail: jmarcinkowski@afm.edu.pl

Centres

Postgraduate Studies (Accountancy; Banking; Business Administration; Educational Administration; English; Environmental Management; Finance; Gender Studies; German; Government; Health Administration; Human Resources; International Business; Journalism; Management; Multimedia; Preschool Education; Protective Services; Psychology; Public Administration; Public Law; Public Relations; Real Estate; Regional Studies; Safety Engineering; Small Business; Social Welfare; Speech Therapy and Audiology; Tourism; Transport Management)

Departments

Foreign Languages (Arabic; Chinese; English; French; German; Italian; Modern Languages; Polish; Russian; Spanish); **Physical Education and Sports** (Physical Education; Sports)

Faculties

Architecture and Fine Arts (Architecture; Building Technologies; Fine Arts; Graphic Design; Interior Design; Painting and Drawing; Town Planning; Urban Studies); **Economics and Management** (Accountancy; Computer Science; Demography and Population; Economics; Education; Environmental Studies; Finance; Information Management; Management; Mathematics; Statistics); **Health and Medical Science** (Cosmetology; Health Sciences; Medicine; Nursing; Physical Therapy); **Humanities** (Anthropology; Arts and Humanities; Cultural Studies; Education; English; English Studies; Philology; Rehabilitation and Therapy; Social Psychology; Sociology); **International Relations** (American Studies; European Studies; International Business; International Relations; International Studies; Oriental Studies; Taxation; Tourism); **Law and Administration** (Administration; Justice Administration; Law; Private Law; Public Administration; Public Law); **Political Science and Communication** (Communication Studies; Film; Gender Studies; Journalism; Mass Communication; Political Sciences; Public Relations; Radio and Television Broadcasting); **Psychology and Family Sciences** (Arabic; Chinese; English; Family Studies; German; Hungarian; Italian; Japanese; Modern Languages; Psychology; Russian; Social Work); **Security Studies** (Civil Security; Occupational Health; Police Studies; Protective Services; Safety Engineering)

History: Founded as Krakowska Szkoła Wyższa im. Andrzeja Frycza Modrzewskiego (Cracow Higher School 'Andrzej Frycz Modrzewski', Cracow) 2000. Acquired present title 2009.

Governing Bodies: Senate

Admission Requirements: Secondary school certificate (matura)

Main Language(s) of Instruction: Polish

International Co-operation: c. 70 agreements with universities in Austria, Bulgaria, Croatia, Egypt, England, Finland, France, Germany, Hungary, Holland, Israel, Italy, Lithuania, Morocco, Russia, Scotland, Serbia, Slovakia, Slovenia, Spain, Sweden, Taiwan, Turkey, Ukraine and USA. Participates in Erasmus Programme.

Accrediting Agencies: Ministry of Science and Higher Education

Degrees and Diplomas: *Licencjat*; *Świadectwo ukończenia studiów podyplomowych*; *Magister*; *Doktor*. Also MBA

Student Numbers *2010-2011*: Total: c. 15,000
Last Updated: 19/09/11

ASESOR LOWER SILESIAN COLLEGE OF PUBLIC SERVICES, WROCŁAW

Dolnośląska Wyższa Szkoła Służb Publicznych "ASESOR" (DWSSP "ASESOR")

ul. Dawida 9/11, 50-527 Wrocław, dolnośląskie
Tel: +48(71) 342-35-07
Fax: +48(71) 342-35-07
EMail: sekretariat@asesor.pl
Website: http://www.asesor.pl

Rektor: Ludmiła Dziewięcka-Bokun (2000-)
Kanclerz: Maria Bokun Tel: +48(71) 343-79-80

International Relations: Bartosz Bokun, Rector's Plenipotentiary for the Bologna Process and International Cooperation

Faculties

Postgraduate Studies (Administration; Advertising and Publicity; Art Management; Fiscal Law; Law; Management; Public

Administration; Welfare and Protective Services); **Public Service** (Administration; International Studies; Protective Services; Public Administration; Social Work)

History: Founded 2000.

Governing Bodies: Senate

Admission Requirements: Secondary school certificate (matura)

Main Language(s) of Instruction: Polish

Accrediting Agencies: Ministry of Science and Higher Education

Degrees and Diplomas: *Licencjat*; *Świadectwo ukończenia studiów podyplomowych*

Last Updated: 13/10/11

ATENEUM UNIVERSITY IN GDAŃSK

Ateneum - Szkoła Wyższa w Gdańsku (A-SW)

ul. Wały Piastowskie 1, 80-855 Gdańsk, pomorskie
Tel: +48(58) 307-45-51
Fax: +48(58) 307-45-51
EMail: ateneum@ateneum.edu.pl
Website: http://www.ateneum.edu.pl

Rector: Waldemar TłokińskiFax: +48(58) 307-45-54
EMail: rektor@ateneum.edu.pl

Faculties

Educational Sciences (Child Care and Development; Educational Sciences; Family Studies; Pedagogy; Speech Therapy and Audiology; Teacher Training); **European Studies, Political Science and Journalism** (Education; European Studies; Journalism; Marketing; Mass Communication; Media Studies; Political Sciences; Rehabilitation and Therapy; Welfare and Protective Services); **Neophilology** (Cultural Studies; English; Italian; Mediterranean Studies; Modern Languages; Philology; Spanish; Translation and Interpretation)

Units

Foreign Languages *(Interfaculty)* (Asian Studies; Chinese; Cultural Studies; French; German; Italian; Latin American Studies; Modern Languages; Norwegian; Russian; Spanish; Swedish); **Physical Education** *(Interfaculty)* (Physical Education; Sports)

Further Information: A traditional and distance education institution.

History: Founded 2004.

Main Language(s) of Instruction: Polish

International Co-operation: Participates in the Erasmus programme.

Degrees and Diplomas: *Licencjat*; *Świadectwo ukończenia studiów podyplomowych*; *Magister*

Student Numbers *2010-2011*: Total: c. 2,500

Last Updated: 12/10/11

B. MARKOWSKIEGO HIGHER SCHOOL OF COMMERCE, KIELCE

Wyższa Szkoła Handlowa im. B. Markowskiego w Kielcach (WSH)

ul. Peryferyjna 15, 25-562 Kielce, świętokrzyskie
Tel: +48(41) 362-60-25
Fax: +48(41) 368-51-29
EMail: info@wsh-kielce.edu.pl
Website: http://www.wsh-kielce.edu.pl

Rektor: Jan Waluszewski (1993-) Tel: +48(41) 368-51-29

Chancellor: Zbigniew Morawiecki
Tel: +48(41) 362-60-25, Fax: +48(41) 362-60-25

International Relations: Krystyna Iwińska-Knop, Assistant Professor Tel: +48 602-755-854

Campuses

Ostrowiec (Transport Management); **Tarnobrzeg** (Economics; International Relations)

Faculties

Administration and Humanities (Accountancy; Administration; Civil Security; Finance; Fire Science; Human Resources; Protective Services; Real Estate); **Economics and Technology** (Construction Engineering; Economics; Management; Transport Engineering)

History: Founded 1993.

Governing Bodies: Senate

Admission Requirements: Secondary school certificate (matura)

Fees: (New Złoty): 1,350-2,425 per semester.

Main Language(s) of Instruction: Polish

Accrediting Agencies: Ministry of Science and Higher Education

Degrees and Diplomas: *Inżynier*, *Licencjat*; *Magister (mgr)*

Last Updated: 26/08/11

BOGDAN JAŃSKI ACADEMY

Wyższa Szkoła Zarządzania i Przedsiębiorczości im. Bogdana Jańskiego w Łomży (WSZIP)

ul. Krzywe Koło 9, 18-400 Łomża, podlaskie
Tel: +48(86) 216-70-50
Fax: +48(86) 216-47-75
EMail: administracja@lomza.janski.edu.pl; dziekanat@lomza.janski.edu.pl
Website: http://www.lomza.janski.edu.pl

Rektor: Kazimierz Korab

Kanclerz: Marian Piwko

Campuses

Chelm (Accountancy; Child Care and Development; Educational Administration; Human Resources; Management; Nursing; Pedagogy; Preschool Education; Real Estate; Safety Engineering; Slavic Languages; Sociology; Town Planning; Transport Management); **Elbag** (Accountancy; Education; Educational Administration; Higher Education; Human Resources; Management; Occupational Health; Pedagogy; Preschool Education; Real Estate; Rehabilitation and Therapy; Safety Engineering; Town Planning); **Krakow** (Education; Management; Political Sciences; Sociology); **Opole** (Accountancy; Development Studies; Educational Administration; Health Sciences; International Relations; Management; Mass Communication; Pedagogy; Preschool Education; Public Relations; Real Estate; Safety Engineering; Social Welfare; Sociology; Town Planning); **Zabrze** (Accountancy; Communication Studies; Development Studies; Human Resources; Information Management; International Relations; Management; Occupational Health; Pedagogy; Preschool Education; Protective Services; Psychology; Public Relations; Real Estate; Safety Engineering; Town Planning)

Faculties

Management (Business Administration; Communication Studies; Economics; Educational Administration; Finance; Health Administration; Human Resources; Information Management; Information Technology; Management; Protective Services; Public Administration; Real Estate; Town Planning); **Social Sciences** (Education; Higher Education; Philosophy; Political Sciences; Preschool Education; Safety Engineering; Social Sciences; Sociology; Teacher Training)

Schools

Management and Entrepreneurship *(Lomza)* (Education; Family Studies; Higher Education; Leisure Studies; Management; Occupational Health; Pedagogy; Real Estate; Rehabilitation and Therapy; Safety Engineering; Sociology; Tourism; Vocational Education)

History: Founded 1993. Formerly known as formerly the Bogdan Jański Academy of Management and Entrepreneurship in Warsaw.

Admission Requirements: Secondary school certificate (Matura)

Main Language(s) of Instruction: Polish

Accrediting Agencies: Ministry of Science and Higher Education

Degrees and Diplomas: *Licencjat*; *Świadectwo ukończenia studiów podyplomowych*; *Magister*

Student Numbers *2010-2011*: Total: c. 7,000

Last Updated: 25/10/11

BUSINESS COLLEGE IN LODZ

Wyższa Szkoła Marketingu i Biznesu w Łodzi (WSMIB)

ul. Klaretyńska 9, 91-117 Łódź, łódzkie
Tel: +48(42) 652-62-66 +48(42) 611-09-52
Fax: +48(42) 652-72-12
EMail: dziekanat@wsmib.edu.pl; rektor@wsmib.edu.pl
Website: http://www.wsmib.edu.pl

Rektor: Szczepan Miłosz

International Relations: Bożena Bobińska, Prorektor
Fax: +48(42) 652-62-66 Ext. 33 EMail: bbobinsk@wsmib.edu.pl

Departments

Postgraduate Studies (Occupational Health; Public Relations; Safety Engineering; Taxation; Transport Management)

Faculties

Finance and Accountancy (Accountancy; Banking; Finance; Insurance; Taxation); **Management** (Business Administration; International Business; International Economics; International Relations; Management; Marketing; Occupational Health; Safety Engineering)

History: Founded 1994.

Governing Bodies: Senate

Academic Year: November to September

Admission Requirements: Secondary school certificate (Świadectwo sojrzałości) and entrance examination

Fees: (New Zloty): c. 3,600 per annum

Main Language(s) of Instruction: Polish, English, German

International Co-operation: With institutions in Austria, Spain, Germany. Participates in the Socrates/Erasmus programme

Accrediting Agencies: Ministry of Science and Higher Education

Degrees and Diplomas: *Licencjat*; *Świadectwo ukończenia studiów podyplomowych*

Student Services: Academic counselling, Canteen, Employment services, Foreign student adviser, Health services, Language programs, Social counselling, Sports facilities

Student Residential Facilities: Yes

Special Facilities: Computer Centre. Language Laboratory

Libraries: c. 4,000 vols. (in Polish and English)

Publications: Debiuty Naukowe Studentow *(biannually)*; Zeszyty Naukowe - 'Studia i Materiałi Kadry Dydaktycznej' *(biannually)*

Press or Publishing House: University Publishing House

Last Updated: 23/10/11

COLLEGE OF APEIRON PUBLIC AND INDIVIDUAL SECURITY IN CRACOW

Wyższa Szkoła Bezpieczeństwa Publicznego i Indywidualnego "Apeiron" w Krakowie

ul. Krupnicza 3, 31-123 Kraków, małopolskie
Tel: +48(12) 422-30-68
Fax: +48(12) 421-67-25
EMail: rektorat@apeiron.edu.pl
Website: http://apeiron.edu.pl/

Rektor: Juliusz Piwowarski

Kanclerz: Barbara Piwowarska

Departments

Postgraduate studies (Administration; Heritage Preservation; Protective Services; Safety Engineering)

Faculties

Administration (Administration; Government; Information Management; Protective Services)

History: Founded 2005.

Fees: (New Złoty): Extramural tuition fee, 12 instalments of 380.

Main Language(s) of Instruction: Polish

Accrediting Agencies: Ministry of Science and Higher Education

Degrees and Diplomas: *Licencjat*; *Świadectwo ukończenia studiów podyplomowych*

Last Updated: 18/10/11

COLLEGE OF COMMUNICATIONS AND MANAGEMENT

Wyższa Szkola Komunikacji i Zarzadzania w Poznaniu (WSKIZ)

ul. Różana 17a, 61-577 Poznań, wielkopolskie
Tel: +48(61) 834-59-01
Fax: +48(61) 834-59-49
EMail: uczelnia@wskiz.pl
Website: http://www.wskiz.edu

Rektor: Eugeniusz Neumann
Tel: +48(61) 834-59-01, Fax: +48(61) 834-59-49

Kanclerz: Andrzej Piekarzewski

International Relations: Agnieszka Piekarzewska, International Relations Coordinator
Tel: +48(61) 834-59-01, Fax: +48(61) 834-59-49
EMail: international@wskiz.edu; apiekarzewska@wskiz.edu

Departments

Postgraduate Studies (Computer Science; Ecology; Economics; Finance; Gerontology; Health Administration; Human Resources; Information Sciences; Information Technology; Management; Mass Communication; Occupational Health; Protective Services; Writing)

Faculties

Automation and Robotics (Automation and Control Engineering; Robotics); **Computer Science** (Computer Networks; Computer Science; Information Technology; Multimedia); **Environmental Protection** (Environmental Engineering; Environmental Studies); **Management** (Accountancy; Finance; Government; Management; Marketing); **Management and Production Engineering** (Computer Engineering; Computer Graphics; Management; Production Engineering; Safety Engineering; Transport Management); **Pedagogy** (Pedagogy; Rehabilitation and Therapy; Social Work; Vocational Counselling)

History: Founded 1997, acquired present status 1999.

Governing Bodies: Senate

Admission Requirements: Secondary school certificate (matura)

Main Language(s) of Instruction: Polish

International Co-operation: With universities in Spain, Germany and Brazil. Participates in the Erasmus programme.

Accrediting Agencies: Ministry of Science and Higher Education

Degrees and Diplomas: *Inżynier*; *Licencjat*; *Świadectwo ukończenia studiów podyplomowych*; *Magister*. Also Executive MBA offered jointly with Tiffin University (USA).

Last Updated: 23/10/11

COLLEGE OF COSMETOLOGY AND HEALTH SCIENCES IN ŁÓDŹ

Wyższa Szkoła Kosmetyki i Nauk o Zdrowiu w Łodzi

ul. Wileńska 53/55, 94-011 Łódź, łódzkie
Tel: +48(42) 687-00-44
Fax: +48(42) 687-00-44
EMail: uczelnia@wyzszaszkolakosmetyki.pl
Website: http://www.wyzszaszkolakosmetyki.pl

Rektor: Stanislaw Dyla

Kanclerz: Edward Kujawa

Departments

Postgraduate Studies (Alternative Medicine)

Programmes

Cosmetology and Health Sciences (Alternative Medicine; Ayurveda; Cosmetology; Health Sciences)

Fees: (New Złoty): 400 per month; Postgraduate studies, 3,200 per semester.

Main Language(s) of Instruction: Polish

Degrees and Diplomas: *Licencjat*; *Świadectwo ukończenia studiów podyplomowych*

Academic Staff *2010-2011*: Total: c. 30

Last Updated: 19/10/11

COLLEGE OF EDUCATION AND THERAPY IN POZNAN

Wyższa Szkoła Edukacji i Terapii w Poznaniu (WSEIT)
ul. Grabowa 22, 61-473 Poznań, wielkopolskie
Tel: +48(61) 832-77-76
Fax: +48(61) 832-77-76
EMail: rekrutacja@wseit.edu.pl
Website: http://www.wseit.edu.pl

Rektor: Kazimiera Milanowska

Kanclerz: Violetta Musa

Departments

Postgraduate Studies (Cosmetology; Paediatrics; Physical Therapy; Rehabilitation and Therapy)

Faculties

Cosmetology (Alternative Medicine; Cosmetology; Podiatry); **Material Engineering - Dental Engineering** (Dental Technology; Materials Engineering); **Pedagogy** (English; Occupational Therapy; Pedagogy; Preschool Education; Speech Therapy and Audiology); **Physical Education** (Physical Education); **Physiotherapy** (Physical Therapy)

History: Founded 2005.

Fees: (New Złoty): 320-850 per semester; Postgraduate programmes, 1,800-2,900 per semester.

Main Language(s) of Instruction: Polish

International Co-operation: Paricipates in the Erasmus programme.

Degrees and Diplomas: *Licencjat*; *Świadectwo ukończenia studiów podyplomowych*

Libraries: c. 4,000 vols

Last Updated: 20/10/11

COLLEGE OF ENTERPRISE AND ADMINISTRATION IN LUBLIN

Wyższa Szkoła Przedsiębiorczości i Administracji w Lublinie (WSPA)
ul. Bursaki 12, 20-150 Lublin, lubelskie
Tel: +48(81) 740-84-10
Fax: +48(81) 740-84-13
EMail: sekretariat@wspa.pl
Website: http://www.wspa.lublin.pl

Rector: Andrzej Miszczuk

Kanclerz: Edyta Truszkowska
Tel: +48(81) 740-84-70 EMail: administracja@wspa.pl

International Relations: Julita Agnieszka Rybczynska, Vice Rector for Vice-Rector for Development and International Exchange
EMail: biuro.karier@wspa.pl

Faculties

Economic and Technical Sciences (Accountancy; Computer Science; Economics; Finance; Management; Transport and Communications); **Social Sciences** (Administration; International Relations; Journalism; Mass Communication; Political Sciences; Social Sciences; Sociology)

History: Founded 1992 as Centrum Kształcenia Menedżerów Przemysłowych (CKMP), acquired present status and title 1998.

Governing Bodies: Senate

Admission Requirements: Secondary school certificate (matura)

Main Language(s) of Instruction: Polish

Accrediting Agencies: Ministry of Science and Higher Education

Degrees and Diplomas: *Inżynier*; *Licencjat*; *Świadectwo ukończenia studiów podyplomowych*; *Magister*

Student Numbers *2010-2011*: Total: c. 4,000

Last Updated: 08/10/11

COLLEGE OF FOREIGN LANGUAGES IN SWIECIE

Wyższa Szkoła Języków Obcych w Świeciu (WSJO)
ul. Chmielniki 2 A, 86-100 Świecie, kujawsko-pomorskie
Tel: +48(52) 333-02-70
Fax: +48(52) 331-27-03
EMail: wsjo@wsjo.edu.pl; wsjodziekanat@wp.pl
Website: http://www.wsjo.edu.pl

Rektor: Liliana Górska EMail: lgorska@ymail.com

Kanclerz: Elzbieta Sternal EMail: elzbietasternal@wp.pl

Faculties

Philology (English; Foreign Languages Education; German; Philology; Russian; Translation and Interpretation)

Further Information: A traditional and distance education institution. Also University of Third Age.

History: Founded 2004.

Main Language(s) of Instruction: Polish

Degrees and Diplomas: *Licencjat*; *Świadectwo ukończenia studiów podyplomowych*; *Magister*

Libraries: Yes

Last Updated: 23/10/11

COLLEGE OF MANAGEMENT 'EDUKACJA'

Wyższa Szkoła Zarządzania 'Edukacja' we Wrocławiu (WSZ)
ul. Krakowska 56/62, 50-425 Wrocław, dolnośląskie
Tel: +48(71) 377-21-00
Fax: +48(71) 377-21-07
EMail: edukacja@edukacja.wroc.pl
Website: http://www.edukacja.wroc.pl

Rektor: Zdzisław Knecht (2008-)

Kanclerz: Bogdan Jan Koprek

International Relations: Aleksandra Kwiatkowska, International Relations Officer

Faculties

Economics *(Kępno)* (Economics); **Management** (Art Therapy; Computer Science; English Studies; International Relations; Journalism; Management; Mass Communication; Parks and Recreation; Pedagogy; Political Sciences; Tourism); **Management** *(Pardubice, Czech Republic)* (Management); **Management** *(Lubin)* (Management); **Tourism** *(Kłodzko)* (Tourism)

History: Founded 1997.

Governing Bodies: Senate

Admission Requirements: Secondary school certificate (Matura) and entrance examination

Fees: (New Złoty): Extramural and postgraduate, c. 290-360 per month

Main Language(s) of Instruction: Polish

International Co-operation: With universities in Czech Republic, France, Spain, Germany, Lithuania, Hungary, Italy, Sweden, Latvia, Portugal, Romania, Greece, Turkey, Belgium. Participates in the Erasmus programme.

Accrediting Agencies: Ministry of Science and Higher Education

Degrees and Diplomas: *Inżynier*, *Licencjat*; *Magister*

Student Residential Facilities: No

Libraries: Central Library

Publications: Kwartalnik Gospodarka Rynek Edukacja *(quarterly)*

Last Updated: 10/10/11

COLLEGE OF PERSONNEL MANAGEMENT IN WARSAW

Wyższa Szkoła Zarządzania Personelem w Warszawie (WSZP)
ul. Dereniowa 52/54, 02-776 Warszawa, mazowieckie
Tel: +48(22) 855-49-16
Fax: +48(22) 855-49-16 Ext. 113
EMail: info@wszp.edu.pl
Website: http://www.wszp.edu.pl

Rektor: Tadeusz Szmidtka

Kanclerz: Janusz Przepiórski

International Relations: Andrzej Waśkiewicz

Departments

Postgraduate studies (Administration; Human Resources; Labour Law; Law; Management; Marketing; Media Studies; Occupational Health; Protective Services; Psychology; Safety Engineering)

Faculties

Management (Human Resources; Management); **National Security** (Protective Services); **Sociology** (Marketing; Media Studies; Social Psychology; Sociology)

Further Information: A traditional and distance education institution.

History: Founded 2001.

Governing Bodies: Senate

Admission Requirements: Secondary school certificate (matura)

Fees: (New Złoty): 2,900-5,900 per annum

Main Language(s) of Instruction: Polish

Accrediting Agencies: Ministry of Science and Higher Education

Degrees and Diplomas: *Licencjat*; *Świadectwo ukończenia studiów podyplomowych*

Last Updated: 25/10/11

COLLEGE OF PHYSIOTHERAPY IN WROCŁAW

Wyższa Szkoła Fizjoterapii we Wrocławiu (WSF)

ul. Tadeusza Kościuszki 4, 50-038 Wrocław, dolnośląskie

Tel: +48(71) 342-50-02

Fax: +48(71) 342-50-02

EMail: sekretariat@wsf.wroc.pl

Website: http://www.wsf.wroc.pl

Rector: Andrzej Bugajski (2002-)

Kanclerz: Andrzej Czamara

International Relations: Agata Hajpel

Programmes

Cosmetology (Cosmetology); **Physiotherapy** (Physical Therapy)

History: Founded 1999.

Governing Bodies: Senate

Admission Requirements: Secondary school certificate (matura)

Fees: (New Złoty): 2,200-2,450 per semester

Main Language(s) of Instruction: Polish

Accrediting Agencies: Ministry of Science and Higher Education; State Accreditation Committee

Degrees and Diplomas: *Licencjat*; *Magister*

Last Updated: 06/10/11

COLLEGE OF SOCIAL AND MEDIA STUDIES IN TORUN

Wyższa Szkoła Kultury Społecznej i Medialnej w Toruniu (WSKSiM)

ul. Św. Józefa 23/35, 87-100 Toruń, kujawsko-pomorskie

Tel: +48(56) 610-72-00

Fax: +48(56) 610-72-01

EMail: wsksim@wsksim.edu.pl

Website: http://www.wsksim.edu.pl

Rector: Krzysztof Bieliński (2007-)

Departments

Postgraduate Studies (Communication Studies; Computer Graphics; Educational Technology; Environmental Management; Environmental Studies; Information Technology; International Relations; Journalism; Management; Media Studies; Multimedia)

Faculties

Computer Science (Computer Graphics; Computer Networks; Computer Science; Data Processing; Information Technology; Multimedia); **Cultural Studies** (Art History; Arts and Humanities; Cultural Studies; European Studies; History; Literature; Philosophy; Tourism); **Journalism and Social communication** (Advertising and Publicity; Journalism; Mass Communication; Media Studies); **Political Sciences** (International Relations; Marketing; Political Sciences; Social Policy)

History: Founded 2001.

Fees: (New Złoty): 1,700-1,900 per semester

Main Language(s) of Instruction: Polish

Accrediting Agencies: State Accreditation Committee (SAC)

Degrees and Diplomas: *Inżynier*; *Licencjat*; *Świadectwo ukończenia studiów podyplomowych*; *Magister*

Last Updated: 07/10/11

COLLEGE OF SOCIAL COMMUNICATIONS IN GDYNIA

Wyższa Szkoła Komunikacji Społecznej w Gdyni (WSKS)

ul. Hryniewickiego 10, 81-365 Gdynia, pomorskie

Tel: +48(58) 661-88-71 +48(58) 661-89-55

Fax: +48(58) 661-89-55

EMail: biuro@wsks.pl

Website: http://www.wsks.pl

Rektor: Andrzej Pawelczyk

Prorektor: Miron Klusak

Departments

Postgraduate Studies (Adult Education; Air Transport; Civics; Educational Administration; Educational Technology; European Studies; Health Sciences; Information Management; Leisure Studies; Marine Transport; Peace and Disarmament; Preschool Education; Rehabilitation and Therapy; Safety Engineering; Tourism; Vocational Counselling)

Faculties

National Security (Air Transport; Information Management; Marine Transport; Peace and Disarmament; Protective Services; Safety Engineering); **Pedagogy** (Adult Education; Child Care and Development; Education; English; Foreign Languages Education; Leisure Studies; Pedagogy; Preschool Education; Rehabilitation and Therapy; Safety Engineering; Tourism); **Political Science** (Government; International Relations; Journalism; Media Studies; Political Sciences; Transport and Communications)

History: Founded 2003.

Main Language(s) of Instruction: Polish

Degrees and Diplomas: *Licencjat*; *Świadectwo ukończenia studiów podyplomowych*

Last Updated: 23/10/11

COLLEGIUM BALTICUM IN SZCZECIN

Szczecińska Szkoła Wyższa Collegium Balticum (WSZ-CB)

ul. Mieszka I 61 C, 71-011 Szczecin, zachodniopomorskie

Tel: +48(91) 483-81-64

Fax: +48(91) 483-05-81

EMail: biuro.rektora@cb.szczecin.pl

Website: http://www.cb.szczecin.pl

Rector: Aleksandra Żukrowska (2008-)

Kanclerz: Dariusz Czekan EMail: kanclerz@cb.szczecin.pl

International Relations: Janusz Ruszkowski

Academies

Foreign Language (English; German; Modern Languages; Russian)

Faculties

Economics (Accountancy; Business Administration; Business Computing; Economics; Finance; Hotel and Restaurant; Human Resources; Industrial and Organizational Psychology; International Business; Labour and Industrial Relations; Management; Marine Transport; Marketing; Public Relations; Real Estate; Tourism; Transport Management); **Education** (Business Administration; Dietetics; Education; Educational Administration; Educational and Student Counselling; Foreign Languages Education; Gender Studies; Information Sciences; Library Science; Management; Media Studies; Nutrition; Occupational Therapy; Parks and Recreation; Pedagogy; Preschool Education; Rehabilitation and Therapy; Social Work; Sports; Teacher Training; Technology Education; Theatre;

Tourism); **Internal Security** (Communication Studies; Criminology; Peace and Disarmament; Police Studies; Protective Services; Safety Engineering; Social and Preventive Medicine; Welfare and Protective Services); **Philology** (Communication Studies; English; German; Philology; Russian; Translation and Interpretation); **Physiotherapy** (Gerontology; Physical Therapy; Rehabilitation and Therapy; Sports); **Political Sciences** (Civil Security; Cultural Studies; Economics; Government; International Economics; International Relations; Leadership; Marketing; Political Sciences; Public Administration; Public Relations; Social Sciences); **Teacher Training** (Business Administration; Business Education; Human Resources; Management; Marketing; Sales Techniques; Teacher Training)

Further Information: Alos Nowogard, Kolobrzeg and Stargard Szczecin campuses. A traditional and distance education institution.

History: Founded 2000.

Governing Bodies: Senate

Admission Requirements: Secondary school certificate (matura)

Main Language(s) of Instruction: Polish

International Co-operation: Participates in the Erasmus programme.

Accrediting Agencies: Ministry of Science and Higher Education

Degrees and Diplomas: *Licencjat*; *Świadectwo ukończenia studiów podyplomowych*; *Magister*

Last Updated: 25/10/11

COLLEGIUM CIVITAS

Collegium Civitas (CC)

Plac Defilad 1, 00-901 Warszawa, mazowieckie
Tel: +48(22) 656-77-62
Fax: +48(22) 656-71-75
EMail: info@collegium.edu.pl
Website: http://www.collegium.edu.pl

Rektor: Edmund Wnuk-Lipiński
EMail: edmund.wnuk-lipinski@collegium.edu.pl

Administrative Officer: Adam Grejcz
Tel: +48(22) 656-71-78 EMail: adam.grejcz@collegium.edu.pl

International Relations: Dariusz Stola, Vice-Rector for International Cooperation
Tel: +48(22) 863-12-25, Fax: +48(22) 863-12-25
EMail: dariusz.stola@collegium.edu.pl

Programmes

Asian Studies (Arabic; Asian Studies; Chinese; Cultural Studies; English; European Studies; Hindi; International Relations; Japanese); **Doctorate Studies** (Political Sciences; Slavic Languages; Sociology); **Human Rights and Genocide Studies** (Human Rights; Jewish Studies); **International Relations** (Communication Studies; European Union Law; History; International Economics; International Law; International Relations; Political Sciences; Social Sciences); **Journalism** (Information Sciences; Journalism; Mass Communication; Media Studies; Radio and Television Broadcasting); **Political Science** (Communication Studies; Cultural Studies; Insurance; International Relations; Journalism; Leadership; Marketing; Media Studies; Political Sciences; Psychology; Public Relations); **Postgraduate Studies** (Communication Studies; Design; Economics; Fashion Design; Fine Arts; Human Resources; Insurance; International Relations; Journalism; Leadership; Political Sciences; Public Relations; Sociology; Theatre); **Sociology** (Advertising and Publicity; Communication Studies; Cultural Studies; Marketing; Media Studies; Public Administration; Social Psychology; Sociology)

History: Founded 1997.

Governing Bodies: Senate

Academic Year: October to June

Admission Requirements: Secondary school certificate (Matura)

Fees: (New Złoty): 3,300-4,950 per semester.

Main Language(s) of Instruction: Polish; English

International Co-operation: Erasmus (Italy, France, Germany, United Kingdom, Hungary)

Accrediting Agencies: National Accreditation Commission; University Accreditation Commission at the Conference of Rectors of Polish Universities

Degrees and Diplomas: *Licencjat*; *Świadectwo ukończenia studiów podyplomowych*; *Magister*; *Doktor*

Student Services: Canteen, Employment services, Foreign student adviser, Foreign Studies Centre, Language programs, Sports facilities

Student Residential Facilities: None

Special Facilities: Palace of Culture and Science; Computer lab; 3 theatres; 2 museums; Concert hall

Libraries: Collegium Civitas Library; Library of the Institute of Philosophy and Sociology

Last Updated: 14/09/11

COPERNICUS UNIVERSITY OF INFORMATION TECHNOLOGY AND MANAGEMENT, WROCLAW

Wyższa Szkoła Informatyki i Zarządzania Copernicus" we Wrocławiu (WSIZ)

ul. Inowrocławska 56, 53-648 Wrocław, dolnośląskie
Tel: +48(71) 795-03-93 +48(71) 795-03-84
Fax: +48(71) 795-03-99 +48(71) 795-03-88
EMail: sekratariat@wsiz.wroc.pl
Website: http://www.wsiz.wroc.pl

Rektor: Adam Maciej Sosnowski
Tel: +48(71)-795-03-80 EMail: asosnowski@wsiz.wroc.pl

Kanclerz: Ewa Kostrzewa
Tel: +48(71) 795-03-92 EMail: e.kostrzewa@wsiz.wroc.pl

International Relations: Małgorzata Zioło, Head of Foreign Languages Department EMail: malgosia@wsiz.wroc.pl

Faculties

Administration (Administration; Environmental Management; European Studies; Public Administration); **Computer Science** (Computer Engineering; Computer Networks; Computer Science); **Physiotherapy** (Physical Therapy); **Postgraduate Studies** (Administration; Administrative Law; Government; Public Administration)

History: Founded 2001.

Main Language(s) of Instruction: Polish

Degrees and Diplomas: *Inżynier*; *Licencjat*; *Świadectwo ukończenia studiów podyplomowych*

Last Updated: 23/10/11

COSINUS HIGHER SCHOOL IN ŁÓDŹ

Wyższa Szkoła COSINUS w Łódźi

ul. Wólczańska 81, 90-515 Łódź, łódzkie
Tel: +48(42) 636-33-66
Fax: +48(42) 636-41-70
Website: http://ws.cosinus.pl/

Rektor: Beata Piotrowska

Kanclerz: Anna Wojtaszek

Departments

Postgraduate studies (Child Care and Development; Education; Human Resources; Police Studies; Public Administration; Rehabilitation and Therapy; Welfare and Protective Services)

Faculties

Administration (Administration; Government; Protective Services; Social Work; Welfare and Protective Services); **Pedagogy** (Child Care and Development; Educational and Student Counselling; Pedagogy; Rehabilitation and Therapy)

History: Founded 2005.

Degrees and Diplomas: *Licencjat*; *Świadectwo ukończenia studiów podyplomowych*

Last Updated: 19/10/11

CRACOW SCHOOL OF BUSINESS AND COMMERCE

Wyższa Szkoła Handlowa w Krakowie (WSH)
ul. Smoleńsk 14, 31-112 Kraków, małopolskie
Tel: +48(12) 422-92-02
Fax: +48(12) 429-18-09
EMail: rektorat@wsh.krakow.pl
Website: http://www.wsh.krakow.pl

Rector: Jerzy Marek Bialkiewicz

Prorector: Joanna Zyra

International Relations: Lidia Białkiewicz

Faculties

International Relations (International Business; International Relations; Law; Political Sciences; Public Relations); **Management** (Accountancy; Administration; Business Administration; Finance; Industrial and Organizational Psychology; Management; Tourism)

History: Founded 1994. A private institution under the juridiction of the Ministry of National Education.

Governing Bodies: Board of Founding

Academic Year: October to September

Admission Requirements: Secondary school certificate (Świadectwo dorzałości) and entrance examination

Fees: (New Złoty): c. 4,700 per annum

Main Language(s) of Instruction: Polish

Accrediting Agencies: Ministry of Science and Higher Education; State Accreditation Commission

Degrees and Diplomas: *Licencjat*; *Świadectwo ukończenia studiów podyplomowych*; *Magister*

Student Services: Academic counselling, Employment services, Language programs, Social counselling, Sports facilities

Special Facilities: Movis Studio. Computer Laboratory

Libraries: WSH Library

Publications: Management and Marketing *(annually)*

Last Updated: 21/10/11

CRACOW SCHOOL OF HEALTH PROMOTION

Krakowska Wyższa Szkoła Promocji Zdrowia (KWSPZ)
ul. Krowoderska 73, 31-158 Kraków, małopolskie
Tel: +48(12) 423-38-40
Fax: +48(12) 633-45-56
EMail: info@kwspz.pl
Website: http://www.kwspz.pl

Rektora: Wiesława Tracz

Kanclerza: Ewa Podobińska

Departments

Postgraduate Studies (Cosmetology; Dietetics; Physical Therapy; Podiatry)

Programmes

Cosmetology (Cosmetology); **Dietetics** (Dietetics); **Physiotherapy** (Physical Therapy); **Tourism and Recreation** (Parks and Recreation; Tourism)

History: Founded 2002.

Degrees and Diplomas: *Licencjat*; *Świadectwo ukończenia studiów podyplomowych*

Special Facilities: Multimedia lecture halls; Computer labs

Last Updated: 17/10/11

CZESTOCHOWA UNIVERSITY OF MANAGEMENT

Wyższa Szkoła Zarządzania w Częstochowie (WSZ)
ul. Rząsawska 40, 42-209 Częstochowa, śląskie
Tel: +48(34) 364-33-72
Fax: +48(34) 364-34-26
EMail: rektorat@wsz.edu.pl
Website: http://www.wsz.edu.pl

Rektor: Andrzej Dziewiątkowski (1998-)

Kanclerz: Maciej Dziewiątkowski
Tel: +48(34) 364-33-82 Ext. 63 EMail: maciek@wsz.edu.pl

International Relations: Iwona Raszka, International Relations Officer
Tel: +48(34) 362-18-36, Fax: +48(34) 362-18-36
EMail: iro@wsz.edu.pl; i.raszka@wsz.edu.pl

Faculties

Management (Educational Administration; Finance; Health Administration; Management; Marketing); **Management and Production Engineering** (Management; Production Engineering); **Nursing** (Midwifery; Nursing); **Pedagogy** (Education; Pedagogy; Social Work); **Postgraduate Studies** (Accountancy; Business Computing; Energy Engineering; Finance; Management; Pedagogy; Sales Techniques)

Further Information: Wyższa Szkoła Inżynierii Rolniczej i Zarządzania w Ropcycach. A distance and traditional education institution.

History: Founded 1995.

Governing Bodies: Senate

Academic Year: October to June (October-January; February-June)

Admission Requirements: Secondary school certificate (Matura)

Fees: (New Złoty): c. 3,600 per annum

Main Language(s) of Instruction: Polish

International Co-operation: With universities in France, Lithuania, Slovakia, Turkey and Italy. Participates in the Erasmus programme.

Accrediting Agencies: Ministry of Science and Higher Education; Association of Management Education 'FORUM'

Degrees and Diplomas: *Inżynier*, *Licencjat*, *Świadectwo ukończenia studiów podyplomowych*; *Magister*

Student Services: Academic counselling, Canteen, Cultural centre, Foreign student adviser, Health services, Language programs, Sports facilities

Libraries: Public Library; University Library; Electronic Library; 10,000 vols

Publications: Scientific Bulletins *(other/irregular)*

Last Updated: 12/10/11

EAST-WEST HIGHER SCHOOL IN ŁÓDŹ

Wschód-Zachód Szkoła Wyższa im. Henryka Jóźwiaka w Łodzi
ul. Rewolucji 1905 r. nr 44 piętro I, pok. 108, 90-213 Łódź, łódzkie
Tel: +48(42) 632-29-29 +48(42) 632-40-15
Fax: +48(42) 632-23-51
EMail: rektorat@wschodzachod.edu.pl
Website: http://www.wschodzachod.edu.pl/

Rektor: Danuta Jedrzejczak

Kanclerz: Adrian Józwiak

Departments

Postgraduate Studies (Accountancy; Banking; English; Ethics; European Studies; Finance; German; International Business; International Economics; International Relations; Translation and Interpretation)

Faculties

Philology (English; German; Greek; Japanese; Philology; Romance Languages; Spanish); **Social Sciences** *(Nowy Sacz)* (Cultural Studies; Education; English; Foreign Languages Education; German; Journalism; Literature; Media Studies; Pedagogy; Philology; Preschool Education; Social Sciences; Social Work; Sociology); **Social Sciences** (American Studies; Cultural Studies; Education; International Business; International Relations; Literature; Middle Eastern Studies; Preschool Education; Social Sciences; Sociology; Theatre); **Social Sciences** *(Leszno - Distance Education)* (Social Sciences)

Further Information: A traditional and distance education institution.

History: Founded 2006.

Main Language(s) of Instruction: Polish

Degrees and Diplomas: *Licencjat*; *Świadectwo ukończenia studiów podyplomowych*
Last Updated: 19/10/11

ECONOMIC-SOCIAL HIGHER SCHOOL IN OSTROŁĘKA

Wyższa Szkoła Ekonomiczno - Społeczna w Ostrołęce (WSES)

ul. Kołobrzeska 15, 07-410 Ostrołęka, mazowieckie
Tel: +48(29) 769-10-34
Fax: +48(29) 769-10-34
EMail: wses@wses.edu.pl
Website: http://www.wses.edu.pl

Rektor: Ireneusz Żuchowski

Kanclerz: Kazimierz Krzysztof Bloch

International Relations: Anna Skonieczna

Departments
Postgraduate Studies (Accountancy; Educational Administration; Human Resources; Public Administration; Safety Engineering)

Faculties
Management (Art History; Business Administration; Computer Science; Economics; English; Geography; German; Government; History; Human Resources; Leisure Studies; Management; Philosophy; Russian; Sociology; Sports Management)

History: Founded 2002.

Fees: (New Złoty): 1,200 per semester

Main Language(s) of Instruction: Polish

International Co-operation: Participates in the Erasmus programme.

Degrees and Diplomas: *Licencjat*; *Świadectwo ukończenia studiów podyplomowych*; *Magister*

Libraries: c. 5,200 vols; 3,400 vols

Academic Staff *2010-2011*: Total 60
STAFF WITH DOCTORATE: Total 4
Last Updated: 20/10/11

ELBLĄG HIGHER SCHOOL OF HUMANITIES AND ECONOMICS

Elbląska Uczelnia Humanistyczno-Ekonomiczna (EUH-E)

ul. Lotnicza 2, 82-300 Elbląg, warmińsko-mazurskie
Tel: +48(55) 239-38-02
Fax: +48(55) 239-38-01
EMail: rektorat@euh-e.edu.pl
Website: http://www.euh-e.edu.pl/

Rektor: Magdalena Dubiella-Polakowska

Kanclerz: Henryk Fall

International Relations: Izabela Seredocha
EMail: promocja@euh-e.edu.pl

Faculties
Administration and Economics (Administration; Economics; Finance; Government; Health Administration; Management; Marketing; Public Administration; Rural Planning; Small Business; Transport Management); **Health Sciences** (Health Sciences; Medicine; Nursing; Physical Therapy; Public Health); **Pedagogy** (Child Care and Development; Health Education; Pedagogy; Social Work)

Programmes
Foreign Language Teaching (Foreign Languages Education); **Nurses and Midwives** *(Postgraduate)* (Midwifery; Nursing); **Postgraduate Studies** (Educational Administration; Pedagogy; Physical Therapy; Preschool Education; Rehabilitation and Therapy; Social Work)

History: Founded 2001.

Governing Bodies: Senate

International Co-operation: With universities in Canada, Germany, Russia, Finland, Bulgaria, Belarus, United Kingdom and Ukraine. Participates in Socrates-Erasmus programmes.

Accrediting Agencies: State Accreditation Committee

Degrees and Diplomas: *Licencjat*; *Świadectwo ukończenia studiów podyplomowych*; *Magister*

Libraries: c. 20,000 vols; 53 periodical subscriptions

Student Numbers *2010-2011*: Total: c. 4,200
Last Updated: 14/09/11

ENGINEERING COLLEGE OF MECHATRONICS IN KATOWICE

Wyższa Szkoła Mechatroniki w Katowicach

ul. 11 listopada 13, 40-387 Katowice, śląskie
Tel: +48(32) 352-03-57
Fax: +48(32) 759-16-17
EMail: info@wsm.katowice.pl
Website: http://mechatronika.edu.pl/

Rektor: Dariusz Szymański

Kanclerz: Jarosław Podolski

Departments
Mechatronics (Automotive Engineering; Computer Engineering; Electronic Engineering; Engineering; Information Technology; Mechanical Engineering); **Postgraduate Studies** (Computer Engineering; Electronic Engineering; Mechanical Engineering)

Degrees and Diplomas: *Inżynier*; *Świadectwo ukończenia studiów podyplomowych*
Last Updated: 17/10/11

ENGINEERING HIGHER SCHOOL OF SAFETY AND ORGANISATION OF WORK, RADOM

Wyższa Inżynierska Szkoła Bezpieczeństwa i Organizacji Pracy w Radomiu (WISBIOP)

ul. Mokra 13/19, 26-600 Radom Radom, mazowieckie
Tel: +48(48) 385-13-14
Fax: +48(48) 385-11-16
EMail: wisbiop@wisbiop.pl
Website: http://www.wisbiop.pl

Rektor: Andrzej Stepien
Tel: +48(48) 385-11-16 Ext. 23 EMail: rektorat@wisbiop.pl

Kanclerz: Ryszard Bródka Tel: +48(48) 385-11-16 Ext.24

Departments
Postgraduate Studies (Environmental Engineering; Labour Law; Safety Engineering; Welfare and Protective Services)

Faculties
Building and Civil Engineering (Building Technologies; Civil Engineering; Environmental Engineering); **Occupational Safety and Health** (Occupational Health; Safety Engineering)

History: Founded 2002.

Degrees and Diplomas: *Inżynier*; *Licencjat*; *Świadectwo ukończenia studiów podyplomowych*

Libraries: Yes
Last Updated: 19/10/11

EUGENIUSZ KWIATKOWSKI SCHOOL OF BUSINESS AND ADMINISTRATION IN GDYNIA

Wyższa Szkoła Administracji i Biznesu im. Eugeniusza Kwiatkowskiego w Gdyni (WSAIB)

ul. Kielecka 7, 81-303 Gdynia, pomorskie
Tel: +48(58) 660-74-00
Fax: +48(58) 621-12-70
EMail: info@wsaib.pl
Website: http://www.wsaib.pl

Rector: Jerzy Młynarczyk (2005-)

Managing Director: Regina Szutenberg
Tel: +48(58) 660-74-31 EMail: r.szutenberg@wsaib.pl

International Relations: Anna Kalejta, International Relations Coordinator Tel: +48(58) 660-74-29 EMail: international@wsaib.pl

Faculties

Law and Administration (Accountancy; Administration; European Union Law; Finance; History of Law; International Law; Labour and Industrial Relations; Law; Safety Engineering; Welfare and Protective Services); **Management** (Economics; Human Resources; Management; Transport Management)

History: Founded 1994.

Governing Bodies: Senate

Admission Requirements: Secondary school certificate (Matura)

Fees: (New Zołty): 1,450-2,700 per semester.

Main Language(s) of Instruction: Polish

Accrediting Agencies: Ministry of Science and Higher Education

Degrees and Diplomas: *Licencjat*; *Świadectwo ukończenia studiów podyplomowych*; *Magister*

Last Updated: 04/10/11

EUROPEAN ACADEMY OF ARTS, WARSAW

Europejska Akademia Sztuk w Warszawie (EAS)

ul. Skazańców 25, 01-532 Warszawa, mazowieckie

Tel: +48(22) 839-93 98 +48(22) 839-93 90

Fax: +48(22) 839-93-90

EMail: dziekanat@eas.edu.pl

Website: http://www.eas.edu.pl

Rector: Antoni Fałat (1992-) Tel: +48(22) 869-91-11

Dyrektor Administracyjny: Aleksandra Iwińska

International Relations: Jadwiga Nash Nasielska, Public Relations Officer

Faculties

Graphic Arts (Architecture; Art Criticism; Art History; Computer Science; English; Fine Arts; French; Graphic Arts; Graphic Design; Information Technology; Painting and Drawing; Photography); **Graphic Design** (Advertising and Publicity; Architecture; Art Criticism; Art History; Design; English; Fine Arts; French; Graphic Design; Information Technology; Multimedia; Painting and Drawing; Photography); **Multimedia Art** (Architecture; Art Criticism; Art History; Design; English; Fine Arts; French; Graphic Arts; Graphic Design; Information Technology; Marketing; Multimedia; Painting and Drawing; Photography; Publishing and Book Trade); **Painting** (Advertising and Publicity; Anatomy; Architecture; Art History; English; Graphic Arts; Graphic Design; Information Technology; Marketing; Painting and Drawing; Sculpture)

History: Founded 1992 as a first private Academy of Arts having a status of University of Arts.

Governing Bodies: Senate

Academic Year: Winter and Spring Semesters

Admission Requirements: Secondary school certificate (matura) and selection of works

Fees: (New Złoty): 1,100 per month

Main Language(s) of Instruction: Polish

Accrediting Agencies: Ministry of Science and Higher Education

Degrees and Diplomas: *Licencjat*; *Magister*

Student Services: Language programs

Special Facilities: Art Gallery

Libraries: Central Library with Internet access

Last Updated: 14/09/11

EUROPEAN HIGHER SCHOOL OF COMPUTER SCIENCE AND ECONOMICS IN WARSAW

Europejska Wyższa Szkoła Informatyczno-Ekonomiczna (EWSIE)

ul. Białostocka 22, 03-741 Warszawa, mazowieckie

Tel: +48(22) 371-03-30

EMail: info@eu.edu.pl; uczelnia@eu.edu.pl

Website: http://www.ewsie.edu.pl/

Rektor: Jerzy G. Isajew
Tel: +48(22) 499-62-36 EMail: biuro@eu.edu.pl

Kanclerz: Dorota M. Kloc-Isajew EMail: kanclerz@eu.edu.pl

Departments

Postgraduate Studies (Administration; Computer Graphics; Government; Information Management; Information Sciences; Multimedia)

Faculties

Administration (Administration; Business Computing; Information Management; Information Technology); **Computer Science** (Business Computing; Computer Graphics; Computer Networks; Computer Science; Data Processing; Information Management; Information Technology; Multimedia; Software Engineering); **Management** (Accountancy; Administration; Advertising and Publicity; Banking; Business Administration; Finance; Human Resources; Information Management; Information Sciences; Insurance; Management; Marketing; Public Relations; Safety Engineering; Transport Management)

History: Founded 2005.

Fees: (New Złoty): 1,250-1,800 per semester

Main Language(s) of Instruction: Polish

Accrediting Agencies: Ministry of Science and Higher Education

Degrees and Diplomas: *Inżynier*; *Licencjat*; *Świadectwo ukończenia studiów podyplomowych*

Last Updated: 24/10/11

EUROPEAN HIGHER SCHOOL OF LAW AND ADMINISTRATION, WARSAW

Europejska Wyższa Szkoła Prawa i Administracji w Warszawie (EWSPA)

ul. Grodzieńska 21/29, 03-750 Warszawa, mazowieckie

Tel: +48(22) 619-02-83 +48(22) 619-90-11 +48(22) 619-28-90

Fax: +48(22) 619-52-40

EMail: dziekanat@ewspa.edu.pl; rekrutacja@ewspa.edu.pl

Website: http://www.ewspa.edu.pl

Rector: Jerzy Wiatr (2008-)
Tel: +48(22) 619-28-90 EMail: rektorat@ewspa.edu.pl

General Director: Katarzyna Zając EMail: rabbit@ewspa.edu.pl

International Relations: Żaneta Frelkowska, Coordinator of Foreign Student's Affairs
Tel: +48(22) 619-24-90 Ext. 35, Fax: +48(22) 619-24-90 Ext. 35
EMail: zf@ewspa.edu.pl

Programmes

Administration (Administration; Business Administration; Government; Public Administration); **International Relations** (European Union Law; International Relations); **Law** *(Postgraduate)* (European Union Law; International Law; Law; Political Sciences); **Postgraduate studies** (Communication Studies; Public Law)

History: Founded 1997.

Governing Bodies: Senate

Admission Requirements: Secondary school leaving certificate (Świadectwo maturalne)

Fees: (New Złoty): Tuition: c. 1,000-2,700 per semester; Foreign students, c. 3,300

Main Language(s) of Instruction: Polish

Accrediting Agencies: Ministry of Science and Higher Education

Degrees and Diplomas: *Licencjat*; *Świadectwo ukończenia studiów podyplomowych*; *Magister*

Student Services: Academic counselling, Canteen, Health services, Language programs, Sports facilities

Special Facilities: Computer Laboratory

Libraries: EWSPA Library

Last Updated: 19/09/11

E. WISZNIEWSKI COLLEGE OF ECONOMICS, WARSAW

Warszawska Wyższa Szkoła Ekonomiczna im. Prof. E. Wiszniewskiego (WWSE)

ul. Szachowa 1, 04-894 Warszawa-Miedzeszyn, mazowieckie

Tel: +48(22) 512-84-44

Fax: +48(22) 205-04-11

EMail: rekrutacja@futurus.org

Website: http://iuczelnia.edu.pl/index.php?option=com_content&view=article&id=47&Itemid=139

Rektor: Agata Wolska-Adamczy

Kanclerz: Robert Gmaj

Faculties

Economic Relations and Management (Accountancy; Banking; Economics; Finance; Human Resources; Management; Marketing; Public Health; Taxation)

History: Founded 1994. Operates in the TUTURUS University Consortium (Konsorcjum Uczelni FUTURUS) since September 2011.

Governing Bodies: Senate; Faculty Council

Academic Year: October to September

Admission Requirements: Secondary school certificate (Matura)

Fees: (New Złoty): 3,600-3,950 per annum

Main Language(s) of Instruction: Polish

International Co-operation: With universities in Ukraine

Accrediting Agencies: Ministry of Science and Higher Education

Degrees and Diplomas: *Licencjat*; *Magister*

Student Services: Canteen, Language programs, Sports facilities

Libraries: c. 7,540 vols

Publications: Scientific Review, Scientific Journal *(quarterly)*

Last Updated: 03/10/11

GDAŃSK COLLEGE OF ADMINISTRATION

Gdańska Wyższa Szkoła Administracji (GWSA)

ul. Wydmy 3, 80-656 Gdańsk, pomorskie

Tel: +48(58) 305-08-12 +48(58) 305-08-89

Fax: +48(58) 305-08-12 Ext. 40

EMail: gwsa@gwsa.pl

Website: http://gwsa.pl

Rektor: Waldemar Polak

Tel: +48(58) 305-08-12 Ext. 33 EMail: rektor@gwsa.pl

Campuses

Olsztyn (Administration; Public Administration); **Slupsk** (Administration; Public Administration)

Departments

Postgraduate Studies (Accountancy; Finance; Management; Occupational Health; Public Administration; Safety Engineering)

Faculties

Administration (Administration; Protective Services; Public Administration; Sociology); **Economics and Social Sciences** (Accountancy; Child Care and Development; Economics; Educational Psychology; European Studies; Management; Pedagogy; Rehabilitation and Therapy; Social Sciences); **Engineering** (Civil Engineering; Environmental Engineering; Occupational Health; Production Engineering; Safety Engineering; Transport Management)

History: Founded 2002.

Main Language(s) of Instruction: Polish

Accrediting Agencies: Ministry of Science and Higher Education; State Accreditation Committee

Degrees and Diplomas: *Inżynier*; *Licencjat*; *Świadectwo ukończenia studiów podyplomowych*; *Magister*

Special Facilities: Auditoriums; Lecture halls; Computer labs

Libraries: Yes

Last Updated: 13/10/11

GDANSK HIGHER SCHOOL OF HUMANITIES KOSZALIN BRANCH

Gdańska Wyższa Szkoła Humanistyczna (GWSH)

ul. Biskupia 24 B, 80-875 Gdańsk, pomorskie

Tel: +48(58) 306-54-78

Fax: +48(58) 306-54-66

EMail: sekretariat@koszalin.gwsh.gda.pl

Website: http://www.bwsh.edu.pl

Rector: Zbigniew Machaliński

Tel: +48(58) 306-63-93, Fax: +48(58) 306-63-93

EMail: rektor@gwsh.gda.pl

Kanclerz: Wiktor Usik

Tel: +48(58) 303-20-00, Fax: +48(58) 303-20-00

EMail: kanclerz@gwsh.gda.pl

International Relations: Monika Mechlińska Pauli, Head, International Cooperation

Tel: +48(58) 306-54-78, Fax: +48(58) 306-63-93

EMail: erasmus@gwsh.gda.pl

Faculties

Administration and Political Sciences (Administration; Government; Political Sciences; Public Administration); **Cultural Studies** (Anthropology; Cultural Studies; European Studies); **European Studies** (Administration; Cultural Studies; Economics; European Studies; Finance; International Business; Marketing; Tourism); **Management** (E-Business/Commerce; European Studies; Finance; Human Resources; Management; Psychology; Sports Management; Transport Management); **Pedagogy** (Education; Pedagogy)

Programmes

Postgraduate studies (Accountancy; Business Administration; Child Care and Development; E-Business/Commerce; Educational Administration; Educational Technology; Ethics; Finance; Foreign Languages Education; Government; Health Education; Health Sciences; Human Resources; Labour Law; Management; Preschool Education; Primary Education; Protective Services; Public Administration; Rehabilitation and Therapy; Safety Engineering; Speech Therapy and Audiology; Taxation)

History: Founded 1994. Formely known as Bałtycka Wyższa Szkoła Humanistyczna w Koszalinie.

Governing Bodies: Senate

Admission Requirements: Secondary school certificate (matura)

Main Language(s) of Instruction: Polish

Accrediting Agencies: Ministry of Science and Higher Education

Degrees and Diplomas: *Licencjat*; *Świadectwo ukończenia studiów podyplomowych*; *Magister*

Last Updated: 09/09/11

GDAŃSK HIGHER SCHOOL OF HUMANITIES, KOSZALIN BRANCH

GDAŃSKA WYżSZA SZKOŁA HUMANISTYCZNA FILIA W KOSZALINIE (GWSH KOSZALIN)

ul. Zwycięstwa 113, 75-601 Koszalin, zachodniopomorskie

Tel: +48(94) 343-10-71

Fax: +48(94) 340-83-85

EMail: sekretariat@koszalin.gwsh.gda.pl

Website: http://koszalin.gwsh.gda.pl/pl

Rektor: Zbigniew Machaliński

Tel: +48(94) 343-10-71, Fax: +48(94) 340-83-85

EMail: kanclerz@koszalin.gwsh.gda.pl;

Kanclerz: Wiktor Usik

Tel: +48(94) 343-10-71, Fax: +48(94) 340-83-85

EMail: kanclerz@koszalin.gwsh.gda.pl

Faculties

Administration (Administration; Cooking and Catering; Government; Hotel and Restaurant; Human Resources; Public Administration; Tourism); **Humanities** (Art Therapy; Arts and Humanities; Education; Health Education; Media Studies; Pedagogy; Preschool Education; Vocational Counselling); **Postgraduate Studies** (Accountancy; Administration; Child Care and Development; E-Business/Commerce; Educational Administration; Educational Technology; Ethics; Finance; Government; Health Administration; Health Sciences; Human Resources; Labour Law; Management; Music Education; Preschool Education; Primary Education; Public Administration; Rehabilitation and Therapy; Speech Therapy and Audiology; Taxation)

History: Founded 2008.

Governing Bodies: Senate

Main Language(s) of Instruction: Polish

Accrediting Agencies: Ministry of Higher Education

Degrees and Diplomas: *Licencjat*; *Świadectwo ukończenia studiów podyplomowych*; *Magister*

GDAŃSK MANAGEMENT COLLEGE

Wyższa Szkoła Zarządzania w Gdańsku (WSZ)

ul. Pelplińska 7, 80-335 Gdańsk, pomorskie
Tel: +48(58) 769-08-00 +48(58) 769-08-10
Fax: +48(58) 769-08-19
EMail: dziekanat@wsz.pl
Website: http://www.wsz.pl

Rektor: Erwin Szneidrowski (2009-) EMail: rektor@wsz.pl

Kanclerz: Marcin Jarosław Geryk
Tel: +48(58) 769-08-80, Fax: +48(58)769-08-89
EMail: marcin.geryk@wsz.pl

International Relations: Żaneta Geryk, Vice-Chancellor
Tel: +48(58) 769-08-80, Fax: +48(58) 769-08-89
EMail: zaneta.geryk@wsz.pl

Departments

Postgraduate Studies (Business Administration; Computer Graphics; Dietetics; Educational Administration; Finance; Human Resources; Management)

Faculties

Administration (Administration; Public Administration); **Environmental Studies** (Environmental Engineering; Environmental Management; Environmental Studies); **Finance and Accounting** (Accountancy; Banking; Finance; Insurance); **Informatics** (Computer Engineering; Computer Graphics; Computer Networks; Computer Science; Information Technology); **Management** (Business Administration; Finance; Industrial and Organizational Psychology; Management); **Physiotherapy** (Alternative Medicine; Health Administration; Health Sciences; Physical Therapy; Rehabilitation and Therapy); **Sociology** (Journalism; Mass Communication; Sociology)

History: Founded 1999.

Fees: (New Złoty): Undergraduate programmes, 2,150-2,600 per semester; Postgraduate programmes, 900-2,100 per semester.

Main Language(s) of Instruction: Polish

International Co-operation: Participates in the Erasmus programme.

Degrees and Diplomas: *Inżynier*, *Licencjat*, *Świadectwo ukończenia studiów podyplomowych*
Last Updated: 25/10/11

GDANSK SCHOOL OF BANKING

Wyższa Szkoła Bankowa w Gdańsku (WSB)

ul. Dolna Brama 8, 80-821 Gdańsk, pomorskie
Tel: +48(58) 323-89-10
Fax: +48(58) 323-89-25
EMail: kancelaria@wsb.gda.pl
Website: http://www.wsb.gda.pl

Rektor: Jan Wiśniewski EMail: rektor@wsb.gda.pl

Chancellor: Emilia Michalska EMail: emilia@wsb.gda.pl

International Relations: Alicja Kaminska, International Relations Officer Tel: +48(58) 323-89-40 EMail: international@wsb.gda.pl

Faculties

Economics and Management *(Gdyni)* (Computer Graphics; Computer Networks; Data Processing; Econometrics; Economics; Information Technology; International Relations; Management; Mass Communication; Multimedia; Psychology); **Finance and Management** (Accountancy; Banking; Finance; Hotel and Restaurant; Human Resources; International Business; Management; Marketing; Psychology; Public Relations; Real Estate; Taxation; Tourism; Transport Management)

History: Founded 1998.

Governing Bodies: Senate

Admission Requirements: Secondary school certificate (matura)

Main Language(s) of Instruction: Polish

International Co-operation: With universities in France, Belgium, Germany, Italy, Switzerland, Slovakia, the Czech Republic, Turkey, Bulgaria, Cyprus, Denmark, UK, Sweden and Norway. Participates in the Erasmus programme.

Accrediting Agencies: State Accreditation Committee

Degrees and Diplomas: *Licencjat*; *Świadectwo ukończenia studiów podyplomowych*; *Magister*. Also MBA
Last Updated: 04/10/11

GIEDROYC COLLEGE OF COMMUNICATIONS AND MEDIA IN WARSAW

Wyższa Szkoła Komunikowania i Mediów Społecznych im. Jerzego Giedroycia (WSKIMS)

ul. Rydygiera 8 (entrance from ul. Broniewski), 01-793 Warszawa, mazowieckie
Tel: +48(22) 833-81-18 +48(22) 833-83-11
Fax: +48(22) 833-83-11
EMail: dziekanat@wskims.edu.pl
Website: http://www.wskims.edu.pl

Rector: Waldemar Dziak

Dyrektor Generalny: Anna Mazurkiewicz
EMail: natka@acn.waw.pl

International Relations: Wojciech Włoch
EMail: wojciechwloch@wp.pl

Faculties

Acting (Acting); **Political Sciences** (Advertising and Publicity; Communication Studies; Journalism; Marketing; Media Studies; Political Sciences; Public Relations; Radio and Television Broadcasting); **Postgraduate Studies** (Communication Studies; Journalism; Marketing; Media Studies; Public Relations; Radio and Television Broadcasting; Translation and Interpretation)

History: Founded 1994.

Governing Bodies: Senate

Admission Requirements: Secondary school certificate (matura)

Main Language(s) of Instruction: Polish

International Co-operation: With universities in Belgium, France, Portugal and the USA. Participates in the Erasmus programme.

Accrediting Agencies: Ministry of Science and Higher Education

Degrees and Diplomas: *Licencjat*; *Świadectwo ukończenia studiów podyplomowych*; *Magister*
Last Updated: 07/10/11

GLIWICE HIGHER SCHOOL OF ENTERPRISE

Gliwicka Wyższa Szkoła Przedsiębiorczości (GWSP)

ul. Bojkowska 37, 44-100 Gliwice, śląskie
Tel: +48(32) 461-21-50
Fax: +48(32) 461-21-50
EMail: info@gwsp.gliwice.pl
Website: http://www.gwsp.gliwice.pl/

Rektor: Tadeusz Grabowiecki
Tel: +48(32) 461-21-43 EMail: rektor@gwsp.gliwice.pl

Kanclerz: Róża Złotecka
Tel: +48(32) 461-21-39 EMail: kanclerz@gwsp.gliwice.pl

International Relations: Milena Gojny, Rector's Plenipotentiary for European Funds and International Cooperation
EMail: fundusze_europejskie@gwsp.gliwice.pl

Chairs

Design (Design; Industrial Design); **Economy** (Advertising and Publicity; Economics; Finance; Government; Human Resources; International Business; Management; Psychology; Real Estate); **Pedagogy** (Art Therapy; Child Care and Development; Educational Administration; Ethics; Foreign Languages Education; Pedagogy; Preschool Education; Safety Engineering; Special Education; Speech Therapy and Audiology; Teacher Trainers Education; Teacher Training); **Philology** (English; Philology; Russian; Tourism)

History: Founded 2005.

Fees: (New Złoty): 1,710-2,850 per semester

Main Language(s) of Instruction: Poland

Degrees and Diplomas: *Licencjat*; *Świadectwo ukończenia studiów podyplomowych*
Last Updated: 17/10/11

HALINA KONOPACKA HIGHER SCHOOL OF PHYSICAL EDUCATION AND TOURISM IN PRUSZKOW

Wyższa Szkoła Kultury Fizycznej i Turystyki im. Haliny Konopackiej (WSKFIT)

ul. Staszica 1, 05-800 Pruszków, mazowieckie
Tel: +48(22) 759-55-36 +48(22) 759-93-20
Fax: +48(22) 759-83-55
EMail: wskfit@wskfit.pl
Website: http://www.wskfit.pl

Rektor: Grzegorz Kazimierz Janicki (1999-)
Tel: +48(22) 759-55-28 EMail: rektor@wskfit.pl

Kanclerz: Ryszard Baecker

International Relations: Jerzy Zieliński Tel: +48 501 186

Departments

Postgraduate Studies (Physical Education; Sports; Sports Management)

Faculties

Administration (Administration; Administrative Law; Economics; Public Administration; Public Law); **Physical Education** (Physical Education); **Tourism and Recreation** (Leisure Studies; Tourism)

Further Information: A

History: Founded 1999, acquired present status and title 2000.

Governing Bodies: Senate

Admission Requirements: Secondary school certificate (matura)

Fees: (New Złoty): 1,650-2,200 per semester.

Main Language(s) of Instruction: Polish

Accrediting Agencies: Ministry of Science and Higher Education; National Accreditation Commission

Degrees and Diplomas: *Licencjat*; *Świadectwo ukończenia studiów podyplomowych*; *Magister*

Last Updated: 23/10/11

HANZEATIC HIGHER SCHOOL OF MANAGEMENT IN SŁUPSK

Wyższa Hanzeatycka Szkoła Zarządzania (WSZ)

ul. Kozietulskiego 6-7, 76-200 Słupsk, pomorskie
Tel: +48(59) 848-28-63
Fax: +48(59) 848-28-67
EMail: rektorat@wsz.slupsk.pl; dziekanat@whsz.slupsk.pl
Website: http://www.whsz.slupsk.pl/

Rector: Eugeniusz Janowicz (2002-)
Tel: +48(59) 848-28-67 EMail: rektor@whsz.slupsk.pl

Kanclerz: Władysław Pędziwiatr
Tel: +48(59) 848-28-68 EMail: kanclerz@whsz.slupsk.pl

Departments

Postgraduate Studies (Educational Administration; Finance; Health Administration; Human Resources; Management; Real Estate; Safety Engineering)

Faculties

Management (Administration; Business Administration; Economics; Finance; Human Resources; Management); **Tourism and Recreation** (Hotel and Restaurant; Leisure Studies; Parks and Recreation; Physical Education; Tourism)

History: Founded 1995 as Wyższa Szkoła Zarządzania w Słupsku (Higher School of Management, Słupsk).

Admission Requirements: Secondary school certificate (Matura)

Fees: 2,150 per semester

Main Language(s) of Instruction: Polish

Accrediting Agencies: Ministry of Science and Higher Education

Degrees and Diplomas: *Licencjat*; *Świadectwo ukończenia studiów podyplomowych*; *Magister*

Last Updated: 25/10/11

HELENA CHODKOWSKA UNIVERSITY OF MANAGEMENT AND LAW IN WARSAW

Wyższa Szkoła Zarządzania i Prawa im. Heleny Chodkowskiej w Warszawie (WSZIM)

al. Jerozolimskie 200, 02-486 Warszawa, mazowieckie
Tel: +48(22) 539-19-00
Fax: +48(22) 539-19-01
EMail: uczelnia@chodkowska.edu.pl; rekrutacja@chodkowska.edu.pl
Website: http://www.chodkowska.edu.pl/

Rector: Piotr Mochnaczewski
Tel: +48(22) 539-19-50, Fax: +48(22) 539-19-51
EMail: rektorat@chodkowska.edu.pl

Dyrektor: Patrycja Wyżlic

International Relations: Anna Korszak, Head of International Relations Office
Tel: +48(22) 539-19-67, Fax: +48(22) 539-19-72
EMail: anna.korszak@chodkowska.edu.pl; international@chodkowska.edu.pl

Departments

Foreign Languages (Chinese; English; French; German; Italian; Modern Languages; Russian; Spanish; Turkish); **Postgraduate Studies** (Construction Engineering; Ecology; Economics; Environmental Management; Insurance; Marketing; Media Studies; Political Sciences; Real Estate)

Faculties

Administration (Administration; Economics; European Studies; Public Administration); **Finance and Accounting** (Accountancy; Banking; Finance; Taxation); **Internal Security** (Computer Networks; Ecology; Economics; Information Technology; Protective Services); **International Relations** (European Studies; International Economics; International Relations; Protective Services); **Law** (Administrative Law; Commercial Law; International Law; Law); **Management** (Communication Studies; Health Administration; Hotel and Restaurant; Human Resources; Industrial and Organizational Psychology; International Economics; Management; Marketing; Public Health; Public Relations; Real Estate; Tourism; Transport Management); **Psychology** (Family Studies; Gender Studies; Industrial and Organizational Psychology; Psychology; Social Psychology)

Further Information: Also campuses in Wrocław, Płońsk, Łódź.

History: Founded 1992. Wyższa Szkoła Zarządzania i Marketingu w Warszawie

Governing Bodies: Senate

Admission Requirements: Secondary school certificate (Matura)

Main Language(s) of Instruction: Polish

International Co-operation: With universities in France, Germany, Netherlands, Italy, Ukraine, USA, Spain. Also participates in the Socrates-Erasmus, Leonardo da Vinci and Jean Monnet programmes

Accrediting Agencies: Ministry of Science and Higher Education

Degrees and Diplomas: *Licencjat*; *Świadectwo ukończenia studiów podyplomowych*; *Magister*. Also MBA

Student Services: Canteen, Foreign student adviser, Language programs, Social counselling, Sports facilities

Libraries: c. 19,000 vols, 150 periodicals

Publications: Promotor *(monthly)*; Spekulator *(monthly)*; Zeszyty Naukowe *(quarterly)*

Last Updated: 12/10/11

HIGHER SCHOOL OF ADMINISTRATION, BIELSKO-BIAŁA

Wyższa Szkoła Administracji w Bielsku-Białej (WSA)

ul. A. Frycza-Modrzewskiego 12, 43-300 Bielsko-Biała, śląskie
Tel: +48(33) 810-01-89
Fax: +48(33) 810-01-89
EMail: wsa@wsa.bielsko.pl
Website: http://www.wsa.bielsko.pl

Rektor: Wiesława Korzeniowska
Tel: +48(33) 810-01-89 EMail: rektor@wsa.bielsko.pl

Dyrektor Administracyjny: Renata Rosowska

Departments

Foreign Languages (English; French; German; Russian; Spanish); **Postgraduate Studies** (Educational Administration; Health Sciences; Primary Education; Public Administration; Safety Engineering; Social Work; Speech Therapy and Audiology)

Faculties

Administration (Administration; Pedagogy; Protective Services; Public Administration); **International Relations** (International Business; International Relations; Preschool Education; Protective Services; Tourism; Transport Management); **Physiotherapy and Pedagogy** (Child Care and Development; Occupational Health; Pedagogy; Physical Therapy; Preschool Education)

History: Founded 1997.

Governing Bodies: Senate

Academic Year: October to September

Admission Requirements: Secondary school certificate (Świadectwo dojrłości)

Fees: (New Złoty): Registration, c. 500; tuition, c. 3,300 per annum

Main Language(s) of Instruction: Polish

Accrediting Agencies: Ministry of Science and Higher Education; State Accreditation Committee

Degrees and Diplomas: *Licencjat*; *Świadectwo ukończenia studiów podyplomowych*; *Magister*

Student Services: Canteen, Sports facilities

Student Residential Facilities: Yes

Special Facilities: Physhiotherapy Workshops; Computer Rooms

Libraries: Main Library, c. 15,678 vols; 33 periodicals

Publications: Scientific Booklets *(3 per annum)*

Last Updated: 19/10/11

HIGHER SCHOOL OF AGRICULTURE, ŁOMŻA

Wyższa Szkoła Agrobiznesu w Łomży (WSA)

ul. Studencka 19, 18-402 Łomża, podlaskie
Tel: +48(86) 216-94-97
Fax: +48(86) 215-11-89
EMail: rektorat@wsa.edu.pl
Website: http://www.wsa.edu.pl

Rector: Roman Zbigniew Engler (1996-)

Pro-Rektor: Zbigniew Puchalski

International Relations: Henryk Porwisiak EMail: dis@wsa.edu.pl

Faculties

Agriculture (Agricultural Business; Agricultural Economics; Agriculture; Dairy; Environmental Management); **Commodity Science** (Cooking and Catering; Food Science; Tourism); **Construction Engineering** (Architecture; Construction Engineering); **Educational Technology and Computer Science** (Computer Science; Educational Technology; Information Technology); **Internal Security** (Protective Services); **Nursing** (Nursing)

History: Founded 1996.

Governing Bodies: Senate

Admission Requirements: Secondary school certificate (matura)

Main Language(s) of Instruction: Polish

Accrediting Agencies: Ministry of Science and Higher Education; State Accreditation Committee

Degrees and Diplomas: *Inżynier*, *Licencjat*, *Magister*

Student Services: Sports facilities

Special Facilities: Auditoriums; Computer Labs

Libraries: Yes

Last Updated: 20/10/11

HIGHER SCHOOL OF APPLIED ARTS, SZCZECIN

Wyższa Szkoła Sztuki Użytkowej w Szczecinie (WSSU)

ul. Kolumba 61, 70-035 Szczecin, zachodniopomorskie
Tel: +48(91) 489-24-47
Fax: +48(91) 489-24-48
EMail: uczelnia@wssu.pl
Website: http://www.wssu.pl

Rektor: Maria Radomska-Tomczuk (1996-)
Tel: +48(91) 489-24-49

Dean: Andrzej Tomczak Tel: +48(91) 489-24-49

International Relations: Danuta Raciborska

Chairs

Graphic Arts (Graphic Arts; Graphic Design; Photography); **Interior Architecture** (Architecture; Communication Arts; Design; Furniture Design; Interior Design; Safety Engineering); **Painting** *(Interdisciplinary)* (Painting and Drawing)

Divisions

Theoretical Subjects *(Interdisciplinary)* (English; Modern Languages)

History: Founded 1995.

Governing Bodies: Senate

Academic Year: October to May (October-January; March-May)

Admission Requirements: Secondary school leaving certificate (Świadectwo maturalne) and presentation of Portfolio with 10-20 Art Works

Fees: (New Złoty): c. 6,000 per annum

Main Language(s) of Instruction: Polish

International Co-operation: With universities in Germany, Spain and Portugal. Participates in the Socrates programme

Accrediting Agencies: Ministry of Science and Higher Education

Degrees and Diplomas: *Licencjat*; *Magister*

Student Numbers *2010-2011*: Total: c. 200

Last Updated: 08/10/11

HIGHER SCHOOL OF ART AND DESIGN, ŁÓDŹ

Wyższa Szkoła Sztuki i Projektowania w Łodzi (WSSIP)

ul. Targowa 65, 90-324 Łódź, łódzkie
Tel: +48(42) 678-05-50
Fax: +48(42) 678-26-71
EMail: info@wssip.edu.pl
Website: http://www.wssip.edu.pl

Rector: Jerzy Derkowski (1998-)
Tel: +48(42) 678-25-89, Fax: +48(42) 678-25-89
EMail: sekretariat.rektor@wssip.edu.pl

Dean: Danuta Wódz Tel: +48(42) 678-05-50

International Relations: Danuta Krauze

Faculties

Architecture (Architecture; Architecture and Planning; Display and Stage Design; Interior Design); **Design** (Clothing and Sewing; Graphic Arts; Graphic Design; Industrial Design; Jewelry Art; Multimedia; Textile Design; Visual Arts); **Film and Photography** (Cinema and Television; Cultural Studies; Film; Fine Arts; Photography)

History: Founded 1998.

Governing Bodies: Senate

Admission Requirements: Secondary school certificate (Matura)

Main Language(s) of Instruction: Polish

Accrediting Agencies: Ministry of Science and Higher Education; National Accreditation Commission

Degrees and Diplomas: *Inżynier*; *Licencjat*; *Świadectwo ukończenia studiów podyplomowych*; *Magister*

Last Updated: 08/10/11

HIGHER SCHOOL OF ARTS AND NATURAL SCIENCES, SANDOMIERZ

Wyższa Szkoła Humanistyczno-Przyrodnicza w Sandomierzu (WSH-P)

ul. Krakowska 26, 27-600 Sandomierz, świętokrzyskie
Tel: +48(15) 832-22-84
Fax: +48(15) 832-60-81Ext. 307
EMail: wshp@wshp.sandomierz.pl
Website: http://www.wshp.sandomierz.pl

Rektor: Tadeusz Studziński
Tel: +48(15) 832-22-84, Fax: +48(15) 832-22-84
EMail: rektorat@wshp.sandomierz.pl

Kanclerz: Ewa Lachor

Departments

Postgraduate Studies (Administration; Art Education; Art Therapy; Behavioural Sciences; Biology; Business Administration; Civics; Computer Science; Cultural Studies; Ecology; Educational Technology; Engineering; Environmental Studies; Geography; Health Sciences; History; Information Management; Information Technology; Management; Mathematics and Computer Science; Music Education; Pedagogy; Polish; Public Administration; Public Law; Public Relations; Rehabilitation and Therapy; Speech Therapy and Audiology)

Faculties

Environmental Studies (Environmental Studies; Plant and Crop Protection); **Humanities** (Archaeology; Arts and Humanities; Cultural Studies; Film; Heritage Preservation; Polish; Rehabilitation and Therapy; Special Education; Speech Therapy and Audiology; Theatre); **Law and Economics** (Administration; Business Administration; Economics; Government; Health Administration; Law; Public Administration); **Management** (Biology; International Business; Management; Mathematics and Computer Science); **Natural Sciences and Mathematics** (Mathematics; Natural Sciences)

History: Founded 1995.

Governing Bodies: Senate

Admission Requirements: Secondary school certificate (Matura)

Fees: (New Złoty): c. 3,000 per annum

Main Language(s) of Instruction: Polish

Accrediting Agencies: Ministry of Science and Higher Education

Degrees and Diplomas: *Licencjat*; *Świadectwo ukończenia studiów podyplomowych*

Student Services: Canteen, Employment services, Foreign student adviser, Language programs, Social counselling, Sports facilities

Libraries: c. 50,000 vols

Publications: Nasza Uczelnia *(monthly)*; Rozprawy Wydziału Humanistycznego *(biennially)*

Last Updated: 22/10/11

HIGHER SCHOOL OF BANKING AND FINANCE, BIELSKO-BIAŁA

Wyższa Szkoła Bankowości i Finansów w Bielsku-Białej (WSBIF)

ul. Tańskiego 5, 43-382 Bielsko-Biała, śląskie
Tel: +48(33) 829-72-12
Fax: +48(33) 829-72-21
EMail: sekretariat@wsbif.edu.pl
Website: http://www.wsbif.edu.pl

Rektor: Jan Ostoj (1999-)
Tel: +48(33) 829-72-14 EMail: janostoj@tlen.pl

Kanclerz: Szarlota Binda
Tel: +48(33) 829-72-12 EMail: szbinda@wsbif.edu.pl

International Relations: Jacek Binda, Pro-Rector
Tel: +48(33) 829-72-13 EMail: jbinda@wsbif.edu.pl

Faculties

Computer Science (Computer Engineering; Computer Graphics; Computer Networks; Computer Science; Data Processing; Fire Science; Information Sciences; Multimedia; Peace and Disarmament; Software Engineering); **Finance and Accounting** (Accountancy; Banking; Economics; Finance; Real Estate; Safety Engineering; Taxation; Tourism; Transport and Communications; Transport Management); **Internal Security** (Police Studies; Protective Services); **Law** (European Union Law; International Law; Law); **Political Sciences** (European Studies; Government; Journalism; Political Sciences; Public Relations; Safety Engineering; Social Work); **Postgraduate studies** (Accountancy; Administration; Banking; Commercial Law; Communication Studies; Computer Networks; Computer Science; Economics; Educational Administration; Finance; Fiscal Law; Health Administration; Information Technology; Law; Real Estate; Taxation)

Further Information: Also distance education.

History: Founded 1995.

Governing Bodies: Senate

Admission Requirements: Secondary school certificate (matura)

Fees: (New Złoty): 1,000-2,500 per semester

Main Language(s) of Instruction: Polish

Accrediting Agencies: Ministry of Science and Higher Education; National Accreditation Commission; International Education Society in London

Degrees and Diplomas: *Inżynier*, *Licencjat*; *Świadectwo ukończenia studiów podyplomowych*; *Magister*

Last Updated: 04/10/11

HIGHER SCHOOL OF BANKING AND FINANCE, KATOWICE

Wyższa Szkoła Bankowości i Finansów w Katowicach (WSBIF)

ul. Ks. Bpa St. Adamskiego 7, 40-069 Katowice, śląskie
Tel: +48(32) 251-96-50
Fax: +48(32) 257-23-54
EMail: info@wsbif.pl
Website: http://www.wsbif.pl

Rektor: Longin Leśniewski EMail: rektorat@wsbif.pl

Kanclerz: Irena Ziomek
Tel: +48(32) 257-78-16 Ext. 7816 EMail: kanclerz@wsbif.pl

Faculties

Economics and Social Sciences (Accountancy; Banking; Computer Science; Economics; English; Finance; Modern Languages; Polish; Protective Services; Public Administration; Real Estate; Social Sciences; Statistics)

History: Founded 1996.

Admission Requirements: Secondary school certificate (matura)

Fees: (New Złoty): 1,465-2,430 per semester

Main Language(s) of Instruction: Polish

International Co-operation: With universities in Switzerland; Participates in the Erasmus programme.

Accrediting Agencies: Ministry of Science and Higher Education

Degrees and Diplomas: *Licencjat*; *Świadectwo ukończenia studiów podyplomowych*

Student Services: Canteen, Handicapped facilities, Language programs, Sports facilities

Student Residential Facilities: Yes

Libraries: Library, 4,500 vols

Publications: Conference Proceedings 'The Structure and Management of a Bank Branch'; Zeszyty Naukowe WSBiF *(biennially)*

Last Updated: 04/10/11

HIGHER SCHOOL OF BUSINESS AND ADMINISTRATION, ŁUKÓW

Wyższa Szkoła Biznesu i Administracji w Łukowie (WSBIA)

ul. Siedlecka 56, 21-400 Łuków, lubelskie
Tel: +48(25) 798-54-01
Fax: +48(25) 798-99-41
EMail: dziekanat@wsbia.edu.pl
Website: http://www.wsbia.edu.pl

Rektor: Jarosław Będkowski (2008-) EMail: rektor@wsbia.edu.pl

Kanclerz: Hanna Będkowska
Tel: +48(25) 644-08-47 EMail: kanclerz@wsbia.edu.pl

Departments
Postgraduate Studies (Alternative Medicine; Development Studies; Health Sciences; Human Resources; Information Management; Information Technology; Insurance; Management; Protective Services; Public Administration; Safety Engineering; Social Work; Transport and Communications; Transport Management)

Institutes
Management and Logistics *(IZIL)* (Accountancy; Economics; Finance; Government; Health Sciences; Industrial Management; Information Technology; Management; Safety Engineering; Transport and Communications; Transport Management); **Political Science and Sociology** *(IPIS)* (Political Sciences; Protective Services; Social Work; Sociology; Vocational Counselling)

History: Founded 2001.

Fees: (New Złoty): 1,775-1,900 per semester.

Main Language(s) of Instruction: Polish

Degrees and Diplomas: *Licencjat*; *Świadectwo ukończenia studiów podyplomowych*

Libraries: c. 5,000 vols

Last Updated: 20/10/11

HIGHER SCHOOL OF BUSINESS AND MANAGEMENT, CIECHANÓW

Wyższa Szkoła Biznesu i Zarządzania - Ciechanów (WSBIZ)

ul. Płońska 57a, 06-400 Ciechanów, mazowieckie
Tel: +48(23) 673-49-49 +48(23) 673-49-09
Fax: +48(23) 673-15-03
EMail: wsbiz@wsbiz.pl
Website: http://www.wsbiz.pl

Rektor: Marian Wozniak

Kanclerz: Stefan Wejs

Departments
Postgraduate studies (Accountancy; Finance; Fiscal Law; Information Management; Information Technology; Taxation)

Faculties
Finance and Accounting (Accountancy; Agricultural Economics; Banking; Computer Science; Economics; English; Finance; Information Technology; Insurance; Law; Management; Mass Communication; Mathematics; Sociology; Statistics; Transport Management)

History: Founded 1998.

Governing Bodies: Senate

Admission Requirements: Secondary school certificate (matura) and entrance examinations

Fees: (New Złoty): 1,500 per semester

Main Language(s) of Instruction: Polish

Accrediting Agencies: Ministry of Science and Higher Education; National Accreditation Commission

Degrees and Diplomas: *Licencjat*; *Świadectwo ukończenia studiów podyplomowych*

Last Updated: 20/10/11

HIGHER SCHOOL OF BUSINESS IN RADOM

Wyższa Szkoła Biznesu im. bpa Jana Chrapka w Radomiu (WSB)

ul. Kolejowa 22, 26-600 Radom, mazowieckie
Tel: +48(48) 363-70-07
Fax: +48(48) 381-77-27
EMail: sekretariat@wsb.com.pl
Website: http://www.wsb.com.pl

Rektor: Krystyna Leśniak-Moczuk
Tel: +48(48) 363-70-07, Ext. 105
EMail: krystyna.lesniak-moczuk@wsb.com.pl

Kanclerz: Ewa Wiśniewska
Tel: +48(48) 363-70-07, Ext. 105
EMail: ewa.wisniewska@wsb.com.pl

International Relations: Katarzyna Głąbicka

Departments
Postgraduate Studies (Accountancy; Business Administration; Communication Studies)

Faculties
Economics and Administration (Accountancy; Administration; Banking; Economics; Finance; Government; Public Administration); **Technical Sciences** (Computer Science; Mechanical Engineering)

History: Founded 1998.

Governing Bodies: Konwent

Admission Requirements: Secondary school certificate (matura)

Fees: (New Złoty): 1,400-1,600 per semester

Main Language(s) of Instruction: Polish

Accrediting Agencies: Ministry of Science and Higher Education

Degrees and Diplomas: *Licencjat*; *Świadectwo ukończenia studiów podyplomowych*

Last Updated: 20/10/11

HIGHER SCHOOL OF BUSINESS, GORZÓW WIELKOPOLSKI

Wyższa Szkoła Biznesu w Gorzowie Wielkopolskim (WSB)

ul. Myśliborska 30, 66-400 Gorzów Wielkopolski, lubuskie
Tel: +48(95) 733-66-67
Fax: +48(95) 733-66-67
EMail: wsb@wsb.gorzow.pl
Website: http://www.wsb.gorzow.pl

Rektor: Maja Kiba-Janiak
Tel: +48(95) 733-66-67, Fax: +48(95) 733-66-67

Kanclerz: Anna Siwko

International Relations: Agnieszka Przybył, International Cooperation Officer
Tel: +48(95) 733-36-96, Fax: +48(95) 733-66-67
EMail: a.przybyl@wsb.gorzow.pl

Departments
Postgraduate Studies (Environmental Management; Human Resources; Management; Occupational Health; Public Administration; Real Estate; Rehabilitation and Therapy; Safety Engineering; Transport Management; Vocational Counselling)

Faculties
Management (Civil Security; Finance; Human Resources; Management; Transport Management); **Sociology** (Advertising and Publicity; Social Problems; Sociology; Vocational Counselling); **Spatial Economy** (Economics; Real Estate; Regional Studies)

Schools
Foreign Languages *(Lingua Academia)* (English; Modern Languages)

History: Founded 1992 as Business Institute, acquired present status and title 1997.

Governing Bodies: Senate

Admission Requirements: Secondary school certificate (matura)

Fees: (New Złoty): 1,500-2,250 per semester

Main Language(s) of Instruction: Polish

Accrediting Agencies: Ministry of Science and Higher Education

Degrees and Diplomas: *Licencjat*; *Świadectwo ukończenia studiów podyplomowych*

Last Updated: 20/10/11

HIGHER SCHOOL OF BUSINESS - NLU, NOWY SĄCZ

Wyższa Szkoła Biznesu - National Louis University w Nowym Sączu (WSB-NLU)

ul. Zielona 27, 33-300 Nowy Sącz, małopolskie
Tel: +48(18) 449-91-00
Fax: +48(18) 449-91-21
EMail: wsb-nlu@wsb-nlu.edu.pl
Website: http://www.wsb-nlu.edu.pl

Rector: Krzysztof Pawłowski

International Relations: Urszula Potoniec-Medon, International Cooperation Officer
Tel: +48(18) 449-91-22 EMail: ulamed@wsb-nlu.edu.pl

Faculties

Chemical and Process Engineering *(Tarnów Branch)* (Chemical Engineering; Economics; English; Management; Marketing; Modern Languages; Production Engineering); **Computer Science** (Computer Networks; Computer Science; Multimedia; Software Engineering); **Financial Management in Russian** (Finance; Management; Russian); **Management** (Advertising and Publicity; Business Administration; Business Computing; E-Business/Commerce; Finance; Hotel Management; Human Resources; Management; Marketing; Public Administration; Tourism); **Management** (International Business; International Relations; Management); **Political Science** (Administration; International Relations; Mass Communication; Media Studies; Political Sciences; Public Administration); **Postgraduate Studies** (Accountancy; Advertising and Publicity; Educational Administration; Finance; Government; Health Administration; Hotel Management; International Relations; Management; Marketing; Media Studies; Psychology; Public Administration; Public Relations; Tourism); **Psychology** (Clinical Psychology; Educational Psychology; Industrial and Organizational Psychology; Psychology); **Social Work** (Communication Studies; Management; Social Work)

Programmes

Business Administration *(MBA)* (Accountancy; Business Administration; Economics; Ethics; Finance; Information Technology; Law; Management; Marketing)

Schools

Foreign Languages (English; German; Italian; Modern Languages; Spanish)

History: Founded 1992.

Governing Bodies: Board of Advisors

Academic Year: October to June

Admission Requirements: Secondary school leaving certificate (Matura) or foreign equivalent

Fees: (New Złoty): Undergraduate tuition fee, 440-675 per programme; Master, 770 per programme; Postgraduate tuition fee,3,400-6,700 per programme; MBA, 29,000 for the whole programme.

Main Language(s) of Instruction: Polish, English, Russian

International Co-operation: With universities in Austria, Bulgaria, Czech Republic, Cyprus, Denmark, Finland, France, Spain, Netherlands, Ireland, Lithuania, Latvia, Germany, Norway, Slovakia, Slovenia, Switzerland, Sweden, Turkey, Ukraine, Hungary. Participates in the Erasmus-LLP programme.

Accrediting Agencies: Ministry of Science and Higher Education; Polish State Accreditation Committee

Degrees and Diplomas: *Inżynier*, *Licencjat*, *Świadectwo ukończenia studiów podyplomowych*; *Magister*. Also Master in Business Administration (MBA), a further 2 yrs following first degree

Student Services: Academic counselling, Canteen, Employment services, Foreign student adviser, Handicapped facilities, Health services, Social counselling, Sports facilities

Student Residential Facilities: For c. 550 students.

Special Facilities: Computer Laboratories. Videoconference room. TV Studio

Libraries: c. 56,000 vols; c. 120 journals; c. 2,890 CD-Roms

Last Updated: 04/10/11

HIGHER SCHOOL OF COMMUNICATIONS, POLITICAL SCIENCE AND INTERNATIONAL RELATIONS IN WARSAW

Wyższa Szkoła Komunikowania, Politologii i Stosunków Międzynarodowych w Warszawie

Al. Jerozolimskie 44 (piętro X, pokój nr 1002), 00-024 Warszawa, mazowieckie
Tel: +48(22) 255-39-52
Fax: +48(22) 255-39-53
EMail: rektorat@wskpism.edu.pl; dziekanat@wskpism.edu.pl
Website: http://www.wskpism.edu.pl/

Head: Aleksandra Burek

Kanclerz: Piotr Nowosad

Departments

Postgraduate Studies (Educational Administration; European Union Law; Pedagogy; Preschool Education; Rehabilitation and Therapy; Safety Engineering; Translation and Interpretation; Vocational Counselling)

Faculties

Air Traffic Service (Air Transport); **International Relations** (International Relations; Tourism; Transport Management); **Journalism** (Chinese; Journalism); **Pedagogy** (Child Care and Development; Educational and Student Counselling; Library Science; Pedagogy; Social Work); **Philology** (English; Japanese; Philology; Russian; Spanish); **Political Sciences** (Administration; Government; Human Resources; Political Sciences; Protective Services)

History: Founded 2005.

Fees: (New Złoty): 3,600-5,951 per annum.

Main Language(s) of Instruction: Polish

Degrees and Diplomas: *Licencjat*; *Świadectwo ukończenia studiów podyplomowych*

Last Updated: 24/10/11

HIGHER SCHOOL OF COMPUTER SCIENCE AND MANAGEMENT, WARSAW

Wyższa Szkoła Informatyki, Zarządzania i Administracji w Warszawie (WSIZIA)

ul. Meksykańska 6, 03-948 Warszawa, mazowieckie
Tel: +48(22) 616-15-66
Fax: +48(22) 672-59-63
EMail: wsizia@wsizia.edu.pl
Website: http://www.wsizia.edu.pl

Rector: Zdzisław Nowakowski (2001-) Tel: +48(22) 672-59-80

Pro-Rector: Sławomir Nowak Tel: +48(22) 672-59-66

International Relations: Slawomir Czepielewski, Vice Rector

Faculties

Administration and Management *(WAiZ)* (Administration; Management); **Computer Science and Telecommunications** *(WIiT)* (Computer Science; Information Technology; Management; Production Engineering; Telecommunications Engineering); **Social Sciences** *(WNS)* (Journalism; Mass Communication; Protective Services; Social Sciences; Transport Management)

Institutes

Postgraduate Studies (Computer Science; Engineering; Film; Journalism; Radio and Television Broadcasting; Safety Engineering)

Further Information: Branches in Góra Kalwaria and Piaseczno

History: Founded 1999.

Governing Bodies: Senate

Admission Requirements: Secondary school certificate (matura)

Fees: (New Złoty): 2,100-2,800 per semester

Main Language(s) of Instruction: Polish

International Co-operation: With universities in Spain, France, Ukraine, Belarus.

Accrediting Agencies: Ministry of Science and Higher Education

Degrees and Diplomas: *Inżynier*, *Licencjat*, *Świadectwo ukończenia studiów podyplomowych*; *Magister*

Student Numbers *2010-2011*: Total: c. 2,000

Last Updated: 07/10/11

HIGHER SCHOOL OF COSMETOLOGY AND HEALTH PROMOTION IN SZCZECIN

Wyższa Szkoła Kosmetologii i Promocji Zdrowia w Szczecinie (WSKIPZ)

ul. Waryńskiego 6, 71-310 Szczecin, zachodniopomorskie
Tel: +48(91) 488-31-17
EMail: psk@data.pl
Website: http://www.wskipz.szczecin.pl

Programmes
Cosmetology (Anatomy; Biochemistry; Chemistry; Cosmetology; Dermatology; Dietetics; Information Technology; Marketing; Microbiology; Pedagogy; Physical Therapy; Physiology; Psychology); **Postgraduate Studies** (Alternative Medicine; Chemistry; Cosmetology; Dietetics; Food Science; Podiatry; Rehabilitation and Therapy)

History: Founded 2006.

Main Language(s) of Instruction: Polish

Degrees and Diplomas: *Licencjat*; *Świadectwo ukończenia studiów podyplomowych*
Last Updated: 21/10/11

HIGHER SCHOOL OF CUSTOMS STUDIES

Wyższa Szkoła Cła i Logistyki w Warszawie (WSCIL)
ul. Jagiellońska 82, 03-301 Warszawa, mazowieckie
Tel: +48(22) 262-88-00
Fax: +48(22) 262-88-01
EMail: sekretariat@wscil.edu.pl
Website: http://www.wscil.edu.pl/

Rektor: Sławomir Wiatr (2001-) EMail: rektor@clo-wsc.edu.pl

Prorektor: Mariusz Edgaro

International Relations: Aleksandra Laskowska, International Relations Officer
Tel: +48(22) 262-88-28
EMail: a.laskowska@wscil.edu.pl; international@wscil.edu.pl

Centres
Postgraduate Studies (Air Transport; European Studies; Human Resources; International Economics; Management; Psychology; Road Transport; Transport and Communications; Transport Management)

Faculties
Transport (European Union Law; International Business; Taxation; Transport and Communications; Transport Management)

History: Founded .

Main Language(s) of Instruction: Polish

International Co-operation: With universities in Czech Republic, Slovenia, France, Croatia, Turkey, Italy, Germany, Bulgaria, Portugal. Participates in the Erasmus programme.

Degrees and Diplomas: *Inżynier*, *Licencjat*; *Świadectwo ukończenia studiów podyplomowych*; *Magister*
Last Updated: 20/10/11

HIGHER SCHOOL OF ECONOMICS AND COMPUTER SCIENCE, CRACOW

Wyższa Szkoła Ekonomii i Informatyki w Krakowie (WSEI)
ul. Św. Filipa 17, 31-150 Kraków, małopolskie
Tel: +48(12) 431-18-90 +48(12) 431-18-82
Fax: +48(12) 431-18-82
EMail: kancelaria@wsei.edu.pl; rekrutacja@wsei.edu.pl
Website: http://www.wsei.edu.pl

Rector: Aleksander Kowalski (2008-)
Tel: +48(12) 431-18-90 Ext. 101 EMail: akowalski@wsei.edu.pl

Kanclerz: Stanisław Kowalski
Tel: +48(12) 431-18-90 Ext. 101, Fax: +48(12) 431-18-90 Ext. 111
EMail: kancelaria@wsei.edu.pl

International Relations: Dagmara Kobiela, International Relations and Promotion Officer
Tel: +48(12) 431-18-90 Ext.131
EMail: bwz@wsei.edu.pl; dkobiela@wsei.edu.pl

Colleges
Postgraduate Studies (Accountancy; Advertising and Publicity; Computer Networks; E-Business/Commerce; Finance; Health Administration; Human Resources; Management; Marketing; Public Administration; Public Relations; Real Estate)

Faculties
Computer Science and Econometrics (Business Computing; Computer Engineering; Computer Networks; Computer Science; Data Processing; Design; E-Business/Commerce; Econometrics; Finance; Information Sciences; Information Technology; Management); **Management** (Accountancy; Advertising and Publicity; Business Administration; E-Business/Commerce; Human Resources; Information Technology; Management; Marketing; Psychology; Real Estate; Sales Techniques; Tourism)

Institutes
Management Studies *(Postgraduate)* (Management)

History: Founded 2000.

Governing Bodies: Senate

Admission Requirements: Secondary school certificate (matura)

Main Language(s) of Instruction: Polish

Accrediting Agencies: Ministry of Science and Higher Education

Degrees and Diplomas: *Inżynier*, *Licencjat*; *Świadectwo ukończenia studiów podyplomowych*. Also ECDL - European Computer Skills Certificate.
Last Updated: 20/10/11

HIGHER SCHOOL OF ECONOMICS AND MANAGEMENT IN ŁÓDŹ

Salezjańska Wyższa Szkoła Ekonomii i Zarządzania w Łodzi (SWSEIZ)
ul. Wodna 34, 90-046 Łódź, łódzkie
Tel: +48(42) 671-85-10
Fax: +48(42) 671-85-09
EMail: rektor@swseiz.lodz.pl
Website: http://www.swseiz.lodz.pl

Rector: Piotr Przesmycki Tel: +48(42) 674-41-28

Dyrektor Administracyjny: Andrzej Borysiak

Departments
Postgraduate Studies (Administration; Banking; Educational Administration; Finance; Government; Health Sciences; Human Resources; Information Management; Labour Law; Safety Engineering)

Faculties
Administration (Administration; Environmental Studies; European Union Law; Justice Administration; Real Estate; Safety Engineering); **Finance and Accounting** (Accountancy; Banking; Finance; Insurance; Management)

History: Founded 1996.

Accrediting Agencies: Ministry of Science and Higher Education

Degrees and Diplomas: *Licencjat*; *Świadectwo ukończenia studiów podyplomowych*. Recruitment for the first year of Licencjat has been suspended.
Last Updated: 18/10/11

HIGHER SCHOOL OF ECONOMICS, PRZEMYSL

Wyższa Szkoła Gospodarcza w Przemyślu (WSG)
ul. Rolnicza 10, 37-700 Przemyśl, podkarpackie
Tel: +48(16) 672-02-31
Fax: +48(16) 672-02-31
EMail: wsg@wsg.edu.pl
Website: http://www.wsg.edu.pl

Rektor: Henryk Fedewicz Tel: +48 605 720 595

Executive Director: Edward Smyk
Tel: +48(16) 678-27-84 EMail: kanclerz@wsg.edu.pl

International Relations: Tadeusz Błaszczyszyn
EMail: sekretariat@wsg.edu.pl

Departments
Postgraduate Studies (Dietetics; Ecology; Economics; Education; Farm Management; Fire Science; Food Technology; Health Administration; Human Resources; Human Rights; Law; Management; Media Studies; Protective Services; Psychology; Safety Engineering; Sociology)

Faculties
Economics (Economics; Information Management; Management; Protective Services); **Food Technology and Analysis** (Cooking and Catering; Food Technology; Nutrition)

History: Founded 2001.

Main Language(s) of Instruction: Polish

Degrees and Diplomas: *Inżynier*; *Licencjat*; *Świadectwo ukończenia studiów podyplomowych*; *Magister*. The Master (Magister) is offered jointly with Politechniką Lubelską w Lublinie.

Last Updated: 21/10/11

HIGHER SCHOOL OF ECONOMICS, STALOWA WOLA

Wyższa Szkoła Ekonomiczna w Stalowej Woli (WSE)

ul. 1 Sierpnia 12, 37-450 Stalowa Wola, podkarpackie
Tel: +48(15) 844-65-43
Fax: +48(15) 844-65-43
EMail: wse@wse.stalowawola.pl
Website: http://www.wse.stalowawola.pl

Rektor: Janusz Bek

Departments

Postgraduate Studies (Accountancy; Art Management; Development Studies; Educational Administration; Environmental Management; Government; Health Administration; Human Resources; International Business; Labour and Industrial Relations; Management; Public Administration; Safety Engineering; Taxation)

Faculties

Economics (Accountancy; Business Administration; Business Computing; Data Processing; Economics; Finance; Government; Human Resources; Information Management; Marketing; Taxation; Tourism)

History: Founded 1997.

Main Language(s) of Instruction: Polish

Accrediting Agencies: Ministry of Science and Higher Education

Degrees and Diplomas: *Licencjat*; *Świadectwo ukończenia studiów podyplomowych*

Academic Staff *2010-2011*: Total: c. 50

Student Numbers *2010-2011*: Total: c. 700

Last Updated: 20/10/11

HIGHER SCHOOL OF ECONOMICS, TOURISM AND SOCIAL SCIENCES, KIELCE

Wyższa Szkoła Ekonomii, Turystyki i Nauk Spolecznych w Kielcach

ul. Ponurego Piwnika 49, 25-666 Kielce, świętokrzyskie
Tel: +48(41) 345-85-88 +48(41) 345-23-57
Fax: +48(41) 345-85-88
EMail: etins@etins.edu.pl
Website: http://www.etins.edu.pl

Rektor: Jan Telus (2001-) EMail: jtelus@etins.edu.pl

Kanclerz: Ryszard Kruk EMail: rkruk@etins.edu.pl

International Relations: Joanna Nowakowska

Departments

Postgraduate Studies (Accountancy; Child Care and Development; Computer Science; Education; Educational Administration; Finance; Health Education; Hotel and Restaurant; Information Technology; Management; Pedagogy; Preschool Education; Rehabilitation and Therapy; Safety Engineering; Social Welfare; Speech Therapy and Audiology; Teacher Training; Tourism; Vocational Counselling)

Faculties

Economics (Accountancy; Economics; Environmental Studies; International Economics; International Relations; Public Administration; Tourism); **Land Management** (Architecture and Planning; Engineering; Real Estate; Town Planning; Urban Studies); **Languages** (English; German; Russian); **Pedagogy** (English; Pedagogy; Preschool Education; Rehabilitation and Therapy; Social Work; Speech Therapy and Audiology); **Public Health** (Alternative Medicine; Cosmetology; Health Sciences; Public Health)

Further Information: A traditional and distance education institution. Also campuses Myślenice in and Krosno.

History: Founded 2001.

Fees: (New Złoty): 220-235 per month (12 installations).

Main Language(s) of Instruction: Polish

International Co-operation: With universities in Slovakia, USA, Greece, Spain, Serbia, Macedonia, Ireland, France, Great Britain, Sweden, Germany, the Czech Republic, Ukraine, Lithuania, Latvia, Hungary, Italy and the Russian Federation. Participates in the Erasmus programme.

Degrees and Diplomas: *Inżynier*; *Licencjat*; *Świadectwo ukończenia studiów podyplomowych*; *Magister*

Last Updated: 20/10/11

HIGHER SCHOOL OF ECONOMY AND MANAGEMENT IN CRACOW

Wyższa Szkoła Gospodarki i Zarządzania w Krakowie (WSGIZ)

ul. Miechowity 6, 31-469 Kraków, małopolskie
Tel: +48(12) 411-07-67
EMail: wsgiz@wsgiz.krakow.pl
Website: http://www.wsgiz.krakow.pl/

Rektor: Waclaw Nelec

Kanclerz: Andrzej Prusek

Departments

Postgraduate Studies (Administration; Educational Administration; Occupational Health; Safety Engineering; Sports Management)

Faculties

Architecture and Art (Architectural and Environmental Design; Architectural Restoration; Architecture; Architecture and Planning; Fine Arts); **Economics** *(Mielec)* (Accountancy; Administration; Business Administration; Economics; Industrial Management; Insurance; International Business; International Economics; Management; Public Administration; Real Estate; Tourism); **Economics and Tourism** (Economics; European Studies; International Business; International Economics; International Relations; Management; Real Estate; Tourism)

History: Founded 2008.

Fees: 1,600 per semester

Main Language(s) of Instruction: Polish

International Co-operation: With universities in Ukraine, France, England, Germany

Degrees and Diplomas: *Inżynier*; *Licencjat*; *Świadectwo ukończenia studiów podyplomowych*

Last Updated: 18/10/11

HIGHER SCHOOL OF ECONOMY ENGINEERING IN SŁUPSK

Wyższa Szkoła Inżynierii Gospodarki w Słupsku (WSBW)

ul. Bałtycka 29, 76-200 Kępice, pomorskie
Tel: +48(59) 841-36-40 +48(59) 842-53-14
Fax: +48(59) 842-53-14
EMail: dziekanat@wsig-slupsk.pl
Website: http://www.wsig-slupsk.pl

Rector: Andrzej Hopfer EMail: rektorat@wsig-slupsk.pl

Courses

Postgraduate Studies (Energy Engineering; Information Sciences; Landscape Architecture; Real Estate; Soil Conservation)

Programmes

Geodesy and Cartography (Information Sciences; Surveying and Mapping); **Spatial Economy** (Energy Engineering; Landscape Architecture; Real Estate; Town Planning)

History: Founded 2003 as Wyższa Szkoła Biznesu Wiejskiego w Warcinie (Wyższa Szkoła Biznesu Wiejskiego w Warcinie).

Degrees and Diplomas: *Licencjat*; *Świadectwo ukończenia studiów podyplomowych*

Last Updated: 15/10/11

HIGHER SCHOOL OF ENGINEERING AND ECONOMICS, RAPCZYCE

Wyższa Szkoła Inżynieryjno - Ekonomiczna z siedzibą w Rzeszowie (WSI-E)

ul. Miłocińska 40, 35-232 Ropczyce, podkarpackie
Tel: +48(17) 866-04-30 +48(17) 8601640 Ext. 32
Fax: +48(17) 866-04-32 +48(17) 8601640 Ext. 32
EMail: info@wsie.edu.pl
Website: http://www.wsie.edu.pl

Rektor: Sylwia Pelc EMail: rektor@wsie.ropczyce.pl

Kanclerz: Jolanta Ptaszek EMail: kanclerz@wsie.ropczyce.pl

International Relations: Stanisław Sosnowski, Vice Rector, International Relations

Departments

Foreign Languages (English; Modern Languages); **Green Areas Management Entrepreneurship** (Horticulture; Management); **Physical Education** (Physical Education); **Postgraduate Studies** (Child Care and Development; Data Processing; Family Studies; Management; Real Estate); **Public Administration** (Administration; Administrative Law; Justice Administration; Public Administration); **Social Sciences** (Family Studies; Social Sciences; Social Work); **Surveying and Real Estate** (Earth Sciences; Information Technology; Real Estate; Surveying and Mapping)

History: Founded 2000.

Governing Bodies: Senate

Admission Requirements: Secondary school certificate (matura)

Main Language(s) of Instruction: Polish

International Co-operation: With universities in USA, Germany, Slovakia, Ukraine. Participates in the Erasmus programme.

Accrediting Agencies: Ministry of Science and Higher Education; National Accreditation Commission (SAC)

Degrees and Diplomas: *Inżynier*, *Licencjat*; *Świadectwo ukończenia studiów podyplomowych*; *Magister*

Student Services: Canteen

Student Residential Facilities: Dormitories

Special Facilities: 9 lecture halls with modern audiovisual equipment; Computer laboratories; Geodesic workroom; Physics and chemistry laboratory; Educational dendrological path;Art Gallery

Libraries: Yes

Last Updated: 07/10/11

HIGHER SCHOOL OF ENTERPRISE AND SOCIAL SCIENCES , OTWOCK

Wyższa Szkoła Przedsiębiorczości i Nauk Społecznych w Otwocku (WSPINS)

ul. Armii Krajowej 13, 05-400 Otwock, mazowieckie
Tel: +44(22) 719-52-15
Fax: +44(22) 719-52-15
EMail: rektorat@wspins.edu.pl
Website: http://www.wspins.edu.pl

Rektor: Andrzej Pietrych
Tel: +48(22) 719-52-10 EMail: rektor@wspins.edu.pl

Departments

Postgraduate Studies (Business Administration; Human Resources; Management; Public Administration; Real Estate)

Faculties

Administration (Administration; Economics; Finance; Public Administration; Taxation); **Management** (Accountancy; Business Administration; Economics; Finance; Human Resources; Management; Real Estate; Small Business; Transport Management); **Spatial Economy** (Environmental Management; Environmental Studies; Real Estate; Town Planning; Waste Management)

Further Information: Also University of the Third Age.

History: Founded 1998.

Fees: (New Złoty): 340-370 per month

Main Language(s) of Instruction: Polish

Accrediting Agencies: Ministry of Science and Education

Degrees and Diplomas: *Inżynier*, *Licencjat*; *Świadectwo ukończenia studiów podyplomowych*. Also MBA

Last Updated: 24/10/11

HIGHER SCHOOL OF ENTREPRENEURSHIP AND MARKETING, CHRZANÓW

Wyższa Szkoła Przedsiębiorczości i Marketingu w Chrzanowie (WSPIM)

ul. Janiny Woynarowskiej 1, 32-500 Chrzanów, małopolskie
Tel: +48(32) 623-51-80 +48(32) 623-38-78
Fax: +48(32) 623-38-78
EMail: wspim@wspim.edu.pl
Website: http://wspim.edu.pl

Rektor: Wiesław Pierzchała
Tel: +48(32) 624-00-72 EMail: rektorat@wspim.edu.pl

Kanclerz: Zbigniew Braś

International Relations: Arkadiusz Potocki, Prorektor
Tel: +48(32) 624-00-72

Departments

Postgraduate Studies (Economics; Educational Administration; Educational Technology; Management; Pedagogy; Rehabilitation and Therapy)

Faculties

Education (Child Care and Development; Education; Pedagogy; Preschool Education; Social Work); **Education Technology and Informatics** (Computer Science; Educational Technology; Media Studies); **Management** (Accountancy; Information Management; Information Technology; Management; Public Administration); **Philology** (English; English Studies; German; Philology; Primary Education); **Sociology** (Advertising and Publicity; Communication Studies; Leadership; Sociology)

History: Founded 1994.

Governing Bodies: Senate

Academic Year: October to June

Admission Requirements: Secondary school certificate (Matura) and entrance examination

Fees: (New Złoty): c. 1,600 per semester; extramural studies, c. 1,200

Main Language(s) of Instruction: Polish, English, German

Accrediting Agencies: Ministry of Science and Higher Education

Degrees and Diplomas: *Licencjat*; *Świadectwo ukończenia studiów podyplomowych*

Libraries: c. 9,000 vols

Publications: Prace Naukowe (Scientific Papers), Publication of research works in economics *(annually)*

Last Updated: 24/10/11

HIGHER SCHOOL OF ENTREPRENEURSHIP, WARSAW

Szkoły Beaty Mydłowskiej

ul. Kaleńska 3, 04-367 Warszawa, mazowieckie
Tel: +48(22) 619-32-25 +48(22) 870-54-29
Fax: +48(22) 870-54-29
EMail: szkolakosmetyczna@neostrada.pl
Website: http://www.szkolymydlowskiej.pl

Rektor: Jerzy Rzytki

Kanclerz: Beata Mydlowska

Departments

Postgraduate Studies (Aesthetics; Cosmetology; Dermatology; Immunology; Microbiology; Nutrition; Physical Therapy; Technology; Toxicology)

Faculties

Cosmetology (Alternative Medicine; Cosmetology; Management)

Fees: (New Złoty): Full-time studies, 3,300 per semester; Part-time studies, 2,800 per semester; Postgraduate studies, 1,950 per semester.

Main Language(s) of Instruction: Polish

Degrees and Diplomas: *Licencjat*; *Świadectwo ukończenia studiów podyplomowych*
Last Updated: 26/10/11

HIGHER SCHOOL OF ENVIRONMENTAL PROTECTION, BYDGOSZCZ

Wyższa Szkoła Ochrony Środowiska w Bydgoszczy (WSOŚ)

ul. Fordońska 120, 85-739 Bydgoszcz, kujawsko-pomorskie
Tel: +48(52) 342-92-90 +48(52) 342-92-85
Fax: +48(52) 345-24-40
EMail: rektor@wss.edu.pl
Website: http://www.wsos.edu.pl

Rector: Barbara Kowalkowska (1998-) EMail: rektor@wsos.edu.pl

Kanclerz: Maria Arndt

International Relations: Szymon Leniec EMail: biuro@wsos.edu.pl

Departments
Postgraduate Studies (Air Transport; Construction Engineering; Energy Engineering; Environmental Management; Environmental Studies; Health Sciences; Heritage Preservation; Safety Engineering; Transport and Communications; Waste Management)

Faculties
Aviation and Aerospace (Aeronautical and Aerospace Engineering; Air Transport); **Environmental Protection** (Environmental Engineering; Environmental Management; Environmental Studies; Landscape Architecture; Peace and Disarmament; Transport Management); **Protection of Cultural Property** (Cultural Studies; Heritage Preservation; Law)

History: Founded 1998.

Governing Bodies: Senate

Academic Year: October to June

Admission Requirements: Secondary school certificate (matura) and entrance examinations

Fees: (New Złoty): c. 900 per quarter

Main Language(s) of Instruction: Polish

International Co-operation: Participates in the Erasmus programme.

Accrediting Agencies: Ministry of Science and Higher Education

Degrees and Diplomas: *Inżynier*; *Licencjat*; *Świadectwo ukończenia studiów podyplomowych*; *Magister*
Last Updated: 23/10/11

HIGHER SCHOOL OF FINANCE AND ADMINISTRATION IN GDAŃSK

Wyższa Szkoła Finansów i Administracji w Sopocie (WSFIA)

ul. Żwirki i Wigury 15, 81-387 Gdańsk-Zaspa, pomorskie
Tel: +48(58) 524-13-00
Fax: +48(58) 524-13-01
EMail: wsfia@skok.pl
Website: http://www.skok.pl/wsfia

Rektor: Wlodzimierz Soinski

Departments
Postgraduate Studies (Business Administration; Business Computing; Health Administration; Information Technology; Labour Law; Management; Mathematics; Taxation)

Programmes
Financial Management (Accountancy; Finance; Management); **IT and Business Management ;** (Business Administration; Business Computing; Information Technology); **Management of Economic Organization** (Business Administration; Management; Protective Services; Transport Management); **Property Management** (Environmental Management; Real Estate); **Psychology in Management** (Psychology)

History: Founded 2001.

Main Language(s) of Instruction: Polish

Accrediting Agencies: State Accreditation Committee

Degrees and Diplomas: *Licencjat*; *Świadectwo ukończenia studiów podyplomowych*
Last Updated: 20/10/11

HIGHER SCHOOL OF FINANCE AND COMPUTER SCIENCE, ŁÓDŹ

Wyższa Szkoła Finansów i Informatyki im. Prof. J. Chechlińskiego (WSFI)

ul. Św. Jerzego 10/12, 91-072 Łódź, łódzkie
Tel: +48(42) 664-93-10
Fax: +48(42) 631-04-60
EMail: dziekanat@wsfi.pl
Website: http://www.wsfi.edu.pl/

Rector: Ewa Maciaszczyk (1997-)

Kanclerz: Maria Jackowska-Fuk

Departments
Postgraduate Studies (Business Administration; Education; Finance; Peace and Disarmament; Psychology; Safety Engineering)

Faculties
Economics *(Kalisz)* (Accountancy; Banking; Business Computing; Computer Science; Economics; English; European Union Law; Finance; German; Psychology; Regional Studies); **Economics** *(Starachowice)* (Economics; English; European Union Law; Finance; German); **Economics and Social Sciences** *(Lodz)* (Accountancy; Banking; Economics; English; Finance; German; Insurance; Social Sciences); **Homeland Security** (English; German; Protective Services); **Science and Management** *(Konin)* (Accountancy; Computer Science; English; Finance; German; Government; Human Resources; Management; Small Business; Taxation)

Further Information: A traditional and distance education institution.

History: Founded 1997.

Governing Bodies: Academic Council

Academic Year: October to June. Also Summer Session

Admission Requirements: Secondary school certificate (Matura) or equivalent, and competitive examination

Fees: (New Złoty): Registration, c. 500; tuition, 3,150 per annum; extramural and evening students, c. 2,835

Main Language(s) of Instruction: Polish, English for Business and Banking courses

Accrediting Agencies: State Accreditation Committee

Degrees and Diplomas: *Inżynier*, *Licencjat*; *Świadectwo ukończenia studiów podyplomowych*

Student Services: Academic counselling, Employment services, Health services, Language programs, Social counselling, Sports facilities

Libraries: Central Library, c. 2,000 vols; 20 periodicals
Last Updated: 20/10/11

HIGHER SCHOOL OF FINANCE AND MANAGEMENT, BIAŁYSTOK

Wyższa Szkoła Finansów i Zarządzania w Białymstoku (WSFIZ)

ul. Ciepła 40, 15-472 Białystok, podlaskie
Tel: +48(85) 678-58-67 +48(85) 678-58-23
Fax: +48(85) 678-59-18
EMail: wsfiz@wsfiz.edu.pl
Website: http://www.wsfiz.edu.pl

Rector: Józef Szabłowski
Tel: +48(85) 678-58-27 EMail: jozef.szablowski@wsfiz.edu.pl

Kanclerz: Anatoliusz Kopczuk
Tel: +48(85) 678-58-58 EMail: anatoliusz.kopczuk@wsfiz.edu.pl

International Relations: Joanna Boboryko, Head, International Relations Office EMail: foreign@wsfiz.edu.pl

Centres
Postgraduate Studies (Accountancy; Banking; Business Administration; Communication Studies; Computer Science; Educational Administration; Educational and Student Counselling; Finance;

Government; Health Administration; Management; Mass Communication; Occupational Health; Psychology; Public Administration; Public Relations; Real Estate; Safety Engineering; Taxation; Tourism; Transport Management)

Faculties
Economic Science *(Ostrow Mazowiecka)* (Accountancy; Banking; Economic and Finance Policy; Economics; Finance; Geography; Information Sciences; International Economics; International Relations; Law; Management; Marketing; Mathematics; Psychology; Social Policy; Sociology; Taxation); **Finance and Informatics** (Accountancy; Banking; Business Computing; Computer Graphics; Computer Science; E-Business/Commerce; Econometrics; Finance; Information Technology; Insurance; Taxation); **Humanities** *(Elk)* (Arts and Humanities; English; Philology; Translation and Interpretation); **Humanities** (Arts and Humanities; English; English Studies; Philology; Polish; Political Sciences); **Management and Marketing** *(Elk)* (Accountancy; Computer Science; Economics; Educational Administration; Educational and Student Counselling; Energy Engineering; Finance; Government; Health Administration; Health Sciences; Hotel and Restaurant; Human Resources; Management; Marketing; Mass Communication; Psychology; Public Administration; Public Relations; Safety Engineering; Social Work; Taxation; Tourism; Transport Management); **Management and Marketing** (Accountancy; Administration; Advertising and Publicity; Computer Graphics; European Studies; Finance; Government; Human Resources; Information Technology; International Business; Leadership; Management; Marketing; Psychology; Sports Management; Welfare and Protective Services); **Spatial Planning** (Administration; Architecture and Planning; Economics; European Studies; Information Sciences; Real Estate; Surveying and Mapping; Town Planning); **Technical Sciences** *(Elk)* (Architecture; Computer Graphics; Electrical Engineering; Engineering)

History: Founded 1993.

Governing Bodies: Senate

Academic Year: October to June (October-February; February-June)

Admission Requirements: Secondary school certificate (matura)

Fees: (New Złoty): 3,500 per annum

Main Language(s) of Instruction: Polish, English

International Co-operation: With universities in Italy, Spain, Finland, Denmark, Germany, Belarus, Ukraine, Estonia, Sweden, Romania, Turkey; Socrates Erasmus Programme

Accrediting Agencies: National Accreditation Committee; Forum

Degrees and Diplomas: *Inżynier*; *Licencjat*; *Świadectwo ukończenia studiów podyplomowych*; *Magister*. Also MBA

Student Services: Academic counselling, Canteen, Employment services, Foreign Studies Centre, Health services, Sports facilities

Student Residential Facilities: Yes

Special Facilities: Movie Studio

Libraries: c. 60,000 vols; 3,000 periodical subscriptions

Publications: "Pomosty - w kregu nauki i biznesu" *(quarterly)*

Academic Staff *2010-2011*	**TOTAL**
FULL-TIME	**230**
STAFF WITH DOCTORATE FULL-TIME	c. **90**
Student Numbers *2010-2011*	
All (Foreign Included)	c. **7,000**
FOREIGN ONLY	**40**

Part-time students, 4,230.
Last Updated: 05/10/11

HIGHER SCHOOL OF FINANCE AND MANAGEMENT, SIEDLCE

Collegium Mazovia Innowacyjna Szkoła Wyższa
ul. Sokołowska 161, 08-110 Siedlce, mazowieckie
Tel: +48(25) 633-30-32
Fax: +48(25) 633-20-51
EMail: info@mazovia.edu.pl
Website: http://www.mazovia.edu.pl/

Rektor: Leszek Gadomski (2008-)
Tel: +48(25) 633 30 32 Ext.11/or 63
EMail: leszek.gadomski@mazovia.edu.pl

Kanclerz: Mariusz Szablowski
Tel: +48(25) 633-30-32 Ext. 6
EMail: mariusz.szablowski@mazovia.edu.pl

International Relations: Mariusz Szabłowski, Chancellor
EMail: info@wsfiz.siedlce.pl

Centres
Entrepreneuship Development (Management)

Departments
Foreign Languages (English; Modern Languages); **Postgraduate Studies** (Accountancy; Construction Engineering; Economics; Environmental Studies; Finance; Government; Information Technology; Landscape Architecture; Management; Public Health; Real Estate)

Faculties
Economics and Management (Accountancy; Administration; Economics; Finance; Law; Management); **Health Sciences** (Health Sciences; Nursing; Public Health); **Technical Sciences** (Civil Engineering; Computer Science; Landscape Architecture; Mathematics)

History: Founded 1999 as Wyższa Szkoła Finansów i Zarządzania w Siedlcach (Higher School of Finance and Management, Siedlce). Acquired present title 2010.

Governing Bodies: Senate

Admission Requirements: Secondary school certificate (matura)

Main Language(s) of Instruction: Polish

International Co-operation: With universities in Romania, Ukraine, Bnelarus, Germany, Mexico.

Accrediting Agencies: Ministry of Science and Higher Education

Degrees and Diplomas: *Inżynier*, *Licencjat*; *Świadectwo ukończenia studiów podyplomowych*; *Magister*

Last Updated: 20/10/11

HIGHER SCHOOL OF FOREIGN LANGUAGES, CZĘSTOCHOWA

Wyższa Szkoła Lingwistyczna w Częstochowie (WSL)
ul. Nadrzeczna 7, 42-200 Częstochowa, śląskie
Tel: +48(34) 365-58-02
Fax: +48(34) 324-59-12
EMail: rekrutacja@wsl.edu.pl
Website: http://www.wsl.edu.pl

Rektor: Cezary Wosiński EMail: wosinski@wsl.edu.pl

International Relations: Anna Berezowska
EMail: international@wsl.edu.pl

Departments
Online Studies (English; German; Pedagogy; Philology; Preschool Education; Teacher Training; Translation and Interpretation); **Postgraduate Studies** (Business Administration; English; Foreign Languages Education; German; Heritage Preservation; Management; Pedagogy; Physical Education; Polish; Rehabilitation and Therapy; Sports; Translation and Interpretation)

Faculties
Journalism and Public Relations - Polish Studies (Cultural Studies; Journalism; Mass Communication; Media Studies; Psychology; Public Relations; Radio and Television Broadcasting); **Pedagogy; Philology** (English; German; Russian)

History: Founded 1992. Acquired present status and title 1996.

Governing Bodies: Senate

Admission Requirements: Secondary school certificate (matura)

Main Language(s) of Instruction: Polish

International Co-operation: Participates in the Erasmus LLP Programme.

Accrediting Agencies: Ministry of Science and Higher Education; State Accreditation Committee

Degrees and Diplomas: *Licencjat*; *Świadectwo ukończenia studiów podyplomowych*; *Magister*

Student Services: Canteen, Health services, Sports facilities

Special Facilities: Language labs with satellite TV; Computer rooms with Internet access

Libraries: Yes

Academic Staff *2010-2011*: Total: c. 140

Student Numbers *2010-2011*: Total: c. 1,600

Last Updated: 07/10/11

HIGHER SCHOOL OF GRUDZIĄDZ

Grudziądzka Szkoła Wyższa (GSW)
ul. Hallera 31, 86-300 Grudziądz, kujawsko-pomorskie
Tel: +48(56) 461-04-23
Fax: +48(56) 461-04-23
EMail: info@gsw.edu.pl
Website: http://www.gsw.edu.pl

Rektor: Krzysztof Schroeder

Kanclerz: Wojciech Rzemieniewski

Departments

Postgraduate Studies (Hygiene; Occupational Health; Safety Engineering)

Faculties

Mechanics and Mechanical Engineering (Electronic Engineering; Environmental Engineering; Mechanical Engineering; Mechanics; Production Engineering); **Political and Social Sciences** (Economic and Finance Policy; Government; Mass Communication; Media Studies; Political Sciences; Protective Services; Social Sciences)

Degrees and Diplomas: *Inżynier*; *Licencjat*; *Świadectwo ukończenia studiów podyplomowych*

Last Updated: 15/10/11

HIGHER SCHOOL OF HEALTH SCIENCES, BYDGOSZCZ

Wyższa Szkoła Nauk o Zdrowiu w Bydgoszczy
ul. Karpacka 54, 85-164 Bydgoszcz, kujawsko-pomorskie
Tel: +48(52) 379-23-52
Fax: +48(52) 379-23-52
EMail: wsnoz.pl@wsnoz.pl; sekretariat@wsnoz.pl
Website: http://www.wsnoz.pl/

Kanclerz: Marek Krzysztof Szarata

Rektor: Bronisław A. Zachara

Departments

Postgraduate studies (Biotechnology; Cosmetology; Health Sciences; Medical Technology; Physical Therapy)

Programmes

Biotechnology (Biotechnology); **Cosmetology** (Cosmetology; Physical Therapy); **Physiotherapy** (Physical Therapy; Rehabilitation and Therapy)

Further Information: A traditional and distance learning institution.

History: Founded 2005.

Main Language(s) of Instruction: Polish

Degrees and Diplomas: *Licencjat*; *Świadectwo ukończenia studiów podyplomowych*

Last Updated: 17/10/11

HIGHER SCHOOL OF HOTEL INDUSTRY, GASTRONOMY AND TOURISM, WARSAW

Wyższa Szkoła Hotelarstwa, Gastronomii i Turystyki w Warszawie (WSHGIT)
ul. Chodakowska 50, 03-816 Warszawa, mazowieckie
Tel: +48(22) 256-88-00 +48(22) 818-15-08
Fax: +48(22) 619-19-10
EMail: wshgit@wshgit.waw.pl
Website: http://www.wshgit.waw.pl

Rektor: Jolanta Mogiła-Lisowska EMail: rektorat@wshgit.waw.pl

Dyrektor Administracyjny: Julian Walczyński
Tel: +48(22) 256-88-11, Fax: +48(22) 619-19-10

International Relations: Marek Piekutowski, Dean of Students
Tel: +48(22) 513-87-89, Fax: +48(22) 619-19-10

Departments

Fundamental Sciences (Ecology; Environmental Management; Environmental Studies; Ethics; Geography; Law; Natural Resources; Psychology; Sociology; Tourism); **Hotel and Catering** (Cooking and Catering; Dietetics; Economics; Food Science; Food Technology; Hotel and Restaurant; Hotel Management; Information Technology; Management; Marketing; Nutrition; Safety Engineering; Tourism); **Recreation and Animation in Tourism** (Development Studies; Health Education; Health Sciences; Physical Education; Physiology; Safety Engineering; Sports; Tourism); **Tourism** (Accountancy; Air Transport; Economics; Finance; Human Resources; Insurance; Law; Management; Marketing; Parks and Recreation; Public Relations; Safety Engineering; Tourism)

History: Founded 1996.

Governing Bodies: Senate

Academic Year: October to September

Admission Requirements: Secondary school certificate (Świadectwo dojrzałeści) and knowledge of foreign languages and geography

Fees: (New Złoty): 420-510 per month

Main Language(s) of Instruction: Polish

Accrediting Agencies: Ministry of Science and Higher Education

Degrees and Diplomas: *Licencjat*; *Świadectwo ukończenia studiów podyplomowych*; *Magister*

Student Services: Academic counselling, Canteen, Cultural centre, Employment services, Health services, Language programs, Nursery care, Social counselling, Sports facilities

Special Facilities: Language Laboratories

Libraries: Central Library

Last Updated: 06/10/11

HIGHER SCHOOL OF HUMAN SCIENCES AND ECONOMICS, BRZEG

Wyższa Szkoła Humanistyczno-Ekonomiczna w Brzegu (WSH-E)
Ul. Młynarska 12, 49-300 Brzeg, opolskie
Tel: +48(77) 416-00-70
Fax: +48(77) 404-46-00
EMail: dziekanat@wshe.edu.pl
Website: http://www.wshe.edu.pl

Rektor: Marian Ścipuro (2008-) EMail: rektorat@wshe.edu.pl

Kanclerz: Stanislaw Widocki EMail: administracja@wshe.edu.pl

Departments

Postgraduate Studies (Anthropology; Art Therapy; Child Care and Development; Computer Education; Cultural Studies; Education; Educational Administration; English; Ethics; Family Studies; Geography; Higher Education; History; Information Technology; Library Science; Music Education; Native Language Education; Occupational Therapy; Pedagogy; Philosophy; Preschool Education; Primary Education; Rehabilitation and Therapy; Safety Engineering; Secondary Education; Singing; Special Education; Speech Therapy and Audiology; Technology Education)

Faculties

History (Archiving; History; Information Management; Information Sciences); **Pedagogy** (Child Care and Development; Civics; Cultural Studies; Educational Administration; Educational and Student Counselling; Family Studies; Media Studies; Pedagogy; Rehabilitation and Therapy; Speech Therapy and Audiology; Vocational Counselling); **Russian Philology** (Philology; Russian)

History: Founded 2001.

Main Language(s) of Instruction: Polish

Degrees and Diplomas: *Licencjat*; *Świadectwo ukończenia studiów podyplomowych*

Last Updated: 21/10/11

HIGHER SCHOOL OF HUMANITIES AND ECONOMICS, SIERADZ

Wyższa Szkoła Humanistyczno-Ekonomiczna w Sieradzu (WSHE)

ul. Mickiewicza 6, 98-200 Sieradz, łódzkie
Tel: +48(42) 828-63-02 +48(42) 828-63-03
Fax: +48(42) 828-63-05
EMail: sieradz@wshe.sieradz.pl
Website: http://www.wshe.sieradz.pl/

Rektor: Jakub Bartoszewski

Kanclerz: Joanna Lisiecka

International Relations: Daria Modrzejewska
EMail: dariamod@tlen.pl

Departments

Postgraduate Studies (Pedagogy; Preschool Education; Teacher Training)

Faculties

Internal Security (Protective Services; Safety Engineering); **Pedagogy** (Pedagogy; Physical Therapy; Preschool Education; Psychology; Rehabilitation and Therapy; Social and Preventive Medicine; Social Work)

History: Founded 2002.

Main Language(s) of Instruction: Polish

Degrees and Diplomas: *Licencjat*; *Świadectwo ukończenia studiów podyplomowych*

Last Updated: 22/10/11

HIGHER SCHOOL OF INFORMATION TECHNOLOGY AND MANAGEMENT, WARSAW

Wyższa Szkoła Informatyki Stosowanej i Zarządzania WIT pod auspicjami Polskiej Akademii Nauk (WSISIZ)

ul. Newelska 6, 01-447 Warszawa, mazowieckie
Tel: +48(22) 348-65-00
Fax: +48(22) 837-71-90
EMail: wit@wit.edu.pl
Website: http://www.wit.edu.pl

Rector: Maciej Krawczak
Tel: +48(22) 348-65-23 EMail: rektor@wit.edu.pl

Prorektor: Barbara Mażbic-Kulma
Tel: +48(22) 348-65-97 EMail: B.Mazbic-Kulma@wit.edu.pl

International Relations: Andrzej Woźniak
Tel: +48(22) 837-35-78, Ext. 471 EMail: a.z.wozniak@wsisiz.edu.pl

Departments

Postgraduate Studies (Computer Graphics; Computer Networks; Computer Science; Data Processing; Economics; Educational Administration; Information Technology; Management; Mathematics; Safety Engineering; Software Engineering)

Faculties

Administration (Accountancy; Administration; Data Processing; E-Business/Commerce; Finance; Government; Information Technology; Management; Multimedia; Public Administration); **Computer Science** (Computer Engineering; Computer Graphics; Computer Networks; Computer Science; Data Processing; Information Technology; Mathematics; Mathematics and Computer Science; Software Engineering; Telecommunications Engineering); **Graphics** (Computer Graphics; Graphic Design; Multimedia); **Management** (Business Computing; Information Management; Information Technology; Management; Psychology)

History: Founded 1996.

Governing Bodies: Senate

Admission Requirements: Secondary school certificate (matura)

Fees: (New Złoty): 1,000-3,300 per semester.

Main Language(s) of Instruction: Polish

International Co-operation: With universities in Czech Republic, Finland, Belarus, Belgium, USA, Slovakia. Participates in the Socrates/Leonardo da Vinci/Erasmus programmes.

Accrediting Agencies: Ministry of Science and Higher Education

Degrees and Diplomas: *Inżynier*; *Licencjat*; *Świadectwo ukończenia studiów podyplomowych*; *Magister*

Last Updated: 07/10/11

HIGHER SCHOOL OF INFORMATION TECHNOLOGY, KATOWICE

Wyższa Szkoła Technologii Informatycznych w Katowicach (WSTI)

ul. Mickiewicza 29, 40-085 Katowice, śląskie
Tel: +48(32) 207-30-70 +48(32) 207-30-80
EMail: info@wsti.pl
Website: http://www.wsti.pl

Rector: Dariusz Badura

Departments

Postgraduate Studies (Advertising and Publicity; Computer Graphics; Computer Networks; E-Business/Commerce; Information Sciences; Information Technology; Multimedia; Photography; Visual Arts)

Programmes

Computer Science (Computer Engineering; Computer Graphics; Computer Networks; Computer Science; Information Technology); **Graphic Design** (English; Fine Arts; Graphic Design; Information Technology; Law; Marketing; Modern Languages)

History: Founded 2003.

Fees: (New Złoty): 1,390 -1,849 per semester

Main Language(s) of Instruction: Polish

Degrees and Diplomas: *Inżynier*; *Licencjat*; *Świadectwo ukończenia studiów podyplomowych*

Last Updated: 24/10/11

HIGHER SCHOOL OF INFRASTRUCTURE AND MANAGEMENT, WARSAW

Wyższa Szkoła Infrastruktury i Zarządzania w Warszawie (WSIIZ)

ul. Rakowiecka 32, 02-532 Warszawa, mazowieckie
Tel: 48(22) 646-20-60
Fax: 48(22) 646-20-60
EMail: rekrutacja@wsiiz.pl
Website: http://ww.wsiiz.pl

Rektor: Krzysztof Florian Wierzbicki
EMail: krzysztof.wierzbicki@licencjat.pl

Kanclerz: Marcin Jaroslaw Geryk

Departments

Postgraduate Studies (Cosmetology; Health Administration; Management; Pharmacy; Physical Therapy; Real Estate)

Faculties

Administration (Administration; Government; Public Administration); **Computer Science** (Computer Engineering; Computer Graphics; Computer Networks; Computer Science; Information Technology); **Cosmetology** (Cosmetology; Health Sciences); **Ecology and Environmental Protection** (Ecology; Environmental Management; Environmental Studies; Waste Management; Water Management); **Management** (Management; Marketing; Small Business); **Spatial Economy** (Construction Engineering; Real Estate; Surveying and Mapping; Town Planning)

History: Founded 2003. Acquired present status 2005.

Fees: (New Złoty): 1,800-2,200 per semester.

Main Language(s) of Instruction: Polish

International Co-operation: Participates in the Erasmus programme.

Degrees and Diplomas: *Inżynier*; *Licencjat*; *Świadectwo ukończenia studiów podyplomowych*

Student Numbers *2010-2011*: Total: c. 600

Last Updated: 23/10/11

HIGHER SCHOOL OF INTEGRATIONAL AND INTERCULTURAL EDUCATION IN POZNAN

Wyższa Szkoła Edukacji Integracyjnej i Interkulturowej w Poznaniu (WSEIII)

ul. Prądzyńskiego 53, 61-527 Poznań, wielkopolskie
Tel: +48(61) 833-05-30
Fax: +48(61) 833-15-43
EMail: rekrutacja@wseiii.pl; dziekanat@wseiii.pl
Website: http://www.wseiii.pl

Rektor: Dariusz Grzybek EMail: rektorat@wseiii.pl

Kanclerz: Luiza Kalupa EMail: luiza.kalupa@wseiii.pl

Departments

Postgraduate Studies (Child Care and Development; Education; Educational Administration; Educational Technology; Ethics; Family Studies; Fine Arts; Foreign Languages Education; Gender Studies; Information Technology; Music; Pedagogy; Philosophy; Preschool Education; Protective Services; Rehabilitation and Therapy; Special Education; Speech Therapy and Audiology; Vocational Counselling)

Faculties

Archaeology (Archaeology); **Dietetics** (Dietetics; Nutrition); **Ethnology** (Anthropology; Communication Studies; Ethnology; International Business; Tourism); **Special Education** (Child Care and Development; Pedagogy; Rehabilitation and Therapy; Special Education; Speech Therapy and Audiology)

Degrees and Diplomas: *Licencjat*; *Świadectwo ukończenia studiów podyplomowych*

Last Updated: 20/10/11

HIGHER SCHOOL OF INTERNATIONAL RELATIONS AND SOCIAL COMMUNICATIONS, CHEŁM

Wyższa Szkoła Stosunków Międzynarodowych i Komunikacji Społecznej w Chełmie (WSSMIKS)

ul. Wojsławicka 8 A, 22-100 Chełm, lubelskie
Tel: +48(82) 560-40-50
Fax: +48(82) 560-31-11
EMail: poczta@wssm.pl
Website: http://www.wssm.pl

Rektor: Michał Gołoś
Tel: +48(82) 560-31-01 EMail: rektorat@wssm.pl

Prorektor: Agnieszka Kasinska-Metryka

Departments

Postgraduate Studies (Accountancy; Administration; Business Administration; English; European Union Law; Finance; Management; Modern Languages)

Faculties

Social Sciences (Administration; Demography and Population; European Union Law; Government; Mass Communication; Media Studies; Protective Services; Social Policy; Social Sciences)

History: Founded 2004.

Fees: (New Złoty): Undergraduate programmes, 1,500 per semester; Graduate programmes, 2,000 per semester.

Main Language(s) of Instruction: Polish

International Co-operation: With universities in Ukraine, Lithuania and Belarus

Degrees and Diplomas: *Licencjat*; *Świadectwo ukończenia studiów podyplomowych*; *Magister*

Libraries: Yes

Last Updated: 24/10/11

HIGHER SCHOOL OF LABOUR PROTECTION MANAGEMENT, KATOWICE

Wyższa Szkoła Zarządzania Ochroną Pracy w Katowicach (WSZOP)

ul. Bankowa 8, 40-007 Katowice, śląskie
Tel: +48(32) 355-97-70
Fax: +48(32) 258-92-64
EMail: dziekanat@wszop.edu.pl
Website: http://www.wszop.edu.pl

Rektor: Marek Trombski EMail: mtrombski@wszop.edu.pl

Kanclerz: Małgorata Sikorska EMail: msikorska@wszop.edu.pl

International Relations: Anna Jakubowska, Vice-Rector
EMail: ajakubowska@wszop.edu.pl

Faculties

Cultural Studies (Advertising and Publicity; Cultural Studies; Journalism; Public Relations; Radio and Television Broadcasting); **English Philology** (Chinese; English; Philology; Spanish; Translation and Interpretation); **Internal safety** (Protective Services; Safety Engineering); **Management** (Health Administration; Human Resources; Industrial and Organizational Psychology; Management; Sales Techniques; Vocational Counselling); **Production Management and Engineering** (Environmental Engineering; Fire Science; Human Resources; Hygiene; Production Engineering; Safety Engineering; Transport Management; Waste Management)

History: Founded 2002.

Main Language(s) of Instruction: Polish

International Co-operation: With universities in Sweden, France, Germany and Ukraine. Participates in the Erasmus programme.

Accrediting Agencies: Ministry of Science and Higher Education; State Accreditation Committee

Degrees and Diplomas: *Inżynier*; *Licencjat*; *Świadectwo ukończenia studiów podyplomowych*; *Magister*

Special Facilities: Laboratories; Multimedia room.

Last Updated: 25/10/11

HIGHER SCHOOL OF LINGUISTICS

Lingwistyczna Szkoła Wyższa w Warszawie (WSJO "AVANS")

ul. Ogrodowa 46/48, 00-876 Warszawa, mazowieckie
Tel: +48(22) 886-50-12
Fax: +48(22) 886-50-14
EMail: avans@avans.com.pl
Website: http://www.lingwistyka.edu.pl

Rektor: Leszek Biedrzycki

Prorektor: Zofia Jancewicz

International Relations: Klinga Irzykowska

Faculties

Linguistics (English; Foreign Languages Education; German; Linguistics; Multimedia; Philology; Russian; Translation and Interpretation)

History: Founded 1999 as Wyższa Szkoła Języków Obcych 'Avans' w Warszawie. 2006 - Lingwistyczna Szkoła Wyższa w Warszawie.

Governing Bodies: Senate

Admission Requirements: Secondary school certificate (matura)

Main Language(s) of Instruction: Polish

Accrediting Agencies: Ministry of Science and Higher Education; State Accreditation Committee

Degrees and Diplomas: *Licencjat*; *Świadectwo ukończenia studiów podyplomowych*

Last Updated: 23/10/11

HIGHER SCHOOL OF MANAGEMENT - THE POLISH OPEN UNIVERSITY, WARSAW

Wyższa Szkoła Zarządzania w Warszawie - Polish Open University (WSZ/POU)

ul. Domaniewska 37a, 02-672 Warszawa, mazowieckie
Tel: +48(22) 853-38-46
Fax: +48(22) 847-22-82
EMail: rektorat@pou.pl
Website: http://www.pou.pl/

Rektor: Zuzanna Kalisiak (2009-)

Dean, Mazowiecki Region: Krzysztof Bartosik
Tel: +48(22) 843-76-92, Fax: +48(22) 853-38-45
EMail: krzysztof.bartosik@pou.pl

Departments

Development Theory of Economics (Economics) *Director*: Kazimierz Niemczycki; **Quantitative Methods in Finance** (Finance) *Director*: Leszek Zaremba

Institutes

Business English (English) *Director*: Kalińska Alicja; **Economics and Management** (Economics; Management) *Director*: Roman Skarżyński; **Finance and Accountancy** (Accountancy; Finance) *Director*: Kukurba Maria; **Human Resources Management** (Human Resources) *Director*: Marian Egeman; **Marketing and Advertising** (Advertising and Publicity; Marketing) *Director*: Białecki Klemens; **Operational Management and Information Systems** (Information Sciences; Operations Research) *Director*: Andrzej Chrzanowski

Programmes

Advertising and Marketing (Advertising and Publicity; Marketing); **Business Administration** (Business Administration); **Business Information Systems** (Business Computing); **Finance and Business Information Systems** (Business Computing; Finance); **Financial Management** (Finance; Management); **Personnel Management** (Human Resources)

History: Founded 1991, acquired present status 2000.

Governing Bodies: Ministry of Science and Higher Education

Academic Year: September to June

Admission Requirements: BA Matriculation good command of Polish. MBA - Bachelor degree, 3 yrs of business experience. English LCCI II. Admission test

Fees: (New Złoty): BA - registration 190, tuition fees for 3 years period: about 12,000; EMBA - registration 200, tuition fees 31,000 (installment plan possibility).

Main Language(s) of Instruction: Polish; English

International Co-operation: With universities in United Kingdom, Greece, France, Portugal, Germany, Turkey, Lithuania, Bulgaria. Also participates in the POLSYS, ALFIT,Tempus, UNDP programmes.

Accrediting Agencies: Ministry of Science and Higher Education; Oxford Brookes University; Association of MBA's (AMBA).

Degrees and Diplomas: *Licencjat*: Business Administration; Business Information Systems; Finance Management; Advertising; Management; Personnel Management; Enterpreneurship and Management; *Magister*: E-Business; Business Administration; Human Resources Management; Strategic Communication in Marketing; Finance Management. Also Executive MBA

Student Services: Academic counselling, Canteen, Cultural centre, Employment services, Foreign student adviser, Language programs, Social counselling

Special Facilities: Multimedia and computer/internet facilities; Wi-Fi.

Libraries: Libraries in two branches in Warsaw and Cracow. Electronic databases accessible via university web page

Publications: The art of management (www.pou.pl/magazyn), Information, analyses and dissemination of up to date trends in management *(monthly)*

Last Updated: 30/08/11

HIGHER SCHOOL OF MANAGEMENT AND COACHING IN WROCŁAW

Wyższa Szkoła Zarządzania i Coachingu we Wrocławiu (WSZIC)

ul. Paderewskiego 35 - Korona Stadionu Olimpijskiego, Wejście nr 7 (przy bramie nr 18), 51-612 Wrocław, dolnośląskie
Tel: +48(50) 405-15-97
EMail: rekrutacja@wszic.pl; biuro@wszic.pl
Website: http://www.wszic.pl/

Rektor: Edward Superlak

Kanclerz: Ewa Panfil

Faculties

Coaching (Cognitive Sciences; Ethics; Leadership; Psychology); **Sports** (Economics; Marketing; Sports; Sports Management)

History: Founded 2005.

Fees: (New Złoty): 3,750 per annum; Postgraduate programmes, 3,800-5,800 per annum.

Main Language(s) of Instruction: Polish

Degrees and Diplomas: *Licencjat*; *Świadectwo ukończenia studiów podyplomowych*

Last Updated: 26/10/11

HIGHER SCHOOL OF MANAGEMENT AND SOCIAL SCIENCES, TYCHY

Wyższa Szkoła Zarządzania i Nauk Społecznych im. ks. Emila Szramka w Tychach (WSZINS)

al. Niepodległości 32, 43-100 Tychy, śląskie
Tel: +48(32) 326-51-04
Fax: +48(32) 326-51-01-03
EMail: rektorat@wszins.tychy.pl; dziekanat@wszins.tychy.pl
Website: http://www.wszins.tychy.pl

Rektor: Stanisław Tomaszek
Tel: +48(32) 326-51-01 EMail: rektor.tomaszek@wszins.tychy.pl

Prorektor: Marek S. Szczepański
EMail: marek.szczepanski@wszins.tychy.pl

International Relations: Jacek Roguski, Rector's Proxy for International Cooperation
Tel: +48(32) 326-51-01 Ext. 200 EMail: j.roguski@wszins.tychy.pl

Centres

Foreign Languages (English; German; Modern Languages)

Departments

Postgraduate Studies (Accountancy; Government; Management; Pedagogy; Preschool Education; Primary Education; Real Estate; Rehabilitation and Therapy)

Faculties

Administration (Administration; Administrative Law; Banking; Commercial Law; Criminal Law; Finance; Fiscal Law; Government; Labour Law; Law; Management; Public Law; Real Estate; Taxation); **Economics and Management** (Accountancy; Banking; Business Computing; Economics; Finance; Leadership; Management; Mathematics; Safety Engineering); **Education** (Art Education; Development Studies; Education; Environmental Studies; Occupational Health; Safety Engineering); **Internal Security** (Human Rights; Protective Services; Public Administration; Social Sciences); **Sociology** (Administration; Clinical Psychology; Criminology; Ethics; Psychology; Social Psychology; Sociology)

History: Founded 1997.

Governing Bodies: Senate

Admission Requirements: Secondary school certificate (Matura)

Fees: (New Złoty): Registration, c. 350, tuition, c. 3,680 per annum; part-time students, c. 2,980 per annum

Main Language(s) of Instruction: Polish

International Co-operation: With universities in Slovakia, Ukraine, Germany, Czech Republic and Scotland. Participates in the Erasmus programme

Accrediting Agencies: Ministry of Science and Higher Education

Degrees and Diplomas: *Licencjat*; *Świadectwo ukończenia studiów podyplomowych*

Last Updated: 25/10/11

HIGHER SCHOOL OF MANAGEMENT, KONIN

Wyższa Szkoła Kadr Menedżerskich w Koninie (WSKM)

ul. Powstańców Wielkopolskich 16a, 62-510 Konin, wielkopolskie
Tel: +48(63) 249-15-15
EMail: dziekanat@wskmkonin.edu.pl
Website: http://wskmkonin.edu.pl

Rektor: Wojciech Chomicz
Tel: +48(63) 249-15-15 Ext. 33 EMail: rektorat@wskmkonin.edu.pl

Kanclerz: Blazej Balewski
Tel: +48(63) 249-15-15 Ext. 30 EMail: blazej@balewski.pl

Departments
Postgraduate Studies (Adult Education; Commercial Law; Economics; Health Education; Management; Occupational Health; Preschool Education; Safety Engineering; Vocational Education)

Faculties
Administration (Administration; Business Administration; Labour Law; Law; Public Administration); **Economics and Management** (Accountancy; Banking; Economics; Finance; Human Resources; Insurance; Management); **Energy** (Energy Engineering; Power Engineering); **Humanities** (Arts and Humanities; Child Care and Development; Education; Pedagogy)

History: Founded 2007.

Fees: (New Złoty): 3,300 per annum

Main Language(s) of Instruction: Polish

Degrees and Diplomas: *Licencjat*; *Świadectwo ukończenia studiów podyplomowych*
Last Updated: 17/10/11

HIGHER SCHOOL OF MANAGEMENT, LEGNICA

Wyższa Szkoła Menedżerska w Legnicy (WSM)
ul. Korfantego 4, 59-220 Legnica, dolnośląskie
Tel: +48(76) 855-16-66
Fax: +48(76) 855-16-24
EMail: sekretariat@wsm.edu.pl
Website: http://www.wsmlca.edu.pl

Rektor: Łukasz Czuma

Kanclerz: Teresa Demecka

Departments
Architecture and Urban Planning (Architecture and Planning; Building Technologies; Landscape Architecture; Town Planning); **Information Technology** (Computer Engineering; Computer Networks; Computer Science; Data Processing; Information Management; Information Technology; Software Engineering); **Law** (Administrative Law; Civil Law; Commercial Law; Constitutional Law; Criminal Law; Environmental Studies; European Union Law; History of Law; International Law; Labour Law; Law; Public Law); **Management and Marketing** (Economics; Management; Marketing; Pedagogy; Sociology); **National Security** (Government; Management; Protective Services; Public Administration; Transport Management); **Philology** (Cultural Studies; English; French; German; History; Italian; Literature; Modern Languages; Philology; Spanish); **Transport** (Transport and Communications; Transport Engineering; Transport Management)

History: Founded 1997.

Fees: (New Złoty): Undegraduate programmes, 1,595-3,055 per semester; Graduate programmes, 2,035-2,660 per semester.

International Co-operation: With universities in France; Italy and Ukraine

Accrediting Agencies: Ministry of Science and Higher Education

Degrees and Diplomas: *Inżynier*, *Licencjat*; *Magister*

Libraries: c. 19,800 vols; 107 periodical subscriptions

Last Updated: 07/10/11

HIGHER SCHOOL OF MANAGEMENT OF THE ENVIRONMENT, TUCHOLA

Wyższa Szkoła Zarządzania Środowiskiem w Tucholi (WSZS)
ul. Pocztowa 13, 89-500 Tuchola, kujawsko-pomorskie
Tel: +48(52) 559-19-87
Fax: +48(52) 559-19-87
EMail: wszs@tuchola.pl
Website: http://www.wszs.tuchola.pl

Rektor: Krzysztof Kannenberg
Tel: +48(52) 559-20-22 EMail: rektorat@tuchola.pl

Kanclerz: Hanna Bronk

Departments
Postgraduate Studies (Accountancy; Finance; Forestry; Landscape Architecture; Tourism)

Programmes
Environmental Engineering (Environmental Engineering); **Forestry** (Forestry); **Landscape Architecture** (Landscape Architecture)

Further Information: Also University of the Third Age and University of First Age.

History: Founded 2003.

Fees: (New Złoty): 1,600-2,400 per semester

Main Language(s) of Instruction: Polish

Degrees and Diplomas: *Inżynier*, *Świadectwo ukończenia studiów podyplomowych*
Last Updated: 25/10/11

HIGHER SCHOOL OF MANAGEMENT, WARSAW

Wyższa Szkoła Menedżerska w Warszawie (WSM)
ul. Kawęczyńska 36, 03-772 Warszawa, mazowieckie
Tel: +48(22) 590-07-00
Fax: +48(22) 818-00-52
EMail: rektorat@mac.edu.pl
Website: http://www.kaweczynska.pl/

Rektor: Brunon Hołyst

Kanclerz: Radosław Dawidziuk
Tel: +48(22) 619-07-58, Ext. 106 EMail: kanclerz@interia.pl

International Relations: Andrzej Dawidziuk
Tel: +48(22) 619-07-58, Ext. 123

Departments
Foreign Languages (English; German; Modern Languages)

Faculties
Applied Science and Technology Security (Computer Engineering; Computer Graphics; Computer Networks; Computer Science; Criminology; Information Management; Information Technology; Safety Engineering; Technology); **Executive** (Accountancy; Health Administration; Management; Marketing; Production Engineering; Real Estate; Safety Engineering); **Law and Administration** (Administration; Administrative Law; Civil Law; Criminal Law; Criminology; Health Sciences; History of Law; Information Management; International Law; Journalism; Law; Protective Services; Public Law; Safety Engineering); **Social Sciences** (Child Care and Development; Education; Educational Administration; Educational Technology; European Studies; International Relations; Journalism; Mass Communication; Pedagogy; Physical Education; Political Sciences; Psychology; Rehabilitation and Therapy; Social Sciences; Social Work; Sociology; Tourism; Vocational Counselling)

Further Information: Also campuses in Ursus, Ciechanów and Bełchatów.

History: Founded 1995, acquired present status 2000.

Governing Bodies: Senate

Admission Requirements: Secondary school certificate (matura)

Main Language(s) of Instruction: Polish

International Co-operation: With universities USA, Belgium, Ukraine, Belarus, Greece.

Accrediting Agencies: Ministry of Science and Higher Education

Degrees and Diplomas: *Inżynier*, *Licencjat*; *Świadectwo ukończenia studiów podyplomowych*; *Magister*
Last Updated: 07/10/11

HIGHER SCHOOL OF MATHEMATICS AND APPLIED INFORMATICS, BIALYSTOK

Wyższa Szkoła Matematyki i Informatyki Użytkowej w Białymstoku (WSMIIU)
ul. Kamienna 17, 15-021 Białystok, podlaskie
Tel: +48(85) 732-30-91 +48(85) 732-30-65
Fax: +48(85) 732-30-65
EMail: wsmiiu@wsmiiu.edu.pl
Website: http://www.wsmiiu.edu.pl

Rector: Zofia Leszczyńska (1995-)

Dean: Dorota Dworzańczyk

Departments
Postgraduate Studies (Computer Science; Information Technology; Mathematics)

Faculties
Informatics (Business Computing; Computer Engineering; Computer Science; Data Processing; Information Technology); **Logistics** (Transport Management); **Mathematics** (Banking; Business Computing; Educational Technology; Mathematics; Mathematics and Computer Science; Primary Education; Secondary Education)

History: Founded 1995, acquired present status and title 1996.

Governing Bodies: Senate

Admission Requirements: Secondary school certificate (matura) and entrance examinations

Fees: (New Złoty): Undergraduate programmes, 640; Postgraduate programmes, 900-1,000 per semester.

Main Language(s) of Instruction: Polish

Accrediting Agencies: Ministry of Science and Higher Education

Degrees and Diplomas: *Licencjat*; *Świadectwo ukończenia studiów podyplomowych*

Last Updated: 23/10/11

HIGHER SCHOOL OF PEDAGOGICS AND TECHNOLOGY, KONIN

Wyższa Szkoła Pedagogiczno Techniczna w Koninie (WSPT)

ul. Chopina 21H, 62-510 Konin, wielkopolskie
Tel: +48(63) 245-70-08
EMail: dziekanat@wspt.pl
Website: http://www.wspt.pl/

Rektor: Krzysztof Gandziarski

Kanclerz: Wanda Musial

Centres
Postgraduate Studies (Accountancy; Administration; Business Administration; Child Care and Development; Computer Graphics; Computer Science; Family Studies; Finance; Fiscal Law; Health Sciences; Information Technology; Mathematics; Multimedia; Pedagogy; Preschool Education; Public Law; Rehabilitation and Therapy; Safety Engineering; Speech Therapy and Audiology; Teacher Training; Vocational Education)

Faculties
Humanities (Arts and Humanities; Education); **Technical Education and Informatics** (Computer Science; Technology Education)

History: Founded 2007.

Degrees and Diplomas: *Licencjat*; *Świadectwo ukończenia studiów podyplomowych*

Last Updated: 18/10/11

HIGHER SCHOOL OF PEDAGOGY OF THE POLISH ASSOCIATION FOR ADULT EDUCATION, WARSAW

Wyższa Szkoła Pedagogiczna TWP w Warszawie (WSP TWP)

ul. Pandy 13, 02-202 Warszawa, mazowieckie
Tel: +48(22) 823-66-23
Fax: +48(22) 823-66-69
EMail: rektorat@wsptwp.eu
Website: http://www.wsptwp.eu/

Rektor: Julian Auleytner

Campuses
Człuchów (English; Information Technology; Modern Languages); **Lublin** (Child Care and Development; Education; English; Health Education; Parks and Recreation; Pedagogy; Preschool Education; Psychology; Rehabilitation and Therapy; Social Sciences; Sports); **Szczecin** (Pedagogy; Political Sciences)

Centres
Distance Learning (Child Care and Development; International Relations; Marketing; Pedagogy; Philology; Political Sciences; Rehabilitation and Therapy; Social Work; Sociology; Speech Therapy and Audiology)

Faculties
Humanities and Social Sciences *(Olsztyn)* (Arts and Humanities; Pedagogy; Social Sciences); **Social and Pedagogical Sciences** *(Katowice)* (English; German; Pedagogy; Russian; Social Sciences; Social Work; Spanish); **Social Sciences** (Education; English; English Studies; German; Italian; Pedagogy; Philology; Political Sciences; Russian; Social Sciences; Sociology; Spanish)

Further Information: Branch Institutes in Człuchów, Lublin, Katowice, Olsztyn, Szczecin, and Wałbrzych

History: Founded 1993 by the Polish Association for Adult Education.

Governing Bodies: Senate

Admission Requirements: Secondary school certificate (Matura)

Fees: (New Złoty): 3,240 -4,160 per annum.

Main Language(s) of Instruction: Polish

International Co-operation: With universities in Austria, Spain, Portugal, Britain, France, Greece, Belgium and Cyprus. Participates in the Socrates/Erasmus programme.

Accrediting Agencies: Ministry of Science and Higher Education; State Accreditation Commission

Degrees and Diplomas: *Licencjat*; *Świadectwo ukończenia studiów podyplomowych*; *Magister*

Libraries: Central Library

Publications: Res Humanae, Scientific magazine *(biannually)*

Last Updated: 07/10/11

HIGHER SCHOOL OF PHYSICAL EDUCATION AND TOURISM, SUPRAŚL

Wyższa Szkoła Wychowania Fizycznego i Turystyki w Supraślu (WSWFIT)

ul. Mickiewicza 49, 15-213 Białystok, podlaskie
Tel: +48(85) 713-15-91
Fax: +48(85) 713-15-92
EMail: wswfit@wswfit.com.pl
Website: http://www.wswfit.com.pl

Rektor: Krzysztof L. Sobolewski (2009-2013)

Programmes
Physical Education (Physical Education); **Sports** (Sports); **Tourism and Recreation** (Parks and Recreation; Tourism)

History: Founded 2001 in Supra. Moved to Białystok 2008.

Fees: (New Złoty): 1,500-1,900 per semester.

Accrediting Agencies: Minister of Education

Degrees and Diplomas: *Magister (mgr)*

Libraries: c. 9,800 vols and 300 periodical subscriptions.

Last Updated: 30/08/11

HIGHER SCHOOL OF PODKARPACIE, JASLO

Podkarpacka Szkoła Wyższa im. bł. ks. Władysława Findysza w Jaśle (PSW W JAŚLE)

ul. Na Kotlinę 8, 38-200 Jasło, podkarpackie
Tel: +48(13) 445-95-13
Fax: +48(13) 445-95-37
EMail: psw@psw.jaslo.pl; dziekanat@psw.jaslo.pl
Website: http://www.psw.jaslo.pl/

Rektor: Stanisław Polański

Kanclerz: Marek Polanski

Departments
Postgraduate Studies (Finance; Management; Marketing; Small Business)

Faculties
Economics (Accountancy; Business Administration; Economics; Hotel and Restaurant; Service Trades; Tourism); **Spatial Economy** (Development Studies; Landscape Architecture; Regional Planning); **Transportation** (Maintenance Technology; Marine Transport; Road Engineering; Transport and Communications; Transport Management)

History: Founded 2001 as Wyższa Szkoła Hotelarstwa i Turystyki w Jaśle (Higher School of Tourism and Hotel Industry, Jasło).

Degrees and Diplomas: *Inżynier*; *Licencjat*; *Świadectwo ukończenia studiów podyplomowych*
Last Updated: 21/10/11

HIGHER SCHOOL OF PUBLIC ADMINISTRATION

Wyższa Szkoła Administracji Publicznej w Szczecinie (WSAP)

ul. Marii Skłodowskiej-Curie 4, 71-332 Szczecin, zachodniopomorskie
Tel: +48(91) 486-15-42 +48(91) 486-15-45
Fax: +48(91) 486-15-44
EMail: biuro@wsap.szczecin.pl
Website: http://www.wsap.szczecin.pl

Rektor: Włodzimierz Puzyna (1995-)
EMail: wpuzyna@wsap.szczecin.pl

Kanclerz: Eugenia Dziedzic
Tel: +48(91) 486-15-48 EMail: rstrzel@wsap.szczecin.pl

International Relations: Thomas Chubar, International Relations Officer Tel: +48(91) 486-15-43 EMail: tomcz@wsap.szczecin.pl

Departments
Postgraduate Studies (Accountancy; Administration; Administrative Law; Finance; Fiscal Law; Government; Justice Administration; Labour Law; Law; Social Work; Taxation)

Programmes
Accounting and Taxation (Accountancy; Taxation); **Euroregional Administration** (Administration; European Union Law); **Justice Administration** (Justice Administration); **Public Administration** (Public Administration); **Taxation** (Taxation)

History: Founded 1995.

Governing Bodies: Senate

Academic Year: October to September

Admission Requirements: Secondary school certificate (Świadectwo dojrzałości)

Fees: (New Złoty): c. 3,420 per annum

Main Language(s) of Instruction: Polish

International Co-operation: With Germany and Ukraine. Paricipates in the Erasmus programme.

Accrediting Agencies: Ministry of Science and Higher Education; National Accreditation Commission

Degrees and Diplomas: *Licencjat*; *Świadectwo ukończenia studiów podyplomowych*

Student Services: Academic counselling, Canteen, Health services, Language programs, Social counselling

Libraries: Central Library
Last Updated: 19/10/11

HIGHER SCHOOL OF PUBLIC ADMINISTRATION, KIELCE

Wyższa Szkoła Administracji Publicznej w Kielcach (WSAP)

ul. Staffa 7, 25-410 Kielce, świętokrzyskie
Tel: +38(41) 330-37-88 +38(41) 368-60-77
Fax: +38(41) 368-66-61 Ext.106
EMail: sekretariat@wsap-kielce.edu.pl
Website: http://www.wsap-kielce.edu.pl

Rektor: Andrzej Bednarz (1999-) EMail: rektor@wsap-kielce.edu.pl

International Relations: Wojciech Kaczmarczyk, Vice-Rector
EMail: prorektor@wsap-kielce.edu.pl

Departments
Postgraduate Studies (Accountancy; Administration; Environmental Management; Finance; Government; Health Sciences; Labour Law; Management; Protective Services; Public Administration; Public Law; Safety Engineering; Welfare and Protective Services)

Faculties
Administration (Administration; European Union Law; Government); **Administration in the Process of European Integration** (Administration; European Union Law; Management)

Programmes
Public Administration (Finance; Information Technology; Law; Psychology; Public Administration; Social Sciences; Sociology)

History: Founded 1999.

Governing Bodies: Senate

Admission Requirements: Secondary school certificate (matura)

Main Language(s) of Instruction: Polish

Accrediting Agencies: Ministry of Science and Higher Education

Degrees and Diplomas: *Licencjat*; *Świadectwo ukończenia studiów podyplomowych*; *Magister*
Last Updated: 19/10/11

HIGHER SCHOOL OF REAL ESTATE, WARSAW

Wyższa Szkoła Gospodarowania Nieruchomościami w Warszawie (WSGN)

ul. Karowa 31, 00-324 Warszawa, mazowieckie
Tel: +48(22) 828-97-34
Fax: +48(22) 828-97-36
EMail: wsgnwar@wsgn.pl
Website: http://www.wsgn.pl

Rektor: Andrzej Bałandynowicz (1997-) Tel: +48(22) 828-97-38

Kanclerz: Karol Bulenda EMail: kbulenda@polan.com.pl

Campuses
Bialystok (Economics; Management; Real Estate)

Centres
Postgraduate studies (Human Resources; Management; Public Relations; Real Estate)

Faculties
Administration (Administration; Protective Services; Public Administration; Safety Engineering); **Economics** (Economics; Management; Real Estate)

Further Information: Branches in Białystok and Gdańsk
History: Founded 1997.
Governing Bodies: Senate

Admission Requirements: Secondary school certificate (matura)

Main Language(s) of Instruction: Polish

Accrediting Agencies: Ministry of Science and Higher Education

Degrees and Diplomas: *Licencjat*; *Świadectwo ukończenia studiów podyplomowych*; *Magister*
Last Updated: 06/10/11

HIGHER SCHOOL OF SAFETY AND SECURITY SERVICES, WARSAW

Wyższa Szkoła Bezpieczeństwa i Ochrony im. Marszałka Józefa Piłsudskiego (WSBIO)

ul. gen. J. Zajączka 7, 01-518 Warszawa, mazowieckie
Tel: +48(22) 856-52-06 Ext.20
EMail: rektorat@wsbio.waw.pl
Website: http://www.wsbio.waw.pl/

Kanclerz: Jacek Pomiankiewicz EMail: rektor@wsbio.waw.pl

Kanclerz: Bogusław Purski

Faculties
Administration (Administration; Civil Security; Criminal Law; Criminology; E-Business/Commerce; Information Management; Protective Services); **Internal Security** (Civil Security; Criminal Law; Fire Science; Law; Protective Services; Transport Management); **National Security** (Economics; Fire Science; Health Sciences; Information Management; Information Sciences; International Law; Medicine; Political Sciences; Protective Services; Public Administration; Public Law; Transport Management)

Further Information: Also Nisku campus.
History: Founded 2005.
Governing Bodies: Senate

Main Language(s) of Instruction: Polish

Accrediting Agencies: Minister of Science and Higher Education; National Accreditation Commission
Degrees and Diplomas: *Licencjat*; *Magister*
Last Updated: 26/10/11

HIGHER SCHOOL OF SAFETY ENGINEERING AND ECOLOGY, SOSNOWIEC

Wyższa Szkoła Inżynierii Bezpieczeństwa i Ekologii (WSE)
ul. Wojska Polskiego 6, 41-200 Sosnowiec, śląskie
Tel: +48(32) 266-20-51
Fax: +48(32) 266-20-53
EMail: dziekanat@wsibie.edu.pl
Website: http://www.wse.sosnowiec.pl

Rektor: Janusz Juras
Kanclerz: Paulina Buczek

Departments
Postgraduate Studies (Environmental Studies; Occupational Health; Safety Engineering)

Faculties
Environmental Protection (Environmental Engineering; Environmental Studies); **Safety Engineering** (Environmental Studies; Occupational Health; Safety Engineering)
History: Founded 2004.
Main Language(s) of Instruction: Polish
Accrediting Agencies: State Accreditation Commission
Degrees and Diplomas: *Inżynier*; *Świadectwo ukończenia studiów podyplomowych*
Last Updated: 23/10/11

HIGHER SCHOOL OF SAFETY, POZNAN

Wyższa Szkoła Bezpieczeństwa z siedzibą w Poznaniu (WSB)
ul. Wyspianskiego 16/4, 60-750 Poznań, wielkopolskie
Tel: +48(61) 670-33-11
EMail: rekrutacja@wsb.net.pl
Website: http://www.wsb.net.pl/

Rektor: Andrzej Zduniak
Tel: +48(61) 851-05-18 Ext. 121 EMail: rektor@wsb.net.pl
Kanclerz: Michal Kwiatkowski
Tel: +48(61) 851-05-18 Ext. 121 EMail: kanclerz@wsb.net.pl

Campuses
Gdansk (Arts and Humanities; Child Care and Development; Education; Food Technology; Higher Education; Journalism; Occupational Health; Pedagogy; Protective Services; Real Estate; Safety Engineering; Social Sciences); **Gliwice** (Arts and Humanities; Child Care and Development; Educational Administration; Information Management; Journalism; Management; Occupational Health; Protective Services; Rehabilitation and Therapy; Safety Engineering; Social Sciences; Social Work)

Faculties
Social Security (Social Welfare; Welfare and Protective Services); **Socio-Economic Sciences** (Arts and Humanities; Child Care and Development; Economics; Education; Educational Administration; Health Administration; Higher Education; Information Management; Journalism; Leadership; Management; Pedagogy; Rehabilitation and Therapy; Safety Engineering; Social Sciences; Social Welfare; Social Work)
History: Founded 2004.
Governing Bodies: Senate
Fees: (New Złoty): 1,950-4,080 per annum
Main Language(s) of Instruction: Polish
Degrees and Diplomas: *Licencjat*; *Świadectwo ukończenia studiów podyplomowych*; *Magister*
Last Updated: 20/10/11

HIGHER SCHOOL OF SOCIAL ADMINISTRATION, WARSAW

Wyższa Szkoła Administracyjno-Społeczna w Warszawie (WSAS)
ul. Grochowska 346/348, 03-838 Warszawa, mazowieckie
Tel: +48(22) 619-14-80
Fax: +48(22) 619-14-80
EMail: biuro@wsas.edu.pl
Website: http://www.wsas.edu.pl

Rektor: Eugeniusz Zieliński
Kanclerz: Tadeusz Okrasa

Departments
Foreign Languages (English; Polish); **Postgraduate Studies** (Administration; Educational Administration; Information Management)

Faculties
Administration (Administration; Business Administration; European Union Law; Government; Protective Services; Public Administration; Welfare and Protective Services); **European Studies** (Administration; Cultural Studies; European Studies); **Internal Security** (Protective Services)
History: Founded 2003.
Fees: (New Złoty): 1,390-1,990 per semester
Main Language(s) of Instruction: Polish
International Co-operation: Participates in the Erasmus programme.
Degrees and Diplomas: *Licencjat*; *Świadectwo ukończenia studiów podyplomowych*; *Magister*
Last Updated: 19/10/11

HIGHER SCHOOL OF SOCIAL AND TECHNICAL SCIENCES, RADOM

Wyższa Szkoła Nauk Społecznych i Technicznych w Radomiu (WSNSIT)
ul. Wodna 13/21, 26-600 Radom, mazowieckie
Tel: +48(48) 344-00-55 +48(48) 363-86-80
Fax: +48(48) 363-86-80
EMail: dziekanat@wsnsit.pl
Website: http://www.wsnsit.pl/

Rektor: Maria Pierzchalska
Tel: +48(48) 360-13-22, Fax: +48(48) 360-13-22
EMail: biurorektora@wsnsit.pl
Kanclerz: Beata Dziadczyk
Tel: +48(48) 344-00-55 Ext.37 EMail: dziadczykb@wsnsit.pl
International Relations: Edgar M. Klus, Development Manager
Tel: +48(48) 344-00-55 Ext.43
EMail: eklusa@wsnsit.pl; internationaloffice@wsnsit.pl

Departments
Foreign Languages (English; Modern Languages); **Postgraduate Studies** (Accountancy; Civil Engineering; Construction Engineering; Cosmetology; Education; Educational Administration; Ethics; Family Studies; Finance; Health Administration; Human Resources; Information Technology; Insurance; Labour Law; Library Science; Management; Mass Communication; Media Studies; Pedagogy; Philosophy; Physical Therapy; Preschool Education; Public Administration; Real Estate; Rehabilitation and Therapy; Safety Engineering; Social Welfare; Social Work; Speech Therapy and Audiology; Sports; Sports Management; Taxation; Transport and Communications)

Faculties
Administration (Administration; Finance; Government; Protective Services; Public Administration; Taxation); **Construction** (Architecture; Construction Engineering; Road Engineering); **Cosmetology** (Alternative Medicine; Cosmetology); **Education** (Education; Educational and Student Counselling; Pedagogy; Preschool Education; Speech Therapy and Audiology; Teacher Training); **Philology** (English; English Studies; French; German; Philology; Russian); **Public Health** (Alternative Medicine; Cooking and Catering; Dental Hygiene; Dietetics; Health Administration; Health Sciences; Nutrition; Public Health)

History: Founded 2007.

Main Language(s) of Instruction: Polish

International Co-operation: Participates in the Erasmus programme.

Degrees and Diplomas: *Inżynier*; *Licencjat*; *Świadectwo ukończenia studiów podyplomowych*; *Magister*

Last Updated: 20/10/11

HIGHER SCHOOL OF SOCIAL SCIENCES, LUBLIN

Wyższa Szkoła Nauk Społecznych z siedzibą w Lublinie (WSNS)

ul. Olchowa 8, 20-355 Lublin, lubelskie
Tel: +48(81) 744-21-13
Fax: +48(81) 463-17-30
EMail: info@wsns.lublin.pl
Website: http://www.wsns.pl

Rektor: Emilia Żerel (2001-) EMail: ezerel@wsns.pl

Kanclerz: Adam Żerel EMail: azerel@wsns.pl

Departments

Postgraduate Studies (Advertising and Publicity; Child Care and Development; Cosmetology; Economics; Marketing; Medicine; Nutrition; Public Relations; Rehabilitation and Therapy; Sociology; Vocational Counselling)

Faculties

Cosmetology in Medicine (Cosmetology); **Dance** (Dance); **Dental Technology** (Dental Technology; Orthodontics); **Dietetics** (Cooking and Catering; Dietetics; Nutrition); **Medical Emergency** (Medicine); **Sociology** (Engineering; Marketing; Political Sciences; Sociology; Vocational Counselling)

History: Founded 2001.

Main Language(s) of Instruction: Polish

Degrees and Diplomas: *Licencjat*; *Świadectwo ukończenia studiów podyplomowych*

Last Updated: 23/10/11

HIGHER SCHOOL OF SOCIAL SCIENCES, MINSK MAZOWIECKI

Wyższa Szkoła Nauk Społecznych im. Ks. Józefa Majki w Mińsku Mazowieckim (WSNS)

ul. Konstytucji 3 Maja 1a ul. Gen. K. Sosnkowskiego 43, 05-300 Mińsk Mazowiecki, mazowieckie
Tel: +48(25) 758-86-45
Fax: +48(22) 670-26-65
EMail: sekretariat@majka.edu.pl
Website: http://www.majka.edu.pl

Rektor: Witold Zdaniewicz
Tel: +48(22) 818-88-50 EMail: rektorat@majka.edu.pl

Kanclerz: Sylwia Cmiel EMail: kanclerz@majka.edu.pl

Departments

Postgraduate Studies (Communication Studies; Education; Educational Administration; Human Resources; Pedagogy; Preschool Education; Psychology; Rehabilitation and Therapy; Safety Engineering; Vocational Education)

Faculties

Pedagogy (Child Care and Development; Leisure Studies; Pedagogy; Preschool Education; Protective Services; Rehabilitation and Therapy; Tourism); **Sociology** (Administration; Mass Communication; Media Studies; Political Sciences; Sociology)

History: Founded 2002.

Governing Bodies: Senate

Main Language(s) of Instruction: Polish

International Co-operation: With universiiteis in Lithuania, Spain, Italy, Hungary , Slovakia. Participates in the Erasmus programme.

Degrees and Diplomas: *Licencjat*; *Świadectwo ukończenia studiów podyplomowych*

Libraries: Yes

Last Updated: 23/10/11

HIGHER SCHOOL OF SPORT COACHES, WARSAW

Wyższa Szkoła Trenerów Sportu (WSTS)

ul. Stokłosy 3 pok. 311A (3 piętro), 02-787 Warszawa, mazowieckie
Tel: +48(22) 490-40-97 +48(22) 490-44-47
EMail: studia@wststorwar.pl
Website: http://wststorwar.pl/

Rektor: Edward Samoraj

Kanclerz: Ryszard Fijalkowski

Programmes

Sports Coaches Training (Dance; Sports; Sports Management)

History: Founded 2009.

Fees: (New Złoty): 3,000 per semester

Main Language(s) of Instruction: Polish

Accrediting Agencies: Minister of Science and Higher Education

Degrees and Diplomas: *Licencjat*; *Świadectwo ukończenia studiów podyplomowych*

Last Updated: 26/10/11

HIGHER SCHOOL OF SPORTS NAMED AFTER KAZIMIERZ GÓRSKI, LODZ

Wyższa Szkoła Sportowa im.Kazimierza Górskiego w Łodzi (WSS)

ul. Milionowa 12, 93-193 Łódź, łódzkie
Tel: +48(42) 254-05-91
EMail: dziekanat@wss.lodz.pl
Website: http://www.wss.lodz.pl/

Kanclerz: Roman Stepien

Kanclerz: Malgorzata Jalkiewicz-Hoffmann

Programmes

Physical Education and Sports (Physical Education; Sports)

History: Founded 2008.

Main Language(s) of Instruction: Polish

Degrees and Diplomas: *Licencjat*; *Świadectwo ukończenia studiów podyplomowych*

Student Services: Canteen, Sports facilities

Last Updated: 19/10/11

HIGHER SCHOOL OF STRATEGIC PLANNING, DĄBROWA GÓRNICZA

Wyższa Szkoła Planowania Strategicznego w Dąbrowie Górniczej (WSPS)

ul Kościelna 6, 41-303 Dąbrowa Górnicza, śląskie
Tel: +48(32) 264-74-75 Ext.25
Fax: +48(32) 264-74-75
EMail: kancelaria@wsps.pl
Website: http://www.wsps.pl

Rektor: Jolanta Dobosz

Kanclerz: Danuta Szopa

Departments

Postgraduate Studies (Environmental Management; Environmental Studies; Epidemiology; Gerontology; Health Administration; Health Sciences; Human Resources; Medicine; Neurological Therapy; Occupational Health; Public Health; Rehabilitation and Therapy; Safety Engineering; Transport Management)

Faculties

Socio-Medical Studies (Cosmetology; Gynaecology and Obstetrics; Medicine; Midwifery; Nursing; Physical Therapy; Public Health; Transport Management)

History: Founded 2004.

Fees: (New Złoty): 1,750-2,300 per semester

Main Language(s) of Instruction: Polish

International Co-operation: With universities in Lithuania, Russia, Ukraine.

Accrediting Agencies: Ministry of Science and Higher Education; National Accreditation Commission

Degrees and Diplomas: *Inżynier*; *Licencjat*; *Świadectwo ukończenia studiów podyplomowych*
Last Updated: 24/10/11

HIGHER SCHOOL OF TEACHER EDUCATION OF THE POLISH TEACHERS TRADE UNION, WARSAW

Wyższa Szkoła Pedagogiczna Związku Nauczycielstwa Polskiego w Warszawie (WSP TWP)
ul. Smulikowskiego 6/8, 00-389 Warszawa, mazowieckie
Tel: +48(22) 330-57-35
Fax: +48(22) 330-57-40
EMail: wsp@wsp.edu.pl
Website: http://www.wsp.edu.pl

Rektor: Stefan Mieszalski
Tel: +48(22) 330-57-35 EMail: rektor@wsp.edu.pl
International Relations: Tadeusz Lewowicki, Pro-Rector
Tel: +48(22) 828-13-57

Chairs

Early Pedagogy (Child Care and Development; English; Pedagogy; Preschool Education); **General Pedagogy and Pedagogy Culture** (Art Management; Cultural Studies; Health Education; Management; Pedagogy; Teacher Training); **Pedagogical Methodology** (Educational Administration; Marketing; Pedagogy); **Pedagogical Work and Social Pedagogy** (Family Studies; Pedagogy; Social Work); **Pedagogy and Psychology** (Pedagogy; Psychology; Rehabilitation and Therapy)

Laboratories

Pedagogical and Psychological Evaluation (Pedagogy; Psychology)

History: Founded 1995 by the Polish Teacher's Association.

Governing Bodies: Senate

Admission Requirements: Secondary school certificate (matura)

Fees: (New Złoty): 1,250-1,750 per semester

Main Language(s) of Instruction: Polish

Accrediting Agencies: Ministry of Science and Higher Education

Degrees and Diplomas: *Licencjat*; *Świadectwo ukończenia studiów podyplomowych*; *Magister*

Special Facilities: Computer lab
Last Updated: 08/10/11

HIGHER SCHOOL OF TELECOMMUNICATION AND COMPUTER SCIENCES, ŚWIDNICA

Wyższa Szkoła Technologii Teleinformatycznych w Świdnicy (WSTT W ŚWIDNICY)
ul. Kliczkowska 34, 58-100 Świdnica, dolnośląskie
Tel: +48(74) 640-03-40 +48(74) 640-03-42
Fax: +48(74) 640-03-41
EMail: dziekanat@wstt.edu.pl
Website: http://www.wstt.edu.pl

Rektor: Tadeusz Jeleniewski

Prorektor: Adam Janiak

Departments

Postgraduate Studies (Administrative Law; Civil Law; Economics; European Union Law; Finance; Government; Law; Management; Social Policy)

Faculties

Computer Sciences (Computer Engineering; Computer Graphics; Computer Networks; Computer Science; Electronic Engineering; Information Technology; Mechanical Engineering); **Economics** (Agricultural Business; Business Administration; Economics; Environmental Management; Management; Social Welfare; Tourism; Transport Management)

History: Founded 2001.

Fees: (New Złoty): 1,770-2,340 per semester

Main Language(s) of Instruction: Polish

Degrees and Diplomas: *Inżynier*; *Licencjat*; *Świadectwo ukończenia studiów podyplomowych*
Last Updated: 24/10/11

HIGHER SCHOOL OF THE NATIONAL ECONOMY, KUTNO

Wyższa Szkoła Gospodarki Krajowej w Kutnie (WSGK)
ul. Lelewela 7, 99-300 Kutno, łódzkie
Tel: +48(24) 355-83-40
Fax: +48(24) 355-83-40
EMail: wsgk@wsgk.com.pl
Website: http://www.wsgk.com.pl

Rektor: Sławomira Białobłocka

Kanclerz: Elżbieta Borowiecka EMail: kanclerz@wsgk.com.pl

Faculties

Administration and Social Sciences (Administration; Administrative Law; Archiving; E-Business/Commerce; Human Resources; Public Administration; Social Sciences; Welfare and Protective Services); **European Studies** (European Studies; International Business; International Relations; Management; Marine Transport; Protective Services; Public Administration; Public Law; Transport and Communications; Transport Management); **Health Sciences** (Health Sciences; Nursing); **Horticulture** (Agricultural Equipment; Agricultural Management; Botany; Farm Management; Fruit Production; Horticulture; Landscape Architecture; Vegetable Production); **Management** (Business Administration; Management; Transport Management); **Rehabilitation and Educational Studies** (Child Care and Development; Educational and Student Counselling; Educational Sciences; Pedagogy; Rehabilitation and Therapy; Special Education; Teacher Training); **Technical Sciences** (Agriculture; Building Technologies; Computer Networks; Computer Science; Engineering; Environmental Engineering; Forestry; Geological Engineering; Information Management; Information Technology; Real Estate; Surveying and Mapping)

History: Founded 1998.

Governing Bodies: Senate

Admission Requirements: Secondary school certificate (matura)

Fees: (New Złoty): 350-420

Main Language(s) of Instruction: Polish

Accrediting Agencies: Ministry of Science and Higher Education; State Accreditation Commission

Degrees and Diplomas: *Inżynier*; *Licencjat*; *Świadectwo ukończenia studiów podyplomowych*; *Magister*
Last Updated: 06/10/11

HIGHER SCHOOL OF TOURISM AND FOREIGN LANGUAGES, WARSAW

Wyższa Szkoła Turystyki i Języków Obcych w Warszawie (WSTIJO)
Al. Prymasa Tysiąclecia 38, 01-242 Warszawa, mazowieckie
Tel: +48(22) 855-47-58
Fax: +48(22) 855-47-58
EMail: dziekanat@wstijo.edu.pl; rekrutacja@wstijo.edu.pl
Website: http://www.wstijo.edu.pl

Rektor: Krystyna Żelazna

Kanclerz: Jadwiga Barbara Moroz

Faculties

Computer Science and Econometrics (Computer Engineering; Computer Networks; Computer Science; Data Processing; Econometrics; Information Sciences; Mathematics; Mathematics and Computer Science; Statistics); **Philology** (English; Philology; Translation and Interpretation); **Sociology and Fashion Management** (Art Management; Fashion Design; French; German; Italian; Sociology; Spanish); **Tourism and Leisure** *(in English)* (Hotel and Restaurant; International Business; Leisure Studies; Management; Mass Communication; Tourism); **Tourism and Leisure** (Farm Management; Hotel and Restaurant; International Business; Leisure Studies; Management; Mass Communication; Tourism)

History: Founded 2003.

Fees: (New Złoty): 3,400-3,800 per annum

Main Language(s) of Instruction: Polish; English

International Co-operation: With universities in Scotland and Turkey. Participates in the Erasmus and Leonardo programmes.

Degrees and Diplomas: *Licencjat*; *Świadectwo ukończenia studiów podyplomowych*; *Magister*
Last Updated: 24/10/11

HIGHER SCHOOL OF TOURISM AND HOTEL INDUSTRY, GDANSK

Wyższa Szkoła Turystyki i Hotelarstwa w Gdańsku (WSTIH)

ul. L. Miszewskiego 12/13, 80-239 Gdańsk, pomorskie
Tel: +48(58) 520-26-14
Fax: +48(58) 348-82-20
EMail: wstih@wstih.edu.pl
Website: http://www.wstih.edu.pl

Rector: Władysław Włodzimierz Gaworecki
Tel: +48(58) 348-82-20

Chancellor - Vice-Rector: Halina Jendrasik

International Relations: Manfred Białk, Rector's Plenipotentiary for International Cooperation and school Publications
Tel: +48(58) 520-26-14 EMail: bialkm@wstih.pl

Departments

Tourism, Recreation and Health (Computer Science; Cosmetology; Dietetics; Economics; Environmental Management; Geography; Health Sciences; Hotel and Restaurant; Human Resources; International Business; Law; Management; Parks and Recreation; Small Business; Tourism)

Further Information: Also University of the Third Age.

History: Founded 1996.

Governing Bodies: Senate

Admission Requirements: Secondary school certificate (Matura)

Main Language(s) of Instruction: Polish

International Co-operation: With universities in Germany, Ukraine, Belarus, Russia. Participates in the Erasmus programme.

Accrediting Agencies: Ministry of Science and Higher Education; State Accreditation Committee

Degrees and Diplomas: *Licencjat*; *Świadectwo ukończenia studiów podyplomowych*; *Magister*

Last Updated: 08/10/11

HIGHER SCHOOL OF TOURISM AND HOTEL MANAGEMENT, ŁÓDŹ

Wyższa Szkoła Turystyki i Hotelarstwa w Łodzi (WSTIH)

Dziekanat:, ul. Słowiańska 1/9, p. 305, 93-101 Łódź, łódzkie
Tel: +48(42) 674-52-74
Fax: +48(42) 632-42-23
EMail: katarzyna.szymanska@wsth.edu.pl; aleksandra.boguszewska@wsth.edu.pl; agnieszka.klepacz@wsth.edu.pl
Website: http://www.wsth.edu.pl

Rektor: Andrzej Stasiak

Campuses

Gostynin (Hotel Management; Tourism)

Departments

Postgraduate Studies (Cooking and Catering; Hotel and Restaurant; Tourism)

Faculties

Tourism and Recreation (Cooking and Catering; English; French; German; Hotel and Restaurant; Italian; Leisure Studies; Modern Languages; Parks and Recreation; Russian; Tourism)

Further Information: Also University of the Third Age.

History: Founded 2000.

Fees: (New Złoty): 350-430 per month

Main Language(s) of Instruction: Polish

International Co-operation: With universities in Russia, Ukraine, Lithuania, Slovakia and Switzerland.

Accrediting Agencies: State Accreditation Commission

Degrees and Diplomas: *Licencjat*; *Świadectwo ukończenia studiów podyplomowych*

Academic Staff *2010-2011*: Total: c. 70

Last Updated: 24/10/11

HIGHER SCHOOL 'TWP' 'WSZECHNICA POLSKA', WARSAW

Wszechnica Polska - Szkoła Wyższa TWP w Warszawie (WP-TWP)

Pałac Kultury i Nauki, X piętro, pok. 1044A, 00-901 Warszawa, mazowieckie
Tel: +48(22) 656-61-92 +48(22) 624-88-35
Fax: +48(22) 624-88-35
EMail: wszechnica@wszechnicapolska.edu.pl; rekrutacja@wszechnicapolska.edu.pl
Website: http://www.wszechnicapolska.ids.pl

Rector: Zdzisław Gajewski (2008-)

Kanclerz: Mirosław Żukowski
Tel: +48(22) 656-61-77, Fax: +48(22) 656-61-77
EMail: mzukowski@wszechnicapolska.edu.pl

Departments

Postgraduate Studies (Accountancy; Banking; Child Care and Development; Computer Science; Education; Finance; Pedagogy; Preschool Education; Safety Engineering; Social and Preventive Medicine; Teacher Training; Technology)

Faculties

Administration (Administration; Mass Communication; Public Relations; Tourism); **Computer Science** (Computer Science); **Education** (Child Care and Development; Education; Pedagogy; Preschool Education; Rehabilitation and Therapy; Social and Preventive Medicine); **Finance and Accounting** (Accountancy; Economic and Finance Policy; Finance; Management; Marketing; Taxation); **Internal security** (Criminal Law; Protective Services); **National Security** (International Relations; Military Science; Protective Services; Transport Management); **Philology** (English; German; Philology; Russian; Spanish); **Public Health** (Cosmetology; Dietetics; Economics; Health Administration; Nutrition; Physical Therapy; Public Health)

History: Founded 2001 by the Polish Association of Adult Education.

Governing Bodies: Senate

Admission Requirements: Secondary school certificate (matura)

Fees: (New Złoty): 3,800-4,800 per annum

Main Language(s) of Instruction: Polish

Accrediting Agencies: Ministry of Science and Higher Education

Degrees and Diplomas: *Inżynier*, *Licencjat*; *Świadectwo ukończenia studiów podyplomowych*; *Magister*

Last Updated: 19/10/11

HIGHER VOCATIONAL SCHOOL , PIŃCZÓW

Wyższa Szkoła Umiejętności Zawodowych w Pińczowie (WSUZ)

ul. 3 maja 17, 28-400 Pińczów, świętokrzyskie
Tel: +48(41) 357-67-50
Fax: +48(41) 357-77-40
EMail: administracja@wsuz.pl
Website: http://www.wsuz.pl

Rektor: Seweryn Kukula EMail: s.kukula@wsuz.pl

Head, Administration: Monika Chmielarska

Faculties

Dietetics (Dietetics); **Environmental Protection** (Ecology; Energy Engineering; Environmental Engineering; Environmental Studies; Tourism; Waste Management); **Nursing** (Health Sciences; Nursing)

History: Founded 2004.

Fees: (New Złoty): 500-1,800 per semester

Main Language(s) of Instruction: Polish

Accrediting Agencies: Minister of Science and Higher Education; National Council for Accreditation of Medical Education

Degrees and Diplomas: *Inżynier*, *Licencjat*; *Świadectwo ukończenia studiów podyplomowych*

Libraries: Over 400 vols

Last Updated: 24/10/11

HIGHER VOCATIONAL SCHOOL OF HEALTH AND BEAUTY TREATMENT, POZNAŃ

Wyższa Szkoła Zdrowia, Urody i Edukacji w Poznaniu (WSZPZIU)

ul. Brzeźnicka 3, 60-133 Poznań, wielkopolskie
Tel: +48(61) 655-85-85
Fax: +48(61) 655-85-70
EMail: dziekanat@wszuie.pl
Website: http://www.uczelniakosmetyczna.pl

Rector: Barbara Raszeja-Kotelba (2008-)

Kanclerz: Aniela Goc

Faculties

Gdyni (Cosmetology; Dietetics; Marketing; Podiatry; Technology); **Poznan** (Cosmetology; Dietetics; English; Marketing; Physical Therapy; Podiatry; Protective Services; Technology); **Szczecinie** (Cosmetology; Dietetics; Marketing; Podiatry; Technology)

History: Founded 2000.

Fees: (New Złoty): 360-550 per month. Postgraduate studies, 1,800-2,800 per semester.

Main Language(s) of Instruction: Polish

Degrees and Diplomas: *Licencjat*; *Świadectwo ukończenia studiów podyplomowych*; *Magister*

Last Updated: 25/10/11

HIGHER VOCATIONAL SCHOOL OF ŁÓDŹ EDUCATIONAL CORPORATION

Wyższa Szkoła Zawodowa Łódzkiej Korporacji Oświatowej w Łodzi (WSZŁKO)

ul. Wólczańska 93, 90-515 Łódź, łódzkie
Tel: +48(42) 636-51-62
Fax: +48(42) 636-51-62
EMail: wszlko@op.pl
Website: http://www.wsz-lko.pl

Rektor: Janusz Baranowski

Kanclerz: Barbara Lukasik

Faculties

Applied Chemistry (Applied Chemistry; Cosmetology; Pharmacy; Technology)

History: Founded 2004.

Fees: (New Złoty): 500-550 per month; Postgraduate programmes, 1-000-1,500 per semester.

Main Language(s) of Instruction: Polish

Degrees and Diplomas: *Inżynier*, *Licencjat*; *Świadectwo ukończenia studiów podyplomowych*

Libraries: Yes

Last Updated: 26/10/11

HIGHER VOCATIONAL SCHOOL OF THE COPPER BASIN, LUBIN

Uczelnia Zawodowa Zagłębia Miedziowego w Lubinie (UZZM)

ul. Odrodzenia 21/23, 59-300 Lubin, dolnośląskie
Tel: +48(76) 749-89-29
Fax: +48(76) 749-89-28
EMail: uzzm@uzzm.pl
Website: http://www.uzzm.pl

Rektor: Jan Anusiak (2008-)

Kanclerz: Lucyna Kubis

Departments

Postgraduate Studies (Industrial Engineering; Occupational Health; Pedagogy; Preschool Education; Rehabilitation and Therapy; Safety Engineering)

Faculties

Management and Social Sciences (Accountancy; Administration; Business Administration; Child Care and Development; Communication Studies; E-Business/Commerce; Education; Finance; Management; Marketing; Pedagogy; Preschool Education; Psychology; Social Sciences); **Technical Sciences** (Automation and Control Engineering; Electrical Engineering; Geology; Industrial Engineering; Management; Mining Engineering; Production Engineering)

History: Founded 2002.

Main Language(s) of Instruction: Polish

International Co-operation: Participates in the Erasmus programme.

Accrediting Agencies: Minister of Science and Higher Education; State Accreditation Committee (SAC)

Degrees and Diplomas: *Inżynier*, *Licencjat*; *Świadectwo ukończenia studiów podyplomowych*

Last Updated: 18/10/11

HIGHER VOCATIONAL SCHOOL, WAŁCZ

Państwowa Wyższa Szkoła Zawodowa w Wałczu (PWSZ)

ul. Bydgoska 50, 78-600 Wałcz, zachodniopomorskie
Tel: +48(67) 250-01-87
Fax: +48(67) 250-01-87
EMail: rektorat@pwsz.eu
Website: http://www.pwszwalcz.org.pl

Rektor: Jolanta Witek EMail: rektor@pwsz.eu

Kanclerz: Jacek Kasiński EMail: kanclerz@pwsz.eu

Institutes

Economics (Accountancy; Banking; Business Computing; E-Business/Commerce; Econometrics; Finance; Information Sciences; Information Technology; Management; Public Administration); **Humanities** (Arts and Humanities; English; German; Russian; Translation and Interpretation); **Physical Education** (Physical Education; Protective Services; Rehabilitation and Therapy; Sports); **Polytechnic** (Automation and Control Engineering; Business Computing; Computer Engineering; Engineering; Management; Production Engineering; Transport Management)

Programmes

Postgraduate Studies (Accountancy; Finance; Foreign Languages Education; Industrial Management; Marketing; Translation and Interpretation)

Degrees and Diplomas: *Inżynier*, *Licencjat*; *Świadectwo ukończenia studiów podyplomowych*

Last Updated: 05/09/11

HIGH SCHOOL OF ENTERPRISE AND REGIONAL DEVELOPMENT IN FALENTY

Wyższa Szkoła Przedsiębiorczości i Rozwoju Regionalnego (WSPIRR)

Falenty-Pałac, 05-090 Raszyn, mazowieckie
Tel: +48(22) 720-05-35
Fax: +48(22) 628-37-63
EMail: wspirr@wspirr.edu.pl
Website: http://www.wspirr.edu.pl

Rector: Edmund Kaca (2002-) EMail: e.kaca@imuz.edu.pl

Kanclerz: Izabela Lubbe

Departments

Postgraduate Studies (Environmental Management; Environmental Studies)

Faculties

Environmental Protection (Environmental Engineering; Environmental Management); **Spatial Planning** (Development Studies; Economics; Regional Planning)

History: Founded 2002.

Fees: (New Zoty); 370 per month.

Main Language(s) of Instruction: Polish

Degrees and Diplomas: *Inżynier*, *Świadectwo ukończenia studiów podyplomowych*

Last Updated: 24/10/11

HOLY CROSS UNIVERSITY IN THE CITY OF KIELCE

Wszechnica Świętokrzyska w Kielcach (WS)

ul. E. Orzeszkowej 15, 25-435 Kielce, świętokrzyskie

Tel: +48(41) 331-12-44

Fax: +48(41) 331-12-44

EMail: ws@ws.edu.pl

Website: http://www.ws.edu.pl

Rektor: Janusz Zdebski

Tel: +48(41) 331-12-44 Ext.101, Fax: +48(41) 331-92-92

Kanclerz: Krzysztof Ludwikowski

International Relations: Justyna Palacz

Tel: +48(41) 331-72-38, Fax: +48(41) 331-72-38

Faculties

Humanities and Teaching (Art Therapy; Arts and Humanities; Child Care and Development; Education; Educational and Student Counselling; English; English Studies; Foreign Languages Education; Pedagogy; Philology; Preschool Education; Rehabilitation and Therapy; Social Work; Translation and Interpretation); **Physical Education and Tourism** (Health Sciences; Hotel Management; Leisure Studies; Physical Education; Physical Therapy; Sports; Tourism)

Further Information: Also Branch in Lublin

History: Founded 1994, acquired present status and title 1999.

Governing Bodies: Senate

Admission Requirements: Secondary school certificate (Matura)

Fees: (New Złoty): c. 1,950 per annum

Main Language(s) of Instruction: Polish, English, German

International Co-operation: With universities in Belgium, Spain, Germany, England, Italy and Cyprus. Participates in the Erasmus programme.

Accrediting Agencies: Ministry of Science and Higher Education; National Accreditation Commission

Degrees and Diplomas: *Licencjat*; *Świadectwo ukończenia studiów podyplomowych*; *Magister*

Student Services: Academic counselling, Handicapped facilities, Sports facilities

Special Facilities: Computer Laboratory

Libraries: WS Library, c. 5,700 vols, 52 periodicals

Publications: Zeszyty Wszechnicy Świętokrzyskiej *(biennially)*

Last Updated: 19/10/11

HUMANISTIC-MANAGER MILENNIUM HIGHER SCHOOL, GNIEZNO

Gnieźnieńska Wyższa Szkoła Humanistyczno-Menedżerska "Milenium" (GWSHM "MILENIUM')

ul. Cieszkowskiego 17, 62-200 Gniezno, wielkopolskie

Tel: +48(61) 428-26-27

Fax: +48(61) 428-26-27

EMail: dziekanat@gwshm.edu.pl

Website: http://www.gwshm.edu.pl

Rektor: Lechosław Gawrecki

Kanclerz: Krzysztof Gawrecki

Faculties

Cultural Studies and Tourism (Cultural Studies; Hotel and Restaurant; Physical Therapy; Rehabilitation and Therapy; Singing; Theatre; Tourism); **Education** (Art Therapy; Education; English; Ethics; Health Sciences; Information Technology; Modern Languages; Pedagogy; Psychology; Rehabilitation and Therapy; Sociology); **Management and Marketing** (Accountancy; Communication Studies; Economics; English; Finance; Human Resources; Information Management; Law; Management; Marketing; Mathematics; Modern Languages; Multimedia; Psychology; Public Administration; Safety Engineering; Small Business; Sociology; Statistics; Transport Management)

History: Founded 2003.

Fees: (New Zloty): 1,500-1,860 per semester

Main Language(s) of Instruction: Polish

Degrees and Diplomas: *Licencjat*; *Świadectwo ukończenia studiów podyplomowych*; *Magister*

Last Updated: 13/10/11

HUMANITAS UNIVERSITY, SOSNOWIEC

Wyższa Szkoła Humanitas w Sosnowcu (WSZIM)

ul. Kilińskiego 43, 41-200 Sosnowiec, śląskie

Tel: +48(32) 363-12-00

Fax: +48(32) 363-12-07

EMail: sekretariat@humanitas.edu.pl; rekrutacja@humanitas.edu.pl

Website: http://www.humanitas.edu.pl/

Rektor: Jerzy Kopel (1999-)

Kanclerz: Aleksander Dudek

Tel: +48(32) 266-40-01, Fax: +48(32) 266-40-01

International Relations: Kazimierz Ślęczka, Vice Rector for Science and International Relations

Faculties

Administration (Administration; Administrative Law; Economics; European Studies; Law; Public Administration; Real Estate; Safety Engineering); **English Philology** (English; Foreign Languages Education; Philology; Translation and Interpretation); **Environmental Protection** (Development Studies; English; Environmental Studies; German; Russian); **European Studies** (Cultural Studies; Economics; European Studies; Media Studies); **Health and Safety** (Health Sciences; Occupational Health; Safety Engineering; Transport Engineering); **History** (Archaeology; Cultural Studies; English; Ethnology; German; History; International Relations; Political Sciences; Russian; Sociology); **Homeland Security** (Administration; Education; Fire Science; Human Resources; Military Science; Pedagogy; Police Studies; Protective Services; Public Administration); **Journalism and Social Communication** (Business Administration; English; German; Journalism; Mass Communication; Radio and Television Broadcasting; Russian); **Management** (Accountancy; Advertising and Publicity; Business Computing; English; Finance; Fire Science; German; Hotel Management; Human Resources; Information Technology; Management; Protective Services; Russian; Safety Engineering; Tourism; Transport Management); **Pedagogy** (Child Care and Development; English; German; Pedagogy; Physical Therapy; Preschool Education; Protective Services; Rehabilitation and Therapy; Russian; Social Work; Teacher Training; Welfare and Protective Services); **Political Sciences** (English; German; Government; Political Sciences; Russian; Social Policy); **Sociology** (Cultural Studies; Demography and Population; English; German; History; Pedagogy; Political Sciences; Russian; Sociology; Statistics)

History: Founded 1997. Wyższa Szkoła Zarządzania i Marketingu w Sosnowcu until 2007

Admission Requirements: Secondary school certificate (Matura)

Main Language(s) of Instruction: Polish

International Co-operation: With universities in Slovenia, Czech Republic, Turkey, Lithuania, Slovakia, Greece, Italy, Portugal, Germany, Spain. Participates in the LLP-Erasmus Programme

Accrediting Agencies: Ministry of Science and Higher Education; National Accreditation Commission

Degrees and Diplomas: *Licencjat*; *Świadectwo ukończenia studiów podyplomowych*; *Magister*

Academic Staff *2010-2011*: Total: c. 350

Last Updated: 06/10/11

IGNATIANUM JESUIT UNIVERSITY OF PHILOSOPHY AND EDUCATION, CRACOW

Akademia Ignatianum w Krakowie

ul. Kopernika 26, 31-501 Kraków, małopolskie

Tel: +48(12) 431-10-37

Fax: +48(12) 423-00-38

EMail: rektorat@ignatianum.edu.pl

Website: http://www.ignatianum.edu.pl

Rektor: Henryk Pietras Tel: +48(12) 629-34-16

Kanclerz: Adolfo Nicolas

Tel: +48(12) 629-34-22 EMail: owoc.m@jezuici.krakow.pl

International Relations: Anna Turlej, International Educational Programs
Tel: +48(12) 443-62-93 EMail: erasmus@ignatianum.edu.pl

Faculties

Education (Administration; Education; Family Studies; Government; Journalism; Leadership; Pedagogy; Political Sciences; Preschool Education; Primary Education; Rehabilitation and Therapy; Social Work; Welfare and Protective Services); **Philosophy** (Anthropology; Communication Studies; Cultural Studies; Ethics; Journalism; Literature; Management; Mass Communication; Media Studies; Philosophy; Religion; Tourism)

History: Founded 1932, acquired present status 1989. Formerly known as Wyższa Szkoła Filozoficzno-Pedagogiczna "Ignatianum", Kraków (Ignatianum Higher School of Philosophy and Pedagogy, Cracow).

Governing Bodies: Senate

Admission Requirements: Secondary School Certificate (Matura) and Entrance examinations

Fees: (New złoty): 100 per semester for full-time studies; 1,300-1,600 per semester for part-time studies; Postgraduate Studies, 1,200-1,500 per semester.

Main Language(s) of Instruction: Polish

International Co-operation: With universities in Germany, Italy, United Kingdom, Spain. Also participates in Youth European Voluntary Service (EVS), Socrates-Erasmus programmes

Accrediting Agencies: Ministry of Science and Higher Education

Degrees and Diplomas: *Licencjat*; *Świadectwo ukończenia studiów podyplomowych*; *Magister*, *Doktor*

Student Services: Canteen, Handicapped facilities, Social counselling, Sports facilities

Publications: Forum Philosophicum; Horizons of Education; Yearbook

Press or Publishing House: University Publishing

Last Updated: 05/10/11

INDEPENDENT UNIVERSITY OF BUSINESS, ADMINISTRATION AND COMPUTER SCIENCE

Prywatna Wyższa Szkoła Biznesu i Administracji w Warszawie (PWSBIA)

ul. Bobrowiecka 9, 00-728 Warszawa, mazowieckie
Tel: +48(22) 559-20-00 +48(22) 559-22-39
Fax: +48(22) 559-22-60 +48(22) 559-21-33
EMail: pwsbia@pwsbia.edu.pl; rekrutacja@pwsbia.edu.pl
Website: http://www.pwsbia.edu.pl

Rector: Tadeusz Koźluk (1991-)
Tel: +48(22) 559-22-05 EMail: rektor@pwsbia.edu.pl

Deputy Rector: Tadeusz Morawski
Tel: +48(22) 559-22-76 EMail: tmor@pwsbia.edu.pl

International Relations: Beata Waliszkiewicz, Head, Foreign Affairs Office
Tel: +48(22) 559-21-12, Fax: +48(22) 559-21-12
EMail: beata.wa@pwsbia.edu.pl

Institutes

Law (Administrative Law; Canadian Studies; Chinese; Civil Law; Comparative Law; Constitutional Law; Criminal Law; Criminology; English; Environmental Studies; European Union Law; Fiscal Law; History of Law; International Law; Japanese; Labour Law; Latin; Law; Public Law)

Programmes

Postgraduate Studies (Commercial Law; Computer Networks; Health Sciences; Information Technology; Management; Multimedia; Public Administration; Public Law)

Schools

Economics and Computer Science (Accountancy; Automation and Control Engineering; Business Computing; Computer Science; Economics; English; Finance; Information Technology; International Economics; Multimedia; Physical Education; Public Administration; Robotics; Social Problems); **Foreign Languages** (Chinese; English; French; German; Italian; Japanese; Modern Languages; Russian); **Modern Diplomacy and Administration** (Administration; Business Administration; Ecology; Economics; English; Environmental Studies; European Studies; International Business; International Relations; Law; Protective Services; Public Administration; Social Psychology; Social Sciences)

History: Founded 1991.

Governing Bodies: President, Senate

Academic Year: September to June

Admission Requirements: Secondary school certificate (Matura), entrance examination and interview

Fees: (New Złoty): Undergraduate, 3,000 per annum; Postgraduate, 4,500 per annum.

Main Language(s) of Instruction: Polish; English

International Co-operation: With universities in Russia, Ukraine, United Kingdom, China, Brazil, Chile.

Accrediting Agencies: Ministry of Science and Higher Education

Degrees and Diplomas: *Inżynier*, *Licencjat*; *Świadectwo ukończenia studiów podyplomowych*; *Magister*

Student Services: Academic counselling, Canteen, Health services, Language programs, Social counselling

Student Residential Facilities: Yes

Special Facilities: Radio Network.

Libraries: UN Depository Library

Publications: Journal of Science, Conferences and Seminars

Last Updated: 26/09/11

INSTITUTE OF COSMETOLOGY AND HEALTH CARE, BIALYSTOK

Kosmetologii i Ochrony Zdrowia w Białymstoku (WSKIOZ)

ul. Krakowska 9, 15-875 Białystok, podlaskie
Tel: +48(85) 749-94-30
Fax: +48(85) 749-94-31
EMail: biuro@wskosm.pl
Website: http://wskioz.edu.pl

Rektor: Zbigniew Puchalski

Kanclerz: Mikolaj Tomulewicz

Departments

Postgraduate Studies (Cosmetology; Gerontology; Health Administration; Physical Therapy; Rehabilitation and Therapy)

Faculties

Biotechnology (Biotechnology); **Cosmetology** (Cosmetology); **Medical Rescue** (Medicine); **Nursing** (Nursing); **Physioteraphy** (Physical Therapy)

Further Information: A traditional and distance education institution.

History: Founded 2003. Formerly known as Wyższa Szkoła Kosmetologii w Białymstoku.

Governing Bodies: Senate

Fees: (New Złoty): Undergraduate programmes, 4,500-6,400 per annum; Graduate programmes, 8,500 per annum.

Main Language(s) of Instruction: Polish; English

Accrediting Agencies: Ministry of National Education and Sport

Degrees and Diplomas: *Licencjat*; *Świadectwo ukończenia studiów podyplomowych*; *Magister*

Last Updated: 23/10/11

INTERNATIONAL UNIVERSITY OF LOGISTICS AND TRANSPORT, WROCŁAW

Międzynarodowa Wyższa Szkoła Logistyki i Transportu we Wrocławiu (MWSLIT)

ul. Sołtysowicka 19B, 51-168 Wrocław, dolnośląskie
Tel: +48(71) 324-68-42
Fax: +48(71) 325-15-61
EMail: uczelnia@msl.com.pl
Website: http://www.msl.com.pl

Rektor: Janusz Zierkiewicz EMail: krawczyk@manager.ae.wroc.pl
Chancellor: Janusz Paweska
International Relations: Ewa Heimrath-Bekier, Vice-Rector
Tel: +48(71) 324-68-42 Ext.125, Fax: +48(71) 322-61-87
EMail: e.heimrath-bekier@msl.com.pl

Programmes
Logistics (Transport Management); **Management** (Management; Transport Management)

History: Founded 2001.
Main Language(s) of Instruction: Polish; English
International Co-operation: With universities in Czech Republic, France, Slovak Republic, Bulgaria, Ukraine. Participates in the Erasmus programme.
Degrees and Diplomas: *Inżynier*; *Licencjat*; *Świadectwo ukończenia studiów podyplomowych*; *Magister*
Last Updated: 17/10/11

JAN ZAMOYSKI COLLEGE OF HUMANITIES AND ECONOMICS, ZAMOŚĆ

Wyższa Szkoła Humanistyczno-Ekonomiczna im. Jana Zamoyskiego z siedzibą w Zamościu (WSZHE)
ul. Koszary 8, 22-400 Zamość, lubelskie
Tel: +48(84) 638-82-00
Fax: +48(84) 638-82-00
EMail: dziekanat@wszh-e.edu.pl
Website: http://www.wszh-e.edu.pl

Rektor: Jan Waszczyński
Kanclerz: Ewa Lipczyńska
International Relations: Janusz Skowron

Departments
Postgraduate Studies (Business Administration; Economics; European Union Law; Health Administration; Human Resources; Management; Public Administration; Public Law; Small Business; Sociology; Tourism)

Faculties
Administrative Sciences and Public Law (Administration; Protective Services; Public Law); **Economics and Social Sciences** (Economics; Social Sciences); **International and European Law** (European Union Law; International Law); **Sociology** (Sociology)

Programmes
Defence Studies *(Intercollegiate)* (Military Science)

History: Founded 1998.
Governing Bodies: Senate
Admission Requirements: Secondary school certificate (matura)
Main Language(s) of Instruction: Polish
International Co-operation: With universities in Belgium, Czech Republic, Lithuania, Slovak Republic, Turkey, Ukraine, USA. Participates in the Erasmus programme.
Accrediting Agencies: Ministry of Science and Higher Education
Degrees and Diplomas: *Licencjat*; *Świadectwo ukończenia studiów podyplomowych*
Student Services: Sports facilities
Libraries: Yes
Last Updated: 21/10/11

JÓZEF RUSIECKI HIGHER SCHOOL, OLSZTYN

Olsztyńska Szkoła Wyższa im. Józefa Rusieckiego (OSW)
ul. Bydgoska 33, 10-243 Olsztyn, warmińsko-mazurskie
Tel: +48(89) 526-04-00
Fax: +48(89) 526-04-00
EMail: osw@osw.olsztyn.p
Website: http://www.osw.olsztyn.pl

Rektor: Henryk Kostyra Tel: 48 (89) 526-04-00
General Dyrektor: Helena Rusiecka Tel: +48(89) 526-87-22
International Relations: Agnieszka Zimnicka

Centres
Body Attitudes (Sports); **Health and Sports** (Health Sciences; Sports)

Colleges
English Language (English)

Faculties
Education (Computer Education; Education; Health Education; Parks and Recreation; Pedagogy; Political Sciences; Protective Services; Tourism); **Physical Education** (Physical Education; Sports); **Physiotherapy** (Physical Therapy); **Public Health** (Public Health)

Programmes
Professional Studies (Child Care and Development; Computer Education; Cosmetology; Dance; Dietetics; Education; Educational Administration; Geography; Library Science; Mathematics Education; Native Language Education; Nutrition; Occupational Therapy; Pedagogy; Physical Education; Rehabilitation and Therapy; Speech Therapy and Audiology; Sports; Vocational Counselling)

Research Laboratories
Central (Physical Education)

History: Founded 1997.
Governing Bodies: Senate
Admission Requirements: Secondary school certificate (matura)
Main Language(s) of Instruction: Polish
Accrediting Agencies: Ministry of Science and Higher Education
Degrees and Diplomas: *Licencjat*; *Świadectwo ukończenia studiów podyplomowych*; *Magister*
Special Facilities: 25
Libraries: c. 25,000 vols; 128 periodical subscriptions (including two foreign ones).
Last Updated: 20/09/11

KASZUBIAN-POMERANIAN HIGHER SCHOOL, WEJHEROWO

Kaszubsko-Pomorska Szkoła Wyższa w Wejherowie (KPSW)
ul. Dworcowa 7, 84-200 Wejherowo, pomorskie
Tel: +48(58) 672-25-50
Fax: +48(58) 672-90-09
EMail: sekretariat@kpsw.pl
Website: http://www.kpsw.pl

Rektor: Jerzy Cyberski
Kanclerz: Bożena Pogorzelska

Faculties
Economy (Accountancy; Banking; Business Administration; Economics; Finance; Human Resources; International Economics; Management; Marketing; Taxation); **Environmental Protection** (Biochemistry; Biology; Business Administration; Environmental Management; Environmental Studies; Geology; Meteorology; Tourism); **Nursing** (Nursing); **Sociology** (Human Resources; Social Sciences; Social Work; Sociology)

Degrees and Diplomas: *Licencjat*; *Świadectwo ukończenia studiów podyplomowych*
Last Updated: 15/10/11

KATOWICE SCHOOL OF ECONOMICS

Górnośląska Wyższa Szkoła Handlowa im. Wojciecha Korfantego (GWSH)
ul. Harcerzy Września 3, 40-659 Katowice, śląskie
Tel: +48(32) 357-05-00 +48(32) 357-05-50
EMail: rektorat@gwsh.pl
Website: http://www.gwsh.pl

Rector: Krzysztof Szaflarski
Dyrektor Administracyjny: Monika Bienek
International Relations: Wacław Petryński
Tel: +48(32) 357-05-41 EMail: w.petrynski@gwsh.pl

Campuses
Bielsko-Biala (Parks and Recreation; Tourism); **Bytom** (Accountancy; Administration; Finance; International Relations;

Management; Pedagogy); **Cieszyn** (Administration; Management); **Jaworzno** (Accountancy; Administration; Finance; Management; Sociology); **Nysa** (Administration; International Relations; Management; Pedagogy); **Vienna** (Accountancy; Administration; Finance; International Relations; Sociology); **Żory** (Accountancy; Administration; Computer Science; Finance; Management; Pedagogy); **Żywiec** (Accountancy; Finance; Management)

Faculties

Management (Accountancy; Administration; Computer Science; Economics; Finance; International Relations; Management; Pedagogy; Psychology; Sociology); **Tourism and Health Promotion** (Cosmetology; Health Sciences; Parks and Recreation; Physical Therapy; Tourism)

Programmes

Doctoral Studies (Economics; Management); **Postgraduate Studies** (Accountancy; Administration; Banking; Business Administration; Communication Studies; Educational Administration; Family Studies; Hotel and Restaurant; Human Resources; Information Management; Journalism; Law; Leadership; Management; Marketing; Medicine; Neurological Therapy; Pedagogy; Psychology; Real Estate; Taxation; Tourism)

History: Founded as 1991 College, acquired present status and title 1994.

Governing Bodies: Senate

Academic Year: October to June

Admission Requirements: Secondary school certificate (Matura) and language tests.

Fees: (New złoty): full time studies, 526 per month; extramural studies, 1,410 per semester

Main Language(s) of Instruction: Polish

International Co-operation: Participates in Socrates programme (Germany, France, United Kingdom, Belgium, Czech Republic, USA, Russian Federation, Ukraine, Belarus)

Accrediting Agencies: Ministry of Science and Higher Education; National Accrediting Commission; Association of Management Education (FORUM); European Council for Business Education (ECBE)

Degrees and Diplomas: *Inżynier*; *Licencjat*; *Świadectwo ukończenia studiów podyplomowych*; *Magister*; *Doktor*. Also Licencjat in Journalism

Student Services: Academic counselling, Canteen, Cultural centre, Employment services, Foreign Studies Centre, Handicapped facilities, Health services, Language programs, Nursery care, Social counselling, Sports facilities

Libraries:c. 25,500 vols, 1,500 audios, videos and CDs, 82 periodical subscriptions

Publications: Zeszyty Naukowe, Scientific papers *(other/irregular)*

Press or Publishing House: Kontrasty, Students's magazine

Last Updated: 19/09/11

KATOWICE SCHOOL OF TECHNOLOGY

Wyższa Szkoła Techniczna w Katowicach (WST)

ul. Rolna 43, 40-555 Katowice, śląskie
Tel: +48(32) 202-50-34 +48(32) 252-28-74
Fax: +48(32) 252-28-75
EMail: wst@wst.com.pl; sekretariat@wst.com.pl
Website: http://www.wst.com.pl

Rektor: Andrzej Grzybowski

Kanclerz: Arkadiusz Holda

International Relations: Malgorzata M. Maloszyce-Tomaszewicz, International Cooperation Coordinators EMail: dwz@wst.com.pl

Departments

Postgraduate Studies (Architectural and Environmental Design; Interior Design; Real Estate; Town Planning)

Faculties

Architecture (Architecture); **Architecture and Town Planning** (Architecture and Planning; Town Planning); **Design** (Design); **Direction** (Cinema and Television; Film; Radio and Television Broadcasting); **Graphics** (Graphic Design); **Interior Design** (Interior Design); **Journalism and Social Communication** (Journalism; Mass Communication); **Spatial Planning** (Architectural and Environmental Design; Economics; Environmental Engineering; Town Planning)

History: Founded 2004.

Fees: (New Zoty): Undergraduate programmes, 1,750-3,800 per semester; Graduate programmes, 3,400 per semester; Postgraduate programmes, 1,800-2,450 per semester.

Main Language(s) of Instruction: Polish

International Co-operation: Participates in the Erasmus programme.

Degrees and Diplomas: *Inżynier*, *Licencjat*; *Świadectwo ukończenia studiów podyplomowych*; *Magister*

Last Updated: 24/10/11

KING STANISŁAW LESZCZYŃSKI HIGHER SCHOOL OF HUMANITIES, LESZNO

Wyższa Szkoła Humanistyczna "im. Króla Stanisława Leszcźńskiego" (WSH)

ul. Królowej Jadwigi 10, 64-100 Leszno, wielkopolskie
Tel: +48(65) 529-47-77
Fax: +48(65) 529-92-62
EMail: infowshl@ck-leszno.com.pl
Website: http://www.wsh-leszno.pl

Rektor: Aleksander Zandecki (2001-)
Tel: +48(65) 529-35-20, Fax: +48(65) 529-35-20
EMail: rektorat@wsh-leszno.pl

Kanclerz: Ryszard Karmoliński

Centres

Postgraduate Studies (Child Care and Development; Cosmetology; Education; Educational Psychology; Ethics; European Studies; Family Studies; Health Sciences; Human Resources; Nutrition; Pedagogy; Preschool Education; Rehabilitation and Therapy; Safety Engineering; Speech Therapy and Audiology; Vocational Counselling; Welfare and Protective Services)

Departments

Foreign Languages (English; French; German; Italian; Modern Languages; Russian; Spanish; Swedish); **Physical Education** (Physical Education; Sports)

Programmes

Cosmetology (Cosmetology); **Dietetics** (Dietetics; Nutrition); **Education** (Education; Educational Psychology; Gerontology; Health Education; Pedagogy; Preschool Education; Psychology; Rehabilitation and Therapy; Speech Therapy and Audiology; Teacher Training); **Homeland Security** (Administration; Government; Protective Services); **Social Work** (Management; Psychology; Social Work); **Sociology** (European Studies; Government; Human Resources; Journalism; Labour and Industrial Relations; Mass Communication; Media Studies; Social Sciences; Sociology)

Further Information: Also distance education.

Degrees and Diplomas: *Licencjat*; *Świadectwo ukończenia studiów podyplomowych*; *Magister*

Last Updated: 06/10/11

KOSZALIN HIGHER SCHOOL OF HUMANITIES

Koszalińska Wyższa Szkoła Nauk Humanistycznych (KWSNH)

ul. Batalionów Chłopskich 79, 75-333 Koszalin, zachodniopomorskie
Tel: +48(94) 341-45-27
Fax: +48(94) 341-45-27
EMail: info@kwsnh.edu.pl
Website: http://www.kwsnh.edu.pl/

Rektor: Adam Moscicki

Departments

Postgraduate Studies (Administration; Education; Ethics; Finance; Foreign Languages Education; Occupational Health; Pedagogy; Philosophy; Preschool Education; Public Administration; Rehabilitation and Therapy; Safety Engineering; Social Work; Taxation; Teacher Training; Vocational Education)

Faculties

Administration (Administration; Environmental Management; European Studies; European Union Law; Government; Modern

Languages; Public Administration); **Education** (Child Care and Development; Education; Protective Services; Vocational Counselling)
History: Founded 2005.
Degrees and Diplomas: *Licencjat*; *Świadectwo ukończenia studiów podyplomowych*
Last Updated: 18/10/11

KOTARBINSKI UNIVERSITY OF INFORMATION TECHNOLOGY AND MANAGEMENT, OLSZTYN

Olsztyńska Wyższa Szkoła Informatyki i Zarządzania im. Prof. Tadeusza Kotarbińskiego (OWSIIZ)

ul. Artyleryjska 3c, 10-165 Olsztyn, warmińsko-mazurskie
Tel: +48(89) 534-32-03
Fax: +48(89) 534-33-20
EMail: owsiiz@owsiiz.edu.pl
Website: http://www.owsiiz.edu.pl

Rektor: Zdzislaw Kowalczyk (2009-)

Chancellor: Janusz Zwirko EMail: janusz.zwirko@owsiiz.edu.pl

International Relations: Izabela Bors-Nasilowska
EMail: Izabela.bors@owsiiz.edu.pl

Centres

New Technologies (Technology)

Faculties

Cultural Studies (Cultural Studies; Journalism; Media Studies); **Economics** (Economics; Finance; Management; Marketing; Small Business); **Economics and Social Sciences** (Accountancy; Business Administration; Business Computing; Finance; Health Administration; Human Resources; International Business; Management; Real Estate); **European Studies** (Business Administration; Cultural Studies; Economics; European Studies; International Relations; Management; Political Sciences; Protective Services); **Informatics and Technology Sciences** (Automation and Control Engineering; Computer Engineering; Computer Networks; Computer Science; Electronic Engineering; Information Management; Information Technology; Mechanical Engineering; Robotics); **Pedagogy** (Human Resources; Pedagogy)

Institutes

Research and Innovation

History: Founded 1990 as Olsztyn School of Management and Administration. Acquired university status and became known as Kotarbinski University of Management in Olsztyn 1996. Acquired present title 2001.

Governing Bodies: Senate; Board

Academic Year: Oct - Feb; Feb - June

Admission Requirements: Secondary school certificate (Świadectwo dojrzałości)

Fees: (New Złoty): 1,550 - 2,050 per semester

Main Language(s) of Instruction: Polish

International Co-operation: with institutions in Belgium, Romania, Turkey, UK, Lithuania, Germany, Ukraine and Russia.

Accrediting Agencies: Ministry of Science and Higher Education

Degrees and Diplomas: *Inżynier*: Mechatronics; Informatics, 3 1/2 yrs; *Licencjat*: Management; Economics; European Studies; Cultural Studies; Pedagogy, 3 yrs. Also Postgraduate studies

Student Services: Academic counselling, Canteen, Employment services, Handicapped facilities, Social counselling, Sports facilities

Student Residential Facilities: Yes

Libraries: c. 18,360 vols

Academic Staff *2009-2010*	**TOTAL**
FULL-TIME	128
PART-TIME	85
STAFF WITH DOCTORATE	
FULL-TIME	103
Student Numbers *2009-2010*	
All (Foreign Included)	1,886
FOREIGN ONLY	1

Part-time students, 1,600.
Last Updated: 08/09/11

KOZMINSKI UNIVERSITY, WARSAW

Akademia Leona Koźmińskiego (WSPIZ)

ul. Jagiellońska 57/59, 03-301 Warszawa, mazowieckie
Tel: +48(22) 519-21-00
Fax: +48(22) 519-23-01
EMail: wspiz@wspiz.edu.pl
Website: http://www.kozminski.edu.pl/

Rektor: Witold T. Bielecki
Tel: +48(22) 519-21-11 EMail: rektorat@kozminski.edu.pl

Dyrektor Administracyjny: Mirosława Łukasiewicz-Kwiatkowska
Tel: +48(22) 519-21-29

International Relations: Valentyna Gumińska, Director, Bureau for International Cooperation
Tel: +48(22) 519-22-89, Fax: +48(22) 519-22-47
EMail: vguminska@kozminski.edu.pl

Colleges

Business Law (Administrative Law; Civil Law; Commercial Law; Constitutional Law; Criminal Law; European Union Law; Fiscal Law; International Law; Law; Private Law); **Management and Finance** (Accountancy; Business Administration; Economics; European Studies; Finance; Government; Human Resources; Information Technology; International Business; International Economics; International Relations; Management; Marketing; Operations Research; Psychology; Public Health; Social Sciences)

Schools

International Business (Business Administration; International Business)

History: Founded 199 as Wyższą Szkołę Przedsiębiorczości i Zarządzania (Academy of Entrepreneurship and Management). Renamed Wyższa Szkoła Przedsiębiorczości i Zarządzania otrzymała imię prof. Leona Koźmińskiego (Leon Kozminski Academy of Entrepreneurship and Management) 1997. Acquired present title 2008.

Governing Bodies: Senate

Academic Year: October to June

Admission Requirements: Secondary school certificate (Matura)

Fees: (New Złoty): 4,500-8,200 per semester

Main Language(s) of Instruction: Polish; English

International Co-operation: With universities in Europe, Canada, US, Mexico, Japan, China , Russia. Participates in the LLP Erasmus programme.

Accrediting Agencies: International accreditation: EQUIS, AMBA and AASCB

Degrees and Diplomas: *Inżynier*, *Świadectwo ukończenia studiów podyplomowych*; *Magister*, *Doktor*. Also MBA; Double Bachelor's degree in Management offered jointly with the Duale Hochschule Baden-Württenberg - Mannheim (Germany).

Student Services: Academic counselling, Canteen, Employment services, Foreign student adviser, Foreign Studies Centre, Handicapped facilities, Health services, Language programs, Sports facilities

Student Residential Facilities: None

Special Facilities: Computer Centre

Libraries: Library, c. 8,000 vols
Last Updated: 08/10/11

KUJAWY AND POMORZE UNIVERSITY, BYDGOSZCZ

Kujawsko-Pomorska Szkoła Wyższa w Bydgoszczy (KPSW)

ul. M. Piotrowskiego 12-14, 85-098 Bydgoszcz, kujawsko-pomorskie
Tel: +48(52) 322-03-22
Fax: +48(52) 322-34-04 Ext. 34
EMail: rekrutacja@kpsw.edu.pl
Website: http://www.kpsw.edu.pl

Rektor: Włodzimierz Jabłoński
Tel: +48(52) 321-11-88, Fax: +48(52) 339-30-22
EMail: rektorat@kpsw.edu.pl

Kanclerz: Roman Czarkowski EMail: r.czarkowski@wp.pl

International Relations: Ryszard Paczuski, Prorektor
EMail: internationaloffice@kpsw.edu.pl

Faculties

Economics and Social Sciences (Accountancy; Banking; Business Administration; Business Computing; Communication Studies; Cooking and Catering; East Asian Studies; Eastern European Studies; Economics; English; Finance; Hotel Management; Human Resources; Information Technology; International Economics; International Relations; Journalism; Mass Communication; Public Relations; Russian; Service Trades; Small Business; Social Policy; Social Sciences; Social Work; Tourism; Transport Economics; Transport Management); **Law and Administration** (Administration; Administrative Law; Business Administration; Environmental Studies; Government; Health Administration; Human Rights; Law; Protective Services; Public Administration; Real Estate; Social Policy; Welfare and Protective Services); **Pedagogy** (Child Care and Development; Criminology; Cultural Studies; Dance; Education; Educational Psychology; Family Studies; Health Education; Human Resources; Music; Pedagogy; Preschool Education; Psychology; Rehabilitation and Therapy; Safety Engineering; Social and Preventive Medicine; Social Psychology; Sociology; Special Education; Visual Arts); **Philology** (English; Philology; Russian; Spanish); **Technology** (Business Computing; Computer Engineering; Computer Graphics; Computer Networks; Computer Science; Data Processing; Engineering; Information Technology; Software Engineering; Sound Engineering (Acoustics))

Programmes

Postgraduate Studies (Administration; Art Education; Child Care and Development; Commercial Law; Communication Studies; Computer Graphics; Cultural Studies; Educational Administration; Ethics; Fine Arts; Foreign Languages Education; Health Sciences; Human Resources; Management; Music; Music Education; Occupational Therapy; Pedagogy; Physical Therapy; Preschool Education; Public Relations; Real Estate; Rehabilitation and Therapy; Small Business; Special Education; Speech Therapy and Audiology; Vocational Education)

History: Founded 2000.

Governing Bodies: Senate

Admission Requirements: Secondary school certificate (matura)

Fees: (Euro): Undergraduate tuition, 650 per semester for programmes in Polish language and 1,000 per semester for programmes in English language; Graduate tuition, 850 per semester.

Main Language(s) of Instruction: Polish

International Co-operation: With universities in United Kingdom and Ukraine; internships are also available in Finland, Germany, Austria, Slovenia and the United Kingdom. Participates in the LLP - Erasmus Programme, Leodardo da Vinci Programme, implements ECTS credits and carries out students and teachers exchange.

Accrediting Agencies: Ministry of Science and Higher Education

Degrees and Diplomas: *Inżynier*; *Licencjat*; *Świadectwo ukończenia studiów podyplomowych*; *Magister*

Special Facilities: Computer laboratories; auditorium; KPU TV.

Libraries: c. 23,000 vols; 86 periodical subscription (including foreign) in the field, including pedagogy, psychology, rehabilitation, economics, law, administration, geodesy.

Academic Staff *2010-2011*: Total: c. 400
Last Updated: 20/09/11

KWIDZYN SCHOOL OF MANAGEMENT

Powiślańska Szkoła Wyższa (WSZ)
ul. 11 Listopada 29, 82-500 Kwidzyn, pomorskie
Tel: +48(55) 279-17-68
Fax: +48(55) 261-31-39
EMail: dziekanat@psw.kwidzyn.edu.pl; rekrutacja@psw.kwidzyn.edu.pl
Website: http://www.wsz.kwidzyn.edu.pl

Rector: Stefan Angielski EMail: rektor@wsz.kwidzyn.edu.pl

Kanclerz: Grzegorz Bakierski

International Relations: Jolanta Sala
Tel: +48 606-317-135 EMail: prorektor@wsz.kwidzyn.edu.pl

Departments

Postgraduate Studies (Accountancy; Business Administration; Educational Administration; Finance; Health Administration; Health Sciences; Human Resources; Labour Law; Law; Management; Pedagogy; Transport Management; Vocational Counselling)

Faculties

Health Sciences (Health Sciences; Medical Auxiliaries; Nursing); **Management** (Accountancy; Computer Science; Development Studies; Economics; Finance; Human Resources; Management; Media Studies; Public Health; Taxation; Tourism; Transport and Communications; Transport Management)

History: Founded 1999. Formelry kwnown as Wyższa Szkoła Zarządzania w Kwidzynie.

Governing Bodies: Senate

Admission Requirements: Secondary school certificate (matura)

Main Language(s) of Instruction: Polish

International Co-operation: With universities in Turkey, Estonia, France, Cezch Republic, Slovenia, Greece, Lithuania, Germany, and Romania. Participates in the Erasmus programme.

Accrediting Agencies: Ministry of Science and Higher Education

Degrees and Diplomas: *Licencjat*; *Świadectwo ukończenia studiów podyplomowych*; *Magister*: Nursing

Last Updated: 18/10/11

ŁAZARSKI UNIVERSITY

Uczelnia Łazarskiego (WSHIP)
ul. Świeradowska 43, 02-662 Warszawa, mazowieckie
Tel: +48(22) 543-54-30
Fax: +48(22) 543-55-55
EMail: uczelnia@lazarski.edu.pl
Website: http://www.lazarski.pl

Rector: Daria Nałęcz (2008-)
Tel: +48(22) 543-54-03 EMail: rektor@lazarski.edu.pl

University Secretary: Krystyna Fórmaniak
Tel: +48(22) 853-75-41 EMail: k.formaniak@lazarski.edu.pl

International Relations: Carolina Borowska, Institutional Coordinator, Erasmus Programme
Tel: +48(22) 543-53-65, Fax: +48(22) 543-53-63
EMail: k.borowska@lazarski.edu.pl

Centres

Postgraduate Studies (Accountancy; Business Administration; E-Business/Commerce; Educational Administration; Film; Human Resources; Labour Law; Law; Management; Marketing; Media Studies; Psychology; Public Administration; Radio and Television Broadcasting; Real Estate; Welfare and Protective Services)

Departments

Foreign Languages (Chinese; English; Foreign Languages Education; French; German; Modern Languages; Polish; Russian; Spanish; Turkish)

Faculties

Economics and Management (Accountancy; American Studies; Banking; Business Administration; E-Business/Commerce; Economics; European Studies; Finance; Human Resources; International Economics; International Relations; Management; Marketing; Operations Research; Small Business; Tourism; Transport Management); **Law and Administration** (Administration; Administrative Law; Civil Law; Commercial Law; Constitutional Law; Criminal Law; Government; History of Law; International Law; Law; Political Sciences; Public Administration; Real Estate)

Programmes

Fitness Studies and Training (Sports)

History: Founded 1993 as Prywatna Wyższa Szkoła Handlowa (Private Higher School of Commerce). Became Wyższa Szkoła Handlu i Prawa(School of Commerce and Law).1997. Renamed Wyższa Szkoła Handlu i Prawa im. Ryszrada Łazarskiego (Ryszard Łazarski Higher School of Commerce and Law, Warsaw) 2000. Acquired present title 2010.

Governing Bodies: Senate

Academic Year: September to June

Admission Requirements: Secondary school certificate (Matura)

Fees: (New Złoty): 1,800-3,696 per semester for programmes taught in Polish and 4,320-5,840 per semester for programmes taught in English.
Main Language(s) of Instruction: Polish, English
International Co-operation: With universities in Belgium, Finland, France, Greece, Spain, Netherlands, Ireland, Lithuania, Malta, Germany, Norway, Portugal, Romania, Slovenia, Sweden, Turkey, Hungary, United Kingdom and Italy. Participates in the Erasmus and Leonardo da Vinci programmes.
Accrediting Agencies: Ministry of Science and Higher Education
Degrees and Diplomas: *Licencjat*; *Świadectwo ukończenia studiów podyplomowych*; *Magister*
Student Services: Health services, Nursery care
Libraries: School Library
Publications: Zeszyty Naukowy WSHiP *(biennially)*

Academic Staff *2010-2011*: Total: c. 250
Last Updated: 06/10/11

LODZ ACADEMY OF INTERNATIONAL STUDIES

Wyższa Szkoła Studiów Międzynarodowych w Łodzi (WSSM)

ul. Brzozowa 3/9, 93-101 Łódź, łódzkie
Tel: +48(42) 684-14-74
Fax: +48(42) 689-72-12
EMail: sekretariat@wssm.edu.pl
Website: http://www.wssm.edu.pl

Rector: Marian Wilk (1997-)
Tel: +48(42) 689-72-20, Fax: +48(42) 689-72-13
EMail: rektor@wssm.edu.pl
Kanclerz: Małgorzata Wilk Tel: +48(42) 689-72-22
International Relations: Wioletta Wilk-Reguła, Vice-Rector for Science and International Relations
Tel: +48(42) 689-72-10 Ext. 160 EMail: viola@wssm.edu.pl

Faculties

International Relations and Business (American Studies; Asian Studies; Business Administration; Chinese; European Studies; European Union Law; Finance; International Business; International Law; International Relations; Journalism; Management; Mass Communication; Media Studies; Political Sciences; Tourism); **Philology** (English; German; Italian; Japanese; Modern Languages; Philology; Spanish)

Programmes

Postgraduate Studies (Translation and Interpretation)
History: Founded 1997.
Governing Bodies: Senate
Admission Requirements: Secondary school certificate (Matura)
Fees: (New Złoty): 500-567 per month; Postgraduate studies, 2,600 per semester.
Main Language(s) of Instruction: Polish
International Co-operation: Participates in the Eramsus programme.
Accrediting Agencies: Ministry of Science and Higher Education
Degrees and Diplomas: *Licencjat*; *Świadectwo ukończenia studiów podyplomowych*; *Magister*, *Doktor*
Student Residential Facilities: Dormitory

Student Numbers *2010-2011*: Total: c. 2,000
Last Updated: 08/10/11

LOWER SILESIAN HIGHER SCHOOL, WROCŁAW

Dolnośląska Szkoła Wyższa we Wrocławiu (DSWE TWP)

ul. Wagonowa 9, 53-609 Wrocław, dolnośląskie
Tel: +48(71) 358-27-00
Fax: +48(71) 358-27-14
EMail: sekret@dswe.wroc.pl
Website: http://www.dswe.pl

Rektor: Robert Kwaśnica (1997-)
Tel: +48(71) 358-27-15 +48(71) 358-27-14,
Fax: +48(71) 358-27-14 EMail: rektorat@dswe.pl
Kanclerz: Czesław Błaszczyk
Tel: +48(71) 358-27-21, Fax: +48(71) 358-27-35
EMail: kanclerz@dswe.pl
International Relations: Bogusława Dorota Gołębniak, Vice-Rector for Research and International Relations
Tel: +48(71) 358-27-15 +48(71) 358-27-25,
Fax: +48(71) 358-27-14 EMail: bwz@dswe.pl

Faculties

Pedagogical Sciences (Education; Family Studies; Pedagogy; Social Work; Special Education); **Social Sciences and Journalism** (Cultural Studies; Ethnology; History; International Relations; Journalism; Mass Communication; Philosophy; Protective Services; Social Sciences); **Technical Sciences** (Earth Sciences; Marine Transport; Surveying and Mapping)

Units

Foreign Languages (English; Modern Languages); **Physical Education** (Physical Education)
Further Information: Also Distance Education Faculty (Klodzo).
History: Founded 1997.
Governing Bodies: Senate
Admission Requirements: Secondary school certificate (matura)
Main Language(s) of Instruction: Polish; English
International Co-operation: With 60 universities; Participates in ERASMUS programme.
Accrediting Agencies: Ministry of Science and Higher Education
Degrees and Diplomas: *Inżynier*; *Licencjat*; *Świadectwo ukończenia studiów podyplomowych*; *Magister*; *Doktor*. Also MBA
Special Facilities: University of the Third Age; Radio "BIT" and Television Studio;
Libraries: over 66,000 vols

Academic Staff *2010-2011*: Total: c. 200
Student Numbers *2010-2011*: Total: c. 8,500
Last Updated: 14/09/11

LUBLIN HIGHER SCHOOL IN RYKI

Lubelska Szkoła Wyższa w Rykach (WSUPIZ)

ul. Warszawska 3b, 08-500 Ryki, lubelskie
Tel: +48(81) 865-70-05
Fax: +48(81) 865-43-54
EMail: dziekanat@lswryki.pl
Website: http://www.lswryki.pl/

Rector: Tadeusz Graca
Tel: +48(81) 865-43-54, Fax: +48(81) 865-43-54 Ext.30
EMail: rektorat@lswryki.pl
Kanclerz: Agnieszka Kacprzak EMail: kanclerz@wsupiz.edu.pl

Departments

Postgraduate Studies (Child Care and Development; Computer Education; Computer Science; Cultural Studies; Education; Educational Administration; Ethics; Health Sciences; Pedagogy; Preschool Education; Primary Education; Protective Services; Rehabilitation and Therapy; Safety Engineering; Special Education)

Faculties

Pedagogy (Computer Education; Educational Administration; Pedagogy; Preschool Education; Protective Services; Rehabilitation and Therapy; Safety Engineering; Teacher Trainers Education)
History: Founded 1997 as Wyższa Szkoła Umiejętności Pedagogicznych i Zarządzania w Rykach (Higher School of Pedagogical Knowledge and Management, Ryki). Acquired present title 2009.
Governing Bodies: Senate
Admission Requirements: Secondary school certificate (Matura)
Fees: (New Złoty): 300-650 per month
Main Language(s) of Instruction: Polish
Accrediting Agencies: Ministry of Science and Higher Education; National Accreditation Commission
Degrees and Diplomas: *Licencjat*; *Świadectwo ukończenia studiów podyplomowych*
Last Updated: 24/10/11

ŁUŻYCE HUMANISTIC HIGHER SCHOOL IN ŻARY

Łużycka Wyższa Szkoła Humanistyczna im. Jana Benedykta Solfy z siedzibą w Żarach (ŁWSH)
ul. 9 - Maja 11, 68-200 Żary, lubelskie
Tel: (068) 363-00-55
Fax: (068) 374-20-40
EMail: lwsh@wp.pl
Website: http://www.lwsh.pl

Rektor: Grzegorz Popow

Kanclerz: Izabela Kumor

Departments

Postgraduate Studies (Accountancy; Computer Engineering; Data Processing; E-Business/Commerce; Electronic Engineering; Finance; Mechanical Engineering)

Faculties

Pedagogy *(Gubinie)* (Educational and Student Counselling; Pedagogy; Preschool Education); **Pedagogy** (Adult Education; Child Care and Development; Education; Educational and Student Counselling; Gerontology; Health Education; Pedagogy; Preschool Education; Safety Engineering; Social and Preventive Medicine; Social Work); **Polish Philology** (Philology; Polish)

History: Founded 2004.

Main Language(s) of Instruction: Polish

Accrediting Agencies: Ministry of Science and Higher Education

Degrees and Diplomas: *Licencjat*; *Świadectwo ukończenia studiów podyplomowych*; *Magister*

Libraries: c. 13,000 vols

Academic Staff *2010-2011*: Total 40

STAFF WITH DOCTORATE: Total 16

Last Updated: 18/10/11

MAŁOPOLSKA HIGHER SCHOOL OF ECONOMICS, TARNÓW

Małopolska Wyższa Szkoła Ekonomiczna w Tarnowie (MWSE)
ul. Waryńskiego 14, 33-100 Tarnów, małopolskie
Tel: +48(14) 688-00-19 +48(14) 688-00-20
Fax: +48(14) 688-00-19 +48(14) 688-00-20
EMail: mwse@mwse.edu.pl
Website: http://www.mwse.edu.pl

Rector: Zenon Muszynski EMail: rektor@mwse.edu.pl

Kanclerz: Zofia Kozioł
EMail: kanclerz@mwse.edu.pl; koziolz@mwse.edu.pl

International Relations: Agnieska Huszno, International Relations Officer EMail: ahuszno@mwse.edu.pl

Faculties

Management and Tourism (Accountancy; Computer Networks; Computer Science; Engineering Management; Finance; Hotel and Restaurant; Hotel Management; Information Technology; Insurance; Leisure Studies; Management; Marketing; Physical Education; Public Administration; Real Estate; Sports; Tourism); **Social Sciences** (Economics; Educational Sciences; English; European Studies; French; German; Italian; Management; Modern Languages; Pedagogy; Preschool Education; Public Administration; Russian; Social Sciences; Spanish)

Programmes

Postgraduate Studies (Accountancy; Business Administration; Education; Educational Administration; Finance; International Business; Management; Real Estate; Speech Therapy and Audiology; Tourism)

History: Founded 1995.

Governing Bodies: Senate

Academic Year: October-July

Admission Requirements: Secondary school certificate (matura) and interview

Fees: (New Złoty): Full-time students, c. 4,000 per annum; part-time students, c. 2,500

Main Language(s) of Instruction: Polish, English

International Co-operation: With universities in Turkey, Spain, Czech Republic, Denmark, Portugal. Participates in the Erasmus programme.

Accrediting Agencies: Ministry of Science and Higher Education

Degrees and Diplomas: *Licencjat*; *Świadectwo ukończenia studiów podyplomowych*; *Magister*. Also Certificates and Licenses.

Student Services: Canteen, Cultural centre, Health services, Language programs, Nursery care, Sports facilities

Student Residential Facilities: Yes

Libraries: c. 22,500 vols

Publications: MWSE Periodicals, Thematic Division: Transformation processes, Finance, Marketing

Last Updated: 20/09/11

MANAGEMENT COLLEGE, SZCZECIN

Wyższa Szkoła Zarządzania w Szczecinie (WSZ)
ul. Dworcowa 20a, 70-900 Szczecin, zachodniopomorskie
Tel: +48(91) 812-80-18
Fax: +48(91) 812-80-18
EMail: rektorat@wsz.szczecin.pl; dziekanat@wsz.szczecin.pl
Website: http://www.wsz.szczecin.pl

Rektor: Adam Rudawski

Dean: Cezary Pawlowski

Departments

Postgraduate Studies (Business Administration; Finance; Human Resources; Management; Marketing; Public Relations)

Faculties

Human Resource Management (Human Resources); **Management and Real Estate Management** (Management; Real Estate); **Marketing, Trade and Services** (Business Administration; Marketing; Service Trades); **Media Management** (Management; Media Studies)

History: Founded 1999.

Governing Bodies: Senate

Admission Requirements: Secondary school certificate (matura)

Fees: (New Złoty): 295 per month

Main Language(s) of Instruction: Polish

Accrediting Agencies: Ministry of Science and Higher Education; National Accreditation Commission

Degrees and Diplomas: *Licencjat*; *Świadectwo ukończenia studiów podyplomowych*

Last Updated: 25/10/11

MARIA SKLODOWSKA-CURIE HIGHER SCHOOL, WARSAW

Uczelnia Warszawska im. Marii Sklodowskiej-Curie (WSDG)
ul. Łabiszyńska 25, 03-204 Warszawa, mazowieckie
Tel: +48(22) 675-88-65
Fax: +48(22) 675-88-66
EMail: informacja@uczelniawarszawska.pl; jolanta.podgrudna@uczelniawarszawska.pl
Website: http://www.uczelniawarszawska.pl

Rektor: Irenusz Michałków (2008-)
Tel: +48(22) 814-35-07, Fax: +48(22) 814-54-41
EMail: rektor@uczelniawarszawska.pl

Pro-Rector: Barbara Smuk

Programmes

Architecture (Architecture); **Computer Science** (Computer Science); **Economics** (Accountancy; Banking; Business Administration; Economics; Finance; Human Resources; Insurance; International Business; International Economics; International Relations; Management; Real Estate; Transport and Communications; Transport Management); **Education** (Child Care and Development; Education; Pedagogy; Preschool Education; Primary Education); **Geodesy and Cartography** (Earth Sciences; Information Sciences; Surveying and Mapping); **Nursing** (Nursing); **Postgraduate Studies** (Accountancy; Human Resources; Leisure

Studies; Management; Pedagogy; Tourism; Vocational Counselling); **Public Health** (Food Science; Health Administration; Health Education; Nutrition; Public Health); **Tourism and Recreation** (Business Administration; Hotel and Restaurant; Leisure Studies; Parks and Recreation; Tourism)

History: Founded 1997.

Governing Bodies: Senate

Admission Requirements: Secondary school certificate (matura)

Fees: (New Złoty): 1,300-2,000 per semester.

Main Language(s) of Instruction: Polish

Accrediting Agencies: Ministry of Science and Higher Education

Degrees and Diplomas: *Inżynier*; *Licencjat*; *Świadectwo ukończenia studiów podyplomowych*; *Magister*

Last Updated: 28/09/11

MASURIAN ACADEMY, OLECKO

Wszechnica Mazurska w Olecku - Wyższa Szkoła na Mazurach Olecko (WM)

pl. Plac Zamkowy 5, 19-400 Olecko, warmińsko-mazurskie
Tel: +48(87) 520-36-44 +48(87) 520-31-33
Fax: +48(87) 520-36-44
EMail: wm@wm.olecko.pl
Website: http://www.wm.olecko.pl

Rektor: Józef Krajewski (1992-) EMail: rektorat@wm.olecko.pl

International Relations: Marzena Łaskowska, International Relations Officer
Tel: +48(87) 520-31-33, Fax: +48(87) 520-36-44
EMail: marzenal@wm.olecko.pl

Faculties

Administration (Administration; Protective Services); **Pedagogy** (Child Care and Development; Media Studies; Pedagogy; Preschool Education; Social Work; Teacher Training); **Physical Education** (Environmental Management; Environmental Studies; Physical Education; Tourism); **Postgraduate Studies** (Child Care and Development; Environmental Engineering; Environmental Studies; Management; Occupational Health; Pedagogy; Physical Education; Physical Therapy; Preschool Education; Public Administration; Rehabilitation and Therapy; Safety Engineering; Social Work; Speech Therapy and Audiology; Sports)

History: Founded 1992.

Governing Bodies: Senate

Admission Requirements: Secondary school certificate (matura)

Main Language(s) of Instruction: Polish

Accrediting Agencies: Ministry of Science and Higher Education

Degrees and Diplomas: *Licencjat*; *Świadectwo ukończenia studiów podyplomowych*; *Magister*

Last Updated: 04/10/11

MAZOVIAN HIGHER SCHOOL OF HUMANITIES AND PEDAGOGICS, ŁOWICZ

Mazowiecka Wyższa Szkoła Humanistyczno-Pedagogiczna w Łowiczu (MWSHP)

ul. Akademicka 1/3, 99-400 Łowicz, łódzkie
Tel: +48(46) 837-43-78
Fax: +48(46) 837-43-92
EMail: sekretariat@mwshp.lowicz.pl
Website: http://www.mwshp.lowicz.pl

Rektor: Wiesław Balcerak (1993-)
Tel: +48(46) 837-43-78, Fax: +48(46) 837-43-92 Ext. 60

Dyrektor Administracyjny: Tadeusz Żaczek
Tel: +48(46) 837-75-76

International Relations: Zbigniew Tomkowski, Prorektor

Faculties

Humanities (Archiving; Arts and Humanities; Comparative Literature; Contemporary History; English; History; Information Management; Italian; Journalism; Literature; Mass Communication; Medieval Studies; Modern History; Philology; Polish; Russian; Social Studies; Speech Therapy and Audiology); **Management and Marketing** (Accountancy; Business Administration; Economics; Finance; Government; Information Management; Management; Marketing); **Pedagogy** (Child Care and Development; Education; Pedagogy; Preschool Education; Primary Education; Protective Services; Rehabilitation and Therapy; Social Work; Vocational Counselling)

Programmes

Postgraduate Studies (Archiving; Business Education; Child Care and Development; Education; Educational Administration; Educational and Student Counselling; History; Information Management; Management; Pedagogy; Preschool Education; Vocational Education)

History: Founded 1993, acquired present status and title 1994.

Governing Bodies: Senate

Admission Requirements: Secondary school certificate (matura) and entrance examinations

Fees: (New Złoty): Undergraduate programmes, 350-370; Postgraduate programmes: 3,200.

Main Language(s) of Instruction: Polish

Accrediting Agencies: Ministry of Science and Higher Education

Degrees and Diplomas: *Licencjat*; *Świadectwo ukończenia studiów podyplomowych*; *Magister*

Student Residential Facilities: 2 Hostels

Special Facilities: Conference Centre

Publications: Masovia Mater, Publication about life at the university and in the region *(biweekly)*; Punjab Studies in the Humanities, Scientific periodical

Last Updated: 20/09/11

MEDICAL HIGHER SCHOOL OF SILESIA IN KATOWICE

Śląska Wyższa Szkoła Medyczna w Katowicach (SWSM)

ul. Mickiewicza 29, 40-085 Katowice (centrum miasta), śląskie
Tel: +48(32) 207-27-00
Fax: +48(32) 207-27-05
EMail: info@swsm.pl
Website: http://www.swsm.pl/

Departments

Postgraduate Studies (Cosmetology; Podiatry)

Programmes

Cosmetology (Cosmetology); **Dietetics** (Dietetics)

History: Founded 2008.

Governing Bodies: Senate

Main Language(s) of Instruction: Polish

Degrees and Diplomas: *Licencjat*; *Świadectwo ukończenia studiów podyplomowych*

Last Updated: 17/10/11

MEDICAL HIGHER SCHOOL, SOSNOWIEC

Wyższa Szkoła Medyczna w Sosnowcu

ul. Wojska Polskiego 6, 41-200 Sosnowiec, śląskie
Tel: +48(32) 291-10-19
Fax: +48(32) 263-40-13 Ext. 219
EMail: wsm.sosnowiec@op.pl
Website: http://www.wsm.sosnowiec.pl/

Rektor: Adam Sipinski

Kanclerz: Danuta Obcowska

Departments

Postgraduate Studies (Family Studies; Gender Studies; Health Administration; Health Sciences; Rehabilitation and Therapy)

Faculties

Health Sciences and Recreation (Arts and Humanities; Gynaecology and Obstetrics; Health Sciences; Hotel Management; Leisure Studies; Medicine; Nursing; Rehabilitation and Therapy; Social Sciences; Tourism)

History: Founded 2007.

Main Language(s) of Instruction: Polish

Accrediting Agencies: Ministry of Science and Higher Education

Degrees and Diplomas: *Licencjat*; *Świadectwo ukończenia studiów podyplomowych*
Last Updated: 21/10/11

MIECZYSLAW ORLOWICZ COLLEGE OF TOURISM AND RECREATION, WARSAW

Wyższa Szkoła Turystyki i Rekreacji im. Mieczysława Orłowicza w Warszawie (WSTIR)
ul. Stokłosy 3, 02-787 Warszawa, mazowieckie
Tel: +48(22) 457-23-86
Fax: +48(22) 834-57-14
EMail: wstir@wstir.edu.pl
Website: http://www.wstir.edu.pl

Rektor: Aleksander Ronikier (1995-) Tel: +48(22) 834-57-14

Kanclerz: Zbigniew Glapa

Departments
Postgraduate Studies (Sports Management)

Faculties
Tourism and Recreation (Air Transport; Hotel and Restaurant; Leisure Studies; Parks and Recreation; Sports; Sports Management; Tourism; Transport and Communications)

History: Founded 1995.

Governing Bodies: Senate

Admission Requirements: Secondary school certificate (Matura)

Fees: (New Złoty): Ful-time programmes, 2,300 per semester; Part-time programmes, 1,600-2,050 per semester.

Main Language(s) of Instruction: Polish

Accrediting Agencies: Ministry of Science and Higher Education

Degrees and Diplomas: *Licencjat*; *Świadectwo ukończenia studiów podyplomowych*
Last Updated: 24/10/11

MIESZKO I COLLEGE OF EDUCATION AND ADMINISTRATION, POZNAŃ

Wyższa Szkoła Pedagogiki i Administracji im. Mieszka I w Poznaniu (WSPIA)
ul. 28 Czerwca 1956 r. 213-215, 61-485 Poznań, wielkopolskie
Tel: +48(61) 832-11-79
EMail: kontakt@wspia.pl; rekrutacja@wspia.pl
Website: http://www.wspia.pl

Rektor: Jerzy Matynia
Tel: +48(61) 835-06-78, Fax: +48(61) 835-06-78

Kanclerz: Janusz Musial

Departments
Postgraduate Studies (Administration; Art Education; Art Therapy; Cultural Studies; Education; Educational Sciences; Health Education; Heritage Preservation; Human Resources; Journalism; Protective Services; Public Relations; Rehabilitation and Therapy; Secretarial Studies; Social Studies; Sports; Sports Management)

Faculties
Administration (Administration; Economics; European Union Law; Public Administration); **Cosmetology** (Cosmetology); **International Relations** (International Relations); **Law** (Law); **Medical Emergency Rescue** (Medicine); **Pedagogy** (Education; Leisure Studies; Pedagogy; Physical Education; Preschool Education; Primary Education; Public Relations; Rehabilitation and Therapy; Social Work; Vocational Counselling); **Philology** (English; German; Philology); **Physical Education** (Physical Education); **Physiotherapy** (Gerontology; Physical Therapy; Rehabilitation and Therapy); **Technical and IT Education** (Educational Technology; Technology Education)

International Co-operation: Participates in the Erasmus Programme

Degrees and Diplomas: *Inżynier*; *Licencjat*; *Świadectwo ukończenia studiów podyplomowych*; *Magister*

Special Facilities: Specialist laboratories and studios; Computer rooms

Libraries: Yes
Last Updated: 23/10/11

NON-PUBLIC HIGHER SCHOOL OF MEDICINE, WROCŁAW

Niepubliczna Wyższa Szkoła Medyczna (NWSM)
ul. Nowowiejska 69, 50-340 Wrocław, dolnośląskie
Tel: +48(71) 322-15-48 +48(71) 786-83-28
Fax: +48(71) 786-83-28
EMail: dziekanat@nwsm.pl
Website: http://www.nwsm.pl

Rektor: Aleksander Koll

Kanclerz: Bartosz Zywirski

Departments
Postgraduate Studies (Cosmetology; Podiatry; Sports)

Faculties
Cosmetology (Cosmetology); **Dietetics** (Dietetics); **Emergency Medical Services** (Health Sciences; Medical Auxiliaries; Medicine); **Public Health** (Public Health)

History: Founded 2006. Formerly known as Niepubliczna Wyższa Szkoła Kosmetyczna (Non-Public Higher School of Cosmetology in Wrocław).

Fees: (New Złoty): Undergraduate studies, 4,500-6,720; Postgraduate studies, 2,400-4,000 per semester

Main Language(s) of Instruction: Polish

Accrediting Agencies: Minister of Science and Higher Education

Degrees and Diplomas: *Licencjat*; *Świadectwo ukończenia studiów podyplomowych*
Last Updated: 25/10/11

NON-STATE HIGHER PEDAGOGICAL SCHOOL, BIAŁYSTOK

Niepaństwowa Wyższa Szkoła Pedagogiczna w Białymstoku (NWSP)
ul. Jana Pawła II, 15-703 Białystok, podlaskie
Tel: +48(85) 742-01-99
Fax: +48(85) 744-26-00
EMail: nwsp@nwsp.bialystok.pl
Website: http://www.nwsp.bialystok.pl

Rektor: Marek Jasiński
Tel: +48(85) 742-01-99 Ext. 11,12,13
EMail: rektorat@nwsp.bialystok.pl

Programmes
Internal security (Peace and Disarmament; Protective Services); **Pedagogy** (Child Care and Development; Graphic Design; Health Education; Pedagogy; Preschool Education; Rehabilitation and Therapy; Social Work); **Postgraduate studies** (Family Studies; Higher Education; Human Resources; Management; Pedagogy; Preschool Education; Primary Education; Psychology; Teacher Training); **Psychology** (Clinical Psychology); **Social Work** (Social Work)

History: Founded 1996.

Governing Bodies: Senate

Admission Requirements: Secondary school certificate (matura)

Fees: (New Zoty): 2,400-3,000 per annum. Postgraduate programmes, 1,600 for 3 semesters.

Main Language(s) of Instruction: Polish

Accrediting Agencies: State Accreditation Commission and the Ministry of National Education Ministry

Degrees and Diplomas: *Licencjat*; *Świadectwo ukończenia studiów podyplomowych*; *Magister*
Last Updated: 20/09/11

OECONOMICUS VOCATIONAL HIGHER SCHOOL, SZCZECIN

Wyższa Szkoła Zawodowa 'Oeconomicus' (WSZ)
plac Jana Kilińskiego 3, 71-414 Szczecin, zachodniopomorskie
Tel: +48(91) 455-34-55
Fax: +48(91) 455-34-71
EMail: rektorat@pte.szczecin.pl
Website: http://www.oe.edu.pl

Rektor: Katarzyna Szumilas

Prorektor: Katarzyna Dadańska

Departments

Postgraduate Studies (Art Education; Art Therapy; Business Education; Communication Arts; Cultural Studies; Education; Educational Administration; Educational and Student Counselling; Health Education; Health Sciences; Labour Law; Management; Marketing; Pedagogy; Preschool Education; Real Estate; Safety Engineering; Vocational Counselling)

Faculties

Economics (Communication Arts; Economics; Hotel and Restaurant; Information Management; Management; Marketing; Occupational Health; Real Estate; Safety Engineering; Tourism); **Education** (Art Criticism; Art Education; Art Therapy; Communication Arts; Education; Health Education; Pedagogy; Preschool Education; Rehabilitation and Therapy; Social and Preventive Medicine; Special Education; Teacher Training)

History: Founded 1999.

Governing Bodies: Senate

Admission Requirements: Secondary school certificate (matura)

Main Language(s) of Instruction: Polish

Accrediting Agencies: Ministry of Science and Higher Education

Degrees and Diplomas: *Licencjat*; *Świadectwo ukończenia studiów podyplomowych*

Libraries: 4,000 vols

Last Updated: 25/10/11

PAWEL WLODKOWIC UNIVERSITY COLLEGE, PŁOCK

Szkoła Wyższa im. Pawła Włodkowica (SWPW)

Al. Kilińskiego 12, budynek A, pokój nr 1, 09-402 Płock, mazowieckie

Tel: +48(24) 366-41-00 +48(24) 366-41-50

Fax: +48(24) 366-41-64

EMail: rekrutacja@wlodkowic.pl; kanclerz@wlodkowic.pl

Website: http://www.wlodkowic.pl

Rektor: Zbigniew Paweł Kruszewski EMail: rektor@wlodkowic.pl

Departments

Administration (Administration; Government); **Computer Science** (Business Computing; Computer Engineering; Computer Graphics; Computer Networks; Computer Science; Data Processing; Engineering; Software Engineering); **Education** (Child Care and Development; Education; Health Education; Pedagogy; Preschool Education; Primary Education); **European studies** (European Studies); **Health and safety** (Health Sciences; Safety Engineering); **Homeland Security** (Protective Services); **Management** (Accountancy; Business Administration; Environmental Management; Finance; Human Resources; Management; Marketing; Real Estate; Small Business); **Nursing** (Nursing); **Physical Education** (Physical Education); **Political Sciences** (Communication Studies; Marketing; Media Studies; Political Sciences; Public Relations); **Social Work** (Social Work)

History: Founded 1992, acquired present status and title 1995.

Governing Bodies: Senate

Academic Year: October - June, February - January

Admission Requirements: Secondary school certificate (Matura)

Fees: (New Złoty): fees 3,000 - 4,000

Main Language(s) of Instruction: Polish

International Co-operation: With institutions in Russia, Lithuania, Germany, the Netherlands, Greece, Italy, Spain, the United States and New Zealand. Paricipate in the Socrates - Erasmus and Leonardo da Vinci programmes.

Accrediting Agencies: Ministry of Science and Higher Education

Degrees and Diplomas: *Inżynier*, *Licencjat*; *Świadectwo ukończenia studiów podyplomowych*; *Magister*

Student Services: Academic counselling, Employment services, Handicapped facilities, Language programs, Sports facilities

Student Residential Facilities: Yes

Libraries: yes

Press or Publishing House: NOVUM

Academic Staff *2010-2011*: Total 450

STAFF WITH DOCTORATE: Total 160

Last Updated: 27/09/11

PEDAGOGICAL ACADEMY, LODZ

Wyższa Szkoła Pedagogiczna w Łodzi (WSP)

ul. Żeromskiego 115, 90-542 Łódź, łódzkie

Tel: +48(42) 630-30-72

Fax: +48(42) 630-30-72

EMail: sekretariat@wsp.lodz.pl

Website: http://www.wsp.lodz.pl

Rektor: Leszek Cezary Szymanski EMail: rektor@wsp.lodz.pl

Chancellor: Malgorzata Cyperling

Departments

Pedagogy (Pedagogy); **Sociology** (Sociology); **Special Education** (Special Education)

History: Founded 2003.

Degrees and Diplomas: *Licencjat*; *Magister*. Pedagogy

Last Updated: 29/08/11

PEDAGOGIUM - HIGHER SCHOOL OF PEDAGOGY AND SOCIAL EDUCATION, WARSAW

Pedagogium - Wyższa Szkoła Pedagogiki Resocjalizacyjnej w Warszawie

ul. Marszałkowska 115, 00-102 Warszawa, mazowieckie

Tel: +48(22) 620-76-54

Fax: +48(22) 620-76-58

EMail: rektorat@pedagogium.edu.pl

Website: http://www.pedagogium.edu.pl

Rector: Marek Konopczyński

Kanclerz: Jacek Budner

Departments

Criminology and Penitentiary Education (Criminology; Forensic Medicine and Dentistry; Human Resources; Law; Sports); **Defense Education and Public Safety** (Civil Security; Protective Services); **Education Rehabilitation** (Art Therapy; Education; Rehabilitation and Therapy; Toxicology); **Education to Information** (Computer Science; Education; Information Sciences); **Foreign Languages** (English; German; Modern Languages; Russian); **Foundations of Education** (Adult Education; Education; Educational Sciences; Information Technology; Pedagogy); **Philosophy and Sociology** (Anthropology; Ethics; Logic; Philosophy; Sociology); **Psychology** (Clinical Psychology; Psychology; Psychotherapy; Social Psychology); **Social Pedagogy and Social Work** (Education; Environmental Studies; Health Education; Social Policy; Social Work)

Programmes

Postgraduate Studies (Art Therapy; Child Care and Development; Gerontology; Pedagogy; Psychology; Rehabilitation and Therapy; Social Work)

History: Founded 2004.

Fees: (New Złoty): 1,600-2,500 per semster

Main Language(s) of Instruction: Polish

Degrees and Diplomas: *Licencjat*; *Świadectwo ukończenia studiów podyplomowych*; *Magister*

Last Updated: 21/09/11

PHILOLOGICAL SCHOOL OF HIGHER EDUCATION

Wyższa Szkoła Filologiczna we Wrocławiu (WSF)

ul. Sienkiewicza 32, 50-335 Wrocław, dolnośląskie

Tel: +48(71) 328-14-14

Fax: +48(71) 322-10-06

EMail: wsf@wsf.edu.pl

Website: http://www.wsf.edu.pl

Rector: Zdzisław Wąsik (2002-) EMail: z.wasik@wsf.edu.pl

Chancellor: Ryszard Opala EMail: r.opala@wsf.edu.pl

International Relations: Anna Zaslona, Erasmus Institutional Coordinator Tel: +48(71) 395-84-73 EMail: a.zaslona@wsf.edu.pl

Programmes

American Studies (American Studies; Communication Studies; Cultural Studies; English; Information Technology); **English** *(Graduate)* (English); **English Philology** (Business Administration; Communication Studies; Cultural Studies; English; English Studies; Foreign Languages Education; Information Technology; Philology; Tourism; Translation and Interpretation); **German** *(Graduate)* (German); **German Philology** (Business Administration; Communication Studies; Cultural Studies; Foreign Languages Education; German; Germanic Studies; Information Technology; Philology; Tourism; Translation and Interpretation); **Graduate Studies** (English; German); **Italian Philology** (Business Administration; Communication Studies; Cultural Studies; Foreign Languages Education; Information Technology; Italian; Philology; Tourism); **Language** (Business Administration; Communication Studies; Cultural Studies; Foreign Languages Education; Information Technology; Modern Languages; Tourism; Translation and Interpretation); **Spanish** *(Graduate)* (Spanish); **Spanish Philology** (Business Administration; Communication Studies; Cultural Studies; Foreign Languages Education; Information Technology; Philology; Spanish; Tourism)

History: Founded 2005.

Fees: (New Złoty): 2,475-2,950 per semester

Main Language(s) of Instruction: Polish

International Co-operation: Participates in the Erasmus programme.

Accrediting Agencies: State Accreditation Committee

Degrees and Diplomas: *Licencjat*; *Magister*

Academic Staff *2010-2011*: Total 57

Last Updated: 05/10/11

PIŁA ACADEMY OF BUSINESS

Wyższa Szkoła Biznesu w Pile (WSB)

al. Niepodległości 2, 64-920 Piła, wielkopolskie

Tel: +48(67) 212-73-10

Fax: +48(67) 212-49-72

EMail: wsb@wsb.pila.pl

Website: http://www.wsb.pila.pl

Rektor: Włodzimierz Okrasa (2008-)

Kanclerz: Urszula Nowak-Roznowska

International Relations: Sylwia Sysko-Romanczuk

Departments

Postgraduate Studies (Accountancy; Administration; Environmental Management; Finance; Hotel and Restaurant; Human Resources; Law; Management; Real Estate; Safety Engineering; Small Business; Tourism; Transport Management)

Faculties

Administration (Administration; Environmental Studies; Finance; Information Technology; Justice Administration; Protective Services; Public Administration; Real Estate; Safety Engineering; Taxation); **Management** (Business Computing; Finance; Human Resources; Management; Psychology; Safety Engineering; Tourism; Transport Management)

History: Founded 1996.

Governing Bodies: Senate

Admission Requirements: Secondary school certificate (matura)

Main Language(s) of Instruction: Polish

International Co-operation: With universities in the Erasmus programme. Participates in the Erasmus programme.

Accrediting Agencies: Ministry of Science and Higher Education

Degrees and Diplomas: *Licencjat*; *Świadectwo ukończenia studiów podyplomowych*; *Magister*

Last Updated: 20/10/11

POLISH-CZECH HIGHER SCHOOL OF BUSINESS AND SPORT - GLACENSE COLLEGIUM, NOWA RUDA

Polsko-Czeska Wyższa Szkoła Biznesu i Sportu "Collegium Glacense" w Nowej Rudzie

ul. Kłodzka 16, 57-402 Nowa Ruda, dolnośląskie

Tel: +48(74) 872-65-65

Fax: +48(74) 872-60-10

EMail: dziekanat@cg.edu.pl

Website: http://www.cg.edu.pl

Rektor: Andrzej Hordyj
Tel: +48(74) 872-66-03 EMail: rektor@cg.edu.pl

Kanclerz: Adam Wegrzyn
Tel: +48(74) 872-81-66 EMail: kanclerz@cg.edu.pl

Departments

Postgraduate Studies (Educational Administration; Government; Management; Modern Languages; Physical Education; Physical Therapy; Small Business)

Faculties

Management (Government; International Business; Management; Production Engineering); **Nursing** (Nursing); **Physical Education** (Physical Education; Sports)

History: Founded 2004.

Main Language(s) of Instruction: Polish

Degrees and Diplomas: *Licencjat*; *Świadectwo ukończenia studiów podyplomowych*

Last Updated: 18/10/11

POLISH-JAPANESE INSTITUTE OF INFORMATION TECHNOLOGY, WARSAW

Polsko-Japońska Wyższa Szkoła Technik Komputerowych, Warsaw (PJWSTK)

ul. Koszykowa 86, 02-008 Warszawa, mazowieckie

Tel: +48(22) 584-45-00

Fax: +48(22) 584-45-01

EMail: pjwstk@pjwstk.edu.pl

Website: http://www.pjwstk.edu.pl

Rector: Jerzy Paweł Nowacki (1994-)

International Relations: Ida Jokisz, Deputy President for International Relations
Tel: +48(22) 584-45-44, Fax: +48(22) 584-45-44
EMail: ida@pjwstk.edu.pl

Programmes

Information Management (Banking; Information Management; International Business; Public Administration); **Information Technology** (Computer Networks; Data Processing; Information Technology; Multimedia; Robotics; Software Engineering); **Interior Design** (Graphic Arts; Interior Design); **Japanese Culture** (Cultural Studies; Japanese); **New Media Art** (Computer Graphics; Visual Arts); **Social Informatics** (Computer Science)

History: Founded 1994, acquired present status 1998.

Governing Bodies: Senate

Academic Year: October to June

Admission Requirements: Secondary school certificate (matura) and entrance examinations (if applicable)

Fees: (New złoty/PNL): Studies in Polish, 1,080 per month; Studies in English, 1,280 per month

Main Language(s) of Instruction: Polish; English

International Co-operation: With universities in United Kingdom, Japan, USA, Italy, Ireland, Finland, Spain, Vietnam, Ukraine, Luxembourg, Canada, Germany. Also participates in the LLP Erasmus programme.

Accrediting Agencies: Ministry of Science and Higher Education

Degrees and Diplomas: *Inżynier*, *Licencjat*; *Magister (M.Sc.)*; *Doktor (PhD)*. Also Postgraduate diplomas and Professional diplomas.

Student Services: Canteen, Foreign student adviser, Handicapped facilities, Language programs

Special Facilities: Career Counselling Office

Libraries: Library, 12,200 vols

Press or Publishing House: Publishing House: Wydawnictwo PJWSTK

Last Updated: 25/08/11

POLONIA UNIVERSITY IN CZĘSTOCHOWA

Akademia Polonijna w Częstochowie (AP)
ul. Pułaskiego 4/6, 42-200 Częstochowa, śląskie
Tel: +48(34) 368-42-00 +48(34) 368-42-01
Fax: +48(34) 324-96-62
EMail: ap@ap.edu.pl
Website: http://www.ap.edu.pl

Rector: Stanisław Łupiński (2009-)
Tel: +48(34) 368-42-01 +48(34) 368-42-70,
Fax: +48(34) 324-96-62
EMail: rector@ap.edu.pl; sekretariat@ap.edu.pl

Kanclerz: Olga Kacprzak
Tel: +48(34) 368-09-21, Fax: +48(34) 324-96-62
EMail: kanclerz@ap.edu.pl

International Relations: Andrzej Kryński, Vice-Rector for International Affairs Tel: +48(34) 368-42-01 EMail: sec@ap.edu.pl

Centres

Ethics *(European)* (Christian Religious Studies; Ethics; History; Logic; Philosophy); **European Information** *(Regional)* (Administration; Business Administration; Economics; Philology); **Research and Projects**; **Scholar and Teacher** (Art Education; Child Care and Development; Information Technology; Management; Pedagogy; Science Education; Teacher Training)

Departments

International Cooperation (Modern Languages; Polish)

Faculties

Health Sciences (Biotechnology; Health Sciences; Nursing); **Interdisciplinary Studies** (Administration; Arts and Humanities; Business Administration; Distance Education; Economics; English; Ethics; Foreign Languages Education; International Relations; Philology; Polish; Translation and Interpretation)

Institutes

Thomas More (International Relations; Literature; Political Sciences)

Programmes

Postgraduate Studies (Administration; Criminal Law; Economics; Educational Administration; English; European Union Law; Foreign Languages Education; Health Administration; Human Resources; Insurance; Labour and Industrial Relations; Law; Management; Pedagogy; Philology; Polish; Protective Services; Public Law; Translation and Interpretation)

Schools

Diplomacy *(Polonia)* (International Relations); **Polish Language and Culture** (Cultural Studies; Polish); **Translators** *(European)* (Translation and Interpretation)

Further Information: Also Third Age University.

History: Founded 1992 as University of Foreign Languages and Economics. Acquired present name and status 2001.

Governing Bodies: Supervisory Board

Academic Year: September to July

Admission Requirements: General Certificate of Secondary School Education (Matura)

Fees: (New Złoty): 1,600-3,000 per semester.

Main Language(s) of Instruction: Polish

International Co-operation: With universities in Europe, North and South America, Asia, Australia. Also participates in Socrates-Erasmus; Erasmus Mundus; Leonardo da Vinci; Phare Ace; Jean Monnet; Socrates-Lingua, and Socrates-Minerva Programme

Accrediting Agencies: Ministry of Science and Higher Education

Degrees and Diplomas: *Licencjat*; *Świadectwo ukończenia studiów podyplomowych*; *Magister*

Student Services: Canteen, Cultural centre, Foreign student adviser, Foreign Studies Centre, Handicapped facilities, Language programs, Nursery care, Sports facilities

Special Facilities: Museum; Art Gallery; Observatory; Movie Studio

Libraries: Library in EIFLE Direct (Electronic Information for Libraries). 4,500 periodicals.

Publications: Glos Akademii (Academy Voice) *(monthly)*; Obserwator *(monthly)*; Poland in Europe *(1-2 per annum)*; Research periodicals on Thomas More; Research publications of respective departments *(biennially)*; Teacher-Work-Experience *(annually)*

Press or Publishing House: EDUCATOR

Last Updated: 07/09/11

POMERANIA GENERAL HIGHER SCHOOL OF HUMANITIES, CHOJNICE

Powszechna Wyższa Szkoła Humanistyczna "Pomerania" w Chojnicach (PWSH "POMERANIA")
ul. Świętopełka 10, 89-620 Chojnice, pomorskie
Tel: +48(52) 334-28-87
Fax: +48(52) 334-28-87
EMail: kasa-pwsh@pomeraniachojnice.edu.pl; administracja@pomeraniachojnice.edu.pl
Website: http://pomeraniachojnice.edu.pl

Rektor: Janusz Gierszewski
EMail: rektor@pomeraniachojnice.edu.pl

Kanclerz: Mariusz Brunka EMail: dyrektorpwsh@chojnice.edu.pl

Departments

Postgraduate Studies (Administration; Child Care and Development; Cultural Studies; Education; Educational Administration; Government; Pedagogy; Philology; Polish; Preschool Education; Public Administration; Regional Studies; Rehabilitation and Therapy; Safety Engineering; Social Work; Speech Therapy and Audiology)

Faculties

Administration (Administration; Criminal Law; Economics; European Union Law; Finance; Fiscal Law; Government; Protective Services; Public Administration; Taxation); **Education** (Education; Health Education; Pedagogy; Preschool Education; Teacher Training)

History: Founded 2004.

Governing Bodies: Senate

Fees: (New Złoty): 1,800-1,900 per semester; Postgraduate programmes, 1,200-1,400 per semester

Main Language(s) of Instruction: Polish

Degrees and Diplomas: *Licencjat*, *Świadectwo ukończenia studiów podyplomowych*

Last Updated: 18/10/11

POMERANIAN HIGHER SCHOOL OF SOCIAL AND TERRITORIAL POLITICS, STAROGARD GDAŃSKI

Pomorska Wyższa Szkoła w Starogardzie Gdańskim (PSWPSW PWSPSIG)
ul. Kościuszki 112/114, 83-200 Starogard Gdański, pomorskie
Tel: +48(58) 563-00-90
Fax: +48(58) 563-00-90
EMail: info@psw.stg.pl
Website: http://www.psw.stg.pl

Rektor: Zdzisław Kordel (2002-) Tel: +48 603 959 669

Kanclerz: Wojciech Lademann Tel: +48(58) 341-64-17

International Relations: Zdzisław Kordel, Rector

Departments

Postgraduate Studies (Accountancy; Child Care and Development; Education; Educational Administration; Finance; Foreign Languages Education; Management; Marketing; Pedagogy; Political Sciences; Preschool Education; Safety Engineering; Vocational Counselling; Vocational Education)

Programmes

Economy (Accountancy; Banking; Business Administration; Economics; Finance; Human Resources; Management; Marketing); **Education** (Education; Health Education; Physical Education; Rehabilitation and Therapy; Social Work); **Logistics** (Business

Administration; Economics; Information Management; Transport Management); **Political Science** (Political Sciences; Public Administration; Social Problems; Sociology)

History: Founded 2001. Formerly known as Pomorska Wyższa Szkoła Polityki Społecznej i Gospodarczej w Starogardzie Gdańskim.

Governing Bodies: Senate

Admission Requirements: Secondary school certificate (matura)

Fees: (New Złoty): 1,750 per semester

Main Language(s) of Instruction: Polish

Accrediting Agencies: Ministry of Science and Higher Education

Degrees and Diplomas: *Inżynier*, *Licencjat*; *Świadectwo ukończenia studiów podyplomowych*

Last Updated: 18/10/11

POMERANIAN SCHOOL OF HIGHER EDUCATION, GDYNIA

Pomorska Wyższa Szkoła Nauk Stosowanych w Gdyni (PWSH)

ul. Opata Hackiego 8-10, 81-213 Gdynia, pomorskie
Tel: +48(58) 783-97-08
Fax: +48(58) 783-97-18
EMail: pwsh@pwsh.edu.pl
Website: http://www.pwsh.edu.pl

Rektor: Anna Uniszewska
Tel: +48(58) 623-09-22 Ext.101 +48(58) 783-97-01
EMail: rektorat@pwsh.edu.pl

Kanclerz: Justyna Kalota
Tel: +48(58) 623-09-55 Ext.121 +48(58) 783-97-21
EMail: kanclerz@pwsh.edu.pl

International Relations: Anna Uniszewska

Departments

Postgraduate Studies (Art Therapy; Child Care and Development; Cultural Studies; Design; Educational Administration; Fashion Design; Marketing; Pedagogy; Preschool Education; Rehabilitation and Therapy; Speech Therapy and Audiology; Teacher Training)

Faculties

Cultural Studies (Computer Graphics; Cultural Studies; Design; Fashion Design; Marketing; Political Sciences; Public Relations); **Pedagogy** (Foreign Languages Education; Information Sciences; Pedagogy; Preschool Education; Protective Services; Rehabilitation and Therapy; Speech Therapy and Audiology; Teacher Training; Vocational Counselling); **Philology** (Cultural Studies; English; English Studies; German; Italian; Modern Languages; Philology; Spanish)

History: Founded 2001.

Main Language(s) of Instruction: Polish

International Co-operation: Paricipates in the Erasmus programme.

Degrees and Diplomas: *Licencjat*; *Świadectwo ukończenia studiów podyplomowych*

Last Updated: 18/10/11

PONTIFICAL FACULTY OF THEOLOGY, WROCLAW

Papieski Wydział Teologiczny we Wrocławiu (PWT WROC)

ul. Katedralna 9, 50-328 Wrocław, dolnośląskie
Tel: +48(71) 322-99-70
Fax: +48(71) 327-12-01
EMail: sekretarz@pwt.wroc.pl
Website: http://www.pwt.wroc.pl

Great Chancellor: Marian Gołębiewski

Secretary-General: Grzegorz Sokołowski

International Relations: Andrzej Tomko, Vice-Rector
Tel: +48(71) 322-99-70 EMail: pwt@pwt.wroc.pl

Institutes

Christian Philosophy (Christian Religious Studies; Philosophy) *Dyrektor*: Jerzy Machnacz; **Church History** (History of Religion) *Direktor*: Mieczysław Kogut; **Practical Theology** (Theology) *Dyrektor*: Waldemar Irek; **Systematic Theology** (Theology) *Dyrektor*: Piotr Liszka

Programmes

Biblical and Modern Languages (English; French; German; Greek (Classical); Hebrew; Italian; Latin); **Postgraduate Studies** (Bible; Ethics; Family Studies; Journalism; Philosophy; Theology; Tourism)

History: Founded 1968. Acquired present status 1989.

Governing Bodies: Senate

Admission Requirements: Secondary School Certificate (matura)

Main Language(s) of Instruction: Polish

Accrediting Agencies: Ministry of Higher Education

Degrees and Diplomas: *Magister*, *Doktor*

Last Updated: 29/08/11

PONTIFICAL UNIVERSITY OF JOHN PAUL II, CRACOW

Uniwersytet Papieski Jana Pawła II w Krakowie (UPJP2)

ul. Kanonicza 25, 31-002 Kraków, małopolskie
Tel: +48(12) 421-84-16
Fax: +48(12) 421-86-26
EMail: rektorat@pat.krakow.pl
Website: http://upjp2.edu.pl/

Rektor: Władysław Zuziak
Tel: +48(12) 421-84-16, Fax: +48(12) 422-86-26
EMail: rektorat@upjp2.edu.pl

Kanclerz: Andrzej Kopicz
Tel: +48(12) 421-68-48 EMail: atmotyka@cyf-kr.edu.pl

International Relations: Wojciech Życiński, S.J., Vice Rector
Tel: +48 608-29-06-83, Tel: +48 (12) 266-06-50
EMail: zyto@sdb.krakow.pl

Deaneries

Inter-Department of Foreign Languages *(Inter-faculty)* (Arabic; Classical Languages; English; French; German; Italian; Modern Languages; Russian; Slavic Languages; Spanish)

Faculties

Canon Law (Canon Law); **History and Heritage** (Ancient Civilizations; Art History; Heritage Preservation; History; History of Religion; Medieval Studies; Museum Studies; Religious Music); **Philosophy** (Arts and Humanities; Ethics; Logic; Metaphysics; Philosophy; Psycholinguistics; Religion); **Social Sciences** (Education; Family Studies; Journalism; Mass Communication; Media Studies; Psychology; Social Sciences; Social Work; Sociology; Theology); **Theology** (Bible; Religious Practice; Theology); **Theology** *(Tarnów)* (Canon Law; History of Religion; Holy Writings; New Testament; Pastoral Studies; Philosophy; Religious Art; Religious Practice; Social Sciences; Social Work; Theology)

Institutes

Bioethics *(Inter-faculty)* (Ethics); **Church Music** *(Interfaculty)* (Religious Music); **Ecumenism and Dialogue** *(Interfaculty)* (Catholic Theology; Cultural Studies; Jewish Studies; Philosophy); **Inter-Department of Physical Education** *(Inter-faculty)* (Physical Education; Sports)

Research Centres

Interdisciplinary *(Copernicus)* (Astronomy and Space Science; Biology; History; Mathematics; Philosophy; Physics; Theology); **Thought of John Paul II** (Philosophy; Theology)

History: Founded 1397 as Faculty of Theology of Jagiellonian University, removed 1954 by the unilateral edict of the communist Cabinet. Trnasformed into Papieska Akademia Teologiczna w Krakowie (Pontifical Academy of Theology, Cracow) 1981 by decree of the Holy Father. Acquired present status and title 2009.

Governing Bodies: Senate

Admission Requirements: Secondary school certificate (matura) and entrance examinations

Main Language(s) of Instruction: Polish

International Co-operation: With universities in Hungary, Germany, Austria, Slovakia,

Accrediting Agencies: Ministry of Science and Higher Education

Degrees and Diplomas: *Licencjat*; *Świadectwo ukończenia studiów podyplomowych*; *Magister*; *Doktor*

Student Services: Academic counselling, Canteen, Cultural centre, Health services, Nursery care, Social counselling, Sports facilities

Libraries: c. 300,000 vols and 3,000 periodicals

Publications: Annalecta Cracoviensia *(annually)*; Folia Historica Cracoviensia *(annually)*; Logos i Ethos *(biennially)*; Patos, Bulletin; Polonia Sacra *(biennially)*; Vita Academica, Bulletin

Academic Staff *2010-2011*: Total: c. 220

Student Numbers *2010-2011*: Total: c. 3,500

. Also 673 students at Tarnów Branch

Last Updated: 29/09/11

POZNAN COLLEGE OF MODERN LANGUAGES

Wyższa Szkoła Języków Obcych im. Samuela Bogumiła Lindego (WSJO/PCML)

ul. Św. Marcin 59, 61-806 Poznań, wielkopolskie

Tel: +48(61) 663-62-64 +48(61) 663-87-06

Fax: +48(61) 663-62-52

EMail: info@wsjo.pl

Website: http://www.wsjo.pl/

Rector: Hubert Orłowski

Registrar: Cezary M. Pieczyński Tel: +48(61) 663-62-90

International Relations: Raphael Szczukiewicz, Head of the Bureau of International Cooperation
Tel: +48(61) 663-62-13, Fax: +48(61) 663-62-90
EMail: rafal.szczukiewicz@wsjo.pl

Departments

English (Applied Linguistics; English; Foreign Languages Education; Philology; Translation and Interpretation); **European Studies** (European Studies); **German** (Applied Linguistics; Foreign Languages Education; German; Philology; Translation and Interpretation); **Physical Education** (Physical Education); **Romance Languages** (Applied Linguistics; Foreign Languages Education; French; Philology; Romance Languages; Translation and Interpretation); **Spanish** (Foreign Languages Education; Philology; Spanish; Translation and Interpretation)

Programmes

Business (Business Administration); **Chinese** (Asian Studies; Chinese); **Japanese** (Asian Studies; Japanese)

Main Language(s) of Instruction: Polish

International Co-operation: With universities in Germany, UK, Ireland, Spain and Turkey. Participates in the Socrates-Erasmus Programme.

Degrees and Diplomas: *Licencjat*; *Świadectwo ukończenia studiów podyplomowych*; *Magister*

Academic Staff *2010-2011*: Total 300

STAFF WITH DOCTORATE: Total 99

Student Numbers *2010-2011*: Total: c. 3,500

Last Updated: 07/10/11

POZNAŃ SCHOOL OF BANKING

Wyższa Szkoła Bankowa w Poznaniu (WSB)

al. Niepodległości 2, 61-874 Poznań, wielkopolskie

Tel: +48(61) 655-33-30

Fax: +48(61) 655-32-27

EMail: info@wsb.poznan.pl

Website: http://www.wsb.poznan.pl

Rector: Beata Filipiak (2010-)
Tel: +48(61) 655-33-78, Fax: +48(61) 855-33-71
EMail: Wladyslaw.Balicki@wsb.poznan.pl

Executive Director: Andrzej Janiak
Tel: +48(61) 655-32-29, Fax: +48(61) 655-32-27
EMail: Janiak@wsb.poznan.pl

International Relations: Joanna Małecka, International Relations Officer
Tel: +48(61) 655-33-91, Fax: +48(61) 655-33-69
EMail: joanna.malecka@wsb.poznan.pl

Campuses

Chorzow (Accountancy; Banking; Business Computing; Computer Graphics; Computer Networks; Computer Science; Data Processing; Econometrics; Finance; Government; Human Resources; Information Technology; International Business; International Relations; Marketing; Mass Communication; Media Studies; Multimedia; Political Sciences; Psychology; Real Estate; Safety Engineering; Sales Techniques; Social Work; Taxation; Tourism; Transport Management)

Faculties

Economics *(Szczecin)* (Accountancy; Banking; Business Computing; Economics; Finance; Human Resources; Management; Marketing; Psychology; Public Administration; Small Business; Taxation; Tourism; Transport Engineering); **Finance and Banking** (Accountancy; Administration; Banking; Business Computing; Computer Science; Econometrics; Economics; English; Finance; Government; International Relations; Management; Marketing; Modern Languages; Physical Education; Taxation)

Further Information: Chorzów

History: Founded 1994.

Governing Bodies: Senate

Admission Requirements: Secondary school certificate (matura)

Main Language(s) of Instruction: Polish

Accrediting Agencies: Ministry of Science and Higher Education

Degrees and Diplomas: *Inżynier*; *Licencjat*; *Świadectwo ukończenia studiów podyplomowych*; *Magister*. Executive MBA

Last Updated: 04/10/11

POZNAN SCHOOL OF COMMERCE AND ACCOUNTING

Wyższa Szkoła Handlu i Rachunkowości (WSZHIR)

ul. 27 Grudnia 7, 61-737 Poznań, wielkopolskie

Tel: +48(61) 864-10-40

Fax: +48(61) 864-10-40

EMail: wshir@wshir.pl

Website: http://www.wshir.pl

Rektor: Maria Chromińska
Tel: +48(61) 866-12-62, Fax: +48(61) 866-12-62
EMail: rektor@wshir.pl

Kanclerz: Janusz Czerny Fax: +48(61) 864-10-40
EMail: kanclerz@wshir.poznan.pl

International Relations: Magdalena Musiał, Chancellor's Assistant (2002-) EMail: magdam@wshir.poznan.pl

Departments

Postgraduate Studies (Accountancy; Administration; Finance; Government; Human Resources; Landscape Architecture; Protective Services; Public Administration; Public Relations; Safety Engineering; Taxation)

Faculties

Accounting (Accountancy; Finance; Health Administration); **Economics** (Business Computing; E-Business/Commerce; Economics; Information Management; International Business; Management; Safety Engineering; Small Business; Sports Management)

History: Founded 1998.

Governing Bodies: Senate; Council of Faculties

Admission Requirements: Secondary school certificate (matura)

Fees: (New Złoty): 1,800-2,100 per semester

Main Language(s) of Instruction: Polish

International Co-operation: Participates in the Erasmus programme

Accrediting Agencies: Ministry of Science and Higher Education

Degrees and Diplomas: *Licencjat*; *Świadectwo ukończenia studiów podyplomowych*

Last Updated: 21/10/11

POZNAN SCHOOL OF LOGISTICS

Wyższa Szkoła Logistyki w Poznaniu (WSL)
ul. E. Estkowskiego 6, 61-755 Poznań, wielkopolskie
Tel: +48(61) 850 47 81851-06-04
Fax: +48(61) 851-06-03
EMail: rektorat@wsl.com.pl
Website: http://www.wsl.com.pl

Rector: Andrzej Korzeniowski EMail: rektor@wsl.com.pl

Kanclerz: Ireneusz Fechner EMail: kanclerz@wsl.com.pl

International Relations: Karol Górski, Head, Research and Co-operation Department Department
Tel: +48(61) 850-47-75 EMail: karol.gorski@wsl.com.pl

Departments

Economics and Marketing (Economics; Marketing; Transport Economics); **Foreign Languages** (English; Modern Languages); **Information and Computer Science** (Computer Science; Information Sciences); **Logistics** (Transport Engineering; Transport Management); **Management** (Accountancy; Finance; Management; Occupational Health; Real Estate; Safety Engineering; Small Business); **Physical Education** (Physical Education; Sports); **Postgraduate Studies** (Health Administration; Management; Safety Engineering; Transport Management)

History: Founded 2001.

International Co-operation: With universities in Germany, Hungary, Finland, UK, Czech Republic, Slovakia, Russia, Belarus. Participates in the Virtual laboratories - success of innovation, Wielkopolska Must Know, Seventh framework, Erasmus and Leonardo Da Vinci programmes.

Degrees and Diplomas: *Inżynier*; *Licencjat*; *Świadectwo ukończenia studiów podyplomowych*; *Magister*
Last Updated: 06/10/11

POZNAŃ TRADE AND COMMERCE COLLEGE

Wyższa Szkoła Handlu i Usług w Poznaniu (WSHIU)
ul. Zwierzyniecka 13-15, 60-813 Poznań, wielkopolskie
Tel: +48(61) 842-70-20
Fax: +48 (61) 843 47 96 Ext. 33
EMail: wshiu@wshiu.poznan.pl
Website: http://www.wshiu.poznan.pl

Rektor: Kamila Wilczyńska
Tel: +48(61) 842-70-20 EMail: rektorat@wshiu.poznan.pl

Kanclerz: Piotr Dwornicki EMail: rektorat@wshiu.poznan.pl

International Relations: Kamila Wilczyńska, Rector of Science Affairs EMail: rektoratwshiu@poczta.onet.pl

Departments

Postgraduate Studies (Business Administration; Business Computing; Education; Educational Administration; Health Administration; Human Resources; Management; Marketing; Occupational Health; Safety Engineering; Tourism)

Faculties

Management (Business Administration; Business and Commerce; Health Administration; Management; Marketing; Protective Services; Safety Engineering; Service Trades; Transport Management); **National Security** (Protective Services; Safety Engineering); **Tourism and Recreation** (Dietetics; Hotel and Restaurant; International Business; Leisure Studies; Tourism)

History: Founded 1997.

Governing Bodies: Senate

Admission Requirements: Secondary school certificate (matura)

Fees: (New Złoty): 2,000 per semester

Main Language(s) of Instruction: Polish

International Co-operation: With universities in Portugal, Turkey, Germany, Hungary and Norway. Participates in the Erasmus Programme.

Accrediting Agencies: Ministry of Science and Higher Education

Degrees and Diplomas: *Licencjat*; *Świadectwo ukończenia studiów podyplomowych*
Last Updated: 21/10/11

PUŁAWY HIGHER SCHOOL

Puławska Szkoła Wyższa (PSW)
ul. Moniuszki 1, 24-100 Puławy, lubelskie
Tel: +48(81) 887-49-49
Fax: +48(81) 888-81-11
EMail: psw@psw.pulawy.pl
Website: http://www.psw.pulawy.pl

Rektor: Janusz Kalbarczyk (2008-) EMail: rektorat@psw.pulawy.pl
Kanclerz: Grażyna Jablonka

Departments

Postgraduate Studies (Education; Gerontology; Human Resources; Management; Pedagogy; Preschool Education; Public Administration; Rehabilitation and Therapy; Safety Engineering; Social Work; Tourism; Vocational Education; Welfare and Protective Services)

Programmes

Administration (Administration; Civil Engineering; Finance; Fiscal Law); **Economics** (Administrative Law; Banking; Computer Science; Econometrics; Economic and Finance Policy; Economics; English; Finance; German; International Business; International Economics; Law; Management; Mathematics; Russian; Statistics); **Pedagogy** (Child Care and Development; Health Education; Health Sciences; Law; Pedagogy; Protective Services; Psychology; Rehabilitation and Therapy; Social and Preventive Medicine); **Physiotherapy** (Physical Therapy; Rehabilitation and Therapy)

History: Founded 1997.

Governing Bodies: Senate

Admission Requirements: Secondary school certificate

Main Language(s) of Instruction: Polish

Accrediting Agencies: Ministry of Science and Higher Education

Degrees and Diplomas: *Licencjat*; *Świadectwo ukończenia studiów podyplomowych*
Last Updated: 18/10/11

RADOM ACADEMY OF ECONOMICS

Wyższa Szkoła Handlowa w Radomiu (WSH)
ul. Domagalskiego 7a, 26-600 Radom, mazowieckie
Tel: +48(48) 363-15-10
Fax: +48(48) 360-10-75 Ext. 26
EMail: kkaca@wsh.pl
Website: http://www.wsh.pl

Rector: Elżbieta Kielska (2008-) EMail: ekielska@wsh.pl

Kanclerz: Gerard Pawel Maj
Tel: +48(48) 340-16-94, Fax: +48(48) 340-16-94
EMail: gmaj@wsh.pl

International Relations: Karolina Komorowska, Head, Department of International Relatons and Student Practice
Tel: +48(48) 363-22-90 Ext.45, Fax: +48(48) 363-22-90 Ext.45
EMail: kkomorowska@wsh.pl; zagranica@wsh.pl

Departments

Postgraduate Studies (Accountancy; Administration; Business Administration; Computer Engineering; Computer Graphics; Computer Networks; Finance; Health Administration; Human Resources; International Business; Law; Management; Marketing; Multimedia; Pedagogy; Preschool Education; Public Law; Real Estate; Safety Engineering; Sales Techniques; Speech Therapy and Audiology; Taxation; Transport Management; Vocational Education)

Faculties

Administration (Administration; Finance; Public Administration; Real Estate); **Informatics** (Computer Graphics; Computer Networks; Computer Science; Information Management; Multimedia); **Internal Security** (Protective Services); **International Relations** (Finance; International Business; International Relations; Tourism; Transport Management); **Journalism and Social Communication** (Advertising and Publicity; Communication Studies; Journalism; Marketing; Mass Communication; Media Studies; Public Relations); **Pedagogy** (Education; English; Pedagogy; Preschool Education; Rehabilitation and Therapy)

History: Founded 1998 as Higher School of Applied Economics and International Trade, acquired present status and title 2000.

Governing Bodies: Senate
Admission Requirements: Secondary school certificate (matura)
Main Language(s) of Instruction: Polish
Accrediting Agencies: Ministry of Science and Higher Education
Degrees and Diplomas: *Inżynier*; *Licencjat*; *Świadectwo ukończenia studiów podyplomowych*; *Magister*
Libraries: c. 14,300 vols; c. 70 periodical subscriptions
Press or Publishing House: University Press
Last Updated: 21/10/11

RADOM HIGHER SCHOOL

Radomska Szkoła Wyższa (RSW)

ul. Zubrzyckiego 2, 26-600 Radom, mazowieckie
Tel: +48(48) 344-12-58
Fax: +48(48) 344-13-97
EMail: wsfib@wsfib.edu.pl
Website: http://rsw.edu.pl/

Rector: Zbigniew Kwaśnik EMail: rektorat@wsfib.edu.pl
Kanclerz: Elżbieta Komosa
International Relations: Magdalena Nowotnik
EMail: magdawiktoria@poczta.onet.pl

Centres
Computer Science (Computer Science); **Economic and Legal Education** (Economics; Law); **European Integration** (European Union Law; Regional Studies); **Foreign Languages** (English; Modern Languages)

Departments
Postgraduate Studies (Computer Science; Safety Engineering; Teacher Training; Vocational Counselling)

Faculties
Economics (Accountancy; Arts and Humanities; Banking; Computer Science; Economics; Engineering; Finance; Geological Engineering; International Economics; International Relations; Law; Management; Marketing; Real Estate; Surveying and Mapping); **Health Sciences** (Anatomy; Biomedicine; Cosmetology; Health Education; Health Sciences; Nursing; Physical Therapy; Physiology; Public Health; Social Work)
History: Founded 1995, acquired present status 1998. Formerly known as Wyższa Szkoła Finansów i Bankowości w Radomiu (Higher School of Finance and Banking, Radom).
Governing Bodies: Senate
Admission Requirements: Secondary school certificate (matura)
Main Language(s) of Instruction: Polish
International Co-operation: Participates in the Erasmus programme.
Accrediting Agencies: Ministry of Science and Higher Education
Degrees and Diplomas: *Inżynier*; *Licencjat*; *Świadectwo ukończenia studiów podyplomowych*
Last Updated: 20/10/11

R. KUDLIŃSKI OLYMPUS HIGHER SCHOOL, WARSAW

Olympus Szkoła Wyższa im. R. Kudlińskiego w Warszawie (WSBFIZ)

ul. Wolność 2a, 01-018 Warszawa, mazowieckie
Tel: +48(22) 636-90-00
Fax: +48(22) 636-65-73
EMail: rektorat@olympus.edu.pl
Website: http://www.olympus.edu.pl

Rektor: Jerzy Kleer (1995-)
Kanclerz: Danuta Lachowiecka
Tel: +48(22) 636-04-78, Fax: +48(22) 838-01-31
EMail: sekretariat@olympus.com.pl
International Relations: Andrzej Kondratowicz, Prorektor
EMail: ak@post.com

Faculties
Economics and Social Sciences (Accountancy; Banking; Economics; Finance; Human Resources; Insurance; Management; Social Sciences; Tourism); **Finance and Accountancy** (Accountancy; Finance); **Foreign languages** (English; English Studies; Modern Languages; Philology; Russian)
Further Information: Also Branch in Bielsko-Biała
History: Founded 1995.
Governing Bodies: Senate
Admission Requirements: Secondary school certificate (matura)
Main Language(s) of Instruction: Polish
Accrediting Agencies: Ministry of Science and Higher Education
Degrees and Diplomas: *Licencjat*; *Świadectwo ukończenia studiów podyplomowych*; *Magister*
Libraries: c. 10,000 vols.
Last Updated: 10/10/11

SCHOOL OF ECONOMICS AND LAW, KIELCE

Wyższa Szkoła Ekonomii i Prawa im. prof. Edwarda Lipińskiego (WSEIP)

ul. Jagiellonska 109 A, 25-734 Kielce, świętokrzyskie
Tel: +48(41) 345-13-13
Fax: +48(41) 345-78-88
EMail: wseip@wseip.edu.pl
Website: http://www.wseip.edu.pl

Rektor: Tadeusz Dziekan Tel: +48(41) 366-93-30
Kanclerz: Andrzej Mroczek
International Relations: Zbigniew Szczepańczyk, Director, International Cooperation
Tel: +48(41) 366-93-62, Fax: +48(41) 345-00-70
EMail: zbigniew@wseip.edu.pl

Departments
Postgraduate Studies (European Studies)

Faculties
Computer Science (Computer Science; Information Management; Information Technology); **Economics and Finance** (Accountancy; Banking; Economic and Finance Policy; Economics; Finance; Information Technology; Public Administration; Real Estate; Tourism; Transport Management); **Health Sciences** (Cosmetology; Gynaecology and Obstetrics; Health Sciences; Medicine; Nursing; Physical Therapy; Public Health); **Law** (Law); **Social Sciences** (Administration; European Studies; Government; Hotel and Restaurant; International Economics; International Relations; Journalism; Mass Communication; Media Studies; Parks and Recreation; Political Sciences; Radio and Television Broadcasting; Social Sciences; Tourism)
History: Founded 1997 as Wyższej Szkoły Ekonomii i Administracji im. prof. Edwarda Lipińskiego w Kielcach (School of Economics and Administration 'E. Lipiński', Kielce). Acquired present title 2007.
Governing Bodies: Rector's Collegium
Admission Requirements: Secondary school certificate (Matura) and qualifying interview
Fees: (New Złoty): c. 1,600-2,500 per annum
Main Language(s) of Instruction: Polish
International Co-operation: Also participates in the Tempus-Phare programme
Accrediting Agencies: Ministry of Science and Higher Education
Degrees and Diplomas: *Inżynier*; *Licencjat*; *Świadectwo ukończenia studiów podyplomowych*; *Magister*. Also MBA
Student Services: Academic counselling, Canteen, Cultural centre, Foreign student adviser, Handicapped facilities, Health services, Language programs, Sports facilities
Libraries: University Library
Publications: Zeszyty Naukowe WSEiA, WSEiA Scientific Papers *(quarterly)*

Academic Staff *2010-2011*: Total 260
Student Numbers *2010-2011*: Total: c. 6,000
Last Updated: 05/10/11

SCHOOL OF GRADUATE STUDIES IN HOTEL MANAGEMENT AND TOURISM, CZESTOCHOWA

Wyższa Szkoła Hotelarstwa i Turystyki w Częstochowie (WSHIT)

ul. Ogrodowa 47, 42-200 Częstochowa, śląskie
Tel: +48(34) 324-15-17
Fax: +48(34) 361-18-57
EMail: wshit@wshit.edu.pl
Website: http://www.wshit.edu.pl

Rektor: Wiesław Gworys

Dyrektor Administracyjny: Henryk Kózmiński

International Relations: Bartłomiej Gworys

Departments

Postgraduate Studies (Food Technology; Hotel and Restaurant; Nutrition; Protective Services; Safety Engineering; Tourism)

Faculties

Education (Education); **Food Technology and Human Nutrition** (Food Technology; Nutrition); **Tourism and Recreation** (Leisure Studies; Tourism)

History: Founded 1999.

Governing Bodies: Senate

Admission Requirements: Secondary school certificate (matura)

Fees: (New Złoty): 1,800-2,000 per semester

Main Language(s) of Instruction: Polish

International Co-operation: With universities in the Russian Federation, Lithuania, Bulgaria, Greece, Cyprus. Participates in the LLP-Erasmus programme.

Accrediting Agencies: Ministry of Science and Higher Education

Degrees and Diplomas: *Inżynier*; *Licencjat*; *Świadectwo ukończenia studiów podyplomowych*; *Magister*

Last Updated: 21/10/11

SCHOOL OF HUMANITIES AND JOURNALISM, POZNAN

Wyższa Szkoła Nauk Humanistycznych i Dziennikarstwa (WSNHID)

ul. gen. Tadeusza Kutrzeby 10, 61-719 Poznań, wielkopolskie
Tel: +48(61) 858-43-70
Fax: +48(61) 858-43-62
EMail: info@wsnhid.pl; rekrutacja@wsnhid.pl
Website: http://www.wsnhid.pl

Rektor: Karol Olejnik (2008-)
Tel: +48(61) 858-43-60, Fax: +48(61) 858-43-62

Chancellor: Małgorzata Wróblewska EMail: kanclerz@wsnhid.pl

International Relations: Karol Olejnik, Head, Department of International Relations

Departments

Postgraduate Studies (Acting; Business Administration; Dance; Design; European Studies; Graphic Design; History; Human Resources; Industrial and Organizational Psychology; Interior Design; Journalism; Labour Law; Leadership; Photography; Psychology; Public Relations; Social Psychology; Tourism)

Faculties

Computer Science (Computer Engineering; Computer Graphics; Computer Networks; Computer Science; Information Technology); **Cultural Studies** (Art Management; Art Therapy; Cultural Studies; Film; Mass Communication; Media Studies; Multimedia; Theatre); **Graphics** (Computer Graphics; Graphic Design); **International Relations** (Arabic; English; French; German; International Business; International Law; International Relations; Italian; Japanese; Modern Languages; Russian; Spanish; Turkish); **Pedagogy** (Pedagogy); **Political Sciences** (Human Resources; Management; Marketing; Political Sciences; Protective Services; Public Administration); **Sociology** (Information Sciences; Social Sciences; Social Work; Sociology)

Programmes

Social Psychology Studies (Journalism; Law; Mass Communication; Real Estate; Social Psychology)

Further Information: Also University of the Third Age and University of the Chidren.

History: Founded 1996.

Governing Bodies: Senate

Admission Requirements: Secondary school certificate (matura)

Main Language(s) of Instruction: Polish

Accrediting Agencies: Ministry of Science and Higher Education

Degrees and Diplomas: *Inżynier*; *Licencjat*; *Świadectwo ukończenia studiów podyplomowych*; *Magister*. Some of the Postgraduate programmes are offered jointly with the School of Social Psychology in Warsaw.

Academic Staff *2010-2011*: Total: c. 250

Student Numbers *2010-2011*: Total: c. 6,000

Last Updated: 07/10/11

SCHOOL OF LAW AND PUBLIC ADMINISTRATION

Wyższa Szkoła Prawa i Administracji, Przemyślu (WSAIZ)

ul. Wybrzeże Ojca Świętego Jana Pawła II 2, 37-700 Przemyśl, podkarpackie
Tel: +48(16) 677-90-50
Fax: +48(16) 677-90-50
EMail: sekretariat.p@wspia.eu
Website: http://www.wsaiz.edu.pl

Rektor: Jerzy Posłuszny (2002-)
Tel: +48(16) 852-90-30 EMail: Jerzy.Posluszny@wsaiz.edu.pl

Dyrektor Administracyjny: Anna Chmielarz
Tel: +48(17) 677-90-60, Fax: +48(17) 679-13-31
EMail: administracja@wspia.eu

International Relations: Maria Pawłucka Tel: +48(16) 678-48-54

Faculties

Administration (Accountancy; Administration; Business Administration; European Studies; Finance; Government; Health Administration; Human Resources; Insurance; Justice Administration; Public Administration; Real Estate; Rehabilitation and Therapy; Social Work; Taxation); **Internal Security** (Peace and Disarmament; Police Studies; Protective Services); **Law** (Administrative Law; Canon Law; Civil Law; Commercial Law; Constitutional Law; Economics; Fiscal Law; History of Law; International Law; Labour Law; Law; Modern Languages; Physical Education; Polish; Psychology; Public Law; Sociology)

History: Founded 1995. Wyższa Szkoła Administracji i Zarządzania w Przemyślu until 2008

Governing Bodies: Senate

Academic Year: October to September

Admission Requirements: Secondary school certificate (Matura) and qualifying interview

Fees: (New Złoty): c. 2,200-3,000 per annum

Main Language(s) of Instruction: Polish, German, English

Accrediting Agencies: Ministry of Science and Higher Education

Degrees and Diplomas: *Licencjat*; *Świadectwo ukończenia studiów podyplomowych*; *Magister*; *Doktor*

Student Services: Academic counselling, Cultural centre, Handicapped facilities, Health services

Student Residential Facilities: Apartments for c. 300 students

Special Facilities: Lecture theatre; Computer room

Libraries: Central Library

Publications: Academic Articles Collection *(annually)*

Academic Staff *2010-2011*: Total: c. 200

Student Numbers *2010-2011*: Total: c. 10,000

Last Updated: 08/10/11

SCHOOL OF MANAGEMENT AND BANKING, POZNAN

Wyższa Szkoła Zarządzania i Bankowości w Poznaniu (WSZIB)
ul. Robocza 4, 61-538 Poznań, wielkopolskie
Tel: +48(61) 835-15-11
Fax: +48(61) 835-19-27
EMail: rekrutacja@wszib.poznan.pl
Website: http://www.wszib.poznan.pl

Rektor: Barbara Kobusiewicz
Tel: +48(61) 835-15-03, Fax: +48(61) 835-15-04

Pro-Rektor: Ryszard Orliński

International Relations: Maria Skibniewska
Tel: +48 603 076 938 EMail: skibniewska_maria@wszib.poznan.pl

Faculties

Administration (Administration; Finance; International Business; Labour Law; Law; Management; Public Administration); **Internal security** (Communication Studies; Leadership; Media Studies; Protective Services); **Management** (Accountancy; Banking; Business Administration; European Union Law; Finance; Human Resources; Information Management; Information Technology; Management; Marketing; Psychology; Transport Management); **Political Sciences** (International Relations; International Studies; Journalism; Leadership; Marketing; Mass Communication; Media Studies; Political Sciences; Protective Services; Public Administration); **Postgraduate Studies** (Business Administration; Mass Communication; Media Studies)

Further Information: The Graduate programmes in Management, Administration and Political Sciences are offered in New York City, USA. A traditional and distance education institution. Also branch in Wrocław.

History: Founded 1992. Ministry accreditation for Master degree studies at the Faculty of Management and Marketing and Faculty of Administration since 1997.

Governing Bodies: Senate

Academic Year: October to July

Admission Requirements: Secondary school certificate (Matura)

Fees: (New Złoty): 1,516-2,195 per semester, depending on type of studies

Main Language(s) of Instruction: Polish

Accrediting Agencies: Ministry of Science and Higher Education

Degrees and Diplomas: *Licencjat*; *Świadectwo ukończenia studiów podyplomowych*; *Magister*

Student Services: Language programs, Sports facilities

Libraries: 9,000 vols

Publications: Forum Naukowe *(quarterly)*

Press or Publishing House: Wydawnictwo Terra

Last Updated: 11/10/11

SCHOOL OF MANAGEMENT AND BANKING, WROCŁAW

WYżSZA SZKOŁA ZARZąDZANIA I BANKOWOSCI WE WROCŁAWIU (WSZIM)

ul. Św. Antoniego 24a, 50-073 Wrocław, dolnośląskie
Tel: +48(71) 344-49-24 +48(71) 344-89-82
Fax: +48(71) 342-25-15
EMail: rekrutacja@wszib.wroc.pl
Website: http://www.wszib.wroc.pl

Rektor: Barbara Kobusiewicz

Prorektor: Stanislaw Kowalczyk

Faculties

Administration (Administration; Business Administration; Finance; International Business; Labour Law; Law; Management; Protective Services; Public Administration); **Internal Security** (Communication Studies; Leadership; Media Studies; Protective Services); **Management** (Accountancy; Advertising and Publicity; Banking; Business Administration; Finance; Human Resources; Information Management; Information Technology; International Business; Management; Marketing; Psychology; Social Work; Transport Management); **Political Sciences** (International Studies; Journalism; Leadership; Marketing; Mass Communication; Political Sciences; Protective Services; Public Administration); **Postgraduate Studies** (Administration; Human Resources; Law; Management; Marketing; Public Administration; Public Relations; Small Business; Tourism)

Further Information: A traditional and distance education institution.

History: Founded 1995. Became a branch of 2001.

Governing Bodies: Senat

Admission Requirements: Secondary school certificate (Matura)

Main Language(s) of Instruction: Polish

Accrediting Agencies: Ministry of Science and Higher Education; National Accreditation Commission

Degrees and Diplomas: *Licencjat*; *Świadectwo ukończenia studiów podyplomowych*; *Magister*

SILESIAN HIGHER SCHOOL OF COMPUTER SCIENCE AND MEDICINE IN CHORZÓW

Śląska Wyższa Szkoła Informatyczno-Medyczna z siedzibą w Chorzowie (SWSIM)
ul. Sportowa 21, 41- 506 Chorzów, śląskie
Tel: +48(32) 246-60-00
Fax: +48(32) 246-60-00 Ext.17
EMail: dziekanat@swsi.edu.pl
Website: http://www.swsim.edu.pl

Rektor: Lech Tomawski
Tel: +48(32) 246-60-00 Ext.15, Fax: +48(32) 246-60-00 Ext.17
EMail: rektorat@swsim.edu.pl

Chancellor: Agnieszka Beberok-Surowiec

Departments

Postgraduate Studies (Film)

Faculties

Computer Graphics (Computer Graphics; Computer Science); **Natural Sciences** (Health Sciences; Natural Sciences; Physical Therapy; Public Health; Safety Engineering)

History: Founded 2002.

Fees: (New Złoty): 290-470 per month.

Main Language(s) of Instruction: Polish

International Co-operation: Participates in the Erasmus programme.

Degrees and Diplomas: *Inżynier*; *Licencjat*; *Świadectwo ukończenia studiów podyplomowych*; *Magister*

Last Updated: 18/10/11

SILESIAN SCHOOL OF ECONOMICS AND LANGUAGES, KATOWICE

Wyższa Szkoła Zarządzania Marketingowego i Języków Obcych w Katowicach (WSZMIJO)
ul. Gallusa 12, 40-594 Katowice, śląskie
Tel: +48(32) 207-92-01
Fax: +48(32) 207-92-13
EMail: info@gallus.pl
Website: http://www.gallus.pl

Rector: Andrzej Limański (1994-) EMail: rektorat@gallus.pl

Dyrektor Administracyjny: Mariusz Krzysztofek
Tel: +48(32) 207-92-82 EMail: Mariusz.Krzysztofek@gallus.pl

International Relations: Katarzyna Mika, Erasmus Institutional Coordinator
Tel: +48(32) 207-92-28, Fax: +48(32) 207-92-28
EMail: jacek.ruszkowski@gallus.pl

Departments

Postgraduate Studies (Administration; Banking; English; German; Hotel and Restaurant; Human Resources; Journalism; Marine Transport; Protective Services; Russian; Safety Engineering; Spanish; Tourism; Translation and Interpretation; Transport Management; Writing)

Faculties
Economic and Engineering (Advertising and Publicity; Economics; Engineering; Finance; Hotel and Restaurant; Human Resources; Information Technology; International Business; Management; Marketing; Police Studies; Protective Services; Safety Engineering; Sales Techniques; Tourism); **Humanities** (Arts and Humanities; English; English Studies; German; Philology; Russian)

History: Founded 1994. Acquired present status in 1998.

Governing Bodies: Senate

Admission Requirements: Secondary School certificate (Matura)

Fees: (New Zoty): Full-time mode, 1,900-1,950; Part-time/evening mode, 1,600-1,800.

Main Language(s) of Instruction: Polish

International Co-operation: Participates in the Erasmus programme

Accrediting Agencies: Ministry of Science and Higher Education

Degrees and Diplomas: *Licencjat*; *Świadectwo ukończenia studiów podyplomowych*; *Magister*

Student Services: Academic counselling, Employment services, Foreign student adviser, Handicapped facilities, Language programs

Student Residential Facilities: Residential Facilities for 190 students

Libraries: c. 15,000 vols.

Last Updated: 12/10/11

SKARBEK UNIVERSITY

Wyższa Szkoła Handlu i Finansów Międzynarodowych w Warszawie (WSHIFM)

Al. Jerozolimskie 65/79, 00-697 Warszawa, mazowieckie
Tel: +48(22) 487-58-75
Fax: +48(22) 487-58-75
EMail: biurorektora@wshifm.edu.pl
Website: http://www.wshifm.edu.pl

Rector: Michal Kelles-Krauz

Kanclerz: Piotr Kusznieruk

International Relations: Edith M. Wirkowska, International Affairs Coordinator
Tel: +48(22) 487-58-75
EMail: international.office@wshifm.edu.pl; ewirkowska@wshifm.edu.pl

Faculties
Economics, Management and Finance (Accountancy; Banking; E-Business/Commerce; Economics; Finance; Human Resources; Management; Marketing; Protective Services; Real Estate; Taxation; Tourism; Transport Management); **Long-Distance Education** (Archiving; Economics; Finance; Government; History; Human Resources; Journalism; Management; Mass Communication; Media Studies; Military Science; Political Sciences; Real Estate; Social Policy; Social Work; Transport Economics; Transport Management); **Tourism** (Air Transport; Business Administration; Cooking and Catering; Hotel and Restaurant; International Relations; Parks and Recreation; Tourism)

History: Founded 1995. Formerly known as Higher School of International Commerce and Finance, Warsaw.

Governing Bodies: Senate

Academic Year: October - September

Admission Requirements: Secondary school certificate (matura)

Fees: (New Złoty): 2,200-3,650 per annum. (Euros): 3,300 studies in English. (US Dollars): BBA and MBA, 4,050

Main Language(s) of Instruction: Polish, English

International Co-operation: With universities in Europe, China, Egypt, India, Korea, Mexico, Morocco, South Africa, Turkey.

Accrediting Agencies: Ministry of Science and Higher Education

Degrees and Diplomas: *Licencjat*; *Świadectwo ukończenia studiów podyplomowych*; *Magister*. Also MBA

Student Services: Academic counselling, Canteen, Employment services, Foreign student adviser, Foreign Studies Centre, Handicapped facilities, Health services, Language programs, Social counselling, Sports facilities

Libraries: over 8,000 vols

Publications: Funkcjonowanie Rynkóow Finansowych w Polsce i na Świecie *(annually)*; Opere et Studio pro Oeconomia *(monthly)*

Student Numbers *2010-2011*	**TOTAL**
All (Foreign Included)	c. **2,000**
FOREIGN ONLY	**200**

Last Updated: 06/10/11

SOCIAL ECONOMIC HIGHER SCHOOL IN GDAŃSK

Wyższa Szkoła Społeczno - Ekonomiczna w Gdańsku (WSSE)

ul. Łagiewniki 3, 80-847 Gdańsk, pomorskie
Tel: +48(58) 301-31-79 Ext.50
Fax: +48(58) 305-65-18
EMail: info@wsse.edu.pl; dziekanat@wsse.edu.pl
Website: http://www.wsse.edu.pl

Rektor: Grażyna Kosiorowska-Gęsicka (2008-)

Vice-Chancellor: Ewa Jarmołowicz

International Relations: Maciej Radłowski

Departments
Postgraduate Studies (Pedagogy; Rehabilitation and Therapy; Teacher Training; Technology Education)

Faculties
Management (Agricultural Management; Human Resources; Management; Marine Transport; Occupational Health; Psychology; Public Administration; Safety Engineering; Transport and Communications; Transport Management; Vocational Counselling); **Pedagogy** (Business Education; Child Care and Development; Educational Administration; Educational and Student Counselling; Educational Technology; Library Science; Occupational Therapy; Pedagogy; Preschool Education; Rehabilitation and Therapy; Speech Therapy and Audiology; Teacher Training)

History: Founded 2001.

Governing Bodies: Senate

Admission Requirements: Secondary school certificate (matura)

Fees: (New Złoty): Full-time, 1,700-1,900 per semester; Part-time, 1,500-1,700 per semester.

Main Language(s) of Instruction: Polish

Accrediting Agencies: Ministry of Science and Higher Education; State Accreditation Committee

Degrees and Diplomas: *Licencjat*; *Świadectwo ukończenia studiów podyplomowych*; *Magister*

Last Updated: 24/10/11

SOPOT HIGHER SCHOOL

Sopocka Szkoła Wyższa (WSFIR)

ul. Kościuszki 47, 81-702 Sopot, pomorskie
Tel: +48(58) 555-83-80
Fax: +48(58) 550-78-80
EMail: rekrutacja@ssw.sopot.pl
Website: http://www.ssw.sopot.pl

Rector: Teresa Martyniuk

Chancellor: Maria Basandowska

International Relations: Janusz Żółkiewicz, Prorector

Campuses
Chojnice (European Studies; International Business; Mass Communication; Media Studies)

Departments
Foreign Languages (English; German; Modern Languages; Swedish); **Physical Education** (Physical Education; Sports)

Faculties

Architecture (Architectural and Environmental Design; Architectural Restoration; Architecture; Design; Interior Design; Landscape Architecture; Town Planning); **Economics and Social Sciences** (Accountancy; Economics; European Studies; Finance; Human Resources; Insurance; International Business; International Relations; Management; Mass Communication; Media Studies; Real Estate; Service Trades; Social Sciences; Taxation; Transport and Communications; Transport Management)

History: Founded 2000. Formerly known as Wyższa Szkoła Finansów i Rachunkowości w Sopocie (Higher School of Finance and Accounting, Sopot).

Main Language(s) of Instruction: Polish

International Co-operation: Participates in the Erasmus programme.

Degrees and Diplomas: *Inżynier*; *Licencjat*; *Świadectwo ukończenia studiów podyplomowych*

Last Updated: 20/10/11

STANISLAW STASZIC COLLEGE OF PUBLIC ADMINISTRATION IN BIALYSTOK

Wyższa Szkoła Administracji Publicznej w Białymstoku (WSAP)

ul. Dojlidy Fabryczne 26, 15-555 Białystok, podlaskie

Tel: +48(85) 732-12-93

Fax: +48(85) 732-12-93

EMail: wsap@wsap.edu.pl

Website: http://www.wsap.bialystok.pl

Rector: Jerzy Marian Kopania (2008-)
Tel: +48(85) 732-26-09 EMail: rektorat@wsap.edu.pl

Dyrektor Administracyjny: Sebastian Roszkowski
Tel: +48(85) 732-12-93 EMail: sroszkowski@wsap.edu.pl

International Relations: Greg Orlowski, Head of the Centre for European Funds and International Cooperation
Tel: +48(85) 732-12-93 Ext. 302
EMail: grzegorz.orlowski@wsap.edu.pl

Departments

Humanities (Applied Linguistics; Arts and Humanities; Computer Science; Cultural Studies; Logic; Mass Communication; Pedagogy; Philosophy; Psychology; Sociology); **International Relations and National Security** (Economic and Finance Policy; Economics; European Studies; History; International Relations; Management; Political Sciences; Protective Services); **Public Administration** (Administration; Civil Law; Criminal Law; Economics; Finance; Government; Public Administration; Public Law; Regional Studies; Social Policy); **Public Health** (Health Administration; Health Sciences; Modern Languages; Physical Education; Public Health)

History: Founded 1996 as a non-profit, self-financing and self-governing academic institution.

Governing Bodies: Senate; WSAP Council

Academic Year: October to June

Admission Requirements: Secondary school certificate (Matura) or foreign equivalent, and health certificate

Fees: (New Złoty): c. 3,000-3,500 per annum

Main Language(s) of Instruction: Polish; English

International Co-operation: Also participates in the JEP Tempus Bis and Erasmus programmes.

Accrediting Agencies: Ministry of Science and Higher Education

Degrees and Diplomas: *Licencjat*; *Świadectwo ukończenia studiów podyplomowych*; *Magister*

Student Services: Academic counselling, Canteen, Employment services, Handicapped facilities, Language programs, Social counselling, Sports facilities

Special Facilities: Historical Park

Libraries: WSAP Library, c. 3,500 vols, 42 periodicals

Publications: WSAPER, Students newspaper

Last Updated: 04/10/11

STARGARDINUM HIGHER SCHOOL, STARGARD SZCZECINSKI

Stargardzka Szkoła Wyższa Stargardinum (SSW STARGARDINUM)

ul. Kazimierza Wielkiego 17, 73-110 Stargard Szczeciński

Tel: +48(91) 577-83-60

Fax: +48(91) 577-83-65

EMail: dziekanat@stargardinum.pl

Website: http://www.stargardinum.pl

Rektor: Miroslaw Zajac

Kanclerz: Tatiana Burdzy

Colleges

Teacher Training *(NKJO)* (English; Foreign Languages Education; German; Teacher Training)

Departments

Postgraduate Studies (Accountancy; Computer Science; Economics; Finance; Information Management; International Business; Journalism; Management; Mass Communication; Media Studies; Political Sciences; Tourism; Transport Economics)

Faculties

Computer Science (Business Computing; Computer Graphics; Computer Networks; Computer Science; Data Processing; E-Business/Commerce; Information Management; Information Technology; Medical Technology; Multimedia); **Economics** (Accountancy; Economics; Finance; Human Resources; International Business; Management; Marketing; Real Estate; Transport Economics; Transport Management); **Journalism** (Journalism; Mass Communication; Media Studies; Multimedia; Photography; Public Relations; Radio and Television Broadcasting; Sociology; Writing)

Further Information: Also Post-secondary vocational school.

Main Language(s) of Instruction: Polish

Degrees and Diplomas: *Inżynier*; *Licencjat*; *Świadectwo ukończenia studiów podyplomowych*

Special Facilities: Computer labs; Lecture hall (200 seats)

Libraries: Yes

Last Updated: 21/10/11

STATE HIGHER VOCATIONAL SCHOOL IN GŁOGÓW

Państwowa Wyższa Szkoła Zawodowa w Głogowie (PWSZ)

ul. Piotra Skargi 5, 67-200 Głogów, dolnośląskie

Tel: +48(76) 835-35-66

Fax: +48(76) 835-35-66

EMail: kontakt@pwsz.glogow.pl

Website: http://www.pwsz.glogow.pl/1/

Rector: Stanisław Czaja
Tel: +48(76) 835-35-82, Fax: +48(76) 835-35-82
EMail: czaja@pwsz.glogow.pl

Kanclerz: Jan Miśko
Tel: +48(76) 832-04-20 EMail: kanclerz@pwsz.glogow.pl

Departments

Foreign Language (English; French; German; Italian; Modern Languages); **Information Technology** (Computer Science; Information Technology); **Physical Education** (Physical Education; Sports); **Post-graduate Studies** (Accountancy; Child Care and Development; Computer Education; Computer Science; Ethics; European Studies; Management; Modern Languages; Philosophy; Real Estate; Rehabilitation and Therapy; Science Education; Social Work; Technology)

Institutes

Economics (Accountancy; Business Administration; Economics; Finance); **Humanities** (Arts and Humanities; Cultural Studies; Pedagogy; Visual Arts); **Science and Technology** (Automation and Control Engineering; Electronic Engineering; Metallurgical Engineering; Robotics; Technology)

History: Founded 2004.

Governing Bodies: Senate

Degrees and Diplomas: *Inżynier*, *Licencjat*; *Świadectwo ukończenia studiów podyplomowych*

Special Facilities: Computer labs

Last Updated: 21/09/11

STATE HIGHER VOCATIONAL SCHOOL IN GNIEZNO

Państwowa Wyższa Szkoła Zawodowa w Gnieźnie (PWSZ)

ul. Ks. Kard. Stefana Wyszyńskiego 38, 62-200 Gniezno, wielkopolskie

Tel: +48(61) 424-29-42

Fax: +48(61) 424-29-42 Ext.33

EMail: sekretariat@pwsz-gniezno.edu.pl

Website: http://www.pwsz-gniezno.edu.pl

Rector: Józef Garbarczyk Tel: +48(61) 424-29-42 Ext. 30

Kanclerz: Mieczyslaw Baranowsk

Departments

Postgraduate Studies (Accountancy; Business Administration; Ecology; Economics; Environmental Management; Environmental Studies; Ethics; Law; Management; Marketing; Public Administration)

Institutes

Electronics and Telecommunications Engineering (Computer Engineering; Computer Networks; Electronic Engineering; Telecommunications Engineering); **Environmental Protection** (Biotechnology; Ecology; Environmental Engineering; Environmental Management); **Informatics** (Automation and Control Engineering; Computer Engineering; Computer Science; Electronic Engineering; Mechanical Engineering); **Management and Production Engineering** (Engineering; Management; Production Engineering; Safety Engineering); **Nursing** (Nursing); **Transport** (Transport and Communications; Transport Management)

History: Founded 2004.

Degrees and Diplomas: *Inżynier*, *Licencjat*; *Świadectwo ukończenia studiów podyplomowych*

Last Updated: 18/10/11

STEFAN BATORY HIGHER SCHOOL OF BUSINESS IN PIOTRKÓW TRYBUNALSKI

Wyższa Szkoła Handlowa im. Króla Stefana Batorego w Piotrkowie Trybunalskim (WSH)

ul. Sienkiewicza 10/12, 97-300 Piotrków Trybunalski, łódzkie

Tel: +48(44)645-21-00

Fax: +48(44)645-21-00

EMail: wsh@piotrkow.edu.pl

Website: http://www.wsh.net.pl

Dean Department of Administrationand International Relations: Lidia Labocha-Kozar

Tel: +48(44)647-50-05, Fax: +48(44)645-21-00

Kanclerz: Agnieszka Dolna

International Relations: Magdalena Dubiel, International Cooperation Officer

Tel: +48(44) 645-21-00 Ext. 27 EMail: biurorektora@wsh.net.pl

Departments

Postgraduate Studies (Accountancy; Administration; Data Processing; Educational Administration; Health Administration; Human Resources; Insurance; International Business; Management; Marketing; Mass Communication; Occupational Health; Protective Services; Public Administration; Public Relations; Real Estate; Road Transport; Safety Engineering; Social Welfare; Taxation; Tourism; Transport Management; Vocational Counselling)

Faculties

Administration (Administration; European Union Law; Government; Human Resources; Insurance; Protective Services; Public Administration; Real Estate; Taxation; Welfare and Protective Services); **International Relations** (Accountancy; Administration; Finance; International Business; International Relations; Journalism; Management; Tourism; Transport Management); **Mechatronics** (Electronic Engineering; Mechanical Engineering); **National Security** (Protective Services)

History: Founded 1997.

Main Language(s) of Instruction: Polish

International Co-operation: With universities in Denmark, Estonia, France, Germany, Hungary, Portugal, Romania, Slovak Republik, Slovenia, Turkey, Hungary. Participates in the Erasmus programmes.

Degrees and Diplomas: *Inżynier*, *Licencjat*; *Świadectwo ukończenia studiów podyplomowych*; *Magister*

Libraries: Yes

Last Updated: 21/10/11

ŚWIĘTOKRZYSKA HIGHER SCHOOL IN KIELCE

Świętokrzyska Szkoła Wyższa w Kielcach

ul. Zagnańska 65, 25-558 Kielce, świętokrzyskie

Tel: +48(41) 362-30-18

Fax: +48(41) 332-74-51

EMail: swietokrzyska.szkola.wyzsza@wp.pl

Website: http://www.ssw.edu.pl/

Rector: Józef Krasuski

Departments

Postgraduate Studies (Child Care and Development; Ecology; Gerontology; Health Administration; Neurological Therapy; Neurology; Pedagogy; Physical Therapy; Preschool Education; Protective Services; Rehabilitation and Therapy; Social and Preventive Medicine; Social Work; Speech Therapy and Audiology; Sports; Welfare and Protective Services)

Faculties

Education and Health (Education; Health Sciences; Pedagogy; Physical Therapy; Protective Services; Public Health; Rehabilitation and Therapy; Social Work)

History: Founded 2003.

Governing Bodies: Senate

Fees: (New Złoty): 2,400-3,700 per annum.

Main Language(s) of Instruction: Polish

Degrees and Diplomas: *Licencjat*; *Świadectwo ukończenia studiów podyplomowych*

Last Updated: 18/10/11

SWSPIZ ACADEMY OF MANAGEMENT

Społeczna Wyższa Szkoła Przedsiębiorczości i Zarządzania (SWSPIZ)

ul. Sienkiewicza 9, 90-113 Łódź, łódzkie

Tel: +48(42) 664-66-66

Fax: +48(42) 636-55-32

EMail: uczelnia@swspiz.pl

Website: http://www.swspiz.pl

Rektor: Roman Patora (1995-)

Public Relations Manager: Jadwiga Gawryś

EMail: international@swspiz.pl

International Relations: Zbigniew Pyszka, International Cooperation Officer EMail: zpyszka@swspiz.pl; dwz@swspiz.pl

Academies

Postgraduate Studies (Advertising and Publicity; Business Administration; Computer Science; Education; English; Health Administration; Health Sciences; Human Resources; Insurance; Management; Psychology; Public Administration; Public Relations; Safety Engineering; Taxation; Teacher Training; Translation and Interpretation; Transport Management)

Departments

Foreign Languages (English; French; German; Modern Languages; Russian)

Faculties

International Studies and Computer Science (Computer Science; English; International Business; International Relations; International Studies; Journalism; Media Studies; Modern Languages; Philology); **Management** (Accountancy; Econometrics; Economics; Education; Finance; Graphic Design; Management; Marketing; Physical Therapy; Psychology; Public Health; Social Sciences; Sociology; Statistics; Transport Management)

Further Information: Also branches in Brodnica, Garwolin, Kolobrzeg, Ostrow Wielkopolski, Skarżysko-Kamienna, Slupsk, Warsaw, Zdunska Wola.

History: Founded 1992 as Higher School of Entrepreneurship and Management, acquired present status and title 1995.

Governing Bodies: Senate

Admission Requirements: Secondary school certificate (Matura) or foreign equivalent and foreign language requirements (Polish, English, German)

Fees: (New Złoty): c. 300-690 per month.

Main Language(s) of Instruction: Polish, English

Accrediting Agencies: Ministry of Science and Higher Education

Degrees and Diplomas: *Inżynier*; *Licencjat*; *Świadectwo ukończenia studiów podyplomowych*; *Magister*; *Doktor*. Also Polish-American Master's degree programme offered with Clark University (USA).

Student Services: Academic counselling, Canteen, Cultural centre, Employment services, Handicapped facilities, Health services, Language programs, Nursery care, Social counselling, Sports facilities

Libraries: c. 11,000 vols, Electronic Library

Publications: Zarządzanie i Marketing, Scientific and Economic Publication *(monthly)*

Last Updated: 27/09/11

THE ACADEMY OF COMPUTER SCIENCE IN ŁÓDŹ

Wyższa Szkoła Informatyki w Łodzi (WSINF)

ul. Rzgowska 17a, 93-008 Łódź, łódzkie

Tel: +48(42) 275-01-00

Fax: +48(42) 640-33-55

EMail: wsinf@wsinf.edu.pl

Website: http://www.wsinf.edu.pl

Rektor: Andrzej Nowakowski

Tel: +48(42) 275-01-16 EMail: Andrzej_Nowakowski@wsinf.edu.pl

Kanclerz: Aniela Bednarek

Tel: +48(42) 275-01-16 EMail: anielab@sk.abis.lodz.pl

International Relations: Anna Ziemecka-Potter, Head, International Projects

Tel: +48(42) 275-01-48 EMail: anna_poteraj@wsinf.edu.pl

Departments

Foreign Languages School of Computer Science (Computer Science; English; German; Modern Languages; Russian)

Faculties

Computer Science and Management (Administration; Artificial Intelligence; Computer Engineering; Computer Science; Engineering; Information Management; Information Sciences; Management; Physics); **Education and Health Promotion** (Cosmetology; Education; Educational Sciences; Health Sciences; Pedagogy; Physical Education; Physical Therapy; Psychology); **Fine Arts and Design** (Computer Graphics; Design; Fine Arts; Interior Design)

History: Founded 1997.

Governing Bodies: Council

Admission Requirements: Secondary school certificate (Matura), entrance examination and interview

Fees: (New Złoty): Registration, c. 500; tuition, c. 300 per month

Main Language(s) of Instruction: Polish

Accrediting Agencies: Ministry of Science and Higher Education

Degrees and Diplomas: *Inżynier*; *Licencjat*; *Świadectwo ukończenia studiów podyplomowych*; *Magister*

Student Services: Academic counselling, Canteen, Cultural centre, Employment services, Foreign student adviser, Foreign Studies Centre, Handicapped facilities, Language programs, Social counselling, Sports facilities

Student Residential Facilities: Yes

Special Facilities: Electronics Laboratory; Telecommunications Laboratory

Libraries: Library

Last Updated: 07/10/11

THE ACADEMY OF COSMETICS AND HEALTH CARE, WARSAW

Wyższa Szkoła Zawodowa Kosmetyki i Pielęgnacji Zdrowia (WSZKIPZ)

ul. Podwale 13, 00-252 Warszawa, mazowieckie

Tel: +48(22) 831-00-81 +48(22) 635-50-09

Fax: +48(22) 635-73-62

EMail: kosmeto@wszkipz.pl

Website: http://www.wszkipz.pl

Rektor: Jacek Arct

Tel: +48(22) 635-14-47, Fax: +48(22) 635-79-23

EMail: rektorat@wszkipz.pl

Kanclerz: Janusz Lewandowski

Tel: +48(22) 831-63-56, Fax: +48(22) 635-79-23

EMail: janusz.lewandowski@wszkipz.pl

International Relations: Sławomir Majewski, Vice-Rector, International Cooperation

Departments

Foreign Languages (English; Modern Languages)

Faculties

Cosmetics and Household Products (Cosmetology); **Cosmetology** (Cosmetology); **Pharmacy Products** (Pharmacy); **Postgraduate Studies** (Alternative Medicine; Chemistry; Cosmetology; Educational and Student Counselling; Health Sciences; Podiatry; Social Welfare; Welfare and Protective Services); **Public Health** (Public Health); **Social Work** (Social Work)

History: Founded 2000.

Governing Bodies: Senate

Admission Requirements: Secondary school certificate (matura)

Fees: (New Złoty): 2,100-5,300 per semester

Main Language(s) of Instruction: Polish

International Co-operation: With universities in UK and Finland. Participates in the Erasmus/Socrates programmes.

Accrediting Agencies: Ministry of Science and Higher Education

Degrees and Diplomas: *Inżynier*; *Licencjat*; *Świadectwo ukończenia studiów podyplomowych*; *Magister*

Academic Staff *2010-2011*: Total: c. 90

Last Updated: 25/10/11

THE ALFRED MEISSNER SCHOOL OF DENTAL ENGINEERING

Wyższa Szkoła Inżynierii Dentystycznej i Nauk Humanistycznych im. prof. Meissnera w Ustroniu (WSID)

ul. Słoneczna 2, 43-450 Ustron, śląskie

Tel: +48(33) 854-40-90

Fax: +48(33) 854-57-77

EMail: wsid@wsid.edu.pl

Website: http://www.wsid.edu.pl

Rektor: Jerzego Zabrzeskiego EMail: sekretariat@wsid.edu.pl

Programmes

Dental Engineering (Dental Technology); **Dental Engineering** *(Graduate)* (Dental Technology; Engineering); **Dental Hygiene** (Dental Hygiene); **Engineering and Dental Technology** (Dental Technology; Engineering); **Environmental Protection** (Environmental Engineering; Environmental Management); **Tourism and Recreation** (Leisure Studies; Tourism)

History: Founded 1999.

Governing Bodies: Senate

Admission Requirements: Secondary school certificate (matura)

Main Language(s) of Instruction: Polish

Accrediting Agencies: Ministry of Science and Higher Education

Degrees and Diplomas: *Inżynier*; *Licencjat*; *Magister*

Last Updated: 23/10/11

THE BIALYSTOK SCHOOL OF ECONOMICS

Wyższa Szkoła Ekonomiczna w Białymstoku (WSE)

ul. Choroszczańska 31, 15-732 Białystok, podlaskie
Tel: +48(85) 652-09-25
Fax: +48(85) 652-09-25
EMail: wse@wse.edu.pl
Website: http://www.wse.edu.pl

Rektor: Mirosława Cywoniuk EMail: rektor@wse.edu.pl

Chairs

Economic Policy, Social and Regional (Economic and Finance Policy; Regional Studies; Social Sciences); **Economics** (Economics); **Finance and Accounting** (Accountancy; Finance); **International Relations** (International Relations); **Management, Marketing and Law** (Law; Management; Marketing); **Occupational Safety and Health** (Occupational Health; Safety Engineering); **Quantitative Methods and Computer Science** (Computer Science; Operations Research); **Sustainable Development and Knowledge-Based Economy** (Development Studies; Economics)

Departments

Foreign Languages (English; German; Modern Languages; Russian); **Physical Education** (Physical Education); **Postgraduate studies** (Business Administration; East Asian Studies; Human Resources; Management; Marketing; Occupational Health; Public Relations; Real Estate; Safety Engineering; Taxation)

History: Founded 1995, acquired present status and title 2001.

Governing Bodies: Senate

Academic Year: October to September

Admission Requirements: Secondary school certificate (Matura) and entrance examinations

Fees: (New Złoty): 2,900-3,400 per annum

Main Language(s) of Instruction: Polish

International Co-operation: With universities in Portugal; Participates in the Erasmus LLP programme.

Accrediting Agencies: Ministry of Science and Higher Education

Degrees and Diplomas: *Licencjat*; *Świadectwo ukończenia studiów podyplomowych*; *Magister*

Student Services: Academic counselling, Canteen, Cultural centre, Employment services, Foreign student adviser, Foreign Studies Centre, Handicapped facilities, Language programs, Sports facilities

Libraries: Library, c. 36,000 vols; 147 periodicals

Publications: Geopolitical and Economic Research on the Central and Eastern Europe *(biennially)*; Studia Regionalne, Central and Eastern Europe Regional Studies *(biennially)*

Last Updated: 05/10/11

THE BOGDAN JAŃSKI ACADEMY

Szkoła Wyższa im. Bogdana Jańskiego (SW)

ul. Chełmska 21a, 00-724 Warszawa, mazowieckie
Tel: +48(22) 851-28-88 +48(22) 851-28-90
Fax: +48(22) 851-28-87
EMail: administracja@warszawa.janski.edu.pl
Website: http://www.janski.edu.pl

Rektor: Kazimierz Korab

Kanclerz: Marian Piwko

Campuses

Chelm (Management; Pedagogy; Sociology); **Cracow** (Education; Management; Parks and Recreation; Political Sciences; Sociology; Tourism); **Elbląg** (International Relations; Management; Parks and Recreation; Tourism); **Opole** (Economics; International Relations; Sociology); **Zabrze** (Environmental Studies; International Relations)

Faculties

Management (Administration; Business Administration; Management); **Social Sciences** (Pedagogy; Philosophy; Political Sciences; Social Sciences; Sociology)

Higher Schools

Management and Entrepreneurship *(Łomża)* (Education; Management; Sociology)

Programmes

Physical Education (Physical Education; Sports)

History: Founded 1993. Formerly known as the Bogdan Jański Academy of Management and Entrepreneurship in Warsaw

Governing Bodies: Senate

Admission Requirements: Secondary school certificate (Matura)

Main Language(s) of Instruction: Polish

Accrediting Agencies: Ministry of Science and Higher Education

Degrees and Diplomas: *Inżynier*; *Licencjat*; *Świadectwo ukończenia studiów podyplomowych*; *Magister*

Student Numbers *2010-2011*: Total: c. 8,000

Last Updated: 27/09/11

THE CARDINAL AUGUST HLOND UNIVERSITY OF EDUCATION IN MYSLOWICE

Górnośląska Wyższa Szkoła Pedagogicna im. kard. A. Hlonda w Mysłowicach (GWSP)

ul. Powstańców 19, 41-400 Mysłowice, śląskie
Tel: +48(32) 225-39-05
Fax: +48(32) 223-81-44
EMail: rektorat@wsew.edu.pl
Website: http://www.wsew.edu.pl

Rector: Mirosław Wójcik

Administrative Officer: Kazimierz Misiołek

International Relations: Luis Ochoa Siguencia

Faculties

Education (Child Care and Development; Education; Pedagogy; Preschool Education); **Public Health** (Dietetics; Gerontology; Health Education; Health Sciences; Hygiene; Medical Auxiliaries; Nutrition; Psychiatry and Mental Health; Public Health); **Social Policy** (Social Policy); **Social Work** (Social Work)

Schools

Postgraduate Studies (Art Education; Child Care and Development; Education of the Gifted; Educational Technology; Family Studies; Pedagogy; Preschool Education; Speech Therapy and Audiology)

History: Founded 1995 as College of Primary School Education, acquired present status and title 2000.

Governing Bodies: Senate

Admission Requirements: Secondary school certificate (matura)

Main Language(s) of Instruction: Polish

Accrediting Agencies: Ministry of Science and Higher Education

Degrees and Diplomas: *Licencjat*; *Świadectwo ukończenia studiów podyplomowych*; *Magister*

Last Updated: 19/09/11

THE COLLEGE SCHOOL OF ECONOMICS AND ARTS IN SKIERNIEWICE

Wyższa Szkoła Ekonomiczno-Humanistycznaim.prof. Szczepana A. Pieniążka (WSEH)

ul. Mazowiecka 1b, 96-100 Skierniewice, łódzkie
Tel: +48(46) 832-11-61 +48(46) 832-51-40
Fax: +48(46) 834-90-91
EMail: informacja@wsehsk.home.pl; rekrutacja@wsehsk.home.pl
Website: http://www.wsehsk.home.pl

Rektor: Zbigniew Wilczyński EMail: rektorat@wsehsk.home.pl

Dyrektor Generalny: Aldona Lipska Tel: +48(46) 832-11-61

Departments

Postgraduate Studies (Administration; Agriculture; Horticulture; Management; Occupational Health; Safety Engineering; Teacher Training; Welfare and Protective Services)

Faculties

Administration (Administration; Administrative Law; Commercial Law; Constitutional Law; Criminal Law; Demography and Population; Economics; Environmental Studies; European Union Law; Finance; Government; Information Technology; International Law; Labour Law; Law; Public Administration; Social Sciences;

Sociology); **Education** (Child Care and Development; Education; Educational and Student Counselling; Pedagogy; Rehabilitation and Therapy); **Horticulture** (Data Processing; Fruit Production; Horticulture; Landscape Architecture; Molecular Biology; Statistics; Vegetable Production); **Management** (Accountancy; Business Administration; Environmental Studies; Finance; Management; Transport and Communications; Transport Management)

Programmes
Foreign Languages (English; French; German; Modern Languages; Polish; Russian)

History: Founded 1996.

Governing Bodies: Senate

Admission Requirements: Secondary school certificate (Matura)

Fees: (New Złoty): 1,938-2,052 per semester.

Main Language(s) of Instruction: Polish

International Co-operation: Also participates in the Tempus programme

Accrediting Agencies: Ministry of Science and Higher Education

Degrees and Diplomas: *Inżynier*; *Licencjat*; *Świadectwo ukończenia studiów podyplomowych*; *Magister*

Libraries: Central Library

Academic Staff *2010-2011*: Total: c. 220
Last Updated: 05/10/11

THE EUROPEAN CAREER COLLEGE IN POZNAN

Wyższa Szkoła Zawodowa Kadry dla Europy (KDE)

ul. Petera Mansfelda 4, 60-855 Poznań, wielkopolskie
Tel: +48(61) 658-24-00
EMail: rekrutacja@kde.edu.pl
Website: http://www.kde.edu.pl

Rektor: Barbara Kochanska
Tel: +48(61) 658-24-50 EMail: b.kochanska@kde.edu.pl

Kanclerz: Andrzej Roszkiewicz

Faculties
Architecture and Urban Planning (Architectural Restoration; Architecture; Architecture and Planning; Town Planning); **Economy** (Accountancy; Agricultural Economics; Economics; Finance; Human Resources; Labour and Industrial Relations; Small Business; Transport and Communications; Transport Management); **Education** (Education; English; Finnish; French; German; Preschool Education; Primary Education; Psychology; Rehabilitation and Therapy; Spanish; Swedish; Vocational Counselling); **European Studies** (European Studies; Management; Protective Services; Public Administration); **Philology** (American Studies; Communication Studies; Danish; English; German; Germanic Languages; Norwegian; Philology; Slavic Languages; Swedish; Translation and Interpretation); **Protection of Cultural Property** (Cultural Studies; Design; Fine Arts; Heritage Preservation; Photography); **Tourism and Recreation** (Economics; Hotel and Restaurant; Leisure Studies; Tourism)

Fees: (New Złoty): c. 400 per month

Main Language(s) of Instruction: Polish

Degrees and Diplomas: *Inżynier*; *Licencjat*; *Świadectwo ukończenia studiów podyplomowych*; *Magister*
Last Updated: 20/10/11

THE GENERAL JERZY ZIĘTEK SILESIAN SCHOOL OF MANAGEMENT

Śląska Wyższa Szkoła Zarządzania im. Generala Jerzego Ziętka w Katowicach (SWSZ)

ul. Z. Krasińskiego 2, 40-952 Katowice, śląskie
Tel: +48(32) 255-34-17 +48(32) 256-40-84
Fax: +48(32) 255-34-17 +48(32) 256-40-84
EMail: admin@swsz.katowice.pl
Website: http://www.swsz.katowice.pl

Rector: Andrzej S. Barczak EMail: rektorat@swsz.katowice.pl

Dyrektor Administracyjny: Agata Fortuna
Tel: +48(32) 255-34-01 Ext. 115
EMail: a.fortuna@swsz.katowice.pl

International Relations: Anna Korzunowicz-Drozd, International Relations Officer
Tel: +48(32) 251-14-49 Ext. 117, Fax: +48(32) 255-34-17 Ext. 117
EMail: a.drozd@swsz.katowice.pl

Campuses
Olkusz (Education; Pedagogy; Preschool Education); **Z.arki** (Accountancy; Administration; Agricultural Economics; Business Administration; Economics; Finance; Government; Human Resources; International Economics; International Relations; Marketing; Service Trades; Small Business; Social Policy; Tourism)

Faculties
Health Sciences *(Tychy)* (Health Sciences; Nursing); **Social Sciences and Technology** (Computer Science; Econometrics; Economics; Education; Environmental Studies; European Studies; Foreign Languages Education; Heritage Preservation; Law; Management; Marketing; Pathology; Physical Education; Psychology; Social Policy; Social Sciences; Statistics; Technology; Transport and Communications; Transport Management)

History: Founded 1993. Acquired present name 2001.

Governing Bodies: Senate

Admission Requirements: Secondary school certificate (Matura) and interview

Fees: (New złoty): 4,500 per annum

Main Language(s) of Instruction: Polish, English

International Co-operation: Participates in Erasmus programme (Germany, Italy), Socrates and Leonardo da Vinci programmes.

Accrediting Agencies: Ministry of Science and Higher Education

Degrees and Diplomas: *Inżynier*; *Licencjat*; *Świadectwo ukończenia studiów podyplomowych*; *Magister*

Student Services: Academic counselling, Canteen, Employment services, Foreign student adviser, Foreign Studies Centre, Health services, Language programs, Sports facilities

Publications: Materiały Konferencyjne, Conference Materials *(biennially)*; Trend, Students' magazine; Zeszyty naukowe, Scientific Papers
Last Updated: 28/09/11

THE JOHN PAUL II CATHOLIC UNIVERSITY OF LUBLIN

Katolicki Uniwersytet Lubelski Jana Pawła II (KUL)

Al. Racławickie 14, 20-950 Lublin, lubelskie
Tel: +48(81) 445-41-01
Fax: +48(81) 445-41-91
EMail: dwz@kul.lublin.pl
Website: http://www.kul.pl/

Rector: Stanisław Wilk (2004-)
Tel: +48(81) 445-41-20, Fax: +48(81) 445-41-23
EMail: rektorat@kul.pl

Pro-Rector, Administration and Finance: Stanisław Zięba
EMail: kancelaria@kul.lublin.pl

International Relations: Sławomir Nowosad, Vice-Rector for Science and International Relations
Tel: +48(81) 445-41-05, Fax: +48(81) 445-41-91
EMail: AGM@kul.pl

Academies
Artes Liberales (Art History; Classical Languages; Cultural Studies; Dutch; Economics; Education; German; History; Journalism; Law; Mass Communication; Musicology; Philology; Philosophy; Psychology; Romance Languages; Slavic Languages; Sociology; Theology)

Centres
Postgraduate Studies (Administration; Child Care and Development; Clinical Psychology; Computer Science; Ethics; Finance; History; Human Resources; International Relations; Journalism; Labour Law; Mass Communication; Museum Studies; Pedagogy; Philology; Philosophy; Polish; Preschool Education; Psychology;

Psychotherapy; Rehabilitation and Therapy; Theology; Transport Management; Welfare and Protective Services)

Colleges

Individual Studies in the Humanities *(Interfaculty)* (Arts and Humanities)

Faculties

Humanities (Art History; Arts and Humanities; Classical Languages; English; English Studies; Geography; German; Greek (Classical); History; Latin; Linguistics; Literature; Modern Languages; Philology; Polish; Romance Languages; Slavic Languages); **Law and Economic Sciences** *(Off-Campus, Stalowa Wola)* (Economics; Law); **Law, Canon Law and Administration** (Administration; Canon Law; European Studies; Law); **Legal and Economic Sciences** *(Off-campus, Tomaszów Lubelski)* (Economics; Law); **Mathematics and Natural Sciences** (Environmental Studies; Landscape Architecture; Mathematics and Computer Science; Natural Sciences); **Philosophy** (Ethics; Logic; Metaphysics; Philosophy); **Social Sciences** (Economics; Journalism; Management; Mass Communication; Pedagogy; Psychology; Sociology); **Social Sciences** *(Off-Campus, Stalowa Wola)* (Pedagogy; Sociology); **Theology** (Ancient Civilizations; Archiving; Bible; Family Studies; History of Religion; Library Science; Museum Studies; Musicology; Pastoral Studies; Religious Practice; Theology)

Institutes

Lexicography (Terminology)

Schools

Foreign Languages (English; French; German; Greek (Classical); Italian; Latin; Modern Languages; Russian; Spanish); **Polish Language and Culture** (Cultural Studies; Polish)

Further Information: Also courses for foreign students: Polish Language and Culture programme, Summer School of Polish language and culture

History: Founded 1918 as a private institution under the patronage of the Polish Episcopate, and approved by the Holy See. 1920, recognized as public school. Authorized by the State to award degrees 1938. Closed 1939 during German occupation and professors arrested. Reopened 1944. Financed by the Polish Episcopate and by gifts. Since 1991, partly subsidized by the government.

Governing Bodies: Academic Senate

Academic Year: October to June (October-February; February-June)

Admission Requirements: Secondary school certificate (Matura) and entrance examinations

Fees: (Euros): Foreign students: Master Degree Studies, 2,000 per annum; Doctoral Studies, 3,000 per annum

Main Language(s) of Instruction: Polish; English

International Co-operation: Participates in the Socrates/Erasmus (Belgium, The Netherlands, Italy, Finland, France, Germany, Hungary, Spain, Switzerland, Latvia, Estonia, Czech Republic, Slovakia, Slovenia) and SOCRATES-Comenius, Leonardo da Vinci and Ceepus programmes

Accrediting Agencies: Ministry of Science and Higher Education

Degrees and Diplomas: *Inżynier*; *Licencjat*; *Świadectwo ukończenia studiów podyplomowych*; *Magister*; *Doktor*

Student Services: Academic counselling, Canteen, Cultural centre, Employment services, Foreign student adviser, Foreign Studies Centre, Handicapped facilities, Health services, Language programs, Sports facilities

Student Residential Facilities: Yes

Special Facilities: University Museum. Art Gallery of 'Scena Plastyczna'; Art Gallery 'Galeria 1'. Theatre

Libraries: University Library, c. 1,800,000 vols; faculty libraries, c. 350,000 vols

Publications: Acta Mediaevalia *(quarterly)*; Ethos *(quarterly)*; Kerygs *(biennially)*; Law-Administration-Church *(quarterly)*; Przegląd Uniwersytecki *(bimonthly)*; Roczniki Filozoficzne *(annually)*; Roczniki Humanistyczne *(annually)*; Roczniki Nauk Prawnych *(annually)*; Roczniki Nauk Społecznych *(annually)*; Roczniki Teologiczne *(annually)*; Studia Norwidiana *(annually)*; Studia Polonijne *(annually)*; Vox Patrum *(quarterly)*; Zeszyty Naukowe KUL *(quarterly)*

Press or Publishing House: Redakcja Wydawnictw KUL. Towarzystwo Naukowe KUL

Last Updated: 19/09/11

THE KAROL GODULA UPPER SILESIAN ACADEMY OF ENTREPRENEURSHIP

Górnośląska Wyższa Szkoła Przedsiębiorczości im. Karola Goduli (GWSP)

ul. Racławicka 23, 41-506 Chorzów, śląskie

Tel: +48(32) 247-25-56 Ext. 11

Fax: +48(32) 247-25-56 Ext. 10

EMail: gwsp@gwsp.edu.pl

Website: http://www.gwsp.edu.pl

Rector: Andrzej Klasik (1999-) Tel: +48(32) 247-25-56 Ext. 10

Kanclerz: Anna Radzikowska

International Relations: Adam Drobnia

Centres

Entrepreneurship and Regional Development (Development Studies; Management)

Departments

Accounting and Finance (Accountancy; Finance); **Creative Economics** (Economics); **Entrepreneurship and Management** (Administration; Gender Studies; Human Resources; Industrial and Organizational Psychology; Management; Public Administration; Real Estate; Small Business; Tourism; Transport Management); **Foreign Languages** (English; Modern Languages); **Information Technology and Econometrics** (Econometrics; Information Technology); **Physical Education** (Physical Education; Sports)

History: Founded 1999.

Governing Bodies: Senate

Admission Requirements: Secondary school certificate (matura)

Main Language(s) of Instruction: Polish; English

International Co-operation: Participates in the Erasmus programme

Accrediting Agencies: Ministry of Science and Higher Education

Degrees and Diplomas: *Licencjat*; *Świadectwo ukończenia studiów podyplomowych*

Last Updated: 13/10/11

THE LOWER SILESIAN COLLEGE OF ENTREPRENEURSHIP AND TECHNOLOGY IN POLKOWICE

Dolnośląska Wyższa Szkoła Przedsiębiorczości i Techniki w Polkowicach (DWSPIT)

ul. Skalników 6b, 59-101 Polkowice, dolnośląskie

Tel: +48(76) 746-53-53

Fax: +48(76) 746-53-52

EMail: sekretariat@dwspit.pl

Website: http://www.dwspit.pl/

Rector: Marian S. Wolański Tel: +48(76) 746-53-53

Chancellor: Włodzimierz Olszewski

Tel: +48(76) 845-20-65, Fax: +48(76) 845-24-80

EMail: w.olszewski@dwspit.polkowice.pl

International Relations: Danuta Berezowska, International Relations Officer

Tel: +48(76) 746-53-44 EMail: d.berezowska@dwspit.pl

Centres

Foreign Language (German; Modern Languages); **Physical Education and Sports** (Physical Education; Sports)

Faculties

Information Technology (Computer Engineering; Computer Networks; Electronic Engineering; Information Technology; Mechanical Engineering); **International Relations** (International Economics; International Relations; Political Sciences; Social Policy); **Mechatronics** (Electronic Engineering; Mechanical Engineering)

History: Founded 2002.

Fees: (New Złoty): 1,250-1,450 per semester

Main Language(s) of Instruction: Polish

International Co-operation: With universities in Poland and Germany. Participates in the Erasmus programme.

Degrees and Diplomas: *Licencjat*; *Świadectwo ukończenia studiów podyplomowych*

Last Updated: 13/10/11

THE MAŁOPOLSKA COLLEGE IN BRZESKO

Małopolska Szkoła Wyższa w Brzesku (MSZW)

ul. Królowej Jadwigi 18, 32-800 Brzesko, małopolskie

Tel: +48(14) 663-31-35

Fax: +48(14) 621-05-56

EMail: studia@mszw.edu.pl

Website: http://mszw.edu.pl/

Rektor: Barbara Garajdura

Kanclerz: Bozena Szoltysek

Departments

Foreign Languages *(Inter-organizational Unit)* (Modern Languages); **Post-graduate Studies** (Education; Pedagogy; Rehabilitation and Therapy; Safety Engineering; Social Work)

Faculties

Applied Sciences *(Tarnow)* (Cosmetology; Education; Protective Services; Rehabilitation and Therapy; Special Education); **Economics and Education** (Child Care and Development; Economics; Education; Pedagogy; Rehabilitation and Therapy; Safety Engineering)

History: Founded 2004.

Governing Bodies: Senate

Main Language(s) of Instruction: Polish

Degrees and Diplomas: *Licencjat*; *Świadectwo ukończenia studiów podyplomowych*

Last Updated: 17/10/11

THE POPE JOHN PAUL II SUWALSKO-MAZURIAN UNIVERSITY IN SUWAŁKI

Wyższa Szkoła Suwalsko-Mazurska im. Papieża Jana Pawła II w Suwałkach (WSS-M)

ul. Marii Skłodowskiej-Curie 5, 16-400 Suwałki, podlaskie

Tel: +48(87) 565-81-28

Fax: +48(87) 565-81-37

EMail: sekretariat@wssm.home.pl

Website: http://www.wssm.home.pl

Rektor: Marek M. Dolata EMail: rektormd@wssm.home.pl

Kanclerz: Jarema Sykulski
Tel: +48(87) 565-81-29 EMail: kanclerz@wssm.home.pl

Departments

Postgraduate Studies (Child Care and Development; Family Studies; Fiscal Law; Management; Pedagogy; Preschool Education; Psychology; Rehabilitation and Therapy; Safety Engineering; Social Problems; Welfare and Protective Services)

Faculties

Administration (Administration; Administrative Law; Civil Law; Economics; English; International Law; Management; Modern Languages; Psychology; Public Administration; Public Law); **Education** (Education; Pedagogy; Physical Education; Primary Education; Rehabilitation and Therapy; Social Work; Tourism)

History: Founded 1997.

Governing Bodies: Senate

Admission Requirements: Secondary school certificate (Matura)

Main Language(s) of Instruction: Polish

Accrediting Agencies: Ministry of Science and Higher Education

Degrees and Diplomas: *Licencjat*; *Świadectwo ukończenia studiów podyplomowych*

Special Facilities: Auditorium for 250 people; Chapel

Academic Staff *2010-2011*: Total: c. 80

Last Updated: 24/10/11

THE POZNAN SCHOOL OF SOCIAL SCIENCES

Wyższa Szkoła Umiejętności Społecznych w Poznaniu (WSUS)

ul. Głogowska 26, 60-734 Poznań, wielkopolskie

Tel: +48(61) 886-28-00

Fax: +48(61) 886-28-29

EMail: wsus@wsus.poznan.pl; dziekanat@wsus.poznan.pl

Website: http://www.wsus.poznan.pl

Rector: Michał Iwaszkiewicz (1997-)
Tel: +48(61) 848-31-57 Ext. 103
EMail: miwaszkiewicz@wsus.poznan.pl

Director: Jacek Woda
Tel: +48(61) 848-31-57 Ext. 128 EMail: jwoda@wsus.poznan.pl

International Relations: Agnieszka Woch, Chancellor
Tel: +48(61) 848-31-57 Ext. 102 EMail: awoch@wsus.poznan.pl

Faculties

Design (Ceramic Art; Design; Display and Stage Design; Fashion Design; Graphic Design; Industrial Design; Jewelry Art); **Information and Library Sciences** (History; Information Sciences; Library Science; Media Studies); **Interior design** (Interior Design); **Journalism and Social Communication** (Journalism; Marketing; Mass Communication; Media Studies; Public Relations); **Law** (Administrative Law; Civil Law; Constitutional Law; Criminal Law; European Union Law; International Law; Law); **Marketing and Management** (Economics; Finance; Management; Marketing; Mathematics; Protective Services; Public Relations; Statistics); **Postgraduate Studies** (Art Management; Electronic Engineering; Information Sciences; Library Science; Media Studies; Real Estate; Safety Engineering)

Schools

Social Skills (Cultural Studies; Graphic Design; Library Science; Management; Speech Studies)

History: Founded 1997.

Governing Bodies: Senate

Admission Requirements: Secondary school certificate (Matura)

Fees: (New Złoty): 3,510-7,560 per annum

Main Language(s) of Instruction: Polish

International Co-operation: Participates in the Erasmus Programme.

Accrediting Agencies: Ministry of Science and Higher Education

Degrees and Diplomas: *Licencjat*; *Świadectwo ukończenia studiów podyplomowych*; *Magister*

Libraries: c. 1,200 vols; c. 15,000 periodical subscriptions

Last Updated: 10/10/11

THE QUEEN JADWIGA SCHOOL OF MANAGEMENT AND ACCOUNTING IN RUDA SLASKA

Wyższa Szkoła Nauk Stosowanych w Rudzie Śląskiej (WSH)

ul. Królowej Jadwigi 18, 41-704 Ruda Śląska, śląskie

Tel: +48(32) 240-71-11

Fax: +48(32) 248-12-92

EMail: uczelnia@wsnsrs.edu.pl

Website: http://www.wsnsrs.edu.pl

Rektor: Adam Sałaniewski

Kanclerz: Dariusz Luboń

Departments

Postgraduate Studies (Health Administration; Protective Services)

Faculties

Health Sciences (Arts and Humanities; Gynaecology and Obstetrics; Health Sciences; Medicine; Nursing); **Management** (Management; Marketing)

History: Change of name in 2008

Governing Bodies: Senate

Main Language(s) of Instruction: Polish

Accrediting Agencies: Ministry of Science and Higher Education

Degrees and Diplomas: *Licencjat*; *Świadectwo ukończenia studiów podyplomowych*
Last Updated: 23/10/11

THE SCHOOL OF HIGHER EDUCATION IN HUMANITIES IN SZCZECIN

Wyższa Szkoła Humanistyczna Towarzystwa Wiedzy Powszechnej w Szczecinie (WSH-TWP)
ul. Broniewskiego 14, 71-528 Szczecin, zachodniopomorskie
Tel: +48(91) 452-84-40 +48(91) 452-84-00
Fax: +48(91) 452-84-40 +48(91) 452-84-00
EMail: wshtwp@wshtwp.pl
Website: http://www.wshtwp.pl/

Rektor: Kazimierz Wenta EMail: rektor@wshtwp.szczecin.pl

Chancellor: Joanna Golczyk

International Relations: Anna Ociesa
EMail: aociesa@wshtwp.szczecin.pl

Centres
Foreign Language Teaching (English; Modern Languages); **Information Sciences Training** (Information Sciences; Information Technology)

Departments
Postgraduate Studies (Child Care and Development; Computer Graphics; Computer Science; Distance Education; Educational Administration; Environmental Studies; Ethics; Health Sciences; Human Resources; Information Technology; Journalism; Library Science; Mass Communication; Pedagogy; Preschool Education; Protective Services; Rehabilitation and Therapy; Safety Engineering; Social Welfare; Social Work; Special Education; Speech Therapy and Audiology; Theatre; Tourism; Vocational Education)

Faculties
Social Sciences (Education; Educational Sciences; History; Journalism; Mass Communication; Pedagogy; Political Sciences; Preschool Education; Social Problems; Social Sciences; Social Studies; Sociology; Teacher Training)

Further Information: Also Center ul. Monte Cassino

History: Founded 1997 as a private Institution of the Polish Association for Adult Education.

Governing Bodies: Senate

Admission Requirements: Secondary school certificate (matura)

Main Language(s) of Instruction: Polish

Accrediting Agencies: Ministry of Science and Higher Education

Degrees and Diplomas: *Licencjat*; *Świadectwo ukończenia studiów podyplomowych*; *Magister*

Student Numbers *2010-2011*: Total: c. 3,000
Last Updated: 21/10/11

THE SCHOOL OF MANAGEMENT AND BANKING, KRAKÓW

Wyższa Szkoła Zarządzania i Bankowości w Krakowie (WSZIB)
al. Kijowska 14, 30-079 Kraków, małopolskie
Tel: +48(12) 635-68-05
Fax: +48(12) 635-68-04
EMail: bbudka@wszib.edu.pl
Website: http://www.wszib.krakow.pl/

Rektor: Włodzimierz Roszczynialski (1998-)
Tel: +48(12) 635-68-35, Fax: +48(12) 661-07-12
EMail: wszib@wszib.edu.pl

Vice Chancellor: Bohdan Makary
Tel: +48 501-220-800 EMail: kanclerz@wszib.krakow.pl

International Relations: Magdalena Kowalska-Musiał
Tel: +48 502-501-301 EMail: magda-kowalska@wszib.krakow.pl

Faculties
Computer Science (Business Computing; Computer Engineering; Computer Graphics; Computer Networks; Computer Science); **Finance and Accounting** (Accountancy; Banking; Finance); **Management** *(Graduate)* (Business Administration; Computer Science; Finance; Health Administration; Human Resources; International Business; Management; Protective Services; Sociology)); **Management** *(Undergraduate)* (Advertising and Publicity; Computer Graphics; E-Business/Commerce; Human Resources; Information Management; Information Technology; Management; Marketing); **Postgraduate Studies** (Accountancy; Administration; Business Administration; Communication Studies; Environmental Management; Health Administration; Human Resources; Information Management; Leadership; Management; Marketing; Media Studies; Psychology; Safety Engineering)); **Sociology** (Communication Studies; Media Studies; Sociology)

History: Founded 1995.

Governing Bodies: Senate

Academic Year: September to June

Admission Requirements: Secondary school certificate (Matura)

Fees: (New Złoty): c. 4,500 per annum

Main Language(s) of Instruction: Polish

Accrediting Agencies: Ministry of Science and Higher Education; Association of Management Education

Degrees and Diplomas: *Inżynier*; *Licencjat*; *Świadectwo ukończenia studiów podyplomowych*; *Magister*. Also MBA

Student Services: Employment services, Foreign student adviser, Health services, Language programs, Sports facilities

Student Residential Facilities: Yes

Special Facilities: Computer Laboratories

Libraries: c. 22,000 vols
Last Updated: 10/10/11

THE SCHOOL OF MANAGEMENT AND MARKETING IN SOCHACZEW

Wyższa Szkoła Zarządzania i Marketingu w Sochaczewie (WSZIM)
ul. Stadionowa 4, 96-500 Sochaczew, mazowieckie
Tel: +48(46) 862-50-80
Fax: +48(46) 862-50-80
EMail: info@wszim-sochaczew.edu.pl
Website: http://www.wszim-sochaczew.edu.pl

Rektor: Wojciech Ciechomski (2002-)
EMail: wojciech.ciechomski@wszim-sochaczew.edu.pl

Dyrektor Administracyjny: Zbigniew Kicka
EMail: zbigniew.kicka@wszim-sochaczew.edu.pl

Departments
Postgraduate Studies (Business Computing; Data Processing; Finance; Human Resources; Transport Management)

Faculties
Computer Science and Econometrics (Business Computing; Computer Science; Data Processing; Econometrics); **Management** (Business Administration; Business Computing; Finance; Human Resources; Information Technology; Management; Transport Management)

Further Information: Also Third Age University.

History: Founded 1997.

Governing Bodies: Senate

Admission Requirements: Secondary school leaving certificate (Świadectwo dojrzałości)

Fees: (New Złoty): c. 350 per month

Main Language(s) of Instruction: Polish

Accrediting Agencies: Ministry of Science and Higher Education

Degrees and Diplomas: *Licencjat*; *Świadectwo ukończenia studiów podyplomowych*. Also Postgraduate programmes offered through the Human Capital Programme (Programu Kapitał Ludzki).

Student Services: Canteen, Social counselling, Sports facilities

Special Facilities: Movie Studio

Publications: Wiadomości
Last Updated: 25/10/11

THE STATE COLLEGE OF COMPUTER SCIENCE AND BUSINESS ADMINISTRATION IN ŁOMŻA

Państwowa Wyższa Szkoła Informatyki i Przedsiębiorczości w Łomży (PWSIIP)
ul. Akademicka 14, 18-400 Łomża, podlaskie
Tel: +48(86) 215-59-53
Fax: +48(86) 215-66-01
EMail: biuro@pwsip.edu.pl
Website: http://www.pwsip.edu.pl

Rector: Robert Charmas Fax: +48(86) 215-59-50 EMail: rektor@pwsip.edu.pl

Kanclerz: Henryk Trojanowski EMail: kanclerz@pwsip.edu.pl

International Relations: Lilianna Rywacka, Head, International Relations Office EMail: lrywacka@pwsip.edu.pl

Programmes
Administration (Administration); **Automation and Robotics** (Automation and Control Engineering; Robotics); **Computer Science** (Computer Science); **Cosmetology** (Cosmetology); **English Philology with Information Technology** (English; Information Technology; Philology); **Food Technology and Human Nutrition** (Food Technology; Nutrition); **Management** (Management); **Nursing** (Nursing); **Physical Education** (Physical Education); **Social Work** (Social Work)

History: Founded 2004.

Governing Bodies: Senate

Degrees and Diplomas: *Inżynier*, *Licencjat*; *Świadectwo ukończenia studiów podyplomowych*
Last Updated: 03/09/11

THE UNIVERSITY OF ARTS AND SCIENCES IN KIELCE

Wyższa Szkoła Umiejętności w Kielcach (WSU)
ul. Wesoła 52, 25-353 Kielce, świętokrzyskie
Tel: +48(41) 344-98-69
Fax: +48(41) 344-98-69
EMail: nauka@wsu.kielce.pl
Website: http://www.wsu.kielce.pl

Rektor: Andrzej Błachut (1997-)

Sekretarka: Katarzyna Mucha-Duda Tel: +48(41) 344-98-67

International Relations: Bożena Zakrzewska Tel: +48(41) 343-21-77

Faculties
Economics (Economics); **English Philology** (English; Philology); **Family Studies** (Family Studies); **Journalism and Social Communication** (Journalism; Mass Communication); **Philosophy** (Philosophy); **Political Sciences** (Political Sciences); **Postgraduate Studies** (Health Sciences; Hotel and Restaurant; Marketing; Occupational Health; Real Estate; Safety Engineering; Tourism; Welfare and Protective Services); **Public Health** (Public Health); **Sociology** (Sociology); **Spatial Economics** (Economics); **Tourism and Recreation** (Parks and Recreation; Tourism)

History: Founded 1995.

Admission Requirements: Secondary school certificate (Matura)

Main Language(s) of Instruction: Polish

International Co-operation: (New Złoty): Full-time, 2,160-3,600 per semester; part-time studies, 1,650-2,940 per semester.

Accrediting Agencies: Ministry of Science and Higher Education

Degrees and Diplomas: *Inżynier*, *Licencjat*; *Świadectwo ukończenia studiów podyplomowych*; *Magister*
Last Updated: 10/10/11

THE UNIVERSITY OF ECONOMICS AND HUMANITIES

Wyższa Szkoła Ekonomiczno-Humanistyczna w Bielsku-Białej (WSEH)
ul. gen. Wł. Sikorskiego 4 i 4c, 43-300 Bielsko-Biała, śląskie
Tel: +48(33) 816 51 69/70
Fax: +48(33) 816-51-70
EMail: wseh@wseh.pl
Website: http://www.wseh.pl

Rektor: Czesław Bugdalski EMail: rektorat@wseh.pl

Kanclerz: Jerzy Dec

International Relations: Jessica Mendrek, Erasmus Coordinator Tel: +48(33) 816-51-69/70 Internal 13 EMail: jmendrek@wseh.pl

Colleges
English Studies (Applied Linguistics; Arts and Humanities; Business Administration; English; English Studies; Film; Foreign Languages Education; German; Media Studies; Philology; Translation and Interpretation); **Social Sciences** (Management; Political Sciences; Social Sciences)

History: Founded 1997 as Higher School of Management and Marketing in Bielsko-Biała, acquired present status and title 2000.

Governing Bodies: Senate

Admission Requirements: Secondary school certificate (matura) and entrance examinations

Fees: (New Złoty): 3,200-3,600 per annum

Main Language(s) of Instruction: Polish

Accrediting Agencies: Ministry of Science and Higher Education; National Accreditation Commission

Degrees and Diplomas: *Licencjat*; *Świadectwo ukończenia studiów podyplomowych*; *Magister*
Last Updated: 20/10/11

THE UNIVERSITY OF ECONOMY IN BYDGOSZCZ

Wyższa Szkoła Gospodarki w Bydgoszczy (WPSTIH)
ul. Garbary 2, 85-229 Bydgoszcz, kujawsko-pomorskie
Tel: +48(52) 348-23-48 +48(52) 567-00-78
Fax: +48(52) 567-00-77
EMail: cwz@byd.pl; rekrutacja@byd.pl
Website: http://www.wsg.byd.pl

Rector: Gabriel Wójcik Tel: +48(52) 567-00-47 +48(52) 567-00-48 EMail: rektorat@byd.pl

International Relations: Łukasz Jasiński, Head, International Cooperation Office Tel: +48(52) 567-00-78, Fax: +48(52) 567-00-78 EMail: lukasz.jasinski@byd.pl; cwz@byd.pl

Departments
Foreign Languages *(Interfaculty Unit)* (English; French; German; Modern Languages; Russian); **Inter-Pedagogical Studies** *(Interfaculty Unit)* (Child Care and Development; Education; Pedagogy; Teacher Training)

Faculties
Health and Tourism (Dietetics; Geography; Health Sciences; Hotel and Restaurant; Physical Education; Physical Therapy; Sports; Tourism); **Management and Engineering** *(Malbork)* (Engineering; Management); **Management and Entrepreneurship** *(Slupsk)* (Management); **Management and Social Sciences** *(Inowrocław)* (Management; Social Sciences); **Social Sciences and Economics** (Accountancy; Applied Linguistics; Commercial Law; Economics; Education; English; Family Studies; Finance; German; History; Management; Philology; Philosophy; Russian; Social Sciences; Sociology; Transport and Communications; Transport Management); **Technology** *(Torun)* (Technology); **Technology** (Architectural Restoration; Architecture; Architecture and Planning; Automation and Control Engineering; Building Technologies; Computer Education; Computer Engineering; Computer Science; Econometrics; Electronic Engineering; Information Sciences; Interior Design; Landscape Architecture; Materials Engineering; Mathematics; Measurement and Precision Engineering; Mechanical Engineering; Physics; Regional Planning; Robotics; Statistics; Structural Architecture; Technology); **Tourism Management** *(Elk)* (Management; Tourism)

History: Founded 1999.

Governing Bodies: Senate

Admission Requirements: Secondary school certificate (matura)

Main Language(s) of Instruction: Polish

International Co-operation: With universities in Austria, Belgium, Belarus, China, Czech Republic, Denmark, Estonia, Finland, France, Netherlands, Spain, Lithuania, Latvia, Morocco, Germany,

Portugal, Russia, Romania, Slovenia, Turkey, Ukraine, Hungary, UK, Italy. Participates in the Erasmus programme.

Accrediting Agencies: Ministry of Science and Higher Education

Degrees and Diplomas: *Inżynier*; *Licencjat*; *Świadectwo ukończenia studiów podyplomowych*; *Magister*. Also professional training and certification programmes.

Libraries: c. 23,000 vols

Student Numbers *2010-2011*: Total: c. 7,000

Last Updated: 06/10/11

THE UNIVERSITY OF MEDICAL SCIENCES IN LEGNICA

Wyższa Szkoła Medyczna LZDZ w Legnicy (WSM LZDZ)

ul. Powstańców Śląskich 3, 59-220 Legnica, dolnośląskie
Tel: +48(76) 724-51-58
Fax: +48(76) 724-51-60
EMail: dziekan@wsmlegnica.pl
Website: http://www.wsmlegnica.pl

Rector: Zbigniew Rykowski
Tel: +48(76) 854-99-35 EMail: rektorat@wsmlegnica.pl

Kanclerz: Aleksander Pekala

Faculties

Emergency Medical (Medicine; Occupational Health; Safety Engineering); **Management** (Health Administration; Management; Marketing); **Nursing** (Nursing)

History: Founded 2004.

Main Language(s) of Instruction: Polish

Accrediting Agencies: Ministry of Science and Higher Education; National Accreditation Commission.

Degrees and Diplomas: *Licencjat*; *Świadectwo ukończenia studiów podyplomowych*; *Magister*

Last Updated: 23/10/11

THE UNIVERSITY OF TRADE IN LODZ

Wyższa Szkoła Kupiecka w Łodzi (WSZK)

ul. Pojezierska 97 B, 91-341 Łódź, łódzkie
Tel: +48(42) 654-73-00 +48(42) 654-73-11
EMail: info@kupiecka.pl
Website: http://www.kupiecka.pl

Rektor: Leszek Czarnota
Tel: +48(42) 654-90-95 EMail: rektor@kupiecka.pl

Dyrektor Administracyjny: Dariusz Krygier
Tel: +48(42) 612-12-89 EMail: dariusz.krygier@kupiecka.pl

International Relations: Wielisław Nowakowski, Director
Tel: +48(42) 651-90-95 EMail: biuro.zagranica@kupiecka.pl

Faculties

Administration (Administration; Civil Law; Commercial Law; Criminal Law; Criminology; European Union Law; Finance; Government; Human Rights; Justice Administration; Labour and Industrial Relations; Labour Law; Law; Marketing; Protective Services; Public Administration; Social Policy; Taxation); **Education** (Adult Education; Child Care and Development; Education; Health Sciences; Rehabilitation and Therapy; Vocational Counselling); **Graphics** (Architecture; Computer Graphics; Graphic Design; Interior Design); **Management** (Banking; Business Administration; Finance; Human Resources; Management; Sales Techniques; Small Business; Transport Management); **Sociology** (Human Resources; Marketing; Public Relations; Sociology)

Further Information: Also Branches in Łódź, Piotrków Trybunalski, Sieradz, Szczecinek, Rawa Mazowiecka and Konin

History: Founded 1994.

Governing Bodies: Scientific Board

Academic Year: October to June (October-January; March-June)

Admission Requirements: Secondary school certificate (Matura) and entrance examination

Fees: (New Złoty): c. 285-504 per month.

Main Language(s) of Instruction: Polish, English

International Co-operation: With universities in Germany, Netherlands, France, Belgium, Canada, UK, Greece, Denmark, USA, Finland, Ukraine, Latvia. Also participates in the Socrates/Erasmus programme

Accrediting Agencies: Ministry of Science and Higher Education

Degrees and Diplomas: *Licencjat*; *Świadectwo ukończenia studiów podyplomowych*; *Magister*

Student Services: Academic counselling, Canteen, Employment services, Foreign student adviser, Foreign Studies Centre, Health services, Language programs, Sports facilities

Student Residential Facilities: Yes

Special Facilities: Computer Laboratories

Publications: Trade Handbook, Professors Articles and Essays *(quarterly)*

Last Updated: 07/10/11

THE WARSAW FAMILY ALLIANCE INSTITUTE OF HIGHER EDUCATION

Wyższa Szkoła Przymierza Rodzin im. Bł. Edmunda Bojanowskiego (SWPR)

ul. Marii Grzegorzewskiej 10, 02-778 Warszawa, mazowieckie
Tel: +48(22) 644-07-97 +48(22) 644-07-55
Fax: +48(22) 644-07-97
EMail: swpr@swpr.edu.pl
Website: http://www.swpr.edu.pl

Kanclerz: Jaroslaw Domanski

Rektor: Elżbieta Mycielska-Dowgiałło

Departments

Postgraduate Studies (Child Care and Development; Communication Studies; Earth Sciences; Ethics; History; Home Economics; Information Sciences; Law; Pedagogy; Philology; Philosophy; Polish; Psychology; Rehabilitation and Therapy; Speech Therapy and Audiology; Teacher Training)

Faculties

Computer Science and Geoscience (Computer Science; Earth Sciences); **Geography** (Geography); **History** (History); **Pedagogy** (Pedagogy); **Polish Philology** (Philology; Polish); **Public Health** (Public Health); **Sociology** (Sociology); **Tourism and Recreation** (Leisure Studies; Parks and Recreation; Tourism)

History: Founded 2001.

Fees: (New Złoty): 1,000-1,550 per semester

Main Language(s) of Instruction: Polish

International Co-operation: State Accreditation Committee

Degrees and Diplomas: *Licencjat*; *Świadectwo ukończenia studiów podyplomowych*

Last Updated: 24/10/11

THE WROCLAW COLLEGE OF HUMANITIES

Wyższa Szkoła Humanistyczna we Wrocławiu (WSH)

ul. Stabłowicka 95, 54-062 Wrocław, dolnośląskie
Tel: +48(71) 354-37-49
Fax: +46(71) 349-06-40 Ext. 49
EMail: wsh@wsh.wroc.edu.pl
Website: http://www.wsh.wroc.edu.pl

Rektor: Robert Dziuba EMail: rektor@wsh.wroc.edu.pl

Kanclerz: Waclaw Laczynski EMail: kanclerz@wsh.wroc.edu.pl

International Relations: Barbara Kobzarska-Bar
EMail: international@wsh.wroc.edu.pl

Departments

Postgraduate Studies (Accountancy; Alternative Medicine; Energy Engineering; Interior Design; Real Estate)

Faculties

Humanities and Art (Arts and Humanities; Fine Arts; Interior Design); **Physical Culture** (Physical Therapy); **Technology and Economics** (Architecture and Planning; Civil Engineering; Economics; Geological Engineering; Surveying and Mapping; Technology; Town Planning)

History: Founded 2002.

Governing Bodies: Senate; Faculty Council
Main Language(s) of Instruction: Polish
International Co-operation: With universities in Estonia, Bulgaria, Lithuania, Germany, Portugal, Hungary, Turkey and Romania. Participates in the Erasmus programme.
Degrees and Diplomas: *Inżynier*; *Licencjat*; *Świadectwo ukończenia studiów podyplomowych*
Last Updated: 21/10/11

TISCHNER EUROPEAN UNIVERSITY

Wyższa Szkoła Europejska im. ks. Józefa Tischnera (WSE / TEU)
ul. Westerplatte, 11, 31-033 Kraków, małopolskie
Tel: +48(12) 683-24-00
Fax: +48(12) 683-24-32
EMail: wse@wse.krakow.pl; rekrutacja@wse.krakow.pl
Website: http://www.wse.krakow.pl

Rector: Jarosław Gowin (2003-)
Tel: +48(12) 683-24-01 +48(12) 683-24-03,
Fax: +48(12) 683-24-14
EMail: rektor@wse.krakow.pl; jgowin@wse.krakow.pl; rektor-at@wse.krakow.pl

Chancellor: Małgorzata Gosek
Tel: +48(12) 683-24-06 EMail: mgosek@wse.krakow.pl

International Relations: Wojciech Michnik, Vice Dean for the direction of international relations and national security
Tel: +483(12) 683-24-81, Fax: +483(12) 683-24-32
EMail: international@wse.krakow.pl

Centres
Modern Foreign Languages (Applied Linguistics; English; Modern Languages; Russian; Teacher Training; Translation and Interpretation); **Postgraduate Studies** (Cultural Studies; European Studies; Family Studies; Finance; Graphic Design; Human Resources; Journalism; Leadership; Management; Marketing; Media Studies; Modern Languages; Occupational Health; Philosophy; Protective Services; Public Relations; Safety Engineering; Translation and Interpretation)

Chairs
European Integration *(Kondrad Adenauer)* (European Studies; International Relations)

Departments
Sociology (Advertising and Publicity; Sociology)

Faculties
International Economic and Political Relations (Asian Studies; Human Resources; International Business; International Economics; International Law; International Relations; Management; Political Sciences; Protective Services; Public Administration; Public Relations); **Sociology and Social Anthropology** (Anthropology; Social Sciences; Sociology)

History: Founded 2003. Acquired current title and status 2007.

Governing Bodies: Rector, Senate

Academic Year: October to June

Admission Requirements: High School Diploma (Świadectwo dojrzałości / Matura) for Bachelor's level study; Bachelor's degree (Licencjat) for Master's level study.

Fees: (Polish Złoty): 1,750 per semester; Postgraduate tuition fee, 5,600 per programme.

Main Language(s) of Instruction: Polish, English

International Co-operation: Participate in the Erasmus programme.

Accrediting Agencies: Państwowa Komisja Akredytacyjna (State Accreditation Commission)

Degrees and Diplomas: *Licencjat*; *Świadectwo ukończenia studiów podyplomowych*; *Magister*

Student Services: Academic counselling, Cultural centre, Employment services, Foreign student adviser, Foreign Studies Centre, Language programs, Social counselling

Student Residential Facilities: Yes. Assistance given to overseas students in finding accommodation.

Publications: Zeszyty Naukowe WSE (Scientific Book of TEU), Articles and works of University faculty on teaching matters at TEU (sociology, international relations etc.) *(annually)*

Academic Staff *2010-2011*	**TOTAL**
FULL-TIME	**50**
PART-TIME	**50**
STAFF WITH DOCTORATE	
FULL-TIME	**20**
PART-TIME	c. **15**
Student Numbers *2010-2011*	
All (Foreign Included)	c. **1,300**
FOREIGN ONLY	**20**

Part-time students, 330.
Last Updated: 05/10/11

TORUŃ HIGHER SCHOOL

Toruńska Szkoła Wyższa (TSW)
Ul. Młodzieżowa 29, 87-100 Toruń, kujawsko-pomorskie
Tel: 056 - 661 07 12
EMail: dziekanat@tsw.home.pl
Website: http://www.tsw.edu.pl

Rektor: Jan Parys

Kanclerz: Ewa Nowakowska

Departments
Postgraduate Programmes (Finance; Insurance; International Business; Marketing; Sales Techniques; Taxation; Transport Management)

Faculties
Administration (Administration); **International Relations** (International Relations); **Pedagogy** (Pedagogy)

History: Founded 2003.

Main Language(s) of Instruction: Polish

Degrees and Diplomas: *Licencjat*; *Świadectwo ukończenia studiów podyplomowych*; *Magister*

Libraries: Yes
Last Updated: 18/10/11

TORUN HIGHER SCHOOL OF ENTREPRENEURSHIP

Toruńska Wyższa Szkoła Przedsiębiorczości (TWSP)
Plac Św. Katarzyny 9, 87-100 Toruń, kujawsko-pomorskie
Tel: +48(56) 652-20-83
EMail: dziekanat@twsp.pl
Website: http://www.twsp.com.pl/

Rektor: Wlodzimierz Wysocki EMail: rektor@twsp.pl

Kanclerz: Bozena Stryjska-Lach EMail: kanclerz@twsp.pl

Departments
Postgraduate Studies (Protective Services; Transport and Communications; Transport Management)

Faculties
Cosmetology (Alternative Medicine; Cosmetology); **Homeland Security** (Protective Services; Safety Engineering; Transport Management); **Logistics** (Information Technology; Transport and Communications; Transport Economics; Transport Management); **Tourism and Recreation** (International Business; Leisure Studies; Nutrition; Tourism)

History: Founded .

Fees: (New Złoty): Full-time, 1,950-3,000 per semester; Part-time, 1,700-2,750 per semester.

Main Language(s) of Instruction: Polish

Degrees and Diplomas: *Inżynier*, *Licencjat*; *Świadectwo ukończenia studiów podyplomowych*
Last Updated: 21/10/11

TORUN SCHOOL OF BANKING

Wyższa Szkoła Bankowa w Toruniu (WSB)
ul. Młodzieżowa 31a, 87-100 Toruń, kujawsko-pomorskie
Tel: +48(56) 660-91-00
Fax: +48(56) 660-91-07
EMail: wsb@wsb.torun.pl
Website: http://www.wsb.torun.pl

Rektor: Jan Głuchowski (1998-)
Tel: +48(56) 660-91-00 Ext. 12 EMail: rektorat@wsb.torun.pl

Kanclerz: Anna Kocikowska
Tel: +48(56) 660-91-07 EMail: kancelar@wsb.torun.pl

International Relations: Anna Kępa, International Relations Officer
Tel: +48(56) 660-92-36, Fax: +48(56) 660-92-07
EMail: international@wsb.torun.pl

Faculties

Finance and Management *(Bydgoszcz)* (Accountancy; Administration; Banking; Business Computing; English; Finance; Government; Human Resources; Management; Marketing; Occupational Health; Psychology; Real Estate; Sales Techniques; Sociology; Taxation; Tourism; Transport and Communications; Transport Management)

Institutes

Economic Practices (Business Administration; Economics; European Union Law; Finance; Human Resources; Information Technology; Law; Management; Modern Languages)

Schools

Banking (Accountancy; Administration; Banking; European Studies; Finance; Management; Parks and Recreation; Sociology; Tourism; Transport Management)

History: Founded 1998.

Governing Bodies: Senate

Admission Requirements: Secondary school certificate (matura)

Main Language(s) of Instruction: Polish; English

International Co-operation: Participates in the Erasmus programme.

Accrediting Agencies: Ministry of Science and Higher Education

Degrees and Diplomas: *Licencjat*; *Świadectwo ukończenia studiów podyplomowych*; *Magister*

Last Updated: 04/10/11

UNIVERSITY COLLEGE OF ENVIRONMENTAL SCIENCES IN RADOM

Prywatna Wyższa Szkoła Ochrony Środowiska w Radomiu (PWSOŚ)
ul. Zubrzyckiego 6, 26-600 Radom, mazowieckie
Tel: +48(48) 383-11-50
Fax: +48(48) 383-11-50
EMail: rektor@pwsos.pl
Website: http://www.pwsos.pl/

Rector: Anatol Peretiatkowicz (1995-)
Tel: +48(48) 382-11-50 Ext.26

Administrative Director: Rafał Ostrowski
Tel: +48(48) 382-11-50 Ext. 38

Centres

Education *(Ostrow Mazowiecka)*

Faculties

Environmental Protection *(Miechow Branch)* (Environmental Studies; Toxicology); **Environmental Protection** (Ecology; Economics; Energy Engineering; Environmental Management; Environmental Studies; Farm Management; Forest Economics; Forest Management; Hygiene; Peace and Disarmament; Public Health; Safety Engineering; Tourism; Transport Engineering; Transport Management; Waste Management; Water Management); **Logistics** (Environmental Studies; Farm Management; Horticulture; Hygiene; Public Health; Safety Engineering; Tourism; Transport and Communications; Transport Management); **Safety and Environmental Protection Work** (Ecology; Economics; Energy Engineering; Environmental Management; Environmental Studies; Farm Management; Horticulture; Hygiene; Occupational Health; Peace and Disarmament; Public Health; Safety Engineering; Tourism; Transport Engineering; Transport Management); **Tourism and Recreation** (Cooking and Catering; Energy Engineering; Environmental Studies; Farm Management; Horticulture; Hotel and Restaurant; Hygiene; Leisure Studies; Parks and Recreation; Peace and Disarmament; Public Health; Safety Engineering; Tourism); **Tourism and Recreation** *(Zakopane)* (Leisure Studies; Parks and Recreation; Tourism)

History: Founded 1993, acquired present status and title 1999.

Governing Bodies: Senate; Council

Academic Year: October to January (October-September; February-January)

Admission Requirements: Secondary school certificate (Matura)

Fees: (New Złoty): Tuition fee, c. 360-480 per month.

Main Language(s) of Instruction: Polish

Accrediting Agencies: Ministry of Science and Higher Education

Degrees and Diplomas: *Inżynier*; *Licencjat*; *Świadectwo ukończenia studiów podyplomowych*; *Magister*

Student Services: Canteen, Health services, Language programs, Sports facilities

Student Residential Facilities: Yes

Libraries: Main Library

Publications: Przeglad Naukowo-Dydaktycny PWSOS, Readings and research reports *(biannually)*

Last Updated: 27/09/11

UNIVERSITY COLLEGE OF TOURISM AND ECOLOGY IN SUCHA BESKIDZKA

Wyższa Szkoła Turystyki i Ekologii w Suchej Beskidzkiej (WSTIE)
ul. Spółdzielców 1, 34-200 Sucha Beskidzka, małopolskie
Tel: +48(33) 874-20-80
Fax: +48(33) 874-46-05
EMail: szkola@wste.edu.pl
Website: http://www.wste.edu.pl

Rector: Janusz Sondel (2001-)

Administrative Officer: Maria Grzechynka Tel: +48(33) 874-47-40

Departments

Postgraduate Degree (Business Computing; Computer Graphics; Computer Networks; Hotel and Restaurant; Information Technology; Management; Media Studies; Multimedia; Public Relations; Software Engineering; Tourism)

Faculties

Computer Science (Computer Science; Data Processing; Information Technology; Software Engineering); **Leisure and Tourism** (Business Administration; Hotel and Restaurant; International Business; Leisure Studies; Management; Tourism); **Social Sciences** (Communication Studies; Government; Management; Political Sciences; Public Relations; Social Sciences)

History: Founded 2001.

Main Language(s) of Instruction: Polish

International Co-operation: With universities in Spain, UK, Hungary, Turkey, Portugal, France, Germany, Italy, Estonia, Latvia, Slovenia. Participates in the Erasmus programme.

Accrediting Agencies: National Accreditation Commission

Degrees and Diplomas: *Inżynier*; *Licencjat*; *Świadectwo ukończenia studiów podyplomowych*; *Magister*. Also undergraduate course and certificates.

Student Residential Facilities: Yes

Special Facilities: Laboratories; Computer Labs

Libraries: Yes

Last Updated: 24/10/11

UNIVERSITY OF BUSINESS AND ENTERPRISE IN OSTROWIEC ŚWIĘTOKRZYSKI

Wyższa Szkoła Biznesu Wyższa Szkoła Biznesu i Przedsiębiorczości w Ostrowcu Świętokrzyskim (WSBIP)

ul. Akademicka 12, 27-400 Ostrowiec Świętokrzyski, świętokrzyskie
Tel: +48(41) 260-40-41
Fax: +48(41) 263-21-10
EMail: info@wsbip.edu.pl; rekrutacja@wsbip.edu.pl
Website: http://www.wsbip.edu.pl

Rector: Bożena Zboina
Tel: +48(41) 260-40-44
EMail: rektorat@wsbip.edu.pl; rektorat@wsbip.edu.pl

Kanclerz: Józef Tyburczy
Tel: +48(41) 260-40-40 Ext.112 EMail: kanclerz@wsbip.edu.pl

International Relations: Marta Dobrowolska-Wesolowska, International Relations Officer and Socrates Erasmus Coordinator
Tel: +48(41) 263-21-10, Fax: +48(41) 263-21-10
EMail: zagranica@wsbip.edu.pl; wesolowska_m@wp.pl

Departments

Pedagogy and Health Science (Education; Health Sciences; Nursing; Parks and Recreation; Pedagogy; Physical Education; Physical Therapy; Public Health; Tourism); **Social and Technical Science** (Economics; Educational Technology; Engineering; Geological Engineering; Information Technology; Metallurgical Engineering; Political Sciences; Protective Services; Social Sciences; Sociology; Surveying and Mapping)

History: Founded 1996 as Higher School of Business. Acquired present title 1998.

Fees: (New Złoty): Undergraduate tuition fee, 2,310-3,600 per annum; Graduate tuition fee, 3,000-4,800 per annum

International Co-operation: With universities in Lithuania, Turkey, Czech Republic, Italy, Hungary. Participates in the Erasmus LLP programme.

Accrediting Agencies: Ministry of Science and Higher Education

Degrees and Diplomas: *Inżynier*; *Licencjat*; *Świadectwo ukończenia studiów podyplomowych*; *Magister*

Libraries: c. 50,000 vols; 109 periodical subscriptions.

Academic Staff *2010-2011*: Total 196
STAFF WITH DOCTORATE: Total 43
Student Numbers *2010-2011*: Total: c. 3,000
Last Updated: 04/10/11

UNIVERSITY OF BUSINESS IN WROCLAW

Wyższa Szkoła Handlowa we Wrocławiu (WSH)

ul. Ostrowskiego 22, 53-238 Wrocław, dolnośląskie
Tel: +48(71) 333-11-12
Fax: +48(71) 333-11-02
EMail: rektorat@handlowa.eu
Website: http://www.handlowa.eu/

Rector: Zdzisław Jagiełło (2008-) EMail: rektor@handlowa.eu

Chancellor: Irena Tomys EMail: kanclerz@handlowa.eu

International Relations: Zbigniew Sebastian, Vice-Rector for International Relations
Tel: +48(71) 333-11-13 EMail: zbigniew.sebastian@handlowa.eu

Departments

Foreign Languages (English; Foreign Languages Education; German; Italian; Modern Languages; Spanish)

Faculties

European Studies (Accountancy; Administrative Law; European Studies; Government; International Business; Management; Public Administration); **Finance** (Accountancy; Engineering; Finance; Taxation); **Internal Security** (Fire Science; Protective Services; Safety Engineering; Transport Management); **Management** (Accountancy; Business Administration; Business Computing; E-Business/Commerce; Finance; Human Resources; Management; Marketing; Public Administration; Service Trades; Small Business; Tourism; Transport Management); **Tourism and Recreation** (Business Administration; Economics; English; Health Administration; Hotel and Restaurant; International Business; Leisure Studies; Management; Marketing; Parks and Recreation; Tourism)

Further Information: Also International Programme Unit

History: Founded 1997.

Governing Bodies: Senate

Admission Requirements: Secondary school certificate (matura)

Main Language(s) of Instruction: Polish; English

International Co-operation: Participates in the Erasmus programme

Accrediting Agencies: Ministry of Science and Higher Education

Degrees and Diplomas: *Licencjat*; *Świadectwo ukończenia studiów podyplomowych*; *Magister*. Also Certificates in foreign languages; MBA

Student Numbers *2010-2011*: Total: c. 4,000
Last Updated: 06/10/11

UNIVERSITY OF BYDGOSZCZ

Bydgoska Szkoła Wyższa z siedzibą w Bydgoszczy (BSW)

ul. Unii Lubelskiej 4C, 85-059 Bydgoszcz, kujawsko-pomorskie
Tel: +48(52) 584-11-43
EMail: uczelnia@bsw.edu.pl
Website: http://bsw.edu.pl/

Rektor: Sławomir Tecław
Tel: +48(52) 584-11-43, Fax: +48(52) 584-11-47
EMail: biuro.rektora@bsw.edu.pl

Kanclerz: Arkadiusz Slowinski

Faculties

Administration (Administration; Environmental Management; Finance; Justice Administration; Management; Public Administration; Public Law; Real Estate); **Construction Engineering** (Civil Engineering; Construction Engineering; Road Engineering); **Cosmetology** (Alternative Medicine; Cosmetology; Dermatology); **Education** (Child Care and Development; Education; Preschool Education; Special Education); **Human Nutrition and Dietetics** (Dietetics; Nutrition; Rehabilitation and Therapy; Sports Medicine); **Logistics** (Transport Management); **National Security** (Protective Services); **Physiotherapy** (Gerontology; Physical Therapy; Rehabilitation and Therapy; Sports Medicine); **Production Management and Engineering** (Business Administration; Energy Engineering; Military Science; Production Engineering; Safety Engineering; Transport and Communications); **Public Health** (Gerontology; Health Administration; Health Sciences; Psychiatry and Mental Health; Psychotherapy; Public Health; Welfare and Protective Services)

History: Founded 2004 as Wyższa Szkoła Informatyki i Nauk Społeczno–Prawnych w Bydgoszczy. Changed name to Wyższa Szkoła Informatyki i Przedsiębiorczości 2007. Acquired present title 2009.

Main Language(s) of Instruction: Polish

Degrees and Diplomas: *Inżynier*, *Licencjat*; *Świadectwo ukończenia studiów podyplomowych*

Last Updated: 25/11/08

UNIVERSITY OF COMPUTER SCIENCE AND ECONOMICS IN OLSZTYN

Wyższa Szkoła Informatyki i Ekonomii Towarzystwa Wiedzy Powszechnej (WSIIE TWP)

ul. Barczewskiego 11, 10-061 Olsztyn, warmińsko-mazurskie
Tel: +48(89) 527-55-45
Fax: +48(89) 353-19-48
EMail: sekretariat@wsiie.olsztyn.pl
Website: http://www.wsiie.olsztyn.pl/

Rektor: Jan Kwiatkowski
Tel: +48(89) 521-89-08, Fax: +48(89) 521-89-08

Kanclerz: Wiesław Nałęcz
Tel: +48(89) 535-19-48, Fax: +48(89) 535-19-48

International Relations: Sylwia Żuk, International Relations Officer
Tel: +48(89) 521-89-08 Ext. 12, Fax: +48(89) 521-89-08 Ext. 138
EMail: sylwia.zuk@wsiie.olsztyn.pl

Campuses

Kętrzyn (Accountancy; Administration; Business Administration; Economics; Educational Sciences; Finance; Pedagogy; Primary Education; Protective Services; Public Administration)

Faculties

Informatics and Economics (Accountancy; Actuarial Science; Banking; Business Administration; Business Computing; Communication Arts; Computer Engineering; Computer Graphics; Computer Networks; Computer Science; Econometrics; Economics; Educational Administration; Educational Technology; Finance; Health Administration; Information Sciences; Information Technology); **Sociology and Pedagogy** (Administration; Art Therapy; Cultural Studies; Educational Psychology; Family Studies; Health Education; Human Resources; Mass Communication; Pedagogy; Primary Education; Protective Services; Public Administration; Public Relations; Rehabilitation and Therapy; Sociology; Speech Therapy and Audiology; Teacher Training; Vocational Counselling)

Further Information: Kętrzyn

History: Founded 1997.

Governing Bodies: Senate

Academic Year: October to September

Admission Requirements: Secondary school certificate (Matura)

Fees: (New Złoty): c. 3,300 per annum

Main Language(s) of Instruction: Polish, English

International Co-operation: Participates in the Erasmus and Leonardo da Vinci programmes.

Accrediting Agencies: Ministry of Science and Higher Education

Degrees and Diplomas: *Licencjat*; *Świadectwo ukończenia studiów podyplomowych*; *Magister*

Student Services: Cultural centre, Employment services, Language programs, Social counselling, Sports facilities

Student Residential Facilities: Yes

Special Facilities: Academic Incubator for Entrepreneurship

Libraries: WSIiE TWP Library

Publications: Silva Rerum

Academic Staff *2010-2011*: Total: c. 100

Last Updated: 06/10/11

UNIVERSITY OF ECOLOGY AND MANAGEMENT IN WARSAW

Wyższa Szkoła Ekologii i Zarządzania w Warszawie (WSEIZ)

ul. Wawelska 14, 02-061 Warszawa, mazowieckie
Tel: +48(22) 825-80-34 +48(22) 825-80-35
Fax: +48(22) 825-80-31
EMail: rekrutacja@wseiz.pl
Website: http://www.wseiz.pl

Rektor: Monika Madej EMail: rektorat@wseiz.pl

Departments

Postgraduate Studies (Ecology; Economics; Energy Engineering; Management; Occupational Health; Safety Engineering; Waste Management); **Tourism** *(Inter-specialty)* (Dietetics; Nutrition; Parks and Recreation; Tourism)

Faculties

Architecture (Architecture; Architecture and Planning; Building Technologies; Construction Engineering; Design; Interior Design; Landscape Architecture; Town Planning); **Ecology** (Computer Education; Ecology; Environmental Management; Environmental Studies; Public Health); **Management** (Engineering; Management; Production Engineering)

History: Founded 1995.

Governing Bodies: Senate; Faculty Councils

Academic Year: October to September

Admission Requirements: Secondary school certificate (Świadectwo dojrzałości); Architecture, drawing examination

Fees: (New Złoty): c. 400-970 per month

Main Language(s) of Instruction: Polish

International Co-operation: Participates in the Erasmus programme.

Accrediting Agencies: Ministry of Science and Higher Education

Degrees and Diplomas: *Inżynier*; *Licencjat*; *Świadectwo ukończenia studiów podyplomowych*; *Magister*

Student Services: Handicapped facilities, Health services, Language programs, Sports facilities

Special Facilities: Plant and Landscape Protection Station

Libraries: University Library; c. 42,000 vols

Academic Staff *2010-2011*: Total 350

STAFF WITH DOCTORATE: Total 186

Student Numbers *2010-2011*: Total: c. 4,000

Last Updated: 05/10/11

UNIVERSITY OF ECONOMICS AND ADMINISTRATION IN BYTOM

Wyższa Szkoła Ekonomii i Administracji w Bytomiu (WSEIA)

ul. A. Frycza-Modrzewskiego, 12, 41-907 Bytom, śląskie
Tel: +48(32) 387-53-61
Fax: +48(32) 286-95-21
EMail: rektorat@wsea.edu.pl
Website: http://www.wsea.edu.pl

Rektor: Mirosław Czapka Tel: +48(32) 387-53-61 Ext.120

International Relations: Luis Ocho Siguencia, Director, Department of International Relations
Tel: +48(32) 387-53-61 Ext.146 EMail: ird_biuro@wsea.edu.pl

Faculties

Administration (Administration; European Studies; Government); **Cosmetology** (Cosmetology); **Economy** (Accountancy; Economics; Environmental Management; Environmental Studies; International Economics; International Relations; Management; Marketing; Occupational Health; Parks and Recreation; Tourism; Transport Economics; Transport Management); **Management and Engineering Production** (Engineering; Engineering Management; Production Engineering; Safety Engineering); **Physiotherapy** (Physical Therapy; Rehabilitation and Therapy); **Politology** (Journalism; Marketing; Political Sciences)

Programmes

Weekend Master Study (Accountancy; Computer Science; Economics; Environmental Management; European Studies; Management; Marketing; Occupational Health; Public Administration; Transport Economics; Transport Management)

History: Founded 1996.

Academic Year: September to May (September-January; February-May)

Fees: (New Złoty): 1,650-2,100 per semester

International Co-operation: With universities in Ukraine, Lithuania, Czech Republic, USA, Slovakia, Italy, Belarus, France. Participates in the Erasmus programme.

Accrediting Agencies: Ministry of Science and Higher Education

Degrees and Diplomas: *Inżynier*; *Licencjat*; *Świadectwo ukończenia studiów podyplomowych*; *Magister*

Last Updated: 05/10/11

UNIVERSITY OF ECONOMICS AND INNOVATION IN LUBLIN

Wyższa Szkoła Ekonomii i Innowacji w Lublinie (WSEI)

ul. Mełgiewska 7-9, 20-209 Lublin, lubelskie
Tel: +48(81) 749-17-77
Fax: +48(81) 749-17-77 +48(81) 749-32-13
EMail: sekretariat@wsei.lublin.pl
Website: http://www.wsei.lublin.pl

Rector: Marek Żmigrodzki

Kanclerz: Teresa Bogacka
Tel: +48(81) 532-59-29, Fax: +48(81) 532-86-26
EMail: oicpl@platon.man.lublin.pl

International Relations: Ewelina Iwanek-Chachaj, International Cooperation Officer

Tel: +48(81) 749-32-49, Fax: +48(81) 749-32-13
EMail: ewelina.iwanek@wsei.lublin.pl

Centres

Postgraduate Studies (Accountancy; Banking; Business Administration; Communication Studies; Computer Graphics; Computer Networks; Cultural Studies; Data Processing; Development Studies; Economics; Environmental Management; Environmental Studies; Family Studies; Finance; Gender Studies; Health Administration; Human Resources; International Business; Labour Law; Management; Media Studies; Pedagogy; Preschool Education; Protective Services; Psychology; Public Health; Public Relations; Real Estate; Rehabilitation and Therapy; Safety Engineering; Small Business; Statistics; Taxation; Teacher Training; Transport and Communications; Welfare and Protective Services)

Faculties

Administration (Administration; European Studies; International Relations; Protective Services; Public Administration); **Economics** (Accountancy; Business Administration; Business Computing; Economics; Finance; International Business; Management; Occupational Health; Real Estate; Safety Engineering; Transport Economics; Transport Management); **Pedagogy and Psychology** (Nursing; Pedagogy; Protective Services; Psychology; Rehabilitation and Therapy; Social Sciences; Social Work); **Transport and Computer Science** (Automotive Engineering; Computer Graphics; Computer Networks; Computer Science; Engineering; Information Technology; Machine Building; Mechanical Engineering; Multimedia; Telecommunications Engineering; Transport and Communications; Transport Engineering; Transport Management)

Governing Bodies: Senate

Accrediting Agencies: State Accreditation Committee

Degrees and Diplomas: *Inżynier*; *Licencjat*; *Świadectwo ukończenia studiów podyplomowych*; *Magister*

Academic Staff *2010-2011*: Total: c. 320
Student Numbers *2010-2011*: Total: c. 10,500
Last Updated: 05/10/11

UNIVERSITY OF FINANCE AND MANAGEMENT IN WARSAW

Wyższa Szkoła Finansów i Zarządzania w Warszawie (WSFIZ)

ul. Pawia 55, 01-030 Warszawa, mazowieckie
Tel: +48(22) 536-54-80
Fax: +48(22) 536-54-64
EMail: rekrutacja@vizja.pl
Website: http://www.vizja.pl

Rector: Maria Sierpińska (2001-)
Tel: +48(22) 536-54-10 EMail: rektorat@vizja.pl

Secretary-General: Marzena Sikorska
Tel: +48(22) 331-89-61 EMail: sikorska@vizja.pl

International Relations: Magdalena Klepacz
Tel: +48 602 113 166
EMail: klepacz@vizja.pl; magda.klepacz@waw.pl

Departments

Doctoral Studies (Economics; Psychology); **Foreign Languages** *(DFL)* (English; French; German; Modern Languages; Russian; Spanish); **Postgraduate Studies** (Accountancy; Advertising and Publicity; Business Administration; Finance; Human Resources; Marketing; Occupational Health; Psychology; Real Estate; Safety Engineering; Transport Management)

Faculties

Administration (Administration; Business Administration; Government; Public Administration); **Finance and Accountancy** (Accountancy; Administration; Banking; Economics; Finance; Government; Insurance; International Economics; International Relations; Management; Public Administration); **Law** (Commercial Law; E-Business/Commerce; European Union Law; Fiscal Law; International Law; Labour Law; Law; Public Administration; Real Estate); **Management** (Accountancy; Advertising and Publicity; Communication Studies; E-Business/Commerce; Human Resources; Information Management; Management; Marketing; Parks and Recreation; Public Administration; Public Relations; Tourism); **Political Sciences** (European Studies; International Relations; Journalism; Management; Mass Communication; Political Sciences); **Psychology** (Clinical Psychology; Forensic Medicine and Dentistry; Industrial and Organizational Psychology; Neurology; Psychology; Psychotherapy; Social Psychology)

Governing Bodies: Senate

Admission Requirements: Secondary school certificate (matura)

Fees: (New Złoty): 3,500-4,400 per annum

Main Language(s) of Instruction: Polish

Accrediting Agencies: Ministry of Science and Higher Education

Degrees and Diplomas: *Licencjat*; *Świadectwo ukończenia studiów podyplomowych*; *Magister*; *Doktor*

Student Residential Facilities: 342 appartements
Last Updated: 06/10/11

UNIVERSITY OF HUMANITIES AND ECONOMICS IN LODZ

Akademia Humanistyczno-Ekonomiczna w Łodzi (AHE)

ul. Rewolucji 1905 r. nr. 64, 90-222 Łódź, łódzkie
Tel: +48(42) 631-50-00
Fax: +48(42) 631-58-88
EMail: uczelnia@ahe.lodz.pl; rekrutacja@ahe.lodz.pl
Website: http://www.ahe.lodz.pl

Rektor: Andrzej Denys

Kanclerz: Kalina Odziemczewska

International Relations: Joanna Kmiecik
EMail: jkmiecik@ahe.lodz.pl

Departments

Arts (Cultural Studies; Graphic Design); **Computer Science, Management and Transport** (Computer Science; Management; Transport and Communications); **Humanities** (Administration; Communication Studies; Journalism; Nursing; Pedagogy; Philology; Polish; Political Sciences)

History: Founded 1995. The largest and oldest non-public and independent University in Poland. Formerly known as Wyższa Szkoła Humanistyczno-Ekonomiczna w Łodzi.

Governing Bodies: Senate

Academic Year: October to June

Admission Requirements: Secondary school certificate (Matura) or equivalent

Fees: (New Złoty): c. 3,720-7,320 per annum

Main Language(s) of Instruction: Polish, English

International Co-operation: Participates in the Socrates, Leonardo da Vinci and Youth for Europe programmes

Accrediting Agencies: Ministry of Science and Higher Education; the State Accreditation Committee

Degrees and Diplomas: *Inżynier*: Transport Engineering; *Licencjat*: Philology; Pedagogy; Journalism and Social Communication; Polish Philology; Administration; Political Science; Nursing; Graphic design; Cultural studies; *Magister*: Philology; Pedagogy; Polish Philology; Political Science; Graphic Design; *Doktor*: Linguistics; Computer Science; Fine Arts. Postgraduate studies are organised by the Centrum Kształcenia Podyplomowego (Postgraduate Studies Centre) and the AHE in Lodz for people with MA and BA titles. These are extramural studies with the lectures taking place during the weekends and run for two or three semesters.

Student Services: Academic counselling, Canteen, Cultural centre, Employment services, Foreign student adviser, Handicapped facilities, Health services, Language programs, Sports facilities

Student Residential Facilities: Yes

Special Facilities: Art Studios

Publications: Civitas Hominibus, Social science *(annually)*; Homo Politicus, Political science *(annually)*; Językoznawstwo, Linguistics *(annually)*; Literaturoznawstwo, Literature *(annually)*; Media - Kultura - Społeczeństwo, Journalism and Social Communication *(annually)*; Studien zur Germanistik, German studies *(annually)*; Zarządzanie Innowacyjne w Gospodarce i Biznesie, Management and marketing *(1-2 per annum)*
Last Updated: 29/08/11

UNIVERSITY OF HUMANITIES AND ECONOMICS IN WŁOCŁAWEK

Wyższa Szkoła Humanistyczno-Ekonomiczna we Włocławku (WSHE/UHEW)

Plac Wolności 1, 87-800 Włocławek, kujawsko-pomorskie
Tel: +48(54) 425-20-07
Fax: +48(54) 425-20-07 Ext.12
EMail: biurorektora@wshe.pl
Website: http://www.wshe.pl

Rektor: Stanisław Kunikowski EMail: rektor@wshe.pl

Kanclerz: Jolanta Mroczkowska

International Relations: Paweł Churski, Prorektor
Tel: +48(54) 231-53-36 EMail: chur@amu.edu.pl

Departments

Foreign Languages (English; Foreign Languages Education; French; German; Italian; Modern Languages; Russian; Spanish); **Information Technology** (Computer Science; Information Technology); **Physical Education** (Physical Education; Sports)

Faculties

Health Sciences (Health Sciences; Nursing; Physical Education); **Pedagogics** (Computer Education; Health Education; Management; Pedagogy; Protective Services; Rehabilitation and Therapy; Social Work; Vocational Counselling); **Social and Technical Sciences** (Accountancy; Administration; Banking; Botany; Ecology; Economics; English; Environmental Studies; Finance; Forestry; French; German; Government; Human Resources; Insurance; Management; Modern Languages; Protective Services; Public Administration; Real Estate; Russian; Social Sciences; Spanish; Transport Management; Wildlife)

History: Founded 1995 as Higher School of Social Work, acquired present status and title 1997.

Governing Bodies: Senate

Admission Requirements: Secondary school certificate (matura)

Main Language(s) of Instruction: Polish

International Co-operation: With universitie in Sweden, Spain, Turkey, Latvia, Portugal and Bulgaria. Participates in Phare II, Erasmus LLP, Leonardo Da Vinci, and Socrates Lingua 1 programmes.

Accrediting Agencies: Ministry of Science and Higher Education; State Accreditation Commission

Degrees and Diplomas: *Inżynier*; *Licencjat*; *Świadectwo ukończenia studiów podyplomowych*; *Magister*

Student Services: Sports facilities

Special Facilities: Theatre 'Brama'. Computer Centre

Libraries: Central Library, c. 52,200 vols; 91 periodical subscriptions.

Publications: Open Lectures; Scientific Debuts of WSHE; Scientific Journals of WSHE; VLADISLAVIA, Journal on Humanities and Economics *(1-2 per annum)*

Press or Publishing House: University Publishing House; Publishing House "Lega"

Last Updated: 06/10/11

UNIVERSITY OF INFORMATION TECHNOLOGY AND MANAGEMENT, RZESZOW

Wyższa Szkoła Informatyki i Zarządzania z siedzibą w Rzeszowie (WSIiZ)

ul. H. Sucharskiego 2, 35-225 Rzeszów, podkarpackie
Tel: +48(17) 866-12-22 +48(17) 866-12-24
Fax: +48(17) 866-12-12
EMail: wsiz@wsiz.rzeszow.pl
Website: http://www.wsiz.rzeszow.pl

Rektor: Tadeusz Pomianek
EMail: tpomianek@wenus.wsiz.rzeszow.pl

Kanclerz: Stanisław Harpula

International Relations: Elżbieta Tylek-Hydryńska, Head, Department of International Relations
Tel: +48(17) 866-12-71, Fax: +48(17) 866-11-28
EMail: ird@wsiz.rzeszow.pl; etylek@wsiz.rzeszow.pl

Centres

Foreign Languages School of Computer Science and Management (Computer Science; English; French; German; Hindi; Japanese; Management; Modern Languages; Persian; Polish; Slavic Languages; Spanish; Swedish); **Postgraduate Studies** (Accountancy; Administration; Banking; Business Administration; Computer Engineering; Computer Networks; Computer Science; Cosmetology; E-Business/Commerce; Educational Administration; Educational and Student Counselling; Educational Technology; Ethics; Family Studies; Finance; Health Sciences; Hotel and Restaurant; Human Resources; Information Sciences; Insurance; International Business; Journalism; Library Science; Management; Marketing; Mass Communication; Multimedia; Occupational Health; Pedagogy; Physical Education; Physical Therapy; Polish; Preschool Education; Protective Services; Public Administration; Public Relations; Radio and Television Broadcasting; Real Estate; Rehabilitation and Therapy; Safety Engineering; Software Engineering; Taxation; Technology; Tourism; Transport Management)

Faculties

Administration and Social Sciences (Administration; Administrative Law; Advertising and Publicity; Computer Graphics; Constitutional Law; Higher Education; Journalism; Law; Media Studies; Protective Services; Public Relations; Social Sciences); **Applied IT** (Artificial Intelligence; E-Business/Commerce; Economics; Electronic Engineering; Information Sciences; Information Technology; Mathematics; Telecommunications Engineering); **Economics** (Economic and Finance Policy; Economics; International Economics; International Relations; Operations Research; Social Policy); **Tourism and Health Sciences** (Cosmetology; Economics; Geography; Health Sciences; Medicine; Parks and Recreation; Physical Therapy; Public Health; Tourism)

History: Founded 1996. Merged with the Wyższa Szkoła Społeczno-Gospodarcza w Tyczynie (Higher School of Social Sciences and Economics, Tyczyn) 2008.

Governing Bodies: Senate

Academic Year: October to September

Admission Requirements: Secondary school certificate (matura)

Fees: (New Złoty): 660-750 per month for EU member students. (Euro): 1,500-1,750 per semester for non-EU member students.

Main Language(s) of Instruction: Polish, English

International Co-operation: With universities in United Kingdom, France, Germany, Finland, Spain, Portugal, Denmark, Slovakia, Netherlands, Ukraine, Serbia, Macedonia, Hungary, USA, Canada, Indian, China, Iran, Malaysia, Turkey, Singapore. Also participates in the Socrates/Erasmus programme.

Accrediting Agencies: Ministry of Science and Higher Education; State Accreditation Committee (SAC)

Degrees and Diplomas: *Licencjat*; *Magister*. Also double degree programmes offered by UITM and USA- and Europe based institutions at no extra charge in the following fields: Information Technology, Computer Graphics and Animation, International Business, Business Administration, MBA, Hospitality Management, Leisure and Tourism, Public Health, Paramedic studies, Journalism and Social Communication, European Studies.

Student Services: Academic counselling, Canteen, Cultural centre, Employment services, Language programs, Sports facilities

Student Residential Facilities: 240 places in dormitories

Special Facilities: 300 seats auditorium hall; 9 lecture halls; 3 Computer Laboratories; Specialized computer labs; Internet access

Libraries: 19,557 vols; 1,403 audiovisual materials

Publications: Przedsiebiorczy Patrioci, Economics and Social problems *(biennially)*; Zeszyty Naukowe, Conference materials, Thematic essays *(quarterly)*

Student Numbers *2010-2011*: Total: c. 10,000

Last Updated: 07/10/11

UNIVERSITY OF TECHNOLOGY AND ENTERPRISE, WŁOCŁAWEK

Wyższa Szkoła Techniki i Przedsiębiorczości we Włocławku (WSTIP)

ul. Łęgska 20, 87-800 Włocławek, kujawsko-pomorskie
Tel: +47(54) 425-11-31 +47(54) 425-11-32
Fax: +47(54) 425-11-40
EMail: dziekanat@wstip.pl; rektorat@wstip.pl
Website: http://www.wstip.wloclawek.pl/

Rektor: Maciej Woropay

Kanclerz: Agnieszka Woropay-Jankowska

Departments

Postgraduate Studies (Energy Engineering; Thermal Engineering)

Faculties

Construction Engineering (Air Transport; Construction Engineering; Road Engineering); **Logistics** (Management; Transport Management); **Technical Education - Computer Science** (Computer Science; Information Technology; Production Engineering; Technology Education); **Transport** (Transport and Communications; Transport Engineering; Transport Management)

History: Founded 2004.

Main Language(s) of Instruction: Polish

Accrediting Agencies: Minister of Education and Sport

Degrees and Diplomas: *Inżynier*, *Świadectwo ukończenia studiów podyplomowych*

Last Updated: 26/10/11

VINCENT POL UNIVERSITY, LUBLIN

Wyższa Szkoła Społeczno-Przyrodnicza im. Wincentego Pola w Lublinie (WSS-P)

ul. Choiny 2, 20-816 Lublin, lubelskie
Tel: +48(81) 740-72-40
Fax: +48(81) 740-25-08
EMail: info@wssp.edu.pl
Website: http://www.wssp.edu.pl

Rektor: Witold Kłaczewski Fax: +48(81) 740-25-09

Kanclerz: Henryk Stefanek

Centres

Green School *(Piotrawin)* (Environmental Studies; Wildlife)

Faculties

Humanities and Social Sciences (Arts and Humanities; Computer Science; Economics; English; Health Education; Management; Parks and Recreation; Pedagogy; Philology; Physical Education; Rehabilitation and Therapy; Social Sciences; Spanish; Special Education; Tourism); **Physiotherapy** (Physical Therapy); **Tourism and Economics** (Econometrics; Economics; Hotel and Restaurant; Information Technology; Tourism)

Schools

Cosmetology (Cosmetology)

History: Founded 2000.

Governing Bodies: Senate

Admission Requirements: Secondary school certificate (matura)

Main Language(s) of Instruction: Polish

International Co-operation: With universities in France, USA, Serbia, Ukraine, Portugal, Hungary, Spain.

Accrediting Agencies: Ministry of Science and Higher Education

Degrees and Diplomas: *Licencjat*, *Świadectwo ukończenia studiów podyplomowych*; *Magister*

Student Services: Sports facilities

Libraries: c. 20,000 vols

Last Updated: 08/10/11

VISTULA UNIVERSITY

Uczelnia Vistula

ul. Stokłosy 3, 02-787 Warszawa, mazowieckie
Tel: +48(22) 457-23-00 +48(22) 457-24-00
Fax: +48(22) 457-23-03
EMail: info@vistula.edu.pl; rekrutacja@vistula.edu.pl
Website: http://www.vistula.edu.pl/

Rector: Krzysztof Rybiński (2010-)
Tel: +48(22) 457-23-70, Fax: +48(22) 457-23-71
EMail: rektorat@vistula.edu.pl

Kanclerz: Arif Erkol
Tel: +48(22) 457-23-37, Fax: +48(22) 457-23-03
EMail: kanclerz@vistula.edu.pl

International Relations: Davut Han Aslan, International Officer
Tel: +48(22) 457-23-16 EMail: leondavuthan@gmail.com

Centres

Postgraduate Studies (Accountancy; Art Management; Banking; Educational Administration; English; Finance; Fiscal Law; Foreign Languages Education; French; German; Information Sciences; International Business; Italian; Journalism; Leadership; Polish; Public Administration; Real Estate; Russian; Spanish; Translation and Interpretation; Waste Management)

Faculties

Business (Accountancy; Air Transport; Banking; Business Administration; Economics; Finance; Hotel and Restaurant; Human Resources; Information Management; Insurance; International Business; International Economics; International Relations; Law; Management; Parks and Recreation; Sports Management; Taxation; Tourism); **Foreign Affairs and Public Relations** (Government; International Relations; Media Studies; Political Sciences; Public Relations; Sociology); **Philology** (Communication Studies; Cultural Studies; English; French; German; Italian; Modern Languages; Philology; Polish; Russian; Spanish; Translation and Interpretation); **Science** (Business Computing; Computer Engineering; Computer Networks; Data Processing; Software Engineering)

History: Founded 1996. Formerly know as Wyższa Szkoła Ekonomiczno-Informatyczna w Warszawie (Higher School of Economics and Information Technology, Warsaw). Acquired present title 2011.

Governing Bodies: Senate

Admission Requirements: Secondary school certificate (matura)

Main Language(s) of Instruction: Polish; English

International Co-operation: With . Participates in the Erasmus programme.

Accrediting Agencies: Ministry of Science and Higher Education

Degrees and Diplomas: *Licencjat*, *Świadectwo ukończenia studiów podyplomowych*; *Magister*

Academic Staff *2010-2011*: Total 210
STAFF WITH DOCTORATE: Total 50
Last Updated: 05/10/11

WAŁBRZYCH HIGHER SCHOOL OF MANAGEMENT AND ENTERPRISE

Wałbrzyska Wyższa Szkoła Zarządzania i Przedsiębiorczości (WWSZIP)

ul. 1-go Maja 131, 58-305 Wałbrzych, dolnośląskie
Tel: +48(74) 848-54-13
Fax: +48(74) 848-60-17
EMail: rektorat@wwszip.pl
Website: http://www.wwszip.pl

Rektor: Rafal Krupski

Kanclerz: Marek Zielinski EMail: zielinski@wwszip.pl

Academies

Local Government (Administration; Administrative Law; Development Studies; Ecology; Environmental Management; Government; Law; Public Administration); **Logistics** (Business Administration; International Business; Transport and Communications; Transport Management)

Campuses

Educational Center *(Świdnica)* (Management)

Departments

Postgraduate Studies (Business Administration; Business Education; Child Care and Development; Education; Environmental Studies; Ethics; Health Sciences; Human Resources; Humanities and Social Science Education; Management; Mathematics Education; Pedagogy; Philosophy; Physical Therapy; Preschool Education; Real Estate; Rehabilitation and Therapy; Safety Engineering; Science Education; Social Sciences; Sociology; Teacher Training; Transport Management)

Faculties

Management, Administration and Computer Science (Accountancy; Administration; Computer Science; Finance; Health Education; Health Sciences; Human Resources; Information Sciences; Justice Administration; Management; Safety Engineering;

Sociology; Tourism); **Social and Health Sciences** (Child Care and Development; Education; Health Sciences; Pedagogy; Physical Therapy; Preschool Education; Social Sciences)

Further Information: Also University of Third Age.

History: Founded 1991, acquired present status and title 1996.

Governing Bodies: Senate

Admission Requirements: Secondary school certificate (matura)

Main Language(s) of Instruction: Polish

Accrediting Agencies: Ministry of Science and Higher Education; State Accreditation Committee

Degrees and Diplomas: *Licencjat*; *Świadectwo ukończenia studiów podyplomowych*; *Magister*

Student Numbers *2010-2011*: Total: c. 3,500

Last Updated: 18/10/11

WARSAW COLLEGE OF PROMOTION

Wyższa Szkoła Promocji w Warszawie (WSP)
al. Jerozolimskie 44, 00-024 Warszawa, mazowieckie
Tel: +48(22) 433-76-15
Fax: +48(22) 433-77-30
EMail: rektorat@wsp.pl
Website: http://www.wsp.pl

Rector: Adam Grzegorczyk

Courses

Business English (English)

Faculties

Management (Management)

Institutes

Advertising (Advertising and Publicity); **Human Resource Management** (Human Resources; Management); **Marketing Activities** (Marketing); **Multimedia Design** (Computer Graphics; Graphic Design; Multimedia); **Political Sciences and Social Marketing** (Marketing; Political Sciences); **Public Relations** (Public Relations)

History: Founded 2001.

Governing Bodies: Senate

Admission Requirements: Secondary school certificate (matura)

Fees: (US Dollars): 4,500 per annum

Main Language(s) of Instruction: Polish

Accrediting Agencies: Ministry of Science and Higher Education

Degrees and Diplomas: *Licencjat*; *Świadectwo ukończenia studiów podyplomowych*; *Magister*

Last Updated: 08/10/11

WARSAW HUMANISTIC HIGHER SCHOOL

Warszawska Wyższa Szkoła Humanistyczna im. Bolesława Prusa
ul. Bema 87, 01-233 Warszawa, mazowieckie
Tel: +48(22) 888-07-87
Fax: +48(22) 456-87-92
EMail: rekrutacja@wwsh.edu.pl; info@wwsh.edu.pl
Website: http://www.wwsh.edu.pl

Rektor: Maciej Dębski

Kanclerz: Wojciech Wiśniewski

Programmes

Cultural Studies (Anthropology; Cultural Studies; History; Philosophy; Public Relations; Religion; Sociology); **Finance and Accounting** *(in collaboration with Szkołą Wyższą im. Króla Władysława Jagiełły)* (Accountancy; Banking; Finance); **Journalism and Social Communication** (Administration; Journalism; Mass Communication; Media Studies; Writing); **Postgraduate Studies** (Administration; Health Administration; Journalism; Media Studies; Public Health; Publishing and Book Trade); **Public Health** *(in collaboration with Szkołą Wyższą im. Króla Władysława Jagiełły)* (Cosmetology; Health Administration; Health Education; Hygiene; Public Health; Social Work)

History: Founded 2002.

Fees: (New Złoty): 4,320-5,800 per annum

Main Language(s) of Instruction: Polish

Accrediting Agencies: National Accreditation Commission

Degrees and Diplomas: *Licencjat*; *Świadectwo ukończenia studiów podyplomowych*; *Magister*

Libraries: c. 5,600 vols; 45 journals and periodical subscriptions

Last Updated: 03/10/11

WARSAW SCHOOL OF COMPUTER SCIENCE

Warszawska Wyższa Szkoła Informatyki (WWSI)
ul. Lewartowskiego 17, 00-169 Warszawa, mazowieckie
Tel: +48(22) 489-64-52/00 +48(22) 489-64-94
Fax: +48(22) 489-64-01
EMail: rekrutacja@wwsi.edu.pl
Website: http://www.wwsi.edu.pl/

Rector: Andrzej Żyławski (2000-)
Tel: +48(22) 489-64-92 EMail: rektorat@wwsi.edu.pl

Prorektor: Halina Wojciechowska EMail: hwojcie@mila.edu.pl

International Relations: Andrzej Żyławski

Departments

Postgraduate studies (Business Computing; Computer Networks; Computer Science; Data Processing; Information Technology; Telecommunications Engineering)

Programmes

Computer Science *(Graduate)* (Computer Engineering; Computer Networks; Computer Science; Information Technology; Management); **Computer Science** *(Undergraduate)* (Computer Networks; Computer Science; Data Processing; Multimedia; Software Engineering; Telecommunications Engineering)

History: Founded 2000.

Governing Bodies: Senate

Admission Requirements: Secondary school certificate (matura)

Fees: (New Złoty): 1,500 per term

Main Language(s) of Instruction: Polish

International Co-operation: Participates in the Erasmus/Socrates Programme

Accrediting Agencies: Ministry of Science and Higher Education

Degrees and Diplomas: *Inżynier*, *Licencjat*; *Świadectwo ukończenia studiów podyplomowych*; *Magister*

Academic Staff *2010-2011*: Total 100

STAFF WITH DOCTORATE: Total 17

Last Updated: 19/10/11

WARSAW SCHOOL OF MANAGEMENT - HIGHER SCHOOL

Warszawska Szkoła Zarządzania - Szkoła Wyższa (WSZ-SW)
ul. Siedmiogrodzka 3a, 01-204 Warszawa, mazowieckie
Tel: +48(22) 862-32-24
Fax: +48(22) 862-32-47
EMail: manage@wsz-sw.edu.pl
Website: http://www.wsz-sw.edu.pl

Rektor: Mieczysław Lubański

Programmes

Management (Administration; Finance; Human Resources; Management; Safety Engineering); **Postgraduate Studies** (Environmental Management; Finance; Health Administration; Human Resources; Information Management; Management; Public Administration; Real Estate)

History: Founded 1992.

Governing Bodies: Council of Patronage

Admission Requirements: Secondary school certificate (matura)

Fees: (New Złoty): c. 2,400 per annum

Main Language(s) of Instruction: Polish, English

International Co-operation: Also participates in the Socrates programme

Accrediting Agencies: Ministry of Science and Higher Education

Degrees and Diplomas: *Licencjat*; *Świadectwo ukończenia studiów podyplomowych*; *Magister*

Student Services: Canteen, Language programs, Sports facilities

Last Updated: 03/10/11

WARSAW SCHOOL OF SOCIAL SCIENCES AND HUMANITIES

Szkoła Wyższa Psychologii Społecznej (SWPS)
ul. Chodakowska 19/31, 03-815 Warszawa, mazowieckie
Tel: +48(22) 517-99-00
Fax: +48(22) 517-99-01
EMail: biuro.rektora@swps.edu.pl
Website: http://www.swps.pl

Rector: Andrzej Eliasz (1996-) EMail: rektor@swps.edu.pl

Director, Administrative Officer: Jacek Bernacik
Tel: +48(22) 517-98-30 EMail: jacek.bernacik@swps.edu.pl

International Relations: Teresa Gardocka
Tel: +48(22) 517-99-28 EMail: tgardocka@swps.edu.pl

Campuses

Katowice (Psychology) *Dean*: Katarzyna Popiolek; **Poznan** (Design; International Relations; Journalism; Law; Psychology; Tourism; Town Planning) *Vice-Dean*: Zdzislaw Kaminski; **Sopot** (Physical Therapy; Psychology; Social Psychology) *Dean*: Bogdan Wojciszke; **Wroclaw** (Arts and Humanities; Clinical Psychology; Cognitive Sciences; Economics; European Studies; Journalism; Mass Communication; Psychology; Social Psychology; Sociology) *Dean*: Dariusz Dolinski

Faculties

Humanities and Social Sciences (Aesthetics; Anthropology; Arts and Humanities; Communication Studies; Cultural Studies; International Relations; Journalism; Management; Media Studies; Philosophy; Political Sciences; Regional Studies; Social Sciences; Sociology) *Dean*: Jacek Wasilewski; **Languages and Literatures** (English; English Studies; Foreign Languages Education; Italian; Linguistics; Literature; Modern Languages; Oriental Studies; Scandinavian Languages; Spanish) *Dean*: Piotr Skurowski; **Law** (Civil Law; Criminal Law; European Union Law; History of Law; Human Rights; International Law; Labour Law; Law; Public Law) *Dean*: Teresa Gardocka; **Psychology** (Behavioural Sciences; Clinical Psychology; Cognitive Sciences; Communication Studies; Economics; Educational Psychology; English; Experimental Psychology; Marketing; Neurological Therapy; Neurosciences; Psychology; Social Psychology) *Dean*: Jerzy Karylowski

History: Founded 1996. Formerly known as Wyższa Szkoła Psychologii Społecznej w Warszawie.

Governing Bodies: Senate

Admission Requirements: Secondary school certificate (matura)

Main Language(s) of Instruction: Polish

Accrediting Agencies: Ministry of Science and Higher Education; State Accreditation Committee

Degrees and Diplomas: *Licencjat*: (Poznan): Journalism; Urban Development; Tourism; Urban Design and Planning; (Sopot Campus): Physiotherapy; (Warsaw Campus): Administration in the Judicial System; Internal Safety; Journalism; English Studies; Scandinavian Studies; Polish Studies; Oriental Studies; Spanish Studies; Cultural Studies; Political Science; Sociology; International Relations; (Wroclaw Campus): Journalism; Graphics; Sociology; *Magister*: (Katowice Campus): Psychology; (Poznan Campus): Law; (Sopot Campus): Psychology; (Warsaw Campus): Psychology; Law; (Wroclaw Campus): Psychology, 5 yrs; *Magister*: (Warsaw Campus): English Studies; Scandinavian Studies; Cultural Studies; Sociology; International Relations; (Wroclaw Campus): Sociology; *Doktor*: Psychology; Cultural Studies; Sociology (Ph.D.); *Doktor habilitowany*: Psychology; Cultural studies. Also CPD Continuing Professional Development programmes.

Last Updated: 30/08/11

WARSAW UNIVERSITY COLLEGE OF TECHNOLOGY AND BUSINESS

Wyższa Szkoła Techniczno-Ekonomiczna w Warszawie (WST-E)
ul. Szachowa 1 (teren Instytutu Łączności), 04-894 Warszawa, mazowieckie
Tel: +48(22) 517-34-50
Fax: +48(22) 815-46-94
EMail: dziekanat@wste.pl
Website: http://www.wste.pl

Rektor: Kornel B. Wydro
Tel: +48(22) 512-86-71, Fax: +48(22) 872-90-75
EMail: rektorat@wste.futurus.org

Kanclerz: Anna Gmaj

Departments

Postgraduate Studies (Information Technology; Management; Telecommunications Engineering; Transport Engineering)

Faculties

Computer Science (Business Computing; Computer Science; Environmental Engineering; Information Sciences; Information Technology; Insurance; Telecommunications Engineering; Transport Engineering); **International Relations** (European Union Law; International Business; International Relations; Real Estate; Transport Management)

History: Founded 2001.

Fees: (New Złoty): Polish students, 3,600-4,050 per annnum. (Euro): International students, 2,200 per annum.

Main Language(s) of Instruction: Polish

Degrees and Diplomas: *Inżynier*, *Licencjat*; *Świadectwo ukończenia studiów podyplomowych*. Also Magister (Master) offered by the Instytutem Radiotelekomunikacji Politechniki Warszawskiej.

Last Updated: 24/10/11

WEST HIGHER SCHOOL OF COMMERCE AND INTERNATIONAL FINANCE, ZIELONA GÓRA

Zachodnia Wyższa Szkoła Handlu i Finansów Międzynarodowych w Zielonej Górze (ZWSHIFM)
Pl. Słowiański 9, 65-069 Zielona Góra, lubuskie
Tel: +48(68) 455-84-52
Fax: +48(68) 455-84-51
EMail: dziekanat@zwshifm.edu.pl
Website: http://zwshifm.edu.pl/

Rektor: Zbigniew Jan Pierożek (2010-) Tel: +48(68) 455-84-53

Chancellor: Tomasz Kosior EMail: kanclerz@zwshifm.zgora.pl

International Relations: Aneta Nosal
Tel: +48(68) 453-58-34 EMail: anetanosal@wp.pl

Departments

Postgraduate Studies (Accountancy; Health Administration; Public Administration; Real Estate)

Faculties

Economics and International Trade (Accountancy; Business Administration; Economics; Finance; Management; Real Estate; Social Policy; Social Work; Welfare and Protective Services)

History: Founded 2002.

Fees: (New Zoty): Full-time studies, 2,000-2,520 per semester; Part-time studies, 1,620-2,380 per semester

Degrees and Diplomas: *Licencjat*; *Świadectwo ukończenia studiów podyplomowych*

Libraries: Yes

Last Updated: 26/10/11

WEST POMERANIAN BUSINESS SCHOOL

Zachodniopomorska Szkoła Biznesu w Szczecinie (ZPSB)

ul. Żołnierska 53, 71-210 Szczecin, zachodniopomorskie
Tel: +48(91) 814-94-10
Fax: +48(91) 814-94-40
EMail: zpsb@zpsb.szczecin.pl; dziekanat@zpsb.szczecin.pl; nabor@zpsb.szczecin.pl
Website: http://www.zpsb.szczecin.pl

Rector: Wojciech Olejniczak (2002-)
Tel: +48(91) 814-94-70
EMail: rektor@zpsb.szczecin.pl; rektor@business-edu.eu

Kanclerz: Jan Majewski
Tel: +48(91) 814-94-60
EMail: kanclerz@zpsb.szczecin.pl; kanclerz@business-edu.eu

International Relations: Jerzy Rozwadowski
Tel: +48(91) 814-94-83, Fax: +48(91) 814-94-54
EMail: international@zpsb.szczecin.pl; international@business-edu.eu

Chairs

Computer Science and Quantitative Methods (Computer Science; Operations Research); **Economics and International Business** (Economics; International Business); **Entrepreneurship** *(Stargard)* (Management); **Entrepreneurship** *(Swinoujscie)* (Management); **European Studies** (European Studies); **Finance and Accounting** (Accountancy; Finance); **Management and Marketing** (Management; Marketing); **Sociology** (Sociology)

Departments

Entrepreneurship *(Kolobrzeg)* (Management); **Entrepreneurship** *(Gryfice)* (Management); **Financial and Management Consultancy** *(Berlin)* (Finance; Management)

Faculties

Economics and Informatics (Computer Science; Economics); **Social Sciences** (Social Sciences)

History: Founded 1993.

Governing Bodies: Senate

Admission Requirements: Secondary school certificate (Matura)

Main Language(s) of Instruction: Polish

Accrediting Agencies: Ministry of Science and Higher Education

Degrees and Diplomas: *Inżynier*; *Licencjat*; *Świadectwo ukończenia studiów podyplomowych*; *Magister*. Also Diploma; Executive and International MBA

Last Updated: 12/10/11

WIELKOPOLSKA HIGHER SCHOOL OF HUMANITIES AND ECONOMICS EDUCATION, JAROCIN

Wielkopolska Wyższa Szkoła Humanistyczno-Ekonomiczna w Jarocinie (WWSHE)

al. Niepodległości 34a, 63-200 Jarocin, wielkopolskie
Tel: +48(62) 505-20-60
Fax: +48(62) 747-28-19
EMail: biuro@wwshe.edu.pl
Website: http://www.wwshe.edu.pl

Rektor: Tadeusz Smoliński (2001-)
Tel: +48(62) 747-85-90 EMail: rektor@wwshe.edu.pl

Chancellor: Krzysztof Gąsiorowski

International Relations: Olga Paleczna, Lecturer
Tel: +48 +48 506-033-394 EMail: olapaleczna@wp.pl

Courses

First Aid (Health Sciences)

Programmes

Administration (Administration; Business Administration; Business Computing); **Electronic Administration** (Administration; Business Computing; Information Management; Information Technology; Management); **Internal Security** (Management; Protective Services; Psychology; Sociology)

History: Founded 2001.

Fees: (New Złoty): 1,290-1,650 per semester

Degrees and Diplomas: *Licencjat*; *Świadectwo ukończenia studiów podyplomowych*

Last Updated: 19/10/11

WIELKOPOLSKA HIGHER SCHOOL OF SOCIAL SCIENCES AND ECONOMICS, SRODA WIELKOPOLSKA

Wielkopolską Wyższa Szkoła Społeczno-Ekonomiczna w Środzie Wielkopolskiej (WWSSE)

ul. Surzyńskich 2, 63-000 Środa Wielkopolska
Tel: +48(61) 222-45-56
Fax: +48(61) 222-45-57
EMail: info@wwsse.pl
Website: http://www.wwsse.pl/

Rektor: Przemyslaw Frackowiak

Kanclerz: Danuta M. Ardelli

International Relations: Monika Ciszewska, Head, Department of International Cooperation

Faculties

Economics (Accountancy; Banking; Business Administration; Economics; Environmental Studies; Finance; Human Resources; Real Estate); **Educational Sciences** (Education; Educational Sciences; Pedagogy; Preschool Education; Rehabilitation and Therapy; Social Welfare; Social Work; Sociology)

Institutes

Computer Science (Computer Science; Mathematics); **Mathematics** (Applied Mathematics; Mathematics; Mathematics Education)

Laboratories

Foreign languages (English; Modern Languages)

History: Founded 2005.

Main Language(s) of Instruction: Polish

Degrees and Diplomas: *Inżynier*, *Licencjat*; *Świadectwo ukończenia studiów podyplomowych*; *Magister*

Last Updated: 21/10/11

WIELKOPOLSKA HIGHER SCHOOL OF TOURISM AND MANAGEMENT, POZNAŃ

Wielkopolska Wyższa Szkoła Turystyki i Zarządzania w Poznaniu (WWSTIZ)

ul. Św. Marcin 40, 61-807 Poznań, wielkopolskie
Tel: +48(61) 851-69-71 +48(61) 855-14-68
Fax: +48(61) 855-14-68
EMail: szkola@wwstiz.pl
Website: http://www.wwstiz.pl

Rektor: Jan Jeszka EMail: rektorat@wwstiz.pl

Departments

Postgraduate Studies (Alternative Medicine; Leisure Studies; Tourism)

Programmes

International Relations (Commercial Law; Economics; European Union Law; Geography; Human Rights; International Business; International Relations; Law; Marketing; Statistics; Transport Management); **Tourism and Leisure Studies** (Accountancy; Art History; Computer Science; Ecology; Economics; English; Environmental Studies; French; Geography; German; Hotel Management; Information Management; Information Technology; Insurance; Law; Leisure Studies; Management; Marketing; Modern Languages; Parks and Recreation; Physical Education; Physiology; Psychology; Russian; Spanish; Tourism)

History: Founded 2003.

Main Language(s) of Instruction: Polish

Degrees and Diplomas: *Licencjat*; *Świadectwo ukończenia studiów podyplomowych*; *Magister*

Libraries: Yes

Last Updated: 19/10/11

WŁADYSŁAW JAGIEŁŁO HIGHER SCHOOL, LUBLIN

Lubelska Szkoła Wyższa im. Władysława Jagiełły (LSB)
ul. Archidiakońska 6, 20-113 Lublin, lubelskie
Tel: +48(81) 441-33-00
Fax: +48(81) 441-33-02
EMail: info@lsb.edu.pl
Website: http://80.55.100.58/˜marek/LSW/index.php?id=3&pm=2

Rektor: Tadeusz Zasępa (1999-)

Dyrektor Administracyjny: Piotr Zieliński Tel: +48(81) 441-53-80

International Relations: Jarosław Dąbrowski

Departments

Postgraduate Studies (Accountancy; Food Technology; Human Resources; International Business; Management; Occupational Health; Safety Engineering)

Faculties

Finance and Accountancy (Accountancy; Finance); **Public Health** (Public Health)

History: Founded 1999.

Governing Bodies: Senate

Admission Requirements: Secondary school certificate (matura)

Fees: (New Złoty): 1,600-1,800 per semester

Main Language(s) of Instruction: Polish

Accrediting Agencies: Ministry of Science and Higher Education

Degrees and Diplomas: *Licencjat*; *Świadectwo ukończenia studiów podyplomowych*

Last Updated: 16/10/11

WROCŁAW HIGHER SCHOOL OF APPLIED INFORMATICS

Wrocławska Wyższa Szkoła Informatyki Stosowanej we Wrocławiu (WWSIS)
ul. Wejherowska 28, pok. 2.09, 53-615 Wrocław, dolnośląskie
Tel: +48(71) 799-19-37 +48(71) 788-94-25
Fax: +48(71) 788-94-29
EMail: dziekanat@horyzont.eu
Website: http://www.horyzont.eu

Rector: Marian Czerwiński EMail: rektor@horyzont.eu

Kanclerz: Iwona Bus EMail: iwona.bus@horyzont.eu

Departments

Postgraduate Studies (Computer Science; English; German; Leisure Studies; Philology; Tourism)

Faculties

Computer Science (Computer Engineering; Computer Graphics; Computer Networks; Computer Science; Information Technology; Software Engineering); **English and German Philology** (English; English Studies; German; Literature; Philology; Teacher Training; Translation and Interpretation); **Tourism and Recreation** (Leisure Studies; Tourism)

History: Founded 2004.

Main Language(s) of Instruction: Polish

International Co-operation: Participates in the Eramus programme

Degrees and Diplomas: *Inżynier*, *Licencjat*; *Świadectwo ukończenia studiów podyplomowych*. Also vocational courses.

Last Updated: 19/10/11

WROCLAW SCHOOL OF BANKING

Wyższa Szkoła Bankowa we Wrocławiu (WSB)
ul. Fabryczna 29-31, 53-609 Wrocław, dolnośląskie
Tel: +48(71) 356-16-10
Fax: +48(71) 356-36-80
EMail: informacja@wsb.wroclaw.pl
Website: http://www.wsb.wroclaw.pl

Rector: Stefan Forlicz EMail: rektorat@wsb.wroclaw.pl

Kanclerz: Marek Natalli
EMail: kanclerz@wsb.poznan.pl; kancelaria@wsb.wroclaw.pl

International Relations: Jarosław Tomaszewski, Director of International Relations Office
Tel: +48(71) 356-16-16, Fax: +48(71) 735-12-65
EMail: jaroslaw.tomaszewski@wsb.wroclaw.pl

Chairs

Accountancy (Accountancy); **Banking** (Banking); **Capital Markets and Insurance** (Economics; Insurance); **Economics** (Economics); **Finance** (Finance); **Human Resources Management** (Human Resources); **International Economic Relations** (International Economics; International Relations); **Logistics** (Transport Management); **Management** (Management); **Marketing** (Marketing); **Public Finance** (Finance; Public Administration); **Quantitative Methods** (Operations Research); **Tourism and Recreation** (Parks and Recreation; Tourism)

Departments

Computer Science (Computer Science); **English Language** (English); **German Language** (German); **Physical Education** (Physical Education; Sports)

History: Founded 1998.

Governing Bodies: Senate

Admission Requirements: Secondary school certificate (matura)

Main Language(s) of Instruction: Polish

International Co-operation: Participates in Eramsus programme

Accrediting Agencies: Ministry of Science and Higher Education

Degrees and Diplomas: *Licencjat*; *Świadectwo ukończenia studiów podyplomowych*; *Magister*. Also MBA and Franklin University MBA

Last Updated: 04/10/11

ZAMOŚĆ UNIVERSITY OF MANAGEMENT AND ADMINISTRATION

Wyższa Szkoła Zarządzania i Administracji w Zamościu (WSZIA)
ul. Akademika 4, 22-400 Zamość, lubelskie
Tel: +48(84) 677-67-09
Fax: +48(84) 677-67-09
EMail: poczta@wszia.edu.pl
Website: http://www.wszia.edu.pl

Rector: Jan Andreasik (1998-)
Tel: +48 33 829 72 80, Fax: +48 33 810-05-87
EMail: rektorat@poczta.wszia.edu.pl; jandreasik@wszia.edu.pl

Kanclerz: Andrzej Łygas

International Relations: Aleksandra Kahan, International Relations Coordinator
Tel: +48(84) 677-67-89, Fax: +48(84) 677-67-10
EMail: akahan@wszia.edu.pl

Faculties

Management and Administration (Administration; Administrative Law; Banking; Building Technologies; Business Computing; Commercial Law; Computer Engineering; Computer Science; Constitutional Law; Construction Engineering; Data Processing; Econometrics; Economics; European Union Law; Finance; Information Technology; Labour Law; Management; Mathematics; Statistics); **Physiotherapy and Pedagogy** (Anaesthesiology; Anatomy; Biochemistry; Biophysics; Dietetics; Economics; Educational Technology; Gynaecology and Obstetrics; Health Administration; Law; Neurology; Nursing; Paediatrics; Pathology; Pedagogy; Physical Therapy; Physiology; Psychiatry and Mental Health; Public Health); **Postgraduate Studies** (Accountancy; Educational Technology; Health Administration; Management)

History: Founded 1997.

Governing Bodies: Senate

Admission Requirements: Secondary school certificate (Matura)

Main Language(s) of Instruction: Polish

International Co-operation: Participates in the Erasmus programme.

Accrediting Agencies: Higher Education Department of the Ministry of National Education and Sport

Degrees and Diplomas: *Inżynier*, *Licencjat*; *Świadectwo ukończenia studiów podyplomowych*; *Magister*

Last Updated: 10/10/11

Portugal

STRUCTURE OF HIGHER EDUCATION SYSTEM

Description:

Higher education includes university and polytechnic education. University education is offered by public, private and cooperative university institutions and polytechnic education is offered by public, private and cooperative non-university institutions. The Portuguese Catholic University was instituted by decree of the Holy See and is recognized by the State of Portugal. Private higher education institutions must be subject to prior recognition by the Ministry of Science, Technology and Higher Education and the Agência de Avaliação e Acreditação do Ensino Superior (Agency for Assessment and Accreditation of Higher Education - A3ES). The two systems of higher education (university and polytechnic) are linked and it is possible to transfer from one to the other. It is also possible to transfer from a public institution to a private one and vice-versa.

Stages of studies:

University level first stage: Licenciado

Since the publication of law 49/2005, in university education, the cycle of studies that leads to the degree of Licenciado with a normal duration of six to eight curricular semesters, corresponds to 180 to 240 credits. In the first cycle of university studies, the degree of Licenciado is conferred to those who, after concluding all the curricular units that integrate the study programme of the licenciatura course, have obtained the established number of credits.

University level second stage: Mestre

Since the publication of law 49/2005, the cycle of studies that leads to the degree of Mestre has a normal length of three to four curricular semesters, corresponding to 90 to 120 credits. In university education, the Mestre degree may also be conferred after an integrated cycle of studies, with 300 to 360 credits and a normal length of 10 to 12 curricular semesters, in cases where the access to the practice of a certain professional activity depends on the length of time established by legal EU standards or results from a stable practice consolidated in the European Union.

In the second cycle of studies of the university and polytechnic institutions, the degree of Mestre is conferred to those who, after concluding all the curricular units that integrate the study programme of the Mestrado course, have obtained the established number of credits and successfully defended in public their dissertation, their project work or their traineeship report.

University level third stage: Doutor

The Doutor (doctorate) degree is only conferred by university institutions. The degree of Doutor (doctorate) is conferred to those who, after concluding all the curricular units that integrate the study programme of the Doutoramento course, have successfully defended their thesis in public.

University level fourth stage: Agregação

This is the highest qualification reserved to holders of the Doutor degree. It requires the capacity to undertake high level research and special pedagogical competence in a specific field. It is awarded after passing specific examinations.

Distance higher education:

Distance higher education is provided by the Universidade Aberta.

ADMISSION TO HIGHER EDUCATION

Admission to university-level studies:

Name of secondary school credential required: Diploma de Especialização Tecnológica

Minimum score/requirement: 9,5

For entry to: Programmes in the same field of study.

Name of secondary school credential required: Diploma de Ensino Secundário

For entry to: All programmes

Alternatives to credentials: Special competitions organized for applicants over 23 who do not hold the Diploma de Ensino Secundário but who have to sit for a special examination (ad hoc exam); candidates already holding a medium / higher level qualification; candidates from other higher education systems.

Entrance exam requirements: Set for the national examinations of secondary school corresponding to the admission tests in accordance with the higher education course the student wishes to attend and obtain the minimum mark required (9,5 in a numerical scale between 0 to 20 marks).

Numerus clausus/restrictions: Each year, the institution (public and private) establishes the number of places available for each course which has to be approved by the Ministry of Science and Higher Education

Other admission requirements: In addition to passing entrance and access tests, students must fulfil particular prerequisites for the chosen course. Universities make their entrance requirements known in a booklet distributed to applicants by the Regional Office of the Direcção-Geral de Ensino Superior which is responsible for placing applicants in courses according to their preference. Vacancies allocated by public institutions are filled by means of a national competition organized by the Direcção-Geral do Ensino Superior. Each private institute fills its places by means of a local competitive examination which they organize.

Foreign students admission:

Entrance exam requirements: Foreign students must have a Secondary-School-Leaving Certificate (certified copy). In order to enter university they must also pass an entrance examination. They must present the notice of approval and length of the programme (if necessary).

Entry regulations: Students of non-EU countries must have a study visa (obtained from the Portuguese consulate in the country of residence) , or provide proof of adequate financial means for the duration of their studies in Portugal.

Health requirements: Health visa.

Language requirements: Students must have a good knowledge of Portuguese. Some universities organize language courses for foreigners. Currently some degree programmes are already taught in English.

RECOGNITION OF STUDIES

Quality assurance system:

The Agência de Avaliação e Acreditação do Ensino Superior (Agency for Assessment and Accreditation of Higher Education - A3ES) was created in 2007 to define and enforce the quality standards of the higher education system; to assess and accredit study cycles and higher education institutions; to promote public disclosure of the assessment and accreditation results.

Bodies dealing with recognition:

Agência de Avaliação e Acreditação do Ensino Superior - A3ES (Agency for Assessment and Accreditation of Higher Education)

Chairman: Alberto Amaral
Rua D. Estefânia 195 - 5.° Esq.
Lisboa 1000-155
Tel: +351 213 511 690
Fax: +351 213 511 691
EMail: a3es@a3es.pt
WWW: http://www.a3es.pt/

Services provided and students dealt with: The A3ES defines and enforces the quality standards of the higher education system, assesses and accredits study cycles and higher education institutions, and promotes public disclosure of the assessment and accreditation results.

NARIC, Direcção-Geral do Ensino Superior (National Academic Recognition Information Centre / Directorate General for Higher Education)

Head: Manuela Paiva
Avenida Duque d'Avila, 137
Lisboa 1069-016
Tel: +351 213 126 000
Fax: +351 213 126 020
EMail: info.naric@dges.mctes.pt
WWW: http://www.naricportugal.pt

Services provided and students dealt with: The Portuguese NARIC is the official information centre for providing information about recognition of foreign qualifications both for academic and professional purpose. The centre is also part of the ENIC network which is made up of the national information centres of the States belonging to the Council of Europe and UNESCO. It provides information to national and foreign students and graduates; higher education institutions; Ministries and other public authorities; professional organizations and employers; ENIC/NARIC centres; national and international organizations.

Special provisions for recognition:

For exercising a profession: Access to regulated professions is subject to recognition by competent authorities according to Law n° 9/2009 of 4 March which transposed Directive 2005/36/EC.

For access to advanced studies and research: Those who meet the following conditions may apply to advanced studies and research:
- Holders of the Licenciado degree or legal equivalent;
- Holders of the Mestre degree or legal equivalent;
- Holders of a foreign academic degree conferred following a 1st cycle of studies organized according to the principles of the Bologna Process by a State that has subscribed this Process;
- Holders of an academic, scientific or professional curriculum vitae that is recognized as attesting the capacity to carry out this cycle of studies by the statutorily competent scientific body of the higher education institution to which they wish to be admitted.

Recognition for university level studies: In Portugal, there are two main decrees on the recognition of foreign higher education qualifications:
- the Decree-Law nr. 283/83 dated 21 June which establishes a system of recognition/equivalence based on the scientific re-evaluation of work carried out with a view to obtaining the foreign degree and on a casuistic assessment of the merit of the foreign higher degrees/diplomas. According to this decree only higher education institutions are incumbent to decide about awarding the equivalence/recognition.
- the Decree-Law nr. 341/07 dated 12 October which sets up a new regime, based on the principle of mutual trust, for the automatic recognition of foreign academic degrees of a level and nature and with objectives that are identical to the degrees of Licenciado, Mestre and Doutor awarded by Portuguese higher education institutions.

NATIONAL BODIES

Ministério da Educação e Ciência - MEC (Ministry of Education and Science)

Minister: Nuno Crato
Estrada das Laranjeiras, 197-205
Lisboa 1649-018
Tel: +351 217 231 000
Fax: +351 217 271 457
EMail: mctes@mctes.gov.pt
WWW: http://www.portugal.gov.pt/pt/os-ministerios/ministerio-da-educacao-e-ciencia.aspx

Role of national body: MEC is the government body responsible for the definition, implementation and evaluation of national policies within Science and Higher Education, as well as for the Information Society.

Direcção-Geral do Ensino Superior - DGES (Directorate General of Higher Education)

Director-General: Vitor Magriço
Avenida Duque d'Avila n°137

Lisboa 1069 016
Tel: +351 213 126 000
Fax: +351 213 126 001
EMail: secretariado@dges.mctes.pt
WWW: http://www.dges.mctes.pt
Role of national body: This Directorate General is a central service of the direct state administration under the responsibility of the Ministry of Science, Technology and Higher Education and it is responsible for the implementation and coordination of the policies regarding higher education, that is incumbent to the Ministry.

Conselho Coordenador dos Institutos Superiores Politécnicos - CCISP (Coordinating Council for Higher Polytechnic Institutes)
President: João Sobrinho Teixeira
Avenida 5 de Outubro 89-3.°
Lisboa 1050-050
Tel: +351 217 928 360
Fax: +351 217 928 369
EMail: ccisp@ccisp.pt
WWW: http://www.ccisp.pt
Role of national body: It is the body that represents all public higher polytechnic institutions.

Conselho de Reitores das Universidades Portuguesas - CRUP (Portuguese Council of University Rectors)
President: António Rendas
Edificio O Campus do Lumiar,
Estrada do Paço do
Lisboa 1649-038
WWW: http://www.crup.pt
Role of national body: It is the body that represents all public universities.

Associação Portuguesa de Ensino Superior Privado - APESP (Portuguese Association of Private Higher Education Institutions)
President: Manuel Damásio
Av. da República, 47 - 1° Dto
Lisboa 1050.188
Tel: +351 217 994860
Fax: +351 217 994 869
EMail: contactos@apesp.pt
WWW: http://www.apesp.pt/
Role of national body: The Portuguese Association of Private Higher Education Institutions is an association, of the officially recognized non-state institutions of higher education, according to the Statute of Private and Co-operative Higher Education and of other applicable legislation.

Agência Nacional para a Gestão do Programa Aprendizagem ao Longo da Vida (National Agency for Lifelong Learning)
Director: Isabel Duarte
Avenida Infante Santo, n°2 Piso 4
Lisboa 1350 178
Tel: +351 213 944 760
Fax: +351 213 944 737
EMail: agencianacional@proalv.pt
WWW: http://www.proalv.pt/
Role of national body: The Agency is a structure created to guarantee the management of the programme of the Lifelong Learning with the aim to contribute to the development of the European Union whilst a knowledge based society.

Data for academic year: 2011-2012
Source: IAU from NARIC, Direcção-Geral do Ensino Superior, Lisboa, 2011. Bodies, 2012.

INSTITUTIONS

PUBLIC INSTITUTIONS

COIMBRA SCHOOL OF NURSING

Escola Superior de Enfermagem de Coimbra
Avenida Bissaya Barreto - Apartado 7001, 3046-851 Coimbra
Tel: +351(239) 487-200
Fax: +351(239) 483-378
EMail: esebb@esebb.pt
Website: http://www.esenfc.pt

Presidente: Maria da Conceição Saraiva da Silva Costa Bento
Tel: +351(239) 802-934 EMail: cbento@esebb.pt

Vice-Presidente: Aida Maria de Oliveira Cruz Mendes

Vice-Presidente: Fernando Manuel Dias Henriques

Courses

Nursing (Anatomy; Microbiology; Nursing; Parasitology; Physiology; Psychology)

History: Founded 2004 following merger of the Escolas Superiores de Enfermagem do Dr. Ângelo da Fonseca and of Bissaya Barreto, .

Main Language(s) of Instruction: Portuguese

Degrees and Diplomas: *Licenciado*; *Mestre*. Also postgraduate diplomas
Last Updated: 28/09/11

INFANTE D. HENRIQUE NAUTICAL SCHOOL

Escola Superior Náutica Infante D. Henrique
Av. Eng. Bonneville Franco, 2780-572 Paço de Arcos
Tel: +351(21) 446-0010
Fax: +351(21) 442-9546
EMail: info@enautica.pt
Website: http://www.enautica.pt

Director Geral: João Manuel Reverendo da Silva (1997-)
Tel: 351(21) 442-6026 EMail: director@enautica.pt

Departments

Maritime Electronic Systems (Marine Engineering); **Maritime Machinery Engineering** (Marine Engineering); **Piloting**; **Port Administration** (Transport Management)

History: Founded 1972. Acquired present status 1985.

Degrees and Diplomas: *Licenciado*; *Mestre*
Last Updated: 19/09/11

LISBON SCHOOL OF NURSING

Escola Superior de Enfermagem de Lisboa
Avenida Prof. Egas Moniz, 1600-190 Lisboa
Tel: +351(21) 791-3400
Fax: +351(21) 795-4729
EMail: esenfcgl@esenfcgl.pt
Website: http://www.esel.pt/esel/pt/

Presidente: Maria Filomena Mendes Gaspar

Courses

Graduate Studies (Community Health; Gynaecology and Obstetrics; Health Administration; Nursing; Paediatrics; Psychiatry and Mental Health; Public Health; Rehabilitation and Therapy; Sociology; Surgery); **Nursing** (Administration; Biochemistry; Biology; Educational Sciences; Ethics; Health Sciences; Management; Medicine; Nursing; Philosophy; Psychology; Sociology)

History: Founded 2004 following merger of Escola Superior de Enfermagem de Artur Ravara; Escola Superior de Enfermagem de Calouste Gulbenkian de Lisboa; Escola Superior de Enfermagem de Francisco Gentil and Escola Superior de Enfermagem de Maria Fernanda Resende.

Degrees and Diplomas: *Licenciado*; *Mestre*; *Doutor*. Also postgraduate diplomas
Last Updated: 28/09/11

LISBON UNIVERSITY INSTITUTE

Instituto Universitário de Lisboa (ISCTE-IUL)
Avenida das Forças Armadas, 1649-026 Lisboa
Tel: +351(217) 903-000
Fax: +351(217) 964-710
EMail: geral@iscte.pt
Website: http://www.iscte.pt

Reitor: Luís Antero Reto
Tel: +351(217) 903-048 EMail: reitor@iscte.pt

International Relations: José Paulo Esperança, Pró-Reitor

Schools

Architecture and Technology (Architecture; Computer Engineering; Electronic Engineering; Information Technology; Management Systems; Software Engineering; Structural Architecture; Telecommunications Engineering; Town Planning); **Business** (Accountancy; Business Administration; Business Computing; Chinese; Economics; Finance; Hotel and Restaurant; Hotel Management; Human Resources; Industrial Engineering; International Business; Management; Marketing; Tourism); **Human and Social Sciences** (Anthropology; Commercial Law; Contemporary History; Cultural Studies; Economics; Ethnology; Finance; Health Sciences; Human Resources; Industrial and Organizational Psychology; Museum Studies; Psychology; Social Psychology; Urban Studies; Visual Arts); **Social and Public Policies** (African Studies; Communication Studies; Cultural Studies; Demography and Population; Educational Administration; Geography (Human); Heritage Preservation; History; Information Technology; International Relations; Labour and Industrial Relations; Modern History; Political Sciences; Public Administration; Social and Community Services; Social Sciences; Social Studies; Sociology)

History: Founded 1972. Acquired present status 2005. Formerly known as Instituto Superior de Ciências do Trabalho e da Empresa (ISCTE).

Academic Year: September to July

Admission Requirements: Secondary school certificate and entrance examination, or recognized foreign equivalent

Fees: (Euros): c. 3,800 per term

Main Language(s) of Instruction: Portuguese, English

Degrees and Diplomas: *Licenciado*; *Mestre*: African Studies: Social and Economic Development in Africa; Development; Local Diversity and World Challenges; Anthropology: Multiculturalism and Identities; Museology: Explanatory Contents; Urban Anthropology; Architecture: Contemporary Architectonic Culture; Public Art; Urban and Architectonic Rehabilitation; Urban Design; Communication, Culture and Information Technology; Demography and Sociology of Population; European Studies: Institutions, Policy and Society; Family and Society; Labour Sciences and Labour Relations; Planning and Evaluation of Development Processes; History of International Relations; History of the Cities: Society and Culture; Human Resources Development Policies; Social and Solidary Economics; Economics and Public Policies; Information Studies and Digital Libraries; Information Systems Management; Telecommunications and Computer Engineering; Integrated Decision Support Systems; New Frontiers of Law; Public Administration and Policies; Risk, Trauma and Society; Social Institutions and Social Justice; Society and Environment; Sociology; Sociology of Migration; *Doutor*: Management; Anthropology; Urban Anthropology; Information Sciences and Technologies; Economics; African Studies; Contemporary and Social History; Social and Organizational Psychology; Social Service; Sociology

Student Services: Canteen, Cultural centre, Employment services, Foreign student adviser, Handicapped facilities, Language programs, Sports facilities

Libraries: c. 35,000 books and c. 2,000 periodicals

Publications: Cidades, Comunidades e Territórios *(biennially)*; Estudos de Gestão; Etnográfica *(biennially)*; Ler História *(biennially)*; Revista Economia Global & Gestão *(biennially)*; Revista Portuguesa de Gestão *(quarterly)*; Revista Portuguesa e Brasileira de Gestão *(quarterly)*; Revista Urbanismo de Origem Portuguesa; Sociologia, Problemas e Práticas, Scientific journal *(3 per annum)*; The Portuguese Journal of Social Sciences (PJSS); Trajectos - Revista de Comunicação, Cultura e Tecnologias de Informação *(biennially)*

Last Updated: 03/10/11

NEW UNIVERSITY OF LISBON

Universidade Nova de Lisboa (UNL)

Campus de Campolide, 1099-085 Lisboa
Tel: +351(21) 371-5642
Fax: +351(21) 371-5645
EMail: reitoria@unl.pt
Website: http://www.unl.pt

Reitor: António Manuel Bensabat Rendas
Tel: +351(21) 371-5632, Fax: +351(21) 371-5614

Faculties

Sciences (Medicine; Rehabilitation and Therapy); **Economics and Management** (Economics; Finance; Management); **Law** (Law); **Science and Technology** (Applied Chemistry; Applied Mathematics; Biochemistry; Bioengineering; Biomedical Engineering; Biotechnology; Ceramics and Glass Technology; Civil Engineering; Computer Engineering; Educational Sciences; Electrical and Electronic Equipment and Maintenance; Energy Engineering; Environmental Engineering; Genetics; Geological Engineering; Geology; Industrial Engineering; Materials Engineering; Mathematics; Mechanical Engineering; Microelectronics; Molecular Biology; Nanotechnology; Physical Engineering; Restoration of Works of Art; Water Management); **Social and Human Sciences** (Anthropology; Archaeology; Art History; Educational Sciences; English; Geography; Germanic Languages; Heritage Preservation; History; International Relations; Library Science; Linguistics; Literature; Mass Communication; Modern Languages; Museum Studies; Music; Philosophy; Political Sciences; Portuguese; Sociology; Translation and Interpretation; Women's Studies)

Institutes

Chemical and Biological Technology (Technology); **Hygiene and Tropical Medicine** (Biomedicine; Tropical Medicine); **Statistics and Information Management** (Information Management; Statistics)

Schools

Public Health (Health Administration; Public Health; Rehabilitation and Therapy)

Further Information: Also branch in Angola

History: Founded 1973. Department structure replaced 1977 by faculties. Enjoys scientific, academic and administrative autonomy and is mainly funded by the Ministry of Science, Technology and Higher Education.

Governing Bodies: Conselho Geral; Colégio de Directores; Conselho de Estudantes; Conselho de Disciplina; Conselho de Gestão; Provedor do Estudante.

Academic Year: October to July (October-February; March-July)

Admission Requirements: Secondary school certificate or recognized foreign equivalent, and entrance examination

Fees: (Euro): c. 900.00 per annum

Main Language(s) of Instruction: Portuguese, English

International Co-operation: with institutions in France, Germany, Italy, Spain.

Degrees and Diplomas: *Licenciado*; *Mestre*; *Doutor*. Also Postgraduate and Specialization courses.

Student Services: Academic counselling, Canteen, Employment services, Foreign student adviser, Foreign Studies Centre, Handicapped facilities, Health services, Language programs, Nursery care, Social counselling, Sports facilities

Student Residential Facilities: Three student residences.

Special Facilities: Art Gallery.

Libraries: Independent library facilities within each academic unit.

Academic Staff *2008-2009*	MEN	WOMEN	**TOTAL**
FULL-TIME	648	453	**1,101**
PART-TIME	300	195	**495**
STAFF WITH DOCTORATE			
FULL-TIME	539	350	**889**
PART-TIME	95	53	**148**
Student Numbers *2008-2009*			
All (Foreign Included)	8,583	8,066	**16,649**
FOREIGN ONLY	419	501	**920**

Last Updated: 08/10/09

OPEN UNIVERSITY

Universidade Aberta (UAB)

Palácio Ceia, Rua da Escola Politécnica, 141-147, 1269-001 Lisboa
Tel: +351(213) 916-300
Fax: +351(213) 916-517
EMail: infosac@univ-ab.pt
Website: http://www.univ-ab.pt

Reitor: Paulo Maria Bastos da Silva DiasPaulo Maria Bastos da Silva Dias (2011-)

Vice-Reitora: Alda Pereira

Departments

Education and Distance Education (Curriculum; Distance Education; Education; Educational Administration; Educational Research; Educational Sciences; Educational Technology; Philosophy of Education; Special Education; Teacher Training); **Graduate Studies** (Art Education; Business Administration; Cinema and Television; Comparative Literature; Computer Science; Cultural Studies; Distance Education; Documentation Techniques; E-Business/Commerce; Education; Educational Administration; Educational and Student Counselling; Educational Technology; Environmental Management; Environmental Studies; European Studies; Food Science; Graphic Arts; Heritage Preservation; History; Information Management; Information Sciences; Library Science; Mathematics; Multimedia; Native Language; Pedagogy; Portuguese; Statistics; Western European Studies; Women's Studies); **Humanities** (African American Studies; American Studies; Archaeology; Art History; Arts and Humanities; Canadian Studies; Comparative Literature; Cultural Studies; English Studies; French Studies; Germanic Studies; History; Literature; Modern Languages; Museum Studies; Native Language; Philosophy; Portuguese; Social Sciences; Writing); **Science and Technology** (Applied Mathematics; Biological and Life Sciences; Chemistry; Computer Engineering; Computer Science; Earth Sciences; Environmental Studies; Materials Engineering; Mathematics; Physics; Statistics; Technology); **Social Sciences and Management** (Asian Studies; Communication Studies; Documentation Techniques; E-Business/Commerce; European Studies; Heritage Preservation; History; Information Sciences; Management; Social Sciences; Social Work)

Further Information: Branches in Coimbra and Porto

History: Founded 1988. The only distance teaching university in Portugal.

Governing Bodies: Assembleia; Senado; Conselho Administrativo

Academic Year: October to July

Admission Requirements: Secondary school certificate or recognized foreign equivalent. Students over 25 with no secondary education may gain admission through examination

Main Language(s) of Instruction: Portuguese

International Co-operation: With universities in Angola, Cape Verde, Mozambique, Guinée-Bissau, Brazil and Timor. Also participates in Erasmus programme.

Accrediting Agencies: European Association of Distance Teaching Universities; European Distance Education Network; International Council for Distance Education; AULP; EUA

Degrees and Diplomas: *Licenciado*: Applied Mathematics; Computer Science; European Studies; History; Management; Modern Languages and Literature; Social Sciences, 4 yrs; *Mestre*: Accounting and Auditing; American Studies; Business Accounting and Finance; English Studies; Educational Administration; Health Communication; Intercultural Relations; Interdisciplinary Studies; Multimedia; Project Management; Quality Management, 2 yrs; *Doutor*: Anthropology; Biology; Biotechnology; Chemistry; Communication Sciences; Computer Science; Economics; Education; Environmental Sciences; Geography; Geosciences; History;

Linguistics; Literature; Management; Mathematics; Philosophy; Physics; Psychology. Teacher Training programmes; Portuguese Language and Culture Studies for foreigners

Student Services: Academic counselling

Student Residential Facilities: None

Special Facilities: Audio, Video and Multimedia studios

Libraries: Yes

Publications: Discursos *(annually)*

Press or Publishing House: Universidade Aberta

Last Updated: 24/01/12

POLYTECHNIC INSTITUTE OF BEJA

Instituto Politécnico de Beja

Apartado 6155, Rua Pedro Soares, Campus do Instituto Politécnico de Beja, 7800-295 Beja

Tel: +351(284) 314-400

Fax: +351(284) 314-401

EMail: geral@ipbeja.pt

Website: http://www.ipbeja.pt

Presidente: Vito Carioca (2009-) EMail: presidente@ipbeja.pt

Schools

Agriculture (Agricultural Engineering; Agriculture; Agronomy; Biology; Environmental Engineering; Food Technology; Forestry; Horticulture; Tropical Agriculture); **Education** (Clinical Psychology; Cognitive Sciences; Continuing Education; Education; English; Fine Arts; French; Gerontology; Mathematics Education; Multimedia; Music Education; Natural Sciences; Physical Education; Portuguese; Preschool Education; Primary Education; Special Education; Sports; Teacher Training); **Health Sciences** (Environmental Management; Nursing; Occupational Health); **Management and Technology** (Business Administration; Civil Engineering; Computer Engineering; Management; Surveying and Mapping; Technology; Tourism; Welfare and Protective Services)

History: Founded 1979.

Main Language(s) of Instruction: Portuguese

International Co-operation: Participates in SOCRATES/ERASMUS

Degrees and Diplomas: *Licenciado*; *Mestre*. Also postgraduate programmes

Special Facilities: Botanical Museum

Last Updated: 29/09/11

POLYTECHNIC INSTITUTE OF BRAGANÇA

Instituto Politécnico de Bragança

Apartado 1038, Campus de Santa Apolónia, 5301-854 Bragança

Tel: +351(273) 303-200

Fax: +351(273) 325-405

EMail: ipb@ipb.pt

Website: http://www.ipb.pt

Presidente: João Alberto Sobrinho Teixeira

Schools

Agriculture *(Escola Superior Agrária de Bragança (ESA))* (Agricultural Engineering; Agriculture; Bioengineering; Biotechnology; Botany; Ecology; Environmental Engineering; Environmental Management; Food Technology; Forestry; Veterinary Science); **Communication, Administration and Tourism** *(Escola Superior de Comunicação, Administração e Turismo (EsACT))* (Communication Studies; Computer Science; Cultural Studies; Information Sciences; Information Technology; Management; Marketing; Multimedia; Public Administration; Tourism); **Education** *(Escola Superior de Educação de Bragança (ESE))* (Art Education; Design; Education; Educational Administration; Educational and Student Counselling; Educational Sciences; English; Environmental Studies; Fine Arts; Foreign Languages Education; Health Education; Information Technology; International Relations; Literacy Education; Music Education; Performing Arts; Physical Education; Preschool Education; Primary Education; Science Education; Social Studies; Spanish; Sports; Technology Education; Translation and Interpretation; Visual Arts); **Health** *(Escola Superior de Saúde de Bragança (ESSa))* (Community Health; Dietetics; Gerontology; Gynaecology and Obstetrics; Health Administration; Health Sciences; Nursing; Pharmacy; Public Health; Rehabilitation and Therapy); **Management and Technology** *(Escola Superior de Tecnologia e Gestão de Bragança (ESTIG))* (Accountancy; Automation and Control Engineering; Automotive Engineering; Bioengineering; Biology; Chemical Engineering; Chemistry; Civil Engineering; Computer Engineering; Computer Networks; Construction Engineering; Electrical and Electronic Engineering; Electronic Engineering; Energy Engineering; Engineering Management; Environmental Engineering; Finance; Industrial Engineering; Information Technology; Management; Mechanical Engineering; Technology)

Further Information: Schools in Bragança and Mirandela

History: Founded 1979. Incorporated Escola Superior de Enfermagem de Bragança.

Main Language(s) of Instruction: Portuguese

Degrees and Diplomas: *Licenciado*; *Mestre*. Also specialization programmes

Last Updated: 29/09/11

POLYTECHNIC INSTITUTE OF CASTELO BRANCO

Instituto Politécnico de Castelo Branco

Avenida Pedro Alvares Cabral 12, 6000-084 Castelo Branco

Tel: +351(272) 339-600

Fax: +351(272) 339-601

EMail: gri.ipcb@ipcb.pt

Website: http://www.ipcb.pt

Presidente: Carlos Manuel Leitão Maia

Vice-Presidente: José Carlos Dias Duarte Gonçalves

Programmes

Tourism, Sports and Services (Hotel Management; Physical Education; Sports; Tourism)

Schools

Agriculture *(ESA)* (Agricultural Engineering; Agriculture; Bioengineering; Food Technology; Nutrition; Veterinary Science); **Applied Arts** *(ESART)* (Cinema and Television; Communication Arts; Design; Fashion Design; Fine Arts; Interior Design; Music; Music Education; Musical Instruments; Performing Arts; Singing; Textile Design); **Education** *(ESE)* (Education; Primary Education); **Graduate** (Agricultural Engineering; Business Administration; Civil Engineering; Construction Engineering; Educational and Student Counselling; English; Environmental Management; Fashion Design; Food Science; Foreign Languages Education; Forest Management; Forestry; French; Fruit Production; Gerontology; Graphic Design; Hydraulic Engineering; Interior Design; Management; Multimedia; Music; Music Education; Performing Arts; Preschool Education; Primary Education; Software Engineering; Soil Conservation; Spanish; Special Education; Sports; Telecommunications Engineering; Textile Design; Veterinary Science; Waste Management; Water Management; Zoology); **Health** *(Dr. Lopes Dias (ESALD))* (Cardiology; Health Sciences; Nursing; Physical Therapy; Pneumology; Public Health; Radiology; Social and Preventive Medicine); **Management** *(Idanha-a-Nova (ESG))* (Accountancy; Finance; Human Resources; Management; Secretarial Studies); **Technology** (Computer Engineering; Electronic Engineering; Engineering; Environmental Engineering; Industrial Engineering; Information Technology; Multimedia; Telecommunications Engineering; Welfare and Protective Services)

History: Founded 1979.

International Co-operation: With universities in Spain, France, Belgium, Denmark, United Kingdom, Finland, Germany, Poland, Czech Republic, Italy, Romania, Slovenia.

Degrees and Diplomas: *Licenciado*; *Mestre*

Student Services: Canteen, Employment services, Foreign Studies Centre, Handicapped facilities, Social counselling, Sports facilities

Publications: Polinfor *(monthly)*

Last Updated: 29/09/11

POLYTECHNIC INSTITUTE OF CÁVADO AND AVE

Instituto Politécnico do Cávado e do Ave
Avenida Dr. Sidónio País, 222, 4750-333 Barcelos
Tel: +351(253) 802-190
Fax: +351(253) 812-281
EMail: geral@ipca.pt
Website: http://www.ipca.pt

Presidente: João Carvalho Tel: +351(253) 812-281

Administrador: Antonio Siva Pereira Tel: +351(253) 802-208

Programmes

Graduate Studies (Accountancy; Banking; Business Administration; Computer Networks; Finance; Industrial Design; Industrial Management; Insurance; Management Systems; Multimedia; Occupational Health; Safety Engineering; Taxation; Transport Management)

Schools

Management (Accountancy; Banking; Finance; Fiscal Law; Management; Taxation; Tourism); **Technology** (Computer Science; Electrical Engineering; Engineering Management; Environmental Engineering; Graphic Design; Industrial Design; Safety Engineering; Systems Analysis; Technology)

History: Founded 1994.

Main Language(s) of Instruction: Portuguese

Degrees and Diplomas: *Diploma de Especialização Tecnológica*; *Licenciado*; *Mestre*. Also postgraduate courses
Last Updated: 30/09/11

POLYTECHNIC INSTITUTE OF COIMBRA

Instituto Politécnico de Coimbra
Avenida Marnoco e Sousa, 30, 3000-271 Coimbra
Tel: +351(239) 791-250
Fax: +351(239) 791-262
EMail: ipc@ipc.pt
Website: http://www.ipc.pt

Presidente: Rui Jorge da Silva Antunes

Administrador: Manuel Filipe Mateus dos Reis

Institutes

Accountancy and Administration (Accountancy; Administration; Business Administration; Business Computing; Public Administration); **Engineering** (Bioengineering; Civil Engineering; Computer Engineering; Electrical Engineering; Electronic Engineering; Engineering; Industrial Engineering; Industrial Management; Mechanical Engineering)

Schools

Agriculture (Agriculture; Animal Husbandry; Biotechnology; Environmental Engineering; Environmental Management; Food Technology; Forest Products; Forestry); **Education** (Communication Arts; Communication Studies; Design; Education; Gerontology; Leisure Studies; Multimedia; Music; Primary Education; Social Studies; Special Education; Sports; Theatre; Tourism); **Health Technology** (Cardiology; Dietetics; Environmental Management; Health Sciences; Nutrition; Pharmacy; Physical Therapy; Pneumology; Public Health; Radiology); **Management and Technology** *(Oliveira do Hospital)* (Administration; Computer Engineering; Finance; Management; Marketing; Safety Engineering; Technology)

History: Founded 1979, acquired present status 1998.

Degrees and Diplomas: *Diploma de Especialização Tecnológica*; *Licenciado*; *Mestre*
Last Updated: 30/09/11

POLYTECHNIC INSTITUTE OF GUARDA

Instituto Politécnico da Guarda
Avenida Dr. Francisco Sá Carneiro, 50, 6301-559 Guarda
Tel: +351(271) 220-111
Fax: +351(271) 222-690
EMail: ipg@ipg.pt
Website: http://www.ipg.pt

Presidente: Constantino Mendes Rei
Tel: +351(271) 220-140, Fax: +351(271) 220-690
EMail: assessoria@ipg.pt

Schools

Education, Communication and Sports (Communication Studies; Cultural Studies; Education; Educational Sciences; Library Science; Modern Languages; Multimedia; Natural Sciences; Physical Education; Preschool Education; Primary Education; Psychology; Public Relations; Social Sciences; Sports); **Health** (Child Care and Development; Community Health; Nursing; Paediatrics; Pharmacy); **Technology and Management** (Accountancy; Arts and Humanities; Civil Engineering; Computer Engineering; Cultural Studies; Environmental Engineering; Human Resources; Management; Marketing; Mathematics; Mechanical Engineering; Modern Languages; Secretarial Studies; Social Sciences; Surveying and Mapping; Technology; Transport Management); **Tourism and Hotel Management** *(Seia)* (Cooking and Catering; Hotel and Restaurant; Hotel Management; Leisure Studies; Tourism)

History: Founded 1980.

Main Language(s) of Instruction: Portuguese

Degrees and Diplomas: *Licenciado*; *Mestre*. Also specialization courses
Last Updated: 29/09/11

POLYTECHNIC INSTITUTE OF LEIRIA

Instituto Politécnico de Leiria
Rua General Norton de Matos, Apartado 4133, 2411-901 Leiria
Tel: +351(244) 830-010
Fax: +351(244) 813-013
EMail: ipleiria@ipleiria.pt
Website: http://www.ipleiria.pt

Presidente: Nuno André Oliveira Mangas Pereira
EMail: presidencia@ipleiria.pt

Vice-Presidente: João Paulo Marques

Schools

Education and Social Sciences *(ESSE-Leiria)* (Chinese; Communication Studies; Cultural Studies; Education; Human Resources; Labour and Industrial Relations; Multimedia; Portuguese; Primary Education; Social Studies; Sports; Translation and Interpretation); **Fine Arts and Design** *(ESTGAD-Caldas da Rainha)* (Ceramic Art; Dance; Design; Fine Arts; Glass Art; Graphic Design; Industrial Design; Multimedia; Radio and Television Broadcasting; Sound Engineering (Acoustics); Theatre); **Health Sciences** *(ESS-Leiria)* (Dietetics; Nursing; Occupational Therapy; Physical Therapy; Speech Therapy and Audiology); **Technology and Management** *(ESTG-Leiria)* (Accountancy; Automotive Engineering; Civil Engineering; Computer Engineering; Computer Networks; Electrical Engineering; Energy Engineering; Environmental Engineering; Finance; Management; Marketing; Mechanical Engineering; Medical Technology; Public Administration; Telecommunications Engineering; Welfare and Protective Services); **Tourism and Maritime Technology** *(ESTG-Peniche)* (Cooking and Catering; Food Technology; Hotel and Restaurant; Hotel Management; Leisure Studies; Marine Biology; Marine Engineering; Tourism)

History: Founded 1980.

Main Language(s) of Instruction: Portuguese

Degrees and Diplomas: *Licenciado*; *Mestre*. Also postgraduate programmes
Last Updated: 29/09/11

POLYTECHNIC INSTITUTE OF LISBON

Instituto Politécnico de Lisboa
Estrada de Benfica, 529, 1549-020 Lisboa
Tel: +351(217) 101-200
Fax: +351(217) 101-235
EMail: webmaster@ipl.pt
Website: http://www.ipl.pt

Presidente: Luís Manuel Vicente Ferreira (2011-)
Tel: +351(217) 101-213

Administrador: António José Carvalho Marques
Tel: +351(217) 786-428

Institutes

Accountancy and Administration *(ISCAL)* (Accountancy; Administration; Management; Public Administration; Taxation); **Engineering** *(ISEL)* (Bioengineering; Chemical Engineering; Civil Engineering; Computer Engineering; Electronic Engineering; Engineering; Mechanical Engineering; Multimedia; Telecommunications Engineering)

Schools

Dance *(ESD)* (Dance); **Education** *(ESELx)* (Education; Educational Administration; Educational Sciences; English; Environmental Studies; Foreign Languages Education; French; Information Technology; Mathematics Education; Music; Music Education; Native Language Education; Portuguese; Preschool Education; Primary Education; Science Education; Secondary Education; Special Education; Visual Arts); **Health Technology** *(ESTeSL)* (Anatomy; Cardiology; Dietetics; Hygiene; Medical Technology; Medicine; Nutrition; Occupational Health; Optical Technology; Orthopaedics; Pathology; Pharmacy; Physical Therapy; Pneumology; Public Health; Radiology); **Music** *(ESML)* (Jazz and Popular Music; Music; Music Theory and Composition; Musical Instruments; Singing); **Social Communication** *(ESCS)* (Advertising and Publicity; Communication Studies; English; Journalism; Marketing; Multimedia; Public Administration; Radio and Television Broadcasting); **Theatre and Cinema** *(ESTC)* (Cinema and Television; Display and Stage Design; Film; Performing Arts; Theatre)

History: Founded 1979, acquired present status 1984.

Main Language(s) of Instruction: Portuguese

Degrees and Diplomas: *Licenciado*; *Mestre*; *Doutor*

Academic Staff *2010-2011*: Total 14,540

Student Numbers *2010-2011*: Total 1,335

Last Updated: 29/09/11

POLYTECHNIC INSTITUTE OF OPORTO

Instituto Politécnico do Porto
Rua Dr. Roberto Frias, 712, 4200-465 Porto
Tel: +351(22) 557-1000
Fax: +351(22) 520-0772
EMail: ipp@ipp.pt
Website: http://www.ipp.pt

Presidente: Vítor Santos
Tel: +351(22) 557-1002 EMail: ippls@mail.telepac.pt

Administrador: Orlando de Freitas Barreira Fernandes
Tel: +351(22) 557-1031 EMail: of@sc.ipp.pt

International Relations: Maria da Fátima Lopes da Silva Morgado
Tel: +351(22) 557-1009, Fax: +351(22) 502-0772
EMail: fatimamorgado@sc.ipp.pt

Institutes

Accountancy and Administration (Accountancy; Administration; Communication Studies; Finance; Information Technology; International Business; Marketing; Taxation; Tourism; Translation and Interpretation; Transport Management); **Engineering** (Automotive Engineering; Chemical Engineering; Civil Engineering; Computer Engineering; Electrical Engineering; Electronic Engineering; Engineering; Environmental Engineering; Measurement and Precision Engineering; Mechanical Engineering; Medical Technology)

Schools

Education (Art Education; Education; Foreign Languages Education; Heritage Preservation; Modern Languages; Music Education; Physical Education; Portuguese; Preschool Education; Primary Education; Social Studies; Sports; Translation and Interpretation; Visual Arts); **Health Technology** (Biochemistry; Educational Sciences; Environmental Management; Occupational Therapy; Pharmacy; Physical Therapy); **Industrial and Management Studies** *(Vila do Conde)* (Advertising and Publicity; Bioengineering; Design; Documentation Techniques; Finance; Graphic Design; Hotel Management; Human Resources; Industrial Design; Industrial Engineering; Industrial Management; Information Technology; Library Science; Mechanical Engineering); **Music and Performing Arts** (Communication Arts; Multimedia; Music; Performing Arts; Theatre); **Technology and Management** *(Felgueiras)* (Business Computing; Computer Engineering; Computer Networks; Management; Safety Engineering; Teacher Training; Technology)

History: Founded 1979.

Main Language(s) of Instruction: Portuguese

Degrees and Diplomas: *Licenciado*; *Mestre*. Also postgraduate programmes

Last Updated: 30/09/11

POLYTECHNIC INSTITUTE OF PORTALEGRE

Instituto Politécnico de Portalegre
Apartado 84, Praça da Município, 7301-901 Portalegre
Tel: +351(245) 301-500
Fax: +351(245) 330-353
EMail: geral@ipportalegre.pt
Website: http://www.ipportalegre.pt

Presidente: Joaquim Mourato
EMail: presidipp@mail.ipportalegre.pt

Programmes

Graduate Studies (Accountancy; Agricultural Engineering; Agriculture; Automation and Control Engineering; Child Care and Development; Civil Engineering; Communication Studies; Community Health; Computer Networks; Continuing Education; Cultural Studies; Education; Electrical Engineering; English; Environmental Management; Food Science; Foreign Languages Education; French; Gerontology; Health Administration; Health Education; Industrial Engineering; Journalism; Landscape Architecture; Management; Mechanical Engineering; Multimedia; Nursing; Occupational Health; Oenology; Paediatrics; Power Engineering; Preschool Education; Primary Education; Psychology; Robotics; Taxation; Tourism; Town Planning; Urban Studies)

Schools

Agriculture *(Elvas)* (Agricultural Engineering; Agriculture; Agronomy; Landscape Architecture; Regional Planning; Rural Planning; Veterinary Science); **Education** (Advertising and Publicity; Art Education; Communication Studies; Cultural Studies; Education; Journalism; Primary Education; Public Relations; Social and Community Services; Tourism); **Health** (Hygiene; Nursing); **Technology and Management** (Accountancy; Advertising and Publicity; Bioengineering; Business Administration; Civil Engineering; Communication Arts; Computer Engineering; Design; Engineering; Environmental Engineering; Industrial Engineering; Industrial Management; Information Technology; Management; Marketing; Multimedia; Technology)

History: Founded 1980.

Degrees and Diplomas: *Licenciado*; *Mestre*. Also specialization and postgraduate programmes

Last Updated: 30/09/11

POLYTECHNIC INSTITUTE OF SANTARÉM

Instituto Politécnico de Santarém
Complexo Andaluz, Apartado 279, 2001-904 Santarém
Tel: +351(243) 309-520
Fax: +351(243) 309-539 +351(243) 309-538
EMail: secretariado@ipsantarem.pt
Website: http://www.ipsantarem.pt

Presidente: Jorge Alberto Guerra Justino (2006-)
EMail: presidente.ips@ipsantarem.pt

Administrador: Pedro Maria Nogueiro Carvalho
EMail: Administracao@Ipsantarem.pt

International Relations: Maria do Céu Martins

Schools

Agriculture (Agricultural Engineering; Agriculture; Animal Husbandry; Environmental Engineering; Food Technology; Fruit Production; Horticulture; Oenology); **Education** (Communication Arts; Communication Studies; Cultural Studies; Education; Educational Administration; Educational and Student Counselling; Fine Arts; Multimedia; Preschool Education; Primary Education; Science Education; Social and Community Services); **Health** (Community Health; Gynaecology and Obstetrics; Nursing; Rehabilitation and Therapy); **Management and Technology** (Accountancy; Advertising and Publicity; Business Administration; Computer Engineering; Computer Networks; Computer Science; Management; Management Systems; Marketing; Multimedia; Public Administration;

Taxation); **Sport** *(Rio Maior)* (Environmental Studies; Physical Education; Sports; Tourism)

History: Founded 1979.

Main Language(s) of Instruction: Portuguese

Degrees and Diplomas: *Licenciado*; *Mestre*. Also postgraduate programmes

Last Updated: 30/09/11

POLYTECHNIC INSTITUTE OF SETÚBAL

Instituto Politécnico de Setúbal

Largo Defensores da República, 1, 2910-470 Setúbal
Tel: +351(265) 548-820
Fax: +351(265) 231-110
EMail: ips@spr.ips.pt
Website: http://www.ips.pt

Presidente: Armando José Pinheiro Marques Pires (2006-)

Administradora: Maria Manuela Silva Gomes Serra

Programmes

Graduate Studies (Accountancy; Aeronautical and Aerospace Engineering; Architectural Restoration; Art Education; Business Administration; Civil Engineering; Communication Arts; Computer Engineering; Electronic Engineering; Energy Engineering; English; Environmental Engineering; Environmental Management; Finance; Foreign Languages Education; Health Sciences; Heating and Refrigeration; Heritage Preservation; Human Resources; Industrial Engineering; Management; Management Systems; Music Education; Nursing; Occupational Health; Physical Therapy; Preschool Education; Primary Education; Production Engineering; Psychiatry and Mental Health; Real Estate; Safety Engineering; Speech Therapy and Audiology; Sports; Surgery; Technology Education; Telecommunications Engineering; Transport Management)

Schools

Business Administration (Accountancy; Business Administration; Finance; Human Resources; Information Technology; Marketing; Transport Management); **Education** (Communication Studies; Cultural Studies; Education; Education of the Handicapped; Heritage Preservation; Physical Education; Primary Education; Sports; Translation and Interpretation); **Health** (Health Sciences; Physical Therapy; Speech Therapy and Audiology); **Technology** *(Barreiro)* (Chemical Engineering; Civil Engineering; Construction Engineering); **Technology** *(Setúbal)* (Automation and Control Engineering; Bioengineering; Computer Engineering; Electronic Engineering; Environmental Engineering; Industrial Engineering; Mechanical Engineering; Safety Engineering)

History: Founded 1979.

Main Language(s) of Instruction: Portuguese

Degrees and Diplomas: *Licenciado*; *Mestre*. Also postgraduate programmes

Last Updated: 30/09/11

POLYTECHNIC INSTITUTE OF THE WEST

Instituto Superior Politécnico do Oeste

Praceta Prof. José Carvalho Mesquita, n° 5 -2° - Urbanização da Conquinha, 2560-299 Torres Vedras
Tel: +351(261) 316-104
Fax: +351(261) 314-084
EMail: informacoes@ispo.pt
Website: http://www.ispo.pt

Courses

Accountancy and Administration (Accountancy; Administration); **Human Resource Management** (Human Resources); **Law** (Law); **Management Computing** (Business Computing); **Postgraduate Studies** (Educational Administration); **Tourism and Hotel Management** (Hotel Management; Tourism)

History: Founded 2005 following merger of the Instituto Superior de Matemática e Gestão and the Instituto Superior de Humanidades e Tecnologias.

Main Language(s) of Instruction: Portuguese

Degrees and Diplomas: *Licenciado*. Also postgraduate courses

Last Updated: 05/10/11

POLYTECHNIC INSTITUTE OF TOMAR

Instituto Politécnico de Tomar

Quinta do Contador, Estrada da Serra, 2300-313 Tomar
Tel: +351(249) 328-100
Fax: +351(249) 328-186
EMail: geral@ipt.pt
Website: http://www.ipt.pt

Presidente: Eugénio Pina de Almeida (2010-)

Vice-Presidente: Miguel Pinto dos Santos

International Relations: Horácio Lopez

Programmes

Graduate Studies (Accountancy; Archaeology; Architectural Restoration; Automation and Control Engineering; Chemical Engineering; Design; Documentation Techniques; Electronic Engineering; Ethnology; Finance; Folklore; Health Administration; Heritage Preservation; Human Resources; Museum Management; Museum Studies; Occupational Health; Photography; Prehistory; Public Administration; Small Business; Tourism; Town Planning; Urban Studies)

Schools

Management (Accountancy; Business Administration; Cultural Studies; Finance; Health Administration; Human Resources; Management; Public Administration; Tourism); **Technology** (Archaeology; Architectural Restoration; Biochemistry; Bioengineering; Chemical Engineering; Civil Engineering; Computer Engineering; Electronic Engineering; Environmental Engineering; Fine Arts; Graphic Arts; Heritage Preservation; Multimedia; Painting and Drawing; Photography; Technology); **Technology** *(Abrantes)* (Cinema and Television; Film; Industrial Design; Industrial Engineering; Industrial Management; Information Technology; Mechanical Engineering; Production Engineering; Technology; Video)

History: Founded 1996.

Main Language(s) of Instruction: Portuguese

Degrees and Diplomas: *Licenciado*; *Mestre*. Also postgraduate and specialization programmes

Last Updated: 30/09/11

POLYTECHNIC INSTITUTE OF VIANA DO CASTELO

Instituto Politécnico de Viana do Castelo

Praça General Barbosa, 4900-347 Viana do Castelo
Tel: +351(258) 809-610
Fax: +351(258) 829-065
EMail: geral@ipvc.pt
Website: http://www.ipvc.pt

Presidente: Rui Alberto Martins Teixeira EMail: ruitx@ipvc.pt

Administradora: Margarida Amorim Pereira
EMail: margaridaamorim@ipvc.pt

Programmes

Graduate Studies (Accountancy; Agriculture; Art Education; Art Management; Banking; Communication Studies; Community Health; Educational Research; English; Environmental Management; Finance; Food Technology; Foreign Languages Education; French; Gerontology; Gynaecology and Obstetrics; Health Education; Health Sciences; Management Systems; Marketing; Mathematics Education; Native Language Education; Nursing; Occupational Health; Oenology; Pedagogy; Portuguese; Preschool Education; Primary Education; Rehabilitation and Therapy; Science Education; Surgery; Transport Management; Veterinary Science)

Schools

Agriculture *(Ponte de Lima)* (Agricultural Economics; Agricultural Engineering; Agriculture; Animal Husbandry; Biotechnology; Botany; Environmental Studies; Food Technology; Rural Planning; Rural Studies; Zoology); **Business Administration** *(Valença)* (Accountancy; Business Administration; Business Computing; Economics; Finance; Marketing; Social Sciences; Taxation; Transport Management); **Education** (Art Education; Cultural Studies; Education; Gerontology; Primary Education); **Health** (Nursing; Occupational Therapy); **Sports and Leisure Studies** (Leisure Studies; Sports); **Technology and Management** (Ceramic Art; Chemical Engineering; Civil Engineering; Computer Engineering;

Computer Networks; Design; Electronic Engineering; Energy Engineering; Environmental Engineering; Food Technology; Industrial Design; Management; Materials Engineering; Multimedia; Technology; Tourism)

History: Founded 1980, acquired present status 1995.

Main Language(s) of Instruction: Portuguese

Degrees and Diplomas: *Licenciado*; *Mestre*. Also postgraduate programmes

Last Updated: 30/09/11

POLYTECHNIC INSTITUTE OF VISEU

Instituto Politécnico de Viseu

Av. Cor. José Maria Vale de Andrade, 3504-510 Viseu

Tel: +351(232) 480-700

Fax: +351(232) 480-750

EMail: ipv@pres.ipv.pt

Website: http://www.ipv.pt

Presidente: Fernando Lopes Rodrigues Sebastião
Tel: +351(232) 480-703, Fax: +351(232) 480-780
EMail: fsebastiao@pres.ipv.pt

Vice-Presidente: Maria Paula Martins de Oliveira Carvalho
EMail: mpcarvalho@pres.ipv.pt

Schools

Agriculture *(ESAV)* (Agricultural Engineering; Agriculture; Agronomy; Animal Husbandry; Botany; Ecology; Floriculture; Food Technology; Landscape Architecture; Meat and Poultry; Oenology; Veterinary Science; Viticulture; Zoology); **Education** *(ESEV)* (Art Education; Communication Arts; Communication Studies; Cultural Studies; Education; Educational Psychology; Environmental Studies; Fine Arts; Foreign Languages Education; Media Studies; Modern Languages; Multimedia; Native Language Education; Natural Sciences; Physical Education; Primary Education; Psychology; Science Education; Social Studies; Sports; Teacher Training; Visual Arts); **Health** *(ESSV)* (Community Health; Gynaecology and Obstetrics; Nursing; Paediatrics; Psychiatry and Mental Health; Rehabilitation and Therapy; Surgery); **Technology and Management - Lamego** *(ESTGL)* (Accountancy; Business Computing; Computer Science; Cultural Studies; Management; Secretarial Studies; Social Work; Technology; Telecommunications Engineering; Tourism); **Technology and Management - Viseu** *(ESTGV)* (Accountancy; Administration; Architectural Restoration; Automation and Control Engineering; Business Administration; Civil Engineering; Computer Engineering; Computer Networks; Electronic Engineering; Energy Engineering; Engineering; Environmental Engineering; Finance; Furniture Design; Heating and Refrigeration; Industrial Engineering; Industrial Management; Information Management; Information Technology; Laboratory Techniques; Marketing; Mechanical Engineering; Multimedia; Technology; Tourism; Wood Technology)

History: Founded 1979, acquired present status 1995.

Main Language(s) of Instruction: Portuguese

Degrees and Diplomas: *Licenciado*; *Mestre*. Also specialization and postgraduate programmes

Last Updated: 30/09/11

SCHOOL OF HOTEL MANAGEMENT AND TOURISM OF ESTORIL

Escola Superior de Hotelaria e Turismo do Estoril

Avenida Condes de Barcelona, 2769-510 Estoril

Tel: +351(21) 004-0700

Fax: +351(21) 004-0719

EMail: info@eshte.pt

Website: http://www.eshte.pt

Presidente: Fernando João Matos Moreira

Vice-Presidente: João Leitão

Courses

Food Production for Restaurants (Food Science; Hotel and Restaurant); **Graduate Studies** (Communication Studies; Cooking and Catering; Cultural Studies; Hotel and Restaurant; Hotel Management; Tourism); **Hotel Management** (Hotel Management); **Leisure and Tourism Management** (Leisure Studies; Tourism); **Tourism Information** (Information Management; Tourism)

History: Founded 1991.

Main Language(s) of Instruction: Portuguese

Degrees and Diplomas: *Licenciado*; *Mestre*. Also postgraduate diplomas. Doutoramento in Tourism in partnership with the Instituto de Geografia e Ordenamento do Território (IGOT)

Last Updated: 28/09/11

SCHOOL OF NURSING OF OPORTO

Escola Superior de Enfermagem do Porto

Rua Dr. António Bernardino de Almeida, 4050-040 Porto

Tel: +351(22) 507 35 00

Fax: +351(22) 509 63 37

EMail: esep@esenf.pt

Website: http://portal.esenf.pt

Presidente do Conselho Directivo: Maria Arminda Mendes Costa (1998-) EMail: arminda@esecp.min-saude.pt

Secretário: Manuel Vieira Mendes
EMail: vmendes@esecp.min-saude.pt

International Relations: Maria do Céu Aguiar Barbieri de Figueiredo EMail: ceu@esecp.min-saude.pt

Courses

Graduate Studies (Nursing); **Nursing** (Anatomy; Biochemistry; Community Health; Health Sciences; Microbiology; Nursing; Parasitology; Pharmacology; Physiology; Psychology; Social Sciences; Surgery)

History: Founded 2007 following merger of Escola Superior de Enfermagem Cidade do Porto, Escola Superior de Enfermagem de D. Ana Guedes and Escola Superior de Enfermagem de São João.

Main Language(s) of Instruction: Portuguese

Degrees and Diplomas: *Licenciado*; *Mestre*. Also specialization and postgraduate diplomas

Last Updated: 28/09/11

TECHNICAL UNIVERSITY OF LISBON

Universidade Técnica de Lisboa (UTL)

Alameda Santo António dos Capuchos, 1, Palácio Centeno, 1169-047 Lisboa

Tel: +351(218) 811-900

Fax: +351(218) 811-991

EMail: utl@reitoria.utl.pt

Website: http://www.utl.pt

Reitora: Helena Pereira

International Relations: Isabel França
EMail: isabel.franca@reitoria.utl.pt

Faculties

Architecture (Architecture; Art Management; Communication Arts; Design; Display and Stage Design; Fashion Design; Industrial Design; Interior Design; Performing Arts; Real Estate; Regional Planning; Town Planning); **Human Kinetics** (Dance; Physical Education; Physical Therapy; Rehabilitation and Therapy; Special Education; Sports; Sports Management; Teacher Training); **Veterinary Science** (Animal Husbandry; Food Science; Veterinary Science)

Institutes

Agronomy (Agricultural Business; Agricultural Economics; Agricultural Engineering; Agronomy; Animal Husbandry; Applied Mathematics; Bioengineering; Biology; Botany; Crop Production; Environmental Studies; Food Science; Forestry; Landscape Architecture; Mathematics; Natural Resources; Oenology; Tropical Agriculture; Viticulture; Zoology); **Economics and Management** *(ISEG)* (Actuarial Science; Applied Mathematics; Business Administration; Development Studies; Econometrics; Economic History; Economics; Finance; Human Resources; Information Technology; Management; Marketing; Mathematics; Real Estate; Social Sciences; Taxation); **Social and Political Sciences** (Administration; African Studies; Anthropology; Human Resources; International Relations; International Studies; Journalism; Mass Communication; Political Sciences; Public Administration; Social and Community Services; Social Work; Sociology); **Technical** (Aeronautical and Aerospace Engineering; Applied Mathematics; Architecture; Bioengineering; Biomedical Engineering; Chemical Engineering; Chemistry; Civil Engineering; Computer Engineering; Electrical and Electronic

Engineering; Engineering Management; Environmental Engineering; Geological Engineering; Hydraulic Engineering; Industrial Engineering; Marine Engineering; Materials Engineering; Mathematics; Mechanical Engineering; Mining Engineering; Naval Architecture; Physical Engineering; Physics; Regional Planning; Town Planning; Water Management)

History: Founded 1930, incorporating 4 previously existing institutions founded between 1830 and 1911. Acquired present status 1989.

Governing Bodies: Assembleia; Senado; Conselho Administrativo

Academic Year: October to July (October-February; March-July)

Admission Requirements: Secondary school certificate, entrance examination according to the fields of study

Main Language(s) of Instruction: Portuguese

International Co-operation: With universities in Europe, USA, Canada, Africa, Latin America and Asia

Degrees and Diplomas: *Licenciado*; *Mestre*; *Doutor*

Student Services: Canteen, Cultural centre, Employment services, Foreign student adviser, Foreign Studies Centre, Health services, Language programs, Nursery care, Social counselling, Sports facilities

Student Residential Facilities: Yes

Libraries: Total, c. 252,000 vols

Publications: Episteme *(biennially)*; Jornal da UTL *(biennially)*

Press or Publishing House: IST Press

Last Updated: 17/10/11

UNIVERSITY OF AVEIRO

Universidade de Aveiro

Campus Universitário de Santiago, 3810-193 Aveiro
Tel: +351(234) 370-211
Fax: +351(234) 370-985
Website: http://www.ua.pt

Reitor: Manuel António Assunção
Tel: +351(234) 370-606, Fax: +351(234) 370-089
EMail: reitoria@ua.pt

Vice-Reitor: Joaquim da Costa Leite

Departments

Biology (Biology; Geology; Science Education); **Ceramics and Glass Engineering** (Ceramics and Glass Technology; Materials Engineering; Nanotechnology); **Chemistry** (Biochemistry; Biotechnology; Chemical Engineering; Chemistry; Marine Engineering); **Civil Engineering** (Civil Engineering); **Communication and Art** (Communication Studies; Design; Information Technology; Multimedia; Music; Music Education); **Economics, Management and Industrial Engineering** (Accountancy; Economics; Environmental Management; Industrial Management; Information Management; Management; Tourism); **Education** (Art Education; Clinical Psychology; Education; Educational Sciences; Educational Technology; Mathematics Education; Pedagogy; Preschool Education; Psychology; Science Education); **Electronics, Telecommunications and Computing** (Automation and Control Engineering; Computer Engineering; Electronic Engineering; Information Technology; Telecommunications Engineering); **Environment and Planning** (Ecology; Environmental Engineering; Geology); **Geoscience** (Biology; Geological Engineering; Geology); **Health Sciences** (Biomedicine; Gerontology; Molecular Biology; Pharmacy; Speech Therapy and Audiology); **Languages and Cultures** (Cultural Studies; International Business; Literature; Modern Languages; Publishing and Book Trade; Translation and Interpretation); **Mathematics** (Applied Mathematics; Mathematics); **Mechanical Engineering** (Mechanical Engineering); **Physics** (Geophysics; Marine Science and Oceanography; Meteorology; Physical Engineering; Physics); **Social Sciences, Policy and Planning** (Administration; Chinese; Government; Higher Education; Management; Political Sciences; Public Administration; Regional Planning; Science Education; Social Policy; Social Sciences; Town Planning)

Institutes

Accounting and Administration *(ISCA-UA)* (Accountancy; Finance; Marketing; Public Administration)

Research Centres

Cell Biology *(CBC)* (Cell Biology); **Ceramic and Composite Materials** *(CICECO)* (Ceramics and Glass Technology; Materials Engineering); **Development of Pedagogic Knowledge in Educational and Training Systems** *(CCPSF)* (Pedagogy); **Didactics and Technology in Teacher Training** *(CDTFF)* (Educational Technology; Pedagogy); **Enterprise Competitiveness** *(CECE)*; **Environmental and Marine Studies** *(CESAM)* (Earth Sciences; Environmental Studies; Marine Science and Oceanography); **Governance and Public Policy** *(CEGOPP)*; **Industrial Minerals and Clays** *(MIA)* (Industrial Engineering; Materials Engineering); **Languages and Cultures** *(CLC)* (Cultural Studies; Modern Languages); **Lithosphere Evolution and Surface Environment** *(ELMAS)* (Earth Sciences; Geology); **Mathematics and Applications** *(MA)* (Applied Mathematics); **Mechanical Technology and Automation** *(TEMA)* (Automation and Control Engineering; Mechanical Engineering); **Optimization and Control** *(CEOC)*; **Organic Chemistry, Natural and Agro-food Products** *(QOPNA)* (Food Technology; Organic Chemistry); **Physics of Layered Semiconductors, Opto-electronics and Disordered Systems** *(FSCOSD)* (Electronic Engineering; Information Technology; Physics)

Research Institutes

Electronics and Telematics Engineering of Aveiro *(IEETA)* (Electronic Engineering; Telecommunications Engineering); **Telecommunications** *(IT)* (Information Technology; Telecommunications Engineering)

Research Units

Communication and Art *(UniCA)* (Communication Studies; Fine Arts)

Schools

Aveiro North School (Production Engineering; Technology); **Design, Production Technology and Management** *(Aveiro Norte (ESAN))* (Design; Industrial Management; Production Engineering); **Health Sciences** *(ESSUA)* (Gerontology; Health Sciences; Nursing; Physical Therapy; Radiology; Speech Therapy and Audiology); **Technology and Management** *(Águeda)* (Administration; Archiving; Business and Commerce; Documentation Techniques; Electronic Engineering; Information Technology; Public Administration)

Further Information: Also Study Abroad programmes

History: Founded 1973.

Governing Bodies: Senado; Assembleia; Conselho

Academic Year: September to July (September-January; February-July)

Admission Requirements: Secondary school certificate and entrance examination

Main Language(s) of Instruction: Portuguese

International Co-operation: Participates in the Erasmus, Socrates, Erasmus Mundus, Alban and Tempus programmes.

Degrees and Diplomas: *Licenciado*: 4-5 yrs; *Mestre*: a further 2 yrs; *Doutor*: a further 3-5 yrs

Student Services: Academic counselling, Canteen, Cultural centre, Employment services, Foreign student adviser, Foreign Studies Centre, Health services, Language programs, Nursery care, Social counselling, Sports facilities

Student Residential Facilities: For c. 900 students

Special Facilities: Art Gallery; Theatre; Multimedia Centre

Libraries: Total, c. 259,450 vols

Publications: Revista LINHAS *(biennially)*

Press or Publishing House: Comissão Editorial

Last Updated: 06/10/11

UNIVERSITY OF BEIRA INTERIOR

Universidade da Beira Interior (UBI)

Convento de Sto António, 6201-001 Covilhã
Tel: +351(275) 319-700
Fax: +351(275) 329-183
EMail: geral@ubi.pt
Website: http://www.ubi.pt

Reitor: João António de Sampaio Rodrigues Queiroz
Tel: +351(275) 319-002, Fax: +351(275) 319-056

Administrador: João Carlos Correia Leitão
Tel: +351(275) 319-037

Centres

Computer Science (Computer Science); **Optics** (Optics)

Faculties

Arts and Humanities (Advertising and Publicity; Cinema and Television; Communication Studies; Design; English; Geography (Human); History; Journalism; Linguistics; Literature; Multimedia; Philosophy; Portuguese; Public Relations; Spanish; Visual Arts); **Engineering** (Aeronautical and Aerospace Engineering; Architecture; Civil Engineering; Computer Engineering; Electrical Engineering; Mechanical Engineering; Paper Technology; Structural Architecture; Textile Technology); **Health Sciences** (Biomedicine; Gerontology; Health Sciences; Medicine; Optometry; Pharmacy); **Science** (Applied Mathematics; Biochemistry; Biotechnology; Chemistry; Industrial Chemistry; Mathematics; Mathematics Education; Paper Technology; Physics); **Social and Human Sciences** (Economics; Education; Health Administration; Management; Marketing; Psychology; Sociology; Sports)

History: Founded 1973 as Instituto Politécnico da Covilhã. Became Instituto Universitário 1979 and acquired present title 1986.

Governing Bodies: Assembleia; Senado; Conselho Administrativo

Academic Year: September to June (September-January; February-June)

Admission Requirements: Secondary school certificate and entrance examination

Main Language(s) of Instruction: Portuguese

Degrees and Diplomas: *Licenciado*: 3 yrs; *Licenciado*: Engineering, 5 yrs; *Licenciado*: Medicine; Architecture, 6 yrs; *Mestre*: a further 2 yrs; *Doutor*: a further 3 yrs

Student Services: Academic counselling, Canteen, Employment services, Foreign Studies Centre, Health services, Social counselling, Sports facilities

Student Residential Facilities: Yes

Special Facilities: Museu de Lanificos (Wool Museum)

Libraries: Central Library, c. 80,000 vols

Publications: À Beira, Humanities; Anais Universitários; Psicologia e Educação; Revista de Gesão e Economia

Last Updated: 06/10/11

UNIVERSITY OF COIMBRA

Universidade de Coimbra (UC)
Paço das Escolas, 3004-531 Coimbra
Tel: +351(239) 859-900
Fax: +351(239) 827-994
EMail: ucadmin@adm.uc.pt
Website: http://www.uc.pt

Reitor: João Gabriel Silva (2011-)
Tel: +351(239) 859-810, Fax: +351(239) 859-813
EMail: gbreitor@uc.pt

Secretary-General: Carlos Lúzio Vaz
Tel: +351(239) 859-920, Fax: +351(239) 827-994
EMail: ucademin@ci.uc.pt

International Relations: Joaquim Ramos de Carvalho, Vice-Rector, International Relations
Tel: +351(239) 857-003 EMail: vr.joaquim.carvalho@uc.pt

Faculties

Economics (Accountancy; Business Administration; Economics; Educational Administration; Environmental Studies; Finance; Health Administration; International Relations; Labour and Industrial Relations; Management; Marketing; Sociology); **Humanities** (Archaeology; Archiving; Art Education; Art History; Classical Languages; Communication Studies; Documentation Techniques; Geography (Human); History; Information Sciences; Journalism; Modern Languages; Native Language; Philosophy; Portuguese; Translation and Interpretation); **Law** (Law; Private Law; Public Administration; Public Law); **Medicine** (Anatomy; Biochemistry; Biomedicine; Biophysics; Cell Biology; Dental Technology; Dentistry; Dermatology; Dietetics; Embryology and Reproduction Biology; Epidemiology; Ergotherapy; Genetics; Health Sciences; Immunology; Medicine; Microbiology; Molecular Biology; Neurology; Nutrition; Occupational Health; Oncology; Ophthalmology; Otorhinolaryngology; Paediatrics; Pathology; Periodontics; Pharmacology; Physiology; Psychiatry and Mental Health; Psychology; Public Health; Radiology; Social and Preventive Medicine; Sports Medicine; Surgery; Toxicology); **Pharmacy** (Pharmacology; Pharmacy); **Psychology and Education** (Cognitive Sciences; Curriculum; Educational Administration; Educational Sciences; Industrial and Organizational Psychology; Neurosciences; Pedagogy; Psychology; Social and Community Services; Special Education; Teacher Trainers Education); **Science and Technology** (Anthropology; Architecture; Biochemistry; Biological and Life Sciences; Biology; Biomedical Engineering; Chemical Engineering; Chemistry; Civil Engineering; Communication Studies; Computer Engineering; Computer Science; Earth Sciences; Electrical Engineering; Electronic Engineering; Environmental Engineering; Geography; Geological Engineering; Geology; Industrial Chemistry; Information Technology; Materials Engineering; Mathematics; Mechanical Engineering; Mining Engineering; Multimedia; Natural Sciences; Physical Engineering; Physics; Technology); **Sports and Physical Education** (Physical Education; Sports)

Institutes

Interdisciplinary Research

Further Information: Also University Hospitals. Courses for foreign students in Portuguese Language and Culture

History: Founded in Lisbon 1290, transferred to Coimbra 1308, returned to Lisbon in 14th century. Permanently established in Coimbra 1537. Reorganized 1772. Operating under the jurisdiction of the Ministry of Science and Higher Education.

Governing Bodies: Assembleia; Senado; Conselho Administrativo

Academic Year: October to July (October-February; March-July)

Admission Requirements: Secondary school certificate and entrance examination

Fees: (Euros): 900.00 per annum

Main Language(s) of Instruction: Portuguese

International Co-operation: With universities in EU,China, USA, Canada, Australia. Also Participates in Socrates; Erasmus; Tempus; ACP and Alfa Coimbra programmes. Also participates in Utrecht Network; Transnational Network and Tordesillas Group

Accrediting Agencies: Ministry of Science, Technology and Higher Education

Degrees and Diplomas: *Licenciado*: Humanities; Economics; Education; Engineering; Law; Mathematics and Computer Science; Natural Sciences; Health Sciences; Pharmacy; Psychology; Social Sciences; Information Sciences; Sports, 4-5 yrs; *Mestre*: Humanities; Economics; Education; Engineering; Law; Mathematics and Computer Science; Natural Sciences; Health Sciences; Pharmacy; Psychology; Social Sciences; Information Sciences; Sports, a further 2 yrs following Licenciatura; *Doutor*: Humanities; Economics; Education; Engineering; Law; Mathematics and Computer Science; Natural Sciences; Health Sciences; Pharmacy; Psychology; Social Sciences; Information Sciences; Sports (PhD), 3-4 yrs

Student Services: Academic counselling, Canteen, Cultural centre, Employment services, Foreign student adviser, Foreign Studies Centre, Handicapped facilities, Health services, Language programs, Nursery care, Social counselling, Sports facilities

Student Residential Facilities: For c. 1,100 students

Special Facilities: Anthropology Museum; Zoology Museum; Botany Museum; Mineralogy Museum; Geology Museum. Observatory; Botanic Garden

Libraries: Central Library, c. 1.5m. vols; specialized Libraries, c. 2m. Vols

Last Updated: 06/10/11

UNIVERSITY OF EVORA

Universidade de Évora (UE)
Apartado 94, Largo dos Colegiais, 2, 7004-516 Évora
Tel: +351(266) 740-800
Fax: +351(266) 740-806
EMail: uevora@uevora.pt
Website: http://www.uevora.pt

Reitor: Carlos Alberto dos Santos Braumann
Tel: +351(266) 740-832

Director: José Ventura
Tel: +351(266) 705-031, Fax: +351(266) 742-870
EMail: jventura@uevora.pt

International Relations: Manuel D'Orey Cancela D'Abreu, Vice-Reitor Tel: +351(266) 740-817 EMail: abreu@uevora.pt

Schools

Social Sciences (Arts and Humanities; Economics; Education; History; Linguistics; Literature; Management; Pedagogy; Philosophy; Psychology; Social Sciences; Sociology; Translation and Interpretation); **Art** (Architecture; Design; Music; Performing Arts; Theatre; Visual Arts); **Nursing** *(São João de Deus)* (Community Health; Gynaecology and Obstetrics; Nursing; Psychiatry and Mental Health); **Science and Technology** (Agricultural Engineering; Biology; Chemistry; Computer Science; Earth Sciences; Environmental Management; Geology; Landscape Architecture; Mathematics; Microbiology; Natural Sciences; Physics; Sports; Veterinary Science; Zoology)

History: Founded 1559 as the University of the Holy Spirit, reopened 1973 as University of Evora. Acquired present status 1979.

Governing Bodies: University Assembly; Rector; Senate; Administrative Council

Academic Year: October to July (October-February; March-July)

Admission Requirements: Secondary school certificate and entrance examination

Main Language(s) of Instruction: Portuguese

International Co-operation: Participates in the Erasmus, Alfa and Leonardo da Vinci Programmes.

Accrediting Agencies: Ministry of Science and Higher Education

Degrees and Diplomas: *Licenciado*: 4-5 yrs; *Mestre*: a further 2 yrs; *Doutor (PhD)*: 3-4 yrs

Student Services: Academic counselling, Canteen, Cultural centre, Foreign Studies Centre, Handicapped facilities, Health services, Language programs, Social counselling, Sports facilities

Student Residential Facilities: For 589 students

Libraries:c. 124,900 vols
Last Updated: 06/10/11

UNIVERSITY OF LISBON

Universidade de Lisboa (UL)

Alameda da Universidade, Cidade Universitária, 1649-004 Lisboa
Tel: +351(217) 967-624
Fax: +351(217) 933-624
EMail: reitoria@reitoria.ul.pt
Website: http://www.ul.pt

Reitor: António Manuel Sampaio da Nóvoa (2006-)
Tel: +351(21) 017-0109 EMail: reitor@reitoria.ul.pt

Administrador: Luís Pedro Gomes Costa Paulitos
EMail: lpaulitos@reitoria.ul.pt

International Relations: Maria Amélia Martins-Loução, Vice-Reitora Tel: +351(21) 011-3462 EMail: maloucao@reitoria.ul.pt

Faculties

Arts and Humanities (African Studies; American Studies; Archaeology; Architectural Restoration; Art History; Arts and Humanities; Asian Studies; Classical Languages; Communication Studies; Cultural Studies; Documentation Techniques; English; English Studies; European Studies; Geography (Human); German; Germanic Studies; Heritage Preservation; History; Information Sciences; Linguistics; Literature; Medieval Studies; Mediterranean Studies; Modern Languages; Native Language; Performing Arts; Philosophy; Portuguese; Regional Studies; Religious Studies; Romance Languages; Slavic Languages; Theatre; Tourism; Translation and Interpretation); **Dental Medicine** (Dental Hygiene; Dental Technology; Dentistry; Oral Pathology; Periodontics); **Fine Arts** (Art Education; Communication Arts; Fine Arts; Furniture Design; Glass Art; Heritage Preservation; Media Studies; Multimedia; Museum Studies; Painting and Drawing; Sculpture); **Law** (Administrative Law; Civil Law; Commercial Law; Constitutional Law; Economics; Fiscal Law; International Law; Labour Law; Law; Private Law; Public Law); **Medicine** (Dietetics; Medicine; Microbiology; Nutrition); **Pharmacy** (Analytical Chemistry; Anatomy; Biochemistry; Biology; Botany; Cell Biology; Chemistry; Embryology and Reproduction Biology; Haematology; Histology; Immunology; Mathematics; Microbiology; Organic Chemistry; Parasitology; Pharmacology; Pharmacy; Physical Chemistry; Physics; Physiology; Statistics; Toxicology; Virology); **Psychology** (Psychology); **Science** (Biochemistry; Biological and Life Sciences; Chemistry; Computer Science; Geology; Mathematics; Natural Sciences; Operations Research; Physics; Science Education; Statistics)

Institutes

Bacteriology *(Câmara Pestana)* (Microbiology; Virology); **Confusius** (Chinese; South Asian Studies); **Education** (Curriculum; Education; Educational Administration; Educational Psychology; Educational Technology; Social Psychology); **Geography and Territorial Planning** (Demography and Population; Geography; Geography (Human); History; Regional Planning; Tourism; Urban Studies); **Geophysics** *(Infante D. Luís)* (Geophysics; Seismology); **Interdisciplinary Research**; **Juridical Cooperation** (Law); **Professional Guidance**; **Social Sciences** (Anthropology; Economics; Geography (Human); History; Political Sciences; Social Psychology; Social Sciences; Sociology)

Further Information: Also Portuguese Language and Culture Department for foreign students

History: Founded 1911, but traces its history back to the University established in Lisbon 1288 and subsequently transferred to Coimbra. A public institution under the jurisdiction of the Ministry of Education. Acquired present status 1992.

Governing Bodies: Senado, comprising 44 members; Assembleia, comprisingc. 300 members

Academic Year: October to July (October-February; March-July)

Admission Requirements: Secondary school certificate and entrance examination

Fees: (Euros): 570-920 per annum

Main Language(s) of Instruction: Portuguese

International Co-operation: With universities worldwide. Also participates in EU programmes, Socrates/Erasmus, Alban, Erasmus Mundos; Leonardo da Vinci; Alfa and Jean Monet and European funded-research programmes.

Degrees and Diplomas: *Licenciado*: African Studies; Applied Mathematics; Applied Statistics; Archaeology; Biology; Biochemical; Chemistry; Classical Studies; Computer Engineering; Education; European Studies; Geography; Geology; Art History; History; Dental Technology; Language Studies; Literature; Culture Studies; Mathematics; Pharmacy; Philosophy; Portuguese Studies; Cultural Studies; Linguistics; Information Technologies; Communication Studies; Chemical Engineering; Translation, 3 yrs; *Licenciado*: Arts and Humanities; Multimedia; Communication Studies; Communication Art; Design; Dentistry; Dietetics; Nutrition; Law; Medicine; Microbiology; Pharmacy; Sculpture; Painting; Psychology, 5-6 yrs; *Licenciado*: Energy Studies; Environment Studies; Physical Engineering; Physics; Meteorology; Oceanography, Geophysical; Microbiology, 4 yrs; *Mestre*: Advanced Biopharmacy and Pharmacokinetics; Food Quality Control and Toxicology; Community Pharmacy; Hospital Pharmacy; Pharmaceutical Technology; Pharmaceutical Chemistry; Art; Patrimony and Restoration; Local Autorities and Culture; Didactics of History; Aesthetics and Philosophy of Art; German Studies; English Studies; Classical studies; Theatre Studies; Romance Studies; Urban Studies; Astronomy; Astrophysics; Biophysics; Preserving Biology; Biochemistry; Plant Biotechnology; Sciences and Engineering of Surfaces; Earth and Life Sciences for Teaching; Earth Sciences and Egineering; Geophysical Science; Bioethics; Deflecting Behavior and Criminal Science; Palliative Care; Emergent Infectious Diseases; Medical Education; Immunology; Legal Medicine and Forensic Science; Microbiology; Neurosciences; Nutrition; Psychiatry; School Health; Contemporary History; History of Africa; History of Discoveries and Expansion; History and Culture of Brazil; History and Contemporary European Culture; History and Pre-Classic Culture; Dentistry; Education; Applied Electrochemistry; Physical Engineering; Geographical Engineering; Geo-Computer Science; Physics for Teaching; Plant Physiology and Biochemistry; Dynamic Geology; Applied Economic Geology; Geology; History and Philosophy of Sciences; Computer Science; Mathematics; Sciences Methodology; Chemistry; Educational Sciences; Psychology; Anatomy; Glass Art; Drawing; Curator Studies; Museology and Museography; Painting; Art Theories; Historical Legal Sciences; Legal Economic Sciences; Legal International Sciences; Legal Entrepreurial Sciences; Legal Criminal Sciences; Intellectual Law; Mathematics; Mathematics for

Teaching; Probability and Statistics; Applied Analytical Chemistry; Chemistry Applied to the Cultural Patrimony; Chemistry for Teaching; Physical Chemistry; Vegetal Secretion and Renewable Natural Resources; Mediaeval History; Modern History; Regional and Local History; Linguistics; Comparative Literature; Prehistory, Archaeology; Literary Theory; Culture Theory and Analysis; Phenomenology and Hermeneutics; Philosophy; Philosophy of Language and of the Mind; Philosophy of Natures and Environment; Philosophy in Portugal; Geography and Local/Regional Planning; Human Geography: Environment Education and Development; Psychology; Science Education; History and Philosophy of Sciences; Computer Science; Computer Science and Education; Operational Research; Social Sciences, a further 2-2 1/2 yrs; *Mestre*: Animal Diversity Conservation; Plant Diversity and Ecosystem Dynamics; Ecology; Management and Modeling of Marine Resources; *Doutor*: Art Sciences; Drawing; Communication Design; Equipment Design; Sculpture; Descriptive Geometry; Painting; Image Theory; Geology; History and Philosophy of Sciences; Computer Science; Mathematics; Sciences Methodology; Chemistry; Educational Sciences; Psychology; Anatomy; Medicine; Biomedic Science; Astronomy; Astrophysics; Biophysics; Biology; Biochemistry; Sea Science; Education; Geographical Engineering; Statistics and Operations Research; Physics; Mathematical Physics, a minimum of 4 yrs, and dissertation. Also specialisation courses: Teacher Training, Portuguese Language and Culture Intensive for Foreign and Portuguese Students; Free Courses (one year)

Student Services: Academic counselling, Canteen, Cultural centre, Employment services, Foreign student adviser, Handicapped facilities, Health services, Language programs, Social counselling, Sports facilities

Student Residential Facilities: Yes

Special Facilities: Natural History Museum; Science Museum; Mineralogy and Geology Museum; Zoology and Anthropology Museum. Laboratory. Botanical Garden

Libraries: Total, c. 450,000 vols

Publications: Anais do Instituto Geofísico Infante D. Luís *(annually)*; Análise Social *(quarterly)*; Anglo-Saxónica; Ariane *(annually)*; Arquivo do Instituto Bacteriológico Câmara Pestana; Arquivo do Museu Bocage; Artis *(annually)*; Cadernos de História de Arte *(annually)*; Cadmo *(annually)*; Clássica; Clio *(annually)*; Delectus Sporarum et Seminum *(annually)*; Dissertações de Doutoramento; Euphrosyne *(annually)*; Finisterra *(biannually)*; Journal of Portuguese Linguistics *(biennially)*; Philosophica *(biannually)*; Polifonia *(annually)*; Portugalae Acta Biologia *(quarterly)*; Portugaliae Historica; Revista da Faculdade de Direito *(annually)*; Revista da Faculdade de Letras *(annually)*; Revista da Faculdade de Medicina *(biennially)*; Revista de Biologia; Revista Lusitana; Revista Portugaliae Zoológica *(other/irregular)*; Românica *(annually)*; Runa; Textos e Pretextos

Last Updated: 06/10/11

UNIVERSITY OF MADEIRA

Universidade da Madeira (UMA)

Colégio dos Jesuítas, Praça do Município, 9000-082 Funchal
Tel: +351(291) 209-400
Fax: +351(291) 209-410
EMail: gabinetedareitoria@uma.pt
Website: http://www.uma.pt

Reitor: José Manuel Nunes Castanheira da Costa

Administradora: Carla Cró Abreu

Vice-Reitor: Gonçalo Nuno Ramos Ferreira de Gouveia

Departments

Arts and Multimedia (Design; Fine Arts; Painting and Drawing; Sculpture); **Biochemistry** (Biochemistry); **Biology** (Biology); **Chemistry** (Chemistry); **Communication, Culture and Organisation** (Communication Studies; Cultural Studies); **Cultural Studies** (Cultural Studies); **Design** (Design); **Economics** (Economics); **Educational Sciences** (Education; Educational Sciences; Primary Education); **Engineering and Computer Science** (Civil Engineering; Computer Engineering; Electronic Engineering; Software Engineering; Telecommunications Engineering); **English and Business Studies** (Business Administration; English Studies); **Interactive Media Design** (Graphic Design; Media Studies; Multimedia); **Management** (Management); **Mathematics** (Applied Mathematics; Mathematics; Mathematics Education); **Nursing** (Nursing); **Physical Education and Sports** (Physical Education; Sports; Sports Management); **Psychology** (Psychology); **Social Services** (Social and Community Services)

Programmes

Graduate Studies (Applied Chemistry; Art Education; Arts and Humanities; Biochemistry; Biological and Life Sciences; Biology; Business Administration; Chemistry; Civil Engineering; Computer Engineering; Computer Networks; Cultural Studies; Curriculum; Economics; Educational Administration; Educational Psychology; Educational Sciences; Electrical Engineering; Environmental Studies; Geology; Gerontology; Linguistics; Mathematics; Mathematics Education; Pedagogy; Physical Education; Physics; Preschool Education; Primary Education; Psychology; Regional Studies; Science Education; Sports; Telecommunications Engineering; Tourism)

Research Centres

Agriculture (Agriculture; Agronomy); **Biology and Geology** (Biology; Geology); **Food and Environmental Studies** (Environmental Studies; Food Science); **Mathematics** (Mathematics)

History: Founded 1988.

Academic Year: October to June

Admission Requirements: Secondary school certificate and entrance examination

Main Language(s) of Instruction: Portuguese

International Co-operation: With universities in Slovenia, Tunisia, Morocco. Also participates in Erasmus and Leonardo programmes.

Degrees and Diplomas: *Licenciado*: 4-5 yrs; *Mestre*; *Doutor*

Student Services: Academic counselling, Canteen, Employment services, Foreign student adviser, Handicapped facilities, Social counselling

Libraries: Yes

Last Updated: 06/10/11

UNIVERSITY OF MINHO

Universidade do Minho (UM)

Largo do Paço, 4704-553 Braga
Tel: +351(253) 601-100 +351(253) 602-100
Fax: +351(253) 616-936 +351(253) 616-936
EMail: sec-reitor@reitoria.uminho.pt
Website: http://www.uminho.pt

Rector: António M. Cunha (2009-2013)
Tel: +351(253) 601-100, Fax: +351(253) 616-936
EMail: amcunha@reitoria.uminho.pt

International Relations: Adriana Lago de Carvalho, Head of International Relations Office
Tel: +351(253) 604-006, Fax: +351(253) 284-930
EMail: adriana@gri.uminho.pt

Centres

Biology *(Gualtar, Braga campus)* (Biochemistry; Biotechnology; Botany; Cell Biology; Microbiology; Molecular Biology; Pharmacy; Plant Pathology; Traditional Eastern Medicine; Zoology); **Computer Sciences and Technologies** *(Gualtar, Braga campus)* (Computer Networks; Computer Science; Logic; Mass Communication); **Earth Sciences** *(Gualtar, Braga campus)*

Institutes

Arts and Humanities *(Gualtar, Braga)* (American Studies; Asian Studies; Classical Languages; Comparative Literature; Cultural Studies; English; Germanic Studies; Linguistics; Literature; Modern Languages; Music; Philosophy; Portuguese; Romance Languages; Slavic Languages; Translation and Interpretation); **Education** *(Gualtar, Braga campus)* (Adult Education; Art Education; Curriculum; Educational Administration; Educational Psychology; Educational Research; Educational Sciences; Educational Technology; Humanities and Social Science Education; Literacy Education; Pedagogy; Philosophy of Education; Physical Education; Psychology; Sociology; Special Education); **Social Sciences** *(Gualtar, Braga campus)* (Anthropology; Archaeology; Communication Studies; Geography (Human); History; Mass Communication; Regional Planning; Rural Planning; Sociology; Town Planning)

Research Centres

Administration and Public Policies Studies *(Gualtar, Braga campus)*; **Algorithms** *(Azurém, Guimarães campus)* (Computer

Engineering; Information Technology); **Applied Microeconomics** *(Gualtar, Braga)* (Economics); **Archaeology Studies** (Landscape Architecture); **Biological Engineering** *(Gualtar, Bragar campus)* (Bioengineering); **Chemistry** *(Gualtar, Braga campus)* (Biochemistry; Chemistry); **Children's Studies** *(Braga, independent building)* (Pedagogy; Physical Education; Preschool Education; Primary Education; Special Education); **Civil Engineering** *(Azurém, Guimarães)* (Building Technologies; Civil Engineering; Construction Engineering; Materials Engineering; Mechanics); **Communication and Society Studies** *(Gualtar, Braga campus)* (Advertising and Publicity; Communication Studies; Journalism; Media Studies; Modern Languages); **Economic Policies** *(Gualtar, Braga campus)* (Economics; International Economics; Political Sciences); **Education Studies** *(Gualtar, Braga campus)* (Education; Educational Psychology); **European, International and Industrial Economics** *(Gualtar, Braga campus)*; **Geography and Planning** *(Azurém, Guimarães)*; **Geological Planning and Resources Valorisation** *(Gualtar, Braga campus)* (Mineralogy; Mining Engineering; Natural Resources; Thermal Engineering); **Historical and Social Sciences** *(Gualtar, Brga)* (Anthropology; Communication Studies; History; Sociology); **History Studies** *(Gualtar, Braga campus)*; **Humanistic Studies** *(Gualtar, Braga)* (Cultural Studies; Literature; Philosophy); **Law Studies** *(Gualtar, Braga campus)* (Law); **Literacy promotion and Child Well-being** (Child Care and Development; Literacy Education); **Management Studies** *(Gualtar, Braga campus)* (Accountancy; Behavioural Sciences; Finance; Human Resources; Management; Marketing); **Mathematics** *(Azurém, Braga campus)*; **Mathematics** *(Gualtar, Braga campus)* (Mathematics); **Mechanical Engineering** *(Azurém, Gualtar campus)* (Automation and Control Engineering; Design; Energy Engineering; Machine Building; Mechanical Engineering; Metal Techniques; Metallurgical Engineering; Production Engineering); **Physics** (Atomic and Molecular Physics; Optics; Physics); **Political Science and International Relations** *(Gualtar, Braga)* (International Relations; Political Sciences); **Polymer Engineering** *(Azurém, Guimarães campus)* (Polymer and Plastics Technology); **Population and Society Studies** *(Azurém, Guimarães)* (Demography and Population; Sociology); **Production and Energy Technologies Interdisciplinary Studies** *(Azurém, Guimarães campus)*; **Production Systems Engineering** *(Azurém, Gualtar campus)* (Economics; Engineering; Human Resources; Management Systems); **Psychology** *(Gualtar, Braga campus)*; **Sociology Studies** *(Gualtar, Braga campus)*; **Surfaces Interface and Behaviour** *(Azurém, Guimarães)* (Materials Engineering); **Textile Sciences and Technology** *(Azurém, Guimarães campus)* (Artificial Intelligence; Automation and Control Engineering; Environmental Engineering; Marketing; Textile Design); **Training of Child Education Professionals** *(Independent Building of the Institute of Child Studies in Braga)* (Pedagogy; Special Education; Teacher Trainers Education)

Research Groups

3 B's- Biomaterials, Biodegradables and Biomimetics *(Azurém, Guimarães campus)*

Schools

Architecture *(Autonomous; Azurém, Guimarães campus)* (Architectural and Environmental Design; Architecture; Architecture and Planning; Civil Engineering; Painting and Drawing; Social Sciences); **Economics and Management** *(Gualtar, Braga)* (Accountancy; Administration; Business and Commerce; Economics; Finance; Human Resources; International Relations; Management; Political Sciences; Public Administration); **Engineering** *(Azurém, Guimarães)* (Bioengineering; Biomedical Engineering; Civil Engineering; Computer Engineering; Electrical and Electronic Engineering; Environmental Engineering; Industrial Engineering; Information Technology; Mechanical Engineering; Polymer and Plastics Technology; Production Engineering; Textile Technology); **Health Sciences** *(Gualtar)* (Community Health; Health Sciences; Medicine; Molecular Biology; Surgery); **Law** *(Braga)* (Administrative Law; Civil Law; Commercial Law; Criminal Law; Law; Private Law; Public Law); **Nursing** (Nursing); **Psychology** (Psychology); **Science** *(Braga)* (Applied Mathematics; Biological and Life Sciences; Biology; Chemistry; Earth Sciences; Mathematics; Mathematics and Computer Science; Physics)

History: Founded 1973 with a structure based on a series of Scientific Pedagogical Units. A State institution under the jurisdiction of the Ministry of Education.

Governing Bodies: Senate; University Assembly; Academic Council; Administrative Council; Cultural Council

Academic Year: September to July (September-February; February- July)

Admission Requirements: Secondary school certificate and entrance examination, or recognized foreign equivalent

Main Language(s) of Instruction: Portuguese

International Co-operation: Participates in the Leonardo da Vinci; Socrates; Alfa; Tempus; Jean Monnet; the 4th Community and 5th Economic Framework Programmes for RTD

Degrees and Diplomas: *Licenciado*; *Mestre*: Biological Engineering; Textile Engineering; Manufacturing Technology; Informatics; Computer Integrated Productions; Environmental Technology; Polymer Engineering; Construction and Heritage Management; Industrial Engineering; Textile Chemistry; Communication Sciences; Education; Psychology; Special Education; Childhood Sociology; Childhood Education; Child Studies; French Language and Literature; English Language and Literature; Portuguese Literature; Literature and Culture; Philosophy; Design and Marketing; Industrial Electronics; Biotechnology; Bioprocess Engineering; Civil Engineering; Textile Engineering; Human Engineering; Mechanical Engineering; Metallurgy Engineering; Municipal Engineering; Project Engineering; Industrial and Business Economics; Economic and Social Studies; Economic Policy; International Economic and Social Relations; Human Resource Management; Accountancy and Administration; Accountancy and Auditing; Health Management and Economy; Economy; Information Systems; Textile Management and Apparel; Materials Engineering; Automobile Technology Engineering; Mould Project and Fabrication; Materials Processing and Characterization; Data Systems and Analytical Processing; Graphic Computation; Physics; Environmental Sciences; Molecular Genetics; Mathematics; Computational Mathematics; Chemistry; Mathematics and Mechanical Applications; Plant Stress Biology; Law and Human Rights; Public Administration; European Studies; Management; Portuguese Culture; Theory of Literature; Linguistics; Luso-German Studies; Bilingual and Intercultural Training; French Studies; International Trade; Virtual Environments; Anthropology; Archaeology; History of Colonization and Migrations: Portugal-Brazil; History of Institutions and Modern and Contemporary Culture; History of Population; Medieval History and Culture; Sociology; Patrimony and Tourism; *Doutor*: Drawing; Materials Science and Technology; Sciences; Juridical Sciences; Economics; Management; Administration; Political Science and International Relations; Engineering; Polymer Science and Engineering; Industrial Electronics; Civil Engineering; Production and Systems Engineering; Mechanical Engineering; Chemical and Biological Engineering; Textile Engineering; Informatics; Information Technology and Systems; Anthropology; Communication Sciences; History; Sociology; Geography; Archaeology; Education; Psychology; Child Studies; Literature; Cultural Studies; Philosophy; Languages; Health Sciences

Student Services: Academic counselling, Canteen, Cultural centre, Foreign student adviser, Foreign Studies Centre, Handicapped facilities, Health services, Language programs, Social counselling, Sports facilities

Student Residential Facilities: Yes

Special Facilities: 'Nogueira da Silva' Museu. Study Centre 'Lusíadas'"Casa Lloyd Braga" Foundation; Archaeology Unit

Libraries: General Library. Library in Guimarães; Institution of Child Stuies; Education Sciences; Braga's Public Library Specialized libraries of the School/Institutes. Braga District Archives, Bibliopolis

Publications: Cadernos de Direito Privado, Specialised magazine(Minho's Juridical Studies Centre) *(quarterly)*; Cadernos de Justiça Administrativa *(biennially)*; Cadernos do NEPS; Colecção Hespérides; Colecção Poliedro; Colectâneas de Pedagogia e Didáctica; Guia do Estudante de História *(annually)*; Monografias em Educação; Revista "Ensinarte", Arts magazine in an educational context(Child Studies Centre) *(3 per annum)*; Revista "Inclusão", Studies on special education (Research Centre for the Training of Professionals in Child Education); Revista Cadernos do Noroeste, Centre of Historical and Social Sciences *(biannually)*; Revista Comunicação e Sociedade (Communication Series of Cadernos do Noroeste) *(biannually)*; Revista Diacrítica *(annually)*; Revista Forum *(biannually)*; Revista Portuguesa de Educação *(biannually)*; Revista PSIAX, Studies on drawing and image (Autonomous Department of Architecture); Revista Psicologia - Teoria, Investigação e Prática *(biannually)*; Revista Scientia Jurídica *(biannually)*; Scientia Ivridica, Specialised magazine(Law) *(3 per annum)*

Last Updated: 07/10/11

UNIVERSITY OF OPORTO

Universidade do Porto (UPORTO)

Praça Gomes Teixeira, 4099-002 Porto
Tel: +351(220) 408-000
Fax: +351(220) 408-186/7
EMail: up@up.pt
Website: http://www.up.pt

Reitor: José Carlos D. Marques dos Santos (1998-2014)
Tel: +351(22) 040-8023, Fax: +351(22) 040 8186/87
EMail: reitor@reit.up.pt

Administrador: Pedro Silva Pinto
Tel: +351(22) 040-8000, Fax: +351(22) 040-8186/87

International Relations: Cristina Gomes Ferreira, Director of International Office
Tel: +351(22) 040-8046, Fax: +351(22) 040-8183
EMail: sri@reit.up.pt

Faculties

Architecture (Architecture; Ecology; Environmental Management; Town Planning; Urban Studies); **Arts and Humanities** (African Studies; American Studies; Arabic; Archaeology; Art History; Bulgarian; Chinese; Coastal Studies; Communication Arts; Contemporary History; Cultural Studies; Danish; Dutch; Education; English; English Studies; Ethics; Finnish; Foreign Languages Education; French; Geography; Geography (Human); German; Grammar; Greek (Classical); Hebrew; Heritage Preservation; Hindi; History; Hungarian; Information Sciences; International Relations; Italian; Japanese; Journalism; Korean; Latin; Linguistics; Literature; Medieval Studies; Modern Languages; Multimedia; Museum Studies; Native Language; Native Language Education; Natural Resources; Persian; Philosophy; Polish; Portuguese; Primary Education; Public Relations; Romance Languages; Romanian; Russian; Secondary Education; Sociology; Spanish; Surveying and Mapping; Swedish; Theatre; Tourism; Translation and Interpretation; Turkish; Women's Studies); **Dentistry** (Dentistry; Oral Pathology; Orthodontics; Periodontics; Surgery); **Economics** (Accountancy; Administration; Business Administration; Econometrics; Economics; Environmental Management; Finance; Health Administration; Human Resources; International Economics; Management; Marketing; Taxation); **Engineering** (Automation and Control Engineering; Bioengineering; Biomedical Engineering; Chemical Engineering; Civil Engineering; Computer Engineering; Construction Engineering; Electrical Engineering; Electronic Engineering; Engineering Management; Environmental Engineering; Geological Engineering; Hydraulic Engineering; Industrial Chemistry; Industrial Design; Industrial Engineering; Information Sciences; Information Technology; Management Systems; Materials Engineering; Mechanical Engineering; Metallurgical Engineering; Mining Engineering; Multimedia; Occupational Health; Petroleum and Gas Engineering; Physical Engineering; Production Engineering; Safety Engineering; Telecommunications Engineering; Thermal Engineering; Town Planning; Transport Economics; Transport Engineering; Transport Management); **Fine Arts** (Art Education; Communication Arts; Design; Graphic Arts; Graphic Design; Industrial Design; Multimedia; Painting and Drawing; Printing and Printmaking; Sculpture); **Law** (Criminal Law; Fiscal Law; Law); **Medicine** (Biomedicine; Cardiology; Epidemiology; Ethics; Forensic Medicine and Dentistry; Gerontology; Health Administration; Health Education; Medicine; Neurosciences; Occupational Health; Oncology; Orthodontics; Psychiatry and Mental Health; Public Health; Social and Preventive Medicine; Sports Medicine; Surgery); **Nutrition and Food Science** (Dietetics; Food Science; Nutrition); **Pharmacy** (Analytical Chemistry; Medical Technology; Pharmacy; Toxicology); **Psychology and Education Sciences** (Adult Education; African Studies; Community Health; Continuing Education; Development Studies; Educational Psychology; Educational Sciences; Higher Education; Psychology; Social Studies; Special Education); **Science** (Agricultural Engineering; Agriculture; Applied Mathematics; Astronomy and Space Science; Biochemistry; Biology; Botany; Cell Biology; Chemistry; Computer Networks; Computer Science; Earth Sciences; Ecology; Engineering; Environmental Engineering; Environmental Studies; Food Science; Food Technology; Genetics; Geology; Landscape Architecture; Marine Biology; Mathematics; Molecular Biology; Natural Resources; Nutrition; Oenology; Physics; Science Education; Urban Studies; Viticulture; Water Management; Water Science); **Sports** (Health Sciences; Leisure Studies; Physical Education; Sports; Sports Management)

Institutes

Biomedical Sciences *(Abel Salazar)* (Acupuncture; Alternative Medicine; Anaesthesiology; Aquaculture; Biology; Biomedicine; Environmental Studies; Forensic Medicine and Dentistry; Genetics; Gerontology; Marine Science and Oceanography; Medicine; Nursing; Oncology; Pathology; Traditional Eastern Medicine; Veterinary Science; Zoology)

History: Founded 1911.

Governing Bodies: University Assembly; Rector; University Senate; Administrative Council; Consultative Board

Academic Year: September to July

Admission Requirements: Secondary school certificate and entrance examination, with admitted students requiring a score of at least 10/20

Fees: (Euros): 972, undergraduate, per annum; 3,580, postgraduate, per annum. Applies to home and international students.

Main Language(s) of Instruction: Portuguese, with some courses in English

International Co-operation: With Universities in Europe, Africa, Latin America and Asia.

Degrees and Diplomas: *Licenciado*: Fine Arts; Science; Nutrition and Food Science; Sport; Law; Economics; Engineering; Arts; Education; Aquatic Science (Bachelor's Degree), 3-4 yrs; *Mestre*: Architecture; Fine Arts; Science; Nutrition and Food Science; Sport; Law; Economics; Engineering; Pharmacy; Arts; Medicine; Dental Medicine; Psychology; Educational Science; Business Administration (Master's Degree), a further 1-2 yrs, and dissertation; *Doutor*: Science; Sport; Economics; Engineering; Arts; Medicine; Psychology; Education Science (PhD), 3-4 yrs

Student Services: Academic counselling, Canteen, Cultural centre, Employment services, Foreign student adviser, Foreign Studies Centre, Handicapped facilities, Health services, Language programs, Nursery care, Social counselling, Sports facilities

Student Residential Facilities: 8 residential halls for 1,216 students.

Special Facilities: Botanical Museum, Fine Art Gallery, Natural History Museum, Observatory, Museum of Medicine, Computer Rooms, Video Studio

Libraries: Faculty libraries.

Press or Publishing House: EDITORA U.P.

Academic Staff *2007-2008*	MEN	WOMEN	TOTAL
FULL-TIME	473	1,229	**1,702**
STAFF WITH DOCTORATE FULL-TIME	1,418	852	**2,270**
Student Numbers *2007-2008*			
All (Foreign Included)	13,896	15,005	**28,901**
FOREIGN ONLY	457	628	**1,085**

Last Updated: 07/10/11

UNIVERSITY OF THE ALGARVE

Universidade do Algarve

Campus da Penha, 8000-139 Faro
Tel: +351(289) 800-100 +351(289) 800-900
Fax: +351(289) 800-072
EMail: info@ualg.pt
Website: http://www.ualg.pt

Reitor: João Pinto Guerreiro EMail: reitor@ualg.pt

Administradora: Maria Cândida Rico Soares Barroso
Tel: +351(289) 800-113, Fax: +351(289) 862-506

International Relations: Maria Isabel Santana da Cruz
Tel: +351(289) 800-121 EMail: micruz@ualg.pt

Departments

Biomedical Sciences and Medicine (Biomedicine; Medicine)

Faculties

Economics (Banking; Criminology; Economics; Finance; Health Administration; Management; Sociology; Tourism); **Human and Social Sciences** (Advertising and Publicity; Anthropology; Archaeology; Arts and Humanities; Biology; Clinical Psychology; Cognitive Sciences; Communication Studies; Cultural Studies; Documentation Techniques; Education; Educational Psychology; Educational Technology; Genetics; Heritage Preservation; History;

Industrial and Organizational Psychology; Literature; Marketing; Modern Languages; Philosophy of Education; Psychology; Psychotherapy; Social Psychology; Social Sciences; Social Studies; Sociology; Statistics; Visual Arts); **Science and Technology** (Agronomy; Applied Mathematics; Biochemistry; Bioengineering; Biology; Biotechnology; Chemistry; Computer Engineering; Electrical Engineering; Environmental Engineering; Landscape Architecture; Marine Biology; Marine Science and Oceanography; Mathematics; Pharmacy; Physics; Telecommunications Engineering)

Institutes

Engineering (Civil Engineering; Electrical and Electronic Engineering; Energy Engineering; Engineering; Environmental Management; Food Technology; Heating and Refrigeration; Mechanical Engineering; Orthopaedics; Surveying and Mapping)

Laboratories

Chemical Analysis *(ITUCCA / Laboratório de Análise Químicas)* (Chemistry); **Instrumentation and Particle Physics** *(LIP)* (Physics); **Marine Geosciences** *(Disepla)* (Earth Sciences; Geology; Marine Science and Oceanography); **Signal Processing and Subaquatic Acoustics** *(SiPLAB, Integrated in the Institute of Systems and Robot Science (ISR/IST), Lisbon)* (Information Technology; Sound Engineering (Acoustics)); **Visual Perception and Image Processing** *(VisLAB)* (Computer Graphics)

Schools

Education and Communication (Child Care and Development; Communication Studies; Education; Educational Technology; Foreign Languages Education; Gerontology; Multimedia; Preschool Education; Primary Education; Secondary Education; Sports; Translation and Interpretation); **Health** *(Faro)* (Dietetics; Nursing; Nutrition; Pharmacy; Physical Therapy; Radiology); **Tourism and Hotel Management** *(Portimão, Faro)* (Accountancy; Hotel Management; Management; Marketing; Tourism)

Further Information: Portuguese language course for students of the Erasmus programme

History: Founded 1979, acquired present status 1991. Two campuses, Penha and Gambelas at Portimão and Vila Real de Santo António.

Governing Bodies: University's Assembly; Senate; Rector and Financial Administration Board

Academic Year: October to July (October-February; March-July)

Admission Requirements: Secondary school certificate and entrance examination

Main Language(s) of Instruction: Portuguese

International Co-operation: With universities in United Kingdom, Germany and Spain.

Degrees and Diplomas: *Licenciado*: 4 yrs; *Mestre*: 1-2 yrs; *Doutor (PhD)*. Also Postgraduate Degree, 1-2 yrs, and European Master

Student Services: Canteen, Foreign Studies Centre, Health services, Language programs, Social counselling, Sports facilities

Student Residential Facilities: Yes

Libraries: c. 91,600 vols, and 3,100 publications in all Algarve University's libraries

Last Updated: 07/10/11

UNIVERSITY OF THE AZORES

Universidade dos Açores

Apartado 1422, 9501-801 Ponta Delgada
Tel: +351(296) 650-000
Fax: +351(296) 650-005
EMail: uac@notes.uac.pt
Website: http://www.uac.pt

Reitor: Jorge Manuel Rosa de Medeiros EMail: reitor@notes.uac.pt

Centres

Agricultural Research and Technology *(Azores)* (Agriculture; Agronomy); **Applied Economic Studies of the Atlantic** (Economics); **Applied Mathematics and Information Technology** (Applied Mathematics; Information Technology); **Biotechnology** *(Azores Centre)* (Biotechnology); **Climate, Meteorology and Global Change** (Meteorology); **Entrepreneurship** (Management); **Gaspar Frutuoso** *(Centro de Estudos Gaspar Frutuoso)* (History); **History** *(Além-Mar)* (History); **Innovation and Sustainability in Engineering and Construction** (Construction Engineering; Engineering); **Law and Economics Studies** (Economics; Law); **Philosophy** (Philosophy); **Physics and Technology Research** (Physics; Technology); **Social Studies** (Social Studies); **Vulcanology and Geological Risks** (Geology; Seismology)

Departments

Agriculture *(Angra do Heroismo)* (Agricultural Engineering; Agriculture; Agronomy; Animal Husbandry; Environmental Engineering; Environmental Management; Food Science; Food Technology; Natural Resources; Nutrition; Pharmacy; Veterinary Science; Water Management; Water Science; Zoology); **Biology** (Biology; Biotechnology; Ecology; Environmental Studies; Health Sciences); **Economics and Management** *(Ponta Delgada)* (Business Administration; Economics; Management; Tourism); **Educational Sciences** *(Ponta Delgada)* (Education; Educational Psychology; Educational Sciences; Pedagogy; Preschool Education; Primary Education; Psychology; Teacher Trainers Education; Toxicology); **Geosciences** *(Ponta Delgada)* (Earth Sciences; Geology; Seismology); **History, Philosophy and Social Sciences** *(Ponta Delgada)* (Cultural Studies; Development Studies; Ethics; European Studies; Heritage Preservation; History; International Relations; International Studies; Museum Studies; Philosophy; Social and Community Services; Social Sciences; Social Work; Sociology); **Mathematics** *(Ponta Delgada)* (Computer Engineering; Computer Networks; Computer Science; Data Processing; Electronic Engineering; Information Management; Mathematics; Multimedia); **Modern Languages and Literature** *(Ponta Delgada)* (Communication Studies; Cultural Studies; Linguistics; Literature; Modern Languages; Public Relations; Social Studies; Translation and Interpretation; Western European Studies); **Oceanography and Fishery** *(Horta)* (Fishery; Marine Science and Oceanography; Tourism); **Technological Sciences and Development** *(Ponta Delgada)* (Architecture; Chemistry; Civil Engineering; Computer Engineering; Construction Engineering; Electronic Engineering; Food Science; Industrial Engineering; Mechanical Engineering; Physics; Public Health)

Schools

Nursing *(Angra do Heroísmo)* (Gerontology; Health Administration; Nursing); **Nursing** *(Ponta Delgada)* (Community Health; Gynaecology and Obstetrics; Nursing)

Further Information: Also Seminário Internacional de Estudos Nemesianos

History: Founded 1976 as College, became University 1980. An autonomous State Institution under the jurisdiction of the Ministry of Education and Culture.

Governing Bodies: Scientific Committee; University Committee

Academic Year: October to July (October-March; March-July)

Admission Requirements: University degree and professional experience, and individual interview

Main Language(s) of Instruction: Portuguese

Degrees and Diplomas: *Licenciado*: 4-5 yrs; *Mestre*; *Doutor*. Also postgraduate degrees

Student Services: Academic counselling, Canteen, Foreign student adviser, Health services, Social counselling, Sports facilities

Student Residential Facilities: Yes

Libraries: c. 185,000 vols

Publications: Arquipélago (Human Sciences, Natural Sciences) *(biannually)*

Last Updated: 07/10/11

UNIVERSITY OF TRAS-OS-MONTES AND ALTO DOURO

Universidade de Trás-os-Montes e Alto Douro (UTAD)

Apartado 1013, Quinta dos Prados, 5001-801 Vila Real
Tel: +351(259) 350-000
Fax: +351(259) 350-480
EMail: reitoria@utad.pt
Website: http://www.utad.pt

Reitor: Carlos Alberto Sequeira

Vice-Rector, Administration and Finance: Carlos Machado dos Santos

Programmes
Graduate Studies (Accountancy; Advertising and Publicity; Agricultural Engineering; Agronomy; American Studies; Archaeology; Biochemistry; Biological and Life Sciences; Biology; Biotechnology; Chemistry; Civil Engineering; Classical Languages; Clinical Psychology; Communication Studies; Community Health; Computer Engineering; Continuing Education; Cultural Studies; Development Studies; Documentation Techniques; Earth Sciences; Economics; Education; Educational Administration; Educational Psychology; Educational Technology; Electronic Engineering; Energy Engineering; English; English Studies; Environmental Engineering; Environmental Management; Environmental Studies; Finance; Fine Arts; Food Science; Foreign Languages Education; Forestry; French; Geography; Geology; German; Gerontology; Gynaecology and Obstetrics; Health Administration; Information Sciences; Information Technology; International Relations; Journalism; Laboratory Techniques; Landscape Architecture; Leisure Studies; Literature; Management; Mathematics Education; Mechanical Engineering; Modern Languages; Multimedia; Native Language Education; Nursing; Oenology; Optics; Optometry; Pedagogy; Philosophy; Physical Education; Physics; Portuguese; Preschool Education; Psychology; Public Relations; Rehabilitation and Therapy; Science Education; Secondary Education; Social and Community Services; Social Work; Special Education; Sports; Statistics; Technology Education; Tourism; Translation and Interpretation; Veterinary Science; Zoology)

Schools
Agrarian and Veterinary Science (Agronomy; Forestry; Landscape Architecture; Veterinary Science; Zoology); **Human and Social Sciences** (Communication Studies; Cultural Studies; Economics; Education; Literature; Management; Modern Languages; Performing Arts; Psychology; Sociology; Theatre); **Life and Environmental Sciences** (Biological and Life Sciences; Biotechnology; Chemistry; Environmental Studies; Genetics; Geology; Health Sciences; Sports); **Nursing** *(Vila Real)* (Child Care and Development; Community Health; Nursing; Paediatrics; Psychiatry and Mental Health; Rehabilitation and Therapy); **Science and Technology** (Engineering; Mathematics; Physics)

History: Founded 1973 as Polytechnic, and admitted first students 1975. Became Instituto Universitario 1979 and acquired present status and title 1986. A State Institution under the jurisdiction of the Ministry of Education and Culture.

Governing Bodies: Assembleia; Senado

Academic Year: October to June (October-January; March-June)

Admission Requirements: Secondary school certificate

Main Language(s) of Instruction: Portuguese

Degrees and Diplomas: *Licenciado*; *Mestre*; *Doutor*

Student Residential Facilities: Yes

Special Facilities: Geology Museum

Libraries: Documentation Centre, c. 36,000 vols

Publications: Anais da UTAD *(annually)*

Last Updated: 07/10/11

PRIVATE INSTITUTIONS

ALMEIDA GARRETT SCHOOL OF EDUCATION

Escola Superior de Educação Almeida Garrett

Palácio de Santa Helena, Largo do Sequeira, 7, 1100-587 Lisboa
Tel: +351(21) 886-2042
Fax: +351(21) 887-2725
EMail: informacoes@eseag.pt
Website: http://www.eseag.pt

Director: Jorge Serrano

Courses
Basic Education (Education; Mathematics; Natural Sciences; Portuguese; Social Sciences); **Environmental Education and Cultural Heritage** (Arts and Humanities; Biology; Cultural Studies; Ecology; English; Environmental Management; Environmental Studies; Ethics; Genetics; Geography (Human); Heritage Preservation; Microbiology; Political Sciences; Social Sciences); **Graduate Studies** (Art Education; Biology; Communication Studies; Demography and Population; Educational Administration; Educational Psychology; Educational Research; Environmental Studies; Geography; Geography (Human); History; Human Rights; Information Technology; Linguistics; Mathematics Education; Native Language Education; Natural Sciences; Pedagogy; Philosophy of Education; Physiology; Portuguese; Preschool Education; Primary Education; Science Education; Social Sciences; Social Studies; Special Education; Teacher Trainers Education; Teacher Training); **Social Education** (Cultural Studies; Development Studies; Ecology; Education; Educational Administration; Educational Technology; English; Environmental Studies; Family Studies; Fine Arts; Food Science; Geography (Human); Gerontology; Health Sciences; Hygiene; Law; Multimedia; Music; Philosophy of Education; Portuguese; Psychology; Public Health; Social Psychology; Social Studies; Social Welfare; Sociology)

History: Founded 1993.

Main Language(s) of Instruction: Portuguese

Degrees and Diplomas: *Licenciado*; *Mestre*. Also specialization courses

Last Updated: 26/09/11

ATLANTIC UNIVERSITY

Universidade Atlântica (UATLA)

Fábrica da Pólvora de Barcarena, 2730-036 Barcarena
Tel: +351(21) 439-8200
Fax: +351(21) 430-2573
EMail: geral@uatlantica.pt
Website: http://www.uatlantica.pt

Reitor: Nelson Lourenço

Secretária-Geral: Natália do Espírito-Santo
Tel: +351(21) 439-8202

Areas
Business Studies (Accountancy; Health Administration; Management; Marketing); **Health** (Health Sciences; Nursing; Nutrition; Physical Therapy; Public Health; Radiology; Speech Therapy and Audiology); **Information and Communication Technology** (Information Technology; Telecommunications Engineering); **Land, Environment and Development** (Environmental Management)

Programmes
Graduate Studies (Anaesthesiology; Communication Arts; Communication Studies; Community Health; Environmental Management; Health Administration; Laboratory Techniques; Management; Marketing; Nursing; Paediatrics; Pharmacy; Radiology; Rehabilitation and Therapy; Respiratory Therapy; Surgery)

History: Founded 1996.

Admission Requirements: Certificado de Habilitações do Ensino Secundario; Prova de Ingresso

Main Language(s) of Instruction: Portuguese

Degrees and Diplomas: *Licenciado*: 4 yrs; *Mestre*. Also Postgraduate studies

Student Services: Canteen, Employment services, Language programs, Sports facilities

Last Updated: 05/10/11

AUTONOMOUS INSTITUTE OF POLYTECHNIC STUDIES

Instituto Superior Autónomo de Estudos Politécnicos (IPA)

Rua de Xabregas, 20-1, 1900-440 Lisboa
Tel: +351(21) 861-0360
Fax: +351(21) 868-6014
EMail: info@ipa.univ.pt
Website: http://www.ipa.univ.pt

Presidente: Alves Vieira EMail: aavieira@ipa.univ.pt

Administrador: Nuno Bento EMail: nbento@ipa.univ.pt

Secretário-geral: Tânia Carraquico EMail: tcarraquico@ipa.univ.pt

Courses
Art (Design; Fine Arts; Multimedia; Music; Photography; Sound Engineering (Acoustics)); **Engineering and Technology** (Civil Engineering; Computer Engineering; Computer Graphics; Computer Science; Mechanical Engineering)
History: Founded 1990.
Main Language(s) of Instruction: Portuguese
Degrees and Diplomas: *Licenciado*. Also postgraduate diplomas
Last Updated: 30/09/11

AUTONOMOUS UNIVERSITY OF LISBON

Universidade Autónoma de Lisboa (UAL)
Palácio dos Condes do Redondo, Rua de Santa Marta, 56, 1169-023 Lisboa
Tel: +351(21) 317-7600
Fax: +351(21) 353-3702
EMail: secgeral@universidade-autonoma.pt
Website: http://www.universidade-autonoma.pt

Reitor: Justino Mendes de Almeida (1992-)
Tel: +351(21) 317-7695
Secretário Geral: Reginaldo Almeida
EMail: ceu-dir@univerdade-autonoma.pt
International Relations: José Victorino
Tel: +351(21) 317-7600, Fax: +351(21) 317-7610
EMail: gci@universidade-autonoma.pt

Departments
Architecture (Architectural and Environmental Design; Architecture; Restoration of Works of Art); **Business Administration** (Accountancy; Business Administration; Business and Commerce; Finance; Management); **Communication Sciences** (Communication Studies; Mass Communication); **Economics and Business** (Business Administration; Economics); **History** (History); **International Relations** (International Relations); **Law** (Criminal Law; European Union Law; History of Law; International Law; Justice Administration; Labour Law; Law; Private Law; Public Law); **Psychology and Sociology** (Psychology; Sociology); **Public Administration and Management** (Business Computing; Management; Public Administration); **Science and Technology** (Applied Mathematics; Computer Engineering; Computer Science; Management; Mathematics; Technology); **Sports Management** (Sports Management); **Translation, Modern Languages and Literature** (Archaeology; Arts and Humanities; Classical Languages; Comparative Literature; History; Linguistics; Literature; Modern Languages; Translation and Interpretation)

Programmes
Graduate Studies (Administrative Law; Archaeology; Architectural Restoration; Architecture; Business Administration; Clinical Psychology; Communication Studies; Computer Engineering; Computer Science; Criminology; Documentation Techniques; Economics; Educational and Student Counselling; Environmental Management; Ethics; Family Studies; Finance; Fiscal Law; Forensic Medicine and Dentistry; Government; Heritage Preservation; History; Industrial and Organizational Psychology; International Relations; Labour Law; Law; Management; Multimedia; Nautical Science; Notary Studies; Peace and Disarmament; Private Law; Psychology; Psychotherapy; Public Administration; Radio and Television Broadcasting; Real Estate; Rehabilitation and Therapy; Social Psychology; Speech Therapy and Audiology; Town Planning; Translation and Interpretation; Urban Studies)
History: Founded 1986.
Governing Bodies: Administrative Board Committee, Scientific Committees
Admission Requirements: School Certificate (in English)
Main Language(s) of Instruction: Portuguese
International Co-operation: With universities in Spain, France, Italy, United Kingdom and Scandinavia.
Accrediting Agencies: APESP, EUA
Degrees and Diplomas: *Licenciado*; *Mestre*; *Doutor*. Also postgraduate programmes
Student Services: Academic counselling, Canteen, Employment services, Health services, Language programs, Nursery care, Social counselling, Sports facilities
Libraries: c. 20,000 vols
Last Updated: 05/10/11

BISSAYA BARRETO INSTITUTE

Instituto Superior Bissaya Barreto
Apartado 7049, 3046-901 Coimbra
Tel: +351(239) 800-450
Fax: +351(239) 800-495
EMail: isbb@isbb.pt
Website: http://www.isbb.pt

Directora: Maria Luísa Ferreira Cabral dos Santos Veiga

Courses
Law *(Undergraduate and postgraduate programme)* (Administration; International Relations; Law; Notary Studies; Public Administration); **Legal and Forensic Sciences** *(Master programme)* (Forensic Medicine and Dentistry; Law); **Management** *(Postgraduate programme)* (Educational Administration; Finance; Human Resources; Labour Law; Management; Marketing; Pharmacy); **Musical Therapy** *(Postgraduate programme)* (Music; Rehabilitation and Therapy); **Pedagogical Supervision** (Curriculum; Educational Sciences; Educational Testing and Evaluation; Pedagogy); **Project Management** *(Postgraduate programme)* (Management); **Public Administration** (Accountancy; Administrative Law; Finance; Law; Management; Public Administration; Social Policy; Social Sciences; Town Planning); **Social Gerontology** *(Master programme)* (Gerontology; Law; Medicine; Psychology; Social Work; Sociology); **Software and Computer Engineering** (Computer Engineering; Software Engineering); **Sport** *(Postgraduate programme)* (Sports; Sports Management)
History: Founded 1993.
Main Language(s) of Instruction: Portuguese
Degrees and Diplomas: *Licenciado*; *Mestre*. Also postgraduate programmes
Last Updated: 03/10/11

CATHOLIC UNIVERSITY OF PORTUGAL

Universidade Católica Portuguesa
Palma de Cima, 1649-023 Lisboa
Tel: +351(217) 214-000
Fax: +351(217) 270-256
EMail: info@reitoria.ucp.pt
Website: http://www.ucp.pt

Reitora: Maria de Glória Garcia (2012-)
International Relations: Maria da Graça Pereira Coutinho
Tel: +351(21) 726-5838, Fax: +351(21) 726-0546
EMail: gcoutinho@reitoria.ucp.pt

Departments
Architecture, Science and Technology *(Viseu)* (Architecture; Technology); **Arts** *(Viseu)* (Arts and Humanities; Classical Languages; Communication Studies; Foreign Languages Education; Heritage Preservation; History; Linguistics; Modern Languages; Native Language Education; Tourism); **Economics, Management and Social Sciences** *(Viseu)* (Economics; Management; Social Sciences)

Faculties
Economics and Business Administration *(Lisboa)* (Business Administration; Economics; Finance); **Economics and Management** *(Oporto)* (Business Administration; Economics); **Education and Psychology** (Education; Educational Psychology; Psychology); **Engineering** *(Sintra)* (Biomedical Engineering; Civil Engineering; Computer Engineering; Engineering; Industrial Engineering; Mechanical Engineering); **Human Sciences** *(Lisboa)* (Arts and Humanities; Communication Studies; Literature; Modern Languages; Portuguese; Social Work; Sociology); **Law** *(Lisboa and Oporto)* (Law); **Philosophy** *(Braga)* (Philosophy); **Social Sciences** *(Braga)* (Social Sciences; Social Work); **Theology** *(Lisboa, Braga and Oporto)* (Theology)

Institutes
Bioethics *(Oporto)* (Ethics); **Canon Law** *(Lisboa)*; **European Studies** *(Lisboa)* (European Studies); **Family Studies** (Family Studies); **Health Sciences** *(Lisboa, Oporto, Viseu)* (Health Sciences;

Nursing); **Oriental Studies** (Oriental Studies); **Political Studies** *(Lisboa)* (Political Sciences)

Research Centres

Applied Studies; **Art Science and Technology**; **Biotechnology and Chemistry** (Biotechnology; Chemistry); **Communication and Culture** (Communication Studies; Cultural Studies); **Conservation and Restoration**; **History of Religion** (History of Religion); **Management and Applied Economics** (Economics; Management); **Management and Economics** (Economics; Management); **Opinion Poll Studies**; **Philosophy** (Philosophy); **Philosophy and Humanities** (Arts and Humanities; Philosophy); **Portuguese Thought**; **Psychology and Education** (Education; Educational Psychology; Psychology); **Religious and Cultural Studies** *(Cardeal Hoeffner Centre)* (Cultural Studies; Religious Studies); **Social Services and Sociology** (Social and Community Services; Sociology); **Studies for Portuguese-Speaking People and Portuguese Culture** (Cultural Studies; Linguistics)

Schools

Biotechnology *(Porto)* (Biotechnology); **Fine Arts** *(Oporto)*

History: Founded 1967, recognized by the Government 1971 as a non-State institution of public interest.

Governing Bodies: Conselho Superior (Board of Trustees)

Academic Year: September to July (September-February; March-July)

Admission Requirements: Secondary school certificate and entrance examination, or recognized foreign equivalent

Main Language(s) of Instruction: Portuguese

International Co-operation: Participates in the Leonardo, Tempus, Jean Monnet Action and Socrates programmes.

Degrees and Diplomas: *Licenciado*: 5 yrs; *Mestre*: a further 2-3 yrs following upon Licenciatura; *Doutor*

Student Services: Canteen, Employment services, Language programs, Social counselling

Student Residential Facilities: Yes

Libraries: John Paul II University Library, c. 320,000 vols; Philosophy (Braga), c. 58,000; Porto; Viseu

Publications: Didaskalia; Direito e Justiça; Economia; Gestão e Desenvolvimento; Humanística e Teologia; Lusitânia Sacra; Máthesis; Povos e Culturas. Gestão e Desenvolvimento; Revista Portuguesa de Filosofia; Revista Portuguesa de Humanidades; Theológica

Last Updated: 16/10/12

COLLEGE OF DECORATIVE ARTS

Escola Superior de Artes Decorativas

Rua João de Oliveira Miguens, 80, 1350-187 Lisboa
Tel: +351(21) 881-4696
Fax: +351(21) 881-4643
EMail: esad.geral@fress.pt
Website: http://www.fress.pt

Directora: Teresa Vale (1996-)

Courses

Conservation and Restoration (Restoration of Works of Art); **Cultural Studies** (Cultural Studies); **Interior Design and Decorative Arts** (Architecture; Design; Interior Design; Painting and Drawing; Sculpture)

History: Founded 1963 as School of Decorative Arts. Acquired present title 1990.

Main Language(s) of Instruction: Portuguese

Degrees and Diplomas: *Licenciado*; *Mestre*. Also curso de Pós-Graduação

Last Updated: 19/09/11

D. DINIS INSTITUTE

Instituto Superior D. Dinis

Av. 1 de Maio, 164, 2430-211 Marinha Grande
Tel: +351(244) 503-800
Fax: +351(244) 503-840
EMail: informacoes@isdom.pt
Website: http://www.isdom.pt

Director: Ercilio Mendes EMail: Ercilio.mendes@isdom.pt

Courses

Accountancy and Administration (Accountancy; Administration; Advertising and Publicity; Business Computing; Marketing; Public Relations); **Design** (Design); **Educational Sciences** (Continuing Education; Educational Administration; Educational Sciences; Special Education; Teacher Trainers Education); **Human Resource Management** (Human Resources; Management); **Industrial Production Engineering** (Production Engineering); **Safety Engineering** (Safety Engineering); **Social Welfare** (Criminology; Gerontology; Social Problems; Social Welfare)

History: Founded 2005 following merger of two institutes of Humanities and Technology and The Institute of Mathematics ad Management of Marinha Grande.

Degrees and Diplomas: *Licenciado*. Also postgraduate programmes

Last Updated: 03/10/11

DOM AFONSO III INSTITUTE

Instituto Superior Dom Afonso III

Convento Espírito Santo, 8100-641 Loulé
Tel: +351(289) 420-480
Fax: +351(289) 420-488
EMail: inuaf-academicos@mail.telepac.pt
Website: http://www.inuaf-studia.pt

Courses

Management (Management); **Management of Bio-Resources** (Environmental Management; Natural Resources); **Marketing and Advertising** (Advertising and Publicity; Marketing); **Multimedia** (Multimedia); **Musical Education** (Music Education); **Physical Education and Sports** (Physical Education; Sports); **Psychology** (Psychology); **Real Estate Management** (Real Estate); **Sustainable Tourism** (Tourism); **Tourism Management**

Programmes

Graduate Studies (Clinical Psychology; Educational Administration; Educational Psychology; Environmental Management; Human Resources; Leisure Studies; Marketing; Multimedia; Music Education; Neurology; Physical Education; Primary Education; Psychology; Real Estate; Secondary Education; Special Education; Sports; Tourism; Welfare and Protective Services)

History: Founded 1997.

Main Language(s) of Instruction: Portuguese

Degrees and Diplomas: *Licenciado*; *Mestre*; *Doutor*. Also postgraduate programmes

Last Updated: 05/10/11

DR. JOSÉ TIMÓTEO MONTALVÃO MACHADO SCHOOL OF NURSING

Escola Superior de Enfermagem Dr. José Timóteo Montalvão Machado

Quinta dos Montalvões - Outeiro Seco, 5400-673 Chaves
Tel: +351(276) 301-690
Fax: +351(276) 301-691
EMail: info@esechaves.pt
Website: http://www.esedjtmm.pt.vu

Presidente: João Batista

Courses

Graduate Studies (Community Health; Gerontology; Health Administration; Nursing; Paediatrics; Psychiatry and Mental Health; Rehabilitation and Therapy; Surgery); **Nursing** (Community Health; Nursing; Surgery)

History: Founded 1993.

Main Language(s) of Instruction: Portuguese

Degrees and Diplomas: *Licenciado*. Also specialization and postgraduate diplomas

Last Updated: 28/09/11

EGAS MONIZ INSTITUTE OF HEALTH SCIENCES

Instituto Superior de Ciências da Saúde Egas Moniz
Campus Universitário, Quinta da Granja, 2829-511 Monte de Caparica
Tel: +351(212) 946-700
Fax: +351(212) 946-868
EMail: iscsem@egasmoniz.edu.pt
Website: http://www.egasmoniz.com.pt/

Director: Manuel Jorge de Queiroz Medeiros (2001-)

Chefe de Secretaria: Margarida Vieira
Tel: +351(212) 946-753, Fax: +351(212) 946-733
EMail: secretaria@egasmoniz.edu.pt

International Relations: Carla Ascenso, Co-ordinator ERASMUS
Tel: +351(212) 946-793 EMail: casacenso@egasmoniz.edu.pt

Courses

Criminal Psychology (Psychology); **Forensic and Criminal Sciences** (Forensic Medicine and Dentistry); **Graduate Studies** (Dental Technology; Dentistry; Forensic Medicine and Dentistry; Nutrition; Pharmacology; Pharmacy; Psychology); **Health Sciences** (Health Sciences); **Nutrition** (Nutrition)

History: Founded 1987.

Governing Bodies: Administration; Director; Scientific Council

Main Language(s) of Instruction: Portuguese

International Co-operation: With universities in United Kingdom and Spain.

Degrees and Diplomas: *Licenciado*: 5-6 yrs; *Mestre*: 18-24 months. Also postgraduate courses

Student Services: Academic counselling, Canteen, Health services

Student Residential Facilities: No.

Special Facilities: No.

Libraries: Yes.

Last Updated: 29/09/11

EGAS MONIZ SCHOOL OF HEALTH

Escola Superior de Saúde Egas Moniz
Campus Universitário, Quinta da Granja, 2829-511 Monte de Caparica
Tel: +351(212) 946-700
Fax: +351(212) 946-868
EMail: essem@egasmoniz.edu.pt
Website: http://www.egasmoniz.com.pt/

Director: José A. de Salis Amaral

Courses

Cardiopneumology (Cardiology; Pneumology); **Clinical Analyses and Public Health** (Public Health); **Dental Prosthetics** (Dental Technology); **Graduate Studies** (Gerontology; Health Administration; Health Education; Molecular Biology; Physical Therapy; Social and Preventive Medicine); **Nursing** (Nursing); **Pathological, Cytological and Thanatological Anatomy** (Anatomy; Cell Biology; Pathology); **Pharmacy** (Pharmacy); **Physical Therapy** (Physical Therapy); **Radiology** (Radiology); **Speech Therapy and Audiology** (Speech Therapy and Audiology)

History: Founded 1999.

Degrees and Diplomas: *Licenciado*; *Mestre*

Last Updated: 29/09/11

FERNANDO PESSOA UNIVERSITY

Universidade Fernando Pessoa (UFP)
Praça 9 de Abril, 349, 4249-004 Porto
Tel: +351(22) 507-1300
Fax: +351(22) 550-8269
EMail: geral@ufp.pt
Website: http://www.ufp.pt

Reitor: Salvato Trigo (1999-)
Tel: +351(22) 507-1346, Fax: +351(22) 550-7682
EMail: strigo@ufp.pt

Vice-Reitora: Manuela Trigo EMail: mmtrigo@ufp.pt

International Relations: Nadine Trigo-Neaves, Director, International Relations Office
Tel: +351(22) 507-1349, Fax: +351(22) 550-7682
EMail: relint@ufp.pt

Faculties

Health Sciences (Dentistry; Health Sciences; Speech Therapy and Audiology); **Human and Social Sciences** (Accountancy; Administration; Advertising and Publicity; Anthropology; Behavioural Sciences; Business Administration; Clinical Psychology; Communication Studies; Comparative Literature; Cultural Studies; Development Studies; Economics; Information Sciences; International Relations; Islamic Studies; Journalism; Management; Marketing; Political Sciences; Psychology; Public Relations; Social Psychology; Social Sciences); **Science and Technology** (Architecture; Civil Engineering; Computer Engineering; Engineering; Environmental Engineering; Environmental Management; Information Technology; Multimedia; Technology; Town Planning)

History: Founded 1994. Acquired present status 1996.

Admission Requirements: Secondary school certificate

Fees: (Euros): 1,800-4,290 per annum

Main Language(s) of Instruction: Portuguese

International Co-operation: Participates in the Socrates/ Leonardo and Projecto Brasil programmes

Degrees and Diplomas: *Licenciado*; *Mestre*; *Doutor*

Student Services: Academic counselling, Canteen, Employment services, Foreign student adviser, Health services, Language programs, Nursery care, Sports facilities

Student Residential Facilities: Yes

Libraries: Central Library

Publications: Anthropológicas *(biannually)*; Revista da UFP *(biannually)*

Student Numbers *2011-2012*: Total 3,440

Last Updated: 07/10/11

PONTE DE LIMA UNIT

UNIDADE DE PONTE DE LIMA (UFP-P. DE LIMA)

Casa da Garrida, Rua Conde de Bertiandos, 4990-078 Ponte de Lima
Tel: +351(258) 741-026
Fax: +351(258) 741-412
EMail: geral.plima@ufp.edu.pt
Website: http://www.ufp.pt

Reitor: Salvato Trigo (1999-) EMail: strigo@ufp.pt

Areas

Business Studies (Accountancy; Business Administration; Public Relations); **Health Sciences** (Health Sciences; Rehabilitation and Therapy)

Research Centres

Applied Anthropology (Anthropology); **Bioengineering and Pharmacology** *(CBFC)* (Bioengineering; Pharmacology); **Communication Studies** (Communication Studies); **Conscience Studies** (Psychoanalysis; Psychology; Psychometrics); **Fiscal and Administrative Studies** *(CETA)* (Fiscal Law; Public Administration); **Hotel and Tourism Studies** *(CETS-HT)* (Hotel and Restaurant; Statistics; Tourism); **International Studies** *(CEALA)* (African American Studies; Latin American Studies); **Internet Literature** *(CETIC)* (Information Technology; Literature); **Minorities Studies** *(CENMIN)* (Demography and Population; Sociology); **Modellization and Environmental Systems Analysis** *(CEMAS)* (Statistics); **Multimedia Resources** *(CEREM)* (Multimedia); **Psychology Studies** *(CEPSI)* (Psychology)

History: Founded 1990.

GALLÉCIA SCHOOL

Escola Superior Gallécia
Largo das Oliveiras, 4902-275 Vila Nova de Cerveira
Tel: +351(251) 794-054
Fax: +651(251) 794-055
EMail: esg@esg.pt
Website: http://www.esg.pt/

Presidente: Mariana Correia

Vice-Presidente: Rui Correia

Courses

Architecture and Urban Planning *(Master programme)* (Architecture; Town Planning); **Arts and Multimedia** (Fine Arts; Multimedia); **Design** (Design; Graphic Design; Industrial Design); **Ecology and Landscape** (Ecology; Landscape Architecture)

History: Founded 1988.

Main Language(s) of Instruction: Portuguese

Degrees and Diplomas: *Licenciado*; *Mestre*: Architecture and Town Planning

Last Updated: 29/09/11

HIGHER SCHOOL OF MUSIC OF GAIA

Conservatório Superior de Música de Gaia

Rua António Ferreira Gomes, 4400-112 Vila Nova de Gaia

Tel: +351(22) 371-2213

Fax: +351(22) 371-2214

EMail: fundacao.crg@netc.pt

Website: http://www.conservatoriodegaia.org/index.php?op=1

Courses

Conducting (Conducting); **Theatrical Singing** (Singing; Theatre)

Degrees and Diplomas: *Licenciado*

Last Updated: 19/09/11

INFANTE D. HENRIQUE UNIVERSITY OF OPORTO

Universidade Portucalense Infante D. Henrique

Rua Dr. António Bernardino de Almeida, 541, 4200 072 Porto

Tel: +351(225) 572-000

Fax: +351(225) 572-010

EMail: up@upt.pt

Website: http://www.upt.pt

Rector: Guilherme Freire Falcão de Oliveira
Tel: +351(225) 572-641, Fax: +351(225) 572-011
EMail: reitoria@upt.pt

Administrative Officer: Fernando Silva e Sousa
Tel: +351(225) 572-635, Fax: +351(225) 572-044
EMail: admin@upt.pt

International Relations: Susana Carvalho
Tel: +351(225) 572-582, Fax: +351(225) 572-010 EMail: ri@upt.pt

Departments

Economics and Management (Accountancy; Administration; Business Administration; Business and Commerce; Economics; Finance; Health Administration; Hotel Management; Industrial Management; International Business; International Economics; Management; Management Systems; Marketing; Taxation); **Education and Heritage** (Administration; Architectural Restoration; Archiving; Art History; Clinical Psychology; Cultural Studies; Educational Administration; Educational and Student Counselling; Educational Psychology; Family Studies; Foreign Languages Education; Geography; Geography (Human); Health Education; Heritage Preservation; Higher Education Teacher Training; History; Humanities and Social Science Education; Information Management; Information Sciences; Latin American Studies; Library Science; Management; Native Language Education; Pedagogy; Portuguese; Preschool Education; Primary Education; Psychology; Science Education; Secondary Education; Social and Community Services; Social Work; Special Education; Teacher Trainers Education; Tourism); **Innovation, Science and Technology** (Applied Mathematics; Business Administration; Computer Engineering; Computer Science; Information Management; Information Technology; Management; Management Systems; Mathematics; Mathematics Education; Software Engineering; Statistics); **Law** (Administrative Law; Arts and Humanities; Commercial Law; Humanities and Social Science Education; Institutional Administration; Labour and Industrial Relations; Law; Public Administration)

History: Founded 1986.

Governing Bodies: General Assembly

Academic Year: September to July

Admission Requirements: Secondary school certificate and entrance examination, or recognized foreign equivalent

Main Language(s) of Instruction: Portuguese

International Co-operation: Participates in Erasmus/Socrates, Leonardo, Alfa and Tempus programmes.

Degrees and Diplomas: *Licenciado*; *Mestre*; *Doutor*. Also Postgraduate courses

Student Services: Academic counselling, Canteen, Cultural centre, Employment services, Foreign student adviser, Foreign Studies Centre, Language programs, Social counselling

Special Facilities: Auditorium

Libraries: 46,000 vols

Publications: Historical Sciences Magazine *(annually)*; Judicial Magazine

Last Updated: 17/10/11

INSTITUTE OF ADMINISTRATION AND LANGUAGES

Instituto Superior de Administração e Línguas (ISAL)

Rua do Comboio, 5, 9050-053 Funchal

Tel: +351(291) 705-705

Fax: +351(291) 705-709

EMail: isal@isal.pt

Website: http://www.isal.pt

Director Geral: José Quaresma

Courses

Accountancy and Finance (Accountancy; Finance); **Business Administration** (Business Administration; Health Administration); **Hotel Management** (Hotel Management; Management; Tourism); **Tourism** (Tourism)

History: Founded 1984, acquired present status 1989.

Main Language(s) of Instruction: Portuguese

Degrees and Diplomas: *Licenciado*. Also postgraduate programmes

Last Updated: 03/10/11

INSTITUTE OF ADMINISTRATION AND MANAGEMENT

Instituto Superior de Administração e Gestão

Rua do Campo Alegre, 1376, 4150-175 Porto

Tel: +351(220) 303-200

Fax: +351(226) 099-223

EMail: isag@isag.pt

Website: http://www.isag.pt

Presidente: Joaquim Alberto Hierro Lopes (1979-)
Tel: +351(22) 609-8825

Gerente: Vitor Ruiz Póvoas Vieira da Costa

International Relations: Vitor Manuel Domingos Tavares

Courses

Business Administration (Accountancy; Business Administration; Finance; Management; Marketing); **Hotel Management** (Hotel and Restaurant; Hotel Management); **Human and Social Sciences** (Economics; History; Modern Languages; Portuguese; Psychology); **Law** (Law); **Mathematics and Computer Science** (Computer Science; Mathematics); **Tourism** (Tourism); **Translation and Interpretation** (Translation and Interpretation)

History: Founded 1979. Merged with the Instituto Superior de Assistentes e Intérpretes - ISAI (Higher Institute of Assistants and Interpreters) 2005.

Main Language(s) of Instruction: Portuguese

Degrees and Diplomas: *Licenciado*; *Mestre*. Also postgraduate and specialization diplomas

Last Updated: 03/10/11

INSTITUTE OF ADMINISTRATION STUDIES

Instituto Superior de Ciências da Administração (ISCAD)
Rua de S. Paulo, 89, 1200-427 Lisboa
Tel: +351(213) 261-440
Fax: +351(213) 261-447
EMail: informacoes@iscad.pt
Website: http://www.iscad.pt/

Diretor: Joel Hasse Ferreira

Courses

Accountancy and Administration (Accountancy; Administration); **Administration and Public Administration** (Administration; Public Administration); **Hotel Management** (Hotel Management; Tourism); **Law** *(First and second cycles)* (Accountancy; Civil Law; Finance; Law; Notary Studies)

History: Founded following the merger of the IESC - Instituto Superior de Estudos de Contabilidade and ISHT - Instituto Superior de Humanidades e Tecnologias.

Main Language(s) of Instruction: Portuguese

Degrees and Diplomas: *Licenciado*; *Mestre*. Also postgraduate diplomas

Last Updated: 03/10/11

INSTITUTE OF ADVANCED STUDIES OF FAFE

Instituto de Estudos Superiores de Fafe (IESF)
Apartado 178, Rua Universitaria-Medelo, 4824-909 Fafe
Tel: +35(253) 509-000
Fax: +35(253) 509-001
EMail: iesf@iesfafe.pt
Website: http://www.iesfafe.pt

Director: Luciano Magalhâes de Sampaio

Schools

Education *(Escola Superior de Educação de Fafe)* (Education; Mathematics; Natural Sciences; Physical Education; Teacher Training); **Technology** *(Escola Superior de Tecnologias de Fafe)* (Accountancy; Business Computing; Computer Science; Management; Technology; Tourism)

Main Language(s) of Instruction: Portuguese

Degrees and Diplomas: *Licenciado*; *Mestre*. Also postgraduate diplomas

Last Updated: 27/09/11

INSTITUTE OF ADVANCED TECHNOLOGIES

Instituto Superior de Tecnologias Avançadas (ISTEC)
Avenida Eng° Arantes e Oliveira, 3/RC, 1900-221 Lisboa
Tel: +351(21) 843-6670 +351(21) 843-6677 +351(21) 843-6678
Fax: +351(21) 848-6063
EMail: secretaria@istec.pt
Website: http://www.istec.pt

Director: José António Carriço (1989-)
Tel: +351(21) 843-6672, Fax: +351(21) 843-6672
EMail: isteclx@esoterica.pt

Director Geral: Artur Salada Ferreira

International Relations: António Fidalgo

Courses

Computer Science *(Lisboa / Porto)* (Computer Networks; Computer Science; Information Technology; Telecommunications Engineering); **Multimedia Engineering** *(Lisboa / Porto)* (Educational Technology; Multimedia)

Departments

Graduate Studies (Computer Graphics; Computer Networks; Information Technology; Multimedia; Software Engineering; Video)

Further Information: Branch in Oporto

History: Founded 1989.

Main Language(s) of Instruction: Portuguese

Degrees and Diplomas: *Licenciado*. Also postgraduate programmes

Last Updated: 05/10/11

INSTITUTE OF BUSINESS AND TOURISM

Instituto Superior de Ciências Empresariais e do Turismo (ISCET)
Rua de Cedofeita, 285, 4050-180 Porto
Tel: +351(222) 053-685
Fax: +351(222) 053-744
EMail: iscet@iscet.pt
Website: http://www.iscet.pt

Presidente: Maria Gabriela de Araújo Guimarães (1995-)

Administrador: Manoel Teixeira Oliveira

International Relations: Maria Gabriela de Araújo Guimarães

Courses

Human Resources Management (Human Resources; Management); **International Business** (International Business); **Law** (Commercial Law; Law); **Marketing and Advertising** (Advertising and Publicity; Marketing); **Social and Organizational Psychology** (Industrial and Organizational Psychology; Psychology; Social Psychology); **Social Services** (Social and Community Services; Social Work); **Tourism** (Tourism)

History: Founded 1990.

Degrees and Diplomas: *Licenciado*; *Mestre*; *Doutor*

Last Updated: 03/10/11

INSTITUTE OF BUSINESS COMMUNICATION

Instituto Superior de Comunicação Empresarial (ISCEM)
Praça do Principe Real, 27, 1250-184 Lisboa
Tel: +351(213) 474-283
Fax: +351(213) 474-288
EMail: info@iscem.pt
Website: http://www.iscem.pt

Presidente: Regina Campos Moreira (1990-)
Tel: +351(21) 233-960 EMail: director@iscem.pt

International Relations: Isabel Canhoto
EMail: isabel.canhoto@iscem.pt

Courses

Business Communication (Business and Commerce; Communication Studies); **Marketing Management** (Management; Marketing)

History: Founded 1990.

Main Language(s) of Instruction: Portuguese

Degrees and Diplomas: *Licenciado*; *Mestre*

Last Updated: 03/10/11

INSTITUTE OF EDUCATION AND LABOUR

Instituto Superior de Educação e Trabalho
Rua Pereira Reis, 399, 4200-448 Porto
Tel: +351(22) 507-3890
Fax: +351(22) 550-6597
EMail: geral@iset.pt
Website: http://www.iset.pt

Presidente: Maria da Conceição Alves Pinto (1993-)

Courses

Education (Cultural Studies; Education; Educational Administration; Social Studies; Special Education)

History: Founded 1993.

Main Language(s) of Instruction: Portuguese

Degrees and Diplomas: *Licenciado*; *Mestre*. Also specialization courses

Last Updated: 03/10/11

INSTITUTE OF EDUCATION AND SCIENCE

Instituto Superior de Educação e Ciências
Alameda das Linhas de Torres, 179, 1750-142 Lisboa
Tel: +351(217) 541-310
Fax: +351(217) 541-319
EMail: info@isec.universitas.pt
Website: http://www.isec.universitas.pt

Presidente: José Reis Jorge

Director Administrativo: António Varão

Schools

Business and Administration (Business Administration; Business and Commerce; Health Administration; Hotel Management; Management; Marketing; Real Estate); **Design and Graphic Arts** (Communication Arts; Communication Studies; Computer Graphics; Design; Graphic Arts; Graphic Design; Information Technology; Photography); **Educational Sciences** (Education; Educational Administration; Mathematics Education; Preschool Education; Primary Education; Social and Community Services; Social Studies; Special Education; Teacher Training); **Science and Technology** (Aeronautical and Aerospace Engineering; Air Transport; Occupational Health; Safety Engineering; Transport Management)

History: Founded in 1991.

Main Language(s) of Instruction: Portuguese

Degrees and Diplomas: *Licenciado*; *Mestre*. Also specialization and postgraduate programmes

Last Updated: 03/10/11

INSTITUTE OF EDUCATIONAL SCIENCES

Instituto Superior de Ciências Educativas (ISCE)

Rua Bento de Jesus Caraça, 12, Serra da Amoreira, 2620-379 Ramada

Tel: +351(219) 347-135

Fax: +351(219) 332-688

EMail: geral@isce.pt

Website: http://www.isce.pt/

Presidente: Felisima Santos Morais (1988-)

International Relations: Isabel Duarte

EMail: gri@isce-odivelas.com

Departments

Education (Communication Arts; Communication Studies; Education; Educational Administration; English; Foreign Languages Education; Higher Education; Information Technology; Music Education; Pedagogy; Preschool Education; Primary Education; Special Education; Speech Therapy and Audiology; Teacher Trainers Education); **Physical Education and Sport** (Physical Education; Sports); **Social and Cultural Studies** (Cultural Studies; Gerontology; Social Studies; Social Work); **Tourism** (Cooking and Catering; Hotel and Restaurant; Hotel Management; Human Resources; Tourism)

History: Founded 1988.

Degrees and Diplomas: *Licenciado*; *Mestre*. Also postgraduate programmes

Last Updated: 03/10/11

INSTITUTE OF ENTRE DOURO AND VOUGA

Instituto Superior de Entre Douro e Vouga (ISVOUGA)

Apartado 132, Rua António de Castro Corte Real, 4520-909 Santa Maria da Feira, Codex

Tel: +351(256) 377-550

Fax: +351(256) 377-559

EMail: secretaria@isvouga.pt; smi@isvouga.pt

Website: http://www.isvouga.pt/

Directora: Maria Teresa de Carvalho Leão

EMail: direccao@isvouga.pt

Chefe de Serviços: Maria Clara Gomes

International Relations: João Nuno Macedo Lameiras

Courses

Accountancy (Accountancy); **Business Administration** (Accountancy; Business Administration; Finance; Taxation); **Law** (Civil Law; Law; Notary Studies); **Marketing, Advertising and Public Relations** (Advertising and Publicity; Marketing; Public Relations); **Production and Industrial Management Engineering** (Industrial Management; Production Engineering)

History: Founded 1990.

Main Language(s) of Instruction: Portuguese

Degrees and Diplomas: *Licenciado*. Also postgraduate diplomas

Last Updated: 03/10/11

INSTITUTE OF FINANCIAL AND FISCAL STUDIES

Instituto de Estudos Superiores Financeiros e Fiscais (IESF)

Edificio Helântia, Avenida Sanatórios, 4405-604 Vila Nova de Gaia

Tel: +351(227) 538-800

Fax: +351(227) 538-870

EMail: info@iesf.pt

Website: http://www.iesf.pt

Director: João Paulo Peixoto EMail: jpp@iesf.pt

Chefe de Secção: Sofia Rodriges

International Relations: João Paulo Seara Peixoto

Courses

Business and Management (Business Administration; Business and Commerce; E-Business/Commerce; Human Resources; International Business; Management; Marketing); **Finance and Taxation** (Accountancy; Commercial Law; Economics; Finance; Information Management; Taxation); **Graduate Studies** (Business Administration; Human Resources; Management; Occupational Health); **Management and Information Systems** (Information Technology; Management Systems)

History: Founded 1990.

Main Language(s) of Instruction: Portuguese

Degrees and Diplomas: *Licenciado*; *Mestre*

Last Updated: 29/09/11

INSTITUTE OF HEALTH STUDIES OF ALTO AVE

Instituto Superior de Saúde do Alto Ave

Quinta de Matos-Geraz do Minho, 4830-316 Póvo de Lanhoso

Tel: +351(253) 639-800

Fax: +351(253) 639-801

EMail: geral@isave.pt

Website: http://www.isave.pt

Presidente: Jónatas Pego

Courses

Clinical Analysis and Public Health (Public Health); **Dental Hygiene** (Dental Hygiene); **Dental Technology** (Dental Technology); **Graduate Studies** (Medical Technology; Radiology); **Nursing** (Nursing); **Occupational Therapy** (Occupational Therapy); **Pharmacy** (Pharmacy); **Physical Therapy** (Physical Therapy); **Radiology** (Radiology); **Speech Therapy** (Speech Therapy and Audiology)

History: Founded 2002.

Main Language(s) of Instruction: Portuguese

Degrees and Diplomas: *Licenciado*. Also specialization and postgraduate programmes

Last Updated: 05/10/11

INSTITUTE OF INFORMATION AND ADMINISTRATION

Instituto Superior de Ciências da Informação e da Administração (ISCIA)

Apartado 292, Avenida Dom Manuel de Almeida Trindade, S. Joana, 3810-448 Aveiro

Tel: +351(234) 423-045

Fax: +351(234) 381-406

EMail: info@iscia.edu.pt

Website: http://www.iscia.edu.pt

Presidente: Armando Teixeira Carneiro

Vice-Presidente: Luis Felipe Neves

Departments

Communication (Communication Studies; Institutional Administration); **Digital Technology** (Computer Science); **Languages and Culture**; **Management and International Relations** (International Relations; Management); **Psychology and Education** (Education; Psychology)

Further Information: Pólo de Aveiro and Pólo de Baião

History: Founded 1990.

Main Language(s) of Instruction: Portuguese

Degrees and Diplomas: *Licenciado*; *Mestre*
Last Updated: 12/10/09

INSTITUTE OF LANGUAGES AND ADMINISTRATION - BRAGANÇA

Instituto Superior de Línguas e Administração de Bragança

Rua Prof. Dr. António Gonçalves Rodrigues, Edificio ISLA, 5300-238 Bragança
Tel: +351(273) 331-434
Fax: +351(273) 324-473
EMail: info@islabraganca.pt
Website: http://www.islabraganca.pt

Directora: Maria da Graça Martins

Courses
Business Computing (Business Computing); **Organizational Psychology** (Industrial and Organizational Psychology); **Physical Education and Leisure Studies** (Leisure Studies; Physical Education)
History: Founded 1965.
Main Language(s) of Instruction: Portuguese
Degrees and Diplomas: *Licenciado*; *Mestre*; *Doutor*
Last Updated: 24/01/08

INSTITUTE OF LANGUAGES AND ADMINISTRATION - LEIRIA

Instituto Superior de Línguas e Administração de Leiria (ISLA)

Rua da Cooperativa, São Romão, 2414-017 Leiria
Tel: +351(244) 820-650
Fax: +351(244) 813-021
EMail: info@islaleiria.pt
Website: http://www.islaleiria.pt

Director: Carlos Francisco Silva

Courses
Business Administration (Business Administration; Management); **Graduate Studies** (Business Administration; Computer Networks; Educational Psychology; Environmental Engineering; Health Sciences; Human Resources; Industrial and Organizational Psychology; Information Technology; Library Science; Management; Multimedia; Nursing; Psychology; Psychotherapy; Safety Engineering; Social Psychology; Social Work; Technology); **Human Resources Management** (Human Resources); **Labour Safety Engineering** (Safety Engineering); **Social and Organizational Psychology** (Industrial and Organizational Psychology; Psychology)
History: Founded 1990.
Degrees and Diplomas: *Licenciado*; *Mestre*. Also postgraduate and specialization programmes
Last Updated: 05/10/11

INSTITUTE OF LANGUAGES AND ADMINISTRATION - LISBON

Instituto Superior de Línguas e Administração de Lisboa (ISLA)

Estrada da Correia, 53, 1500-210 Lisboa
Tel: +351808-203-544
EMail: elpme@lx.isla.pt
Website: http://www.isla.pt

Courses
Business Administration (Business Administration); **Business Computing** (Business Computing); **Graduate Studies** (Banking; Business Administration; Business Computing; Finance; Human Resources; Labour Law; Management; Management Systems; Marketing); **Hotel Management** (Hotel Management); **Human Resources and Organizational Management** (Business Administration; Human Resources; Management); **Information Systems, Web and Multimedia** (Computer Networks; Information Technology; Multimedia); **Marketing, Publicity and Public Relations** (Advertising and Publicity; Marketing; Public Relations); **Safety Management and Civil Protection** (Civil Security; Welfare and Protective Services); **Secretariat and Corporate Communications** (Secretarial Studies); **Tourism** (Tourism)
History: Founded 1962.
Main Language(s) of Instruction: Portuguese
Degrees and Diplomas: *Licenciado*; *Mestre*. Also postgraduate programmes
Last Updated: 05/10/11

INSTITUTE OF LANGUAGES AND ADMINISTRATION - SANTARÉM

Instituto Superior de Línguas e Administração - Santarém (ISLA)

Largo Cândido dos Reis, Edificio do Antigo Hospital de Santarém, 2000-241 Santarém
Tel: +351(243) 305-880
Fax: +351(243) 326-261
EMail: info@islasantarem.pt
Website: http://www.islasantarem.pt

Director: Valter Martins Vairinhos

Courses
Graduate Studies (Business Administration; Computer Networks; Educational Psychology; Environmental Engineering; Health Sciences; Human Resources; Industrial and Organizational Psychology; Information Technology; Library Science; Management; Multimedia; Nursing; Psychology; Psychotherapy; Safety Engineering; Social Psychology; Social Work; Technology); **Human Resources Management** (Human Resources; Management); **Labour Safety Engineering** (Safety Engineering)
History: Founded 1984.
Main Language(s) of Instruction: Portuguese
Degrees and Diplomas: *Licenciado*; *Mestre*. Also postgraduate and specialization programmes
Last Updated: 05/10/11

INSTITUTE OF LANGUAGES AND ADMINISTRATION - VILA NOVA DE GAIA

Instituto Superior de Línguas e Administração de Vila Nova de Gaia (ISLA)

Rua Cabo Borges, 55, 4430-646 Vila Nova de Gaia
Tel: +351(223) 772-980
Fax: +351(223) 757-989
EMail: info@mail.islgaia.pt
Website: http://www.islagaia.pt

Director: António Lencastre Godinho

Courses
Business Administration (Business Administration); **Graduate Studies** (Business Administration; Computer Networks; Educational Psychology; Environmental Engineering; Health Sciences; Human Resources; Industrial and Organizational Psychology; Information Technology; Library Science; Management; Multimedia; Nursing; Psychology; Psychotherapy; Safety Engineering; Social Psychology; Social Work; Technology); **Human Resources Management** (Human Resources); **Information Systems and Multimedia Management** (Information Management; Multimedia); **Labour Safety Engineering** (Safety Engineering); **Psychology** (Industrial and Organizational Psychology; Psychology); **Tourism** (Tourism)
History: Founded 1989.
Degrees and Diplomas: *Licenciado*; *Mestre*. Also postgraduate and specialization programmes
Last Updated: 05/10/11

INSTITUTE OF MAIA

Instituto Superior da Maia (ISMAI)

Av. Carlos Oliveira Campos, Avioso S. Pedro, 4475-690 Castelo da Maia
Tel: +351(229) 866-000
Fax: +351(229) 825-331
EMail: info@ismai.pt
Website: http://www.ismai.pt

Presidente: José Manuel Matias de Azevedo
Vice-Presidente: Fernando Hernâni Bento

International Relations: António Malcata Julião

Programmes

Licenciatura (Accountancy; Business Administration; Business Computing; Communication Studies; Computer Networks; Criminology; Electronic Engineering; Fine Arts; Human Resources; Information Technology; Law; Management; Marketing; Multimedia; Physical Education; Psychology; Public Relations; Safety Engineering; Software Engineering; Sports; Sports Management; Telecommunications Engineering; Tourism); **Mestrado** (Business Administration; Clinical Psychology; Development Studies; Educational Psychology; Health Sciences; Heritage Preservation; Human Resources; Industrial and Organizational Psychology; Management; Marketing; Neurological Therapy; Occupational Health; Physical Education; Primary Education; Psychology; Psychotherapy; Secondary Education; Sports; Sports Management; Tourism)

History: Founded 1990.

Degrees and Diplomas: *Licenciado*; *Mestre*; *Doutor*. Also postgraduate programmes

Last Updated: 03/10/11

INSTITUTE OF MANAGEMENT

Instituto Superior de Gestão

Rua Vitorino Nemésio, 5, Ameixoeira, 1750-306 Lisboa

Tel: +351(21) 751-3700

Fax: +351(21) 757-3966

EMail: informacoes@isg.pt

Website: http://www.isg.pt

Director: Miguel Varela

Secretário-Geral: Alexandre Safont Tavares

Courses

Economics (Economics); **Graduate Studies** (Accountancy; Business Administration; Educational Administration; Finance; Human Resources; Information Management; Information Technology; International Business; Labour Law; Management; Marketing; Public Administration; Taxation; Transport Management); **Human Resources Management** (Human Resources; Management); **Management** (Management); **Marketing** (Marketing)

History: Founded 1978.

Main Language(s) of Instruction: Portuguese

Degrees and Diplomas: *Licenciado*; *Mestre*. Also specialization and postgraduate programmes

Last Updated: 05/10/11

INSTITUTE OF PAÇOS DE BRANDÃO

Instituto Superior de Paços de Brandão

Avenida Escolar - Apartado 99, 4535-906 Paços de Brandão

Tel: +351(227) 449-277

Fax: +351(227) 451-009

EMail: geral@ispab.pt

Website: http://www.ispab.pt

Presidente: José Manuel Carmo da Silva

Courses

Chemical Engineering (Chemical Engineering); **Graduate Studies** (Communication Studies; Environmental Management; Finance; Management; Marketing; Safety Engineering); **Management and Accountancy** (Accountancy; Management); **Marketing, Advertising and Public Relations** (Advertising and Publicity; Marketing; Public Relations)

History: Founded 1990.

Main Language(s) of Instruction: Portuguese

Degrees and Diplomas: *Licenciado*. Also postgraduate programmes

Last Updated: 05/10/11

INSTITUTE OF SOCIAL SERVICES OF OPORTO

Instituto Superior de Serviço Social do Porto

Avenida Dr Manuel Teixeira, 370, 4460-362 Senhora da Hora

Tel: +351(22) 957-7210

Fax: +351(22) 957-7219

EMail: geral@isssp.pt

Website: http://www.isssp.pt/

Presidente: José Alberto Falcão dos Reis (2006-)

Chefe de Serviços: Ermelinda de Sousa Ferreira

Departments

Graduate Studies (Cultural Studies; Gerontology; Health Sciences; Social and Community Services; Social Policy; Social Sciences; Social Studies); **Social Gerontology** (Gerontology; Health Sciences; Law; Psychology; Sociology); **Social Services** (Economics; Law; Psychology; Social and Community Services; Social Work; Sociology)

History: Founded 1956.

Main Language(s) of Instruction: Portuguese

Degrees and Diplomas: *Licenciado*; *Mestre*. Also postgraduate programmes

Last Updated: 05/10/11

INSTITUTE OF THE NEW PROFESSIONS

Instituto Superior de Novas Profissões (INP)

Campus Universitário da Ameixoeira, Rua Vitorino Nemésio, 5, Ameixoeira, 1750-306 Lisboa

Tel: +351(217) 508-010

Fax: +351(217) 508-020

EMail: inp@inp.pt

Website: http://www.inp.pt

Director: Miguel Varela EMail: direccaoinp@inp.pt

Courses

Business Administration and Commerce (Business Administration; Business and Commerce); **Communication** (Communication Arts; Communication Studies; Marketing; Public Relations); **Graduate Studies** (Advertising and Publicity; Business Administration; Communication Studies; Cultural Studies; Marketing; Media Studies; Secretarial Studies; Tourism; Transport Management); **Journalism**; **Public Relations and Publicity** (Advertising and Publicity; Public Relations); **Secretarial Studies in Management and Administration** (Secretarial Studies); **Tourism** (Hotel Management; Tourism)

History: Founded 1964.

Main Language(s) of Instruction: Portuguese

Degrees and Diplomas: *Licenciado*; *Mestre*. Also postgraduate programmes

Last Updated: 05/10/11

INSTITUTE OF VISUAL ARTS, DESIGN AND MARKETING

Instituto de Artes Visuais, Design e Marketing

Avenida D. Carlos I, 4, 1200-649 Lisboa

Tel: +351(213) 939-600

Fax: +351(213) 939-610

EMail: iade@iade.pt

Website: http://www.iade.pt

Presidente das Escolas Universitárias do IADE: Carlos A. M. Duarte

Programmes

Graduate (Advertising and Publicity; Cinema and Television; Communication Arts; Design; Industrial Design; Marketing; Multimedia; Photography; Visual Arts)

Schools

Advertising and Publicity (Advertising and Publicity); **Design** (Design); **Marketing** (Marketing); **Photography** (Photography; Visual Arts)

Further Information: Edifício D. Carlos and Palácio Quintela campuses. Also Portuguese courses for foreign students

History: Founded 1969.

Main Language(s) of Instruction: Portuguese

Degrees and Diplomas: *Licenciado*; *Mestre*. Also specialization courses

Last Updated: 29/09/11

INSTITUTE PF EDUCATIONAL SCIENCES OF FELGUEIRAS

Instituto Superior de Ciências Educativas de Felgueiras
Rua Dr. Luís Gonzaga F. Moreira, 4610-177 Felgueiras
Tel: +351(255) 318-550
Fax: +351(255) 312-529
EMail: isce-felgueiras@pedago.pt
Website: http://isce-felgueiras.com

Departments

Education (Communication Studies; Education; Educational Administration; English; Foreign Languages Education; Information Technology; Music Education; Pedagogy; Preschool Education; Primary Education; Spanish; Special Education; Teacher Trainers Education; Visual Arts); **Social and Cultural Studies** (Cultural Studies; Social Studies); **Sports** (Sports); **Tourism** (Rehabilitation and Therapy; Tourism)

History: Founded 1991.

Main Language(s) of Instruction: Portuguese

Degrees and Diplomas: *Licenciado*; *Mestre*

Last Updated: 12/10/09

JOÃO DE DEUS SCHOOL OF EDUCATION

Escola Superior de Educação de João de Deus
Avenida Álvares Cabral, 69, 1269-094 Lisboa
Tel: +351(21) 396-8154
Fax: +351(21) 396-7183
EMail: ese@escolasjoaodeus.pt
Website: http://www.ese-jdeus.edu.pt

Director: António Ponces de Carvalho (1988-)

Courses

Basic Education (Communication Studies; Cultural Studies; Design; Education; Educational Psychology; Environmental Studies; Geography (Human); Health Education; History; Information Technology; Linguistics; Literacy Education; Mathematics Education; Music Education; Natural Sciences; Pedagogy; Physics; Primary Education; Science Education; Visual Arts); **Educational Sciences** *(Graduate studies (Master))* (Art Education; Educational Administration; Educational Sciences; Literacy Education; Pedagogy; Special Education); **Postgraduate Studies** (Gerontology; Oncology); **Pre-school Education** (Preschool Education); **Social Gerontology** (Anthropology; Behavioural Sciences; Biology; Community Health; Demography and Population; Gerontology; Health Sciences; Leisure Studies; Psychiatry and Mental Health; Psychology; Social Psychology; Social Studies; Statistics; Tourism); **Teacher Training** *(Graduate studies (Master))* (Education; Preschool Education; Teacher Training)

History: Founded 1988.

Main Language(s) of Instruction: Portuguese

Degrees and Diplomas: *Licenciado*; *Mestre*; *Doutor*. Also specialization and postgraduate courses

Last Updated: 26/09/11

LUSIADA UNIVERSITY OF LISBON

Universidade Lusíada de Lisboa (ULA)
Rua da Junqueira 188-198, 1349-001 Lisboa
Tel: +351(213) 611-500
Fax: +351(213) 638-307
EMail: info@lis.ulusiada.pt
Website: http://www.lis.ulusiada.pt

Reitor: Diamantino Freitas Gomes Durão
EMail: reitoria@lis.ulusiada.pt

Faculties

Architecture and Arts (Architecture; Arts and Humanities; Design; Environmental Engineering; Industrial Design; Visual Arts); **Economics and Business Studies** (Accountancy; Advertising and Publicity; Business Administration; Computer Engineering; Computer Science; Economics; Electronic Engineering; Health Administration; Human Resources; Management; Marketing; Sports Management; Tourism); **Humanities and Social Sciences** (Art History; Arts and Humanities; Civil Security; Communication Arts; History; International Relations; Jazz and Popular Music; Leisure Studies; Multimedia; Music; Performing Arts; Social Sciences; Sports Management); **Law** (International Relations; Law; Political Sciences; Psychology)

Institutes

Environmental Law (Environmental Management; Law); **Postgraduate**; **Psychology and Educational Sciences** (Art Education; Clinical Psychology; Educational Sciences; Health Education; Industrial and Organizational Psychology; Music; Neurological Therapy; Primary Education; Psychology; Secondary Education; Special Education); **Research and Development**; **Social Services** (Gerontology; Social and Community Services)

History: Founded 1986.

Governing Bodies: Board of Directors

Academic Year: September to July

Admission Requirements: Secondary school certificate and entrance examination or foreign equivalent

Main Language(s) of Instruction: Portuguese

International Co-operation: Participates in the Erasmus programme

Degrees and Diplomas: *Licenciado*: 4-5 yrs; *Mestre*: a further 2 yrs; *Doutor*: a further 3 yrs. Also postgraduate programmes

Libraries: Yes

Publications: Lusiada *(quarterly)*

Last Updated: 07/10/11

LUSIADA UNIVERSITY OF ANGOLA

UNIVERSIDADE LUSÍADA DE ANGOLA
Largo do Lumeji n°11-12, Luanda, Angola
Tel: +244(222) 37-03-46
EMail: geral@ulangola.net
Website: http://www.ulangola.net

Faculties

Architecture and Arts; **Business Administration**; **Engineering** (Automation and Control Engineering; Computer Engineering; Electronic Engineering; Energy Engineering; Engineering; Textile Technology)

Further Information: Also branches in Benguela and Cabinda

History: Founded 1999.

Main Language(s) of Instruction: Portuguese

Degrees and Diplomas: *Licenciado*; *Mestre*

LUSIADA UNIVERSITY OF OPORTO

UNIVERSIDADE LUSÍADA DO PORTO
Rua Dr. Lopo de Carvalho, 4369-006 Porto
Tel: +351(22) 557-0880
Fax: +351(22) 557-0897
EMail: info@por.ulusiada.pt
Website: http://www.por.ulusiada.pt

Faculties

Architecture and Arts (Architecture; Design; Fine Arts; Industrial Design); **Economics and Business** (Applied Mathematics; Business Administration; Business and Commerce; Economics; Human Resources; Management); **Law** (Criminology; International Relations; Law)

Institutes

Psychology and Educational Sciences (Educational Sciences; Psychology)

History: Founded 1991.

Main Language(s) of Instruction: Portuguese

Degrees and Diplomas: *Licenciado*; *Mestre*; *Doutor*

LUSIADA UNIVERSITY OF VILA NOVA DE FAMALIÇÃO
UNIVERSIDADE LUSÍADA DE VILA NOVA DE FAMALIÇÃO
Largo Tinoco de Sousa, Edifício da Lapa, 4760-108 Vila Nova de Famalição
Tel: +351(22) 309-200
Fax: +351(22) 376-363
EMail: info@fam.ulusiada.pt
Website: http://www.fam.ulusiada.pt

Reitora: Rosa Moreira EMail: dina@fam.ulusiada.pt

Faculties
Architecture and Fine Arts (Architecture; Design); **Economic and Business Studies** (Accountancy; Business Administration; Economics; Marketing); **Engineering and Technology** (Civil Engineering; Computer Engineering; Electronic Engineering; Industrial Engineering; Mathematics; Mechanical Engineering; Textile Technology)

History: Founded 1991.

Main Language(s) of Instruction: Portuguese

Degrees and Diplomas: *Licenciado*; *Mestre*: Architecture; Design; Management; Economics; Marketing; Engineering and Technology; *Doutor*: Architecture; Design; Economics; Engineering and Industrial Management. Also postgraduate and specialization diplomas

LUSOPHONE UNIVERSITY OF HUMANITIES AND TECHNOLOGIES

Universidade Lusófona de Humanidades e Tecnologias (ULHT)
Campo Grande, 376, 1749-024 Lisboa
Tel: +351(217) 515-500
Fax: +351(217) 577-006
EMail: informacoes@ulusofona.pt
Website: http://www.ulusofona.pt

Reitor: Mário Moutinho Tel: +351(217) 515-575

Administrador: Manuel Almeida Damásio
Tel: +351(217) 570-550
EMail: administracao@ulusofona.pt; mdamasio@ulusofona.pt

International Relations: Teresa do Rosario Damásio, Head, International Office
Tel: +351(217) 515-565, Fax: +351(217) 515-534
EMail: trdamasio@ulusofona.pt

Faculties
Aeronautics (Aeronautical and Aerospace Engineering; Air Transport); **Biomedical Sciences** (Biochemistry; Biology; Biomedicine; Health Sciences; Immunology); **Economics and Management** (Accountancy; Business Administration; Economics; Human Resources; Management; Sports Management; Taxation); **Engineering and Natural Sciences** (Bioengineering; Biology; Biotechnology; Chemistry; Civil Engineering; Electrical and Electronic Engineering; Electronic Engineering; Energy Engineering; Engineering; Engineering Management; Environmental Engineering; Food Science; Food Technology; Geology; Industrial Engineering; Industrial Management; Marine Science and Oceanography; Mathematics; Physics; Real Estate; Science Education); **Health Sciences and Technology** (Cosmetology; Dermatology; Health Administration; Health Sciences; Nutrition; Pharmacology; Pharmacy; Public Health); **Human and Social Sciences** (Development Studies; Educational Sciences; European Studies; Geography (Human); Gerontology; History; International Relations; Museum Studies; Political Sciences; Regional Planning; Religious Studies; Social and Community Services; Social Policy; Social Work; Sociology; Tourism; Town Planning; Translation and Interpretation; Urban Studies; Water Management); **Law** (Commercial Law; Criminology; Law; Maritime Law; Taxation); **Philosophy, Mathematics and Cognitive Sciences** (Cognitive Sciences; Philosophy; Science Education); **Physical Education and Sports** (Leisure Studies; Physical Education; Primary Education; Secondary Education; Sports); **Political Sciences, Portuguese Speaking Countries and International Relations** (European Studies; Government; International Business; International Economics; International Relations; Political Sciences; Portuguese; Psychology; Religious Studies); **Psychology** (Educational Psychology; Human Resources; Industrial and Organizational Psychology; Neurology; Psychology; Psychotherapy); **Veterinary Medicine** (Veterinary Science)

Institutes
Education (Documentation Techniques; Education; Educational Administration; Educational and Student Counselling; Geography; Geography (Human); History; Library Science; Special Education); **Security Studies** (Civil Security; Protective Services)

Schools
Administration (Administration; Commercial Law; Finance; Leadership; Public Administration; Public Law); **Communication Sciences, Arts and Information Technologies** (Advertising and Publicity; Architecture; Art Education; Art Management; Cinema and Television; Communication Arts; Communication Studies; Computer Engineering; Computer Science; Contemporary History; Cultural Studies; Design; Documentation Techniques; Graphic Arts; Graphic Design; Health Administration; Information Sciences; Information Technology; Journalism; Marketing; Multimedia; Photography; Political Sciences; Public Relations; Special Education; Technology Education; Translation and Interpretation; Writing); **Fine Arts** (Architectural Restoration; Design; Heritage Preservation; Interior Design; Music; Painting and Drawing; Sculpture; Theatre)

History: Founded 1993.

Governing Bodies: Board of Directors

Academic Year: October to June

Main Language(s) of Instruction: Portuguese

International Co-operation: Participates in Socrates, Tempus, Leonardo and Alfa programmes, and also with various European countries. Also agreements with universities in USA, Canada, South Africa, Brazil, Cost Rica, Mexico, Colombia, Argentina, Venezuela, Chile

Accrediting Agencies: Departamento do Ensino Superior (DESUP); Ministério da Ciencia, Tecnología e Encino Superior

Degrees and Diplomas: *Diploma de Especialização Tecnológica*; *Licenciado*; *Mestre*; *Doutor*

Student Services: Canteen, Employment services, Foreign student adviser, Handicapped facilities, Language programs, Social counselling, Sports facilities

Student Residential Facilities: Yes

Special Facilities: Audiovisual Pos-production and Multimedia Centre; TV and Sound Studio; 2 Multimedia Laboratories; Linear Editing room; 4 Auditoria; Fitness Centre

Libraries: Main Library

Publications: Afreudite, Lusophone journal of applied and pure psychoanalysis; Babilonia, Lusophone journal of language, culture and translation; Caderno Sociomuseologica, Art and socio-musuem studies; Campus Social, Lusophone journal of social sciences; Malha Urbana, Lusophone journal of town planning; Metacrítica, Philosophics journal; Res-Publica, Lusophone journal for political science and international relations; Revista Lusófona de Ciêncas da Educação, Lusophone journal of education sciences; Revista Lusófona de Ciêncas da Mente e do Comportamento, Lusophone journal of behavioural science; Revista Lusófona de Ciências das Religiões, Lusophone journal of religious studies; Revista Lusófona de Ciêncas e Tecnologias da Saúde, Lusophone journal of health sciences and technology; Revista Lusófona de Humanidades e Tecnologias, Lusophone journal for humanities and technology

Last Updated: 17/10/11

LUSOPHONE UNIVERSITY OF PORTO

Universidade Lusófona do Porto
Rua Augusto Rosa, n° 24, 4000-098 Porto
Tel: +351(22) 207-3230
Fax: +351(22) 207-3237
EMail: informacoes@ulp.pt
Website: http://www.ulp.pt

Reitor: Fernando dos Santos Neves EMail: reitoria@ulp.pt

Faculties
Aeronautics (Aeronautical and Aerospace Engineering; Air Transport); **Architecture and Urbanism** (Architecture; Regional Planning; Town Planning); **Communication, Arts and Information Technology** (Communication Arts; Communication Studies; Computer Engineering; Cultural Studies; Information Technology;

Modern Languages; Multimedia; Translation and Interpretation); **Economics and Management** (Economics; Human Resources; Industrial Design; Information Management; Management; Public Administration); **Health Sciences and Technology** (Gerontology; Health Sciences; Medical Technology); **Law** (Law); **Natural Sciences, Engineering and Technology** (Automation and Control Engineering; Civil Engineering; Electronic Engineering; Energy Engineering; Environmental Engineering; Safety Engineering; Systems Analysis); **Psychology** (Psychology); **Social and Human Sciences** (European Studies; International Relations; Political Sciences; Public Administration; Religious Studies; Sociology)

Institutes

Education (Educational Administration; Educational Sciences; Social and Community Services; Social Studies); **Educational Psychology** (Clinical Psychology; Educational Psychology); **Languages** (English; Modern Languages)

Main Language(s) of Instruction: Portuguese

Degrees and Diplomas: *Licenciado*; *Mestre*; *Doutor*

Last Updated: 17/10/11

MANUEL TEIXEIRA GOMES INSTITUTE

Instituto Superior Manuel Teixeira Gomes

Avenida Miguel Bombarda, 15, 8500-508 Portimão

Tel: +351(282) 450-430

Fax: +351(282) 450-439

EMail: informacoes@ismat.pt

Website: http://www.ismat.pt

Administrator: Damásio Manuel

Courses

Accountancy (Accountancy); **Business Administration** (Business Administration); **Communication Design** (Communication Arts; Design); **Computer Engineering** (Computer Engineering); **Graduate Studies** (Accountancy; Architecture; Business Administration; Community Health; Design; Educational and Student Counselling; Gynaecology and Obstetrics; Industrial and Organizational Psychology; Information Technology; Library Science; Management; Neurology; Nursing; Psychology; Psychotherapy; Taxation; Tourism); **Human Resources Management** (Human Resources); **Law** (Law); **Physical Education and Sports** (Physical Education; Sports); **Psychology** (Psychology)

History: Founded 1993. Acquired present status 2004.

Degrees and Diplomas: *Licenciado*; *Mestre*. Also postgraduate programmes

Last Updated: 05/10/11

MARIA ULRICH EARLY CHILDHOOD EDUCATORS' SCHOOL

Escola Superior de Educadores de Infância Maria Ulrich

Rua do Jardim à Estrela, 16, 1350-184 Lisboa

Tel: +351(21) 392-9560

Fax: +351(21) 392-9569

EMail: esei.mu@telepac.pt

Website: http://www.eseimu.pt

Presidente: Ana Maria de Jesus Levy Aires

International Relations: Maria Júlia Assis Lopes

EMail: esei@um.mail.telepac.pt

Courses

Education (Art Education; Cognitive Sciences; Preschool Education; Primary Education; Special Education); **Graduate Studies** (Preschool Education; Primary Education; Special Education)

History: Founded 1954.

Degrees and Diplomas: *Licenciado*; *Mestre*

Last Updated: 28/09/11

MIGUEL TORGA INSTITUTE

Instituto Superior Miguel Torga

Largo da Cruz de Celas, 1, 3000-132 Coimbra

Tel: +351(239) 488-030

Fax: +351(239) 488-031

EMail: ismt@ismt.pt

Website: http://www.ismt.pt

Courses

Accountancy and Auditing (Accountancy); **Business Computing** (Business Computing); **Communication Design** (Communication Arts; Design; Graphic Design); **Computer Science** (Computer Science); **Corporate Communication** (Communication Studies); **Human Resources Management** (Human Resources; Management); **Management** (Accountancy; Finance; Human Resources; Management; Marketing); **Multimedia** (Multimedia); **Psychology** (Psychology); **Social Communication** (Communication Studies; Social Studies); **Social Work** (Social and Community Services; Social Work)

Programmes

Graduate Studies (Clinical Psychology; Computer Networks; Computer Science; Gerontology; Human Resources; Industrial and Organizational Psychology; Psychoanalysis; Psychology; Psychotherapy; Social and Community Services; Social Psychology; Social Work)

History: Founded 1937.

International Co-operation: Participates in the Erasmus programme

Degrees and Diplomas: *Licenciado*; *Mestre*; *Doutor*. Also postgraduate and specialization programmes

Last Updated: 05/10/11

PIAGET INSTITUTE - ALMADA UNIVERSITY CAMPUS

Instituto Piaget - Campus Universitário de Almada

Quinta da Arreinela de Cima, 2800-305 Almada

Tel: +351(212) 946-250

Fax: +351(212) 946-251

EMail: info@almada.ipiaget.org

Website: http://www.ipiaget.org/almada/

Higher Institutes

Intercultural and Interdisciplinary Studies *(Instituto Superior de Estudos Interculturais e Transdisciplinares (ISEIT))* (Communication Studies; Computer Engineering; Food Technology; Management; Marketing; Music; Nutrition; Physical Therapy; Psychology; Safety Engineering; Sociology)

Higher Schools

Education *(Escola Superior de Educação (ESE))* (Education; Music Education; Primary Education)

Programmes

Graduate Studies (Art Education; Clinical Psychology; Cultural Studies; Educational Administration; Educational Psychology; Gerontology; Information Technology; Musical Instruments; Physical Education; Physical Therapy; Preschool Education; Primary Education; Safety Engineering; Secondary Education; Singing; Social Psychology; Special Education; Sports)

History: Founded 1986.

Degrees and Diplomas: *Licenciado*; *Mestre*. Also Postgraduate Diplomas

Last Updated: 27/09/11

PIAGET INSTITUTE - MACEDO DE CAVALEIROS ACADEMIC CAMPUS

Instituto Piaget - Campus Académico de Macedo de Cavaleiros

Rua Dr. António Oliveira Cruz, 5340-257 Macedo de Cavaleiros

Tel: +351(278) 420-040

Fax: +351(278) 425-430

EMail: info@macedo.ipiaget.org

Website: http://www.ipiaget.org/macedo-cavaleiros/

Higher Schools

Education *(Escola Superior de Educação (ESE)/Nordeste)* (Education; Educational Technology; Music Education; Social Studies); **Health Sciences** *(Escola Superior de Saúde (ESS))* (Health Sciences; Nursing; Physical Therapy; Public Health)

Programmes

Graduate Studies (Communication Disorders; Community Health; Educational Administration; Gerontology; Hygiene; Information

Technology; Nursing; Nutrition; Occupational Health; Pedagogy; Physical Therapy; Preschool Education; Primary Education; Public Health; Special Education; Speech Therapy and Audiology)

History: Founded 1990.

Degrees and Diplomas: *Licenciado*; *Mestre*. Also Postgraduate Diplomas

Last Updated: 28/09/11

PIAGET INSTITUTE - MIRANDELA UNIVERSITY CAMPUS

Instituto Piaget - Campus Universitário de Mirandela
Avenida 25 de Abril, 5370-202 Mirandela
Tel: +351(278) 200-150
Fax: +351(278) 265-203
EMail: info@mirandela.ipiaget.org
Website: http://www.ipiaget.org/mirandela/

Higher Institutes

Intercultural and Interdisciplinary Studies *(Instituto Superior de Estudos Interculturais e Transdisciplinares (ISEIT))* (Civil Engineering; Communication Studies; Engineering; Marketing; Music; Sociology; Visual Arts)

Programmes

Graduate Studies (Architectural Restoration; Banking; Conducting; Heritage Preservation; Insurance; Music; Musical Instruments; Physical Education; Primary Education; Secondary Education; Singing; Sociology; Sports; Visual Arts)

History: Founded 1997.

Degrees and Diplomas: *Licenciado*; *Mestre*. Also Postgraduate Diplomas

Last Updated: 28/09/11

PIAGET INSTITUTE - SANTO ANDRÉ UNIVERSITY CAMPUS

Instituto Piaget - Campus Universitário de Santo André
Bairro das Flores, Apartado 38, 7500-999 Vila Nova de Santo André
Tel: +351(269) 708-710
Fax: +351(269) 708-717
EMail: info@standre.ipiaget.org
Website: http://www.ipiaget.org/santo-andre/

Higher Institutes

Intercultural and Interdisciplinary Studies *(Instituto Superior de Estudos Interculturais e Transdisciplinares (ISEIT))* (Engineering; Environmental Studies; Hotel Management; Human Resources; Occupational Health; Petroleum and Gas Engineering; Physical Therapy; Safety Engineering; Tourism)

Programmes

Graduate Studies (Development Studies; Environmental Management; Information Technology; Occupational Health; Social Studies)

History: Founded 2002.

Degrees and Diplomas: *Licenciado*; *Mestre*. Also Postgraduate Diplomas

Last Updated: 28/09/11

PIAGET INSTITUTE - SILVES ACADEMIC CAMPUS

Instituto Piaget - Campus Académico de Silves
Enxerim, 8300-025 Silves
Tel: +351(282) 440-170
Fax: +351(282) 440-171
EMail: info@silves.ipiaget.org
Website: http://www.ipiaget.org/silves/

Higher Schools

Health Sciences *(Escola Superior de Saúde (ESS))* (Health Sciences; Nursing; Pharmacy; Physical Therapy)

Programmes

Graduate Studies (Educational Administration; Health Education; Nursing; Physical Therapy; Special Education; Surgery)

History: Founded 2002.

Degrees and Diplomas: *Licenciado*; *Mestre*. Also Postgraduate Diplomas

Last Updated: 28/09/11

PIAGET INSTITUTE - VILA NOVA DE GAIA ACADEMIC CAMPUS

Instituto Piaget - Campus Académico de Vila Nova de Gaia
Alameda Jean Piaget, Gulpilhares, 4405-678 Vila Nova de Gaia
Tel: +351(227) 537-600
Fax: +351(227) 537-681
EMail: info@gaia.ipiaget.org
Website: http://www.ipiaget.org/vn-gaia/

Higher Schools

Education *(Escola Superior de Educação (ESE))* (Education; English; Foreign Languages Education; Music Education; Physical Education; Preschool Education; Primary Education; Spanish); **Health Sciences** *(Escola Superior de Saúde (ESS))* (Dietetics; Health Sciences; Nursing; Pharmacy; Physical Therapy; Radiology)

Programmes

Graduate Studies (Educational Administration; Gynaecology and Obstetrics; Information Technology; Multimedia; Music Education; Nursing; Occupational Health; Pharmacy; Physical Education; Physical Therapy; Preschool Education; Primary Education; Special Education; Surgery)

History: Founded 1988.

Degrees and Diplomas: *Licenciado*; *Mestre*. Also Postgraduate Diplomas

Last Updated: 28/09/11

PIAGET INSTITUTE - VISEU UNIVERSITY CAMPUS

Instituto Piaget - Campus Universitário de Viseu
Estrada do Alto do Gaio, Galifonge, Lordosa, 3515-776 Viseu
Tel: +351(232) 910-100
Fax: +351(232) 910-180
EMail: info@viseu.ipiaget.org
Website: http://www.ipiaget.org/viseu/

Higher Institutes

Intercultural and Interdisciplinary Studies *(Instituto Superior de Estudos Interculturais e Transdisciplinares (ISEIT))* (Cultural Studies; Management; Music; Performing Arts; Psychology)

Higher Schools

Education *(Escola Superior de Educação (ESE))* (Education; English; Foreign Languages Education; Music Education; Nutrition; Spanish); **Health Sciences** *(Escola Superior de Saúde (ESS))* (Health Sciences; Nursing; Nutrition; Physical Therapy)

Programmes

Graduate Studies (Art Education; Clinical Psychology; Conducting; Cultural Studies; Education; Educational Psychology; Gerontology; Industrial and Organizational Psychology; Information Technology; Music Education; Musical Instruments; Nursing; Physical Education; Physical Therapy; Preschool Education; Primary Education; Rehabilitation and Therapy; Singing; Social Psychology; Special Education; Sports; Tourism)

History: Founded 1993.

Degrees and Diplomas: *Licenciado*; *Mestre*. Also Postgraduate Diplomas

Last Updated: 28/09/11

POLYTECHNIC AND UNIVERSITY COOPERATIVE

Cooperativa de Ensino Superior Politécnico e Universitário
R. Central de Gandra, 1317, 4585-116 Gandra
Tel: +351(224) 157-100
Fax: +351(224) 157-102
EMail: info@cespu.pt
Website: http://www.cespu.pt

President: António Manuel de Almeida Dias

Vice-President: Joaquim Manuel Merino da Rocha e Sousa

Degrees and Diplomas: *Licenciado*; *Mestre*. Also Postgraduate programmes

Last Updated: 18/10/11

INSTITUTE OF HEALTH SCIENCES - NORTH

INSTITUTO SUPERIOR DE CIÊNCIAS DA SAÚDE-NORTE

Rua Central de Gandra, 1317, Vilarinho de Cima, 4585-116 Gandra-Paredes

Tel: +351(224) 157-100

Fax: +351(224) 157-101

EMail: info@cespu.pt

Website: http://www.cespu.pt

Director: Jorge Brandão Proença EMail: jorge.proenca@cespu.pt

Departments

Dentistry (Dental Technology; Dentistry; Oral Pathology; Orthodontics; Periodontics; Surgery); **Pharmaceutical Sciences** (Cosmetology; Dermatology; Pharmacology); **Physical Education, Health and Sport** (Physical Education; Sports; Sports Medicine); **Postgraduate Studies** (Administration; Anatomy; Biochemistry; Biomedicine; Biotechnology; Cardiology; Cosmetology; Dental Technology; Dentistry; Dermatology; Forensic Medicine and Dentistry; Health Sciences; Management; Medicine; Nursing; Nutrition; Occupational Health; Pathology; Pharmacy; Physical Therapy; Pneumology; Psychology; Radiology; Rehabilitation and Therapy; Speech Therapy and Audiology; Sports); **Psychology** (Clinical Psychology; Educational Psychology; Gerontology; Neurosciences; Psychology); **Science** (Biochemistry; Biomedicine; Environmental Management; Environmental Studies; Food Science; Forensic Medicine and Dentistry; Health Sciences; Nutrition; Toxicology; Water Science)

History: Founded 1989.

Main Language(s) of Instruction: Portuguese

Degrees and Diplomas: *Licenciado*; *Mestre*. Also postgraduate programmes

POLYTECHNIC INSTITUTE OF HEALTH OF THE NORTH

INSTITUTO POLITÉCNICO DE SAÚDE DO NORTE

Rua Central de Gandra, 1317, 4585-116 Gandra

Tel: +351(224) 157-100

Fax: +351(224) 157-102

EMail: info@cespu.pt

Website: http://www.cespu.pt

Director: Jorge Brandão Proença EMail: jorge.proenca@cespu.pt

Schools

Health Sciences - Vale do Ave *(Escola Superior de Saúde do Vale do Ave)* (Cardiology; Neurology; Nursing; Pharmacy; Physiology; Pneumology; Podiatry; Public Health); **Health Sciences - Vale do Sousa** *(Escola Superior de Saúde do Vale do Sousa)* (Anatomy; Dental Technology; Nursing; Pathology; Physical Therapy; Podiatry)

Degrees and Diplomas: *Licenciado*; *Mestre*. Also Postgraduate programmes

POLYTECHNIC INSTITUTE OF GAYA

Instituto Superior Politécnico Gaya

Avenida dos Descobrimentos, 333, Santa Marinha, 4400-103 Vila Nova de Gaia

Tel: +351(223) 745-730

Fax: +351(220) 134-479

EMail: info@ispgaya.pt; secretaria@ispgaya.pt

Website: http://www.ispgaya.pt

Presidente: João de Freitas Ferreira EMail: jfreitas@ispgaya.pt

Courses

Graduate Studies (Art Education; Child Care and Development; Computer Networks; Energy Engineering; Environmental Engineering; Gerontology; Health Education; Human Resources; Industrial and Organizational Psychology; Preschool Education; Social and Community Services)

Schools

Education *(Escola Superior de Educação de Santa Maria)* (Education; Primary Education); **Science and Technology** (Accountancy; Automation and Control Engineering; Business Administration; Business Computing; Computer Engineering; Electronic Engineering; Environmental Engineering; Industrial Engineering; Industrial Management; Management; Mechanical Engineering; Telecommunications Engineering); **Social and Community Development** (Development Studies; Public Administration; Social and Community Services; Social Work; Tourism)

History: Founded 1988.

Main Language(s) of Instruction: Portuguese

Degrees and Diplomas: *Licenciado*; *Mestre*. Also postgraduate courses

Last Updated: 05/10/11

PORTUGUESE INSTITUTE OF ADMINISTRATION AND MARKETING OF AVEIRO

Instituto Português de Administração e Marketing de Aveiro

Rua das Cardadeiras - Esgueira, 3800-125 Aveiro

Tel: +351(234) 400-180

Fax: +351(234) 424-967

EMail: ipam@ipam.pt

Website: http://www.ipam.pt

Director IPAM Porto e Aveiro: Daniel Sá
EMail: daniel.sa@ipam.pt

Courses

Consumer Studies (Consumer Studies); **Marketing Management** (Management; Marketing)

History: Founded 1989.

Degrees and Diplomas: *Licenciado*; *Mestre*. Also postgraduate programmes

Last Updated: 30/09/11

PORTUGUESE INSTITUTE OF ADMINISTRATION AND MARKETING OF LISBON

Instituto Português de Administração e Marketing de Lisboa

Avenida Marechal Gomes da Costa 21, 1800-255 Lisboa

Tel: +351(218) 360-030

Fax: +351(218) 360-039

EMail: ipam@ipam.pt

Website: http://www.ipam.pt

Presidente da Direcção do IPAM: Filipe Ferrão
EMail: ferrao.filipe@ipam.pt

Director IPAM Lisboa: Luís Liz EMail: luis.liz@ipam.pt

Courses

Consumer Studies (Consumer Studies); **Marketing Management** (Management; Marketing)

History: Founded 1984.

Main Language(s) of Instruction: Portuguese

Degrees and Diplomas: *Licenciado*; *Mestre*. Also postgraduate programmes

Last Updated: 30/09/11

PORTUGUESE INSTITUTE OF ADMINISTRATION AND MARKETING OF MATOSINHOS

Instituto Português de Administração e Marketing de Matosinhos

Avenida da República, 594, 4450-238 Matosinhos

Tel: +351(229) 398-080

Fax: +351(219) 382-800

EMail: ipam@ipam.pt

Website: http://www.ipam.pt

Director IPAM Porto e Aveiro: Daniel Sá
EMail: daniel.sa@ipam.pt

Courses
Marketing Management (Management; Marketing)
History: Founded 1984.
Main Language(s) of Instruction: Portuguese
Degrees and Diplomas: *Licenciado*; *Mestre*. Also postgraduate programmes
Last Updated: 30/09/11

RIBEIRO SANCHES SCHOOL OF HEALTH

Escola Superior de Saúde Ribeiro Sanches
Rua do Telhal aos Olivais, n8 - 8a, 1900-693 Lisboa
Tel: +351(212) 621-060
EMail: informacoes@erisa.pt
Website: http://www.erisa.pt

Diretora: Adelina Motta da Cruz

Courses
Clinical Analysis and Public Health (Public Health); **Graduate Studies** (Child Care and Development; Community Health; Gynaecology and Obstetrics; Health Sciences; Immunology; Laboratory Techniques; Molecular Biology; Nursing; Paediatrics; Public Health; Radiology; Social and Preventive Medicine); **Nursing** (Nursing); **Pharmacy** (Pharmacy); **Radiology** (Radiology)
Degrees and Diplomas: *Licenciado*; *Mestre*. Also specialization and postgraduate diplomas
Last Updated: 29/09/11

SAINT JOSEPH OF CLUNY SCHOOL OF NURSING

Escola Superior de Enfermagem de São José de Cluny
Rampa da Quinta de Sant'Ana 22, Madeira, 9050-282 Funchal
Tel: +351(291) 743-444
Fax: +351(291) 743-626
EMail: geral@esesjcluny.pt
Website: http://www.esesjcluny.pt

Presidente: Irmã Maria Berta da Fonseca Soares

Courses
Graduate Studies (Communication Studies; Health Administration; Information Technology; Nursing; Pedagogy; Psychology); **Nursing** (Anatomy; Anthropology; Biochemistry; Biophysics; Epidemiology; Ethics; Microbiology; Nursing; Nutrition; Pathology; Pharmacology; Physiology; Psychology; Sociology)
History: Founded 1940.
Main Language(s) of Instruction: Portuguese
Degrees and Diplomas: *Licenciado*. Also post-licenciatura de especialização courses
Last Updated: 12/10/09

SANTA MARIA TEACHER TRAINING COLLEGE

Escola Superior de Educação de Santa Maria
Rua de Guerra Junqueira, 597-621, 4150-389 Porto
Tel: +351(22) 607-6830
Fax: +351(22) 607-3301
EMail: esesm@asm.mail.pt
Website: http://www.esesantamaria.com

Directora: Isabel Carvalho (1981-)
Tel: +351(22) 607-6837 EMail: esesm-dir@asm.mail.pt

Courses
Educational Management (Educational Administration); **Pre-primary Education** (Preschool Education)
History: Founded 1981.
Main Language(s) of Instruction: Portuguese
Degrees and Diplomas: *Licenciado*. Also postgraduate courses
Last Updated: 06/10/09

SCHOOL OF ART AND DESIGN

Escola Superior de Artes e Design
Avenida Calouste Gulbenkian, 4460-268 Senhora da Hora Matosinhos
Tel: +351(22) 957-8750
Fax: +351(22) 955-2643
EMail: info@esad.pt
Website: http://www.esad.pt

Director: Vitor Carvalho (1997-)

Courses
Art (Fine Arts; Jewelry Art; Multimedia); **Design** (Communication Arts; Design; Industrial Design; Interior Design); **Graduate Studies** (Communication Arts; Industrial Design; Interior Design)
History: Founded 1989.
Degrees and Diplomas: *Licenciado*; *Mestre*
Last Updated: 19/09/11

SCHOOL OF ARTS OF OPORTO

Escola Superior Artística do Porto
Largo de S. Domingos, 80, 4050-545 Porto
Tel: +351(22) 339-2130
Fax: +351(22) 339-2139
EMail: secretaria@esap.pt; geral@esap.pt
Website: http://www.esap.pt

Presidente: António Manuel da Silva Martins Teixeira

Courses
Animation and Cultural Production (Communication Arts; Cultural Studies; Fine Arts); **Cinema and Audiovisual** (Cinema and Television); **Cultural Management** (Art Management; Cultural Studies); **Design and Multimedia Communication** (Communication Arts; Design; Multimedia); **Fine Arts** (Fine Arts); **Theatre - Interpretation and Staging** (Acting; Display and Stage Design; Theatre); **Visual Arts - Photography** (Photography; Visual Arts)
Further Information: Also branch in Guimarães
History: Founded 1982.
Main Language(s) of Instruction: Portuguese
Degrees and Diplomas: *Licenciado*; *Mestre*; *Doutor*
Last Updated: 19/09/11

SCHOOL OF EDUCATION OF PAULA FRASSINETTI

Escola Superior de Educação de Paula Frassinetti
Rua Gil Vicente, 138-142, 4000-255 Porto
Tel: +351(22) 557-3420
Fax: +351(22) 550-8485
EMail: secretaria@esefrassinetti.pt
Website: http://www.esefrassinetti.pt

Director: José Luís de Almeida Gonçalves
Tel: +351(22) 557-3423 EMail: dir@esefrassinetti.pt

Chefe de Secção: Olivia da Silva Cunha Tel: +351(22) 557-3427

International Relations: Júlio Pereira de Sousa
Tel: +351(22) 783-268 EMail: julioepsousa@mail.telepac.pt

Courses
Graduate Studies (Educational Sciences; Literacy Education; Pedagogy; Preschool Education; Primary Education; Social and Community Services; Special Education; Teacher Training)

Departments
Basic Education (Primary Education); **Social Education** (Social Work); **Special Education** (Special Education)
History: Founded 1988.
Main Language(s) of Instruction: Portuguese
Degrees and Diplomas: *Licenciado*; *Mestre*. Also Pós-Graduações
Last Updated: 26/09/11

SCHOOL OF EDUCATION OF TORRES NOVAS

Escola Superior de Educação de Torres Novas
Quinta do Sto. António, 2350 Torres Novas
Tel: +351(249) 824-892
Fax: +351(249) 812-647
EMail: esetn@mail.telepac.pt
Website: http://www.esetn.pt

Director: João Paulo do Canto Rosa Moreira Lopes Fernandes

Administrador: Paulo Alexandre Santos Ferreira
EMail: paulo.ferreira@esetn.pt

Departments
Arts and Crafts (Handicrafts); **Educational Sciences**; **Information and Commmunication Technology** (Information Technology); **Languages and Literature** (Literature; Modern Languages); **Pedagogy and Teacher Training** (Leisure Studies; Pedagogy; Physical Education; Teacher Training); **Science and Mathematics** (Mathematics; Natural Sciences); **Social Sciences** (Social Sciences)

History: Founded 1988.

Main Language(s) of Instruction: Portuguese

Degrees and Diplomas: *Licenciado*; *Mestre*. Also postgraduate and specialization courses
Last Updated: 06/10/09

SCHOOL OF HEALTH OF ALCOITÃO

Escola Superior de Saúde do Alcoitão
Rua Conde Barão, 2649-506 Alcabideche
Tel: +351(21) 460-7450
Fax: +351(21) 460-7459
EMail: geral@essa.pt
Website: http://www.essa.pt

Director: António Duarte Amaro (1998-)

Administrador: José Manuel Henriques de Campos

International Relations: António Manuel Fernandes Lopes

Courses
Occupational Therapy (Occupational Therapy); **Physical Therapy** (Physical Therapy); **Speech Therapy** (Speech Therapy and Audiology)

History: Founded in 1966. Acquired present status 1994.

Main Language(s) of Instruction: Portuguese

Degrees and Diplomas: *Licenciado*; *Mestre*. Also postgraduate diplomas
Last Updated: 28/09/11

SCHOOL OF HEALTH OF THE PORTUGUESE RED CROSS

Escola Superior de Saúde da Cruz Vermelha Portuguesa
Av. de Ceuta 1, Edificio Urbiceuta 6° piso, 1350-125 Lisboa
Tel: +351(21) 361-6790
Fax: +351(21) 361-6799
EMail: secretaria@esscvp.eu
Website: http://www.esscvp.eu

Presidente: Luis Aires de Sousa

Courses
Health Studies (Cardiology; Gynaecology and Obstetrics; Health Administration; Nursing; Occupational Therapy; Physical Therapy; Pneumology; Radiology)

History: Founded 1993.

Main Language(s) of Instruction: Portuguese

Degrees and Diplomas: *Licenciado*; *Mestre*. Also specialization and postgraduate diplomas
Last Updated: 28/09/11

SCHOOL OF NURSING OF SANTA MARIA

Escola Superior de Enfermagem de Santa Maria
Travessa Antero Quental, 173/175, 4049-024 Porto
Tel: +351(225) 098-664
Fax: +351(225) 095-060
EMail: geral@esenfsm.pt
Website: http://www.esenfsm.pt

Presidente: Maria de Fátima Moreira Lopes Ferreira
EMail: conselho.direccao@esenfsm.pt

Vice-Presidente: Joaquina Patrício de Oliveira

Courses
Graduate Studies (Gynaecology and Obstetrics; Health Administration; Health Sciences; Nursing); **Nursing** (Nursing)

History: Founded 1952. Acquired present status 1991.

Main Language(s) of Instruction: Portuguese

Degrees and Diplomas: *Licenciado*. Also post-licenciatura de especialização courses
Last Updated: 28/09/11

SCHOOL OF NURSING OF SÃO FRANCISCO DAS MISERICÓRDIAS

Escola Superior de Enfermagem São Francisco das Misericórdias
Rua de Santa Marta 56, 1169-023 Lisboa
Tel: +351(21) 712-0913
Fax: +351(21) 716-1076
EMail: esesfm@esesfm.pt
Website: http://www.esesfm.pt

Directora: João Paulo Batalim Nunes EMail: esesfm@netcabo.pt

Chefe de Secção: Rosa Fernandes

International Relations: João Paulo Batalim Nunes
EMail: jpbn@cheerful.com

Courses
Nursing (Nursing)

History: Founded 1991.

Main Language(s) of Instruction: Portuguese

Degrees and Diplomas: *Licenciado*. Also specialization and postgraduate diplomas
Last Updated: 28/09/11

SCHOOL OF NURSING OF THE PORTUGUESE RED CROSS, OLIVEIRA DE AZEMÉIS

Escola Superior de Enfermagem da Cruz Vermelha de Oliveira de Azeméis
Rua Padre Joaquim Ferreira Salgado, Apartado 1002, 3720-277 Oliveira de Azeméis
Tel: +351(256) 661-430
Fax: +351(256) 661-439
EMail: secretaria@esecvpoa.com
Website: http://www.esecvpoa.com/netpa/page

Courses
Health Sciences (Gynaecology and Obstetrics; Health Administration; Health Sciences; Nursing; Psychiatry and Mental Health; Surgery)

History: Founded 2002.

Main Language(s) of Instruction: Portuguese

Degrees and Diplomas: *Licenciado*. Also post-licenciatura de especialização courses
Last Updated: 28/09/11

SCHOOL OF REAL ESTATE STUDIES

Escola Superior de Actividades Imobiliárias (ESAI)
Edifício Coopemi, Pr. Eduardo Mondlane, 7 C, 1900-677 Lisboa
Tel: +351(21) 839-2000
Fax: +351(21) 839-2060
EMail: esai@esai.pt
Website: http://www.esai.pt

Presidente: Leandro Pereira

Secretária Geral: Carla Freitas

Courses

Real Estate and Management (Management; Real Estate)

History: Founded 1990.

Main Language(s) of Instruction: Portuguese

Degrees and Diplomas: *Licenciado*; *Mestre*

Last Updated: 19/09/11

SCHOOL OF TECHNOLOGY AND FINE ARTS OF LISBON

Escola Superior de Tecnologias e Artes de Lisboa

Rua de Sto. Amaro 34, 1200-803 Lisboa
Tel: +351(213) 964-806
Fax: +351(213) 950-567
EMail: estal@estal.pt
Website: http://www.estal.pt

Presidente: Nuno Lobo Moreira

Courses

Communication Design (Communication Arts); **Cultural and Artistic Education** *(Beja)* (Art Education; Cultural Studies); **Jazz and Modern Music** (Jazz and Popular Music); **Performing Arts** (Performing Arts); **Postgraduate** (Computer Graphics; Computer Networks; Design; Industrial Design; Performing Arts)

History: Founded 1990.

Main Language(s) of Instruction: Portuguese

Degrees and Diplomas: *Licenciado*. Also postgraduate diplomas

Last Updated: 29/09/11

THE PORTUGUESE SCHOOL OF BANK MANAGEMENT

Instituto Superior de Gestão Bancária

Avenida Barbosa du Bocage, 87-R/C, 1050-030 Lisboa
Tel: +351(217) 916-210
Fax: +351(217) 955-234
EMail: isgb@isgb.pt
Website: http://www.isgb.pt

Presidente: Luís Vilhena da Cunha
Tel: +351(21) 793-0077, Fax: +351(21) 797-2917

Courses

Banking Management (Banking; Management); **Graduate Studies** (Banking; Business and Commerce; Finance; Management; Management Systems); **Information Management** (Information Management)

History: Founded 1991.

Degrees and Diplomas: *Licenciado*. Also postgraduate programmes

Last Updated: 05/10/11

UNIVERSITY INSTITUTE OF PSYCHOLOGICAL, SOCIAL AND LIFE SCIENCES

Instituto Universitário de Ciências Psicológicas, Sociais e da Vida

Rua Jardim do Tabaco, 34, 1149-041 Lisboa
Tel: +351(21) 881-1700
Fax: +351(21) 886-0954
EMail: info@ispa.pt
Website: http://www.ispa.pt

Reitor: Rui Pais de Oliveira EMail: reitor@ispa.pt

Secretário-Geral: José João Amoreira
EMail: secretario.geral@ispa.pt

Vice-Reitor: Francisco José Brito Peixoto
EMail: vice-reitor@ispa.pt

Courses

Community Development (Social and Community Services); **Graduate Studies** (Clinical Psychology; Educational Psychology; Educational Sciences; Industrial and Organizational Psychology; Psychology; Social Psychology); **Psychology** (Psychology); **Rehabilitation and Social Insertion** (Rehabilitation and Therapy; Social and Community Services)

History: Founded 1962 as Instituto de Ciências Pedagógicas. Renamed Instituto Superior de Psicologia Aplicada (ISPA) 1964. Acquired present status and title 2009.

Main Language(s) of Instruction: Portuguese

Degrees and Diplomas: *Licenciado*; *Mestre*; *Doutor*

Last Updated: 19/09/11

UNIVERSITY SCHOOL OF FINE ARTS OF COIMBRA

Escola Universitária das Artes de Coimbra (EUAC)

Campus Universitário da Arca, Lordemão, 3020-210 Coimbra
Tel: +351(239) 497-400
Fax: +351(239) 838-533
EMail: info@arca.pt
Website: http://www.arca.pt

Director: Carlos Sá Furtado (2004-)

Courses

Architecture (Architecture); **Communication Arts** (Communication Arts); **Design** (Furniture Design; Industrial Design; Interior Design); **Fine Arts** (Fine Arts); **Graduate Studies** (Architecture; Art Education; Communication Arts; Fine Arts; Graphic Design; Technology Education; Visual Arts)

History: Founded 1992.

Main Language(s) of Instruction: Portuguese

Degrees and Diplomas: *Licenciado*; *Mestre*

Last Updated: 29/09/11

VASCO DA GAMA UNIVERSITY SCHOOL

Escola Universitária Vasco da Gama

Mosteiro de São Jorge de Milreu, Estrada da Conraria, 3040-714 Castelo Viegas
Tel: +351(239) 444-444
Fax: +351(239) 437-628
EMail: geral@euvg.net
Website: http://www.euvg.net

Presidente: Luís Malheiro Vilar EMail: lmvilar@euvg.net

Secretário-Geral: Silvério de Sousa Mendes
EMail: ssousamendes@euvg.net

Departments

Architecture and Landscape Architecture (Architecture; Landscape Architecture); **Veterinary Science** (Veterinary Science)

History: Founded 2001.

Main Language(s) of Instruction: Portuguese

Degrees and Diplomas: *Licenciado*; *Mestre*

Last Updated: 29/09/11

Qatar

STRUCTURE OF HIGHER EDUCATION SYSTEM

Description:

Post-secondary education is provided by the government, government-owned companies, and private for-profit and not-for-profit providers. The University of Qatar, which is comprised of six colleges, is the only state academic institution. It is autonomous in both academic and financial matters. Its resources come from credits granted by the State. Its governing body is the University Board of Regents (advising on priorities, policies and quality).

Stages of studies:

University level first stage: Bachelor's degree
Bachelor's degree courses last for four years except in Engineering where they last for five years. All courses follow a credit system (between 12 and 18 credits per semester).

University level second stage: MBA and Diplomas
MBA courses last for 2 years after the Bachelor's degree. Postgraduate Diploma courses last between two and five semesters.

ADMISSION TO HIGHER EDUCATION

Admission to university-level studies:

Name of secondary school credential required: Al-Thanawiya Aama Qatari

Minimum score/requirement: 75% in the scientific track and 80% in the literary track. For admission to the Engineering and Administration Faculties, students must obtain 75%.

Alternatives to credentials: Commercial Secondary Examinations: Only the top achievers in these exams may proceed to the Faculty of Administration and Economics.
Technical or Industrial Secondary Examinations: Only the top achievers in these exams may proceed to the Faculty of Engineering.

Foreign students admission:

Quotas: 10 to 25% of places are reserved for foreign students.

Entrance exam requirements: Foreign students should have a High School Certificate or a recognized equivalent.

Language requirements: A good knowledge of Arabic is required for all major subjects, except Engineering courses, which are taught in English.

RECOGNITION OF STUDIES

Bodies dealing with recognition:

Institutional Standards Office, SEC

Director: Ahmed Al Ganahi
PO Box 35111
Doha
Tel: +974 456 0823
Fax: +974 427 0598
EMail: info@sec.gov.qa
WWW: http://www.english.education.gov.qa/section/sec/hei/iso

NATIONAL BODIES

Ministry of Education

Minister: Saad bin Ibrahim al-Mahmud
PO Box 80
Doha

Tel: +974 333444
Fax: +974 413886
WWW: http://www.moe.edu.qa/

Supreme Education Council - SEC
Secretary-General: Saad Bin Ibrahim Al Mahmoud
P. O Box 35111
Doha
Tel: +974 455 9362
Fax: +974 455 9380
EMail: info@sec.gov.qa
WWW: http://www.sec.gov.qa/
Role of national body: The Supreme Education Council determines education policy in Qatar. It monitors the progress of education reform efforts and oversees the Education and Evaluation Institutes, approving the Institutes' budgets and appointing the directors of each. The Supreme Education Council also approves the contracts for the Independent Schools.

Higher Education Institute, SEC
Chair: HH Sheikh Tamim Bin Hamad ben Khalifa Al Thani
PO Box 35111
Doha
Tel: +974 4456-07000
Fax: +974 4427-0492
EMail: aljanahi@sec.gov.qa
WWW: http://www.sec.gov.qa/En/SECInstitutes/HigherEducationInstitute/Pages/home.aspx
Role of national body: Through a variety of scholarship programmes, the Higher Education Institute (HEI) aims at supporting the development of higher, technical and vocational education by offering a variety of scholarship programmes so that students are able to pursue higher education and be prepared for the tasks they will face in applying to and attending top colleges and universities both locally and around the world.

Data for academic year: 2006-2007
Source: IAU from Qatar University, 2006. Bodies, 2012.

INSTITUTION

PUBLIC INSTITUTION

IAU UNIVERSITY OF QATAR (QU)

PO Box 2713, Al-Jameaa Street, Doha, al-Dafna
Tel: +974 485-2222
Fax: +974 483-5111
EMail: postmaster@qu.edu.qa
Website: http://www.qu.edu.qa

President: Sheikha Al-Misnad (2003-)
Tel: +974 485-2055, Fax: +974 483-5111
EMail: president@qu.edu.qa

Vice-President and Chief Financial Officer: Humaid A. Al-Madfa
Tel: +974 483-5055, Fax: +974 483-5222

Vice-President and Chief Academic Officer: Sheikha Jabor Al-Thani
Tel: +974 485-2083, Fax: +974 483-5222
EMail: vpacademic@qu.edu.qa

Colleges
Arts and Sciences (Arabic; Arts and Humanities; Biological and Life Sciences; Chemistry; Earth Sciences; Health Sciences; Information Sciences; Mass Communication; Mathematics; Modern Languages; Physics; Social Sciences); **Business and Economics** (Accountancy; Economics; Finance; Information Technology; Management; Marketing); **Education** (Art Education; Education; Educational Psychology; Educational Sciences; Physical Education; Psychology; Sports); **Engineering** (Chemical Engineering; Civil Engineering; Computer Engineering; Computer Science; Electrical Engineering; Industrial Engineering; Mechanical Engineering; Structural Architecture); **Law** (Law); **Pharmacy** (Pharmacy); **Sharia** (Islamic Law; Islamic Studies; Law)

Programmes
Arabic for Non-Native Speakers (Arabic); **International Affairs** (International Relations; International Studies)

Research Centres
Environmental Studies (Arts and Humanities; Documentation Techniques; History); **Gas Processing** (Petroleum and Gas Engineering)

History: Founded 1973 as Faculties of Education, acquired present status and title 1977. A State institution with academic and financial autonomy. Financially supported by the government.

Governing Bodies: Board of Regents

Academic Year: September to June (September-January; February-June)

Admission Requirements: Secondary school certificate (Thanawiya Aama) or recognized foreign equivalent

Main Language(s) of Instruction: Arabic, and English in some programmes

International Co-operation: With universities and institutions in Europe, USA, Africa, Middle East

Degrees and Diplomas: *Bachelor's Degree*: Administration and Economics, min. 125 credit hours; *Bachelor's Degree*: Arts ans Science, 120-125 credit hours; *Bachelor's Degree*: Engineering, 139 credit hours; *Bachelor's Degree*: Islamic Studies, 120 credit hours; *Bachelor's Degree*: Law, 123 credit hours; *Bachelor's Degree*: Pharmacy, 170 credit hours; *MBA*: Business and Economics, 36 credit hours; *Postgraduate Diploma*: Early Childhood Education; Special Education; Primary Educator Preparation Programme; Secondary Education; Teacher Assistant Programme, 27-30 credit hours. Master's Degree in Education (Educational Leadership and Special Education), 33 credit hours

Student Services: Academic counselling, Canteen, Cultural centre, Foreign student adviser, Health services, Nursery care, Social counselling, Sports facilities

Student Residential Facilities: For 1000 foreign students

Special Facilities: Oceanographic Research Vessel; MV Mukhtabar Albihar; Material Science Unit; Central Laboratories Unit; GIS Unit

Libraries: 351,418 vols (Arabic, 229,279; English, 122,139)

Publications: Book of Abstracts (Engineering) *(biennially)*; Bulletin of the Faculty of Education *(annually)*; Bulletin of the Faculty of Humanities and Social Sciences *(annually)*; Bulletin of the Faculty of Islamic Studies *(annually)*; Engineering Journal of Qatar University *(annually)*; Fruits of Knowledge (Public lectures) *(annually)*; Journal of Administrative Sciences and Economics *(annually)*; Qatar University Science Journal *(annually)*

Last Updated: 29/11/11

Romania

STRUCTURE OF HIGHER EDUCATION SYSTEM

Description:

Higher education in Romania is offered in both public and private higher education institutions. These include universities, academies and colleges organized in specialized departments. In accordance with its objectives, university education comprises: short term higher education offered by university colleges (3 years), long term higher education (4 to 6 years); postgraduate higher education (1 to 2 years) and doctorate studies. Public and private accredited higher education institutions are coordinated by the Ministry of Education, Research and Youth. University autonomy is fully guaranteed. Private higher education is an alternative to public education. It is subject to an accreditation process. Accredited private institutions may obtain state support. Since 2004, the Bologna process is being implemented in Romania.

Stages of studies:

University level first stage: *Diploma de Licenta; Diploma de Inginer; Diploma de urbanist, Diploma de arhitect*
The first stage of university-level study comprises short-term (3 years) or long-term degrees (4 to 6 years, according to the field of study).

University level second stage: *Diploma de Master; Certificat de atestare a competentelor profesionale*
The second stage is composed of diplomas awarded after one to two years of studies which may include research work.

University level third stage: *Diploma de Doctor*
The Doctorate is the highest postgraduate stage of specialization and lasts for 3 years. There are scientific and professional Doctorates. Extra-mural courses can also be offered in main foreign languages. Candidates who have passed the examination for the Doctor's degree (Doctorate) are awarded the Diplomã de Doctor în Stiințe.

University level fourth stage: *Atestat de studii postdoctorale*
Postdoctoral programmes are for people who have obtained a Doctorate 5 years at most prior to admission to the programme and want to improve their knowledge by studying at another institution than where they obtained their Doctorate. Postdoctoral studies have a duration of 1 year.

Distance higher education:
A National Centre for Open Distance Education has been created in all universities.

ADMISSION TO HIGHER EDUCATION

Admission to university-level studies:

Name of secondary school credential required: Diplomă de Bacalaureat

Minimum score/requirement: 6

For entry to: University

RECOGNITION OF STUDIES

Quality assurance system:

All accredited courses of studies and credentials obtained from a public or private higher education institution are recognized by the State.

Bodies dealing with recognition:

Centrul Naţional de Recunoaştere şi Echivalare a Diplomelor (National Centre for Diploma Recognition)

Director: Gianina Chirazi
Ministry of Education, Research, Youth and Sports
Str. Gen. Berthelot 28-30
Sector 1
Bucharest 010168
Tel: +40(21) 405 6322
Fax: +40(21) 313 1013
WWW: http://www.cnred.edu.ro
Deals with credential recognition for entry to institution: yes
Deals with credential recognition for entry to profession: yes

NATIONAL BODIES

Ministerul Educaţiei, Cercetării, Tineretului şi Sportului (Ministry of Education, Research, Youth and Sport)

Minister: Ecaterina Andronescu
Str. Gen. Berthelot 28-30
Sector 1
Bucharest 010168
Tel: +40(21) 405 6200
WWW: http://www.edu.ro
Role of national body: Management of the national system of education and research (cf. Government Decision no. 223/2005 on the organization and functioning of the Ministry).

Agenţia Română de Asigurare a Calităţii în Învăţământul Superior - ARACIS (Romanian Agency for Quality Assurance in Higher Education)

President: Ioan Curtu
Secretary-General: Mihai Aristotel Ungureanu
Str. Spiru Haret
nr. 12
Bucharest 010176
Tel: +40(21) 206 7600
Fax: +40(21) 312 7135
EMail: mail@aracis.ro
WWW: http://www.aracis.ro/
Role of national body: ARACIS, in the accreditation field, has the following tasks: a) to develop regularly the methodology and standards of accreditation for programmes and higher education providers to be approved by the Ministry; b) to assess, upon request or of its own initiative, higher education providers and their programmes to propose authorization, according to which the Ministry will develop the legislative provision for the establishment of higher education institutions.
In the field of quality assurance; ARACIS has, among others, the following tasks: a) to develop and regularly review national standards and performance indicators to assess and ensure higher education quality; b) to cooperate with the Ministry and ARACIP to develop policies and actions to improve higher education quality in Romania; c) to organize consultations with HEIs to put forwad the priorities in the field of quality assurance; d) to develop its own procedures for external quality assessment; e) to conclude agreements for the provision of external quality assessment; f) to cooperate with other similar foreign agencies to develop and implement effective measures to improve higher education quality; etc.

Data for academic year: 2011-2012
Source: IAU from the National Centre for Diploma Recognition, Ministry of Education, Research, Youth and Sport, 2011. Bodies, 2012.

INSTITUTIONS

PUBLIC INSTITUTIONS

1 DECEMBER 1918 UNIVERSITY OF ALBA IULIA

Universitatea 1 Decembrie 1918 din Alba Iulia (UAB)
Gabriel Bethlen Street nr. 5, 510009 Alba Iulia
Tel: +40(258) 80-61-30
Fax: +40(258) 81-26-30
EMail: cond@uab.ro
Website: http://www.uab.ro

Rector: Moise Ioan Achim (2004-)
Tel: +40(258) 81-15-12, Fax: +40(258) 81-03-67
EMail: achimmoise@yahoo.com

Director, Administration: Gheorghe Marculet (1999-)
Tel: +40(258) 81-03-67, Fax: +40(258) 81-03-67

International Relations: Mircea Risteiu, Director of the International Relations and European Integration Department
Tel: +40(258) 80-60-42, Fax: +40(258) 80-60-42
EMail: relint@uab.ro; risteiuexamen@uab.ro

Faculties
History and Philology (Archaeology; English; French; Heritage Preservation; History; Literature; Museum Studies; Philology; Prehistory; Romanian); **Law and Social Sciences**; **Orthodox Theology** (Literature; Pastoral Studies; Romanian; Social Work; Theology); **Sciences** (Accountancy; Banking; Business Administration; Business and Commerce; Computer Science; Economics; Electronic Engineering; Environmental Engineering; Finance; Management; Management Systems; Marketing; Service Trades; Surveying and Mapping; Tourism)

History: Founded 1991.

Admission Requirements: Secondary school leaving certificate (Bacalaureat) or recognized equivalent, and entrance examination

Main Language(s) of Instruction: Romanian

International Co-operation: Participates in Erasmus/Socrates student and teaching staff exchange programmes, International Reserarch programmes (FP6-CAENTI Project)

Accrediting Agencies: Ministry of Education and Research

Degrees and Diplomas: *Diploma de Licență*; *Diplomă de Master*; *Diplomă de Doctor*. Also certificates of continuing education studies

Student Services: Academic counselling, Canteen, Cultural centre, Employment services, Foreign student adviser, Foreign Studies Centre, Health services, Language programs, Nursery care, Social counselling, Sports facilities

Student Residential Facilities: Yes

Special Facilities: Museum

Libraries: University Library; Museum Library

Publications: Acta Universitatis Apulensis, Series: Philologica, Jurispridentua, Paedagogica, Psychologica, Mathematics-Informatics, Asistenta Sociala, Historica *(annually)*; Bulletin of Students' Research Groups *(annually)*; Journal of Mathematics and Informatics *(annually)*; Procont ALBA IULIA *(biannually)*; RevCad Journal *(annually)*

Last Updated: 08/09/11

ALEXANDRU IOAN CUZA POLICE ACADEMY OF BUCHAREST

Academia de Poliție 'Alexandru Ioan Cuza' din București
Aleea Privighetorilor Street, nr. 1A, Sector 1, 014031 București
Tel: +40(21) 317-55-23
Fax: +40(21) 317-55-17
EMail: secretar@academiadepolitie.ro
Website: http://www.academiadepolitie.ro/

Rector, Chestor principal de Poliție: Iamandiloan Liviu Taut
Tel: +40(21) 317-55-23 Ext: 17,100
EMail: ioan.taut@academiadepolitie.ro

Secretar SefSecretar Sef: Marius Chervase

Faculties
Archive Studies (Archiving); **Firefighting** (Construction Engineering; Engineering; Fire Science); **Police Training** (Civil Security)

History: Created in 1991. Acquired current title and statue 2004.

Admission Requirements: Entrance exam

Main Language(s) of Instruction: Romanian

Accrediting Agencies: National Council for Academic Assessment and Accreditation; Ministry of the Interior and Administration

Degrees and Diplomas: *Diploma de Licență*; *Diplomă de Master*; *Diplomă de Doctor*

Last Updated: 13/09/11

ALEXANDRU IOAN CUZA UNIVERSITY OF IAȘI

Universitatea Alexandru Ioan Cuza din Iași (UAIC)
Bulevardul Carol nr. 11, 700506 Iași
Tel: +40(232) 20-10-10
Fax: +40(232) 20-12-01
EMail: rectorat@uaic.ro
Website: http://www.uaic.ro

Rector: Vasile Ișan
Tel: +40(232) 20-10-11 EMail: birou_senat@uaic.ro

General Manager: Bogdan-Eduard Pleșcan

International Relations: Henri Luchian, Vice-Rector
Tel: +40(232) 20-10-13 EMail: hluchian@uaic.ro

Centres
European Studies (Anthropology; Economics; European Studies; Medieval Studies; Modern History)

Faculties
Biology (Agricultural Engineering; Biological and Life Sciences; Biology; Biotechnology; Ecology; Environmental Studies; Food Technology; Genetics; Molecular Biology; Natural Sciences); **Chemistry** (Biochemistry; Biological and Life Sciences; Chemistry; Computer Science; Environmental Studies; Natural Sciences; Science Education); **Computer Science** (Computer Science); **Economics and Business Administration** (Business Administration; Economics); **Geography and Geology** (Environmental Studies; Geochemistry; Geography; Geological Engineering; Geology; Meteorology; Rural Planning; Soil Science; Surveying and Mapping; Tourism); **History** (Archaeology; Archiving; Art History; Cultural Studies; European Studies; Hebrew; History; International Relations; Jewish Studies; Mediterranean Studies; Museum Studies; Restoration of Works of Art; Tourism); **Law** (Commercial Law; Criminal Law; European Union Law; International Law; Law); **Letters** (American Studies; Arts and Humanities; Communication Studies; Comparative Literature; Cultural Studies; English; Foreign Languages Education; French; French Studies; German; Germanic Studies; Italian; Journalism; Latin; Linguistics; Literature; Modern Languages; Multimedia; Romanian; Russian; Spanish; Terminology; Translation and Interpretation; Writing); **Mathematics** (Computer Science; Mathematics; Mathematics and Computer Science; Mechanics; Statistics); **Orthodox Theology** (Bible; History of Religion; Holy Writings; Orthodox Theology; Pastoral Studies; Religious Art; Theology); **Philosophy and Social-Political Sciences** (Philosophy; Political Sciences; Social Sciences); **Physical Education and Sports** (Leisure Studies; Physical Education; Physical Therapy; Sports; Sports Management); **Physics** (Physics); **Psychology and Education Sciences** (Adult Education; Clinical Psychology; Communication Studies; Educational Sciences; Human Resources; Management; Pedagogy; Preschool Education; Primary Education; Psychology; Psychotherapy; Special Education); **Roman-Catholic Theology** (Catholic Theology; Theology)

Further Information: Also International Summer Courses in Romanian Language and Civilization (first 3 weeks of July)

History: Founded 1860 as University of Iași on former Mihail Sturdza Academy created 1835, named after Alexandru Ioan Cuza, the Ruler of the Union. In 1937 two branches of the Faculty of Agricultural Sciences (Electro-Technical Education and Technological Chemistry) were reorganized within the 'Gheorghe Asachi'

Polytechnic Institute of Iași and became an independent institution. A State Institution.

Governing Bodies: Senate

Academic Year: September to June (September-February; February-June)

Admission Requirements: Secondary school certificate (Bacalaureat) and entrance examination

Main Language(s) of Instruction: Romanian

International Co-operation: With universities in Belgium, Bulgaria, Canada, Chile, China, France, Germany, Greece, Hungary, Israel, Italy, Japan, Republic of Moldova, Netherlands, Norway, Singapore, Spain, Switzerland, Tunisia, Turkey, Ukraine and USA. Also participates in the Socrates programme.

Accrediting Agencies: Ministry of Education and Research

Degrees and Diplomas: *Diploma de Licență*; *Diplomă de Master*; *Diplomă de Doctor*. Also postgraduate Diplomas 1-2 yrs

Student Services: Academic counselling, Canteen, Cultural centre, Foreign student adviser, Foreign Studies Centre, Health services, Language programs, Sports facilities

Student Residential Facilities: Yes

Special Facilities: National History Museum; Museum of Palaeontology; Museum of Crystallography. Botanical Garden. Marine Biology Research Unit of Agigea-Constanța and Biological Research Unit of Potoci-Neamț

Libraries: Central Library; faculty libraries, total, c. 2.7m. vols

Publications: Annales scientifiques de l'Université, Academic Research Papers *(annually)*; Lassyer Beltrage zur Germanistik (in German) *(annually)*; Quality Assurance Review *(annually)*; Slavonic Studies *(annually)*; Studia Antiqua et Archaeologica, P *(annually)*; V. Adamachi, Natural Sciences Review *(annually)*; Yearbook of 'A.D. Xenopol' Institute of History *(annually)*

Press or Publishing House: Alexandru Ioan Cuza University Press

Academic Staff *2010-2011*: Total 823

Student Numbers *2010-2011*: Total 37,492

Last Updated: 16/09/11

AUREL VLAICU UNIVERSITY OF ARAD

Universitatea Aurel Vlaicu din Arad (UAV)

P.O. Box 2/158, Bvd. Revoluției nr. 77, 310130 Arad
Tel: +40(257) 28-30-10
Fax: +40(257) 28-00-70
EMail: rectorat@uav.ro
Website: http://www.uav.ro/

Rector: Lizica Mihuț (2008-)

General Secretary: Nicoleta Dumitrascu

International Relations: Florentina Muntean, Vice-Rector, International Relations EMail: florentina.munteanu@uav.ro

Departments

Continuing Education *(Ziridava)*; **Open and Distance Learning**

Faculties

Applied Sciences (Biology; Chemistry; Mathematics; Mathematics and Computer Science); **Design** (Design); **Economic Studies** (Accountancy; Finance; Management; Marketing); **Educational Sciences and Social Work** (Educational Sciences; Social Work); **Engineering** (Computer Engineering; Engineering Management; Industrial Engineering; Industrial Management; Mechanical Engineering); **Food Engineering, Tourism and Environment Protection** (Environmental Studies; Food Technology; Tourism); **Humanities and Social Sciences** (English; German; Modern Languages; Romanian; Social Sciences); **Physical Education and Sports** (Physical Education; Sports); **Theology** (Theology)

Institutes

Economics (Economics); **European Studies** (European Studies); **Research**; **Technology and Business**

History: Founded 1812 as Pedagogical Institute, became Faculty of Technical Engineers 1972, and acquired present status and title 1990, with various Faculties and Departments being added gradually.

Governing Bodies: Senate, comprising 49 members.

Academic Year: October to June (October-January; February-June)

Admission Requirements: Secondary school certificate (Bacalaureat) or recognized equivalent, and entrance examination

Main Language(s) of Instruction: Romanian

International Co-operation: LLP/ Erasmus – Italy, Portugal, Germany, France, Belgium, Spain, Cyprus, Czech Republic, Slovakia, Poland, Denmark, Hungary and Turkey.

Accrediting Agencies: Ministry of Education and Research

Degrees and Diplomas: *Diploma de Licență*; *Diplomă de Master*. Also specialisation programmes in Engineering.

Student Services: Academic counselling, Foreign student adviser, Foreign Studies Centre, Health services, Language programs, Social counselling, Sports facilities

Student Residential Facilities: Yes

Special Facilities: Museums. Art Galleries. Cinemas. Theatres and Concert Halls.

Libraries: 200,000 vols

Publications: Akademos *(annually)*; Educația Plus *(annually)*; Electrotechnical, Electronics, Automatic Control and Computer), Scientific Bulletin *(annually)*; Food Science and Technology, Scientific Bulletin *(annually)*; Mechanical, Scientific Bulletin *(annually)*; Teologia *(quarterly)*; Textile, Scientific Bulletin *(annually)*

Press or Publishing House: University Publishing House

Academic Staff *2007-2008*	MEN	WOMEN	TOTAL
FULL-TIME	132	112	**244**
PART-TIME	–	–	**114**
STAFF WITH DOCTORATE			
FULL-TIME	84	57	**141**
Student Numbers *2007-2008*			
All (Foreign Included)	–	–	**15,138**

Last Updated: 08/09/11

BABEȘ-BOLYAI UNIVERSITY OF CLUJ-NAPOCA

Universitatea Babeș-Bolyai din Cluj-Napoca (UBB)

Strada Mihail Kogălniceanu nr. 1, 400084 Cluj-Napoca
Tel: +40(264) 40-53-22 +40(264) 40-53-69
Fax: +40(264) 59-19-06
EMail: staff@staff.ubbcluj.ro
Website: http://www.ubbcluj.ro

Rector: Ioan Aurel Pop (2012-)
Tel: +40(264) 40-53-00, Fax: +40(264) 59-19-06
EMail: rector@ubbcluj.ro

International Relations: Toader Nicoara, Prorector, International Relations
Tel: +40(264) 42-97-62 EMail: nicoara.toader@ubbcluj.ro

Centres

Languages Studies *(LINGUA and ALPHA)* (Modern Languages)

Departments

Teacher Training (Teacher Training)

Faculties

Biology and Geology (Biology; Geology); **Business** (Business Administration); **Chemistry and Chemical Engineering** (Chemical Engineering; Chemistry); **Economics and Business Management** (Business Administration; Cooking and Catering; Economics; Management; Tourism); **Environmental Sciences** (Environmental Studies); **European Studies** (European Studies); **Geography** (Geography); **Greek Catholic Theology** (Catholic Theology; Theology); **History and Philosophy** (Ancient Civilizations; Archaeology; History; Logic; Modern History; Philosophical Schools; Philosophy; Political Sciences; Social Work; Sociology); **Law** (Law); **Letters** (Arts and Humanities; Classical Languages; French; Hungarian; Linguistics; Literature; Romance Languages; Romanian; Slavic Languages; Spanish; Theatre); **Mathematics and Computer Science** (Mathematics and Computer Science); **Orthodox Theology** (Orthodox Theology); **Physical Education and Sports** (Physical Education; Sports); **Physics** (Electrical Engineering; Mechanical Engineering; Nuclear Physics; Optics; Physics; Solid State Physics; Special Education; Thermal Physics); **Political,**

Administrative and Communication Sciences (Communication Studies; Journalism; Political Sciences; Public Administration); **Protestant Theology** (Theology); **Psychology and Educational Sciences** (Educational Sciences; Psychology); **Roman Catholic Theology** (Catholic Theology; Theology); **Sociology and Social Work** (Social Work; Sociology); **Theatre and Television**

Sections

Distance Learning (Administration; Arts and Humanities; Business Administration; Communication Studies; Economics; Educational Sciences; Ethnology; Finance; History; International Relations; Management; Marketing; Political Sciences; Psychology; Social and Community Services; Statistics)

History: Founded 1959 by the merging of the Universitatea 'Victor Babeş' (founded 1919), and the Universitatea 'Bolyai Janos', (founded 1945). A State Institution.

Governing Bodies: University Senate, comprising 77 members; Senate Board, comprising 8 members; Faculty Councils

Academic Year: September to June (September-January; February-June)

Admission Requirements: Secondary school certificate (Bacalaureat) or equivalent, and entrance examination

Fees: (US Dollars): Foreign students, c. 320 per month

Main Language(s) of Instruction: Romanian, Hungarian, German, English, French

International Co-operation: Participates in the Phare, Tempus, Copernicus, Peco and Socrates programmes

Accrediting Agencies: Ministry of Education and Research

Degrees and Diplomas: *Diploma de Licenţă*: 4-5 yrs; *Diplomă de Master*: Language and Literature; Cultural Studies; Applied Modern Languages; International Relations and European Studies; Cultural Studies; Business Administration; Physical Education and Sport; Theology; Environmental Science; Dramatic Arts; Law; History; Communication Sciences; International Relations and European Studies; Political Sciences; Philosophy; Sociology; Social Assistance; Psychology; Educational Sciences; Communication Sciences; Political Sciences; Administrative Sciences; Mathematics; Physics; Chemistry and Chemical Engineering; Geography; Biology; Geology; Business Administration; Economics and International Bussiness; Economics; Finance; Accountancy; Management; Marketing; Cybernetics, Statistics and Economic Informatics; *Diplomă de Doctor*. Also Postdoctoral Studies programme in Psychotherapy and Applied Mental Health.

Student Services: Academic counselling, Canteen, Cultural centre, Employment services, Foreign Studies Centre, Health services, Social counselling, Sports facilities

Student Residential Facilities: For c. 700 students

Special Facilities: Botany Museum; Zoology Museum; Palaeontology Museum; Mineralogy Museum. Botanical Garden

Libraries: Central University Library, 3.5m. vols; 8 specialized libraries, c. 1m

Publications: Colocvia; Contribuţii Botanice; Matematica; Studia Universitatis 'Babeş-Bolyai' (13 series)

Press or Publishing House: University Press

Student Numbers *20102011*: Total: c. 50,000
Last Updated: 23/04/12

BANAT'S UNIVERSITY OF AGRICULTURAL SCIENCES AND VETERINARY MEDICINE OF TIMIŞOARA

Universitatea de Ştiinte Agricole şi Medicină Veterinară a Banatului din Timişoara (USAMVBT)

Calea Aradului no, 119, 300645 Timişoara
Tel: +40(256) 49-40-23
Fax: +40(256) 20-02-96
EMail: usabtm@mail.dnttm.ro
Website: http://www.usab-tm.ro

Rector: Alexandru Pavel Moisuc
Tel: +40(256) 27-70-09, Fax: +40(256) 20-02-96
EMail: alex_moisuc@yahoo.com

Secretar şef: Enikö Nădăşan
Tel: +40(256) 27-72-22 EMail: eniko.nadasan@usab-tm.ro

International Relations: Horia Cernescu, Prorector and Coordonator International Relations
Tel: +40(256) 27-70-73
EMail: Horia.Cernescu@fmvt.ro; rel_int_usamvbt@gmail.ro

Departments

Teacher Training and Social and Human Sciences

Faculties

Agricultural Management (Agricultural Business; Agricultural Economics; Agricultural Engineering; Agricultural Management; Agriculture; Agronomy; Animal Husbandry; Rural Studies; Tourism); **Agriculture** (Agricultural Engineering; Agricultural Equipment; Agriculture; Agrobiology; Biology; Biotechnology; Environmental Engineering; Plant and Crop Protection); **Animal Husbandry and Biotechnology** (Animal Husbandry; Biotechnology; Fishery); **Food Technology** (Biochemistry; Food Science; Food Technology; Safety Engineering); **Horticulture and Forestry** (Agricultural Engineering; Forestry; Genetics; Horticulture; Landscape Architecture); **Veterinary Science** (Veterinary Science)

History: Founded 1945 as Faculty of Timişoara Technical Institute, became an independent Institution and acquired present status and title 1948.

Governing Bodies: Senat

Academic Year: September to July (September-January; February-July)

Admission Requirements: Secondary school certificate (Bacalaureat) or foreign equivalent, and entrance examination for foreign students

Fees: (US Dollars): Foreign students, c. 320 per annum

Main Language(s) of Instruction: Romanian

Accrediting Agencies: Ministry of Education and Research

Degrees and Diplomas: *Diploma de Licenţă*: Agronomy; Environmental Engineering; Biology; Engineering; Geodesy; Horticulture; Biotechnology; Forestry; Agricultural Engineering and Management; Agro-food Engineering and Management; Veterinary Medicine; Industrial engineering; Animal Husbandry; *Certificat de atestare a competentelor profesionale*: Safety Eng.; Vet. Medicine; Animal Protection; Agric. Ecology; Epidemiology, Statistics and Vet. Prognostic; Pharmacy and Toxicology; Nutrition; Vet./Admin. Law; Management; Vet. Forensic Medicine; Food Safety; Traceability in Vet. Medicine; Public Health; *Diplomă de Master*: Agricultural Sciences; Veterinary Medicine; Agricultural Management; Animal Husbandry and Biotechnology; *Diplomă de Doctor*: Agriculture; Horticulture and Forestry; Agricultural Management; Veterinary Medicine; Food Technology; Animal Breeding and Biotechnology

Student Services: Academic counselling, Canteen, Cultural centre, Foreign student adviser, Foreign Studies Centre, Health services, Language programs, Social counselling, Sports facilities

Student Residential Facilities: Yes

Special Facilities: Biological Garden. Experimental Station

Libraries: Central Library, 191,114 vols

Publications: Agricultura Banatului, Scientific Articles *(monthly)*; Lucrări ştiinţifice, Faculty scientific papers *(annually)*

Press or Publishing House: Agroprint Publishing House
Last Updated: 20/09/11

BUCHAREST ACADEMY OF ECONOMIC STUDIES

Academia de Studii Economice din Bucureşti (ASE)

Piaţa Romană nr. 6, Sectorul 1, Postal office 22, 010374 Bucureşti
Tel: +40(21) 319-19-00
Fax: +40(21) 319-18-99
EMail: rectorat@crc.ase.ro
Website: http://www.ase.ro/engl_site/index.asp

Rector: Ion Gh. Rosca (2004-)
Tel: +40(21) 319-19-19 EMail: Ion.Rosca@ase.ro

Chief Secretary: Adina Dragomir
Tel: +40(21) 319-19-65, Fax: +40(21) 319-18-99
EMail: Adina.Dragomir@ase.ro

Vice-Rector, Co-ordinating Administrative, Patrimonial and Financial Activities: Ion Plumb
Tel: +40(21) 319-20-22, Fax: +40(21) 319-18-99
EMail: Ion.Plumb@ase.ro

International Relations: Viorel Lefter, Vice-Rector, International relations and European Integration
Tel: +40(21) 319-20-25, Fax: +40(21) 319-20-25
EMail: Viorel.Lefter@ase.ro

Faculties

Accounting and Management Information Systems (Accountancy; Business Administration; Finance; Information Management; Information Sciences; Law); **Agrifcultural Food Production and Environment Economics** *(AEE)* (Agricultural Business; Agricultural Economics; Economics; Environmental Studies; Food Technology); **Business Administration** *(in Foreign Languages)* (Business Administration); **Commerce** (Business Administration; Business and Commerce; Marketing; Service Trades; Tourism); **Economic Cybernetics, Statistics and Informatics** *(ECSI)* (Business Computing; Computer Science; Economics; Mathematics; Statistics); **Economics** (Economics); **Finance, Insurance, Banking and Stock Exchange** *(FIBSE)* (Banking; Business Administration; Finance; Insurance); **International Business and Economics** *(IBE)* (International Business); **Management** (Business Administration; Economics; Management; Philosophy; Political Sciences; Public Administration; Sociology); **Marketing** (Business Administration; Marketing)

Graduate Schools

Management - SPPM *(Romanian-Canadian MBA Programme)* (Business Administration; Management)

Institutes

Economic Development - INDE *(Romanian-French MBA Programme)*

Programmes

Management Mindset *(Romanian-German MBA Programme)*

History: Founded 1913 as Academy of Advanced Commercial and Industrial Studies, acquired present status and title 1967. Also branch in Buzău.

Governing Bodies: Senate

Admission Requirements: Secondary school certificate (bacalaureat) and entrance examination

Fees: (Lei): for Romanian students: 14,000,000 per annum; (US Dollars): for foreign students 320 per month

Main Language(s) of Instruction: Romanian, English, French, German

International Co-operation: Participates in the Tempus and Phare programmes

Accrediting Agencies: Ministry of Education and Research

Degrees and Diplomas: *Diploma de Licenţă*; *Diplomă de Master*, *Diplomă de Doctor*

Student Services: Academic counselling, Cultural centre, Employment services, Foreign student adviser, Foreign Studies Centre, Health services, Language programs, Social counselling, Sports facilities

Libraries: c. 749,846 volumes; 1,250 reference works, 146 journals, Computer Labs

Publications: Comparative Management *(quarterly)*; Dialogos, Literature *(biennially)*; Economic Informatics *(quarterly)*; Economics *(biennially)*; Public Management and Administration *(annually)*; Romanian Economic Journal *(biennially)*; Scientific Bulletin *(annually)*

Last Updated: 29/01/10

BUCHAREST NATIONAL UNIVERSITY OF ARTS

Universitatea Nationala de Arte din Bucureşti (UNA)
General Budişteanu Street nr. 19, Sectorul 1, 010773 Bucureşti
Tel: +40(21) 312-5197
Fax: +40(21) 312-5429
EMail: rectorat@unarte.org
Website: http://unarte.org

Rector: Ruxandra Demetrescu (2006-)

Chancellor: Catalin Balescu
Tel: +40(21) 312-2753 EMail: balescu@unarte.ro

International Relations: Raluca Ionescu, International Relations Coordinator Tel: +40(21) 316-8864, Fax: +40(21) 316-8864

Faculties

Art History and Theory (Aesthetics; Art Criticism; Art History; Restoration of Works of Art); **Decorative Arts and Design** (Art Management; Ceramic Art; Display and Stage Design; Fashion Design; Glass Art; Graphic Arts; Handicrafts; Industrial Design; Jewelry Art; Religious Art; Textile Design; Weaving); **Fine Arts** (Computer Graphics; Engraving; Handicrafts; Painting and Drawing; Photography; Printing and Printmaking; Sculpture; Video; Visual Arts)

History: Founded 1864 as Academia de Belle Arte, acquired present status and title 1998 (Previously known as Universitatea de Arta din Bucureşti) All course durations recently changed to be brought into line with the Bologna Process.

Governing Bodies: University Senate

Academic Year: October to July (October-January; February-July)

Admission Requirements: Secondary school certificate (Bacalaureat) and entrance examination

Fees: (Euro): 1,000 per annum (50% of available places are state-funded)

Main Language(s) of Instruction: Romanian

Accrediting Agencies: Ministry of Education and Research

Degrees and Diplomas: *Diploma de Licenţă*; *Diplomă de Master*, *Diplomă de Doctor (PhD)*

Student Services: Academic counselling, Foreign student adviser, Foreign Studies Centre, Health services, Language programs, Sports facilities

Student Residential Facilities: For c. 400 students

Special Facilities: Art Gallery, Museum, Dark Room

Libraries: Biblioteca Universităţii de Arte, c. 60,000 vols

Academic Staff *2010-2011*	**TOTAL**
FULL-TIME	**300**
PART-TIME	c. **50**
Student Numbers *2010-2011*	
All (Foreign Included)	c. **1,000**
FOREIGN ONLY	**50**

Last Updated: 15/02/10

CAROL DAVILA UNIVERSITY OF MEDICINE AND PHARMACY OF BUCHAREST

Universitatea de Medicină şi Farmacie Carol Davila din Bucureşti (UMF 'C.DAVILA')
Dionisie Lupu Street nr. 37, Sectorul 1, 020022 Bucureşti
Tel: +40(21) 210-31-09
Fax: +40(21) 211-02-76
EMail: postmaster@univermed-cdgm.ro
Website: http://www.umf.ro/

Rector: Florian Popa (1992-)
Tel: +40(21) 211-40-86, Ext. 214, Fax: +40(21) 638-30-10

Faculties

Dentistry (Anaesthesiology; Anatomy; Behavioural Sciences; Biochemistry; Biology; Biophysics; Chemistry; Dental Technology; Dentistry; Dermatology; Embryology and Reproduction Biology; Endocrinology; Forensic Medicine and Dentistry; Genetics; Gynaecology and Obstetrics; Microbiology; Neurology; Nutrition; Ophthalmology; Oral Pathology; Organic Chemistry; Orthodontics; Orthopaedics; Otorhinolaryngology; Paediatrics; Pathology; Periodontics; Physical Therapy; Physics; Psychiatry and Mental Health; Public Health; Radiology; Rehabilitation and Therapy; Statistics; Surgery); **Medicine** (Anatomy; Biochemistry; Biology; Biophysics; Cardiology; Chemistry; Dermatology; Epidemiology; Forensic Medicine and Dentistry; Gastroenterology; Genetics; Gerontology; Gynaecology and Obstetrics; Haematology; Health Administration; Hygiene; Immunology; Marketing; Medicine; Microbiology; Modern Languages; Nephrology; Neurology; Nursing; Occupational Health; Oncology; Ophthalmology; Optics; Organic Chemistry; Orthopaedics; Otorhinolaryngology; Paediatrics; Parasitology; Pathology; Pharmacology; Physical Education; Physics; Plastic Surgery;

Psychiatry and Mental Health; Public Health; Radiology; Rehabilitation and Therapy; Rheumatology; Sports; Statistics; Surgery; Urology); **Midwifery and Nursing** (Health Sciences; Medical Auxiliaries; Midwifery; Nursing); **Pharmacy** (Anatomy; Applied Mathematics; Biochemistry; Biology; Biotechnology; Cell Biology; Chemistry; Computer Science; Hygiene; Inorganic Chemistry; Laboratory Techniques; Management; Marketing; Microbiology; Nutrition; Organic Chemistry; Pedagogy; Pharmacology; Pharmacy; Physical Chemistry; Physiology; Statistics; Toxicology)

History: Founded 1857 as National School of Medicine and Surgery, by Carol Davila, became School of Medicine and Pharmacy of the University of Bucharest, 1869, detached as separate Institute 1948 as Institute of Medicine and Pharmacy. Acquired present status and title 1989. A State Institution.

Governing Bodies: Senate; Executive Committee of Senate

Academic Year: October to July (October-February; February-July)

Admission Requirements: Secondary school certificate (Bacalaureat), or foreing equivalent and competitive entrance examination

Fees: (US Dollars): Tuition, foreign students, 360-380 per month

Main Language(s) of Instruction: Romanian or English

International Co-operation: With universities in Belgium, Denmark, France, Germany, Greece, Lithuania, Spain, United Kingdom. Also participates in Erasmus programme

Accrediting Agencies: Ministry of Education and Research

Degrees and Diplomas: *Diploma de Licenţă*; *Certificat de atestare a competentelor profesionale*; *Diplomă de Master*: Public Health Adminsitration; Biophysics and Cell Biotechnology; Endodontics; Biostatistics; Dentistry; Oral Implantology; *Diplomă de Doctor*: Leadership; Bioethics; Scientific Research Law; Biostatistics

Student Services: Academic counselling, Canteen, Cultural centre, Foreign student adviser, Foreign Studies Centre, Health services, Language programs, Nursery care, Social counselling, Sports facilities

Special Facilities: Anatomy Museum

Libraries: Central Library, 723,000 vols; faculty libraries

Publications: The International Scientific Journal, Indexed by the Institute for Scientific Information (Philadelphia); The Journal of Cellular and Molecular Medicine, Scientific journal of the Davila University *(monthly)*

Press or Publishing House: Carol Davila University Press

Last Updated: 07/09/11

CONSTANŢA MARITIME UNIVERSITY

Universitatea Maritimă din Constanţa (UMC)

Mircea cel Bătrân Street nr. 104, 900663 Constanţa

Tel: +40(241) 66-47-40

Fax: +40(241) 61-72-60

EMail: info@imc.ro

Website: http://www.cmu-edu.eu/

Rector: Cornel Panait (2008-)
Tel: +40(241) 66-47-40, Ext.108, Fax: +40(241) 61 72 60
EMail: cornel.panait@gaod.ro

Registrar: Edith Padineanu
Tel: +40 (241) 66-47-40 Ext.111, Fax: +40(241) 61 72 60
EMail: edithpadineanu@imc.ro

International Relations: Eugen Bârsan, Vice-Rector for Research and International Relations
Tel: +40(241) 66-47-40 Ext.128, Fax: +40(241) 61-72-60
EMail: ebirsan@inbox.com

Faculties

Naval Electromechanics (Electrical and Electronic Engineering; Marine Engineering; Mechanical Engineering; Telecommunications Engineering) *Dean*: George Caruntu; **Navigation and Naval Transport** (Marine Transport; Nautical Science) *Dean*: Ghiorghe Batranca

Further Information: Also organizes life-long learning courses and IMO courses.

History: Founded as a maritime school 1972. Became merchant marine institute of higher education 1990. Acquired current title and status 2000.

Governing Bodies: Managerial Board of the University Senate

Academic Year: October to July (October-January; March-July)

Admission Requirements: Secondary school certificate (Baccalaureat) or equivalent

Fees: (Euro): Romanian students, 600 per annum; (US Dollars): Foreign students, 3,400 per annum

Main Language(s) of Instruction: Romanian, English

International Co-operation: with institutions in Bulgaria, Germany and UK.

Accrediting Agencies: Ministry of Education and Research; National Council for Academic Assessment and Accreditation

Degrees and Diplomas: *Diploma de Licenţă*: Navigation and Naval Transport; Electromechanics; Electronics; *Diplomă de Master*: Management; Maritime Law; Radiocommunications; Electromechanics; Maritime Safety; Transport; *Diplomă de Doctor*: Mechanical Engineering

Student Services: Academic counselling, Canteen, Employment services, Foreign student adviser, Foreign Studies Centre, Health services, Language programs, Social counselling, Sports facilities

Student Residential Facilities: Hostel for c. 500 students

Special Facilities: Nautical Centre; Navigation Complex Simulator; GMDSS Simulator; LNG Simulator; Potential Incident Simulator Control and Evaluation System

Libraries: 35,000 vols, journals and specific didactic materials

Publications: Annals of Constanta Maritime University, Scientific works by academics and PhD candidates from European and American maritime institutions. *(annually)*; Journal of Marine Technology and Environment, Developments in the field of maritime technology *(biannually)*; Naval Transports, Professional journal. *(3 per annum)*

Press or Publishing House: Nautica Publishing House

Academic Staff *2010-2011*	**TOTAL**
FULL-TIME	**90**
PART-TIME	**100**
STAFF WITH DOCTORATE	
FULL-TIME	**50**
PART-TIME	c. **30**

Student Numbers *2010-2011*	
All (Foreign Included)	c. **5,500**
FOREIGN ONLY	**50**

Part-time students, 2,250.

Last Updated: 15/09/11

CONSTANTIN BRÂNCUŞI UNIVERSITY OF TÂRGU-JIU

Universitatea Constantin Brâncuşi din Târgu-Jiu

Calea Eroilor Street nr. 30, Târgu-Jiu

Tel: +40(253) 21-43-07

Fax: +40(253) 21-57-94

EMail: univ@utgjiu.ro

Website: http://www.utgjiu.ro

Rector: Adrian Gorun EMail: rector@utgjiu.ro

Secretar şef: Alina Drăghescu

International Relations: Otilia Simion EMail: ri@utgjiu.ro

Departments

Distance Learning (Accountancy; Administration; Banking; Economics; Finance; Law; Management; Service Trades; Tourism); **Mathematics** (Mathematics); **Teacher Training**

Faculties

Arts and Social Sciences; **Economics and Business Administration** (Accountancy; Banking; Business Administration; Business Computing; Economics; Finance; Management; Marketing; Tourism); **Engineering** (Automation and Control Engineering; Energy Engineering; Engineering; Engineering Management; Environmental Engineering; Industrial Engineering; Systems Analysis); **Law and Letters** (Law; Private Law; Public Law); **Physical Education and Sports**

History: Founded 1992, incorporating existing College of Engineering, a branch of University of Craiova.

Academic Year: October to July (October-February; March-July)

Admission Requirements: Secondary school certificate (Baca-laureat) or recognized equivalent, and entrance examination

Fees: None

Main Language(s) of Instruction: Romanian

International Co-operation: Participates in the Tempus and Phare programmes

Accrediting Agencies: Ministry of Education

Degrees and Diplomas: *Diploma de Licenţă*; *Diplomă de Master*; *Diplomă de Doctor*

Student Services: Academic counselling, Canteen, Cultural centre, Employment services, Foreign Studies Centre, Health services, Nursery care, Social counselling, Sports facilities

Student Residential Facilities: For c. 220 students

Publications: Analele Universităţii 'Constantin Brâncuşi' *(annually)*

Press or Publishing House: Editura Universităţii

Last Updated: 20/09/11

EFTIMIE MURGU UNIVERSITY OF REŞIŢA

Universitatea Eftimie Murgu din Reşiţa (UEMR)
Piaţa Traian Vuia nr, 1-4, 320085 Reşiţa
Tel: +40(255) 21-02-27
Fax: +40(255) 21-02-30
EMail: rector@uem.ro
Website: http://www.uni-resita.eu/

Rector: Doina Frunzaverde

Administrative Director: Teodor Gavriş Tel: +40(255) 21-51-35

International Relations: Andrada Nagy
Tel: +40(255) 21-81-69, Fax: +40(255) 22-22-12
EMail: birelex@uem.ro

Departments

Open Distance Learning (Marketing; Public Administration); **Teacher Training**

Faculties

Business Studies and Administration (Accountancy; Business and Commerce; Economic History; Marketing; Physical Education; Public Administration; Religious Studies; Social Work; Tourism) *Dean*: Gheorghe Popovici; **Engineering** (Computer Engineering; Economics; Electronic Engineering; Engineering; Engineering Management; Machine Building; Materials Engineering; Mechanical Engineering; Technology) *Dean*: Sava Ianici

History: Founded 1971. Acquired present status and title 1992.

Governing Bodies: Senate; Teachers Board

Academic Year: October to June (October-January; February-June)

Admission Requirements: High school degree and entrance examination

Fees: (Euro): 300 per annum

Main Language(s) of Instruction: Romanian

International Co-operation: With universities in Germany, France, Belgium, Greece, Poland, Italy

Accrediting Agencies: Ministry of Education and Research

Degrees and Diplomas: *Diploma de Licenţă*: Economics Engineering; (ING.EC.); Machine Building Technology; Welding Technology; Materials Science; Computer Science; Electromechanics (ING); Marketing; Business and Commerce; Tourism (EC); Social Work; Public Administration; Religious Studies and History; *Diplomă de Master*, *Diplomă de Doctor (Ph.D.)*

Student Services: Academic counselling, Canteen, Cultural centre, Foreign student adviser, Foreign Studies Centre, Health services, Language programs, Nursery care, Social counselling, Sports facilities

Special Facilities: None

Libraries: Library; E-Library

Publications: Anale UEMR *(biennially)*; Modus Vivendi *(biennially)*; Revista de Asistenta Sociala *(biennially)*; Robotică şi Management *(quarterly)*

Press or Publishing House: Yes

Last Updated: 19/09/11

GEORGE ENESCU UNIVERSITY OF ARTS OF IAŞI

Universitatea de Arte George Enescu din Iaşi
Horia Street nr, 7-9, 700126 Iaşi
Tel: +40(232) 21-25-49 +40(232) 21-25-48
Fax: +40(232) 21-25-51 +40(232) 21-66-37
EMail: enescu@arteiasi.ro
Website: http://www.arteiasi.ro

Rector: Viorel Munteanu EMail: munteanu@arteiasi.ro

Director-General, Administration: Dumitru Spătaru
Tel: +40(232)27-61-62

International Relations: Felicia Balan
Tel: +40(232) 21-25-48, Fax: +40(232) 21-66-37
EMail: feliciabalan@arteiasi.ro; feliciabalan7@yahoo.com

Faculties

Composition, Musicology, Music Pedagogy and Drama (Acting; Conducting; Jazz and Popular Music; Music Education; Music Theory and Composition; Musicology; Performing Arts; Religious Music; Theatre); **Fine Arts, Decorative Arts and Design** (Aeronautical and Aerospace Engineering; Art Criticism; Art Education; Art History; Design; Fashion Design; Fine Arts; Graphic Design; Industrial Design; Painting and Drawing; Restoration of Works of Art; Sculpture; Textile Design; Visual Arts); **Music Performance** (Musical Instruments; Opera; Performing Arts; Singing)

Research Centres

Aesthetics and Artistic Creation (Aesthetics; Fine Arts); **Fine Arts Preservation and Restoration** *(CREART)* (Fine Arts; Restoration of Works of Art); **The Art of Theatre, Study and Creation** (Theatre); **The Knowledge of Music** (Music)

History: Founded 1860 as Higher School of Music and Theatre of Iaşi. Reorganized 1931 as 'George Enescu' Academy of Arts of Iaşi, and acquired present status and title 1990.

Governing Bodies: Senate

Academic Year: September to July (September-April; May-July)

Admission Requirements: Secondary school certificate (Baca-laureat) and entrance examination

Fees: (US Dollars): Registration, c. 40; tuition, c. 1,000 per annum

Main Language(s) of Instruction: Romanian

International Co-operation: Participates in the Socrates/Erasmus programme

Accrediting Agencies: Ministry of Education

Degrees and Diplomas: *Diploma de Licenţă*; *Diplomă de Master*: Music Performance; Music Education; Theatrology; Fine Arts Decorative Arts and Design; *Diplomă de Doctor*: Music Education; Theatrology; Fine Arts Decorative Arts and Design

Student Services: Canteen, Cultural centre, Health services, Language programs, Nursery care, Sports facilities

Student Residential Facilities: Yes

Special Facilities: Art Gallery. Communication and Information Technology Centre

Libraries: Central Library, c. 200,000 vols

Publications: Arta *(monthly)*; Artes *(annually)*; Byzantion *(annually)*

Last Updated: 16/09/11

GH. ASACHI TECHNICAL UNIVERSITY OF IAŞI

Universitatea Tehnică Gh. Asachi din Iaşi (UTI)
Bulevardul Dimitrie Mangeron no, 67, 700050 Iaşi
Tel: +40(232) 27-86-83 +40(232) 27-86-80
Fax: +40(232) 27-86-28
EMail: international@tuiasi.ro
Website: http://www.tuiasi.ro

Rector: Ion Giurma Tel: +40(232) 21-23-22

Secretar ştiinţific: Dan Gelu Galuşcă Tel: +40(232) 21-23-28

International Relations: Horia-Nicolai Teodorescu, Pro-Rector, International Relations
Tel: +40(232) 27-86-28, Fax: +40(232) 27-86-28

Centres

Continuing Education and Training; **Public and Private Business Administration** *(Regional)* (E-Business/Commerce;

Maintenance Technology; Management; Marketing; Production Engineering; Transport Management)

Departments

Management Informatisation (Business Computing; Computer Science; Management); **Teacher Training** (Educational Sciences; Teacher Training)

Faculties

Architecture *(G.M. Cantacuzino)* (Architecture; Restoration of Works of Art); **Automation and Computer Engineering** (Automation and Control Engineering; Computer Engineering; Computer Science); **Chemical Engineering and Environmental Protection** (Biotechnology; Chemical Engineering; Economics; Environmental Engineering; Inorganic Chemistry; Molecular Biology; Organic Chemistry; Printing and Printmaking); **Construction and Installation Engineering** (Agricultural Engineering; Building Technologies; Civil Engineering; Construction Engineering; Development Studies; Industrial Engineering; Transport Engineering); **Electrical Engineering, Power Engineering and Applied Informatics** (Computer Science; Electrical Engineering; Power Engineering); **Electronics, Telecommunications Engineering and Information Technology** (Electronic Engineering; Information Technology; Telecommunications Engineering); **Hydrology, Geodesy and Environmental Engineering** (Environmental Engineering; Geology; Hydraulic Engineering; Sanitary Engineering; Water Science); **Machine Manufacturing and Industrial Management** (Industrial Management; Machine Building; Mechanics); **Materials Science and Engineering** (Materials Engineering; Metal Techniques; Metallurgical Engineering); **Mechanical Engineering** (Agriculture; Automotive Engineering; Electronic Engineering; Food Technology; Mechanical Engineering; Mechanics; Robotics); **Textile and Leather Technology** (Leather Techniques; Textile Design; Textile Technology)

History: Founded 1912. Reorganized 1937, when the Electrotechnical School and the Section of Technological Chemistry of 'Alexandru Ioan Cuza' University of Iaşi became the 'Gh. Asachi' Polytechnic Institute of Iaşi, to which the Faculty of Agricultural Sciences was attached a year later. Acquired present status and title 1993. A State Institution enjoying autonomy in academic matters and financed by the Government.

Governing Bodies: Senate; Faculty Councils

Academic Year: October to June (October-January; March-June)

Admission Requirements: Secondary school certificate (Bacalaureat) and entrance examination

Fees: (US Dollars): Foreign students, 320 per month. No fees for Romanian and Moldavian students

Main Language(s) of Instruction: Romanian, English, French

International Co-operation: With universities in Austria, Belgium, Germany, Denmark, Spain, France, Greece, United Kingdom, Italy, Netherlands, Portugal. Also participates in Erasmus, Socrates, Leonardo da Vinci, COST, FP6 Programmes.

Accrediting Agencies: Ministry of Education and Research; National Council of Evaluation and Accrediting

Degrees and Diplomas: *Diploma de Licenţă*; *Certificat de atestare a competentelor profesionale*; *Diplomă de Master*; *Diplomă de Doctor*

Student Services: Academic counselling, Cultural centre, Employment services, Foreign student adviser, Health services, Language programs, Sports facilities

Student Residential Facilities: Yes

Libraries: Library, 1.1m. vols; 5 branch libraries

Publications: Buletinul Institutului Politehnic din Iaşl *(quarterly)*; Iaşi Polytechnic Magazine *(biennially)*; Monitorul, Bulletin; Romanian Review of Textile-Leather Engineering *(quarterly)*

Press or Publishing House: 'Gheorghe Asachi' Publishing House

Last Updated: 16/09/11

GHEORGHE DIMA MUSIC ACADEMY OF CLUJ-NAPOCA

Academia de Muzică Gheorghe Dima din Cluj-Napoca (AMGD)

I.C. Brătianu Street nr. 25, 400079 Cluj-Napoca
Tel: +40(264) 59-12-41 +40(264) 59-12-42
Fax: +40(264) 59-38-79
EMail: conscluj@gmail.com
Website: http://www.amgd.ro

Rector: Adrian Pop
Tel: +40(264) 59-38-79 EMail: aurelmarc012000@yahoo.com

International Relations: Roxana Huza
Tel: +40(295) 59-12-43, Ext: 113, Fax: +40(295) 59-38-79
EMail: roxanahuza@amgd.ro

Departments

Distance Learning (Music Education; Musical Instruments)

Faculties

Instrumental Performance (Musical Instruments); **Music** *(Piatra Neamţ)* (Music; Music Education); **Music Theory** (Conducting; Music; Music Education; Music Theory and Composition; Musicology); **Scenic Art** (Theatre)

History: Founded 1919 as Conservatory, became Academy of Music and Drama 1931, reorganized as Conservatory 1950, and acquired present status and title 1990.

Governing Bodies: Senate

Academic Year: October to June (October-February; February-June)

Admission Requirements: Secondary school certificate (Bacalaureat)

Fees: (US Dollars): foreign students, 470 per month; (Euros): Romanian students, 350-750 per annum

Main Language(s) of Instruction: Romanian, also courses in English, French, Italian, German

International Co-operation: With universities in Germany, Greece, Italy and United Kingdom

Accrediting Agencies: Ministry of Education and Research

Degrees and Diplomas: *Diploma de Licenţă*; *Diplomă de Master*; *Diplomă de Doctor*

Student Services: Academic counselling, Foreign student adviser, Foreign Studies Centre, Health services, Sports facilities

Student Residential Facilities: For 180 students

Libraries: Musical Library, c. 144,110 vols; 21,625 recordings

Publications: Studii de muzicologie *(annually)*

Press or Publishing House: Media Musica Publishing House

Last Updated: 09/09/11

GRIGORE T. POPA UNIVERSITY OF MEDICINE AND PHARMACY OF IAŞI

Universitatea de Medicină şi Farmacie Grigore T. Popa din Iaşi (UMF GR.T.POPA)

Universităţii Street nr. 16,
700115 Iaşi
Tel: +40(232) 221-18-18
Fax: +40(232) 221-18-20
EMail: rectorat@umfiasi.ro
Website: http://www.umfiasi.ro

Rector: Vasile Astarastoae (2008-)

Director General Administrative: Dana Drugus
EMail: ddrugus@DirGen.umfiasi.ro

International Relations: Dragos Pieptu, Vice-Rector
Fax: +40(232) 226-46-70 EMail: dpieptu@ChPla.umfiasi.ro

Faculties

Biomedical Engineering (Biomedical Engineering); **Dentistry** (Dentistry) *Dean*: Norina Consuela Forna; **Medicine** (Laboratory Techniques; Medicine; Midwifery; Nursing; Physical Therapy; Radiology; Rehabilitation and Therapy) *Dean*: Doina Azoicai; **Pharmacy** (Pharmacy) *Dean*: Monica Hancianu

Higher Schools

Postgraduate Studies

Research Centres

Diagnosis and Therapeutic Techniques in Gastroenterology (Gastroenterology); **Endocrinology** (Endocrinology); **Implant and Prosthesis Bioengineering** (Dental Technology)

Further Information: Also courses in English and in French for foreing students in Medicine

History: Founded 1879, as Faculty of 'Al. I. Cuza' University of Iaşi, detached as separate Institution 1948. Acquired present status and title 1992, named after Grigore T. Popa. A State Institution.

Academic Year: October to July (October-January; February-July)

Admission Requirements: Secondary school certificate (Bacalaureat), or recognized foreign equivalent and competitive entrance examination

Main Language(s) of Instruction: Romanian, English

International Co-operation: With universities in Belgium, France, Germany, Greece, Italy, Portugal, Spain, United Kingdom. Also participates in Socrates/Erasmus programme

Accrediting Agencies: Ministry of Education and Research; National Council for Academic Evaluation and Accreditation

Degrees and Diplomas: *Diploma de Licenţă*: Bioengineering, 4 yrs; *Diploma de Licenţă*: Pharmacy, 5 yrs; *Diplomă de Doctor*: Dentistry and Stomatology; Medicine, 6 yrs

Student Services: Academic counselling, Canteen, Cultural centre, Employment services, Foreign student adviser, Foreign Studies Centre, Handicapped facilities, Health services, Language programs, Nursery care, Social counselling, Sports facilities

Student Residential Facilities: For 2,147 students

Special Facilities: Computer Centre; Language Centre. Multimedia Laboratory

Libraries: Central Library, c. 380,000 vols

Press or Publishing House: University Publishing House

Academic Staff *2010-2011*: Total 1,000

STAFF WITH DOCTORATE: Total 500

Student Numbers *2010-2011*: Total: c. 8,500

Last Updated: 16/09/11

I.L. CARAGIALE UNIVERSITY OF DRAMA AND CINEMA OF BUCHAREST

Universitatea de Artă Teatrală şi Cinematografică I.L. Caragiale din Bucureşti (UATC)

Matei Voevod Street nr. 75-77, Sectorul 2, Bucureşti
Tel: +40(21) 252-80-20
Fax: +40(21) 252-58-81
EMail: rector@unatc.ro
Website: http://www.unatc.ro

Rector: Gelu Colceag Tel: +40(21) 252-81-25

Director General Administrative: Gheorghe Bălăşoiu
Tel: +40(21) 252-74-57

International Relations: Manuela Cernat, Pro-Rector, International Relations

Faculties

Theatre (Acting; Aesthetics; Art Criticism; Art Management; Dance; Display and Stage Design; Theatre)

Schools

Film (Cinema and Television; Film; Multimedia; Photography; Radio and Television Broadcasting; Video; Visual Arts)

History: Founded 1950 as Cinematographic Art Institute, merged with Dramatic Art Institute 1954 and acquired present title 1997.

Governing Bodies: Senate

Academic Year: October to June (October-January; January-June)

Admission Requirements: Secondary school certificate (Bacalaureat) and entrance examination

Fees: (US Dollars): Foreign students, c. 760 per month

Main Language(s) of Instruction: Romanian

Accrediting Agencies: Ministry of Education

Degrees and Diplomas: *Diploma de Licenţă*; *Diplomă de Master*: Theater; Film; *Diplomă de Doctor*: Theater; Film; Media Studies

Student Services: Cultural centre, Foreign student adviser, Foreign Studies Centre, Sports facilities

Special Facilities: Theatre Studio; Film Studio

Libraries: Main Library, 80,000 vols

Last Updated: 09/09/11

ION IONESCU DE LA BRAD UNIVERSITY OF AGRICULTURAL SCIENCES AND VETERINARY MEDICINE OF IAŞI

Universitatea de Ştiinţe Agricole şi Medicină Veterinară Ion Ionescu de la Brad din Iaşi' (USAMV IASI)

Aleea Mihail Sadoveanu nr. 3, 700490 Iaşi
Tel: +40(232) 27-49-33 +40(232) 21-30-69
Fax: +40(232) 26-06-50
EMail: rectorat@uaiasi.ro
Website: http://www.uaiasi.ro

Rector: Gerard Jităreanu (2004-)
Tel: +40(232) 21-30-71 EMail: gerardj@uaiasi.ro

Director-General (Administration): Adrian Neagu
EMail: dga@uaiasi.ro

International Relations: Gheorghe Savuta, Head, Office of International Relations
Tel: +40(744) 40-75-00, Fax: +40(232) 40-73-67
EMail: gsavuta@uaiasi.ro

Faculties

Agriculture (Agricultural Economics; Agriculture; Agronomy; Biology; Engineering Management; Food Technology); **Animal Husbandry** (Animal Husbandry; Fishery; Zoology); **Horticulture** (Horticulture; Landscape Architecture); **Veterinary Science** (Veterinary Science)

History: Founded 1912 as Faculty of Science of 'Alexandru Ioan Cuza' University of Iaşi. Reorganized 1951 as Agronomical Institute of Iaşi, named after Ion Ionescu de la Brad 1956. Faculty of Veterinary Medicine set up within the institute 1961. Reorganized 1992 as 'Ion Ionescu de la Brad' Agronomical University of Iaşi, and acquired present title 1996.

Governing Bodies: Senate

Academic Year: October to July (October-January; February-July)

Admission Requirements: Secondary school certificate (Bacalaureat) or recognized equivalent

Fees: (US Dollars): Foreign students, 320 per annum

Main Language(s) of Instruction: Romanian

International Co-operation: Participates in the Socrates, Copernicus and Leonardo da Vinci programmes

Accrediting Agencies: Ministry of Education and Research; National Council of Evaluation and Accrediting

Degrees and Diplomas: *Diploma de Licenţă*; *Diplomă de Master*; *Diplomă de Doctor (PhD)*. Also technical qualification, 3 yrs

Student Services: Academic counselling, Canteen, Cultural centre, Employment services, Foreign student adviser, Health services, Language programs, Sports facilities

Student Residential Facilities: For 1,445 students

Libraries: University Library, 111,828 vols

Publications: Agriculture *(annually)*; Animal Husbandry *(annually)*; Horticulture *(annually)*; Veterinary Medicine *(annually)*

Last Updated: 16/09/11

ION MINCU UNIVERSITY OF ARCHITECTURE AND URBANISM

Universitatea de Arhitectură şi Urbanism Ion Mincu (UAUIM)

Academiei Street nr, 18-20, 010014 Bucureşti
Tel: +40(21) 313-54-82
Fax: +40(21) 312-39-54
EMail: mac@iaim.ro
Website: http://www.iaim.ro

President: Emil Barbu Popescu (2008-) Tel: +40(21) 307-71-59

Rector: Stefan Scafa Udriste

Secretar şef: Lucia Vlad
Tel: +40(21) 307-71-36 EMail: secretarsef@iaim.ro

International Relations: Beatrice-Gabriela Jöger, International Relations Officer
Tel: +40(21) 307-71-13, Fax: +40(21) 312-39-54
EMail: bgjoger@yahoo.com

Centres
Research (Architectural and Environmental Design; Architectural Restoration; Architecture; Landscape Architecture; Structural Architecture; Town Planning)

Faculties
Architecture (Architectural Restoration; Architecture; Structural Architecture; Technology); **Interior Design** (Furniture Design; Industrial Design; Interior Design); **Urbanism** (Architecture and Planning; Environmental Studies; Landscape Architecture; Public Administration; Town Planning; Urban Studies)

Schools
Postgraduate Studies (Architectural Restoration; Architecture; Architecture and Planning; Town Planning)

History: Founded 1892 as Higher School, became an independent School of Architecture 1904. Reorganized as Academy 1932, incorporated with Polytechnic School 1938, reorganized as Institute of Architecture 'Ion Mincu' 1953, and acquired present status and title 2000.

Governing Bodies: Senate

Academic Year: October to July (October-January; February-July)

Admission Requirements: Secondary school certificate (Bacalaureat), and entrance examination

Fees: (US Dollars): Foreign students, c. 2,080 per annum

Main Language(s) of Instruction: Romanian

International Co-operation: Participates in the Socrates/Erasmus programme

Accrediting Agencies: Ministry of Education and Research

Degrees and Diplomas: *Diploma de Licență*; *Certificat de atestare a competentelor profesionale*: Fire Safety Management; Integrated Concept of Design; Implementation and Operation of Buildings; *Diplomă de Master*, *Diplomă de Doctor (PhD)*

Student Services: Canteen, Cultural centre, Foreign student adviser, Foreign Studies Centre, Health services, Social counselling, Sports facilities

Student Residential Facilities: For c. 550 students

Special Facilities: University Museum

Libraries: University Library

Publications: Library Bulletin *(annually)*

Last Updated: 07/09/11

IULIU HAȚIEGANU UNIVERSITY OF MEDICINE AND PHARMACY OF CLUJ-NAPOCA

Universitatea de Medicină și Farmacie Iuliu Hațieganu din Cluj-Napoca (UMF)

Emil Isac Street nr. 3, 400023 Cluj-Napoca
Tel: +40(264) 40-68-29
Fax: +40(264) 59-72-57
EMail: dri@umfcluj.ro
Website: http://www.umfcluj.ro

Rector: Constantin Ciuce
Tel: +40(264) 40-68-41, Fax: +40(264) 59-42-89
EMail: cciuce@umfcluj.ro; rectoratumf@umfcluj.ro

Secretar Rector: Mihai Gudea
Tel: +40(264) 40-68-41, Fax: +40(264) 59-42-89
EMail: rectoratumf@umfcluj.ro; mgudea@umfcluj.ro

International Relations: Cristina Ghervan, Director, International Relations Tel: +40(264) 40-68-29, Fax: +40(264) 59-72-57

Faculties
Dentistry (Dental Hygiene; Dentistry; Radiology; Rehabilitation and Therapy; Stomatology; Surgery); **Medicine** (Anatomy; Biochemistry; Biophysics; Cell Biology; Computer Science; Dermatology; Diabetology; Embryology and Reproduction Biology; Endocrinology; Epidemiology; Forensic Medicine and Dentistry; Genetics; Gerontology; Health Administration; Histology; Immunology; Medicine; Midwifery; Molecular Biology; Nephrology; Nursing; Nutrition; Occupational Health; Pathology; Pharmacology; Physical Therapy; Physiology; Public Health; Radiology; Rehabilitation and Therapy; Rheumatology; Statistics; Toxicology); **Pharmacy** (Biochemistry; Botany; Chemistry; Cosmetology; Dermatology; Laboratory Techniques; Mathematics; Mathematics and Computer Science; Organic Chemistry; Pharmacology; Pharmacy; Physical Chemistry; Toxicology)

History: Founded 1875 as School, became Faculty of Medicine of the University of Cluj 1948. Acquired present status and title 1948. A State Institution.

Governing Bodies: Senat

Academic Year: October to July (October-February; February-July)

Admission Requirements: Secondary school certificate (Bacalaureat) or foreign equivalent, and entrance examination

Fees: (US Dollars): Foreign students, 360 per month

Main Language(s) of Instruction: Romanian, English, French

International Co-operation: With universities in France, Georgia, Germany, Greece, Hungary, Italy, South Africa, Spain, United Kingdom, USA. Also participates in the Socrates, and Erasmus programmes, Ceepus and AUF

Accrediting Agencies: Ministry of Education and Research; National Council of Evaluation and Accreditation

Degrees and Diplomas: *Diploma de Licență*; *Diplomă de Master*, *Diplomă de Doctor*. Also Potsgraduate and Continuing Education degree Programmes

Student Services: Canteen, Cultural centre, Foreign Studies Centre, Health services, Nursery care, Social counselling, Sports facilities

Student Residential Facilities: Yes

Special Facilities: History of Medicine and Pharmacy Museum

Libraries: Central Library, 560,830 vols

Publications: Clujul Medical *(quarterly)*

Last Updated: 15/09/11

LUCIAN BLAGA UNIVERSITY OF SIBIU

Universitatea Lucian Blaga din Sibiu

Bulevardul Victoriei nr. 10, 550024 Sibiu
Tel: +40(269) 21-60-62
Fax: +40(269) 21-04-92
EMail: rectorat@ulbsibiu.ro
Website: http://www.ulbsibiu.ro

Rector: Constantin Oprean
Tel: +40(269) 21-81-65, Fax: +40(269) 21-78-87
EMail: rector@ulbsibiu.ro

General Administrativ Director: Vasile Motoc
Tel: +40(269) 21-81-65, Fax: +40(269) 21-78-87
EMail: administratie@ulbsibiu.ro

Departments
Distance Education (Agriculture; Banking; Business Administration; Computer Science; Criminal Law; Economics; Engineering; European Union Law; Finance; French; German; History; Industrial Engineering; Information Technology; Insurance; Journalism; Law; Literature; Management; Mass Communication; Mathematics; Mathematics and Computer Science; Mechanical Engineering; Political Sciences; Private Law; Public Administration; Romanian; Service Trades; Statistics; Tourism)

Faculties
Agriculture, Food Technology and Environment Protection (Agricultural Engineering; Agricultural Management; Agriculture; Biotechnology; Environmental Engineering; Environmental Studies; Food Technology); **Economics** (Accountancy; Business Administration; Economics; Finance; Insurance; International Business; Marketing; Public Relations; Service Trades; Small Business; Tourism); **Engineering** *(Hermann Oberth)* (Computer Science; Electrical Engineering; Engineering; Information Technology; Machine Building; Mechanical Engineering; Production Engineering; Safety Engineering; Telecommunications Engineering; Textile Technology); **History and Heritage Preservation** *(Nicolae Lupu)* (Architectural Restoration; Fashion Design; History); **Journalism** (Journalism; Mass Communication; Philosophy; Public Relations); **Law and Administrative Sciences** *(Simion Bărnuțiu)* (Administration; Law; Public Administration); **Letters** (American Studies; Arts and Humanities; Communication Studies; Cultural Studies; English; French; German; Information Sciences; Library Science; Literature; Philology; Romance Languages; Theatre; Translation and Interpretation); **Medicine** *(Victor Papilian)* (Dental Technology; Dentistry; Medicine; Nursing); **Orthodox Theology** *(Andrei Șaguna)*

(Orthodox Theology; Theology); **Political Science, International Relations and Security Studies** (European Studies; International Relations; Peace and Disarmament; Political Sciences; Protective Services); **Protestant Theology** (Protestant Theology; Theology); **Science** (Applied Mathematics; Biology; Chemistry; Computer Science; Ecology; Education; Environmental Studies; Human Resources; Leadership; Mathematics; Mathematics and Computer Science; Mathematics Education; Physical Education; Physics; Psychology; Social Work; Sociology; Sports)

Further Information: Also Teaching Hospital. Intensive Romanian Language and Civilization courses

History: Founded 1976 as Institute of Higher Learning. Acquired present status 1990 and title 1995, named after Lucian Blaga.

Governing Bodies: Senate

Academic Year: October to July (October-February; February-July)

Admission Requirements: Secondary school certificate (Bacalaureat) and entrance examination

Fees: (US Dollars): 1,350-2,700 per annum; Foreign students, c. 1,920 per semester

Main Language(s) of Instruction: Romanian

International Co-operation: Participates in the Tempus programme

Accrediting Agencies: Ministry of Education and Research

Degrees and Diplomas: *Diploma de Licenţă*; *Diplomă de Master*; *Diplomă de Doctor*

Student Residential Facilities: Yes

Libraries: Total, c. 1m vols

Publications: 'Acta Universitatis Cibiniensis'; Buletinul ştiinţific *(annually)*; 'Saeculum' (Literary magazine); 'Sibiul Universitar'

Press or Publishing House: Sibiu University Press

Last Updated: 19/09/11

MICHAEL THE BRAVE NATIONAL ACADEMY OF INFORMATION

Academia Naţională de Informaţii 'Mihai Viteazul'
Şoseaua Odăi Streer nr. 20, sector 1, Bucureşti
Tel: +40(21) 410-65-50
Fax: +40(21) 310-47-50
EMail: ani@sri.ro
Website: http://www.animv.ro

Rector: Gheorghe Teodoru Stephan

Faculties

Intelligence Studies (Civil Security; Communication Studies; Information Sciences; Psychology; Public Relations)

Programmes

Postgraduate Studies (Business Administration; Information Management; Information Sciences; Military Science)

History: Founded 1992.

Degrees and Diplomas: *Diploma de Licenţă*: Psychology and Information Sciences; Communication, Public Relations and Information Sciences; *Certificat de atestare a competentelor profesionale*; *Diplomă de Master*: Business Administration; Management Education in Safety Culture; National Security Information Management; Management of information in Combating Terrorism; *Diplomă de Doctor*: Military Science and Information

Last Updated: 13/09/11

MIRCEA CEL BATRAN NAVAL ACADEMY, CONSTANŢA

Academia Navala Mircea cel Batran, Constanţa
Fulgerului Street nr, 1, 900218 Constanţa
Tel: +40(241) 62-62-00
Fax: +40(241) 64-30-96
EMail: relpub@anmb.ro
Website: http://www.anmb.ro

Director: Chitac Vergil (2010-)
Tel: +40(241) 64-30-96 EMail: rector@anmb.ro

Director, Administration: Petrariu Gheorghe
Tel: +40(241) 66-63-92, Fax: +40(241) 63-86-01

Departments

Foreign Languages (English; French; German; Modern Languages); **Life-Long Learning and Technology Tranfer** (Technology)

Faculties

Merchant Marine (Computer Science; Mathematics; Nautical Science; Naval Architecture; Transport Management); **Naval Studies** (Behavioural Sciences; Communication Studies; Electronic Engineering; Marine Engineering; Nautical Science)

Further Information: Also 2 research centres

History: Founded 1872 as School, became institute 1973, and acquired present status and title 1990.

Academic Year: October to July (October-January; March-July)

Admission Requirements: Secondary school certificate (Bacalaureat) or equivalent

Fees: None

Main Language(s) of Instruction: Romanian

International Co-operation: With institutions in Turkey; Netherlands; USA; Greece; France; Spain; Ukraine; Bulgaria; Italy

Accrediting Agencies: Ministry of Education and Research

Degrees and Diplomas: *Diploma de Licenţă*: Engineering; *Diplomă de Master*. Also undergraduate certificates

Student Services: Employment services, Health services, Social counselling, Sports facilities

Student Residential Facilities: For c. 580 students

Special Facilities: Museum

Libraries: c. 300,000 vols

Press or Publishing House: Institute Publishing House

Last Updated: 13/09/11

NATIONAL UNIVERSITY OF MUSIC OF BUCHAREST

Universitatea Nationala de Muzică din Bucureşti (UNMB)
Ştirbei Vodă Streer nr, 33, Sectorul 1, 010102 Bucureşti
Tel: +40(21) 314-63-41
Fax: +40(21) 315-83-96
EMail: rectorat@unmb.ro
Website: http://www.unmb.ro

Rector: Dan Dediu-Sandu Fax: +40(21) 314-63-41
EMail: dan.dediu@unmb.ro

Administrative Director: Gheorghe Mihaila
Tel: +40(21) 313-58-87, Fax: +40(21) 313-58-87
EMail: dga@unmb.ro

International Relations: Lucia Costinescu
Tel: +40(21) 313-58-89, Fax: +40(21) 313-58-89
EMail: international@unmb.ro

Faculties

Composition, Musicology and Pedagogy *Dean*: Teodor Ţuţuianu; **Performing Arts** (Musical Instruments; Opera; Performing Arts; Singing) *Dean*: Serban Dimitrie Soreanu

History: Founded 1864 as Royal Conservatoire of Music, reorganized as 'Ciprian Porumbescu' Academy of Music 1948, and acquired present status and title 2000.

Governing Bodies: Senate; Faculty Councils

Academic Year: October to July

Admission Requirements: Secondary school certificate (Bacalaureat)

Fees: (US Dollars): undergraduate: 470 per month; postgraduate: 495

Main Language(s) of Instruction: Romanian, English, French, Italian, Germany

International Co-operation: Participates in Socrates-Erasmus with universities in Austria, Finland, Germany, Italy, Netherlands, Norway, Portugal, Sweden and United Kingdom.

Accrediting Agencies: National Council of Academic Accreditation

Degrees and Diplomas: *Diploma de Licență*: Music; *Diplomă de Master*: Music; *Diplomă de Doctor*: Music (PhD)

Student Services: Academic counselling, Foreign student adviser, Health services, Language programs, Social counselling, Sports facilities

Student Residential Facilities: Yes

Libraries: Central Library, 250,000 vols; Sound Library, 23,465 recording items

Publications: Akademos, Musicological Research *(biannually)*; Musicological Studies

Academic Staff *2009-2010*	**TOTAL**
FULL-TIME	**130**
STAFF WITH DOCTORATE	
FULL-TIME	c. **100**
Student Numbers *2009-2010*	
All (Foreign Included)	c. **1,200**
FOREIGN ONLY	**40**

Last Updated: 09/09/11

NATIONAL UNIVERSITY OF PHYSICAL EDUCATION AND SPORTS OF BUCHAREST

Universitatea Națională de Educație Fizică și Sport din București (UNEFS)

Constantin Noica Street nr. 140, Sector 6, 060057 București
Tel: +40(21) 316-41-07
Fax: +40(21) 312-04-00
EMail: secretariat@unefs.ro
Website: http://www.unefs.ro

Rector: Viorel Cojocaru (2008-)
Tel: +40(21) 316-41-07 EMail: rector@unefs.ro

Director Departamentul de Comunicare și Relații Externe: Sabina Macovei EMail: dcre@unefs.ro

International Relations: Vasilica Grigore, Vice Rector
EMail: prorector@unefs.ro

Faculties

Physical Education and Sports (Physical Education; Sports); **Physical Therapy** *(Military)* (Physical Therapy)

Laboratories

Interdisciplinary Research (Biochemistry; Biology; Biomedical Engineering; Computer Science; Education; Engineering; Physics)

Further Information: Also courses for foreign students

History: Founded 1922 as the National Institute of Physical Education, separated in to two institutes 1929, gained university status 1937 and present title 1992.

Governing Bodies: Senate

Academic Year: October to June (October-January; February-June)

Admission Requirements: Secondary school certificate (Bacalaureat)

Fees: (US Dollars): c. 320 per month; extramural courses, c. 320; Doctorate, c. 340

Main Language(s) of Instruction: Romanian

Accrediting Agencies: Ministry of Education and Research

Degrees and Diplomas: *Diploma de Licență*; *Diplomă de Master*, *Diplomă de Doctor*. Also Coach Qualification, 3 yrs

Student Services: Health services, Sports facilities

Student Residential Facilities: For c. 460 students

Special Facilities: Academy Museum

Libraries: Main Library, c. 152,000 vols

Publications: Discobolul *(quarterly)*

Student Numbers *2012-2013*: Total 1,451

Last Updated: 11/03/13

NATIONAL UNIVERSITY OF POLITICAL STUDIES AND PUBLIC ADMINISTRATION

Școala Națională de Studii Politice și Administrative (SNSPA)

Povernei Street Nr. 6, District 1, 010643 București
Tel: +40(21) 312-25-35
Fax: +40(21) 312-25-35
EMail: rectorat@snspa.ro
Website: http://www.snspa.ro

Rector: Remus Pricopie (2012-2017)
Tel: +40(21) 312-25-35, Fax: +40(21) 312-25-35
EMail: remus.pricopie@comunicare.ro; remus_pricopie@yahoo.com;

Head-Secretary: Sorin Dragnea
Tel: +40(21) 318-08-95, Fax: +40(21) 312-25-35
EMail: dragneas@snspa.ro

International Relations: Liliana Popescu, Pro-rector
Tel: +40(21) 318-08-97 (1115), Fax: +40(21) 312-25-35
EMail: liliana.popescu2008@gmail.com

Departments

International Relations and European Integration (Economic and Finance Policy; Economics; European Studies; International Business; International Relations; Peace and Disarmament); **Teacher Training** *(DPPD)* (Teacher Trainers Education; Teacher Training)

Faculties

Communications and Public Relations (Communication Studies; Public Relations); **Management** (Management); **Political Sciences** (Political Sciences); **Public Administration** (Administration; Public Administration)

Programmes

Distance Learning (Communication Studies; Mass Communication; Political Sciences; Public Administration; Public Relations); **Doctorate** (Administration; Mass Communication; Political Sciences; Sociology)

History: Founded 1991.

Governing Bodies: Senate

Academic Year: October to September

Admission Requirements: Baccalaureate degree

Fees: (Lei): from 2,000 to 18,600 per year

Main Language(s) of Instruction: Romanian, French, English

International Co-operation: Participates in the Erasmus, Socrates and Leonardo Programmes.

Accrediting Agencies: Romanian Agency for Quality Assurance in Higher Education

Degrees and Diplomas: *Diploma de Licență*: Political Science; Public Administration; Management; Communication and Public Relations, 3 yrs; *Diplomă de Master*: Political Science; Public Administration; Communication and Public Relations; International Relations, a further 2 yrs; *Diplomă de Doctor*: Political Science; Public Administration; Communication and Public Relations; Sociology (PhD), a further 3 yrs

Student Services: Academic counselling, Canteen, Foreign student adviser, Handicapped facilities, Language programs, Social counselling

Student Residential Facilities: For c. 550 students

Special Facilities: IT Lab, Internet Access, Multimedia

Libraries: c. 19,500 vols.

Publications: Occasional Papers *(other/irregular)*

Press or Publishing House: Comunicare.ro

Academic Staff *2011-2012*	MEN	WOMEN	TOTAL
FULL-TIME	71	62	**133**
PART-TIME	40	20	**60**
STAFF WITH DOCTORATE			
FULL-TIME	78	24	**102**
PART-TIME	40	20	c. **60**
Student Numbers *2011-2012*			
All (Foreign Included)	2,280	5,315	c. **7,595**

Part-time students, 1,440. **Distance students**, 910. **Evening students**, 0.

Last Updated: 08/08/12

NORTH UNIVERSITY OF BAIA-MARE

Universitatea de Nord Baia-Mare (UNBM)

Dr. Victor Babeş Street no. 62/A, 430083 Baia-Mare, Maramures
Tel: +40(262) 21-89-22
Fax: +40(262) 27-61-53
Website: http://www.ubm.ro

Rector: Dan Călin Peter (2004-) EMail: dan.calin.peter@ubm.ro

Director-General, Administration: Vasile Aniţaş
Tel: +40(262) 40-12-68, Fax: +40(262) 27-61-53
EMail: vasile.anitas@ubm.ro

International Relations: Ramona Demarcsek
Tel: +40(262) 21-89-22, Fax: +40(262) 27-61-53
EMail: ramona@ubm.ro

Faculties

Engineering (Computer Engineering; Electrical Engineering; Energy Engineering; Engineering Management; Environmental Engineering; Industrial Engineering; Information Technology; Machine Building; Mechanical Engineering; Telecommunications Engineering); **Humanities** (Anthropology; Applied Linguistics; Arts and Humanities; Canadian Studies; Catholic Theology; Christian Religious Studies; Communication Studies; English; Ethnology; French; German; Information Sciences; Journalism; Literature; Modern Languages; Orthodox Theology; Painting and Drawing; Peace and Disarmament; Philology; Philosophy; Romanian; Social Work; Translation and Interpretation); **Mineral Resources and Environment** (Agricultural Engineering; Civil Engineering; Environmental Engineering; Environmental Studies; Industrial Engineering; Materials Engineering; Mining Engineering; Natural Resources; Petroleum and Gas Engineering; Surveying and Mapping); **Sciences** (Biochemistry; Biology; Business Administration; Chemistry; Computer Science; Economics; Food Technology; Management; Mathematics; Mathematics and Computer Science; Physics; Public Administration)

Further Information: Also 5 research centres

History: Founded 1961 as Teacher Training Institute of Baia Mare, reorganized 1969 as Institute of Sub-Engineers, 1974 as Institute of Higher Education and passed under the patronage of the Polytechnic Institute of Cluj Napoca as Institute of Sub-Egineers. Regained Autonomy 1990 as Institute of Higher Education of Baia Mare. Acquired present status 1991 by Governmental Decree and title 1996. A State Institution enjoying considerable autonomy in both academic and financial matters.

Governing Bodies: Senate

Academic Year: October to June (October-February; February-June)

Admission Requirements: Secondary school certificate (Bacalaureat)

Fees: (US Dollars): Registration, 250-350 per annum

Main Language(s) of Instruction: Romanian

International Co-operation: With universities in: Belgium, France, Germany, Greece, the Netherlands. Also participates in Tempus, Leonardo da Vinci and Socrates programmes

Accrediting Agencies: Ministry of Education and Research

Degrees and Diplomas: *Diploma de Licenţă*; *Certificat de atestare a competentelor profesionale*: Engineering; *Diplomă de Master*: Ethnology and Social Anthropology; Language and Popular Culture; Romanian Literature and European Modernism; Canadian Studies; Supervision in Social Work; Translation; Applied Linguistics; Ethnotourism; Human Rights, Democracy, Peace and Tolerance; Industrial Engineering; Mechanical Engineering; Electrical Engineering; Energy Engineering; Environmental Engineering; Mathematics Educations; Mathematics and Computer Sciences; Biology - Biochemistry; Methods of Analysis of Environmental Quality and Product; Chemistry Education; European Project Management; Business Administration; Nanostructured Systems Analysis; *Diplomă de Doctor*: Mechanical Engineering; Philology; Mathematics

Student Services: Academic counselling, Canteen, Foreign Studies Centre, Health services, Social counselling, Sports facilities

Student Residential Facilities: For 850 students

Libraries: Biblioteca Universităţii, c. 250,000 vols

Publications: Scientific Bulletin *(annually)*

Press or Publishing House: University Press

Academic Staff *2010-2011*: Total 210

STAFF WITH DOCTORATE: Total 120

Student Numbers *2010-2011*: Total: c. 5,500

Distance students, 40.

Last Updated: 12/09/11

OVIDIUS UNIVERSITY OF CONSTANŢA

Universitatea Ovidius din Constanţa

Bulevardul Mamaia nr.124, 900527 Constanţa
Tel: +40(241) 606-400
Fax: +40(241) 619-040
EMail: rectorat@univ-ovidius.ro
Website: http://www.univ-ovidius.ro

Rector: Victor Ciupina
Tel: +40(241) 61-90-40 EMail: vciupina@univ-ovidius.ro

Vice-Rector: Victor Ploae EMail: vploae@univ-ovidius.ro

Departments

Distance Learning Centre (Economics; History; Law; Mathematics and Computer Science; Mechanical Engineering; Natural Sciences; Public Administration) *Director*: Adriana Manea; **Modern Languages** (English; German; Italian; Romanian; Russian; Spanish; Turkish); **Teachers Training** (English; French; Graphic Arts; Music; Pedagogy; Robotics; Sports)

Faculties

Arts (Fine Arts; Music; Performing Arts; Theatre); **Civil Engineering** (Civil Engineering; Construction Engineering; Hydraulic Engineering; Rural Planning); **Dentistry** (Dentistry; Pharmacy); **Economics** (Accountancy; Banking; Finance; Information Management; International Economics; Service Trades; Tourism); **History and Politican Sciences** (History; International Relations; Political Sciences); **Law and Administration** (Law; Public Administration; Sociology); **Letters** (American Studies; English; French; Italian; Journalism; Modern Languages; Romanian; Spanish); **Mathematics and Computer Science** (Mathematical Physics; Mathematics; Mathematics and Computer Science); **Mechanical and Marine Engineering** (Energy Engineering; Industrial Engineering; Marine Engineering; Mechanical Engineering; Mechanical Equipment and Maintenance; Metal Techniques; Naval Architecture; Thermal Physics); **Medicine** (Anatomy; Gastroenterology; Hepatology; Medicine; Surgery); **Natural Sciences and Agriculture**; **Pharmacy** (Pharmacy); **Physics, Chemistry and Petroleum Processing Technology**; **Psychology and Educational Sciences**; **Sports and Physical Education** (Physical Education; Sports); **Theology** (Orthodox Theology; Pastoral Studies; Religion; Theology)

History: Founded 1961.

Governing Bodies: Senate

Academic Year: October to June

Admission Requirements: Secondary school certificate (Bacalaureat), one-year Romanian preparation course and entrance examination

Fees: (US Dollars): 3,200-7,600 per annum (undergraduate programmes); 3,400-8,000 for graduate programmes

Main Language(s) of Instruction: Romanian

International Co-operation: Participates in the Black Sea Universities Network (BSUN)

Accrediting Agencies: Ministry of Education and Research

Degrees and Diplomas: *Diploma de Licenţă*: Letters, Theology, History, Law and Public Administration, Economics, Physics, Chemistry, Petroleum Technology, Mathematics and Informatics, Natural Sciences, Sports, Medicine, Dentistry, Arts, Pedagogy; Petroleum Technology, Agriculture, Mechanical Engineering, Civil Engineering; *Diplomă de Master*: Letters, Theology, History, Law, Economics, Physics, Chemistry, Petroleum Technology, Mathematics and Informatics, Natural Sciences, Medicine, Dentistry; *Diplomă de Doctor*: Letters, History, Economics, Mathematics and Informatics, Natural Sciences, Medicine (PhD). Also postgraduate Diplomas

Student Services: Canteen, Cultural centre, Foreign student adviser, Health services, Language programs, Sports facilities

Student Residential Facilities: For 1,000 students
Special Facilities: Computer Centre. Multimedia Laboratory
Libraries: Central Library, c. 500,000 vols; 2,000 periodicals
Publications: Annals, In all fields *(annually)*
Last Updated: 09/09/11

PETROLEUM AND GAS UNIVERSITY OF PLOIEŞTI

Universitatea Petrol-Gaze din Ploieşti (UPG)
PO Box 52, Bulevardul Bucureşti nr. 39, 100680 Ploieşti
Tel: +40(244) 57-31-71
Fax: +40(244) 57-58-47
EMail: rectorat@upg-ploiesti.ro
Website: http://www.upg-ploiesti.ro

Rector: Vlad Ulmanu (2004-) EMail: vulmanu@upg-ploiesti.ro

President of the Administrative Council: Niculae Napoleon Antonescu EMail: nnantonescu@upg-ploiesti.ro

International Relations: Liviu Dumitrascu, Prorector
Tel: +40(244) 57-52-15, Fax: +40(244) 57-58-47
EMail: ldumitrascu@upg-ploiesti.ro

Departments

Open and Distance Learning (Accountancy; Automation and Control Engineering; Chemical Engineering; Economics; Educational Sciences; Environmental Engineering; Finance; Management; Modern Languages; Petroleum and Gas Engineering; Philology)

Faculties

Arts and Sciences (Administration; Chemistry; Cultural Studies; English; French; Mathematics and Computer Science; Modern Languages; Philology; Physics; Secretarial Studies); **Economics** (Accountancy; Computer Science; Economics; Finance; Management); **Mechanical and Electrical Engineering** (Automation and Control Engineering; Economics; Electrical Engineering; Electronic Engineering; Machine Building; Mechanical Engineering; Mechanical Equipment and Maintenance); **Petroleum Engineering and Gas Engineering** (Geology; Petroleum and Gas Engineering; Production Engineering); **Petroleum Refining and Petrochemistry** (Applied Chemistry; Chemical Engineering; Chemistry; Environmental Engineering)

Institutes

Economics (Economics)

Schools

Postgraduate *(Paneuropean)*

History: Founded 1948 as Petroleum and Gas Institute of Bucharest. Moved to Ploieşti 1973 and acquired present status and title 1994.
Governing Bodies: Senate
Academic Year: October to July (October-February; February-July)
Admission Requirements: Secondary school certificate (Bacalaureat)
Fees: (US Dollars): Foreign students, c. 320-340 per month
Main Language(s) of Instruction: Romanian (English for PhD and postgraduate studies)
International Co-operation: With universities in France, Germany, Spain, United Kingdom, China, Vietnam. Participates in Erasmus, Comenius and Leonardo programmes
Accrediting Agencies: National Council for Academic Assessment and Accreditation (N.C.A.A.A.)
Degrees and Diplomas: *Diploma de Licenţă*; *Certificat de atestare a competentelor profesionale*; *Diplomă de Master*, *Diplomă de Doctor*
Student Services: Canteen, Cultural centre, Foreign Studies Centre, Health services, Language programs, Social counselling, Sports facilities
Student Residential Facilities: For c. 2,500 students
Libraries: Central Library, c. 300,000 vols
Publications: Buletinul Universităţii Petrol-Gaze din Ploieşti *(biannually)*
Press or Publishing House: University of Ploieşti Publishing House
Last Updated: 19/09/11

PETRU MAIOR UNIVERSITY OF TÂRGU-MUREŞ

Universitatea Petru Maior din Târgu-Mureş
Nicolae Iorga Street nr. 1, 540088 Târgu-Mureş
Tel: +40(265) 26-22-75
Fax: +40(265) 26-22-75
EMail: rectorat@upm.ro
Website: http://www.upm.ro

Rector: Liviu Marian (2004-)
Tel: +40(265) 26-22-75, Fax: +40(265) 26-22-75
EMail: liviu.marian@ea.upm.ro

International Relations: Antonia Suciu (2000-)
Tel: +40(265) 21-18-38, Fax: +40(265) 21-18-38
EMail: suciu@upm.ro

Departments

Open and Distance Learning Education *(ODL)* (Accountancy; Business Administration; Business and Commerce; Management; Philology; Public Administration) *Director*: Maria Georgescu; **Teacher Training** *(Trainers for European Integration)* (Teacher Training) *Director*: Emilia Albu

Faculties

Economics, Juridical and Administrative Sciences (Accountancy; Administration; Banking; Business Administration; Business and Commerce; Economics; Finance; Health Administration; Human Resources; Law; Management; Public Administration; Service Trades; Tourism) *Dean*: Zsuzsanna Szabo; **Engineering** (Automation and Control Engineering; Computer Engineering; Computer Graphics; Economics; Electrical Engineering; Electronic Engineering; Energy Engineering; Engineering; Engineering Management; Environmental Engineering; Industrial Design; Industrial Engineering; Machine Building; Mechanical Engineering; Production Engineering; Safety Engineering) *Dean*: Mircea Dulau; **Science and Letters** (English; European Studies; French; Gender Studies; History; International Relations; Literature; Mathematics and Computer Science; Natural Sciences; Philology; Romanian) *Dean*: Iulian Boldea

History: Founded 1960 as a Public Institution.
Governing Bodies: Senate
Academic Year: October to July
Admission Requirements: High school certificate (Bacalaureat)
Fees: (Euro): Self-financing students, 350-600 per annum
Main Language(s) of Instruction: Romanian
International Co-operation: With universities in Austria; Belgium; Denmark; Greece; Hungary; Ireland; Italy; Netherlands; Slovak Republic; Slovenia; Spain; United Kingdom. Also participates in the Socrates, Erasmus, Minerva, Leonardo da Vinci and CEEPUS programmes
Accrediting Agencies: National Council for Accreditation and Academic Evaluation
Degrees and Diplomas: *Diploma de Licenţă*: Accountancy; Computer Science; History; Management; Mathematics; Philology; Administration; Science (Licentiat); Law; *Diplomă de Master*: Engineering; Economics; Business Administration; Juridical Consulting; Human Resources Management; Project Management; Sanitary System Management; Gender Studies; History of Literature; European Construction; *Diplomă de Doctor*: Philology. Diplomă de Inginer, 4 yrs (Bologna System)
Student Services: Academic counselling, Canteen, Cultural centre, Health services, Sports facilities
Student Residential Facilities: Yes
Libraries: Central Library, 130,329 vols
Publications: Buletinul Ştiinţific al Universităţii 'Petru Maior' *(annually)*; Studia Universitatis - Filologia *(annually)*; Studia Universitatis - Istoria *(annually)*
Press or Publishing House: Editura Universităţii 'Petru Maior'

Academic Staff *2010-2011*	TOTAL
FULL-TIME	150
PART-TIME	50
STAFF WITH DOCTORATE	
FULL-TIME	80
PART-TIME	c. 20
Student Numbers *2010-2011*	
All (Foreign Included)	c. 6,000
FOREIGN ONLY	20

Part-time students, 1,400. **Distance students**, 60.
Last Updated: 20/09/11

POLITECHNIC UNIVERSITY OF BUCHAREST

Universitatea Politehnica din Bucureşti (PUB/UPB)

Splaiul Independenţei Street, nr. 313, Sectorul 6, 060042 Bucureşti
Tel: +40(21) 402-91-00
Fax: +40(21) 318-10-01
EMail: dci@rectorat.pub.ro
Website: http://www.pub.ro

Rector: Ecaterina Andronescu
Tel: +40(21) 318-1000 EMail: e_andronescu@rectorat.pub.ro

Secretar Sef: Gabriel Iacobescu
Tel: +40(21) 410-7270, Fax: +40(21) 318 1003

International Relations: Marian Gheorghe, Vice-Rector
Tel: +40(21) 402-9872, Fax: +40(21) 318-1006
EMail: m_gheorghe@rectorat.pub.ro

Faculties

Aerospace Engineering (Aeronautical and Aerospace Engineering) *Dean*: Stelian Galetuse; **Applied Chemistry and Materials Sciences** (Applied Chemistry; Materials Engineering) *Dean*: Horia Iovu; **Applied Engineering Sciences** (Engineering) *Dean*: Constantin Udriste; **Automatic Control and Computers** (Automation and Control Engineering; Computer Science); **Biotechnical Systems** (Agricultural Engineering; Agricultural Equipment; Biotechnology; Food Technology); **Electrical Engineering** (Electrical Engineering); **Electronics, Telecommunications and Information Technology** (Electronic Engineering; Information Technology; Telecommunications Engineering); **Energetics** (Energy Engineering); **Engineering and Management of Technological Systems** (Technology); **Engineering in Foreign Languages** (Foreign Languages Education); **Materials Science and Engineering** (Materials Engineering); **Mechanical and Mechatronics Engineering** (Electronic Engineering; Mechanical Engineering); **Transports** (Transport Engineering)

History: Has been teaching courses in Engineering since 1818, founded 1867 as School of Bridges, Roads and Mines. Reorganized as Polytechnic School of Bucharest 1948, with some faculties detached as separate institutions. Acquired present status and title 1965. A State Institution.

Governing Bodies: Senate

Academic Year: October to July (October-February; February-July)

Admission Requirements: Secondary school certificate (Bacalaureat) and entrance examination

Fees: (US Dollars): Foreign students, tuition, c. 320 per month

Main Language(s) of Instruction: Romanian, English, French, German (for Faculty of Engineering Sciences)

Accrediting Agencies: Ministry of Education and Research

Degrees and Diplomas: *Diploma de Licenţă*: Engineering; *Diplomă de Master*: Engineering, a further 1-2 yrs; *Diplomă de Doctor (PhD)*: a further 3-4 yrs

Student Services: Canteen, Health services, Social counselling, Sports facilities

Student Residential Facilities: For c. 12,000 students

Libraries: Central Library, c. 1.35m. vols; libraries of the faculties

Publications: Buletinul Universităţii Politehnice din Bucureşti (in English, French, German and Russian) *(biannually)*

Press or Publishing House: Litografia U.P.B

Last Updated: 17/02/10

POLYTECHNIC UNIVERSITY OF TIMIŞOARA

Universitatea Politehnica din Timişoara (UPT)

Piaţa Victoriei nr. 2, 300006 Timişoara
Tel: +40(256) 40-30-00
Fax: +40(256) 40-30-21
EMail: rector@rectorat.upt.ro
Website: http://www.upt.ro

Rector: Nicolae Robu (2004-) EMail: nicolae.robu@rectorat.upt.ro

Secretar şef: Alexandru Gaşpar
Tel: +40(256) 40-30-08, Fax: +40(256) 40-30-28
EMail: alexandru.gaspar@rectorat.upt.ro

International Relations: Radu Vasiu
EMail: radu.vasiu@rectorat.upt.ro

Centres

Distance Education (Computer Engineering; Distance Education; Multimedia)

Departments

Communication and Foreign Languages (Communication Studies; Modern Languages); **Continuing Education** (Continuing Education; Engineering); **Mathematics** (Mathematics); **Teachers Training** (Pedagogy; Teacher Training)

Faculties

Architecture (Architecture; Architecture and Planning); **Automation and Computer Engineering** (Automation and Control Engineering; Computer Engineering; Computer Science); **Civil Engineering** (Bridge Engineering; Building Technologies; Civil Engineering; Construction Engineering; Industrial Engineering; Railway Engineering; Road Engineering; Surveying and Mapping); **Electronic and Electroenergetics Engineering** (Electronic Engineering; Energy Engineering); **Electronics and Telecommunications** (Electronic Engineering; Telecommunications Engineering); **Engineering** *(Hunedoara)* (Engineering; Materials Engineering; Mechanical Engineering; Mechanics; Metal Techniques; Metallurgical Engineering; Polymer and Plastics Technology; Technology); **Hydrotechnical Engineering** (Environmental Engineering; Environmental Studies; Hydraulic Engineering; Sanitary Engineering; Waste Management); **Industrial Chemistry and Environmental Engineering** (Chemical Engineering; Engineering Management; Environmental Engineering; Industrial Chemistry; Inorganic Chemistry; Leather Techniques; Organic Chemistry; Waste Management); **Management in Production and Transportation** (Industrial and Production Economics; Production Engineering; Transport Engineering); **Mechanical Engineering** (Automation and Control Engineering; Automotive Engineering; Building Technologies; Electronic Engineering; Hydraulic Engineering; Instrument Making; Machine Building; Materials Engineering; Mathematics and Computer Science; Measurement and Precision Engineering; Mechanical Engineering; Mechanical Equipment and Maintenance; Mechanics; Metal Techniques; Production Engineering; Robotics; Technology; Thermal Physics)

Further Information: Also courses for foreign students

History: Founded 1920, as Polytechnical School of Timişoara by a Royal Decree of King Ferdinand of Romania. Reorganized 1948 as Polytechnic Institute of Timişoara and 'Traian Vuia' Polytechnical Institute 1970. Acquired present status 1991 and present title 1996. A State institution.

Governing Bodies: Senate; Council of Administration

Academic Year: September to July (September-January; February-July)

Admission Requirements: Secondary school certificate (Bacalaureat) or equivalent, and entrance examination

Main Language(s) of Instruction: Romanian, German, English, French

International Co-operation: With universities in: Belarus, Belgium, Chile, Finland, Germany, Hungary, Japan, Moldova, Netherlands, Portugal, Slovenia, United Kingdom, USA, France, Czech Republic, Serbia and Montenegro, Italy, Russian Federation.

Accrediting Agencies: Ministry of Education and Research, and National Council for Academic Evaluation and Accreditation

Degrees and Diplomas: *Diploma de Licenţă*; *Diplomă de Master*; *Diplomă de Doctor (PhD)*. Also postgraduate Diplomas (a further 1-2 yrs)

Student Services: Academic counselling, Canteen, Cultural centre, Health services, Language programs, Sports facilities

Student Residential Facilities: For 5,668 students

Libraries: Central Library, c. 672,000 vols

Publications: Annual Summary Research *(annually)*; Buletinul Ştiinţific *(biannually)*

Press or Publishing House: 'Politehnica' Publishing House

Academic Staff *2009-2010*: Total 900
STAFF WITH DOCTORATE: Total 240

Student Numbers *2009-2010*: Total: c. 15,000

Last Updated: 20/09/11

STEFAN CEL MARE UNIVERSITY OF SUCEAVA

Universitatea Ştefan cel Mare din Suceava (USV)
Universităţii Street, nr, 13, 720229 Suceava
Tel: +40(230) 21-61-47
Fax: +40(230) 52-00-80
EMail: rectorat@usv.ro
Website: http://www.usv.ro

Rector: Valentin Popa (2011-)
Tel: +40(230) 52-00-81 EMail: rector@usv.ro

Vice-Rector: Emanuel N. Diaconescu
Tel: +40(230) 52-00-81 EMail: iadina@usv.ro

International Relations: Sanda Maria Ardeleanu, International Relations Tel: +40(230) 52-03-16 EMail: relint@usv.ro

Departments

Teacher Training *Director*: Carmen Balan

Faculties

Economic Sciences and Public Administration (Accountancy; Banking; Business Administration; Business and Commerce; Economics; Finance; Law; Management; Public Administration; Secretarial Studies; Service Trades; Tourism) *Dean*: Elena Hlaciuc; **Educational Sciences** *Director*: Rodica Nagy; **Electrical Engineering and Computer Science** (Automation and Control Engineering; Computer Science; Electrical Engineering; Electronic Engineering; Energy Engineering) *Dean*: Stefan-Gheorghe Pentiuc; **Food Engineering** (Food Science; Food Technology) *Director*: Sonia Gutt; **Forestry** (Forestry) *Dean*: Sergiu-Andrei Horodnic; **History and Geography** *Dean*: Stefan Purici; **Letters and Communication Sciences** (Communication Studies; English; French; German; Italian; Public Relations; Romanian; Slavic Languages; Spanish) *Dean*: Mircea Diaconu; **Mechanical Engineering, Mechatronics and Management** (Electronic Engineering; Machine Building; Mechanical Engineering) *Dean*: Ioan Mihai; **Physical Education and Sport** *Dean*: Petru Ghrvan

History: Founded in 1963 as Pedagogical Institute. In 1976 became Faculty of Letters and Sciences. In the same year, Technical Faculty is founded. In 1990 obtained current title, comprising 4 faculties. Further faculties added over the following years.

Governing Bodies: Senate

Academic Year: October to July (October-January; February-July)

Admission Requirements: Secondary school certificate (Bacalaureat) and proficiency in Romanian.

Fees: (Euros): Romanian and other EU students, 450-500 per annum; non-EU students, (US Dollars): 320-340 per month

Main Language(s) of Instruction: Romanian

International Co-operation: With universities in Poland; Ireland; United Kingdom; Mexico; Greece; Austria; Spain; Portugal; Brazil; Germany; France; Belgium; Ukraine; Italy; Moldova; Denmark; Czech Republic; Turkey; Albania; Netherlands; Hungary; Bulgaria; Latvia; Norway; Finland; Russia; Slovak Republik and Cyprus

Accrediting Agencies: Ministry of Education and Research

Degrees and Diplomas: *Diploma de Licenţă*: Accounting; Economics and International Business; Management; Finance; Business Administration; Statistics and Economics Informatics; Administrative Sciences; English; French (Language/Literature); History; Geography; Philosophy; Kinesthiology; Physical Education and Sport; Education Sciences; Mechanical Engineering; Electrical Engineering; Forestry: Food Engineering; Philology; *Diplomă de Master*: Mechanical Engineering; Philology; Electrical Engineering; Economics; Forestry; Geography; History; Management; Communication Studies; Public Relations; Public Administration; *Diplomă de Doctor*: Computer and Information Technology; Philology; Engineering Materials; Electrical Engineering; Electronics and Telecommunications Engineering; Mechanical Engineering; History; Forestry (PhD)

Student Services: Academic counselling, Canteen, Employment services, Foreign student adviser, Health services, Language programs, Sports facilities

Student Residential Facilities: 4 student hostels for 800 students

Special Facilities: Observatory; Art Gallery

Libraries: c 271,000 vols

Publications: Acta Mechanica *(annually)*; Acta Tribologica *(annually)*; Advances in Electrical and Computer Engineering *(biannually)*; ANADISS *(annually)*; Atelier de Traduction *(biannually)*; Distributed Systems *(annually)*; European Trends and Perspectives in Physical Education and Sport *(biannually)*; Inter Litteras et Terras *(biannually)*; La Lettre 'R' *(biannually)*; Limbaje si Comunicare *(biannually)*; Mecatronica *(annually)*; Messages, Sages and Ages *(biannually)*; Omul si Mitul; Proceedings of the International Conference on Development and Application Systems *(annually)*; Proceedings of VAREHD *(biannually)*; University's Annals, Sections: Mechanical Engineering; Electrical Engineering; Philology; Food Engineering; Economic Sciences and Public Administration; Education Sciences; Philosophy and Humanities; Geography; Forestry; Philosophy and Humanities; Physical Education and Sport *(annually)*

Press or Publishing House: Suceava University Publishing House

Academic Staff *2008-2009*	MEN	WOMEN	TOTAL
FULL-TIME	186	156	**342**
PART-TIME	16	8	**24**
STAFF WITH DOCTORATE			
FULL-TIME	101	111	**212**
PART-TIME	5	–	**5**
Student Numbers *2008-2009*			
All (Foreign Included)	6,546	6,258	**12,804**
FOREIGN ONLY	82	126	**208**

Distance students, 2,469.
Last Updated: 13/09/11

TECHNICAL UNIVERSITY OF CIVIL ENGINEERING OF BUCHAREST

Universitatea Tehnică de Construcţii din Bucureşti (TUCEB)
Bulevardul Lacul Tei nr. 124, Sectorul 2, 020396 Bucureşti
Tel: +40(21) 242-1208
Fax: +40(21) 242-0781
EMail: iro@utcb.ro
Website: http://www.utcb.ro

Rector: Johan Neuner (2004-)
Tel: +40(21) 242-1161, Fax: +40(21) 242-0272
EMail: neuner@utcb.ro

Registrar: Laurentiu Rece
Tel: +40(21) 243-3650 EMail: secretariat@utcb.ro; rece@utcb.ro

International Relations: Iacint Manoliu
Tel: +40(21) 242-9350, Fax: +402(21) 242-0866
EMail: manoliu@utcb.ro

Faculties

Building Services (Construction Engineering; Electrical and Electronic Engineering; Energy Engineering; Mechanical Engineering); **Civil, Industrial and Agricultural Engineering** (Building Technologies; Civil Engineering; Construction Engineering; Engineering Management; Industrial Engineering; Town Planning); **Engineering taught in Foreign Languages** (Civil Engineering; Construction Engineering; Engineering; English; French); **Geodesy** (Surveying and Mapping); **Hydrotechnics** (Hydraulic Engineering; Sanitary Engineering); **Railways, Roads and Bridges** (Civil Engineering; Road Engineering; Transport Engineering); **Technological Equipment** (Mechanical Engineering; Technology)

History: Founded 1818 as School for Land Surveyors, Reorganized as School of Bridges and Roads 1864 and Polytechnic School of Bucharest 1921. Became independent Institution 1948. Acquired present title 1994.

Governing Bodies: Senate; Faculty Councils

Academic Year: October to July (October-February; March-July)

Admission Requirements: Secondary school certificate (Bacalaureat) or equivalent

Fees: (US Dollars): Foreign students, 320 per month; postgraduate students, 340

Main Language(s) of Instruction: Romanian, English and French (for Department of Engineering in Foreign Languages and Communication)

International Co-operation: With universities in France, Italy, Belgium, Netherlands, United Kingdom, Germany, Denmark, Finland, Sweden, Portugal, Spain, Greece, Austria

Accrediting Agencies: Ministry of Education and Research

Degrees and Diplomas: *Diploma de Licenţă*: Construction Engineering; Hydraulic Engineering; Civil Engineering; Thermal Engineering; Electrical Engineering; Automation and Robotics; Equipment Technology and Mechanical Engineering; Geodesy; *Diplomă de Doctor*: Construction Engineering; Hydraulic Engineering; Civil Engineering; Machine Building; Electrical Engineering; Industrial Engineering; Geodesy (PhD)

Student Services: Canteen, Cultural centre, Health services, Sports facilities

Student Residential Facilities: For c. 2,455 students

Libraries: c. 530,000 vols

Press or Publishing House: Conspres

Last Updated: 07/09/11

TECHNICAL UNIVERSITY OF CLUJ-NAPOCA

Universitatea Tehnică din Cluj-Napoca (UTC-N)

Constantin Daicoviciu Street nr. 15, 400020 Cluj-Napoca

Tel: +40(264) 40-12-00 +40(264) 40-12-48

Fax: +40(264) 59-20-55

EMail: utcluj@utcluj.ro

Website: http://www.utcluj.ro

Rector: Radu Munteanu (2003-)

Tel: +40(264) 40-12-02 EMail: Radu.Munteanu@mas.utcluj.ro

General Manager: Horia Ardeleanu

Tel: +40(264) 40-12-07 EMail: horia.ardeleanu@staff.utcluj.ro

International Relations: Vasile Topa, Director, Office of International Relations

Tel: +40(264) 40-12-14 EMail: Vasile.Topa@et.utcluj.ro

Faculties

Architecture and Town Planning (Architecture and Planning; Town Planning); **Automation and Computer Science** (Automation and Control Engineering; Computer Engineering; Computer Science); **Civil Engineering** (Civil Engineering; Construction Engineering; Industrial Engineering; Railway Engineering; Transport Engineering); **Electrical Engineering** (Electrical and Electronic Engineering; Power Engineering); **Electronics and Telecommunications** (Electrical and Electronic Engineering; Telecommunications Engineering); **Equipment Engineering** (Building Technologies); **Machine Building** (Building Technologies; Computer Engineering; Engineering Management; Industrial Engineering; Machine Building; Mechanical Engineering; Mechanics; Physical Engineering; Production Engineering; Robotics); **Materials Science and Engineering** (Engineering Management; Industrial Engineering; Materials Engineering; Mechanical Engineering; Mechanics; Metal Techniques; Polymer and Plastics Technology); **Mechanical Engineering** (Agricultural Engineering; Measurement and Precision Engineering; Mechanical Engineering; Mechanics; Road Engineering; Road Transport)

Further Information: Also 14 research centres

History: Founded 1922 as Electromechanical Institute, became Mechanical Institute 1948, Polytechnical Institute 1953, and acquired present status and title 1992. A State Institution enjoying academic autonomy.

Governing Bodies: Senate

Academic Year: October to July (October-January; February-July)

Admission Requirements: Secondary school certificate (Bacalaureat) and entrance examination

Fees: (Euro): State financed students, tuition, none; Romanian students, 400 per annum; foreign students, 350 per month

Main Language(s) of Instruction: Romanian, English, German

International Co-operation: With universities in Austria, Belgium, Denmark, Finland, France, Germany, Greece, Ireland, Italy, Portugal, Spain, Netherlands and United Kingdom

Accrediting Agencies: National Council for Academic Evaluation and Accreditation

Degrees and Diplomas: *Diploma de Licenţă*: Architecture and Urbanism; Automation and Computer Science; Civil Engineering; Machine Building; Electronics, Telecommunications and Information Technology; Electrical Engineering; Mechanics; Materials Science and Engineering; *Diplomă de Doctor*

Student Services: Canteen, Cultural centre, Foreign student adviser, Health services, Language programs, Sports facilities

Student Residential Facilities: Yes

Special Facilities: TV Studio.

Libraries: UTC-N Library

Publications: Acta Technica Napocensis *(biennially)*; Automation Computers and Applied Mathematics *(biennially)*; Electromotion *(quarterly)*; Logi A, Architecture *(annually)*

Academic Staff *2011-2012*: Total: c. 600

Student Numbers *2011-2012*: Total: c. 12,000

Last Updated: 12/09/11

TRANSYLVANIA UNIVERSITY OF BRAŞOV

Universitatea Transilvania din Braşov

Bulevardul Eroilor nr. 29, 500036 Braşov

Tel: +40(268) 14-25-76

Fax: +40(268) 14-46-34

EMail: rector@unitbv.ro

Website: http://www.unitbv.ro

Rector: Ion Visa Tel: +40(268) 41-20-88, Fax: +40(268) 41-05-25

Secretar şef: Mihaela Augusta Balan

Tel: +40(268) 41-30-00 EMail: secretar-sef@unitbv.ro

International Relations: Marina Cionca, Prorector for International Relations

Tel: +40(268) 41-05-64, Fax: +40(268) 41-05-58

EMail: prorector-rel.internationale@unitbv.ro

Departments

Continuing Education (Arabic; Banking; Business Administration; Computer Science; English; Environmental Management; European Union Law; Finance; French; German; Health Sciences; Information Technology; Management; Marketing; Nutrition; Paediatrics; Pathology; Romanian; Russian; Safety Engineering; Technology; Translation and Interpretation; Transport Management); **Distance Education** (Accountancy; Art Therapy; Banking; Cultural Studies; Economics; Energy Engineering; English; Environmental Studies; Finance; French; Industrial Engineering; Information Sciences; International Business; Library Science; Literature; Management; Marketing; Modern Languages; Pedagogy; Physical Education; Preschool Education; Primary Education; Psychology; Service Trades; Sports; Tourism; Wood Technology)

Faculties

Construction Engineering (Building Technologies; Civil Engineering; Construction Engineering); **Economics** (Accountancy; Banking; Business Administration; Business Computing; Economics; Finance; International Business; International Relations; Law; Management; Marketing; Service Trades; Small Business; Sociology; Tourism); **Electrical Engineering and Computer Science** (Automation and Control Engineering; Computer Engineering; Computer Science; Electrical and Electronic Engineering; Electrical and Electronic Equipment and Maintenance; Information Technology; Mathematics; Software Engineering; Telecommunications Engineering); **Food and Tourism** (Agricultural Equipment; Food Science; Food Technology; Hotel and Restaurant; Tourism); **Forestry** (Forest Management; Forestry; Surveying and Mapping); **Law and Sociology**; **Letters**; **Materials Science and Engineering** (Chemistry; Materials Engineering); **Mathematics and Computer Science** (Computer Science; Mathematics; Mathematics and Computer Science); **Mechanical Engineering** (Agricultural Equipment; Automotive Engineering; Electrical and Electronic Equipment and Maintenance; Food Technology; Machine Building; Mechanical Engineering; Mechanical Equipment and Maintenance; Mechanics; Optometry; Transport Engineering); **Medicine** (Medical Auxiliaries; Medicine); **Music** (Art Therapy; Music; Music Education; Music Theory and Composition; Musical Instruments; Opera; Singing); **Physical Education and Sports**; **Psychology and Educational Sciences**; **Technological Engineering**; **Wood Technology** (Forest Management; Forest Products; Furniture Design; Industrial Engineering; Wood Technology)

Further Information: Also preparatory year of Romanian language for students from the Republic of Moldova

History: Founded1940. Incorporating the Institute of Silviculture 1948, and the Institute of Mechanics 1949. Reorganized 1956 as Polytechnic Institute. Developed 1959 with Faculty of Wood Industry and Faculty of Mechanical Manufacturing Technology 1964 and incorporating the Pedagogical Institute of Braşov 1971. Acquired present status and title 1971. A State Institution.

Governing Bodies: Senate

Academic Year: October to July (October-February; February-July)

Admission Requirements: Secondary school certificate (Bacalaureat) and entrance examination

Fees: (US Dollars): c. 3,200-5,000 per annum

Main Language(s) of Instruction: Romanian, English

International Co-operation: Participates in the Socrates, Tempus, Fullbright, Leonardo da Vinci, and Copernicus programmes

Accrediting Agencies: Ministry of Education; National Council of Academic Accreditation

Degrees and Diplomas: *Diploma de Licenţă*; *Diplomă de Master*; *Diplomă de Doctor*. Also Teaching Qualification, Secondary level, 3 yrs

Student Services: Academic counselling, Cultural centre, Employment services, Foreign student adviser, Foreign Studies Centre, Language programs, Social counselling, Sports facilities

Student Residential Facilities: Yes

Special Facilities: Zoology Museum

Libraries: Central Library and faculty Libraries, total, 680,000 vols

Publications: Buletinul Universităţii 'Transilvania' (Bulletin of Transylvania University of Brasov), Series B: Mathematics, Physics, Chemistry, Medicine, Philology *(annually)*; Buletinul Universităţii 'Transilvania' (Bulletin of Transylvania University of Brasov), Series A: Mechanics, Electrotechnics and Electronics, Materials Processing, Wood Industry, Silviculture *(annually)*

Press or Publishing House: 'Transilvania' University Press

Student Numbers *2009-2010*: Total: c. 23,000

Last Updated: 12/09/11

UNIVERSITY DUNĂREA DE JOS OF GALAŢI

Universitatea Dunărea de Jos din Galaţi
Domnească Street nr. 47, 800008 Galaţi
Tel: +40(236) 41-36-02
Fax: +40(236) 46-13-53
EMail: rectorat@ugal.ro
Website: http://www.ugal.ro

Rector: Viorel Mînzu (2006-)

Director-General of Administration: Romeu Horghidan

International Relations: Sanda Cruceanu
Tel: +40(336) 13-01-09, Fax: +40(236) 46-13-53
EMail: sanda.cruceanu@ugal.ro

Departments

Continuing Education and Technology Transfer (Continuing Education; Technology); **Distance Education**; **Teacher Training** (Education; Teacher Training)

Faculties

Arts (Arts and Humanities); **Computer Science** (Automation and Control Engineering; Computer Engineering; Computer Science; Information Technology); **Economics and Business Administration** (Accountancy; Administration; Business Administration; Econometrics; Economics; Finance; Law; Management; Sociology); **Electrical and Electronic Engineering**; **Engineering** *(Braila)* (Engineering; Mechanical Engineering; Mechanical Equipment and Maintenance; Technology); **Food Science and Engineering** (Biochemistry; Biotechnology; Food Science); **History, Philosophy and Theology** (History; Philosophy; Theology); **Humanities, Economics and Engineering** *(Cross-border)* (Arts and Humanities; Economics; Engineering); **Juridical, Social and Political Sciences; Law, Social and Political Sciences** (Law; Political Sciences; Social Sciences); **Letters** (Modern Languages); **Mechanical Engineering** (Construction Engineering; Machine Building; Mechanical Engineering; Mechanical Equipment and Maintenance; Mechanics; Robotics; Thermal Physics); **Medicine and Pharmacy** (Medicine; Pharmacy); **Metallurgy and Materials Science** (Materials Engineering; Metallurgical Engineering; Polymer and Plastics Technology); **Physical Education and Sports** (Physical Education; Sports); **Science and Environment** (Chemistry; Computer Science; Environmental Studies; Mathematics; Physics); **Shipbuilding** (Automation and Control Engineering; Computer Science; Electrical Engineering; Electronic Engineering; Information Technology; Marine Engineering; Naval Architecture)

Further Information: Also division in Cahul - Moldova

History: Founded 1951 as Naval and Mechanical Engineering Institute. Reorganized 1953 when the Institute of Fish Breeding and Fishing Technology located in the city of Constanţa merged with the Naval Institute of Galaţi as Technical Institute of Galaţi. Became Polytechnical Institute of Galaţi 1957. Acquired present status 1974 when the Polytechnical Institute and the College of Education merged, and present title 1989, named after the historical name of the area around the City of Galaţi. A State Institution responsible to the Ministry of Education. Also branch in Brăila.

Governing Bodies: Senate; Academic Council

Academic Year: October to July (October-February; February-July)

Admission Requirements: Secondary school certificate (Bacalaureat) and entrance examination

Main Language(s) of Instruction: Romanian, French

International Co-operation: With universities in France, Germany, Italy, Spain, United Kingdom. Also participates in Socrates, Tempus, Copernicus programmes

Accrediting Agencies: Ministry of Education and Research

Degrees and Diplomas: *Diploma de Licenţă*; *Diplomă de Master*: Environmental Engineering; Food Engineering; Engineering Management; Applied Sciences Engineering; Language and Literature; Mathematics; Physics; Chemistry; Quality Management in Science; Finance; Marketing; Economics and International Affairs; Management; Cybernetics, Statistics and Economic; Accountancy; Economics; History; Philosophy; Theology; Administration; Law; Physical Education and Sport; Mechanical Engineering; Industrial Engineering; Naval Architecture; Electrical Engineering; Electronics and Telecommunications Engineering; Systems Engineering; Computer Science and Information Technology; Materials Engineering; *Diplomă de Doctor*: Industrial Engineering; Food Engineering; Chemistry; Mechanical Engineering; Electrical Engineering; Systems Engineering; Computers and Information Technology; Materials Engineering; Economics; Management; Philology; History (PhD)

Student Services: Canteen, Cultural centre, Foreign student adviser, Health services, Language programs, Sports facilities

Student Residential Facilities: For 3,000 students

Special Facilities: Television Studio

Libraries: Central Library, c. 600,000 vols

Last Updated: 16/09/11

UNIVERSITY OF AGRICULTURAL SCIENCES AND VETERINARY MEDICINE OF BUCHAREST

Universitatea de Ştiinţe Agronomice şi Medicină Veterinară din Bucureşti (USAMVB)
Bulevardul Mărăşti nr. 59, 011464 Bucureşti
Tel: +40(21) 318-25-64
Fax: +40(21) 318-25-67
EMail: post@info.usamv.ro
Website: http://www.usab.ro

Rector: Stefan Diaconescu
Tel: +40(21) 224-22-66, Fax: +40(21) 224-28-15
EMail: diacstef@agral.usamv.ro

Director: Niculae Dobrescu
Tel: +40(21) 224-36-14, Fax: +40(21) 224-28-15
EMail: dobrescu@info.usamv.ro

International Relations: Florin Stănică, Prorector Probleme Studenţeşti, Relaţii Interne şi internaţionale
Tel: +40(21) 318-03-66, Fax: +40(21) 318-28-88

Departments

Distance Learning

Faculties
Agriculture (Agricultural Management; Agriculture; Biology; Forestry; Plant and Crop Protection; Soil Science); **Animal Science** (Agriculture; Animal Husbandry; Aquaculture; Ecology; Fishery; Food Science; Food Technology; Zoology); **Biotechnology** (Biotechnology); **Horticulture** (Horticulture; Landscape Architecture); **Land Amelioration and Environmental Engineering** (Environmental Engineering; Environmental Management; Environmental Studies; Rural Studies; Surveying and Mapping); **Management, Economic Engineering in Agriculture and Rural Development** (Agricultural Economics; Agricultural Engineering; Agricultural Management; Rural Planning); **Veterinary Medicine** (Food Technology; Safety Engineering; Veterinary Science)

Further Information: Also branches in Slatina and Calarasi.

History: Founded 1852 as Agricultural Institute in Pantelimon, reorganized 1867 as Central School of Agriculture and Silviculture located in Herăstrău. The Silviculture department became independent as The Agricultural School of Herăstrău 1893. Reorganized several times and became Agricultural Institute of Bucharest 1948, named after Nicolae Bălcescu 1952, University of Agricultural Sciences 1992 and acquired present title 1995. A State Institution.

Governing Bodies: Senate; Faculty Councils

Academic Year: October to July (October-January; February-July)

Admission Requirements: Secondary school certificate (Bacalaureat), health certificate and entrance examination

Main Language(s) of Instruction: Romanian

International Co-operation: With universities in France, United Kingdom, Italy, Denmark, Germany, Spain and Portugal.

Accrediting Agencies: Ministry of Education and Research

Degrees and Diplomas: *Diploma de Licenţă*; *Diplomă de Master*; *Diplomă de Doctor*

Student Services: Academic counselling, Canteen, Employment services, Foreign student adviser, Health services, Language programs, Nursery care, Social counselling, Sports facilities

Student Residential Facilities: For c. 2,400 students

Special Facilities: 5 Experimental Farms. Botanic Garden

Libraries: Central Library, 460,000 vols

Publications: Agricultorul Roman *(monthly)*; Lucrări ştiinţifice, Scientific Work Abstracts *(annually)*; Tanarul Agricultor *(monthly)*

Student Numbers *2009-2010*: Total: c. 16,000
Last Updated: 23/11/10

UNIVERSITY OF AGRICULTURAL SCIENCES AND VETERINARY MEDICINE OF CLUJ-NAPOCA

Universitatea de Ştiinţe Agricole şi Medicină Veterinară Cluj-Napoca (USAMV CLUJ)
Calea Mănăştur nr. 3-5, 400372 Cluj-Napoca
Tel: +40(264) 59-63-84
Fax: +40(264) 59-37-92
EMail: contact@usamvcluj.ro
Website: http://www.usamvcluj.ro

Rector: Doru Pamfil
Tel: +40(264) 59-63-84, Fax: +40(264) 59-37-92
EMail: rector@usamvcluj.ro

Secretar şef: Mărioara Morar
Tel: +40(264) 59-63-84 EMail: morarmm@personal.ro

International Relations: Daniel Cap
Tel: +40(264) 59-93-46 EMail: int.rel@usamvcluj.ro

Faculties
Agriculture (Agricultural Business; Agricultural Economics; Agricultural Engineering; Agricultural Equipment; Agricultural Management; Agriculture; Agrobiology; Agronomy; Analytical Chemistry; Applied Chemistry; Biochemistry; Biology; Biophysics; Environmental Engineering; Environmental Management; Environmental Studies; Food Science; Food Technology; Industrial Chemistry; Inorganic Chemistry; Irrigation; Mountain Studies; Organic Chemistry; Physical Chemistry; Plant and Crop Protection; Soil Conservation; Soil Management; Soil Science); **Animal Science and Biotechnology** (Animal Husbandry; Apiculture; Aquaculture; Biochemistry; Biology; Biotechnology; Cattle Breeding; Fishery; Food Technology; Genetics; Microbiology; Molecular Biology; Physiology; Plant Pathology; Sericulture; Zoology); **Horticulture** (Agricultural Economics; Biochemistry; Biology; Biophysics; Biotechnology; Botany; Cell Biology; Engineering Management; Floriculture; Food Science; Forestry; Fruit Production; Genetics; Horticulture; Landscape Architecture; Natural Resources; Nutrition; Rural Planning; Surveying and Mapping; Vegetable Production; Viticulture); **Veterinary Science** (Anatomy; Biotechnology; Cell Biology; Dentistry; Embryology and Reproduction Biology; Entomology; Epidemiology; Genetics; Gynaecology and Obstetrics; Histology; Immunology; Microbiology; Nutrition; Pathology; Pharmacology; Pharmacy; Physiology; Radiology; Toxicology; Veterinary Science)

History: Founded 1869 as School of Agriculture, became Institution of Higher Education 1906, Faculty 1938 and Institute 1948. Acquired present status and title 1995. A State Institution.

Governing Bodies: Senate, Faculty Council

Academic Year: October to July

Admission Requirements: Secondary school leaving certificate (Bacalaureat). No exam for overseas students

Fees: (US Dollars): Foreign students, 320 per month

Main Language(s) of Instruction: Romanian

International Co-operation: Participates in Socrates/Erasmus, CEEPUS, Leonardo da Vinci programmes and Phare Projects

Accrediting Agencies: Academic Evaluation and Accreditation Council

Degrees and Diplomas: *Diploma de Licenţă*: Agriculture; Horticulture; Animal Husbandry; Biotechnology; Veterinary Medicine; *Diplomă de Master*; *Diplomă de Doctor*: Agriculture; Horticulture; Animal Husbandry; Biotechnology (PhD); Veterinary Medicine (PhD)

Student Services: Academic counselling, Canteen, Foreign student adviser, Health services, Language programs, Social counselling, Sports facilities

Student Residential Facilities: For 1,200 students

Special Facilities: Anatomy Museum, Pisciculture Museum, Agrobotany Museum

Libraries: c. 165,000 vols; 50,000 periodicals, Computer Labs

Publications: Agricultura *(biennially)*; Buletin Stiintific al USAMV seria Agricultura si Horticultura *(annually)*; Buletin Stiintific al USAMV seria Zootehnie, Biotehnologii si Medicina Veterinara *(annually)*; Buletin Universităţii de Ştiinte Agricole si Medicina Veterinară Cluj-Napoca *(biennially)*; Clujul Medical Veterinar *(biennially)*; Hameiul si Planete Medicinale *(annually)*; Index Sminum - Hortus Agrobotanicus Napocensis *(annually)*; Scientia Parasitologica *(biennially)*
Last Updated: 12/09/11

UNIVERSITY OF ART AND DESIGN OF CLUJ-NAPOCA

Universitatea de Artă si Design din Cluj-Napoca (AAV)
Piaţa Unirii Street, nr. 31, 400098 Cluj-Napoca
Tel: +40(264) 51-15-77
Fax: +40(264) 59-28-90
Website: http://www.uad.ro/

Rector: Radu Solovastru
Tel: +40(264) 59-81-90, Fax: +40(264) 59-28-90
EMail: tehnic@uartdcluj.ro

Chief secretary: Anamaria Bocean
Tel: +40(264) 59-15-77, Fax: +40(264) 59-28-90
EMail: secretarsef@uad.ro

International Relations: Anamaria Tataru, International Relations Coordinator
Tel: +40(264) 59-50-21, Fax: +40(264) 59-28-90
EMail: relint@uad.ro

Faculties
Decorative Arts and Design (Ceramic Art; Design; Glass Art; Textile Design) *Dean*: Alexandru Alaemoreanu; **Fine Arts** (Art Education; Graphic Arts; Painting and Drawing; Photography; Restoration of Works of Art; Sculpture; Video)

Research Centres

Creative Exploration in Art and Design *(Centre for Excellency)* (Design; Fine Arts; Visual Arts)

Further Information: University Colleges at Bistrita and Sighisoara

History: Founded 1926 as Higher School of Fine Arts, moved to Timişoara 1932. Reorganized as Romanian Institute of Arts 1948, and as Academia de Artă Vizuale Ioan Andreescu din Cluj-Napoca 1990. Acquired present status and title 2002.

Governing Bodies: Senate; Faculty Councils; Academic Board

Admission Requirements: Secondary school certificate (Bacalaureat) and competitive entrance examination

Main Language(s) of Instruction: Romanian

International Co-operation: With universities in Austria, Belgium, Czech Republic, Craotia, France, Germany, Great Britain, Greece, Hungary, Italy, Ireland, Netherlands, Moldova, Sweden, USA. ERASMUS; CEEPUS;

Accrediting Agencies: Ministry of Education and Research

Degrees and Diplomas: *Diploma de Licenţă*; *Diplomă de Master*; *Diplomă de Doctor*. Also Certificate in 3 yrs offered at Bistrita and Sighisoara

Special Facilities: Artistic studios; Workshops

Libraries: c. 50,000 vols; Rare collection

Last Updated: 09/09/11

UNIVERSITY OF BUCHAREST

Universitatea din Bucureşti (UNIBUC)

Bulevardul Mihail Kogălniceanu 36-46, Sectorul 5,
050107 Bucureşti
Tel: +40(21) 307-73-00
Fax: +40(21) 313-17-60
EMail: info@unibuc.ro
Website: http://www.unibuc.ro

Rector: Ioan Panzaru (1996-)
Tel: +40(21) 307-73-02 EMail: panzaru@unibuc.ro

Secretar şef: Maria Prună
Tel: +40(21) 307-73-12, Fax: +40(21) 307-73-59
EMail: maria@secretariat.unibuc.ro

International Relations: Carmen Bătătorescu
Tel: +40(21) 307-73-22, Fax: +40(21) 314-09-42
EMail: externe@unibuc.ro

Chairs

Intercultural and Interreligious Exchanges *(UNESCO)* (Cultural Studies; Management)

Faculties

Administration and Business (Administration; Business Administration; Human Resources; Labour and Industrial Relations; Management; Public Administration; Public Relations; Secretarial Studies); **Baptist Theology** (Modern Languages; Romanian; Social Work; Theology); **Biology** (Biochemistry; Biology; Ecology); **Chemistry** (Biotechnology; Chemistry; Physical Chemistry; Radiophysics); **Foreign Languages and Literature** (American Studies; Arabic; Bulgarian; Canadian Studies; Chinese; Classical Languages; Czech; Dutch; English; French; French Studies; German; Hungarian; Italian; Japanese; Korean; Linguistics; Literature; Medieval Studies; Modern Languages; Persian; Philology; Polish; Portuguese; Romance Languages; Romanian; Russian; Serbocroatian; Slavic Languages; Spanish; Swedish; Translation and Interpretation; Turkish); **Geography** (Environmental Studies; Geography; Meteorology; Surveying and Mapping; Water Science); **Geology and Geophysics** (Geological Engineering; Geology; Geophysics; Mineralogy; Paleontology); **History** (Ancient Civilizations; Archaeology; Art History; Contemporary History; European Studies; History; International Relations; Medieval Studies; Modern History); **Journalism and Communication Sciences** (Advertising and Publicity; Anthropology; Canadian Studies; Human Resources; Journalism; Mass Communication; Multimedia; Public Relations); **Law** (Commercial Law; Constitutional Law; Criminal Law; European Union Law; International Law; Labour and Industrial Relations; Law; Private Law; Public Administration; Public Law); **Letters** (Administration; Communication Studies; Comparative Literature; Ethnology; European Studies; Information Sciences; International Relations; Library Science; Linguistics; Literature; Management; Mass Communication; Modern Languages; Philology; Public Relations; Romanian; Secretarial Studies); **Mathematics and Computer Science** (Applied Mathematics; Astronomy and Space Science; Computer Science; Design; Information Technology; Mathematics; Mathematics and Computer Science; Mechanics; Physics); **Open and Distance learning** *(CREDIS)*; **Orthodox Theology** (Bible; Cultural Studies; English; French; Orthodox Theology; Pastoral Studies; Philology; Religious Art; Romanian; Social Work; Theology); **Philosophy** (Cultural Studies; Ethics; Logic; Philosophical Schools); **Physics** (Atomic and Molecular Physics; Biophysics; Electronic Engineering; Laser Engineering; Mathematical Physics; Mechanics; Meteorology; Optics; Physics; Polymer and Plastics Technology; Solid State Physics); **Political Sciences** (Political Sciences); **Primary and Preschool Education Pedagogy**; **Psychology and Educational Sciences** (Education; Educational and Student Counselling; Educational Psychology; Educational Sciences; Pedagogy; Psychology; Psychotherapy; Teacher Training); **Roman Catholic Theology** (Catholic Theology; Social Work); **Sociology and Social Work**; **Technology** *(CREDIS)*

History: Founded 1694 by Prince Constantin Basarab Brâncoveanu as Sfantul Sava Princiary Academy, established as University 1864, reorganized 1948. Present structure adopted 1990. A State Institution.

Governing Bodies: Administrative Council; Senate; Executive Board

Academic Year: October to July (October-December; February-July)

Admission Requirements: Secondary school certificate (Bacalaureat) and competitive entrance examination

Fees: (US Dollars): Foreign students, 320 per month

Main Language(s) of Instruction: Romanian

International Co-operation: With universities in Austria, Belgium, France, Germany, Italy, Spain, Sweden, United Kingdom. Alos participates in Socrates-Erasmus, Leonardo da Vinci, Aimos, Tempra, Copernicus programmes. UNESCO-Cousteau Ecotechnic Chair

Accrediting Agencies: Ministry of Education and Research; National Council for Academic Assesment and Accreditation

Degrees and Diplomas: *Diploma de Licenţă*; *Certificat de atestare a competentelor profesionale*; *Diplomă de Master*; *Diplomă de Doctor (PhD)*

Student Services: Academic counselling, Canteen, Employment services, Foreign student adviser, Health services, Language programs, Social counselling, Sports facilities

Student Residential Facilities: For c. 4,000 students

Special Facilities: University Museum. 'Dimitrie Brândză' Botanical Garden

Libraries: Central Library; libraries of the faculties and institutes, total, c. 2m. vols

Publications: Analele Universitaţii Bucureşti, Ten series published in Romanian, English, French *(annually)*; Arta Botanica Horti Bucurestiensia, Journal of Botany, published in English, French and Romanian *(annually)*

Press or Publishing House: Tipografia Universităţii Bucureşti; 'Ars Docendi' Press

Last Updated: 07/09/11

UNIVERSITY OF CRAIOVA

Universitatea din Craiova (UCV)

Strada Alexandru Ioan Cuza Street nr, 13, 200585 Craiova
Tel: +40(251) 41-43-98
Fax: +40(251) 41-16-88
EMail: rectorat@central.ucv.ro
Website: http://www.central.ucv.ro

Rector: Ion Vladimirescu (2004-) Tel: +40(251) 41-43-98

Prorector: Dan Popescu
Tel: +40(251) 41-90-15 EMail: danpopescu@central.ucv.ro

International Relations: Nicolae Panea, Prorector
Tel: +40(251) 41-70-47, Fax: +40(251) 41-70-47
EMail: relint@central.ucv.ro; npanea@yahoo.com

Departments

Applied Foreign Languages (English; French; German; Modern Languages; Romanian); **Applied Mathematics** (Applied Mathematics); **Teacher Training** (Teacher Training)

Faculties

Agriculture (Agronomy) *Dean*: Dan Badescu; **Automatics, Computer Science** (Automation and Control Engineering; Computer Engineering; Electrical and Electronic Engineering); **Chemistry** (Chemistry); **Economics and Business Administration** (Accountancy; Business and Commerce; Computer Science; Economics; Finance; International Economics; International Relations; Management; Marketing; Statistics); **Electromechanics, Environments and Industrial Informatics** (Automation and Control Engineering; Electrical and Electronic Engineering; Engineering; Environmental Engineering; Mechanical Engineering); **Electrotechnics Engineering** (Aeronautical and Aerospace Engineering; Automation and Control Engineering; Electrical and Electronic Equipment and Maintenance; Electrical Engineering; Energy Engineering; Power Engineering)); **Engineering and Management of Technological Systems** *(Drobeta-Turnu Severin)*; **History, Philosophy and Geography**; **Horticulture** (Biology; Environmental Engineering; Food Technology; Horticulture); **Law and Administrative Sciences** *(Nicolae Titulescu)* (Administration; Law); **Letters** (Arts and Humanities; Classical Languages; Communication Studies; Design; Educational Sciences; Fine Arts; Linguistics; Literature; Modern Languages; Music; Political Sciences; Social Sciences; Theatre; Translation and Interpretation); **Mathematics and Informatics** (Computer Science; Mathematics); **Mechanics** (Engineering; Engineering Management; Industrial Engineering; Materials Engineering; Mechanical Engineering); **Physical Education and Sports** (Alternative Medicine; Sports); **Physics** (Physics); **Social Sciences** (Social Sciences); **Technological Systems Management and Engineering** *(Dobreta-Turnu Severin)* (Engineering Management; Environmental Engineering; Industrial Engineering; Marine Engineering; Mechanical Engineering); **Theology** (Social Work; Theology)

Units

Drobeta Turnu Severin *(Drobeta Turnu Severin)*

History: Founded 1947 as Institute, became university 1966 and independent institution 1990. A State institution. Financed by the State, also receives financial support for research from industry. Also branch in Drobeta - Turnu Severin.

Governing Bodies: Senate

Academic Year: October to July (October-January; February-July)

Admission Requirements: Secondary school certificate (Bacalaureat) or equivalent, and entrance examination

Fees: (Euro): residents, 250-850 per annum; (US Dollars): foreigners, 3,200-3,400 per annum

Main Language(s) of Instruction: Romanian, English, French

International Co-operation: Participates in the Socrates programme

Accrediting Agencies: National Council for Academic Evaluation and Accrditation

Degrees and Diplomas: *Diploma de Licenţă*; *Diploma de Licenţă*: Arts and Humanities; Social and Political Sciences; *Diplomă de Master*, *Diplomă de Master*: Agronomy; Chemistry; Horticulture; Complex Electromechanical Systems; Electrical Engineering; Energy Engineering; Engineering Sciences; Mechanical Engineering; Industrial Engineering; MaterialScience and Engineering; History; Philosophy; Sociology; Geography; Political Sciences; Law; Administration; Management; Economics; Accountancy; Finance; International Economic Relations;Economic Cybernetics and Statistics; Mathematics and Informatics; Physics; Orthodox Theology; Physical Education and Sport; System and Computer Science; *Diplomă de Doctor*: Agronomy; Chemistry; Automatic Systems; Computer Science; Electrical Engineering; Energy Engineering; Electronic Engineering; Engineering Sciences; Mechanical Engineering; Industrial Engineering; MaterialScience and Engineering; History; Horticulture; Law; Mathematics; Philology; Physics; Management; Economics; Accountancy; Finance; International Economic Relations;Economic Cybernetics and Statistics

Student Services: Academic counselling, Canteen, Cultural centre, Employment services, Foreign student adviser, Foreign Studies Centre, Health services, Language programs, Sports facilities

Student Residential Facilities: For 4,000 students

Special Facilities: 'Teleuniversitatea' TV Station

Libraries: c. 1.1m. vols

Publications: Analele Universităţii *(annually)*

Press or Publishing House: Universitaria Publishing House

Student Numbers *2010-2011*: Total: c. 32,000

Last Updated: 15/09/11

UNIVERSITY OF DRAMATIC ART OF TÂRGU-MUREŞ

Universitatea de Artă Teatrală din Târgu-Mureş

Köteles Samuel Street nr. 6, 540057 Târgu-Mureş

Tel: +40(265) 26-62-81 +40(265) 26-03-62

Fax: +40(265) 26-62-81

EMail: uat@uat.ro; admitere@uat.ro

Website: http://www.uat.ro

Rector: Attila Gáspárik

Faculties

Music (Music); **Theatre** *(in Romanian and Hungarian)* (Acting; Dance; Display and Stage Design; Performing Arts; Theatre)

History: Founded in Cluj 1946, moved to Târgu-Mureş 1954. Acquired present status and title 2002.

Governing Bodies: Senate

Academic Year: October to July (October-January; January-July)

Admission Requirements: Secondary school certificate (Bacalaureat)

Main Language(s) of Instruction: Romanian, Hungarian

International Co-operation: With universities in Hungary.

Accrediting Agencies: Ministry of Education and Research

Degrees and Diplomas: *Diploma de Licenţă*: Acting; Pupetry; Choreography; Theater; Scenography and Artistic Events; *Diplomă de Master*: Theater; Art Directing; Dramatic Writing; Speak and language in Performing Arts; Contemporary Performance Direction; *Diplomă de Doctor*: Theatre

Special Facilities: Theatre Studio

Libraries: c. 40,000 vols

Last Updated: 20/09/11

UNIVERSITY OF MEDICINE AND PHARMACY OF CRAIOVA

Universitatea de Medicină şi Farmacie din Craiova (UMFCV)

Strada Petru Rareş no, 2-4,
200349 Craiova

Tel: +40(251) 52-24-58

Fax: +40(251) 59-30-77

EMail: eu-office@umfcv.ro

Website: http://www.umfcv.ro/

Rector: Adrian Săftoiu
Tel: +40(251) 12-24-58 EMail: rectorat@umfcv.ro

Director General Administrative: Mihai Caragea
EMail: dga@umfcv.ro

Faculties

Dentistry (Dentistry); **Medicine** (Medicine; Rehabilitation and Therapy); **Midwifery and Nursing** (Midwifery; Nursing); **Pharmacy** (Pharmacy)

History: Founded as faculty 1970, acquired present status and title 1998.

Governing Bodies: Senate; Senate Bureau; Faculty Councils

Academic Year: October to July (October-February; March-July)

Admission Requirements: Secondary school certificate (Bacalaureat), or foreign equivalent

Fees: (US Dollars): Romanian students, 600 per annum; foreign students, 360-380 per month

Main Language(s) of Instruction: Romanian, English

International Co-operation: With universities in Belgium, France, Germany, Greece, Italy, Netherlands, Portugal and Spain

Accrediting Agencies: Ministry of Education and Research

Degrees and Diplomas: *Diploma de Licență*; *Diplomă de Master*: Health Administration; Medical Biostatistics; Prosthetics; Nursing; Pharmacology and Toxicology; *Diplomă de Doctor (Ph.D.)*

Student Services: Academic counselling, Canteen, Cultural centre, Employment services, Foreign student adviser, Foreign Studies Centre, Health services, Language programs, Social counselling, Sports facilities

Libraries: University Library

Publications: Craiova medicală, National Medical Journal *(quarterly)*

Press or Publishing House: Editura medicală universitară

Last Updated: 16/09/11

UNIVERSITY OF MEDICINE AND PHARMACY OF TÂRGU-MUREȘ

Universitatea de Medicină și Farmacie din Târgu-Mureș (UMF)

Gheorghe Marinescu Street nr. 38,
540000 Târgu-Mureș
Tel: +40(265) 21-55-51
Fax: +40(265) 21-04-07
EMail: rectorat@umftgm.ro
Website: http://www.umftgm.ro

Rector: Constantin Copotoiu (2000-) Tel: +40(265) 21-31-27

Cancelar: Aurel Nirestean EMail: cancelar@umftgm.ro

International Relations: Angela Borda, International Relations Officer Tel: +40(265) 21-51-33, Fax: +40(265) 21-04-07

Colleges

Nursing (Nursing) *Head*: Alexandru Șchiopu

Faculties

Dentistry (Dentistry) *Dean*: Mircea Suciu; **Medicine** (Dietetics; Laboratory Techniques; Medical Auxiliaries; Medicine; Nutrition) *Dean*: Leonard Dobreanu; **Pharmacy** (Pharmacy) *Dean*: Daniela Muntean

History: Founded 1945 as a section of the Faculty of Medicine of the University of Cluj. Acquired present status and title 1947.

Governing Bodies: Senate

Academic Year: October to July (October-December; January-July)

Admission Requirements: Secondary school certificate (Baccalaureat) and entrance examination

Fees: State scholarships for 45% of the students, according to professional training and social aspects; (US Dollars): 800 for faculty; 300 for college per annum

Main Language(s) of Instruction: Romanian, Hungarian

International Co-operation: With universities in Poland. Participates in Erasmus, Tempus and Leonardo da Vinci programmes.

Accrediting Agencies: Ministry of Education

Degrees and Diplomas: *Diploma de Licență*; *Certificat de atestare a competentelor profesionale*; *Diplomă de Master*; *Diplomă de Doctor*. Also Medical Assistant qualification

Student Services: Academic counselling, Canteen, Cultural centre, Foreign Studies Centre, Health services, Social counselling, Sports facilities

Student Residential Facilities: Yes

Special Facilities: Anatomy Museum; History of Medicine Museum. Audiovisual, Multimedia, and Medical Computing Laboratories. Botanical Garden; Garden of Medicinal Herbs

Libraries: Central Library, c. 275,000 vols; departmental libraries, c. 105,000

Publications: Revista de Medicină și Farmacie *(quarterly)*

Press or Publishing House: Univ.Med.Pharm

Academic Staff *2008-2009*	MEN	WOMEN	TOTAL
FULL-TIME	191	233	**424**
STAFF WITH DOCTORATE			
FULL-TIME	–	–	**75**
PART-TIME	–	–	**334**
Student Numbers *2008-2009*			
All (Foreign Included)	–	–	**3,567**
FOREIGN ONLY	–	–	**83**

Last Updated: 20/09/11

UNIVERSITY OF ORADEA

Universitatea din Oradea

C.P. nr. 114, Oficiul Postal 1, Universitatii Street nr. 1,
410087 Oradea
Tel: +40(259) 40-81-13 +40(259) 43-28-30
Fax: +40(259) 43-27-89
EMail: rectorat@uoradea.ro
Website: http://www.uoradea.ro

Rector: Cornel Antal (2004-)
Tel: +40(259) 43-28-89 EMail: cantal@uoradea.ro

General Director of Administration: Gordan Mircea
Tel: +40(259) 40-81-02 EMail: mgordan@uoradea.ro

International Relations: Carmen Buran, Head, International Relations Department
Tel: +40(259) 46-76-42, Fax: +40(259) 46-76-42
EMail: driie@uoradea.ro; cburan@uoradea.ro

Departments

Distance Learning *(ID)*; **Lifelong Learning** (Continuing Education); **Teacher Training** *(DPPPD)*

Faculties

Architecture and Construction (Architecture; Construction Engineering; Sanitary Engineering; Surveying and Mapping); **Economics**; **Electrical Engineering and Information Technology** (Computer Science; Electrical Engineering; Electronic Engineering; Information Technology; Technology); **Energy Engineering** (Electrical Engineering; Energy Engineering; Thermal Engineering); **Engineering Management and Technology** (Engineering; Machine Building; Mechanics); **Environmental Protection** (Agriculture; Chemistry; Computer Science; Environmental Engineering; Forestry; Physics); **History, Geography and International Relations** (Archaeology; Architecture and Planning; Art History; Environmental Studies; European Studies; Geography; History; International Relations; Tourism); **Legal Sciences** (Private Law; Public Law); **Letters** (English; French; German; Literature; Modern Languages; Romanian); **Medicine and Pharmacy** (Anatomy; Biochemistry; Dentistry; Medicine; Microbiology; Neurology; Pharmacology; Pharmacy; Physiology; Psychiatry and Mental Health; Radiology); **Music** (Music); **Orthodox Theology** (Orthodox Theology); **Physical Education and Sports** (Physical Education; Physical Therapy; Sports); **Political Science and Communication Studies** (Journalism; Political Sciences); **Sciences** (Biology; Chemistry; Mathematics; Physics); **Social Sciences** (Social Sciences); **Textiles and Leatherwork** (Leather Techniques; Textile Design; Textile Technology); **Visual Arts** (Fine Arts; Visual Arts)

History: Founded 1963 as Pedagogical Institute. Reorganized 1975 with one Faculty. Became Technical University 1990 and acquired present title 1991. A State Institution.

Governing Bodies: Senate

Academic Year: October - June

Admission Requirements: Secondary school certificate (Bacalaureat) and entrance examination

Fees: (US Dollars): 3,200 - 3,800 per annum

Main Language(s) of Instruction: Romanian, English

International Co-operation: With universities in Austria, Belgium, Brazil, Bulgaria, Canada, Czech Republic, China, Congo, Croatia, Denmark, Finland, France, Germany, Greece, Iceland, Italy, Japan, Latvia, Macedonia, United Kingdom, Mexico, Moldova, Norway, Netherlands, Poland, Portugal, Russia, San Marino, Slovakia, Slovenia, Spain, USA, Sweden, Taiwan, Turkey, Ukraine, Hungary

Accrediting Agencies: Ministry of Education and Research

Degrees and Diplomas: *Diploma de Licență*; *Certificat de atestare a competentelor profesionale*; *Diplomă de Master*; *Diplomă de Doctor*: Electrical Engineering; Industrial Engineering; Energy

Engineering; Economics; Medicine; Biology; History; Geography; Philology; Sociology

Student Services: Academic counselling, Canteen, Cultural centre, Foreign student adviser, Health services, Language programs, Social counselling, Sports facilities

Student Residential Facilities: Yes

Special Facilities: 3 MW Geothermal Plant. Research Laboratory. Art Gallery

Libraries: c. 211,505 vols, computer labs

Publications: Oradea Medical Magazine *(annually)*

Press or Publishing House: Oradea University Press

Last Updated: 19/09/11

UNIVERSITY OF PETROŞANI

Universitatea din Petroşani (UPET)

Universitatii Street nr. 20, 332006 Petroşani
Tel: +40(254) 54-25-80 +40(254) 54-33-82
Fax: +40(254) 54-34-91
EMail: international@upet.ro
Website: http://www.upet.ro

Rector: Emil Pop Fax: +40(254) 54-29-94 EMail: rector@upet.ro

Secretary General: Maria Zapartan
Tel: +40(254) 54-90-10, Fax: +40(254) 54-90-10
EMail: zapartan@upet.ro

Faculties

Mechanical and Electrical Engineering (Automation and Control Engineering; Computer Engineering; Electrical Engineering; Energy Engineering; Industrial Engineering; Mechanical Engineering; Transport Engineering); **Mining Engineering** (Civil Engineering; Economics; Environmental Engineering; Geological Engineering; Mineralogy; Mining Engineering; Surveying and Mapping); **Science** (Accountancy; Banking; Business and Commerce; Business Computing; Management; Mathematics; Physics; Public Administration; Sociology; Tourism)

History: Founded 1864 as Coal Institute. Incorporated former Brad Institute of Mining 1952. Incorporated former Bucharest Institute of Mining 1957. Reorganized as Technical University 1991. Acquired present status and title 1995.

Governing Bodies: Senate

Academic Year: October to July (October-February; March-July)

Admission Requirements: High school certificate

Fees: (Euro): Foreign students, 3,200 per annum; (Lei): Romanian Students, 1,500 per annum

Main Language(s) of Instruction: Romanian

International Co-operation: With universities in Belgium, Bulgaria, Czech Republic, Croatia, Egypt, France, Germany, Hungary, Italy, Moldova, Namibia, Poland, Russia, Slovakia, Slovenia, Ukraine, USA. Participates in Socrates/ Erasmus Programme and Leonardo Da Vinci Programme.

Accrediting Agencies: Agenţia Română de Asigurare A Calităţii în învăţământul Superior (ARACIS)

Degrees and Diplomas: *Diploma de Licenţă*; *Certificat de atestare a competentelor profesionale*: Mechanical and Electrical Engineering; Mining Engineering; Computer Science; Electronics and Communication; *Diplomă de Master*: Strategic Management; Finance-Banking; Information Systems Management; Social Policy and Social Protection; Mining Engineering; Mechancial and Electrical Engineering; *Diplomă de Doctor*: Mining, Petroleum and Gas Engineering; Industrial Engineering; Electrical Engineering; Automation and Control Engineering (PhD)

Student Services: Academic counselling, Canteen, Cultural centre, Employment services, Foreign student adviser, Foreign Studies Centre, Health services, Language programs, Social counselling, Sports facilities

Student Residential Facilities: For over 1,200 students

Special Facilities: Mining Museum

Libraries: Central Library, over 300,000 vols

Publications: Annals of the University of Petroşani (in English, French, German), Four sections: Physics, Mining Engineering, Electrical Engineering; Mechanical Engineering; Economics *(annually)*; Revista Minelor, Fundamental Research publication of the Mining faculty *(monthly)*; Universitaria Ropet *(annually)*

Press or Publishing House: Universitas Publishing House

Academic Staff *2010-2011*	**TOTAL**
FULL-TIME	300
PART-TIME	50
STAFF WITH DOCTORATE	
FULL-TIME	150
PART-TIME	c. 25
Student Numbers *2010-2011*	
All (Foreign Included)	c. 7,000
FOREIGN ONLY	30

Distance students, 1,600.

Last Updated: 19/09/11

UNIVERSITY OF PITEŞTI

Universitatea din Piteşti (UPIT)

Piaţa Vasile Milea 1, 110040 Piteşti
Tel: +40(348) 45-31-00
Fax: +40(348) 45-31-23
EMail: info@upit.ro
Website: http://www.upit.ro

Rector: Gheorghe Barbu EMail: gheorghe.Barbu@upit.ro

Secretar Şef: Găvan Smaranda

International Relations: Dumitru Chirlesan, Pro-Rector, International Relations and European Integration
Tel: +40(248) 21-88-04 EMail: dumitru.chirlesan@upit.ro

Faculties

Economics (Accountancy; Agricultural Economics; Banking; Business Administration; Business and Commerce; Economics; Finance; Hotel and Restaurant; Human Resources; International Business; Management; Marketing; Tourism); **Educational Sciences** (Education); **Electronics, Communications and Computers** (Computer Engineering; Electrical Engineering; Electronic Engineering; Software Engineering; Telecommunications Engineering); **Legal and Administrative Sciences** (Administration; Commercial Law; European Union Law; International Law; Law; Public Administration); **Letters** (Arts and Humanities; English; French; Literature; Modern Languages; Romance Languages; Romanian; Spanish; Translation and Interpretation); **Mathematics and Computer Science** (Applied Mathematics; Computer Science; Information Technology; Mathematics; Mathematics and Computer Science); **Mechanics and Technology** (Engineering; Industrial Engineering; Materials Engineering; Mechanical Engineering; Mechanics; Technology); **Orthodox Theology** (Orthodox Theology); **Physical Education and Sports** (Leisure Studies; Physical Education; Physical Therapy; Sports; Tourism); **Science** (Biology; Chemistry; Ecology; Horticulture; Natural Sciences; Physics); **Social Sciences** (Social Sciences)

History: Founded 1962 as Pedagogic Institute, acquired present status and title 1990. A University enjoying academic autonomy.

Governing Bodies: Senate

Academic Year: October to July (October-February; February-July)

Admission Requirements: Secondary school certificate (Bacalaureat)

Main Language(s) of Instruction: Romanian, English, French

International Co-operation: With universities in: Denmark, France, Germany, Greece, Portugal, Spain, United Kingdom, Serbia and Montenegro. Also participates in Leonardo, Grundtvig, Minerva, Erasmus/Socrates programmes

Accrediting Agencies: Ministry of Education and Research

Degrees and Diplomas: *Diploma de Licenţă*; *Diplomă de Master*: Business Administration; Human Resources; Banking; Finance; Economics; Management; Computer Science; Information Technology; Applied Mathematics; Mathematics; Educational Management; Electronic Engineering and Intelligent Systems; Electronic Systems for Industrial Process Management; Electronic Systems and Distributed Parallel Processing; French Literature; Romanian; Translation (French and English); Literary Linguistics (English); Medical Biology; Ecology and Environment Protection; Physics and Chemistry of Materials; Materials and Nuclear Technologies; Plant Protection; Public Administration in the Context of European

Integration; Legal Assistance of the Enterprise; Community and International Legal Institutions; Romanians and Romania in the European Context; Ethics of public policies; Sports; Tourism and Leisure Activities; *Diplomă de Doctor*: Biology; Electronics and Telecommunications; Physical Education and Sports; Mechanical Engineering; Industrial Engineering; Materials Science; Romanian; Romanian Literature; French Literature; Computer Science; Mathematics. Also Postgraduate Master degree.

Student Services: Academic counselling, Canteen, Cultural centre, Employment services, Foreign student adviser, Foreign Studies Centre, Handicapped facilities, Health services, Language programs, Nursery care, Social counselling, Sports facilities

Student Residential Facilities: For 1,048 students

Special Facilities: Zoology Museum; History Museum. Language Laboratory

Libraries: Central University Library, c. 185,000 vols

Publications: Mathematics and Computer Science Pedagogy *(biannually)*; Metrology *(biannually)*; Physical Education and Sport Pedagogy *(biannually)*; The Scientific Bulletin (Series: Automobile, Machine Engineering, Applied Electronics, Applied Mechanics) *(biannually)*

Last Updated: 19/09/11

UNIVERSITY OF THE WEST OF TIMIŞOARA

Universitatea de Vest din Timişoara (UVT)

Bulevardul Vasile Pârvan no, 4, 300223 Timişoara
Tel: +40(256) 59-21-11
Fax: +40(256) 59-23-10
EMail: secretariat@rectorat.uvt.ro
Website: http://www.uvt.ro

Rector: Ioan Talpoş
Tel: +40(256) 59-21-68, Fax: +40(256) 59-23-10
EMail: ioan.talpos@rectorat.uvt.ro

Secretar Şef: Mihaela Răduţă
Tel: +40(256) 59-21-69, Fax: +40(256) 59-22-41
EMail: mraduta@rectorat.uvt.ro

International Relations: Florin Foltean, Prorector
Tel: +40(256) 59-21-13, Fax: +40(256) 59-23-13
EMail: florin.foltean@rectorat.uvt.ro

Departments

Continuing and Distance Education *(DECIDD)* (Continuing Education; Distance Education); **Teacher Training** (Teacher Training)

Faculties

Arts and Design (Art Education; Ceramic Art; Design; Fashion Design; Fine Arts; Graphic Design; Industrial Design; Interior Design; Painting and Drawing; Photography; Restoration of Works of Art; Sculpture; Textile Design; Video; Visual Arts); **Chemistry, Biology, Geography**; **Economics and Business Administration**; **Law and Administrative Sciences** (Administration; Civil Law; Commercial Law; Criminal Law; European Union Law; Fiscal Law; Law; Public Administration; Public Law); **Letters, History and Theology** (Arts and Humanities; Classical Languages; Comparative Literature; English; French; German; History; Italian; Linguistics; Literature; Orthodox Theology; Pastoral Studies; Philology; Romance Languages; Romanian; Serbocroatian; Slavic Languages; Theology); **Mathematics and Informatics** (Applied Mathematics; Artificial Intelligence; Business Computing; Computer Science; Mathematics; Mathematics and Computer Science; Software Engineering); **Music** (Acting; Conducting; Music; Music Education; Musical Instruments; Singing; Theatre); **Physical Education and Sports**; **Physics** (Applied Physics; Computer Science; Engineering; Optics; Physics; Solid State Physics); **Political Science, Philosophy and Communication Sciences**; **Sociology and Psychology**

Further Information: Also Scientific Research Centres active in the field of Artistic Creation, Excellence in Science, Artistic Excellence

History: Founded 1948 as Institute of Education, acquired present status and tile 1962. A State Institution.

Governing Bodies: Senate

Academic Year: October to May (October-January; February-May). Also Summer Session (July)

Admission Requirements: Secondary school certificate (Bacalaureat) or equivalent, and entrance examination

Fees: (US Dollars): Undergraduate students, c. 320-790 per month, postgraduate students, c. 340-810; doctoral students, c. 360-830

Main Language(s) of Instruction: Romanian

International Co-operation: Participates in the Socrates/Erasmus, Tempus and Leonardo da Vinci programmes

Accrediting Agencies: Ministry of Education and Research

Degrees and Diplomas: *Diploma de Licenţă*; *Diplomă de Master*; *Diplomă de Doctor (PhD)*

Student Services: Academic counselling, Foreign student adviser, Foreign Studies Centre, Health services, Language programs, Sports facilities

Student Residential Facilities: Yes

Special Facilities: Observatory. Video Studio. Seismical Station. Research Centres

Libraries: Central Library, c. 1m. vols

Publications: Analele Universităţii de Vest din Timişoara, Faculties series *(annually)*

Press or Publishing House: University Publishing House

Last Updated: 20/09/11

VALACHIA UNIVERSITY OF TÂRGOVIŞTE

Universitatea Valahia din Târgovişte

Bd. Carol I, Nr. 2, 130024 Târgovişte
Tel: +40(245) 20-61-01
Fax: +40(245) 21-76-92
EMail: rectorat@valahia.ro
Website: http://www.valahia.ro

Rector: Ion Cucui (1992-) EMail: icucui@valahia.ro

International Relations: Delia Popescu, Director, Department for International Relations
Tel: +40(245) 21-18-09, Fax: +40(245) 21-18-09
EMail: relint@valahia.ro

Departments

Distance Learning and Continuing Education

Faculties

Economics; **Electrical Engineering** (Electrical Engineering); **Environmental Engineering and Biotechnology** (Agronomy; Biotechnology; Environmental Engineering; Food Technology); **Humanities** (Arts and Humanities); **Juridical, Social and Political Sciences** (Journalism; Law; Political Sciences; Preschool Education; Primary Education; Public Administration; Social Sciences); **Materials Engineering, Mecatronics and Robotics** (Engineering; Materials Engineering; Mechanical Engineering; Robotics); **Sciences and Arts**; **Theology** (Pastoral Studies; Theology)

History: Founded 1992 on former University College of Technology and Economics.

Governing Bodies: Senate

Academic Year: October to July (October-February; March-July)

Admission Requirements: Secondary school certificate (Bacalaureat) or recognized equivalent, and entrance examination

Main Language(s) of Instruction: Romanian

International Co-operation: Participates in the Tempus, Socrates, Copernicus and Peco programmes

Accrediting Agencies: Ministry of Education and Research

Degrees and Diplomas: *Diploma de Licenţă*; *Certificat de atestare a competentelor profesionale*; *Diplomă de Master*; *Diplomă de Doctor*

Student Services: Canteen, Cultural centre, Foreign Studies Centre, Social counselling, Sports facilities

Student Residential Facilities: For c. 300 students

Special Facilities: Printing Museum

Libraries: c. 5,000 vols

Publications: Analele Universităţii 'Valahia' *(annually)*

Press or Publishing House: Publishing House

Last Updated: 20/09/11

VASILE ALECSANDRI UNIVERSITY OF BACĂU

Universitatea Vasile Alecsandri din Bacău (UB)

Calea Mărăşeşti 157, 600115 Bacău
Tel: +40(234) 54-24-11
Fax: +40(234) 54-57-53
EMail: rector@ub.ro
Website: http://www.ub.ro

Rector: Valentin Nedeff Tel: +40(234) 13-47-12

International Relations: Silvia Leonte
Tel: +40(234) 57-69-01, Fax: +40(234) 57-69-01
EMail: relint@ub.ro

Departments

Distance Education *(DIDFR)* (Distance Education); **Research, Technology Transfer, Postgraduate Studies, Continuing Education and PhD** (Applied Physics; Business Administration; Chemistry; Communication Studies; Cultural Studies; Energy Engineering; Engineering; Environmental Management; Food Technology; Health Sciences; Industrial Engineering; Information Sciences; Journalism; Linguistics; Literature; Machine Building; Mechanics; Solid State Physics); **Teacher Training** (Education; Teacher Training)

Faculties

Arts and Humanities (Arts and Humanities; Communication Studies; Cultural Studies; Education; English; French; History; Journalism; Literature; Modern Languages; Political Sciences; Public Relations; Romanian; Social Sciences); **Economical Sciences**; **Engineering** (Chemical Engineering; Computer Engineering; Electronic Engineering; Energy Engineering; Engineering; Engineering Management; Environmental Engineering; Food Technology; Industrial Design; Industrial Engineering; Information Technology; Mechanical Engineering; Robotics); **Science**; **Science of Movement, Sports and Health**

Further Information: Also Romanian language courses for foreign students

History: Founded 1961 on former Teacher Training Institute, acquired present status 1990.

Governing Bodies: Senate

Academic Year: October to July (October-February; February-July)

Admission Requirements: Secondary school certificate (Bacalaureat) and entrance examination(for some of specializations)

Main Language(s) of Instruction: Romanian

International Co-operation: Participates in Socrates, Tempus, Copernicus and Leonardo da Vinci programmes

Accrediting Agencies: National Council for Academic Evaluation and Accreditation

Degrees and Diplomas: *Diploma de Licenţă*; *Certificat de atestare a competentelor profesionale*; *Diplomă de Master*: 2 yrs; *Diplomă de Doctor*

Student Services: Canteen, Foreign student adviser, Health services, Language programs, Sports facilities

Student Residential Facilities: Yes

Libraries: Total, c. 250,000 vols (3 department libraries for Mathematics and Economics, French, English)

Publications: Studii şi cercetări ştiinţifice *(annually)*

Last Updated: 09/09/11

VICTOR BABES UNIVERSITY OF MEDICINE AND PHARMACY OF TIMISOARA

Universitatea de Medicină şi Farmacie Victor Babes din Timişoara (UMFT)

Piata Eftimie Murgu 2, 300041 Timişoara
Tel: +40(256) 29-33-89
Fax: +40(256) 49-06-26
EMail: rectorat@umft.ro
Website: http://www.umft.ro

Rector: Marius Raica (2012-)
Tel: +40(256) 29-33-89, Fax: +40(256) 49-06-26

Secretary General: Ionel Puia Tel: +40(256) 24-11-17

International Relations: Carmen Bunu, Head of International Relations Department
Tel: +40(256) 22-04-82, Fax: +40(256) 22-04-82
EMail: relint@umft.ro; cbunu@umft.ro

Faculties

Dental Medicine (Anaesthesiology; Dental Technology; Dentistry; Health Education; Oral Pathology; Orthodontics; Periodontics; Radiology; Rehabilitation and Therapy; Surgery); **Medicine** (Anatomy; Biochemistry; Biophysics; Cardiology; Cell Biology; Child Care and Development; Computer Science; Dermatology; Endocrinology; Epidemiology; Gastroenterology; Genetics; Gynaecology and Obstetrics; Haematology; Histology; Hygiene; Immunology; Medical Auxiliaries; Medicine; Microbiology; Midwifery; Modern Languages; Molecular Biology; Nephrology; Neurology; Nursing; Orthopaedics; Otorhinolaryngology; Paediatrics; Parasitology; Pathology; Pharmacology; Philosophy; Physical Education; Physical Therapy; Physiology; Plastic Surgery; Psychiatry and Mental Health; Public Health; Radiology; Rehabilitation and Therapy; Romanian; Surgery; Urology); **Pharmacy** (Cosmetology; Pharmacy)

Further Information: Also 15 Teaching Hospitals and Clinics

History: Founded 1945. A State Institution.

Governing Bodies: Senate

Academic Year: October to July (October-February; March-July)

Admission Requirements: High school certificate (Bacalaureat) and entrance examination

Fees: (US Dollars): Foreign students, 360 per month; Doctor of Specialization, 380 per month; Medical undergraduate, 380 per month; Language test, 320 per month

Main Language(s) of Instruction: Romanian, English, French

International Co-operation: With universities in France, Germany, Spain, Italy and Belgium.

Accrediting Agencies: Ministry of Education and Research

Degrees and Diplomas: *Diploma de Licenţă*; *Certificat de atestare a competentelor profesionale*; *Diplomă de Doctor (PhD)*

Student Services: Academic counselling, Canteen, Foreign student adviser, Health services, Language programs, Nursery care, Sports facilities

Student Residential Facilities: For c. 2,450 students

Libraries: Total, 198,342 vols

Publications: Cercetări experimentale medico-chirurgicale *(quarterly)*; Timişoara medicalia *(quarterly)*

Academic Staff *2010-2011*: Total 720
STAFF WITH DOCTORATE: Total 310
Student Numbers *2010-2011*: Total: c. 3,200
Last Updated: 20/09/11

PRIVATE INSTITUTIONS

AVRAM IANCU UNIVERSITY OF CLUJ-NAPOCA

Universitatea Avram Iancu din Cluj-Napoca (UAI)

Ilie Măcelaru Street no. 1A, Cluj-Napoca
Tel: +40(264) 45-00-50
EMail: uai.rectorat@gmail.com
Website: http://www.uai-cluj.ro/

Rector: Achim Mihu

Secretary: Oana Moldovan

Faculties

Management and Economics (Economics; Management); **Physical Education and Sports**; **Social and Political Sciences** (Anthropology; Political Sciences; Social Sciences)

History: Founded 1992. Acquired present status 2008.

Main Language(s) of Instruction: Romanian

Degrees and Diplomas: *Diploma de Licenţă*; *Diplomă de Master*
Last Updated: 27/09/11

ANDREI SAGUNA UNIVERSITY OF CONSTANŢA

Universitatea Andrei Şaguna din Constanţa
Alexandru Lăpuşneanu Street, nr. 13, 900916 Constanţa
Tel: +40(241) 662-520 +40(241) 510-500
Fax: +40(241) 662-520
EMail: contact@andreisaguna.ro
Website: http://www.andreisaguna.ro/

Rector: Aurel Papari

Faculties

Communication Studies and Political Sciences (Communication Studies; Political Sciences); **Economics** (Accountancy; Banking; Business Computing; Economics; Finance; Management); **Law and Administrative Sciences** (Accountancy; Administrative Law; Civil Law; Commercial Law; Constitutional Law; Criminal Law; Demography and Population; Economics; History of Law; Human Resources; International Law; Labour Law; Law; Management; Modern Languages; Public Administration; Public Law; Sociology); **Navigation and Marine Transport** (Marine Transport); **Psychosociology** (Psychology; Social Sciences; Social Work; Sociology)

History: Created 1992. Acquired status 2005.

Admission Requirements: Bacalaureat (or equivalent secondary school certificate) for undergraduate programmes; Licenţă (or equivalent Bachelor level degree) for Master's programme; Entrance exam

Main Language(s) of Instruction: Romanian

Degrees and Diplomas: *Diploma de Licenţă*; *Diplomă de Master*. Also Postgraduate courses.

Last Updated: 26/09/11

APOLLONIA UNIVERSITY OF IAŞI

Universitatea Apollonia din Iaşi
Păcurari Street nr. 11, 700511 Iaşl
Tel: +40(232) 21-03-10
Fax: +40(232) 21-03-10
EMail: secretariat.md@univapollonia.ro
Website: http://www.univapollonia.ro

President: Vasile Burlui

Faculties

Communication Sciences (Communication Studies); **Dentistry** (Dental Technology; Dentistry)

History: Founded 1991. Acquired present status 2002.

Admission Requirements: Entrance exam

Main Language(s) of Instruction: Romanian

Accrediting Agencies: Ministry of Education

Degrees and Diplomas: *Diploma de Licenţă*: Dentistry; Optometry. Medicina Dentara: 6yrs

Special Facilities: Specialist laboratories

Libraries: c. 16,000 vols including periodicals

ARTIFEX UNIVERSITY OF BUCHAREST

Universitatea Artifex din Bucureşti
Economu Cezarescu Street nr. 47, sector 6, 060754 Bucureşti
Tel: +40(21) 222-62-49 +40(21) 212-62-55
Fax: +40(21) 212-61-55
EMail: universitate@artifex.org.ro
Website: http://www.artifex.org.ro/

Rector: Dan Cruceru

Faculties

Finance and Accounting (Accountancy; Banking; Finance) *Dean*: Cristian-Marian Barbu; **Management and Marketing** *Dean*: Constantin Coderie

History: Created 1992. Acquired status 2005.

Governing Bodies: University Senate.

Admission Requirements: Bacalaureat (or equivalent secondary school certificate) for undergraduate programmes; Licenţă (or equivalent Bachelor level degree) for Master's programme.

Main Language(s) of Instruction: Romanian

Degrees and Diplomas: *Diploma de Licenţă*: Management; Marketing; Finance and Banking; Accountancy and Information Management; Economics, Tourism and Service Trades; *Diplomă de Master*: Small and Medium Business Management; Marketing and Business Communication; Financial Management, Banking and Insurance (CURSURI DE MASTERAT Complementary Masters Courses); Strategic Marketing; Organisational Management; Finance, Banking and Capital Markets

Last Updated: 22/09/11

ATHENAEUM UNIVERSITY OF BUCHAREST

Universitatea Athenaeum din Bucureşti
Giuseppe Garibaldi Street nr. 2A, sector 2, 020223 Bucureşti
Tel: +40(21) 230-57-38 +40(21) 230-57-26
Fax: +40(21) 231-74-18
EMail: secretariat@univath.ro
Website: http://www.univath.ro/

Rector: Emilia Vasile EMail: rector@univath.ro

Departments

Economics (Business Administration; Economics; Finance; Marketing); **Public Administration** (Public Administration)

History: Created 1990. Acquired status 2005.

Governing Bodies: University Senate

Admission Requirements: Bacalaureat (or equivalent secondary school certificate) for undergraduate programmes; Licenţă (or equivalent Bachelor level degree) for Master's programme.

International Co-operation: Participate in Erasmus prgramme.

Degrees and Diplomas: *Diploma de Licenţă*: Economics; Public Administration, 3-4 yrs; *Diplomă de Master*: International Accounting and Financial Audit; Banking Risks / Insurance and Reinsurance; Internal Audit of Public Institutions; Public Administration and European Integration, 1 1/2 yrs. Also offers online degrees and double degrees in Finance and Business Administration with universities in USA and France.

Libraries: Yes

Academic Staff *2007-2008*: Total: c. 10

Student Numbers *2007-2008*: Total: c. 1,600

Last Updated: 22/09/11

BIOTERRA UNIVERSITY OF BUCHAREST

Universitatea Bioterra din Bucureşti
pavilionul central, Gârlei Street nr, 81, Sector 1, Bucureşti
Tel: +40(21) 490-61-28 +40(21) 490-61-27
Fax: +40(21) 490-61-28
EMail: georgiane22@yahoo.com
Website: http://www.bioterra.ro/

President: Ion Nicolae
Tel: +40(21) 269-34-47, Fax: +40(21) 269-34-38
EMail: nicolaebio@yahoo.com

Rector: Floarea Nicolae EMail: nicolaebio@yahoo.com

International Relations: Iliuta Patrascu, Pro-Rector Social Affairs and International Relations
Tel: +40(21) 269-34-47, Fax: +40(21) 269-34-38

Faculties

Agrotourism Management (Agriculture; Tourism); **Food Engineering** (Brewing; Dairy; Food Science; Food Technology; Horticulture; Meat and Poultry); **Food Production Control and Expertise** (Food Technology); **Law**

Further Information: Also campuses in Alexandria; Slobozia and Buzau

History: Founded 1994 and acquired present status and title 2002.

Governing Bodies: University Senate

Admission Requirements: High school diploma

Fees: (Euro): 300 per annum

Main Language(s) of Instruction: Romanian

International Co-operation: With universities in Canada, Italy, France, Poland and Egypt.

Accrediting Agencies: National Agency of Academic Accreditation

Degrees and Diplomas: *Diploma de Licenţă*; *Diplomă de Master*: Community Security and Terrorism; Performance Management in

Rural Tourism, Food Services and Consumer Protection; Food Safety, Consumer Protection and Environmental Protection

Student Services: Academic counselling, Canteen, Cultural centre, Health services, Language programs, Nursery care, Social counselling, Sports facilities

Student Residential Facilities: Yes

Libraries: 3 Libraries, c. 20,000 vols

Publications: Bulletin of Scientific Information *(annually)*; Research and Scientific Works *(annually)*

Press or Publishing House: Bioterra University Printing Department

Last Updated: 21/09/11

BOGDAN-VODĂ UNIVERSITY OF CLUJ-NAPOCA

Universitatea Bogdan-Vodă din Cluj-Napoca
Grigore Alexandrescu Street nr. 26A RO, 400560 Cluj-Napoca
Tel: +40(264) 598-787
Fax: +40(264) 591-830
EMail: ubv@ubv.ro
Website: http://www.ubv.ro/

Rector: Dumitru Purdea

Faculties

Economics (Accountancy; Banking; Finance; Information Technology; Management; Marketing); **Law** (Civil Law; Commercial Law; Criminal Law) *Dean*: Ioan Santai; **Physical Education and Sport** *(Baia Mare)* (Philosophy of Education; Sports; Sports Management) *Dean*: Gheorghe Neta

Further Information: Also Baia Mare campus.

Governing Bodies: University Senate.

Admission Requirements: Bacalaureat (or equivalent secondary school certificate) for undergraduate programmes; Licenţă (or equivalent Bachelor level degree) for Master's programme.

Fees: (Euro): 500 per annum

Main Language(s) of Instruction: Romanian

Degrees and Diplomas: *Diploma de Licenţă*: Management; Finance and Banking; Accountancy and Management; Information Technology; Law; Physical Education and Sports; *Diplomă de Master*: Audit and Control (in collaboration with the "December 1, 1,918" Alba Iulia); Business Administration; Human Resources Management; Administrative Management; Credit and Companies Management;Health Administration; Criminology; Administrative and Labour Relations Law; Sports Management

Libraries: Yes.

Last Updated: 22/09/11

CONSTANTIN BRÂNCOVEANU UNIVERSITY OF PITEŞTI

Universitatea Constantin Brâncoveanu din Piteşti
Calea Bascovului Street nr. 2A, 11005 Piteşti
Tel: +40(248) 21-26-27 +40(248) 61-33-08
Fax: +40(248) 22-10-98
EMail: pitesti@univcb.ro
Website: http://www.univcb.ro

Rector: Alexandru Puiu (2004-) EMail: rectorat_ucb@yahoo.com

Pro-Rector: Marius Gust

International Relations: Tudorel Popescu, Head of International Relations Office
Tel: +40(248) 61-00-88
EMail: tudorel.popescu@gmail.com; ireoffice@univcb.ro

Faculties

Administration and Communication *(Braila)* (Administration; Communication Studies); **Finance and Accountancy** *(Piteşti)* (Accountancy; Finance) *Dean*: Silvia Dugan; **Law, Administration and Communication Studies** *(Piteşti)* (Administration; Communication Studies; Law) *Dean*: Gabriel Pârvu; **Management, Marketing and Business** *(Piteşti)* (Business Administration; Economics; Management; Marketing) *Dean*: Radu Gabriel Pârvu; **Management, Marketing and Business** *(Braila)* (Business Administration; Management; Marketing) *Dean*: Elena Enache; **Management, Marketing and Business** *(Ramnicu-Valcea)* (Business Administration; Management; Marketing) *Dean*: Iuliana Ciochina

Further Information: Branches in Brăila and Râmnicu Vâlcea.

History: Founded 1991, acquired present status and title 2002.

Academic Year: October to September

Admission Requirements: Secondary school certificate (Bacalaureat), and entrance examination

Fees: (Lei): full time,1,500; part time, 1,300

Main Language(s) of Instruction: Romanian

Accrediting Agencies: Ministry of Education and Research; Romanian Agency for Quality Assurance in Higher Education

Degrees and Diplomas: *Diploma de Licenţă*; *Diplomă de Master*

Student Services: Academic counselling, Canteen, Cultural centre, Employment services, Health services, Language programs, Social counselling, Sports facilities

Student Residential Facilities: Yes

Libraries: Central Library

Press or Publishing House: Economic

Academic Staff *2010-2011*	**TOTAL**
FULL-TIME	150
PART-TIME	80
STAFF WITH DOCTORATE	
FULL-TIME	120
PART-TIME	c. 50
Student Numbers *2010-2011*	
All (Foreign Included)	c. 6,700

Part-time students, 1,300.

Last Updated: 27/09/11

DANUBE UNIVERSITY OF GALAŢI

Universitatea Danubius din Galaţi
B-dul Galati nr. 3, 800654 Galaţi
Tel: +40(236) 36-00-38
Fax: +40(236) 46-00-38
EMail: rectorat@univ-danubius.ro
Website: http://www.univ-danubius.ro

Rector: Benone Puşcă
Tel: +40(372) 36-11-02, Fax: +40(372) 36-12-90
EMail: benonepusca@univ-danubius.ro

Director General Administrative: Georgeta Dragomir
EMail: gretadragomir@univ-danubius.ro

Faculties

Administrative Sciences (Administration); **Communication Studies** (Communication Studies; Public Relations); **Distance Education and Low Frequency** (Banking; Communication Studies; Economics; European Studies; Finance; International Relations; Law; Public Relations; Service Trades; Tourism); **Economics** (Accountancy; Banking; Business Administration; Business and Commerce; Communication Studies; Economics; Finance; Tourism); **International Relations and European Studies** (European Studies; International Relations) *Dean*: Anisoara Popa; **Law** (Administrative Law; Civil Law; Commercial Law; Constitutional Law; Criminal Law; European Union Law; Fiscal Law; International Law; International Relations; Law; Management; Private Law; Public Law)

History: Created 1992. Acquired status 2002.

Governing Bodies: University Senate

Admission Requirements: Bacalaureat (or equivalent secondary school certificate) for undergraduate programmes; Licenţă (or equivalent Bachelor-level degree) for postgraduate programmes.

Main Language(s) of Instruction: Romanian

International Co-operation: With Université Jean Monnet Saint-Etienne, France

Degrees and Diplomas: *Diploma de Licenţă*; *Diplomă de Master*: Community Law; Criminal Science; European Law;and Public Administration; Private and Public Financial Management; Business Financial Management; Financial Management - Banking and Business Communication. Also distance learning, degrees in 5 yrs

Libraries: c. 25,000 vols; 2,000 periodical subscriptions
Last Updated: 26/09/11

DIMITRIE CANTEMIR CHRISTIAN UNIVERSITY OF BUCHAREST

Universitatea Creştină Dimitrie Cantemir din Bucureşti
Splaiul Unirii Street nr. 176, Sectorul 4, Bucureşti
Tel: +40(21) 330-79-00 +40(21) 330-79-11 +40(21) 330-79-14
Fax: +40(21) 330-87-74
EMail: office@ucdc.ro
Website: http://www.ucdc.ro/

Rector: Corina Dumitrescu
Tel: +40(21) 330-84-90 EMail: rectorat@ucdc.ro

Faculties

Economic Science *(Cluj)*; **Finance, Banking and Accounting** *(Braşov)* (Accountancy; Banking; Finance); **Finance, Banking and Accounting** (Accountancy; Banking; Finance); **Foreign Languages and Literatures**; **History** (History); **International Economic Relations** (Banking; Business Administration; Commercial Law; English; French; German; International Business; International Economics; International Law; Law; Marketing; Mathematics; Statistics); **International Economic Relations** *(Braşov)* (Accountancy; Economics; International Business; International Relations; Management); **Law** *(Cluj)*; **Law and Administration** (Administration; Law; Public Administration); **Political Sciences** (International Relations; Political Sciences; Public Administration; Sociology); **Tourism and Geography** *(Sibiu)*; **Tourism and Trade Management** *(Constantza)* (Business and Commerce; Management; Modern Languages; Tourism); **Tourism and Trade Management** (Business and Commerce; Management; Modern Languages; Tourism); **Tourism and Trade Management** *(Timişoara)* (Business and Commerce; Management; Modern Languages; Tourism); **Tourism and Trade Management** *(Sibiu)*

History: Created in 1990. Acquired current status 2002.

Governing Bodies: Management Board

Admission Requirements: Bacalaureat (or equivalent secondary school certificate) for undergraduate; Licenţă (or equivelent) for postgraduate.

Fees: (Euro): 200 to 500 per annum

Main Language(s) of Instruction: Romanian

Degrees and Diplomas: *Diploma de Licenţă*; *Diplomă de Master*
Last Updated: 02/02/10

DIMITRIE CANTEMIR UNIVERSITY OF TÂRGU-MUREŞ

Universitatea Dimitrie Cantemir din Municipiul Târgu-Mureş
Bodoni Sandor Street nr. 3-5, 540082 Târgu-Mureş
Fax: +40(365) 401-127 +40(365) 401-129
EMail: office@cantemir.ro
Website: http://www.cantemir.ro/

Rector: Viorel Beju

International Relations: Mihai Voda, Head of International Relations Office
Tel: +40(365) 80-18-22, Fax: +40(365) 40-11-25
EMail: mmvoda@yahoo.com; mihaivoda@cantemir.ro

Faculties

Economics (Accountancy; Banking; Business Administration; Economics; English; Finance; Hotel and Restaurant; Insurance; Management; Marketing; Service Trades; Statistics; Tourism); **Geography** (Environmental Management; Geography; Management; Tourism); **Law** (Administrative Law; Civil Law; Commercial Law; Constitutional Law; Criminal Law; English; European Union Law; International Law; Law; Private Law; Public Law); **Psychology and Educational Sciences** (Educational Sciences; Psychology)

History: Created 1991. Acquired status 2005.

Governing Bodies: University Senate

Admission Requirements: Bacalaureat (or equivalent secondary school certificate) for undergraduate programmes.

Fees: (Lei): 330 per annum

Main Language(s) of Instruction: Romanian

Degrees and Diplomas: *Diploma de Licenţă*; *Diplomă de Master*

Student Residential Facilities: Yes.

Libraries: Yes.
Last Updated: 08/02/10

DRĂGAN EUROPEAN UNIVERSITY OF LUGOJ

Universitatea Europeană Drăgan din Lugoj (UED)
Ion Huniade Street nr. 2, 305500 Lugos
Tel: +40(256) 359-198
Fax: +40(256) 359-198
EMail: ued@deu.ro
Website: http://www.universitateaeuropeanadragan.ro/

Rector: Nicu Trandafir (2001-)
Tel: +40(256) 35-91-98
EMail: rectorat@deu.ro; nicu.trandafir@deu.ro

Administrative Officer: Daniela Blaj
Tel: +40(256) 35-91-98 EMail: daniela.blaj@deu.ro

International Relations: Astrid Costantea, Head, International Relations Department

Faculties

Economics (Banking; Business Computing; Economics; Finance; International Business; International Relations; Management; Public Administration); **Law** (Administrative Law; Private Law; Public Law) *Dean*: Alexandru Crişan

History: Founded 1992. Acquired present status 2003.

Governing Bodies: Senate, Faculty Council

Academic Year: 2 semesters of 14 weeks starting in October

Admission Requirements: Bacalaureat

Fees: (Euro): 450 per annum

Main Language(s) of Instruction: Romanian

Accrediting Agencies: Ministry of Education and Research, National Council of Academic Evaluation and Accreditation

Degrees and Diplomas: *Diploma de Licenţă*; *Diplomă de Master*: Criminal Investigation Management; Public Administration and Minors Rights Protection

Student Services: Canteen, Cultural centre, Handicapped facilities, Health services, Language programs

Student Residential Facilities: Yes

Libraries: Yes

Publications: Annals - Economics Series *(biannually)*; Cyberneticus *(biannually)*; Studium Legis *(biannually)*
Last Updated: 26/09/11

EMANUEL UNIVERSITY OF ORADEA

Universitatea Emanuel din Oradea (EUO)
Nufărului Street nr, 87, 410597 Oradea
Tel: +40(259) 42-66-92
Fax: +40(259) 42-66-92
EMail: contact@emanuel.ro
Website: http://www.emanuel.ro

Rector: Paul Negruţ (2004-)
Tel: +40(259) 40-56-00
EMail: pauln@emanuel.ro; rectorat@emanuel.ro

Secretar Şef: Marcela Tundrea
Tel: +40(259) 42-66-92
EMail: marcela.tundrea@emanuel.ro; secretariat@emanuel.ro

Programmes

Distance Education

Schools

Management *(Brian Griffiths)* (Business Administration; Management) *Dean*: Sebastian Vaduva; **Pastoral Theology** (Music; Pastoral Studies; Social and Community Services; Theology) *Dean*: Marius David Cruceru

History: Founded 1990 under the jurisdiction of the Romanian Baptist Church, acquired present status 2002.

Governing Bodies: Board of Trustees

Academic Year: October to June

Admission Requirements: Secondary school certificate (Baccalaureat) and admission examination

Fees: (US Dollars): Tuition, 320 per month (Scholarship available upon request)

Accrediting Agencies: Ministry of Education and Research; National Council for Academic Evaluation and Accreditation

Degrees and Diplomas: *Diploma de Licență*: Pastoral Theology; Management; Music Education; Social Work; Language and Literature; *Diplomă de Master*: Pastoral Theology and Missiology; Business Administration; Music; Social and Community Services

Student Services: Academic counselling, Canteen, Employment services, Foreign student adviser, Health services, Language programs, Social counselling

Student Residential Facilities: For 260 students

Libraries: c. 60,100 vols

Publications: Perichoresis, Theological Journal

Academic Staff *2010-2011*	**TOTAL**
FULL-TIME	**40**
PART-TIME	**20**
STAFF WITH DOCTORATE	
FULL-TIME	**20**
PART-TIME	c. **15**
Student Numbers *2010-2011*	
All (Foreign Included)	c. **350**

Last Updated: 26/09/11

GEORGE BACOVIA UNIVERSITY OF BACĂU

Universitatea George Bacovia din Bacău (UGB)

Pictor Aman Street nr, 96, 600164 Bacău

Tel: +40(234) 51-64-48

Fax: +40(234) 51-64-48

EMail: rectorat@ugb.ro

Website: http://www.ugb.ro

Rector: Toader Gherasim

Tel: +40(234) 56-26-00 EMail: rector@ugb.ro

General Manager: Viorica Cisca

International Relations: Liviu Drugus EMail: ldrugus@ugb.ro

Departments

Distance and Part-time Learning (Accountancy; Banking; Data Processing; Finance; Management; Marketing; Public Administration; Social Work)

Faculties

Finance and Accountancy (Accountancy; Banking; Business Computing; Computer Science; Data Processing; Finance); **Law and Administration** (Administration; Business Administration; Law; Public Administration; Social Work); **Management, Marketing** (Management; Marketing; Public Administration)

History: Founded 1992. Acquired present status 2002.

Degrees and Diplomas: *Diploma de Licență*; *Diplomă de Master*

Last Updated: 22/09/11

GEORGE BARIȚIU UNIVERSITY OF BRAȘOV

Universitatea George Barițiu din Brașov (UGB)

Lunii Street nr. 6, Brașov

Tel: +40(268) 31-99-48

Fax: +40(268) 31-98-06

EMail: univgbar@email.ro

Website: http://www.universitateagbaritiu.ro/

President: Neculai Patrascu

EMail: neculai.patrascu@universitateagbaritiu.ro

Faculties

Economics (Accountancy; Business Administration; Business Computing; Economics; Tourism); **Law** (Civil Law; Criminal Law; European Union Law; Law); **Physical Education and Sports** (Physical Education; Sports)

Further Information: Also campuses in Ploiesti, Buzau, Focsani and Miercurea Ciuc.

History: Founded 1990. Acquired present status 2002.

Degrees and Diplomas: *Diploma de Licență*; *Diplomă de Master*: Community Law and Politics of European Integration; Criminology; Civil Law; Tourism; Accountancy and Auditing; Accountancy Consulting

Academic Staff *2008-2009*: Total: c. 200

Student Numbers *2008-2009*: Total: c. 6,000

Last Updated: 09/02/10

GHEORGHE CRISTEA ROMANIAN UNIVERSITY OF SCIENCES AND ARTS

Universitatea Română de Științe și Arte Gheorghe Cristea

B-dul Energeticienilor 9 E, Bloc M1, sector 3, 032091 București

Tel: +40(21) 346-16-41

Fax: +40(21) 346-16-41

EMail: ugc@ugc.ro

Website: http://www.ugc.ro

Rector: Lidia Cristea (2000-) EMail: ugc_rector@ugc.ro

Secretary-General: Cristina Vilculescu

Tel: +40(21) 346-90-49 EMail: drept@ugc.ro

International Relations: Tudor Geangoș

Tel: +40(21) 346-90-49 EMail: ugc_rei@ugc.ro

Faculties

Arts and Science (Arts and Humanities; Communication Studies; Dance; English; French; Natural Sciences; Performing Arts; Political Sciences; Public Relations); **Economics, Law and Administration** (Administration; Banking; Economics; Finance; Law)

History: Founded 1990. Acquired present status 2002.

Governing Bodies: Senatul Universității; Consilillul de Administrație

Academic Year: October to September

Admission Requirements: Bacalaureat

Main Language(s) of Instruction: Romanian

International Co-operation: Hungary; Lithuania; Turkey; Poland; Slovenia; Moldavia; Spain; France; Greece; Germany; Serbia and Montenegro

Accrediting Agencies: Consiliul Național de Evaluare Academică și Acreditare

Degrees and Diplomas: *Diploma de Licență*; *Diplomă de Master*

Student Services: Canteen, Language programs, Sports facilities

Libraries: c. 70,000 vols

Publications: Euroglob, Review of Economics and International Relations Studies *(biannually)*; The Danube River, Environment and Education, Review of Environmental Studies *(biannually)*; Universalia, Review of Ethno-linguistics *(biannually)*

Last Updated: 22/09/11

HYPERION UNIVERSITY OF BUCHAREST

Universitatea Hyperion din București

Calea Călărașilor 169, Sector 3, 030615 București

Tel: +40(21) 321-46-67

Fax: +40(21) 321-62-96

EMail: rectorat@hyperion.ro

Website: http://www.hyperion.ro

President: Ion Spânulescu

Vice-President: Iulian Cârtână

International Relations: Anca Gheorghiu

Tel: +40(21) 323-83-09, Fax: +40(21) 323-83-09

EMail: ancagheorghiu@hyperion.ro

Faculties

Arts (Arts and Humanities); **Economics** (Accountancy; Banking; Business Administration; Business Computing; Economics; International Business; Management; Service Trades; Tourism); **Electronics, Automation and Applied Informatics** (Automation and Control Engineering; Computer Science; Electronic Engineering; Engineering); **History and Geography** (Geography; History); **Journalism** (Journalism); **Law and Public Administration** (Law; Public Administration); **Letters and Foreign Languages** (Arts and Humanities; Chinese; French; Italian; Japanese; Literature; Modern Languages; Romanian); **Mathematics and Computer Science**

(Computer Science; Mathematics); **Physics** (Physics); **Political Sciences, Sociology and International Relations** (International Relations; Political Sciences; Sociology); **Psychology** (Psychology)

History: Founded 1990 as Fundaţia Universitară Hyperion. Acquired present status and title 2002.

Governing Bodies: Ministry of Education and Research

Academic Year: October to July

Admission Requirements: Secondary school certificate (Diplomă de Bacalaureat)

Fees: (Euros): 3,200 per annum

Main Language(s) of Instruction: Romanian

International Co-operation: With Universities in France, Italy, Moldova, Japan, Hungary, Ukraine, China and Thailand

Accrediting Agencies: Ministry of Education and Research; Consiliul National de Evaluare Academica si Acreditare (CNEAA)

Degrees and Diplomas: *Diploma de Licenţă*; *Diplomă de Master*

Student Services: Academic counselling, Canteen, Employment services, Handicapped facilities, Health services, Language programs, Sports facilities

Student Residential Facilities: Yes

Special Facilities: Movie studio

Libraries: Hyperion Central Library

Publications: Hyperion Scientific Journal *(biennially)*; Journal of Cinematographic Studies *(biannually)*

Press or Publishing House: "Victor" Publishing House

Last Updated: 21/09/11

INSTITUTE OF BUSINESS ADMINISTRATION OF BUCHAREST

Institutul de Administrare a Afacerilor din Municipiul Bucuresti

Griviţei Street nr. 8-10, Sector 1, 010731 Bucureşti
Tel: +40(213) 12-59-34 +40(213) 19-64-40

Faculties

Business Administration (Business Administration)

History: Founded 2009.

Main Language(s) of Instruction: Romanian

Degrees and Diplomas: *Diplomă de Master (MBA)*

Last Updated: 28/09/11

MIHAI EMINESCU UNIVERSITY OF TIMIŞOARA

Universitatea Mihai Eminescu din Timişoara

Bv. Revolutiei Street nr. 19, 300579 Timişoara
Tel: +40(256) 466-360 +40(256) 482-084
Fax: +40(256) 510-500
EMail: secretariat@umet.ro
Website: http://www.umet.ro

Rector: Alexandru Lucian Stroia

Faculties

Hotel and Tourism Management (Hotel and Restaurant; Hotel Management; Tourism); **Modern Languages** (Literature; Romance Languages); **Psychology and Social Welfare** (Psychology; Social Welfare)

Main Language(s) of Instruction: Romanian

Degrees and Diplomas: *Diploma de Licenţă*; *Diplomă de Master*

Last Updated: 15/02/10

MIHAIL KOGALNICEANU UNIVERSITY OF IAŞI

Universitatea Mihail Kogălniceanu din Municipiul Iaşi (UKM)

Băluşescu Street nr.2, cartier Tătăraşl, 700309 Iaşi
Tel: +40(232) 475-165
Fax: +40(232) 279-821
EMail: rectorat@umk.ro
Website: http://www.umk.ro/

Rector: Genoveva Vrabie (2001-) Tel: +40(232) 21-24-16

Faculties

Communication Studies and Public Relations (Communication Studies; Public Relations); **Geography** (Geography); **International Relations and European Studies** (European Studies; International Relations); **Law** (Civil Law; English; French; Law; Private Law; Public Law)

History: Created 1990. Acquired present status 2005.

Governing Bodies: University Senate.

Admission Requirements: Bacalaureat (or equivalent secondary school certificate) for undergraduate programmes; Licenţă (or equivalent Bachelor level degree) for Master's programme.

Fees: (Lei): c. 1,800 per annum for all programmes.

Main Language(s) of Instruction: Romanian

Degrees and Diplomas: *Diploma de Licenţă*; *Diplomă de Master*

Last Updated: 26/09/11

NICOLAE TITULESCU UNIVERSITY OF BUCHAREST

Universitatea Nicolae Titulescu din Bucureşti (UNT)

Calea Văcăreşti nr. 185, Sectorul 4, 040051 Bucureşti
Tel: +40(21) 330-90-32
Fax: +40(21) 330-86-06
EMail: office@univnt.ro
Website: http://www.univnt.ro

Rector: Ion Neagu
Tel: +40(21) 330-82-99
EMail: ineagu@univnt.ro; rectorat@univnt.ro

Secretar şef: Carmen Rizea
Tel: +40(21) 330-86-04 EMail: crizea@inivnt.ro

International Relations: Amelia Jiglau EMail: ama@univnt.ro

Faculties

Economics (Accountancy; Banking; Finance; Marketing); **Law** (Law); **Social Science and Administration** (Public Administration; Social and Community Services; Social Sciences)

Graduate Schools

Law, Economics and Public Administration (Accountancy; Finance; Law; Public Administration)

History: Founded 1990, acquired present status 2002.

Governing Bodies: Senate

Academic Year: October to September

Admission Requirements: Secondary school certificate (Bacalaureat) and entrance examination

Fees: (US Dollars): 400-500

Main Language(s) of Instruction: Romanian

Degrees and Diplomas: *Diploma de Licenţă*; *Diplomă de Master*; *Diplomă de Doctor*

Student Services: Academic counselling, Canteen, Health services, Language programs, Social counselling, Sports facilities

Special Facilities: Criminology Laboratory

Libraries: c. 13,568 vols

Publications: Analele Universităţii 'Nicolae Titulescu', Scientific research of staff *(annually)*; Lex et Scientia, Scientific work of staff and students *(annually)*; Studii juridice şi economice, Research in Law and Economics *(annually)*

Last Updated: 21/09/11

PARTIUM CHRISTIAN UNIVERSITY OF ORADEA

Universitatea Crestina Partium din Oradea

Primăriei Street, nr. 36, 410209 Oradea
Tel: +40(259) 41-82-44
EMail: partium@partium.ro
Website: http:www.partium.ro

Rector: János-Szatmári Szabolcs

Faculties

Arts (Arts and Humanities; Fine Arts; Music); **Economics** (Economics; Leadership); **Humanities and Social Studies** (Arts and Humanities; Social Sciences)

History: Founded 1990. Acquired present status 2008.
Main Language(s) of Instruction: Romanian
Degrees and Diplomas: *Diploma de Licență*; *Diplomă de Master*
Last Updated: 27/09/11

PETRE ANDREI UNIVERSITY OF IAŞI

Universitatea Petre Andrei din Iaşi (UPA)
Voda Grigore Ghica 13, 700469 Iaşi
Tel: +40(232) 21-04-74 +40(232) 21-72-50
Fax: +40(232) 21-72-50 +40(232) 21-04-74
EMail: dir@upa.ro
Website: http://www.upa.ro/

Rector: Doru Tompea (2009-2013)
Tel: +40 232 214 858, Fax: +40 232 214 858 EMail: office@upa.ro

Secretary-General: Daniel Sandru
Tel: +40 740 212 582, Fax: +40 232 214 858
EMail: danielsandru@upa.ro

International Relations: Sorina Postolea, Assistant Coordinator, Department of International Relations
Tel: +40(741) 92-19-20, Fax: +40(232) 21-48-58
EMail: sorinapostolea@yahoo.com

Faculties

Economics (Economics); **Law** (Law); **Political and Administrative Sciences** (Administration; Political Sciences); **Psychology and Educational Sciences** (Educational Sciences; Psychology); **Social Work and Sociology** (Social Work; Sociology)

Further Information: Study centres in: Piatra Neamţ, Botoşani, Bacău, Focşani, Suceava, Roman and Tecuci.
History: Founded 1990. Acquired present status 2002.
Governing Bodies: Senate; Sentate Bureau; Rectorat
Academic Year: October to February; February to June
Admission Requirements: Secondary school certificate (Diplomă de Bacalaureat) or equivalent.
Fees: (Lei): 2,200 per annum
Main Language(s) of Instruction: Romanian
International Co-operation: Participates in Minerva, Erasmus, Leonardo da Vinci and Jean Monnet programmes
Accrediting Agencies: Agenția Română de Asigurare a Calității în Învățământul Superior (ARACIS)

Degrees and Diplomas: *Diploma de Licență*: Law; Psychology, Social Work, Sociology, Political Science, Finance and Banking, Commercial, Tourism and Services Economics, Accounting, Information Technology in Management; *Diplomă de Master*: Communication, Creativity and Psycho-Social Skills in Organisations; Psychological Assessment and Recovering Psychotherapies; Educational Counselling and Intervention for Educational and Vocational Guidance; European Financial ManagementBank Operations and ManagementPublic Management and FinancesManagement of Insurance and ReinsuranceAuditing and Financial Management; European Law, Business Law, Criminal Science, Public Government Law; Human Resources Management; Clinical Psychology; Family Psychotherapy and Counselling; Political Psychology and Leadership in Government; Psychological Testing and Measuring; Project Management; Psycho-Social Counselling; Psycho-Sociology of Information and Private Security; Drug Counselling; Therapy and Social Reinsertion through Probation; Conflict Mediation and Negotiation; Child Protection; Educational Management; Psycho-Sociology in Prison Management

Student Services: Academic counselling, Employment services, Handicapped facilities, Social counselling
Student Residential Facilities: Upon request.
Special Facilities: 12 auditoria, 9 laboratories.
Libraries: c. 6,000 vols; access to other academic libraries in the city
Publications: Economy 21, Research articles in economics. *(biannually)*; Journal of Juridical Studies, Research articles in law. *(biannually)*; 'Petre Andrei University Annals - 'Social Sciences', Periodical devoted to research and studies by university staff. *(annually)*

Academic Staff *2010-2011*	**TOTAL**
FULL-TIME	**110**
PART-TIME	**50**
STAFF WITH DOCTORATE	
FULL-TIME	**c. 50**

Student Numbers *2010-2011*	
All (Foreign Included)	**c. 5,900**
FOREIGN ONLY	**60**

Last Updated: 27/09/11

ROMANIAN-AMERICAN UNIVERSITY OF BUCHAREST

Universitatea Româno-Americana din Bucuresti
Blvd. Expozitiei nr. 1B, Sectorul 1, 012101 Bucureşti
Tel: +40(21) 202-95-18
Fax: +40(21) 222-35-66
EMail: relatii.publice@rau.ro
Website: http://www.rau.ro

Rector: Ion Smedescu
Tel: +40(21) 312-32-70 EMail: rector@rau.ro

Faculties

Domestic and International Tourism Economics (Economics; Tourism); **European Economical Studies** (Economics; European Studies; International Relations); **Finance, Banking, Domestic and International Business** (Accountancy; Banking; Finance; International Business); **IT Management Systems**; **Law** (Law); **Management-Marketing** (Management; Marketing)

International Co-operation: With universities in the USA, Europe and Brazil
Degrees and Diplomas: *Diploma de Licență*; *Diplomă de Master*
Student Services: Canteen, Language programs, Sports facilities
Student Residential Facilities: Yes
Libraries: Yes
Last Updated: 21/09/11

ROMANIAN-GERMAN UNIVERSITY OF SIBIU

Universitatea Româno-Germană din Sibiu
Calea Dumbrăvii Street, nr. 28-30, 550324 Sibiu
Tel: +40(269) 233-568 +40(269) 401-002
Fax: +40(269) 233-576
EMail: rectorat@roger-univ.ro
Website: http://www.roger-univ.ro/

Rector: Hortensia Gorski EMail: hortensia.gorski@roger-univ.ro
Secretarul Sef: Maria Troanca

Faculties

Economics (Accountancy; Banking; Economics; Finance; Management; Marketing; Mathematics; Tourism); **Engineering** (Electrical Engineering; Electronic Engineering; Energy Engineering; Engineering); **Law and Public Administration** (Administrative Law; Criminal Law; Private Law)

History: Created in 1998. Acquired status 2005.
Governing Bodies: University Senate.
Admission Requirements: Bacalaureat (or equivalent secondary school certificate) for undergraduate programmes; Licență (or equivalent Bachelor level degree) for Master's programme.
Fees: (Lei): 1,500 - 1,600 per annum.
International Co-operation: With universities in: Austria, France, Germany, Spain.
Degrees and Diplomas: *Diploma de Licență*; *Diplomă de Master*
Libraries: c. 18,000 vols in various languages.
Last Updated: 27/09/11

SPIRU HARET UNIVERSITY OF BUCHAREST

Universitatea Spiru Haret din Bucureşti
Ion Ghica Street nr. 13, Sector 3, 030045 Bucureşti
Tel: +40(21) 314-99-31 +40(21) 312-23-01
Fax: +40(21) 314-95-25
EMail: info@spiruharet.ro
Website: http://www.spiruharet.ro

Rector: Aurelian Gh. Bondrea (2008-) EMail: rector@spiruharet.ro

International Relations: Emilia Bondrea, Vice-Rector, International Relations
Tel: +40(21) 314-39-03, Fax: +40(21) 312-00-36
EMail: ushcls@spiruharet.ro

Campuses

Blaj (Banking; Business Administration; Computer Science; Economics; Finance; Mathematics); **Brasov** (Administration; Law; Management; Pedagogy; Psychology); **Câmpulung-Muscel** (Accountancy; Banking; Business Administration; Business Computing; Finance); **Constanta** (Accountancy; Finance; Law; Public Administration); **Craiova** (Accountancy; Business Computing; Finance; Law; Public Administration); **Ramnicu-Valcea** (Accountancy; Finance; Law; Public Administration)

Faculties

Architecture (Architecture); **Arts** (Acting; Arts and Humanities; Music; Theatre); **Finance and Banking** (Banking; Finance); **Financial and Management Accountancy** (Accountancy; Finance; Management); **Geography** (Geography); **History, Museology and Archiving** (Archiving; History; Museum Studies); **International Relations, History and Philosophy** (European Studies; History; International Relations; Philosophy; Political Sciences); **Journalism, Communication and Public Relations** (Communication Studies; Journalism; Public Relations); **Law and Public Administration**; **Letters** (Arts and Humanities; Germanic Languages; Literature; Modern Languages; Oriental Languages; Romanian; Slavic Languages); **Marketing and International Business** (International Business; Marketing); **Mathematics and Computer Science** (Computer Science; Mathematics; Mathematics and Computer Science); **Physical Education and Sports** (Physical Education; Physical Therapy; Sports); **Sociology and Psychology** (Psychology; Sociology); **Veterinary Science** (Veterinary Science)

Degrees and Diplomas: *Diploma de Licenţă*; *Certificat de atestare a competentelor profesionale*; *Diplomă de Master*
Last Updated: 21/09/11

TIBISCUS UNIVERSITY OF TIMIŞOARA

Universitatea Tibiscus din Timişoara
Daliei Street nr. 1A,
300558 Timişoara
Tel: +40(256) 20-29-31 +40(256) 20-29-32
Fax: +40(256) 20-29-30
EMail: rectorat@tibiscus.ro
Website: http://www.tibiscus.ro

Rector: Cornel Haranguš (1999-) EMail: charangus@tibiscus.ro

Chief Secretary: Cristiana Maghear EMail: augusta@tibiscus.ro

International Relations: Corina Hiller, Director, Department of International Relations
Tel: +40(256) 22-06-89, Fax: +40(256) 22-06-89
EMail: cmusuroi@tibiscus.ro

Faculties

Computer Science and Applied Informatics (Computer Science); **Design** (Design; Fine Arts); **Economics** (Accountancy; Administration; Business Administration; Economics; International Business; Marketing); **Journalism, Communication and Modern Languages** (Advertising and Publicity; Communication Studies; Journalism; Mass Communication; Media Studies; Modern Languages; Public Relations); **Law and Public Administration** (European Union Law; Law; Public Administration); **Music** (Music; Musical Instruments); **Physical Education and Sport** (Physical Education; Sports); **Psychology** (Clinical Psychology; Human Resources; Psychology)

History: Founded 1991. Acquired present status 2002.

Governing Bodies: University Senate

Admission Requirements: Bacalaureat (or equivalent) for undergraduate programmes;

Main Language(s) of Instruction: Romanian

Degrees and Diplomas: *Diploma de Licenţă*; *Diplomă de Master*
Last Updated: 27/09/11

TITU MAIORESCU UNIVERSITY OF BUCHAREST

Universitatea Titu Maiorescu din Bucureşti (UTM)
Dâmbovnicului Street nr, 22, sector 4, 040041 Bucureşti
Tel: +40(21) 311-22-97
Fax: +40(21) 316-16-46
EMail: rectorat@utm.ro
Website: http://www.utm.ro

Rector: Iosif R. Urs (2008-) EMail: rector@utm.ro

Registrar: Antigona Camelia Iordana EMail: secretar.sef@utm.ro

International Relations: Iulia Alecu, Head of International Relations Department
Tel: +40(21) 316-16-43, Fax: +40(21) 316-16-43
EMail: international@utm.ro; iulia.alecu@utm.ro

Centres

Psychological Counselling and Career Orientation *Director*: Ioana Panc

Departments

Distance Learning *(Branches in: Piteşti, Curtea de Argeş, Tulcea, Turnu Măgurele, Resiţa, Piatra Neamţ, Slatina, Vălenii de Munte, Roşiorii de Vede, Călăraşi, Urziceni, Ulmeni, Târgu Jiu)* (Computer Science; Economics; Law; Psychology) *Director*: Madalina Voiculescu; **International Relations and Community Programmes** *Head*: Iulia Alecu; **Lifelong Learning Education** *Director*: Valentin Pau; **Scientific Research** *Director*: Andrei Firica; **Teacher Training** (Teacher Training) *Director*: Mihai Puiu

Faculties

Computer Sciences and Technology (Computer Science; Information Sciences; Information Technology) *Dean*: Emil Creţu; **Economic Sciences** (Accountancy; Banking; Business Administration; Economics; Finance; Insurance) *Dean*: Florin Văduva; **Economic Sciences** *(Tâgu Jiu)* (Economics) *Dean*: Pârgaru Ion Ion; **Law** (Civil Law; Commercial Law; Criminal Law; European Union Law; Fiscal Law; International Law; International Relations; Labour Law; Law; Private Law; Public Administration; Public Law) *Dean*: Smaranda Angheni; **Law** *(Tâgu Jiu)* (Law) *Dean*: Dan Voinea; **Medicine and Dentistry** (Dental Technology; Medical Technology; Medicine; Nursing) *Dean*: Dan Florin Ungureanu; **Psychology** (Behavioural Sciences; Cognitive Sciences; Educational Psychology; Human Resources; Industrial and Organizational Psychology; Psychology; Social Psychology) *Dean*: Viorel Iulian Tănase; **Social and Political Sciences** (Political Sciences; Social Sciences)

Foundations

Education and Science *(Titu Maiorescu) President*: Iosif R. Urs

History: Founded 1990. Acquired present title 2002.

Governing Bodies: Senate

Academic Year: October to July

Admission Requirements: Bacalaureat; for Licenta programme, questionnaire and interview; for Master programme, questionnaire only.

Fees: (Euro): Licenta, 450-1,500 per annum for European Citizens; 1,000 per month for Nursing programmes and 1,300 per month for Dental Technology; 400-700 per month for non-EU students. Master's degree, 300-600 per semester. Doctor's degree, 375-1,000 per semester for EU students; 300-800 per month for non-EU students. Distance Learning programmes, 420-520 per annum.

Main Language(s) of Instruction: Romanian

International Co-operation: With universities in France, Spain, Austria, Denmark, Norway, Great Britain, Latvia,Turkey, USA and Moldova

Accrediting Agencies: Romanian Agency for Quality Assurance in Higher Education (ARACIS)

Degrees and Diplomas: *Diploma de Licenţă*: Finance and Banking; Accountancy and Business Computing; Business Administration; Computer Science; Commerce, Tourism and Services Trade; Law; Public Administration; Psychology; Medicine; Dentistry; Medical Auxiliary; Dental Technology; *Certificat de atestare a competentelor profesionale*: Political Science; European Studies; International Relations and Diplomacy; Risk Evaluation in Occupational Safety and Health; *Diplomă de Master*: Dentistry; Human Resources Psychology; Communication Techniques and Psychology; Educational

Psychology and Counselling; Financial Management; Business Funding Policies; Finance, Audit and Accountancy; Banking and Insurance; International and European Law; Penal Science; Conflict Mediation in Law; Community Law; Banking Law; Civil Law; *Diplomă de Doctor*: Law

Student Services: Academic counselling, Cultural centre, Employment services, Foreign student adviser, Foreign Studies Centre, Handicapped facilities, Health services, Language programs, Nursery care, Social counselling, Sports facilities

Libraries: Avram Filipas library; over 40,000 vols.

Publications: Annals of Titu Maiorescu University, Scientific papers writen by professors from the Faculty of Law and from other legal education institutions throughout the country and abroad *(annually)*

Press or Publishing House: University Publishing House

Academic Staff *2009-2010*	MEN	WOMEN	TOTAL
FULL-TIME	160	237	**397**
STAFF WITH DOCTORATE			
FULL-TIME	46	42	**88**
Student Numbers *2009-2010*			
All (Foreign Included)	6,980	7,620	**14,600**
FOREIGN ONLY	91	77	**168**

Distance students, 6,950.

Last Updated: 21/09/11

UNIVERSITY OF ECOLOGY OF BUCHAREST

Universitatea Ecologica din București

Bd. Vasile Milea nr. 1G, Sector 6, 061341 București
Tel: +40(21) 316-79-32
Fax: +40(21) 316-63-37
EMail: rectorat@ueb.ro
Website: http://www.ueb.ro

Rector: Alexandru Ticlea Tel: +40(21) 384-53-57

Secretar Șef: Mariana Dumitru

Faculties

Communication Science (Advertising and Publicity; Communication Studies; Mass Communication; Media Studies; Public Relations; Social Psychology; Sociology); **Ecology and Environmental Protection** (Ecology; Environmental Studies; Natural Sciences); **Economics** (Banking; Business Administration; Finance; Management); **Law and Administrative Sciences** (Administration; Law); **Managerial Engineering** (Engineering; Engineering Management; Environmental Engineering); **Physical Education and Sport** (Physical Education; Sports); **Psychology** (Educational Psychology; Experimental Psychology; Psychology)

History: Created 1990. Obtained current status 2003.

Governing Bodies: Senate

Admission Requirements: Bacalaureat (or equivalent secondary school certificate) for undergraduate programmes; Licență (or equivalent Bachelor's degree) for postgraduate programmes.

Main Language(s) of Instruction: Romanian

International Co-operation: ERASMUS; Central and East European Universities Network

Degrees and Diplomas: *Diploma de Licență*; *Diplomă de Master*: Law; Economic Science; Ecology and Environmental Protection; Engineering and Management; Physical Education and Sport; Psychology; Public Relations

Student Services: Canteen, Cultural centre, Language programs, Sports facilities

Libraries: Yes. Law library. Online library for Management Faculty.

Publications: The Journal of Economy and Environment; The Romanian Journal of Environmental Law, in Romanian and French; The Romanian Journal of Labour Law

Last Updated: 21/09/11

VASILE GOLDIȘ WEST UNIVERSITY OF ARAD

Universitatea de Vest Vasile Goldiș din Arad

Bulevardul Revoluției nr, 81, Arad
Tel: +40(257) 28-03-35
Fax: +40(257) 28-08-10
EMail: rectorat@uvvg.ro
Website: http://www.uvvg.ro/site/

Rector: Aurel Ardelean Fax: +40(257) 28-08-10

General Administrative Manager: Isabela Alic

Faculties

Computer Science (Computer Science); **Economics** (Accountancy; Banking; Business Administration; Business and Commerce; Business Computing; Finance; Management; Marketing; Service Trades; Tourism); **Engineering** (Engineering); **Humanities, Political and Administrative Sciences** (Administration; Arts and Humanities; Communication Studies; English; European Studies; French; German; History; International Relations; Jewish Studies; Journalism; Literature; Modern Languages; Multimedia; Philosophy; Political Sciences; Public Administration; Public Relations; Romanian); **Law** (Law); **Medicine, Pharmacy, and Dentistry** (Dental Technology; Dentistry; Gastroenterology; Medical Auxiliaries; Medicine; Midwifery; Orthopaedics; Pharmacology; Pharmacy; Psychiatry and Mental Health; Radiology; Rehabilitation and Therapy; Social and Preventive Medicine; Urology); **Natural Sciences** (Biology; Ecology; Environmental Studies; Geography; Natural Sciences); **Physical Training and Sport** (Physical Education; Sports); **Psychology** (Psychology)

International Co-operation: With universities and higher education institutions in Australia, Brazil, France, Germany, Italy, UK, Poland, Portugal, Republic of Moldavia, Slovakia, Sweden, Taiwan and USA. Agreements with European Universities Association (EUA), European Federation of Schools (FEDE), Danube's Rectors Conference (DRC), European Medical School Association AMSE, Association of the Universities from the Carpathian Region ACRU. Signatory of The Magna Charta Universitatum. Participation in ERASMUS, LINGUA, COMENIUS, LEONARDO DA VINCI, SECAL and Fullbright Scholarships Porgrammes.

Degrees and Diplomas: *Diploma de Licență*; *Diploma de Licență*; *Diplomă de Master*; *Diplomă de Doctor*. Common Doctorate Programmes, in Medicine, Organised With the faculties of Medicine from a number of German Universities (Tubingen, Heidelberg, Frankfurt, Wiesbaden, Rottenburg) but also with University of Caen (France) and Tesedik Samuel University (Hungary).

Last Updated: 22/09/11

Russian Federation

STRUCTURE OF HIGHER EDUCATION SYSTEM

Description:

Higher education is provided by state and non-state higher education institutions (HEIs). Approximately half of state HEI students pay for their studies. In non-state HEIs all students have to pay tuition fees. Higher education falls within the jurisdiction of the Ministry of Education and Science. The Federal Service of Supervision in Education and Science is responsible for quality assurance in education and recognition of international credentials. There are three levels of higher education: 1) incomplete higher education (2 years at least); 2) 4-year programmes leading to the Bakalavr degree, the first final university degree; 3) postgraduate studies with a duration of 1-2 years leading to the Specialist Diploma or the Magistr degree. HEIs are authorized to award the Magistr degree after the completion of 2 years of study or the Specialist Diploma after 1 year of study following the Bakalavr degree. Scientific degrees in Russia traditionally include two levels of doctoral degrees: the Candidate of Sciences (the first level, equivalent to PhD) and the Doctor of Sciences (the second, post doctoral level). The Federal Agency for Education finances a certain number of state HEIs. The rest are financed by other Ministries or local authorities.

Stages of studies:

University level first stage:

The first stage consists of at least a two-year higher education study programme. On leaving the university, students may ask for the Diploma O Nepolnom Vysshem Obrazovanii (Diploma of Incomplete Higher Education) which entitles them to obtain jobs that require some HE training but not a degree, and to continue their studies.

University level second stage: *Bakalavr*

Bakalavr (Bachelor's) degree programmes last for at least 4 years of full-time university-level study. The programmes are elaborated in accordance with the State Educational Standards which regulate 50% of the content, the remaining 50% being developed by the university. The programmes include professional and special courses in science, humanities and socio-economic disciplines, professional training, completion of a final research paper/project and sitting for State final exams. Having obtained the Bakalavr degree, students may apply to enter the Magistr programmes or continue their studies in the framework of the Specialist Diploma programmes. The Bakalavr degree is awarded in all fields except medicine after defending a diploma project prepared under the guidance of a supervisor and sitting for final exams. In medicine, the first stage lasts for six years.

University level third stage: *Magistr, Specialist Diploma*

Holders of the Bakalavr degree are admitted to the Specialist Diploma and Magistr programmes. Access to these programmes is competitive. The Magistr degree is awarded after successful completion of two years of full-time study. Students must complete advanced studies, prepare and defend a thesis and sit for final examinations.The Specialist Diploma can be earned in two ways: by completion of at least one year's study after the Bakalavr programme or upon completion of five to six years' continuous study beyond the Attestat o Srednem (Polnom) Obshchem Obrazovanii. The Specialist Diploma is a professional qualification that gives the right to exercise a profession and to apply for doctoral programmes. It is conferred after students have completed advanced studies, prepared and defended a thesis and sat for final examinations.

University level fourth stage: *Kandidat Nauk (Aspirantura programmes), Doktor Nauk (Doktorantura programmes)*

Access to the Aspirantura is competitive. Applicants must hold a Specialist Diploma or a Magistr degree. Studies last for 3 years. The Aspirantura programmes train for research and teaching activities. Students must learn research and teaching methods, ICTs, and pass qualifying (Kandidat Nauk) exams in certain fields of study. After carrying out independent research, preparing and defending a dissertation in public, they are awarded the Kandidat Nauk scientific degree. The Doctor Nauk programme duration is not fixed (from 5 to 15 years). It follows the Kandidat Nauk degree. The Doctor Nauk scientific degree is awarded after the public defence of a dissertation. It is a type of post doctoral qualification.

Distance higher education:
Distance learning is regarded as ICT utilisation for provision of a wide variety of education programmes or parts (blocks) of programmes in higher professional education, vocational education, school education, lifelong education and upgrading.

ADMISSION TO HIGHER EDUCATION

Admission to university-level studies:

Name of secondary school credential required: Attestat o Srednem (Polnom) Obshchem Obrazovanii

Minimum score/requirement: satisfactory

Name of secondary school credential required: Diplom o Srednem Professionalnom Obrazovanii (Higher Vocational Education Diploma)

For entry to: 3rd or 4th semesters when transfer of profiling courses is counted, and to the first year when the student enters a different field of study.

Alternatives to credentials: Diplom o Nachalnom Professional'nom Obrasovanii (lower post-secondary vocational education diploma) conferred after programmes with duration of 2 and more years.

Other admission requirements: Compulsory competitive institutional exams/tests, Uniform State Exam.

Foreign students admission:

Definition of foreign student: A student who does not have Russian citizenship.

Quotas: Around 8,000 state scholarships are annually offered for foreign students.

Entrance exam requirements: Students must hold the Secondary School Leaving Certificate or its equivalent. There are compulsory pre-academic programmes for those who are not proficient in Russian or/and for those with weak pre-university training. They must successfully pass entrance exams/tests. Foreign applicants entering universities should not be older than 28 (35 for doctoral studies in Aspirantura).

Entry regulations: Student visa and financial guarantees.

Health requirements: A medical certificate confirming that the student is in good health and a HIV test are required. Candidates must have a Medical Insurance Policy (approx. 200 US dollars/year).

Language requirements: Good knowledge of Russian

RECOGNITION OF STUDIES

Quality assurance system:

Licensing in non-university level education is the prerogative of the local authorities. It includes a formal assessment by a visiting expert group to ensure that an educational establishment meets the state and local requirements, including facilities, sanitation, equipment, staff, etc. Each new programme must also be assessed and licensed. Accreditation allows the institution to issue state recognized diplomas. Accreditation is carried out by federal ministry-founders of respective institutions in cooperation with local/municipal authorities. Licensing and accreditation in lower post-secondary vocational education is carried out by local authorities. The procedures are more or less the same as for non-university level HEIs.
University level HEIs also have to pass licensing and accreditation procedures, carried out by the Federal Service for Supervision in Education and Science. Licensing: assessment of the compliance of educational facilities, laboratory equipment, expertise of teaching staff, and teaching material with State requirements; Accreditation: recognition (confirmation for the next term) of the State accreditation status of the HEI according to its type (higher education institution) and kind (institute, academy, university) with the prescribed list of educational programmes of higher professional education according to which the institution has the right to issue diplomas. Non-accredited HEIs issue their own non-state diplomas.

Bodies dealing with recognition:

Division of Licensing, Accreditation and Supervision in Education

Head: Viktor Kruglov
Federal Service for Supervision in Education and Science
Shabolovka Street 33

Moscow 115162
Tel: +7(495) 954 5127
Fax: +7(495) 954 5127
EMail: license@ministry.ru

National Accreditation Agency of Russia, Federal Service for Supervision in Education and Science
Director: Denis V. Ponomarev
2 Lenin Square
Yoshkar-Ola, Republic of Marii El 424000
Tel: +7(836) 241 6194
Fax: +7(836) 241 3884
EMail: postmaster@nica.ru
WWW: http://www.nica.ru/

Higher Attestation Committee
Head: Mihail Kirpichnikov
Sadovo-Suharevskaya Ul 16, K-51, GSP-4
Moscow 127994
Tel: +7(495) 608 7286
Fax: +7(495) 608 7286
WWW: http://vak.ed.gov.ru/

National Information Centre on Academic Recognition and Mobility
Director: Gennady Lukichev
Officer: Valery Mitrofanov
Mikluho-Maklaya Street 6
Moscow 117198
Tel: +7(495) 958 2881/ 955 0818
Fax: +7(495) 434 1511/ 9582 881
EMail: RussianENIC@sci.pfu.edu.ru
WWW: http://www.russianenic.ru

Special provisions for recognition:

Recognition for university level studies: Licensing and state accreditation (with procedures of self-evaluation and external assessment)/ HEI which has successfully passed these procedures is granted the right to isue state diplomas.

For access to advanced studies and research: Accredited HEIs may apply to the Higher Attestation Commission (HAC) to obtain the right to provide advanced studies (Aspirantura and Doctorantura) and train researchers. The right is granted when HAC requirements are met.

For exercising a profession: Applicants have to obtain a recognition certificate of all foreign qualification, degree, title or diploma at the Federal Service for Supervision in Education and Science. This certificate facilitates employers' decisions for access to a profession.

NATIONAL BODIES

Ministry of Education and Science
Minister: Dmitrij Viktorovich Livanov
Tverskaya Street 11
Moscow 125993
Tel: +7(495) 539 5519
Fax: +7(495) 629 0891
WWW: http://www.mon.gov.ru
Role of national body: The Ministry is responsible for state policy and legal regulation in education, R&D, innovation activities and youth policy, coordination and control of other bodies in the education and research fields.

Federal Agency on Education

Head: Nikolai Bulaev
Ljusinovskaya ul. 51
Moscow 115998
Tel: +7(495) 237 9763
Fax: +7(495) 236 0171
EMail: bicab@ed.gov.ru
WWW: http://www.ed.gov.ru

Role of national body: The Federal Agency on Education manages the state property, implements education and youth development policies, funds HEIs, proposes further development of HEIs.

Federal Service for Supervision in Education and Science

Head: Lubov Glebova
Sadovaya-Sukharevskaya 16
Moscow 127994
Tel: +7(495) 608 6158
Fax: + +7(495) 608 6158
EMail: akkred@ministry.ru
WWW: http://www.obrnadzor.gov.ru

Role of national body: The Federal Service for Supervision in Education and Science supervises and controls the implementation of the legislation in education, R&D and youth policy. It is responsible for the quality assurance policy, the licensing of education institutions and programmes.

Russian Rectors' Union

President: Viktor Sadovnitchy
Secretary-General: Olga Kashirina
V-234, Leninskije Gory, M.V. Lomonosov MSU, Main building, room 1001-1003
Moscow 119992
Tel: +7(495) 939 2032
Fax: +7(095) 939 2032
EMail: office@rsr-online.ru
WWW: http://www.rsr-online.ru

Role of national body: Observation of state policy, projection on further development of HE and research, examination of legislative drafts, participation in lawmaking in contact with the State Duma and the Senate, cooperation with associations of employers and international and other national rectors' unions.

Association of Non-State Higher Education Institutions

Director: Valerii Kapustin
ul. Radio, 22, office 225
Moscow 105005
Tel: +7(495) 925 0380
Fax: +7(495) 925 0380
EMail: info@anvuz.ru;anvuz@anvuz.ru
WWW: http://www.anvuz.ru/

Role of national body: Coordinates cooperation and joint activities of private HEIs aimed to further development of HE and research.

Association of Russian Higher Education Institutions

President: Viktor Savinykh
4 Gorokhovsky per.
Moscow 105064
Tel: +7(495) 261 3152/ 236 9821
Fax: +7(495) 267 4681/ 261 3089
EMail: SVP@miigaik.ru

Role of national body: Coordinates cooperation and joint activities of State HEIs aimed to further development of HE and research.

Data for academic year: 2008-2009
Source: IAU from National Information Centre on Academic Recognition and Mobility, Ministry of Education and Science of the Russian Federation, 2008. Bodies, 2012.

INSTITUTIONS

PUBLIC INSTITUTIONS

ACADEMY OF CHOIR SINGING NAMED AFTER V.S. POPOV

Akademija Khorovogo Iskusstva im. V.S. Popova
ul. Festival'naja 2, Moskva 125565
Tel: +7(495) 988-99-56
EMail: info@axu.ru
Website: http://www.axu.ru/

Rector: Nikolai Nikolaevich Azarov

Programmes
Acting (Acting); **Conducting** (Conducting); **Music** (Music; Music Theory and Composition); **Singing** (Singing)
History: Created 1991.
Degrees and Diplomas: *Specialist Diploma*; *Kandidat Nauk*
Last Updated: 31/07/12

ACADEMY OF CIVIL PROTECTION

Akademija Graždanskoj Zašity
Khimki, 141435 Moskovskaja oblast'
Tel: +7(495) 575-4847
Fax: +7(495) 575-9555
EMail: agz@mchs.gov.ru
Website: http://www.amchs.ru/

Rector: Sergei Anatolievich Shljakov

Programmes
Civil Protection (Military Science; Protective Services)
History: Created 1933.
Degrees and Diplomas: *Bakalavr*, *Specialist Diploma*
Last Updated: 14/04/11

ACADEMY OF ECONOMIC SECURITY

Akademija Ekonomičeskoj Bezopasnosti
ul. Kol'skaja, 2, Moskva 129329
Tel: +7(499) 189-97-96 +7(499) 993-36-84
Fax: +7(499) 186-61-10
EMail: academy@bk.ru; info@econsafety.ru
Website: http://www.econsafety.ru/

Rector: Alik Galimzjanovich Khabibulin

Programmes
Financial Security (Accountancy; Banking; Economics; Finance; Fiscal Law; International Law; Taxation)
History: Created 1996.
Degrees and Diplomas: *Specialist Diploma*
Last Updated: 31/07/12

ACADEMY OF FEDERAL SECURITY SERVICE OF THE RUSSIAN FEDERATION

Akademija Federalnoj Sluzby okhrany Rossijskoj Federatsii
ul. Priborostroitelnaja, n d. 35, Orjol 302034
Tel: +7(4862) 54-97-63 +7(4862) 54-97-64
Fax: +7(4862) 54-13-25
EMail: ycheba@academ.msk.rsnet.ru
Website: http://academ.msk.rsnet.ru/

Rector: Viktor Mikhailovich Shchekotikhin

Programmes
Communication (Communication Studies); **Information Technology** (Computer Graphics; Information Sciences; Information Technology; Telecommunications Services)
History: Formerly Akademija Federal'nogo Agenctva Pravitel'stvennoj Svjazi I Informacii pri Presidente Rossijskoj Federacii and Akademija Služby Special'noj Svjazi I Informacii pri Federal'noj Sluzbe Ohrany Rossijskoj Federacii. Acquired current title 2003.
Degrees and Diplomas: *Bakalavr*, *Specialist Diploma*
Last Updated: 14/04/11

ACADEMY OF LAW AND MANAGEMENT OF THE FEDERAL PENAL SERVICE

Akademija Prava i Upravlenija Federalnoj Služby Ispolnenija Nakazanij
ul. Sennaja 1, Rjazan 390036
Tel: +7(4912) 27-21-12
Fax: +7(4912) 27-21-12
EMail: apu-fsin@mail.ru
Website: http://apu-fsin.ru/

Rector: Aleksandr Aleksandrovich Krymov

Faculties
Economics (Accountancy; Economics; Finance; Taxation); **Law** (Law); **Management** (Management); **Psychology** (Psychology; Social Psychology)
History: Formerly known as Akademija Prava i Upravlenija Ministerstva Justicii Rossijskoj Federacii (Academy of Law and Management of the Russian Federation Ministry of Justice).
Degrees and Diplomas: *Bakalavr*, *Specialist Diploma*; *Magistr*
Last Updated: 31/07/12

ACADEMY OF MANAGEMENT OF INTERNAL AFFAIRS OF THE RUSSIAN FEDERATION

Akademija Upravlenja MVD Rossii Federatsii
ul. Zoii i Aleksandra Kosmodem'janskih 8, Moskva 125171
Tel: +7(499) 150-1034
Fax: +7(495) 150-1763
EMail: amvd@mail.ru
Website: http://www.amvd.ru/

Rector: Vladimir V. Gordienko (2006-)

Programmes
Law (Law); **Military Studies** (Military Science; Police Studies)
History: Founded 1929. Acquired present status 1954.
Governing Bodies: Council
Academic Year: September to June
Main Language(s) of Instruction: Russian
Accrediting Agencies: Management Department of International Cooperation of the Interior Ministry of Russia
Degrees and Diplomas: *Specialist Diploma*
Student Services: Academic counselling, Canteen, Cultural centre, Employment services, Foreign student adviser, Foreign Studies Centre, Health services, Language programs, Social counselling, Sports facilities
Student Residential Facilities: Hostel
Special Facilities: Museum; Art Gallery; Movie Studio
Libraries: 2 libraries, 837,086 vols
Publications: Akademicheskiye Vesti, Academy newspaper *(monthly)*
Last Updated: 30/06/11

ACADEMY OF SOCIAL EDUCATION

Akademija Social'nogo Obrazovanija (KSUI)
ul. Isaeva 12, Kazan,
420039 Tatarstan
Tel: +7(843) 555-61-77
Fax: +7(843) 542-63-24
EMail: info@aso-ksui.ru
Website: http://www.aso-ksui.ru/

Rector: Iskandar Mukhametzyanov (2005-)
Tel: +7(843) 555-61-76, Fax: +7(843) 542-63-24
EMail: ishm@inbox.ru;

International Relations: Elvira Rafikova, Head, Department of International Exchange
Tel: +7(843) 542-62-24, Fax: +7(843) 542-62-24
EMail: rafelle@mail.ru

Faculties

Law *(Kazan, Elabuga)* (Civil Law; Criminal Law; Criminology; Law); **Pedagogy and Psychology** *(Kazan, Zelenodolsk)* (Educational Psychology; Pedagogy; Psychology); **Social and Economic Studies** *(Kazan, Arsk, Buinsk, Elabuga, Zelenodolsk)* (Cultural Studies; Human Resources; Marketing; Public Relations; Social Work)

Further Information: Also Branches in 5 towns: Zelenodolsk, Buinsk, Arsk, Tetjushy, Elabuga. Also Distance Learning Centre and Information Technology Centre.

History: Founded 1993 as Kazan Social and Juridical Institute. Acquired present status and title 2004.

Governing Bodies: Academic Senate; Chancellor's Office

Academic Year: September to July

Admission Requirements: Secondary school certificate (Attestat o srednem obrazovanii)

Fees: (Russian Rubles): 25,000 per annum

Main Language(s) of Instruction: Russian

International Co-operation: The University participates in the Tempus programmes with other institutions based in France, Germany, Italy and Great Britain.

Accrediting Agencies: Ministry of Education

Degrees and Diplomas: *Specialist Diploma*: 5 yrs (full-time) - 6 yrs (part-time); *Kandidat Nauk*: 3 yrs and defense of thesis (dissertation)

Student Services: Academic counselling, Canteen, Cultural centre, Foreign student adviser, Foreign Studies Centre, Health services, Language programs, Sports facilities

Student Residential Facilities: Hostel for 30 students

Special Facilities: Radio studio

Libraries: Yes

Publications: Kazan Pedagogical Journal, Academic Psychological and Pedagogical Journal: Methodology, Theory *(monthly)*

Last Updated: 31/07/12

ACADEMY OF THE FEDERAL SECURITY ADMINISTRATION OF THE RUSSIAN FEDERATION

Akademija Federalnoj Služby Bezopasnosti Rossii
prosp. Mičurinskij 70,
Moskva 119602
Tel: +7(495) 931-3300 +7(495) 931-10-11
Fax: +7(495) 931-0222
EMail: info@academy.fsb.ru
Website: http://www.academy.fsb.ru/

Rector: Viktor Vasilievich Ostroukhov

Programmes

Law (Criminology; Law; Police Studies)

History: Created 1921.

Degrees and Diplomas: *Bakalavr*, *Specialist Diploma*

Last Updated: 14/04/11

ADMIRAL USHAKOV MARITIME STATE UNIVERSITY

Gosudarstvennyj Morskoj Universitet im. Admirala F.F. Ušakova (NSMA)
prosp. Lenina 93, Novorossijsk, 353918 Krasnodar Region
Tel: +7(8617) 717-525
Fax: +7(8617) 717-525
EMail: mail@nsma.ru
Website: http://www.nsma.ru

Rector: Sergey Kondratyev (2012-)
Tel: +7(8617) 767-800 EMail: sikondr@gmail.com

International Relations: Alexander Fayvisovich, Vice-Rector
Tel: +7(8617) 767-839 EMail: faivisovich@nsma.ru

Faculties

Economics and Management (Accountancy; Banking; Cultural Studies; Economics; Finance; International Economics; Management; Transport Management); **International and Marine Law** (International Law; Maritime Law); **Marine Engineering** (Electrical Engineering; Maintenance Technology; Marine Engineering); **Water Transport Operations and Navigation** (Marine Transport)

History: Founded 1975. Previuosly known as Novorossijskaja Gosudarstvennaja Morskaja Akademija (Novorossijsk State Maritime Academy). Acquired current title and status 2005.

Governing Bodies: Academic Board

Academic Year: September to June

Admission Requirements: Secondary school certificate (Attestat o srednem obrazovanii)

Main Language(s) of Instruction: Russian

Degrees and Diplomas: *Bakalavr*, *Specialist Diploma*; *Kandidat Nauk*; *Doktor Nauk*

Student Services: Academic counselling, Canteen, Cultural centre, Employment services, Health services, Language programs, Social counselling, Sports facilities

Student Residential Facilities: Yes

Special Facilities: Museum. Marine Simulators. Computer Centre

Libraries: c. 270,000 vols; 180 periodical subscriptions

Academic Staff *2010-2011*	**TOTAL**
FULL-TIME	**232**
PART-TIME	**97**
STAFF WITH DOCTORATE	
FULL-TIME	**44**
Student Numbers *2012-2013*	
All (Foreign Included)	**4,946**

Last Updated: 11/03/13

ADYGEJA STATE UNIVERSITY

Adygejskij Gosudarstvennyj Universitet
ul. Pervomajskaja 208, Majkop, 385000 Respublika Adygeja
Tel: +7(8772) 57-17-10 +7(8772) 59-38-76
Fax: +7(8772) 57-02-73
EMail: adsu@adygnet.ru
Website: http://www.adygnet.ru

Rector: Rashid D. Hunagov (1996-)

Faculties

Adygej Philology and Culture (Cultural Studies; Native Language; Philology; Russian); **Economics** (Accountancy; Economics; Management); **Foreign Languages** (Arabic; English; Foreign Languages Education; French; German); **History** (History); **Law** (Civil Law; Criminal Law; Law); **Mathematics and Computer Science** (Computer Science; Mathematics); **Natural Sciences** (Biology; Chemistry; Geography); **Pedagogy** (Educational Psychology; Primary Education; Psychology); **Philology** (Literature; Philology); **Physics** (Computer Science; Engineering; Industrial Management; Information Technology; Physics)

History: Founded 1940, acquired present status 1992.

Degrees and Diplomas: *Bakalavr*, *Specialist Diploma*

Last Updated: 12/03/12

ALL-RUSSIAN ACADEMY OF FOREIGN TRADE

Vserossijskaja Akademija Vnešnej Torgovli
ul. Pudovkina 4a, Moskva 119285
Tel: +7(495) 143-1235
Fax: +7(495) 938-2258
EMail: info@vavt.ru
Website: http://www.vavt.ru

Rector: Sergej Sinelnicov-Murylev EMail: sinel@vavt.ru

Centres

Foreign Languages (English; French; German; Italian; Modern Languages; Spanish)

Departments

Foreign Trade Management (Accountancy; Business Administration; Econometrics; Economics; Management; Statistics); **International Commerce** (Banking; Finance; International Business; International Economics); **International Economics** (Accountancy; Banking; International Business; International Economics; Taxation); **International Law** (Civil Law; Commercial Law; European Union Law; International Law; Law; Private Law)

Programmes

Postgraduate Studies (Civil Law; Commercial Law; European Union Law; International Economics; International Law; Private Law)

Schools

Business *(Department of Professional Programmes)* (Business Administration; Finance; International Business; Management; Marketing)

History: Created 1931.

Degrees and Diplomas: *Bakalavr*, *Magistr*
Last Updated: 25/11/11

ALL-RUSSIAN DISTANCE EDUCATION INSTITUTE OF FINANCE AND ECONOMICS

Vserossijskij Zaočnyj Finansovo-Ekonomičeskij Institut
ul. Oleko Dundiča 23, GSP-2, Moskva 121807
Tel: +7(495) 144-8519
Fax: +7(495) 144-8559
EMail: main@vzfei.ru
Website: http://www.vzfei.ru

Rector (Acting): Lanskikh Anatoly Nikolaevič

Vice-Rector: Rogozenkov Aleksandr Vasilevič

Faculties

Accountancy and Statistics (Accountancy; Banking; Statistics); **Continuing Education** (Economics); **Finance and Credit** (Banking; Finance; Insurance; Taxation); **Management and Marketing** (Government; Management; Marketing; Public Administration; Sociology)

Programmes

Postgraduate Studies (Accountancy; Banking; Finance; Marketing)

Further Information: 21 branches throughout the Russian Federation

History: Founded 1930 as Central Distance Institute of Financial and Economic Sciences.

Academic Year: September to June

Admission Requirements: Secondary school certificate (Dokument o polnom srednem obrazovanii)

Main Language(s) of Instruction: Russian

International Co-operation: With institutions in Belarus; Canada; Czech Republic; Denmark; Finland; Germany; Kazakhstan; Spain; Sweden; USA; Uzbekistan

Degrees and Diplomas: *Specialist Diploma*: 5 yrs; *Kandidat Nauk*: 3 yrs; *Doktor Nauk*: Economics

Libraries: c. 1 m. vols

Press or Publishing House: Economic Education
Last Updated: 25/11/11

ALL-RUSSIAN STATE TAX ACADEMY OF THE RUSSIAN FEDERATION FINANCE MINISTRY

Vserossijskaja Gosudarstvennaja Nalogavaja Akademija Ministerstva Finansov Rossijskoj Federatsii
4-j Vešnjakovskij per., Moskva 109456
Tel: +7(495) 371-10-06
Fax: +7(495) 371-10-06
EMail: vgna_r@aha.ru; umuvgna@mail.ru
Website: http://www.vgna.ru/

Rector: Alla P. Balakina

Faculties

Finance and Economics (Accountancy; Banking; Economics; Finance; Human Resources; Industrial and Organizational Psychology; Taxation); **Information Technology** (Applied Mathematics; Business and Commerce; Computer Networks; Information Technology); **Law** (Administrative Law; Civil Law; Commercial Law; Criminal Law; Criminology; International Law; Law)

History: Created 1996.

Degrees and Diplomas: *Bakalavr*, *Specialist Diploma*
Last Updated: 15/03/12

ALL-RUSSIAN STATE UNIVERSITY OF CINEMATOGRAPHY NAMED AFTER S.A. GERASIMOV

Vserossijskij Gosudarstvennyj Universitet Kinematografii im. S.A. Gerasimova (VGIK)
ul. Vi'gelma Pika, 3, Moskva 129226
Tel: +7(499) 181-04-10 +7(499) 181-36-68
Fax: +7(499) 181-80-74
EMail: mail@vgik.info
Website: http://www.vgik.info

Rector: Vladimir S. Malyshev (2007-)

Faculties

Acting (Acting); **Cinema Studies and Screenwriting** (Cinema and Television; Film; Writing); **Cinematography** (Cinema and Television; Film); **Design** (Display and Stage Design); **Film Direction** (Cinema and Television; Film); **Multimedia** (Film; Multimedia); **Production and Economics** (Economics; Film)

History: Founded 1919. Acquired present status 2008.

Governing Bodies: Council

Admission Requirements: Secondary school certificate

Main Language(s) of Instruction: Russian

Degrees and Diplomas: *Specialist Diploma*; *Kandidat Nauk*

Student Services: Academic counselling, Canteen, Cultural centre, Foreign student adviser, Foreign Studies Centre, Health services, Language programs, Nursery care, Sports facilities

Student Residential Facilities: Yes

Special Facilities: Movie Studio. Art pavilion. Theatres

Libraries: Yes
Last Updated: 13/03/12

ALMETIEVSK STATE INSTITUTE OF MUNICIPAL SERVICE

Al'metievskij Gosudarstvennyj Institut Munitsipalnoj Služby
ul. M. Džalilja 9, Al'metievsk, 423450 Respublika Tatarstan
Tel: +7(8553) 45-80-71
Fax: +7(8553) 45-80-75
EMail: rector-agims@mail.ru
Website: http://agims.ru/

Rektor: Il'jas R. Salakhov

Faculties

Continuing Education; **Economics and Management** (Accountancy; Economics; Management); **Psychology and Pedagogy** (Computer Science; Information Technology; Linguistics; Pedagogy; Philology; Psychology); **State and Municipal Management** (Management; Public Administration)

History: Created 1996.

Degrees and Diplomas: *Bakalavr*, *Specialist Diploma*
Last Updated: 31/07/12

ALMETIEVSK STATE OIL INSTITUTE

Al'metievskij Gosudarstvennij Neftianoj Institut
ul. Lenina 2, Al'metievsk, 423450 Respublika Tatarstan
Tel: +7(8553) 31-00-06 +7(8553) 31-00-04
Fax: +7(8553) 43-88-35
EMail: info@agni-rt.ru; alni@rambler.ru
Website: http://www.agni-rt.ru/

Rector: Aleksandr Aleksandrovich Emekeev
EMail: rektor@agni-rt.ru; Alni@rambler.ru

Faculties

Economics and Management (Economics; Engineering Management; Management); **Energy and Automation** (Applied Chemistry; Applied Mathematics; Energy Engineering; Heating and Refrigeration; Information Technology); **Mechanical Engineering** (Engineering Management; Mechanical Engineering; Transport Management); **Oil and Gas Engineering** (Geological Engineering; Metallurgical Engineering; Petroleum and Gas Engineering)

History: Created 1992.

Degrees and Diplomas: *Bakalavr*; *Specialist Diploma*; *Magistr*
Last Updated: 31/07/12

ALTAJ ACADEMY OF ECONOMICS AND LAW (INSTITUTE)

Altajskaja Akademija Ekonomiki i Prava (Institut)
Komsomol'skij prosp. 86, Barnaul, 656038 Altaijskij kraj
Tel: +7(3852) 24-48-08 +7(3852) 66-81-80
Fax: +7(3852) 24-48-08
EMail: adm@aael.altai.ru
Website: http://www.aael.altai.ru

Rektor: Leonid V. Ten

Faculties

Economics (Accountancy; Economics; Finance; Management; Mathematics)

Programmes

Law (Law)

History: Created 1995.

Degrees and Diplomas: *Bakalavr*; *Specialist Diploma*; *Magistr*
Last Updated: 31/07/12

ALTAJ STATE ACADEMY OF FINE ARTS AND CULTURE

Altajskaja Gosudarstvennaja Akademija Iskusstv i Kul'tury
ul. Jurina 277, Barnaul, 656055 Altaijskij kraj
Tel: +7(3852) 54-73-68 +7(3852) 54-73-52
Fax: +7(3852) 54-73-57
EMail: oo@altgaki.org; rector@altgaki.org
Website: http://www.altgaki.org/

Rector: Anatolij Stepanovič Kondykov

Faculties

Choreography (Dance); **Fine Arts** (Acting; Cultural Studies; Fine Arts; Speech Studies; Theatre; Tourism); **Information Technology and Design** (Architecture; Design; Information Technology; Literature; Modern Languages; Museum Studies; Social Psychology); **Music** (Music; Music Education; Music Theory and Composition; Musical Instruments)

History: Created 1974. Previously known as Altajskij Gosudarstvennyj Institut Iskusstv i Kul'tury (Altaj State Institute of Fine Arts and Culture). Acquired current title 2005.

Degrees and Diplomas: *Bakalavr*; *Specialist Diploma*; *Magistr*
Last Updated: 20/01/12

ALTAJ STATE TECHNICAL UNIVERSITY NAMED AFTER I. I. POLZUNOVA

Altajskij Gosudarstvennyj Tehničeskij Universitet im. I. I. Polzunova (ALTSTU)
prosp. Lenina 46, Barnaul, 656038 Altaijskij kraj
Tel: +7(3852) 260-917
Fax: +7(3852) 367-864
EMail: ntsc@desert.secna.ru
Website: http://www.altstu.ru//

Rector: Lec Aleksandrovich Korshunov EMail: altstu@altrrc.ru

Faculties

Automotive Engineering (Automotive Engineering; Machine Building; Road Transport); **Civil Engineering** (Building Technologies; Civil Engineering; Construction Engineering; Road Engineering); **Economics and Regional Development Management** (Economics; Engineering; Finance; Industrial Management; Labour and Industrial Relations); **Food Industry** (Food Science; Food Technology); **Humanities** (Advertising and Publicity; Arts and Humanities; Regional Studies; Social Work); **Information Technology and Business** (Business and Commerce; Business Computing; Information Technology; Instrument Making; International Economics; Materials Engineering); **Mechanical Engineering** (Industrial Engineering; Mechanical Engineering); **Physical Engineering** (Physical Engineering); **Power Engineering** (Electrical Engineering; Energy Engineering; Power Engineering; Water Management); **Social and Cultural Services and Tourism** (Cultural Studies; Tourism)

Institutes

Architecture and Design (Architecture; Design); **Textiles and Light Industry** (Textile Technology)

Further Information: Branches also in Bijsk, Rubtsovsk.

History: Founded 1942. Acquired present status and title 1992.

Governing Bodies: University Board

Academic Year: September to July (September-January; February-July)

Admission Requirements: Secondary school certificate (Attestat o srednem obrazovanii)

Main Language(s) of Instruction: Russian

Degrees and Diplomas: *Bakalavr*; *Specialist Diploma*; *Magistr*; *Kandidat Nauk*; *Doktor Nauk*

Student Services: Academic counselling, Canteen, Cultural centre, Handicapped facilities, Health services, Social counselling, Sports facilities

Student Residential Facilities: For 2,500 students

Special Facilities: University history Museum.

Libraries: Central Library, c. 1,2m. vols

Distance students,3,269. **Evening students**, 1,872.
Last Updated: 30/06/11

ALTAJ STATE UNIVERSITY

Altajskij Gosudarstvennyj Universitet (AGU)
pr. Lenina 61, Barnaul, 656099 Altaijskij kraj
Tel: +7(3852) 66-75-84
Fax: +7(3852) 66-76-26
EMail: rector@asu.ru
Website: http://www.asu.ru

Rector: Sergei Valentinovich Zemljukov

Faculties

Art (Fine Arts; Music); **Biology** (Biochemistry; Biology; Biotechnology; Botany; Ecology; Zoology); **Chemistry** (Analytical Chemistry; Chemistry; Inorganic Chemistry; Organic Chemistry; Physical Chemistry); **Geography** (Ecology; Environmental Management; Geography; Tourism); **History** (Archiving; History; International Relations); **Journalism** (Journalism; Publishing and Book Trade); **Law** (Civil Law; Constitutional Law; Criminal Law; Criminology; International Law; Labour Law; Law); **Mathematics** (Applied Mathematics; Computer Science; Mathematics); **Pedagogy** (Computer Education; Educational Technology; Pedagogy); **Philology** (Linguistics; Literature; Modern Languages; Philology); **Physics and Technology** (Applied Mathematics; Physics; Radiophysics; Systems Analysis); **Political Science** (Political Sciences; Religious Studies; Theology); **Psychology** (Clinical Psychology; Psychology; Social Psychology); **Sociology** (Advertising and Publicity; Social Work; Sociology)

Institutes

International Institute for Economics, Management and Information Systems (Business Computing; Economic History; Management)

Further Information: Also branches in Mikhajlovskoe, Rubtsovsk, Belokurikha, Bijsk, Kamen'-na-Obi, Slavgorod

History: Founded 1973.

Governing Bodies: Academic Council

Academic Year: September to July

Admission Requirements: Secondary education certificate (Attestat o srednem obrazovanii) and entrance examination

Main Language(s) of Instruction: Russian

International Co-operation: With Universities in Canada, China, Czech Republic, France, Germany, United Kingdom, Mongolia, Sweden, USA. Also participates in Tempus and INTAS programmes

Degrees and Diplomas: *Bakalavr*; *Specialist Diploma*; *Magistr*; *Kandidat Nauk*; *Doktor Nauk*

Student Services: Academic counselling, Canteen, Cultural centre, Employment services, Foreign student adviser, Health services, Social counselling, Sports facilities

Student Residential Facilities: Yes

Special Facilities: Art Gallery; Research Laboratories; Botanical Gardens; Multimedia Centre; Museums

Libraries: Total, c. 1.5 m. vols. Media Library with Internet Access

Publications: Chemistry and Plant Raw Materials *(quarterly)*; Izvestija AGU (The Proceedings of the ASU) *(quarterly)*; Turcsaninowia *(quarterly)*

Last Updated: 31/07/12

ALTAJ STATE UNIVERSITY OF AGRICULTURE

Altajskij Gosudarstvennyj Agrarnyj Universitet

prosp. Krasnoarmejskij 98, Barnaul,
656099 Altaijskij kraj
Tel: +7(3852) 628-396
Fax: +7(3852) 229-778
EMail: rector@asau.ru
Website: http://www.asau.ru/

Rector: Sergei Vladimirovich Makarychev EMail: makar@asau.ru

Faculties

Agroengineering (Agricultural Economics; Agricultural Engineering; Agricultural Equipment); **Agronomy** (Agronomy; Botany; Forestry; Plant and Crop Protection; Soil Conservation); **Economics** (Accountancy; Agricultural Business; Agricultural Economics; Agricultural Management; Economics; Finance; Information Technology; Management; Marketing); **Environmental Studies** (Ecology; Environmental Management; Environmental Studies; Surveying and Mapping); **Veterinary Medicine** (Veterinary Science)

History: Created 1943.

Degrees and Diplomas: *Bakalavr*; *Specialist Diploma*; *Magistr*; *Kandidat Nauk*

Last Updated: 31/07/12

ALTAJ STATE UNIVERSITY OF MEDICINE

Altajskij Gosudarstvennyj Medicinskij Universitet

prosp. Lenina 40, Barnaul,
656038 Altaijskij kraj
Tel: +7(3852) 36-88-48 +7(3852) 36-61-13 +7(3852) 36-72-34
Fax: +7(3852) 36-60-91 +7(3852) 36-60-84
EMail: rector@agmu.ru
Website: http://www.agmu.ru

Rector: Valerij Mikhailovich Brjukhanov

Faculties

Health Administration (Health Administration); **Medicine** (Gynaecology and Obstetrics; Medicine; Midwifery; Surgery); **Nursing** (Midwifery; Nursing); **Paediatrics** (Paediatrics); **Pharmacy** (Pharmacology; Pharmacy); **Preventive Medicine** (Ecology; Epidemiology; Social and Preventive Medicine); **Stomatology** (Orthodontics; Otorhinolaryngology; Stomatology)

History: Created 1954

Degrees and Diplomas: *Specialist Diploma*

Last Updated: 20/01/12

AMUR HUMANITIES-PEDAGOGY STATE UNIVERSITY

Amurskij Gumanitarno-Pedagogičeskij Gosudarstvennyj Universitet

ul. Kirova, Korp. 2, part 2, Komsomol'sk-na-Amure,
681000 Khabarovskaja oblast'
Tel: +7(42172) 460-39
Fax: +7(42172) 461-49
EMail: mail@amgpgu.kms.ru
Website: http://amgpgu.kms.ru/

Rector: Alexandr Shumyeiko (2005-)
EMail: rector@amgpgu.kms.ru

Vice-Rector: Alexander Nikitin

International Relations: Andrey Koshkin, Vice-Rector, International Affairs EMail: apkosh@mail.ru

Faculties

Economics (Economics); **Geography and Natural Studies** (Biology; Ecology; Environmental Studies; Geography; Regional Studies); **History and Law** (History; Law); **Physics and Mathematics** (Mathematics; Physics); **Technology and Design** (Design; Technology)

Institutes

Pedagogy and Psychology (Clinical Psychology; Educational Psychology; Pedagogy; Preschool Education; Primary Education; Social Psychology; Speech Therapy and Audiology; Sports Management); **Philology** (Chinese; English; French; German; Japanese; Korean; Literature; Marketing; Native Language; Philology; Russian; Translation and Interpretation)

History: Founded in 1954 as Komsomolsk-na-Amure State Pedagogical Institute. Became Komsomol'skij-na-Amure Gosudarstvennyj Pedagogičeskij Universitet (Komsomolsk-na-Amure State Pedagogical University) in 1999. Acquired current title and status 2006

Governing Bodies: University Council

Academic Year: September to June (September-January; February-June)

Admission Requirements: Secondary school certificate (Attestat o Srednem Obshchem Obrazovanii)

Fees: (Russian Rubles): Residents, 32,000-40,000 per annum; Non-residents, (Euros): 1,400-1,700

Main Language(s) of Instruction: Russian

International Co-operation: With universities in China, United Kingdom, Vietnam, Japan

Accrediting Agencies: Ministry of Education and Science

Degrees and Diplomas: *Bakalavr*: 4 yrs; *Bakalavr*: 4 yrs; *Bakalavr*: 4 yrs; *Specialist Diploma*: 5 yrs; *Kandidat Nauk*: a further 2-3 yrs; *Kandidat Nauk*: a further 2-3 yrs. Certificate of Additional Vocational Training after graduating from the Department of Extracurricular Activities

Student Services: Academic counselling, Canteen, Cultural centre, Employment services, Foreign student adviser, Foreign Studies Centre, Health services, Language programs, Nursery care, Social counselling, Sports facilities

Student Residential Facilities: yes - shared, furnished accommodation

Special Facilities: Museum of University history and awards; art gallery; laboratories; computer rooms

Libraries: 4 reading rooms; traditional library; e-library; access to Moscow University e-library

Publications: Bulletin of Students' and Young Researchers' Scientific Society *(biennially)*; Far East 21st Century, Publication of the annual University conference *(annually)*; Higher Education in the period of Modernization: Experience, problems and perspectives, Research papers on education and innovations in the domain *(annually)*; Technology, Research papers on technology *(biennially)*

Last Updated: 31/03/09

AMUR STATE MEDICAL ACADEMY

Amurskaja Gosudarstvennaja Meditsinskaja Akademija
ul. Gorkogo 95, Blagoveščensk, 675000 Amurskaja oblast'
Tel: +7(4162) 526-828
Fax: +7(4162) 527-407
EMail: agma@amur.ru; agma@nm.ru
Website: http://www.amursma.ru/

Rector: Vladimir Dorovskih

Faculties
Medicine (Medicine); **Paediatrics** (Paediatrics)

History: Founded 1952 as Blagoveščensk Medical Institute, acquired present status and title 1995.

Governing Bodies: Academic Council

Academic Year: September to June

Main Language(s) of Instruction: Russian

International Co-operation: With universities in Japan and China

Accrediting Agencies: Federal Egency on Healthcare and Social Development of Russia Federation

Degrees and Diplomas: *Specialist Diploma*

Student Services: Academic counselling, Cultural centre, Health services, Language programs, Social counselling, Sports facilities

Student Residential Facilities: 8 students' hostels (2,500 persons capacity)

Special Facilities: 2 Conference Halls; 26 hospitals outpatient clinics and dispensaries (4,053 beds)

Libraries: c. 270,000 vols and journals

Press or Publishing House: Amurskaja Meditsina - Academy newspaper

Last Updated: 14/04/11

AMUR STATE UNIVERSITY

Amurskij Gosudarstvennyj Universitet (AMSU)
Ignatjevskoje šosse 21, Blagoveščensk, 675027 Amurskaja oblast'
Tel: +7(4162) 39-45-01
Fax: +7(4162) 39-45-25
EMail: master@amursu.ru
Website: http://www.amursu.ru

Rector: Andrei Plutenko

Faculties
Design and Technology (Clothing and Sewing; Design; Fashion Design; Painting and Drawing; Textile Design); **Economics** (Economics; Finance; International Economics; Management; Taxation; Tourism); **Energy Engineering** (Energy Engineering; Production Engineering); **Engineering and Physics** (Environmental Engineering; Geological Engineering; Laser Engineering; Physics; Safety Engineering); **International Relations** (Chinese; History; International Relations); **Law** (Civil Law; Constitutional Law; Criminal Law; Law); **Mathematics and Computer Science** (Applied Mathematics; Computer Science; Information Technology; Mathematics); **Philology** (English; German; Journalism; Philology; Russian; Translation and Interpretation); **Social Work** (Educational and Student Counselling; Psychology; Religious Studies; Social Psychology; Social Work; Sociology)

History: Founded 1975 as a branch of Khabarovsk Polytechnic University. Acquired present status and title 1994.

Governing Bodies: University Council

Academic Year: September to June

Admission Requirements: Secondary school certificate or equivalent

Main Language(s) of Instruction: Russian

International Co-operation: With universities in Germany, USA, Korea, China.

Accrediting Agencies: Ministry of Education

Degrees and Diplomas: *Bakalavr*, *Specialist Diploma*; *Magistr*

Special Facilities: Museum. Art gallery. Theatre. Innovation centre.

Libraries: c. 2,255,535 vols

Last Updated: 31/07/12

ANGARSK STATE TECHNICAL ACADEMY

Angarskaja Gosudarstvennaja Tehničeskaja Akademija
ul. Čajkovskogo 60, Angarsk, 665835 Irkutskaja oblast'
Tel: +7(3955) 67-34-17 +7(3955) 67-18-32
Fax: +7(3955) 67-18-32
EMail: ivc@agta.ru; web@agta.ru
Website: http://www.agta.ru/

Rector: Artem Viktorovich Badennikov

Faculties
Cybernetics Engineering (Automation and Control Engineering; Computer Science; Electronic Engineering; Mathematics; Physics; Robotics); **Management and Business** (Accountancy; Economics; Environmental Management; Finance; Industrial Management; Marketing); **Technology** (Chemical Engineering; Civil Engineering; Industrial Engineering; Technology; Transport Management)

History: Created 1991 as Angarskij State Tekhnologičeskij Institute (Angarsk State Technological Institute). Acquired current title and status 2000.

Degrees and Diplomas: *Specialist Diploma*; *Kandidat Nauk*

Last Updated: 15/04/11

ARMAVIR STATE PEDAGOGICAL ACADEMY

Armavirskaja Gosudarstvennaja Pedagogičeskaja Akademija
ul. Roza Ljuksemburg 159, Armavir, 352901 Krasnodarskij Kraj
Tel: +7(86137) 33560
Fax: +7(86137) 33420
EMail: umo_agpu@mail.ru; rektoragpu@mail.ru
Website: http://www.agpu.net/

Rector: Ambartsum Robertovich Galustov
EMail: rektoragpu@mail.ru

Faculties
Applied Computer Studies, Mathematics and Physics (Applied Mathematics; Applied Physics; Computer Science; Mathematics; Mathematics Education; Physics; Science Education); **Foreign Languages** (English; Foreign Languages Education; Linguistics); **History** (History; Humanities and Social Science Education); **Peda-Pyschology** (Educational Psychology; Pedagogy; Psychology; Social Work; Special Education); **Philology** (Cultural Studies; Journalism; Teacher Training); **Technology and Entrepreneurship** (Business Education; Design; Ecology; Economics; Management; Teacher Training; Technology)

History: Created 1839. Previously known as Armavirskaja Gosudarstvennaja Pedagogičeskaja Akademija. Acquired Academy status 2003.

Degrees and Diplomas: *Bakalavr*, *Specialist Diploma*

Last Updated: 30/06/11

ARZAMAS STATE PEDAGOGICAL INSTITUTE

Arzamaskij Gosudarstvennyj Pedagogičeskij Institut
ul. Karla Marksa 36, Arzamas 607220
Tel: +7(83147) 41553
Fax: +7(83147) 41553
EMail: agpi@nts.ru
Website: http://agpi.info/index.php

Rector: Evgenij Pavlovič Titkov

Programmes
Education (Education)

Degrees and Diplomas: *Specialist Diploma*

ASTRAHAN INSTITUTE OF ARCHITECTURE AND CIVIL ENGINEERING

Astrahanskij Inženerno-Stroitel'nyj Institut
ul. Tatičseva 18, Astrakhan, 414056 Astrahhanskaja oblast'
Tel: +7(8510) 251-468
Fax: +7(8510) 121-468
EMail: buildinst@mail.ru
Website: http://www.aisi.nm.ru

Rector: Adolf Sapožnikov (1992-)
Tel: +7 (8510) 251-468, Fax: +7 (8512) 251-468

Pro-Rector: Vladimir Svintsov Tel: +7(8512) 251-887

International Relations: Tatiana Zolina

Faculties

Applied Geology (Engineering; Environmental Studies; European Languages; Geology; Mathematics) *Dean*: Andrei Kurdjuk; **Architecture** *Dean*: Gennadi Akhmedov; **Engineering** (Building Technologies; Chemistry; Civil Engineering; Computer Engineering; Computer Science; Cultural Studies; Economics; Electrical and Electronic Engineering; Electrical Engineering; Engineering; Environmental Engineering; Environmental Studies; European Languages; Fire Science; Geology; Management; Mathematics; Mechanical Engineering; Physics; Psychology; Safety Engineering; Sociology; Taxation) *Dean*: Adolf Sapozhnikov; **Gas, Heating Supply and Ventilation** *Dean*: Nickolai Shishkin; **Industrial and Civil Engineering** *Dean*: Adolf Sapozhnikov; **Water Supply and Water Removal** *Dean*: Ljudmila Boronina

History: Founded 1992.

Governing Bodies: University Council

Academic Year: September to July

Admission Requirements: Secondary school certificate (Attestat o srednem obrazovanii) and entrance examination

Fees: (Russian Rubles): c. 16,800 per annum

Main Language(s) of Instruction: Russian

International Co-operation: With universities in India

Accrediting Agencies: Ministry of Education

Degrees and Diplomas: *Bakalavr*: All faculties except Architecture, 4 yrs; *Specialist Diploma*: All faculties, 5-6 yrs

Student Services: Academic counselling, Canteen, Employment services, Language programs, Nursery care, Sports facilities

Student Residential Facilities: Yes

Libraries: c. 70,000 vols

Publications: Collection of Scientific and Methodical Publications *(3 per annum)*; 'The Architect' *(monthly)*

ASTRAHAN STATE MEDICAL ACADEMY

Astrahanskaja Gosudarstvennaja Medicinskaja Akademija (ASMA)

ul. Bakinskaja 121, Astrakhan, 414000 Astrahhanskaja oblast'
Tel: +7(8512) 227-023
Fax: +7(8512) 227-016
EMail: agma@astranet.ru
Website: http://agma.astranet.ru/

Rector: Khalil Mingalievich Galimzyanov (2007-)
Tel: +7(8512) 227-023, Fax: +7(8512) 394-130

Pro-Rector: Halil Galimzyanov
Tel: +7(8512) 227-023, Fax: +7(8512) 394-130

International Relations: Tatyana Kirillova, Dean of Faculty of Foreign Students Tel: +7(8512) 306-018, Fax: +7(8512) 306-018

Faculties

Advanced Training for Doctors and Postgraduate Training (Medicine) *Dean*: Anatoliy Serdyukov; **Health Care** (Medicine) *Dean*: Vladimir Ryubkin; **Medicine** (Medicine) *Dean*: Ludmila Sentyurova; **Nursery Service** *Dean*: Luciya Bahmutova; **Paediatrics** (Paediatrics) *Dean*: Gennadiy Harchenko; **Pharmacy** *Dean*: Bronislav Feldman; **Teaching Medicine to Foreign Students** (Health Education) *Dean*: Tatyana Kirillova

History: Founded 1918 as Medical Department of Astrahan University, became State Medical Institute (independent) 1922 and acquired present status and title 1995.

Governing Bodies: Rectorate; Deans Office; Head of Chairs

Academic Year: September to July

Admission Requirements: Secondary school certificate (Attestat o srednem obrazovanii)

Fees: (Russian Rubles): c. 25,000 per annum (most students are exempted from fees); foreign students (US Dollars), c. 1,500 per annum

Main Language(s) of Instruction: Russian

Degrees and Diplomas: *Kandidat Nauk*: Medicine; Therapy; Surgery: Paediatrics, 3-5 yrs

Student Services: Academic counselling, Canteen, Cultural centre, Employment services, Foreign student adviser, Foreign Studies Centre, Handicapped facilities, Health services, Language programs, Nursery care, Social counselling, Sports facilities

Student Residential Facilities: 5 students hostels

Special Facilities: Astrahan State Medical Academy History Museum; Military Glory of the Medical Workers Museum; Anatomy Museum

Libraries: c. 700,000 vols

Publications: Research Handbook of ASMA *(annually)*

Press or Publishing House: Publishing Centre of the Academy

ASTRAHAN STATE MUSIC CONSERVATORY (ACADEMY)

Astrahanskaja Gosudarstvennaja Konservatorija (Akademija)

ul. Sovetskaja 23, Astrakhan, 414000 Astrahhanskaja oblast'
Tel: +7(8512) 22-57-69 +7(8512) 22-68-81
Fax: +7(8512) 22-93-11
EMail: lira@veriga.ru
Website: http://www.astracons.ru/

Rector: Alexandr Valentinovich Mostykanov

Programmes

Music (Conducting; Music; Music Theory and Composition; Musical Instruments; Musicology; Singing)

History: Founded 1969, acquired present status and title of Academy 2010.

Governing Bodies: Board of trustees

Academic Year: September to June

Admission Requirements: Musical College Certificate

Main Language(s) of Instruction: Russian

Degrees and Diplomas: *Specialist Diploma*; *Kandidat Nauk*

Student Services: Academic counselling, Foreign student adviser, Health services, Language programs, Social counselling, Sports facilities

Student Residential Facilities: Yes

Special Facilities: Sound Laboratory. Concert Halls

Libraries: c. 1,1 m. vols. c. 27,000 scientific books

Press or Publishing House: Editorial Publishing Department
Last Updated: 15/04/11

ASTRAHAN STATE TECHNICAL UNIVERSITY

Astrahanskij Gosudarstvennyj Tehničeskij Universitet (ASTU)

ul. Tatiščeva 16, Astrakhan, 414025 Astrahhanskaja oblast'
Tel: +7(8512) 250-923
Fax: +7(8512) 256-427
EMail: astu@astu.org
Website: http://www.astu.org/

Rector: Yuri Timofeevich Pimenov

Deputy-Rector: Mikhail Nikolaevich Pokusaev
Tel: +7(8512) 256-409

International Relations: Vladimir Grigorevich Bukin, Pro-Rector, Internaional Affairs
Tel: +7(8512) 251-490, Fax: +7(8512) 251-490
EMail: interoffice@astmail.astranet.ru

Faculties

Automation and Computer Facilities (Automation and Control Engineering; Computer Engineering); **Biology and Nature Management** (Biology; Ecology; Environmental Management); **Chemistry and Technology** (Chemical Engineering; Chemistry; Technology); **Correspondence Studies; Fisheries** (Fishery); **Law** (Law); **Marine Power Engineering** (Marine Science and Oceanography; Power Engineering); **Mechanics** (Mechanics)

Institutes

Economics (Economics)

Further Information: Russian Courses for foreign students. Study Abroad programmes

History: Founded 1930, acquired present status 1994.

Academic Year: September to July (September-January; February-July)

Admission Requirements: Secondary school certificate (Attestat o sredem obrazovanii)

Fees: (US Dollars): Preparatory Faculty for foreign students, c. 800 per annum; study of speciality c. 1,000; study of a field, c. 1,100; Master's degree, c. 1,200-1,500; postgraduate studies, c. 2,000-3,500; Training course, c. 1,500-2,500; Russian language courses, c. 80 per month

Main Language(s) of Instruction: Russian

Degrees and Diplomas: *Bakalavr*: 4 yrs; *Specialist Diploma*: 5 yrs; *Magistr*: a further 2 yrs

Student Services: Academic counselling, Canteen, Cultural centre, Employment services, Foreign student adviser, Foreign Studies Centre, Handicapped facilities, Health services, Language programs, Social counselling, Sports facilities

Student Residential Facilities: For c. 2,890 students

Special Facilities: University Museum

Libraries: c. 501,000 vols

Press or Publishing House: Inform-publishing Centre

ASTRAHAN STATE UNIVERSITY

Astrahanskij Gosudarstvennyj Universitet

ul. Taticševa 20a, Astrakhan, 414056 Astrahhanskaja oblast'
Tel: +7(8512) 610-890
Fax: +7(8512) 251-718
EMail: aspu@aspu.ru
Website: http://www.aspu.ru

Rector: Aleksandr Pavlovič Lunyev

Provost: Galina Stefanova EMail: firstpro@aspu.ru

International Relations: Nikolay Khurchak, Head, International Relations Department EMail: nikolay.khurchak@gmail.com

Institutes

Business Language and Professional Communciation (Foreigners Education; Modern Languages; Philology; Primary Education); **Humanities** (Architecture; Business Administration; Communication Studies; Design; Economics; History; Law; Management); **Natural Sciences** (Agronomy; Biology; Chemistry; Geography; Geology); **Pedagogy, Psychology, and Sociak Work** (Pedagogy; Physical Education; Psychology; Social Work); **Physico-Mathematical Institute of Innovative Development** (Electronic Engineering; Information Technology; Mathematics; Physics)

History: Created 1932. Acquired current status 2002.

Governing Bodies: Rectorate

Admission Requirements: Secondary school certificate

Fees: (Russian Rubles): 14,500 - 29,100 per semester

Main Language(s) of Instruction: Russian

International Co-operation: with institutions in Russia, Germany, USA, China. TEMPUS programme

Degrees and Diplomas: *Bakalavr*: 4 yrs; *Specialist Diploma*: 5 yrs; *Magistr*: a further 2 yrs; *Kandidat Nauk*: 3 yrs

Student Residential Facilities: 6 hostels

Academic Staff *2010-2011*	MEN	WOMEN	TOTAL
FULL-TIME	180	506	**686**
PART-TIME	151	158	**309**
STAFF WITH DOCTORATE			
FULL-TIME	39	41	**80**
PART-TIME	69	24	**93**
Student Numbers *2010-2011*			
All (Foreign Included)	5,800	8,321	**14,121**
FOREIGN ONLY	230	144	**374**

Part-time students, 6,306. **Distance students**, 230. **Evening students**, 654.

Last Updated: 29/09/11

AZOV-BLACK SEA STATE AGRO-ENGINEERING ACADEMY

Azovo-Černomorskaja Gosudarstvennaja Agroinženernaja Akademija (ACHGAA)

ul. Lenina 21, Zernograd, 347740 Rostovskaja oblast'
Tel: +7(86359) 417-43
Fax: +7(86359) 343-55
EMail: achgaa@zern.donpac.ru
Website: http://www.achgaa.ru

Rector: Mikhail Taranov EMail: achaa@zern.donpac.ru

Faculties

Agricultural Technology (Agricultural Business; Agricultural Engineering; Agricultural Equipment; Agronomy); **Economics** (Accountancy; Economics; Management); **Engineering** (Agricultural Engineering; Electrical Engineering; Heating and Refrigeration; Power Engineering; Thermal Engineering); **Transport** (Automotive Engineering; Road Transport; Transport Engineering; Transport Management)

History: Founded 1930 as Institute of Mechanical Engineers of Socialist Crop Farming. Successively reorganised into Azov-Black Sea Institute of Mechanical Engineers of Agriculture (1934), Azov-Black Sea Institute of Mechanization of Agriculture (1938), Azov-Black Sea State AgroEngineering Academy (1995), State Higher Educational Establishment of Professional Training "Azov-Black Sea State AgroEngineering Academy" (2001). Acquired present status and title 2003.

Governing Bodies: Ministry of Agriculture of Russian Federation

Academic Year: September to July

Admission Requirements: Secondary School Ccertificate (attestat o srednem obrazovanii) or diploma of secondary specialized/vocational/technical education (Diplom o Srednem Spetsialnom obrazonavii); Entrance examination (Common State Examination)

Main Language(s) of Instruction: Russian

International Co-operation: With Institutions in Germany, France, Hungary

Accrediting Agencies: Ministry of Education of Russian Federation

Degrees and Diplomas: *Bakalavr*, *Specialist Diploma*: 5 yrs

Student Services: Academic counselling, Canteen, Cultural centre, Foreign student adviser, Health services, Language programs, Social counselling, Sports facilities

Student Residential Facilities: Five youth hostels for 1,500 students

Special Facilities: Museum; Internet Club "Kompas"

Libraries: 275,375 vols (in Russian, in English, in German and in French)

Last Updated: 30/06/11

BAIKAL STATE UNIVERSITY OF ECONOMICS AND LAW

Baikalskij Gosudarstvennij Universitet Ekonomiki I Prava

ul. Lenina 11, Irkutsk, 664003
Irkutskaja oblast'
Tel: +7(3952) 241-055
Fax: +7(3952) 241-200
EMail: info@isea.ru
Website: http://www.bnu.ru/eng/

Rector: M. A. Vinokurov

International Relations: Olga Onoshko, Vice-Rector International Cooperation
Tel: +7(3952) 211-228, Fax: +7(3952) 242-944
EMail: olga@isea.ru

Programmes

Economics (Economics); **Finance** (Finance); **Information Technology** (Information Technology); **Law** (Law)

History: Formerly known as Irkutskaja Gosudarstvennaja Ekonomičeskaja Akademija (Irkutsk State Academy of Economics).

BALTIC FEDERAL UNIVERSITY NAMED AFTER EMMANUEL KANT

Baltijskij Federalnyj Universitet im. Immanuila Kanta
ul. A. Nevskogo 14, Kaliningrad 236041
Tel: +7(4012) 465-917
Fax: +7(4012) 465-813
EMail: rector@kantiana.ru; ikuksa@kantiana.ru; esmirnova@kantiana.ru
Website: http://www.kantiana.ru

Rector: Andrey Klemešev
EMail: AKlemeshev@kantiana.ru; rector@kantiana.ru

Faculties
Bioecology (Biology; Botany; Chemistry; Ecology; Plant and Crop Protection; Zoology); **Economics** (Economics; Finance; Management; Marketing); **Geography and Geoecology** (Ecology; Geography; Tourism); **History** (Cultural Studies; History; Philosophy; Political Sciences; Sociology); **Law** (Commercial Law; Criminal Law; European Union Law; International Law; Law); **Linguistics and Intercultural Communication** (Foreign Languages Education; International Studies; Linguistics; Modern Languages); **Mathematics** (Applied Mathematics; Computer Science; Mathematics); **Medicine** (Medicine; Midwifery; Nursing; Pharmacy; Stomatology); **Philology and Journalism** (Baltic Languages; Journalism; Literature; Philology; Russian; Slavic Languages); **Physical Education and Sport** (Physical Education; Sports); **Physics** (Applied Physics; Physics; Radiophysics; Telecommunications Engineering); **Psychology and Social Work** (Clinical Psychology; Experimental Psychology; Psychology; Social Work); **Service and Tourism** (Hotel and Restaurant; Tourism; Transport Management)

Institutes
Modern Educational Technology (Educational Psychology; Educational Sciences; Pedagogy)

History: Founded 1947. Formerly known as Kaliningradskij Gosudarstvennyj Universitet (Kaliningrad State University) and Rossijskij Gosudarstvennyj Universitet imeni Immanuila Kanta (State University of Russia named after Emmanuel Kant). Acquired current title 2010.

Governing Bodies: Academic Council

Academic Year: September to June (September-January; February-June)

Admission Requirements: Secondary school certificate (Attestat o srednem obrazovanii) and entrance examination

Main Language(s) of Instruction: Russian

Degrees and Diplomas: *Bakalavr*; *Specialist Diploma*: 5 yrs; *Magistr*; *Kandidat Nauk*: a further 3 yrs and thesis; *Doktor Nauk*: by thesis after Kandidat

Student Residential Facilities: For 1,200 students

Special Facilities: Botanical Garden; Kant museum; Internet Centre

Libraries: Central Library, c. 650,000 vols

Last Updated: 28/04/11

BALTIC STATE FISHING FLEET ACADEMY

Baltijskaja Gosudarstvennaja Akademija Rybopromyslovogo Flota (BGA)
ul. Molodjozšnaja 6, Kaliningrad 236029
Tel: +7(112) 217-204
Fax: +7(112) 516-690
EMail: bugakova@bga.gazinter.net; kanzabga@bga.gazinter.net
Website: http://www.bgarf.ru/

Rector: Aleksandr Pimošenko (1985-)
EMail: rektor@bga.gazinter.net

Vice-Rector: Vadim Kalašnik Tel: +7(112) 551-616

International Relations: Alexey Pozdnyakov
Tel: +7(112) 275-070 EMail: bgaio@mail.ru

Departments
Business Administration *Head*: Vladimir Ovčarenko; **Data Processing and Control Systems** (Automation and Control Engineering; Data Processing) *Head*: Vladimir Pleškov; **English** *Head*: Emilia Sopova; **History, Philosophy and Social Studies** (History; Philosophy; Social Studies) *Head*: Ali Salihov; **Marine Radio Engineering Systems** (Marine Engineering; Radio and Television Broadcasting) *Head*: Arseny Kologrivov; **Marine Safety** *Head*: Vyačeslav Efentiev; **Marketing and Commerce** (Business and Commerce; Marketing) *Head*: Levan Gamkrelidze; **Mathematics** (Applied Mathematics; Mathematics) *Head*: Galina Bokareva; **Mechanical Engineering** (Mechanical Engineering) *Head*: Andrey Osnyač; **Metal Technology and Ship Repair** (Metal Techniques; Naval Architecture) *Head*: Alexander Pimošenko; **Navigation** (Nautical Science) *Head*: Vitaly Bukaty; **Physics** (Physics) *Head*: Nikolai Sinyavsky; **Refrigeration Technology, Electrical Equipment and Ship Control Systems** (Automation and Control Engineering; Electrical and Electronic Equipment and Maintenance; Heating and Refrigeration) *Head*: Yuri Slastihin; **Ship Propulsion Plants** (Marine Engineering) *Head*: Victor Odintsov; **Theory and Ship Operations** (Nautical Science) *Head*: Vitaly Kulagin; **Theory of Economics** (Economics) *Head*: Yuri Matočkin; **Theory of Radio Technology** (Radio and Television Broadcasting) *Head*: Anatoly Karlov; **Transport Management** (Marine Transport; Road Transport; Transport Management) *Head*: Leonid Meiler

Faculties
Business Administration (Business Administration; Business and Commerce; Management; Marketing) *Dean*: Alexey Serbulov; **Distance Learning** (Business Administration; Nautical Science; Radio and Television Broadcasting; Transport Management) *Dean*: Georgy Grošev; **Marine Engineering** (Marine Engineering) *Dean*: Victor Barannikov; **Navigation** (Nautical Science) *Dean*: Vitaly Bondarev; **Radio Engineering** (Telecommunications Engineering) *Dean*: Vladimir Kozulov

Further Information: Also Maritime Lyceum

History: Founded 1966.

Governing Bodies: Academic Council

Academic Year: September to June

Admission Requirements: Secondary school certificate (Attestat o srednem obrazovanii) or equivalent

Fees: (Dollars): 750-800 per annum; foreign students, 750-1,000 per annum

Main Language(s) of Instruction: Russian

International Co-operation: With universities in Germany, Poland, Sweden

Accrediting Agencies: Ministry of Education; London Institute of Marine Engineers, Science and Technology

Degrees and Diplomas: *Specialist Diploma*: Marketing; Commerce; Management; Automation Control Systems, 5 yrs; *Specialist Diploma*: Operation of Marine Power Plants; Techniques and Physics of Low Temperatures; Maintenance of Transport Radio Equipment, 51/2 yrs

Student Services: Academic counselling, Canteen, Cultural centre, Foreign student adviser, Foreign Studies Centre, Health services, Language programs, Sports facilities

Student Residential Facilities: Yes

Special Facilities: Museum

Libraries: C. 386,000 vols

Publications: Education Topics *(annually)*; Refrigeration Installations *(annually)*

BALTIC STATE TECHNICAL UNIVERSITY NAMED AFTER D.F. USTINOV 'VOENMEH'

Baltijskij Gosudarstvennyj Tehničeskij Universitet im. D.F. Ustinova 'Voenmeh'
1-ja Krasnoarmejskaja 1, Sankt-Peterburg 190005
Tel: +7(812) 316-23-94 +7(812) 314-37-86
Fax: +7(812) 316-24-09 +7(812) 314-37-86
EMail: komdep@bstu.spb.su; center@bstu.spb.su
Website: http://www.voenmeh.ru/

Rector: Konstantin Mikhailovich Ivanov EMail: rector@bstu.spb.su

Faculties
Aerospace (Aeronautical and Aerospace Engineering); **Arms and Weapon Systems** (Military Science); **Information and Guidance Systems** (Information Technology; Telecommunications Engineering); **International Communication** (Humanities and Social Science Education; Linguistics; Political Sciences); **International**

Industrial Management (Industrial Management; International Business); **Mechatronics and Control** (Automation and Control Engineering; Electronic Engineering; Mechanical Engineering); **Physics and Technics** (Physics); **Rocketry and Aircraft** (Aeronautical and Aerospace Engineering)

Further Information: Branch also in Bishkek, Kyrgyzstan.

History: Founded 1875 as Technical School. Reformed 1932 as Military Institute of Mechanics, and acquired present status and title 1992.

Academic Year: September to June (September-December; Februay-June)

Admission Requirements: Secondary school certificate (Attestat o srednem obrazovanii)

Main Language(s) of Instruction: Russian

Degrees and Diplomas: *Bakalavr*, *Specialist Diploma*; *Magistr*, *Kandidat Nauk*

Student Services: Canteen, Health services, Language programs, Sports facilities

Student Residential Facilities: For c. 1,800 students

Special Facilities: University Historical Museum

Libraries: c. 1.1m. vols

Last Updated: 19/01/12

BARNAUL LAW INSTITUTE OF THE MINISTRY OF INTERNAL AFFAIRS OF RUSSIA

Barnaulskij Juridičeskij Institut MVD Rossii

ul. Čkalova 49, Barnaul 656099

Tel: +7(3852) 368-836

Fax: +7(3852) 242-211

Website: http://www.buimvd.ru/

Rector: Vladimir Mihajlovič Semenov

Programmes

Law (Criminology; Law; Police Studies)

Degrees and Diplomas: *Specialist Diploma*

BARNAUL STATE PEDAGOGICAL UNIVERSITY

Barnaulskij Gosudarstvennyj Pedagogičeskij Universitet

ul. Molodežnaja 55, Barnaul 656031

Tel: +7(3852) 368-277

Fax: +7(3852) 260-836

Website: http://www.bspu.secna.ru

Rector: Vladimir Lopatkin

Programmes

Education (Education)

History: Founded 1967.

BASHKIR ACADEMY OF PUBLIC ADMINISTRATION AND MANAGEMENT UNDER THE AUSPICES OF THE PRESIDENT OF BASHKORTOSTAN REPUBLIC

Baškirskaja Akademija Gosudarstvennoj Služby i Upravlenija pri Prezidente Respubliki Baškorstortan (BAPAM)

ul. Frunze 40, Ufa, 450000 Respublika Bashkortosan

Tel: +7(3472) 721-077

Fax: +7(3472) 727-448

EMail: ciabagsu@yandex.ru

Website: http://www.bagsu.rb.ru

Rector: Ildar Gimaev

Vice-Rector: Sergei Lavrontjev Tel: +7(3472) 728-610

International Relations: Sharifyan Samirkhanov
Tel: +7(3472) 736-521

Departments

Postgraduate Studies (Administrative Law; Constitutional Law; Economics; Political Sciences; Social Psychology; Social Sciences)

Faculties

Higher Qualification Learning; **Law**; **Professional Retraining** (Accountancy; Information Sciences; Marketing; Real Estate); **Public Administration and Management** (Accountancy; Computer Science; Economics; Finance; Law; Marketing; Modern Languages; Political Sciences; Psychology; Public Administration; Sociology)

Programmes

Specialist Training

History: Founded 1991, acquired present status 1994.

Governing Bodies: Academy Council

Academic Year: September to June

Admission Requirements: Secondary school certificate

Fees: (Russian Rubles): c. 27,000 per annum

Main Language(s) of Instruction: Russian

Accrediting Agencies: Ministry of General and Professional Education

Student Services: Academic counselling, Canteen, Foreign student adviser, Language programs

Publications: Economics and Management *(monthly)*

BASHKIR STATE AGRARIAN UNIVERSITY

Baškirskij Gosudarstvennyj Agrarnyj Universitet (BGAU)

ul. 50 Let Oktjabrja 34, Ufa, 450001 Respublika Bashkortosan

Tel: +7(3472) 280-898

Fax: +7(3472) 286-811

EMail: bgau@ufanet.ru

Website: http://www.bsau.ru

Head: Vladimir Nedorezkov Tel: +7(3472) 289-177

Deputy-Rector: Rafkat Gaisin
Tel: +7(3472) 281-511, Fax: +7(3472) 281-511
EMail: gaisin@ufanet.ru

International Relations: Nurutdin Taipov, Deputy Rector
Tel: +7(3472) 526-214 EMail: taipov@ufanet.ru

Departments

Farm Mechanization (Agricultural Equipment; Farm Management) *Head*: Fanil Gabdrafikov

Faculties

Agronomy *Head*: Denis Andrianov; **Animal Product Technologies** *Head*: Rinat Gadiev; **Economics** *Head*: Rashit Hannanov; **Electrical Engineering and Automation** *Head*: Rustam Aipov; **Food Technologies** (Brewing; Dairy; Food Science; Food Technology; Meat and Poultry) *Dean*: Vagiz Fashutdinov; **Forestry and Landscape Management** *Head*: Vladimir Konovalov; **Veterinary Science** *Head*: Vasilij Kirilov

History: Founded 1930, acquired present status 1993.

Governing Bodies: Council

Academic Year: September to June

Admission Requirements: Secondary school certificate and entrance examination

Main Language(s) of Instruction: Russian

International Co-operation: With universities in Germany, Poland

Accrediting Agencies: Ministry of Education

Degrees and Diplomas: *Specialist Diploma*: 5 yrs

Student Services: Academic counselling, Canteen, Cultural centre, Employment services, Foreign student adviser, Foreign Studies Centre, Handicapped facilities, Health services, Language programs, Nursery care, Social counselling, Sports facilities

Student Residential Facilities: Yes

Special Facilities: Training Farm. Experimental Forestry

Libraries: Central Library, 700,000 vols

Publications: 'Kolos' Newspaper, Scientific Newspaper *(bimonthly)*; Works, Publication of Scientific Studies *(quarterly)*

BASHKIR STATE MEDICAL UNIVERSITY

Baškirskij Gosudarstvennyj Meditsinskij Universitet (BSMU)

ul. Lenina 3, Ufa, 450000 Respublika Bashkortosan
Tel: +7(347) 273-39-68
Fax: +7(347) 272-37-51
EMail: rectorat@bgmy.ru; info@bgmy.ru
Website: http://www.bgmy.ru/

Rector: Valentin Nikolaevish Pavlov

Faculties

General Medicine (Medicine); **Medical-prophylactic** (Medicine); **Nursing** (Nursing); **Paediatrics** (Paediatrics); **Pharmacy** (Pharmacy); **Stomatology** (Dentistry; Stomatology)

Further Information: Also Research Laboratories

History: Founded 1932, acquired present status 1998.

Governing Bodies: Russian Ministry of Public Health

Academic Year: September to August

Admission Requirements: Secondary school certificate (Attestat o srednem obrazovanii), or equivalent

Main Language(s) of Instruction: Russian; English

International Co-operation: Students Exchange and cooperation programmes with univertsities in Germany, England, Turkey, Norway.

Accrediting Agencies: Ministry of Public Health

Degrees and Diplomas: *Specialist Diploma*: Medicine; Dentistry; Paediatrics; Pharmacy; Microbiology; Social work, 4-6 yrs

Student Services: Canteen, Cultural centre, Employment services, Foreign student adviser, Foreign Studies Centre, Health services, Language programs, Sports facilities

Student Residential Facilities: Two hostels respectively offering 521 places and 460 places (80 are reserved for Post-graduates students

Libraries: Central Library, c. 506,722 units vols including 332,634 scientific editions, 279,235 educational editions and 20.92 university issues). Reading rooms get 287 periodicals. 4 specialized reading halls with 252 seats. Electronic catalogue accessible through the Internet

Publications: Medizinskiy Vestnik Bashkortostana, Scientific medical journal *(bimonthly)*

Last Updated: 22/09/11

BASHKIR STATE PEDAGOGICAL UNIVERSITY NAMED AFTER M. AKMULLA

Baškirskij Gosudarstvennyj Pedagogičeskij Universitet im. M Akmully

ul. Oktjabrskaja Revoljucija 3-a, Ufa,
450000 Respublika Bashkortosan
Tel: +7(3472) 225-805
Fax: +7(3472) 229-034
Website: http://www.bspu.ru/

Rector: Raul Mirvaevitch Asadullin

Pro-Rector for Academic Affairs: Maksim Vladimirovitch Mikhailov

International Relations: M.A. Mananov

Programmes

Education (Education)

Degrees and Diplomas: *Bakalavr*: Pedagogy; Natural History; Ecology; *Specialist Diploma*: Applied Informatics; Genetics; Archiving; Museum Studies; Modern Language Teaching; Translation; Computing; Music Teaching; Art Teaching; Preschool Education and Psychology; Elementary Education; Pedagogy and Psychology; Social Pedagogy; Mathematics; Physics; Chemistry; Biology; Geography; Law; Cultural Studies; Environmental Studies; *Magistr*: Pedagogy

Last Updated: 20/07/09

BASHKIR STATE UNIVERSITY

Baškirskij Gosudarstvennyj Universitet

ul. Zaki Validi 32, Ufa, 450074 Respublika Bashkortosan
Tel: +7(347) 273-67-34 +7(347) 273-32-87
Fax: +7(347) 273-67-34 +7(347) 273-67-78
EMail: rector@bsu.bashedu.ru
Website:http: //www.bashedu.ru

Rector: Akhat Gazizjanovich Mustafin

Faculties

Baškir Philology and Journalism (Journalism; Philology); **Biology** (Biochemistry; Biology; Biotechnology; Botany; Physiology; Plant Pathology; Zoology); **Chemistry** (Analytical Chemistry; Chemistry; Inorganic Chemistry; Organic Chemistry; Physical Chemistry); **Economics** (Accountancy; Business and Commerce; Economics; Finance; International Business; Management; Marketing; Taxation); **Geography** (Geography; Geology; Water Science); **Geology** (Geology); **History** (Archaeology; Ethnology; History; Medieval Studies); **Mathematics** (Applied Mathematics; Mathematics; Systems Analysis); **Philology and Journalism** (Journalism; Literature; Oriental Languages; Philology; Russian); **Physics** (Applied Physics; Atomic and Molecular Physics; Electronic Engineering; Geophysics; Mechanics; Physical Engineering; Physics; Radiophysics); **Romance-German Philology** (Comparative Literature; English; French; German; Romance Languages)

History: Founded 1957. Placed under the authority of the Russian State Committee of Higher Education. Financed by the State.

Governing Bodies: Ministry of Higher Education

Academic Year: September to July (September-January; February-July)

Admission Requirements: Secondary education certificate (Attestat o srednem obrazovanii) and entrance examination

Main Language(s) of Instruction: Russian

Degrees and Diplomas: *Bakalavr*, *Specialist Diploma*; *Magistr*, *Kandidat Nauk*; *Doktor Nauk*

Student Services: Academic counselling, Canteen, Employment services, Foreign student adviser, Health services, Language programs, Nursery care, Sports facilities

Student Residential Facilities: Yes

Special Facilities: Biological Museum; 'Prof. Kjekbajev' Memorial Museum; Museum of Ethnography

Libraries: University Library, 2m. vols

Last Updated: 19/01/12

BELGOROD STATE AGRICULTURAL ACADEMY

Belgorodskaja Gosudarstvennaja Sel'skohozjajstvennaja Akademija (BSAA)

ul. Vavilova 1, Pos. Maiskii, Belgorod 308503
Tel: +7(4722) 391-174 +7(4722) 392-179
Fax: +7(4722) 391-174 +7(4722) 392-262
EMail: info@bsaa.edu.ru
Website: http://www.bsaa.edu.ru

Rector: Aleksandr Tur'janskij (2002-)

Vice-Rector: Pavel Breslavets Tel: +7(4722) 392-205

International Relations: Tatiana Litvinenko, Head of International Department EMail: bsaa-inter@mail.ru

Faculties

Accountancy and Finance (Accountancy; Finance); **Agricultural Engineering** (Agricultural Engineering; Agricultural Equipment); **Agronomy** (Agriculture; Agronomy); **Economics and Management** (Accountancy; Agricultural Economics; Agricultural Management); **Technology of Animal Husbandry** (Animal Husbandry; Cattle Breeding); **Veterinary Medicine** (Veterinary Science)

History: Founded 1978, acquired present status 1994.

Governing Bodies: Russian Ministry of Education; Russian Ministry of Agriculture

Academic Year: September to mid-June

Admission Requirements: Complete Secondary Education Certificate or equivalent

Fees: (Russian Roubles): 33,300-48,400 per annum

Main Language(s) of Instruction: Russian

International Co-operation: The University participates in the Appolo, Deula, DBV, Logo, WISE programmes

Accrediting Agencies: Russian Ministry of Education

Degrees and Diplomas: *Bakalavr*: 4 yrs; *Specialist Diploma*: 5 yrs

Student Services: Academic counselling, Canteen, Cultural centre, Foreign student adviser, Language programs, Nursery care, Social counselling, Sports facilities

Student Residential Facilities: Hostels

Special Facilities: Museum; Veterinary Clinic

Libraries: C

Last Updated: 25/11/08

BELGOROD STATE TECHNICAL UNIVERSITY NAMED AFTER V.G. SHOUKHOV

Belgorodskij Gosudarstvennij Tehnologičeskij Universitet im. V.G. Shuhova

ul. Kostjukova 46, Belgorod 308012
Tel: +7(4722) 554-103 +7(4722) 542-087
Fax: +7(4722) 557-139
EMail: rect@intbel.ru
Website: http://www.bstu.ru

Rector: Anatolij Gridčin (1970-) EMail: rector@intbel.ru

Vice-Rector for Education: A. Rudyčev

International Relations: Aleksandr Šapovalov
Tel: +7(4722) 543-947 EMail: umoc@intbel.ru

Departments

Machines Construction (Automation and Control Engineering; Building Technologies; Machine Building); **Power Energy** (Energy Engineering; Power Engineering)

Institutes

Architecture and Constructions (Architecture; Building Technologies; Civil Engineering; Construction Engineering; Industrial Engineering; Safety Engineering; Town Planning); **Building Materials Study** (Building Technologies; Chemical Engineering; Materials Engineering); **Ecological Engineering** (Ecology; Environmental Engineering; Environmental Management; Heating and Refrigeration; Safety Engineering); **Economics and Management** (Accountancy; Economics; Finance; International Economics; Management; Marketing); **Information Technologies and Management Systems** (Automation and Control Engineering; Computer Science; Information Technology; Software Engineering); **Road Constructions** (Construction Engineering; Machine Building; Road Engineering; Road Transport; Transport Engineering); **Technological Equipment and Complexes** (Automation and Control Engineering; Mechanical Equipment and Maintenance)

Programmes

Part-time and Distance Training; **Pre-Courses Studies** (Biology; Chemistry; Computer Science; Mathematics; Physics; Russian)

History: Founded 1957. Formerly Belgorodska Gosudarstvennaja Akademija Stroitelnyh Materialov (Belgorod State Technological Academy of Building Materials).

Academic Year: September to June (September-January; February-June)

Admission Requirements: Secondary school certificate (Attestat o srednem obrazovanii) or professional education diploma.

Fees: (US Dollars): c. 1,100-1,700 per annum

Main Language(s) of Instruction: Russian

Accrediting Agencies: Federal Agency for Education and Science

Degrees and Diplomas: *Bakalavr*, *Specialist Diploma*: 3-6 yrs; *Magistr*, *Kandidat Nauk (PhD)*: a further 3 yrs following Specialist's Diploma; *Doktor Nauk*: a further 3 yrs following PhD

Student Services: Academic counselling, Canteen, Cultural centre, Employment services, Foreign student adviser, Foreign Studies Centre, Health services, Language programs, Social counselling, Sports facilities

Student Residential Facilities: For c. 3,500 students

Libraries: c. 1,300,000 vols

Publications: Vestnik of BSTU *(biennially)*

BELGOROD STATE UNIVERSITY

Belgorodskij Gosudarstvennyj Universitet (BSU)

ul. Studenčeskaja 12, Belgorod 308007
Tel: +7(0722) 341-532 +7(0722) 301-211
Fax: +7(0722) 341-477
EMail: info@bsu.edu.ru
Website: http://www.bsu.edu.ru

Rector: Leonid Yakovlevič Djatčenko (1990-)
EMail: Rector@bsu.edu.ru

First Vice-Rector: Tatiana Valerovna Balabanova
EMail: ViceRectorFirst@bsu.edu.ru

Faculties

Economics (Accountancy; Economics; Finance); **Education** *(pre-school and primary levels)* (Education; Preschool Education; Primary Education); **Germanic and Romance Languages** (Germanic Languages; Philology; Romance Languages); **History** (History); **Law** (Law); **Medicine** (Medicine); **Natural Sciences and Geography** (Geography; Natural Sciences); **Philology** (English; French; German; Literature; Philology; Russian); **Physical Education** (Physical Education); **Physics and Mathematics** (Mathematics; Physics); **Primary and Pre-School Education**; **Sociology and Psychology**

Institutes

Economics and Management (Economics; Management)

Research Institutes

Pedagogy and Psychology (Pedagogy; Psychology); **Philology** (Philology); **Regional Studies** (Regional Studies); **Science** (Natural Sciences); **Socio-Political Problems** (Political Sciences; Social Problems)

Further Information: Also Teaching Hospitals and Courses for Foreign Students

History: Founded 1876 as Pedagogical Academy, acquired present status and title 1996.

Governing Bodies: Academic Council

Academic Year: September to June (September-January; February-June)

Admission Requirements: Secondary school certificate (Attestat o srednem obrazovanii)

Main Language(s) of Instruction: Russian

Degrees and Diplomas: *Bakalavr*: 4 yrs; *Magistr*: a further 1-2 yrs; *Kandidat Nauk (PhD)*: a further 3-4 yrs

Student Services: Canteen, Cultural centre, Foreign Studies Centre, Health services, Nursery care, Social counselling, Sports facilities

Student Residential Facilities: For c. 5,320 students

Special Facilities: History of the University Museum; Zoology Museum

Libraries: Central Library, c. 550,000 vols

Publications: BSU Scientific Records

Press or Publishing House: BSU Publishing House

BIJSK STATE PEDAGOGICAL UNIVERSITY NAMED AFTER V.M.SHUKSHINA

Bijskij Gosudarstvennyj Pędagogičeskij Universitet im. V.M. Šukšina

ul. Korolenko 53, Bijsk, 659333 Altajskij kraj
Tel: +7(3854) 244-451 +7(3854) 240-436
Fax: +7(3854) 245-137
EMail: rektor@bigpi.biysk.ru
Website: http://www.bigpi.biysk.ru

Rector: Valeriya Petrovna Nikishaeva Tel: +7(3854) 240-610

Secretary: Raissa Komarova

International Relations: Oleg Zayakin
Tel: +7(3854) 240-710 EMail: aaa@bigpi.biysk.ru

Colleges

Information Technology (Accountancy; Information Management; Information Technology; Statistics) *Director*: Michael Tolokonnikov

Faculties

Additional Professions (Computer Science; Conducting; Crafts and Trades; Educational Administration; Music; Singing) *Dean*: Tatyana Tkachenko; **Arts and Design** *Dean*: Valeriy Borzov; **Education** (Education; Educational Sciences; Special Education) *Dean*: Nina Belyaeva; **Foreign Languages** (Chinese; English; German; Linguistics; Modern Languages) *Dean*: Lyudmila Ulanskaya; **Geography and Natural Sciences** *Dean*: Viktor Vazhov; **History and Law** (Archaeology; Civil Law; Constitutional Law; Criminal Law; History; History of Law; Law) *Dean*: Olga Potapchuk; **Music and Education** *Dean*: Alexander Kakovkin; **Philology** (English; History; Linguistics; Literature; Philology) *Dean*: Ludmila Chirkova; **Physics and Mathematics** (Applied Mathematics; Applied Physics; Computer Science; Mathematics; Mathematics Education; Physics; Systems Analysis) *Dean*: Michael Starovikov; **Psychology** (Education; Experimental Psychology; Psychology) *Dean*: Lyudmila Mokretsova; **Technology and Professional Education** (Accountancy; Administration; Building Technologies; Business Administration; Crafts and Trades; Management; Marketing; Small Business; Technology) *Dean*: Yuriy Nikitin

History: Founded 1939, acquired present status 2005.

Governing Bodies: University Council

Academic Year: September to June (September-January; February-June)

Admission Requirements: Secondary school certificate and entrance examination

Fees: (Russian Roubles): 22,000 per annum

Main Language(s) of Instruction: Russian

International Co-operation: Participates in DAAD fund, Fullbright and Irex programmes.

Degrees and Diplomas: *Magistr*: Arts (MA); Education (MEd); Philology (MPh); Psychology (MPsh), 5 yrs

Student Services: Academic counselling, Canteen, Cultural centre, Employment services, Foreign student adviser, Foreign Studies Centre, Health services, Language programs, Nursery care, Social counselling, Sports facilities

Student Residential Facilities: Yes

Special Facilities: Museums. Internet Centre.

Libraries: 370,063 vols.

Publications: Pedagog, Research Papers of Staff *(monthly)*

Press or Publishing House: Scientific Publishing Centre

BIRSK STATE SOCIO-PEDAGOGICAL ACADEMY

Birskaja Gosudarstvennaja Sotsial'no-Pedagogičeskaja Akademija

ul. Internacionalnaja 10, Birsk 452320

Tel: +7(34714) 264-55

Fax: +7(37414) 264-51

Website: http://www.birsk.ru/

Rector: Salavat Usmanov

Programmes

Education (Education)

History: Created 1939. Previously known as Birskij Gosudarstvennyj Pedagogičeskij Institut (Birsk State Pedagogical Institute)

Degrees and Diplomas: *Specialist Diploma*

Last Updated: 30/03/09

BLAGOVECHSHENSK STATE PEDAGOGICAL UNIVERSITY

Blagovečšenskij Gosudarstvennyj Pedagogičeskij Universitet (BSPU)

ul. Lenina 104, Blagoveščensk, 675000 Amurskaja oblast'

Tel: +7(4162) 524-164

Fax: +7(4162) 524-164

EMail: rektorat@bgpu.ru

Website: http://www.bgpu.ru

Rector: Yury Pavlovich Sergienko (1999-)
Tel: +7(4162) 376-149, Fax: +7(4162) 524-164
EMail: rector@bgpu.ru

First Vice-Rector: Yury Malinovsky Tel: +7(4162) 448-686

International Relations: Nikolai Vladimirovich Kukharenko, Head of Foreign Affairs Office
Tel: +7(4162) 375-781 EMail: inter.bspu@gmail.com

Departments

Foreign Languages *Head*: Elena Ivashchik; **History and Philology** *Head*: Dmitry Bolotin; **Industry and Pedagogics** (Clothing and Sewing; Crafts and Trades; Household Management; Industrial Design; Technology) *Head*: Irina Kiyashko; **Natural Sciences and Geography** (Agrobiology; Analytical Chemistry; Applied Chemistry; Biochemistry; Biology; Botany; Entomology; Geography; Geology; Inorganic Chemistry; Mineralogy; Organic Chemistry; Paleontology; Zoology) *Head*: Irina Trofimova; **Pedagogics and Elementary Education** *Head*: Tatiana Plotnikova; **Physical Culture and Sports** (Physical Education; Sports) *Head*: Nickolay Daryin; **Physics and Mathematics** (Computer Engineering; Computer Science; Information Technology; Mathematics; Physics) *Head*: Vladimir Karatsuba; **Psychology and Pedagogics** (Advertising and Publicity; Management; Pedagogy; Psychology; Public Relations; Translation and Interpretation) *Head*: Svetlana Zueva

History: Founded 1930. Acquired present status and title 1996.

Academic Year: September to July

Admission Requirements: School certificate (in Language of country) and other minimum requirements for first year entry. Foreign students have to pass the TORFL (Test of Russian as a Foreign Language)

Fees: (Russian Roubles): 35,000-55,000 per annum

Main Language(s) of Instruction: Russian

International Co-operation: With universities in China, USA, Germany, France. Also Joint Bachelor's degree with Heihe Institute (China). Goethe Center established with the help of DAAD (German Service of Academic Exchanges) 1996.

Accrediting Agencies: Federal Education Agency

Degrees and Diplomas: *Bakalavr*: Philology (Russian), 4 yrs; *Specialist Diploma*: Arts and Crafts; Clothing Design; Materials Design and Technology; Technology of Ready-Made Garments; Teacher-Psychologist; Manager and Translator in Business Economics; Physics and Mathematics Teaching; Computer Sciences and Mathematics Teaching; Physics and Computer Science Teaching; Computer and Translation in IT Sphere Teaching; Mathematics-Programming; Engineering; Geography and Biology Teaching; Psychologist in Corrective Educational Institutions; Foreign Languages, Interpretation Teaching; English; French; German; Chinese; Physical Culture Education; Physical Culture and Sports; Life Security, 5 yrs; *Specialist Diploma*: Biology and Chemsitry Teaching; History Teaching; Russian Language and Literature Teaching; Russian as Foreign Language; Elementary School Teaching; Teacher-Logopedist; Pre-chool Pedagogics and Psychology Teaching; Oligophrenopedagogics, ching; *Magistr*: Pedagogics, a further 1 yr

Student Services: Academic counselling, Canteen, Cultural centre, Employment services, Foreign student adviser, Foreign Studies Centre, Health services, Language programs, Social counselling, Sports facilities

Student Residential Facilities: 5 dormitories

Special Facilities: Insect museum; Archaeological museum; Archaeological Laboratory; Spectral Analysis Laboratory; Molecular Biology Laboratory; Water Laboratory; Hetero-organic Compounds Laboratory; Materilas Electro Spark Coating Laboratory; Geoinformation Technologies Laboratory; Humanistic Pedagogics Laboratory

Libraries: c. 700,000 vols.

Student Numbers *2007-2008*	MEN	WOMEN	**TOTAL**
All (Foreign Included)	2,100	4,100	**6,200**
FOREIGN ONLY	360	190	**550**

Part-time students, 170.

Last Updated: 26/11/08

BORISOGLEBSK PEDAGOGICAL STATE INSTITUTE

Borisoglebskij Gosudarstvennyj Pedagogičeskij Institut
ul. Narodnaja 43, Borisoglebsk, 397160 Voronežskaja oblast'
Tel: +7(47354) 6-26-01
Fax: +7(47354) 6-26-01
EMail: bgpi@mail.ru
Website: http://www.bgpi.ru/

Rector: Mikhail Jakovlevich Pachshenko

Faculties

Biology (Biology; Ecology; Zoology); **History and Philology** (History; Humanities and Social Science Education; Literature; Native Language Education; Philology; Russian); **Physics and Mathematics** (Applied Mathematics; Mathematics; Mathematics Education; Physics; Science Education); **Preschool Education** (Preschool Education); **Primary Education** (Native Language Education; Pedagogy; Primary Education; Science Education)

History: Created 1940.

Degrees and Diplomas: *Bakalavr*; *Specialist Diploma*

Last Updated: 15/04/11

BRATSK STATE UNIVERSITY

Bratskij Gosudarstvennyj Universitet (BRSU)
ul. Makarenko 40, Bratsk, 665709 Irkutsk Region
Tel: +7(3953) 325-300
Fax: +7(3953) 332-008
EMail: rector@brstu.ru
Website: http://www.brstu.ru

Rector: Sergey Vladimirovič Belokobyl'skiy (2003-)

Vice-Rector: Petr Mikhailovich Ogar
Tel: +7(3953) 325-302 EMail: ogar@brstu.ru

International Relations: Dmitriy Yur'evich Kobzov, International Department Chief
Tel: +7(3953) 325-493, Fax: +7(3953) 377-992
EMail: interdep@brstu.ru

Colleges

Pedagogy (Pedagogy) *Director*: Lyubov Nikolaevna Slaikovskaya; **Pulp and Paper Industry** (Paper Technology) *Director*: Vladimir Petrovich Kalinnikov

Faculties

Building Engineering *Dean*: Alexander Alexandrovich Zinov'ev; **Distance Education** (Arts and Humanities; Automation and Control Engineering; Building Technologies; Economics; Forestry; Management; Mechanics; Natural Sciences; Paper Technology; Pedagogy; Power Engineering) *Dean*: Oleg Vasil'evich Kulikov; **Economics and Management** (Accountancy; Advertising and Publicity; Banking; Business and Commerce; Business Computing; Economics; Finance; Industrial Management; Management; Marketing; Public Administration; Social and Community Services; Tourism) *Dean*: Mikhail Pavlovich Glebov; **Humanities and Pedagogy** (Arts and Humanities; History; Law; Pedagogy; Psychology) *Dean*: Sergey Alexeevich Soldatov; **Magistracy** (Automation and Control Engineering; Construction Engineering; Forestry; Machine Building; Maintenance Technology; Management; Power Engineering; Technology; Telecommunications Engineering; Transport and Communications) *Dean*: Elena Al'bertovna Chevskaya; **Mechanics** (Automotive Engineering; Machine Building; Mechanical Engineering; Mechanics) *Dean*: Sergey Alexeevich Zen'kov; **Natural Sciences** (Applied Mathematics; Ecology; Information Sciences; Information Technology; Mathematics; Natural Sciences; Vocational Education) *Dean*: Alla Dmitrievna Sinegibskaya; **Post-Graduate Education** (Automation and Control Engineering; Building Technologies; Data Processing; Ecology; Economics; Education; Electrical Engineering; Engineering; Fire Science; Forestry; History; Industrial and Organizational Psychology; Industrial Design; Machine Building; Maintenance Technology; Management; Mathematics; Mathematics and Computer Science; Mechanical Engineering; Pedagogy; Power Engineering; Robotics; Rural Planning; Town Planning; Wood Technology) *Chief*: Elena Stepanova Yudina; **Power Engineering and Automation** (Automation and Control Engineering; Civil Engineering; Computer Science; Electrical Engineering; Industrial Engineering; Power Engineering; Technology) *Dean*: Svetlana Mikhailovna Ignat'eva; **Specialists' Training** (Accountancy; Advertising and Publicity; Banking; Business Administration; Business and Commerce; Finance; Management; Marketing) *Head*: Lyudmila Alexandrovna Kaverzina; **Timber Industry** (Engineering; Forest Products; Forestry; Landscape Architecture; Wood Technology) *Dean*: Elena Mikhailovna Runova

Programmes

Short Course Education (Arts and Humanities; Automation and Control Engineering; Building Technologies; Economics; Forestry; Management; Mechanics; Natural Sciences; Paper Technology; Pedagogy; Power Engineering) *Dean*: Nadezdha Alexeevna Shitukhina

Further Information: Also branch in Ulst-Ilimsk City

History: Founded 1956 as a branch of Irkutsk Polytechnic Institute. Reorganised into Bratsk industrial Institute 1980. Acquired university status and renamed Bratsk State Technical University 1999. Acquired present title 2004.

Governing Bodies: Academic Council

Academic Year: September to June

Admission Requirements: Secondary school certificate and entrance examination

Fees: (Russian Roubles): 18,400-43,000 per annum

Main Language(s) of Instruction: Russian; English

International Co-operation: None

Accrediting Agencies: Ministry of Education; Federal Agency on Education

Degrees and Diplomas: *Bakalavr*: 4 yrs; *Specialist Diploma*: 5 yrs; *Magistr*: 6 yrs; *Kandidat Nauk*: a further 3 yrs; *Doktor Nauk*: System Analysis, Control Data Processing, 3 yrs following Kandidat Nauk

Student Services: Academic counselling, Canteen, Cultural centre, Employment services, Foreign student adviser, Health services, Language programs, Social counselling, Sports facilities

Student Residential Facilities: Yes

Special Facilities: Center for Improvement of Professional Skills and Additional Training in Different Branches of Industry; Center for Quality of Education Assessment; Timber Facilities

Libraries: Yes

Publications: Mechancial Engineers to XXI Century, Collected Articles *(annually)*; Quality of Vocational Training, Collected Articles *(annually)*; Works of the Bratsk State University. Series: Economy and Social Economic Region Development, Collected Articles *(annually)*; Works of the Bratsk State University. Series: Humanitarian and Social Problems, Collected Articles *(annually)*; Works of the Bratsk State University. Series: Natural and Engineering Sciences, Collected Articles *(annually)*

Academic Staff *2008-2009*	MEN	WOMEN	TOTAL
FULL-TIME	132	185	**317**
PART-TIME	61	19	**80**
STAFF WITH DOCTORATE			
FULL-TIME	113	57	**170**
PART-TIME	16	15	**31**
Student Numbers *2008-2009*			
All (Foreign Included)	5,058	6,037	**11,095**
FOREIGN ONLY	9	–	**9**

Part-time students, 2,015. **Distance students**, 4,494. **Evening students**, 56.

Last Updated: 25/11/08

BRYANSK STATE ACADEMY OF AGRICULTURE

Brjanskaja Gosudarstvennaja Sel'skohozjajstvennaja Akademija
Kokino, Vigoničskij District, 243365 Brjanskaja oblast'
Tel: +7(8341) 243-21
Fax: +7(8341) 243-81
Website: http://www.bgsha.com

Rector: Egor Pavlovič Vaščekin

Programmes

Agriculture (Agriculture)

Degrees and Diplomas: *Specialist Diploma*

BRYANSK STATE ENGINEERING ACADEMY

Brjanskaja Gosudarstvennaja Inženerno-Tehnologičeskaja Akademija

prosp. Stanke Dimitrova 3, Brjansk 241037
Tel: +7(4832) 64-99-12
Fax: +7(4832) 74-60-08
EMail: mail@bgita.ru
Website: http://www.bgita.ru/

Rector: Vladimir Igorevič Mikrin

Faculties

Building Technology (Building Technologies; Transport Engineering); **Ecology Engineering** (Environmental Engineering; Safety Engineering); **Economics** (Economics; Environmental Management; Finance; Industrial Management; Management; Public Administration); **Forestry** (Forest Management; Forestry; Parks and Recreation); **Mechanical Engineering Technology** (Machine Building; Mechanical Engineering)

History: Founded 1930 as Institute of Forestry Engineering, acquired present title 1960.

Admission Requirements: Secondary education certificate (Attestat o srednem obrazovanii)

Degrees and Diplomas: *Bakalavr*; *Specialist Diploma*; *Magistr*; *Kandidat Nauk*

Libraries: c. 350,000 vols

Last Updated: 15/04/11

BRYANSK STATE TECHNICAL UNIVERSITY

Brjanskij Gosudarstvennyj Tehničeskij Universitet

bul. 50-letija Oktjabrja 7, Brjansk 241035
Tel: +7(4832) 560-905
Fax: +7(4832) 562-939
EMail: rector@tu-bryansk.ru; staff@tu-bryansk.ru
Website: http://www.tu-bryansk.ru

Rector: Aleksandr Valer'evich Lagerev EMail: rector@tu-bryansk.ru

Faculties

Economics and Management (Accountancy; Economics; English; Finance; French; German; Information Management; Management; Marketing; Sociology; Translation and Interpretation); **Information Technology** (Computer Science; Information Technology); **Mechanical Technology** (Machine Building; Mechanical Engineering); **Power and Electronics Engineering** (Electronic Engineering; Physics; Power Engineering; Telecommunications Engineering; Telecommunications Services)

Further Information: Also branch in Ludinovo

History: Founded 1929 as Brjansk Transport Engineering Institute, acquired present status and title 1996.

Governing Bodies: University Council

Academic Year: September to July (September-January; February-July)

Admission Requirements: Secondary school certificate (Attestat o srednem obrazovanii)

Main Language(s) of Instruction: Russian

Degrees and Diplomas: *Bakalavr*; *Specialist Diploma*; *Magistr*

Student Services: Canteen, Cultural centre, Employment services, Health services, Language programs, Social counselling, Sports facilities

Student Residential Facilities: For c. 1,300 students

Special Facilities: History of the University Museum

Libraries: c. 600,000 vols

Last Updated: 15/04/11

BRYANSK STATE UNIVERSITY NAMED AFTER I.G.PETROVSKY

Brjanskij Gosudarstvennyj Universitet im. I.G. Petrovskogo

ul. Bežickaja 14, Brjansk 241036
Tel: +7(4832) 66-65-24 +7(4832) 66-67-15
Fax: +7(4832) 66-65-38
EMail: bryanskgu@mail.ru
Website: http://www.brgu.ru/

Rector: Andrey Antyukhov

Pro-Rector: Sergey Mikhalchenko

Faculties

Foreign Languages (English; Foreign Languages Education; French; German; Modern Languages; Translation and Interpretation); **Geography and Natural Science** (Botany; Chemistry; Ecology; Geography; Zoology); **History and International Relations** (History; International Relations); **Law** (Law); **Philology** (Journalism; Literature; Philology; Russian); **Physics and Mathematics** (Mathematics; Physics); **Social Education** (Art Education; Mathematics; Native Language Education; Pedagogy; Russian); **Sports and Physical Education** (Physical Education; Sports)

Institutes

Socio-Economics (Advertising and Publicity; Design; Economics; Finance; Psychology; Public Law; Technology)

Further Information: Also branch in Novozybkov

History: Founded 1930 in Novozynkov as Agro-Pedagogical Institute, transferred to Bryansk 1976, acquired present status 2001. Formerly Brjanskij Gosudarstvennyj Pedagogičeskij Universitet.

Academic Year: September to July

Admission Requirements: Attestat o srednem obrazovanii; Russian language knowledge

Main Language(s) of Instruction: Russian

International Co-operation: With universities in Poland, Bulgaria, Hungary, Germany, France

Degrees and Diplomas: *Bakalavr*; *Specialist Diploma*; *Magistr*; *Kandidat Nauk*; *Doktor Nauk*

Student Services: Academic counselling, Canteen, Foreign student adviser, Health services, Social counselling, Sports facilities

Student Residential Facilities: Yes

Special Facilities: Archaeological Museum; Museum of the University History; Art Gallery

Libraries: 800,000 vols (including magazines)

Publications: Problemy Slavyanovedeniya, Scientific Yearbook *(annually)*; Vestnik Bryanskogo Gosudarstvennogo Universiteta, Scientific Magazine *(quarterly)*

Press or Publishing House: Izdatelstvo BGU

Last Updated: 15/04/11

BURJAT STATE ACADEMY OF AGRICULTURE

Burjatskaja Gosudarstvennaja Sel'skohozjajstvennaja Akademija (BGSHA)

ul. Puškina 8, Ulan-Ude, 670024 Burjatija
Tel: +7(3012) 442-133
Fax: +7(3012) 442-133
EMail: bgsha@bgsha.ru
Website: http://www.bgsha.ru

Rector: Aleksandr P. Popov
Tel: +7(3012) 442-611 EMail: rector@bgsha.ru

Vice-Rector: Maria Tumanova
Tel: +7(3012) 442-847, Fax: +7(3012) 217-018
EMail: tumanova@bgsha.ru

International Relations: Zoya Yampilova
Tel: +7(3012) 442-799 EMail: yampilova@bgsha.ru

Faculties

Agronomy *Dean*: Gennadiy Čelpanov; **Animal Husbandry** (Animal Husbandry; Apiculture; Cattle Breeding) *Dean*: Ivan Kalašnikov; **Economics** (Accountancy; Agricultural Business; Agricultural Economics; Agricultural Management; Economics; Finance) *Dean*: Irina Doržieva; **Farm Mechanization** (Agricultural Engineering; Farm Management) *Dean*: Sergei Ešeev; **Veterinary Science** (Veterinary Science) *Dean*: Čimit Sandanov

History: Founded 1931 as Agropedagogical Institute, acquired present status and title 1995.

Governing Bodies: Academic Board

Academic Year: September to July (September-December; February-June)

Admission Requirements: Secondary school certificate (Attestat o sredem obrazovanii), or equivalent (Attestat o sredem specialnom)

Fees: (US Dollars): 1,300 per annum

Main Language(s) of Instruction: Russian

International Co-operation: With universities in Mongolia, China. Also participates in Tempus, TACIS (Sweden, Finland, Germany, France, Netherlands)

Accrediting Agencies: Ministry of Education

Degrees and Diplomas: *Bakalavr*: Agroecology; Agronomy, 3 yrs; *Specialist Diploma*: Animal Husbandry; Veterinary Science, Agronomy; Agroecology; Land Management; Economics; Management; Commerce; Accounting and Finance; Agricultural Engineering and Farm Mechanization; Non-Traditional Sources of energy; Technology of Livestock Products, 5 yrs; *Kandidat Nauk*: Animal Husbandry; Agronomy; Agroecology; Veterinary Medicine, a further 3-4 yrs. Also Doctor's Degree

Student Services: Academic counselling, Canteen, Cultural centre, Employment services, Foreign student adviser, Health services, Language programs, Social counselling, Sports facilities

Student Residential Facilities: Yes

Special Facilities: Anatomy Museum. Also Clinic for Small Animals, Scientific Laboratories

Libraries: Central Libray, c. 580,000 vols

BURJAT STATE UNIVERSITY

Burjatskij Gosudarstvennyj Universitet

ul. Smolina 24a, Ulan-Ude, 670000 Burjatija
Tel: +8(3012) 211-580 +8(3012) 213-646
Fax: +8(3012) 210-588
EMail: univer@bsu.ru
Website: http://www.bsu.ru/

Rector: Stepan V. Kalmykov (1993-)

Faculties

Chemistry (Chemistry; Geology; Inorganic Chemistry; Organic Chemistry); **Economics and Management** (Economics; Management; Public Administration); **Foreign Languages** (English; French; German; Modern Languages; Translation and Interpretation); **Geography and Biology** (Biology; Botany; Ecology; Environmental Management; Geography; Natural Resources; Zoology); **History** (History); **Law** (Civil Law; Constitutional Law; Criminal Law; History of Law; Law); **Medicine** (Immunology; Medicine; Midwifery; Pharmacology; Pharmacy; Sports Medicine; Surgery; Traditional Eastern Medicine); **Oriental Studies** (Archaeology; Asian Studies; Ethnology; History; Middle Eastern Studies; Oriental Languages); **Philology** (Advertising and Publicity; Journalism; Linguistics; Literature; Philology; Russian); **Physical Education, Sport and Tourism** (Physical Education; Sports; Sports Management; Tourism); **Physics and Technology** (Computer Science; Information Technology; Machine Building; Physics; Technology); **Social Work and Psychology** (Psychology; Social Work)

Institutes

Mathematics and Computer Science (Applied Mathematics; Computer Science; Information Technology; Mathematics); **Pedagogy** (Education; Humanities and Social Science Education; Pedagogy; Philology; Preschool Education; Primary Education; Psychology; Technology)

Further Information: Also Russian language courses for foreign students

History: Founded 1932 as Pedagogical Institute, acquired present status and title 1995 by merging with local branch of Novosibirsk University.

Governing Bodies: Academic Council

Academic Year: September to July (September-January; February-July)

Admission Requirements: Secondary school certificate (Attestat o srednem obrazovanii) or equivalent, and entrance examination

Main Language(s) of Instruction: Russian, Burjat

Degrees and Diplomas: *Bakalavr*, *Specialist Diploma*: 5 yrs; *Magistr*, *Kandidat Nauk*: a further 3-4 yrs; *Doktor Nauk*: 3 yrs following Kandidat

Student Services: Canteen, Cultural centre, Employment services, Foreign Studies Centre, Health services, Nursery care, Social counselling, Sports facilities

Student Residential Facilities: For c. 6,500 students

Special Facilities: Agricultural and Biological Station

Libraries: c. 850,000 vols

Press or Publishing House: Publishing Office

Last Updated: 15/04/11

CHAJKOVSKIJ STATE INSTITUTE OF PHYSICAL TRAINING

Čajkovskij Gosudarstvennyj Institut Fizičeskoj Kul'tury

ul. Lenina 67, Čaikovskij, 617764 Permskaja oblast'
Tel: +7(34241) 243-00 +7(34241) 239-17
Fax: +7(34241) 239-17
EMail: ifk@mail.ru
Website: http://www.hna.permlink.ru

Rector: Anatolij Danilov (1980-)

Vice-Rector: Sergey Gorbunov
Tel: +7(34241) 233-29 EMail: kohta_ed@mail.ru

Faculties

Specialisation (Management; Pedagogy) *Dean*: Fanis Mukchamityanov; **Sports** (Physical Education; Sports) *Dean*: Eugenie Kirillov

History: Founded in 1980 as branch of Chelyabinsk Institute of Physical Culture; acquired present status and title 1996.

Governing Bodies: University Administration; Faculties

Academic Year: September-July

Admission Requirements: Secondary school certificate (Attestat o Srednem (Polnom) Obshchem Obrazovanii) or incomplete higher education diploma (Diplom o Nepolnom Visshem Obrazovanii)

Fees: (Russian Rubles): 15,000 per term

Main Language(s) of Instruction: Russian

International Co-operation: none

Accrediting Agencies: Federal Service for Supervision in Education and Science

Degrees and Diplomas: *Bakalavr*: Physical Culture; Physical Culture and Sport, 4 yrs; *Specialist Diploma*: Physical Culture and Sport; Safety and Teaching; Sports Management and Finance, 5 yrs

Student Services: Academic counselling, Canteen, Cultural centre, Handicapped facilities, Health services, Language programs, Social counselling, Sports facilities

Student Residential Facilities: Student hostel

Special Facilities: Biomechanics laboratories, computer centre

Libraries: Lending and reference libraries

CHECHEN STATE PEDAGOGICAL INSTITUTE

Čečenskij Gosudarstvennyj Pedagogičeskij Institut

ul. Kievskaja. 33, Groznyj 364914
Tel: +7(8712) 332-403
Fax: +7(8712) 332-407
EMail: chechgpi@mail.ru
Website: http://www.birsk.ru/

Rector: Behan Hazbulatov

Programmes

Education (Education)

Degrees and Diplomas: *Specialist Diploma*

CHECHEN STATE UNIVERSITY

Čečenskij Gosudarstvennyj Universitet

ul. A. Šeripova 32, Groznyj 364907
Tel: +7(8712) 234-089 +7(8712) 222-304
Fax: +7(8712) 234-089
EMail: chechen.st.univ@list.ru; mail@chesu.ru
Website: http://www.chesu.ru/

Rector: Zaurbek Aslanbekovich Saidov

Faculties

Agrotechnology (Agronomy); **Biology and Chemistry** (Biology; Botany; Chemistry; Inorganic Chemistry; Microbiology; Organic Chemistry; Physical Chemistry; Physiology); **Chechen Studies and Philology** (Acting; Folklore; Journalism; Linguistics; Literature; Native Language; Pedagogy; Philology; Psychology; Russian);

Economics (Accountancy; Economics; Taxation); **Finance and Economics** (Banking; Business and Commerce; Economics; Finance; Marketing); **Foreign Languages** (English; French; German; Literature; Philology; Translation and Interpretation); **Geography and Geoecology** (Ecology; Geography; Tourism); **History** (Cultural Studies; History; Political Sciences); **Horticulture and Viticulture** (Agricultural Equipment; Animal Husbandry; Horticulture; Plant and Crop Protection; Veterinary Science; Viticulture); **Law** (Law); **Mathematics and Computer Science** (Computer Science; Mathematics); **Medicine** (Medicine; Midwifery; Nursing; Pharmacology; Surgery); **Physics** (Physics; Radiophysics); **State Administration** (Administration; Management; Public Administration)

History: Founded 1972 as Čečeno-Inguš State University, acquired present title 1995.

Governing Bodies: University Council

Academic Year: September to July

Admission Requirements: Secondary school certificate (Attestat o srednem obrazovanii) and entrance examination

Fees: None

Main Language(s) of Instruction: Russian

Degrees and Diplomas: *Specialist Diploma*

Student Residential Facilities: Yes

Special Facilities: Literary Museum. Alpinarium. Mountainous Geographic Research Station

Libraries: c. 800,000 vols

Publications: History (Collection of Scientific Papers) *(annually)*; Mathematics (Collection of Scientific Papers) *(annually)*; Physics (Collection of Scientific Papers) *(annually)*; Romance and Germanic Philology (Collection of Scientific Papers) *(annually)*; Russian and Vainah Philology (Collection of Scientific Papers) *(annually)*

Press or Publishing House: Press House affiliated to Rostov University Publishing House

Last Updated: 19/04/11

CHELYABINSK LAW INSTITUTE OF THE MINISTRY OF INTERNAL AFFAIRS OF RUSSIA

Čeljabinskij Juridičeskij Institut MVD of Rossii

ul. Libedinskogo 41, Čeljabinsk 454081
Tel: +7(351) 772-73-07
Fax: +7(351) 772-52-33
EMail: admin@chelurid.ru
Website: http://www.chelurid.ru/

Rector: Viktor Ivanovich Gorkun

Programmes

Law (Law)

History: Created 1996

Degrees and Diplomas: *Specialist Diploma*

Last Updated: 20/01/12

CHELYABINSK STATE ACADEMY OF CULTURE AND ARTS

Čeljabinskaja Gosudarstvennaja Akademija Kul'tury i Iskusstv

ul. Ordžonikidze 36a, Čeljabinsk 454090
Tel: +7(3512) 263-8932
Fax: +7(3512) 727-7613
EMail: info@chgaki.ru
Website: http://www.chgaki.ru

Rektor: Vladimir Rušanin (2001-)

First Vice Rector: Nadezhda Sobolenko
EMail: sobolenko@chgaki.ru

International Relations: Bozor Safaraliyev, Head of International Relations Department
Tel: +7(3512) 263-9535, Fax: +7(3512) 263-9534
EMail: mic@chgaki.ru

Faculties

Applied Arts *Dean*: Anatoly Chebotarev; **Choreography** *Dean*: Victor Panferov; **Cultural Science** (Cultural Studies) *Dean*: Tatiana Yershova; **Documents Communication** (Documentation Techniques) *Dean*: Tatiana Rubanova; **Musical Education** *Dean*: Elina Bolodurina; **Musical Performing** (Music) *Dean*: Natalia Yeremina; **Theatre, Cinema and TV** (Cinema and Television; Theatre) *Dean*: Maria Sharonina

History: Founded 1968. Acquired present status 1999.

Academic Year: September to June

Main Language(s) of Instruction: Russian

Degrees and Diplomas: *Specialist Diploma*: 5 yrs

Student Services: Academic counselling, Canteen, Health services, Social counselling, Sports facilities

Student Residential Facilities: 2 students' hostels

Special Facilities: Recording Studio; Computing Laboratories

Libraries: 2 libraries; 1 reading room; Free internet access

Last Updated: 27/11/08

CHELYABINSK STATE ACADEMY OF MEDICINE

Čeljabinskaja Gosudarstvennaja Medicinskaja Akademija (CHSMA)

ul. Vorovskogo 64, Čeljabinsk 454092
Tel: +7(351) 232-73-82
Fax: +7(351) 232-73-69
EMail: kanc@chelsma.ru
Website: http://www.chelsma.ru/

Rector: Ilya Il'ich Dolgushin

Faculties

Medicine (Medicine); **Nursing** (Health Administration; Midwifery; Nursing; Social Work); **Paediatrics** (Paediatrics); **Pharmacy** (Pharmacy); **Stomatology** (Stomatology)

History: Founded 1944

Main Language(s) of Instruction: Russian

Degrees and Diplomas: *Bakalavr*; *Specialist Diploma*

Last Updated: 20/09/11

CHELYABINSK STATE AGROENGINEERING ACADEMY

Čeljabinskaja Gosudarstvennaja Agroinženernaja Akademija

prosp. Lenina 75, Čeljabinsk 454080
Tel: +7(351) 266-6530
Fax: +7(351) 266-6535
EMail: mail@csaa.ru
Website: http://www.csaa.ru/

Rector: Yuri Borisovich Chetyrkin

Faculties

Agricultural Technology (Agricultural Engineering; Agricultural Equipment); **Agro-Ecology** *(Miaskoe)* (Agriculture; Ecology); **Economics** (Accountancy; Agricultural Business; Agricultural Economics; Agricultural Management; Economics); **Electrification and Automation** (Automation and Control Engineering; Electrical Engineering)

History: Founded 1936. Previously known as Čeljabinskij Gosudarstvennyj Agroinženernyj Universitet. Acquired current title 2007.

Academic Year: September to June (September-January; February-June)

Admission Requirements: Secondary school certificate (Attestat o srednem obrazovanii)

Main Language(s) of Instruction: Russian

Degrees and Diplomas: *Bakalavr*, *Specialist Diploma*; *Magistr*

Special Facilities: Training Farm

Libraries: Central Library, 400,000 vols; Specialized Libraries, 100,000

Publications: Vestinik Universiteta *(quarterly)*

Last Updated: 30/06/11

CHELYABINSK STATE PEDAGOGICAL UNIVERSITY

Čeljabinskij Gosudarstvennyj Pedagogičeskij Universitet (CSPU)

ul. Lenina 69, Čeljabinsk 454080
Tel: +7(3512) 335-781
Fax: +7(3512) 367-753
EMail: cspi@cspi.urc.ac.ru
Website: http://www.cspu.chel.su

Rector: Vitali Viktorovič Latušin (2001-)
EMail: latushin@cspi.urc.ac.ru

Faculties

Computer Science (Computer Science); **Foreign Languages** (English; French; German; Philology); **History** (History); **Mathematics** (Mathematics); **Pedagogy** (Pedagogy); **Philology** (Literature; Philology); **Physics** (Physics); **Preschool Education** (Preschool Education); **Primary Education** (Primary Education); **Psychology** (Psychology); **Science and Technology** (Anatomy; Biology; Ecology; Geography; Physiology; Technology; Zoology); **Social Education** (Social Work)

History: Founded 1934. Acquired present status 1995.

Main Language(s) of Instruction: Russian

CHELYABINSK STATE UNIVERSITY

Čeljabinskij Gosudarstvennyj Universitet (CSU)

ul. Bratiev Kashirinykh 129, Čeljabinsk 454021
Tel: +7(351) 247-92-19
Fax: +7(351) 799-71-25
EMail: kazantsv@csu.ru
Website: http://www.csu.ru

Rector: Andrey Yu. Shatin (2003-)
Tel: +7(351) 799-71-07, Fax: +7(351) 420-925
EMail: rector@csu.ru

Vice-Rector: Alexey Shumakov
Tel: +7(351) 799-7125 EMail: shumakov@csu.ru

International Relations: Aleksandr Kazantsev, Director, Institute of International Education
Tel: +7(351) 799-7125, Fax: +7(351) 799-7125

Faculties

Biology (Bioengineering; Biology; Microbiology); **Chemistry** (Analytical Chemistry; Chemistry; Physical Chemistry); **Continuing Education** (Continuing Education); **Ecology** (Ecology); **Economics and Finance** (Economics; Finance; Library Science); **Eurasia and the East** (Asian Studies; Oriental Studies); **History** (Archaeology; Ethnology; History; History of Societies; Modern History; Philosophy); **Journalism**; **Law** (Law); **Linguistics** (German; Linguistics; Modern Languages; Romance Languages); **Management** (Management); **Mathematics** (Mathematics); **Philology** (Folklore; Journalism; Literature; Philology; Russian; Turkish); **Physics** (Electronic Engineering; Physics; Radiophysics); **Social Sciences** (Health Administration; Health Sciences; History of Societies; Political Sciences; Social Sciences; Social Work; Sociology)

Institutes

Business Administration (Business Administration); **Economics** (Economics); **International Education** (Education; International Studies); **Problems of Access to Higher Education** (Educational Sciences; Higher Education); **Psychology and Pedagogy** (Pedagogy; Psychology)

History: Founded 1976, a State Institution under the authority of the Committee for Science and Higher Education. Financed by the State.

Governing Bodies: Scientific Council

Academic Year: September to July

Admission Requirements: Secondary school certificate (Attestat o srednem obrazovanii) and entrance examination

Fees: (Russian Rubles): 50,000

Main Language(s) of Instruction: Russian

Accrediting Agencies: Ministry of Education

Degrees and Diplomas: *Bakalavr*: Physics; Mathematics; Ecology; Economics; Management; Applied Mathematics and Computers, 4 yrs; *Specialist Diploma*: International Communication; Pedagogics and Psychology; Special Psychology; Finance and Credit; Accountancy; Economy; Public Management; Business Management; Commputer Safety; Automation; Regional Studies; Social Work; Customs; Mathematics; Applied Mathematics and Computer Science; Physics; Chemistry; Biology; Microbiology; Bioecology; Radiophysics and Electronics; Political Science; Psychology; History; Study of Arts; Law; Journalism; Philology; Translation, 5 yrs; *Magistr*: Mathematics; Applied Mathematics; Physics; Economics; *Kandidat Nauk*: Economics; Pedagogy; Philology; Physics and Mathematics; History; Philosophy; Law, by thesis; *Doktor Nauk*: History; Mathematics; Pedagogy; Physics and Mathematics; Philology. Also degree of Professor

Student Services: Academic counselling, Canteen, Foreign student adviser, Foreign Studies Centre, Handicapped facilities, Health services, Language programs, Social counselling, Sports facilities

Student Residential Facilities: Yes

Special Facilities: History and Art Centre of Arkaim; Museum of Archaeology; Museum of Ethnology

Libraries: c. 685,000 vols

Publications: Universiteckaja Naberežnaja *(monthly)*; Vestnik

Press or Publishing House: Prinitng and Publication Department

Last Updated: 07/04/08

CHEREPOVETS STATE UNIVERSITY

Čerepoveckij Gosudarstvennyj Universitet (CHSU)

prosp. Lunacharskogo 5, Čerepovec, 162600 Volgogradskaja oblast'
Tel: +7(8202) 556-597
Fax: +7(8202) 557-049
EMail: chsu@chsu.ru
Website: http://www.chsu.ru

Rector: Vladimir S. Gryzlov (1993-) EMail: rector@chsu.ru

First Pro-Rector: Evgeni V. Eršov
Tel: +7(8202) 556-419, Fax: +7(8202) 556-597

International Relations: Victor Prihodskij, Rector's Assistant
Tel: +7(921) 137-9012, Fax: +7(8202) 556-597
EMail: interdep@chsu.ru

Faculties

Mathematics and Natural Sciences (Chemistry; Mathematics; Natural Sciences; Physics) *Dean*: Nadežda Belyaeva; **Metallurgy** (Health Sciences; Machine Building; Maintenance Technology; Metallurgical Engineering) *Dean*: Alexander Stepanov; **Social and Economic Science** (Cultural Studies; Economics; History of Societies; Modern Languages; Natural Sciences; Philosophy; Physical Education; Russian; Social Sciences) *Dean*: Svetlana Kondraškina

Institutes

Engineering *Director*: Alexander Kuzminov; **Engineering and Economics** (Accountancy; Civil Engineering; Ecology; Economics; Engineering; Human Resources; Industrial Engineering; Management; Real Estate) *Director*: Valery Plašenko; **Humanities** (Archaeology; Art History; Arts and Humanities; Classical Languages; Comparative Literature; Design; Fine Arts; History; Linguistics; Literature; Modern Languages; Painting and Drawing; Philosophy; Public Relations; Religious Studies; Translation and Interpretation) *Director*: Alexander Černov; **Information Technology** (Computer Science; Information Technology) *Director*: Konstantin Harahnin; **Innovations and Life-long Education** (Education) *Director*: Tatiana Vorobiyova; **Pedagogy and Psychology** (Anatomy; Biology; Botany; Ecology; Education; Health Sciences; Medicine; Natural Sciences; Paediatrics; Pedagogy; Physiology; Psychology) *Director*: Vladimir Maralov

History: Founded 1957, acquired present status 1996, incorporating the State Institute of Technology and the Pedagogical Institute.

Governing Bodies: Academic council

Academic Year: September to June (September-January; February-June)

Admission Requirements: Complete Secondary school education certificate

Fees: (Russian Rubles): c. 30,000-50,000 per annum

Main Language(s) of Instruction: Russian

International Co-operation: With the Raahe School of Engineering and Business of Oulu Univerity of Applied Sciences, Finland

Accrediting Agencies: Federal Agency for Education and Science

Degrees and Diplomas: *Bakalavr*: 4 yrs; *Specialist Diploma*: 5 yrs; *Magistr*: a further 2 yrs; *Kandidat Nauk*: a further 3-4 yrs following kandidat

Student Services: Academic counselling, Canteen, Cultural centre, Employment services, Handicapped facilities, Health services, Social counselling, Sports facilities

Student Residential Facilities: For 1,500 students

Special Facilities: Museum. Observatory

Libraries: c. 500,000 vols; over 300 periodical subscriptions

Publications: Monograph; University Proceedings, Collection of Scientific Papers writen by University Teachers *(quarterly)*

Press or Publishing House: Editorial and Publishing Department

Academic Staff *2007-2008*: Total: c. 500

Student Numbers *2007-2008*: Total: c. 9,500

Last Updated: 09/12/08

CHITA STATE MEDICAL ACADEMY

Čitinskaja Gosudarstvennaja Medicinskaja Akademija (CHGMA (CHSMA))

ul. Gorkogo 39a, Chita 672090
Tel: +7(3022) 354-324
Fax: +7(3022) 323-058
EMail: macadem@mail.chita.ru
Website: http://www.medacadem.chita.ru

Rector: Anatolij Vas. Govorin Tel: +7(3022) 354-163

Pro-Rector: Natalia F. Šilnikova Tel: +7(3022) 324-362

Departments

Nursing *Dean*: Yelena A. Tzeluba

Faculties

Dentistry *Dean*: Aleksey G. Shapovalov; **Medicine** (Medicine) *Dean*: Sergey V. Yuntsev; **Paediatrics** *Dean*: Alexandra S. Pančenko

History: Founded 1953. Acquired present title 1995 and status 2005.

Governing Bodies: Health Ministry

Admission Requirements: Secondary school certificate (Attestat o srednem obrazovanii) and unified state examination examination

Fees: (US Dollars): Foreign students, c. 2,000 per annum

Main Language(s) of Instruction: Russian

International Co-operation: With universities in Mongolia and China

Accrediting Agencies: Ministry of Education

Degrees and Diplomas: *Specialist Diploma*: Dentistry; Nursing, 5 yrs; *Specialist Diploma*: General Medicine; Paediatrics, 6 yrs

Student Services: Academic counselling, Canteen, Cultural centre, Employment services, Health services, Sports facilities

Student Residential Facilities: For c. 1,400 students and staff

Special Facilities: Anatomy Museum

Libraries: c. 264,000 vols

Publications: Zabaikalskij Medicinskij Vestnik, Publication for Advances in Medical Research *(quarterly)*

Press or Publishing House: Publishing Cente of ChGMA

Academic Staff *2008-2009*	MEN	WOMEN	**TOTAL**
FULL-TIME	106	231	**337**
PART-TIME	11	8	**19**
STAFF WITH DOCTORATE			
FULL-TIME	90	139	**229**

Student Numbers *2008-2009*			
All (Foreign Included)	838	1,775	**2,613**
FOREIGN ONLY	1	1	**2**

Part-time students, 143.

Last Updated: 02/12/08

CHITA STATE UNIVERSITY

Čitinskij Gosudarstvennyj Universitet

ul. Aleksandro-Zavodskaja 30, Chita 672039
Tel: +7(83022) 264-393
Fax: +7(83022) 261-459
EMail: info@chita.ru
Website: http://www.techuniv.chita.ru

Rector: Jurij N. Reznik (1993-)

Vice-Rector: N.M. Filipov Tel: +7(83022) 235-894

International Relations: V.A. Abramov Tel: +7(83022) 262-438

Departments

Civil Engineering (Civil Engineering); **Distance Education**; **Human Sciences** (Social Sciences); **Law** (Law); **Mechanics** (Mechanics); **Mining** (Mining Engineering); **Power Engineering** (Power Engineering)

History: Founded 1994 as Polytechnic Institute, acquired present status and title 1995. Formerly Čitinskij Gosudarstvennyj Tehničeskij Universitet.

Academic Year: September to June (September-January; February-June)

Admission Requirements: Secondary school certificate (Attestat zrelosti)

Main Language(s) of Instruction: Russian

Degrees and Diplomas: *Bakalavr*: 4 yrs; *Magistr*: a further 2 yrs; *Kandidat Nauk*: 3 yrs

Student Residential Facilities: For c. 1,200 students

Special Facilities: Geological Museum

Libraries: c. 308,125 vols

Publications: Conference Digests; Conference Proceedings

Press or Publishing House: Publishing House

CHUVASH STATE AGRICULTURAL ACADEMY

Čuvašskaja Gosudarstvennaja Sel'skohozjajstvennaja Akademija

ul. Karla Marksa 29, Čeboksary 428003
Tel: +7(8352) 622-334 +7(8652) 622-325
Fax: +7(8352) 622-334 +7(8352) 623-837
EMail: info@academy21.ru; academy21ru@gmail.com
Website: http://www.academy21.ru

Rector: Nikolay Kirilovič Kirilov (1991-) EMail: academy29@mail.ru

Faculties

Agronomy (Agronomy; Crop Production; Plant and Crop Protection; Soil Science); **Biotechnology** (Biotechnology); **Economics** (Agricultural Business; Agricultural Economics; Agricultural Management; Economics; Information Technology); **Engineering** (Agricultural Engineering; Agricultural Equipment; Machine Building); **Farm Mechanization** (Agricultural Engineering); **Veterinary Medicine** (Animal Husbandry; Veterinary Science)

History: Founded 1931, acquired present status and title 1995.

Governing Bodies: Scientific Council

Academic Year: September to June (September-January; February-June)

Admission Requirements: Secondary school certificate (Attestat o srednem obrazovanii)

Main Language(s) of Instruction: Russian, Čuvaš

Degrees and Diplomas: *Bakalavr*, *Specialist Diploma*

Student Residential Facilities: For c. 1,000 students

Special Facilities: History of Academy Museum; Museum of Soils. Experimental Farm

Publications: Proceeding of Scientific Conferences *(annually)*

Press or Publishing House: Editorial and Publishing Department

Last Updated: 30/06/11

CHUVASH STATE PEDAGOGICAL UNIVERSITY NAMED AFTER I.J. JAKOVLEVA

Čuvašskij Gosudarstvennyj Pedagogičeskij Universitet im. I.Ja. Jakovleva

ul. Karla Marksa 38, Čeboksary 428000
Tel: +7(8352) 62-03-12 +7(8352) 62-34-64
Fax: +7(8352) 62-03-12
EMail: rektorat@chgpu.edu.ru
Website: http://www.chgpu.edu.ru/

Rector: Boris Gurevich Mironov

Faculties

Art and Design (Art Education; Art History; Design; Fine Arts; Painting and Drawing; Sculpture); **Čuvaš Philology** (Literature; Native Language; Native Language Education); **Education and Psychology** (Education; Educational Psychology; Primary Education; Psychology); **Foreign Languages** (English; Germanic Languages; Romance Languages; Translation and Interpretation); **History** (History; Humanities and Social Science Education); **Management** (Business Computing; Economics; Information Technology; Management); **Mathematics and Physics** (Computer Science; Mathematics; Mathematics and Computer Science; Physics; Science Education); **Music Education** (Music; Music Education; Music Theory and Composition; Musical Instruments; Singing); **Natural Sciences and Environmental Design** (Biology; Chemistry; Environmental Management; Environmental Studies; Geography; Landscape Architecture); **Physical Education** (Physical Education; Sports); **Preschool Education, Special Education and Psychology** (Preschool Education; Psychology; Special Education; Speech Therapy and Audiology); **Russian Philology** (Cultural Studies; Linguistics; Literature; Philology; Russian); **Technology** (Business Education; Clothing and Sewing; Fashion Design; Mechanical Engineering; Technology Education)

History: Founded 1930, acquired present status 1998.

Governing Bodies: Council

Academic Year: September to June

Admission Requirements: Secondary school certificate and entrance examination

Main Language(s) of Instruction: Russian

Accrediting Agencies: Ministry of Education

Degrees and Diplomas: *Bakalavr*; *Specialist Diploma*; *Kandidat Nauk*; *Doktor Nauk*

Student Residential Facilities: Yes

Last Updated: 20/01/12

CHUVASH STATE UNIVERSITY NAMED AFTER I.M. ULJANOVA

Čuvašskij Gosudarstvennyj Universitet im. I.L.Ul'janova

prosp. Moskovskij 15, Čeboksary 428015
Tel: +7(8352) 58-30-36
Fax: +7(8352) 45-02-79
EMail: office@chuvsu.ru; muha21@mail.ru; aav@chuvsu.ru
Website: http://www.chuvsu.ru

Rector: Vsevolod Georgievič Agakov EMail: agakov@chusvu.ru

Faculties

Applied Mathematics, Physics and Information Technology (Actuarial Science; Applied Mathematics; Computer Networks; Computer Science; Mathematics; Mechanics; Physics; Systems Analysis; Thermal Physics); **Chemistry and Pharmacology** (Analytical Chemistry; Chemistry; Inorganic Chemistry; Organic Chemistry; Pharmacology; Physical Chemistry); **Čuvaš Philology and Culture** (Cultural Studies; Literature; Native Language; Philology); **Design and Computer Technology** (Computer Engineering; Computer Science; Design; Information Technology); **Economics** (Economics); **Economics and Management** (Accountancy; Banking; Business Computing; Economics; Finance; International Economics; Management; Marketing); **Electrical Engineering** (Automation and Control Engineering; Electrical and Electronic Equipment and Maintenance; Electrical Engineering; Technology); **Fine Arts** (Fine Arts; Music; Musicology; Singing; Theatre); **Foreign Languages** (Cultural Studies; Germanic Languages; Linguistics; Modern Languages; Romance Languages; Translation and Interpretation); **History and Geography** (Archaeology; Ecology; Ethnology; Geography; History); **Information Technology and Computer Science** (Computer Science; Information Technology); **Journalism** (Journalism); **Law** (Law); **Machine Building and Civil Engineering** (Automation and Control Engineering; Civil Engineering; Machine Building; Technology); **Medicine** (Gynaecology and Obstetrics; Medicine; Midwifery; Nursing; Paediatrics; Physical Therapy; Stomatology; Surgery); **Philology** (Foreign Languages Education; Linguistics; Literature; Philology; Russian); **Physics and Engineering** (Engineering; Physics); **Power Engineering** (Agricultural Engineering; Automation and Control Engineering; Electrical Engineering; Power Engineering); **Radiotechnics and Electronics** (Automation and Control Engineering; Computer Science; Electronic Engineering; Engineering Drawing and Design; Microelectronics)

History: Founded 1967.

Governing Bodies: Academic Council

Academic Year: September to July (September-January; February-July)

Admission Requirements: Secondary school certificate (Attestat o srednem obrazovanii)

Main Language(s) of Instruction: Čuvaš, Russian

Accrediting Agencies: Federal Agency of Science and Education

Degrees and Diplomas: *Bakalavr*; *Specialist Diploma*; *Magistr*; *Kandidat Nauk*; *Doktor Nauk*

Student Services: Academic counselling, Canteen, Cultural centre, Employment services, Foreign student adviser, Foreign Studies Centre, Handicapped facilities, Health services, Language programs, Nursery care, Social counselling, Sports facilities

Student Residential Facilities: Yes

Special Facilities: Museums: I.N. Uljanov; Ethnography; Archaeology; Anatomy; Computer Centre

Libraries: 2 m.vols

Press or Publishing House: Čuvaš University Publishing House

Last Updated: 20/01/12

DAGESTAN STATE ACADEMY OF AGRICULTURE

Dagestanskaja Gosudarstvennaja Sel'skohozjajstvennaja Akademija

ul. Gadzšjev 180, Mahačkala 367032
Tel: +7(8722) 682-470
Fax: +7(8722) 682-419
Website: http://dgsha.iwt.ru/

Rector: Sejiduljah Gabibukkaevič Hanmagomedov

Programmes

Agriculture (Agriculture)

DAGESTAN STATE ACADEMY OF MEDICINE

Dagestanskaja Gosudarstvennaja Medicinskaja Akademija

ul. Lenina 1, Mahačkala 367012
Tel: +7(8722) 670-794
Fax: +7(8722) 681-280
Website: http://www.dgma.ru/

Rector: Abdurahman Osmanovič Osmanov

International Relations: Albert Bulač, Vice-Rector

Programmes

Medicine (Medicine)

DAGESTAN STATE INSTITUTE OF NATIONAL ECONOMY OF THE DAGESTAN REPUBLIC

Dagestanskij Gosudarstvennyj Institut Narodnogo Hozyaistva Pravitel'stva Respublika Dagestan

ul. D. Ataeva, 5, Mahačkala 367008
Tel: +7(8722) 63-24-60
Fax: +7(8722) 63-24-60
EMail: dginh@yandex.ru; dginh_re@mail.ru
Website: http://www.dginh.ru/

Rector: Yahya Bučaev

Faculties
Accountancy and Audit (Accountancy); **Computer Science** (Business Computing; Computer Science; Systems Analysis); **Finance and Credit** (Banking; Finance; Taxation); **Foreign Languages** (Linguistics; Modern Languages; Translation and Interpretation); **Law** (Law); **Management** (Management)

History: Founded 1991.

Governing Bodies: Council

Academic Year: September to June

Admission Requirements: Secondary school certificate (Attestat o Polnom Srednem Obshchem Obrazovanii) and entrance examination

Main Language(s) of Instruction: Russian

International Co-operation: With universities in Turkey

Accrediting Agencies: Ministry of Education

Degrees and Diplomas: *Bakalavr*; *Specialist Diploma*

Student Services: Academic counselling, Canteen, Cultural centre, Employment services, Foreign student adviser, Health services, Language programs, Nursery care, Social counselling, Sports facilities

Student Residential Facilities: For 100 students

Special Facilities: Movie Studio. Internet Hall

Libraries: Central Library, 38,000 vols and Electronic Catalogue

Publications: Collection of Scientific Articles *(annually)*

Last Updated: 26/09/11

DAGESTAN STATE PEDAGOGICAL UNIVERSITY

Dagestanskij Gosudarstvennyj Pedagogičeskij Universitet
ul. Jaragskogo 57, Mahačkala 367003
Tel: +7(8722) 670-928
Fax: +7(8722) 670-926
Website: http://www.dgpu.ru/

Rector: Sejih Ismailov

Programmes
Education (Education)

DAGESTAN STATE TECHNICAL UNIVERSITY

Dagestanskij Gosudarstvennyj Tekhničeskij Universitet
70, Imam Shamil Avenue, Mahačkala 367015
Tel: +7(8722) 623-761
Fax: +7(8722) 623-797
EMail: dstu@dstu.ru
Website: http://www.dstu.ru

Rector: Tagir Abdurašidovič Ismailov (2006-)
Fax: +7(8722) 623-761

Vice-Rector: Kadi Gasanov
Tel: +7(8722) 629-353, Fax: +7(8722) 623-782

International Relations: Inga Khalimbekova
Fax: +7(8722) 623-761

Faculties
Architecture and Construction *Dean*: Abakar Abakarov; **Correpsondence Tuition 2** (Communication Studies; Computer Science; Economics; Electronic Engineering; Energy Engineering; Engineering; Environmental Engineering; Geology; Instrument Making; Management; Optical Technology; Safety Engineering; Telecommunications Engineering; Welfare and Protective Services) *Dean*: Arbuli Magomedov; **Correspondence Tuition 1** *Dean*: Magomednabi Azaev; **Engineering and Economics** (Economics; Engineering; Management) *Dean*: Abdulžafar Akaev; **Finance and Audit** (Economics; Finance; Management) *Dean*: Makhmud Amiraliev; **Humanities and Social Sciences** (Arts and Humanities; Service Trades; Social Sciences; Tourism) *Dean*: Gulnara Alieva; **Hydroengineering** (Environmental Engineering; Geology; Hydraulic Engineering; Safety Engineering) *Dean*: Marina Kotenko; **Informatics and Management** *Dean*: Emran Iliyasov; **Information Systems** *Dean*: Tadzhidin Sarkarov; **Law and Customs Affair** *Dean*: Nadir Sanaev; **Public and Municipal Management** *Dean*: Nurmagomed Surakatov; **Radio Engineering** *Dean*: Shirali Yusufov; **Skill Improvement and Personnel Retraining** (Economics; Management) *Dean*: Aishat Shakhmaeva; **Technology** (Biotechnology; Chemical Engineering; Food Technology; Technology) *Dean*: Ammakadi Rabadanov; **Transport** *Dean*: Gusein Magomedov

Further Information: Branches in Caspiysk, Kizlyar, Derbent

History: Founded in 1972 on the base of Dagestan State University and the branch of Leningrad Shipbuilding Institute.

Academic Year: September to July

International Co-operation: With universities in France. Participates in Tempus programme

Degrees and Diplomas: *Bakalavr*: Innovation Technology; Petroleum and Gas Engineering;, 4 yrs; *Specialist Diploma*: Chemical and Biotechnology; Technology; Electronic and Radio Engineering; Telecommunication; Computer Engineering; Civil Engineering; Software Engineering; Marketing and Management; Humanities and Social Sciences; Economics; Service and Tourism; Energetics; Transport; Transportation; Instrument and Optical engineering; Architecture and Construction; Machine Building; Public Relations, Documentation Techniques, 5 yrs; *Kandidat Nauk*: Biology; Physics & Mathematics; Philology; Sociology; Economics; Technology; Chemistry; Arts; Philosophy; Law; History; Agriculture, 3-4 yrs; *Doktor Nauk*: Technology; Economics, 3-4 yrs

Student Services: Academic counselling, Canteen, Cultural centre, Employment services, Foreign student adviser, Health services, Language programs, Social counselling, Sports facilities

Student Residential Facilities: Hostels for 1,325 persons

Libraries: 1 m. vols

Publications: Vestnik DGTU. Gumanitarnye Nauki, Humanities *(annually)*; Vestnik DGTU. Technicheskie Nauki, Technology *(annually)*

Academic Staff *2007-2008*	MEN	WOMEN	TOTAL
FULL-TIME	339	226	**565**
PART-TIME	183	70	**253**
STAFF WITH DOCTORATE			
FULL-TIME	403	4	**407**
PART-TIME	232	5	**237**
Student Numbers *2007-2008*			
All (Foreign Included)	6,857	3,528	**10,385**
FOREIGN ONLY	16	10	**26**

Part-time students, 4,977.

Last Updated: 10/12/08

DAGESTAN STATE UNIVERSITY

Dagestanskij Gosudarstvennyj Universitet
ul. Gadghieva, 43a, Mahačkala 3670000
Tel: +7(8722) 67-61-52
Fax: +7(8722) 68-23-26
EMail: dgu@dgu.ru
Website: http://www.dgu.ru

Rector: Murtazali Khulataevich Rabadanov

Faculties
Arab Philology (Arabic; Philology); **Biology** (Biochemistry; Biology; Biophysics; Botany; Forestry; Soil Science; Zoology); **Chemistry** (Chemistry); **Cultural Studies** (Acting; Cultural Studies; Library Science); **Foreign Languages** (English; French; German); **History** (History); **Mathematics** (Mathematics); **Physics** (Physics); **Psychology** (Psychology)

History: Founded 1957.

Governing Bodies: Academic Council

Academic Year: September to July

Admission Requirements: Secondary education certificate (Attestat o srednem obrazovanii) and entrance examination

Fees: None

Degrees and Diplomas: *Specialist Diploma*: 5 yrs; *Magistr*, *Kandidat Nauk*: a further 3 yrs and thesis; *Doktor Nauk*: by thesis after Kandidat

Last Updated: 22/09/11

DIPLOMATIC ACADEMY OF THE MINISTRY OF FOREIGN AFFAIRS OF THE RUSSIAN FEDERATION

Diplomatičeskaja Akademija Ministerstva Innostrannyh Del Rossijskoj Federacii
ul. Ostoženka 53/2, Moskva 119992
Tel: +7(495) 246-1844
Fax: +7(495) 244-1878
EMail: info.rector@dipacademy.ru
Website: http://www.dipacademy.ru

Rector: Alexander Panov (2006-)
Tel: +7(495) 245-3386 EMail: alexander.panov@dipacademy.ru

Vice-Rector: Evgeny Sadchikov
Tel: +7(499) 245-0603, Fax: +7(499) 246-0960

International Relations: Evgeny Bazhanov, Pro-Rector
Tel: +7(495) 608-9461, Fax: +7(495) 608-9466

Departments

Improvement of Professional Skills *(Higher International Studies) Director*: Nikolai K. Tikhomirov; **International Relations** *(Evening)* (International Relations) *Director*: Vladimir F. Stratanovich; **International Relations** (International Relations) *Director*: Tatyana M. Morozova; **World Economy and International Economic Relations** (International Economics) *Director*: Marina E. Kazatchkova

Institutes

Contemporary International Studies (International Studies) *Director*: Evgeni P. Bazhanov

History: Founded 1934, acquired present status 1974. A leading Educational Institution providing basic and advanced training for diplomats and other specialists in international relations.

Academic Year: September to June

Admission Requirements: State certificate of Higher Education

Fees: (US Dollars): Contemporary International Studies, 3,300-3,900 per annum; other diplomas, 4,600; Foreign students, 6,000

Main Language(s) of Instruction: Russian

Accrediting Agencies: Ministry of Foreign Affairs; Ministry of Education

Degrees and Diplomas: *Specialist Diploma*: International Economics; International Relations (Specialist), 3 yrs; *Kandidat Nauk*: International Relations; International Economics; International Law; Political Science (Candidate of Science), 3 yrs; *Doktor Nauk*: International Relations; International Economics; International Law; Political Science (Doctor of Science), 3 yrs. Also Honorary Doctor of the Diplomatic Academy

Student Services: Academic counselling, Canteen, Cultural centre, Foreign student adviser, Foreign Studies Centre, Health services, Language programs, Social counselling, Sports facilities

Student Residential Facilities: Yes

Special Facilities: Directorate of Technical Means of Education; Art Gallery; Museum

Libraries: Central Library, 400,000 vols

Publications: C.I.S. Yearbook, Collection of Articles *(annually)*; Diplomatic Yearbook, Topical Issues From Foreign Policies to History of Diplomacy *(annually)*; Scholarly Works of the DA, Collection of Articles *(quarterly)*; Works of Young Scholars of the DA, Collection of Articles *(annually)*

Press or Publishing House: "Vostok-Zapad ("East West") Publishing House

Academic Staff *2007-2008*	MEN	WOMEN	TOTAL
FULL-TIME	60	110	**170**
PART-TIME	10	5	**15**
STAFF WITH DOCTORATE			
FULL-TIME	80	50	**130**
PART-TIME	10	5	c. **15**
Student Numbers *2007-2008*			
All (Foreign Included)	350	200	c. **550**
FOREIGN ONLY	60	15	**75**

Part-time students, 290. **Evening students,** 270.

Last Updated: 03/12/08

DON STATE TECHNICAL UNIVERSITY

Donskoj Gosudarstvennyj Tekhničeskij Universitet
pl. Gagarina 1, Rostov-na-Donu 344000
Tel: +7(863) 273-85-11
Fax: +7(863) 232-79-53
EMail: office@dstu.edu.ru; reception@dstu.edu.ru
Website: http://www.dstu.edu.ru/

Rector: Besik Chokhoevich Meskhi EMail: reception@donstu.ru

Faculties

Air Transport, Services and Maintenance (Aeronautical and Aerospace Engineering; Air Transport; Hydraulic Engineering; Maintenance Technology; Transport Engineering; Transport Management); **Automation, Robotics, and Control** (Automation and Control Engineering; Electrical Engineering; Industrial Management; Measurement and Precision Engineering; Robotics); **Communications and Multimedia** (Communication Studies; Mass Communication; Multimedia); **Computer Science** (Applied Mathematics; Computer Engineering; Computer Science; Information Technology; Multimedia); **Engineering Technology and Equipment** (Engineering; Machine Building; Metal Techniques; Polymer and Plastics Technology); **Humanities and Social Sciences** (Cultural Studies; Educational Testing and Evaluation; History; Philosophy; Physical Education; Public Relations); **Innovative Business and Management** (Economics; Engineering Management; International Economics; Management; Marketing; Tourism); **Instrument and Technical Regulation** (Biomedical Engineering; Instrument Making; Measurement and Precision Engineering; Safety Engineering); **Machinery and Agriculture Equipment** (Agricultural Engineering; Agricultural Equipment; Computer Engineering; Computer Graphics; Food Technology; Materials Engineering; Mechanics); **Mechanical Engineering** (Machine Building; Mechanical Engineering; Thermal Engineering); **Nanotechnology and Composite Materials** (Materials Engineering; Metal Techniques; Metallurgical Engineering; Nanotechnology); **Safety and Environmental Engineering** (Aquaculture; Environmental Engineering; Fire Science; Safety Engineering; Water Science)

Further Information: Branches also in Azov, Taganrog, Volgodonsk.

History: Created 1930. Acquired current title and status 2010 after merging with Rostovskaja-na-Donu Gosudarstvennaja Akademija Sel'ckohozajstvennogo Mašinostroenija (Rostov State Academy of Mechanical Agricultural Engineering) and Institut Upravlenija i Innovatsionnoj Promyšlennosti (Institute for Management and Innovative Industry).

Degrees and Diplomas: *Bakalavr*, *Specialist Diploma*; *Magistr*

Last Updated: 28/02/12

DON STATE UNIVERSITY OF AGRICULTURE

Donskoj Gosudarstvennyj Agrarnyj Universitet
Pos. Persjanovka, Oktjabrskj, 346493 Rostovskaja oblast'
Tel: +7(86360) 351-50
Fax: +7(86360) 361-50
EMail: dongau@mail.ru
Website: http://www.dongau.ru

Rector: Anatolij Ivanovič Baranikov

Programmes

Agriculture (Agriculture)

DUBNA INTERNATIONAL UNIVERSITY FOR NATURE, SOCIETY AND MAN

Meždunarodnyj Universitet Prirody, Obščestva i Čeloveka, Dubna
ul. Universitetskaja 19, Dubna, 141980 Moskovskaja oblast'
Tel: +7(49621) 910-01 +7(49621) 907-01
Fax: +7(49621) 907-68 +7(49621) 907-70
EMail: rector@uni-dubna.ru; msv@uni-dubna.ru
Website: http://www.uni-dubna.ru

Rector: Dmitrii Vladimirovich Fursaev EMail: rector@uni-dubna.ru

International Relations: Svetlana P. Ivanova
Tel: +7(09621) 650-89, Fax: +7(09621) 658-51

Faculties
Economics and Management (Administration; Economics; Management; Social Work); **Natural Sciences and Engineering** (Applied Mathematics; Astronomy and Space Science; Biophysics; Chemistry; Computer Science; Earth Sciences; Ecology; Environmental Studies; Geochemistry; Geophysics; Nanotechnology; Nuclear Physics; Physics); **Social Sciences and Humanities** (Civil Law; Clinical Psychology; Criminal Law; Experimental Psychology; Linguistics; Psychology; Public Law; Social Sciences; Sociology)

Institutes
Systems Analysis and Management (Automation and Control Engineering; Computer Engineering; Information Technology; Management; Software Engineering; Systems Analysis)

Further Information: Branches also in Dmitrov, Dzerzhinskij (Ugresha branch), Protvino, and Kotel'niki.

History: Founded 1994.

Governing Bodies: Scientific Council

Academic Year: September to June (September-January; February-June)

Admission Requirements: Secondary school certificate (Attestat o srednem/polnom obščem obrazovanii) or equivalent (Diplom o srednem profesionalom obrazovanii)

Main Language(s) of Instruction: Russian, English

Degrees and Diplomas: *Bakalavr*: 4 yrs; *Specialist Diploma*: a further yr following Bakalavr; *Magistr*: a further 2 yrs following Bakalavr; *Kandidat Nauk*: a further 3 yrs following Specialist's Diploma or Magistr

Student Services: Canteen, Cultural centre, Health services, Sports facilities

Student Residential Facilities: For c. 685 students

Libraries: c. 105,000 vols

Publications: Vestnik universiteta 'Dubna', Magazine *(quarterly)*

Press or Publishing House: IMA Press-Print

Last Updated: 23/06/11

EAST SIBERIAN INSTITUTE OF THE RUSSIAN FEDERATION MINISTRY OF INTERNAL AFFAIRS

Vostočno-Sibirskij Institut MVD Rossijskoj Federatsii

ul. Lermontova, 110, Irkutsk, 664074 Irkutskaja oblast'
Tel: +7(3952) 41-09-82 +7(3952) 41-09-89
Fax: +7(3952) 41-19-53
EMail: admin@esi.irk.ru
Website: http://www.esi.irk.ru

Rector: Anatolij V. Chernov

Programmes
Law (Civil Security; Criminal Law; Criminology; Law; Police Studies)

History: Created 1993.

Degrees and Diplomas: *Specialist Diploma*

Last Updated: 15/03/12

EAST SIBERIAN STATE ACADEMY OF CULTURE AND ARTS

Vostočno-Sibirskaja Gosudarstvennaja Akademija Kul'tury i Iskusstv (VSGAKI)

ul. Tereshkovoj 1, Ulan-Ude, 670031 Burjatija
Tel: +7(3012) 23-23-45
Fax: +7(3012) 23-33-22
EMail: vsgaki-umu@mail.ru; info@vsgaki.ru
Website: http://www.vsgaki.ru/

Rector: Raisa Ivanovna Pshenichnikova (1995-)

Faculties
Arts (Acting; Fine Arts; Handicrafts; Performing Arts); **Humanities and Cultural Studies** (Cultural Studies; Ethnology; History; Modern Languages; Pedagogy; Philosophy; Physical Education)

Institutes
Cultural Studies and Tourism (Cultural Studies; Fine Arts; Museum Studies; Tourism); **Dance** (Dance); **Information Technology, Management, and Economics** (Economics; Information Technology; Management; Marketing); **Music** (Music)

Further Information: Also Preparatory Courses for foreign students. Branches in Čita, Irkutsk, Jakutsk and Kisil

History: Founded 1960 as a Librarian Training Institute. Reorganized into Institute of Culture 1964, acquired present title 1995.

Governing Bodies: Ministry of Culture and Mass Communications

Academic Year: September to July (September-January; February-July)

Admission Requirements: Attestat o sredem obrazovanii or Diplom o sredem spetsialnom obrazovanii or equivalent for foreign students; Akademicheskaya spravka for undergraduates; Diplom o sredem specialnom obrazovanii for graduates

Main Language(s) of Instruction: Russian

International Co-operation: With universities in Mongolia and China

Accrediting Agencies: Ministry of Education

Degrees and Diplomas: *Bakalavr*, *Specialist Diploma*; *Kandidat Nauk*

Student Services: Academic counselling, Canteen, Cultural centre, Employment services, Foreign student adviser, Health services, Language programs, Social counselling, Sports facilities

Student Residential Facilities: Two dormitories for 952 students

Special Facilities: Digital sound recording Studio 'GESER'. Photovideo laboratory. Scores Library, Bibliographic Museum

Libraries: 454,683 vols

Last Updated: 22/09/11

EAST SIBERIAN STATE ACADEMY OF EDUCATION

Vostočno-Sibirskaja Gosudarstvennaja Akademija Obrazovanija

Nižnjaja Naberežnaja 6, Irkutsk, 664011 Irkutskaja oblast'
Tel: +7(3952) 24-10-97 +7(3952) 24-03-89
Fax: +7(3952) 24-05-59
EMail: mail@vsgao.ru
Website: http://www.vsgao.com/

Rector: Aleksandr Viktorovič Gavriljuk

Programmes
Education (Art Education; Education; Humanities and Social Science Education; Information Technology; Mathematics Education; Music Education; Pedagogy; Science Education)

Further Information: Branch also in Ust'-Ilimsk.

History: Created 1909. Previously known as Irkutskij Gosudarstvennyj Pedagogičeskij Universitet (Irkutsk State Pedagogical University). Acquired current title 2009.

Degrees and Diplomas: *Bakalavr*, *Specialist Diploma*; *Magistr*

Last Updated: 17/01/12

EAST SIBERIAN STATE UNIVERSITY OF TECHNOLOGY

Vostočno-Sibirskij Gosudarstvennyj Tehnologičeskij Universitet (ESSUT)

ul. Ključevskaja 40b, Ulan-Ude, 670013 Burjatija
Tel: +7(3012) 431-415
Fax: +7(3012) 431-415
EMail: office@esstu.ru; public@esstu.ru
Website: http://www.esstu.ru

Rector: Vladimir Evgen'evič Saktoev (1997-)
EMail: rector@esstu.ru

Faculties
Construction (Building Technologies; Civil Engineering; Construction Engineering; Heating and Refrigeration; Industrial Engineering; Real Estate); **Electrical Engineering** (Automation and Control Engineering; Computer Science; Electrical and Electronic Equipment and Maintenance; Electrical Engineering; Electronic Engineering; Thermal Engineering); **Mechanical Engineering** (Aeronautical and Aerospace Engineering; Automotive Engineering; Machine Building; Mechanical Engineering; Mechanical Equipment and Maintenance; Metal Techniques; Metallurgical Engineering);

Services, Technology and Design (Analytical Chemistry; Chemistry; Fashion Design; Inorganic Chemistry; Leather Techniques; Packaging Technology; Physics; Textile Technology)

Institutes

Economics and Law (Accountancy; Administration; Banking; Civil Law; Constitutional Law; Criminal Law; Economics; Environmental Engineering; Finance; Human Resources; International Economics; Law; Management; Marketing; Taxation); **Food Engineering and Biotechnology** (Agricultural Engineering; Bioengineering; Biomedical Engineering; Biomedicine; Biotechnology; Botany; Chemistry; Computer Graphics; Cooking and Catering; Engineering; Food Science; Food Technology; Meat and Poultry); **Sustainable Development** (Advertising and Publicity; Anthropology; Applied Mathematics; Archiving; Arts and Humanities; Communication Studies; Cultural Studies; Ecology; Economics; English; European Languages; History; Linguistics; Philosophy; Physical Education; Political Sciences; Public Relations; Regional Studies; Sociology)

History: Founded 1962 as East Siberian State Institute of Technology. Acquired present status 1994.

Governing Bodies: Scientific Council

Academic Year: September to June

Admission Requirements: Secondary School Certificate and entrance examinations

Main Language(s) of Instruction: Russian

International Co-operation: With universities in China, Mongolia

Degrees and Diplomas: *Bakalavr*: 4 yrs; *Specialist Diploma*: 5 yrs; *Magistr*: 6 yrs. Postgraduate courses: 3 yrs (full time), 4 yrs (part time)

Student Services: Canteen, Cultural centre, Health services, Language programs, Sports facilities

Student Residential Facilities: Yes

Libraries: c. 877,700 vols; 63,560 periodical subscriptions

Publications: Collected Scientific Articles *(annually)*; Scientific Works, Collection on Various Fields of Study *(annually)*

Last Updated: 25/11/11

EKATERINBURG STATE THEATRE INSTITUTE

Ekaterinburgskij Gosudarstvennyj Teatralnyj Institut

ul. Vajnera 2, Ekaterinburg, 6200114 Sverdlovskaja oblast'

Tel: +7(3432) 717-645

Fax: +7(3432) 517-531

Website: http://www.theatre.ural.ru

Rector: Vladimir Babenko

Programmes

Theatre (Theatre)

ELEC STATE UNIVERSITY NAMED AFTER I.A. BUNIN

Eleckij Gosudarstvennyj Universitet im.I.A. Bunina

ul. Lenina 91, Elec, 399740 Lipeckaja oblast'

Tel: +7(07467) 221-93 +7(07467) 262-95

Fax: +7(07467) 204-63

EMail: nauka@elsu.ru

Website: http://www.elsu.ru/

Rector: Valerij P. Kuzovlev

Programmes

Education (Education)

FAR EASTERN FEDERAL UNIVERSITY

Dal'nevostočnyj Federalnyj Universitet (FENU)

ul. Sukhanova 8, Vladivostok, 690950 Primorskij kraj

Tel: +7(4232) 433-280

Fax: +7(4232) 432-315

EMail: office@dip.dvgu.ru; rectorat@dvgu.ru

Website: http://www.dvgu.ru

Rector: Vladimir Vladmirovic Miklushenskij (2010-)

EMail: rectorat@dvgu.ru

Academies

Ecology, Marine Biology and Biotechnology (Biochemistry; Biology; Biotechnology; Ecology; Marine Biology; Soil Science)

Institutes

Chemistry and Applied Ecology (Chemistry; Ecology); **Environmental Sciences** (Environmental Studies; Geography; Geophysics); **Foreign Languages** (English; Germanic Languages; Romance Languages); **History, Philosophy and Cultural Studies** (Cultural Studies; History; Philosophy); **International Studies of the Pacific Rim Region** *(Vladivostok)* (International Relations; Political Sciences; Public Administration); **International Tourism and Hospitality** (Hotel Management; Tourism); **Law** (Law); **Management and Business** (Business Administration; Business and Commerce; Economics; International Economics; Management); **Mass Media** (Mass Communication); **Mathematics and Computer Science** (Computer Science; Mathematics); **Pedagogy and Education** (Education; Pedagogy); **Physical Education and Sports** (Physical Education; Sports); **Physics and Information Technologies** (Geology; Information Technology; Physical Engineering; Physics); **Psychology and Social Sciences** (Psychology; Social Sciences); **Russian Language and Literature** (Literature; Russian)

Further Information: Also Branch in Hakodate, Japan; Russia Branches in Arseniev, Artyom, Mikhailovka, Nakhodka, Partizansk, Spassk-Dalny, Ussuriisk and Law Institute Branch at Petropavlovsk-Kamchatsky. Also Russian Language Courses offered to foreign students by FENU Russian School for International Students

History: Founded 1899 as Institute of Oriental Studies, became Dal'nevostočnyj Gosudarstvennyj Universitet (Far Eastern National University) in 1920. Merged with Tihookeanskij Gosudarstvennyj Ekonomičeskij Universitet (Pacific State University of Economics). Acquired current title and status 2010.

Governing Bodies: Academic Council

Academic Year: September to July (September-January; February-July)

Admission Requirements: Secondary school certificate (Attestat o srednem obrazovanii) and entrance examination

Main Language(s) of Instruction: Russian

International Co-operation: With universities in China, Japan, USA and Australia

Degrees and Diplomas: *Bakalavr*; *Specialist Diploma*; *Magistr*; *Kandidat Nauk*: a further 3 yrs and thesis; *Doktor Nauk*: by thesis after Kandidat

Student Services: Canteen, Health services, Sports facilities

Student Residential Facilities: For c. 2,360 students

Special Facilities: FENU Scientific Museum

Libraries: c. 1,021,000 vols

Publications: Far Eastern State University *(quarterly)*; News of the Institute of Oriental Studies of Far Eastern State University *(annually)*

Press or Publishing House: FESU Publishing House

Last Updated: 14/04/11

FAR EASTERN LAW INSTITUTE OF THE MINISTRY OF INTERNAL AFFAIRS OF RUSSIA

Dal'nevostočnyj Juridičeskij Institut MVD Rossii

per. Kazarmennyj 15, Khabarovsk 680020

Tel: +7(4212) 23-77-40 +7(4212) 21-56-26 +7(4212) 21-57-86

Fax: +7(4212) 21-55-79

EMail: dvui@mail.redcom.ru

Website: http://www.dvui.ru/

Rector: Andrej Sergevich Bakhta

Programmes

Law (Law)

History: Founded 1921. Acquired present status 1998.

Academic Year: September to July

Main Language(s) of Instruction: Russian

Accrediting Agencies: Ministry of Internal Affairs; Ministry of Education and Science

Degrees and Diplomas: *Specialist Diploma*

Student Services: Canteen, Cultural centre, Health services, Sports facilities
Last Updated: 19/04/11

FAR EASTERN STATE ACADEMY FOR SOCIAL SCIENCES AND THE HUMANITIES

Dal'nevostočnaja Gosudarstvannaja Sotsial'no-Gumanitarnaja Akademija
ul. Širokaja 70a, Birobidžan 679015
Tel: +7(42622) 4-01-46 +7(42622) 4-64-69 +7(42622)4-66-75
Fax: +7(42622) 4-01-46 +7(42622) 4-66-75
EMail: rectorat@dvgsgu.ru
Website: http://www.dvgsga.ru/

Rector: Lev Solomnovich Grinkrug

Faculties
Economics, Management and Law (Economics; Finance; Law; Management); **Geography and Environmental Studies** (Biology; Ecology; Environmental Studies; Geography); **Mathematics and Information Science** (Computer Science; Information Technology; Mathematics; Mathematics Education); **Philology, History and Journalism** (English; History; Journalism; Literature; Philology; Russian; South and Southeast Asian Languages); **Social Education and Psychology** (Pedagogy; Psychology); **Socio-Cultural Activities and Services** (Advertising and Publicity; Design; Fine Arts; Philosophy; Physical Education; Social Work; Sociology; Sports)

History: Created 1989. Previously known as Birobidžan State Pedagogical Institute (Birobidžanskij Gosudarstvennyj Pedagogičeskij Institut). Obtained current title 2005.

Degrees and Diplomas: *Bakalavr*, *Specialist Diploma*; *Magistr*
Last Updated: 19/01/12

FAR EASTERN STATE ACADEMY OF ARTS

Dal'nevostočnaja Gosudarstvennaja Akademija Iskusstv
ul. Petra Velikogo 3a, Vladivostok, 690990 Primorskij kraj
Tel: +7(4232) 264-922
Fax: +7(4232) 264-922
EMail: dvgai@mail.primorye.ru
Website: http://www.dv-art.ru/

Rector: Andrei Matveevich Chugunov

Faculties
Art (Fine Arts; Painting and Drawing); **Music** (Music); **Theatre** (Acting; Theatre)

History: Founded 1962.

Governing Bodies: Academic Council

Academic Year: September to June (September-January; February-June)

Admission Requirements: Secondary school certificate (Attestat o srednem obrazovanii), or equivalent

Main Language(s) of Instruction: Russian

Degrees and Diplomas: *Specialist Diploma*

Student Services: Academic counselling, Canteen, Sports facilities

Student Residential Facilities: For c. 250 students

Publications: Collected Scientific Papers 'Culture of Russian Far East and Asian Pacific Area Nations : East-West' *(annually)*
Last Updated: 15/04/11

FAR EASTERN STATE ACADEMY OF ECONOMICS AND MANAGEMENT

Dal'nevostočnaja Gosudartvennai Akademija Economik I Upravlenija
Okeanskij prosp. 19, Vladivostok, 690950 Primorskij kraj
Tel: +7(4232) 269-843
Fax: +7(4232) 265-089
EMail: web@psue.ru
Website: http://www.fesaem.ru

Rector: Viktor G. Belkin

Programmes
Economics (Economics); **Management** (Management)

FAR EASTERN STATE ACADEMY OF PHYSICAL EDUCATION

Dal'nevostočnaja Gosudarstvennaja Akademija Fizičeskoj Kultury
bul. Amurskij 1, Khabarovsk 680028
Tel: +7(4212) 305-677
Fax: +7(4212) 305-677
Website: http://www.dwgafk.narod.ru

Rector: V.P. Kargapolov (1973-)

Vice-Rector: Vladimir Ph. Liguta Tel: +7(4212) 308-728

International Relations: Victor D. Polycarpov, Vice-Rector
Tel: +7(4212) 305-935

Faculties
Distance Education (Distance Education); **Pedagogy** (Pedagogy) *Head*: Victor Nesterov; **Physical Education** (Physical Education) *Head*: Gennady Ilemkov; **Rehabilitation and Therapy** (Rehabilitation and Therapy) *Head*: Victor Nesterov; **Staff Development** (Staff Development)

History: Founded 1967 as Institute, acquired present status 1998.

Governing Bodies: Rectorate; Scientific Council

Academic Year: September to July

Admission Requirements: Secondary school certificate (Attestat o srednem obrazovanii)

Main Language(s) of Instruction: Russian

International Co-operation: With universities of China and Republic of Korea

Accrediting Agencies: Ministry of Education

Degrees and Diplomas: *Bakalavr*: 4 yrs; *Specialist Diploma*: 5 yrs; *Specialist Diploma*: Physical Culture, 5 yrs; *Magistr*: a further 2 yrs

Student Services: Academic counselling, Canteen, Cultural centre, Employment services, Foreign student adviser, Foreign Studies Centre, Handicapped facilities, Health services, Language programs, Nursery care, Social counselling, Sports facilities

Student Residential Facilities: Hostel

Special Facilities: University Museum

Libraries: c. 20,000 vols

FAR EASTERN STATE TECHNICAL FISHERIES UNIVERSITY (DALRYBVTUZ)

Dal'nevostočnyj Gosudarstvennyj Tekhničeskij Rybohozjajstvennyj Universitet (FESTFU)
ul. Lugovaja 52-b, Vladivostok, 690087 Primorskij kraj
Tel: +7(4232) 440-306
Fax: +7(4232) 442-432
EMail: fish75@yandex.ru
Website: http://www.dalrybvtuz.ru

Rector: Georgy Nikolaevič Kim

Vice-president: Ivan Sergejevič Karpušin
Tel: +7(4232) 440-176 EMail: karpushin5@mail.ru

International Relations: Anna Alexandrovna Polozova, Head of International Department
Tel: +7(4232) 441-928, Fax: +7(4232) 441-928
EMail: omsdti@mail.primorye.ru

Centres
Asian-Pacific Countries (Asian Studies; Chinese; Cultural Studies; Korean; Pacific Area Studies; Vietnamese) *Director*: Irina Arnoldovna Mamayeva; **Russian-Japanese Technological Studies** (Technology) *Director*: Alexander Ivanovich Vasil'yev

Institutes
Applied Biotechnology *Director*: Olesya Viktorovna Kuznetsova; **Distance Education** (Distance Education) *Director*: Vladimir Kubajevič Dosmagambetov; **Economics and Management** (Accountancy; Banking; Economics; Finance; Management; Marketing) *Director*: Sergey Borisovich Burkhanov; **Fishery and Aquaculture** *(Experimental)* (Aquaculture; Fishery) *Director*: Anatoly Nikolayevich Boitsov; **Food and Refrigerating Engineering**

Director: Grigorij Spiridonovič Phillipov; **International Studies** (Aquaculture; Economics; Fishery; Food Technology; Management) *Director*: Lyudmila L'vovna Arbuzova; **Navigation** (Marine Transport) *Director*: Alexej Fiodorovič Burkov; **Pre-College Training** (Fishery) *Director*: Elena Sergeevna Melnikova; **Regional** (Food Science; Marine Transport; Nautical Science) *Director*: Anatolij Ivanovič Yushin

Further Information: Also 3 regional branch located in the Far East of Russia: Nakhodka, Sakhalin, Slavyanka and Bol'shoi Kamen'.

History: Founded 1930, acquired present status and title 1997.

Governing Bodies: Head of the Federal Agency of Russian Federation for Fisheries; Federal Agency of Russian Federation for Fisheries; Rector and Vice-president of FESTFU

Academic Year: September to July (September-December; January-June)

Admission Requirements: Secondary school certificate (Attestat o polnom srednem obrazovanii) and entrance examination; translated secondary school certificate for international students

Fees: (Russian Rubles): Application (once) fee, 200; registration fee, 2 per 1 day of staying in Russia; visa prolongation 600 (once in a year); accommodation, 1,500 month. (US Dollars): tuition fee, c. 2,000 annum depending on Programme

Main Language(s) of Instruction: Russian

International Co-operation: With universities in People's Republic of China (Dalian, Harbin, Shaghai), Republic of Korea, Republic of Uzbekistan

Accrediting Agencies: Ministry of Education and Science of Russian Federation

Degrees and Diplomas: *Bakalavr*: 4 yrs; *Specialist Diploma*: 5 yrs; *Kandidat Nauk*: 2-4 yrs following Specialist's Diploma; *Doktor Nauk*: a further 3 yrs following Kandidat Nauk

Student Services: Academic counselling, Canteen, Cultural centre, Employment services, Foreign Studies Centre, Language programs, Social counselling, Sports facilities

Special Facilities: University Museum; Aquaculture Centre

Libraries: c. 1m. Vols

Publications: Scientific Works of Dalrybvtuz *(annually)*; University's "Compas" *(monthly)*

Academic Staff *2008-2009*	**TOTAL**
FULL-TIME	**1,195**
Student Numbers *2008-2009*	
All (Foreign Included)	**8,200**
FOREIGN ONLY	**312**

Part-time students, 3,056.

Last Updated: 10/12/08

FAR EASTERN STATE TECHNICAL UNIVERSITY

Dal'nevostočnyj Gosudarstvennyj Tekhničeskij Universitet

ul. Puškinskaja 10, Vladivostok, 690950 Primorskij kraj
Tel: +7(4232) 265-118
Fax: +7(4232) 266-988
EMail: festu@festu.ru
Website: http://www.festu.ru

Rector: Gennady P. Turmov (1992-) EMail: turmov@festu.ru

Vice-Rector: Anvir A. Fatkulin Tel: +7(4232) 261-000

International Relations: Peter P. Unru, Vice-Rector
Tel: +7(4232) 261-689 EMail: unru@festu.ru

Institutes

Architecture, Art and Design (Architecture; Design) *Director*: Elena A. Erysheva; **Civil Engineering** (Building Technologies; Civil Engineering; Construction Engineering; Environmental Engineering; Hydraulic Engineering) *Director*: Valeri I. Maksimenko; **Economics and Management** (Economics; Industrial and Production Economics; Management; Management Systems; Public Relations; Social Work) *Director*: Evgeny A. Gnezdilov; **Engineering and Social Ecology** (Ecology; Environmental Engineering) *Director*: Valerii I. Petuhov; **Humanities** (Anthropology; Arts and Humanities; Cultural Studies; Foreign Languages Education; Germanic Languages; Modern Languages; Pedagogy; Philosophy) *Director*: Yelena Y. Gorodetskaya; **Information Science and Radio-electronics** (Automation and Control Engineering; Computer Science; Electronic Engineering; Information Technology; Optics; Power Engineering; Telecommunications Services) *Director*: Viktor V. Petrosiants; **International Politics and Law** (Civil Law; International Law; International Relations; International Studies; Political Sciences; Public Administration; Public Law) *Director*: Natalia N. Menšenina; **Maritime Studies** (Marine Engineering; Naval Architecture) *Director*: Nikolay I. Voskovčuk; **Mechanics, Automation and Advanced Technologies** (Automotive Engineering; Materials Engineering; Mechanical Engineering; Mechanics; Metal Techniques; Road Transport; Transport Management; Wood Technology) *Director*: Anatoly A. Popovič; **Mine Studies** (Earth Sciences; Ecology; Geology; Geophysics; Mining Engineering; Surveying and Mapping) *Director*: Viktor I. Čebotkevič; **Natural Sciences** (Applied Mathematics; Energy Engineering; Natural Sciences; Solid State Physics; Thermal Physics) *Director*: Boris V. Golcev; **Oriental Studies** (Chinese; East Asian Studies; Japanese; Korean; Oriental Languages; Oriental Studies) *Director*: Olga P. Bolotina

Further Information: Wide range of non-degree and supplementary training programs

History: Founded 1899 as Institute, acquired present status and title 1992.

Governing Bodies: Academic Council

Academic Year: September to July (September-February; March-July)

Admission Requirements: Secondary school certificate (Attestat o srednem obrazovanii). TORFL test (First Level) for international students

Fees: (Russian Rubles): 25,000 per annum

Main Language(s) of Instruction: Russian

International Co-operation: With universities in China, USA, Republic of Korea, Japan, United Kingdom, Germany.

Accrediting Agencies: Ministry of Education

Degrees and Diplomas: *Bakalavr*: 4 yrs; *Specialist Diploma*: 5 yrs; *Magistr*: a further 1-2 yrs; *Kandidat Nauk*: 3 yrs; *Doktor Nauk*: a further 2-4 yrs

Student Services: Canteen, Cultural centre, Employment services, Health services, Language programs, Sports facilities

Student Residential Facilities: Yes

Special Facilities: History Museum; Geology Museum. TV Channel. Students' Radio Station. Pushkin Theatre

Libraries: c. 2.3 m. vols

Publications: Pacific Science Review Journal, Jointly with Kangnam University, Korea *(biannually)*

Press or Publishing House: FESTU Publishers

FAR EASTERN STATE TRANSPORT UNIVERSITY

Dal'nevostočnyj Gosudarstvennyj Universitet Putej Soobščenija (DVGUPS)

ul. Seryševa 47, Khabarovsk 680021
Tel: +7(4212) 359-516
Fax: +7(4212) 34-0808
EMail: root@festu.khv.ru
Website: http://www.festu.khv.ru

Rector: Viktor Grigorenko (1989-) Tel: +7(4212) 343-076

First Vice-Rector: Sergei Ivanilov
Tel: +7(4212) 35-9501, Fax: +7(4212) 64-7314
EMail: ivanilov@festu.khv.ru

International Relations: Serguei Tretiak, Director
Tel: +7(4212) 64-7297, Fax: +7(4212) 64-7269
EMail: tretjak@festu.khv.ru

Faculties

Electric Power Industry (Electrical Engineering) *Dean*: Svetlana Petuhova; **Humanities** (Law; Psychology; Social Work; Tourism) *Dean*: Vladimir Sadov; **Natural Sciences** (Applied Mathematics; Computer Science; Optical Technology; Physics; Telecommunications Engineering) *Dean*: Evgeniy Kravčenko

Institutes
Administration, Automation and Telecommunications (Administration; Automation and Control Engineering; Information Sciences; Maintenance Technology; Telecommunications Engineering) *Rector*: Vladimir Pelmenev; **Economics** (Accountancy; Business and Commerce; Finance; International Business; Management; Marketing; Transport Economics) *Rector*: Vitaliy Podoba; **Power Drafting and Mobile Transportation Facilities** (Railway Transport; Transport and Communications) *Rector*: Yuriy Gamolya; **Transportation Industry Construction** (Civil Engineering; Construction Engineering; Real Estate; Transport Engineering; Water Management) *Rector*: Pavel Krasovsky

Schools
Business Administration *(Division of International Cooperation Center)* (Accountancy; Business Administration; Finance; Management; Marketing) *Dean*: Serguei Tretiak

History: Founded 1939, acquired present status 1979.

Governing Bodies: University Council

Academic Year: September to June

Admission Requirements: School Certificate, Entrance Examination

Fees: (US Dollars): Tuition, 900 per annum

Main Language(s) of Instruction: Russian

International Co-operation: Russian-American Academic Programme; Russian-Chinese Academic Programme

Accrediting Agencies: Ministry of Higher Vocational Education

Degrees and Diplomas: *Bakalavr*: Business; Engineering; Law, 4 yrs; *Specialist Diploma*: Business; Engineering; Law, 5 yrs; *Magistr*: Business; Engineering; Law, 6 yrs; *Kandidat Nauk*: Business; Engineering; Philosophy, 3 yrs; *Doktor Nauk*: Business; Engineering, 3 yrs

Student Services: Academic counselling, Canteen, Cultural centre, Employment services, Foreign student adviser, Foreign Studies Centre, Health services, Language programs, Nursery care, Social counselling, Sports facilities

Student Residential Facilities: Yes

Special Facilities: Museum, Students Theatre

Libraries: Main Library; Reading Halls; Branch Divisions; c. 845,075 vols

Publications: Scientific Reports Bulletin, Compendium *(annually)*

FAR EASTERN STATE UNIVERSITY OF AGRICULTURE

Dal'nevostočnyj Gosudarstvennyj Agrarnij Universitet (FESAU)

ul. Politehničeskaja 86, Blagoveščensk, 675005 Amurskaja oblast'
Tel: +7(4162) 52-64-81 +7(4162) 52-17-27
Fax: +7(4162) 52-64-81 +7(4162) 52-62-80
EMail: umo@dalgau.ru; dalgau_umo@mail.ru
Website: http://www.dalgau.ru

Rector: Ivan Vasil'evič Bumbar

Institutes
Agricultural Electrification and Automation (Agricultural Engineering; Agricultural Equipment; Electrical and Electronic Equipment and Maintenance; Information Sciences; Physics); **Agricultural Technology** (Agricultural Engineering; Agricultural Equipment; Machine Building; Maintenance Technology; Mechanical Equipment and Maintenance); **Agronomy and Ecology** (Agronomy; Ecology; Plant and Crop Protection; Soil Science); **Civil Engineering** (Civil Engineering; Irrigation; Natural Resources; Water Management); **Finance and Economics** (Accountancy; Business Administration; Economics; Management; Marketing); **Forestry** (Forestry; Wood Technology); **Humanities** (Chinese; Cultural Studies; English; French; German; History; Japanese; Latin; Philosophy; Physical Chemistry; Sports); **Technology** (Biochemistry; Chemistry; Food Science; Food Technology; Mathematics; Organic Chemistry); **Veterinary Medicine and Animal Husbandry** (Animal Husbandry; Veterinary Science; Zoology)

Further Information: Also branch in Birobidjan.

History: Founded 1950. Acquired present status 1993.

Academic Year: September to August

Admission Requirements: School leaving certificate or college degree

Degrees and Diplomas: *Bakalavr*; *Specialist Diploma*; *Kandidat Nauk*; *Doktor Nauk*

Student Services: Academic counselling, Canteen, Cultural centre, Foreign student adviser, Health services, Nursery care, Sports facilities

Student Residential Facilities: Yes

Special Facilities: Museum

Libraries: 400,000 vols

Publications: Amur Researcher *(biennially)*; Science to Production *(annually)*; Students' Research to Production *(annually)*; The Collection of Scientific Publications *(1-2 per annum)*

Press or Publishing House: FESAU Publishing House

Last Updated: 15/04/11

FAR EASTERN STATE UNIVERSITY OF MEDICINE

Dal'nevostočnyj Gosudarstvennyj Medicinskij Universitet

ul. Muravieva-Amyrskogo, 35, Khabarovsk 680000
Tel: +7(4212) 30-53-11
Fax: +7(4212) 32-55-92
EMail: rec@mail.fesmu.ru
Website: http://www.fesmu.ru/

Rector: Vladmimir Petrovich Molochnyj

Faculties
Medicine (Medicine); **Paediatrics** (Paediatrics); **Pharmacology** (Pharmacology); **Stomatology** (Stomatology)

History: Created 1929.

Degrees and Diplomas: *Specialist Diploma*

Last Updated: 19/04/11

FINANCE UNIVERSITY UNDER THE RUSSIAN FEDERATION GOVERNMENT

Finansovyj Universitet pri Pravitel'stve Rossijskoj Federacii

prosp. Leningradskij 49, Moskva 125993
Tel: +7(499) 943-98-55 +7(499) 943-98-29
Fax: +7(499) 157-70-70
EMail: academy@fa.ru
Website: http://www.fa.ru/

Rector: Mikhail A. Eskindarov (2006-)

Faculties
Accounting (Accountancy); **Finance and Credit** (Banking; Finance; Insurance; Management); **Financial Management** (Finance; Management); **International Economic Relations** (International Economics; International Relations); **International Economics** (International Economics); **International Finance** (Finance; International Business); **Law** (Law); **Management** (Management); **Mathematics** (Applied Linguistics; Mathematics); **Sociology and Polical Science** (Political Sciences; Sociology); **Taxation** (Taxation)

Higher Schools
Law (Law); **State Management** (Administration)

Institutes
Business Administration; **Continuing Education**; **Continuing Teacher Education**; **Economic and Financial Research**; **Economic Security and Strategic Planning**; **Innovation**; **Short Programmes** (Business Administration); **State and Civil Society**

Schools
International Business (Business Administration)

Further Information: Also Colleges of Professional Training in Finance and Economics in 11 towns of Russia

History: Founded 1918, incorporating two existing institutes. Formerly known as Finansovaja Akademija pri Pravitel'stve Rossijskoj Federacii. Acquired current title 2010.

Governing Bodies: Academic Council; Rectorate

Academic Year: September to June (September-January; February-June)

Admission Requirements: Secondary school certificate (Attestat o srednem obrazovanii)

Fees: (US Dollars): Foreign, 6,000 per annum; residents, graduate students, 5,500-6,500 per annum

Main Language(s) of Instruction: Russian

International Co-operation: With universities in France, Belarus, Ukraine, USA, Germany, Poland, United Kingdom, Portugal, Luxembourg, Switzerland, Bulgaria, Austria, Spain, China and Italy

Accrediting Agencies: Ministry of Education

Degrees and Diplomas: *Bakalavr*; *Specialist Diploma*; *Magistr (MBA)*. Also postgraduate qualifications

Student Services: Academic counselling, Canteen, Cultural centre, Employment services, Foreign student adviser, Foreign Studies Centre, Health services, Language programs, Social counselling, Sports facilities

Student Residential Facilities: Yes.

Special Facilities: Numismatic Museum. Art gallery. Concert and events Hall. Cinema. 2 Theatres. Choreographic and singing studios. Academic Council Hall

Libraries: Total, c. 1 m. vols

Last Updated: 23/02/12

FIRST MOSCOW STATE MEDICAL UNIVERSITY NAMED AFTER I.M.SECHENOV

Pervyj Moskovskij Gosudarstvennyj Medicinskij Universitet imeni I.M. Sečenova

ul. Trubetskaja 8, bldg. 1-2, Moskva 119991
Tel: +7(499) 248-05-53
Fax: +7(499) 248-01-81
EMail: mma-sechenov@mtu-net.ru
Website: http://www.mma.ru

Rector: Petr Vitalyevich Glybochko (2010-)
EMail: rektorat@mma.ru

Vice-Rector: Sergey V. Grachev
Tel: +7(499) 248-31-22, Fax: +7(499) 248-48-93
EMail: grachev@mmascience.ru

International Relations: Lyudmila V. Mikheeva
Tel: +7(499) 248-47-77, Fax: +7(499) 248-47-77
EMail: id@mmascience.ru

Faculties

Dentistry (Dentistry) *Dean*: Irina M. Makeeva; **Foreign Students Training** (Medicine; Pharmacy) *Dean*: Renat N. Alyautdin; **Medicine** (Medicine) *Dean*: Nadezhda S. Podchernayeva; **Military Medicine** (Medicine) *Dean*: Pulito V.M.; **Nursing** (Nursing) *Dean*: Alexey Yu. Brazhnikov; **Pharmacy** (Pharmacy) *Dean*: Ivan I. Krasniuk; **Postgraduate Professional Education I** (Pharmacy) *Dean*: Elena A. Maksimkina; **Postgraduate Professional Education II** (Medicine) *Dean*: Lyudmila U. Yudina; **Postgraduate Professional Education III** (Social and Preventive Medicine) *Dean*: Ekaterina I. Akimova; **Preventive Medicine** (Social and Preventive Medicine) *Dean*: Jurij V. Nesvizhsky; **Public Health Management** (Public Health) *Dean*: Sergey G. Boyarsky

Research Centres

Medicine and Medical Education (Medicine) *Director*: Nikolay N. Potekaev; **Molecular Medicine** (Medicine) *Director*: Mihail A. Paltsev; **Parasitology and Tropical Medicine** (Parasitology; Tropical Medicine) *Director*: Vladimir P. Sergiev; **Pharmacy** (Pharmacy) *Director*: Irina A. Samylina; **Phtisiopulmonology** (Pneumology) *Director*: Mihail I. Perelman; **Postgraduate Professional Education IV** (Paediatrics) *Dean*: Ekaterina I. Alekseyeva; **Public Health Management I** (Public Health) *Co-director*: Vladimir Z. Kučerenko; **Public Health Management II** (Public Health) *Co-director*: Lyudmila E. Syrtsova

History: Founded 1758 as Faculty of Medicine of Moscow University. Became Institute 1930, and acquired present status and title 1990.

Governing Bodies: Scientific Council (Academic Board), Rectorate

Academic Year: September to July (September-January; February-July)

Admission Requirements: Secondary school certificate (Attestat o srednem obrazovanii) and entrance examination

Fees: (US Dollars): Foreign students, 1,700-5,000 per annum

Main Language(s) of Instruction: Russian, English, French

International Co-operation: With universities in Austria, Germany, Hungary, The Netherlands, Norway, Serbia, Montenegro, France, United Kingdom, USA

Accrediting Agencies: Ministry of Education

Degrees and Diplomas: *Specialist Diploma*: Medicine; Pharmacy; Dentistry; Nursing; Preventive Medicine, 5-6 yrs; *Kandidat Nauk*: Medicine; Pharmacy; Medical Education (PhD), a further 3 yrs; *Doktor Nauk*: Medicine; Pharmacy; Medical Education, by thesis after Kandidat

Student Residential Facilities: Yes

Special Facilities: Museums: University History; Medical Schools; Anatomy; Pathology; Surgery and Anatomy; General Hygiene; Skin and Venereal Diseases; Biology; Histology; Physiology; Forensic Medicine

Libraries: c. 5 m. vols

Publications: 'Farmacia', Medical Journal *(bimonthly)*; 'Istoricheskiy Vestnik MMA', Almanac *(quarterly)*; 'Medsestra', Medical Journal *(bimonthly)*; 'Vrach', Medical Journal *(monthly)*

Last Updated: 06/04/12

GLAZOV STATE PEDAGOGICAL INSTITUTE

Glazovskij Gosudarstvennyj Pedagogičeskij Institut

ul. Pervomaiskaja 25, Glazov, 427621 Udmurt Republic
Tel: +7(34141) 558-57
Fax: +7(34141) 559-49
EMail: ggpi@ggpi.org
Website: http://www.ggpi.org/news.php

Rector: Alexei Miroshnichenko (2004-)

Vice-Rector: Mikhail Babushkin
Tel: +7(34141) 558-66 EMail: ggiudm@udmnet.ru

International Relations: Anatoly Kazarinov, Vice-Rector, Scientific Research
Tel: +7(34141) 532-29 EMail: prorector1@ggpi.glazov.net

Departments

Foreign Languages *Dean*: Vera Shirokikh; **History** *Dean*: Andrei Makurin; **Pedagogics** (Education; Pedagogy) *Head*: Marina Zakharishtcheva; **Philology** *Dean*: Vyacheslav Zakharov; **Physics** (Physics; Science Education) *Dean*: Valery Maier; **Social and Computer Technologies** (Computer Science; Information Technology) *Dean*: Renat Kamalov

History: Founded 1915 as a Boys School then became a Teacher Training School. Acquired current status and title in 1939.

Governing Bodies: Council of three Vice-Rectors headed by Rector

Academic Year: September-June

Admission Requirements: Secondary school certificate (Attestat o Srednem Obshchem Obrazovanii) and entrance examination

Fees: (Russian Rubles): 26,000 per annum

Main Language(s) of Instruction: Russian

Accrediting Agencies: Federal Agency on Education

Degrees and Diplomas: *Specialist Diploma*: all disciplines, 5 yrs

Student Services: Academic counselling, Canteen, Cultural centre, Health services, Language programs, Social counselling, Sports facilities

Student Residential Facilities: Yes

Special Facilities: Museum of Ethnology

Libraries: yes

GORNO-ALTAISK STATE UNIVERSITY

Gorno-Altajskij Gosudarstvennyj Universitet (GASU)

ul. Lenkina 1, Gorno-Altajsk 649000
Tel: +7(38822) 264-39
Fax: +7(38822) 267-35
EMail: root@gasu.gorny.ru
Website: http://www.gasu.ru

Rector: Jurij V. Tabakaev (1990-)
Tel: +7(38822) 225-67, Fax: +7(38822) 267-35
EMail: office@gasu.ru

Deputy Rector: Olga A. Goncharova
Tel: +7(38822) 663-95, Fax: +7(38822) 267-35
EMail: prorector@gasu.ru

International Relations: Viktor N. Lukjanenko, International Office Director Tel: +7(38822) 663-20 EMail: sci@gasu.ru

Colleges

Agriculture (Agriculture; Agronomy; Farm Management; Veterinary Science) *Dean*: Vladimir G. Ždanov

Faculties

Agriculture (Agriculture; Agronomy; Veterinary Science) *Dean*: Lyudmila I. Surtayeva; **Biology and Chemistry** (Biology; Chemistry) *Dean*: Vera N. Aleinikova; **Economics** (Accountancy; Economics; Management) *Dean*: Evgenie E. Švakov; **Foreign Languages** (English; German; Modern Languages) *Dean*: Tatiana V. Derbeneva; **Geography** (Geography; Tourism) *Dean*: Alexei V. Bondarenko; **History** (Archaeology; History) *Dean*: Tatiana S. Pustogačeva; **Law** *Dean*: Vera S. Ivanova; **Philology** (Literature; Modern Languages; Mongolian; Philology; Russian; Turkish) *Dean*: Tatjana N. Nikonova; **Physics and Mathematics** (Computer Science; Mathematics; Physics) *Dean*: Ivan B. Davydkin; **Psychology and Educational Sciences** (Education; Psychology) *Dean*: Olga V. Ostapovič

History: Founded 1949 as Teacher's Training College, acquired present status and title 1993.

Governing Bodies: Rector's Council; Learned Council

Academic Year: September to June (September-December; February-June)

Admission Requirements: Secondary school certificate (Attestat o srednem obrazovanii)

Fees: (Russian Rubles): 30,000-40,000 per annum; foreign students 35,000-45,000 per annum

Main Language(s) of Instruction: Russian

International Co-operation: With universities in USA, Belgium, Mongolia

Accrediting Agencies: Federal Agency of Education

Degrees and Diplomas: *Specialist Diploma*: 5 yrs; *Kandidat Nauk*: a further 3 yrs

Student Services: Academic counselling, Canteen, Cultural centre, Employment services, Foreign student adviser, Foreign Studies Centre, Handicapped facilities, Health services, Language programs, Nursery care, Sports facilities

Student Residential Facilities: For 1,100 students

Special Facilities: Geographical Museum; Zoological Museum; Archaeological Museum. Biological Garden. German Cultural Centre

Libraries: Gorno-Altaisk University Library, c. 315,000 vols

Press or Publishing House: Gorno-Altaisk University Press

GORSKY STATE UNIVERSITY OF AGRICULTURE

Gorskij Gosudarstvennyj Agrarnij Universitet

ul. Kirova 37, Vladikavkaz, 362040 Respublika Severnaja Osetija-Alanija
Tel: +7(8672) 53-23-04 +7(8672) 53-90-04
Fax: +7(8672) 53-02-49
EMail: ggau@globalalania.ru; info@gorskigau.ru
Website: http://www.gorskigau.ru/

Rector: Viktor Khamitsevich Temiraev EMail: rector@gorskigau.ru

Faculties

Agricultural Machinery (Agricultural Equipment); **Agronomy** (Agronomy; Botany; Crop Production; Ecology; Forest Management; Forestry; Plant and Crop Protection; Plant Pathology; Soil Management); **Automotive Engineering** (Automotive Engineering; Machine Building; Maintenance Technology; Mechanical Equipment and Maintenance); **Biotechnology** (Biotechnology); **Economics** (Accountancy; Agricultural Economics; Economics; Marketing); **Engineering Management** (Agricultural Management; Animal Husbandry; Engineering Management; Zoology); **Law** (Law); **Taxation** (Agricultural Business; Agricultural Economics; Farm Management; Taxation); **Veterinary Medicine** (Veterinary Science; Zoology)

History: Created 1918.

Degrees and Diplomas: *Bakalavr*, *Specialist Diploma*

Last Updated: 16/03/12

GROZNY STATE PETROLEUM TECHNOLOGICAL UNIVERSITY NAMED AFTER ACADEMICIAN M.D. MILLIONSHCHIKOV

Groznenskij Gosudarstvennyj Neftjanoj Teckhničeskij Universitet im. Akademika M.D. Millionščhikova

ul Avtorkhanova d.14/53, Groznyj 364051
Tel: +7(8712) 22-31-20 +7(8712) 22-36-19 +7(8712) 22-28-26
Fax: +7(8712) 22-36-07
EMail: umoggni@yandex.ru
Website: http://gsoi.ru/

Rector: Hasan E. Taimaskhanov

Faculties

Automation and Applied Informatics (Automation and Control Engineering; Electrical and Electronic Engineering; Information Sciences); **Civil Engineering** (Architecture; Civil Engineering; Heating and Refrigeration; Industrial Engineering; Surveying and Mapping); **Economics and Management** (Applied Mathematics; Economics; Industrial Management; Management; Taxation); **Engineering and Ecocomics** *(Gudermes)* (Business Computing; Economics; Engineering); **Geological Engineering** (Ecology; Geological Engineering; Geology; Geophysics; Petroleum and Gas Engineering; Petrology); **Humanities** (History; Law; Modern Languages; Native Language; Philosophy; Political Sciences; Russian; Sociology; Sports); **Petrochemistry** (Machine Building; Mechanics; Petroleum and Gas Engineering; Transport Engineering); **Petroleum and Gas Engineering** (Chemical Engineering; Chemistry; Environmental Engineering; Food Technology; Hydraulic Engineering; Oenology; Organic Chemistry; Petroleum and Gas Engineering; Physical Chemistry; Safety Engineering)

History: Created 1920. Previously known as Groznenskij Neftjanoj Institut (Grozny Institute of Oil Industry). Acquired current title 2002.

Degrees and Diplomas: *Bakalavr*, *Specialist Diploma*

Last Updated: 20/01/12

HABAROVSK STATE ACADEMY OF ECONOMICS AND LAW

Khabarovskaja Gosudarstvennaja Akademija Ekonomiki i Prava

ul. Tihookeanskaja 134, Khabarovsk 680042
Tel: +7(4212) 224-879 +7(4212) 224-906
Fax: +7(4212) 744-782
EMail: IRO-ksael@rambler.ru
Website: http://www.ael.ru

Rector: Vladimir A. Lihobabin (1996-) EMail: rector@ael.ru

International Relations: Tatjana V. Malovichko
Tel: +7(4212) 224-906

Centres

Auditing (Accountancy); **Banking** (Banking); **Business and Foreign Languages** (Business Administration; Modern Languages); **Computer Technologies** (Computer Science; Information Technology); **Finance** (Finance); **Further Professional Education for Workers of Trade Entreprises and Public Catering** *(Krai)*; **Risk Management and Property Estimation** (Insurance); **State Procurement**; **Tax Consulting**

Faculties

Auditing (Accountancy; Economics; Information Technology; Statistics); **Commerce** (Business Administration; Business and Commerce; Economics); **Finance** (Banking; Finance; Insurance); **International Economic Relations** (Advertising and Publicity; Business and Commerce; Communication Studies; Economics; International Economics; Marketing; Modern Languages); **Law** (Administrative Law; Arts and Humanities; Civil Law; Criminal Law; History of Law; Law); **Management** (Administration; Economics;

Hotel and Restaurant; Human Resources; Information Sciences; Insurance; Management; Mathematics; Tourism)

Programmes
Graduate Studies

Research Centres
Economics; **Student**

Further Information: Also 4 dissertation councils on candidate of economics degree and 1 dissertation council on doctor of philosophy degree.

History: Founded 1970 as Institute, merged with Law and Commerce branches of Moscow State Academy and Moscow Commercial University, and acquired present title 1994.

Governing Bodies: Academic Council; Trustee Board

Academic Year: September to June (September-January; February-June)

Admission Requirements: Secondary school certificate (Attestat o srednem obrazovanii); TORFL (I certificate level)

Main Language(s) of Instruction: Russian

Degrees and Diplomas: *Specialist Diploma*: 3-5 yrs; *Magistr*: a further 2 yrs; *Kandidat Nauk*: a further 1 1/2-2 yrs; *Doktor Nauk*: a further 3-5 yrs

Student Services: Canteen, Cultural centre, Health services, Social counselling, Sports facilities

Student Residential Facilities: For c. 600 students

Special Facilities: Theatres; Concert Halls

Libraries: 438,709 vols; scientific literature, 56,882 vols; textbooks, 368,939 vols; belles-lettres, 12,810 vols; foreign literature, 1,447 vols; periodical subscriptions, 327 journals and 412 sets.

HABAROVSK STATE INSTITUTE OF ARTS AND CULTURE

Khabarovskij Gosudarstvennyj Institut Iskusstv i Kul'tury

ul. Krasnorečenskaja 112, Khabarovsk 680045
Tel: +7(4212) 36-07-17 +7(4212) 36-48-59
Fax: +7(4212) 36-30-39
EMail: hgiik@pochta.ru
Website: http://www.hgiik.ru/

Rector: Sergei Nesterovich Skorinov

Faculties
Fine Arts (Acting; Dance; Fine Arts; Music; Singing); **Social and Cultural Studies** (Cultural Studies; Documentation Techniques; Library Science; Philology; Philosophy; Psychology)

History: Created 1968.

Degrees and Diplomas: *Specialist Diploma*
Last Updated: 20/01/12

HABAROVSK STATE PEDAGOGICAL UNIVERSITY

Khabarovskij Gosudarstvennyj Pedagogičeskij Universitet

ul. Karla Marksa 68, Khabarovsk 680000
Tel: +7(4212) 304-504
Fax: +7(4212) 210-100
EMail: khspu@khspu.ru
Website: http://www.khspu.ru

Rector: Mihail Ivanović Kostenko

Vice-Rector: Ludmila Nikitina EMail: science@khpsu.ru

International Relations: Tamara Mungalova
Tel: +7(4212) 305-877

Faculties
Arts and Graphics (Arts and Humanities; Graphic Arts); **Biology and Chemistry** (Biology; Chemistry); **Continuing Education**; **History** (History); **International Education** (International and Comparative Education); **Oriental Languages** (Oriental Languages); **Physical Training** (Physical Education); **Physics and Mathematics** (Mathematics; Physics); **Russian Language and Literature** (Literature; Russian); **Special Psychology and Pedagogy** (Pedagogy; Psychology)

Institutes
Linguistics and Cross Cultural Communication (Cultural Studies; Linguistics); **Psychology and Management** (Management; Psychology)

History: Founded 1934, acquired present status and title 1994.

Academic Year: September to July

Admission Requirements: Secondary school certificate (Attestat o srednem obrazovanii)

Main Language(s) of Instruction: Russian

Student Services: Academic counselling, Canteen, Cultural centre, Foreign student adviser, Foreign Studies Centre, Health services, Language programs, Social counselling, Sports facilities

Student Residential Facilities: Yes

Special Facilities: Art Gallery.

Libraries: c. 500,000 vols

HIGHER SCHOOL OF MUSIC OF THE SAHA REPUBLIC (JAKUTIJA) (INSTITUTE)

Vyssaja Škola Muzyki Respubliki Saha (Jakutija) (Institut)

Pokrovskij trakt, 16km, Yakutsk 677013
Tel: +7(4112) 31-60-03 +7(4112) 31-60-01
Fax: +7(4112) 31-60-03 +7(4112) 31-60-01
EMail: vshkolamus@mail.ru
Website: http://www.vschoolmus.ru/

Rector: Ivan Ivanovich Naumov

Programmes
Music (Conducting; Music; Music Education; Music Theory and Composition; Musical Instruments; Singing)

History: Created 1993.

Academic Year: September to June

Admission Requirements: Entrance examination and audition (preslušivane)

Fees: None

Main Language(s) of Instruction: Russian

Accrediting Agencies: Ministry of Culture

Degrees and Diplomas: *Specialist Diploma*

Student Services: Academic counselling, Canteen, Handicapped facilities, Health services, Language programs, Social counselling, Sports facilities

Student Residential Facilities: Yes

Special Facilities: Art Gallery

Libraries: Main Library
Last Updated: 12/03/12

HIGHER SCHOOL OF THEATRE (INSTITUTE) NAMED AFTER M.S. SHCHEPKIN

Vyssee Teatralnoje Učilišče (Institute) im. M.S. Ščepkina

6/2, Neglinnaya, str 1/2, Moskva 109012
Tel: +7(495) 624-52-25 +7(495) 623-76-75
Fax: +7(495) 923-18-80
EMail: schepkinschool@mtu-net.ru
Website: http://schepkin.maly.ru/

Rector: Boris Nikolajevič Lyubimov (2007-)

Departments
Acting (Acting); **Art Criticism** (Art Criticism); **Philosophy and History of Culture** (Cultural Studies; Philosophy); **Rhythmical and State Motion** (Dance; Performing Arts; Theatre); **Stage Speech Training** (Acting)

Further Information: Also Russian Language courses for foreign students

History: Founded 1809, acquired present status and title 1943.

Governing Bodies: Academic Council

Academic Year: September to June (September-January; February-June)

Admission Requirements: Secondary school certificate (Attestat o srednem obrazovanii)

Main Language(s) of Instruction: Russian

Degrees and Diplomas: *Specialist Diploma*; *Magistr*

Student Services: Canteen, Health services

Student Residential Facilities: Yes

Libraries: c. 49,000 vols

Last Updated: 13/03/12

HUMANITARIAN INSTITUTE OF TELEVISION AND BROADCASTING NAMED AFTER M.A.LITOVČIN

Gumanitarnyj Institut Televidenija i Radioveščanija im. M.A. Litovčina

Brodnikov per. 3, Moskva 109180
Tel: +7(495) 238-5548 +7(495) 238-1975
Fax: +7(495) 238-5548
Website: http://www.gift.ru

Rector: Valentin V. Lazutkin

Programmes

Television and Broadcasting (Radio and Television Broadcasting)

INGUSH STATE UNIVERSITY

Ingušskij Gosudarstvennyj Universitet

ul. Pervomajskaja, 15a, pos. Gagarin, Magas, 366700 Republic of Ingushetia
Tel: +7(873) 222-38-52 +7(873) 222-38-54
Fax: +7(873) 222-38-54
EMail: ing_gu@mail.ru
Website: http://www.inggu.ru/

Rector: Arsamak Martazanov (2001-)

Faculties

Agricultural Engineering (Agricultural Engineering; Agricultural Equipment; Agriculture; Agronomy; Animal Husbandry; Crop Production; Veterinary Science); **Chemistry and Biology** (Biochemistry; Biology; Chemistry; Inorganic Chemistry; Organic Chemistry; Physiology; Zoology); **Economics and Accountancy** (Accountancy; Business and Commerce; Economics; Management); **Finance** (Banking; Finance; Taxation); **History** (History; Philosophy); **Law** (Civil Law; Criminal Law; Law; Public Law); **Medicine** (Anaesthesiology; Cardiology; Dermatology; Medicine; Paediatrics); **Philology** (English; French; German; Linguistics; Literature; Native Language; Philology; Russian); **Physics and Mathematics** (Applied Mathematics; Computer Science; Mathematics; Physics; Statistics)

History: Founded 1994.

Academic Year: September to June

Admission Requirements: Secondary school certificate (Attestat o srednem obrazovanii) and entrance examination

Main Language(s) of Instruction: Russian

Accrediting Agencies: Ministry of Education

Degrees and Diplomas: *Bakalavr*; *Specialist Diploma*

Last Updated: 17/01/12

INSTITUTE OF AUTOMOBILE TECHNOLOGIES AND MANAGEMENT

Institut Avtomobilnyj Tekhnologij I Upravlinija (MAMI)

ul. B.Semenovskaja, 38, Moskva 105839
Tel: +7(495) 223-05-34
EMail: yvm@mami.ru; ankin@mami.ru
Website: http://iatu.info

Rector: Jurij Viktorovich Maksimov

Programmes

Automobile Technology (Automotive Engineering)

History: Created 1997.

Degrees and Diplomas: *Specialist Diploma*

Last Updated: 13/01/12

INSTITUTE OF RUSSIAN LANGUAGE NAMED AFTER A.S. PUSHKIN

Gosudarstvennyj Institut Russkogo Jazyka im A.S. Puškina

ak. Volgina, 6, Moskva 117485
Tel: +7(495) 335-0800
Fax: +7(495) 330-8565
EMail: inbox@pushkin.edu.ru
Website: http://www.pushkin.edu.ru

Rector: Yuri E. Prokhorov
Tel: +7(495) 174-6281, Fax: +7(495) 371-1322
EMail: rector@guu.ru

INTERNATIONAL INSTITUTE FOR HUMANITIES AND LINGUISTICS

Meždunarodnyj Gumanitarno-lingvističeskij Institut (IIHL)

ul. Bol'šaja Čerjomuškinskaja 17a, Moskva 117447
Tel: +7(495) 127-2391
EMail: mgli@mfua.ru
Website: http://www.mgli.ru

Rector: Galina Zabelina (1994-)
Tel: +7(495) 123-90-35 EMail: Zabelin.a.G@mfua.ru

Administrative Officer: Mara Kistalova
EMail: Kistalova.M@mfua.ru

International Relations: Gulnara Akataeva, Deputy Dean
EMail: Akataeva.G@mfua.ru

Faculties

Management; **Management of Organisation**; **Russian as a Foreign Language**; **Theory and Methods of Teaching of Foreign Languages and Cultures**; **Translation theory and practice** (Translation and Interpretation)

History: Founded 1989. Received full accreditation from Russian Ministry of education 1998. Formerly known as Rossijskij Universitet Innovacij (Institut)/Russian University of Innovations (Institute).

Governing Bodies: President; Rector

Admission Requirements: Secondary school certificate (Certifikat o srednem obrazovanii)

Fees: (Russian Rubles): 85,000 per annum

Main Language(s) of Instruction: Russian

Accrediting Agencies: Russian Ministry of Education (Federal'naja Sluzhba Nadsory v Sfere obrazovanija I Nauki)

Degrees and Diplomas: *Bakalavr*: Linguistics; Management; *Specialist Diploma*: Foreign Language Teaching; Translation; Russian as a Foreign Language; Management of Organisation

Student Services: Canteen, Cultural centre, Employment services, Foreign student adviser, Foreign Studies Centre, Health services, Language programs, Sports facilities

Special Facilities: Movie studio; IT labs

Libraries: Over 50,000 vols

Academic Staff *2008-2009*	MEN	WOMEN	TOTAL
FULL-TIME	20	60	**80**
Student Numbers *2008-2009*			
All (Foreign Included)	51	266	**317**
FOREIGN ONLY	–	–	**1**

Part-time students, 116. **Distance students**, 8. **Evening students**, 85.

Last Updated: 05/01/09

IRKUTSK STATE ACADEMY OF AGRICULTURE

Irkutskaja Gosudarstvennaja Sel'skohozjajstvennaja Akademija

pos. Molodyozhny, Irkutsk, 664038 Irkutskaja oblast'
Tel: +7(3952) 399-330
Fax: +7(3952) 399-418
Website: http://www.isaa.narod.ru

Rector: Alexandr Dolgopolov

Pro-Rector: Viktor Rykov Tel: +7(3952) 399-491

International Relations: Larisa Mironez, Head, International Department Tel: +7(3952) 399-440 EMail: intrel@yandex.ru

Faculties

Agronomy (Agrobiology; Agronomy; Crop Production; Ecology; Environmental Studies; Floriculture; Fruit Production; Harvest Technology; Horticulture; Plant and Crop Protection; Plant Pathology; Soil Conservation; Soil Management; Vegetable Production) *Dean*: Anatoli Abramov; **Economics** (Accountancy; Agricultural Business; Agricultural Economics; Agricultural Equipment; Agricultural Management; Applied Mathematics; Banking; Computer Engineering; Data Processing; Farm Management; Finance; Management Systems; Marketing; Statistics; Systems Analysis; Taxation) *Dean*: Yaroslav Ivan'o; **Energy** (Automation and Control Engineering; Electrical and Electronic Engineering; Electrical Engineering; Energy Engineering; Engineering Management; Industrial Engineering; Power Engineering; Thermal Engineering) *Dean*: Marina Buzunova; **Mechanization** *Dean*: Nikolai Stepanov; **Wild Life Management** (Biology; Cell Biology; Forest Economics; Forest Management; Forest Products; Forestry; Wildlife) *Dean*: Oled Zharov; **Zoological Engineering** (Animal Husbandry; Apiculture; Cattle Breeding; Chemistry; Dairy; Food Science; Genetics; Histology; Meat and Poultry; Microbiology; Parasitology; Plant Pathology; Veterinary Science; Zoology) *Dean*: Tsydenzhap Ludypov

Institutes

Agrarian Sciences *(Trans-Baikal) Director*: Anatoli Vershinin

History: Founded 1934 as the East Siberian Institute. Acquired status 1995

Governing Bodies: Academy Administration

Academic Year: September to June (2 semesters)

Admission Requirements: Secondary school certificate (Attestat o srednem obrazovanii) and entrance examination

Fees: (Russian Rubles): 30,000 per annum

Main Language(s) of Instruction: Russian

International Co-operation: With universities in Germany; Japan; France; Mongolia; China; Poland

Degrees and Diplomas: *Specialist Diploma*: 5-6 yrs

Student Services: Academic counselling, Canteen, Cultural centre, Foreign student adviser, Health services, Nursery care, Social counselling, Sports facilities

Student Residential Facilities: 8 hostels

Special Facilities: Training Farms (Dairy and Meat Production, Hunting), Veterinary Clinic, Laboratories, Museum of Wildlife Management, History Museum

Libraries: 504,814 vols

IRKUTSK STATE LINGUISTIC UNIVERSITY

Irkutskij Gosudarstvennyj Lingvističeskij Universitet

ul. Lenina 8, Irkutsk, 664000 Irkutskaja oblast'
Tel: +7(3952) 242-977
Fax: +7(3952) 243-244
EMail: islu@islu.irk.ru
Website: http://www.islu.ru

Rector: Grigori Voskoboinik (2000-)
Tel: +7(3952) 242-598 EMail: voskoboinik@islu.irk.ru

Vice-Rector for Academic Programmes: Anna Y. Suslova
Tel: +7(3952) 242-598 EMail: aysuslova@islu.irk.ru

International Relations: Julia N. Kuznetsova
Tel: +7(3952) 243-249, Fax: +7(3952) 243-249
EMail: inter@islu.irk.ru

Centres

Postgraduate Studies; **Preschool Education** *Head*: Olga Hamaeva; **Russian-Japanese Education** (East Asian Studies; Heritage Preservation; Japanese; Philology; Russian) *Director*: Svetlana Bogdanova; **Scientific Research on Language and Teacher Training** *Head*: Valentina Levit; **Teaching Materials** *Head*: Angelika Matienko

Colleges

Translators, Interpreters and Managers *Head*: Vladimir Nazarov

Departments

In-Service Retraining Programmes *Head*: Galina Ageeva; **Modern English** (American Studies; Education; English; Linguistics; Translation and Interpretation) *Head*: Angelika Matienko; **Modern German** (German; Linguistics; Teacher Training; Translation and Interpretation) *Head*: Svetlana Hahalova; **Oriental Languages** (Chinese; Information Technology; Japanese; Korean; Oriental Languages; Speech Studies; Translation and Interpretation) *Head*: En Ok Kim; **Pre-institutional Training** *(Siberian Region) Head*: Irina Kuzina; **Romance Languages** (French; Italian; Linguistics; Romance Languages; Spanish) *Head*: Tatjana Kalentieva

Faculties

Distance Education (English; French; German; Teacher Training; Translation and Interpretation) *Dean*: Natalija Torunova; **Foreign Languages and Social Sciences** (Advertising and Publicity; Business Administration; Modern Languages; Pedagogy; Philology; Preschool Education; Public Relations) *Dean*: Zhanna Igumnova

Laboratories

Cognitive Linguistics (Linguistics); **Eurasian Cultures and Languages** (Cultural Studies; Eastern European Studies; Eurasian and North Asian Languages); **Inter-university Teacher Trainers Education**; **Modern Aspects of Teacher Training** (Pedagogy; Teacher Training); **New Technologies for Teaching Foreign Languages** (Foreign Languages Education); **Social Psychology**; **Systematic Research on Language and Speech**

History: Founded 1948 as Teacher Training Institute of Foreign Languages, acquired present status and title 1996.

Governing Bodies: Ministry of Education

Academic Year: September to July (September-December; January-July)

Admission Requirements: Secondary school certificate (Attestat o srednem obrazovanii) or equivalent (Diploma o srednem specialnom obrazovanii) and entrance examination

Fees: (Dollars): 700 per annum

Main Language(s) of Instruction: Russian, English, German, French

International Co-operation: Participates in TACIS Tempus programme

Accrediting Agencies: Ministry of Education

Degrees and Diplomas: *Bakalavr*: Russian; English; German; French; Spanish; Chinese; Korean; Japanese (DIB), 4 yrs; *Specialist Diploma*: Russian; English; German; French; Spanish; Chinese; Korean; Japanese (DIS, DVS), 5 yrs; *Magistr*: Russian; German; Romance Languages; Oriental Languages; Linguistics (DIM), 6 yrs; *Kandidat Nauk*: German; Romance Languages; Oriental Languages (DIM), 3 yrs

Student Services: Academic counselling, Canteen, Cultural centre, Employment services, Foreign student adviser, Foreign Studies Centre, Health services, Language programs, Sports facilities

Student Residential Facilities: For 2,055 students

Special Facilities: Museum

Libraries: 379,722 vols

Publications: ISLU Collection *(other/irregular)*; Vestnik *(other/irregular)*

IRKUTSK STATE RAILWAY UNIVERSITY

Irkutskij Gosudarstvennyj Universitet Putej Soobščenija

ul. Černyševskogo 15, Irkutsk,
664074 Irkutskaja oblast'
Tel: +7(3952) 432-607
Fax: +7(3952) 434-846
Website: http://www.iriit.irk.ru

Rector: Andrej Pavlovič Homenko

Programmes

Railway Engineering (Railway Engineering); **Transport Management** (Transport Management)

History: Formerly known as Irkutskij Institut Inženernoj Železnodorožnogo Transporta

IRKUTSK STATE TECHNICAL UNIVERSITY

Irkutskij Gosudarstvennyj Tehničeskij Universitet (ISTU)

ul. Lermontova 83, Irkutsk, 664074 Irkutskaja oblast'
Tel: +7(3952) 405-200
Fax: +7(3952) 405-100
EMail: info@istu.edu
Website: http://www.istu.edu

Rector: Ivan Mikhailovič Golovnykh (2000-) Tel: +7(3952) 405-000

Administrative Officer: Nina Petrovna Safonova

International Relations: Oleg Vladimirovič Repetsky, Deputy Rector

Faculties

Architecture (Architectural and Environmental Design; Architectural Restoration; Architecture) *Dean*: Valery Vasiljevič Kozlov; **Business and Management** (Business Administration; Economics; Finance; Industrial Management; International Economics; Management) *Dean*: Gennady Efimovič Dykusov; **Chemical Engineering and Metallurgy** (Automation and Control Engineering; Chemical Engineering; Food Technology; Materials Engineering; Metallurgical Engineering; Mineralogy; Oenology; Production Engineering) *Dean*: Elena Valentinova Zelinskaya; **Civil Engineering and Municipal Planning** (Civil Engineering; Construction Engineering; Heating and Refrigeration; Industrial Engineering; Real Estate; Road Engineering; Road Transport; Water Management) *Dean*: Viktor Romanovič Čupin; **Computer Science** (Computer Networks; Computer Science; Data Processing; Information Sciences; Information Technology) *Dean*: Aleksandr Vasiljevič Petrov; **Evening and Distance Education** *Dean*: Viktor Vladimirovič Elšin; **Fine Arts** (Crafts and Trades; Cultural Studies; Design; Fine Arts) *Dean*: Širškov Igor Alexandrovič; **Geology, Geological Data Processing and Geological Ecology** (Data Processing; Environmental Studies; Geological Engineering; Geology; Information Technology; Mineralogy; Petroleum and Gas Engineering; Surveying and Mapping) *Dean*: Vladislav Vasilievič Neskoromnyh; **Law, Sociology and Mass Media** (Advertising and Publicity; Journalism; Law; Psychology; Social Work; Sociology) *Dean*: Artur Victorovič Harinskii; **Mining Engineering** (Automation and Control Engineering; Mineralogy; Mining Engineering; Robotics; Safety Engineering; Surveying and Mapping) *Dean*: Boris Leonidovič Talgamer; **Power Engineering** (Electrical and Electronic Engineering; Electrical Engineering; Energy Engineering; Power Engineering; Thermal Engineering) *Dean*: Vadim Valentinovič Fedčišin; **Technology and Computerization of Mechanical Engineering** (Automation and Control Engineering; Information Technology; Machine Building; Materials Engineering; Mechanical Engineering; Production Engineering; Robotics) *Dean*: Vladimir Petrovič Koltcov; **Transportation Systems** (Aeronautical and Aerospace Engineering; Air Transport; Automotive Engineering; Civil Engineering; Road Transport; Transport Engineering) *Dean*: Igor Nikolaevič Gušev

Further Information: Also Russian Courses for foreign students

History: Founded 1930, acquired present status and title 1993.

Academic Year: September to June (September-January; February-June)

Admission Requirements: Secondary school certificate (Attestat o srednem obrazovanii)

Fees: (US Dollars): 1,000-1,500 per annum

Main Language(s) of Instruction: Russian

Degrees and Diplomas: *Bakalavr*: 4 yrs; *Specialist Diploma*: Engineering; Technology, 1 further yr; *Magistr*: a further 1 yr; *Kandidat Nauk*: a further 3-4 yrs; *Doktor Nauk*: a further 3 yrs following Kandidat

Student Services: Academic counselling, Canteen, Cultural centre, Foreign student adviser, Health services, Language programs, Social counselling, Sports facilities

Student Residential Facilities: Yes

Special Facilities: University History Museum; Mineralogy Museum. Youth Art Gallery. Dance Studio. Educational TV Channel and TV Studio

Libraries: c. 1.2 m. vols

Publications: Collection of Scientific Works: Geology, Search and Prospecting of Ore and Mineral Deposits *(annually)*; Collection of Scientific Works: Ore Dressing *(annually)*

Press or Publishing House: Irkutsk State Technical University Publishing House

IRKUTSK STATE UNIVERSITY

Irkutskij Gosudarstvennyj Universitet (ISU)

ul. Karla Marksa 1, Irkutsk,
664003 Irkutskaja oblast'
Tel: +7(3952) 243-453
Fax: +7(3952) 242-238
EMail: smirnov@isu.ru
Website: http://www.isu.ru

Rector: Alexandre Smirnov

Vice-Rector for Academic Affairs: Igor I. Gutnik
Tel: +7(3952) 243-215 EMail: gutnik@admin.isu.ru

International Relations: Sergei Šunin
Tel: +7(3952) 202-284, Fax: +7(3952) 242-249
EMail: bogatova@admin.isu.runnet.ru

Faculties

Biology and Soil Science (Biology; Ecology; Physiology; Soil Science) *Dean*: Natalia Granina; **Business and Management** *(Extramural and Distant Training)* (Business and Commerce; Economics; Management) *Dean*: Margarita Šilverskič; **Chemistry** (Analytical Chemistry; Chemistry; Inorganic Chemistry; Organic Chemistry; Physical Chemistry) *Dean*: Aleksandr Safronov; **Geography** (Geography; Meteorology; Water Science; Wildlife) *Dean*: Alla Argučintseva; **Geology** (Geochemistry; Geology; Petroleum and Gas Engineering; Surveying and Mapping) *Dean*: Svetlana Primina; **History** (Archaeology; Ethnology; History; International Relations; Political Sciences) *Dean*: Serguei Kuznetsov; **International** (Business and Commerce; Linguistics) *Dean*: Valentina Andruhova; **Management** *(Siberian-American)* (Human Resources; International Studies; Management; Marketing) *Dean*: Aleksandr Diogenov; **Philology and Journalism** (Journalism; Literature; Philology; Russian) *Dean*: Anatoli Sobennikov; **Physics** (Electronic Engineering; Physics; Radiophysics) *Dean*: Jurij Parfenov; **Psychology** (Psychology; Speech Therapy and Audiology) *Dean*: Igor Konopak; **Service and Advertising** (Advertising and Publicity; Cultural Studies; Household Management; Social Studies; Tourism) *Dean*: Vera Karnauhova; **Social Sciences** (Regional Studies; Social Work; Sociology) *Dean*: Vladimir Rešetnikov

Institutes

Law (Civil Law; Constitutional Law; Criminal Law; International Law; Law) *Dean*: Oleg Ličičan; **Mathematics and Economics** (Applied Mathematics; Econometrics; Economics; Mathematics) *Dean*: Oleg Vasiliev

History: Founded 1918.

Governing Bodies: Academic Council; Faculty Councils

Academic Year: September to July (September-January; February-July)

Admission Requirements: Secondary education certificate (Attestat o srednem obrazovanii) and entrance examination

Fees: None

Main Language(s) of Instruction: Russian

International Co-operation: With universities in Germany, Netherlands.

Accrediting Agencies: Ministry of Education

Degrees and Diplomas: *Bakalavr*: 4 yrs; *Specialist Diploma*: 5 yrs; *Magistr*: 2 yrs following Bakalavr; *Kandidat Nauk*: a further 3 yrs and thesis; *Doktor Nauk*: by thesis after Kandidat

Student Services: Academic counselling, Canteen, Cultural centre, Foreign student adviser, Health services, Language programs, Social counselling, Sports facilities

Special Facilities: Baikal Museum; Zoology Museum. Herbarium of Eastern Siberia. Observatory. Botanical Garden. Baikal Biological Station

Libraries: Regional Scientific Library, c. 3m. vols

Publications: Scientific Papers of the ISU, Physics, Chemistry, Biology *(annually)*; Scientific Papers of Young Researchers of the ISU, Ecological Problems of the Eastern Regions *(annually)*

IRKUTSK STATE UNIVERSITY OF MEDICINE

Irkutskij Gosudarstvennyj Meditsinskij Universitet

ul. Krasnogo Vosstanija 1, Irkutsk, 664003 Irkutskaja oblast'
Tel: +7(3952) 24-38-25 +7(3952) 24-30-66 +7(3952) 24-35-97
Fax: +7(3952) 24-38-25
EMail: administrator@ismu.baikal.ru
Website: http://www.ismu.baikal.ru/

Rector: Igor Vladimirovich Malov

Faculties

Medicine (Anatomy; Dermatology; Gynaecology and Obstetrics; Medicine; Neurology; Oncology; Ophthalmology; Orthopaedics; Otorhinolaryngology; Pathology; Psychiatry and Mental Health; Surgery; Urology; Venereology); **Paediatrics** (Gynaecology and Obstetrics; Immunology; Paediatrics; Physiology; Radiology); **Pharmacy** (Biochemistry; Inorganic Chemistry; Organic Chemistry; Pharmacology; Pharmacy; Toxicology); **Postgraduate Studies**; **Preventive Medicine** (Biology; Epidemiology; Hygiene; Microbiology; Pathology; Social and Preventive Medicine); **Stomatology** (Histology; Physiology; Stomatology)

Institutes

Nursing (Nursing)

Further Information: Also Teaching Hospital

History: Founded 1919 as Department within Irkuck University, became independent 1930. Acquired present status 1995.

Governing Bodies: Academic Council

Academic Year: September to June (September-January; February-June)

Admission Requirements: Secondary school certificate (Attestat o srednem obrazovanii)

Main Language(s) of Instruction: Russian

Degrees and Diplomas: *Specialist Diploma*; *Kandidat Nauk*

Student Residential Facilities: For c. 200 foreign students

Special Facilities: History of the University Museum; Anatomy Museum; Museum of Forensic Medicine

Libraries: c. 560,000 vols

Last Updated: 27/01/12

ISHIM STATE PEDAGOGICAL INSTITUTE

Išimskij Gosudarstvennyj Pedagogičeskij Institut

ul. Lenina 1, Išim, 627400 Tjumenskaja oblast'
Tel: +7(34-551) 219-41
Fax: +7(34-551) 239-39
EMail: igpi@ishim.ru
Website: http://www.ishim.ru

Rector: Nikolaj Stepanovic Gusel'nikov

Programmes

Education (Education)

IVANOVO STATE ACADEMY OF AGRICULTURE

Ivanovskaja Gosudarstvennaja Sel'skohozjajstvennaja Academija (IGSHA)

ul. Sovetskaja, 45, Ivanovo 153467
Tel: +7(4932) 300-603
Fax: +7(4932) 328-144
EMail: ivgsha@tpi.ru
Website: http://ivgsha.tpi.ru

Rector: V.F. Tzarev (1999-)

Vice-Rector: V.V. Pronin
Tel: +7(4932) 325-376 EMail: proninvv63@mail.ru

International Relations: V.V. Kolobova, Assistant of Vice-Rector
EMail: kolobovavv@mail.ru

Faculties

Agrotechnology (Agricultural Engineering; Agriculture) *Dean*: V.A Sokolov; **Economics** (Economics) *Dean*: A.D. Shuvalov; **Mechanization in Agriculture** (Agricultural Equipment) *Dean*: U.I. Chernov; **Veterinary Medicine and Biotechnology in Animal Husbandry** (Animal Husbandry; Biotechnology; Veterinary Science) *Dean*: V.P. Fedotov

History: Founded 1930, on the basis of the Agricultural Department of Ivanovo-Voznesensk Polytechnic Institute in 1918. Acquired present status 1996.

Governing Bodies: Rector's council; Academic council; Dean's council.

Academic Year: September to July

Admission Requirements: Secodnary School Certificate (Attestat)

Fees: (Russian Rubles): 30,000 Rubles per annum or 15,000 per term for Russian citizens; 50,000 per annum or 25,000 per term for foreign citizens.

Main Language(s) of Instruction: Russian

International Co-operation: Scientific cooperation agreement with Agriculture Academies of Serbia and Belorussia; program LOGO in cooperation with Germany

Degrees and Diplomas: *Bakalavr*: Economics; Agriculture; Machinery and Technology, 4 yrs; *Specialist Diploma*: Veterinary, 5 yrs; *Kandidat Nauk*: 3 yrs

Student Services: Academic counselling, Canteen, Cultural centre, Employment services, Foreign student adviser, Foreign Studies Centre, Health services, Language programs, Nursery care, Sports facilities

Student Residential Facilities: Dormitory

Special Facilities: Museum; Arboretum; Experimental Field; Training Farm.

Libraries: 4 Libraries: 2 Scientific Libraries, Library with Popular Literature and Fiction, Reading-Hall with Internet Access.

Publications: Collection of Scientific Works, Articles on main problems of agriculture, veterinary medicine, agronomy, organization of the use of land, mechanization in agriculture, economy of agroindustrial complex *(annually)*; Monographs of Academy scientists, Agro-industrial problems *(annually)*

Academic Staff *2007-2008*	MEN	WOMEN	TOTAL
FULL-TIME	281	313	**594**
PART-TIME	18	41	**59**
Student Numbers *2007-2008*			
All (Foreign Included)	1,145	1,009	**2,154**
FOREIGN ONLY	17	3	**20**

Part-time students, 1,300.

Last Updated: 10/12/08

IVANOVO STATE ACADEMY OF ARCHITECTURE AND CIVIL ENGINEERING

Ivanovskaja Gosudarstevennaja Arhitekturno-Stroitel'naja Akademija

ul. 8 Marta 20, Ivanovo 153002
Tel: +7(0932) 329-755
Fax: +7(0932) 371-942
EMail: rektor@igasu.ru
Website: http://www.igasa.ru

Rector: Sergey Fedosov

Programmes

Architecture (Architecture); **Civil Engineering** (Civil Engineering); **Economics** (Economics)

IVANOVO STATE MEDICAL ACADEMY

Ivanovskaja Gosudarstevennaja Medicinskaja Akademija

prosp. Fridriha Engelsa 8, Ivanovo 153462
Tel: +7(0932) 301-766
Fax: +7(0932) 326-604
EMail: adm@isma.ivanovo.ru
Website: http://www.isma.ivanovo.ru

Rector: Rudol'f R. Šiljaev

Secretary-General: Y. V. Nikolaenkov Tel: +7(0932) 327-742

International Relations: S.B. Nazarov Tel: +7(0932) 325-042

Centres

Research

Colleges
Medicine (Medicine)

Faculties
Medicine (Medicine); **Nursing** (Nursing); **Paediatrics** (Paediatrics)

Laboratories
Biochemistry (Biochemistry); **Blood Physiology** (Physiology); **Electron Microscopy** (Atomic and Molecular Physics); **Microcirculation**; **Morphology** (Anatomy)

History: Founded 1930, acquired present status 1994.

Governing Bodies: Ministry of Public Health of the Federation of Russia

Academic Year: September to July (September-January; February-July)

Admission Requirements: Secondary school certificate (Attestat o poldnom srednem obrazovanii)

Main Language(s) of Instruction: Russian

Degrees and Diplomas: *Specialist Diploma*: Medicine, 6 yrs

Student Services: Academic counselling, Canteen, Cultural centre, Employment services, Foreign Studies Centre, Health services, Social counselling, Sports facilities

Student Residential Facilities: For c. 1,190 students

Special Facilities: History of Academy Museum

Libraries: c. 570,000 vols

IVANOVO STATE TEXTILE ACADEMY

Ivanovskaja Gosudarstvennaja Tekstil'naja Akademija (IGTA)

prosp. F. Engelsa 21, Ivanovo 153000
Tel: +7(4932) 32-93-63 +7(4932) 35-78-60
Fax: +7(4932) 41-21-08 +7(4932) 32-93-63
EMail: rector@igta.ru; vvl@igta.ru; umu@igta.ru
Website: http://www.igta.ru/

Rector: Grigorij Ilich Chistoborodov
EMail: rector@igta.ru; ilyich@igta.ru

Faculties
Clothing Manufacturing (Clothing and Sewing; Fashion Design; Textile Design; Textile Technology); **Design and Cultural Service** (Clothing and Sewing; Fashion Design); **Economics and Management** (Accountancy; Administration; Banking; Economics; Human Resources; Management; Marketing); **Mechanical Engineering and Automation** (Automation and Control Engineering; Engineering; Machine Building; Maintenance Technology; Mechanical Engineering); **Textile Technology** (Safety Engineering; Textile Technology)

Further Information: Branch in Vichuga, Kineshma, Krasnodar, Nizhnij Novgorod, Rjazan, Teikovo.

History: Founded 1918 as Ivanovo Polytechnic Institute. Became independent 1930, and acquired present status and title 1994.

Governing Bodies: Academy Council, comprising 60 members

Academic Year: September to July (September-January; February-July)

Admission Requirements: Secondary school certificate (Attestat o srednem obrazovanii)

Main Language(s) of Instruction: Russian

International Co-operation: With universities in Belarus, China, Italy, Mongolia, Pakistan, Poland, Romania and Uzbekistan. Also participates in the DAAD, Soros Foundation, New Horizons and Gold Bar Award Programmes

Accrediting Agencies: Ministry of Education

Degrees and Diplomas: *Bakalavr*; *Specialist Diploma*; *Magistr*; *Kandidat Nauk*

Student Services: Academic counselling, Canteen, Cultural centre, Foreign student adviser, Foreign Studies Centre, Health services, Language programs, Social counselling, Sports facilities

Special Facilities: History of the Academy Museum. Art Gallery. Movie Studio

Libraries: 757,454 vols

Last Updated: 17/01/12

IVANOVO STATE UNIVERSITY

Ivanovskij Gosudarstvennyj Universitet

ul. Ermaka 39, Ivanovo 153025
Tel: +7(4932) 32-62-10 +7(4932) 35-64-28
Fax: +7(4932) 32-46-77 +7(4932) 32-66-00
EMail: rector@ivanovo.ac.ru
Website: http://www.ivanovo.ac.ru

Rector: Vladimir Nikolajevič Yegorov (2000-)

Faculties
Biology and Chemistry (Biology; Chemistry); **Economics** (Economics; Information Technology; Management); **History** (History); **Law** (Civil Law; Commercial Law; Constitutional Law; Criminal Law; Labour Law; Law); **Mathematics** (Computer Science; Mathematics); **Philology** (Advertising and Publicity; Journalism; Linguistics; Literature; Philology; Slavic Languages); **Physics** (Physics); **Romance-German Philology** (English; French; German; Latin; Philology; Romance Languages); **Sociology and Psychology** (Psychology; Social Work; Sociology)

Further Information: Branch in Derbent.

History: Founded 1974.

Governing Bodies: Academic Council

Academic Year: September to July

Admission Requirements: Secondary school certificate (Attestat o srednem obrazovanii) and entrance examination

Main Language(s) of Instruction: Russian

Accrediting Agencies: Ministry of Education and Science

Degrees and Diplomas: *Bakalavr*, *Specialist Diploma*; *Magistr*, *Kandidat Nauk*; *Doktor Nauk*

Student Services: Academic counselling, Canteen, Cultural centre, Foreign student adviser, Foreign Studies Centre, Health services, Sports facilities

Student Residential Facilities: Yes

Special Facilities: History of the University Museum; Literature Museum; Zoology Museum; Biology Museum; Botany Garden

Libraries: University Library; Foreign Literature and Languages Library; total, 745,139 vols

Publications: Ivanovo State University Bulletin *(quarterly)*; Liquid Crystals and their Application *(quarterly)*; Women in Russian Society *(quarterly)*

Press or Publishing House: Ivanovo State University Publishing House

Last Updated: 17/01/12

IVANOVO STATE UNIVERSITY OF CHEMISTRY AND TECHNOLOGY

Ivanovskij Gosudarstvennyj Himikotehnologičeskij Universitet

prosp. Fridriha Engelsa 7, Ivanovo 153460
Tel: +7(4932) 329-241
Fax: +7(4932) 329-502
EMail: root@isuct.ru
Website: http://www.isuct.ru

Rector: Oskar Koifman (1998-) Fax: +7(0932) 417-995
EMail: rektor@isuct.ru

Vice-Rector for Administration: Valentin Šarnin
Tel: +7(0932) 329-500 EMail: sharn@isuct.ru

International Relations: Valentina Ivanova Borisova
EMail: borisova@isuct.ru

Colleges
Chemistry (Chemistry) *Head*: Yuri Čistyakov

Faculties
Chemical Engineering and Cybernetics (Automation and Control Engineering; Chemical Engineering) *Dean*: Alexander Labutin; **Chemistry of Solids and Rational Use of Nature** (Chemistry) *Dean*: Lev Kudin; **Humanities** (Arts and Humanities; History; Modern Languages; Philosophy; Physical Education; Political Sciences; Russian) *Dean*: Elena Raskatova

History: Founded 1918 as Polytechnic Institute, acquired present title 1998.

Academic Year: September to June (September-January; February-June)

Admission Requirements: Secondary school certificate (Attestat o srednem obrazovanii), or equivalent, and entrance examination

Main Language(s) of Instruction: Russian

Degrees and Diplomas: *Bakalavr*: 4 yrs; *Specialist Diploma*: Engineering, Technology, 3 yrs; *Magistr*: a further 2 yrs; *Kandidat Nauk*: a further 3 yrs following Magistr

Student Services: Canteen, Cultural centre, Employment services, Foreign student adviser, Foreign Studies Centre, Health services, Social counselling, Sports facilities

Libraries: Information Centre, c. 653,000 vols

IVANOVO STATE UNIVERSITY OF POWER ENGINEERING

Ivanovskij Gosudarstvennyj Energetičeskij Universitet (IGEU (ISPU))

ul. Rabfakovskaja 34, Ivanovo 153003
Tel: +7(4932) 326-448
Fax: +7(4932) 269-696
EMail: office@ispu.ru
Website: http://www.ispu.ru

President: Sergey V. Tararykin (2006-)
Tel: +7(4932) 327-243 EMail: tsv@ispu.ru

Administrative Vice-President: Dmitriy V. Tupitsin
Tel: +7(4932) 269-898 EMail: dvt@ispu.ru

International Relations: Nataliya A. Dudareva, Head, International Relations Department Tel: +7(4932) 269-864 EMail: ield@mail.ru

Faculties

Distance Education (Automation and Control Engineering; Electrical Engineering; Heating and Refrigeration; Industrial Engineering; Power Engineering) *Head*: Nikolay I. Dupovkin; **Economics and Management** (Economics; Management; Public Relations; Sociology) *Head*: Alexander M. Karyakin; **Electroengineering** (Automation and Control Engineering; Electrical Engineering; Electronic Engineering; Power Engineering) *Head*: Alexander F. Sorokin; **Electromechanical Engineering** (Automation and Control Engineering; Electrical Engineering; Electronic Engineering; Industrial Engineering; Machine Building; Mechanical Engineering; Mechanics; Metal Techniques) *Head*: Valeri P. Shishkin; **Engineering and Physics** (Engineering; Nuclear Engineering; Physics; Power Engineering; Safety Engineering) *Head*: Sergey G. Andrianov; **Heat Engineering** (Automation and Control Engineering; Energy Engineering; Heating and Refrigeration; Nuclear Engineering; Power Engineering) *Head*: Sergey B. Pletnikov; **Information and Computer Science** (Applied Mathematics; Computer Science; Documentation Techniques; Information Management; Information Sciences; Information Technology; Software Engineering; Systems Analysis) *Head*: Vladimir M. Kokin; **International Students** (Documentation Techniques; Economics; Electrical and Electronic Engineering; Industrial Design; Industrial Management; Information Sciences; Machine Building; Mechanical Engineering; Nuclear Engineering; Power Engineering; Public Relations; Sociology; Software Engineering; Thermal Engineering; Water Science) *Head*: Vera A. Falina; **Professional Development for University Teachers** (Computer Science; Economics; Electronic Engineering; Engineering; Heating and Refrigeration; Information Sciences; Management; Mechanical Engineering; Physics) *Head*: Nadezhda N. Babanova

History: Founded 1918 as Ivanovo-Voznesensk Polytechnical Institute, acquired present status and title 1993.

Governing Bodies: ISPU Scientific Council; Federal Education Agency of Russian Federation

Academic Year: September to June (September-February; February-June)

Admission Requirements: Secondary education certificate (Attestat o srednem obrazovanii)

Fees: (RUB): full-time students, 46,000 per annum; part-time students (by correspondence), 26,000 per annum; full-time international students, 62,000 per annum; full-time post-graduate students, 54,000 per annum; full-time post-graduate international students, 70,000 per annum.

Main Language(s) of Instruction: Russian

International Co-operation: With universities in USA, Germany, France, Kazakstan, Norway, Tajikistan.

Accrediting Agencies: Federal Education Agency of Russian Federation

Degrees and Diplomas: *Bakalavr*: Automation and Management; Heat Power Engineering, Electrical Engineering; Electromechanics and Electrical Technologies; Electrical Power Engineering; Information Systems and Computer Science, 4 yrs; *Specialist Diploma*: Offered in all fields., 5 yrs; *Magistr*: Automatic Electromechanical Complexes and Systems; Electrical Engineering, Electromechanics and Electrical Technologies; Electromechanical Systems of Autonomous Projects; Environment Protection in Heat Power Engineering; Automation of Power Systems, 6 yrs (or two years after Bakalavr); *Kandidat Nauk*: Computer Networks; Computer Graphics; Nuclear Engineering; Power Engineering; Industrial Engineering; Chemical Engineering; Economics; Finance; Sociology, a furhter 3 yrs; *Kandidat Nauk*: Machine Building; Physics; Heat Engineering; Technology; Electrical and Electronic Engineering; Information Technology; Information Management; Automation and Control Engineering; Management; Mathematics and Computer Science; Software Engineering, a further 3 yrs; *Doktor Nauk*: Electrical Engineering; Automationand Control Engineering; Computer Graphics; Power Engineering; Industrial Engineering, a further 3 yrs

Student Services: Canteen, Cultural centre, Foreign student adviser, Health services, Language programs, Sports facilities

Student Residential Facilities: For c. 1,400 students

Special Facilities: Museum; Television Studio; Russian-French Resource Centre

Libraries: 1.9 m. vols

Publications: Vestnik IGEU *(quarterly)*

Press or Publishing House: ISPU Publishing House

Academic Staff *2008-2009*	MEN	WOMEN	TOTAL
FULL-TIME	280	173	**453**
PART-TIME	32	13	**45**
Student Numbers *2008-2009*			
All (Foreign Included)	2,794	1,488	**4,282**
FOREIGN ONLY	38	2	**40**

Part-time students, 2,924. **Distance students**, 2,818.

Last Updated: 20/05/11

IZHEVSK STATE AGRICULTURAL ACADEMY

Iževskaja Gosudarstvennaja Sel'skohozjajstvennaja Akademija (IZHSAA)

ul. Studenčeskaja 11, Iževsk, 426069 Udmurtskaja Respublika
Tel: +7(3412) 589-948
Fax: +7(3412) 589-947
EMail: info@izhgsha.ru
Website: http://www.izhgsha.ru

Rector: Aleksandr Ivanović Lyubimov (2002-)
EMail: akmarov@izhgsha.ru

Faculties

Agroengineering (Agricultural Engineering; Agricultural Equipment); **Agronomy** (Agriculture; Agronomy; Ecology); **Animal Science** (Animal Husbandry; Zoology); **Economics** (Agricultural Economics; Agricultural Management; Economics; Farm Management; Management); **Farm Electrification and Automation** (Agricultural Engineering; Automation and Control Engineering; Farm Management); **Forestry** (Forestry); **Veterinary Medicine** (Veterinary Science)

History: Founded 1954 as Iżesk Agricultural Institute (comprising 3 faculties). Reoganized 1995 as Iżesk Agricultural Academy (9 faculties).

Governing Bodies: Rectorate

Academic Year: September to June

Admission Requirements: Entrance examination

Main Language(s) of Instruction: Russian

International Co-operation: None

Accrediting Agencies: Ministry of Education of Russian Federation

Degrees and Diplomas: *Bakalavr*; *Specialist Diploma*; *Magistr*

Student Services: Academic counselling, Canteen, Employment services, Foreign student adviser, Foreign Studies Centre, Health services, Language programs, Social counselling, Sports facilities

Student Residential Facilities: Yes

Special Facilities: Soil and Mineral Museum; Museum of History of the Academy

Libraries: 532,325 vols

Last Updated: 26/09/11

IZHEVSK STATE MEDICAL ACADEMY

Iževskaja Gosudarstvennaja Medicinskaja Akademija (ISMA)

ul. Revoljucionnaja 199, Iževsk, 426034 Udmurtskaja Respublika
Tel: +7(3412) 526-201
Fax: +7(3412) 558-167
EMail: rector@igma.udm.ru
Website: http://www.users.mark-itt.ru

Rector: Nilolay Strelkov (1992-)

Pro-Rector: Evgenij Butolin Tel: +7(3412) 485-797

International Relations: Alevtina Soboleva, Executive Director
Tel: +7(3412) 788-201, Fax: +7(3412) 757-421
EMail: asmi@igma.udm.ru

Faculties

Advanced Studies for Doctors (Anaesthesiology; Dentistry; Epidemiology; Forensic Medicine and Dentistry; Gynaecology and Obstetrics; Health Sciences; Laboratory Techniques; Neurology; Paediatrics; Psychiatry and Mental Health; Surgery) *Dean*: Antonina Sannikova; **Dentistry** (Dental Technology; Dentistry) *Dean*: Aleksandr Perminov; **General Medicine** (Anaesthesiology; Cardiology; Dermatology; Endocrinology; Gastroenterology; Gynaecology and Obstetrics; Haematology; Hepatology; Medicine; Nephrology; Neurology; Oncology; Ophthalmology; Otorhinolaryngology; Pneumology; Radiology; Rehabilitation and Therapy; Rheumatology; Tropical Medicine; Urology; Venereology) *Dean*: Vladimir Bryndin; **Nursing** (Nursing) *Dean*: Natalija Popova; **Paediatrics** (Paediatrics; Surgery) *Dean*: Viktor Pozdeev

History: Founded 1933, acquired present status and title 1995.

Governing Bodies: Rectorate

Academic Year: September to June

Admission Requirements: Secondary school certificate (Attestat o srednem obrazovanii) and qualifying interview

Fees: (US Dollars): 1,200 per annum

Main Language(s) of Instruction: Russian

Accrediting Agencies: Ministry of Health of the Russian Federation

Degrees and Diplomas: *Specialist Diploma*: Stomatology; Paediatrics; Management and Patients Care; General Medicine, 6 yrs

Student Services: Canteen, Foreign student adviser, Foreign Studies Centre, Health services, Language programs, Nursery care, Sports facilities

Student Residential Facilities: Yes

Special Facilities: Museums: University History; Anatomy; Criminology

Libraries: c. 250,000 vols

Publications: Collection of Scientific Articles; Medical Bulletin, Newspaper

IZHEVSK STATE TECHNICAL UNIVERSITY

Iževskij Gosudarstvennyj Tekhničeskij Universitet (ISTU)

ul. Studenčeskaja 7, Iževsk, 426069 Udmurtskaja Respublika
Tel: +7(3412) 585-338
Fax: +7(3412) 588-852
Website: http://www.istu.ru/

Rector: Boris Yakimovich Fax: +7(3412) 585-358

Vice-Rector: Alexander Elenskiy
Tel: +7 (3412) 588-852 EMail: disso@istu.ru

International Relations: Ella Sosnovich, Head
Tel: +7(3412) 592-555, Fax: +7(3412) 592-555
EMail: inter@istu.ru

Faculties

Advanced Technologies and Automobiles (Automotive Engineering; Chemical Engineering; Chemistry; Materials Engineering; Mechanical Equipment and Maintenance; Metal Techniques; Metallurgical Engineering; Robotics; Technology) *Dean*: Yuri Puzanov; **Advertising and Design** (Advertising and Publicity; Design; Graphic Design; Industrial Design; Technology) *Dean*: Mikhail Chernykh; **Applied Mathematics** *Dean*: Ivan Rusyak; **Civil Engineering** (Architecture; Building Technologies; Civil Engineering; Construction Engineering; Economics; Geological Engineering; Mechanics) *Dean*: Grigory Pervushin; **Computer Science** (Automation and Control Engineering; Computer Engineering; Computer Science; Data Processing; Economics; Information Technology; Safety Engineering; Software Engineering) *Dean*: Mikhail Senilov; **Economics, Law and Humanities** (Administration; Arts and Humanities; Cultural Studies; Economics; English; French; German; Law; Linguistics; Management; Philosophy; Political Sciences; Public Administration; Social Psychology; Sociology) *Dean*: Rail Galiakhmetov; **Engineering Pedagogics** (Engineering; Pedagogy) *Dean*: Yury Shikhov; **Heat Engineering** (Heating and Refrigeration; Power Engineering; Water Management) *Dean*: Valeriy Didenko; **Instrumentation Engineering** (Electrical Engineering; Instrument Making; Laser Engineering; Radio and Television Broadcasting; Safety Engineering; Telecommunications Engineering) *Dean*: Yury Demakov; **Management and Marketing** (Accountancy; Banking; Business and Commerce; Economics; Finance; Industrial and Production Economics; Management; Marketing; Technology) *Dean*: Alexey Shchenyatskiy; **Mechanical Engineering** (Automotive Engineering; Machine Building; Mechanical Engineering; Mechanics) *Dean*: Yury Bryzgalov; **Postgraduate Education** (Accountancy; Aeronautical and Aerospace Engineering; Automotive Engineering; Civil Engineering; Computer Engineering; Computer Graphics; Computer Networks; Computer Science; Data Processing; Economics; Finance; Heating and Refrigeration; Human Resources; Information Management; Instrument Making; Maintenance Technology; Management; Power Engineering; Production Engineering; Safety Engineering; Technology Education; Telecommunications Engineering) *Dean*: Yury Turygin; **Quality Management** *Dean*: Viktor Klekovkin; **Sports** (Sports; Sports Management; Sports Medicine) *Dean*: Ildus Gibadullin

Further Information: Also branches in Votkinsk, Sarapul, Tčaikovsky, Glazov and Kambarka

History: Founded 1952 as Institute, acquired present status 1993.

Governing Bodies: Academic Board

Academic Year: September to July (September-January; February-July)

Admission Requirements: Secondary school certificate (Svidetelistvo o srednem obrazovanii)

Fees: (US Dollars): c. 1,300 per annum; postgraduate students, c. 2,500

Main Language(s) of Instruction: Russian

Degrees and Diplomas: *Bakalavr*: 4 yrs; *Specialist Diploma*: 5 yrs; *Magistr*: a further 2 yrs; *Kandidat Nauk*: a further 3 yrs by thesis; *Doktor Nauk*: by thesis

Student Services: Canteen, Cultural centre, Foreign student adviser, Health services, Nursery care, Sports facilities

Student Residential Facilities: Yes (Hostels)

Special Facilities: Sports Camp on Kama River

Libraries: over 730,000 vols

Publications: Vestnik ISTU *(quarterly)*

Press or Publishing House: Publishing House of ISTU

Academic Staff *2008-2009*	**TOTAL**
FULL-TIME	**850**
PART-TIME	**150**
STAFF WITH DOCTORATE	
FULL-TIME	**500**
PART-TIME	c. **100**
Student Numbers *2008-2009*	
All (Foreign Included)	c. **23,500**
FOREIGN ONLY	**70**

Distance students, 7,450. **Evening students**, 1,850.

Last Updated: 24/11/08

JAKUTSK STATE ACADEMY OF AGRICULTURE

Jakutskaja Gosudarstvennaja Sel'skohozjajstvennaja Akademija

ul. Krasil'nikova, 15, Jakutsk, 677891 Respublika Saha (Jakutija)
Tel: +7(4112) 257-993
Fax: +7(4112) 257-813
EMail: yagsha@mail.sakha.ru
Website: http://www.agrocademy.com

Rector: Leonid Vladimirov

Programmes

Agriculture (Agriculture)

JAROSLAVL STATE ACADEMY OF AGRICULTURE

Jaroslavskaja Gosudarstvennaja Sel'skohozjajstvennaja Akademija

Tutaevskoje Sosse 58, Jaroslavl 150042
Tel: +7(4852) 56-80-25 +7(4852) 98-51-53
Fax: +7(4852) 56-80-25
EMail: info@yaragrovuz.ru
Website: http://yaragrovuz.ru/

Rector: Petr Dugin

Faculties

Economics (Accountancy; Agricultural Business; Economics; Information Technology; Mathematics); **Engineering** (Agricultural Engineering; Agricultural Equipment; Machine Building; Maintenance Technology); **Technology** (Agricultural Equipment; Agriculture; Agrobiology; Agronomy; Biotechnology; Ecology; Plant and Crop Protection; Veterinary Science; Zoology)

History: Created 1977.

Degrees and Diplomas: *Bakalavr*, *Specialist Diploma*

Last Updated: 17/01/12

JAROSLAVL STATE INSTITUTE OF THEATRE

Jaroslavskij Gosudarstvennyj Teatralnyj Institut

ul. Pervomaiskaja 43, Jaroslavl 150000
Tel: +7(4852) 31-41-14 +7(4852) 30-75-69
Fax: +7(4852) 72-81-11
EMail: admin@theatrins-yar.ru
Website: http://www.theatrins-yar.ru/

Rector: Sergei Filippovich Kutsenko

Departments

Music Education (Music; Music Education); **Puppet Theatre** (Theatre); **Theatre** (Acting; Theatre)

History: Created 1980.

Degrees and Diplomas: *Bakalavr*, *Specialist Diploma*

Last Updated: 27/01/12

JAROSLAVL STATE MEDICAL ACADEMY

Jaroslavskaja Gosudarstvennaja Medicinskaja Akademija

ul. Revoljucionnaja 5, Jaroslavl 150000
Tel: +7(4852) 305-641
Fax: +7(4852) 729-142
EMail: rector@yma.ac.ru
Website: http://www.yma.ac.ru/

Rector: Aleksej Vladimirovich Pavlov

Faculties

Medicine (Medicine); **Paediatric Medicine** (Paediatrics); **Pharmacy** (Pharmacology; Pharmacy); **Stomatology** (Dentistry; Stomatology)

Institutes

Postgraduate Education

History: Founded 1944.

Degrees and Diplomas: *Specialist Diploma*: 5-6 yrs

Last Updated: 10/11/11

JAROSLAVL STATE PEDAGOGICAL UNIVERSITY

Jaroslavskij Gosudarstvennyj Pedagogičeskij Universitet (YSPU)

ul. Respublikanskaja 108, Jaroslavl 150000
Tel: +7(4852) 305-661
Fax: +7(4852) 305-112
EMail: rector@yspu.yar.ru
Website: http://www.yspu.yar.ru

Rector: Vladimir Afanasyev (1989-)

Vice-Rector: Viktor Vlasov
Tel: +7(4852) 305-671 EMail: vlasov@yspu.yar.ru

International Relations: Mihail Novikov
Tel: +7(4852) 305-596, Fax: +7(4852) 305-596
EMail: novikov@yspu.yar.ru

Faculties

Defectology (Child Care and Development; Education; Education of the Handicapped; Educational Psychology) *Dean*: Mihail Kalugin; **Foreign Languages** (Foreign Languages Education; Modern Languages) *Dean*: Lidia Afanasyeva; **History** (Education; History; Teacher Trainers Education) *Dean*: Andrey Sokolov; **History and Geography** (Geography; History) *Dean*: Nikolai Runov; **Pedagogy** (Education; Educational Sciences; Pedagogy; Teacher Trainers Education) *Dean*: Lev Zaytsev; **Physical Culture and Sports** (Education; Physical Education; Sports; Teacher Trainers Education) *Dean*: Alexander Vikulov; **Physics and Mathematics** (Education; Mathematics; Physics; Teacher Trainers Education) *Dean*: Elena Žohova; **Russian Philology and Culture** (Cultural Studies; Philology; Russian) *Dean*: Albert Vasilevsky; **Social Management** *(Special Faculty)* (Management; Social Sciences; Social Work) *Dean*: Andrei Simanovsky

Institutes

Pedagogy and Psychology (Educational Psychology; Pedagogy; Psychology) *Director*: Mihail Rožkov

History: Founded 1908, acquired present status and title 1995.

Governing Bodies: University and Faculty Councils

Academic Year: September to June

Admission Requirements: Secondary school certificate (Attestat o srednem obrazovanii) and entrance examination

Fees: (US Dollars): 600 per semester

Main Language(s) of Instruction: Russian

International Co-operation: Participates in TACIS and DAAD international exchange programmes

Accrediting Agencies: Ministry of Education

Degrees and Diplomas: *Bakalavr*: 4 yrs; *Specialist Diploma*: 5 yrs; *Magistr*: a further 2 yrs

Student Services: Academic counselling, Canteen, Foreign student adviser, Health services, Language programs, Sports facilities

Student Residential Facilities: Yes

Special Facilities: Museum; Observatory; Video Studio; Computer and Sound Laboratories

Libraries: c. 1,2 m. vols

Publications: Sbornik Naučnyč Trudov Molodyh Učenyh (Collection of Scientific Works by Young Scientists), For higher education specialists *(annually)*; Tesisy Dokladov Vystuplenii na Konferentsii Pamyati K.D. Ušinskogo (Summaries of Reports at the Conference Dedicated to K.D. Ushinsky), For higher education specialists *(annually)*; Yaroslavsky Pedagogičesky Vestnik (Yaroslavl Pedagocial Messenger), For higher education specialists and school teachers *(quarterly)*

JAROSLAVL STATE TECHNICAL UNIVERSITY

Jaroslavskij Gosudarstvennyj Tehničeskij Universitet

Moskovskij prosp. 88, Jaroslavl 150053
Tel: +7(4852) 44-87-93 +7(4952) 44-07-21
Fax: +7(4852) 44-87-93
EMail: rector@ystu.ru; krainovaa@ystu.ru; fishelsonnf@ystu.ru
Website: http://www.ystu.ru/

Rector: Aleksandr Anatolevich Lomov

Faculties
Architecture and Construction (Architecture; Construction Engineering); **Automobile Engineering** (Automotive Engineering); **Chemical Technology** (Chemical Engineering; Physical Chemistry; Polymer and Plastics Technology); **Engineering Economics** (Applied Mathematics; Business Computing; Economics; Engineering Management; Information Sciences; Management); **Humanities** (History; Modern Languages; Philosophy; Political Sciences; Sports); **Mechanical Engineering** (Machine Building; Mechanical Engineering)

History: Created 1944.

Degrees and Diplomas: *Bakalavr*; *Specialist Diploma*; *Magistr*
Last Updated: 27/01/12

JUGRA STATE UNIVERSITY

Jugorskij Gosudarstvennyj Universitet
ul. Chekhova, 16, Khanty-Mansijsk, 628012 Tjumenskaja oblast', Khanty-Mansijskij avt. okrug-Jugra
Tel: +7(3467) 35-75-04 +7(3467)35-77-32
Fax: +7(3467) 35-77-67
EMail: ugrasu@ugrasu.ru
Website: http://www.ugrasu.ru/

Rector: Tat'jana Dmitrievna Karminkskaja

Institutes
Environmental Studies (Applied Chemistry; Chemistry; Ecology; Environmental Management; Environmental Studies; Geology; Geophysics); **Humanities** (Journalism; Law; Linguistics; Native Language; Philology; Social Work); **Management and Economics** (Accountancy; Banking; Economic History; Finance; Management; Taxation; Tourism); **Management Systems and Information Technology** (Applied Mathematics; Business Computing; Computer Engineering; Information Technology; Management Systems); **Polytechnic** (Building Technologies; Chemistry; Civil Engineering; Industrial Engineering; Maintenance Technology; Physics; Transport Engineering; Transport Management)

History: Created 2001.

Degrees and Diplomas: *Bakalavr*; *Specialist Diploma*; *Magistr*
Last Updated: 16/03/12

KABARDINO-BALKARIAN STATE AGRICULTURAL ACADEMY NAMED AFTER V.M. KOKOV

Kabardino-Balkarskaja Gosudarstvennaja Sel'skohozjajstvennaja Akademija im. V.M. Kokova
prosp. Lenina 1b, Nalčik 360030
Tel: +7(8662) 47-41-77 +7(8662) 40-66-65
Fax: +7(8662) 47-12-74 +7(8662) 40-66-65
EMail: info@kbsaa.ru
Website: http://www.kbsha.ru/

Rector: Boris Hažmuratovič Žerukov (1981-)

Faculties
Accountancy and Auditing (Accountancy); **Agronomy** (Agronomy); **Animal Husbandry** (Animal Husbandry); **Commerce and Trade** (Business and Commerce); **Economics** (Agricultural Economics; Agricultural Management; Economics); **Finance** (Business Computing; Economics; Finance; Management); **Food Technology** (Food Technology); **Humanities** (Arts and Humanities; History; Modern Languages; Philosophy; Physical Education); **Landscape Planning** (Landscape Architecture); **State and Municipal Management** (Administration; Human Resources; Management); **Veterinary Science** (Veterinary Science)

History: Founded 1981, acquired present status and title 1995.

Academic Year: September to June (September-December; February-June)

Admission Requirements: Secondary school certificate (Attestat o srednem obrazovanii)

Main Language(s) of Instruction: Russian

Degrees and Diplomas: *Bakalavr*; *Specialist Diploma*; *Magistr*; *Kandidat Nauk*

Student Services: Academic counselling, Canteen, Cultural centre, Health services, Social counselling, Sports facilities

Special Facilities: Biological Garden. Experimental Farm
Last Updated: 27/01/12

KABARDINO-BALKARIAN STATE UNIVERSITY

Kabardino-Balkarskij Gosudarstvennyj Universitet
ul. Černiševskogo 173, Nalčik 360004
Tel: +7(8662) 4225-60
Fax: +7(8662) 4225-62
Website: http://www.kbsu.ru

Rector: Barasby Sulejmanovic Karamurzov (1994-)

Administrative Officer: Hazesha Talievich Taov
Tel: +7(8662) 42-52-58

International Relations: Barasby Sulejmanovic Karamurzov
Fax: +7(095) 3379-955

Colleges
Communal Constructing *Head*: Resuan Gisovich Bekulov; **Design** *Head*: Svetlana Mahtievna Kozuhovskaya; **Medical** *Head*: Hadezhda Hakimovna Deppueva; **Pedagogy** *Head*: Nina Harunovna Baichikueva; **Polytechnic** *Head*: Anatoly Muhamedovich Nartokov; **Statistics, Economics and Informational Technologies** *Head*: Rosa Aleksandrovna Harchenko

Faculties
Applied Mathematics and Control Systems (Applied Mathematics; Automation and Control Engineering) *Dean*: Michail Hasanbievich Abregov; **Biology** (Biology) *Dean*: Safarbi Hasanbievich Shchagapsoev; **Chemistry** (Biology; Chemistry) *Dean*: Muhamed Husenovich Ligidov; **Economics** (Economics) *Dean*: Rita Vanoevna Gurfova; **Engineering and Constructing** *Dean*: Umar Danjalovich Batirov; **History** (History); **Information and Management** *Dean*: Yurri Kalimetovich Tlostanov; **Law** (Law) *Dean*: Angela Zaurbievna Dolova; **Medicine** (Medicine) *Dean*: Ruslan Maksidovich Zahohov; **Microelectronics and Computer Technologies** (Computer Science; Microelectronics) *Dean*: Ruslan Shahbanovich Teshev; **Pedagogy** *Dean*: Artur Zhabagievich Nasipov; **Physical Culture and Sports** (Physical Education; Sports) *Dean*: Alsan Oskerhanovich Kozhemov; **Physics** (Physics) *Dean*: Anatoly Akhubekov

Institutes
Philology (English; French; German; Russian; Slavic Languages) *Dean*: Rashid Sultanovich Alikaev; **Social - Humanity Studies** (History; Service Trades; Social Work; Tourism) *Dean*: Hamitbi Borisovich Mamsirov; **Upgrading Qualifications** *Head*: Svetlana Muhamedovna Tohova

History: Founded 1957 on the basis of a Pedagogical Institute, established 1932.

Governing Bodies: Academic Council

Academic Year: September to June (September-January; February-June)

Admission Requirements: Secondary education certificate (Attestat o srednem obrazovanii) and entrance examination

Fees: None

Main Language(s) of Instruction: Russian

International Co-operation: Spain; Hungary; Japan; Ukraine; Turkey; Syria; Jordan; USA; Pakistan; South Korea; Denmark

Degrees and Diplomas: *Specialist Diploma*: 5 yrs; *Kandidat Nauk*: a further 3 yrs and thesis; *Doktor Nauk*: by thesis after Kandidat

Student Residential Facilities: Yes

Special Facilities: Biological Garden

Libraries: c. 200,000 vols

Publications: Scientific Transactions

KALININGRAD INSTITUTE OF LAW OF THE MINISTRY OF INTERNAL AFFAIRS OF RUSSIA

Kaliningradskij Juridičeskij Institut MVD Rossii
Moskvskij prosp. 8, Kaliningrad 236006
Tel: +7(4012) 46-18-02 +7(4012) 46-24-06
Fax: +7(4012) 46-18-02
EMail: postmaster@ptskl.baltnet.ru
Website: http://www.klimvd.ru/

Rector: Vitalij Mikhailovich Bocharov

Programmes
Law (Law)

History: Created 1953.

Degrees and Diplomas: *Specialist Diploma*

Last Updated: 27/01/12

KALININGRAD STATE TECHNICAL UNIVERSITY

Kaliningradskij Gosudarstvennyj Tekhničeskij Universitet (KSTU)

Sovietskij prospect 1, Kaliningrad 236022

Tel: +7(4012) 595-201

EMail: rector@klgtu.ru

Website: http://www.klgtu.ru

Rector: Viktor Evgen'evic Ivanov Fax: +7(4012) 916-846

International Relations: Anatoly Zagorodniy
Tel: +7(4012) 595-226, Fax: +7(4012) 595-226
EMail: zag@klgtu.ru

Faculties
Biological Resources and Use of Nature *Dean*: Konstantin Tylik; **Commercial Fishery** *Dean*: Gennadiy Dolin; **Economics** *Dean*: Victor Murov; **Fundamental Sciences** (Applied Mathematics; Chemistry; Mathematics; Physics) *Dean*: Gorbatchev; **Humanities** (Arts and Humanities; Cultural Studies; English; German; History; Law; Modern Languages; Pedagogy; Russian; Social Sciences; Spanish; Sports) *Dean*: Oleg Arkhangelsky; **Mechanics and Technology** *Dean*: Vladimir Erlichman; **Naval and Power Engineering** (Civil Engineering; Electrical Engineering; Heating and Refrigeration; Marine Engineering; Power Engineering) *Dean*: Boris Pimenov; **Production Automation and Control** *Dean*: Alexander Kogan; **Upgrading** (Continuing Education) *Dean*: Vladimir Pukhov

Institutes
European Klaus Mehnert (Cultural Studies; Economics; English; European Studies; European Union Law; French; German; International Relations; Political Sciences; Russian; Social Policy) *Director*: Anatoliy Zagorodniy

History: Founded 1930 as State Technical Institute for Fisheries and Economy in Moscow. Became Kaliningrad State Technical Institute for Fishery Industry and Economy in Kaliningrad. Acquired present status and title 1994.

Governing Bodies: Scientific Council

Academic Year: September to June (September-December; February-June)

Admission Requirements: Secondary School Certificate

Main Language(s) of Instruction: Russian

International Co-operation: 65 cooperation agreements

Degrees and Diplomas: *Bakalavr*: 4 yrs; *Specialist Diploma*: 5-5 1/2 yrs; *Magistr*: 1 1/2-2 yrs. Also professional retraining and professional upgrading certificate

Student Services: Academic counselling, Canteen, Cultural centre, Employment services, Foreign student adviser, Foreign Studies Centre, Health services, Language programs, Nursery care, Social counselling, Sports facilities

Special Facilities: Historical Museum with the Art gallery; Hydro biological Museum; Ichthyologic Museum

Libraries: 500,000 vols

Academic Staff *2007-2008*	**TOTAL**
FULL-TIME	**1,200**
Student Numbers *2007-2008*	
All (Foreign Included)	**7,000**
FOREIGN ONLY	**160**

Last Updated: 27/11/08

KALMIC STATE UNIVERSITY

Kalmyckij Gosudarstvennyj Universitet (KSU)

ul. Puškina 11, Elista Kalmikija-Halmg 358000

Tel: +7(84722) 534-31

Fax: +7(84722) 537-29

EMail: uni@kalmsu.ru

Website: http://www.kalmsu.ru

Rector: German M. Borlikov

Faculties
Agriculture (Agriculture); **Biology** (Biology); **Philology** (Philology); **Physics and Mathematics** (Mathematics; Physics)

History: Founded 1970.

Governing Bodies: Academic Council

Academic Year: September to July

Admission Requirements: Secondary education certificate (Attestat o srednem obrazovanii) and entrance examination

Fees: None

Degrees and Diplomas: *Specialist Diploma*: 5 yrs; *Kandidat Nauk*: a further 3 yrs and thesis; *Doktor Nauk*: by thesis after Kandidat

KALUGA STATE PEDAGOGICAL UNIVERSITY NAMED AFTER K. CIOLKOVSKY

Kalužskij Gosudarstvennyj Pedagogičeskij Universitet im. K. Ciolkovskogo (KSPU)

ul. Stepan Razin 26, Kaluga 248023

Tel: +7(0842) 576-120

Fax: +7(0842) 571-078

EMail: rector@kspu.kaluga.ru

Website: http://www.kspu.kaluga.ru

Rector: Vladimir Alekseevich Lyitkin

Secretary-General: Natalja Bedlinskaja

International Relations: Ljubov Mejanikova

Centres
Medical Psychology (Psychology)

Faculties
Biology and Chemistry (Biology; Chemistry; Ecology; Geography) *Kandidat*: Tamara Ilchenko; **Education** (Education; Primary Education); **Engineering and Pedagogics** (Engineering; Physical Education; Technology) *Kandidat*: Irina Kaznacheeva; **Foreign Languages** (English; French; German; Modern Languages) *Kandidat*: Elena Shchoseva; **History** (History; Social Sciences) *Kandidat*: Maxim Kazak; **Philology** (Literature; Philology; Russian) *Kandidat*: Lyudmila Alekseeva; **Physics and Mathematics** (Mathematics; Physics) *Kandidat*: Anatoliy Kulikov; **Primary Education** *Kandidat*: Nina Shtreker; **Psychology** (Psychology) *Kandidat*: Irina Krasnoshchochenko

Institutes
Social Relations *Kandidat*: Olga Lytkina

Further Information: Also Research Centres

History: Founded 1786 as National School, reorganized as Pedagogical Institute 1948, and acquired present status and title 1994.

Governing Bodies: Scientific Council

Academic Year: September to June (September-January; February-June)

Admission Requirements: Secondary school certificate (Attestat o srednem obrazovanii)

Main Language(s) of Instruction: Russian

Degrees and Diplomas: *Bakalavr*: 4-5 yrs; *Specialist Diploma*: 5 yrs; *Specialist Diploma*: Teaching, 3 yrs; *Magistr*: 6 yrs

Special Facilities: History of the University Museum

Libraries: c. 550,500 vols

Publications: Scientific Papers *(annually)*

Press or Publishing House: Publishing Department

KAMCHATKA STATE TECHNICAL UNIVERSITY

Kamčatskij Gosudarstvennyj Tekhničeskij Universitet

ul. Ključevskaja 35, Petropavlovsk-Kamčatskij, 683003 Kamčatskij Kraj

Tel: +7(4152) 30-09-33

Fax: +7(4152) 42-05-01

EMail: kamchatgtu@kamchatgtu.ru

Website: http://www.kamchatgtu.ru

Rector: Aleksandr Jakovlevich Isakov

Faculties
Economics and Management (Accountancy; Economics; Management); **Fisheries** (Aquaculture; Ecology; Environmental Management; Fishery; Water Management); **Information Technology** (Applied Mathematics; Computer Science; Information Technology; Physics); **Naval Engineering** (Heating and Refrigeration; Marine Engineering; Marine Transport; Naval Architecture)

History: Created 1987 as Petropavlovsk-Kamčatskoje Vyssee Inženernoe Morskoe Učilišče (Petropavlovsk-Kamchatskij School of Naval Engineering). Acquired current title and status 2000.

Degrees and Diplomas: *Bakalavr*, *Specialist Diploma*
Last Updated: 27/02/12

KAMCHATKA STATE UNIVERSITY NAMED AFTER VITUS BERING

Kamčatskij Gosudarstvennyj Universitet im. Vitusa Beringa (VBKSU)

ul. Pogranichnaja 4, Petropavlovsk-Kamčatskij, 683032 Kamčatskij Kraj
Tel: +7(4152) 433-743
Fax: +7(4152) 410-833
EMail: kgpu@kamgpu.ru
Website: http://www.kamgpu.ru/

Rector: Marina V. Sushchova (1992-)

International Relations: Elena B. Vesna EMail: vesna@kamgpu.ru

Faculties
Advanced Professional Training *Dean*: Melaniya V. Kuzmina; **Extra-mural Studies** (Ecology; Education; History; Literature; Psychology; Russian) *Dean*: Galina Y. Akhmatova; **Foreign Languages** (Education; Foreign Languages Education; Translation and Interpretation) *Dean*: Irene N. Hohlova; **Philology** (Education; Journalism; Literature; Native Language; Philology; Russian) *Dean*: Natalya G. Iyinskaja; **Physics and Mathematics** (Computer Education; Education; Geography; Geology; Geophysics; Mathematics Education; Physics) *Dean*: Anatoliy A. Ustinov; **Psychology** (Cultural Studies; Education; Psychology) *Dean*: Elena V. Prozorova; **Social Studies** (Economics; Education; Geography; History) *Dean*: Dmitry V. Chaplygin

History: Founded 1958 as Kamchatka Teachers Training Institute. Previously known as Kamčatskij Gosudarstvennyj Pedagogičeskij Universitet (Kamčatka State University of Education). Acquired present title and status in 2005

Academic Year: September to June

Admission Requirements: Secondary school certificate (Attestat o srednem obrazovanii)

Fees: (Russian Rubles): 16,000 - 27,000 per annum

Main Language(s) of Instruction: Russian

International Co-operation: With universities in Japan, China, Korea, USA, Germany, United Kingdom and France.

Degrees and Diplomas: *Specialist Diploma*: Foreign Languages; History and Geography; Mathematics and Computer Science; Psychology; Russian Language and Literature; Translation and Interpreting; Psychology; French; Tourism; Computer Sciences, 5 yrs

Student Services: Academic counselling, Canteen, Cultural centre, Employment services, Foreign student adviser, Health services, Language programs, Sports facilities

Special Facilities: Movie Studio; Museum; Internal TV network; Music Studio

Libraries: c. 480,000 vols

Publications: KRASEC Journal, Collection of scientific works of Kamchatka Regional Association of Scientific-Educational Centres *(biennially)*

KAMSK STATE ACADEMY OF ENGINEERING AND ECONOMICS

Kamskaja Gosudarstvennaja Inženerno-Ekonomičeskaja Akademija (INEKA)

prosp. Mira 68/19, Naberežnje Čelny, 423810 Respublika Tatarstan
Tel: +7(8552) 39-71-40 +7(8552) 39-71-37
Fax: +7(8552) 39-59-72 +7(8552) 38-34-39
EMail: ineka@ineka.ru; umo@ineka.ru
Website: http://www.ineka.ru/

Rector: Vladimir Georgievich Shabakov EMail: shibakov@ineka.ru

Faculties
Automation and Advanced Technologies (Machine Building; Metallurgical Engineering); **Automotive Engineering** (Automotive Engineering; Design; Electrical and Electronic Engineering; Food Technology; Hydraulic Engineering; Interior Design; Machine Building; Maintenance Technology; Transport Engineering); **Building** (Building Technologies; Civil Engineering; Industrial Engineering; Road Engineering; Road Transport; Safety Engineering); **Economics** (Accountancy; Advertising and Publicity; Economics; Finance; Management; Marketing; Public Relations; Transport Management)

Further Information: Branch also in Chistopol'.

History: Created 1980 as Kamskij Gosudarstvennyj Politehničeskij Institut (Kamsk State Polytechnic Institute). Acquired current title and status 2001.

Degrees and Diplomas: *Bakalavr*, *Specialist Diploma*; *Magistr*
Last Updated: 27/01/12

KARACHAEVO-CHERKESSK STATE INSTITUTE OF TECHNOLOGY

Karačaevo-Čerkesskij Gosudarstvennyj Tehnologičeskij Institut

ul. Stavropolskaja 36, Čerkessk 369000
Tel: +7(8782) 29-35-01 +7(8782) 29-35-03 +7(8782) 29-35-32
Fax: +7(8782) 29-35-32
EMail: pk_kchgta@kchgta.ru
Website: http://www.kchgta.ru/

Rector: Askerbij Dzhiraslanovich Mambetov
EMail: rector@kchgta.ru

Faculties
Fine Arts and Design (Environmental Studies; Fashion Design; Landscape Architecture)

Institutes
Agriculture (Agriculture; Production Engineering; Veterinary Science); **Applied Mathematics and Information Technology** (Applied Mathematics; Computer Science; Information Technology; Modern Languages); **Construction and Electrical Engineering** (Construction Engineering; Electrical Engineering; Information Technology); **Economics** (Accountancy; Economics; Finance; Psychology; Taxation); **Industrial Engineering** (Automotive Engineering; Ecology; Industrial Engineering; Machine Building; Physics); **Management** (Management; Marketing); **Medicine** (Medicine)

History: Created 1971 as Karačaevo-Čerkessk National Institute of Technology. Became Karačaevo-Čerkesskij Gosudarstvennyj Tehnologičeskij Institut (Karachaevo-Cherkessk State Institute of Technology). Acquired current title and status 2003.

Degrees and Diplomas: *Bakalavr*, *Specialist Diploma*
Last Updated: 27/01/12

KARACHAEVO-CHERKESSK STATE UNIVERSITY NAMED AFTER U.D. ALIEV

Karačaevo-Čerkesskij Gosudarstvennyj Universitet im. U.D. Alieva

ul. Lenina 29, Karačaevsk 369202
Tel: +7(87879) 2-20-13
Fax: +7(87879) 2-80-68
EMail: kcsu@mail.ru
Website: http://kchgu.ru/

Rector: Burkhan Njurchukovich Tambiev

Faculties
Arts and Graphic Design (Art Education; Crafts and Trades; Design; Fine Arts; Graphic Arts; Landscape Architecture; Painting and Drawing); **Economics and Management** (Accountancy; Business Computing; Economics; Finance; Management); **History** (History); **Music Education** (Conducting; Music; Music Education; Singing); **Natural Sciences and Geography** (Biology; Chemistry; Ecology; Education; Geography; Humanities and Social Science Education; Science Education); **Philology** (German; Journalism; Literature; Native Language; Philology; Russian); **Physical**

Education (Physical Education; Sports; Tourism); **Physics and Mathematics** (Applied Mathematics; Computer Education; Computer Science; Mathematics; Mathematics Education; Physics; Science Education); **Psychology** (Educational Psychology; Psychology)

History: Founded in 1940, acquired present status and title 1994. Formerly Karačaevo-Čerkesskij Gosudarstvennyj Pedagogičeskij Universitet.

Academic Year: September to July

Admission Requirements: Secondary school certificate (Attestat o srednem obrazovanii)

Main Language(s) of Instruction: Russian

Degrees and Diplomas: *Bakalavr*, *Specialist Diploma*; *Magistr*

Last Updated: 27/01/12

KARELIAN STATE PEDAGOGICAL ACADEMY

Karel'skaja Gosudarstvennaja Pedagogičeskaja Akademija

ul. Puškinskaja, 17, Petrozavodsk, 185680 Respublika Karelija
Tel: +7(8142) 78-30-29 +7(8412) 78-05-41
Fax: +7(8142) 78-30-29
EMail: rector@kspu.karelia.ru
Website: http://kspu.karelia.ru/

Rector: Sergey Pavlovich Grippa EMail: grippa@kspu.karelia.ru

Faculties

Foreign Languages (English; Finnish; French; German); **History and Philology** (History; Literature; Philology; Russian); **Natural Sciences and Geography** (Biology; Chemistry; Ecology; Geography; Science Education; Zoology); **Physical Education** (Physical Education; Sports); **Physics and Mathematics** (Computer Networks; Mathematics; Mathematics Education; Physics; Science Education); **Preschool Education** (Preschool Education); **Primary Education** (Mathematics Education; Native Language Education; Primary Education; Science Education); **Psychology** (Educational Psychology; Psychology); **Technology** (Art Education; Design; Fine Arts; Home Economics Education; Industrial Arts Education; Technology)

History: Founded 1931, acquired title of Karelskij Gosudarstvennyj Pedagogičeskij Universitet (Karelian State Pedagogical University) and status 1996. The Faculty has been training social workers since 1999. Acquired current title and status 2004.

Governing Bodies: Academic Council

Academic Year: September to June

Admission Requirements: Secondary school certificate (Attestat o srednem obrazovanii) and three entrance examinations

Fees: None

Main Language(s) of Instruction: Russian

International Co-operation: With universities in Finland, Sweden, USA, France

Degrees and Diplomas: *Bakalavr*, *Specialist Diploma*

Student Services: Academic counselling, Canteen, Cultural centre, Health services, Social counselling, Sports facilities

Student Residential Facilities: Yes

Special Facilities: Museum. Centre for New Information Technologies. TV Studio

Libraries: Central Library, 465,000 vols

Last Updated: 06/04/12

KAZAN (VOLGA REGION) FEDERAL UNIVERSITY

Kazanskij (Privolžskij) Federalnyj Universitet (KFU)

ul. Kremlyovskaya 18, Kazan, 420008 Tatarstan
Tel: +7(8432) 92-76-00
Fax: +7(8432) 92-74-18
EMail: inter@ksu.ru
Website: http://www.ksu.ru

Rector: Ilshat Rafkatovich Gafurov (2010-)
Tel: +7(8432) 92-69-77, Fax: +7(8432) 92-44-48
EMail: rector@ksu.ru

President: Myakzyum Salakhov
Tel: +7(8432) 33-79-34, Fax: +7(8432) 92-44-48
EMail: Myakzyum.Salakhov@ksu.ru

International Relations: Andrei Krylov, Head of International Office
Tel: +7(8432) 38-73-21, Fax: +7(8342) 92-74-18
EMail: Andrei.Krylov@ksu.ru

Faculties

Biology and Soil Science (Agricultural Education; Biochemistry; Biology; Genetics; Microbiology; Molecular Biology; Physiology); **Economics** (Business Education; Economics; Management; Private Administration; Public Administration); **Journalism and Sociology** (Humanities and Social Science Education; Journalism; Media Studies; Multimedia; Radio and Television Broadcasting; Sociology); **Law** (Administrative Law; Civics; Civil Law; Commercial Law; Comparative Law; Constitutional Law; Criminal Law; European Union Law; Fiscal Law; History of Law; Human Rights; International Law; Labour Law; Law; Private Law; Public Law)

Institutes

Chemistry *(A.Butlerov)* (Analytical Chemistry; Applied Chemistry; Chemistry; Inorganic Chemistry; Organic Chemistry; Physical Chemistry); **Finance and Economics** (Accountancy; Banking; Finance; Taxation); **Geography and Ecology** (Environmental Management; Geography; Meteorology; Surveying and Mapping; Tourism); **Geology and Oil and Gas Technology** (Geochemistry; Geological Engineering; Geology; Geophysics); **History** (Art History; History; Museum Studies); **Mathematics and Information Technologies** (Applied Mathematics; Computer Education; Computer Science; Information Management; Information Technology; Statistics); **Mechanics and Mathematics** *(N.Lobachevsky)* (Mathematics; Mathematics Education; Mechanics); **Pedagogy and Psychology** (Educational Psychology; Psychology; Social Psychology; Teacher Training); **Philology and Arts** *(Tatar Languages)* (Applied Linguistics; Art Education; English; Foreign Languages Education; Grammar; Music Education; Native Language; Philology; Phonetics; Russian; Spanish; Translation and Interpretation); **Physical Culture, Sports and Regenerative Medicine** (Physical Education; Physical Therapy; Rehabilitation and Therapy); **Physics** (Astronomy and Space Science; Astrophysics; Atomic and Molecular Physics; Mathematical Physics; Nuclear Physics; Optics; Physics; Radiophysics; Solid State Physics; Thermal Physics)

History: Founded 1804 as Kazan State University. Acquired current title and status 2010. The main centre of higher education for a vast Volga Region (Povolzhskii Federal District). Created on the basis of Kazan State University, Tatar State University of Humanities and Education, Kazan State Finance and Economics Institute, and Yelabuga State University of Education.

Governing Bodies: Rector; Academic Council; Supervisory Council; Board of Trustees

Academic Year: Sept to Feb; Feb to June. (July-Aug – summer holidays, no regular classes, only Russian language summer schools for overseas students.)

Admission Requirements: Russian students, the results of the Unified State Exam; for international students, secondary school diploma and secondary school examination results. For all categories of students the results in basic subjects for the certificate of secondary education or USE are expected to be equal to no less than 80% of the maximum grade attainable.

Fees: (RUB): 60,000 per annum

Main Language(s) of Instruction: Russian

International Co-operation: With institutions in Germany, China, Korea, Japan, Spain, Finland, Belgium, USA

Accrediting Agencies: Ministry of Higher Education

Degrees and Diplomas: *Bakalavr*: 4 yrs; *Specialist Diploma*: 5 yrs; *Magistr*: a further 2 yrs after Bakalavr; *Kandidat Nauk*: a further 3 yrs following Specialist's Diploma; *Doktor Nauk*

Student Services: Academic counselling, Canteen, Cultural centre, Foreign student adviser, Health services, Language programs, Social counselling, Sports facilities

Student Residential Facilities: 11 dormitories for c. 9,000 students. Well-equipped, new infrastructure, wireless communication

Special Facilities: Museums : University History; Zoology; Geology; Ethnography; Archaeology. Observatory. Computer Service

Libraries: 4 librarues, c. 5m. vols

Academic Staff *2009-2010*	MEN	WOMEN	TOTAL
FULL-TIME	–	–	**2,894**
PART-TIME	–	–	**704**
STAFF WITH DOCTORATE			
FULL-TIME	–	–	**2,144**
Student Numbers *2009-2010*			
All (Foreign Included)	13,444	27,999	**41,443**
FOREIGN ONLY	266	389	**655**

Part-time students, 14,240. **Evening students**, 728.
Last Updated: 20/05/11

KAZAN INSTITUTE OF THE MINISTRY OF INTERNAL AFFAIRS OF RUSSIA

Kazanskij Juridičeskij Institut MVD RF
Orenburgskij trakt, 128, Kazan, 420059 Tatarstan
Tel: +7(843) 277-80-77 +7(843) 278-93-50
Fax: +7(843) 570-27-05
EMail: kuitatarstan@mail.ru
Website: http://www.kuimvd.ru/

Rector: Foat Kanafievich Zinnurov

Programmes

Law (Commercial Law; Criminology; Justice Administration; Law; Police Studies)

History: Founded 1974. Acquired present status and title 1999.

Governing Bodies: Ministry of Internal Affairs

Academic Year: September to July

Admission Requirements: Secondary school certificate

Main Language(s) of Instruction: Russian

International Co-operation: None

Accrediting Agencies: None

Degrees and Diplomas: *Bakalavr*; *Specialist Diploma*

Student Services: Academic counselling, Canteen, Cultural centre, Health services, Language programs, Sports facilities

Student Residential Facilities: 22 rooms

Special Facilities: Museum

Libraries: 5 libraries

Publications: Collection of Scientific Works *(annually)*

Last Updated: 17/01/12

KAZAN STATE ACADEMY OF VETERINARY MEDICINE NAMED AFTER N.E. BAUMAN

Kazanskaja Gosudarstvennaja Akademija Veterinarnoj Meditsiny im. N.E. Baumana
Sibirskij trakt 35, Kazan, 420074 Tatarstan
Tel: +7(843) 273-96-46 +7(843) 273-97-14
Fax: +7(843) 273-97-14 +7(843) 273-97-84
EMail: study@ksavm.senet.ru
Website: http://www.ksavm.senet.ru

Rector: Galimzjan Fazylzjanovich Kabirov

Faculties

Biotechnology (Animal Husbandry; Biotechnology; Zoology); **Veterinary Medicine** (Veterinary Science)

History: Founded 1873, acquired present title 1995.

Governing Bodies: Academic Council; Scientific Council

Academic Year: September to June (September-January; February-June)

Admission Requirements: Secondary school certificate (Attestat o srednem obrazovanii)

Main Language(s) of Instruction: Russian

Degrees and Diplomas: *Specialist Diploma*

Last Updated: 27/01/12

KAZAN STATE AGRARIAN UNIVERSITY

Kazanskij Gosudarstvenij Agrarnij Universitet (KSAU)
ul. Karla Marksa, 65, Kazan, 420015 Tatarstan
Tel: +7(843) 2366-522
Fax: +7(843) 2366-651
EMail: info@ksha.ru
Website: http://www.kazgau.ru

Rector: Dzhaudat Faizrakhmanov

Pro-rector: Larisa Tinchurina
Tel: +7(843) 236-6752 EMail: ltinchurina@mail.ru

International Relations: Olga Shmeleva
Tel: +7 (843) 236-6471, Fax: +7 (843) 236-6471
EMail: olga.ksha@mail.ru

Faculties

Agriculture/ Agronomy (Agriculture; Agronomy) *Dean*: Radik Safin; **Forestry and Ecology** (Ecology; Forestry) *Dean*: Aynur Puryaev

Institutes

Economics, Management and Accounting *Director*: Farit Mukhametgaliev; **Mechanization and Technical Service** (Maintenance Technology; Mechanical Equipment and Maintenance) *Director*: Bulat Ziganshin

History: Founded 1922 following the integration of the Agricultural School of Polytechnic Institute and the Forestry School of the Kazan University. Acquired Academy status 1995. Acquired present status and title 2006. Formerly known as Kazanskaja Gosudarstvennaja Sel'skohozjajstvennaja Akademija (Kazan State Academy of Agriculture).

Academic Year: September to August

Admission Requirements: Secondary school certificate; Unified State Examination

Fees: (Russian Rubles): 24,000-40,000 per annum

Main Language(s) of Instruction: Russian

International Co-operation: Academic exchange programmes with the USA, Germany; International internship programmes for Students in the USA, Great Britain, Germany, Netherlands, Sweden, Denmark, Switzerland, Finland, Canada

Accrediting Agencies: Federal State Administration "National accrediting agency in the sphere of education"

Degrees and Diplomas: *Bakalavr*: Agronomy, Forestry and Ecology, Economics and Management, Accounting, Mechanization and Technical Service, 4; *Specialist Diploma*: Agronomy, Forestry and Ecology, Economics and Management, Accounting, Mechanization and Technical Service, 6 yrs

Student Services: Canteen, Cultural centre, Employment services, Health services, Language programs, Nursery care, Social counselling, Sports facilities

Student Residential Facilities: Hostels

Special Facilities: Museum of the University

Libraries: over 400,000 vols

Publications: "Vestnik- Kazan GAU", Scientific Publication *(quarterly)*

Press or Publishing House: None

Academic Staff *2007-2008*	MEN	WOMEN	TOTAL
FULL-TIME	58	77	**135**
PART-TIME	13	5	**18**
STAFF WITH DOCTORATE			
FULL-TIME	127	62	**189**
PART-TIME	23	10	**33**
Student Numbers *2007-2008*			
All (Foreign Included)	3,158	2,200	**5,358**

Part-time students, 3,100. **Distance students**, 2,258.
Last Updated: 10/12/08

KAZAN STATE ENERGETICS UNIVERSITY

Kazanskij Gosudarstvennyj Energetičeskij Universitet
ul. Krasnosel'skaja 51, Kazan, 420066 Tatarstan
Tel: +7(843) 519-42-02
Fax: +7(843) 562-43-25
EMail: kgeu@kgeu.ru
Website: http://www.kgeu.ru/

Acting Rector: Edvard Junusovich Abdullazjanov

Faculties

Power Engineering (Power Engineering)

Institutes

Economics and Social Technology (Cultural Studies; Documentation Techniques; Economics; History; Journalism; Library

Science; Management; Sociology; Technology Education); **Electrical and Electronic Engineering** (Electrical and Electronic Engineering); **Thermal Engineering** (Thermal Engineering)

History: Founded 1967.

Main Language(s) of Instruction: Russian

Degrees and Diplomas: *Bakalavr*; *Specialist Diploma*; *Magistr*

Student Residential Facilities: 1 hostel for 650 students

Last Updated: 27/01/12

KAZAN STATE FINANCE AND ECONOMICS INSTITUTE

Kazanskij Gosudarstvennyj Finansovo-Ekonomičeskij Institut (KSFEI)

ul. Butlerova 4, Kazan, 420012 Tatarstan
Tel: +7(8432) 367-180
Fax: +7(8432) 382-782
EMail: econom@ksfei.ru
Website: http://www.ksfei.ru

Rector: Shamil Valitov (2007-)
Tel: +7(8432) 646-247; +7(8432) 911-310,
Fax: +7(8432) 383-054 EMail: rector@ksfei.ru

Vice-Rector: Ildar Khairoullin

International Relations: Alsu Akhmetshina
Tel: +7(8432) 911-313, Fax: +7(8432) 383-054
EMail: alsu@ksfei.ru

Faculties

Correspondence Education *Dean*: Andrei Dašin; **Economics of Enterprise** (Accountancy; Business Administration; Economics; Labour and Industrial Relations; Management; Marketing) *Dean*: Svetlana Meleshchenko; **Finance and Credit** (Banking; Business Administration; Finance) *Dean*: Kamil Harisov; **General Economics** (Business Administration; Economics; History; Law; Mathematics and Computer Science; Philosophy; Political Sciences; Sociology; Statistics; Technology) *Dean*: Oleg Bodrov; **Management** *Dean*: Milyausha Biktemirova

Research Centres

Retraining Specialists with Higher Education (Business Administration; Management) *Dean*: Valentina Toropova

History: Founded 1931.

Governing Bodies: Academic Board

Academic Year: September to June

Admission Requirements: Secondary school certificate (Attestat o srednem obrazovanii) and entrance examination

Fees: (Russian Rubles): c. 62,200 per annum

Main Language(s) of Instruction: Russian

International Co-operation: DAAD, American Councils' UGRAD Programme, Partnerships with institutions in USA, Sweden and France

Degrees and Diplomas: *Bakalavr*: 4 yrs; *Magistr*: a further 2 yrs; *Kandidat Nauk*: a further 3 yrs by thesis; *Doktor Nauk*: a further 3 yrs by thesis

Student Services: Academic counselling, Canteen, Employment services, Foreign student adviser, Health services, Language programs, Social counselling, Sports facilities

Student Residential Facilities: For 643 students

Special Facilities: Museum

Libraries: c. 350,000 vols

Publications: Vestnik KGFEI, Scientific journal of KGFEI *(quarterly)*

Press or Publishing House: Publishing Department

Academic Staff *2007-2008*	**TOTAL**
FULL-TIME	**642**
Student Numbers *2007-2008*	
All (Foreign Included)	**5,216**
FOREIGN ONLY	**20**

Part-time students, 2,047.

Last Updated: 26/11/08

KAZAN STATE MUSIC CONSERVATORY (ACADEMY)

Kazanskaja Gosudarstvennaja Konservatorija (Akademija) (KSC)

ul. Bolšaja Krasnaja 38, Kazan, 420015 Tatarstan
Tel: +7(843) 236-55-33 +7(843) 236-59-62
Fax: +7(843) 236-56-41
EMail: kgk-dekanat@mail.ru
Website: http://www.kazanconservatoire.ru/

Rector: Rubin Kabirovich Abdoullin EMail: pavana511@gmail.com

Departments

Choir Conducting (Conducting); **Folk Instruments** (Musical Instruments); **Orchestral Music** (Music); **Piano** (Music; Musical Instruments); **Tatar Musical Art** (Music); **Theory and Composition** (Music Theory and Composition); **Vocal Art** (Singing)

History: Founded 1945. Previously known as Kazanskaja Gosudarstvennaja Konservatorija (Kazan State Music Conservatory). Acquired current title and status 2004.

Governing Bodies: University Council

Academic Year: September to June

Admission Requirements: Secondary school certificate (Svidetelstvo) or Diplom from Musical College

Main Language(s) of Instruction: Russian, Tatar

Degrees and Diplomas: *Specialist Diploma*

Last Updated: 27/01/12

KAZAN STATE TECHNICAL UNIVERSITY NAMED AFTER A.N. TUPOLEV

Kazanskij Gosudarstvennyj Tehničeskij Universitet im. A.N. Tupoleva

ul. Karla Marksa 10, Kazan, 420111 Tatarstan
Tel: +7(843) 238-4110
Fax: +7(843) 292-2141
EMail: icd@kai.ru
Website: http://www.kai.ru

Rector: Gennady L. Degtyarev (1987-) Tel: +7(843) 238-4110

International Relations: Ravil R. Agishev

Faculties

Aircraft Engineering (Aeronautical and Aerospace Engineering); **Aircraft Engines** (Aeronautical and Aerospace Engineering); **Automation and Electronic Instruments Making** (Automation and Control Engineering; Electronic Engineering; Instrument Making); **Humanitarian Studies** (Development Studies); **Informatics and Technical Cybernetics** (Automation and Control Engineering; Computer Science); **Management and Business Studies** (Business Administration; Business and Commerce; Management); **Radio Engineering and Telecommunications** (Radiophysics; Telecommunications Engineering)

History: Founded 1932.

Academic Year: September to June

Admission Requirements: Secondary school certificate (Attestat o srednem obrazovanii/Diplom o srednem specialnom obrazovanii)

Fees: (US Dollars): c. 2,000-4,000 per annum

Main Language(s) of Instruction: Russian

Degrees and Diplomas: *Bakalavr*: 4 yrs; *Specialist Diploma*: Engineering, Technology, a further 1 1/2 yrs; *Magistr*: a further 2 yrs; *Kandidat Nauk*: 3 yrs following Bakalavr's; *Doktor Nauk*: 3 yrs following Kandidat

Student Services: Canteen, Cultural centre, Employment services, Foreign Studies Centre, Handicapped facilities, Health services, Social counselling, Sports facilities

Student Residential Facilities: For c. 2,000 students

Special Facilities: University History Museum

Libraries: Scientific Library, c. 1m. vols

Publications: Russian Aeronautics, In Russian and English *(quarterly)*

Press or Publishing House: KSTU Publishing House

KAZAN STATE UNIVERSITY OF ARCHITECTURE AND CIVIL ENGINEERING

Kazanskij Gosudarstvennij Arhitekturno-Stroitelnij Universitet (KGASU)

ul. Zelenaja 1, Kazan, 420043 Tatarstan
Tel: +7(843) 510-46-01
Fax: +7(843) 238-79-72
EMail: rector@ksaba.ru
Website: http://www.ksaba.ru

Rector: Valerij Nikolaevich Kuprijanov (1988-)

Vice-Rector: Vladimir Nikolaevich Suchkov
Tel: +7(843) 510-46-02 EMail: info@ksaba.ru

International Relations: Vera Alekseevna Kuznetsova
Tel: +7(843) 510-46-48 EMail: interksaba@mail.ru

Faculties

Construction (Construction Engineering) *Dean*: Vladimir Sergeevich Agafonkin; **Construction Technology** (Building Technologies) *Dean*: Rashid Kurbangalievič Nizamov; **Correspondence Engineering** (Engineering) *Dean*: Munir Abdullovič Valiullin; **Engineering Systems and Ecology** (Ecology; Engineering Management; Heating and Refrigeration; Water Science) *Dean*: Rais Semigullovich Safin

Institutes

Advanced Training (Design; Heating and Refrigeration) *Director*: Vladimir Nikolaevič Sučkov; **Architecture and Design** (Architectural and Environmental Design; Architecture; Interior Design) *Ditrector*: Yevguenij Mikhailovič Udler; **Economy and Building Management** *Director*: Gulsina Mansurovna Zadigullina; **Transport** (Engineering; Mathematics and Computer Science; Production Engineering; Transport Engineering) *Director*: Aleksander Iosifovich Brechman

History: Founded 1930. Acquired present status and title 2005. Formerly known as Kazanskaja Gosudarstvennaja Arhitekturno-Stroitel'naja Akademija (Kazan State Academy of Architecture and Civil Engineering).

Governing Bodies: Academic Council; Rector

Academic Year: September to June (September-January; February-June)

Admission Requirements: Secondary school certificate or equivalent and admission test

Fees: (Euros): 1,700-2,300 per annum

Main Language(s) of Instruction: Russian, Tatar

International Co-operation: With universities in Israel, USA, Italy, Austria, United Kingdom and Switzerland. Also participates in Fullbright programmes and programmes of the Getty Foundation.

Accrediting Agencies: Federal Educational Agency

Degrees and Diplomas: *Bakalavr*: Architecture, 4 1/2 yrs; *Bakalavr*: Civil Engineering, 4 yrs; *Specialist Diploma*: Architectural and Artistic Specialities, 6 yrs; *Specialist Diploma*: Building Design, 5 1/2 yrs; *Magistr*: Architecture, a further 2 ys; *Magistr*: Civil Engineering, a further 2 yrs; *Kandidat Nauk*: Science

Student Services: Academic counselling, Canteen, Cultural centre, Employment services, Foreign student adviser, Foreign Studies Centre, Handicapped facilities, Health services, Language programs, Nursery care, Social counselling, Sports facilities

Student Residential Facilities: Yes.

Special Facilities: Academy Museum; Research Laboratories; Health Centre; Polyclinic

Libraries: Scientific Library, c. 570,000 vols.

Publications: Collection of Reports at the Republic Scientific and Technological Conference on Architecture and Civil Engineering, Articles by Tatarstan researchers; KGASU News, Journal of Science and Technology *(quarterly)*

Press or Publishing House: KGASU Publishing House

KAZAN STATE UNIVERSITY OF CULTURE AND ARTS

Kazanskaja Gosudarstvennaja Universitet Kul'tury i Iskusstv

Orenburgskij trakt 3, Kazan, 420059 Tatarstan
Tel: +7(8432) 775-836
Fax: +7(8432) 775-907
EMail: info@kazguki.ru
Website: http://www.kazguki.ru

Rector: Rifkat Jusupov (1996-)

Vice-Rector: Tatjana Dunaeva Tel: +7(8432) 375-527

International Relations: Dinara Jusupova

Faculties

Culture and Culture Management (Cultural Studies; Social Studies); **Drama** (Theatre); **Library and Information Sciences** (Information Sciences; Library Science); **Music** (Music)

History: Founded 1969 as a branch of Leningrad Institute of Culture, became independent 1974. Acquired present status and title 1996.

Governing Bodies: Scientific Council

Academic Year: September to June (September-January; February-June)

Admission Requirements: Secondary school certificate (Attestat o srednem obrazovanii), or equivalent (Diplom o srednem specialnom obrazovanii)

Main Language(s) of Instruction: Russian

Degrees and Diplomas: *Specialist Diploma*: 5 yrs; *Kandidat Nauk*: a further 3 yrs

Student Residential Facilities: For c. 450 students

Libraries: c. 130,000 vols

Publications: Proceedings of Scientific Conferences *(annually)*

Press or Publishing House: Grand-Dan

KAZAN STATE UNIVERSITY OF MEDICINE

Kazanskij Gosudarstvennyj Medicinskij Universitet (KSMU)

ul. Butlerova 40, Kazan, 420012 Tatarstan
Tel: +7(8432) 360-652
Fax: +7(8432) 360-393
EMail: rector@kgmu.kcn.ru
Website: http://kcn.ru/tat.ru/education/med.univ/

Rector: Nail Amirov

Vice-Rector: Aleksei Sozinov

International Relations: Irina Karamysheva
Tel: +7(8432) 367-744 EMail: ikaramysheva@hotmail.com

Faculties

Dentistry (Dentistry); **General Medicine** (Medicine; Nursing; Pharmacy; Social and Preventive Medicine; Social Work); **Nursing**; **Paediatrics** (Paediatrics); **Pharmacy**

History: Founded 1814, acquired present status 1995.

Academic Year: September to July

Admission Requirements: Secondary school certificate (Attestat o srednem obrazovanii) and entrance examination

Main Language(s) of Instruction: Russian; English (courses for foreign students)

Accrediting Agencies: Ministry of Education and Ministry of Health

Degrees and Diplomas: *Specialist Diploma*: 5-7 yrs

Student Services: Canteen, Cultural centre, Foreign Studies Centre, Health services, Language programs, Social counselling, Sports facilities

Student Residential Facilities: Yes

Special Facilities: University Museum

KAZAN STATE UNIVERSITY OF TECHNOLOGY

Kazanskij Gosudarstvennyj Tekhnologičeskij Universitet

ul. Karla Marksa 68, Kazan, 420015 Tartastan
Tel: +7(8432) 365-768
Fax: +7(8432) 365-768
EMail: oms@kstu.ru
Website: http://www.oms.kstu.ru/

Rector: Sergei G. Diakonov (1988-)
Tel: +7(8432) 314-202, Fax: +7(8432) 314-202
EMail: office@kstu.ru

Vice-Rector: German Diakonov
Tel: +7(8432) 367-534, Fax: +7(8432) 367-534
EMail: guerman@kstu.ru

Institutes
Chemical and Oil Engineering (Energy Engineering; Mechanical Engineering; Wood Technology) *Head*: Valery Alayev; **Control, Automation and Software Technologies** (Automation and Control Engineering; Computer Engineering; Electrical Engineering) *Head*: Victor Fafurin; **Food Technology and Biotechnologies** *Head*: Minsagir Nurtdinov; **Light Industry, Fashion and Design Technology** *Head*: Ludmila Abutalipova; **Management, Economics, Law and Humanitarian and Social Sciences** (Economics; Management; Social Work) *Head*: Nailia Valeeva; **Oil and Chemistry** *Head*: German S. Diakonov; **Polymer Studies** *Head*: Alexandr Kochnev

History: Founded 1890 as Kazan Industrial School. Became Kazan Polytechnic Institute 1919, Kazan Chemical Institute 1930 and Kazan Institute of Chemical Engineering 1933. Acquired current title and status 1992.

Governing Bodies: University Council

Academic Year: September to June (September-January; February-June)

Admission Requirements: Undergraduate: Attestat o Srednem Obshchem Obrazovanii (secondary school certificate) or equivalent; For Doctor Nauk, candidates must hold a Kandidat Nauk degree

Main Language(s) of Instruction: Russian

Accrediting Agencies: Ministry of Education and Science

Degrees and Diplomas: *Bakalavr*: 4 yrs; *Specialist Diploma*: 5-5.5 yrs; *Magistr*: a further 2 yrs; *Doktor Nauk*: High-molecular Compounds; Physical Chemistry; Technology of Organic Substances; Theory and Methods of Professional Training, 3 yrs following on from Kandidat Nauk

Student Services: Academic counselling, Canteen, Cultural centre, Employment services, Foreign student adviser, Foreign Studies Centre, Health services, Language programs, Nursery care, Social counselling, Sports facilities

Libraries: c. 2m. vols

Publications: Vestnik KSTU, Research by university scientists *(biennially)*

KEMEROVO STATE AGRICULTURAL INSTITUTE

Kemerovskij Gosudartsvennyj Sel'skokhozajstvennyj Institut (KEMGAKI)

ul. Markovtseva, 5, Kemerovo 650056
Tel: +7(3842) 73-76-56 +7(3842) 73-43-59
Fax: +7(3842) 73-40-23
EMail: ksai@ksai.ru
Website: http://www.ksai.ru/

Rector: Viktor I. Mjalenko EMail: rector@ksai.ru

Faculties
Agricultural Technology (Agricultural Equipment; Agronomy; Animal Husbandry; Botany; Crop Production; Ecology; Soil Science; Veterinary Science; Zoology); **Economics** (Accountancy; Business Computing; Economics; Finance; Information Technology); **Engineering** (Agricultural Engineering; Maintenance Technology; Mechanical Equipment and Maintenance; Mechanics; Transport Management); **Pedagogy** (Arts and Humanities; Biology; Chemistry; History; Modern Languages; Physical Education; Science Education)

History: Created 1982 as Kemerovo branch of Novosibirsk Agricultural Institute. Acquired current title and status 2002.

Degrees and Diplomas: *Bakalavr*, *Specialist Diploma*

Last Updated: 30/01/12

KEMEROVO STATE MEDICAL ACADEMY

Kemerovskaja Gosudarstvennaja Medicinskaja Akademija (KEMSMA)

ul. Vorošilov 22-a, Kemerovo 650029
Tel: +7(3842) 73-48-56 +7(3842) 73-48-55
Fax: +7(3842) 73-48-56 +7(3842) 73-48-55
EMail: kemsma@kemsma.ru
Website: http://www.kemsma.ru

Rector: Valeryij Mikhailovich Ivoilov EMail: rector@kemsma.ru

Faculties
Dentistry (Dentistry) *Dean*: Oleg Aleksejevich Shevchenko; **Medicine** (Medicine) *Dean*: Yurij Ivanovich Burago; **Paediatrics** (Paediatrics) *Dean*: Galina Petrovna Torochkina; **Pharmacy** (Pharmacy) *Dean*: Vadim Vasiljevich Shkarenda; **Preventive Medicine** (Social and Preventive Medicine) *Dean*: Yelena Vladimirovna Kos'kina

History: Founded 1956, acquired present title 1995.

Governing Bodies: Academic Council

Academic Year: September to June (September-January; February-June)

Admission Requirements: Secondary school certificate (Attestat o srednem obrazovanii)

Main Language(s) of Instruction: Russian

Accrediting Agencies: Ministry of Education

Degrees and Diplomas: *Specialist Diploma*

Student Services: Academic counselling, Canteen, Employment services, Health services, Nursery care, Social counselling, Sports facilities

Student Residential Facilities: For c. 1,600 students

Special Facilities: Museum of the History of KEMSMA

Libraries: 400,948 vols

Press or Publishing House: Publishing Department

Last Updated: 17/01/12

KEMEROVO STATE UNIVERSITY

Kemerovskij Gosudarstvennyj Universitet

ul. Krasnaja 6, Kemerovo 650043
Tel: +7(3842) 583-912
EMail: rector@kemsu.ru; inter@kemsu.ru
Website: http://www.kemsu.ru

Rector: Irina Al'bertovna Sviridova EMail: rector@kemsu.ru

Campuses
Anžero-Sudženskk (Economics; Information Sciences; Law; Mathematics; Pedagogy); **Belovo** (Accountancy; Economics; Finance; History; Law; Psychology); **Novokuznetsk** (Ecology; Economics; History; Information Technology; Law; Mathematics; Modern Languages; Natural Sciences; Philosophy; Physical Education; Psychology; Tourism); **Prokopevsk** (Administration; Management; Modern Languages; Physical Education; Psychology; Social Welfare; Sports); **Yurga** (Accountancy; Economics; Information Technology; Law; Physical Education; Sports; Taxation)

Faculties
Biology (Biology; Botany; Ecology; Genetics; Natural Sciences; Physiology; Zoology); **Chemistry** (Analytical Chemistry; Chemistry; Inorganic Chemistry; Organic Chemistry; Physical Chemistry); **Economics** (Banking; Economics; Finance; International Economics; Management; Marketing; Taxation); **History and International Relations** (Archaeology; History; International Relations; Modern Languages); **Law** (Administrative Law; Constitutional Law; Criminal Law; Criminology; Labour Law; Law; Philosophy; Private Law; Public Law); **Mathematics** (Mathematics; Mathematics and Computer Science); **Philology and Journalism** (Folklore; Journalism; Linguistics; Literature; Philology; Russian); **Physics** (Physics); **Political Science and Sociology** (Economics; Political Sciences; Sociology); **Romance and German Philology** (English; French; German; Romance Languages; Translation and Interpretation); **Sociology and Psychology** (Psychology; Social Work; Sociology); **Sports and Physical Education** (Physical Education; Sports)

Further Information: Also Russian language courses for foreign students; Study Abroad programmes

History: Founded 1954, acquired present status and title 1974.

Governing Bodies: Academic Council

Academic Year: September to July (September-January; February-July)

Admission Requirements: Secondary education certificate (Attestat o srednem obrazovanii) and entrance examination

Main Language(s) of Instruction: Russian

Degrees and Diplomas: *Bakalavr*, *Specialist Diploma*: 5 yrs; *Magistr*, *Kandidat Nauk*: a further 3 yrs and thesis; *Doktor Nauk*: by thesis following Kandidat Nauk

Student Services: Academic counselling, Canteen, Cultural centre, Foreign Studies Centre, Health services, Sports facilities

Student Residential Facilities: For c. 4,900 students

Special Facilities: Museums: Archaeology; Zoology; History of Kuzbass Party Organization. Astronomy Complex. University Radio System. University TV System

Libraries: Scientific Library, 1m. vols

Last Updated: 11/04/11

KEMEROVO STATE UNIVERSITY OF CULTURE AND ARTS

Kemerovskij Gosudarstvennyj Universitet Kul'tury i Iskusstv (KEMGUKI)

ul. Voroshilova 17, Kemerovo 650029

Tel: +7(3842) 732-808

Fax: +7(3842) 732-808

EMail: tvorchestvo2006@mail.ru

Website: http://www.art.kemerovonet.ru/

Rector: Ekaterina Kudrina (1995-) Tel: +7(3842) 732-967

Vice-Rector: Marina Povarich Tel: +7(3842) 732-983

International Relations: Valery Ponomaryov Tel: +7(3842) 734-599

Faculties

Cultural Studies (Cultural Studies; Graphic Design; Leisure Studies; Management; Museum Management; Social and Community Services) *Dean*: Natalia Puvljuck; **Dance Education** (Dance) *Dean*: Galina Feshkova; **Information Technology** *Dean*: Galina Bragina; **Musical Art** (Conducting; Jazz and Popular Music; Music; Music Theory and Composition; Musical Instruments; Performing Arts; Singing) *Dean*: Olga Guseva; **Producing and Acting Arts** (Acting; Dance; Photography; Radio and Television Broadcasting; Visual Arts) *Dean*: Lyudmila Udovitskaja

History: Founded 1970 as Institute of Culture, became Institute of Arts and Culture 1994, Academy of Culture and Arts in 1994. Acquired present title 2004.

Governing Bodies: Academic Council

Academic Year: September to June

Admission Requirements: Secondary school certificate (Attestat o srednem obrazovanii) and entrance examination

Fees: (Russian Rubles): Up to 20,000 for 3% of full-time students; up to 15,000 for 25% distance students. Free for most students.

Main Language(s) of Instruction: Russian

Degrees and Diplomas: *Bakalavr*: Musical Instruments, 3 yrs; *Specialist Diploma*: 5 yrs; *Kandidat Nauk*: Philosophy and Cultural Studies; Social and Cultural Studies; Museum Studies; Information Technology and Librarianship, a further 3 yrs

Student Services: Academic counselling, Canteen, Cultural centre, Health services, Language programs, Nursery care, Social counselling, Sports facilities

Student Residential Facilities: For 950 students

Special Facilities: Museum. Art Gallery. Video Studio. Concert Hall

Libraries: Central Library, 268,282 vols

Publications: Cultural Studies *(annually)*

KEMEROVO TECHNOLOGICAL INSTITUTE OF FOOD INDUSTRY

Kemerovskij Tehnologičeskij Institut Piščevoj Promyšlennosti

bul. Stroitelej 47, Kemerovo 650056

Tel: +7(3842) 73-40-40 +7(3842) 73-42-16

Fax: +7(3842) 39-68-81

EMail: office@kemtipp.ru

Website: http://www.kemtipp.ru

Rector: Vladimir Petrovich Justratov (1993-)
EMail: rector@kemtipp.ru

Faculties

Economics (Cooking and Catering; Economics; Hotel and Restaurant; Industrial and Production Economics); **Mechanics** (Automation and Control Engineering; Engineering; Food Technology; Heating and Refrigeration; Mechanics; Technology); **Technology** (Food Science; Food Technology; Meat and Poultry)

History: Founded 1972.

Governing Bodies: Council, comprising 47 members

Academic Year: September to June (September-January; February-June)

Admission Requirements: Certificate of secondary education (Attestat o srednem obrazovanii)

Main Language(s) of Instruction: Russian

Accrediting Agencies: Department of Accreditation and Licensing of Ministry of Education

Degrees and Diplomas: *Bakalavr*; *Specialist Diploma*; *Magistr*; *Kandidat Nauk*; *Doktor Nauk*

Student Services: Academic counselling, Canteen, Cultural centre, Handicapped facilities, Health services, Nursery care, Social counselling, Sports facilities

Student Residential Facilities: For c. 2,000 students

Libraries: Scientific Libraries, total, c. 590,000 vols

Last Updated: 16/01/12

KHAKASSIJAN STATE UNIVERSITY NAMED AFTER N.F. KATANOV

Khakasskij Gosudarstvennyj Universitet im. N.F. Katonova (KSU)

prosp. Lenina 92, Abakan 655017

Tel: +7(3902) 24-30-18 +7(3902) 22-40-43

Fax: +7(3902) 24-33-64 +7(3902) 22-40-43

EMail: univer@khsu.ru; anjushin@inbox.ru

Website: http://www.khsu.ru

Rector: Ol'ga Vladimirovna Shtygasheva

Colleges

Agriculture (Accountancy; Agronomy; Building Technologies; Fishery; Veterinary Science; Zoology); **Medicine** (Medicine); **Music** (Conducting; Music Education; Musical Instruments; Singing); **Pedagogical Education, Computer Science and Law** (Archiving; Computer Science; Law; Pedagogy; Preschool Education; Primary Education)

Institutes

Arts (Fine Arts; Music Education); **Computer Science and Telematics** (Computer Engineering; Information Management; Information Sciences; Information Technology; Software Engineering); **Continuing Pedagogical Education** (Pedagogy; Preschool Education; Primary Education; Psychology); **Economics and Management** (Accountancy; Economics; Finance; Management); **History and Law** (History; Law); **Medicine, Psychology and Social Sciences** (Medicine; Psychology; Social Sciences); **Natural Sciences and Mathematics** (Biology; Botany; Chemistry; Civil Security; Ecology; Environmental Studies; Mathematics; Mathematics Education; Physics; Zoology); **Philology** (Germanic Languages; Journalism; Literature; Philology; Romance Languages; Russian); **Sajan-Altay Turkology** (Literature; Native Language); **Service and Design Technologies** (Technology)

History: Founded 1939, acquired present status and title 1994.

Governing Bodies: University Council

Academic Year: September to June (September-December; February-June)

Admission Requirements: Secondary school certificate (Attestat o srednem obščem obrazovanii) or equivalent (Diplom o srednem profesionalom obrazovanii)

Main Language(s) of Instruction: Russian

Accrediting Agencies: Federal Agency of Education

Degrees and Diplomas: *Bakalavr*; *Specialist Diploma*; *Magistr*; *Kandidat Nauk*

Student Services: Academic counselling, Canteen, Cultural centre, Employment services, Foreign student adviser, Foreign Studies Centre, Health services, Language programs, Social counselling, Sports facilities

Student Residential Facilities: For 1,000 students

Special Facilities: Archaeology Museum

Libraries: Central Library, c. 815,000 vols

Press or Publishing House: University Publishing House
Last Updated: 17/01/12

KHANTY-MANSIJSK STATE MEDICAL ACADEMY

Khanty-Mansijskaja Gosudarstvennaja Meditsinskaja Akademija

ul. Mira, 40, Khanty-Mansijsk, 628011 Tjumenskaja oblast', Khanty-Mansijskij avt. okrug-Jugra
Tel: +7(467) 32-45-88
Fax: +7(467) 32-45-88
EMail: hmgmi2006@mail.ru
Website: http://www.hmsmi.ru/

Rector: Fedor Igorevich Petrovskij

Programmes

Medical Technology (Laboratory Techniques; Medical Technology); **Medicine** (Medicine); **Nursing** (Midwifery; Nursing)

History: Created 1994.

Degrees and Diplomas: *Specialist Diploma*
Last Updated: 16/03/12

KIROV STATE MEDICAL ACADEMY

Kirovskaja Gosudarstvennaja Medicinskaja Akademija (KSMA)

ul. Karla Marksa 112, Kirov 610027
Tel: +7(8332) 690-976
Fax: +7(8332) 690-734
EMail: ivc@kirovgma.ru
Website: http://www.kirovgma.ru/

Rector: Igor Sheshunov (2003-)

First Pro-Rector: Oleg Lavrov

International Relations: Vladimir Golovin
Tel: +7(8332) 693-208 EMail: golovin_vladimir@list.ru

Faculties

Food Expertise and Economics (Food Science; Food Technology; Nutrition) *Dean*: Nikolai Odintsov; **Further Professional Training for Medical Practioners** (Anaesthesiology; Cardiology; Dermatology; Immunology; Medicine; Neurology; Oncology; Ophthalmology; Paediatrics; Psychiatry and Mental Health; Radiology; Surgery) *Dean*: Anatoly Kislichko; **Internal Medicine** *(Affiliated Faculty also in Syktyvkar)* (Gynaecology and Obstetrics; Rehabilitation and Therapy; Surgery; Traditional Eastern Medicine) *Dean*: Sergey Ashikhmin; **Paediatrics** (Paediatrics) *Dean*: Vladimir Belyakov; **Pre-school Education** *(subjects required for entry into KSMA)* (Anatomy; Biology; Chemistry; Computer Science; Cultural Studies; English; French; German; Latin; Physics; Physiology) *Dean*: Vladimir Kudryavtsev; **Social Work and Nursing** (Aesthetics; Anthropology; Comparative Sociology; Demography and Population; Developmental Psychology; Economics; Ethics; Ethnology; Family Studies; Foreign Languages Education; History; Industrial and Organizational Psychology; Management; Mathematics; Natural Sciences; Nursing; Pedagogy; Philosophy; Psychology; Social Policy; Social Work; Sociology; Statistics; Women's Studies) *Dean*: Marina Zlokazova

History: Founded 1987 as Perm State Medical Institute, reorganized as Kirov State Medical Institute 1993, and acquired present status and title 1999.

Governing Bodies: Scientific Council; Central Methodological Council; Rector's Advisory Board

Academic Year: September to June

Admission Requirements: Secondary school certificate (Attestat ob obrazovanii) and entrance examination

Fees: (US Dollars): 1,800-2,000 for foreign students; no tuition fees for Russian students

Main Language(s) of Instruction: Russian

Accrediting Agencies: Ministry of Health; Ministry of Education

Degrees and Diplomas: *Specialist Diploma*: Internal Medicine; Paediatrics, 6 yrs; *Specialist Diploma*: Sociology and Social Work, 5 yrs. Also postgraduate Certificates that confirm clinical qualification of practical physicians, surgeons, anesthesiologists and specialists. One-year internships courses for all graduates and two-year residency courses for Internal Medicine graduates

Student Services: Academic counselling, Canteen, Cultural centre, Foreign student adviser, Foreign Studies Centre, Health services, Language programs, Nursery care, Sports facilities

Student Residential Facilities: For c. 700 students

Special Facilities: Anatomy Museum; Museum of the Committee of International Relations; Bekhterev Museum

Libraries: c. 140,000 vols; audio-visual library

Publications: Journal of Vyatka Medicine *(quarterly)*

KOMI STATE PEDAGOGICAL INSTITUTE

Komi Gosudarstvennyj Pedagogičeskij Institut

ul. Kommunističeskaja 25, Syktyvkar 167982
Tel: +7(8212) 214-481 +7(8212) 24-30-20 +7(8212) 21-46-14
Fax: +7(8212) 214-481
EMail: kgpi@kgpi.ru
Website: http://www.kgpi.ru/

Rector: Mikhail Dimitriovich Kitaigorodskij (2011-)

Faculties

Foreign Languages (English; French; German); **Geography and Biology** (Anatomy; Biology; Geography; Physiology; Zoology); **Mathematics and Physics** (Computer Science; Mathematics; Physics); **Pedagogy and Primary Education** (Education; Educational Psychology; Native Language Education; Pedagogy; Preschool Education; Primary Education; Special Education; Speech Therapy and Audiology); **Philology** (Cultural Studies; Literature; Native Language; Russian); **Technology and Business** (Agricultural Engineering; Agricultural Equipment; Business Education; Computer Engineering; Electrical and Electronic Equipment and Maintenance; Machine Building; Maintenance Technology; Mechanical Engineering; Road Transport; Technology Education)

History: Created 1931.

Degrees and Diplomas: *Bakalavr*; *Specialist Diploma*
Last Updated: 30/01/12

KOMSOMOL'SK-ON-AMUR STATE TECHNICAL UNIVERSITY

Komsomol'skij-na-Amure Gosudarstvennyj Techničeskij Universitet

prosp. Lenina 27, Komsomol'sk-na-Amure, 681013 Khabarovskaja oblast'
Tel: +7(42172) 323-04
Fax: +7(42172) 361-50
EMail: office@knastu.ru
Website: http://www.knastu.ru

Rector: Jury Kabaldin

Faculties

Aircraft and Naval Engineering (Aeronautical and Aerospace Engineering; Marine Engineering); **Civil Engineering** (Civil Engineering); **Distance Education**; **Electrical Engineering** (Electrical Engineering); **Market Economics** (Economics); **Mechanical Engineering** (Mechanical Engineering)

KOSTROMA STATE ACADEMY OF AGRICULTURE

Kostromskaja Gosudarstvennaja Sel'skohozjajstvennaja Akademija (KSAA)

p/o Karavaevo-1, Kostroma, 157930 Kostromskaja oblast'
Tel: +7(0942) 541-263
Fax: +7(0942) 543-423
EMail: mobot@ksaa.edu.ru
Website: http://www.ksaa.edu.ru

Rector: Vladimir Il'ich Vorob'ev

Vice-Rector: Galina Nikolaevna Sharlamova
Tel: +7(0942) 541-203

International Relations: Vadim Mironovich Ignatov

Centres

Cattle Breeding (Animal Husbandry; Cattle Breeding)

Faculties

Agricultural Business (Agricultural Business); **Architecture and Building** (Architecture; Building Technologies); **Economics** (Economics); **Farm Automation** (Automation and Control Engineering); **Farm Mechanization** (Agricultural Equipment); **Veterinary Science** (Veterinary Science)

Laboratories

Flax (Crop Production)

Further Information: Also 2 Experimental Farms

History: Founded 1949, acquired present status and title 1994.

Academic Year: October to July (October-January; February-July)

Admission Requirements: Secondary school certificate (Attestat o srednem obrazovanii) or equivalent

Main Language(s) of Instruction: Russian

Degrees and Diplomas: *Specialist Diploma*: 5 yrs; *Kandidat Nauk*: a further 3 yrs

Student Services: Academic counselling, Canteen, Cultural centre, Employment services, Health services, Nursery care, Social counselling, Sports facilities

Student Residential Facilities: For c. 640 students

Special Facilities: History of the Academy Museum. Students' Theatre. Film Studio

Libraries: Total, c. 447,600 vols

Publications: Kostroma State Academy Collection of Works

Press or Publishing House: Publishing House

KOSTROMA STATE UNIVERSITY NAMED AFTER N.A. NEKRASOV

Kostromskoj Gosudarstvennyj Universitet im. N.A. Nekrasova

ul. 1st May 14, Kostroma, 156601 Kostromskaja oblast'

Tel: +7(4942) 31-82-91

Fax: +7(4942) 31-13-22

EMail: ksu@ksu.edu.ru

Website: http://ksu.edu.ru/

Rector: Nikolay M. Rassadin (1990-)

Faculties

Foreign Languages (English; French; German); **Graphic Art** (Art Education; Fine Arts); **History** (History; Philosophy; Political Sciences); **Law** (Law); **Music Education** (Music Education; Singing); **Natural Sciences** (Biomedicine; Botany; Chemistry; Geography; Zoology); **Pedagogy and Psychology** (Educational Technology; Pedagogy; Primary Education; Social Psychology; Social Work; Special Education); **Philology** (Folklore; Journalism; Literature; Native Language; Philology; Russian); **Physical Education** (Physical Education; Sports); **Physics and Mathematics** (Applied Mathematics; Computer Science; Information Sciences; Information Technology; Mathematics; Physics); **Technology and Services** (Small Business; Technology; Technology Education)

Institutes

Economics (Accountancy; Business Computing; Economics; Finance; Management; Marketing)

Further Information: Branches in Kirovsk, Shar'ja.

History: Established 1949 as Kostroma State Teacher Training Institute; 1994 became Kostroma State Teacher Training University; acquired present title 1999.

Governing Bodies: Academic Council

Academic Year: September to June

Admission Requirements: Attestat o Srednem (Polnom) Obshchem Obrazovanii and entrance examination

Main Language(s) of Instruction: Russian

International Co-operation: With Germany, Czech Republic, Poland

Accrediting Agencies: National Accreditation Agency of Russia, Federal Service for Supervision in Education and Science

Degrees and Diplomas: *Bakalavr*; *Specialist Diploma*; *Magistr*; *Kandidat Nauk*

Student Services: Academic counselling, Canteen, Cultural centre, Employment services, Foreign student adviser, Foreign Studies Centre, Health services, Language programs, Social counselling, Sports facilities

Student Residential Facilities: Yes

Libraries: yes

Press or Publishing House: Publishing House of Kostroma State University

Last Updated: 17/01/12

KOSTROMA STATE UNIVERSITY OF TECHNOLOGY

Kostromskoj Gosudarstvennyj Tehnologičeskij Universitet (KSTU)

ul. Dzeržinskogo 17, Kostroma, 156005 Kostromskaja oblast'

Tel: +7(0942) 314-814

Fax: +7(0942) 317-008

EMail: info@kstu.edu.ru

Website: http://www.kstu.edu.ru

Rector: Wladyslav N. Krotov (2000-) EMail: rector@kstu.edu.ru

Vice-Rector: Andrei P. Bolotney
Tel: +7(0942) 312-550 EMail: vicerector@kstu.edu.ru

International Relations: Viktor P. Kalashnik, Vice-Rector
Tel: +7(0942) 578-398, Fax: +7(0942) 578-398
EMail: inter@kstu.edu.ru

Centres

Arts (Arts and Humanities) *Head*: Tatjana A. Jelshina; **Business** (Business and Commerce) *Director*: Lubov A. Bekeneva; **New Information Technologies** (Information Technology) *Director*: Oleg J. Tolstov

Departments

Scientific Research (Natural Sciences) *Head*: Rostislav V. Korabelnikov

Faculties

Automated Systems and Technologies (Automation and Control Engineering; Computer Science; Information Management; Technology) *Dean*: Vladimir G. Drozdov; **Evening and Distance Education** (Accountancy; Administration; Automation and Control Engineering; Clothing and Sewing; Economics; Government; Industrial Management; Law; Machine Building; Production Engineering; Textile Technology) *Dean*: Anatoly I. Suljatjev; **Forestry Engineering** (Forestry; Wood Technology) *Dean*: Vladimir P. Čulkov; **Humanities** *Dean*: Albina I. Evstratova; **Industrial Economics** (Accountancy; Administration; Banking; Commercial Law; Economics; Finance; Government; Industrial Management) *Dean*: Margarita I. Berkovič; **Mechanical Engineering** (Graphic Design; Machine Building; Materials Engineering; Mechanical Engineering) *Dean*: Vladimir A. Sadov; **Technology** (Clothing and Sewing; Technology; Textile Design; Textile Technology; Weaving) *Dean*: Valerii A. Tyagunov

Further Information: Also courses for foreign students

History: Founded 1932 as Textile Institute, acquired present status and title 1995.

Governing Bodies: Council

Academic Year: September to June (September-January; February-June)

Admission Requirements: Secondary education certificate (Attestat o srednem obrazovanii)

Main Language(s) of Instruction: Russian

Degrees and Diplomas: *Bakalavr*: 4 yrs; *Specialist Diploma*: Engineering, Technology, a further 1 yr; *Magistr*: a further 1-2 yrs; *Kandidat Nauk*: Technical Sciences, a further 2-3 yrs; *Doktor Nauk*: a further 2 yrs

Student Services: Canteen, Cultural centre, Foreign student adviser, Foreign Studies Centre, Health services, Nursery care, Social counselling, Sports facilities

Student Residential Facilities: For 1,360 students

Special Facilities: Museum of the Institute's History. Movie and Video Studio

Libraries: University Library, c. 500,000 vols

Publications: Research Notes on Problems Linked to Russian Flax

Press or Publishing House: Publishing Department

KOVROV STATE ACADEMY OF TECHNOLOGY NAMED AFTER V.A. DEGTJAREV

Kovrovskaja Gosudarstvennaja Tehnologičeskaja Akademija im. V.A. Degtjareva (KGTA)

ul. Majakovskogo 19, Kovrov, 601910 Vladimirskaja oblast'
Tel: +7(49232) 3-14-81 +7(49232) 5-36-69 +7(49232) 3-21-60
Fax: +7(49232) 3-21-60 +7(49232) 3-14-81
EMail: ksta@dksta.ru; karekt@kc.ru; vsp@dksta.ru
Website: http://www.dksta.ru/

Rector: Dimitrij Yurevich Poljanskij

Faculties
Automation and Electronics (Automation and Control Engineering; Computer Science; Electronic Engineering; Instrument Making; Measurement and Precision Engineering; Robotics); **Economics and Management** (Economics; Industrial and Organizational Psychology; Industrial Management; Management); **Mechanical Engineering** (Automotive Engineering; Computer Engineering; Computer Networks; Machine Building; Mechanical Engineering); **Physics and Technology** (Ecology; Environmental Management; Hydraulic Engineering; Laser Engineering; Optical Technology; Physics; Safety Engineering)

History: Founded 1952 as branch of Vladimir Polytechnic Institute. Reorganized as Krovov Technological Institute 1991. Acquired present status and title 1996.

Governing Bodies: Scientific Council

Academic Year: September to June

Admission Requirements: Secondary school certificate (Attestat o srednem obrazovanii)

Main Language(s) of Instruction: Russian

Degrees and Diplomas: *Bakalavr*, *Specialist Diploma*; *Magistr*

Special Facilities: History Museum of the Academy; Museum of Small Arms.

Libraries: Central Library, c. 147,000 vols (including 10,600 vols of Scientific Literature and 2,700 vols of Foreign Issues); Library of Orthodox Literature
Last Updated: 30/01/12

KRASNODAR MUNICIPAL MEDICAL INSTITUTE OF HIGHER NURSING EDUCATION

Krasnodarskij Municipalnij Medicinskij Institut Vysšego Sestrinskogo Obrazovanija

Ul. Komsomolskaja 46, Krasnodar 350063
Tel: +7(861) 262-4522
Fax: +7(861) 262-4522
EMail: inso@mail.ru
Website: http://www.kmmivso.com

Rector: Konstantin V. Shapovalov EMail: dek2007@yandex.ru

Secretary of Scientific Union: Erik K. Arutjunov
Tel: +7(861) 262-5123

International Relations: Valentina A. Sokol
Tel: +7(861) 262-2089

Programmes
Nursing (Nursing) *Dean*: Urij Borisov
History: Founded 1991. Acquired present status 1996.

Governing Bodies: Rector; Prorector; Deans

Admission Requirements: School Certificate and Entrance Examination (in Russian Language and Biology)

Fees: (Russian Rubles): 26,000 per annum. (US Dollars): c. 1,000

Main Language(s) of Instruction: Russian

Accrediting Agencies: Ministry of Education and Science of the Russian Republic

Degrees and Diplomas: *Specialist Diploma*: Nursing, 5 yrs

Student Services: Academic counselling, Canteen, Cultural centre, Foreign student adviser, Foreign Studies Centre, Health services, Nursery care, Social counselling, Sports facilities

Special Facilities: Museum; Movie Studio; Concert/Meeting Hall

Libraries: Yes. Internet; Electronic Books.

Academic Staff *2007-2008*	MEN	WOMEN	**TOTAL**
FULL-TIME	22	125	**147**
STAFF WITH DOCTORATE			
FULL-TIME	12	9	**21**
PART-TIME	5	–	**5**
Student Numbers *2007-2008*			
All (Foreign Included)	57	900	**957**
FOREIGN ONLY	2	–	**2**

Part-time students, 461. **Distance students**, 300. **Evening students**, 196.
Last Updated: 26/11/08

KRASNODAR STATE UNIVERSITY OF CULTURE AND ARTS

Krasnodarskij Gosudarstvennyj Universitet Kul'tury i Iskusstv

ul. 40 Let Pobedy 33, Krasnodar 350072
Tel: +7(861) 257-76-32 +7(861) 274-22-43
Fax: +7(861) 257-76-32
EMail: kguki@list.ru
Website: http://kguki.info/

Rector: Nikolai Nikolaevich Shadjuk

Academies
Art and Industry (Design; Fine Arts; Graphic Arts; Graphic Design; Interior Design; Painting and Drawing); **Folk Culture** (Dance; Folklore; Music)

Conservatories
Music (Conducting; Music; Music Education; Music Theory and Composition; Musical Instruments; Singing)

Faculties
Advertising (Advertising and Publicity; Marketing); **Broadcasting** (Cinema and Television; Film; Radio and Television Broadcasting); **Cultural Studies** (Cultural Studies); **Economics and Management** (Economics; Management); **Information and Library Science** (Documentation Techniques; Information Sciences; Library Science); **Law** (Administrative Law; Civil Law; Criminal Law; Criminology; Labour Law; Law; Public Law); **Linguistics and Intercultural Communication** (Communication Studies; Linguistics; Modern Languages; Translation and Interpretation); **Music and Humanities** (Conducting; Cultural Studies; Educational Psychology; Music; Musicology); **Theatre Arts** (Acting; Theatre)

History: Founded 1967 as Institute of Culture, acquired present status and title 1993.

Governing Bodies: Academic Council

Academic Year: September to June (September-January; February-June)

Admission Requirements: Secondary school certificate (Attestat o srednem obrazovanii)

Main Language(s) of Instruction: Russian

Degrees and Diplomas: *Bakalavr*, *Specialist Diploma*; *Kandidat Nauk*

Student Services: Academic counselling, Canteen, Cultural centre, Health services, Sports facilities

Special Facilities: Student Theatre

Libraries: 204,380 vols

Press or Publishing House: Press House
Last Updated: 31/01/12

KRASNODAR UNIVERSITY OF THE MINISTRY OF INTERNAL AFFAIRS OF RUSSIA

Krasnodarskij Universitet MVD Rossii

ul. Jaroslavskaja 128, Krasnodar 350005
Tel: +7(861) 258-42-86 +7(861) 258-40-03
Fax: +7(861) 258-42-86
EMail: yimc@krn.mvd.ru
Website: http://www.krdu-mvd.ru/

Rector: Jurij A. Agafonov

Programmes
Computer Science (Business Computing; Computer Networks); **Economics** (Economics); **Law** (Law)

History: Created 2006.

Degrees and Diplomas: *Bakalavr*; *Specialist Diploma*
Last Updated: 02/02/12

KRASNOJARSK STATE ACADEMY OF MUSIC AND ARTS

Krasnojarskaja Gosudarstvennaja Akademija Muzyki i Teatra

ul. Lenina 22, Krasnojarsk 600049
Tel: +7(3912) 233-502 +7(3912) 230-309
Fax: +7(3912) 233-502
Website: http://www.kgamit.narod.ru/

Rector: Konstantin A. Jakobson

Programmes

Fine Arts (Fine Arts); **Music** (Music)

KRASNOJARSK STATE INSTITUTE FOR TRADE AND ECONOMICS

Krasnojarskij Gosudarstvennyj Torgovo-Ekonomičeskij Institut

ul. L. Prušinskoj 2, Krasnojarsk 660075
Tel: +7(391) 221-81-67
Fax: +7(391) 221-17-74
EMail: omk@kgtei.ru; kgtei@kgtei.ru
Website: http://www.kgtei.ru/

Rector: Jury L. Alexsandrov

Faculties

Accounting (Accountancy); **Commerce and Trade** (Business and Commerce); **Economics and Management** (Economics; Management; Marketing); **Food Technology** (Food Technology; Hotel and Restaurant)

History: Created 1979.

Degrees and Diplomas: *Bakalavr*; *Specialist Diploma*; *Magistr*
Last Updated: 20/09/11

KRASNOJARSK STATE INSTITUTE OF FINE ARTS

Krasnojarskij Gosudarstvennyj Khudožestvennyj Institut

pros. Mira 98, Krasnojarsk 600017
Tel: +7(3912) 27-85-11 +7(3912) 27-82-80
Fax: +7(3912) 27-85-11
EMail: kghi@list.ru
Website: http://www.kghi.ru/

Rector: Alexsandr Pokrovskiy

Programmes

Fine Arts (Ceramic Art; Fine Arts; Graphic Arts; Interior Design; Painting and Drawing; Sculpture)

History: Created 1987.

Degrees and Diplomas: *Specialist Diploma*
Last Updated: 02/02/12

KRASNOJARSK STATE MEDICAL UNIVERSITY NAMED AFTER PROF. V.F. JASENETSKIJ

Krasnojarskij Gosudarstvennyj Meditsinskij Universitet im. profesora V.F. Voino-Jasenetskogo

ul. Partizana Železnjaka 1,
Krasnojarsk 660022
Tel: +7(3912) 277-678
Fax: +7(3912) 237-835
Website: http://krasgmu.ru/news.php

Rector: Ivan Pavlovich Artyukhov EMail: rektorKGMU@rambler.ru

Faculties

Basic Medicine (Anatomy; Biology; Chemistry; Embryology and Reproduction Biology; Histology; Hygiene; Medical Technology; Medicine; Microbiology; Pathology; Physiology; Surgery); **Medicine** (Dermatology; Gynaecology and Obstetrics; Immunology; Medicine; Midwifery; Ophthalmology; Psychiatry and Mental Health; Public Health; Rehabilitation and Therapy; Surgery; Venereology); **Nursing** (Nursing); **Paediatrics** (Paediatrics); **Pharmacy** (Pharmacology); **Pre-University Education**

Institutes

Postgraduate Education; **Stomatology** (Stomatology)

History: Founded 1942 with roots in the Krasnojarsk Medical College, established 1890. Acquired present status 1994. Previously known as Krasnojarskaja Gosudarstvennaja Medicinskaja Akademija

Governing Bodies: Rectorate

Academic Year: September to June (September-January; February-June)

Admission Requirements: Secondary education certificate (Attestat o srednem obrazovanii)

Main Language(s) of Instruction: Russian

International Co-operation: With universities in Japan.

Degrees and Diplomas: *Specialist Diploma*: Medicine, 6 yrs; *Kandidat Nauk*: Medicine, a further 3 yrs; *Doktor Nauk*: Medical Sciences

Student Services: Academic counselling, Cultural centre, Employment services, Nursery care, Social counselling, Sports facilities

Student Residential Facilities: For c. 1,600 students

Special Facilities: Museum of Human Anatomy

Libraries: c. 500,000 vols

Publications: Physician *(monthly)*

Press or Publishing House: Publishing House
Last Updated: 31/03/09

KRASNOJARSK STATE PEDAGOGICAL UNIVERSITY

Krasnojarskij Gosudarstvennyj Pedagogičeskij Universitet

Lebedevoj 89, Krasnojarsk 660049
Tel: +7(3912) 235-877
Fax: +7(3912) 222-892
EMail: kspu@kspu.ru
Website: http://www.kspu.ru

Rector: Nikolaj I. Drozdov (1997-)

Vice-Rector: Mihail I. Bordukov

International Relations: Oxsana P. Tychenko
Tel: +7(3912) 224-280

Faculties

Foreign Languages *Dean*: Tatjana L. Batura; **Geography** *Dean*: Lubov U. Larionova; **History** *Dean*: Samuil I. Kangun; **Natural Sciences** *Dean*: Vladimir G. Fadeev; **Pedagogy and Child Psychology** *Dean*: Aleksey V. Gladilin; **Pedagogy and Psychology** *Dean*: Alexander A. Yarulov; **Physical Education** *Dean*: Sergey L. Sadyrin; **Primary Education** *Dean*: Yakov M. Kofman; **Russian Language and Literature** *Dean*: Galina A. Yakubailik; **Special Needs Education** *Dean*: Aleksey A. Dmitriev

Institutes

Mathematics, Physics and Computer Science *Director*: Nikolay I. Pak

History: Founded 1932. Acquired present status 1993.

Academic Year: September to May

Admission Requirements: Secondary school certificate

Fees: (Russian Rubles): 10,000-20,000 per annum

Main Language(s) of Instruction: Russian

International Co-operation: With universities in Germany; USA; China; Korea; Mongolia; Japan

Accrediting Agencies: Ministry of Education

Degrees and Diplomas: *Specialist Diploma*: 5 yrs

KRASNOJARSK STATE UNIVERSITY OF AGRICULTURE

Krasnojarskij Gosudarstvennyj Agrarnyj Universitet (KSAU)

prosp. Mira 90, Krasnojarsk 600049
Tel: +7(3912) 273-609
Fax: +7(3912) 273-609
EMail: info@kgau.ru
Website: http://www.kgau.ru

Rector: Nikolai Tsuglenok (1995-) EMail: rector@kgau.ru

Vice-Rector: Vasiliy Matushev
Tel: +7(3912) 274-778, Fax: +7(3912) 270-386
EMail: prorector@kgau.ru

International Relations: Galina Tsuglenok, Vice-Rector
Tel: +7(3912) 278-652, Fax: +7(3912) 278-652
EMail: galina@kgau.ru

Centres

Foreign Languages (Modern Languages) *Head*: Natalia Antonova

Departments

Lifelong Education (Continuing Education) *Head*: Tatyana Beketova

Divisions

Administration and Legal Administration *Head*: Sergey Ivanov; **Development Administration** (Administration) *Head*: Tatiana Bastron; **Educational Administration** (Educational Administration) *Head*: Evgenia Sorokataya; **Financial Economic Administration** (Administration; Economics; Finance) *Head*: Olga Dyačenko; **Human Resources** (Human Resources) *Head*: Natalia Shestova; **Information Technology Administration** (Information Technology) *Head*: Nikolay Ambrosenko

Institutes

Agrobusiness and Food Processing Industry (Food Technology) *Director*: Nadezhda Velichko; **Agronomy and Ecology Management** (Agriculture; Agronomy; Ecology) *Director*: Vladimir Ivchenko; **Applied Biotechnology and Veterinary Medicine** *Director*: Tamara Lefler; **Court Expert Examination and Law** *(Extra-mural)* (Law) *Director*: Natalia Tsuglenok; **Economics and Finance** *Dean*: Maria Ozerova; **Energetics and Energetics Resources Management** (Agricultural Engineering; Mechanical Engineering) *Director*: Sergey Shachmatov; **Engineering System Control** (Agricultural Equipment) *Director*: Andrey Vishnyakov; **Innovative Development** *Director*: Valeriy Danilin; **International Management Business** (Human Resources; International Business; Management) *Dean*: Natalia Antonova; **Juridical Studies** (Law) *Dean*: Natalia Sazonova; **Land Use Planning, Cadasters and Nature Planning** (Architecture and Planning; Rural Planning; Town Planning) *Dean*: Igor Danilin; **Management and Agrobusiness** (Business Administration; Management) *Dean*: Zinaida Shaporova; **Personality Development and Professional Self Determination** (Psychology) *Director*: Valentina Ivanova; **Scientific Research and System Analysis** *Head*: Galina Tsuglenok; **Specialists Advanced Training and Re-training** *Director*: Natalia Kozulina

History: Founded 1952. Acquired present status 1991.

Governing Bodies: Ministry of Agriculture

Academic Year: September to July

Admission Requirements: Secondary school certificate

Fees: (Russian Rubles): full-time, 30,000-50,000; part-time, 15,000-30,000

Main Language(s) of Instruction: Russian

Accrediting Agencies: Ministry of Education and Science

Degrees and Diplomas: *Bakalavr*: 4 yrs; *Specialist Diploma*: 5 yrs; *Magistr*: 6 yrs; *Kandidat Nauk*: 3/4 yrs (Part-time/full time); *Doktor Nauk*

Student Services: Handicapped facilities, Nursery care

Student Residential Facilities: Hotel

Special Facilities: Museum

Libraries: 360,442 vols; databases, 34,155 entries; e-catalog, 17,424 entries

Publications: Bulletin of KSAU, Scientific Publications *(other/irregular)*; Collection of articles, presented at scientific conferences *(annually)*

Press or Publishing House: Publishing House of KSAU

Student Numbers *2007-2008*	MEN	WOMEN	**TOTAL**
All (Foreign Included)	2,244	4,019	**6,263**
FOREIGN ONLY	21	15	**36**

Part-time students, 7,012.

Last Updated: 26/11/08

KUBAN INSTITUTE OF INTERNATIONAL BUSINESS AND MANAGEMENT

Kubanskij Institut Meždunarodnogo Predprinimatelstva i Menedžmenta (KIIB&M)

ul. Kubano Naberežnaya 3, Krasnodar 350063
Tel: +7(861) 268-54-72 +7(861) 262-37-41
Fax: +7(861) 268-54-72
EMail: info@kimpim-krasnodar.ru; kimpim@bk.ru
Website: http://www.kimpim-krasnodar.ru/

Rector: Lyudmila Yakovlevna Chikarina

Faculties

Finance and Economics (Economics; Finance); **International Economics and Management** (International Economics; Management); **Tourism Management** (Tourism)

History: Founded 1992.

Admission Requirements: Secondary school certificate (Attestat o srednem obrazovanii) and entrance examination

Main Language(s) of Instruction: Russian

Accrediting Agencies: Ministry of Education

Degrees and Diplomas: *Bakalavr*, *Specialist Diploma*

Student Services: Academic counselling, Canteen, Cultural centre, Employment services, Foreign student adviser, Foreign Studies Centre, Handicapped facilities, Health services, Language programs, Social counselling, Sports facilities

Student Residential Facilities: None

Libraries: Central Library, 50,000 vols

Publications: Globus; Issues on Transitional Economics *(quarterly)*

Last Updated: 20/09/11

KUBAN STATE MEDICAL UNIVERSITY

Kubanskij Gosudarstvennyj Medicinskij Universitet (KGMU)

ul. Sedina 4, Krasnodar 350063
Tel: +7(861) 268-36-84
Fax: +7(861) 262-73-74
EMail: corpus@ksma.kubannet.ru
Website: http://www.ksma.ru

Rector: Mikhail Cherkasov EMail: cherkasov@ksma.ru

International Relations: Andrey Redko, Vice-Rector
Tel: +7(861) 268-55-51

Programmes

Medicine (Medicine; Pharmacy; Stomatology)

History: Founded 1920. Acquired present status and title 2005. Formerly known as Kubanskaja Gosudarstvennaja Medicinskaja Akademija (Kuban State Medical Academy).

Governing Bodies: Federal Agency of Public Health and Social Development of the Russian Federation

Admission Requirements: Secondary school certificate or equivalent; Certificate of preparatory department

Main Language(s) of Instruction: Russian

Degrees and Diplomas: *Specialist Diploma*: Medicine, 6 yrs; *Specialist Diploma*: Stomatology; Pharmacy, 5 yrs

Student Services: Employment services, Foreign Studies Centre, Handicapped facilities, Language programs

Special Facilities: Museum; Laboratories; Stomatology, Midwifery and Gynaecology Clinics

Libraries: Medical Library

Publications: Medik Kubani *(monthly)*

Student Numbers *2007-2008*	**TOTAL**
All (Foreign Included)	**4,025**
FOREIGN ONLY	**425**

Part-time students, 275.
Last Updated: 09/12/08

KUBAN STATE UNIVERSITY

Kubanskij Gosudarstvennyj Universitet (KUBSU)
ul. Stavropolskaja 149, Krasnodar 350040
Tel: +7(861) 219-9502
Fax: +7(861) 219-9517
EMail: rector@kubsu.ru
Website: http://www.kubsu.ru

Rector: Vladimir A. Babeshko (1982-) Tel: +7(861) 269-9504

Pro-Rector: Alexander G. Ivanov
Tel: +7(861) 269-9507, Fax: +7(861) 269-9520
EMail: ivanov@kubsu.ru

International Relations: Anatoly V. Pinkachenko
Tel: +7(861) 269-9534, Fax: +7(861) 269-9534
EMail: interdep@mail.kubsu.ru

Faculties

Applied Mathematics (Applied Mathematics; Computer Science; Economics; Operations Research) *Dean*: Yuri V. Koltsov; **Architecture and Design** (Architecture; Design; Textile Design) *Dean*: Svetlana Y. Kochetkova; **Art and Graphics** (Fine Arts; Graphic Arts; Graphic Design; Painting and Drawing) *Dean*: Yuri V. Korobko; **Biology** (Aquaculture; Biochemistry; Biology; Biotechnology; Genetics; Microbiology; Natural Resources; Physiology; Zoology) *Dean*: Vladimir Y. Nagalevsky; **Chemistry** (Analytical Chemistry; Chemistry; Food Technology; Inorganic Chemistry; Organic Chemistry; Physical Chemistry) *Dean*: Vitaly D. Buikliskу; **Economics** (Accountancy; Economic and Finance Policy; Economics; International Economics; Labour and Industrial Relations; Marketing) *Dean*: Igor V. Shevchenko; **Engineering Physics** (Bioengineering; Electronic Engineering; Medical Technology; Physics; Radiophysics) *Dean*: Nikolay A. Yakovenko; **Geography** (Earth Sciences; Ecology; Geography; Social Studies; Tourism) *Dean*: Mikhail Y. Belikov; **Geology** (Geology; Geophysics) *Dean*: Vasily I. Popkov; **History** (History; International Relations; Philosophy; Sociology) *Dean*: Ruslan M. Achagu; **Journalism** (Journalism; Printing and Printmaking; Radio and Television Broadcasting) *Dean (Acting)*: Nadezhda P. Kravchenko; **Law** (Civil Law; Criminal Law; Labour Law; Law; Public Law) *Dean*: Igor A. Nikolajchuk; **Management** (Administration; Management; Political Sciences) *Dean*: Alexander M. Ždanovsky; **Mathematics** (Mathematics) *Dean*: Grigory F. Sokol; **Philology** (Philology) *Dean*: Valery P. Abramov; **Romance and Germanic Philology** (English; French; German; Greek; Linguistics; Literature; Modern Languages; Philology; Romance Languages; Spanish; Translation and Interpretation) *Dean*: Vladimir I. Tkhorik; **Social Pedagogy, Psychology and Communication Sciences** (Preschool Education; Primary Education; Public Relations; Social Sciences) *Dean*: Veronika M. Grebennikova

History: Founded 1920. Acquired present status 1924.

Governing Bodies: Academic Council

Academic Year: September to July

Admission Requirements: Secondary school certificate (Attestat o srednem obrazovanii) and entrance examination

Fees: None for Russian students

Main Language(s) of Instruction: Russian; some courses in English

Degrees and Diplomas: *Bakalavr*: 4 yrs; *Specialist Diploma*: 5 yrs; *Magistr*: 6 yrs; *Kandidat Nauk*: a further 3 yrs and thesis; *Doktor Nauk*: 3 yrs by thesis. Also undergraduate vocational training 1 yr and 10 months - 3 yrs and 10 months.

Student Services: Canteen, Cultural centre, Foreign student adviser, Foreign Studies Centre, Health services, Language programs, Sports facilities

Student Residential Facilities: Yes

Special Facilities: History Museum; Art Gallery; Geophysical Test Ground

Libraries: 5 Libraries, total, c. 1m. vols

Publications: Ecological Bulletin of Research Centres of the Black Sea Economic Cooperation *(quarterly)*; Human Society Management *(quarterly)*; Linguistics and Literary Criticism Essays; Philological Journal *(monthly)*

KUBAN STATE UNIVERSITY OF AGRICULTURE

Kubanskij Gosudarstvennyj Agrarnyj Universitet (KUBSAU)
ul. Kalinina 13, Krasnodar 350044
Tel: +7(861) 221-5942
Fax: +7(861) 221-5885
EMail: vckubgau@mail.kuban.ru
Website: http://www.kubagro.ru

Rector: Alexander Trubilin (2007-)

Vice-Rector: Sergey Reznichenko Tel: +7(861) 221-58-32

International Relations: Anastasia Oskina
Tel: +7(861) 221-5902 EMail: interkubagro@yandex.ru

Faculties

Accountancy (Accountancy) *Dean*: Sergey Bondarenko; **Agronomy** (Agricultural Engineering; Agronomy) *Dean*: Alexey Radionov; **Applied Informatics, Information Systems and Technology** *Dean*: Sergey Kurnosov; **Construction Engineering** *Dean*: Viktor Taratuta; **Ecology** (Ecology) *Dean*: Andrei Iniukin; **Economics** (Economics) *Dean*: Vladimir Gaiduk; **Energy and Electrification** (Agriculture; Electrical Engineering; Energy Engineering) *Dean*: Grigory Perekotiy; **Finance and Credit** *Dean*: Valery Bout; **Fruit Production, Vegetable Production and Viticulture** *Dean*: Sergey Gorlov; **Land Management and Land Cadastre** *Dean*: Andrei Gavriuchov; **Law** (Civil Law; Criminal Law; Law) *Dean*: Vladimir Zelensky; **Mechanical Engineering** *Dean*: Sergey Sydorenko; **Plant and Crop Protection** (Plant and Crop Protection) *Dean*: Alexander Devyatkin; **Processing Food Technology** (Food Technology) *Dean*: Ludmila Donchenko; **State and Municipality Management** *Dean*: Vladimir Koudryakov; **Taxes and Taxation** *Dean*: Alexei Mohov; **Veterinary** (Veterinary Science) *Dean*: Alexander Kavunnik; **Water Management and Melioration** (Water Management; Water Science) *Dean*: Vasily Tkachenko; **Zoo Technology and Management** (Management; Technology; Zoology) *Dean*: Sergey Smirnov

Further Information: Also two Research Institutions: Applied and Experimental Ecology and Biotechnological Processing

History: Founded in 1922 as Kuban Agricultural Institute. Acquired current status and title 1991

Governing Bodies: Academic Council

Admission Requirements: Secondary school certificate (Attestat o Srednem (Polnom) Obshchem Obrazovanii) or Higher Vocational Education Diploma (Diplom o Srednem Professionalnom Obrazovanii) or equivalent

Main Language(s) of Instruction: Russian

International Co-operation: Participates in the Erasmus Mundus "External Cooperation Window" programme

Accrediting Agencies: Federal Service for Supervision in the Sphere of Education and Science

Degrees and Diplomas: *Bakalavr*: Agriculture, 4 yrs; *Specialist Diploma*: Agronomy, Agrotechnology, Selection and Genetics of Agriculture; Plant and Crop Protection, Agricultural Chemistry, Soil Science; Fruit Production, Vegetable Production and Viticulture; Zoo technology and Management; Processing Food Technology; Applied Informatics, Information Systems and Technology; State and Municipality Management, Pedagogy; Energetic and Electrification for Agriculture; Melioration, Water Providing; Law; Veterinary Medicine; Mechanical Engineering; Ecology; Construction Engineering, Architecture Engineering; Land Management and Land Cadastre; Accountancy, Analysis and Audit; Finance and Credit; Taxes and Taxation, 5 yrs; *Magistr*: Agriculture, 2 yrs following Bakalavr

Student Services: Academic counselling, Cultural centre, Foreign student adviser, Foreign Studies Centre, Health services, Language programs, Social counselling, Sports facilities

Student Residential Facilities: Hostel accommodation for c. 9,500 students

Special Facilities: Museum; Botanical garden

Libraries: c. 1,1m. vols

Publications: The Works of Kuban State Agrarian University, Research journal *(biannually)*

Student Numbers *2007-2008*	MEN	WOMEN	TOTAL
All (Foreign Included)	–	–	**18,000**
FOREIGN ONLY	8	–	**8**

Distance students, 9,000.

Last Updated: 11/12/08

KUBAN STATE UNIVERSITY OF PHYSICAL EDUCATION, SPORT AND TOURISM

Kubanskij Gosudarstvenny Universitet Physicheskoi Kultury, Sporta i Turisma (KSUPHEST)

Ul. Budjonnogo, 161, Krasnodar 350015
Tel: +7(861) 255-3517
Fax: +7(861) 255-3573
EMail: doc@kgafk.ru
Website: http://www.kgafk.ru

Rector: Sultan Medzhidovich Akhmetov Tel: +7(8612) 553-573

Vice-Rector: Aleksei Aleksandrovich Tarasenko
EMail: tarasenko@kgafk.ru

International Relations: Gaik Derenikovich Alexanyants, Vice-Rector
Tel: +7(861) 255-3585, Fax: +7(861) 255-3585
EMail: ag@kgafk.ru

Centres

Employment Promoting *Director*: Irina Guseva; **Information Technology** *Head*: Oleg Rugin

Colleges

Humanities *Head*: Leonid Shiyan; **Medicine** (Medicine) *Head*: Marija Bykova

Departments

Post-Graduate and Doctorate Courses, Dissertation Board *Head*: Ludmila Prosoedova

Faculties

Adaptive and Health-Related Physical Education (Business Administration; Health Education; Physical Education; Rehabilitation and Therapy) *Dean*: Alla Ahromova; **Economics and Management** (Economics; Management) *Dean*: Ludmila Vacalova; **Foreign Students Preparatory Programme** *Dean*: Svetlana Kazarina; **Pedagogics and Psychology** *Dean*: Boris Kurdyukov; **Physical Education** (Physical Education) *Dean*: Vasilii Thorev; **Physical Education, Sports, Service and Tourism** *(Correspondence)* (Physical Education; Public Relations; Service Trades; Sports; Tourism) *Dean*: Alexander Zolotarev; **Qualification and Staff Upgrading** (Dance; Management; Pedagogy; Physical Education; Preschool Education; Psychology; Public Relations; Social and Community Services; Social Welfare; Sports; Tourism) *Dean*: Olga Kostyukova; **Service and Tourism** (Public Relations; Service Trades; Social and Community Services; Tourism) *Dean*: Sviatoslav Evtushenko; **Sports** (Sports) *Dean*: Elena Yeryomina; **University Preparatory Programme** (Higher Education; Vocational Education) *Dean*: Andzhela Rugina

Research Centres

Physical Education and Sport Problems *(Scientific) Head*: Anatoliy Pogrebnoy

History: Founded 1969. Formerly known as Kubanskaja Gosudarstvennaja Akademija Fizičeskoj Kul'tury (Kuban State Academy of Sports).

Academic Year: September to June

Admission Requirements: Secondary school Certificate (Dokument o srednem (polnom) obcshem obrazovanii)

Fees: (Russian Rubles): 20,000 per semester

Main Language(s) of Instruction: Russian

International Co-operation: With Universities in USA, Greece, Switzerland, Chine, Great Britain, Hungary, Belorussia, Kenya, Palestine, Sudan, Jordan, Cameroon, Armenia, Ethiopia

Degrees and Diplomas: *Bakalavr*: 4 yrs; *Specialist Diploma*: Humanitarian Sciences; Education and Pedagogics; Economics and Management; Service, Culture and Arts, 5 yrs; *Magistr*: a further 2 yrs

Student Residential Facilities: 3 student residences

Libraries: over 57,000 vols

Academic Staff *2007-2008*	MEN	WOMEN	TOTAL
FULL-TIME	106	104	**210**
PART-TIME	14	16	**30**
STAFF WITH DOCTORATE			
FULL-TIME	72	79	**151**
PART-TIME	24	25	**49**
Student Numbers *2007-2008*			
All (Foreign Included)	2,520	2,480	**5,000**
FOREIGN ONLY	135	15	**150**

Part-time students, 250. **Distance students**, 2,000.

Last Updated: 08/12/08

KUBAN STATE UNIVERSITY OF TECHNOLOGY

Kubanskij Gosudarstvennyj Tehnologičeskij Universitet (KUBSUT)

ul. Moskovskaja 2,
Krasnodar 350072
Tel: +7(8612) 558-401
Fax: +7(8612) 576-592
EMail: adm@kgtu.kuban.ru
Website: http://www.kubsut.ru

Rector: Anatoly A. Petrik (1984-) Tel: +7(8612) 556-549

International Relations: Jurij S. Zvjagolsky Tel: +7(8612) 558-347

Centres

International Commerce Education (Business Education; Engineering; International Business; Technology); **Social and Humanist Studies** (Humanities and Social Science Education; Social Studies)

Faculties

Bakery Technology (Cooking and Catering; Food Technology); **Chemical Technology** (Chemical Engineering); **Computer Engineering** (Automation and Control Engineering; Computer Engineering; Information Technology); **Construction Engineering** (Construction Engineering); **Economics** (Accountancy; Banking; Business Administration; Finance; Industrial Management); **Food Production Technology** (Food Technology); **Mechanics and Mechanical Engineering** (Mechanical Engineering; Mechanics); **Motor and Highway Engineering** (Civil Engineering; Road Engineering; Transport Engineering); **Power Engineering, Oil and Gas Technology** (Petroleum and Gas Engineering; Power Engineering)

Further Information: Also Russian Language Courses for foreign students. Branches in Armavir and Novorosisk

History: Founded 1918, acquired present status and title 1993.

Governing Bodies: Academic Council

Academic Year: September to June (September-January; February-June)

Admission Requirements: Secondary school certificate (Attestat o srednem obrazovanii)

Fees: (US Dollars): c. 800-1,500 per annum

Main Language(s) of Instruction: Russian

Degrees and Diplomas: *Bakalavr*: 4 yrs; *Specialist Diploma*: Engineering, Technology, 1 further yr; *Magistr*: a further 2 yrs; *Kandidat Nauk*: 3 yrs; *Doktor Nauk*: 3 yrs

Student Services: Academic counselling, Canteen, Cultural centre, Employment services, Foreign Studies Centre, Health services, Social counselling, Sports facilities

Student Residential Facilities: For c. 3,000 students

Libraries: Scientific Library, c. 1m. vols

Publications: Food Technology *(biennially)*; Proceedings of Higher Education Institutions

KURGAN STATE ACADEMY OF AGRICULTURE NAMED AFTER T.S. MALTSEV

Kurganskaja Gosudarstvennaja Sel'skohozjajstvennaja Akademija im. T.S. Mal'tseva

Lesnikogo, Ketovskij raion, 641300 Kurganskaja oblast'
Tel: +7(352) 4-41-40
Fax: +7(352) 4-41-40 +7(352) 4-43-70
EMail: nikols@mail.ksaa.zaural.ru; rectorat@mail.ksaa.zaural.ru
Website: http://www.ksaa.kurgan.ru

Rector: Pavel Efimovich Podgorbunskikh

Faculties

Agronomy (Agronomy; Botany; Ecology; Plant and Crop Protection; Soil Conservation; Soil Science); **Biotechnology** (Biotechnology); **Economics** (Accountancy; Agricultural Business; Agricultural Economics; Banking; Economics; Finance); **Engineering** (Agricultural Engineering; Civil Engineering; Industrial Design); **Technology** (Agricultural Engineering; Agricultural Equipment)

History: Created 1944.

Degrees and Diplomas: *Bakalavr*; *Specialist Diploma*
Last Updated: 16/01/12

KURGAN STATE UNIVERSITY

Kurganskij Gosudarstvennyj Universitet

ul. Gogol 25, Kurgan, 640669 Kurganskaja oblast'
Tel: +7(35222) 432-652
Fax: +7(35222) 432–51
EMail: rector@kgsu.ru
Website: http://www.kgsu.ru

Rector: Oleg Ivanovich Buhtijarov (2002-)
EMail: buhtoyarov@kgsu.ru

First Vice-Rector: Boris S. Shalyutin
Tel: +7(35222) 433-220 EMail: shalutin@kgsu.ru

International Relations: Alexander P. Kuznetsov, Vice Rector
Tel: +7(35222) 433-380 EMail: kuznecov@kgsu.ru

Faculties

Economics (Banking; Economics; Finance; Marketing) *Dean*: Vyačeslav Semyonov; **History** (Cultural Studies; History; Philosophy) *Dean*: Gennadiy Pavlutskih; **Law** *Dean*: Roman Skinderev; **Mathematics and Information Technology** (Information Sciences; Mathematics) *Dean*: Anna Zvereva; **Natural Sciences** (Biology; Chemistry; Ecology; Geography; Natural Sciences; Physics) *Dean*: Oleg Filisteev; **Pedagogy** (Child Care and Development; Pedagogy) *Dean*: Gennadiy Fedosimov; **Philology** (English; French; German; Modern Languages; Philology; Russian) *Dean*: Galina Levčenko; **Psychology, Valeology and Sport** (Pedagogy; Physical Education; Physiology; Psychology) *Dean*: Vitaliy Gryaznykh; **Technology** (Mechanical Engineering; Power Engineering; Safety Engineering) *Dean*: Vladimir Kurdyukov; **Transport Systems** (Automotive Engineering; Transport and Communications) *Dean*: Valeriy Piven

Laboratories

Archaeology (Archaeology) *Head*: Stepan Shilov; **Physical Chemistry of Heterogeneous Systems** (Physical Chemistry) *Head*: Boris Vorontsov; **Physiology of Extreme Conditions** *Head*: Alexander Kuznetsov; **Practical Psychology of Education** (Educational Psychology) *Head*: Raisa Ovcharova

History: Founded 1995, incorporating the Kurgan Pedagogical Institute and Kurgan Mechanical Engineering Institute.

Governing Bodies: Academic Council

Academic Year: September to June (September-January; February-June)

Admission Requirements: Secondary school certificate (Attestat o srednem obrazovanii)

Fees: (US Dollars): 800-1,200 per annum

Main Language(s) of Instruction: Russian

Accrediting Agencies: Ministry of Education and Science

Degrees and Diplomas: *Bakalavr*: 4 yrs; *Specialist Diploma*: 5 yrs; *Kandidat Nauk*; *Doktor Nauk*

Student Services: Academic counselling, Canteen, Cultural centre, Employment services, Foreign Studies Centre, Handicapped facilities, Health services, Language programs, Social counselling, Sports facilities

Student Residential Facilities: 4 dormitories for 1,500 students

Special Facilities: Museum of Natural History; Röntgen Anatomy Museum. Biological Garden

Libraries: Central Library, c. 895,000 vols

Publications: Collected Scientific Papers *(quarterly)*

Press or Publishing House: Publishing Division

KURSK STATE ACADEMY OF AGRICULTURE NAMED AFTER PROF. I.I. IVANOV

Kurskaja Gosudarstvennaja Sel'skohozjajstvennaja Akademija im. Professora I.I. Ivanova (KSAA)

ul. Karla Marksa 70, Kursk 305034
Tel: +7(0712) 531-330
Fax: +7(0712) 538-436
EMail: academy@kgsha.ru
Website: http://www.kgsha.ru

Rector: Vladimir D. Muha

Departments

Agronomy (Agricultural Business; Agronomy; Botany; Crop Production; Farm Management; Food Science; Plant and Crop Protection; Soil Science); **Animal Products**; **Economics** (Accountancy; Agricultural Economics; Economics; Finance; International Economics; Taxation); **Engineering**; **Veterinary Science**

History: Founded 1951 as Kursk Agricultural Institute, acquired present status and title 1994.

Accrediting Agencies: Ministry of Higher Education

KURSK STATE MEDICAL UNIVERSITY

Kurskij Gosudarstvennyj Medicinskij Universitet (KSUU)

ul. Karla Marksa 3, Kursk 305041
Tel: +7(4712) 225-612
Fax: +7(0712) 567-399
EMail: main@kgmu.kursknet.ru
Website: http://www.kgmu.kursknet.ru

Rector: Alexei Ivanovich Lazarev Fax: +7(4712) 513-798

International Relations: Yurij Iobidze
Tel: +7(0712) 565-462, Fax: +7(0712) 565-462
EMail: ksmu46-inter@rambler.ru

Faculties

Biotechnology *Dean*: Lyudmila Lazurina; **Clinical Psychology** (Clinical Psychology; Psychology) *Dean*: Tatiana Vasilenko; **Dentistry** (Dentistry) *Dean*: Yurij Tkatchenko; **Economy and Management of Public Health** (Economics; Health Administration; Management; Public Health) *Dean*: Swetlana Spichak; **Foreign Students Training** *Dean*: Ludmila Severianova; **Medicine** (Medicine) *Dean*: Vladimir Kharchenko; **Nursing and Paediatrics** (Nursing; Paediatrics) *Dean*: Yurij Lyashev; **Pharmaceutical Studies** (Pharmacy) *Dean*: Yurij Sukhomlinov; **Post-diploma Education** *Dean*: Sergey Sumin; **Pre-diploma Education** *Dean*: Alexandr Artemiev; **Preventive Medicine** *Dean*: Alexandr Chernih; **Social Work** (Social Work) *Dean*: Tatiana Vasilenko

History: Founded 1935. Acquired present status and title 1993.

Governing Bodies: Academic Council; Scientific Council

Academic Year: September to June

Admission Requirements: Secondary school certificate or equivalent

Main Language(s) of Instruction: Russian, English

International Co-operation: With universities in Israel, USA, Germany.

Degrees and Diplomas: *Specialist Diploma*: Biotechnology; Economics; Management; Psychology; Social Work, 5 yrs; *Magistr*:

Pharmacy, 5 yrs; *Doktor Nauk*: Medicine; Preventive Medicine, 6 yrs; *Doktor Nauk*: Stomatology, 5 yrs

Student Services: Academic counselling, Canteen, Foreign student adviser, Foreign Studies Centre, Language programs, Social counselling, Sports facilities

Student Residential Facilities: 5 hostels (3 hostels for foreign students)

Special Facilities: University History Museum

Libraries: 3 Libraries

Publications: Scientific Research Bulletin *(biennially)*

KURSK STATE UNIVERSITY

Kurskij Gosudarstvennyj Universitet (KGPU)

ul. Radischeva 33, Kursk 305000

Tel: +7(4712) 560-264

Fax: +7(4712) 513-649

EMail: kurskgu@kursk-uni.ru

Website: http://www.kursk-uni.ru

Rector: Vyacheslav Gvozdev (1995-)

Deputy-Rector: Nikolaj Grebenkov Tel: +7(4712) 700-563

International Relations: Elena Mikhailina
Tel: +7(4712) 513-503, Fax: +7(4712) 561-439
EMail: keep-in-touch@yandex.ru

Faculties

Computer Science *Dean*: Vitalij Kudinov; **Economics** (Accountancy; Economics; Finance; Management; Marketing) *Dean*: Victor Kriulin; **Education and Psychology** *Dean*: Marina Lukina; **Fine Arts** (Art Education; Design; Fine Arts; Interior Design; Painting and Drawing) *Dean*: Victor Zhilin; **Foreign Languages** (English; French; German; Modern Languages) *Dean*: Nikolaj Smakhtin; **History** (History; Humanities and Social Science Education; Psychology; Religion) *Dean*: Igor Plaksin; **Labour Education** (Labour and Industrial Relations) *Dean*: Anatolij Vratskij; **Law** (Labour Law; Private Law; Public Law) *Dean*: Vladimir Zakharov; **Natural Sciences** (Biology; Chemistry; Environmental Studies; Geography; Natural Sciences; Science Education; Social and Community Services; Tourism) *Dean*: Irina Balabina; **Performing Arts** (Music; Music Education; Performing Arts) *Dean*: Elena Kirnosova; **Philology** *Dean*: Yurij Philippov; **Philosophy, Sociology and Cultural Studies** *Dean*: Ludmila Koroleva; **Physical Education and Sports** (Physical Education; Sports) *Dean*: Tatiana Skoblikova; **Physics and Mathematics** *Dean*: Vyachaslav Melentev; **Religious Education and Theology** *Dean*: Anatolij Korzinkin; **Special Education** (Education of the Handicapped; Special Education; Speech Therapy and Audiology) *Dean*: Tamara Bugaeva

Further Information: Also Summer School for foreign students (2-4 weeks), in Russian Language and Culture, History and Orthodox Church

History: Founded 1934, acquired present status and title 2003. Formerly known as Kurskij Gosudarstvennyj Pedagogičeskij Universitet.

Governing Bodies: Academic Senate

Academic Year: September to June

Admission Requirements: Secondary school certificate (Attestat o srednem obrazovanii)

Main Language(s) of Instruction: Russian

Accrediting Agencies: Ministry of Education and Science of the Russian Federation

Degrees and Diplomas: *Bakalavr*: 4 yrs; *Specialist Diploma*: Education, 5 yrs; *Magistr*: 2 yrs; *Kandidat Nauk*; *Doktor Nauk*

Student Services: Academic counselling, Canteen, Cultural centre, Employment services, Foreign student adviser, Foreign Studies Centre, Health services, Language programs, Social counselling, Sports facilities

Student Residential Facilities: Yes

Special Facilities: Zoology Museum; Biology Museum; Archeology Museum. Observatory. Art Studio. TV and Computer Centres

Libraries: Central Library, c. 600,000 vols

Publications: Uchenye zapiski *(quarterly)*

Academic Staff *2007-2008*	**TOTAL**
FULL-TIME	**655**
PART-TIME	**228**
STAFF WITH DOCTORATE	
FULL-TIME	**438**
Student Numbers *2007-2008*	
All (Foreign Included)	**9,919**
FOREIGN ONLY	**201**

Part-time students, 3,662. **Evening students**, 128.

Last Updated: 27/11/08

KUZBASS STATE PEDAGOGICAL ACADEMY

Kuzbasskaja Gosudarstvennaja Pedagogičeskaja Akademija

ul. Pionerskij 13, Novokuzneck, 654027 Kemerovskaja oblast'

Tel: +7(3843) 74-18-60

Fax: +7(3843) 74-18-60

EMail: rector@kuzspa.ru; kuzspa@yandex.ru

Website: http://www.kuzspa.ru

Rector: Sergej Mikhailovich Redlih

Faculties

Biology and Geography (Biology; Geography; Teacher Training); **Foreign Languages** (Foreign Languages Education; Modern Languages); **History** (History; Teacher Training); **Pedagogical Psychology** (Educational Psychology; Pedagogy); **Physical Education** (Physical Education; Sports); **Physics and Mathematics** (Mathematics; Mathematics Education; Physics; Science Education); **Preschool Education** (Preschool Education; Special Education); **Primary Education** (Primary Education); **Russian Language and Literature** (Literature; Native Language Education; Russian); **Technology** (Technology; Technology Education)

History: Created 1939. Previously known as Novokuzneckij Gosudarstvennyj Pedagogičeskij Institut (Novokuzneck State Pedagogical Institute). Acquired current title and status 2002.

Degrees and Diplomas: *Specialist Diploma*

Last Updated: 22/09/11

KUZBASS STATE TECHNICAL UNIVERSITY

Kuzbasskij Gosudarstvennyj Tehničeskij Universitet

ul. Vesennjaja 28, Kemerovo 650026

Tel: +7(3842) 583-073

Fax: +7(3842) 361-687

EMail: gdb@kuzstu.ac.ru

Website: http://www.kuzstu.ac.ru

Rector: Viktor Venjaminovich Kurehin (1993-)
Tel: +7(3842) 233-014

Provost: Valerij Ivanovič Nesterov

International Relations: Sergej Dmitrjevich Jevmenov, Vice-Rector Tel: +7(3842) 231-926

Centres

Expertise (Technology); **New Information Technology** (Information Technology); **Technical Design** *(Nature)* (Industrial Design)

Faculties

Mechanical Engineering (Mechanical Engineering); **Mine Construction** (Mining Engineering); **Mining Electromechanical Engineering** (Electrical Engineering; Mining Engineering); **Mining Engineering** (Mining Engineering)

Laboratories

Geodynamics (Geophysics); **Protection of the Environment** (Ecology)

History: Founded 1950 as Mining Institute, became Polytechnic 1965, and acquired present status and title 1993.

Academic Year: September to June (September-January; February-June)

Admission Requirements: Secondary education certificate (Attestat o srednem obrazovanii)

Main Language(s) of Instruction: Russian

Degrees and Diplomas: *Bakalavr*: 4 yrs; *Specialist Diploma*: Engineering, Technology, 5 yrs; *Magistr*: a further 1-2 yrs

Student Services: Academic counselling, Canteen, Cultural centre, Foreign student adviser, Health services, Language programs, Social counselling, Sports facilities

Student Residential Facilities: For c. 1,400 students

Special Facilities: History Museum

Libraries: Scientific and Technical Library, c. 551,000 vols

Publications: Educational Handbooks; Scientific 'Works'

Press or Publishing House: University Printing House

LAW INSTITUTE (MOSCOW)

Juridičeskij Institut (Moskva)
Malyj Karetnyj per. 11/13, str 2, Moskva 127051
Tel: +7(495) 771-29-37
EMail: 1994@1994.ru

Rector: Oleg Pavlovich Popov

Programmes

Law (Law)

History: Created 1991.

Degrees and Diplomas: *Bakalavr*, *Specialist Diploma*
Last Updated: 27/01/12

LENINGRAD STATE UNIVERSITY NAMED AFTER A.S. PUSHKIN

Leningradskij Gosudarstvennyj Universitet im. A.S. Puškina
Peterburgskoe šosse 10, Pushkin, Sankt-Peterburg 196605
Tel: +7(812) 466-65-58
Fax: +7(812) 466-49-99
EMail: pushkin@lengu.ru
Website: http://lengu.ru/pages/main.php

Rector: Vyaceslav N. Skvortsov

Faculties

Arts (Art History; Arts and Humanities; Design; Fashion Design; Graphic Design; Music; Music Theory and Composition; Musicology; Painting and Drawing); **Economics and Finance** (Accountancy; Banking; Economics; Finance; Government; Public Administration); **Foreign Languages** (English; French; German; Grammar; Latin; Literature; Modern Languages; Philology; Phonetics; Speech Studies; Translation and Interpretation); **History and Social Sciences** (History; Museum Studies; Social Sciences); **Law** (Law); **Linguistics and Intercultural Communication** (Communication Studies; Linguistics; Translation and Interpretation); **Mathematics and Computer Science** (Applied Mathematics; Applied Physics; Archiving; Documentation Techniques; Information Sciences; Mathematics; Mathematics and Computer Science; Mathematics Education; Physics; Science Education; Systems Analysis); **Natural Sciences, Geography and Tourism** (Biology; Biotechnology; Ecology; Geography; Histology; Science Education; Tourism); **Philology**; **Philosophy** (Anthropology; Logic; Philosophy; Religion); **Physical Training** (Hygiene; Physical Education; Sports; Sports Management; Sports Medicine); **Psychology and Pedagogy** (Clinical Psychology; Educational Psychology; Pedagogy; Preschool Education; Primary Education; Psychology; Secondary Education; Social and Community Services); **Special Pedagogy and Psychology** (Education of the Handicapped; Psychology; Special Education)

History: Founded 1993 as Sankt Petersburskij Gosudarstvennyj Oblastnoj Universitet. Acquired present status and title 1996.

Governing Bodies: Academic Council

Admission Requirements: Secondary school certificate (Attestat o srednem obrazovanii)

Main Language(s) of Instruction: Russian

International Co-operation: With universities in Germany and USA

Degrees and Diplomas: *Bakalavr*, *Specialist Diploma*; *Magistr*

Student Services: Canteen, Employment services, Health services, Language programs, Social counselling, Sports facilities

Student Residential Facilities: Yes

Special Facilities: Art Gallery. Greenhouse. Conservatory. Botanical Gardens; Rosarium

Libraries: c. 650,000 vols
Last Updated: 30/03/12

LIPECK STATE PEDAGOGICAL UNIVERSITY

Lipeckij Gosudarstvennyj Pedagogičeskij Universitet
ul. Lenina 42, Lipeck 398020
Tel: +7(4742) 32-83-03
Fax: +7(4742) 32-83-03
EMail: rector@lspu.lipetsk.ru
Website: http://www.lspu.lipetsk.ru/

Rector: Pavel G. Bugakov

Faculties

Graphic Art (Computer Graphics; Design; Fine Arts; Graphic Arts); **History** (Cultural Studies; Economics; History); **Information Technology** (Business Computing; Information Technology; Management; Mathematics; Sociology); **Linguistics and Intercultural Communication** (Communication Studies; Cultural Studies; English; French; German; Linguistics); **Modern Languages** (English; French; German); **Natural Sciences** (Botany; Chemistry; Ecology; Geography; Physiology; Zoology); **Pedagogy and Psychology** (Biological and Life Sciences; Educational Psychology; Pedagogy; Psychology); **Philology** (Linguistics; Literature; Native Language Education; Russian); **Physical Education and Sport** (Physical Education; Sports); **Physics, Mathematics and Computer Science** (Applied Mathematics; Computer Science; Information Technology; Mathematics; Physics; Telecommunications Services); **Technology** (Technology Education)

Institutes

Culture and Art (Art Education; Fine Arts; Music Education)

History: Created 1949.

Degrees and Diplomas: *Bakalavr*, *Specialist Diploma*; *Magistr*
Last Updated: 09/02/12

LIPECK STATE TECHNICAL UNIVERSITY

Lipeckij Gosudarstvennyj Tehničeskij Universitet (LSTU)
ul. Moskovskaja 30, Lipeck 398055
Tel: +7(0742) 328-232
Fax: +7(0742) 310-473
EMail: mailbox@stu.lipetsk.su; root@stu.lipetsk.ru
Website: http://www.lstu.lipetsk.ry

Rector: Mihail Kuprianov (2000-)

Pro-Rector: Pavel Vnukov

International Relations: Vladimir Meshcheriakov
Tel: +7(0742) 318-373

Faculties

Applied Physics and Technology (Applied Physics; Biomedical Engineering; Energy Engineering; Metal Techniques; Physical Engineering; Thermal Engineering) *Dean*: Vladimir Dozhdikov; **Automation and Computer Science** (Applied Mathematics; Automation and Control Engineering; Computer Science; Electrical and Electronic Equipment and Maintenance; Electrical Engineering) *Dean*: Anatolij Pogodaev; **Civil Engineering** (Architecture; Civil Engineering; Construction Engineering; Industrial Engineering; Road Engineering) *Dean*: Vladimir Babkin; **Economics** (Accountancy; Industrial Management; Management) *Dean*: Aleksandr Zaitsev; **Mechanical Engineering** *Dean*: Aleksandr Zhiltsov; **Metallurgy** (Analytical Chemistry; Chemical Engineering; Metallurgical Engineering; Thermal Physics) *Dean*: Sergej Lebedev; **Part-Time and Correspondence** *Dean*: Evgenij Ivannikov; **Social Sciences** *Dean*: Viktor Dolgov; **Transport Engineering** (Automotive Engineering; Railway Transport; Transport Economics; Transport Engineering; Transport Management) *Dean*: Vladimir Loginov

History: Founded 1956, acquired present status and title 1994.

Academic Year: September to May

Admission Requirements: Secondary school certificate (Attestat o srednem obrazovanii) and entrance examination

Fees: (Russian Rubles): 20,808-30,600 per annum

Main Language(s) of Instruction: Russian, some courses in English

Accrediting Agencies: Ministry of Education

Degrees and Diplomas: *Specialist Diploma*: 5 yrs

Student Services: Academic counselling, Canteen, Cultural centre, Employment services, Foreign student adviser, Health services, Language programs, Social counselling, Sports facilities

Student Residential Facilities: Yes

Special Facilities: Museum. Art Gallery

Libraries: c. 800,000 vols

LITERATURE INSTITUTE NAMED AFTER A.M. GORKY

Literaturnyj Institut im. A.M. Gorkogo

bul. Tverskoj 25, Moskva 103104

Tel: +7(495) 202-8422

Fax: +7(495) 202-7688

EMail: rectorat@litinstitut.ru

Website: http://www.filine.centro.ru/gorky

Rector: Sergej Esin
Tel: +7(495) 203-0101, Fax: +7(495) 202-8422

Pro-Rector: Lev Skvorcov Tel: +7(495) 291-5333

International Relations: Sergej Tolkachov Tel: +7(495) 203-0041

Departments

Creative Writing (Literature; Writing); **Literature** (Literature)

History: Founded 1933.

Academic Year: September to June (September-December; February-June)

Admission Requirements: Secondary school certificate (Attestat o srednem obrazovanii) and entrance examination

Main Language(s) of Instruction: Russian

Degrees and Diplomas: *Bakalavr*: 4 yrs; *Specialist Diploma*: Writer's Workshop, 2 yrs; *Magistr*: a further 1-2 yrs; *Kandidat Nauk*: a further 3 yrs

Student Residential Facilities: For c. 30 students

Libraries: c. 250,000 vols

Press or Publishing House: Publishing House

MAGNITOGORSK STATE CONSERVATORY

Magnitogorskaja Gosudarstvennaja Konservatoria

ul. Gryzanova 22, Magnitogorsk 455036

Tel: +7(3511) 371-375

Fax: +7(3511) 217-914

Website: http://www.mgk.maginfo.net

Rector: Natal'ja Nik. Veremeenko Tel: +7(3511) 372-712

Programmes

Education (Education); **Music** (Music)

MAGNITOGORSK STATE TECHNICAL UNIVERSITY NAMED AFTER G.I. NOSOVA

Magnitogorskij Gosudarstvennyj Tehničeskij Universitet im. G.I. Nosova

prosp. Lenin, 38, Magnitogorsk 455000

Tel: +7(3519) 23-57-55 +7(3519) 29-84-02

Fax: +7(3519) 29-84-26 +7(3519) 23-57-59

EMail: umu@magtu.ru; mgtu@magtu.ru

Website: http://www.magtu.ru/

First Vice-Rector: Valery Mihaylovich Kolokolstev
EMail: kwm@magtu.ru

Faculties

Architecture and Building (Architecture; Construction Engineering; Heating and Refrigeration; Road Engineering); **Automation and Computing Techniques** (Automation and Control Engineering; Computer Engineering; Computer Science; Electronic Engineering; Microelectronics; Technology); **Chemistry and Metallurgy** (Chemical Engineering; Educational Psychology; Metallurgical Engineering; Pedagogy; Physical Chemistry); **Economics and Law** (Accountancy; Business Administration; Economics; Law; Management; Marketing; Taxation); **Mechanics and Machine-Building** (Building Technologies; Mechanics; Transport Engineering); **Mining Technology and Transport** (Mining Engineering; Transport Management); **Power Engineering** (Electrical Engineering; Mechanics; Power Engineering; Technology)

Further Information: Branch in Beloretsk.

History: Founded 1934. Acquired present status and title 1998.

Governing Bodies: Academic Council

Academic Year: September to June

Admission Requirements: Secondary School Certificate.

Main Language(s) of Instruction: Russian

Accrediting Agencies: Ministry of Education

Degrees and Diplomas: *Bakalavr*, *Specialist Diploma*; *Magistr*, *Kandidat Nauk*

Student Services: Academic counselling, Cultural centre, Employment services, Health services, Language programs, Social counselling, Sports facilities

Student Residential Facilities: 833 student rooms.

Special Facilities: Museum. Movie Studio. Laboratories (computer, information technologies, scientific research, mechanical and liquid metals, bacterological, raw materials resources)

Libraries: c. 1,1m. vols.

Last Updated: 16/01/12

MAGNITOGORSK STATE UNIVERSITY

Magnitogorskij Gosudarstvennyj Universitet

ul. Lenina 114, Magnitogorsk 455043

Tel: +7(3511) 351-532 +7(3511) 354-666

Fax: +7(3511) 359-232

EMail: masu@masu.ru

Website: http://www.masu.ru

Rector: Valentin F. Romanov

Vice-Rector: Vladimir P. Semenov

International Relations: Vladimir P. Semenov

Faculties

Arts (Fine Arts); **Computer Science** (Computer Science); **Foreign Languages** (English; French; German; Modern Languages); **History** (History); **Infant Care Education** (Child Care and Development); **Pedagogy** (Pedagogy); **Philology** (Philology); **Physics and Mathematics** (Mathematics; Physics); **Psychology** (Psychology); **Technology** (Technology)

History: Founded 1932.

Academic Year: September to June (September-January; February-June)

Admission Requirements: Secondary school certificate (Attestat o srednem obrazovanii) or equivalent, and entrance examination

Main Language(s) of Instruction: Russian

Degrees and Diplomas: *Specialist Diploma*: 5 yrs; *Magistr*: Infant Care Education; *Kandidat Nauk*: a further 3-4 yrs

Student Services: Academic counselling, Canteen, Cultural centre, Employment services, Foreign Studies Centre, Health services, Social counselling, Sports facilities

Special Facilities: Institute Museum. Art Gallery

Publications: Annual Collection of Scientific Reports *(annually)*; Problems of History, Philology and Culture *(annually)*

Press or Publishing House: Printing Complex

MARIJ STATE PEDAGOGICAL INSTITUTE

Marijskij Gosudarstvennyj Pedagogičeskij Institut

ul. Kommunističeskaja 44, Joškar-Ola 424002

Tel: +7(8362) 551-744

Fax: +7(8362) 554-312

Website: http://www.mgpi.mari.ru

Rector: Valerian Alek Egorov

Secretary-General: Elvira Ivanovna Saveljeva
Tel: +7(8362) 554-419

Departments

Education I (Education; Primary Education); **Education II** (Education; Preschool Education); **Foreign Languages** (English; French; German; Modern Languages); **History and Philology** (History; Philology); **Physical Education** (Physical Education); **Physics and Mathematics** (Mathematics; Physics); **Technology and Management** (Management; Technology)

Further Information: Also Russian language courses for foreign students

History: Founded 1931, acquired present status 1933.

Academic Year: September to July (September-January; February-July)

Admission Requirements: Secondary school certificate (Attestat o srednem obrazovanii)

Main Language(s) of Instruction: Russian

Libraries: c. 472,000 vols

MARIJ STATE TECHNICAL UNIVERSITY

Marijskij Gosudarstvennyj Tehničeskij Universitet

pl. Lenina 3, Joškar-Ola 424000
Tel: +7(8362) 45-53-44 +7(8362) 45-30-45
Fax: +7(8362) 41-08-72
EMail: analitic@marstu.net
Website: http://www.marstu.net/

Rector: Evgenij Mikhailovich Romanov EMail: rector@marstu.net

Faculties

Civil Engineering (Civil Engineering); **Ecology** (Ecology); **Economics** (Economics); **Forestry Engineering** (Forestry); **Forestry** (Forestry); **Information Technology and Computer Science** (Computer Science; Information Sciences); **Machine Construction** (Machine Building); **Management and Law** (Law; Management; Marketing); **Radio Engineering** (Electronic Engineering; Telecommunications Engineering); **Water Science** (Natural Resources; Water Management; Water Science)

History: Founded 1932 as Povolzsky Forestry Institute, acquired present status and title 1995.

Academic Year: September to May (September-December; February-May)

Admission Requirements: Secondary school certificate (Attestat o srednem obrazovanii)

Main Language(s) of Instruction: Russian, English

Degrees and Diplomas: *Bakalavr*, *Specialist Diploma*; *Magistr*; *Kandidat Nauk*; *Doktor Nauk*

Student Residential Facilities: For c. 3,000 students

Special Facilities: Museum. Multimedia Laboratory. Biological Garden

Libraries: 1m. vols

Last Updated: 09/02/12

MARIJ STATE UNIVERSITY

Marijskij Gosudarstvennyj Universitet (MARSU)

pl. Lenina 1, Joškar-Ola 424001
Tel: +7(8362) 425-920
Fax: +7(8362) 454-581
EMail: postmaster@marsu.ru
Website: http://www.marsu.ru

Rector: Vitali I. Makarov (1998-) EMail: rector@marsu.ru

First Vice-Rector: Vitaly Ivanov Tel: +7(8362) 426-585

International Relations: Andrey A. Yarygin, Vice-Rector
Tel: +7(8362) 720-705, Fax: +7(8362) 736-333
EMail: andrey@marsu.ru

Faculties

Biology and Chemistry (Biology; Chemistry; Ecology; Psychology) *Dean*: Mikhail Grigoryev; **Culture and Arts** (Cultural Studies; Fine Arts; Folklore; Library Science) *Dean*: Oleg Gerasimov; **Economics** (Accountancy; Agricultural Economics; Econometrics; Economic and Finance Policy; Economic History; Economics) *Dean*: Kavyi Shakirov; **Electrical Power and Energetics** (Electrical and Electronic Equipment and Maintenance; Energy Engineering) *Dean*: Leonid Rybakov; **History and Philology** (History; Journalism; Philology; Regional Studies; Russian) *Dean*: Sergey Starikov; **International Relations** *Dean*: Zory Zorina; **Law** (Law) *Dean*: Anatoly Lomonosov; **Physics and Mathematics** (Applied Mathematics; Mathematics; Physics) *Dean*: Gabtelnur Sitnikov

Institutes

Agriculture (Agriculture; Dairy; Harvest Technology; Meat and Poultry; Plant and Crop Protection; Soil Science) *Director*: Gubeidulla Yunusov; **Finno-Ugric Studies** (Archaeology; Ethnology; Eurasian and North Asian Languages) *Director*: Oleg Tikhonov; **Open Education** *(Distance Learning Centre)* (Accountancy; Economics; Latin American Studies; Management) *Director*: Alexander Kosov

History: Founded 1972.

Governing Bodies: Academic Councils

Academic Year: September to July

Admission Requirements: Secondary school certificate (Attestat o srednem obščem obrazovanii) and entrance examination

Fees: None

Main Language(s) of Instruction: Russian

International Co-operation: With universities in Finland, Sweden. Also partcipates in Tempus.

Accrediting Agencies: Ministry of Education

Degrees and Diplomas: *Specialist Diploma*: 5 yrs; *Kandidat Nauk*: Finno-Ugric Languages; Agriculture, a further 3 yrs by thesis; *Doktor Nauk*: Finno-Ugric Languages; Agriculture, by thesis following Kandidat

Student Services: Academic counselling, Canteen, Cultural centre, Employment services, Foreign student adviser, Foreign Studies Centre, Health services, Language programs, Social counselling, Sports facilities

Student Residential Facilities: Yes

Special Facilities: Zoological Museum; Archaeological Museum; History of the University Museum. Agrobiology Station. Computer Centre; Internet Centre.

Libraries: c. 650,000 vols

Publications: Archaeography Bulletin (in Russian), Research on historical documents, ancient texts, archives *(quarterly)*

Press or Publishing House: Marij State University Press

MARITIME STATE UNIVERSITY

Morskoj Gosudarstvennyj Universitet (MSU)

ul. Verhneportovaja 50-a, Vladivostok, 690059 Primorskij kraj
Tel: +7(4232) 414-968
Fax: +7(4232) 414-968 +7(4232) 517-639
EMail: office@msun.ru
Website: http://www.msun.ru

Rector: Sergey A. Ogay (2008-)

First Vice-Rector: Vladimir F. Gamanov

International Relations: Evgeny N. Malyavin, Vice-Rector for International Affairs
Tel: +7(4232) 301-274, Fax: +7(4232) 301-282

Institutes

Aquatics (Physical Education; Sports); **Automatics and IT** (Automation and Control Engineering; Data Processing; Electrical Engineering; Maintenance Technology; Mechanical Engineering; Telecommunications Engineering); **East Asia** (Chinese; East Asian Studies; Japanese; Korean; Translation and Interpretation); **Humanities** (Arts and Humanities; Pedagogy; Psychology; Social Sciences); **International Education**; **International Educational Programmes**; **Management** (Economics; English; Management; Translation and Interpretation; Transport Management); **Maritime Academy** (Automation and Control Engineering; Electrical Engineering; Law; Marine Transport; Nautical Science; Power Engineering; Transport and Communications); **Maritime Physics and Engineering**; **Maritime Technology** (Food Technology; Machine Building; Marine Engineering; Mechanical Engineering; Naval Architecture; Petroleum and Gas Engineering; Transport Management); **Open Maritime Education**; **Post-Graduate Professional Education**; **Sea Protection** (Safety Engineering); **Social and Political Management** (Human Resources; Management; Social Problems; Sociology)

Further Information: Also Mutlilevel Education provided through: Basic Vocational Education programmes, Secondary Professional Education Programmes; Water Transport Personnel Re-training provided through Upgrading Qualifications Programmes/Continuing Education Courses (Branches in Nakhodka, Primorsky Krai, Blagoveshchensk, Amurskaya Oblast, Sakhalinskaya Oblast); Representation in Khabarovsk.

History: Founded 1890. Higher education institution status obtained 1944. Acquired present status and title 2001.

Governing Bodies: Academic Council

Academic Year: September to July

Admission Requirements: Certificate of completed general Secondary Education (Attestat o Srednem (Polnom) Obshchem Obrazovanii)

Main Language(s) of Instruction: Russian

International Co-operation: With Republic of Korea, Japan, China, Vietnam, USA. Member of IAMU (International Association of Maritime Universities, GlobalMET (Global Marine Education and Training Association), AMFUF (Asia Maritime and Fisheries Universities Forum), GPE (Global Partners in Education), CLARINET (Coastal Linkage of Academic and Research Institution's Network in Northeast Asia)

Degrees and Diplomas: *Bakalavr*: 4 yrs; *Specialist Diploma*: 5-5 1/2 yrs; *Magistr*: 6 yrs; *Doktor Nauk*: Shipbuilding Technology; Ship Repair Technology and Shipbuilding Organisation; Marine Power Plants and their Elements (Main and Auxiliary)

Student Services: Academic counselling, Canteen, Cultural centre, Employment services, Foreign Studies Centre, Health services, Nursery care, Social counselling, Sports facilities

Student Residential Facilities: For 2,850 students

Special Facilities: Museum; Training-and-cargo ships; Bridge and Engine-room Simulators

Libraries: Central Library, c. 482,000 vols

Press or Publishing House: University Publishing House

Academic Staff *2008-2009*	MEN	WOMEN	**TOTAL**
FULL-TIME	163	170	**333**
PART-TIME	80	84	**164**
Student Numbers *2008-2009*			
All (Foreign Included)	3,183	1,297	**4,480**

Distance students, 272.

Last Updated: 21/11/08

MATI-RUSSIAN STATE TECHNOLOGICAL UNIVERSITY

MATI-Rossijskij Gosudarstvennyj Tehnologičeskij Universitet

ul. Orshanskaya 3, Moskva 121552
Tel: +7(495) 141-1940
Fax: +7(495) 141-1950
EMail: intdep@mati.edu.ru
Website: http://www.mati.ru

Rector: Anatoly Petrov Tel: +7(495) 149-0930

First Vice-Rector: Alexandr Kirillianchik

International Relations: Aleksandr S. Grabilnikov
EMail: grabilnikov@mati.ru

Faculties

Aerospace Engineering (Aeronautical and Aerospace Engineering); **Aerospace Technology** (Aeronautical and Aerospace Engineering; Materials Engineering; Metal Techniques; Metallurgical Engineering); **Applied Mathematics and Information Technology** (Applied Mathematics; Computer Engineering; Computer Science; Data Processing; Information Technology; Software Engineering); **Composite Materials Science and Technology** (Materials Engineering); **Economics** (Accountancy; Economics; Management; Marketing); **International Education** (Foreigners Education; International and Comparative Education) *Dean*: Sergei Silantiev; **Radio Engineering and Electronics, Avionics** (Automation and Control Engineering; Electrical and Electronic Engineering; Telecommunications Engineering)

Schools

Ecology

History: Founded 1932. Former Moscow Aviation Technology University named after K.E. Tziolkovsky'.

Governing Bodies: University Board

Academic Year: September to June (September-January; February-June)

Admission Requirements: Secondary school certificate (Attestat o srednem obrazovanii)

Fees: (US Dollars): 3,000-4,500 per annum

Main Language(s) of Instruction: Russian

International Co-operation: With universities in United Kingdom, Netherlands, USA, Republic of Korea, China, Vietnam and India.

Accrediting Agencies: Ministry of Education

Degrees and Diplomas: *Bakalavr*: 4 yrs; *Magistr*: 6 yrs; *Kandidat Nauk*: a further 3 yrs following Magistr. Engineer, 5 1/2 yrs

Student Services: Academic counselling, Canteen, Cultural centre, Foreign student adviser, Foreign Studies Centre, Health services, Language programs, Social counselling, Sports facilities

Student Residential Facilities: Yes

Libraries: University Library, c. 700,000 vols

Publications: University Annual Proceedings *(annually)*

MAYKOP STATE TECHNOLOGICAL INSTITUTE

Maykopskij Gosudarstvennyj Tehnologičeskij Institute

ul. Pjervomaiskaja 191, Majkop, 385000 Respublika Adygeja
Tel: +7(8772) 52-31-31 +7(8772) 57-04-04
Fax: +7(8772) 52-31-31 +7(8772) 52-16-24
EMail: info@mkgtu.ru
Website: http://www.mkgtu.ru/

Rector: Khasret Ramazonovich Blyagoz

Faculties

Agricultural Technology (Agricultural Engineering; Agricultural Equipment; Agronomy; Crop Production; Farm Management; Soil Conservation; Soil Science); **Ecology** (Ecology; Environmental Management; Forestry; Natural Resources; Parks and Recreation); **Engineering and Economics** (Economics; Engineering; Hotel Management; Tourism; Transport Economics); **Finance and Economics** (Banking; Economics; Finance; Taxation); **International Education** (Russian); **Management** (Economics; Management); **New Social Technologies** (Educational Psychology; English; French; Law; Museum Management; Public Relations; Social Policy; Social Sciences; Tourism); **Technology** (Building Technologies; Chemistry; Civil Law; Criminal Law; Food Technology; Inorganic Chemistry; Machine Building; Physical Chemistry; Physics; Technology)

Institutes

Medicine (Medicine; Surgery; Veterinary Science)

History: Founded 1993.

Governing Bodies: Council

Academic Year: September to July

Admission Requirements: Secondary school certificate (Attestat o srednem obrazovanii) or equivalent

Main Language(s) of Instruction: Russian

Degrees and Diplomas: *Bakalavr*; *Specialist Diploma*; *Kandidat Nauk*; *Doktor Nauk*

Student Services: Academic counselling, Canteen, Cultural centre, Employment services, Foreign student adviser, Health services, Social counselling, Sports facilities

Student Residential Facilities: For 270 students

Special Facilities: Botanical Garden

Libraries: Central Library, c. 532,000 vols

Last Updated: 10/02/12

MICHURINSK STATE AGRARIAN UNIVERSITY

Mičurinskij Gosudarstvennyj Agranyj Universitet

ul. Internacionalnaja 101, Mičurinsk, 393740 Tambovskaja oblast'
Tel: +7(07545) 531-37
Fax: +7(07545) 526-35
EMail: mgau@mich.ru
Website: http://www.mgau.ru

Rector: Anatolij Ivanovich Zavražnov (1985-)

Prorector: Stanislav Ivanovich Polevšikov
Tel: +7(07545) 523-95, Fax: +7(07545) 526-35

International Relations: Andrej Ivanovich Kuzin
Tel: +7(07545) 546-62, Fax: +7(07545) 546-62

Faculties

Agronomy (Agronomy) *Dean*: Nikolaj Nikolajevič Babič; **Animal Husbandry** (Agricultural Engineering; Animal Husbandry) *Dean*: Vasilij Stepanovič Suškov; **Economics** (Accountancy; Economics; Finance; Law; Taxation) *Dean*: Vadim Vasiljevič Smykov; **Engineering** (Agricultural Engineering; Agricultural Equipment; Engineering) *Dean*: Nikolaj Vladimirovuč Mihejev; **Fruit and Vegetable Production** (Crop Production; Fruit Production) *Dean*: Yurij Victorovič Trunov; **Humanities** (Arts and Humanities; Business and Commerce; Public Administration; Public Relations) *Dean*: Marina Lvovna Alemasova

Laboratories

Biotechnology (Biotechnology; Fruit Production) *Director*: Alexandr Mihajlovič Tarasov; **Dwarf Apple Rootstock Selection** (Fruit Production) *Director*: Alexandr Vasiljevič Verzilin; **Ecological Testing** (Ecology) *Director*: Vladimir Mihajlovič Lapuškin; **Wheat Selection** (Plant and Crop Protection) *Director*: Mihail Alexandrovič Jakovlev

History: Founded 1931 as Institute, acquired present status and title 1999.

Academic Year: September to July (September-January; February-July)

Admission Requirements: Secondary school certificate (Attestat o srednem obrazovnaii) or equivalent (Diplom o srednem-specialnom obrazovanii)

Main Language(s) of Instruction: Russian

International Co-operation: With universities in Germany, Finland, Hungary, Netherlands, Switzerland.

Accrediting Agencies: Ministry of Agriculture

Degrees and Diplomas: *Bakalavr*: 4 yrs; *Specialist Diploma*: a further 1 yr; *Kandidat Nauk*: Agricultural Sciences, a further 3 yrs; *Doktor Nauk*: Agricultural Sciences, a further 3 yrs following Kandidat Nauk

Student Services: Academic counselling, Canteen, Cultural centre, Health services, Language programs, Social counselling, Sports facilities

Student Residential Facilities: For 1,200 students

Special Facilities: Botanical Garden. University History Museum. Movie Studio.

Libraries: c. 400,000 vols

Publications: Vesti MGAU *(monthly)*; Vestnik MičGAU, Scientific Publication on Agricultural, Economic, and Human Sciences *(1-2 per annum)*

MICHURINSK STATE PEDAGOGICAL INSTITUTE

Mičurinskij Gosudarstvennyj Pedagogičeskij Institut

ul. Sovetskaja 274, Mičurinsk, 393740 Tambovskaja oblast'
Tel: +7(47545) 5-26-45 +7(47545) 5-22-25 +7(47545) 5-33-23
Fax: +7(47545) 5-08-28 +7(47545) 5-67-48
EMail: mgpi_lab@mich.ru; mgpi2@mich.ru
Website: http://www.michgpi.ru/

Rector: Vladimir Nikolaevich Jatsenko

Faculties

Biology (Agriculture; Biology; Chemistry; Ecology; Environmental Studies; Science Education; Zoology); **Philology** (Literature; Philology; Russian); **Primary Education** (Preschool Education; Primary Education)

History: Created 1939.

Degrees and Diplomas: *Specialist Diploma*

Last Updated: 21/02/12

MILITARY AVIATION ENGINEERING UNIVERSITY

Voennij Aviacionnij Inženernyj Universitet

ul. Staryjkh Bol'ševikov, 54A, Voronež, 394064 Voronežskaja oblast'
Tel: +7(473) 226-38-05 +7(473) 226-18-88 +7(473) 226-60-13
Fax: +7(473) 226-47-52 +7(473) 226-18-88
EMail: vvvaiu@vvvaiu.vrn.ru
Website: http://www.vaiu.ru/

Rector: Genagij V. Zibrov

Programmes

Engineering (Aeronautical and Aerospace Engineering; Air Transport; Military Science)

History: Created 1949. Previously known as Voronežskij Voennij Aviacionnij Inženernyj Institut (Voronezh Military Aviation Engineering Institute).

Degrees and Diplomas: *Specialist Diploma*

Last Updated: 12/03/12

MORDOVIAN STATE PEDAGOGICAL INSTITUTE

Mordovskij Gosudarstvennyj Pedagogičeskij Institut (MGPI)

ul. Studenčeskaja, Saransk, 430007 Mordovia
Tel: +7(8342) 321-925
Fax: +7(8342) 323-178
Website: http://www.moris.ru

Rector: Viktor Mironovich Makushkin (1992-) Tel: +7(8342) 331-336

Registrar: Marina Anatoljevnovna Korkina Tel: +7(8342) 331-336

Faculties

Biology and Chemistry (Biology; Chemistry; Organic Chemistry; Zoology); **Foreign Languages** (English; German; Modern Languages); **History and Law** (Archaeology; History; Law); **Pedagogy** (Music Education; Pedagogy; Primary Education); **Philology** (Linguistics; Modern Languages; Native Language; Philology; Russian); **Physical Education** (Physical Education); **Physics and Mathematics** (Applied Physics; Computer Science; Mathematics; Physics; Science Education); **Preschool Education** (Education; Preschool Education); **Special Education** (Education of the Handicapped; Special Education)

History: Founded 1962.

Governing Bodies: Institute Council

Academic Year: September to June (September-January; February-June)

Admission Requirements: Secondary school certificate (Attestat o srednem obrazovanii) or equivalent

Fees: (Russian Rubles): c. 6,500 per annum

Main Language(s) of Instruction: Russian

Degrees and Diplomas: *Specialist Diploma*: 5 yrs. Also Teaching Certificate, 3 yrs

Student Services: Canteen, Cultural centre, Health services, Sports facilities

Student Residential Facilities: For c. 1,130 students

Special Facilities: Mordovian Museum; Zoology Museum

Libraries: Institute Library, c. 437,000 vols

Press or Publishing House: MGPI Publishing House

MORDOVIAN STATE UNIVERSITY NAMED AFTER N.P. OGAREV

Mordovskij Gosudarstvennyj Universitet im. N.P. Ogareva

ul. Bolševiskaja 68, Saransk, 430005 Mordovia
Tel: +7(8342) 24-48-88
Fax: +7(8342) 32-75-27
EMail: rector@mrsu.ru
Website: http://www.mrsu.ru

Rector: Sergei Mikhailovich Vdovin

Faculties

Architecture (Architecture; Civil Engineering; Engineering Drawing and Design; Industrial Engineering; Industrial Management; Transport Engineering); **Biology** (Biochemistry; Biology; Biotechnology; Ecology; Genetics; Molecular Biology; Zoology); **Economics** (Accountancy; Administration; Agricultural Economics; Agricultural Management; Business Computing; Economics; Finance; Human Resources; Management; Marketing; Taxation; Transport Management); **Electronic Engineering** (Electronic Engineering; Industrial Engineering; Microelectronics); **Foreign Languages** (Engineering

Management; French; German; Philology; Romance Languages; Translation and Interpretation); **Geography** (Ecology; Environmental Studies; Geography; Landscape Architecture; Surveying and Mapping; Tourism); **Law** (Civil Law; Criminal Law; Criminology; European Union Law; History of Law; International Law; Law); **Light Technology** (Electrical Engineering); **Mathematics** (Applied Mathematics; Computer Science; Mathematics; Mechanics; Pedagogy); **Philology** (Journalism; Literature; Philology; Russian)

Further Information: Branches also in Kovylkino, Ruzaevka.

History: Founded 1931 as Mordovian State Teachers' Training Institute, acquired status 1957.

Governing Bodies: Academic Council

Academic Year: September to July

Admission Requirements: Secondary school certificate (Attestat o srednem obrazovanii) and entrance examination

Main Language(s) of Instruction: Russian

International Co-operation: With universities in Finland, Great Britain, Germany, Hungary, Sweden, Spain

Accrediting Agencies: Ministry of General Professional Education

Degrees and Diplomas: *Bakalavr*; *Specialist Diploma*; *Magistr*; *Kandidat Nauk*; *Doktor Nauk*

Student Services: Academic counselling, Canteen, Cultural centre, Employment services, Foreign student adviser, Foreign Studies Centre, Health services, Language programs, Social counselling, Sports facilities

Student Residential Facilities: Yes

Special Facilities: Eight Museums, including those of S.D. Aerzya, N.P. Ogarev. Observatory. Botanical Garden

Libraries: Scientific Library, c. 2m. vols

Last Updated: 13/01/12

MOSCOW AGRICULTURAL ACADEMY NAMED AFTER K.A.TIMIRJAZEVA

Moskovskaja Sel'skohozjajstvennaja Akademija im. K.A.Timirjazeva

ul. Timirzevskaja 49, Moskva 127550
Tel: +7(495) 976-0480
Fax: +7(495) 976-2910
EMail: info@timacad.ru
Website: http://www.timacad.ru

Rector: Vladimir Moiseevich Bautin

Programmes

Agriculture (Agriculture)

MOSCOW CITY TEACHER TRAINING UNIVERSITY

Moskovskij Gorodskoj Pedagogičeskij Universitet (MGPU)

2-y Selskokhozyastvenny pr.4-1, Moskva 129226
Tel: +7(499) 181-26-16
Fax: +7(499) 181-65-52
EMail: rectorat@mgpu.ru; info@mgpu.ru
Website: http://www.mgpu.ru

Rector: Alexander G. Kutuzov (2012-) EMail: rectorat@mgpu.ru

Pro-Rector: Elena Nikolaevna Gevorkian
EMail: Gevorcian@mgpu.ru

International Relations: Viktoria Kosteva, Head International Cooperation Department
Tel: +7(499) 694-52-62 EMail: vmkosteva@gmail.com

Campuses

Samara (Economics; Law; Modern Languages; Psychology)

Departments

Art (Art Education); **Economics** (Economics; Management; Marketing); **Law** (Civil Law; Law; Public Law); **Music** (Music); **Special Pedagogy** (Special Education); **Technology and Design** (Design; Handicrafts; Management; Technology)

Institutes

Foreign Languages (Arabic; Chinese; English; French; German; Italian; Japanese; Modern Languages); **Humanitarian Sciences** (History; Literature; Philology; Public Relations; Russian); **Leading Managers in Pedagogy Preparation** (Educational Administration); **Mathematics and Informatics** (Computer Science; Mathematics); **Natural Sciences** (Biology; Chemistry; Ecology; Geography); **Pedagogy and Psychology of Education** (Pedagogy; Preschool Education; Primary Education); **Psychology, Sociology and Social Relations** (Psychology; Social Work; Sociology); **Scientific Research for Education in the Russian Capital** (Mathematics; Natural Sciences); **Sports** (Sports)

History: Founded 1995.

Governing Bodies: University Council

Academic Year: September to June

Admission Requirements: Secondary school certificate (Attestat o srednem obrazovanii), United State Exam (EGE) with notes in three or four subjects depending on the chosen Major

Fees: (US Dollars): 2,500-5,000 per annum

Main Language(s) of Instruction: Russian

International Co-operation: None

Accrediting Agencies: Ministry of Education and Science of the Russian Federation

Degrees and Diplomas: *Bakalavr*; *Specialist Diploma*: 5 yrs; *Magistr*; *Kandidat Nauk*; *Doktor Nauk*

Student Services: Academic counselling, Canteen, Cultural centre, Employment services, Foreign student adviser, Health services, Language programs, Social counselling, Sports facilities

Student Residential Facilities: Hostel (c. 70 beds)

Special Facilities: 19 scientific laboratories in the framework of the Scientific Research Institute for the Education of the Capital (NIISO); 21 buildings in Moscow fully equipped with PCs and PC classes linked to a general University net as well as to all necessary laboratory equipment, language classes, presentation rooms; electronic audimax's

Libraries: 760,000 vols; 360 periodical subscriptions; access to electronic networks, e.g. MARS (Interlibrary analytical collection of articles); Russian courier scientific files delivery system; E-Library (127 scientific journals); UIS Russia; Easdt View (82 titles); archive of scientific periodicals (30,000 vols.)

Publications: Vestnik MGPU, Scientific journal, issued for every major science (e.g. Philology series, Psychology series, etc.) *(quarterly)*

Press or Publishing House: University Publishing House

Academic Staff *2010-2011*	MEN	WOMEN	**TOTAL**
FULL-TIME	304	599	**903**
PART-TIME	137	140	**277**
STAFF WITH DOCTORATE			
FULL-TIME	243	417	**660**
PART-TIME	111	112	**223**

Student Numbers *2012-2013*			
All (Foreign Included)	–	–	**16,051**

Last Updated: 14/02/13

MOSCOW INSTITUTE OF ARCHITECTURE (STATE ACADEMY)

Moskovskij Arhitekturnyj Institut (Gosudarstvennaja Akademija) (MARCHI)

ul. Roždestvenka 11, Moskva 103754
Tel: +7(495) 924-7990
Fax: +7(495) 921-1240
EMail: marhi@marhi.ru
Website: http://www.miarch.edunet.ru

Rector: Alexander P. Kudrjavcev (1987-) Fax: +7(495) 924-7990
EMail: rector@marhi.ru

Vice-Rector in Charge of Curriculum: German Y. Orlov
Tel: +7(495) 924-7951, Fax: +7(495) 921-3522

International Relations: Ilja G. Ležava Tel: +7(495) 923-2091

Faculties

Foreign Students; **Fundamental Studies** (Aesthetics; Architecture and Planning; Art History; Building Technologies; Ecology; Economics; Painting and Drawing; Philosophy; Sculpture; Structural Architecture; Town Planning; Transport Engineering); **General Studies** (Architecture; Art History; Cultural Studies; Foreign Languages Education; History; Mathematics; Mechanics; Painting and Drawing; Physical Education; Surveying and Mapping); **Specialized Studies** (Architectural Restoration; Architecture and Planning; Environmental Studies; Landscape Architecture; Regional Planning; Town Planning)

History: Founded 1804 as Architectural College of Kremlin, acquired present title 1933, and present status 1994.

Governing Bodies: Academic Councils

Academic Year: September to July (September-January; February-July)

Admission Requirements: Secondary education certificate (Attestat o srednem obrazovanii) and entrance examination

Fees: (US Dollars): Foreign students, 2,000-4,000 per annum

Main Language(s) of Instruction: Russian

Degrees and Diplomas: *Bakalavr*: Architecture, 4 yrs; *Specialist Diploma*: Architecture, Environmental Design, a further 2 years; *Kandidat Nauk*: Architecture, a further 3-4 yrs. Diplomas recognized by the British Royal Institute of Architects

Student Services: Academic counselling, Canteen, Foreign Studies Centre, Health services, Language programs, Social counselling, Sports facilities

Student Residential Facilities: For c. 600 students

Special Facilities: Museum of Moscow Institute of Architecture. Art Gallery

Libraries: c. 280,000 vols; rare book division

Publications: *(annually)*; Architectural Science in MARCHI *(annually)*

Press or Publishing House: Ladja Publishing House

MOSCOW INSTITUTE OF AVIATION (TECHNICAL UNIVERSITY)

Moskovskij Aviacionnyj Institut (Tehničeskij Universitet)

Volokolamskoje šosse 4, Moskva 125993
Tel: +7(495) 158-0465
Fax: +7(495) 158-2977
EMail: aet@mai.ru
Website: http://www.mai.ru/english/

Rector: Alexandr Matveenko

International Relations: Alexander Kalliopin, Vice-Rector
EMail: intdep@mai.ru

Faculties

Aerospace Engineering (Aeronautical and Aerospace Engineering); **Aircraft Engineering** (Aeronautical and Aerospace Engineering); **Aircraft Engines** (Aeronautical and Aerospace Engineering); **Aircraft Radio-Electronic Equipment** (Aeronautical and Aerospace Engineering; Telecommunications Engineering); **Applied Mathematics and Physics** (Applied Mathematics; Physics); **Applied Mechanics** (Mechanical Engineering; Mechanics); **Control Systems, Informatics and Electrical Power Engineering** (Automation and Control Engineering; Electrical Engineering; Power Engineering); **Economics and Management** (Economics; Management); **Humanities** (Arts and Humanities); **Robotics** (Automation and Control Engineering; Robotics)

History: Founded 1930.

Governing Bodies: Academic Council

Academic Year: September to July

Admission Requirements: Secondary School Certificate or equivalent

Fees: (US Dollars): Main course, 3,600 per annum

Main Language(s) of Instruction: Russian

International Co-operation: With universities in Germany and France.

Degrees and Diplomas: *Diplom o Nepolnom Visshem Obrazovanii (Incomplete Higher Education Diploma)*: Aeronautical and Aerospace Engineering; Automation and Control Engineering; Computer Engineering; Electrical and Electronic Engineering; Avionics, 5 1/2 yrs; *Magistr*: Aeronautical and Aerospace Engineering; Automation and Control Engineering; Computer Engineering; Electrical and Electronic Engineering; Avionics (ME), a further 2 yrs

Special Facilities: Arts Centre. Research Laboratories.

Libraries: c. 2,984,000 vols.

MOSCOW INSTITUTE OF OPEN EDUCATION

Moskovskij Institut Otkrytogo Obrazovanija

Aviatsionnyj per. 6, Moskva 125167
Tel: +7(499) 151-44-11
Fax: +7(499) 151-69-97
EMail: mioo-avia@mail.ru
Website: http://www.mioo.ru

Rector: Aleksei L'vovich Semenov

Programmes

Education (Education; Educational Administration; Educational Psychology; Educational Technology; Humanities and Social Science Education; Pedagogy; Preschool Education; Primary Education; Science Education; Secondary Education; Special Education; Technology Education)

History: Created 1938.

Degrees and Diplomas: *Specialist Diploma*
Last Updated: 20/08/12

MOSCOW INSTITUTE OF PHYSICS AND TECHNOLOGY (STATE UNIVERSITY)

Moskovskij Fiziko-Tekhničeskij Institut (Gosudarstvennyj Universitet)

Institutskij per. 9, Dolgoprudny, 141700 Moskovskaja oblast'
Tel: +7(495) 408-5700
Fax: +7(495) 408-6869
EMail: rector@mipt.ru
Website: http://www.mipt.ru

Rector: Nikolay N. Kudryavtsev (2002-)

Vice-Rector: Yuri N. Volkov
Tel: +7(495) 576-4177 EMail: yvolkov@mipt.ru

International Relations: Svetlana I. Trofimova
Tel: +7(495) 408-7563 EMail: intoff@oms.mipt.ru

Faculties

Aeromechanics and Flying Techniques (Aeronautical and Aerospace Engineering; Automation and Control Engineering; Data Processing; Information Technology; Mathematical Physics; Mathematics; Mechanical Engineering; Mechanics; Physical Engineering; Sound Engineering (Acoustics)) *Dean*: Victor V. Vyshinsky; **Aerophysics and Space Research** (Aeronautical and Aerospace Engineering; Air Transport; Astronomy and Space Science; Automation and Control Engineering; Electrical Engineering; Mathematics; Mechanics; Metallurgical Engineering; Operations Research; Physics; Power Engineering; Technology; Thermal Physics) *Dean*: Sergey S. Negodyaev; **Control and Applied Mathematics** (Applied Mathematics; Automation and Control Engineering; Computer Science; Economics; Information Technology; Mathematical Physics; Mathematics) *Dean*: Alexandr A. Shananin; **General and Applied Physics** (Applied Physics; Physics) *Dean*: Mikhail R. Trunin; **Innovation and High Technology** *Dean*: Valery E. Krivtsov; **Molecular and Biological Physics** (Biology; Biophysics; Chemistry; Ecology; Information Technology; Mathematics; Mathematics and Computer Science; Molecular Biology; Physics) *Dean*: Ivan N. Groznov; **Physical and Quantum Electronics** (Electronic Engineering; Microelectronics; Nanotechnology; Physical Engineering; Physics; Radiophysics; Technology) *Dean*: Pavel A. Todua; **Problems of Physics and Power Engineering** (Applied Physics; Ecology; Electronic Engineering; Energy Engineering; Mathematics; Optics; Physics; Power Engineering; Technology) *Dean*: Alexey G. Leonov; **Radio Engineering and Cybernetics** (Automation and Control Engineering; Computer Engineering; Computer Science; Data Processing; Electronic Engineering; Engineering; Information Management; Information Technology; Optical Technology; Radiophysics; Safety Engineering;

Software Engineering; Technology; Telecommunications Engineering) *Dean*: Sergey N. Ganchev

History: Founded 1951.

Academic Year: September to June (September-January; February-June)

Admission Requirements: Secondary school certificate (Attestat o srednem obrazovanii) and entrance examination

Fees: (Russian Rubles): Bachelor's degree, 120,000 per annum; Master's degree 135,000 per annum

Main Language(s) of Instruction: Russian

Accrediting Agencies: Ministry of Education and Sciences of the Russian Federation, Federal Agency of Education

Degrees and Diplomas: *Bakalavr*: Applied Mathematics and Physics; Informatics and Computer Science; Systems Analysis and Management, 4 yrs; *Magistr*: Applied Mathematics and Physics; Informatics and Computer Science; Systems Analysis and Management, a further 2 yrs; *Kandidat Nauk*: Mathematics; Informatics; Natural Sciences; Engineering, a further 3 yrs; *Doktor Nauk*: Mathematics; Informatics; Natural Sciences; Engineering, a further 3-4 yrs following Kandidat

Student Services: Academic counselling, Canteen, Cultural centre, Employment services, Foreign student adviser, Foreign Studies Centre, Health services, Language programs, Social counselling, Sports facilities

Student Residential Facilities: For 4,700 students and 600 post-graduate students

Special Facilities: History Museum.

Libraries: Central Library, c. 740,000 vols

Publications: PhysTech Journal *(quarterly)*; Proceedings of the Scientific Conference *(annually)*

Last Updated: 24/11/08

MOSCOW POWER ENGINEERING INSTITUTE

Moskovskij Energetičeskij Institut

ul. Krasnokazarmennaja 14, Moskva 111250
Tel: +7(495) 362-5645
Fax: +7(495) 362-8918
EMail: uvs@mpei.ru
Website: http://www.mpei.ru

Rector: Sergey Vladimirovich Serebriannikov (2005-2015)
Tel: +7(495) 362-5650 EMail: serebrianniksv@mpei.ru

Vice-Rector: Igor S. Samsonov
Tel: +7(495) 362-5133 EMail: samsonovIS@mpei.ru

International Relations: V.N. Zamolodchikov, Vice-Rector, International Relations

Campuses

Smolensk (Accountancy; Administration; Computer Science; Economics; Electrical Engineering; Electronic Engineering; Management; Power Engineering); **Volžskij** (Electrical Engineering; Power Engineering)

Faculties

Professional Skills Upgrading for Professors and Specialists

Institutes

Arts and Humanities (Accountancy; Art Management; Design; Finance); **Computer Science and Automatics Engineering** (Computer Science); **Electrical Engineering** (Electrical Engineering); **Electrical Power Engineering** (Electrical Engineering; Power Engineering); **Electrical Power Engineering and Mechanics** (Mechanical Engineering; Power Engineering); **Power Engineering Efficiency Problems** (Power Engineering); **Radio Engineering and Electronics** (Telecommunications Engineering); **Technology, Economics and Business**; **Thermal and Nuclear Power Engineering** (Nuclear Engineering; Thermal Engineering)

History: Founded 1930, acquired present status and title 2010.

Academic Year: September to July

Admission Requirements: Secondary school certificate (Attestat o srednem obrazovanii) and Uniform State Exam (Edinyj Gosudarstvennyj Ekzamen)

Fees: (US Dollars): 3,300-5,000 per annum; graduate, 4,000-6,000

Main Language(s) of Instruction: Russian. Also some specialities in English.

International Co-operation: With universities in Germany, Norway, Poland, France, Peru, China, Vietnam, etc.

Degrees and Diplomas: *Bakalavr*: Science, 4 yrs; *Magistr*: Science, 6 yrs; *Kandidat Nauk*: Science, a further 3 yrs; *Doktor Nauk*: Science, 3 yrs following Kandidat Nauk

Student Services: Academic counselling, Canteen, Cultural centre, Employment services, Foreign student adviser, Foreign Studies Centre, Health services, Language programs, Nursery care, Social counselling, Sports facilities

Student Residential Facilities: Yes

Special Facilities: Museum.

Libraries: Total, 2,100,000 vols

Academic Staff *2010-2011*: Total 1,300
STAFF WITH DOCTORATE: Total 920

Student Numbers *2012-2013*: Total: c. 12,000

Last Updated: 11/03/13

MOSCOW REGION STATE INSTITUTE FOR THE HUMANITIES

Moskovskij Gosudarstvennyj Oblastnoj Gumanitarnyj Institut

ul. Zelznaja 22, Orehovo-Zuevo 142611
Tel: +7(4964) 25-67-67 +7(4964) 25-78-75
Fax: +7(4964) 25-78-82
EMail: mgogi_rektor@mail.ru
Website: http://www.mgogi.ru/

Rector: Nadja Gennad'evna Jusupova

Faculties

Computer Science (Business Computing; Computer Science); **Educational Psychology** (Educational Psychology; Pedagogy; Social Psychology); **Foreign Languages** (English; Foreign Languages Education; Germanic Languages; Modern History; Romance Languages); **History** (History); **Law** (Law); **Natural and Mathematical Sciences** (Anatomy; Biology; Biotechnology; Botany; Computer Education; Ecology; Mathematics; Mathematics Education; Medicine; Pharmacology; Physics; Physiology); **Pedagogy** (Computer Education; Educational Psychology; Pedagogy; Preschool Education; Primary Education; Science Education; Teacher Training); **Pharmacy** (Pharmacy); **Philology** (Literature; Philology; Russian)

History: Created 1940. Previously known as Orehovo-Zuevskij Gosudarstvennyj Pedagogičeskij Institut (Orehovo-Zuevo State Pedagogical Institute). Acquired current title 2009.

Degrees and Diplomas: *Bakalavr*; *Specialist Diploma*

Last Updated: 24/02/12

MOSCOW REGIONAL INSTITUTE FOR SOCIAL AND ECONOMIC STUDIES

Moskovskij Regional'nyj Institut Vyssego Social'no-Economičeskogo Obrazovanija (MRSEI)

ul. Škol'naja 77, Vidnoe, 142700 Moskovskaja oblast'
Tel: +7(495) 541-8068
Fax: +7(495) 547-0916
EMail: mail@mrsei.ru
Website: http://www.mrsei.ru/

Rector: Vladimir I. Kačnev (1994-)

Secretary: Anastasija Snegirkova Tel: +7 (495) 547-0914

International Relations: Svetlana Ivanova, Head of Foreign Languages Tel: +7 (495) 547-1453

Centres

Methodology of Scientific Investigation *Director*: Vladimir Kačnev

Departments

Accounting and Audit (Accountancy) *Head*: Lyudmila Ermakova; **Design** (Graphic Design) *Head*: Stanislav Šappo; **Economic Theory** *Head*: Yurij Šedko; **Foreign Languages** (English; German) *Head*: Svetlana Ivanova; **General Psychology** (Psychology) *Head*:

Vladimir Čvyakin; **Humanities** (Economic History; Philosophy; Political Sciences; Sociology) *Head*: Boris Tebiev; **Management and Marketing** (Economics; Management) *Head*: Sergei Kim; **National Economy** *Head*: Evgenij Tatarskij; **Pedagogy and Psychology** (Pedagogy; Psychology) *Head*: Olga Knyazeva; **Secondary Vocational Training** *Head*: Irina Mezenceva

Laboratories

Moscow Regional Economy *Head*: Sergei Kim

History: A public higher education institution, the Institute was created to train specialists in social and economic disciplines.

Academic Year: September to June

Admission Requirements: attestat o srednom obrazovanii, diplom o načalnom/nopolnom vyssem obrazovanii

Fees: (Russian Rubles): 21,000-41,000 per annum

Main Language(s) of Instruction: Russian

Accrediting Agencies: Federal Service for Supervision in Education and Science

Degrees and Diplomas: *Bakalavr*, *Specialist Diploma*

Student Residential Facilities: none

Libraries: 32,234 vols

Publications: Ekonomika Podmoskovja, Efficiency of regional economy *(biennially)*; Ekonomika v Škole, Economics teaching in secondary schools *(biennially)*; Praktičeskaja psikhologia, psikhoanaliz *(biennially)*

Press or Publishing House: IPA Press (International Pedagogical Academy)

MOSCOW REGIONAL PEDAGOGICAL UNIVERSITY

Moskovskij Pedagogičeskij Oblastnoj Universitet (MGOU)

ul. Radio 10-a, Moskva 105005
Tel: +7(495) 261-2228
Fax: +7(495) 261-2228
EMail: rectorat@mgou.ru
Website: http://www.mgou.ru

Rector: Vladimir Pasechnik

Pro-Rector: Serguei Dembitski Tel: +7(495) 261-02-87

International Relations: Pavel Khromenkov
EMail: international@mgou.ru

Faculties

Art and Folk Crafts *Dean*: Alexey Viktovski; **Defectology** *(Psychology for Retarded People)* (Education; Health Sciences) *Dean*: Robert Amasyants; **History, Political Science and Law** (Arts and Humanities) *Dean*: Nickolay Smolensky; **Mathematics and Physics** (Mathematics and Computer Science; Natural Sciences) *Dean*: Anatoly Bugrimov; **Military Education** (Welfare and Protective Services) *Dean*: Vladimir Masyuk; **Physical Culture** *Dean*: Vladimir Maslov; **Psychology**; **Russian Philology** (Arts and Humanities) *Dean*: Lev Koposov; **Technology and Business** (Service Trades; Technology) *Dean*: Nickolay Lavrov

Institutes

Economy and Law *Director*: Ludmilia Chistokhodova; **Linguistics and Intercultural Communication** (Arts and Humanities) *Director*: Galina Tugolukova; **Natural Studies** *(Nature and Ecology)* *Director*: Alexander Konichev

History: Founded 1931 as Moscow Pedagogical University, acquired present status and title 2002.

Governing Bodies: Board of Directors

Academic Year: September to June

Admission Requirements: Secondary school certificate (Attestat o srednem obrazovanii) and entrance examination

Fees: (Russian Rubles): 13,000-75,000 per annum

Main Language(s) of Instruction: Russian

International Co-operation: With universities in Germany, France, Czech Republic, Switzerland.

Degrees and Diplomas: *Diplom o Nepolnom Visshem Obrazovanii (Incomplete Higher Education Diploma)*: 5 yrs; *Kandidat Nauk*: a further 3 yrs; *Doktor Nauk*: Science

Student Services: Academic counselling, Canteen, Cultural centre, Employment services, Foreign student adviser, Foreign Studies Centre, Health services, Language programs, Social counselling, Sports facilities

Student Residential Facilities: Yes

Special Facilities: Minerology Museum; Art gallery; Movie Studio

Libraries: Total, c. 1m.vols

Publications: Pedagogical and Managing Staff, Magazine of problems of pedagogical and additional education *(3 per annum)*; Philosophy Issues, Magazine on philosophy and related spheres *(other/irregular)*; Problems of Linguistics and Intercultural Communication *(3 per annum)*

MOSCOW STATE ACADEMIC INSTITUTE OF FINE ARTS NAMED AFTER I. SURIKOV

Moskovskij Gosudarstvennyj Akademičeskij Hudožestvennyj Institut im. I. Surikova

per. Tovarišeski 30, Moskva 109904
Tel: +7(495) 912-3932
Fax: +7(495) 912-1875
EMail: artinst@online.ru
Website: http://www.pencil.nm.ru

Rector: Anatolij Andreevich Bichukov

International Relations: Elena A. Guseva Tel: +7(495) 912-5672

Programmes

Fine Arts (Fine Arts)

MOSCOW STATE ACADEMY OF ART AND INDUSTRY NAMED AFTER S.G. STROGANOV

Moskovskaja Gosudarstvennaja Khudožestvenno-Promyšlennaja Akademija im. S.G. Stroganova

Volokolamskoje šosse 9, Moskva 125080
Tel: +7(499) 158-26-05
Fax: +7(499) 158-26-05
EMail: ychebnoe@mail.ru
Website: http://mghpu.ru/

Rector: Sergei Vladimirovich Kurasov

Faculties

Design (Communication Studies; Design; Furniture Design; Industrial Design; Textile Design); **Monumental and Decorative Arts and Crafts** (Ceramic Art; Glass Art; Graphic Arts; Interior Design; Painting and Drawing; Sculpture); **Restoration** (Art History; Restoration of Works of Art)

History: Created 1945. Previously known as Moskovskij Gosudarstvennyj Hudožestvenno-Promyšlennyj Universitet (Moscow State University of Art Industry). Acquired current title 1992.

Degrees and Diplomas: *Bakalavr*, *Specialist Diploma*; *Magistr*

Last Updated: 23/02/12

MOSCOW STATE ACADEMY OF CHOREOGRAPHY

Moskovskaja Gosudarstvennaja Akademija Horeografii

ul. 2-ja Frunzenskja 5, Moskva 119146
Tel: +7(499) 242-86-11
Fax: +7(499) 242-86-11
EMail: balletacademy@yandex.ru; mgah-bia@yandex.ru
Website: http://www.balletacademy.ru

Rector: Marja Konstantinova Leonova
EMail: balletacademy-rectorat@yandex.ru

Programmes

Dance (Art Management; Dance)

History: Founded 1773.

Degrees and Diplomas: *Specialist Diploma*

Last Updated: 16/01/12

MOSCOW STATE ACADEMY OF FINE CHEMICAL TECHNOLOGY

Moskovskaja Gosudarstvennaja Akademija Tonkoj Himičeskoj Tehnologii

prosp. Vernabskogo 86, Moskva 117571
Tel: +7(495) 437-7155
Fax: +7(495) 434-8711
EMail: mitht@mitht.ru
Website: http://www.mitht.ru

Rector: Vladimir S. Timofeev

Departments

Humanities (Arts and Humanities)

Faculties

Biotechnology and Organic Synthesis (Biotechnology; Chemistry); **Chemistry and Technology of Rare Elements and Materials for Electronics** (Chemistry; Electronic Engineering; Technology); **Management, Economics and Ecology** (Ecology; Economics; Management); **Natural Sciences** (Natural Sciences); **Polymer Chemistry, Physics and Processing Technology** (Chemistry; Physics; Polymer and Plastics Technology; Technology)

History: Founded 1900.

Degrees and Diplomas: *Bakalavr*: Science, 4 yrs; *Specialist Diploma*: 5 1/2 yrs; *Magistr*: Science, a further 2 yrs; *Kandidat Nauk*: 3 yrs; *Doktor Nauk*: 3 yrs

MOSCOW STATE ACADEMY OF GAS AND OIL

Moskovskaja Gosudarstvennaja Akademija Nefti i Gaza

prosp. Leninskij 65, Moskva 117917
Tel: +7(495) 135-8906
Fax: +7(495) 135-8895
Website: http://www.saog.ru

Rector: Albert I. Vladimirov

Vice-Rector: Oleg I. Koroljov

International Relations: Oleg I. Koroljov

Faculties

Chemical Technology and Ecology (Applied Chemistry; Ecology); **Computer Engineering and Automatics** (Automation and Control Engineering; Computer Engineering); **Economics, Management and Law** (Economics; Law; Management); **Engineering Mechanics** (Mechanical Engineering; Mechanics); **Oil and Gas Fields Exploitation** (Petroleum and Gas Engineering); **Oil and Gas Geology and Geophysics** (Geology; Geophysics); **Pipeline Systems** (Construction Engineering)

History: Founded 1930.

MOSCOW STATE ACADEMY OF GEOLOGICAL PROSPECTING

Moskovskaja Gosudarstvennaja Geologorazvedočnaja Akademija

ul. Mikluho-Maklaja 23, Moskva 117873
Tel: +7(495) 433-6256
Fax: +7(495) 433-4144
EMail: msgpa@msgpa.edu.ru
Website: http://www.msgpa.edu.ru

Rector: Leonid G. Grabčak

International Relations: Mihail A. Emelin Tel: +7(495) 433-6511

Faculties

Economics (Economics); **Equipment for Geological Prospecting and Mining** (Geological Engineering; Mining Engineering); **Geological Prospecting** (Geological Engineering); **Geophysics** (Geophysics); **Hydrogeology**

History: Founded 1918.

MOSCOW STATE ACADEMY OF LAW

Moskovskaja Gosudarstvennaja Juridičeskaja Akademija

Sadovaya-Kudrinskyja Str., 9, Moskva 123995
Tel: +7(495) 245-9972
Fax: +7(495) 254-9869
EMail: msal@msal.ru
Website: http://www.msal.ru

President: Oleg E. Kutafin (1993-) Fax: +7(495) 254-9972

First Vice-President: Victor V. Blazheev
Tel: +7(495) 244-8520, Fax: +7(495) 244-0457

International Relations: Valentin N. Soloviev
Tel: +7(495) 244-8543, Fax: +7(495) 254-4423

Centres

Professional Development *Head*: Alexander Slivko

Chairs

Administrative Law (Administrative Law) *Head*: Lev Popov; **Advocacy and Notary Services** (Justice Administration; Law; Notary Studies) *Head*: Anatoliy Koucherena; **Agricultural and Ecological Law** (Law) *Head*: Grigoriy Bystrov; **Business Law** *Head*: Inna Ershova; **Civil Law and Family Law** (Civil Law; Law) *Head*: Victor Mozolin; **Civil Procedure** (Civil Law) *Head*: Victor Blazheev; **Computer Science** (Computer Science) *Head*: Victor Elkin; **Constitutional and Municipal Law of Russia** (Constitutional Law; Law) *Head*: Oleg kutafin; **Constitutional Law and Foreign Countries** (Constitutional Law; International Law) *Head*: Boris Strashoon; **Criminal Law** *Head*: Aleksey Rarog; **Criminal Procedure** (Criminal Law) *Head*: Polina Loupinskaya; **Criminalistics** *Head*: Evgeniy Ishenko; **Criminology** (Criminology) *Head*: Vladimir Eminov; **Economics** *Head*: Evgeniy Borisov; **English Language** (English) *Head*: Galina Ermolenko; **European Union Law** *Head*: Sergey Kashkin; **Financial Law and Accountancy** (Accountancy; Law) *Head*: Olga Gorbounova; **Foreign Languages** (French; German; Latin; Spanish) *Head*: Nina Rastorgoueva; **International Private Law** *Head*: Galina Dmitrieva; **International Public Law** (International Law; Public Law) *Head*: Kamil Bekiashev; **Labour and Social Security Law** *Head*: Kantemir Gousov; **Philosophy** (Philosophy) *Head*: Viacheslav Kirillov; **Physical Training** (Physical Education) *Head*: Victor Kuznetsov; **Political Science** *Head*: Gennadiy Bouyrboulis; **State and Legal History** *Head*: Igor Isaev; **State and Legal Theory** *Head*: Orest Martyshin

Courses

Preparatory Courses *Director*: Irina Smolskaya

Departments

Postgraduate Studies *Head*: Tamara Zhmourova

Divisions

Kirov Branch *Director*: Samvel Kochoi; **Magadan Branch** *Director*: Tatiana Souspitsina; **Vologda Branch** *Director*: Konstantin Grouzdev

Faculties

Continuous Studies *Dean*: Maria Mirzojan; **Distance Studies** (Distance Education) *Dean*: Andrey Ostroumov; **Full-time Studies** *Dean*: Nikolay Kouvyrchenkov; **Part-time Studies** *Dean*: Maria Varlen

Institutes

Orenbourg *Director*: Michail Polshkov; **Prosecutors** *Director*: Evgeniy Maksimov

Further Information: Also Preparatory Courses. Study Abroad programmes

History: Founded 1931, acquired present status and title 1993.

Governing Bodies: Academy Council

Academic Year: September to June

Admission Requirements: Secondary school certificate (Attestat o srednem obrazovanii) or equivalent, and entrance examination

Fees: (US Dollars): Russian and CIS students, 1,500-5,000; Other students, 2,900-5,500 per annum (vary according to courses)

Main Language(s) of Instruction: Russian

International Co-operation: With universities in France, Germany, Kazakhstan, Republic of Korea, United Kingdom, Ukraine, USA, Vietnam.

Accrediting Agencies: Ministry of Education and Science

Degrees and Diplomas: *Specialist Diploma*: Civil Law; Criminal Law; International Law, 5 yrs; *Kandidat Nauk*: Administrative Law; Advocacy; Agricultural Law; Arbitration Procedure; Business Law; Civil Law; Civil Procedure; Constitutional Law; Computer Science; Criminal Enforcement and Criminology; Criminal Procedure; Criminalistics and Forensic Expertise (PhD, LLM); Criminal Investigation; Ecological Law; European Law; Family Law; Financial Law; Judicial

Authority; History of Law; International Law; International Private Law; Labour Law; Municipal Law; Social Security Law; State and Legal Theory (PhD, LLM), a further 3 yrs; *Doktor Nauk*: Administrative Law; Advocacy; Agricultural Law; Arbitration Procedure; Business Law; Civil Law; Civil Procedure; Constitutional Law; Computer Science; Criminal Enforcement and Criminology; Criminal Procedure; Criminalistics and Forensic Expertise (LLD), a furher 3 yrs; *Doktor Nauk*: Criminal Investigation; Ecological Law; European Law; Family Law; Financial Law; Judicial Authority; History of Law; International Law; International Private Law; Labour Law; Municipal Law; Social Security Law; State and Legal Theory (LLD), a further 3 yrs

Student Services: Academic counselling, Canteen, Cultural centre, Employment services, Foreign student adviser, Foreign Studies Centre, Handicapped facilities, Health services, Language programs, Social counselling, Sports facilities

Student Residential Facilities: Yes.

Special Facilities: Computer rooms.

Libraries: c. 400,000 vols.

Publications: Lex Russica, Law journal *(quarterly)*

Press or Publishing House: Publishing House Jurist

MOSCOW STATE ACADEMY OF PHYSICAL EDUCATION

Moskovskaja Gosudarstvennaja Akademija Fizičeskoj Kul'tury (MGAFK)

ul. Šosseinaja 33, Malahovka, 140032 Moskovskaja oblast
Tel: +7(495) 501-5545
Fax: +7(495) 501-2236
EMail: mos.gafk@mtu-net.ru
Website: http://www.infosport.ru/mgafk

Rector: Sergej Germanovich Seiranov (1997-)

Pro-Rector: Aleksandr Vasiljevich Portnov Tel: +7(495) 501-6011

International Relations: Ljudmila Filipovna Zueva
Tel: +7(495) 501-7372

Colleges

Humanities (Physical Education; Psychology; Sports Management; Sports Medicine)

Departments

Athletics (Physical Education; Psychology; Sports; Sports Management; Sports Medicine); **Gymnastics** (Sports); **Management, Economy and History of Sports** (Law; Physical Education; Sports; Sports Management); **Methods of Physical Education and Sports Training** (Education; Physical Education; Sports); **Recreational Technology** (Leisure Studies; Physical Education; Physiology; Psychology; Rehabilitation and Therapy); **Soccer and Hockey** (Physical Education; Psychology; Sports; Sports Management; Sports Medicine); **Sports Games** (Physical Education; Psychology; Sports; Sports Management; Sports Medicine); **Sports Medicine** (Physical Education; Physical Therapy; Psychology; Sports Medicine); **Swimming, Rowing and Equestrian Sports** (Physical Education; Psychology; Sports; Sports Management; Sports Medicine); **Weightlifting and Wrestling** (Physical Education; Psychology; Sports; Sports Management; Sports Medicine); **Winter Sports** (Physical Education; Sports Management; Sports Medicine)

Faculties

Physical Education (Anatomy; Physical Education; Physiology; Psychology; Sports Management; Sports Medicine)

Institutes

Information Technology (Information Technology; Physical Education; Sports); **Physical Education** (Physical Education)

History: Founded 1931 as Department, became independent Institution 1933, and acquired present status and title 1994.

Governing Bodies: Ministry of Physical Education, Sports and Tourism

Academic Year: September to June (September-December; February-June)

Admission Requirements: Secondary school certificate (Attestat o srednem obrazovanii)

Fees: (US Dollars): 2,500-4,000 per annum

Main Language(s) of Instruction: Russian

Degrees and Diplomas: *Specialist Diploma*: Physical Education; Adaptive Physical Education, 4 yrs; *Kandidat Nauk*: Pedagogical Sciences, a further 3 yrs

Student Services: Academic counselling, Canteen, Health services, Sports facilities

Student Residential Facilities: For c. 150 students

Special Facilities: Sports Museum

Libraries: Central Library, 218,000 vols

Publications: Materials of Scientific Conferences of Students *(annually)*; Scientific Anthology of Moscow State Academy of Physical Education *(annually)*; Theory and Practice of Physical Education *(monthly)*

Press or Publishing House: 'SportAcademPress' Publishing House

MOSCOW STATE ACADEMY OF VETERINARY MEDICINE AND BIOTECHNOLOGY

Moskovskaja Gosudarstvennaja Akademija Veterinarnoj Mediciny i Biotehnologii

ul. Akademika Skrjabina 23, Moskva 109472
Tel: +7(495) 377-9117
Fax: +7(495) 377-4939
EMail: rector@mgavm.ru
Website: http://www.mgavm.ru

Rector: Evguenij Voronin

Programmes

Biotechnology (Biotechnology); **Veterinary Science** (Veterinary Science)

MOSCOW STATE ACADEMY OF WATER TRANSPORT

Moskovskaja Gosudarstvennaja Akademija Vodnogo Transporta

No 2, Building 1, Novodanilovskaya naberezhnaya, Moskva 117105
Tel: +7(495) 633-16-35
Fax: +7(495) 633-16-02
EMail: mgavt@mail.ru
Website: http://www.msawt.ru/

Rector: Vladimir Ivanovich Kostin

Faculties

Economics and Management (Business Administration; Engineering Management; Human Resources; Management); **Marine Engineering** (Marine Engineering; Marketing); **Navigation, Maintenance of Fleet and Waterways** (Marine Transport; Nautical Science); **Waterways, Ports and Port Equipment** (Hydraulic Engineering; Marine Engineering; Marine Transport; Marketing)

Institutes

Law (Law; Maritime Law)

History: Founded 1979. Acquired present status 1993.

Academic Year: September to June

Admission Requirements: Secondary school certificate

Main Language(s) of Instruction: Russian

Accrediting Agencies: Ministry of Education and Science

Degrees and Diplomas: *Bakalavr*, *Specialist Diploma*; *Kandidat Nauk*

Student Services: Academic counselling, Employment services, Foreign Studies Centre, Health services, Sports facilities

Student Residential Facilities: Yes

Special Facilities: Museum

Libraries: 189,416 vols

Last Updated: 16/01/12

MOSCOW STATE AUTOMOBILE AND HIGHWAY ENGINEERING INSTITUTE (TECHNICAL UNIVERSITY)

Moskovskij Gosudarstvennyj Avtomobilno-Dorožnyj Institut (Tehničeskij Universitet) (MADI)

prosp. Leningradskij 64, Moskva 125829
Tel: +7(495) 1516-412
Fax: +7(495) 1518-965
EMail: info@madi.ru
Website: http://www.madi.ru

Rector: Vjačeslav M. Pričod'ko EMail: lukanin@madi.ru

First Vice-Rector: Vjačeslav M. Prihodko
Tel: +7(495) 1550-404, Fax: +7(495) 1517-911
EMail: prih@madi.ru

International Relations: Kjazim H. Akmaev, Vice-Rector
Tel: +7(495) 1513-991, Fax: +7(495) 1513-991
EMail: akmaev@madi.ru

Centres

Russian Coordination for Foreign Students Education *(Ministry of Education of Russia)*; **Russian Language for Foreign Students** (Russian)

Faculties

Bridge and Transport Tunnels (Civil Engineering; Transport Engineering); **Economics** (Economics); **Energy-Ecology** (Ecology; Energy Engineering); **Highway and Airport** (Air Transport; Civil Engineering; Road Engineering); **Humanities** (Arts and Humanities); **Machine Design and Mechanical Engineering** (Industrial Design; Mechanical Engineering); **Management** (Management); **Military and Sports** (Military Science; Sports); **Natural Sciences** (Natural Sciences); **Preparatory Studies** *(For foreign students)*; **Pre-School Teacher Training** (Preschool Education); **Road Building and Technological Machines** (Machine Building; Road Engineering); **Road Transport** (Road Transport); **Teacher Trainers Education** (Teacher Trainers Education); **Training Specialists in Road Transport** (Road Transport)

Institutes

Transport (Transport and Communications)

Research Institutes

Energy-Ecological Problems (Ecology; Energy Engineering); **Humanitarian** (Human Rights); **Management and Safety** (Management; Safety Engineering); **Mechanical Engineering** (Mechanical Engineering); **Nature Studies** (Natural Resources); **Social and Economic Aspects of Transport** (Economics; Social Studies; Transport and Communications); **Technology of Machines Maintenance** (Maintenance Technology; Mechanical Equipment and Maintenance)

Units

International Association for Automotive and Road Engineering Education *(IAAREE)* (Automotive Engineering; International Relations; Road Engineering)

Further Information: Also branches in Mahačla and Bronnitzy

History: Founded 1930, acquired present status and title 1992.

Governing Bodies: University Council

Academic Year: September to June (September-January; February-June)

Admission Requirements: Secondary school certificate (Attestat o sredem obrazovanii)

Fees: (US Dollars): 1,500-2,250 per annum

Main Language(s) of Instruction: Russian

Accrediting Agencies: Ministry of Education of the Russian Federation

Degrees and Diplomas: *Bakalavr*: 4 yrs; *Specialist Diploma*: Engineering, Technology, a further 1 1/2 yrs; *Magistr*: Science, a further 2 yrs; *Doktor Nauk*

Student Services: Academic counselling, Canteen, Foreign Studies Centre, Health services, Sports facilities

Student Residential Facilities: For c. 3,500 students

Special Facilities: History of the University Museum

Libraries: Madi-Tu Library, c. 1,3m. vols

Publications: University Proceedings *(annually)*

Press or Publishing House: Madi-Tu Publishing House

MOSCOW STATE FORESTRY UNIVERSITY

Moskovskij Gosudarstvennyj Universitet Lesa (MGUL)

ul. Pervaja Instituckaja 1, Mytišči, 141005 Moskovskaja oblast
Tel: +7(498) 687-41-48
Fax: +7(495) 583-73-42
EMail: rektor@mgul.ac.ru; priem@mgul.ac.ru
Website: http://www.mgul.ac.ru

Rector: Viktor Georgievič Sanaev
EMail: rector@mgul.ac.ru; vsanaev@mgul.ac.ru

Faculties

Economics and Foreign Relations (Accountancy; Agricultural Economics; Economics; Finance; International Relations; Management; Marketing); **Electronics and Technical Systems** (Applied Mathematics; Computer Science; Electronic Engineering; Mathematics; Physics; Technology); **Forestry Technology** (Forest Management; Forest Products; Forestry); **Humanities** (Cultural Studies; Educational Psychology; History; Law; Literature; Modern Languages; Pedagogy; Philosophy; Russian; Translation and Interpretation); **Landscape Architecture** (Architectural and Environmental Design; Landscape Architecture); **Mechanical and Chemical Wood Technology** (Applied Chemistry; Forest Products; Wood Technology); **Military and Sports Training** (Military Science; Sports)

Schools

Management and Business *(International)* (Business and Commerce; Management)

Further Information: Also Russian Language Courses for foreign students.

History: Founded 1919 as Moscow Forest Engineering Institute, acquired present status and title 1968.

Governing Bodies: Board of Directors; Scientific Council

Academic Year: September to July (September-January; February-July)

Admission Requirements: Secondary school certificate (Attestat o srednem obrazovanii) or equivalent (Technical Diploma)

Main Language(s) of Instruction: Russian

Degrees and Diplomas: *Bakalavr*, *Specialist Diploma*; *Magistr*, *Kandidat Nauk*; *Doktor Nauk*

Student Services: Academic counselling, Canteen, Cultural centre, Foreign Studies Centre, Health services, Nursery care, Social counselling, Sports facilities

Student Residential Facilities: For c. 3,000 students

Special Facilities: University Museum

Libraries: c. 600,000 vols

Last Updated: 13/01/12

MOSCOW STATE HUMANITARIAN UNIVERSITY NAMED AFTER M.A. SHOLOKHOV

Moskovskij Gosudarstvennyj Gumanitarnij Universitet im. M.A. Šolohova (MGGU)

ul. Verhnjaja Radiščevskaja 16-18, Moskva 109240
Tel: +7(495) 915-5053
Fax: +7(495) 915-5053
EMail: mgopu@mgopu.ru
Website: http://www.mgopu.ru

Rector: Jury G. Kruglov (1987-)
Tel: +7(495) 915-5512, Fax: +7(495) 915-5512

Vice-Principal (Pro-Rector): Alexander I. Nizhnikov

International Relations: Oleg P. Poplevin
Tel: +7(495) 915-5515 Ext. 2-31, Fax: +7(495) 915-3928
EMail: ums@mgopu.ru

Faculties

Education (Education) *Head*: Valeriy Borisov

History: Founded 1951 as Moscow State Distance Teacher Training Institute. Reorganised as Moscow State Open Teacher Training University (Moskovskij Gosudarstvennyj Otkrytyj Pedagogičeskij

Universitet) 1995. Named after M.A. Sholohova 2000. Acquired present title 2006.

Governing Bodies: Academic Council

Academic Year: September to June

Admission Requirements: School leaving certificate or diploma of secondary vocational school; entrance examination

Fees: (Russian Rubles): 35,000 per semester

Main Language(s) of Instruction: Russian

International Co-operation: With institutions in United Kingdom, Germany, Israel, Spain, China, Poland, Republic of Korea, Syria, Finland, Countries of CIS

Accrediting Agencies: Federal service for the supervision of education and science of Russia

Degrees and Diplomas: *Diplom o Nepolnom Visshem Obrazovanii (Incomplete Higher Education Diploma)*; *Bakalavr*: Philology Education; Linguistics; Pedagogy; Artistic Education; Physico-mathematical Education; Natural Science Education; Technological Education; Socio-economic Education, 4 yrs; *Magistr*: Philology Education; Linguistics; Pedagogy; Artistic Education; Physico-mathematical Education; Natural Science Education; Technological Education; Socio-economic Education, a further 2 yrs; *Kandidat Nauk*: 3 yrs; *Doktor Nauk*: 3 yrs

Student Services: Academic counselling, Canteen, Cultural centre, Employment services, Foreign student adviser, Foreign Studies Centre, Handicapped facilities, Language programs, Social counselling, Sports facilities

Student Residential Facilities: No

Special Facilities: Sholokhov museum; Sholokhov scientific centre; Institute of education informatization; Inter-University centre of Pedagogical Innovations

Libraries: Joint library of the University; Branch libraries

Publications: Collections, Collections of scientific articles *(annually)*; Herald of the MGGU, Collections of scientific articles *(quarterly)*

Press or Publishing House: Taganka publishing house

Academic Staff *2007-2008*	MEN	WOMEN	**TOTAL**
FULL-TIME	493	697	**1,190**
PART-TIME	123	175	**298**
STAFF WITH DOCTORATE			
FULL-TIME	–	–	**825**
PART-TIME	–	–	**590**
Student Numbers *2007-2008*			
All (Foreign Included)	11,750	19,050	**30,800**
FOREIGN ONLY	190	395	**585**

Part-time students, 8,120. **Distance students**, 12,210. **Evening students**, 10,470.

Last Updated: 08/12/08

MOSCOW STATE INDUSTRIAL UNIVERSITY

Moskovskij Gosudarstvennyj Industrialnyj Universitet (MSIU)

ul. Avtozavodskaja 16, Moskva 115280
Tel: +7(495) 675-5237
Fax: +7(495) 674-6392
EMail: topstaff@msiu.ru
Website: http://www.msiu.ru

Rector: Victor A. Demin

International Relations: Alexander D. Sedykh
Tel: +7(495) 675-2256 EMail: asedykh@msiu.ru

Departments

Post-graduate (Applied Mathematics; Automotive Engineering; Civil Law; Commercial Law; Economics; Information Technology; Machine Building; Management; Materials Engineering; Metallurgical Engineering; Physics; Public Law)

Faculties

Applied Mathematics and Technical Physics (Applied Mathematics; Information Technology; Materials Engineering; Physics); **Automotive Engineering** (Automotive Engineering; Machine Building); **Economics, Management and Information Technology** (Accountancy; Economics; Finance; Human Resources; Information Technology; Management); **Law** (Civil Law; History of Law; Law; Public Law)

History: Founded 1960, acquired present status and title 1996.

Governing Bodies: University Administration; University Academic Council

Academic Year: September to June

Main Language(s) of Instruction: Russian

Accrediting Agencies: Coordination Council for Independent Public Professional Accreditation (CC IPPA)

Degrees and Diplomas: *Bakalavr*: 4 yrs; *Specialist Diploma*: 5 yrs; *Magistr*: 2 yrs; *Kandidat Nauk*: 3 yrs; *Doktor Nauk*

Student Services: Academic counselling, Canteen, Cultural centre, Employment services, Foreign student adviser, Health services, Social counselling, Sports facilities

Student Residential Facilities: No

Special Facilities: No

Libraries: c. 500,000 vols

Publications: Izvestija MGIU (Proceedings of MSIU), Natural Sciences, Engineering Sciences, Information Technology, Social Sciences, Liberal Arts *(quarterly)*; Mashinostrojenije I Inzhnernoje Obrazovanije, Machine Building and Engineering Education *(quarterly)*

Academic Staff *2007-2008*	MEN	WOMEN	**TOTAL**
FULL-TIME	268	197	**465**
PART-TIME	210	99	**309**
STAFF WITH DOCTORATE			
FULL-TIME	218	105	**323**
PART-TIME	141	55	**196**
Student Numbers *2007-2008*			
All (Foreign Included)	–	–	**7,000**

Distance students, 20,000.

Last Updated: 27/11/08

MOSCOW STATE INSTITUTE OF BUSINESS MANAGEMENT

Moskovskij Gosudarstvennyj Institut Delovogo Administrirovanija (MSIBA)

1140, Moskva, Zelenograd 124460
Tel: +7(495) 530-94-42
Fax: +7(495) 530-94-42
EMail: info@miba.ru
Website: http://www.miba.ru

Rector: Tamara Kostina (2004-)
Tel: +7(495) 530-94-55 EMail: kostina@miba.ru

Administrative Officer: Elena Nosova

International Relations: Valeriy Surinskiy, Pro-Rector for International Co-operation
Tel: +7(495) 530-94-31 EMail: surinsky@miba.ru

Departments

Postgraduate Studies (Economics; Management) *Head*: Nina Blinkova

Faculties

Economics and Management (Accountancy; International Economics; Management) *Dean*: Galina Kolpakova; **Extra-Mural Studies** (Accountancy; Management; Private Law; Public Law) *Dean*: Eugeny Sutiagin; **Law** (Private Law; Public Law) *Dean*: Margarita Tokmovtseva

History: Founded 1992 as Moscow College of Business Administration. Acquired present status and title 1997.

Governing Bodies: Academic Council

Academic Year: September to June

Admission Requirements: Secondary school certificate

Fees: (Russian Rubles): 600-1,200 per month

Main Language(s) of Instruction: Russian

International Co-operation: With universities in Japan, Sweden, USA, Germany, United Kingdom

Degrees and Diplomas: *Bakalavr*: Management; Economics, 4 yrs; *Specialist Diploma*: Management; International Economics; Accountancy; Law, 5 yrs. Also postgraduate studies in Economics and National Economy Management (Labour Economics, Organization and Management of Companies; Innovative Management)

Student Services: Academic counselling, Canteen, Cultural centre, Employment services, Health services, Language programs, Social counselling, Sports facilities

Student Residential Facilities: None

Special Facilities: Movie Studio

Libraries: Yes

Publications: Business, Collected articles *(annually)*; Open Society. Sustainable Development, Collected articles *(annually)*; The Day of Science, Collected articles *(annually)*

MOSCOW STATE INSTITUTE OF ELECTRONIC TECHNOLOGY (TECHNICAL UNIVERSITY)

Moskovskij Gosudarstvennyj Institut Elektronnoj Tehniki (Tehničeskij Universitet)

ul. Zelenograd Alleja, Moskva 103498

Tel: +7(495) 531-4441

Fax: +7(495) 530-2233

EMail: netadm@miee.ru

Website: http://www.miee.ru

Rector: Jurij A. Chaplygin (1998-)

Pro-Rector: Aleksei S. Pospelov

International Relations: Jurij T. Buharov
Tel: +7(495) 534-0264 EMail: postmaster@mocnit.zgrad.su

Faculties

Automatics and Electronic Engineering (Automation and Control Engineering; Electronic Engineering; Information Sciences; Information Technology); **Electronics and Computer Technology** (Automation and Control Engineering; Biomedical Engineering; Computer Science; Electronic Engineering; Microelectronics); **Evening Studies** (Business Administration; Computer Engineering; Computer Science; Econometrics; Electronic Engineering; Management; Materials Engineering; Microelectronics); **Information Technology and Microelectronics** (Computer Science; Electronic Engineering; Information Sciences; Microelectronics); **Law** (Civil Law; Higher Education Teacher Training; Labour Law; Public Law); **Microdevices and Engineering Cybernetics** (Applied Mathematics; Artificial Intelligence; Communication Studies; Computer Engineering; Computer Science; Electronic Engineering; Information Technology; Mathematics; Microelectronics; Software Engineering); **Physics and Chemistry** (Chemistry; Electronic Engineering; Materials Engineering; Microelectronics; Physics); **Psychology** (Educational Psychology; Psychology; Social Psychology)

Institutes

Economics and Management (Econometrics; Economics; Finance; Information Management; Marketing); **International Business Education** (Business Administration; Business Education; International Business)

History: Founded 1965.

Governing Bodies: Board of Deans; Academic Council

Academic Year: September to June (September-January; January-June)

Admission Requirements: Secondary school certificate (Attestat o srednem obrazovanii)

Main Language(s) of Instruction: Russian

Degrees and Diplomas: *Bakalavr*: 4 yrs; *Specialist Diploma*: Engineering; Technology, 5 yrs; *Magistr*: Further 2 yrs Following Bakalavr; *Kandidat Nauk*: a further 3 yrs

Student Services: Canteen, Cultural centre, Health services, Language programs, Sports facilities

Student Residential Facilities: For c. 2,000 students

Libraries: c. 672,000 vols

Publications: Naučno-Tehničeskij Sbornik, Research Publications *(annually)*

MOSCOW STATE INSTITUTE OF ELECTRONICS AND MATHEMATICS (TECHNICAL UNIVERSITY)

Moskovskij Gosudarstvennyj Institut Elektroniki i Matematiki (Tehničeskij Universitet) (MIEM)

per. Bolšoy Trjohsvjatitelsky 3/12, Moskva 109028

Tel: +7(495) 917-9089

Fax: +7(495) 916-2807

EMail: unims@miem.edu.ru

Website: http://www.miem.edu.ru

Rector: Dmitry Bykov (1990-)

Vice-Rector: Vladimir Kapyrin Tel: +7(495) 917-1386

International Relations: Igor Borodulin
Tel: +7(495) 917-0750, Fax: +7(495) 917-0750
EMail: bin@miem.edu.ru

Faculties

Automatics and Computer Engineering (Automation and Control Engineering; Computer Engineering; Software Engineering); **Economics and Mathematics**; **Electronics** (Electronic Engineering); **Informatics and Telecommunications** (Automation and Control Engineering; Computer Science; Engineering Drawing and Design; Telecommunications Engineering); **Mathematics** (Applied Mathematics; Computer Science; Mathematics)

History: Founded 1962, acquired present status and title 1993.

Governing Bodies: Board of Trustees

Academic Year: September to June (September-January; February-June)

Admission Requirements: Secondary school certificate (Attestat o srednem obrazovanii) and entrance examination

Main Language(s) of Instruction: Russian

Degrees and Diplomas: *Bakalavr*: Economics and Management, 4 yrs; *Specialist Diploma*: 5 1/2 yrs; *Doktor Nauk (PhD)*

Student Services: Academic counselling, Canteen, Employment services, Foreign student adviser, Health services, Language programs, Social counselling, Sports facilities

Special Facilities: Russian National Multimedia Centre

Libraries: Central Library

MOSCOW STATE INSTITUTE OF INTERNATIONAL RELATIONS (UNIVERSITY)

Moskovskij Gosudarstvennyj Institut Meždunarodnyh Otnošenij (Universitet) (MGIMO)

76 Vernadskogo prospekt, Moskva 119454

Tel: +7(495) 434-0089

Fax: +7(495) 434-9061

EMail: pr@mgimo.ru

Website: http://www.mgimo.ru

Rector: Anatoliy Torkunov (1992-)
Tel: +7(495) 434-9174 EMail: tork@mgimo.ru

Pro-rector for International and Public Relations: Andrey Silantyev
Tel: +7(495) 433-2175, Fax: +7(495) 434-1402
EMail: asilantiev@hotmail.com

International Relations: Roman Kotov
Tel: +7(495) 434-9288, Fax: +7(495) 434-1402
EMail: kotovs.family@gmail.com

Departments

Master Degree Studies *Director*: Anton Oleynov; **Postgraduate Studies** *Director*: Natalya Polyakova

Faculties

Basic Training *(Preparatory Faculty - FBP) Dean*: Sergey Monin; **Complementary Professional Education** (Education) *Dean*: Tatiana Polyanova; **International Business and Administration** (Administration; Business and Commerce; International Business) *Dean*: Vladimir Shitov; **International Economics Relations** *(MEO)* (Business and Commerce; Business Computing; Finance; International Economics; International Relations) *Dean*: Anatoliy Kholopov; **International Journalism** *(MJ)* (Journalism; Mass Communication; Public Relations; Sociology) *Dean*: Yaroslav Skvortsov; **International Law** *(MP)* (European Union Law; International Law; Private

Law; Public Law) *Dean*: Gennadiy Tolstopyatenko; **International Relations** *(MO) Dean*: Yuriy Bogaturov; **Political Sciences** *(FP)* (Comparative Politics; Political Sciences) *Dean*: Aleksey Voskresenskiy

Institutes

Administration *(International)* (Administration) *Director*: Robert Engibaryan; **Energy Politics and Diplomacy** *(International) Director*: Valeriy Salygin; **European Law** *(IEP)* (European Union Law) *Director*: Tamara Shashikhina; **European Studies** *(Russian European College - REK)* (European Studies) *Director*: Mark Entin; **External Economic Links** *(IVES)* (Business and Commerce; Management; Marketing) *Director*: Valeriy Chasovoy

Further Information: All graduate programmes are Bologna Process compatible

History: Founded 1944. Acquired present status 1994.

Governing Bodies: Academic Senate

Academic Year: September to June

Admission Requirements: Secondary school certificate (Attestat o srednem (polnom) obschem obrazovanii), Unified State Examination in Russia (Sertifikat Edinogo gosudarstvennogo ekzamena (EGE)).

Fees: (Russian Rubles): 196,000-432,000 per annum

Main Language(s) of Instruction: Russian

International Co-operation: With Universities in USA, Canada, Cuba, Venezuela, Chile, United Kingdom, France, Spain, Germany, Greece, Italy, Cyprus, Norway, The Netherlands, Portugal, Finland, Switzerland, Sweden, Azerbaidjan, Belarus, Armenia, Bulgaria, Hungary, Georgia, Latvia, Lithuania, Moldova, Poland, Serbia, Slovakia, Ukraine, Czech Republic, Israel, Jordan, UAE, Syria, Kazakhstan, Kyrgyzstan, Tajikistan, Uzbekistan, Brunei, Vietnam, India, Iran, People's Republic of China; Republic of Korea; Mongolia; Singapore; Taiwan; Japan; Egypt; Mozambique; South Africa

Degrees and Diplomas: *Bakalavr*; *Specialist Diploma*; *Magistr*; *Kandidat Nauk*; *Doktor Nauk*

Student Services: Academic counselling, Canteen, Cultural centre, Employment services, Foreign student adviser, Foreign Studies Centre, Health services, Language programs, Social counselling, Sports facilities

Student Residential Facilities: 4 dormitories (1 on campus, 3 in the city)

Special Facilities: Museum of History; Photo, video studio; drama and vocal studios (Cultural centre)

Libraries: I.G. Tyulin Library (700,000 vols); 55 languages, also Manuscripts museum

Academic Staff *2007-2008*	**TOTAL**
FULL-TIME	**1,000**
STAFF WITH DOCTORATE FULL-TIME	c. **200**
Student Numbers *2007-2008*	
All (Foreign Included)	c. **6,000**
FOREIGN ONLY	**800**

Evening students, 200.

Last Updated: 02/12/08

MOSCOW STATE INSTITUTE OF METALLURGY - EVENING STUDIES

Moskovskij Gosudarstvennyj Večernij Metallurgičeskij Institut

Lefortovskij val 26, Moskva 112250
Tel: +7(495) 361-1480
Fax: +7(495) 361-1446
EMail: mgvmi-mail@mtu-net.ru
Website: http://www.mgvmi.ru

Rector: Gennadij N. Elanskij

Programmes

Economics (Economics); **Mechanical Engineering** (Mechanical Engineering); **Metallurgical Engineering** (Metallurgical Engineering)

MOSCOW STATE INSTITUTE OF RADIO ENGINEERING, ELECTRONICS AND AUTOMATION (TECHNICAL UNIVERSITY)

Moskovskij Gosudarstvennyj Institut Radiotekhniki Elektroniki i Avtomatiki (Tekhničeskij Universitet)

prosp. Vernadskogo 78, Moskva 119454
Tel: +7(495) 433-0066
Fax: +7(495) 434-8665
EMail: mirea@mirea.ru
Website: http://www.mirea.ru

Rector: Alexander Sigov
Tel: +7(495) 433-0044, Fax: +7(495) 434-9287

International Relations: Ala A. Čekmazova
Tel: +7(495) 434-9276 EMail: chekmazova@mirea.ru

Faculties

Computer Science (Computer Engineering; Computer Networks; Computer Science; Software Engineering; Telecommunications Engineering) *Dean*: Serge Kovalenko; **Cybernetics** (Applied Mathematics; Automation and Control Engineering; Electronic Engineering; Robotics) *Dean*: Mikhail Romanov; **Economy and Management** (Banking; Economics; Finance; Management) *Dean*: Alexander Bolšakov; **Electronics** (Electronic Engineering; Materials Engineering; Microelectronics; Physics; Solid State Physics) *Dean*: Andrey Vasilev; **Radio-Engineering Systems** (Design; Electrical and Electronic Engineering; Electronic Engineering; Radiophysics; Technology; Telecommunications Engineering) *Dean*: Vladimir Bitiukov

Further Information: Also Partner Institution in Dubna City, Moscow Region, offering programmes in Industrial Electronics and Computer Science.

History: Founded 1947. Acquired present status 1993.

Academic Year: September to June

Admission Requirements: Secondary school certificate

Fees: (Russian Rubles): 55,000 per annum

Main Language(s) of Instruction: Russian

International Co-operation: With universities in France, Italy, Ireland

Accrediting Agencies: Federal Association for Education and Science Supervision (Rosobrnadzor)

Degrees and Diplomas: *Specialist Diploma*: Economics, 5 yrs; *Specialist Diploma*: Engineering; Mathematics; Computer Security, 5 1/2 yrs

Student Services: Academic counselling, Canteen, Cultural centre, Employment services, Foreign student adviser, Foreign Studies Centre, Health services, Language programs, Social counselling, Sports facilities

Student Residential Facilities: None

Special Facilities: Museum

Libraries: c. 1,1m. Vols

Publications: MIREA Scientific Bulletin *(quarterly)*

Press or Publishing House: Yes

MOSCOW STATE LINGUISTIC UNIVERSITY

Moskovskij Gosudarstvennyj Lingvističeskij Universitet (MSLU)

ul. Ostozhenka 38, Moskva 119034
Tel: +7(499) 245-0612
Fax: +7(499) 246-8366
EMail: info@linguanet.ru
Website: http://www.linguanet.ru

Rector: Irina Ivanovna Khaleeva (1986-)
Tel: +7(499) 246-8603
EMail: khaleeva@linguanet.ru; rector@linguanet.ru

International Relations: Vladimir Shleg, Vice-Rector
Tel: +7(499) 766-4395, Fax: +7(499) 246-2807
EMail: shleg@linguanet.ru

Centres

Academic Mobility; **Account Analysis and Audit**; **Armenian Language and Culture**; **Austrian Studies**; **Azerbaijani Language**

and Culture; **British Language and Culture**; **Business Incubator for Scientific Personnel**; **Canadian Language and Culture**; **CIS States Language and Culture**; **Distance Education**; **Dutch Language and Culture**; **Educational Technologies for Intercultural Communication**; **Federal Centre for Foreign Specialists Training**; **Fundamental and Applied Speech Studies**; **Gender Studies**; **German Language and Culture**; **Ibero-American Programs**; **Information Centre for International Security**; **International Francophone Studies**; **Inter-University Reading and Information Culture Studies**; **Italian Language and Culture**; **Japanese Language and Culture**; **Kazakh Language and Culture**; **Kirghiz Language and Culture**; **Language and Culture of the Grand Duchy of Luxemburg**; **Law Innovation** *(Study Centre)*; **Lingua-Interface Training and Research**; **Linguistic Education Quality Assessment**; **Moldavian Language and Culture**; **Russian Language and Culture**; **Social Studies**; **Spanish Language and Culture**; **Turkish Language and Culture**; **Ukrainian Language and Culture**; **World Culture** *(Ethno Genesis)*

Faculties
Correspondance Education; **Economics and Law** (Economics; Law); **Foreign Student Education**; **French Language** (French); **German Language** (German); **Humanities and Applied Sciences** (Arts and Humanities; Computer Science; Economics; Linguistics; Mathematics); **Intercultural Communication** *(within Advance Language Training Institute)* (Communication Studies); **Translation and Interpretation** (Translation and Interpretation)

Institutes
Advanced Language Training; **Applied and Mathematical Linguistics**; **CIS States Languages** *(International)*; **Foreign Languages** *(Maurice Thorez)* (Modern Languages); **International Relations and Social and Political Sciences** (International Relations; Political Sciences; Social Sciences)

Schools
Business *(International)* (Business Administration); **Translation and Interpretation** *(within Advance Language Training Institute)* (Translation and Interpretation)

Further Information: The University teaches 36 foreign languages, has 23 main programs and areas of training. Also provides Russian language courses for foreign students.

History: Founded 1930.

Governing Bodies: University Council

Academic Year: September to June

Admission Requirements: Secondary school certificate (Attestat o srednem obrazovanii) and entrance examination.

Main Language(s) of Instruction: Russian, English, German, French, Spanish, Italian, Scandinavian languages, Portuguese, Chinese, Japanese, Korean, Arabic

International Co-operation: with 79 institutions in 36 countries.

Degrees and Diplomas: *Bakalavr*, *Magistr*

Student Services: Canteen, Cultural centre

Special Facilities: Computer Training Laboratory; Press Centre; TV Centre; 3-D Centre

Press or Publishing House: REMA Publishing House

Academic Staff *2010-2011*	**TOTAL**
FULL-TIME	**1,015**
PART-TIME	**452**
Student Numbers *2010-2011*	
All (Foreign Included)	**10,354**
FOREIGN ONLY	**354**

Last Updated: 30/09/11

MOSCOW STATE MUSIC CONSERVATORY
Moskovskaja Gosudarstvennaja Konservatorija

ul. Boshaja Nikitskaja 13, Moskva 125009
Tel: +7(495) 229-0959
Fax: +7(495) 290-2273
EMail: rector@mosconsv.ru
Website: http://www.mosconsv.ru

Rector: Tigran Abramovich Alikhanov

Vice-Rector: Vladimir Suhanov Tel: +7(495) 251-5190

International Relations: Vladimir Vladimirovich Sukhanov, Vice-Rector, International
Tel: +7(495) 629-9736, Fax: +7(495) 785-1914
EMail: sukhanov@mosconsv.ru

Programmes
Music (Music)

MOSCOW STATE MUSIC INSTITUTE NAMED AFTER A.G. SHNITKE
Moskovskij Gosudarstvennyj Institut Muzyki im. A.G. Shnitke

ul. Maršala Sokolova 10, Moskva 123060
Tel: +7(499) 194-83-89 +7(499) 194-12-35
Fax: +7(499) 1194-83-89
EMail: info@schnittke-mgim.ru
Website: http://www.schnittke-mgim.ru/

Rector: Aleksandr Leontevich Detjarev

Programmes
Music (Conducting; Music; Music Education; Music Theory and Composition; Musical Instruments; Musicology; Opera; Singing)

History: Created 1993. Formerly known as Moskovskij Gosudarstvennyj Muzykalnyj College.

Degrees and Diplomas: *Bakalavr*, *Specialist Diploma*; *Magistr*

Last Updated: 23/02/12

MOSCOW STATE OPEN UNIVERSITY
Moskovskij Gosudarstvennyj Otkrytyj Universitet

ul. Korčagina 22, Moskva 129805
Tel: +7(495) 683-77-58
Fax: +7(495) 683-42-86
EMail: msou_energy@list.ru
Website: http://www.msou.ru

Rector: Edouard Ovanesovich Tsaturyan (2005-)
EMail: rector@msou.ru

Faculties
Applied Mathematics (Applied Mathematics; Computer Science); **Automechanics** (Automotive Engineering; Maintenance Technology; Road Transport); **Building** (Building Technologies; Civil Engineering; Heating and Refrigeration; Industrial Engineering); **Business and Administration** (Accountancy; Administration; Management); **Chemical Engineering** (Chemical Engineering); **Computing and Radioelectronics** (Computer Engineering; Computer Science; Electrical and Electronic Engineering; Microelectronics); **Economics and Administration of Mining and Metallurgy** (Accountancy; Administration; Economics; Management); **Energy** (Energy Engineering); **International Economic Relations** (International Economics); **Law** (Law); **Linguistics and Intercultural Communication** (Linguistics); **Machine Building** (Machine Building; Maintenance Technology); **Management and Economic Policy** (Economics; Management); **Mining and Oil** (Ecology; Mining Engineering; Petroleum and Gas Engineering)

History: Created 1992. Acquired current status 2005.

Degrees and Diplomas: *Specialist Diploma*: 5 yrs

Last Updated: 22/09/11

MOSCOW STATE PEDAGOGICAL UNIVERSITY
Moskovskij Pedagogičeskij Gosudarstvennyj Universitet

ul. M. Pirogovskaja 1, Moskva 119882
Tel: +7(495) 246-0123
Fax: +7(495) 248-0162
EMail: rector.mpgu@ru.net
Website: http://www.mpgu.edu

Rector: Viktor L. Matrosov (1986-) Tel: +7(495) 246-6011

Programmes
Biology and Chemistry (Biology; Chemistry) *Dean*: Anastacia Romanova; **Chemistry** (Chemistry) *Dean*: Harry Kasiev; **Education of the Handicapped** (Education of the Handicapped) *Dean*: Boris Pussanov; **Fine Arts** (Fine Arts) *Dean*: Evgenii Šorohov; **Geography** (Geography) *Dean*: Viktor Dronov; **History** (History) *Dean*: Peter Saveliev; **Management** (Management) *Dean*: Alexander

Karachev; **Mathematics** (Mathematics) *Dean*: Sergei Zjdanov; **Modern Languages** (Modern Languages) *Dean*: Ludmila Kovaleva; **Music** (Music) *Dean*: Yurii Stepnyak; **Pedagogy and Psychology** (Pedagogy; Psychology) *Dean*: Vitalii Slastenin; **Physical Education** (Physical Education) *Dean*: Igor Zaporov; **Physics** (Physics); **Preschool Education** (Preschool Education) *Dean*: Ludmila Pozdnyak; **Primary Education** (Primary Education) *Dean*: Valentina Danilova; **Russian** (Russian) *Dean*: Alevtina Deikina; **Slavic Languages** (Slavic Languages) *Dean*: Margarita Samoilova; **Sociology** (Sociology) *Dean*: Olga Šušarina

Further Information: Also Russian Language courses for foreign students

History: Founded 1872 as Moscow Higher Women's Courses. Previously part of the former Second Moscow State University, founded 1917. Acquired present status and title 1989. Formerly Moskovskij Gosudarstvennyj Pedagogičeskij Universitet.

Governing Bodies: Special Pedagogical Board

Academic Year: September to July (September-January; February-June)

Admission Requirements: Secondary education certificate (Attestat o srednem obrazovanii) and entrance examination

Main Language(s) of Instruction: Russian

Degrees and Diplomas: *Bakalavr*: 4 yrs; *Specialist Diploma*: 5 yrs; *Magistr*: a further 2 yrs; *Kandidat Nauk*: a further 3 yrs; *Doktor Nauk*: a further 3 yrs following Kandidat

Student Services: Academic counselling, Canteen, Cultural centre, Employment services, Foreign Studies Centre, Health services, Social counselling

Student Residential Facilities: For c. 4,000 students

Special Facilities: 2 Agro-Biological Stations. Observatory

Libraries: Central Library, c. 1.3m. vols; libraries of the faculties

Publications: Collection of Scientific Works *(annually)*; Pedagogičesky Universitet (Pedagogical University)

Press or Publishing House: 'Prometheus Publishing House

MOSCOW STATE REGIONAL SOCIO-HUMANITARIAN INSTITUTE

Moskovskij Gosudarstvennyj Oblastnoj Sotsial'no-Gumanitarnyj Institut

ul. Zeljonaja 30, Kolomna, 140410 Moskovskaja oblast'
Tel: +7(496) 615-13-30 +7(496) 613-41-46
Fax: +7(496) 613-42-58
EMail: mgosgi@gmail.com
Website: http://www.kolomna-kgpi.ru/

Rector: Aleksei Borisovich Mazurov

Faculties

Economics (Business and Commerce; Economics; Management); **Foreign Languages** (English; Foreign Languages Education; French; German; Translation and Interpretation); **History, Management, and Tourism** (History; Management; Public Administration; Tourism); **Law** (Administrative Law; Civil Law; Constitutional Law; Criminal Law; Fiscal Law; History of Law; International Law); **Mathematics, Physics, Chemistry, and Computer Science** (Chemistry; Computer Education; Computer Science; Ecology; Mathematics; Mathematics Education; Physics; Science Education); **Pedagogy** (Art Education; Fine Arts; Pedagogy; Preschool Education; Primary Education; Special Education; Speech Therapy and Audiology); **Philology** (Literature; Music Education; Philology; Russian); **Physical Education and Sports** (Physical Education; Sports); **Psychology** (Pedagogy; Psychology; Social Psychology); **Technology** (Technology; Technology Education)

History: Founded 1939, acquired present status and title of Kolomenskij Gosudarstvennyj Pedagogičeskij Institut (Kolomna State Pedagogical Institute) 1953. Acquired current title 2009.

Governing Bodies: Scientific Council

Academic Year: September to June

Admission Requirements: Secondary school certificate (Attestat o srednem obrazovanii) and entrance examination

Main Language(s) of Instruction: Russian

Accrediting Agencies: Ministry of Education

Degrees and Diplomas: *Specialist Diploma*

Student Services: Canteen, Cultural centre, Health services, Language programs, Sports facilities

Student Residential Facilities: Yes

Publications: Narodny Uchitel *(monthly)*

Press or Publishing House: Kolomna Pedagogical Institute Press

Last Updated: 16/01/12

MOSCOW STATE REGIONAL UNIVERSITY

Moskovskij Gosudarstvennyj Oblastnoj Universitet (MGOU)

ul. Radio 10a, Moskva 105005
Tel: +7(495) 261-15-11
Fax: +7(495) 261-22-28
EMail: rectorat@mgou.ru
Website: http://www.mgou.ru/

Rector: Pavel Nikolievich Khromenkov

Faculties

Arts and Crafts (Art Education; Crafts and Trades; Design; Music Education; Painting and Drawing); **Biology and Chemistry** (Analytical Chemistry; Biology; Botany; Chemistry; Ecology; Organic Chemistry; Zoology); **Economics** (Economics; Management; Mathematics; Public Administration; Small Business; Social Sciences); **Geography and Ecology** (Ecology; Geography; Geology); **History, Political Science, and Law** (Ancient Civilizations; History; Humanities and Social Science Education; Law; Political Sciences); **Law** (Civil Law; Criminal Law; Law; Public Law); **Linguistics** (Applied Linguistics; English; Eurasian and North Asian Languages; Germanic Languages; Indic Languages; Linguistics; Romance Languages; Translation and Interpretation); **Physical Education** (Physical Education; Sports); **Physics and Mathematics** (Computer Education; Computer Science; Mathematical Physics; Physics; Science Education); **Psychology** (Psychology; Social Psychology; Social Work); **Romance and Germanic Languages** (English; German; Philology; Romance Languages); **Russian Philology** (Literature; Native Language Education; Philology; Russian); **Safety Engineering** (Environmental Management; Safety Engineering); **Special Education** (Education of the Handicapped; Educational Psychology; Special Education); **Technology and Entrepreneurship** (Business Education; Small Business; Technology Education)

Further Information: Branches in Noginsk, Fryazino

History: Created 1931.

Degrees and Diplomas: *Bakalavr*, *Specialist Diploma*; *Magistr*

Last Updated: 16/01/12

MOSCOW STATE SOCIO-HUMANITIES INSTITUTE

Moskovskij Gosudarstvennyj Sotsialno-Gumanitarnyj Institut (MII)

ul. Losinoostrovskaja 49, Moskva 107150
Tel: +7(499) 160-92-00
Fax: +7(499) 160-22-05
EMail: info@mgsgi.ru
Website: http://www.mgsgi.ru/

Rector: Vagif Deirushovich Bairamov (2006-)

Faculties

Applied Mathematics and Information Science (Applied Mathematics; Computer Science; Information Sciences); **Economics** (Economics); **Foreign Languages** (English; German; Linguistics; Modern Languages; Translation and Interpretation); **Law** (Law); **Publishing** (Publishing and Book Trade)

Laboratories

Psychology of Special Education (Psychology; Special Education)

History: Founded 1990. Previously known as Moskovskij Institut-Internat dlja Invalidov s Narušeniem Oporno-Dvigatelnoj Sistemy (Moscow Institute-Internate for the Motor Disabled), and Moskovskij Gosudarstvennyj Sotsialno-Gumanitarnyj Institut dlia Invalidov s Narušeniem Oporn-Dvigatelnoj Sistemy (Moscow State Social-Humanities Institute for the Motor Disabled). Acquired current title 2005.

Governing Bodies: Academic Council

Academic Year: September to May (September-December; February-May)

Admission Requirements: Secondary education certificate (Attestat o srednem obrazovanii)

Fees: None

Main Language(s) of Instruction: Russian

Degrees and Diplomas: *Specialist Diploma*

Student Residential Facilities: For c. 225 students

Libraries: c. 9,000 vols

Publications: Collection of Works on Special Education *(annually)*

Press or Publishing House: MII Publishing House

Last Updated: 23/02/12

MOSCOW STATE TECHNICAL UNIVERSITY 'MAMI'

Moskovskij Gosudarstvennyj Tehničeskij Universitet 'MAMI'

ul. B. Semenovskaja 38, Moskva 105839
Tel: +7(495) 369-0780
Fax: +7(495) 369-0149
EMail: yvm@mami.ru
Website: http://www.mami.ru

Rector: Anatolij L. Karunin (1988-) Fax: +7(495) 369-2832

Secretary-General: Aleksandr V. Lepjoškin
Tel: +7(495) 369-9501, Fax: +7(495) 369-5891

International Relations: Jury V. Maksimov
Tel: +7(495) 369-9153, Fax: +7(495) 918-2975

Boards Of Study

Automated Machine-Tool Systems and Tools (Automation and Control Engineering) *Head*: Anatolij M. Kuznecov; **Automation and Control** (Automation and Control Engineering) *Dean*: Valerij I. Charitonov; **Automation and Microprocessors** (Automation and Control Engineering; Microelectronics) *Head*: Valerij I. Charitonov; **Automobile and Tractor Engines** (Automotive Engineering) *Head*: Vadim F. Kutenev; **Automobiles** (Automotive Engineering) *Head*: Anatolij L. Karunin; **Automobiles and Tractors** (Automotive Engineering) *Dean*: Anatolij P. Marinkin; **Auto-Tractors Power Machinery** (Automotive Engineering; Power Engineering) *Head*: Viktor I. Korotkov; **Car Body Construction and Pressure Processing** (Automotive Engineering; Building Technologies) *Head*: Nikolaj F. Shpunkin; **Complex Automation of Mechanical Engineering** (Automation and Control Engineering; Industrial Engineering; Mechanical Engineering) *Head*: Sergej A Zajcev; **Design** (Industrial Design) *Head*: Aleksandr Sorokin; **Design and Technology** (Industrial Design; Technology) *Dean*: Viktor M. Zujev; **Ecology and Safety** (Ecology; Safety Engineering) *Head*: Boris N. Njunin; **Economics** (Economics; Machine Building; Management; Marketing; Production Engineering) *Dean*: Nikolaj T. Katanaev; **Electronics and Computerized Electro-Mechanical Systems** (Electrical and Electronic Engineering) *Head*: Boris I. Petlenko; **Energy Machine and Device Building** (Automotive Engineering; Energy Engineering; Machine Building) *Dean*: Viktor I. Korotkov; **Equipment Design and Automobiles** (Automotive Engineering; Design) *Head*: Anatolij L. Karunin; **Machines and Foundry Technology** (Mechanical Engineering; Metal Techniques) *Head*: Anatolij P. Truhov; **Marketing and Management** (Management; Marketing) *Head*: Valentina I. Kravcova; **Materials Resistance** (Materials Engineering) *Head*: Nikolaj A. Kramskoy; **Philosophy and Psychology** *Head*: Marina A. Kukartzeva; **Production Organization, Planning and Economy of Machine Building Industry** (Automotive Engineering; Building Technologies; Industrial and Production Economics) *Head*: Nikolaj F. Spunkin; **Standardization, Metrology and Certification** (Measurement and Precision Engineering) *Head*: Sergej A. Zajcev; **Technology and Automation of Mechanical Assembly Production** (Automation and Control Engineering; Mechanical Equipment and Maintenance; Technology) *Head*: Boris V. Šandrov; **Tractors** (Automotive Engineering) *Head*: Valerij M. Šaripov; **Transport Gas Turbine Engines** (Transport Engineering) *Head*: Jurij S. Kustarev

Faculties

Engineering Management (Engineering Management) *Dean*: Mihail A. Krescenko; **Machine Building** (Machine Building) *Dean*: Ivan T. Prilepin; **Mechanics and Technology** (Mechanics; Technology) *Dean*: Sergey N. Ivannikov

History: Founded 1939, acquired present status and title 1997.

Governing Bodies: Senate

Academic Year: September to July (September-January; February-July)

Admission Requirements: Secondary school certificate (Attestat o srednem obrazovanii) and entrance examination

Fees: (US Dollars): 1,400 per annum

Main Language(s) of Instruction: Russian

Degrees and Diplomas: *Bakalavr*: 4 yrs; *Specialist Diploma*: Engineering, Technology, 5 yrs; *Magistr*: a further 2 yrs; *Kandidat Nauk*: Engineering, a further 3 yrs

Student Services: Canteen, Employment services, Foreign student adviser, Health services, Sports facilities

Student Residential Facilities: For 1,750 students

Special Facilities: University Museum

Libraries: 1m. vols

Publications: Collections of Reports; Works of the Scientific and Technical Conferences

MOSCOW STATE TECHNICAL UNIVERSITY NAMED AFTER N.E. BAUMAN

Moskovskij Gosudarstvennyj Tehničeskij Universitet im. N.E. Baumana

ul. 2-ja Baumanskaja 5, Moskva 107005
Tel: +7(495) 263-6391
Fax: +7(495) 263-6707
EMail: bauman@bmstu.ru
Website: http://www.bmstu.ru

Rector: Igor Borisovič Fedorov (1991-)

Centres

Rehabilitation for the Deaf

Faculties

Biomedical Engineering (Biomedical Engineering); **Engineering Business and Management** (Business and Commerce; Engineering Management); **Fundamental Sciences** (Natural Sciences); **Information Science and Control Engineering** (Automation and Control Engineering; Information Sciences); **Manufacturing Engineering** (Production Engineering); **Power Engineering** (Power Engineering); **Radioelectronics and Laser Technology** (Electronic Engineering; Laser Engineering); **Robotics and Integrated Automation** (Automation and Control Engineering; Robotics); **Social Sciences and Humanities** (Arts and Humanities; Social Sciences); **Special-purpose Engineering** (Machine Building)

Institutes

Applied Mathematics and Mechanics (Applied Mathematics; Mechanics); **Biomedical Engineering** (Biomedical Engineering); **Information Science and Control Systems** (Automation and Control Engineering; Information Sciences); **Manufacturing Processes Automation** (Automation and Control Engineering; Industrial Engineering); **Power Engineering** (Power Engineering); **Radio Electronics and Laser Technology** (Electronic Engineering; Laser Engineering); **Special-purpose Engineering** (Engineering); **Structural Materials and Technological Processes** (Materials Engineering; Technology)

Further Information: Also branch in Kaluga. Russian Language courses for foreign students

History: Founded 1830.

Academic Year: September to June

Admission Requirements: Secondary education certificate (Attestat o srednem obrazovanii) and entrance examination

Main Language(s) of Instruction: Russian

International Co-operation: Participates in T.I.M.E., Tempus, Intas and Copernicus programmes

Degrees and Diplomas: *Bakalavr*: 4 yrs; *Specialist Diploma*: 6 yrs; *Magistr*: a further 2 yrs following Bakalavr

Student Services: Cultural centre, Foreign Studies Centre, Handicapped facilities, Health services, Social counselling, Sports facilities

Student Residential Facilities: For c. 5,000 students

Special Facilities: History of Science and Techology in Russia Museum

Libraries: c. 2.4m. Vols

Publications: Izvestja Vuzov (Institutions News); Series: Mechanical Engineering; Vestnik MGTU, Series: Instrumental Engineering, Mechanical Engineering

Press or Publishing House: BMSTU PRESS

MOSCOW STATE TECHNICAL UNIVERSITY OF CIVIL AVIATION

Moskovskij Gosudarstvennyj Tehničeskij Universitet Graždanskoj Aviacii (MSTUCA)

20 Kronshtadtskij Boulevard, A-493, GSP-3, Moskva 125993
Tel: +7(495) 459-0707
Fax: +7(495) 457-1201
EMail: rectorat@mstuca.ru
Website: http://www.mstuca.ru

Rector: Vladimir G. Vorobyov (1983-)

International Relations: Aleksandr V. Prokhorov, Dean
Tel: +7(495) 458-7626, Fax: +7(495) 458-7626
EMail: dfct@mstuca.ru

Faculties

Applied Mathematics and Computer Engineering (Applied Mathematics; Computer Engineering) *Dean*: Viktor V. Solometsev; **Aviation Systems** (Aeronautical and Aerospace Engineering) *Dean*: Yuri P. Artiomenko; **Management and Public Relations** (Management; Public Relations) *Dean*: Olga V. Repina; **Mechanical Engineering** (Mechanical Engineering) *Dean*: Yuri M. Chinuchin

History: Founded 1971 as Moscow Institute of Civil Aviation Engineers, acquired present status and title 1993.

Governing Bodies: Scientific Council

Academic Year: September to June (September-January; February-June)

Admission Requirements: Secondary school certificate (Attestat o srednem obrazovanii)

Fees: (US Dollars): 2,000-2,800 per annum. Includes accomodation and medical insurance

Main Language(s) of Instruction: Russian

Degrees and Diplomas: *Bakalavr*: Techniques and Technology, 4 yrs; *Specialist Diploma*: Engineering, Technology; Management; Public Relations, 5-5 1/2 yrs; *Magistr*: Techniques and Technology, 6 yrs

Student Services: Academic counselling, Canteen, Cultural centre, Foreign student adviser, Foreign Studies Centre, Health services, Social counselling, Sports facilities

Student Residential Facilities: Yes

Special Facilities: Museum

Libraries: c. 850,000 vols

Publications: Scientific Issues *(monthly)*

MOSCOW STATE TEXTILE UNIVERSITY NAMED AFTER A.N. KOSYGIN

Moskovskij Gosudarstvennyj Tekstil'nyj Universitet im. A.N. Kosygina (MGTU)

ul. Malaja Kalužskaja 1, Moskva 119991
Tel: +7(495) 954-7073
Fax: +7(495) 952-1440
EMail: office@msta.ac.ru
Website: http://www.msta.ac.ru

Rector: Sergei Nikolaev (1970-) Tel: +7(495) 954-7533

International Relations: Alexandr Frolov, Vice-Rector
Tel: +7(495) 954-3971

Centres

Computer (Computer Science) *Director*: Konstantin Kobrakov; **Scientific-Technical Information** (Information Sciences) *Director*: Konstantin Kobrakov

Departments

General Studies (Mathematics; Modern Languages; Physical Education; Physics; Russian) *Director*: Alexandr Cernikov

Faculties

Applied Arts (Fashion Design; Handicrafts; Interior Design; Jewelry Art; Textile Design) *Dean*: Tatiana Kozlova; **Chemical Technology** (Chemical Engineering; Safety Engineering) *Dean*: Valentin Safonov; **Economics and Management** (Industrial Management; Leadership; Marketing) *Dean*: Ludmila Zernova; **Information, Automation and Energetics** (Computer Engineering; Power Engineering) *Dean*: Anatoly Pojkov; **Mechanical Engineering** (Technology; Textile Technology) *Dean*: Sergei Jhin; **Textile Machine Design** (Mechanical Engineering) *Dean*: Anatoly Jaskin

Further Information: Also courses for foreign students

History: Founded 1919 as Textile Institute, reorganized as Academy 1991, acquired present status and title 1999.

Academic Year: September to June (September-January; February-June)

Admission Requirements: Secondary school certificate (Attestat o srednem obrazovanii) or equivalent

Fees: (US Dollars): 2,000-3,000 per annum

Main Language(s) of Instruction: Russian

International Co-operation: With universities in The Netherlands, China, Pakistan, Japan, Mongolia, Iran.

Accrediting Agencies: Ministry of Education

Degrees and Diplomas: *Bakalavr*: Technology; Machine Building; Chemistry, 4 yrs; *Specialist Diploma*: Engineering; Technology; Management; Chemistry; Applied Arts, 5 yrs; *Magistr*: Technology; Machine Building; Chemistry, 6 yrs; *Kandidat Nauk*: Technology; Chemistry; Applied Arts; Economics, 2-3 yrs

Student Services: Academic counselling, Canteen, Cultural centre, Employment services, Foreign Studies Centre, Health services, Nursery care, Social counselling, Sports facilities

Student Residential Facilities: For 2,000 students

Special Facilities: Museum. Art Gallery.

Libraries: Central Library, 800,000 vols

Publications: Vestnik MGTU *(biennially)*

Press or Publishing House: Moskovskaja Pravda Printing House

MOSCOW STATE UNIVERSITY NAMED AFTER M.V. LOMONOSOV

Moskovskij Gosudarstvennyj Universitet im. M.V. Lomonosova (MSU)

Leninskie Gory, Moskva 119992
Tel: +7(495) 939-1000
Fax: +7(495) 939-0126
EMail: admission@rector.msu.ru
Website: http://www.msu.ru

Rector: Viktor Antonovich Sadovnichy (1992-)
EMail: info@rector.msu.ru

Vice-Rector: Victor Kruzhalin
Tel: +7(495) 939-3889, Fax: +7(495) 939-0847
EMail: kruz@rector.msu.ru

International Relations: Alexandre Sidorovich, Vice-Rector
Tel: +7(495) 939-4809, Fax: +7(495) 939-0069
EMail: sidorovich@rector.msu.ru

Centres

International Education *(Pre-Graduate)* (Education; Russian) *Director*: Vladimir Kochetov; **International Laser** (Physics) *Director*: Vladimir Shuvalov; **Research Computing** (Automation and Control Engineering; Computer Science; Information Sciences; Information Technology) *Director*: Aleksander Tikhonravov

Colleges

French *(French University College)* (French; History; Law; Literature; Sociology) *Director*: François-Xavier Nerard

Departments
Art (Dance; Fine Arts; Music; Opera; Theatre) *Dean*: Aleksander Lobodanov; **Bioengineering and Bioinformatics** (Bioengineering; Information Technology) *Dean*: Vladimir Skulachev; **Biology** (Biology) *Dean*: Mikhail Gusev; **Chemistry** (Chemistry) *Dean*: Valery Lunin; **Computing Mathematics and Cybernetics** (Automation and Control Engineering; Mathematics and Computer Science) *Dean*: Jevgeny Moiseev; **Continuing Education** (Cultural Studies; Economics; History; Philosophy; Political Sciences; Sociology) *Dean*: Dmitry Klementyev; **Economics** (Economics; Statistics) *Dean*: Vasily Kolesov; **Foreign Languages** (European Languages; Linguistics; Modern Languages; Slavic Languages; Translation and Interpretation) *Dean*: Svetlana Ter-Minasova; **Fundamental Medicine** (Anatomy; Biochemistry; Chemistry; Medicine; Pharmacology) *Dean*: Vsevolod Tkachuk; **Geography** (Geography) *Dean*: Nikolay Kasimov; **Geology** (Geology) *Dean*: Dmitry Puscharovsky; **History** (Ancient Civilizations; Anthropology; Archaeology; Art History; Classical Languages; Eastern European Studies; History; Medieval Studies; Modern Languages) *Dean*: Sergey Karpov; **Journalism** (Journalism; Media Studies; Publishing and Book Trade; Radio and Television Broadcasting) *Dean*: Yasen Zasursky; **Law** (Criminology; Law) *Dean*: Alexander Golichenkov; **Materials Science** (Materials Engineering) *Dean*: Jury Tretyakov; **Mechanics and Mathematics** (Applied Mathematics; Mathematics; Mechanics) *Dean*: Oleg Lupanov; **Pedagogy** (Pedagogy) *Dean*: Nikolay Rozov; **Philology** (Classical Languages; Folklore; Germanic Languages; Linguistics; Literature; Philology; Romance Languages; Russian; Slavic Languages) *Dean*: Marina Remneva; **Philosophy** (Logic; Philosophy; Political Sciences) *Dean*: Vladimir Mironov; **Physics** (Astrophysics; Electronic Engineering; Geophysics; Nuclear Physics; Physics; Radiophysics) *Dean*: Vladimir Trukhin; **Psychology** (Pedagogy; Psychology) *Dean*: Aleksander Dontsov; **Sociology** (Political Sciences; Sociology) *Dean*: Vladimir Dobren'kov; **Soil Science** (Soil Science) *Dean*: Sergey Shoba; **State Government** (Economics; Government; Management; Philosophy) *Dean*: Aleksey Surin; **World Politics** *Dean*: Andrey Kokoshin

Higher Schools
Business (Management) *Director*: Oleg Vihanskiy

Institutes
Anthropology Research *(Anuchin)* (Anthropology) *Director*: Vladimir Chtekov; **Asian and African Studies** (African Languages; African Studies; Asian Studies; Economics; History; Oriental Languages; Political Sciences) *Director*: Mihail Meyer; **Astronomy** *(P.K. Shernberg)* (Astronomy and Space Science) *Director*: Anatoly Cherepaschuk

Research Institutes
Additional Education (Cultural Studies; Economics; History; Political Sciences; Sociology) *Director*: Aleksander Mikhalev; **Mechanics** (Mechanics) *Director*: Yury Okunev; **Nuclear Physics** *(D.V. Skobel'tsyn)* (Nuclear Physics) *Director*: Mikhail Panasuk; **Physical and Chemical Biology** *(A.N. Belozersky)* (Biochemistry; Physical Chemistry) *Director*: Vladimir Skulachev

Further Information: Also branches in Astana, Kazakhstan, and Sevastopol, Ukraine

History: Founded 1755 by M.V. Lomonosov, and acquired present status 1992.

Governing Bodies: Academic Council

Academic Year: September to July (September-January; February-July)

Admission Requirements: Secondary school certificate (Attestat o srednem obrazovanii) and entrance examination. Pregraduate course certificate for foreign students

Fees: (US Dollars): 2,000-8,500 per annum

Main Language(s) of Instruction: Russian; English

International Co-operation: With more than 75 universities in USA, Europe and Asia.

Degrees and Diplomas: *Bakalavr*: Economics; Management (BSc; BA), 4 yrs; *Specialist Diploma*: 5 yrs; *Magistr (MSc; MA)*: a further 2 yrs; *Kandidat Nauk (PhD)*: a further 3 yrs following Master; *Doktor Nauk (DSc)*: 3 yrs following Kandidat Nauk

Student Services: Academic counselling, Canteen, Cultural centre, Employment services, Foreign student adviser, Foreign Studies Centre, Handicapped facilities, Health services, Language programs, Nursery care, Social counselling, Sports facilities

Student Residential Facilities: Yes

Special Facilities: Zoology Museum; Soil Science Museum; History of the University Museum; Anthropology Museum; Earth Sciences Museum; Museum of Rare Books. Botanical Garden; Internet Centre

Libraries: Gorki Scientific Library

Publications: Vestnik MGU, 20 series

Press or Publishing House: MSU Press and Publishing House

MOSCOW STATE UNIVERSITY OF AGRICULTURAL ENGINEERING NAMED AFTER B.P. GORJACHKIN

Moskovskij Gosudarstvennyj Agroinženernyj Universitet im. B.P. Gorjačkina

ul. Timirjazevskaja 58, Moskva 127550
Tel: +7(499) 976-05-94
Fax: +7(499) 976-43-96
EMail: r.msau@msau.ru
Website: http://www.msau.ru

Rector: Aleksandr Mitrofanovich Sysoev

Faculties
Agricultural Machines (Agricultural Engineering; Agricultural Management); **Agrotechnology** (Agricultural Equipment; Engineering Drawing and Design; Machine Building); **Economics** (Accountancy; Agricultural Economics; Agricultural Management; Business Computing); **Energy Engineering** (Chemistry; Energy Engineering; Heating and Refrigeration; Physical Therapy)

History: Created 1930.

Degrees and Diplomas: *Bakalavr*; *Specialist Diploma*; *Magistr*
Last Updated: 13/01/12

MOSCOW STATE UNIVERSITY OF APPLIED BIOTECHNOLOGY

Moskovskij Gosudarstvennyj Universitet Prikladnoj Biotehnologii (MSUAB)

ul. Talalihina 33, Moskva 109316
Tel: +7(495) 676-1910
Fax: +7(495) 676-1423
EMail: rector@msaab.ru
Website: http://www.msaab.ru

Rector: Evgeny I. Titov

President: Iosif A. Rogov

International Relations: Olga A. Legonkova
Tel: +7(495) 677-0743, Fax: +7(495) 672-248

Faculties
Applied Biotechnology (Applied Chemistry; Biotechnology; Dairy; Fishery; Food Science; Food Technology; Meat and Poultry; Packaging Technology); **Bioengineering** (Agricultural Equipment; Bioengineering; Industrial Design); **Biotechnological Systems Automation** (Automation and Control Engineering; Biotechnology; Computer Engineering; Information Technology; Software Engineering); **Engineering and Economics**; **Refrigeration Engineering and Technology** (Environmental Engineering; Heating and Refrigeration; Hydraulic Engineering; Physics; Safety Engineering; Technology); **Veterinary Science and Sanitation** (Anatomy; Biology; Microbiology; Molecular Biology; Parasitology; Sanitary Engineering; Toxicology; Veterinary Science; Virology)

Institutes
Food Protein and Ecology (Ecology; Food Science)

Laboratories
Electro-Physical Methods of Food Processing (Electronic Engineering; Food Technology); **Polymers Processing for Food Industry Research** (Polymer and Plastics Technology); **Reliability and Technical Diagnosis of New Agroindustrial Techniques** (Safety Engineering; Technology)

History: Founded 1930 as Chemical and Technological Institute of Meat Industry, reorganized as Technological Institute of Meat and Dairy Industry 1954, and acquired present status and title 1996.

Governing Bodies: Academic Board

Academic Year: September to June (September-January; February-June)

Admission Requirements: Secondary education certificate (Attestat o srednem obrazovanii)

Fees: (US Dollars): 1,800-2,000 per annum

Main Language(s) of Instruction: Russian

Degrees and Diplomas: *Bakalavr*: 4 yrs; *Specialist Diploma*: 5 yrs; *Magistr*: 1 further yr; *Kandidat Nauk*: 3 further yrs; *Doktor Nauk*: 3 further yrs

Student Services: Academic counselling, Cultural centre, Foreign student adviser, Social counselling, Sports facilities

Student Residential Facilities: For c. 1,800 students

Special Facilities: History Museum of the University

Libraries: Central Library, c. 600,000 vols

Publications: Food Industry, Magazine *(monthly)*; Meat Industry, Magazine *(monthly)*; Reports of the Russian Agricultural University

Press or Publishing House: Publishing Department

MOSCOW STATE UNIVERSITY OF CIVIL ENGINEERING

Moskovskij Gosudarstvennyj Stroitel'nyj Universitet (MGSU)

26, Jaroslavskoe sh., Moskva 129337
Tel: +7(499) 183-4438
Fax: +7(499) 183-4438
EMail: kanz@mgsu.ru
Website: http://www.mgsu.ru

Rector: Valeriy Ivanovich Telichenko
Tel: +7(499) 183-5338, Fax: +7(499) 183-5338
EMail: rector@mgsu.ru; telichenko@mgsu.ru

International Relations: Valdimir I. Gagin, Vice-Rector
Tel: +7(499) 183-3201, Fax: +7(499) 183-3201
EMail: kin@mgsu.ru; gagin@mgsu.ru

Institutes

Basic Sciences (Applied Mathematics; History; Mathematics; Mechanics; Modern Languages; Natural Sciences; Philosophy; Political Sciences; Psychology; Russian; Sociology) *Head*: Valdimir N. Sidorov; **Construction and Architecture** *Dean*: Nikolai Senin; **Economics, Management and Information Systems of Civil Engineering and Real Estate** (Automation and Control Engineering; Civil Engineering; Computer Science; Data Processing; Economics; Engineering Management; Industrial Management; Information Sciences; Information Technology; Real Estate) *Head*: Inessa Lukmanova; **Infrastructure of Civil Engineering** (Automation and Control Engineering; Building Technologies; Civil Engineering; Construction Engineering; Engineering; Heating and Refrigeration; Machine Building; Materials Engineering; Mechanical Engineering; Mechanical Equipment and Maintenance; Petroleum and Gas Engineering; Town Planning; Urban Studies) *Head*: Vladimir G. Vozikov; **Power, Water Resources System and Environmental Construction** *Director*: Mikail Zertsalov

History: Founded 1921.

Governing Bodies: Ministry of Education; Federal Agency of Education

Academic Year: September to June

Admission Requirements: Secondary school certificate; Professional College Certificate

Main Language(s) of Instruction: Russian

International Co-operation: With universities in Germany, United Kingdom, Poland, Vietnam and China

Accrediting Agencies: Russian Accreditation Agency

Degrees and Diplomas: *Bakalavr*: Construction; Applied Mechanics (B.Sc.), 4 yrs; *Specialist Diploma*: Heat and Gas Supply and Ventilation; Water Management; Waste Management; Construction Engineering; Building Design; Real Estate; Automation and Control Engineering; Computer-Aided Design Systems; Applied Mathematics; Environmental Engineering; (Eng); Management; Industrial Management; Industrial Economics; Building Technologies; Mechanical Technologies; Maintenance Technologies; Materials Technologies; Industrial Engineering; Civil Engineering; Hydraulic Engineering; Urban Engineering (Eng.), 5 yrs; *Magistr*: Construction; Applied Mechanics (M.Sc.), a further 2 yrs; *Kandidat Nauk*: Building Structures and Constructions; Heating and Refrigeration; Water Management; Building Materials; Hydraulic Power Constructions; Hydraulic Engineering; Building Production Technology and Organisation; Labour Protection; Fire and Industrial Safety (Ph.D.); Economics and Management in Civil Engineering; Architecture; Urban Engineering; Geology, Geocryology and Soil Science; Geomechanics, Destruction of Rocks; Geotechnology; Land Mangement, Cadastre and Soil Monitoring of the Grounds; Geodesy; Geoecology (Ph.D.); Mathematics; Mechancis; Ecology; Engineering; Geometry; Computer Graphics; Civil Engineering; Industrial Management; Machine Building; Electromechanics and Electrical Instruments; Electrotechnical Complexes and Systems (Ph.D.); Systems Analysis, Information Mangement and Information Processing; Automation and Management of Technological Processes and Production; Computer-Aided Design Systems; Industrial Heat-and Power Engineering; Metallurgical Engineering (Ph.D.), 3 yrs; *Doktor Nauk*: Automation and Management of Technological Processes and Production; Computer-Aided Designs Systems; Power Installation Based on Renewable Energy; Building Structures and Constructions; Bases, Foundations and Underground Constructions (D.Sc.); Building Materials and Products; Hydraulic Power Construction; Building Production Technology and Organisation; Building Mechanics; Economics and Management in Civil Engineering; Geodesy (D.Sc.); Mechanics of Deformable Bodies; Machines, Units and Processes (Civil Engineering); Industrial Management; Machine Building; Systems Analysis, Information Management and Information Processing (D.Sc.), 3 yrs

Student Services: Academic counselling, Canteen, Cultural centre, Employment services, Foreign student adviser, Foreign Studies Centre, Health services, Language programs, Social counselling, Sports facilities

Student Residential Facilities: Hostel

Special Facilities: Museum; Internet Club; Culture Palace

Libraries: 1,707,131 vols. (of which 924,111 scientifc vols and 848,546 normative vols); Electronic library, 25,000 vols

Publications: Herald of MSUCE, Journal; International Journal for Computational Civil and Structural Engineering; Real Estate: economy, management, Journal

Academic Staff *2007-2008*	**TOTAL**
FULL-TIME	**1,512**
STAFF WITH DOCTORATE FULL-TIME	**664**
Student Numbers *2007-2008*	
All (Foreign Included)	**17,376**
FOREIGN ONLY	**521**

Part-time students, 3,825. **Distance students**, 1,477. **Evening students**, 1,709.

Last Updated: 20/11/08

MOSCOW STATE UNIVERSITY OF CULTURE AND ARTS

Moskovskij Gosudarstvennyj Universitet Kul'tury i Iskusstv

ul. Bibliotečnaja 7, Khimki, 141406 Moskovskaja oblast'
Tel: +7(495) 570-04-77
Fax: +7(495) 570-04-44
EMail: kanc@mguki.ru
Website: http://www.mguki.ru/

Rector: Ramazan Abdulatipov

Faculties

Choreography (Dance); **Folk Culture and Arts** (Cultural Studies; Design; Fine Arts); **Socio-Cultural Studies** (Cultural Studies; Music); **Theatre** (Acting; Theatre)

Institutes

Culture and Musicology (Cultural Studies; Music; Musicology); **Economics, Management and Law** (Economics; Law; Management); **Information Sciences** (Information Sciences; Library Science); **Mass Media** (Advertising and Publicity; Cinema and Television; Journalism; Radio and Television Broadcasting; Video); **Music** (Music)

Further Information: 12 Regional Branches in European, Asian and Arctic regions of Russia

History: Founded 1930 as Librarian Institute, became Moscow State Institute of Culture 1959, and acquired present status and title 1994.

Governing Bodies: University Council

Academic Year: September to June

Admission Requirements: Secondary school certificate (Attestat o srednem obrazovanii), or equivalent

Main Language(s) of Instruction: Russian

International Co-operation: With universities in Netherlands; France; Vietnam; Belarus. Also participates in UNESCO/UNITWIN

Accrediting Agencies: Ministry of Culture; Ministry of Education

Degrees and Diplomas: *Bakalavr*, *Specialist Diploma*; *Magistr*

Student Services: Academic counselling, Canteen, Cultural centre, Foreign student adviser, Foreign Studies Centre, Health services, Language programs, Social counselling, Sports facilities

Student Residential Facilities: Yes

Special Facilities: Museum. Art Galleries

Libraries: University Library

Publications: Scientific Information Journal *(monthly)*; Vestnik *(quarterly)*

Last Updated: 22/09/11

MOSCOW STATE UNIVERSITY OF DESIGN AND TECHNOLOGY

Moskovskij Gosudarstvennyj Universitet Dizajna i Tekhnologii (MGUDT)

ul. Sadovničevskaja 33, Moskva 115035
Tel: +7(495) 951-58-01
Fax: +7(495) 953-02-97
EMail: mgalp.msk@ru.net
Website: http://www.mgudt.ru

Rector: Valerij Savel'evich Belgorodskij

Faculties

Chemical Technology and Industrial Ecology (Analytical Chemistry; Chemical Engineering; Ecology; Inorganic Chemistry; Organic Chemistry; Physical Chemistry; Polymer and Plastics Technology); **Mechanical Engineering** (Automation and Control Engineering; Electrical and Electronic Engineering; Information Technology; Machine Building; Mechanical Engineering; Mechanics)

Institutes

Design (Fashion Design; Industrial Chemistry; Landscape Architecture; Painting and Drawing); **Economics and Management** (Accountancy; Economics; Management; Mathematics); **Social Sciences** (Management; Modern History; Philosophy; Psychology; Russian; Sociology; Sports); **Technology** (Clothing and Sewing; Computer Science; Information Sciences; Leather Techniques; Materials Engineering; Physics; Technology; Textile Design; Textile Technology)

History: Founded 1930 as Moscow Technological Institute of Light Industry (MTILI). Acquired present status 1999.

Admission Requirements: Secondary school certificate and entrance examination

Main Language(s) of Instruction: Russian

International Co-operation: With universities in USA, Germany, United Kingdom, Israel

Accrediting Agencies: Ministry of Higher Education

Degrees and Diplomas: *Bakalavr*, *Specialist Diploma*; *Magistr*

Student Services: Academic counselling, Canteen, Cultural centre, Foreign student adviser, Health services, Language programs, Nursery care, Social counselling, Sports facilities

Student Residential Facilities: For 2,000 students

Special Facilities: Theatre

Libraries: c. 360,000 vols

Academic Staff	MEN	WOMEN	TOTAL
STAFF WITH DOCTORATE			
FULL-TIME	117	86	**203**
PART-TIME	46	36	**82**

Last Updated: 23/02/12

MOSCOW STATE UNIVERSITY OF ECONOMICS, STATISTICS AND INFORMATICS

Moskovskij Gosudarstvennyj Universitet Ekonomiki, Statistiki i Informatiki (MESI)

ul. Nežinskaja 7, Moskva 119501
Tel: +7(495) 442-7155
Fax: +7(495) 442-6558
EMail: info@mesi.ru
Website: http://www.mesi.ru

Rector: Vladimir P. Tihomirov (1991-)
Tel: +7(495) 442-6577 EMail: vpt@rector.mesi.ru

First Vice-Rector: Aleksandr V. Horoshilov
Tel: +7(495) 442-8533, Fax: +7(495) 442-7122
EMail: akhor@rector.mesi.ru

International Relations: Nikolay L. Pasholikov
Tel: +7(495) 442-2366, Fax: +7(495) 442-2366
EMail: npasholikov@staff.mesi.ru

Campuses

Astrakhan *Director*: Rustam S. Aseinov; **Belgorod** *Director*: Sergei V. Tsvetkov; **Derbent** *Director*: Bilal G. Gasanov; **Kaliningrad** *Director*: Oleg D. Mishin; **Krasnoyarsk** *Director*: Eugeni P. Vasiliev; **Minsk** *(Belarus) Director*: Sergei N. Maliachenko; **Ryazan** *Director*: Vladimir Iv. Lyadov; **Tver** *Director*: Irina V. Tretiakova; **Ust-Kamenogorsk** *(Kazakhstan) Director*: Olga Iv. Vidova; **Yaroslavl** *Director*: Marina V. Makarova; **Yerevan** *(Armenia) Director*: Migran Ab. Shakhzadeyan

Colleges

MESI *Director*: Olga V. Prikhodko

Faculties

Economics and Finance *Director*: Vitaly G. Minashkin

Institutes

Computer Technology *Director*: Yuri F. Telnov; **Law and Humanities** *Director*: Pavel Feodorov; **Management** *Director*: Larisa A. Dantchenok; **Master's Programmes** *Dean*: Eleonora V. Vergeles; **Professional Development** *Dean*: Natalia A. Dmitrievskaya; **Statistics and Econometrics** *Director*: Vladimir S. Mhitarian

History: Founded 1932, acquired present status and title 1996.

Governing Bodies: Academic Council; University Council

Academic Year: September to July

Admission Requirements: Secondary education certficate (Attestat o srednem obrazovanii) and entrance examination

Fees: (US Dollars): 2,520-3,480 per annum

Main Language(s) of Instruction: Russian, English (special courses)

International Co-operation: With universities in Netherlands; Germany; Poland; Austria; Australia; Bulgaria; Greece; USA; Tunisia; China; Vietnam; Israel; India; Lebanon; Mongolia; Peru; Armenia; Georgia; Kazakhstan; Latvia; Lithuania; Tajikistan; Uzbekistan; Ukraine

Accrediting Agencies: Ministry of Education and Science of Russian Federation

Degrees and Diplomas: *Bakalavr*: 4 yrs; *Specialist Diploma*: 5 yrs; *Magistr*: a further 2 yrs; *Kandidat Nauk*: a further 3 yrs; *Doktor Nauk*: a further 3 yrs at least following Kandidat Nauk

Student Services: Academic counselling, Canteen, Employment services, Foreign student adviser, Foreign Studies Centre, Health services, Language programs, Nursery care, Social counselling, Sports facilities

Student Residential Facilities: Yes

Libraries: Central Library, c. 300,000 vols; E-Library

Publications: E-Learning World, Journal of Distance Education; Journal of Distance Education *(biennially)*; Open Education, Educational Journal; Periodical Scientific Reports

MOSCOW STATE UNIVERSITY OF ENGINEERING ECOLOGY

Moskovskij Gosudarstvennyj Universitet Inženernoj Ekologii

ul. Staraja Basmannaja 21/4, Moskva 107884
Tel: +7(495) 267-0701
Fax: +7(495) 261-4961
EMail: michm@msuie.ru
Website: http://www.msuie.ru

Rector: Mihail Generalov

International Relations: Anatolij G. Rjauzov

Faculties

Chemical and Biological Engineering (Biotechnology; Chemical Engineering); **Chemical Apparatus Manufacturing** (Industrial Chemistry; Machine Building); **Cryogenic Engineering** (Heating and Refrigeration); **Engineering Cybernetics** (Automation and Control Engineering); **Engineering** (Engineering); **Humanities and Engineering Economics** (Engineering Management; Humanities and Social Science Education; Industrial and Production Economics)

History: Founded 1920.

MOSCOW STATE UNIVERSITY OF ENVIRONMENTAL ENGINEERING

Moskovskij Gosudarstvennyj Universitet Prirodoobustroistva

19, Pryanishnikova Street, Moskva 127550
Tel: +7(499) 976-29-62 +7(499) 976-29-79
Fax: +7(499) 976-10-46
EMail: mailbox@msuee.ru
Website: http://www.msuee.ru/

Rector: Dmitri Vjacheslavovich Kozlov

Faculties

Construction Engineering (Civil Engineering; Construction Engineering; Hydraulic Engineering); **Ecology and Environmental Studies** (Ecology; Environmental Studies; Landscape Architecture; Rural Planning); **Economics** (Business Computing; Economics; Management); **Environmental Engineering and Water Management** (Advertising and Publicity; Environmental Engineering; Public Relations; Rural Planning; Water Management); **Mechanization** (Machine Building; Transport Engineering; Transport Management)

History: Created 1930.

Governing Bodies: Scientific Council

Academic Year: September to July

Admission Requirements: Certificate of Secondary Education, Entrance Examination

Main Language(s) of Instruction: Russian

International Co-operation: None

Degrees and Diplomas: *Bakalavr*; *Specialist Diploma*; *Magistr*; *Kandidat Nauk*

Student Services: Academic counselling, Canteen, Cultural centre, Employment services, Foreign student adviser, Foreign Studies Centre, Health services, Language programs, Social counselling, Sports facilities

Student Residential Facilities: Hostels

Special Facilities: Museum

Libraries: Yes

Last Updated: 13/01/12

MOSCOW STATE UNIVERSITY OF FOOD PRODUCTION

Moskovskij Gosudarstvennyj Universitet Piščevyh Proizvodstv (MGUPP)

Volokolamskoe šosse 11, Moskva 125080
Tel: +7(495) 158-7168
Fax: +7(495) 158-0371
EMail: traubenberg@mgupp.ru
Website: http://www.msafp.ru

President-Rector: Vyačeslav Tužilkin (1990-)

Secretary-Referent: Tatiana Gorbatuk

International Relations: Evgenij A. Prokofjev
Tel: +7(495) 158-7159

Faculties

Alternative Forms of Study, Economics and Business Management (Accountancy; Automation and Control Engineering; Biotechnology; Business Administration; Economics; Food Science; Food Technology; Information Technology)

Institutes

Economics and Business Management (Accountancy; Business Administration; Economics; Industrial Management; Information Sciences; Marketing); **Equipment, Automation and Information Technology** (Automation and Control Engineering; Computer Science; Data Processing; Engineering; Food Science; Food Technology; Industrial Engineering; Information Management; Information Technology; Maintenance Technology; Materials Engineering; Packaging Technology); **Food Quality, Technology and Production Management** (Biotechnology; Food Technology; Industrial and Production Economics; Nutrition; Production Engineering; Technology)

History: Founded 1931 as Institute of Bakery Engineering, became independent 1941 and acquired present status and title 1996.

Academic Year: September to June (September-January; February-June)

Admission Requirements: Secondary school certificate (Attestat o srednem obrazovanii)

Fees: (Russian Rubles): 8,800-17,600 per annum

Main Language(s) of Instruction: Russian

Degrees and Diplomas: *Bakalavr*: Science, 4 yrs; *Specialist Diploma*: Engineering, Technology, 1 further yr; *Magistr*: Science, a further 2 yrs; *Kandidat Nauk*: 3 yrs; *Doktor Nauk*: a further 2 yrs

Student Services: Foreign student adviser, Language programs, Sports facilities

Special Facilities: Museum

Libraries: Scientific and Technical Library, total, c. 1m. vols

Publications: Vestnik Universiteta

Press or Publishing House: Publication Complex

MOSCOW STATE UNIVERSITY OF GEODESY AND CARTOGRAPHY

Moskovskij Gosudarstvennyj Universitet Geodezii i Kartografii

Gorokhovsky per. 4, Moskva 105064
Tel: +7(499) 261-55-69 +7(499) 267-43-45
Fax: +7(499) 267-46-81
EMail: studydep@miigaik.ru; aoi@miigaik.ru
Website: http://www.miigaik.ru

Rector: Vasillij Aleksandrovich Malinninkov
EMail: rector@miigaik.ru

Faculties

Applied Cosmology (Astronomy and Space Science; Computer Graphics; Ecology; Environmental Management; Natural Resources); **Cartography** (Geography; Surveying and Mapping); **Cartography and Geoinformatics** (Surveying and Mapping); **Economics and Management** (Economics; Management); **Geodesy** (Astronomy and Space Science; Geography; Geological Engineering; Surveying and Mapping); **Humanities** (Arts and Humanities; Modern Languages; Social Sciences); **Land Management** (Architectural and Environmental Design; Environmental Management; Town Planning); **Optical Instruments Design** (Design; Optical Technology; Optics); **Photogrammetry** (Astronomy and Space Science; Computer Graphics; Optometry; Photography)

Further Information: Also branch in Kirov.

History: Founded 1779 as Moscow Institute of Geodesy, Aerial Surveying and Cartography, acquired present status and title 1993.

Governing Bodies: Scientific Council, comprising 58 members

Academic Year: September to June (September-January; February-June)

Admission Requirements: Secondary school certificate (Attestat o srednem obrazovanii)

Main Language(s) of Instruction: Russian

Degrees and Diplomas: *Bakalavr*, *Specialist Diploma*; *Magistr*, *Kandidat Nauk*; *Doktor Nauk*

Student Services: Academic counselling, Canteen, Cultural centre, Employment services, Foreign Studies Centre, Health services, Sports facilities

Student Residential Facilities: For c. 1,000 students

Special Facilities: Geodetical Museum (unique and rare atlases, maps, charts, etc)

Libraries: c. 1.5m. vols

Last Updated: 11/01/12

MOSCOW STATE UNIVERSITY OF INSTRUMENT ENGINEERING AND COMPUTER SCIENCE

Moskovskij Gosudarstvennyj Universitet Priborostroenija i Informatiki

ul. Stromynka 20, Moskva 107846

Tel: +7(495) 268-0001

Fax: +7(495) 268-0291

EMail: omc@mgupi.ru

Website: http://www.mgupi.ru

Rector: Igor Vladimirovich Golubyatnikov

International Relations: Galina A. Slastikhina

Faculties

Artificial Intelligence Engineering Systems (Artificial Intelligence); **Automobile Engineering and Instrumentation Technology** *(Serpuhov)* (Automotive Engineering; Instrument Making); **Computer Science and Instrumentation** *(Servjev Posad)* (Computer Science; Instrument Making); **Electronics, Computer Science and Engineering** (Computer Science; Electronic Engineering; Engineering); **Humanities** (Arts and Humanities); **Information Technology and Computer-Integrated Manufacturing Processes** *(Kasýra)* (Automation and Control Engineering; Industrial Engineering; Information Technology); **Materials Science and Technology** (Materials Engineering; Technology); **Mechanical Engineering Technology** *(Himki)* (Mechanical Engineering); **Radioelectronics and Instrumentation Technology** (Electronic Engineering; Instrument Making; Telecommunications Engineering)

History: Founded 1936. Previously known as Moskovskaja Gosudarstvennaja Akademija Priborostroenija i Informatiki (Moscow State Academy of Instrumentation Technology and Informatics). Acquired current title 2005.

Last Updated: 08/01/10

IAU MOSCOW STATE UNIVERSITY OF MEDICINE AND DENTISTRY

Moskovskij Gosudarstvennyj Medico-Stomatologičeskij Universitet (MSUMD)

ul. Delegatskaja 20/1, Moskva 127473

Tel: +7(495) 684-49-86

Fax: +7(495) 973-32-59

EMail: msmsu@msmsu.ru

Website: http://www.msmsu.ru

Rector: Oleg O. Yanushevich (2007-)

Dean of Postgraduate Education: Sergey T. Sokhov
Tel: +7(495) 609-65-20
EMail: drsokhov@tushino.com; Sokhov2@msmsu.ru

International Relations: Solomon A. Rabinovich, Vice-Rector, International Relations EMail: rabinovich@msmsu.ru

Faculties

Advanced Training in Medicine and Dentistry (Dentistry; Medicine); **Clinical Psychology** (Clinical Psychology); **Dentistry I** (Dentistry); **Economics and Management in Health Care** (Health Administration); **Medical and Dental Auxiliaries Training** *(Auxiliary Personnel)* (Dental Hygiene; Dentistry; Medical Auxiliaries; Paramedical Sciences); **Medicine I** (Medicine); **Penitentiary Medicine** (Medicine)

Schools

Nursing (Nursing); **Postgraduate Studies** (Cardiology; Dentistry; Epidemiology; Gastroenterology; Gynaecology and Obstetrics; Immunology; Ophthalmology; Paediatrics; Venereology)

Further Information: Also 86 academic research departments and 2 research institutes

History: Founded 1922 as Moscow Medical Stomatology Institute, acquired present status and title 1999.

Governing Bodies: University Council

Academic Year: September to June

Admission Requirements: Secondary school certificate (attestat o srednem obrazovanii)

Main Language(s) of Instruction: Russian

Accrediting Agencies: Ministry of Public Health and Social Policy; Ministry of Science and Education of the Russian Federation

Degrees and Diplomas: *Specialist Diploma*: Dentistry; Medical Psychology, 5 yrs; *Specialist Diploma*: Dentistry, 2 yrs following first degree; *Specialist Diploma*: Medicine, 6 yrs; *Kandidat Nauk*: Medical Sciences, 3 yrs; *Doktor Nauk*: Medical Sciences, a further 3 yrs

Student Services: Canteen, Health services, Language programs

Student Residential Facilities: 3 student hostels

Special Facilities: Museum of MGMSU's History

Libraries: Total, 500,000 vols; 19,000 periodical subscriptions

Press or Publishing House: MSUMD Publishing House

Last Updated: 29/04/11

MOSCOW STATE UNIVERSITY OF MINING ENGINEERING

Moskovskij Gosudarstvennyj Gornyj Universitet

prosp. Leninskij 6, Moskva 119991

Tel: +7(499) 230-25-05

Fax: +7(499) 237-31-63

EMail: ud@msmu.ru

Website: http://www.msmu.ru/

Rector: Andrei Vladimirovich Korchak Tel: +7(495) 236-6525

Faculties

Coal Mining (Industrial Management; Mining Engineering); **Electromechanics in Mining Engineering** (Electrical Engineering; Mechanics); **Informatics and Automated Systems** (Automation and Control Engineering); **Ore and Non-Ore Deposits Exploitation** (Mining Engineering); **Physical Engineering** (Physical Engineering)

History: Founded 1918.

Degrees and Diplomas: *Bakalavr*, *Specialist Diploma*; *Magistr*

Last Updated: 23/02/12

MOSCOW STATE UNIVERSITY OF PRINTING ARTS

Moskovskij Gosudarstvennyj Universitet Pečati (MGUP)

ul. Prjanišnikova 2a, Moskva 127550

Tel: +7(495) 976-4070

Fax: +7(495) 976-0635

EMail: info@mgup.ru

Website: http://www.mgup.ru

Rector: Konstantin Valerevich Antipov EMail: mgup@mail.cat.ru

Faculties

Advertising and Public Relations (Advertising and Publicity; Public Relations); **Economics and Management** (Economics; Management); **Graphic Arts** (Design; Graphic Arts); **Information Technology and Media** (Information Technology; Media Studies; Printing and Printmaking; Technology); **Printing Machinery and Printing Technology** (Graphic Arts; Printing and Printmaking); **Publishing, Economics and Book Trade** (Economics; Journalism; Publishing and Book Trade)

Institutes

Printing Arts *(St Petersburg)* (Graphic Arts; Graphic Design; Printing and Printmaking; Publishing and Book Trade)

Further Information: Also Preparatory Faculty for foreign students (INCORVUZ-MSAPA Training Centre). Branch Establishment: State Engineering University of Armenia in Yerevan.

History: Founded 1930, acquired present status and title 1997.

Governing Bodies: Academic Council

Academic Year: September to June

Admission Requirements: Secondary school certificate (Attestat o srednem obrazovanii)

Fees: (US Dollars): 1,800-3,000 per annum

Main Language(s) of Instruction: Russian

Degrees and Diplomas: *Bakalavr*: 4 yrs; *Specialist Diploma*: 1 further yr following Bakalavr; *Magistr*: a further 2 yrs following Bakalavr; *Kandidat Nauk*: a further 3 yrs following Specialist of Magistr; *Doktor Nauk*: a further 5 yrs following Specialist of Kandidat Nauk

Student Services: Academic counselling, Canteen, Cultural centre, Foreign student adviser, Health services, Language programs, Social counselling, Sports facilities

Special Facilities: Museum. Art Gallery. Demo Centres

Libraries: c. 1.9m. Vols

Publications: Problems of Graphic Arts Industry and Publishing *(quarterly)*; The World of Printing Arts and Publishing *(monthly)*

Last Updated: 11/04/11

MOSCOW STATE UNIVERSITY OF PSYCHOLOGY AND EDUCATION

Moskovskij Gorodskoj Universitet Psihologo-Pedagogičeskij Universitet (MSUPE)

ul. Sretenka 29, Moskva 127051
Tel: +7(495) 632-9433
Fax: +7(495) 632-9252
EMail: mgppi2001@mail.ru
Website: http://www.mgppu.ru

Rector: Vitaly Rubtsov (1996-)

Chief Provost, Provost for Academic Affairs: Arkady Margolis Tel: +7(495) 923-3848 EMail: amargolis@mail.ru

International Relations: Galina Gabuniya, Pro-Rector, Provost for International Relations

Colleges

Social Education (Pedagogy) *Head*: Marina Shumskikh

Faculties

Clinical and Special Psychology (Clinical Psychology; Psychology) *Dean*: Tatiana Meshkova; **Counselling Psychology** (Clinical Psychology; Psychology) *Dean*: Fyodor Vasilyuk; **Distance Education** *Dean*: Bronius Aismontas; **Foreign Languages** (Communication Studies; Cultural Studies; Linguistics) *Dean*: Tatiana Turanskaya; **Information Technology** (Computer Science; Information Technology) *Dean*: Lev Kuravsky; **Legal Psychology** (Law; Psychology) *Dean*: Yelena Dozorteva; **Psychology of Education** (Developmental Psychology; Educational Psychology; Psychology) *Dean*: Marina Yegorova; **Social Education** (Pedagogy) *Dean*: Vladimir Torokhty; **Social Psychology** (Psychology; Social Psychology) *Dean*: Mikhail Kondratiev; **State and Municipal Management** *Dean*: Marina Kovtunovich

Programmes

Emergency Psychological Aid *(Postgraduate)* (Psychology) *Head*: O. Vihristuk

History: Founded 1997. Previously known as Moskovskij Gosudartsvennyj Universitet Psihologo I Obrazovanija. Acquired present status and title 2002.

Governing Bodies: Noard of Academics

Academic Year: September to June

Admission Requirements: General Certificate of Secondary Education (Attestat o srednem obrazovanii) and entrance examination

Fees: (Russian Rubles): Full time students, c. 45,000 per term; part time students, c. 29,000 per term

Main Language(s) of Instruction: Russian

International Co-operation: With universities in France, Italy, Germany, USA, Japan, Switzerland

Accrediting Agencies: Ministry of Education and Science; Federal Service for Supervision in Education and Science

Degrees and Diplomas: *Bakalavr*: Psychology, 4 yrs; *Specialist Diploma*: Psychology; Social Pedagogy; Linguistics; Information Technology, 5 yrs; *Kandidat Nauk*: Developmental Psychology; Acmeology, a further 3-4 yrs. Secondary Diploma in Psychology (a further 3 1/2 yrs)

Student Services: Academic counselling, Canteen, Employment services, Foreign student adviser, Handicapped facilities, Health services, Language programs, Sports facilities

Student Residential Facilities: No

Special Facilities: Research Laboratories. Toy Museum.

Libraries: c. 350,000 vols

Publications: Cultural-Historical Psychology *(quarterly)*; Moscow Journal of Psychotherapy *(1-2 per annum)*; Psychological Science and Education, Educational psychology, developmental psychology, school psychology *(quarterly)*

Academic Staff *2007-2008*	MEN	WOMEN	TOTAL
FULL-TIME	73	206	**279**
PART-TIME	104	111	**215**
STAFF WITH DOCTORATE			
FULL-TIME	54	108	**162**
PART-TIME	84	80	**164**
Student Numbers *2007-2008*			
All (Foreign Included)	1,416	4,451	**5,867**
FOREIGN ONLY	18	76	**94**

Part-time students, 1,430. **Distance students**, 192. **Evening students**, 1,243.

Last Updated: 21/11/08

MOSCOW STATE UNIVERSITY OF RAILWAY ENGINEERING

Moskovskij Gosudarstvennyj Universitet Putej Soobščenija (MIIT)

ul. Obraztsova, 9/9, Moskva 127994
Tel: +7(495) 681-31-77
Fax: +7(495) 681-13-40
EMail: tsa1783@mail.ru; tu@miit.ru
Website: http://www.miit.ru/

Rector: Boris Lievin (1997-)

Academies

Russian Academy of Transport (Transport and Communications; Transport Engineering; Transport Management); **Russian Open Academy of Transport** (Transport and Communications; Transport Engineering; Transport Management)

Faculties

Environmental Protection (Environmental Engineering; Environmental Studies)

Institutes

Control Systems, Telecommunications and Electrification; **Economics and Finance** (Applied Mathematics; Business and Commerce; Economics; Finance; Information Sciences; Management); **Humanities** (Advertising and Publicity; Journalism; Psychology; Service Trades; Sociology); **Information Technology** (Information Technology); **Law** (Law); **Rail Operation and Information Technologies** (Railway Engineering; Railway Transport); **Railtrack Construction and Structures** (Railway Engineering; Railway Transport); **Transport Engineering** (Power Engineering; Railway Engineering; Thermal Engineering; Transport Engineering)

History: Founded 1896 as an Engineering School, reorganized as Institute of Communication 1913, and acquired present status and title 1993.

Academic Year: September to June (September-December; February-June)

Admission Requirements: Secondary school certificate (Attestat o srednem obrazovanii)

Main Language(s) of Instruction: Russian

International Co-operation: With universities in France; Germany; Latvia; Mongolia; China; Poland; Bulgaria; USA; Vietnam; Korea; Slovak Republic; Canada; Finland; Iran; Spain; Cuba; Syria; Norway; Czech Republic; Switzerland; Sweden; Serbia; Myanmar

Degrees and Diplomas: *Bakalavr*, *Specialist Diploma*; *Magistr*, *Kandidat Nauk*; *Doktor Nauk*

Student Services: Academic counselling, Canteen, Cultural centre, Employment services, Foreign student adviser, Foreign Studies Centre, Health services, Language programs, Social counselling, Sports facilities

Student Residential Facilities: For c. 15,000 students

Special Facilities: History of the University Museum

Libraries: c. 2m. vols
Last Updated: 30/03/12

MOSCOW STATE UNIVERSITY OF TECHNOLOGY (STANKIN)

Moskovskij Gosudarstvennyj Tehnologičeskij Universitet (Stankin)

Vadkovskij per. 1, Moskva 127055
Tel: +7(499) 973-30-66 +7(495) 973-39-30
Fax: +7(499) 973-38-85 +7(495) 973-38-36
EMail: rector@stankin.ru
Website: http://www.stankin.ru

Rector: Sergei Nikolaevich Grigor'ev

Faculties

Economics and Management (Economics; Finance; Industrial Management; Management); **Engineering Technologies and Equipment** (Ecology; Engineering; Environmental Engineering; Instrument Making; Machine Building; Technology); **Information Technology and Systems Management** (Applied Mathematics; Computer Networks; Computer Science; Information Technology; Robotics)

History: Founded 1930 as Moscow Machine Tools and Tooling Institute, acquired present status and title 1992.

Academic Year: September to June (September-January; February-June)

Admission Requirements: Secondary education certificate (Attestat o srednem obrazovanii)

Main Language(s) of Instruction: Russian

Degrees and Diplomas: *Bakalavr*, *Specialist Diploma*; *Magistr*

Student Services: Academic counselling, Canteen, Cultural centre, Employment services, Foreign Studies Centre, Handicapped facilities, Health services, Language programs, Nursery care, Social counselling, Sports facilities

Student Residential Facilities: For c. 1,000 students

Libraries: 1.5m. Vols

Press or Publishing House: Stankin Press
Last Updated: 13/01/12

MOSCOW STATE UNIVERSITY OF TECHNOLOGY AND MANAGEMENT NAMED AFTER K.G. RAZUMOVSKIJ

Moskovskij Gosudarstvennyj Universitet Technologii I Unpravlenija im. K.G. Razumovskogo (MGUTU)

Zemljanoy val 73, Moskva 109004
Tel: +7(495) 915-03-40
Fax: +7(495) 915-08-15
EMail: rektorat@mgutm.ru
Website: http://www.mgutm.ru/

Rector: Valentina Ivanova

Institutes

Bioecology and Fishery (Ecology; Environmental Studies; Fishery; Heating and Refrigeration; Limnology); **Design and Packaging Production** (Design; Packaging Technology; Painting and Drawing; Sculpture); **Economics and Business** (Accountancy; Business and Commerce; Economics; Marketing); **Food Technology** (Brewing; Cosmetology; Food Science; Food Technology; Inorganic Chemistry; Oenology); **Law** (Civil Law; Criminal Law; History of Law; International Law; Justice Administration; Labour Law; Law; Public Law); **Management** (Accountancy; Economics; Finance; Management); **Management and Technology** (Engineering Drawing and Design; Food Technology; Industrial Management; Information Technology; Management); **Social Studies and Humanities** (Advertising and Publicity; Cultural Studies; Economics; Educational Psychology; English; French; German; Histology; Latin; Pedagogy; Philosophy; Political Sciences; Psychology; Public Law; Sociology; Sports); **Systems Innovation and Automation** (Automation and Control Engineering; Industrial Engineering; Mathematics; Physics); **Technology Management** (Analytical Chemistry; Food Technology; Organic Chemistry; Physical Chemistry; Plant Pathology)

Further Information: Also Institute of Personnel Professional Retraining and Institute of Information Technologies and Improvement of Professional Skills of the personnel.

History: Founded 1953 as All-union Correspondence Institute of Food Industry. Became Moscow State Institute of Food Industry 1993, and acquired present status and title 2003. Formerly known as Moskovskaja Gosudarstvennaja Tehnologičeskaja Akademija (Moscow State Technological Academy).

Academic Year: September to June

Admission Requirements: Secondary school certificate (Attestat o srednem obrazovanii) with minimum required for first year entry; Entrance examinations

Main Language(s) of Instruction: Russian

Accrediting Agencies: Federal Education Agency (Rosobnadzor), Minsitry of Education and Science of the Russian Federation

Degrees and Diplomas: *Bakalavr*, *Specialist Diploma*; *Kandidat Nauk*

Student Services: Academic counselling, Canteen, Cultural centre, Employment services, Foreign student adviser, Foreign Studies Centre, Handicapped facilities, Language programs, Nursery care, Social counselling, Sports facilities

Student Residential Facilities: Yes

Special Facilities: Information Technologies Centre

Libraries: 300,000 vols

Publications: Materials of Science Methodology, Compilation of reports and theses *(annually)*
Last Updated: 12/01/12

MOSCOW TECHNICAL UNIVERSITY OF COMMUNICATION AND INFORMATICS

Moskovskij Tehničeskij Universitet Svjazi i Informatiki

ul. Avjamotornaja 8, Moskva 111024
Tel: +7(495) 273-8917 +7(495) 273-2762
Fax: +7(495) 273-1713 +7(495) 274-0032
EMail: mtuci@mtuci.ru
Website: http://www.mtuci.ru

Rector: Vagan V. Šahgildjan (1987-)

Secretary of the Council: Tatjana V. Zotova
Tel: +7(495) 273-3503

International Relations: Igor A. Zaharov, Vice-Rector
Tel: +7(495) 273-3674, Fax: +7(495) 274-0032
EMail: ird@mruci.ru

Faculties

Automation and Postal Services Computerization (Automation and Control Engineering; Postal Services); **Economics and Management** (Economics; Management); **Multichannel Telecommunications** (Telecommunications Engineering); **Radiocommunication, Broadcasting and TV** (Radio and Television Broadcasting); **Radioengineering** (Automation and Control Engineering; Electronic Engineering; Telecommunications Engineering); **Telecommunications and Informatics** (Computer Engineering; Information Technology; Telecommunications Engineering)

Further Information: Also Branch in Rostov-on-Don

History: Founded 1921 as Electrotechnical Institute, acquired present status and title 1992.

Academic Year: September to May (September-December; February-May)

Admission Requirements: Secondary school certificate (Attestat o srednem obrazovanii) or equivalent (Diplom o srednem specialnom obrazovanii)

Fees: (US Dollars): 2,000-2,500 per annum

Main Language(s) of Instruction: Russian

Degrees and Diplomas: *Bakalavr*: 4 yrs; *Specialist Diploma*: Engineering, Technology, 1 further yr; *Magistr*: 2 yrs following Bakalavr's; *Kandidat Nauk*: 3 yrs; *Doktor Nauk*: 3 yrs

Student Services: Academic counselling, Canteen, Employment services, Foreign Studies Centre, Health services, Sports facilities

Libraries: Central Library, c. 897,000 vols

Press or Publishing House: Informsvjazizdat Publishing House

MOSCOW UNIVERSITY OF THE MINISTRY OF INTERNAL AFFAIRS OF THE RUSSIAN FEDERATION

Moskovskij Universitet MVD Rossijskij Federacii
ul. Akademika Volgina 12, Moskva 117437
Tel: +7(495) 336-22-44
Fax: +7(495) 336-62-88
EMail: support@mosu-mvd.com
Website: http://www.mosu-mvd.com/

Rector: Nikolai Victorovich Rumjantsev

Programmes

Law (Law); **Military Studies** (Military Science)

History: Created 1975.

Degrees and Diplomas: *Bakalavr*, *Specialist Diploma*

Last Updated: 13/01/12

MURMANSK STATE TECHNICAL UNIVERSITY

Murmanskij Gosudarstvennyj Tehničeskij Universitet
ul. Sportivnaja 13, Murmansk 183010
Tel: +7(8152) 557-119
Fax: +7(8152) 557-119
Website: http://www.mstu.edu.ru

Rector: Aleksandr P. Galjanov
Tel: +7(8152) 562-051, Fax: +7(8152) 232-492

First Vice-Rector: Viktor F. Štykov Tel: +7(8152) 565-973

Centres

Continuing Education

Colleges

Economics (Economics)

Faculties

Distance Education; **Electromechanics** (Electrical Engineering; Mechanical Engineering; Mechanics); **Finance** (Accountancy; Banking; Finance); **Humanities** (Arts and Humanities; Foreign Languages Education; History; Philosophy; Psychology; Russian; Sociology); **Law** (Civil Law; Criminal Law; International Law; Law); **Management and Economics** (Advertising and Publicity; Business and Commerce; Economics; Management; Marketing); **Marine Engineering** (Marine Engineering); **Natural Sciences** (Ecology; Geology; Mineralogy; Mining Engineering; Natural Sciences; Petroleum and Gas Engineering; Water Management); **Navigation** (Automation and Control Engineering; Nautical Science; Software Engineering); **Social and Economic Education** *(Distance Education)* (Business Education); **Technology** (Biology; Chemistry; Food Technology; Technology)

Further Information: Also preparatory Courses

History: Founded 1950 as Marine Engineering College, acquired present status and title 1996.

Admission Requirements: Secondary school certificate (Attestat o srednem obrazovanii) or equivalent

Fees: (Russian Rubles): c. 13,000-14,000 per annum

Main Language(s) of Instruction: Russian

Degrees and Diplomas: *Bakalavr*: Science, 4 yrs; *Specialist Diploma*: 5-5 1/2 yrs; *Magistr*: Science; *Kandidat Nauk*

Special Facilities: University Museum. Training Ship

Libraries: c. 350,000 vols

Publications: Vestnik MGTU

Press or Publishing House: Publishing Department

MURMANSK STATE UNIVERSITY FOR THE HUMANITIES

Murmanskij Gosudarstvennyj Gumanitarny Universitet (MSPU)
ul. Kapitana Egorova 15, Murmansk 183720
Tel: +7(8152) 21-38-01 +7(8152) 21-39-49
Fax: +7(8152) 45-27-52
EMail: mshu@mshu.edu.ru
Website: http://www.mshu.edu.ru/

Rector: Andrei Mikhailovich Sergeev

Faculties

Art Education, Technology and Design (Art Education; Design; Fine Arts; Music Education; Technology; Technology Education); **History and Social Sciences** (History; Humanities and Social Science Education; Philosophy; Social Work; Sociology); **Natural Sciences and Physical Education** (Biology; Chemistry; Ecology; Geography; Physical Education; Public Health; Science Education; Sports); **Pedagogy and Psychology** (Education; Educational Psychology; Pedagogy; Preschool Education; Psychology; Special Education; Speech Therapy and Audiology); **Philology, Journalism, and Intercultural Communication** (Communication Studies; Foreign Languages Education; International Relations; Journalism; Linguistics; Philology; Translation and Interpretation); **Physics and Mathematics Education** (Applied Mathematics; Computer Education; Information Technology; Mathematics; Mathematics Education; Physics; Science Education)

History: Founded 1939 as Murmanskij Gosudarstvennyj Pedagogičeskij Institut (Murmansk State Pedagogical Institute). Was also known as Murmanskij Gosudarstvennyj Pedagogičeskij Universitet (Murmansk State Pedagogical University). Acquired title 2003.

Governing Bodies: Academic Council

Academic Year: September to June (September-January; February-June)

Admission Requirements: Secondary school certificate (Attestat o polnom sredem obrazovanii), or equivalent (Diplom o sredem specialnom obrazovanii), or equivalent; entrance examination

Main Language(s) of Instruction: Russian

International Co-operation: With universities in Finland and Norway

Degrees and Diplomas: *Bakalavr*, *Specialist Diploma*; *Magistr*; *Kandidat Nauk*

Student Services: Academic counselling, Canteen, Cultural centre, Employment services, Foreign student adviser, Foreign Studies Centre, Health services, Language programs, Social counselling, Sports facilities

Student Residential Facilities: Students' hostel for 520 persons

Special Facilities: Museum for Regional Education, History and Culture. Educational TV Studio

Libraries: c. 450,000 vols and periodical subscriptions. Wide range of books in foreign Languages (English, German, French, Finnish, Norwegian, Swedish)

Press or Publishing House: Publishing House

Last Updated: 24/02/12

NABEREZHNJE CHELNY INSTITUTE OF SOCIAL AND EDUCATIONAL TECHNOLOGY AND RESOURCES

Naberežnočelninskij Gosudarstvennyj Institut Sotsial'no-Pedagogičeskikh Tekhnologij i Resursov
ul. Nizametdinova, 28, Naberežnje Čelny, 423806 Respublika Tatarstan
Tel: +7(8552) 46-62-16 +7(8552) 46-96-02
Fax: +7(8552) 46-62-16
EMail: ngpi@tatngpi.ru
Website: http://www.tatngpi.ru/

Rector: Fairuza Zufarovna Mustafina

Faculties
Graphic Art (Art Education; Design; Fine Arts); **History and Management** (History; Management); **Mathematics and Computer Science** (Computer Education; Computer Science; Mathematics; Mathematics Education); **Modern Languages** (English; Foreign Languages Education; French; German); **Natural Science and Geography** (Biology; Geography; Science Education; Tourism); **Philology** (Native Language; Native Language Education; Philology; Russian); **Preschool Education** (Preschool Education; Social Psychology); **Primary Education** (Educational Psychology; Pedagogy; Primary Education)

History: Created 1990. Previously known as Naberežno Čelninskij Gosudarstvennyj Pedagogičeskij Institut (Naberezhnje Chelny State Pedagogical Institute). Acquired current title 2011.

Degrees and Diplomas: *Specialist Diploma*
Last Updated: 24/02/12

NABEREZHNJE CHELNY STATE INSTITUTE OF TRADE AND TECHNOLOGY

Naberežnočelninskij Gosudarstvennyj Torgovo-Tekhnologičeskij Institut

Moskovskij prosp., 95, Naberežnje Čelny, 423812 Respublika Tatarstan
Tel: +7(8552) 58-79-82 +7(8552) 58-70-79
Fax: +7(8552) 58-79-70
EMail: into@ngtti.ru; tti.nc@edu.tatar.ru
Website: http://ngtti.ru/

Rector: Viktor Semenovich Suvorov

Faculties
Management (Management; Marketing; Public Relations); **Technology and Trade** (Business and Commerce; Food Technology; Technology)

History: Created 2004.

Degrees and Diplomas: *Bakalavr*, *Specialist Diploma*
Last Updated: 24/02/12

NATIONAL NUCLEAR RESEARCH UNIVERSITY

Natsional'nyj Issledovatel'skij Jadernyj Universiter 'MIFI' (MEPHI)

Kaširskoe šosse 31, Moskva 115409
Tel: +7(495) 323-94-25
Fax: +7(495) 324-21-11
EMail: rector@mephi.ru
Website: http://www.mephi.ru

Rector: Mikhail Niklaevich Strikhanov

Faculties
Automation and Electronics (Electronic Engineering; Microelectronics; Physics); **Cybernetics and Information Security** (Applied Mathematics; Automation and Control Engineering; Computer Science; Mathematics and Computer Science); **Experimental and Theoretical Physics** (Bioengineering; Biomedical Engineering; Nuclear Physics; Physical Engineering; Solid State Physics); **Physical Engineering** (Materials Engineering; Nuclear Engineering; Nuclear Physics; Physical Engineering; Thermal Physics); **Technology Management and Economics** (Economics; Engineering Management; Human Resources; Industrial Management; Information Technology; Management)

Higher Schools
Physics (Laser Engineering; Microwaves; Physics)

History: Founded 1942. Previously known as Moskovskij Inženerno-Fizičeskij Institut (Gosudarstvennyj Universitet) (Moscow Engineering Physics Institute (State University)). Acquired current title 2009.

Academic Year: September to June (September-January; February-June)

Admission Requirements: Secondary education certificate (Attestat o srednem obrazovanii)

Main Language(s) of Instruction: Russian, English

Degrees and Diplomas: *Bakalavr*, *Specialist Diploma*; *Magistr*, *Kandidat Nauk*

Student Services: Academic counselling, Canteen, Employment services, Foreign student adviser, Health services, Language programs, Social counselling, Sports facilities

Student Residential Facilities: For 600 students

Libraries: c. 1m. vols
Last Updated: 19/03/12

NATIONAL RESEARCH UNIVERSITY "HIGHER SCHOOL OF ECONOMICS"

Natsional'nyj Issledovatel'skij Universitet "Vyssaja Skola Ekonomiki"

ul. Myasnitskaya, 20, Moskva 101000
Tel: +7(495) 628-96-71
Fax: +7(495) 628-96-71
EMail: nobidina@hse.ru; hse@hse.ru
Website: http://www.hse.ru/

Rector: Yaroslav Kuzminov (1992-) EMail: gecrec@hse.ru

Faculties
Applied Political Science (Political Sciences); **Business Computing** (Applied Mathematics; Business Computing; Computer Science); **Economics** (Economics); **History** (History); **International Economics and Politics** (International Economics; Political Sciences); **Law** (International Law; Private Law; Public Law); **Management** (Management); **Mathematics** (Mathematics); **Media Communication** (Communication Studies; Journalism; Media Studies); **Philology** (Linguistics; Philology); **Philosophy** (Cultural Studies; East Asian Studies; Esoteric Practices; Philosophy); **Psychology** (Psychology); **Sociology** (Sociology); **State and Municipal Administration** (Government; Public Administration)

Graduate Institutes
Urban Studies (Town Planning; Urban Studies)

Institutes
Economics and Finance *(International)* (Economic History; Finance); **Education Development** (Educational Research; Educational Sciences); **Innovation Management** (Management)

Further Information: Branches also in St. Petersburg, Nizhny Novgorod and Perm.

History: Founded 1992. Acquired present status and title 2009.

Governing Bodies: Academic board

Academic Year: September to June

Main Language(s) of Instruction: Russian

Degrees and Diplomas: *Bakalavr*, *Specialist Diploma*; *Magistr*, *Kandidat Nauk*; *Doktor Nauk*

Student Services: Academic counselling, Canteen, Employment services, Foreign student adviser, Health services, Language programs, Social counselling, Sports facilities

Student Residential Facilities: Yes

Libraries: c. 10,000 vols; c. 7,000 magazines and journals
Last Updated: 13/03/12

NATIONAL STATE UNIVERSITY OF PHYSICAL EDUCATION, SPORT AND HEALTH NAMED AFTER P.F. LESGAFT

Natsional'nyj Gosudarstvennyj Universitet Fizičeskoj Kul'tury, Sporta i Zdorovja im. P.F. Lesgafta (LNSU)

ul. Dekabristov 35, Sankt-Peterburg 190121
Tel: +7(812) 714-41-13
Fax: +7(812) 714-10-84
EMail: rectorlesgaft@mail.ru
Website: http://www.lesgaft.spb.ru

Rector: Vladimir A. Tajmazov (2000-)

Centres
Medical Care (Medicine; Sports Medicine)

Faculties
Adaptive PE (Midwifery); **Coaching** (Sports); **Economics, Management and Law** (Economics; Law; Management; Sports Management); **Pedagogy** (Pedagogy; Physical Education); **Postgraduate Studies** (Natural Sciences; Sports)

Institutes
Physical Education

Further Information: Branches also in Bryansk, Monchegorsk.

History: Founded 1896 as Legsaft Courses. Formerly known as Lesgaft Institute of Physical Education (1919-1992), Lesgaft Academy of Physical Education (1992-2005), Lesgaft University of Physical Education and/or Saint-Petersburg State Academy of Physical Education (Sankt-Peterburgskaja Gosudarstvennaja Akademija Fizičeskoj Kul'tury) in our own publications (2005-2008). Acquired present title 2008.

Governing Bodies: Rector's Division; Academic Council

Academic Year: September to June

Admission Requirements: Secondary School Diploma; Entrance Examination

Main Language(s) of Instruction: Russian

Degrees and Diplomas: *Bakalavr*, *Specialist Diploma*; *Magistr*

Student Services: Academic counselling, Canteen, Cultural centre, Foreign student adviser, Foreign Studies Centre, Health services, Language programs, Nursery care, Social counselling, Sports facilities

Special Facilities: Stadium; Sport Base (St. Petersburg suburb); Water Sport base; 4 sports Halls; Swimming-pool

Libraries: National Library of Physical Education (over 100,000 vols)

Last Updated: 13/01/12

NATIONAL UNIVERSITY OF SCIENCE AND TECHNOLOGY 'MISIS'

Natsional'nyj Issledovatel'skij Tekhnologičeskij Universitet 'MISiS' (MISIS)

prosp. Leninskij 4, Moskva 119049

Tel: +7(495) 955-0032

Fax: +7(495) 236-2105

EMail: kancela@misis.ru; akochetov@usr.misis.ru; trav@misis.ru; yurchuk@misis.ru; elui@misis.ru

Website: http://www.misis.ru

Rector: Dmitry Livanov (2007-)

EMail: livanovdv@misis.ru; rectorat@misis.ru

Faculties
Distance Education (Computer Science; Electronic Engineering; Management; Metallurgical Engineering; Microelectronics)

Institutes
Economics and Management (Business Computing; Economics; Industrial Management; Management; Small Business); **Environmental Technology and Engineering** (Analytical Chemistry; Environmental Engineering; Environmental Management; Metallurgical Engineering; Natural Resources; Thermal Physics); **Information Technology and Automated Control Systems** (Applied Mathematics; Automation and Control Engineering; Computer Science; Information Technology); **New Materials and Nanotechnology** (Applied Physics; Computer Science; Materials Engineering; Nanotechnology; Physical Chemistry; Physics; Solid State Physics)

Further Information: MISIS has 4 University branches in Elektrostahl (Moscow region), Stary Oskol (Belgorod Regio), Novotroitsk (Orenburg region), and Vyksa (Nizhniy-Novgorod region); informative-consulting centers in Tula, Cherepovets, Izhevsk, Nizhnii Tagil, Kulebaki, Ryazan, Kolchugino, Podolsk, and Tver as well as Distance learning Department.

History: Founded 1918 as a course offered at the Metallurgical Faculty of Moscow Mining Academy (MMA). Became Moscow Institute of Steel (MIS), separated from MMA, became an independent institution of Higher Education 1930. Merged with Institute of Non-Ferrous Metals and Gold to become the Moscow Institute of Steel and Alloys 1962, and became Gosudarstvennyj Technologicheskij Universitet "Moskovskij Institut Stali i Splavov" in 1993. Acquired current title and status in 2009.

Governing Bodies: Senate

Academic Year: September to June (September-January; February-June)

Admission Requirements: secondary (higher) education at institution of further education

Fees: (Russian Roubles): 60,000-180,000 per annum depending on specialty and degree programme

Main Language(s) of Instruction: Russian

International Co-operation: With universities in Germany, France, UK, Norway, Italy, USA, Sweden, Poland, Czech Republic, Poland, Bulgaria.

Accrediting Agencies: Federal Service of Supervision in Education and Science

Degrees and Diplomas: *Bakalavr*, *Specialist Diploma*; *Magistr*; *Kandidat Nauk*; *Doktor Nauk*

Student Services: Academic counselling, Canteen, Cultural centre, Foreign student adviser, Foreign Studies Centre, Health services, Language programs, Nursery care, Social counselling, Sports facilities

Student Residential Facilities: Four dormitories

Special Facilities: University museum; concert hall (1200 seats); student theatre

Libraries: over 1,2m. Vols; electronic library access

Last Updated: 05/05/11

NIZHNEVARTOVSK STATE UNIVERSITY FOR THE HUMANITIES

Nižnevartovsk Gosudarstvennyj Gumanitarskij Universiter

ul. Lenina 56, Nižnevartovsk, 628605 Tjumenskaja oblast', Khanty-Mansijskij avt. okrug-Jugra

Tel: +7(3466) 44-39-50 +7(3466) 44-40-30

Fax: +7(3466) 45-18-05

EMail: nggu@nggu.ru; nggu@wsmail.ru

Website: http://www.nggu.ru/

Rector: Sergei Ivanovich Gorlov

Faculties
Art and Design (Architecture; Art Education; Design; Fine Arts); **Cultural Studies and Services** (Cultural Studies; Music Education; Philosophy; Social Sciences; Tourism); **Economics and Management** (Business and Commerce; Economics; Management); **Humanities** (Archiving; Documentation Techniques; History; Linguistics; Mass Communication; Modern Languages; Philology; Public Relations; Russian; Translation and Interpretation); **Information Technology and Mathematics** (Computer Education; Computer Science; Information Technology; Mathematics; Mathematics Education); **Natural Science and Geography** (Ecology; Environmental Studies; Geography); **Pedagogy and Psychology** (Educational Psychology; Pedagogy; Preschool Education; Primary Education); **Physical Education and Sport** (Physical Education; Sports)

History: Founded 1988 as a branch of the Tobolsk Pedagogical Institute. Became Nižnevartovsk Gosudarstvennyj Pedagogičeskij Institut (Nizhnevartovsk State Pedagogical Institute) in 1992. Acquired currents and title in 2005.

Academic Year: September to June (September-January; February-June)

Admission Requirements: Secondary school certificate (Attestat o srednem obrazovanii)

Main Language(s) of Instruction: Russian

Degrees and Diplomas: *Bakalavr*, *Specialist Diploma*; *Magistr*; *Kandidat Nauk*

Student Residential Facilities: For c. 120 students

Libraries: Main Library, c. 161,000 vols

Press or Publishing House: Publishing House

Last Updated: 12/01/12

NIZHNIJ TAGIL STATE SOCIO-PEDAGOGICAL ACADEMY

Nižnetagilskaja Gosudarstvennaja Socialno-Pedagogičeskaja Academija (NTGSPA)

ul. Krasnogvardejskaja 57, Nižnij Tagil, 622031 Sverdlovskaja oblast'

Tel: +7(3435) 255-300 +7(3435) 253-644

Fax: +7(3435) 254-800

EMail: office@ntspi.ru

Website: http://www.ntspi.ru

Rector: Vladimir Ivanovich Smirnov (1989-)

Vice-Rector for Academic Affairs: Lyudmila Petrovna Filatova Tel: +7(3435) 255-301

International Relations: Sergej Aleksandrovich Nozdrin, Vice Rector for Science Tel: +7(3435) 255-310

Faculties

Chemistry and Biology (Biology; Chemistry; Ecology; Geography) *Dean*: Eleonora Vasilyevna Meling; **Elementary Education** (Pre-school Education; Primary Education) *Dean*: Marina Valentinovna Lomayeva; **Fine Arts** (Art Education; Fine Arts; Visual Arts) *Dean*: Larisa Petrovna Lebedeva; **Foreign Languages** (English; French; German; Modern Languages) *Dean*: Elena Vladimirovna Yuzhaninova; **Health and Safety** *Head*: Elena Anatolyevna Feschenko; **History and Social Studies** (Documentation Techniques; History; Social Studies) *Dean*: Akhat Minigareyevich Ganiyev; **Mass Communication** (Mass Communication) *Dean*: Anna Borisnova Ryaposova; **Performing Arts** (Dance; Music; Performing Arts; Theatre) *Dean*: Irina Aleksandrovna Startseva; **Physics and Mathematics** (Computer Education; Information Technology; Mathematics; Physics) *Head*: Sergej Ervinovich Potoskuyev; **Russian Language and Literature** (Literature; Russian) *Dean*: Olga Ivanovna Sidorova; **Social Work** (Social and Community Services; Social Welfare; Social Work) *Dean*: Liliya Igorevna Kirillova; **Technologies and Engineering** (Engineering; Home Economics Education; Technology; Technology Education) *Dean*: Nadezhda Mikhailovna Komarova

Further Information: Also Preparatory Courses and Professional Orientation programme, Post graduate Education

History: Founded 1939 as Pedagogical College, acquired present status and title 1952. Formerly known as Nižnetagilskij Gosudarstvennyj Pedagogičeskij Institut.

Governing Bodies: Academic Council

Academic Year: September to June (September-December; January-June)

Admission Requirements: Secondary school certificate (Attestat o srednem obrazovanii), or equivalent (srednem specialnom, diplom tehnikuma)

Fees: (Russian Rubles): 25,000 per semester

Main Language(s) of Instruction: Russian

Accrediting Agencies: Ministry of Education and Science of the Russian Federation

Degrees and Diplomas: *Bakalavr*: Art Education; Biology; Chemistry; Computer Education; Dance; Documentation Techniques; Fine Arts; Geography; Health Education; History; Home Economics Education; Information Technology; Literature; Mass Communication; Mathematics; Modern Languages: English; French; German; Music; Occupational Health; Performing Arts; Physics; Preschool Education; Primary Education; Russian; Social and Community Services; Social Studies; Social Welfare; Technology Education; Technology; Theatre; Visual Arts, 4 yrs; *Magistr*: Pedagogy; Linguistics; History, a further 2 yrs. Diplomas of certified specialists; continuing professional education; post-graduate education in pedagogy, Russian, History of Russia and teaching methodology of physics

Student Services: Academic counselling, Canteen, Employment services, Health services, Language programs, Social counselling, Sports facilities

Student Residential Facilities: 3 hostels for 1.000 students

Special Facilities: Museum; Video Studio; Resource Centre and Laboratories; Plant and Crop experimental Facility

Libraries: Rresearch library, over 80.000 vols of scientific, fiction, referential literature and periodicals

Publications: Scholarly Notes, A collection of articles on philosophy, pedagogy, linguistics, history *(annually)*

Press or Publishing House: Publishing House of the Academy

Academic Staff *2007-2008*	MEN	WOMEN	**TOTAL**
FULL-TIME	64	258	**322**
PART-TIME	12	46	**58**
STAFF WITH DOCTORATE			
FULL-TIME	111	443	**554**
PART-TIME	15	60	**75**
Student Numbers *2007-2008*			
All (Foreign Included)	378	2,146	**2,524**

Part-time students, 1,722.

Last Updated: 05/12/08

NIZHNY NOVGOROD ACADEMY OF THE MINISTRY OF INTERNAL AFFAIRS OF RUSSIA

Nižegorodskaja Akademija MVD Rossii

Ankudinovskoje šosse 3, Nižnij Novgorod 603144

Tel: +7(8312) 65-5787

Fax: +7(8312) 64-3018

EMail: na@namvd.nnov.ru

Website: http://www.namvd.nnov.ru

Rector: Vjacheslav I. Kanygin

Degrees and Diplomas: *Specialist Diploma*: 5 yrs

NIZHNY NOVGOROD STATE ACADEMY OF AGRICULTURE

Nižegorodskaja Gosudarstvennaja Sel'skohozjajstvennaja Akademija

ul. Gagarina 97, Nižnij Novgorod 603107

Tel: +7(8312) 660-730

Fax: +7(8312) 660-684

EMail: root@agri.sci-nnov.ru

Website: http://www.agri.sci-nnov.ru

Rector: Vitalij Konstantinovič Khlustov Tel: +7(8312) 663-460

Programmes

Agriculture (Agriculture); **Economics**

NIZHNY NOVGOROD STATE LINGUISTIC UNIVERSITY NAMED AFTER N.A. DOBROLJUBOV

Nižegorodskij Gosudarstvennyj Lingvističeskij Universitet im. N.A. Dobroljubova (LUNN)

ul. Minina 31-a, Nižnij Novgorod 603155

Tel: +7(8312) 361-840

Fax: +7(8312) 362-049

EMail: interoff@lunn.sci-nnov.ru

Website: http://www.lunn.sci-nnov.ru

Rector: Gennadij P. Rjabov (1988-)
Tel: +7(8312) 361-575 EMail: ryabov@lunn.sci-nnov.ru

First Vice-Rector: Lev A. L'vov
Tel: +7(8312) 361-470 EMail: ivov@lunn.sci-nnov.ru

Vice-Rector: Vladimir G. Tikhonov EMail: vgt@lunn.ru

International Relations: Anatolij G. Aniščenko
Tel: +7(8312) 362-049 EMail: eac@lunn.sci-nnov.ru

Faculties

Economics; **English Language** (Advertising and Publicity; Business Administration; Education; English; Foreign Languages Education; Hotel Management; International Relations; Linguistics; Public Relations; Secretarial Studies; Tourism); **French Language** (Education; Foreign Languages Education; French; Linguistics); **German Language** (Education; Foreign Languages Education; German; Linguistics); **Philology** (Literature; Native Language; Philology); **Translation and Interpreting** (Banking; Finance; Journalism; Linguistics; Translation and Interpretation)

Further Information: Courses for foreign students. The University also runs programmes in Nabereżnye Čelny (194 students, 58 of them distance students), Kazan (128 students, 19 of them distance students), Lipetsk (102 students) and Vladimir, 22 students)

History: Founded 1937, acquired present status and title 1994.

Governing Bodies: University Council

Academic Year: September to June (September-December; January-June)

Admission Requirements: Secondary school certificate (Attestat o srednem obrazovanii) or equivalent

Fees: (Russian Rubles): c. 33,000 per annum; foreign students, (US Dollars), 80-225 per week

Main Language(s) of Instruction: Russian

Degrees and Diplomas: *Bakalavr*: 4 yrs; *Magistr*: a further 1-2 yrs; *Kandidat Nauk*: a further 2-3 yrs

Student Services: Academic counselling, Canteen, Cultural centre, Employment services, Foreign Studies Centre, Health services, Language programs, Social counselling

Student Residential Facilities: Yes

Special Facilities: Russian History and Culture Museum

Libraries: c. 450,000 vols

Publications: Linguistics and Philology Monographs *(annually)*; Research Papers

Press or Publishing House: Printing House

NIZHNY NOVGOROD STATE MEDICAL ACADEMY

Nižegorodskaja Gosudarstvennaja Medicinskaja Akademija

Minin and Požarsky sq. 10/1, Nižnij Novgorod 603005

Tel: +7(8312) 390-943 +7(8312) 390-643

Fax: +7(8312) 390-943

EMail: nnsma@sandy.ru

Website: http://www.n-nov.mednet.com

Rector: Vyačeslav V. Škarin (2002-)

Vice-Rector, Training Division: Gennadij A. Bulanov
Tel: +7(8312) 390-643

International Relations: Mikhail M. Khilov
Tel: +7(8312) 199-820, Fax: +7(8312) 199-820
EMail: fois-ngma@list.ru; marketing.nnsma@gmail.com

Centres

Continuing Education and Professional Specialist Training *Vice-Rector*: Jurij N. Filippov

Faculties

Dentistry (Dentistry) *Dean*: Evgenij N. Žulev; **General Medicine** (Medicine) *Dean*: Aleksandr N. Kuznecov; **Health Sciences** *(International Students) Dean*: Elena I. Erlykina; **Nursing Higher Education** *Dean*: Tatyana V. Pozdeyeva; **Paediatrics** (Paediatrics) *Dean*: Arkady V. Leonov; **Pharmacy** *Dean*: Svetlana V. Kononova; **Preventive Medicine** (Social and Preventive Medicine) *Dean*: Arkady V. Leonov

Institutes

Skin and Venereal Diseases (Dermatology; Venereology) *Director*: Nikolaj K. Nikulin

Laboratories

Research *Head*: Irina V. Muhina

Research Institutes

Applied and Fundamental Medicine

Further Information: Also 28 Teaching Hospitals

History: Founded as faculty of Nižnij Novgorod Universitet 1920. Became independent 1930. Acquired present status and title 1994.

Academic Year: September to June (September-January; February-June)

Admission Requirements: Certificate of full/general secondary education or equivalent (Attestat o srednem/polnom obschem obrazovanii)

Fees: (Russian Rubles): 21,000-40,000 per annum. (US Dollars): Foreign students, 1,900-3,700; (US Dollars), Internship, Clinical Residency, PhD Programme, 2,300-3,500

Main Language(s) of Instruction: Russian, English for foreign students

International Co-operation: Essen University (Germany); Nice University Sophia Antipolis (France)

Degrees and Diplomas: *Specialist Diploma*: Dentistry; Nursing Higher Education; Pharmacy, 5 yrs; *Specialist Diploma*: General Medicine; Paediatrics; Preventive Medicine, 6 yrs; *Kandidat Nauk*: a further 3 yrs by thesis. Also postgraduate studies, Internship, a further yr; Clinical Residency, a further 3 yrs

Student Services: Academic counselling, Canteen, Cultural centre, Employment services, Foreign student adviser, Foreign Studies Centre, Health services, Language programs, Social counselling, Sports facilities

Student Residential Facilities: For c. 2,000 students

Special Facilities: Academy Museum; Anatomy Museum

Libraries: c. 500,000 vols

Publications: Nizhny Novgorod Medical Journal *(quarterly)*

Press or Publishing House: Publishing House

NIZHNY NOVGOROD STATE MUSIC CONSERVATORY (ACADEMY) NAMED AFTER M.I. GLINKA

Nižegorodskaja Gosudarstvennaja Konservatorija (Akademija) im. M. I. Glinka

ul. Piskunova 40, Nižnij Novgorod 603605

Tel: +7(831) 419-40-23 +7(831) 419-40-46

Fax: +7(831) 419-40-46

EMail: education.nngk@mail.ru; nngk@mail.ru

Website: http://nnovcons.ru

Rector: Edouard Fertelmeister

Faculties

Conducting (Conducting); **Folk Instruments** (Music; Performing Arts); **Musicology and Composition** (Musicology); **Orchestra** (Music; Musical Instruments; Performing Arts); **Piano** (Musical Instruments); **Singing** (Singing)

History: Founded 1946.

Governing Bodies: Academic Council

Academic Year: September to June (September-January; February-June)

Admission Requirements: Secondary school certificate (Attestat o sredem obrazovanii) or equivalent (Diploma o sredem profesionalnom obrazovanii), and entrance examination

Main Language(s) of Instruction: Russian

International Co-operation: With universities in Germany, Austria, China

Accrediting Agencies: Ministry of Culture

Degrees and Diplomas: *Bakalavr*; *Specialist Diploma*; *Magistr*

Student Services: Academic counselling, Canteen, Cultural centre, Foreign student adviser, Health services, Sports facilities

Student Residential Facilities: For 320 students

Special Facilities: Museum; Sound Laboratory

Libraries: Yes

Last Updated: 12/01/12

NIZHNY NOVGOROD STATE PEDAGOGICAL UNIVERSITY

Nižegorodskij Gosudarstvennyj Pedagogičeskij Universitet (NNSPU)

ul. Uljanova 1, Nižnij Novgorod 603950

Tel: +7(831) 439-00-84

Fax: +7(831) 436-44-46

EMail: nnspu@nnspu.ru

Website: http://nnspu.ru

Acting Rector: Lev Shaposhnikov

Faculties

Astronomy (Astronomy and Space Science); **Economic Theory** (Economics); **Educational Psychology** (Educational Psychology); **Esthetics** (Fine Arts); **Foreign Languages** (Modern Languages); **General Pedagogy** (Pedagogy); **History** (Archaeology; History; History of Religion; Modern History; Religion) *Dean*: Radislav Kaurkin; **Mathematics, Informatics and Physics** (Astrophysics; Computer Science; Mathematics; Mathematics Education; Physics) *Dean*: Elena Perevozschikova; **Natural Sciences and Geography** (Anatomy; Biology; Botany; Ecology; Geography; Inorganic Chemistry; Natural Sciences; Organic Chemistry; Zoology) *Dean*: Natalia Koposova; **Philology** (Literature; Native Language Education; Philology; Russian) *Dean*: Galina Samoylova; **Philosophy** (Philosophy); **Philosophy and Theology** (Orthodox Theology; Philosophy; Religion; Theology) *Head*: Oleg Parilov; **Physical Culture** (Physical Education); **Physical Training** (Anatomy; Biological and Life Sciences; Physical Education; Sports; Sports Medicine) *Dean*: Vitaly Skitnevsky; **Physics** (Astrophysics; Physics; Science Education); **Psychology** (Psychology); **Psychology and Education** (Modern Languages; Preschool Education; Primary Education; Psychology; Teacher Trainers Education) *Dean*: Alecksandr Dmitriev; **Russian Language and Culture**; **Technology and Economics** (Crafts and Trades; Economics; Industrial Arts Education; Industrial Design; Machine Building; Management; Marketing; Technology; Technology Education) *Dean*: Sofia Shevchenko; **World Russian Culture** (Cultural Studies; Russian)

Further Information: Also preparatory Courses for foreign students and distance training programmes

History: Founded 1911. Reorganised as Pedagogical Institute 1918. Acquired present status and title 1993.

Governing Bodies: Rector's Committee (Rector, Vice-rectors and their assistants). University Scientific Council (Academic Council), comprising 55 members

Academic Year: September to July

Admission Requirements: Secondary school certificate (Attestat o srednem obrazovanii) or equivalent, and entrance examination

Fees: (US Dollars): c. 1,000-3,000 per annum

Main Language(s) of Instruction: Russian

International Co-operation: Federal Service for Supervision of Education and Science

Degrees and Diplomas: *Bakalavr*; *Specialist Diploma*

Student Services: Canteen, Employment services, Foreign student adviser, Health services, Language programs, Social counselling, Sports facilities

Student Residential Facilities: 2 university student hostels

Special Facilities: Observatory. Two Museums

Libraries: C. 650,000 vols

Student Numbers *2007-2008*: Total: c. 10,000

Last Updated: 08/12/08

NIZHNY NOVGOROD STATE TECHNICAL UNIVERSITY

Nižegorodskij Gosudarstvennyj Tehničeskij Universitet imeni R.E. Alekseevich (NSTU)

ul. Minina 24, Nižnij Novgorod 603600
Tel: +7(831) 436-23-25
Fax: +7(831) 436-94-75
EMail: rektorat@nntu.nnov.ru
Website: http://www.nntu.nnov.ru/

Rector: Sergei Mihkailovich Dmitriev
EMail: tishkov@nntu.sci-nnov.ru

Faculties

Applied Mathematics (Applied Mathematics); **Applied Physics** (Applied Physics); **Automobile Engineering** (Automotive Engineering); **Economics** (Economics); **Electrical Engineering** (Electrical Engineering); **Mechanical Engineering and Automated Manufacturing Processes** (Automation and Control Engineering; Industrial Engineering; Mechanical Engineering); **Metallurgy** (Metallurgical Engineering); **Naval Engineering** (Marine Engineering); **Physical Chemistry** (Physical Chemistry); **Radio Electronics and Engineering Cybernetics** (Automation and Control Engineering; Telecommunications Engineering); **Sociology and Economics** (Economics; Sociology)

History: Founded 1917, acquired present status and title 1991.

Degrees and Diplomas: *Bakalavr*; *Specialist Diploma*; *Magistr*

Last Updated: 26/09/11

NIZHNY NOVGOROD STATE UNIVERSITY NAMED AFTER N.I. LOBACHEVSKY

Nižegorodskij Gosudarstvennyj Universitet im N.I. Lobachevskogo (NNGU)

prosp. Gagarina 23, GSP - 20, Nižnij Novgorod 603950
Tel: +7(8312) 658-490
Fax: +7(8312) 658-592
EMail: rector@unn.ac.ru
Website: http://www.unn.ac.ru

Rector: Roman Strongin (2003-)
Tel: +7(8312) 659-015, Fax: +7(8312) 345-125

International Relations: Alexandre Groudzinski
EMail: aog@unn.ac.ru

Faculties

Biology (Biology) *Dean*: Aleksandr P. Veselov; **Chemistry** (Chemistry) *Dean*: Aleksej Gushchin; **Computational Mathematics and Cybernetics** (Automation and Control Engineering; Computer Engineering; Mathematics and Computer Science) *Dean*: Viktor Gergel; **Economics** (Economics) *Dean*: Jurij Trifonov; **Finance** (Finance) *Dean*: Vjačeslav N. Jasenev; **History** (History) *Dean*: Jevgenij Molev; **International Relations** (International Relations) *Dean*: Oleg Kolobov; **Law** (Law) *Dean*: Petr Milkov; **Management and Business** *(Higher)* (Business and Commerce; Management) *Dean*: Aleksandr Groudzinski; **Mechanics and Mathematics** (Mathematics; Mechanics) *Dean*: Aleksandr Lyubimov; **Philology** (Philology) *Dean*: Lyudmila Ruchina; **Physical Education and Sports** (Physical Education; Sports) *Dean*: Vadim Kuzmin; **Physics** (Physics) *Dean*: Kirill Markov; **Radio Physics** (Physics) *Dean*: Arkadij Jakimov; **Social Sciences** (Social Sciences) *Dean*: Vladimir Blonin

Schools

General and Applied Physics *(Advanced)* (Applied Physics; Physics) *Dean*: Mikhail Tokman

History: Founded 1916, acquired present status and title 1918.

Governing Bodies: Academic Council

Academic Year: September to June (September-January; February-June)

Admission Requirements: Secondary school certificate (Attestat o srednem obrazovanii) and entrance examination

Fees: For all international students (a limited number of State-funded tuition-free places is available to Russian students with the best score on entrance exams)

Main Language(s) of Instruction: Russian

Degrees and Diplomas: *Bakalavr*: 4 yrs; *Specialist Diploma*: 5 yrs; *Magistr*: a further 2 yrs; *Kandidat Nauk*: a further 3 yrs and thesis; *Doktor Nauk*: by thesis after Kandidat

Special Facilities: Zoology Museum; University Museum; Botanical Garden; Innovation Technology Centre; Internet Centre.

Libraries:c. 2m. Vols

Publications: Vestnik Nizhegorodskogo Gosudarstvennogo Universiteta

NIZHNY NOVGOROD STATE UNIVERSITY OF ARCHITECTURE AND CIVIL ENGINEERING

Nižegorodskij Gosudarstvennyj Arhitekturno-Stroitel'nyj Universitet

ul. Iljinskaja 65, Nižnij Novgorod 603950
Tel: +7(8312) 340-291
Fax: +7(8312) 305-348
EMail: srec@nngasu.ru
Website: http://www.nngasu.ru

Rector: Evgeny Vasilievich Koposov (2006-)
EMail: koposov@nngasu.ru

Vice-Rector: Vladimir Nikolaevich Bobylev Tel: +7(8312) 306-495

International Relations: Alexander Vasilievich Paleev, Vice-Rector
Tel: +7(8312) 333-370 EMail: iro@nngasu.ru

Centres

Pre-University Training and Education of Foreign Students (Russian) *Deputy Director*: Viktor Y. Azarov

Departments

Ecologically Safe Development of Large Regions - the Volga Basin *(UNESCO Chair)* (Ecology; Heritage Preservation; Soil Conservation; Water Management) *Acting Head*: Alexander Nikolaevich Kosarikov

Faculties

Engineering (Building Technologies; Chemistry; Computer Graphics; Engineering; Geophysics; Information Technology; Materials Engineering; Mathematics; Mechanical Engineering; Physics; Surveying and Mapping) *Head*: Nikolai M. Konnov

Institutes

Architecture and Urban Development (Architectural and Environmental Design; Architecture; Engineering; Fine Arts; Graphic Arts; Industrial Design; Landscape Architecture; Road Engineering; Surveying and Mapping; Town Planning; Transport Engineering; Urban Studies) *Director*: Evgenij K. Nikolsky; **Arts and Humanities** (Arts and Humanities; Cultural Studies; Development Studies; Educational Technology; Fine Arts; Graphic Arts; Health Education; Interior Design; Medicine; Pedagogy; Psychology; Social Sciences;

Sociology) *Director*: Yuri A. Lebedev; **Civil Engineering** (Building Technologies; Construction Engineering; Hydraulic Engineering; Mechanical Engineering; Structural Architecture; Wood Technology) *Director*: Alexander I. Kolesov; **Continuing Education** *Director*: Vladislav V. Borodachev; **Economics and Law** (Accountancy; Civil Law; Law; Management; Real Estate) *Director*: Vyacheslav J. Kolesov; **Engineering and Ecological Systems and Installations** (Ecology; Engineering; Environmental Engineering; Environmental Management; Heating and Refrigeration; Power Engineering; Waste Management; Water Management) *Director*: Boris B. Lampsi; **International Law, Management and Economics** (Banking; Economics; Finance; Institutional Administration; International Law; Management; Marketing) *Director*: Igor V. Arzhenovsky

Research Institutes

Social Education and Human Ecology (Ecology; Social Studies) *Director*: Yuri A. Lebedev

Further Information: Also Russian Courses for foreign students

History: Founded 1930 as Institute, acquired present status and title 1997.

Governing Bodies: Scientific Board

Academic Year: September to June (September-January; February-June)

Admission Requirements: Secondary school certificate (Attestat o srednem obrazovanii) or equivalent, and entrance examination (for Russian speaking candidates) or Certificate of completed one year entrance level programme, including Russian as Foreign Language

Fees: (US Dollars): 1,600-2,000 per annum

Main Language(s) of Instruction: Russian, English and German in the Institute of International Law and Management

International Co-operation: With universities in Germany, Netherlands, France and Malta.

Accrediting Agencies: Federal Agency for Education of Ministry of Education and Science of the Russian Federation

Degrees and Diplomas: *Bakalavr*: 4 yrs; *Specialist Diploma*: 5-6 yrs; *Magistr*: Science, 6 yrs; *Kandidat Nauk*: 8 yrs; *Doktor Nauk*: 11 yrs

Student Services: Academic counselling, Canteen, Cultural centre, Foreign Studies Centre, Health services, Language programs, Sports facilities

Student Residential Facilities: Yes (Hostel)

Special Facilities: History of the University Museum; TV and Video Studio

Libraries: Central and Specialized Libraries, total, c. 1m. vols

Publications: Abstracts of international and National Conferences; Issues of Multilevel Architectural and Civil Engineering Education *(annually)*

Press or Publishing House: Publishing Centre

NORILSK INSTITUTE OF INDUSTRY

Norilskij Industrialnyj Institut (NII)

ul. 50-letija Oktjabrja 7, Norilsk 663310
Tel: +7(3919) 421-632
Fax: +7(3919) 421-741
EMail: skachkov.nii@norcom.ru; norvuz.nii@norcom.ru
Website: http://www.norcom.ru/users/norvuz.nii

Rector: Arsentij Kolegov (1995-)

Vice-Rector: Vladimir Zabusov Tel: +7(3915) 421-609

International Relations: Mihail Skačkov

Faculties

Economics and Engineering (Accountancy; Business Administration; Economics; Finance; Information Management; Management) *Dean*: Vitaly Kurovsky; **Mining and Metallurgy** (Heating and Refrigeration; Metallurgical Engineering; Mining Engineering; Water Management) *Dean*: Vladimir Korovkin; **Power Engineering and Technological Equipment** (Automation and Control Engineering; Machine Building; Metallurgical Engineering; Power Engineering) *Dean*: Victor Černoby; **Technology** (Technology) *Dean*: Nickolai Davidov

History: Founded 1961. Acquired present status 1991.

Academic Year: September to June

Admission Requirements: Secondary school certificate

Fees: None

Main Language(s) of Instruction: Russian

International Co-operation: With universities in Finland

Accrediting Agencies: Ministry of Education

Student Services: Academic counselling, Canteen, Cultural centre, Employment services, Foreign student adviser, Handicapped facilities, Health services, Language programs, Nursery care, Social counselling, Sports facilities

Student Residential Facilities: Yes

Special Facilities: Museum; Movie Studio

Libraries: c. 350,000 vols

NORTH CAUCASUS ACADEMY OF PUBLIC ADMINISTRATION

Severo-Kavkazskaja Akademija Gosudarstvennoj Služby

ul. Puškinskaja 70, Rostov-na-Donu 344007
Tel: +7(8632) 402-723
Fax: +7(8632) 406-115
EMail: kanc@skags.ru; academy@skags.ru
Website: http://www.skags.ru

Rector: Vassilij V. Rudoi

Departments

Economic Theory and Entrepreneurship; **Philosophy** (Logic; Modern History; Philosophical Schools; Philosophy); **Politology and Ethnopolitics**; **State and Municipal Management** (Industrial Management; Management Systems; Public Administration)

Faculties

Management (Business Administration; Human Resources; Management; Public Administration)

Institutes

International Economics (Economic and Finance Policy; Economic History; International Economics; Marketing; Taxation); **Law** (Administrative Law; Civil Law; Commercial Law; International Law; Law)

History: Founded 1992, acquired present status and title 1995.

Governing Bodies: Academic Council

Academic Year: September to July

Admission Requirements: Secondary school certificate (Attestat o srednem obrazovanii) and entrance examination

Fees: (Russian Rubles): Law and International Economics Institutes, c. 12,000 per annum

Main Language(s) of Instruction: Russian

Degrees and Diplomas: *Bakalavr*, *Specialist Diploma*: International Economics; Law; State and Municipal Management; *Doktor Nauk*

Student Services: Academic counselling, Canteen, Cultural centre, Employment services, Health services, Language programs, Social counselling, Sports facilities

Student Residential Facilities: Student Hostel

Special Facilities: Laboratory of Regional Managers

Libraries: Central Library

Publications: North-Caucasian Yuridichesky Vestnik *(3 per annum)*; State and Municipal Management *(quarterly)*

Last Updated: 07/12/11

NORTH CAUCASUS MINING AND METALLURGICAL INSTITUTE (STATE UNIVERSITY OF TECHNOLOGY)

Severo-Kavkazskij Gorno-Metallurgičeskij Institut (Gosudarstvennyj Tekhnologičeskij Universitet)

ul. Nikolaeva 44, Vladikavkaz, 362021 Respublika Severnaja Osetija-Alanija
Tel: +7(8672) 40-71-01 +7(8672) 40-71-50
Fax: +7(8672) 40-72-03
EMail: info@skgmi-gtu.ru
Website: http://www.skgmi-gtu.ru/

Rector: Nikolai Evgen'evich Shubin

Faculties

Architecture and Civil Engineering (Architecture; Civil Engineering; Road Engineering; Road Transport; Transport Management); **Economics and Management** (Economics; History; Management; Political Sciences; Sociology); **Electromechanics** (Electrical Engineering; Mechanical Engineering); **Electronic Engineering** (Electronic Engineering; Physics); **Finance and Economics** (Accountancy; Economics; Finance; Taxation); **Food Technology** (Brewing; Food Technology); **Geology and Mining Engineering** (Geology; Mining Engineering); **Information Technology** (Business and Commerce; Computer Science; Information Technology); **Law** (Law); **Metallurgy** (Metallurgical Engineering)

History: Founded 1931. Previously known as Severo-Kavkazskij Gosudarstvennyj Tehnologičeskij Universitet (North Caucasus State University of Technology). Acquired current title and status 2003.

Degrees and Diplomas: *Bakalavr*, *Specialist Diploma*; *Magistr*
Last Updated: 16/03/12

NORTH CAUCASUS STATE INSTITUTE OF ARTS

Severo-Kavkazskij Gosudarstvennyj Institut Iskusstv

prosp. Lenina 1, Nalčik 360000
Tel: +7(8662) 40-89-01
Fax: +7(8662)47-26-48
EMail: mail@skgii.ru
Website: http://www.skgii.ru/

Rector: Anatoliy Rahaev (2005-)

Colleges

Culture and Art (Acting; Cinema and Television; Cultural Studies; Dance; Design; Library Science; Museum Studies; Music Education; Music Theory and Composition; Musical Instruments; Singing)

Further Information: Also Courses for foreign students

History: Founded 1989 as Higher School of Arts, acquired present status and title 1995.

Academic Year: September to June (September-January; February-June)

Admission Requirements: Secondary school certificate (Attestat o srednem obrazovanii) or special equivalent for some faculties

Main Language(s) of Instruction: Russian

Degrees and Diplomas: *Bakalavr*, *Specialist Diploma*; *Magistr*, *Kandidat Nauk*

Student Services: Academic counselling, Canteen, Cultural centre, Employment services, Health services, Nursery care, Social counselling, Sports facilities

Student Residential Facilities: For 600 students

Special Facilities: Museum; Theatre Studios

Libraries: Central Library

Publications: All Russia Scientific Conferences on Culture; Institute Annual Conferences *(annually)*
Last Updated: 07/12/11

NORTH CAUCASUS STATE TECHNICAL UNIVERSITY

Severo-Kavkazskij Gosudarstvennyj Tekhničeskij Universitet (NCSTU)

prosp. Kulakova 2, Stavropol, 355029 Stavropol'skij kraj
Tel: +7(8652) 956-932 +7(8652) 956-808
Fax: +7(8652) 956-808
EMail: info@ncstu.ru
Website: http://www.ncstu.ru

Rector: Boris Mihailovich Sinelnikov (1987-)

Faculties

Civil Engineering (Architecture; Building Technologies; Civil Engineering; Construction Engineering); **Economics and Finance** (Accountancy; Banking; Business and Commerce; Finance; Management; Real Estate; Taxation); **Electronics, Nanotechnologies and Chemical Industry** (Chemical Engineering; Electronic Engineering; Nanotechnology); **Food Production and Biotechnology** (Biotechnology; Food Science; Food Technology); **Humanities** (Communication Studies; Cultural Studies; Design; Education; Linguistics; Modern Languages; Pedagogy; Psychology; Social Work; Sociology; Tourism; Translation and Interpretation); **Information Technologies and Telecommunications** (Applied Mathematics; Computer Engineering; Computer Science; Information Management; Information Sciences; Information Technology; Mathematics); **Law** (Criminal Law; History of Law; Philosophy; Private Law; Public Law); **Oil and Gas** (Geology; Geophysics; Mineralogy; Mining Engineering; Petroleum and Gas Engineering); **Power Engineering, Machine Building and Transport** (Automotive Engineering; Electrical Engineering; Energy Engineering; Mechanical Engineering; Transport Engineering; Transport Management)

History: Founded 1971. Acquired present status and title 1994. Formerly known as Stavropolskij Gosudarstvennyj Tehničeskij Universitet (Stavropol State Technical University).

Admission Requirements: Secondary School Certificate

Main Language(s) of Instruction: Russian; English

International Co-operation: With universities in Colombia, Czech Republic, Germany and Poland

Accrediting Agencies: Ministry of Education and Science of Russian Federation, Federal Education Agency. Educational Institutions Licensing, Certification and Accreditation Office

Degrees and Diplomas: *Bakalavr*, *Specialist Diploma*; *Magistr*, *Kandidat Nauk*

Student Services: Academic counselling, Canteen, Cultural centre, Employment services, Foreign student adviser, Foreign Studies Centre, Handicapped facilities, Health services, Language programs, Nursery care, Social counselling, Sports facilities

Student Residential Facilities: 3 hostels; hotel
Libraries: 840,000 vols; electronic catalogue, 120,450 entries
Last Updated: 26/01/12

NORTH EASTERN FEDERAL UNIVERSITY

Severo-Vostočnyj Federalnyj Universitet im. M.K. Ammasova

ul. Berlinskogo 58, Jakutsk, 677891 Respublika Saha (Jakutija)
Tel: +7(4112) 49-68-10
Fax: +7(4112) 36-14-53
Website: http://www.ysu.ru/

Rector: Evgenija Mikhailova Isaevna (1998-)
EMail: rector-svfu@ysu.ru

President: Anatolij Nikolaevich Alekseev EMail: prezident@ysu.ru

Faculties

Biology and Geography (Analytical Chemistry; Biochemistry; Biology; Chemistry; Ecology; Geography; Organic Chemistry; Physical Chemistry; Science Education); **Engineering and Technology** (Architecture; Building Technologies; Construction Engineering; Engineering; Engineering Drawing and Design; Heating and Refrigeration; Technology; Town Planning); **Geology and Surveying** (Geology; Geophysics; Surveying and Mapping); **History** (Archaeology; Ethnology; History; Political Sciences); **Law** (Law; Private Law; Public Law); **Mining** (Mining Engineering; Safety Engineering); **Philology** (Journalism; Linguistics; Literature; Modern Languages; Native Language Education; Philology; Russian); **Road Transport** (Automotive Engineering; Road Transport; Transport Engineering)

Institutes

Economics and Finance (Economics; Finance); **Foreign Philology and Regional Studies** (Modern Languages); **Mathematics and Computer Science** (Computer Science; Mathematics); **Medicine** (Medicine; Paediatrics; Pharmacy; Stomatology); **North Eastern Culture and Languages** (Cultural Studies; Native Language; Slavic Languages); **Physical Education and Sport** (Physical Education; Sports); **Physics and Engineering** (Information Technology; Metallurgical Engineering; Nuclear Physics; Physics; Radiophysics; Science Education; Thermal Engineering); **Psychology** (Psychology); **Teacher Training** (Computer Education; Educational Psychology; Pedagogy; Preschool Education; Primary Education; Teacher Training; Technology Education); **Technology** *(Neryungri)* (Applied Mathematics; Energy Engineering; Engineering Management; Finance; Geology; Mathematics; Mining Engineering; Russian; Technology; Transport Engineering; Transport Management; Water Management)

Further Information: Also Polytechnical Institute (Myrnyj)

History: Founded 1934 as Pedagogical Institute. Became Jakutskij Gosudarstvennyj Universitet (Jakutsk State University) in 1956. Acquired current title and status 2010.

Governing Bodies: Academic Council

Academic Year: September to July (September-February; February-July)

Admission Requirements: Secondary education certificate (Attestat o srednem obrazovanii) and entrance examination

Main Language(s) of Instruction: Russian

Degrees and Diplomas: *Bakalavr*; *Specialist Diploma*; *Magistr*; *Kandidat Nauk*

Student Services: Academic counselling, Canteen, Cultural centre, Employment services, Foreign Studies Centre, Health services, Social counselling, Sports facilities

Student Residential Facilities: For c. 3,500 students

Special Facilities: Museum of Human Anatomy; Museum of Legal Medicine; Museum of Domestic Animals Anatomy; Museum of Geology and Zoology; Museum of Archaeology. Art Gallery. Music Club

Libraries: Main Library and Specialized Libraries, total, 1,066,967 vols

Press or Publishing House: Editorial-Publishing Department

Last Updated: 08/04/11

NORTH OSSETIAN STATE ACADEMY OF MEDICINE

Severo-Osetinskaja Gosudarstvennaja Medicinskaja Akademia

ul. Puškinskaja 40, Vladikavkaz, 362019 Respublika Severnaja Osetija-Alanija
Tel: +7(8672) 53-77-28 +7(8672) 28-02-22
Fax: +7(8672) 53-03-97 +7(8672) 53-77-28
EMail: nosma@dol.ru; sogma@yandex.ru; sogma.rso@gmail.com
Website: http://www.sogma.ru

Rector: Tamara Magometovna Gatagonova (2007-)

Faculties

Medical-prophylactic Studies (Dental Hygiene; Dietetics; Epidemiology; Nutrition; Occupational Health; Parasitology; Public Health; Virology); **Medicine** (Gynaecology and Obstetrics; Medicine; Surgery); **Nursing** (Midwifery; Nursing); **Paediatrics** (Paediatrics); **Pharmacy** (Pharmacology; Pharmacy); **Stomatology** (Dentistry; Orthodontics; Stomatology)

Further Information: Also Russian courses for foreign students

History: Founded 1939, acquired present status and title 1995.

Academic Year: September to June (September-January; February-June)

Admission Requirements: Secondary school certificate (Attestat o srednem obrazovanii)

Main Language(s) of Instruction: Russian

Degrees and Diplomas: *Specialist Diploma*

Student Services: Academic counselling, Canteen, Cultural centre, Foreign Studies Centre, Handicapped facilities, Health services, Social counselling, Sports facilities

Student Residential Facilities: For c. 2,500 students

Special Facilities: Anatomy Museum; Biology Museum; History of Medicine Museum

Libraries: Academy Library, c. 420,000 vols

Last Updated: 16/03/12

NORTH OSSETIAN STATE PEDAGOGICAL INSTITUTE

Severo-Osetinskij Gosudarstvennyj Pedagogičeskij Institut

ul. Karla Marksa, 36, Vladikavkaz, 362003 Respublika Severnaja Osetija-Alanija
Tel: +7(8672) 75-15-36 +7(8672) 64-98-14
Fax: +7(8672) 54-96-20
EMail: sogpi@mail.ru
Website: http://www.sogpi.org/

Rector: Lyudmila Aslanbekovna Kuchieva

Faculties

Educational Psychology (Educational Psychology; Social Welfare); **Linguistics** (Foreign Languages Education; Linguistics; Literature; Modern Languages; Native Language Education; Pedagogy)); **Management** (Management); **Physical Education** (Physical Education); **Special Education** (Educational Administration; Educational Psychology; Preschool Education; Primary Education; Special Education; Speech Therapy and Audiology)

History: Created 2001.

Degrees and Diplomas: *Bakalavr*, *Specialist Diploma*

Last Updated: 16/03/12

NORTH OSSETIAN STATE UNIVERSITY NAMED AFTER K. L. KHETAGUROV

Severo-Osetinskij Gosudarstvennyj Universitet im. K. L. Khetagurova (NOSU)

ul. Vatutina 46, Vladikavkaz, 362025 Respublika Severnaja Osetija-Alanija
Tel: +7(8672) 53-50-96 +7(8672) 54-68-14
Fax: +7(8672) 53-50-96
EMail: sogu@teacher-edu.ru
Website: http://www.nosu.ru

Rector: Valerij Sozanov

Departments

Foreign Languages (English; Foreign Languages Education; French; German; History; Linguistics; Literature; Modern Languages; Philology; Russian)

Faculties

Arts (Acting; Cinema and Television; Fine Arts; Graphic Arts; Graphic Design; Music; Painting and Drawing; Performing Arts; Theatre); **Biology and Technology** (Anatomy; Biology; Botany; Earth Sciences; Food Technology; Hygiene; Physiology; Soil Science; Zoology); **Chemical Technology** (Analytical Chemistry; Chemistry; Inorganic Chemistry; Organic Chemistry; Physical Chemistry; Technology); **Dentistry** (Dentistry); **Economics** (Accountancy; Banking; Business and Commerce; Economics; Finance; Management; Marketing; Statistics; Taxation); **Education** (Education; Educational Psychology; Pedagogy; Preschool Education; Primary Education; Psychology; Social Psychology; Speech Therapy and Audiology); **Geography and Geoecology** (Development Studies; Ecology; Geography; Geography (Human); Tourism); **History** (Ancient Civilizations; Archaeology; History; Medieval Studies; Modern History; Oriental Studies; Political Sciences); **International Relations** (Arabic; English; French; German; International Economics; International Relations; Linguistics; Persian; Spanish; Turkish); **Journalism** (Advertising and Publicity; Journalism; Mass Communication; Public Relations; Radio and Television Broadcasting; Speech Studies); **Law** (Civil Law; Commercial Law; Criminal Law; Criminology; History of Law; Labour Law; Law); **Management** (Business Administration; Business and Commerce; Economics; Management; Marketing); **Mathematics** (Applied Mathematics; Computer Science; Information Technology; Mathematics; Mathematics Education; Systems Analysis); **Ossetian Philology** (Linguistics; Literature; Oriental Languages; Philology; Russian); **Pharmacy** (Pharmacology; Pharmacy); **Physical Education and Sports** (Anatomy; Physical Education; Physiology; Sports); **Physics and Technology** (Astronomy and Space Science; Astrophysics; Electronic Engineering; Mathematical Physics; Nanotechnology; Physics; Solid State Physics; Textile Design); **Psychology and Sociology** (Advertising and Publicity; Educational Psychology; Marketing; Psychology; Social Psychology; Social Work; Sociology); **Russian Philology** (English; French; German; Literature; Modern Languages; Philology; Russian); **Social Work** (Education; Health Sciences; Psychology; Social Work); **Training and Retraining** (Cultural Studies; Economics; English; German; Government; Information Technology; Management; Marketing; Modern Languages; Tourism)

History: Founded 1920 as Terek Institute of Education, acquired present status and title 1969.

Governing Bodies: Chancellor's Council (Rektorat); Scientific Council (Učeny Sovet)

Academic Year: September to June (September-February; February-June)

Admission Requirements: Secondary education certificate (Attestat o srednem obrazovanii) and entrance examination

Main Language(s) of Instruction: Russian

Degrees and Diplomas: *Bakalavr*; *Specialist Diploma*; *Magistr*; *Kandidat Nauk*: 3-4 yrs; *Doktor Nauk*: 3 yrs

Student Services: Academic counselling, Canteen, Cultural centre, Foreign student adviser, Foreign Studies Centre, Language programs, Sports facilities

Student Residential Facilities: Yes

Special Facilities: Zoology Museum; Archaeology Museum; Geography Museum; Museum of the Great Patriotic War 1941-1945. Movie Studio TV SOGU, TV NOSU, Radio and TV Compagny

Libraries: Scientific Library, c. 600,000 vols

Last Updated: 16/03/12

NORTHERN (ARCTIC) FEDERAL UNIVERSITY

Severnyj (Arktičeskij) Federalnyj Universitet (AGTU)

Nabereznaja Severnoj Dviny 17, Arkhangelsk 163002
Tel: +7(8182) 21-89-20
Fax: +7(8182) 28-76-14
EMail: public@narfu.ru
Website: http://narfu.ru/

Rector: Yelena Vladimirovna Kudryashova (1997-)
EMail: rector@narfu.ru

Institutes

Civil Engineering and Architecture (Architecture; Civil Engineering; Construction Engineering; Geological Engineering; Mathematics; Road Engineering; Road Transport); **Economics** (Accountancy; Economics; Finance; Industrial Management; Management); **Forestry Engineering** (Ecology; Forest Management; Forest Products; Forestry; Furniture Design; Wood Technology); **Information and Space-based Processing** (Applied Mathematics; Computer Education; Information Technology; Telecommunications Engineering; Telecommunications Services); **Law and Entrepreneurship** (Arts and Humanities; Civil Engineering; Constitutional Law; Criminal Law; Criminology; Labour Law; Law; Philosophy; Social Sciences); **Oil and Gas** (Petroleum and Gas Engineering); **Theoretical and Applied Chemistry** (Applied Chemistry; Chemistry); **Translation and Interpretation** (Translation and Interpretation)

History: Founded 1929 as Arhangelskij Gosudarstvennyj Tehničeskij Universitet (Archangel State Technical University). Acquired present status and title 2009.

Governing Bodies: Scientific Council

Academic Year: September to June (September-January; February-June)

Admission Requirements: Secondary school certificate (Attestat o polnomobščem obrazovanii) and entrance examination

Main Language(s) of Instruction: Russian

Degrees and Diplomas: *Bakalavr*: 4 yrs; *Specialist Diploma*: 5 yrs; *Kandidat Nauk*: a further 3 yrs

Student Services: Canteen, Cultural centre, Health services, Nursery care, Social counselling, Sports facilities

Student Residential Facilities: Yes

Special Facilities: University Museum. Arboretum

Libraries: c. 600,000 vols

Last Updated: 12/04/11

NORTHERN STATE MEDICAL UNIVERSITY

Severnyj Gosudarstvennyj Medicinskij Universitet (NSMU)

Troitsky prosp. 51, Arkhangelsk 163000
Tel: +7(8182) 285-791
Fax: +7(8182) 286-595
EMail: info@nsmu.ru
Website: http://www.nsmu.ru

Rector: Pavel I. Sidorov (1993-)
Tel: +7(8182) 285-791 EMail: pshiatr@nsmu.ru

Vice-Rector, Strategic Development: Aleksandr M. Vjazmin
Tel: +7(8182) 285-761 EMail: vyazmin@nsmu.ru

International Relations: Yury A. Sumarokov, Vice Rector, International Relations Tel: +7(8182) 285-759 EMail: sumja@nsmu.ru

Programmes

Adaptive Physical Training (Physical Education; Public Health); **Clinical (Medical) Psychology** (Clinical Psychology; Psychology); **Dentistry** (Dentistry); **Ecology** (Ecology); **Economics and Finance** (Economics; Finance); **General Medicine** (Medicine); **Information Technology** (Information Technology); **Management** (Management); **Medical Prophylactics** (Epidemiology; Social and Preventive Medicine); **Nursing** (Nursing); **Paediatrics** (Paediatrics); **Pharmacy** (Pharmacy); **Public Health** *(Master)* (Medicine); **Social Work** (Social Work); **Tourism and Hospitality** (Hotel and Restaurant; Tourism)

Further Information: University College; Preparatory Faculty for Foreign Students

History: Founded 1932 as Arkhangelsk Medical Institute. Changed name to Arkhangelsk State Medical Academy 1994. Acquired present status and title 2000.

Governing Bodies: Academic Council

Academic Year: September to July (September-January; February-July)

Admission Requirements: Secondary School Certificate (Attestat) or equivalent; entrance examination

Main Language(s) of Instruction: Russian; English

International Co-operation: With universities in Norway, Sweden, Finland, Poland, Denmark, Germany and USA

Accrediting Agencies: Federal Agency on Health Care and Social Development (under Ministry of Health Care and Social Development); Federal Service on Supervision in the field of Education and Science (under Ministry of Education and Science)

Degrees and Diplomas: *Diplom o Srednem Professionalnom Obrazovanii (Higher Vocational Education Diploma)*: 2-4 yrs; *Diplom o Nepolnom Visshem Obrazovanii (Incomplete Higher Education Diploma)*: 2-4 yrs; *Specialist Diploma*: 5-6 yrs; *Kandidat Nauk*: a further 3 yrs; *Doktor Nauk*: a further 3 yrs. Also Medicine Certificates (sertifikat spetsialista po okonchaniju internatura,1yr; sertifikat spetsialista po okonchaniju ordinatura, 2 yrs)

Student Services: Academic counselling, Canteen, Cultural centre, Employment services, Foreign student adviser, Foreign Studies Centre, Health services, Language programs, Nursery care, Social counselling, Sports facilities

Student Residential Facilities: Three student dormitories. Also room for short time staying guests. Annex for doctors attending postgraduate programmes

Special Facilities: Museum of Anatomy; Museum of Anthropology; Museum of Mental Patient's Art

Libraries: Scientific Library of the NSMU

Publications: Human Ecology (Ekologija Cheloveka), Scientific articles on medical, educational, social and environmental issues relating to ecology. *(monthly)*

Press or Publishing House: NSMU Publishing Centre

Last Updated: 27/01/12

NORTHWEST ACADEMY OF PUBLIC ADMINISTRATION

Severo-Zapadnaja Akademija Gosudarstvennoj Služby

Vasil'ievskiji Ostrov, Sredny pr. 57, Sankt-Peterburg 199178
Tel: +7(812) 323-5092
Fax: +7(812) 323-5092
EMail: interdep@nwags.ru
Website: http://www.szags.ru

Rector: Alexander S. Gorshkov EMail: dp@nwags.ru

Premier Prorector: Alexander S. Turgaev EMail: dp@nwags.ru

International Relations: Eduard S. Shevchenko, Head of International Department EMail: Interdep@nwags.ru

Departments

Civil Servants and Professional Training and Retraining *Dean*: Valentina N. Kotelnikova; **Economics and Finance** *Dean*: Vladimir V. Zasiad'-Volk; **International Relations** *Dean*: Yurij N. Polokhalo;

Law *Dean*: Tatiana M. Polyakova; **Social Technologies** *Dean*: Tatiana G. Grinenko

Institutes

International Business and Law *Director*: Elena L. Bogdanova

History: Founded 1991 as North-Western Personnel Training Centre. Acquired present status and title 1995.

Governing Bodies: Rector office

Admission Requirements: Secondary School Certificate

Fees: (Euros): 2,000 per annum

Main Language(s) of Instruction: Russian

International Co-operation: With universities in Europe.

Degrees and Diplomas: *Specialist Diploma (Manager)*: 5-6 yrs

Student Services: Academic counselling, Canteen, Foreign student adviser, Health services, Language programs, Social counselling, Sports facilities

Special Facilities: Museum of Public Administration

Libraries: c. 360,000 vols

NORTHWEST STATE TECHNICAL UNIVERSITY

Severo-Zapadnyj Zaočnyj Tehničeskij Universitet

ul. Milionnaja 5, Sankt-Peterburg 191186
Tel: +7(812) 335-2626
Fax: +7(812) 571-6016
EMail: office@nwpi.ru
Website: http://www.nwpi.ru

Rector: Alexander A. Kondratyev

First Vice-Rector: Vladimir Vorontsov Tel: +7(812) 335-2667

Institutes

Energy (Electrical Engineering; Energy Engineering; Heating and Refrigeration; Industrial Engineering; Thermal Engineering); **Information Systems and Computer Engineering** (Computer Engineering; Computer Networks; Information Management; Information Technology); **Instrument Engineering and Systems Safety** (Ecology; Environmental Engineering; Environmental Management; Geology; Measurement and Precision Engineering; Medical Technology; Psychiatry and Mental Health; Psychology; Safety Engineering); **Intelligent Electronic Systems** (Artificial Intelligence; Electrical and Electronic Engineering); **Machine Building** *(Technological Institute)* (Chemical Engineering; Inorganic Chemistry; Materials Engineering; Metal Techniques; Metallurgical Engineering; Organic Chemistry; Production Engineering); **Management of Production and Innovation** (Economics; Engineering Management; Finance; Management; Modern Languages; Physical Education; Social Sciences; Transport Management); **Road Transport** (Management; Road Transport; Transport Engineering; Transport Management)

Further Information: Also 35 Study-Advice Branches in different regions of Russia and NIS

History: Founded 1930 as North West Extra Mural Polytechnical Institute. Acquired present status 2000.

Governing Bodies: Council

Academic Year: September to June (September-January; February-June)

Admission Requirements: Secondary school certificate (Attestat o srednem obrazovanii)

Main Language(s) of Instruction: Russian

Accrediting Agencies: Ministry of Education

Degrees and Diplomas: *Bakalavr*: 4 yrs; *Specialist Diploma*: 5 yrs; *Magistr*: Engineering, a further 2 yrs; *Kandidat Nauk (PhD)*: a further 3 yrs following Magistr

Student Services: Canteen, Foreign student adviser, Foreign Studies Centre, Language programs

Student Residential Facilities: Yes

Libraries: Central Library, 1.2m. vols; Scientific Library, 200,000 vols

Last Updated: 26/01/12

NOVGOROD STATE UNIVERSITY

Novgorodskij Gosudarstvennyj Universitet (NOVSU)

ul. Bolšaja, ul. B. Sankt-Peterburgskaja 41, Veliky Novgorod 173003
Tel: +7(8162) 627-244
Fax: +7(8162) 624-110
EMail: tel@novsu.ru
Website: http://www.novsu.ac.ru

Rector: Viktor Veber (2008-) EMail: viktor.veber@novsu.ru

Vice-Rector for Academic Affairs: Sergey Gudilov
Tel: +7(8162) 627-887 EMail: sergey.gudilov@novsu.ru

International Relations: Mikhail Pevzner, Vice Rector for International Relations
Tel: +7(8162) 623-707, Fax: +7(8162) 623-707
EMail: mikhail.pevzner@novsu.ru

Faculties

Architecture, Fine Arts and Construction (Architectural and Environmental Design; Architecture; Civil Engineering; Construction Engineering; Design; Fashion Design; Fine Arts; Industrial Design; Industrial Engineering; Machine Building; Materials Engineering; Metal Techniques) *Dean*: Tatiana Kauda; **Engineering and Technology** (Automation and Control Engineering; Automotive Engineering; Engineering; Heating and Refrigeration; Industrial Engineering; Power Engineering; Technology) *Dean*: Valery Emelyanov

Institutes

Agriculture and Natural Resources *Director*: Anna Kozina; **Continuous Pedagogical Education** *Director*: Alexander Shirin; **Economics and Administration** *Director*: Pavel Nikiforov; **Electronic and Information Systems** (Applied Mathematics; Computer Engineering; Design; Electronic Engineering; Engineering; Information Sciences; Mathematics; Microelectronics; Physics; Radiophysics; Software Engineering; Technology) *Director*: Boris Seleznev; **Humanities** *Director*: Anatoly Donchenko; **Medical Education** *Deputy Director*: Vladimir Soloyev

History: Founded 1993 through the merger of Pedagogical and Polytechnic Institutes of Veliky Novgorod. The Novgorod Agricultural Academy was later included.

Governing Bodies: Federal Education Agency.

Academic Year: September to June

Main Language(s) of Instruction: Russian

Accrediting Agencies: Federal Education and Science Supervision Service

Degrees and Diplomas: *Bakalavr*, *Specialist Diploma*; *Magistr*

Student Services: Academic counselling, Canteen, Cultural centre, Employment services, Foreign student adviser, Foreign Studies Centre, Health services, Language programs, Nursery care, Social counselling, Sports facilities

Last Updated: 03/12/08

NOVOCHERKASSK STATE ACADEMY OF LAND CONSERVATION

Novočerkasskaja Gosudarstvennaja Meliorativnaja Akademija

ul. Puškinkaja 111, Novočerkassk 346428
Tel: +7(8635) 22-21-70
Fax: +7(8635) 22-44-59
EMail: rekngma@magnet.ru
Website: http://www.ngma.su/

Rector: Pavel Aleksandrovich Mikheev

Faculties

Civil Engineering (Civil Engineering; Fire Science); **Economics and Management** (Agricultural Economics; Agricultural Management; Economics; Management; Water Management); **Forestry** (Forestry; Landscape Architecture; Parks and Recreation); **Land Planning** (Rural Planning); **Mechanical Engineering** (Agricultural Equipment; Marine Transport; Mechanical Engineering; Mechanical Equipment and Maintenance; Transport Engineering); **Water Management** (Environmental Management; Water Management)

History: Created 1930.

Degrees and Diplomas: *Bakalavr*, *Specialist Diploma*

Last Updated: 24/02/12

NOVOSIBIRSK STATE ACADEMY OF ARCHITECTURE AND FINE ARTS

Novosibirskaja Gosudarstvennaja Arhitekturno-Hudožestvennaja Akademija (NSAAFA)

prosp. Krasnyj 38, Novosibirsk, 630099 Novosibiraskaja oblast'
Tel: +7(383) 227-08-83
Fax: +7(383) 203-52-30
EMail: oko@ngaha.ru
Website: http://www.ngaha.ru/

Rector: Gennadij Pustovetov (1989-) EMail: rektor@ngaha.ru

Departments

Postgraduate Education *Head*: Irina Verešagina

Faculties

Architecture (Architectural and Environmental Design; Architectural Restoration; Architecture; Landscape Architecture; Regional Planning; Rural Planning; Structural Architecture; Town Planning); **Fine Arts** (Design; Fine Arts)

History: Founded 1907 as Department of Tomsk Technological Institute, reorganized 1930 as branch of Siberian Civil Engineering Institute and 1989 as branch of Novosibirsk Architectural Institute (NAHRI). Acquired present status and title 1996.

Governing Bodies: Council

Academic Year: September to June (September-January; February-June)

Admission Requirements: Upper secondary school certificate (Attestat o polnom srednem obrazovanii), and entrance examination

Fees: (US Dollars): Foreign students, 2,500 per annum

Main Language(s) of Instruction: Russian

Degrees and Diplomas: *Bakalavr*: 4 1/2 yrs; *Specialist Diploma*; *Magistr*: a further 1 1/2 yrs; *Kandidat Nauk*: a further 3 yrs; *Doktor Nauk*: by thesis following Kandidat

Student Services: Canteen, Cultural centre, Foreign student adviser, Foreign Studies Centre, Language programs, Social counselling, Sports facilities

Student Residential Facilities: For c. 300 students

Special Facilities: Museum of the History of Siberian Architecture. Art Gallery

Libraries: Library, 55,250 vols

Publications: Annual issue of scientific articles *(annually)*; PRO, Magazine of Architecture and Design *(monthly)*

Press or Publishing House: Publishing Office

Last Updated: 18/04/11

NOVOSIBIRSK STATE AGRARIAN UNIVERSITY

Novosibirskij Gosudarstvennyj Agrarnyj Universitet

ul. Dobroljubova 160, Novosibirsk, 630039 Novosibiraskaja oblast'
Tel: +7(3832) 673-811
Fax: +7(3832) 673-922
Website: http://www.nsau.edu.ru

Rector: Anatoly Kondratov (1987-)

Administrative Officer: Marina Stepanova Tel: +7(3832) 670-510

International Relations: Yury Blynsky, Vice Rector
Tel: +7(3832) 670-688, Fax: +7(3832) 673-910

Faculties

Agronomy (Accountancy; Agronomy; Biotechnology; Ecology; Genetics) *Head*: Alexey Marmulev; **Economics** (Accountancy; Economics) *Dean*: Victor Lukyanenko; **Law** (Law) *Dean*: Borik Mkrtchan; **Municipal and Public Administration** (Public Administration) *Dean*: Anatoly Pičugin; **Plant Protection** (Biology; Plant and Crop Protection) *Dean*: Vera Tsvetkova; **Training** (Biology; Chemistry; English; Mathematics; Physics; Russian) *Dean*: Ivan Degtyarenko; **Veterinary Science** (Veterinary Science) *Dean*: Sergey Mager; **Zoological Engineering** (Animal Husbandry; Biotechnology; Genetics; Zoology) *Dean*: Šamil Nugaev

Institutes

Agriculture I *(Kemerovo)* (Agriculture) *Director*: Victor Myalenko; **Agriculture II** *(Tomsk)* (Agriculture) *Director*: Nikolay Šipilin; **Distance Education and Advanced Training** (Accountancy; Agricultural Engineering; Agricultural Equipment; Agronomy; Economics; Veterinary Science; Zoology) *Director*: Vladimir Medvedčikov; **Engineering** (Agricultural Engineering; Agricultural Equipment; Electrical Engineering; Transport Engineering) *Director*: Gennady Krohta

Research Institutes

Cattle Breeding (Cattle Breeding) *Director*: Anatoly Nezvitin; **Veterinary Genetics** (Biology; Genetics; Veterinary Science) *Director*: Valery Petučov

History: Founded 1936, acquired present status and title 1991.

Governing Bodies: Science and Engineering Council

Academic Year: September to June

Admission Requirements: Secondary school certificate (Attestat o srednem obrazovanii) and entrance examination

Fees: (Russian Rubles): 12,000-15,000 per annum; foreign students, (US Dollars), 1,500-2,500

Main Language(s) of Instruction: Russian

Accrediting Agencies: Ministry of Agriculture

Degrees and Diplomas: *Specialist Diploma*: 5 yrs; *Kandidat Nauk*: 3 yrs; *Doktor Nauk*: 2 yrs

Student Residential Facilities: Yes

Special Facilities: Experimental training farm

Libraries: University Library

Publications: Agrarnyj Vestnik *(monthly)*; Collection of Scientific Articles *(3 per annum)*

NOVOSIBIRSK STATE CONSERVATORY (ACADEMY) NAMED AFTER M.I. GLINKA

Novosibirskaja Gosudarstvennaja Konservatorija (Akademija) im. M.I. Glinki

ul. Sovetskaja 31, Novosibirsk, 630099 Novosibiraskaja oblast'
Tel: +7(383) 22-25-22 +7(383) 222-42-16 +7(383) 222-43-47
Fax: +7(383) 223-95-37
EMail: info@conservatoire.ru
Website: http://www.conservatoire.ru/

Rector: Konstantin Mikhailovich Kurlenija

Programmes

Music (Conducting; Music; Music Education; Music Theory and Composition; Musical Instruments; Musicology; Singing)

History: Created 1956.

Degrees and Diplomas: *Bakalavr*; *Specialist Diploma*; *Magistr*

Last Updated: 24/02/12

NOVOSIBIRSK STATE MEDICAL UNIVERSITY

Novosibirskij Gosudarstvennyj Medicinskij Universitet (NSMA)

prosp. Krasnyj 52, Novosibirsk, 630091 Novosibiraskaja oblast'
Tel: +7(383) 222-32-04 +7(383) 222-13-80
Fax: +7(383) 222-32-04 +7(383) 222-13-80
EMail: rector@ngmu.ru; rectorngmu@yandex.ru; abiturient@ngmu.ru
Website: http://www.ngmu.ru/

Rector: Igor Olegovich Marinkin EMail: rector@ngmu.ru

Faculties

Clinical Psychology (Clinical Psychology; Psychiatry and Mental Health; Psychology; Psychotherapy); **Management** (Health Administration; Nursing); **Medicine** (Endocrinology; Gynaecology and Obstetrics; Immunology; Medicine; Microbiology; Midwifery; Oncology; Pharmacology; Surgery); **Medicine and Prophylactics** (Biology; Genetics; Health Administration; Hygiene; Medicine; Physics); **Paediatrics** (Paediatrics); **Pharmacy** (Pharmacology; Pharmacy); **Social Work** (Social Work); **Stomatology** (Dentistry; Stomatology)

Further Information: Postgraduate Medical Training in 58 medical disciplines and Training in non-medical disciplines.

History: Founded 1935 as Novosibirsk Medical Institute. Acquired title of Novosibirskaja Gosudarstvennaja Medicinskaja Akademija (Novosibirsk State Medical Academy) in 1999. Acquired current title in 2005.

Governing Bodies: The Academy Administration

Academic Year: September to June (September-January; February-June)

Admission Requirements: Secondary school certificate (Attestat o srednem obrazovanii)

Main Language(s) of Instruction: Russian

Degrees and Diplomas: *Specialist Diploma*; *Kandidat Nauk*; *Doktor Nauk*

Student Services: Academic counselling, Canteen, Foreign student adviser, Foreign Studies Centre, Health services, Language programs, Sports facilities

Student Residential Facilities: 2 student hostels for 1,300 students

Special Facilities: Medical Museum.

Libraries: Total, c. 400,000 vols

Last Updated: 12/01/12

NOVOSIBIRSK STATE PEDAGOGICAL UNIVERSITY

Novosibirskij Gosudarstvennyj Pedagogičeskij Universitet

ul. Viljuiskaja 28, Novosibirsk, 630126 Novosibiraskaja oblast'
Tel: +7(3832) 680-054
Fax: +7(3832) 681-161
EMail: root@nspu.ru
Website: http://www.nspu.ru

Rector: Aleksej Gerasjov
Tel: +7(383) 276-80-135 EMail: rector@nspu.nsu.ru

Vice-Rector: Ludmila Barahtenova
Tel: +7(383) 276-80-161, Fax: +7(383) 276-80-161

International Relations: Olga Novosjolova
Tel: +7(383) 276-92-357

Faculties

Arts *Dean*: Vitalij Elagin; **Foreign Languages** *Dean*: Ekarterina Kostina; **History** *Dean*: Oleg Kationov; **Mathematics** (Computer Education; Education; Mathematics) *Dean*: Alfat Hasanov; **Natural Sciences** *Dean*: Aleksandr Prosenko; **Physical Education** *Dean*: Oleg Endropov; **Physics** *Dean*: Oleg Chashin; **Preschool Education** *Dean*: Arna Geytzi; **Primary Education** *Dean*: Svetlana Belovolova; **Psychology** *Dean*: Ilja Votčin; **Technology and Business** *Dean*: Valerij Krašeninikov

Institutes

Advertising and Public Relations *Director*: Gennadii Terebilo; **Philology, Media and Psychology** *Director*: Elena Buligina

History: Founded 1935, acquired present status and title 1994.

Academic Year: September to June

Admission Requirements: Secondary school certificate (Attestat o srednem obrazovanii) or college certificate

Main Language(s) of Instruction: Russian

Degrees and Diplomas: *Specialist Diploma*: Teaching, 5 yrs; *Kandidat Nauk*: 3 yrs

Student Services: Academic counselling, Canteen, Cultural centre, Foreign student adviser, Health services, Social counselling, Sports facilities

Student Residential Facilities: 4 student hostels

Special Facilities: University Museum. Art Gallery. Computer Classes

Libraries: Central Library, 1 m. vols

Last Updated: 27/11/08

NOVOSIBIRSK STATE TECHNICAL UNIVERSITY

Novosibirskij Gosudarstvennyj Tehničeskij Universitet (NSTU)

prosp. Karla Marksa 20, Novosibirsk, 630092 Novosibiraskaja oblast'
Tel: +7(383) 3465-001
Fax: +7(383) 3460-209
EMail: rector@nstu.ru
Website: http://www.nstu.ru

Rector: Nikolay V. Pustovoi (2005-)

Vice-Rector: Gennady I. Rastorgouev EMail: firstpro@adm.nstu.ru

International Relations: Jevgenij B. Tsoi, Vice-Rector
EMail: ebcoi@nstu.ru

Faculties

Aircraft Studies (Aeronautical and Aerospace Engineering; Air Transport); **Applied Mathematics and Computer Science** (Applied Mathematics; Computer Science); **Automation and Computer Engineering** (Automation and Control Engineering; Computer Engineering; Computer Science); **Business** (Business Administration; Business and Commerce; Economics; Finance; Management; Marketing; Taxation); **Energy Engineering** (Chemistry; Energy Engineering; Heating and Refrigeration; Safety Engineering; Thermal Engineering); **Humanities** (Advertising and Publicity; Linguistics; Peace and Disarmament; Philology; Psychology; Regional Studies; Social Work; Sociology); **Law** (Constitutional Law; Criminal Law; International Law; Law; Private Administration); **Mechanical Engineering** (Engineering Drawing and Design; Machine Building; Mechanical Engineering; Mechanics); **Mechatronics and Automotive Engineerng** (Automotive Engineering; Mechanics); **Physical Engineering** (Engineering; Physical Engineering; Physics); **Radio- and Electronic Engineering** (Electronic Engineering; Telecommunications Engineering)

Institutes

Social Rehabilitation (Fine Arts; Mathematics; Natural Sciences)

History: Founded 1950 as Institute of Electrical Engineering; acquired present status and title 1992.

Governing Bodies: Rector and Scientific Council

Academic Year: September to June (September-January; February-June)

Admission Requirements: Secondary education certificate (Attestat o srednem obrazovanii)

Fees: (Russian Rubles): Russian students, 30,000-46,000 per annum; foreign students, 52,000-58,000

Main Language(s) of Instruction: Russian

International Co-operation: With universities in Germany, France, China, Republic of Korea; Mongolia

Accrediting Agencies: Ministry of Education

Degrees and Diplomas: *Bakalavr*: Science (BSc), 4 yrs; *Specialist Diploma*: Engineering, Technology, 5 yrs; *Magistr*: Science and Engineering (MSc), a further 2 yrs; *Kandidat Nauk*: Science and Engineering (CandSc), 3 yrs; *Doktor Nauk*: Science and Engineering (DSc)

Student Services: Academic counselling, Canteen, Cultural centre, Foreign student adviser, Foreign Studies Centre, Handicapped facilities, Health services, Language programs, Nursery care, Social counselling, Sports facilities

Student Residential Facilities: Yes

Special Facilities: Museum of the University History. Art Gallery. TV Studio

Libraries: Scientific Library, c. 1,013,330. Vols

Publications: Problems of Higher Technical Education *(annually)*; Scientific Bulletin *(biennially)*; Scientific Works *(quarterly)*

Last Updated: 11/04/11

NOVOSIBIRSK STATE UNIVERSITY

Novosibirskij Gosudarstvennyj Universitet (NSU)

ul. Pirogova 2, Novosibirsk, 630090 Novosibiraskaja oblast'
Tel: +7(383) 363-4001
Fax: +7 (383) 363-4001
EMail: sei@lab.nsu.ru
Website: http://www.nsu.ru

Rector: Vladimir A. Sobyanin (2007-)
Tel: +7(383) 330-3244, Fax: +7(383) 330-3255
EMail: rector@nsu.ru

Vice-Rector for Education: Natalia V. Dulepova
Tel: +7(383) 363-4053, Fax: +7(383) 330-2237
EMail: dnv@nsu.ru

International Relations: Evgeny I. Sagaidak
Tel: +7(383) 363-4418, Fax: +7(383) 363-4418

Centres

International Educational Programmes (Russian)

Departments

Economics (Business Administration; Economics; Finance; Law; Management; Sociology); **Foreign Languages** (Foreign Languages Education; Linguistics; Translation and Interpretation); **Geology and Geophysics** (Crystallography; Geochemistry; Geology; Geophysics; Mineralogy; Paleontology; Petroleum and Gas Engineering; Surveying and Mapping); **Humanities** (African Studies; Anthropology; Archaeology; Ethnology; Germanic Languages; History; Oriental Studies; Philology; Romance Languages; Russian); **Information Technology** (Computer Engineering; Computer Networks; Computer Science; Information Technology; Mathematics and Computer Science; Software Engineering); **Journalism** (Journalism; Radio and Television Broadcasting); **Law** (Civil Law; Criminal Law; International Law; Law); **Mechanics and Mathematics** (Applied Mathematics; Computer Science; Mathematics; Mathematics and Computer Science; Mechanics; Software Engineering); **Medicine** (Cardiology; Immunology; Medicine; Oncology; Paediatrics; Surgery; Virology); **Natural Sciences** (Biochemistry; Biology; Cell Biology; Chemistry; Ecology; Genetics; Histology; Inorganic Chemistry; Molecular Biology; Organic Chemistry; Physical Chemistry; Physiology; Zoology); **Philosophy** (Philosophy); **Physics** (Atomic and Molecular Physics; Laser Engineering; Optics; Physics; Radiophysics; Solid State Physics; Thermal Physics); **Psychology** (Psychology)

Further Information: Also Study Abroad programmes. Russian Language School

History: Founded 1959 together with the Novosibirsk Scientific Centre (NSC) - Siberian Branch of USSR Academy of Sciences to develop Eastern regions of Russia. Scientific Research Division (SRD) founded 1969.

Governing Bodies: Rectorat

Academic Year: September-January; February-June

Admission Requirements: Secondary school certificate and entrance examination.

Fees: (Euros): 3,300 - 3,700 per annum

Main Language(s) of Instruction: Russian

International Co-operation: With universities in Germany, Italy, USA, China, Japan, France, Republic of Korea, Spain,Belgium, Kazakhstan, Singapore, Taiwan, Switerland

Accrediting Agencies: Ministry of Education and Science

Degrees and Diplomas: *Bakalavr*: 4 yrs; *Specialist Diploma*: 5 yrs; *Magistr*: 2 yrs; *Kandidat Nauk*: a further 3 yrs and thesis; *Doktor Nauk*

Student Residential Facilities: 11 dormitories.

Special Facilities: Observatory; Research sections and laboratories; Geological and Biological field camps (for summer field expeditions); Museum NSU History Museum of Geology

Libraries: c. 880,162 vols

Academic Staff *2011-2012*	MEN	WOMEN	TOTAL
FULL-TIME	171	289	**460**
PART-TIME	1,325	426	**1,751**
STAFF WITH DOCTORATE			
FULL-TIME	99	119	**218**
PART-TIME	1,122	305	**1,427**
Student Numbers *2011-2012*			
All (Foreign Included)	3,394	3,421	**6,815**
FOREIGN ONLY	–	–	**329**

Part-time students, 68. **Evening students**, 496.

Last Updated: 29/09/11

NOVOSIBIRSK STATE UNIVERSITY OF ARCHITECTURE AND CIVIL ENGINEERING

Novosibirskij Gosudarstvennyj Arhitekturno-Stroitel'nyj Universitet (NSUACE (SIBSTRIN))

ul. Leningradskaja 113, Novosibirsk, 630008 Novosibiraskaja oblast'

Tel: +7(3832) 664-125

Fax: +7(3832) 604-083

EMail: uungas@sibstrin.ru

Website: http://www.sibstrin.ru/

Rector: Arkady Petrovič Yanenko (1989-) EMail: rector@sibstrin.ru

Vice-Rector: Stanislav Victorovich Linovsky
Tel: +7(3832) 660-974 EMail: linovsky@sibstrin.ru

International Relations: Victor Yakovlevich Melnik
Tel: +7(3832) 664-359, Fax: +7(3832) 664-359
EMail: in_dec@sibstrin.ru

Departments

Architecture and Construction *Dean*: Dmitrij Abramenkov; **Construction Economics and Management** (Accountancy; Administration; Economics; Finance; Industrial Management; Labour and Industrial Relations; Management Systems; Marketing; Public Administration; Real Estate) *Dean*: Mikhail Soppa; **Construction Technology** (Automation and Control Engineering; Construction Engineering; Environmental Engineering; Industrial Engineering; Information Technology; Materials Engineering) *Dean*: Vladimir Chichkanov; **Environmental Engineering** (Heating and Refrigeration; Hydraulic Engineering; Industrial Engineering; Soil Science; Water Science) *Dean*: Yelena Garshina; **Evening and Distance Education** (Architecture and Planning; Building Technologies; Civil Engineering; Construction Engineering; Economics; Heating and Refrigeration; Industrial Design; Management; Mechanical Engineering; Real Estate; Urban Studies; Water Management; Water Science) *Dean*: Vladimir Gvozdev; **First Stage of Higher Education** (Chemistry; Geology; Mathematics; Mineralogy; Physics; Statistics) *Dean*: Yuriy Chyorniy; **Foreign Students** (Architecture; Engineering; Sociology; Water Management) *Dean*: Victor Melnik

Institutes

Distance Education (Construction Engineering; Economics; Management) *Director*: Evgeniy Timoshenko; **Economics and Management** (Accountancy; Administration; Economics; Finance; Industrial Management; Labour and Industrial Relations; Management; Marketing; Public Administration; Real Estate) *Director*: Vladimir Balikoyev; **Humanities** (Arts and Humanities; English; Ethics; French; German; Logic; Modern History; Modern Languages; Philosophy; Psychology; Russian; Sociology) *Director*: Yuriy Kasantsev

Further Information: Also 5 branches in Mirny, Udachny, Aihal, Lensk, Aldan.

History: Founded 1930 as Siberian Contruction Institute (Sibstrin), acquired present status 1998.

Governing Bodies: Academic Council, Rectorate

Admission Requirements: Secondary school certificate

Fees: (Roubles): 50,0,000 per annum. Postgraduate and Doctorate, 75,000

Main Language(s) of Instruction: Russian

Accrediting Agencies: Ministry of Education

Degrees and Diplomas: *Bakalavr*: 4 yrs; *Magistr*: a further 2 yrs. Also Inzhener 5-6 yrs

Student Services: Canteen, Employment services, Foreign student adviser, Health services, Language programs, Social counselling, Sports facilities

Student Residential Facilities: For 1,820 students

Special Facilities: University Museum. Siberian Regional Centre for Scientific Research

Libraries: Central Library, 650,000 vols.

Publications: Izvestiya vuzov. Stroitelstvo, Theoretical Publication in Civil Engineering, Architecture and Ecology *(monthly)*; NSUACE Scientific Journal, Theoretical and Scientific Journal in Natural Science, Engineering, Technologies and Arts *(3 per annum)*

NOVOSIBIRSK STATE UNIVERSITY OF ECONOMICS AND MANAGEMENT

Novosibirskij Gosudarstvennij Universitet Ekonomiki i Upravlemija

ul. Kamenskaja 56, Novosibirsk, 630099 Novosibiraskaja oblast'

Tel: +7(383) 224-5955

Fax: +7(383) 224-5910

EMail: rector@nsaem.ru

Website: http://www.nsaem.ru

Rector: Jurij V. Gusev

Departments
Economics (Economics); **Finance** (Finance); **Law** (Law); **Management** (Management)

History: Formerly known as Novosibirsk State Academy of Economics and Management (Novosibirskaja Gosudarstvennaja Akademija Ekonomiki i Upravlenija).
Last Updated: 02/12/08

NOVOSIBIRSK STATE WATER TRANSPORT ACADEMY

Novosibirskaja Gosudarstvennaja Akademija Vodnogo Transporta
ul. Ščetinkina 33, Novosibirsk, 630099 Novosibiraskaja oblast'
Tel: +7(383) 222-64-68 +7(383) 222-24-28 +7(383) 222-13-46
Fax: +7(383) 222-64-68 +7(383) 222-49-76
EMail: nfo@nsawt.ru; ngavt@ngs.ru
Website: http://www.nsawt.ru/

Rector: Igor Anatolevich Ragulin EMail: rector@nsawt.ru

Faculties
Electromechanics (Chemistry; Electrical Engineering; Engineering Drawing and Design; Mechanical Engineering; Physics); **Hydrotechnics** (Ecology; Hydraulic Engineering); **Navigation** (Marine Engineering; Nautical Science); **Port Operations and Management** (Economics; Marine Transport); **Ship Mechanics** (Marine Engineering; Marine Transport; Mechanical Engineering)

History: Founded 1951 as Novosibirsk Water Transport Engineering Institute. Acquired present status and title 1994.

Governing Bodies: Academic Council

Academic Year: September to June

Admission Requirements: Entrance Examination

Main Language(s) of Instruction: Russian

Degrees and Diplomas: *Bakalavr*, *Specialist Diploma*
Last Updated: 24/02/12

NOVOURALSKY STATE INSTITUTE OF TECHNOLOGY

Novoural'skij Gosudarstvennyj Tehnologičeskij Institut
ul. Lenina 85, Novoural'sk, 624133 Sverdlovskaja oblast'
Tel: +7(34370) 949-51
Fax: +7(34370) 950-25
EMail: rector@nsti.ru
Website: http://www.nsti.ru/

Rector: Nikolaj A. Nosyrev

Programmes
Engineering (Accountancy; Economics; Engineering; Engineering Management; Technology)

History: Created 1952

Degrees and Diplomas: *Bakalavr*, *Specialist Diploma*
Last Updated: 20/09/11

OBNINSK STATE TECHNICAL UNIVERSITY FOR NUCLEAR POWER ENGINEERING

Obninskij Gosudarstvennyj Tehničeskij Universitet Atomnoj Energetiki
Studgorodok, Obninsk, 249020 Kaluga Region
Tel: +7(08439) 773-33
Fax: +7(08439) 108-22
EMail: info@iate.obninsk.ru
Website: http://www.iate.obninsk.ru

Rector: Nikolaj Salnikov (2001-)

Secretary General: Karina Petrosova
EMail: karina@iate.obninsk.ru

International Relations: Vladimir Artisyuk, Vice-President
EMail: artisyuk@iate.obninsk.ru

Faculties
Advanced Specialists' Training (Nuclear Engineering; Psychology) *Dean*: Valeriy Tkachenko; **Cybernetics** (Computer Science) *Dean*: Aleksandr Antonov; **Economics** (Economics; Psychology; Sociology) *Dean*: Vladimir Tyabin; **Evening Education** (Computer Science; Economics; Electrical and Electronic Engineering; Psychology; Sociology) *Dean*: Olga Gulina; **Natural Sciences** (Applied Mathematics; Applied Physics; Biological and Life Sciences; Chemistry; Hydraulic Engineering; Nuclear Engineering; Physics) *Dean*: Sergej Burukhin; **Nuclear Industry** (Chemical Engineering; Energy Engineering; Materials Engineering; Nuclear Engineering) *Dean*: Lidia Zhugan

Research Laboratories
Nuclear Engineering (Nuclear Engineering) *Director*: Vladilena Abramova; **Nuclear Reactors** (Nuclear Engineering) *Director*: Yurii Kazansky; **PUSK** (Nuclear Engineering; Nuclear Physics) *Director*: Yurii Korovin

Further Information: Russian Language courses for foreign students

History: Founded 1953 as a branch of Moscow Engineering and Physics Institute. Became Obninsk Institute for Nuclear Power Engineering 1985. Acquired state technical university status 2002.

Academic Year: September to June (September-January; February-June)

Admission Requirements: Secondary school certificate (Attestato srednem obrazovanii)

Fees: (Russian Rubles): 20,000 (irregular courses); 30,000 (regular courses) for Kandidat Nauk

Main Language(s) of Instruction: Russian

International Co-operation: No

Degrees and Diplomas: *Bakalavr*: Computer Science and Technology; Applied Mathematics; Physics; Physics of Atmosphere, 4 yrs; *Specialist Diploma*: Material Diagnostics and Control; Information Technology; Ecology and Environmental Monitoring; Psychology; Financial and Informational Management; Nuclear Medicine, 5 yrs; *Specialist Diploma*: Nuclear Power Plants and facilities; Physical processes in Nuclear Reactors; Material Science; Methods of Experimental Physics; Computer Science; Automatic Control System; Applied Mathematics, 5 1/2 yrs; *Magistr*: Computer Science and Technology; Management and Control of Nuclear Materials, 6 yrs; *Kandidat Nauk*: Mathematics; Physics; Nuclear Engineering; Automation and Control Engineering; Electronic Engineering; Computer Science and Technology; Information Systems; Management and Economics; Mathematical Methods in Economics, a further 3-4 yrs

Student Services: Academic counselling, Canteen, Cultural centre, Employment services, Foreign student adviser, Health services, Language programs, Social counselling, Sports facilities

Student Residential Facilities: Dormitories

Libraries: 1,292,420 vols; 2,002 Russian periodicals and subscriptions; 5 foreign periodicals and subscriptions

Publications: Nuclear Energetics, Communications of Universities *(bimonthly)*

OMSK ACADEMY OF THE MINISTRY OF INTERNAL AFFAIRS OF RUSSIA

Omskaja Akademija MVD Rossiiskoj Federatsij
prosp. Komarova 7, Omsk, Omskaja oblast'
Tel: +7(3812) 15-1560
Fax: +7(3812) 15-0560
EMail: academy@omamvd.ru
Website: http://www.omamvd.ru/

Rector: Boris Borisovich Bulatov

Programmes
Law (Criminal Law; Criminology; Law; Military Science; Police Studies)

History: Created 1920.

Degrees and Diplomas: *Specialist Diploma*
Last Updated: 24/02/12

OMSK STATE AGRARIAN UNIVERSITY

Omskij Gosudarstvennyj Agrarnyj Universitet

pl. Instituckaja 2, Omsk, 644008 Omskaja oblast'
Tel: +7(3812) 652-145
Fax: +7(3812) 651-735
EMail: adm@omgau.ru
Website: http://www.omgau.ru

Rector: Nikolaj M. Kolychev (1994-)

Faculties

Agricultural Chemistry and Soil Science (Agriculture; Ecology; Soil Science) *Dean*: Igor Bobrenko; **Agricultural Engineering** (Agricultural Engineering; Agricultural Equipment) *Dean*: Pavel Čupin; **Agronomy** (Agronomy; Forestry; Horticulture; Plant and Crop Protection; Viticulture) *Dean*: Victor Tarakanov; **Food Processing** (Food Technology) *Dean*: Vladimir Ivanov; **Humanities** (Arts and Humanities; Modern Languages; Sociology) *Dean*: Vladimir Slabodtsky; **Land Use Planning** (Rural Planning) *Dean*: Nikolaj Mičailov; **Natural Resources Engineering** (Natural Resources; Water Management) *Dean*: Evgenij Petrov

Institutes

Animal Husbandry *Dean*: Sergeij Borisenko; **Economics and Finance** *Dean*: Vitalij Petsevič; **Food Certification and Quality Control** *Dean*: Gennadij Kopylov; **Veterinary Science** *(Previously Omskij Gosudarstvennyj Veterinarnyj Institut)* (Animal Husbandry; Veterinary Science) *Director*: Genadij Khonin

History: Founded 1918, acquired present status and title 1994. In 2005 added the Omskij Gosudarstvennyj Veterinarnyj Institut

Academic Year: October to July (October-January; February-July)

Admission Requirements: Secondary school certificate (Attestat o srednem obrazovanii) and entrance examination

Main Language(s) of Instruction: Russian

Degrees and Diplomas: *Specialist Diploma*: 5 yrs; *Kandidat Nauk*: a further 3-4 yrs

Student Services: Canteen, Cultural centre, Health services, Sports facilities

Student Residential Facilities: For c. 4,900 students

Special Facilities: University Museum. Botanical Garden

Libraries: c. 630,000 vols

Publications: Vestnik OmGAU (Magazine) *(quarterly)*

Press or Publishing House: Publishing House

OMSK STATE INSTITUTE OF SERVICES

Omskij Gosudarstvennyj Institut Servisa

ul. Pevtsova, 13, Omsk, 644099 Omskaja oblast'
Tel: +7(3812) 24-21-91 +7(3812) 23-44-62
Fax: +7(3812) 24-94-45 +7(3812) 24-21-91
EMail: rector@omgis.ru
Website: http://www.omgis.ru/

Rector: Dmitrij Pavlovich Maevskij

Faculties

Art and Technology (Clothing and Sewing; Design; Landscape Architecture; Service Trades; Technology; Textile Design; Textile Technology); **Economics** (Accountancy; Economics; Management); **Tourism and Applied Information Technoloby** (Business Computing; Home Economics; Household Management; Information Technology; Management; Secretarial Studies; Tourism)

History: Founded 1977 as Institute of Consumer Services. Acquired present title 1997.

Academic Year: September to June

Admission Requirements: Secondary school certificate (Attestat o srednem obrazovanii)

Main Language(s) of Instruction: Russian

Degrees and Diplomas: *Bakalavr*, *Specialist Diploma*; *Magistr*

Student Services: Academic counselling, Canteen, Cultural centre, Employment services, Foreign Studies Centre, Health services, Social counselling, Sports facilities

Student Residential Facilities: For c. 450 students

Special Facilities: Art Gallery

Libraries: c. 210,000 vols

Last Updated: 24/02/12

OMSK STATE MEDICAL ACADEMY

Omskaja Gosudarstvennaja Medicinskaja Akademija (OSMA)

ul. Lenina 12, Omsk, 644099 Omskaja oblast'
Tel: +7(3812) 233-289
Fax: +7(3812) 234-632
EMail: intdept@omsk-osma.ru
Website: http://www.omsk-osma.ru

Rector: Alexander Novikov (1997-) EMail: omsk@omsk-osma.ru

Vice-Rector: Alexander Patiutov Tel: +7(3812) 232-502

International Relations: Victor Akulinin
Tel: +7(3812) 230-414 EMail: Akulinin@omsk-osma.ru

Faculties

Dentistry (Dentistry) *Dean*: Valerii Suntsov; **Medicine** (Medicine) *Dean*: Constantine Kozlov; **Paediatrics** (Paediatrics) *Dean*: Nikolai Sobotyuck; **Pharmacy** *Dean*: Vyacheslav Batuhtin; **Preventive Medicine** (Social and Preventive Medicine) *Dean*: Igor Sočoško

Further Information: Also Teaching Hospitals

History: Founded 1920. Acquired present status 1994.

Governing Bodies: Council

Academic Year: September to June (September-January; February-June)

Admission Requirements: Secondary school certificate (Attestat o srednem obrazovanii)

Fees: (Russian Rubles): c. 30,000 per annum

Main Language(s) of Instruction: Russian

Degrees and Diplomas: *Specialist Diploma*: Dentistry; Social and Preventive Medicine, 5 yrs; *Specialist Diploma*: Medicine; Paediatrics, 6 yrs; *Specialist Diploma*: Pharmacy, 5-5 1/2 yrs

Student Services: Academic counselling, Canteen, Cultural centre, Employment services, Foreign student adviser, Foreign Studies Centre, Handicapped facilities, Health services, Language programs, Nursery care, Social counselling, Sports facilities

Student Residential Facilities: Yes

Special Facilities: Museum of Anatomy; Museum of Pathological Anatomy; Biology Museum

Libraries: c. 550,000 vols

Publications: Theses of Medical Student Conferences *(annually)*

OMSK STATE PEDAGOGICAL UNIVERSITY

Omskij Gosudarstvennyj Pedagogičeskij Universitet (OSPU)

Naberezhnaya Tukhachevskogo 14, Omsk, 644099 Omskaja oblast'
Tel: +7(3812) 243-795
Fax: +7(3812) 243-795
EMail: common@omsk.edu
Website: http://dic.omgpu.omsk.edu

Rector: Konstantin A. Churkin EMail: omgpu@omsk.edu

Administrative Officer: Sergei Shirobokov
EMail: sshirob@omgpu.omsk.edu

International Relations: Nikita Brinyov, Deputy Director

Faculties

Chemistry and Biology (Biology; Chemistry; Environmental Engineering; Health Sciences; Information Technology; Natural Resources); **Computer Science** (Computer Science; English; Management); **Economics and Management** (Business Administration; Economics; Management; Marketing); **Fine Arts** (Design; Fine Arts; Music Education); **Foreign Languages** (Chinese; English; French; German; Literature); **Geography** (Business Administration; Geography; Social and Community Services; Tourism); **History** (History; Law); **Mathematics** (Economics; Mathematics; Mathematics and Computer Science); **Philology**; **Philosophy**; **Physics** (Business and Commerce; Computer Science; Physics; Technology; Technology Education); **Pre-School Pedagogy** (Pedagogy; Preschool Education; Psychology; Speech Therapy and Audiology); **Primary Education** (Pedagogy; Primary Education); **Psychology and Pedagogy** (Pedagogy; Psychology; Social Work)

History: Founded 1932, acquired present status and title 1993.

Governing Bodies: Rector; Vice-Rector; Deans of the Faculties

Academic Year: September to June (September-February; February-June)

Admission Requirements: Secondary school certificate (Attestat o srednem obrazovanii)

Fees: (Rubles): foreign students, 1,100 per annum (Bachelor's Programme or Russian Language Preparatory Course)

Main Language(s) of Instruction: Russian

International Co-operation: With universities in USA, Germany, Canada, France

Accrediting Agencies: Ministry of Education of the Russian Federation

Degrees and Diplomas: *Bakalavr*: Physics; Chemistry; Biology; Environmental Studies; Pedagogy; Practical Psychology, 4 yrs; *Specialist Diploma*: Mathematics; Computer Science; Physics; Chemistry; Biology; Geography; Psychology; Pedagogy; History; Primary Education; Philology; Fine Arts; Foreign Languages; Special Education; Pre-school Education; Economics; Management; Philosophy, 5 yrs; *Magistr*: Pedagogy; Natural Sciences; Physics; Mathematics; Philology; Economics; Social Sciences, a further 2 yrs; *Kandidat Nauk*: Mathematics; Biology; Environmental Studies; Russian History; Archeology; Economics; Management; Philosophy; Literature; Folklore; Russian; German; Comparative Linguistics; Pedagogy; Psychology; Geography, a further 3 yrs; *Doktor Nauk*: Russian History; Philosophy; Russian Literature; Pedagogy; Education; Mathematics Education; Computer Education (PhD), a further 5-6 yrs

Student Services: Academic counselling, Canteen, Cultural centre, Employment services, Foreign student adviser, Foreign Studies Centre, Health services, Language programs, Social counselling, Sports facilities

Libraries: Yes

Publications: Humanities, Scientific Journal *(annually)*; Natural Sciences and Environment Studies, Scientific Journal *(annually)*

OMSK STATE TECHNICAL UNIVERSITY

Omskij Gosudarstvennyj Tehničeskij Universitet

prosp. Mira 11, Omsk, 644050 Omskaja oblast'
Tel: +7(3812) 653-343
Fax: +7(3812) 652-698
EMail: info@omgtu.ru
Website: http://www.omgtu.ru

Rector: Nikolaj S. Zhilin

Vice-Rector: Gennadij Boyarkin
Tel: +7(3812) 653-017, Fax: +7(3812) 653-017

International Relations: Viatcheslav Solomin
Tel: +7(3812) 656-492, Fax: +7(3812) 656-492

Departments

Aerospace (Aeronautical and Aerospace Engineering; Environmental Engineering); **Automation** (Automation and Control Engineering; Computer Networks; Computer Science; Information Technology; Robotics; Systems Analysis); **Chemical Polygraphy** (Automation and Control Engineering; Environmental Engineering; Technology); **Economics and Management** (Administration; Economics; Management; Marketing); **Electrotechnical Engineering** (Electrical and Electronic Equipment and Maintenance; Electrical Engineering; Electronic Engineering; Information Technology; Power Engineering); **Humanities** (Advertising and Publicity; Design; Public Relations; Publishing and Book Trade; Social Welfare); **Machine Building** (Machine Building; Technology); **Mechanical Techology** (Automotive Engineering; Hydraulic Engineering; Mechanical Engineering; Safety Engineering; Technology; Transport Management); **Radio Engineering** (Electronic Engineering; Industrial Engineering; Telecommunications Engineering); **Thermal Energy**

History: Founded as Machine Building Institute 1942, acquired present status and title 1993.

Academic Year: September to June

Admission Requirements: Secondary School Certificate

Main Language(s) of Instruction: Russian

Degrees and Diplomas: *Bakalavr*: 4-5 yrs; *Specialist Diploma*: 4-5 yrs

Student Services: Academic counselling, Canteen, Cultural centre, Foreign student adviser, Health services, Language programs, Social counselling, Sports facilities

Special Facilities: OSTU Museum.

Publications: Omsk Scientific Bulletin, Magazine *(quarterly)*

Press or Publishing House: Publishing House

OMSK STATE TRANSPORT UNIVERSITY

Omskij Gosudarstvennyj Universitet Putej Soobščenija (OSTU (OMGUPS))

prosp. Karl Marx 35, Omsk, 644046 Omskaja oblast'
Tel: +7(3812) 314-219 +7(3812) 314-213
Fax: +7(3812) 314-219 +7(3812) 314-213
EMail: omgups@omgups.ru
Website: http://www.omgups.ru

Rector: Il'ham I. Galijev (1999-)

Pro-Rector: Alexander Volodin Tel: +7(3812) 310-600

International Relations: Alexander Tetter EMail: umu@omgups.ru

Departments

Foundation Studies *Dean*: Sergei Krochin; **Postgraduate Studies** *Dean*: Irina Razdobarova; **Scientific Research** (Natural Sciences; Transport and Communications) *Dean*: Sergei Shantarenko; **Upgrading of Engineering Qualification** (Engineering) *Dean*: Nikolai Gorbachev

Faculties

Automation, Telecommunication and Information Technology *Dean*: Aleksei Kogut; **Correspondence Courses** *Dean*: Vladislav Isakov; **Electro-Mechanics** (Electrical Engineering; Mechanical Engineering; Railway Engineering) *Dean*: Tatyana Komjakova; **Management and Economics** (Business and Commerce; Economics; Finance; International Business; Management; Marketing; Public Relations; Taxation; Tourism) *Dean*: Sergei Vetrov; **Mechanics** (Mechanical Engineering; Mechanics) *Dean*: Boris Sergeev; **Thermal Energy** (Energy Engineering; Environmental Engineering; Railway Engineering; Railway Transport; Thermal Engineering) *Dean*: Pavel Blinov

History: Founded 1900, acquired present status and title 1997.

Governing Bodies: Ministry of Transport; Ministry of Education

Academic Year: September to June

Admission Requirements: Secondary school certificate (Attestat o srednem polnom obshem obrazovanii) and entrance examination

Fees: (Rubles): 70,000 per annum

Main Language(s) of Instruction: Russian

International Co-operation: Participates in the Tempus programme

Degrees and Diplomas: *Bakalavr*: Engineering; Business Administration, 4 yrs; *Specialist Diploma*: Engineering; Business Administration, 5 yrs; *Magistr*: Engineering; Business Administration, 6 yrs

Student Services: Academic counselling, Canteen, Cultural centre, Employment services, Foreign student adviser, Foreign Studies Centre, Health services, Language programs, Sports facilities

Student Residential Facilities: Student Hostels

Special Facilities: University Museum

Libraries: c. 850,000 vols

Press or Publishing House: Publishing House

Academic Staff *2007-2008*	MEN	WOMEN	**TOTAL**
FULL-TIME	202	140	**342**
PART-TIME	28	25	**53**
STAFF WITH DOCTORATE			
FULL-TIME	157	69	**226**
PART-TIME	26	17	**43**
Student Numbers *2007-2008*			
All (Foreign Included)	2,778	1,699	**4,477**
FOREIGN ONLY	–	–	**379**

Part-time students, 3,558.

Last Updated: 12/12/08

OMSK STATE UNIVERSITY

Omskij Gosudarstvennyj Universitet (OMSU)
prosp. Mira 55a, Omsk, 644077 Omskaja oblast'
Tel: +7(3812) 642-587
Fax: +7(3812) 285-581 +7(3812) 647-444
EMail: gering@omsu.omskreg.ru
Website: http://www.univer.omsk.ru

Rector: Genadij Gering (1996-)
Tel: +7(3812) 268-422, Fax: +7(3812) 268-422

Senior Vice-Rector: Mihail Koroshevsky
Tel: +7(3812) 631-598 EMail: hmv@univer.omsk.su

International Relations: Vitaliy Issers
Tel: +7(3812) 225-725 EMail: interdep@unievr.omsk.su

Centres

Business Education (Banking; Business Education; Economics; Finance; Law; Management; Marketing; Psychology; Social Work) *Director*: Elena Eremenko; **Internet** (Computer Science) *Director*: Leonid Eremeev; **Science and Education Foundation** *Director*: Valerij Gagarin

Divisions

Computer Science *Head*: Alexander Guts

Faculties

Chemistry (Analytical Chemistry; Chemistry; Inorganic Chemistry; Organic Chemistry; Physical Chemistry) *Dean*: Irina Vlasova; **Culture and Arts** (Conducting; Cultural Studies; Dance; Fine Arts; Folklore; Library Science; Music Theory and Composition; Singing) *Dean*: Nina Genova; **Economics** (Accountancy; Banking; Economics; Finance; Government; Management; Marketing; Taxation) *Dean*: Ludmila Ivanova; **Foreign Languages** (English; Foreign Languages Education; French; German; Linguistics; Philology; Translation and Interpretation) *Dean*: Natalija Gičeva; **History** (Cultural Studies; History; Museum Studies; Prehistory; Regional Studies; Sociology; Theology) *Dean*: Aleksej Jakub; **International Business** (International Business; International Economics; Marketing) *Dean*: Valerij Čuhlomin; **Law** (Civil Law; Criminal Law; Labour Law; Law) *Dean*: Oleg Dmitriev; **Mathematics** (Applied Mathematics; Mathematics) *Dean*: Vladimir Nikolaev; **Philology** (Applied Linguistics; Journalism; Linguistics; Philology; Russian) *Dean*: Nikolaj Misjurov; **Physics** (Applied Mathematics; Applied Physics; Electronic Engineering; Physics; Radiophysics) *Dean*: Klementiy Jugai; **Psychology** (Educational Psychology; Psychology; Social Psychology) *Dean*: Ludmila Dementiy; **Theology** (History; Religious Studies; Theology) *Dean*: Dmitriy Sinelnikov

Further Information: Also Affiliated Centres in Kazakhstan and Uzbekistan

History: Founded 1974.

Governing Bodies: Scientific Council of the University

Academic Year: September to July

Admission Requirements: Secondary education certificate (Attestat o srednem obrazovanii) and entrance examination

Fees: (Russian Rubles): Full-time students, 5,100-21,900 per semester; part-time students, 3,600-11,100

Main Language(s) of Instruction: Russian

International Co-operation: With Universities in Australia, USA.

Accrediting Agencies: Ministry of General and Professional Education of the Russian Federation

Degrees and Diplomas: *Bakalavr*: Business Administration; Law; Theology, 4 yrs; *Specialist Diploma*: 5 yrs; *Kandidat Nauk*: Chemistry; Economics; History; Law; Mathematics; Philology; Physics, a further 3 yrs and thesis; *Doktor Nauk*: National History; Russian Language, a further 2 yrs following Kandidat

Student Services: Academic counselling, Canteen, Cultural centre, Employment services, Foreign student adviser, Foreign Studies Centre, Health services, Language programs, Sports facilities

Student Residential Facilities: Yes

Special Facilities: University Museum; Archaeology Museum; National Park at Butakovo; Chemical Laboratories; Students' Theatre "Poisk"

Libraries: Total, 508,680 vols

Press or Publishing House: Izdatelstvo Omskogo Gosuniversiteta

OREL STATE AGRARIAN UNIVERSITY

Orlovskij Gosudarstvennyj Agrarnyj Universitet
ul. Generala Rodina, 69, Orel, 302019 Orlovskaja oblast'
Tel: +7(4862) 45-40-79 +7(4862) 45-40-64
Fax: +7(4862) 45-40-79 +7(4862) 45-40-64
EMail: pnv@orel.ru; umo1@orelsau.ru
Website: http://www.orelsau.ru

Rector: Nikolaj Vasiljevič Parakhin (1994-)

Faculties

Agricultural Technology and Energy (Agricultural Engineering; Agricultural Equipment; Electrical and Electronic Equipment and Maintenance; Maintenance Technology); **Agrobusiness and Ecology** (Agricultural Business; Agricultural Economics; Ecology; Environmental Management; Plant and Crop Protection); **Biotechnology and Veterinary Science** (Animal Husbandry; Dairy; Meat and Poultry; Veterinary Science; Zoology); **Economics** (Accountancy; Agricultural Business; Economics; Finance; Information Technology; International Economics); **Engineering** (Agricultural Engineering; Agricultural Equipment; Civil Engineering; Electrical Engineering; Engineering; Industrial Engineering; Landscape Architecture); **Humanities and Science** (History; Mathematics; Philosophy; Physics; Russian; Sports)

History: Founded 1975, acquired present status and title 1999.

Academic Year: September to May (September-December; February-May)

Admission Requirements: Secondary school certificate (Attestat o srednem obrazovanii)

Main Language(s) of Instruction: Russian

Degrees and Diplomas: *Bakalavr*, *Specialist Diploma*; *Magistr*

Student Services: Academic counselling, Canteen, Cultural centre, Health services, Sports facilities

Libraries: c. 310,000 vols

Last Updated: 20/04/12

OREL STATE INSTITUTE OF ARTS AND CULTURE

Orlovskij Gosudarstvennyj Institut Isskustv i Kul'tury
ul. Leskova, 15, Orel, 302020 Orlovskaja oblast'
Tel: +7(4862) 41-61-91
Fax: +7(4862) 41-64-9
EMail: orart@orel.ru
Website: http://www.ogiik.orel.ru

Rector: Nikolaj A. Parshikov

Faculties

Arts and Culture (Conducting; Dance; Film; Fine Arts; Music; Singing; Theatre); **Documentation Studies** (Archiving; Documentation Techniques; Histology; Information Technology; Literature; Modern Languages; Museum Studies); **Social Science and Cultural Studies** (Cultural Studies; Economics; Educational Psychology; Management; Social Work; Sports)

History: Created 1972.

Degrees and Diplomas: *Bakalavr*, *Specialist Diploma*

Last Updated: 16/04/12

OREL STATE INSTITUTE OF ECONOMY AND TRADE

Orlovskij Gosudarstsvennyj Institut Ekonimiki I Torgovli (OGIET (OSIET))
ul.Oktyabrskaja 12, Orel, 302028 Orlovskaja oblast'
Tel: +7(4862) 43-51-63 +7(4862) 43-54-88 +7(4862) 43-50-78
Fax: +7(4862) 43-51-63 +7(4862) 43-33-36
EMail: ogiet@ogiet.ru; ogiet@orel.ru
Website: http://www.orelgiet.ru/

Rector: Nina Lygina

Faculties

Accountancy and Information Technology (Accountancy; Business Computing); **Business and Advertising** (Advertising and Publicity; Business and Commerce; Public Relations; Tourism); **Economics** (Economics); **Management** (Management; Marketing); **Technology** (Food Science; Food Technology)

History: Founded 1961 as Centre of the Institute of Soviet Trade, acquired present status and title 1991.

Governing Bodies: Scientific Council, comprising 30 members

Academic Year: September to July

Admission Requirements: Secondary school certificate (Attestat o srednem obrazovanii) or equivalent (Diplom srednego tehničeskogo obrazovanija)

Main Language(s) of Instruction: Russian

International Co-operation: None

Accrediting Agencies: Ministry of Education and Science; Federal Agency on Education

Degrees and Diplomas: *Bakalavr*; *Specialist Diploma*; *Magistr*

Student Services: Canteen, Cultural centre, Employment services, Health services, Language programs, Sports facilities

Student Residential Facilities: For 700 students

Special Facilities: Computer Centre; Museum of History; Quality Management Centre; Marketing and Employement Centre

Libraries: Institute Library, c. 116,311 vols

Press or Publishing House: Orel IGIET Publishing House

Last Updated: 12/01/12

OREL STATE UNIVERSITY

Orlovskij Gosudarstvennyj Universitet (OSU)
ul. Komsomolskaja 95, Orel, 302026 Orlovskaja oblast'
Tel: +7(4862) 777-318
Fax: +7(4862) 777-318
EMail: rector@univ-orel.ru
Website: http://www.univ-orel.ru/

Rector: Fjodor Stepanovič Avdeev (1993-)

Rector's Assistant: Valentina Fefelova

International Relations: Yelena Alekseeva, Pro-Rector, Distance Education International Affairs
Tel: +7(4862) 777-359, Fax: +7(4862) 777-359
EMail: alekseeva@univ-orel.ru

Centres
Conflict Resolution

Departments
Postgraduate Studies

Faculties
Aesthetic Education (Fine Arts; Performing Arts); **Document Science and Education** (Archiving; Documentation Techniques; Mathematics Education; Music Education; Native Language Education; Pedagogy; Primary Education); **Economics and Management** (Business Computing; Economics; Human Resources; Management; Real Estate); **Foreign Languages** (Foreign Languages Education; Linguistics; Translation and Interpretation); **Graphic Arts** (Art Education; Design; Fashion Design; Graphic Arts; Handicrafts; Painting and Drawing; Sculpture; Textile Design); **History** (Cultural Studies; Education; History); **Law** (Law); **Natural Sciences** (Biology; Chemistry; Ecology; Environmental Management; Genetics; Geography; Hotel Management; Landscape Architecture; Plant Pathology; Science Education; Soil Science; Tourism; Zoology); **Pedagogy and Psychology** (Educational and Student Counselling; Educational Psychology; Pedagogy; Psychology; Special Education); **Philology** (Advertising and Publicity; Journalism; Literature; Philology; Public Relations; Russian); **Philosophy** (Philosophy; Physical Education; Political Sciences; Religious Studies; Sociology; Sports; Theology); **Physics and Mathematics** (Applied Mathematics; Computer Science; Mathematical Physics; Mathematics; Mathematics Education; Physics); **Pre-University Training** *(for overseas students)*; **Professional Education**; **Social Pedagogy and Social Work** (Educational Psychology; Peace and Disarmament; Psychology; Social Work); **Technology, Business and Services** (Design; Education; Technology)

Institutes
Medicine (Anaesthesiology; Anatomy; Cardiology; Gynaecology and Obstetrics; Immunology; Medicine; Neurology; Ophthalmology; Paediatrics; Pathology; Pharmacy; Radiology; Surgery); **Student Research and Innovation**

Research Centres
Globalization and European Law; **Nanotechnology**

Research Institutes
Legal Problems; **Natural Sciences**; **Pedagogy and Psychology**; **Philology**; **Provincial Culture Problems**

History: Founded 1931 as Pedagogical Institute, acquired present status and title 1996.

Governing Bodies: Senate

Academic Year: September to July

Admission Requirements: Secondary school certificate (Attestat o srednem obrazovanii), for undergraduate degree. Undergraduate degree required for Magistr.

Fees: (Russian Rubles): 22,000 to 61,000 per annum.

Main Language(s) of Instruction: Russian

International Co-operation: With universities in France, Belgium, Germany, China.

Degrees and Diplomas: *Bakalavr*: 4-5 yrs; *Specialist Diploma*: 5-6 yrs; *Magistr*: a further 2 yrs; *Kandidat Nauk*: a further 3 yrs; *Doktor Nauk*

Student Residential Facilities: 4 hostels for 2,000 students.

Libraries: c. 1,042,125 vols.

Academic Staff *2010-2011*	MEN	WOMEN	**TOTAL**
FULL-TIME	259	533	**792**
PART-TIME	68	81	**149**
STAFF WITH DOCTORATE			
FULL-TIME	171	354	**525**
PART-TIME	75	65	**140**
Student Numbers *2010-2011*			
All (Foreign Included)	3,326	8,530	**11,856**
FOREIGN ONLY	62	52	**114**

Part-time students, 3,547. **Evening students**, 170.

Last Updated: 18/10/11

ORENBURG STATE MEDICAL ACADEMY

Orenburgskaja Gosudarstvennaja Medicinskaja Akademija
ul. Sovetskaja 6, Orenburg 460000
Tel: +7(3532) 77-61-03 +7(3532) 77-94-08
Fax: +7(3532) 77-94-08 +7(3532) 77-24-59
EMail: orgma@esoo.ru
Website: http://orgma.ru/

Rector: Victor Mikhailovich Boyev

Programmes
Medicine (Clinical Psychology; Health Administration; Medicine; Psychology; Stomatology)

History: Founded 1944.

Academic Year: September to June

Admission Requirements: Secondary school certificate (Attestat o srednem obščem obrazovanii)

Main Language(s) of Instruction: Russian

Degrees and Diplomas: *Specialist Diploma*; *Kandidat Nauk*

Student Services: Academic counselling, Canteen, Cultural centre, Employment services, Foreign Studies Centre, Health services, Social counselling, Sports facilities

Student Residential Facilities: For c. 3,000 students

Special Facilities: Academy History Museum

Press or Publishing House: Publishing House

Last Updated: 12/01/12

ORENBURG STATE PEDAGOGICAL UNIVERSITY

Orenburgskij Gosudarstvennyj Pedagogičeskij Universitet (OSPU)
ul. Sovetskaja 19, Orenburg 460844
Tel: +7(3532) 77-24-52 +7(3532) 77-68-39
Fax: +7(3532) 77-24-52 +7(3532) 77-68-39
EMail: ospu@ospu.ru
Website: http://www.ospu.ru/

Rector: Svetlana Aleksandrovna Aleshina

Faculties

Foreign Languages (English; Foreign Languages Education; French; German); **History** (History; Humanities and Social Science Education); **Philology** (Journalism; Linguistics; Literature; Native Language Education; Philology; Russian; Speech Studies); **Physics and Mathematics** (Computer Education; Computer Science; Mathematics; Mathematics Education; Physics; Science Education); **Preschool and Primary Education** (Art Education; Preschool Education; Primary Education); **Psychology** (Educational Psychology; Psychology); **Social Pedagogics** (Educational Psychology; Social Psychology)

Institutes

Physical Education and Sport (Physical Education; Sports); **Science and Economics** (Analytical Chemistry; Biology; Botany; Business Education; Chemistry; Ecology; Economics; Geography; Humanities and Social Science Education; Management; Plant Pathology; Science Education; Zoology)

History: Founded 1919. Became institute 1930. Acquired University status 1996.

Governing Bodies: Rectorat

Admission Requirements: Secondary school-leaving certificate

Main Language(s) of Instruction: Russian

International Co-operation: With universities in Kazakhstan

Accrediting Agencies: Ministry of Education and Science

Degrees and Diplomas: *Bakalavr*, *Specialist Diploma*; *Magistr*

Student Residential Facilities: 3 students hostels

Special Facilities: Zoological Museum; Archeological Museum; Museum of the University's History

Libraries: 870,000 vols

Last Updated: 24/02/12

ORENBURG STATE UNIVERSITY

Orenburgskij Gosudarstvennyj Universitet (OGU)

prosp. Pobedy 13, Orenburg 460018
Tel: +7(3532) 77-67-70
Fax: +7(3532) 72-37-01 +7(3532) 77-67-70
EMail: post@mail.osu.ru
Website: http://www.osu.ru

Rector: Vladimir Petrovich Kovalevskij EMail: vpk@mail.osu.ru

Faculties

Applied Biotechnology and Engineering (Bioengineering; Biotechnology; Chemical Engineering); **Architecture and Civil Engineering** (Architecture; Building Technologies; Civil Engineering; Construction Engineering; Design; Road Engineering; Town Planning; Transport Engineering); **Chemistry and Biology** (Applied Chemistry; Biochemistry; Biology; Chemistry; Ecology; Microbiology; Soil Science); **Earth Sciences** (Ecology; Environmental Management; Geography; Geological Engineering; Geology); **Economics and Management** (Advertising and Publicity; Business and Commerce; Economics; Home Economics; Human Resources; International Economics; Management; Marketing; Tourism); **Electronic Engineering** (Electronic Engineering; Energy Engineering; Industrial Design); **Finance** (Accountancy; Economics; Finance; Taxation); **Humanities and Social Science** (Cultural Studies; History; Philosophy; Psychology; Religious Studies); **Information Technology** (Business Computing; Computer Networks; Computer Science; Information Technology; Software Engineering; Systems Analysis); **Journalism** (Advertising and Publicity; Journalism; Media Studies; Public Relations); **Law** (Law); **Mathematics** (Applied Mathematics; Computer Science; Information Technology; Mathematics); **Philology** (Foreign Languages Education; Linguistics; Philology; Translation and Interpretation); **Physics** (Biophysics; Electronic Engineering; Physics; Radiophysics); **Transport Engineering** (Automotive Engineering; Transport Engineering; Transport Management)

Institutes

Aerospace (Aeronautical and Aerospace Engineering; Machine Building)

Further Information: Branches in Akbulak, Bugursulan, Buzuluk, Kumertau, Orsk, Ufa.

History: Founded 1971 as Orenburg Branch of Samara Polytechnic, acquired present status and title 1996.

Governing Bodies: Academic Council

Academic Year: September to June

Admission Requirements: High School/Professional certificate (attestat o srednem/srednem specialnom obrazovanii) and entrance examination

Main Language(s) of Instruction: Russian

Degrees and Diplomas: *Bakalavr*, *Specialist Diploma*; *Magistr*

Student Residential Facilities: For c. 1,420 students

Special Facilities: OSU History Museum Memorial Museum of Geological Studies; Southern Urals Cossack History Museum. Art Gallery

Libraries: 610,000 vols

Last Updated: 24/02/12

ORENBURG UNIVERSITY OF AGRICULTURE

Orenburgskij Gosudarstvennyj Agrarnyj Universitet

ul. Čeljuskintsev, 18, Orenburg 460795
Tel: +7(3532) 77-52-30
Fax: +7(3532) 77-52-30 +7(3532) 72-57-06
EMail: orensau@mail.ru
Website: http://www.orensau.ru/

Rector: Vladimir Vasiliievich Karakulev

Faculties

Agronomy (Agronomy); **Economics** (Economics); **Engineering** (Engineering); **Forestry** (Forestry); **Information Technology** (Information Technology); **Law** (Law); **Veterinary Medicine** (Veterinary Science)

Further Information: Branches also in Adamovka (Orenburg oblast), Buzulk, Ilek, Stepanovskij, Sorochinsk.

History: Created 1930.

Degrees and Diplomas: *Bakalavr*, *Specialist Diploma*; *Magistr*

Last Updated: 12/01/12

PACIFIC STATE UNIVERSITY

Tikhookeanskij Gosudarstvennyj Universitet (KSTU)

ul. Tikhookeanskaja 136, Khabarovsk 680035
Tel: +7(4212) 37-51-86 +7(4212) 72-06-84
Fax: +7(4212) 72-06-84
EMail: khstu@khstu.ru
Website: http://www.khstu.ru

Rector: Sergei N. Ivančeko (2002-) EMail: rector@khstu.ru

Faculties

Architecture and Design (Architecture; Design; Fine Arts; Town Planning); **Civil Engineering** (Bridge Engineering; Civil Engineering; Construction Engineering; Heating and Refrigeration; Hydraulic Engineering; Road Engineering; Water Management); **Economics and Management** (Economics; Finance; Management; Marketing); **Humanities and Social Sciences** (Cultural Studies; Linguistics; Modern Languages; Philology; Philosophy; Political Sciences; Psychology; Regional Studies; Russian; Social Work; Sociology; Tourism); **Information Technologies** (Computer Graphics; Computer Science; Electrical and Electronic Engineering; Information Technology); **Law** (Law); **Natural and Computer Sciences** (Applied Linguistics; Chemistry; Computer Science; Mathematics; Mechanics; Physics); **Natural Resources and Environmental Studies** (Biotechnology; Chemical Engineering; Ecology; Environmental Management; Forest Management; Forest Products; Forestry; Natural Resources; Wood Technology); **Transport** (Automotive Engineering; Maintenance Technology; Transport Engineering)

History: Founded 1958 as Polytechnic Institute. In 1992 became Habarovskij Gosudarstvennyj Tehničeskij Universitet (Habarovsk State University of Technology). Acquired current title 2005.

Governing Bodies: Academic Council

Academic Year: September to July (September-January; February-July)

Fees: None

Main Language(s) of Instruction: Russian

International Co-operation: With universities in China, South Korea, Germany, Japan

Degrees and Diplomas: *Bakalavr*; *Specialist Diploma*; *Magistr*; *Kandidat Nauk*

Student Services: Canteen, Cultural centre, Foreign student adviser, Foreign Studies Centre, Health services, Language programs, Sports facilities

Special Facilities: Museum. Theatre. Music Studio. Dance Studio.

Libraries: Central Library

Last Updated: 15/03/12

PENZA STATE AGRICULTURAL ACADEMY

Penzenskaja Gosudarstvennaja Sel'skokhozjajstvenaja Akademija

ul. Botaničeskaja 30, Penza, 440014 Penzenskaja oblast'
Tel: +7(8412) 62-83-54 +7(841) 62-83-59
Fax: +7(8412) 62-83-54
EMail: sha_penza@mail.ru
Website: http://pgsha.penza.net/

Rector: Vladimir Dmitrievich Korotnev

Faculties

Agronomy (Agronomy; Plant and Crop Protection; Plant Pathology; Soil Management); **Economics** (Accountancy; Agricultural Economics; Business Computing; Economics; Farm Management; Finance; Management); **Engineering** (Agricultural Engineering; Agricultural Equipment; Automotive Engineering; Crop Production; Engineering; Farm Management); **Technology** (Animal Husbandry; Crop Production; Food Technology; Technology)

History: Founded 1951, acquired present status and title 1995.

Governing Bodies: Academic Board

Academic Year: September to July (September-January; February-July)

Admission Requirements: Secondary school certificate (Attestat o srednem obrazivanii) or equivalent

Main Language(s) of Instruction: Russian

Degrees and Diplomas: *Bakalavr*; *Specialist Diploma*

Student Services: Academic counselling, Canteen, Cultural centre, Employment services, Foreign student adviser, Foreign Studies Centre, Handicapped facilities, Health services, Language programs, Nursery care, Social counselling, Sports facilities

Student Residential Facilities: For 1,500 students (3 hostels)

Special Facilities: Experimental Farm. Machinery Park. Preventive Clinic

Libraries: c. 325,000 vols

Last Updated: 12/01/12

PENZA STATE PEDAGOGICAL UNIVERSITY NAMED AFTER V.G. BELINSKIJ

Penzenskij Gosudarstvennyj Pedagogičeskij Universitet im. V.G. Belinskogo

ul. Lermontova 37, Penza, 440026 Penzenskaja oblast'
Tel: +7(8412) 54-83-62 +7(8412) 54-84-20 +7(8412) 56-35-53
Fax: +7(8412) 56-25-66
EMail: rector@spu-penza.ru
Website: http://www.spu-penza.ru/

Rector: Vladimir Ivanovich Korotov

Faculties

Economics, Management, and Law (Applied Linguistics; Business and Commerce; Economics; Law; Management); **Foreign Languages** (English; Foreign Languages Education; French; Germanic Languages; Pedagogy); **History** (Archaeology; History; Humanities and Social Science Education); **Mathematics and Physics** (Computer Education; Computer Science; Mathematics; Mathematics Education; Physics; Science Education); **Natural Sciences** (Biochemistry; Biology; Botany; Chemistry; Ecology; Geography); **Physical Education** (Physical Education; Sports); **Primary and Special Education** (Primary Education; Special Education); **Psychology** (Psychology); **Russian Language and Literature** (Journalism; Literature; Native Language Education; Pedagogy; Russian); **Sociology and Social Work** (Philosophy; Political Sciences; Social Work; Sociology)

History: Founded 1939 as Teachers Training Institute, acquired present status and title 1994.

Admission Requirements: Secondary school certificate (Attestat o srednem obrazovanii) and entrance examinations

Main Language(s) of Instruction: Russian

Accrediting Agencies: Ministry of Education

Degrees and Diplomas: *Bakalavr*; *Specialist Diploma*; *Magistr*

Student Residential Facilities: Yes

Special Facilities: Natural Science Museum; History Museum; Art Gallery; Movie Studio

Press or Publishing House: University Publishing House

Last Updated: 24/02/12

PENZA STATE TECHNICAL ACADEMY

Penzenskij Gosudarstvennaja Tekhnologičeskaja Akademija

Bajhdukova Proezd / ul Gagarina, 1-a 11, Penza, 440605 Penzenskaja oblast'
Tel: +7(8412) 49-54-41
Fax: +7(8412) 49-60-86
EMail: info@pgta.ru; rector@pgta.ru
Website: http://www.pgta.ru

Rector: Vasilij Borisovich Moiseev EMail: rector@pgta.ru

Faculties

Educational Technology (Biotechnology; Information Technology; Linguistics); **Industrial Economics and Computing** (Applied Mathematics; Biotechnology; Economics; Industrial Management; Information Technology); **Industrial Technology** (Computer Networks; Construction Engineering; Food Technology; Industrial Management; Information Technology; Machine Building)

History: Created 1959 as Penzenskij Gosudarstvennyj Teckhnologičeskij Institut. Acquired current title 2004. Previously known as Penzenskij Gosudarstvennyj Tehničeskij Universitet (Penza State Technical University).

Degrees and Diplomas: *Bakalavr*; *Specialist Diploma*; *Magistr*; *Kandidat Nauk*

Last Updated: 11/04/11

PENZA STATE UNIVERSITY

Penzenskij Gosudarstvennyj Universitet (PGU)

ul. Krasnaja 40, Penza, 440026 Penzenskaja oblast'
Tel: +7(8412) 56-35-11
Fax: +7(8412) 56-51-22
EMail: mvb@pnzgu.ru; gerand@pnzgu.ru; cnit@pnzgu.ru
Website: http://www.pnzgu.ru

Rector: Vladimir Volchikhin (1999-)

Faculties

Computer Science (Automation and Control Engineering; Business Computing; Computer Education; Computer Graphics; Computer Science; Data Processing; Documentation Techniques; Information Management; Information Technology; Software Engineering); **Economics and Management** (Accountancy; Economics; Finance; Management; Marketing); **Information Technology and Systems** (Biomedical Engineering; Information Technology; Instrument Making; Measurement and Precision Engineering; Safety Engineering); **Law** (Criminal Law; History of Law; International Law; Labour Law; Private Law; Public Law); **Natural Sciences, Nanotechnology, and Radio Electronics** (Applied Mathematics; Environmental Engineering; Mathematics; Microelectronics; Nanotechnology; Physics; Radiophysics; Translation and Interpretation); **Transport Engineering** (Machine Building; Mechanical Engineering; Mechanical Equipment and Maintenance; Transport Engineering)

Institutes

Medicine (Medicine; Pharmacy)

History: Founded 1943. Acquired present status and title 1998.

Governing Bodies: Rector; Pro-Rectors

Academic Year: September to July

Admission Requirements: Secondary school certificate and entrance examination

Main Language(s) of Instruction: Russian

International Co-operation: With universities in China, Germany, Syria, India and Pakistan

Accrediting Agencies: Ministry of Education and Science

Degrees and Diplomas: *Bakalavr*; *Specialist Diploma*; *Magistr*

Student Services: Academic counselling, Canteen, Cultural centre, Foreign student adviser, Foreign Studies Centre, Handicapped facilities, Health services, Language programs, Nursery care, Social counselling, Sports facilities

Student Residential Facilities: Five Hostels

Special Facilities: Universtiy Museum; Television Centre; Laboratories

Libraries: c. 2,5m. Vols.
Last Updated: 16/04/12

PENZA STATE UNIVERSITY OF ARCHITECTURE AND CONSTRUCTION

Penzenskij Gosudarstvennyj Universitet Arhitektury I Stroitelstva (PGUAS)

ul. G. Titova 28, Penza, 440028 Penzenskaja oblast'
Tel: +7(8412) 49-72-77
Fax: +7(8412) 49-72-77
EMail: office@pguas.ru
Website: http://www.pguas.ru/

Rector: Yuri Petrovich Skachkov

Faculties

Architecture (Architectural and Environmental Design; Architecture; Fashion Design; Interior Design; Town Planning); **Technology** (Building Technologies; Chemistry; Construction Engineering; Materials Engineering)

Institutes

Automobile and Road Transport (Automotive Engineering; Transport and Communications; Transport Engineering; Transport Management); **Civil Engineering** (Civil Engineering; Construction Engineering; Design; Engineering; Industrial Engineering; Painting and Drawing; Road Engineering); **Ecological Engineering** (Ecology; Environmental Engineering; Environmental Management; Heating and Refrigeration); **Economics and Management** (Economics; Management; Management Systems; Marketing)

History: Founded 1958 as Civil Engineering Institute, acquired present status and title 2003.

Governing Bodies: Board of Trustees

Academic Year: September to June

Admission Requirements: Secondary school certificate (Attestat o srednem obrazovanii)

Main Language(s) of Instruction: Russian

International Co-operation: With universities in Germany, China, Vietnam, USA, India, Pakistan.

Degrees and Diplomas: *Bakalavr*, *Specialist Diploma*; *Magistr*

Student Services: Academic counselling, Canteen, Cultural centre, Employment services, Foreign Studies Centre, Health services, Language programs, Sports facilities

Student Residential Facilities: 3 students hostels

Special Facilities: Museum of the University

Libraries: c. 450,000 vols
Last Updated: 16/04/12

PEOPLES' FRIENDSHIP UNIVERSITY OF RUSSIA

Rossijskij Universitet Družby Narodov (RUDN)

ul. Mikluho-Maklaja 6, Moskva 117198
Tel: +7(495) 787-3803
Fax: +7(495) 434-7016
EMail: dcio@rudn.ru
Website: http://www.pfu.edu.ru/

Rector: Vladimir Mikhailovič Filippov (2005-)
Tel: +7(495) 434-7027, Fax: +7(495) 433-7379
EMail: rector@rudn.ru

International Relations: Gulnara Amangueldinovna, Vice-Rector for International Affairs
Tel: +7(495) 434-70-16 Ext. 10-06, Fax: +7(495) 434-70-16
EMail: krasnova@pfu.edu.ru; n.odintsova@rudn.ru

Faculties

Agriculture (Agricultural Economics; Agricultural Equipment; Agriculture; Agronomy; Animal Husbandry; Veterinary Science); **Ecology** (Ecology); **Economics** (Accountancy; Business and Commerce; Economics; Finance; Law; Management; Marketing); **Engineering** (Architecture; Automation and Control Engineering; Business Administration; Construction Engineering; Electrical and Electronic Engineering; Engineering; Machine Building; Mechanical Engineering; Mining Engineering; Power Engineering; Technology); **Foreign Languages and General Education** *(Preparatory Studies)* (Modern Languages); **Humanities and Social Sciences** (Arts and Humanities; Social Sciences); **Law** (Law); **Medicine** (Dentistry; Medicine; Pharmacy); **Philology** (Philology); **Science** (Natural Sciences)

History: Founded 1960. Open mainly to students from developing countries but including c. 25 per cent Russian students. Degrees and diplomas are the same as those awarded by other Russian Universities. Financed by the State and by organizations which took part in the foundation of the University.

Governing Bodies: University Council, including student representatives, Rectorate

Academic Year: September to July

Admission Requirements: Secondary school certificate, advanced level or equivalent

Fees: (US Dollars): Foreign students, 1,200-3,500 per annum

Main Language(s) of Instruction: Russian

International Co-operation: With more than 140 universities worldwide

Degrees and Diplomas: *Bakalavr*: Civil Engineering; Mining Engineering; Ecology; Law; International Relations (BSc); History; Philosophy; Sociology; Political Science; Physics; Mathematics; Applied Mathematics; Computer Science; Chemistry; Management; Marketing; Finance; Business and Commerce; Philology; Linguistics; Journalism; Agronomy; Architecture; Power Engineering (BSc), 4 yrs; *Specialist Diploma*: Economics; Management; Public Relations; Radiophysics; and Electronics; Medicine; Pharmacy; Dentistry; International Relations, 5 yrs; *Magistr*: Mining Engineering; Ecology; Law; International Relations (MSc), a further 2 yrs; *Magistr*: Sociology; Political Science; Physics; Mathematics; Applied Mathematics; Computer Science; Chemistry; Management; Marketing; Finance; Business and Commerce; Philology; Linguistics; Journalism; Agronomy; Architecture; Power Engineering; Civil Engineering, a further 2 yrs following Bakalavr; *Kandidat Nauk*: Agriculture; Architecture; Arts and Humanities; Economics; Business Administration; Engineering; Medicine; Pharmacy; Dentistry; Law; Mathematics; Physics; Chemistry; Applied Mathematics and Computer Science, Ecology (Ph.D.), a further 3 yrs following Magistr; *Doktor Nauk*: Agriculture; Architecture; Arts and Humanities; Economics; Business Administration; Engineering; Medicine; Pharmacy; Dentistry; Law; Mathematics; Physics; Chemistry; Applied Mathematics and Computer Science; Ecology (Dr. Sc.)

Student Services: Academic counselling, Canteen, Cultural centre, Employment services, Foreign student adviser, Foreign Studies Centre, Health services, Language programs, Social counselling, Sports facilities

Student Residential Facilities: Yes

Special Facilities: Museum: History of the University; Anatomy; Geology; Antique Civilizations. TV Channel

Libraries: Scientific Library of the University, c. 1.6m. vols

Publications: Bulletin, Series on Economics, Law, International Relations, Sciences, Humanities *(quarterly)*
Last Updated: 20/03/12

PERM NATIONAL RESEARCH POLYTECHNIC UNIVERSITY

Permskij Natsional'nyj Gosudarstvennyj Issledovatel'skij Politekhničeskij Universitet (PSTU)

Komsomolskij prosp. 29, k. 225, Perm' 614990
Tel: +7(342) 219-80-68
Fax: +7(342) 219-80-67
EMail: rector@pstu.ru
Website: http://www.pstu.ac.ru

Rector: Anatolij Aleksandrovich Tashkinov

Faculties

Aerospace (Aeronautical and Aerospace Engineering; Hydraulic Engineering; Polymer and Plastics Technology); **Applied Mathematics and Mechanics** (Applied Mathematics; Applied Physics; Mechanics; Physics); **Automobile and Road Building** (Automotive Engineering; Machine Building; Road Engineering; Road Transport); **Chemical Engineering** (Biotechnology; Chemical Engineering; Chemistry); **Civil Engineering** (Architecture; Building Technologies; Civil Engineering; Heating and Refrigeration; Real Estate; Waste Management); **Electrical Engineering** (Electrical Engineering); **Humanities** (Administration; Applied Linguistics; Cultural Studies; Economics; Finance; History; Industrial Management; Linguistics; Management; Marketing; Modern Languages; Political Sciences; Sociology); **Mechanical Engineering** (Mechanical Engineering; Metallurgical Engineering; Thermal Engineering); **Mining and Oil Industries** (Electrical and Electronic Equipment and Maintenance; Geology; Mining Engineering; Petroleum and Gas Engineering)

Further Information: Branches also in Berezniki, Lys'va, Chaikovskij.

History: Founded 1953 as a Polytechnical Institute, acquired status and title of Permskij Gosudarstvennyj Tekhničeskij Universitet (Perm State Technical University) in 1992. Acquired current title 2011.

Governing Bodies: Academic Board

Academic Year: September to June

Admission Requirements: Secondary school certificate (Attestat o srednem obrazovanii)

Main Language(s) of Instruction: Russian

Accrediting Agencies: Ministry of Education

Degrees and Diplomas: *Bakalavr*, *Specialist Diploma*; *Magistr*

Student Residential Facilities: Yes

Special Facilities: Historical-Cultural Complex

Libraries: c. 1.3m vols

Last Updated: 11/01/12

PERM STATE ACADEMY OF AGRICULTURE NAMED AFTER D.N. PRIANISHNIKOV

Permskaja Gosudarstvennaja Sel'skokhozjajstvennaja Akademija im. Akademika D.N. Prjanišhnikov

ul. Kommunističeskaja 23, Perm', 614600 Permskij kraj
Tel: +7(342) 212-53-94
Fax: +7(342) 212-53-94
EMail: psaa@perm-edu.ru
Website: http://www.psaa.ru

Rector: Andrej Alekseevich Belykh

Faculties

Agrotechnology and Forestry (Agricultural Equipment; Botany; Crop Production; Forest Products; Forestry; Plant and Crop Protection); **Applied Computer Science** (Computer Science; Information Technology); **Architecture and Engineering** (Agricultural Engineering; Agricultural Equipment; Architecture; Civil Engineering; Maintenance Technology; Mechanical Engineering); **Economics, Commerce and Finance** (Accountancy; Agricultural Business; Agricultural Economics; Agricultural Equipment; Business and Commerce; Economics; Finance; Management); **Land Management** (Philosophical Schools; Physics; Surveying and Mapping); **Soil Science, Agrochemistry, and Ecology** (Chemistry; Ecology; Soil Science); **Veterinary Medicine** (Animal Husbandry; Veterinary Science; Zoology)

History: Created 1930.

Degrees and Diplomas: *Bakalavr*, *Specialist Diploma*; *Magistr*

Last Updated: 16/04/12

PERM STATE ACADEMY OF MEDICINE NAMED AFTER E.A. WAGNER

Permskaja Gosudarstvennaja Meditsinskaja Akademija im. Akademika E.A. Vagnera

ul. Petropavlovskaja, 26, Perm', 614990 Permskij kraj
Tel: +7(342) 217-10-31
Fax: +7(342) 217-10-30
EMail: med@psma.ru; rector@psma.ru
Website: http://www.psma.ru

Rector: Irina P. Korjukina

Faculties

Dentistry (Dental Hygiene; Dentistry; Oral Pathology; Orthodontics; Periodontics; Stomatology); **Medicine** (Gynaecology and Obstetrics; Medicine; Surgery); **Nursing** (Nursing); **Paediatrics** (Paediatrics)

History: Founded 1916, acquired present status 2006.

Academic Year: September to July

Admission Requirements: Secondary school certificate

Main Language(s) of Instruction: Russian

International Co-operation: IFMSA, DAAD, Open Society Institution, Fulbright, Erasmus

Accrediting Agencies: Ministry of Education of Russian Federation; Federal Agency of Public Health and Social Development of Russian Federation

Degrees and Diplomas: *Specialist Diploma*

Student Services: Academic counselling, Canteen, Cultural centre, Foreign student adviser, Foreign Studies Centre, Handicapped facilities, Health services, Language programs, Social counselling, Sports facilities

Student Residential Facilities: Yes

Special Facilities: Museums: Morphology; Anatomy; University History; Military History; Surgery

Last Updated: 16/04/12

PERM STATE INSTITUTE OF ARTS AND CULTURE

Permskij Gosudarstvennyj Institut Iskusstv i Kul'tury

ul. Gazety 'Zvezda', 18, Perm', 614000 Permskij kraj
Tel: +7(342) 212-45-93 +7(342) 210-10-08
Fax: +7(342) 212-17-63
EMail: rectorat@psiac.ru
Website: http://www.psiac.ru/

Rector: E.A. Malyanov

Faculties

Art (Fine Arts; Music; Music Education; Musical Instruments; Painting and Drawing; Singing); **Art Education** (Acting; Art Education; Conducting; Dance; Theatre); **Cultural Studies** (Acting; Cultural Studies; Management; Theatre); **Information Sciences** (Documentation Techniques; Information Sciences; Information Technology; Library Science)

History: Created 1975.

Degrees and Diplomas: *Bakalavr*, *Specialist Diploma*

Last Updated: 27/02/12

PERM STATE NATIONAL RESEACH UNIVERSITY

Permskij Gosudarstvennyj National'nyj Issledovatel'skij Universitet

ul. Bukireva 15, Perm', 614990 Permskij kraj
Tel: +7(342) 237-17-93 +7(342) 239-63-26
Fax: +7(342) 237-16-11
EMail: info@psu.ru
Website: http://www.psu.ru

Rector: Igor Yur'evich Makarikhin EMail: rector@psu.ru

Faculties

Biology (Biology; Botany; Ecology; Immunology; Microbiology; Water Management; Zoology); **Chemistry** (Analytical Chemistry; Chemistry; Inorganic Chemistry; Organic Chemistry; Physical Chemistry); **Economics** (Accountancy; Business Computing; Economics; Finance; International Business; Management; Marketing); **Geography** (Geography; Meteorology; Tourism; Water Science); **Geology** (Geological Engineering; Geology; Geophysics; Mineralogy; Mining Engineering; Petroleum and Gas Engineering); **History and Political Studies** (History; Political Sciences); **Law** (Civil Law; Constitutional Law; Criminal Law; European Union Law; Fiscal Law; International Law; Labour Law; Law; Social Work); **Mathematics and Mechanical Engineering** (Applied Mathematics; Information Technology; Mathematics; Mechanical Engineering; Mechanics); **Modern Languages and Literature** (Foreign

Languages Education; Germanic Languages; Literature; Modern Languages; Romance Languages); **Philology** (Journalism; Literature; Philology; Russian; Slavic Languages); **Philosophy and Sociology** (Clinical Psychology; Philosophy; Political Sciences; Sociology); **Physics** (Electronic Engineering; Physics; Telecommunications Engineering)

Further Information: Also Russian language courses for foreign students

History: Founded 1916. Previously known as Permskij Gosudarstvennyj Universitet (Perm State University). Acquired current title and status 2011.

Governing Bodies: Academic Council

Academic Year: September to July

Admission Requirements: Secondary education certificate (Attestat o srednem obrazovanii) and entrance examination

Main Language(s) of Instruction: Russian

Degrees and Diplomas: *Bakalavr*; *Specialist Diploma*; *Magistr*; *Kandidat Nauk*; *Doktor Nauk*

Student Services: Academic counselling, Canteen, Cultural centre, Employment services, Foreign Studies Centre, Handicapped facilities, Health services, Nursery care, Social counselling, Sports facilities

Student Residential Facilities: Yes

Special Facilities: History of the University Museum; Archaeological Museum; Botanical Museum; Zoology Museum; Mineralogy Museum; Paleontology and Engineering Geology Museum

Libraries: c. 1.5m. vols

Last Updated: 16/04/12

PERM STATE PEDAGOGICAL UNIVERSITY

Permskij Gosudarstvennyj Pedagogičeskij Universitet (PSPU)

ul. Sibirskaja, 24, Perm', 614990 Permskij kraj
Tel: +7(3422) 127-253
Fax: +7(3422) 127-019
EMail: postmaster@pspu.ac.ru
Website: http://www.pspu.ac.ru

Rector: Andrei Kolesnikov (2003-) EMail: kolesnikov@pspu.ru

Faculties

Child Psychology and Pedagogy (Pedagogy; Preschool Education; Special Education; Speech Therapy and Audiology); **Foreign Languages** (English; Foreign Languages Education; French; German; Philology); **History** (Cultural Studies; History; Humanities and Social Science Education); **Information Science and Economics** (Computer Education; Computer Science; Economics; Information Technology); **Mathematics** (Applied Mathematics; Mathematics; Mathematics Education); **Music** (Music; Music Education); **Natural Science** (Anatomy; Botany; Chemistry; Science Education; Zoology); **Philology** (Linguistics; Literature; Native Language Education; Philology; Russian; Slavic Languages); **Physical Education** (Health Education; Physical Education; Rehabilitation and Therapy; Sports); **Physics** (Computer Education; Computer Science; Physics; Science Education); **Primary Education** (Pedagogy; Primary Education; Teacher Training); **Psychology** (Psychology)

Further Information: PSPU alo hosts: Regional Centre for New Information Technologies in Educaiton; Regional Centre for Ecological Education; Institute fo Komi-Pernian Language, Traditional Culture and History; Centre for Ethnolinguistics of Pern Region; Centre for Scottish Culture; Branch of Russian Academy of Education; Branch of Russian Academy of Apiculture; Branch of History and Archaeology Institute of the Ural Department of Russian Academy of Science; Branch of Russian Psychological Association and Pern Committee of Russian Heraldic Association.

History: Founded 1919 as Institute of People's Education. Reorganised as Pern Pedagogical Institute 1921. Acquired present status 1994.

Governing Bodies: Conference of the members of University Staff (academic and other) and students; Scientific Council of the University

Academic Year: September to June

Admission Requirements: Certificate of secondary (complete) comprehensive education or secondary professional education; United State Exam Certificate; or equivalent

Main Language(s) of Instruction: Russian

International Co-operation: With Universities in United Kingdom, the Netherlands, Germany, Belgium, France (Tempus-Tacsi Joint Educational Projects, Cooperation Agreements)

Degrees and Diplomas: *Bakalavr*; *Specialist Diploma*; *Magistr*; *Kandidat Nauk*; *Doktor Nauk*

Student Services: Academic counselling, Canteen, Employment services, Foreign student adviser, Health services, Language programs, Social counselling, Sports facilities

Student Residential Facilities: 3 student hostels

Special Facilities: Ethnography and Archaeology Museum; Zoological and Botanical Museum; Biological Research Station; Laboratory "Mathematical Modeling of Pedagogical Systems and Processes"; Laboratory of Archaeology, Anthropology and Trasology; Laboratory of Psychophysical and Social Development of Preschool Age Children; Education Psychology Laboratory; Differential Psychology Laboratory; Laboratory of Organic Synthesis and Analysis; Laboratory of Physical Training

Libraries: 802,630 vols (185,963 academic monographs, 341,373 textbooks and study manuals, 107,924 fiction publications, 167,370 periodical subscriptions), reding rooms, computer equipment

Last Updated: 16/04/12

PERM STATE PHARMACEUTICAL ACADEMY

Permskaja Gosudarstvennaja Farmatsevtičeskaja Akademija

ul. Polevaja, 2, Perm', 614990 Permskij kraj
Tel: +7(342) 233-52-12
Fax: +7(342) 233-55-01
EMail: perm@pfa.ru
Website: http://www.pfa.ru/

Rector: Tatjana Fedorovna Odegova

Faculties

Postgraduate Studies (Pharmacy)

Programmes

Pharmacy (Pharmacy)

Further Information: Also Preparatory Courses for foreign students

History: Founded 1937, acquired present status and title 1995.

Governing Bodies: Scientific Council

Academic Year: September to June (September-January; February-June)

Admission Requirements: Secondary school certificate (Attestat o srednem obrazovanii)

Fees: None

Main Language(s) of Instruction: Russian

Degrees and Diplomas: *Specialist Diploma*: Pharmacy

Special Facilities: Biological Garden

Libraries: 250,000 vols

Last Updated: 20/09/11

PETERSBURG STATE TRANSPORT UNIVERSITY

Peterburgskij Gosudarstvennyj Universitet Putej Soobščenija

Moskovskij prosp. 9, Sankt-Peterburg 190031
Tel: +7(812) 310-25-21 +7(812) 310-17-24
Fax: +7(812) 315-26-21
EMail: pochta@pgups.edu
Website: http://www.pgups.ru/

Rector: Valerij I. Kovalev

Faculties

Bridge and Tunnel Construction (Bridge Engineering; Civil Engineering; Industrial Engineering; Transport Engineering); **Civil Engineering** (Civil Engineering); **Economics and Social Management** (Accountancy; Economics; Management; Marketing; Transport Management); **Electrical Engineering** (Electrical

Engineering); **Electromechanical Engineering** (Electrical and Electronic Engineering; Hydraulic Engineering; Railway Engineering; Railway Transport); **Mechanical Engineering** (Mechanical Engineering; Railway Engineering); **Transport Management** (Railway Transport; Transport Management)

Further Information: Also preparatory faculty, part-time and evening departments

History: Founded 1809 as Institute of Railway Engineers.

Degrees and Diplomas: *Bakalavr*; *Specialist Diploma*; *Magistr*; *Kandidat Nauk*

Libraries: 1,300,000 vols; 397 periodical subscriptions

Last Updated: 02/03/12

PETROZAVODSK STATE MUSIC CONSERVATORY (ACADEMY) NAMED AFTER A.K. GLAZUNOV

Petrozavodskaja Gosudarstvennaja Konservatorija (Akademija) im. A.K. Glazunova

ul. Leningradskaja, 16, Petrozavodsk,
185031 Respublika Karelija
Tel: +7(8142) 70-60-06 +7(8412) 76-93-88
Fax: +7(8142) 70-60-06
EMail: rcons@karelia.ru
Website: http://conservatory.karelia.ru/

Rector: Vladimir A. Solovjev (2002-)

Departments

Chamber Music and Accompaniment (Music); **Choir Conducting** (Conducting); **Drama** (Theatre); **Finno-Ugrian Music** (Music); **History of Music** (Musicology); **Piano** (Musical Instruments); **Russian Folk Instruments** (Folklore); **String Instruments** (Musical Instruments); **Theory of Music and Composition** (Music Education; Music Theory and Composition); **Vocal Music** (Singing); **Woodwind, Brass and Percussion Instruments** (Musical Instruments)

History: Founded 1967 as a branch of Saint-Petersburg State Conservatoire, became independent institution 1991.

Governing Bodies: Academic Council

Academic Year: September to June (September-January; February-June)

Admission Requirements: Secondary school certificate (Attestat o srednem obrazovanii) or equivalent (Diplom muzykalnogo učilišča)

Main Language(s) of Instruction: Russian, English, Korean

Degrees and Diplomas: *Specialist Diploma*

Student Residential Facilities: For 640 students

Libraries: General Library, 71,460 vols; Music Library, 41,840 vols; 15,350 records

Last Updated: 06/04/12

PETROZAVODSK STATE UNIVERSITY

Petrozavodskij Gosudarstvennyj Universitet (PETRSU)

prosp. Lenina, 33, Petrozavodsk, 185640 Respublika Karelija
Tel: +7(8142) 78-51-40
Fax: +7(8142) 71-10-00
EMail: office@psu.karelia.ru
Website: http://petrsu.karelia.ru/

Rector: Anatoly V. Voronin
EMail: rectorat@psu.karelia.ru; rector@psu.karelia.ru; voronin@psu.karelia.ru

Faculties

Agrotechnology (Agricultural Equipment; Agriculture; Agronomy; Animal Husbandry; Zoology); **Baltic and Finnish Philology and Culture** (Baltic Languages; Philology); **Ecology and Biology** (Biology; Botany; Chemistry; Ecology; Molecular Biology; Plant Pathology; Zoology); **Economics** (Accountancy; Economics; Management); **Engineering** (Architecture; Civil Engineering; Engineering Management; Mechanical Engineering; Water Management); **Forestry and Wood Technology** (Forest Products; Forestry; Paper Technology; Wood Technology); **Geology and Mining** (Geology; Geophysics; Mining Engineering); **History** (History); **Law** (Civil Law; Constitutional Law; Criminal Law; International Law; Law); **Mathematics** (Applied Mathematics; Mathematics); **Medicine** (Gynaecology and Obstetrics; Medicine; Midwifery; Paediatrics; Pharmacology; Pharmacy; Surgery); **Philology** (Classical Languages; German; Journalism; Literature; Philology; Russian; Scandinavian Languages); **Physics** (Electronic Engineering; Physics); **Political and Social Sciences** (International Relations; Modern Languages; Political Sciences; Social Work; Sociology); **Tourism** (Tourism)

History: Founded 1940 with four Faculties, some of which were later reorganized or replaced by others in order to adapt the structure of the University to the particular needs of the country.

Governing Bodies: Academic Council

Academic Year: September to July (September-January; February-July)

Admission Requirements: Secondary education certificate (Attestat o srednem obrazovanii) and entrance examination

Fees: None for Russian Federation citizens

Main Language(s) of Instruction: Russian

International Co-operation: With universities in Finland, Sweden, Norway, USA

Degrees and Diplomas: *Bakalavr*; *Specialist Diploma*; *Magistr*; *Kandidat Nauk*; *Doktor Nauk*

Student Services: Academic counselling, Canteen, Employment services, Foreign student adviser, Foreign Studies Centre, Health services, Language programs, Social counselling, Sports facilities

Student Residential Facilities: Yes

Special Facilities: Geology Museum. Geo-Botany Museum. Botanical Gardens. Theatre Studio.

Libraries: c. 1,003,797 vols

Last Updated: 06/04/12

PRIMORSKY STATE ACADEMY OF AGRICULTURE

Primorskaja Gosudarstvennaja Sel'skokhozjajstvennaja Akademija (PSAA)

ul. Bljukhera 44, Ussurijsk,
692510 Primorskij kraj
Tel: +7(4234) 26-54-60 +7(4234) 26-37-46
Fax: +7(4234) 26-54-60
EMail: pgsa@rambler.ru
Website: http://www.primacad.ru

Rector: Andrei Edwardovich Komin

Institutes

Animal Husbandry and Veterinary Science (Animal Husbandry; Veterinary Science); **Economics and Business** (Accountancy; Agricultural Business; Economics); **Farm Mechanization** (Agricultural Equipment); **Forestry** (Forestry); **Humanities** (Economics; History; Modern Languages; Philosophy; Physical Education; Social Sciences); **Land Management and Farming** (Agronomy; Crop Production; Environmental Studies; Soil Science; Water Science); **Soil Sciences and Environmental Engineering** (Agricultural Management; Agrobiology; Ecology; Environmental Engineering; Soil Science; Water Management; Water Science)

History: Founded as Primorsky Agricultural Institute 1957. Acquired present name and status 1995.

Governing Bodies: Ministry of Agriculture

Academic Year: September to June

Admission Requirements: Secondary school certificate

Main Language(s) of Instruction: Russian

Degrees and Diplomas: *Bakalavr*; *Specialist Diploma*; *Doktor Nauk*

Student Residential Facilities: Yes

Special Facilities: Experimental Training Farm, Music studio

Libraries: 380,000 vols

Last Updated: 27/02/12

PSKOV LAW INSTITUTE OF THE FEDERAL PENITENTIARY SERVICE

Pskovskij Juridičeskij Institut Federal'noj Služby Ispolnenija Nakazanij

Zonal'noe Shosse 28, Pskov 180014
Tel: +7(8112) 62-31-41 +7(8112) 62-31-67
Fax: +7(8112) 62-31-41
EMail: pui_fsin@ellink.ru
Website: http://www.puifsin.ru/

Rector: Aleksei Alekseevich Chistjakov

Programmes

Law (Criminology; Law; Military Science)

History: Created 1992.

Degrees and Diplomas: *Bakalavr*, *Specialist Diploma*

Last Updated: 27/02/12

PSKOV STATE UNIVERSITY

Pskovskij Gosudarstvennyj Universitet

pl. Lenina 2, Pskov 180760
Tel: +7(8112) 75-29-46
Fax: +7(8112) 75-34-90
EMail: info@pskgu.ru
Website: http://www.pskgu.ru

Rector: Jurij Anatol'evich Dem'janenko

Faculties

Computer Science (Applied Mathematics; Computer Science; Information Technology; Physics); **Educational Technology** (Educational Technology); **Electrical Engineering** (Electrical Engineering; Energy Engineering); **Engineering** (Building Technologies; Civil Engineering); **Finance and Economics** (Economics; Finance); **Foreign Languages** (English; French; German); **History** (Archaeology; History; Museum Studies); **Law** (Law); **Management** (Management); **Mechanical Engineering** (Mechanical Engineering); **Natural Sciences and Geography** (Botany; Chemistry; Ecology; Geography; Plant and Crop Protection; Zoology); **Philology** (Literature; Philology; Russian); **Physics and Mathematics** (Mathematics; Mathematics Education; Physics); **Psychology** (Educational Psychology; Psychology; Social Psychology); **Technology and Design** (Design; Fine Arts; Technology)

History: Created 2011 from Pskov State Pedagogical University named after Kirov, and Pskov State Polytechnic Institute.

Degrees and Diplomas: *Bakalavr*, *Specialist Diploma*

Last Updated: 27/02/12

PUSHCHINO STATE INSTITUTE FOR NATURAL SCIENCE

Puščinskij Gosudarstvennyj Estestvenno-Naučnyj Institut

prosp. Nauki 3, Puščino, 142290 Moskovskaja oblast'
Tel: +7(4967) 73-18-57 +7(4967) 73-25-38 +7(4967) 73-26-79
Fax: +7(4967) 73-27-11
EMail: nir_pushgu@itaec.ru
Website: http://www.pushgu.ru

Rector: Mikhail Borisovich Beinstein (2006-)

Faculties

Astrophysics and Radio-astronomy (Astrophysics; Physics; Radiophysics); **Cell Biophysics** (Biochemistry; Biophysics; Cell Biology); **Mathematics and Biology** (Biology; Mathematics); **Microbiology and Biotechnology** (Biochemistry; Biotechnology; Genetics; Microbiology; Molecular Biology); **Physio-chemical Biology and Biotechnology** (Biochemistry; Biological and Life Sciences; Biotechnology; Microbiology; Pharmacology; Physical Chemistry); **Physiology and Biophysics** (Biophysics; Neurosciences; Physiology); **Soil Sciences, Ecology and Environmental Studies** (Biochemistry; Ecology; Environmental Studies; Plant Pathology; Soil Science)

History: Founded 1992 as Puščinskij Gosudarstvennyj Universitet (Pushchino State University). Acquired current title 2011. A postgraduate Institution.

Governing Bodies: Scientific Board

Academic Year: September to June (September-January; February-June)

Admission Requirements: Bachelor's degree; Diploma of higher education

Main Language(s) of Instruction: Russian

Degrees and Diplomas: *Magistr*, *Kandidat Nauk*

Student Residential Facilities: For c. 240 students

Libraries: c. 700,000 vols

Last Updated: 05/04/12

IAU PYATIGORSK STATE LINGUISTIC UNIVERSITY

Pjatigorskij Gosudarstvennyj Lingvističeskij Universitet (PSLU)

prosp. Kalinina 9, Pjatigorsk, 357532 Stavropol'skij kraj
Tel: +7(8793) 400-000
Fax: +7(8793) 400-110
EMail: rector@pglu.ru
Website: http://www.pglu.ru

Rector: Alexander Pavlovich Gorbunov (2005-)
Tel: +7(8793) 400-505, Fax: +7(8793) 400-110
EMail: gorbunov@pglu.ru

Vice-Rector, Administration: Alexander Kolyadin
Tel: +7(8793) 400-133, Fax: +7(8793) 400-602
EMail: kolyadin@pglu.ru

International Relations: Viktor Evgenyevich Mishin, Director, International Relations and Programmes
Tel: +7(8793) 400-427, Fax: +7(8793) 400-527
EMail: mishin@pglu.ru

Departments

Postgraduate Studies *(Doctoral School)* (Education; Educational Technology; Germanic Languages; History; International Relations; Linguistics; Peace and Disarmament; Pedagogy; Political Sciences; Romance Languages) *Director*: Evgenia Vartanova

Faculties

English and Germanic Languages (Applied Linguistics; English; German; Germanic Languages; Linguistics) *Dean*: Dina Akselroud; **English and Romance Languages** (English; French; Hotel and Restaurant; Italian; Linguistics; Romance Languages; Tourism) *Dean*: Irina Akopyants; **French and English Languages** (English; French; Linguistics; Parks and Recreation; Sports; Tourism) *Dean*: Alexander Moiseev; **German and English Languages** (Advertising and Publicity; English; German; Linguistics; Tourism) *Dean*: Tatiana Yanukyan; **Government and Public Administration** (English; French; German; Government; Human Resources; Islamic Theology; Management; Oriental Studies; Orthodox Theology; Public Administration); **International Relations** (Arabic; English; French; Greek; International Law; International Relations; Journalism; Public Relations; Turkish); **Philology** *(Russian Language and Literature)* (English; Foreign Languages Education; French; German; Philology; Russian; Spanish); **Psychology** (Psychology); **Spanish and English Languages** (English; Information Technology; Linguistics; Spanish; Tourism)

Institutes

Extended Educational Programmes *(Life Long Learning)* (Accountancy; Foreign Languages Education; Graphic Arts; Information Management; Management; Marketing; Social Psychology); **Integral Programmes for Higher and Postgraduate Education** *(Qualification upgrading)*

Schools

Business (Business Administration; Business and Commerce); **Translating and Interpreting** (Arabic; Chinese; English; French; German; Linguistics; Polish; Spanish; Translation and Interpretation)

Further Information: Also Russian language for International students (full year, short-term, semester). Test of Russian Foreign Language (TORFL). Study Abroad programmes

History: Founded in 1939 as Pyatigorsk State Teachers Training College. Became Pyatigorsk State Pedagogical Institute of Foreign Languages in 1961. Acquired current title and status 1995

Governing Bodies: University Council

Academic Year: September to June

Admission Requirements: Russian Students, Secondary school certificate (Svidetelstvo ob obrazovanii) and results of Common National Examination (CNE); International Students, Secondary school certificate and Test of Russain as a Foreign Language (TORFL), minimum 1st level.

Fees: ((Rubles): 79,000 per annum

Main Language(s) of Instruction: Russian

International Co-operation: with institutions in France, Germany, Spain, China, USA, Egypt, Belgium

Accrediting Agencies: Federal Agency of Education and Science

Degrees and Diplomas: *Bakalavr*: Psychology; Linguistics; Philology; Management; Conflict Resolution; International Law (BA), 4 yrs; *Specialist Diploma*: Advertising and Publicity; Government and Public Administration; Personnel Management; Organizational Management; Theology; Foreign Languages and Cultures Education; Translation and Interpretation; Russian as a Foreign Language; Intercultural Communications in Customs Affairs; Hospitality Service and Tourism; Intercultural Communication in Tourism; Intercultural Communication in Commerce; Applied Linguistics; International Relations; International Journalism; Public Relations; Recreation and Sports and Health Tourism; Information Protection Technology, 5 yrs; *Magistr*: Linguistics (MA), a further 2 yrs; *Kandidat Nauk*: Philosophy; Philology; Linguistics; Pedagogy; Teaching Technologies; Psychology; Political Science; International Relations, a further 3 yrs

Student Services: Academic counselling, Canteen, Cultural centre, Employment services, Foreign student adviser, Foreign Studies Centre, Health services, Language programs, Nursery care, Social counselling, Sports facilities

Student Residential Facilities: 5 campus dormitories for 1,600 students

Special Facilities: Film Studio; TV Studio; Computer Labs; Audio-training labs; Museum

Libraries: University Library c. 732.00 vols

Publications: Caucasus Philology *(biannually)*; PSLU Herald, Scientific research journal on linguitics and social science *(quarterly)*

Press or Publishing House: PSLU Publishing House

Academic Staff *2008-2009*	MEN	WOMEN	TOTAL
FULL-TIME	123	418	**541**
PART-TIME	24	3	**27**
STAFF WITH DOCTORATE			
FULL-TIME	109	255	**364**
PART-TIME	24	3	**27**
Student Numbers *2008-2009*			
All (Foreign Included)	929	4,530	**5,459**
FOREIGN ONLY	81	53	**134**

Part-time students, 950. **Evening students**, 333.
Last Updated: 30/03/12

PYATIGORSK STATE PHARMACEUTICAL ACADEMY

Pjatigorskaja Gosudarstvennaja Farmacevtičeskaja Akademija

prosp. Kalinina 11, Pjatigorsk, 357532 Stavropol'skij kraj
Tel: +7(8793) 32-44-74 +7(8793) 32-92-66
Fax: +7(8793) 32-92-67
EMail: farmnauka@mail.ru; sprorector@pgfa.ru
Website: http://www.pgfa.ru/

Rector: Mikhail Vital'evich Gavrilin

Programmes

Pharmacy (Pharmacology; Pharmacy)

History: Created 1943.

Degrees and Diplomas: *Specialist Diploma*
Last Updated: 27/02/12

RJAZAN STATE RADIO ENGINEERING UNIVERSITY

Rjazanskij Gosudarstvennyj Radiotekhničeskij Universitet (RSREA)

ul. Gagarina, 59/1, Rjazan 390005
Tel: +7(4912) 46-03-03
Fax: +7(4912) 92-22-15
EMail: rgrtu@rsreu.ru
Website: http://www.rgrta.ryazan.ru

Rector: Viktor Sergeevich Gurov
EMail: rector@rsreu.ru; gurov.v.s@rsreu.ru

Faculties

Automation *Dean*: Anatoliy Bobikov; **Computer Technology** (Applied Mathematics; Computer Science; Information Technology; Mathematics and Computer Science; Mechanics); **Electronics** (Electronic Engineering; Laser Engineering; Physics); **Engineering Economics** (Administration; Ecology; Econometrics; Economics; Engineering Management; Environmental Management; Finance); **Information Technology** (Computer Science; Graphic Design; Information Technology; Mathematics); **Radio Engineering** (Radiophysics; Telecommunications Engineering)

Institutes

Humanities (History; Law; Philosophy; Political Sciences)

Further Information: Branches also in Znamensk, Sasovo.

History: Founded 1951, acquired title of Rjazanskaja Gosudarstvennaja Radiotehničeskaja Akademija (Rjazan State Radio Engineering Academy) in 1993. Acquired current title 2006.

Governing Bodies: Academic Board

Academic Year: September to June

Admission Requirements: Secondary school certificate (Attestat o srednem obrazovanii) and entrance examination

Main Language(s) of Instruction: Russian

Degrees and Diplomas: *Bakalavr*; *Specialist Diploma*; *Magistr*; *Kandidat Nauk*; *Doktor Nauk*

Student Services: Academic counselling, Canteen, Cultural centre, Employment services, Foreign student adviser, Foreign Studies Centre, Health services, Language programs, Sports facilities

Student Residential Facilities: Yes

Special Facilities: Museum. Radio studio

Libraries: c. 700,000 vols
Last Updated: 11/01/12

RJAZAN STATE UNIVERSITY NAMED AFTER S.A. JESENIN

Rjazanskij Gosudarstvennyj Universitet im. S.A. Jesenina (RSPU)

ul. Svoboda 46, Rjazan 390000
Tel: +7(4912) 28-04-83 +7(4912) 28-03-89
Fax: +7(4912) 28-14-35
EMail: rsu@rsu.edu.ru
Website: http://www.rsu.edu.ru/

Rector: Irina Mikhailovna Sheina

Faculties

Economics (Accountancy; Economics); **History and International Relations** (Advertising and Publicity; Art Education; History; International Relations); **Law and Political Sciences** (Administrative Law; Civil Law; Commercial Law; Constitutional Law; Criminal Law; Criminology; Fiscal Law; Labour Law; Law; Political Sciences); **Natural Sciences** (Biology; Chemistry; Ecology; Geography; Science Education; Tourism); **Physical Education and Sport** (Physical Education; Sports); **Physics and Mathematics** (Computer Science; Mathematics; Mathematics Education; Physics; Science Education); **Russian Philology and Culture** (Art Education; Cultural Studies; Journalism; Literature; Music Education; Native Language; Philology; Public Relations; Russian; Theology); **Sociology and Management** (Human Resources; Management; Sociology)

Institutes

Modern Languages (Chinese; English; Foreign Languages Education; French; German; Japanese; Linguistics; Modern Languages; Spanish; Traditional Eastern Medicine); **Psychology, Pedagogy**

and Social Work (Pedagogy; Preschool Education; Primary Education; Psychology; Social Work; Speech Therapy and Audiology)

History: Founded 1853 as College for Women, became Pedagogical University 1918 and aRjazanskij Gosudarstvennyj Pedagogičeskij Universitet (Rjazan State Pedagogical University) in 1994. Acquired current title and status 2011.

Governing Bodies: University Administration

Academic Year: September to June

Admission Requirements: Secondary school certificate (Attestat o srednem obščem obrazovanii)

Main Language(s) of Instruction: Russian, English

International Co-operation: With universities in Germany, USA, Japan.

Accrediting Agencies: Federal Agency of Education

Degrees and Diplomas: *Bakalavr*; *Specialist Diploma*; *Magistr*; *Kandidat Nauk*; *Doktor Nauk*

Student Services: Academic counselling, Canteen, Employment services, Foreign student adviser, Foreign Studies Centre, Health services, Language programs, Sports facilities

Student Residential Facilities: Yes

Special Facilities: Museum. Observatory. Movie studio

Libraries: Main Library, 755,510 vols; specialized libraries

Last Updated: 05/04/12

RJAZAN STATE UNIVERSITY OF AGROTECHNOLOGY NAMED AFTER P.A. KOSTYČEV

Rjazanskij Gosudarstvennyj Agrotekhnologičeskij Universitet im. P.A. Kostyčeva

ul. Kostyčeva 1, Rjazan 390044

Tel: +7(4912) 35-35-01

Fax: +7(4912) 34-30-96 +7(4912) 34-08-42

Website: http://www.rgatu.ru/

Rector: Nikolai Vladmirovich Byshov

Faculties

Agriculture and Ecology (Agronomy; Ecology; Forestry; Plant and Crop Protection; Soil Science); **Economics** (Business Computing; Economics; Management; Social Work); **Engineering** (Agricultural Engineering; Agricultural Equipment; Maintenance Technology; Physics); **Finance** (Accountancy; Finance); **Road Transport** (Road Engineering; Road Transport; Transport Engineering); **Technology** (Dairy; Food Technology); **Veterinary Medicine and Biotechnology** (Biology; Biotechnology; Veterinary Science; Zoology)

History: Created 1949 as Rjazanskij Sel'skohozjajstvennyj Institut im. P.A. Kostyčeva (Rjazan Agricultural Institute named after P.A. Kostyčev. Become Rjazanskaja Gosudarstvennaja Sel'skohozjajstvennaja Akademija im. P.A. Kostyčeva (Rjazan State Academy of Agriculture named after P.A. Kostyčev) in 1995. Acquired current title 2008.

Degrees and Diplomas: *Bakalavr*; *Specialist Diploma*; *Magistr*

Last Updated: 27/02/12

RJAZAN STATE UNIVERSITY OF MEDICINE NAMED AFTER I.P. PAVLOV

Rjazanskij Gosudarstvennyj Meditsinskij Universitet im. akademika I.P.Pavlova

ul. Vysokovol'tnaja 9, Rjazan 390026

Tel: +7(4912) 98-40-67 +7(4912) 46-08-00

Fax: +7(4912) 46-08-08

EMail: rzgmu@rzgmu.ru

Website: http://www.rzgmu.ru/

Rector: Roman Evgenevich Kalinin EMail: rector@rzgmu.ru

Faculties

Dentistry (Dentistry; Stomatology); **General Medicine** (Health Administration; Medicine; Psychology; Surgery); **Pharmacy** (Pharmacy)

History: Founded 1943. Acquired current title 1950 to mark 100th anniversary of the birth of Nobel prize winner Pavlov and was moved to his hometown of Ryazan.

Governing Bodies: Rector; Vice-Rectors

Academic Year: September-June

Admission Requirements: Secondary school certificate (Attestat o Srednem (Polnom) Obshchem Obrazovanii); Entrance examination

Main Language(s) of Instruction: Russian, English, French

International Co-operation: With universities in Germany

Accrediting Agencies: Ministry of Education and Science

Degrees and Diplomas: *Specialist Diploma*

Student Services: Canteen, Cultural centre, Foreign student adviser, Foreign Studies Centre, Health services, Sports facilities

Special Facilities: Botanical Garden; Conference facilities; Anatomy museum; Vivarium; Botanical Garden; Theatre; Puppet theatre; Art Gallery

Libraries: c. 765,000 vols, internet

Last Updated: 05/04/12

ROSTOV LAW INSTITUTE OF THE RUSSIAN MINISTRY OF INTERNAL AFFAIRS

Rostovskij Juridiceskij Institut MVD Rossii (RJI)

ul. Marsala Eremenko 83, Rostov-na-Donu 344015

Tel: +7(863) 278-6017 +7(863) 278-6490

EMail: info@ruimvd.ru

Website: http://www.ruimvd.ru

Rector: Gennady Barkovsky

Faculties

Law (Administrative Law; Criminal Law; Criminology; Law)

History: Founded 1961. Acquired present status and title 1998.

Governing Bodies: Institute Administration Departments

Academic Year: September to July

Admission Requirements: School certificate

Fees: None

Main Language(s) of Instruction: Russian

International Co-operation: With universities in USA, Germany, Hungary, Canada, United Kingdom, Ukraine, Moldova

Accrediting Agencies: Ministry of Education and Science

Degrees and Diplomas: *Specialist Diploma*; *Magistr (MSc)*; *Doktor Nauk (PhD)*

Student Services: Academic counselling, Canteen, Cultural centre, Employment services, Health services, Language programs, Social counselling, Sports facilities

Student Residential Facilities: Yes.

Special Facilities: Museum.

Libraries: General and professional library

Publications: Creation, Literature publications *(biennially)*; Lawyer, Federal, scientific journal *(quarterly)*; Philosophy of Law, Federal, scientific journal *(quarterly)*

Press or Publishing House: Rostovskij Juridiceskij Institut MVD Rossii Publishing Department

Last Updated: 02/03/12

ROSTOV STATE ECONOMICS UNIVERSITY 'RINKH'

Rostovskij Gosudarstvennyj Ekonomičeskij Universitet 'RINX'

ul. Bol'shaja Sadovaja 69, Rostov-na-Donu 344002

Tel: +7(863) 240-1304

Fax: +7(863) 240-4344

EMail: rector@rsue.ru; main@rsue.ru

Website: http://www.rsue.ru/

Rector: Nikolai Gennadievich Kuznetsov EMail: rector@rsue.ru

Faculties

Accountancy (Accountancy; Statistics; Taxation); **Commerce and Marketing** (Advertising and Publicity; Business Administration; Business and Commerce; Economics; Marketing; Safety Engineering; Taxation; Transport Management); **Finance** (Finance); **Information Technology and Management** (Business Administration; Business Computing; Human Resources; Information Management; Information Technology; Management); **Law** (Law; Taxation); **Linguistics and Journalism** (Journalism; Linguistics;

Regional Studies); **National and International Economics** (Business Administration; Economics; International Economics; Management)

Further Information: Also Branches in Azov, Čerkesk, Georgievsk, Salsk, Matveevo-Kurgan, Millerovo, Bataysk, Yesk, Aksay, Kislovodsk, Stavropol, Derbent and Mahatčkala.

History: Founded 1931, acquired present title 1996.

Academic Year: September to June (September-January; February-June)

Main Language(s) of Instruction: Russian

Degrees and Diplomas: *Bakalavr*; *Specialist Diploma*; *Magistr*; *Kandidat Nauk*; *Doktor Nauk*

Student Services: Canteen, Cultural centre, Health services, Sports facilities

Student Residential Facilities: For 400 students

Last Updated: 19/12/11

ROSTOV STATE MEDICAL UNIVERSITY

Rostovskij Gosudarstvennyj Meditsinskij Universitet

Nahičevanskij per. 29, Rostov-na-Donu 344022

Tel: +7(863) 250-42-00 +7(863) 250-41-93

Fax: +7(863) 201-43-90

EMail: okt@rostgmu.ru

Website: http://www.rostgmu.ru/

Rector: Aleksei Alekseevich Savis'ko

Programmes

Medicine (Laboratory Techniques; Medical Auxiliaries; Medical Technology; Medicine; Midwifery; Nursing; Paediatrics; Paramedical Sciences; Pharmacy; Stomatology)

History: Created 1930.

Degrees and Diplomas: *Bakalavr*; *Specialist Diploma*

Last Updated: 28/02/12

ROSTOV STATE MUSIC CONSERVATORY (ACADEMY) NAMED AFTER S.V RACHMANINOV

Rostovskaja Gosudarstvennaja Konservatorija (Akademija) im. S.V. Rakhmaninova

prosp. Budjennovskij 23, Rostov-na-Donu 344007

Tel: +7(863) 262-36-14 +7(863) 262-46-45

Fax: +7(863) 262-35-84

EMail: rostcons@aaanet.ru

Website: http://www.rostcons.ru

Rector: Aleksandr S. Danilov (1988-)

Faculties

Orchestral studies (Conducting; Music; Music Education; Music Theory and Composition; Musical Instruments); **Piano and Vocal studies** (Musical Instruments; Singing)

History: Founded 1967 as Rostov Musical Pedagogical Institute. Became Rostov State Music Conservatory 1992. Acquired present status and title 2004.

Governing Bodies: Rectorat

Academic Year: September to June

Admission Requirements: Secondary school certificate or diploma of a college of Music

Main Language(s) of Instruction: Russian, English

Degrees and Diplomas: *Specialist Diploma*; *Magistr*

Student Services: Academic counselling, Canteen, Foreign student adviser, Health services, Language programs, Social counselling, Sports facilities

Student Residential Facilities: Student Hostel

Special Facilities: Phonotheque, Recording Studio

Libraries: Over 300,000 vols

Last Updated: 06/03/12

ROSTOV STATE UNIVERSITY OF CIVIL ENGINEERING

Rostovskij Gosudarstvennyj Stroitel'nyj Universitet (RSUCE)

ul. Socialističeskaja 162, Rostov-na-Donu 344022

Tel: +7(863) 227-73-81 +7(863) 263-65-35

Fax: +7(863) 227-73-81 +7(863) 227-75-92

EMail: rgsu@rgsu.ru; demchenko@rgsu.ru

Website: http://www.rgsu.ru

President: Viktor Ivanovich Shumeiko (2008-)

Rector: Vladimir Stefanovich Vagin

Chief of International Education and Cooperation Department: Alexander Victorivich Kaklugin
Tel: +7(8632) 634-589 EMail: inter@rgsu.donpac.ru

International Relations: Taisiya Anatolievna Kudinova, Head of Department Tel: +7(8632) 277-594, Fax: +7(8632) 277-594

Institutes

Construction Technologies and Materials (Building Technologies; Chemistry; Geological Engineering; Physics); **Ecological Systems Engineering** (Environmental Engineering; Heating and Refrigeration; Production Engineering; Safety Engineering; Water Management); **Economics and Management** (Accountancy; Advertising and Publicity; Economics; Finance; Management; Marketing; Surveying and Mapping); **Industrial and Civil Engineering** (Civil Engineering; Heritage Preservation; Industrial Engineering; Information Management; Information Technology; Management; Real Estate; Restoration of Works of Art); **Road Transport Engineering** (Automotive Engineering; Bridge Engineering; Road Engineering; Safety Engineering; Transport Engineering; Transport Management); **Technology and Materials Engineering** (Automation and Control Engineering; Construction Engineering; Materials Engineering; Production Engineering; Technology); **Urban Development and Architecture** (Architecture; Civil Engineering; Environmental Engineering; Town Planning; Urban Studies)

Further Information: Also programmes in Azov and Taganrog, and 21 research laboratories

History: Founded 1944, acquired present status and title 1997.

Academic Year: September to June (September-January; February-June)

Admission Requirements: Secondary school certificate (Attestat o srednem obrazovanii)

Main Language(s) of Instruction: Russian. Also some special courses in English

International Co-operation: With universities in Germany, Mexico, China, Turkey.

Accrediting Agencies: Ministry of Education and Science

Degrees and Diplomas: *Bakalavr*; *Specialist Diploma*; *Magistr*; *Kandidat Nauk*; *Doktor Nauk*

Student Services: Academic counselling, Canteen, Cultural centre, Employment services, Foreign student adviser, Foreign Studies Centre, Health services, Language programs, Social counselling, Sports facilities

Student Residential Facilities: For c. 1,000 students

Special Facilities: Historical Museum. Concert hall. Movie Studio.

Libraries: Total, 700,000 vols

Publications: Izvestiya *(quarterly)*

Press or Publishing House: RSBU Publishing House

Last Updated: 20/01/12

ROSTOV STATE UNIVERSITY OF RAILWAY COMMUNICATIONS

Rostovskij Gosudarstvennyj Universitet Putej Soobščenija

pl. Rostovskogo Strelkogo Polka Narodnogo Opolchenija, 2, Rostov-na-Donu 344038

Tel: +7(863) 230-21-80 +7(863) 245-03-81

Fax: +7(863) 245-06-13

EMail: oav@rgups.ru; timoshek@rgups.ru; up_del@rgups.ru

Website: http://www.rgups.ru

Rector: Vladimir I. Kolesnikov (1996-) EMail: rek@rgups.ru

Faculties

Automation and Telecommunications Engineering (Automation and Control Engineering; Telecommunications Engineering); **Construction Engineering** (Construction Engineering); **Economics, Management, and Law** (Economics; Law; Management); **Electromechanical Engineering** (Electronic Engineering; Mechanical Engineering); **Energy Engineering** (Energy Engineering; Physics); **Humanities** (History; Modern Languages; Pedagogy; Philosophy; Political Sciences; Psychology; Social Work; Sociology; Sports; Tourism); **Power Engineering** (Power Engineering); **Road-Building Machines** (Building Technologies; Machine Building; Road Engineering); **Transport Management** (Transport Management)

Further Information: Branches also in Bataisk, Vladikavkaz, Volgograd, Liski, Kamensk-Shakhtinskij, Tikhoretsk, Krasnodar, Kropotkin, Mineralnyje Vody, Tuapse.

History: Founded 1929 as Institute of Railway Engineers, acquired present status and title 1993.

Governing Bodies: Scientific Council, Rectorate

Academic Year: September to June (September-January; February-June)

Admission Requirements: Secondary school certificate (Attestat o srednem obrazovanii)

Main Language(s) of Instruction: Russian, English, German, French

International Co-operation: With universities in Poland, Germany, United Kingdom. Also participates in the German Academic Exchange Service programme, LINK. Special arrangements with Open University Business School, United Kingdom.

Accrediting Agencies: Ministry of Education

Degrees and Diplomas: *Bakalavr*; *Specialist Diploma*; *Magistr*; *Kandidat Nauk*

Student Services: Academic counselling, Canteen, Cultural centre, Employment services, Foreign student adviser, Foreign Studies Centre, Health services, Language programs, Nursery care, Social counselling, Sports facilities

Special Facilities: Museum of Transport History

Libraries: c. 670,000 vols

Press or Publishing House: Publishing House

Last Updated: 11/01/12

RUSSIAN ACADEMY OF MUSIC NAMED AFTER GNESINYH

Rossijskaja Akademija Muzyki im. Gnesinyh

ul. Povarskaja 30/36,
Moskva 121069
Tel: +7(095) 691-56-62
Fax: +7(095) 690-49-08
EMail: priem@gnesin-academy.ru; mailbox@gnesin-academy.ru
Website: http://www.gnesin-academy.ru/

Rector: Galina Vasilevna Mayarovskaja

Programmes

Composition (Music Theory and Composition); **Conducting** (Conducting); **Folk Instruments** (Musical Instruments); **Musical Art** (Performing Arts); **Musical Interpretation** (Performing Arts); **Musicology** (Musicology); **Sound Production** (Sound Engineering (Acoustics)); **Vocal Arts** (Singing)

History: Founded 1944.

Governing Bodies: Academic Council of the Academy

Main Language(s) of Instruction: Russian

International Co-operation: With universities in USA, Korea, China, Serbia, Finland, Germany.

Degrees and Diplomas: *Bakalavr*; *Specialist Diploma*; *Magistr*; *Kandidat Nauk*

Student Services: Canteen, Foreign student adviser, Language programs

Last Updated: 22/09/11

RUSSIAN ACADEMY OF PAINTING, SCULPTURE AND ARCHITECTURE

Rossijskaja Akademija Živopisi, Vajanija i Zodčestva Il'i Glazunova

ul. Mjasnitskaja 21, Moskva 101000
Tel: +7(495) 621-07-02
Fax: +7(495) 623-06-34
EMail: academy.glazunov@gmail.com
Website: http://www.glazunov-academy.ru

Rector: Ilya Sergeevich Glazunov

Faculties

Architecture (Architecture); **History of Art** (Art History); **Painting** (Painting and Drawing); **Restoration** (Restoration of Works of Art); **Sculpture** (Sculpture)

History: Founded 1987 to replace the Emperor School of Painting, Sculpture and Architecture of Russia.

Academic Year: October to July

Admission Requirements: Secondary school Certificate (Attestat)

Fees: None

Main Language(s) of Instruction: Russian

Accrediting Agencies: Ministry of Education and Science

Degrees and Diplomas: *Specialist Diploma*

Student Services: Academic counselling, Canteen, Cultural centre, Handicapped facilities, Health services, Social counselling

Special Facilities: Museum of National Art for Training and Education

Libraries: More than 52,000 vols; Depositary

Last Updated: 05/04/12

RUSSIAN ACADEMY OF PUBLIC ADMINISTRATION OF THE PRESIDENT OF THE RUSSIAN FEDERATION

Rossijskaja Akademija Gosudarstvennoj Služby pri Prezidente Rossijskoj Federacii

prosp. Vernadskogo 84, Moskva 119606
Tel: +7(495) 436-9924
Fax: +7(495) 434-5700
EMail: atsareva@ur.rags.ru
Website: http://www.rags.ru

Rector: Andrei M. Margolin

Programmes

Postgraduate *(Magistr)* (Administration; Business Computing; Economics; Human Resources; Information Technology; Law; Management; Political Sciences; Psychology; Sociology); **Undergraduate** *(Bakalavr)* (Administration; Advertising and Publicity; Business Computing; Computer Science; Design; Economics; History; Human Resources; Information Technology; International Relations; Law; Management; Political Sciences; Psychology; Service Trades; Sociology)

History: Created 1991.

Degrees and Diplomas: *Bakalavr*; *Specialist Diploma*; *Magistr*; *Kandidat Nauk*; *Doktor Nauk*

Last Updated: 07/12/11

RUSSIAN BALLET ACADEMY NAMED AFTER A.J. VAGANOVA

Akademija Russkogo Baleta im. A J. Vaganovoj

ul. Zodčego Rossi 2, Sankt-Peterburg 191023
Tel: +7(812) 710-42-46 +7(812) 312-17-02
Fax: +7(812) 315-53-90
EMail: academy@vaganova.ru
Website: http://www.vaganova.ru/

Rector: Vera Dorofeeva (2004-)

Programmes

Dance (Dance)

History: Founded by Imperial Decree by the Empress Anna in 1738, the first classes were taught by Jean-Baptiste Lande in the Winter Palace.

Academic Year: September to June

Degrees and Diplomas: *Bakalavr*; *Specialist Diploma*; *Magistr*; *Kandidat Nauk*

Last Updated: 31/07/12

RUSSIAN CUSTOMS ACADEMY

Rossijskaja Tamožennaja Akademija

Komsomolskij prosp, 4, Lubertsi, 140009 Moskovskaja oblast'
Tel: +7(495) 559-00-33 +7(495) 500-13-63
Fax: +7(495) 503-77-36
EMail: rta_2009@mail.ru
Website: http://rta.customs.ru

Rector: Victor S. Chechevatov

Faculties

Customs Management (Taxation); **Economics** (Economics); **Law** (Law)

Further Information: Also branches in St Petersburg, Vladivostok, Rostov-on-Don

History: Created 1993.

Main Language(s) of Instruction: Russian

International Co-operation: With institutions in CIS countries

Degrees and Diplomas: *Specialist Diploma*

Student Services: Academic counselling, Employment services, Foreign student adviser, Foreign Studies Centre, Sports facilities

Last Updated: 10/01/12

RUSSIAN DISTANCE EDUCATION INSTITUTE OF TEXTILE AND LIGHT INDUSTRY

Rossijskij Zaočnyj Institut Tekstil'noj i Legkoj Promyšlennosti (GOU VPO)

ul. Narodnogo Opolčenija 38 Korp 2, Moskva 123298
Tel: +7(499) 943-63-80
Fax: +7(499) 943-63-80
EMail: umu-roszitlp@bk.ru; vvk58@bk.ru
Website: http://www.roszitlp.com/

Rector: Mijhail Ivanovich Semin

Faculties

Economics and Management (Accountancy; Economics; Human Resources; Industrial Management; Management; Marketing; Small Business); **Fashion Industry** (Clothing and Sewing; Fashion Design; Textile Design); **Technology** (Clothing and Sewing; Leather Techniques; Technology); **Textile Technology** (Textile Technology)

History: Founded 1932. Acquired present status 2002.

Academic Year: September to June

Admission Requirements: Secondary school certificate (Attestat o srednem obrazovanii)

Main Language(s) of Instruction: Russian

Degrees and Diplomas: *Bakalavr*; *Specialist Diploma*; *Kandidat Nauk*

Student Services: Canteen, Health services

Last Updated: 28/02/12

RUSSIAN LAW ACADEMY OF THE RUSSIAN FEDERATION MINISTRY OF JUSTICS

Rossijskaja Pravovaja Akademija Ministerstva Justitsii Rossijskoj Federatsii

ul. Azovskaja 2, korp 1, Moskva 117638
Tel: +7(499) 613-47-54
Fax: +7(499) 613-47-54
EMail: rpa@rpa-mjust.ru
Website: http://www.rpa-mu.ru

Rector: Sergei Ivanovich Gerasimov

Programmes

Law (Criminal Law; Criminology; Law)

History: Founded 1970, acquired present status and title 1991. 14 affiliations throughout Russia (St. Petersburg, Kazan, Khabarovsk, etc.). Also known as Gosudarstvennoye obrazovatelnoye uchrezhdeniye vysshego professionalnogo obrazovaniya "Rossiyskaya Pravovaya Akademiya Ministerstva Ustitzii Rossiyskoy Federatzii"/ State-owned educational institution of higher professional learning "The Russian Federation Ministry of Justice Russian Law Academy".

Governing Bodies: Academic Council

Academic Year: September to June

Admission Requirements: Secondary school certificate (Attestat o srednem obrazovanii) and entrance examination

Fees: Free of Charge

Main Language(s) of Instruction: Russian

International Co-operation: With universities in France, Germany, Austria, Switzerland

Degrees and Diplomas: *Bakalavr*; *Specialist Diploma*; *Kandidat Nauk*; *Doktor Nauk*

Student Services: Academic counselling, Canteen, Employment services, Foreign student adviser, Language programs, Social counselling, Sports facilities

Student Residential Facilities: Dorms for Lawyers Refresher Faculty

Libraries: Central Library

Last Updated: 03/04/12

RUSSIAN NATIONAL RESEARCH MEDICAL UNIVERSITY NAMED AFTER N.I. PIROGOV

Rossijskij Natsional'nyj Issledovatel'skij Meditsinskij Universitet im. N.I. Pirogova

ul. Ostrovitjanova 1, Moskva 117997
Tel: +7(495) 434-6129
Fax: +7(495) 434-0329
EMail: rsmu@rsmu.ru; iao@rsmu.ru
Website: http://www.rsmu.ru

Acting Rector: Natal'ja Valentinovna Polunina

Faculties

Biology (Biology); **Dentistry** (Dentistry; Stomatology); **Medicine** (Medicine); **Paediatrics** (Paediatrics); **Pharmacy** (Pharmacy); **Psychology** (Psychology)

History: Founded 1906 as Faculty, became independent institution 1930. Known as Rossijskij Gosudarstvennyj Medicinskij Universitet (Russian State Medical University) from 1991. Acquired current title 2011.

Governing Bodies: Academic Board

Academic Year: September to July (September-January; February-July)

Admission Requirements: Secondary school certificate (Attestat o srednem obrazovanii)

Main Language(s) of Instruction: Russian

Degrees and Diplomas: *Bakalavr*; *Specialist Diploma*; *Kandidat Nauk*: 5 yrs

Student Services: Academic counselling, Canteen, Cultural centre, Employment services, Foreign Studies Centre, Health services, Social counselling, Sports facilities

Student Residential Facilities: For c. 2,500 students

Special Facilities: History of the University Museum; Pirogov Museum

Libraries:c. 1m. vols

Press or Publishing House: Publishing Department

Last Updated: 19/12/11

RUSSIAN STATE ACADEMY OF INTELLECTUAL PROPERTY

Rossijskaja Gosudarstvennaja Akademija Intellektual'noj Sobstvennosti

ul. Miklukho-Maklaja, 55a, Moskva 117279
Tel: +7(495) 330-10-83
Fax: +7(495) 330-10-83
EMail: inst@rgiis.ru
Website: http://rgiis.ru/

Rector: Ivan Anatol'evich Bliznets

Faculties

Law (Civil Law; History of Law; Law; Public Law); **Management** (Management)

History: Created 1968. Previously known as Rossijskij Institut Intellektualnoj Sobstvennosti (Russian Institute of Intellectual Property). Acquired current title 2006.

Degrees and Diplomas: *Bakalavr*; *Specialist Diploma*; *Magistr*

Last Updated: 28/02/12

RUSSIAN STATE AGRARIAN UNIVERSITY – MOSCOW AGRICULTURAL ACADEMY NAMED AFTER K.A. TIMIRYAZEV

Rossijskij Gosudarstvennyj Agrarny Universitet – Moskovskaya Selskohosyaistvennaya Akademiya imeni K.A. Timiryezeva (RSAU-MTAA)

ul. Timirjazevskaja 49, Moskva 127550

Tel: +7(495) 976-04-80

Fax: +7(495) 976-04-28

EMail: info@timacad.ru

Website: http://www.timacad.ru

Rector: Vladimir Bautin

Faculties

Accounting and Finance (Accountancy; Banking; Business Computing; E-Business/Commerce; Econometrics; Finance; Mathematics; Statistics; Taxation); **Agricultural Chemistry, Soil Science and Ecology** (Agriculture; Agronomy; Analytical Chemistry; Biology; Chemistry; Ecology; Forestry; Geology; Immunology; Inorganic Chemistry; Microbiology; Organic Chemistry; Physical Chemistry; Soil Management; Soil Science; Surveying and Mapping); **Agronomy** (Agricultural Business; Agriculture; Agronomy; Biotechnology; Cattle Breeding; Crop Production; Genetics; Meteorology; Plant and Crop Protection); **Economics** (Agricultural Business; Agricultural Economics; Agricultural Management; International Economics; Management; Marketing); **Horticulture and Landscape Architecture** (Biotechnology; Botany; Crop Production; Floriculture; Horticulture; Landscape Architecture; Vegetable Production; Viticulture); **Humanities and Education** (Arts and Humanities; Cultural Studies; Educational Psychology; English; Foreign Languages Education; French; German; Government; History; Modern Languages; Pedagogy; Philosophy of Education; Physical Education; Psychology; Public Relations; Russian; Sociology; Speech Studies; Tourism); **Technology** (Agriculture; Food Technology; Production Engineering); **Zooengineering** (Agricultural Engineering; Cattle Breeding; Zoology)

Graduate Schools

Agro-Business (Agricultural Business); **Management** (Management)

Further Information: Also includes the Center of Extension and Information Support for Agro-Industrial Complex of Russia, the Center of Pre-University Orientation training, Linguistic Educational Center, Educational and Methodical Center "Audit", Educational, Research and Consultative Center "The Forest Experimental Station", Facilities Management Administration, and other Departments and Production Divisions; Affiliate institution in Kaluga City

History: Founded 1865 as Petrovskaya academy of agriculture and forestry. Reorganized 1917. Acquired present status and title 2005. Formerly known as Timirjazev Moskovskaja Sel'skohozjajstvennaja Akademija (Timirjazev Moscow Academy of Agriculture).

Governing Bodies: Rector; Vice-Rectors

Academic Year: September to July (September-January;February-July)

Admission Requirements: Secondary school certificate (Attestat o srednem obrazovanii)

Main Language(s) of Instruction: Russian

International Co-operation: With more than 30 Universities and Scientific Centres in 25 countries. Scientific and technical cooperation programmes with Universities in Germany, the Netherlands, USA, Denmark, and China. Participates in TEMPUS-TACIS European Union programmes; Erasmus Mundus External Cooperation Window

Accrediting Agencies: Russian Ministry of Education

Degrees and Diplomas: *Bakalavr*; *Specialist Diploma*; *Magistr*

Student Services: Academic counselling, Canteen, Cultural centre, Employment services, Foreign student adviser, Foreign Studies Centre, Health services, Language programs, Social counselling, Sports facilities

Student Residential Facilities: University Residence

Special Facilities: Four training and research farms ("Druzhba", Yaroslavskaya region; "Mummovskoe", Saratov region; "Kalina", Tambov region; "Mikhailovskoe", Moscow region); Museum of History of RSAU-MTAA; Museum of Minerals and Geology; V.R.Williams Soil-Agronomic Museum; Horse Breeding Museum; Museum of the Chair of Animal Anatomy, Histology and Embryology; Bee-keeping Museum and Training and research apiary; the V. Mikhelson Meteorological Observatory; Recreation centre; Field Experimental Station (the N. Timofeev Selection Station); Botanical and Dendrological gardens; Preventive clinic; Laboratories; Studios

Libraries: N. Zheleznov Central Scientific Library, c. 1 m. vols

Last Updated: 30/03/12

RUSSIAN STATE DISTANCE EDUCATION UNIVERSITY OF AGRICULTURE

Rossijskij Gosudarstvennyj Agrarnyj Zaočnij Universitet

ul. Juliusa Fuchika, 1, Balašiha, 143900 Moskovskaja oblast'

Tel: +7(495) 521-24 64

Fax: +7(495) 521-24 56

EMail: mail@rgazu.ru; osojnova@yandex.ru

Website: http://www.rgazu.ru

Rector: Vladimir Anatol'evich Dubovik

Faculties

Agronomy (Agronomy; Botany; Chemistry; Geology; Plant and Crop Protection; Plant Pathology; Soil Management); **Animal Husbandry** (Animal Husbandry); **Ecology** (Ecology); **Economics** (Accountancy; Economics; Finance; Management); **Mechanical Engineering** (Agricultural Equipment; Engineering; Machine Building; Maintenance Technology)

Institutes

Commerce, Management, and Innovative Technology (Business and Commerce; Business Computing; Information Technology; Management)

History: Created 1930.

Degrees and Diplomas: *Bakalavr*; *Specialist Diploma*; *Magistr*

Last Updated: 03/04/12

RUSSIAN STATE HUMANITIES UNIVERSITY

Rossijskij Gosudarstvennyj Gumanitarnyj Universitet

pl. Mjusskaja 6, Moskva 125993

Tel: +7(499) 250-6511

Fax: +7(499) 250-0809

EMail: rsuh@rsuh.ru; zabotkina@rggu.ru

Website: http://rggu.com/

Rector: Efim Iosifovič Pivovar (2011-) EMail: rggu@rggu.ru

International Relations: Vera Zabotkina, Vice-Rector, Innovative International Projects EMail: zabotkina@rggu.ru

Centres

Archive Studies (Archiving) *Director*: Aleksandr J. Afanasiev; **Comparative Studies of World Religions** (Comparative Religion; Religion) *Director*: Nikolay V. Šaburov; **Hebrew and Bible Studies** (Bible; Hebrew) *Director*: Mark S. Kupovetsky; **Historical Anthropology** (Anthropology; History) *Director*: Julia V. Tkačenko; **Information and Computer Studies** (Computer Science; Information Management) *Director*: Vadim B. Kravčenko; **Management Problems Studies** (Management) *Director*: Farida Ju. Čanhjeva; **Russian as a Foreign Language** (Russian) *Director*: Valentina Ja. Trufanova; **Russian-Canadian Science and Education** *('Moscow-Quebec')* (International and Comparative Education) *Director*: Tatyana Mogilevskaja; **Russian-Mexican Science and Education** *Director*: Galina G. Eršova; **Russian-Swedish Science and Education** (International and Comparative Education) *Director*: Tamara A. Salyčeva; **World History** (History) *Director*: Aleksandr O. Čubarjan

Divisions
Social Anthropology (Anthropology; Social Sciences) *Director*: Valery A. Tiškov

Faculties
Art History (Art History; Fine Arts) *Dean*: Irina V. Bacanova; **Economics** (Economics) *Dean*: Yilia N. Nesterenko; **History and Archives** (Ancient Books; Archiving; History) *Dean*: Aleksandr B. Bezborodov; **History and Philology** (History; Modern Languages; Philology) *Dean*: Pavel P. Škarenkov; **History, Political Science and Law** (History; Law; Political Sciences) *Dean*: Aleksandr P. Logunov; **Information Protection** *Dean*: Vladimir S. Anašin; **Linguistics** (Artificial Intelligence; Linguistics; Oriental Languages) *Dean*: Maksim A. Krongauz; **Management** (Management) *Dean*: Nadežda I. Arhipova; **Philosophy** (Philosophy) *Dean*: Valery D. Gubin; **Scientific, Technical and Film/Photo/Sound Archives** (Archiving) *Dean*: Vladimir M. Magidov

Institutes
Economy, Management and Law (Economics; Law; Management) *Director*: Nadežda I. Arhipova; **European Cultures** (Cultural Studies; European Studies) *Director*: Valerja Ju. Kudrjavceva; **Higher Research in Humanities** *Dean*: Sergey D. Serebryanny; **History and Archives** (Archiving; History; Law; Political Sciences; Technology) *Dean*: Aleksandr B. Bezborodov; **Media Studies** (Media Studies) *Director*: Andrey J. Afanasiev; **Oriental Cultures** (Cultural Studies; Oriental Studies) *Director*: Ilja S. Smirnov; **Psychology** (Psychology) *Director*: Elena E. Kravcova; **Russian History** (History) *Director*: Andrey I. Fursov

Schools
Archives (Archiving) *Director*: Ljudmila I. Demina; **Contemporary Arts** (Fine Arts) *Director*: Ekaterina A. Mellina

Further Information: International Exchange programmes

History: Founded 1991.

Governing Bodies: Rectorate; Scientific Board

Academic Year: September to June (September-January; February-June)

Admission Requirements: Secondary school certificate (Attestat o srednem obrazovanii). Basic Russian

Fees: (US Dollars): 6,000 per annum for overseas students.

Main Language(s) of Instruction: Russian

Degrees and Diplomas: *Bakalavr*: 4 yrs; *Specialist Diploma*: 5 yrs; *Magistr*: a further 2 yrs after Bakalavr; *Kandidat Nauk*: a further 3 yrs

Student Services: Academic counselling, Canteen, Employment services, Foreign Studies Centre, Health services, Social counselling, Sports facilities

Student Residential Facilities: Yes

Libraries: c. 1.7m. Vols

Publications: Logos: filosofsko-literaturnyi zhurnal; Mjussa; The Moscow Linguistic Journal; Trudy Istoriko - Arhivnogo Instituta; Universum; Vestnik RGGU; Vestnik gumanitarnih nauki

Press or Publishing House: The RGGU Publishing Centre

Academic Staff *2008-2009*	**TOTAL**
FULL-TIME	**1,117**
PART-TIME	**710**
Student Numbers *2010-2011*	
All (Foreign Included)	**34,211**

Note: Student statistics include branches.
Last Updated: 10/05/11

RUSSIAN STATE HYDRO-METEOROLOGICAL UNIVERSITY

Rossijskij Gosudarstvennyj Gidrometeorologičeskij Universitet (RSHU)
prosp. Malookhtinskij 98, Sankt-Peterburg 195196
Tel: +7(812) 444-4163
Fax: +7(812) 444-6090
EMail: rector@rshu.ru
Website: http://www.rshu.ru

Rector: Lev Karlin (1988-)

Secretary-General: Galina M. Veretennikova
Tel: +7(812) 444-4136

International Relations: Anatoliy Bogush, Vice Rector for International Relations Tel: +7(812) 444-5636 EMail: bogush@rshu.ru

Faculties
Ecology and Environmental Physics (Ecology; Environmental Studies; Mathematics; Mechanics; Physics); **Economics and Socio-Humanitarian Sciences** (Econometrics; Economic and Finance Policy; Economic History; Economics; Industrial and Production Economics; International Economics; Management; Modern Languages; Physical Education; Public Relations; Russian; Small Business); **Hydrology** (Geological Engineering; Hydraulic Engineering; Water Management; Water Science); **Meteorology** (Meteorology); **Oceanography** (Coastal Studies; Marine Science and Oceanography; Meteorology)

History: Founded 1930 as Moscow Hydrometeorological Institute. Became High Military Hydrometeorological Institute of the Red Army in 1941 and evacuated to Leninabad in October. Returned from evacuation to Moscow in 1943, transferred to Leningrad in 1944 and became the Leningrad Hydrometeorological Institute in 1945. Following an Agreement between the government and the World Meteorological Organization (WMO) in 1995 the institution received the status of a regional meteorological educational centre of the WMO. Renamed Russian State Hydrometeorological University in 1998. Became a signatory of the Magna Charta Universitatum in 2006.

Governing Bodies: Rector and Academic Council

Academic Year: September to June (September-January; February-June)

Admission Requirements: Secondary school certificate (attestat o srednem obrazovanii)

Fees: (Russian Rubles): 70,000 - 80,000 per annum

Main Language(s) of Instruction: Russian

International Co-operation: Cooperation with universities in Finland, Sweden, Norway, Poland, Germany, France, UK, Spain, Portugal, China, USA. Participates in Tacis, Tempus, Intas, NorFA, UNESCO Chair, UNITWIN, VCP of WMO, Erasmus Mundus, DAAD, Nordic Council.

Accrediting Agencies: Ministry of Education and Science of the Russian Federation, WMO

Degrees and Diplomas: *Bakalavr*: Hydro-meteorology; Ecology; Environmental Studies (BSc), 4 yrs; *Specialist Diploma*: Meteorology; Oceanography; Hydrology; Management; Geo-ecology; Public Relations; Economics (MSc), 5 yrs; *Magistr*: Hydrometeorology; Ecology and Natural Resource Management, a further 2 yrs; *Doktor Nauk*: 4 yrs. Also PhD courses (3 yrs). The Bachelor's degree programme in Hydrometeorology is taught in English

Student Services: Academic counselling, Canteen, Employment services, Foreign student adviser, Foreign Studies Centre, Health services, Language programs, Sports facilities

Student Residential Facilities: Yes

Libraries: c. 350,000 vols.

Publications: Proceedings of RSHU, Scientific articles *(quarterly)*

Academic Staff *2010-2011*	MEN	WOMEN	**TOTAL**
FULL-TIME	350	400	**750**
STAFF WITH DOCTORATE			
FULL-TIME	110	90	**200**
Student Numbers *2010-2011*			
All (Foreign Included)	2,400	2,720	**5,120**
FOREIGN ONLY	180	140	**320**

Distance students, 1,800.
Last Updated: 18/10/11

RUSSIAN STATE PEDAGOGICAL UNIVERSITY NAMED AFTER HERZEN

Rossijskij Gosudarstvennyj Pedagogičeskij Universitet im. A.I. Herzena (HSPU)
nab. Reki Moiki, 48, Sankt-Peterburg 191186
Tel: +7(812) 570-08-60
Fax: +7(812) 312-02-22
EMail: postmaster@herzen.spb.ru
Website: http://www.herzen.spb.ru

Rector: Valerij Pavlovich Solomin EMail: vps@herzen.spb.ru

Faculties

Biology (Anatomy; Biology; Botany; Physiology; Science Education; Zoology); **Chemistry** (Analytical Chemistry; Chemistry; Inorganic Chemistry; Organic Chemistry; Physical Chemistry; Science Education); **Economics** (Economics; Marketing); **Fine Arts** (Fine Arts; Museum Studies; Painting and Drawing); **Foreign Languages** (English; Foreign Languages Education; German; Philology; Phonetics; Romance Languages; Spanish; Translation and Interpretation); **Geography** (Ecology; Environmental Studies; Geography; Geology); **Health and Safety** (Health Sciences); **Human Philosophy** (Advertising and Publicity; Aesthetics; Cultural Studies; Ethics; Philosophy); **Information Technology** (Computer Education; Computer Science; Educational Technology; Information Technology); **Law** (Civil Law; Criminal Law; International Law; Law; Public Law); **Management** (Educational Administration; Human Resources; Management); **Mathematics** (Computer Science; Mathematics; Mathematics Education); **Music** (Music; Music Education; Singing); **Pedagogy** (Educational Psychology; Pedagogy; Social Work; Sociology); **Philology** (Philology; Russian); **Physical Education** (Physical Chemistry; Sports); **Physics** (Applied Mathematics; Astronomy and Space Science; Electronic Engineering; Physics; Science Education); **Russian as a Foreign Language** (Russian); **Social Science** (History; Political Sciences; Religious Studies; Social Sciences; Sociology); **Special Education** (Education of the Handicapped; Special Education); **Technology and Entrepreneurship** (Business Education; Design; Small Business; Technology; Technology Education)

Further Information: Also Russian language courses for foreign students. Campuses also in Vyborg, Makhachkala (Dagestan), and Volkhov.

History: Founded 1797 as a Hospice also educating orphans, reorganized as Women's Pedagogical Institute 1903, and acquired present status and title 1991.

Governing Bodies: University Council

Academic Year: September to June (September-January; February-June)

Admission Requirements: Secondary school certificate (Attestat o srednem obrazovanii)

Main Language(s) of Instruction: Russian

International Co-operation: With universities in the USA; Germany; Finland; Poland; Korea.

Accrediting Agencies: Ministry of Education and Science

Degrees and Diplomas: *Bakalavr*; *Specialist Diploma*; *Magistr*; *Kandidat Nauk*; *Doktor Nauk*

Student Services: Academic counselling, Canteen, Cultural centre, Employment services, Foreign student adviser, Foreign Studies Centre, Handicapped facilities, Health services, Language programs, Sports facilities

Student Residential Facilities: Yes

Special Facilities: Zoology Museum; Geology Museum. Observatory. University Museum. Art Gallery.

Libraries: Main library, c. 3 m. vols, including rare publications

Last Updated: 10/01/12

RUSSIAN STATE SOCIAL UNIVERSITY

Rossijskij Gosudarstvennyj Sotsial'nyj Universitet

ul. Vel'gel'ma Pika, 4/1, Moskva 129226
Tel: +7(495) 187-60-25
Fax: +7(495) 783-71-25
EMail: info@mgsu.info; info@rgsu.net
Website: http://www.rgsu.net

Rector: Vasily I. Žukov (1989-)

Faculties

Arts and Cultural Studies (Cultural Studies; Fine Arts; Sociology); **Computer Technology**; **Foreign Languages** (Arts and Humanities; Education; Pedagogy; Translation and Interpretation); **Humanities** (Arts and Humanities; Cultural Studies; Journalism; Political Sciences; Public Relations); **Information Technology** (Applied Mathematics; Computer Science; Information Technology); **Insurance and Economics** (Arts and Humanities; Economics; Finance; Insurance; Law; Management; Taxation); **Labour Security** (Ecology; Environmental Management; Parks and Recreation; Safety Engineering); **Law** (Law); **Management** (Management); **Medicine and Rehabilitation Technology** (Medical Technology; Medicine; Rehabilitation and Therapy); **Psychology** (Psychology); **Social Medicine and Adapted Physical Education** (Nursing; Parks and Recreation; Physical Education; Sports; Tourism); **Social Work and Pedagogy** (Family Studies; Pedagogy; Psychology; Social Work; Sociology); **Sociology** (Sociology)

History: Founded 1991. Previously known as Moskovskij Gosudarstvennyj Socialnyj Universitet (Moscow State Social University). Acquired current title 2005.

Admission Requirements: Secondary school certificate (Attestat o srednem obrazovanii) and entrance examination

Main Language(s) of Instruction: Russian

International Co-operation: With universities in Bulgaria, United Kingdom, Hungary, Vietnam, Germany, Spain, Canada, China, South Korea, Latvia, Mongolia, Norway, Poland, Switzerland, USA, Finland, France, Estonia.

Degrees and Diplomas: *Bakalavr*; *Specialist Diploma*; *Magistr*; *Kandidat Nauk*; *Doktor Nauk*

Student Services: Academic counselling, Canteen, Cultural centre, Employment services, Foreign student adviser, Foreign Studies Centre, Health services, Language programs, Nursery care, Social counselling, Sports facilities

Student Residential Facilities: Yes.

Special Facilities: Museum of the History of RGSU. Video Studio. Music Studio. Theatre Club. Ballet Studio. Recording Studio. Photo Studio.

Libraries: Scientific Library, c. 167,000 vols; French Library, c. 13,670 vols

Last Updated: 30/03/12

RUSSIAN STATE UNIVERSITY FOR PHYSICAL EDUCATION, SPORT, YOUTH AND TOURISM

Rossijskij Gosudarstvennyj Universitet Fizičeskoj Kul'tury, Sporta, Molodeži i Turizma

Sirenevij bul. 4, Moskva 105122
Tel: +7(495) 961-31-11
Fax: +7(495) 961-31-11
EMail: info@sportedu.ru
Website: http://www.sportedu.ru/

Rector: Aleksandr Nikolaevich Bleer

Institutes

Humanities (Advertising and Publicity; Computer Science; Economics; Management; Psychology; Public Relations; Social Work; Theatre); **Physical Education and Sports** (Physical Education; Sports; Sports Management); **Tourism, Recreation, Rehabilitation and Fitness** (Ecology; Parks and Recreation; Rehabilitation and Therapy; Sports; Tourism)

History: Founded 1918. Previously known as Rossijskaja Gosudarstvennaja Akademija Fizičeskoj Kul'tury (Russian State Academy of Physical Education). Acquired present title and status 2011.

Governing Bodies: Academic Board

Academic Year: September to June (September-January; February-June)

Admission Requirements: Secondary school certificate (Attestat o srednem obrazovanii)

Main Language(s) of Instruction: Russian

International Co-operation: Participates in the American Consortium on Cultural and Academic Exchange programme. The Academy is represented in the European College of Sports Science (ECSS); European Committee on Physical Education in ENSSHE

Degrees and Diplomas: *Bakalavr*; *Specialist Diploma*; *Magistr*; *Kandidat Nauk*; *Doktor Nauk*

Student Services: Canteen, Cultural centre, Foreign student adviser, Foreign Studies Centre, Health services, Language programs, Social counselling, Sports facilities

Student Residential Facilities: For c. 1,000 students

Special Facilities: Museum of Sports History

Libraries: c. 600,000 vols

Last Updated: 05/04/12

RUSSIAN STATE UNIVERSITY OF OIL AND GAS NAMED AFTER I.M. GUBKIN

Rossijskij Gosudarstvennyj Universitet Nefti i Gaza im. I.M. Gubkina

Leninskij prosp. 65, Moskva 119991
Tel: +7(499) 233-92-25
Fax: +7(499) 135-88-95
EMail: com@gubkin.ru
Website: http://www.gubkin.ru

Rector: Viktor Georgievich Martynov

Faculties

Automation and Computer Engineering (Applied Mathematics; Automation and Control Engineering; Computer Engineering; Computer Science; Electrical Engineering; Mathematics; Measurement and Precision Engineering); **Chemical Engineering and Ecology** (Chemical Engineering; Ecology; Inorganic Chemistry; Organic Chemistry; Petroleum and Gas Engineering; Petrology; Physical Chemistry); **Economics and Management** (Economics; Engineering Management; Industrial Management; Management); **Engineering, Construction and Operation of Pipeline Systems** (Thermal Engineering; Thermal Physics); **Geology and Geophysics of Oil and Gas** (Geology; Geophysics; Petroleum and Gas Engineering); **Humanities** (Foreigners Education; History; Philosophy; Political Sciences; Russian; Sports); **Law** (Administrative Law; Commercial Law; Law); **Mechanical Engineering** (Environmental Engineering; Environmental Management; Mechanical Engineering; Mechanics; Metallurgical Engineering; Safety Engineering); **Oil and Gas Fields** (Petroleum and Gas Engineering; Physics)

History: Created 1930.

Degrees and Diplomas: *Bakalavr*; *Specialist Diploma*; *Magistr*; *Kandidat Nauk*; *Doktor Nauk*

Last Updated: 20/03/12

RUSSIAN STATE UNIVERSITY OF TOURISM AND SERVICE

Rossijskij Gosudarstvennyj Universitet Turisma i Servisa

ul. Glavnaja, 99, Pushkinskaja rajon, pos. Čerkizovo, 141221 Moskovskaja oblast'
Tel: +7(495) 993-33-17
Fax: +7(495) 993-33-17
EMail: prorektor-umr@mail.ru
Website: http://www.rguts.ru/

Rector: Alexandr Alekseevich Fedulin

Faculties

Economics (Economics); **Law and Social Work** (Law; Social Work); **Services** (Environmental Management; Information Technology; Machine Building; Radio and Television Broadcasting); **Technology and Design** (Design; Fine Arts; Technology); **Tourism and Hospitality** (Advertising and Publicity; Cultural Studies; Food Technology; Home Economics; Hotel and Restaurant; Hotel Management; Linguistics; Tourism)

History: Created 1993 as Gosudarstvennaja Akademija Sfery Byta i Uslug (State Academy of Service). Became Moskovskij Gosudarstvennyj Universitet Servisa (Moscow State University of Service) in 1999. Acquired current title 2007. Created to deliver multilevel education in the fields of tourism and the service industries as well as training and retraining for professionals.

International Co-operation: With universities in Switzerland, United Kingdom, Hungary. Also participates in TEMPUS, TASIS, SOCRATES, DAAD and ERASMUS programmes

Degrees and Diplomas: *Bakalavr*, *Specialist Diploma*: 5 yrs; *Magistr*, *Kandidat Nauk*

Student Services: Academic counselling, Canteen

Last Updated: 20/03/12

RUSSIAN STATE UNIVERSITY OF TRADE AND ECONOMICS

Rossijskij Gosudarstvennyj Torgovo-Economičeskij Universitet (RGTEU)

ul. Smol'naya, 36, Moskva 125993
Tel: +7(495) 458-94-79 +7(495) 458-94-77
Fax: +7(495) 458-72-47
EMail: rektorat@rsute.ru
Website: http://www.rsute.ru

Rector: Sergei Baburin (2002-)

Faculties

Commerce and Marketing (Advertising and Publicity; Business and Commerce; Marketing; Social Sciences; Transport Management); **Finance and Economics** (Accountancy; Finance; Taxation); **Hospitality and Restaurant Business** (Hotel and Restaurant; Hotel Management; House Arts and Environment; Tourism); **Information Technology** (Archiving; Business Computing; Documentation Techniques; Information Technology); **International Economics and Trade** (Communication Studies; English; French; German; International Business; International Economics; Spanish; Taxation; Translation and Interpretation); **Law** (Administrative Law; Civil Law; Commercial Law; Constitutional Law; Criminal Law; Justice Administration; Law; Notary Studies); **Management** (Economics; Human Resources; Management; Public Administration); **Social Technologies** (Administration; Advertising and Publicity; Graphic Design; Landscape Architecture; Political Sciences; Psychology; Public Relations; Sociology)

History: Founded 1930 as Economic Correspondence Studies Institute, acquired present status 1995 and title 2002.

Governing Bodies: Academic Council

Academic Year: September to July (September-January; February-July)

Admission Requirements: Secondary school certificate (Attestat o srednem obrazovanii)

Main Language(s) of Instruction: Russian

International Co-operation: With institutions in Belarus, China, France, Germany, United Kingdom, Kyrgyzstan, Moldova, Ukraine, USA.

Accrediting Agencies: n

Degrees and Diplomas: *Bakalavr*, *Specialist Diploma*; *Magistr*, *Kandidat Nauk*. Diploma of Specialist in conjunction with Ecole Supérieure de Commerce de Lyon (France).

Student Services: Academic counselling, Canteen, Employment services, Foreign student adviser, Nursery care, Social counselling, Sports facilities

Special Facilities: Museum

Libraries: Main Library, 880,000 vols

Last Updated: 20/03/12

RUSSIAN STATE VOCATIONAL-PEDAGOGICAL UNIVERSITY

Rossijskij Gosudarstvennyj Professionalno-Pedagogičeskij Universitet (RGPPU)

ul. Mašinostroitelej 11, Ekaterinburg, 620012 Sverdlovskaja oblast'
Tel: +7(343) 338-44-47
Fax: +7(343) 338-44-42
EMail: mail@rsvpu.ru
Website: http://www.rsvpu.ru

Rector: Gennadij M. Romantsev (1993-)
EMail: Gennadi.Romantsev@rsvpu.ru

Institutes

Art (Art Education; Ceramic Art; Cinema and Television; Computer Graphics; Fashion Design; Film; Fine Arts; Graphic Design; Interior Design; Sound Engineering (Acoustics)); **Economics and Management** (Economics; Management; Marketing); **Linguistics** (Linguistics; Modern Languages; Philology; Russian); **Mechanical Engineering** (Mechanical Engineering); **Power Engineering and Computer Science** (Computer Science; Power Engineering); **Psychology** (Educational Psychology; Psychology); **Sociology and Law** (Archiving; Documentation Techniques; Law; Sociology)

History: Founded 1979 as Institute, acquired present status and title 2008.

Governing Bodies: Academic Board

Academic Year: September to June (September-December; February-June)

Admission Requirements: Secondary school certificate (Attestat o srednem obrazovanii)

Main Language(s) of Instruction: Russian

Degrees and Diplomas: *Bakalavr*, *Specialist Diploma*; *Magistr*, *Kandidat Nauk*; *Doktor Nauk*

Student Services: Academic counselling, Canteen, Cultural centre, Employment services, Foreign Studies Centre, Health services, Social counselling, Sports facilities

Libraries: Central Library, c. 425,500 vols

Last Updated: 30/03/12

RUSSIAN UNIVERSITY OF CHEMICAL TECHNOLOGY NAMED AFTER D.I MENDELEEV

Rossijskij Khimiko-Tehnologičeskij Universitet im. D.I. Mendeleeva (RHTU)

pl. Mijusskaja 9, Moskva 125047
Tel: +7(499) 978-86-24 +7(499) 978-49-61
Fax: +7(499)609-29-64
EMail: rector@muctr.ru; priem@muctr.ru
Website: http://www.muctr.ru

Rector: Vladimir A. Kolesnikov (2006-) EMail: rector@muctr.ru

Departments

Ceramics and Glass Technology *(Silicate Chemical Technology Faculty)* (Ceramics and Glass Technology)

Faculties

Chemical Engineering Technology (Chemical Engineering); **Ecology Engineering** (Ecology; Environmental Studies); **Economics** (Economics); **Engineering Physics and Chemistry** (Chemical Engineering; Physical Engineering); **General Studies** (Analytical Chemistry; Chemical Engineering; Chemistry; Computer Graphics; Computer Science; Design; Electrical Engineering; Foreign Languages Education; Inorganic Chemistry; Mathematics; Mechanics; Organic Chemistry; Physical Chemistry; Physics; Teacher Training); **High Resource Saving and Information Technology** (Computer Engineering; Computer Science); **Humanities** (History; History of Law; Philosophical Schools; Russian; Sports); **Inorganic Materials Technology** (Materials Engineering); **Organic Materials and Chemico-Pharmaceutical Agents Technology** (Materials Engineering); **Polymer Chemical Technology** (Polymer and Plastics Technology); **Silicate Chemical Technology** (Applied Chemistry)

Institutes

Sustainable Development (Ecology; Environmental Studies)

Further Information: Branch also in Novomoskovsk (Tula oblast).

History: Founded 1920.

Governing Bodies: Rectorate

Academic Year: September to June (September-January; February-June)

Admission Requirements: Secondary school certificate (Attestat o srednem obrazovanii) or equivalent

Main Language(s) of Instruction: Russian

Degrees and Diplomas: *Bakalavr*; *Specialist Diploma*; *Magistr*; *Kandidat Nauk*

Student Services: Academic counselling, Canteen, Cultural centre, Employment services, Foreign student adviser, Health services, Social counselling, Sports facilities

Student Residential Facilities: For c. 5,000 students

Special Facilities: History Museum

Libraries: c. 1.7m. vols

Last Updated: 11/01/12

RUSSIAN UNIVERSITY OF ECONOMICS NAMED AFTER G.V. PLEKHANOV

Rossijskij Ekonomičeskij Universitet im. G.V. Plekhanova

Stremjannyj per. 36, Moskva 117997
Tel: +7(495) 236-44-43 +7(495) 958-28-65
Fax: +7(495) 958-27-54
EMail: rector.con@rea.ru
Website: http://www.rea.ru

Rector: Viktor Ivanovich Grishin

Faculties

Business (Business Administration; Economics; International Business; Management); **Economics and Mathematics** (Applied Mathematics; Mathematical Physics; Statistics); **Engineering Economics** (Engineering Management); **Finance** (Banking; Finance; Insurance; Management; Taxation); **Information Sciences** (Business Computing; Computer Science; Information Technology); **International Economic Relations** (International Economics; International Relations; Modern Languages); **Management** (Administration; Management); **Marketing** (Advertising and Publicity; Marketing; Transport Management); **Political Sciences and Law** (Commercial Law; International Law; Law; Political Sciences; Sociology); **Public Service, Labour and Employment** (Service Trades); **Trade Economics** (Business and Commerce; Economics)

Higher Schools

Sport and Tourism (Sports; Sports Management; Tourism)

Institutes

International Business School (International Business)

Further Information: Affiliates in: Taškent, Voronež, Nižnevartovsk, Krasnodar. Also Courses for foreign students; Study Abroad programmes

History: Founded 1907 as Moscow Commerce Institute, became Rossijskaja Ekonomičeskaja Akademija im. G.V. Plehanova (Russian Academy of Economics named after G.V. Plehanov) in 1991. Acquired current title and status 2010.

Academic Year: September to June (September-January; February-June)

Admission Requirements: Secondary school certificate (Attestat o srednem obrazovanii)

Main Language(s) of Instruction: Russian

Degrees and Diplomas: *Bakalavr*; *Specialist Diploma*; *Magistr*; *Kandidat Nauk*

Student Services: Canteen, Cultural centre, Employment services, Foreign Studies Centre, Handicapped facilities, Health services, Nursery care, Sports facilities

Student Residential Facilities: For c. 600 students

Special Facilities: History of Russian Entrepreneurship Museum. Movie Studio

Last Updated: 05/04/12

RUSSIAN UNIVERSITY OF THEATRE ART

Rossijskij Universitet Teatral'nogo Iskusstva

Malyj Kislovskij per. 6, Moskva 125009
Tel: +7(495) 695-49-86
Fax: +7(495) 691-91-84
EMail: umo@gitis.net; info@gitis.net
Website: http://www.gitis.net/

Rector: Karina Levonovna Melik-Pašaeva

Faculties

Acting (Acting); **Ballet** (Dance); **Directing**; **History of Theatre and Criticism** (Art Criticism; Art History); **Musical Theatre** (Theatre); **Production** (Theatre); **Stage Design** (Display and Stage Design); **Variety** (Theatre)

Further Information: Also Special Summer and Winter courses

History: Founded 1878 as Rossijskaja Akademija Teatralnogo Iskusstva (Russian Theatre Academy). Acquired current title and status 2011.

Academic Year: September to June

Admission Requirements: Secondary school certificate (Diplom srednei obše obrazovtelnoi školi)

Main Language(s) of Instruction: Russian

Degrees and Diplomas: *Specialist Diploma*; *Magistr*; *Kandidat Nauk*

Special Facilities: Student Theatre

Last Updated: 05/04/12

RYBINSK STATE ACADEMY OF AVIATION TECHNOLOGY

Rybinskaja Gosudarstvennaja Aviatsionnaja Tehnologičeskaja Akademija im. P.A. Solov'eva

ul. Puškina 53, Rybinsk 152934
Tel: +7(4855) 28-04-70 +7(4855) 28-04-72
Fax: +7(4855) 21-39-64
EMail: root@rgata.ru
Website: http://www.rgatu.ru/

Rector: Valerij Alekseevich Poletaev EMail: rector@rgata.ru

Colleges

Aviation (Air Transport)

Faculties

Aerospace Engineering (Aeronautical and Aerospace Engineering); **Aircraft Engineering** (Aeronautical and Aerospace Engineering; Air Transport; Physics); **Economics** (Business Computing; Economics; Management); **Radio Engineering, Electronics and Informatics** (Computer Science; Telecommunications Engineering)

History: Founded 1955, acquired present status and title 1994.

Academic Year: September to June (September-January; February-June)

Admission Requirements: Secondary school certificate (Attestat o srednem obrazovanii), and entrance examination

Main Language(s) of Instruction: Russian

Degrees and Diplomas: *Bakalavr*; *Specialist Diploma*; *Magistr*; *Kandidat Nauk*; *Doktor Nauk*

Student Services: Academic counselling, Canteen, Cultural centre, Health services, Social counselling, Sports facilities

Special Facilities: History of the Academy Museum

Libraries: c. 482,000 vols

Last Updated: 11/01/12

SAHALIN STATE UNIVERSITY

Sahalinskij Gosudarstvennyj Universitet

Lenina Street, 290, Yuzhno-Sakhalinsk, 693008 Sakhalin Region
Tel: +7(4242) 424-357
Fax: +7(4242) 429-945
EMail: admin@sakhgu.ru
Website: http://www.sakhgu.ru/

Rector: Boris Misikov (1998-)
Tel: +7(4242) 420-868 EMail: rector@sakhgu.ru

Vice-Rector: Vladimir Voloshin
Tel: +7(4242) 424-515 EMail: vice-rector@sakhgu.ru

International Relations: Victor Korsunov
Tel: +7(4242) 741-071, Fax: +7(4242) 741-071
EMail: vkorsunov@sakhgu.ru

Colleges

Alexandrovsk-Sakhalinskij Campus (Arts and Humanities; Education; English; Humanities and Social Science Education; Mathematics; Music; Pedagogy; Physical Education; Primary Education; Psychology; Russian); **Arts** (Acting; Dance; Literature; Singing; Theatre); **Education** (Education; English; Humanities and Social Science Education; Mathematics; Music; Pedagogy; Preschool Education; Primary Education; Psychology; Russian)

Departments

Geoecology and Management (Ecology; Environmental Management); **Mathematics, Physics and Computer Science** (Computer Science; Mathematics; Physics); **Natural Resources and Petroleum Engineering** (Natural Resources; Petroleum and Gas Engineering); **Physics** (Education; Physics; Science Education); **Services and Tourism** (Service Trades; Tourism); **Surveying and Mapping** (Surveying and Mapping)

Faculties

Natural Sciences (Biology; Geography; Natural Sciences)

Institutes

Economics and Oriental Studies (Cultural Studies; East Asian Studies; Economics; Finance; Foreign Languages Education; Japanese; Korean; Oriental Studies; Philology); **Education** (Education; Educational Psychology; Pedagogy; Physical Education; Preschool Education; Primary Education; Psychology; Sports); **History, Sociology and Management** (Government; History; Management; Philosophy; Sociology); **Law** (Administrative Law; Criminal Law; Labour Law; Law; Public Law); **Philology** (English; Foreign Languages Education; Germanic Languages; Journalism; Linguistics; Literature; Native Language Education; Philology; Romance Languages; Russian; Speech Therapy and Audiology; Translation and Interpretation); **Technology** (Business Education; Occupational Health; Technology; Technology Education)

History: Founded 1949 as Teachers' Training College. Became State Pedagogical Institute 1954 and acquired present status and title 1998.

Governing Bodies: Academic Council of SSU; Councils of Institutes

Academic Year: September to June

Admission Requirements: Secondary education certificate (attestat o srednem obrazovanii) and entrance examination, testing

Main Language(s) of Instruction: Russian

Accrediting Agencies: Ministry of Education and Science of the Russian Federation

Degrees and Diplomas: *Bakalavr*: 4 yrs; *Specialist Diploma*: 5 yrs

Student Services: Canteen, Cultural centre, Employment services, Foreign student adviser, Health services, Language programs, Sports facilities

Student Residential Facilities: For 700 residents

Special Facilities: Archaeology Museum

Libraries: Central Library, 534,000 vols

Publications: Proceedings of Annual Scientific Conference *(annually)*; Report on Research Activity of SSU *(annually)*

Last Updated: 02/03/12

SAINT-PETERSBURG INSITUTE OF TRADE AND ECONOMICS

Sankt-Peterburgskij Torgovo-Ekonomičeskij Institut

ul. Novorossijskaja 50, Sankt-Peterburg 194021
Tel: +7(812) 297-7806
Fax: +7(812) 247-4342
EMail: rector@ice.spb.ru
Website: http://www.spbtei.ru

Faculties

Distance Education (Accountancy; Business Administration; Economics; Food Technology); **Engineering** (Engineering); **Finance and Economics** (Accountancy; Economics); **Management and Business Technology** (Management; Technology); **Trade and Expertise in Consumer Goods** (Consumer Studies; Crafts and Trades)

Further Information: Also Graduate School

History: Founded 1930 as Leningrad Institute of Soviet Trade (LIST).

Degrees and Diplomas: *Specialist Diploma*; *Magistr*

Last Updated: 27/01/12

SAINT-PETERSBURG INSTITUTE OF MECHANICAL ENGINEERING

Sankt-Peterburgskij Institut Mašinostroenija (Vtuz LMZ)

pr. Poljustrovskij 14, Sankt-Peterburg 195197
Tel: +7(812) 540-0154
Fax: +7(812) 540-0159
EMail: lmz-vtuz@mail.wplus.net; info@zavod-vtuz.ru
Website: http://www.zavod-vtuz.ru/

Rector: Yuri Mikhaelovich Zubarev

Faculties

Automotive Engineering (Automation and Control Engineering; Automotive Engineering; Chemistry); **Economics** (Ecology; Economic History; Economics; Management; Philosophy; Small Business); **Energy Engineering** (Energy Engineering; Nuclear Engineering); **Mechanical Engineering** (Machine Building; Mechanical Engineering); **Technology** (Machine Building; Metal Techniques; Metallurgical Engineering; Technology); **Turbine**

Engineering (Engineering; Heating and Refrigeration; Hydraulic Engineering)

History: Founded 1925.

Governing Bodies: Academic Council

Admission Requirements: Secondary school certificate

Main Language(s) of Instruction: Russian

Accrediting Agencies: Ministry of Education

Degrees and Diplomas: *Specialist Diploma*

Student Services: Academic counselling, Canteen, Cultural centre, Employment services, Foreign student adviser, Foreign Studies Centre, Handicapped facilities, Health services, Language programs, Social counselling, Sports facilities

Student Residential Facilities: Yes

Special Facilities: Museum, Theatre; Movie Studio, Internet facilities

Last Updated: 19/12/11

SAINT-PETERSBURG STATE ACADEMIC INSTITUTE OF PAINTING, SCULPTURE AND ARCHITECTURE NAMED AFTER I.E. REPIN

Sankt-Peterburgskij Gosudarstvennyj Akademičeskij Institut Živopisi, Skulptury i Arhitektury im. I.E. Repina

Universiteckaja nap. 17, Sankt-Peterburg 199034

Tel: +7(812) 323-72-45

Fax: +7(812) 323-65-48

EMail: artacademy@artacademy.spb.ru; artsacademy.spb@gmail.com

Website: http://www.artsacademy.ru/

Rector: Semyon Mikhailovskij

Departments

Sculpture (Restoration of Works of Art; Sculpture); **Theory and History of Art** (Art History)

Faculties

Architecture (Architecture); **Graphic Arts** (Graphic Arts; Painting and Drawing; Printing and Printmaking); **Painting** (Painting and Drawing)

History: Founded 1757. Acquired present status and title 1947.

Academic Year: October to June

Admission Requirements: School leaving certificate and special art preparation (showing art works)

Main Language(s) of Instruction: Russian

Degrees and Diplomas: *Specialist Diploma*

Student Services: Canteen, Cultural centre, Foreign student adviser, Foreign Studies Centre, Health services, Language programs, Nursery care, Sports facilities

Special Facilities: Museum. Art Gallery.

Libraries: Science and students' libraries

Last Updated: 29/02/12

SAINT-PETERSBURG STATE ACADEMY OF FORESTRY ENGINEERING NAMED AFTER S.M. KIROV

Sankt-Peterburgskaja Gosudarstvennaja Lesotehničeskaja Akademija im. S.M. Kirova

per. Institutskij 5, Sankt-Peterburg 194021

Tel: +7(812) 670-9246

Fax: +7(812) 670-9221

EMail: info@ftacademy.ru; public@ftacademy.ru

Website: http://www.ftacademy.ru/

Rector: Andrey V. Selichovkin

Tel: +7(812) 550-0690, Fax: +7(812) 550-0866

Vice-Rector for Administration: Nikolai V. Tsymbal

Faculties

Chemical Technology and Biotechnology (Biotechnology; Chemical Engineering; Energy Engineering; Petroleum and Gas Engineering); **Economics and Management** (Economics; Management); **Forest Technology** (Forestry; Mechanical Engineering); **Forestry** (Biology; Botany; Computer Science; Ecology; Environmental Management; Forest Products; Forestry; History; Law; Natural Resources; Soil Science); **Forestry Engineering** (Agricultural Engineering; Forestry; Hydraulic Engineering; Marine Transport; Mathematics; Physical Education); **Landscape Architecture** (Landscape Architecture); **Mechanical Wood Technology** (Automation and Control Engineering; Engineering Management; Measurement and Precision Engineering; Wood Technology)

Further Information: Also Faculty of Vocational Education

History: Founded as Forest School in 1803. Later reorganized into the Academy

Academic Year: September to June

Admission Requirements: Secondary school certficate

Fees: (US Dollars): c. 2,600 per annum; postgraduate study, c. 2,800

Main Language(s) of Instruction: Russian

International Co-operation: With universities in Finland, Sweden, Denmark, Germany, France

Accrediting Agencies: Ministry of Education and Science

Degrees and Diplomas: *Bakalavr*: 6 yrs; *Specialist Diploma*: 5 yrs; *Magistr*: 6 yrs; *Kandidat Nauk*: 3 yrs after Magister; *Doktor Nauk*

Student Services: Academic counselling, Canteen, Employment services, Foreign student adviser, Foreign Studies Centre, Health services, Language programs, Social counselling, Sports facilities

Special Facilities: Forest Entomology Museum; Zoology and Hunting Museum. Botanical and Dendrological gardens

Libraries: 1,5 million vols

Publications: Collected reports of young scientists *(annually)*

Last Updated: 01/03/12

SAINT-PETERSBURG STATE ACADEMY OF VETERINARY MEDICINE

Sankt-Peterburgskaja Gosudarstvennaja Veterinarnaja Akademija (SPBGAVM)

ul. Černigovskaja 5, Sankt-Peterburg 196084

Tel: +7(812) 298-3631

Fax: +7(812) 388-3631

EMail: mail@spbgavm.ru; akvetzoo@list.ru

Website: http://www.spbgavm.ru

Rector: Anatoly A. Stekolnikov (2003-) EMail: mail@spbgavm.ru

Vice-Rector: Sergei Kovalev

Departments

Agronomy and Botany (Agronomy; Botany; Veterinary Science); **Animal Anatomy** (Anatomy; Veterinary Science; Zoology); **Biochemical and Organic Chemistry** (Biochemistry; Organic Chemistry); **Economics, Organization and Management of Agricultural Production** (Agricultural Economics; Agricultural Management; Crop Production); **Foreign Languages** (English; Foreign Languages Education; French; German; Modern Languages); **General and Special Surgery** (Surgery; Veterinary Science); **Histology and General Biology** (Biology; Histology); **History and Economic Theory** (Economics; History); **Microbiology, Virology and Immunology** (Immunology; Microbiology; Virology); **Pathophysiology** (Pathology; Physiology); **Philosophy and Political Sciences** (Philosophy; Political Sciences); **Physical Education** (Physical Education; Sports); **Veterinary Biology and Life Safety in Emergency Situations** (Biology; Physical Therapy; Physics; Radiology; Veterinary Science)

History: Founded 1808.

Governing Bodies: Ministry of Agriculture of the Russian Federation

Academic Year: September to June

Admission Requirements: Secondary School Certificate of Certificate of Professional Education

Fees: (Russian Rubles): c. 16,000 per semester; foreign students, c. 30,000 per semester

Main Language(s) of Instruction: Russian

International Co-operation: Federal Service in the field of Education and Science

Degrees and Diplomas: *Specialist Diploma*: 5 yrs

Student Services: Academic counselling, Canteen, Cultural centre, Health services, Social counselling, Sports facilities

Special Facilities: Museums (Anatomy, Pathological Anatomy, Veterinary-Sanitary Medicine)

Libraries: Yes

Publications: Questions of Veterinary Legislation *(quarterly)*; Veterinary Review, Magazine *(quarterly)*

Press or Publishing House: Publishing House of SPbGAVM

Academic Staff *2007-2008*	MEN	WOMEN	TOTAL
FULL-TIME	106	100	**206**
PART-TIME	5	11	**16**
STAFF WITH DOCTORATE			
FULL-TIME	80	14	**94**
PART-TIME	10	6	**16**

Student Numbers *2007-2008*			
All (Foreign Included)	408	1,379	**1,787**
FOREIGN ONLY	17	19	**36**

Distance students, 296.

Last Updated: 29/02/12

SAINT-PETERSBURG STATE AGRARIAN UNIVERSITY

Sankt-Peterburgskij Gosudarstvennyj Agrarnyj Universitet

Peterburgskoe šosse, 2, Pushkin,
Sankt-Peterburg 196600
Tel: +7(812) 470-04-22
Fax: +7(812) 465-05-05
EMail: spbgau@mail.ru; agro@spbgau.ru
Website: http://www.spbgau.spb.ru

Rector: Viktor Efimov (2005-)

Departments

Distance Education (Agricultural Economics; Agricultural Engineering; Agricultural Equipment; Agricultural Management; Agrobiology; Agronomy; Automation and Control Engineering; Banking; Economics; Finance; Horticulture; Law; Plant and Crop Protection; Viticulture; Zoology); **Energy** (Agricultural Engineering; Automation and Control Engineering; Electrical Engineering; Energy Engineering; Mathematics; Physics; Power Engineering); **Horticulture and Ornamental Horticulture** (Horticulture; Landscape Architecture; Viticulture); **Land Management** (Computer Science; Economics; Environmental Management; Rural Planning; Surveying and Mapping); **Plant Protection and Quarantine** (Plant and Crop Protection); **Soil Science and Agroecology** (Agronomy; Applied Chemistry; Ecology; Soil Science)

Faculties

Agricultural Construction (Agricultural Equipment; Civil Engineering; Industrial Engineering); **Agronomy** (Agricultural Business; Agriculture; Agronomy; Animal Husbandry; Biotechnology; Botany; Cattle Breeding); **Economics** (Accountancy; Agricultural Economics; Agricultural Management; Banking; Finance; Marketing); **Engineering and Technology** (Agricultural Engineering; Agricultural Equipment; Agricultural Management; Animal Husbandry; Automotive Engineering; Engineering; Mechanical Equipment and Maintenance); **Law** (Civil Law; Commercial Law; Constitutional Law; Criminal Law; Law; Political Sciences; Sociology); **Management** (Agricultural Management; Hotel and Restaurant; Hotel Management; Industrial Management; Information Technology; Management; Marketing; Public Administration; Small Business; Tourism; Transport Management); **Zooengineering** (Animal Husbandry; Aquaculture; Cattle Breeding; Food Technology; Zoology)

Programmes

Humanities and Education (Architectural Restoration; Arts and Humanities; Cultural Studies; Heritage Preservation; Modern Languages; Museum Studies; Pedagogy; Philosophy; Russian)

History: Founded 1904 as Agricultural Courses, acquired present status and title 1992.

Governing Bodies: Rectorate; Scientific Council

Academic Year: September to July

Admission Requirements: Secondary school certificate (Attestat o srednem obrazovanii), college diploma and entrance examinations

Main Language(s) of Instruction: Russian

Degrees and Diplomas: *Bakalavr (B.Sc.)*: 4 yrs; *Specialist Diploma*: 1 further yr; *Kandidat Nauk (Ph.D.)*: a further 3 yrs by thesis

Student Services: Academic counselling, Canteen, Foreign student adviser, Health services, Language programs, Sports facilities

Student Residential Facilities: Yes

Special Facilities: Museums

Libraries: Central Library, 750,000 vols

Publications: Scientific Reports *(annually)*

Academic Staff *2011-2012*: Total: c. 500

Student Numbers *2011-2012*: Total: c. 4,500

Last Updated: 29/02/12

SAINT-PETERSBURG STATE CHEMICAL AND PHARMACEUTICAL ACADEMY

Sankt-Peterburgskaja Gosudarstvennaja Himiko-Farmacevtičeskaja Academija (SPHFA)

ul. Prof. Popova 14,
Sankt-Peterburg 197022
Tel: +7(812) 234-5729
Fax: +7(812) 234-6044
EMail: info@pharminnotech.com; info@spcpa.ru
Website: http://www.spcpa.ru

Rector: Igor Narkevič
EMail: rector@spcpa.ru; rectorat.main@pharminnotech.com

First Vice-Rector: Eugenia N. Kirillov
EMail: Eugenia.Kirillova@pharminnotech.com

International Relations: Anton O. Karasavidi, Vice-Rector of the International Student and International Relations
Tel: +7(812) 234-4232
EMail: Anton.Karasavidi@pharminnotech.com

Faculties

Biotechnology (Biotechnology; Industrial Chemistry); **Pharmacy** (Pharmacology; Pharmacy); **Preparatory** (Biology; Botany; Chemistry; Mathematics; Physics; Russian)

Schools

Graduate Studies (Analytical Chemistry; Biochemistry; Biotechnology; Industrial Chemistry; Microbiology; Organic Chemistry; Pharmacology; Pharmacy; Toxicology)

Further Information: Also Russian courses for foreign students. Courses for teachers of Russian as a foreign language.

History: Founded 1919, acquired present status and title 1996.

Academic Year: September to July (September-December; February-July)

Admission Requirements: Secondary school certificate (Attestat o srednem obrazovanii) or equivalent

Main Language(s) of Instruction: Russian

Accrediting Agencies: Ministry of Health; Ministry of Education

Degrees and Diplomas: *Specialist Diploma*: Pharmacy; Biotechnology, 5-7 yrs; *Magistr*: Pharmacy; Biotechnology, 5 yrs; *Kandidat Nauk*: Pharmacy; Biotechnology, a further 3 yrs

Student Services: Academic counselling, Canteen, Foreign student adviser, Foreign Studies Centre, Health services, Language programs, Social counselling, Sports facilities

Student Residential Facilities: Yes

Libraries: c. 300,000 vols

Publications: Aptekarsky Prospect *(monthly)*; Phyto Remedium *(quarterly)*; Young Pharmacy *(annually)*

Last Updated: 01/03/12

SAINT-PETERSBURG STATE CONSERVATORY NAMED AFTER N.A.RIMSKY-KORSAKOV (ACADEMY)

Sankt-Peterburgskaja Gosudarstvennaja Konservatorija im. N.A.Rimskogo-Korsakova (Akademija)

pl. Teatralnaja 3, Sankt-Peterburg 190000
Tel: +7(812) 312-2129
Fax: +7(812) 312-9104
EMail: rectorat@conservatory.ru
Website: http://www.conservatory.ru

Rector: Michael Gantvarg Tel: +7(812) 312-2129

Departments

Interfaculty (Arts and Humanities; Modern Languages; Physical Education; Russian; Social Sciences)

Faculties

Composition and Conducting (Conducting; Music Theory and Composition; Musical Instruments); **Directing** (Dance; Singing; Theatre); **Folk Instruments** (Jazz and Popular Music; Musical Instruments); **Musicology** (Music; Music Theory and Composition; Musical Instruments; Musicology; Singing); **Orchestra** (Music; Performing Arts); **Piano** (Musical Instruments); **Vocal Art** (Singing)

History: Founded 1862, acquired present status and title 1918.

Academic Year: September to July

Admission Requirements: Secondary school certificate

Main Language(s) of Instruction: Russian

International Co-operation: With universities in Switzerland, Scotland, Germany, Norway, USA, Korea, Finland.

Degrees and Diplomas: *Specialist Diploma*: 5 yrs; *Kandidat Nauk*: a further 3 yrs following Specialist's Diploma

Student Services: Canteen, Foreign student adviser, Foreign Studies Centre, Health services, Social counselling, Sports facilities

Student Residential Facilities: 2 hostels

Special Facilities: Museum

Libraries: Central Library
Last Updated: 01/03/12

SAINT-PETERSBURG STATE ELECTROTECHNICAL UNIVERSITY 'LETI'

Sankt-Peterburgskij Gosudarstvennyj Elektrotehničeskij Universitet 'LETI'

ul. Prof. Popova 5, Sankt-Peterburg 197376
Tel: +7(812) 346-4487
Fax: +7(812) 346-2758
EMail: eltech@eltech.ru; root@post.etu.spb.ru
Website: http://www.eltech.ru

Rector: Vladimir Kutuzov EMail: VMKutuzov@eltech.ru

Vice-Rector for Administration: Sergey V. Mamistov
EMail: SVMamistov@mail.eltech.ru

Faculties

Computer and Information Technology (Applied Mathematics; Automation and Control Engineering; Computer Engineering; Computer Graphics; Computer Science; Information Management; Mathematics; Software Engineering; Systems Analysis); **Economics and Management** (Business Computing; Economics; Information Management; Information Technology; Management); **Electrical Engineering and Automation** (Automation and Control Engineering; Electrical Engineering; Electronic Engineering; Marine Transport; Power Engineering; Robotics); **Electronics** (Electronic Engineering; Laser Engineering; Mathematics; Microelectronics; Physical Engineering; Physics); **Humanities** (History; Modern Languages; Philosophy; Political Sciences; Public Relations; Russian; Social Studies; Sociology); **Instrumentation and Biotechnological Engineering** (Biotechnology; Engineering Drawing and Design; Environmental Engineering; Laser Engineering; Physical Chemistry; Physical Education; Safety Engineering; Sound Engineering (Acoustics); Sports); **Radio Engineering and Telecommunications** (Astronomy and Space Science; Electronic Engineering; Radio and Television Broadcasting; Telecommunications Engineering; Video)

Further Information: Also Preparatory courses for foreign students; Continuing Education and In Service Education for Academic Staff faculties

History: Founded 1886 as Engineering College of Post and Telegraph. Became Imperial Institute 1891 and acquired present status and title 1992.

Academic Year: September to June (September-January; February-June)

Admission Requirements: Secondary school certificate (Attestato srednem obrazovanii) or equivalent

Main Language(s) of Instruction: Russian, English

Degrees and Diplomas: *Bakalavr*: 4 yrs; *Specialist Diploma*: 5 1/2 yrs; *Magistr*: 2 yrs following Bakalavr's; *Kandidat Nauk*: a further 3 yrs; *Doktor Nauk*: by thesis following Kandidat

Student Services: Academic counselling, Canteen, Cultural centre, Employment services, Foreign Studies Centre, Health services, Social counselling, Sports facilities

Special Facilities: History of the University Museum. A. Popov Museum

Libraries: Central Library, c. 1m. vols

Publications: Izvestija ETU *(quarterly)*

Press or Publishing House: Publishing House
Last Updated: 29/02/12

SAINT-PETERSBURG STATE INSTITUTE OF PSYCHOLOGY AND SOCIAL WORK

Sankt-Peterburgskij Gosudarstvennyj Institut Psihologii i Socialnoj Raboty

Vasilievsky ostrov, 55, 6 Liniya, Sankt-Peterburg 199178
Tel: +7(812) 323-0784 +7(812) 327-1425
Fax: +7(812) 323-0784
EMail: info@gipsr.ru
Website: http://www.psysocwork.ru

Rector: Yuri Platonov Tel: +7(812) 323-0780

Programmes

Applied Psychology (Developmental Psychology; Educational Psychology; Industrial and Organizational Psychology; Psychology; Social Psychology); **Graduate and Postgraduate Studies** (Educational Psychology; Psychology; Social Psychology; Social Work); **Social Work** (Family Studies; Social and Community Services; Social Psychology; Social Work)

History: Founded 1992, acquired present status 1999.

Academic Year: September to June

Main Language(s) of Instruction: Russian

Degrees and Diplomas: *Bakalavr*: 4 yrs; *Specialist Diploma*: 5 yrs; *Magistr*; *Kandidat Nauk*; *Doktor Nauk*

Student Residential Facilities: Yes
Last Updated: 28/02/12

SAINT-PETERSBURG STATE INSTITUTE OF TECHNOLOGY (TECHNICAL UNIVERSITY)

Sankt-Peterburgskij Gosudarstvennyj Tehnologičeskij Institut (Tehničeskij Universitet) (SPSIT)

prosp. Moskovskij 26, Sankt-Peterburg 190013
Tel: +7(812) 259-4839
Fax: +7(812) 259-4839
EMail: office@technolog.edu.ru
Website: http://technolog.edu.ru

Rector: Nikolay Vasilievich Lisitsin (1985-)
Tel: +7(812) 710-1356 EMail: rector@technolog.edu.ru

International Relations: Alexey Kudryashov, Head of International Department
Tel: +7(812) 494-9377, Fax: +7(812) 315-1434
EMail: international@technolog.edu.ru

Faculties

Advanced Training for University Teachers (Analytical Chemistry; Higher Education; Inorganic Chemistry; Organic Chemistry); **Biotechnology** (Biotechnology; Environmental Engineering; Microbiology; Organic Chemistry); **Chemistry of Substances and Materials** (Analytical Chemistry; Chemistry; Inorganic Chemistry;

Organic Chemistry; Physical Chemistry); **Distance Learning** (Chemistry; Computer Science; Information Sciences; Technology); **Economics and Management** (Economics; Finance; History; Human Resources; Industrial Engineering; Management; Marketing; Modern Languages; Philosophy; Physical Education; Russian; Sociology; Statistics); **Engineering** (Chemical Engineering; Energy Engineering; Nuclear Engineering; Physics); **Information Technology and Control** (Applied Mathematics; Chemical Engineering; Computer Graphics; Electronic Engineering; Information Technology); **Mechanical Engineering** (Engineering Drawing and Design; Mechanical Engineering; Robotics)

History: Founded 1828. Acquired current status 2002.

Governing Bodies: Rectorat

Academic Year: September-January; February-June

Admission Requirements: Secondary education certificate (Attestat o srednem obrazovanii)

Fees: (Roubles): 100,000 per annum

Main Language(s) of Instruction: Russian

International Co-operation: With universities in Germany, Korea, Denmark, Algeria, China, Finland, France, other CIS countries

Degrees and Diplomas: *Bakalavr*: 4 yrs; *Specialist Diploma*: 5 1/2 yrs; *Magistr*: 2 yrs; *Kandidat Nauk*: 3 yrs; *Doktor Nauk*: from 5 yrs

Student Residential Facilities: For c. 3,820 students

Special Facilities: St. Petersburg State Institute of Technology Museum

Libraries: 1,000,000 vols

Press or Publishing House: 'Syntes' Publishing company

Academic Staff *2011-2012*	**TOTAL**
FULL-TIME	**495**
PART-TIME	**11**
STAFF WITH DOCTORATE	
FULL-TIME	**120**
PART-TIME	**3**
Student Numbers *2011-2012*	
All (Foreign Included)	c. **6,000**
FOREIGN ONLY	**200**

Distance students, 40.

Last Updated: 29/09/11

SAINT-PETERSBURG STATE MARINE TECHNICAL UNIVERSITY

Sankt-Peterburgskij Gosudarstvennyj Morskoj Tehničeskij Universitet

ul. Locmanskaja 3, Sankt-Peterburg 190008
Tel: +7(812) 495-0227
Fax: +7(812) 495-0227
EMail: inter@smtu.ru
Website: http://www.smtu.ru

Rector: Konstantin P. Borisenko EMail: rector@smtu.ru

International Relations: K. V. Roždestvenskij
Tel: +7(812) 114-2932

Faculties

Business and Management (Accountancy; Banking; Business Administration; Economics; Finance; Industrial and Organizational Psychology; Management; Small Business; Taxation); **Marine Electronics and Control Systems** (Computer Engineering; Computer Networks; Electronic Engineering; Marine Engineering; Transport Engineering); **Marine Engineering** (Automation and Control Engineering; Electrical Engineering; Electronic Engineering; Marine Engineering; Mechanical Engineering); **Natural Sciences, Social Sciences and Humanities** (Applied Mathematics; Arts and Humanities; Chemistry; Computer Graphics; Cultural Studies; History; Law; Materials Engineering; Mathematics; Mechanical Engineering; Modern Languages; Natural Sciences; Philosophy; Physical Education; Physics; Political Sciences; Russian; Social Sciences); **Naval Architecture and Ocean Engineering** (Marine Engineering; Marine Science and Oceanography; Naval Architecture)

Further Information: Branch in Severodvinsk. Also courses for foreign students

History: Founded 1930 as Shipbuilding Institute, acquired present status and title 1991.

Governing Bodies: Administrative Academic Council

Academic Year: September to June (September-January; February-June)

Admission Requirements: Secondary school certificate (Attestat o srednem obrazovanii) or equivalent

Main Language(s) of Instruction: Russian

Degrees and Diplomas: *Bakalavr*: 4 yrs; *Specialist Diploma*: 5 1/2 yrs; *Specialist Diploma*: 5 yrs; *Magistr*: Science, a further 1-2 yrs; *Kandidat Nauk*: a further 3-4 yrs

Student Services: Academic counselling, Canteen, Foreign Studies Centre, Health services, Social counselling

Libraries: c. 1m. vols

Press or Publishing House: Publishing Department

Last Updated: 27/02/12

SAINT-PETERSBURG STATE MEDICAL ACADEMY NAMED AFTER I.I. MECHNIKOV

Sankt-Peterburgskaja Gosudarstvennaja Medicinskaja Akademija im. I.I. Mečnihova

pr. Piskarjovskij 47, Sankt-Peterburg 195067
Tel: +7(812) 534-9609
Fax: +7(812) 740-1524
EMail: mechnik@gmail.com
Website: http://www.mechnik.spb.ru

Rector (Acting): Alexander Leela Tel: +7(812) 543-5014

Vice-Rector for Administration (Acting): Pavel Korovchenko
Tel: +7(812) 543-9547

International Relations: Natalia Denisenko, Provost (Acting)
Tel: +7(812) 543-5432, Fax: +7(812) 543-5432
EMail: spbgma_fiu@front.ru

Faculties

Advanced Nursing Education (Medicine; Nursing); **Medicine** (Anaesthesiology; Anatomy; Biochemistry; Biophysics; Community Health; Dentistry; Dermatology; Embryology and Reproduction Biology; Endocrinology; Forensic Medicine and Dentistry; Genetics; Gynaecology and Obstetrics; Histology; Hygiene; Immunology; Latin; Medicine; Microbiology; Modern Languages; Nephrology; Neurology; Nursing; Oncology; Orthopaedics; Paediatrics; Pathology; Pedagogy; Pharmacology; Physical Education; Physical Therapy; Physiology; Pneumology; Psychology; Public Health; Radiology; Russian; Surgery; Urology; Venereology; Virology); **Preventive Medicine** (Epidemiology; Health Administration; Hygiene; Medicine; Public Health; Social and Preventive Medicine); **Social Professions** (Hygiene; Medicine; Social Sciences)

Further Information: Also Faculty of General Medicine for Foreign Students, Preparatory Faculty and Faculty training and professional Retraining

History: Founded 1907 as Psychoneurological Institute, renamed 1946 as Leningrad Medical Institute of Sanitary and Hygiene. Acquired present status and title 1994.

Academic Year: September to June

Admission Requirements: Secondary school certificate

Main Language(s) of Instruction: Russian, English

International Co-operation: With universities in Sweden, Finland, USA, Canada and Germany

Accrediting Agencies: Ministry of Education and Science of the Russian Federation, Ministry of Health

Degrees and Diplomas: *Specialist Diploma*: Medicine; Surgery, 2-3 yrs; *Doktor Nauk*: Medicine; Surgery, 6 yrs. Also specialisations in Medicine, 2-3 yrs

Student Services: Academic counselling, Canteen, Cultural centre, Foreign student adviser, Health services, Language programs, Social counselling, Sports facilities

Student Residential Facilities: Yes

Libraries: More than 600,000 vols, computer centre

Publications: Vestnik Sankt-Peterburgskoi Gosudarstvennoi Medicinskoi Akademii *(quarterly)*

Academic Staff *2007-2008*	MEN	WOMEN	TOTAL
FULL-TIME	246	342	**588**
PART-TIME	109	97	**206**
STAFF WITH DOCTORATE			
FULL-TIME	–	–	**447**
PART-TIME	–	–	**85**
Student Numbers *2007-2008*			
All (Foreign Included)	2,224	2,507	**4,731**
FOREIGN ONLY	400	114	**514**

Part-time students, 536. **Evening students**, 145.
Last Updated: 01/03/12

SAINT-PETERSBURG STATE MEDICAL ACADEMY OF PAEDIATRICS

Sankt-Peterburgskaja Gosudarstvennaja Pediatričeskaja Medicinskaja Akademija (SPBGPMA)

ul. Litovskaja 2, Sankt-Peterburg 194100
Tel: +7(812) 295-06-46
Fax: +7(812) 295-40-85
EMail: spb@gpma.ru
Website: http://www.gpma.ru/

Rector: Vladimir V. Levanovich EMail: gpma@gpma.ru

Faculties
Clinical Psychology (Clinical Psychology); **General Medicine** (Medicine); **Pediatrics** (Paediatrics); **Stomatology** (Stomatology)

History: Organized as a clinical paediatric hospital 1905. Became the Research Institute of Maternity and Child Welfare 1925. Acquired present status 1995.

Governing Bodies: Federal Agency of Public Health Services and Social Development.

Academic Year: From September to June

Admission Requirements: High school certificate; entrance examinations

Main Language(s) of Instruction: Russian; English

International Co-operation: With universities in 70 countries

Accrediting Agencies: Ministry of Health Care

Degrees and Diplomas: *Specialist Diploma*: 5 - 6 yrs; *Kandidat Nauk*; *Doktor Nauk*. Also Post-graduate course certificate and more than 40 specializations

Student Services: Cultural centre, Health services, Language programs, Nursery care, Social counselling, Sports facilities

Student Residential Facilities: 4 hostels

Special Facilities: 25 laboratories, 2 Museums

Libraries: 600,000 vols

Publications: Vestnik Pediatricheskoj Akademij *(quarterly)*

Press or Publishing House: University Publishing House

Last Updated: 20/09/11

SAINT-PETERSBURG STATE MINING INSTITUTE NAMED AFTER G.V. PLEKHANOV

Sankt-Peterburgskij Gosudarstvennyj Gornyj Institut im. G.V. Plekhanova (SPMI (TU))

Vasilevskii ostrov 21, Linija 2, Sankt-Peterburg 199106
Tel: +7(812) 328-8200
Fax: +7(812) 321-4081
EMail: rectorat@spmi.ru
Website: http://www.spmi.ru

Rector: Vladimir S. Litvinenko (1994-) Tel: +7(812) 327-7360

First Vice-Rector: Natalia V. Pashkevich
Tel: +7(812) 328-4077, Fax: +7(812) 328-4077
EMail: slm@spmi.ru

International Relations: Vladimir T. Borzenkov
Tel: +7(812) 328-8248, Fax: +7(812) 328-8248
EMail: ums@spmi.ru

Departments
Oil and Gas (Geology; Petroleum and Gas Engineering; Petrology)

Faculties
Chemistry and Metallurgy (Automation and Control Engineering; Biotechnology; Energy Engineering; Engineering Management; Environmental Engineering; Industrial Engineering; Metallurgical Engineering; Mining Engineering; Physical Chemistry; Thermal Physics); **Economics** (Accountancy; Administration; Business Computing; Industrial Management; Management); **Geological Surveying** (Crystallography; Geochemistry; Geological Engineering; Geology; Geophysics; Mineralogy; Mining Engineering; Paleontology; Petroleum and Gas Engineering; Petrology; Seismology); **Humanities** (Computer Engineering; Computer Science; English; French; German; History; Literature; Mathematics; Modern Languages; Philology; Philosophy; Physical Education; Physics; Psychology; Russian; Sociology); **Mining and Electromechanics** (Construction Engineering; Electrical and Electronic Engineering; Explosive Engineering; Geological Engineering; Hydraulic Engineering; Machine Building; Mechanical Engineering; Transport Engineering); **Underground Space Development** (Building Technologies; Construction Engineering; Geological Engineering; Mechanics; Physics; Surveying and Mapping)

Schools
Mountain Studies (Ecology; Environmental Engineering; Environmental Management; Explosive Engineering; Geochemistry; Geology; Mineralogy; Mining Engineering; Mountain Studies; Natural Resources; Safety Engineering)

Further Information: Also Correspondence School and Faculty of Vocational Education

History: Founded 1773. Acquired present status 1991.

Governing Bodies: Academic Council

Academic Year: September to June (September-December; February-June)

Admission Requirements: Secondary education certificate (Attestat o srednem obrazovanii)

Fees: (US Dollars): Russian Students, free of charge except Contract Training, 2,500 per annum; foreign students, Bachelor's Degree, 3,200 per annum, Master's Degree, 3,500 per annum, Postgraduate, 5,000 per annum

Main Language(s) of Instruction: Russian

International Co-operation: With universities in Germany, France, Austria, Poland, Bulgaria, Finland, Sweden, United Kingdom, Romania, Italy, Nepal, Angola, USA, Canada, Cuba, China, Mongolia, Republic of Korea

Accrediting Agencies: The Ministry of Education and Sciences of the Russian Federation

Degrees and Diplomas: *Bakalavr*: Technical Sciences; Engineering; Economy; Management, 4 yrs; *Specialist Diploma*: Engineering, Technology, Economy; Management, 5 yrs; *Magistr*: Engineering, Technology, Economy; Management, a further 2 yrs after Bakalavr; *Kandidat Nauk*: Engineering, Technology, Economy; Management, a further 3-4 yrs; *Doktor Nauk*: Engineering, Technology, Economy; Management

Student Services: Academic counselling, Canteen, Cultural centre, Employment services, Foreign student adviser, Foreign Studies Centre, Health services, Language programs, Social counselling, Sports facilities

Student Residential Facilities: 5 hostels in the centre of St. Petersburg

Special Facilities: The Mining Museum; Conference Halls; Research and Education Centre; Laboratory Complex; Physical Education Centre; Industrial Training Grounds; Video Studio

Libraries: The Mining Library; the Library of the Russian Mineralogical Society

Publications: Proceedings of the Mining Institute, Publications on research in Mineral and Raw-Material Sector; Publications of the Institute's researchers, under and Postgraduate students *(quarterly)*; Proceedings of the Russian Mineralogical Society, Publications on research in Mineral and Raw-Material Sector; Publications of the Institute's researchers, under and Postgraduate students *(annually)*

Last Updated: 28/02/12

SAINT-PETERSBURG STATE POLYTECHNIC UNIVERSITY

Sankt-Peterburgskij Gosudarstvennyj Politehničeskij Universitet (SPBSPU)

ul. Politehničeskaja 29, Sankt-Peterburg 195251
Tel: +7(812) 534-1002
Fax: +7(812) 534-1365
EMail: office@spbstu.ru
Website: http://www.spbstu.ru

Rector: Vladimir Glukhov
Tel: +7(812) 247-1616, Fax: +7(812) 552-7882
EMail: rector@spbstu.ru

Vice-Rector for Administration: S. Romanov
Tel: +7(812) 247-2088, Fax: +7(812) 247-2088
EMail: Mail@ums.stu.neva.ru

International Relations: Dmitry G. Arseniev, Vice-Rector for International Affairs Tel: +7(812) 534-1001

Departments

Innovation (Industrial Management; Management)

Faculties

Economics and Management (Accountancy; Business Administration; Business and Commerce; Economics; Engineering Management; Environmental Management; Finance; International Economics; Management; Marketing; Social Sciences); **Electromechanical** (Electrical Engineering; Mechanical Engineering; Power Engineering); **Engineering and Construction** (Civil Engineering; Construction Engineering; Energy Engineering; Engineering; Environmental Engineering; Hydraulic Engineering; Landscape Architecture; Materials Engineering); **Foreign Languages** (Cultural Studies; English; Germanic Languages; Linguistics; Modern Languages; Romance Languages); **Humanities** (Arts and Humanities; Educational Psychology; Engineering; History; International Studies; Law; Philosophy; Political Sciences; Psychology; Russian; Social Sciences; Sociology); **Integrated Security** (Civil Security; Physical Education); **Law** (Civil Law; Constitutional Law; Criminal Law; Criminology; History of Law; International Law; Law); **Management and Information Technology** (Artificial Intelligence; Information Technology; Management; Social and Community Services); **Mechanical Engineering** (Automation and Control Engineering; Engineering Drawing and Design; Information Technology; Machine Building; Mechanical Engineering; Printing and Printmaking; Production Engineering; Structural Architecture); **Medical Physics and Bioengineering** (Applied Physics; Bioengineering; Biomedical Engineering; Biotechnology; Cell Biology; Medical Technology; Nanotechnology; Physics); **Physico-Technical** (Astrophysics; Physical Engineering; Solid State Physics); **Physics and Mechanics** (Applied Mathematics; Applied Physics; Biophysics; Engineering; Mathematics; Mechanical Engineering; Nuclear Physics; Physical Engineering; Physics; Thermal Physics); **Power Engineering** (Energy Engineering; Heating and Refrigeration; Industrial Engineering; Nuclear Engineering; Power Engineering; Thermal Engineering); **Radiophysics** (Applied Physics; Electronic Engineering; Nanotechnology; Optics; Radiophysics; Solid State Physics); **Technical Cybernetics** (Automation and Control Engineering; Computer Engineering; Computer Networks; Computer Science; Environmental Engineering; Information Technology; Software Engineering); **Technologies and Materials Research** (Applied Chemistry; Applied Physics; Chemistry; Laser Engineering; Metal Techniques; Metallurgical Engineering; Nanotechnology; Organic Chemistry; Physical Chemistry)

Graduate Schools

Management *(International)* (Business Administration; International Business; International Economics; International Relations; Management)

Institutes

International Education Programmes (Applied Mathematics; Applied Physics; Artificial Intelligence; Computer Graphics; Cultural Studies; Foreigners Education; Information Technology; International Relations; International Studies; Linguistics; Literature; Mathematics; Regional Studies; Russian)

Research Institutes

Robotics and Technical Cybernetics (RTC) (Automation and Control Engineering; Electronic Engineering; Robotics)

Further Information: Also International Education programmes

History: Founded 1899 as St. Petersburg Politechnic Institute, acquired present title 1994.

Governing Bodies: Academic Council, comprising 80 members

Academic Year: September to July (September-January; February-June; June-July)

Admission Requirements: Secondary education certificate (Attestat o srednem obrazovanii) and entrance examination

Fees: None. Fees for foreigners and some local students

Main Language(s) of Instruction: Russian, English

International Co-operation: Participates in ERASMUS, Finnish-Russian Student Exchange Programmes

Degrees and Diplomas: *Bakalavr*: 4 yrs; *Specialist Diploma*: a further 1 1/2 yrs; *Magistr*: 2 yrs following Bakalavr's; *Kandidat Nauk*: a further 3 yrs; *Doktor Nauk*

Student Services: Academic counselling, Canteen, Cultural centre, Foreign student adviser, Foreign Studies Centre, Health services, Language programs, Social counselling, Sports facilities

Student Residential Facilities: For 2,000 students

Special Facilities: History Museum; Technology Museum. Theatre

Libraries: Main Library, c. 3.5m. vols

Publications: Nauchno-technicheskie Vedomosty *(quarterly)*

Press or Publishing House: 'Polytechnic'Publishing House

Academic Staff *2010-2011*: Total: c. 550
Student Numbers *2010-2011*: Total: c. 16,900
Distance students, 4,160. **Evening students**, 4,200.
Last Updated: 27/02/12

SAINT-PETERSBURG STATE TECHNOLOGICAL UNIVERSITY OF PLANT POLYMERS

Sankt-Peterburgskij Gosudarstvennyj Tehnologičeskij Universitet Rastitelnyh Polimerov (TUPP)
ul. Ivana Černyh 4, Sankt-Peterburg 198095
Tel: +7(812) 786-5744
Fax: +7(812) 786-8600
EMail: mail@gturp.spb.ru
Website: http://www.gturp.spb.ru

Rector: Pavel Lukanin

Vice-Rector for Academic Affairs: Evgeny V. Khardikov

Departments

Energy and Industry (Energy Engineering; Heating and Refrigeration; Power Engineering; Thermal Engineering); **Engineering and Environment** (Biotechnology; Chemical Engineering; Ecology; Energy Engineering; Environmental Management; Natural Resources; Waste Management); **Mechanics of Automated Production** (Automation and Control Engineering; Industrial Engineering; Mechanical Engineering)

Faculties

Automated Process Control Systems (Applied Mathematics; Automation and Control Engineering; Computer Science; Electrical Engineering; Power Engineering); **Chemical Engineering** (Chemical Engineering; Packaging Technology; Paper Technology; Polymer and Plastics Technology; Wood Technology); **Economics and Management** (Accountancy; Banking; Business and Commerce; Economics; Finance; Industrial Management; Taxation; Transport Management); **Humanities** (Advertising and Publicity; Design; Heritage Preservation; Museum Studies; Public Relations)

Schools

Correspondence Studies (Automation and Control Engineering; Biotechnology; Chemical Engineering; Cultural Studies; Economics; Energy Engineering; Engineering Management; Finance; Heating and Refrigeration; Industrial Management; Management; Natural Resources; Petroleum and Gas Engineering; Thermal Engineering; Transport Management; Wood Technology); **Evening Education** (Applied Mathematics; Automation and Control Engineering; Biotechnology; Chemical Engineering; Computer Science; Design; Energy Engineering; Environmental Engineering; Finance; Industrial Design; Industrial Engineering; Industrial Management; Management; Packaging Technology; Power Engineering; Printing and Printmaking; Thermal Engineering; Transport Management)

Further Information: Special courses for foreign students. Study Abroad programmes

History: Founded 1931, acquired present status and title 1993. The former Leningrad Technological Insitute of the Pulp and Paper Industry

Governing Bodies: Scientific Council

Academic Year: September to June (September-January; February-June)

Admission Requirements: Secondary school certificate (Attestat o srednem obrazovanii)

Main Language(s) of Instruction: Russian

Degrees and Diplomas: *Bakalavr*: 4 yrs; *Specialist Diploma*: 1 1/2 yrs following Bakalavr's Diploma; *Magistr*: a further 2 yrs

Student Services: Academic counselling, Canteen, Cultural centre, Foreign Studies Centre, Health services, Social counselling, Sports facilities

Student Residential Facilities: For c. 2,000 students

Special Facilities: History Museum. Art Gallery. Movie Studio

Libraries: c. 1m. vols

Press or Publishing House: Publishing and Editing Unit

Academic Staff *2010-2011*: Total: c. 300

Student Numbers *2010-2011*: Total: c. 5,000

Last Updated: 27/02/12

SAINT-PETERSBURG STATE THEATRE ARTS ACADEMY

Sankt-Peterburgskaja Gosudarstvennaja Akademija Teatralnogo Iskusstva

ul. Mokhovaja 34, Sankt-Peterburg 191028
Tel: +7(812) 273-07-51
Fax: +7(812) 273-03-83 +7(812) 272-24-79
EMail: rector@tart.spb.ru
Website: http://www.tart.spb.ru

Rector: Lev Sundstrem (1993-)

Departments

Drama (Acting; Cinema and Television; Music; Performing Arts; Theatre; Video); **Puppetry** (Performing Arts; Technology; Theatre); **Stage Design and Stage Design Technology** (Display and Stage Design; Theatre); **Theatre Studies** (Theatre)

History: Founded 1779. Acquired present status 1993.

Governing Bodies: Academic Council

Academic Year: September to July (September-January; February-July)

Admission Requirements: Secondary school certificate (Attestat zrelosti) and entrance examination

Degrees and Diplomas: *Bakalavr*; *Specialist Diploma*; *Magistr*; *Kandidat Nauk*

Student Services: Canteen, Foreign Studies Centre, Health services, Social counselling, Sports facilities

Student Residential Facilities: For c. 230 students

Special Facilities: "On Mohovaya " Academy Theatre; Exhibition Hall

Libraries: c. 300,000 vols

Last Updated: 19/03/12

SAINT-PETERSBURG STATE UNIVERSITY

Sankt-Peterburgskij Gosudarstvennyj Universitet

Universiteckaja nab. 7/9, Sankt-Peterburg 199034
Tel: +7(812) 328-2000
Fax: +7(812) 325-8736 +7(812) 326-4976
EMail: rector@pu.ru
Website: http://www.spbu.ru

Rector: Nikolay M. Kropachev (2009-2014)
Tel: +7(812) 328-9701, Fax: +7(812) 325-8736
EMail: office@jurfak.spb.ru

Head of the Public Relations Office: Marina Maximova
Tel: +7(812) 328-0402, Fax: +7(812) 328-0402
EMail: m.maximova@econ.pu.ru

International Relations: Konstantin Platonov, Deputy Vice-Rector for International Affairs
Tel: +7(812) 326-4943, Fax: +7(812) 328-1346
EMail: platonov@ir.pu.ru

Departments

Military Education (Military Science); **Physical Education and Sports** (Physical Education; Sports)

Faculties

Applied Mathematics (Applied Mathematics; Computer Science); **Arts** (Architectural and Environmental Design; Cinema and Television; Design; Fine Arts; Graphic Design; Music; Musical Instruments; Painting and Drawing; Performing Arts; Restoration of Works of Art; Sculpture; Theatre); **Biology** (Biology; Soil Science); **Chemistry** (Chemistry); **Economics** (Accountancy; Economics; Finance; Insurance; Statistics); **Geography and Geo-ecology** (Ecology; Geography; Geology); **Geology** (Earth Sciences; Geology); **History** (Archaeology; Art History; History; Modern History); **International Relations** (International Relations); **Journalism** (Journalism); **Law** (Administrative Law; Civil Law; Commercial Law; Criminal Law; Criminology; International Law; Labour Law; Law); **Liberal Arts and Sciences** *(Smolny College of Liberal Arts and Sciences)* (Anthropology; Art History; Cultural Studies; Economics; Film; History; Human Rights; International Relations; Islamic Studies; Literature; Modern Languages; Music; Performing Arts; Philosophy; Political Sciences; Sociology; Theatre; Video); **Mathematics and Mechanics** (Mathematics; Mechanical Engineering); **Medicine** (Dentistry; Medical Technology; Medicine); **Oriental Studies** (African Studies; Asian Studies; Middle Eastern Studies; Oriental Languages); **Philology and Arts** (Arts and Humanities; Classical Languages; Philology); **Philosophy and Political Science** (Aesthetics; Cultural Studies; Ethics; Philosophy; Political Sciences; Psychology); **Physics** (Physics); **Political Sciences** (Political Sciences); **Psychology** (Psychology); **Sociology** (Sociology; Urban Studies)

Graduate Schools

Management (Management)

Institutes

Linguistic Studies (Linguistics; Terminology); **Management** (Management); **Russian Humanities**

Research Institutes

Astronomy (Astronomy and Space Science); **Biology** (Biology); **Chemistry** (Chemistry); **Complex Social Research** (Social Studies); **Computational Mathematics and Control Process** (Applied Mathematics); **Earth's Crust** (Earth Sciences; Geology); **Geography** (Geography); **Information Technologies** (Information Technology; Software Engineering); **Mathematics and Mechanics** (Mathematics; Mechanical Engineering); **Physics** (Physics); **Physiology** (Physiology); **Radiophysics** (Physics; Radiophysics)

Further Information: Also campus in Peterhof

History: Founded 1724 as part of the Russian Acadmy of Science.; closed between 1765 and 1819. Reopened 1819 with present title.

Governing Bodies: Academic Council; Faculty Councils

Academic Year: September to July (September-January; February-July)

Admission Requirements: Secondary school certificate (Attestat o srednem obrazovanii) and entrance examination

Main Language(s) of Instruction: Russian; English

International Co-operation: With more than 190 Universities in Europe, America and Asia. Participates in the following programmes: Erasmus Mundus External Cooperation Window (cooperation with the following universities: University of Turku, Finland (Coordinator); University of Algarve, Portugal; University of Bologna, Italy; University of Deusto, Spain; University of Göttingen, Germany; Humboldt University Berlin, Germany; University of Leuven, Belgium; Middle East Technical University, Turkey); Tempus (cooperation with the following universities: Helsinki University, Finland; Hamburg University, Germany; London University, Great Britain; Cambridge University, Great Britain; Nijmegen University, the Netherlands; Amsterdam University, the Netherlands; Kalmar University, Sweden; Nancy University, France; Bialystok Technical University, Poland); First (cooperation with the following universities: Turku University, Joensuu University, Tampere University, Finland); Cross-Border University (cooperation with the following universities: Helsinki University, Joensuu University, Kuopio University, Tampere University, Lappeenranta Technical University).

Degrees and Diplomas: *Bakalavr*: 4 yrs; *Specialist Diploma*: 5 yrs; *Magistr*: a further 2 yrs; *Kandidat Nauk*: a further 3 yrs and thesis; *Doktor Nauk*: by thesis after Kandidat

Student Services: Academic counselling, Canteen, Cultural centre, Employment services, Foreign student adviser, Health services, Language programs, Social counselling, Sports facilities

Student Residential Facilities: Yes

Special Facilities: Dmitry Mendeleev Museum and Archives; Museum of the History of the University; Botanical Garden; Mineralogical Museum

Libraries: Gor'kij Scientific Library, c. 7m. vols; faculty libraries

Publications: Vestnik Sankt-Petersburgskogo Universiteta *(quarterly)*

Press or Publishing House: SPB University Press

Academic Staff *2010-2011*	**TOTAL**
FULL-TIME	**3,900**
PART-TIME	**1,500**
STAFF WITH DOCTORATE	
FULL-TIME	**2,200**
PART-TIME	**470**
Student Numbers *2010-2011*	
All (Foreign Included)	c. **30,000**
FOREIGN ONLY	**1,500**

Distance students, 2,900. **Evening students**, 4,800.

Last Updated: 27/02/12

SAINT-PETERSBURG STATE UNIVERSITY OF AEROSPACE INSTRUMENTATION

Sankt-Peterburgskij Gosudarstvennyj Universitet Aerokosmičeskogo Priborostroenija

ul. Bolshaja.Morskaja 67, Sankt-Peterburg 190000
Tel: +7(812) 312-0937
Fax: +7(812) 312-0658
EMail: int@aanet.ru
Website: http://www.aanet.ru

Rector: Anatolij A. Ovodenko (1999-)

Vice-Rector: Vitaly Khimenko

International Relations: Oksana Mukhina, Head of Department, International Cooperation

Faculties

Additional and Secondary Professional Education; **Aerospace Instruments and Systems** (Aeronautical and Aerospace Engineering; Computer Science); **Computer Systems and Programming** (Computer Networks; Computer Science; Information Technology); **Economics** (Accountancy; Business Computing; E-Business/Commerce; Economics; Finance; International Relations; Management); **Humanities** (History; Modern Languages; Philosophy; Physical Education; Political Sciences; Sports); **Information Systems and Data Protection** (Information Sciences; Information Technology); **Innovation and Basic Masters Training** (Applied Mathematics; Mathematics; Mechanics; Meteorology; Physics); **Intellectual Control Systems and Nanotechnologies** (Electrical Engineering; Measurement and Precision Engineering; Nanotechnology; Nuclear Engineering; Power Engineering; Thermal Engineering); **Law** (Civil Law; Commercial Law; Criminal Law; Criminology; International Law; Law); **Military Education** (Military Science); **Radio Engineering, Electronics and Communications** (Electronic Engineering; Optical Technology; Optics; Telecommunications Engineering)

Further Information: Also Russian Language courses

History: Founded 1941, acquired present title 1993.

Governing Bodies: Rectorat

Academic Year: September - January; February - June

Admission Requirements: Secondary school certificate (Diplom o srednem obrazovanii) or equivalent (Diplom o srednem specialnom obrazovanii)

Fees: (Roubles): 35,000 to 70,000 per semester

Main Language(s) of Instruction: Russian

International Co-operation: with institutions in France, Belgium, USA, Poland, Germany, Italy, Spain, China, Republic of Korea, Canada

Degrees and Diplomas: *Bakalavr*: 4 yrs; *Specialist Diploma*: 5 yrs; *Magistr*: 2 yrs after Bakalavr

Student Residential Facilities: For c. 7,000 students

Libraries: c. 950,000 vols

Academic Staff *2010-2011*	**TOTAL**
FULL-TIME	c. **800**
Student Numbers *2010-11*	
All (Foreign Included)	c. **13,000**
FOREIGN ONLY	**560**

Last Updated: 30/09/11

SAINT-PETERSBURG STATE UNIVERSITY OF ARCHITECTURE AND CIVIL ENGINEERING

Sankt-Peterburgskij Gosudarstvennyj Arhitekturno-Stroitel'nyj Universitet (SPUACE)

ul. 2-aja Krasnoarmejskaja 4, Sankt-Peterburg 190005
Tel: +7(812) 316-4819
Fax: +7(812) 316-3261
EMail: rector@spbgasu.ru
Website: http://www.spbgasu.ru

Rector: Evgenij Rybnov EMail: rybnov@spbgasu.ru

Faculties

Architecture (Architecture; Town Planning; Urban Studies); **Automobile and Transport Engineering** (Automotive Engineering; Transport and Communications; Transport Engineering; Transport Management); **Civil Engineering** (Architectural Restoration; Building Technologies; Civil Engineering; Construction Engineering; Materials Engineering); **Economics and Management** (Economics; Management); **Environmental Engineering and Protection** (Applied Mathematics; Energy Engineering; Environmental Engineering; Heating and Refrigeration; Water Management)

Further Information: Russsian Language courses for foreign students

History: Founded 1832, acquired present status and title 1993.

Governing Bodies: Academic Council

Academic Year: September to June (September-January; February-June)

Admission Requirements: Secondary school certificate (Attestat o srednem obrazovanii)

Main Language(s) of Instruction: Russian

International Co-operation: With universities in Finland, Germany, Poland, Austria, USA, China

Accrediting Agencies: Ministry of Education

Degrees and Diplomas: *Bakalavr*, *Specialist Diploma*; *Magistr*, *Kandidat Nauk*

Student Services: Academic counselling, Canteen, Employment services, Foreign student adviser, Health services, Social counselling, Sports facilities

Student Residential Facilities: For 1,597 students

Special Facilities: University History Museum

Libraries: c. 1m. vols

Publications: Scientific Papers *(biannually)*

Press or Publishing House: Publishing Department

Last Updated: 19/12/11

SAINT-PETERSBURG STATE UNIVERSITY OF CINEMA AND TELEVISION

Sankt-Peterburgskij Gosudarstvennyj Universitet Kino i Televidenija

ul. Pravdy, 13, Sankt-Peterburg 191119
Tel: +7(812) 315-74-83 +7(812) 315-70-04
Fax: +7(812) 315-01-72
EMail: rektorat@liki.spb.ru
Website: http://www.gukit.ru/

Rector: Aleksandr D. Evmenov

Departments
Mass Communication (Advertising and Publicity; Journalism; Mass Communication; Public Administration; Public Relations); **Multimedia Equipment** (Computer Graphics; Film; Multimedia; Photography; Video)

Faculties
Audiovisual Equipement (Cinema and Television; Electronic Engineering; Nanotechnology; Radio and Television Broadcasting; Sound Engineering (Acoustics); Video)

Institutes
Economics and Management (Accountancy; Economics; Management); **Screen Arts** (Cinema and Television; Computer Graphics; Film; Multimedia; Theatre)

Schools
Photo and Material Recording Technologies (Biotechnology; Chemical Engineering; Environmental Management; Natural Resources; Photography; Polymer and Plastics Technology; Sound Engineering (Acoustics))

History: Founded 1918. Acquired present status 1998.

Fees: (Rubles): c. 150,000 per annum

Main Language(s) of Instruction: Russian

International Co-operation: with universities in UK, Denmark, France, Hungary

Accrediting Agencies: Federal Ministry of Education

Degrees and Diplomas: *Bakalavr*: 4 yrs; *Specialist Diploma*: 5 yrs; *Magistr*

Student Services: Academic counselling, Canteen, Employment services, Foreign student adviser, Foreign Studies Centre, Health services, Social counselling, Sports facilities

Special Facilities: Film museum

Libraries: 2 libraries, 20 film studios

Academic Staff *2010-2011*	MEN	WOMEN	**TOTAL**
FULL-TIME	250	350	**600**
PART-TIME	50	30	**80**
STAFF WITH DOCTORATE			
FULL-TIME	–	–	**160**
PART-TIME	–	–	c. **50**
Student Numbers *2010-2011*			
All (Foreign Included)	2,500	3,500	c. **6,000**
FOREIGN ONLY	50	15	**65**

Distance students, 2,100. **Evening students**, 580.

Last Updated: 27/02/12

SAINT-PETERSBURG STATE UNIVERSITY OF CIVIL AVIATION

Sankt-Peterburgskij Gosudarstvennyj Universitet Grazhdanskoj Aviatsii

ul. Pilotov 38, Sankt-Peterburg 196210
Tel: +7(812) 104-1818
Fax: +7(812) 104-1863
EMail: info@academiaga.ru
Website: http://www.academiaga.ru/

Rector: Mikhail Yurevich Smurov (2004-) Tel: +7(812) 704-1511

International Relations: Yuri Michalczewski, Vice-Rector for International Relations Tel: +7(812) 704-1514

Departments
Air Freight and Airport Management (Air Transport; Transport Management); **Aviation Management** (Air Transport; Economics; Human Resources; Management); **Engineering and Technology** (Aeronautical and Aerospace Engineering; Automation and Control Engineering; Computer Science; Engineering; Safety Engineering)

Faculties
Flight Operations (Aeronautical and Aerospace Engineering; Air Transport); **Humanities** (Communication Studies; Economics; History; Human Resources; Modern Languages; Philosophy; Physical Education; Physiology; Psychology; Social Studies); **Law** (Civil Law; Commercial Law; Criminal Law; Criminology; International Law; Labour Law; Law)

Institutes
Air Navigation (Air Transport; Meteorology); **Economics and Management of Transport Systems** (Air Transport; Applied Mathematics; Economics; Transport Management); **Executives and Industry Professionals** (Aeronautical and Aerospace Engineering; Air Transport)

History: Previously known as Akademija Graždanskoj Aviacii (Academy of Civil Aviation). Founded in 1930. Acquired current title and status 2004.

Governing Bodies: Scientific Council

Main Language(s) of Instruction: Russian

Degrees and Diplomas: *Specialist Diploma*: 5 yrs; *Kandidat Nauk*; *Doktor Nauk*

Last Updated: 27/02/12

SAINT-PETERSBURG STATE UNIVERSITY OF CULTURE AND ARTS

Sankt-Peterburgskij Gosudarstvennyj Universitet Kul'tury i Iskusstv

Dvorcovaja Nab.2, Sankt-Peterburg 191186
Tel: +7(812) 314-1121 +7(812) 312-9521
Fax: +7(812) 312-5333
EMail: pk@spbguki.ru
Website: http://www.spbguki.ru/

Rector: Alexander Thurgau

Centres
Director and Producer Skills Studies (Theatre)

Departments
Cultural Studies and Sociology (Art Management; Cultural Studies; Political Sciences; Sociology); **Culture of the Family and Childhood** (Child Care and Development; Cultural Studies; Educational Psychology; Family Studies; Pedagogy; Psychology; Social Studies; Tourism); **History of World Culture** (Art History; Communication Studies; Cultural Studies); **Library and Information** (Documentation Techniques; Information Management; Information Technology; Library Science); **Museology and Cultural Heritage** (Art Management; Cultural Studies; Heritage Preservation; Museum Studies; Tourism); **Pop Music** (Jazz and Popular Music; Music; Musical Instruments)

Faculties
Arts (Art Education; Cinema and Television; Conducting; Cultural Studies; Film; Fine Arts; Jazz and Popular Music; Music; Music Theory and Composition; Musical Instruments; Performing Arts; Photography; Singing; Speech Studies; Theatre; Video); **Information Technology** (Business Computing; Computer Engineering; Computer Graphics; Computer Science; Economics; Information Technology; Law; Social Studies); **Management and Economics** (Advertising and Publicity; Economics; Management; Small Business; Tourism); **Socio-Cultural Technologies** (Cultural Studies; Social Studies)

History: Founded 1918.

Degrees and Diplomas: *Specialist Diploma*

Last Updated: 27/02/12

SAINT-PETERSBURG STATE UNIVERSITY OF ECONOMICS AND FINANCE

Sankt-Peterburgskij Gosudarstvennyj Universitet Ekonomiki i Finansov

ul. Sadovaja 21, Sankt-Peterburg 191023
Tel: +7(812) 310-3823
Fax: +7(812) 110-5674
EMail: rector@finec.ru
Website: http://www.finec.ru/

Rector: Igor A. Maksimtsev (2006-)

Vice-Rector: Alexandre Karlik
Tel: +7(812) 310-3409 EMail: karlik@finec.ru

International Relations: Elena Tarasenko
Tel: +7(812) 315-8134, Fax: +7(812) 710-5644
EMail: tarasenko@finec.ru

Departments

Economic Theory and Politicy (Economic and Finance Policy; Economics; International Economics); **General Economics** (Applied Mathematics; Economic and Finance Policy; Economics; History; Philosophy; Physical Education; Political Sciences); **Statistics, Accountancy and Economic Analysis** (Accountancy; Economic and Finance Policy; Management; Statistics)

Faculties

Commerce and Marketing (Business and Commerce; Economics; Management; Marketing; Transport Management); **Economics and Management** (Economics; Industrial Management; International Economics; Management); **Economics of Labour and Personnel Management** (Commercial Law; Economics; Human Resources; Sociology); **Finance, Credit and International Economic Relations** (Banking; Finance; Insurance; International Economics; International Relations); **Humanities** (Communication Studies; English; German; Literature; Modern Languages; Public Relations; Romance Languages; Russian; Scandinavian Languages; Translation and Interpretation); **Regional Studies, Computer Science, Tourism and Mathematical Methods** (Applied Mathematics; Computer Science; Cultural Studies; Econometrics; Information Sciences; Regional Studies; Social Studies; Tourism)

Schools

Law (Civil Law; Commercial Law; Constitutional Law; Criminal Law; History of Law; Law)

Further Information: Also Russian Language Courses for foreign students

History: Founded 1930 as Leningrad Finance and Economics Institute, acquired present status and title 1991.

Governing Bodies: Scientific Council

Academic Year: September to June (September-December; February-June)

Admission Requirements: Secondary education certificate (Attestat o srednem obrazovanii) for Bakalavr degree and Specialist programmes; Bakalavr degree for Magistr Programme

Main Language(s) of Instruction: Russian

International Co-operation: with 91 institutions. Russian-French Bachelor programme "Licence en Economie et Gestion" in partnership with the University Pierre Mendes-France (Grenoble, France) with the support of Ministry of Foreign Affairs of France. Russian-German programme "Master of International Business Administration Hamburg-St.Petersburg" in partnership with the University of Hamburg with the support of DAAD. Russian-French Master programme "Master of International Business - Corporate Finance, Control & Project Management" in partnership with the University Paris-Dauphine (Paris, France) with the support of Ministry of Foreign Affairs of France. European Master programme "Economy of Enterprise and International Integration" in partnership with the University Pierre Mendes-France (Grenoble, France), Krakow Economic University (Poland), University La Sapienza (Roma, Italy) with the support of European Union (TEMPUS). Participates in the ERASMUS programme with institutions in France, Spain, Italy, Finland, Romania.

Degrees and Diplomas: *Bakalavr*: 4 yrs; *Specialist Diploma*: 5 yrs; *Magistr*: 2 years following Bachelor or Specialist; *Kandidat Nauk*: Economics; Social Sciences; Management; Linguistics; Law, a further 3 yrs; *Doktor Nauk*: Economics; Social Sciences; Management; Linguistics; Law, a further 3 yrs. Also international dual-Bachelor degree programmes with institutions in France, Germany. European Masters with several institutions.

Student Services: Academic counselling, Canteen, Cultural centre, Employment services, Foreign student adviser, Foreign Studies Centre, Health services, Language programs, Social counselling, Sports facilities

Student Residential Facilities: For c. 2,350 students

Special Facilities: University History Museum

Libraries: Yes

Publications: Collection of Scientific Articles *(annually)*; Economist, Journal

Press or Publishing House: Publishing House

Academic Staff *2008-2009*	**TOTAL**
FULL-TIME	c. **1,200**
Student Numbers *2008-2009*	
All (Foreign Included)	**7,823**
FOREIGN ONLY	**399**

Part-time students, 520. **Distance students**, 1,408. **Evening students**, 1,848.

Last Updated: 27/02/12

SAINT-PETERSBURG STATE UNIVERSITY OF ENGINEERING AND ECONOMICS

Sankt-Peterburgskij Gosudarstvennyj Inženerno-Ekonomičeskij Universitet

ul. Marata 27, Sankt-Peterburg 191002

Tel: +7(812) 602-2323

Fax: +7(812) 712-0607

EMail: rector@engec.ru; dept.kancel@engec.ru

Website: http://www.engec.ru

Rector: Olga Goncharuk Tel: +7(812) 118-5003

Departments

Information Systems in Economics and Management (Applied Mathematics; Business Computing; Economics; Information Management; Information Technology; Management; Statistics); **Logistics** (Economics; Industrial Management; Management; Taxation; Transport and Communications; Transport Economics; Transport Management)

Faculties

Business and Finance (Accountancy; Banking; Business Administration; Business and Commerce; Finance; Insurance; International Business; Management); **Economics and Management in the Chemical Industry and Environmental Management** (Accountancy; Business Administration; Chemical Engineering; Economics; Environmental Management; Management; Natural Resources; Petroleum and Gas Engineering); **Engineering Economics and Management** (Economics; Engineering; Finance; German; Industrial Engineering; Industrial Management; Management; Mechanical Engineering; Russian; Safety Engineering); **Humanities** (Arts and Humanities; Demography and Population; English; Germanic Languages; History; Pedagogy; Political Sciences; Psychology; Romance Languages; Sociology); **Law and Economic Security** (Administrative Law; Civil Law; Commercial Law; Criminal Law; Economics; Law); **Management** (Business Administration; Economics; Human Resources; International Business; International Economics; Management; Marketing); **Media Industry** (Advertising and Publicity; Film; Journalism; Mass Communication; Media Studies; Multimedia; Public Relations; Radio and Television Broadcasting; Russian); **Regional Economics and Management** (Business Administration; Economics; Health Administration; Management; Public Administration; Real Estate; Sports Management; Town Planning); **Tourism and Hotel Management** (Cultural Studies; Hotel and Restaurant; Hotel Management; Physical Education; Service Trades; Social and Community Services; Tourism)

Higher Schools

Economics and Management (Economics; International Economics; Management)

Institutes

E-learning Training and Information Technologies (Distance Education; Information Technology); **Fundamental and Applied Researches** (Economics; Industrial Management); **Improvement of Professional Skills** (Staff Development); **Innovation Management** (Industrial Management; International Business; Management)

History: Founded as Higher Commercial Courses in St Petersburg 1906. Reorganised into the Institute of National Economy as an industrial cycle of an administrative-financial department 1919. Became the Leningrad Institute of Engineering and Economics 1930. Became Academy of Engineering and Economics. Acquired university status 2000.

Governing Bodies: Academic Council

Academic Year: September to July (September-December; February-June)

Admission Requirements: Secondary School Certificate

Main Language(s) of Instruction: Russian

Accrediting Agencies: Ministry of Higher and Professional Education

Degrees and Diplomas: *Bakalavr*: 4 yrs; *Specialist Diploma*: 5 yrs; *Magistr*: 6 yrs; *Kandidat Nauk*: a further 3 yrs

Student Services: Academic counselling, Canteen, Cultural centre, Foreign student adviser, Foreign Studies Centre, Health services, Language programs, Sports facilities

Student Residential Facilities: University Hostels

Special Facilities: University Museum; Informational-Computing Center; Language Laboratory; Auditoriums

Libraries: Central Library, 750,000 vols

Academic Staff *2011-2012*: Total: c. 1,000

Student Numbers *2011-2012*: Total: c. 28,000

Last Updated: 28/02/12

SAINT-PETERSBURG STATE UNIVERSITY OF INFORMATION TECHNOLOGY, MECHANICS AND OPTICS

Sankt-Peterburgskij Gosudarstvennyj Universitet Informacionnyh Tehnologij, Mehaniki i Optiki

Kronverkskii proezd 49, Sankt-Peterburg 197101
Tel: +7(812) 232-9704
Fax: +7(812) 232-0574
EMail: org@mail.ifmo.ru; rector@ifmo.ru
Website: http://www.ifmo.ru

Rector: V. N. Vasilev EMail: vasilev@mail.ifmo.ru

Vice-Rector for Administration: Yuri Kolesnikov EMail: kolesnikov@mail.ifmo.ru

Academies

Management Techniques (Business Computing; Computer Graphics; Design; Law; Management; Management Systems; Modern Languages; Software Engineering; Town Planning; Translation and Interpretation)

Departments

Computer Technology and Management (Applied Mathematics; Automation and Control Engineering; Computer Networks; Computer Science; Educational Technology; Electrical and Electronic Engineering; Electrical and Electronic Equipment and Maintenance; Electrical Engineering; Information Technology; Management Systems; Measurement and Precision Engineering); **Entrepreneurship** (Information Management; Management; Management Systems); **Optical Information Systems and Technology** (Automation and Control Engineering; Information Technology; Optical Technology; Optics); **Photonics and Opto-Informatics** (Applied Physics; Optics)

Faculties

Humanities (Arts and Humanities; Business Administration; Cultural Studies; Econometrics; Economics; Environmental Management; Finance; History; Management; Marketing; Modern Languages; Philosophy); **Information and Communication Technologies** (Information Technology; Optical Technology; Optics; Software Engineering; Telecommunications Engineering); **Information Technology and Programming** (Computer Engineering; Information Technology; Software Engineering); **Natural Sciences** (Mathematics; Mechanics; Natural Sciences; Physics); **Physics Engineering** (Biomedical Engineering; Electronic Engineering; Energy Engineering; Laser Engineering; Mechanics; Optics; Physical Engineering; Solid State Physics); **Precision Mechanics and Technology** (Computer Graphics; Electronic Engineering; Materials Engineering; Measurement and Precision Engineering; Nanotechnology)

Institutes

International Business and Law (Economic and Finance Policy; International Business; International Economics; International Law; International Relations; Taxation; Transport Management); **Refrigeration and Biotechnology** (Applied Mathematics; Automation and Control Engineering; Biochemistry; Biotechnology; Business and Commerce; Chemistry; Computer Graphics; Computer Science; Cultural Studies; Dairy; Ecology; Economic and Finance Policy; Economics; Electrical and Electronic Engineering; Engineering Drawing and Design; Environmental Management; Food Science; Food Technology; Heating and Refrigeration; History; Inorganic Chemistry; Mathematics; Mechanics; Metal Techniques; Microbiology; Modern Languages; Organic Chemistry; Philosophy; Physical Education; Physics; Safety Engineering)

History: Founded 1900 as St. Petersburg School of Craft Crown Prince Nicholas. Formerly known as St. Petersburg State Institute of Exact Mechanics and Optics (Technical University). Acquired present status 1994 and current title 2003.

Degrees and Diplomas: *Bakalavr*, *Specialist Diploma*; *Magistr*

Academic Staff *2011-2012*: Total 800

STAFF WITH DOCTORATE: Total 650

Student Numbers *2011-2012*: Total: c. 9,000

Last Updated: 28/02/12

SAINT-PETERSBURG STATE UNIVERSITY OF MEDICINE NAMED AFTER ACADEMICIAN I.P. PAVLOVA

Sankt-Peterburgskij Gosudarstvennyj Medicinskij Universitet im. akademika I.P. Pavlova

ul. L. Tolstogo 6/8, Sankt-Peterburg 197022
Tel: +7(812) 234-0821
Fax: +7(812) 234-0125
EMail: pr@spb-gmu.ru
Website: http://www.spb-gmu.ru/

Rector (Acting): Sergei Yashin

International Relations: Salman Al-Shukri, Vice-Rector for International Affairs Tel: +7(812) 346-3413

Departments

Paediatrics (Paediatrics); **Sports Medicine** (Sports Medicine)

Faculties

Adaptive Physical Training (Physical Education); **Dentistry** (Dental Technology; Dentistry); **Postgraduate Training** (Medicine)

Institutes

Nursing Education (Nursing)

Schools

Medicine (Cardiology; Cosmetology; Dentistry; Dermatology; Endocrinology; Gastroenterology; Gynaecology and Obstetrics; Haematology; Immunology; Medical Technology; Medicine; Nephrology; Neurology; Oncology; Ophthalmology; Otorhinolaryngology; Physical Therapy; Pneumology; Psychotherapy; Radiology; Rheumatology; Surgery; Urology; Venereology)

History: Founded 1897 as St. Petersburg Women's Medical Institute. Acquired present title 1994.

Degrees and Diplomas: *Specialist Diploma*; *Kandidat Nauk*; *Doktor Nauk*

Last Updated: 28/02/12

SAINT-PETERSBURG STATE UNIVERSITY OF REFRIGERATION AND FOOD ENGINEERING

Sankt-Peterburgskij Gosudarstvennyj Universitet Nizkotemperaturnyh i Piščevyh Tehnologij

ul. Lomonosova 9, Sankt-Peterburg 191002
Tel: +7(812) 315-36-17
Fax: +7(812) 315-36 17
EMail: refr@gunipt.spb.ru
Website: http://www.gunipt.edu.ru/

Rector: Alexander Baranenko EMail: rector@gunipt.spb.ru

Faculties

Economics and Ecology Management (Ecology; Economics); **Food Engineering** (Food Technology); **Food Technology** (Dairy; Meat and Poultry); **Refridgeration Technology** (Heating and Refrigeration; Mechanical Equipment and Maintenance); **Refrigeration and Air Conditioning** (Heating and Refrigeration)

History: Founded 1931, acquired present status 1999.

Governing Bodies: Scientific Board

Academic Year: September to June (September- January; February-June)

Admission Requirements: Secondary school certificate

Main Language(s) of Instruction: Russian

International Co-operation: With universities in Finland, Sweden, South Korea, Germany, Austria, Belgium, Switzerland, Bulgaria, China

Degrees and Diplomas: *Bakalavr*; *Specialist Diploma*; *Magistr*; *Kandidat Nauk*

Student Services: Academic counselling, Canteen, Cultural centre, Foreign student adviser, Health services, Language programs, Sports facilities

Student Residential Facilities: Yes

Libraries: Central Library, 1m. Vols

Publications: Scientific Transaction of the SURFE *(annually)*

Last Updated: 22/09/11

SAINT-PETERSBURG STATE UNIVERSITY OF TECHNOLOGY AND DESIGN

Sankt-Peterburgskij Gosudarstvennyj Universitet Tekhnologii i Dizajna

ul. Bolšaja Morskaja 18, Sankt-Peterburg 191186
Tel: +7(812) 315-7525
Fax: +7(812) 311-9584
EMail: postmaster@sutd.ru
Website: http://www.sutd.ru

Rector: Alexei V. Demidov EMail: rector@sutd.ru

Departments

Applied Chemistry and Ecology (Applied Chemistry; Chemical Engineering; Chemistry; Ecology; Environmental Studies; Nanotechnology; Physical Chemistry; Polymer and Plastics Technology; Textile Design; Textile Technology)

Faculties

Information Technology and Engineering (Automation and Control Engineering; Computer Science; Engineering Drawing and Design; Mathematics; Mechanical Engineering; Production Engineering); **Science and Humanities** (Arts and Humanities; History; Literature; Mathematics; Modern Languages; Natural Sciences; Philosophy; Physical Education; Physics; Russian; Social Work)

Institutes

Applied Arts (Design; Handicrafts; Painting and Drawing; Sculpture); **Arts and Design** (Aesthetics; Art History; Interior Design; Painting and Drawing); **Business Communication** (Advertising and Publicity; Graphic Design; Industrial Design; Information Technology; Tourism); **Continuing Professional Education** (Construction Engineering; Crafts and Trades; Textile Design; Textile Technology); **Costume Design** (Fashion Design); **Economics and Business** (Economics; Finance; Human Resources; Management; Marketing); **Environmental Design** (Architectural and Environmental Design; Landscape Architecture); **Graphic Design** (Advertising and Publicity; Design; Graphic Design); **Management and Foreign Economic Affairs** (Accountancy; International Economics; Management); **Printing** *(North-West Institute of Printing (APIS))* (Printing and Printmaking); **Professional Pedagogy** *(Northwest Professional Pedagogical Institute)* (Economics; Educational Psychology; Interior Design; Management; Pedagogy); **Textile and Fashion** (Fashion Design; Textile Design; Textile Technology)

Further Information: Also Research Laboratories; Research and Education Centres. Russian courses for foreign students

History: Founded 1828 as St. Petersburg Practical Technological Institute.

Academic Year: September to June (September-December; February-June)

Admission Requirements: Secondary education certificate (Attestat o srednem obrazovanii)

Main Language(s) of Instruction: Russian

International Co-operation: With universities in United Kingdom, France and Finland

Accrediting Agencies: Federal Agency of Education, Russian Federation

Degrees and Diplomas: *Bakalavr*: 4 yrs; *Specialist Diploma*: 5 yrs; *Magistr (MA; MTech.)*: a further 2 yrs; *Kandidat Nauk (PhD)*: a further 3 yrs

Student Services: Canteen, Employment services, Foreign student adviser, Health services, Language programs, Nursery care, Sports facilities

Student Residential Facilities: Yes

Special Facilities: Museum; Innovation Centre

Libraries: c. 600,000 vols

Publications: Proceedings of the University *(quarterly)*

Press or Publishing House: Publishing and Printing Centre (House)

Last Updated: 24/02/12

SAINT-PETERSBURG STATE UNIVERSITY OF TELECOMMUNICATIONS NAMED AFTER PROF. BONCH-BRUEVICH

Sankt-Peterburgskij Gosudarstvennyj Universitet Telekommunikacij imeni professora Bonch-Bruevicha (SPBSUT)

Naberežnaja Reki Mojki 61, Sankt-Peterburg 191186
Tel: +7(812) 315-8910
Fax: +7(812) 315-3227
EMail: rector@sut.ru
Website: http://www.sut.ru

Rector: Sergey Bachevsk EMail: bachevskiy@inbox.ru

Vice-Rector for Administration: Victor Y. Cherenkov

First Vice-Rector, Vice-President for Academic Affairs: Georgy Mashkov EMail: MashkovGM@sut.ru

International Relations: Oleg Zolotokrylin, Vice-Rector for Education and International Cooperation
Tel: +7(812) 315-0112, Fax: +7(812) 315-0112
EMail: o.zolotokrylin@sut.ru

Faculties

Communication Networks, Switching Systems and Computer Engineering (Automation and Control Engineering; Computer Engineering; Computer Networks; Information Management; Telecommunications Engineering; Telecommunications Services); **Communication Technology and Biomedical Electronics** (Automation and Control Engineering; Computer Graphics; Electronic Engineering; Materials Engineering; Microelectronics); **Economics and Management** (Business Administration; Communication Studies; Economics; Information Technology; Management); **Humanities** (Cultural Studies; History; Modern Languages; Philosophy; Physical Education; Political Sciences; Russian; Social Sciences); **Information Systems and Technology** (Information Sciences; Information Technology); **Multi Channel Telecommunication Systems** (Information Technology; Optical Technology; Telecommunications Engineering); **Radio, Television and Multimedia Technology** (Computer Engineering; Electronic Engineering; Information Technology; Measurement and Precision Engineering; Multimedia; Radio and Television Broadcasting; Telecommunications Engineering; Video)

History: Founded 1930 by Decree of the Council of People's Commissars of the USSR as Leningrad Electro-technical Institute of Communications. Acquired present status and title 1993.

Governing Bodies: Academic Council; Rectorate

Academic Year: September to June

Admission Requirements: Secondary school certificate (Attestat o srednem (polnom) obrazovanii)

Fees: (Russian Rubles): 74,000-84,000 per annum

Main Language(s) of Instruction: Russian

International Co-operation: With universities in Germany, France, Finland

Accrediting Agencies: Ministry of Education of Russian Federation

Degrees and Diplomas: *Bakalavr*: 4 yrs; *Specialist Diploma*: 5 yrs; *Magistr*: 2 yrs; *Kandidat Nauk (PhD)*: 3 yrs

Student Services: Academic counselling, Canteen, Employment services, Foreign student adviser, Foreign Studies Centre, Health services, Language programs, Social counselling, Sports facilities

Student Residential Facilities: Student Hostels

Special Facilities: Movie Studio

Student Numbers *2011-2012*: Total: c. 6,000

Last Updated: 24/02/12

SAINT-PETERSBURG STATE UNIVERSITY OF WATERWAYS COMMUNICATIONS

Sankt-Peterburgskij Gosudarstvennyj Universitet Vodnykh Kommunikacij

ul. Dvinskaja 5/7, Sankt-Peterburg 198035
Tel: +7(812) 251-1221
Fax: +7(812) 251-0114
EMail: rektor@spbuwc.ru
Website: http://www.spbuwc.ru/

Rector: Sergei Olegovich Baryshnikov

Faculties

Cargo Handling and Electrical Engineering (Electrical Engineering; Marine Engineering); **Economics and Finance** (Management; Marketing; Transport Economics); **Humanities** (Communication Studies; Cultural Studies; International Business; Tourism); **Hydraulic Engineering** (Hydraulic Engineering; Marine Engineering; Marine Transport; Natural Resources); **Information Technology** (Computer Science); **Law** (Civil Law; Criminal Law); **Ship Engineering** (Marine Engineering; Naval Architecture); **Ship Navigation** (Nautical Science)

History: Founded 1809 as Institute of Engineers. Acquired present status and title 1993.

Governing Bodies: University Council

Academic Year: September to July

Admission Requirements: Secondary school certificate

Main Language(s) of Instruction: Russian, English

Degrees and Diplomas: *Bakalavr*; *Specialist Diploma*; *Magistr*

Student Services: Academic counselling, Canteen, Foreign student adviser, Foreign Studies Centre, Health services, Language programs, Social counselling, Sports facilities

Student Residential Facilities: Students' hostel

Special Facilities: Museum

Libraries: c. 1,000,000 vols.

Last Updated: 19/12/11

SAINT-PETERSBURG UNIVERSITY OF THE MINISTRY OF INTERNAL AFFAIRS OF RUSSIA

Sankt-Peterburgskij Universitet MVD Rossii

ul. Ljotčika Piljutova 1, Sankt-Peterburg 198206
Tel: +7(812) 744-7000
Fax: +7(812) 144-7042
EMail: mail@univermvd.ru
Website: http://www.univermvd.ru

Rector: Kudin A. Vasili

Departments

Accounting, Auditing and Analysis (Accountancy); **Administration** (Administration); **Administrative Law** (Administrative Law); **Civil Law** (Civil Law); **Civil Procedure** (Civil Law); **Constitutional and International Law** (Constitutional Law; International Law); **Criminal Law** (Criminal Law); **Criminology** (Criminology); **Economics and Management of Social and Economic Processes** (Economics; Management; Social Policy); **Finance and Taxation** (Finance; Taxation); **Fire Science** (Fire Science); **Foreign Languages** (Modern Languages); **Forensic Medicine and Investigations** (Forensic Medicine and Dentistry); **History of State and Law** (Government; History of Law; Law); **Legal Psychology** (Psychology); **Logistics** (Transport Management); **Philosophy and Sociology** (Philosophy; Sociology); **Physical Training and Applied Arts** (Graphic Arts; Handicrafts; Physical Education); **Police Studies** (Police Studies); **Psychology** (Clinical Psychology; Educational Psychology; Experimental Psychology; Psychiatry and Mental Health; Psychology; Psychotherapy); **Russian Language** (Russian); **Social Psychology** (Social Psychology); **Special Events and Special Equipment**; **Special Information Technology and Information Security** (Information Technology)

History: Founded 1998.

Degrees and Diplomas: *Specialist Diploma*

Last Updated: 27/01/12

SAMARA STATE ACADEMY OF AGRICULTURE

Samarskaja Gosudarstvennaja Sel'skohozjajstvennaja Akademija (SSAA)

ul. Ucebnaja, 2, Kinel' 446442
Tel: +7(84663) 4-61-31 +7(84663) 4-62-31 +7(84663) 4-64-31
Fax: +7(84663) 4-61-31
EMail: ssaa-samara@mail.ru
Website: http://www.ssaa.ru/

Rector: Vladimir A. Milutkin EMail: rektor-ssaa@inbox.ru

Faculties

Agronomy (Agronomy; Botany; Crop Production; Ecology; Horticulture; Irrigation; Landscape Architecture; Plant and Crop Protection; Soil Management); **Biotechnology and Veterinary Medicine** (Biotechnology; Veterinary Science; Zoology); **Economics** (Accountancy; Agricultural Business; Agricultural Economics; Agricultural Management; Finance; Information Technology; Marketing); **Engineering** (Agricultural Engineering; Agricultural Equipment; Mechanical Equipment and Maintenance); **Technology** (Agricultural Equipment; Biochemistry; Chemistry; Technology)

History: Founded 1922. Acquired current name and status 1991.

Governing Bodies: Scientific Council

Academic Year: September-December; February-May

Admission Requirements: Secondary School Certificate (Attestat Zrelosti)

Fees: None

Main Language(s) of Instruction: Russian

International Co-operation: With universities in Germany, Poland, Canada; Participates in USDA Faculty Exchange Programme, TACIS, DAAD

Accrediting Agencies: Federal Service for Supervision in Education and Science

Degrees and Diplomas: *Bakalavr*; *Specialist Diploma*; *Magistr*; *Kandidat Nauk*

Student Services: Academic counselling, Canteen, Cultural centre, Employment services, Health services, Language programs, Social counselling, Sports facilities

Student Residential Facilities: Yes

Special Facilities: University History Museum

Libraries: yes

Last Updated: 07/12/11

SAMARA STATE ACADEMY OF CULTURE AND ARTS

Samarskaja Gosudarstvennaja Akademija Kul'tury i Iskusstv

ul. Frunze 167, Samara 443010
Tel: +7(846) 332-76-54 +7(846) 333-25-22
Fax: +7(846) 333-22-30
EMail: mail@smrgaki.ru
Website: http://www.smrgaki.ru/

Rector: Elleonora Aleksandrovna Kurlenko

Institutes

Contemporary Art and Communications (Acting; Dance; Fine Arts; Music Education; Theatre); **Cultural Studies** (Advertising and Publicity; Cultural Studies; Linguistics; Public Relations; Social Welfare); **Information and Communication Technologies** (Documentation Techniques; Information Management; Information Sciences; Information Technology; Library Science); **Music** *(Conservatory)* (Conducting; Music; Musical Instruments; Singing)

History: Created 1971.

Degrees and Diplomas: *Specialist Diploma*
Last Updated: 20/03/12

SAMARA STATE ACADEMY OF SOCIAL SCIENCES AND HUMANITIES

Povolzhskaya Gosudarstvennaja Socialno-Gumanitarnaja Akademija (SSPU)

ul. Gorkogo 65/67, Samara 443099
Tel: +7(846) 333-6457
Fax: +7(846) 269-6444
EMail: rectorat@pgsga.ru
Website: http://www.pgsga.ru/

Rector: Igor V. Veršinin

Vice-Rector for Administration: Sergey G. Tsyrkulov

International Relations: Valeria Bondareva, Head of International Department
Tel: +7(846) 296-6416, Fax: +7(846) 296-6416
EMail: val1965@mail.ru

Departments

Primary Education (Education; Educational Psychology; Pedagogy; Preschool Education; Primary Education); **Psychology** (Educational Psychology; Industrial and Organizational Psychology; Psychology; Social Psychology); **Special Education** (Special Education; Speech Therapy and Audiology)

Faculties

Art Education (Art Education; Computer Graphics; Conducting; Cultural Studies; Dance; Design; Fine Arts; Graphic Arts; Interior Design; Music Theory and Composition; Musical Instruments; Painting and Drawing; Sculpture; Singing); **Economics** (Economics); **Foreign Languages** (American Studies; Cultural Studies; English; English Studies; Foreign Languages Education; French; French Studies; German; Germanic Studies; Linguistics; Translation and Interpretation); **History** (Archaeology; History); **Management** (Business Administration; Management); **Mathematics, Physics and Computer Science** (Applied Mathematics; Computer Science; Information Technology; Mathematics; Mathematics Education; Physics); **Natural Sciences** (Anatomy; Biological and Life Sciences; Biology; Botany; Chemistry; Ecology; Geography; Natural Sciences; Physiology; Zoology); **Philology** (Journalism; Linguistics; Literature; Native Language Education; Philology; Russian); **Physical Education and Sports** (Physical Education; Sports)

History: Founded 1911 as Samara Pedagogical Institute. Formerly known as Samara State Pedagogical University. Acquired present title 2009.

Governing Bodies: University Administration

Academic Year: September to July

Admission Requirements: Secondary school certificate (Attestat o sredem obščem obrazovanii) and entrance examinations

Fees: (US Dollars): 2,000-3,000 per annum

Main Language(s) of Instruction: Russian

International Co-operation: With Universities in Germany, France, Czech Republic, Italy and USA

Accrediting Agencies: Ministry of Education of Russian Federation

Degrees and Diplomas: *Specialist Diploma*: 5 yrs; *Kandidat Nauk*: 3 yrs; *Doktor Nauk*: 5 yrs

Student Services: Academic counselling, Canteen, Cultural centre, Employment services, Foreign student adviser, Foreign Studies Centre, Health services, Language programs, Social counselling, Sports facilities

Student Residential Facilities: Yes

Special Facilities: Zoological Museum; Botanic Laboratories; Archeological Laboratory; History Museum

Libraries: Main Library

Publications: Departmental Scientific Journals *(annually)*; University Scientific Journal *(annually)*

Press or Publishing House: University Publishing House

Academic Staff *2010-2011*	**TOTAL**
FULL-TIME	**600**
STAFF WITH DOCTORATE FULL-TIME	c. **320**
Student Numbers *2010-2011*	
All (Foreign Included)	**10,000**
FOREIGN ONLY	**20**

Part-time students, 3,800.
Last Updated: 02/03/12

SAMARA STATE AEROSPACE UNIVERSITY

Samarskij Gosudarstvennyj Aerokosmičeskij Universitet

Moskovskoe Šose 34, Samara 443086
Tel: +7(846) 335-1826
Fax: +7(846) 335-1836
EMail: ssau@ssau.ru
Website: http://www.ssau.ru

Rector: Evgueni V. Šahmatov
Tel: +7(846) 267-4301 EMail: shakhm@ssau.ru

Vice-Rector for Administration: Dmitry Ustinov
EMail: dsu@ssau.ru

International Relations: Vladimir D. Bogatyrev, Vice-Rector for Educational and International Activities
Tel: +7(846) 267-4303 EMail: teach@ssau.ru

Centres

Certification

Departments

Air Transport Engineering (Air Transport; Electrical and Electronic Equipment and Maintenance; Mechanical Equipment and Maintenance); **Radio Engineering** (Bioengineering; Biomedical Engineering; Electrical and Electronic Engineering; Nanotechnology)

Faculties

Aircraft Construction (Aeronautical and Aerospace Engineering; Air Transport; Safety Engineering); **Aircraft Engines** (Aeronautical and Aerospace Engineering; Heating and Refrigeration; Mechanical Engineering); **Economics and Management** (Economics; Management); **Engineering and Technology** (Aeronautical and Aerospace Engineering; Engineering)

Institutes

Computer Science (Applied Mathematics; Computer Science; Electronic Engineering; Mathematics; Physics; Software Engineering); **Energy and Transport** (Air Transport; Energy Engineering; Transport Engineering); **Printing** (Printing and Printmaking; Publishing and Book Trade)

Further Information: Campus in Togliatti. Also Department of Distance Education, Department of Basic Training and Basic Sciences, Institute of Continuing Professional Education. Research centres and institutes

History: Founded 1942 as Kuibyšev Aviation Institute, acquired present status and title 1992.

Academic Year: September to June (September-January; February-June)

Admission Requirements: Secondary school certificate (Attestat o srednem obrazovanii)

Main Language(s) of Instruction: Russian

Degrees and Diplomas: *Bakalavr*: 5 1/2 yrs; *Specialist Diploma*: 5 1/2 yrs; *Magistr*: 5 1/2 yrs; *Kandidat Nauk*: 3 yrs; *Doktor Nauk*: a further 3 yrs

Student Services: Canteen, Cultural centre, Health services, Sports facilities

Student Residential Facilities: For c. 3,000 students

Special Facilities: Museum of Aviation Engines History; Aviation Museum

Libraries: c. 1,100,000 vols

Publications: Vestnik Samarskogo Aerosmicheskogo Universiteta, Scientific developments results *(quarterly)*

Press or Publishing House: Publishing House of Samara State Aerospace University

Last Updated: 02/03/12

SAMARA STATE MEDICAL UNIVERSITY

Samarskij Gosudarstvennyj Medicinskij Universitet

ul. Chapaevskaja 89, Samara 443099
Tel: +7(8462) 321-634
Fax: +7(8462) 332-976
EMail: info@samsmu.ru
Website: http://www.samsmu.samara.ru

Rector: Gennady P. Kotelnikov (1998-)

Vice-Rector for Administration: Sergei Vyrmaskin

Faculties

Clinical Psychology (Clinical Psychology; Social and Preventive Medicine); **Dentistry** (Dental Technology; Dentistry; Social and Preventive Medicine; Stomatology; Surgery); **Economics and Health Management** (Health Administration; Public Health); **General Medicine** (Medicine); **Paediatrics** (Child Care and Development; Paediatrics); **Pharmacy** (Pharmacology; Pharmacy); **Preventive Medicine** (Epidemiology; Hygiene; Social and Preventive Medicine)

Institutes

Continuing Education (Medicine); **Dentistry** (Dentistry); **Haematology, Transfusion and Intensive Care** (Haematology); **Nursing Education** (Nursing); **Ophtalmology** (Ophthalmology); **Pathology** (Pathology); **Rehabilitation Medicine** (Rehabilitation and Therapy)

Research Institutes

Experimental Medicine and Biotechnology (Biotechnology; Medicine); **Hygiene and Human Ecology** (Environmental Studies; Hygiene; Microbiology; Public Health; Toxicology); **Non-Ionising Radiations** (Nuclear Physics; Optical Technology; Optics; Surgery)

Further Information: Also Teaching Hospital

History: Founded 1919, acquired present status and title 1993.

Academic Year: September to June (September-January; February-June)

Admission Requirements: Secondary school certificate (Attestat o srednem obrazovanii)

Main Language(s) of Instruction: Russian

International Co-operation: With Linkoping University, Sweden.

Degrees and Diplomas: *Specialist Diploma*: Dentistry; General Medicine; Paediatrics; Pharmacy, 6 yrs; *Specialist Diploma*: Higher Nursing Education; Medical Psychology, 5 yrs; *Specialist Diploma*: Public Health, 5-6 yrs; *Kandidat Nauk*: Health Sciences, By thesis following Diploma; *Doktor Nauk*: Health Sciences, By thesis following Kandidat

Student Services: Academic counselling, Canteen, Cultural centre, Foreign student adviser, Foreign Studies Centre, Health services, Language programs, Nursery care, Social counselling, Sports facilities

Student Residential Facilities: Yes

Special Facilities: Anatomy Museum; Pathology Museum

Libraries: Central Library, 580,000 vols

Publications: Annals of Traumatology and Orthopaedics *(bimonthly)*

Last Updated: 02/03/12

SAMARA STATE NAYANOVA MUNICIPAL UNIVERSITY

Samarskij Gosugarstvennyi Municipal'nyj Universitet Najanovoi

ul. Molodogvardejcev 196, Samara 443001
Tel: +7(846) 242-4790
Fax: +7(846) 242-3853
EMail: mnu@nayanova.edu
Website: http://www.nayanova.edu

Rector: Marina V. Najanova

Departments

Chemistry and Biology (Biological and Life Sciences; Chemistry; Computer Science; Ecology; Environmental Studies; Mathematics; Organic Chemistry; Physics)

Faculties

Arts (Theatre); **Economics** (Accountancy; Economics; Statistics); **Management** (Industrial Management; Management); **Mathematics and Computer Science** (Applied Mathematics; Computer Science; Mathematics; Mathematics and Computer Science); **Philosophy** (Literature; Philosophy)

Schools

+International Relations (Accountancy; Advertising and Publicity; Communication Studies; International Relations; Sociology; Statistics); **+Law** (Civil Law; Criminal Law; History of Law; Law)

History: Founded 1988.

Degrees and Diplomas: *Specialist Diploma*

Last Updated: 01/03/12

SAMARA STATE REGIONAL ACADEMY (NAJANOVA)

Samarskaja Gosudarstvennaja Oblastnaja Akademija (Najanovoj)

ul. Čapaevskaya 186, Samara 443010
Tel: +7(846) 242-47-90
Fax: +7(846) 242-47-90
EMail: mnu@nayanova.edu
Website: http://www.nayanova.edu

Rector: Maria Venediktovna Najanova

Faculties

Art (Acting; Dance; Singing; Theatre); **Biology and Chemistry** (Biology; Chemistry; Ecology; Environmental Studies); **Economics** (Accountancy; Economics); **International Relations** (Advertising and Publicity; International Relations; Public Relations); **Law** (Civil Law; Criminal Law; Law); **Management** (Human Resources; Management); **Mathematics and Computer Science** (Applied Mathematics; Computer Science; Information Technology; Mathematics); **Philosophy** (Literature; Philosophy)

History: Created 1988 as Samarskij Gosudarstvennyj Oblastnyj Universitet (Najanovoj). Acquired current title 2010.

Degrees and Diplomas: *Bakalavr*, *Specialist Diploma*

Last Updated: 09/03/12

SAMARA STATE TECHNICAL UNIVERSITY

Samarskij Gosudarstvennyj Tehničeskij Universitet (SAMGTU (SSTU))

ul. Molodogvardeickaja, d. 244, Glavnyj Korpus, Samara 443100
Tel: +7(846) 278-4302
Fax: +7(846) 278-4400
EMail: rector@samgtu.ru
Website: http://www.samgtu.ru

Rector: Dmitrij Evgenevich Bykov

Faculties

Automation and Information Technology (Applied Mathematics; Artificial Intelligence; Automation and Control Engineering; Computer Engineering; Computer Graphics; Computer Networks; Data Processing; Electrical and Electronic Engineering; Electronic Engineering; Information Management; Information Technology; Mathematics; Measurement and Precision Engineering; Microelectronics; Microwaves; Operations Research; Robotics; Software Engineering; Systems Analysis; Telecommunications Engineering); **Chemical Technology** (Analytical Chemistry; Applied Chemistry; Bioengineering; Chemical Engineering; Chemistry; Environmental Engineering; Industrial Chemistry; Inorganic Chemistry; Organic Chemistry; Physical Chemistry; Sanitary Engineering); **Economics** (Economics); **Electrical Engineering** (Automation and Control Engineering; Electrical and Electronic Engineering; Electrical Engineering; Energy Engineering; Industrial Engineering; Industrial Maintenance; Maintenance Technology; Power Engineering); **Engineering Technologies** (Automation and Control Engineering; Explosive Engineering; Industrial Engineering; Polymer and Plastics Technology; Rubber Technology; Safety Engineering; Sanitary Engineering); **Food Processing Industry** (Bioengineering; Brewing; Food Science; Food Technology; Oenology); **Heat Power** (Automation and Control Engineering; Energy Engineering; Heating and Refrigeration; Thermal Engineering); **Humanities** (Advertising and Publicity; Arts and Humanities; English; Journalism; Marketing; Mass Communication; Media Studies; Psychology; Public Relations); **Machine-Building and Motor Transport** (Automation and Control Engineering; Automotive Engineering; Instrument Making; Machine Building; Measurement and Precision Engineering; Mechanical Engineering; Physical Engineering; Road Transport); **Oil Technology** (Ecology; Environmental Management; Environmental Studies; Geological Engineering; Natural Resources; Petroleum and Gas Engineering); **Physical Technology** (Materials Engineering; Measurement and Precision Engineering; Metal Techniques; Metallurgical Engineering; Physical Engineering; Production Engineering)

History: Founded 1914. Acquired present status 1992.

Governing Bodies: Academic Senate

Academic Year: September to July

Admission Requirements: Secondary School Certificate

Main Language(s) of Instruction: Russian

International Co-operation: With universities in Great Britain, Germany. Participates in the TEMPUS programme

Accrediting Agencies: the Federal Service of Supervion in Education and Science of the Russian Federation (Rosobnadzor)

Degrees and Diplomas: *Bakalavr*; *Specialist Diploma*; *Magistr*

Student Services: Canteen, Cultural centre, Employment services, Health services, Language programs, Nursery care, Social counselling, Sports facilities

Student Residential Facilities: Dormitories for 1,335 students

Special Facilities: Museum of the History of Samara State Technical University; Geological Museum

Libraries: Academic Library, 11,750,000 vols; Access to electronic databases and resources; Accees to over 100 computer workstations

Publications: Vestnik SamGTU Seriya " Fiziko-matematocheskiye nauki", Journal *(biweekly)*; Vestnik SamGTU Seriya "Mathematicheskaya", Journal *(biweekly)*; Vestnik SamGTU Seriya "Psikhologo-pedagogicheskiye nauki", Journal *(biweekly)*; Vestnik SamGTU Seriya "Tekhnicheskiye nauki", Journal *(biweekly)*

Last Updated: 19/12/11

SAMARA STATE UNIVERSITY

Samarskij Gosudarstvennyj Universitet

ul. Akademika Pavlova 1, Samara 443011

Tel: +7(846) 334-54-02

Fax: +7(846) 334-54-17

EMail: rector@ssu.samara.ru

Website: http://www.ssu.samara.ru

Rector: Igor Aleksandrovich Noskov

Faculties

Biology (Biology; Botany; Zoology); **Chemistry** (Chemistry); **History** (History); **Law** (Law); **Management and Economics** (Economics; Management); **Mechanics and Applied Mathematics** (Applied Mathematics; Mathematics; Mechanics); **Philology** (English; German; Linguistics; Philology; Russian); **Physics** (Physics); **Psychology** (Educational and Student Counselling; Pedagogy; Psychology; Social Psychology); **Sociology** (Social Studies; Sociology)

History: Founded 1969.

Governing Bodies: Academic Council

Academic Year: September to July

Admission Requirements: Secondary school certificate (Attestat o srednem obrazovanii) and entrance examination

Fees: None

Main Language(s) of Instruction: Russian

Degrees and Diplomas: *Bakalavr*; *Specialist Diploma*; *Magistr*; *Kandidat Nauk*; *Doktor Nauk*

Student Services: Academic counselling, Cultural centre, Employment services, Foreign student adviser, Language programs, Social counselling, Sports facilities

Student Residential Facilities: For 3,720 students

Special Facilities: Biological Garden

Libraries: 806,171 vols

Publications: Philosophy and Culture; Samarsky Universitet *(monthly)*; Samarsky Zemsky Sbornik *(biannually)*; Vestnik SamGU *(quarterly)*

Last Updated: 22/09/11

SAMARA STATE UNIVERSITY OF ARCHITECTURE AND CIVIL ENGINEERING

Samarskij Gosudarstvennyj Arkhitekturno-Stroitel'nyj Universitet

ul. Molodogvardejskaja 194, Samara 443001

Tel: +7(846) 242-1784

Fax: +7(846) 332-1965

EMail: sgasu@sgasu.smr.ru

Website: http://www.sgasu.smr.ru/

Rector: Michael I. Balzannikov (2002-) Fax: +7(846) 242-1784

Institutes

Architecture and Design (Architectural and Environmental Design; Architecture; Fashion Design; Graphic Design; Industrial Design; Interior Design; Landscape Architecture; Town Planning); **Construction** (Automation and Control Engineering; Building Technologies; Business Administration; Civil Engineering; Construction Engineering; Electrical Engineering; Industrial Engineering; Marketing; Materials Engineering; Mechanical Engineering; Production Engineering; Road Engineering; Town Planning; Transport and Communications); **Ecology and Life Support Engineering Systems** (Engineering; Environmental Studies; Hydraulic Engineering; Petroleum and Gas Engineering; Safety Engineering; Water Management); **Economics and Management** (Business Administration; Communication Studies; Economics; Engineering; Information Sciences; Information Technology; Linguistics; Management; Russian; Safety Engineering; Social and Community Services; Tourism; Translation and Interpretation)

Further Information: Also preliminary training before university entry, Lyceum of Architecture and Civil Engineering, preparatory courses

History: Founded 1930 as Civil Engineering Institute, acquired present title 2004. Formerly known as Samara State Academy of Architecture and Civil Engineering.

Governing Bodies: Academic Board

Academic Year: September to June (September-January; February-June)

Admission Requirements: Secondary education certificate (Attestat o srednem obrazovanii)

Main Language(s) of Instruction: Russian

Degrees and Diplomas: *Bakalavr*; *Magistr*; *Kandidat Nauk*; *Doktor Nauk*

Student Services: Academic counselling, Canteen, Cultural centre, Employment services, Foreign student adviser, Foreign Studies Centre, Health services, Language programs, Social counselling, Sports facilities

Student Residential Facilities: For c. 1,500 students

Special Facilities: Academy Museum

Libraries: 667,490 vols; 110,000 periodical subsciptions

Last Updated: 02/03/12

IAU SAMARA STATE UNIVERSITY OF ECONOMICS

Samarskij Gosudarstvennyj Ekonomičeskij Universitet

ul. Sovetskoj Armii 141, Samara 443090

Tel: +7(846) 222-4981

Fax: +7(846) 222-0953

EMail: ecun@sseu.ru; intercentre@sseu.ru

Website: http://www.sseu.ru/

Rector: Gabibulla Rabadanovich Khasaev
Tel: +7(846) 224-1542, Fax: +7(846) 224-0953
EMail: rector@sseu.ru

Vice-Rector: Vladimir A. Piskunov
Tel: +7(846) 224-06-69 EMail: piskunov@sseu.ru

International Relations: Svetlana Komarova, Head of International Collaboration EMail: komarova@sseu.ru

Institutes

Commerce, Marketing and Services (Advertising and Publicity; Business and Commerce; Business Computing; Cooking and Catering; E-Business/Commerce; Marketing; Service Trades; Transport Management); **Control Systems** (Accountancy; Economics; Industrial Management; Management; Statistics); **Economics and Enterprise Management** (Agricultural Economics; Agricultural Management; Econometrics; Economics; Human Resources; Management); **Law** (Civil Law; Commercial Law; Criminal Law; Law); **National Economy** (Banking; Economics; Finance; Natural Resources; Statistics); **Theoretical Economics and International Economic Relations** (Economics; International Economics)

History: Founded 1931 as Kuibyshevskij Planovyj Institut (Kubyshev Institue of Economic Planning). In 1994 became Samarskaja Gosudarstvennaja Ekonomičeskaja Akademija (Samara State Academy of Economics), and obtained current title and status 2005.

Governing Bodies: Academic Council

Academic Year: September to June

Admission Requirements: Attestat o Srednem (Polnom) Obshchem Obrazovanii (Secondary school certificate) and entrance examination

Fees: (Russian Rubles): 60,000 per annum

Main Language(s) of Instruction: Russian

International Co-operation: With universities in USA, Germany, UK

Accrediting Agencies: Federal Service for Supervision in Education and Science

Degrees and Diplomas: *Bakalavr*: 4 yrs; *Specialist Diploma*: National Economy; Finance and Credit; Statistics; Economic Theory; World Economy; Law; Marketing; Commerce; Service; Management; Information Technologies; Labour Economy; Personnel Management; Accounting and Audit; Agricultural Business and Economics, 5 yrs; *Magistr*: a further 2 yrs

Student Services: Academic counselling, Canteen, Cultural centre, Employment services, Foreign student adviser, Language programs, Social counselling, Sports facilities

Student Residential Facilities: 3 dormitories

Libraries: Founded in 1,931, one of the oldest in the city. Houses 860,000 editions, 4 reading halls, journals collection, computer rooms

Publications: Vestnik of SSEU, Collection of research articles written by SSEU staff *(other/irregular)*; Vestnik of Young Scientists, Collection of research articles written by young researchers, students and postgraduates of SSEU *(biennially)*

Press or Publishing House: SSEU Publishing House

Student Numbers *2011-2012*: Total: c. 12,000

Last Updated: 02/03/12

SAMARA STATE UNIVERSITY OF TRANSPORT

Samarskij Gosudarstvennyj Universitet Putej Soobščenija (SAMGAPS)

1-yj Bezymjannyj per., d.18, Samara 443066
Tel: +7(846) 262-4112
Fax: +7(846) 262-3076
EMail: rektorat@samiit.ru
Website: http://www.samgups.ru/

Rector: Alexander V. Kovtunov (2002-)

Faculties

Electrical Engineering (Electrical Engineering)

Institutes

Management and Economics (Accountancy; Economics; Human Resources; Management; Transport Economics; Transport Management); **Transport Engineering** (Transport Engineering); **Transport Structure and Vehicles** (Construction Engineering; Railway Engineering)

History: Founded 1973, previously known as Samarskij Institut Inženerov Železnodorožnogo Transporta (Samara Institute for Railway Engineers) and acquired current name in 2002

Governing Bodies: Academic Council

Academic Year: September to June (September-January; February-June)

Admission Requirements: Secondary school certificate (Attestat o srednem obrazovanii) and entrance examination

Main Language(s) of Instruction: Russian

International Co-operation: TEMPUS; DAAD

Accrediting Agencies: Federal Service for Supervision in Education and Science

Degrees and Diplomas: *Bakalavr*, *Specialist Diploma*; *Magistr*, *Kandidat Nauk*

Student Services: Academic counselling, Canteen, Cultural centre, Employment services, Foreign student adviser, Health services, Language programs, Social counselling, Sports facilities

Student Residential Facilities: For c. 1,600 students

Special Facilities: Museum of Rail Transport History; student theatre

Libraries: c. 500,000 vols

Last Updated: 21/11/11

SARATOV LAW INSTITUTE OF THE MINISTRY OF INTERNAL AFFAIRS OF RUSSIA

Saratovskij Juridičeskij Institut MVD Rossijskoij Federatsii

ul. Sokolovaja 339, Saratov 410034
Tel: +7(8452) 37-92-13
Fax: +7(8452) 64-27-77
EMail: suimvd@overta.ru
Website: http://www.suimvd.ru/

Rector: Valerij Jurevich Nazarov

Faculties

Forensics (Criminology; Forensic Medicine and Dentistry; Police Studies); **Law** (Law); **Law Enforcement** (Criminology; Police Studies)

History: Created 1925.

Degrees and Diplomas: *Bakalavr*, *Specialist Diploma*

Last Updated: 21/04/11

SARATOV STATE AGRARIAN UNIVERSITY NAMED AFTER N.I. VAVILOV

Saratovskij Gosudarstvennyj Agrarnyj Universitet im. N.I. Vavilova (SGAU/SSAU)

pl. Teatralnaja 1, Saratov 410012
Tel: +7(8452) 233-292
Fax: +7(8452) 264-781
EMail: rector@sgau.ru
Website: http://www.sgau.ru/

Rector: Nikolaj I. Kuznetsov (2003-)

Faculties

Agricultural Market (Agricultural Business; Food Science; Food Technology); **Agricultural Mechanization and Electrification** (Agricultural Equipment); **Agronomy** (Agricultural Economics; Agronomy; Crop Production; Ecology; Environmental Management; Horticulture; Natural Resources; Plant and Crop Protection; Plant Pathology; Viticulture); **Finance and Economics** (Accountancy; Economics; Finance; Information Technology); **Forestry** (Forest Management; Forestry; Landscape Architecture; Soil Conservation); **Management and Agrobusiness** (Agricultural Business; Agricultural Economics; Agricultural Management); **Veterinary Medicine and Biotechnology** (Animal Husbandry; Aquaculture; Biotechnology; Veterinary Science; Water Science; Zoology)

History: Founded 1998 through a merging of former Saratov State Academy of Agriculture, Saratov State Agroengineering University and Saratov State Academy of Veterinary Medicine and Biotechnology, named after N.I. Vavilova.

Academic Year: September to June (September-January; February-June)

Admission Requirements: Secondary school certificate (Attestat o srednem obrazovanii), or equivalent

Fees: (US Dollars): foreign students: 1,200-1,500 per annum

Main Language(s) of Instruction: Russian, English, German, French

Accrediting Agencies: Ministry of Agriculture and Food

Degrees and Diplomas: *Bakalavr*; *Specialist Diploma*; *Magistr*; *Kandidat Nauk*; *Doktor Nauk*

Student Services: Academic counselling, Canteen, Cultural centre, Employment services, Health services, Nursery care, Social counselling, Sports facilities

Student Residential Facilities: For 3,156 students

Special Facilities: University Museum

Libraries: c. 1,531,944 vols

Publications: Pedagogical Works *(annually)*; Research Papers Volumes *(annually)*

Press or Publishing House: Publishing Department

Last Updated: 26/04/11

SARATOV STATE JURIDICAL ACADEMY

Saratovskaja Gosudarstvennaja Juridičeskaja Akademija

ul. Černyševskogo 104, Saratov 410056
Tel: +7(8452) 29-92-02
Fax: +7(8452) 20-56-58
EMail: post@sgap.ru
Website: http://www.sgap.ru

Rector: Sergej Borisovich Surovov

Programmes

Law (Law); **Linguistics** (Linguistics); **Political Studies** (Political Sciences)

History: Founded 1931as Saratovskaja Gosudarstvennaja Akademija Prava. Aacquired present status 2011.

Academic Year: September to June

Main Language(s) of Instruction: Russian

International Co-operation: With universities in Germany, USA, Spain, France

Degrees and Diplomas: *Bakalavr*, *Specialist Diploma*; *Magistr*

Student Services: Academic counselling, Canteen, Cultural centre, Foreign student adviser, Health services, Language programs, Nursery care, Sports facilities

Student Residential Facilities: Yes

Libraries: 750,000 vols

Last Updated: 19/03/12

SARATOV STATE MEDICAL UNIVERSITY NAMED AFTER V. I. RAZUMOVSKIJ

Saratovskij Gosudarstvennyj Medicinskij Universitet im. V. I. Razumovskij

Bolshaya Kazachia Str., 112, Saratov 410712
Tel: +7(8452) 66-97-77 +7(8452) 66-97-79
Fax: +7(8452) 51-15-34
EMail: meduniv@sgmu.ru
Website: http://www.sgmu.ru

Rector: Vladimir M. Popkov

Faculties

Dentistry (Dentistry); **Medicine** (Medicine); **Nursing** (Nursing); **Paediatrics** (Paediatrics); **Pharmacy** (Pharmacy); **Public Health** (Public Health)

History: Founded 1909. Acquired present status and title 2002.

Degrees and Diplomas: *Specialist Diploma*

Last Updated: 19/12/11

SARATOV STATE MUSIC CONSERVATORY (ACADEMY) NAMED AFTER L.V. SOBINOVA

Saratovskaja Gosudarstvennaja Konservatorija (Akademija) im. L.V. Sobinova (SGK)

prosp. Kirova 1, Saratov 410012
Tel: +7(8452) 230-976 +7(8452) 231-864
Fax: +7(8452) 272-653
EMail: sgk@freeline.ru
Website: http://www.sarcons.ru/

Rector: Lev Isaevich Shugom

Faculties

Performing Arts (Acting; Cinema and Television; Performing Arts); **Theatre** (Theatre); **Theory of Music** (Music; Music Theory and Composition; Musicology)

History: Founded 1912, acquired present status 1918.

Governing Bodies: Scientific Board

Academic Year: September to June (September-January; February-June)

Admission Requirements: Secondary school certificate; Musical College Diploma for Theoretical and Performing Arts

Main Language(s) of Instruction: Russian

Accrediting Agencies: Ministry of Education; Ministry of Culture

Degrees and Diplomas: *Bakalavr*, *Specialist Diploma*; *Kandidat Nauk*; *Doktor Nauk*

Student Services: Cultural centre, Foreign Studies Centre, Health services, Language programs, Sports facilities

Student Residential Facilities: Yes

Special Facilities: Recording Studio; Movie Studio

Libraries: 202,000 vols

Last Updated: 19/12/11

SARATOV STATE SOCIO-ECONOMIC UNIVERSITY

Saratovskij Gosudarstvennyj Socialno-Ekonomičeskij Universitet (SGSEU)

ul. Radiščeva 89, Saratov 410003
Tel: +7(8452) 755-212
Fax: +7(8452) 755-212
EMail: rector@ssea.runnet.ru
Website: http://www.seun.ru

Rector: Vladimir A. Dines Tel: +7(8452) 756-173

First Vice-Rector: Mihail V. Popov
Tel: +7(8452) 756-110 EMail: popov@ssea.runnet.ru

International Relations: Anatoliy A. Sinyagin, Vice-Rector
Tel: +7(8452) 279-109 EMail: sinyagin@ssea.runnet.ru

Departments

Computer Science and Information Technology (Applied Mathematics; Banking; Business Computing; Computer Science; Ecology; Information Technology)

Faculties

Economics and Accountancy (Accountancy; Applied Mathematics; Computer Science; Information Management; Management; Software Engineering; Statistics); **Economics and Management** (Business and Commerce; Economics; Management; Marketing; Public Administration); **Economics and Services** (Communication Studies; Economic History; Law; Psychology; Public Relations; Social and Community Services; Sociology; Tourism); **Extra-Mural Studies** (Accountancy; Administrative Law; Finance; Food Technology; Law; Management; Marketing; Taxation); **Finance and Credit** (Banking; Computer Science; Economic and Finance Policy; Finance; Taxation); **Humanities** (Communication Studies; Cultural Studies; Economics; Education; Educational Psychology; English; French; German; History; Modern Languages; Pedagogy; Philosophy; Physical Education; Political Sciences; Psychology; Public Relations; Sociology; Spanish; Sports; Translation and Interpretation); **Law** (Administrative Law; History of Law; Law; Private Law; Public Law; Taxation)

Institutes

Continuing Professional Education; **Distance Learning** (Accountancy; Finance; Law; Management; Statistics)

Further Information: Branches in Astrahan, Balacovo, Balašov

History: Founded 1931, acquired present title 1999. The University commemorated its 70th anniversary 2001, came out successfully through evaluation (a certification, a licensing, an accrediting), which was carried out by the Ministry of Education of the Russian Federation.

Governing Bodies: Board of Academics (Rector, Vice-Rectors and Deans)

Academic Year: September to June (September-January; February-June)

Admission Requirements: Notification. Medical certificate. Passport. 6 Photos. Certificate of education (attestat o srdnem obrazovanii)

Main Language(s) of Instruction: Russian; English

International Co-operation: With universities in the United Kingdom, USA, Canada, France, Ukraine. Also participates in Tempus, Tacis, DAAD, ACTR, Eurasia, Soros and Fulbright programmes

Accrediting Agencies: Ministry of Education

Degrees and Diplomas: *Specialist Diploma*: 5 yrs; *Kandidat Nauk*: Administrative Law; Financial Law; Informational Law; Theory and Methods of Professional Education; Economic Sociology and Demography; Political Institutes; Ethnological and Political Conflictology; National and Political Processes and Technology; Native History; Economic Theory; Economics and Management of the National Economy; finance; Currency and Credit; Business Accountancy; Statistics; Mathematical and Instrumental Methods in Economics, a further 3 yrs; *Doktor Nauk*: Administrative Law; Financial Law; Informational Law; Theory and Methods of Professional Education; Economic Sociology and Demography; Political Institutes; Ethnological and Political Conflictology; National and Political Processes and Technology; Native History; Economic Theory; Economics and Management of the National Economy; Finance; Currency and Credit; Business Accountancy; Statistics; Mathematical and Instrumental Methods in Economics, a further 2-4 yrs

Student Services: Academic counselling, Canteen, Cultural centre, Employment services, Foreign student adviser, Foreign Studies Centre, Health services, Language programs, Social counselling, Sports facilities

Student Residential Facilities: Yes

Special Facilities: History Museum. Virtual Subsidiary of the Russian Museum

Libraries: c. 600,000 vols

Publications: Vestnik SGSEU, Economics *(biannually)*

Press or Publishing House: Publishing Centre

Last Updated: 27/01/12

SARATOV STATE TECHNICAL UNIVERSITY NAMED AFTER Y.A GAGARIN

Saratovskij Gosudarstvennyj Tehničeskij Universitet im. Ju. A. Gagarina (SSTU)

ul. Politehničeskaja 77, Saratov 410054
Tel: +7(8452) 52-64-98
Fax: +7(8452) 50-75-63
EMail: rectorat@sstu.ru; lgv@sstu.ru
Website: http://www.sstu.ru/

Rector: Igor Pleve (2008-)

Faculties

Architecture and Civil Engineering (Architecture; Civil Engineering); **Automobile Engineering** (Automotive Engineering; Road Transport; Transport Management); **Electronic Engineering and Instrument Making** (Automation and Control Engineering; Computer Engineering; Electronic Engineering; Instrument Making; Software Engineering; Technology); **Electronic Industrial Management** (Business and Commerce; Economics; Engineering; Industrial Management; Management; Transport Economics); **Power Engineering** (Electrical Engineering; Power Engineering); **Social Management** (Arts and Humanities; Ecology; Economics; Gender Studies; Management; Safety Engineering; Social Sciences); **Transport Construction** (Hydraulic Engineering; Road Engineering; Road Transport; Transport Management)

Institutes

Technology *(City of Engels)* (Chemical Engineering; Fashion Design; Mechanical Engineering; Software Engineering); **Technology and Management** *(Balakovo)* (Civil Engineering; Information Technology; Management; Mechanical Engineering; Social Studies; Technology)

Schools

Russian Language *(International)* (Cultural Studies; History; Russian)

Further Information: Also APTECH Computer Training Centre; Microsoft IT Academy; Softline IT Academy

History: Founded 1930, acquired present status 1992.

Governing Bodies: Academic Board

Academic Year: September to June

Admission Requirements: Secondary school certificate (Attestat o srednem obrazovanii)

Main Language(s) of Instruction: Russian; English (for international curricula)

International Co-operation: Participates in the Tempus programme (United Kingdom, Germany, Belgium, USA, Ireland, France)

Accrediting Agencies: Federal Education Agency

Degrees and Diplomas: *Bakalavr*, *Specialist Diploma*; *Magistr*, *Kandidat Nauk*. Also short-term courses certificates

Student Services: Academic counselling, Canteen, Cultural centre, Employment services, Foreign student adviser, Foreign Studies Centre, Handicapped facilities, Health services, Language programs, Nursery care, Social counselling, Sports facilities

Student Residential Facilities: Yes

Special Facilities: Museum

Libraries: 2 m. vols.

Publications: Sociological Journal *(quarterly)*; Vestnik of SSTU, Scientific Journal on research and Innovation *(monthly)*

Academic Staff	MEN	WOMEN	TOTAL
PART-TIME	–	-64	0

Last Updated: 07/12/11

SARATOV STATE UNIVERSITY NAMED AFTER N.G. CHERNYSHESKIJ

Saratovskij Gosudarstvennyj Universitet im. N.G. Černyšeskogo

ul. Astrahanskaja 83, Saratov 410001
Tel: +7(8452) 26-16-96 +7(8451) 51-92-26
Website: http://www.sgu.ru/

Rector: Leonid Yurevich Kossovich (2003-) EMail: rector@sgu.ru

Faculties

Biology (Biology); **Computer Science and Information Technology** (Computer Networks; Information Technology); **Economics** (Banking; Economics; Finance; Management; Marketing); **Geography** (Geography); **Geology** (Geology); **Law** (Law); **Mechanics and Mathematics** (Computer Science; Mathematical Physics; Mathematics; Mechanical Engineering); **Nanotechnology and Biomedical Technology** (Biotechnology; Nanotechnology; Solid State Physics); **Nonlinear Processes** (Geophysics); **Philosophy** (Philosophy); **Physics** (Physics); **Psychology** (Psychology); **Sociology** (Sociology)

Institutes

Balashov *(Balashov)* (Biology; Ecology; Economics; Mathematics; Modern Languages; Pedagogy; Physical Education; Physics; Psychology; Social Welfare); **Pedagogy** (Art Criticism; Art History; Cultural Studies; Educational Psychology; English; Fine Arts; French; German; Pedagogy; Physical Education; Primary Education; Special Education; Theatre)

History: Founded 1909.

Governing Bodies: Academic Council

Academic Year: September to July

Admission Requirements: Secondary education certificate (Attestat o srednem obrazovanii) and entrance examination

Degrees and Diplomas: *Bakalavr*, *Specialist Diploma*: 5 yrs; *Magistr*, *Kandidat Nauk*: a further 3 yrs and thesis

Student Services: Canteen, Cultural centre, Employment services, Foreign Studies Centre, Health services, Nursery care, Sports facilities

Special Facilities: Geological Museum; Zoological Museum; Museum of Russian History. Biological Garden

Libraries: c. 3m. vols

Publications: Saratovskij Universitet

Press or Publishing House: Publishing House
Last Updated: 11/04/11

SCHOOL-STUDIO (INSTITUTE) NAMED AFTER V.I. NEMIROVICH-DANCHENKO OF THE MOSCOW ART ACADEMY THEATRE NAMED AFTER A.P. CHEKHOV

Škola-Studija (Institut) im. V.I. Nemiroviča-Dančenko pri Moskovskom Khudožestvennom Akademičeskom Teatre im. A.P. Čekhov

ul. Tverskaja 6/1, Building 7, Moskva 125009
Tel: +7(495) 629-3936
Fax: +7(495) 692-5767
EMail: public@mxat-school.ru
Website: http://www.mhatschool.theatre.ru

Rector: Anatolij Mironovich Smeljanskij

Programmes

Acting (Acting; Film); **Performing Arts Management** (Art Management; Performing Arts; Theatre); **Stage and Costume Design** (Design; Display and Stage Design; Theatre)

History: Founded 1943. Formerly Škola-Studija pri Moskovskij Hudožestveniyj Teatr.

Governing Bodies: Ministry of Culture

Academic Year: September to July

Admission Requirements: Secondary School Certificate or equivalent

Main Language(s) of Instruction: Russian

International Co-operation: With universities in Sweden, USA

Accrediting Agencies: Ministry of Education

Degrees and Diplomas: *Bakalavr*, *Specialist Diploma*

Student Services: Canteen, Foreign student adviser, Foreign Studies Centre, Language programs

Student Residential Facilities: Yes.

Libraries: Main Library

Last Updated: 24/01/12

SEVERSK STATE TECHNOLOGICAL ACADEMY

Severskaja Gosudarstvennaja Tehnologičeskaja Akademija

prosp. Kommunisticeskij 65, Seversk, 636036 Tomskaja oblast'
Tel: +7(3822) 77-95-29
Fax: +7(3822) 77-95-29
EMail: secretary@ssti.ru
Website: http://www.ssti.ru/

Rector: Aleksandr N. Zhiganov (1987-)

Vice-Rector: Boris M. Kerbel EMail: akbm@ssti.ru

International Relations: Mikhail D. Noskov EMail: nmd@ssti.ru

Faculties

Electrical Engineering and Automation (Automation and Control Engineering; Electrical and Electronic Equipment and Maintenance; Electrical Engineering; Electronic Engineering; Nuclear Physics; Physical Education; Physics; Power Engineering); **Management of Technology** (Accountancy; Applied Mathematics; Arts and Humanities; Computer Science; Economics; History; Mathematics; Operations Research; Philosophy; Political Sciences; Psychology; Social Work; Sociology); **Technology** (Chemical Engineering; Chemistry; Machine Building; Materials Engineering; Modern Languages; Technology)

History: Previously known as Seversk State Institute of Technology. Created 1959 as part of Tomsk Polytechnic Institute, became an Institute in 2001 and eventually was certified an Academy in 2005.

Academic Year: September to June

Admission Requirements: Secondary school certificate, Specialised Secondary Education

Fees: None

Main Language(s) of Instruction: Russian

International Co-operation: With Germany and United Kingdom

Accrediting Agencies: Ministry of Education and Science

Degrees and Diplomas: *Specialist Diploma*: 5-5 1/2 yrs

Student Services: Academic counselling, Canteen, Employment services, Foreign Studies Centre, Health services, Language programs, Social counselling, Sports facilities

Student Residential Facilities: None

Special Facilities: None

Libraries: c. 110,000 items

Publications: Nuclear Fuel Cycle, Scientific Journal *(annually)*; Technology and Automation Nuclear Power, Scientific Journal *(annually)*

Press or Publishing House: Seversk State Technology Academy Publishing House

Last Updated: 26/01/12

SHADRINSK STATE PEDAGOGICAL INSTITUTE

Šadrinskij Gosudarstvennyj Pedagogičeskij Institut

ul. K. Libkneht 3, Šadrinsk, 641800 Kurganskaja oblast'
Tel: +7(35253) 63-502
Fax: +7(35253) 63-502
EMail: shgpi@list.ru
Website: http://www.shgpi.edu.ru

Rector: L. I. Ponomareva

Departments

Education (Education; Educational Psychology; Music Education; Pedagogy; Preschool Education; Primary Education; Psychology); **Graphic Arts** (Art Education; Design; Fine Arts; Graphic Arts); **History and Law** (Education; History; Law); **Informatics** (Computer Science; Economics; Engineering; Mathematics; Science Education; Software Engineering); **Physical Education** (Physical Education); **Physics and Mathematics** (Biology; Geography; Mathematics Education; Physics; Science Education); **Russian and Western European Philology** (Cultural Studies; English; Foreign Languages Education; French; German; History; Journalism; Linguistics; Native Language Education; Russian; Translation and Interpretation); **Social Education** (Law; Service Trades; Social Work; Tourism); **Special Education and Psychology** (Educational Psychology; Psychology; Special Education; Speech Therapy and Audiology); **Technology and Entrepreneurship** (Business Education; Teacher Training; Technology Education)

History: Founded 1939.

Degrees and Diplomas: *Bakalavr*, *Magistr*

Last Updated: 02/03/12

SHUYA STATE PEDAGOGICAL UNIVERSITY

Šuiskij Gosudarstvennyj Pedagogičeskij Universitet

ul. Kooperativnaja 24, Shuja, 155908 Ivanovskaja oblast'
Tel: +7(49351) 3-04-63
Fax: +7(49351) 3-04-63
EMail: sgpu@sspu.ru
Website: http://www.sspu.ru/

Rector: Aleksej Aleksandrovich Mikhailov EMail: rektorat@mail.ru

Faculties

Arts (Art Education; Cultural Studies; Fine Arts; Folklore; Literature); **Geography and Environmental Studies** (Biology; Ecology; Geography; Science Education); **History and Philology** (English; French; German; Literature; Pedagogy; Religious Studies; Russian); **Pedagogy and Psychology** (Pedagogy; Preschool Education; Primary Education; Psychology; Special Education; Speech Therapy and Audiology); **Physical Education** (Physical Education; Sports); **Social Sciences and Humanities** (Economics; Law; Management); **Technology** (Business and Commerce; Computer Science; Ecology; Household Management; Marketing; Mathematics; Mathematics Education; Physics; Protective Services; Science Education; Technology)

Further Information: Also Branches in Azovskaya Settlement, Kineshma, Ivanovo.

History: Founded 1815, acquired present status 1996.

Academic Year: September to June

Admission Requirements: Secondary school certificate and entrance examination

Main Language(s) of Instruction: Russian

Degrees and Diplomas: *Bakalavr*; *Specialist Diploma*; *Magistr*

Student Services: Academic counselling, Canteen, Cultural centre, Employment services, Health services, Social counselling, Sports facilities

Student Residential Facilities: Yes

Special Facilities: Computer Labs

Libraries: 2 centralised libraries

Last Updated: 16/03/12

SIBERIAN ACADEMY OF PUBLIC ADMINISTRATION

Sibirskaja Akademija Gosudarstvennoj Služby (SAGS (SAPA))

Ul. Nižegorodskaya 6, Novosibirsk, 630102 Novosibiraskaja oblast'

Tel: +7(383) 210-1767 +7(383) 210-1240

Fax: +7(383) 210-1098

EMail: pechenkina@sapa.nsk.su; common@sapa.nsk.su; musychenko@sapa.nsk.su

Website: http://www.sapanet.ru/

Rector: Jevgenij A. Bojko (1991-) EMail: boyko@sapa.nsk.su

Faculties

Economics (Banking; Economics; Finance; Taxation); **Jurisprudence** (Law; Psychology); **State and Municipal Management** *(SMM)* (Human Resources; Management; Public Administration; Public Relations)

History: Founded 1991 as Siberian Personnel Training Center. Acquired present status and title 1995. SAPA is managed by the Federal Agency on Education of the Ministry of Education and Science of the Russian Federation.

Governing Bodies: Academic Board

Academic Year: September to June

Admission Requirements: Secondary school certificate (Attestat) and entrance examination

Fees: (Russian Rubles): full-time students, 54,000 per annum; part-time students, 35,000 per annum

Main Language(s) of Instruction: Russian

International Co-operation: With Association of Netherlands Municipalities and its international agency VNG International (TACIS project); with partners in Czech and Ukrainian (MATRA project), in France (Institutes of Regional Administration (IRA) in Nantes, Lilles and Lyons and National Center of Territory State Service in Paris) and in Germany (Bavarian School of Management).

Accrediting Agencies: Federal Supervisory Service of the Ministry of Education and Science of the Russian Federation

Degrees and Diplomas: *Specialist Diploma*: Finance and Credit; Jurisprudence; Public and Municipal Management, Personnel Management, 5 yrs

Student Services: Academic counselling, Canteen, Cultural centre, Employment services, Health services, Language programs, Social counselling, Sports facilities

Student Residential Facilities: 3 hostels in the center of Novosibirsk

Special Facilities: Arts Club; Concert Hall

Libraries: 367,018 vols, Periodical Journals, Reference Audiovisual CDs, DVDs, Videos and audiocassettes; Official publications - legislative documents, policy documents, discussions documents, statistics and reports produced by central governments, their departments and organisations

Publications: Proceedings of SAPA, Scientific papers, reports *(bimonthly)*; Vestnik SibAGS, Informational and Analytical Edition *(quarterly)*

Press or Publishing House: Publishing House of SAPA

Last Updated: 26/04/11

SIBERIAN FEDERAL UNIVERSITY

Sibirskij Federalinyj Universitet

prosp. Svobodnyj 79, Krasnojarsk 660041

Tel: +7(391) 244-82-13

Fax: +7(391) 244-86-25

EMail: info@sfu-kras.ru

Website: http://www.sfu-kras.ru

Rector: Evgenij Aleksandrovich Vaganov EMail: rector@sfu-kras.ru

Chairs

UNESCO

Institutes

Architecture and Design (Architecture; Graphic Design; Painting and Drawing; Sculpture); **Business Management and Economics** (Business Administration; Business Computing; Economics; Marketing); **Economics, Management and Environmental Studies** (Accountancy; Economics; Environmental Management; International Economics); **Education, Psychology and Sociology** (Education; Educational and Student Counselling; Educational Psychology; Pedagogy); **Engineering** (Building Technologies; Civil Engineering; Construction Engineering; Industrial Engineering; Road Engineering); **Fundamental Biology and Biotechnology** (Biology; Biophysics; Biotechnology); **Humanities** (Advertising and Publicity; Cultural Studies; Fine Arts; History; Information Technology; Museum Studies; Philosophy); **Information and Space Technology** (Computer Science; Information Sciences; Information Technology); **Law** (Law); **Mathematics** (Mathematics); **Military Studies** (Military Science); **Mining, Geology, and Geotechnology** (Geology; Mineralogy; Mining Engineering); **Non-Ferrous Metals and Materials Science** (Metallurgical Engineering); **Oil and Gas** (Petroleum and Gas Engineering); **Philology and Language Communication** (European Languages; Journalism; Linguistics; Literature; Philology; Russian; Translation and Interpretation); **Physical and Radio Engineering** (Laser Engineering; Physical Engineering; Radiophysics; Telecommunications Engineering); **Physical Education, Sport and Tourism** (Physical Education; Sports; Tourism); **Polytechnic** (Electrical Engineering; Energy Engineering; Environmental Engineering; Food Technology; Mechanical Engineering; Robotics)

History: Founded 1969 as Krasnojarskij Gosudarstvennyj Universitet (branch of the Novosibirsk State University and Tomsk State University). Acquired current status and title 2006 when formed as Federal University with: Krasnojarskij Gosudarstvennyj Tehničeskij Universitet, Krasnojarskaja Gosudarstvennaja Arhitekturno-Stroitel'naja Akademija, and Gosudarstvennyj Universitet Tsvetnykh Metallov i Zolota.

Governing Bodies: Academic Council; Board of Trustees

Academic Year: September to July (September-December; January-July)

Admission Requirements: Secondary school certificate (Attestat o srednem obrazovanii) and entrance examination

Main Language(s) of Instruction: Russian

Accrediting Agencies: Ministry of Education

Degrees and Diplomas: *Bakalavr*; *Specialist Diploma*; *Magistr*; *Kandidat Nauk*: a further 3 yrs; *Doktor Nauk*: by thesis

Student Services: Academic counselling, Canteen, Cultural centre, Foreign student adviser, Foreign Studies Centre, Health services, Language programs, Sports facilities

Student Residential Facilities: Yes

Libraries: Yes

Press or Publishing House: Izdatelstvo Krasnojarskogo Universiteta

Last Updated: 22/09/11

SIBERIAN LAW INSTITUTE OF THE RUSSIAN FEDERATION FSDC

Sibirskij Yuridičeskij Institut FSKN Rossii

ul. Rokossovsky, 20, Krasnojarsk 660131

Tel: +7(391) 224-87-81

Fax: +7(391) 220-25-46

EMail: post@sibli.ru

Website: http://www.sibli.ru/

Rector: Dmitrij Dmitrievich Nevirko

Departments

Administrative Law (Administrative Law); **Civil Law** (Civil Law); **Criminal Law and Criminology** (Criminal Law; Criminology); **Criminal Process** (Criminal Law; Criminology); **Criminology** (Criminology); **Foreign Languages** (Modern Languages); **Humanities, Social and Economic Sciences** (Arts and Humanities; Economics; Social Sciences); **Information Technology** (Information Technology); **Operational Military and Physical Training** (Military Science; Physical Education); **Operational-Investigative Activities** (Military Science); **State and Legal Disciplines** (Government; Law)

History: founded 1993, acquired present status 1999

Academic Year: September - August

Main Language(s) of Instruction: Russian

Accrediting Agencies: The Ministry of Internal Affairs of the Russian Federation

Degrees and Diplomas: *Specialist Diploma*

Student Services: Academic counselling, Canteen, Cultural centre, Health services, Sports facilities

Student Residential Facilities: 340 places

Libraries: c. 210,000 vols

Last Updated: 24/01/12

SIBERIAN STATE ACADEMY OF GEODESY

Sibirskaja Gosudarstvennaja Geodezičeskaja Akademija (SSGA)

ul. Plahotnogo 10, Novosibirsk, 630108 Novosibiraskaja oblast'
Tel: +7(383) 343-3937
Fax: +7(383) 343-3060
EMail: rektorat@ssga.ru
Website: http://www.ssga.ru

Rector: Alexander P. Karpik (1993-)
Tel: +7(383) 343-2534 EMail: rector@ssga.ru

Vice-Rector, Administration: Vyacheslav Roldugin
Tel: +7(383) 361-0180

International Relations: Igor A. Musihin
Tel: +7(383) 343-2539, Fax: +7(383) 343-2539
EMail: igor_musihin@mail.ru

Institutes

Cadastre and Geographic Information Systems (Earth Sciences; Engineering; Surveying and Mapping; Welfare and Protective Services); **Geodesy and Management** (Business Administration; Computer Engineering; Management; Surveying and Mapping); **Optics and Optical Technologies** (Optical Technology; Optics; Surveying and Mapping); **Remote Sensing and Environmental Management** (Earth Sciences; Environmental Management; Environmental Studies; Surveying and Mapping; Welfare and Protective Services)

Further Information: Also Institute of Distance Education

History: Founded 1933.

Governing Bodies: Academic Council

Academic Year: September to July (September-January; February-July)

Admission Requirements: Secondary school certificate and entrance examination

Fees: (US Dollars): preparatory course, 2,200 per annum

Main Language(s) of Instruction: Russian

International Co-operation: Germany, China, Mongolia

Degrees and Diplomas: *Bakalavr*: 4 yrs; *Specialist Diploma*: 4-5 yrs or 2 yrs after B.Sc.; *Specialist Diploma*: Engineering, 6 ys; *Magistr*: a further 2 yrs following Bakavr; *Kandidat Nauk*: Science (PhD), a further 3 yrs and thesis; *Doktor Nauk*: Science, by thesis after Kandidat

Student Services: Academic counselling, Canteen, Cultural centre, Foreign student adviser, Health services, Language programs, Social counselling, Sports facilities

Student Residential Facilities: 2 dormitories

Special Facilities: Planetarium; Museum; Surveying Training Ground

Libraries: 267,000 vols and 600 rare books

Publications: Vestnik of SSGA, Proceedings of the Conferences held at SSGA *(annually)*

Academic Staff *2007-2008*	MEN	WOMEN	**TOTAL**
FULL-TIME	148	202	**350**
STAFF WITH DOCTORATE			
FULL-TIME	109	27	**136**
Student Numbers *2007-2008*			
All (Foreign Included)	2,038	6,933	**8,971**
FOREIGN ONLY	–	–	**45**

Distance students, 3,545. **Evening students**, 824.

Last Updated: 25/01/12

SIBERIAN STATE AEROSPACE UNIVERSITY

Sibirskij Gosudarstvennyj Aerokosmičeskij Universitet

prosp. im. Gazetj 'Krasnojarskij Rabočij' 31, Krasnojarsk 660014
Tel: +7(391) 291-9063
Fax: +7(391) 262-7238
EMail: ums@sibsau.ru
Website: http://www.sibsau.ru/

Rector: Igor V. Kovalev EMail: rector@sibsau.ru

First Vice-Rector – Vice-Rector for Development: Vladimir A. Kureshov EMail: kureshov@sibsau.ru

International Relations: Anna A. Voroshilov, Vice-Rector, International Cooperation

Faculties

Civil Aviation and Customs Affairs (Aeronautical and Aerospace Engineering; Air Transport; Electrical and Electronic Equipment and Maintenance; Engineering; Taxation); **Engineering and Economics** (Accountancy; Computer Science; Economics; Finance; Management; Marketing); **Humanities** (Advertising and Publicity; Arts and Humanities; Computer Graphics; Cultural Studies; English; History; Human Resources; Labour and Industrial Relations; Law; Literature; Management; Marketing; Modern Languages; Philosophy; Public Relations; Russian; Social Sciences); **Mechanical Engineering and Mechatronics** (Electronic Engineering; Engineering Drawing and Design; Mechanical Engineering; Power Engineering; Robotics); **Physical Education and Sport** (Physical Education; Sports)

Higher Schools

Business *(International Higher Business School)* (Accountancy; Banking; Business and Commerce; Finance; Human Resources; Insurance; Management; Marketing)

Institutes

Computer Science and Telecommunications (Computer Science; Information Technology; Software Engineering; Systems Analysis; Telecommunications Engineering); **Space Research and High Technologies** (Aeronautical and Aerospace Engineering; Heating and Refrigeration; Machine Building; Mechanical Engineering; Metal Techniques; Nanotechnology; Physics); **Space Technology** (Aeronautical and Aerospace Engineering)

Further Information: Also Russian Courses for foreign students. Student Exchange programmes

History: Founded 1959, acquired present university status and title 2002.

Governing Bodies: Governing Council; Scientific Council

Academic Year: September to May (September-December; February-May)

Admission Requirements: Secondary school certificate (Attestat o srednem obrazovanii)

Main Language(s) of Instruction: Russian

Degrees and Diplomas: *Bakalavr*: 4 yrs; *Specialist Diploma*: 5 1/2 yrs; *Magistr*: 6 1/2 yrs; *Kandidat Nauk*: a further 3 yrs; *Doktor Nauk*

Student Services: Canteen, Cultural centre, Health services, Sports facilities

Student Residential Facilities: For 3,000 students

Special Facilities: Academy Museum

Libraries: Central Library, 253,000 vols

Last Updated: 26/01/12

SIBERIAN STATE AUTOMOBILE AND TRANSPORT ACADEMY

Sibirskaja Gosudarstvennaja Avtomobilno-Dorožnaja Akademija (SIBADI)

prosp. Mira 5, Omsk, 644080 Omskaja oblast'
Tel: +7(3812) 650-322
Fax: +7(3812) 650-322
EMail: info@sibadi.org
Website: http://www.sibadi.org/

Rector: Viktor A. Sal'nikov (1999-) EMail: rector@sibadi.org

Faculties

Automobile Transport and Economy (Transport Economics; Transport Management); **Civil Engineering** (Administration; Architecture; Civil Engineering; Management; Town Planning); **Economics and Management** (Economics; Industrial Management; Management); **Road Machinery** (Mechanical Engineering; Road Transport); **Roads and Bridges** (Bridge Engineering; Civil Engineering; Road Engineering; Road Transport)

History: Founded 1930.

Academic Year: September to June

Admission Requirements: Secondary school certificate (Attestat o srednem obrazovanii)

Fees: (Russian Rubles): c. 40,000 per annum

Main Language(s) of Instruction: Russian

Degrees and Diplomas: *Bakalavr*; *Specialist Diploma*; *Magistr*

Student Services: Canteen, Cultural centre, Nursery care, Sports facilities

Student Residential Facilities: Yes

Special Facilities: Academy History Museum

Libraries: c. 660,000 vols

Last Updated: 26/04/11

SIBERIAN STATE INDUSTRIAL UNIVERSITY

Sibirskij Gosudarstvennyj Industrial'nyj Universitet (SIBSIU)

ul. Kirova 42, Novokuzneck, 654007 Kemerovskaja oblast'
Tel: +7(3843) 463-502 +7(3843) 784-470
Fax: +7(3843) 465-792
EMail: rector@sibsiu.ru
Website: http://www.sibsiu.ru

Rector: Sergej P. Mochalov (2008-)
Tel: +7(3843) 463-502 EMail: spm@sibsiu.ru

Vice-Rector, Administration: Andrej Stolboushkin
Tel: +7(3843) 774-017 EMail: stanyr@list.ru

Faculties

Natural Sciences (Analytical Chemistry; Chemistry; Graphic Design; Mathematics; Metallurgical Engineering; Physical Chemistry; Physics)

Institutes

Economics and Management (Accountancy; Administration; Advertising and Publicity; Banking; Economic and Finance Policy; Economics; Finance; History; Labour and Industrial Relations; Law; Management; Marketing; Mining Engineering; Modern Languages; Pedagogy; Philosophy; Political Sciences; Psychology; Social Work; Sociology); **Engineering** (Architecture; Building Technologies; Engineering; Heating and Refrigeration; Materials Engineering; Real Estate; Sanitary Engineering; Structural Architecture; Water Management); **Engineering and Transport** (Mechanical Engineering; Metal Techniques; Metallurgical Engineering; Transport Management); **Information Technology and Automated Systems** (Automation and Control Engineering; Computer Engineering; Computer Science; Electrical Engineering; Electronic Engineering; Industrial Engineering; Information Management; Information Technology; Mechanical Engineering); **Metallurgy and Materials** (Ecology; Metal Techniques; Metallurgical Engineering; Physics; Thermal Physics); **Mining and Geosystems** (Earth Sciences; Ecology; Geology; Mining Engineering)

Further Information: Also long- or short-term Russian Language courses for International Students

History: Founded 1930. Acquired present status 1998.

Governing Bodies: Rector; Rector's Council; Academic Council

Academic Year: September to July (September-January; February-July)

Admission Requirements: Secondary school certificate or equivalent, with translation) ; Results of TORFL (1st certificate Level)

Fees: (Russian Rubles): 31,500-53,900

Main Language(s) of Instruction: Russian

Accrediting Agencies: Ministry of Education of the Russian Federation

Degrees and Diplomas: *Bakalavr*: 4 yrs; *Specialist Diploma*: 5 yrs; *Magistr*: 2 yrs; *Kandidat Nauk*: 3 yrs; *Doktor Nauk*

Student Services: Academic counselling, Canteen, Cultural centre, Employment services, Foreign student adviser, Foreign Studies Centre, Health services, Language programs, Sports facilities

Student Residential Facilities: Dormitories for up to 1,500 students

Special Facilities: Geological Museum; Museum of the University's History

Libraries: Yes

Publications: Izvestija Vuzov. Chernaja Metallurgija *(monthly)*

Academic Staff *2007-2008*	**TOTAL**
FULL-TIME	**660**
STAFF WITH DOCTORATE FULL-TIME	**350**
Student Numbers *2007-2008*	
All (Foreign Included)	**13,368**
FOREIGN ONLY	**20**

Part-time students, 3,930.

Last Updated: 25/01/12

SIBERIAN STATE MEDICAL UNIVERSITY

Sibirskij Gosudarstvennyj Medicinskij Universitet (SGMU)

ul. Moskovskij Trakt 2, Tomsk 634050
Tel: +7(3822) 530-423
Fax: +7(3822) 533-309
EMail: office@ssmu.ru
Website: http://www.ssmu.ru

Rector: Vaycheslav Novitskiy

Faculties

Advanced Training and Professional Development; **Biomedicine** (Biomedicine); **Clinical Psychology, Psychotherapy and Social Work** (Clinical Psychology; Psychology; Psychotherapy; Social Work); **Health Administration and Economics** (Health Administration); **Medicine** (Medicine; Surgery); **Nursing** (Nursing); **Paediatrics** (Paediatrics); **Pharmacy** (Pharmacology; Pharmacy)

History: Founded 1878. Acquired present status 1992.

Governing Bodies: Academic Council

Academic Year: September to June

Admission Requirements: Secondary school certificate

Main Language(s) of Instruction: Russian

International Co-operation: With universities in the USA, United Kingdom, Germany, the Netherlands

Accrediting Agencies: Ministry of Health Care; Ministry of Higher Education

Degrees and Diplomas: *Specialist Diploma*: Pharmacy; Health Administration; Social Work; Psychology, 5 yrs; *Kandidat Nauk*; *Doktor Nauk*. Also Medical Doctor (MD) 6 yrs

Student Services: Academic counselling, Canteen, Employment services, Foreign student adviser, Foreign Studies Centre, Health services, Language programs, Nursery care, Social counselling, Sports facilities

Student Residential Facilities: Yes

Special Facilities: Anatomy Museum; Forensic Medicine Museum; Pathology and Anatomy Museum

Libraries: c. 1,000,000 vols

Publications: Bulletin of Siberian Medicine *(quarterly)*; Magazine of Gastroenterology and Hepatology *(quarterly)*; Magazine of Microsurgery and Plastic Surgery *(quarterly)*
Last Updated: 20/09/11

SIBERIAN STATE TECHNOLOGICAL UNIVERSITY

Sibirskij Gosudarstvennyj Tehnologičeskij Universitet (SIB.STU)

prosp. Mira 82, Krasnojarsk 660049
Tel: +7(391) 266-0388
Fax: +7(391) 227-2373
EMail: sibstu@sibstu.kts.ru
Website: http://www.sibgtu.ru/

Rector: Viktor Vladimirovich Ogurtsov

Departments

Chemical Engineering *(Distance Studies)* (Automation and Control Engineering; Chemical Engineering; Economics); **Forestry** *(Distance Studies)* (Forestry)

Faculties

Automation and Information Technology (Automation and Control Engineering; Computer Engineering; Electrical Engineering; Information Technology; Physics; Software Engineering); **Chemical Engineering** (Analytical Chemistry; Chemical Engineering; Inorganic Chemistry; Organic Chemistry; Physical Chemistry; Polymer and Plastics Technology); **Economics** (Accountancy; Applied Mathematics; Finance; Forest Management; Forestry; Human Resources; Industrial Chemistry; Industrial Management; Management); **Forestry** (Cattle Breeding; Crop Production; Ecology; Environmental Studies; Forest Management; Forestry); **Forestry Engineering** (Agricultural Engineering; Forestry; Mathematics and Computer Science; Water Management); **Humanities** (Arts and Humanities; Cultural Studies; Economics; History; Industrial and Organizational Psychology; Law; Linguistics; Management; Modern Languages; Pedagogy; Philosophy; Physical Education; Political Sciences; Psychology; Social Work; Sociology; Translation and Interpretation); **Mechanical Engineering** (Agricultural Equipment; Environmental Engineering; Mechanical Engineering; Mechanics); **Processings of Natural Compounds** (Biotechnology; Chemical Engineering; Ecology; Measurement and Precision Engineering; Natural Resources; Paper Technology)

History: Founded 1930, reorganized as Krasnoyarsk State Technological Academy 1994, acquired present name and status 1997.

Governing Bodies: Scientific Council

Academic Year: September to June

Admission Requirements: Secondary school certificate and entrance examination

Main Language(s) of Instruction: Russian

International Co-operation: With universities in France, United Kingdom, USA, Spain, Poland, Ukraine, Netherlands. Also participates in Copernicus.

Degrees and Diplomas: *Bakalavr*; *Specialist Diploma*; *Magistr*; *Kandidat Nauk*; *Doktor Nauk*

Student Services: Academic counselling, Canteen, Cultural centre, Employment services, Foreign student adviser, Foreign Studies Centre, Health services, Language programs, Social counselling, Sports facilities

Student Residential Facilities: Yes

Special Facilities: Museum: University History; Biology. Botanical Gardens. Scientific Labs

Libraries: Central Library, 900,000 vols
Last Updated: 25/01/12

SIBERIAN STATE TRANSPORT UNIVERSITY

Sibirskij Gosudarstvennyj Universitet Putej Soobščenija (SGUPS)

ul. D. Kovalchuk, 191, Novosibirsk, 630049 Novosibiraskaja oblast'
Tel: +7(383) 328-04-70
Fax: +7(383) 226-79-78
EMail: public@stu.ru
Website: http://www.stu.ru/

Rector: Vladimir D. Vereskun

Vice-Rector, Administration: Oleg Vasiliev

International Relations: Vladimir Nekhoroshkov, Pro-Rector, International Cooperation

Faculties

Bridges and Tunnels Construction (Bridge Engineering; Civil Engineering); **Business Information Systems** (Business Computing; Information Technology); **Construction Machinery** (Civil Engineering; Road Engineering); **Distance Education**; **Engineering and Economics** (Economics; Engineering Management); **Human Resources Management** (Human Resources); **Industrial and Civil Engineering** (Building Technologies; Civil Engineering; Industrial Engineering); **International Economics and Law** (International Economics; International Law); **Railway Construction** (Railway Engineering; Railway Transport); **Railway Transport Management** (Industrial Management)

Further Information: Branches also at Belovo, Novoaltaisk, Tomsk.

History: Created in 1932 as Novosibirskij Putejsko-Stroitelnyj Institut Inzhenerov Zheleznodorozhnogo Transporta. Acquired current title and status 1997.

Main Language(s) of Instruction: Russian

Degrees and Diplomas: *Bakalavr*; *Specialist Diploma*; *Kandidat Nauk*; *Doktor Nauk*
Last Updated: 25/01/12

SIBERIAN STATE UNIVERSITY OF PHYSICAL EDUCATION

Sibirskij Gosudarstvennyj Universitet Fizičeskoj Kul'tury (SIBGUFK)

ul. Maslennikova 144, Omsk, 644009 Omskaja oblast'
Tel: +7(3812) 36-42-74
Fax: +7(3812) 36-56-54
EMail: rector@sibsport.ru
Website: http://www.sibsport.ru/

Rector: Vladimir Mikhalev (1991-) Tel: +7(3812) 365-654

Colleges

Physical Education (Physical Education)

Departments

Anatomy, Physiology, Sports Medicine and Hygiene (Anatomy; Hygiene; Physiology; Sports Medicine); **Biomedical Foundations of Physical Education and Sports** (Biomedicine; Physical Education; Sports); **Foreign Languages** (Modern Languages); **Management, Economics and Law of Physical Education** (Physical Education; Sports; Sports Management); **Pedagogy** (Pedagogy); **Philosophy and History** (History; Philosophy); **Physical Education Teaching Methods** (Pedagogy; Physical Education); **Psychology** (Educational Psychology; Psychology); **Public Relations** (Public Relations); **Theoretical and Applied Physics and Mathematics** (Applied Mathematics; Applied Physics; Mathematics; Physics); **Theory and History of Physical Education and Sports** (Physical Education; Sports); **Theory and Methodology of Adaptive Physical Education** (Physical Education); **Theory and Methodology of Sports** (Sports; Sports Management); **Theory and Methods of Athletics** (Sports); **Theory and Methods of Boxing, Fencing and Martial Arts** (Sports); **Theory and Methods of Cycling and Skating** (Sports); **Theory and Methods of Football and Hockey** (Sports); **Theory and Methods of Gymnastics** (Sports); **Theory and Methods of Life Safety**; **Theory and Methods of Navigation** (Nautical Science; Sports); **Theory and Methods of Skiing** (Sports); **Theory and Methods of Sports and Recreation Activities** (Parks and Recreation; Sports); **Theory and Methods of Tourism and Socio-Cultural Services** (Cultural Studies; Tourism)

Further Information: Branches in Kemerovo, Nadym, Krasnojarsk, and Berezovsky

History: Founded 1950, acquired present status and title 2003.

Governing Bodies: Academic Council

Academic Year: September to June (September-January; February-June)

Admission Requirements: Secondary school certificate (Attestat o srednem obrazovanii) or equivalent, and sports achievement not lower than 2nd sporting grade

Main Language(s) of Instruction: Russian

Degrees and Diplomas: *Bakalavr*; *Specialist Diploma*; *Magistr*; *Kandidat Nauk*; *Doktor Nauk*

Student Services: Canteen, Employment services, Health services, Sports facilities

Student Residential Facilities: For c. 400 students

Special Facilities: Museum

Libraries: Total, c. 252,000 vols

Last Updated: 02/03/12

SIBERIAN STATE UNIVERSITY OF TELECOMMUNICATIONS AND INFORMATICS

Sibirskij Gosudarstvennyj Universitet Telekommunikacij i Informatiki

ul. Kirova 86, Novosibirsk, 630102 Novosibiraskaja oblast'

Tel: +7(383) 269-8202

Fax: +7(383) 269-8203

EMail: info@sibsutis.ru

Website: http://www.sibsutis.ru

Rector: Boris Ryabko EMail: rectorat@sibsutis.ru

Campuses

Buryat *(Buryat branch)*

Faculties

Automated Telecommunications (Electrical Engineering; Measurement and Precision Engineering; Safety Engineering; Telecommunications Engineering); **Computer Science and Computer Engineering** (Applied Mathematics; Automation and Control Engineering; Computer Engineering; Computer Networks; Computer Science; Information Management; Mathematics; Software Engineering; Telecommunications Engineering); **Distance Education** (Economics; Information Sciences; Telecommunications Engineering); **Engineering and Economics** (Accountancy; Economic and Finance Policy; Economics; Finance; Industrial Management; Marketing); **Humanities** (History; Modern Languages; Philosophy; Physical Education; Political Sciences; Psychology; Russian; Sociology; Sports); **Mobile Communications and Multimedia** (Computer Graphics; Information Management; Information Technology; Multimedia; Radio and Television Broadcasting; Safety Engineering); **Multiservice Telecommunications Systems** (Computer Networks; Electrical and Electronic Engineering; Electronic Engineering; Nanotechnology; Optics)

Institutes

Communications and Information Technology *(Ural Institute of Communications and Information Technology (Branch))* (Communication Studies; Computer Science; Information Technology); **Infocomm** *(Khabarovsk Institute of Infocomm (branch))* (Information Sciences; Information Technology)

Further Information: Also Russian Language courses for foreign students

History: Founded 1953. Branch in Habarovsk. Colleges in: Ekaterinburg, Ulan-Ude and Novosibirsk.

Governing Bodies: Academic Council

Academic Year: September to June (September-January; February-June)

Admission Requirements: Secondary school certificate (Attestat ob okončanii srednei školy)

Main Language(s) of Instruction: Russian

Degrees and Diplomas: *Bakalavr*; *Specialist Diploma*; *Magistr*; *Kandidat Nauk*; *Doktor Nauk*

Student Services: Academic counselling, Handicapped facilities, Health services, Social counselling, Sports facilities

Student Residential Facilities: For c. 1,500 students

Libraries: Central Library

Last Updated: 25/01/12

SMOLENSK STATE ACADEMY OF MEDICINE

Smolenskaja Gosudarstvennaja Medicinskaja Akademija

ul. Krupskok, 28, Smolensk 214019

Tel: +7(4812) 55-02-75

Fax: +7(4812) 52-01-51

EMail: adm@sgma.info

Website: http://www.sgma.info

Rector: Igor Otvagin

Faculties

Dentistry (Dentistry; Oral Pathology; Orthodontics; Stomatology); **Higher Nursing Education** (Nursing; Public Health); **Medicine** (Anatomy; Cardiology; Gastroenterology; Gynaecology and Obstetrics; Medicine; Physiology; Pneumology; Rehabilitation and Therapy; Rheumatology; Surgery); **Paediatrics** (Gynaecology and Obstetrics; Paediatrics; Surgery); **Pharmacy** (Chemistry; Pharmacology; Pharmacy)

Further Information: Also Courses for foreign students

History: Founded 1920 as department of Smolensk University, became an independent Institution 1930. Acquired present status 1993.

Governing Bodies: Academic Council

Academic Year: September to June (September-January; February-June)

Admission Requirements: Secondary school certificate (Attestat o srednem obrazovanii)

Main Language(s) of Instruction: Russian

Degrees and Diplomas: *Bakalavr*, *Specialist Diploma*

Student Services: Academic counselling, Canteen, Cultural centre, Employment services, Foreign Studies Centre, Health services, Nursery care, Social counselling, Sports facilities

Student Residential Facilities: For c. 500 students

Special Facilities: 2 Museums

Libraries: Scientific Library, c. 500,000 vols

Last Updated: 02/03/12

SMOLENSK STATE ACADEMY OF PHYSICAL EDUCATION, SPORTS AND TOURISM (INSTITUTE)

Smolenskaja Gosudarstvennaja Akademija Fizičeskoj Kul'tury, Sporta i Turisma (SGAPCST)

pr. Gagarina 23, Smolensk, 214018 Smolanskaja oblast'

Tel: +7(4812) 59-92-91

Fax: +7(4812) 59-92-91

EMail: smolakademsport@mail.ru; akademsport@sci.smolensk.ru

Website: http://www.sgafkst.ru/

Rector: Georgij Nikolaevich Grets

Faculties

Physical Culture and Recreational Technologies (Physical Education; Sports; Sports Management; Tourism); **Physical Culture and Sports** (Physical Education; Sports; Tourism)

History: Founded 1950. Previously known as Smolenskij Gosudarstvennyj Institut Fizičeskoj Kul'tury. Acquired current title and status 2005.

Governing Bodies: Scientific Board

Academic Year: September to June (September-December; January-June)

Admission Requirements: Secondary school certificate (Attestat o srednem obrazovanii)

Main Language(s) of Instruction: Russian

Degrees and Diplomas: *Bakalavr*, *Specialist Diploma*; *Magistr*

Student Services: Canteen, Employment services, Health services, Sports facilities

Student Residential Facilities: For c. 2,000 students

Special Facilities: Academy Museum

Libraries: Yes

Academic Staff: Total 100

Last Updated: 02/03/12

SMOLENSK STATE AGRICULTURAL ACADEMY

Smolenskaja Gosudarstvennaja Sel'skohozjajstvennaja Akademija (Institut)

ul. Bolšaja Sovetckaja 10/2, Smolensk 214000
Tel: +7(4812) 38-30-32 +7(4812) 38-18-18
Fax: +7(4812) 38-22-41
EMail: sgsha@smoltelecom.ru
Website: http://www.sgsha.ru/

Rector: Anatoly R. Kamošenkov (2001-)

Faculties

Economics (Accountancy; Agricultural Economics; Agricultural Management; Arts and Humanities; Business Administration; Classical Languages; Economics; English; French; German; Information Technology; Latin; Management; Marketing; Mathematics; Modern Languages); **Engineering and Technology** (Agricultural Business; Agricultural Engineering; Agricultural Equipment; Agriculture; Agronomy; Animal Husbandry; Crop Production; Ecology); **Zooengineering and Veterinary Medicine** (Animal Husbandry; Biotechnology; Cattle Breeding; Physical Education; Veterinary Science)

History: Founded as a Smolensk branch of the Moscow Agricultural Academy 1974. Became Smolensk Institute of Agriculture 1990 and Smolensk State Agricultural Academy 2006.

Academic Year: September to August

Main Language(s) of Instruction: Russian

Accrediting Agencies: Ministry of Agriculture

Degrees and Diplomas: *Bakalavr*; *Specialist Diploma*; *Magistr*

Student Services: Academic counselling, Canteen, Cultural centre, Employment services, Health services, Language programs, Social counselling, Sports facilities

Special Facilities: Zoological museum

Libraries: c. 150,000 vols

Last Updated: 02/03/12

SMOLENSK STATE INSTITUTE OF FINE ARTS

Smolenskij Gosudarstvennyj Institut Iskusstv

ul. Rumjantseva, 8, Smolensk, 214020 Smolenskaja oblast'
Tel: +7(4812) 31-02-88 +7(4812) 31-74-42
Fax: +7(4812) 31-02-88
EMail: sgii@admin.smolensk.ru
Website: http://sgii.smolgrad.ru/

Rector: Elena Vladimirovna Gorbylova

Faculties

Arts (Acting; Art Education; Dance; Design; Fine Arts; Music; Music Education; Musical Instruments; Performing Arts; Singing; Theatre); **Cultural Studies** (Architectural Restoration; Cultural Studies; Information Management; Information Sciences; Library Science; Museum Studies; Social Studies)

History: Founded 1961.

Degrees and Diplomas: *Bakalavr*; *Specialist Diploma*

Last Updated: 24/01/12

SMOLENSK STATE UNIVERSITY

Smolenskij Gosudarstvennyj Universitet

ul. Prževalskogo 4, Smolensk 214000
Tel: +7(812) 38-31-57 +7(812) 38-28-23
Fax: +7(812) 38-31-57
EMail: rectorat@smolgu.ru
Website: http://www.smolgu.ru/

Rector: Evgenij V. Kodin

Faculties

Fine Arts and Technical Drawing (Design; Fashion Design; Fine Arts; Graphic Design; Painting and Drawing); **Foreign Languages** (English; French; German; Translation and Interpretation); **History** (History; Law); **Management** (Computer Science; Economics; Management; Mathematics; Sociology); **Natural Sciences** (Biology; Botany; Chemistry; Ecology; Geography; Tourism; Zoology); **Peda-Sociology** (Pedagogy; Psychology; Social Work); **Philology** (Journalism; Literature; Philology; Russian); **Physics and Mathematics** (Computer Education; Mathematics; Mathematics Education; Pedagogy; Physics); **Primary and Special Education** (Pedagogy; Primary Education; Special Education)

History: Founded 1918 as branch of Smolensk State University. Acquired present status and title 1998. Was known as Smolenskij Gosudarstvennyj Pedagogičeskij Universitet (Smolensk State Pedagogical University). Acquired current title 2006.

Governing Bodies: University Council

Academic Year: September to July (September-January; February-July)

Admission Requirements: Secondary school certificate (Attestato srednem/polnom obrazovanii)

Main Language(s) of Instruction: Russian

International Co-operation: With universities in Germany, USA

Accrediting Agencies: Ministry of Education

Degrees and Diplomas: *Bakalavr*; *Specialist Diploma*; *Magistr*; *Kandidat Nauk*

Student Services: Canteen, Cultural centre, Foreign student adviser, Foreign Studies Centre, Handicapped facilities, Health services, Language programs, Sports facilities

Student Residential Facilities: For c. 2,000 students

Special Facilities: Museum of Literature

Libraries: 730,000 vols

Publications: Collected Papers; Filologeskije Zapiski (Notes on Philology) *(annually)*

Last Updated: 07/12/11

SOCHI STATE UNIVERSITY FOR TOURISM AND RECREATION

Sočinskij Gosudarstvennyj Universitet Turizma i Kurortnogo Dela

ul. Soveckaja 26a, Soči, 354000 Krasnodarskij Kraj
Tel: +7(8622) 64-84-82 +7(8622) 64-84-84 +7(8622) 64-85-03
Fax: +7(8622) 64-84-82 +7(8622) 64-87-90
EMail: university@sutr.ru
Website: http://www.sutr.ru/

Rector: Galina Maksimovna Romanovna

Faculties

Civil Engineering and Ecology (Civil Engineering; Ecology); **Economics** (Economics); **Law** (Law); **Sport** (Sports); **Tourism and Health Recreation** (Tourism); **Tourism Business** (Business Administration; Tourism)

Further Information: Also Russian courses for foreign students

History: Founded 1989 as branch of Kuban State University, became independent 1992.

Admission Requirements: Secondary school certificate (Attestat o srednem obrazovanii) and entrance examination

Main Language(s) of Instruction: Russian

Degrees and Diplomas: *Bakalavr*; *Specialist Diploma*: 5 yrs

Student Residential Facilities: For c. 20 students

Libraries: c. 87,900 vols

Publications: Selected Research

Last Updated: 26/04/11

SOLIKAMSK STATE PEDAGOGICAL INSTITUTE

Solikamskij Gosudarstvennyj Pedagogičeskij Institut

ul. Severnaja 44, Solikamsk 618500
Tel: +7(34253) 24-172
Fax: +7(34253) 24-209
EMail: institut@solgpi.ru
Website: http://www.solgpi.ru/

Faculties

Education (Art Education; Education; Health Education; Mathematics Education; Pedagogy; Physical Education; Primary Education; Social Sciences); **Humanities** (Arts and Humanities; Cultural Studies; Foreign Languages Education; History; Hotel and Restaurant; Journalism; Literature; Native Language; Native Language Education; Preschool Education; Russian; Social Studies; Tourism); **Natural Sciences and Mathematics** (Biomedicine; Environmental Studies; Mathematics; Mathematics and Computer Science; Natural

Sciences; Physics); **Psychology** (Educational Psychology; Pedagogy; Preschool Education; Psychology; Speech Therapy and Audiology)

History: Created 1991.

Degrees and Diplomas: *Specialist Diploma*
Last Updated: 24/01/12

SOUTHERN FEDERAL UNIVERSITY

Južnyj Federalnyj Universitet (SFU)

ul. B.Sadovaja 105/42, Rostov-na-Donu 344006
Tel: +7(863) 263-84-98
Fax: +7(863) 263-87-23
EMail: rectorat@sfedu.ru
Website: http://www.sfedu.ru/

Rector: Vladislav Georgievich Zakharevich (2007-)

Senior Vice-Rector, Academic: Igor Uznarodov
EMail: imuznarodov@sfedu.ru

International Relations: Sergey Alexandrovich Duzhikov, Vice-Rector, International Relations EMail: duzhikov@sfedu.ru

Faculties

Architecture (Architecture; Design; Environmental Studies; Landscape Architecture; Regional Planning; Town Planning); **Arts** (Arts and Humanities); **Arts and Graphics** (Art History; Fashion Design; Fine Arts; Graphic Arts; Industrial Design; Painting and Drawing; Photography); **Automation and Computer Science** (Mathematics; Operations Research; Systems Analysis); **Biology and Soils** (Anatomy; Biochemistry; Biological and Life Sciences; Biology; Biotechnology; Botany; Cell Biology; Genetics; Microbiology; Molecular Biology; Neurosciences; Physiology; Zoology); **Chemistry** (Applied Chemistry; Chemistry; Inorganic Chemistry; Organic Chemistry; Physical Chemistry); **Economic and Social Systems Management** (Economics; Management); **Economics** (Accountancy; Administration; Banking; Economics; Finance; Interior Design; Management; Marketing; Taxation); **Economics, Management and Law** (Economics; Law; Management); **Electronics and Electronic Equipment Engineering** (Electronic Engineering; Microelectronics; Power Engineering; Technology; Telecommunications Engineering); **Geology and Geography** (Geography; Geology; Geophysics; Marine Science and Oceanography; Mineralogy); **High Technologies** (Information Technology; Instrument Making; Systems Analysis); **History** (Ancient Civilizations; Contemporary History; History; Medieval Studies; Modern History; Prehistory); **Information Security** (Information Management; Information Technology); **Law** (Administrative Law; Air and Space Law; Civil Law; Commercial Law; Comparative Law; Constitutional Law; Criminal Law; European Union Law; History of Law; Human Rights; International Law; Labour Law; Law; Private Law; Public Law); **Mathematics and Informatics** (Applied Mathematics; Mathematics; Operations Research; Statistics); **Mathematics, Mechanics and Computer Science** (Applied Mathematics; Computer Science; Mathematics; Mechanics; Operations Research; Statistics); **Natural Science** (Biology; Chemistry); **Pedagogic and Practical Psychology** (Educational Psychology; Pedagogy; Psychology); **Philology** (Grammar; Linguistics; Literature; Modern Languages; Philology; Phonetics); **Philology and Journalism** (Comparative Literature; English; French; German; Germanic Languages; Grammar; Journalism; Linguistics; Mass Communication; Philology; Phonetics; Russian; Slavic Languages; Spanish; Speech Studies; Terminology); **Philosophy and Cultural Studies** (Cultural Studies; European Studies; Philosophy); **Physical Culture and Sports** (Sports Management); **Physics** (Applied Physics; Atomic and Molecular Physics; Mathematical Physics; Mechanics; Nuclear Physics; Optics; Physics; Radiophysics; Solid State Physics); **Physics** (Applied Physics; Physics); **Psychology** (Clinical Psychology; Developmental Psychology; Educational Psychology; Experimental Psychology; Industrial and Organizational Psychology; Psychology; Social Psychology); **Radio Engineering** (Electronic Engineering; Microelectronics); **Regional Studies** (Cultural Studies; Philosophy; Political Sciences; Regional Studies; Sociology); **Social and Political Science** (Political Sciences; Sociology)

Institutes

Architecture and Arts (Architecture; Design; Fine Arts); **Economic and Foreign Economic Relations** (Social Sciences); **Law and Management** (Social Sciences); **Pedagogy** (Education; Pedagogy; Teacher Training); **Technology** *(Taganrog)* (Technology)

History: Previously known as Rostovskij Gosudarstvennyj Universitet (Rostov State University). Created 2006 from merger between Rostovskij Gosudarstvennyj Universitet (founded 1915), Rostovskaja Gosudarstvennaja Arhitekturno-Hudožestvennaja Akademija (Rostov State Academy of Architecture and Arts), founded 1944, Rostovskij Gosudarstvennyj Pedagogičeskij Universitet (Rostov State Pedagogical University), founded 1931 and Taganrogskij Gosudarstvennyj Radiotehničeskij Universitet (Taganrog State University of Radio Engineering), founded 1952.

Governing Bodies: Academic Council, Rectorat

Academic Year: September to July (September-December; February-May)

Admission Requirements: Secondary education certificate and entrance examination

Fees: Free for Russian students. See website for more fee details.

Main Language(s) of Instruction: Russian, some classes taught in English

International Co-operation: With universities in Germany, Poland, United Kingdom and USA.

Degrees and Diplomas: *Bakalavr*: 4 yrs; *Specialist Diploma*; *Magistr*: a further 2 yrs; *Kandidat Nauk*: 3 yrs; *Doktor Nauk*: 3 yrs

Student Services: Academic counselling, Canteen, Employment services, Foreign student adviser, Foreign Studies Centre, Health services, Language programs, Sports facilities

Student Residential Facilities: For c. 2,800 students

Special Facilities: Biology Museum; Geology Museum; History Museum. Botanical Garden.

Libraries: Central Library, c. 4 m. vols; c. 750,000 periodicals; access to multiple electronic networks

Publications: Ekonomicheskij Vestnik *(quarterly)*; Izvestja SKNC *(quarterly)*; Philologicheskij *(quarterly)*

Press or Publishing House: University Press

Academic Staff *2009-2010*	MEN	WOMEN	TOTAL
FULL-TIME	5,832	4,180	**10,012**
PART-TIME	935	964	**1,899**
STAFF WITH DOCTORATE			
FULL-TIME	235	159	**394**
Student Numbers *2009-2010*			
All (Foreign Included)	23,076	21,570	**44,646**
FOREIGN ONLY	206	198	**404**

Part-time students, 16,747. **Evening students**, 3,188.
Last Updated: 25/10/10

SOUTHERN URAL STATE INSTITUTE FOR THE ARTS NAMED AFTER P.I. TCHAIKOVSKY

Južno-Ural'skij Gosudarstvennyj Institut Iskusstv im. P.I. Čaikovskogo

ul. Plehanova 41, Čeljabinsk 454000
Tel: +7(351) 263-34-61 +7(351) 263-35-43 +7(351) 263-35-95
Fax: +7(351) 263-34-61
EMail: chgim@mail.ru
Website: http://www.chgim.ru/

Rector: Pavel Ivanovich Kostenok EMail: rector_chgim@mail.ru

Programmes

Music (Music; Music Theory and Composition; Musical Instruments; Singing); **Music Education** (Music Education)

History: Created 1994 as Čeljabinskij Musikalno-Pedagogičeskij Institut. Later became Čeljabinskij Institut Musiki im P.I. Tchaikovskogo Institut (Chelyabinsk Music Institute named after P.I. Tchaikovsky). Acquired current title 2010.

Degrees and Diplomas: *Specialist Diploma*
Last Updated: 20/01/12

SOUTHERN URAL STATE UNIVERSITY

Južno-Uralskij Gosudarstvennyj Universitet

prosp. Lenina 76, Čeljabinsk 454080
Tel: +7(3512) 335-882
Fax: +7(3512) 347-408
EMail: webmaster@urc.ac.ru
Website: http://www.tu-chel.ac.ru

Rector: German P. Vjatkin (1986-)

Vice-Rector: Gennadij G. Mihailov Tel: +7(3512) 339-556

International Relations: Dmitrij G. Sherbakov
Tel: +7(3512) 656-504

Faculties

Aircraft and Spacecraft (Aeronautical and Aerospace Engineering); **Applied Mathematics and Physics** (Applied Mathematics; Physics); **Architecture and Construction** (Architecture; Construction Engineering); **Automation and Mechanics** (Automation and Control Engineering; Mechanical Engineering); **Automobiles and Tractors** (Automotive Engineering); **Commerce** (Business and Commerce); **Economics and Law** (Economics; Law); **Economics and Management** (Economics; Management); **Electronics** (Electronic Engineering); **Linguistics** (Linguistics); **Management** *(International)* (Management); **Mechanical Technology** (Mechanical Engineering); **Metallurgy** (Metallurgical Engineering); **Physical Education and Sports** (Physical Education; Sports); **Power Engineering** (Power Engineering); **Psychology** (Psychology); **Services and Light Industry**

Further Information: Branches in: Zlatovst, Kyštym, Mjas. Also Russian language courses for foreign students. Study Abroad programmes. Numerous Research Centres

History: Founded 1943 as Institute of Mechanical Engineering, acquired present status and title 1997.

Academic Year: September to June (September-December; February-June)

Admission Requirements: Secondary school certificate (Attestat o srednem obrazovanii) or equivalent

Main Language(s) of Instruction: Russian

Degrees and Diplomas: *Bakalavr*: 4 yrs; *Specialist Diploma*: Engineering, Technology, 5 yrs; *Kandidat Nauk*: a further 2-3 yrs

Student Services: Academic counselling, Canteen, Cultural centre, Employment services, Foreign Studies Centre, Health services, Social counselling, Sports facilities

Special Facilities: History of the University Museum

Libraries: Research Library, c. 2m. vols

Press or Publishing House: Publishing House

SOUTH RUSSIAN STATE TECHNICAL UNIVERSITY

Južno-Rossijskij Gosudarstvennyj Tehničeskij Universitet (SRSTU (NPI))

ul. Prosveščenija 132, Novočerkassk, 346428 Rostovskaja oblast'
Tel: +7(86352) 555-14
Fax: +7(86352) 272-69
EMail: rektorat@npi-tu.ru
Website: http://www.srstu.novoch.ru

Rector: Vladimir Grigorievich Perederij (1998-)

Faculties

Building (Architectural Restoration; Building Technologies; Civil Engineering; Environmental Engineering; Environmental Management; Mechanics; Water Management); **Chemical Engineering** (Ceramic Art; Chemical Engineering; Chemistry; Food Science; Organic Chemistry; Physical Chemistry; Technology); **Electromechanics, Mechatronics and Technology** (Electrical and Electronic Engineering; Mechanical Equipment and Maintenance; Mechanics); **Energy Engineering** (Energy Engineering); **Humanities and Socio-Economic Education** (Cultural Studies; Design; Economics; History; Law; Management; Philosophy; Physical Education; Psychology; Public Administration; Sociology); **Information Technology and Management** (Business Computing; Computer Science; Information Management; Information Technology); **Mechanical Engineering** (Automotive Engineering; Computer Engineering; Computer Graphics; Machine Building; Materials Engineering; Mechanical Engineering; Road Transport; Technology); **Mining and Geology** (Ecology; Environmental Management; Geological Engineering; Geology; Mineralogy; Mining Engineering; Petroleum and Gas Engineering); **Open and Distance Learning**; **Physics and Mathematics** (Applied Mathematics; Applied Physics; Mathematics; Mechanics; Physics)

Institutes

International Education (Cultural Studies; English; French; German; Russian); **Military Education** (Military Science)

Further Information: Also branches in: Rostov-on-Don, Kamensk-Šakhtinskij, Georgievsk, Majkop, Šakhty, Volgodonsk, Belaja Kalitva, and Novošakhtinsk

History: Founded 1907 on the basis of Warsaw Polytechnical Institute.

Governing Bodies: Ministry of Education and Science

Academic Year: September to June (September-December; February-June)

Admission Requirements: Secondary education certificate (Attestat o srednem obrazovanii)

Main Language(s) of Instruction: Russian

International Co-operation: With universities in China, Germany, France.

Accrediting Agencies: Ministry of Education and Science

Degrees and Diplomas: *Bakalavr*: 4 yrs; *Specialist Diploma*; *Magistr*: 6 yrs; *Kandidat Nauk*; *Doktor Nauk*

Student Services: Canteen, Cultural centre, Employment services, Foreign student adviser, Foreign Studies Centre, Handicapped facilities, Health services, Language programs, Nursery care, Social counselling, Sports facilities

Student Residential Facilities: For 7,370 students

Special Facilities: Museums: University History; Mineralogy

Libraries: Total, 3.1m. Vols

Publications: 'Electromechanica' *(quarterly)*; 'Izvestia Severokavkazskogo naučnogo centra vyssy školy' *(quarterly)*

Press or Publishing House: Publishing House

Last Updated: 08/04/11

SOUTH RUSSIAN STATE UNIVERSITY OF ECONOMICS AND SERVICES

Južno-Rossijskij Gosudarstvennyj Universitet Ekonomiki i Servisa

ul. Ševčenko 147, Šahty, 346500 Rostovskaja oblast'
Tel: +7(86362) 220-37 +7(86362) 270-69
Fax: +7(86362) 254-91
EMail: mail@sssu.ru
Website: http://www.sssu.ru

Rector: Anatolij G. Sapronov

Departments

Scientific Research (Automation and Control Engineering; Computer Engineering; Engineering; Sociology)

Faculties

Banking and Finance; **Economics** (Accountancy; Economics; Finance; Management); **Management**; **Marketing**; **Philosophy**; **Radio-Mechanics** (Automotive Engineering; Electronic Engineering; Maintenance Technology; Textile Design; Transport Management); **Social Humanities** (Hotel Management; Tourism); **Technology** (Fashion Design; Leather Techniques; Technology; Textile Design; Textile Technology)

Further Information: Also courses for foreign students. 11 Educational Workshops; Computer equipped laboratories and classrooms

History: Founded 1969, acquired present status and title 1999.

Governing Bodies: University Council

Academic Year: September to June (September-January; February-June)

Admission Requirements: Secondary school certificate (Attestat o srednem obrazovanii)

Fees: (US Dollars): Foreign students, c. 1,200-2,000 per annum

Main Language(s) of Instruction: Russian

International Co-operation: Agreements with Algeria, Canada, China, France, Germany, Hungary, India, Nepal, Netherlands, Portugal, Spain, United Kingdom

Degrees and Diplomas: *Diplom o Nepolnom Visshem Obrazovanii (Incomplete Higher Education Diploma)*: 2 yrs; *Bakalavr*: 4 yrs; *Specialist Diploma*: 5 yrs. Also Postgraduate courses, 3 yrs

Student Services: Academic counselling, Canteen, Cultural centre, Handicapped facilities, Health services, Social counselling, Sports facilities

Student Residential Facilities: Yes

Libraries: c. 1.8m. Vols

Publications: Collection of Scientific Works of Academic Staff and Postgraduate Students *(annually)*; Methodical Directions *(monthly)*; Thesis from Reports of Scientific-Practical Conferences *(annually)*

Press or Publishing House: Publishing Department

SOUTHWESTERN STATE UNIVERSITY

Jugo-Zapadnyj Gosudarsternnyj Universitet
ul. 50-let Oktjabrja 94, Kursk 305040
Tel: +7(4712) 50-48-00 +7(4712) 50-48-20
Fax: +7(4712) 50-48-29
EMail: rector@swsu.ru
Website: http://www.swsu.ru

Rector: Sergei Gennadievich Emel'janov

Campuses

Mining Engineering *(Zheleznogorsk)* (Mining Engineering)

Faculties

Architecture and Building (Architecture; Civil Engineering; Industrial Engineering; Landscape Architecture; Rural Planning; Surveying and Mapping; Town Planning; Waste Management; Water Management); **Computer Science** (Applied Mathematics; Biomedical Engineering; Computer Networks; Computer Science; Information Technology; Mathematics; Telecommunications Engineering; Telecommunications Services); **Economics** (Accountancy; Business and Commerce; Economics; Finance; International Economics; Management); **Innovation and Management** (Automotive Engineering; Engineering Management; Machine Building; Materials Engineering; Mechanics; Physics); **Law** (Civil Law; Commercial Law; Constitutional Law; Criminal Law; History of Law; Labour Law; Law); **Linguistics and Intercultural Communication** (Applied Linguistics; Communication Studies; Cultural Studies; International Studies; Linguistics); **Public Administration and International Relations** (International Relations; Public Administration); **Technology and Design** (Analytical Chemistry; Chemistry; Design; Environmental Management; Industrial Design; Inorganic Chemistry; Organic Chemistry; Physical Chemistry)

History: Created 1964 as Kurskij Politekhnicheskij Institut (Kursk Polytechnic Institute), then became Gosudarstvennyj Tehničeskij Universitet (Kursk State Technical University). Acquired current title 2010.

Degrees and Diplomas: *Bakalavr*, *Specialist Diploma*; *Magistr*

Last Updated: 16/01/12

STATE ACADEMY FOR FIRE SERVICE OF THE MINISTRY OF INTERNAL AFFAIRS OF THE RUSSIAN FEDERATION

Akademija Gosudarstvennoj Protivopožarnoj Služby MVD Rossijskoij Federatsii
ul. Borisa Galuškina 4, Moskva 129366
Tel: +7(495) 682-12-11 +7(495) 686-45-27
Fax: +7(495) 683-76-77
EMail: info@academygps.ru
Website: http://www.academygps.ru/

Rector: Ivan Mikhailovich Teterin

Programmes

Firefighting (Fire Science)

History: Created 1936.

Degrees and Diplomas: *Specialist Diploma*

Last Updated: 14/04/11

STATE ACADEMY OF SLAVONIC CULTURE

Gosudarstvennaja Akademija Slavjanskoj Kul'tury (GASK / SASK)
ul. Geroev Panfilovcev 39, Moskva 125373
Tel: +7(495) 948-2510; +7(495) 948-9501
Fax: +7(495) 948-9200
EMail: info@gask.ru
Website: http://www.gask.ru/

Rector: Alla Konenkova (2006-)

International Relations: Maria Zhylenko, Pro-Rector

Bureaus

Office of Slavonic Culture *(Obnisk, correspondence course only)* (Communication Studies; English; Foreign Languages Education; Psychology) *Director*: Marina Trofimova

Campuses

Slavonic Culture *(Tver)* (Art Criticism; Art History; Cultural Studies; Eastern European Studies; Folklore) *Director*: Igor Pobedash

Faculties

Artistic Creative Folk Work (part of Institute of Dancing) (Folklore) *Dean*: Ludmila Mikheeva; **Artistic Culture** (Art Criticism; Art History; Painting and Drawing) *Dean*: Igor Ovasapov; **Choreography (part of Institute of Dancing)** (Dance) *Dean*: Valentina Degt'areva; **Cultural Studies** *Dean*: Georgij Melnikov; **Linguistics** (Communication Studies; English; Foreign Languages Education) *Dean*: Olga Gourjanova; **Musical Arts** *Dean*: Vladimir Selivokhin; **Philology** (Native Language; Philology; Russian; Slavic Languages) *Dean*: Igor Kaliganov; **Psychology** *Dean*: Alexander Sukharev; **Vocal Art** *Dean*: Valentina Sharonova

History: Founded 1992.

Governing Bodies: Rector; Council of Founders

Academic Year: September to July

Admission Requirements: Attestat o Srednem Obshchem Obrazovanii (Secondary school certificate)

Fees: (Russian Rubles): 25,000-40,000 Free tuition for some students depending on entrance examination marks

Main Language(s) of Instruction: Russian

International Co-operation: With universities in Poland, Slovak Republic, Bulgaria

Accrediting Agencies: Federal Service for Supervision in Education and Science

Degrees and Diplomas: *Specialist Diploma*: All disciplines, 3-5 yrs (6 yrs for distance courses); *Kandidat Nauk*: Cultural Studies; Philosophy of Culture, 3-4 yrs; *Doktor Nauk*: Cultural Studies; Philosophy of Culture, 3-4 yrs

Student Services: Academic counselling, Canteen, Cultural centre, Handicapped facilities, Health services, Language programs, Social counselling, Sports facilities

Student Residential Facilities: none

Special Facilities: Creative workshops

Libraries: yes

Publications: Bulletin of Slavonic Cultures *(annually)*

STATE CLASSICAL ACADEMY NAMED AFTER MAIMONEDES

Gosudarstvennaja Klassičeskaja Akademija im. Majmonida
ul. Bol'šaja Bronnaja 6, Moskva 103104
Tel: +7(495) 959-45-84
Fax: +7(495) 951-76-12
EMail: sciekogan@mail.ru
Website: http://www.gka.ru/

Rector: Irina Veronika Rafailovna

Faculties

International Music Culture (Music; Music Education; Music Theory and Composition; Musical Instruments; Singing); **Mathematics and Computer Science** (Applied Mathematics; Computer Science; Mathematics); **Medicine** (Medicine; Psychology; Stomatology); **Philology** (English; Foreign Languages Education; German; Literature; Native Language; Native Language Education;

Philology); **Philosophy and Law** (Criminal Law; International Law; Law; Notary Studies; Philosophy)
History: Created 1991.
Degrees and Diplomas: *Specialist Diploma*
Last Updated: 19/01/12

STATE MARINE ACADEMY NAMED AFTER ADMIRAL MAKAROV

Gosudarstvennaja Morskaja Akademija im. Admirala S.O. Makarova (AMSMA)
Kosaja Linija 15A, Sankt-Peterburg 199106
Tel: +7(812) 322-1934
Fax: +7(812) 322-7807
EMail: gmamak@mail.wplus.net
Website: http://www.gma.sp.ru

President: Ivan Kostylev

International Relations: Elena Kozlova
Tel: +7(812) 322- 6083, Fax: +7(812) 322-0682

Colleges
Maritime Training *(Makarov) Head*: Sergey Aizinov

Divisions
Post-Graduate Studies *Head*: Viktoria Kutay

Faculties
Arctic Studies (Arctic Studies) *Dean*: Vladimir Porjadkov; **Distance Education** *Dean*: Peter Thomson; **Electrical Engineering** *Dean*: Viktor Romanovsky; **International Transport Management** *Dean*: Jury Panteleev; **Marine Engineering** *Dean*: Aleksandr Punda; **Navigation** (Nautical Science) *Dean*: Ruben Zaharjan; **Radio Engineering** (Radiophysics) *Dean*: Mihail Solodovničenko

Institutes
Management and Economics (Leadership; Management) *Director*: Aleksandr Jalovenko

History: Founded 1876. Acquired present status 1990.
Academic Year: October to June
Admission Requirements: Secondary school certificate and entrance examination
Fees: (US Dollar): 2,000-3,500 per annum
Main Language(s) of Instruction: Russian
International Co-operation: With maritime universities in Bulgaria, Germany, Latvia, the Netherlands, Poland, USA
Accrediting Agencies: Ministry of Higher Education; Ministry of Transport
Degrees and Diplomas: *Specialist Diploma*: Electrical Engineering; Marine Engineering; Navigation, 5 1/2 yrs
Student Services: Academic counselling, Canteen, Cultural centre, Foreign student adviser, Health services, Language programs, Nursery care, Sports facilities
Student Residential Facilities: Yes
Special Facilities: Museum. Observatory. Movie Studio
Publications: Makarovets *(quarterly)*

STATE MUSIC AND PEDAGOGICAL INSTITUTE

Gosudarstvennyj Muzikalno-Pedagogičeskij Institut
ul. Marksistkaja 36, Moskva 109147
Tel: +7(495) 911-9605
Fax: +7(495) 911-9293
Website: http://www.ippolitovka.hotbox.ru

Rector: A. A. Korsakovich

Pro-Rector for Academic Affairs: G. L. Bogdanova
Tel: +7(495) 911-9601

Programmes
Conducting (Conducting); **Music** (Music); **Music Education** (Music Education); **Singing** (Singing)

STATE RURAL INSTITUTE NAMED AFTER CYRILL AND METHOD

Krest'yanskij Gosudarstvennyj Institut imeni Kirilla i Mefodija
prosp. Kirova 73, Luga, 188230 Leningradskaja oblast'
Tel: +7(81372) 2-37-79 +7(81372) 2-24-39 +7(81372) 2-14-02
Fax: +7(81372) 2-06-84
EMail: kgu@luga.ru
Website: http://www.kgu.luga.ru/

Rector: Vjacheslav Pavlovich Timofeev

Programmes
Accounting (Accountancy; Economics; Management); **Biotechnology** (Biotechnology); **Finance** (Banking; Finance); **Law** (Law); **Philology** (Philology); **Science Teaching** (Biology; Science Education)

History: Created 1991. Previously known as Krest'yanskij Gosudarstvennyj Institut imeni Kirilla i Mefodija (State Rural Institute named after Cyrill and Method). Acquired current title 2006.
Degrees and Diplomas: *Specialist Diploma*
Last Updated: 02/02/12

STATE SPECIALIZED INSTITUTE OF ARTS

Gosudarstvennyj Specializirovannyj Institut Iskusstv
prosp. Rezervnyj 10/12, Moskva 121165
Tel: +7(499) 249-33-80
Fax: +7(499) 249-33-80
EMail: rektorat-gsii@yandex.ru
Website: http://gsii.org/

Rector: Alexander Nikolaevich Jakupov

Faculties
Fine Arts (Design; Fine Arts; Painting and Drawing); **Music** (Music; Music Theory and Composition; Musical Instruments; Singing); **Theatre** (Acting; Theatre)

History: Founded 1991. Acquired present status 2005.
Academic Year: September to June
Admission Requirements: Secondary school certificate; entrance examination for special programmes
Main Language(s) of Instruction: Russian
Degrees and Diplomas: *Specialist Diploma*
Student Services: Academic counselling, Canteen, Employment services, Foreign student adviser, Handicapped facilities, Health services, Language programs, Social counselling
Libraries: Yes
Last Updated: 19/01/12

STATE UNIVERSITY - HIGHER SCHOOL OF ECONOMICS

Gosudarstvennyj Universitet - Vyssaja Škola Ekonomiki
Kočnovskij pr. 3, Moskva 125319
Tel: +7(495) 928-9290
Fax: +7(495) 928-7931
EMail: hse@hse.ru
Website: http://www.hse.ru

Rector: Jaroslav I. Kuz'minov

Programmes
Economics (Economics)

STATE UNIVERSITY OF LAND USE PLANNING

Gosudarstvennyj Universitet po Zemleustrojstvu (GUZ)
ul. Kazakova 15, Moskva 105064
Tel: +7(495) 261-3146
Fax: +7(495) 261-9545
EMail: office@guz.ru; info@guz.ru
Website: http://www.guz.ru

Rector: Sergej Nikolajevich Volkov EMail: volkov@guz.ru

Pro-Rector: Nikolai Konokotin
Tel: +7(495) 261-4482 EMail: konokotin@guz.ru

International Relations: Andrei Shimkevich, Pro-Rector
Tel: +7(495) 261-1069 EMail: interdep@guz.ru

Faculties

Architecture (Architecture) *Head*: Ivan Ivanov; **Land Cadastre** (Architecture and Planning; Real Estate) *Head*: Tatiana Koševeleva; **Land Use Planning** (Architecture and Planning; Surveying and Mapping) *Head*: Timur Papaskiry; **Law** (Law) *Head*: Irina Širokorad; **Urban Cadastre** (Real Estate; Structural Architecture; Town Planning) *Head*: Albert Junusov

History: Founded 1779 as Surveying School.

Governing Bodies: Scientist Council

Academic Year: September to July

Admission Requirements: Secondary school certificate and entrance examination

Fees: Depends on speciality

Main Language(s) of Instruction: Russian

International Co-operation: With universities in Germany and France

Accrediting Agencies: Federal Agency of Education and Science Ministry

Degrees and Diplomas: *Bakalavr*: Land Use Planning and Cadastres, 4 yrs; *Specialist Diploma*: 5 yrs; *Magistr*: Land Use Planning and Cadastres, a further 2 yrs; *Kandidat Nauk*: a further 3 yrs; *Doktor Nauk*: a further 3 yrs

Student Services: Academic counselling, Canteen, Cultural centre, Employment services, Foreign student adviser, Foreign Studies Centre, Health services, Language programs, Nursery care, Social counselling, Sports facilities

Student Residential Facilities: 2 Student Houses; Hotel Complex

Special Facilities: Museum; Art Gallery

Libraries: c. 430,000 vols

Publications: Land Use Planner *(monthly)*; Land Use Planning *(monthly)*; Research Papers of the University

Press or Publishing House: Koloss; University Publishing House

STATE UNIVERSITY OF MANAGEMENT

Gosudarstvennyj Universitet Upravlenija (SUM)

prosp. Rjazanskij 99, Moskva 109542
Tel: +7(495) 371-13-22
Fax: +7(495) 371-69-47
EMail: inf@guu.ru
Website: http://www.guu.ru

Rector: Viktor Anatol'evich Kozbanenko (2011-)
EMail: rector@guu.ru; rectorat@guu.ru

Institutes

Civil Service (Institutional Administration; Public Administration); **Federal and Municipal Management** (Management; Marketing; Public Administration; Urban Studies); **Financial Management** (Accountancy; Banking; Finance; Management); **Foreign Languages** (Modern Languages); **Innovations and Logistics** (Industrial Management); **International Business** (International Business); **Management and Entrepreneurship in the Social Sphere** (Management); **Management in Chemistry and Metallurgy** (Chemical Engineering; Industrial Management; Metallurgical Engineering); **Management in Civil Engineering and Project Management** (Business Administration; Construction Engineering; Industrial Management; Real Estate); **Management in Power Engineering** (Energy Engineering; Industrial Management; Production Engineering); **Management Information Systems** (Information Management; Information Technology; Operations Research; Secretarial Studies); **Management of Migration Processes** (Management); **New Economy Problems Management** (Economics; Finance); **Russian-Dutch Faculty of Marketing** (Marketing); **Sociology and Personnel Management** (Advertising and Publicity; Public Relations; Sociology); **Taxes and Tax Management** (Information Technology; Management; Taxation); **Tourism and Market Development** (Hotel Management; Service Trades; Tourism); **Training of Academic-Teaching and Academic Personnel** (Cultural Studies; Economics; Management; Psychology; Sociology); **Transport Management** (Transport Economics; Transport Management); **World and National Economics** (Economics; International Economics; Management)

Further Information: Also branch in Obninsk (Kaluga)

History: Founded 1919, acquired present status and title 1998.

Governing Bodies: Academic Council

Academic Year: September to June (September-January; February-June)

Admission Requirements: Secondary school certificate (Attestat o srednem obrazovanii) and entrance examination

Main Language(s) of Instruction: Russian

International Co-operation: With universities in Germany, United Kingdom, Netherlands, Finland.

Accrediting Agencies: Ministry of Education

Degrees and Diplomas: *Specialist Diploma*: Business Administration, Social Sciences, 5 yrs; *Magistr*: Business Administration, a further 3-4 yrs; *Kandidat Nauk*: Business Administration, Social Sciences, a further 3-4 yrs; *Doktor Nauk*: Business Administation, Social Sciences, a further 3-4 yrs

Student Services: Academic counselling, Canteen, Cultural centre, Employment services, Foreign student adviser, Foreign Studies Centre, Handicapped facilities, Health services, Language programs, Nursery care, Social counselling, Sports facilities

Student Residential Facilities: Yes

Special Facilities: TV-Studio

Libraries: c. 1m. vols

Press or Publishing House: Publishing House

Last Updated: 29/03/12

STATE UNIVERSITY - TEACHING, RESEARCH AND PRODUCTION COMPLEX

Gosudarstvennyj Universitet – Učebno-Naučno-Proizvodstvennyj Kompleks

Naugorskoe šosse 29, Orel, 302020 Orlokskaja oblast'
Tel: +7(4862) 42-00-24
Fax: +7(4862) 41-66-84
EMail: admin@ostu.ru
Website: http://gu-unpk.ru/

Rector: Vjacheslav A. Golenkov

Faculties

Economics and Management (Advertising and Publicity; Economics; Human Resources; International Business; Management; Public Relations; Small Business; Transport Management); **Finance** (Accountancy; Finance; International Economics; Statistics; Taxation); **Food Biotechnology** (Food Science; Food Technology; Hotel and Restaurant; Tourism); **Light Industry** (Food Technology; Maintenance Technology; Textile Technology); **Natural Sciences** (Applied Mathematics; Chemistry; Ecology; Environmental Management; Mathematics; Physics); **New Technologies and Automation of Production** (Electronic Engineering; Industrial Management; Machine Building; Mechanical Engineering; Mechanics; Robotics); **Physical Education and Sport** (Physical Education; Sports); **Technology and Design Technology** (Industrial Design; Machine Building)

History: Founded 1954 as branch of Moscow Instrumental Institute, became independent 1993, and became Orlovskij Gosudarstvennyj Tehničeskij Universitet (Orel State Technical University) in1995. Acquired current title 2010.

Academic Year: September to June (September-January; February-June)

Admission Requirements: Secondary education certificate (Attestat o srednem obrazovanii)

Degrees and Diplomas: *Bakalavr*, *Specialist Diploma*; *Magistr*, *Kandidat Nauk*

Student Services: Academic counselling, Canteen, Cultural centre, Foreign Studies Centre, Health services, Social counselling, Sports facilities

Libraries: c. 386,000 vols

Last Updated: 16/04/12

STATE UNIVERSITY OF THE RUSSIAN FEDERATION FINANCE MINISTRY

Gosudarsvennyj Universitet Ministerstva Finansov Rossijskoj Federatsii

Zlatoustinskij Malyj per 7, str. 1, Moskva 101990
Tel: +7(495) 621-624-58-24
Fax: +7(495) 621-624-58-24
EMail: info@gumf.ru
Website: http://www.gumf.ru/

Acting Rector: Jelena V. Markina

Faculties
Accounting (Accountancy); **Applied Computer Science and Mathematics** (Applied Mathematics; Business Computing; Computer Science); **Finance** (Economics; Finance); **International Economic Relations** (Economics; International Economics; Tourism); **Law** (Law); **Management** (Management)

History: Founded 1988. Previously known as Akademija Budžeta i Kaznačejstva Ministerstva Finansov Rossijskoj Federacii (Budget and Treasury Academy of the Finance Ministry of the Russian Federation). Acquired current title 2003.

Governing Bodies: Ministry of Finance; Ministry of Education

Academic Year: September to July

Admission Requirements: School Certificate, Bachelor's Diploma

Main Language(s) of Instruction: Russian

Degrees and Diplomas: *Bakalavr*, *Specialist Diploma*; *Magistr*

Student Services: Academic counselling, Canteen, Health services, Language programs, Social counselling, Sports facilities

Libraries: c. 53,900 vols and Magazines

Last Updated: 30/07/12

STAVROPOL STATE AGRARIAN UNIVERSITY

Stavropolskij Gosudarstvennyj Agrarnyj Universitet (SSAU)

per. Zootehničeskij 12, Stavropol, 355017 Stavropol'skij kraj
Tel: +7(8652) 352-282
Fax: +7(8652) 715-815
EMail: inf@stgau.ru
Website: http://www.stgau.ru

Rector: Vladimir I. Truhachev (1998-) EMail: rector@stgau.ru

Departments
Electricity (Electrical Engineering)

Divisions
Training Management

Faculties
Accountancy and Finance (Accountancy; Finance); **Agronomy** (Agronomy; Rural Planning; Town Planning; Viticulture); **Economics** (Agricultural Business; Business Administration; Business Computing; Economics; International Economics; Management; Marketing; Public Administration; Staff Development); **Electrification and Automation of Agriculture** (Agricultural Engineering; Agricultural Equipment); **Plant Protection** (Landscape Architecture; Natural Resources; Plant and Crop Protection); **Technology Management** (Agricultural Engineering); **Veterinary Medicine** (Veterinary Science)

Schools
Graduate (Accountancy; Agricultural Economics; Agricultural Engineering; Agricultural Equipment; Agricultural Management; Agriculture; Analytical Chemistry; Animal Husbandry; Banking; Biochemistry; Biology; Biotechnology; Cattle Breeding; Chemistry; Crop Production; Demography and Population; Ecology; Economics; Engineering; Entomology; Finance; Food Technology; Heating and Refrigeration; International Economics; Management; Mathematics; Metaphysics; Microbiology; Nanotechnology; Parasitology; Pedagogy; Philosophy; Physics; Physiology; Plant and Crop Protection; Sociology; Statistics; Thermal Physics; Virology; Zoology)

Further Information: Also distance learning study programmes.

History: Founded 1930. Acquired present status 2001.

Governing Bodies: Scientific Council

Academic Year: September to June

Admission Requirements: Secondary school certificate (Attestat o srednem obrazovanii)

Fees: Free of charge

Main Language(s) of Instruction: Russian

International Co-operation: With universities in Germany, Austria, Italy, Republic of Poland, Czech Republic, Slovac Republic, The Netherlands, Danemark

Accrediting Agencies: Ministry of Agriculture of the Russian Federation

Degrees and Diplomas: *Bakalavr*, *Specialist Diploma*: 5 yrs; *Kandidat Nauk*; *Doktor Nauk*

Student Services: Academic counselling, Canteen, Cultural centre, Foreign student adviser, Language programs, Sports facilities

Special Facilities: Museum

Libraries: Yes

Press or Publishing House: Agrarian University Publishing House

Academic Staff *2007-2008*	**TOTAL**
FULL-TIME	**702**
STAFF WITH DOCTORATE FULL-TIME	**645**
Student Numbers *2007-2008*	
All (Foreign Included)	**6,659**
FOREIGN ONLY	**2**

Part-time students, 5,082. **Distance students**, 2,595. **Evening students**, 662.

Last Updated: 05/01/12

STAVROPOL STATE MEDICAL ACADEMY

Stavropolskaja Gosudarstvennaja Medicinskaja Akademija (SSMA)

ul. Mira 310, Stavropol, 355017 Stavropol'skij kraj
Tel: +7(8652) 352-331 +7(8652) 352-524
Fax: +7(8652) 356-185
EMail: postmaster@stgma.ru
Website: http://www.stgma.ru

Rector: Valentina Nikolaevna Muraveva

Faculties
Dentistry (Dentistry); **Medicine** (Medicine); **Paediatrics** (Paediatrics)

Further Information: Also courses for foreign students

History: Founded 1937. Acquired present status 1994.

Governing Bodies: Scientific Council

Academic Year: September to June (September-January; February-June)

Admission Requirements: Secondary school certificate (Attestat o srednem obrazovanii)

Main Language(s) of Instruction: English, Russian

Degrees and Diplomas: *Specialist Diploma*; *Magistr*, *Kandidat Nauk*; *Doktor Nauk*

Student Services: Academic counselling, Canteen, Cultural centre, Foreign student adviser, Foreign Studies Centre, Health services, Nursery care, Social counselling, Sports facilities

Student Residential Facilities: For 2,000 students

Libraries: c. 400,000 vols

Publications: Medical Bulletin of North Caucasus *(quarterly)*

Last Updated: 19/12/11

STAVROPOL STATE UNIVERSITY

Stavropolskij Gosudarstvennyj Universitet

ul. Puškina 1, Stavropol, 355009 Stavropol'skij kraj
Tel: +7(8652) 357-265
Fax: +7(8652) 354-033
EMail: stavsu@stavsu.ru
Website: http://www.stavsu.ru

Rector: Vladimir Šapovalov

Vice-Rector for Administration: Anatoly Vasilenko

Departments
Foreign Languages I (English; Foreign Languages Education; French; German; Germanic Studies; International Economics); **Foreign Languages II** (English; English Studies; Foreign Languages Education; French Studies; German; Germanic Studies; Translation and Interpretation); **Higher Education Pedagogy and Psychology** (Curriculum; Educational Psychology; Educational Technology; Higher Education; Pedagogy; Physical Education; Psychology; Sports); **History and Philosophy of Science** (Natural Sciences; Philosophy); **Information Technology** (Applied Mathematics; Computer Graphics; Computer Networks; Computer Science; Educational Technology; Information Technology; Multimedia; Software Engineering); **Medico-Biological-Chemical Studies** (Anatomy; Applied Chemistry; Biochemistry; Biology; Biophysics; Botany; Cell Biology; Chemistry; Entomology; Genetics; Industrial Chemistry; Inorganic Chemistry; Organic Chemistry; Pharmacology; Pharmacy; Physical Chemistry; Physiology; Zoology); **Military Studies** (Military Science); **Philosophy** (Anthropology; Logic; Philosophical Schools; Philosophy); **Physical Education** (Physical Education; Sports); **Political History** (History; Political Sciences); **Political Science and Sociology** (International Relations; Political Sciences; Sociology); **Psychology** (Clinical Psychology; Developmental Psychology; Educational Psychology; Experimental Psychology; Pedagogy; Primary Education; Psychology; Social Psychology; Speech Therapy and Audiology); **Social Philosophy and Ethnology** (Ethnology; Philosophy; Philosophy of Education; Social Sciences; Social Studies)

Faculties
Arts (Art Education; Conducting; Music; Music Theory and Composition; Musicology; Singing); **Economics** (Accountancy; Administration; Banking; Business and Commerce; E-Business/ Commerce; Economics; Finance; Home Economics; Human Resources; Institutional Administration; Insurance; International Business; International Economics; Labour and Industrial Relations; Management; Marketing; Real Estate; Regional Studies; Social Work; Taxation); **Geography** (Ecology; Geography; Geography (Human); Natural Resources; Surveying and Mapping); **History** (Ancient Civilizations; Archaeology; Comparative Sociology; Contemporary History; Ethics; Ethnology; History; Logic; Medieval Studies; Modern History; Philosophy; Prehistory; Social Policy; Sociology); **Law** (Administrative Law; Civil Law; Commercial Law; Comparative Law; Constitutional Law; Criminal Law; Criminology; Fiscal Law; History of Law; Human Rights; International Law; Labour Law; Law; Notary Studies); **Philology and Journalism** (Cultural Studies; Information Management; Information Technology; Journalism; Library Science; Linguistics; Literature; Mass Communication; Media Studies; Philology; Radio and Television Broadcasting; Russian; Slavic Languages); **Physical Education** (Physical Education; Sports; Sports Management); **Physics and Mathematics** (Applied Mathematics; Applied Physics; Astronomy and Space Science; Astrophysics; Atomic and Molecular Physics; Computer Science; Mathematics; Mathematics and Computer Science; Nuclear Physics; Optics; Physics; Systems Analysis); **Professional Upgrading** (Educational Administration; Pedagogy; Psychology); **Romance and Germanic Languages** (Applied Linguistics; Communication Studies; Comparative Literature; Computer Education; English; French; German; Germanic Languages; Grammar; Latin; Linguistics; Literature; Native Language; Phonetics; Psycholinguistics; Romance Languages; Speech Studies; Terminology; Translation and Interpretation; Writing)

History: Founded 1930. Acquired present status 1996.
Governing Bodies: Academic Council
Academic Year: September to July
Admission Requirements: Secondary school certificate (Attestat o srednem obrazovanii) and entrance examination
Main Language(s) of Instruction: Russian
Accrediting Agencies: Ministry of Education
Degrees and Diplomas: *Bakalavr*: 4 yrs; *Specialist Diploma*: 5 yrs; *Magistr*: History, 6 yrs; *Kandidat Nauk*
Student Services: Academic counselling, Canteen, Cultural centre, Employment services, Foreign student adviser, Foreign Studies Centre, Health services, Language programs, Nursery care, Social counselling, Sports facilities
Student Residential Facilities: Yes
Special Facilities: Laboratories
Last Updated: 05/01/12

STERLITAMAK STATE PEDAGOGICAL ACADEMY NAMED AFTER ZAINAB BIISHEVOJ

Sterlitamakskaja Gosudarstvennaja Pedagogičeskaja Akademija im. Zainab Biševoj

pr. Lenina 49, Sterlitamak 453103
Tel: +7(3473) 437-329 +7(3473) 436-843
Fax: +7(3473) 439-418
EMail: sspa@sspa.bashtel.ru
Website: http://sspa.edu.ru

Rector: Ilgiz Rajanovich Kyzyrgilov

Faculties
Bashkir Philology (Modern Languages; Native Language; Philology); **Economics and Management** (Economics; Finance; Management); **History** (History; Humanities and Social Science Education); **Mathematics and Natural Sciences** (Biology; Chemistry; Computer Science; Mathematics; Mathematics Education; Physics; Science Education); **Pedagogy and Psychology** (Educational and Student Counselling; Music Education; Pedagogy; Primary Education); **Philology** (Germanic Languages; Journalism; Linguistics; Literature; Native Language; Philology; Russian); **Technology and Entrepreneurship** (Small Business; Technology)

History: Founded 1954. Previously known as Sterlitamakskij Gosudarstvennyj Pedagogičeskij Institut (Sterlitamak State Pedagogical Institute). Acquired current title 2003.
Governing Bodies: Ministry of General and Professional Education of Russian Federation
Academic Year: September to June (September-January; February-June)
Admission Requirements: Secondary school certificate (Attestat o srednem obrazovanii)
Fees: None
Main Language(s) of Instruction: Russian
Degrees and Diplomas: *Bakalavr*, *Specialist Diploma*
Student Services: Canteen, Cultural centre, Health services, Language programs, Sports facilities
Libraries: Main Library, 410,000 vols
Last Updated: 19/12/11

STIEGLITZ STATE ACADEMY OF ART AND DESIGN, SAINT-PETERSBURG

Sankt-Peterburgskaja Gosudarstvennaja Hudožestvenno-Promyšlennaja Akademija im A. L. Štiglitsa (SSAAD)

per. Soljanoj 13, Sankt-Peterburg 191028
Tel: +7(812) 273-3804
Fax: +7(812) 272-8446
EMail: spbghpa@mail.ru
Website: http://www.spbghpa.ru/

Rector: Alexander Palmin (2009-)
Vice-Rector: Ninel Kozhemyakina
International Relations: Galina Sirenko, Head, International Relations Department
Tel: +7(812) 579-5296, Fax: +7(812) 579-5296
EMail: stieglitzspghpa@mail.ru

Faculties
Design (Design; Fashion Design; Furniture Design; Graphic Design; Industrial Design); **Monumental and Decorative Arts** (Art History; Ceramic Art; Fine Arts; Glass Art; Graphic Arts; Metal Techniques; Painting and Drawing; Restoration of Works of Art; Textile Design)

History: Founded 1876 as Central College of Technical Drawing, became Higher Education Institution 1948 known as Leningrad College of Art and Design. Acquired present status and title 1994.
Governing Bodies: Academic Council
Academic Year: Sep - Dec; Jan - June
Admission Requirements: Applicants are required to submit a portfolio of up to eight pieces of work. Personal works evaluation, four examinations in painting, drawing, composition, Russian language test.

Fees: (RUB): Overseas students, preliminary courses: one year, 190.000 (painting, drawing, composition, Russian language); Bakalavr, 240.000 per annum;Magistr, 240.000 per annum; Spetsialist, 240.000 per annumPost-graduate courses, 150.000 per annum.

Main Language(s) of Instruction: Russian

International Co-operation: With art institutions in Finland, Germany, Israel, France, China, Armenia

Degrees and Diplomas: *Bakalavr*: 4 yrs; *Specialist Diploma*: 6 yrs; *Magistr*: a further 2 yrs

Student Residential Facilities: Yes

Special Facilities: Museum of Applied Art

Libraries: Academy Library, 150,000 vols

Academic Staff *2010-2011*	MEN	WOMEN	TOTAL
FULL-TIME	80	170	**250**
PART-TIME	19	13	**32**
STAFF WITH DOCTORATE			
FULL-TIME	5	4	**9**
Student Numbers *2010-2011*			
All (Foreign Included)	307	1,211	**1,518**
FOREIGN ONLY	7	34	**41**

Last Updated: 20/05/11

SURGUT STATE PEDAGOGICAL UNIVERSITY

Surgutskij Gosudarstvennyj Pedagogičeskij Universitet

ul. 50 let VLKSM, Surgut, 628417 Tjumenskaja oblast', Khanty-Mansijskij avt. okrug-Jugra
Tel: +7(3462) 31-94-34
Fax: +7(3462) 31-94-38
EMail: office@surgpu.ru; statistics@surgpu.ru
Website: http://www.surgpu.ru/

Rector: Nadezhda V. Konoplina EMail: rector@surgpu.ru

Faculties

Humanities and Social Sciences (Archiving; Documentation Techniques; History; Tourism); **Management** (Economics; Human Resources; Management); **Philology** (Engineering Management; French; German; Journalism; Literature; Philology; Russian); **Physical Education and Sports** (Physical Education; Sports); **Psychology and Pedagogy** (Pedagogy; Preschool Education; Primary Education; Psychology); **Social and Cultural Studies** (Cultural Studies; Design; Fine Arts)

History: Created 1986. Previously known as Surgutskij Gosudarstvennyj Pedagogičeskij Institut (Surgut State Pedagogical Institute). Acquired current title 2009.

Degrees and Diplomas: *Bakalavr*, *Specialist Diploma*

Last Updated: 18/04/11

SURGUT STATE UNIVERSITY OF THE KHANTY-MANSIJSK AUTONOMOUS OKRUG

Surgutskij Gosudarstvennyj Universitet Khanty-Mansijskogo avtonomnogo okruga - Yugry (SURGU)

ul. Energetikov 14, Surgut, 628412 Tjumenskaja oblast', Khanty-Mansijskij avt. okrug-Jugra
Tel: +7(3462) 76-29-01 +7(3462) 76-29-10
Fax: +7(3462) 76-29-29
EMail: info@pr.surgu.ru; rector@surgu.ru
Website: http://www.surgu.ru/

Rector: Sergey M. Kosenok EMail: rector@surgu.ru

Faculties

Automation and Telecommunications (Computer Science; Engineering Management; Information Technology; Physics; Telecommunications Engineering); **Biology** (Biology; Ecology; Environmental Studies); **Building** (Building Technologies; Civil Engineering; Construction Engineering; Mathematical Physics); **Chemical Technology** (Analytical Chemistry; Chemistry; Fire Science; Petrology); **Economics** (Accountancy; Banking; Economics; Finance); **Education** (Education; Pedagogy; Technology Education); **History** (Cultural Studies; History; Museum Studies; Restoration of Works of Art; Theology); **Information Technology** (Applied Mathematics; Computer Science; Information Technology; Systems Analysis); **Law** (Law); **Linguistics** (English; German; Linguistics; Translation and Interpretation); **Management** (Economics; Human Resources; Management; Public Administration); **Medicine** (Gynaecology and Obstetrics; Medicine; Midwifery; Paediatrics); **Physical Education** (Physical Education; Sports; Sports Management); **Postgraduate Medicine** (Medicine; Paediatrics); **Psychology** (Clinical Psychology; Psychology); **Social Studies** (Advertising and Publicity; Political Sciences)

Institutes

Medicine (Medicine)

Research Institutes

Research Institute for Nature and Environment of the North

History: Founded in 1993. Became University of Khanty-Maniisky Autonomous Okrug in March 1995. Acquired current title and status 1995.

Governing Bodies: Academic Council

Academic Year: September to July

Admission Requirements: Attestat o Srednem (Polnom) Obshchem Obrazovanii (Secondary School Certificate)

Main Language(s) of Instruction: Russian

Accrediting Agencies: Federal Service for Supervision in Education and Science

Degrees and Diplomas: *Bakalavr*, *Specialist Diploma*; *Magistr*

Student Residential Facilities: Yes

Special Facilities: Museum of History, science labs, film studio, theatre, radio station

Libraries: c. 400,000 vols. incl. 600 periodicals. 4 faculty libraries

Press or Publishing House: University Publishing House

Last Updated: 21/11/11

SYKTYVKAR STATE UNIVERSITY

Syktyvkarskij Gosudarstvennyj Universitet

pr. Oktjabrskij 55, Syktyvkar 167001
Tel: +7(8212) 436-820 +7(8212) 311-907
Fax: +7(8212) 436-820
EMail: tim@syktsu.ru
Website: http://www.syktsu.ru/

Rector: Vasilij N. Zadorožnyj EMail: rektor@syktsu.ru

Centres

Sustainable Development of the North

Faculties

Arts (Design; Fine Arts); **Chemistry and Biology** (Biology; Chemistry; Ecology); **Extra-mural Studies** (Economics; Law; Psychology); **Finance and Economics** (Accountancy; Banking; Economics; Finance; Management; Taxation); **History and International Relations** (Advertising and Publicity; Archaeology; Ethnology; History; International Relations; Political Sciences); **Humanities** (Cultural Studies; English; French; History; Philology; Philosophy; Political Sciences; Sociology); **Information Systems and Technology** (Business Computing; Information Technology); **Law** (Civil Law; Criminal Law; History of Law; Law); **Management** (Economics; Management; Marketing); **Mathematics** (Applied Mathematics; Computer Science; Mathematics); **Philology** (Ancient Books; Folklore; History; Journalism; Linguistics; Literature; Russian); **Physics** (Geology; Physics; Radiophysics); **Psychology, Social Work and Physical Education** (Ecology; Physical Education; Psychology; Social Work; Sports)

Further Information: Also Russian courses for foreign students

History: Founded 1972.

Governing Bodies: Academic Council

Academic Year: September to July (September-January; February-July)

Admission Requirements: Secondary education certificate (Attestat o srednem obrazovanii) and entrance examination

Main Language(s) of Instruction: Russian

Degrees and Diplomas: *Bakalavr*, *Specialist Diploma*: 5 yrs; *Magistr*, *Kandidat Nauk*: a further 3 yrs and thesis

Student Services: Academic counselling, Canteen, Social counselling, Sports facilities

Student Residential Facilities: For c. 1,240 students

Special Facilities: Museum of the Komi Region; Zoology Museum; Archaeology Museum. Biological Garden

Libraries: c. 520,000 vols

Publications: Rubež *(quarterly)*

Press or Publishing House: Syktyvkar State University Press

Last Updated: 26/04/11

TAGANROG STATE PEDAGOGICAL INSTITUTE NAMED AFTER A.P. CHEKHOV

Taganrogskij Gosudarstvennyj Pedagogičeskij Institut im. A.P. Čekhova (TSPI/TGPI)

ul. Iniciativnaja 48, Taganrog, 347936 Rostov

Tel: +7(8634) 601-812

Fax: +7(8634) 603-417

EMail: rector@tgpi.ru

Website: http://www.tgpi.ru

Rector: Irina V. Golubeva

Faculties

Art Education (Art Education; Art History; Music Education; Singing); **Business and Information Science** (Economics; Information Sciences; Management); **Foreign Languages** (Engineering Management; French; German); **History and Law** (Archaeology; Civil Law; Criminal Law; History; Law; Paleontology); **Pedagogy and Basic Education** (Mathematics Education; Pedagogy; Primary Education; Russian; Speech Therapy and Audiology); **Physics and Mathematics** (Mathematics; Physical Education; Physics); **Psychology** (Educational Psychology; Pedagogy); **Russian Language and Literature** (Linguistics; Literature; Russian)

History: Founded 1955. Acquired current name 2011.

Admission Requirements: Secondary school certificate (Attestat)

Main Language(s) of Instruction: Russian

Accrediting Agencies: Russian Federal Agency for Education

Degrees and Diplomas: *Bakalavr*, *Specialist Diploma*: 5 yrs; *Kandidat Nauk*

Student Services: Academic counselling, Cultural centre, Employment services, Foreign student adviser, Health services, Language programs, Nursery care, Social counselling, Sports facilities

Special Facilities: None

Libraries: Taganrog State Pedagogical Institute Library

Publications: Journal of Taganrog State Pedagogical Institute *(biannually)*

Last Updated: 07/12/11

TAMBOV STATE PEDAGOGICAL INSTITUTE OF MUSIC NAMED AFTER S.V. RACHMANINOFF

Tambovskij Gosudarstvennyj Muzykalno-Pedagogičeskij Institut imeni S.V. Rachmaninov

ul. Sovetskaja 87, Tambov 392000

Tel: +7(752) 725-220 +7(752) 751-799

Fax: +7(752) 723-383

EMail: tgmpi@tmb.ru; rector@tgmpi.tmb.ru

Website: http://www.rachmaninov.ru/

Faculties

Higher Professional Education (Art Education; Conducting; Music; Musical Instruments; Musicology; Performing Arts; Singing)

Programmes

Postgraduate Studies (Music; Music Theory and Composition)

History: Founded 1882, acquired present status 1996.

Governing Bodies: Rectorate

Academic Year: September to july

Admission Requirements: Secondary school certificate (Attestat o srednem obrazovanii)

Main Language(s) of Instruction: Russian

International Co-operation: Ministry of Education of Russian Federation

Degrees and Diplomas: *Bakalavr*: Music, 4 yrs; *Magistr*: Music, 6 yrs

Student Services: Academic counselling, Canteen, Cultural centre, Foreign student adviser, Health services, Language programs

Special Facilities: History of Institute Museum. Concert Hall. Digital Sound Studio. Rachmaninov Memorial Estate

Publications: Works of Rachmaninov Institute *(annually)*

Last Updated: 04/01/12

TAMBOV STATE TECHNICAL UNIVERSITY

Tambovskij Gosudarstvennyj Tekhničeskij Universitet (TSTU)

ul. Sovetskaja 106, Tambov, 392000 Tambovskaja oblast'

Tel: +7(4752) 63-10-19

Fax: +7(4752) 63-06-43

EMail: nach_umu@nnn.tstu.ru; tstu@admin.tstu.ru

Website: http://www.tstu.ru

Rector: Sergei Vladimirovich Mischenko
EMail: rector@rector.tstu.ru

Faculties

Architecture and Civil Engineering (Architecture; Civil Engineering; Construction Engineering; Economics; Road Engineering); **Engineering Cybernetics** (Engineering); **Humanities** (Computer Science; History; Law; Philology; Philosophy; Public Relations; Russian); **Information Technology** (Computer Graphics; Design; Information Management; Information Sciences; Information Technology; Systems Analysis); **International Education** (Foreign Languages Education; International Studies; Russian); **Power Engineering** (Agricultural Equipment; Electrical Engineering; Electronic Engineering; Industrial Design; Power Engineering); **Transport and Agricultural Service** (Agricultural Engineering; Agricultural Equipment; Maintenance Technology; Transport and Communications; Transport Management)

Institutes

Economics and Production Management (Accountancy; Banking; Business Administration; Business and Commerce; Business Computing; Economics; Finance; Management; Marketing); **Technological** (Chemical Engineering; Engineering; Environmental Engineering; Food Science; Food Technology; Organic Chemistry; Production Engineering; Technology)

Further Information: Also Correspondence Faculty; Pre-university Training Faculty

History: Founded 1958 as Tambov Chemical Engineering Institute, acquired present status and title 1993.

Governing Bodies: Administrative Board; Academic Council

Academic Year: September to June (September-January; February-June)

Admission Requirements: Secondary school certificate (Attestat o srednem obrazovanii) or equivalent

Main Language(s) of Instruction: Russian

International Co-operation: With universities in Australia, Austria, India, Vietnam, Canada, China, Denmark, France, Germany, Japan, Spain, United Kingdom, Italy, Finland, Slovak Republic, Norway, Ukraine.

Degrees and Diplomas: *Bakalavr*; *Specialist Diploma*; *Magistr*; *Kandidat Nauk*; *Doktor Nauk*

Student Services: Academic counselling, Canteen, Cultural centre, Employment services, Foreign student adviser, Foreign Studies Centre, Health services, Language programs, Social counselling, Sports facilities

Special Facilities: University Museum. Exhibition Hall. TV-Studio

Libraries: Scientific Library, c. 1 500.000 vols

Last Updated: 16/03/12

TAMBOV STATE UNIVERSITY NAMED AFTER G.R. DERZHAVIN

Tambovskij Gosudarstvennyj Universitet im. G.R. Deržavina

ul. Internatsional'naja 33, Tambov, 392622 Tambovskaja oblast'

Tel: +7(4752) 72-34-40 +7(4752) 72-70-76 +7(4752) 72-43-72

Fax: +7(4752) 72-36-31

EMail: rector@tsu.tmb.ru; priem1@tsu.tmb.ru

Website: http://www.tsu.tmb.ru

Rector: Vladislav M. Jurev (1995-) EMail: rector@tsu.tmb.ru

Academies

Economics and Management (Accountancy; Administration; Banking; Economics; Finance; International Economics; Management; Marketing); **History** (Heritage Preservation; History; Museum Studies); **Law** (Civil Law; Comparative Law; Criminal Law; History of Law; Law; Public Law); **Pedagogy and Psychology** (Developmental Psychology; Educational Psychology; Pedagogy; Primary Education; Psychology; Social Psychology); **Philology and Journalism** (English; French; German; Grammar; Linguistics; Modern Languages; Philology; Phonetics; Romance Languages; Speech Studies); **Physics, Mathematics and Computer Science** (Computer Science; Mathematics; Physics; Statistics; Systems Analysis); **Social Work**; **Sociology** (Sociology)

Faculties

Information Resources (Archiving; Documentation Techniques; Information Sciences; Library Science); **Physical Education and Sports** (Physical Education; Sports); **Preparatory Studies for Foreign Students**; **Psychology** (Developmental Psychology; Educational Psychology; Psychology; Social Psychology); **Russian Language and Literature** (Grammar; Journalism; Linguistics; Literature; Philology; Phonetics; Russian; Speech Studies)

Institutes

Culture and Arts (Acting; Conducting; Dance; Folklore; Music; Music Education; Musical Instruments; Singing; Theatre); **Natural Sciences** (Analytical Chemistry; Anatomy; Biochemistry; Biology; Botany; Chemistry; Crystallography; Geography; Geology; Mineralogy)

Research Centres

Biochemistry of Natural Compounds (Biochemistry); **Ethics in Russian Philosophy** (Ethics; Philosophy); **Regional Economics** (Economics); **Social and Cultural Activities and Regional Context** (Cultural Studies; Regional Studies)

History: Founded 1930 as Pedagogical Institute. Acquired present status and title 1994 by merging with Institute of Culture.

Academic Year: September to June (September-January; February-June)

Admission Requirements: Secondary school certificate (Attestat o srednem obrazovanii)

Main Language(s) of Instruction: Russian

Degrees and Diplomas: *Bakalavr*; *Specialist Diploma*; *Magistr*; *Kandidat Nauk*; *Doktor Nauk*

Student Services: Academic counselling, Canteen, Cultural centre, Employment services, Foreign Studies Centre, Health services, Language programs, Social counselling, Sports facilities

Student Residential Facilities: For c. 2,000 students

Special Facilities: Russian Folk Museum; Zoological Museum; Museum of Physics History. Theatre Studio

Libraries: c. 900,000 vols

Last Updated: 16/03/12

THE RUSSIAN PRESIDENTIAL ACADEMY OF NATIONAL ECONOMY AND PUBLIC ADMINISTRATION

Rossijskaja Akademija Narodnogo Khozjajstva i Gosudarstvennoj Sluzby pri Presidente Rossijskoj Federacii

prosp. Vernadskogo 82, Moskva 119571
Tel: +7(495) 434-8389
Fax: +7(495) 433-2485
EMail: rector@ane.ru
Website: http://www.ane.ru

Rector: Vladimir Aleksandrovič Mau (2007-) EMail: mau@ane.ru

Vice-Rector: Elena Karpukhina
EMail: bell@ane.ru; karpuhina@anx.ru

International Relations: Leonid Todorov, Counselor for International Relations Tel: +7(495) 142-3994 EMail: todorov@anx.ru

Campuses

Krasnogorsk (Business Administration; Business and Commerce; Economics; Finance; Management; Marketing)

Centres

International Projects

Faculties

Business Technology; **Economics** (Economics); **Finance and Banking** (Banking; Finance); **Law** *(M.M. Speranskii)*; **Real Estate Economics** (Management; Real Estate); **Social and Economic Science** (Economics; Social Sciences); **State Management** (Administration; Management; Political Sciences; Public Administration)

Higher Schools

Corporate Management; **Finance and Management**; **International Business** (International Business; Management; Marketing); **Russian-German Higher School of Management** (Management)

Institutes

Business and Business Management; **Business and Economics** (Business Administration; Economics); **Management and Marketing** (Management; Marketing)

Schools

Moscow School of Social and Economic Science (Economics; Social Sciences)

Further Information: Branches throughout the Russian Federation.

History: Created 1991.

International Co-operation: With universities in United Kingdom, Germany, France, the Netherlands, Italy and Spain. Also projects with the World Bank, EBRD, the National Training Foundation, the British Council, USAID, TACIS. The Academy is member of the European Federation of Management Development (EFMD).

Accrediting Agencies: Ministry of Education

Degrees and Diplomas: *Bakalavr*; *Magistr*; *Kandidat Nauk*; *Doktor Nauk*

Student Services: Canteen, Health services, Sports facilities

Student Residential Facilities: Yes

Special Facilities: Computer Laboratories

Libraries: The Library of the Academy: c. 200,000 vols., monographs and course texts; c. 200 journals and periodical subscriptions. The Library of the Moscow School of Social and Economic Sciences of the Academy: c. 15,000 vols., monographs and course texts; over 180 journals and periodical subscriptions.

Publications: Business Academy Journal, Publication on Business Education; Business Navigator, Publication on Management trends

Press or Publishing House: Delo (Publishing company of the Academy)

Last Updated: 19/01/12

THEATRE INSTITUTE NAMED AFTER BORIS SHCHUKIN

Teatralnyj Institut im. Borisa Ščukina

Bolshoi Nikolopeskovskii pereulok, 12a, Moskva 119002
Tel: +7(499) 241-56-44 +7(499) 241-78-23
Fax: +7(499) 241-56-44
EMail: ossovskaya_mp@mail.ru
Website: http://htvs.ru/

Rector: Evgeniy Vladimirovich Knyazev

Programmes

Theatre (Acting; Theatre)

History: Founded 1914 by Stanislavsky's disciples. Previously known as Vyssee Teatralnoje Učilišče im. B.V. Ščukina (Theatre School named after B.V. Shchukin).

Academic Year: September to June

Admission Requirements: Secondary school certificate (Attestat o srednem obrazovanii)

Main Language(s) of Instruction: Russian

Degrees and Diplomas: *Bakalavr*; *Specialist Diploma*; *Magistr*

Student Services: Academic counselling, Foreign Studies Centre

Student Residential Facilities: For c. 90 students

Libraries: c. 40,000 vols

Last Updated: 12/03/12

TJUMEN LAW INSTITUTE OF THE RUSSIAN FEDERATION MINISTRY OF INTERNAL AFFAIRS

Tjumenskij Juridičeskij Institut MVD Rossijskoj Federatsii

ul. Amurskaja 75, Tjumen 625049
Tel: +7(3452) 59-54-03 +7(3452) 59-84-04
Fax: +7(3452) 59-84-19 +7(3452) 59-85-12
EMail: radar17@yandex.ru; radar17@rambler.ru
Website: http://www.tuimvd.ru/

Rector: Nikolai Vasil'evich Jadszhin

Programmes

Law (Law)

History: Created 1977.

Degrees and Diplomas: *Bakalavr*, *Specialist Diploma*
Last Updated: 02/03/12

TJUMEN STATE ACADEMY OF AGRICULTURE

Tjumenskaja Gosudarstvennaja Sel'skohozjajstvennaja Akademija

ul. Respubliki 7, Tjumen 625003
Tel: +7(3452) 461-650
Fax: +7(3452) 461-650
EMail: acadagro@tmn.ru
Website: http://www.tsaa.ru/

Rector: Nikolai V. Abramov
Tel: +7(3452) 461-743, Fax: +7(3452) 467-647

Vice-Rector for Administration: Grigorii Filisyuk

Institutes

Agricultural Technology (Agriculture; Agronomy; Applied Chemistry; Biology; Chemistry; Crop Production; Ecology; Environmental Management; Horticulture; Philosophy; Soil Science; Surveying and Mapping; Viticulture); **Biotechnology and Veterinary Medicine** (Anatomy; Animal Husbandry; Aquaculture; Biotechnology; Cattle Breeding; Fishery; Foreign Languages Education; Parasitology; Physiology; Veterinary Science); **Distance Education**; **Economics and Finance** (Accountancy; Agricultural Management; Economics; Environmental Management; Finance; Management; Mathematics; Natural Resources; Social Sciences; Statistics); **Mechanical Engineering** (Agricultural Engineering; Agricultural Equipment; Engineering; Food Technology; Forestry; Mechanical Engineering; Physics; Wood Technology)

History: Founded 1881 as Institute of Agriculture, acquired present name 1959.

Governing Bodies: Scientific Council

Admission Requirements: Secondary school certificate and entrance examination

Main Language(s) of Instruction: Russian

International Co-operation: With University of Nebraska at Lincoln (USA) and University of Saskatchewan (Canada)

Accrediting Agencies: Ministry of Education, Ministry of Agriculture

Degrees and Diplomas: *Specialist Diploma*: Agriculture, 5 yrs; *Kandidat Nauk*: Agriculture, a further 3 yrs

Student Services: Academic counselling, Canteen, Foreign student adviser, Language programs, Sports facilities

Student Residential Facilities: Yes

Special Facilities: Academy History Museum
Last Updated: 04/01/12

TJUMEN STATE ACADEMY OF ARCHITECTURE AND CIVIL ENGINEERING

Tjumenskaja Gosudarstvennaja Arkhitekturno-Stroitel'naja Akademija

ul. Lunačarskogo 2, Tjumen 625001
Tel: +7(3452) 461-010 +7(3452) 462-051
Fax: +7(3452) 462-390
EMail: info@tgasu.ru
Website: http://www.tgasu.ru/

Rector: Victor M. Chikishev EMail: rektorat@tgasu.ru

Departments

Architecture and Civil Engineering (Architectural and Environmental Design; Architecture; Civil Engineering; Heating and Refrigeration; Interior Design; Structural Architecture; Thermal Engineering); **Economics and Management** (Accountancy; Business and Commerce; Economics; Management; Marketing; Transport Management); **Engineering Networks and Facilities** (Computer Networks; Engineering); **Highway** (Civil Engineering; Road Engineering); **Municipal Management and Services** (Arts and Humanities; Law; Public Administration; Social Sciences)

History: Founded 1971.

Degrees and Diplomas: *Bakalavr*, *Magistr*, *Kandidat Nauk*
Last Updated: 04/01/12

TJUMEN STATE ACADEMY OF INTERNATIONAL ECONOMICS, MANAGEMENT AND LAW (INSTITUTE)

Tjumenskaja Gosudarstvennaja Akademija Mirovoj Ekonomiki, Upravlenija i Prava (Institut) (TIIEL)

ul. 30 Let Pobedy 102, Tjumen 625051
Tel: +7(3452) 33-25-31
Fax: +7(3452) 35-88-16
EMail: adm@tiiel.ru
Website: http://www.tiiel.ru

Rector: Victor Novikov

Faculties

Economics (Accountancy; Economics; Human Resources; Management; Marketing; Taxation); **Law** (Administrative Law; Commercial Law; Constitutional Law; History of Law; Human Rights; International Law; Labour Law; Law; Private Law; Public Law); **Management** (Management; Marketing; Mathematics and Computer Science; Regional Studies)

Further Information: Also Correspondence Studies Department

History: Founded 1992. Became an international institute 1997 and acquired present status 1999.

Governing Bodies: Department of Education and Sciences of the Tjumen Region

Academic Year: September to July

Main Language(s) of Instruction: Russian and English

International Co-operation: With universities in United Kingdom and USA.

Degrees and Diplomas: *Specialist Diploma*; *Kandidat Nauk*

Student Services: Academic counselling, Canteen, Cultural centre, Foreign student adviser, Health services, Language programs, Social counselling, Sports facilities

Student Residential Facilities: For 350 students.

Libraries: Reading Halls; Electronic catalogue
Last Updated: 22/12/11

TJUMEN STATE ACADEMY OF MEDICINE

Tjumenskaja Gosudarstvennaja Medicinskaja Akademija (TGMA)

ul. Odesskaja 54, Tjumen 625023
Tel: +7(3452) 20-62-00
Fax: +7(3452) 20-62-00
EMail: tgma@tyumsma.ru
Website: http://www.tyumsma.ru/

Rector: Eduard Kašuba

Faculties

Medicine (Medicine); **Nursing** (Nursing); **Paediatrics** (Paediatrics); **Pharmacy** (Pharmacy); **Stomatology** (Stomatology)

History: Founded 1963. Acquired present status 1993.

Governing Bodies: Ministry of Health

Academic Year: September to June

Admission Requirements: Secondary school certificate (attestat)

Main Language(s) of Instruction: Russian

International Co-operation: No

Accrediting Agencies: Ministry of Health

Degrees and Diplomas: *Specialist Diploma*

Student Services: Academic counselling, Canteen, Cultural centre, Employment services, Foreign student adviser, Foreign Studies Centre, Health services, Language programs, Nursery care, Social counselling, Sports facilities

Student Residential Facilities: Yes

Special Facilities: Museum

Libraries: 150,000 vols

Last Updated: 26/09/11

TJUMEN STATE OIL AND GAS UNIVERSITY

Tjumenskij Gosudarstvennyj Neftegazovyj Universitet (TGNGU)

ul. Vologarskogo 38, Tjumen 625000
Tel: +7(3452) 25-69-71 +7(3452) 25-69-32
Fax: +7(3452) 25-69-71 +7(3452) 25-69-28
EMail: sag@tsogu.ru
Website: http://www.tsogu.ru

Rector: Vladimir V. Novoselov EMail: general@tsogu.ru

Institutes

Cybernetics, Informatics and Communication (Automation and Control Engineering; Computer Science; Information Technology; Robotics); **Geology, Gas and Oil** (Geology; Petroleum and Gas Engineering); **Humanities** (Arts and Humanities; Cultural Studies; History; Modern Languages; Philosophy; Physical Education; Religious Studies; Russian; Social Work; Sociology); **Industrial Technology and Engineering** (Engineering; Industrial Engineering; Machine Building; Technology); **Management and Business** (Economics; Industrial Management; Management; Marketing); **Transport** (Transport and Communications; Transport Management)

Further Information: Also 18 branches in the Tyumen region and 12 Research Institutes

History: Founded 1963, acquired present status 1994.

Academic Year: September to July

Admission Requirements: Secondary school certificate and entrance examination

Main Language(s) of Instruction: Russian

International Co-operation: Tempus, Tacis, DAAD, SABIT

Degrees and Diplomas: *Bakalavr*, *Specialist Diploma*; *Magistr*

Student Services: Academic counselling, Canteen, Cultural centre, Employment services, Health services, Language programs, Nursery care, Social counselling, Sports facilities

Student Residential Facilities: Yes

Special Facilities: Museum. Art Gallery. Movie Studio

Libraries: Central Library, 1,800,000 vols

Last Updated: 19/04/11

TJUMEN STATE UNIVERSITY

Tjumenskij Gosudarstvennyj Universitet

ul. Semakova 10, Tjumen 625003
Tel: +7(3452) 464-061 +7(3452) 461-798
Fax: +7(3452) 361-930
EMail: president@utmn.ru
Website: http://www.utmn.ru/

Rector: Gennady Chebotarev Fax: +7(3452) 464-061

President: Gennady Kutsev

Head of Staff Department: Tatjana Lysova Tel: +7(3452) 461-231

International Relations: Nina Sivakova Fax: +7(3452) 461-798 EMail: nsivakova@utmn.ru

Institutes

Continuing Professional Education (Accountancy; Business Administration; Economics; Finance; Law); **Distance Education**; **Human Sciences** (Ancient Civilizations; Archaeology; Contemporary History; Documentation Techniques; English; French; German; History; Information Management; International Relations; Journalism; Linguistics; Literature; Medieval Studies; Philology; Philosophy; Publishing and Book Trade; Russian; Translation and Interpretation); **Law, Economics and Management** (Accountancy; Administrative Law; Banking; Civil Law; Communication Studies; Constitutional Law; Criminal Law; Economics; Finance; Government; Insurance; International Business; International Economics; International Law; Labour Law; Law; Management; Marketing; Mathematics; Modern Languages; Public Administration; Sociology; Statistics; Taxation; Transport Management); **Mathematics, Science and Information Technology** (Anatomy; Applied Physics; Biology; Biotechnology; Botany; Chemistry; Communication Studies; Cultural Studies; Ecology; Environmental Studies; Genetics; Geography; Geography (Human); Information Technology; Inorganic Chemistry; Landscape Architecture; Mathematics; Mathematics and Computer Science; Modern Languages; Nanotechnology; Natural Resources; Physical Chemistry; Physics; Software Engineering; Surveying and Mapping; Tourism; Zoology); **Physical Education** (Leisure Studies; Physical Education; Sports; Sports Management); **Psychology and Pedagogy** (Art Education; Biological and Life Sciences; Biomedicine; Educational Psychology; Educational Research; Fine Arts; Music Education; Pedagogy; Psychology; Social Psychology)

Further Information: Also Russian courses for foreign students

History: Founded 1930. Acquired present status and title 1973.

Governing Bodies: Academic Council

Academic Year: September to June (September-January; February-June)

Admission Requirements: Secondary education certificate (Attestat o srednem obrazovanii) and entrance examination

Main Language(s) of Instruction: Russian

Accrediting Agencies: Federal Service of Supervision in the Sphere of Education and Science

Degrees and Diplomas: *Bakalavr*, *Specialist Diploma*: 5 yrs; *Magistr*, *Kandidat Nauk*: a further 3 yrs; *Doktor Nauk*: by thesis after Kandidat

Student Services: Academic counselling, Canteen, Cultural centre, Health services, Sports facilities

Student Residential Facilities: Yes

Special Facilities: Biological Museum; Archaeological Museum

Libraries: University Library, c. 1 m. vols; Department of Rare Books

Press or Publishing House: Isdatelstvo

Last Updated: 22/12/11

TOBOLSK STATE SOCIAL PEDAGOGICAL ACADEMY NAMED AFTER D. I. MENDELEEV

Tobolskaja Gosudarstvennaja Sotsialno-Pedagogičeskaja Akademija

ul. Znamenskogo 58, Tobolsk, 626150 Tjumenskaja oblast'
Tel: +7(3456) 25-15-88 +7(3456) 25-31-78
Fax: +7(3456) 25-15-88
EMail: tgspa@tgspa.ru
Website: http://www.tgspa.ru

Rector: Sergej V. Slinkin EMail: rector@tgspa.ru

Vice-Rector, Administration: Viktoria Tikhonova

Faculties

Biology and Chemistry (Biology; Chemistry; Ecology; Science Education); **Graphic Arts** (Art Education; Design); **History** (History; Humanities and Social Science Education); **Pedagogy** (Pedagogy; Preschool Education; Primary Education); **Philology** (Engineering Management; Germanic Languages; Journalism; Literature; Native Language Education; Romance Languages; Russian); **Physics and Mathematics** (Computer Education; Computer Science; Information Technology; Mathematics; Mathematics Education; Physics; Science Education); **Professional Education** (Hotel and Restaurant; Physical Education; Preschool Education; Primary Education; Tourism); **Service and Trades** (Cultural Studies; Economic History; Museum Studies; Philosophy; Sociology; Tourism); **Socio–Psychology** (Educational Psychology; Pedagogy; Psychology)

History: Founded 1939 as Tobolskij Gosudarstvennyj Pedagogičeskij Institut. Acquired present status and title 2004.

Governing Bodies: Rectorate

Academic Year: September to June

Admission Requirements: Attestat o Srednem (Polnom) Obshchem Obrazovanii (school certificate)

Fees: (Russian Rubles): 16,650 per annum; 8,325 per semester

Main Language(s) of Instruction: Russian

International Co-operation: With universities in USA, Germany, United Kingdom

Accrediting Agencies: State Department of Education

Degrees and Diplomas: *Diplom o Srednem Professionalnom Obrazovanii (Higher Vocational Education Diploma)*; *Bakalavr*; *Specialist Diploma*; *Magistr*

Student Services: Academic counselling, Canteen, Cultural centre, Employment services, Foreign student adviser, Language programs, Nursery care, Social counselling, Sports facilities

Student Residential Facilities: Hostel

Special Facilities: Museum. Art Gallery. Movie Studio. Laboratories. Computer clubs

Libraries: Main library

Publications: Mendeleevskiye Ohteniya, Scientific works *(annually)*; Vestnik TGPI, Scientific works *(annually)*

Press or Publishing House: Publishing Laboratory

Last Updated: 26/04/11

TOL'JATTI STATE UNIVERSITY

Tol'jattinskij Gosudarstvennij Universitet

ul. Belorusskaja 14, Tol'jatti, 445667 Samarskaja oblast'
Tel: +7(8482) 546-399
EMail: office@tltsu.ru
Website: http://www.tltsu.ru

Rector: Mikhail M. Krishtal
Tel: +7(8482) 280-125, Fax: +7(8482) 539-522

International Relations: Elena Kargina
Tel: +7(8482) 546-399 EMail: international@tltsu.ru

Faculties

Electrical Engineering (Electrical and Electronic Equipment and Maintenance; Electrical Engineering; Electronic Engineering; Mechanical Equipment and Maintenance; Power Engineering); **Fine, Decorative and Applied Arts** (Design; Fine Arts; Graphic Arts; Handicrafts; Painting and Drawing; Sculpture); **Law** (Civil Law; Criminal Law; Law); **Mathematics and Informatics** (Applied Mathematics; Computer Engineering; Computer Science; Mathematics); **Physical Education and Sports** (Physical Education; Sports); **Teacher Training** (Education; Industrial Arts Education; Pedagogy; Preschool Education; Teacher Training)

Institutes

Automotive and Mechanical Engineering (Agricultural Equipment; Automotive Engineering; Computer Science; Engineering Drawing and Design; Heating and Refrigeration; Mechanical Engineering; Mechanical Equipment and Maintenance; Metal Techniques); **Chemistry and Engineering Ecology** (Chemistry; Ecology; Environmental Engineering; Food Technology; Industrial Chemistry); **Civil and Building Engineering** (Civil Engineering; Design; Heating and Refrigeration; Industrial Engineering; Petroleum and Gas Engineering; Town Planning; Water Management); **Continuing Education**; **Finance, Economics and Management** (Accountancy; Economics; Finance; Management); **Humanities** (Foreign Languages Education; German; History; Journalism; Philology; Philosophy; Psychology; Romance Languages; Russian; Sociology; Translation and Interpretation); **Military Training**; **Physics and Engineering** (Automation and Control Engineering; Materials Engineering; Mechanical Engineering; Nanotechnology; Physics)

Further Information: Also 23 Research Laboratories and 3 Affiliated Colleges. Russian language courses for foreign students

History: Founded 1952 as branch of Kuibišev Industrial Institute, became Togliatti Polytechnical Institute 1967, and acquired present status and title 1995. Formerly Tol'jattinskij Politehničeskij Institut.

Academic Year: September to June (September-January; February-June)

Admission Requirements: Secondary school certificate (Attestat o srednem obrazovanii)

Main Language(s) of Instruction: Russian, English

Degrees and Diplomas: *Bakalavr*; *Specialist Diploma*; *Magistr*; *Kandidat Nauk*

Libraries: Central Library, c. 250,000 vols; Art Library, 16,000 vols

Press or Publishing House: Izdatelskaja Gruppa

Last Updated: 22/12/11

TOMSK POLYTECHNIC UNIVERSITY

Tomskij Politekhničeskij Universitet

pr. Lenina 30, Tomsk 634034
Tel: +7(3822) 415-620 +7(3822) 563-470
Fax: +7(3822) 563-823 +7(3822) 563-865
EMail: tpu@tpu.edu.ru
Website: http://www.tpu.ru

Rector: Petr S. Chubik
Tel: +7(3822) 563-823 EMail: rector@tpu.ru; chubik@tpu.ru

Vice-Rector for Academic Affairs: Egor G. Yazikov
Tel: +7(3822) 563-814, Fax: +7(3822) 563-908
EMail: yazikoveg@tpu.ru

International Relations: Alexander I. Čučalin, Vice-Rector for Academic and International Affairs
Tel: +7(3822) 563-406, Fax: +7(3822) 563-406
EMail: chai@tpu.ru

Centres

Cybernetics (Automation and Control Engineering) *Director*: Mikhail A. Sonkin

Faculties

Applied Physics and Engineering (Applied Physics; Automation and Control Engineering; Chemical Engineering; Electronic Engineering; Engineering; Nuclear Engineering; Nuclear Physics; Safety Engineering) *Dean*: Vladimir Ilič Boiko; **Chemistry and Chemical Engineering** (Automation and Control Engineering; Bioengineering; Biotechnology; Chemical Engineering; Chemistry; Inorganic Chemistry; Organic Chemistry) *Dean*: Valeriy Matveevič Pogrebenkov; **Computer Science and Engineering** (Computer Engineering; Computer Science; Engineering) *Dean*: Sergej Anatolyevic Gajvoroskij; **Economics and Management** (Accountancy; Business and Commerce; Economics; Environmental Engineering; Environmental Management; Management; Marketing) *Dean*: Nikolay Ivanovic Gvozdev; **Electrophysics and Electronic Equipment** (Biomedical Engineering; Biotechnology; Electronic Engineering; Industrial Engineering; Information Technology; Instrument Making; Laser Engineering; Measurement and Precision Engineering; Microelectronics; Optical Technology; Physics; Safety Engineering) *Dean*: Gennadij Sergeevic Yevtushenko; **Humanities** (Advertising and Publicity; Arts and Humanities; Communication Studies; Cultural Studies; History; Law; Management; Philosophy; Psychology; Regional Studies; Social Studies; Social Work; Sociology; Tourism) *Dean*: Vitaly Georgervič Rubanov; **Mechanical Engineering** (Applied Physics; Automation and Control Engineering; Materials Engineering; Mechanical Engineering; Metal Techniques; Robotics; Technology) *Dean*: Rostislav Ivanovič Dedyukh; **Natural Sciences and Mathematics** (Applied Mathematics; Foreign Languages Education; Inorganic Chemistry; Materials Engineering; Mathematical Physics; Mathematics; Nanotechnology; Natural Sciences; Physics) *Dean*: Jurij Ivanovic Tyurin; **Physical Culture and Sports**; **Thermal Power Engineering** (Automation and Control Engineering; Heating and Refrigeration; Hydraulic Engineering; Nuclear Engineering; Thermal Engineering) *Dean*: Geniy V. Kuznetsov

Institutes

Continuing Professional Development; **Distance Learning** (Accountancy; Administration; Automation and Control Engineering; Chemical Engineering; Computer Networks; Computer Science; Cultural Studies; Economics; Electrical Engineering; Heating and Refrigeration; Information Management; Information Technology; Management; Mechanical Engineering; Metal Techniques; Natural Resources; Power Engineering; Public Relations; Safety Engineering; Social Studies; Social Work; Software Engineering; Tourism; Translation and Interpretation); **Electrical Engineering** (Electrical Engineering); **Engineering Entrepreneurship** (Business Administration; English; International Business; Management); **Geology and Oil & Gas Industries** (Environmental Engineering; Geological Engineering; Geology; Geophysics; Mining Engineering; Natural Resources; Petroleum and Gas Engineering); **International Education and Language Communication** (Communication Studies; English; European Languages; Foreign Languages Education; German; Linguistics; Modern Languages; Oriental Languages;

Russian; Translation and Interpretation); **Technology** *(Yurga)* (Technology)

Research Institutes

High Voltage (Power Engineering); **Non-Destructive Testing**; **Nuclear Physics** (Nuclear Physics)

Further Information: Branches in Jurga and Seversk, campus in Cyprus. Also Russian Language courses for foreign students

History: Founded 1896 as Technological Institute, acquired present title 1991 and status of National Research University 2009.

Academic Year: September to July (September-January; February-July)

Admission Requirements: Secondary school certificate (Attestat)

Main Language(s) of Instruction: Russian, English

Degrees and Diplomas: *Bakalavr*: 4 yrs; *Specialist Diploma*: one further yr; *Magistr*: a further 2 yrs; *Doktor Nauk*: a further 3 yrs following Magistr

Student Services: Academic counselling, Canteen, Cultural centre, Employment services, Foreign Studies Centre, Handicapped facilities, Nursery care, Social counselling, Sports facilities

Student Residential Facilities: For c. 4,640 students

Special Facilities: History of the University Museum; Museum of Mineralogy. Movie Studio

Libraries: c. 2.7m. vols

Publications: Tomsky Polytehnik *(annually)*

Press or Publishing House: Publishing House

Last Updated: 04/02/10

TOMSK STATE PEDAGOGICAL UNIVERSITY

Tomskij Gosudarstvennyj Pedagogičeskij Universitet (TSPU)

Kievskaya 60, Tomsk 634041
Tel: +7(3822) 521-767
Fax: +7(3822) 446-826
EMail: rector@tspu.edu.ru
Website: http://www.tspu.edu.ru/

Rector: Valerij V. Obuhov (2000-) Tel: +7(3822) 443-644

Vice-Rector for Administration: Igor B. Medvedev
EMail: Medvedev@tspu.edu.ru

Faculties

Chemistry and Biology (Biology; Botany; Chemistry; Ecology; Inorganic Chemistry; Organic Chemistry; Science Education); **Economics and Management** (Civil Law; Economics; Home Economics; Law; Management; Tourism); **Foreign Languages** (Cognitive Sciences; Cultural Studies; English; Foreign Languages Education; Grammar; Linguistics; Modern Languages; Philology; Romance Languages; Russian; Terminology; Translation and Interpretation); **History, Geography and Philology** (Archaeology; Ethnology; Geography; History; Literacy Education; Native Language Education; Philology); **Pedagogy** (Education; Pedagogy; Preschool Education; Primary Education; Teacher Trainers Education); **Physical Training and Sports** (Physical Education; Sports); **Physics and Mathematics** (Computer Science; Mathematics; Physics); **Psychology, Public Relations and Advertising** (Advertising and Publicity; Pedagogy; Psychology; Public Relations); **Technology and Enterpreneurship** (Management; Mechanics; Safety Engineering; Technology; Wood Technology)

Institutes

Culture (Art Education; Computer Science; Cultural Studies; Educational Psychology; Fine Arts; History; Medicine; Modern Languages; Music Education; Pedagogy; Philosophy; Physiology; Psychology; Religious Studies; Social Sciences; Speech Studies)

History: Founded 1902 at the Royal Command of His Majesty Emperor Nicolas II as Teachers' Institute. Became Tomsk State Pedagogical Institute. Acquired present status and title 1995.

Governing Bodies: Academic Council

Academic Year: September to June

Admission Requirements: Seconday school certificate or equivalent

Main Language(s) of Instruction: Russian; English

International Co-operation: With universities in Poland, Japan and USA

Accrediting Agencies: Federal Service for Supervision of Education and Science of Russian Education

Degrees and Diplomas: *Bakalavr*: 4 yrs; *Specialist Diploma*: 5 yrs; *Kandidat Nauk*: a further 3 yrs; *Doktor Nauk*

Student Services: Academic counselling, Canteen, Cultural centre, Employment services, Foreign student adviser, Foreign Studies Centre, Health services, Language programs, Nursery care, Social counselling, Sports facilities

Student Residential Facilities: Dormitory

Special Facilities: Museums; Art Gallery

Libraries: Electronic Catalogue

Publications: "Vestnik of Tomsk State Pedagogical University", Scientific journal for publications in English and Russian from all over the world *(monthly)*

Press or Publishing House: TSPU Publishing House

Last Updated: 22/12/11

TOMSK STATE UNIVERSITY

Tomskij Gosudarstvennyj Universitet

ul. Lenina, 36, Tomsk 634050
Tel: +7(3822) 529-852
Fax: +7(3822) 529-585
EMail: rector@tsu.ru
Website: http://www.tsu.ru

Rector: Georgij V. Majer

International Relations: Sergey N. Kirpotin
Tel: +7(3822) 529-644 EMail: Kirp@ums.tsu.ru

Colleges

Arts and Culture (Cultural Studies; Fine Arts; Library Science; Museum Studies; Musical Instruments; Singing)

Faculties

Agriculture and Ecology *(International)* (Agricultural Management; Agriculture; Agronomy; Ecology; Environmental Studies; Industrial Management; Natural Resources; Plant and Crop Protection); **Applied Mathematics and Cybernetics** (Applied Mathematics; Computer Networks; Information Management; Information Sciences); **Biology and Soil Science** (Architectural and Environmental Design; Biology; Ecology; Forestry; Soil Science); **Chemistry** (Chemistry; Environmental Management; Natural Resources); **Computer Studies** (Computer Networks; Information Technology; Mathematics and Computer Science); **Economics** (Economics); **Foreign Languages** (Foreign Languages Education; Modern Languages; Translation and Interpretation); **Geology and Geography** (Environmental Management; Geochemistry; Geography; Geology; Meteorology; Natural Resources; Water Science); **History** (Archaeology; Ethnology; History; Information Management; Information Sciences; International Relations; Regional Studies); **Journalism** (Journalism); **Management** *(International)* (Documentation Techniques; Information Management); **Mathematics and Mechanics** (Mathematics; Mechanics); **Philology** (Philology); **Philosophy** (Logic; Philosophy; Political Sciences; Social Studies; Social Work); **Physics** (Astronomy and Space Science; Information Technology; Physics); **Physics and Engineering** (Industrial Design; Mechanics; Physics; Robotics; Technology); **Psychology** (Clinical Psychology; Management; Psychology; Public Relations); **Radio-Physics** (Applied Physics; Automation and Control Engineering; Electronic Engineering; Laser Engineering; Optical Technology; Optics)

Schools

Business (Banking; Business and Commerce; Economics; International Relations; Law; Statistics); **Law** (Law)

History: Founded 1878.

Governing Bodies: Academic Council

Academic Year: September to July

Admission Requirements: Secondary school certificate (Attestat o srednem obrazovanii)

Main Language(s) of Instruction: Russian

Degrees and Diplomas: *Bakalavr*: 4 yrs; *Specialist Diploma*: 1 further yr; *Magistr*: 1 further yr; *Kandidat Nauk*: a further 3 yrs and thesis; *Doktor Nauk*: by thesis after Kandidat
Special Facilities: Museums; Observatory; Siberian botanical garden
Libraries: c. 4 m. vols
Last Updated: 21/12/11

TOMSK STATE UNIVERSITY OF CIVIL ENGINEERING

Tomskij Gosudarstvennyj Arhitekturno-Stroitelnyj Universitet
pl. Soljanaja 2, Tomsk 634003
Tel: +7(3822) 753-930
Fax: +7(3822) 753-922
Website: http://www.tsuab.ru

First Vice-Rector: Sergey Yuschube Tel: +7(3822) 653-382

Departments

Engineering and Environment (Environmental Studies; Heating and Refrigeration; Occupational Health; Water Management; Water Science); **Mechanics** (Agricultural Equipment; Mechanics; Road Transport); **Road Construction** (Bridge Engineering; Civil Engineering; Ecology; Geological Engineering; Road Engineering; Surveying and Mapping); **Vocational Education** (Surveying and Mapping)

Faculties

Architecture (Architectural and Environmental Design; Architectural Restoration; Architecture; Engineering Drawing and Design); **Civil Engineering** (Building Technologies; Civil Engineering; Metal Techniques; Painting and Drawing; Real Estate; Sculpture; Wood Technology); **Economics and Management** (Economics; Industrial Management; Town Planning); **Forestry** *(Forestry Institute)* (Automation and Control Engineering; Electronic Engineering; Forestry; Wood Technology); **General Education** (Applied Mathematics; Chemistry; English; French; German; History; Mathematics; Mechanics; Philosophy; Physics); **Geoinformation Technology and Inventory** (Surveying and Mapping); **Preparatory** (Architecture; Construction Engineering)

History: Created 1952. Acquired present title 1997.

Degrees and Diplomas: *Bakalavr*; *Specialist Diploma*; *Magistr*
Last Updated: 22/12/11

TOMSK STATE UNIVERSITY OF CONTROL SYSTEMS AND RADIOELECTRONICS

Tomskij Gosudarstvennyj Universitet Sistem Upravlenija i Radioelektroniki (TUCSR)
pr. Lenina 40, Tomsk 634050
Tel: +7(3822) 053-051
Fax: +7(3822) 513-262
Website: http://www.tusur.ru

Rector: Yuri Shurygin (2009-) EMail: office@tusur.ru

Vice-Rector for Administration: Oleg E. Trojan
EMail: toe@main.tusur.ru

Colleges

Informatics, Electronics and Management (Electronic Engineering)

Faculties

Advanced Training; **Computer Systems** (Automation and Control Engineering; Computer Networks; Computer Science; Electronic Engineering; Graphic Design; Mechanical Engineering; Safety Engineering); **Control Systems** (Automation and Control Engineering; Data Processing; Mathematics); **Distance Learning**; **Economics** (Applied Mathematics; Computer Science; Statistics); **Electronic Engineering** (Electronic Engineering; Physics); **Extramural and Evening Education**; **Human Sciences** (Cultural Studies; History; Modern Languages; Philosophy; Physical Education; Social Work; Sociology; Sports); **Innovation Technologies** (Electronic Engineering); **Law** (Civil Law; Criminal Law; Law); **Radio Design** (Industrial Design); **Radio Engineering** (Electronic Engineering; Telecommunications Engineering)

Further Information: Also Russian language courses for foreign students

History: Founded 1962 on the basis of the radioengineering faculty of the Tomsk Politechnical Institute. Acquired present title 1997.

Academic Year: September to June (September-January; February-June)

Admission Requirements: Secondary school certificate (Attestat o srednem obrazovanii) and entrance examination

Main Language(s) of Instruction: Russian

Degrees and Diplomas: *Bakalavr*: 4 yrs; *Specialist Diploma*: 1 further yr; *Magistr*: 3 yrs; *Kandidat Nauk*: 3 yrs

Student Services: Academic counselling, Canteen, Employment services, Foreign Studies Centre, Handicapped facilities, Health services, Social counselling, Sports facilities

Special Facilities: History of the University Museum

Libraries: c. 750,000 vols

Press or Publishing House: Publishing House of the TUCSR
Last Updated: 21/12/11

TULA STATE PEDAGOGICAL UNIVERSITY NAMED AFTER LEV TOLSTOY

Tulskij Gosudarstvennyj Pedagogičeskij Universitet im. Lva Tolstogo (TGPU/TSPU)
pr. Lenina 125, Tula, 300026 Tulskaja oblast'
Tel: +7(4872) 333-646
Fax: +7(4872) 357-807
EMail: tgpu@tula.net
Website: http://www.tsput.ru/

Rector: Nadežda A. Šaidenko (2007-)

Provost: Aleksandr P. Plotnikov Tel: +7(872) 352-161

International Relations: Žanna E. Fomičeva
Tel: +7(4872) 355-474 EMail: interdept@tspu.tula.ru

Centres

New Educational Systems and Technology (Educational Research; Technology)

Departments

Foreign Languages (English; French; German; Modern Languages; Philology; Phonetics; Romance Languages; Translation and Interpretation); **Mathematics, Physics and Informatics** (Computer Science; Information Technology; Mathematics; Physics)

Faculties

Arts, Social Sciences and Humanities (Child Care and Development; Cultural Studies; Education; Educational Psychology; Ethics; Pedagogy; Philosophy; Political Sciences; Primary Education; Psychology; Religion; Religious Studies; Social Sciences; Sociology; Theology); **History and Law** (Archaeology; History; Law); **International** *(Pre-university training)* (Arts and Humanities; Foreigners Education; Mathematics Education; Native Language; Philology; Russian; Science Education); **Psychology** (Educational Psychology; Psychology); **Russian Philology and Documentation** (Linguistics; Literature; Philology; Russian); **Science, Physical Education and Tourism** (Agronomy; Biochemistry; Biology; Biomedicine; Botany; Chemistry; Cultural Studies; Ecology; Environmental Studies; Geography; Hygiene; Inorganic Chemistry; Natural Sciences; Organic Chemistry; Physical Education; Physiology; Psychology; Science Education; Sports; Sports Medicine; Tourism; Zoology); **Technology, Economics and Agriculture** (Agricultural Engineering; Agricultural Equipment; Economics; Environmental Management; Human Resources; Management; Pedagogy; Technology)

Further Information: Also Special Units, i.e. Teaching Hospitals, Courses for foreign students, Study Abroad Programmes etc.

History: Founded 1938 as Institute, acquired present status and title 1994.

Academic Year: September to June (September-January; February-June)

Admission Requirements: High school certificate (Attestat o srednem polnom obscem obrazovanii) or equivalent and entrance examination

Main Language(s) of Instruction: Russian, English, German, French

International Co-operation: With universities in Denmark; France; USA; Germany; Poland; Slovak Republic

Accrediting Agencies: Ministry of Education

Degrees and Diplomas: *Bakalavr*: 4 yrs; *Magistr*: 1-2 yrs; *Kandidat Nauk*: a further 3 yrs

Student Services: Academic counselling, Canteen, Cultural centre, Employment services, Health services, Social counselling, Sports facilities

Student Residential Facilities: Yes

Special Facilities: Planetarium. Biological and Agricultural Research Station. Museums. Herbarium.

Libraries: Central Library, 600,000 vols; Specialized Libraries, 265,900 vols.

Press or Publishing House: Publishing Centre of Tula State Pedagogical University

Student Numbers *2010-2011*: Total 5,777
Last Updated: 20/12/11

TULA STATE UNIVERSITY

Tulskij Gosudarstvennyj Universitet

pr. Lenina 92, Tula, 300600 Tulskaja oblast'
Tel: +7(4872) 33-42-98
Fax: +7(4872) 33-13-05
EMail: info@tsu.tula.ru; imc@tsu.tula.ru
Website: http://www.tsu.tula.ru

Rector: Michail Vasilievich Gryazev

Faculties

Automated Control Systems (Electrical and Electronic Engineering; Optical Technology; Optics; Telecommunications Engineering); **Cybernetics** (Computer Science; Robotics); **Economics and Management** (Administration; Business Computing; Economics; Finance; Information Sciences; International Economics; Management); **Humanities** (Cultural Studies; Design; History; Journalism; Linguistics; Modern Languages; Philosophy; Political Sciences; Psychology; Sociology; Theology; Translation and Interpretation); **Law** (Law); **Mechanical Engineering** (Mechanical Engineering); **Mechanices and Mathematics** (Applied Mathematics; Mathematics; Mechanics); **Mechanics and Engineering** (Machine Building; Mechanical Engineering); **Mining and Construction** (Architecture; Civil Engineering; Construction Engineering; Environmental Management; Geological Engineering; Mining Engineering); **Natural Sciences** (Biotechnology; Chemistry; Metallurgical Engineering; Physics); **Physical Education, Sport and Tourism** (Physical Education; Sports; Tourism); **Transport and Technological Systems** (Computer Graphics; Food Technology; Transport Engineering)

Further Information: Also Russian language courses for foreign students

History: Founded 1930 as Tula Mechanical Institute, incorporating Tula Mining Institute 1963. Became Tula State Technical University 1992, and acquired present title 1995.

Academic Year: September to May (September-December; February-May)

Admission Requirements: Secondary school certificate (Attestat o srednem obrazovanii)

Main Language(s) of Instruction: Russian, English, French, German

International Co-operation: With universities in USA, Germany (DAAD, IREX, Fullbright, American Councils, Open Society Institute)

Accrediting Agencies: Ministry of Education and Science

Degrees and Diplomas: *Bakalavr*: 4 yrs; *Specialist Diploma*: 5 yrs; *Magistr*, *Kandidat Nauk*; *Doktor Nauk*

Student Services: Academic counselling, Canteen, Cultural centre, Employment services, Foreign Studies Centre, Handicapped facilities, Health services, Nursery care, Social counselling, Sports facilities

Student Residential Facilities: For c. 800 students

Special Facilities: University Museum. Theatre Studio.

Libraries: Central and Specialized Libraries, total, c. 3.5m. vols

Publications: Collected Works *(annually)*; TSU Scientific News *(quarterly)*

Press or Publishing House: Publishing Department
Last Updated: 06/12/11

TVER STATE AGRICULTURAL ACADEMY

Tverskaja Gosudarstvennaja Sel'skohozjajstvennaja Academija

ul. Vasilevskogo, 7, pos. Saharovo, Tver, 170904 Tverskaja oblast'
Tel: +7(4222) 53-12-33 +7(4222) 53-10-66
Fax: +7(4222) 53-12-36 +7(4222) 53-18-23
EMail: rybalco@tvcom.ru
Website: http://www.tvgsha.ru

Rector: Oleg R. Balayan EMail: 110@tvcom.ru

Faculties

Economics (Economics; Management); **Engineering** (Agricultural Business; Agricultural Engineering; Agricultural Equipment; Engineering; Engineering Drawing and Design; Physics); **Technology** (Agriculture; Agronomy; Animal Husbandry; Applied Chemistry; Aquaculture; Biology; Botany; Cattle Breeding; Chemistry; Crop Production; Veterinary Science)

History: Founded 1972.

Degrees and Diplomas: *Bakalavr*, *Specialist Diploma*
Last Updated: 20/12/11

TVER STATE MEDICAL ACADEMY

Tverskaja Gosudarstvennaja Medicinskaja Akademija (TSMA)

ul. Soveckaja 4, Tver, 170100 Tverskaja oblast'
Tel: +7(4822) 317-779
Fax: +7(4822) 345-759
EMail: info@tvergma.ru
Website: http://www.tvergma.ru/

Rector: Mikhail N. Kalinkin (2008-)

Vice-Rector: Denis V. Kileynikov
Tel: +7 (4822) 359-870, Fax: +7 (4822) 359-870
EMail: kileynikovdenis@mail.ru

International Relations: Dmitry V. Bajenov, Vice-Rector
Tel: +7 (4822) 345-714, Fax: +7 (4822) 345-714
EMail: bajenovd@mail.ru

Faculties

Advanced Nursing Education (Nursing); **Dentistry** (Dental Hygiene; Dental Technology; Dentistry; Oral Pathology; Orthodontics; Periodontics; Plastic Surgery; Stomatology); **General Medicine** (Anaesthesiology; Anatomy; Applied Physics; Biochemistry; Biology; Cardiology; Chemistry; Dermatology; Diabetology; Dietetics; Endocrinology; Epidemiology; Gastroenterology; Gerontology; Gynaecology and Obstetrics; Haematology; Hepatology; Histology; Hygiene; Latin; Medical Parasitology; Medicine; Microbiology; Modern Languages; Nephrology; Neurology; Oncology; Ophthalmology; Orthopaedics; Otorhinolaryngology; Pathology; Physiology; Plastic Surgery; Pneumology; Psychiatry and Mental Health; Psychotherapy; Public Health; Radiology; Rheumatology; Social and Preventive Medicine; Social Sciences; Surgery; Treatment Techniques; Tropical Medicine; Urology; Venereology; Virology); **Paediatrics** (Biochemistry; Dentistry; Dermatology; Endocrinology; Orthopaedics; Paediatrics; Radiology; Social and Preventive Medicine; Surgery); **Pharmacy** (Pharmacy); **Postgraduate Studies** (Anaesthesiology; Cardiology; Dental Technology; Dermatology; Endocrinology; Gastroenterology; Gynaecology and Obstetrics; Immunology; Medicine; Neurology; Nursing; Oncology; Ophthalmology; Orthodontics; Orthopaedics; Paediatrics; Periodontics; Pharmacy; Physical Therapy; Pneumology; Psychiatry and Mental Health; Public Health; Radiology; Surgery; Tropical Medicine; Urology)

History: Founded 1936 as Leningrad Stomatological medical Institute. Transferred from Leningrad to the city of Kalinin, became the Kalinin Medical Institute 1954. Acquired present status 1994. Formerly known as Kalinin State Medical Academy.

Governing Bodies: Federal Agency for Public Health and Social Development

Academic Year: September to June

Admission Requirements: Secondary Education Certificate

Fees: (Russian Rubles): 60,000 per annum

Main Language(s) of Instruction: Russian; English

International Co-operation: Pilot Project " Health Care Reforms in Tver Region"-a programme of the World Bank; Project "Tver Regional Programme of noncommunicable disease prevention"-CINDI programme-WHO; Programme "Public Health School" (Public Health School of Israel); TEMPUS/TACIS- Project " PROFI " "Optimization of Processes in Financial Management" (1999-2001); TEMPUS/TACIS-Project " CROSSUM " (2002-2004); TACIS Project MTP "Raising of the managers' proficiency level" (2004)

Accrediting Agencies: National Accrediting Agency for Education

Degrees and Diplomas: *Specialist Diploma*: 5-6 yrs; *Magistr*: 5 yrs

Student Services: Academic counselling, Canteen, Cultural centre, Employment services, Foreign student adviser, Foreign Studies Centre, Handicapped facilities, Health services, Language programs, Nursery care, Social counselling, Sports facilities

Student Residential Facilities: 4 Hostels for 1,840 students

Special Facilities: Clinical Departments (c. 6,000 beds); Stomatological Polyclinic; 2 Centres of new Medical Technologies.

Libraries: Over 520,000 vols of foreign and Russian literature

Publications: Verkhnevoljsky Medicinsky Jurnal *(bimonthly)*

Academic Staff *2007-2008*	MEN	WOMEN	**TOTAL**
FULL-TIME	263	250	**513**
PART-TIME	34	20	**54**
STAFF WITH DOCTORATE			
FULL-TIME	65	20	**85**
Student Numbers *2007-2008*			
All (Foreign Included)	1,703	2,093	**3,796**
FOREIGN ONLY	753	349	**1,102**

Part-time students, 394.

Last Updated: 20/12/11

TVER STATE TECHNICAL UNIVERSITY

Tverskoj Gosudarstvennyj Tehničeskij Universitet
nab. Afanasija Nikitina 22, Tver, 170026 Tverskaja oblast'
Tel: +7(4822) 526-335
Fax: +7(4822) 316-292
EMail: common@tstu.tver.ru
Website: http://www.tstu.tver.ru

Rector: Boris Palyuh

First Vice-Rector: A. I. Matveev Tel: +7(822) 314-112

International Relations: Valery L. Sourinsky Tel: +7(822) 314-307

Faculties

Chemical Engineering (Applied Chemistry; Biotechnology; Chemical Engineering; Chemistry; Measurement and Precision Engineering; Polymer and Plastics Technology); **Distance Learning** (Accountancy; Civil Engineering; Environmental Management; Food Technology; Information Management; Information Technology; Natural Resources; Psychology; Sociology; Tourism); **Engineering** (Applied Physics; Automation and Control Engineering; Electrical Engineering; Energy Engineering; Engineering; Engineering Drawing and Design; Mechanical Engineering; Power Engineering; Production Engineering; Road Engineering; Transport Engineering); **Engineering and Construction** (Architecture and Planning; Civil Engineering; Ecology; Industrial Engineering; Mathematics; Safety Engineering; Surveying and Mapping; Town Planning); **Information Technology** (Applied Mathematics; Automation and Control Engineering; Biomedical Engineering; Computer Engineering; Computer Science; Information Technology; Software Engineering; Technology); **International Academic Cooperation** (Biology; Chemistry; Computer Science; Economics; Engineering Drawing and Design; Geography; Mathematics; Physics; Russian); **Natural Resources and Environmental Engineering** (Environmental Engineering; Geology; Mechanics; Mining Engineering; Natural Resources; Physics; Technology)

Programmes

Management and Social Communication (Accountancy; Advertising and Publicity; Business Computing; Economics; Human Resources; Insurance; Management; Philosophy; Physical Education; Psychology; Public Relations; Road Transport; Sociology; Sports; Tourism; Transport Management)

Further Information: Also Institute of Continuing Professional Education

History: Founded 1922 as Moscow Peat Institute, moved to Tver 1958. Acquired present title 1994.

Academic Year: September to June (September-January; February-June)

Admission Requirements: Secondary school certificate (Attestat o srednem obrazovanii)

Main Language(s) of Instruction: Russian

Degrees and Diplomas: *Bakalavr*, *Specialist Diploma*; *Magistr*, *Kandidat Nauk*

Student Services: Academic counselling, Canteen, Cultural centre, Employment services, Foreign Studies Centre, Health services, Sports facilities

Student Residential Facilities: For c. 1,200 students

Special Facilities: Memory Museum

Libraries: Central Library, c. 2m. vols

Press or Publishing House: Publishing House

Last Updated: 20/12/11

TVER STATE UNIVERSITY

Tverskoj Gosudarstvennyj Universitet (TSU)
ul. Željabova 33, Tver, 170100 Tverskaja oblast'
Tel: +7(4822) 342-452
Fax: +7(4822) 321-274
EMail: rector@tversu.ru
Website: http://www.university.tversu.ru

Rector: Andrew Belotserkovsky

International Relations: Yuri Orlov, Vice-Rector for Information Tel: +7(4822) 347-562 EMail: IT@tversu.ru

Departments

Inter-Faculty of Foreign Languages (English; Foreign Languages Education; French; German); **Management and Sociology** (Documentation Techniques; Management; Political Sciences; Public Relations; Regional Studies; Sociology); **Russian as a Foreign Language** (Finnish; Grammar; Russian; Social Studies; Spanish; Translation and Interpretation; Writing)

Faculties

Applied Mathematics and Cybernetics (Applied Mathematics; Computer Engineering; Computer Science; Economics; Information Technology; Mathematics and Computer Science; Software Engineering; Statistics); **Biology** (Anatomy; Applied Chemistry; Applied Physics; Biology; Biomedicine; Botany; Ecology; Physiology; Zoology); **Chemical Technology** (Analytical Chemistry; Biochemistry; Chemical Engineering; Chemistry; Inorganic Chemistry; Organic Chemistry; Pharmacology; Physical Chemistry); **Economics** (Accountancy; Banking; Econometrics; Economic and Finance Policy; Economics; Finance; Marketing; Mathematics and Computer Science; Statistics); **Education** (Education; Educational Psychology; History; Mathematics Education; Music Education; Native Language Education; Natural Sciences; Orthodox Theology; Pedagogy; Preschool Education; Primary Education; Science Education; Teacher Training); **Foreign Languages and International Communication** (Communication Studies; English; French; German; Modern Languages; Philology; Translation and Interpretation); **Geography and Geo-ecology** (Ecology; Geography; Geography (Human); Surveying and Mapping; Tourism); **History** (Archaeology; Archiving; Cultural Studies; History; Museum Studies; Philosophy); **Mathematics** (Applied Mathematics; Computer Science; Logic; Mathematics); **Philology** (Advertising and Publicity; Applied Linguistics; Documentation Techniques; Information Management; Journalism; Linguistics; Literature; Philology; Publishing and Book Trade; Russian); **Physical Education** (Leisure Studies; Physical Education; Sports; Sports Management); **Psychology and Social Work** (Clinical Psychology; Industrial and Organizational Psychology; Psychology; Social Psychology; Social Work)

Schools

Law (Administrative Law; Civil Law; Constitutional Law; Criminal Law; Law; Taxation); **Physics and Techniques** (Applied Physics; Electronic Engineering; Physics; Radiophysics)

Further Information: Branches in Rzhev and Nelidovo. Russian language courses for foreign students. Study Abroad programme

History: Founded 1917 as a private Pedagogical Institute, became Kalinin State University 1971, and acquired present title 1991.

Academic Year: September to June (September-December; January-June)

Admission Requirements: Secondary school certificate (Attestat o srednem obrazovanii)

Main Language(s) of Instruction: Russian

International Co-operation: With universities in Finland, France, Germany, USA, Bulgaria and Germany. Also participates in the Tempus programme.

Accrediting Agencies: Ministry of Education and Science

Degrees and Diplomas: *Bakalavr*: 4 yrs; *Specialist Diploma*: 5 yrs; *Magistr*: 6 yrs. Also postgraduate study programme (3 yrs)

Student Services: Academic counselling, Canteen, Employment services, Foreign student adviser, Health services, Language programs, Social counselling, Sports facilities

Student Residential Facilities: For 1,124 students

Special Facilities: University Museum. Botanical Garden

Libraries: c. 850,000 vols

Last Updated: 19/12/11

TYUMEN STATE ACADEMY OF ARTS, CULTURE AND SOCIAL TECHNOLOGIES

Tjumenskaja Gosudarstvennaja Akademija Iskusstv, Kul'tury I Socialno-Tehnologij

ul. Respubliki 19, Tjumen 625003
Tel: +7(3452) 246-498 +7(3452) 240-715
Fax: +7(3452) 240-715
EMail: tgiik-rektorat@mail.ru
Website: http://www.tsiac.ru/academy

Rector: Igor G. Shishkin Tel: +7(3452) 297-049

Vice-Rector for Academic Affairs: Irina G. Fomichev
Tel: +7(3452) 297-054

Institutes

Architecture, Design and Visual Arts (Architectural and Environmental Design; Architecture; Design; Graphic Design; Multimedia; Textile Design; Visual Arts); **Intellectual and Information Technology** (Information Sciences; Library Science; Media Studies); **Museum of Fine Arts and Technology** (Art History; Fine Arts; Handicrafts; History; Museum Studies; Painting and Drawing); **Music, Theater and Dance** (Conducting; Dance; Music; Music Education; Music Theory and Composition; Musical Instruments; Singing; Theatre); **Socio-Cultural Communications** *(Service Institute)* (Cultural Studies; Economics; Foreign Languages Education; Hotel and Restaurant; Hotel Management; Law; Pedagogy; Physical Education; Tourism)

History: Founded 1956 as Tyumen School of Music. Renamed Tyumen Art College 1998. Acquired present title 2009.

Degrees and Diplomas: *Specialist Diploma*

Last Updated: 04/01/12

TYVA STATE UNIVERSITY

Tyvinskij Gosudarstvennyj Universitet (TYVGU)

ul. Lenina 36, Kyzyl, 667000 Respublika of Tyva
Tel: +7(39422) 21969 +7(39422) 38378
Fax: +7(39422) 21969 +7(39422) 38378
EMail: tgu@tuva.ru
Website: http://www.tuvsu.ru

Rector: Sergei Ondar
Tel: +7(39422) 38452, Fax: +7(39422) 21969

Colleges

Education (Education; Primary Education; Teacher Training)

Faculties

Agriculture (Agriculture; Agronomy; Bioengineering; Biotechnology; Cattle Breeding; Crop Production); **Childhood Education** (Child Care and Development; Education); **Economics** (Accountancy; Economics; Management); **Education** (Education; English; Foreign Languages Education; Literature); **Engineering and Technology** (Automotive Engineering; Civil Engineering; Construction Engineering; Engineering; Road Engineering; Town Planning; Transport Engineering); **Environmental-Geographical Studies** (Anatomy; Biology; Chemistry; Ecology; Environmental Studies; Genetics; Geography; Geography (Human); Microbiology; Physiology; Zoology); **History** (Archaeology; Archiving; History); **Philology** (English; Folklore; Foreign Languages Education; Linguistics; Literature; Philology; Russian); **Physical Education and Sports** (Physical Education; Sports); **Physics and Mathematics** (Mathematics; Physics); **Upgrading and Retraining of Personnels**

Institutes

Pedagogy (Education; Pedagogy)

Schools

Graduate Studies (Agriculture; Animal Husbandry; Cultural Studies; Ecology; Economics; Geology; History; History of Law; Law; Management; Native Language; Physical Education; Russian; Social Psychology; Sports); **Law** (Civil Law; Constitutional Law; Criminal Law; History of Law; Law)

History: Founded 1996 incorporating previously exisiting Institutions.

Academic Year: September to July

Admission Requirements: High school diploma and transcript; Russian passport; health certificate; United states exam

Fees: (Rubles): 31,000

International Co-operation: With universities in China, Germany, Mongolia

Accrediting Agencies: Federal Agency of the Russian Federation for Education

Degrees and Diplomas: *Specialist Diploma*: 5 yrs; *Kandidat Nauk*: 3 yrs

Student Services: Canteen, Foreign student adviser, Health services, Language programs, Sports facilities

Special Facilities: Ecological Museum

Libraries: Yes

Academic Staff *2007-2008*	MEN	WOMEN	**TOTAL**
FULL-TIME	67	241	**308**
STAFF WITH DOCTORATE FULL-TIME	–	–	**232**
Student Numbers *2007-2008*			
All (Foreign Included)	1,191	2,272	**3,463**
FOREIGN ONLY	6	2	**8**

Last Updated: 12/12/11

UDMURT STATE UNIVERSITY

Udmurtskij Gosudarstvennyj Universitet (UDSU)

ul. Universitetskaja 1, Iževsk, 426034 Udmurtskaja Respublika
Tel: +7(3412) 68-1610
Fax: +7(3412) 68-5866
EMail: inter@uni.udm.ru; rector@udsu.ru
Website: http://www.udsu.ru

Faculties

Biology and Chemistry (Analytical Chemistry; Biology; Botany; Chemistry; Ecology; Inorganic Chemistry; Physical Chemistry; Physiology; Zoology); **Foreign Languages for Specific Purposes** (Communication Studies; Cultural Studies; Foreign Languages Education; Grammar; History; Linguistics; Mathematics and Computer Science; Modern Languages; Natural Sciences; Philosophy; Phonetics; Physical Education; Political Sciences; Russian; Sociology; Terminology; Translation and Interpretation); **Geography** (Environmental Management; Geography; Natural Resources; Surveying and Mapping); **History** (History; International Relations; Political Sciences; Regional Studies); **Information Technologies and Computer Engineering** (Computer Engineering; Information Technology; Mathematics and Computer Science; Software Engineering); **Journalism** (Journalism; Media Studies); **Mathematics** (Applied Mathematics; Astronomy and Space Science; Computer Science; Mathematics; Mathematics and Computer Science; Mechanics; Operations Research; Software Engineering); **Medical Biotechnology** (Biochemistry; Biotechnology; Immunology; Molecular Biology); **Philology** (Linguistics; Philology; Russian; Speech Studies); **Physical Education** (Physical Education; Sports); **Physics and Energetics** (Astrophysics; Electronic Engineering; Materials Engineering; Mathematical Physics; Nanotechnology; Nuclear Engineering; Physics; Power Engineering; Radiophysics; Thermal Physics); **Sociology and Philosophy** (Anthropology; Cultural Studies; Educational Sciences; Ethnology; Gender Studies; Philosophy; Political Sciences; Sociology; Urban Studies); **Udmurt philology** (English; Finnish; Foreign Languages Education; German; Hungarian; Literature; Philology; Russian)

Institutes

Art and Design (Art History; Computer Graphics; Design; Fashion Design; Fine Arts; Handicrafts; Industrial Design; Music; Painting and Drawing; Performing Arts; Sculpture); **Civil Protection** (Environmental Management; Welfare and Protective Services); **Economics and Management** (Accountancy; Administration; Banking; Business and Commerce; Econometrics; Finance; Government; International Business; International Economics; Labour and Industrial Relations; Management; Mathematics and Computer Science; Taxation); **Foreign Languages and Literature** (English; German; Phonetics; Romance Languages; Terminology; Translation and Interpretation); **Law, Social Management and Security** (Civil Law; Criminal Law; Criminology; Ecology; Economics; Finance; International Law; Law; Private Law; Social Sciences); **Oil and Gas** (Geology; Industrial Management; Mining Engineering; Petroleum and Gas Engineering; Petrology); **Pedagogy, Psychology and Social Technologies** (Clinical Psychology; Computer Networks; Cultural Studies; Educational Psychology; Engineering; Experimental Psychology; Handicrafts; Household Management; Multimedia; Pedagogy; Psychology; Social and Preventive Medicine; Social Psychology; Social Studies; Speech Therapy and Audiology); **Social Communications** (Advertising and Publicity; Communication Studies; Cultural Studies; History; Political Sciences; Public Relations; Publishing and Book Trade; Service Trades; Social Studies; Tourism)

Further Information: Also courses of Russian as a Foreign Language

History: Founded 1931 as a Pedagogical Institute, acquired present title 1971.

Governing Bodies: Academic Council

Academic Year: September to June

Admission Requirements: Secondary school certificate (Attestat o srednem obrazovanii) and entrance examination

Fees: (Russian Rubles): 4,690-11,724 per annum; foreign students, 5,628-14,070

Main Language(s) of Instruction: Russian

Degrees and Diplomas: *Bakalavr*: 3-4 yrs; *Specialist Diploma*: 5 yrs; *Magistr*: 2 yrs; *Kandidat Nauk*: a further 3 -4 yrs and thesis; *Doktor Nauk*: 2 yrs by thesis following Kandidat Nauk

Student Services: Canteen, Cultural centre, Employment services, Foreign Studies Centre, Health services, Language programs, Sports facilities

Student Residential Facilities: For c. 2,500 students

Special Facilities: Archaeological Museum. Art Gallery. Biological Garden

Libraries: 1,061,121 vols

Last Updated: 12/12/11

UFA STATE ACADEMY OF ARTS NAMED AFTER ZAGIRA ISMAGILOVA

Ufimskaja Gosudarstvennaja Akademija Iskusstv imeni Zagira Ismagilova

ul. Lenina 14, Ufa, 45008 Respublika Bashkortosan
Tel: +7(347) 272-49-83
Fax: +7(347) 272-49-83
EMail: rector@ufaart.ru; asf-amina@yandex.ru
Website: http://ufaart.ru/

Rector: Amina Shafikova

Faculties

Baškir Music (Folklore; Music; Musical Instruments; Musicology); **Fine Arts** (Art History; Design; Display and Stage Design; Fine Arts; Graphic Arts; Painting and Drawing; Sculpture); **Music** *(Conservatory)* (Conducting; Jazz and Popular Music; Music; Music Theory and Composition; Musical Instruments; Musicology; Singing; Sound Engineering (Acoustics)); **Theatre** (Acting; Art History; Dance; Performing Arts; Theatre)

History: Founded 1968 as Ufa State Institute of Arts. Acquired present status and title 2003.

Academic Year: September to July

Admission Requirements: Secondary school certificate (Attestat o srednem obrazovanii)

Main Language(s) of Instruction: Russian, English

Accrediting Agencies: Ministry of Education of Russian Federation

Degrees and Diplomas: *Bakalavr*, *Specialist Diploma*

Student Services: Academic counselling, Canteen, Cultural centre, Health services, Language programs, Social counselling, Sports facilities

Student Residential Facilities: Yes

Special Facilities: Concert Halls. Drama Theatre. Exhibition Hall. Movie Studio. Sound Recording Studio

Last Updated: 06/12/11

UFA STATE AVIATION TECHNICAL UNIVERSITY

Ufimskij Gosudarstvennyj Aviacionnyj Tehničeskij Universitet

ul. Marksa 12, Ufa, 450000 Respublika Bashkortosan
Tel: +7(347) 272-63-07
Fax: +7(347) 272-29-18
EMail: admin@ugatu.ac.ru; office@ugatu.su
Website: http://www.ugatu.ac.ru

Rector: Murat B. Guzairov
Tel: +7(3472) 722-215, Fax: +7(3472) 728-169
EMail: guzairov@rb.ru

Faculties

Aircraft Engines (Aeronautical and Aerospace Engineering; Air Transport); **Aircraft Instrument Making** (Aeronautical and Aerospace Engineering; Electrical and Electronic Equipment and Maintenance; Electrical Engineering; Electronic Engineering; Engineering; Instrument Making); **Aviation Technological Systems** (Aeronautical and Aerospace Engineering; Automation and Control Engineering; Materials Engineering; Mechanical Engineering; Metal Techniques; Metallurgical Engineering; Nanotechnology); **Computer Science and Robotics** (Automation and Control Engineering; Computer Science; Mathematics and Computer Science; Robotics); **Humanities** (Arts and Humanities; Communication Studies; Cultural Studies; History; Linguistics; Philosophy; Psychology); **Protection in Emergency Situations** (Fire Science; Physical Education; Safety Engineering); **Science** (Chemistry; Computer Science; Mathematics; Natural Sciences; Physics)

Institutes

Aviation Technologies (Aeronautical and Aerospace Engineering); **Computer** (Computer Engineering); **Economics and Management** (Business and Commerce; Economics; Finance; Information Technology; Leadership; Management; Marketing; Taxation); **Electrochemical Treatment Theory and Technology** (Electrical and Electronic Engineering; Technology); **Information Communication Technologies** (Communication Studies; Information Technology); **Management, System Analysis, Robotics and Mechatronics** (Management; Robotics; Systems Analysis); **Research into Physical and Technical Material Work, Renovation and Welding**; **Research into Physics of Perspective Materials** (Physics); **Tribotechnology and Lubrication**

History: Founded 1932 as Institute, acquired present status and title 1992.

Governing Bodies: Academic Council

Academic Year: September to June (September-January; February-June)

Admission Requirements: Secondary school certificate (Attestat o srednem obrazovanii)

Main Language(s) of Instruction: Russian

Degrees and Diplomas: *Bakalavr*: 4 yrs; *Specialist Diploma*: 5-5 1/2 yrs; *Magistr*: 6 yrs; *Kandidat Nauk*: a further 3 yrs

Student Residential Facilities: For c. 2,000 students

Special Facilities: History of the University Museum; Aircraft Engines Museum

Libraries: c. 1.06m. Vols

Publications: Aeroengine Tests; Complex Systems Control; Control and Design of Information and Cybernetic Systems; Control Problems in Complex Systems; Control Systems of Power Installations and Energy Conversion Complexes; Economic Systems Control; Machining Optimization of Structural Materials; Strength of Parts in Aviation Systems; Surface: Technological Aspects of Units Strength; Theory and Analysis of Dynamic Processes in Thermal Engines

Press or Publishing House: 'Daurja' Publishing Centre

Last Updated: 06/12/11

UFA STATE PETROLEUM TECHNICAL UNIVERSITY

Ufimskij Gosudarstvennyj Neftjanoj Tehničeskij Universitet

ul. Kosmanavtov 1, Ufa, 450062 Respublika Bashkortosan
Tel: +7(3472) 431-910
Fax: +7(3472) 431-910
EMail: info@rusoil.ru
Website: http://www.ugntu.ru

Rector: Airat Mingazovič Shammazov (1999-)
Tel: +8(3472) 420-370, Fax: +8(3472) 431-419
EMail: info@rusoil.net

Pro-Rector: Ildus Ibragimov EMail: bakhtizin@rusoil.net

International Relations: Ekaterina Kotova
Tel: +8(3472) 431-830, Fax: +8(3472) 431-830
EMail: foredu@rusoil.net

Faculties

Architecture and Civil Engineering (Applied Chemistry; Applied Linguistics; Applied Physics; Architecture; Building Technologies; Civil Engineering; Engineering Drawing and Design; Engineering Management; Industrial Management; Mechanics; Water Management); **Humanities and Social Sciences** (Cultural Studies; Economics; History; Modern Languages; Philology; Philosophy; Physical Education; Polish; Public Law; Russian; Social Sciences); **Industrial Processes Automation** (Computer Engineering; Computer Networks; Electrical Engineering); **Mechanical Engineering** (Fire Science; Mechanical Engineering; Mechanics; Safety Engineering); **Oil Mining** (Geology; Geophysics; Mining Engineering; Petroleum and Gas Engineering; Physics); **Pipeline Transportation** (Petroleum and Gas Engineering); **Technology** (Analytical Chemistry; Biochemistry; Chemical Engineering; Chemistry; Ecology; Organic Chemistry; Petroleum and Gas Engineering; Physical Chemistry; Safety Engineering; Technology)

Institutes

Economics (Accountancy; Banking; Economics; Engineering Management; Finance; Industrial Management; Management; Taxation)

Further Information: Branches also in Oktjabrskij, Salavat, and Sterlitamak.

History: Founded 1948 as Ufa Petroleum Institute, acquired present status and title 1993.

Governing Bodies: University Senate

Academic Year: September to June (September-January; February-June)

Admission Requirements: Secondary school certificate (Attestat o srednem obrazovanii)

Fees: (US Dollars): 1,000-3,000 per annum

Main Language(s) of Instruction: Russian

Accrediting Agencies: Russian Ministry of Education and Science

Degrees and Diplomas: *Bakalavr*: Science, 4 yrs; *Specialist Diploma*: Engineering in Architecture, 6 yrs; *Specialist Diploma*: Engineering; Technology, 5 yrs; *Magistr*: Science, 6 yrs; *Kandidat Nauk*: 3 yrs; *Doktor Nauk*: 2-3 yrs

Student Services: Academic counselling, Canteen, Cultural centre, Foreign student adviser, Foreign Studies Centre, Health services, Language programs, Nursery care, Social counselling, Sports facilities

Student Residential Facilities: For c. 3,032 students

Special Facilities: Geological Museum; Historical Museum

Libraries: Total: 1,062,462; Scientific Library: 475,967; Training Library: 562,789; Fiction: 29,706

Press or Publishing House: Editorial and Publishing Office

Last Updated: 11/04/11

UHTA STATE TECHNICAL UNIVERSITY

Uhtinskij Gosudarstvennyj Tehničeskij Universitet

ul. Pervomajskaja 13, Uhta, 169400 Respublika Komi
Tel: +7(82147) 339-36 +7(82147) 336-70
Fax: +7(82147) 337-82
EMail: info@ugtu.net
Website: http://www.ugtu.net

Rector: Nikolai D. Tshadaya (1980-) EMail: rector@ugtu.net

Vice-Rector, Economic Affairs: Arkady Emeksuzyan
EMail: aemeksuzyan@ugtu.net

First Vice-Rector: Yaroslav Tsunevsky
Tel: +7(82147) 336-70 EMail: yatsunevskiy@ugtu.net

Departments

Architectural and Civil Engineering (Architecture; Building Technologies; Civil Engineering; Hydraulic Engineering; Structural Architecture; Thermal Engineering); **Oil and Gas** (Analytical Chemistry; Chemistry; Geology; Geophysics; Hydraulic Engineering; Organic Chemistry; Petroleum and Gas Engineering)

Faculties

Economics and Management (Banking; Economics; Finance; Management); **Forestry** (Agricultural Equipment; Engineering; Forest Products; Forestry; Mechanics; Wood Technology); **Geological Prospecting** (Geochemistry; Geological Engineering; Geology; Geophysics; Mineralogy; Petroleum and Gas Engineering); **Humanities** (Arts and Humanities; Cultural Studies; History; Law; Modern Languages; Philosophy; Political Sciences; Public Relations; Sociology); **Information Technology** (Applied Mathematics; Automation and Control Engineering; Chemistry; Electrical Engineering; Information Technology; Mathematics and Computer Science; Physics)

Institutes

Advanced Studies *(Extra-mural)* (Accountancy; Finance; Human Resources; Management; Mining Engineering; Petroleum and Gas Engineering; Safety Engineering; Tourism); **Oil and Gas Research and Design** (Petroleum and Gas Engineering); **Physical Education and Sports** (Physical Education; Sports)

Further Information: Branches in Vorkuta and Usinsk.

History: Founded 1967 on the basis of the Evening Faculty of Moscow Institute of Petrochemical and Gas Industry. Acquired present status 1999.

Governing Bodies: Academic Council; Federal Education Agency

Academic Year: September to June

Admission Requirements: Secondary school certificate (Attestat o srednem obrazovanii)

Fees: (Russian Rubles): 20,000-50,000 per annum

Main Language(s) of Instruction: Russian

Degrees and Diplomas: *Bakalavr*: 4 yrs; *Specialist Diploma*: 5 yrs; *Magistr*: 6 yrs; *Kandidat Nauk*

Student Services: Canteen, Cultural centre, Employment services, Health services, Language programs, Social counselling, Sports facilities

Special Facilities: History of the Institute Museum; Geological Museum; TV Studio; Sanatorium

Libraries: c. 275,000 vols

Press or Publishing House: University Publishing House

Student Numbers *2008-2009*: Total: c. 7,000
Last Updated: 06/12/11

ULJANOVSK HIGHER SCHOOL OF CIVIL AVIATION (INSTITUTE)

Ul'janovskoje Vyssee Aviacionnoe Učilišče Graždanskoj Aviacii (Institut)
ul. Možajskogo 8/8, Uljanovsk 432071
Tel: +7(8422) 39-80-33 +7(8422) 39-81-23
Fax: +7(8422) 44-54-45
EMail: uvau@list.ru
Website: http://www.uvauga.ru/

Rector: Sergei Ivanovich Krasnov

Faculties

Air Traffic Control (Air and Space Law; Air Transport; Transport Management); **Air Transport Personnel Training** (Air Transport; Transport Management)

History: Founded 1935 as School, acquired present status and title 2004.

Governing Bodies: Academic Board

Academic Year: September to July (September-January; February-July)

Admission Requirements: Secondary school certificate (Attestat o srednem obrazovanii) or equivalent

Main Language(s) of Instruction: Russian

Degrees and Diplomas: *Bakalavr*, *Specialist Diploma*

Student Services: Academic counselling, Canteen, Cultural centre, Employment services, Foreign Studies Centre, Health services, Social counselling, Sports facilities

Student Residential Facilities: Yes

Special Facilities: Civil Aviation Museum

Libraries: c. 144,000 vols
Last Updated: 09/03/12

ULJANOVSK STATE ACADEMY OF AGRICULTURE

Ul'janovskaja Gosudarstvennaja Sel'skohozjajstvennaja Akademija
bul. Novij Venec 1, Uljanovsk 432063
Tel: +7(8422) 314-272
Fax: +7(8422) 443-072
EMail: ugsha@yandex.ru
Website: http://www.ugsha.ru/

Rector: Alexander Dozorova

First Vice-Rector: Vitaly Isaichev EMail: isaichev@ugsha.ru

Chairs

Humanities (Arts and Humanities; Cultural Studies; Economics; Education; History of Law; Modern Languages; Pedagogy; Philosophy; Physical Education; Psychology; Sociology)

Colleges

Agricultural Technology and Business (Accountancy; Agricultural Business; Agricultural Economics; Agricultural Engineering; Agriculture; Agronomy; Crop Production; Economics; Environmental Management; Meat and Poultry; Natural Resources; Surveying and Mapping; Veterinary Science)

Departments

Agronomy (Agricultural Management; Agriculture; Agronomy; Biology; Botany; Chemistry; Crop Production; Soil Science; Surveying and Mapping; Technology); **Biotechnology** (Agricultural Engineering; Animal Husbandry; Aquaculture; Biotechnology; Cattle Breeding; Water Science); **Continuing Education** (Agricultural Business; Agricultural Engineering; Agriculture)

Faculties

Economics (Accountancy; Agricultural Business; Banking; Computer Science; Economics; Finance; Management; Statistics); **Engineering** (Agricultural Engineering; Agricultural Equipment; Animal Husbandry; Energy Engineering; Engineering; Materials Engineering; Mathematics; Mechanical Engineering; Physics; Safety Engineering); **Veterinary Medicine** (Anatomy; Ecology; Microbiology; Parasitology; Pharmacology; Physiology; Veterinary Science; Virology; Zoology)

History: Founded 1943.

Degrees and Diplomas: *Bakalavr*, *Specialist Diploma*; *Magistr*, *Kandidat Nauk*
Last Updated: 06/12/11

ULJANOVSK STATE PEDAGOGICAL UNIVERSITY

Ul'janovskij Gosudarstvennyj Pedagogičeskij Universitet
pl. 100-Letija so dnja roždenija V. I. Lenina 4, Uljanovsk 432700
Tel: +7(8422) 312-527
Fax: +7(8422) 312-474
Website: http://ulspu.ru/

Vice-Rector, Administration: Victor G. Bezborodov

Faculties

Education (Education; Educational Psychology; Pedagogy; Primary Education); **Foreign Languages** (English; Foreign Languages Education; French; German; Germanic Studies; Linguistics; Pedagogy); **Geography and Natural Sciences** (Biology; Botany; Chemistry; Ecology; Education; Entomology; Geography; Physiology; Science Education; Zoology); **History** (History; Museum Studies; Social Sciences); **Law** (Civil Law; Criminal Law; Law; Public Law); **Pedagogy, Psychology and Management** (Educational Psychology; Pedagogy; Preschool Education; Psychology); **Philology** (Literature; Russian); **Physical Education and Sports** (Physical Education; Sports); **Physics and Mathematics** (Computer Science; Mathematics; Mathematics Education; Physics); **Technology and Enterprise** (Engineering; Technology; Technology Education)

History: Created 1932.

Degrees and Diplomas: *Bakalavr*, *Specialist Diploma*; *Magistr*, *Kandidat Nauk*
Last Updated: 06/12/11

ULJANOVSK STATE TECHNICAL UNIVERSITY

Ul'janovskij Gosudarstvennyj Tehničeskij Universitet
ul. Severnyj Venec 32, Uljanovsk 432027
Tel: +7(8422) 430-643
Fax: +7(8422) 430-237
EMail: rector@ulstu.ru
Website: http://www.ulstu.ru

Rector: Alexandr D. Gorbokonenko (2000-)

Centres

International Collaboration in Higher Education (Higher Education); **New Information Technology**; **Scientific Research** (Natural Sciences)

Faculties

Civil Engineering (Civil Engineering; Construction Engineering); **Economics and Mathematics** (Applied Mathematics; Chemistry; Natural Sciences; Physics); **Humanities** (Arts and Humanities; Cultural Studies; Foreign Languages Education; History; Management; Modern Languages; Philosophy; Physical Education; Political Sciences; Russian; Sociology); **Information Systems and Technology** (Computer Engineering; Computer Networks; Information Technology); **Machine Building** (Machine Building; Mechanical Engineering; Road Transport); **Power Engineering** (Electrical Engineering; Power Engineering; Thermal Engineering); **Radio Engineering** (Telecommunications Engineering)

Institutes

Aircraft Technology and Management (Aeronautical and Aerospace Engineering; Management)

Schools

Business (Business and Commerce)

Further Information: Also branch in Dimitrovgrad.

History: Founded 1957 as Evening Polytechnic Institute, acquired present status and title 1994.

Academic Year: September to July (September-December; February-July)

Admission Requirements: Secondary school certificate (Attestat o srednem obrazovanii) or equivalent

Fees: (US Dollars): Foreign students: 1,200-1,500 per annum

Main Language(s) of Instruction: Russian

Degrees and Diplomas: *Bakalavr*; *Specialist Diploma*; *Magistr*; *Kandidat Nauk*: Science; *Doktor Nauk*: Science

Student Services: Canteen, Cultural centre, Foreign student adviser, Foreign Studies Centre, Health services, Sports facilities

Student Residential Facilities: Yes

Special Facilities: Museum of the University History. Student Theatre. Cultural Centre Concert Hall

Libraries: 1,230,000 vols

Publications: Proceedings of Scientific Conferences *(annually)*; Vestnik Uliyanovskogo Gosudarstvennogo Tehničeskogo Universiteta *(quarterly)*

Press or Publishing House: University Printing House

Last Updated: 11/04/11

ULJANOVSK STATE UNIVERSITY

Ul'janovskij Gosudarstvennyj Universitet (UIGU(USU))

ul. Tolstogo 42, Uljanovsk 432970
Tel: +7(8422) 412-088
Fax: +7(8422) 412-340
EMail: contact@ulsu.ru
Website: http://www.ulsu.ru

Rector: Boris Kostishko

President: Jurij Polyanskov (1988-) EMail: rector@ulsu.ru

First Vice-Rector: Nectarios T. Gurin
Tel: +7(8422) 412-091, Fax: +7(8422) 412-818

Colleges

Automotive (Accountancy; Automotive Engineering; Computer Networks; Economics; Industrial Engineering; Mechanical Engineering; Metal Techniques; Road Transport; Safety Engineering); **Medicine** (Dental Technology; Dentistry; Medicine; Midwifery; Nursing; Physical Education; Social and Preventive Medicine); **Music** (Conducting; Music; Music Theory and Composition; Musical Instruments; Performing Arts; Singing)

Departments

Ecology (Biology; Chemistry; Ecology; Forestry); **Engineering Physics - High Technology** (Materials Engineering; Physics; Radiophysics); **Foreign Languages and Professional Communication** (English; English Studies; Foreign Languages Education; French; Geography (Human); German; History; International Relations; Linguistics; Russian; Social Sciences; Tourism; Translation and Interpretation); **Linguistics and International Collaboration** (Communication Studies; Foreign Languages Education; International Relations; Linguistics; Translation and Interpretation); **Mathematics and Information Technology** (Aeronautical and Aerospace Engineering; Applied Mathematics; Automation and Control Engineering; Information Technology; Mathematics; Mathematics and Computer Science; Mechanics; Operations Research; Software Engineering; Telecommunications Engineering); **Physical Training and Rehabilitation** (Physical Education; Rehabilitation and Therapy)

Faculties

Culture and Arts (Advertising and Publicity; Archiving; Conducting; Cultural Studies; Design; Documentation Techniques; Fine Arts; Folklore; Graphic Arts; Interior Design; Library Science; Linguistics; Music; Musical Instruments; Performing Arts; Philology; Public Relations); **Finance and Accounting** (Accountancy; Business Computing; Economics; Finance); **Humanities** *(Zavolzhskiy Economics Faculty of Humanities)* (Accountancy; Banking; Economics; Law; Management; Social Welfare); **Humanities and Social Technologies** (Arts and Humanities; Philosophy; Political Sciences; Psychology; Social Work; Sociology; Tourism); **Management** (Human Resources; Management); **Medicine** (Anaesthesiology; Anatomy; Clinical Psychology; Dentistry; Dermatology; Gynaecology and Obstetrics; Medicine; Neurology; Occupational Health; Oncology; Orthopaedics; Paediatrics; Pathology; Physical Therapy; Physiology; Psychiatry and Mental Health; Public Health; Radiology; Rehabilitation and Therapy; Surgery; Urology; Venereology); **Postgraduate Medical and Pharmaceutical Education** (Community Health; Health Education; Nursing; Pharmacy); **Russian-American** (Comparative Politics; Cultural Studies; Economics; International Business; Management; Social Studies)

Institutes

Economics and Business (Accountancy; Banking; Business and Commerce; Business Computing; Economics; Finance; Human Resources; International Economics; Management); **International Relations** (Advertising and Publicity; Applied Mathematics; Computer Science; Economics; Foreign Languages Education; International Relations; Linguistics; Management; Tourism); **Medicine, Environmental and Physical Education** (Biological and Life Sciences; Biology; Chemistry; Ecology; Environmental Management; Forest Economics; Forestry; Health Sciences; Medicine; Natural Resources; Nursing; Paediatrics; Pharmacy; Physical Education); **Open Education** *(Also Modern open college (FALCON))* (Accountancy; Banking; Economics; Insurance; Law; Management; Social Welfare; Software Engineering)

Schools

Business (Business Computing; Economics; Human Resources; Management); **Law** (Law; Taxation); **Russian-German** (Applied Mathematics; German; Germanic Studies; Management; Mathematics and Computer Science; Physics)

Further Information: Also branch in Dimitrovgrad

History: Founded 1988. Acquired present status 1995.

Governing Bodies: Academic Council

Academic Year: September to July

Admission Requirements: Secondary School Certificate (Attestat o srednem obrazovanii)

Main Language(s) of Instruction: Russian

International Co-operation: With universities in the USA, Germany, Korea, United Kingdom, Finland, Italy

Accrediting Agencies: Ministry of Education

Degrees and Diplomas: *Bakalavr*: 3-4 yrs; *Specialist Diploma*; *Magistr*: a further 2 yrs

Student Services: Academic counselling, Canteen, Cultural centre, Employment services, Foreign student adviser, Foreign Studies Centre, Health services, Language programs, Nursery care, Social counselling

Student Residential Facilities: None

Special Facilities: Museum. Movie studio. Archeological Virtual Museum

Libraries: Yes

Publications: Vestnik

Last Updated: 06/12/11

URAL ACADEMY OF PUBLIC ADMINISTRATION

Uralskaja Akademija Gosudarstvennoj Služby

ul. 8-th Marta 66, Ekaterinburg, 620219 Sverdlovskaja oblast'
Tel: +7(343) 257-2040
Fax: +7(343) 257-4427
EMail: vladimir.lockutov@uapa.ru
Website: http://www.uapa.ru

Rector: Vladimir Loskutov
Tel: +7(343) 257-2040 EMail: vladimir.loskutov@uapa.ru

Vice-Rector: Vjačeslav Skorobogatsky
Tel: +7(343) 257-1602 EMail: vyacheslav.skorobogatsky@uapa.ru

Departments

Accounting, Auditing and Analysis (Accountancy; Economics; Finance; Insurance; International Economics; Statistics; Taxation); **Computer Science and Mathematics** (Applied Mathematics; Econometrics; Information Technology; Mathematics and Computer Science; Statistics); **Criminal Law** (Criminal Law; Criminology); **Economic Theory** (Economics); **Economics and Management** (Banking; Economics; Finance; Management; Social Policy; Taxation); **Foreign Languages** (English; French; German; Latin); **Graduate Studies** (Administrative Law; Applied Mathematics; Civil Law; Commercial Law; Constitutional Law; Criminal Law; Criminology; Economics; History of Law; International Law; Labour Law; Law; Management; Philosophy; Political Sciences; Private Law; Public Administration); **Personnel Management** (Human Resources; Industrial and Organizational Psychology; Management); **Philosophy and Political Sciences** (Cultural Studies; History; Logic; Philosophy; Political Sciences; Sociology); **Physical Education** (Physical Education; Sports); **Private Law** (Accountancy; Economics; Management; Private Law; Taxation); **Public Administration** (Government; Human Resources; Political Sciences; Public Administration; Public Relations; Social Policy); **Social Security** (Labour Law; Social Welfare); **State Law** (Administrative Law; Constitutional Law; Finance; International Law; Law; Taxation); **Theory and Practice of Management** (Accountancy; Cultural Studies; Ethics; Industrial and Organizational Psychology; Law; Management; Marketing; Psychology; Public Relations; Taxation)

History: Founded 1991, acquired present title and status 1994.

Admission Requirements: School certificat (Attestat Zrelosty)

Main Language(s) of Instruction: Russian

Accrediting Agencies: Ministry of General and Professional Education of the Russian Federation

Degrees and Diplomas: *Specialist Diploma*: 5-6 yrs; *Magistr*

Student Services: Academic counselling, Canteen, Cultural centre, Health services, Language programs, Sports facilities

Special Facilities: Art Gallery. Movie Studio. Internet

Libraries: Main Library, c. 240,000 vols; c. 250,000 periodicals

Publications: Chinovnik, Magazine dealing with public administration and law. Contains articles by professors of UrAPA, civil servants and foreign specialists *(quarterly)*

Last Updated: 07/12/11

URAL FEDERAL UNIVERSITY NAMED AFTER THE FIRST PRESIDENT OF RUSSIA B.N. YELTSIN

Uralskij Federalnyj Universitet im. Pervogo Presidenta Rossii B.N. Yeltsina

ul. Mira 19, Ekaterinburg, 620002 Sverdlovskaja oblast'
Tel: +7(343) 375-93-40 +7(343) 374-03-62
Fax: +7(343) 374-38-84
EMail: info@ustu.ru; international_office@ustu.ru
Website: http://www.ustu.ru

Rector: Viktor Anatolevich Koksharov
Tel: +7(343) 374-0362 +7(343) 45-03,
Fax: +7(343) 374-0362 +7(343) 45-03 EMail: rectorat@ustu.ru

International Relations: Maxim Khomyakov, Vice-Rector for International Relations
Tel: +7(343) 374-54-34
EMail: international_office@ustu.ru; maxim.khomyakov@usu.ru

Graduate Schools

Economics and Management (Business and Commerce; Economics; Information Technology; Management)

Institutes

Chemical and Technology (Chemical Engineering; Chemistry; Organic Chemistry; Physical Chemistry); **Civil Engineering** (Architecture; Civil Engineering; Construction Engineering; Heating and Refrigeration; Water Management); **Educational Information Technology** *(Distance Learning)* (Business and Commerce; Computer Science; Economics; Electronic Engineering; Human Resources; Information Technology; Management; Metallurgical Engineering); **Fundamental Education**; **Further Education and Vocational Training**; **Humanities and Art** (Archiving; Art History; Cultural Studies; Fine Arts; Folklore; German; History; Journalism; Library Science; Literature; Museum Studies; Philology; Romance Languages; Russian; Tourism); **Materials Science and Metallurgy** (Materials Engineering; Metallurgical Engineering); **Mathematics and Computer Science** (Computer Science; Mathematics; Software Engineering); **Mechanics and Machine Building** (Automotive Engineering; Information Technology; Machine Building; Mechanical Engineering; Mechanical Equipment and Maintenance); **Military Technical Education and Security**; **Natural Sciences** (Astronomy and Space Science; Biology; Chemistry; Ecology; Environmental Studies; Information Technology; Physics; Radiophysics); **Physical Education, Sport and Youth Policy** (Physical Education; Sports Management); **Physics and Technology** (Applied Mathematics; Applied Physics; Information Technology; Physical Engineering; Physics; Radiophysics); **Power Engineering** *(Ural)* (Applied Mathematics; Energy Engineering; Nuclear Engineering; Thermal Engineering); **Public Administration and Entrepreneurship** (Advertising and Publicity; Business Computing; Management; Small Business); **Radioelectronics and Information Technology** (Computer Engineering; Information Management; Information Technology; Microwaves; Telecommunications Engineering; Telecommunications Services); **Social and Political Sciences** (International Relations; Philosophy; Political Sciences; Psychology; Sociology)

Further Information: Branches also in: Nižnyj Tagil, Kamensk-Uralskij, Alapaevsk, Verkhnjaja Salda, Irbit, Krasnoturinsk, Krasnouralsk, Nevjansk, Pervouralsk, Serov, Sredenuralsk, and Čusovoj.

History: Founded 1920 as Ural State Technical University (Uralskij Gosudarstvennyj Tehničeskij Universitet). Acquired current title and status 2011 after merger with Uralskij Gosudarstvennyj Universitet im. A.M. Gorkogo (Ural State University named after A.M. Gorky).

Governing Bodies: Rectorate; Senate

Academic Year: September - December; January - June

Admission Requirements: Undergraduate, Secondary school certificate (Attestat o srednem obrazovanii); Postgraduate, undergraduate degree; knowledge of Russian.

Fees: (Russian Rubles): Undergraduate, 87,500 to 150,000 per annum; Postgraduate, 110,000 per annum.

Main Language(s) of Instruction: Russian

International Co-operation: Participates in Tempus, Erasmus, FP7, Network Collaboration of the Arctic, CIS University Network, University Network of Shanghai; also with institutions in France, Germany, Mongolia, China, South Korea

Degrees and Diplomas: *Bakalavr*: 4 yrs; *Specialist Diploma*: 5 yrs; *Magistr*: a further 2 yrs; *Kandidat Nauk*: Physical and Mathematical Sciences; Chemical Sciences; Biological Sciences; Technical Sciences; History; Economics; Philosophy; Language and Literature; Pedagogy; Arts; Psychology; Social Sciences; Political Sciences; Cultural Studies; Earth Sciences, a further 3 yrs following Magistr; *Doktor Nauk*: Physical and Mathematical Sciences; Chemical Sciences; Biological Sciences; Technical Sciences; HistoryEconomics; Philosophy; Language and Literature; Pedagogy; Arts; Psychology; Social Sciences; Political Sciences; Cultural Studies; Earth Sciences

Student Services: Academic counselling, Canteen, Cultural centre, Employment services, Foreign student adviser, Foreign Studies Centre, Health services, Language programs, Social counselling, Sports facilities

Special Facilities: Kourovka Observatory; B.U.Kashkin Museum of Modern Art; Archaeology Museum; Manufacturing Facility (including power station and Center of High Technologies in Machine Building); Biological Station; Botanical Gardens; Depository of Antiquities (one of the world's largest collections of Russian black-letter books and manuscripts dating from the 15th centuriy); University Museum; TV StudioSport Facilities (including several gyms, swimming pool and football stadium)

Libraries: c. 3m. vols; electronic databases; electronic archive; rare books collection from 17th and 19th century. Also serves for all other institutions in the Ural region.

Publications: Analitika i Kontrol (Analitics and Control), Peer-reviewed journal dedicated to analytical chemistry and control. *(quarterly)*; Izvestia. Ural Federal University Journal, Peer-reviewed university research journal, and includes four series: 'Problesm of Education, Science and Culture', 'Humanities', 'Social Sciences', 'Mathematics'. *(quarterly)*; Universitetskoe Upravlenie: praktika i analiz (University Management: Practice and Analysis), Specialized research periodical, dedicated to the university management and administration *(monthly)*; Vestnik Uralskogo Federalnogo Universiteta. Serya Ekonomika i Upravlenie (Bulletin of Ural Federal University. Economics and Management), Peer-reviewed journal dedicated to management and economic issues. *(quarterly)*; Voprosy Onomastiki (Questions of Onomastics), Peer-reviewed journal covering problems of theoretical, regional, and applied onomastics and terminology. *(annually)*

Press or Publishing House: Za industrialnie Kadry – Uralskiy Universitet

Academic Staff *2011-2012*	**TOTAL**
FULL-TIME	**3,005**
PART-TIME	**1,669**
STAFF WITH DOCTORATE	
FULL-TIME	**1,881**
PART-TIME	**925**
Student Numbers *2011-2012*	
All (Foreign Included)	**44,323**
FOREIGN ONLY	**1,007**

Part-time students, 19,361.
Last Updated: 14/05/12

URAL LAW INSTITUTE OF THE RUSSIAN FEDERATION MINISTRY OF INTERNAL AFFAIRS

Uralskij Juridiceskij Institut MVD Rossijskoj Federatsii
ul. Korepina 66, Ekaterinburg, 620057 Sverdlovskaja oblast'
Tel: +7(343) 331-70-80 +7(343) 379-09-30
Fax: +7(343) 331-70-84
EMail: evsh@ural-mvd.ru
Website: http://www.ural-mvd.ru/

Rector: Aleksandr Ivanovich Guk

Programmes
Law (Civil Security; Criminology; Law)

History: Created 1991.

Degrees and Diplomas: *Specialist Diploma*

Last Updated: 09/03/12

URAL STATE ACADEMY OF ARCHITECTURE AND ARTS

Uralskaja Gosudarstvennaja Arhitekturno-Hudožestvennaja Akademija
ul. Karl Liebknecht 23, Ekaterinburg, 620075 Sverdlovskaja oblast'
Tel: +7(343) 371-33-69
Fax: +7(343) 371-5732
EMail: webmaster@usaaa.ru
Website: http://www.usaaa.ru

Rector: Sergei Postnikov EMail: postnikov@usaaa.ru

Vice-Rector for Administration: Pavel A. Pozdnyakov
Tel: +7(343) 371-6541 EMail: ahr@usaaa.ru

Departments
Education (Architecture; Art Education; Education; Graphic Design); **Graduate Studies** (Architectural and Environmental Design; Industrial Design; Textile Design)

Faculties
Architecture (Architectural and Environmental Design; Architectural Restoration; Architecture; Regional Planning; Town Planning); **Continuing Professional Education** (Advertising and Publicity; Architectural and Environmental Design; Design; Fashion Design; Interior Design; Textile Design); **Preparatory** (Architecture; Art Education; Fine Arts)

Institutes
Fine Arts (Computer Graphics; Fine Arts; Handicrafts; Interior Design; Painting and Drawing; Sculpture); **Urban Studies** (Architecture; Communication Studies; Computer Science; Economics; Environmental Engineering; Social Studies; Town Planning)

Schools
Design (Architectural and Environmental Design; Design; Graphic Design; Industrial Design; Textile Design)

History: Founded 1972, acquired present status and title 1996.

Governing Bodies: Academic Council

Academic Year: September to July (September-December; January-July)

Admission Requirements: Secondary school certificate (Attestat o srednem obrazovanii)

Main Language(s) of Instruction: Russian

Degrees and Diplomas: *Bakalavr*: 4 yrs; *Specialist Diploma*: 6 yrs; *Magistr*: 6 yrs

Student Residential Facilities: Yes

Special Facilities: Museum of History of Architecture and Technology in the Urals

Libraries: 100,000 vols

Publications: Architecton *(quarterly)*

Press or Publishing House: 'Architecton' Publishing House

Last Updated: 02/12/11

URAL STATE ACADEMY OF LAW

Uralskaja Gosudarstvennaja Juridičeskaja Akademija
ul. Komsomol'skaja 21, Ekaterinburg, 62066 Sverdlovskaja oblast'
Tel: +7(343) 374-43-63
Fax: +7(343) 374-50-34
EMail: rektorat@usla.ru
Website: http://www.usla.ru

Rector: Vladimir Bagel

Vice-Rector for Administration: Vladimir Gribanov
EMail: rektorat.ahr@usla.ru

Departments
Administrative Law (Administrative Law; Law); **Business Law** (Commercial Law); **Civil Law** (Civil Law); **Civil Procedure** (Civil Law); **Constitutional Law** (Constitutional Law); **Constitutional Law of Foreign Countries and International Law** (Constitutional Law; International Law); **Criminal Law** (Criminal Law); **Criminal Procedure** (Criminal Law); **Ecological and Land Law** (Ecology; Law); **Economic Theory** (Economic and Finance Policy); **Employment and Labour Law and Social Security** (Labour Law; Social Welfare); **Financial Law** (Economic and Finance Policy; Finance; Law); **Foreign Languages** (English; Foreign Languages Education; German); **History of State and Law** (History of Law; History of Societies; Political Sciences); **Legal Information Technology** (Information Technology; Law); **Legal Psychology and Forensic Examination** (Criminology; Psychology); **Municipal and International Law** (International Law; Public Law); **Philosophy and Sociology** (Philosophy; Sociology); **Prosecution** (Law; Public Law); **Social Law, State and Municipal Service** (Social and Community Services; Social Sciences; Social Studies); **Theory and Practice of Management** (Management); **Theory of State and Law** (Government; Law)

Further Information: Also department of postgraduate studies

History: Founded 1931 as Sverdlovsk Institute of Law, acquired present status and title 1992.

Governing Bodies: Academic Board

Academic Year: September to June (September-January; February-June)

Admission Requirements: Secondary school certificate (Attestat o srednem obrazovanii)

Main Language(s) of Instruction: Russian

Degrees and Diplomas: *Specialist Diploma*: 5 yrs; *Kandidat Nauk*: Law, a further 3 yrs; *Doktor Nauk*: Law, 3 yrs

Student Services: Academic counselling, Canteen, Cultural centre, Employment services, Health services, Sports facilities

Libraries: c. 800,000 vols

Publications: Russian Law Journal

Press or Publishing House: USA Law Press

Last Updated: 01/12/11

URAL STATE ACADEMY OF PHYSICAL EDUCATION

Uralskaja Gosudarstvennaja Akademija Fizičeskoj Kul'tury (URALGAFK)
ul. Ordžonikidze 1, Čeljabinsk 454111
Tel: +7(351) 237-0565
Fax: +7(351) 237-0576
Website: http://www.uralgufk.ru/

Rector: Leonid Kulikov

Colleges
Physical Education (Physical Education; Sports)

Departments
Anatomy (Anatomy); **Biochemistry** (Biochemistry); **Distance Learning** (Sports); **Gymnastics and Recreational Swimming**

(Sports); **Mathematics, Physics and Information Technology** (Information Technology; Mathematics; Physics); **Pedagogy** (Pedagogy); **Physiology** (Physiology); **Theory of Physical Education and Biomechanics** (Physical Education)

Faculties
Economics, Law and Humanities (Arts and Humanities; Economics; Law); **Health Technology and Sports Medicine** (Medical Technology; Sports Medicine); **Summer Sports** (Sports); **Winter Sports** (Sports)

Institutes
Economics (Economics); **Tourism and Socio-Cultural Services** (Cultural Studies; Social Studies; Tourism)

Degrees and Diplomas: *Bakalavr*; *Specialist Diploma*; *Magistr*; *Kandidat Nauk*
Last Updated: 02/12/11

URAL STATE ACADEMY OF VETERINARY MEDICINE

Uralskaja Gosudarstvennaja Akademija Veterinarnoj Mediciny
ul. Gagarina 13, Troitsk, 457100 Čeliabinsk region
Tel: +7(35163) 200-10
Fax: +7(35163) 204-72
EMail: tvi_t@mail.ru; tvi@chel.surnet.ru
Website: http://www.usavm.ac.ru/

Rector: Victor G. Litovchenko

First Vice-Rector: Aleksandr Ivanovich Kuznecov
Tel: +8(35163) 204-72

Colleges
Agriculture *(Trinity College of Agriculture)* (Agricultural Economics; Agricultural Engineering; Agricultural Equipment; Agriculture; Agronomy; Biotechnology; Economics)

Departments
Commodity Studies (Agricultural Business; Agricultural Economics; Chemistry; Crafts and Trades; Food Science; Food Technology; Inorganic Chemistry; Laboratory Techniques; Organic Chemistry; Store Management); **Postgraduate Studies** (Animal Husbandry; Ecology; Pedagogy; Pharmacy; Physiology; Veterinary Science; Zoology)

Faculties
Biotechnology (Agricultural Engineering; Animal Husbandry; Biological and Life Sciences; Biology; Biophysics; Botany; Chemistry; Ecology; Genetics; History; Mathematics and Computer Science; Pedagogy; Philosophy; Physical Education; Physics; Sports); **Veterinary Medicine** (Anatomy; Histology; Microbiology; Modern Languages; Parasitology; Pharmacology; Physiology; Surgery; Veterinary Science; Virology; Zoology)

Schools
Graduate (Animal Husbandry; Ecology; Physiology; Veterinary Science; Zoology)

Further Information: Also specialized councils

History: Founded 1930, acquired present title 1999. Integrated Trinity College of Agriculture 2004.

Governing Bodies: Scientific Council

Academic Year: September to June (September-January; February-June)

Admission Requirements: High School Education Diploma (diplom ob polnom sredenem obrazovanii); Secondary Special Diploma (diplom o sredmem specialnom obrazovanii)

Fees: Variable

Main Language(s) of Instruction: Russian

Accrediting Agencies: Department of Education of Ministry of Agriculture and Forestry

Degrees and Diplomas: *Specialist Diploma*: Biological Ecology; Animal Husbandry; Science Commodities; Agricultural Production; Veterinary Surgery, 5 yrs

Student Services: Academic counselling, Canteen, Cultural centre, Employment services, Foreign student adviser, Health services, Language programs, Social counselling, Sports facilities

Student Residential Facilities: 7 student Hostels

Special Facilities: History Museum; Anatomy Museum; Biology and Ecology Museum; Pathological Physiology Museum

Libraries: 420,150 vols

Academic Staff *2007-2008*	MEN	WOMEN	**TOTAL**
FULL-TIME	153	76	**229**
PART-TIME	2	11	**13**
STAFF WITH DOCTORATE			
FULL-TIME	84	58	**142**
PART-TIME	2	11	**13**
Student Numbers *2007-2008*			
All (Foreign Included)	1,175	778	**1,953**
FOREIGN ONLY	28	18	**46**

Distance students, 1,624.
Last Updated: 02/12/11

URAL STATE AGRICULTURAL ACADEMY

Uralskaja Gosudarstvennaja Sel'skohozjajstvennaja Akademija
ul. Karla Liebknecht 42, Ekaterinburg, 620075 Sverdlovskaja oblast'
Tel: +7(3432) 513-336
Fax: +7(3432) 512-480
EMail: academy@usaca.ru
Website: http://www.usaca.ru
Rector: Irina Melilotus Tel: +7(343) 371-33-63

Faculties
Agronomy (Agronomy); **Animal Husbandry** (Animal Husbandry); **Economics** (Economics); **Engineering** (Engineering); **Veterinary Science** (Veterinary Science)

History: Founded 1940.

Governing Bodies: Scientific Council

Academic Year: September to June (September-January; February-June)

Admission Requirements: Secondary school certificate (Attestat o srednem obrazovanii) or equivalent

Main Language(s) of Instruction: Russian

Degrees and Diplomas: *Bakalavr*: 4 yrs; *Magistr*: a further 1-2 yrs

Student Services: Canteen, Cultural centre, Health services, Sports facilities

Special Facilities: History of the Academy Museum. Training Farm

Libraries: c. 450,000 vols

Publications: Agrovestnik *(monthly)*

Press or Publishing House: Publishing House

Last Updated: 01/12/11

URAL STATE FOREST ENGINEERING UNIVERSITY

Uralskij Gosudarstvennyj Lesotehničeskij Universitet (USFEU)
ul. Sibirskij trakt 37, Ekaterinburg, 620100 Sverdlovskaja oblast'
Tel: +7(343) 254-6506
Fax: +7(343) 254-6225
EMail: general@usfeu.ru
Website: http://www.usfeu.ru/

Rector: Andrew Mehrentseva (2011-) EMail: rector@usfeu.ru

Centres
Ural Forest Teknopark

Departments
Scientific Work (Science Education)

Faculties
Accounting, Analysis, and Economic Security (Accountancy; Economics); **Complementary Education** (Educational Sciences); **Correspondence Studies** (Ecology; Engineering; Forest Management; Management; Mechanical Equipment and Maintenance; Road Engineering; Social and Community Services; Tourism; Wood Technology); **Ecological Engineering** (Ecology; Engineering); **Economics of Forest Business** (Agricultural Business; Forest Management); **Economics of Transport and Logistics**

(Economics; Information Management; Management; Transport Economics; Transport Management); **Forestry Engineering** (Automation and Control Engineering; Forestry; Transport and Communications); **Humanities** (Arts and Humanities; Social and Community Services; Social Sciences; Tourism); **Logging Machinery** (Maintenance Technology; Mechanical Equipment and Maintenance; Transport and Communications; Wood Technology); **Wood Technology** (Automation and Control Engineering; Wood Technology)

Institutes

Biotechnology and Nanomaterials (Biotechnology; Nanotechnology); **Eco-toxicology** (Ecology; Toxicology); **Life's Quality** (Service Trades); **Road Transport** (Road Transport); **Scientific Research** (Road Transport)

History: Founded 1930 as Ural State Institute of Forestry Engineering. Acquired present status 2001.

Governing Bodies: Scientific Council

Academic Year: September to June (September to January; February to June)

Admission Requirements: Secondary school certificate (Attestat o srednem obrazovanii)

Fees: (Russian Rubles): 25,000-30,000 per semester depending on speciality

Main Language(s) of Instruction: Russian

International Co-operation: With universities in Switzerland, Finland, Germany, Slovakia, Czech Republic, China, Hungary, India, Cyprus, USA. Also participates in INTAS.

Accrediting Agencies: Ministry of Education and Science of Russian Federation

Degrees and Diplomas: *Bakalavr*: Road Transport; Information Systems in Economics; Management and Economics; Construction; Protection of Environment; Technology; Logging and Woodworking Equipment; Forest Business, 4 yrs; *Specialist Diploma*: Ecology; Mechanical Equipment; Maintenance; Forest Management; Wood Technology; Management; Forestry Engineering; Tourism, 5 yrs; *Magistr*: Road Transport; Management; Forest Business; Woodworking Enterprises Technology and Equipment, 2 yrs

Student Services: Academic counselling, Canteen, Cultural centre, Foreign student adviser, Handicapped facilities, Health services, Language programs, Nursery care, Social counselling, Sports facilities

Student Residential Facilities: Yes

Special Facilities: Museum. Vigorov Garden of Medicinal Plants. Educational-Industrial Workshop. Ural educational-experimental forest plant USFEU. Forest Academy for school children

Libraries: Central Library, c. 850,000 vols

Publications: Proceedings *(annually)*

Academic Staff	MEN	WOMEN	**TOTAL**
STAFF WITH DOCTORATE			
FULL-TIME	231	250	**481**
Student Numbers *2007-2008*			
All (Foreign Included)	2,824	2,277	**5,101**
FOREIGN ONLY	9	6	**15**

Part-time students, 4,289. **Distance students**, 9. **Evening students**, 134.

Last Updated: 01/12/11

URAL STATE MEDICAL ACADEMY

Uralskaja Gosudarstvennaja Medicinskaja Akademija
ul. Repina 32, Ekaterinburg, 620213 Sverdlovskaja oblast'
Tel: +7(343) 371-3490
Fax: +7(343) 371-6400
EMail: usma@usma.ru
Website: http://www.usma.ru/

Rector: A. P. Yastrebov

Pro-Rector for Academic Affairs: B. G. Yuškov

Programmes

Medicine (Anaesthesiology; Anatomy; Biochemistry; Biology; Botany; Cardiology; Chemistry; Dentistry; Endocrinology; Forensic Medicine and Dentistry; Gynaecology and Obstetrics; Immunology; Medicine; Neurology; Nursing; Oncology; Ophthalmology; Orthopaedics; Paediatrics; Pathology; Pharmacology; Pharmacy; Psychiatry and Mental Health; Psychology; Social and Preventive Medicine; Social Work; Stomatology; Surgery; Urology)

History: Created 1930 as Sverdlovsk State Medical Institute. Acquired present status and title 1995.

Degrees and Diplomas: *Bakalavr*; *Specialist Diploma*; *Kandidat Nauk*

Last Updated: 01/12/11

URAL STATE MINING UNIVERSITY

Uralskij Gosudarstvennyj Gornyj Universitet
ul. Kuibyševa 30, Ekaterinburg, 620144 Sverdlovskaja oblast'
Tel: +7(343) 257-25-47
Fax: +7(343) 251-48-38
EMail: rector@ursmu.ru
Website: http://www.ursmu.ru/

Rector: Nikolaj P. Kosarev

Faculties

Geology (Geology); **Geophysics** (Geophysics); **Mining Engineering** (Automation and Control Engineering; Mining Engineering); **Mining Engineering and Economy** (Economics; Mining Engineering); **Mining Technology** (Mining Engineering)

History: Founded 1917. Previously known as Uralskaja Gosudarstvennaja Gorno-Geologičeskaja Akademija (Ural State Academy of Mining and Geology). Acquired current title 2004.

Academic Year: October to June

Admission Requirements: Secondary school certificate and examinations and test in Russian

Main Language(s) of Instruction: Russian

Degrees and Diplomas: *Bakalavr*; *Specialist Diploma*; *Magistr*; *Kandidat Nauk*; *Doktor Nauk*

Student Services: Academic counselling, Canteen, Cultural centre, Employment services, Foreign student adviser, Health services, Social counselling, Sports facilities

Student Residential Facilities: Yes

Special Facilities: The Urals Geological Museum

Last Updated: 21/11/11

URAL STATE MUSIC CONSERVATORY NAMED AFTER M.P. MUSSORGSKY

Uralskaja Gosudarstvennaja Konservatorija im. M.P. Musorgskogo
pr. Lenina 26, Ekaterinburg, 620014 Sverdlovskaja oblast'
Tel: +7(3432) 517-180
Fax: +7(3432) 517-369
EMail: mail@uralcons.org
Website: http://www.uralcons.org/

Rector: Valerij Dmitievich Shkarupa

Departments

Humanities (Arts and Humanities; Social Studies)

Faculties

Instrumental Performance (Music; Musical Instruments; Performing Arts); **Vocal and Choral Art, Musicology, Composition and Musical Sound Producing** (Conducting; Music; Music Theory and Composition; Musicology; Singing; Sound Engineering (Acoustics))

Schools

Graduate (Music; Music Education)

History: Founded 1934. Acquired present title and status 1946.

Academic Year: September to July

Admission Requirements: Diploma of a Musical College or special music School

Main Language(s) of Instruction: Russian, English

Degrees and Diplomas: *Specialist Diploma*: 5 yrs; *Kandidat Nauk*

Student Services: Academic counselling, Canteen, Cultural centre, Foreign student adviser, Health services, Language programs, Social counselling, Sports facilities

Student Residential Facilities: For c. 340 students

Special Facilities: Sound recording studio

Last Updated: 01/12/11

URAL STATE PEDAGOGICAL UNIVERSITY

Uralskij Gosudarstvennyj Pedagogičeskij Universitet

pr. Kosmonavtov 26, GSP-135, Ekaterinburg, 620017
Sverdlovskaja oblast'
Tel: +7(343) 336-1400
Fax: +7(343) 336-1242
EMail: uspu@uspu.ru
Website: http://www.uspu.ru

Rector: Boris M. Igoshev Tel: +7(3432) 341-302

Vice-Rector: V. V. Korkunov Tel: +7(3432) 343-348

Departments

Biology and Geography (Biology; Environmental Studies; Geography); **Mathematics** (Computer Science; Mathematics); **Russian Language and Literature** (Comparative Literature; Literature; Russian; Slavic Languages); **Sociology** (Philosophy; Political Sciences; Sociology)

Faculties

Economics (Accountancy; Business Administration; Economics; Management; Marketing); **History** (History); **Law** (Law); **Life Safety** (Welfare and Protective Services); **Physical Education and Sports** (Leisure Studies; Physical Education; Sports; Sports Management); **Social Education** (Pedagogy; Social Studies); **Tourism and Hospitality Services** (Hotel and Restaurant; Tourism)

Institutes

Basic Psychology and Teacher Education (Education; Psychology; Teacher Training); **Computer Science and Information Technology** (Computer Science; Information Technology); **Foreign Languages** (Classical Languages; Modern Languages); **Fundamental Social and Humanities Education** (Humanities and Social Science Education); **Music and Art Education** (Art Education; Fine Arts; Music; Music Education); **Pedagogy and Child Psychology** (Child Care and Development; Education; Educational Psychology; Pedagogy; Preschool Education; Psychology); **Personnel Development and Management** (Human Resources; Management); **Philology, Cultural and Intercultural Communication** (Communication Studies; Cultural Studies; Philology); **Physics and Technology** (Physics; Technology); **Psychology** (Education; Psychology); **Special Education** (Education of the Gifted; Education of the Handicapped; Special Education)

History: Founded 1930 as Pedagogical Institute, acquired present status and title 1993.

Governing Bodies: Academic Council

Academic Year: September to June (September-December; February-June)

Admission Requirements: Secondary school certificate (Attestat o srednem obrazovanii)

Main Language(s) of Instruction: Russian

Accrediting Agencies: Ministry of Education of the Russian Federation

Degrees and Diplomas: *Bakalavr*: 4 yrs; *Specialist Diploma*: 5 yrs; *Magistr*: a further 1-2 yrs; *Kandidat Nauk*. Also Postgraduate Education, 3 yrs

Student Services: Academic counselling, Canteen, Cultural centre, Employment services, Foreign student adviser, Health services, Language programs, Social counselling, Sports facilities

Student Residential Facilities: For c. 5,000 students

Special Facilities: University History Museum

Libraries: c. 800,000 vols

Last Updated: 01/12/11

URAL STATE UNIVERSITY NAMED AFTER A.M. GORKY

Uralskij Gosudarstvennyj Universitet im. A.M. Gorkogo (USU)

ul. Lenina 51, Ekaterinburg, 620083 Sverdlovskaja oblast'
Tel: +7(3432) 557-401
Fax: +7(3432) 557-401
EMail: kontakt@usu.ru; doc_office@usu.ru
Website: http://www.usu.ru

President: Vladimir E. Tretjakov (1993-)
Tel: +7(3432) 557-420, Fax: +7(3432) 556-583
EMail: Vladimir.Tretjakov@usu.ru

First Vice-Rector: Dmitri V. Bugrov
Tel: +7(3432) 555-960, Fax: +7(3432) 555-964
EMail: Dmitry.Bugrov@usu.ru

Departments

Biology (Biology; Botany; Ecology; Natural Resources; Physiology; Zoology); **Chemistry** (Analytical Chemistry; Chemistry; Molecular Biology; Organic Chemistry; Physical Chemistry); **Culture and Art Studies** (Art Education; Art History; Cultural Studies); **International Relations** (African Studies; International Relations; Linguistics; Oriental Studies; Regional Studies; Slavic Languages); **Management and Enterprise** (Business Computing; Management; Public Administration); **Mathematics and Mechanics** (Mathematics; Mathematics and Computer Science; Mechanics); **Physics** (Astronomy and Space Science; Information Sciences; Information Technology; Measurement and Precision Engineering; Nanotechnology; Physics; Surveying and Mapping); **Psychology** (Clinical Psychology; Psychology); **Public Relations and Advertising** (Advertising and Publicity; Public Relations)

Faculties

+Economics (Economics; Management); **+History** (Ancient Civilizations; Archaeology; Archiving; Ethnology; History; History of Law; Management; Medieval Studies; Tourism); **+Philology** (Germanic Languages; Philology; Romance Languages; Russian); **+Philosophy** (Aesthetics; Anthropology; Linguistics; Philosophy; Religious Studies); **+Political Sciences and Sociology** (Political Sciences; Social Work; Sociology); **In-service Training** (Natural Sciences)

Schools

+Journalism (Journalism; Radio and Television Broadcasting; Russian); **Graduate** (Biology; Chemistry; Cultural Studies; Earth Sciences; Economics; History; Mathematics; Pedagogy; Philology; Philosophy; Physics; Political Sciences; Sociology; Technology)

History: Founded 1920.

Governing Bodies: Academic Council; Board of Trustees

Academic Year: September to June (September-January; February-June)

Admission Requirements: Certificate of medium general or medium professional education or certificate of initial professional training

Main Language(s) of Instruction: Russian

International Co-operation: Participates in Tempus-TACIS; DAAD; Usaid; Irex; Unesco Chairs

Accrediting Agencies: Ministry of Education

Degrees and Diplomas: *Bakalavr*: 4 yrs; *Specialist Diploma*: 5 yrs; *Magistr*: a further 2 yrs; *Kandidat Nauk*: a further 3 yrs; *Doktor Nauk*: 3 yrs

Student Services: Academic counselling, Canteen, Cultural centre, Employment services, Foreign student adviser, Foreign Studies Centre, Health services, Language programs, Social counselling, Sports facilities

Student Residential Facilities: Yes

Special Facilities: Botanical Garden. Observatory. Biological station

Libraries: 1,064,789 vols. Department of Rare Books

Publications: University Management: practice and analysis *(quarterly)*

Last Updated: 01/12/11

URAL STATE UNIVERSITY OF ECONOMICS

Uralskij Gosudarstvennyj Ekonomičeskij Universitet (USUE)

8 Marta / Narodnoi Voli 62/45, GSP-985, Ekaterinburg, 620219
Sverdlovskaja oblast'
Tel: +7(343) 257-9140
Fax: +7(343) 257-7147
EMail: usue@usue.ru; press@usue.ru
Website: http://www.usue.ru

Rector: Mihail Fedorov (2005-)
Tel: +7(343) 257-0246, Ext 3-00 EMail: rector@usue.ru

First Vice-Rector: Maksim Maramygin
EMail: maram_m_s@mail.ru

International Relations: Oleg Oshkordin, Vice-Rector for International and Youth Programmes
Tel: +7(343) 251-9620 EMail: vnj@usue.ru

Faculties

Commerce, Supply and Services (Advertising and Publicity; Agricultural Management; Animal Husbandry; Business and Commerce; Cooking and Catering; Economics; Food Technology; Hotel and Restaurant; Hotel Management; Marketing; Safety Engineering; Tourism; Transport Management); **Economics** (Business Computing; Economics; Environmental Studies; Health Administration; Human Resources; Industrial Management; Information Management; Labour and Industrial Relations; Law; Management; Marketing); **Finance and Law** (Accountancy; Advertising and Publicity; Banking; Finance; Insurance; Law; Psychology; Sociology; Taxation); **Management and Computer Science** (Business Computing; Computer Science; Economics; Information Technology; Management; Management Systems; Public Administration)

History: Founded 1967 as Sverdlovsk Institute of National Economy. Acquired present title 1994.

Governing Bodies: Council

Academic Year: September to June (September-January; February-June)

Admission Requirements: Secondary school certificate (Attestat o srednem obrazovanii) and entrance examination (Edinyi Gosudarstvennyi Eksamen)

Fees: (Russian Rubles): Faculty of Finance, 70,000 per annum; Faculty of Management and International Economics Relations, 65,000 per annum; other faculties 60,000 per annum

Main Language(s) of Instruction: Russian

International Co-operation: BRIDGE (UK) - 3 projects - Finance, Logistics and Corporative Governance

Accrediting Agencies: Federal Service for Supervision of Education and Science (http://obrnadzor.gov.ru)

Degrees and Diplomas: *Bakalavr*: 3 yrs; *Specialist Diploma*: 5 yrs; *Magistr*: 2 yrs

Student Services: Academic counselling, Canteen, Cultural centre, Employment services, Foreign student adviser, Health services, Social counselling, Sports facilities

Student Residential Facilities: For c. 1,500 students

Special Facilities: History of the University Museum

Libraries: c. 750,000 vols

Publications: Proceeding of the Ural State University of Economics *(quarterly)*

Academic Staff *2007-2008*	MEN	WOMEN	**TOTAL**
FULL-TIME	115	342	**457**
PART-TIME	76	40	**116**
STAFF WITH DOCTORATE			
FULL-TIME	–	–	**271**
Student Numbers *2007-2008*			
All (Foreign Included)	4,120	12,852	**16,972**
FOREIGN ONLY	–	–	**68**

Part-time students, 2. **Distance students**, 2,219.

Last Updated: 01/12/11

URAL STATE UNIVERSITY OF RAILWAY TRANSPORT

Uralskij Gosudarstvennyj Universitet Putej Soobščenija
ul. Kolmogorova 66, Ekaterinburg, 620034 Sverdlovskaja oblast'
Tel: +7(343) 370-0285 +7(343) 245-3467
Fax: +7(343) 245-3467
EMail: webmaster@usurt.ru
Website: http://www.usurt.ru

Rector: Aleksandr V. Jefimov (1992-) EMail: rector@usurt.ru

International Relations: Marina Zhuravskaya, Vice-Rector
Tel: +7(343) 245-3339, Fax: +7(343) 370-0285
EMail: MZhuravskaya@cca.usurt.ru

Departments

Postgraduate Studies (Railway Transport; Telecommunications Engineering; Transport Management)

Faculties

Building (Bridge Engineering; Civil Engineering; Railway Engineering); **Economics** (Accountancy; Business Administration; Business and Commerce; Economics; History; Human Resources; Information Technology; International Economics; Management; Modern Languages; Philosophy; Physical Education; Political Sciences; Railway Transport; Sociology; Transport and Communications; Transport Economics; Transport Management); **Electrotechnics** (Applied Mathematics; Automation and Control Engineering; Electrical Engineering; Electronic Engineering; Information Technology; Mechanical Engineering; Railway Engineering; Railway Transport); **Mechanical Engineering** (Electronic Engineering; Industrial Design; Mechanical Engineering); **Transport Power Supply** (Automation and Control Engineering; Electrical and Electronic Engineering; Railway Transport; Transport Management); **Transport Processes** (Environmental Engineering; Railway Transport; Safety Engineering; Transport Management)

History: Founded 1956 as Urals Electromechanical Institute for Railway Engineers, acquired present status and title 1999.

Governing Bodies: Senate

Academic Year: September to June

Admission Requirements: Secondary school certificate (Attestat o srednem obrazovanii) and entrance examination

Main Language(s) of Instruction: Russian

Degrees and Diplomas: *Bakalavr*: 4 yrs; *Specialist Diploma*: 5 yrs; *Magistr*: a further 3 yrs; *Kandidat Nauk*

Student Services: Canteen, Cultural centre, Employment services, Foreign student adviser, Health services, Language programs, Sports facilities

Student Residential Facilities: For c. 2,300 students

Special Facilities: History of the Academy Museum

Libraries: c. 600,000 vols

Publications: Research Review *(biennially)*

Last Updated: 30/11/11

VELIKIJE LUKI STATE ACADEMY OF PHYSICAL CULTURE AND SPORT

Velikolukskaja Gosudarstvennaja Akademija Fizičeskij Kulturny i Sporta
pl. Jubilejnaja 4, Velikje Lukij, 182100 Pskovskaja oblast'
Tel: +7(81153) 393-88
Fax: +7(81153) 393-88
EMail: vlgifc@ellink.ru; rectorat@vlgafc.ru
Website: http://www.vlgafc.ru/

Rector: Ruslan Gorodnichev (1997-) EMail: vlgafc-rector@allink.ru

Faculties

Day Course Study (Pedagogy; Physical Education; Physiology; Psychology; Sports); **Distance Education**

History: Founded 1970, previously known as Velikolukskij Gosudarstvennyj Fizieeskoj Kul'tury Institut, acquired present status 2003

Governing Bodies: Council

Academic Year: September to June

Admission Requirements: Secondary school certificate (Attestat o srednem obrazovanii)

Main Language(s) of Instruction: Russian

Accrediting Agencies: Federal Service for Supervision of Education and Science

Degrees and Diplomas: *Bakalavr*, *Specialist Diploma*: 5 yrs; *Magistr*

Student Services: Academic counselling, Cultural centre, Health services, Social counselling, Sports facilities

Student Residential Facilities: Yes

Libraries: c. 79,000 vols

Publications: Research Yearbook *(annually)*

Last Updated: 18/04/11

VELIKIJE LUKI STATE AGRICULTURAL ACADEMY

Velikolukskaja Gosudarstvennaja Sel'skohozjajstvennaja Akademija (VGSA)

pl. Lenina 1, Velikje Lukij, 182112 Pskovskaja oblast'
Tel: +7(81153) 376-71
Fax: +7(81153) 376-71
EMail: vgsha@mart.ru
Website: http://www.vgsa.ru

Rector: Vladimir V. Morozov
Tel: +7(81153) 718-30 EMail: rektor@mart.ru

Vice-Rector for Administration: Aleksandr Fomčenko

International Relations: Julia Fedorova
Tel: +7(81153) 754-23 EMail: nauka@mart.ru

Faculties

Agroecology (Agriculture; Animal Husbandry; Ecology; Plant and Crop Protection); **Economics** (Accountancy; Arts and Humanities; Banking; Business and Commerce; Computer Science; Economics; Finance; Information Technology; Management; Social Sciences; Taxation); **Engineering** (Agricultural Engineering; Agricultural Equipment; Animal Husbandry; Engineering; Maintenance Technology; Mathematics; Mechanical Engineering; Physics); **Livestock Technology** (Animal Husbandry; Cattle Breeding; Dairy; Physical Education; Sports; Veterinary Science; Zoology)

History: Founded 1957. Acquired present title and status 1994.

Academic Year: September to August

Admission Requirements: Secondary school certificate (Attestat o srednem obrazovanii) and entrance examination

Main Language(s) of Instruction: Russian

Accrediting Agencies: Ministry of General and professional Education

Degrees and Diplomas: *Specialist Diploma*: 5 yrs

Student Residential Facilities: Yes

Special Facilities: Museum

Libraries: c. 380,000 vols

Publications: Collections of Scientific Works; Reports of Scientific Publications

Last Updated: 30/11/11

VJATKA STATE AGRICULTURAL ACADEMY

Vjatskaja Gosudarstvennaja Sel'skohozjajstvennaja Akademija

pr. Oktjabrskij 133, Kirov 610017
Tel: +7(8332) 548-633
Fax: +7(8332) 548-633
EMail: info@vgsha.info
Website: http://www.vgsha.info

Rector: Sergej L. Zhdanov

Vice-Rector for Administration: V.A. Likhanov

Faculties

Agronomy (Agricultural Business; Agronomy; Applied Chemistry; Botany; Cattle Breeding; Crop Production; Horticulture; Landscape Architecture; Plant and Crop Protection; Soil Science; Surveying and Mapping); **Biology** (Apiculture; Biochemistry; Biology; Cattle Breeding; Ecology; Fishery; Physiology; Zoology); **Economics** (Accountancy; Applied Mathematics; Banking; Economics; Finance; History; Information Technology; Management; Marketing; Philosophy; Political Sciences; Statistics); **Engineering** (Agricultural Engineering; Agricultural Equipment; Automotive Engineering; Materials Engineering; Mathematics; Mechanical Engineering; Mechanical Equipment and Maintenance; Physics); **Veterinary Science** (Veterinary Science)

History: Founded 1930, acquired present status and title 1994. Formerly known as Kirov Agricultural Institute.

Governing Bodies: Scientific Council

Academic Year: September to August (September-January; February-August)

Admission Requirements: Secondary school certificate (Attestat o srednem obrazovanii) and entrance examination

Fees: None

Main Language(s) of Instruction: Russian

Degrees and Diplomas: *Specialist Diploma*

Student Residential Facilities: For c. 2,650 students

Special Facilities: History of the Academy Museum

Libraries: c. 420,000 vols

Publications: Didactic Papers *(annually)*; Scientific Papers *(annually)*

Last Updated: 30/11/11

VJATKA STATE HUMANITARIAN UNIVERSITY

Vjatskij Gosudarstvennyj Gumanitarnnij Universitet (VGPU)

ul. Krasnoarmejckaja, d.26, Kirov 610002
Tel: +7(8332) 678-975
Fax: +7(8332) 375-169
EMail: entrance@vshu.kirov.ru; vshu@vshu.kirov.ru
Website: http://www.vshu.kirov.ru/

Rector: Valeri Teodorovich Yungbludt EMail: rector@vshu.kirov.ru

Faculties

Chemistry (Chemistry; Ecology); **Computer Science, Mathematics and Physics** (Computer Science; Mathematics; Physics); **Economics** (Accountancy; Business and Commerce; Economics; Marketing); **History** (History); **Humanities** (Publishing and Book Trade; Social Work; Tourism); **Law** (Law); **Linguistics** (Foreign Languages Education; Germanic Studies; Linguistics; Philology; Romance Languages; Translation and Interpretation); **Management** (Government; Human Resources; Management); **Natural Sciences and Geography** (Biology; Ecology; Geography); **Pedagogy** (Pedagogy; Preschool Education; Primary Education); **Philology** (Journalism; Philology); **Philosophy and Cultural Studies** (Advertising and Publicity; Cultural Studies; Philosophy; Sociology); **Physical Education** (Physical Education; Sports); **Psychology** (Psychology); **Technology and Design** (Design; Fine Arts; Technology; Technology Education)

History: Founded 1914 as Pedagogical School, became Institute 1918. Acquired present status and title 1995. Formerly Vjatskij Gosudarstvennyj Pedagogičeskij Universitet.

Academic Year: September to June (September-January; February-June)

Admission Requirements: Secondary school certificate (Diplom o srednem obrazovanii)

Fees: (Russian Rubles): 10,000 per annum

Main Language(s) of Instruction: Russian

International Co-operation: With universities in Cyprus. Also participates in Tempus

Degrees and Diplomas: *Bakalavr*, *Specialist Diploma*: 5 yrs; *Magistr*, *Kandidat Nauk*: 3-4 yrs; *Doktor Nauk*: 1-3 yrs

Student Services: Academic counselling, Canteen, Cultural centre, Foreign Studies Centre, Handicapped facilities, Health services, Language programs, Social counselling, Sports facilities

Special Facilities: Observatory. Botanical Garden. Museum

Libraries: University Library

Publications: Vestnik VGPU *(biennially)*

Press or Publishing House: Publishing House

Last Updated: 26/04/11

VJATKA STATE UNIVERSITY

Vjatskij Gosudarstvennyj Universitet (VYATSTU)

ul. Moskovskaja 36, Kirov 610000
Tel: +7(8332) 64-69-17 +7(8332) 64-39-91
Fax: +7(8332) 64-65-71 +7(8332) 64-39-91
EMail: rectorat@vyatsu.ru
Website: http://www.vyatsu.ru/

Rector: Valentin Nikolaevich Pugach
EMail: rector@vyatsu.ru; pugach@vyatsu.ru

Faculties

Applied Mathematics and Telecommunications Engineering (Applied Mathematics; Computer Science; Telecommunications Engineering; Telecommunications Services); **Automation and Computer Science** (Automation and Control Engineering;

Computer Science; Electrical and Electronic Engineering; Information Technology; Software Engineering; Telecommunications Engineering); **Automation and Machine Building** (Automation and Control Engineering; Machine Building; Materials Engineering; Mechanical Equipment and Maintenance; Metal Techniques); **Biology** (Bioengineering; Biology; Biotechnology; Food Technology; Microbiology); **Chemistry** (Biotechnology; Chemistry; Inorganic Chemistry; Organic Chemistry; Physical Chemistry); **Civil Engineering and Architecture** (Architectural and Environmental Design; Architecture; Civil Engineering; Construction Engineering; Ecology; Machine Building); **Economics and Management** (Business and Commerce; Business Computing; Economics; Information Technology; Management); **Electrical Engineering** (Computer Networks; Electrical Engineering; Energy Engineering; Hydraulic Engineering; Industrial Management; Power Engineering; Thermal Engineering); **Humanities** (Cultural Studies; History; Journalism; Law; Linguistics; Modern Languages; Philosophical Schools; Psychology; Sociology; Sports; Traditional Eastern Medicine); **Law** (Criminal Law; History of Law; Law; Public Law)

History: Founded 1962, acquired present status and title 1994.

Governing Bodies: Board of trustees

Academic Year: September to June

Admission Requirements: Secondary school certificate (Attestat o srednem obrazovanii) or foreign equivalent

Main Language(s) of Instruction: Russian, English, German

Degrees and Diplomas: *Bakalavr*; *Specialist Diploma*; *Kandidat Nauk*; *Doktor Nauk*

Student Services: Academic counselling, Canteen, Cultural centre, Employment services, Foreign student adviser, Foreign Studies Centre, Health services, Language programs, Social counselling, Sports facilities

Student Residential Facilities: Yes

Special Facilities: University Museum. University Hospital

Libraries: c. 1m. vols

Last Updated: 09/03/12

VLADIMIR LAW INSTITUTE OF THE FEDERAL PENITENTIARY SERVICE

Vladimirskij Juridiceskij Institut Federal'noj Služby Ispolnenija Nakazanij

ul. Bol'šaja Nižegorodkaja 67-e, Vladimir 600020
Tel: +7(4922) 32-31-64 +7(4922) 32-39-97
Fax: +7(4922) 32-28-93
EMail: vui@vui.vladinfo.ru; uchebotdel@vui.vladinfo.ru
Website: http://vui-fsin.ru/

Rector: Sergei Nikolaevich Emel'janov

Programmes

Law (Justice Administration; Law; Social Work)

History: Created 1996. Previously known as Vladimirskij Juridiceskij Institut Ministerstva Justicii Rossijskoj Federacii (Vladimir Law Institute of the Russian Federation Justice Ministry). Acquired current title 2005.

Degrees and Diplomas: *Bakalavr*; *Specialist Diploma*

Last Updated: 12/03/12

VLADIMIR STATE UNIVERSITY FOR THE HUMANITIES

Vladimirskij Gosudarstvennyj Gumanitarnyj Universitet

pr. Stroitelej 11, Vladimir 600024
Tel: +7(4922) 337-302
Fax: +7(4922) 341-819
EMail: rector@vladggu.ru
Website: http://www.vladggu.ru

Rector: Victor Trofimovich Malygin

Faculties

Arts and Art Education (Art Education; Design; Fine Arts; Graphic Design; Music; Music Education; Restoration of Works of Art); **History** (Ancient Civilizations; History); **Law** (Law); **Modern Languages** (English; Foreign Languages Education; French; German); **Natural Sciences and Geography** (Anatomy; Botany; Chemical Engineering; Ecology; Geography; Physiology; Zoology); **Philology** (Literature; Russian); **Physical Education** (Physical Education; Sports); **Physics and Mathematics** (Computer Science; Information Technology; Mathematics; Mathematics and Computer Science; Physics; Science Education); **Primary Education** (Preschool Education; Primary Education); **Psychology** (Educational Psychology; Psychology); **Social and Special Education** (Educational Psychology; Pedagogy; Special Education); **Technology and Economics** (Economics; Management; Technology; Technology Education)

History: Founded 1912 as Pedagogical School became Institute of Education 1939, State Pedagogical Institute 1950, Vladimirskij Gosudarstvennyj Pedagogičeskij Universitet (Vladimir State Pedagogical University) 1993. Acquired current title and status 2008.

Academic Year: September to June (September-January; February-June)

Admission Requirements: Secondary school certificate (Attestat o srednem obrazovanii) and entrance examination

Main Language(s) of Instruction: Russian

Degrees and Diplomas: *Bakalavr*; *Specialist Diploma*; *Magistr*; *Kandidat Nauk*

Student Services: Academic counselling, Canteen, Cultural centre, Employment services, Foreign Studies Centre, Health services, Social counselling, Sports facilities

Student Residential Facilities: For 1,800 students

Libraries: Central Library, 600,000 vols

Publications: Conference Material; Research Reports *(annually)*

Press or Publishing House: University Publishing House

Last Updated: 26/04/11

VLADIMIR STATE UNIVERSITY NAMED AFTER ALEKSANR GRIGOREVICH AND NIKOLAI STOLETOVY

Vladimirskij Gosudarstvennyj Universitet im. Aleksandra Grigor'evicha i Nikolaja Stoletovykh

ul. Gor'kogo 87, Vladimir 600000
Tel: +7(4922) 53-25-75 +7(4922) 33-52-42
Fax: +7(4922) 53-25-75 +7(4922) 33-52-42
EMail: rector@vlsu.ru; oid@vlsu.ru
Website: http://www.vlsu.ru

Rector: Valentin Vasilievich Morozov EMail: rector@vlsu.ru

Faculties

Law (Civil Law; Criminal Law; Law)

Institutes

Applied Mathematics and Computer Science, Bio-and Nanotechnology (Applied Mathematics; Applied Physics; Biology; Biotechnology; Ceramics and Glass Technology; Chemistry; Computer Networks; Ecology; Nanotechnology; Pharmacy; Physics; Polymer and Plastics Technology; Soil Science); **Art** (Dance; Design; Fine Arts; Graphic Design; Music; Restoration of Works of Art); **Economics and Management** (Banking; Business Computing; Finance; Management; Marketing); **Humanities** (Advertising and Publicity; Archaeology; Cultural Studies; Educational Psychology; History; Journalism; Modern Languages; Museum Studies; Philosophy; Psychology; Public Relations; Regional Studies; Sociology; Special Education); **Innovation Technology** (Biomedical Engineering; Computer Science; Construction Engineering; Information Technology; Machine Building; Mechanics; Radiophysics; Telecommunications Engineering); **Pedagogy** (Anatomy; Botany; Ecology; Economics; English; Foreign Languages Education; French; Geography; German; History; Humanities and Social Science Education; Literature; Mathematics; Mathematics Education; Pedagogy; Philology; Preschool Education; Primary Education; Russian; Technology Education; Zoology); **Physical Education** (Physical Education; Sports); **Small and Medium-Size Business**

Further Information: Also Department for foreign students

History: Founded 1963.

Academic Year: September to June (September-January; February-June)

Admission Requirements: Secondary school certificate (Attestat o srednem obrazovanii) or equivalent

Main Language(s) of Instruction: Russian

Degrees and Diplomas: *Bakalavr*; *Specialist Diploma*; *Magistr*; *Kandidat Nauk*; *Doktor Nauk*
Student Residential Facilities: Yes
Libraries: Electronic library
Last Updated: 15/03/12

VLADIVOSTOK STATE MEDICAL UNIVERSITY

Vladivostokskij Gosudarstvennyj Meditsinskij Universitet
pr. Ostrjakova 2, Vladivostok, 690600 Primorskij kraj
Tel: +7(4232) 42-97-78 +7(4232) 45-17-36
Fax: +7(4232) 45-17-19 +7(4232) 42-97-50
EMail: mail@vgmu.ru
Website: http://www.vgmu.ru

Rector: Valentin B. Shumatov

Faculties

Clinical Psychology (Clinical Psychology; Neurological Therapy; Psychiatry and Mental Health; Psychology); **Medicine** (Medicine; Surgery); **Nursing** (Midwifery; Nursing); **Paediatrics** (Paediatrics); **Pharmacy** (Pharmacy); **Stomatology** (Dentistry; Stomatology)
History: Created 1958.
Degrees and Diplomas: *Specialist Diploma*
Last Updated: 15/03/12

VLADIVOSTOK STATE UNIVERSITY OF ECONOMICS AND SERVICES

Vladivostockij Gosudarstvennyj Universitet Ekonomiki i Servisa (VSUES)
ul. Gogolja 41, Vladivostok, 690600 Primorskij kraj
Tel: +7(4232) 455-630
Fax: +7(4232) 429-158 +7(4232) 404-154
EMail: rectorat@vvsu.ru; international@vvsu.ru
Website: http://www.vvsu.ru

President: Gennadiy Lazarev (1988-)
Tel: +7(4232) 257-954, Fax: +7(4232) 422-144
EMail: gennadiy.lazarev@vvsu.ru

Vice-Rector, Economics and Finance: Olga V. Mitina
EMail: olga.mitina@vvsu.ru

International Relations: Natalia Zhukova
Tel: +7(4232) 404-035, Fax: +7(4232) 429-158
EMail: international@vvsu.ru

Departments

Graduate Studies (Accountancy; Banking; Business Administration; Business and Commerce; Computer Science; Economics; Finance; International Business; International Economics; Management; Marketing; Tourism)

Schools

Computer Science, Innovation and Business Systems (Accountancy; Automotive Engineering; Business Computing; Computer Graphics; Computer Science; Ecology; Electronic Engineering; Environmental Management; Environmental Studies; Information Technology; International Economics; Mathematics); **Distance and Correspondence Education** (Accountancy; Banking; Business and Commerce; Cooking and Catering; Cultural Studies; Design; Documentation Techniques; Economics; Finance; Food Technology; Hotel and Restaurant; Hotel Management; Human Resources; Information Technology; Management; Marketing; Philosophy; Psychology; Public Administration; Taxation; Tourism; Translation and Interpretation); **Foreign Languages** (American Studies; Chinese; English; International Relations; Japanese; Korean; Linguistics; Modern Languages; Regional Studies; Russian; Southeast Asian Studies); **International Business and Economics** (Business and Commerce; International Business; International Economics; Marketing; Taxation); **Law and Management** (Accountancy; Administrative Law; Business Administration; Business and Commerce; Civil Law; Commercial Law; Constitutional Law; Criminal Law; Documentation Techniques; Economics; Finance; History of Law; Human Resources; International Economics; International Law; Labour Law; Law; Management; Mathematics; Philosophy; Political Sciences; Private Law; Public Administration; Social Work; Taxation); **Service, Fashion and Design** (Architectural and Environmental Design; Cooking and Catering; Cultural Studies; Design; Fashion Design; Fine Arts; Hotel and Restaurant; Hotel Management; Industrial Design; Service Trades; Sports; Technology; Tourism)
Further Information: Also Artem and Nakhodka branches
History: Founded 1967, by the Ministry of Light Industry and Services. Acquired present status 1996.
Academic Year: September to June (September-January; February-June)
Admission Requirements: Secondary school certificate (Attestat o sredenem obrazovanii)
Main Language(s) of Instruction: Russian
International Co-operation: With universities in China, Republic of Korea and Japan
Accrediting Agencies: Ministry of Education of the Russian Federation
Degrees and Diplomas: *Bakalavr*: 4 yrs; *Specialist Diploma*: 5 yrs; *Magistr*, *Kandidat Nauk*: 3 yrs; *Doktor Nauk*: a further 3 yrs. Also Certificate of the Faculty of Russian Language for Foreigners
Student Services: Academic counselling, Canteen, Cultural centre, Employment services, Foreign student adviser, Foreign Studies Centre, Health services, Language programs, Social counselling, Sports facilities
Student Residential Facilities: Yes
Libraries: c. 800,000 vols; c. 430,000 periodicals
Last Updated: 29/11/11

VOLGA REGION STATE ACADEMY OF PHYSICAL CULTURE, SPORT AND TOURISM

Povolžskaja Gosudarstvennaja Akademija Fizičeskoj Kul'tury, Sporta i Turizma
ul. Gor'kovskoje Shosse, 26, Kazan, 420004 Tartastan
Tel: +7(8552) 71-24-22 +7(8552) 71-24-46
Fax: +7(8552) 71-24-22
EMail: kamgafksit@mail.ru; otvsekretar@mail.ru
Website: http://sportacadem.ru

Rector: Yusip Digansheevich Jakubov

Programmes

Physical Education (Physical Education); **Sport** (Sports); **Tourism** (Tourism)
Further Information: Branch also in Nabereznje Čelny.
History: Founded 1974. Acquired current status 2008. Previously known as Kamskij Gosudarstvennyj Institut Fizičeskoj Kul'tury (Kama State Institute of Physical Culture). Acquired current title 2010.
Main Language(s) of Instruction: Russian
Degrees and Diplomas: *Specialist Diploma*
Student Services: Academic counselling, Canteen, Cultural centre, Employment services, Foreign student adviser, Foreign Studies Centre, Health services, Language programs, Social counselling, Sports facilities
Student Residential Facilities: Yes
Libraries: yes
Last Updated: 16/01/12

VOLGA REGION STATE UNIVERSITY OF TELECOMMUNICATIONS AND INFORMATICS

Povolžskij Gosudarstvennyj Universitet Telekommunikaci i Informatiki
ul. L'va Tolstogo 23, Samara 443010
Tel: +7(846) 333-58-56 +7(846) 332-49-15
Fax: +7(846) 332-48-64
EMail: pgati@mail.samtel.ru; sai@psati.ru
Website: http://www.psuti.ru/

Rector: Vladimir A. Andreev EMail: andreev@psati.ru

Faculties

Information Systems and Technology (Business Computing; Computer Science; E-Business/Commerce; Information Technology; Modern Languages; Public Relations; Telecommunications Engineering); **Telecommunications** (Mathematics; Philosophy;

Physics; Radio and Television Broadcasting; Telecommunications Services); **Telecommunications and Radio Engineering** (Economics; Radio and Television Broadcasting; Telecommunications Engineering)

Further Information: Branches also in Kazan, Orenburg, Stavropol.

History: Founded 1956. Previously known as Povolžskaja Gosudarstvennaja Akademija Telekommunikaci i Informatiki (Volga Region State Academy of Telecommunications and Informatics). Acquired current title 2008.

Governing Bodies: Academic Council

Academic Year: September to July (September-January; February-July)

Admission Requirements: Secondary education certificate (Attestat o srednem obrazovanii) and entrance examination

Main Language(s) of Instruction: Russian

Degrees and Diplomas: *Bakalavr*; *Specialist Diploma*; *Magistr*; *Kandidat Nauk*

Student Residential Facilities: Yes

Libraries: c. 500,000 vols

Last Updated: 11/01/12

VOLGA STATE ACADEMY OF WATER TRANSPORT

Volžskaja Gosudarstvennaja Akademija Vodnogo Transporta

ul. Nesterova 5, Nižnij Novgorod 603600
Tel: +7(8314) 197-813
Fax: +7(8314) 197-858
EMail: vgavt@aqua.sci-nnov.ru
Website: http://www.vgavt-nn.ru/

Rector: Valery I. Mineev EMail: mineyev@aqua.sci-nnov.ru

Departments

Electromechanical Engineering (Computer Science; Electrical Engineering; Marine Engineering; Marine Transport; Mechanical Engineering; Physics)

Faculties

Economics and Management (Accountancy; Banking; Economics; Finance; Marketing; Mathematics; Transport Management); **Navigation, Marine Transport and Nautical Science** (Foreign Languages Education; Marine Transport; Nautical Science; Physical Education; Sports); **Shipbuilding, Hydraulic and Environmental Protection** (Ecology; Environmental Management; Hydraulic Engineering; Marine Engineering; Marine Transport; Materials Engineering; Structural Architecture)

Schools

Law (Civil Law; Criminal Law; Engineering; Foreign Languages Education; Government; Law; Philosophy; Social Sciences)

Further Information: Branches: Astrakhan, Kazan, Samara and Perm

History: Founded 1930.

Degrees and Diplomas: *Bakalavr*; *Specialist Diploma*

Last Updated: 29/11/11

VOLGOGRAD ACADEMY OF THE MINISTRY OF INTERNAL AFFAIRS OF THE RUSSIAN FEDERATION

Volgogradskaja Akademija MVD Rossii

ul. Istoričeskaja 130, Volgograd 400089
Tel: +7(8442) 54-76-77 +7(8442) 35-02-90 +7(8442) 48-36-84
Fax: +7(8442) 54-76-77
EMail: va@va-mvd.ru; academy@va-mvd.ru
Website: http://va-mvd.ru/modules.php?name=News

Rector: Vladimir Ivanovich Tretjakov EMail: va-mvd@va-mvd.ru

Programmes

Law (Law)

History: Founded 1967. Acquired present status 2000.

Governing Bodies: Academic Council

Academic Year: September to July

Main Language(s) of Instruction: Russian

International Co-operation: With universities in USA

Accrediting Agencies: Ministry of Education and Science

Degrees and Diplomas: *Bakalavr*: Operational Investigation;Law, 4 yrs; *Specialist Diploma*: Jurisprudence/Criminal Law;Forensic Science, 5 yrs; *Kandidat Nauk*. Also 2-year diploma in Operational Investigation

Student Services: Canteen, Cultural centre, Employment services, Health services, Language programs, Sports facilities

Student Residential Facilities: Cadet dormitories

Libraries: 662,890 vols. including rare collections, 245 journals

Publications: Vector, Research methodology and legal journal *(biennially)*

Last Updated: 18/04/11

VOLGOGRAD ARTS INSTITUTE NAMED AFTER P. A. SEREBRJAKOV

Volgogradskij Institut Iskusstv im. P. A. Serebrjakova

ul. Mira 5a, Volgograd 400131
Tel: +7(8442) 33-43-85
Fax: +7(8442) 33-43-85 +7(8442) 33-43-86
EMail: vmii_priem@mail.ru
Website: http://www.serebryakovka.ru/

Rector: Dmitrij R. Arutunov

Programmes

Design (Design; Fine Arts); **Music** (Conducting; Music; Music Education; Music Theory and Composition; Musical Instruments; Musicology; Singing)

History: Created 1996 as Volgogradskij Municipalnyj Institut Iskusstv (Volgograd Municipal Institute of Fine Arts). Acquired current title and status 2009.

Degrees and Diplomas: *Specialist Diploma*

Last Updated: 19/04/11

VOLGOGRAD STATE AGRICULTURAL ACADEMY

Volgogradskaja Gosudarstvennaja Sel'skohozjajstvennaja Akademija

Universitetskij prospect 26, Volgograd 400002
Tel: +7(8442) 41-17-84 +7(8442) 41-10-94 +7(8442) 41-17-55
Fax: +7(8442) 41-10-85
EMail: vgsha@vgsha.ru; vgsxa@avtlg.ru
Website: http://www.vgsha.ru/

Rector: Aleksei Semenovich Ovchinnikov

Faculties

Agriculture Electrification (Agricultural Equipment); **Agriculture Mechanization** (Agricultural Equipment); **Agronomy** (Agronomy; Crop Production; Ecology; Plant and Crop Protection; Soil Management); **Animal Husbandry** (Animal Husbandry; Veterinary Science; Zoology); **Ecology and Soil Improvement** (Ecology; Soil Science); **Economics** (Economics)

History: Founded 1944.

Admission Requirements: School or College Certificate

Main Language(s) of Instruction: Russian

Degrees and Diplomas: *Bakalavr*, *Specialist Diploma*

Student Services: Canteen, Cultural centre, Foreign student adviser, Health services, Sports facilities

Student Residential Facilities: 6 student hostels

Special Facilities: Museum of Academy History; Vivarium

Libraries: Library: 613,585 vols; with 220 seats

Last Updated: 12/03/12

VOLGOGRAD STATE MEDICAL UNIVERSITY

Volgogradskij Gosudarstvennyj Medicinskij Universitet
1, pl. Pavshikh Bortsov 1, Volgograd 400131
Tel: +7(8442) 383-028
Fax: +7(8442) 408-140
EMail: cved@volgmed.ru
Website: http://www.volgmed.ru

Rector: Vladimir Ivanovič Petrov EMail: rector@volgmed.ru

International Relations: A. A. Spasov
Tel: +7(8442) 383-028, Fax: +7(8442) 383-028
EMail: foreign@volgmed.ru

Centres
Acupuncture (Acupuncture)

Colleges
Advanced Medical Studies (Anaesthesiology; Cardiology; Community Health; Dentistry; Family Studies; Gynaecology and Obstetrics; Hygiene; Paediatrics; Pharmacology; Surgery)

Faculties
Dentistry (Dental Technology; Dentistry); **Medical Biochemistry** (Biochemistry; Biology; Cell Biology; Chemistry); **Medicine** (Anatomy; Computer Science; Dental Technology; Dermatology; Ecology; Embryology and Reproduction Biology; Epidemiology; Ethics; Forensic Medicine and Dentistry; Gynaecology and Obstetrics; Health Sciences; Histology; Hygiene; Immunology; Law; Mathematics; Medicine; Microbiology; Neurology; Oncology; Ophthalmology; Otorhinolaryngology; Pathology; Philosophy; Physics; Physiology; Pneumology; Psychiatry and Mental Health; Psychology; Radiology; Rehabilitation and Therapy; Sociology; Sports Medicine; Surgery; Urology; Virology); **Paediatrics** (Child Care and Development; Paediatrics); **Pharmacy** (Botany; Pharmacology; Pharmacy; Toxicology); **Social Work and Clinical Psychology** (Clinical Psychology; Orthopaedics; Social Work)

Institutes
Pharmacology (Pharmacology); **Rheumatology** (Rheumatology)

Further Information: Also Departments for International Students and Foundation Studies; Research Laboratories

History: Founded 1935. Acquired Academy status 1993. Acquired present status of University 2003.

Governing Bodies: Scientific Council

Academic Year: September to June (September-January; February-June)

Admission Requirements: Secondary school certificate (Attestat o srednem obrazovanii)

Main Language(s) of Instruction: Russian

Degrees and Diplomas: *Specialist Diploma*: Dentistry; Pharmacy, 5 yrs; *Specialist Diploma*: Medicine, 6 yrs; *Kandidat Nauk*: 3 yrs following Specialist's Diploma; *Doktor Nauk*

Student Services: Canteen, Cultural centre, Foreign student adviser, Foreign Studies Centre, Health services, Language programs, Social counselling, Sports facilities

Student Residential Facilities: For c. 1,000 students

Special Facilities: History of the Volgograd State Medical University Museum

Libraries: c. 630,000 vols

Publications: Vestnik of VolSMU, Morphology, Pathology, Pharmacology, Ecology, Obstetrics and Gynecology, Therapy, Surgery, etc. *(quarterly)*

Press or Publishing House: University Publishing House

Last Updated: 28/11/11

VOLGOGRAD STATE PEDAGOGICAL UNIVERSITY

Volgogradskij Gosudarstvennyj Pedagogičeskij Universitet
pr. Lenina 27, Volgograd 400013
Tel: +7(8442) 302-816
Fax: +7(8442) 241-378 +7(8442) 241-369
EMail: dvi@vspu.ru
Website: http://www.vspu.ru

Rector: N.K. Sergeev EMail: rector@vspu.ru; nks@vspu.ru

Colleges
Teacher Training (Foreign Languages Education; Pedagogy; Primary Education; Secondary Education; Teacher Training)

Departments
Chemistry and Chemistry Education (Chemistry; Science Education); **Economics, Social Geography and Geography Education** (Economics; Geography (Human)); **Educational Psychology and Development** (Educational Psychology); **Geography and Natural Sciences** (Geography; Natural Sciences); **History Education** (Civics; History); **History of Russia** (History); **Law** (Law); **Mathematics, Informatics and Physics** (Computer Science; Mathematics; Mathematics Education; Physics; Science Education); **Mechanical Engineering, Safety and Life Safety Education** (Mechanical Engineering; Safety Engineering); **Pedagogy** (Pedagogy); **Philosophy and Political Science** (Philosophy; Political Sciences); **Psychology and Social Work** (Psychology; Social Work); **Social Pedagogy** (Pedagogy); **Social Work** (Social Work); **Technology and Services** (Technology); **Theory and History of Culture** (Cultural Studies)

Divisions
Arts and Graphics Education (Art Education; Graphic Arts; Graphic Design); **Music Education** (Music Education)

Faculties
Design (Design); **Economics and Management** (Economics; Human Resources; Management); **General History** (History); **History and Law** (History; Law); **Language Studies for Foreign Students** (English; Foreign Languages Education; German; Russian); **Mathematics** (Computer Education; Computer Science; Mathematics; Mathematics Education); **Philology** (English; German; Linguistics; Literature; Philology; Russian); **Physical Education and Life** (Physical Education)

Institutes
Art Education (Design; Fine Arts; Graphic Arts; Music; Sculpture); **Foreign Languages** (Chinese; English; French; German; Modern Languages; Spanish); **In-Service Training**; **Personality-Oriented Education** (Continuing Education; Philosophy of Education; Vocational Education); **Preschool, Primary and Special Education** (Preschool Education; Primary Education; Special Education)

History: Founded 1931. Acquired present status 1992.

Governing Bodies: University Management Board; University Council

Academic Year: September to June (September-February; February-June)

Admission Requirements: Secondary school certificate (Attestat o srednem obrazovanii) or equivalent

Main Language(s) of Instruction: Russian; English

International Co-operation: With universities in China, Germany, USA, Netherlands, Denmark, United Kingdom, Czech Republic and France

Accrediting Agencies: Ministry of Education

Degrees and Diplomas: *Bakalavr (B.A.; B.Sc.)*: 4 yrs; *Magistr (M.A.; M.Sc.)*: a further 2 yrs; *Kandidat Nauk (Ph.D.)*: a further 3 yrs; *Doktor Nauk*: a further 3 yrs followin Kandidat

Student Services: Academic counselling, Canteen, Cultural centre, Employment services, Foreign student adviser, Foreign Studies Centre, Handicapped facilities, Health services, Language programs, Social counselling, Sports facilities

Student Residential Facilities: 3 dormitories

Special Facilities: 5 Museums

Libraries: c. 810,000 vols

Publications: Izvestiya of the Volgograd State Pedagogical University *(biennially)*

Press or Publishing House: Peremena Publishing House

Last Updated: 28/11/11

VOLGOGRAD STATE PHYSICAL EDUCATION ACADEMY

Volgogradskaja Gosudarstvennaja Akademija Fizičeskoj Kul'tury

pr. Lenina 78, Volgograd 400005
Tel: +7(8442) 230-195
Fax: +7(8442) 236-672
EMail: vgafk@vlink.ru
Website: http://www.vgafk.ru

Rector: Aleksandr Shamardin (2004-)

Departments

Anatomy (Anatomy; Biology; Ecology); **Foreign Languages** (English; Foreign Languages Education; French; German; Modern Languages); **Natural Sciences and Information Technology** (Computer Science; Information Technology; Mathematics; Natural Sciences; Physics; Statistics); **Part-time Education** (Higher Education; Physical Education; Sports Medicine; Teacher Trainers Education); **Philosophy** (Cultural Studies; History; Law; Philosophy; Political Sciences; Sociology); **Physiology** (Biochemistry; Chemistry; Physiology); **Postgraduate Education** (Higher Education; Physical Education; Sports Medicine; Teacher Trainers Education); **Sports Medicine, Hygiene and Medical Physical Education** (Hygiene; Occupational Therapy; Physical Therapy; Rehabilitation and Therapy; Sports Medicine); **Theory and History of Physical Education and Sport** (Physical Education; Sports)

History: Founded 1960, acquired present status 1996.

Governing Bodies: Scientific Council

Academic Year: September to July (September-January; February-July)

Admission Requirements: Secondary school certificate (Attestat zrelosty) and good ranking in the chosen sport

Main Language(s) of Instruction: Russian

International Co-operation: With universities in Germany. Also participates in DAAD.

Degrees and Diplomas: *Bakalavr*: 4 yrs; *Specialist Diploma*: Theatrical and Holiday Entertainments Production; Education and Psychology; Management; Adaptive Physical Education; Sports and Physical Education, 5 yrs; *Magistr*: Sports and Physical Education, a further 2 yrs; *Kandidat Nauk*: Sports Pedagogy, a further 3 yrs

Student Services: Academic counselling, Canteen, Cultural centre, Employment services, Foreign student adviser, Foreign Studies Centre, Health services, Social counselling, Sports facilities

Student Residential Facilities: For 250 students

Special Facilities: Sports Museum

Libraries: 215,697 vols

Publications: Scientific Papers of Teaching Staff *(annually)*

Press or Publishing House: Publishing House

Academic Staff *2007-2008*	MEN	WOMEN	TOTAL
FULL-TIME	99	118	**217**
PART-TIME	15	9	**24**
STAFF WITH DOCTORATE			
FULL-TIME	70	65	**135**
PART-TIME	9	6	**15**
Student Numbers *2007-2008*			
All (Foreign Included)	1,177	779	**1,956**
FOREIGN ONLY	8	3	**11**

Distance students, 498.

Last Updated: 28/11/11

VOLGOGRAD STATE TECHNICAL UNIVERSITY

Volgogradskij Gosudarstvennyj Tehničeskij Universitet

pr. Lenina 28, Volgograd 400131
Tel: +7(8442) 340-076
Fax: +7(8442) 344-121
EMail: rector@vstu.ru
Website: http://www.vstu.ru

Rector: Ivan Alexandrovič Novakov (1987-)

International Relations: Aleksandr Valentinovič Navrotskij
Tel: +7(8442) 344-121 EMail: navrotskiy@vstu.ru

Faculties

Automobile and Tractor Engineering (Automotive Engineering); **Automobile Transport** (Automotive Engineering; Road Transport; Transport Management); **Chemical Engineering** (Agricultural Engineering; Agricultural Equipment; Analytical Chemistry; Automation and Control Engineering; Biochemistry; Biotechnology; Chemical Engineering; Chemistry; Electrical and Electronic Engineering; Environmental Engineering; Environmental Management; Food Science; Food Technology; Inorganic Chemistry; Mathematics; Mechanics; Molecular Biology; Organic Chemistry; Physical Chemistry; Physics; Polymer and Plastics Technology; Technology; Textile Design; Textile Technology); **Economics and Management** (Advertising and Publicity; Applied Mathematics; Computer Science; Economics; Finance; International Business; International Economics; Management; Marketing); **Electronics and Computer Science** (Artificial Intelligence; Computer Engineering; Computer Graphics; Computer Networks; Data Processing; Electronic Engineering; Information Sciences; Physics; Systems Analysis); **Food Engineering** (Applied Chemistry; Chemistry; Dairy; Electrical and Electronic Engineering; Environmental Management; Food Technology; Mathematics; Meat and Poultry; Mechanics; Natural Resources; Physics); **Mechanical Engineering** (Automation and Control Engineering; Computer Graphics; Machine Building; Mechanical Engineering); **Postgraduate Studies** (Advertising and Publicity; Business Computing; Computer Networks; Computer Science; Data Processing; Economics; Information Technology; Management); **Structural Materials Technology** (Design; Materials Engineering; Metal Techniques; Metallurgical Engineering)

Further Information: Branches in Volzhsky and Kamyshin.

History: Founded 1930, acquired present status and title 1993.

Governing Bodies: University Board

Academic Year: September to July (September-January; February-July)

Admission Requirements: Secondary school certificate (Attestat o polnom srednem obrazovanii) or equivalent

Fees: (Russian Rubles): 30,000-45,000 per annum

Main Language(s) of Instruction: Russian

Accrediting Agencies: Ministry of Education

Degrees and Diplomas: *Bakalavr*: 4 yrs; *Specialist Diploma*: a further 1 1/2-2 yrs; *Magistr*: a further 2 yrs; *Kandidat Nauk*: a further 3-4 yrs

Student Services: Academic counselling, Canteen, Cultural centre, Employment services, Foreign Studies Centre, Health services, Language programs, Social counselling, Sports facilities

Student Residential Facilities: For 2,000 students

Special Facilities: History Museum; Museum of Scientific and Technical Advancement

Libraries: Central Library, 1.2 m. vols

Last Updated: 28/11/11

VOLGOGRAD STATE UNIVERSITY

Volgogradskij Gosudarstvennyj Universitet (VOLSU)

pr. Universitetskij 100, Volgograd 400062
Tel: +7(8442) 40-55-47 +7(8442) 46-02-79
EMail: ob.otdel@volsu.ru; priem@volsu.ru; rector@volsu.ru
Website: http://www.volsu.ru

Rector: Oleg Vasilyevich Inshakov (1996-) EMail: rector@volsu.ru

Vice-Rector for Academic Affairs: Sergei Grigoryevich Sidorov
EMail: urprorector@volsu.ru

International Relations: Pavel V. Timachev, Director of International Office EMail: oms@volsu.ru

Campuses

Uryupinsk (Banking; Finance; History; Law; Management; Philology)

Faculties

Law (Civil Law; Criminal Law; Criminology; Human Rights; International Law; Law); **Management and Regional Economy** (Business Computing; Economics; Management); **Mathematics and Information Technology** (Applied Mathematics; Computer Science; Information Technology; Mathematics); **Natural Sciences** (Biology; Ecology; Environmental Management; Natural Resources; Physical Education; Psychology); **Philosophy, History,**

International Relations and Social Technologies (Archaeology; History; International Relations; Philosophy; Political Sciences; Social Work; Sociology)

Institutes

Humanities *(Volžskij)* (Applied Mathematics; Banking; Ecology; Economics; Environmental Management; Finance; History; Information Technology; Law; Philology; Psychology; Regional Studies); **Philology and Intercultural Communication** (Documentation Techniques; English; German; Journalism; Linguistics; Literature; Philology; Publishing and Book Trade; Russian; Translation and Interpretation); **Physics and Telecommunications** (Laser Engineering; Physics; Telecommunications Engineering; Telecommunications Services); **World Economy and Finances** (Accountancy; Banking; Economic and Finance Policy; Finance; International Business; International Economics; Taxation)

Further Information: Also Study Abroad programmes

History: Founded 1980.

Governing Bodies: University Council

Academic Year: September to June (September-January; February-June)

Admission Requirements: Secondary school certificate (Attestat o srednem obrazovanii) and entrance examination. Interview for applicants who pay tuition fees

Fees: (US Dollars): 1,400-4,000 per 5 yrs; foreign students, 1,150-3,150 per annum

Main Language(s) of Instruction: Russian, English, German, French

Accrediting Agencies: Ministry of Education

Degrees and Diplomas: *Bakalavr*, *Specialist Diploma*; *Magistr*; *Kandidat Nauk*

Student Services: Academic counselling, Canteen, Cultural centre, Employment services, Foreign student adviser, Foreign Studies Centre, Health services, Language programs, Social counselling, Sports facilities

Student Residential Facilities: For 950 students

Special Facilities: Borkovsky Museum; Archaelogy Museum; Russian Military Cadets Museum; Ethnography Museum; University History Museum; Numismatic Museum

Libraries: Central Library, c. 650,000 vols; Rare Book Department, c. 5,000; Mathematics and Physics Library, c. 82,000; Literature and Linguistics Library, c. 271,000; Economics Department Library, c. 274,703; Affiliate Libraries, c. 5,400; Foreign Literature Department, c. 11,900

Publications: Proceedings of International Conferences *(annually)*; Proceedings of the Annual Scientific Conference *(annually)*; Topical Publications of VSU *(biannually)*

Press or Publishing House: Vologograd Universtiy Press

Last Updated: 12/04/11

VOLGOGRAD STATE UNIVERSITY OF ARCHITECTURE AND CIVIL ENGINEERING

Volgogradskij Gosudarstvennyj Arkhitekturno-Stroitelnyj Universitet (VOLGGASU)

ul. Akademicheskaya 1, Volgograd 400074
Tel: +7(8442) 974-872
Fax: +7(8442) 974-933
EMail: info@vgasu.ru; ias@vgasu.ru
Website: http://www.vgasu.ru

Rector: Sergey Yuryevich Kalashnikov
EMail: kalashnikovs@mail.ru; rektor@vgasu.ru

Institutes

Architecture and Civil Engineering (Architectural and Environmental Design; Architecture; Building Technologies; Civil Engineering; Construction Engineering; Engineering; Interior Design; Landscape Architecture; Painting and Drawing; Rural Planning; Sculpture; Town Planning); **Civil Engineering and Technologies** *(Affiliate institute, Volzhsky)* (Civil Engineering; Construction Engineering; Machine Building; Materials Engineering; Road Engineering; Rural Planning; Town Planning); **Distance Education** (Architecture; Civil Engineering; Environmental Engineering; Industrial and Production Economics; Transport Engineering); **Ecology** (Civil Security; Environmental Engineering; Fire Science; Geological Engineering; Heating and Refrigeration; Petroleum and Gas Engineering; Safety Engineering; Solid State Physics; Thermal Engineering); **Economics and Law** (Banking; Economics; Finance; Industrial and Production Economics; Institutional Administration; Law; Management; Private Administration); **Sebryakovsky** *(Affiliate institute)* (Banking; Building Technologies; Construction Engineering; Finance; Industrial and Production Economics); **Traffic Engineering** (Bridge Engineering; Road Engineering; Transport Engineering)

History: Founded 1951, acquired present title and status 2003.

Academic Year: September to June

Admission Requirements: Secondary school certificate (Attesta o srednem obrazovanii)

Main Language(s) of Instruction: Russian

International Co-operation: With universities in the USA, Germany and Canada

Accrediting Agencies: Ministry of Education and Science of the Russian Federation

Degrees and Diplomas: *Bakalavr (BSc)*: 4 yrs; *Specialist Diploma*: 5 yrs; *Magistr*: Civil Engineering; Transport Engineering; Ecology, a further 2 yrs; *Kandidat Nauk*: Technical Science; Physics; Mathematics; Geology, 3 yrs following upon Specialist's Diploma; *Doktor Nauk*: Physics; Geology; Structural Mechanics, 3 yrs after Kandidat Nauk

Student Services: Academic counselling, Canteen, Cultural centre, Employment services, Foreign student adviser, Foreign Studies Centre, Health services, Language programs, Social counselling, Sports facilities

Student Residential Facilities: Yes

Libraries: c. 950,000 vols

Publications: Internet-Vestnik VSUACE, Scientific and Technical mutli-topic Internet Journal *(biannually)*; Vestnik VolGASU, Scientific and Technical Journal *(quarterly)*

Press or Publishing House: Editorial and Publication Department of VolgGASU

Last Updated: 28/11/11

VOLOGDA INSTITUTE OF LAW AND ECONOMICS OF THE FEDERAL PENITENTIARY SERVICE

Vologodskij Institut Prava i Ekonomiki Federalnoj Služby Ispolnenija Nakazanij

ul. Četina, 2, Vologda 160002
Tel: +7(8172) 530-173
Fax: +7(8172) 518-248
EMail: vipe.vologda@mail.ru; ono-vipe@mail.ru
Website: http://www.vipe-fsin.ru/

Rector: Viktor V. Popov

Faculties

Engineering and Economics (Economics; Engineering); **Law** (Law); **Psychology** (Psychology)

History: Created 1979. Previously known as Vologodskij Institut Prava I Economiki, Ministerstva Justicii Rossii (Vologda State Institute of Law and Economics, Ministry of Justice of the Russian Federation)

Degrees and Diplomas: *Bakalavr*, *Specialist Diploma*

Last Updated: 18/04/11

VOLOGDA STATE DAIRY-FARMING ACADEMY NAMED AFTER N. V. VERESHCHAGIN

Vologodskaja Gosudarstvennaja Moločnokhozyaistvennaja Akademija im. N. V. Vereshchagina (VGMKHA)

ul. Šmidt 2, Vologda 160555
Tel: +7(8172) 525-730
Fax: +7(8172) 761-069
EMail: academy@molochnoe.ru
Website: http://www.molochnoe.ru

Rector: Nikolai Malkov Gurievič

Vice-Rector: Andrej Kuzin

Colleges

Technology (Agricultural Engineering; Dairy; Engineering; Technology)

Faculties

Agronomy and Forestry (Agriculture; Agronomy; Botany; Forestry; Physical Education); **Economics** (Accountancy; Agricultural Business; Banking; Crop Production; Economics; Finance; History; Marketing; Philosophy; Statistics); **Engineering** (Agricultural Business; Agricultural Engineering; Agricultural Equipment; Engineering; Mathematics; Mechanical Engineering; Physics); **Technology** (Agricultural Equipment; Applied Chemistry; Chemistry; Dairy; Measurement and Precision Engineering; Modern Languages; Technology); **Veterinary Medicine** (Anatomy; Microbiology; Physiology; Veterinary Science; Zoology); **Zooengineering** (Agricultural Engineering; Animal Husbandry; Cattle Breeding)

History: Created 1911 as Vologodskij Moločnohozyaistvennii Institut. Became Vologodskij Selskohozyaistvennii Institut in 1930. Obtained current status and title 1995.

Main Language(s) of Instruction: Russian

Degrees and Diplomas: *Specialist Diploma*; *Magistr*; *Kandidat Nauk*

Student Services: Canteen, Sports facilities

Student Residential Facilities: 7 residences for c. 2,000 students

Special Facilities: Specialised workshops

Libraries: c. 450,000 vols

Last Updated: 28/11/11

VOLOGDA STATE PEDAGOGICAL UNIVERSITY

Vologodskij Gosudarstvennyj Pedagogičeskij Universitet

ul. S. Orlova 6, Vologda 160035
Tel: +7(8172) 721-683
Fax: +7(8172) 722-550
EMail: common@uni-vologda.ac.ru
Website: http://www.vologda-uni.ru/

International Relations: Lilia A. Berseneva
EMail: oms-vologda@rambler.ru

Faculties

Applied Mathematics and Computer Technologies (Applied Mathematics; Computer Engineering); **Continuing Education** (Advertising and Publicity; Design; Management; Music; Parks and Recreation; Pedagogy; Psychology; Public Relations; Social Work; Sports; Tourism); **Foreign Languages and Cultures** (Cultural Studies; English; Ethnology; Foreign Languages Education; French; German; Modern Languages; Philosophy); **History** (Economics; History; Management); **Law** (Civil Law; Constitutional Law; Criminal Law; International Law; Law; Political Sciences); **Musical Education** (Music; Music Education; Music Theory and Composition; Musical Instruments; Singing); **Natural Sciences and Geography** (Anatomy; Botany; Chemistry; Ecology; Geography; Hygiene; Physiology; Zoology); **Philology** (Communication Studies; Journalism; Literature; Philology; Russian); **Physical Education** (Physical Education; Sports; Sports Medicine); **Physics and Mathematics** (Computer Engineering; Computer Science; Mathematics; Mathematics Education; Physics); **Social Work, Pedagogy and Psychology** (Educational Psychology; Pedagogy; Psychology; Social Work)

History: Created 1912. Acquired present status 1995.

Degrees and Diplomas: *Bakalavr*; *Magistr*

Last Updated: 28/11/11

VOLOGDA STATE TECHNICAL UNIVERSITY

Vologodskij Gosudarstvennyj Tehničeskij Universitet (VSTU)

ul. Lenina 15, Vologda 160000
Tel: +7(8172) 724-645
Fax: +7(8172) 720-292
EMail: vagor@vstu.edu.ru
Website: http://www.vstu.edu.ru

Rector: Leonid Sokolov
EMail: rector_s@mh.vstu.edu.ru; sokolov@vstu.edu.ru

Colleges

Engineering (Accountancy; Automation and Control Engineering; Automotive Engineering; Business and Commerce; Computer Networks; Computer Science; Economics; Engineering; Information Management; Information Technology; Insurance; Production Engineering)

Departments

Civil Engineering (Aeronautical and Aerospace Engineering; Agricultural Engineering; Architectural and Environmental Design; Architecture; Civil Engineering; Engineering Drawing and Design; Heating and Refrigeration; Industrial Engineering; Materials Engineering; Road Engineering; Town Planning); **Electricity** (Automation and Control Engineering; Electrical Engineering; Engineering Management; Information Technology; Mechanical Engineering)

Faculties

Distance Education (Accountancy; Automotive Engineering; Banking; Business Administration; Construction Engineering; Economics; Electrical Engineering; Environmental Engineering; Finance; Information Technology; Management; Mechanical Engineering; Power Engineering; Production Engineering; Public Administration; Water Management); **Ecology** (Chemistry; Ecology; Environmental Studies; Geological Engineering; Geology; Natural Resources; Safety Engineering; Surveying and Mapping; Town Planning; Water Management); **Economics** (Accountancy; Banking; Business Administration; Economics; Finance; Management; Small Business; Transport Management); **Humanities** (Arts and Humanities; Communication Studies; Cultural Studies; Law; Linguistics; Modern Languages; Philosophy; Physical Education; Social Sciences; Tourism; Translation and Interpretation); **Production Management and Innovative Technologies** (Automation and Control Engineering; Automotive Engineering; Engineering Drawing and Design; Engineering Management; Machine Building; Management; Mechanical Engineering; Mechanical Equipment and Maintenance; Production Engineering; Safety Engineering; Wood Technology)

Further Information: Also Interbranch Training Centre and Retrainings of personnel.

History: Founded 1966 as a branch of the Leningrad North-West Correspondence Institute. Became independent Vologda Polytechnic Institute 1975. Acquired present status and title 1999.

Academic Year: September to June

Admission Requirements: School certificate or foreign equivalent

Main Language(s) of Instruction: Russian

Accrediting Agencies: Federal Agency of Education

Degrees and Diplomas: *Diplom o Srednem Professionalnom Obrazovanii (Higher Vocational Education Diploma)*; *Specialist Diploma*; *Magistr*; *Kandidat Nauk*

Student Services: Academic counselling, Canteen, Cultural centre, Employment services, Foreign student adviser, Health services, Language programs, Social counselling, Sports facilities

Student Residential Facilities: Yes.

Special Facilities: Museum. Art gallery.

Libraries: 20,000 new editions, 20 newspapers; 122 magazine titles, annually.

Publications: Alkonost, Literature magazine *(annually)*; Magazine of University Science *(annually)*

Last Updated: 28/11/11

VORONEZH INSTITUTE OF THE MINISTRY OF THE INTERIOR OF THE RUSSIAN FEDERATION

Voronežskij Institut MVD Rossii

prosp. Patriotov 53, Voronež, 394065 Voronežskaja oblast'
Tel: +7(4732) 476-707
Fax: +7(4732) 476-707
EMail: mail@vimvd.ru; vorhmscl@comch.ru
Website: http://www.imvd.vrn.ru

Rector: Aleksandr Viktorovich Simonenko

Faculties

Law (Law); **Radio Technology** (Information Technology; Telecommunications Engineering; Telecommunications Services)

History: Created 1972.

Degrees and Diplomas: *Specialist Diploma*

Last Updated: 19/04/11

VORONEZH STATE ACADEMY OF ARTS

Voronežskaja Gosudarstvennaja Akademija Iskusstv

ul. Generala Lizjukova, 42, Voronež, 394053 Voronežskaja oblast'

Tel: +7(473) 266-14-81 +7(473) 266-16-72

EMail: rector@vsaa.ru

Website: http://www.artacademy.vrn.ru/

Rector: Viktor Semenov

Faculties

Music (Conducting; Music; Musical Instruments; Musicology; Performing Arts; Singing); **Painting** (Fine Arts; Painting and Drawing); **Theatre** (Acting; Performing Arts; Theatre)

History: Created 1971.

Degrees and Diplomas: *Bakalavr*; *Magistr*; *Kandidat Nauk*

Last Updated: 28/11/11

VORONEZH STATE ACADEMY OF FORESTRY ENGINEERING

Voronežskaja Gosudarstvennaja Lesotehničeskaja Akademija (VGLTA/VSAFE)

ul. 8 Timirjazeva, Voronež, 394613 Voronežskaja oblast'

Tel: +7(4732) 538-411

Fax: +7(4732) 537-847

Website: http://www.vglta.vrn.ru

Rector: Vladimir Bugakov (2005-) EMail: rectorat@vglta.vrn.ru

Vice-Rector: Nikolai Matseev
Tel: +7(4732) 538-004, Fax: +7(4732) 538-004

International Relations: V. M. Bugakov
Tel: +7(4732) 538-670 EMail: interdept@vglta.vrn.ru

Programmes

Economics and Management (Business Administration; Economics; International Business; Management); **Forestry** (Applied Physics; Botany; Chemistry; Computer Engineering; Ecology; Forestry; Landscape Architecture; Physics); **Forestry Engineering** (Forest Management; Machine Building; Mechanical Engineering; Transport Management); **Mechanical Engineering and Management in Forestry** (Forest Economics; Forest Management; Furniture Design; Heating and Refrigeration; Wood Technology); **Wood Processing Technology** (Forest Biology; Forest Economics; Forest Management; Forestry; Wood Technology)

Further Information: Also preparatory courses for foreign students

History: Founded 1918 as Forestry and Agriculture Institute, acquired present status and title 1994.

Governing Bodies: Education and Scientific Board

Academic Year: September to July (September-January; January-July)

Admission Requirements: Secondary school certificate (Attestat o srednem obrazovanii)

Fees: (US Dollars): c. 1,750 per annum, including accommodation

Main Language(s) of Instruction: Russian

Degrees and Diplomas: *Bakalavr*; *Specialist Diploma*; *Kandidat Nauk*; *Doktor Nauk*

Student Services: Academic counselling, Canteen, Cultural centre, Foreign student adviser, Foreign Studies Centre, Health services, Language programs, Social counselling, Sports facilities

Student Residential Facilities: For c. 1,700 students

Special Facilities: Experimental Forest. Arboretum. Ecology Laboratory; Modified Wood Laboratory.

Libraries: c. 700,000 vols

Publications: Sbornyk nautchnyh trudov, Scientific Articles; Conference Materials; Abstracts of Conference Papers *(annually)*

Press or Publishing House: Za Lesnyii Kadry

Academic Staff *2007-2008*	**TOTAL**
FULL-TIME	335
PART-TIME	28
STAFF WITH DOCTORATE	
FULL-TIME	268

Student Numbers *2007-2008*	
All (Foreign Included)	4,069
FOREIGN ONLY	155

Part-time students, 651.

Last Updated: 25/11/11

VORONEZH STATE ACADEMY OF TECHNOLOGY

Voronežskaja Gosudarstvennaja Tehnologičeskaja Akademija

pr. Revoljucii 19, Voronež, 394017 Voronežskaja oblast'

Tel: +7(4732) 554-267

Fax: +7(4732) 554-267

EMail: post@vgta.vrn.ru

Website: http://www.vgta.vrn.ru

Rector: Evgenij Tčertov EMail: ched@vgta.vrn.ru

Faculties

Automation and Technological Processes (Automation and Control Engineering; Technology); **Continuing Education**; **Ecology and Chemical Technology** (Ecology; Industrial Chemistry); **Economics** (Economics); **Food Technology** (Food Technology); **Humanities** (Arts and Humanities); **Meat and Dairy Products** (Dairy; Meat and Poultry); **Technology** (Technology)

History: Founded 1930, acquired present status and title 1994.

Academic Year: September to June (September-January; February-June)

Admission Requirements: Secondary school certificate (Attestat o sredem obrazovanii)

Main Language(s) of Instruction: Russian

Degrees and Diplomas: *Bakalavr*: 4 yrs; *Specialist Diploma*: 5 yrs; *Magistr*: a further 2 yrs; *Kandidat Nauk*: 3 yrs; *Doktor Nauk*: a further 2 yrs

Student Services: Academic counselling, Foreign Studies Centre, Handicapped facilities, Health services, Sports facilities

Student Residential Facilities: For c. 1,980 students

Special Facilities: History of the Academy Museum

Libraries: c. 820,000 vols

Press or Publishing House: Press Service

Last Updated: 25/11/11

VORONEZH STATE AGRICULTURAL UNIVERSITY NAMED AFTER EMPEROR PETER I

Voronežskij Gosudarstvennyj Agrarnyj Universitet im. Imperatora Petra I

ul. Mičurina 1, Voronež, 394087 Voronežskaja oblast'

Tel: +7(4732) 538-651

Fax: +7(4732) 538-651

EMail: main@vsau.ru

Website: http://www.vsau.ru

Rector: Vjacheslav Ivanovich Kotarev

Faculties

Accounting and Finance (Accountancy; Applied Mathematics; Finance; Taxation); **Agrochemistry and Soil Science** (Agronomy; Soil Science); **Agroengineering** (Agricultural Engineering; Agricultural Equipment); **Agronomy, Agricultural Chemistry and Ecology** (Agronomy; Botany; Crop Production; Ecology; Fruit Production; Horticulture; Soil Science; Vegetable Production); **Economics and Management** (Agricultural Economics; Farm Management; Management; Marketing); **Humanities and Law** (History; Law; Modern Languages; Philosophy; Physical Education; Social Psychology); **Land Management and Planning** (Landscape Architecture; Rural Planning; Waste Management; Water Management); **Veterinary Science and Animal Husbandry** (Animal Husbandry; Veterinary Science)

History: Founded 1912 as Centre for Agricultural Study. Acquired present status and title 1991.

Governing Bodies: Academic Council

Academic Year: September to July (September-February; February-July)

Admission Requirements: Secondary school certificate (Attestat zrelosti) and entrance examination

Main Language(s) of Instruction: Russian

International Co-operation: Participates in the Tacis and Tempus programmes. Also collaborates with DAAD, APOLLO, LOGO

Degrees and Diplomas: *Bakalavr*; *Specialist Diploma*; *Magistr*

Student Services: Canteen, Cultural centre, Foreign Studies Centre, Health services, Sports facilities

Student Residential Facilities: For 75% of the students

Special Facilities: Museum. Botanical Garden

Libraries: Scientific Library, c. 1 m. vols

Last Updated: 15/03/12

VORONEZH STATE MEDICAL ACADEMY NAMED AFTER N.N. BURDENKO

Voronežskaja Gosudarstvennaja Medicinskaja Akademija im. N.N. Burdenko (VSMA)

Studencheskaja 10, Voronež, 394036 Voronežskaja oblast'
Tel: +7(4732) 593-806
Fax: +7(4732) 530-398
EMail: canc@vsma.ac.ru
Website: http://www.vsma.ac.ru

Rector: Igor Yesaulenko (2000-)

Director of IIMEC: Alexey Morozov
Tel: +7(473) 253-12-22, Fax: +7(473) 253-03-98
EMail: mfsurgery@mail.ru

International Relations: Tatyana Endovitskaya, Deputy Director for International Relations of IIMEC
Tel: +7(473) 253-03-98, Fax: +7(473) 253-03-98
EMail: foreign@vsma.ac.ru

Faculties

Dentistry (Dentistry); **Medicine** (Anaesthesiology; Biomedicine; Cardiology; Dermatology; Diabetology; Endocrinology; Epidemiology; Forensic Medicine and Dentistry; Gastroenterology; Gynaecology and Obstetrics; Haematology; Medical Auxiliaries; Medical Parasitology; Medical Technology; Medicine; Nephrology; Neurology; Oncology; Ophthalmology; Orthopaedics; Otorhinolaryngology; Pathology; Pneumology; Podiatry; Psychiatry and Mental Health; Respiratory Therapy; Rheumatology; Speech Therapy and Audiology; Urology; Venereology); **Paediatrics** (Paediatrics); **Pharmacy** (Pharmacy); **Preventive Medicine** (Medicine)

Institutes

Advanced Nursing (Nursing); **International Institute of Medical Education and Cooperation** *(IIMEC)* (Medicine; Optometry; Public Health; Rehabilitation and Therapy); **Postgraduate Medical Education** (Medicine)

History: Founded 1802 as a university department Voronezh University. Became independent Medical Institute 1930 and acquired present status and title 1994.

Governing Bodies: Academic Council

Academic Year: September-December; February-June

Admission Requirements: Secondary school certificate (Attestat o sredem obrazovanii), with over 50% in biology, chemistry and physics. Overseas students must take entrance examination in natural sciences and Russian language.

Fees: (US Dollars): Higher professional education: General Medicine, 3,000; Pediatrics, 3,000; Pharmacy 3,000; Dentistry, 3,500; Nursing, 2,000.Secondary professional education: Nursing, 2,000; Pharmacy, 1,900; Prosthetic dentistry, 1,900.English medium course in General Medicine: 1-3 years, 3,700; 4-6 years, 3,000.Internship course in the specialties: Therapy, 3,000; Surgery, 3,000; Dentistry, 3,400; Pharmacy, 3,000.Residency course: Therapy, 3,100; Surgery, 3,100; Dentistry, 3,400 (all fees per annum).

Main Language(s) of Instruction: Russian, English

International Co-operation: Erasmus Mundus

Accrediting Agencies: Federal Service for Supervision in Education and Science

Degrees and Diplomas: *Specialist Diploma*: General Medicine (MD); Paediatrics (MD), 6 yrs; *Specialist Diploma*: Pharmacy; Stomatology (MD), 5 yrs; *Kandidat Nauk*: General Medicine (PhD); Paediatrics; Stomatology, 3-4 yrs. Doctor of Science in Medicine

Student Services: Canteen

Student Residential Facilities: Yes.

Special Facilities: Museum of Academy's History; Anatomy Museum; Biological Museum; Laser Centre; Internet Centre

Libraries: 667,782 vols

Academic Staff *2010-2011*	MEN	WOMEN	**TOTAL**
FULL-TIME	213	412	**625**
PART-TIME	64	65	**129**
STAFF WITH DOCTORATE			
FULL-TIME	164	282	**446**
PART-TIME	45	33	**78**
Student Numbers *2010-2011*			
All (Foreign Included)	1,143	3,657	**4,800**
FOREIGN ONLY	235	101	**336**

Part-time students, 537.

Last Updated: 05/05/11

VORONEZH STATE PEDAGOGICAL UNIVERSITY

Voronežskij Gosudarstvennyj Pedagogičeskij Universitet

ul. Lenina 86, Voronež, 394043 Voronežskaja oblast'
Tel: +7(732) 555-747
Fax: +7(732) 555-446
EMail: aspo@vspu.ac.ru; pk@vspu.ac.ru
Website: http://www.vspu.ac.ru

Rector: Aleksandr Sergevich Potapov EMail: rectorat@vspu.ac.ru

Faculties

Art Education (Art Education; Conducting; Fine Arts; Music; Music Education; Singing); **Cultural Studies and Art** (Art Education; Cultural Studies; Design; Preschool Education); **Educational Psychology and Pedagogy** (Educational Psychology; Pedagogy; Primary Education); **Foreign Languages** (English; French; German); **History** (Administration; Archaeology; Economics; History; Social Studies); **Natural Sciences and Geography** (Anatomy; Biology; Chemistry; Ecology; Environmental Management; Geography; Microbiology; Physiology; Plant Pathology); **Physical Education** (Physical Education; Sports); **Physics and Mathematics** (Computer Education; Mathematics; Physics; Technology; Technology Education); **Russian Language and Literature** (Literature; Russian)

History: Founded 1931, acquired present status 1993.

Governing Bodies: Academic Council

Academic Year: September to June

Admission Requirements: Secondary school certificate

Fees: (US Dollars): 900-1,000 per annum

Main Language(s) of Instruction: Russian

International Co-operation: With universities in France

Accrediting Agencies: Ministry of Education

Degrees and Diplomas: *Bakalavr*; *Specialist Diploma*; *Magistr*; *Kandidat Nauk*

Student Services: Academic counselling, Canteen, Foreign student adviser, Foreign Studies Centre, Health services, Language programs, Nursery care, Social counselling, Sports facilities

Student Residential Facilities: Yes

Special Facilities: Museum. Research Biostation

Libraries: Central Library, 525,986 vols

Publications: Educational Technologies *(annually)*; Proceedings of VGPU, Different Fields of Research *(annually)*

Last Updated: 26/04/11

VORONEZH STATE TECHNICAL UNIVERSITY

Voronežskij Gosudarstvennyj Tekhničeskij Universitet

prosp. Moskovskij 14, Voronež, 394026 Voronežskaja oblast'
Tel: +7(4732) 21-09-19 +7(732) 46-26-67
Fax: +7(4732) 46-42-65
EMail: rector@vorstu.ru
Website: http://www.vorstu.ru/

Rector: Vladimir Romanovich Petrenko

Faculties

Automation and Electromechanics (Automation and Control Engineering; Electrical and Electronic Equipment and Maintenance; Information Technology; Power Engineering); **Automation and Robotics Engineering** (Applied Mathematics; Automation and Control Engineering; Computer Science; Machine Building; Robotics); **Aviation** (Aeronautical and Aerospace Engineering; Air Transport); **Engineering Economics** (Engineering Management; Health Administration; Human Resources; Industrial Management); **Physics** (Chemistry; Ecology; Environmental Management; History; Metal Techniques; Metallurgical Engineering; Physics; Political Sciences); **Radio Engineering** (Electronic Engineering; Telecommunications Engineering); **Science and Humanities** (Civil Security; Health Administration; Information Technology; Philosophy; Systems Analysis)

Programmes

Arts and Humanities (Arts and Humanities); **Computer Science** (Computer Science); **Earth Sciences** (Earth Sciences); **Economics** (Economics); **Electronic Engineering** (Electronic Engineering); **Law** (Law); **Mathematics** (Mathematics); **Natural Sciences** (Biological and Life Sciences; Chemistry); **Physics** (Physics)

History: Founded 1918.

Degrees and Diplomas: *Bakalavr*; *Specialist Diploma*; *Magistr*

Last Updated: 15/03/12

VORONEZH STATE UNIVERSITY

Voronežskij Gosudarstvennyj Universitet (VSU)

Universiteckaya ploshad 1, Voronež, 394006 Voronežskaja oblast'
Tel: +7(4732) 207-522 +7(4732) 208-674
Fax: +7(4732) 208-755 +7(4732) 208-972
EMail: office@main.vsu.ru
Website: http://www.vsu.ru

Rector: Dmitrij Endovitsij
Tel: +7(4732) 208-522, Fax: +7(4732) 208-972
EMail: rector@vsu.ru

Faculties

Applied Mathematics, Computer Science and Mechanics (Applied Mathematics; Automation and Control Engineering; Computer Science; Mechanics; Operations Research; Software Engineering); **Biology** (Agrobiology; Analytical Chemistry; Biochemistry; Biology; Biophysics; Biotechnology; Botany; Ecology; Genetics; Microbiology; Physiology; Soil Science; Zoology); **Chemistry** (Analytical Chemistry; Chemistry; Inorganic Chemistry; Organic Chemistry; Physical Chemistry; Polymer and Plastics Technology); **Computer Science** (Computer Science; Information Technology); **Economics** (Accountancy; Applied Mathematics; Economic and Finance Policy; Economics; Finance; Human Resources; Information Technology; International Economics; Management; Marketing); **Geography and Ecology** (Ecology; Environmental Management; Environmental Studies; Geography; Natural Resources; Regional Studies; Rural Planning); **Geology** (Geological Engineering; Geology; Geophysics; Hydraulic Engineering; Mineralogy; Paleontology; Petrology); **History** (Ancient Civilizations; Archaeology; History; Medieval Studies; Modern History; Political Sciences; Sociology); **International Relations** (International Business; International Economics; International Relations; Regional Studies); **Journalism and Media Studies** (Advertising and Publicity; Design; Journalism; Media Studies; Radio and Television Broadcasting); **Law** (Administrative Law; Civil Law; Constitutional Law; Criminal Law; Criminology; European Union Law; Government; International Law; Labour Law; Law); **Mathematics** (Mathematics; Operations Research; Surveying and Mapping); **Pharmacy** (Pharmacology; Pharmacy); **Philology** (Arts and Humanities; Folklore; Linguistics; Literature; Native Language; Philology; Russian; Slavic Languages); **Philosophy and Psychology** (Cultural Studies; Metaphysics; Pedagogy; Philosophy; Psychology; Social Psychology); **Physics** (Electronic Engineering; Mathematical Physics; Nuclear Physics; Optics; Physics; Radiophysics; Solid State Physics); **Romance and Germanic Philology** (Cultural Studies; English; French; German; Germanic Languages; Linguistics; Philology; Romance Languages; Translation and Interpretation)

Institutes

International Education *(For Foreign Students)* (Arts and Humanities; Russian; Science Education)

Further Information: Also Research Institutes, Centres and Laboratories

History: Founded 1918.

Governing Bodies: Academic Council

Academic Year: September to July

Admission Requirements: Secondary school certificate and admission test.

Main Language(s) of Instruction: Russian, English

International Co-operation: With universities in USA. Also participates in the Tempus/Tacis, IREX, INTAS and DAAD programmes;

Degrees and Diplomas: *Bakalavr (BS;BA)*: 4 yrs; *Specialist Diploma*: Applied Mathematics and Information Sciences; Mechanics; Software and Information Systems Management; Applied Mathematics in Jurisprudence; Biology; Soil Science; Chemistry; Information Systems and Technology; Economics; Management; Labour Economy; Hydroecology and Engineering Geology; Ecological Ecology; Geological Survey and Exploration; History; Political Science; Sociology; International Relations; World Economics; Journalism; Advertising; Public Relations; Law; Mathematics; Pharmacy; Philology; National Economy; Financing and Credit; Accountancy, Analysis and Audit; Marketing; Mathematical Methods in Economics; Management; State and Municipal Management; Human Resources Management; Geography; Ecology; Environmental Studies; Geology; Physics; Psychology; Philosophy; Cultural Studies; Social Pedagogy; Physics; Radiophysics; Radiophysics and Electronics; Nanotechnology in Electronics; Microelectronics and Semiconductor Devices; Theory and Methods of Teaching Foreign Languages; Translation and Interpretation; Theoretical and Applied Linguistics, 5 yrs; *Magistr*: Applied Mathematics and Information Sciences; Biology; Chemistry; Economics; Management; Geology; Journalism; Mathematics; Philology; Physics; Radiophysics (MS;MA), a further 2 yrs following Bakalavr; *Kandidat Nauk*: Differential Equations; Physical Chemistry; Electrochemistry; Lithology; Geophysics; Radiophysics; Physics of Semiconductors; Processing of Information; Pedagogy; National Hystory; General History; Archeology; Political Institutions; Conflictology (PhD); Philosophy; Physiology and Biochemistry; Soil Sciences; Biophysics; Biochemistry; Law; Botany; Entomology; Ecology; Theoretical Physics; Optics; Physics of Condensed Matters; Russian; Theory of Language; Inorganic Chemistry; Mathematical Analysis (PhD); Russian Literature; Foreign Literature; Economics; Economics and Management; ; Accountancy; Statistics; Germanic Languages; Roman Languages; Physical Geography; Economic Geography; Geoecology; Journalism; Analytical Chemistry; Organic Chemistry (PhD), a further 3 yrs and thesis; *Doktor Nauk*: Differential Equations; Physical Chemistry; Electrochemistry; Lithology; Geophysics; Radiophysics; Physics of Semiconductors; Processing of Information; Pedagogy; National Hystory; General History; Archeology; Political Institutions; Conflictology; Philosophy; Physiology and Biochemistry; Soil Sciences; Biophysics; Biochemistry; Law; Botany; Entomology; Ecology; Theoretical Physics; Optics; Physics of Condensed Matters; Russian; Theory of Language; Inorganic Chemistry; Mathematical Analysis; Russian Literature; Foreign Literature; Economics; Economics and Management; ; Accountancy; Statistics; Germanic Languages; Roman Languages; Physical Geography; Economic Geography; Geoecology; Journalism; Analytical Chemistry; Organic Chemistry (DS), by thesis following PhD

Student Services: Academic counselling, Canteen, Cultural centre, Employment services, Foreign student adviser, Foreign Studies Centre, Health services, Language programs, Social counselling, Sports facilities

Student Residential Facilities: For c. 3,500 students

Special Facilities: Museums: History; Archaeology; Soil Science; Geology; Zoology. Botanical Garden. Biosphere Preserve. Innovation Centre for New Technologies. Internet Centre

Libraries: University Library, c. 3m. vols

Publications: Condensed Mediums and Phase Boundary Scope *(quarterly)*; Sorption and Chromatographical Processes *(quarterly)*; Vestnic VGU, Series on Physics and Mathematics, Biology and Chemistry, Geology, Geography and Geoecology, Humanities, Higher Education

Press or Publishing House: Voronezh State University Publishing House

Last Updated: 25/11/11

VORONEZH STATE UNIVERSITY OF ARCHITECTURE AND CIVIL ENGINEERING

Voronežskij Gosudarstvennyj Arkhitekturno-Stroitel'nyj Universitet

ul. 20-Letija Oktjabrja 84, Voronež, 394006 Voronežskaja oblast'
Tel: +7(473) 76-39-75 +7(473) 71-59-05
Fax: +7(473) 71-59-05
EMail: rector@vgasu.vrn.ru
Website: http://edu.vgasu.vrn.ru

Rector: Igor S. Surovtsev (1987-)

Faculties

Architecture (Architecture; Design); **Civil Engineering** (Civil Engineering); **Civil Engineering and Technology** (Civil Engineering; Technology); **Distance Education** (Civil Engineering); **Economics and Construction** (Construction Engineering; Economics; Engineering Management; Industrial Management); **Humanities** (Arts and Humanities); **Mechanical Engineering and Highway Construction** (Mechanical Engineering; Road Engineering); **Systems Engineering and Structures** (Building Technologies; Engineering)

Further Information: Also courses for foreign students

History: Founded 1930, acquired present title 2000.

Governing Bodies: Academic Council

Academic Year: September to June (September-January; February-June)

Admission Requirements: Secondary school certificate (Attestat zrelosti) or equivalent

Main Language(s) of Instruction: Russian

Degrees and Diplomas: *Bakalavr*; *Specialist Diploma*; *Magistr*; *Kandidat Nauk*; *Doktor Nauk*

Student Services: Academic counselling, Canteen, Cultural centre, Employment services, Foreign Studies Centre, Health services, Social counselling, Sports facilities

Student Residential Facilities: For 7,000 students

Special Facilities: Historical Museum; Research and Strategy Laboratory; Computer Technology Centre

Libraries: 457,447 vols; 285 periodical subscriptions; access to electronic networks

Press or Publishing House: Press Department

Last Updated: 15/03/12

WESTERN URAL INSTITUTE OF ECONOMICS AND LAW

Zapadno-Ural'skij Institut Ekonomiki i Prava

ul. Sibirskaja, 35, Perm' 614000
Tel: +7(342) 212-76-86 +7(342) 212-54-93
Fax: +7(342) 212-76-86
EMail: zuiep@mail.ru
Website: http://www.wuiel.ru/

Rector: Jelena A. Oracheva

Faculties

Economics (Economics; Finance; Taxation); **Law** (Law); **Management** (Human Resources; Management)

History: Created 1994.

Degrees and Diplomas: *Bakalavr*, *Specialist Diploma*

Last Updated: 18/04/11

YAROSLAVL STATE UNIVERSITY NAMED AFTER P.G.DEMIDOV

Jaroslavskij Gosudarstvennyj Universitet im. P.G. Demidova (YRSU)

Ul. Sovetskaya 14, Yaroslavl 150000
Tel: +7(4852) 728-256
Fax: +7(4852) 255-787
EMail: rectorat@uniyar.ac.ru
Website: http://www.uniyar.ac.ru

Rector: Alexander Rusakov (1983-)
Tel: +7(4852) 797-701, Fax: +7(4852) 728-256
EMail: alex@yars.free.net

Assistant, Rector: Natalia Paykova Tel: +7(4852) 728-256

International Relations: Albina Ergorova, Director
Tel: +7(4852) 725-138, Fax: +7(4852) 797-746
EMail: albina@uniyar.ac.ru; depint@uniyar.ac.ru

Faculties

Biology and Ecology (Biochemistry; Biological and Life Sciences; Biology; Botany; Chemistry; Ecology; Microbiology; Physiology; Zoology) *Head*: Avtandil V. Eremeishvili; **Economics** (Accountancy; Banking; Business Administration; Economics; Finance; Management; Taxation) *Head*: Ludmila B. Parfenova; **History** (Art Management; Contemporary History; History; Medieval Studies; Museum Studies) *Dean*: Vladimir P. Fedyuk; **Law** (Civil Law; Criminal Law; History of Law; Law) *Head*: Ludmila N. Tarusina; **Mathematics** (Applied Mathematics; Computer Science; Mathematics; Operations Research) *Head*: Valery G. Durnev; **Mathematics and Computer Technology** (Applied Mathematics; Mathematics and Computer Science; Software Engineering; Systems Analysis) *Head*: Pavel G. Parfenov; **Physics** (Applied Physics; Atomic and Molecular Physics; Nuclear Physics; Physics; Radiophysics) *Head*: Alexandr N. Kuznetsov; **Psychology** (Developmental Psychology; Educational Psychology; Psychology; Social Psychology) *Head*: Anatoly V. Karpov; **Social and Political Sciences** (Political Sciences; Social Policy; Social Sciences; Social Welfare; Sociology) *Head*: Gadgy M. Nažmutdinov

Further Information: Also Russian language courses for foreign students

History: Founded 1803 as Academy of Higher Sciences; became Demidov Lyceum in 1834; Demidov Law Lyceum in 1868; Jaroslavl State University in 1918. Acquired current title and status 1995.

Governing Bodies: Academic Council

Academic Year: September to July (September-December; January-July)

Admission Requirements: Secondary education certificate (Attestat o srednem obrazovanii) and entrance examination

Fees: (Russian Rubles): 40,000-105,000 per annum

Main Language(s) of Instruction: Russian

International Co-operation: With universities in Finland, France, Germany and USA.

Accrediting Agencies: Federal Agency for Education

Degrees and Diplomas: *Bakalavr*: 4 yrs; *Specialist Diploma*: 5 yrs; *Magistr*: 2 yrs after Bakalavr; *Kandidat Nauk*: a further 3 yrs; *Doktor Nauk*: by thesis after Kandidat

Student Services: Academic counselling, Canteen, Employment services, Foreign student adviser, Foreign Studies Centre, Health services, Language programs, Social counselling, Sports facilities

Student Residential Facilities: Yes

Special Facilities: Internet Center. Movie Studio

Libraries: 777,894 vols. 369 periodical subscriptions.

Publications: Aktualnye Problemy Physiki *(annually)*; Ekonomicheskiy Vestnik, Bulletin on Economics *(annually)*; Juridicheskie zapiski, Juridical Notes *(annually)*; Modelirovanie i Analiz Informatzionnych System, Modelling and Analysis of Information Systems *(1-2 per annum)*; Sovremenye Problemy Matematiki i Informatiki *(annually)*

Academic Staff *2008-2009*	**TOTAL**
FULL-TIME	**346**
PART-TIME	**90**
STAFF WITH DOCTORATE	
FULL-TIME	**78**
Student Numbers *2008-2009*	
All (Foreign Included)	**7,430**

Last Updated: 24/11/08

ZABAIKAL STATE HUMANITARIAN PEDAGOGICAL UNIVERSITY NAMED AFTER N.G. CHERNISHEVSKY

Zabaikalskij Gosudarstvennyj Gumanitarno-Pedagogičeskij Universitet im. N.G. Černyševskogo (ZABGPU)

ul. Babuškina 129,
Chita 672007
Tel: +7(3022) 26-73-17 +7(3022) 35-56-89
Fax: +7(3022) 26-73-17
EMail: rektorchita@mail.ru; asimatov@mail.ru
Website: http://www.zabspu.ru/

Rector: Ivan Ivanovich Katanayev

Faculties

Culture and Art (Cultural Studies; Design; Fine Arts; Museum Management; Museum Studies; Music; Music Education); **History** (History; Humanities and Social Science Education; Political Sciences); **Law** (Civil Law; Criminal Law; Economics; Law; Management); **Modern Languages** (Chinese; English; Foreign Languages Education; French; German; Linguistics; Modern Languages; Philology); **Natural Sciences** (Anatomy; Biology; Chemistry; Community Health; Ecology; Geography; Physiology; Science Education); **Pedagogy** (Pedagogy; Preschool Education; Primary Education; Special Education); **Philology** (Foreign Languages Education; Journalism; Literature; Mongolian; Philology; Russian); **Physical Education** (Physical Education; Sports Management; Sports Medicine); **Physics and Mathematics** (Applied Mathematics; Computer Education; Computer Science; Mathematics; Mathematics Education; Physics; Science Education); **Psychology** (Educational Psychology; Psychology); **Social Work** (Pedagogy; Philosophy; Social Work; Sociology); **Technology** (Business Education; Educational Administration; Technology Education)

History: Founded 1938. Previously known as Zabaikalskij Gosudarstvennyj Pedagogičeskij Universitet (Zabaikal State Pedagogical University). Acquired current title 2003.

Academic Year: September to June

Admission Requirements: Secondary school certificate

Main Language(s) of Instruction: Russian

Degrees and Diplomas: *Bakalavr*, *Specialist Diploma*

Student Services: Academic counselling, Canteen, Cultural centre, Foreign student adviser, Foreign Studies Centre, Health services, Language programs, Social counselling, Sports facilities

Student Residential Facilities: Yes

Special Facilities: Museum of Public Education

Libraries: 561,000 vols

Last Updated: 12/03/12

PRIVATE INSTITUTIONS

ACADEMIC INSTITUTE OF APPLIED ENERGY

Akademičeskij Institut Prikladnoj Energetiki

ul. Industrial'naja, d.46,
Nižnevartovsk,
628600 Tjumenskaja oblast', Khanty-Mansijskij avt. okrug-Jugra
Tel: +7(3466) 63-13-48 +7(3466) 63-12-87 +7(3466) 63-18-46
Fax: +7(3466) 63-12-87
EMail: nv.aipe@gmail.com
Website: http://aipe-nv.ru

Rector: Yuri Zakharovich Kovalev

Programmes

Applied Computing (Business Computing; Computer Engineering; Computer Science)

History: Created 2002.

Degrees and Diplomas: *Bakalavr*, *Specialist Diploma*

Last Updated: 12/01/12

ACADEMIC LAW INSTITUTE

Akademičeskij Pravovoj Institut

ul. Znamenka 10, Moskva 119841
Tel: +7(495) 691-8825
Fax: +7(495) 691-8574
EMail: apu@apu.edu.ru; ovorlova@mailfrom.ru
Website: http://www.apu.edu.ru/

Rector: N.Yu Khamaneva

Departments

Civil Law (Civil Law); **Criminal Law** (Criminal Law); **International Law** (International Law); **Public Law** (Public Law); **Theory and History of State and Law** (History of Law)

Further Information: Branches also in Rjazan and Anapa.

History: Founded 1993 as Akademičeskij Pravovoj Universitet pri Institute Gosudarstva i Prava Rossijskoj Akademii Nauk (Academic Law University (Institute of Law of the Russian Academy of Science)). Acquireed current title 1999.

Degrees and Diplomas: *Specialist Diploma*: Law

Last Updated: 30/07/12

ACADEMY OF INNOVATION MANAGEMENT (INSTITUTE)

Akademija Menedžmenta Innovacij (Institut)

ul. 2-ja Rybinskaja, d.13, Moskva 107113
Tel: +7(495) 973-25-26
EMail: info@mosobrsouz.ru
Website: http://www.mosobrsouz.ru

Rector: Sergej Borisovich Kalmykov

Programmes

Accounting (Accountancy); **Health Management** (Health Administration); **Management** (Educational Administration; Management; Sports Management)

History: Created 1992.

Degrees and Diplomas: *Bakalavr*, *Specialist Diploma*

Last Updated: 14/04/11

ACADEMY OF LABOUR AND SOCIAL RELATIONS

Akademija Truda i Social'nyh Otnošenij (ATISO (ALSR))

ul. Lobačevskogo 90, Moskva 119454
Tel: +7(499) 432-3375
Fax: +7(499) 432-3370
EMail: umu_309@mail.ru; info@atiso.ru
Website: http://www.atiso.ru

Rector: Evgenij Mikhailovich Kozhokin EMail: rector@atiso.ru

Departments

Correspondance Studies (Applied Mathematics; Information Technology; Modern Languages; Philosophy; Physical Education; Political Sciences; Russian; Sociology)

Faculties

International Economics, Finance and Insurance (Economics; Finance; Insurance; International Economics); **Law** (Administration; Civil Law; Commercial Law; Criminal Law; Criminology; International Law; Labour Law; Law); **Social Sciences and Economics** (Economics; Human Resources; Industrial and Production Economics; Management)

Further Information: Also Russian language training for international students

History: Non-governmental organisation founded 1919 by the Federation of Independent Trade Unions of Russia. Acquired present status 1990.

Governing Bodies: Academic Council

Academic Year: September to July

Admission Requirements: Secondary school certificate or equivalent

Main Language(s) of Instruction: Russian

International Co-operation: With universities in China, CIS countries, Germany, Japan, Switzerland, Vietnam

Degrees and Diplomas: *Bakalavr, Specialist Diploma; Magistr*

Student Services: Academic counselling, Canteen, Employment services, Foreign student adviser, Foreign Studies Centre, Language programs, Sports facilities

Student Residential Facilities: Students' Hostel

Special Facilities: Radio and TV Studio; Computer Classes; Conference Hall;

Libraries: c. 700,000 vols

Publications: Labour and Social Relations ("Trud i sotsialnye otnosheniya"), Magazine summarising scientific and practical experience of researchers. Published in Russian *(quarterly)*

Last Updated: 30/06/11

ACADEMY OF LAW AND MANAGEMENT (INSTITUTE)

Akademija Prava i Upravlenija (Institut)
ul Sadovniki, d.2, Moskva 115487
Tel: +7(495) 271-66-52
Fax: +7(495) 271-66-52
EMail: sekretar@academprava.ru
Website: http://www.academprava.ru

Rector: Timofei Nikolaevich Radko

Faculties

Applied Computer Science (Computer Science; Information Technology); **Law** (Law); **Management** (Accountancy; Linguistics; Management; Psychology; Tourism)

History: Created 1997.

Degrees and Diplomas: *Bakalavr, Specialist Diploma*

Last Updated: 26/09/11

ACADEMY OF MARKETING AND SOCIAL INFORMATION TECHNOLOGY

Akademija Marketinga i Social'no-Informacionnyh Tehnologij - IMSIT
ul. Ziposkaja, 5, Krasnodar 350010
Tel: +7(861) 252-25-81 +7(861) 278-22-83
Fax: +7(861) 252-25-81 +7(861) 278-22-83
EMail: info-imsit@mail.ru; imsit@imsit.ru
Website: http://www.imsit.ru

Rector: Sultan N. Jakaev

Faculties

Accounts and Finance (Accountancy; Finance; Taxation); **Computer Science and Information Technology** (Computer Science; Information Technology; Technology)); **Management** (Administration; Economics; Engineering Management; Human Resources; Management); **Marketing, Tourism, and International Business** (African Studies; American Studies; European Studies; International Business; International Economics; Latin American Studies; Marketing; Philology; Public Relations; Regional Studies; Tourism)

Institutes

Eurpean (Business and Commerce; European Studies; Finance; Hotel Management; Insurance; Marketing; Sports Management; Tourism); **Finance** (Banking; Finance); **Information Technology and Innovation** (Computer Science; Information Technology)

Further Information: Branch also in Novosibirsk

History: Created 1994 as Institut Marketinga i Social'no-Informacionnyh Tehnologij (Institute of Marketing and Social-Information Technology). Acquired current title and status 2001.

Degrees and Diplomas: *Bakalavr, Specialist Diploma*

Last Updated: 12/01/12

ACADEMY OF SOCIO-ECONOMIC DEVELOPMENT (INSTITUTE)

Akademija Sotsialno-Ekonomičeskogo Razvitija (Institut)
ul. Ostrjakova 3, Moskva 125057
Tel: +7(495) 107-38-75 +7(495) 505-77-14
Fax: +7(495) 107-38-75
EMail: info@as-ed.ru
Website: http://www.as-ed.ru

Rector: Aleksandr G. Sharov

Faculties

Ecology and Environmental Studies (Ecology; Environmental Studies); **Electronic Engineering** (Electrical and Electronic Engineering; Electrical and Electronic Equipment and Maintenance); **Finance and Credit** (Banking; Finance); **Law** (Law); **Management** (Management); **Psychology; State and Municpal Administration** (Administration; Public Administration)

History: Created 1996 as Academy 'Continent'. Acquired current title and status 2007.

Degrees and Diplomas: *Bakalavr, Specialist Diploma*

Last Updated: 14/04/11

ALTAJ ECONOMIC AND LAW INSTITUTE

Altajskij Ekonomiko-Juridičeskij Institut
Prosp Krasnoarmejskij, 108, Barnaul, 656015 Altaiskij kraj
Tel: +7(3852) 62-66-86
Fax: +7(3852) 62-56-71
EMail: rector@aeli.altai.ru; institut@aeli.altai.ru
Website: http://aeli.altai.ru/

Rector: Victor Ivanovič Stepanov (1993-)
EMail: rector@aeli.altai.ru

Faculties

Economics (Economics; Finance; Management); **Law** (Administrative Law; Civil Law; Criminal Law; Law)

History: Founded in 1993 as the affiliation of Tomsk Higher Economics and Law College. In 1995 was renamed into the Altai Higher Economics and Law College. In 1996 was renamed into Altai Economics and Law Institute.

Governing Bodies: Academic Council

Academic Year: September - June

Admission Requirements: High school certificate and entrance tests

Degrees and Diplomas: *Bakalavr, Specialist Diploma*

Special Facilities: Criminology Museum

Libraries: 50,000 vols

Last Updated: 31/07/12

ARMAVIR FINANCE AND ECONOMICS INSTITUTE

Armavirskij Finansovo-Economičeskij Institut
ul. Kirova 127, Armavir, 352905 Krasnodarskij Krai
Tel: +7(86137) 466-44
EMail: afei@mail.ru
Website: http://www.afei.ru

Rector: Evgenij D. Aksaev

Programmes

Economics and Finance

ARMAVIR LINGUISTIC SOCIAL INSTITUTE

Armavirskij Lingvističeskij Sotsialnyj Institut
ul. Kirova 22-24, Armavir, 352901 Krasnodarskij Krai
Tel: +7(86137) 334-41 +7(86137) 334-35
Fax: +7(86137) 334-51
EMail: alsi@itech.ru
Website: http://www.alu.itech.ru

Rector: Fatima Nurdinova Avanesova

Faculties

Economics (Accountancy; Economics); **Law** (Civil Law; Criminal Law; Law; Public Law); **Linguistics** (English; French; German; Latin; Linguistics; Philology; Spanish); **Public Relations** (Advertising and Publicity; Public Relations)

History: Founded 1992, previously known as Armavirskij Lingvističeskij Universitet. Acquired current title 2002.

Governing Bodies: Scientific council; Rectorate

Academic Year: September to June (September-January; January-June)

Admission Requirements: Secondary school certificate (Attesta o srednem obrazovanii, or foreign equivalent) and entrance examination

Main Language(s) of Instruction: Russian

Accrediting Agencies: Ministry of Education of the Russian Federation

Degrees and Diplomas: *Bakalavr*, *Specialist Diploma*

Student Services: Academic counselling, Canteen, Cultural centre, Employment services, Foreign student adviser, Foreign Studies Centre, Health services, Language programs, Nursery care, Social counselling, Sports facilities

Student Residential Facilities: For c. 150 students

Special Facilities: Computer classrooms

Libraries: c. 30,000 vols

Distance students, 408.

Last Updated: 30/06/11

ARMAVIR SOCIAL ORTHODOX INSTITUTE

Armavirskij Pravoslavno-Social'nyj Institut (APSI)
ul. Lunačarskogo 185, Armavir, 352905 Krasnodarskij Kraj
Tel: +7(86137) 74-338
Fax: +7(86137) 74-194
EMail: apsi@bk.ru
Website: http://www.ap-si.ru/

Rektor: Sergej P. Tokar (1993-)

Vice-Rector: Evgenij Fedotenkov

International Relations: Evgenij Fedotenkov, Vice-Rector

Faculties

Applied Information Science (Information Sciences) *Dean*: Olga Matukh; **Jurisprudence** *Dean*: Natalia Tarasyan; **Postgraduate Studies** (Anthropology; Cultural Studies; Philosophy; Religious Studies) *Director*: Anna Shuster; **Psychology** (Psychology) *Dean*: Tatiana Demidova; **Religious Science** (Religion; Religious Studies) *Dean*: Pavel Kalinin

History: Founded in 1993.

Governing Bodies: Council of Founders

Admission Requirements: Attestat o Srednem Obshchem Obrazovanii (Secondary school certificate)

Fees: (Russian Rubles): 25,000 per annum

Main Language(s) of Instruction: Russian

Accrediting Agencies: Ministry of Education and Science

Degrees and Diplomas: *Specialist Diploma*: Jurisprudence; Psychology; Religious Science; Economics; Information Science; Accounting, 5 yrs; *Kandidat Nauk*: Religious Science; Philosophic Anthropology; Cultural Philosophy, a further 3 yrs plus thesis

Student Services: Academic counselling, Canteen, Cultural centre, Employment services, Health services, Nursery care, Social counselling, Sports facilities

Student Residential Facilities: none

Special Facilities: Icon-painting School

Libraries: yes

BALTIC INSTITUTE OF ECOLOGY, POLITICS AND LAW

Baltijskij Institut Ekologii, Politiki i Prava
17-ja Linija, V.O., d. 4-6, Sankt-Peterburg 199034
Tel: +7(812) 327-71-07 +7(812) 327-60-94
Fax: +7(812) 327-79-74
EMail: info@buepl.ru; vkarmazinenko@buepl.ru
Website: http://www.buepl.spb.ru

Rector: Evgenij Davidovich Reife EMail: rector@buepl.ru

Faculties

Business Administration (Accountancy; Economics; Finance; Management); **Design** (Design; Fashion Design; Interior Design); **Environmental Sciences** (Ecology; Environmental Management; Natural Resources); **Law** (Law); **Performing Arts** (Acting; Theatre); **Psychology** (Psychology)

History: Created 1993. Acquire current status 2008.

Degrees and Diplomas: *Bakalavr*, *Specialist Diploma*

Last Updated: 15/04/11

BALTIC INSTITUTE OF ECONOMICS AND FINANCE

Baltijskij Institut Ekonomiki i Finansov
ul. Generala Ozerova 57, Kaliningrad 236040
Tel: +7(0112) 275-062 +7(0112) 275-463
Fax: +7(0112) 275-062
EMail: info@bief.ru
Website: http://www.bief.ru

Rector: Albert G. Mnacakanjan

BALTIC INSTITUTE OF FOREIGN LANGUAGES AND INTERNATIONAL COOPERATION

Baltijskij Institut Inostrannyh Jazykov i Meždunarodnogo Sotrudničestva
ul. Millionnaja 6, Sankt-Peterburg 191186
Tel: +7(812) 110-6756
Fax: +7(812) 110-6756 +7(812) 312-9981
Website: http://www.buflic.bu.spb.ru

Rector: Evgenij D. Reife

Programmes

Foreign Languages and International Cooperation (Foreign Languages Education; International Relations)

BALTIC INTERNATIONAL INSTITUTE OF TOURISM

Baltijskij Meždunarodnyj Institut Turizma
prosp. Morskojskij 29, Sankt-Peterburg 197042
Tel: +7(812) 235-5066
Fax: +7(812) 230-0115
EMail: bmit@mail.wplus.net
Website: http://www.bmit.spb.ru

Rector: Tamara I. Vlasova

Programmes

Finance and Banking (Banking; Finance); **Management** (Management); **Tourism** (Tourism)

BELGOROD LAW INSTITUTE OF THE MINISTRY OF THE INTERIOR OF THE RUSSIAN FEDERATION

Belgorodskij Juridičeskij Institut Ministerstva Vnutrennij del Rossijskoj Federatsii
ul. Gor'kogo, 71, Belgorod 308024
Tel: +7(4722) 55-71-13
Fax: +7(4722) 55-53-31
EMail: bui@belgtts.ru
Website: http://www.belui.ru/

Rector: Igor Filippov Amelchakov

Faculties

Law (Law); **Law Enforcement** (Criminology; Police Studies)

History: Create 1997. Previously known as Belgorodskaja Vysshaja Shkola Militsii (Belogord Higher School of Military Training).

Degrees and Diplomas: *Specialist Diploma*

Last Updated: 15/04/11

IAU BELGOROD UNIVERSITY OF COOPERATION, ECONOMICS AND LAW

Belgorodskij Universitet Kooperacii, Ekonomika i Prava (BUCC)
ul. Sadovaja 1116a, Belgorod 308023
Tel: +7(4722) 264-389
Fax: +7(4722) 260-848
EMail: rector@bukep.ru
Website: http://www.bukep.ru/

Rector: Vitalij Ivanovich Teplov (2007-)

First Vice-Rector for Academic Affairs: Elena Vitalievna Isaenko
Tel: +7(4722) 265-297, Fax: +7(4722) 265-297
EMail: educate@bukep.ru; acad@bukep.ru

International Relations: Elizaveta Evgenievna Tarasova, First Vice-Rector for Research
Tel: +7(4722) 260-747, Fax: +7(4722) 260-747
EMail: research@bukep.ru; tarasova@bukep.ru

Faculties

Computer Education and Information Protection (Business Computing; Computer Science; Information Sciences; Software Engineering); **Customs** (Taxation); **Economics** (Economics); **Finance and Accounting** (Accountancy; Finance); **Law** (Law); **Management** (Archiving; Documentation Techniques; Government; Management; Marketing; Psychology; Social Work); **Secondary Vocational Education** (Accountancy; Advertising and Publicity; Archiving; Banking; Business and Commerce; Cooking and Catering; Documentation Techniques; Economics; Food Technology; Hotel and Restaurant; Information Sciences; Law; Photography; Service Trades; Social Welfare; Tourism); **Technology** (Advertising and Publicity; Cooking and Catering; Design; Food Science; Food Technology; Service Trades; Tourism)

History: Founded 1978, acquired present status 1996. Previously known as Belgorod University of Consumer Cooperatives (Belgorodskij Universitet Potrebitelskoj Kooperacii).

Governing Bodies: Learned Council; Rector

Academic Year: September - June

Main Language(s) of Instruction: Russian

Accrediting Agencies: State Accreditation

Degrees and Diplomas: *Bakalavr*: 4 yrs; *Specialist Diploma*: 5 yrs; *Magistr*: 2 yrs after Bakalavr; *Kandidat Nauk*: 3 yrs; *Doktor Nauk*: 4 yrs

Student Services: Academic counselling, Canteen, Cultural centre, Employment services, Foreign student adviser, Foreign Studies Centre, Health services, Language programs, Social counselling, Sports facilities

Student Residential Facilities: For 1,221 students

Special Facilities: Museum of History of Consumer Co-operatives

Libraries: 647,000 vols, 252 periodical subscriptions, 356 vols.

Academic Staff *2010-2011*	**TOTAL**
FULL-TIME	**334**
PART-TIME	**3**
STAFF WITH DOCTORATE	
FULL-TIME	**36**
Student Numbers *2010-2011*	
All (Foreign Included)	**23,773**

Last Updated: 06/06/11

BLACK SEA HUMANITARIAN ACADEMY

Černomorskaja Gumanitarnaja Akademija (CHGA)
ul. Ordžonikidze 10A, Soči, 354000 Krasnodarskij Kraj
Tel: +7(8622) 62-08-29
Fax: +7(8622) 62-08-29
EMail: chga@inbox.ru
Website: http://www.chga.sochi.ru/

Rector: Galina A. Berulava

Faculties

Economics (Accountancy; Economics; Finance; International Economics; Taxation); **Information Technology** (Computer Engineering; Information Technology; Transport Engineering); **Law** (Law); **Management, Resort Services and Tourism**

History: Previously known as Institut Ekonomiki, Prava i Sociologii (Institute of Economics, Law and Sociology)

Admission Requirements: Attestat o Srednem Pol'nom Obrazovanii

International Co-operation: with Germany and USA

Accrediting Agencies: Ministry of Education and Science of the Russian Federation

CHELYABINSK INSTITUTE OF ECONOMICS AND LAW NAMED AFTER M.V. LADOSHINA

Čeljabinskij Institut Ekonomiki i Prava im M.V. Ladošina
ul. Energetikov 63, Čeljabinsk 454135
Tel: +7(351) 253-54-15 +7(351) 253-54-12
Fax: +7(351) 253-54-15
EMail: info@chiep.ru
Website: http://www.chiep.ru/

Rector: Galina Ivanovna Ladoshina

Faculties

Business and Law (Accountancy; Economics; Finance; International Economics; Journalism; Law; Linguistics; Management; Public Relations; Translation and Interpretation)

History: Created 1996. Previously known as Čeljabinskij Institut Ekonomiki i Prava (Chelyabinsk Institute of Economics and Law). Acquired current title 2003.

Degrees and Diplomas: *Bakalavr*, *Specialist Diploma*

Last Updated: 19/01/12

DONSKOI LAW INSTITUTE

Donskoj Juridičeskij Institut
ul. Oborony 49, Rostov-na-Donu 344008
Tel: +7(8632) 339-767
Fax: +7(8632) 359-944
EMail: dui@aaanet.ru
Website: http://www.dui.ru

Rector: E.I. Dulimov

Programmes

Law (Law)

EAST EUROPEAN INSTITUTE OF PSYCHOANALYSIS

Vostočno-Evropejskij Institut Psihoanaliza (EEPI)
Bol'šoj prosp., Petrogrdskaja Storona 18a, Sankt-Peterburg 197198
Tel: +7(812) 235-28-57 +7(812) 235-11-39
Fax: +7(812) 235-28-57
EMail: rector@oedipus.ru
Website: http://veip.oedipus.ru/

Rector: Mihail Reshetnikov

Faculties

Psychology and Psychoanalysis (Clinical Psychology; Philosophy; Psychoanalysis; Psychology; Psychotherapy)

History: Created 1991.

Governing Bodies: Scientific Council

Academic Year: September to July

Admission Requirements: Complete School Education for Psychology, Complete Higher Education for Psychoanalysis

Main Language(s) of Instruction: Russian

International Co-operation: Ministry of Education

Degrees and Diplomas: *Specialist Diploma*: Psychoanalysis, 3 yrs; *Specialist Diploma*: Psychology, 5 yrs

Student Services: Academic counselling, Foreign student adviser, Nursery care

Student Residential Facilities: None.

Special Facilities: Sigmund Freud's Dreams Museum. Modern Art Gallery. Movie club

Libraries: More than 10,000 vols in Russian and English

Publications: Books on Psychology and Psychoanalysis, Classical and modern works; Psychoanalytical Bulletin *(biennially)*

Press or Publishing House: Publishing House

Last Updated: 25/11/11

EASTERN HUMANITIES ACADEMY FOR ECONOMICS AND LAW

Vostočnaja Ekonomiko-Juridičeskaja Gumanitarnaja Akademija
ul. Mubarjakova, 3, Ufa, 450092 Respublika Bashkortosan
Tel: +7(347) 241-55-71
Fax: +7(347) 241-55-50 +7(347) 241-55-51
EMail: minnibaev@vegu.ru; ace@vegu.ru; masalimov@vegu.ru
Website: http://www.vegu.ru/

Rector: Evgenij Kadyrovich Minnibaev EMail: minnibaev@vegu.ru

Institutes

Economics, Management, and Information Science (Business Computing; Computer Engineering; Computer Science; Economics; Management; Marketing); **Law** (International Relations; Law); **Psychology, Socio-Cultural Work and Journalism** (Cultural Studies; Design; Folklore; Journalism; Pedagogy; Philology; Physical Chemistry; Preschool Education; Primary Education; Psychology; Social Work; Special Education; Tourism)

Further Information: Branches also in Al'metevsk, Moscow, Naberezhnye Chelny, Samara, Sochi, Sterlitamak, Tol'jatti, Tomsk.

History: Created 1993. Previously known as Vostočnyj Institut Ekonomiki, Gumanitarnyh Nauk, Upravlenija i Prava (Eastern Institute of Economics, Humanitarian Science, Management and Law). Acquired current title 2008.

Degrees and Diplomas: *Bakalavr*, *Specialist Diploma*; *Magistr*
Last Updated: 12/03/12

EASTERN INSTITUTE

Vostočnyj Institut
Tuchkov pereulok, d. 11/5, Sankt-Peterburg 199053
Tel: +7(812) 320-9733
Fax: +7(812) 320-9733
EMail: info@orientalinstitute.ru
Website: http://www.orientalinstitute.ru/

Rector: Konstantin Edwardovich Khmelevskij

Programmes

Chinese (Chinese); **Japanese** (Japanese)

History: Created 1994.

Degrees and Diplomas: *Bakalavr*, *Specialist Diploma*
Last Updated: 18/04/11

EASTERN SIBERIAN INSTITUTE OF ECONOMICS AND LAW

Vostočno-Sibirskij Institut Ekonomiki i Prava
ul. Baikalskaja, 258a, Irkutsk, 664050 Irkutskaja oblast'
Tel: +7(3952) 35-06-87
Fax: +7(3952) 35-71-44
EMail: mail@esiel.ru
Website: http://www.esiel.ru/

Rector: Aleksandr Nikolaevich Trukhin

Faculties

Accounting and Finance (Accountancy; Finance); **Law** (Law); **Management and Tourism** (Management; Tourism)

History: Created 1997.

Degrees and Diplomas: *Bakalavr*, *Specialist Diploma*
Last Updated: 22/09/11

ESSENTUKI INSTITUTE OF MANAGEMENT, BUSINESS AND LAW

Essentukskij Institut Upravlenija, Biznesa i Prava
ul. Ermolova 2, Essentuki, 357600 Stavropol'skij kraj
Tel: +7(87934) 62-600 +7(87934) 63-383
Fax: +7(78934) 62-600
EMail: eimbp@esstel.ru
Website: http://www.eimbl.webjump.com
Rector: Anatolij V. Aralov

Programmes

Business and Commerce; **Law**; **Management**

EURO-ASIAN INSTITUTE OF MANAGEMENT AND BUSINESS

Evrpejsko-Aziatskij Institut Upravlenija i Predprinimatel'stva
ul. Shchorsa, 54a, Ekaterinburg, 620142 Sverdlovskaja oblast'
Tel: +7(343) 260-76-14
Fax: +7(343) 260-76-12
EMail: info@ame.ru
Website: http://www.ame.ru

Rector: Vladimir A. Bulanichev

Programmes

Business and Management (Business Administration; Business and Commerce; Economics; Management; Marketing)

History: Created 1992. Previously known as Akademija Upravlenja i Predprinimatel'stva (Institut) (Academy of Management and Business (Institute)). Acquired current title 2004.

Degrees and Diplomas: *Bakalavr*, *Specialist Diploma*
Last Updated: 31/07/12

FAR EAST INSTITUTE OF MANAGEMENT, BUSINESS AND LAW

Dal'nevostočnaja Institut Upravlenija, Biznesa i Prava
ul. Viluiskaja 25, Petropavlovsk-Kamčatskij, 683003 Kamčatskij Kraj
Tel: +7(4152) 42–34–69 +7(4152) 42–54–90
Fax: +7(4152) 42-34-69 +7(4152) 42-54-90
EMail: rectordvf@mail.ru
Website: http://www.diubp.ru/

Rector: Vladimir I. Dvorcov

Faculties

Economics (Accountancy; Economics; Finance)

History: Founded 1991. Previously known as Dal'nevostočnaja Akademija Upravlenija, Biznesa i Prava.

Degrees and Diplomas: *Specialist Diploma*

Student Services: Employment services

Libraries: c. 18,000 vols
Last Updated: 15/04/11

FAR EASTERN INSTITUTE OF LAW AND JURISPRUDENCE

Dal'nevostočnyj Institut Zakonodatel'stva i Pravovedenija
ul. Angarskaja 11, Khabarovsk 680006
Tel: +7(4212) 364-405
Fax: +7(4212) 362-074
Website: http://www.dvizip.ru

Rector: Nikolaj M. Rudjakov

Programmes

Law (Law)

FIRST MOSCOW LAW INSTITUTE

Pervyj Moskovskij Juridičeskij Institut
ul. Sadovo-Kudrinskaja, 9, Moskva 105005
Tel: +7(499) 261-9091
Fax: +7(499) 267-3070 +7(499) 267-3100
EMail: pmui@pmui.ru
Website: http://www.pmui.ru

Rector: Maria Varlen (2008-) Tel: +7(499) 267-3070

Pro-Rector, Academic Affairs: Natalia Sokolova
Tel: +7(499) 267-9784

International Relations: Aelita Smolyachenko, International Relations Officer

Institutes

Law (Administrative Law; Civil Law; Commercial Law; Comparative Law; Constitutional Law; Criminal Law; International Law; Labour Law; Private Law; Public Law)

History: Founded 1992. Acquired present status 1996.

Governing Bodies: Rectorate

Academic Year: Sep - Dec; Feb - July

Admission Requirements: Attestat o Srednem Obrazovanii (Secondary School Leaving Certificate) and Edinyj Gosudarstvennyj Ekzamen (Unified National Examination)

Fees: (RUB): 140,000 per annum

Main Language(s) of Instruction: Russian

Accrediting Agencies: Federal Education and Science Supervision Agency

Degrees and Diplomas: *Bakalavr*; *Specialist Diploma*; *Magistr*

Student Residential Facilities: Hostel accommodation.

Libraries: 45,115 vols

Academic Staff *2010-2011*	MEN	WOMEN	TOTAL
FULL-TIME	8	17	**25**
PART-TIME	–	7	**7**
STAFF WITH DOCTORATE			
FULL-TIME	1	5	**6**
Student Numbers *2010-2011*			
All (Foreign Included)	231	254	**485**

Distance students, 195. **Evening students**, 116.

Last Updated: 20/05/11

FRANCO-RUSSIAN INSTITUTE OF BUSINESS ADMINISTRATION

Franko-Rossijskij Institut Delovogo Administrirovanija (FRIBA)

prosp. Lenina 129, Obninsk, 249030 Kaluga Region
Tel: +7(8439) 346-43
Fax: +7(8439) 408-88
EMail: fridas@obninsk.ru
Website: http://www.fridas.ru

Rector: Anatolij Sotnikov (1993-)

Deputy Rector: Valerij Patsula Tel: +7(8439) 658-57

International Relations: Julia Rastopchina
Tel: +7(8439) 733-51 EMail: abc@obninsk.ru

Centres

Business Training (Business and Commerce) *Director*: Olga Kolossova; **Education** (English; Foreign Languages Education; Russian) *Director*: Julia Rastopčina; **Pre-University Training** *Director*: Galina Rygina

Faculties

Management (Management; Marketing; Public Relations) *Dean*: Valerij Patsula

History: Founded 1993.

Governing Bodies: Administration Board

Academic Year: September to July

Admission Requirements: Secondary school certificate and entrance examination

Fees: (Russian Rubles): 43,000 per annum

Main Language(s) of Instruction: Russian

Accrediting Agencies: Ministry of Education

Degrees and Diplomas: *Bakalavr*: 4 yrs; *Specialist Diploma*: 5 yrs

Student Services: Academic counselling, Canteen, Employment services, Foreign student adviser, Language programs

Student Residential Facilities: For 80 students

Libraries: 80,000 vols

HIGHER SCHOOL OF MODERN EDUCATION (INSTITUTE)

Vysšaja Škola Sovremennogo Obrazovanija (Institut)

Malyi Golovin per. 14/17, Moskva 107045
Tel: +7(495) 607-40-73 +7(495) 607-25-64
Fax: +7(495) 607-40-73
EMail: school-so@mail.ru
Website: http://www.school-so.ru

Rector: Vera Ivanovna Šlenkina

Programmes

Economics (Economics)

History: Founded 1997.

Admission Requirements: Secondary School Certificate

Main Language(s) of Instruction: Russian, English

Accrediting Agencies: Ministry of Education of the Russian Federation

Degrees and Diplomas: *Specialist Diploma*: Economics, 5 yrs. Also Certificate of Interpreter

Student Services: Academic counselling, Canteen, Foreign student adviser, Health services, Language programs, Sports facilities

Student Residential Facilities: Yes

Libraries: 4,650 vols

Last Updated: 18/04/11

HUMANITARIAN INSTITUTE

Gumanitarnyj Institut

1-aja Mytiščinskaja, 8, d. 23, Moskva 129626
Tel: +7(495) 978-80-67 +7(495) 682-21-73
Fax: +7(495) 682-21-73
EMail: rektorat@huminst.ru; abitur@huminst.ru
Website: http://www.huminst.ru/

Rector: Aleksandr Mikhajlovich Shakhrai

Faculties

Economics (Economics; Management); **Information Technology** (Business Computing; Information Technology); **Law** (Law); **Linguistics** (Linguistics; Translation and Interpretation); **Psychology** (Industrial and Organizational Psychology; Psychology; Social Psychology)

Further Information: Also Branch in Nizhnij Novgorod, Ulan Ude, Shakkty.

History: Created 1995.

Degrees and Diplomas: *Bakalavr*; *Specialist Diploma*; *Kandidat Nauk*

Last Updated: 17/01/12

INSTITUTE FOR THE HISTORY OF CULTURE

Institut Istorii Kul'tur

ul. Južnobutovskaja, 53, Moskva 113042
Tel: +7(495) 968-69-21
Fax: +7(495) 968-69-21
EMail: unic@dol.ru
Website: http://www.unic.dol.ru

Rector: Evgenij Anatolievich Ermolin

INSTITUTE FOR THE HUMANITIES AND INFORMATION TECHNOLOGY

Institut Gumanitarnogo Obrazovanija i Informatsionnykh Tekhnologij

ul. 9-ja Parkovaja, 48, kor. 5. Bil.2, Moskva 105264
Tel: +7(495) 603-85-77
Fax: +7(495) 603-80-44
EMail: rektorat@igumo.ru; capital@igumo.ru
Website: http://www.igumo.ru

Rector: Marina Vladimirovna Volynkina

Faculties

Advertising and Public Relations (Advertising and Publicity; Public Relations); **Design** (Design; Graphic Design; Interior Design); **Economy** (Accountancy; Economics; Finance; Human Resources; Management; Marketing; Taxation); **Foreign Languages** (English; Foreign Languages Education; Germanic Languages; Linguistics; Philology; Romance Languages; Translation and Interpretation); **Information Technology** (Applied Mathematics; Business Computing; Computer Science; Information Management; Information Technology); **Journalism** (Journalism); **Law** (Civil Law; Criminal Law; Law); **Management** (Management; Small Business); **Psychology** (Clinical Psychology; Psychology; Social Psychology); **Theatre** (Acting; Art Education; Theatre)

History: Created 1996. Previously known as Institut Humanitarnogo Obrazovanija (Institute of Humanitarian Education). Acquired current title 2008.

Degrees and Diplomas: *Bakalavr*; *Specialist Diploma*

Last Updated: 19/01/12

INSTITUTE OF BUSINESS AND LAW - MOSCOW

Institut Biznesa i Prava - Moskva

Olimpijskij prosp. 30, Moskva 129272
Tel: +7(495) 215-55-57
Fax: +7(495) 215-14-55
Website: http://www.st7.ru

Rector: Edvard Aramovich Abgarjan

Programmes
Business and Law (Business Administration; Law)

INSTITUTE OF BUSINESS AND LAW - SAINT PETERSBURG

Institut Biznesa i Prava - Sankt-Peterburg
ul. Lomonosova 9, of. 1631, Sankt-Peterburg 191002
Tel: +7(812) 315-37-37
Fax: +7(812) 325-04-13
EMail: info@ibl.ru
Website: http://www.ibl.ru

Rector: Viktor L. Vasilenok

Programmes
Business and Law (Business Administration; Law)

INSTITUTE OF BUSINESS AND POLICY

Institut Biznesa i Politiki
ul. Aleksandra Solzhenitsyna, 13, str. 13, Moskva 109004
Tel: +7(495) 912-06-46 +7(495) 912-90-19
Fax: +7(495) 912-90-19
EMail: priem@ibp-m.ru
Website: http://ibp-portal.ru/

Rector: Igor Vitalevich Demichev

Faculties
Economics and Management (Economics; Management); **Foreign Languages** (Linguistics; Modern History); **Law** (Law); **Political Science** (Cultural Studies; Political Sciences); **Practical Psychology** (Psychology)

History: Created 1994.

Degrees and Diplomas: *Bakalavr*, *Specialist Diploma*
Last Updated: 24/01/12

INSTITUTE OF BUSINESS CAREERS

Institut Delavoj Kar'ery
prosp. Volgogradskij, 12, Moskva 105264
Tel: +7(495) 361-7444
Fax: +7(495) 361-7444
EMail: info@ideka.ru
Website: http://www.ideka.ru

Rector: Valerij Alekseevich Nazarov

INSTITUTE OF BUSINESS INFRASTRUCTURE

Institut Infrastruktury Predprininatel'stva
ul. Altuf'evskoe shosse, 27a, Moskva 127106
Tel: +7(499) 201-13-56 +7(499) 500-61-55
Fax: +7(499) 201-13-56 +7(499) 500-61-55
EMail: iip@noiip.ru
Website: http://noiip.ru/iip/

Rector: Tomara Vasil'evna Bogomolova

Programmes
Accounting (Accountancy); **Law** (Law); **State and Municipal Management** (Administration)

History: Created 1995.

Degrees and Diplomas: *Bakalavr*, *Specialist Diploma*
Last Updated: 26/01/12

INSTITUTE OF BUSINESS, PSYCHOLOGY AND MANAGEMENT

Institut Biznesa, Psikhologii i Upravlenija
ul. Zoi Kosmodem'janskoj, 2, Khimki, 141400 Moskovskaja oblast'
Tel: +7(495) 572-57-95 +7(455) 572-04-44
Fax: +7(495) 573-21-10
EMail: info@ibpu.ru
Website: http://www.ibpu.ru

Rector: Tomara Borisovna Solomatina

Faculties
Customs (Taxation); **Economics and Management** (Business and Commerce; Economics; Information Technology; Management); **Social Sciences and Humanities** (Design; Pedagogy; Psychology; Social Work)

History: Created 1997.

Degrees and Diplomas: *Bakalavr*, *Specialist Diploma*; *Magistr*
Last Updated: 26/01/12

INSTITUTE OF CIVILIZATION

Institut Tsivilizatsii
ul. Gastello, 79, Vladikavkaz, 362003 Respublika Severnaja Osetija-Alanija
Tel: +7(8672) 52-82-70 +7(8672) 55-34-67
Fax: +7(8672) 52-82-70
EMail: inci2001@inci.ru; info@inci.ru
Website: http://www.inci.ru/

Rector: Vladimir Georgievich Gamaonov

Programmes
Business Information Technology (Business Computing; Information Technology); **Public Relations** (Public Relations)

History: Created 2000.

Degrees and Diplomas: *Specialist Diploma*
Last Updated: 16/03/12

INSTITUTE OF COMMERCE AND LAW

Institut Kommercii i Prava
Bol'shoj Fackelny per 38, Moskva 109147
Tel: +7(495) 912-54-18 +7(495) 911-39-35 +7(495) 912-15-06
Fax: +7(495) 912-54-18
EMail: ukip@nm.ru
Website: http://nouikip.ru/

Rector: Vsevolod Borisovich Ershov

Programmes
Accountancy (Accountancy); **Business and Commerce** (Business and Commerce); **Economics** (Economics); **Finance and Banking** (Banking; Finance); **Management** (Management)

Further Information: Branch in Tol'jatti.

History: Created 1991.

Degrees and Diplomas: *Specialist Diploma*
Last Updated: 19/01/12

INSTITUTE OF ECONOMIC LAW

Institut Pravovoj Economiki
ul. Narimanovskaja, d.22, k.1, Moskva 107564
Tel: +7(499) 162-90-11
Fax: +7(495) 162-02-02
EMail: max11167@mail.ru
Website: http://www.ipe.ru

Rector: Kirill Evgenevich Bratsev

Programmes
Accounting (Accountancy); **Economics** (Economics); **Management** (Management); **State and Municipal Administration** (Public Administration)

History: Created 1998.

Degrees and Diplomas: *Bakalavr*, *Specialist Diploma*
Last Updated: 22/09/11

INSTITUTE OF ECONOMICS AND CULTURE - MOSCOW

Institut Ekonomiki i Kul'tury - Moskva
ul. Budajskogo, 3, Moskva 129128
Tel: +7(495) 187-1294
Fax: +7(495) 187-9973
Website: http://www.ieac.ru/

Rector: Suliko N. Stolejnikova

Programmes
Cultural Studies (Cultural Studies); **Economics** (Economics)

INSTITUTE OF ECONOMICS AND ENTREPRENEURSHIP

Institut Ekonomiki i Predprinimatelstva
ul. Dubninskaja 16, Office 216, Moskva 127540
Tel: +7(499) 946-89-12
Fax: +7(499) 946-89-12
EMail: inep@inep.ru
Website: http://www.inep.ru

Rector: Julia Sokolova

Faculties

Economics and Management (Accountancy; Administration; Business Computing; Economics; Management; Marketing; Taxation); **Law** (Administrative Law; Civil Law; Constitutional Law; Criminal Law; History; Law)

Further Information: Branch in Orekhovo-Zuevo.

History: Created 1994.

Degrees and Diplomas: *Bakalavr*, *Specialist Diploma*; *Magistr*

Last Updated: 19/01/12

INSTITUTE OF ECONOMICS AND FINANCE

Institut Ekonomiki i Finansov (IEF)
ul. Tankista Khrustitskogo 94, Sankt-Peterburg 198217
Tel: +7(812) 703-36-70 +7(812) 756-04-00
Fax: +7(812) 756-00-89
EMail: ief@ief-spb.ru
Website: http://www.ief-spb.ru/

Rector: Alija S. Rumyantzeva

Programmes

Accounting (Accountancy); **Economics** (Economics); **Finance and Credit** (Finance); **International Economics** (International Economics); **Management** (Management); **Marketing** (Marketing)

History: Founded 1992. Acquired present status 1997.

Degrees and Diplomas: *Bakalavr*, *Specialist Diploma*

Last Updated: 24/01/12

INSTITUTE OF ECONOMICS AND LAW - VORONEZH

Institut Ekonomiki i Prava - Voronezh
ul. K. Marksa, 43, Voronež, 394000 Voronežskaja oblast'
Tel: +7(4732) 226-552 +7(4732) 522-481
Fax: +7(4732) 551-880
EMail: info@iep-km.ru
Website: http://www.iep-km.ru

Rector: Islamabade Gedzhievich Amrakhov
EMail: vedomstvo@rambler.ru

International Relations: Naimat Nadirali Ragimova, First Prorector

Faculties

Economics and Law *Dean*: Galina Pevchenko

History: Founded 1997.

Governing Bodies: Rector

Academic Year: September to July

Admission Requirements: Secondary school certificate (in Russian)

Fees: (Euro): 1,000 per annum

Main Language(s) of Instruction: Russian

Degrees and Diplomas: *Specialist Diploma*: Finance and Credit; Civil Law; Automobile Sevice; Socio-cultural Service, 5 yrs

Student Services: Academic counselling, Canteen, Cultural centre, Employment services, Foreign student adviser, Foreign Studies Centre, Health services, Nursery care, Social counselling, Sports facilities

Special Facilities: Movie Studio

Libraries: Yes

Academic Staff *2007-2008*	**TOTAL**
FULL-TIME	**26**
PART-TIME	**14**
STAFF WITH DOCTORATE	
FULL-TIME	**26**
Student Numbers *2007-2008*	
All (Foreign Included)	c. **500**

Last Updated: 12/12/08

INSTITUTE OF ECONOMICS AND MANAGEMENT

Institut Ekonomiki i Upravlenija
ul. Moskovskaja, 10, Pyatigorsk 357500
Tel: +7(8793) 32-66-87
Fax: +7(8793) 32-66-87
EMail: info.ineu@gmail.ru
Website: http://www.ineu.ru

Rector: Viktor Misostovich Vazagov

Faculties

Economics (Accountancy; Banking; Business Computing; Economics; Finance; Management; Mathematics; Taxation); **Law** (Civil Law; Criminal Law; History of Law; Law)

History: Founded 1990 as branch of Moscow Commercial Academy, acquired present status and title 1996.

Governing Bodies: Non-state High Schools Association (ANVUZ)

Academic Year: September to June (September-January; January-June)

Admission Requirements: Secondary school certificate (Attestat o srednem obrazovanii)

Main Language(s) of Instruction: Russian

Accrediting Agencies: Ministry of General and Professional Education

Degrees and Diplomas: *Bakalavr*, *Specialist Diploma*

Student Services: Academic counselling, Canteen, Cultural centre, Employment services, Language programs, Social counselling, Sports facilities

Last Updated: 17/01/12

INSTITUTE OF ECONOMICS AND MANAGEMENT OF KUBAN REGION STATE MEDICAL ACADEMY

Institut Ekonomiki i Upravlenija Kubanskoj Gosudarstvennoj Medicinskoj Akademii
ul. Sedina 4, Krasnodar 350063
Tel: +7(8612) 68-48-74
Fax: +7(8612) 68-73-74
EMail: admkgma@ksma.kubannet.ru
Website: http://www.ksma.kubanent.ru

Rector: Vladimir Vladimirovich Latkin

Programmes

Economics (Economics); **Management** (Management); **Medicine** (Medicine)

INSTITUTE OF ECONOMICS AND PUBLIC RELATIONS

Institut Ekonomiki i Svjazej Soobščenija (IEPR)
ul. Krzhizhanovskogo, d15, k2, Moskva 117218
Tel: +7(495) 788-09-29
Fax: +7(495) 772-67-05
Website: http://www.unepr.ru/

Rector: Oleg Aleksandrovich Bryksin

Faculties

International Economics (International Economics); **Management**; **Public Relations** (Public Relations)

Degrees and Diplomas: *Specialist Diploma*: International Economics; Enterprise Management; Public Relations, 5 yrs

Last Updated: 22/01/09

INSTITUTE OF ECONOMICS, LAW AND NATURAL SCIENCES - KRASNODAR

Institut Ekonomiki, Prava i Estestvennyh Special'nostej - Krasnodar
ul. Stavropolskaja 149, Krasnodar 350640
Tel: +7(8612) 337-502
EMail: inep@mail.kuban.ru
Website: http://inep.kuban.ru/

Rector: V.A. Narskij

Programmes
Accountancy (Accountancy); **Design** (Design); **Ecology** (Ecology); **Law** (Law); **Linguistics** (Linguistics); **Mathematical Methods and Business Operation Studies** (Mathematics)

INSTITUTE OF ECONOMICS, MANAGEMENT AND LAW

Institut Ekonomiki, Upravlenija i Prava
ul. Moskovskaja, 42, Kazan, 420111 Tartastan
Tel: +7(8432) 293-61-69
Fax: +7(8432) 292-61-59
EMail: rector@ieml.ru
Website: http://www.ieml.ru

Rector: Vitalij G. Timirjasov

Programmes
Accounting (Accountancy); **Economics** (Economics); **Law** (Law); **Management** (Management); **Marketing** (Marketing)

Further Information: Branches in Naberezhnje Chelny, Al'me-t'evsk, Bugul'ma, Zelenodol'sk, Nizhnekamsk, Novocheboksark, Chistopol.

History: Created 1994.

Degrees and Diplomas: *Specialist Diploma*
Last Updated: 17/01/12

INSTITUTE OF ECONOMICS, SOCIAL POLICY AND LAW

Institut Rynočnoj Ekonomiki, Social'noj Politiki i Prava
Zolotorožskij val 11, Moskva 109033
Tel: +7(495) 362-91-34
Fax: +7(495) 362-67-89
EMail: info@irespip.ru
Website: http://www.irespip.ru

Rector: Viktor P. Nelaev

INSTITUTE OF FOREIGN LANGUAGES

Institut Inostrannykh Jazykov, Sankt-Peterburg (IFL)
12-ja Linija V.O., d.13, Sankt-Peterburg 199178
Tel: +7(812) 320-97-73
Fax: +7(812) 320-97-73
EMail: ifl@ifl.ru; iflspb@mail.wplus.net
Website: http://www.ifl.ru

Rector: Olga Igorevna Brodovich

Programmes
Linguistics (English; French; German; Linguistics; Modern Languages; Spanish; Translation and Interpretation)

History: Founded 1991, acquired present status 1998.

Governing Bodies: Academic Council

Academic Year: September to June

Admission Requirements: Secondary school certificate or equivalent

Main Language(s) of Instruction: Russian

Accrediting Agencies: Ministry of Education

Degrees and Diplomas: *Bakalavr*; *Specialist Diploma*

Student Services: Academic counselling, Social counselling

Student Residential Facilities: Yes

Libraries: Main Library

Publications: Vestnik Instituta Inostrannyh Jazykov, Issues of Philology; Translation Studies; Foreign Language Teaching Methods *(3 per annum)*
Last Updated: 26/01/12

INSTITUTE OF GLOBAL ECONOMY AND COMPUTER SCIENCE

Institut Mirovoj Ekonomiki i Informatizacii
ul. Tverskaja 5/6, Moskva 103009
Tel: +7(495) 267-55-16
Fax: +7(495) 267-96-39
EMail: iwei_wai@mtu-net.ru
Website: http://www.iwei.az.ru

Rector: Jelena Halevinskaja

Programmes
Computer Science (Computer Science); **International Business** (International Business)

INSTITUTE OF HUMANITIES AND ECOLOGY

Gumanitarno-Ekologičeskij Institut
6-oj Monetčikovskij per. 19, Moskva 113054
Tel: +7(499) 237-32-88 +7(499) 237-35-17
Fax: +7(499) 237-37-28
EMail: gek_inst@mail.ru; info@mgeu.ru
Website: http://www.mgeu.ru/

Rektor: Ljudmila Egorovna Pikalova

Faculties
Design (Design; Fashion Design; Interior Design; Landscape Architecture); **Management** (Environmental Management; Hotel Management; Management; Marketing; Tourism)

History: Created 1993.

Degrees and Diplomas: *Bakalavr*; *Specialist Diploma*
Last Updated: 20/01/12

INSTITUTE OF INFORMATION TECHNOLOGY, ECONOMY AND MANAGEMENT

Institut Informacionoj Technologij, Ekonomiki I Menedžmenta
ul. Mira, 36a, Klin, 141600 Moskovskaja oblast'
Tel: +7(499) 230-24-54 +7(49624) 3-13-13
Fax: +7(499) 230-24-54 +7(49624) 3-13-13
EMail: iitem@narod.ru
Website: http://www.iitem.ru/

Rector: Jurij Nikolaevich Kostin

Departments
Economics and Management (Economics; Management); **Finance and Accounting** (Accountancy; Finance); **Information Technology** (Business Computing; Information Technology)

History: Created 1996.

Degrees and Diplomas: *Bakalavr*; *Specialist Diploma*
Last Updated: 30/01/12

INSTITUTE OF INTERNATIONAL BUSINESS EDUCATION

Institut Meždunarodnogo Biznes Obrazovanija (IBE (IMBO))
Zelenograd, proezd 4806, d. 5, Moskva 124498
Tel: +7(499) 272-41-90
Fax: +7(499) 272-41-90
EMail: support@imbo.ru; lyakovleva@imbo.ru
Website: http://www.imbo.ru/

Rector: Ljubov' V. Jakovleva EMail: lyakovleva@ibe.miee.ru

Programmes
Management (International Business; Management)

History: Created 1992.

Degrees and Diplomas: *Bakalavr*
Last Updated: 17/01/12

INSTITUTE OF INTERNATIONAL ECONOMIC COOPERATION

Institut Meždunarodnyh Ekonomiceskih Svjazej
Mosfilmovskaja ul. 35-1, Moskva 119330
Tel: +7(495) 147-55-11
Fax: +7(495) 143-86-71
EMail: imes@sumail.ru
Website: http://www.imes-iier.ru/

Rector: Tatiana Bogomolova

Departments
International Relations (International Relations)

INSTITUTE OF INTERNATIONAL ECONOMIC RELATIONS

Institut Meždunarodnykh Ekonomičeskikh Otnošenij
ul. Moskovskaja, 38, Khimki, 141400 Moskovskaja oblast'
Tel: +7(495) 573-66-42 +7(495) 573-66-43
Fax: +7(495) 573-15-97
EMail: admin@vpo-imeo.ru
Website: http://www.vpo-imeo.ru/

Rector: Suren Ashotovich Sarkisjan

Programmes
Economics (Economics; French; German; Information Technology; International Economics; Italian; Mathematical Physics; Spanish)

History: Created 1998.

Degrees and Diplomas: *Bakalavr*
Last Updated: 26/01/12

INSTITUTE OF INTERNATIONAL LAW AND ECONOMICS NAMED AFTER A.S. GRIBOEDOV

Institut Meždunarodnogo Prava i Ekonomiki im. A.S. Griboedova
Bld. 21, Entuziastov highway, Moskva 111123
Tel: +7(495) 673-7371
Fax: +7(495) 673-7379
EMail: info@iile.ru
Website: http://www.iile.ru

Rector: Pavel Pavlovich Pilipienko
Tel: +7(495) 673-7372 EMail: pavelpilipenko@yandex.ru

First Pro-Rector: Efim M. Kopaigorodsky
Tel: +7(495) 673-7413, Fax: +7(495) 673-7413

Faculties
Economics (Accountancy; Banking; Economics; Finance; Management) *Dean*: Nataliya P. Golovina; **Journalism** (Advertising and Publicity; Journalism; Public Relations) *Dean*: Jury V. Troškin; **Law** (Civil Law; Criminal Law; International Law; Law) *Dean*: Nikolay K. Potockiy; **Linguistics** *Dean*: Larisa N. Talalova

Further Information: Seven branches in: Murmansk, Lipetsk, Uljanovsk, Petrozavodsk, Vologda, Kaluga, Nižnevartovsk.

History: Founded 1993.

Governing Bodies: Board of Trustees; Academic Council

Academic Year: September to June (September-January; February-June)

Admission Requirements: Secondary school certificate

Fees: (US Dollars): 1,000-5,000 per annum

Main Language(s) of Instruction: Russian

Degrees and Diplomas: *Bakalavr*: 4 yrs; *Specialist Diploma*: a further 1 yr

Student Services: Academic counselling, Canteen, Cultural centre, Employment services, Foreign Studies Centre, Health services, Language programs, Social counselling, Sports facilities

Special Facilities: Criminalistic Laboratory

Libraries: c. 250,000 vols
Last Updated: 24/11/08

INSTITUTE OF INTERNATIONAL LAW, ECONOMICS, HUMANITARIAN SCIENCES AND MANAGEMENT NAMED AFTER K.V. ROSSINSKOGO

Institut Meždunarodnogo Prava, Ekonomikii, Gumanitarnyh Nauk i Upravlenija im. K.V. Rossinskogo
ul. 2-j proedzd Stasova, 48, Krasnodar 350011
Tel: +7(861) 233-64-48 +7(861) 227-16-92
Fax: +7(861) 233-64-48 +7(861) 227-16-92
EMail: ross-inst@mail.ru
Website: http://www.rossinsky.ru/

Rector: Viktor Nikolaevich Dubrov

Faculties
Economics and Management (Accountancy; Administration; Computer Science; Economics; Finance; Management; Mathematics); **Law** (Constitutional Law; International Law; Law)

Programmes
Humanities (Ecology; English; French; German; History; Journalism; Linguistics; Modern Languages; Pedagogy; Philology; Philosophy; Physical Education; Psychology; Spanish; Sports)

History: Created 1992.

Degrees and Diplomas: *Bakalavr*, *Specialist Diploma*
Last Updated: 26/01/12

INSTITUTE OF INTERNATIONAL RELATIONS

Institut Meždunorodnyh Svjazej
ul. Karla Libknekhta 33, Ekaterinburg, 620075 Sverdlovskaja oblast'
Tel: +7(343) 371-18-95 +7(343) 371-19-70
Fax: +7(343) 371-18-95
EMail: ims@ims-ural.ru; pr@ims-ural.ru
Website: http://www.ims-ural.ru/

Rector: Ol'ga Georgievich Skvortsov

Faculties
International Economic Relations (Advertising and Publicity; Economics; International Relations; Public Relations); **Linguistics** (Communication Disorders; English; French; German; Linguistics; Translation and Interpretation)

Further Information: Branch in Kamensk-Uralskij

History: Created 1994.

Degrees and Diplomas: *Bakalavr*, *Specialist Diploma*
Last Updated: 19/01/12

INSTITUTE OF INTERNATIONAL TRADE AND LAW

Institut Meždunarodnoj Torgovli i Prava
ul. Kastanaevskaja 59, korp. 2, Moskva 121108
Tel: +7(495) 144-01-25
Fax: +7(495) 144-01-35
EMail: imtp@imtp.ru
Website: http://www.imtp.ru/

Rector: Oleg Jurevich Gavrjushin

Faculties
Economics (Economics; International Economics); **Law** (International Law; Law); **Management** (Management)

History: Created 1996.

Admission Requirements: Secondary school certificate

Main Language(s) of Instruction: Russian

Degrees and Diplomas: *Bakalavr*, *Specialist Diploma*
Last Updated: 26/01/12

INSTITUTE OF JOURNALISM AND CREATIVE LITERACY

Institut Žurnalistiki i Literaturnogo Tvorčestva
Kostjanskij per 13, Moskva 103045
Tel: +7(495) 691-51-25 +7(495) 691-50-87
Fax: +7(495) 691-59-36
EMail: iglt@iglt.ru
Website: http://www.iglt.ru

Rector: Leonid E. Bezin

Programmes

Journalism (Journalism; Writing)

History: Created 1995.

Degrees and Diplomas: *Specialist Diploma*

Last Updated: 17/01/12

INSTITUTE OF LANGUAGES AND CULTURE NAMED AFTER LEO TOLSTOY

Institut Jazykov i Kul'tur Im.L'va Tolstogo

ul. Khabarovskaja, 18a, Moskva 107589

Tel: +7(495) 466-32-65

Fax: +7(495) 466-32-65

EMail: leotolstoy_inst@rambler.ru

Website: http://www.leotolstoyinstitute.ru/

Rector: Marija Dmitrievna Tikhonycheva

Faculties

Cultural Studies (Cultural Studies); **International and Regional Relations** (Asian Studies; European Studies; International Relations; Oriental Studies; Political Sciences; Regional Studies); **Modern Languages** (Bulgarian; Chinese; English; French; German; Italian; Japanese; Linguistics; Modern Languages; Serbocroatian; Slavic Languages; Spanish; Translation and Interpretation; Turkish)

History: Created 1994.

Degrees and Diplomas: *Bakalavr, Specialist Diploma*

Last Updated: 26/01/12

INSTITUTE OF LAW AND BUSINESS

Institut Pravovedenija i Predprinimatelstva (IPP)

ul. Malaya, 8, Pushkin, Sankt-Peterburg 196600

Tel: +7(812) 470-08-00 +7(812) 465-28-13

Fax: +7(812) 470-08-00

EMail: ipp@mail.ptl.ru

Website: http://www.ippspb.ru/

Rector: Tatiana Kozlova

Faculties

Law (Administrative Law; Civil Law; Criminal Law); **Management** (Economic History; Management; Tourism)

History: Founded 1994, acquired present status and title 1997.

Academic Year: September to July

Admission Requirements: Secondary school certificate (Attestat o srednem obrazovanii) and entrance examination

Main Language(s) of Instruction: Russian

Accrediting Agencies: Ministry of Education

Degrees and Diplomas: *Bakalavr, Specialist Diploma; Magistr*

Student Services: Academic counselling, Canteen, Cultural centre, Employment services, Foreign student adviser, Health services, Language programs, Social counselling, Sports facilities

Student Residential Facilities: Yes

Special Facilities: Criminology Laboratory. Computer Centre

Libraries: c. 31,000 vols

Last Updated: 30/03/12

INSTITUTE OF MANAGEMENT AND BUSINESS

Institut Menedžmenta i Biznesa

ul. Avtozavodskaja, 16, Moskva 115280

Tel: +7(495) (495) 627-35-97 +7(495) 674-62-78

Fax: +7(495) (495) 627-35-97 +7(495) 674-62-78

EMail: ujva@msiu.ru; mor-z@msiu.ru

Website: http://www.i-m-b.ru

Rector: Jurij Serafimovich Avraamov

Faculties

Economics and Management (Business Computing; Economics; Information Technology; Management)

History: Created 1996.

Degrees and Diplomas: *Bakalavr, Specialist Diploma*

Last Updated: 12/01/12

INSTITUTE OF MANAGEMENT AND BUSINESS

Institut Upravlenija i Biznesa

ul. Kazbekova 39a, Mahačkala 367009

Tel: +7(8722) 69-53-65

Fax: +7(8722) 69-53-66

EMail: institut@xtreem.ru

Rector: Magomagazi Kamilovich Kamilov

Programmes

Design (Design; Fashion Design; Graphic Design); **Finance and Credit** (Banking; Economics; Finance); **Law** (Law)

History: Created 1993.

Degrees and Diplomas: *Specialist Diploma*

Last Updated: 12/03/12

INSTITUTE OF MANAGEMENT AND COMPUTER SCIENCE

Institut Upravlenija i Informatiki

ul Zogre, 24/b, Moskva 123060

Tel: +7(499) 198-43-29 +7(499)198-43-28

Fax: +7(499) 198-43-28

EMail: info@mosiui.ru

Website: http://www.mosiui.ru/

Rector: Sergei Aleksandrovich Larionov

Faculties

Advertising (Advertising and Publicity); **Applied Computer Science** (Business Computing; Computer Science); **Design** (Design); **Management** (Management); **Psychology** (Psychology); **Public Relations** (Public Relations); **Tourism** (Tourism)

History: Created 2004.

Degrees and Diplomas: *Bakalavr, Specialist Diploma; Magistr*

Last Updated: 26/01/12

INSTITUTE OF MANAGEMENT AND LAW

Institut Upravlenija i Prava

ul. Artjukhinoj, 6/1, Moskva 109390

Tel: +7(495) 221-34-75

Fax: +7(495) 221-34-75

EMail: info@iup.com.ru

Website: http://www.iup.com.ru

Rector: Ivan Mikhailovich Aleksandrov
EMail: alexandrov@iup.com.ru

Faculties

Economics (Accountancy; Economics; Finance); **Law and Psychology** (Law; Psychology); **Management** (Management)

History: Created 2002.

Degrees and Diplomas: *Bakalavr, Specialist Diploma*

Last Updated: 26/01/12

INSTITUTE OF MANAGEMENT AND MARKET

Institut Menedžmenta i Rynka

ul. Mira, 19, Ekaterinburg, 620002 Sverdlovskaja oblast'

Tel: +7(3432) 741-646

Fax: +7(3432) 741-646

EMail: umc@uicde.ru

Website: http://www.uicde.ru

Rector: Nikolaj Ivanovich Vernov

INSTITUTE OF MANAGEMENT, BUSINESS AND LAW

Institut Upravlenija, Biznesa i Prava

ul. M. Nagibina, Rostov-na-Donu 344068

Tel: +7(8632) 38-69-33

Fax: +7(8632) 45-45-65

EMail: iubip@iubip.ru

Website: http://www.iubip.ru

Rector: Imran Gurru Ogly Akperov EMail: rector@iubip.ru

Academies
Economics and Business (Economic History; Modern Languages; Philology); **Law** (Law); **Management** (Business Administration; Business and Commerce; Economics; Law; Management; Psychology)

History: Created 1991.

Degrees and Diplomas: *Bakalavr, Specialist Diploma*
Last Updated: 26/01/12

INSTITUTE OF MANAGEMENT, INFORMATION AND BUSINESS

Institut Upravlenija, Informacii i Biznesa
ul. Senjukova 15, Ukhta, 169300 Respublika Komi
Tel: +7(8216) 743-707
Fax: +7(8216) 744 324
EMail: mibi@ugtu.net
Website: http://www.mibirk.ru/

Rector: Vladimir S. Hain

Departments
Business (Business Administration); **Finance** (Finance); **Information Management** (Documentation Techniques; Information Management); **Modern Languages** (Modern Languages)

History: Created 1996.

Degrees and Diplomas: *Specialist Diploma*
Last Updated: 27/01/12

INSTITUTE OF MANAGEMENT, MARKETING AND FINANCE

Institut Menedžmenta, Marketinga i Finansov (IMM&F)
ul. K. Marksa, d.67, Voronež, 394030 Voronežskaja oblast'
Tel: +7(732) 532-611 +7(732) 598-293
Fax: +7(732) 532-611
EMail: info@immf.ru
Website: http://www.immf.ru/

Rector and Executive Director: Olga Anatolievna Zaitzeva (1991-)

Faculties
Accountancy (Accountancy); **Economics** (Economics); **Finance and Credit** (Banking; Finance); **Foreign Languages** (Modern Languages); **Humanities** (Arts and Humanities); **Law** (Law); **Management** (Management); **Marketing** (Marketing); **Mathematics and Computer Science** (Computer Science; Mathematics); **Personnel Management** (Human Resources; Management)

History: Founded 1991, acquired present status and title 1997.

Academic Year: September to June

Admission Requirements: Secondary school certificate (Attestat o srednem obrazovanii)

Fees: (Russian Rubles): 7,000 per semester

Main Language(s) of Instruction: Russian

Accrediting Agencies: Ministry of General Education

Degrees and Diplomas: *Bakalavr*: Management; Economics, 4 yrs; *Specialist Diploma*: Accountancy; Mathematical Methods in Economics; Advertizing; Documentation; Finance and Credit; Management; Marketing; Personnel Management, 5 yrs. Also Certificates in English; Translator in Business Communication

Student Services: Academic counselling, Canteen, Cultural centre, Health services, Language programs

Special Facilities: Drama Studio, Dance Studio

Libraries: c. 32,000 vols

Publications: Journal of Scientific Works, Lectures and Students Articles *(monthly)*

Last Updated: 18/04/11

INSTITUTE OF MODERN ARTS

Institut Sovremennogo Iskusstva
ul. 1812 y., 10, korp 2, Moskva 121601
Tel: +7(495) 145-9297
Fax: +7(495) 145-9844
EMail: isi@ipc.ru
Website: http://www.ipc.ru/~isi

Rector: I.N. Suholet

Programmes
Acting; **Design**; **Directing**; **Directing Dancing**; **Journalism**; **Singing**; **Teaching Dancing**

INSTITUTE OF MODERN TECHNOLOGY AND ECONOMICS

Institut Sovremennyh Tehnologij i Ekonomiki
ul. Krasnaja 91, Krasnodar 350000
Tel: +7(861) 274-34-12 +7(861) 277-75-83
Fax: +7(861) 274-34-11
EMail: tuk@23mail.ru; vs@simankov.ru
Website: http://www.kuban-istek.ru/

Rector: Vladimir Sergevich Simankov EMail: vs@simankov.ru

Programmes
Economics (Economics); **Management** (Management); **Technology** (Technology)

History: Created 1995.

Degrees and Diplomas: *Bakalavr, Specialist Diploma*
Last Updated: 26/01/12

INSTITUTE OF NATURAL SCIENCES AND ECOLOGY

Institut Jestestvennyh Nauk i Ecologii
ul. Masksimova 4, Moskva 123098
Tel: +7(495) 196-53-11
Fax: +7(495) 192-77-45
Website: http://www.inse.kiae.ru

Rector: Spartak T. Beljaev

Programmes
Ecology (Ecology); **Natural Sciences** (Natural Sciences)

INSTITUTE OF PRACTICAL ORIENTAL STUDIES

Institut Praktičeskogo Vostokovedenija
pr. Nakhimovskij, d.32, Moskva 117218
Tel: +7(499) 124-07-22
Fax: +7(499) 124-01-04
EMail: info@ipos-msk.ru; ipv@ipos-msk.ru
Website: http://www.ipos-msk.ru

Rector: Andrej L. Fedorin

Programmes
Oriental Studies (African Languages; African Studies; Oriental Languages; Oriental Studies)

History: Created 1993.

Degrees and Diplomas: *Bakalavr, Magistr*
Last Updated: 22/09/11

INSTITUTE OF PROFESSIONAL EVALUATION

Institut Professional'noj Ocenki
Leningradskij prosp. 49, Moskva 125468
Tel: +7(495) 943-9549
Fax: +7(495) 943-9469
EMail: ipo@ocenka.net
Website: http://www.ocenka.net

Rector: Marina A. Fedotova

INSTITUTE OF PROFESSIONAL INNOVATIONS

Institut Profesional'nyh Innovacij
prosp Rjazanskij, 86/1, Moskva 109542
Tel: +7(495) 972-79-75 +7(495) 971-15-13
Fax: +7(495) 971-15-13
EMail: inprofin@mail.ru
Website: http://www.inprofin.ru

Rector: Aleksandr Anatolevich Khuriev

Programmes
Business Administration (Economic History; Management); **Law** (Law); **Psychology** (Educational Psychology; Pedagogy; Psychology)

History: Created 1996.

Degrees and Diplomas: *Bakalavr*; *Specialist Diploma*
Last Updated: 26/01/12

INSTITUTE OF PROGRAMME SYSTEMS 'UNIVERSITY OF PERESLAVL'

Institut Programmnyh Sistem-"Universitet Goroda Pereslavlya"
ul. Sovetskaja 2, Pereslavl-Zalesskij, 152140 Jaroslavskaja oblast'
Tel: +7(0853) 598-242
Fax: +7(0853) 520-865
EMail: adm@u.pereslavl.ru
Website: http://www.u.pereslavl.ru

Rector: Al'fred K. Ajlamazjan

Programmes
Computer Engineering (Computer Engineering); **Systems Analysis** (Systems Analysis)

INSTITUTE OF PSYCHOLOGY AND PEDAGOGY

Institut Psikhologii i Pedagogiki
ul. Sel'skohozjajstvennaja 13, Moskva 129226
Tel: +7(495) 963-03-68 +7(495) 963-32-77
Fax: +7(495) 963-32-77
EMail: ppsy@bk.ru; info@ppsy.ru
Website: http://www.ppsy.ru

Rector: Natal'ja Emannuilovna Matveeva

Programmes
Pedagogy (Pedagogy); **Psychology** (Psychology)

History: Created 1995.

Degrees and Diplomas: *Specialist Diploma*
Last Updated: 17/01/12

INSTITUTE OF PSYCHOLOGY AND PSYCHOANALYSIS

Institut Praktičeskoj Psihologii i Psihoanaliza
ul. Jaroslavskaja 13, Moskva 129366
Tel: +7(495) 282-74-06
Fax: +7(495) 282-11-14
Website: http://www.psychol.ras.ru

Rector: Jelena A. Spirkana

Programmes
Psychoanalysis (Psychoanalysis); **Psychology** (Psychology)

INSTITUTE OF REAL ESTATE AND CONSTRUCTION BUSINESS

Institut Nedviženosti i Stroitel'nogo Biznesa
Jaroslavskoe shosse, 26, Moskva 129337
Tel: +7(495) 235-6603
Fax: +7(495) 235-5707
EMail: recbi@mail.ru
Website: http://inisb.ru

Rector: Evgenij Leonidonich Miturev

INSTITUTE OF SOCIAL AND HUMAN SCIENCES

Institut Social'nyh i Gumanitarnyh Znanij
ul. Profsouznaja, 13/17, Kazan, 420011 Tatarstan
Tel: +7(8482) 98-37-20
Fax: +7(8482) 98-36-05
EMail: info@isgz.ru
Website: http://www.isgz.ru

Rector: Nikolaj V. Ponomarjov

Programmes
Social Sciences (Social Sciences)

INSTITUTE OF SPECIAL PEDAGOGY AND PSYCHOLOGY

Institut Special'noj Pedagogiki i Psihologii
ul. Bol'šaja Zelenina 30, Sankt-Peterburg 197110
Tel: +7(812) 167-03-48
Fax: +7(812) 325-57-11
EMail: rector@rwiufc.spb.ru
Website: http://www.rwiufc.sbp.ru

Rector: Lujdmila Mihajlovna Shipicyna

Programmes
Pedagogy (Pedagogy); **Psychology** (Psychology)

INSTITUTE OF STATE ADMINISTRATION

Institut Gosurdarstvennogo Administrirovanija (IGA)
Leninskij prosp.80, Moskva 117261
Tel: +7(495) 131-95-24
Fax: +7(495) 131-91-88
EMail: info@iga.ru
Website: http://www.iga.ru

Rector: Valerij A. Tarakanov (1993-)
Tel: +7(495) 760-6717 EMail: vat40@mail.ru

First Deputy Rector: Aleksandr V. Tarakanov
Tel: +7(495) 726-2796 EMail: tarakanov66@mail.ru

International Relations: Elena V. Lavrina
Tel: +7(915) 282-4567 EMail: elenalavrina@gmail.ru

Faculties
Economics and Administration *Dean*: Michael Danilov; **Juridical Studies** (Administration; Law; Public Administration) *Dean*: Aleksandr Kuzmin; **Psychology and Pedagogy** *(Yakytsk, Ulan-Ude, Orenburg, Kazan, Frankfurt am Main - Distance Education))* (Pedagogy; Psychology) *Dean*: Vladimir Inshakov

History: Founded 1994. Acuired present status 1995.

Academic Year: September to June

Admission Requirements: Secondary School Certificate

Main Language(s) of Instruction: Russian

International Co-operation: With universities in Germany

Accrediting Agencies: Federal Accreditation Agency

Degrees and Diplomas: *Bakalavr*: 4 yrs; *Specialist Diploma*: 5 yrs; *Kandidat Nauk*; *Doktor Nauk*

Student Services: Academic counselling, Canteen, Foreign student adviser, Language programs, Social counselling, Sports facilities

Special Facilities: Movie Studio

Libraries: Yes

Publications: Collected Scientific Articles, Law, Economics, Management, Ecology, Psychology, Pedagogy *(1-2 per annum)*

Academic Staff *2007-2008*	MEN	WOMEN	**TOTAL**
FULL-TIME	24	20	**44**
PART-TIME	27	16	**43**
STAFF WITH DOCTORATE			
FULL-TIME	4	3	**7**
PART-TIME	7	4	**11**

Student Numbers *2007-2008*			
All (Foreign Included)	828	1,107	**1,935**
FOREIGN ONLY	25	26	**51**

Part-time students, 105. **Distance students**, 1,700. **Evening students**, 130.

Last Updated: 27/11/08

INSTITUTE OF TECHNOLOGY AND BUSINESS

Institut Tekhnologii i Biznesa (ITIB)
ul. Dalnjaija, 14, Nakhodka, 692900 Primorskij kraj
Tel: +7(4236) 62-39-24 +7(4236) 62-35-72
Fax: +7(4236) 62-39-24
EMail: post@itib.ru
Website: http://www.itib.ru

Rector: Raisa Shakirovna Govorukha (2000-)

Programmes
Economics (Economics); **Information Technology** (Information Technology); **Management** (Management); **Marketing** (Marketing)
Further Information: The Lyceum, which is the Institute's affiliate, provides high school education for children and prepares them for further education.
History: Founded 1993.
Academic Year: September to June
Admission Requirements: Certifcate of Secondary Education (Attestat o srednem obrazovanii), tests
Main Language(s) of Instruction: Russian
Accrediting Agencies: Department of Licensing, Accreditation and Certification
Degrees and Diplomas: *Bakalavr*, *Specialist Diploma*
Student Services: Academic counselling, Canteen, Employment services, Health services, Language programs
Student Residential Facilities: Yes
Libraries: Main Library
Last Updated: 17/01/12

INSTITUTE OF THE RESTORATION OF WORKS OF ART

Institut Iskusstva Restavracii
Godorok im. Baumana 3, korp. 4, Moskva 105037
Tel: +7(495) 767-28-49 +7(495) 767-29-48
Fax: +7(495) 767-28-49
EMail: info@resvuz.ru
Website: http://www.resvuz.ru/

Rector: Aleksandr Viktorovich Danilin

Programmes
Restoration of Works of Art (Restoration of Works of Art)
History: Created 1991.
Degrees and Diplomas: *Bakalavr*, *Specialist Diploma*
Last Updated: 26/01/12

INSTITUTE OF WORLD CIVILIZATIONS

Institut Mirovoj Civilizacii
1-yj Basmannij per., 3 bil. 1, Moskva 107078
Tel: +7(499) 261-11-26 +7(499) 261-43-08
Fax: +7(499) 261-13-85
EMail: wci.imc@rambler.ru
Website: http://www.imc-i.ru/

Rector: Aleksandr Borisovich Kurdjumov

Programmes
Business Computing (Business Computing); **Economics** (Economics); **Law** (Law); **Management** (Management); **Politics** (Political Sciences); **Psychology** (Psychology); **Regional Studies** (Regional Studies); **Tourism** (Tourism)
History: Created 1999.
Degrees and Diplomas: *Bakalavr*, *Specialist Diploma*
Last Updated: 26/01/12

INTERNATIONAL ACADEMY OF BUSINESS AND BANKING (INSTITUTE)

Meždunarodnaja Akademija Biznesa i Bankovskogo Dela (Institut)
bul. Primorskij 25, Tol'jatti, 445057 Samarskaja oblast'
Tel: +7(8482) 407-100
Fax: +7(8482) 407-456
EMail: info@taom.ru
Website: http://www.iabb.edu.ru

Rector: Andrej E. Volkov

Programmes
Design (Design); **Economics and Information Technology** (Economics; Information Technology); **Finance and Banking** (Banking; Finance); **Law** (Law); **Linguistics** (Linguistics); **Management** (Management)

INTERNATIONAL ACADEMY OF BUSINESS AND MANAGEMENT

Meždunarodnaja Akademija Biznesa i Upravlenija
5-j proezd Mar'inoj Rošči, 15a, Moskva 129594
Tel: +7(495) 688-88-63
Fax: +7(495) 688-88-63
EMail: info@mabiu.ru; davidova.alla@list.ru
Website: http://www.mubiu.ru

Rector: Vladimir I. Dobren'kov

Institutes
Computer Science (Computer Science; Information Sciences; Information Technology); **Design and Advertising** (Advertising and Publicity; Fashion Design; Graphic Design); **Economics and Management** (Economics; Management; Public Administration); **Information and Innovative Technology** (Information Technology); **International Relations and Economics** (International Business; International Relations; Translation and Interpretation); **Law** (Law)
History: Founded 1994. Previously known as Meždunarodnyj Universitet Biznesa i Upravlenija (International University of Business and Management). Acquired current title 1998.
Academic Year: September to July
Admission Requirements: Secondary school certificate (Attestat o srdnem obrazovanii) or equivalent
Main Language(s) of Instruction: Russian
Degrees and Diplomas: *Bakalavr*, *Specialist Diploma*; *Magistr*
Student Services: Canteen, Health services, Language programs, Sports facilities
Last Updated: 20/09/11

INTERNATIONAL BANKING INSTITUTE

Meždunarodnyj Bankovskij Institut
Nevsky prosp. 58, Sankt-Peterburg 191011
Tel: +7(812) 311-5309
Fax: +7(812) 311-1219
EMail: ibi@metrocom.ru
Website: http://www.ibi.spb.ru

President: Victor N. Veniaminov
Administrative Officer: Igor N. Zaharov Tel: +7(812) 315-5794
International Relations: Sergej I. Sidorenko, Vice-President
Tel: +7(812) 314-3310 EMail: ssi@ibi.metrocom.ru

Faculties
Banking and Finance (Accountancy; Banking; Finance; Information Management; International Economics; Management; Marketing) *Dean*: Vadim Fattahov; **Distance Education** *Dean*: Nikolay Karpuhin; **Professional Retraining** *Dean*: Nikolay Tsarev
History: Founded 1991.
Governing Bodies: Board of Trustees
Academic Year: September to June
Admission Requirements: Secondary school certificate (Attestat o srednem obrazovanii) and entrance examination
Fees: (US Dollars): 1,800 per annum
Main Language(s) of Instruction: Russian, English
International Co-operation: Joint programmes: MBA together with Stockholm University, GAAP course of International Association of Bookkeepers (UK). Also participates in TACIS, TEMPUS.
Accrediting Agencies: Ministry of Education of the Russian Federation
Degrees and Diplomas: *Bakalavr (BSc)*: 4 yrs; *Specialist Diploma (DS)*: 5 yrs; *Magistr (MBA)*: 6 yrs
Student Services: Academic counselling, Employment services, Foreign student adviser, Foreign Studies Centre, Language programs, Social counselling, Sports facilities
Student Residential Facilities: Yes
Special Facilities: Training Bank. Stock Exchange Technology Centre. Art Gallery
Libraries: Main Library
Publications: Collection of Academic Articles *(annually)*

INTERNATIONAL INDEPENDENT UNIVERSITY OF ENVIRONMENTAL AND POLITICAL SCIENCES

Meždunarodnyj Nezavisimyj Ekologo-Politologičeskij Universitet (Institut) (MNEPU (IIUEPS))

ul. Kosmonavta Volkova, 20, Moskva 127299
Tel: +7(495) 231-4450
Fax: +7(495) 159-1727
EMail: info@mnepu.ru
Website: http://www.mnepu.ru

President: Stanislav A. Stepanov (2008-)
Tel: +7(495) 231-44-50 Ext. 103 EMail: president@mnepu.ru

Rector: Sergey S. Stepanov (2008-)
Tel: +7(495) 231-44-50 Ext. 195 EMail: stepanov@mnepu.ru

International Relations: Olga V. Ivchenko
Tel: +7(495) 231-44-50 Ext. 121 EMail: cip@mnepu.ru

Centres

Complementary Programmes *Director*: Vjacheslav N. Eresjko; **Sciences Programmes** (Natural Sciences) *Director*: Irina N. Makarova; **University Entry Training** *Director*: Olga Yu. Spiridonova

Colleges

Environmental Studies *Director*: Olga Yu. Spiridonova

Departments

American-Russian Business Institute *(ARBI) Director*: Olga V. Ivchenko; **Environment** *Dean*: Nikolay N. Marfenin; **Foreign Languages** (Philosophy; Translation and Interpretation) *Dean*: Yevgeniy V. Dmitriyev; **Law** *Dean*: Evgeniy A. Karpov; **Management, Finance and State Management** *(MFGU) Dean*: Galina N. Chilikina; **Nizhnij Novgorod Branch of IIUEPS** *(Specialization)* (Economics; Law) *Director*: Vladimir V. Presnjakov; **Penza Branch of IIUEPS** *(Specialization; PF MNEPU)* (Business Administration; Economics; Environmental Studies; Law; Philology; Psychology) *Rector*: Ljudmila M. Hurnova; **Social Communications** *(FSC)* (Journalism; Psychology; Public Relations; Social Sciences) *Dean*: Sergey N. Fedotov; **World Economy and International Relations** *(MEMO)* (Accountancy; Banking; Economics; Finance; International Relations) *Dean*: Leonid L. Fituni

Divisions

Management and Service in International Environmental Tourism *(MesMET) Director*: Galina N. Chilikina; **Political Science** *Director*: Natalja V. Ezhokova

Institutes

Ecological Professional Retraining *(MIEPP) Director*: Arkadiy T. Nikitin; **Information Technology** *Director*: Olga Ye. Matiunina; **Open Education** (Economics; Environmental Studies; Law) *Director*: Irina V. Mcrtumova

Further Information: Also Moscow Environmental Educational Complex (MEOC). Branches in Baikonur (Kazakhstan), Omsk, Makhachkala (Dagestan)

History: Founded 1992. At present IIUEPS is one of the leaders among 400 non-governmental Higher Education bodies in the Russian Federation because leading national scientists work at the university. It has 2 branches and several representations. Besides that, universities in Russia and in CIS countries were established with its support.

Governing Bodies: Scientific Council; Guardian Council

Academic Year: September to June

Admission Requirements: School certificate, passport, medical certificate, good results at admission tests and interview.

Fees: (Rubles): 22,000-36,000 per semester (depending on Department)

Main Language(s) of Instruction: Russian

International Co-operation: With universities in USA, Great Britain, Switzerland, Greece, Serbia and Montenegro

Accrediting Agencies: Ministry of Education and Science of the Russian Federation

Degrees and Diplomas: *Bakalavr*: 4 yrs full-time; 5 yrs part-time; *Magistr*: 5 yrs full-time; 6 yrs part-time; *Kandidat Nauk*: Economy; Law (PhD), 3 yrs full-time; 4 yrs part-time

Student Services: Academic counselling, Canteen, Cultural centre, Foreign student adviser, Health services, Language programs, Sports facilities

Student Residential Facilities: Student hostel

Libraries: Over 56,000 books; computers

Publications: Bulletin of Environmental Education in Russia *(quarterly)*; Proceedings of Eco-medical Annual International Seminar "Environmental Health Studies. Life Quality Management", Annual edition of an international seminar on Eco-medicine *(annually)*; Russia in The Surrounding World, Analytic annual publication dealing with problems of the environment *(annually)*

Academic Staff *2007-2008*	MEN	WOMEN	**TOTAL**
FULL-TIME	–	–	**350**
STAFF WITH DOCTORATE			
FULL-TIME	80	60	**140**
Student Numbers *2007-2008*			
All (Foreign Included)		–	**5,300**

Last Updated: 08/12/08

INTERNATIONAL INSTITUTE OF COMPUTER TECHNOLOGIES

Meždunarodnyj Institut Kompjuternykh Tekhnologij

ul Solnechnaja, d.29b, Voronež, 394026 Voronežskaja oblast'
Tel: +7(4732) 39-25-00 +7(4732) 39-25-01
Fax: +7(4732) 21-00-69 +7(4732) 239-25-01
EMail: vuz@iict.ru; mathy@mail.ru
Website: http://www.iict.ru/

Rector: Anatolij I. Shijanov EMail: rector@iict.ru

Faculties

Economics (Economics; Finance; Management; Psychology); **Energy Engineering** (Energy Engineering; Heating and Refrigeration; Nuclear Engineering; Power Engineering); **Information Systems** (Computer Science; Information Technology)

History: Created 1992.

Degrees and Diplomas: *Bakalavr*, *Specialist Diploma*

Last Updated: 14/02/12

INTERNATIONAL INSTITUTE OF COMPUTER TECHNOLOGY

Meždunarodnyj Institut Komp'juternyh Tehnologij

Moskovskij prosp. 14, Voronež, 394026 Voronežskaja oblast'
Tel: +7(0732) 52-63-17
Fax: +7(0732) 52-9835
EMail: mathu@mail.ru
Website: http://www.mikt.boom.ru

Rector: Anatolij I. Šijanov

Programmes

Computer Technology (Computer Science; Technology)

INTERNATIONAL INSTITUTE OF ECONOMICS AND LAW

Meždunarodnyj Institut Ekonomiki i Prava

Rubtsoskaja nab. 3, building 1, Saltykovka Village 107082
Tel: +7(495) 232-2894
Fax: +7(495) 232-2894
Website: http://www.miep.ru

Rector: M. A. Alekseeva Tel: +7(495) 232-2892

Vice-Rector: F. L. Šarov

Programmes

Business and Commerce; **Economics**; **Finance and Banking**; **Law**; **Management** (Management); **Marketing**

INTERNATIONAL INSTITUTE OF MANAGEMENT

Meždunarodnij Institut Upravlenija

ul. Urickogo 43, Arkhangelsk 163060
Tel: +7(8182) 266-183 +7(8182) 266-090
Fax: +7(8182) 237-403
Website: http://www.miuarh.ru

Rector: Anatolij N. Ežov

Programmes

Accountancy (Accountancy); **Finance and Banking** (Banking; Finance); **Management**

INTERNATIONAL INSTITUTE OF MANAGEMENT "LINK"

Meždunarodnyj Institut Menedžmenta "LINK"
ul. Moskovskaja 8/1, Žukovskij, 140180 Moskovskaja oblast'
Tel: +7(495) 781-26-36
Fax: +7(495) 781-26-38
EMail: info@ou-link.ru
Website: http://www.ou-link.ru/

Rector: Sergei A. Shchennikov (1992-) EMail: rector@ou-link.ru

International Relations: Andrei Šuinov, Deputy Rector, International Affairs EMail: ashuinoiv@ou-link.ru

Faculties

Linguistics (Linguistics; Modern Languages); **Management** (Management)

Further Information: Branches also in Moscow, Sarov.

History: Founded 1992, licensed as a higher education enterprise and received state accreditation 1997.

Governing Bodies: Board of Directors

Academic Year: September to May for non-distance courses; Distance course enrolment in November and May

Admission Requirements: Secondary School Certificate for non-distance courses; Undergraduate degree for distance courses

Main Language(s) of Instruction: Russian

Accrediting Agencies: Ministry of Education and Science of the Russian Federation

Degrees and Diplomas: *Bakalavr*; *Specialist Diploma*; *Magistr*

Last Updated: 16/01/12

INTERNATIONAL LAW INSTITUTE

Meždunarodnyj Juridičeskij Institut
ul Kashenkin lug, d.4, Moskva 127427
Tel: +7(495) 610-20-00 +7(495) 610-28-00
Fax: +7(495) 935-82-56
EMail: priem@lawinst.ru
Website: http://www.lawacademy.ru/

Rector: Vladimir Bukov

Programmes

Law (Justice Administration; Law)

History: Created 1992. Previously known as Meždunarodnyj Juridičeskij Institut pri Ministerstve Justicii Rossijskoj Federacii (International Law Institute of the Ministry of Justice of the Russian Federation). Acquired current title 2009.

Degrees and Diplomas: *Bakalavr*, *Specialist Diploma*

Last Updated: 14/02/12

INTERNATIONAL MANAGEMENT INSTITUTE ST PETERSBURG

Sankt-Peterburgskij Meždunarodnyj Institut Menedžmenta
Vasil'evskij Ostrov, 9-ja linija, 50/A, Sankt-Peterburg 199004
Tel: +7(812) 325-19-09 +7(812) 320-61-72
Fax: +7(812) 325-63-48
EMail: office@imisp.ru
Website: http://www.imisp.ru/

Rector: Sergej Mordovin

Programmes

Management (Management)

History: Created 1989.

Degrees and Diplomas: *Bakalavr*

Last Updated: 02/03/12

INTERNATIONAL MARKET INSTITUTE

Meždunarodnyj Institut Rynka (IMI)
ul. Želyabova, d.21, Samara 443030
Tel: +7(846) 336-53-54 +7(846) 266-40-00
Fax: +7(846) 336-90-36
EMail: imi@imi-samara.ru
Website: http://www.imi-samara.ru/

Rector: Vadim G. Chumak

Faculties

Economics and Management (Business Computing; Economics; Management); **Linguistics** (Linguistics; Translation and Interpretation); **Public Administration** (Public Administration)

History: Founded 1994.

Governing Bodies: Board of Trustees; Board of Founders

Academic Year: September to June

Admission Requirements: High school certificate and entrance examinations

Main Language(s) of Instruction: Russian

Accrediting Agencies: Federal Ministry of Common and Vocational Education

Degrees and Diplomas: *Bakalavr*, *Specialist Diploma*

Student Services: Academic counselling, Canteen, Employment services, Health services, Language programs, Sports facilities

Student Residential Facilities: None

Libraries: Yes

Last Updated: 22/09/11

INTERNATIONAL SLAVIC INSTITUTE

Meždunarodnyj Slavjanskij Institut (MSI)
Godovikova str. 9, build. 25, Moskva 129085
Tel: +7(495) 687-03-39 +7(495) 602-46-76
Fax: +7(495) 687-03-39 +7(495) 602-46-76 +7(495) 602-46-84
EMail: intslavinst@mtu-net.ru
Website: http://www.slavinst.ru/

Rector: Kim A. Smirnov (1993-)

Faculties

Acting (Acting; Theatre); **Design** (Design; Fashion Design; Fine Arts; Information Technology; Landscape Architecture); **Economics and Administration** (Administration; Economics; Management); **Foreign Languages** (Foreign Languages Education; Linguistics; Modern Languages); **Law** (Civil Law; Criminal Law; Law); **Psychology** (Law; Linguistics; Psychology); **Vocal Arts** (Singing)

History: Founded 1993.

Academic Year: September to June

Main Language(s) of Instruction: Russian

Accrediting Agencies: Ministry of Education

Degrees and Diplomas: *Specialist Diploma*

Student Services: Academic counselling, Canteen, Foreign student adviser, Language programs

Student Residential Facilities: None

Special Facilities: Art Gallery; Concert Hall

Libraries: c. 10,000 vols.

Publications: Vestnik *(biennially)*

Last Updated: 16/01/12

INTERNATIONAL UNIVERSITY IN MOSCOW

Meždunarodnyj Universitet v Moskve (IUM)
prosp. Leningradskogo 17, Moskva 125040
Tel: +7(495) 251-6438
Fax: +7(495) 251-6438
EMail: kastrel@interun.ru
Website: http://www.ium.edu

President: Sergej N. Krasavchenko
Tel: +7(495) 956-6990, Fax: +7(495) 250-4049
EMail: popov@interun.ru

Vice-Rector: Tatjana Kastrel

International Relations: Viktor V. Raitarovsky
EMail: nnovikov@ium.edu

Departments
Art Management

Faculties
Humanities; **Law**; **Management** (Administration; Banking; Business Administration; Economics; Finance; International Economics; Management; Marketing; Public Administration)

Graduate Schools
Business Administration

Programmes
Postgraduate

History: Founded 1991.

Governing Bodies: Board of Trustees; Senate

Academic Year: September to June

Admission Requirements: Secondary school certificate (Attestat o srednem obrazovanii) or equivalent

Fees: (US Dollars): 3,000-4,000 per annum

Main Language(s) of Instruction: Russian, English

Accrediting Agencies: Ministry of Education; European Council for Business Education

Degrees and Diplomas: *Bakalavr*: Science, 4 yrs; *Specialist Diploma*: Science, 5 yrs; *Magistr*: Science, 6 yrs; *Doktor Nauk*: Science, 3 yrs

Student Services: Academic counselling, Canteen, Cultural centre, Employment services, Foreign student adviser, Foreign Studies Centre, Health services, Language programs, Nursery care, Sports facilities

Student Residential Facilities: Yes

Special Facilities: Two Art Galleries

Publications: Socratic Readings *(annually)*; Vestnik *(quarterly)*

INTERNATIONAL UNIVERSITY OF BUSINESS AND NEW TECHNOLOGIES

Meždunarodnyj Universitet Biznesa i Novykh Tekhnologij (Institut) (IUBNT)
Pervomajskaja, 7, Yaroslavl 150003
Tel: +7(4852) 250-525
Fax: +7(4852) 320-962
EMail: org@mubint.ru
Website: http://www.mubint.ru

President and Rector: Valerie S. Ivanov (1992-)

First Vice-Rector: Mihail Irodnov
Tel: +7(4852) 736-906 EMail: irodov@mubint.ru

International Relations: Natalia Bagrova
Tel: +7(4852) 320-270, Fax: +7(4852) 320-270
EMail: interdept@mubint.ru

Departments
Accountancy *Head*: Alexsandr Perfiliev; **Computer Science** *Head*: Tatjana Nikitina; **Economics and Management of Gas and Oil Industries** (Economics; Management) *Head*: Iosif Mayorov; **Finance and Credit** *Head*: Vitalii Nekludov; **History of Law** *Head*: Vladimir Laitman; **Management** *Head*: Ludmila Gainutdinova; **Marketing** *Head*: Nikolai Goldobin; **Public Law** *Head*: Andrei Lyshnikov; **Public Relations** *Head*: Valentin Stepanov; **Theory of Economics** *Head*: Galina Rodina

Institutes
Commerce *Head*: Nikolai Voronets; **Information Technology** *Head*: Vladimir Veitsman; **Linguistics** *Head*: Svetlana Potapova; **State and Municipal Administration** *Head*: Lidia Leontieva

Further Information: Branches in Kostroma and Vologda. 32 representative offices in Yaroslavl, Ivanovo, Vologda, Kostroma, Archangelsk regions.

History: Founded 1992. One of the first non-state universities in the Russian Federation. Acquired present status 2003.

Governing Bodies: Academic Council

Academic Year: September to July

Admission Requirements: Secondary school certificate and entrance examinations or tests (depending on field of study)

Fees: (Russian Rubles): Full-time: 32,600-38,600 per annum; part-time 16,200-18,800

Main Language(s) of Instruction: Russian

International Co-operation: With universities in the United Kingdom, Germany. Also participates in Tempus/Tacis programme.

Accrediting Agencies: Russian Federation Ministry of Education and Science

Degrees and Diplomas: *Specialist Diploma*: Finance and Banking; Accountancy; Management; Taxation; Information Technology; Linguistics; Law, 5 yrs

Student Services: Academic counselling, Canteen, Cultural centre, Employment services, Foreign student adviser, Foreign Studies Centre, Health services, Language programs, Social counselling, Sports facilities

Student Residential Facilities: Yes

Libraries: Yes

IRKUTSK INSTITUTE OF INTERNATIONAL TOURISM

Irkutskij Institut Meždunarodnogo Turizma
ul Lermontova 80, Irkutsk, 664074 Irkutskaja oblast'
Tel: +7(3952) 39-81-71
Fax: +7(3952) 39-79-38
EMail: institut@iimt.ru
Website: http://www.iimt.ru/

Rector: Ol'ga Nikolaevna Shcherbakova

Departments
Customs and Excise (Taxation); **Economics and Financial Management** (Business Administration; Economics; Finance); **Hospitality Management and Tourism** (Hotel and Restaurant; Hotel Management; Tourism)

History: Created 2004.

Degrees and Diplomas: *Specialist Diploma*

Last Updated: 19/01/12

KALININGRAD INSTITUTE OF MANAGEMENT

Kaliningradskij Institut Upravlenija
ul. Litovskij val. 38, lit A1, Kaliningrad 394000
Tel: +7(4012) 45-25-35 +7(4012) 46-94-23 +7(4012) 45-12-23
Fax: +7(4012) 45-25-35
EMail: nabor@kvshu39.ru; kramarenko-anatolij@rambler.ru
Website: http://www.kvshu39.ru/

Rector: Vladimir Manvelovich Manukjan

Programmes
Economics (Economics); **Management** (Management)

History: Created 1993. Previously known as Kaliningradskaja Vyssšaja Škola Upravlenija (Kaliningrad Higher School of Management). Acquired current title 2009.

Degrees and Diplomas: *Bakalavr*, *Specialist Diploma*

Last Updated: 27/01/12

KAMSK INSTITUTE

Kamskij Institut
prosp. Mira, 76, Naberežnje Čelny, 423818 Respublika Tatarstan
Tel: +7(8552) 56-55-38
Fax: +7(8552) 54-82-43
EMail: kaminstitut@yandex.ru
Website: http://www.kam-institut.ru/

Rector: Rimma Vladimirovna Daraselija

Faculties
Ecology (Ecology); **Economics** (Economics; Management)

History: Created 1995.

Degrees and Diplomas: *Specialist Diploma*

Last Updated: 16/01/12

KAMSK INSTITUTE OF ART AND DESIGN

Kamskij Institut Iskusstv i Dizajna
prosp. Chulman, 112, Naberežnje Čelny, 423826 Respublika Tatarstan
Tel: +7(8552) 32-98-20 +7(8552) 72-61-15 +7(8552)
Fax: +7(8552) 32-98-20 +7(8552) 72-61-15
EMail: kamkiid@rambler.ru
Website: http://www.kiid.ru/

Rector: El'mira Gandulovna Akhmetshina

Faculties

Design (Fashion Design; Graphic Design; Industrial Design; Interior Design; Landscape Architecture)

History: Created 2003.

Degrees and Diplomas: *Specialist Diploma*
Last Updated: 16/01/12

KAMSK INSTITUTE OF HUMANITARIAN AND ENGINEERING TECHNOLOGY

Kamskij Institut Gumanitarnyh i Inženernyh Tehnologij
ul. im. Vadima Sivkova, 12a, Iževsk, 426003 Udmurtskaja Respublika
Tel: +7(3412) 51-17-60 +7(3412) 50-16-07
Fax: +7(3412) 51-17-60 +7(3412) 51-17-27
EMail: kigit@udm.ru; kigit@bk.ru
Website: http://www.kigit.ru/

Rector: Ol'ga Alexandrovna Degteva

Faculties

Architecture and Design (Architecture; Computer Graphics; Design; Graphic Design; Industrial Design; Interior Design; Landscape Architecture); **Continuing Professional Education** (Design; Ecology; Economics; Finance; Information Technology; Petroleum and Gas Engineering); **Economics and Communication** (Accountancy; Advertising and Publicity; Economic History; Finance; Journalism; Management; Public Relations; Social Work); **Oil and Gas Engineering** (Petroleum and Gas Engineering)

Programmes

Humanities and Engineering Technology (Arts and Humanities; Engineering; Technology)

History: Created 1993.

Degrees and Diplomas: *Bakalavr*, *Specialist Diploma*; *Magistr*
Last Updated: 16/01/12

KHAKASSIJAN INSTITUTE OF BUSINESS

Khakasskij Institut Biznesa
ul. Puškina 190, korp. 1, Abakan 665004
Tel: +7(3902) 35-51-50 +7(3902) 35-49-60
Fax: +7(3902) 35-49-60
EMail: khakib@khakib.abakannet.ru
Website: http://www.khakib.ru

Rector: Svetlana Artemovna Cypysheva

Faculties

Economics and Management (Accountancy; Economics; Finance; Management; Marketing)

History: Founded 1993.

Governing Bodies: Academic Council

Academic Year: September to June

Main Language(s) of Instruction: Russian

Degrees and Diplomas: *Bakalavr*, *Specialist Diploma*

Student Services: Academic counselling, Canteen, Cultural centre, Health services, Language programs, Social counselling, Sports facilities

Student Residential Facilities: For c. 160 students

Libraries: Central Library: c. 55,000 vols
Last Updated: 17/01/12

KISLOVODSK HUMANITARIAN-TECHNICAL INSTITUTE

Kislovodskij Gumanitarno-Tehničeskij Institut
prosp. Pobedy 37a, Kislovodsk 357700
Tel: +7(87937) 2-83-33
Fax: +7(87937) 2-83-33
EMail: admin@kgti.ru; rector@kgti.ru
Website: http://www.kgti.ru/

Rector: Boris Ramazanovich Gochijaev

Faculties

Economics and Business Administration (Accountancy; Business Administration; Economics; Finance; Management); **Engineering** (Applied Mathematics; Automation and Control Engineering; Electrical and Electronic Equipment and Maintenance; Radio and Television Broadcasting; Telecommunications Engineering); **Law** (Law)

Programmes

Management (Management)

History: Created 1993.

Degrees and Diplomas: *Bakalavr*, *Specialist Diploma*
Last Updated: 30/01/12

KISLOVODSK INSTITUTE OF ECONOMICS AND LAW

Kislovodskij Institut Ekonomiki i Prava (KIEP)
ul. Roza Luksemburg 42, Kislovodsk 357700
Tel: +7(86537) 519-84
Fax: +7(86537) 423-15
EMail: kiep@kiep.ru
Website: http://www.kiep.ru

Rector: Aznaur S. Dudov Tel: +7(86537) 618-04

Vice-Rector: H. H. Dudova Tel: +7(86537) 618-17

International Relations: Natalia I. Gerasimova, Pro-Rector
Tel: +7(86537) 705-77

Departments

Economics (Accountancy; Banking; Computer Science; Economics; Finance; Management; Mathematics; Taxation); **Law**; **Philology** *(Courses for foreign students)* (English; French; German; Latin; Philology; Russian)

Further Information: All fields of study are suggested to foreign students. At the KIEL the postgraduate study act on 3 economic and 2 law specializations

History: Founded 1994, acquired present status and title 1997.

Governing Bodies: Institute Administration

Academic Year: September to June

Admission Requirements: Secondary school certificate (Attestat o srednem obrazovanii), or equivalent

Fees: (Russian Rubles): Tuition, c. 1,300; fees, c. 9,500 per annum; foreign students (US Dollars), c. 1,400

Main Language(s) of Instruction: Russian, English

Degrees and Diplomas: *Specialist Diploma*: 5 yrs; *Kandidat Nauk (PhD)*: 2-3 yrs

Student Services: Academic counselling, Canteen, Cultural centre, Employment services, Foreign student adviser, Foreign Studies Centre, Handicapped facilities, Health services, Language programs, Nursery care, Social counselling, Sports facilities

Special Facilities: Museum

Libraries: Main Library, c. 10,000 vols

KURSK INSTITUTE OF MANAGEMENT, ECONOMICS AND BUSINESS

Kurskij Institut Menedžmenta, Ekonomiki i Biznesa
ul. Radishcheva 35, Kursk 305000
Tel: +7(4712) 56-16-32 +7(4712) 56-16-28
Fax: +7(4712) 56-86-51
EMail: lector@znanie.kurskcity.ru
Website: http://www.mebik.ru/

Rector: Galina P. Okorokova

Faculties
Economics (Accountancy; Economics; Finance; International Economics; Management); **Management and Public Relations** (Advertising and Publicity; Human Resources; Management; Public Relations)
Further Information: Branches in Zheleznogorsk, Rylsk.
History: Created 1994.
Degrees and Diplomas: *Bakalavr*; *Specialist Diploma*; *Magistr*
Last Updated: 13/01/12

KUZBASS INSTITUTE OF ECONOMICS AND LAW

Kuzbasskij Institut Ekonomiki i Prava
ul. 40 let Oktjabrja, 2, Kemerovo 650001
Tel: +7(3842) 31-08-79
Fax: +7(3872) 31-34-33
EMail: kiel@kiel.ru
Website: http://www.kiel.ru/

Rector: Alexsandr I. Shcherbakov

Programmes
Economics and Law (Economics; Law)
History: Created 1994.
Degrees and Diplomas: *Specialist Diploma*
Last Updated: 09/02/12

LAW INSTITUTE (ST PETERSBURG)

Juridičeskij Institut (Sankt-Peterburg)
ul. Gavanskaja, 3, Sankt-Peterburg 199106
Tel: +7(812) 322-18-08 +7(812) 325-46-25
Fax: +7(812) 325-3887
EMail: lawinst-spb@mail.ru; main@lawinst.ru
Website: http://www.lawinst-spb.ru

Rector: Marija Borisovna Revnova

Programmes
Law (Law)
History: Created 1992.
Degrees and Diplomas: *Bakalavr*; *Specialist Diploma*
Last Updated: 15/04/11

LIBERAL ARTS UNIVERSITY (INSTITUTE)

Gumanitarnyj Universitet (Institut)
ul. Studenčeskaja 19, Ekaterinburg, 620049 Sverdlovskaja oblast'
Tel: +7(343) 374-5190
Fax: +7(343) 383-4666
EMail: lau@r66.ru
Website: http://www.gu.ur.ru

Rector: Lev Zaks EMail: rectorgu@r66.ru
Vice-Rector: Irina Koscheyeva EMail: prorector@gu.ur.ru
International Relations: Irina Fridman EMail: ms@gu.epn.ru

Departments
Broadcast Journalism (Journalism) *Dean*: Svetlana Balmaeva; **Computer Technology** (Computer Science; Economics) *Dean*: Alexander Agenosov; **Contemporary Dance** (Dance) *Director*: Lev Zaks; **Economics** (Accountancy; Business Administration; Finance; Management; Marketing) *Dean*: Sergey Mitsek; **European Area Studies and Linguistics** *Dean*: Tamara Sobko; **Fashion Design** (Fashion Design) *Dean*: Lev Zaks; **Law** *Dean*: Alexey Semitko; **Social Psychology** *Dean*: Elena Perelygina; **Sociology** *Dean*: Harold Zborovsky
History: Founded 1990. Acquired present status 1998.
Admission Requirements: Secondary school certificate
Fees: Vary according to Departments.
Main Language(s) of Instruction: Russian
Degrees and Diplomas: *Bakalavr*: Journalism, 4 yrs; *Specialist Diploma*: 5 yrs; *Kandidat Nauk*: Industrial Management and Economics; Finance; Banking and Credit; Religious Studies; Philosophical Anthropology; Philosophy of Culture; Theory and History of State and Law; History of Law Studies; Social Psychology; Sociology of Culture, 3 yrs
Student Residential Facilities: Yes
Libraries: Yes

LIPECK ECOLOGY-HUMANITARIAN INSTITUTE

Lipeckij Ekologo-Gumanitarnyj Institut (LEHI)
ul. Internacional'naja 5a, Lipeck 398600
Tel: +7(0742) 72-25-01
Fax: +7(0742) 77-92-41
EMail: legi@lipetsk.ru
Website: http://www.ligi.ligipetsk.ru

Rector: Jurij Ja. Filonenko
Prorector: Victor Filonenko

Faculties
Economics (Computer Science; Ecology; Economic and Finance Policy; Marketing) *Dean*: Sufia Demkina; **Humanitarian Studies** (Arts and Humanities; Ecology; Teacher Training) *Dean*: Valerij Birjukov
History: Founded in 1995.
Admission Requirements: School certificate; certificate of specialized secondary education entrance (if available); entrance examinations.
Main Language(s) of Instruction: Russian
Degrees and Diplomas: *Bakalavr*: Economics, 4 yrs; *Bakalavr*: Philology, 5 yrs
Student Residential Facilities: Yes.
Libraries: Yes
Publications: Environmental Problems of the Black-Earth Zone *(biennially)*; Vivat Ecology! *(quarterly)*
Press or Publishing House: LEHI publishing house

METROPOLITAN INSTITUTE OF TRANSLATORS

Stoličnyj Institut Perevodčikov
ul. 14-ja Parkovaja, 8, Moskva 105203
Tel: +7(495) 989-63-28
Fax: +7(495) 989-63-28
EMail: info@sip-vuz.ru
Website: http://www.sip-vuz.ru/

Rector: Tamara Vasil'evna Zhuravleva

Programmes
Foreign Language Teaching (Foreign Languages Education); **Linguistics** (Linguistics); **Translation and Interpretation** (Translation and Interpretation)
History: Created 1999.
Degrees and Diplomas: *Bakalavr*; *Specialist Diploma*
Last Updated: 23/02/12

MODERN UNIVERSITY OF HUMANITIES

Sovremennaja Gumanitarnaja Akademija (MUH)
ul. Koževničeskaja 3, Moskva 113114
Tel: +7(095) 235-1233
Fax: +7(095) 235-8851
EMail: ird@muh.ru
Website: http://www.muh.ru

President, SHA: Mikhail P. Karpenko (1992-)
Rector, WGA: Valery Tarakanov EMail: rectorat@muh.ru

Faculties
Computer Science (Artificial Intelligence; Computer Graphics; Computer Networks; Data Processing; Information Management; Information Sciences; Mathematics; Operations Research; Software Engineering; Systems Analysis); **Economics** (Accountancy; Business and Commerce; Economics; International Business; Marketing); **Law** (Administration; Civil Law; Criminal Law; International Law; Law); **Linguistics** (Foreign Languages Education; Linguistics; Translation and Interpretation); **Management** (Finance; Industrial Management; International Business; Management; Tourism); **Psychology**

Schools

Graduate (Accountancy; Automation and Control Engineering; Civil Law; Commercial Law; Computer Networks; Constitutional Law; Demography and Population; Economics; European Union Law; History of Law; Industrial and Organizational Psychology; Industrial Management; International Law; Law; Management; Marketing; Mathematics and Computer Science; Parks and Recreation; Philosophy; Private Law; Psychology; Social Policy; Social Psychology; Sociology; Software Engineering; Statistics; Technology; Tourism; Transport Management)

Further Information: Branches in the Russian Federation, Ukraine, Belarus, Armenia, Moldova, Kazakhstan, Tajikistan, Israel, Peru, Kyrgyzstan, Latvia, Lithuania, Mongolia

History: Founded 1992 as a Distance Education Institution, acquired present status 1994.

Governing Bodies: Board of Trustees

Academic Year: September to May

Admission Requirements: Secondary school certificate (Attestat o srednem obrazovanii) and entrance examination

Main Language(s) of Instruction: Russian

International Co-operation: With universities in United Kingdom, USA and France.

Accrediting Agencies: Ministry of Education, UK National Academic Recognition and Information Centre (NARIC)

Degrees and Diplomas: *Bakalavr*: 4 yrs; *Specialist Diploma*: 5 yrs; *Magistr*: a further 2 yrs; *Kandidat Nauk*: 2-4 yrs following Magistr

Student Services: Academic counselling, Canteen, Cultural centre, Employment services, Foreign student adviser, Foreign Studies Centre, Handicapped facilities, Health services, Language programs, Nursery care, Social counselling, Sports facilities

Special Facilities: Educational Satelite TV. Virtual University. Computer Training Rooms

Libraries: c. 5m. vols

Publications: Law and Education, Magazine *(monthly)*; MUH Scientific Journal, Magazine *(monthly)*; Telecommunications and Information Technology in Education, Magazine *(monthly)*

Last Updated: 24/01/12

MOSCOW ACADEMY OF ECONOMICS AND LAW

Moskovskaja Akademija Ekonomiki i Prava (MAEL)

Varšavskoje šosse, 23, Moskva 117105
Tel: +7(495) 958-1432
Fax: +7(495) 958-1432
EMail: info@mael.ru
Website: http://www.mael.ru

Rector: Vladimir Buyanov (1997-)

Vice-Rector: Oleg Zaitsev

International Relations: Mikael Chatberachvili, Advisor of Rector Tel: +7(495) 952-4520

Institutes

Economics (Accountancy; Banking; Finance; Management) *Director*: Leon Mikailov; **Law** *(Moscow) Director*: Valeri Zipunov

History: Founded 1993. Acquired present status and title 2000.

Governing Bodies: Academic Board

Academic Year: September to July

Fees: (US Dollars): 1,500-1,700 per annum

Main Language(s) of Instruction: Russian

International Co-operation: With universities in Poland.

Accrediting Agencies: Ministry of Education

Degrees and Diplomas: *Bakalavr*: Economics; Law, 4 yrs; *Specialist Diploma*: Economics; Law, 5-6 yrs

Student Services: Academic counselling, Canteen, Health services, Language programs, Sports facilities

Publications: Economics, Business, Environment *(biennially)*

MOSCOW AKADEMY OF EDUCATION NATALIA NESTEROVA ACADEMY

Moskovskaja Akademija Obrazovanija Natalii Nesterovoj

Varšavskoe šosse 38, Moskva 115230
Tel: +7(495) 787-22-87
Fax: +7(495) 787-22-87
EMail: zlvik@nesterova.ru; info@nesterova.ru; chernnad@yandex.ru
Website: http://www.nesterova.ru

Rector: Natal'ja V. Nesterova

Faculties

Choreography (Dance); **Communications** (Advertising and Publicity; Journalism; Literature; Public Relations); **Design and Technology** (Art History; Art Management; Design; Fashion Design; Fine Arts; Graphic Design); **Economics and Management** (Economics; Finance; Management; Marketing); **Film and TV Studies** (Acting; Cinema and Television; Film); **Humanities** (Civil Law; Commercial Law; International Law; Law; Linguistics; Translation and Interpretation); **Information Technology** (Computer Science; Information Technology); **Painting** (Graphic Arts; Painting and Drawing); **Practical Psychology** (Educational Psychology; Psychology; Social Work); **Tourism and Hotel Management** (Hotel Management; Tourism)

History: Founded 1990. Formerly Novyj Gumanitarnyj Universitet 'Natalii Nesterovoj' (Institut) and Universitet 'Natalii Nesterovoj'. Previously known as Akademija Natalii Nesterovoj (Natalia Nesterova Academy). Acquired current title in 2006.

Main Language(s) of Instruction: Russian

Degrees and Diplomas: *Bakalavr*; *Specialist Diploma*; *Magistr*; *Kandidat Nauk*

Last Updated: 31/07/12

MOSCOW BANK INSTITUTE

Moskovskij Bankovskij Institut

ul. Profsojuznaja 18, korp. 2, Moskva 117292
Tel: +7(495) 125-0627
Fax: +7(495) 125-0724
EMail: mbi_umo@mail.ru
Website: http://www.mbinst.ru

Director: Natalia R. Geronina Tel: +7(495) 125-0724

Colleges

Banking (Banking)

Programmes

Economics (Economics)

Governing Bodies: Ministry of Higher Education

Academic Year: September-July

Admission Requirements: Secondary school certificate and entrance examination

Main Language(s) of Instruction: Russian

Degrees and Diplomas: *Bakalavr*: 4 yrs

Student Services: Academic counselling, Canteen, Cultural centre, Foreign student adviser, Health services, Language programs, Nursery care, Social counselling, Sports facilities

MOSCOW ECONOMICS AND LAW INSTITUTE

Moskovskij Ekonomico-Pravovoj Institut (ELIM)

ul. Permskaja 1-1, Moskva 107143
Tel: +7(499) 167-1563 +7(499) 167-0120
Fax: +7(499) 167-7068
EMail: pmsu@yandex.ru
Website: http://www.mepi77.com

Rector: Igor V. Volkov (2004-) Tel: +7(499) 167-8321

Vice Rector: Tatiana Y. Prokofieva Tel: +7(499) 167-7326

International Relations: Karina M. Ivanova Tel: +7(499) 167-7060 EMail: krn25@yandex.ru

Faculties

Accountancy and Audit (Accountancy; Economics) *Dean*: Oleg M. Tolmachev; **Law** (Law) *Dean*: Anatoliy N. Kustov; **Management**

(Administration; Business Administration; Management) *Dean*: Valdimir M. Yurov

History: Founded 1995. Received accreditation 2000.

Admission Requirements: School certificate; Entrance Examination

Fees: (Russian Rubles): 24,000-48,000 per annum

Main Language(s) of Instruction: Russian

Accrediting Agencies: Russian Ministry of Education

MOSCOW ECONOMICS-FINANCE INSTITUTE

Moskovskij Ekonomiko-Finansovyj Institut
ul. P. Romanova 7, str. 2, Moskva 109193
Tel: +7(495) 279-3442
Fax: +7(495) 279-4917
EMail: mefi@mail.ru
Website: http://www.mefi.ru

Rector: Viktor Sidor Pavlenko

Programmes

Economics and Finance (Economics; Finance)

Degrees and Diplomas: *Specialist Diploma*: 5 yrs; *Kandidat Nauk*: Constitutional Law, Municipal Law; Economic Theory; Economics and Management of National Economy, 3 yrs

Student Services: Academic counselling, Canteen, Language programs, Nursery care

Student Residential Facilities: Yes

Libraries: Library; e-library

Publications: Problemi MSU, Economy, Law, Politics, history, investigation practice, statistics, regional news *(bimonthly)*

Press or Publishing House: ASI-Moscow

Academic Staff *2007-2008*	MEN	WOMEN	TOTAL
FULL-TIME	14	21	**35**
PART-TIME	3	7	**10**
STAFF WITH DOCTORATE			
FULL-TIME	8	12	**20**
PART-TIME	2	5	**7**
Student Numbers *2007-2008*			
All (Foreign Included)	670	710	**1,380**
FOREIGN ONLY	3	–	3

Part-time students, 600. **Evening students**, 390.

Last Updated: 09/12/08

MOSCOW ECONOMICS-LINGUISTICS INSTITUTE

Moskovskij Ekonomico-Lingvističeskij Institut
1st Kotlyakovskij per, d.1, Moskva 109044
Tel: +7(495) 660-81-50 +7(495) 660-81-60
Fax: +7(495) 734-91-55
EMail: info@meli.ru
Website: http://www.meli.ru/

Rector: Andrej L. Lomakin

Programmes

Economics and Linguistics (Economics; Linguistics)

MOSCOW FINANCE AND LAW UNIVERSITY

Moskovskij Finansovo-Juridičeskij Universitet (MFUA)
Ul Bolshaya Cheromushkinskaya 17A, Moskva 117447
Tel: +7(499) 127-94-03
Fax: +7(499) 127-94-03
EMail: shedrotkina.s@mfua.ru
Website: http://www.mfua.ru

Rector: Aleksey Zabelin (1989-) EMail: zabelin.a@mfua.ru

Faculties

Business and Information Technology (Accountancy; Business Computing; Design; Information Technology; Management; Taxation); **Business and Law** (Advertising and Publicity; Commercial Law; Finance; International Economics; Law; Management); **Economics and Law** (Accountancy; Documentation Techniques; Economics; Finance; International Economics; Law; Marketing); **Economics and Management** (Business and Commerce; Business Computing; Economics; Landscape Architecture; Law; Management); **Humanities** (Finance; Journalism; Law; Political Sciences; Psychology; Taxation; Translation and Interpretation); **Information Technology** (Business Computing; Information Technology; Law; Management); **Law and Economics** (Economics; Law)

History: Founded 1989 with the support of the Moscow Government, Association of International Education and Leading Universities of Russia, 16 branches all over Russia. Received full accreditation, from Russian Ministry of Education 1998. Previously known as Moskovskaja Finansovo-Juridičeskaja Akademija (Moscow Finance and Law Academy). Acquired current title 2009

Governing Bodies: Board of Guardians

Academic Year: September to June

Admission Requirements: Secondary school certificate (Attestat o srednem Obrazovanii) or equivalent

Main Language(s) of Instruction: Russian

Accrediting Agencies: Russian Ministry of Education (Federal'naja Sluzhba no Natsory I Sfere Obrazovani i Naukh)

Degrees and Diplomas: *Bakalavr*; *Specialist Diploma*; *Magistr*

Student Services: Canteen, Cultural centre, Employment services, Foreign student adviser, Foreign Studies Centre, Health services, Language programs, Sports facilities

Student Residential Facilities: Facilities for 1,000 students

Special Facilities: Movie studio; IT labs;

Libraries: c. 280,000 vols

Last Updated: 13/01/12

MOSCOW HUMANITARIAN ECONOMICS INSTITUTE

Moskovskij Gumanitarno-Ekonomičeskij Institut
Leninskij prosp d8. str 16, Moskva 119049
Tel: +7(499) 237-41-06 +7(499) 237-55-403595
Fax: +7(499) 237-56-60
EMail: mgei@mail.ru
Website: http://mgei.ru/

Rector: Ljubov Anisimovna Demidova

Faculties

Economics and Management (Economics; Management); **Humanities** (Advertising and Publicity; Design; International Relations; Journalism; Psychology; Public Relations; Tourism); **Law** (Law; Taxation)

History: Created 1994.

Degrees and Diplomas: *Specialist Diploma*

Last Updated: 20/01/12

MOSCOW INSTITUTE OF ADVERTISING, TOURISM AND SHOW BUSINESS

Moskovskij Institut Reklamy, Turizma i Show-Biznesa
ul. Malaja Semjonovskaja, 11/2, str. 7, Moskva 115008
Tel: +7(499) 369-50-41
Fax: +7(499) 369-50-41
EMail: anika-igorg@yandex.ru
Website: http://www.mirtshb.ru/

Rector: Igor Georgievich Anikanov

Faculties

Advertising (Advertising and Publicity); **Cinema and Television** (Cinema and Television; Film); **Cultural Service and Tourism** (Tourism); **Management** (Management); **Show Business** (Acting; Radio and Television Broadcasting; Theatre)

Further Information: Branches in Brjansk, Volzhskij.

History: Created 1996.

Degrees and Diplomas: *Specialist Diploma*

Last Updated: 17/01/12

MOSCOW INSTITUTE OF ECONOMICS AND LAW

Moskovskij Ekonomiko-Pravovoj Institut (MEPI)

ul. Permskaya, 1, structure, 1, Moskva 107143

Tel: +7(495) 167-70-68

Fax: +7(495) 167-70-68

EMail: mepirector@yandex.ru

Website: http://www.mepi77.com/

Rector: Tatiana Yurievna Prokofieva

Faculties

Economics and Management (Accountancy; Economics; Finance; Management); **Law** (Law)

History: Created 2000.

Fees: (Russian Rubles): 5,500 per month (full time students)

Degrees and Diplomas: *Bakalavr*, *Specialist Diploma*

Student Services: Canteen, Health services

Libraries: Yes

Last Updated: 31/03/11

MOSCOW INSTITUTE OF ECONOMICS, MANAGEMENT AND LAW

Moskovskij Institut Ekonomiki, Menedžmenta i Prava

ul. Novopeschnnaja, 3, 12, Moskva 125057

Tel: +7(495) 155-9512

Fax: +7(495) 155-9512

EMail: miemp@miemp.ru

Website: http://www.miemp.ru

President: Sergej Ivanovic Dmitraško EMail: inter@miemp.ru

MOSCOW INSTITUTE OF ECONOMICS, MANAGEMENT AND LAW

Moskovskij Institut Ekonomiki, Menedžmenta i Prava (MIEML)

2 Kozhukhovsky pr. 12, Moskva 115432

Tel: +7(495) 783-6848

Fax: +7(495) 783-6849

EMail: inter@miemp.ru

Website: http://www.miemp.ru

President: Nikolay G. Malyshev (2002-)
Tel: +7(495) 783-6818, Fax: +7(495) 783-6819
EMail: malyshev@miemp.ru

Rector: Natalya M. Kondratenko
Tel: +7(095) 783-6818, Fax: +7(095) 783-6819
EMail: nkondratenko@miemp.ru

International Relations: Igor N. Shapkin, Deputy Director
Tel: +7(495) 783-6843, Fax: +7(495) 783-6819
EMail: ishapkin@miemp.ru

Faculties

Economics and Finance *Dean*: Marina A. Balashova; **Law** *Dean*: Maria U. Iroshnikova; **Management** (Administration; Business Administration; Computer Science; Hotel and Restaurant; Management; Marketing; Public Administration; Tourism) *Dean*: Elena S. Khripunova

Further Information: MIEML offers different forms of learning, including full-time and part-time programmes (evening, non-resident and weekend schedules). Postgraduate school. MIEML has branches in 10 cities and towns all over the country (Ryazan, Nizhny Novgorod, Voronezh, Rostov-on-Don, Penza, Tula, Krasnodar, Perm', Chernogolovka, Sergiyev Posad). State Diploma of the Russian Federation.

History: Founded 1993.

Governing Bodies: Council of Founders

Academic Year: September to June

Admission Requirements: Secondary school certificate

Fees: (Euros): 90,000 per annum

Main Language(s) of Instruction: Russian

International Co-operation: With universities in USA

Accrediting Agencies: Ministry of Education

Degrees and Diplomas: *Bakalavr (BBA)*: 4 yrs; *Specialist Diploma*: 5 yrs (fuul-time) -6 yrs (part-time)

Student Services: Academic counselling, Canteen, Cultural centre, Employment services, Foreign student adviser, Foreign Studies Centre, Health services, Language programs, Nursery care, Social counselling, Sports facilities

Student Residential Facilities: Yes

Special Facilities: Art studio "KVN", movies studio

Libraries: Yes

Publications: Dom 12, Student's newspaper *(monthly)*

Press or Publishing House: Dom 12

Academic Staff *2008-2009*	MEN	WOMEN	**TOTAL**
FULL-TIME	–	–	**307**
PART-TIME	–	–	**336**
STAFF WITH DOCTORATE			
FULL-TIME	–	–	**202**
PART-TIME	–	–	**195**
Student Numbers *2008-2009*			
All (Foreign Included)	7,920	16,800	**24,720**
FOREIGN ONLY	147	312	**459**

Part-time students, 11,862. **Distance students**, 3,113. **Evening students**, 3,924.

Last Updated: 25/11/08

MOSCOW INSTITUTE OF ECONOMICS, POLITICS AND LAW

Moskovskij Institut Ekonomiki, Politiki i Prava

ul. 5 Kožuhovskaja 26, Moskva 109193

Tel: +7(495) 277-3302

Fax: +7(495) 277-3813

Website: http://www.miepl.ru

Rector: Andrij I. Šilov

Programmes

Economics (Economics); **Finance** (Finance); **Law** (Law)

MOSCOW INSTITUTE OF ENTREPRENEURSHIP AND LAW

Moskovskij Institut Predprinimatelstva i Prava

ul. Staropetrovskij proezd 1a, Moskva 125130

Tel: +7(495) 786-78-03 +7(495) 786-78-00

Fax: +7(495) 786-78-04

EMail: rector@mipp.ru

Website: http://www.mipp.ru

Rector: Oleg Aleksandrovich Rykhlov

Programmes

Banking (Banking); **Business and Commerce** (Business and Commerce); **Economics** (Economics); **Management** (Management)

Further Information: Branches in Buinaksk, Derbent, Makhachkala, Mineralnye Vody, Novosibirsk, Norilsk, Orenburg, Penza, Prague, Rostov-na-Donu, Bishkek, Ekaterinburg, Karakol, Osh, Sergiev Posad, Sochi, Stavropol, Tiraspol.

History: Created 1995.

Degrees and Diplomas: *Bakalavr*, *Specialist Diploma*

Last Updated: 12/01/12

MOSCOW INSTITUTE OF FINANCE AND ECONOMICS

Moskovskij Finansovo-Ekonomičeskij Institut

ul. Novomoskovskaja 15a, str. 1, Moskva 129075

Tel: +7(495) 616-45-23

Fax: +7(495) 616-45-23

EMail: rectorat@mfei.ru

Website: http://www.mfei.ru/

Rector: Nikolai Nikolaevich Stoljarov

Faculties

Economics and Financial Management (Accountancy; Economics; Finance)

History: Created 1993 as Finansovaja Akademija pri Pravitel'stve Rossijskoj Federacii (Finance Academy of the Russian Federation Government).

Degrees and Diplomas: *Bakalavr*, *Specialist Diploma*
Last Updated: 23/02/12

MOSCOW INSTITUTE OF FINANCE AND LAW

Moskovskij Finansovo-Pravovoi Institut (MFPI)
ul. Letčika Babuškina, d. 6, str. 2, Moskva 129344
Tel: +7(495) 470-81-43
Fax: +7(499) 909-18-22
Website: http://www.mfpi-vyz.ru/

Rector: Igor Vitalevich Konstandi (2004-)

Programmes

Accounting and Audit (Accountancy); **Economics** (Economics); **Law** (Law); **Management** (Management); **Tax** (Taxation)

History: Created 199. Previously known as Moskovskij Institut Buhgalterskogo Učjota i Audita (Moscow Institute of Accountancy and Audit).

Governing Bodies: Academic Council, Rector

Admission Requirements: Secondary School Certificate

Fees: (Rub): 2,870 - 7,290 per month.

Main Language(s) of Instruction: Russian

Accrediting Agencies: Ministry of Higher Education

Degrees and Diplomas: *Specialist Diploma*; *Kandidat Nauk*

Student Services: Cultural centre, Language programs, Sports facilities

Libraries: Yes

Last Updated: 23/07/10

MOSCOW INSTITUTE OF FOREIGN LANGUAGES

Moskovskij Institut Inostrannykh Jazykov
prosp. Ladožskaja 9/8, Moskva 105005
Tel: +7(495) 632-25-33
Fax: +7(495) 632-25-33
EMail: rector@gaudeamus.ru; inter@gaudeamus.ru
Website: http://www.gaudeamus.ru/

Rector: Emma Volodarskaja EMail: rector@gaudeamus.ru

Faculties

Foreign Languages (Foreign Languages Education; Philology); **International Economics** (International Economics); **International Tourism** (Tourism); **Language and Culture** (Cultural Studies; Modern Languages; Philology); **Law** (Law); **Regional Geography** (International Studies; Regional Studies); **Translation** (English; Translation and Interpretation)

History: Created 1995.

Degrees and Diplomas: *Bakalavr*, *Specialist Diploma*
Last Updated: 26/01/12

MOSCOW INSTITUTE OF INTERNATIONAL ECONOMICS RELATIONS

Moskovskij Institut Meždunarodnyh Ekonomičeskih Otnošenij
ul. Gabričevskogo 3, Korp. 3, Moskva 123367
Tel: +7(495) 956-1714
Fax: +7(495) 912-5608
Website: http://www.mimeo.ru

Rector: Konstantin S. Lekomcev

Programmes

International Economics Relations (International Economics; International Relations)

MOSCOW INSTITUTE OF LAW

Moskovskij Institut Prava
ul Jablochkova, 8a, Moskva 127254
Tel: +7(495) 610-31-12 +7(495) 610-28-57
Fax: +7(495) 610-28-57
EMail: info@mip-vuz.ru
Website: http://www.mip-vuz.ru/

Rector: Oleg Petrovich Kireev

Programmes

Economics (Economics; Management; Psychology); **Law** (Law)

History: Created 1994.

Degrees and Diplomas: *Bakalavr*, *Specialist Diploma*
Last Updated: 24/02/12

MOSCOW INSTITUTE OF LINGUISTICS

Moskovskij Institut Lingvistiki
Novomoskovskaja, d.15a, Moskva 115184
Tel: +7(495) 616-2641 +7(495) 616-3701
Fax: +7(495) 616-3610
EMail: info@inyaz-mil.ru; uo@inyaz-mil.ru
Website: http://www.inyaz-mil.ru

Rector: Livinu Mikhailovich Terentij

Faculties

International Management (Accountancy; Finance; Management); **Linguistics and Intercultural Communication** (Chinese; English; German; Linguistics; Philology; Spanish; Translation and Interpretation); **Tourism and Hospitality Management** (Hotel Management; Tourism)

History: Created 1996. Acquired status 2009.

Degrees and Diplomas: *Bakalavr*, *Magistr*
Last Updated: 30/08/11

MOSCOW INSTITUTE OF MUNICIPAL ECONOMY AND CONSTRUCTION

Moskovskij Institut Kommunalnogo Hozyajstva i Stroitel' stva
ul. Srednyaya Kalitnikovskaya, 30, Moskva 109029
Tel: +7 (495) 678-3205 +7(495) 670-7180
Fax: +7(495) 670-7180
EMail: mikhis-lab@bk.ru
Website: http://www.mikhis.ru

Rector: Aleksandr Anatol'evič Kal'gin
Tel: +7(495) 678-3205, Fax: +7(495) 678-3205
EMail: mikhis-rektor@mail.ru

Faculties

Automated Systems (Automation and Control Engineering) *Dean*: Anatolij Ivanovich Dotsenko; **Engineering, Systems and Ecology** (Ecology; Engineering) *Dean*: Eugene Maxutovich Avdolimov; **Industrial and Civil Engineering** (Civil Engineering; Industrial Engineering) *Dean*: Mikhail Vasilevich Berlinov; **Industrial Economics and Management** (Business Administration; Management) *Dean*: Sergey Mikhailovich Yarovenko; **Technology** (Technology) *Dean*: Vladimir Vasilevich Baev; **Urban and Highway Construction** (Road Engineering; Urban Studies) *Dean*: Vladimir Ivanovich Rimshin

Degrees and Diplomas: *Specialist Diploma*: 5 yrs
Last Updated: 10/12/08

MOSCOW INSTITUTE OF SOCIAL SCIENCE AND LIBERAL ARTS

Moskovskij Sotsial'no-Gumanitarnyj Institut
Dubininskja, 57 str. 2, Office 2115, Moskva 115054
Tel: +7(495) 626-26-41
Fax: +7(495) 626-26-41
EMail: msgi@inbox.ru
Website: http://www.msgi.info/

Rector: Evgenij Vazgenovich Oganesjan

International Relations: Gulzhan Gubareva, Head of Innovation and Development EMail: gubareva@msgi.info

Programmes

Economics (Economics); **Educational Psychology** (Educational Psychology); **Management** (Management); **Psychology** (Psychology); **Public and Municipal Administration** (Administration; Public Administration); **Special Education** (Education of the Handicapped; Special Education; Speech Therapy and Audiology)

Further Information: Branches in Aprelevka, Egorievsk, Kazan, Kamensk Shakhtinsky, Nefteyugansk, Novomoskovsk, Rzhev, Taganrog, and Yaroslavl.

History: Created 1996 to train professionals in public administration, social services, and business.

Degrees and Diplomas: *Bakalavr*, *Specialist Diploma*

Academic Staff *2010-2011*: Total 340

Student Numbers *2010-2011*: Total: c. 7,000

Last Updated: 03/09/12

MOSCOW INSTITUTE OF WORLD ECONOMY AND INTERNATIONAL RELATIONS

Moskovskij Institut Mirovoj Ekonomika i Meždunarodnykh Otnošenij

ul. Gabrichevskaja, 3/3, Moskva 123367

Tel: +7(499) 151-05-83 +7(499) 747-71-15

Fax: +7(499) 151-05-83

EMail: info@mimemo.ru

Website: http://www.mimemo.ru

Rector: Andrei Nikolaevich Batenev

Programmes

Business Computing (Business Computing); **Economics** (Economics; International Economics); **Law** (Law); **Management** (Management)

History: Created 1994.

Degrees and Diplomas: *Bakalavr*, *Specialist Diploma*

Last Updated: 26/01/12

MOSCOW INTERNATIONAL HIGHER SCHOOL OF BUSINESS "MIRBIS" (INSTITUTE)

Moskovskaja Meždunarodnaja Vysšaja Škola Biznesa "MIRBIS" (Institut) (MIRBIS)

ul. Marksistskaja, 34/7, Moskva 109147

Tel: +7(495) 921-41-88 +7(495) 921-41-80

Fax: +7(495) 237-34-30 +7(495) 662-78-82

EMail: info@mirbis.ru

Website: http://www.mirbis.ru

Rector: Stanislav Leonidovich Savin EMail: rector@mirbis.ru

Faculties

International Business (Business Administration; Economics; International Economics; Management; Marketing)

History: Created 1998.

Degrees and Diplomas: *Bakalavr*, *Specialist Diploma*; *Magistr*

Last Updated: 23/02/12

MOSCOW NEW LAW INSTITUTE

Moskovskij Novyj Juridičeskij Institut

ul. Sabovničeskaja 67, bdlg. 2, Moskva 113035

Tel: +7(495) 951-9672

Fax: +7(495) 951-2626

Website: http://www.mnyi.ru

Rector: Aleksandr M. Jakovlev

First Vice-Rector: N. A. Batarčuk

Programmes

Law (Law)

MOSCOW OPEN INSTITUTION OF LAW

Moskovskij Otkrytyj Juridičeskij Institut (MOYI)

Solnečnogorsk 141506

Tel: +7(495) 941-84-68

Fax: +7(495) 941 84-69

EMail: oji@yandex.ru

Website: http://www.oji.ru/

Rector: Natalia Victorovana Maiorova
EMail: rektor760@hotmail.com

President: Alexander Marusov
Tel: +7(495) 166-28-51, Fax: +7(495) 166-28-52

International Relations: Victor Fersht EMail: fersht@narod.ru

Faculties

Law *Dean*: Anatoliy Voloshko

History: Created 2001. Acquired status 2004.

Fees: (Rubels): 24,000 per annum

Main Language(s) of Instruction: Russian

International Co-operation: with institutions in Israel

Degrees and Diplomas: *Bakalavr*: 4-5 yrs; *Specialist Diploma*: 5-6 yrs; *Kandidat Nauk*: 3 yrs

Student Services: Academic counselling, Canteen, Employment services, Handicapped facilities, Health services, Nursery care, Social counselling, Sports facilities

Student Residential Facilities: For 50 students

Libraries: c. 87,000 books; c. 1,590 periodical subscriptions; c. 12,000 e-books

Academic Staff *2007-2008*	**TOTAL**
FULL-TIME	**65**
PART-TIME	**35**
Student Numbers *2007-2008*	
All (Foreign Included)	**1,050**

Last Updated: 11/01/08

MOSCOW PSYCHOLOGY AND SOCIAL INSTITUTE

Moskovskij Psihologo-Social'nyj Institut

4 Roshchinskij proezd, 9A, Moskva 115191

Tel: +7(495) 232-10-69

Fax: +7(495) 232-10-68

EMail: mpsi@col.ru

Website: http://www.mpsu.ru/

Rector: Svetlana K. Bondypeva

Faculties

Economics, Management, and Tourism (Economics; Management; Marketing; Mathematics; Tourism); **Information Technology** (Information Technology; Mathematics and Computer Science); **Law** (Commercial Law; Constitutional Law; Criminal Law; Fiscal Law; Law; Private Law); **Linguistics** (Foreign Languages Education; Linguistics; Social Work); **Psychology** (Clinical Psychology; Educational Psychology; Pedagogy; Psychology; Social Psychology); **Speech Therapy** (Special Education; Speech Therapy and Audiology)

History: Created 1995.

Degrees and Diplomas: *Bakalavr*, *Specialist Diploma*

Last Updated: 24/02/12

MOSCOW REGION INSTITUTE OF MANAGEMENT AND LAW

Moskovskij Oblastnoj Institut Upravlenija i Prava

ul. Permovajskaja, 14, Ivanteevka, 141280 Moskvskaja Oblast'

Tel: +7(49653) 6-24-25

Fax: +7(49653) 6-15-71

EMail: moiup@mail.ru

Website: http://www.moiup.ru

Rector: Suren S. Mkrtchjan (1996-)

Faculties

Economics (Accountancy; Economics; Finance); **Law** (Civil Law; Criminal Law; Law; Notary Studies); **Management** (Management)

History: Founded 1996. Formerly known as Ivanteevskij Institut Upravlenija i Prava (Invanteevskij Institute of Management and Law).

Governing Bodies: Rector; Prorector for Scienctific Affairs; Prorector for Educational Affairs

Academic Year: September to July

Admission Requirements: Secondary School Leaving Certificate (Attestat)

Main Language(s) of Instruction: Russian

International Co-operation: With universities in Belorussia and Finland.

Accrediting Agencies: Ministry of Education and Science

Degrees and Diplomas: *Bakalavr*; *Specialist Diploma*

Student Services: Academic counselling, Canteen, Cultural centre, Employment services, Foreign student adviser, Health services, Nursery care, Social counselling, Sports facilities

Student Residential Facilities: Dormitory

Libraries: Yes

Last Updated: 13/01/12

MOSCOW REGIONAL INSTITUTE OF MANAGEMENT

Moskovskij Oblastnoi Institut Upravlenija

šosse Entuziastov 59, Balašiha 143900

Tel: +7(495) 521-21-50 +7(495) 521-70-54 +7(495) 521-40-27

Fax: +7(495) 521-70-54 +7(495) 521-40-27

EMail: moiu@mail.ru

Website: http://www.moiu.ru/

Rector: Tat'jana Evgeneva Chernyshova

Programmes

Law (Law); **Management** (Management)

History: Created 1992. Previously known as Institut Biznesa, Prava i Informacionnyh Tehnologij (Institute of Business, Law and Information Technology). Acquired current title 2005.

Degrees and Diplomas: *Bakalavr*; *Specialist Diploma*

Last Updated: 24/01/12

MOSCOW SOCIAL OPEN ACADEMY

Moskovskaja Otkrytaja Social'naja Akademija (MOSU)

Zel'ev pereulok, d.11, Moskva 107392

Tel: +7(499) 785-55-68

Fax: +7(499) 785-55-58

EMail: info@mosa.su; info@mosu.ru

Website: http://www.mosu.ru

Rector: Ivan G. Bezuglov

Faculties

Design (Design; Fashion Design; Graphic Arts; Graphic Design); **Finance and Economics** (Accountancy; Business Computing; Economics; Finance; Management); **Law** (Law); **Modern Languages** (Chinese; English; French; German; Italian; Spanish); **Psychology** (Psychology); **Special Education** (Education of the Handicapped; Special Education; Speech Studies); **Toursim** (Tourism)

Further Information: Branches in Maikop, Astrakhan', Bijsk, Volgodonsk, Voronezh, Kaliningrad, Elista, Cherkessk, Joshkar-Ola, Mineralnyje Vody, Novyj Urengoj, Nojabrs'k, Penza, Pskov, Tambov, Ust'-Ilimsk.

History: Created 1992 as Moskovskij Otkrytyj Social'nyj Universitet (Moscow Social Open University). Acquired current title and status 2002.

Degrees and Diplomas: *Bakalavr*; *Specialist Diploma*; *Magistr*

Last Updated: 12/01/12

MOSCOW TECHNOLOGICAL INSTITUTE "WTU"

Moskovskij Tekhnologičeskij Institut "VTU" (MTI WTU)

ul. Kedrova 8, korp.2, Moskva 115432

Tel: +7(495) 500-0306

Fax: +7(495) 500-0306

EMail: open@mti.edu.ru

Website: http://mti.edu.ru

President: Nikolay Malyshev (1998-)
Tel: +7(495) 783-6848, Fax: +7(495) 783-6819

Rector: Grigorij Bubnov

International Relations: Evgeniy Pluzhnik, First Pro-Rector
Tel: +7(495) 648-6226, Fax: +7(495) 648-6226
EMail: E_pluzhnik@mti.edu.ru

Faculties

Economics and Management (Accountancy; Banking; Business Administration; E-Business/Commerce; Economics; Finance; Human Resources; Industrial and Production Economics; Industrial Management; International Economics; Leadership; Management; Private Administration; Public Administration; Small Business; Taxation); **Techniques and Modern Technology** (Building Technologies; Electrical and Electronic Equipment and Maintenance; Energy Engineering; Engineering Management; Environmental Engineering; Food Technology; Industrial Engineering; Information Management; Information Sciences; Information Technology; Maintenance Technology; Safety Engineering; Thermal Engineeering)

Further Information: Branches in Taganrog, Volgograd, Penza, Ryazan, Nizhny Novgorod, Orenburg, Rostov-on-Don, Sankt-Peterburg.

History: Created 1997. Also offers e-learning and other distance courses.

Governing Bodies: CouncilCouncil of Founders

Academic Year: September to June

Admission Requirements: Secondary School Certifcate.

Fees: (Rub): 60,000 per annum

Main Language(s) of Instruction: Russian

International Co-operation: with institutions in USA.

Degrees and Diplomas: *Bakalavr*: 4-4 1/2 yrs; *Magistr*: a further 2 yrs

Student Services: Academic counselling, Canteen, Cultural centre, Employment services, Foreign student adviser, Health services, Language programs, Social counselling

Student Residential Facilities: Yes

Special Facilities: Art studio, movie studio

Libraries: Yes

Academic Staff *2011-2012*	MEN	WOMEN	TOTAL
FULL-TIME	–	–	**20**
PART-TIME	–	–	**120**
STAFF WITH DOCTORATE			
FULL-TIME	–	–	**56**
Student Numbers *2011-2012*			
All (Foreign Included)	3,358	3,327	**6,685**
FOREIGN ONLY	612	835	**1,447**

Part-time students, 5,560. **Distance students**, 1,106.

Last Updated: 17/07/12

MOSCOW TRANSPORT INSTITUTE

Moskovskij Transportnyj Institut

Leningradskij prosp. 64, Moskva 125319

Tel: +7(499) 155-07-14 +7(499) 155-01-68

Fax: +7(499) 151-03-61

EMail: noy-mti@yandex.ru

Website: http://www.nou-mti.ru/

Rector: Vladimir Borisovich Borisevich

Programmes

Transport Studies (Transport and Communications; Transport Management)

History: Created 1995.

Degrees and Diplomas: *Specialist Diploma*
Last Updated: 24/02/12

MOSCOW UNIVERSITY FOR THE HUMANITIES

Moskovskij Gumanitarnyj Universitet (MOSGU)
ul. Yunosti 5/1, Moskva 111395
Tel: +7(499) 374-53-60
Fax: +7(499) 374-53-60
EMail: mosgu.icd@mail.ru
Website: http://www.mosgu.ru

Rector: Igor Mihailovich Ilyinskij (1994-)
Tel: +7(499) 374-52-80, Fax: +7(499) 374-52-80

Pro-Rector for International Relations and Education: Evgeniy A. Belyi Tel: +7(499) 374-67-97 EMail: ebelyi@mosgu.ru

International Relations: Ekaterina Andreychenko, Head of International Cooperation Department (2009-)
Tel: +7(499) 374-53-60, Fax: +7(499) 374-53-60

Colleges

Humanities (Accountancy; Advertising and Publicity; Banking; Business Computing; Economics; Law; Management; Marketing)

Faculties

Advertising (Advertising and Publicity; Design; Marketing; Mass Communication); **Economics and Management** (Economics; Finance; International Economics; Mathematics); **International Relations** (International Relations); **Law** (Civil Law; Criminal Law; Human Rights; International Law; Law); **Postgraduate Training and Doctorate Studies**; **Psychology and Social Work** (Human Resources; Psychology; Social Work); **Tourism and Cultural Studies** (Cultural Studies; Tourism)

Further Information: Research Institute for Humanities; UNESCO International Institute of Youth for the Culture of Peace and Democracy; The Centre of Information and Computer Technologies; Irida non-governmental comprehensive secondary school

History: Founded 1944. Acquired present title and status 2008.

Academic Year: September to June

Admission Requirements: Common state examination certificate (Edinij gosudarstvennij ekzamen), entrance exam.

Fees: (Euros): 2,000 - 3,500 per annum

Main Language(s) of Instruction: Russian

International Co-operation: With universities in France, Austria, Germany, UK, Sweden, China, Netherlands

Accrediting Agencies: Ministry of Education and Science

Degrees and Diplomas: *Specialist Diploma*: Advertising; Management and Economics; Law; International Relations; Tourism and Cultural Studies;Psychology and Social Work, 5 yrs full time/6 yrs part time

Student Services: Academic counselling, Canteen, Cultural centre, Employment services, Foreign student adviser, Foreign Studies Centre, Health services, Language programs, Social counselling, Sports facilities

Student Residential Facilities: Yes

Special Facilities: Movie studio; Theatre; Cultural Centre

Libraries: Yes

Publications: Knowledge. Understanding. Skills, Humanitarian Science Magazine *(quarterly)*; Science works of Moscow University for Humanities, Humanitarian Science *(quarterly)*

Press or Publishing House: University Publishing House

Academic Staff *2007-2008*	**TOTAL**
FULL-TIME	**550**
PART-TIME	**441**
STAFF WITH DOCTORATE	
FULL-TIME	**353**
PART-TIME	**183**
Student Numbers *2007-2008*	
All (Foreign Included)	c. **10,000**

Last Updated: 06/06/11

MOSCOW UNIVERSITY NAMED AFTER E.R. DASHKOVA

Moskovskij Gumanitarnyj Institut im. E.R. Daškovoj
ul. Leskova 6, Korp B, Moskva 127349
Tel: +7(495) 909-9101
Fax: +7(495) 909-7920
EMail: dashkova@starlink.ru
Website: http://www.dashkova.ru

Rector: Larisa V. Tychinina (1992-) Tel: +7(495) 229-0519

Executive Director: V. V. Tychinin

International Relations: Zciegniew Iwanowski, Pro-Rector
EMail: iwanowski@dashkova.ru

Departments

Economics and Law (Accountancy; Banking; Civil Law; Criminal Law; Industrial Management) *Dean*: Vladimir Melnikov; **Journalism** (Advertising and Publicity; Journalism) *Dean*: Nadezhda Kostikova; **Linguistics** (Linguistics); **Management** (Management); **Philology** (Philology); **Protection of Information** (Information Management); **Psychology and Intercultural Communication** (Psychology; Translation and Interpretation) *Dean*: Natalya Begunkova

History: Founded 1992.

Academic Year: September to July

Admission Requirements: Secondary school certificate (Attestat o srednem obrazovanii) or equivalent

Fees: (Euros): 1,000

Main Language(s) of Instruction: Russian

Accrediting Agencies: Ministry of Science and Education

Degrees and Diplomas: *Specialist Diploma*: 5-6 yrs

Student Services: Canteen, Health services, Language programs, Sports facilities

Libraries: Yes

MOSCOW UNIVERSITY OF INDUSTRY AND FINANCE

Moskovskaja Finansovo-Promyšlennaja Akademija (MFPA)
ul. Meschanskaya 9/14, Moskva 129090
Tel: +7(495) 681-0103
Fax: +7(495) 681-0103
EMail: inter@mfpa.ru
Website: http://www.mfpa.ru

Rector: Yuri Rubin
Tel: +7(495) 684-5060, Fax: +7(495) 684-5060
EMail: yrubin@mfpa.ru

First Vice-Rector: Vladimir Lednev
Tel: +7(495) 158-1442, Fax: +7(495) 158-1442
EMail: vlednev@mfpa.ru

International Relations: Erika Rubina EMail: ERubina@mfpa.ru

Faculties

Finance (Accountancy; Finance; Taxation); **Informatics** (Information Technology); **International Economics** (International Economics); **Law** (Law); **Management** (Management)

History: Founded 1995 as Moskovskij Meždunarodnyj Institut Ekonometriki, Informatiki, Finansow i Prava/Moscow International Institute of Econometrics, Informatics, Finance and Law, acquired present status and title 2005.

Academic Year: October to July

Admission Requirements: Secondary school certificate (Attestat o srednem obrazovanii)

Fees: (US Dollars): 2,050 per semester

Main Language(s) of Instruction: Russian

Accrediting Agencies: Ministry of Education

Degrees and Diplomas: *Bakalavr*: 4 yrs; *Specialist Diploma*: 5 yrs; *Magistr*: a further 2 yrs following Bakalavr; *Kandidat Nauk*: a further 3 yrs

Student Services: Academic counselling, Canteen, Employment services, Foreign student adviser, Foreign Studies Centre, Health services, Language programs, Nursery care, Social counselling, Sports facilities

Student Residential Facilities: Yes

Libraries: Central library, electronic library

Academic Staff *2007-2008*	**TOTAL**
FULL-TIME	**212**
PART-TIME	**121**
STAFF WITH DOCTORATE	
FULL-TIME	**124**
PART-TIME	**98**
Student Numbers *2007-2008*	
All (Foreign Included)	**22,588**
FOREIGN ONLY	**183**

Last Updated: 25/11/08

MOSCOW UNIVERSITY TOURO

Moskovskij Universitet Turo

Podsosenskij per. 20/12, Moskva 105062
Tel: +7(495) 917-33-11
Fax: +7(495) 917-53-48
EMail: admin@touro.ru
Website: http://www.touro.ru

Rector: Renee Lekač (1991-) Tel: +7(495) 917-4052

Vice-Rector: Svetlana Pavlova
Tel: +7(495) 917-41-69 EMail: pavlovas@touro.ru

International Relations: Michael Glatt, Vice-Rector
Tel: +7(495) 917-33-22 EMail: glatt@touro.ru

Programmes

Business Administration (Banking; Business Administration; Finance; Information Technology; Marketing); **Business Management** (Business Administration; Management); **Health Sciences** (Health Administration; Health Sciences; Medicine; Public Health; Safety Engineering); **Law** (Business Education; Commercial Law; Finance; Law)

History: Founded 1991. Acquired present status 1994.

Admission Requirements: Secondary school certificate, TOEFL score 500, and entrance examination

Fees: (US Dollars): 3,000 per semester

Main Language(s) of Instruction: English

International Co-operation: With universitites in USA

Accrediting Agencies: Ministry of Education; Middle States Association of Colleges and Schools

Degrees and Diplomas: *Bakalavr*: Business Management (BSc), 3 1/2-4 yrs; *Magistr*: Business Administration; Banking; Marketing; Information Technology (MBA), 15 months following Bakalavr. Bakalavr and Magistr equivalent to Bachelor's and Master's Degrees

Student Services: Canteen, Sports facilities

Special Facilities: Movie Studio

Libraries: c. 45,000 vols, virtual library

MOSOW INSTITUTE OF PHYSICAL EDUCATION AND SPORT

Moskovskij Institut Fizičeskoj Kul'tury i Sporta

ul. Tashkentskaja, 26/2, Moskva 109472
Tel: +7(495) 372-00-31
Fax: +7(495) 372-00-31
EMail: mifkis-org@yandex.ru
Website: http://www.mifkis.ru/

Rector: Vladislav Viktorovich Kalinkin

Programmes

Physical Education (Educational Psychology; Physical Education; Teacher Training; Tourism); **Sport** (Sports; Sports Management)

History: Created 1999.

Degrees and Diplomas: *Bakalavr*, *Specialist Diploma*

Last Updated: 05/04/12

MURMANSK ACADEMY OF ECONOMICS AND LAW

Murmanskij Akademija Ekonomiki i Prava

ul. Poljarnoj Pravdy, 8,
Murmansk 183025
Tel: +7(8152) 44-04-49
Fax: +7(8152) 44-04-49
EMail: rectorat@maem.ru
Website: http://maem.ru/

Rector: Natalja Nikolaevna Shchebarova

Faculties

Economics and Finance (Accountancy; Banking; Economics; Finance; Insurance); **Natural Sciences** (Administration; Business Computing; Information Technology; Management)

History: Created 1994 as Murmanskij Institut Ekonomiki i Prava (Murmansk Institute of Economics and Law). Acquired current title and status 2006.

Degrees and Diplomas: *Bakalavr*, *Specialist Diploma*; *Magistr*

Last Updated: 24/02/12

MURMANSK HUMANITIES INSTITUTE

Murmanskij Gumanitarnyj Institut (MHI)

Oktiabrskaya 3a, Murmansk 183038
Tel: +7(8152) 45-55-46
Fax: +7(8152) 45-52-58
EMail: info@mginet.ru
Website: http://www.mginet.ru

Rector: Valerija Shergalina (1994-)

Vice-Rector for Academic Affairs: Anatoliy Tretiakovich

International Relations: Elena Skiotis, Head of International Relations Office Tel: +7(8152) 45-88-32 EMail: skiotis@mginet.ru

Faculties

Economics (Accountancy; Administration; Business and Commerce; Economics; Finance; Insurance; Management; Marketing) *Dean*: Elena Anasenko; **Foreign Languages and Journalism** (Journalism; Linguistics; Literature; Modern Languages; Public Relations; Teacher Training; Translation and Interpretation; Writing) *Dean*: Galina Smirnova; **Law** (Comparative Law; Criminal Law; European Union Law; History of Law; Human Rights; International Law; Labour Law; Law; Notary Studies; Private Law; Public Law) *Dean*: Vyačeslav Boltuškin; **Psychology** (Psychology; Social Work) *Dean*: Inna Khrapenko

History: Created in 1994 as a branch of Moscow Open Social University and there were only two faculties – the Faculty of Law and the Faculty of Economics. In 1995 the Faculty of Foreign Languages and the Faculty of Psychology were established. In 1996 the branch was transformed into the non-governmental educational establishment "Murmansk Humanities Institute". In 1995 the Faculty of Journalism was established. Since 2002, the institution has offered postgraduate studies in the fields of economics, law and psychology.

Governing Bodies: Rectorat; Academic Council

Academic Year: September-January; February-June

Admission Requirements: Certificate of completed secondary Education (Attestat O Polnom Srednem Obrasovanii); national examination certificates in 3 required subjects (as regulated by the Ministry of Education and Science in accordance with the fields of studies within higher education)

Fees: (Russian Rubles): 32,000-57,000 per annum

Main Language(s) of Instruction: Russian

Accrediting Agencies: National Accreditation Agency

Degrees and Diplomas: *Bakalavr*: 4-5 yrs; *Specialist Diploma*: 5-6 yrs; *Kandidat Nauk*: 3-4 yrs

Student Residential Facilities: None

Libraries: Yes

Press or Publishing House: MHI Publishing House

Academic Staff *2010-2011*	MEN	WOMEN	TOTAL
FULL-TIME	24	56	80
PART-TIME	8	18	26
STAFF WITH DOCTORATE			
FULL-TIME	15	40	55
PART-TIME	6	7	13
Student Numbers *2010-2011*			
All (Foreign Included)	455	1,423	1,878

Part-time students, 1,070. **Evening students**, 11.

Last Updated: 29/04/11

NATIONAL INSTITUTE OF BUSINESS

Natsional'nyj Institut Biznesa
ul. Junosti 5/1, Moskva 111395
Tel: +7(495) 374-7510
Fax: +7(495) 374-7510
Website: http://www.nib.webzone.ru

Rector: Sergej I. Plaksij

Programmes

Business Administration (Business Administration; Business and Commerce)

NEVSKY INSTITUTE OF MANAGEMENT AND DESIGN

Nevskij Institut Upravlenija i Dizajna
8 Linija, d.83/A, Vasilevskij ostrov, Sankt-Peterburg 199178
Tel: +7(812) 328-53-29 +7(812) 328-10-64
Fax: +7(812) 328-53-39
EMail: info@euro-expert.ru
Website: http://euroexpert.spb.ru

Rector: Sergei Anatol'evich Surmilov

Programmes

Commerce (Business Administration; Business and Commerce; E-Business/Commerce; Hotel and Restaurant; Real Estate; Tourism; Transport Management); **Design**; **Psychology** (Psychology)

History: Created 1996. Acquired status 2008.

Degrees and Diplomas: *Bakalavr*: Design; Commerce; Psychology; *Specialist Diploma*: Design; Commerce; Psychology

Last Updated: 08/03/10

NEW SIBERIAN UNIVERSITY

Novyj Sibirskij Universitet
ul. Suhanovskaja, 6a, Novosibirsk, 630020 Novosibiraskaja oblast'
Tel: +7(3832) 747-221
Fax: +7(3832) 747-221
EMail: nsu@nsu.gcom.ru
Website: http://www.nsu.gcom.ru

Rector: Nadežda Dmitrievna Vavilina

NIZHNY NOVGOROD COMMERCIAL INSTITUTE

Nižegorodskij Kommerčeskij Institut (NKI)
prosp. Lenina 27, Nižnij Novgorod 603950
Tel: +7(8312) 45-33-32
Fax: +7(8312) 40-30-03
EMail: nki@nki.nnov.ru
Website: http://www.nnki.ru/

Rector: Natalja Sumtsova (1992-)

International Relations: Alexander Vatrasov
Tel: +7(8312) 40-09-10 EMail: vatrasov@nki.nnov.ru

Faculties

Commerce (Business and Commerce) *Dean*: Olga Chkalova; **Crisis Management and Information Technology** (Information Technology; Management) *Dean*: Evgeny Suchkov; **Finance, Credit, Accountancy and Audit** (Accountancy; Banking) *Dean*: Vladimir Zharinov

History: Founded 1898, acquired present status and title 1991.

Academic Year: September-June

Admission Requirements: Attestat o Srednem (Polnom) Obshchem Obrazovanii (Secondary School Certificate)

Main Language(s) of Instruction: Russian

International Co-operation: With universities in UK, Germany, Cyprus, USA, Canada

Degrees and Diplomas: *Specialist Diploma*: 5-6 yrs

Student Services: Academic counselling, Canteen, Cultural centre, Employment services, Foreign student adviser, Health services, Language programs, Social counselling, Sports facilities

Student Residential Facilities: Yes

Special Facilities: Movie studio, Video studio

Libraries: Central Library

NIZHNY NOVGOROD INSTITUTE OF MANAGEMENT AND BUSINESS

Niżegorodskij Institut Menedžmenta i Biznesa
Okskij S'jezd 4, Nižnij Novgorod 603600
Tel: +7(8312) 33-02-51
Fax: +7(8312) 33-76-34
EMail: roman@nimb.nnov.ru
Website: http://www.inforis.ru

Rector: Aleksandr P. Jegoršin

Programmes

Business Administration and Management

NORTH CAUCASUS INSTITUTE OF BUSINESS, ENGINEERING AND INFORMATION TECHNOLOGIES

Severo-Kavkazskij Institut Biznesa, Inženernykh i Informatsionnykh Tekhnologij
ul. Dzeržinskogo, 62/1, Armavir, 352900 Krasnodarskij Kraj
Tel: +7(86137) 3-76-10 +7(86137) 3-31-44
Fax: +7(86137) 3-31-44
EMail: info@skibiit.ru
Website: http://www.skibiit.ru

Rector: Irina Evgen'evna Aksaeva

Faculties

Accounting and Finance (Accountancy; Finance); **Economics and Management** (Economics; Management); **Law** (European Union Law; International Law; Law)

History: Created 1992.

Degrees and Diplomas: *Bakalavr*, *Specialist Diploma*

Last Updated: 02/03/12

NORTH CAUCASUS SOCIAL INSTITUTE

Severo-Kavkazskij Sotsial'nyj Institut
ul. Dovatortsev 38, Stavropol, 355000 Stavropol'skij kraj
Tel: +7(8652) 244-065 +7(8652) 267-412
Fax: +7(8652) 244-065
EMail: rektorat@sksi.ru; abitur-sksi@mail.ru; rektorat-sksi@yandex.ru
Website: http://www.sksi.ru

Rector: Evgeny N. Shiyanov (1991-)
Tel: +7(8652) 244-005 EMail: rektorat@sksi.ru

Vice-Rector: Julia E. Ledeneva Tel: +7(8652) 244-065

International Relations: Alexander Fedorovskiy, Vice-Rector
Tel: +7(8652) 945-348, Fax: +7(8652) 244-065

Faculties

Economics (Accountancy; Banking; Business Administration; Business and Commerce; Finance; Management; Taxation); **Information Systems and Technology** (Applied Mathematics; Computer Networks; Computer Science; Information Sciences; Information Technology); **Law** (Civil Law; Commercial Law; Criminal Law; Criminology; Forensic Medicine and Dentistry; History of Law; Insurance; International Law; Labour Law; Law; Notary Studies; Private Law; Real Estate); **Socio-Psychology** (Advertising and Publicity; Arts and Humanities; Educational Psychology; Hotel and Restaurant; Linguistics; Modern Languages; Psychology; Social Sciences; Social Work; Teacher Training; Tourism)

History: Founded in 1992 as a branch of Moscow Open Social University and became a non-state educational institute in 1997.

Academic Year: September-June

Admission Requirements: Attestat o Srednem (Polnom) Obshchem Obrazovanii (secondary school certificate)

Fees: (Russian Rubles): 27,000 - 34,000

Main Language(s) of Instruction: Russian

Accrediting Agencies: Federal Service for Supervision in Education and Science

Degrees and Diplomas: *Specialist Diploma*: Applied Informatics; Psychology; Law; Publishing; Theory and Methods of Foreign Language Teaching; Translation and Theory; Intercultural Communication; Business Administration; Social Work; Pedagogics and Psychology; Social Pedagogy; Economics and National Economy Administration; Social Philosophy; Historical, Typological and Comparative Linguistics; Theory and History of Law and State; Law; General Pedagogy; Theory and History of Professional Education; Psychology; Social Sciences; Social and Cultural Services and Tourism; Advertising; Finance and Credit; Taxes and Taxation; Accounting, Analysis and Audit; Marketing; Commerce; Economics and Enterprise; Management in Food Technology; Building; City Economy; Trade and Catering; State and Municipal Management; Personnel Administration; Organisational Management; Service, 5 yrs

Student Services: Academic counselling, Cultural centre, Employment services, Foreign student adviser, Health services, Language programs, Social counselling, Sports facilities

Student Residential Facilities: none

Libraries: yes

Press or Publishing House: Izdatelstvo "Severo-Kavkazskiy Sotsialnyj Institut"

Academic Staff *2007-2008*	MEN	WOMEN	TOTAL
FULL-TIME	75	52	**127**
PART-TIME	37	27	**64**
STAFF WITH DOCTORATE			
FULL-TIME	–	–	**85**
PART-TIME	–	–	**48**
Student Numbers *2007-2008*			
All (Foreign Included)	1,137	1,017	**2,154**

Part-time students, 824. **Distance students**, 125.

Last Updated: 26/01/12

NORTH-EASTERN STATE UNIVERSITY

Severo-Vostočnyj Gosudarstvennyj Universitet

Portovaya St. 13, Magadan 685000

Tel: +7(4132) 639-343

Fax: +7(4132) 634-237

EMail: rector@svgu.ru

Website: http://www.svgu.ru

Rector: Anatolij Ivanovich Shirokov

Faculties

Management, Economics and Finance (Accountancy; Economics; Finance; Management); **Mathematics and Natural Sciences** (Biology; Computer Science; Mathematics; Physics); **Pedagogy** (Physical Education; Preschool Education; Primary Education; Sports; Teacher Training); **Philology** (English; German; Literature; Russian); **Sociology and Humanities** (History; Law; Psychology; Sociology)

Institutes

Polytechnic (Automotive Engineering; Civil Engineering; Geology; Mechanics; Mining Engineering; Physical Education; Road Transport; Sports; Surveying and Mapping)

History: Created in 1960 as Magadanskij Gosudarstvennyj Pedagogicheskij Institut. Changed named to Severnyj Meždunarodnyj Universitet v Magadane in 1998. Acquired current title and status in 2007.

Governing Bodies: International Board of Trustees, comprising representatives of co-founding Universities

Academic Year: September to June (September-January; February-June)

Admission Requirements: Secondary school certificate (Attestat srednego obrazovanja)

Main Language(s) of Instruction: Russian

International Co-operation: Germany, USA and Japan

Accrediting Agencies: Ministry of Education

Degrees and Diplomas: *Bakalavr*: 4-5 yrs; *Specialist Diploma*: 5 yrs; *Kandidat Nauk*: a further 3-4 yrs

Student Services: Canteen, Cultural centre, Employment services, Foreign student adviser, Foreign Studies Centre, Health services, Language programs, Social counselling, Sports facilities

Student Residential Facilities: For c. 500 students

Special Facilities: Museum. TV Studio

Libraries: Central Library, c. 300,000 vols

Publications: Ideas, Hypotheses, Research, Publications of the postgraduates and young researchers *(annually)*; Translation and Translators, Almanac of the publications on translation studies *(annually)*

Press or Publishing House: Publishing House

Last Updated: 26/04/11

NORTH INSTITUTE OF BUSINESS

Severnyj Institut Predprinimatel'stva

ul. Suvorova, 2, Arkhangelsk 163045

Tel: +7(8182) 24-28-82 +7(8182) 65-46-52

Fax: +7(8182) 24-29-20

EMail: nel2007@yandex.ru; sip@atnet.ru

Website: http://www.nousip.ru/

Rector: Sergej Anatolevich Kochegarov

Programmes

Business (Business Administration; Business and Commerce; Management; Marketing); **Law** (Civil Law; Law)

History: Created 1993.

Degrees and Diplomas: *Specialist Diploma*

Last Updated: 02/03/12

NORTH OSSETIAN INSTITUTE OF ECOLOGY AND CIVIL PROTECTION

Severo-Osetinskij Institut Ekologii i Bezopasnosti Zhiznedejatel'nosti

prosp. Kosta, 101, Vladikavkaz, 362035 Respublika Severnaja Osetija-Alanija

Tel: +7(8672) 74-93-36

Fax: +7(8672) 74-93-36

EMail: soiebg@yandex.ru

Website: http://www.inst-ecology.ru

Rector: Ivan Davydovich Alborov

Programmes

Civil Protection (Civil Security); **Environmental Protection** (Civil Security; Ecology; Environmental Management); **Transport Management** (Transport Management)

History: Created 2000.

Degrees and Diplomas: *Specialist Diploma*

Last Updated: 16/03/12

NOVOSIBIRSK HUMANITARIAN INSTITUTE

Novosibirskij Gumanitarnyj Institut (NHI)

ul. Sovetskaya, 23, Novosibirsk, 630099 Novosibiraskaja oblast'

Tel: +7(3832) 183-533 +7(3832) 183-552

Fax: +7(3832) 183-552

EMail: rectorat@mail.ru

Website: http://www.novgi.ru

Rector: Jevgenij A. Sokolkov (1993-)

Faculties

Economics; Law; Psychology

History: Founded 1993, licensed 1995, acquired present status and title 1998.

Governing Bodies: Board of Trustees; Academic Council

Academic Year: September to June

Admission Requirements: Secondary school certificate (Attestat o srednem obrazovanii) or College certificate and entrance examination

Main Language(s) of Instruction: Russian

Accrediting Agencies: Ministry of Higher Education

Degrees and Diplomas: *Bakalavr.* 5 yrs

Student Services: Academic counselling, Employment services, Handicapped facilities, Language programs, Social counselling

Libraries: c. 35,000 vols

Publications: The development of the Humanitarian in Siberia, Scientific Proceeding *(annually)*

NOVOSIBIRSK INSTITUTE OF ECONOMICS AND MANAGEMENT

Novosibirskij Institut Ekonomiki i Menedžmenta
ul. Vybornaja 126, Novosibirsk, 630048 Novosibiraskaja oblast'
Tel: +7(3882) 49-5739
Fax: +7(3882) 46-1084
EMail: niem@niem.siberia.net
Website: http://www.siberia.net

Rector: Jurij N. Odrov

Programmes

Economics and Management

NOVOSIBIRSK INSTITUTE OF ECONOMICS, PSYCHOLOGY AND LAW

Novosibirskij Institut Ekonomiki, Psihologii i Prava
ul. Narodnaja 10, Novosibirsk, 630075 Novosibiraskaja oblast'
Tel: +7(3832) 10-6702
Fax: +7(3832) 46-3930
EMail: nki-info@mail.ru
Website: http://www.nki.ru

Rector: Dmitrij O. Gusev

Programmes

Economics, Psychology and Law

OPEN INSTITUTE OF LAW, VLADIVOSTOK

Otkrytyj Juridičeskij Institut, Vladivostok (OJI)
11, Aleutskaya str., Vladivostok, 690091 Primorskij kraj
Tel: +7(4232) 96-25-89 +7(4232) 96-25-84
Fax: +7(4232) 96-25-84
EMail: oji-vl@mail.ru
Website: http://www.oji.ru

Rector: Dmitij Afanas'evich Turchin

Faculties

Informatics (Computer Science); **Law** (Law); **Management and Economics** (Accountancy; Economics; Management); **Psychology** (Psychology)

Further Information: The Division of Distance Education Technologies and Foreign Students also has offices in the Moscow region (Russia), Honolulu (HI, USA), Seattle (WA, USA), Nicosia (Cyprus) and Tel-Aviv (Israel).

History: Founded 2001. Acquired present status 2004.

Governing Bodies: Board of Trustees

Academic Year: September to June

Admission Requirements: A complete secondary education certificate (nalichie polnogo srednego obrazovania).

Fees: None (students training expenditures are compensated by the independent trade unions)

Main Language(s) of Instruction: Russian

Degrees and Diplomas: *Specialist Diploma*

Student Services: Academic counselling, Canteen, Cultural centre, Employment services, Foreign student adviser, Foreign Studies Centre, Handicapped facilities, Health services, Language programs, Social counselling, Sports facilities

Special Facilities: Computer laboratories; Forensic Science Laboratory; Video Studio

Libraries: c. 4,900 vols; online library

Last Updated: 16/04/12

ORENBURG INSTITUTE OF ECONOMICS AND CULTURE

Orenburgskij Institut Ekonomiki i Kul'tury
ul.Tomilinskaja 249, Orenburg, 460005 Orenburgskaja oblast'
Tel: +7(3532) 75-45-50 +7(3532) 75-22-58
Fax: +7(3532) 75-53-21
EMail: iik-08@mail.ru
Website: http://oreniik.moy.su/

Rector: Nadežda Morgunova

Departments

Economics and Management (Economics; Management); **Finance and Credit** (Banking; Finance); **Humanities and Intercultural Communications** (Communication Studies; Cultural Studies; Ethics; Political Sciences; Speech Studies); **Natural Sciences and Mathematics** (Mathematics; Natural Sciences); **Philology and Modern Languages** (English; German; Linguistics; Philology); **Social Work and Pedagogy** (Pedagogy; Social Work)

History: Created 1995.

Degrees and Diplomas: *Bakalavr*, *Specialist Diploma*; *Magistr*

Last Updated: 20/04/12

PEOPLES' FRIENDSHIP INSTITUTE OF THE CAUCASUS

Institut Družby Narodov Kavkaza
prosp Karla Marksa, 7, Stavropol, 355008 Stavropol'skij kraj
Tel: +7(8652) 28-25-00 +7(8652) 28-47-60
Fax: +7(8652) 28-25-00
EMail: idnk@mail.ru
Website: http://www.idnk.stavropol.ru

Rector: Tat'jana Sergeevna Ledovich

Departments

Applied Information Technology (Information Technology)

Faculties

Economics (Economics; Management); **International Relations** (International Relations; Modern Languages; Peace and Disarmament; Political Sciences; Public Relations); **Law** (Law); **Psychology** (Educational Psychology; Psychology; Social Psychology); **Theology** (Theology)

Further Information: Branches in Budennovsk, Svetlograd.

History: Created 1996.

Degrees and Diplomas: *Bakalavr*, *Specialist Diploma*; *Magistr*

Last Updated: 19/01/12

PERM INSTITUTE OF MUNICIPAL MANAGEMENT (HIGHER SCHOOL OF PRIVATIZATION AND ENTREPRENEURSHIP)

Permskij Institut Munitsipal'nogo Upravlenija (Vyssaja Škola Privatizacii i Predprinimatelstva)
Jaroslavskoe shosse, 170, Perm'
Tel: +7(342) 212-75-35 +7(342) 201-73-94
Fax: +7(342) 212-75-35 +7(342) 212-63-30
EMail: pimy-info@yandex.ru; info@pimy.ms
Website: http://www.pimy.ms/

Rector: Lidija Anatol'evna Sergeeva

Programmes

Economics and Management (Economics; Management); **Finance and Credit** (Banking; Finance)

History: Created 1992 as Vyssaja Škola Privatizacii i Predprinimatelstva (Institut) (Higher School of Privatization and Entrepreneurship (Institute)). Acquired current title and status 2009.

Degrees and Diplomas: *Specialist Diploma*

Last Updated: 13/03/12

PETERSBURG INSTITUTE OF JUDAISM

Peterburgskij Institut Judaiki
ul. Harčenko, 4, Sankt-Peterburg 194100
Tel: +7(812) 449-52-50 +7(812) 449-52-51
Fax: +7(812) 449-52-50
EMail: info@pijs.ru
Website: http://www.pijs.ru

Rector: Dmitrij Arkad'evich El'jashevich

Faculties
History (History; Jewish Studies; Judaic Religious Studies); **Philology** (German; Hebrew; Jewish Studies; Judaic Religious Studies; Philology)

History: Created 1989 as Peterburgskij Evrejskij Universitet. Acquired current title and status 1992.

Degrees and Diplomas: *Bakalavr, Specialist Diploma*
Last Updated: 06/04/12

REGIONAL OPEN SOCIAL INSTITUTE

Regional'nyj Otkrytyj Social'nyj Institut
ul. Majakovskogo, d.85, Kursk 305009
Tel: +7(4712) 34-38-48 +7(4712) 34-38-45
Fax: +7(4712) 34-38-48
EMail: mail@rosi-edu.ru
Website: http://www.rosi-edu.ru

Rector: Vladimir N. Petrov

Faculties
Communication Studies (Communication Studies; Linguistics; Pedagogy; Psychology; Tourism; Translation and Interpretation); **Economics** (Banking; Economics; Finance; Management); **Information Technologies and Computer Science** (Business Computing; Computer Science; Information Technology); **Law** (Civil Law; Criminal Law; Law; Public Law)

History: Created 1994.

Degrees and Diplomas: *Bakalavr, Specialist Diploma*
Last Updated: 11/01/12

ROSTOV INSTITUTE FOR ENTREPRENEUR PROTECTION

Rostovskij Institut Zaščity Predprinimatelja
prosp. Budennovskij, 86, lit A, Rostov-na-Donu 344018
Tel: +7(863) 234-34-34
Fax: +7(863) 234-34-34
EMail: rizp@donpac.ru; rektorat@rizp.ru
Website: http://www.rizp.ru/

Rector: Aleksandr Vladimirovich Parshin

Faculties
Economics (Accountancy; Economic History; Marketing; Taxation); **Law** (Law)

History: Created 1993.
Degrees and Diplomas: *Bakalavr, Specialist Diploma*
Last Updated: 27/01/12

RUSSIAN ACADEMY OF BARRISTERS AND NOTARIES (INSTITUTE)

Rossijskaja Akademija Advokatury i Notariata (Institut)
Malyj Polujaroslavskij per. 3/5, Moskva 107120
Tel: +7(495) 917-24-78 +7(495) 917-20-52
Fax: +7(495) 916-30-67
EMail: info@raa.ru; pkraan@yandex.ru; raa@hotmail.ru
Website: http://www.raa.ru

Rector: Gasan Mirzojev (1996-)

Faculties
Law (Law; Notary Studies)

History: Founded 1995. Acquired present status and title 2008.

Admission Requirements: Secondary School Certificate

Main Language(s) of Instruction: Russian

Degrees and Diplomas: *Bakalavr, Magistr*

Student Services: Canteen, Cultural centre, Employment services, Health services, Sports facilities
Last Updated: 11/01/12

RUSSIAN ACADEMY OF ENTREPRENEURSHIP

Rossijskaja Akademija Predprinimatelstva
ul. Radio 14, Moskva 105005
Tel: +7(499) 265-62-61
Fax: +7(499) 267-67-81 +7(495) 632-24-26
EMail: info@rusacad.ru; priem@rusacad.ru
Website: http://www.rusacad.ru/

President: Vladimir Balabanov
EMail: rector@rusacad.ru; office@rusacad.ru

Programmes
Accountancy and Auditing (Accountancy); **Economics** (Economics; International Economics); **Finance and Credit** (Banking; Finance; Insurance; Taxation); **Human Resources** (Human Resources); **Law** (Law); **Management** (Business Administration; Management); **Marketing** (Marketing); **Public Relations** (Public Relations)

History: Created 1991.

Degrees and Diplomas: *Bakalavr, Specialist Diploma; Magistr*
Last Updated: 27/02/12

RUSSIAN-BRITISH INSTITUTE OF MANAGEMENT

Russko-Britanskij Institut Upravlenija
ul Voroshilova 12, Čeljabinsk 454014
Tel: +7(351) 742-22-10 +7(351) 742-65-49 +7(351) 742-22-72
Fax: +7(351) 742-22-10
EMail: info@rbiu.ru
Website: http://www.rbiu.ru/

Rector: Tat'jana Vasilevna. Usynina
EMail: Menshikova.V.M@rbiu.ru

Higher Schools
Design (Computer Graphics; Fashion Design; Graphic Design; Interior Design; Landscape Architecture); **Management** (Business Computing; Economics; Finance; Human Resources; Information Technology; Management); **Tourism** (Hotel and Restaurant; Hotel Management; Tourism)

History: Created 1992 as Čeljabinskij Gumanitarnyj Institut (Chelyabinsk Humanitarian Institute). Acquired current title 2008.

Degrees and Diplomas: *Bakalavr, Specialist Diploma*
Last Updated: 20/01/12

RUSSIAN CHRISTIAN ACADEMY FOR THE HUMANITIES

Russkaja Khristianskaja Gumanitarnaja Akademija
Nab. Reki Fontanki, 15, Sankt-Peterburg 191023
Tel: +7(812) 314-35-21
Fax: +7(812) 571-30-75
EMail: info@rhga.ru
Website: http://www.rhga.ru/

Rector: Dmitrij Kirillovich Burlaka EMail: rector@rhga.ru

Faculties
International Culture and Languages (Asian Studies; Chinese; English; Finnish; German; Italian; Japanese; Latin American Studies; Philology; Romance Languages; Spanish; Turkish); **Philosophy, Theology and Religious Studies** (Cultural Studies; Philosophy; Religious Studies; Theology); **Psychology and Philosophy** (Pedagogy; Philosophy; Psychology)

History: Created 1993. Previously known as Rossijskij Hristianskij Gumanitarnyj Institut (Russian Christian Humanitarian Institute).

Degrees and Diplomas: *Bakalavr, Specialist Diploma; Magistr*
Last Updated: 28/02/12

RUSSIAN INSTITUTE MANAGEMENT NAMED AFTER V.P. CHERNOV

Rossijskij Institut Upravlenija im. V.P. Černova

ul. Grina 1, Korp. 3, Moskva 117216
Tel: +7(495) 713-10-72
Fax: +7(495) 713-34-09
EMail: riminfo@tantal-sov.ru
Website: http://www.tantal.ru/

Rector: Valerij Vital'evich Galaktionov

Programmes

Business and Management (Accountancy; Business Administration; Economics; Law; Management)

History: Created 1997 as Rossijskij Institut Biznesa i Upravlenija (Russian Institute of Business and Management). Acquired current title 2004.

Degrees and Diplomas: *Bakalavr*
Last Updated: 28/02/12

RUSSIAN INTERNATIONAL ACADEMY OF TOURISM

Rossijskaja Meždunarodnaja Akademija Turizma (RIAT)

ul. Octyabrskaja 10, mikrorajon Skhodnja, Khimki, 141420 Moskovskaja oblast'
Tel: +7(495) 574-22-88
Fax: +7(495) 574-16 36
EMail: rector@rmat.ru; license@rmat.ru; info@rmat.ru
Website: http://www.rmat.ru/

Rector: Igor Zorin (1981-) EMail: rector@rmat.ru

Institutes

Central Tourism Training *(Practical Training)* (Tourism); **Tourism** *(Moscow)* (Tourism); **Tourism Innovation and Research** (Tourism); **Tourism Management** (Tourism)

Programmes

Tourism (Business Administration; Food Technology; Hotel and Restaurant; Hotel Management; Marketing; Tourism)

Further Information: Also branches in Barnaul, Yerevan (Armenia), Vladimir, Naberezhnyje Chelny, Volokolamsk, Voskresensk, Vjazma, Dmitrov, Odintsovskij, Kazan, Kalingrad, Kaluzhskij, Petrozavodsk, Konakovo, Magnitogorsk, Pavlovskij Posad, Pskov, Pjatigorsk, Sochi, Tula.

History: Founded 1969 as Central Tourism School, reorganized as Institute for Advanced Education on Tourism Organizations Workers 1981, as Institute of Tourism 1991, and acquired present status and title 1993.

Governing Bodies: Senate; Scientific Council

Academic Year: September to June (September-January; February-June)

Admission Requirements: Secondary school certificate (Attestat o srednem obrazovanii) and entrance examination

Main Language(s) of Instruction: Russian, English

International Co-operation: With universities in Spain; Greece; USA; China; Germany; Malta; Czech Republic and Poland

Accrediting Agencies: Ministry of Education

Degrees and Diplomas: *Bakalavr*, *Specialist Diploma*; *Magistr*, *Kandidat Nauk*

Student Residential Facilities: For 600 students

Special Facilities: TV-Multimedia Laboratory

Libraries: c. 316,000 vols

Publications:
Last Updated: 10/01/12

RUSSIAN NEW UNIVERSITY

Rossijskij Novyj Universitet (RNU/ROSNOU)

Radio Street 22, Moskva 105005
Tel: +7(495) 105-0383 +7(495) 263-7065
Fax: +7(495) 105-0381
Website: http://www.rosnou.ru

Rector: Vladimir Zernov EMail: rector@rosnou.ru

Vice-Rector for Education: Evgeney Palkin

International Relations: Anna Biryukova EMail: diesa@rosnou.ru

Faculties

E-learning (Accountancy; Economics; Hotel Management; Information Technology; Law; Pedagogy; Psychology; Social and Community Services; Tourism); **Finance and Economics** (Accountancy; Banking; Economics; Management) *Dean*: Tatjana M. Regent; **Foreign Languages and Intercultural Communication** *Dean*: Uliyana T. Ivanova; **Humanitarian Science Technologies** (Literature; Public Relations; Russian; Social Work) *Dean*: Olga Y. Ivanova; **Information Systems and Technology** *Dean*: Andrey S. Kryukovsky; **Law** (Civil Law; Commercial Law; International Law; Law) *Dean*: Mihail R. Šagalov; **Psychology** *Dean*: Elena V. Lobanova; **Tourism and Hotel Management** (Advertising and Publicity; Hotel Management; Social and Community Services; Tourism) *Dean*: Natalja S. Morozova

Further Information: Regional branches in 27 cities in the country (12 subsidiaries, 26 representative offices)

History: Founded 1991. Acquired present status 2006.

Governing Bodies: Rector's Council; Scientific Council

Academic Year: September to June

Admission Requirements: Secondary school certificate

Fees: (Euros): 2,200 per annum

Main Language(s) of Instruction: Russian

International Co-operation: Participates in American Councils of international education; DAAD programmes; TEMPUS; EduFrance

Accrediting Agencies: Ministry of Education

Degrees and Diplomas: *Bakalavr*: Business Administration; Information Systems in Economics; Information Systems in Management; Management; Finance and Banking; Accountancy; World Economics; Taxation; State Law; Tourism and Hotel Management; *Specialist Diploma*: Information Systems in Economics; Information Systems in Management; Management; Finance and Banking; Accountancy; World Economics; Taxation; State Law; Criminal Law; Civil Law; International Law; Commercial Law; Pedagogy and Psychology; Psychological Consulting; Practical and Clinical Psychology; Tourism and Hotel Management; Social and Cultural Services; International and Domestic Tourism; Advertising; Foreign Languages and Intercultural Communication; Interpretation and Translation, 5 yrs; *Magistr*: Information Systems in Economics; Information Systems in Management; Management; Finance and Banking; Accountancy; World Economics; Taxation; State Law; Criminal Law; Civil Law; International Law; Commercial Law; Pedagogy and Psychology

Student Services: Academic counselling, Canteen, Cultural centre, Employment services, Foreign student adviser, Foreign Studies Centre, Health services, Language programs, Social counselling, Sports facilities

Student Residential Facilities: Yes

Special Facilities: Music Studio

Libraries: c. 150,000 vols; electronic library

Publications: RNU Proceedings *(quarterly)*

RUSSIAN SCHOOL OF PRIVATE LAW

Rossijskaja Škola Častnogo Prava (Institut)

ul. Ilinka 8, bldg. 2, Moskva 103132
Tel: +7(495) 606-37-28 +7(495) 606-51-98
Fax: +7(495) 606-37-28
EMail: mail@schoolprivlaw.ru; 6063728@mail.ru
Website: http://www.privlaw.ru

Rector: Aleksandr L'vovich Makovskij

Programmes

Law (Law)

History: Created 1994.

Degrees and Diplomas: *Magistr*
Last Updated: 03/04/12

RUSSIAN UNIVERSITY OF COOPERATION

Rossijskij Universitet Kooperatsii

ul. V. Vološinoj 12/30, Mytišči, 141014 Moskovskaja oblast'
Tel: +7(495) 582-93-71
Fax: +7(495) 582-93-71
EMail: rector@ruc.su
Website: http://www.ruc.su/

Rector: Vladimir A. Krivoshei EMail: rektor@ruc.su

Faculties

Accounting and Applied Informatics (Accountancy; Business Computing; Finance; Information Technology; Management; Taxation); **Economics** (Accountancy; Banking; Economics; Finance; Information Technology; Insurance; Management; Taxation); **International Economic Relations** (Accountancy; Advertising and Publicity; Banking; Finance; Insurance; International Economics; Management; Marketing; Secretarial Studies; Taxation; Translation and Interpretation); **Law and Customs** (Administrative Law; Commercial Law; Law; Private Law; Public Law; Taxation); **Trade and Catering** (Cooking and Catering; Hotel and Restaurant; Hotel Management; Service Trades)

Further Information: Includes 22 branches, including Cheboksary, Saransk, Volga, Volgograd, Kazan, Krasnodar, Bashkir cooperative institutions (branches)

History: Created 1913. Previously known as Moskovskij Universitet Potrebitel'skoj Kooperacii (Moscow University of Consumers' Cooperative Societies). Acquired present title and status 2006.

Degrees and Diplomas: *Bakalavr*; *Specialist Diploma*
Last Updated: 20/03/12

RYAZAN INSTITUTE OF MANAGEMENT AND LAW

Rjazanskij Institut Upravlenija i Prava
ul. Poletaeva 25/2, Rjazan 390035
Tel: +7(4912) 98-46-36
Fax: +7(4912) 98-46-36
EMail: nou@riup.ryazan.ru

Rector: Maksim Vital'evich Vojlošnikov

Programmes

Economics (Economics); **Law** (Law)

History: Created 1995.

Degrees and Diplomas: *Bakalavr*; *Specialist Diploma*
Last Updated: 27/02/12

SACRED IOANN BOGOLSLOV ORTHODOX INSTITUTE

Pravoslavnyj Institut 'Svjatogo Ionna Bogoslova'
per. Chernyshevskogo, 11a, Moskva 127030
Tel: +7(495) 681-59-57 +7(495) 681-19-14
Fax: +7(495) 681-19-14
EMail: g-ekaterina-v@mail.ru
Website: http://www.rpi.su/

Rector: Ruslan Nikolaevich Eremeev

Programmes

Economics (Economics); **Fine Arts** (Fine Arts); **History** (History; Humanities and Social Science Education); **Journalism** (Journalism); **Orthodox Theology** (Orthodox Theology; Religious Studies; Theology); **Psychology** (Psychology)

History: Created 1993. Previously known as Rossijskij Pravoslavnyj Institut 'Svjatogo Ionna Bogoslova' (Sacred Ioann Bogolslov Russian Orthodox Institute). Acquired current title 2010.

Degrees and Diplomas: *Bakalavr*; *Specialist Diploma*
Last Updated: 28/02/12

IAU SAINT PETERSBURG UNIVERSITY OF MANAGEMENT AND ECONOMICS

Sankt-Peterburgskij Universitet Upravlenija i Ekonomiki
pr. Lermontovskij, d.44, Lit. A, Sankt-Peterburg 190103
Tel: +7(812) 575-03-00
Fax: +7(812) 575-02-70
EMail: rector@spbume.ru
Website: http://www.spbume.ru

Rector: Victor Gnevko

Pro-Rector for Development and International Affairs: Viktoria Marich
Tel: +7(812) 313-39-44, Fax: +7(812) 575-02-70
EMail: v.marich@spbume.ru

International Relations: Tatiana S. Avetikyan, Head of the Department of International Cooperation and Academic Mobility
Tel: +7(812)) 313-02-43, Fax: +7(812)) 313-02-43
EMail: inter@spbume.ru

Faculties

Economics and Finance (Accountancy; Economics; Finance; Information Management; Management); **Information Systems and Technologies** (Information Management; Information Technology; Mathematics and Computer Science); **Law** (History of Law; Human Rights; International Law; Justice Administration; Labour Law; Law; Notary Studies; Private Law; Public Health); **Management** (Administration; Business and Commerce; Human Resources; Labour and Industrial Relations; Labour Law; Management; Marketing; Retailing and Wholesaling); **Pre-Higher Education** (Accountancy; Banking; Business and Commerce; Computer Science; Economics; Insurance; Tourism); **Service and Cross-cultural Communication** (Hotel and Restaurant; Linguistics; Modern Languages; Museum Studies; Tourism); **Social Management** (Communication Studies; Educational Sciences; Information Management; Library Science; Mass Communication; Psychology; Secretarial Studies; Social Work; Sociology)

History: Founded 1991 as Institut Upravlenija i Ekonomiki. Sankt-Peterburgskaja Akademija Upravlenija i Ekonomiki (Saint Petersburg Academy of Management and Economics). Acquired current title 2005.

Governing Bodies: Rectorat

Academic Year: Sept - Jan; Feb to June

Admission Requirements: Attestat o Srednem (Polnom) Obshchem Obrazovanii (school leaving certificate), Unified State Exam, or entrance examination.

Fees: (RUB): 20,000 to 50,000 per semester

Main Language(s) of Instruction: Russian

International Co-operation: with institutions in UK, Finland, Latvia, Ghana, Turkmenistan, Kazakhstan.

Degrees and Diplomas: *Bakalavr*: Advertising and Public Relations; Psychology; Documentation and Archival Science; Linguistics; Publishing; Social Work; Pedagogy; Museology and Protection of Objects of Cultural and Natural Heritage; Economics; Information Security; Applied Computer Science; Management; Commerce; Jurisprudence; Foreign Languages; Tourism; Cross-Cultural Communications; Hotel Service; Mathematics and Natural Science; Information Technologies, 3 - 4 1/2 yrs; *Specialist Diploma*: Applied Computer Science; Management; Commerce; Jurisprudence; Foreign Languages; Tourism; Cross-Cultural Communications; Hotel Service; Mathematics and Natural Science; Information Technologies; Psychology; Documentation and Archival Science; Linguistics; Publishing; Social Work; Pedagogy; Museology and Protection of Objects of Cultural and Natural Heritage; Economics; Information Security, 5 yrs; *Magistr*: Economics; Applied Computer Science; Management; Commerce; Psychology; Linguistics; Tourism; Jurisprudence, a further 2 - 2 1/2 yrs; *Kandidat Nauk*: Economics; Management; Psychology; Law, 3 - 4 yrs; *Doktor Nauk*: Economics

Student Services: Academic counselling, Canteen, Employment services, Health services, Language programs, Sports facilities

Special Facilities: Museum, Criminalistics Laboratory, Laboratory of Theoretic Informatics, Laboratory of Innovative Educational Technologies, Laboratory of Applied, Social and Organizational Psychology, Student Scientific Society, Psychological Training Exercises Office, School of Newly Qualified Scientists, Students Law Consultation Office

Libraries: 526,477 vols; 479 periodical subscriptions; access to electronic networks

Publications: Economics and Management; Scholarly Notes; Sociology and Law; The Manager

Press or Publishing House: University Publishing House

Academic Staff *2011-2012*	MEN	WOMEN	**TOTAL**
FULL-TIME	225	300	**525**
PART-TIME	270	357	**627**
STAFF WITH DOCTORATE			
FULL-TIME	53	70	**123**
PART-TIME	34	45	**79**
Student Numbers *2011-2012*			
All (Foreign Included)	9,916	8,795	**18,711**
FOREIGN ONLY	81	89	**170**

Part-time students, 8,400. **Distance students**, 1,500. **Evening students**, 3,500.

Last Updated: 23/05/12

SAINT-PETERSBURG HUMANITARIAN UNIVERSITY OF TRADE UNIONS

Sankt-Peterburgskij Gumanitarnyj Universitet Profsojuzov (SPBUHSS)

ul. Fučika 15, Sankt-Peterburg 192238
Tel: +7(812) 269-1936 +7(812) 327-2728
Fax: +7(812) 269-5966
EMail: info@gup.ru
Website: http://www.gup.ru

Rector: Alexander Zapesotsky EMail: rector@gup.ru

Faculties

Arts (Art Criticism; Art History; Business and Commerce; Conducting; Dance; Folklore; Modern Languages; Multimedia; Performing Arts; Sound Engineering (Acoustics); Theatre); **Conflict Studies** (Advertising and Publicity; Cultural Studies; Economics; Labour and Industrial Relations; Law; Linguistics; Management; Multimedia; Psychology; Public Relations; Social Studies; Social Work); **Culture** (Advertising and Publicity; Communication Studies; Cultural Studies; History; Journalism; Linguistics; Literature; Philosophy; Physical Education; Psychology; Public Relations; Russian; Social Psychology; Social Work); **Economics** (Business and Commerce; Business Computing; Economics; English; German; Hotel Management; Leisure Studies; Management; Mathematics and Computer Science; Romance Languages; Sports)

Schools

Law (Civil Law; Labour Law; Law; Public Law)

Further Information: Branches: Almaty Branch; Vladivostok Branch; Kirov Branch; Krasnoyarsk Branch; Moscow regional branch of the Institute of Arts and Information Technology; Murmansk Branch; Sevastopol Branch; Samara Branch; Yakutsk Branch (Sakha Republic)

History: Founded 1926. Acquired present status and title 1991.

Governing Bodies: University Administration

Academic Year: September to June (September-December; January-June)

Admission Requirements: Secondary general education or secondary professional education certificate; medical certificate

Main Language(s) of Instruction: Russian

International Co-operation: With universities in United Kingdom, USA, Switzerland, Germany and Estonia

Accrediting Agencies: Ministry of Education of the Russian Federation

Degrees and Diplomas: *Specialist Diploma*: Art Criticism; Choreography; Multimedia; Theatre; Audio Direction; Translation and Interpretation; Journalism; Linguistics and Intercultural Communication; Computer Science in Welfare Sphere; Psychology; Advertising; Public Relations; Social Work; Welfare and Protective Services; Law; Management; Business and Commerce; Business Computing; Welfare Services and Tourism; Business Economics and Management; Hotel Management; Sports; Conflict Studies, 5 yrs; *Kandidat Nauk*: Cultural Studies; Pedagogics; Art Criticism; Jurisprudence; Economics (PhD), 3-5 yrs; *Doktor Nauk*: Philosophy; Pedagogy, 3-4 yrs. Also Senior doctoral degree in Philosophy and Pedagogy, 3-5 yrs

Student Services: Academic counselling, Canteen, Cultural centre, Employment services, Foreign student adviser, Foreign Studies Centre, Handicapped facilities, Health services, Language programs, Nursery care, Social counselling, Sports facilities

Student Residential Facilities: Dormitory; Hostel for visitors and guests

Special Facilities: 15 multimedia and computer laboratories; Multimedia centre; 4 language laboratories; Music studio; TV Studio; internet café; theatre and concert complex

Libraries: c. 550,000 vols; 449 periodical subscriptions; 32 foreign subscriptions; 75 newspapers; 374 magazines

Press or Publishing House: University Publishing House

Last Updated: 24/02/12

SAINT-PETERSBURG INSTITUTE OF ECONOMICS AND MANAGEMENT

Sankt-Peterburgskij Institut Ekonomiki i Upravlenija

ul. Bolshaja Pushkarskaja, 35, Sankt-Peterburg 197101
Tel: +7(812) 230-49-72 +7(812) 232-00-45
Fax: +7(812) 230-49-72
EMail: info@spbiem.ru
Website: http://www.spbiem.ru

Rector: Vladislav V. Baldesov

Programmes

Accounting (Accountancy); **Banking** (Banking); **Economics** (Economics); **Finance** (Finance); **Insurance** (Insurance); **Logistics** (Transport Management); **Management** (Management)

History: Create 1994.

Degrees and Diplomas: *Bakalavr*, *Specialist Diploma*; *Magistr*

Last Updated: 07/12/11

SAINT-PETERSBURG INSTITUTE OF HOSPITALITY

Sankt-Peterburgskij Institut Gostepriimstva (SPIH)

Bogatyrskij prosp. 24/1, Sankt-Peterburg 195197
Tel: +7(812) 643-50-00
Fax: +7(812) 643-50-00
EMail: spig@spig.spb.ru; faculty@spig.spb.ru
Website: http://www.myspig.ru/

Rector: Irina Asanova (2001-)

Departments

Applied Psychology (Industrial and Organizational Psychology; Psychology); **Economics and Finance** (Economics; Finance); **Management and Marketing** (Management; Marketing); **Mathematics and Computer Science** (Information Technology; Mathematics); **Tourism and Hospitality** (Hotel and Restaurant; Hotel Management; Tourism)

History: Founded 1994.

Academic Year: September to July

Admission Requirements: School-leaving certificate

Main Language(s) of Instruction: Russian

Degrees and Diplomas: *Bakalavr*, *Specialist Diploma*

Student Services: Academic counselling, Canteen, Cultural centre, Employment services, Foreign student adviser, Health services, Language programs, Social counselling, Sports facilities

Student Residential Facilities: Hostel

Special Facilities: None

Libraries: c. 8,000 vols.

Last Updated: 02/03/12

SAINT-PETERSBURG INSTITUTE OF INTERNATIONAL ECONOMIC RELATIONS, ECONOMICS AND LAW

Sankt-Peterburgskij Institut Vnešneekonomičeskih Svjazej, Ekonomiki i Prava

prosp. Liteinyi 42, Sankt-Peterburg 191014
Tel: +7(812) 273-2049
Fax: +7(812) 273-5390
EMail: pravlenie@znanie.spb.ru
Website: http://www.ivesep.spb.ru

Rector: Sergej Klimov

Departments

Management (Management); **Transport Management and Logistics**

Faculties

Economics (Accountancy; Banking; Business and Commerce; Business Computing; Economics; Finance; Industrial Management; International Economics; Management; Small Business; Town Planning; Transport Management); **Humanities** (Advertising and Publicity; Arts and Humanities; History; Linguistics; Modern Languages; Philosophy; Physical Education; Psychology; Public

Relations; Social Psychology; Translation and Interpretation); **Law** (Civil Law; Criminal Law; Law; Public Law)

Schools
International Relations (International Relations; International Studies; Regional Studies)

Further Information: Also Department for Continuing Education

History: Founded 1994.

Degrees and Diplomas: *Bakalavr*, *Specialist Diploma*; *Magistr*
Last Updated: 27/01/12

SAINT-PETERSBURG INSTITUTE OF MANAGEMENT AND LAW

Sankt-Peterburgskij Institut Upravlenija i Prava
g. Kronštadt, ul. Vs. Viŝnevskogo 5, Sankt-Peterburg 189640
Tel: +7(812) 275-5330
Fax: +7(812) 275-5353
EMail: spiup@mail.ru
Website: http://www.spigl.ru

Rector: Vladimir N. Dezkin

First Vice-Rector: Olga Petko

Departments
Information Systems and Technology (Computer Graphics; Computer Networks; Computer Science; Design; Engineering; Industrial Engineering; Information Technology; Management; Multimedia; Operations Research; Software Engineering); **Psychology** (Educational Psychology; Experimental Psychology; Industrial and Organizational Psychology; Occupational Health; Psychology; Social Psychology)

Faculties
Economics (Accountancy; Banking; Commercial Law; Economics; Finance; Insurance; International Economics; Labour Law; Marketing; Statistics; Taxation); **International Management and Tourism** (Cooking and Catering; Hotel and Restaurant; Hotel Management; Management; Tourism; Transport Management); **Management** (Administration; Administrative Law; Civil Law; Constitutional Law; Demography and Population; Economics; Engineering Management; Finance; Government; Human Resources; Information Technology; Labour Law; Logic; Management; Political Sciences; Statistics)

Schools
Law (Civil Law; Criminal Law; International Law; Public Law)

Further Information: Branches in Pskov and Novgorod

Degrees and Diplomas: *Bakalavr*, *Specialist Diploma*
Last Updated: 27/01/12

SAMARA ACADEMY OF HUMANITIES

Samarskaja Gumanitarnaja Akademija (SAGA)
ul. 8th Radial 2, Samara 443001
Tel: +7(846) 926-2640
Fax: +7(846) 926-2326
EMail: saga@samgum.ru
Website: http://www.samgum.ru

Rector: Natal'ja Yu. Vorornina (1992-) EMail: gum@saminfo.ru

First Vice-Rector: Sergej I. Golenkov
Tel: +7(8462) 162-358, Fax: +7(8462) 162-793
EMail: golenkov@samgum.ru

International Relations: Eugene Eu. Stefanski
Tel: +7(8462) 162-793

Departments
Interfaculty (Arts and Humanities; Modern Languages; Natural Sciences; Theology)

Faculties
Economics (Accountancy; Business Administration; Taxation); **Philosophy** (Philosophy); **Psychology** (Industrial and Organizational Psychology; Psychology; Social Psychology)

Schools
Law (Civil Law; Commercial Law; Criminal Law; European Union Law; History of Law; Human Rights; International Law; Law; Private Law)

History: Founded 1992. Accredited by the Ministry of Education and Science as "Institute" 1997. Acquired present status and title 2000.

Governing Bodies: Board of Founders; Academy Board; Academy Senate

Academic Year: September to July

Admission Requirements: Secondary school certificate (Attestat sredem polnom obrazovanii) or equivalent

Main Language(s) of Instruction: Russian

International Co-operation: With universities in China.

Accrediting Agencies: Ministry of Education and Science

Degrees and Diplomas: *Specialist Diploma*: 5 yrs; *Magistr*

Student Services: Canteen, Foreign student adviser, Foreign Studies Centre, Handicapped facilities, Language programs, Sports facilities

Student Residential Facilities: For 140 students.

Libraries: 77,484 vols including 20,296 scientific books, 55,580 educational books; 137 journal subscriptions 18,758 records (including 8,751 scientific articles) in the electronic library catalogue
Last Updated: 02/03/12

SAMARA INSTITUTE OF BUSINESS AND MANAGEMENT

Samarskij Institut Biznesa i Upravlenija
ul. Kuibyšev 81, Samara 443099
Tel: +7(846) 333-51-80 +7(846) 332-02-76
Fax: +7(846) 332-82-53
EMail: znanie@samibm.ru; znanie@samtel.ru
Website: http://www.samibm.ru/

Rector: Anatolij Leont'evich Zadorozhnyj

Faculties
Economics and Management (Economics; Management); **Law** (Law)

History: Created 1998.

Degrees and Diplomas: *Bakalavr*, *Specialist Diploma*

Student Services: Academic counselling, Canteen, Cultural centre, Employment services, Handicapped facilities, Health services, Social counselling, Sports facilities
Last Updated: 19/03/12

SAMARA MEDICAL INSTITUTE "REAVIZ"

Samarskij Medicinskij Institut "Reaviz"
ul. Čapajevskaja 227, Samara 443001
Tel: +7(846) 333-54-51 +7(846) 270-49-47
Fax: +7(846) 270-49-47
EMail: mail@reaviz.ru
Website: http://www.reaviz.ru/

Rector: Nikolai Aleksandrovich Lysov

Faculties
Medicine (Health Administration; Medicine; Midwifery; Nursing; Surgery); **Pharmacy** (Pharmacy); **Stomatology** (Stomatology)

History: Created 1993.

Degrees and Diplomas: *Specialist Diploma*
Last Updated: 28/02/12

SERGIEVO-POSAD HUMANITARIAN INSTITUTE

Sergievo-Posadskij Gumanitarnyj Institut
Moskovskoe shosse, 12a, Sergievo Posad, 141300 Moskvoskaja oblast'
Tel: +7(496) 547-29-22 +7(496) 547-94–67
Fax: +7(496) 547-29-22
EMail: spgi@sphi.ru
Website: http://www.sphi.ru

Rector: Natal'ja Je. Tolstaja

Faculties
Economics (Accountancy; Economics; Finance; Management); **Law** (Civil Law; Criminal Law; Law); **Psychology** (Psychology)

History: Created 1994.

Degrees and Diplomas: *Bakalavr*, *Specialist Diploma*

Last Updated: 02/03/12

SIBERIAN ACADEMY OF FINANCE AND BANKING

Sibirskaja Akademija Finansov i Bankovskogo Dela
ul. Polzunova, 7, Novosibirsk, 630051 Novosibiraskaja oblast'
Tel: +7(383) 279-7383
Website: http://www.safbd.ru/

Rector: Natal'ja V. Fadejkina EMail: rektor@nnet.ru

Vice-Rector, Administration: Dmitry Safronov

Departments
Accounting and Auditing (Accountancy; Banking; Taxation); **Economics and Human Resources** (Economics; Human Resources); **Finance and Credit** (Banking; Finance; Taxation); **Foreign Languages** (English; Modern Languages); **Management and Control of Innovation** (Management); **Mathematics and Computer Science** (Computer Engineering; Mathematics and Computer Science; Software Engineering); **Philosophy, Pedagogy and Psychology** (Pedagogy; Philosophy; Psychology)

Schools
Graduate (Accountancy; Banking; Economics; Finance; Management; Marketing; Statistics)

History: Created 1992. Acquired present status and title 2007.

Degrees and Diplomas: *Bakalavr*, *Magistr*

Last Updated: 25/01/12

SIBERIAN INDEPENDENT INSTITUTE

Sibirskij Nezavisimyj Institut
ul. Severnaya, 23/1, Novosibirsk, 630082 Novosibiraskaja oblast'
Tel: +7(383) 203-35-31 +7(383) 203-34-41
Fax: +7(383) 203-35-31
EMail: adm@isuni.ru
Website: http://www.isuni.ru/

Rector: Aleksandr Revuzenko EMail: revuzh@isuni.ru

Faculties
Business (Accountancy; Finance; Human Resources; Management; Marketing; Transport Management); **Economics and Finance** (Economics; Finance); **Modern Languages** (Chinese; English; French; German; Linguistics; Spanish; Swedish; Translation and Interpretation); **Psychology** (Psychology)

History: Created 1992.

Degrees and Diplomas: *Bakalavr*, *Specialist Diploma*; *Magistr*

Last Updated: 19/12/11

SIBERIAN INSTITUTE OF BUSINESS AND INFORMATION TECHNOLOGY

Sibirskij Institut Biznesa i Informatsionnykh Tekhnologij
ul. 24 Severnaja, 196, Omsk, 644116 Omskaja oblast'
Tel: +7(3812) 68-00-77 +7(3812) 62-59-89
Fax: +7(3812) 62-59-89
EMail: post@sano.ru
Website: http://sibit.sano.ru/

Rector: Oleg Vladimirovich Volokh

Faculties
Economics and Management (Business Computing; Economics; Human Resources; Information Technology; Management)

History: Created 1996.

Degrees and Diplomas: *Bakalavr*, *Specialist Diploma*

Last Updated: 17/01/12

SIBERIAN INSTITUTE OF BUSINESS, MANAGEMENT AND PSYCHOLOGY

Sibirskij Institut Biznesa, Upravlenija i Psikhologii
ul. Moskovskaja 7A, Krasnojarsk 660037
Tel: +7(391) 264-55-29 +7(391) 278-60-20
Fax: +7(391) 264-55-29
EMail: info@sibup.ru
Website: http://www.sibup.ru/

Rector: Vladimir F. Zabuga

Faculties
Economics (Accountancy; Applied Mathematics; Computer Science; Economics; International Economics; Linguistics; Management; Mathematics and Computer Science); **Law** (Civil Law; Criminal Law; Law; Public Law); **Psychology** (Physical Education; Psychology; Social Sciences; Sports)

History: Founded 1995. Acquired present status 2010.

Degrees and Diplomas: *Bakalavr*, *Specialist Diploma*

Last Updated: 25/01/12

SIBERIAN UNIVERSITY OF CONSUMER COOPERATIVES

Sibirskij Universitet Potrebitel'skoj Kooperacii
prosp. K. Marksa 26, Novosibirsk, 630087 Novosibiraskaja oblast'
Tel: +7(3832) 46-5531
Fax: +7(3832) 46-1354
EMail: procorr@sibupk.nsk.su; common@sibupk.nsk.su
Website: http://www.sibupk.nsk.su

Rector: Vladimir V. Stepanov (2011-) EMail: rector@sibupk.nsk.su

Faculties
Commerce (Advertising and Publicity; Business and Commerce; History; Marketing; Philosophy; Physical Education; Sports); **Economics** (Computer Science; Economics; Industrial and Production Economics; Mathematics; Modern Languages; Pedagogy; Psychology; Regional Studies; Statistics); **Finance and Accountancy** (Accountancy; Finance; Management; Taxation); **Socio-Technological** (Cooking and Catering; Hotel and Restaurant; Technology; Tourism)

Schools
Graduate (Accountancy; Constitutional Law; Cooking and Catering; Economics; Food Technology; Geography (Human); Government; History of Law; Hotel and Restaurant; Industrial Management; Law; Management; Marketing; Statistics; Tourism); **Law** (Civil Law; Constitutional Law; Criminal Law; Criminology; Government; History of Law; International Law; Law)

History: Founded 1956.

Degrees and Diplomas: *Bakalavr*, *Specialist Diploma*

Last Updated: 24/01/12

SLAVIC BUSINESS INSTITUTE NAMED AFTER K.V. NECHAEV

Slavjanskij Delovoj Institut i.m. K.V. Nechaeva (SBI)
ul Dobrolubov, 16/2,
Moskva 127254
Tel: +7(495) 618-05-30 +7(495) 618-06-57
Fax: +7(495) 618-06-63
EMail: sldi@mail.ru; mail@sldi.ru
Website: http://www.sldi.ru/

Rector: Anatolij Mironovich Smeljanskij

Faculties
Economics (Accountancy; Business and Commerce; Economics; Information Technology); **Information Technology** (Economics; Information Technology); **Law** (Law)

History: Founded 1992.

Academic Year: September to June

Admission Requirements: Secondary school certificate (Attestat o srednem obrazovanii)

Main Language(s) of Instruction: Russian

Degrees and Diplomas: *Bakalavr*, *Specialist Diploma*; *Magistr*

Student Services: Academic counselling, Canteen, Cultural centre, Employment services, Health services, Language programs, Social counselling, Sports facilities

Student Residential Facilities: Off-campus building in Moscow

Special Facilities: No

Libraries: Yes. c. 10,000 vols

Last Updated: 02/03/12

SMOLENSKY UNIVERSITY FOR THE HUMANITIES

Smolenskij Gumanitarnyj Universitet (Institut)
ul. Gercena, 2, Smolensk 214014
Tel: +7(0812) 683-335
Fax: +7(0812) 683-335
EMail: shu@shu.ru
Website: http://www.shu.ru

Rector: Nikolaj E. Mažar

Faculties

Information Technology, Design, and Economics (Business Computing; Design; Economics; Finance; Information Technology; Management; Taxation); **International Tourism and Modern Languages** (Engineering Management; Food Technology; Geography; German; Philology; Philosophy; Tourism); **Psychology and Law** (Law; Physical Education; Psychology)

History: Created 1992.

Degrees and Diplomas: *Bakalavr*, *Specialist Diploma*; *Magistr*

Last Updated: 19/12/11

SOCHI INSTITUTE OF ECONOMICS AND INFORMATION TECHNOLOGIES

Sočinskij Institut Ekonomiki i Informacionnykh Tehnologij
ul. Junyh Lenincev 5, Soči, 354000 Krasnodarskij Kraj
Tel: +7(8622) 55-72-79 +7(8622) 55-74-41 +7(8622) 55-72-75
Fax: +7(8622) 55-72-75
EMail: sieit@sieit.ru; sieit2010@yandex.ru
Website: http://www.sieit.ru/

Rector: Gennadij V. Turovcev

Programmes

Computer Science (Computer Networks); **Information Technology** (Information Technology); **Management** (Management)

Degrees and Diplomas: *Specialist Diploma*

Last Updated: 26/04/11

SOUTH RUSSIAN HUMANITIES INSTITUTE

Južno-Rossijskij Gumanitarnyj Institut (URGI)
ul. Bol. Sadovaja. 101 of. 19, Rostov-na-Donu 34400
Tel: +7(8632) 441-281 +7(8632) 673-437
Fax: +7(8632) 650-236
EMail: urgi-ofic@info-don.ru
Website: http://www.urgi.ru

Rector: Victor O. Pigulevsky

Vice-Chancellor: Ludmila Miskaya

International Relations: Vladimir Romer, Chair

Faculties

Advertising and Communication (Advertising and Publicity; Communication Studies) *Head*: Alexander Ovrutsky; **Business and Commerce** (Business and Commerce; Economics) *Head*: Roman Shehivtsev; **Design** (Design) *Head*: Alexander Surin; **Philosophical Schools** (Philosophical Schools; Philosophy) *Head*: Miskaya Ludmila; **Psychology** (Psychology) *Head*: Tatyana Sinchenko; **Public Law** (Law; Public Law) *Head*: Anatoly Mayboroda

Governing Bodies: Academic Council

Academic Year: September to June

Fees: (Russian Rubles): 26,000 per annum

Main Language(s) of Instruction: Russian, English

Accrediting Agencies: Ministry of Education

Student Services: Academic counselling, Canteen, Employment services, Foreign student adviser, Foreign Studies Centre, Health services, Language programs, Social counselling, Sports facilities

Student Residential Facilities: Yes

Special Facilities: Art Gallery. Movie Studio.

Libraries: Yes

Press or Publishing House: FOLIANT

SOUTHDAG INSTITUTE

Institut JužDag
ul. Sovetskaja 11, Derbent, 368600 Respublika Dagestan
Tel: +7(87240) 2-33-80
Fax: +7(87240) 4-20-94
EMail: alpan@derbent.ru

Rector: Nariman O. Osmanov

Programmes

Economics (Economics); **Law** (Law); **Linguistics** (Linguistics); **Logistics** (Transport Management); **Physical Education** (Physical Education); **Primary Education** (Primary Education); **Russian Teaching** (Literature; Native Language Education; Russian); **Science Education** (Biology; Science Education)

History: Created 1993.

Degrees and Diplomas: *Specialist Diploma*

Last Updated: 26/01/12

SOUTHERN INSTITUTE OF MANAGEMENT

Južnyj Institut Menedžmenta (JIM)
ul. Stavropol'skaja 216, Krasnodar 350040
Tel: +7(861) 233-88-59 +7(861) 233-39-38
Fax: +7(861) 233-88-59
EMail: rektorat@uim.ru; info@uim.ru
Website: http://www.uim.ru

Rector: Vladimir F. Lazovskij (1993-)
EMail: Vladimir.lazovsky@uim.ru

Faculties

Management, Economics and Law (Accountancy; Economics; Finance; Law; Management; Marketing; Tourism)

Higher Schools

International Business (Economics; International Business; Linguistics; Management; Marketing; Modern Languages)

History: Founded 1993. Acquired present status 1994. Received accreditation 2003.

Academic Year: September to July

Admission Requirements: High school Diploma (Attestat)

Main Language(s) of Instruction: Russian

Degrees and Diplomas: *Bakalavr*, *Specialist Diploma*; *Magistr*

Libraries: c. 220,100 vols.

Last Updated: 26/01/12

SOUTHERN SAKHALIN INSTITUTE OF ECONOMICS, LAW AND COMPUTER SCIENCE

Južno-Sahalinskij Institut Ekonomiki, Prava i Informatiki
Kommunisticheskij prosp. 72, Južno-Sakhalinsk 693000
Tel: +7(4242) 42-33-52 +7(4242) 42-29-67
Fax: +7(4242) 42-05-97
EMail: rector@sakhiepi.ru
Website: http://www.sakhiepi.ru

Rector: En Bok Kan

Faculties

Economics (Accountancy; Economics; Finance); **Engineering** (Automation and Control Engineering; Electrical Engineering; Energy Engineering; Engineering; Engineering Management; Power Engineering); **Information Technology and Computer Science**

(Applied Mathematics; Business Computing; Computer Science; Information Technology); **Law** (Administrative Law; Civil Law; Commercial Law; Criminal Law; Criminology; Labour Law; Law); **Management** (Management; Marketing; Tourism); **Modern Languages** (Chinese; English; French; German; Japanese; Korean; Linguistics; Philology; Spanish)

History: Created 1993.

Degrees and Diplomas: *Bakalavr*, *Specialist Diploma*
Last Updated: 27/01/12

ST TIKHON'S ORTHODOX UNIVERSITY FOR THE HUMANITIES

Pravoslavnyj Svjato-Tikhonovskij Gumanitarnyj Universitet
ul. Novokuznetskaja 23/5a, Moskva 115184
Tel: +7(495) 953-51-41
Fax: +7(495) 953-56-97 +7(495) 131-93-90
EMail: pstbi@pstbi.ru; max11167@mail.ru; pstbi@ccas.ru
Website: http://www.pstbi.ru

Rector: Vladimir Vorobiev (1992-) EMail: recpstbi@ccas.ru

Faculties

Church Arts (Handicrafts; Painting and Drawing; Religious Art; Religious Studies; Restoration of Works of Art); **Church Music** (Conducting; Music Theory and Composition; Musicology; Religious Music; Singing); **Computer Science and Applied Mathematics** (Applied Mathematics; Computer Science); **History** (Archaeology; Cultural Studies; History; Holy Writings; Religious Education; Religious Studies); **Missionary Studies** (Missionary Studies); **Philology** (Ancient Languages; History; History of Religion; Linguistics; Literature; Modern Languages; Oriental Languages; Philology; Phonetics; Religious Studies); **Social Sciences** (Economic History; Sociology); **Teacher Training** (Teacher Training); **Theology** (Comparative Religion; History of Religion; Holy Writings; Pastoral Studies; Theology)

History: Founded 1992 as Pravoslavnyj Svjato-Tihonovskij Bogoslavskij Institut (St Tikhon's Orthodox Theological Institute) a private institute. Acquired current title and status 2004.

Governing Bodies: Academic Council

Academic Year: September to June (September-January; January-June)

Admission Requirements: Secondary school certificate (Attestat o srednem obrazovanii) and entrance examination

Main Language(s) of Instruction: Russian

International Co-operation: With universities in Germany and Netherlands

Degrees and Diplomas: *Bakalavr*, *Specialist Diploma*; *Magistr*

Student Services: Academic counselling, Canteen, Cultural centre, Employment services, Health services, Language programs, Social counselling, Sports facilities

Special Facilities: Museum. Archives on Modern History of the Russian Orthodox Church. Internet. Concert Hall

Libraries: c. 60,000 vols
Last Updated: 05/04/12

STAVROPOL INSTITUTE NAMED AFTER V.D. CHURSIN

Stavropolskij Institut im. V.D. Čursina
ul. Roza Ljuksemburg 59, Stavropol, 355000 Stavropol'skij kraj
Tel: +7(8652) 23-27-23
Fax: +7(8652) 23-27-23
EMail: institut@vuz-chursin.ru
Website: http://www.vuz-chursin.ru

Rector: Polina V. Čursina

Programmes

Law (Administrative Law; Arts and Humanities; Civil Law; Commercial Law; Constitutional Law; Criminal Law; Criminology; Cultural Studies; Ecology; English; Ethics; Fiscal Law; French; History; History of Law; History of Religion; Human Rights; International Law; Labour Law; Latin; Law; Linguistics; Logic; Notary Studies; Pedagogy; Philosophy; Political Sciences; Psychology; Public Law; Religious Studies; Sociology; Sports); **Management** (Accountancy; Administration; Banking; Business and Commerce; Business Computing; Finance; French; German; Insurance; International Economics; Management; Marketing; Russian; Sports; Taxation)

History: Founded 1992.

Admission Requirements: Secondary school certificate (Attestat o srednem obrazovanii) and entrance examination

Main Language(s) of Instruction: Russian

Degrees and Diplomas: *Specialist Diploma*: 5 yrs

Student Services: Academic counselling, Canteen, Cultural centre, Health services, Language programs, Social counselling, Sports facilities

Student Residential Facilities: Yes

Libraries: Main Library, c. 250,000 vols
Last Updated: 19/03/12

STAVROPOL INSTITUTE OF FINANCE AND ECONOMICS

Stavropolskij Finansovo-Ekonomičeskij Institut
ul. Lenina, 267, Stavropol, 355003 Stavropol'skij kraj
Tel: +7(8652) 352-462
Fax: +7(8652) 371-101
EMail: sfeisk@mail.ru
Website: http://sfeisk.ru/

Rector: Vil' V. Hisamudinov

Programmes

Accounting and Audit (Accountancy); **Economics** (Economics); **Finance and Credit** (Banking; Finance; Insurance; Management)

History: Created 1993.

Degrees and Diplomas: *Bakalavr*, *Specialist Diploma*
Last Updated: 19/12/11

TAGANROG INSTITUTE OF MANAGEMENT AND ECONOMICS

Taganrogskij Institut Upravlenija i Ekonomiki (TMEI)
ul. Petrovskaja 45, Taganrog, 374900 Rostov
Tel: +7(8634) 383-360
Fax: +7(8634) 383-360
EMail: info@tmei.ru
Website: http://www.tmei.ru/

Rector: Sergey Y. Avakov

Faculties

Economics (Accountancy; Economics; Finance; International Economics; Management); **Law** (Civil Law; Criminal Law; Law; Public Law); **Psychology and Communications** (Advertising and Publicity; Psychology; Public Relations)

History: Founded 1994.

Governing Bodies: Ministry of Education

Admission Requirements: Secondary school certificate and entrance examination

Main Language(s) of Instruction: Russian

Degrees and Diplomas: *Bakalavr*, *Specialist Diploma*; *Magistr*

Student Services: Academic counselling, Canteen, Cultural centre, Language programs, Social counselling, Sports facilities

Libraries: Yes

Publications: Collection of scientific works *(annually)*
Last Updated: 07/12/11

TISBI UNIVERSITY OF MANAGEMENT

Universitet Upravlenija TISBI (TISBI)
ul. Mushtari 13, Kazan, 420012 Tatarstan
Tel: +7(843) 236-9297 +7(843) 236-9539
Fax: +7(843) 236-9297
EMail: tisbi@tisbi.ru
Website: http://www.tisbi.org/

Rector: Nella M. Pruss (1992-)
Tel: +7(843) 236-9244 EMail: rector@tisbi.ru;

Vice-Rector for Academic Affairs: Galina Akhmina
Tel: +7(843) 299-4300

International Relations: Evguenia Belyaeva, Vice-Rector, International Cooperation
Tel: +7(843) 238-6875 EMail: rgarifullina@tisbi.ru

Departments

Postgraduate Studies (Law)

Faculties

Economics (Banking; Economics; Finance; Industrial and Production Economics; Taxation); **Extramural Studies** (Computer Science; Economics; Law; Management); **Humanities** (Hotel Management; International Relations; Service Trades; Social Work; Tourism); **Information Technologies** (Business Computing; Information Technology); **Law** (European Union Law; International Law; Law); **Management** (Business Computing; Management; Maritime Law; Small Business); **Secondary Professional Education** (Accountancy; Design; Economics; Law; Transport Management)

Institutes

Continuing Education

History: Founded 1992 as the Tatar Institute Business Promotion, and became Akademija Upravlenija TISBI (TISBI Academy of Management) in 2003. Acquired current title 2011.

Governing Bodies: Rectorate

Academic Year: Sep-Dec; Jan-Mar; Apr-June

Admission Requirements: Secondary school certificate (Attestat o srednem obrazovanii) and entrance examination; Unified State Exam

Fees: (Russian Rubles): 17,000 - 26,500 per 6 months full-time; 15,000 - 20,000 per 6 months part-time.

Main Language(s) of Instruction: Russian

International Co-operation: with institutions in USA, China, The Netherlands, Germany, Belgium, Turkey, Scotland, Israel, Mongolia, Ukraine, Kazakhstan, Kyrgyzstan

Accrediting Agencies: Ministry of Education

Degrees and Diplomas: *Bakalavr*: 4-5 yrs; *Magistr*: a further 2-2 1/2 yrs; *Kandidat Nauk*: 3-4 yrs

Special Facilities: IT Centre

Libraries: 200,000 vols

Academic Staff *2010-2011*	MEN	WOMEN	**TOTAL**
FULL-TIME	111	322	**433**
PART-TIME	48	68	**116**
STAFF WITH DOCTORATE			
FULL-TIME	34	69	**103**
PART-TIME	38	25	**63**
Student Numbers *2010-2011*			
All (Foreign Included)	–	–	**4,402**
FOREIGN ONLY	9	2	**11**

Part-time students, 1,729. **Distance students**, 1,587.

Last Updated: 18/10/11

TOGLIATTI ACADEMY OF MANAGEMENT

Tol'jattinskaja Akademija Upravlenija (TAM)
Primorskij Bul'var, 25, Tol'jatti, 445057 Samarskaja oblast'
Tel: +7(8482) 40-71-00 +7(8482) 73-60-50 +7(8482) 73-60-60
Fax: +7(8482) 40-74-56
EMail: info@taom.ru
Website: http://www.taom.ru

Rector: Igor V. Bogdanov EMail: ibogdanov@taom.ru

Departments

Applied Information Technology (Business Computing; Information Technology); **Applied Mathematics** (Applied Mathematics; Mathematics); **Design** (Design); **Finance and Economics** (Economics; Finance); **Management** (Management); **Modern Languages** (Modern Languages); **Physical Education** (Physical Education); **Public Relations** (Public Relations)

History: Founded 1993as the Bank College. Became Academy of Business and Banking 1993. Acquired present title 2001.

Governing Bodies: Board of Trustees; Academic Council

Academic Year: September to July (September-December; January-April; May-July)

Admission Requirements: School Education Certificate or equivalent

Main Language(s) of Instruction: Russian (Some programmes are offered in English)

International Co-operation: With universities in Hungary, India, Poland, USA

Degrees and Diplomas: *Bakalavr*, *Specialist Diploma*

Student Services: Academic counselling, Canteen, Cultural centre, Employment services, Foreign student adviser, Health services, Language programs, Social counselling, Sports facilities

Student Residential Facilities: Residence Hall

Special Facilities: Museum of Academy history; Design and Media Studios

Libraries: c. 46,000 vols; Internet access; Automated informational library's system; Free access to periodical resources of Oxford University

Last Updated: 16/03/12

TOMSK INSTITUTE OF ECONOMICS AND LAW

Tomskij Ekonomiko-Juridičeskij Institut
Moskovskij Trakt 2g, Tomsk 634050
Tel: +7(3822) 52-96-55 +7(3822) 52-76-13
Fax: +7(3822) 52-76-13
EMail: infocenter@mail.ru; priemcom@teui.ru
Website: http://teui.ru/

Rector: Vladimir V. Tirskij EMail: rector@teui.ru

Departments

Economics (Economics); **Law** (Law)

History: Created 1992.

Degrees and Diplomas: *Bakalavr*

Last Updated: 02/03/12

TVER INSTITUTE OF ECOLOGY AND LAW

Tverskoj Institut Ekologii i Prava
ul. Kalinina, 23, Tver, 170001 Tverskaja oblast'
Tel: +7(4822) 42-06-55
Fax: +7(4822) 42-06-55
EMail: tiep2000@mail.ru
Website: http://www.tiep.ru/

Rector: Igor' Davydovich Lel'chitskij

Faculties

Ecology (Ecology); **Economics and Management** (Economics; Management); **Law** (Law); **Psychology** (Psychology)

History: Created 1995.

Degrees and Diplomas: *Bakalavr*, *Specialist Diploma*

Last Updated: 02/03/12

TVER INSTITUTE OF ECONOMICS AND MANAGEMENT

Tverskoj Institut Ekomiki i Menedžmenta
prosp Pobedy, 27, Tver, 170008 Tverskaja oblast'
Tel: +7(4822) 34-53-08 +7(4822) 34-28-69 +7(4822) 43-03-088
Fax: +7(4822) 34-28-69
EMail: tvinm@tvcom.ru; info@tvertiem.ru
Website: http://tvertiem.ru/

Rector: Nadezhda Valer'evna Pilipchuk

Departments

Finance and Credit (Banking; Economics; Finance; Management); **Mondern Languages** (Modern Languages)

History: Created 1995.

Degrees and Diplomas: *Bakalavr*, *Specialist Diploma*

Last Updated: 02/03/12

UNIVERSITY OF THE RUSSIAN ACADEMY OF EDUCATION

Universitet Rossijskoj Akademija Obrazovanija (URAE)
ul. Bol'šaja Poljanka 58, Moskva 119180
Tel: +7(499) 237-43-02
Fax: +7(499) 238-26-28
EMail: umu@urao.edu
Website: http://www.urao.edu

Rector: Mikhail Nikolaevich Berulava EMail: rector@urao.edu

Faculties

Arts (Art History; Design; Fine Arts; Music Theory and Composition; Painting and Drawing); **Computer Science** (Computer Science); **Economics and Business** (Accountancy; Banking; Business Administration; Economics; Finance; Management; Marketing; Public Administration); **Educational Psychology** *(Psychology of under-achieving children)* (Clinical Psychology; Economics; Educational Psychology; Social Psychology; Zoology); **Foreign Languages** (Classical Languages; Foreign Languages Education; Linguistics; Phonetics; Translation and Interpretation); **Geography and Regional Politics** (Geography; Regional Planning); **History and Cultural Science** (Ancient Civilizations; Contemporary History; Cultural Studies; Documentation Techniques; History; Media Studies; Medieval Studies; Visual Arts); **Journalism** *(Specialized industrial journalism - Nižny Novgorod branch)* (Ethics; Journalism); **Law** (Canon Law; Criminal Law; Family Studies; History; Labour Law; Law; Notary Studies; Public Law); **Natural Sciences** (Biophysics; Ecology; Energy Engineering; Geochemistry; Natural Sciences); **Philology** (Linguistics; Literature; Philology; Phonetics; Psycholinguistics; Terminology); **Philosophy** (Ethics; History; Logic; Metaphysics; Philosophical Schools; Philosophy)

History: Founded 1994. Acquired present status 2002.

Academic Year: September to June

Admission Requirements: Secondary school certificate (Attestat o srednem obrazovanii) or equivalent

Main Language(s) of Instruction: Russian

Degrees and Diplomas: *Bakalavr*; *Specialist Diploma*; *Magistr*. Also Certificates

Student Services: Academic counselling, Canteen, Cultural centre, Employment services, Foreign student adviser, Handicapped facilities, Health services, Language programs, Social counselling, Sports facilities

Student Residential Facilities: Yes

Special Facilities: Education Museum. Conference Centre

Libraries: Total, c. 150,000 vols

Last Updated: 16/03/12

UPPER VOLGA INSTITUTE

Institut "Verhnevolž'je"
ul. Sovetskaja, d.36, Tver, 170100 Tverskaja oblast'
Tel: +7(4822) 35-86-92
Fax: +7(4822) 35-86-53
EMail: uvitver@inbox.ru; uppervolga@inbox.ru
Website: http://www.uppervolga.ru

Rector: Irina N. Aksenova (1993-)

Departments

Economics and Management (Economics; Management); **Humanities and Natural Sciences** (Arts and Humanities; Natural Sciences); **Law** (Law); **Psychology** (Psychology)

History: Founded 1993. A private, non-state institution of higher education. Acquires present status and title 1995.

Governing Bodies: Rector

Academic Year: September to June

Admission Requirements: Secondary school certificate or equivalent

Main Language(s) of Instruction: Russian

International Co-operation: With universities in USA.

Accrediting Agencies: Ministry of Education

Degrees and Diplomas: *Bakalavr*, *Specialist Diploma*

Student Services: Academic counselling, Employment services, Social counselling

Special Facilities: Laboratory of Information Technology

Libraries: Total: c. 3,000 vols

Publications: Annual Conferences Report, Professors' publications *(annually)*

Last Updated: 26/09/11

URAL INSTITUTE FOR THE HUMANITIES

Uralskij Gumanitarnyj Institut (UIH)
ul. Komsomolskaya 63, Ekaterinburg, 620078 Sverdlovskaja oblast'
Tel: +7(343) 375-9106 +7(343) 378-8192
Fax: +7(343) 375-3048
EMail: uhi@ural.ru
Website: http://www.urgi.ural.ru

Principal: Mikhail N. Denisevich (1994-) Tel: +7(343) 375-3048

President: Veniamin Alekseyev

Programmes

Accounting, Analysis and Auditing (Accountancy; Taxation); **Applied Computer Science in Economics** (Business Computing; Computer Science; Information Technology); **Business Management** (Human Resources; International Business; Management; Marketing; Tourism); **Finance and Credit** (Banking; Finance; Insurance); **Law** (Civil Law; Law); **Psychology** (Developmental Psychology; Industrial and Organizational Psychology; Psychology; Psychotherapy); **Theory and Practice of Translation** (Translation and Interpretation)

History: Founded 1994 under the patronage of Ural Academy of Sciences, Ural Technical University (UGTU-UPI), Academy (VEGU).

Governing Bodies: Ural Academy of Sciences (Ekaterinburg), Ural Technical University (UGTU-UPI) (Ekaterinburg), Academy (VEGU) (Ufa).

Academic Year: September to June

Admission Requirements: Secondary School Certificate; Entrance Examination

Fees: (Russain Rubles): 60,000 per annum

Main Language(s) of Instruction: Russian, English, German, French

International Co-operation: With Universities in France, Germany and China

Accrediting Agencies: Ministry of Education of Russia

Degrees and Diplomas: *Specialist Diploma*: 5 yrs

Student Services: Canteen, Foreign Studies Centre, Language programs, Sports facilities

Student Residential Facilities: None

Special Facilities: None

Libraries: 251,600 vols

Publications: Translation and Comparative Linguistics *(biannually)*

Press or Publishing House: Annals of Ural Institute for the Humanities (Newspaper)

Academic Staff *2007-2008*	MEN	WOMEN	**TOTAL**
FULL-TIME	15	26	**41**
PART-TIME	12	14	**26**
STAFF WITH DOCTORATE			
FULL-TIME	7	18	**25**
PART-TIME	8	18	**26**
Student Numbers *2007-2008*			
All (Foreign Included)	970	2,881	**3,851**

Part-time students, 2,992. **Evening students**, 200.

Last Updated: 30/11/11

URAL INSTITUTE OF BUSINESS

Uralskij Institut Biznesa
pereulok Tsentralnogo Rynka, d.6, Ekaterinburg, 620214 Sverdlovskaja oblast'
Tel: +7(343) 376-45-30 +7(351) 264-36-87
Fax: +7(351) 264-36-88
EMail: barenn@mail.ru; urib@inset.ru
Website: http://urib.info/

Rector: Aleksandr Maksimovich Minjaila

Departments

Accounting (Accountancy); **Applied Computing** (Business Computing; Computer Science; Information Technology); **Commerce** (Business Administration; Business and Commerce); **Economics and Management** (Economics; Management); **Theology and Humanities** (Arts and Humanities; Theology)

History: Created 1998.

Degrees and Diplomas: *Bakalavr*, *Specialist Diploma*

Last Updated: 26/09/11

URAL INSTITUTE OF COMMERCE AND LAW

Uralskij Institut Kommertsii i Prava

ul. Lunačarskogo 81, Ekaterinburg, 620075 Sverdlovskaja oblast'

Tel: +7(343) 350-45-35 +7(343) 358-99-22

Fax: +7(343) 388-10-38

EMail: uicp@uicp.e-burg.ru

Website: http://www.uicp.e-burg.ru

Rector: Gennadij G. Smirnov EMail: rector@uicp.e-burg.ru

Programmes

Economics (Accountancy; Banking; Commercial Law; Economics; Management); **Law** (Law)

History: Created 1994.

Degrees and Diplomas: *Bakalavr*, *Specialist Diploma*

Last Updated: 19/04/11

URAL INSTITUTE OF ECONOMICS, MANAGEMENT AND LAW

Uralskij Institut Ekonomiki, Upravlenija i Prava

ul. Lunačarskogo 194, Ekaterinburg, 620055 Sverdlovskaja oblast'

Tel: +7(3432) 613-007 +7(3432) 615-958

Fax: +7(3432) 613-007

Website: http://www.urep.ru

Rector: Ali Asadov (2006-)

Departments

Administrative and Financial Law (Administration; Commercial Law; Economic and Finance Policy; Environmental Studies; Finance; Taxation); **Applied Informatics** (Artificial Intelligence; Computer Graphics; Computer Networks; Computer Science; Data Processing; Information Technology; Telecommunications Engineering); **Business Accounting, Analysis and Audit** (Accountancy; Finance; Leadership; Management Systems; Marketing; Taxation); **Civil Law** (Civil Law; Commercial Law; Insurance; Labour Law; Private Law); **Communication and Cultural Studies** (Communication Arts; Communication Studies; Cultural Studies; Russian); **Constitutional Law, State and Law Theory** (Constitutional Law; International Law; Law); **Economic Theory** (Economic and Finance Policy); **Enterprise Economy** (Advertising and Publicity; Consumer Studies; Hotel Management; Human Resources; Industrial and Organizational Psychology; Leadership; Management; Management Systems; Marketing; Real Estate; Tourism; Transport Management); **Finance and Credit** (Banking; Economic and Finance Policy; Finance); **Foreign Languages** (English; Foreign Languages Education; German); **History** (Civil Law; Economics; History; History of Law; Management); **Mathematics and Natural Sciences** (Applied Mathematics; Ecology; Econometrics; Finance; Mathematics; Natural Sciences; Operations Research); **Physical Education** (Physical Education); **Public Law Studies** (Criminal Law; Criminology; Forensic Medicine and Dentistry; Public Law); **Social, Political and Psychological Studies** (Ethics; History of Law; Logic; Pedagogy; Philosophy; Political Sciences; Psychology; Social Studies; Sociology); **World Economy** (Economic and Finance Policy; International Economics)

Further Information: Branches: Kurgan; Nizhny Tagil; Lesnoi; Kamensk-Uralsky; Polevskoi; Zlatoust; Krasnoturinsk; The Ural Technical School of Economics and Law

History: Founded in 1992 by associate professors and professors of Economics faculty of Urals State University and the Urals State Law Academy.

Governing Bodies: Board of Founders

Admission Requirements: School certificate and entrance examinations.

Main Language(s) of Instruction: Russian

Degrees and Diplomas: *Specialist Diploma*: 5 yrs

Student Services: Cultural centre, Employment services, Health services

Libraries: Yes

Last Updated: 30/11/11

URAL INSTITUTE OF FINANCE AND LAW

Uralskij Finansovo-Juridičeskij Institut

ul. Karla Libknekhta, d.1, Ekaterinburg, 620075 Sverdlovskaja oblast'

Tel: +7(343) 371-21-29

Fax: +7(343) 371-92-86

EMail: urfji@mail.ru

Website: http://www.urfji.com

Rector: Vladislav I. Nazarov

Faculties

Finance (Finance); **Law** (Law)

History: Created 1995.

Degrees and Diplomas: *Specialist Diploma*

Last Updated: 22/09/11

URAL INSTITUTE OF MARKETING

Uralskij Institut Fondovogo Rynka

ul. Sibirskij trakt, 35, Ekaterinburg, 620032 Sverdlovskaja oblast'

Tel: +7(343) 254-62-38

Fax: +7(343) 261-60-98

EMail: info@uifr.ru

Website: http://www.uifr.ru

Rector: V. Chashchin

Programmes

Finance and Economics (Accountancy; Banking; Business Administration; Consumer Studies; Economics; Finance; Management; Marketing)

History: Created 1993.

Degrees and Diplomas: *Specialist Diploma*

Last Updated: 30/11/11

VJATKA SOCIAL-ECONOMICS INSTITUTE

Vjatskij Social'no-Economičeskij Institut

Bolševikov prosp. 91, Kirov 610002

Tel: +7(8332) 670-235

Fax: +7(8332) 670-235

EMail: vsei@vsei.ru

Website: http://www.vsei.ru

Rector: Vladimir Sizov EMail: rektor@vsei.ru

Faculties

Economics and Management (Banking; Computer Science; Economics; Finance; Foreign Languages Education; Management; Taxation); **Humanities** (Biomedicine; Civil Law; Criminal Law; Design; Government; History of Law; Law; Philosophy; Psychology)

History: Founded 1993.

Admission Requirements: Secondary School Certificate (Attestat) or College Diploma; Entrance Examination

Main Language(s) of Instruction: Russian

Degrees and Diplomas: *Bakalavr*: On-campus, 4 yrs; Distance, 5 yrs; *Specialist Diploma*: On-campus, 5 yrs; Distance, 6 yrs

Student Services: Academic counselling, Canteen, Employment services, Foreign Studies Centre, Health services, Language programs, Sports facilities

Libraries: Library and Electronic Library

Publications: Interregional Scholars Group - Problems of Neoeconomy, Academic and Research Publications *(quarterly)*

Last Updated: 29/11/11

VLADIKAVKAZ FASHION INSTITUTE

Vladikavkazskij Institut Mody
prosp. Mira, 54, Vladikavkaz, 362040 Respublika Severnaja Osetija-Alanija
Tel: +7(8672) 44-58-25 +7(8672) 53-19-95
Fax: +7(8672) 53-19-95
EMail: institutmody@mail.ru

Rector: Zinaida Georgievna Tomaeva

Programmes
Fashion Design (Advertising and Publicity; Clothing and Sewing; Fashion Design; Interior Design)

History: Created 1997.

Degrees and Diplomas: *Specialist Diploma*
Last Updated: 16/03/12

VLADIKAVKAZ INSTITUTE OF ECONOMICS, MANAGEMENT ANF LAW

Vladikavkazskij Institut Ekonomiki, Upravlenija i Prava
ul. S. Tabolova, 8, Vladikavkaz, 362011 Respublika Severnaja Osetija-Alanija
Tel: +7(8672) 51-99-00 +7(8672) 51-92-55
Fax: +7(8672) 51-99-00
EMail: vieup@inbox.ru

Rector: Larisa Muradinovna Balikoeva

Programmes
Economics (Economics); **Law** (Law); **Linguistics** (Linguistics); **Public Relations** (Public Relations)

History: Created 1996.

Degrees and Diplomas: *Specialist Diploma*
Last Updated: 16/03/12

VLADIKAVKAZ INSTITUTE OF MANAGEMENT

Vladikavkazskij Institut Upravlenija (VIU (VIM))
ul. Borodinskaja, 14, Vladikavkaz, 362025 Respublika Severnaja Osetija-Alanija
Tel: +7(8672) 54-15-80
Fax: +7(8672) 54-15-80
EMail: viu-online@mail.ru
Website: http://www.viu-online.ru

Rector: Zita I. Salbieva EMail: salbieva@rambler.ru

Programmes
Business Administration (Business Administration; Management); **Customs Affairs** (Taxation); **Finance and Credit** (Banking; Finance); **Law** (Law)

History: Founded 1996. Acquired present status 2000.

Academic Year: September to June

Admission Requirements: General certificate of school education

Main Language(s) of Instruction: Russian

Degrees and Diplomas: *Specialist Diploma*

Student Services: Academic counselling, Canteen, Cultural centre, Employment services, Foreign student adviser, Health services, Language programs, Nursery care, Social counselling, Sports facilities
Last Updated: 16/03/12

VLADIMIR INSTITUTE OF BUSINESS

Vladimirskij Institut Biznesa
ul. Dvorjanskaja, 27a, korp 7, Vladimir 600001
Tel: +7(4922) 32-22-69 +7(4922) 32-40-79 +7(4922) 32-22-34
Fax: +7(4922) 32-22-34
EMail: all@vib.vladimir.ru
Website: http://www.vib33.ru/

Rector: Olga P. Zvjagintseva

Faculties
Economics and Finance (Accountancy; Economic History; Finance); **Management and Information Technology** (Business Administration; Business Computing; Information Technology; Management; Marketing)

History: Created 1997.

Degrees and Diplomas: *Specialist Diploma*
Last Updated: 15/03/12

VOLGA REGION INSTITUTE OF BUSINESS

Povolžskij Institut Biznesa
ul. Galaktionovskaja 141, Samara 443010
Tel: +7(846) 332-42-19 +7(846) 278-43-80
Fax: +7(846) 334-23-27 +7(846) 372-86-52
EMail: pib1993@mail.ru
Website: http://www.pib-samara.ru/

Rector: Alevtina A. Prohorenko

Programmes
Management (Economics; Management; Marketing)

History: Created 1993.

Degrees and Diplomas: *Bakalavr*; *Specialist Diploma*
Last Updated: 05/04/12

VOLGOGRAD INSTITUTE OF ECONOMICS, SOCIOLOGY AND LAW

Volgogradskij Institut Ekonomiki, Sotsiologii i Prava (VIESP)
Pr. Universitetskij, 64, Volgograd 400011
Tel: +7(8442) 466-839
Fax: +7(8442) 465-867
EMail: viesp@viesp.ru
Website: http://www.viesp.ru

Rector: Vitalij Jusupov Tel: +7(8442) 465-867

Vice-Rector on Academic Affairs: Andrej Jusupov
Tel: +7(8442) 466-837, Fax: +7(8442) 466-837

Faculties
Economics and Management (Accountancy; Advertising and Publicity; Banking; Business Administration; Consumer Studies; Economic History; Economics; Finance; Human Resources; Information Management; Management; Marketing; Tourism; Transport Management); **Law** (Administrative Law; Constitutional Law; Criminal Law; Fiscal Law; Law; Philosophy; Private Law; Public Law; Sociology)

History: Founded 1993 as Volgograd Branch of Moscow Institute of Economics, Politics and Law. Acquired present title 1995. Acquired present status 2000.

Governing Bodies: Rector's Board; Academic Council.

Academic Year: September to June (September-January; February-June); Also Summer session in July-August

Admission Requirements: Secondary school leaving certificate (Attestat o Srednem Obrazovanii)

Fees: None

Main Language(s) of Instruction: Russian

Accrediting Agencies: The Federal Supervision Service in the Sphere of Education and Science

Degrees and Diplomas: *Diplom o Srednem Professionalnom Obrazovanii (Higher Vocational Education Diploma)*: 2 1/2 yrs; *Bakalavr*: 4 yrs; *Specialist Diploma*: 5 yrs

Student Services: Academic counselling, Canteen, Cultural centre, Employment services, Foreign student adviser, Foreign Studies Centre, Health services, Language programs, Social counselling, Sports facilities

Student Residential Facilities: None

Special Facilities: Computer Classroom; Poetic Art Museum

Libraries: Yes

Publications: Philosophy of Social Communications, Theoretical Scientific Journal *(quarterly)*; Scientific Proceedings, Scientific Conference Release *(annually)*

Press or Publishing House: VIESP's Publishing Office
Last Updated: 28/11/11

VOLZHSKY UNIVERSITY NAMED AFTER V.N. TATISCHEV (INSTITUTE)

Volžskij Universitet im. V.N. Tatiščeva (VUIT)

ul. Leningradskaja, 16, Tol'jatti, 445020 Samarskaja oblast'
Tel: +7(8482) 48-76-11
Fax: +7(8482) 46-65-89
EMail: info@vuit.ru
Website: http://www.vuit.ru

Rector: Vladimir A. Jakušin (2000-)

Vice-Rector, Academic: Alexander Nemtsev
Tel: +7(8482) 40-18-91

International Relations: Ekaterina A. Moločkova, Head of International Affairs Department
Tel: +7(8482) 48-73-07, Fax: +7(8482) 48-73-07
EMail: molochkovaea@vuit.ru

Colleges
Environmental Control and Efficient Use of Natural Resources (Environmental Studies; Natural Resources); **Maintenance of Computing Machinery and Multicomputer Systems** (Computer Engineering; Maintenance Technology)

Departments
Ecology (Biology; Ecology; Natural Resources; Natural Sciences); **Social Technologies** (Child Care and Development; Journalism)

Faculties
Computer Science and Telecommunications (Applied Mathematics; Computer Science; Information Technology; Telecommunications Engineering); **Economics** (Accountancy; Banking; Economics; Finance; Management; Marketing); **Further Education** (Accountancy; Computer Science; Ecology; Information Technology; Law; Management; Modern Languages; Secretarial Studies); **Humanities** (Acting; Arts and Humanities; German; Literature; Modern Languages; Performing Arts; Philology; Romance Languages; Russian; Social Sciences)

Programmes
Postgraduate (Computer Networks; Criminal Law; Criminology; Economics; Germanic Languages; Law; Management; Mathematics; Telecommunications Engineering)

Schools
Law (Civil Law; Constitutional Law; Criminal Law; History of Law; International Law; Law)

History: Founded in 1995

Governing Bodies: Academic Council

Academic Year: September-July

Admission Requirements: Entrance exam

Main Language(s) of Instruction: Russian

International Co-operation: With universities in Germany, Bulgaria, Czech Republic, Portugal

Accrediting Agencies: Federal Service for Supervision in Education and Science

Degrees and Diplomas: *Specialist Diploma*: Information systems in Industry; Applied Mathematics; Computers, Systems and Networks; Philology; Performing Arts; Journalism; Ecology; Environmental Management; Law; Finance and Credit; Accounting, Analysis and Audit; Organisational Management; Marketing; Taxes and Taxation; Information Science and Telecommunications; Mechatronics, 5-6 yrs. Also various vocational diplomas

Student Services: Academic counselling, Canteen, Cultural centre, Foreign student adviser, Foreign Studies Centre, Health services, Language programs, Nursery care, Social counselling, Sports facilities

Special Facilities: Actors' studio; Law service; Internet laboratories; Multimedia rooms; Health Spa "Russkiy Bor"

Libraries: 2 libraries, 3 reading rooms

Publications: Faculty, Educational journal of the Social Technologies department *(biennially)*; Museum Newspaper, Local journal produced by the Museum of Local Lore in Togliatti *(monthly)*; Volžshky University, Newspaper about the scientific, scholarly, cultural and educational life on the university *(bimonthly)*

Press or Publishing House: Volžshky University Publishing House

Academic Staff *2007-2008*	**TOTAL**
FULL-TIME	**136**
PART-TIME	**81**
Student Numbers *2007-2008*	
All (Foreign Included)	**5,092**
FOREIGN ONLY	**22**

Last Updated: 29/11/11

VORONEZH INSTITUTE OF ECONOMICS AND SOCIAL MANAGEMENT

Voronežskij Institut Ekonomiki i Sotsial'nogo Upravlenija

ul. Pomjalovskogo, 27, Voronež, 394036 Voronežskaja oblast'
Tel: +7(473) 253-16-23
Fax: +7(473) 253-16-23
EMail: viesm@vmail.ru
Website: http://www.viesm.vrn.ru/

Rector: Raisa Il'inicha Mel'nikova

Faculties
Economics and Management (Economics; Management); **State and Municipal Management** (Administration; Management; Political Sciences)

Programmes
Social Management (Management; Social Sciences)

History: Created 1995.

Degrees and Diplomas: *Bakalavr*, *Specialist Diploma*
Last Updated: 12/03/12

VORONEZH INSTITUTE OF HIGH TECHNOLOGIES

Voronežskij Institut Vysokikh Tekhnologij

ul. Lenina, 73a, Voronež, 394043 Voronežskaja oblast'
Tel: +7(4732) 72-73-98 +7(4732) 72-73-63
Fax: +7(4732) 72-73-98
EMail: office@vivt.ru
Website: http://www.vivt.ru/

Rector: Jakov E. L'vovich

Programmes
Fire Science (Fire Science); **Information Technology** (Computer Science; Information Technology); **Management** (Business Computing; Human Resources; Management); **Tourism** (Tourism)

History: Created 1992.

Degrees and Diplomas: *Bakalavr*, *Specialist Diploma*; *Magistr*
Last Updated: 21/02/12

WEST SIBERIAN INSTITUTE OF FINANCE AND LAW

Zapadno-Sibirskij Institut Finansov i Prava

ul. Permskaja, 25, Nižnevartovsk, 628600 Tjumenskaja oblast', Khanty-Mansijskij avt. okrug-Jugra
Tel: +7(3466) 45-75-30
Fax: +7(1466) 45-75-30
EMail: zsifip@nptus.ru
Website: http://www.zsifip.ru/

Rector: Sergei Georgievich Izmailov

Faculties
Economics and Law (Accountancy; Criminal Law; Economics; Finance; Law; Management)

History: Created 1997.

Degrees and Diplomas: *Bakalavr*, *Specialist Diploma*
Last Updated: 12/01/12

Printed in China